1994

65th Edition

INTERNATIONAL

MOTION PICTURE

ALMANAC

Editor: BARRY MONUSH

British Editor: WILLIAM PAY

Canadian Editor: PATRICIA THOMPSON

Quigley Publishing Company, Inc.

159 West 53rd Street, New York, N.Y. 10019

●

(212) 247-3100

Foreword

As Hollywood applauded its highest figures yet for summer releases—over $2.1 billion—the fact remained that threatrical showings had long ceased to reign as the major financial intake of feature films. Theatre attendance was now responsible for only 25% of domestic revenues, as opposed to 80% in 1980. However, a diverse selection of popular movies, chief among them the $300 million-plus smash "Jurassic Park," proved that the lure of moviegoing remained strong.

—BARRY MONUSH

65th Edition
INTERNATIONAL
MOTION PICTURE ALMANAC
For 1994
ISSN: 0074-7084
ISBN: 0-900610-48-4

Table of Contents

ALPHABETICAL INDEX OF SUBJECTS

Individual listings for the following sections are not included in this index: Services, Distributors of 16 mm Films, Non-theatrical Distributors, Buying and Booking Services, The Industry in Great Britain and Canada. For these see separate sections.

A

B

C

N

O

P

11A

U

V

W

Y

Z

The Year in Review

There was much good fortune to be spread around as 1992 showed a profit increase of nearly 60% for five major studios: Walt Disney, Warner Bros., Fox, Inc., Sony Pictures Entertainment (Columbia/TriStar), and Paramount. There was more good news to come as the summer of 1993 set box office records, passing the previous record holding season, summer '89, with revenues of more than $2 billion.

Universal Pictures led the pack during this lucrative summer season with the phenomenally successful dinosaur thriller "Jurassic Park." Adapted from the smash best seller by Michael Crichton, directed by reliable hit-maker Steven Spielberg, and boasting the most talked-about special effects of their time, the movie was guaranteed to strike it rich and did, breaking one record after another. These records included the biggest opening weekend in movie history (approx. $48 million), largest single day total ($17.6 million), and shortest time to reach the $200 million mark (23 days). By the end of August "Jurassic" had taken in more than $300 million U.S. dollars and was still posting impressive returns as Autumn arrived. The movie's magic touch continued throughout Europe where it grossed an amazing $287 million by mid-September with plenty more to come. "Jurassic Park's" final total will place it in the number two spot on the U.S. box office chart of all-time hits, second to Universal and Steven Spielberg's earlier triumph, "E.T. The Extra-Terrestrial."

There were many other success stories during the year. The crowning touch on Clint Eastwood's critical and commercial success "Unforgiven" (Warner Bros.) was a pair of Academy Awards—for best picture of 1992 and best director. The brooding, anti-violence Western had captured several critics' citations and continued to lure steady audiences since its August 1992 opening. By the following summer the film had passed the $100 million mark. No sooner had "Unforgiven" finished its run when Eastwood appeared in Columbia/Castle Rock's thriller "In the Line of Fire" and had a second $100 million hit on his hands.

The Walt Disney Company did the unthinkable by surpassing the triumph of its 1991 animated feature "Beauty and the Beast," with an even bigger box office hit, "Aladdin." Aided by another award-winning Alan Menken score, state-of-the-art animation, and the vocal talents of Robin Williams, the Arabian Nights fantasy became the movie to see during the holiday season and the highest grossing movie released in 1992 ($215,700,000 as of Labor Day '93). Disney's other big news was its surprise purchase of the independent company Miramax Films for a figure estimated between $60–$80 million. Under the new agreement Miramax would function as a division of Disney's Buena Vista Pictures Distribution, but still maintain operations as its own production, marketing and distribution company.

The film that no doubt helped to increase Disney's interest in buying the NY-based indie was Miramax's incredibly successful "The Crying Game." Bolstered by some of the most favorable reviews of the year and a secret "twist" in the story that had everyone talking but not giving anything away, the British-Irish political thriller/love story went far beyond anyone's wildest expectations making $62.5 million. In the Winter of 1993 the company scored another unexpected hit with the Mexican drama "Like Water for Chocolate." With more than $16 million earned in 6 months' time the movie stood a good chance of becoming the all-time top-grossing foreign-language film to play in America. In addition to Miramax's Australian dance film "Strictly Ballroom" ($11,660,000), other independent money makers included the Samuel Goldwyn Company's latest Kenneth Branagh adaptation of Shakespeare, "Much Ado About Nothing"

($20,000,000 as of Labor Day '93), and New Line Cinema's grim, inner-city drama "Menace II Society" ($27,000,000).

Among the other box office winners for the various majors were: Paramount's romantic drama "Indecent Proposal" ($106,100,000) and the Tom Cruise vehicle from the top best seller "The Firm" ($147,680,000 by Labor Day '93); Columbia Pictures' bizarre stylized version of "Bram Stoker's Dracula" ($82,500,000), the Tom Cruise–Jack Nicholson courtroom drama "A Few Good Men" (Castle Rock, $141,220,000) and Bill Murray's comic-fantasy "Groundhog Day" ($70,820,000); Warner Bros.' big budget update of the tv series "The Fugitive" starring Harrison Ford ($133,000,000 by Labor Day '93 and still going strong), Steven Seagal's biggest action adventure to date, "Under Siege" ($83,570,000), the Kevin Costner–Whitney Houston love story "The Bodyguard" ($121,950,000), "Dave" the political satire starring Kevin Kline ($63,110,000), and "Free Willy" the most popular feature from the studio's new Family Entertainment division ($67,150,000, Labor Day '93); 20th Century Fox's Macaulay Culkin sequel "Home Alone 2: Lost in New York" ($171,710,000) and the colonial adventure "The Last of the Mohicans" ($70,100,000); TriStar's Sylvester Stallone's highscale adventure "Cliffhanger" ($82,120,000), and the romantic comedy of the year "Sleepless in Seattle" with Tom Hanks and Meg Ryan ($110,100,000, Labor Day '93); and Universal's Oscar-winning showcase for Al Pacino, "Scent of a Woman" ($62,770,000).

Unfortunately there was little of this money coming into the industry's two perpetually problem-plagued majors: MGM and Orion. While MGM showed decent but unremarkable $20 million-plus figures on both "Untamed Heart" and "Benny & Joon," there was nothing but bad news for Orion. Finally unleashing three of its long-on-the-shelf titles, "Love Field," "Married to It," and "The Dark Half," the company had major disappointments with each. Hoping to get back into current film production,

and not just concentrate on distributing older titles, Orion Pictures formed a joint venture with Metromedia Co. under the name Orion Productions Co. to help finance its new product.

MGM left its long-established base of Culver City and moved into its new headquarters in Santa Monica, eventually dismissing chairman Alan Ladd, Jr. and replacing him with former Paramount head Frank Mancuso, Jr. in hopes of injecting some new life into the ailing business. Credit Lyonnais, the French bank which owns MGM, provided the studio with a $190 million credit facility in the spring of 1993 and then followed with another $210 million that summer. Operating plans included reviving the dormant United Artists division. Unfortunately the first new UA feature "Son of the Pink Panther" had a quick demise.

Ted Turner and the Turner Broadcasting System were eager to enter the moviemaking business and offered between $415–$500 million to purchase New Line Cinema Corp. In addition TBS would also assume some $50 million in existing debt from the film company. At the same time Turner also hoped to take over Castle Rock Entertainment. The company was asking for $100 million plus the assumption of approximately $100 million more in liabilities. Final negotiations were underway in September of '93.

Most theatre chains still refused to book films given an "NC-17" rating despite hopes that this revamping of the previous "X" would put an end to such resistance. A handful of independent "art-house" movies were content to receive the "NC-17" and play minimal bookings. These included two Australian productions, "Wide Sargasso Sea" (Fine Line Features) and "Romper Stomper" (Academy Entertainment), and the controversial Harvey Keitel police drama "Bad Lieutenant" (Aries Films). On the other hand, several movies chose to edit footage to lessen the rating from "NC-17" to an "R" including Louis Malle's "Damage" (New Line Cinema), the Madonna vehicle "Body of Evidence" (MGM), MGM's erotic love story "The Lover," the offbeat drama "Boxing Helena" (Orion Classics), John Woo's action thriller "Hard Target" (Universal) and the Brad Pitt road movie "Kalifornia" (Gramercy Pictures). In July 1993 brief rating explanations for all rated movies were offered to the public by way of MovieFone. This way moviegoers could find out why the current releases were rated as they were.

In December 1992 Loews' 19th Street Theatre in Manhattan premiered the first live-action interactive film, "I'm Your Man." During the 20 minute short three color codes would flash on the screen at certain points during the action asking for a decision to advance the plot. Audience members would then respond by pressing the corresponding color button of their choice on a pistol grip attached to the arm of each seat. After tallying the votes electronically the film would continue its story according to what the majority had dictated by pressing their buttons. This experimental movie continued its run in U.S. theatres throughout 1993.

Minor Oscar controversies erupted prior to the actual spring ceremonies. The Academy voted to dispense with two traditional categories—documentary short and live-action short, feeling that both "have long ceased to reflect the realities of theatrical motion picture distribution." An unexpected outcry from various filmmakers and Academy members caused the rapid reinstatement of both categories. There was, however, no bending to the decision to eliminate one of the year's foreign-language film nominees from the voting ballot. "A Place in the World" was disqualified after it was discovered that the movie was not a Uruguayan film as originally stated but primarily Argentine. A lawsuit on behalf of the film's director was brought against the Academy but dismissed by the court. On Oscar night only four nominees, instead of the customary five, were read from the nominations list.

Motion Picture Industry

EXHIBITION

THEATRE GROSSES, 1950–1992:

U.S. Box Office Receipts in Relation to Personal Consumption Expenditures

SOURCES: U.S. Dept. of Commerce, Office of Business Economics, National Income Division and the Motion Picture Association of America. (Latest revisions included.)

	1950	1951	1952	1953	1954	1955	1956	1957	1958	1959	1960
Admissions to U.S. motion picture theatres (millions $)	1,376	1,310	1,246	1,187	1,228	1,326	1,394	1,126	992	958	951
Percentage of total U.S. personal consumption expenditures (%)	0.72	0.64	0.58	0.52	0.52	0.52	0.52	0.40	0.34	0.31	0.29
Percentage of total U.S. recreation expenditures (%)	12.34	11.33	10.30	9.33	9.39	9.42	9.31	7.34	6.27	5.51	5.20
Percentage of total U.S. spectator amusement expenditures (%)	77.26	76.34	75.29	73.96	73.44	73.63	73.41	68.04	64.50	60.98	59.22

	1961	1962	1963	1964	1965	1966	1967	1968	1969	1970	1971
Admissions to U.S. motion picture theatres (millions $)	921	903	904	913	927	964	989	1,045	1,099	1,162	1,170
Percentage of total U.S. personal consumption expenditures (%)	0.27	0.25	0.24	0.23	0.21	0.23	0.22	0.20	0.19	0.19	0.18
Percentage of total U.S. recreation expenditures (%)	4.72	4.41	4.07	3.71	3.51	3.34	3.20	3.11	2.98	2.86	2.74
Percentage of total U.S. spectator amusement expenditures (%)	56.68	54.86	53.43	51.81	51.19	50.13	48.79	46.71	48.59	48.00	47.74

	1972	1973	1974	1975	1976	1977	1978	1979	1980	1981	1982
Admissions to U.S. motion picture theatres (millions $)	1,644	1,524	1,909	2,115	1,742	2,376	2,811	2,946	2,750	2,966	3,453
Percentage of total U.S. personal consumption expenditures (%)	0.22	0.20	0.28	0.26	0.27	0.56	0.54	—	—	—	—
Percentage of total U.S. recreation expenditures (%)	3.03	3.50	4.10	3.84	4.12	—	—	—	2.56	2.45	2.73
Percentage of total U.S. spectator amusement expenditures (%)	47.01	50.77	53.99	51.81	53.36	34.8	35.8	—	42.7	43.2	45.7

	1983	1984	1985	1986	1987	1988	1989	1990	1991	1992
Admissions to U.S. motion picture theatres (millions $)	3,766	4,156	3,749	3,778	4,252	4,458	5,033	5,021	4,803	4,871
Percentage of total U.S. personal consumption expenditures (%)	—	—	—	—	—	—	—	—	—	—
Percentage of total U.S. recreation expenditures (%)	2.66	2.50	2.43	1.97	2.03	—	—	—	—	—
Percentage of total U.S. spectator amusement expenditures (%)	45.6	45.8	3.85	3.78	3.69	—	—	—	—	—

NUMBER OF THEATRES:

There were a total of 25,105 screens (including drive-ins) in the U.S. at the end of 1992, an increase of 2.2 percent from the 24,570 in 1991. Although there was a 4% drop in the number of drive-in screens to 872 in 1992, compared with 908 in 1991, the number of indoor screens was once again on the rise: up 2.4 percent in 1992 to 24,233, as compared to 23,662 in 1991.

US THEATRE CIRCUITS:

There are 33 circuits in the U.S. with 100 screens or more, as of May 1993. Largest in size at most recent count was United Artists Theatre Circuit with 2,312 screens. UA is followed by American Multi-Cinema with 1,628 screens; Cineplex Odeon (1,614); Carmike (1,570); and General Cinema Theatres (1,355).

ADMISSION PRICES:

Admission prices continued to rise in 1992, averaging $5.052 for the year, an increase of 3.3% compared to the 1991 average of $4.892. Since 1980, admission prices have risen by 87.7%, from $2.691. In New York City the top price is now $7.50.

ATTENDANCE:

Total theatre admissions at U.S. theatres in 1992 were 964.2 million, falling below the one billion mark for the second year in a row. The figure compares with 981.9 million in 1991, representing a decrease of 1.8 percent.

THEATRE GROSSES 1982-1992
(Figures in Millions of Dollars)

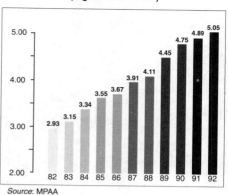

Source: MPAA

ADMISSION PRICES 1982-1992
(Figures in Dollars)

Source: MPAA

THEATRE ADMISSIONS 1982-1992
(Figures in Millions)

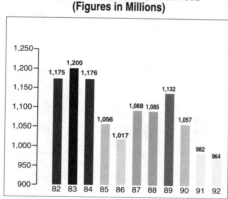

Source: MPAA

A study conducted by the Motion Picture Association of America, Inc. showed the following:

National probability sample: 2,004 adults age 18 and over,
257 teenagers, 12 to 17
Total 2,261

Admissions by Age Groups

Age:	1992	Percent of Total Yearly Admissions 1991	1990	Percent of Resident Civilian Population as of 1/91
12–15 yrs.	12%	12%	11%	7%
16–20	15	19	20	8
21–24	11	12	11	7
25–29	11	12	14	10
30–39	19	19	20	21
40–49	15	13	12	16
50–59	7	5	5	11
60 and over	8	8	7	20
	100%	100%	100%	100%
12–17	18%	17%	18%	10%
18 and over	82	83	82	90

Attendees under 30 continue to be the dominant force in movie-going, despite their share of total attendance having decreased: 49% in 1992, versus 55% in 1991.

Age groups showing the greatest discrepancy between proportion of yearly admissions and proportion in the population are as follows:

Age Group	1992	Percent of Total Yearly Admissions 1991	1990	1991 Percent Population
12–29 years	49%	54%	56%	32%
12–39 years	68	73	76	53
16–39	56	61	65	47
40 and over	30	27	24	47

Moviegoers (age 12 and over)
Frequency of Attendance

	Total Public Age 12 & Over			Adult Public Age 18 & Over			Teenagers Age 12 to 17		
	1992	1991	1990	1992	1991	1990	1992	1991	1990
Frequent (at least once a month)	27%	21%	23%	24%	18%	22%	47%	43%	45%
Occasional (once in 2 to 6 months)	33	34	31	32	33	30	40	44	38
Infrequent (less than once in 6 months)	11	12	12	11	13	12	6	5	8
Never	28	32	33	31	36	36	3	6	5
Not reported	1	1	1	1	1	—	3	2	3

Total Moviegoing Public Frequency
(based on moviegoers only)

	1992	1991	1990
Frequent	38%	31%	36%
Occasional	47	51	47
Infrequent	15	18	18

Moviegoing Adults

	1992	1991	1990
Frequent	36%	28%	33%
Occasional	48	52	48
Infrequent	17	20	20

Moviegoing Teenagers

	1992	1991	1990
Frequent	51%	47%	49%
Occasional	43	48	41
Infrequent	6	5	9

Marital Status—Adults

	Married			Single		
	1992	1991	1990	1992	1991	1990
Frequent	19%	14%	16%	32%	24%	26%
Occasional	33	32	32	32	34	30
Infrequent	13	15	15	9	9	9
Never	35	38	36	26	32	35

Single persons continue to be more frequent moviegoers than married persons.

Adults With Children Under 18

	1992	1991	1990
Frequent	25%	18%	22%
Occasional	40	40	39
Infrequent	13	16	15
Never	22	26	23

Adults Without Children

	1992	1991	1990
Frequent	24%	18%	20%
Occasional	28	28	26
Infrequent	10	10	11
Never	38	43	43

Education

	Less Than High School			High School Completed			At Least Some College		
	1992	1991	1990	1992	1991	1990	1992	1991	1990
Frequent	11%	6%	11%	19%	14%	17%	31%	24%	27%
Occasional	21	17	19	31	32	30	37	38	34
Infrequent	11	10	9	10	15	13	12	12	13
Never	57	67	60	39	38	40	20	26	26

Sex

	Age 12 and Over						Age 18 and Over					
	Male			Female			Male			Female		
	1992	1991	1990	1992	1991	1990	1992	1991	1990	1992	1991	1990
Frequent	29%	23%	25%	26%	19%	21%	28%	21%	23%	21%	16%	17%
Occasional	33	36	32	36	31	31	31	35	32	34	31	30
Infrequent	10	12	12	11	12	12	11	13	12	12	12	13
Never	27	28	30	27	37	35	30	31	33	32	40	39

As in previous years, more males than females tend to be frequent moviegoers.
NOTE: Certain tables may not add to 100% due to rounding of percentages.

PRODUCTION

NUMBER OF FILMS:

Total theatrical releases by all companies in 1992 were 484, including 53 reissues. Of the new 431 pictures for the year 141 came from member companies of the Motion Picture Association of America and the remaining 290 from independent distributors. The total number of films for the year was up from the 448 released in 1991, which included 33 reissues. The number of new films from MPAA members was down by 9, however, from the 150 released in 1991.

TOP-GROSSING FEATURES:

A total of 36 pictures released by MPAA members took in film rentals of $20 million or more in 1992, compared to 30 in 1991, 1990 and 1989. (For titles of the winners see "Top-Grossing Features" in the Awards and Poll Winners section of this book.)

PRODUCTION COSTS:

According to industry estimates, the average feature production cost of the major U.S. companies has increased many times since the beginning of World War II. In 1941, average cost per feature was $400,000. In 1949, this had risen to more than $1,000,000. The average negative cost of theatrical film in 1972 was $1,890,000. In 1974 it was more than $2,500,000 and in 1976, $4,000,000. In 1978 it jumped to $5,000,000. In 1980 it was placed at $8,500,000 and 1981 at $10,000,000. In 1982 it reached $11,300,000 and in 1983, $11,800,000. In 1984 it was estimated to have risen to $14,410,000 and to $16,780,000 in 1985. In 1986 it rose again to $17,450,000 and in 1987 to $20,100,000. The upward trend was reversed, however, in 1988 when the figure dropped by 10 per cent to $18.1 million. In 1989 it rose again to $23,454,000, an increase of nearly 30% and to $26,783,200 in 1990, a 14.2 increase. 1991 saw a slight decrease of 2.4% with the average cost at $26,135,500. The cost jumped 10.4% in 1992 with the average figure at $28,858,300.

PRINTS AND ADVERTISING COSTS OF NEW FEATURES:

Total U.S. marketing costs (prints and advertising) increased 11.5 percent in 1992 to $13,456,000 over the $12,064,000 recorded for 1991. In 1980 the combined marketing costs were $4,329,000. Thus the figure has risen by more than 210.8% in ten years.

EMPLOYMENT:

The average number of full- and part-time employees in the industry was 382,800 in 1992, compared to 388,600 in 1991, 394,500 in 1990, 377,000 in 1989, 354,200 in 1988, 231,156 in 1987 and 219,356 in 1986, 220,967 in 1985, 218,122 in 1984 and 210,733 in 1983. The figure was 216,000 in 1982 and stayed steady at 222,000 in 1979, 1980 and 1981. The average number of full- and part-time employees was 213,000 in 1978; 210,000 in 1977; 205,000 in 1976; 204,000 in 1975; 203,000 in 1974; 204,000 in 1973; 199,000 in 1972; 201,000 in 1971; 210,000 in 1970; 202,000 in 1969; 194,000 in 1968; 193,000 in 1967; 187,000 in 1966; 181,000 in 1965; 176,000 in 1964; 175,000 in 1963; 174,000 in 1962; 183,000 in 1961; 192,000 in 1960; and 184,000 in 1959.

Wages and salaries in 1929 were $308,000,000 and $339,000,000 in 1939. By 1942, payroll had risen to $410,000,000 and in 1943 to $459,000,000. In 1944, it was $509,000,000; in 1945, $552,000,000; in 1946, $679,000,000; in 1947, $649,000,000; in 1948, $655,000,000; in 1949, $659,000,000; in 1950, $651,000,000; in 1951, $668,000,000; in 1952, $684,000,000; in 1953, $678,000,000; in 1956, $800,000,000; in 1957, $795,000,000; in 1958, $756,000,000; in 1959, $789,000,000; in 1960, $754,000,000; in 1961, $833,000,000; in 1962, $805,000,000; in 1963, $806,000,000; in 1964, $864,000,000; in 1965, $967,000,000; in 1966, $1,039,000,000; in 1967, $1,100,000,000; in 1968, $1,172,000,000; in 1969, $1,278,000,000; in 1970, $1,274,000,000; in 1971, $1,277,000,000; in 1972, $1,343,000,000; in 1973, $1,429,000,000; in 1974, $1,575,000,000; in 1975, $1,662,000,000; in 1976, $1,887,000,000; in 1977, $2,133,000,000; in 1978, $2,449,000,000; in 1979, $2,879,000,000; in 1980, $3,076,000,000; in 1981, $3,418,000,000; in 1982, $3,604,000,000; in 1983, $3,985,000,000; in 1984, $4,416,000,000; in 1985, $4,862,000,000; in 1986, $5,141,000,000; in 1987, $5,980,000,000; in 1988, $6,445,000,000.

INDUSTRY FILM RATING SYSTEM:

On November 1, 1968, member companies of the Motion Picture Association put into effect a voluntary film program with all pictures released after that date to carry one of four identifying rating symbols on all prints, trailers, advertising and at theatre box offices. The four categories were originally "G" for general audiences; "M" for adults and mature young people, on which parental discretion is advised; "R" for attendance restricted to persons over 16, unless accompanied by parent or adult guardian and "X" pictures to which no one under 16 is to be admitted. On March 1, 1970, the "M" rating was changed to "GP" (all ages admitted—parental guidance) and later this was changed to "PG." In 1984 a new rating was introduced: PG-13, for films which parents are cautioned to give special guidance for children under 13 years of age.

In September of 1990 the "X" rating was changed to "NC-17," or "No Children Under 17," in hopes or removing the pornographic connotation of the "X."

In 1992 the Classification and Rating Administration rated 616 films, a slight increase over the 614 rated the year before. The pattern of film ratings issued has not varied significantly over the past three years.

In 1992 ratings were as follows: 18 rated "G"; 87 "PG"; 114 "PG-13"; 390 "R"; 7 "NC-17/X." This compares with 1991 as follows: 14 "G"; 86 "PG"; 119 "PG-13"; 374 "R"; and 21 "NC-17/X."

Since the ratings began in 1968 the totals through 1992 for each category are as follows: 984 rated "G"; 3,165 "PG"; 741 "PG-13"; 5,625 "R"; and 401 "X" or "NC-17."

Awards and Polls

* **NATIONAL AND INTERNATIONAL AWARDS, 1992**

* **COMPLETE ACADEMY AWARDS, 1927–PRESENT**

* **COMPLETE DIRECTORS GUILD OF AMERICA AWARDS**

* **QP MONEY-MAKING STARS 1933–92**

* **TOP-GROSSING FILMS**

Award and Poll Winners: 1992

ACADEMY AWARD WINNERS OF 1992

The Academy of Motion Picture Arts and Sciences was founded in May, 1927, in Hollywood with 36 charter members including production executives and cinema luminaries. Its aims included a determination to raise the standards of production educationally, culturally and scientifically.

In the years since its inception this non-subsidized organization has grown to embrace 14 principal branches of film making.

Voting for the Academy Awards of Merit is done by the entire membership with each of the 13 branches creating its own procedure and conducting individual nominations in the manner best suited to its special requirements. The final nominating ballot from each branch is limited to a maximum of five entrants.

The eligible voting breakdown is as follows: actors comprise by far the largest branch. There are 1,354 actors, 293 art directors and costume designers, 146 cinematographers, 292 directors, 201 film editors, 234 musicians, 247 short film makers, 375 in the sound branch, and 383 writers. The 374 executives, 410 producers, 324 public relations executives, and 441 members at large only nominate for best picture. The only nominations that are made by the Academy as a whole are those for best picture.

The 5,074 voting members of the Academy are eligible to vote for the winners in most categories. However, no member is allowed to vote in the documentary, short film and foreign-language categories unless he certifies that he has seen all nominees.

After nominations have been closed the Academy holds screenings of the nominated films in order that eligible voters can review them. A final ballot is then prepared and sent to the Academy membership. These ballots are marked and returned to Price Waterhouse and Company, certified public accountants, who prepare the tabulation. The names of the winners are announced only at the annual Academy Awards presentation ceremonies.

Excluding foreign language and documentary films, 237 movies were eligible for nomination for the 65th Annual Academy Awards. To be eligible, a film had to be exhibited in 35m or a larger format at theaters in the Los Angeles area for seven consecutive days starting no later than Dec. 31, 1992. Entries submitted for the best foreign-language film award must have been released commercially in their countries of origin between Nov. 1, 1991, and Oct. 31, 1992, and selected by a recognized organization to represent those nations. The films need not have been distributed in the U.S., but to be eligible in most other categories, including best picture, they must have met the requirements applicable to all other films.

Awards of the Academy of Motion Picture Arts and Sciences for 1992, made March 29, 1993 at the Dorothy Chandler Pavilion were as follows:

BEST PICTURE
"Unforgiven," Warner Bros. Production, WB; Clint Eastwood, producer.

BEST FOREIGN LANGUAGE FILM
"Indochine," Paradis Films/La Générale d'Images/BAC Films/Orly Films/Dine Cinq production, Sony Pictures Classics (France).

BEST DIRECTOR
Clint Eastwood, "Unforgiven."

BEST ACTOR
Al Pacino, "Scent of a Woman." Universal Pictures production, Universal.

BEST ACTRESS
Emma Thompson, "Howards End." Merchant Ivory production, Sony Pictures Classics.

BEST SUPPORTING ACTOR
Gene Hackman, "Unforgiven."

BEST SUPPORTING ACTRESS
Marisa Tomei, "My Cousin Vinny," 20th Century Fox production, 20th Century Fox.

BEST ORIGINAL SCREENPLAY
Neil Jordan, "The Crying Game," Palace Pictures production, Miramax.

BEST SCREENPLAY ADAPTATION
Ruth Prawer Jhabvala, "Howards End."

BEST CINEMATOGRAPHY
Philippe Rousselot, "A River Runs Through It," Columbia Pictures production, Columbia; Robert Redford, Patrick Markey, producers.

BEST FILM EDITING
Joel Cox, "Unforgiven."

BEST ORIGINAL SCORE
Alan Menken, "Aladdin," Walt Disney Pictures production, Buena Vista.

BEST ORIGINAL SONG
"Whole New World," from "Aladdin." Music by Alan Menken, lyric by Tim Rice.

BEST ART DIRECTION
Luciana Arrighi, art direction; **Ian Whittaker,** set decoration; "Howards End."

BEST COSTUME DESIGN
Eiko Ishioka, "Bram Stoker's Dracula," Columbia Pictures production, Columbia; Francis Ford Coppola, Fred Fuchs, Charles Mulvehill, producers.

BEST SOUND
Chris Jenkins, Doug Hemphill, Mark Smith, Simon Kaye, "The Last of the Mohicans," 20th Century Fox production, 20th Century Fox.

BEST SOUND EFFECTS EDITING
Tom C. McCarthy, David E. Stone, "Bram Stoker's Dracula."

BEST MAKEUP
Greg Cannom, Michele Burke, Matthew W. Mungle, "Bram Stoker's Dracula."

BEST VISUAL EFFECTS
Ken Ralston, Doug Chiang, Doug Smythe, Tom Woodruff, "Death Becomes Her," Universal Pictures production, Universal.

BEST SHORT FILMS
(Animated)
"Mona Lisa Descending a Staircase," Joan C. Gratz production; Gratz, producer.
(Live-Action)
"Omnibus," Lazennec tout court/Le CRRAV production; Sam Karmann, producer.

BEST DOCUMENTARIES
(Feature)
"The Panama Deception," Empowerment Project production; Barbara Trent, David Kasper, producers.
(Short Subject)
"Educating Peter," State of the Art Inc. production; Thomas C. Goodwin, Gerardine Wurzburg, producers.

HONORARY ACADEMY AWARD
Federico Fellini, "in recognition of his cinematic accomplishments that have thrilled and entertained worldwide audiences."

JEAN HERSHOLT HUMANITARIAN AWARD
Audrey Hepburn, for her UNICEF work. **Elizabeth Taylor,** for her support of AIDS research.

GORDON E. SAWYER AWARD
(Statuette)
Erich Kaestner, "whose technical contributions have brought credit to the motion picture industry."

ACADEMY AWARD OF MERIT
(Statuette)
Chadwell O'Connor of O'Connor Engineering Laboratories for "the concept and engineering of the fluid-damped camera-head for motion picture photography."

SCIENTIFIC OR TECHNICAL AWARDS
(Voted by Academy Board of Governors)

Scientific and Engineering Award
(Academy Plaque)

Loren Carpenter, Rob Cook, Ed Catmull, Tom Porter, Pat Hanrahan, Tony Apodacca and **Darwyn Peachy** for development of "RenderMan" software providing the means to digitally create scenes or elements that may be composited with other footage.

Clause Wiedemann and **Robert Orban** for the design, and **Dolby Laboratories** for the development, of the Dolby "Container," a stereo five-band audio processor that limits signals in selected bands, then removes resulting harmonics, allowing creative use of an analog soundtrack with increased dynamic range.

Ken Bates for design and development of the Bates Decelerator System, which provides a means for significantly increasing the safety of very high stunt falls.

Al Mayer for camera design; **Iain Neil** and **George Kraemer** for optical design; **Hans Spirawski** and **Bill Eslick** for opto-mechanical design; and **Don Earl** for technical support in developing the Panavision System 65 Studio Sync Sound Reflex Camera for 65m motion picture photography.

Douglas Trumbull for concept; **Geoffrey Williamson** for movement design; **Robert Auguste** for electronic design; and **Edmund DiGiulio** for camera system of the CP-65 Showscan Camera System for 65m motion picture photography (first modern 65m camera developed in 25 years).

Arriflex Corp., Otto Blaschek and the **engineering department of the ARRI, Austria**, for the design and development of the Arriflex 765 Camera System for 65m motion picture photography.

Technical Achievement Award
(Academy Certificate)

Ira Tiffen, Tiffen Manufacturing, for production of the Ultra Contrast Filter Series for motion picture photography, which provides a graded range of contrast reduction filters with excellent consistency over the entire frame area.

Robert R. Burton, Audio Rents Inc., for development of the Model S-27 4-Band Splitter/Combiner, a method of processing soundtrack by allowing the sound mixer to work on separate bands of the audio spectrum.

Iain Neil for optical design, and **Kaz Fudano**, for mechanical design of the Panavision Slant Focus Lens, which allows for the focus plane to be tipped and rotated so that near and far objects can be simultaneously brought into focus.

Tom Brigham, for the original concept and pioneering work; and **Douglas Smythe** and the **computer graphics department of Industrial Light & Magic** for development and first implementation in feature motion pictures of the MORF system for digital metamorphosis of high resolution images. The MORF system made practical the creation of metamorphosis and transformation effects for films.

MEDAL OF COMMENDATION

(Medallion)

Petro Vlahos "in appreciation for outstanding service and dedication in upholding the high standards of the Academy of Motion Picture Arts & Sciences."

DIRECTORS GUILD OF AMERICA AWARDS 1992

Film Director's Award: CLINT EASTWOOD, Unforgiven

D.W. Griffith Life Achievement Award: SIDNEY LUMET

Documentary Directors: JOSEPH BERLINGER and BRUCE SINOFSKY, Brother's Keeper

(for a complete list of DGA winners see page 42A)

NATIONAL BOARD OF REVIEW OF MOTION PICTURES AWARDS 1992

The group is the oldest organization to give film awards, beginning with its Exceptional Photoplay Committee awards in 1917. It is also the first chronologically to vote its awards each year.

Best Picture: HOWARDS END

Best Director: JAMES IVORY, Howards End

Best Actor: JACK LEMMON, Glengarry Glen Ross

Best Actress: EMMA THOMPSON, Howards End

Best Supporting Actor: JACK NICHOLSON, A Few Good Men

Best Supporting Actress: JUDY DAVIS, Husbands and Wives

Best Foreign Film: INDOCHINE

Special Awards: SHIRLEY TEMPLE BLACK (life achievement), JAYE DAVIDSON of The Crying Game (most auspicious debut)

NATIONAL SOCIETY OF FILM CRITICS AWARDS 1992

Best Picture: UNFORGIVEN

Best Director: CLINT EASTWOOD, Unforgiven

Best Actor: STEPHEN REA, The Crying Game

Best Actress: EMMA THOMPSON, Howards End

Best Supporting Actor: GENE HACKMAN, Unforgiven

Best Supporting Actress: JUDY DAVIS, Husbands and Wives

Best Screenplay: DAVID WEBB PEOPLES, Unforgiven

Best Cinematography: ZHAO FEI, Raise the Red Lantern

Best Foreign Film: RAISE THE RED LANTERN

Best Documentary: AMERICAN DREAM

Special Citation (for expanding the possibilities of experimental filmmaking): ANOTHER GIRL, ANOTHER PLANET

NEW YORK FILM CRITICS CIRCLE AWARDS 1992

Best Picture: THE PLAYER

Best Director: ROBERT ALTMAN, The Player

Best Actor: DENZEL WASHINGTON, Malcolm X

Best Actress: EMMA THOMPSON, Howards End

Best Supporting Actor: GENE HACKMAN, Unforgiven

Best Supporting Actress: MIRANDA RICHARDSON, Enchanted April, The Crying Game, and Damage

Best Screenplay: NEIL JORDAN, The Crying Game

Best Foreign Film: RAISE THE RED LANTERN

Best Cinematography: JEAN LEPINE, The Player

Best Documentary: BROTHER'S KEEPER

Best New Director: ALLISON ANDERS, Gas Food Lodging

LOS ANGELES FILM CRITICS AWARDS 1992

Best Picture: UNFORGIVEN

Best Director: CLINT EASTWOOD, Unforgiven

Best Actor: CLINT EASTWOOD, Unforgiven

Best Actress: EMMA THOMPSON, Howards End

Best Supporting Actor: GENE HACKMAN, Unforgiven

Best Supporting Actress: JUDY DAVIS, Husbands and Wives

Best Screenplay: DAVID WEBB PEOPLES, Unforgiven

GOLDEN GLOBE AWARDS 1992—MOTION PICTURES

Best Motion Picture—Drama: SCENT OF A WOMAN

Best Actor—Drama: AL PACINO, Scent of a Woman

Best Actress—Drama: EMMA THOMPSON, Howards End

Best Motion Picture—Comedy or Musical: THE PLAYER

Best Actor—Comedy or Musical: TIM ROBBINS, The Player

Best Actress—Comedy or Musical: MIRANDA RICHARDSON, Enchanted April

Best Director: CLINT EASTWOOD, Unforgiven

Best Supporting Actor: GENE HACKMAN, Unforgiven

Best Supporting Actress: JOAN PLOWRIGHT, Enchanted April

Best Foreign-Language Film: INDOCHINE

Best Screenplay: BO GOLDMAN, Scent of a Woman

Best Original Score: ALAN MENKEN, Aladdin

Best Original Song: WHOLE NEW WORLD from Aladdin (music: Alan Menken; lyrics: Tim Rice)

Special Award: ROBIN WILLIAMS (voice of the Genie), Aladdin
Cecil B. DeMille Award: LAUREN BACALL

WRITERS GUILD OF AMERICA AWARDS 1992

Best Original Screenplay: NEIL JORDAN, The Crying Game
Best Adapted Screenplay: MICHAEL TOLKIN, The Player

BRITISH ACADEMY OF FILM AND TELEVISION ARTS (BAFTA) AWARDS (1992)

Michael Balcon Award for Outstanding British Contribution to Cinema: KENNETH BRANAGH

Film Production and Performance

Best Film: HOWARDS END, Ismail Merchant, James Ivory
David Lean Award for Direction: ROBERT ALTMAN, The Player
Best Original Screenplay: WOODY ALLEN, Husbands and Wives
Best Adapted Screenplay: MICHAEL TOLKIN, The Player
Best Actor in a Leading Role: ROBERT DOWNEY, JR., Chaplin
Best Actress in a Leading Role: EMMA THOMPSON, Howards End
Best Actor in a Supporting Role: GENE HACKMAN, Unforgiven
Best Actress in a Supporting Role: MIRANDA RICHARDSON, Damage
Best Original Film Music: DAVID HIRSCHFELDER, Strictly Ballroom
Best Non-English Language Film: RAISE THE RED LANTERN, Chiu Fu-Sheng, Zhang Yimou
Best Short Film: OMNIBUS, Anne Bennett, Sam Karmann
Best Short Animated Film: DAUMIER'S LAW, Ginger Gibbons, Geoff Dunbar
Alexander Korda Award for Best British Film: THE CRYING GAME, Steven Woolley, Neil Jordan

CANNES FILM FESTIVAL PRIZES: 1993

Palm d'Or (shared): THE PIANO (Jane Campion, Australia), and FAREWELL TO MY CONCUBINE (Chen Kaige, China)
Best Director: MIKE LEIGH, Naked (Britain)
Best Actor: DAVID THEWLIS, Naked
Best Actress: HOLLY HUNTER, The Piano

Grand Jury Prize: FAR AWAY, SO CLOSE (Wim Wenders, Germany)
Jury Prize (shared): RAINING STONES (Ken Loach, Britain) and PUPPET MASTER (Hou Hsiao-hsien, Taiwan)
Camera d'Or (Best First Feature): SCENT OF GREEN PAPAYA (Tran Anh Hung, French)
Camera d'Or Special Mention: FRIENDS (Elaine Proctor, South Africa/Britain)
Palme d'Or for Best Short Subject: COFFEE AND CIGARETTES: SOMEWHERE IN CALIFORNIA (Jim Jarmusch, U.S.)
Technical Achievement in Images and Sound—Feature: MAZEPPA (Jean Gargonne and Vincent Arnardi, France)
Technical Achievement in Images and Sound—Short Subject: THE SINGING TROPHY (Grant Lahood, New Zealand)
International Critics' Prize: FAREWELL TO MY CONCUBINE (for "its incisive analysis of the political and cultural history of China and for its brilliant combination of the spectacular and the intimate.")

AMERICAN FILM INSTITUTE LIFE ACHIEVEMENT AWARD 1993: Elizabeth Taylor

Past recipients: John Ford (1973), James Cagney (1974), Orson Welles (1975), William Wyler (1976), Bette Davis (1977), Henry Fonda (1978), Alfred Hitchcock (1979), James Stewart (1980), Fred Astaire (1981), Frank Capra (1982), John Huston (1983), Lillian Gish (1984), Gene Kelly (1985), Billy Wilder (1986), Barbara Stanwyck (1987), Jack Lemmon (1988), Gregory Peck (1989), Sir David Lean (1990), Kirk Douglas (1991), Sidney Poitier (1992).

QP MONEY-MAKING STARS OF 1992

In the 1992 annual poll of circuit exhibitors in the United States, conducted by Quigley Publications, these stars were voted the Top Ten:

Tom Cruise	1
Mel Gibson	2
Kevin Costner	3
Jack Nicholson	4
Macaulay Culkin	5
Whoopi Goldberg	6
Michael Douglas	7
Clint Eastwood	8
Steven Seagal	9
Robin Williams	10

The runners up: (11) Sharon Stone; (12) Michelle Pfeiffer; (13) Harrison Ford; (14) Danny DeVito; (15) Steve Martin; (16) Michael Keaton; (17) Sean Connery; (18) Joe Pesci; (19) Demi Moore; (20) Eddie Murphy; (21) Billy Crystal; (22) Daniel Day-Lewis; (23) Julia Roberts; (24) Dana Carvey; (25) Al Pacino.

(for a complete list of Quigley Money-Making winners see page 43A)

THE HISTORY OF OSCAR

Oscar, the golden symbol of fame conferred by the Academy of Motion Picture Arts and Sciences, in its present form, has reached full maturity. Long since his first appearance on the scene of glory in Hollywood, his birth, origins and history have become confused in tradition and much elaborated myth.

Oft beset by perplexed inquiries in the years between, Motion Picture Almanac set about research for the purpose of presenting for the industry the truth about Oscar.

Oscar was nameless when he came into the world as an award symbol the year the Academy was founded, 1927, and he remained so for four years, known then just as "the statuette."

The idea for a statuette originated at a meeting of the first board of governors of the Academy. Cedric Gibbons, then executive art director for Metro-Goldwyn-Mayer, after hearing discussions of certificates, scrolls, medals and plaques, urged that the awards should be represented by a figure of dignity and individual character which recipients would be proud to display. While he talked he sketched a figure and design. It was Oscar's first picture. The drawing was adopted and sent for execution in the round to George Stanley, a Los Angeles sculptor. From his hands came the Oscar who has been growing in fame ever since.

The golden figure was still without a name that day in 1931 when Mrs. Margaret Herrick, former executive secretary of the Academy, reported for her first day's work as librarian. A copy of the statuette stood on an executive's desk and she was formally introduced to it as the foremost member of the organization.

She regarded it a moment. "He reminds me," she observed, "of my Uncle Oscar."

Nearby sat a newspaper columnist and the next day his syndicated copy contained the line "Employees have affectionately dubbed their famous statuette 'Oscar'." From that day on he has been Oscar.

On the other hand, two-time Oscar winner Bette Davis has long maintained that it was she who named the statuette after her first husband, Harmon Oscar Nelson Jr.

On May 6, 1929, first year awards were presented—for achievements of 1927–28—eleven "Oscars" were presented by the Academy. Since that day the number of statuettes given the annual "choice few" has increased. During the intervening years a total of several hundred golden knights have gone to persons contributing "best achievements" in motion pictures.

The trophy is fully protected by copyright and is produced by only one manufacturer, licensed by the Academy. Use of the statuette or reproduction of it in any manner is prohibited, without written permission of the Academy.

VITAL STATISTICS

- **NAME:** Oscar.
- **DATE OF BIRTH:** January 1929.
- **CURRENT COST:** Approximately $350.
- **CONTENTS:** Britannia metal, copper plate, nickel plate, gold plate. (Except from 1942 to 1944, when Oscar was made of plaster. Winners were later presented with the real thing.)
- **HEIGHT:** 13½ inches (including pedestal).
- **WEIGHT:** 8½ pounds (including pedestal).
- **CREATOR:** MGM art director Cedric Gibbons, who went on to win 11 of the statuettes he designed.
- **MAKER:** R.S. Owens, Chicago, Ill.
- **MEMORABLE ERROR:** The only engraving mistake ever made was on the 1938 Best Actor statuette given to Spencer Tracy for "Boy's Town." The citation read, "Best Actor: Dick Tracy."
- **INTERESTING FACTS:** The Academy holds all the rights on the statue and recipients pledge never to sell their statuette except back to the Academy.

Between 1936 and 1939 members of the Board of the Academy had to pay for Oscar statues out of their own pockets as the Academy was short of funds.

Supporting players did not receive full statues until 1943. Instead they won plaques.

The only Oscar winner ever to present an Oscar to himself was Irving Berlin, when in 1942 he gave himself the Best Song award for "White Christmas."

- **MOST NOMINATED FILM:** All About Eve (1950), 14 (won 5).
- **MOST AWARDED FILM:** Ben-Hur (1959), 11.
- **MOST AWARDED PERSON:** Walt Disney, 30 (24 regular and 6 honorary).
- **MOST AWARDED PERFORMER:** Katharine Hepburn (4 best actress awards: Morning Glory, Guess Who's Coming to Dinner, The Lion in Winter, On Golden Pond). Also most nominated performer (12).
- **BEST PICTURE FACTS:** Only silent film to win Oscar: Wings (1927–28); First sound film to win: The Broadway Melody (1928–29); First color film to win: Gone With the Wind (1939); First sequel to win: The Godfather Part II (1974); First remake to win: Mutiny on the Bounty (1935); First non-Hollywood film to win: Hamlet (1948). Only films to win top 5 awards in single year (picture, director, actor, actress, screenplay): It Happened One Night (1934), One Flew Over the Cuckoo's Nest (1975) and The Silence of the Lambs (1991).
- **CEREMONY DATA: First presentation,** May 16, 1929, awards handed out at banquet at Hollywood Roosevelt Hotel. **First presentation in theater setting** (Grauman's Chinese) March 2, 1944. **First radio broadcast** of ceremony: April 3, 1930 over KNX Radio (1-hour). **First telecast:** March 19, 1953 over NBC-TV from Pantages in Hollywood, and NBC Theater in NY. **First color telecast:** April 18, 1966 over ABC-TV from Santa Monica Civic Auditorium.
- **ACTOR FACTS:** Oscar Ties: Best Actor: 1931–32: Wallace Beery (The Champ) tied with Fredric March (Dr. Jekyll and Mr. Hyde); Best Actress: 1968: Katharine Hepburn (The Lion in Winter) and Barbra Streisand (Funny Girl). Only actor to direct himself into an Academy Award: Laurence Olivier (1948, Hamlet); First person nominated as producer, director, actor and screenwriter: Orson Welles (1941, Citizen Kane). First posthumous acting winner: Peter Finch (1976, Network)
- **STRANGE REMARKS:** MGM screenwriter Frances Marion, (The Champ), viewing the very first Oscar statuette in 1929, said it was a "perfect symbol of the picture business: a powerful athletic body clutching a gleaming sword, with half his head, that part which held his brains, completely sliced off."

COMPLETE ACADEMY AWARDS WINNERS 1927-1991

Productions, players, directors and craftspersons named for superior merit by the Academy of Motion Picture Arts and Sciences, from inception of the awards through 1991.

1927/1928

Production: Wings, Paramount.
Actor: Emil Jannings in The Way Of All Flesh, and The Last Command, Paramount.
Actress: Janet Gaynor in Seventh Heaven, Street Angel, and Sunrise, Fox.
Direction: Frank Borzage, Seventh Heaven.
Direction (comedy): Lewis Milestone, Two Arabian Knights, United Artists.
Writing (original story): Ben Hecht, Underworld, Paramount.
Writing (adaptation): Benjamin Glazer, Seventh Heaven.
Writing (title): Joseph Farnham, Fair Co-Ed, Laugh, Clown, Laugh, and Telling The World, Metro-Goldwyn-Mayer.
Cinematography: Charles Rosher, Karl Struss, Sunrise.
Art Direction: William Cameron Menzies, The Dove, and The Tempest, United Artists.
Engineering Effects: Roy Pomeroy, Wings.
Artistic Quality of Production: Sunrise.
SPECIAL AWARDS
Warner Brothers, for producing The Jazz Singer, the pioneer talking picture, which has revolutionized the industry.
Charles Chaplin, for versatility and genius in writing, acting, directing and producing The Circus.

1928/1929

Production: Broadway Melody, Metro-Goldwyn-Mayer.
Actor: Warner Baxter in In Old Arizona, Fox.
Actress: Mary Pickford in Coquette, United Artists.
Direction: Frank Lloyd, The Divine Lady, First National.
Writing (achievement): Hans Kraly, The Patriot, Paramount.
Cinematography: Clyde De Vinna, White Shadows In The South Seas, Metro-Goldwyn-Mayer.
Art Direction: Cedric Gibbons, The Bridge Of San Luis Rey, Metro-Goldwyn-Mayer.

1929/1930

Production: All Quiet On The Western Front, Universal.
Actor: George Arliss in Disraeli, Warner Brothers.
Actress: Norma Shearer in The Divorcée, Metro-Goldwyn-Mayer.
Direction: Lewis Milestone, All Quiet On The Western Front.
Writing (achievement): Frances Marion, The Big House, Metro-Goldwyn-Mayer.
Cinematography: Willard Van Der Veer, Joseph T. Rucker, With Byrd At The South Pole, Paramount.
Art Direction: Herman Rosse, King Of Jazz, Universal.
Sound Recording: Douglas Shearer, The Big House.

1930/1931

Production: Cimarron, RKO Radio.
Actor: Lionel Barrymore in A Free Soul, Metro-Goldwyn-Mayer.
Actress: Marie Dressler in Min And Bill, Metro-Goldwyn-Mayer.
Direction: Norman Taurog, Skippy, Paramount.
Writing (original story): John Monk Saunders, The Dawn Patrol, Warner Brothers.
Writing (adaptation): Howard Estabrook, Cimarron.
Cinematography: Floyd Crosby, Tabu, Paramount.
Art Direction: Max Ree, Cimarron.
Sound Recording: Paramount Studio Sound Department.

1931/1932

Production: Grand Hotel, Metro-Goldwyn-Mayer.
Actor: Fredric March in Dr. Jekyll And Mr. Hyde, Paramount. Wallace Beery in The Champ, Metro-Goldwyn-Mayer.
Actress: Helen Hayes in The Sin Of Madelon Claudet, Metro-Goldwyn-Mayer.
Direction: Frank Borzage, Bad Girl, Fox.
Writing (original story): Frances Marion, The Champ.
Writing (adaptation): Edwin Burke, Bad Girl.

Cinematography: Lee Garmes, Shanghai Express, Paramount.
Art Direction: Gordon Wiles, Transatlantic, Fox.
Sound Recording: Paramount Studio Sound Department.
Short Subjects (cartoon): Flowers And Trees, Disney, United Artists.
Short Subjects (comedy): The Music Box, Roach, Metro-Goldwyn-Mayer.
Short Subjects (novelty): Wrestling Swordfish, Sennett-Educational.
SPECIAL AWARD
Walt Disney, for the creation of Mickey Mouse.

1932/1933

Production: Calvacade, Fox.
Actor: Charles Laughton in The Private Life of Henry VIII, London Films, United Artists.
Actress: Katharine Hepburn in Morning Glory, RKO Radio.
Direction: Frank Lloyd, Calvacade.
Writing (original story): Robert Lord, One Way Passage, Warner Brothers.
Writing (adaptation): Sarah Y. Mason, Victor Heerman, Little Women, RKO Radio.
Cinematography: Charles Bryant Lang, Jr., A Farewell To Arms, Paramount.
Art Direction: William S. Darling, Calvacade.
Sound Recording: Harold C. Lewis, A Farewell To Arms.
Assistant Director: Charles Dorian, Metro-Goldwyn-Mayer; Gordon Hollingshead, Warner Brothers; Dewey Starkey, RKO Radio; Charles Barton, Paramount; Scott Beal, Universal; Fred Fox, United Artists; William Tummel, Fox.
Short Subjects (cartoon): The Three Little Pigs, Disney, United Artists.
Short Subjects (comedy): So This Is Harris, RKO Radio.
Short Subjects (novelty): Krakatoa, Educational

1934

Production: It Happened One Night, Columbia.
Actor: Clark Gable in It Happened One Night.
Actress: Claudette Colbert in It Happened One Night.
Direction: Frank Capra, It Happened One Night.
Writing (original story): Arthur Caesar, Manhattan Melodrama, Metro-Goldwyn-Mayer.
Writing (adaptation): Robert Riskin, It Happened One Night.
Cinematography: Victor Milner, Cleopatra, Paramount.
Art Direction: Cedric Gibbons, Frederic Hope, The Merry Widow, Metro-Goldwyn-Mayer.
Sound Recording: Paul Neal, One Night Of Love, Columbia.
Film Editing: Conrad Nevrig, Eskimo, Metro-Goldwyn-Mayer.
Assistant Director: John Waters, Viva Villa, Metro-Goldwyn-Mayer.
Music (score): Louis Silvers, One Night Of Love.
Music (song): Herb Magidson (lyrics), Con Conrad (music), The Continental from The Gay Divorcee, RKO Radio
Short Subjects (cartoon): The Tortoise And The Hare, Disney.
Short Subjects (comedy): La Cucaracha, RKO Radio.
Short Subjects (novelty): City Of Wax, Educational.
SPECIAL AWARD
Shirley Temple, presented in grateful recognition of her outstanding contribution to screen entertainment during the year 1934.

1935

Production: Mutiny On The Bounty, Metro-Goldwyn-Mayer.
Actor: Victor McLaglen in The Informer, RKO Radio.
Actress: Bette Davis in Dangerous, Warner Brothers.
Direction: John Ford, The Informer.
Writing (original story): Ben Hecht, Charles MacArthur, The Scoundrel, Paramount.
Writing (best written screenplay): Dudley Nichols, The Informer.
Cinematography: Hal Mohr, A Midsummer Night's Dream, Warner Brothers.
Art Direction: Richard Day, The Dark Angel, Goldwyn, United Artists.
Sound Recording: William Steinkampf, Naughty Marietta, Metro-Goldwyn-Mayer.
Film Editing: Ralph Dawson, A Midsummer Night's Dream.
Assistant Director: Clem Beauchamp, Paul Wing, Lives Of A Bengal Lancer, Paramount.
Music (score): Max Steiner, The Informer.
Music (song): Al Dubin (lyrics), Harry Warren (music), Lullaby Of Broadway from Golddiggers Of 1935, Warner Brothers.
Dance Direction: Dave Gould, I've Got A Feeling You're Falling number from Broadway Melody Of 1936, Metro-Goldwyn-Mayer. Straw Hat number from Folies Bergere, 20th Century, United Artists.
Short Subjects (cartoon): Three Orphan Kittens, Disney, United Artists.
Short Subjects (comedy): How To Sleep, Metro-Goldwyn-Mayer.

Short Subjects (novelty): Wings Over Mt. Everest, Gaumont British, Educational.
SPECIAL AWARD
David Wark Griffith for his distinguished creative achievements as director and producer and his invaluable initiative and lasting contributions to the progress of the motion picture arts.

1936

Production: The Great Ziegfeld, Metro-Goldwyn-Mayer.
Actor: Paul Muni in The Story Of Louis Pasteur, Warner Brothers.
Actress: Luise Rainer in The Great Ziegfeld.
Supporting Actor: Walter Brennan in Come And Get It, Goldwyn, United Artists.
Supporting Actress: Gale Sondergaard in Anthony Adverse, Warner Brothers.
Direction: Frank Capra, Mr. Deeds Goes To Town, Columbia.
Writing (original story): Pierre Collings, Sheridan Gibney, The Story Of Louis Pasteur.
Writing (best written screenplay): Pierre Collings, Sheridan Gibney, The Story Of Louis Pasteur.
Cinematography: Tony Gaudio, Anthony Adverse.
Art Direction: Richard Day, Dodsworth, Goldwyn, United Artists.
Sound Recording: Douglas Shearer, San Francisco, Metro-Goldwyn-Mayer.
Film Editing: Ralph Dawson, Anthony Adverse.
Assistant Director: Jack Sullivan, The Charge Of The Light Brigade, Warner Brothers.
Music (score): Leo Forbstein, Anthony Adverse.
Music (song): Dorothy Fields (lyrics), Jerome Kern (music), The Way You Look Tonight from Swing Time, RKO Radio.
Dance Direction: Seymour Felix, A Pretty Girl Is Like A Melody number from The Great Ziegfeld.
Short Subjects (cartoon): Country Cousin, Disney, United Artists.
Short Subjects (color): Give Me Liberty, Warner Brothers.
Short Subjects (1-reel): Bored Of Education, Roach, Metro-Goldwyn-Mayer.
Short Subjects (2-reel): The Public Pays, Metro-Goldwyn-Mayer.
SPECIAL AWARDS
The March Of Time, for its significance to motion pictures and for having revolutionized one of the most important branches of the industry—the newsreel.
W. Howard Greene and Harold Rosson, for the color cinematography of the Selznick International production, The Garden Of Allah.

1937

Production: The Life Of Emile Zola, Warner Brothers.
Actor: Spencer Tracy in Captains Courageous, Metro-Goldwyn-Mayer.
Actress: Luise Rainer in The Good Earth, Metro-Goldwyn-Mayer.
Supporting Actor: Joseph Schildkraut in The Life Of Emile Zola.
Supporting Actress: Alice Brady in In Old Chicago, 20th Century Fox.
Direction: Leo McCarey, The Awful Truth, Columbia.
Writing (original story): Robert Carson, William A. Wellman, A Star Is Born, Selznick, United Artists.
Writing (best written screenplay): Norman Reilly Raine, Heinz Herald, Geza Herczeg, The Life Of Emile Zola.
Cinematography: Karl Freund, The Good Earth.
Art Direction: Stephen Goosson, Lost Horizon, Columbia.
Sound Recording: Thomas T. Moulton, Hurricane, Goldwyn, United Artists.
Film Editing: Gene Milford, Gene Havlick, Lost Horizon.
Assistant Director: Robert Webb, In Old Chicago.
Music (score): Charles Previn, One Hundred Men And A Girl, Universal.
Music (song): Harry Owens (lyrics and music), Sweet Leilani from Waikiki Wedding, Paramount.
Dance Direction: Hermes Pan, Fun House number from A Damsel in Distress, RKO Radio.
Short Subjects (cartoon): The Old Mill, Disney, RKO Radio.
Short Subjects (color): Penny Wisdom, Metro-Goldwyn-Mayer.
Short Subjects (1-reel): Private Life Of The Gannets, Educational.
Short Subjects (2-reel): Torture Money, Metro-Goldwyn-Mayer.
Irving G. Thalberg Memorial Award: Darryl F. Zanuck.
SPECIAL AWARDS
The Museum of Modern Art Film Library, for making available to the public the means of studying the development of the motion picture as one of the major arts.
Mack Sennett, for his lasting contribution to the comedy technique of the screen.
Edgar Bergen, for his outstanding comedy creation, Charlie McCarthy.
W. Howard Greene, for the color cinematography of A Star Is Born.

1938

Production: You Can't Take It With You, Columbia.
Actor: Spencer Tracy in Boys' Town, Metro-Goldwyn-Mayer.
Actress: Bette Davis in Jezebel, Warner Brothers.
Supporting Actor: Walter Brennan in Kentucky, 20th Century-Fox.
Supporting Actress: Fay Bainter in Jezebel.
Direction: Frank Capra, You Can't Take It With You.
Writing (original story): Dore Schary, Eleanore Griffin, Boys' Town.
Writing (adaptation): W.P. Lipscomb, Cecil Lewis, Ian Dalrymple, Pygmalion, Metro-Goldwyn-Mayer.
Writing (best written screenplay): George Bernard Shaw, Pygmalion.
Cinematography: Joseph Ruttenberg, The Great Waltz, Metro-Goldwyn-Mayer.
Art Direction: Carl Weyl, The Adventures Of Robin Hood, Warner Brothers.
Sound Recording: Thomas T. Moulton, The Cowboy And The Lady, Goldwyn, United Artists.
Film Editing: Ralph Dawson, The Adventures Of Robin Hood.
Music (best score): Alfred Newman, Alexander's Ragtime Band, 20th Century-Fox.
Music (original score): Erich Wolfgang Korngold, The Adventures Of Robin Hood.
Music (song): Leo Robin (lyrics), Ralph Rainger (music), Thanks For The Memory from Big Broadcast Of 1938, Paramount.
Short Subjects (cartoon): Ferdinand the Bull, Disney, RKO Radio.
Short Subjects (1-reel): That Mothers Might Live, Metro-Goldwyn-Mayer.
Short Subjects (2-reel): Declaration of Independence, Warner Brothers.
Irving G. Thalberg Memorial Award: Hal B. Wallis.
SPECIAL AWARDS
Deanna Durbin and Mickey Rooney, for their significant contribution in bringing to the screen the spirit and personification of youth, and as juvenile players setting a high standard of ability and achievement.
Harry M. Warner, in recognition of patriotic service in the production of historical short subjects presenting significant episodes in the early struggle of the American people for liberty.
Walt Disney, for Snow White And The Seven Dwarfs, recognized as a significant screen innovation which has charmed millions and pioneered a great new entertainment field for the motion picture cartoon.

1939

Production: Gone With The Wind, Selznick.
Actor: Robert Donat in Goodbye, Mr. Chips, Metro-Goldwyn-Mayer.
Actress: Vivien Leigh in Gone With The Wind.
Supporting Actor: Thomas Mitchell in Stagecoach, Wanger, United Artists.
Supporting Actress: Hattie McDaniel in Gone With The Wind.
Direction: Victor Fleming, Gone With The Wind.
Writing (original story): Lewis R. Foster, Mr. Smith Goes To Washington, Columbia.
Writing (best written screenplay): Sidney Howard, Gone With The Wind.
Cinematography (black-and-white): Gregg Toland, Wuthering Heights, Goldwyn, United Artists.
Cinematography (color): Ernest Haller, Ray Rennahan, Gone With The Wind.
Art Direction: Lyle Wheeler, Gone With The Wind.
Sound Recording: Bernard B. Brown, When Tomorrow Comes, Universal.
Film Editing: Hal C. Kern, James E. Newcom, Gone With The Wind.
Music (best score): Richard Hageman, Franke Harling, John Leipold, Leo Shuken, Stagecoach.
Music (original score): Herbert Stothart, The Wizard Of Oz, Metro-Goldwyn-Mayer.
Music (song): E. Y. Harburg (lyrics), Harold Arlen (music), Over The Rainbow from The Wizard Of Oz.
Short Subjects (cartoon): The Ugly Duckling, Disney RKO Radio.
Short Subjects (1-reel): Busy Little Bears, Paramount.
Short Subjects (2-reel): Sons Of Liberty, Warner Brothers.
Irving G. Thalberg Memorial Award: David O. Selznick.
SPECIAL AWARDS
Douglas Fairbanks (Commemorative Award), recognizing the unique and outstanding contribution of Douglas Fairbanks, first President of the Academy, to the international development of the motion picture.
The Technical Company, for its contributions in successfully bringing three-color feature production to the screen.
Motion Picture Relief Fund, acknowledging the outstanding services to the industry during the past year of the Motion Picture Relief Fund and its progressive leadership.
Judy Garland, for her outstanding performance as a screen juvenile during the past year.

William Cameron Menzies, for outstanding achievement in the use of color for the enhancement of dramatic mood in the production of Gone With The Wind.

1940

Production: Rebecca, Selznick, United Artists
Actor: James Stewart in The Philadelphia Story, Metro-Goldwyn-Mayer.
Actress: Ginger Rogers in Kitty Foyle, RKO Radio.
Supporting Actor: Walter Brennan in The Westerner, Goldwyn, United Artists.
Supporting Actress: Jane Darwell in The Grapes Of Wrath, 20th Century-Fox.
Direction: John Ford, The Grapes Of Wrath.
Writing (original story): Benjamin Glazer, John S. Toldy, Arise, My Love, Paramount.
Writing (original screenplay): Preston Sturges, The Great McGinty, Paramount.
Writing (best written screenplay): Donald Ogden Stewart, The Philadelphia Story.
Cinematography (black-and-white): George Barnes, Rebecca.
Cinematography (color): George Perrinal, The Thief Of Bagdad, Korda, United Artists.
Art Direction (black-and-white): Cedric Gibbons, Paul Groesse, Pride And Prejudice, Metro-Goldwyn-Mayer.
Art Direction (color): Vincent Korda, The Thief Of Bagdad.
Sound Recording: Douglas Shearer, Strike Up The Band, Metro-Goldwyn-Mayer.
Film Editing: Anne Bauchens, North West Mounted Police, Paramount.
Special Effects: Lawrence Butler (photographic), Jack Whitney (sound), The Thief Of Bagdad.
Music (best score): Alfred Newman, Tin Pan Alley, 20th Century-Fox.
Music (original score): Leigh Harline, Paul J. Smith, Ned Washington, Pinocchio, Disney, RKO Radio.
Music (song): Ned Washington (lyrics), Leigh Harline (music), When You Wish Upon A Star, from Pinocchio.
Short Subjects (cartoon): The Milky Way, Metro-Goldwyn-Mayer.
Short Subjects (1-reel): Quicker 'N A Wink, Metro-Goldwyn-Mayer.
Short Subjects (2-reel): Teddy, The Rough Rider, Warner Brothers.
SPECIAL AWARDS
Bob Hope, in recognition of his unselfish services to the Motion Picture Industry.
Colonel Nathan Levinson, for his outstanding services to the industry and the Army which made possible the present efficient mobilization of the Motion Picture Industry facilities for the production of Army training films.

1941

Production: How Green Was My Valley, 20th Century-Fox.
Actor: Gary Cooper in Sergeant York, Warner Brothers.
Actress: Joan Fontaine in Suspicion, RKO Radio.
Supporting Actor: Donald Crisp in How Green Was My Valley.
Supporting Actress: Mary Astor in The Great Lie, Warner Brothers.
Direction: John Ford, How Green Was My Valley.
Writing (original story): Harry Segall, Here Comes Mr. Jordan, Columbia.
Writing (original screenplay): Herman J. Mankiewicz, Orson Welles, Citizen Kane, Mercury, RKO Radio.
Writing (best written screenplay): Sidney Buchman, Seton I. Miller, Here Comes Mr. Jordan.
Cinematography (black-and-white): Arthur Miller, How Green Was My Valley.
Cinematography (color): Ernest Palmer, Ray Rennahan, Blood And Sand, 20th Century-Fox.
Art Direction (black-and-white): Richard Day, Nathan Juran, How Green Was My Valley.
Art Direction (color): Cedric Gibbons, Urie McCleary, Blossoms In The Dust, Metro-Goldwyn-Mayer.
Interior Decorator (black-and-white): Thomas Little, How Green Was My Valley.
Interior Decoration (color): Edwin B. Willis, Blossoms In The Dust.
Sound Recording: Jack Whitney (general service), That Hamilton Woman, Korda, United Artists.
Film Editing: William Holmes, Sergeant York.
Special Effects: Farclot Edouart, Gordon Jennings (photographic), Louis Mesenkop (sound), I Wanted Wings, Paramount.
Music (scoring dramatic picture): Bernard Herrmann, All That Money Can Buy, RKO Radio.
Music (scoring musical picture): Frank Churchill, Oliver Wallace, Dumbo, Disney, RKO Radio.
Music (song): Oscar Hammerstein II (lyrics), Jerome Kern (music), The Last Time I Saw Paris from Lady Be Good, Metro-Goldwyn-Mayer.
Short Subjects (cartoon): Lend A Paw, Disney, RKO Radio.
Short Subjects (1-reel): Of Pups And Puzzles, Metro-Goldwyn-Mayer.

Short Subjects (2-reel): Main Street On The March, Metro-Goldwyn-Mayer.
Irving G. Thalberg Memorial Award: Walt Disney.
SPECIAL AWARDS
Churchill's Island, Canadian National Film Board, citation for distinctive achievement.
Rey Scott, for his extraordinary achievement in producing Kukan. The British Ministry of Information, for Target For Tonight.
Leopold Stokowski and his associates, for their unique achievement in the creation of a new form of visualized music in Fantasia.
Walt Disney, William Garity, John N. A. Hawkins and the RCA Manufacturing Company, for their outstanding contribution to the advancement of the use of sound in motion pictures through the production of Fantasia.

1942

Production: Mrs. Miniver, Metro-Goldwyn-Mayer.
Actor: James Cagney in Yankee Doodle Dandy, Warner Brothers.
Actress: Greer Garson in Mrs. Miniver.
Supporting Actor: Van Heflin in Johnny Eager, Metro-Goldwyn-Mayer.
Supporting Actress: Teresa Wright in Mrs. Miniver.
Direction: William Wyler, Mrs. Miniver.
Writing (original story): Emeric Pressburger, The Invaders, Ortus, Columbia.
Writing (original screenplay): Ring Lardner, Jr., Michael Kanin, Woman Of The Year, Metro-Goldwyn-Mayer.
Writing (best written screenplay): Arthur Wimperis, George Froeschel, James Hilton, Claudine West, Mrs. Miniver.
Cinematography (black-and-white): Joseph Ruttenberg, Mrs. Miniver.
Cinematography (color): Leon Shamroy, The Black Swan, 20th Century-Fox.
Art Direction (black-and-white): Richard Day, Joseph Wright, This Above All, 20th Century-Fox.
Art Direction (color): Richard Day, Joseph Wright, My Gal Sal, 20th Century-Fox.
Interior Decoration (black-and-white): Thomas Little, This Above All.
Interior Decoration (color): Thomas Little, My Gal Sal.
Sound Recording: Nathan Levinson, Yankee Doodle Dandy.
Film Editing: Daniel Mandell, The Pride Of The Yankees, Goldwyn, RKO Radio.
Special Effects: Gordon Jennings, Farciot Edouart, William L. Pereira (photographic), Louis Mesenkop (sound), Reap The Wild Wind, Paramount.
Music (scoring dramatic or comedy picture): Max Steiner, Now Voyager, Warner Brothers.
Music (scoring musical picture): Ray Heindorf, Heinz Roemheld, Yankee Doodle Dandy.
Music (song): Irving Berlin (lyrics and music), White Christmas from Holiday Inn, Paramount.
Short Subjects (cartoon): Der Fuehrer's Face, Disney, RKO Radio.
Short Subjects (1-reel): Speaking Of Animals And Their Families, Paramount.
Short Subjects (2-reel): Beyond The Line Of Duty, Warner Brothers.
Documentary (short subject): Kokoda Front Line, Australian News Information Bureau. Battle of Midway, U.S. Navy, 20th Century-Fox. Moscow Strikes Back, Artkino.
Documentary (feature length): Prelude To War, U.S. Army Special Services.
Irving G. Thalberg Memorial Award: Sidney Franklin.
SPECIAL AWARDS
Charles Boyer for his progressive cultural achievement in establishing the French Research Foundation in Los Angeles.
Noel Coward for his outstanding production achievement in In Which We Serve.
Metro-Goldwyn-Mayer Studio, for its achievement in representing the American Way of Life in the production of the Andy Hardy series of films.

1943

Production: Casablanca, Warner Brothers.
Actor: Paul Lukas in Watch On The Rhine, Warner Brothers.
Actress: Jennifer Jones in The Song Of Bernadette, 20th Century Fox.
Supporting Actor: Charles Coburn in The More The Merrier, Columbia.
Supporting Actress: Katina Paxinou in For Whom The Bell Tolls, Paramount.
Direction: Michael Curtiz, Casablanca.
Writing (original story): William Saroyan, The Human Comedy, Metro-Goldwyn-Mayer.
Writing (original screenplay): Norman Krasna, Princess O'Rourke, Warner Brothers.
Writing (best written screenplay): Julius J. Epstein, Philip G. Epstein, Howard Koch, Casablanca.
Cinematography (black-and-white): Arthur Miller, The Song Of Bernadette.

Cinematography (color): Hal Mohr, W. Howard Greene, The Phantom Of The Opera, Universal.
Art Direction (black-and-white): James Basevi, William Darling, The Song Of Bernadette.
Art Direction (color): Alexander Golitzen, John B. Goodman, The Phantom Of The Opera.
Interior Decoration (black-and-white): Thomas Little, The Song Of Bernadette.
Interior Decoration (color): R.A. Gausman, Ira Webb, The Phantom Of The Opera.
Sound Recording: Stephen Dunn, This Land Is Mine, RKO Radio.
Film Editing: George Amy, Air Force, Warner Brothers.
Special Effects: Fred Sersen (photographic), Roger Herman (sound), Crash Dive, 20th Century-Fox.
Music (scoring dramatic or comedy picture): Alfred Newman, The Song Of Bernadette.
Music (scoring musical picture): Ray Heindorf, This Is The Army, Warner Brothers.
Music (song): Mack Gordon (lyrics), Harry Warren (music), You'll Never Know from Hello, Frisco, Hello, 20th Century-Fox.
Short Subjects (cartoon): Yankee Doodle Mouse, Metro-Goldwyn-Mayer.
Short Subjects (1-reel): Amphibious Fighters, Paramount.
Short Subjects (2-reel): Heavenly Music, Metro-Goldwyn-Mayer.
Documentary (short subject): December 7th, U.S. Navy.
Documentary (feature length): Desert Victory, British Ministry of Information.
Irving G. Thalberg Memorial Award: Hal B. Wallis.
SPECIAL AWARD
George Pal, for the development of novel methods and techniques in the production of short subjects known as Puppetoons.

1944

Production: Going My Way, Paramount.
Actor: Bing Crosby in Going My Way.
Actress: Ingrid Bergman in Gaslight, Metro-Goldwyn-Mayer.
Supporting Actor: Barry Fitzgerald in Going My Way.
Supporting Actress: Ethel Barrymore in None But the Lonely Heart, RKO Radio.
Direction: Leo McCarey, Going My Way.
Writing (original story): Leo McCarey, Going My Way.
Writing (original screenplay): Lamar Trotti, Wilson, 20th Century-Fox.
Writing (best written screenplay): Frank Butler, Frank Cavett, Going My Way.
Cinematography (black-and-white): Joseph La Shelle, Laura, 20th Century-Fox.
Cinematography (color): Leon Shamroy, Wilson.
Art Direction (black-and-white): Cedric Gibbons, William Ferrari, Gaslight.
Art Direction (color): Wiard Ihnen, Wilson.
Interior Decoration (black-and-white): Edwin B. Willis, Paul Huldschinsky, Gaslight.
Interior Decoration (color): Thomas Little, Wilson.
Sound Recording: E. H. Hansen, Wilson.
Film Editing: Barbara McLean, Wilson.
Special Effects: A. Arnold Gillespie, Donald Jahraus, Warren Newcombe (photographic), Douglas Shearer (sound), Thirty Seconds Over Tokyo, Metro-Goldwyn-Mayer.
Music (scoring dramatic or comedy picture): Max Steiner, Since You Went Away, Selznick, United Artists.
Music (scoring musical picture): Morris Stoloff, Carmen Dragon, Cover Girl, Columbia.
Music (song): Johnny Burke (lyrics), James Van Heusen (music), Swinging On A Star from Going My Way.
Short Subjects (cartoon): Mouse Trouble, Metro-Goldwyn-Mayer.
Short Subjects (1-reel): Who's Who In Animal Land, Paramount.
Short Subjects (2-reel): I Won't Play, Warner Brothers.
Documentary (short subject): With The Marines At Tarawa, U.S. Marine Corps.
Documentary (feature length): The Fighting Lady, U.S. Navy, 20th Century-Fox.
Irving G. Thalberg Memorial Award: Darryl F. Zanuck.
SPECIAL AWARDS
Margaret O'Brien, outstanding child actress of 1944.
Bob Hope, for his many services to the Academy, a Life Membership in the Academy of Motion Picture Arts and Sciences.

1945

Production: The Lost Weekend, Paramount.
Actor: Ray Milland in The Lost Weekend.
Actress: Joan Crawford in Mildred Pierce, Warner Brothers.
Supporting Actor: James Dunn in A Tree Grows In Brooklyn, 20th Century-Fox.
Supporting Actress: Anne Revere in National Velvet, Metro-Goldwyn-Mayer.
Direction: Billy Wilder, The Lost Weekend.
Writing (original story): Charles G. Booth, The House On 92nd Street, 20th Century-Fox.
Writing (original screenplay): Richard Schweizer, Marie-Louise, Praesens Films.

Writing (best written screenplay): Charles Brackett, Billy Wilder, The Lost Weekend.
Cinematography (black-and-white): Harry Stradling, The Picture Of Dorian Gray, Metro-Goldwyn-Mayer.
Cinematography (color): Leon Shamroy, Leave Her To Heaven, 20th Century-Fox.
Art Direction (black-and-white): Wiard Ihnen, Blood On The Sun, Cagney, United Artists.
Art Direction (color): Hans Dreier, Ernst Fegte, Frenchman's Creek, Paramount.
Interior Decoration (black-and-white): A. Roland Fields, Blood On The Sun.
Interior Decoration (color): Sam Comer, Frenchman's Creek.
Sound Recording: Stephen Dunn, The Bells of St. Mary's, Rainbow, RKO Radio.
Film Editing: Robert J. Kern, National Velvet.
Special Effects: John Fulton (photographic), Arthur W. Johns (sound), Wonder Man, Beverly Productions, RKO Radio.
Music (scoring dramatic or comedy picture): Miklos Rozsa, Spellbound, Selznick, United Artists.
Music (scoring musical picture): Georgie Stoll, Anchors Aweigh, Metro-Goldwyn-Mayer.
Music (song): Oscar Hammerstein II (lyrics), Richard Rodgers (music), It Might As Well Be Spring from State Fair, 20th Century-Fox.
Short Subjects (cartoon): Quiet, Please, Metro-Goldwyn-Mayer.
Short Subjects (1-reel): Stairway To Light, Metro-Goldwyn-Mayer.
Short Subjects (2-reel): Star In The Night, Warner Brothers.
Documentary (short subject): Hitler Lives?, Warner Brothers.
Documentary (feature length): The True Glory, Governments of Great Britain and the United States.
SPECIAL AWARDS
Walter Wanger, for his six years' service as President of the Academy of Motion Picture Arts and Sciences.
Peggy Ann Garner, outstanding child actress of 1945.
The House I Live In, tolerance short subject; produced by Frank Ross and Mervyn LeRoy; directed by Mervyn LeRoy; screenplay by Albert Maltz; song The House I Live In, music by Earl Robinson, lyrics by Lewis Allen; starring Frank Sinatra; released by RKO Radio.

1946

Production: The Best Years Of Our Lives, Goldwyn, RKO Radio.
Actor: Fredric March in The Best Years Of Our Lives.
Actress: Olivia de Havilland in To Each His Own, Paramount.
Supporting Actor: Harold Russell in The Best Years Of Our Lives.
Supporting Actress: Anne Baxter in The Razor's Edge, 20th Century-Fox.
Direction: William Wyler, The Best Years Of Our Lives.
Writing (original story): Clemence Dane, Vacation From Marriage, London Films, Metro-Goldwyn-Mayer.
Writing (original screenplay): Muriel Box, Sydney Box, The Seventh Veil, J. Arthur Rank, Sydney Box, Ortus, Universal.
Writing (best written screenplay): Robert E. Sherwood, The Best Years Of Our Lives.
Cinematography (black-and-white): Arthur Miller, Anna And The King of Siam, 20th Century-Fox.
Cinematography (color): Charles Rosher, Leonard Smith, Arthur Arling, The Yearling, Metro-Goldwyn-Mayer.
Art Direction (black-and-white): Lyle Wheeler, William Darling, Anna And The King Of Siam.
Art Direction (color): Cedric Gibbons, Paul Groesse, The Yearling.
Interior Decoration (black-and-white): Thomas Little, Frank E. Hughes, Anna And The King Of Siam.
Interior Decoration (color): Edwin B. Willis, The Yearling.
Sound Recording: John Livadary, The Jolson Story, Columbia.
Film Editing: Daniel Mandell, The Best Years Of Our Lives.
Special Effects: Thomas Howard (photographic), Blithe Spirit, J. Arthur Rank, Noel Coward, Cineguild, United Artists.
Music (scoring dramatic or comedy picture): Hugo Friedhofer, The Best Years Of Our Lives.
Music (scoring musical picture): Morris Stoloff, The Jolson Story.
Music (song): Johnny Mercer (lyrics), Harry Warren (music), On The Atchison, Topeka And Santa Fe from The Harvey Girls, Metro-Goldwyn-Mayer.
Short Subjects (cartoons): The Cat Concerto, Metro-Goldwyn-Mayer.
Short Subjects (1-reel): Facing Your Danger, Warner Brothers.
Short Subjects (2-reel): A Boy And His Dog, Warner Brothers.
Documentary (short subject): Seeds Of Destiny, U.S. War Department.
Irving G. Thalberg Memorial Award: Samuel Goldwyn.
SPECIAL AWARDS
Laurence Olivier, for his outstanding achievement as actor, producer and director in bringing Henry V to the screen.
Harold Russell, for bringing hope and courage to his fellow veterans through his appearance in The Best Years Of Our Lives.
Ernst Lubitsch, for his distinguished contributions to the art of the motion picture.
Claude Jarman, Jr., outstanding child actor of 1946.

1947

Production: Gentleman's Agreement, 20th Century-Fox.
Actor: Ronald Colman in A Double Life, Kanin Productions, Universal-International.
Actress: Loretta Young in The Farmer's Daughter, RKO Radio.
Supporting Actor: Edmund Gwenn in Miracle On 34th Street, 20th Century-Fox.
Supporting Actress: Celeste Holm in Gentleman's Agreement.
Direction: Elia Kazan, Gentleman's Agreement.
Writing (original story): Valentine Davies, Miracles On 34th Street.
Writing (original screenplay): Sidney Sheldon, The Bachelor And The Bobby Soxer, RKO Radio.
Writing (best written screenplay): George Seaton, Miracle On 34th Street.
Cinematography (black-and-white): Guy Green, Great Expectations, J. Arthur Rank, Universal-International.
Cinematography (color): Jack Cardiff, Black Narcissus, J. Arthur Rank, Universal-International.
Art Direction (black-and-white): John Bryan, Great Expectations.
Art Direction (color): Alfred Junge, Black Narcissus.
Set Decoration (black-and-white): Wilfred Shingleton, Great Expectations.
Set Decoration (color): Alfred Junge, Black Narcissus.
Sound Recording: Gordon Sawyer, The Bishop's Wife, Goldwyn, RKO Radio.
Film Editing: Francis Lyon, Robert Parrish, Body And Soul, Enterprise Productions, United Artists.
Special Effects: A. Arnold Gillespie, Warren Newcombe (visual), Douglas Shearer, Michael Steinore (audible), Green Dolphin Street, Metro-Goldwyn-Mayer.
Music (scoring dramatic or comedy picture): Dr. Miklos Rozsa, A Double Life.
Music (scoring musical picture): Alfred Newman, Mother Wore Tights, 20th Century-Fox.
Music (song): Ray Gilbert (lyrics), Allie Wrubel (music), Zip-A-Dee-Doo-Dah from Song Of The South, Disney, RKO Radio.
Short Subjects (cartoon): Tweetie Pie, Warner Brothers.
Short Subjects (1-reel): Goodbye Miss Turlock, Metro-Goldwyn-Mayer.
Short Subjects (2-reel): Climbing The Matterhorn, Monogram.
Documentary (short subject): First Steps, United Nations Division of Films and Visual Information.
Documentary (feature length): Design For Death, RKO Radio.
SPECIAL AWARDS
James Baskette, for his able and heart-warming characterization of Uncle Remus in Song Of The South, friend and story teller to the children of the world.
Bill And Coo, in which artistry and patience blended in a novel and entertaining use of the medium of motion pictures.
Shoe Shine, for the high quality of this film.
Colonel William N. Selig, Albert E. Smith, Thomas Armat and George K. Spoor, film pioneers.

1948

Production: Hamlet, J. Arthur Rank, Two Cities, Universal-International.
Actor: Laurence Olivier in Hamlet.
Actress: Jane Wyman in Johnny Belinda, Warner Brothers.
Supporting Actor: Walter Huston in The Treasure Of The Sierra Madre, Warner Brothers.
Supporting Actress: Claire Trevor in Key Largo, Warner Brothers.
Direction: John Huston, The Treasure Of The Sierra Madre.
Writing (motion picture story): Richard Schweizer, David Wechsler, The Search, Praesens Film, Metro-Goldwyn-Mayer.
Writing (best written screenplay): John Huston, The Treasure Of The Sierra Madre.
Cinematography (black-and-white): William Daniels, The Naked City, Mark Hellinger Productions, Universal-International.
Cinematography (color): Joseph Valentine, William V. Skall, Winton Hoch, Joan Of Arc, Sierra Pictures, RKO Radio.
Art Direction (black-and-white): Roger K. Furse, Hamlet.
Art Direction (color): Hein Heckroth, The Red Shoes, J. Arthur Rank, Archers, Eagle-Lion.
Set Decoration (black-and-white): Carmen Dillon, Hamlet.
Set Decoration (color): Arthur Lawson, The Red Shoes.
Costume Design (black-and-white): Roger K. Furse, Hamlet.
Costume Design (color): Dorothy Jeakins, Karinska, Joan Of Arc.
Sound Recording: Thomas T. Moulton, The Snake Pit, 20th Century-Fox.
Film Editing: Paul Weatherwax, The Naked City.
Special Effects: Paul Eagler, J. McMillan Johnson, Russell Shearman, Clarence Slifer (visual), Charles Freeman, James G. Stewart (audible), Portrait Of Jennie, The Selznick Studio.
Music (scoring dramatic or comedy picture): Brian Easdale, The Red Shoes.
Music (scoring musical picture): Johnny Green, Roger Edens, Easter Parade, Metro-Goldwyn-Mayer.
Music (song): Jay Livingston, Ray Evans (lyrics and music), Buttons And Bows from The Paleface, Paramount.
Short Subjects (cartoon): The Little Orphan, Metro-Goldwyn-Mayer.

Short Subjects (1-reel): Symphony Of A City, 20th Century-Fox.
Short Subjects (2-reel): Seal Island, Disney, RKO Radio.
Documentary (short subject): Toward Independence, U.S. Army.
Documentary (feature length): The Secret Land, U.S. Navy, Metro-Goldwyn-Mayer.
Irving G. Thalberg Memorial Award: Jerry Wald.
SPECIAL AWARDS
Monsieur Vincent, (French), voted by the Academy Board of Governors as the most outstanding foreign language film released in the United States during 1948. Brandon.
Ivan Jandl, for the outstanding juvenile performance of 1948 in The Search.
Sid Grauman, master showman, who raised the standard of exhibition of motion pictures.
Adolph Zukor, a man who has been called the father of the feature film in America, for his services to the industry over a period of forty years.
Walter Wanger, for distinguished service to the industry in adding to its moral stature in the world community by his production of the picture Joan Of Arc.

1949

Production: All The King's Men, A Robert Rossen Production, Columbia.
Actor: Broderick Crawford in All The King's Men.
Actress: Olivia de Haviland in The Heiress, Paramount.
Supporting Actor: Dean Jagger in Twelve O'Clock High, 20th Century-Fox.
Supporting Actress: Mercedes McCambridge in All The King's Men.
Direction: Joseph L. Mankiewicz, A Letter To Three Wives, 20th Century-Fox.
Writing (motion picture story): Douglas Morrow, The Stratton Story, Metro-Goldwyn-Mayer.
Writing (best written screenplay): Joseph L. Mankiewicz, A Letter To Three Wives.
Writing (story and screenplay): Robert Pirosh, Battleground, Metro-Goldwyn-Mayer.
Cinematography (black-and-white): Paul C. Vogel, Battleground.
Cinematography (color): Winton Hoch, She Wore A Yellow Ribbon, Argosy Pictures Corporation, RKO Radio.
Art Direction (black-and-white): Harry Horner, John Meehan, The Heiress.
Art Direction (color): Cedric Gibbons, Paule Groesse, Little Women, Metro-Goldwyn-Mayer.
Set Decoration (black-and-white): Emile Kuri, The Heiress.
Set Decoration (color): Edwin B. Willis, Jack D. Moore, Little Women.
Costume Design (black-and-white): Edith Head, Gile Steele, The Heiress.
Costume Design (color): Leah Rhodes, Travilla, Marjorie Best, Adventures Of Don Juan, Warner Brothers.
Sound Recording: Thomas T. Moulton, Twelve O'Clock High.
Film Editing: Harry Gerstad, Champion, Screen Plays Corporation, United Artists.
Special Effects: Mighty Joe Young, ARKO Productions, RKO Radio.
Music (scoring dramatic or comedy picture): Aaron Copland, The Heiress.
Music (scoring musical picture): Roger Edens, Lennie Hayton, On The Town, Metro-Goldwyn-Mayer.
Music (song): Frank Loesser (lyrics and music), Baby, It's Cold Outside from Neptune's Daughter, Metro-Goldwyn-Mayer.
Short Subjects (cartoon): For Scent-Imental Reasons, Warner Brothers.
Short Subjects (1-reel): Aquatic House-Party, Paramount.
Short Subjects (2-reel): Van Gogh, Cinema Distributors.
Documentary (short subject): A Chance To Live, March Of Time, 20th Century-Fox. So Much For So Little, Warner Brothers Cartoons, Inc.
Documentary (feature length): Daybreak In Udi, British Information Services.
SPECIAL AWARDS
The Bicycle Thief (Italian), voted by the Academy Board of Governors as the most outstanding foreign language film released in the United States during 1949. Burstyn.
Bobby Driscoll, as the outstanding juvenile actor of 1949.
Fred Astaire, for his unique artistry and his contributions to the technique of musical pictures.
Cecil B. De Mille, distinguished motion picture pioneer, for 37 years of brilliant showmanship.
Jean Hersholt, for distinguished service to the Motion Picture Industry.

1950

Production: All About Eve, 20th Century-Fox.
Actor: Jose Ferrer in Cyrano de Bergerac, A Stanley Kramer Production, United Artists.
Actress: Judy Holliday in Born Yesterday, Columbia.
Supporting Actor: George Sanders in All About Eve.
Supporting Actress: Josephine Hull in Harvey, Universal-International.

Direction: Joseph L. Mankiewicz, All About Eve.
Writing (motion picture story): Edna and Edward Anhalt, Panic In The Streets, 20th Century-Fox.
Writing (screenplay): Joseph L. Mankiewicz, All About Eve.
Supporting Actress: Josephine Hull in Harvey, Universal-International.
Direction: Joseph L. Mankiewicz, All About Eve.
Writing (motion picture story): Edna and Edward Anhalt, Panic In The Streets, 20th Century-Fox.
Writing (screenplay): Joseph L. Mankiewicz, All About Eve.
Writing (story and screenplay): Charles Brackett, Billy Wilder, D. M. Marshman, Jr., Sunset Boulevard, Paramount.
Cinematography (black-and-white): Robert Krasker, The Third Man, Selznick Enterprises in association with London Films., Ltd., Selznick Releasing Organization, Inc.
Cinematography (color): Robert Surtees, King Solomon's Mines, Metro-Goldwyn-Mayer.
Art Direction (black and white): Hans Dreier, John Meehan, Sunset Boulevard.
Cinematography (color): Robert Surtees, King Solomon's Mines, Metro-Goldwyn-Mayer.
Art Direction (black-and-white): Hans Dreier, John Meehan, Sunset Boulevard.
Art Direction (color): Hans Dreier, Walter Tyler, Samson and Delilah, Cecil B. De Mille, Paramount.
Set Decoration (black-and-white): Sam Comer, Ray Moyer, Sunset Boulevard.
Set Decoration (color): Sam Comer, Ray Moyer, Samson and Delilah.
Costume Design (black-and-white): Edith Head, Charles LeMaire, All About Eve.
Costume Design (color): Edith Head, Dorothy Jeakins, Eloise Jenssen, Gile Steel, Gwen Wakeling, Samson And Delilah.
Sound Recording: All About Eve, 20th Century-Fox Sound Department.
Film Editing: Ralph E. Winters, Conrad A. Nervig, King Solomon's Mines.
Special Effects: Destination Moon, George Pal Productions, Eagle Lion Classics.
Music (music score of a dramatic or comedy picture): Franz Waxman, Sunset Boulevard.
Music (scoring musical picture): Adolph Deutsch, Roger Edens, Annie Get Your Gun, Metro-Goldwyn-Mayer.
Music (song): Ray Evans, Jay Livingston (lyrics and music), Mona Lisa from Captain Carey, USA, Paramount.
Short Subjects (cartoon): Gerald McBoing-Boing, United Productions of America, Columbia.
Short Subjects (1-reel): Grandad of Races, Warner Brothers.
Short Subjects (2-reel): In Beaver Valley, Disney, RKO Radio.
Documentary (short subject): Why Korea?, 20th Century-Fox, Movietone.
Documentary (feature length): The Titan: Story Of Michelangelo, Michelangelo Company, Classics Picture, Inc.
Irving G. Thalberg Memorial Award: Darryl F. Zanuck.
SPECIAL AWARDS
The Walls Of Malapaga (Franco-Italian), voted by the Board of Governors as the most outstanding foreign language film released in the United States in 1950.
George Murphy, for his services in interpreting the film industry to the country at large.
Louis B. Mayer, for distinguished service to the motion picture industry.

1951

Production: An American In Paris, Metro-Goldwyn-Mayer.
Actor: Humphrey Bogart in The African Queen, Horizon, United Artists.
Actress: Vivien Leigh in A Streetcar Named Desire, Feldman, Warner Brothers.
Supporting Actor: Karl Malden in A Streetcar Named Desire.
Supporting Actress: Kim Hunter in A Streetcar Named Desire.
Direction: George Stevens, A Place In The Sun, Paramount.
Writing (motion picture story): Paul Dehn, James Bernard, Seven Days To Noon, Boulting Brothers, Mayer, Kingsley, Distinguished Films.
Writing (screenplay): Michael Wilson, Harry Brown, A Place In The Sun.
Writing (story and screenplay): Alan Jay Lerner, An American In Paris.
Cinematography (black-and-white): William C. Mellor, A Place In The Sun.
Cinematography (color): Alfred Gilks, John Alton, An American In Paris.
Art Direction (black-and-white): Richard Day, A Streetcar Named Desire.
Art Direction (color): Cedric Gibbons, Preston Ames, An American In Paris.
Set Decoration (black-and-white): George James Hopkins, A Streetcar Named Desire.
Set Decoration (color): Edwin B. Willis, Keogh Gleason, An American In Paris.
Costume Design (black-and-white): Edith Head, A Place In The Sun.

Costume Design (color): Orry-Kelly, Walter Plunkett, Irene Sharaff, An American In Paris.
Sound Recording: The Great Caruso, Metro-Goldwyn-Mayer Sound Department, Douglas Shearer, Sound Director.
Film Editing: William Hornbeck, A Place In The Sun.
Special Effects: When Worlds Collide, Paramount.
Music (music score of a dramatic or comedy picture): Franz Waxman, A Place In The Sun.
Music (scoring musical picture): Johnny Green, Saul Chaplin, An American In Paris.
Music (song): Johnny Mercer (lyrics), Hoagy Carmichael (music), In The Cool, Cool, Cool Of The Evening from Here Comes The Groom, Paramount.
Short Subjects (cartoon): Two Mouseketeers, Metro-Goldwyn-Mayer.
Short Subjects (1-reel): World Of Kids, Warner Brothers.
Short Subjects (2-reel): Nature's Half Acre, Disney, RKO Radio.
Documentary (short subject): Benjy, Paramount.
Documentary (feature length): Kon-Tiki, Artfilm, RKO Radio.
Irving G. Thalberg Memorial Award: Arthur Freed.
SPECIAL AWARDS
Rashomon (Japanese), voted by the Board of Governors as the most outstanding foreign language film released in the United States during 1951. Harrison.
Gene Kelly, in appreciation of his versatility as an actor, singer, director and dancer, and specifically for his brilliant achievements in the art of choreography on film.

1952

Production: The Greatest Show On Earth, Cecil B. De Mille, Paramount.
Actor: Gary Cooper in High Noon, Kramer, United Artists.
Actress: Shirley Booth in Come Back, Little Sheba, Hal Wallis, Paramount.
Supporting Actor: Anthony Quinn in Viva Zapata!, 20th Century-Fox.
Supporting Actress: Gloria Grahame in The Bad And The Beautiful, Metro-Goldwyn-Mayer.
Direction: John Ford, The Quiet Man, Argosy Pictures, Republic.
Writing (motion picture story): Fredric M. Frank, Theodore St. John, Frank Cavett, The Greatest Show On Earth.
Writing (screenplay): Charles Schnee, The Bad And The Beautiful.
Writing (story and screenplay): T. E. B. Clarke, The Lavender Hill Mob, J. Arthur Rank, Ealing Studios, Universal-International.
Cinematography (black-and-white): Robert Surtees, The Bad And The Beautiful.
Cinematography (color): Winton C. Hoch, Archie Stout, The Quiet Man.
Art Direction (black-and-white): Cedric Gibbons, Edward Carfagno, The Bad And The Beautiful.
Art Direction (color): Paul Sheriff, Moulin Rouge, Romulus Films, United Artists.
Set Decoration (black-and-white): Edwin B. Willis, Keogh Gleason, The Bad And The Beautiful.
Set Decoration (color): Marcel Vertes, Moulin Rouge.
Costume Design (black-and-white): Helen Rose, The Bad And The Beautiful.
Costume Design (color): Marcel Vertes, Moulin Rouge.
Sound Recording: Breaking The Sound Barrier, London Films, United Artists.
Film Editing: Elmo Williams, Harry Gerstad, High Noon.
Special Effects: Plymouth Adventure, Metro-Goldwyn-Mayer.
Music (music score of a dramatic or comedy picture): Dmitri Tiomkin, High Noon.
Music (scoring musical picture): Alfred Newman, With A Song In My Heart, 20th Century-Fox.
Music (song): Ned Washington (lyrics and music), Dmitri Tiomkin (music), High Noon from High Noon.
Short Subjects (cartoon): Johann Mouse, Metro-Goldwyn-Mayer.
Short Subjects (1-reel): Light In The Window, Art Films, 20th Century-Fox.
Short Subjects (2-reel): Water Birds, Disney, RKO Radio.
Documentary (short subject): Neighbours, National Film Board of Canada, Mayer-Kingsly.
Documentary (feature length): The Sea Around Us, RKO Radio.
Irving G. Thalberg Memorial Award: Cecil B. De Mille.
SPECIAL AWARDS
Forbidden Games (French), best foreign language film first released in the United States during 1952. Times.
George Alfred Mitchell, for the design and development of the camera which bears his name and for his continued and dominant presence in the field of cinematography.
Joseph M. Schenck for long and distinguished service to the Motion Picture Industry.
Merian C. Cooper, for his many innovations and contributions to the art of motion pictures.
Harold Lloyd, master comedian and good citizen.
Bob Hope, for his contribution to the laughter of the world.

1953

Production: From Here To Eternity, Columbia.

Actor: William Holden in Stalag 17, Paramount.
Actress: Audrey Hepburn in Roman Holiday, Paramount.
Supporting Actor: Frank Sinatra in From Here To Eternity.
Supporting Actress: Donna Reed in From Here To Eternity.
Direction: Fred Zinnemann, From Here To Eternity.
Writing (motion picture story): Ian McLellan Hunter, Roman Holiday.
Writing (screenplay): Daniel Taradash, From Here To Eternity.
Writing (story and screenplay): Charles Brackett, Walter Reisch, Richard Breen, Titanic, 20th Century-Fox.
Cinematography (black-and-white): Burnett Guffey, From Here To Eternity.
Cinematography (color): Loyal Griggs, Shane, Paramount.
Art Direction (black-and-white): Cedric Gibbons, Edward Carfagno, Julius Caesar, Metro-Goldwyn-Mayer.
Art Direction (color): Lyle Wheeler, George W. Davis, The Robe, 20th Century-Fox.
Set Decoration (black-and-white): Edwin B. Willis, Hugh Hunt, Julius Caesar.
Set Decoration (color): Walter M. Scott, Paul S. Fox, The Robe.
Costume Design (black-and-white): Edith Head, Roman Holiday.
Costume Design (color): Charles Le Maire, Emile Santiago, The Robe.
Sound Recording: From Here To Eternity, Columbia Studio Sound Department, John P. Livadary, Sound Director.
Film Editing: William Lyon, From Here To Eternity.
Special Effects: The War Of The Worlds, Paramount.
Music (music score of a dramatic or comedy picture): Bronislau Kaper, Lili, Metro-Goldwyn-Mayer.
Music (scoring musical picture): Alfred Newman, Call Me Madam, 20th Century-Fox.
Music (song): Paul Francis Webster (lyrics), Sammy Fain (music), Secret Love from Calamity Jane, Warner Brothers.
Short Subjects (cartoon): Toot, Whistle, Plunk And Boom, Disney, Buena Vista.
Short Subjects (1-reel): The Merry Wives Of Windsor Overture, Metro-Goldwyn-Mayer.
Short Subjects (2-reel): Bear Country, Disney, RKO Radio.
Documentary (short subject): The Alaskan Eskimo, Disney, RKO Radio.
Documentary (feature length): The Living Desert, Disney, Buena Vista.
Irving G. Thalberg Memorial Award: George Stevens.
SPECIAL AWARDS
Pete Smith, for his witty and pungent observations on the American scene in the series of Pete Smith Specialties.
The 20th Century-Fox Film Corporation, in recognition of their imagination, showmanship and foresight in introducing the revolutionary process known as CinemaScope.
Joseph I. Breen, for his conscientious, open-minded and dignified management of the Motion Picture Production Code.
Bell and Howell Company, for their pioneering and basic achievements in the advancement of the Motion Picture Industry.

1954

Production: On The Waterfront, Horizon-American, Columbia.
Actor: Marlon Brandon in On The Waterfront.
Actress: Grace Kelly in The Country Girl, Perlberg-Seaton, Paramount.
Supporting Actor: Edmond O'Brien in The Barefoot Contessa, Figaro, United Artists.
Supporting Actress: Eva Marie Saint in On The Waterfront.
Direction: Elia Kazan, On The Waterfront.
Writing (motion picture story): Philip Yordan, Broken Lance, 20th Century-Fox.
Writing (screenplay): George Seaton, The Country Girl.
Writing (story and screenplay): Bud Schulberg, On The Waterfront.
Cinematography (black-and-white): Boris Kaufman, On The Waterfront.
Cinematography (color): Milton Krasner, Three Coins In The Fountain, 20th Century-Fox.
Art Direction (black-and-white): Richard Day, On The Waterfront.
Art Direction (color): John Meehan, 20,000 Leagues Under The Sea, Disney, Buena Vista.
Set Decoration (color): Emile Kuri, 20,000 Leagues Under The Sea.
Costume Design (black-and-white): Edith Head, Sabrina, Paramount.
Costume Design (color): Sanzo Wada, Gate Of Hell, Daiei, Harrison.
Sound Recording: The Glenn Miller Story, Universal-International Sound Department, Leslie I. Carey, Sound Director.
Film Editing: Gene Milford, On The Waterfront.
Special Effects: 20,000 Leagues Under The Sea.
Music (music score of a dramatic or comedy picture): Dimitri Tiomkin, The High And The Mighty, Wayne-Fellows, Warner Brothers.
Music (scoring musical picture): Adolph Deutsch, Saul Chaplin, Seven Brides For Seven Brothers, Metro-Goldwyn-Mayer.
Music (song): Sammy Cahn (lyrics and music), Jule Styne (music), Three Coins In The Fountain from Three Coins In The Fountain.
Short Subjects (cartoon): When Magoo Flew, United Productions of America, Columbia.

Short Subjects (1-reel): This Mechanical Age, Warner Brothers.
Short Subjects (2-reel): A Time Out Of War, Carnival Productions.
Documentary (short subject): Thursday's Children, British Information Services, World Wide-Morse.
Documentary (feature length): The Vanishing Prairie, Disney, Buena Vista.
SPECIAL AWARDS
Gate Of Hell (Japanese), Best foreign language film of 1954.
Bausch and Lomb Optical Company, for their contributions to the advancement of the motion picture industry.
Kemp R. Niver, for the development of the Renovare Process.
Greta Garbo, for unforgettable performances.
Danny Kaye, for his unique talents, his service to the Academy, the motion picture industry, and the American people.
Jon Whitely, for his outstanding juvenile performance in The Little Kidnappers.
Vincent Winter, for his outstanding juvenile performance in The Little Kidnappers.

1955

Best Picture: Marty, Steven, United Artists.
Actor: Ernest Borgnine in Marty.
Actress: Anna Magnani in The Rose Tattoo, Hal Wallis, Paramount.
Supporting Actor: Jack Lemmon in Mister Roberts, Orange, Warner Brothers.
Supporting Actress: Jo Van Fleet in East of Eden, Warner Brothers.
Direction: Delbert Mann, Marty.
Writing (motion picture story): Daniel Fuchs, Love Me Or Leave Me, Metro-Goldwyn-Mayer.
Writing (screenplay): Paddy Chayefsky, Marty.
Writing (story and screenplay): William Ludwig, Sonya Levien, Interrupted Melody, Metro-Goldwyn-Mayer.
Cinematography (black-and-white): James Wong Howe, The Rose Tattoo.
Cinematography (color): Robert Burks, To Catch A Thief, Paramount.
Art Direction (black-and-white): Hal Pereira, Tambi Larsen, The Rose Tattoo.
Art Direction (color): William Flannery, Jo Mielziner, Picnic, Columbia.
Set Decoration (black-and-white): Sam Comer, Arthur Krams, The Rose Tattoo.
Set Decoration (color): Robert Priestly, Picnic.
Costume Design (black-and-white): Helen Rose, I'll Cry Tomorrow, Metro-Goldwyn-Mayer.
Costume Design (color): Charles Le Maire, Love Is A Many-Splendored Thing, 20th Century-Fox.
Sound Recording: Oklahoma! Todd-AO Sound Department, Fred Hynes, Sound Director.
Film Editing: Charles Nelson, William A. Lyon, Picnic.
Music (music score of a dramatic or comedy picture): Alfred Newman, Love Is A Many-Splendored Thing from Love Is A Many-Splendored Thing.
Music (scoring musical picture): Robert Russell Bennett, Jay Blackton, Adolph Deutsch, Oklahoma! Rodgers and Hammerstein, Magna.
Music (song): Paul Francis Webster (lyrics), Sammy Fain (music), Love Is A Many-Splendored Thing.
Short Subjects (cartoon): Speedy Gonzales, Warner Brothers.
Short Subjects (1-reel): Survival City, 20th Century-Fox.
Short Subjects (2-reel): The Face Of Lincoln, University of Southern California, Cavalcade.
Documentary (short subject): Men Against The Arctic, Disney, Buena Vista.
Documentary (feature length): Helen Keller In Her Story, Hamilton.
SPECIAL AWARD
Samurai (Japanese), best foreign language film of 1955. Toho.

1956

Best Picture: Around The World In 80 Days, Todd, United Artists.
Actor: Yul Brynner in The King And I, 20th Century-Fox.
Actress: Ingrid Bergman in Anastasia, 20th Century-Fox.
Supporting Actor: Anthony Quinn in Lust For Life, Metro-Goldwyn-Mayer.
Supporting Actress: Dorothy Malone in Written On The Window, Universal-International.
Direction: George Stevens, Giant, Productions, Warner Brothers.
Foreign Language Film Award: La Strada, Ponti-De Laurentiis, Trans-Lux (Italy).
Writing (motion picture story): Robert Rich (Dalton Trumbo), The Brave One, King Brothers, RKO Radio.
Writing (screenplay-adapted): James Poe, John Farrow, S. J. Perelman, Around The World In 80 Days.
Writing (screenplay-original): Albert Lamorisse, The Red Balloon, Films Montsouris, Lopert.
Cinematography (black-and-white): Joseph Ruttenberg, Somebody Up There Likes Me, Metro-Goldwyn-Mayer.
Cinematography (color): Lionel Lindon, Around The World In 80 Days.

31A

Art Direction (black-and-white): Somebody Up There Likes Me, Cedric Gibbons, Malcolm F. Brown (art direction), Edwin B. Willis, F. Keogh Gleason (set decoration).
Art Direction (color): The King And I, Lyle R. Wheeler, John DeCuir (art direction), Walter M. Scott, Paul S. Fox (set decoration).
Costume Design (black-and-white): Jean Louis, The Solid Gold Cadillac, Columbia.
Costume Design (color): Irene Sharaff, The King And I.
Sound Recording: The King And I, 20th Century-Fox Sound Department.
Film Editing: Gene Ruggiero, Paul Weatherwax, Around The World In 80 Days.
Special Effects: John Fulton, The Ten Commandments, Motion Picture Associates, Paramount.
Music (music score of a dramatic or comedy picture): Victor Young, Around The World In 80 Days.
Music (scoring musical picture): Alfred Newman, Ken Darby, The King And I.
Music (song): Ray Evans, Jay Livingston (lyrics and music), Whatever Will Be, Will Be (Que Sera, Que Sera) from The Man Who Knew Too Much, Filwite, Paramount.
Short Subjects (cartoon): Mister Magoo's Puddle Jumper, UPA, Columbia.
Short Subjects (1-reel): Crashing The Water Barrier, Warner Brothers.
Short Subjects (2-reel): The Bespoke Overcoat, Romulus.
Documentary (short subject): The True Story Of The Civil War, Camera Eye.
Documentary (feature length): The Silent World, Filmad-F.S.J.Y.C., Columbia.
Irving G. Thalberg Memorial Award: Buddy Adler.
Jean Hersholt Humanitarian Award: Y. Frank Freeman.
SPECIAL AWARD
Eddie Cantor, for distinguished service to the film industry.

1957

Best Picture: The Bridge On The River Kwai, Horizon, Columbia.
Actor: Alec Guinness in The Bridge On The River Kwai.
Actress: Joanne Woodward in The Three Faces Of Eve, 20th Century-Fox.
Supporting Actor: Red Buttons in Sayonara, Goetz, Warner Brothers.
Supporting Actress: Miyoshi Umeki in Sayonara.
Direction: David Lean, The Bridge On The River Kwai.
Foreign Language Film Award: The Nights Of Cabiria, De Laurentiis, Lopert Films (Italy).
Writing (screenplay based on material from another medium): Pierre Boulle, The Bridge On The River Kwai.
Writing (story and screenplay written directly from the screen): George Wells, Designing Woman, Metro-Goldwyn-Mayer.
Cinematography: Jack Hildyard, The Bridge On The River Kwai.
Art Direction: Sayonara, Ted Haworth (art direction), Robert Priestley (set decoration).
Costume Design: Orry-Kelly, Les Girls, Siegel, Metro-Goldwyn-Mayer.
Sound Recording: Sayonara, Warner Brothers Studio Sound Department, George R. Groves, Sound Director.
Film Editing: Peter Taylor, The Bridge On The River Kwai.
Special Effects: Walter Rossi, The Enemy Below, 20th Century-Fox.
Music (scoring): Malcolm Arnold, The Bridge On The River Kwai.
Music (song): Sammy Cahn (lyrics), James Van Heusen (music), All The Way from The Joker Is Wild, A.M.B.L., Paramount.
Short Subjects (cartoon): Birds Anonymous, Warner Brothers.
Short Subjects (live action): The Wetback Hound, Disney, Buena Vista.
Documentary (feature length): Albert Schweitzer, Hill and Anderson, de Rochemont.
Jean Hersholt Humanitarian Award: Samuel Goldwyn.
SPECIAL AWARDS
Charles Brackett, for outstanding service to the Academy.
B. B. Kahane, for distinguished service to the Motion Picture Industry.
Gilbert M. ("Broncho Billy") Anderson, motion picture pioneer, for his contributions to the development of motion pictures as entertainment.
The Society of Motion Picture and Television Engineers, for their contributions to the advancement of the Motion Picture Industry.

1958

Best Picture: Gigi, Freed, Metro-Goldwyn-Mayer.
Actor: David Niven in Separate Tables, Clifton, United Artists.
Actress: Susan Hayward in I Want To Live, Figaro, United Artists.
Supporting Actor: Burl Ives in The Big Country, Anthony-World-wide, United Artists.
Supporting Actress: Wendy Hiller in Separate Tables.
Direction: Vincente Minnelli, Gigi.
Foreign Language Film Award: My Uncle, Specta-Gray-Alter, Films del Centaure, Continental (France).
Writing (screenplay based on material from another medium): Alan Jay Lerner, Gigi.

Writing (story and screenplay written directly from the screen): Nathan E. Douglas, Harold Jacob Smith, The Defiant Ones, Kramer, United Artists.
Cinematography (black-and-white): Sam Leavitt, The Defiant Ones.
Cinematography (color): Joseph Ruttenberg, Gigi.
Art Direction: William A. Horning, Preston Ames (art direction), Henry Grace, Keogh Gleason (set decoration), Gigi.
Costume Design: Cecil Beaton, Gigi.
Sound: South Pacific, Todd-AO Sound Department, Fred Hynes, Sound Director.
Film Editing: Adrienne Fazan, Gigi.
Special Effects: Tom Howard, tom thumb, George Pal, Metro-Goldwyn-Mayer.
Music (score of a dramatic or comedy picture): Dimitri Tiomkin, The Old Man And The Sea, Hayward, Warner Brothers.
Music (scoring musical picture): Andre Previn, Gigi.
Music (song): Alan Jay Lerner (lyrics), Frederick Loewe (music), Gigi from Gigi.
Short Subjects (cartoon): Knighty Knight Bugs, Warner Brothers.
Short Subjects (live action): Grand Canyon, Disney, Buena Vista.
Documentary (short subject): AMA Girls, Disney, Buena Vista.
Documentary (feature length): White Wilderness, Disney, Buena Vista.
Irving G. Thalberg Memorial Award: Jack L. Warner.
SPECIAL AWARD
Maurice Chevalier, for his contributions to the world of entertainment for more than half a century.

1959

Best Picture: Ben-Hur, Metro-Goldwyn-Mayer.
Actor: Charlton Heston in Ben-Hur.
Actress: Simone Signoret in Room At The Top, Romulus, Continental.
Supporting Actor: Hugh Griffith in Ben-Hur.
Supporting Actress: Shelley Winters in The Diary of Anne Frank, 20th Century-Fox.
Direction: William Wyler, Ben-Hur.
Foreign Language Film Award: Black Orpheus, Dispatfilm & Gemme Cinematografica, United Artists (Brazil).
Writing (screenplay based on material from another medium): Neil Paterson, Room At The Top.
Writing (story and screenplay written directly from the screen): Russell Rouse, Clarence Greene (story), Stanley Shapiro, Maurice Richlin, (screenplay), Pillow Talk, Arwin, Universal-International.
Cinematography (black and white): William C. Mellor, The Diary of Anne Frank.
Cinematography (color): Robert L. Surtees, Ben-Hur.
Art Direction (black-and-white): The Diary Of Anne Frank, Lyle R. Wheeler, George W. Davis (art direction), Walter M. Scott, Stuart A. Reiss (set decoration).
Art Direction (color): Ben-Hur, William A. Horning, Edward Carfagno (art direction), Hugh Hunt (set decoration).
Costume Design (black-and-white): Orry-Kelly, Some Like It Hot, Ashton, Mirisch, United Artists.
Costume Design (color): Elizabeth Haffenden, Ben-Hur.
Sound: Ben-Hur, Metro-Goldwyn-Mayer Studio Sound Department, Franklin E. Milton, Sound Director.
Film Editing: Ralph E. Winters, John D. Dunning, Ben-Hur.
Sound Effects: Ben-Hur, A. Arnold Gillespie, Robert MacDonald (visual effects), Milo Lory (audible effects).
Music (music score of a dramatic or comedy picture): Miklos Rozsa, Ben-Hur.
Music (scoring musical picture): Andre Previn, Ken Darby, Porgy And Bess, Goldwyn, Columbia.
Music (song): Sammy Cahn (lyrics), James Van Heusen (music), High Hopes from A Hole In The Head, Sincap, United Artists.
Short Subjects (cartoon): Moonbirds, Storyboard, Harrison.
Short Subjects (live action): The Golden Fish, Les Requins, Columbia.
Documentary (short subject): Glass, Netherlands Government, Arthur-Go.
Documentary (feature length): Serengeti Shall Not Die, Okapia-Film, Transocean-Film.
Jean Hersholt Humanitarian Award: Bob Hope.
SPECIAL AWARDS
Lee de Forest, for his pioneering inventions which brought sound to motion pictures.
Buster Keaton, for his unique talents which brought immortal comedies to the screen.

1960

Best Picture: The Apartment, Mirisch, United Artists.
Actor: Burt Lancaster in Elmer Gantry, Lancaster-Brooks, United Artists.
Actress: Elizabeth Taylor in Butterfield 8, Afton-Linebrook, Metro-Goldwyn-Mayer.

Supporting Actor: Peter Ustinov in Spartacus, Bryna, Universal-International.
Supporting Actress: Shirley Jones in Elmer Gantry.
Direction: Billy Wilder, The Apartment.
Foreign Language Film Award: The Virgin Spring, Svensk Filmindustri, Janus (Sweden).
Writing (screenplay based on material from another medium): Richard Brooks, Elmer Gantry.
Writing (story and screenplay written directly for the screen): Billy Wilder, I.A.L. Diamond, The Apartment.
Cinematography (black and white): Freddie Francis, Sons And Lovers, Company of Artists, 20th Century-Fox.
Cinematography (color): Russell Metty, Spartacus.
Art Direction (black-and-white): The Apartment, Alexander Trauner (art direction), Edward G. Boyle (set decoration).
Art Direction (color): Spartacus, Alexander Golitzen, Eric Orbom (art direction), Russell A. Gausman, Julia Heron (set decoration).
Costume Design (black-and-white): Edith Head, Edward Stevenson, The Facts Of Life, Panama & Frank, United Artists.
Costume Design (color): Valles and Bill Thomas, Spartacus.
Sound: The Alamo, Samuel Goldwyn Studio Sound Department, Gordon E. Sawyer, Sound Director; Todd-AO Sound Department, Fred Hynes, Sound Director.
Film Editing: Daniel Mandell, The Apartment.
Special Effects: The Time Machine, Gene Warren, Tim Baar (visual effects), Galaxy, Metro-Goldwyn-Mayer.
Music (music score of a dramatic or comedy picture): Ernest Gold, Exodus, Carlyle-Alpina, United Artists.
Music (scoring musical picture): Morris Stoloff, Harry Sukman, Song Without End (The Story Of Franz Liszt), Goetz-Vidor, Columbia.
Music (song): Manos Hadjidakis (lyrics and music), Never On Sunday from Never On Sunday, Melinafilm, Lopert.
Short Subjects (cartoon): Munro, Rembrandt, Film Representations.
Short Subjects (live action): Day Of The Painter, Little Movies, Kingsley-Union.
Documentary (short subject): Giuseppina, Hill, Schoenfeld.
Documentary (feature length): The Horse With The Flying Tail, Disney, Buena Vista.
Jean Hersholt Humanitarian Award: Sol Lesser.
SPECIAL AWARDS
Gary Cooper, for his many memorable screen performances and the international recognition he, as an individual, has gained for the motion picture industry.
Stan Laurel, for his creative pioneering in the field of cinema comedy.
Hayley Mills, for Pollyanna, the most outstanding juvenile performance during 1960.

1961

Best Picture: West Side Story, Mirisch, B & P, United Artists.
Actor: Maximilian Schell in Judgment At Nuremberg, Kramer, United Artists.
Actress: Sophia Loren in Two Women, Champion-Les Films Marceau-Cocinor, Societe Generale De Cinematographic, Embassy.
Supporting Actor: George Chakiris in West Side Story.
Supporting Actress: Rita Moreno in West Side Story.
Direction: Robert Wise, Jerome Robbins, West Side Story.
Foreign Language Film Award: Through A Glass Darkly, Svensk Filmindustri, Janus (Sweden).
Writing (screenplay based on material from another medium): Abby Mann, Judgment At Nuremberg.
Writing (story and screenplay written directly for the screen): William Inge, Splendor In The Grass, NBI, Warner Brothers.
Cinematography (black and white): Eugen Shuftan, The Hustler, Robert Rossen, 20th Century-Fox.
Cinematography (color): Daniel L. Fapp, West Side Story.
Art Direction (black-and-white): The Hustler, Harry Horner (art direction), Gene Callahan (set decoration).
Art Direction (color): West Side Story, Boris Leven (art direction), Victor A. Gangelin (set decoration).
Costume Design (black-and-white): Piero Gherardi, La Dolce Vita, Riama, Astor.
Costume Design (color): Irene Sharaff, West Side Story.
Sound: West Side Story, Todd-AO Sound Department, Fred Hynes, Sound Director; Samuel Goldwyn Sound Department, Gordon E. Sawyer, Sound Director.
Film Editing: Thomas Stanford, West Side Story.
Special Effects: The Guns Of Navarone, Bill Warrington (visual effects), Vivian C. Greenham (audible effects), Foreman, Columbia.
Music (music score of a dramatic or comedy picture): Henry Mancini, Breakfast At Tiffany's, Jurow-Shepherd, Paramount.
Music (scoring musical picture): Saul Chaplin, Johnny Green, Sid Ramin, Irwin Kostal, West Side Story.
Music (song): Johnny Mercer (lyrics), Henry Mancini (music), Moon River from Breakfast At Tiffany's.
Short Subjects (cartoon): Ersatz, Zagreb, Herts-Lion International.
Short Subjects (live action): Seawards The Great Ships, Templar, Schoenfeld.
Documentary (short subjects): Project Hope, MacManus, John & Adams, Ex-Cell-O, Klaeger.

Documentary (feature length): Le Ciel Et La Boue (Sky Above And Mud Beneath), Ardennes, J. Arthur Rank.
Irving G. Thalberg Memorial Award: Stanley Kramer.
SPECIAL AWARDS
William L. Hendricks, for his outstanding patriotic service in the conception, writing and production of the Marine Corps Film, A Force In Readiness, which has brought honor to the Academy and the motion picture industry.
Jerome Robbins, for his brilliant achievements in the art of choreography on film in "West Side Story."
Fred L. Metzler, for his dedication and outstanding service to the Academy of Motion Picture Arts and Sciences.

1962

Best Picture: Lawrence Of Arabia, Horizon, Spiegel, Lean, Columbia.
Actor: Gregory Peck in To Kill A Mockingbird, Universal-International, Pakula-Mulligan, Brentwood.
Actress: Anne Bancroft in The Miracle Worker, Playfilms, United Artists.
Supporting Actor: Ed Begley in Sweet Bird Of Youth, Roxbury, Metro-Goldwyn-Mayer.
Supporting Actress: Patty Duke in The Miracle Worker.
Direction: David Lean, Lawrence Of Arabia.
Foreign Language Film Award: Sundays And Cybele, Terra-Fides-Orsay, Trocadero, Columbia (France).
Writing (screenplay based on material from another medium): Horton Foote, To Kill A Mockingbird.
Writing (story and screenplay written directly for the screen): Ennio De Concini, Alfredo Giannetti, Pietro Germi, Divorce—Italian Style, Lux-Vides-Galatea, Embassy.
Cinematography (black and white): Jean Bourgoin, Walter Wottitz, The Longest Day, Zanuck, 20th Century-Fox.
Cinematography (color): Fred A. Young, Lawrence of Arabia.
Art Direction (black-and-white): To Kill A Mockingbird, Alexander Golitzen, Henry Bumstead (art direction), Oliver Emert (set decoration).
Art Direction (color): Lawrence Of Arabia, John Box, John Stoll (art direction), Dario Simoni (set decoration).
Costume Design (black-and-white): Norma Koch, What Ever Happened To Baby Jane? Seven Arts, Aldrich, Warner Brothers.
Costume Design (color): Mary Wills, The Wonderful World Of The Brothers Grimm, Metro-Goldwyn-Mayer, Cinerama.
Sound: Lawrence Of Arabia, Shepperton Studio Sound Department, John Cox, Sound Director.
Film Editing: Anne Coates, Lawrence Of Arabia.
Special Effects: The Longest Day, Robert MacDonald (visual effects), Jacques Maumont (audible effects).
Music (score—substantially original): Maurice Jarre, Lawrence Of Arabia.
Music (score—adaptation or treatment): Ray Heindorf, Meredith Wilson's The Music Man, Warner Brothers.
Music (song): Johnny Mercer (lyrics), Henry Mancini (music), Days Of Wine And Roses from Days Of Wine and Roses, Manulis-Jalem, Warner Brothers.
Short Subjects (cartoon): The Hole, Storyboard, Brandon.
Short Subjects (live action): Heureux Anniversaire (Happy Anniversary), CAPAC, Atlantic.
Documentary (short subject): Dylan Thomas, TWW, Janus.
Documentary (feature length): Black Fox, Image, Heritage.
Jean Hersholt Humanitarian Award: Steve Broidy.

1963

Best Picture: Tom Jones, Woodfall, United Artists, Lopert.
Actor: Sidney Poitier in Lilies Of The Field, Rainbow, United Artists.
Actress: Patricia Neal in Hud, Salem-Dover, Paramount.
Supporting Actor: Melvyn Douglas in Hud.
Supporting Actress: Margaret Rutherford in The V.I.P.s Metro-Goldwyn-Mayer.
Direction: Tony Richardson, Tom Jones.
Foreign Language Film Award: Federico Fellini's 8½, Cineriz, Embassy (Italy).
Writing (screenplay based on material from another medium): John Osborne, Tom Jones.
Writing (best story and screenplay written directly for the screen): James R. Webb, How The West Was Won, Metro-Goldwyn-Mayer, Cinerama.
Cinematography (black and white): James Wong Howe, Hud.
Cinematography (color): Leon Shamroy, Cleopatra, 20th Century-Fox, MCL, WALWA.
Art Direction (black-and-white): Gene Callahan, America America, Athena, Warner Brothers.
Art Direction (color): John DeCuir, Jack Martin Smith, Hilyard Brown, Herman Blumenthal, Elven Webb, Maurice Pelling, Boris Juraga (art direction), Walter M. Scott, Paul S. Fox, Ray Moyer (set decoration), Cleopatra.
Costume Design (black-and-white): Piero Gherardi, Federico Fellini's 8½.
Costume Design (color): Irene Sharaff, Vittorio Nino Novarese, Renie, Cleopatra.

Sound: How The West Was Won, Metro-Goldwyn-Mayer Studio Sound Department, Franklin E. Milton, Sound Director.
Sound Effects: It's A Mad, Mad, Mad, Mad World, Walter G. Elliott, Casey, United Artists.
Film Editing: Harold F. Kress, How The West Was Won.
Special Effects: Emil Kosa, Jr., Cleopatra.
Music (score—substantially original): John Adddison, Tom Jones.
Music (score—adaptation or treatment): Andre Previn, Irma La Douce, Mirisch-Phalanx, United Artists.
Music (song): Sammy Cahn (lyrics), James Van Heusen (music), Call Me Irresponsible from Papa's Delicate Condition, Amro, Paramount.
Short Subjects (cartoon): The Critic, Pintoff-Crossbow, Columbia.
Short Subjects (live action): An Occurrence At Owl Creek Bridge, Films Du Centaure, Filmartic, Cappagariff, Janus.
Documentary (short subject): Chagall, Auerbach, Flag.
Documentary (feature length): Robert Frost: A Lover's Quarrel With The World, WGBH Educational Foundation.
Irving G. Thalberg Memorial Award: Sam Spiegel.

1964

Best Picture: My Fair Lady, Warner Brothers.
Actor: Rex Harrison in My Fair Lady.
Actress: Julie Andrews in Mary Poppins, Disney, Buena Vista.
Supporting Actor: Peter Ustinov in Topkapi, Filmways, United Artists.
Supporting Actress: Lila Kedrova in Zorba The Greek, International Classics.
Direction: George Cukor, My Fair Lady.
Foreign Language Film Award: Yesterday, Today And Tomorrow, Champion-Concordia (Italy).
Writing (screenplay adapted from another medium): Edward Anhalt, Becket, Wallis, Paramount.
Writing (original story and screenplay): Story by S. H. Barnett. Screenplay by Peter Stone, Frank Tarloff. Father Goose, Universal.
Cinematography (black and white): Walter Lassally, Zorba The Greek.
Cinematography (color): Harry Stradling, My Fair Lady.
Art Direction (black-and-white): Vassilis Fotopoulos, Zorba The Greeek.
Art Direction (color): Gene Allen, Cecil Beaton, Art Directors; George James Hopkins, Set Decorator; My Fair Lady.
Costume Design (black-and-white): Dorothy Jeakins, The Night Of The Iguana, Seven Arts, Metro-Goldwyn-Mayer.
Costume Design (color): Cecil Beaton, My Fair Lady.
Film Editing: Cotton Warburton, Mary Poppins.
Music (original score): Richard M. Sherman, Robert B. Sherman, Mary Poppins.
Music (scoring—adaptation or treatment): Andre Previn, My Fair Lady.
Music (song): Music and lyrics by Richard M. Sherman and Robert B. Sherman, Chim Chim Cher-ee from Mary Poppins.
Short Subjects (cartoon): The Pink Phink, Mirisch-Geoffrey, United Artists.
Short Subjects (live action): Casals Conducts, Thalia.
Sound: My Fair Lady, Warner Brothers Studio Sound Department, George R. Groves, Sound Director.
Sound Effects: Goldfinger, Eon, United Artists, Norman Wanstall.
Special Visual Effects: Peter Ellenshaw, Hamilton Luske, Eustace Lycett, Mary Poppins.
Documentary (feature): World Without Sun, Columbia.
Documentary (short subject): Nine From Little Rock, USIA, Guggenheim.
SPECIAL AWARDS
William Tuttle, for his outstanding make-up achievement for 7 Faces Of Dr. Lao.

1965

Best Picture: The Sound Of Music, Argyle Enterprises, 20th Century-Fox.
Actor: Lee Marvin in Cat Ballou, Hecht, Columbia.
Actress: Julie Christie in Darling, Anglo-Amalgamated, Embassy.
Supporting Actor: Martin Balsam in A Thousand Clowns, Harrel, United Artists.
Supporting Actress: Shelley Winters in A Patch Of Blue, Berman-Green, Metro-Goldwyn-Mayer.
Direction: Robert Wise, The Sound Of Music.
Foreign Language Film Award: The Shop On Main Street, Ceskoslovensky (Czechoslovakia).
Writing (screenplay based on material from another medium): Robert Bolt, Doctor Zhivago, Sostar, Metro-Goldwyn-Mayer.
Writing (original story and screenplay): Frederic Raphael, Darling.
Cinematography (black-and-white): Ernest Laszlo, Ship Of Fools, Columbia.
Cinematography (color): Freddie Young, Doctor Zhivago.
Art Direction (black-and-white): Robert Clatworthy, Art Director; Joseph Kish, Set Decorator; Ship Of Fools.

Art Direction (color): John Box, Terry Marsh, Doctor Zhivago.
Costume Design (black-and-white): Julie Harris, Darling.
Costume Design (color): Phyllis Dalton, Doctor Zhivago.
Film Editing: William Reynolds, The Sound Of Music.
Music (original score): Maurice Jarre, Doctor Zhivago.
Music (scoring—adaptation or treatment): Irwin Kostal, The Sound Of Music.
Music (song): Paul Francis Webster (lyrics), Johnny Mandel (music), The Shadow Of Your Smile from The Sandpiper, Filmways-Venice, Metro-Goldwyn-Mayer.
Short Subjects (cartoon): The Dot And The Line, Metro-Goldwyn-Mayer.
Short Subjects (live action): The Chicken, Renn, Pathe Contemporary.
Sound: The Sound Of Music, 20th Century-Fox Studio Sound Department, James P. Corcoran, Sound Director; Todd-AO Sound Department, Fred Hynes, Sound Director.
Sound Effects: The Great Race, Patricia-Jalem-Reynard, Warner Brothers, Tregoweth Brown.
Special Visual Effects: John Stears, Thunderball, Broccoli-Saltzman-McClory, United Artists.
Documentary (feature): The Eleanor Roosevelt Story, Glazier, American International.
Documentary (short subject): To Be Alive! Johnson Wax.
Irving G. Thalberg Memorial Award: William Wyler.
Jean Hersholt Humanitarian Award: Edmond L. DePatie.
SPECIAL AWARDS
Bob Hope, for unique and distinguished service to the motion picture industry and the Academy.

1966

Best Picture: A Man For All Seasons, Highland, Columbia.
Actor: Paul Scofield in A Man For All Seasons.
Actress: Elizabeth Taylor in Who's Afraid Of Virginia Woolf? Chenault, Warner Brothers.
Supporting Actor: Walter Matthau in The Fortune Cookie, Phalanx-Jalem-Mirisch, United Artists.
Supporting Actress: Sandy Dennis in Who's Afraid Of Virginia Woolf?
Direction: Fred Zinnemann, A Man For All Seasons.
Foreign Language Film Award: A Man And A Woman, Les Films 13 (France).
Writing (screenplay—based on material from another medium): Robert Bolt, A Man For All Seasons.
Writing (original story and screenplay): A Man And A Woman. Story by Claude Lelouch. Screenplay by Pierre Uytterhoeven and Claude Lelouch.
Cinematography (black-and-white): Haskell Wexler, Who's Afraid Of Virginia Woolf?
Cinematography (color): Ted Moore, A Man For All Seasons.
Art Direction (black-and-white): Richard Sylbert, Art Director; George James Hopkins, Set Decorator; Who's Afraid Of Virginia Woolf?
Art Direction (color): Jack Martin Smith, Dale Hennesy, Art Directors; Walter M. Scott, Stuart A. Reiss, Set Decorators; Fantastic Voyage, 20th Century-Fox.
Costume Design (black-and-white): Irene Sharaff, Who's Afraid Of Virginia Woolf?
Costume Design (color): Elizabeth Haffenden, Joan Bridge, A Man For All Seasons.
Film Editing: Fredric Steinkamp, Henry Berman, Stewart Linder, Frank Santillo, Grand Prix, Douglas-Lewis-Frankenheimer-Cherokee, Metro-Goldwyn-Mayer.
Music (original score): John Barry, Born Free, Open Road, Atlas, Columbia.
Music (adaptation or treatment): Ken Thorne, A Funny Thing Happened On The Way To The Forum, Frank, United Artists.
Music (song): Don Black (lyrics), John Barry (music), Born Free from Born Free.
Short Subjects (cartoon): Herb Alpert And The Tijuana Brass Double Feature, Hubley.
Short Subjects (live action): Wild Wings, British Transport, Manson.
Sound: Grand Prix, Metro-Goldwyn-Mayer Studio Sound Department, Franklin E. Milton, Sound Director.
Sound Effects: Gordon Daniel, Grand Prix.
Special Visual Effects: Art Cruickshank, Fantastic Voyage.
Documentary (short subject): A Year Toward Tomorrow, Sun Dial for the Office of Economic Opportunity.
Documentary (feature): The War Game, British Film Institute, Pathe Contemporary.
Irving G. Thalberg Memorial Award: Robert Wise.
Jean Hersholt Humanitarian Award: George Bagnall.
SPECIAL AWARDS
Y. Frank Freeman, for unusual and outstanding service to the Academy during his thirty years in Hollywood.
Yakima Canutt, for achievements as a stunt man and for developing safety devices to protect stunt men everywhere.

1967

Best Picture: In The Heat Of The Night, Mirisch, United Artists.

34A

Actor: Rod Steiger in In The Heat Of The Night.
Actress: Katharine Hepburn in Guess Who's Coming To Dinner, Kramer, Columbia.
Supporting Actor: George Kennedy in Cool Hand Luke, Jalem, Warner Brothers-Seven Arts.
Supporting Actress: Estelle Parsons in Bonnie And Clyde, Tatira-Hiller, Warner Brothers-Seven Arts.
Directing: Mike Nichols, The Graduate, Nichols-Turman, Embassy.
Foreign Language Film Award: Closely Watched Trains, Barrandov, Sigma II (Czechoslovakia).
Writing (screenplay—based on material from another medium): Stirling Silliphant, In The Heat Of The Night.
Writing (original story and screenplay): William Rose, Guess Who's Coming To Dinner.
Cinematography: Burnett Guffey, Bonnie And Clyde.
Art Direction: John Truscott, Edward Carrere, Art Directors; John W. Brown, Set Decorator; Camelot, Warner Brothers-Seven Arts.
Costume Design: John Truscott, Camelot.
Film Editing: Hal Ashby, In The Heat Of The Night.
Music (original score): Elmer Bernstein, Thoroughly Modern Millie, Hunter, Universal.
Music (adaptation or treatment): Alfred Newman, Ken Darby, Camelot.
Music (song): Music and lyrics by Leslie Bricusse, Talk To The Animals from Doctor Dolittle, Apjac, 20th Century-Fox.
Short Subjects (cartoon): The Box, Murakami, Wolf, Brandon.
Short Subjects (live action): A Place To Stand, T.D.F., Columbia.
Sound: In The Heat Of The Night, Samuel Goldwyn Studio Sound Department.
Sound Effects: John Poyner, The Dirty Dozen, MKH, Metro-Goldwyn-Mayer.
Special Visual Effects: L. B. Abbott, Doctor Dolittle.
Documentary (short subject): The Redwoods, King.
Documentary (feature): The Anderson Platoon, French Broadcasting System.
Irving G. Thalberg Memorial Award: Alfred Hitchcock.
Jean Hersholt Humanitarian Award: Gregory Peck.

1968

Best Picture: Oliver! Romulus Films, Ltd., Columbia.
Actor: Cliff Robertson in Charly, An American Broadcasting Company-Selmur Pictures Production, Cinerama.
Actress: Katharine Hepburn in The Lion In Winter, Haworth Productions, Ltd., Avco Embassy. Barbra Streisand in Funny Girl, Rastar Productions, Columbia.
Supporting Actor: Jack Albertson in The Subject Was Roses, Metro-Goldwyn-Mayer.
Supporting Actress: Ruth Gordon in Rosemary's Baby, William Castle Enterprises Production, Paramount.
Direction: Carole Reed, Oliver!
Foreign Language Film Award: War and Peace, A Mosfilm Production (Russia).
Writing (story and screenplay written directly for the screen): Mel Brooks, The Producers, A Sidney Glazier Production, Avco Embassy.
Writing (screenplay—based on material from another medium): James Goldman, The Lion In Winter.
Cinematography: Pasqualino De Santis, Romeo & Juliet, A Franco Zeffirelli Production, B.H.E. Film-Verona Produzione S.r.l.-Dino De Laurentiis Cinematographica S.p.A. Production, Paramount.
Art Direction: John Box, Terence Marsh, Art Directors; Vernon Dixon, Ken Muggleston, Set Decorators; Oliver!
Costume Design: Danilo Donati, Romeo & Juliet.
Film Editing: Frank P. Keller, Bullitt, A Solar Production, Warner Brothers-Seven Arts.
Music (original score): John Barry, A Lion In Winter.
Music (score of musical picture—original or adaptation): John Green, Oliver!
Music (song): Alan and Marilyn Bergman (lyrics), Michel Legrand (music), The Windmills Of Your Mind from The Thomas Crown Affair, A Mirisch-Solar-Simkoe Production, United Artists.
Short Subjects (cartoon): Winnie The Pooh And The Blustery Day, Walt Disney Productions, Buena Vista Distribution Company.
Short Subjects (live action): Robert Kennedy Remembered, Guggenheim Productions, National General.
Sound: Shepperton Studio Sound Department, Oliver!
Special Visual Effects: 2001: A Space Odyssey, A Polaris Production, Metro-Goldwyn-Mayer.
Documentary (feature): Journey Into Self, Western Behavioral Sciences Institute.
Documentary (short subjects): Why Man Creates, Saul Bass & Associates.
Jean Hersholt Humanitarian Award: Martha Raye.
SPECIAL AWARDS
John Chambers, for his outstanding make-up achievement for Planet Of The Apes.
Onna White, for her outstanding choreography achievement for Oliver!

1969

Best Picture: Midnight Cowboy, A Jerome Hellman-John Schlesinger Production, United Artists.
Actor: John Wayne in True Grit, A Hal Wallis Production, Paramount.
Actress: Maggie Smith in The Prime of Miss Jean Brodie, 20th Century-Fox Productions, Ltd.
Supporting Actor: Gig Young in They Shoot Horses, Don't They? A Chartoff-Winkler-Pollack Production, ABC Pictures Presentation, Cinerama.
Supporting Actress: Goldie Hawn in Cactus Flower, Frankovich Productions, Columbia.
Direction: John Schlesinger, Midnight Cowboy.
Foreign Language Film Award: Z, A Reggane-O.N.C.I.C. Production (Algeria).
Writing (screenplay—based on material from another medium): Waldo Salt, Midnight Cowboy.
Writing (original story and screenplay): William Goldman, Butch Cassidy And The Sundance Kid, a George Roy Hill-Paul Monash Production, 20th Century-Fox.
Cinematography: Conrad Hall, Butch Cassidy And The Sundance Kid.
Art Direction: John DeCuir, Jack Martin Smith, Herman Blumenthal, Art Directors; Walter M. Scott, George Hopkins, Raphael Bretton, Set Decorators; Hello, Dolly! Chenault Productions, 20th Century-Fox.
Costume Design: Margaret Furse, Anne Of A Thousand Days, A Hal Wallis-Universal Pictures, Ltd. Production, Universal.
Film Editing: Françoise Bonnot, Z.
Music (original score): Burt Bacharach, Butch Cassidy And The Sundance Kid.
Music (score): Lennie Hayton, Lionel Newman, Hello, Dolly!
Music (song): Hal David (lyrics), Burt Bacharach (music), Raindrops Keep Fallin' On My Head from Butch Cassidy And The Sundance Kid.
Short Subjects (cartoon): It's Tough To Be A Bird, Walt Disney Productions, Buena Vista Distribution Company.
Short Subjects (live action): The Magic Machines, Fly-By-Night Productions, Manson Distributing.
Sound: Jack Solomon, Murray Spivack, Hello, Dolly!
Special Visual Effects: Robbie Robertson, Marooned, A Frankovich-Sturges Production, Columbia.
Documentary (feature): Artur Rubinstein—The Love Of Life, A Midem Production.
Documentary (short subject): Czechoslovakia 1968, Sanders-Fresco Film Makers, United States Information Agency.
Jean Hersholt Humanitarian Award: George Jessel.
SPECIAL AWARD
Cary Grant, for his unique mastery of the art of screen acting with the respect and affection of his colleagues.

1970

Best Picture: Patton, 20th Century-Fox.
Actor: George C. Scott in Patton.
Actress: Glenda Jackson in Women In Love, A Larry Kramer-Martin Rosen Production, United Artists.
Supporting Actor: John Mills in Ryan's Daughter, Faraway Productions, A.G., Metro-Goldwyn-Mayer.
Supporting Actress: Helen Hayes in Airport, A Ross Hunter-Universal Production, Universal.
Directing: Franklin J. Schaffner, Patton.
Foreign Language Film Award: Investigation Of A Citizen Above Suspicion, A Vera Films S.p.A. Production (Italy).
Writing (screenplay—based on material from another medium): Ring Lardner, Jr., M*A*S*H, Aspen Productions, 20th Century-Fox.
Writing (original story and screenplay): Francis Ford Coppola, Edmund H. North, Patton.
Cinematography: Freddie Young, Ryan's Daughter.
Art Direction: Urie McCleary, Gil Parrondo, Art Directors; Antonio Mateos, Pierre-Louis Thevenet, Set Decorators; Patton.
Costume Design: Nino Novarese, Cromwell, An Irving Allen, Ltd., Production, Columbia.
Film Editing: Hugh S. Fowler, Patton.
Music (original score): Francis Lai, Love Story, Love Story Producing Company Production, Paramount.
Music (original song score): The Beatles, Let It Be, A Beatles-Apple Production, United Artist.
Music (song): Robb Royer, James Griffin (lyrics), Fred Karlin (music), For All We Know from Lovers And Other Strangers, An ABC Pictures Production, Cinerama.
Short Subjects (cartoon): Is It Always Right To Be Right? Stephen Bosustow Productions, Lester A. Schoenfeld Films.
Short Subjects (live action): The Resurrection Of Broncho Billy, University of Southern California Department of Cinema, Universal.
Sound: Douglas Williams, Don Bassman, Patton.
Special Visual Effects: A. D. Flowers, L. B. Abbott, Tora! Tora! Tora! 20th Century-Fox.
Documentary (feature): Woodstock, A Wadleigh-Maurice, Ltd. Production.
Documentary (short subject): Interviews With My Lai Veterans, Laser Film Corporation.

35A

Irving G. Thalberg Memorial Award: Ingmar Bergman.
Jean Hersholt Humanitarian Award: Frank Sinatra.
SPECIAL AWARDS
Lillian Gish, for superlative artistry and for distinguished contribution to the progress of motion pictures.
Orson Welles, for superlative artistry and versatility in the creation of motion pictures.

1971

Best Picture: The French Connection, D'Antoni Productions, 20th Century-Fox.
Actor: Gene Hackman in The French Connection.
Actress: Jane Fonda in Klute, Gus Production, Warner Brothers.
Supporting Actor: Ben Johnson in The Last Picture Show, BBS Productions, Columbia.
Supporting Actress: Cloris Leachman in The Last Picture Show.
Directing: William Friedkin, The French Connection.
Foreign Language Film Award: The Garden Of The Finzi-Continis, Gianni Hecht Lucari-Arthur Cohn (Italy).
Writing (screenplay—based on material from another medium): Ernest Tidyman, The French Connection.
Writing (original story and screenplay): Paddy Chayefsky, The Hospital, Gottfried-Chayefsky, Arthur Hiller, United Artists.
Cinematography: Oswald Morris, Fiddler On The Roof, Mirisch-Cartier, United Artists.
Art Direction: John Box, Ernest Archer, Jack Maxted, Gil Parrondo, Art Directors; Set Decorator, Vernon Dixon; Nicholas And Alexandra, Horizon, Columbia.
Costume Design: Yvonne Blake, Antonio Castillo, Nicholas And Alexandra.
Film Editing: Jerry Greenberg, The French Connection.
Music (original score): Michel Legrand, Summer Of '42, Mulligan-Roth, Warner Brothers.
Music (adaptation or treatment): John Williams, Fiddler On The Roof.
Music (song): Isaac Hayes for Theme From Shaft, Shaft Productions. Metro-Goldwyn-Mayer.
Short Subjects (cartoon): The Crunch Bird, Petok, Regency.
Short Subjects (live action): Sentinels Of Silence, Paramount.
Sound: Gordon K. McCallum, David Hildyard, Fiddler On The Roof.
Special Visual Effects: Danny Lee, Eustace Lycett, Alan Maley, Bedknobs And Broomstocks, Disney, Buena Vista.
Documentary (short subject): Sentinals Of Silence.
Documentary (feature): The Hellstrom Chronicle, Wolper, Cinema 5.
SPECIAL AWARDS
Charles Spencer (Charlie) Chaplin, for his unique contribution to motion pictures.

1972

Best Picture: The Godfather, Albert S. Ruddy Production, Paramount.
Actor: Marlon Brando in The Godfather.
Actress: Liza Minnelli in Cabaret, ABC Pictures Production, Allied Artists.
Supporting Actor: Joel Grey in Cabaret.
Supporting Actress: Eileen Heckart in Butterflies Are Free, Frankovich Productions, Columbia.
Directing: Bob Fosse, Cabaret.
Foreign Language Film Award: The Discreet Charm Of The Bourgeoisie, Serge Silberman Productions (France).
Writing (screenplay—based on material from another medium): Mario Puzo, Francis Ford Coppola, The Godfather.
Writing (original story and screenplay): Jeremy Larner, The Candidate, Redford-Ritchie Production, Warner Brothers.
Cinematography: Geoffrey Unsworth, Cabaret.
Art Direction: Rolf Zehetbauer, Jurgen Kiebach, Art Directors; Set Decorator, Herbert Strabel, Cabaret.
Costume Design: Anthony Powell, Travels With My Aunt, Fryer Productions, Metro-Goldwyn-Mayer.
Film Editing: David Bretherton, Cabaret.
Music (original score): Charles Chaplin, Raymond Rasch, Larry Russell, Limelight, Columbia.
Music (adaptation): Ralph Burns, Cabaret.
Music (song): Al Kasha, Joel Hirschhorn, for The Morning After, The Poseiden Adventure, Irwin Allen Production, 20th Century-Fox.
Short Subjects (animated): A Christmas Carol, Richard Williams Production, ABC Film Services.
Short Subjects (live action): Norman Rockwell's World . . . An American Dream, Concepts Unlimited, Columbia.
Sound: Robert Knudson, David Hildyard, Cabaret.
Special Visual Effects: L. B. Abbott, A. D. Flowers, The Poseidon Adventure.
Documentary (short subject): This Tiny World, Charles Hugeunot van der Linden Production.
Documentary (feature): Marjoe, Cinema X, Cinema 5 Production.
Jean Hersholt Humanitarian Award: Rosalind Russell.
SPECIAL AWARDS
Charles S. Boren, leader for 38 years of the industry's enlightened labor relations and architect of its policy of nondiscrimination.

Edward G. Robinson, who achieved greatness as a player, a patron of the arts, a dedicated citizen . . . in sum, a Renaissance man.

1973

Best Picture: The Sting, Universal-Bill/Phillips-George Roy Hill Film Production, Zanuck/Brown Presentation, Universal.
Actor: Jack Lemmon in Save The Tiger, Filmways-Jalem-Cirandinha Productions, Paramount.
Actress: Glenda Jackson in A Touch Of Class, Brut Productions, Avco Embassy.
Supporting Actor: John Houseman in The Paper Chase, Thompson-Paul Productions, 20th Century-Fox.
Supporting Actress: Tatum O'Neal in Paper Moon, Directors Company Production, Paramount.
Directing: George Roy Hill, The Sting.
Foreign Language Film Award: Day For Night, Les Films Du Carrosse-P.E.C.F.-P.I.C. Production (France).
Writing (screenplay—based on material from another medium): William Peter Blatty, The Exorcist, Hoya Productions, Warner Brothers.
Writing (original story and screenplay): David S. Ward, The Sting.
Cinematography: Sven Nykvist, Cries And Whispers, Svenska Filministitutet-Cinematograph AB Production, New World Pictures.
Art Direction: Harry Bumstead, Art Director; Set Decorator, James Payne, The Sting.
Costume Design: Edith Head, The Sting.
Film Editing: William Reynolds, The Sting.
Music (original score): Marvin Hamlisch, The Way We Were, Rastar Productions, Columbia.
Music (adaptation): Marvin Hamlisch, The Sting.
Music (song): Marvin Hamlisch, music; Allan and Marilyn Bergman, lyrics; The Way We Were from The Way We Were.
Short Subject (animated): Frank Film, Frank Mouris Production.
Short Subject (live action): The Bolero, Allan Miller Productions.
Sound: Robert Knudson, Chris Newman, The Exorcist, Hoya Productions, Warner Brothers.
Documentary (short subject): Princeton: A Search For Answers, Krainin-Sage Productions.
Documentary (feature): The Great American Cowboy, Keith Merrill, Rodeo Films Production.
Jean Hersholt Humanitarian Award: Lew Wasserman.
Irving G. Thalberg Memorial Award: Lawrence Weingarten.
SPECIAL AWARDS
Henri Langlois, for his devotion to the art of film, his massive contributions in preserving its past and his unswerving faith in its future.
Groucho Marx, in recognition of his brilliant creativity and for the unequaled achievements of the Marx Brothers in the art of motion picture comedy.

1974

Best Picture: The Godfather, Part II, A Coppola Company Production, Paramount.
Actor: Art Carney in Harry And Tonto, 20th Century-Fox.
Actress: Ellen Burstyn in Alice Doesn't Live Here Anymore, Warner Brothers.
Supporting Actor: Robert De Niro in The Godfather, Part II.
Supporting Actress: Ingrid Bergman in Murder On The Orient Express, G. W. Films, Paramount.
Directing: Francis Ford Coppola, The Godfather, Part II.
Foreign Language Film Award: Amarcord, F.C.-P.E.C.F. Production (Italy).
Writing (screenplay—based on material from another medium): Francis Ford Coppola, Mario Puzo, The Godfather, Part II.
Writing (original story and screenplay): Robert Towne, Chinatown, Robert Evans Production, Paramount.
Cinematography: Fred Koenekamp, The Towering Inferno, Irwin Allen Productions, 20th Century-Fox/Warner Brothers.
Art Direction: Dean Tavoularis, Angelo Graham; Set Decorator, George R. Nelson, The Godfather, Part II.
Costume Design: Theoni V. Aldredge, The Great Gatsby, David Merrick Productions, Paramount.
Film Editing: Harold F. Kress, Carl Kress, The Towering Inferno.
Music (original score): Nino Rota, Carmine Coppola, The Godfather, Part II.
Music (adaptation): Nelson Riddle, The Great Gatsby.
Music (song): Al Kasha, Joel Hirschhorn, We May Never Love Like This Again, from The Towering Inferno.
Short Subjects (animated): Closed Mondays, Lighthouse Productions.
Short Subjects (live action): One-Eyed Men Are Kings, C.A.P.A.C. Productions.
Sound: Ronald Pierce, Melvin Metcalfe, Sr., Earthquake, Universal-Mark Robson-Filmmakers Group Production, Universal.
Documentary (short subject): Don't, R.A. Films.
Documentary (feature): Hearts And Minds, Touchstone-Audjeff-BBS Production.
Jean Hersholt Humanitarian Award: Arthur Krim.

Jean Renoir, for his outstanding contributions to the world of cinema.
Howard Hawks, for his career-long directorial genius.

1975

Best Picture: One Flew Over The Cuckoo's Nest, A Fantasy Films Production, United Artists.
Actor: Jack Nicholson in One Flew Over The Cuckoo's Nest.
Actress: Louise Fletcher in One Flew Over The Cuckoo's Nest.
Supporting Actor: George Burns in The Sunshine Boys, A Ray Stark Production, Metro-Goldwyn-Mayer.
Supporting Actress: Lee Grant in Shampoo, Rubeeker Productions, Columbia.
Directing: Milos Forman, One Flew Over The Cuckoo's Nest.
Foreign Language Film Award: Dersu Uzala, A Mosfilms Studios Production (U.S.S.R.).
Writing (screenplay adapted from another medium): Lawrence Hauben, Bo Goldman, One Flew Over The Cuckoo's Nest.
Writing (original screenplay): Frank Pierson, Dog Day Afternoon, Warner Bros.
Cinematography: John Alcott, Barry Lyndon, A Hawk Films, Ltd. Production, Warner Bros.
Art Direction: Ken Adam, Roy Walker; Set Decoration, Vernon Dixon, Barry Lyndon.
Costume Design: Ulla-Britt Soderlund, Milena Canonero, Barry Lyndon.
Film Editing: Verna Fields, Jaws, A Universal-Zanuck/Brown Production, Universal.
Music (original score): John Williams, Jaws.
Music (adaptation): Leoanrd Rosenman, Barry Lyndon.
Music (song): Keith Carradine, I'm Easy, from Nashville, an ABC Entertainment-Jerry Weintraub-Robert Altman Production, Paramount.
Short Subject (live action): Bert Salzman, Angel And Big Joe, Bert Salzman Productions.
Short Subject (animated): Bob Godfrey, Great, Grantstern Ltd., and British Lion Films, Ltd.
Documentary (feature): The Man Who Skied Down Everest, A Crawley Films Presentation.
Documentary (short subject): The End Of The Game, Opus Films Limited.
Sound: Robert L. Hoyt, Roger Herman, Earl Madery, John Carter, Jaws.
Sound Effects: The Hindenburg, A Robert Wise-Filmakers Group-Universal Production, Universal, Peter Berkos.
Visual Effects: The Hindenburg, Albert Whitlock, Glen Robinson.
SPECIAL AWARD
Irving G. Thalberg Memorial Award: Mervyn LeRoy.

1976

Best Picture: Rocky, Robert Chartoff-Irwin Winkler Production, United Artists.
Actor: Peter Finch in Network, Howard Gottfried/Paddy Chayefsky Production, Metro-Goldwyn-Mayer/United Artists.
Actress: Faye Dunaway in Network.
Supporting Actor: Jason Robards in All The President's Men, Wildwood Enterprises Production, Warner Brothers.
Supporting Actress: Beatrice Straight in Network.
Directing: John G. Avildsen, Rocky.
Foreign Language Film Award: Black And White In Color, Arthur Cohn Production/Société Ivoirienne De Cinema (Ivory Coast).
Writing (original screenplay): Paddy Chayefsky, Network.
Writing (screenplay adapted from another medium): William Goldman, All The President's Men.
Cinematography: Haskell Wexler, Bound For Glory, The Bound For Glory Company Production, United Artists.
Art Direction: George Jenkins; Set Decoration, George Gaines, All The President's Men.
Costume Design: Danilo Donati, Fellini's Casanova, P.E.A.-Produzioni Europee Associate S.P.A. Production, Universal.
Film Editing: Richard Halsey, Scott Conrad, Rocky.
Music (original score): Jerry Goldsmith, The Omen, 20th Century-Fox Productions, Ltd., 20th Century-Fox.
Music (adaptation): Leonard Rosenman, Bound For Glory.
Music (song): Evergreen, from A Star Is Born. Music by Barbra Streisand. Lyrics for Paul Williams.
Short Subject (animated): Leisure, Film Australia Production.
Short Subjects (live action): In The Region Of Ice, American Film Institute Production.
Documentary (feature): Harlan County, U.S.A., Cabin Creek Films.
Sound: Arthur Piantadosi, Les Fresholtz, Dick Alexander, Jim Webb, All The President's Men.
SPECIAL AWARDS
Visual Effects: King Kong, Dino De Laurentiis Production, Paramount, Carlo Rambaldi, Glen Robinson, Frank Van der Veer.
Logan's Run, Saul David Production, Metro-Goldwyn-Mayer, L. B. Abbott, Glen Robinson, Matthew Yuricich.

1977

Best Picture: Annie Hall, A Jack Rollins-Charles H. Joffe Production, United Artists.

Actor: Richard Dreyfuss in The Goodbye Girl, A Ray Stark Production, Metro-Goldwyn-Mayer, United Artists.
Actress: Diane Keaton in Annie Hall.
Supporting Actor: Jason Robards in Julia, 20th Century-Fox.
Supporting Actress: Vanessa Redgrave in Julia.
Directing: Woody Allen, Annie Hall.
Foreign Language Film Award: Madame Rosa, A Lira Films Production (Italy).
Writing (screenplay—based on material from another medium): Alvin Sargent, Julia.
Writing (original story and screenplay): Woody Allen, Marshall Brickman, Annie Hall.
Cinematography: Vilmos Zsigmond, Close Encounters Of The Third Kind, Close Encounters Productions, Columbia.
Art Direction: John Barry, Norman Reynolds, Leslie Dilley, Art Directors; Roger Christian, Set Decorator; Star Wars, 20th Century-Fox.
Costume Design: John Mollo, Star Wars.
Film Editing: Paul Hirsch, Marcia Lukas, Richard Chew, Star Wars.
Music (original score): John Williams, Star Wars.
Music (song): Joseph Brooks, You Light Up My Life from You Light Up My Life, The Session Company, Columbia.
Music (adaptation): Jonathan Tunick, A Little Night Music, A Sascha-Wien Film Production, Elliott Kastner, New World Pictures.
Short Subjects (animated): Sand Castle, National Film Board of Canada.
Short Subjects (live action): I'll Find A Way, National Film Board of Canada.
Sound: Don MacDougall, Ray West, Bob Minkler, Derek Ball, Star Wars.
Visual Effects: John Stears, John Dykstra, Richard Edlund, Grant McCune, Robert Blalack, Star Wars.
Documentary (feature): Who Are The DeBolts? And Where Did They Get Nineteen Kids? Korty Films, Charles M. Schulz Creative Associates, Sanrio Films.
Documentary (short subject): Gravity Is My Enemy, A John Joseph Production.
Irving G. Thalberg Memorial Award: Walter Mirisch.
Jean Hersholt Humanitarian Award: Charlton Heston.
SPECIAL AWARDS
Frank E. Warner, for special achievements in sound editing for Close Encounters Of The Third Kind.
Benjamin Burt, Jr., for creating the robot voices for Star Wars.

1978

Best Picture: The Deer Hunter, EMI/Michael Cimino, Universal.
Actor: John Voight in Coming Home, United Artists.
Actress: Jane Fonda in Coming Home.
Supporting Actor: Christopher Walken in The Deer Hunter.
Supporting Actress: Maggie Smith in California Suite, Rastar, Columbia.
Directing: Michael Cimino, The Deer Hunter.
Foreign Language Film Award: Get Out Your Handkerchiefs, A Les Films, Ariane-C.A.P.A.C. Production (France).
Writing (screenplay—based on material from another medium): Oliver Stone, Midnight Express.
Writing (screenplay—written directly for the screen): Story; Nancy Dowd; Screenplay; Waldo Salt and Robert C. Jones, Coming Home.
Cinematography: Nestor Almendros, Days Of Heaven.
Art Direction: Paul Sylvet, Edwin O'Donovan; Set Director; George Gaines; Heaven Can Wait.
Costume Design: Anthony Powell, Death On The Nile.
Film Editing: Peter Zinner, The Deer Hunter.
Music (original score): Giorgio Moroder, Midnight Express.
Music (adapted score): Joe Renzetti, The Buddy Holly Story.
Music (song): Paul Jabara, Last Dance from Thank God It's Friday.
Short Subjects (animated): Eunice Macaulay, John Weldon, Special Delivery.
Short Subjects (live action): Taylor Hackford, Teenage Father.
Sound: Richard Portman, William McCaughey, Aaron Rochin, Darin Knight, The Deer Hunter.
Documentary Films (feature): Scared Straight, Arnold Shapiro, Producer.
Documentary Film (short subject): The Flight Of The Gossamer Condor, Jacqueline Phillips Shedd, Ben Shedd, Producers.
Jean Hersholt Humanitarian Award: Leo Jaffe.
HONORARY AWARDS
Walter Lantz, for bringing joy and laughter to every part of the world through his unique animated motion pictures.
Laurence Olivier, for the full body of his work, for the unique achievements of his career, and his lifetime of contributions to the art of film.
King Vidor, for his incomparable achievements as a cinematic creator and innovator.
The Museum of Modern Art Film Department, for the contribution it made to the public's perception of movies as an art form.
SPECIAL ACHIEVEMENT AWARD
Les Bowie, Colin Chivers, Denys Coop, Roy Field, Derek Meddings, and Zoran Perisic, for the visual effects in Superman.

1979

Best Picture: Kramer vs. Kramer, Stanley Jaffe Productions, Columbia.
Actor: Dustin Hoffman for Kramer vs. Kramer.
Actress: Sally Field in Norma Rae, A 20th Century-Fox Production, 20th Century-Fox.
Supporting Actor: Melvyn Douglas in Being There, A Lorimar Film-Und Fernsehproduction GmbH Production, United Artists.
Supporting Actress: Meryl Streep in Kramer vs. Kramer.
Directing: Robert Benton for Kramer vs. Kramer.
Foreign Language Film Award: The Tin Drum, A Franz Seitz Film/Bioskop Film/Artemis Film/Hallelujah Film/GGB 14, KG/Argos Films Production (West Germany).
Writing (screenplay based on material from another medium): Robert Benton for Kramer vs. Kramer.
Writing (screenplay written directly for the screen): Story and screenplay by Steve Tesich for Breaking Away, A 20th Century-Fox Production.
Cinematography: Vittorio Storaro for Apocalypse Now, Omni Zoeotrope Production, United Artists.
Art Direction: Phillip Rosenberg, Tony Walton, Art Directors; Edward Stewart, Gary Bring, Set Decorators; All That Jazz, A Columbia/20th Century-Fox Production.
Costume Design: Albert Wolsky, All That Jazz.
Film Editing: Alan Heim, All That Jazz.
Music (original score): Georges Delerue, A Little Romance, A Pan Arts Production, Otion Pictures.
Music (adapted score): Ralph Burns, All That Jazz.
Music (original song): Music, David Shire; lyrics, Norman Gimbel, It Goes Like It Goes from Norma Rae.
Short Subjects (animated): Every Child, National Film Board of Canada, Derek Lamb, Producer.
Short Subjects (live action): Board And Care, Ron Ellis Films, Sarah Pillsbury and Ron Ellis, Producers.
Documentary (feature): Best Boy, Only Child Motion Pictures. Ira Wohl, Producer.
Documentary (short subject): Paul Robeson: Tribute To An Artist, A Janus Film, Saul J. Turell, Producer.
Visual Effects: H. R. Giger, Carlo Rambaldi, Brian Johnson, Nick Allder, Denys Ayling for Alien, 20th Century-Fox Production, 20th Century-Fox, Ltd.
Sound: Walter Murch, Mark Berger, Richard Beggs, Nat Boxer, Apocalypse Now.
SPECIAL AWARDS
Jean Hersholt Humanitarian Award: Robert S. Benjamin.
Irving G. Thalberg Memorial Award: Ray Stark.
HONORARY AWARDS
Sir Alec Guinness
Hal Ellias
SPECIAL ACHIEVEMENT AWARD
Alan Solet for The Black Stallion, Sound Effects Editing.
ACADEMY AWARD OF MERIT
Mark Serrueier for Moviola.

1980

Best Picture: Ordinary People, Wildwood Enterprises Production, Paramount, Ronald L. Schwary, Producer.
Actor: Robert De Niro in Raging Bull, Robert Chartoff-Irwin Winkler Production, United Artists.
Actress: Sissy Spacek in Coal Miner's Daughter, Bernard Schwartz-Universal Pictures Production, Universal.
Supporting Actor: Timothy Hutton in Ordinary People.
Supporting Actress: Mary Steenburgen in Melvin and Howard, Linson/Phillips/Demme-Universal Pictures Production, Universal.
Directing: Robert Redford, Oridnary People.
Foreign Language Film Award: Moscow Does Not Believe In Tears, Mosfilm Studio Production (U.S.S.R.).
Writing (original screenplay): Bo Goldman, Melvin And Howard.
Writing (screenplay adaptation): Alvin Sargent, Ordinary People.
Cinematography: Tess, Geoffrey Unsworth, Ghislain Cloquet.
Art Direction: Pierre Guffroy, Jack Stephens, Tess.
Costume Design: Anthony Powell, Tess.
Film Editing: Thelma Schoonmaker, Raging Bull.
Music (original score): Michael Gore, Fame, Metro-Goldwyn-Mayer.
Music (original song): Music by Michael Gore, lyrics by Dean Pitchford, Fame from Fame.
Short Subjects (animated): The Fly, Pannonia Film, Budapest.
Short Subjects (live action): The Dollar Bottom, Rocking Horse Films, Ltd., Paramount, Lloyd Phillips, Producer.
Documentary (feature): From Mao To Mozart: Isaac Stern In China, Hopewell Foundation, Murray Lerner, Producer.
Documentary (short subject): Karl Hess: Toward Liberty, Halle/Ladue Inc. Roland Halle, Peter W. Ladue, Producers.
Sound: The Empire Strikes Back, Lucasfilm Ltd. Production, 20th Century-Fox. Bill Varney, Steve Maslow, Greg Landaker, Peter Sutton.
SPECIAL ACHIEVEMENT AWARDS
Brian Johnson, Richard Edlund, Dennis Murren, and Bruce Nicholson, for the visual effects in The Empire Strikes Back.

HONORARY AWARD
Henry Fonda, the consummate actor, in recognition of his brilliant accomplishments and enduring contributions to the art of motion pictures.

1981

Best Picture: Chariots Of Fire, Enigma Productions, The Ladd Company/Warner Bros. David Puttnam, Producer.
Actor: Henry Fonda in On Golden Pond, Associated Films, Universal.
Actress: Katharine Hepburn in On Golden Pond.
Supporting Actor: John Gielgud in Arthur, Orion Pictures, Warner Bros.
Supporting Actress: Maureen Stapleton in Reds, J.R.S., Paramount Pictures.
Directing: Warren Beatty, Reds.
Foreign Language Film Award: Mephisto, Mafilm-Objektiv Studio (Hungary).
Writing (original screenplay): Colin Welland, Chariots Of Fire.
Writing (screenplay adaptation): Ernest Thompson, On Golden Pond.
Cinematography: Vittorio Storaro, Reds.
Art Direction: Norman Reynolds, Leslie Dilley, Art Directors; Michael Ford, Set Director. Raiders Of The Lost Ark, Lucasfilm Productions, Paramount.
Costume Design: Milena Canonero, Chariots Of Fire.
Film Editing: Michael Kahn, Raiders Of The Lost Ark.
Music (original score): Vangelis, Chariots Of Fire.
Music (original song): Music and Lyrics Burt Bacharach, Carole Bayard Sager, Christopher Cross, Peter Allen. Arthur's Theme (Best That You Can Do), from Arthur.
Short Subjects (animated): Crac, Société Radio-Canada, Frederic Back, Producer.
Short Subjects (live action): Violet, The American Film Institute, Paul Kemp, Shelley Levinson, Producers.
Sound: Bill Varney, Steve Maslow, Greg Landaker, Roy Charman, Raiders Of The Lost Ark.
Visual Effects: Richard Edlund, Kit West, Bruce Nicholson, Joe Johnston, Raiders Of The Lost Ark.
Documentary (feature): Genocide, Arnold Schwartzman Productions, Arnold Schwartzman, Rabbi Marvin Hier, Producers.
Documentary (short subject): Noble Enterprise. Nigel Noble, Producer.
Makeup: Rick Baker, Am American Werewolf in London, Lycanthrope/Polygram/Universal Pictures, Universal.
Honorary Award: Barbara Stanwyck, an artist of impeccable grace and beauty, a dedicated actress, and one of the great ladies of Hollywood.
Irving G. Thalberg Memorial Award: Albert R. (Cubby) Broccoli.
Jean Hersholt Humanitarian Award: Danny Kaye.
SPECIAL AWARDS
Joseph B. Walker
Fuji Photo Film Company Ltd.
SPECIAL ACHIEVEMENT AWARD
Richard L. Anderson, Benjamin P. Burtt, Jr., for sound effects editing, Raiders of the Lost Ark.

1982

Best Picture: Gandhi, an Indo-British Films Production, Columbia, Richard Attenborough, Producer.
Actor: Ben Kingsley in Gandhi.
Actress: Meryl Streep in Sophie's Choice, an ITC Entertainment presentation of a Pakula-Barish Production, Universal/AFD.
Supporting Actor: Louis Gossett, Jr., in An Officer and a Gentleman, a Lorimar Production in association with Martin Elfand, Paramount.
Supporting Actress: Jessica Lange in Tootsie, a Mirage/Punch Production, Columbia.
Directing: Richard Attenborough, Gandhi.
Foreign Language Film Award: Volver A Empezar, Nickel Odeon, S.A. Production (Spain).
Writing (original screenplay): John Briley, Gandhi.
Writing (screenplay adaptation): Constantin Costa-Gavras, Donald Stewart, Missing.
Cinematography: Billy Williams, Ronnie Taylor, Gandhi.
Art Direction: Stuart Craig, Bob Laing, Art Directors; Michael Seirton, Set Director. Gandhi.
Costume Design: John Mullo, Bhanu Athaiya, Gandhi.
Film Editing: John Bloom, Gandhi.
Music (original score): John Williams, E.T. The Extra-Terrestrial, a Universal Pictures Production, Universal.
Music (original song score and adaptation or adaptation score): Henry Mancini, Leslie Bricusse, song score; Henry Mancini, adaptation, Victor/Victoria a Metro-Goldwyn-Mayer Production, MGM/UA.
Music (original song): Up Where We Belong, from An Officer And A Gentleman. Music by Jack Nitzsche and Buffy Sainte-Marie. Lyrics by Will Jennings.
Short Subjects (animated): Tango, Film Polski. Zbigniew Rybczynski, Producer.
Short Subjects (live action): A Shocking Accident, Flamingo Pictures Ltd. Christine Oestreicher, Producer.

Sound: Robert Knudson, Robert Glass, Don Digirolamo, Gene Cantamessa, E.T. The Extra-Terrestrial.
Visual Effects: Carlo Rambaldi, Dennis Muren, Kenneth F. Smith, E.T.: The Extra-Terrestrial.
Documentary (feature): Just Another Missing Kid, Canadian Broadcasting Corp. John Zaritsky, Producer.
Documentary (short subject): If You Love This Planet, National Film Board of Canada. Edward Le Lorrain and Terri Nash, Producers.
Makeup: Quest For Fire, an International Cinema Corp. Production, 20th Century-Fox (credits in controversy).
Honorary Award: Mickey Rooney.
Jean Hersholt Humanitarian Award: Walter Mirisch.
SPECIAL AWARDS
Gordon E. Sawyer Award (Academy statuette) John O. Aalberg for his technological contributions.
Academy Award of Merit (Academy statuette) August Arnold and Erich Kaestner for the concept and engineering of the first operational 35mm, hand-held, spinning mirror reflex, motion picture camera.

1983

Best Picture: Terms Of Endearment, a James L. Brooks Production, Paramount, James L. Brooks, Producer.
Actor: Robert Duvall in Tender Mercies, an EMI presentation of an Antron Media Production, Universal/AFD.
Actress: Shirley MacLaine in Terms Of Endearment.
Supporting Actor: Jack Nicholson in Terms Of Endearment.
Supporting Actress: Linda Hunt in The Year Of Living Dangerously, a Freddie Fields presentation of a Metro-Goldwyn-Mayer Production, MGM/UA.
Directing: James L. Brooks, Terms Of Endearment.
Cinematography: Fanny and Alexander, Cinematograph AB for the Swedish Film Institute/the Swedish Television SVT 1, Sweden/Gaumont, France Personafilm and Tobias Filmkunst, BRD production, Embassy.
Foreign Language Film Award: Fanny and Alexander (Sweden).
Writing (original screenplay): Horton Foote, Tender Mercies.
Writing (screenplay adaptation): James L. Brooks, Terms Of Endearment.
Art Direction: Anna Asp, Art Director; Susanne Lingheim, Set Director. Fanny and Alexander.
Costume Design: Marik Vos, Fanny and Alexander.
Film Editing: Glenn Farr, Lisa Fruchtman, Stephen A. Rotter, Douglas Stewart, Tom Rolf, The Right Stuff, a Robert Chartoff-Irwin Winkler Production, The Ladd Company through Warner Bros.
Music (original score): Bill Conti, The Right Stuff.
Music (original song score or adaptation score): Michel Legrand, Alan and Marilyn Bergman, Yentl, original song score, a United Artists/Ladbroke Feature/Harwood Production, MGM/UA.
Music (original song): Flashdance . . . What A Feeling from Flashdance. Music by Giorgio Moroder: Lyrics by Keith Forsey and Irene Cara.
Short Subjects (animated): Sundae in New York, Motionpicker Prods., Jimmy Picker, Producer.
Short Subjects (live action): Boys and Girls, Atlantis Films Ltd., Janice L. Platt, Producer.
Sound: Mark Berger, Tom Scott, Randy Thorn, David MacMillan, The Right Stuff.
Visual Effects: Richard Edlund, Dennis Muren, Ken Ralston, Phil Tippet, Return Of The Jedi, Lucasfilm Ltd. Production, Twentieth Century-Fox.
Documentary (feature): He Makes Me Feel Like Dancin', Edgar J. Scherick Associates Production, Emile Ardolino, Producer.
Documentary (short subject): Flamenco At 5:15, National Film Board of Canada, Cynthia Scott, Adam Symansky, Producers.
Honorary Award: Hal Roach, in recognition of his unparalleled record of distinguished contributions to the motion picture art form.
Jean Hersholt Humanitarian Award: M.J. (Mike) Frankovich.
SPECIAL AWARDS
Gordon E. Sawyer Award (Academy statuette) Dr. John G. Frayne, for outstanding contributions toward the advancement of the technology of sound in motion pictures.
Academy Award of Merit (Academy statuette) Dr. Kurt Larche, for the research and development of xenon short-arc discharge lamps for motion picture projection.

1984

Best Picture: Amadeus, a Saul Zaentz Company production, Orion. Saul Zaentz, producer.
Actor: F. Murray Abraham, Amadeus.
Actress: Sally Field, Places in the Heart, a Tri-Star Pictures production.
Supporting Actor: Dr. Haing S. Ngor, The Killing Fields, a Goldcrest Film & Television International/International Film Investors L.P. production, Warner Bros.
Supporting Actress: Peggy Ashcroft, A Passage to India, a G. W. Films Ltd. production, Columbia.

Directing: Milos Forman, Amadeus.
Foreign Language Film Award: Dangerous Moves, an Arthur Cohn production (Switzerland).
Writing (original screenplay): Robert Benton, Places in the Heart.
Writing (screenplay adaptation): Peter Shaffer, Amadeus.
Cinematography: Chris Menges, The Killing Fields.
Art Direction: Patrizia von Brandenstein, art direction; Karel Cerny, set decoration; Amadeus.
Costume Design: Theodor Pistek, Amadeus.
Film Editing: Jim Clark, The Killing Fields.
Music (original score): Maurice Jarre, A Passage To India.
Music (original song score): Prince, Purple Rain, a Purple Films Co. production, Warner Bros.
Music (song): I Just Called To Say I Love You, from The Woman In Red, (Orion). Music and lyrics by Stevie Wonder.
Short Subjects (animated): Charade, a Sheridan College Production, Jon Minnis, producer.
Short Subjects (live action): Up, Pyramid Films, Mike Hoover, producer.
Sound: Mark Berger, Tom Scott, Todd Boekelheide, Chris Newman, Amadeus.
Visual Effects: Dennis Muren, Michael McAlister, Lorne Peterson, George Gibbs, Indiana Jones and the Temple of Doom, a Lucasfilm production, Paramount.
Documentary (feature): The Times Of Harvey Milk, Black Sand Educational Productions, Inc., Robert Epstein and Richard Schmiechen, producers.
Documentary (short subject): The Stone Carvers, Paul Wagner Productions, Marjorie Hunt, Paul Wagner, producers.
Honorary Award: James Stewart.
Jean Hersholt Humanitarian Award: David L. Wolper.
SPECIAL AWARDS
Gordon E. Sawyer Award (Academy statuette) Linwood G. Dunn, for outstanding contributions toward the advancement of the science or technology of motion pictures.

1985

Best Picture: Out Of Africa, Universal Pictures Ltd. production, Universal. Sydney Pollack, producer.
Actor: William Hurt, The Kiss Of The Spider Woman, H. B. Filmes production in association with Sugarloaf Films, Island Alive, later distributed by Island Pictures.
Actress: Geraldine Page, The Trip To Bountiful, Bountiful production. Island Pictures.
Supporting Actor: Don Ameche, Cocoon, Fox/Zanuck-Brown production, 20th Century-Fox.
Supporting Actress: Anjelica Huston, Prizzi's Honor, ABC Motion Pictures production, 20th Century-Fox.
Directing: Sydney Pollack, Out Of Africa.
Foreign Language Film Award: The Official Story, Historias Cinematograficas/Cinemania and Progress Communications production, Almi, (Argentina).
Writing (original screenplay): Earl Wallace, William Kelley, screenplay; William Kelley, Pamela Wallace, Earl W. Wallace, story; Witness. Edward S. Feldman production, Paramount.
Writing (screenplay adaptation): Kurt Luedtke, Out of Africa.
Cinematography: David Watkin, Out Of Africa.
Art Direction: Stephen Grimes, art direction; Josie MacAvin, set decoration; Out Of Africa.
Costume Design: Emi Wada, Ran, Greenwich Film/Nippon Herlad Films/Herald Ace Production, Orion Classics.
Film Editing: Thom Noble, Witness.
Music (original score): John Barry, Out Of Africa.
Music (original song): Say You, Say Me, from White Nights, New Visions production, Columbia. Music and lyric by Lionel Richie.
Short Subjects (animated): Anna & Bella, The Netherland. Cilia Van Dijk, producer.
Short Subjects (live action): Molly's Pilgrims, Phoenix Films, Jeff Brown, producer.
Sound: Chris Jenkins, Gary Alexander, Larry Stenswold, Peter Handford, Out Of Africa.
Visual Effects: Ken Ralston, Ralph McQuarrie, Scott Farrar, David Berry, Cocoon.
Documentary (feature): Broken Rainbow, Earthworks Films production. Maria Florio, Victoria Mudd, producers.
Documentary (short subject): Witness to War: Dr. Charlie Clements, Skylight Picture production. David Goodman, producer.
Honorary Awards: Paul Newman, in recognition of his many memorable and compelling screen performances and for his personal integrity and dedication to his craft.
Alex North, in recognition of his brilliant artistry in the creation of memorable music for motion pictures.
Jean Hersholt Humanitarian Award: Charles (Buddy) Rogers.

1986

Best Picture: Platoon, Hemdale Film production, Orion. Arnold Kopelson, producer.
Actor: Paul Newman, The Color Of Money, Touchstone Pictures production in association with Silver Screen Partners II, Buena Vista.

Actress: Marlee Matlin, Children Of A Lesser God, Burt Sugarman Production, Paramount.
Supporting Actor: Michael Caine, Hannah And Her Sisters, Jack Rollins and Charles H. Joffe Production, Orion.
Supporting Actress: Dianne Wiest, Hannah And Her Sisters.
Directing: Oliver Stone, Platoon.
Foreign Language Film Award: The Assault, Fons Rademakers Prod. B. V. for Cannon Group Holland, Cannon (The Netherlands).
Writing (original screenplay): Woody Allen, Hannah And Her Sisters.
Writing (screenplay adaptation): Ruth Prawer Jhabvala, A Room With A View, Merchant Ivory production, Cinecom Pictures.
Cinematography: Chris Menges, The Mission, Warner Bros./Goldcrest and Kingsmere production, Warner Bros.
Art Direction: Gianni Quaranta, Brian Ackland-Snow, art direction; Brian Savegar, Elio Altramura, set decoration, A Room With A View.
Costume Design: Jenny Beavan, John Bright, A Room With A View.
Film Editing: Claire Simpson, Platoon.
Music (original score): Herbie Hancock, 'Round Midnight, Warner Bros. production, Warner Bros.
Music (original song): Take My Breath Away, from Top Gun, Don Simpson and Jerry Bruckheimer production, Paramount. Music by Giorgio Moroder; lyric by Tom Whitlock.
Short Subjects (animated): A Greek Tragedy, CineTe pvba. Linda Van Tulden, William Thijssen, producers.
Short Subjects (live action): Precious Images, Calliope Films Inc. Chuck Workman, producer.
Sound: John (Doc) Wilkinson, Richard Rogers, Charles (Bud) Grenzbach, Simon Kaye, Platoon.
Visual Effects: Robert Skotak, Stan Winston, John Richardson, Suzanne Benson, Aliens.
Documentary (feature): Artie Shaw: Time Is All You've Got, Bridge Film production. Brigitte Berman, producer. Down And Out In America, Joseph Feury production. Joseph Feury, Jilton Justice, producers.
Documentary (short subject): Women—For America, for the World, Educational Film & Video Project. Vivienne Verdon-Roe, producer.
Makeup: Chris Walas, Stephan Dupuis, The Fly, Brooksfilms Ltd. production, 20th Century-Fox.
Honorary Award: Ralph Bellamy, for his unique artistry and his distinguished service to the profession of acting.
Irving G. Thalberg Memorial Award: Steven Spielberg.

1987

Best Picture: The Last Emperor, a Hemdale Film production, Columbia. Jeremy Thomas, producer.
Actor: Michael Douglas, Wall Street, Oaxatal production, 20th Century Fox.
Actress: Cher, Moonstruck, Patrick Palmer and Norman Jewison production, MGM.
Supporting Actor: Sean Connery, The Untouchables, Art Linson production, Paramount.
Supporting Actress: Olympia Dukakis, Moonstruck.
Directing: Bernardo Bertolucci, The Last Emperor.
Foreign Language Film Award: Babette's Feast, Panorama Film Int. production in cooperation with Nordisk Film and the Danish Film Institute, Orion Classics (Denmark).
Writing (original screenplay): John Patrick Shanley, Moonstruck.
Writing (screenplay adaptation): Mark Peploe, Bernardo Bertolucci, The Last Emperor.
Cinematography: Vittorio Storaro, The Last Emperor.
Art Direction: Ferdinando Scarfiotti, art direction; Bruno Cesari, Osvaldu Desideri, set decoration, The Last Emperor.
Costume Design: James Acheson, The Last Emperor.
Film Editing: Gabriella Cristiani, The Last Emperor.
Music (original score): Ryuichi Sakamoto, David Byrne, Cong Su, The Last Emperor.
Music (original song): (I've Had) The Time Of My Life, from Dirty Dancing, Vestron Pictures production in association with Great American Films Limited Partnership, Vestron. Music by Franke Previte, John DeNicola, Donald Markowitz; lyric by Franke Previte.
Short Subjects (animated): The Man Who Painted Trees, Societe Radio-Canada/Canadian Broadcasting Corp., Frederic Back, producer.
Short Subjects (live action): Ray's Male Heterosexual Dance Hall, Chanticleer Films, Jonathan Sanger, Jana Sue Memel, producers.
Sound: Bill Rowe, Ivan Sharrock, The Last Emperor.
Visual Effects: Dennis Muren, William George, Harley Jessup, Kenneth Smith, Innerspace, Warner Bros. production, Warner Bros.
Documentary (feature): The Ten-Year Lunch: The Wit And Legend Of The Algonquin Round Table, Aviva Films production, Aviva Slesin, producer.
Documentary (short subject): Young at Heart, Sue Marx Films Inc. production, Sue Marx, Pamela Conn, producers.

Makeup: Rick Baker, Harry and the Hendersons, Universal/Amblin Entertainment production, Universal.
Irving G. Thalberg Memorial Award: Billy Wilder.

1988

Best Picture: Rain Man, Guber-Peters Co. production, United Artists. Mark Johnson, producer.
Actor: Dustin Hoffman, Rain Man.
Actress: Jodie Foster, The Accused, Jaffe-Lansing production, Paramount.
Supporting Actor: Kevin Kline, A Fish Called Wanda, Michael Shamberg-Prominent Features production, MGM.
Supporting Actress: Geena Davis, The Accidental Tourist, Warner Bros. production, Warner Bros.
Directing: Barry Levinson, Rain Man.
Foreign Language Film Award: Pelle The Conqueror, Per Holst/Kaerne Films production, Miramax Films (Denmark).
Writing (original screenplay): Ronald Bass, Barry Morrow, screenplay; Barry Morrow, story; Rain Man.
Writing (screenplay adaptation): Christopher Hampton, Dangerous Liaisons, NFH Limited production from Lorimar Film Entertainment & Warner Bros., Warner Bros.
Cinematography: Peter Biziou, Mississippi Burning, Frederick Zollo production, Orion.
Art Direction: Stuart Craig, art direction; Gerard James, set decoration; Dangerous Liaisons.
Costume Design: James Acheson, Dangerous Liaisons.
Film Editing: Arthur Schmidt, Who Framed Roger Rabbit, Amblin Entertainment and Touchstone Pictures production, Buena Vista.
Music (original score): Dave Grusin, The Milagro Beanfield War, Robert Redford/Moctesuma Esparza production, Universal.
Music (original song): Let The River Run, from Working Girl, 20th Century Fox production, 20th Century Fox. Music and lyric by Carly Simon.
Short Subjects (animated): Tin Toy, Pixar, John Lasseter, producer.
Short Subjects (live action): The Appointments of Dennis Jennings, Schooner Prods. Inc., Dean Parisot, Steven Wright, producers.
Sound: Les Fresholtz, Dick Alexander, Vern Poore, Willie D. Burton, Bird, Malpaso production, Warner Bros.
Sound Effects Editing: Charles L. Campbell, Louis L. Edemann, Who Framed Roger Rabbit.
Visual Effects: Ken Ralston, Richard Williams, Edward Jones, George Gibbs, Who Framed Roger Rabbit.
Documentary (feature): Hotel Terminus: The Life And Times Of Klaus Barbie, The Memory Pictures Co. production, Marcel Ophuls, producer.
Documentary (short subject): You Don't Have To Die, Tiger Rose production in association with Filmworks Inc., William Guttentag, Malcolm Clarke, producers.
Makeup: Ve Neill, Steve La Porte, Robert Short, Beetlejuice, Geffen Film Co. production, Geffen/Warner Bros.
Honorary Oscar: Eastman Kodak.
SPECIAL AWARDS
Gordon E. Sawyer Award (Academy statuette) Gordon Henry Cook.
National Film Board of Canada.
Richard Williams.

1989

Best Picture: Driving Miss Daisy, Warner Bros., Zanuck, Co. production; Richard D. Zanuck, Lili Fini Zanuck, producers.
Actor: Daniel Day Lewis, My Left Foot, Miramax, Ferndale/Granada production; Noel Pearson, producer.
Actress: Jessica Tandy, Driving Miss Daisy.
Supporting Actor: Denzel Washington, Glory, Tri-Star Pictures production, Tri-Star.
Supporting Actress: Brenda Fricker, My Left Foot.
Directing: Oliver Stone, Born on the Fourth of July, Universal, Kitman Ho & Ixtian production; A. Kitman Ho, Oliver Stone, producers.
Foreign Language Film Award: Cinema Paradiso, Cristaldifilm/Films Ariane production, Miramax (Italy).
Writing (original screenplay): Tom Schulman, Dead Poets Society, Buena Vista, Touchstone Pictures production, in association with Silver Screen Partners IV; Steven Haft, Paul Junger Witt, Tony Thomas, producers.
Writing (screenplay adaptation): Alfred Uhry, Driving Miss Daisy.
Cinematography: Freddie Francis, Glory.
Art Direction: Anton Furst, art direction; Peter Young, set decoration; Batman, Guber-Peters production, Warner Bros.
Costume Design: Phyllis Dlaton, Henry V, Renaissance Films production, in association with BBC, Samuel Goldwyn Co.
Film Editing: David Brenner, Joe Hutshing, Born on the Fourth of July.
Music (original score): Alan Menken, The Little Mermaid, Walt Disney Pictures production, in association with Silver Screen Partners IV, Buena Vista.
Music (original song): Under The Sea, from The Little Mermaid. Music by Alan Menken, lyric by Howard Ashman.

Short Subjects (animated): Balance, Lauenstein production, Christoph Lauenstein, Wolfgang Lauenstein, producers.

Short Subjects (live action): Work Experience, North Inch Production Ltd., James Hendrie, producer.

Sound: Donald O. Mitchell, Gregg C. Rudloff, Elliott Tyson, Russell Williams II, Glory.

Sound Effects Editing: Ben Burtt, Richard Hymns, Indiana Jones And The Last Crusade, Lucasfilm Ltd. production, Paramount.

Visual Effects: John Bruno, Dennis Muren, Hoyt Yeatman, Dennis Skotak, The Abyss, Gale Anne Hurd production, 20th Century Fox.

Documentary (feature): Common Threads: Stories From The Quilt, Telling Pictures and The Couturie Co. production, Robert Epstein, Bill Couturie, producers.

Documentary (short subject): The Johnstown Flood, Guggenheim Productions, Inc. production, Charles Guggenheim, producer.

Makeup: Manlio Rocchetti, Lynn Barber, Kevin Haney, Driving Miss Daisy.

Honorary Oscar: Akira Kurosawa.

SPECIAL AWARDS

Gordon E. Sawyer Award (Academy statuette) Pierre Angenieux.
Jean Hersholt Humanitarian Award, Howard W. Koch.

1990

Best Picture: Dances With Wolves, Orion, Tig production; Jim Wilson, Kevin Costner, producers.

Actor: Jeremy Irons, Reversal Of Fortune, Reversal Films production; Warner Bros.

Actress: Kathy Bates, Misery, Castle Rock Entertainment production, Columbia.

Supporting Actor: Joe Pesci, Goodfellas, Warner Bros. production, Warner Bros.

Supporting Actress: Whoopi Goldberg, Ghost, Howard W. Koch production, Paramount.

Directing: Kevin Costner, Dances With Wolves.

Foreign Language Film Award: Journey of Hope, A Catpics/Condor Features production (Switzerland).

Writing (original screenplay): Bruce Joel Rubin, Ghost.

Writing (screenplay adaptation): Michael Blake, Dances With Wolves.

Cinematography: Dean Semier, Dances With Wolves.

Art Direction: Richard Sylbert, art direction; Rick Simpson, set decoration; Dick Tracy. Touchstone Pictures production, Buena Vista. Music and lyric by Stephen Sondheim.

Costume Design: Franca Squaricapino, Cyrano de Bergerac, Hachette Premiere production, Orion Classics (France).

Film Editing: Neil Travis, Dances With Wolves.

Music (original score): John Barry, Dances With Wolves.

Music (original song): Sooner Or Later (I Always Get My Man), from Dick Tracy.

Short Subjects (animated): Creature Comforts, Aardman Animations Ltd. production, Nick Park, producer.

Short Subjects (live action): The Lunch Date, Adam Davidson production, Adam Davidson, producer.

Sound: Russell Williams II, Jeffrey Perkins, Bill W. Benton, Greg Watkins, Dances With Wolves.

Sound Effects Editing: Cecelia Hall, George Watters II, The Hunt For Red October, Mace Neufeld/Jerry Sherlock production, Paramount.

Visual Effects: Eric Brevig, Rob Bottin, Tim McGovern, Alex Funke, Total Recall, Special Achievement Award.

Documentary (feature): American Dream, Cabin Creek production, Barbara Kopple, Arthur Cohn, producers.

Documentary (short subject): Days Of Waiting, Mouchette Films production, Steven Okazaki, producer.

Makeup: John Caglione Jr., Doug Drexler, Dick Tracy.

Honorary Oscar: Sophia Loren and Myrna Loy.

SPECIAL AWARDS

Gordon E. Sawyer Award (Academy statuette) Stefan Kudelski.
Academy Award of Merit (Academy statuette) Eastman Kodak Co.
Scientific or Technical Awards (Academy Plaque) Bruce Wilton and Carlos Icinkoff of Mechanical Concepts. Engineering Dept. of Arnold & Richter. Fuji Photo Film Co. Ltd. Manfred G. Michelson of Technical Film Systems. John W. Lang, Walter Hrastnik and Charles J. Watson of Bell & Howell Co.

Technical Achievement Award (Academy Certificate) William L. Blowers of Belco Associates and Thomas F. Denove, Iain Neil, Takuo Miyagishima and Panavision. Christopher S. Gilman and Harvey Hubert Jr. of the Diligen Dwarves Effects. Jim Graves of J&G Enterprises. Bengt O. Orhall, Kenneth Lund, Bjorn Selin and Kjell Hogberg of AB Film-Teknik. Richard Mula and Pete Romano of HydroImage. Dedo Weigert of Dedo Weigert Film. Dr. Fred Kolb Jr., Paul Preo, Peter Baldwin and Dr. Paul Kiankhooy and the Lightmaker Co.

Medal of Commendation Roderick T. Ryan, Don Trumbull and Geoffrey H. Williamson.

1991

Best Picture: The Silence of the Lambs, Strong Heart/Demme Production, Orion; Edward Saxon, Kenneth Utt and Ron Bozman, producers.

Actor: Anthony Hopkins, The Silence of the Lambs.

Actress: Jodie Foster, The Silence of the Lambs.

Supporting Actor: Jack Palance, City Slickers, Castle Rock Entertainment in association with Nelson Entertainment presentation of a Face production, Columbia.

Supporting Actress: Mercedes Ruehl, The Fisher King, Hill/Obst production, Tri-Star.

Directing: Jonathan Demme, The Silence of the Lambs.

Foreign Language Film Award: Mediterraneo, Pentafilm S.p.A./A.M.A. Film S.r.l. production (Italy), Miramax.

Writing (original screenplay): Callie Khouri, Thelma & Louise, Percy Main production, MGM.

Writing (screenplay adaptation): Ted Tally, The Silence of the Lambs.

Cinematography: Robert Richardson, JFK.

Art Direction: Dennis Gassner, art direction; Nancy Haigh, set decoration; Bugsy, TriStar Pictures production, TriStar.

Costume Design: Albert Wolsky, Bugsy.

Film Editing: Joe Hutshing, Pietro Scalia, JFK.

Music (original score): Alan Menken, Beauty and the Beast, Walt Disney Pictures production, Buena Vista.

Music (original song): Beauty and the Beast, from Beauty and the Beast. Music by Alan Menken, lyric by Howard Ashman.

Short Subjects (animated): Manipulation, Tandem Films production; Daniel Greaves, producer.

Short Subjects (live action): Session Man, Chanticleer Films production; Daniel Greaves, producer.

Sound: Tom Johnson, Gary Rydstrom, Gary Summers, Lee Orloff, Terminator 2: Judgment Day. Mario Kassar production of a Pacific Western production in association with Lightstorm Entertainment, TriStar (from Carolco).

Sound Effects Editing: Gary Rydstrom, Gloria S. Borders, Terminator 2: Judgment Day.

Visual Effects: Dennis Muren, Stan Winston, Gene Warren Jr., Robert Skotak, Terminator 2: Judgment Day.

Documentary (feature): In the Shadow of the Stars, Light-Saraf Films production; Allie Light, Irving Saraf, producers.

Documentary (short subject): Deadly Deception: General Electric, Nuclear Weapons and Our Environment, Women's Educational Madia Inc. production; Debra Chasnoff, producer.

Makeup: Stan Sinston, Jeff Dawn, Terminator 2: Judgment Day.

Honorary Oscar: Satyajit Ray.

SPECIAL AWARDS

Gordon E. Sawyer Award (Academy statuette) Ray Harryhausen.
Academy Award of Merit (Academy statuette) Eastman Kodak Co.
Scientific or Technical Awards (Academy Plaque) Iain Neil, Albert Saiki, Panavision Inc. Georg Thoma, Heinz Feierlein, and the engineering department of Sachtler AG. Harry J. Baker. Guido Cartoni. Ray Feeney, Richard Keeney, and Richard J. Lundell. Faz Fazakas, Brian Henson, Dave Housman, Peter Miller, and John Stephenson. Mario Celso. Randy Cartwright, David B. Coons, Lem Davis, Thomas Hahn, James Houston, Mark Kimball, Peter Nye, Michael Shantzis, David F. Wolf, and the Walt Disney Feature Animation Department. George Worrall.
Technical Achievement Award (Academy Certificate) Robert W. Stoler Jr. James Doyle. Dick Cavdek, Steve Hamerski, and Otto Namenz Intl. Inc. Ken Robings and Clairmont Camera. Century Precision Optics.
Award of Commendation (Special Plaque) Pete Comandine, Richard T. Dayton, Donald Hagans and Richard T. Ryan of YCM Laboratories.
Medal of Commendation (Medallion) Richard J. Stumpf and Joseph Westheimer.

41A

DIRECTORS GUILD OF AMERICA AWARDS 1948–49 TO 1991

(formerly Screen Directors Guild Awards)

The only instances in history when DGA and Oscar direction prizes didn't match were in 1968, when Anthony Harvey received the DGA for "The Lion in Winter" but Carol Reed won the Oscar for "Oliver!"; 1972, when Francis Coppola won the DGA for "The Godfather," but Bob Fosse was the Oscar winner for "Cabaret," and 1985, when Steven Spielberg was the DGA recipient for "The Color Purple," but Sydney Pollack took the Oscar for "Out of Africa."

1948–49: *Quarterly Awards* to FRED ZINNEMANN for The Search; HOWARD HAWKS for Red River; ANATOLE LITVAK for The Snake Pit; JOSEPH L. MANKIEWICZ for A Letter to Three Wives. *Annual Award* to JOSEPH L. MANKIEWICZ.

1949–50: *Quarterly Awards* to MARK ROBSON for The Champion; ALFRED L. WERKER for Lost Boundaries; ROBERT ROSSEN for All the King's Men; CAROL REED for The Third Man. *Annual Award* to ROBERT ROSSEN.

1950–1951: *Quarterly Awards* to BILLY WILDER for Sunset Boulevard; JOHN HUSTON for The Asphalt Jungle; JOSEPH L. MANKIEWICZ for All About Eve; VINCENTE MINNELLI for Father's Little Dividend. *Annual Award* to JOSEPH L. MANKIEWICZ for All About Eve.

1951: *May–July* to ALFRED HITCHCOCK for Strangers on a Train; *August–October* to GEORGE STEVENS for A Place in the Sun; *November–December* to VINCENTE MINNELLI for An American in Paris. *Annual Award* to GEORGE STEVENS for A Place in the Sun.

1952: *Quarterly Awards* to CHARLES CRICHTON for The Lavender Hill Mob; JOSEPH MANKIEWICZ for Five Fingers; FRED ZINNEMANN for High Noon; JOHN FORD for The Quiet Man. *Annual Award* to JOHN FORD.

1953: *Most Outstanding Directorial Achievement:* FRED ZINNEMANN for From Here to Eternity; *Outstanding Directorial Achievements:* CHARLES WALTERS for Lili; WILLIAM WYLER for Roman Holiday, GEORGE STEVENS for Shane, BILLY WILDER for Stalag 17. *Motion Picture Critic Award:* BOSLEY CROWTHER, New York Times.

1954: *Most Outstanding Directorial Achievement:* ELIA KAZAN for On The Waterfront; *Outstanding Directorial Achievement:* GEORGE SEATON for The Country Girl, ALFRED HITCHCOCK for Rear Window, BILLY WILDER for Sabrina, WILLIAM WELLMAN for The High and the Mighty; *Motion Picture Critic Award:* HAROLD V. COHEN, Pittsburgh *Post-Gazette.*

1955: *Most Outstanding Directorial Achievement:* DELBERT MANN for Marty; *Outstanding Directorial Achievement:* JOHN STURGES for Bad Day at Black Rock, JOHN FORD and MERVYN LEROY for Mister Roberts, ELIA KAZAN for East of Eden, JOSHUA LOGAN for Picnic. *Motion Picture Critic Award:* JOHN ROSENFIELD, Dallas *Morning Evening Star.*

1956: *Most Outstanding Directorial Achievement;* GEORGE STEVENS for Giant; *Outstanding Directorial Achievement:* MICHAEL ANDERSON for Around the World in 80 Days, WILLIAM WYLER for Friendly Persuasion, KING VIDOR for War and Peace, WALTER LANG for The King and I. *Motion Picture Critic Award:* FRANCIS J. CARMODY, Washington *News. D.W. Griffith Award:* KING VIDOR.

1957: *Outstanding Directorial Achievement:* DAVID LEAN for The Bridge On the River Kwai; JOSHUA LOGAN for 12 Angry Men; SIDNEY LUMET for 12 Angry Men; MARK ROBSON for Peyton Place, and BILLY WILDER for Witness for the Prosecution. *Motion Picture Critic Award,* HOLLIS ALPERT and ARTHUR KNIGHT, critics for The Saturday Review.

1958: *Grand Award for Direction:* VINCENTE MINNELLI for Gigi; *D.W. Griffith Award for creative achievement in the film industry:* FRANK CAPRA; *Motion Picture Critic Award:* PHILIP K. SCHEUER, critic of the Los Angeles Times; *Special Award:* LOUELLA PARSONS; *Best Directed Non-English-Speaking Film;* RENE CLAIR for Gates of Paris (French).

1959: *Grand Award for Direction:* WILLIAM WYLER, Ben-Hur; *Most Outstanding Directorial Achievement:* Ben-Hur; *Motion Picture Critic Award:* JOHN E. FITZGERALD, entertainment editor of Our Sunday Visitor, a Sunday Supplement distributed by Catholic weeklies.

1960: *Grand Award for Direction:* BILLY WILDER, The Apartment; *Motion Picture Critic Award:* PAUL BECKLEY, New York Herald Tribune; *Special Award of Honorary Membership:* Y. FRANK FREEMAN.

1961: *Directors Award:* ROBERT WISE, JEROME ROBBINS, West Side Story; *Critics Award:* John Beaufort of the Christian Science Monitor.

1962: *Director's Awards:* DAVID LEAN, Lawrence of Arabia.

1963: *Film Director's Award:* TONY RICHARDSON, Tom Jones; *Motion Picture Critic's Award:* PAINE KNICKERBOCKER, San Francisco Chronicle.

1964: *Film Director's Award:* GEORGE CUKOR, My Fair Lady; *Motion Picture Critic's Award:* JAMES MEADE, The San Diego Union.

1965: *Film Director's Award:* ROBERT WISE, The Sound of Music; *Critics Award:* SAM LESNER, Chicago Daily News; *D.W. Griffith Award:* WILLIAM WYLER.

1966: *Film Director's Award:* FRED ZINNEMANN, A Man for All Seasons.

1967: *Film Director's Award:* MIKE NICHOLS, The Graduate.

1968: *Film Director's Award:* ANTHONY HARVEY, The Lion in Winter; *D.W. Griffith Award:* ALFRED HITCHCOCK.

1969: *Film Director's Award:* JOHN SCHLESINGER, Midnight Cowboy; *D. W. Griffith Award:* FRED ZINNEMANN.

1970: *Film Director's Award:* FRANKLIN SCHAFFNER, Patton.

1971: *Film Director's Award:* WILLIAM FRIEDKIN, The French Connection.

1972: *Film Director's Award:* FRANCIS FORD COPPOLA, The Godfather.

1973: *Film Director's Award:* GEORGE ROY HILL, The Sting.

1974: *Film Director's Award:* FRANCIS FORD COPPOLA, The Godfather, Part II.

1975: *Film Director's Award:* MILOS FORMAN, One Flew Over the Cuckoo's Nest.

1976: *Film Director's Award:* JOHN G. AVILDSEN, Rocky.

1977: *Film Director's Award:* WOODY ALLEN, Annie Hall.

1978: *Film Director's Award:* MICHAEL CIMINO, The Deer Hunter.

1979: *Film Director's Award:* ROBERT BENTON, Kramer Vs. Kramer.

1980: *Film Director's Award:* ROBERT REDFORD, Ordinary People.

1981: *Film Director's Award:* WARREN BEATTY, Reds.

1982: *Film Director's Award:* SIR RICHARD ATTENBOROUGH, Gandhi.

1983: *Film Director's Award:* JAMES BROOKS, Terms of Endearment; *Robert B. Aldrich Service Award (honorary):* ROBERT WISE.

1984: *Film Director's Award:* MILOS FORMAN, Amadeus; *D.W. Griffith Award for Life Achievement:* BILLY WILDER.

1985: *Film Director's Award:* STEVEN SPIELBERG, The Color Purple; *D.W. Griffith Award for Life Achievement:* JOSEPH L. MANKIEWICZ; *Robfert B. Aldrich Award (honorary):* George Sidney.

1986: *Film Director's Award:* OLIVER STONE, Platoon; *D.W. Griffith Award for Life Achievement:* ELIA KAZAN; *Frank Capra Award (to an assistant director or unit production manager for outstanding service to the industry):* HENRY E. "BUD" BRILL.

1987: *Film Director's Award:* BERNARDO BERTOLUCCI, The Last Emperor; *D.W. Griffith Award for Lifetime Achievement:* ROBERT E. WISE; *Robert B. Aldrich Award (for work on behalf of the guild):* SHELDON LEONARD.

1988: *Film Director's Award:* BARRY LEVINSON, Rain Man; *Honorary Life Award:* SIDNEY LUMET; *Robert B. Aldrich Award (for work on behalf of the guild):* GILBERT CATES; *Special DGA Award:* U.S. Representative ROBERT J. MRAZEK (D-NY) who with SIDNEY R. YATES (D-IL) authored National Film Preservation Act of 1988.

1989: *Film Director's Award:* OLIVER STONE, Born on the Fourth of July; *D.W. Griffith Award for Lifetime Achievement:* INGMAR BERGMAN; *Robert B. Aldrich Award (for work on behalf of the guild):* GEORGE SCHAEFER; *Frank Capra Achievement Award (for assistant directors and unit production managers):* STANLEY ACKERMAN.

1990: *Film Director's Award:* KEVIN COSTNER, Dances with Wolves; *Frank Capra Achievement Award:* HOWARD KOCH; *Honorary Life Membership:* GILBERT CATES; *Franklin J. Schaffner Achievement Award:* MORTIMER & CHESTER O'BRIEN; *Robert B. Aldrich Service Award:* LARRY AUERBACH AND MILT FELSEN.

1991: *Film Director's Award:* JONATHAN DEMME, The Silence of the Lambs; *D.W. Griffith Life Achievement Award:* AKIRA KUROSAWA; *Honorary Life Membership:* CHARLES CHAMPLIN.

QP MONEY-MAKING STARS OF 1933–1991

1991: (1) Kevin Costner; (2) Arnold Schwarzenegger; (3) Robin Williams; (4) Julia Roberts; (5) Macaulay Culkin; (6) Jodie Foster; (7) Billy Crystal; (8) Dustin Hoffman; (9) Robert De Niro; (10) Mel Gibson.

1990: (1) Arnold Schwarzenegger; (2) Julia Roberts; (3) Bruce Willis; (4) Tom Cruise; (5) Mel Gibson; (6) Kevin Costner; (7) Patrick Swayze; (8) Sean Connery; (9) Harrison Ford; (10) Richard Gere.

1989: (1) Jack Nicholson; (2) Tom Cruise; (3) Robin Williams; (4) Michael Douglas; (5) Tom Hanks; (6) Michael J. Fox; (7) Eddie Murphy; (8) Mel Gibson; (9) Sean Connery; (10) Kathleen Turner.

1988: (1) Tom Cruise; (2) Eddie Murphy; (3) Tom Hanks; (4) Arnold Schwarzenegger; (5) Paul Hogan; (6) Danny De Vito; (7) Bette Midler; (8) Robin Williams; (9) Tom Selleck; (10) Dustin Hoffman.

1987: (1) Eddie Murphy; (2) Michael Douglas; (3) Michael J. Fox; (4) Arnold Schwarzenegger; (5) Paul Hogan; (6) Tom Cruise; (7) Glenn Close; (8) Sylvester Stallone; (9) Cher; (10) Mel Gibson.

1986: (1) Tom Cruise; (2) Eddie Murphy; (3) Paul Hogan; (4) Rodney Dangerfield; (5) Bette Midler; (6) Sylvester Stallone; (7) Clint Eastwood; (8) Whoopi Goldberg; (9) Kathleen Turner; (10) Paul Newman.

1985: (1) Sylvester Stallone; (2) Eddie Murphy; (3) Clint Eastwood; (4) Michael J. Fox; (5) Chevy Chase; (6) Arnold Schwarzenegger; (7) Chuck Norris; (8) Harrison Ford; (9) Michael Douglas; (10) Meryl Streep.

1984: (1) Clint Eastwood; (2) Bill Murray; (3) Harrison Ford; (4) Eddie Murphy; (5) Sally Field; (6) Burt Reynolds; (7) Robert Redford; (8) Prince; (9) Dan Aykroyd; (10) Meryl Streep.

1983: (1) Clint Eastwood; (2) Eddie Murphy; (3) Sylvester Stallone; (4) Burt Reynolds; (5) John Travolta; (6) Dustin Hoffman; (7) Harrison Ford; (8) Richard Gere; (9) Chevy Chase; (10) Tom Cruise.

1982: (1) Burt Reynolds; (2) Clint Eastwood; (3) Sylvester Stallone; (4) Dudley Moore; (5) Richard Pryor; (6) Dolly Parton; (7) Jane Fonda; (8) Richard Gere; (9) Paul Newman; (10) Harrison Ford.

1981: (1) Burt Reynolds; (2) Clint Eastwood; (3) Dudley Moore; (4) Dolly Parton; (5) Jane Fonda; (6) Harrison Ford; (7) Alan Alda; (8) Bo Derek; (9) Goldie Hawn; (10) Bill Murray.

1980: (1) Burt Reynolds; (2) Robert Redford; (3) Clint Eastwood; (4) Jane Fonda; (5) Dustin Hoffman; (6) John Travolta; (7) Sally Field; (8) Sissy Spacek; (9) Barbra Streisand; (10) Steve Martin.

1979: (1) Burt Reynolds; (2) Clint Eastwood; (3) Jane Fonda; (4) Woody Allen; (5) Barbra Streisand; (6) Sylvester Stallone; (7) John Travolta; (8) Jill Clayburgh; (9) Roger Moore; (10) Mel Brooks.

1978: (1) Burt Reynolds; (2) John Travolta; (3) Richard Dreyfuss; (4) Warren Beatty; (5) Clint Eastwood; (6) Woody Allen; (7) Diane Keaton; (8) Jane Fonda; (9) Peter Sellers; (10) Barbra Streisand.

1977: (1) Sylvester Stallone; (2) Barbra Streisand; (3) Clint Eastwood; (4) Burt Reynolds; (5) Robert Redford; (6) Woody Allen; (7) Mel Brooks; (8) Al Pacino; (9) Diane Keaton; (10) Robert De Niro.

1976: (1) Robert Redford; (2) Jack Nicholson; (3) Dustin Hoffman; (4) Clint Eastwood; (5) Mel Brooks; (6) Burt Reynolds; (7) Al Pacino; (8) Tatum O'Neal; (9) Woody Allen; (10) Charles Bronson.

1975: (1) Robert Redford; (2) Barbra Streisand; (3) Al Pacino; (4) Charles Bronson; (5) Paul Newman; (6) Clint Eastwood; (7) Burt Reynolds; (8) Woody Allen; (9) Steve McQueen; (10) Gene Hackman.

1974: (1) Robert Redford; (2) Clint Eastwood; (3) Paul Newman; (4) Barbra Streisand; (5) Steve McQueen; (6) Burt Reynolds; (7) Charles Bronson; (8) Jack Nicholson; (9) Al Pacino; (10) John Wayne.

1973: (1) Clint Eastwood; (2) Ryan O'Neal; (3) Steve McQueen; (4) Burt Reynolds; (5) Robert Redford; (6) Barbra Streisand; (7) Paul Newman; (8) Charles Bronson; (9) John Wayne; (10) Marlon Brando.

1972: (1) Clint Eastwood; (2) George C. Scott; (3) Gene Hackman; (4) John Wayne; (5) Barbra Streisand; (6) Marlon Brando; (7) Paul Newman; (8) Steve McQueen; (9) Dustin Hoffman; (10) Goldie Hawn.

1971: (1) John Wayne; (2) Clint Eastwood; (3) Paul Newman; (4) Steve McQueen; (5) George C. Scott; (6) Dustin Hoffman; (7) Walter Matthau; (8) Ali MacGraw; (9) Sean Connery; (10) Lee Marvin.

1970: (1) Paul Newman; (2) Clint Eastwood; (3) Steve McQueen; (4) John Wayne; (5) Elliott Gould; (6) Dustin Hoffman; (7) Lee Marvin; (8) Jack Lemmon; (9) Barbra Streisand; (10) Walter Matthau.

1969: (1) Paul Newman; (2) John Wayne; (3) Steve McQueen; (4) Dustin Hoffman; (5) Clint Eastwood; (6) Sidney Poitier; (7) Lee Marvin; (8) Jack Lemmon; (9) Katharine Hepburn; (10) Barbra Streisand.

1968: (1) Sidney Poitier; (2) Paul Newman; (3) Julie Andrews; (4) John Wayne; (5) Clint Eastwood; (6) Dean Martin; (7) Steve McQueen; (8) Jack Lemmon; (9) Lee Marvin; (10) Elizabeth Taylor.

1967: (1) Julie Andrews; (2) Lee Marvin; (3) Paul Newman; (4) Dean Martin; (5) Sean Connery; (6) Elizabeth Taylor; (7) Sidney Poitier; (8) John Wayne; (9) Richard Burton; (10) Steve McQueen.

1966: (1) Julie Andrews; (2) Sean Connery; (3) Elizabeth Taylor; (4) Jack Lemmon; (5) Richard Burton; (6) Cary Grant; (7) John Wayne; (8) Doris Day; (9) Paul Newman; (10) Elvis Presley.

1965: (1) Sean Connery; (2) John Wayne; (3) Doris Day; (4) Julie Andrews; (5) Jack Lemmon; (6) Elvis Presley; (7) Cary Grant; (8) James Stewart; (9) Elizabeth Taylor; (10) Richard Burton.

1964: (1) Doris Day; (2) Jack Lemmon; (3) Rock Hudson; (4) John Wayne; (5) Cary Grant; (6) Elvis Presley; (7) Shirley MacLaine; (8) Ann-Margret; (9) Paul Newman; (10) Jerry Lewis.

1963: (1) Doris Day; (2) John Wayne; (3) Rock Hudson; (4) Jack Lemmon; (5) Cary Grant; (6) Elizabeth Taylor; (7) Elvis Presley; (8) Sandra Dee; (9) Paul Newman; (10) Jerry Lewis.

1962: (1) Doris Day; (2) Rock Hudson; (3) Cary Grant; (4) John Wayne; (5) Elvis Presley; (6) Elizabeth Taylor; (7) Jerry Lewis; (8) Frank Sinatra; (9) Sandra Dee; (10) Burt Lancaster.

1961: (1) Elizabeth Taylor; (2) Rock Hudson; (3) Doris Day; (4) John Wayne; (5) Cary Grant; (6) Sandra Dee; (7) Jerry Lewis; (8) William Holden; (9) Tony Curtis; (10) Elvis Presley.

1960: (1) Doris Day; (2) Rock Hudson; (3) Cary Grant; (4) Elizabeth Taylor; (5) Debbie Reynolds; (6) Tony Curtis; (7) Sandra Dee; (8) Frank Sinatra; (9) Jack Lemmon; (10) John Wayne.

1959: (1) Rock Hudson; (2) Cary Grant; (3) James Stewart; (4) Doris Day; (5) Debbie Reynolds; (6) Glenn Ford; (7) Frank Sinatra; (8) John Wayne; (9) Jerry Lewis; (10) Susan Hayward.

1958: (1) Glenn Ford; (2) Elizabeth Taylor; (3) Jerry Lewis; (4) Marlon Brando; (5) Rock Hudson; (6) William Holden; (7) Brigitte Bardot; (8) Yul Brynner; (9) James Stewart; (10) Frank Sinatra.

1957: (1) Rock Hudson; (2) John Wayne; (3) Pat Boone; (4) Elvis Presley; (5) Frank Sinatra; (6) Gary Cooper; (7) William Holden; (8) James Stewart; (9) Jerry Lewis; (10) Yul Brynner.

1956: (1) William Holden; (2) John Wayne; (3) James Stewart; (4) Burt Lancaster; (5) Glenn Ford; (6) Dean Martin & Jerry Lewis; (7) Gary Cooper; (8) Marilyn Monroe; (9) Kim Novak; (10) Frank Sinatra.

1955: (1) James Stewart; (2) Grace Kelly; (3) John Wayne; (4) William Holden; (5) Gary Cooper; (6) Marlon Brando; (7) Dean Martin & Jerry Lewis; (8) Humphrey Bogart; (9) June Allyson; (10) Clark Gable.

1954: (1) John Wayne; (2) Martin & Lewis; (3) Gary Cooper; (4) James Stewart; (5) Marilyn Monroe; (6) Alan Ladd; (7) William Holden; (8) Bing Crosby; (9) Jane Wyman; (10) Marlon Brando.

1953: (1) Gary Cooper; (2) Martin & Lewis; (3) John Wayne; (4) Alan Ladd; (5) Bing Crosby; (6) Marilyn Monroe; (7) James Stewart; (8) Bob Hope; (9) Susan Hayward; (10) Randolph Scott.

1952: (1) Martin & Lewis; (2) Gary Cooper; (3) John Wayne ; (4) Bing Crosby; (5) Bob Hope; (6) James Stewart; (7) Doris Day; (8) Gregory Peck; (9) Susan Hayward; (10) Randolph Scott.

1951: (1) John Wayne; (2) Martin & Lewis; (3) Betty Grable; (4) Abbott & Costello; (5) Bing Crosby; (6) Bob Hope; (7) Randolph Scott; (8) Gary Cooper; (9) Doris Day; (10) Spencer Tracy.

1950: (1) John Wayne; (2) Bob Hope; (3) Bing Crosby; (4) Betty Grable; (5) James Stewart; (6) Abbott & Costello; (7) Clifton Webb; (8) Esther Williams; (9) Spencer Tracy; (10) Randolph Scott.

1949: (1) Bob Hope; (2) Bing Crosby; (3) Abbott & Costello; (4) John Wayne; (5) Gary Cooper; (6) Cary Grant; (7) Betty Grable; (8) Esther Williams; (9) Humphrey Bogart; (10) Clark Gable.

1948: (1) Bing Crosby; (2) Betty Grable; (3) Abbott & Costello; (4) Gary Cooper; (5) Bob Hope; (6) Humphrey Bogart; (7) Clark Gable; (8) Cary Grant; (9) Spencer Tracy; (10) Ingrid Bergman.

1947: (1) Bing Crosby; (2) Betty Grable; (3) Ingrid Bergman; (4) Gary Cooper; (5) Humphrey Bogart; (6) Bob Hope; (7) Clark Gable; (8) Gregory Peck; (9) Claudette Colbert; (10) Alan Ladd.

1946: (1) Bing Crosby; (2) Ingrid Bergman; (3) Van Johnson; (4) Gary Cooper; (5) Bob Hope; (6) Humphrey Bogart; (7) Greer Garson; (8) Margaret O'Brien; (9) Betty Grable; (10) Roy Rogers.

1945: (1) Bing Crosby; (2) Van Johnson; (3) Greer Garson; (4) Betty Grable; (5) Spencer Tracy; (6) Humphrey Bogart, Gary Cooper; (7) Bob Hope; (8) Judy Garland; (9) Margaret O'Brien; (10) Roy Rogers.

1944: (1) Bing Crosby; (2) Gary Cooper; (3) Bob Hope; (4) Betty Grable; (5) Spencer Tracy; (6) Greer Garson; (7) Humphrey Bogart; (8) Abbott & Costello; (9) Cary Grant; (10) Bette Davis.

1943: (1) Betty Grable; (2) Bob Hope; (3) Abbott & Costello; (4) Bing Crosby; (5) Gary Cooper; (6) Greer Garson; (7) Humphrey Bogart; (8) James Cagney; (9) Mickey Rooney; (10) Clark Gable.

1942: (1) Abbott & Costello; (2) Clark Gable; (3) Gary Cooper; (4) Mickey Rooney; (5) Bob Hope; (6) James Cagney; (7) Gene Autry; (8) Betty Grable; (9) Greer Garson; (10) Spencer Tracy.

1941: (1) Mickey Rooney; (2) Clark Gable; (3) Abbott & Costello; (4) Bob Hope; (5) Spencer Tracy; (6) Gene Autry; (7) Gary Cooper; (8) Bette Davis; (9) James Cagney; (10) Spencer Tracy.

1940: (1) Mickey Rooney; (2) Spencer Tracy; (3) Clark Gable; (4) Gene Autry; (5) Tyrone Power; (6) James Cagney; (7) Bing Crosby; (8) Wallace Beery; (9) Bette Davis; (10) Judy Garland.

1939: (1) Mickey Rooney; (2) Tyrone Power; (3) Spencer Tracy; (4) Clark Gable; (5) Shirley Temple; (6) Bette Davis; (7) Alice Faye; (8) Errol Flynn; (9) James Cagney; (10) Sonja Henie.

1938: (1) Shirley Temple; (2) Clark Gable; (3) Sonja Henie; (4) Mickey Rooney; (5) Spencer Tracy; (6) Robert Taylor; (7) Myrna Loy; (8) Jane Withers; (9) Alice Faye; (10) Tyrone Power.

1937: (1) Shirley Temple; (2) Clark Gable; (3) Robert Taylor; (4) Bing Crosby; (5) William Powell; (6) Jane Withers; (7) Fred Astaire and Ginger Rogers; (8) Sonja Henie; (9) Gary Cooper; (10) Myrna Loy.

1936: (1) Shirley Temple; (2) Clark Gable; (3) Fred Astaire and Ginger Rogers; (4) Robert Taylor; (5) Joe E. Brown; (6) Dick Powell; (7) Joan Crawford; (8) Claudette Colbert; (9) Jeanette MacDonald; (10) Gary Cooper.

1935: (1) Shirley Temple; (2) Will Rogers; (3) Clark Gable; (4) Fred Astaire and Ginger Rogers; (5) Joan Crawford; (6) Claudette Colbert; (7) Dick Powell; (8) Wallace Beery; (9) Joe E. Brown; (10) James Cagney.

1934: (1) Will Rogers; (2) Clark Gable; (3) Janet Gaynor; (4) Wallace Beery; (5) Mae West; (6) Joan Crawford; (7) Bing Crosby; (8) Shirley Temple; (9) Marie Dressler; (10) Norma Shearer.

1933: (1) Marie Dressler; (2) Will Rogers; (3) Janet Gaynor; (4) Eddie Cantor; (5) Wallace Beery; (6) Jean Harlow; (7) Clark Gable; (8) Mae West; (9) Norma Shearer; (10) Joan Crawford.

TOP-GROSSING FILMS

Top-grossing attractions in the United States, as selected by Quigley Publications, for the last 14 years follow.

1992: Aladdin, Buena Vista—John Musker, Ron Clements, producers; **Alien 3**, 20th Century Fox—Gordon Carroll, David Giler, Walter Hill; **Basic Instinct**, TriStar—Alan Marshall; **Batman Returns**, Warner Bros.—Denise Di Novi, Tim Burton; **Beethoven**, Universal—Joe Medjuck, Michael C. Gross; **The Bodyguard**, Warner Bros.—Lawrence Kasdan, Jim Wilson, Kevin Costner; **Boomerang**, Paramount—Brian Grazer, Warrington Hudlin; **Bram Stoker's Dracula**, Columbia—Francis Ford Coppola, Fred Fuchs, Charles Mulvehill; **Bugsy**, Mark Johnson, Barry Levinson, Warren Beatty; **Death Becomes Her**, Universal—Robert Zemeckis, Steve Starkey; **Far and Away**, Universal—Brian Grazer, Ron Howard; **Father of the Bride**, Buena Vista—Nancy Meyers, Carol Baum, Howard Rosenman; **A Few Good Men**, Columbia—David Brown, Rob Reiner, Andrew Schienman; **Fried Green Tomatoes**, Universal—Jon Avnet, Jordan Kerner; **The Hand That Rocks the Cradle**, Buena Vista—David Madden; **Home Alone 2: Lost in New York**, 20th Century Fox—John Hughes; **Honey I Blew Up the Kid** Buena Vista—Dawn Steel, Edward S. Feldman; **Housesitter**, Universal—Brian Grazer; **JFK**, Warner Bros.—A. Kitman Ho, Oliver Stone; **The Last Boy Scout**, Warner Bros.—Joel Silver, Michael Levy; **The Last of the Mohicans**, 20th Century Fox—Michael Mann, Hunt Lowry; **A League of Their Own**, Columbia—Robert Greenhut, Elliot Abbott; **Lethal Weapon 3**, Warner Bros.—Richard Donner, Joel Silver; **My Cousin Vinny**, 20th Century Fox—Dale Launer, Paul Schiff; **Patriot Games**, Paramount—Mace Neufeld, Robert Rehme; **The Prince of Tides**, Columbia—Barbra Streisand, Andrew Karsch; **Sister Act**, Buena Vista—Ted Schwartz; **Sneakers**, Universal—Walter F. Parkes, Lawrence Lasker; **Under Siege**, Warner Bros.—Arnon Milchan, Steven Seagal, Steven Reuther; **Unforgiven**, Warner Bros.—Clint Eastwood; **Unlawful Entry**, 20th Century Fox—Charles Gordon; **Wayne's World**, Paramount—Lorne Michaels; **White Men Can't Jump**, 20th Century Fox—Don Miller, David Lester.

1991: The Addams Family, Paramount—Scott Rudin, producer; **Awakenings**, Columbia—Walter F. Parkes, Lawrence Lasker; **Backdraft**, Universal—Richard B. Lewis, Pen Densham, John Watson; **Beauty and the Beast**, Columbia—Don Hahn; **Boyz N the Hood**, Columbia—Steve Nicolaides; **Cape Fear**, Universal—Barbara De Fina; **City Slickers**, Columbia—Irby Smith; **Doc Hollywood**, Warner Bros.—Susan Solt, Deborah D. Johnson; **Hook**, TriStar—Kathleen Kennedy, Frank Marshall, Gerald R. Molen; **Hot Shots**, 20th Century Fox—Bill Badalato; **My Girl**, Columbia—Brian Grazer; **The Naked Gun 2½: The Smell of Fear**, Paramount—Robert K. Weiss; **New Jack City**, Warner Bros.—Doug McHenry, George Jackson; **101 Dalmatians** (reissue), Buena Vista; **Robin Hood: Prince of Thieves**, Warner Bros.—John Watson, Pen Densham, Richard B. Lewis; **The Rocketeer**, Buena Vista—Lawrence Gordon, Charles Gordon, Lloyd Levin; **The Silence of the Lambs**, Orion—Edward Saxon, Kenneth Utt, Ron Bozman; **Sleeping With the Enemy**, 20th Century Fox—Leonard Goldberg; **Star Trek VI: The Undiscovered Country**, Paramount—Ralph Winter, Steven-Charles Jaffe; **Teenage Mutant Ninja Turtles II: The Se-** cret of the Ooze, New Line Cinema—Thomas K. Gray, Kim Dawson, David Chan; **Terminator 2: Judgment Day**, TriStar—James Cameron; **Thelma & Louise**, MGM—Ridley Scott, Mimi Polk; **What About Bob?**, Buena Vista—Laura Ziskin.

1990: Another 48 Hrs., Paramount—Lawrence Gordon, Robert D. Wachs, producers; **Arachnophobia**, Buena Vista—Kathleen Kennedy, Richard Vane; **Back to the Future Part III**, Universal—Bob Gale, Neil Canton; **Bird on a Wire**, Universal—Rob Cohen; **Born on the Fourth of July**, Universal—A. Kitman Ho, Oliver Stone; **Dances With Wolves**, Orion—Jim Wilson, Kevin Costner; **Days of Thunder**, Paramount—Don Simpson, Jerry Bruckheimer; **Dick Tracy**, Buena Vista—Warren Beatty; **Die Hard 2**, 20th Century Fox—Lawrence Gordon, Joel Silver, Charles Gordon; **Driving Miss Daisy**, Warner Bros.—Richard D. Zanuck, Lili Fini Zanuck; **Edward Scissorhands**, 20th Century Fox—Denise Di Novi, Tim Burton; **Flatliners**, Columbia—Michael Douglas, Rick Bieber; **Ghost**, Paramount—Lisa Weinstein; **The Godfather Part III**, Paramount—Francis Ford Coppola; **Hard to Kill**, Warner Bros.—Gary Adelson, Joel Simon, Bill Todman Jr.; **Home Alone**, 20th Century Fox—John Hughes; **The Hunt for Red October**, Paramount—Mace Neufeld; **Kindergarten Cop**, Universal—Ivan Reitman, Brian Grazer; **Misery**, Columbia—Andrew Scheinman, Rob Reiner; **Presumed Innocent**, Warner Bros.—Sydney Pollack, Mark Rosenberg; **Pretty Woman**, Buena Vista—Arnon Milchan, Steven Reuther; **Problem Child**, Universal—Robert Simonds; **Teenage Mutant Ninja Turtles**, New Line Cinema—Kim Dawson, Simon Fields, David Chan; **Three Men and a Little Lady**, Buena Vista—Ted Field, Robert W. Cort; **Total Recall**, Tri-Star—Buzz Fietshans, Ronald Shusett.

1989: The Abyss, 20th Century Fox—Gale Anne Hurd, producer; **Back to the Future Part II**, Universal—Bob Gale, Neil Canton; **Batman**, Warner Bros.—Jon Peters, Peter Guber; **Beaches**, Buena Vista—Bonnie Bruckheimer-Martell, Bette Midler, Margaret Jennings South; **Black Rain**, Paramount—Stanley R. Jaffe, Sherry Lansing, Michael Douglas; **Dead Poets Society**, Buena Vista—Steven Haft, Paul Junger Witt, Tony Thomas; **Field of Dreams**, Universal—Lawrence Gordon, Charles Gordon; **Ghostbusters II**, Columbia—Ivan Reitman; **Harlem Nights**, Paramount—Robert D. Wachs, Mark Lipsky; **Honey, I Shrunk the Kids**, Buena Vista—Penney Finkelman Cox; **Indiana Jones and the Last Crusade**, Paramount—Robert Watts; **Lethal Weapon 2**, Warner Bros.—Richard Donner, Joel Silver; **The Little Mermaid**, Buena Vista—Howard Ashman, John Musker; **Look Who's Talking**, TriStar—Jonathan D. Krane; **Major League**, Paramount—Chris Chesser, Irby Smith; **National Lampoon's Christmas Vacation**, Warner Bros.—John Hughes, Tom Jacobson; **Parenthood**, Universal—Brian Grazer; **Pet Sematary**, Paramount—Richard Rubinstein; **Rain Man**, United Artists—Mark Johnson; **Sea of Love**, Universal—Martin Bregman, Louis Stroller; **Star Trek V: The Final Frontier**, Paramount—Harve Bennett; **Steel Magnolias**, Tri-Star—Ray Stark; **Turner and Hooch**, Buena Vista—Raymond Wagner; **Twins**, Universal—Ivan Reitman; **Uncle Buck**, Universal—John Hughes, Tom Jacobson; **The War of the Roses**, 20th Century Fox—James L. Brooks, Arnon Milchan; **When Harry Met Sally. . .**, Columbia—Rob Reiner, Andrew Scheinman.

1988: Beetlejuice, Warner Bros.—Michael Bender, Larry Wilson, Richard Hashimoto, producers; **Big**, 20th Century Fox—James L. Brooks, Robert Greenhut; **Bull Durham**, Orion—Thom Mount, Mark Burg; **Cocktail**, Buena Vista—Ted Field, Robert W. Cort; **Colors**, Orion—Robert Solo; **Coming to America**, Paramount—George Folsey, Jr., Robert D. Wachs; **Crocodile Dundee II**, Paramount—John Cornell, Jane Scott; **Die Hard**, 20th Century Fox—Lawrence Gordon, Joel Silver; **A Fish Called Wanda**, MGM/UA—Michael Shamberg; **Good Morning, Vietnam**, Buena Vista—Mark Johnson, Larry Brezner; **Moonstruck**, MGM/UA—Patrick Palmer, Norman Jewison; **The Naked Gun**, Paramount—Robert K. Weiss; **A Nightmare on Elm Street 4: The Dream Master**, New Line—Robert Shaye, Rachel Talalay; **Rain Man**, MGM/UA—Mark Johnson; **Rambo III**, Tri-Star—Buzz Feitshans; **Scrooged**, Paramount—Richard Donner, Art Linson; **Three Men and a Baby**, Buena Vista—Ted Field, Robert W. Cort; **Twins**, Universal—Ivan Reitman; **Who Framed Roger Rabbit**, Buena Vista—Robert Watts, Frank Marshall; **Willow**, MGM/UA—Nigel Wool.

1987: Beverly Hills Cop II, Paramount—Don Simpson and Jerry Bruckheimer, producers; **Dirty Dancing**, Vestron—Linda Gottlieb; **Dragnet**, Universal—David Permut, Robert K. Weiss; **Fatal Attraction**, Paramount—Stanley Jaffe, Sherry Lansing; **Full Metal Jacket**, Warner Bros.—Stanley Kubrick; **La Bamba**, Columbia—Taylor Hackford, Bill Borden; **Lethal Weapon**, Warner Bros.—Richard Donner, Joel Silver; **The Living Daylights**, MGM/UA—Albert R. Broccoli, Michael G. Wilson; **A Nightmare on Elm Street 3: Dream Warriors**, New Line—Robert Shaye; **Outrageous Fortune**, Buena Vista—Ted Field, Robert W. Cort; **Planes, Trains and Automobiles**, Paramount—John Hughes; **Platoon**, Orion—Arnold Kopelson; **Predator**, 20th Century Fox—Lawrence Gordon, Joel Silver; **Robocop**, Orion—Arne Schmidt; **The Secret of My Success**, Universal—Herbert Ross; **Snow White and the 7 Dwarfs**, Buena Vista (reissue); **Stakeout**, Buena Vista—Jim Kouf, Cathleen Summers; **Three Men and a Baby**, Buena Vista—Ted Field, Robert W. Cort; **Throw Momma From the Train**, Orion—Larry Brezner; **The Untouchables**, Paramount—Art Linson; **The**

44A

Witches of Eastwick, Warner Bros.—Neil Canton, Peter Guber, Jon Peters.

1986: Aliens, 20th Century Fox—Gale Anne Hurd, producer; **An American Tail**, Universal—Don Bluth, John Pomeroy, Gary Goldman; **Back To School**, Orion—Chuck Russell; **Cobra**, Warner Bros.—Menahem Golan, Yoram Globus; **The Color of Money**, Buena Vista—Irving Axelrod, Barbara De Fina; **The Color Purple**, Warner Bros.—Steven Spielberg, Kathleen Kennedy, Frank Marshall, Quincy Jones; **Crocodile Dundee**, Paramount—John Cornell; **Down and Out in Bevery Hills**, Buena Vista—Paul Mazursky; **Ferris Bueller's Day Off**, Paramount—John Hughes, Tom Jacobson; **The Golden Child**, Paramount—Edward S. Feldman, Robert D. Wachs; **Heartbreak Ridge**, Warner Bros.—Clint Eastwood; **The Karate Kid Part II**, Columbia—Jerry Weintraub; **Legal Eagles**, Universal—Ivan Reitman; **Out of Africa**, Universal—Sydney Pollack; **Police Academy 3: Back in Training**, Warner Bros.—Paul Maslansky; **Poltergeist II**, MGM-UA—Mark Victor, Michael Grais; **Ruthless People**, Buena Vista—Michael Peyser; **Stand By Me**, Columbia—Bruce A. Evans, Raymold Gideon, Andrew Scheinman; **Star Trek IV: The Voyage Home**, Paramount—Harve Bennett; **Top Gun**, Paramount—Don Simpson, Jerry Bruckheimer.

1985: Back to the Future, Universal—Bob Gale, Neil Canton, producers; **Beverly Hills Cop**, Paramount—Don Simpson, Jerry Bruckheimer; **Cocoon**, 20th Century Fox—Richard Zanuck, David Brown, Lili Fine Zanuck; **Fletch**, Universal—Alan Greisman, Peter Douglas; **The Goonies**, Warner Bros.—Richard Donner, Harvey Bernhard; **The Jewel of the Nile**, 20th Century Fox—Michael Douglas; **National Lampoon's European Vacation**, Warner Bros.—Matty Simmons; **Pale Rider**, Warner Bros.—Clint Eastwood; **Police Academy 2: Their First Assignment**, Warner Bros.—Paul Maslansky; **Rambo: First Blood Part II**, Tri-Star—Buzz Feitshans; **Rocky IV**, MGM/UA—Robert Chartoff, Irwin Winkler; **Spies Like Us**, Warner Bros.—Brian Grazer, George Folsey, Jr.; **A View to a Kill**, MGM/UA—Albert R. Broccoli, Michael Wilson; **Witness**, Paramount—Edward S. Feldman.

1984: Beverly Hills Cop, Paramount—Don Simpson, Jerry Bruckheimer, producers; **Footloose**, Paramount—Lewis J. Rachmil, Craig Zadan; **Ghostbusters**, Columbia—Ivan Reitman; **Gremlins**, Warner Bros.—Michael Finnell; **Greystoke: The Legend of Tarzan, Lord of the Apes**, Warner Bros.—Hugh Hudson, Stanley S. Canter; **Indiana Jones and the Temple of Doom**, Paramount—Robert Watts; **The Karate Kid**, Columbia—Jerry Weintraub; **The Natural**, Tri-Star—Mark Johnson; **Police Academy**, Warner Bros.—Paul Maslansky; **Purple Rain**, Warner Bros.—Robert Cavallo, Joseph Rufallo, Steven Fargnoli; **Romancing the Stone**, 20th Century Fox—Michael Douglas; **Scarface**, Universal—Martin Bregman; **Splash**, Buena Vista—Brian Grazer; **Star Trek III: The Search for Spock**, Paramount—Harve Bennett; **Sudden Impact**, Warner Bros.—Clint Eastwood; **Terms of Endearment**, Paramount—James L. Brooks; **Tightrope**, Warner Bros.—Clint Eastwood, Fritz Manes; **2010**, MGM/UA—Peter Hyams.

1983: Best Friends, Warner Bros.—Norman Jewison and Patrick Palmer, producers; **The Big Chill**, Columbia—Michael Shamberg; **Blue Thunder**, Columbia—Gordon Carroll; **The Dark Crystal**, Universal—David Lazer; **48 Hrs.**, Paramount—Lawrence Gordon and Joel Silver; **Flashdance**, Paramount—Don Simpson and Jerry Bruckheimer; **Gandhi**, Columbia—Richard Attenborough; **High Road to China**, Warner Bros.—Fred Weintraub; **Jaws 3-D**, Universal—Robert Hitzig; **Mr. Mom**, 20th Century-Fox—Lynn Loring and Lauren Shuler; **National Lampoon's Vacation**, Warner Bros.—Matty Simmons; **Never Say Never Again**, Warner Bros.—Jack Schwartzman; **Octopussy**, MGM/UA—Albert R. Broccoli; **Porky's II: The Next Day**, 20th Century-Fox—Don Carmody and Bob Clark; **Psycho II**, Universal—Hilton A. Green; **Return of the Jedi**, 20th-Fox—Howard Kazanjian; **Risky Business**, Warner Bros.—Jon Avnet and Steve Tisch; **Staying Alive**, Paramount—Robert Stigwood and Sylvester Stallone; **Sudden Impact**, Warner Bros.—Clint Eastwood; **Superman III**, Warner Bros.—Pierre Spengler; **Terms of Endearment**, Paramount—James L. Brooks; **Tootsie**, Columbia—Sydney Pollack and Dick Richards; **The Toy**, Columbia—Phil Feldman; **Trading Places**, Paramount—Aaron Russo; **Twilight Zone—The Movie**, Warner Bros.—Steven Spielberg and John Landis; **The Verdict**, 20th-Fox—Richard D. Zanuck and David Brown; **WarGames**, MGM/UA—Harold Schneider.

1982: Absence of Malice, Columbia—Sydney Pollack, producer; **Annie**, Columbia—Ray Stark; **The Best Little Whorehouse in Texas**, Universal—Thomas L. Miller, Edward K. Milkis, Robert L. Boyett; **Chariots of Fire**, Warner Bros.—David Puttnam;

Conan the Barbarian, Universal—Buzz Feitshans, Raffaella De Laurentiis; **E.T.: The Extra-Terrestrial**, Universal—Steven Spielberg, Kathleen Kennedy; **Firefox**, Warner Bros.—Clint Eastwood; **First Blood**, Orion—Buzz Feitshans; **Friday the 13th, Part III**, Paramount—Frank Mancuso, Jr.; **Modern Problems**, 20th Century-Fox—Alan Greisman, Michael Shamberg; **Neighbors**, Columbia—Richard D. Zanuck, David Brown; **An Officer and a Gentleman**, Paramount—Martin Elfand; **On Golden Pond**, Universal—Bruce Gilbert; **Poltergeist**, MGM/UA—Steven Spielberg, Frank Marshall; **Porky's**, 20 Century-Fox—Don Carmody, Bob Clark; **Raiders of the Lost Ark**, Paramount—Frank Marshall; **Reds**, Paramount—Warren Beatty; **Richard Pryor Live on the Sunset Strip**, Columbia—Richard Pryor; **Rocky III**, MGM/UA—Robert Chartoff, Irwin Winkler; **Sharky's Machine**, Warner Bros.—Hank Moonjean; **Star Trek II: The Wrath of Khan**, Paramount—Robert Sallin; **Taps**, 20th Century-Fox—Stanley R. Jaffe, Howard Jaffe; **Time Bandits**, Embassy—Terry Gilliam; **Tron**, Buena Vista—Donald Kushner; **Young Doctors in Love**, 20th Century-Fox—Jerry Bruckheimer.

1981: Any Which Way You Can, Warner Bros.—Fritz Manes, producer; **Arthur**, Warner Bros./Orion—Robert Greenhut; **Bustin' Loose**, Universal—Richard Pryor and Michael Glick; **Cannonball Run**, 20th Century-Fox—Albert S. Ruddy; **Cheech and Chong's Nice Dreams**, Columbia—Howard Brown; **Clash of the Titans**, MGM/UA—Charles H. Schneer and Ray Harryhausen; **Endless Love**, Universal/Polygram—Dyson Levell; **Excalibur**, Warner Bros./Orion—John Boorman; **Flash Gordon**, Universal—Dino De Laurentiis; **For Your Eyes Only**, United Artists—Albert R. Broccoli; **Four Seasons**, Universal—Martin Bergman; **The Fox and the Hound**, Buena Vista—Wolfgang Reitherman; **The Great Muppet Caper**, Universal/AFD—David Lazer and Frank Oz; **Nine to Five**, 20th Century-Fox—Bruce Gilbert; **Raiders of the Lost Ark**, Paramount—Frank Marshall; **Seems Like Old Times**, Columbia—Ray Stark; **Stir Crazy**, Universal—Hannah Weinstein; **Stripes**, Columbia—Ivan Reitman and Dan Goldberg; **Superman II**, Warner Bros.—Pierre Spengler; **Tarzan, the Ape Man**, UGM/UA—Bo Derek; **Time Bandits**, Embassy—Terry Gilliam.

1980: Airplane, Paramount—Jon Davison, producer; **All That Jazz**, 20th Century-Fox—Daniel Melnick; **The Black Hole**, Buena Vista—Ron Miller; **The Black Stallion**, United Artists—Fred Roos and Tom Sternberg; **The Blue Lagoon**, Columbia—Randal Kleiser and Richard Franklin; **The Blues Brothers**, Universal—Bernie Brillstein and Robert K. Weiss; **Brubaker**, 20th Century-Fox—Ron Silverman; **Caddyshack**, Warner Bros.—Douglas Kenney; **Chapter Two**, Columbia—Ray Stark; **Cheech and Chong's Next Movie**, Universal—Howard Brown; **Coal Miner's Daughter**, Universal—Bernard Schwartz; **Dressed To Kill**, Filmways—George Litto; **The Electric Horseman**, Columbia—Ray Stark; **The Empire Strikes Back**, 20th Century-Fox—Gary Kurtz; **Friday the 13th**, Paramount—Sean Cunningham; **The Jerk**, Universal—William E. McEuen and David V. Picker; **Kramer vs. Kramer**, Columbia—Stanley R. Jaffe; **Little Darlings**, Paramount—Stephen J. Friedman; **1941**, Universal—Buzz Feitshans; **Private Benjamin**, Warner Bros.—Nancy Meyers, Charles Shyer and Harvey Miller; **The Rose**, 20th Century-Fox—Marvin Worth and Aaron Russo; **The Shining**, Warner Bros.—Stanley Kubrick; **Smokey and the Bandit II**, Universal—Hank Moonjean; **Star Trek—The Motion Picture**, Paramount—Gene Roddenberry; **Stir Crazy**, Columbia—Hannah Weinstein; **Urban Cowboy**, Paramount—Robert Evans and Irving Azoff.

1979: Alien, 20th Century-Fox—Gordon Carroll, David Giler and Walter Hill, producers; **The Amityville Horror**, American-International—Ronald Saland and Elliot Gresinger; **Apocalypse Now**, United Artists—Francis Coppola; **California Suite**, Columbia—Ray Stark; **The China Syndrome**, Columbia—Michael Douglas; **The Deer Hunter**, Universal—John Peverall; **Escape from Alcatraz**, Paramount Robert Daley; **Every Which Way But Loose**, Warner Bros.—Robert Daley; **The In-Laws**, Warner Bros.—Arthur Hiller and William Sackheim; **Love at First Bite**, American-International—Joel Freeman; **The Main Event**, Warner Bros.—Jon Peters and Barbra Streisand; **Meatballs**, Paramount—Dan Goldberg; **Manhattan**, United Artists—Charles H. Joffe; **Moonraker**, United Artists—Albert Broccoli; **The Muppet Movie**, Associated Film Distribution—Jim Henson; **Rocky II**, United Artists—Robert Chartoff and Irwin Winkler; **Star Trek—The Motion Picture**, Paramount Gene Roddenberry; **Starting Over**, Paramount—Alan J. Pakula and James L. Brooks; **Superman**, Warner Bros.—Pierre Spengler, **"10,"** Warner Bros.—Blake Edwards and Tony Adams.

International Film Festivals and Markets

Listed alphabetically by country. Exact dates vary from year to year but months indicated are generally the same.

AUSTRALIA
Sydney (June)
Melbourne (June)
Brisbane (August–September)

AUSTRIA
Viennale (Vienna) (October)

BELGIUM
Brussels Intl. Film (January); Animated Films (February); Fantastic Films (March)
Cinema Expo. Intl. (Brussels) (June)
Intl. Flanders Fest. (Ghent) (October)

BRAZIL
Brasilia (July)
Branco Nacional Instl. (Rio de Janiero) (September)
Sao Paulo (October–November)

BURKINA FASO
Pan African Film Fest. (Quagadougou) (February–March)

CANADA
Films on Art (Montreal) (March)
Intl. Short Film Fest. (Montreal) (March)
Banff TV Fest. (June)
Montreal World Film Festival (August–September)
Toronto (Festival of Festivals) (September)
Vancouver (October)

COLOMBIA
Cartagena (February)

CUBA
Havana (December)

CZECHOSLOVAKIA
Prague Golden TV Fest. (June)

DENMARK
Odense (July–August)
Copenhagen (September)

EGYPT
Cairo (December)

ENGLAND
Animation Festival (Cardiff) (March)
Lesbian & Gay Film Fst. (London) (March)
Brighton (May)

Southampton (June)
Cambridge (July)
Birmingham Film & TV (October)
Leeds (October)
London Film Festival (November)

FINLAND
Tampere Film Festival (March)
Midnight Sun (Sodankyla) (June)
Helsinki (September)

FRANCE
Avoriaz Fest. of Fantasy Films (January)
Nordic Film Festival (Rouen) (March)
Cognac Thriller Fest. (April)
Cannes Film Festival (May)
Annecy Animation Fest. (June)
Deauville (September)

GERMANY
Berlin (February)
Stuttgart Cartoon Film Fest. (March)
Strasbourg (March)
Short Film Days (Oberhausen) (April)
Munich (June)
Potsdam (June)
Cologne (September)
Hof (October–November)
Mannheim (November

GREECE
Thessolonki (November)

HONG KONG
Kowloon (April)

INDIA
Indian Intl. Film Fest. (January)

IRELAND
Dublin (March)
Cork (October)

ISRAEL
Jerusalem (July)

ITALY
San Remo (March)
Verona (April)
Turin (April)
Milan Horror Fest. (May–June)
Pesaro (June)
Mystfest (Cattolica) (June)
Bergamo (July)

Taormina (Sicily) (July)
Venice (September)
Pordenone (Silents) (October)
Mifed (Milan) (October)
Torino (November)

JAPAN

Hiroshima Animation Fest. (August)
Tokyo (September–October)

MEXICO

Meustra del Cine Mexicano (Guadalajara)
(March)

NETHERLANDS

Rotterdam (January–February)
Dutch Film Days (Utrecht) (September)

NEW ZEALAND

Wellington (July)

NORWAY

Norwegian Short Film Fest. (Grimstad) (June)
Norwegian Film Fest. (Haugesund) (August)

POLAND

Warsaw (May, October)
Polish Film Fest. (Gdansk) (November)

PORTUGAL

Porto Fantasporto/Fantasy Film Fest.
(February)
Troia (June)

PUERTO RICO

Puerto Rico Intl. (November)

RUSSIA

St. Petersburg (February); Festival of Festivals
(June)
Indept. Film Fest. (Sotchi) (May)
Moscow (July)

SCOTLAND

Edinburgh (August)

SPAIN

Madrid (Imagfic) (April)
San Sebastian (September)
Sitges Fantasy & Horror (Barcellona)
(October)
Valencia (October

SWEDEN

Gothenburg (January)
Kaleidoscope (Stockholm) (April)
Stockholm (November)

SWITZERLAND

Intl. Electronic Cinema (June)
Vevey (July)

Locarno (August)
Geneva (October)

TAIWAN

Taipei Intl. Film Fest. (December)

TURKEY

Istanbul (April)

UNITED STATES

Palm Springs (January)
Show Biz Expo East (New York) (January)
Sundance Film Festival (Park City, Utah)
(January)
NATPE (January)
Miami (February)
Aspen (shorts) (February)
American Film Market (Santa Monica)
(February–March)
Portland (February–March)
Natl. Assn. of Broadcasters (Las Vegas)
(March)
Santa Barbara Film Fest. (March)
Asian American (San Francisco) (March)
New Directors/New Films (New York) (March)
NATO/Showest (Las Vegas (March)
Cleveland (April)
Worldwest Houston (April)
AFI Film Festival (San Francisco) (April)
Chicago Latino Fest. (April, September–
October)
Blackworks (Oakland) (April)
USA Film Fest. (Dallas) (April)
Rivertown Intl. (Minneapolis) (April–May)
San Francisco (April–May)
Philadelphia (May)
Human Rights Watch Fest. (May—NY)
(October—LA)
Los Angeles Asian Pacific American Intl.
(May)
American Film & Video (Chicago) (May)
Seattle Intl. (May–June)
Florida Film Fest. (Orlando) (May)
AFI/L.A. Film Fest. (June)
Black Film Festival (Newark) (June)
Showbiz Expo West (Los Angeles) (June)
Gay & Lesbian (San Francisco) (June)
Telluride (Colorado) (September)
Boston (September)
New York (September–October)
Mill Valley (October)
Cinequest (San Jose) (October)
Chicago (October)
Denver (October)
Showeast (Atlantic City) (October)
Los Angeles Animation (October)
Berkshire Fest. (Great Barrington, MA)
(October)
Sarasota French Film (November)
Fort Lauderdale (November)
Women in Film (Los Angeles)

ON MICROFILM

MOTION PICTURE HERALD

MOTION PICTURE DAILY

These historically invaluable trade journals of the Motion Picture industry published by Quigley Publishing Company from 1915 to 1972 have been recorded on microfilm by Brookhaven Press and are now available for immediate delivery.

MOTION PICTURE HERALD
1915-1972 (77 reels)

MOTION PICTURE DAILY
1930-1972 (39 reels)

For price and further information call (608) 781-0850 or order from:

BROOKHAVEN PRESS
Box 2287
La Crosse, WI 54602

SPECIFICATIONS: 35mm positive microfilm, silver halide at a reduction of approximately 17X (meeting ANSI/NMA standards).

Who's Who

In The Entertainment World

A

AAMES, WILLIE: Actor. r.n. William Upton. b. Los Angeles, CA, July 15, 1960.
PICTURES: Scavenger Hunt, Hog Wild, Paradise, Zapped!, Cut and Run, Killing Machine.
TELEVISION: *Guest*: Courtship of Eddie's Father, The Odd Couple. *Series*: We'll Get By, Swiss Family Robinson, Eight Is Enough, The Edge of Night, We're Movin' (host), Charles in Charge. *Movies*: Frankenstein: The True Story, Unwed Father, The Family Nobody Wanted, Eight is Enough: A Family Reunion, An Eight is Enough Wedding. *Special* : Runaway on the Rouge River.

AARON, PAUL: Director. Broadway shows include Salvation, Paris Is Out, '70 Girls '70, Love Me Love My Children.
PICTURES: A Different Story, A Force of One, Deadly Force, Maxie.
TELEVISION: Movies: The Miracle Worker, Thin Ice, Maid in America, When She Says No, Save the Dog!, In Love and War.

AARON, ROY H.: Executive. b. Los Angeles, CA, April 8, 1929. e. UC Berkeley, BA; USC, LLB. Attorney in L.A. law firm of Pacht, Ross, Warne, Bernhard & Sears (1957–78). Joined Plitt Companies in 1978 as sr. v.p. & gen. counsel. In 1980 named pres. & chief operating officer of Plitt Theatres, Inc. and related Plitt companies. 1985–present, pres. & CEO of Showscan Corp.

ABARBANEL, SAM X.: Producer, Writer, Publicist. b. Jersey City, NJ, March 27, 1914. e. Cornell U., U. of Illinois, B.S. 1935. Newspaperman in Chicago before joining NY exploitation dept. of Republic, then to studio as asst. publicity director. W.W.II in Europe with 103rd Div. After war independent publicist and producer. Co-prod. Argyle Secrets, 1948. Co-wrote orig. s.p., co-produced U.A.'s Prehistoric Women, 1950. Exec. prod. U.A.'s Golden Mistress. In 1963 to Spain as associate prod. MGM's Gunfighters of Casa Grande, and Son of Gunfighter. Formed own co. in Spain, 1966. Produced Narco Men. Co-authored, prod. Last Day of War (MGM Int'l.). Orig. & co-s.p. Avco's Summertime Killer, 1972. Co-founder of the Publicists Guild in Hollywood.

ABEND, SHELDON: Executive. b. New York, NY, June 13, 1929. Maritime Labor-Rel. Negotiator, 1954–56; chmn., Maritime Union, 1954–56; head, exec. dir. Authors' Research Co. rep. estates deceased authors, est. 1957. indep. literary negotiator, CC films, A.A.P., RKO General Inc., David O. Selznick, 7 Arts, Warner Bros., 1959–65; pres. American Play Co. Inc., Century Play Co. Inc., 1961–present; est. Million Dollar Movie Play Library, 1962; pres. Amer. Literary Consultants est. 1965; exec. v.p. Chantec Enterprises Inc. 1969–72. Marketing literary consultant for Damon Runyon Estate. Copyright analyst and literary rights negotiator, United Artists Corp. Founder and chmn., Guild for Author's Heirs, 1970–72, Literary negotiator and prod. consultant for Robert Fryer, 1972. Founder, Copyright Royalty Co. for Authors' Heirs, 1974; copyright consultant, Films, Inc. 1975; literary agent for Bway. play, Chicago, 1975. Owner of 53 classic RKO motion pictures for the non-theatrical markets, distributed by Films, Inc. Revived publishing of Damon Runyon stories in quality paperback. Published Cornell Woolrich mystery stories—all prod. by Alfred Hitchcock for TV & motion pictures, 1976. 1978, assoc. prod. of film, Why Would I Lie?; Originator of Million Dollar Movie Book Theatre and Million Dollar Movie Sound Track Co., 1980; assoc. prod. of Bdwy revival, Shanghai Gesture, 1981. Publ. 5 Cornell Woolrich books owned by S. Abend, 1982–83; Co-authored book, The Guardians; 1985, Romance of the Forties by Damon Runyon, 1986; 1985, founder and pres. American Concerts, Inc. and American Theatre Collections, Inc.; Pub. Into the Night by Cornell Woolrich. Packaged m.p. Bloodhounds of Broadway 1988; co-author s.p. Ultimate Demand; 1990, stage adapt. of Bloodhounds of Broadway, Madam La Gimp. exec. prod.

adapt. of Corneli Woolrich stories for TV and movies. 1990 won landmark copyright case before U.S. Supreme Court protecting Woolrich estate, also affecting other deceased authors, songwriters and their copyright renewals of their work. 1992, acquired Damon Runyon copyrights. 1993 Guys & Dolls handbook published by Viking.

ABRAHAM, F. MURRAY: Actor. b. Pittsburgh, PA, Oct. 24, 1939. r.n. Fahrid Murray Abraham. Attended U. of Texas, 1959–61; trained for stage at Herbert Berghof Studios with Uta Hagen. Stage debut in Los Angeles in The Wonderful Ice Cream Suit, 1965. New York debut in The Fantasticks, 1966.
THEATER: Antigone (NYSF, 1982), Uncle Vanya, The Golem (NYSF), Madwoman of Chaillot, Twelfth Night, Macbeth, A Midsummer's Night Dream, Waiting for Godot, King Lear.
PICTURES: They Might Be Giants (debut, 1971), Serpico, The Prisoner of 2nd Avenue, The Sunshine Boys, All the President's Men, The Ritz, Madman, The Big Fix, Scarface, Amadeus (Acad. Award, 1984), The Name of the Rose, Slipstream, The Favorite, Russicum, The Betrothed, An Innocent Man, Beyond the Stars, Eye of the Widow, The Bonfire of the Vanities, Cadence, Mobsters, National Lampoon's Loaded Weapon 1, By the Sword, Last Action Hero, Sweet Killing.
TELEVISION: *Series*: Love of Life. *Movies*: Sex and the Married Woman, A Season of Giants, Journey to the Center of the Earth. *Guest*: Kojak, All in the Family. *Mini-Series*: Marco Polo, Dream West. *Special*: Largo Desolato.

ABRAHAMS, JIM: Producer, Writer, Director. b. Milwaukee, WI, May 10, 1944. e. U. of Wisconsin. Former private investigator. 1971, with friends David and Jerry Zucker, opened the Kentucky Fried Theatre in Madison, WI, a multimedia show specializing in live improvisational skits mixed with video-taped and film routines and sketches, with the threesome writing and appearing in most. Opened new theatre in Los Angeles in 1972 and developed large following. Co-wrote, co-dir., co-exec. produced TV series Police Squad!
PICTURES: The Kentucky Fried Movie (co-s.p. with Zuckers), Airplane! (co-dir., co-exec. prod., co-s.p. with Zuckers), Top Secret! (co-dir., co-s.p., with Zuckers), Ruthless People (co-dir. with Zuckers), Big Business (dir.), The Naked Gun (exec. prod., co-s.p.), Cry-Baby (co-exec. prod.), Welcome Home Roxy Carmichael (dir.), The Naked Gun 2-1/2 (co-exec. prod.), Hot Shots! (dir., co-s.p.), Hot Shots Part Deux!. (dir., co-s.p.).

ABRAHAMS, MORT: Producer. b. New York, NY. Dir. programming, prod., NTA, 1958–60; exec. prod. Cooga Mooga Prod. Inc., 1960–61. Producer: Target, The Corruptors 1961, Route 66, 1962–63; writer TV shows, 1963–64; prod., Kraft Suspense Theatre, 1965; prod., Man from U.N.C.L.E., 1965–66; exec. v.p., APJAC Prod. 1966. Assoc. prod.: Doctor Dolittle, Planet of the Apes, Goodbye, Mr. Chips; Prod.: Planet of the Apes; 1969, v.p. in chg. of prod., Rastar Prods.: 1971–74 exec. prod. American Film Theatre & v.p. Ely Landau Org. in chg. West Coast prod. Exec. prod.: Luther, Homecoming, Man in the Glass Booth; The Greek Tycoon, Hopscotch,; exec. in chg. prod.: The Chosen, Beatlemania; exec. prod.: The Deadly Game; Separate Tables, Mr. Halpern and Mr. Johnson; prod.: Arch of Triumph; exec. prod.: The Holcraft Covenant; prod., Seven Hours to Judgment. Member of Facultyand producer-in-residence, Center for Advanced Film and TV Studies of A.F.I.

ACKERMAN, BETTYE: Actress. b. Cottageville, SC, Feb. 28, 1928. e. Columbia U., 1948–52. Taught dancing 1950–54.
PLAYS: No Count Boy, 1954; Tartuffe, Sophocles' Anti-gone, and Oedipus at Colonus, The Merchant of Venice.
PICTURES: Face of Fire, Rascal, Ted & Venus.
TELEVISION: Alcoa Premiere, Alfred Hitchcock Presents, Perry Mason, Breaking Point, Dr. Maggie Graham on Ben Casey series for five yrs., Hope-Chrysler Theatre, Bonanza,

FBI Story, Mannix, Ironsides, Medical Center, regular on Bracken's World, Columbo, Sixth Sense, Heat of Anger, Return to Peyton Place, (6 months 1972) Rookies, Barnaby Jones, Police Story, Gunsmoke, Harry O, Streets of San Francisco, S.W.A.T., Petrocelli, Wonder Woman, Police Woman, Chips, 240-Robert, The Waltons, Dynasty, Falcon Crest, Me and Mom, Trapper John M.D. Movies: Companions in Nightmare, A Day for Thanks on Walton's Mountain, Confessions of a Married Man.

RECORDS: Salome & School for Scandal.

ACKLAND, JOSS: Actor. b. London, England, Feb. 29, 1928. e. Central Sch. of Speech Training & Dramatic Art. Spent time in Central Africa as a tea planter. Over 400 TV appearances. Autobiography: I Must Be in There Somewhere.

PICTURES: Seven Days to Noon, Crescendo, Trecolonne in Cronaca, The House That Dripped Blood, The Happiness Cage, Villain, England Made Me, The Black Windmill, S.P.Y.S, The Little Prince, Royal Flash, Operation Daybreak, Who Is Killing the Great Chefs of Europe, Saint Jack, The Apple, Rough Cut, Lady Jane, A Zed and Two Noughts, The Sicilian, White Mischief, To Kill a Priest, It Couldn't Happen Here, Lethal Weapon 2, The Hunt for Red October, Object of Beauty, Bill and Ted's Bogus Journey, The Palermo Connection, Once Upon a Crime, The Mighty Ducks, Project Shadowchaser, Nowhere to Run, Where the Wolves Howl.

TELEVISION: Movies/Specials: Queenie, Shadowlands, The Man Who Lived at the Ritz, A Quiet Conspiracy, The Secret Life of Ian Fleming, Jekyll and Hyde, First and Last, A Murder of Quality, A Woman Named Jackie, Ashenden, Voices in the Garden, Young Indiana Jones.

THEATRE: The Old Vic (3 yrs.), Mermaid Theatre (artistic dir., 3 yrs.); Hotel in Amsterdam, Jorrocks Come as You Are, The Collaborators, A Streetcar Named Desire, The Madras House, Captain Brassbound's Conversion, Never the Sinner, Henry IV Parts I & II, Peter Pan (dramatic & musical version), A Little Night Music, Evita, etc.

ADAM, KEN: Art director, Prod. Designer. b. Berlin, Germany, Feb. 5, 1921. e. St. Pauls Sch.; London; London U., student of architecture. 6 years war service as RAF pilot. Ent. m.p. ind. as draughtsman 1947 (This Was a Woman). Art dir.: The Devil's Pass, Soho Incident, Around the World in 80 Days. Prod. Designer: Spin a Dark Web, Night of the Demon, Gideon's Day, The Angry Hills, Beyond This Place. Production Designer: The Rough and the Smooth, In the Nick, Let's Get Married, Trials of Oscar Wilde, Dr. No, Sodom and Gomorrah, In the Cool of the Day, Dr. Strangelove, Goldfinger, Woman of Straw, Thunderball, The Ipcress File, Funeral in Berlin, You Only Live Twice, Chitty Chitty Bang Bang, Goodbye Mr. Chips, The Owl and the Pussycat, Diamonds Are Forever, Sleuth, The Last of Sheila, Barry Lyndon (Acad. Award, 1975), Madam Kitty, The Seven Percent Solution, The Spy Who Loved Me, Moonraker, Pennies from Heaven (visual consult., assoc. prod.), King David, Agnes of God, Crimes of the Heart, The Deceivers, Dead-Bang, The Freshman, The Doctor, Company Business, Undercover Blues, Addams Family Values.

ADAMS, BROOKE: Actress. b. New York, NY, Feb. 8, 1949. e. H.S. of Performing Arts; Inst. of American Ballet; Lee Strasberg. Made professional debut at age of six in Finian's Rainbow. Worked steadily in summer stock and TV until age 18. After hiatus resumed acting career.

THEATER: Split, Key Exchange, Linda Hur, The Heidi Chronicles, Lost in Yonkers. Helps run small summer theater upstate NY.

PICTURES: The Lords of Flatbush, Shock Waves (Death Corps), Days of Heaven, Invasion of the Body Snatchers, Cuba, A Man a Woman and a Bank, Tell me a Riddle, Utilities, The Dead Zone, Almost You, Key Exchange, The Stuff, Man on Fire, The Unborn, Gas Food Lodging.

TELEVISION: Movies: F. Scott Fitzgerald and the Last of the Belles, The Daughters of Joshua Cabe Return, James Dean, Who is the Black Dahlia?, Murder on Flight 502, Nero Wolfe (pilot), Lace, Haunted, Special People, Lace II, The Lion of Africa, Bridesmaids, Sometimes They Come Back, The Last Hit. Specials: Paul Reiser: Out on a Whim. Series: O.K. Crackerby. Pilot: A Girl's Life. Guest: Kojack, Family, Police Woman, Moonlighting.

ADAMS, CATLIN: Actress, Director. r.n. Barab. b. Los Angeles, CA, October 11, 1950. Began career as actress then studied directing at American Film Institute. Directorial debut: Wanted: The Perfect Guy (Emmy-winning ABC Afterschool Special). Also directed Little Shiny Shoes (short, written and prod. with Melanie Mayron), Stolen: One Husband (TV).

THEATER: Safe House, Scandalous Memories, Dream of a Blacklisted Actor, The Candy Store, Ruby Ruby Sam Sam.

PICTURES: As Actress: The Jerk, The Jazz Singer. Director: Sticky Fingers (also co-s.p., co-prod.).

TELEVISION: Specials: How to Survive the 70's and Maybe Even Bump into a Little Happiness, She Loves Me She Loves Me Not. Guest: thirtysomething. Series: Square Pegs. Movie: Panic in Echo Park.

ADAMS, DON: Actor. b. New York, NY, April 13, 1926. Won Arthur Godfrey talent contest. Was nightclub impressionist before starting in TV.

PICTURES: The Nude Bomb, Jimmy the Kid, Back to the Beach.

TELEVISION: Series: Perry Como's Kraft Music Hall, Bill Dana Show, Get Smart (3 Emmy Awards, 2 Clio Awards), The Partners, Don Adams' Screen Test, Three Times Daley, Inspector Gadget, Check It Out!. Movies: The Love Boat, Get Smart Again!

ADAMS, EDIE: Actress, Singer. b. Kingston, PA, April 16, 1927. r.n. Edith Elizabeth Enke. e. Juilliard Sch. of Music, Columbia Sch. of Drama.

STAGE: NY: Wonderful Town, 1952–54; Lil Abner, 1956–57 (Tony Award), Mame.

TELEVISION: Series: Ernie in Kovacsland, The Ernie Kovacs Show (1952–3), The Ernie Kovacs Show (1956), The Chevy Show, Take a Good Look (panelist), Here's Edie, The Edie Adams Show. Movies: Evil Roy Slade, Return of Joe Forrester, Superdome, Fast Friends, Make Me an Offer, A Cry for Love, Ernie Kovacs' Between the Laughter. Guest: Miss U.S. Television, Three to Get Ready, Kovacs on the Corner, Kovacs Unlimited, Jack Paar, Ed Sullivan Show, Perry Como Show, Pat Boone Show, G.E. Theatre, Colgate Comedy House, Dinah Shore Show, Palace, Bob Hope Show. Special: Cinderella.

PICTURES: The Apartment, Lover Come Back, Call Me Bwana, It's a Mad Mad Mad Mad World, Under the Yum Yum Tree, Love With the Proper Stranger, The Best Man, Made in Paris, The Oscar, The Honey Pot, Up in Smoke, The Happy Hooker Goes Hollywood.

ADAMS, GERALD DRAYSON: Writer. b. Winnipeg, Manitoba. e. Oxford U. Export exec. 1925–30; literary agt. 1931–45. Member: Screen Writers' Guild.

PICTURES: Magnificent Rogue, Plunderers, Gallant Legion, Big Steal, Dead Reckoning, Battle of Apache Pass, Son of Ali Baba, Flaming Feather, Flame of Araby, Lady from Texas, Steel Town, Untamed, Frontier, Duel at Silver Creek, Princess of the Nile, Three Young Texans, Gambler from Natchez, Wings of the Hawk, Between Midnight and Dawn, Taza Son of Cochise, Gambler from Natchez, Chief Crazy Horse, Golden Horde, Prince Who Was a Thief, Sea Hornet, Three Bad Sisters, Duel on the Mississippi, Black Sleep, War Drums, Gun Brothers, Affair in Reno, Frontier Rangers, Gold Glory & Custer, Kissin Cousins, Harem Scarem.

TELEVISION: Maverick, G.E. Theatre, Northwest Passage, Broken Arrow, Cheyenne, 77 Sunset Strip.

ADAMS, JULIE: Actress. r.n. Betty May Adams. b. Waterloo, IA, Oct. 17, 1926. e. jr. coll., Little Rock, AK. Coll. dramatics; m.p. debut in Red Hot and Blue (as Betty Adams); Star of Tomorrow, 1953.

PICTURES: Red Hot and Blue (debut, 1949), The Dalton Gang, Crooked River, Hostile Country, West of the Brazos, Colorado Ranger, Fast on the Draw, Marshal of Heldorado. As Julie Adams: Hollywood Story, Finders Keepers, Bend of the River, Bright Victory, Treasure of Lost Canyon, Horizons West, Lawless Breed, Mississippi Gambler, Man From the Alamo, The Stand of Apache River, Wings of the Hawk, The Creature From the Black Lagoon, Francis Joins the WACS, The Looters, One Desire, Private War of Major Benson, Six Bridges to Cross, Away All Boats, Four Girls in Town, Slim Carter, Slaughter on 10th Avenue, Tarawa Beachhead, Gunfight at Dodge City, Raymie, Underwater City, Tickle Me, Valley of Mystery, The Last Movie, McQ, Psychic Killer, The Wild McCullochs, Killer Inside Me, Goodbye Franklin High, The Fifth Floor, Black Roses.

TELEVISION: Series: Yancy Derringer, General Hospital, The Jimmy Stewart Show, Code Red, Capitol. Movies: The Trackers, Go Ask Alice, Code Red, Backtrack. Guest: Murder She Wrote.

ADAMS, MASON: Actor. b. NY, NY, Feb. 26, 1919. e. U. Wisconsin. B.A., 1940; M.A., 1941. Trained for stage at Neighborhood Playhouse. Began on radio in 1946, spending nearly two decades in title role of Pepper Young's Family. Broadway debut: Get Away Old Man (1943).

THEATER: Career Angel, Public Relations, Violet, Shadow of My Enemy, Inquest, The Sign in Sidney Brustein's Window, Tall Story, The Trial of the Catonsville Nine, Foxfire, Checking Out, Danger Memory, The Day Room, The Rose Quartet.

PICTURES: God Told Me To, Raggedy Ann and Andy (voice), Northstar, The Final Conflict, F/X, Toy Soldiers, Son-in-Law.

TELEVISION: Series: Lou Grant (1977–1982), Morningstar/Eveningstar, Knight and Dave. Movies: The Deadliest Season, And Baby Makes Six, The Shining Season, Flamingo Road, The Revenge of the Stepford Wives, The Kid with the Broken Halo, Adam, Passions, Solomon Northrup's Odyssey, The Night They Saved Christmas, Who is Julia?, Under Siege, Rage of Angels: The Story Continues, Perry Mason, Jonathan: The Boy Nobody Wanted, Buying a Landslide.

ADAMS, MAUD: Actress. r.n. Maud Wikstrum. b. Lulea, Sweden, Feb. 12, 1945. Formerly a model. Film debut: as model in The Boys in the Band.
PICTURES: The Christian Licorice Store, U-Turn, Mahoney's Estate, The Man With the Golden Gun, Rollerball, Killer Force, The Merciless Man, Tattoo, Octopussy, Target Eagle, Jane and the Lost City, The Women's Club, A Man of Passion, The Favorite, Soda Cracker.
TELEVISION: Movies: Big Bob Johnson and His Fantastic Speed Circus, The Hostage Tower, Playing for Time, Nairobi Affair. Series: Chicago Story, Emerald Point, N.A.S.

ADAMS, TONY: Producer. b. Dublin, Ireland, Feb. 15, 1953. Began career as asst. to dir. John Boorman and was associated with Burt Reynolds prior to joining Blake Edwards as a prod., 1971. Then president, Blake Edwards Entertainment; Pres. & CEO, The Blake Edwards Company, 1988.
PICTURES: Assoc. Prod.: Return of the Pink Panther; The Pink Panther Strikes Again. Exec. Prod.: Revenge of the Pink Panther. Prod.: "10"; S.O.B.; Victor-Victoria; Trail of the Pink Panther; Curse of the Pink Panther, The Man Who Loved Women, Micki & Maude, That's Life, A Fine Mess, Blind Date, Sunset, Skin Deep, Switch, Son of the Pink Panther.
TELEVISION: Julie Andrews (series and specials), Justin Case, Peter Gunn, Julie.

ADDISON, JOHN: Composer. b. West Chobham, Surrey, England, March 16, 1920. e. Wellington and Royal Coll. of Music. Entered m.p. ind. in 1948. Professor, Royal Coll. of Music, 1948–53. Member of bd. of gov. of Mo. Pic. Academy 1980–9.
PICTURES: Seven Days to Noon, The Man Between, The Maggie, Make Me An Offer, Privates Progress, Reach for the Sky, Lucky Jim, I Was Monty's Double, Carlton Brown of the F. O., The Entertainer, School for Scoundrels, A Taste of Honey, The Loneliness of the Long Distance Runner, Tom Jones (Acad. Award, Grammy Award), Guns at Batasi, Girl With Green Eyes, The Loved One, Torn Curtain, A Fine Madness, I Was Happy Here, The Honey Pot, Smashing Time, The Charge of the Light Brigade, Start the Revolution Without Me, Country Dance (U.S.: Brotherly Love), Mr. Forbush and the Penguins, Sleuth, Luther, Dead Cert, Ride a Wild Pony, Seven-Per-Cent Solution, Swashbuckler, Joseph Andrews, A Bridge Too Far (Brit. Acad. Anthony Asquith Award), .The Pilot, High Point, Strange Invaders, Grace Quigley, Code Name: Emerald, To Die For.
BALLETS: Carte Blanche (at Sadlers Wells and Edinburgh Fest.), Cat's Cradle (Marquis de Cuevas, Paris, Monte Carlo).
PLAYS: The Entertainer, The Chairs, Luther, Midsummer Night's Dream, The Broken Heart, The Workhouse Donkey, Hamlet, Semi-Detached, The Seagull, Saint Joan of the Stockyards, Listen to the Mockingbird, Cranks (revue), Antony & Cleopatra, I Claudius, Twelfth Night, Bloomsbury, Antony and Cleopatra (LA Theatre Centre).
TELEVISION: Sambo and the Snow Mountains, Detective, Hamlet, The Search for Ulysses, Way of the World, Back of Beyond, Black Beauty, The Bastard, Deadly Price of Paradise, Love's Savage Fury, Like Normal People, The French Atlantic Affair, Mistress of Paradise, Eleanor First Lady of The World, Charles and Diana: A Royal Love Story, Mail Order Bride, Thirteen at Dinner, Dead Man's Folly, Mr. Boogedy, Something in Common, Firefighter, Amazing Stories, Bride of Boogedy, Strange Voices. Mini-series: Centennial, Pearl, Ellis Island, Beryl Markham: A Shadow on the Sun, Phantom of the Opera. Series: Nero Wolfe, Murder She Wrote (Emmy Award).
STAGE MUSICALS: The Amazons, Popkiss.

ADELMAN, GARY: Executive. b. Los Angeles, CA, March 16, 1944. e. California State U., Long Beach State Coll. 1969, asst. dir. on feature, The Masterpiece; assoc. prod. on The Candy Snatchers. Produced first feature film, The Severed Arm, 1974. Assisted Winston Hock in development of 3-D process, 1975. 1976–93, pres. & COO of Monarch Prods. Post-prod. consultant for Jerry Gross Organization. 1983, founder and partial owner of New Image Releasing, Inc., new prod. & dist. co. Had post of secty./treas. 1987, named v.p., chg. prod., All-American Group. 1990, assoc. prod. on Nobody's Perfect.

ADELMAN, JOSEPH A.: Executive. b. Winnipeg, Manitoba, Can., Dec. 27, 1933. e. NYU, B.A., 1954; Harvard Law Sch., J.D., 1957, graduated cum laude. Attorney, United Artists Corp., New York, 1958; named west coast counsel, Hollywood, 1964; named exec. asst. to the v.p. in charge of prod. 1968; named v.p., west coast business and legal affairs, 1972; appointed executive v.p., Association of Motion Pictures and Television Producers, 1977; appointed v.p. in chg. of business affairs, Paramount Pictures Corp., 1979; co-founder and exec. v.p. Kidpix, Inc. since 1984; founder and CEO of Kidpix Theaters Corp. since 1985; appointed senior v.p. for business/legal affairs, Color Systems Technology, Inc. 1986; named pres. of CST Entertainment, 1987. Appointed managing dir., Broadway Video Entertainment, 1990. CEO, Intl. Entertainment Enterprises 1991. Admitted to NY, California and U.S. Supreme Court bars; member, Phi Beta Kappa; Alumni

Achievement Award, NYU, 1982; American Bar Association; Los Angeles Copyright Society; Academy of Motion Picture Arts and Sciences; bd. of dirs., AMPTP, 1969–1979; National Assn. of Television Programming Executives.; bd. of trustees, Theatre Authority, 1970–9.

ADELSON, GARY: Producer. b. 1954. e. UCLA (B.A.). Son of Merv Adelson. Joined Lorimar Prods. 1970 as prod. asst. on TV movie Helter Skelter. 1989: formed Adelson/Baumgarten Prods. with Craig Baumgarten.
TELEVISION: Helter Skelter (prod. asst.); Sybil (assoc. prod.); Eight Is Enough (prod.); The Blue Knight (prod.); Exec. prod.: Too Good To Be True, Our Family Business, Cass Malloy, John Steinbeck's The Winter of Our Discontent, Lace, Detective in the House, Lace II, Studio 5B (series), Glitz.
PICTURES: The Last Starfighter (prod.), The Boy Who Could Fly, In The Mood, Tap, Hard to Kill, Nowhere to Run.

ADELSON, MERV: Producer. b. Los Angeles, CA, Oct. 23, 1929. e. UCLA. Pres., Markettown Builders Emporium, Las Vegas 1953–63; mgr. partner Paradise Dev. 1958–; pres. Realty Holdings 1962–; Bd. chmn., Lorimar Inc. 1969–86; chmn. bd. dirs. & CEO. Lorimar Telepictures 1986–.
PICTURES: Twilight's Last Gleaming, The Choirboys, Who Is Killing the Great Chefs of Europe?, Avalanche Express, The Big Red One.
TELEVISION: The Waltons, Eight Is Enough, Dallas, Kaz, The Waverly Wonders, Knots Landing, Sybil, A Man Called Intrepid, The Blue Knight, Helter-Skelter.

ADJANI, ISABELLE: Actress. b. Germany, June 27, 1955.
PICTURES: Faustine and the Beautiful Summer, The Slap, The Story of Adele H. (Acad. Award nom.), The Tenant, Barocco, Violette and Francois, The Driver, Nosferatu—The Vampire, The Bronte Sisters, Clara et les chics types, Possession, Quartet, Next Year If All Goes Well, One Deadly Summer, Antonieta, Deadly Circuit, Subway, Ishtar, Camille Claudel (also co-prod.; Acad. Award nom.), Toxic Affair.

ADLER, ALLEN: Executive Producer. b. New York, NY, 1946. e. Princeton U., B.A.; Harvard Business Sch., M.B.A. Started with Standard & Poor's Inter-Capital; then joined Alan Hirschfield at American Diversified Enterprises; next to Columbia Pictures 1973 as corporate officer. 1979, named sr. v.p., Columbia. 1981, teamed with Daniel Melnick in IndieProd Co.
PICTURE: Making Love.

ADLON, PERCY: Director, Writer, Producer. b. Munich, Germany, June 1, 1935. e. Munich Univ. m. Eleonore Adlon, with whom he has worked on several film projects. Created more than forty tv documentaries.
PICTURES: Celeste, The Last Five Days (dir. only), The Swing, Sugarbaby, Bagdad Cafe, Rosalie Goes Shopping, Salmonberries, Younger and Younger.
TELEVISION: The Gurdian and His Poet (Adolf Grimme Award).

ADRIAN, IRIS: Actress, r.n. Iris Adrian Hostetter. b. Los Angeles, CA, May 29, 1913. Dancer, on stage NY and abroad in Follies of 1931; m.p. debut in MGM two-reel color films.
PICTURES: incl. Smart Woman, Out of the Storm, Paleface, Sky Dragon, There's a Girl in My Heart, Tough Assignment, Once a Thief, Always Leave Them Laughing, Stop That Cab, My Favorite Spy, Varieties on Parade, G.I. Jane, The Racket, Carson City, Take the High Ground, Fast & Furious, Crime Wave, Devil's Harbor, Carnival Rock, The Buccaneer, Blue Hawaii, The Errand Boy, Fate is the Hunter, That Darn Cat, The Odd Couple, The Love Bug, Freaky Friday.

AGAR, JOHN: Actor. b. Chicago, IL, Jan. 31, 1921. In service W.W.II.
PICTURES: Fort Apache (debut, 1948), Adventure in Baltimore, I Married a Communist, Sands of Iwo Jima, She Wore a Yellow Ribbon, Breakthrough, Woman on Pier 13, Magic Carpet, Along the Great Divide, Woman of the North Country, Man of Conflict, Bait, Rocket Man, Shield for Murder, Golden Mistress, Revenge of the Creature, Hold Back Tomorrow, Tarantula, Star in the Dust, The Lonesome Trail, The Mole People, Flesh and the Spur, Daughter of Dr. Jekyll, Cavalry Command, The Brain from Planet Arous, Attack of the Puppet People, Ride a Violent Mile, Joe Butterfly, Jet Attack, Frontier Gun, Invisible Invaders, Raymie, Hand of Death, Lisette, Journey to the 7th Planet, Of Love and Desire, The Young and the Brave, Law of the Lawless, Stage to Thunder Rock, Young Fury, Waco, Johnny Reno, Curse of the Swamp Creature, Zontar: The Thing from Venus, Women of the Prehistoric Planet, St. Valentine's Day Massacre, Big Jake, Chisum, King Kong, Perfect Victims, Miracle Mile, Nightbreed.

AGUTTER, JENNY: Actress. b. Taunton, Devonshire, England, Dec. 20, 1952; e. Elmhurst Ballet Sch. m.p. debut East of Sudan, 1964. Emmy for best supporting actress, 1971; Variety Club of Grt. Britain Most Promising Artiste Award

1971; BAFTA best supporting actress award for Equus, 1976.
PICTURES: East of Sudan, Ballerina (TV in U.S.), Gates of Paradise, Star!, I Start Counting, Walkabout, The Railway Children, Logan's Run, The Eagle Has Landed, Equus, Dominique, China 9 Liberty 37, The Riddle of the Sands, Sweet William, The Survivor, Amy, An American Werewolf in London, Secret Places, Dark Tower, King of the Wind, Dark Man, Child's Play 2, Freddie as F.R.O. 7 (voice).
PLAYS: School for Scandal, Rooted, Arms and the Man, The Ride Across Lake Constance, The Tempest, Spring Awakening, Hedda, Betrayal. Member, Royal Shakespeare Co.—King Lear, Arden of Taversham, The Body. Breaking the Silence, Shrew (Los Angeles), 1986.
TELEVISION: The Great Mr. Dickens, The Wild Duck, The Cherry Orchard, The Snow Goose (Emmy Award, 1972), As Many as Are Here Present, A War of Children, The Man in the Iron Mask, A House in Regent Place, There's Love and Dove, Kiss Me and Die, A Legacy, The Waiting Room, Six Million Dollar Man, School Play, The Mayflower, Voyage of the Pilgrims, Beulah Land, Love's Labour's Lost, This Office Life, Magnum, The Two Ronnies, Silas Marner, The Twilight Zone, Murder She Wrote, No a Penny More Not a Penny Less, Dear John, The Equalizer, The Outsiders, Breaking the Code.

AIELLO, DANNY: Actor. b. New York, NY, June 20, 1933.
THEATER: Lampost Reunion (Theatre World Award), Wheelbarrow Closers, Gemini, Knockout, The Floating Light Bulb, Hurlyburly, The House of Blue Leaves.
PICTURES: Bang the Drum Slowly (debut, 1973), The Godfather Part II, The Front, Fingers, Blood Brothers, Defiance, Hide in Plain Sight, Ft. Apache the Bronx, Chu Chu and the Philly Flash, Deathmask, Once Upon a Time in America, Old Enough, The Purple Rose of Cairo, Key Exchange, The Protector, The Stuff, Radio Days, The Pick-Up Artist, Man on Fire, Moonstruck, The January Man, Crack in the Mirror, Do the Right Thing, Russicum, Harlem Nights, Jacob's Ladder, Once Around, Hudson Hawk, The Closer, 29th Street, Ruby, Mistress, The Cemetery Club, The Pickle.
TELEVISION: Movies: The Last Tenant, Lovey: A Circle of Children Part 2, A Question of Honor, Blood Feud, Lady Blue, Daddy, Alone in the Neon Jungle, The Preppie Murder. Series: Lady Blue. Special: Family of Strangers.

AIMEE, ANOUK: Actress. r.n. Françoise Soyra Dreyfus. b. Paris, France, April 27, 1932. Studied dancing at Marseilles Opera, acting at Bauer-Therond dramatic school, Paris.
PICTURES: La Maison Sous la Mer (debut, 1946), La Fleur de l'age, Les Amants De Verone, The Golden Salamander, Noche de Tormenta, Le Rideau Cramoisi, The Man Who Watched the Trains Go By, Contraband Spain, Forever My Heart, Les Mauvaises Rencontres, Ich Suche Dich, Nina, Stresemann, Pot Bouille, Montparnasse 19, Tous Peuvent Me Tuer, Le Tete Contre Les Murs, The Journey, Les Dragueurs, La Dolce Vita, Le Farceur, Lola, L'Imprevu, Quai Notre-Dame, Il Giudizio Universale, Sodom and Gomorrah, Les Grand Chemins, 8-1/2, Il Terrorista, Il Successo, Liola, Le Voci Bianche, La Fuga, La Stagione del Nostro Amore, A Man and a Woman (Acad. Award nom.), Lo Sacandalo, Il Morbidonne, Un Soir Un Train, The Model Shop, Justine, The Appointment, Si C'Etait d Refaire, Mon Premier Amour, Salto nel Vuoto (Leap Into the Void), Tragedy of a Ridiculous Man, What Makes David Run?, Le General de l'Armee Morte, Success is the Best Revenge, Viva la Vie, A Man and A Woman: 20 Years Later, TArrivederci e Grazie, La Table Tournante, The House of the Lord, Bethune: The Making of a Hero, Rabbit Face.

AKINS, CLAUDE: Actor. b. Nelson, GA, May 25, 1918. e. Northwestern U. Worked as salesman in Indiana before joining Barter Theatre for season. Came to New York; appeared in The Rose Tattoo. Spent several seasons with touring cos. Dinner Theater, Chicago, Houston, Jacksonville in Special Occasions, Goodbye Ghost, You Ought to Be in Pictures, Traveler in the Dark (L.A. Mark Taper Forum).
PICTURES: From Here to Eternity, Bitter Creek, The Raid, The Caine Mutiny, Human Jungle, Shield for Murder, The Sea Chase, Johnny Concho, The Sharkfighters, Hot Summer Night, The Kettles on Old Macdonald's Farm, The Lonely Man, Joe Dakota, The Defiant Ones, Onionhead, Rio Bravo, Don't Give Up the Ship, Porgy and Bess, Hound Dog Man, Yellowstone Kelly, Comanche Station, Inherit the Wind, Merrill's Marauders, How the West Was Won, Black Gold, A Distant Trumpet, The Killers, Ride Beyond Vengeance, Return of the Seven, Waterhole #3, The Devil's Brigade, The Great Bank Robbery, Flap, A Man Called Sledge, Skyjacked, Battle for the Planet of the Apes, Timber Tramps, Tentacles, Monster in the Closet, The Curse, Falling From Grace, Pushed Too Far, Seasons of the Heart, Trilogy of Fear.
TELEVISION: Series: Movin' On, Nashville '99, B.J. and the Bear, The Misadventures of Sherif Lobo, Legmen. Guest: Police Story, Cannon, McCloud, Marcus Welby, M.D., Mannix, The Streets of San Francisco, Murder She Wrote, Hotel, Love Boat, In the Heat of the Night, Hunter. Mini-series: The Rhinemann Exchange, Dream West, Celebrity. Movies: Lock Stock and Barrel, River of Mystery, Night Stalker, Norliss

Tapes, Death Squad, In Tandem, Medical Story, Eric, Kiss Me Kill Me, Yesterday's Child, Killer on Board, Tarantulas: The Deadly Cargo, Little Mo, B.J. and the Bear (pilot), Murder in Music City, Ebony Ivory and Jade, Concrete Cowboys, Desperate Intruder, The Baron and the Kid, If It's Tuesday It Still Must Be Belgium, Mothers Daughters and Lovers, Grass Roots, Gambler IV. Special: Sherlock Holmes and the Incident at Victoria Falls.

ALBECK, ANDY: Executive. b. U.S.S.R., Sept. 25, 1921. Industry career began in 1939 with Columbia Pictures Intl. 1947, Central Motion Picture Exchange. 1949, Eagle Lion Classics, Inc. Joined UA in 1951 in intl. dept., functioning in the area of operations. After filling a number of key posts, named asst. treas. in 1970. In 1972 became v.p. of UA and its subsidiary, UA Broadcasting, Inc. 1973, appt. pres. of UA Broadcasting and in 1976 named sr. v.p.—operations. Named UA Corp. pres. & chief exec. officer in 1978. Retired, 1981.

ALBERGHETTI, ANNA MARIA: Singer, Actress. b. Pesaro, Italy, May 15, 1936; d. Daniele Alberghetti, cellist. Concert debut in 1948 in Pesaro, then toufed Italy, Scandinavia, Spain; Am. debut Carnegie Hall, 1950, sang with NY Philharmonic Society, Phila. Symphony, on television. Broadway stage debut: Carnival, 1962. (Tony Award for best actress).
PICTURES: The Medium (debut, 1951), Here Comes the Groom, The Stars Are Singing, Last Command, Duel at Apache Wells, Ten Thousand Bedrooms, Cinderfella.
TELEVISION: Guest: Toast of the Town, Cavalcade of Stars, Arthur Murray Show, Bob Hope, Eddie Fisher, Red Skelton, Dinah Shore, Desilu Playhouse, G.E. Theatre, Chevy Show, Dupont Show, Voice of Firestone, Colgate Hour, Climax, Loretta Young, Ford Jubilee, Perry Como.

ALBERT, EDDIE: Actor. r.n. Eddie Albert Heimberger. b. Rock Island, IL, April 22, 1908. e. U. of Minnesota. Father of actor Edward Albert. Radio NBC.
BROADWAY: Brother Rat, Say Darling, The Music Man, Room Service, The Boys from Syracuse, Seven Year Itch, Our Town, No Hard Feelings, Reuben Reuben, Miss Liberty, You Can't Take It With You.
PICTURES: Brother Rat (debut, 1938), On Your Toes, Four Wives, Brother Rat and a Baby, Angel from Texas, My Love Came Back, Dispatch from Reuter's, Four Mothers, The Wagons Roll at Night, Out of the Fog, Thieves Fall Out, The Great Mr. Nobody, Treat 'em Rough, Eagle Squadron, Ladies' Day, Lady Bodyguard, Bombadier, Strange Voyage, Rendezvous With Annie, Perfect Marriage, Smash-Up, Time Out of Mind, Hit Parade of 1947, Dude Goes West, You Gotta Stay Happy, Fuller Brush Girl, You're in the Navy Now, Meet Me After the Show, Carrie, Actors and Sin, Roman Holiday (Acad. Award nom.), Girl Rush, I'll Cry Tomorrow, Oklahoma!, Attack, Teahouse of the August Moon, The Sun Also Rises, The Joker is Wild, Orders to Kill, Gun Runners, The Roots of Heaven, Beloved Infidel, The Young Doctors, Two Little Bears, Madison Avenue, Who's Got the Action?, The Longest Day, Captain Newman M.D., Miracle of the White Stallions, The Party's Over, Seven Women, The Heartbreak Kid (Acad. Award nom.), McQ, The Take, The Longest Yard, Escape to Witch Mountain, The Devil's Rain, Hustle, Whiffs, Birch Interval, Moving Violation, Yesterday, The Concorde-Airport 79, Foolin' Around, How to Beat the High Cost of Living, Take This Job and Shove It, Yes Giorgio, Dreamscape, Stitches, Head Office, The Big Picture, Brenda Starr.
TELEVISION: Series: Leave It To Larry, Nothing But the Best, Saturday Night Revue, Green Acres, Switch!, Falcon Crest. Movies & Specials: The Yeagers, Benjamin Franklin, The Borrowers, Killer Bees, Nutcracker, Anything Goes, Crash, The Word, Evening in Byzantium, Pirates Key, Living in Paradise, Oklahoma Dolls, The Plan, Peter and Paul, Goliath Awaits, Concord, Beyond Witch Mountain, Rooster, Demon Murder Case, Coalfire, In Like Flynn, Dress Gray, Mercy or Murder?, War and Remembrance, Return to Green Acres, The Girl from Mars. Guest: The Fall Guy, Love Boat, Highway to Heaven, Falcon Crest, Murder She Wrote, thirtysomething, Ray Bradbury Theatre, Twilight Zone, Time Trax, Golden Palace.

ALBERT, EDWARD: Actor. b. Los Angeles, CA, Feb. 20, 1951. e. UCLA. Son of actor Eddie Albert and late actress Margo. Was prod. asst. on Patton in Spain. Has appeared with father on radio and TV shows. Is photographer and has exhibited work in L.A.
PICTURES: The Fool Killer (debut, 1965), Wild Country, Butterflies Are Free, Forty Carats, Midway, The Domino Principle, Purple Taxi, The Greek Tycoon, When Time Ran Out, The Squeeze, Galaxy of Terror, Butterfly, The House Where Evil Dwells, A Time to Die, Ellie, Getting Even (a.k.a. Hostage: Dallas), Distortions, Terminal Entry, The Rescue, Mind Games, Fist Fighter, Shoot Fighter, Fight to the Death, Guarding Tess.
TELEVISION: Series: The Yellow Rose, Falcon Crest. Host: Viva, Different Point of View, On Call. Guest: Beauty and the Beast, Houston Knights, Murder She Wrote, Police Story, Hitchhiker, The Love Boat, The Rookies. Movies: Killer

Bees, Death Cruise, The Millionaire, Silent Victory: The Kitty O'Neil Story, Black Beauty, Blood Feud, The Girl from Mars, Sight Unseen, Body Language. *Mini-Series*: The Last Convertible. *Specials*: Daddy Can't Read, Orson Welles' Great Mysteries (BBC).
THEATRE: Room Service, Our Town, The Glass Menagerie, Hamlet.

ALBRIGHT, LOLA: Actress. b. Akron, OH, July 20, 1925. e. Studied piano 12 years. Switchboard operator and stenographer NBC; stenographer with WHAM and bit player; photographers' model. Screen debut in The Pirate, 1948.
PICTURES: The Pirate, Easter Parade, Girl from Jones Beach, Tulsa, Champion, Good Humor Man, Bodyhold, When You're Smiling, Sierra Passage, Killer That Stalked New York, Arctic Flight, Silver Whip, Treasure of Ruby Hills, Magnificent Matador, Tender Trap, Monolith Monsters, Pawnee, Oregon Passage, A Cold Wind in August, Kid Galahad, Joy House, Lord Love a Duck, The Way West, Where Were You When the Lights Went Out?, The Impossible Years, The Money Jungle.
TELEVISION: *Series*: Peter Gunn, Peyton Place. *Guest*: Switch, The Eddie Capra Mysteries, Quincy, Airwolf. *Movies*: How I Spent My Summer Vacation, Delta County USA, Terraces.

ALCAINE, JOSE LUIS: Cinematographer. b. Tangier, Algeria, Dec. 26, 1938. e. Spanish Cinema Sch., Madrid. After graduation joined Madrid's Studio Moros doing commercials.
PICTURES: El Puente, El Sur, Taseo, Rustlers' Rhapsody, Bluebeard Bluebeard, Women on the Verge of a Nervous Breakdown, The Mad Monkey, Tie Me Up Tie Me Down, Ay Carmela, Lovers.

ALDA, ALAN: Actor, Writer, Director r.n. Alphonso D'Abruzzo b. New York, NY, Jan. 28, 1936. e. Fordham U., 1956. Son of actor Robert Alda. Studied at Cleveland Playhouse on Ford Foundation Grant; performed with Second City, then on TV in That Was The Week That Was. For work as director, writer and actor on M*A*S*H won 5 Emmys, 2 Writers Guild Awards, 3 Directors Guild Awards, 6 Golden Globes, 7 People's Choice Awards, Humanitas Award (for Writing).
THEATER: *Bdwy*: Only in America, The Owl and The Pussycat, Purlie Victorious, Fair Game For Lovers (Theatre World Award), The Apple Tree (Tony Award nom.), Jake's Women (Tony Award nom.), *London*: Our Town.
PICTURES: Gone Are The Days (debut, 1963), Paper Lion, The Extraordinary Seaman, Jenny, The Moonshine War, The Mephisto Waltz, To Kill a Clown, Same Time Next Year, California Suite, The Seduction of Joe Tynan (also s.p.), The Four Seasons (also dir., s.p.), Sweet Liberty (also dir., s.p.), A New Life (also dir., s.p.), Crimes and Misdemeanors (D.W. Griffith Award, NY Film Critics Award), Betsy's Wedding (also dir., s.p.), Whispers in the Dark, Manhattan Murder Mystery.
TELEVISION: *Series*: That Was the Week That Was, M*A*S*H (11 years). *Movies*: The Glass House, Playmates, Isn't It Shocking?, Kill Me If You Can (Emmy nom.), And the Band Played On. *Specials*: Free to Be You and Me, 6 Rms Riv Vu (also dir.); Created series We'll Get By and The Four Seasons. *Guest*: Phil Silvers Show, The Nurses, Route 66, Trials of O'Brien, Coronet Blue, Carol Burnet Show. *Pilots*: Where's Everett, Higher and Higher.

ALDREDGE, THEONI V.: Costume designer. b. Salonika, Greece, Aug. 22, 1932. m. actor Tom Aldredge. e. American School, Athens; Goodman Theatre School, Chicago, 1949–52.
PICTURES: You're A Big Boy Now, No Way to Treat a Lady, Uptight, Last Summer, I Never Sang for My Father, Promise at Dawn, The Great Gatsby (Acad. Award), Network, Semi-Tough, The Cheap Detective, The Fury, Eyes of Laura Mars (Sci Fi. Acad. Honor), The Champ, The Rose, Can't Stop the Music, Circle of Two, Loving Couples, A Change of Seasons, Middle Age Crazy, Rich and Famous, Annie, Monsignor, Ghostbusters, Moonstruck, We're No Angels, Stanley & Iris, Other People's Money, Addams Family Values.
THEATRE: *Bdwy*: Sweet Bird of Youth, That Championship Season, Sticks and Bones, Two Gentlemen of Verona, A Chorus Line, Annie (Tony Award), Ballroom, Much Ado About Nothing, Barnum (Tony Award), Dream Girls, Woman of the Year, Onward Victoria, La Cage aux Folles (Tony Award), 42nd Street, Merlin, Private Lives, The Corn is Green, The Rink, Blithe Spirit, Chess, Gypsy, Oh Kay!, The Secret Garden, High Rollers.

ALEANDRO, NORMA: Actress. b. Buenos Aires, Argentina, Dec. 6, 1936. Sister is actress Maria Vaner. As child, performed in parents, in theater troupe. In Argentina performed in every theatrical genre and epoch. Was also director. Has written published short stories (1986) and poems and screenplay for Argentinian film, Los Herederos. Was in exile in Uruguay (18 months) and Spain 1976–82 because of the military junta in Argentina. Before exile had made 12 films; after return in 1982 starred in theatre and 7 films.
THEATER: U.S.: About Love and Other Stories (one-woman show), toured South America, then at La Mama and later off-Bdwy at Public Theater (1986); The Senorita of Tacna

(written for her by Mario Vargas-Llosa, 1987).
PICTURES: The Official Story (best actress award, Cannes Film Fest. 1986), Gaby: A True Story (Acad. Award nom.), Cousins, Vital Signs, The Tombs.
TELEVISION: *Movies*: Dark Holiday, One Man's War.

ALEXANDER, JANE: Actress. b. Boston, MA, Oct. 28, 1939. r.n. Jane Quigley. m. director Edwin Sherin. Mother of actor Jace Alexander. e. Sarah Lawrence Coll., U. of Edinburgh. Stage career includes appearances on Broadway; at Arena Stage, Washington D.C.; Kennedy Center, D.C.; Music Center, L.A.; and Shakespeare Festival at Stamford, Conn.
THEATER: *NY*: The Great White Hope (Tony & Theatre World Awards, 1969), 6 Rms Riv Vu, Find Your Way Home, Hamlet, The Heiress, First Monday in October, Goodbye Fidel, Losing Time, Monday After the Miracle, Old Times, Night of the Iguana, Approaching Zanzibar, Shadowlands, The Visit, The Sisters Rosensweig.
PICTURES: The Great White Hope (debut, 1970), A Gunfight, The New Centurions, All the President's Men, The Betsy, Kramer vs. Kramer, Brubaker, Night Crossing, Testament, City Heat, Square Dance, Sweet Country, Glory.
TELEVISION: *Movies*: Welcome Home Johnny Bristol, Miracle on 34th St., This is the West That Was, Death Be Not Proud, Eleanor and Franklin, Eleanor and Franklin: The White House Years, A Circle of Children, Lovey: A Circle of Children Part II, A Question of Love, Playing for Time (Emmy Award), In the Custody of Strangers, When She Says No, Calamity Jane, Malice in Wonderland, Blood & Orchids, In Love and War, Open Admissions, A Friendship in Vienna, Daughter of the Streets, Stay the Night. *Specials*: Mountain View, A Marriage: Georgia O'Keeffe and Alfred Stieglitz. *Pilot*: New Year.

ALEXANDER, JASON: Actor. r.n. Jay Scott Greenspan. b. Newark, NJ, Sept. 23, 1959. e. Boston Univ.
PICTURES: The Burning (debut, 1981), Brighton Beach Memoirs, The Mosquito Coast, Pretty Woman, White Palace, Jacob's Ladder, I Don't Buy Kisses Anymore, Coneheads, North.
THEATRE: NY: Merrily We Roll Along, Forbidden Broadway, The Rink, Personals, Stop the World, Light Up the Sky, Broadway Bound, Jerome Robbins' Broadway (Tony, Drama Desk & Outer Critics' Circle Awards), Accomplice. Regional: Give 'em Hell Harry.
TELEVISION: *Series*: E/R, Everything's Relative, Seinfeld. *Movies*: Senior Trip, Rockabye, Favorite Son. *Guest*: Newhart, Dream On. *Special*: Sexual Healing.

ALEXANDER, RALPH: Executive. Began career with Universal Pictures in sales, 1949; various sls. jobs with 20th Century Fox and Lorimar. 1981–82, v.p., theatrical foreign sls., Filmway Pictures; 1982–84, v.p., sls for Latin America & Southeast Asia, Embassy Pictures Intl. 1984, exec. v.p., multimedia foreign sls. for Robert Meyers Intl. Nov., 1985, joined Dino De Laurentiis Corp. as intl. sls. dir. in chg. all foreign sls. theatrical and ancillary rights except tv. 1986, promoted to v.p., intl. sls., DEG; pres. marketing and sales, Kings Road Intl.—1989; joined Scotti Bros. Pictures as pres. intl. sales and marketing, 1989.

ALGAR, JAMES: Producer, Writer, Director. b. Modesto, CA, June 11, 1912. e. Stanford U., B.A., M.A. journalism. Entire career since 1934 with Walt Disney Prods. Wrote and co-produced Great Moments with Mr. Lincoln; New York World's Fair; Circarama, America the Beautiful, Circle Vision 1958 Brussels World's Fair, Disneyland, Hall of Presidents, Disney World, Florida. Shares in nine Oscars.
DOCUMENTARIES: war. health. True-Life Adventures: Seal Island, The Living Desert, Vanishing Prairie, The African Lion, Secrets of Life.
FEATURES: Animator: Snow White; Director: Fantasia, Bambi, Wind in the Willows, Ichabod & Mr. Toad, Ten Who Dared, The Incredible Journey, Gnome-Mobile, White Wilderness, Rascal, The Legend of Lobo, The Jungle Cat, Run Cougar Run.
TELEVISION: Producer: Run Light Buck, Run, The Not So Lonely Lighthouse Keeper, One Day on Beetle Rock, Wild Heart, Along the Oregon Trail, The Best Doggoned Dog in the World, One Day at Teton Marsh, Solomon, the Sea Turtle, Manado the Wolverine, Wild Geese Calling, Two Against the Arctic, Bayou Bay, Secrets of the Pond, Boy Who Talked to Badgers, Big Sky Man.

ALIN, MORRIS: Editor, Writer, Publicist, Lyricist. e. City Coll. of New York. Came into m.p. industry, auditor of Hunchback of Notre Dame, roadshow oper., 1924; asst. sls. prom. mgr. Universal, 1926–27; slsmn., Universal, 1927; assoc. editor. The Distributor, MGM publication, 1927; editor, 1928–33; writer, publicist, MGM Studio, 1933–34; writer, publicist, Hollywood, New York, 1935–38; rej. Universal. 1938, editor, Progress: (Univ. publication); Twice winner of award, International Competition on Industrial Journalism; Senior publicist and Progress editor, Universal, 1961–67; editor Enterprise Press, 1968; member, executive Enterprise Press 1973; American Guild of Authors and Composers, American Society of Composers, Authors and Publishers, National Academy of Popular Music, and Motion Picture Pioneers.

ALLAND, WILLIAM: Producer. b. Delmar, DE, March 4, 1916. e. Baltimore. Acted in semi-professional groups; with Orson Welles' Mercury Theatre as actor, stage mgr.; asst. prod. Mercury Theatre radio series; actor, dialogue dir., Citizen Kane; act., Macbeth; U.S. Air Force, W.W.II; then radio writer; prod., Universal, 1952.
PICTURES: The Raiders, Flesh and Fury, Stand At Apache River, It Came From Outer Space, The Lawless Breed, Creature From The Black Lagoon, Johnny Dark, This Island Earth, Dawn At Socorro, Four Guns To The Border, Chief Crazy Horse, Revenge Of The Creature, Tarantula, The Creature Walks Among Us, This Island Earth, The Mole People, Gun for a Coward, Land Unknown, Deadly Mantis, Mole People, The Lady Takes a Flyer, As Young As We Are, The Party Crashers, Colossus of New York, Raw Wind in Eden, The Space Children, Look In Any Window (also dir.), The Lively Set, The Rare Breed.

ALLEN, COREY: Director, Actor. r.n. Alan Cohen. b. Cleveland, OH, June 29, 1934. e. UCLA, 1951–54; UCLA law sch. 1954–55. Actor turned dir. starred in Oscar-winning UCLA student film, appeared in 20 plays at Players Ring, Players Gallery and other L.A. theaters. Films as actor: Rebel Without a Cause, Key Witness, Sweet Bird of Youth, Private Property, Party Girl, The Chapman Report; TV: Perry Mason, Alfred Hitchcock Presents. With partner John Herman Shaner, prod. Freeway Circuit Theatre. Led Actors Workshop with actor Guy Stockwell for 10 years.
PICTURES: Director: The Erotic Adventures of Pinocchio, Thunder and Lightning, Avalanche.
TELEVISION: Series Director: This is the Life, Mannix, High Chaparral, Dr. Kildare, Streets of San Francisco (DGA nom.), Ironside, Barnaby Jones, Police Woman, Rockford Files, Quincy, Dallas, Lou Grant, McClain's Law, Family Hovak, T.J. Hooker, Paper Chase: The Second Year, Hill Street Blues (Emmy), Sonny Spoon, Supercarrier, Pilots: Man Undercover, Capitol, Simon and Simon, Whiz Kids, Murder She Wrote, Star Trek: The Next Generation. Unsub. Movies: See the Man Run, Cry Rape!, Yesterday's Child (co-dir.), Stone (pilot), Man in the Santa Claus Suit, The Return of Frank Cannon, The Murder of Sherlock Holmes, Code Name: Foxfire (pilot), Brass, Destination America, Beverly Hills Cowgirl Blues, The Last Fling, Ann Jillian Story.

ALLEN, DAYTON: Performer. b. New York, NY, Sept. 24, 1919. e. Mt. Vernon H.S. Motion picture road shows, 1936–40; disc jockey, WINS, N.Y., 1940–41; writer, vaudeville comedy bits, 1941–45; then radio comic, puppeteer and voices; TV since 1948; film commercials; shows include voices on Terrytoons, Deputy Dawg, Heckle & Jeckle, Lancelot Link: Secret Chimp, Lariat Sam, Oaky Doky, Bonny Maid Varieties, Howdy Doody, Jack Barry's Winky Dink, The Steve Allen Show. 130 Dayton Allen 5 minute shows (synd.). Acted in film The Cotton Club.

ALLEN, DEBBIE: Actress, Choreographer. b. Houston, TX, Jan. 16, 1950. Sister of actress Phylicia Rashad. e. Howard U.
THEATER: Ti-Jean and His Brothers (debut, 1972), Purlie, Raisin, Ain't Misbehavin', West Side Story (revival), Sweet Charity (revival, Tony Award, 1986), Carrie (choreographer).
PICTURES: The Fish That Saved Pittsburgh (1979), Fame, Ragtime, Jo Jo Dancer Your Life is Calling.
TELEVISION: Series: The Jim Stafford Show (1975), 3 Girls 3, Fame (series; 3 Emmys as choreographer, 1 nom. as actress), A Different World (prod., dir.). Mini-Series: Roots—The Next Generation. Movies: The Greatest Thing That Almost Happened, Ebony, Ivory and Jade, Women of San Quentin, Celebrity, Polly-Comin' Home (dir.), Stompin' at the Savoy (also dir.). Specials: Ben Vereen—His Roots, Loretta Lynn in Big Apple Country, Texaco Star Theater—Opening Night, The Kids from Fame, John Schneider's Christmas Holiday, A Tribute to Martin Luther King Jr.—A Celebration of Life, Motown Returns to the Apollo, The Debbie Allen Special (also dir., chor.), Sinbad Live (Afros and Bell Bottoms), Academy Awards (choreographer: 1991–93).

ALLEN, DEDE: Film editor. r.n. Dorothea Carothers Allen b. Cleveland, OH, 1924. Once a messenger at Columbia Pictures, moved to editing dept., then to commercials and features.
PICTURES: Odds Against Tomorrow (1959), The Hustler, America America, Bonnie and Clyde, Rachel Rachel, Alice's Restaurant, Little Big Man, Slaughterhouse 5, Serpico, Night Moves, Dog Day Afternoon, The Missouri Breaks, Slapshot, The Wiz, Reds (also exec. prod.), Harry and Son, Mike's Murder, The Breakfast Club, Off Beat, The Milagro Beanfield War (co-ed.), Let It Ride (co-ed.), Henry and June. The Addams Family.

ALLEN, JAY PRESSON: Writer, Producer. r.n. Jacqueline Presson. b. Fort Worth, TX, March 3, 1922. m. prod. Lewis M. Allen. Playwright: The First Wife, The Prime of Miss Jean Brodie, Forty Carats, Tru (also dir.).
PICTURES: Writer: Marnie, The Prime of Miss Jean

Brodie, Cabaret, Travels with My Aunt, Funny Lady, Just Tell Me What You Want (also prod.), It's My Turn (exec. prod. only), Prince of the City (also exec. prod.), Deathtrap (also exec. prod.).
TELEVISION: Family (creator), Clinic, Hothouse.

ALLEN, JOAN: Actress. b. Rochelle, IL, Aug. 20, 1956. Founding member of Steppenwolf Theatre Co., in Chicago where she performed in over 20 shows including A Lesson from Aloes, Three Sisters, The Miss Firecracker Contest, Cloud 9, Balm in Gilead, Fifth of July, Reckless, Earthly Possessions, Off Broadway in The Marriage of Bette and Boo, And a Nightingale Sang (Clarence Derwent, Drama Desk, Outer Critics' Circle and Theatre World Awards). Broadway debut: Burn This (1987, Tony Award), The Heidi Chronicles.
PICTURES: Compromising Positions (debut, 1985), Manhunter, Peggy Sue Got Married, Tucker: The Man and His Dream, In Country, Ethan Frome, Searching for Bobby Fischer, Josh and S.A.M.
TELEVISION: Special: All My Sons. Mini-Series: Evergreen. Movie: Without Warning: The James Brady Story.

ALLEN, KAREN: Actress. b. Carrollton, IL, Oct. 5, 1951. e. George Washington U., U. of Maryland. Auditioned for theatrical company in Washington, DC and won a role in Saint, touring with it for 7 months. Spent several years with Washington Theatre Laboratory Co. Moved to NY, acting in student films at NYU and studying acting with Lee Strasberg at Theatre Institute.
THEATER: NY: Monday After the Miracle (Broadway debut, 1982; Theatre World Award), Extremities, The Miracle Worker, The Country Girl. Williamstown (MA) Theatre: Tennessee Williams - A Celebration, The Glass Menagerie.
PICTURES: National Lampoon's Animal House (debut, 1978), Manhattan, The Wanderers, Cruising, A Small Circle of Friends, Raiders of the Lost Ark, Shoot the Moon, Split Image, Until September, Starman, The Glass Menagerie, Backfire, Scrooged, Animal Behavior, Secret Places of the Heart, Sweet Talker, Exile, Malcolm X, The Sandlot, Ghost in the Machine.
TELEVISION: Movies: Lovey: A Circle of Children Part II, Secret Weapon, Challenger, Voyage. Guest: Alfred Hitcock Presents (1986). Mini-Series: East of Eden.

ALLEN, LEWIS: Director. b. Shropshire, England, Dec. 25, 1905. e. Tettenhall Coll., Staffs, Eng. Exec. in chg. of N.Y. & London prod. for Gilbert Miller; actor & stage dir. N.Y. & England; dir. (N.Y.) Laburnum Grove, Amazing Doctor Clitterhouse, Ladies & Gentlemen; (London) The Women, studied m.p. prod. at Paramount 2 yrs.; appt. dir. with debut of The Uninvited 1943.
PICTURES: Our Hearts Were Young and Gay, The Unseen, Those Endearing Young Charms, The Perfect Marriage, The Imperfect Lady, Desert Fury, So Evil My Love, Sealed Verdict, Chicago Deadline, Valentino, Appointment with Danger, At Sword's Point, Suddenly, A Bullet For Joey, Illegal, Another Time Another Place, Whirlpool.
(Died: 1986)

ALLEN, LEWIS M.: Producer. b. Berryville, VA, 1922. e. Univ. of VA. m. writer-producer Jay Presson Allen.
PICTURES: The Connection, The Balcony, Lord of the Flies, Fahrenheit 451, The Queen (exec. prod.), Fortune and Men's Eyes, Never Cry Wolf, 1918 (exec. prod.), Valentine's Day (exec. prod.), Swimming to Cambodia, O.C. & Stiggs (exec. prod.), End of the Line (co-prod.), Miss Firecracker (exec. prod.), Lord of the Flies (exec. prod., remake).

ALLEN, MEL: TV commentator. b. Birmingham, AL, Feb. 14, 1913. e. U. of Alabama, A.B. 1932; U. Alabama Law Sch., LL.B. 1936. Started as sportscaster in Birmingham, while in law school; speech instructor in U. Ala. 1935–37; to N.Y. 1937, as staff announcer CBS to 1943; served in U.S. Army W.W.II in infantry until the war ended, then before discharge was transferred to work on NBC Army Hour; sportscasting throughout U.S., joined N.Y. Yankees, 1946, concurrently narrating many shorts incl. How to Make a Yankee, appearing on radio & video and in Babe Ruth Story; sports commentator Fox Movietonews; voted best sportscaster in Motion Picture Daily-Fame radio. TV polls; Monitor, NBC; NCAA TV College Football, NBC; World Series (1938–64), CBS-NBC; Rose Bowl (1951–62), NBC; Sports Broadcasters Hall Of Fame.

ALLEN, NANCY: Actress. b. New York, NY, June 24, 1950. e. H.S. Performing Arts, N.Y.
PICTURES: The Last Detail, Carrie, I Wanna Hold Your Hand, 1941, Home Movies, Dressed to Kill, Blow Out, Strange Invaders, The Buddy System, The Philadelphia Experiment, The Last Victim (Forced Entry), Not for Publication, Terror in the Aisles, Sweet Revenge, Robocop, Poltergeist III, Out of the Dark, Limit Up, Robocop 2, Robocop 3.
TELEVISION: Movies: The Gladiator, Memories of Murder, Acting on Impulse.

ALLEN, REX: Actor. b. Wilcox, AZ, Dec. 31, 1922. e. Wilcox H.S., 1939. Vaudeville & radio actor; WLS, Chicago, 5 yrs.; was

rodeo star appearing in shows through U.S.
PICTURES: Arizona Cowboy, Hills of Oklahoma, Under Mexicali Stars, Thunder in God's Country, Rodeo King & the Senorita, I Dream of Jeannie, Last Musketeer, South Pacific Trail, Old Overland Trail, Down Laredo Way, Phantom Stallion, For the Love of Mike, Tomboy and the Champ; narr., Walt Disney films incl. The Incredible Journey.
TELEVISION: Guest: Perry Como Special. Voice only: commercials, Wonderful World of Color. Series: Frontier Doctor, Five Star Jubilee.

ALLEN, STEVE: Performer. b. New York, NY, Dec 26, 1921. m. actress Jayne Meadows. U.S. Army 1942; radio shows, Los Angeles; TV, N.Y., 1950.
TELEVISION: Series: The Steve Allen Show (1950–2), Songs for Sale, Talent Patrol, What's My Line, Steve Allen Show, Tonight, Steve Allen Show (1956–61), (1962–4), (1964–7), I've Got a Secret, Steve Allen Comedy Hour (1967), Steve Allen Show (1967–9), I've Got a Secret (1972–3) Steve Allen's Laugh Back, Meeting of Minds, Steve Allen Comedy Hour (1980–1), Life's Most Embarrassing Moments. Movies: Now You See It Now You Don't, Stone, The Gossip Columnist. Mini-Series: Rich Man Poor Man.
PICTURES: Down Memory Lane, I'll Get By, The Benny Goodman Story, The Big Circus, College Confidential, Don't Worry We'll Think of a Title, Warning Shot, Where Were You When the Lights Went Out?, The Comic, The Sunshine Boys, Heart Beat, Amazon Women on the Moon, Great Balls of Fire!, The Player.
COMPOSER OR LYRICIST: This Could Be the Start of Something Big, Pretend You Don't See Her, South Rampart St. Parade, Picnic, Houseboat, On the Beach, Sleeping Beauty, Bell Book and Candle, Gravy Waltz, Impossible; Score for Broadway musical Sophie, and TV musicals: The Bachelor, and Alice in Wonderland.
AUTHOR: Fourteen For Tonight, Steve Allen's Bop Fables, The Funny Men, Wry On the Rocks, The Girls on the Tenth Floor, The Question Man, Mark It and Strike It, Not All of Your Laughter, Not All of Your Tears, Bigger Than a Breadbox, A Flash of Swallows, The Wake, Princess Snip-Snip and the Puppykittens, Curses, Schmock-Schmock!, Meeting of Minds, Ripoff, Meeting of Minds-Second Series, Rip-off, Explaining China, The Funny People, Talk Show Murders, Beloved Son: Story of the Jesus Cults, More Funny People, How To Make a Speech and How To Be Funny, Murder on the Glitter Box, The Passionate Non-smoker's Bill of Rights, Dumbth and 81 Ways to Make Americans Smarter, Murder in Manhattan, Steve Allen on the Bible, Religion and Morality, The Public Hating, Murder in Vegas, Hi-Ho Steverino! My Adventures in the Wonderful Wacky World of TV, The Murder Game, More Steve Allen on the Bible, Religion & Morality Book II.

ALLEN, WOODY: Actor, Director, Writer. r.n. Allan Stewart Konigsberg. b. New York, NY, Dec. 1, 1935. e. student NYU, 1953; City Coll. NY, 1953. Began writing comedy at age 17, contributing to various magazines (Playboy, New Yorker) and top TV comedy shows incl. Sid Caesar (1957), Art Carney (1958–59), Herb Shriner (1953). Appeared in nightclubs since 1961 and as a jazz musician at Michael's Pub, NY. Special Award, Berlin Film Fest., 1975. Academy Awards: Annie Hall (Best Director and Original Screenplay), Hannah and Her Sisters (Best Original Screenplay).
BOOKS: Getting Even, Without Feathers, Side Effects.
STAGE: Author: Play It Again, Sam (also star), Don't Drink The Water, The Floating Lightbulb.
PICTURES: Actor-Screenplay: What's New Pussycat?, What's Up Tiger Lily? (also dubbed and compiled footage); assoc. prod.), Casino Royale (actor only). Director, screenplay and actor: Take the Money and Run, Bananas, Play It Again Sam (actor, s.p. only), Everything You Always Wanted to Know About Sex* But Were Afraid to Ask, Sleeper, Love and Death, The Front (actor only), Annie Hall, Interiors (dir., s.p. only), Manhattan, Stardust Memories, A Midsummer Night's Sex Comedy, Zelig, Broadway Danny Rose, The Purple Rose of Cairo (dir., s.p. only), Hannah and Her Sisters, Radio Days (dir., s.p., narrator only), September (dir., s.p. only), King Lear (actor only), Another Woman (dir., s.p. only), New York Stories (Oedipus Wrecks segment), Crimes and Misdemeanors, Alice (dir., s.p. only), Scenes From a Mall (actor only), Shadows and Fog, Husbands and Wives, Manhattan Murder Mystery.
TELEVISION: Specials: Gene Kelly in New York New York, Woody Allen's First Special (also writer), The Woody Allen Special (also writer), Plimpton . . . Did You Hear the One About . . . ? Guest: Hullabaloo, Andy Williams, Hippodrome, Kraft Music Hall.

ALLEY, KIRSTIE: Actress. b. Wichita, KS, Jan. 12, 1955. m. actor Parker Stevenson. e. KS State U., U. of Kansas. On L.A. stage in Cat on a Hot Tin Roof.
PICTURES: Star Trek II—The Wrath of Khan, Blind Date, Champions, Runaway, Shoot to Kill, Loverboy, Look Who's Talking, Madhouse, Sibling Rivalry, Look Who's Talking Too, Look Who's Talking 3.

TELEVISION: Series: Masquerade, Cheers (Emmy Award, 1991). Movies: Sins of the Past, A Bunny's Tale, Stark: Mirror Image, Prince of Bel Air, Infidelity. Mini-Series: North and South (also Book II). Guest: The Love Boat, The Hitchhiker.

ALLYSON, JUNE: Actress. r.n. Ella Geisman. b. Westchester, NY, Oct. 7, 1917. Started as chorus girl. Voted one of ten top money-making stars in Motion Picture Herald-Fame poll, 1955.
BROADWAY: Sing Out the News, Panama Hattie, Best Foot Forward, 40 Carats, No No Nanette (national co.).
PICTURES: Best Foot Foward (debut, 1943), Girl Crazy, Thousands Cheer, Meet the People, Two Girls and a Sailor, Music for Millions, Her Highness and the Bellboy, The Sailor Takes a Wife, Two Sisters From Boston, Till the Clouds Roll By, Secret Heart, High Barbaree, Good News, The Bride Goes Wild, The Three Musketeers, Words and Music, Little Women, The Stratton Story, Meet the People, Reformer and the Redhead, Right Cross, Too Young to Kiss, Girl in White, Battle Circus, Remains to be Seen, Executive Suite, Glenn Miller Story, Woman's World, Strategic Air Command, The Shrike, McConnell Story, Opposite Sex, You Can't Run Away From It, Interlude, My Man Godfrey, Stranger In My Arms, They Only Kill Their Masters.
TELEVISION: Series: DuPont Show With June Allyson. Guest: Murder She Wrote, Misfits of Science. Movies: See the Man Run, Letters from Three Lovers, Curse of the Black Widow, Vega$, Three on a Date, The Kid With the Broken Halo. Special: 20th Century Follies.

ALMODÓVAR, PEDRO: Director, Writer. b. La Mancha, Spain, Sept. 25, 1951. Grew up in Calzada de Calatrava. At 17 moved to Madrid where worked 10 years for telephone co. while writing comic strips and articles for underground newspapers and working as actor with independent theater co., Los Goliardos. Upon the end of Francoist repression in 1975, made Super-8 experimental films starring friends: Screw, Screw Me Tim. Wrote fiction, sang with rock band, published pornographic fotonovela (Todo Tuya), and created character of porn star, Patty Diphusa, whose fictionalized confessions he published under female pseudonym.
PICTURES: Pepi, Lucy, Bom, and Other Girls on the Heap (1980, cost $30,000), Labyrinth of Passion, Dark Habits, What Have I Done to Deserve This? Matador, Law of Desire, Women on the Verge of a Nervous Breakdown, Tie Me Up! Tie Me Down!, High Heels.

ALMOND, PAUL: Producer, Director, Writer. b. Montreal, Canada, April 26, 1931. e. McGill U., Balliol Coll., Oxford U. 1954–66 produced and directed over a hundred television dramas in Toronto, London, N.Y., and Hollywood; prod., dir., s.p., Isabel 1968, Act of the Heart; Etrog (dir.; best Canadian feature); Journey; Ups and Downs; Captive Hearts (dir.), The Dance Goes On (s.p., prod., dir.).

ALONSO, MARIA CONCHITA: Actress, Singer. b. Cuba, 1957. Family moved to Venezuela when she was five. 1971, named Miss Teenager of the World. 1975, Miss Venezuela. Appeared in four feature films and 10 soap operas before coming to U.S. Recorded several albums as singer, 4 gold albums, 1 platinum.
PICTURES: Fear City, Moscow on the Hudson, Touch and Go, A Fine Mess, Extreme Prejudice, The Running Man, Colors, Vampire's Kiss, Predator 2, McBain, House of the Spirits, Roosters.
TELEVISION: An American Cousin (RAI mini-series). Specials: Viva Miami!, The Night of the Super Sounds (host). Guest: One of the Boys. Movie: Teamster Boss: The Jackie Presser Story.

ALONZO, JOHN A: Cinematographer, Director. b. Dallas, TX, 1934.
PICTURES: Bloody Mama, Vanishing Point, Harold and Maude, Get to Know Your Rabbit, Lady Sings the Blues, Sounder, Pete 'n' Tillie, Hit, The Naked Ape, Conrack, Chinatown, Farewell My Lovely, The Fortune, I Will . . . I Will . . . For Now, Once Is Not Enough, The Bad News Bears, Black Sunday, Beyond Reason, Close Encounters of the Third Kind (addtl. photog.), Which Way Is Up?, Casey's Shadow, FM (dir. only), The Cheap Detective, Norma Rae, Tom Horn, Back Roads, Zorro the Gay Blade, Blue Thunder, Cross Creek, Scarface, Out of Control, Terror in the Aisles, Runaway, Jo Jo Dancer Your Life Is Calling, Nothing in Common, 50 Years of action, Real Men, Overboard, Physical Evidence, Steel Magnolias, Internal Affairs, The Guardian, Navy SEALS, Housitter, Cool World, Meteor Man, Clifford.
TELEVISION: Champions: A Love Story, Belle Star (also dir.), Blinded By the Light (also dir.), The Kid From Nowhere (also dir.), Roots: The Gift, Knights of the City.

ALTERMAN, JOSEPH GEORGE: Executive. b. New Haven, CT., Dec. 17, 1919. e. Wesleyan U., B.A., 1942; Inst. for Organization Management, Yale U. 1957–59. Exec. assist., Sound-Scriber Corp., 1945–48; district mgr., Industrial Luncheon Service, 1948–55; asst. secretary and admin. Secretary, Theatre Owners of America, 1955; Exec. dir. and vice pres., Natl. Assn. of Theatre Owners, 1966; Exec. v.p. COMPO.,

1970. Retired Sept. 1988 from NATO. Consultant m.p. industry conventions and meetings. Chmn. bd. governors, Institute for Learning in Retirement.

ALTMAN, ROBERT: Director, Writer, Producer. b. Kansas City, MO, Feb. 20, 1925. e. U. of Missouri. Started by making industrial films before dir. first indept. feature in 1957.
PICTURES: *Director:* The Delinquents (also s.p., prod.), The James Dean Story (also s.p., co-prod.) Countdown, That Cold Day in the Park, M*A*S*H, Brewster McCloud, McCabe & Mrs. Miller (also co-s.p.), Images (also s.p.), The Long Goodbye, Thieves Like Us (also co-s.p.), California Split (also prod.), Nashville (also prod.), Buffalo Bill and the Indians Or Sitting Bull's History Lesson (also co-s.p., prod.), The Late Show (prod. only), Welcome to L.A. (prod. only), Three Women (also s.p., prod.), A Wedding (also co-s.p., prod.), Remember My Name (prod. only), Quintet (also co-s.p., prod.), A Perfect Couple (also co-s.p., prod.), Rich Kids (prod. only), Health (also co-s.p., prod.), Popeye, Come Back to the Five and Dime Jimmy Dean Jimmy Dean, Streamers (also co-prod.), Secret Honor (also prod.), Fool for Love, Beyond Therapy (also co-s.p.), O.C. and Stiggs (also co-prod.), Aria (dir. sequence), Vincent & Theo, The Player, Short Cuts (also co-s.p.), Mrs. Parker and the Round Table (prod.).
TELEVISION: *Series* (dir., writer, &/or prod. episodes): Roaring Twenties, Bonanza, Bus Stop, Combat, Kraft Mystery Theatre, The Gallant Men (pilot).*Specials:* The Laundromat, Tanner '88 (also co-prod.; Emmy Award for dir. episode The Boiler Room, 1989), The Dumb Waiter, The Room, The Real McTeague. *Movie:* The Caine Mutiny Court-Martial (also co-prod.).
THEATRE: *NY:* Two By South, Come Back to the Five and Dime Jimmy Dean Jimmy Dean.

ALVARADO, TRINI: Actress. b. New York, NY, 1967. e. Fordham U. m. actor Robert McNeill. Began performing at age 7 as flamenco dancer with her parents' troupe. Prof. acting debut at 9 in stage musical Becca.
PICTURES: Rich Kids (debut, 1989), Times Square, Mrs. Soffel, Sweet Lorraine, Satisfaction, The Chair, Stella, American Blue Note, The Babe, American Friends.
THEATRE: Runaways, Yours Anne, Maggie Magalita, I Love You I Love You Not, Reds, The Magic Show, Godspell.
TELEVISION: *Movies:* Dreams Don't Die, Prisoner Without a Name, Nitti. *Specials:* Private Contentment, Unicorn Tales, A Movie Star's Daughter, Stagestruck, Sensibility and Sense. *Guest:* Kay O'Brien, Kate and Allie.

ALVIN, JOHN: Actor. r.n. John Alvin Hoffstadt; b. Chicago, IL, Oct. 24, 1917. e. Pasadena Playhouse, CA. Attended Morgan Park Military Acad. On radio Chicago & Detroit; on N.Y. stage Leaning on Letty, Life of the Party. Screen debut 1944 in Destination Tokyo. Under contract four years to Warner Bros., featured in 25 films.
PICTURES: Objective Burma, Destination Tokyo, San Antonio, Beast With Five Fingers, Night and Day, Cheyenne, Missing Women, Two Guys from Texas, Bold Frontiersman, Train to Alcatraz, Shanghai Chest, Carrie, April In Paris, Roughly Speaking, The Very Thought of You, Shadow of a Woman, Three Strangers, Romance on the High Seas, Torpedo Alley, Irma La Douce, Marnie, Inside Daisy Clover, Legend of Lylah Clare, They Shoot Horses Don't They?, They Call Me Mr. Tibbs, Somewhere in Time.
TELEVISION: Meet Millie, Burns and Allen, Death Valley Days, Asphalt Jungle, Climax, Dragnet, Jack Benny Show, My Three Sons, The Texan, Adventures in Paradise, Rawhide, Rifleman, Omnibus, Wells Fargo, Alfred Hitchcock, Mannix, I Spy, Legend of Lizzie Borden, All in the Family, McDuff, Lineup, My Favorite Husband, Family Affair, Get Smart, The Incredible Hulk, The Lucy Show, Ironside, Nightstalker, MASH, Lou Grant Show, Hart to Hart, Yellow Rose, Dennis the Menace (2 Hour Pilot), Murder She Wrote, Monster Squad, House of Evil, Aftermath, General Hospital, Starsky & Hutch, Policewoman, Amazing Stories, Capitol, Passions, The Quest, Visions/KCET, Rachel Sweet Rachel, Swallows Came Back, Return to Green Acres, Moving Target, From Out of the Night, The Walkers, The Bold and the Beautiful.

AMATEAU, ROD: Director. b. New York, NY, Dec. 20, 1927. Staff writer, CBS radio; stage mgr., Lux Radio Theatre; Universal, 1941; junior writer, 20th Century-Fox; then test dir., second unit dir.
TELEVISION: *Series:* Schlitz Playhouse of Stars, Four Star Playhouse, General Electric Theatre, Private Secretary, Dennis Day Show, Lassie, Ray Milland Show, Bob Cummings Show, Burns & Allen Show (also prod.), Dobie Gillis. *Movies:* Uncommon Valor, High School U.S.A., Swimsuit (prod.).
PICTURES: The Statue, Where Does It Hurt?, The Wilby Conspiracy, Drive-In, Lovelines, Garbage Pail Kids (also s.p., prod.), Sunset (story only).

AMECHE, DON: Actor. b. Kenosha, WI, May 31, 1908. r.n. Dominick Amici. e. Columbia Coll., U. of Wisconsin. In stock; on radio (incl. Chase & Sanborn Hour, The Bickersons). 1938 appeared in Beauty (short at World's Fair). In television from 1951; on Broadway in Silk Stockings (1955), Holiday For Lovers, Goldilocks, 13 Daughters, Henry Sweet Henry, Our Town.
PICTURES: Sins of Man (debut, 1936), Ladies in Love, One in a Million, Ramona, Love is News, Fifty Roads to Town, Love Under Fire, You Can't Have Everything, In Old Chicago, Happy Landing, Josette, Gateway, Alexander's Ragtime Band, Midnight, Swanee River, The Three Musketeers, The Story of Alexander Graham Bell, Lillian Russell, Down Argentine Way, Four Sons, That Night in Rio, Kiss the Boys Goodbye, Moon Over Miami, The Feminine Touch, Confirm or Deny, The Magnificent Dope, Girl Trouble, Heaven Can Wait, The Happy Land, Something to Shout About, Wing and a Prayer, Greenwich Village, It's in the Bag, Guest Wife, So Goes My Love, That's My Man, Sleep My Love, Slightly French, A Fever in the Blood, Ring Around the World, Picture Mommy Dead, Suppose They Gave a War & Nobody Came, The Boatniks, Trading Places, Cocoon (Acad. Award, supp. actor, 1985), Harry and the Hendersons, Coming to America, Things Change (Venice Film Fest. Award, 1988), Cocoon: The Return, Odd Ball Hall, Oscar, Folks!, Homeward Bound: The Incredible Journey (voice).
TELEVISION: *Series:* Take a Chance (emcee), Holiday Hotel, Coke Time With Eddie Fisher (host), International Showtime (host 1961–65) *Movies:* Shadow Over Elveron, Gidget Gets Married, A Masterpiece of Murder, Pals. *Guest:* The Love Boat, Climax. *Pilot:* Not in Front of the Kids.

AMES, LEON: Actor. r.n. Leon Wycoff. b. Portland, IN, Jan. 20, 1903. Aviator; with Champlin Players, Lansford, PA, in stock and on stage; plays include: Tobacco Road, Male Animal, Land Is Bright; m.p. debut in Murders in the Rue Morgue, 1932; owner & vice-pres. Studio City Ford Co.
PICTURES: Meet Me in St. Louis, Thirty Seconds Over Tokyo, Yolanda and the Thief, Merton of the Movies, On an Island With You, Velvet Touch, Date With Judy, Battleground, Ambush, Big Hangover, Little Women, Dial 1119, Happy Years, Alias a Gentleman, Watch the Birdie, Cattle Drive, On Moonlight Bay, It's a Big Country, Angel Face, By the Light of the Silvery Moon, Let's Do It Again, Sabre Jet, Peyton Place, From the Terrace, Absent Minded Professor, Son of Flubber, Misadventures of Merlin Jones, The Monkey's Uncle, On a Clear Day You Can See Forever, Tora! Tora! Tora!, Testament, Jake Speed, Peggy Sue Got Married.
TELEVISION: *Series:* Life with Father, Frontier Judge, Father of the Bride, Mr. Ed. *Guest:* Bewitched, Maggie.

AMES, LOUIS B.: Executive. b. St. Louis, MO, Aug. 9, 1918. e. Washington U., St. Louis. m. Jetti Preminger. Began as music consultant and staff director of musical programs for NBC; music dir. 1948, WPIX; 1951 appt. program mgr., WPIX; assoc. prod., Today, NBC TV, 1954; feature editor Home, 1957; Adm.-prod. NBC Opera, 1958; dir. cultural prog. N.Y. World's Fair, 1960–63; dir. RCA Pavillion, N.Y. World's Fair, 1963–65; 1966 dir., Nighttime, TV; 1969, dir. of programming N.W. Ayer & Sons, Inc. 1973 Mgr. Station Services, Television Information Office. NYC.

AMIEL, JON: Director. b. London, England. e. Cambridge. Was in charge of the Oxford & Cambridge Shakespeare Co., then literary mngr. for Hamptead Theatre Club where he started directing. Became story edit. for BBC, then director.
PICTURES: Romance Romance, Silent Twins, Queen of Hearts, Tune in Tomorrow, Sommersby.
TELEVISION: A Sudden Wrench, Gates of Gold, Busted, Tandoori Nights (series; also prod.), The Singing Detective (mini-series).

AMIS, SUZY: Actress. b. Oklahoma City, OK, Jan. 5, 1962. m. actor Sam Robards. At 16 was introduced on the Merv Griffin Show by Eileen Ford whose modeling agency she worked for, as "The Face of the Eighties." After modeling and living in Europe, made film debut in Fandango (1985). Off-Broadway debut: Fresh Horses (Theatre World Award).
PICTURES: Fandango, The Big Town, Plain Clothes, Rocket Gibraltar, Twister, Where the Heart Is, Rich in Love, Watch It, The Ballad of Little Jo.

AMOS, JOHN: Actor. b. Newark, NJ, Dec. 27, 1941. e. East Orange H.S., Colorado State U, Long Beach City Col. Inducted as honorary Master Chief Petty Officer in U.S. Navy 1993. Worked as professional football player, social worker (heading the Vera Institute of Justice in NY), and advertising copywriter before writing television comedy material (for the Leslie Uggams Show) and performing as stand-up comedian in Greenwich Village. Has also dir. theatre with Bahamian Rep. Co. Starred in L.A. in Norman Is That You? and Master Harold...And the Boys, Split Second, The Emperor Jones, Broadway: Tough to Get Help. NYSF: Twelfth Night. Off-Bdwy: The Past is the Past. Regional: Fences, Halley's Comet (also writer). Artistic dir.: John Harms Theatre, Englewood, NJ.
PICTURES: Vanishing Point (debut, 1971), The World's Greatest Athlete, Let's Do It Again, Touched By Love, The Beastmaster, Dance of the Dwarfs, American Flyers, Coming to America, Lock Up, Die Hard 2, Ricochet, Two Evil Eyes

(The Black Cat), Mac, Night Trap (Mardi Gras for the Devil). TELEVISION: *Series*: Mary Tyler Moore, The Funny Side, Maude, Good Times, Hunter, South by Southwest. *Mini-Series*: Roots. *Movies*: The President's Plane is Missing, Future Cop, Cops and Robin, Willa, Alcatraz—The Whole Shocking Story, Bonanza-the Next Generation. *Pilots*: Clippers, 704 Hauser Street; many guest appearances incl. Bill Cosby Show, Love American Style, Sanford and Son, The Love Boat, Cosby Show. *Special*: Without a Pass.

AMSTERDAM, MOREY: Producer, Writer, Composer, Musician, Actor. b. Chicago, IL, Dec. 14, 1914. e. U. of California, Berkeley. Boy soprano. Radio KPO. Night club performer, Chicago, 1929; comedian, singer, musician. Rube Wolf Orchestra; comedian, Optimistic Doughnuts Program, 1930; writer, performer with, Al Pearce Gang, 1932; writer, MGM, 1937; co-writer, m.p. Columbia, Universal; writer, performer, USO Shows, 1942–43; Owner, the Playgoers-club; v.p. International Pictures.
TELEVISION: *Series*: Stop Me If You've Heard This One, Morey Amsterdam Show, Broadway Open House, Battle of the Ages, Who Said That?, Keep Talking, Dick Van Dyke Show. Can You Top This? (also exec. prod.). *Movies*: Sooner or Later, Side By Side.
PICTURES: It Came From Outer Space, Machine Gun Kelly, Murder Inc., Beach Party, Muscle Beach Party, Don't Worry . . . We'll Think of a Title, The Horse in the Gray Flannel Suit, Won Ton Ton the Dog Who Saved Hollywood.
SONGS: Rum and Còca Cola, Why Oh Why Did I Ever Leave Wyoming, Yak A Puk, etc.

ANDERSON, GERRY: Hon. F.B.K.S., Producer, Director, Writer. b. London, England, 1929. Ent. ind. 1946. Chmn./man. dir. Gerry Anderson Productions, Ltd. Over 320 pictures produced for TV worldwide. 1981 Co-founded Anderson Burr Pictures. 1982 prod. Terrahawks in association with London Weekend Television; second series, Terrahawks, 1984; Space Police pilot for series in assoc. with TVS, 1985–6; Dick Spanner stop motion series for Channel Four 1987. Entered commercials as a dir.: numerous commercials incl. Royal Bank of Scotland, Children's World, Domestos, Shout, Scotch Tape, etc. 1992 Anglo Russian Cartoon Series Astro Force and lecture tour An Evening with Garry Anderson.
TELEVISION: *Series*: Supercar, Fireball OL5, Stingray, Thunderbirds, Captain Scarlet, Joe 90, UFO, Space 1999, Terrahawks, Dick Spanner.
PICTURES: Thunderbirds Are Go, Thunderbird 6, Journey to the Far Side of the Sun.

ANDERSON, HARRY: Actor. b. Newport, RI, Oct. 14, 1952. m. actress-magician Leslie Pollack. Performed magic show prior to plays at Oregon Shakespeare Festival. Also opening act for Kenny Rogers, Debbie Reynolds and Roger Miller in Las Vegas. Owner of magic shop in Ashland OR. Received Stage Magician of Year Award, National Acad. of Magician Arts and Sciences.
PICTURE: The Escape Artist.
TELEVISION: *Series*: Night Court (Emmy nom.), Our Time, Dave's World. *Movies*: Spies, Lies and Naked Thighs; The Absent-minded Professor, Stephen King's It. *Guest*: Cheers, The Tonight Show, David Letterman, Saturday Night Live, Wil Shriner. *Specials*: Comic Relief, Harry Anderson's Sideshow (also exec. prod., writer), Comic Relief II, The Best of Gleason, Magic with the Stars, Nell Carter: Never Too Old to Dream, Hello Sucker.

ANDERSON, J. WAYNE: Executive. b. Clifton Forge, VA, Feb. 19, 1947. e. USA Signal School (1965–67); USN Service Schools (1967). USMC, 1965–69; opened and operated 1st military 35mm m.p. theatre, DaNang, Vietnam, 1967–69; R/C Theatres , dist. mgr., 1971–75; v.p., 1976–83; pres./COO, 1983–present; bd. of dirs. Maryland Permanent Bank & Trust co., 1988–present, chairman, 1992–present.
MEMBER: NATO, bd. of dirs., 1987–present, technical advancement committee, 1981–present; Inter-Society for the Enhancement of Theatrical Presenation, 1986–present; Huntsman bd. of dirs., 1979–83; pres., 1982–83; NRA, 1970–life; Will Rogers Inst., 1988–present; Presidential Task Force, 1990–life.

ANDERSON, KEVIN: Actor. b. Illinois, Jan. 13, 1960. e. Goodman School. Member of Chicago's Steppenwolf Theatre where he starred in Orphans. Moved with the play when it transferred to New York (1985) and later starred in the London production, as well as the film version.
THEATER: *NY*: Orphans (Theatre World Award), Moonchildren, Brilliant Tracers, Orpheus Descending. *London*: Sunset Boulevard.
PICTURES: Risky Business, Pink Nights, A Walk on the Moon, Orphans, Miles from Home, In Country, Sleeping With the Enemy, Liebestraum, Hoffa, The Night We Never Met, Rising Sun.
TELEVISION: *Movie*: Orpheus Descending. *Special*: Hale the Hero.

ANDERSON, LINDSAY: Director (cinema & theatre), Writer. b. Bangalore, India, April 17, 1923; e. Cheltenham Coll., Wadham Coll., Oxford (classical scholar). Ent. ind. 1948 as writer-director in charge industrial film prod., also contributing editor and co-founder independent film quarterly Sequence (1947–52). Wrote Making a Film 1951; About John Ford (1981). Principal doc. films: Meet the Pioneers, Three Installations, Wakefield Express, O Dreamland, Thursday's Children (with Guy Brenton; co-s.p., co-dir.; Acad. Award, best short subj. 1954), Every Day Except Christmas (Venice Grand Prix, 1957), March to Aldermaston, The Singing Lesson (Documentary Studio, Warsaw). Founder mem. Free Cinema group. National Film Theatre 1956–9.Artistic director, Royal Court theatre 1969–70. Associate, 1970–76.
TELEVISION: Five episodes Robin Hood series, commercials, 1959–75. 1978 Dir. The Old Crowd. 1986 Free Cinema, Buston Keaton: A Hard Act to Follow (narrator); 1986–87: music videos for Carmel; 1988: Movie Masterclass My Darling Clementine, Glory! Glory! (HBO); John Ford (Omnibus BBC, 1992).
PLAYS: The Long and the Short and the Tall, Billy Liar, The Fire Raisers, Diary of a Madman, Sergeant Musgrave's Dance, The Cherry Orchard, Inadmissible Evidence (at Contemporary Theatre, Warsaw), In Celebration, The Contractor, Home, The Changing Room, The Farm, Life Class, What the Butler Saw, The Sea Gull, The Bed Before Yesterday, The Kingfisher, Alice's Boys, Early Days, Hamlet, The Cherry Orchard, Playboy of the Western World, In Celebration (N.Y.), Hamlet (Washington, DC), Holiday, The March on Russia, Jubilee (British Tour, 1990), Stages.
PICTURES: This Sporting Life, The White Bus, If..., O Lucky Man!, In Celebration, Chariots of Fire (actor only), Britannia Hospital, If You Were There, The Whales of August, Blame It On the Bellboy (voice only), Is That All There Is?.

ANDERSON, LONI: Actress. b. St. Paul, MN, Aug. 5. 1946. e. U. of Minnesota. Taught school before acting.
TELEVISION: *Series*: WKRP in Cincinnati, Partners in Crime, Easy Street. *Specials*: Christmas in Opryland, Shaun Cassidy Special, Bob Hope specials, etc. *Movies*: The Magnificent Magnet of Mesa, Three on a Date, The Jayne Mansfield Story, Sizzle, Country Gold, My Mother's Secret Life, A Letter to Three Wives, Stranded, Necessity, A Whisper Kills, Too Good to Be True, Sorry Wrong Number, Coins in the Fountain, White Hot: The Mysterious Murder of Thelma Todd, The Price She Paid.
PICTURES: Stroker Ace, The Lonely Guy (cameo), All Dogs Go to Heaven (voice), Munchie.

ANDERSON, MELISSA SUE: Actress. b. Berkeley, CA, Sept. 26, 1962. Took up acting at suggestion of a dancing teacher. Did series of commercials; guest role in episode of Brady Bunch; episode of Shaft. Gained fame as Mary Ingalls on Little House on the Prairie series (Emmy nom.).
PICTURES: Happy Birthday to Me, Chattanooga Choo Choo, Dead Men Don't Die.
TELEVISION: *Series*: Little House on the Prairie. *Movies*: Little House on the Prairie (pilot), The Loneliest Runner, James at 15 (pilot), Survival of Dana, Midnight Offerings, Advice to the Lovelorn, An Innocent Love, First Affair, Dark Mansions. *Special*: Which Mother is Mine? (Emmy, 1980).

ANDERSON, MICHAEL: Director. b. London, England, Jan. 30, 1920. e. France, Germany, Spain. Ent. m.p. industry as actor, 1936.
PICTURES: Private Angelo (co-dir., 1949), Waterfront, Hell Is Sold Out, Night Was Our Friend, Will Any Gentleman?, The Dam Busters, 1984, Around the World in 80 Days, Yangtse Incident (Battle Hell), Chase a Crooked Shadow, Shake Hands with the Devil, The Wreck of the Mary Deare, All the Fine Young Cannibals, The Naked Edge, Flight From Ashiya, Monsieur Cognac, Operation Crossbow, The Quiller Memorandum, Shoes of the Fisherman, Pope Joan, Dr. Savage, Conduct Unbecoming, Logan's Run, Orca, Dominique, Muder By Phone, Second Time Lucky, Separate Vacations, Sword of Gideon, Jeweller's Shop, Millenium.
TELEVISION: The Martian Chronicles, Young Catherine, Regina Vs. Nelles, The Sea Wolf.

ANDERSON, MICHAEL, JR.: Actor. b. London, England, Aug. 6, 1943. Son of dir. Michael Anderson. Ent. films as child actor, 1954.
TELEVISION: *Series*: The Monroes. *Mini-Series*: Washington Behind Closed Doors, The Martian Chronicles. *Movies*: The House That Would Not Die, In Search of America, The Family Rico, The Daughters of Joshua Cabe, Coffee Tea or Me? Shootout in a One-Dog Town, Kiss Me Kill Me, The Million Dollar Face, Making of a Male Model, Love Leads the Way.
PICTURES: The Moonraker, Tiger Bay, The Sundowners, In Search of the Castaways, Play It Cool, Reach For Glory, Greatest Story Ever Told, Dear Heart, Major Dundee, The Glory Guys, The Sons of Katie Elder, The Last Movie, Logan's Run.

9

ANDERSON, RICHARD: Actor. b. Long Branch, NJ, Aug. 8, 1926. U.S. Army, W.W.II. Began acting career in summer theatre in Santa Barbara and Laguna Playhouse where spotted by MGM executives who signed him to six-yr. contract. Appeared in 26 films for MGM before leaving studio. Spokesperson for Kiplinger Washington Letter since 1985.
PICTURES: 12 O'Clock High, The People Against O'Hara, Scaramouche, The Story of Three Loves, Escape from Fort Bravo, Forbidden Planet, Paths of Glory, The Long Hot Summer, Compulsion, Seconds, Tora! Tora! Tora!, Macho Callahan, Doctors' Wives, Play It As It Lays, The Honkers, The Player.
TELEVISION: *Series*: Mama Rosa, Bus Stop, The Lieutenant, Perry Mason, Dan August, The Six Million Dollar Man, The Bionic Woman (Emmy nom.), Dynasty, Cover-Up. *Guest*: Ironside, The Big Valley, Mannix, My Friend Tony, The Mod Squad, Land of the Giants, The FBI, Gunsmoke. *Movies*: Along Came a Spider, Kane & Abel, The Return of the Six Million Dollar Man and the Bionic Woman, Pearl, Perry Mason Returns, Hoover vs. the Kennedys, Eminment Domain, Danger High, Stranger on My Land. The Bionic Showdown: The Six Million Dollar Man & The Bionic Woman (also co-prod.), Return of the Six Million Dollar Man and the Bionic Woman III.

ANDERSON, RICHARD DEAN: Actor. b. Minneapolis, MN, Jan. 23, 1950. Planned to become professional hockey player. Became a street mime and jester. Performed with his own rock band, Ricky Dean and Dante.
PICTURES: Young Doctors in Love, Odd Jobs.
TELEVISION: *Series*: General Hospital (1976–81), Seven Brides for Seven Brothers, Emerald Point N.A.S., MacGyver. *Movies*: Ordinary Heroes, In the Eyes of a Stranger, Through the Eyes of a Killer.

ANDERSON, SYLVIA: Producer, Writer (Pinewood Studios). b. London, England. e. London U. Entered m.p. ind. 1960. First pub. novel, Love and Hisses. UK rep for Home Box Office of America.
TELEVISION: series created include: Thunderbirds, U.F.O.; Space 1999.

ANDERSON, WILLIAM H.: Producer; Member of Bd. of Dir. Walt Disney Productions. b. Utah, October 12, 1911. e. Compton Coll. Firestone Rubber Co.; Universal Credit Co.; Walt Disney Prods. 42 years.
PICTURES: Old Yeller, Swiss Family Robinson, Happiest Millionaire, The Computer Wore Tennis Shoes, Barefoot Executive, $1,000,000 Duck, Superdad, Strongest Man in the World, Apple Dumpling Gang, Treasure of Matecumbe, Shaggy D.A.
TELEVISION: Zorro Series 1958–59; 1959–60, Wonderful World of Disney: Zorro, Texas John Slaughter, Daniel Boone, The Swamp Fox, Pop Warner Football (1960–61), Johnny Shiloh, Mooncussers, 1962–63; Bristle Face, The Scarecrow of Romney Marsh (1963–64); The Legend of Young Dick Turpin (1965–66); Willie and the Yank (1966–67); A Boy Called Nuthin', The Young Loner (1967–68); The Wacky Zoo of Morgan City (1970–71); The Mystery of Dracula's Castle (1972–73); The Bull from the Sky, (co-prod.; 1975–76); Great Sleeping Bear Sled Dog Race, (co-prod. 1976–77).

ANDERSSON, BIBI: Actress. b. Stockholm, Sweden, Nov. 11, 1935. e. Royal Dramatic Theatre School.
PICTURES: (for director Ingmar Bergman) Smiles of a Summer Night (1955), The Seventh Seal, Wild Strawberries, Brink of Life, The Magician, The Devil's Eye, Not to Mention All These Women, Persona; other films: My Sister My Love, Le Vio A Passion, Black Palm Trees, Story of a Woman, Duel at Diablo, The Kremlin Letter, The Passion of Anna, I Never Promised You a Rose Garden, Quintet, The Concorde: Airport '79, Enemy of the People, Exposed, Babette's Feast, Fordring Sagare.
TELEVISION: Wallenberg—A Hero's Story.

ANDES, KEITH: Actor. b. Ocean City, NJ, July 12, 1920. e. Temple U., Oxford. U. Radio work; on Broadway in Winged Victory, Kiss Me Kate, Maggie, Wildcat.
PICTURES: Farmer's Daughter, Clash By Night, Blackbeard the Pirate, Split Second, Key Man, Life at Stake, Second Greatest Sex, Away All Boats, Pillars of the Sky, Back from Eternity, The Girl Most·Likely, Damn Citizen, Model for Murder, Surrender - Hell!, Hells Bloody Devils, And Justice for All.
TELEVISION: *Series*: This Man Dawson, Glynis, Search.

ANDRESS, URSULA: Actress. b. Berne, Switzerland, Mar. 19, 1936.
PICTURES: Dr. No, Four For Texas, Fun in Acapulco, She, Tenth Victim, What's New Pussycat?, Nightmare in the Sun, Up to His Ears, Once Before I Die, The Blue Max, Casino Royale, Anyone Can Play, The Southern Star, Perfect Friday, Red Sun, Scaramouche, The Sensuous Nurse, Slave of the Cannibal God, Tigers in Lipstick, The Fifth Musketeer, Clash of the Titans, Class Meeting.

TELEVISION: *Mini-Series*: Peter the Great. *Series*: Falcon Crest. *Movies*: Man Against the Mob.

ANDREWS, ANTHONY: Actor. b. London, England, 1948.
PICTURES: Operation Daybreak, Under the Volcano, The Holcroft Covenant, The Second Victory, The Lighthorsemen, Hanna's War, Lost in Siberia.
TELEVISION: A Beast With Two Backs, Romeo and Juliet, A War of Children, QB VII, Upstairs Downstairs, Danger UXB, Brideshead Revisitéd, Ivanhoe, The Scarlet Pimpernel, Sparkling Cyanide, A.D., Bluegrass, Suspicion, The Woman He Loved, Columbo Goes to the Guillotine, Daniel Steel's Jewels.

ANDREWS, JULIE: Actress, Singer. r.n. Julia Wells. b. Walton-on-Thames. England. Oct 1, 1935. m. dir. Blake Edwards. debut, Eng. Starlight Roof Revue London Hippodrome, 1948.
PLAYS: NY: The Boy Friend, My Fair Lady, Camelot, Putting It Together.
PICTURES: Mary Poppins (debut, 1964; Academy Award), The Americanization of Emily, The Sound of Music (Acad. Award nom.), Hawaii, Torn Curtain, Thoroughly Modern Millie, Star!, Darling Lili, The Tamarind Seed, "10," S.O.B, Victor/Victoria (Acad. Award nom.), The Man Who Loved Women, That's Life, Duet for One, A Fine Romance.
TELEVISION: *Specials*: High Tor, Julie and Carol at Carnegie Hall, The Julie Andrews Show, An Evening with Julie Andrews and Harry Belafonte, The World of Walt Disney, Julie and Carol at Lincoln Center, Julie on Sesame Street, Julie Andrews' Christmas Special, Julie and Dick in Covent Garden, Julie Andrews and Jackie Gleason Together, Julie Andrews—My Favorite Things, Julie Andrews—The Sound of Christmas, Julie and Carol: Together Again. *Series*: The Julie Andrews Hour (1972–3; Emmy Award for Best Variety Series), Julie. *Movie*: Our Sons.
AUTHOR: Mandy, Last of the Really Great Whangdoodles (1973).

ANGERS, AVRIL: Actress, Comedienne, Singer. b. Liverpool, England, April 18. Stage debut at age of 14; screen debut in 1947 in Lucky Mascot.
PICTURES: Miss Pilgrim's Progress, Don't Blame the Stork, Women Without Men, Green Man, Devils of Darkness, Be My Guest, Three Bites of the Apple, The Family Way, Two a Penny, The Best House in London, Staircase, There's a Girl in My Soup, Forbush and the Penguins, Gollocks, Confessions of a Driving Instructor, Dangerous Davies.
TELEVISION: How Do You View, Friends and Neighbors, Dear Dotty, Holiday Town, Charlie Fainsbarn Show, Arthur Askey Show, All Aboard, The Gold Hunter, Bob Monkhouse Show, Before The Fringe, Hudd, Coronation Street, Dick Emery Show, Dad's Army, Bright Boffins, The More We are Together, The Millionairess, Liver Birds, Looks Familiar, No Appointment Necessary, The Songwriters, All Creatures Great and Small, Coronation Concert, Minder, Smuggler, Just Liz, Give Up a Clue, Are You Being Served, Trelawney of the Wells, Cat's Eye, C.A.B., Rude Health.
PLAYS: The Mating Game, Cockie, Murder at the Vicarage, Little Me, Norman, Is That You?, Blithe Spirit, Oklahoma!, Gigi, The Killing of Sister George, Cards on the Table, When We Are Married, Cinderella, Easy Virtue, Post Mortem, Crazy for You.

ANHALT, EDWARD: Writer. b. New York, NY. Mar. 28, 1914. e. Columbia U.
PICTURES: Panic in the Streets (Acad. Award, orig. story), Red Mountain, Member of the Wedding (also prod.), My Six Convicts, Eight Iron Men, Not as a Stranger, The Pride and the Passion, The Young Lions, In Love and War, The Restless Years, The Sins of Rachel Cade, The Young Savages, Girls Girls Girls, A Girl Named Tamiko, Wives and Lovers, Becket (Acad. Award, adapt. s.p.), The Satan Bug, Boeing-Boeing, Hour of the Gun, In Enemy Country, The Boston Strangler, Madwoman of Chaillot, Jeremiah Johnson, Man in the Glass Booth, Luther, Escape to Athena, Green Ice, Holcroft Covenant.
TELEVISION: Peter the Great, QB VII, Contract on Cherry Street, Day That Christ Died, The Neon Empire, The Take, Alexander the Great, The Life and Times of Santa Claus, The Apostles.

ANNAKIN, KENNETH: Director, Writer. b. Yorkshire, Eng., Aug. 10, 1915. Worked with Experimental Theatre and as documentary filmmaker.
PICTURES: Holiday Camp (debut, 1948), Broken Journey, Here Come the Huggetts, Miranda, Quartet (co-dir.), Vote for Huggett, Double Confession, Trio (co-dir.), The Huggetts Abroad, Hotel Sahara, Outpost in Malaya (Planter's Wife), Story of Robin Hood, The Sword and the Rose, The Seekers (Land of Fury), You Know What Sailors Are, Value for Money, Three Men in a Boat, Loser Takes All, Across The Bridge, Third Man on the Mountain, Swiss Family Robinson, Very Important Person, The Hellions, Crooks Anonymous, The Longest Day (co-dir.), The Fast Lady, The Informers, Those Magnificent Men in Their Flying Machines (also co-s.p.), Battle of the Bulge, The Long Duel (also prod.), The

Biggest Bundle of Them All, Monte Carlo or Bust (Those Daring Young Men in Their Jaunty Jalopies; also s.p., prod.), Call of the Wild, Paper Tiger, The Fifth Musketeer, Cheaper to Keep Her, The Pirate Movie, The New Adventures of Pippi Longstocking (also s.p., co-prod.), Genghis Khan.

ANNAUD, JEAN-JACQUES: Writer, Director. b. Draveil, France, Oct. 1, 1943. Began career as film director in French army, making educational pictures. Also directed 500 commercials. Received 1989 cinema prize from French Acad. for career's work.
PICTURES: Black and White in Color (Acad. Award, Best Foreign Film, 1977); Coup de Tete (dir. only); Quest for Fire (dir. only; Cesar Award, best film & dir., 1982); The Name of the Rose (dir. only; Cesar Award, best foreign film, 1987), The Bear (dir., co-s.p.: Cesar Award, best dir., 1989), The Lover. (dir. only).

ANN-MARGRET: Actress, singer. r.n. Ann-Margret Olsson. b. Valsjobyn, Sweden, April 28, 1941. m. Roger Smith, actor, dir., prod. e. grad., New Trier H.S., Winnetka, IL, attended Northwestern U. Radio shows, toured with band; worked with George Burns, Sahara, Las Vegas. TV debut, Jack Benny Show, April, 1961.
PICTURES: Pocketful of Miracles (debut, 1961), State Fair, Bye Bye Birdie, Viva Las Vegas, Kitten With a Whip, The Pleasure Seekers, Bus Riley's Back in Town, Once A Thief, The Cincinnati Kid, Made in Paris, Stagecoach, The Swinger, Murderer's Row, The Prophet, The Tiger and the Pussycat, Rebus, Criminal Affair, RPM, C. C. & Company, Carnal Knowledge, The Outside Man, The Train Robbers, Tommy, The Last Remake of Beau Geste, The Twist, Joseph Andrews, The Cheap Detective, Magic, The Villain, Middle Age Crazy, I Ought To Be in Pictures, Lookin' to Get Out, The Return of the Soldier, Twice in a Lifetime, 52 Pick-up, A Tiger's Tail, A New Life, Newsies, Grumpy Old Men.
TELEVISION: Specials: Ann-Margret Show, From Hollywood With Love, Dames at Sea, Swing Out Sweet Land, When You're Smiling, Ann-Margret Smith, Ann-Margret Olsson, Memories of Elvis, Rhinestone Cowgirl, Hollywood Movie Girls. Movies: Who Will Love My Children?, A Streetcar Named Desire, The Two Mrs. Grenvilles, Our Sons. Mini-Series: Queen.

ANSARA, MICHAEL: Actor. b. Lowell, MA, April 15, 1922. e. Pasadena Playhouse. Served in U.S. Army; then summer stock, little theatre, road shows.
PICTURES: Soldiers Three, Only the Valiant, The Robe, Julius Caesar, Sign of the Pagan, Bengal Brigade, New Orleans Uncensored, Diane, Lone Ranger, Sol Madrid, Daring Game, Dear Dead Delilah, The Bears and I, Mohammad Messenger of God, The Manitou, Gas, Access Code, Knights of the City. Lethal (KGB: The Secret War).
TELEVISION: Series: Broken Arrow, Law of the Plainsman, Buck Rogers in the 25th Century. Mini-Series: Centennial. Guest: The Westerner, Lost in Space, Simon and Simon, Gavilan, George Burns Comedy Week, Hunter, Hardcastle and McCormick. Movies: How I Spent My Summer Vacation, Powderkeg, A Call to Danger, Ordeal, Shootout in a One-Dog Town, Barbary Coast, The Fantastic World of D.C. Collins.

ANSPACH, SUSAN: Actress. b. New York, NY, Nov. 23, 1945. e. Catholic U., Washington, DC. After school returned to N.Y. and in 3 years had performed in 11 Bdwy and off-Bdwy prods. Moved to Los Angeles and entered films.
PICTURES: The Landlord, Five Easy Pieces, Play It Again Sam, Blume in Love, The Big Fix, Running, The Devil and Max Devlin, Gas, Montenegro, Misunderstood, Blue Monkey, Into the Fire, Blood Red, Back to Back, Heaven and Earth.
TELEVISION: Movies: I Want to Keep My Baby, The Secret Life of John Chapman, Rosetti & Ryan, Mad Bull, The Last Giraffe, Portrait of an Escort, The First Time, Deadly Encounter. Mini-Series: Space. Series: The Yellow Rose, The Slap Maxwell Story.

ANSPAUGH, DAVID: Director. b. Decatur, IN, Sept. 24, 1946. e. Indiana U., 1965–70; U. of Southern CA, 1974–76. School teacher, Aspen, CO 1970–74. Awards for Hill Street Blues: Emmys for Outstanding Drama Series: 1982–83; DGA 1982, Golden Globes, 1981–82.
PICTURES: Hoosiers, Fresh Horses, Rudy.
TELEVISION: Series: Hill St. Blues (assoc. prod. 1980–81; prod.-dir. 1981–82; prod.-dir. 1983–84, dir. 1985); St. Elsewhere (dir.), Miami Vice (dir.).Movies: Deadly Care, In the Company of Darkness.

ANTHONY, TONY: Actor, Producer, Writer. b. Clarksburg, WV, Oct. 16, 1939. e. Carnegie Mellon.
PICTURES: Force of Impulse, Pity Me Not, The Wounds of Hunger, A Stranger in Town, The Stranger Returns, A Stranger in Japan, Come Together, Blindman, Pete Pearl and the Pole, Let's Talk About Men, Get Mean, Treasure of the Four Crowns, Comin' at Ya, For Better or For Worse.

ANTON, SUSAN: Actress. b. Oak Glen, CA, Oct. 12, 1950. Concert & night club singer. Country album & single Killin'

Time went top 10 on Country charts, received Gold Record in Japan. On Bdwy in Hurlyburly (debut, 1985), The Will Rogers Follies. Off-Bdwy in X-mas a Go-Go. 1992, hon. chmn. of Amer. Cancer Soc., Calif. Special Olympics, & hon. capt. U.S. Woman's Olympic Volleyball Team..
PICTURES: Goldengirl, Spring Fever, Cannonball Run II, Options (cameo), Making Mr. Right, Lena's Holiday.
TELEVISION: Series: Stop Susan Williams (Cliff Hangers), Presenting Susan Anton. Movie: The Great American Beauty Contest. Guest: Quantum Leap, Blossom, Murder She Wrote, Night Court, The Famous Teddy Z, Circus of the Stars.

ANTONIO, LOU: Actor, Writer, Producer, Director. b. Oklahoma City, OK, Jan. 23. e. U. of OK.
THEATER: Actor: The Buffalo Skinner (Theatre World Award), The Girls of Summer, The Good Soup, The Garden of Sweets, Andorra, The Lady of the Camellias, The Ballad of the Sad Cafe, Ready When You Are, C.B. Dir.: Private Lives (w Taylor/Burton).
PICTURES: Actor: The Strange One, Splendor in the Grass, America America, Hawaii, Cool Hand Luke, The Phynx. Also: Mission Batangas (s.p.); Micki and Maude (exec. prod.).
TELEVISION: Actor: Series: Snoop Sisters; Dog and Cat; Making It. Piece of Blue Sky, The Power and the Glory, Danny Thomas Hour, Partners in Crime, Sole Survivor, Where the Ladies Go, Star Trek. Director: Mini-Series: Rich Man, Poor Man (co-dir.). Movies: Lanigan's Rabbi, Someone I Touched, Something for Joey, The Girl in the Empty Grave, The Critical List, Silent Victory—The Kitty O'Neil Story, A Real American Hero, Breaking Up Is Hard to Do, The Contender, We're Fighting Back, The Star Maker, Something So Right, A Good Sport, Threesome, Rearview Mirror, Face to Face, The Outside Woman (also prod.), Dark Holiday (also exec. prod.), Between Friends, Mayflower Madam, One Terrific Guy, Pals, 13 at Dinner, This Gun for Hire, Lies Before Kisses, The Last Prostitute, The Rape of Dr. Willis, A Taste for Killing, Nightmare in the Daylight.

ANTONIONI, MICHELANGELO: Director, Writer. b. Ferrara, Italy, Sept. 29, 1913. e. Bologna U. Film critic on local paper, then script writer and asst. director. First films as a director were short documentaries including: Gente del Po (1947), N.U., Roma-Montevideo, Oltre l'oblio, L'Amorosa menzogna, Superstizione, Bomarzo, . . . Chung Kuo.
PICTURES: Dir.-Writer: Story of a Love Affair (feature debut as dir., 1950), The Vanquished, Love in the City (segment: When Love Fails), The Lady Without Camelias, Le Amiche (The Girl Friends), Il Grido (The Outcry), L'Avventura, The Night, The Eclipse, The Red Desert, Three Faces of a Woman (dir. only), Blow-Up (Acad. Award nom. for best dir.), Zabriskie Point, The Passenger, The Oberwald Mystery, Identification of a Woman, The Crew.

ANTONOWSKY, MARVIN: Executive. b. New York, NY, Jan. 31, 1929. e. City Coll. of New York, B.A., M.B.A. Joined Kenyon and Eckhart in 1957 for which was media research dir.; named marketing v.p. With Norman, Craig, & Kummel as v.p., mktg. services. 1965, became v.p. in chg. of media research and spot buying at J. Walter Thompson. In 1969 joined ABC-TV as v.p. in chg. research. Left to become v.p. in chg. of programming at NBC-TV. 1976, sr. v.p., Universal-TV. 1979, joined Columbia Pictures as pres., mktg. & research. Rejoined MCA/Universal Pictures as pres, mktg., Nov. 1983. Formed Marvin Antonowsky & Assoc. marketing consultancy firm, 1989. Rejoined Columbia Pictures in 1990 as exec. v.p. and asst. to chmn.

APFEL, EDWIN R.: Executive. b. New York, NY, Jan. 2, 1934. e. Franklin and Marshall Coll., B.A., 1955. Mktg. exec.: Metro-Goldwyn-Mayer, Verve Records, Embassy Pictures. Free-lance copywriter. 1990, writer, Edward R. Murrow: This Reporter, Amer. Masters (PBS). 1992, council member, WGA East.

APTED, MICHAEL: Director. b. Aylesbury, Eng., Feb. 10, 1941. e. Cambridge. Broke into show business at Granada TV in England in early 1960s as trainee, researcher, and finally director. By 1965 was producer-director for local programs and current affairs; then staff drama dir. for TV series, plays and serials. In late 1960s left Granada to freelance.
PICTURES: Triple Echo, Stardust, The Squeeze, Agatha, Coal Miner's Daughter, Continental Divide, Gorky Park, Firstborn, Kipperbang, Bring on the Night, 28 Up (35 Up), Critical Condition, Gorillas in the Mist, Class Action, Thunderheart, Incident at Oglala, Bram Stoker's Dracula (co-exec. prod. only).
TELEVISION: Poor Girl, High Kampf, Highway Robbery, Kisses at 50, The Collection (Intl. Emmy Award 28-Up, (award winning documentary), Ptang Yang, The Long Way Home (doc.), My Life and Times, Criminal Justice (co-exec. prod.), Murder Without Motive (co-exec. prod.), Intruders (co-exec. prod.).

ARCAND, DENYS: Director. b. Deschambault, Quebec, Canada, June 25, 1941. e. U. of Montreal, 1963. While still history

student, co-prod. Seul ou avec D'Autres (1962). Joined National Film Board of Canada, where began making documentary shorts (Champlain, Les Montrealistes and La Route de l'ouest) forming a trilogy dealing with colonial Quebec. In 1970 socio-political doc. about Quebec textile workers, On Est au Coton, generated controversy resulting in the NFB banning film until 1976.
PICTURES: On Est au Coton (doc.), Un Maudite Galette (1st fiction feature, 1971). Dir.-Writer: Quebec: Duplessisz et Apres... (doc.), Rejeanne Padovani, Gina, Le Crime d'Ovide Plouffe, The Decline of the American Empire, Night Zoo (actor only), Jesus of Montreal (Cannes Film Fest. jury prize, 1989), Leolo (actor only), Unidentified Human Remains and the True Nature of Love.
TELEVISION: Duplessis (s.p., 1977 series), Empire Inc. (series, dir.).

ARCHER, ANNE: Actress. b. Los Angeles, CA. Daughter of actress Marjorie Lord and actor John Archer. Married Terry Jastrow, TV network sports producer-director and pres. Jack Nicklaus Prods.
THEATER: A Coupla White Chicks Sitting Around Talking (off-Bdwy, 1981), Les Liaisons Dangereuses (Williamstown Fest., 1988).
PICTURES: The Honkers (debut, 1972), Cancel My Reservation, The All-American Boy, Trackdown, Lifeguard, Paradise Alley, Good Guys Wear Black, Hero at Large, Raise the Titanic, Green Ice, Waltz Across Texas, The Naked Face, Too Scared to Scream, The Check Is in the Mail, Fatal Attraction, Love at Large, Narrow Margin, Eminent Domain, Patriot Games, Body of Evidence, Family Prayers, Short Cuts.
TELEVISION: Series: Bob and Carol and Ted and Alice, The Family Tree, Falcon Crest. Movies: The Blue Knight, The Mark of Zorro, The Log of the Black Pearl, A Matter of Wife...and Death, The Dark Side of Innocence, Harold Robbins' The Pirate, The Sky's No Limit, A Different Affair, A Leap of Faith, The Last of His Tribe, Nails, Jane's House. Mini-Series: Seventh Avenue.

ARCHER, JOHN: Actor. r.n. Ralph Bowman, b. Osceola, NB, May 8, 1915. e. U. of Southern California. Won Jesse L. Lasky Gateway to Hollywood talent quest; m.p. debut in Flaming Frontiers 1938; on N.Y. stage also.
PICTURES: White Heat, After Nightfall, Destination Moon, Big Trees, Yank in Indo-China, Sound Off, Rodeo, Sea Tiger, The Stars Are Singing, Dragon's Gold, No Man's Woman, Emergency Hospital, Apache Rifles.

ARCHERD, ARMY: Columnist, TV commentator. r.n. Armand Archerd, b. New York, NY, Jan. 13, 1922. e. UCLA, grad. '41, U.S. Naval Academy Post Graduate Sch., 1943. Started as usher at Criterion Theatre, N.Y., while in high school. After grad. UCLA, worked at Paramount studios before entering Navy, Lt., joined AP Hollywood bureau 1945, Herald-Express, Daily Variety as columnist, 1953. M.C. Hollywood premieres, Emmys and Academy Awards. President, founder Hollywood Press Club, awards from Masquers, L.A. Press Club, Hollywood Foreign Press Club, and Newsman of the Year award from Publicists Guild, 1970; Movie Game. TV series: People's Choice, co-host. 1987 received Hollywood Women's Press Club Man of the Year Award.

ARDANT, FANNY: Actress. b. Monte Carlo, 1949. Majored in political science in college. Served a 5-year apprenticeship in the French theater acting in Polyeucte, Esther, The Mayor of Santiago, Electra and Tete d'Or. After TV debut in Les Dames de la Cote, went on to star in films by Truffaut who became her mentor.
PICTURES: Les Chiens, Les uns et les Autres, The Woman Next Door, Life is a Novel, Confidentially Yours, Benevenuta, Desire, Swann in Love, Love Unto Death, Les Enrages, L'Ete Prochain, Family Business, Melo, The Family, Three Sisters, Australia, Pleure pas My Love, Afraid of the Dark, Amok.

ARDOLINO, EMILE: Producer, Director. b. New York, NY e. Queens Coll. Actor in touring co. of The Fantasticks. Filmed sequences for Oh, Calcutta. Began career as dir. and prod. of Dance in America and Live From Lincoln Center series for Public TV 1975–81 before feature film debut as dir. Dirty Dancing (1988).
PICTURES: Director: He Makes Me Feel Like Dancin' (also prod., Acad. and Emmy Award-winning doc., Peabody, Christopher, Cine Golden Eagle Awards, 1983), Dirty Dancing, Chances Are, Three Men and a Little Lady, Sister Act, The Nutcracker.
TELEVISION: Dance in America (prod., dir. 28 progs. include. Nuryev and the Joffrey Ballet in Tribute to Nijinsky, Choreography By Balanchine IV (1979 Emmy), The Spellbound Child (DGA Award), Live From Lincoln Center (incl. New York City Ballet in Tribute to George Balanchine, Stravinsky and Balanchine: Genius Has a Birthday; The Saint of Bleeker Street), Baryshnikov at the White House, Mass by Leonard Bernstein, When Hell Freezes Over I'll Skate, Rumplestiltskin (Fairie Tale Theatre), Alice at the Palace, The

Dance and The Railroad, A Midsummer Night's Dream, Good Morning Mr. Orwell, The Rise and Rise of Daniel Rocket (dir.).

ARGENTO, DARIO: Director, Writer. b. Rome, Italy, 1943. Son of prod. Salvatore Argento.
PICTURES: Oggi a Me . . . Domani a Te (s.p.), The Five Man Army (co-s.p.), Metti una Sera a Cena (s.p.), Bird With the Crystal Plumage (dir., s.p.), Cat O'Nine Tails (dir., s.p., story), Four Flies on Grey Velvet (dir., s.p.), Deep Red (dir., s.p.), Suspiria (dir., s.p., music), Dawn of the Dead (co-s.p., music), Inferno (dir., s.p., story), Tenebrae (dir., s.p., story), Creepers (dir., prod., s.p.), Demons (prod., s.p.), Demons 2: The Nightmare is Back (s.p., prod.), Opera (Terror at the Opera; dir., s.p.), La Chiesa (prod., s.p., story), Two Evil Eyes ("The Black Cat"; dir., prod., s.p.), Innocent Blood (actor), Trauma (dir., prod., co-s.p.).

ARKIN, ALAN: Actor, Director, b. New York, NY, March 26, 1934. e. Los Angeles City Col., Los Angeles State Col., Bennington (VT) Col. m. actress-author Barbara Dana. Father of actor Adam Arkin. Was member of folk singing group The Tarriers; then one of the original members of Chicago's Second City improvosational group. Directed short films T.G.I.F., People Soup. Author: Tony's Hard Work Day, The Lemming Condition, Halfway Through the Door, The Clearing, Some Fine Grandpa.
THEATER: Off-Bdwy: Second City, Man Out Loud, From the Second City. Broadway: Enter Laughing (Tony & Theatre World Awards, 1963), Luv. Director: Eh?, Little Murders, White House Murder Case (Obie Award), Joan of Lorraine, Rubbers and Yanks Three, The Sunshine Boys, The Sorrows of Stephen, Room Service.
PICTURES: Calypso Heat Wave (debut, 1957), The Russians Are Coming The Russians Are Coming (Golden Globe Award, Acad. Award nom.), Woman Times Seven, Wait Until Dark, Inspector Clouseau, The Heart Is a Lonely Hunter (NY Film Critics Award, Acad. Award nom.), Popi, The Monitors, Catch-22, Little Murders (also dir.), Deadhead Miles, Last of the Red Hot Lovers, Freebie and the Bean, Rafferty and the Gold Dust Twins, Hearts of the West (NY Film Critics Award), The 7 Per Cent Solution, Fire Sale (also dir.), The In-Laws (also exec. prod.), The Magician of Lublin, Simon, Improper Channels, Chu Chu and the Philly Flash, Full Moon High, The Last Unicorn (voice), The Return of Captain Invincible, Joshua Then and Now, Bad Medicine, Big Trouble, Coupe de Ville, Edward Scissorhands, Havana, The Rocketeer, Glengarry Glen Ross, Indian Summer, So I Married an Axe Murderer.
TELEVISION: Series: Harry. Movies: The Defection of Simas Kurdirka, The Other Side of Hell, A Deadly Business, Escape from Sobibor, Cooperstown, Taking the Heat. Specials: The Love Song of Barney Kempinski, The Fourth Wise Man, A Matter of Principle, Fay (pilot; dir.), Twigs (dir.), The Emperor's New Clothes (Faerie Tale Theatre), The Visit (Trying Times; dir.), The Boss (Trying Times; dir.), Necessary Parties (also co-writer, co-prod.). Guest: East Side/West Side, St. Elsewhere.

ARKOFF, SAMUEL Z.: Producer, Motion Picture executive. Chairman & president of the Samuel Z. Arkoff Company (formed 1980) and Arkoff Int'l Pictures (formed 1981). b. Fort Dodge, IA, June 12, 1918. e. U. of Colorado, U. of Iowa, Loyola U. Law Sch. m. Hilda Rusoff. U.S.A.F. cryptographer W.W.II. Cofounder American Releasing, 1954, and American International Pictures, 1955. Pres. and chmn. of bd. American International Pictures until 1979. Named with partner James H. Nicholson as Producers of the Year in 1963 by Allied States Association of Motion Picture Theatre Owners and in 1964 as Master Showmen of the Decade by the Theatre Owners of America. Also named Producers of the Year at the Show-A-Rama VIII, and in 1966 and 1967 voted among top ten producers in exhibitor ratings by the independent theatre owners. Named Commendatore of the Order of Merit by President of Republic of Italy, in Rome 1970. In 1971 he and Nicholson named Pioneers of the Year by the Foundation of the Motion Picture Pioneers, Inc. Since appointment in 1973, has served as intl. v.p. of Variety Clubs Intl. Vice pres., Permanent Charities Committee. Member of the bd. of Trustees of Loyola Marymount U., Los Angeles, in 1979. Honored by a retrospective on 25th anniversary of AIP at Museum of Modern Art, July–Sept., 1979.
PRODUCTION CREDITS: The House of Usher, Pit and the Pendulum, Tales of Terror, Master of The World, Premature Burial, Panic in the Year Zero, The Raven, Beach Party, Haunted Palace, Comedy of Terrors, Bikini Beach, Masque of the Red Death, Muscle Beach Party, Pajama Party Tomb of Ligeia, Wild Angels, Devil's Angels, The Trip, Three in the Attic, Wild in the Streets, The Oblong Box, Scream and Scream Again, Murders in the Rue Morgue, Cry of the Banshee, Bloody Mama, Wuthering Heights, Dr. Phibes, Frogs, Blacula, Dillinger, Heavy Traffic, Hennessy, Cooley High, Food of the Gods, Futureworld, Great Scout and Cathouse Thursday, Land that Time Forgot, People that Time Forgot, At the Earth's Core, Island of Dr. Moreau, Our

Winning Season, The Amityville Horror, Chomps, Dressed to Kill, How to Beat the High Cost of Living, The Final Terror.

ARKUSH, ALLAN: Director. b. Jersey City, NJ, Apr. 30, 1948. e. Franklin & Marshall, NYU. Film Sch. With New World Pictures as film, music and trailer editor 1974–9. Co-directed Hollywood Boulevard and Death Sport and was 2nd unit dir. of Grand Theft Auto before directing on own. Dir. rock videos with Bette Midler & Mick Jagger, Elvis Costello, Christine McVie.
PICTURES: Hollywood Boulevard (co-dir.), Deathsport (co-dir.), Rock 'n' Roll High School, Heartbeeps, Get Crazy, Caddyshack II.
TELEVISION: Series: Fame, St. Elsewhere, L.A. Law, Moonlighting (Emmy nom., 1987), Shannon's Deal (spv. prod.), Tattinger's, Twilight Zone, Mann & Machine, I'll Fly Away, Middle Ages, Johnny Bago. Pilots: The Bronx Zoo, Capital News (prod.), Parenthood (co-exec. prod.), Body of Evidence, Do the Strand (prod.).

ARLEDGE, ROONE: Executive. b. Forest Hills, NY, July 8, 1931. e. Columbia U. Entered industry with Dumont Network in 1952; joined U.S. Army, 1953, serving at Aberdeen Proving Ground in Maryland, where produced and directed radio programs. Joined NBC in 1954 where held various production positions. In 1960 went to ABC TV; 1964, named v.p. in chg. of ABC Sports. Created ABC's Wide World of Sports in April, 1961. Named pres. of ABC News in 1968; pres. of ABC News and Sports, 1977. Holds four George Foster Peabody Awards for sports reporting; 19 Emmy awards.

ARLING, ARTHUR E.: Cinematographer. b. Missouri, Sept. 2, 1906. e. N.Y. Inst. of Photography. Entered m.p. Fox studio 1927 as asst. cameraman, 2nd cameraman 1931; operative cameraman on Gone With the Wind which won the Academy Award for technicolor photography 1939. Lt. Comdr. U.S.N.R., W.W.II; received Academy Award as dir. of photography on The Yearling 1946. Member: Amer. Soc. of Cinematographers.
PICTURES: Homestretch, Captain from Castile, Mother Was a Freshman, You're My Everything, Wabash Avenue, My Blue Heaven, Call Me Mister, Belles on Their Toes, The Glass Slipper, Three for the Show, Love Me or Leave Me, I'll Cry Tomorrow, Ransom, Great American Pastime, Tammy & the Bachelor, Pay the Devil, Story of Ruth, Pillow Talk, Lover Come Back, Notorious Landlady, Boys Night Out, My Six Loves.

ARMSTRONG, BESS: Actress. b. Baltimore, MD, Dec. 11, 1953. m. producer John Fiedler. e. Brown U.
PICTURES: The House of God, The Four Seasons, Jekyll and Hyde Together Again, High Road to China, Jaws 3-D, Nothing in Common, Second Sight, Mother Mother.
TELEVISION: Series: On Our Own, All is Forgiven, Married People. Movies: Getting Married, How to Pick Up Girls, Walking Through the Fire, 11th Victim, Barefoot in the Park, This Girl for Hire, Lace. Special: Barefoot in the Park.

ARMSTRONG, GILLIAN: Director. b. Melbourne, Australia, Dec. 18, 1950. e. Swinburne Coll. Among 1st class in dirs. course at National Aust. Film & TV School, Sydney. Worked as art dir. on a number of films. Dir. numerous shorts (One Hundred a Day, The Singer and the Dancer) and documentaries (A Busy Kind of Bloke, Bingo Bridesmaids and Braces) before turning to features.
PICTURES: My Brilliant Career (Australian Film Inst. Award), Starstruck, Mrs. Soffel, Hard to Handle, High Tide, Fires Within, The Last Days of Chez Nous.

ARMSTRONG, GORDON: Executive. b. East Orange, NJ, Nov. 26, 1937. e. Arizona State U., graduate studies at NYU. Entered ind. as newspaper contact for MGM (1960–63); with Allan, Foster, Ingersoll and Weber 1963–70 as acct. exec.; joined 20th Century-Fox in 1970 as nat. pub. dir. In 1975 appt. dir. of adv.-pub.-promo. for Dino De Laurentiis Corp. In 1978, became vice pres., worldwide marketing for the company; 1980, named v.p., adv.-pub.-prom., Universal Pictures; 1984, named exec. v.p., mktg. MCA Recreation. 1990, pres. Entertainment Marketing Group. 1991, pres. mktg., Morgan Creek Prods. 1992, DeLaurentiis Communications mktg. consultant.

ARNALL, ELLIS GIBBS: Lawyer, executive. b. Newnan, GA, March 20, 1907. e. Mercer U., U. of the South, A.B. 1928, D.C.L. 1947; U. of Georgia LL.B. 1931; Atlanta Law Sch., LL.D. 1941; Piedmont Coll., LL.D 1943; Bryant Coll., LL.D. 1948. Georgia state representative from Coweta County, 1936–38; asst. Attorney-General (Ga.) 1938–42; Attorney-General (Ga.) 1942–43; Governor of Ga. 1943–47; pres. Dixie Life Insurance Co.; pres. Columbus National Life Insurance Co. senior mem. law firm Arnall, Golden & Gregory; pres. Georgia State Jr. Chamber of Commerce 1939; trustee U. of South; author of The Shore Dimly Seen 1946. What The People Want 1948; member U.S. Natl. Com. on UNESCO; member U.S. delegation to 4th annual conference UNESCO, Paris, France, 1949. Member: SIMPP (Pres. 1948); 1952 on leave as dir. Office of Price Stabilization,

Washington; back to SIMPP, Sept. 1952; pres. Ind. Film Prod. Export Corp., 1953; member bd. of dir., exec. com., U.S. Nat'l Comm. for UNESCO 1964–65, trustee, Mercer U. 1964–68; chmn. bd. Coastal States Life Insurance Co., chmn. bd. National Association of Life Companies. Member Academy Motion Picture Arts & Sciences; vice chmn., Sun Life of America Group, Inc.

ARNAZ, JR., DESI: Actor, Singer. b. Los Angeles, CA, Jan. 19, 1953. Son of Lucille Ball and Desi Arnaz. Sister is actress Lucie Arnaz. Gained fame as rock singer and musician with the Dino, Desi and Billy group. Video: A Day at the Zoo. Regional theatre includes Sunday in New York, Grease, Promises Promises, Alone Together, I Love My Wife, Is There Life After High School?
PICTURES: Red Sky at Morning (debut, 1971), Marco, Billy Two Hats, Joyride, A Wedding, House of the Long Shadows, The Mambo Kings.
TELEVISION: Series: Here's Lucy, Automan. Movies: Mr. & Mrs. Bo Jo Jones, Voyage of the Yes, She Lives, Having Babies, Flight to Holocaust, Black Market Baby, To Kill a Cop, The Courage and the Passion, How to Pick Up Girls, Crisis in Mid-Air, Gridlock, Advice to the Lovelorn, The Night the Bridge Fell Down. Guest: The Love Boat, Fantasy Island, Paul Reiser: Out on a Whim, Matlock.

ARNAZ, LUCIE: Actress. b. Los Angeles, CA, July 17, 1951. Daughter of Lucille Ball and Desi Arnaz. m. actor Laurence Luckinbill. Brother is actor Desi Arnaz Jr. Broadway: They're Playing Our Song (Theatre World Award), Lost in Yonkers. National touring companies: Whose Life is It Anyway?, Educating Rita, My One and Only, Social Security. Nightclubs: Lucie Arnaz—Latin Roots, Irving Berlin in Concert—In Sicily.
PICTURES: Billy Jack Goes to Washington, The Jazz Singer, Second Thoughts.
TELEVISION: Series: Here's Lucy, The Lucy Arnaz Show, Sons and Daughters. Pilot: One More Try. Movies: Who is the Black Dahlia, The Mating Season, The Washington Mistress, Who Gets the Friends? Special: Lucy & Desi: A Home Movie (host, co-exec. prod., co-dir.).

ARNELL, PETER: Producer. b. Bridgeport, CT, Oct. 11, 1918. e. U. of Michigan, A.B. Pub. dir., prog., WJLS, Beckley, WV; m.c. & disc jockey, WPEN, Philadelphia; actor, announcer, N.Y.; creator of Rate Your Mate, Name's the Same; creator & prod. of Wheel of Fortune, Balance Your Budget, I'll Buy That, Take a Guess, What's in a Word? prod. Chance for Romance, Celebrity Talent Scouts, Face the Facts, Talent Scouts, Take My Word, Ernie Kovacs' Take a Good Look.

ARNESS, JAMES: Actor. b. Minneapolis, MN, May 26, 1923. e. Beloit Coll. Brother of actor Peter Graves. Served in U.S. Army; worked in advertising, real estate.
PICTURES: The Farmer's Daughter (debut 1947), Battleground, Wagon Master, Man from Texas, People Against O'Hara, Iron Man, The Thing, Carbine Williams, Hellgate, Big Jim McLain, Horizons West, Lone Hand, Island in the Sky, Veils of Bagdad, Hondo, Her Twelve Men, Them, Many Rivers to Cross, Flame of the Islands, Sea Chase, The First Travelling Saleslady, Gun the Man Down.
TELEVISION: Series: Gunsmoke (20 years), How the West Was Won, McClain's Law. Movies: The Macahans, The Alamo: 13 Days to Glory, Gunsmoke: Return to Dodge, Red River, Gunsmoke: The Last Apache, Gunsmoke: To the Last Man, Gunsmoke: The Long Ride (also exec. prod.). Mini-Series: How the West Was Won.

ARNOLD, DANNY: Writer, Producer, Actor. r.n. Arnold Rothman; b. New York, NY, Jan. 23, 1925. Appeared in summer stock, night clubs, vaudeville; entered m.p. ind. as sound effects ed., Columbia, 1944–46; then legit., night clubs, vaudeville, 1946–50. Appeared in m.p. Breakthrough, Inside the Walls of Folsom Prison, Sailor Beware, Jumping Jacks, Scared Stiff, Stars Are Singing.; featured on Martin and Lewis TV show 2 yrs., and wrote their Comedy Hours to 1953.
PICTURES: The Caddy (co-s.p., story), Desert Sands (co-s.p.), Fort Yuma (story, s.p.), Rebel in Town (story, s.p.), Outside the Law (s.p.), THe War Between Men and Women (co-s.p., prod.).
TELEVISION: Writer: Bewitched. Writer & Dir.: The Real McCoys, The Wackiest Ship in the Army, That Girl, My World and Welcome to It (Emmy Award), Barney Miller (Emmy Award), Joe Bash, Stat.

ARNOLD, EDDY: Singer. b. Henderson, TN, May 15, 1918. Radio performer, Nashville, TN; recording star since 1946; records include That's How Much I Love You, Anytime, Bouquet of Roses (on the Country Music charts longer than any record in the history of country music), Make the World Go Away. Holds the record for most Country Records on the charts. Series: Eddy Arnold Show (1952–3), Eddy Arnold Time, Eddy Arnold Show (1956), The Kraft Music Hall (1967–71). Hosted Music from the Land, Tonight Show, more than 20 specials. Elected to Country Music Hall of Fame (1966); Entertainer of the Year (1967), Pioneer Award from Acad. of

Country Music (1984), President's Award from Songwriter's Guild (1987).

ARNOLD, ROSEANNE: Actress. formerly Roseanne Barr. b. Salt Lake City, UT, Nov. 3, 1952. e. dropped out of high sch. to hitchike across country landing in a Colorado artists' colony at 18. After marrying and raising 3 children, working as a window dresser and part-time cocktail waitress in Denver, began performing in punk bars, biker bars and Unitarian Church coffee-house. Also prod. showcase for women performers, Take Back the Mike at U. of Boulder. 1983 won Denver Laff-Off. Moved to Los Angeles where performed at The Comedy Store, and showcased on TV special Funny and The Tonight Show. Autobiography: My Life as a Woman (1989).
PICTURES: She-Devil (debut, 1989), Look Who's Talking Too (voice), Freddy's Dead, Even Cowgirls Get the Blues.
TELEVISION: Specials: Fast Copy, Rodney Dangerfield-It's Not Easy Bein' Me, Live From Minneapolis: Roseanne, Roseanne Arnold, Live From Trump Castle. Series: Roseanne (also co-exec. prod.; Peabody & Golden Globe Awards), The Jackie Thomas Show (co-exec. prod, guest). Movies: Backfield in Motion, The Woman Who Loved Elvis (also co-exec. prod.).

ARNOW, TED J.: Executive. b. Brooklyn, NY. e. St. Johns U., Washington and Lee U. Served as dir. of recreation for 262nd General Hospital in Panama. Veteran of over 50 yrs. in amusement industry. Was v.p. for adv., pub., & promo. for Loew's Theatres. Member: Motion Picture Pioneers, Variety Clubs, Will Rogers Hospital; former pres. of AMPA (Assoc. M.P. Advertisers). Retired.

ARQUETTE, PATRICIA: Actress. b. 1968. Sister is actress Rosanna Arquette. Studied acting with Milton Katselis.
PICTURES: A Nightmare on Elm Street III, Far North, The Indian Runner, Prayer of the Rollerboys, Ethan Frome, Trouble Bound, Inside Monkey Zetterland, True Romance.
TELEVISION: Movies: Daddy, Dillinger, Wildflower. Guest: The Edge (Indan Poker), thirtysomething, Tales From the Crypt.

ARQUETTE, ROSANNA: Actress. b. New York, NY, Aug. 10, 1959. Granddaughter of humorist Cliff Arquette (Charlie Weaver). Sister is actress Patricia Arquette. Debut as teenage daughter on TV series Shirley (1979).
PICTURES: More American Graffiti, Gorp, S.O.B., Baby It's You, Off the Wall, The Aviator, Desperately Seeking Susan, Silverado, After Hours, 8 Million Ways To Die, Nobody's Fool, Amazon Women on the Moon, The Big Blue, New York Stories (Life Lessons), Flight of the Intruder, Wendy Cracked a Walnut, The Linguini Incident, Fathers and Sons, Nowhere to Run.
TELEVISION: Series: Shirley. Movies: Having Babies II, The Dark Secret of Harvest Home, Zuma Beach, The Ordeal of Patty Heart, A Long Way Home, The Wall, The Executioner's Song, Johnny Belinda, One Cooks the Other Doesn't, The Parade, Survival Guide, Promised a Miracle, Sweet Revenge, Separation, Son of the Morning Star, Black Rainbow, In the Deep Woods. Specials: Mom and Dad Can't Hear Me, A Family Tree (Trying Times), The Wrong Man.

ARTHUR, BEATRICE: Actress. r.n. Bernice Frankel. b. New York, NY, May 13, 1926. Franklin Inst. of Sciences & Art. Studied with Erwin Piscator at New School for Social Research; first stage role was Lysistrata; professional stage debut in Dog Beneath the Skin, 1947. Gas, Yerma, No Exit, Six Characters in Search of an Author. Stock appearances include Personal Appearance, Candlelight, Love or Money, The Voice of the Turtle.
THEATER: The Taming of the Shrew, (1948) The Owl and the Pussycat, The Threepenny Opera (1953 revival), The ShoeString Revue, What's the Rush?, Nature's Way, Ulysses in Nighttown, Gay Divorcee, Fiddler on the Roof, Mame (Tony Award, 1966), The Floating Light Bulb, Night of the 100 Stars.
PICTURES: That Kind of Woman, Lovers and Other Strangers, Mame, History of the World Part I.
TELEVISION: Debut: Once Upon a Time (1951), Numerous guest appearances. Series: Caesar's Hour, Maude (Emmy Award, 1977), Amanda's, Golden Girls (Emmy Award, 1988). Specials: All Star Gala at Ford's Theater (host), Jay Leno's Family Comedy Hour. Movie: My First Love.

ARTHUR, KAREN: Director. b. Omaha, NB, Aug. 24, 1941. 1950–68: ballet dancer, choreographer and musical comedy singer, dancer and actress. 1968–75: actress, film, TV and theatre.
PICTURES: Actress: A Guide for the Married Man, Winning. As director: Legacy (1975, International Film Critics Award, Best First Film, Josef Von Sternberg Award), The Mafu Cage, Lady Beware.
TELEVISION: Movies: Charleston, Victims for Victims: The Theresa Saldana Story (Christopher Award), A Bunny's Tale, The Rape of Richard Beck, Evil in Clear River (Christopher Award), Cracked Up, Bridge to Silence, Blue Bayou, Fall from Grace, Bump in the Night, Shadow of a Doubt, The Secret, Return to Eden, The Jacksons: An American Dream. Mini-

Series: Crossings. Pilots: Tin Man. Episodes: Rich Man Poor Man Book II, Emerald Point, Boone, Two Marriages, Hart to Hart, Remington Steele, Cagney & Lacey (Emmy Award, best dir. dramatic episode, 1985).

ARTZ, BOB: Theatre executive. b. Spokane, WA, Aug 21, 1946 e., B.T.A. Pasadena Playhouse College of Theatre Arts. Began in 1968 as doorman; then asst. mgr to mgr. with National General Theatre Corporation. Joined Plitt Theatres in 1978 as dist. mgr and ad/pub. director, West Coast. Joined General Cinema Theatres in 1986 as reg. marketing dir.; Western region. Became dir., film marketing in 1993.
MEMBER: Variety Club, Life Member: Pasadena Playhouse Alumni & Assoc.

ASH, RENE: Producer. b. Brussels, Belgium, March 14, 1939; e. U. of Omaha. Member of the Publicists Guild since 1968; Eastern v.p. of Pub Guild 1973–1981; Author of The Film Editor in Motion Pictures & Television; employed with I.A.T.S.E. 1968–1979, prior to which was assoc. editor, Greater Amusements; various articles published in foreign film magazines; editor-in-chief, Backstage 1979–80; pres., Cinereal Pictures, 1984–85; co-pres., Eagle Films Corp., since 1985.

ASHER, JANE: Actress. b. London, England, April 5, 1946.
PICTURES: Mandy, Greengage Summer (a.k.a. Loss of Innocence), The Girl in the Headlines, Masque of the Red Death, Alfie, Deep End, The Buttercup Chain, Henry the Eighth and His Six Wives (from the BBC series), Runners, Dream Child, Paris By Night.
TELEVISION: Movies/Specials: Brideshead Revisited, Voyage 'Round My Father, East Lynne, The Mistress, Wish Me Luck, Tonight at 8:30, The Volunteer.

ASHLEY, ELIZABETH: Actress. b. Ocala, FL, Aug. 30, 1939. e. Studied ballet LA State U 1957–58; grad. Neighborhood Playhouse, 1961. Author: Postcards From the Road.
THEATER: Take Her She's Mine (1962 Tony & Theatre World Awards), The Highest Tree, Barefoot in the Park, Ring 'Round the Bathtub, The Skin of Our Teeth, Legend, Cat on a Hot Tin Roof (Bdwy revival), Caesar and Cleopatra, Agnes of God, The Milk Train Doesn't Stop Here Anymore, When She Danced.
PICTURES: The Carpetbaggers (debut, 1964), Ship of Fools, The Third Day, The Marriage of a Young Stockbroker, Paperback Hero, Golden Needles, Rancho DeLuxe, 92 in the Shade, Great Scout and Cathouse Thursday, Coma, Windows, Paternity, Split Image, Dragnet, Vampire's Kiss, Dangerous Curves, Lost Memories.
TELEVISION: Series: Evening Shade. Movies: Harpy, The Face of Fear, When Michael Calls, Second Chance, The Heist, Your Money or Your Wife, The Magician, One of My Wives is Missing, The War Between the Tates, A Fire in the Sky, Svengali, He's Fired She's Hired, Stagecoach, Warm Hearts Cold Feet, The Two Mrs. Grenvilles, Blue Bayou, Reason for Living: The Jill Ireland Story, Love and Curses . . . and All That Jazz, In the Best Interest of the Children. Pilot: Tom and Joann. Guest: Miami Vice, Hunter, Murder She Wrote, B.L. Stryker.

ASHLEY, JOHN: Actor, Producer. r.n. John Atchley. b. Kansas City, MO, Dec. 25, 1934. e. Oklahoma State U., B.A., 1956. Career started in Tulsa Little Theatre, 1956.
PICTURES: Dragstrip Girl (debut, 1957), Motorcycle Gang, Suicide Battalion, Beach Party, How to Stuff a Wild Bikini.
TELEVISION: Series: Straightaway. Guest: Men of Annapolis, Sheriff of Cochise, Frontier Doctor, Matinee Theatre, Jefferson Drum. Movie: Something is Out There (co-exec. prod.). Series Prod: The A-Team, Werewolf.

ASHTON, JOHN: Actor.
PICTURES: Oh God!, Breaking Away, Borderline, Honky Tonk Freeway, Adventures of Buckaroo Banzai, Beverly Hills Cop, National Lampoon's European Vacation, The Last Resort, King Kong Lives, Some Kind of Wonderful, Beverly Hills Cop II, She's Having a Baby, Midnight Run, I Want to Go Home, Curly Sue.
TELEVISION: Series: Dallas, Breaking Away, Hardball. Guest: M*A*S*H*, Police Squad!, The Twilight Zone. Movies: Elvis and the Beauty Queen, A Death in California, The Deliberate Stranger, I Know My First Name is Steven, Dirty Work, Stephen King's The Tommyknockers. Mini-Series: The Rhinemann Exchange.
THEATRE: The Last Meeting of the Knights of the White Magnolia (L.A. Drama Critics Circle Award), True West (Drama-Logue Award).

ASNER, EDWARD: Actor. b. Kansas City, KS, Nov. 15, 1929. e. U. of Chicago, where affiliated with campus acting group. Served two years with U.S. Army in France. Returned to Chicago to join Playwright's Theatre Club. Moved to N.Y.; Broadway debut in Face of a Hero. Appeared off-Broadway (Ivanov, Threepenny Opera, Legend of Lovers, The Tempest, Venice Preserved), in stock, and with NY Shakespeare Festival (1960) and American Shakespeare Festival (1961), returned to Bdwy in Born Yesterday (1989). In 1961 moved to Hollywood to become active in films and TV. National pres. Screen Actors Guild (1981–85), Prod. TV & feature projects through his company, Quince. Winner of numerous humanitarian awards.

PICTURES: Kid Gallahad, The Slender Thread, The Satan Bug, The Venetian Affair, El Dorado, Gunn, Change of Habit, Halls of Anger, They Call Me Mister Tibbs, The Todd Killings, Skin Game, Gus, Fort Apache—The Bronx, O'Hara's Wife, Daniel, Moon Over Parador (cameo), JFK, Happily Ever After (voice).

TELEVISION: Series: Slattery's People, The Mary Tyler Moore Show (3 Emmy Awards), Lou Grant (2 Emmy Awards), Off the Rack, The Bronx Zoo, The Trials of Rosie O'Neill, Fish Police (voice), Hearts Afire. Movies: The Doomsday Flight, Daughter of the Mind, The House on Greenapple Road, The Old Man Who Cried Wolf, The Last Child, They Call It Murder, Haunts of the Very Rich, The Police Story, The Girl Most Likely To . . . , The Imposter, Death Scream, Hey I'm Alive, Life and Assassination of the Kingfish, The Gathering, The Family Man, A Small Killing, Anatomy of an Illness, Vital Signs, Kate's Secret, The Christmas Star, A Friendship in Vienna, Not a Penny More Not a Penny Less, Good Cops Bad Cops, Switched at Birth, Silent Motive, Yes Virginia There Is a Santa Claus, Cruel Doubt. Mini-series: Rich Man Poor Man (Emmy Award), Roots (Emmy Award), Tender Is the Night.

ASPEL, MICHAEL: Radio/TV Presenter. b. London, England. Entered industry 1957. Early career: BBC Radio as actor/presenter. BBC TV as announcer/newsreader. Presentations incl: Miss World, Crackerjack, Give Us A Clue, Family Favourites, Child's Play, ITV Telethon 1988 & 1990, Aspel and Company, This Is Your Life.

ASSANTE, ARMAND: Actor. b. New York, NY, Oct. 4, 1949. e. American Acad. of Dramatic Arts. Appeared with regional theatre groups incl. Arena Stage (D.C.), Long Wharf (New Haven), and Actor's Theatre of Louisville. On Broadway in Boccaccio, Comedians, Romeo and Juliet, Kingdoms. Off-Bdwy in Why I Went Crazy, Rubbers, The Beauty Part, Lake of the Woods, Yankees 3 Detroit 0.

PICTURES: Lords of Flatbush (debut, 1974), Paradise Alley, Prophecy, Little Darlings, Private Benjamin, Love and Money, the Jury, Unfaithfully Yours, Belizaire the Cajun, The Penitent, Animal Behavior, Q & A, Eternity, The Marrying Man, The Mambo Kings, 1492: Conquest of Paradise, Hoffa, Fatal Instinct.

TELEVISION: Movies: Human Feelings, Lady of the House, The Pirate, Sophia Loren—Her Own Story, Rage of Angels, Why Me?, A Deadly Business, Stranger in My Bed, Hands of a Stranger, Jack the Ripper, Passion and Paradise, Fever. Mini-Series: Napoleon and Josephine: A Love Story, Evergreen. Series: The Doctors (1975).

ASSEYEV, TAMARA: Producer. e. Marymont College; UCLA (MA, theatre arts). Began career as asst. to Roger Corman, working on 8 films with him. In 1967 started to produce films independently. Then co-produced films with Alex Rose, starting with Drive-In. In 1966 at 24, became youngest member of Producers Guild of Amer. Member: Costume Council, LA City Museum; founding member LA Museum of Contemporary Art.

PICTURES: The Wild Racers, Paddy, The Arousers, The History of Atlantic Records, Co-produced with Ms. Rose: Drive-In, I Wanna Hold Your Hand, Big Wednesday, Norma Rae.

TELEVISION: Movies (exec. prod.): Penalty Phase, After the Promise, A Shadow on the Sun (also prod., actress), The Secret Life of Kathy McCormick, The Hijacking of the Achille Lauro (also prod.), Murder By Moonlight.

ASTIN, JOHN: Actor. b. Baltimore, MD, March 30, 1930. e. Washington and Jefferson Coll., Washington Drama Sch.; Johns Hopkins U., grad. B.A., U. of Minnesota Graduate School. Father of actors Sean and Mackenzie Astin. First prof. job., Off-Broadway, Threepenny Opera; Broadway debut, Major Barbara; dir., co-prod., A Sleep of Prisoners, Phoenix Theatre; during 1955–59, did voices in cartoons, commercials. Prod. & dir. short subject Prelude.

TELEVISION: Series: I'm Dickens . . . He's Fenster, The Addams Family, The Pruitts of Southampton, Operation Petticoat, Mary, The Addams Family (voice for animated series). Guest: Batman, The Flying Nun, Bonanza, Odd Couple, Night Gallery, Partridge Family, Police Woman, Love Boat, Night Court. Specials: Harry Anderson's Sideshow, Halloween With the Addams Family. Movies: Two on a Bench, Evil Roy Slade, Skyway to Death, Only with Married Men, The Dream Makers, Operation Petticoat (also dir.), Rossetti and Ryan: Men Who Love Women (dir. only). Pilots: Phillip and Barbara, Ethel is an Elephant.

STAGE: The Cave Dwellers, Ulysses in Nighttown, Tall Story, Lend Me a Tenor, H.M.S. Pinafore.

PICTURES: The Pusher (debut, 1958), West Side Story, That Touch of Mink, Move Over Darling, The Wheeler

Dealers, The Spirit is Willing, Candy, Viva Max!, Bunny O'Hare, Get to Know Your Rabbit, Every Little Crook and Nanny, The Brothers O'Toole, Freaky Friday, National Lampoon's European Vacation, Body Slam, Teen Wolf Too, Return of the Killer Tomatoes, Night Life, Gremlins 2, Stepmonster.

ASTIN, SEAN: Actor. b. Santa Monica, Feb. 25, 1971. Son of actors John Astin and Patty Duke. First acting job at 7 opposite mother in Afterschool Special Please Don't Hit Me Mom. Brother of actor Mackenzie Astin. Directed short film On My Honor.

PICTURES: The Goonies (debut, 1985), White Water Summer, Like Father Like Son, Staying Together, The War of the Roses, Memphis Belle, The Willies, Toy Soldiers, Encino Man, Where the Day Takes You, Rudy.

TELEVISION: Movies: The Rules of Marriage, The Brat Patrol. Pilot: Just Our Luck.

THEATRE: Lone Star (L.A.).

ATHERTON, WILLIAM: Actor. b. New Haven, CT, June 30, 1947. While in high school became youngest member of Long Wharf Theatre Co. Given scholarship to Pasadena Playhouse; then switched to Carnegie Tech Sch. of Drama in 1965. In college years toured with USO prods in Europe and in stock and industrial shows. Came to NY. where first prof. job was in natl. co. of Little Murders.

PICTURES: The New Centurions (debut, 1972), Class of '44, The Sugarland Express, The Day of the Locust, The Hindenburg, Looking for Mr. Goodbar, Ghostbusters, Real Genius, No Mercy, Die Hard, Die Hard 2, Grim Prairie Tales, Oscar.

THEATER: The House of Blue Leaves, The Basic Training of Pavlo Hummel, The Sign in Sidney Brustein's Window, Suggs (Theatre World Award), Rich and Famous, Passing Game, Happy New Year, The American Clock, Three Acts of Recognition, The Caine Mutiny Court-Martial, Child's Play, Loco Motives.

TELEVISION: Mini-Series: Centennial. Movies: Tomorrow's Child, Malibu, Intrigue, Buried Alive, Diagnosis of Murder, Chrome Soldiers. Guest: The Equalizer, Twilight Zone, Murder She Wrote, Tales From the Crypt.

ATKINS, CHRISTOPHER: Actor. b. Rye, NY, Feb. 21, 1961. e. Dennison U., Ohio. Early modelling jobs; theatrical film debut in The Blue Lagoon (1980).

PICTURES: The Blue Lagoon, The Pirate Movie, A Night in Heaven, Beaks, Mortuary Academy, Listen to Me, Shakma, King's Ransom, Dracula Rising, Eye of the Camera, Exchange Lifeguards, A Bullet Down Under.

TELEVISION: Movies: Child Bride of Short Creek, Secret Weapons, Fatal Charm. Series: Dallas. Guest: The Black Stallion. Also: The Black Rose, Miami Killer, The Floating Outfit.

ATTENBOROUGH, DAVID: Broadcaster. b. London, England, May 8, 1926; e. Wyggeston Sch., Leicester; Clare Coll., Cambridge. Early career, editor in educational publishing house, ent. BBC-TC Sept. 1952. Prod. Zoo Quest series, Travellers Tales, Adventure and other prog., travel, Eastward with Attenborough, The Tribal Eye, Life on Earth, The Living Planet, The First Eden, The Trials of Life. Controller BBC-2, 1965–68; Dir. of Prog. BBC-TV, 1969–72.

ATTENBOROUGH, SIR RICHARD (SAMUEL), Kt 1976; CBE. 1967: Actor, Producer, Director. b. Cambridge, England, Aug. 29, 1923. m. 1945 Sheila Beryl Grant Sim. e. Wyggeston Grammar Sch., Leicester. Leverhulme Scholarship to Royal Acad. of Dramatic Art, 1941 (Bancroft Medal). First stage appearance Ah Wilderness (Palmers Green, 1941). West End debut in Awake and Sing (1942), then The Little Foxes, Brighton Rock. Joined RAF, 1943; seconded to RAF Film Unit, and appeared in training film Journey Together, 1945; demobilized, 1946. Returned to stage, 1949, in The Way Back (Home of the Brave), To Dorothy a Son, Sweet Madness, The Mousetrap (original cast: 1952–54), Double Image, The Rape of the Belt. 1959 formed Beaver Films with Bryan Forbes; 1960 formed Allied Film Makers.

PICTURES: Actor: In Which We Serve (debut, 1942), Schweik's New Adventures, The Hundred Pound Window, Journey Together, A Matter of Life and Death (Stairway to Heaven), School for Secrets (Secret Flight), The Man Within (The Smugglers), Dancing With Crime, Brighton Rock (Young Scarface), London Belongs to Me (Dulcimer Street), The Guinea Pig, The Lost People, Boys in Brown, Morning Departure (Operation Disaster), Hell Is Sold Out, The Magic Box, Gift Horse (Glory at Sea), Father's Doing Fine, Eight O'Clock Walk, The Ship That Died of Shame, Private's Progress, The Baby and the Battleship, Brothers in Law, The Scamp, Dunkirk, The Man Upstairs, Sea of Sand (Desert Patrol), Danger Within (Breakout), I'm All Right Jack, Jet Storm, SOS Pacific, The Angry Silence (also co-prod.), The League of Gentlemen, Only Two Can Play, All Night Long, The Dock Brief (Trial & Error), The Great Escape, Seance on a Wet Afternoon (also prod.; San Sebastian Film Fest. & Brit. Acad. Awards for Best Actor), The Third Secret, Guns at

Batasi (Brit. Acad. Award), The Flight of the Phoenix, The Sand Pebbles (Golden Globe Award), Dr. Dolittle (Golden Globe Award), The Bliss of Mrs Blossom, Only When I Larf, The Magic Christian, David Copperfield (TV in U.S.), The Last Grenade, A Severed Head, Loot, 10 Rillington Place, Ten Little Indians, Rosebud, Brannigan, Conduct Unbecoming, The Chess Players, The Human Factor, Jurassic Park. *Producer:* Whistle Down the Wind, The L-Shaped Room. Director: Oh! What a Lovely War (also prod.; 16 Intl. Awards incl. Golden Globe and BAFTA UN Award), Young Winston (Golden Globe), A Bridge Too Far (Evening News Best Drama Award, 1977), Magic, Gandhi (also prod.; 8 Oscars, 5 BAFTA Awards, 5 Golden Globes, DGA Award, 1982), A Chorus Line, Cry Freedom (Berlinale Kamera, 1987), Chaplin, Shadowlands (also prod.).

AUBERJONOIS, RENE: Actor. b. New York, NY, June 1, 1940. e. attended Carnegie Mellon U.
THEATER: Dark of the Moon, Beyond the Fringe, Tartuffe, King Lear, Fire, Julius Caesar, Charley's Aunt, Coco (Tony Award, 1970), Tricks, The Ruling Class, Twelfth Night, The Good Doctor (Tony nom.), Break a Leg, The New York Idea, Every Good Boy Deserves Favor; Richard III, The Misanthrope, Flea in Her Ear, Big River (Tony nom.), Metamorphosis, City of Angels (Tony nom.).
PICTURES: Lilith (debut, 1964), Petulia, MASH, Brewster McCloud, McCabe and Mrs. Miller, Pete 'n Tillie, Images, Hindenberg, The Big Bus, King Kong, Eyes of Laura Mars, Where the Buffalo Roam, The Last Unicorn (voice), 3:15, Walker, Police Academy 5: Assignment Miami Beach, My Best Friend is a Vampire, The Little Mermaid (voice), The Feud, Star Trek VI: The Undiscovered Country (unbilled), The Player, Little Nemo (voice), The Ballad of Little Jo.
TELEVISION: *Series:* Benson, Star Trek: Deep Space Nine. *Movies:* The Birdmen, Shirts/Skins, Panache, Dark Secret of Harvest Home, More Wild Wild West, Smoky Mountain Christmas, The Christmas Star, Fire, Gore Vidal's Billy the Kid, Longarm, A Connecticut Yankee in King Arthur's Court, Absolute Strangers, Ned Blessing: The True Story of My Life, Wild Card. *Mini-Series:* The Rhineman Exchange. *Specials:* Faerie Tale Theatre (The Frog Prince, Sleeping Beauty), King Lear, Legend of Sleepy Hollow, Fort Necessity, Incident at Vichy, The Booth, The Cask of Amontillado, Ashenden (BBC), The Lost Language of Cranes (BBC).

AUBREY, JAMES T., JR.: Executive. b. La Salle, IL, Dec. 14, 1918. e. Princeton U., 1941. m. Phyllis Thaxter. U.S. Air Force, 1941–45; salesman, Street and Smith, Condé Nast Pub., 1946–47; account exec., KNX, Los Angeles, 1948; account exec., KNXT, 1951; sales mgr., then gen. mgr., KNXT and CTPN, 1952. Man. network prog., Hollywood CBS-TV, 1956; V.P. programs and talent, ABC-TV 1957; v.p. CBS. 1958; exec. v.p. CBS-TV, 1959; pres. CBS-TV, 1959. In 1969–73 MGM pres.; now indep. prod.
PICTURES: Futureworld (prod.), The Hunger, Hostage (co-exec. prod.).

AUDRAN, STEPHANE: Actress. b. Versailles, France, Nov. 8, 1938. Former wife of French star Jean-Louis Trintignant and director Claude Chabrol.
PICTURES: Les Cousins (debut under direction of Chabrol, 1959), Les Bonnes Femmes, Bluebeard, The Third Lover, Six in Paris, The Champagne Murders, Les Biches, La Femme Infidele, The Beast Must Die, The Lady in the Car, Le Boucher, Without Apparent Motive, Dead Pigeon on Beethoven Street, La Rupture, Just Before Nightfall, The Discreet Charm of the Bourgeoisie, Blood Wedding, The Devil's Advocate, Le Cri de Couer, Vincent Francois Paul and the Others, The Blackbird (U.S. film debut), Ten Little Indians, Silver Bears, Eagle's Wing, The Big Red One, Coup de Torchon (Clean Slate), La Cage ux Folles III: The Wedding, Cop au vin, Babette's Feast, Seasons of Pleasure, Faceless, Body-To-Body, Sons, Manika: The Girl Who Lived Twice, Quiet Days in Clichy, Mass in C Minor, Poulet au Vinaigre.
TELEVISION: Mistral's Daughter, The Blood of Others, The Sun Also Rises, Poor Little Rich Girl: The Barbara Hutton Story, Champagne Charlie.

AUERBACH, NORBERT T.: Executive. b. Vienna, 1923. Educated in U.S. and served with U.S. Army Intelligence in Europe during W.W.II. Joined m.p. business in 1946 after grad. UCLA. (business admin.). First asst. dir. at Service Studios in CA. Moved to N.Y. to join domestic sales dept. of Film Classics. Joined Columbia Pictures in foreign dept. In 1950 assigned to Paris office, where remained for over decade, except for 18 mos. in Portugal as mgr. Returned to Paris in 1953 and filled number of exec. sls. positions for Columbia, ultimately rising to continental mgr. 1961, left Columbia to produce films in France. Resumed career in dist., as continental mgr at Paris office of United Artists. In 1966 returned to prod. to make The Thief of Paris. 1967, joined Seven Arts Prods. heading theatrical and TV sls. operations in Paris. When Seven Arts acquired Warner Bros., he became continental sls. mgr. for Warners in Paris. 1968, set up European prod. and dist. org. for CBS Cinema Center Films,

operating from London. 1972, moved to L.A. as v.p., foreign mgr. for CCF. Returned to London in 1973 to be consultant in prod. and dist. Rejoined UA in 1977 as sls. mgr. for Europe and the Middle East. Named sr. v.p. & foreign mgr. in 1978. Named pres. & COO, Jan. 1981; pres., CEO, Feb. 1981. Co-pres., United Int'l Pictures, London, till 1982. In 1983 formed packaging and financing Co., Eliktra, Inc. 1982, acting pres. and chief exec. officer of Almi Distribution Corp. Now Almi consultant, Exec. v.p. American Screen Co.

AUGUST, BILLE: Director. b. Denmark, 1948. e. trained in advertising photography, Danish Film School, grad. 1971, cinematography. As cinematographer shot: Miesta ei voi raiskata (Men Can't Be Raped), Karleken, The Grass is Singing. Became dir. 1978 with short Kim G. and dramas for Danish TV.
PICTURES: Honnnig Maane (also sp.), Zappa (also s.p.), Twist and Shout (also s.p.), Pelle the Conquerer (also s.p.), The Best Intentions (Cannes Film Festival Palm d'Or Award, 1992), House of the Spirits.

AUMONT, JEAN PIERRE: Actor. b. Paris, France, Jan. 5, 1909. e. Conservatoire of Drama. Roles French stage and films. In 1943 enlisted in Free French Army. Film debut, Jean de la Lune, 1932.
PICTURES: Hotel du Nord, Assignment in Brittany, The Cross of Lorraine, Heartbeat, Song of Scheherazade, Siren of Atlantis, Affairs of a Rogue, Wicked City, Lili, Life Begins Tomorrow, Gay Adventure, Charge of the Lancers, Hilda Crane, The Seventh Sin, John Paul Jones, The Enemy General, The Devil at 4 O'Clock, Carnival of Crime, Five Miles to Midnight, Cauldron of Blood, Castle Keep, Day for Night, Turn the Other Cheek, The Happy Hooker, Mahogany, Catherine & Co., Entire Days Among the Trees, Cat and Mouse, Blackout, Two Solitudes, Something Short of Paradise, Nana, Sweet Country, The Free Frenchman, Senso, A Star for Two, Becoming Colette.
U.S. STAGE: Tovarich, Incident at Vichy, Hostile Witness, Carnival, Camino Real, Murderous Angels, Gigi, A Talent for Murder.
TELEVISION: Sins, Windmills of the Gods, A Tale of Two Cities, Young Indiana Jones.

AURELIUS, GEORGE M.: Executive. b. Grasston, MN, Sept. 16, 1911. e. U. of Minnesota. Ent. m.p. ind. 1927 as usher Finkelstein & Ruben, St. Paul; asst. mgr. 1929–30; to Warner Theatres, New York 1931; mgr. Moss' Broadway; Minnesota Amusement Co. 1932–41; city mgr. Publix-Rickards-Nace. Paramount-Nace Theatres, Tucson, Ariz. 1941–46; v.p. ABC Theas. of Arizona, Inc. 1949–67; pres. ABC North Central Theatres, Inc., 1967–72; v.p., ABC Intermountain Theatres, Inc., v.p. ABC Theatres of California, Inc. 1972–1974; Mgmt. Consulting and ShoWest Convention & Trade Show since 1975, named exec. dir., 1979. Retired 1985.

AUSTIN, RAY: Director, Writer, Producer. b. London, England, Dec. 5, 1932. Has written, produced and directed many TV series, specials and movies.
TELEVISION: Director of series: Avengers, The Champions, Department S, Randall & Hopkirk, Ugliest Girl in Town, Journey into the Unknown, Magnum P.I., Simon and Simon, House Calls, Kings Crossing, Fall Guy, Lime Street, Spencer for Hire. Writer: Randall & Hopkirk, Department S (also prod.). Producer-Director: The Perfumed Garden. Director: It's the Only Way to Go, Fun and Games, Space 1999, New Avengers, Hawaii Five-O, Sword of Justice, Webb, Barnaby Jones, Hardy Boys, Wonder Woman, Salvage, B.J. and the Bear, Hart to Hart, The Yeagers, Man Called Sloane, From Here to Eternity, Bad Cats, Westworld, Tales of the Gold Monkey (2-hr. pilot), The Return of the Man from U.N.C.L.E. Director-Writer: Black Beauty, Zany Adventures of Robin Hood, The Master, Hart to Hart (series), V, Air Wolf, Lime Street (pilot and episodes); Spenser for Hire (several episodes); Magnum P.I. (season premiere 2-hr. episode); Return of the Six Million Dollar Man (pilot); Our House (episodes), Dirty Dozen, Alfred Hitchcock Presents, A Fine Romance.
PICTURES: Virgin Witches, House of the Living Dead.

AUTANT-LARA, CLAUDE: Director. Began career as scenic designer for French films in early 1920s; then asst. dir. to Rene Clair. First solo venture experimental film, 1923; in Hollywood, 1930–32. dir. Parlor, Bedroom and Bath, Incomplete Athlete.
PICTURES: Devil in the Flesh, Seven Deadly Sins (seq.), Red Inn, Oh Amelia, Game of Love, Ciboulette, Red and the Black.

AUTEUIL, DANIEL: Actor. b. Algeria, Jan. 24, 1950. Parents were lyric opera singers in roving troupe. Lived in Avignon. Performed in Amer. prod. in Paris of Godspell. Then did musical comedy for 2 years. Provided voice of baby for French print of U.S. film Look Who's Talking.
PICTURES: L'Aggression/Sombres Vacanes, Attention Les Yeaux, La Nuit de Saint-Germain des Pres, Monsieuer Papa, L'Amour Viole (Rape of Love), Les Heroes n'ont pas froid aux oreilles, A Nous Deux, Bete Mais Discipline, Les Sous-

Doues, La Banquiere, Clara et les chic types, Men Prefer Fat Girls, Pour 100 briques t'as plus rien maintentant, Que les gros salaires levent le doigt!!!, L'Indic, P'tit Con, The Beast, L'Arbalete, Palace, L'Amour en Douce, Jean de Florette, Manon of the Spring, Romuald and Juliette (Mama There's a Man in Your Bed), A Few Days With Me, My Life is Hell, L'Elegant Criminel, Un Coeur en Hiver (A Heart in Winter), Ma Saison Preferee (My Favorite Season).

AUTRY, GENE: Actor. b. Tioga, TX, Sept. 29, 1907. Railroad telegrapher at Sapulba, OK, 1925; became radio singer and recording artist (Columbia Records) 1928; screen debut 1934 at Mascot Pictures (later became Republic) as screen's first singing cowboy. Starred in 89 feature films and 91 half hour TV films. The Gene Autry Show, 1950–55. Formed Flying A Productions, produced Annie Oakley, The Range Rider, Buffalo Bill, Jr. and Adventures of Champion TV series. Wrote or co-wrote over two hundred songs, recorded 635 records, has 12 Gold Records, and 6 platinum records, including all-time best seller, Rudolph the Red-Nosed Reindeer. Voted top money making Western star 1937–42, and in top Western stars 1936, 1946–54; first Western star to be in top ten money makers from 1939–42. Served in U.S.A.A.F. as flight officer, 1942–45; on USO tour overseas 3 mos.; immediately thereafter resumed radio career with former sponsor, the Wm. Wrigley Co., formed Gene Autry Productions, Inc., star of Madison Square Garden Rodeo first in 1940; composed & recorded song Here Comes Santa Claus; owner 4 radio stations, California Angels baseball team and chairman of the board of Gene Autry Western Heritage Museum.

AVALON, FRANKIE: Entertainer. r.n. Francis Thomas Avalone. b. Philadelphia, PA, Sept. 18, 1940. e. South Philadelphia H.S. Trumpet prodigy age 9 yrs. Recording contract, Chancellor Records, Inc., 1957; Gold Record: Venus 1959; Gold Album: Swingin' on a Rainbow, 1959.
TELEVISION: Series: Easy Does It... Starring Frankie Avalon. Guest: Ed Sullivan, Perry Como, Pat Boone, Arthur Murray, Dick Clark Shows, Milton Berle, Golden Circle Spectacular, Dinah Shore Show, Steve Allen Show, The Patty Duke Show, Hullabaloo, Happy Days.
PICTURES: Jamboree (debut, 1957), Guns of the Timberland, The Alamo, Alakazam the Great (voice), Voyage to the Bottom of the Sea, Sail a Crooked Ship, Panic in the Year Zero, Beach Party, The Castilian, Operation Bikini, Bikini Beach, Pajama Party, Muscle Beach Party, How to Stuff a Wild Bikini, Beach Blanket Bingo, Ski Party, I'll Take Sweden, Sgt. Deadhead, Dr. Goldfoot and the Bikini Machine, Fireball 500, The Million Eyes of Su-Muru, Skidoo, Horror House, The Take, Grease, Back to the Beach, Troop Beverly Hills.

AVEDON, DOE: Actress. b. Old Westbury, NY, 1928. Bookkeeper; then actress.
BROADWAY: Young and the Fair, My Name Is Aquilon.
PICTURES: High and the Mighty, Deep in My Heart, The Boss.
TELEVISION: Series: Big Town.

AVERBACK, HY: Director. b. 1925. Theatrical dir. before turning to TV. Formerly actor and radio announcer on Jack Paar Show (1947), Let's Talk Hollywood, Bob Hope Show.
PICTURES: As actor: The Benny Goodman Story, Four Girls in Town, How to Succeed in Business Without Really Trying. Director: Chamber of Horrors (also prod.); Where Were You When the Lights Went Out?, I Love You Alice B. Toklas, The Great Bank Robbery, Suppose They Gave a War & Nobody Came, Where the Boys Are—1984.
TELEVISION: Actor: Saturday Night Revue (1953–4), Meet Corliss Archer (also prod.), Tonight, Our Miss Brooks. Director: The Brothers, The Real McCoys, Donna Reed Show, Tom Ewell Show (prod.), Mrs. G. Goes to College (prod., dir.), Bus Stop, Dick Powell Show, Ensign O'Toole, Burke's Law, Man From U.N.C.L.E., F Troop (exec. prod.), The Flying Nun, McMillan and Wife, Colombo, McCloud (also prod.), M*A*S*H, Friends, The New Maverick, Anna and the King, Needles and Pins, Movin' On, Look Out World, The Night Rider, A Guide for the Married Woman, The Girl, The Gold Watch, and Dynamite; She's in the Army Now, At Ease (also prod.), The Four Seasons.

AVILDSEN, JOHN G.: Director, Cinematographer, Editor. b. Chicago, IL, Dec. 21, 1935. m. actress Tracy Brooks Swope. e. NYU. After service in Army made film with friend, Greenwich Village Story, then joined ad agency to write and produce film commercials. Entered m.p. industry as ass't cameraman on Below the Hill, followed with prod. mgr. job on Italian film made in U.S. Then made first theatrical short, Smiles. Asst. dir: Black Like Me; prod. mgr.: Mickey One, Una Moglie Americana; 2nd unit dir.: Hurry Sundown. Produced, photographed & edited a short, Light, Sound, Diffuse. Returned to industry to make films for ad agencies before resuming theatrical career.
PICTURES: Turn on to Love (debut feature, dir., photo.), Out of It (assoc. prod., dir. of prod., photo.), Sweet Dreams (aka Okay, Bill; also photo., edit.), Guess What We Learned in School Today? (also photo., edit.), Joe (also photo.), Cry Uncle (also photo., edit.), The Stoolie (also photo.), Save the Tiger, W. W. and the Dixie Dancekings, Foreplay (also edit., photo.), Rocky (Acad. Award for best director, 1976), Slow Dancing in the Big City (also prod., edit.), The Formula, Neighbors (also supv. edit.), Traveling Hopefully (documentary), A Night in Heaven (also edit.), The Karate Kid (also edit.), The Karate Kid: Part II (also edit.), Happy New Year, For Keeps (also edit.), Lean On Me (also co-edit.), The Karate Kid Part III (also co-edit.), Rocky V (also co-edit.), The Power of One (also edit.), Cowboy Up, 8 Seconds to Glory.
TELEVISION: From No House to Options House (2 On the Town, Emmy Award).

AVNET, JON: Producer, Director. b. Nov. 17, 1949. e. U. of PA, Sarah Lawrence Coll. Began career as director of off-Bdwy. prods. Produced and directed low-budget film, Confusion's Circle, which brought a directing fellowship at American Film Institute. Joined Weintraub/Heller Prods. as assoc. prod., where met Steve Tisch, with whom formed Tisch/Avnet Prods. Formed Avnet/Kerner Co., 1986.
PICTURES: Checkered Flag or Crash (assoc. prod.), Outlaw Blues (assoc. prod.), Prod.: Coast to Coast, Risky Business, Deal of the Century (exec. prod.), Less Than Zero, Men Don't Leave, Funny About Love, Fried Green Tomatoes (also dir., co-s.p.), The Mighty Ducks, The Three Musketeers (co-exec. prod.), Significant Other.
TELEVISION: Producer: No Other Love, Homeward Bound, Prime Suspect, Something So Right, Silence of the Heart, Calendar Girl Murders, Call to Glory (pilot and series), The Burning Bed, In Love and War (also exec. prod.), Between Two Women (also dir., co-s.p.) Exec. Prod.: Side By Side, My First Love, Breaking Point, Do You Know the Muffin Man?, Heatwave, Backfield in Motion, The Nightman, The Switch, For Their Own Good.

AXEL, GABRIEL: Director. b. 1918. e. France, then studied acting at Danish National Conservatory. Returned to France where joined the Paris theater co. of Louis Jouvet as stagehand. Worked as actor in Copenhagen boulevard theater where made directing debut. Went on to dir. Danish TV, mostly classic plays.
PICTURES: The Red Mantle (1967), Danish Blue, Babette's Feast (Acad. Award, 1988), Christian (also s.p.).

AXELMAN, ARTHUR: Executive. b. Philadelphia, PA, Dec. 10, 1944. e. Florida Atlantic U., B.A., 1969. Entered NY offices of William Morris Agency, June 1972; transferred to Bev. Hills offices, 1976, as literary agent. Founded company's original TV Movie dept., 1977. Appointed v.p. in 1980, sr. v.p. in 1991. Among clients represented while overseeing network sales, negotiation, packaging, development, etc. of some 100 TV movies have been EMI TV, Bob Banner, Edward S. Feldman, Lee Grant, Thom Mount, Edward Anhalt, Zev Braun, Marvin Worth, Gilbert Cates, Jerry London, Jeremy Kagan, Dick Berg, Patty Duke, Finnegan-Pinchuk Prods.

AXELROD, GEORGE: Playwright, writer, prod., dir. b. New York, NY, June 9, 1922. Stage mgr., summer stock, 1940–41; radio writer, 1941–52; writer, novels: Beggar's Choice, Blackmailer; co-writer, nightclub musical: All About Love, 1951.
BROADWAY: The Seven Year Itch, Will Success Spoil Rock Hunter?, Visit to a Small Planet, Once More with Feeling, Goodbye Charlie.
PICTURES: Writer: Phfft, The Seven Year Itch, Bus Stop, Breakfast at Tiffany's, The Manchurian Candidate (also co-prod.), Paris When It Sizzles (also prod.), How to Murder Your Wife, Lord Love a Duck (also dir., prod.), The Secret Life of an American Wife (also dir., prod.), The Lady Vanishes, The Holocroft Covenant, The Fourth Protocol.

AXELROD, JONATHAN: Writer. b. New York, NY, July 9, 1950. Stepson of writer George Axelrod. Started as on-set "gofer" before writing screenplays. 1977–80, v.p. primetime drama dev., ABC Entertainment; 1980–82, v.p. exec. dir. in chg. dev. ABC Ent.; 1983–85 exec. v.p., Columbia Pictures TV; 1985–87, pres. New World Pictures; 1987–, co-owner, Camden Artists; 1989, exe. v.p. Ventura Entertainment Group. Pres. & CEO Ventura M.P. Group. Exec. Prod. of Hollywood Detective series.
PICTURES: The Dirty Movie, Every Little Crook and Nanny.

AYKROYD, DAN: Actor, Writer. b. Ottawa, Canada, July 1, 1952. m. actress Donna Dixon. Member of Toronto Co. of Second City Theater. Worked as mgr. Club 505, after-hours Toronto nightclub 1970–73. Performed and recorded (Briefcase Full of Blues, Made in America) with John Belushi as the Blues Brothers. Co-owner Hard Rock Cafe, NY.
TELEVISION: Coming Up Rosie (Canada), Saturday Night Live 1975–79 (writer and performer; Emmy Award for writing: 1977). Steve Martin's Best Show Ever (performer, writer). Guest: Tales from the Crypt (Yellow).
PICTURES: Love at First Sight (debut, 1977; also co-s.p.), Mr. Mike's Mondo Video, 1941, The Blues Brothers (also co-s.p.), Neighbors, It Came From Hollywood, Doctor Detroit,

Trading Places, Twilight Zone—The Movie, Indiana Jones and the Temple of Doom (cameo), Ghostbusters (also co-s.p.), Nothing Lasts Forever, Into the Night, Spies Like Us (also co-s.p.), One More Saturday Night (exec. prod. only), Dragnet (also co-s.p.), The Couch Trip, The Great Outdoors, Caddyshack II, My Stepmother is an Alien, Ghostbusters II (also co-s.p.), Driving Miss Daisy (Acad. Award nom.), Loose Cannons, Nothing But Trouble (also dir., s.p.), Masters of Menace, My Girl, This is My Life, Sneakers, Chaplin, Coneheads (also co-s.p.), My Girl 2.

AYRES, GERALD: Producer, Writer. e. Yale U. where had four plays produced. Became Broadway play doctor and then joined Columbia Pictures as freelance reader. Named story editor; exec. asst. to v.p. Mike Frankovich; then v.p. in chg. creative affairs in Hollywood. Left in 1970 to become independent. Formed Acrobat Films.
   PICTURES: Producer: Cisco Pike, The Last Detail, Foxes (also s.p.), Rich and Famous (s.p. only; WGA Award, 1981).
   TELEVISION: Movies (writer): Stormy Weathers (co-writer), Crazy in Love (ACE Award nom.).

AYRES, LEW: Actor. b. Minneapolis, MN, Dec. 28, 1908. Toured Mexico with own orchestra; then with Henry Halstead's Orchestra. Served as medical corpsman & asst. chaplain W.W.II.
   PICTURES: The Sophmore (debut, 1929), The Kiss, All Quiet on the Western Front, Common Clay, East is West, Doorway to Hell, Up for Murder, Many a Slip, Spirit of Notre Dame, Heaven on Earth, Impatient Maiden, Night World, Okay America, State Fair, Don't Bet on Love, My Weakness, Cross Country Cruise, Let's Be Ritzy, She Learned About Sailors, Servants' Entrance, Lottery Lover, Silk Hat Kid, Leathernecks Have Landed, Panic on the Air, Shakedown, Lady Be Careful, Murder With Pictures, The Crime Nobody Saw, Last Train from Madrid, Hold 'Em Navy, King of the Newsboys, Scandal Street, Holiday, Rich Man Poor Girl, Young Dr. Kildare (and subsequent series), Spring Madness, Ice Follies of 1939, Broadway Serenade, These Glamour Girls, The Golden Fleecing, Maisie Was a Lady, Fingers at the Window, Dark Mirror, Unfaithful, Johnny Belinda, The Capture, New Mexico, No Escape, Donovan's Brain, Altars to the East (also dir., prod.), narrator), Advise and Consent, The Carpetbaggers, The Biscuit Eater, The Man, Battle for the Planet of the Apes, End of the World, Damien-Omen II, Battlestar Galactica.
   TELEVISION: Series: Frontier Justice (host), Lime Street. Movies: Hawaii Five-O (pilot), Marcus Welby M.D. (pilot), Earth II, She Waits, The Stranger, The Questor Tapes, Heatwave, Francis Gary Powers, Suddenly Love, Salem's Lot, Letters from Frank, Reunion, Of Mice and Men, Under Siege.

AZNAVOUR, CHARLES: Singer, Songwriter, Actor. b. Paris, France, May 22, 1924. r.n. Shahnour Varenagh Aznavourian. Studied dance and drama as a child and was performing at the age of 10. Encouraged by Edith Piaf, became one of France's leading performers by the mid-1950s and an international concert star by the 1970s. Has also composed music for film.
   PICTURES: Adieu Cherie (1947), C'est arrive a 36 Chandelles, Les Dragueurs, Shoot the Piano Player, Le testament d'Orphee, Le Passage du Rhin, Un taxi pour Tobrouk, Horace 62, Tempo di Roma, Les Quatres Verites, Le Rat'd Amerique, Pourquoi Paris?, Paris in August, Candy, The Games, The Adventurers, The Blockhouse, Ten Little Indians, The Twist, Sky Riders, Ciao Les Mecs, The Tin Drum, The Magic Mountain, The Hatter's Ghosts, What Makes David Run?, Long Live Life!, Mangeclous, Friend to Friend, Il Maestro, Double Game.

BABENCO, HECTOR: Director. b. Buenos Aires, Argentina, Feb. 7, 1946. Early years spent in Mar del Plata. Left home at 17 and traveled throughout European capitals for 8 years working as a writer, house-painter, salesman, and, in Rome, as an extra at Cinecitta. Moved to Sao Paulo, Brazil where he made several short documentaries. First feature film, Rei Da Noite (1976).
   PICTURES: Rei Da Noite (King of the Night), Lucio Flavio—Passageioro Da Agonia, Pixote (also s.p.), Kiss of the Spider Woman, Ironweed, Besame Mucho (prod. only), At Play in the Fields of the Lord (also co-s.p.).

BACALL, LAUREN: Actress. r.n. Betty Bacall Perske. b. New York, NY, Sept. 16, 1924. e. American Acad. Dram. Arts. Was m. late Humphrey Bogart, Jason Robards. Started as fashion model before appearing on stage in such plays as Johnny Two-by-Four, Franklin Street.
   BROADWAY: Bdwy: Cactus Flower, Goodbye Charlie, Applause (Tony Award, best actress in musical), Woman of the Year. London/Australia: Sweet Bird of Youth.
   PICTURES: To Have and Have Not (debut, 1944), Two Guys From Milwaukee (cameo), Confidential Agent, The Big Sleep, Dark Passage, Key Largo, Young Man with a Horn, Bright Leaf, How to Marry a Millionaire, Woman's World, Cobweb, Blood Alley, Written on the Wind, Designing

Women, Gift of Love, Flame over India, Shock Treatment, Sex and the Single Girl, Harper, Murder on the Orient Express, The Shootist, Health, The Fan, Appointment with Death, Mr. North, Misery, A Star for Two, All I Want for Christmas.
   TELEVISION: Specials: The Girls in Their Dresses, Blithe Spirit, The Petrified Forest, Applause, Bacall on Bogart. Movies: Perfect Gentlemen, Dinner at Eight, The Portrait, A Foreign Field.

BACH, CATHERINE: Actress. b. Warren, Ohio, March 1, 1954.
   PICTURES: The Midnight Man, Thunderbolt and Lightfoot, Hustle, Cannonball Run II, Tunnels (Criminal Act), Music City Blues, Driving Force, Street Justice.
   TELEVISION: Series: The Dukes of Hazzard (1979–85), The Dukes (cartoon, voice). Guest on many specials. Movies: Matt Helm, Strange New World, Murder in Peyton Place, White Water Rebels.

BACHARACH, BURT: Composer-Conductor-Arranger. b. Kansas City, MO, May 12, 1928. e. McGraw U., Mannes Sch. of Music, Music Acad. of the West. Studied with composers Darius Milhaud, Henry Cowell, and Bohuslav Martinu. Has conducted for Marlene Dietrich, Vic Damone. As a performer albums include: Burt Bacharach; Futures, Man! His Songs. Book: The Bacharach-David Song Book (1978).
   THEATER: Promises Promises (Tony Award, best score, 1969).
   PICTURES: Lizzie, The Sad Sack, The Blob, Country Music Holiday, The Man Who Shot Liberty Valance, Wives and Lovers, Who's Been Sleeping in My Bed?, Send Me No Flowers, A House Is Not a Home, What's New Pussycat?, Alfie, Promise Her Anything, Casino Royale, The April Fools, Butch Cassidy and the Sundance Kid (2 Acad. Awards for best orig. score & song: Raindrops Keep Fallin' on My Head), Something Big, Lost Horizon, Arthur (Acad. Award for best song: Arthur's Theme), Night Shift, Best Defense, Baby Boom, Arthur 2 on the Rocks.
   TELEVISION: Special: Singer Presents Burt Bacharach (Emmy Award for Best Variety Special, 1971).

BACK, LEON B.: Exhibitor. b. Philadelphia, PA, Oct. 23, 1912. e. Johns Hopkins U., B.E., 1932; U. of Baltimore, LL.B., 1933. Entered m.p. ind. as mgr. for Rome Theatres, Baltimore, Md., 1934; booker, ass't buyer, 1936; ass't to gen. mgr. 1939; U.S. Navy 1944–46; v.p., gen. mgr., Rome Theatres, 1946; Allied MPTO of Md. 1952–55; nat'l dir. Allied States, 1952–55; nat'l secy. 1954; Pres. NATO of Maryland 1969–80; Pres. USO Council, Greater Baltimore 1969–75; Chairman, board of trustees, Employees Benefit Trust for Health & Welfare Council of Central Maryland, 1970–79.

BACON, KEVIN: Actor. b. Philadelphia, PA, July 8, 1958. m. actress Kyra Sedgwick. Studied at Manning St. Actor's Theatre. Apprentice at Circle-in-the-Square in N.Y. Bdwy. debut in Slab Boys with Sean Penn. Narrated short film A Little Vicious.
   THEATER: Bdwy: Slab Boys. Off-Bdwy: Getting Out (debut), Album, Forty Deuce (Obie award), Poor Little Lambs, Flux, Men Without Dates, The Author's Voice, Loot, Road, Spike Heels.
   PICTURES: National Lampoon's Animal House (debut, 1978), Starting Over, Hero at Large, Friday the 13th, Only When I Laugh, Forty Deuce, Diner, Footloose, Enormous Changes at the Last Minute, Quicksilver, White Water Summer, End of the Line, Planes Trains and Automobiles, She's Having a Baby, Criminal Law, The Big Picture, Tremors, Flatliners, Queens Logic, He Said/She Said, Pyrates, JFK, A Few Good Men, The Air Up There.
   TELEVISION: Movies: The Gift, The Demon Murder Case, The Tender Age (The Little Sister), Lemon Sky. Series: Search for Tomorrow, The Guiding Light. Special: Mr. Roberts.

BADHAM, JOHN: Director. b. Luton, Eng., Aug. 25, 1939, raised in Alabama. e. Yale U., B.A.; Yale Drama School, M.F.A. Brother of actress Mary Badham. Landed first job at Universal Studio mailroom; later was Universal tour guide, a casting dir. and assoc. prod. to William Sackheim. Made trailers and TV episodes. Twice nominated for Emmy Awards for TV movies.
   PICTURES: The Bingo Long Travelling All-Stars and Motor Kings (debut 1976), Saturday Night Fever, Dracula, Whose Life Is It Anyway?, Blue Thunder, War Games, American Flyers, Short Circuit, Stakeout (also exec. prod.), Disorganized Crime (exec. prod. only), Bird on a Wire, The Hard Way, Point of No Return, Another Stakeout (also exec. prod.).
   TELEVISION: Movies: Night Gallery (assoc. prod. only), Neon Ceiling (assoc. prod. only), The Impatient Heart, Isn't It Shocking?, The Law, The Gun, Reflections of Murder, The Godchild, The Keegans, Relentless: Mind of a Killer (co-exec. prod.only). Series: The Senator (also assoc. prod.).

BAILEY, JOHN: Cinematographer. b. Moberly, MO, August 10, 1942. m. film editor Carol Littleton. e. U. of Santa Clara, Loyola U., U.S.C., U. of Vienna. Lecturer, American Film Institute, 1982 and 84.

PICTURES: Premonition, End of August, Legacy, The Mafu Cage (visual consult.), Boulevard Nights, Winter Kills (add. photog.), American Gigolo, Ordinary People, Honky Tonk Freeway, Continental Divide, Cat People, That Championship Season, Without a Trace, The Big Chill, Racing With the Moon, The Pope of Greenwich Village, Mishima, Silverado, Crossroads, Brighton Beach Memoirs, Light of Day, Swimming to Cambodia, Vibes, The Accidental Tourist, My Blue Heaven, The Search for Signs of Intelligent Life in the Universe (also dir.), A Brief History of Time, Groundhog Day, In the Line of Fire, China Moon (dir.).
TELEVISION: Battered, City in Fear.

BAILEY, ROBIN: Actor. b. Hucknail (Nottingham), Eng., Oct. 5, 1919. e. Henry Mellish School, Nottingham.
STAGE: Barrets of Wimpole Street, Theatre Royal, Nottingham, 1938.
PICTURES: School for Secrets (1946), Private Angelo, Portrait of Clare, His Excellency, Gift Horse, Folly to Be Wise, Single Handed, Sailor of the King, The Young Lovers, For Better, For Worse, Catch Us If You Can, The Whisperers, Spy with a Cold Nose, You Only Live Twice, The Eliminator, Blind Terror, Down by the Riverside, Nightmare Rally, The Four Feathers, Jane and the Lost City.
TELEVISION: Olive Latimer's Husband, Seven Deadly Sins, The Power Game, Public Eye, Person to Person, Troubleshooters, Armchair Theatre, Split Level, The Newcomers, Discharge of Trooper Lusby, Brett, Owen M.D., Solidarity, General Hospital, Murder Must Advertise, Vienna 1900, Justice, The Pallisers, The Couch, Way of the World, Upstairs, Downstairs, Walk with Destiny, North and South, A Legacy, The Velvet Glove, Crown Court, Took and Co., The Good Companions, Cupid's Darts, Sorry, I'm a Stranger Here Myself, Call My Bluff, Jane, Potter, Tales from a Long Room, Sharing Time, Bleak House, Charters and Caldicott, Looks Familiar, On Stage, Rumpole of the Bailey, I Didn't Know You Cared, Number 27, Tinniswood's North Country, Tales From Hollywood.

BAIO, SCOTT: Actor. b. New York, NY, Sept. 22, 1961. Started career at 9 doing commercials and voice-overs.
PICTURES: Bugsy Malone, Skatetown USA, Foxes, Zapped!, I Love New York.
TELEVISION: Series: Blansky's Beauties, Who's Watching the Kids?, Happy Days, Joanie Loves Chachi, Charles in Charge, Baby Talk. Specials: Luke Was There, Muggsy, Stoned, How to Be a Man, Gemini, The Truth About Alex. Guest: Hotel, The Fall Guy, Full House. Movies: The Boy Who Drank Too Much, Senior Trip, Alice in Wonderland.

BAKER, BLANCHE: Actress. r.n. Blanche Garfein. b. New York, NY, Dec. 20, 1956. Daughter of actress Carroll Baker and dir. Jack Garfein. e. Wellesley, Coll., studied acting with Uta Hagen. Acting debut, White Marriage, Yale Repertory Co. (1978), Regional Theater. Bwdy. debut in Lolita (1981).
PICTURES: The Seduction of Joe Tynan (debut, 1979), French Postcards, Sixteen Candles, Raw Deal, Cold Feet, The Handmaid's Tale, Livin' Large, Bum Rap.
TELEVISION: Mini-Series: Holocaust (Emmy Award, supp. actress, 1978). Movies: Mary and Joseph, The Day the Bubble Burst, The Awakening of Candra, Nobody's Child. Special: Romeo & Juliet.

BAKER, CARROLL: Actress. b. Johnstown, PA, May 28, 1931. e. schools there and St. Petersburg (FL) Junior Coll. Career started as dancer in nightclubs. Actors' Studio N.Y. Stage debut: Escapade. Then, All Summer Long. Autobiography: Baby Doll.
PICTURES: Easy to Love (debut, 1953), Giant, Baby Doll, The Big Country, But Not for Me, The Miracle, Bridge to the Sun, Something Wild, How the West Was Won, The Carpetbaggers, Station Six Sahara, Cheyenne Autumn, The Greatest Story Ever Told, Sylvia, Mister Moses, Harlow, Jack of Diamonds, The Sweet Body of Deborah, Paranoia, A Quiet Place to Kill, Captain Apache, The Harem, Honeymoon, My Father's Wife, Andy Warhol's Bad, The World is Full of Married Men, Watcher in the Woods, Star 80, The Secret Diary of Sigmund Freud, Native Son, Ironweed, Red Monarch, Kindergarten Cop, Blonde Fist, Cybereden.
TELEVISION: Specials: Rain, On Fire, Sharing Time, Coward's: What Mad Pursuit. Guest: Tales from the Crypt. Movies: Hitler's SS: Portrait in Evil, On Fire, Judgment Day: The John List Story, Men Don't Tell.

BAKER, DIANE: Actress. b. Hollywood, CA, Feb. 25, 1938. e. USC.
PICTURES: The Diary of Anne Frank (debut, 1959), The Best of Everything, Journey to the Center of the Earth, Tess of the Storm Country, The Wizard of Baghdad, Hemingway's Adventures of a Young Man, 300 Spartans, Nine Hours to Rama, Stolen Hours, The Prize, Straight Jacket, Marnie, Mirage, Sands of Beersheba, The Horse in the Grey Flannel Suit, Krakatoa—East of Java, Baker's Hawk, The Pilot, The Silence of the Lambs, The Closer.
TELEVISION: Series: Here We Go Again. Movies: Dangerous Days of Kiowa Jones, Trial Run, The D.A.: Murder

One, The Old Man Who Cried Wolf, Do You Take This Stranger?, Sarge: The Badge or the Cross, Congratulations It's a Boy!, A Little Game, Killer By Night, Police Story (pilot), A Tree Grows in Brooklyn, The Dream Makers, The Last Survivors, Fugitive Family, The Haunted, Perry Mason: The Case of the Heartbroken Bride. Mini-Series: The Blue and the Gray.

BAKER, GEORGE: Actor, Writer. b. Varna, Bulgaria, April 1, 1931. e. Lancing College, Sussex. Stage debut Deal Repertory Theatre, 1946. Film debut The Intruder, 1953.
PICTURES: Dam Busters, Ship That Died of Shame, Woman for Joe, Extra Day, Feminine Touch, A Hill in Korea, No Time for Tears, These Dangerous Years, Tread Softly Stranger, Lancelot and Guinevere, Curse of the Fly, Mister Ten Per Cent, Goodbye Mr. Chips, Justine, The Executioners, On Her Majesty's Secret Service, A Warm December, The Fire Fighters, The Spy Who Loved Me, Thirty-nine Steps, A Nightingale Sang in Berkeley Square, Hopscotch, North Sea Hijack (ffolkes), For Queen and Country.
TELEVISION: Fan Show, Ron Raudell's programme 1956, Guinea Pig, Death of a Salesman, The Last Troubadour, The Square Ring, Nick of the River, Mary Stuart, Probation Officers, Far Away Music, It Happened Like This, Boule de Suif, Maigret, Zero One, Rupert Henzau, Miss Memory, Any Other Business, The Navigators, Common Ground, Alice, The Queen and Jackson, The Big Man Coughed and Died, Up and Down, Call My Bluff, The Baron, St. Patrick, Love Life, Seven Deadly Virtues, The Prisoner, The Sex Games, Z Cars, Paul Temple, Candida, Fenn Street, Man Outside, The Persuaders, Main Chance, Ministry of Fear, Bowler, Voyage in the Dark, Dial M for Murder, Zodiac, The Survivors, I, Claudius, Print Out, Goodbye, Darling, Chinese Detective, Triangle, Minder, Hart to Hart, Goodbye Mr. Chips, Woman of Substance, The Bird Fancier, Robin of Sherwood, Time after Time, If Tomorrow Comes, Coast to Coast, Dead Head, The Canterville Ghost, Room at the Bottom, Ruth Rendell Mysteries (From Doon With Death; adap.), Journey's End, No Job for a Lady.
WRITER: The Fatal Spring, Imaginary Friends, Going for Broke, The Marches of Wales, The Hopkins, Just a Hunch, Sister, Dear Sister, From Doom With Death, Mouse in the Corner, The Strawberry Tree, Talking About Mira Beau.

BAKER, JOE DON: Actor. b. Groesbeck, TX, Feb. 12, 1936. e. North Texas State Coll., B.B.A., 1958. Began career on N.Y. stage, in Marathon 33 and Blues for Mr. Charlie. L.A. stage in The Caine Mutiny Court Martial.
PICTURES: Cool Hand Luke (debut, 1967), Guns of the Magnificent Seven, Adam at Six A.M., Wild Rovers, Welcome Home Soldier Boys, Junior Bonner, Walking Tall, Charley Varrick, The Outfit, Golden Needles, Mitchell, Framed, Checkered Flag or Crash, Speedtrap, The Pack, Wacko, Joysticks, The Natural, Fletch, Getting Even (Hostage Dallas), The Living Daylights, The Killing Time, Leonard Part 6, Criminal Law, The Children, Cape Fear, The Distinguished Gentleman, Reality Bites.
TELEVISION: Movies: Mongo's Back in Town, That Certain Summer, To Kill a Cop, Power, The Abduction of Kari Swenson, Edge of Darkness (BBC mini-series), Defrosting the Fridge (BBC), Citizen Cohn, Complex of Fear. Series: Eischeid. Guest: In the Heat of the Night.

BAKER, KATHY: Actress. B. Midland, TX, June 8, 1950. Raised in Albuquerque, NM. e. UC/Berkeley. Stage debut in San Francisco premiere of Fool for Love, won Obie and Theatre World Awards for New York debut in same. Also appeared in Desire Under the Elms, Aunt Dan and Lemon.
PICTURES: The Right Stuff (debut, 1983), Street Smart (Natl. Society of Film Critics Award, supp. actress, 1987), Permanent Record, A Killing Affair, Clean and Sober, Jacknife, Dad, Mr. Frost, Edward Scissorhands, Article 99, Jennifer Eight, Mad Dog and Glory.
TELEVISION: Series: Picket Fences. Movies: Nobody's Child, The Image, One Special Victory. Guest: Amazing Stories.

BAKER, RICK: Makeup Artist, Performer. b. Binghamton, NY, Dec. 8, 1950. Started as assist. to makeup artist Dick Smith before creating his own designs in 1972. Frequent film appearances in makeup, usually as gorillas. Worked on Michael Jackson's video Thriller.
PICTURES: Actor: The Thing With Two Heads, King Kong, The Kentucky Fried Movie, Madhouse, The Incredible Shrinking Woman, Into the Night. Makeup Design: Zebra Force, The Incredible Melting Man, Star Wars (2nd unit), It Lives Again, The Howling (consultant), Funhouse, An American Werewolf in London (Acad. Award, 1981), Videodrome, Greystoke: The Legend of Tarzan Lord of the Apes (also costume design), Ratboy, Harry and the Hendersons (Acad. Award, 1987), It's Alive III: Island of the Alive, Coming to America, Gorillas in the Mist (also assoc. prod.), Missing Link. Other: Tanya's Island (beast design), The Double McGuffin (story), Starman (transformation scenes), Cocoon (consultant), My Science Project (Tyrannosaurus Rex se-

quences consultant), Max My Love (chimpanzee consultant), Gremlins 2: The New Batch (co-prod., f/x supervisor).
TELEVISION: Makeup Design: *Series*: Werewolf, Beauty and the Beast. *Movies*: The Autobiography of Miss Jane Pittman (Emmy Award), An American Christmas Carol, Something Is Out There.

BAKER, ROBERT H.: Television programmer. b. Springfield, OH, Oct. 14, 1943. e. Kent State U.A., 1965 (broadcasting); Michigan State U. M.A. 1966 (TV/radio management). Disc jockey, newsman, anchor at various Ohio and Mich. AM and FM stations 1960–66. Storer Broadcasting Co.: local-regional acct. exec WSPD-TV, 1966–69; Storer TV Sales, national rep, 1969–72; WSPD-TV national sales mgr. 1972–74 and gen. sales mgr 1974–75. Owner-gen. mgr. WBIS-AM (Bristol, CT), 1975–76. Sales mgr KDKA-TV Pittsburgh 1976–79; Television Bureau of Advertising markting sales exec 1979–81; v.p. local sales 1981–86; exec. v.p. operations 1986–88. Mgr. Planning & development for Nashville Network, 1989–1991. Dir. of Operations, Country Music TV 1991–present. Mem.: National Speakers Assn. (and TN chap.) 1988–present.

BAKER, ROBERT S.: Producer. b. London, 1916. Entered industry 1937 as assistant director. 1939–46: Army Film Unit. Produced 50 films including Crossplot, Sea of Sand.
TELEVISION: Produced: The Saint (1962–69), Gideon's Way. Directed: The Treasure of Monte Cristo, Hellfire Club, The Siege of Sidney Street, Jack the Ripper. Producer: The Persuaders, 1976–78: Return of the Saint. Devised: Return to Treasure Island. Exec. prod.: The Saint in Manhattan.

BAKER, ROY: Producer, Director. b. London. e. Lycée Corneille, Rouen; City of London School. Ass't dir. with Gainsborough 1934–40; served in Army 1940–46.
PICTURES: Operation Disaster, Don't Bother to Knock, Inferno, One That Got Away, A Night to Remember, The Singer Not the Song, Flame in the Streets, Quartermass and the Pit, The Anniversary, Vampire Lovers, Dr. Jekyll and Mr. Hyde, Asylum (Paris Grand Prize), Seven Golden Vampires.
TELEVISION: The Human Jungle, The Saint, Gideon's Way, The Baron, The Avengers, The Champions, Department S., The Persuaders, Danger UXB, Minder.

BAKER, DR. WILLIAM F.: Television. b. 1944. e. Case Western Reserve U., B.A., M.A., Ph.D. Began broadcasting career in Cleveland while still a student. Joined Scripps-Howard Broadcasting, 1971. Joined Group W as v.p. and general mgr., WJZ-TV, 1978; served as pres. and CEO, Group W Productions; pres. of Group W. Television, 1979; chmn., Group W Satellite Communications, 1981; 1983, carried Explorers Club flag to top of world, becoming one of few in history to visit both North and South Poles; April 1987, appointed pres. and CEO, WNET/Thirteen, N.Y. PBS station.

BAKSHI, RALPH: Animator, Writer, Director. b. Haifa, Palestine, Oct. 29, 1938. Began career at Terrytoons at age 18 as cell painter and animator, then creative dir. 1966, headed Paramount Cartoons. Pres., Bakshi Prods.
PICTURES: *Director*: Fritz the Cat (also s.p.), Heavy Traffic (also s.p.), Coonskin (also s.p.), Wizards (also s.p., prod.), The Lord of the Rings, American Pop (also co-prod.), Hey Good Lookin' (also s.p., prod.), Fire and Ice (also co-prod.), Cool World.
TELEVISION: Mighty Mouse: The New Adventures (creator), This Ain't Bebop (Amer. Playhouse, dir., s.p.).

BAKULA, SCOTT: Actor. b. St. Louis, MO, Oct. 9. e. Kansas Univ.
TELEVISION: *Series*: Gung Ho, Eisenhower & Lutz, Quantum Leap (Emmy Noms., Golden Globe Award). *Movies*: The Last Fling, An Eye for an Eye, In the Shadow of a Killer.
PICTURES: Sibling Rivalry, Necessary Roughness, Color of Night.
THEATRE: *NY*: Marilyn: An American Fable, Three Guys Naked from the Waist Down, Romance/Romance (Tony Award nom.). *L.A.*: Nite Club Confidential.

BALABAN, BOB: Actor. b. Chicago, IL, Aug. 16, 1945. Began working with Second City troupe while still in high school. Attended Colgate U. and NYU while appearing on Broadway in Plaza Suite.
PICTURES: Midnight Cowboy, Me Natalie, The Strawberry Statement, Catch-22, Making It, Bank Shot, Report to the Commissioner, Close Encounters of the Third Kind, Girlfriends, Altered States, Prince of the City, Absence of Malice, Whose Life Is It Anyway?, 2010, In Our Hands (doc.), End of the Line, Parents (dir. debut), Dead-Bang, Alice, Little Man Tate, Bob Roberts, My Boyfriend's Back (dir. only), Greedy.
STAGE: You're a Good Man Charlie Brown, The Inspector General, Who Wants to Be the Lone Ranger?, The Basic Training of Pavlo Hummel, The Children, The White House Murder Case, Some of My Best Friends, The Three Sisters, The Boys Next Door, Speed-the-Plow, Some Americans Abroad.
TELEVISION: *Movies*: Marriage: Year One, The Face of Fear. *Director*: Tales From the Darkside, Amazing Stories, Penn & Teller's Invisible Thread.

BALDWIN, ADAM: Actor. b. Chicago, IL, Feb. 27, 1962. While in high school in Winnetka, was chosen by director Tony Bill for role in My Bodyguard.
PICTURES: My Bodyguard (debut, 1980), Ordinary People, D.C. Cab, Reckless, Bad Guys, 3:15, Full Metal Jacket, The Chocolate War, Cohen and Tate, Next of Kin, Predator 2, Guilty By Suspicion, Radio Flyer, Where the Day Takes You, Deadbolt, Bitter Harvest, Eight Hundred Leagues Down the Amazon, Cold Sweat.
THEATRE: Album (Chicago).
TELEVISION: *Movies*: Off Sides, Poison Ivy, Welcome Home Bobby, Murder in High Places, Cruel Doubt.

BALDWIN, ALEC: Actor. b. Massapequa, NY, April 3, 1958. m. actress Kim Basinger. e. George Washington U., NYU. Brother of actors Stephen, William and Daniel Baldwin. Trained at Lee Strasberg Theatre Inst. and with Mira Rostova, Elaine Aiken. Started career in daytime TV on The Doctors.
THEATER: A Midsummer Night's Dream, The Wager, Summertree, A Life in the Theatre (Hartman), Study in Scarlet (Williamstown), Loot (Theatre World Award, 1986), Serious Money, Prelude to a Kiss, A Streetcar Named Desire.
PICTURES: Forever Lulu (debut, 1987), She's Having a Baby, Beetlejuice, Married to the Mob, Working Girl, Talk Radio, Great Balls of Fire!, The Hunt for Red October, Miami Blues, Alice, The Marrying Man, Prelude to a Kiss, Glengarry Glen Ross, Malice, The Getaway.
TELEVISION: *Series*: The Doctors (1980–2), Cutter to Houston, Knots Landing. *Movies*: Sweet Revenge, Love on the Run, Dress Gray, The Alamo: 13 Days to Glory. *Guest*: Hotel, Saturday Night Live.

BALDWIN, WILLIAM: Actor. b. Massapequa, NY, 1963. e. SUNY/Binghamton. Studied political science, working for a period in Washington on staff of rep. Thomas J. Downey. Brother of actors Alec, Stephen and Daniel Baldwin.
PICTURES: Born on the Fourth of July (debut, 1989), Internal Affairs, Flatliners, Backdraft, Three of Hearts, Sliver.
TELEVISION: *Movie*: The Preppie Murder.

BALE, CHRISTIAN: Actor. b. Pembrokeshire, Wales, Jan. 30, 1974. Acting debut at age 9 in U.S. Pac-man commercial. London stage debut following year in The Nerd.
PICTURES: Empire of the Sun, Land of Faraway, Henry V, Newsies, Swing Kids.
TELEVISION: *Specials/Movies*: Heart of the Country (BBC), Anastasia: The Mystery of Anna (U.S.), Treasure Island (released theatrically in U.K.), A Murder of Quality.

BALLARD, CARROLL: Director. b. Los Angeles, Oct. 14, 1937. e. UCLA.
PICTURES: The Black Stallion, Never Cry Wolf, The Nutcracker, Wind.

BALLARD, KAYE: Actress. b. Cleveland, OH, Nov. 20, 1926. r.n. Catherine Gloria Balotta. Began career as impressionist-singer-actress, toured vaudeville. 17 recordings incl. The Fanny Brice Story, Peanuts, Oklahoma (w/ Nelson Eddy).
TELEVISION: *Series*: Henry Morgan's Great Talent Hunt, The Perry Como Show, The Mothers-in-Law, The Doris Day Show, The Steve Allen Comedy Hour, What a Dummy. *Movies*: The Dream Merchants, Alice in Wonderland. Guest appearances incl. over 100 spots on The Tonight Show.
PICTURES: The Girl Most Likely, A House is Not a Home, Which Way to the Front?, The Ritz, Freaky Friday, Falling in Love Again, Pandemonium, Tiger Warsaw, Modern Love, Eternity.
THEATRE: Three to Make Ready, Carnival, Molly, The Pirates of Penzance, Hey Ma It's Me, Working 42nd Street at Last, Chicago, Touch & Go (London), Nymph Errant (concert version), Hello Dolly, She Stoops to Conquer, Funny Girl, High Spirits.

BALLHAUS, MICHAEL: Cinematographer. b. Berlin, Germany, August 5, 1935.
PICTURES: Deine Zartlichkeiten, Two of Us, Whity, Beware of a Holy Whore, Tschetan, The Indian Boy, The Bitter Tears of Petra von Kant, Fox and his Friends, Mother Kusters Goes to Heaven, Summer Guests, Satan's Brew, I Only Want You To Love Me, Adolf and Marlene, Chinese Roulette, Bolweiser (The Stationmaster's Wife), Willie and the Chinese Cat, Women in New York, Despair, The Marriage of Maria Braun, Germany in Autumn, German Spring, The Uprising, Big and Little, Malou, Looping, Baby It's You Friends and Husbands, Dear Mr. Wonderful, Magic Mountain, Edith's Diary, Aus der Familie der Panzereschen, The Autograph, Heartbreakers, Old Enough, Reckless, After Hours, Under the Cherry Moon, The Color of Money, The Glass Menagerie, Broadcast News, The House on Carroll Street, The Last Temptation of Christ, Working Girl, Dirty Rotten Scoundrels, The Fabulous Baker Boys, GoodFellas, Postcards from the Edge, Guilty by Suspicion, What About Bob?, The Mambo Kings, Bram Stoker's Dracula, The Age of Innocence, Quiz Show.

BALSAM, MARTIN: Actor. b. New York, NY, Nov. 4, 1919. e. New School for Social Research. Daughter is actress Talia Bal-

sam. NY stage debut Ghost for Sale, 1941.
THEATER: Lamp at Midnight, The Wanhope Building, High Tor, A Sound of Hunting, Macbeth, Sundown Beach, The Closing Door, You Know I Can't Hear You When the Water's Running (Tony Award, 1968), Cold Storage (Obie Award).
PICTURES: On the Waterfront (debut, 1954), Twelve Angry Men, Time Limit, Marjorie Morningstar, Al Capone, Middle of the Night, Psycho, Ada, Breakfast at Tiffany's, Cape Fear, The Conquered City, Who's Been Sleeping in My Bed?, The Carpetbaggers, Youngblood Hawke, Seven Days in May, Harlow, The Bedford Incident, A Thousand Clowns (Acad. Award, actor, 1965), After the Fox, Hombre, Me Natalie, The Good Guys and the Bad Guys, Trilogy, Catch 22, Tora Tora Tora, Little Big Man, The Anderson Tapes, Confessions of a Police Captain, The Man, The Stone Killer, Summer Wishes Winter Dreams, The Taking of Pelham One Two Three, Murder on the Orient Express, Mitchell, All The President's Men, Two-Minute Warning, The Sentinel, Silver Bears, Cuba, There Goes the Bride, The Salamander, The Goodbye People, Innocent Prey, St. Elmo's Fire, Death Wish III, The Delta Force, Private Investigations, Two Evil Eyes (The Black Cat), Cape Fear (1991).
TELEVISION: Series: Archie Bunker's Place. Guest: Actors Studio Theatre, US Steel Hour, Mr. Peepers, Alfred Hitchcock Presents, arrest and Trial. Movies: Hunters Are For Killing, The Old Man Who Cried Wolf, Night of Terror, A Brand New Life, Six Million Dollar Man, Trapped Beneath the Sea, Miles to Go Before I Sleep, Death Among Friends, The Lindbergh Kidnapping Case, Raid on Entebbe, Contract on Cherry Street, The Storyteller, Siege, Rainbow, The Millionaire, The Seeding of Sarah Burns, House on Garibaldi Street, Aunt Mary, Love Tapes, People vs. Jean Harris, Little Gloria, Happy at Last, I Want to Live, Murder in Space, Kids Like These. Mini-Series: Space, Queenie. Specials: Cold Storage, Grown Ups.

BANCROFT, ANNE: Actress. r.n. Anna Maria Italiano. b. New York, NY, Sept. 17, 1931. m. director-comedian Mel Brooks. e. American Acad. of Dramatic Arts. Acting debut on TV, Studio One as Anne Marno in Torrents of Spring; many TV shows.
THEATER: Two For the Seasaw (Tony Award, Theatre World Award: 1958), The Miracle Worker (Tony Award, 1960), Mother Courage, The Devils, A Cry of Players, Golda, Duet For One, Mystery of the Rose Bouquet.
PICTURES: Don't Bother to Knock (debut, 1952), Tonight We Sing, Treasure of the Golden Condor, Kid from Left Field, Gorilla at Large, Demetrius and the Gladiators, The Raid, New York Confidential, Life in the Balance, The Naked Street, The Last Frontier, Walk the Proud Land, Nightfall, The Restless Breed, The Girl in Black Stockings, The Miracle Worker (Academy Award, 1962), The Pumpkin Eater, The Slender Thread, Seven Women, The Graduate, Young Winston, The Prisoner of Second Avenue, The Hindenburg, Lipstick, Silent Movie, The Turning Point, Fatso (also dir., s.p.), The Elephant Man, To Be or Not to Be, Garbo Talks, Agnes of God, 'night Mother, 84 Charing Cross Road, Torch Song Trilogy, Bert Rigby You're a Fool, Honeymoon in Vegas, Love Potion No. 9, Point of No Return, Mr. Jones, Malice.
TELEVISION: Mini-series: Jesus of Nazareth, Marco Polo, Specials: I'm Getting Married, Annie and the Hoods, Annie: The Women in the Life of a Man (also dir.; Emmy Award for Best Variety Special, 1970), Mrs. Cage. Movie: Broadway Bound.

BAND, ALBERT: Producer, Director. b. Paris, France, May 7, 1924. e. Lyceum Louis le Grand, won French-English Literature Prize 1938; entered film industry as cutter Pathe Lab.; prod. ass't to John Huston at MGM; first screen credit adaptation Red Badge of Courage novel; first direction, The Young Guns; formed Maxim Productions, Inc., Sept. 1956; prod. Recently formed Albert Band Intl. Prods., Inc.
PICTURES: The Young Guns, I Bury the Living, Face of Fire, The Avenger, Grand Canyon Massacre, The Tramplers, The Hellbenders (prod. only), A Minute to Pray a Second to Die, Little Cigars, Dracula's Dog, She Came to the Valley, Metalstorm: The Destruction of Jared-Syn, Swordkill, Buy and Cell (exec. prod. only), Troll, Terrorvision, Ghoulies II, Robotjox.

BAND, CHARLES: Producer-Director. b. Los Angeles, CA, 1951. e. Overseas Sch. of Rome. Son of Albert Band. Formed Media Home Ent., 1978; formed Empire Ent., 1983; formed Full Moon Ent., 1988.
PICTURES: Prod.: Mansion of the Doomed, Cinderella, End of the World, Laserblast, Fairytales, Swordkill, Dungeonmaster, Eliminators. Dir.-Prod.: Crash, Parasite, Metalstorm, Trancers, Pulsepounders, Meridian (Kiss of the Beast), Crash & Burn, Trancers II, Dr. Mordrid. Exec. Prod.: Tourist Trap, Day Time Ended, Ghoulies, Re-Animator, Zone Troopers, Troll, Terrorvision, Crawlspace, Dolls, From Beyond, The Caller, Spellcaster, Cellar Dweller, Ghoulies II, Enemy Territory, Deadly Weapon, Robot Jox, Prison, Buy & Cell, Ghost Town, Catacombs, Arena, Puppet Master, Shadowzone, Puppet Master II, The Pit and the Pendulum, Suspecies,

Puppet Master III, Arcade, Dollman, Netherworld, Bad Channels, Trancers III.

BANDERAS, ANTONIO: Actor. b. Malaga, Spain, 1960. e. School of Dramatic Art, Malaga. Moved to Madrid in 1981 where he made his stage debut in Los Tarantos. Other theatre incl. The City and the Dogs, Daughter of the Air, The Tragedy of Edward II of England.
PICTURES: Labyrinth of Passion (debut, 1982), Pestanas Positzas, El Senor Galindez, El Caso Almeria, The Stilts, Casa Cerrado, La Corte de Faraon, Requiem por un Campesino Espanol, 27 Hours, Matador, Asi Como Habian Sido, Law of Desire, The Pleasure of Killing, Baton Rouge, Women on the Verge of a Nervous Breakdown, Si Te Dicen Que Cai, Tie Me Up Tie Me Down, Contra el Viento, The Mambo Kings, Going South Shopping, A Man Named Benito, Philadelphia, House of the Spirits.
TELEVISION: The Happy Woman.

BANDY, MARY LEA: Director, Dept. of Film, Museum of Modern Art. b. Evanston, IL, June 16, 1943. e. Stanford U., B.A., 1965. Asst. editor, Harry Abrams and Museum of Modern Art. Administrator (1978–80) and since 1980 director, Dept. of Film, Museum of Modern Art. Editor of MOMA film publications incl.: Rediscovering French Film (1983). Member: Advisory Board, AFI's National Center for Preservation of Film and Video; Film Advisory Comm., American Federation of Arts; Advisory Comm. on Film, Japan Society; Advisory Comm. NY State Motion Picture and Television Advisory Board. Co-president, National Alliance of Media Arts Center, 1986–87, 1987–88. Bd. mem.: Intl. Film Seminars, Collective For Living Cinema, MacDowell Colony.

BANJERJEE, VICTOR: Actor. b. Calcutta, India, Oct. 15, 1946. Was instrumental in forming the first Screen Extras Union in India, presently founding secretary. Won international recognition for A Passage to India (1985). Stage: Pirates of Penzance (at 5), An August Requiem (director, 1981), Desert Song, Godspell.
PICTURES: The Chess Players (debut). In India: Hullabaloo, Madhurban, Tanaya, Pratidan, Prarthana, Dui Prithri, Kalyug, Arohan, Jaipur Junction (German), A Passage to India, Foreign Body, The Home and the World, Hard to Be a God, Bitter Moon, World Within World Without.
TELEVISION: Dadah Is Death, Foreign Body.

BANNEN, IAN: b. Actor. b. Airdrie, Scotland, June 29, 1928. Early career Shakespeare Memorial Theatre (now RSC), Stratford-on-Avon. Film debut Battle Hell (1956).
STAGE: A View From the Bridge, The Iceman Cometh, Long Days Journey Into Night, Sergeant Musgrave's Dance. Royal Shakespeare Thea. Co. 1961–62: Toys in the Attic, Hamlet, As You Like It (with Vanessa Redgrave), Romeo and Juliet, Othello, The Blood Knot, Devil's Disciple, The Iceman Cometh, Hedda Gabler, Translations (Drama Critics Award, 1981); Riverside Mermaid Theatres, 1983; Moon for the Misbegotten (London, Boston, Broadway); All My Sons.
PICTURES: Private's Progress, Miracle in Soho, The Third Key, Behind the Mask, A Tale of Two Cities, The French Mistress, Carlton-Browne of the F.O., Man in Cocked Hat, Macbeth, The Risk, Station Six Sahara, Psyche 59, Rotten to the Core, Mister Moses, The Hill, Flight of the Phoenix (Acad. Award nom.), Penelope, Sailor From Gibraltar, Lock Up Your Daughters!, Too Late the Hero, The Deserter, Fright, Doomwatch, The Offence (BAFTA nom.), The Macintosh Man, The Driver's Seat, The Voyage, Bite the Bullet, From Beyond the Grave, Watcher in the Woods, Eye of the Needle, Night Crossing, Gandhi, Gorky Park, Defense of the Realm, Lamb, Hope and Glory (BAFTA nom.), The Courier, Ghost Dad, Crossing the Line (The Big Man), George's Island, Damage, A Pin for the Butterfly.
TELEVISION: Johnny Belinda, Jane Eyre, Jesus of Nazareth, Tinker, Tailor, Soldier, Spy, Fifteen Streets, Murder in Eden, Ashenden, Uncle Vanya, The Sound and the Silence, The Treaty, Doctor Finlay.

BANNER, BOB: Producer, Director. b. Ennis, TX, Aug. 15, 1921. e. Southern Methodist U., B.A., 1939–43; Northwestern U., M.A., 1946–48. U.S. Naval Reserve 1943–46; faculty, Northwestern U., 1948–50; staff dir., NBC-TV in Chicago, 1949–50; dir., Garroway at Large, 1949–50; prod. & dir., Fred Waring Show, 1950–53; dir. Omnibus. Metropolitan Opera Prod., 1953; Nothing But the Best (prod. dir.), 1953; Omnibus, 1953–54; Dave Garroway Show, 1953–54; (prod. dir); Dinah Shore Show, 1954–57; exec. prod. Garry Moore Show; exec. prod., Carol & Co., 1963; Jimmy Dean Show, 1963–66; Calamity Jane, Once Upon A Mattress, 1964; The Entertainers, 1965; Carol × 2, 1966; Kraft Summer Music Hall, 1966, Carol & Co., Ice Follies, Carol Burnett Show, Peggy Fleming at Madison Square Garden, 1967; John Davidson at Notre Dame, Here's Peggy Fleming; Peggy Fleming at Sun Valley, The American West of John Ford; Love! Love! Love!— Hallmark Hall of Fame; To Europe with Love. Pres., Bob Banner Assocs. Visiting Prof.: Southern Methodist U.

TELEVISION: *Movies*: Warning Shot, Mongo's Back in Town, The Last Survivors, Journey From Darkness, My Sweet Charlie, Bud and Lou, Yes Virginia There is a Santa Claus, Crash Landing, With Murder in Mind, The Sea Wolf. *Specials*: Peggy Fleming Visits the Soviet Union. Perry Como's Lake Tahoe Holiday, Perry Como's Christmas In Mexico, Perry Como's Hawaiian Holiday, Perry Como's Spring In New Orleans. Daily Variety Series: Don Ho Show; Perry Como Las Vegas Style, Perry Como's Christmas in Austria, Jr. Almost Anything Goes, All-Star Anything Goes, Peggy Fleming and Holiday on Ice at Madison Square Garden; Julie Andrews, One Step Into Spring; Leapin' Lizards, It's Liberace; Perry Como's Easter By The Sea, Ford Motor Company's 75th Anniversary; Gift of Music; Specials starring Bob Hope, Julie Andrews, Andy Williams; Los Angeles Music Center 25th Anniversary. Series: Almost Anything Goes, Solid Gold; Star Search; It's Showtime at the Apollo, Uptown Comedy Club.

BAR, JACQUES JEAN LOUIS: Executive. Producer, Exhibitor. b. Chateauroux, France, Sept. 12, 1921. e. Lycées Lakanal and Saint Louis, France. Formed Cité-Films S.A., 1947; CIPRA in assoc. with MGM, 1961; S.C.B., Bourges, 8 cinemas; S.C.M., Le Mans, 9 cinemas. Hollywood films: Bridge to the Sun, Once A Thief, Guns for San Sebastian. Prod. 57 films in France, Spain, Italy, Switzerland, Japan and Brazil 1948–89.
PICTURES: Where the Hot Wind Blows, Bridge to the Sun, Riffifi in Tokyo, A Very Private Affair, Swordsmen of Siena, Monkey in Winter, The Turfist, Any Number Can Win, The Day and the Hour, Joy House, Guns for San Sebastian, Last Known Address, The Homecoming, Dancing Machine, The Candidate, Once a Thief.

BARBEAU, ADRIENNE: Actress. b. Sacramento, CA, June 11, 1947. e. Foothill Col.
TELEVISION: *Series*: Maude. *Movies*: The Great Houdinis, Having Babies, Red Alert, Return to Fantasy Island, Crash, Someone's Watching Me!, The Darker Side of Terror, The Top of the Hill, Valentine Magic on Love Island, Tourist, Charlie and the Great Balloon Chase, Seduced, Bridge Across Time, Blood River, Double Crossed, The Burden of Proof, The Parsley Garden. *Guest*: FBI, Head of the Class, Love Boat, Hotel, Twilight Zone, Murder She Wrote, Dream On.
PICTURES: The Fog, Cannonball Run, Escape From New York, Swamp Thing, Creepshow, The Next One, Back to School, Open House, Two Evil Eyes, Cannibal Women & the Avocado Jungle of Death.
THEATRE: *Bdwy*: Fiddler on the Roof, Grease (Tony nom., Theatre World Award). *L.A.*: Women Behind Bars, Strange Snow, Pump Boys & Dinettes, Drop Dead. *Canadian Premiere*: Lost in Yonkers. Regional: Love Letters, Best Little Whorehouse in Texas.

BARBER, FRANCES: Actress. b. Wolverhampton, Eng., May 13, 1957. e. Bangor U.; grad. studies in theatre, Cardiff U. Stage experience with fringe theaters including improvisational troupe Hull Truck Theatre Company, Glasgow Citizens and Tricycle Theatre (Killburn) before joining Royal Shakespeare Co. (Camille, Hamlet).
PICTURES: The Missionary, A Zed and Two Noughts, White City, Castaway, Prick Up Your Ears, Sammy and Rosie Get Laid, We Think the World of You, The Grasscutter, Chamber à part.
TELEVISION: Clem, Jackie's Story, Home Sweet Home, Flame to the Phoenix, Reilly, Ace of Spies, Those Glory, Glory Days; Hard Feelings, Behaving Badly, The Nightmare Years.

BARBERA, JOSEPH R.: Executive. b. New York, NY, Mar. 24, 1911. e. NYU, American Institute of Banking. After school joined Irving Trust Co. in N.Y.; started submitting cartoon drawings to leading magazines selling one to Collier's. Left banking to seek career in cartooning. Joined Van Buren Associates as sketch artist, later going to work in animation dept. of MGM Studios. At MGM met William Hanna, who became his lifelong business associate. Made first animated short together in 1937, starting the famous Tom & Jerry series which they produced for 20 years. Left MGM in 1957 to form Hanna-Barbera Productions to make cartoons for TV. Series have included Yogi Bear, Huckleberry Hound, The Flintstones, The Jetsons and Scooby-Doo. Hanna-Barbera became a subsidiary of Taft Ent. Co. in 1968 with both men operating studio under long-term agreements with Taft. Taft and the studio was sold to Great American Broadcasting, 1988. Hanna-Barbera Prods. acquired by Turner Bdcstg. System, 1991. Barbera is co-founder, chmn. Co-exec. produced 1993 tv movie I Yabba Dabba Do! Company entered theatrical production with Hey There It's Yogi Bear, 1964. Then A Man Called Flintstone, Charlotte's Web, C.H.O.M.P.S., Heidi's Song and Jetsons: The Movie. Co-Exec. Prod. on live-action movie of The Flintstones.

BARBOUR, ALAN G.: Writer, Editor, Publisher. b. Oakland, CA, July 25, 1933. e. Rutgers U. m. Catherine Jean Callovini, actress, teacher, American Acad. of Dramatic Arts, American Mime Theatre. U.S. Army, worked as computer programmer.

Formed Screen Facts Press in 1963, Screen Facts Magazine. Compiled, edited: The Serials of Republic, The Serials of Columbia, Great Serial Ads, The B Western, Serial Showcase, Hit the Saddle, The Wonderful World of B-Films, Days of Thrills and Adventure, Serial Quarterly, Serial Pictorial, Karloff—A Pictorial History, Errol Flynn—A Pictorial Biography, A Pictorial History of the Serial, A Thousand and One Delights, Cliffhanger, The Old-Time Radio Quiz Book. Direct Mktg. Div., RCA Records. Mgr., A & R, RCA, BMGVideo Club.

BARBOUR, MALCOLM: Executive. b. London, England, May 3, 1934. e. Radley Coll., Oxford, England, Columbia Coll. At NBC was press info. asst., 1958–59; asst. magazine ed., 1959–62; assoc. mag. ed., 1962–64; sr. mag. ed., 1964–65; mgr. of magazine pub., National Broadcasting Co., 1965–67; pub. mgr., Buena Vista, 1967–68; Eastern story ed., Walt Disney Prod., 1968–69; dir. of adv. & pub. relations, Buena Vista, 1969. Partner, Producers Creative Services, 1976–79. President, The International Picture Show, 1980–81 (Tim Conway comedies The Billion Dollar Hobo and They Went That-A-Way & That-A-Way; Slayer. Distributor: Soldier of Orange, The Magic of Lassie, The Visitor, etc.). President, Barbour/Langley Productions, 1982–present. Producer, Geraldo Rivera specials: American Vice, Innocence Lost, Sons of Scarface, Murder: Live from Death Row, Satan Worship. Producer, Jack Anderson specials. Writer-Producer, Cocaine Blues. Co-screenplay, P.O.W. The Escape (Cannon Films). *Executive producer*: Cops, Code 3, Inside the KGB, Cop Files, Strange World.

BARDOT, BRIGITTE: Actress. b. Paris, France, Sept. 28, 1934. r.n. Camille Javal. e. Paris Conservatory. Studied ballet, before becoming model. Studied acting with Rene Simon. On stage in L'Invitation au Chateau. Awarded French Legion of Honor, 1985. Active in the movement to preserve endangered animals. Auctioned her jewels and mementos from her film career, raising $500,000 to create an animal protection foundation, June 1987.
PICTURES: Le Trou Normand (debut, 1952), Nanina la Fille san Voiles, Les Dents Longues, Act of Love, Le Portrait de Son Pere, Royal Affairs in Versailles, Tradita, Le Fils de Caroline Cherie, Helen of Troy, Futures Vedettes, Les Grandes Maneuvres, Doctor at Sea, La Lumiere d'En Face (The Light Across the Street), Cette Sacre Gamine (Mam'zelle Pigalle), Mi Figlio Nerone, En Effeuillant la Marguerite (Please Mr. Balzac), The Bride is Much Too Beautiful, And God Created Woman, Une Parisienne, The Night Heaven Fell, En Cas de Malheur, Le Femme et le Pantin, Babette Goes to War, Come Dance With Me, La Verite (The Truth), La Bride sur le Cou, Les Amours Celebres, A Very Private Affair, Love on a Pillow, Contempt, A Ravishing Idiot, Dear Brigitte, Viva Maria, Masculine-Feminine, Two Weeks in September, Spirits of the Dead, Shalako, Les Femmes, L'Ours et la Poupee, Les Novices, Boulevard du Rhum (Rum Runner), Les Petroleuses (The Legend of Frenchie King), Ms. Don Juan, L'Historie Tres Bonne et Tres Joyeuse de Colinot Troussechemise.

BARE, RICHARD L.: Producer, Director. b. Turlock, CA. Dir. for Warner: Smart Girls Don't Talk, Flaxy Martin, This Side of the Law, House Across the Street, This Rebel Breed, Girl on the Run, Return of Frontiersman; SDG Best Dir. TV award, 1959; author, The Film Director (Macmillan), 1971. Pres., United National Film Corp.
TELEVISION: 77 Sunset Strip, Maverick, So This is Hollywood, The Islanders, Dangerous Robin, This Rebel Breed, Twilight Zone, Bus Stop, Adventures in Paradise, The Virginian, Kraft Theatre, Run For Your Life, Green Acres series, Farraday and Son, Westwind.
PICTURES: Dir.-Prod.-Writer: Wicked Wicked, Story of Chang & Eng, City of Shame, Sudden Target, Purple Moon.

BAREN, HARVEY M.: Executive. b. New York, NY, Nov. 25, 1931. e. State U. of New York. Served in U.S. Army, 1952–54; United Artists Corp., 1954–59 (contract dept., print dept., booker—N.Y. branch); asst. to general sls. mgr., Magna Pictures Corp., 1959–61; road show mgr., national sales coordinator, 20th Century-Fox, 1961–71; asst. general sales manager, Allied Artists Pictures, 1971–79; v.p., gen. sls. mgr., Nat'l. Screen Service, 1978–79; v.p., gen. sls. mgr., Cannon Pictures, 1979–80. 1980, pres. of Summit Feature Distributors; 1983, exec. V.P., dir., MGM/UA Classics; 1986,joined New Century/Vista as v.p., sls. admin. 1991, pres. Sea Movies Inc.

BARENHOLTZ, BEN: Executive. b. Oct. 5, 1935. Whimsically describes ed. as Balcony U. Asst. manager: RKO Bushwick, Brooklyn, 1959–60. Manager: Village Theatre (Fillmore East), N.Y., 1966–68. Owner-operator: Elgin Cinema, 1968–72. President-owner: Libra Film Corp., 1972–84. 1984–1992, vp & partner: Circle Releasing (which launched and distributed The Family Game, Therese, Blood Simple and prod. Raising Arizona). Pres. Barenholtz Prods. Inc.
PICTURES: *Exec. Prod.*: Miller's Crossing, Barton Fink, Cheat.

BARISH, KEITH: Producer. b. Los Angeles, CA. Background in finance. Founded Keith Barish Prods. in 1979. 1984–88 in partnership with Taft Broadcasting Co., Entertainment Div. Founder and chmn. of Planet Hollywood. Appeared in film Last Action Hero.
PICTURES: *Exec. prod.*: Endless Love, Sophie's Choice (prod.), Kiss Me Goodbye, Misunderstood, 9½ Weeks, Big Trouble in Little China, Light of Day (prod.), The Running Man, The Monster Squad, Ironweed (prod.), The Serpent and the Rainbow, Her Alibi, Firebirds, The Fugitive (co-prod.).
TELEVISION: Movie: A Streetcar Named Desire (exec. prod.).

BARKER, BOB (Robert William): TV host. b. Darrington, WA, Dec. 12. e. Springfield Central H.S., Drury Coll. News writer, announcer, disc jockey KTTS until 1949. News editor, staff announcer, Station WWPG; wife, Dorothy Jo. Emcee, Truth or Consequences, 1956. Pres. Bob Barker Prod., Inc., M.C. Miss USA Pageant, CBS-TV, since 1967, M.C. Miss Universe Pageant, CBS-TV since 1967, M.C. Rose Parade, since 1970. Prod.-M. C. Pillsbury Bakeoff, since 1970 CBS. Prod. Lucky Pair, syndicated. M.C. & exec. prod., Price Is Right-CBS, since 1972; Narrator, 500 Festival Parade, Indianapolis 1969–81.

BARKER, CLIVE: Writer, Director. b. Liverpool, England, 1952. e. Liverpool Univ. Moved to London at twenty-one, forming theatre company. Began writing short stories which were subsequently published as Books of Blood (Vols. 1–3 & Vols. 4–6). Novels: Damnation Game, Weaveworld, The Great and Secret Show, Imajica, The Thief of All Ways.
PICTURES: Rawhead Rex (from his story), Transmutations (from his story), Hellraiser (dir., s.p.; from his novella The Hellbound Heart), Hellbound: Hellraiser II (co-exec. prod., from his characters), Nightbreed (dir., s.p.; from his novel Cabal), Sleepwalkers (actor), Hellraiser III: Hell on Earth (exec. prod.; from his characters), Candyman (exec. prod.; from his story The Forbidden).

BARKER, MICHAEL W.: Executive. b. Nurnberg, Germany, Jan. 9, 1954. e. U. of Texas at Austin, B.S. in intl. communications, 1976. Joined Films Inc. 1979–80, then MGM/UA 1980–83. Co-founder of Orion Classics, a div. of Orion Pictures Corp., v.p. sales and marketing, 1983–92. Member, bd. of dir. Independent Feature Project. 1992, co-pres., Sony Pictures Classics.

BARKETT, STEVE: Actor, director, producer, film editor. b. Oklahoma City, OK, Jan. 1, 1950. Exhibited and scored over 52 feature length classic silent films 1966–1968 as dir. of two film series at the Okla. Art Ctr. and Science and Arts Fdn, prior to coming to LA in 1970. Toured in stage prod 1971–1972: Pajama Tops, Winnie the Pooh. Exec in several nontheatrical releasing cos, incl. Independent Film Associates and Thunderbird Films. From 1968 to 1974 was active in film preservation and restoration work on early silent and sound films. 1978 founded The Hollywood Book and Poster Company. Est. The Nautilus Film Co, 1978. Founded and operated Capt. Nemo's Video (1985–1987). Co-wrote and performed with Tricia Drake (Schiotis), 42 episodes of Capt. Nemo's Video Review for radio (1987).
PICTURES: Actor only: The Egyptians are Coming, Corpse Grinders, Dillinger, Night Caller, Cruise Missile, Beverly Hills Vampire, Wizard of the Demon Sword. Prod, director, s.p., ed. only: Collecting, The Fisherman. S.P.: The Ed. only: Hurricane Express. Spcl. Fx. only: Warlords. Actor, dir., s.p., prod. and ed: The Movie People; Cassavetes, The Aftermath, Angels of Death, Empire of the Dark. Actor, f/x: Dark Universe.

BARKIN, ELLEN: Actress. b. Bronx, NY, Apr. 16, 1954. e. Hunter Coll.; Actors Studio.
THEATER: Irish Coffee (debut, Ensemble Studio Theatre), Shout Across the River, Killings Across the Last, Tobacco Road, Extremities, Eden Court.
PICTURES: Diner (debut, 1982), Tender Mercies, Daniel, Eddie and the Cruisers, Harry and Son, The Adventures of Buckaroo Banzai, Enormous Changes at the Last Minute, Terminal Choice, Desert Bloom, Down By Law, The Big Easy, Siesta, Made in Heaven (unbilled), Sea of Love, Johnny Handsome, Switch, Man Trouble, Mac, This Boy's Life, Into the West.
TELEVISION: *Series*: Search for Tomorrow. *Movies*: Kent State, We're Fighting Back, Parole, Terrible Joe Moran, Act of Vengeance, Clinton and Nadine. *Special*: Faerie Tale Theatre (The Princess Who Never Laughed).

BARNHOLTZ, BARRY: Executive. b. St. Louis, MO, Oct. 12, 1945. e. California State U., Northridge; U. of Southern California; UCLA; W.L.A.U. (studied law). Concert promotions in So. Calif. 1963–71; with Medallion TV as v.p. in chg. sls.; Barnholtz Organization, representing independent prod. cos. for feature films for cable. Founder, sr. v.p. of Vidmark Inc., and Trimark Films.

BARR, ANTHONY: Producer, Director, Actor. r.n. Morris Yaffe. b. St. Louis, MO, March 14, 1921. e. Washington U., B.S. 1942. Actor, asst. stage mgr., 1944–46; stage mgr., Katherine Dunham Dancers, 1946–47; teacher, actor, dir. in chg. Film Actors' Workshop, Professional Theatre Workshop, Hollywood; v.p. current prime time series, ABC-TV; v.p., current dramatic program production, CBS-TV; v.p., CBS Entertainment Prods.
BROADWAY: Jacobowsky and the Colonel, Winters' Tale, Embezzled Heaven.
PICTURES: Actor: People Against O'Hara, Border Incident, The Hollywood Story, The Mozart Story. Co-prod.: Dime with a Halo.
TELEVISION: Director: Art Linkletter's Houseparty, About Faces. Assoc. dir.: Climax, Shower of Stars. Prod.: Climax, Summer Studio One. Assoc. prod.: Climax, Playhouse 90, Pursuit, G.E. Theatre, The Law and Mr. Jones, Four-Star.
BOOK: Acting for the Camera, 1982.

BARRAULT, MARIE-CHRISTINE: Actress. b. Paris, France, March 21, 1944. m. director Roger Vadim.
PICTURES: My Night at Maud's, The Daydreamer, Lancelot of the Lake, The Aspern Papers, Les Intrus, La Famille Grossfeld, John Glueckstadt, Cousin Cousine (Acad. Award nom.), By the Tennis Courts, L'Etat Sauvage, Perceval, The Medusa Touch, Tout est a nous, Femme Entre Chien et Loup, Ma Cherie, Stardust Memories, Table for Five, Josephs Tochter, A Love in Germany, Les Mots Pour le Dire, Swann in Love, Grand Piano, Prisonnieres, Un Eté de orages, Necessary Love.

BARRETT, RONA: News correspondent b. New York, NY, Oct. 8, 1936. e. NYU (communications major). Created the column, Rona Barrett's Young Hollywood, which led to featured column in 1960 in Motion Picture Magazine and a nationally syndicated column distributed to 125 newspapers by the North American Newspaper Alliance. Turned to TV; initial appearances on ABC Owned Stations in 5 cities, providing two-minute reports for local newscasts. Resulted in Dateline Hollywood a network morning prog., co-hosted by Joanna Barnes. In 1969 created first daily syndicated TV news segment for Metromedia. 1975, became arts and entertainment editor for ABC's Good Morning America. 1980, joined NBC News. Publ. and exec. editor, newsletter, The Rona Barrett Report. 1985, pres., Rona Barrett Enterprises, Inc., sr. corresp., Entertainment Tonight; Mutual Radio Network. 1988: creator of original novels for television, for NBC prods. Appeared in films Sextette, An Almost Perfect Affair.

BARRIE, BARBARA: Actress. b. Chicago, IL, May 23, 1931. e. U. of TX, B.F.A., 1953. Trained for stage at Herbert Berghof Studio. NY stage debut, The Wooden Dish (1955). Published book Lone Star in 1990.
THEATER: The Crucible, American Shakespeare Fest., Stratford, CT 1958–59, The Beaux Stratagem, The Taming of the Shrew, Conversations in the Dark, All's Well That Ends Well, Happily Never After, Horseman Pass By, Company, The Selling of the President, The Prisoner of Second Avenue, The Killdeer, California Suite, Big and Little, Isn't It Romantic, Torch Song Trilogy, Fugue.
PICTURES: Giant (debut, 1956), The Caretakers, One Potato Two Potato (best actress, Cannes Film Fest, 1964), The Bell Jar, Breaking Away (Acad. Award nom.), Private Benjamin, Real Men, End of the Line, The Passage.
TELEVISION: *Series*: Love of Life, Diana (1973), Barney Miller (1975–76), Breaking Away, Tucker's Witch, Reggie, Double Trouble, Love of Life. *Guest appearances*: Ben Casey, The Fugitive, Dr. Kildare, Alfred Hitchcock Presents, The Defenders, Mary Tyler Moore Show, Lou Grant, Trapper John, M.D., Babes, Kojak, Island Son, thirtysomething. *Movies*: Tell Me My Name, Summer of My German Soldier, To Race the Wind, The Children Nobody Wanted, Not Just Another Affair, Two of a Kind, The Execution, Vital Signs, Winnie, My First Love, Guess Who's Coming for Christmas? *Specials*: To Be Young Gifted and Black, Barefoot in the Park, What's Alan Watching?. *Mini-Series*: 79 Park Avenue, Backstairs at the White House, Roots: The Next Generation.

BARRON, ARTHUR RAY: Executive. b. Mt. Lake, MN, July 12, 1934. e. San Diego State U. 1956–60, B.S. Accounting. Certified public acc't, Calif., 1960. Coopers & Lybrand, 1960–63; Desilu Productions, Inc., 1963–67; v.p. finance and administration, Paramount Television, 1967–70 v.p. finance, Paramount Pictures Corp., 1970; sr. v.p. finance and admin., 1971; exec. v.p., finance & admin., 1974; exec. v.p. 1980; exec. v.p., Gulf & Western Industries, entertainment & communications group, 1983; promoted to pres., 1984–Feb., 1988. Chmn, Time Warner Enterprises, 1990.

BARRY, GENE: Actor. r.n. Eugene Klass. b. New York, NY, June 14, 1919. e. New Utrecht H.S., Brooklyn.
BROADWAY: Rosalinda, Catherine Was Great, Happy Is Larry, Bless You All, The Would-Be Gentleman, La Cage aux Folles (Tony Award nom.).
PICTURES: Atomic City (debut, 1952), Girls of Pleasure Island, War of the Worlds, Those Redheads from Seattle,

Alaska Seas, Red Garters, Naked Alibi, Soldier of Fortune, Purple Mask, Houston Story, Back from Eternity, China Gate, 27th Day, 40 Guns, Thunder Road, Hong Kong Confidential, Maroc 7, Subterfuge, The Second Coming of Suzanne, Guyana: Cult of the Damned.

TELEVISION: *Series:* Our Miss Brooks, Bat Masterson, Burke's Law, The Name of the Game. *Movies:* Prescription Murder, Istanbul Express, Do You Take This Stranger?, The Devil and Miss Sarah, Ransom for Alice!, A Cry for Love, The Girl the Gold Watch and Dynamite, Adventures of Nellie Bly, Turn Back the Clock. *Mini-Series:* Aspen.

BARRY, JOHN: Composer, arranger, conductor. b. York, England, 1933. Artist and prod., CBS Records.

PICTURES: Beat Girl, Never Let Go, The L-Shaped Room, The Amorous Mr. Prawn, From Russia With Love, Seance on a Wet Afternoon, Zulu, Goldfinger, The Ipcress File, The Knack, King Rat, Mister Moses, Thunderball, The Chase, Born Free (2 Acad. Awards for Score & Song, 1966), The Wrong Box, You Only Live Twice, Petulia, The Lion in Winter (Acad. Award, 1968), Midnight Cowboy, The Appointment, On Her Majesty's Secret Service, Monte Walsh, The Last Valley, They Might Be Giants, Murphy's War, Walkabout, Diamonds Are Forever, Mary Queen of Scots, Alice's Adventures in Wonderland, The Public Eye (Follow Me), A Doll's House, The Tamarind Seed, The Dove, The Man With the Golden Gun, The Day of the Locust, Robin and Marian, King Kong, The Deep, The Betsy, Hanover Street, Moonraker, The Black Hole, Starcrash, Game of Death, Raise the Titanic, Somewhere in Time, Inside Moves, Touched By Love, Body Heat, The Legend of the Lone Ranger, Frances, Hammett, High Road to China, Octopussy, The Golden Seal, Mike's Murder, Until September, The Cotton Club, A View to a Kill, Jagged Edge, Out of Africa (Acad. Award, 1985), Howard the Duck, Peggy Sue Got Married, The Living Daylights, Hearts of Fire, Masquerade, A Killing Affair, Dances With Wolves (Acad. Award, 1990), Chaplin, Indecent Proposal.

TELEVISION: Elizabeth Taylor in London, Sophia Loren in Rome.

BARRYMORE, DREW: Actress. b. Los Angeles, CA, Feb. 22, 1975. Daughter of John Barrymore, Jr. At 11 months was in first commercial.

PICTURES: Altered States, E.T.: The Extra Terrestrial, Firestarter, Irreconcilable Differences, Cat's Eye, See You in the Morning, Far From Home, No Place to Hide, Waxwork II, Poison Ivy, Motorama, Doppelganger, Bad Girls.

TELEVISION: *Series:* 2000 Malibu Road. *Movies:* Bogie, Suddenly Love, Babes in Toyland, Conspiracy of Love, The Sketch Artist, Guncrazy, The Amy Fisher Story. *Specials:* Disneyland's 30th Anniversary, Night of 100 Stars II, Con Sawyer and Hucklemary Finn, 15 & Getting Straight.

BARRYMORE, JOHN DREW: Actor. b. Beverly Hills, CA, June 4, 1932. e. St. John's Military Acad., various public and private schools. p. late John Barrymore, Delores Costello. Father of actress Drew Barrymore. Many TV appearances.

PICTURES: Sundowners (debut, 1950), High Lonesome, Big Night, Thunderbirds, While the City Sleeps, Shadow on the Window, Never Love a Stranger, High School Confidential, Night of the Quarter Moon, The Cossacks, The Night They Killed Rasputin, War of the Zombies.

BART, PETER: Executive. b. Martha's Vineyard, MA, July 24, 1932. e. Swarthmore Coll. and The London School of Economics. Eight years as corrp. for New York Times and wrote for such magazines as Harper's, The Atlantic, Saturday Review, etc. Joined Paramount Pictures in 1965. Named exec. ass't. to Robert Evans, exec. in charge of world-wide prod. Appointed v.p. Resigned 1973 to develop and produce own films for Para. Appointed pres. Lorimar Films, 1978. Resigned, 1979, to be independent producer. 1983, joined MGM as sr. v.p., prod., m.p. div. Resigned, 1985, to be indep. prod. Editor, Variety. Novels: Author-Thy Kingdom Come (1983); Destinies (1979), Fade Out.

PICTURES: Islands in the Stream, Fun with Dick and Jane (prod.), Revenge of the Nerds (exec. prod.), Youngblood (prod.), Revenge of the Nerds II (prod.).

BARTEL, PAUL: Director, Writer, Actor. b. New York, NY, Aug. 6, 1938. e. UCLA, B.A. At 13 spent summer working at UPA Cartoons. Later at UCLA won acting and playwriting awards and prod. animated and doc. films. Awarded Fulbright schl. to study film dir. at Centro Sperimentale di Cinematografia in Rome where dir. short Progetti (presented Venice Fest., 1962). Then at Army Pictorial Center, L.I. City. Asst. dir. military training films and writer-dir. monthly news doc. series, Horizontos for U.S. Information Agency. Directed short film The Naughty Nurse. Appeared in 1984 short film Frankenweenie.

PICTURES: *Actor:* Hi Mom!, Private Parts (dir. debut), Big Bad Mama (2nd unit. dir. only), Death Race 2000 (dir. only), Cannonball (also dir., co-s.p.), Eat My Dust!, Hollywood Boulevard, Grand Theft Auto, Mr. Billion, Piranha, Rock 'n'

Roll High School, Heart Like a Wheel, Eating Raoul (also dir., s.p.), Trick or Treats, White Dog, Get Crazy, Not for Publication (also dir., s.p.), Lust in the Dust (dir. only), Into the Night, Sesame Street Presents Follow That Bird, Chopping Mall, Killer Party, The Longshot (dir. only), Munchies, Amazon Women on the Moon, Mortuary Academy, Out of the Dark (also exec. prod.), Scenes From the Class Struggle in Beverly Hills (also dir., s.p.), Pucker Up and Bark Like a Dog, Far Out Man, Gremlins 2: The New Batch, The Pope Must Die, Liquid Dreams, Desire and Hell at Sunset Motel, Posse, Grief.

TELEVISION: *Actor:* Alfred Hitchcock Presents, Fame, L.A. Law, Acting on Impulse (movie). *Director:* Amazing Stories (The Secret Cinema, Gershwin's Truck; also writer, actor), The Hustler of Muscle Beach.

BARTKOWIAK, ANDRZEJ: Cinematographer. b. Lodz, Poland, 1950. Attended Polish Film School. Moved to US in 1972, gaining experience in TV commercials and low-budget features. Protege of Sidney Lumet, for whom did several pictures.

PICTURES: Deadly Hero, Prince of the City, Deathtrap, The Verdict, Daniel, Terms of Endearment, Garbo Talks, Prizzi's Honor, The Morning After, Power, Nuts, Twins, Q&A, Hard Promises, A Stranger Among Us, Falling Down.

BARTLETT, HALL: Producer, Director, Writer. b. Kansas City, MO, Nov. 27, 1925. e. Yale U., B.A. 1942. U.S. Naval Reserve 1942–47; formed Hall Bartlett Productions, 1952; Author: The Rest of Our Lives.

PICTURES: prod. Navajo (winner of 27 nat'l awards & Festival of Brit. Award at Edinburgh); prod., s.p. Crazy-legs (winner of 9 nat'l awards, including Parents Mag. Gold Medal); prod., dir., s.p. Unchained (winner of Parents Mag. Gold Medal, Brotherhd. award of Nat'l Con. of Christians and Jews); prod., dir., s.p. Durango; prod. dir. s.p. Zero Hour, All the Young Men, Sol Madrid; photog., prod., Changes; prod. dir. Winner of the Sans Sebastian Festival, The Sandpit Generals, prod., dir., s.p. Comeback, Love Is Forever.

BARUCH, RALPH M.: Executive. b. Frankfurt, Germany, Aug. 5, 1923. e. The Sorbonne, Administrative aide, SESAC, Inc. 1944–48; account exec., DuMont Television Network, 1948–52; Eastern sales mgr., Consolidated Television Films, 1953–54; account exec., CBS Films, 1954; account supervisor, 1957; dir. intl. sales, 1959; v.p., CBS Enterprises, 1961–70; pres. Viacom Enterprises, 1971; pres., Viacom International, 1979; named chmn. & member of office of CEO, Viacom Intl. (1983–7), now consultant; pres., International Radio Television Society; chmn., Rewrite Committee (Communications Act), NCTA; former member of the bd. dirs. and former chmn., Pay Cable Committee, NCTA; chmn. NCTA Public Policy Planning Committee; gov. (NY), fellow of International Council of the National Academy of Television Arts Sciences. Immediate past chmn., Chmn. Emeritus of Natl. Acad. of Cable Progmg. Memb., bd. of trustees of Museum of TV & Radio. 1988, Sr. Fellow of the Freedom Forum at Col. U. Exec. committee memb., Carnegie Hall.

BARWOOD, HAL: Writer, Producer, Director. e. U. of Southern California Sch. of Cinema. Has written scripts in collaboration with Matthew Robbins, Barwood branching out into producing with Corvette Summer in 1978 and directing with Warning Sign in 1985.

PICTURES: Screen plays, all with Robbins: The Sugarland Express, The Bingo Long Traveling All-Stars and Motor Kings, MacArthur, Corvette Summer (also prod.), Dragonslayer (also prod.), Warning Sign (also dir.).

BARYSHNIKOV, MIKHAIL: Dancer, Actor. b. Riga, Latvia, Jan. 27, 1948. Joined Kirov Ballet, Leningrad, 1969–74; defected to U.S. With American Ballet Theatre 1974–78; New York City Ballet Company 1978–79; named director of the American Ballet Theatre. Bdwy stage debut, Metamorphosis (1989).

PICTURES: The Turning Point, That's Dancing!, White Nights, Dancers, Company Business, The Cabinet of Dr. Ramirez.

TELEVISION: Baryshnikov at the White House (Emmy Award, 1979), Bob Hope on the Road to China, Baryshnikov on Broadway (Emmy Award, 1980), AFI Salute to Fred Astaire, Baryshnikov in Hollywood, AFI Salute to Gene Kelly, David Gordon's Made in USA, All Star Gala at Ford's Theater, Dance in America: Baryshnikov Dances Balanchine (Emmy Award, 1989).

BASCH, BUDDY: Print Media Syndicater, Publicist, Producer. b. South Orange, NJ, June 28, 1922. e. Columbia U. Began career as youngest radio editor in U.S. at 15, since written for national mags, syndicates, wire services, and newspapers. Edited and published "Top Hit Club News"-7 years. Joined Donahue and Coe 1940 on m.p. accounts, U.S. Army in Europe 1942–45. 1945–67: own publicity and promotion office, working on m.p. company accounts and stars such as

Burl Ives, Dinah Shore, Tony Martin, Danny Kaye, Peter Lorre, Tony Bennett, Gloria De Haven, McGuire Sisters, Rhonda Fleming, Sammy Davis, Jr., Anna Maria Alberghetti, Polly Bergen, Meyer Davis, The Beatles, Glenn Miller and Tommy Dorsey Orchestras. Produced many shows for radio, TV and stage in New York, Newark, Chicago, Hartford. Asst. to publisher, The Brooklyn Eagle 1962. 1966 formed Buddy Basch Feature Syndicate, covering assignments on show business, travel and general subjects for N.Y. Daily News, A.P., Grit Magazine, Travel/Holiday, Frontier Magazine, Kaleidoscope, True, United Features, Gannett Westchester-Rockland Newspapers, Bergen (NJ) Record, Argosy, N.A.N.A., Womens' News Service, Today Magazine, Christian Science Monitor, New York Post, Inflight Magazine, Deseret News, California Canadian, Diversion. Member: Friars Club since 1959. Organized & appointed permanent chairman, VIP Reception and Security for Friars luncheons and dinners since 1970. Served as Chairman of Elections (6 times). Member of Admission Comm. and House Committee. Contributing ed. Friars Epistle.

BASINGER, KIM: Actress. b. Athens, GA, Dec. 8, 1953. m. actor Alec Baldwin. e. Neighborhood Playhouse. Began career as a Breck shampoo model (as her mother had been) then as a Ford model in New York. Pursued singing career under the nom-de-chant, Chelsea.
PICTURES: Hard Country (debut, 1981), Mother Lode, Never Say Never Again, The Man Who Loved Women, The Natural, Fool for Love, 9½ Weeks, No Mercy, Blind Date, Nadine, My Stepmother is an Alien, Batman, The Marrying Man, Final Analysis, Cool World, The Real McCoy, The Getaway.
TELEVISION: Series: Dog and Cat, From Here to Eternity. Mini-Series: From Here to Eternity. Movies: Dog and Cat (pilot), The Ghost of Flight 401, Katie: Portrait of a Centerfold, Killjoy. Guest: Starsky and Hutch, The Bionic Woman, Charlie's Angels, The Six Million Dollar Man.

BASS, SAUL: Director, Producer. b. New York, NY, May 8, 1920. e. Arts Students League. Pres., Saul Bass/Herb Yager & Assoc. Directed short films, m.p. titles/prologues/epilogues, TV commercials. Directorial feature debut in 1974 with Phase IV.
PICTURES: Shorts: The Searching Eye, From Here to There, Why Man Creates (Academy Award), Notes on the Popular Arts (AA nomination), The Solar Film (AA nomination), Bass on Titles, Quest. Titles: Carmen Jones, The Man With The Golden Arm, Around the World in 80 Days, Bonjour Tristesse, Cowboy, Vertigo, Anatomy of a Murder, Psycho, Spartacus, Exodus, West Side Story, Advise and Consent, Walk on the Wild Side, It's a Mad Mad Mad Mad World, Bunny Like Is Missing, That's Entertainment Part 2, The Human Factor, Broadcast News, Big, The War of the Roses, Goodfellas, Cape Fear.

BASSETT, ANGELA: Actress. b. New York, NY, Aug. 16, 1958. Moved to St. Petersburg, FL, at 5 yrs. old. e. Yale.
PICTURES: F/X (debut, 1986), Kindergarten Cop, Boyz N the Hood, City of Hope, Innocent Blood, Malcolm X, Passion Fish, What's Love Got to Do With It.
TELEVISION: Movies: Line of Fire: The Morris Dees Story, The Jacksons: An American Dream. Guest: Cosby Show, 227, thirtysomething, Tour of Duty, Equal Justice.
THEATRE: Bdwy: Ma Rainey's Black Bottom, Joe Turner's Come and Gone. Off-Bdwy: Colored People's Time, Antigone, Black Girl, Henry IV Part 1. Regional: Beef No Chicken.

BASSETT, LINDA: Actress. Extensive career in the English theatre.
THEATER: Began with Interplay Community Theatre Company. In 1977 joined Belgrade Theater-in-Education Company in Coventry as actress, writer, and director. 1982, joined Joint Stock Theatre Group for workshop production of Caryl Churchill's' Fen (London and Public Theater, NY). Starred in Abel's Sister (London), The Cherry Orchard, Medea, Woyceck, The Bald Prima Donna and George Dandin with Leicester Haymarket Studio Season. Aunt Dan and Lemon (London and NY).
PICTURES: Debut as Gertrude Stein in Waiting for the Moon, Leave to Remain, Paris By Night.
TELEVISION: Traffik.

BATEMAN, JASON: Actor. b. Rye, NY, Jan. 14, 1969. Brother of actress Justine Bateman. Son of prod.-theatrical mgr. Kent Bateman. Started career in commercials until cast in Little House on the Prairie at 12 (1981).
PICTURES: Teen Wolf Too, Necessary Roughness, Breaking the Rules.
TELEVISION: Series: Little House on the Prairie, Silver Spoons, It's Your Move, Valerie (Valerie's Family, The Hogan Family). Movies: The Fantastic World of D.C. Collins, The Thanksgiving Promise, Can You Feel Me Dancing, The Bates Motel, Moving Target, A Taste for Killing. Mini-Series: Robert Kennedy and His Times. Specials: Just a Little More Love, Candid Camera: Eat! Eat! Eat!

BATEMAN, JUSTINE: Actress, b. Rye, NY, Feb. 19, 1966. Brother is actor Jason Bateman. Father, prod.-theatrical mgr. Kent Bateman.
PICTURES: Satisfaction, The Closer, Primary Motive, Deadbolt, The Night We Never Met.
TELEVISION: Series: Family Ties. Guest: Tales from the Dark Side, One to Grow On, It's Your Move, Glitter. Movies: Right to Kill?, Family Ties Vacation, Can You Feel Me Dancing?, The Fatal Image, In the Eyes of a Stranger, The Hunter. Specials: First the Egg, Whatta Year . . . 1986, Fame Fortune and Romance, Candid Camera: Eat! Eat! Eat!, Merry Christmas Baby.
THEATRE: Lulu, Self-Storage, The Crucible, Love Letters, Carnal Knowledge, Speed-the-Plow.

BATES, ALAN: Actor. b. Allestree, Derbyshire, England, Feb. 17, 1934. e. Herbert Strutt Grammar Sch.; after natl. service with the RAF studied at RADA with Albert Finney, Peter O'Toole and Tom Courtenay. Professional stage debut 1955 with the Midland Theatre Co. in You and Your Wife.
STAGE: London stage: The Mulberry Tree, Look Back in Anger (also NY, Moscow), Long Day's Journey Into Night, Poor Richard, Richard III, In Celebration, Hamlet, Butley (also NY; Tony Award, 1973), The Taming of the Shrew, Life Class, Otherwise Engaged, Stage Struck, A Patriot for Me, One for the Road, Victoria Station, Dance of Death, Yonadab, Melon, Much Ado About Nothing, Ivanov, Stages, The Showman.
PICTURES: The Entertainer (debut, 1960), Whistle Down the Wind, A Kind of Loving, The Caretaker (The Guest), The Running Man, Nothing But the Best, Zorba the Greek, Georgy Girl, King of Hearts, Far From the Madding Crowd, The Fixer (Acad. Award nom.), Women in Love, Three Sisters, The Go-Between, A Day in the Death of Joe Egg, Impossible Object (Story of a Love Story), Butley, In Celebration, Royal Flash, An Unmarried Woman, The Shout, The Rose, Nijinsky, Quartet, The Return of the Soldier, Britannia Hospital, The Wicked Lady, Duet for One, A Prayer for the Dying, We Think the World of You, Mr. Frost, Hamlet, Force Majeure, Dr. M (Club Extinction), Shuttlecock, Secret Friends, Silent Tongue, Losing Track.
TELEVISION: The Thug, A Memory of Two Mondays, The Jukebox, The Square Ring, The Wind and the Rain, Look Back in Anger, Three on a Gasring, Duel for Love, A Hero for Our Time, Plaintiff & Defendant, Two Sundays, The Collection, The Mayor of Casterbridge, The Trespasser, Very Like a Whale, Voyage Round My Father, An Englishman Abroad, Separate Tables, Dr. Fischer of Geneva, One for the Road, Pack of Lies, 102 Boulevard Haussmann, Unnatural Pursuits.

BATES, KATHY: Actress. b. Memphis, TN, June 28, 1948. e. S. Methodist U. Regional theatre incl. D.C. and Actor's Theatre in Louisville.
PICTURES: Taking Off (debut, 1971), Straight Time, Come Back to the 5 & Dime Jimmy Dean Jimmy Dean, Two of a Kind, Summer Heat, My Best Friend is a Vampire, Arthur 2 on the Rocks, Signs of Life, High Stakes (Melanie Rose), Men Don't Leave, Dick Tracy, White Palace, Misery (Academy Award, Golden Globe & Chicago Film Critics Awards, 1990), At Play in the Fields of the Lord, Fried Green Tomatoes, Shadows and Fog, Road to Mecca, Prelude to a Kiss, Used People, A Home of Our Own, North.
THEATRE: Vanities (Off-Bdwy debut, 1976), Semmelweiss, Crimes of the Heart, The Art of Dining, Goodbye Fidel (Bdwy. debut, 1980), Chocolate Cake and Final Placement, Fifth of July, Come Back to the 5 & Dime Jimmy Dean Jimmy Dean, 'night Mother (Tony nom., Outer Critics Circle Award), Two Masters: The Rain of Terror, Curse of the Starving Class, Frankie and Johnny in the Clair de Lune (Obie, L.A. Drama Critics Award), The Road to Mecca.
TELEVISION: Movies: Johnny Bull, No Place Like Home, Roe vs. Wade, Hostages. Mini-Series: Murder Ordained, The Stand. Guest: The Love Boat, St. Elsewhere, Cagney and Lacey, L.A. Law, China Beach.

BATTY, PETER: Producer, Director, Writer. b. Sunderland, England, June 18, 1931. e. Bede Grammar Sch. and Queen's Coll., Oxford. Feature-writer both sides Atlantic 1954–58. Joined BBC TV 1958 dir. short films. Edited Tonight programme 1963–4. Exec. prod. ATV 1964–68. Awarded Grand Prix for doc. at 1965 Venice and Leipzig festivals. Official entries 1970 and 1971 San Francisco and Melbourne festivals. Nominated Intl. Emmy, 1986. Own company since 1968 prod. TV specials, series, commercials.
TELEVISION: The Quiet Revolution, The Big Freeze, The Katanga Affair, Sons of the Navvy Man, The Fall and Rise of the House of Krupp, The Road to Suez, The Suez Affair, Battle for the Desert, Vietnam Fly-In, The Plutocrats, The Aristocrats, Battle for Cassino, Battle for the Bulge, Birth of the Bomb, Search for the Super, Operation Barbarossa, Farouk: Last of the Pharaohs, Superspy, Spy Extraordinary, Sunderland's Pride and Passion, A Rothschild and His Red Gold, The World of Television, The Story of Wine, The Rise and Rise of Laura Ashley, The Gospel According to Saint Michael, Battle for Warsaw, Battle for Dien Bien Phu, Nuclear

25

Nightmares. A Turn Up in A Million, Il Poverello, Swindle!, The Algerian War, Fonteyn and Nureyev: The Perfect Partnership, The Divided Union, A Time for Remembrance, Swastika Over British Soil. Contributed 6 episodes to Emmy-winning World at War series.

BAUER, STEVEN: Actor. b. Havana, Cuba, Dec. 2, 1956. r.n. Steve Echervarria. Moved with family to Miami at age 3. e. Miami Dade Jr. Coll. where studied acting. Breakthrough came with selection for role in Que Pasa U.S.A.? for Public TV. Signed by Columbia TV and moved to California.
PICTURES: Scarface, Thief of Hearts, Running Scared, The Beast, Wildfire, Gleaming the Cube, Bloody Murder!, Raising Cain.
TELEVISION: Series: Wiseguy. Guest: The Rockford Files, From Here to Eternity, One Day at a Time, Hill Street Blues. Movies: Doctors' Private Lives, She's in the Army Now, Nichols and Dymes, An Innocent Love, Sword of Gideon, Sweet Poison, False Arrest, Drive Like Lightning. Mini-Series: Drug Wars: The Camarena Story.

BAUM, MARTIN: Executive. b. New York, NY, March 2, 1924. President, ABC Pictures; previously partner Baum & Newborn Theatrical Agency; head of West Coast office General Artists Corp., head of m.p. dept., Ashley Famous Agency; President of Martin Baum Agency; sr. exec. v.p. Creative Management Associations; president Optimus Productions, Inc., producing Bring Me the Head of Alfredo Garcia, The Wilby Conspiracy, and The Killer Elite. Partners with Michael Ovitz, Ron Meyer, Rowland Perkins, Bill Haber in Creative Artists Agency, Inc.

BAUMGARTEN, CRAIG: Executive. b. Aug. 27, 1949. Partner in independent prod. co., New America Cinema. Joined Paramount Pictures as prod. exec.; named v.p., prod. In 1980 went to Keith Barish Prods., of which was pres. three years. In 1983 appt. exec. v.p. & exec. asst. to the pres. & CEO, Columbia Pictures. Resigned 1985; joined Lorimar Motion Pictures as pres. Joined 20th Century Fox m.p. div. as exec. v.p. of production Oct. 1987. Resigned. 1989 formed Adelson/Baumgarten Prods. with Gary Adelson. Co-Producer: Hart to Kill, Universal Soldier, Nowhere to Run.

BAXTER, BILLY: Executive. b. New York, NY, Feb. 8, 1926. e. Holy Cross, 1948. Mgr., Ambassador Brokerage Group, Albany, 1957–58; Bill Doll & Co., 1959–63; organ., prod., radio show, Earl Wilson Celebrity Column, 1962; prod. Broadway show, Mandingo, with Franchot Tone, 1962; dir. of promotion, spec. events, Rumrill Ad Agency, 1963–64; dir. of promotion, exploitation, Landau Co., 1964–65; dir. of adv. and pub., Rizzoli Co., 1965–66. Consultant on special events to the Philip Morris Corp. and American Express.
PICTURES: Coprod.: Love and Anarchy, Daughters-Daughters, Outrageous, One Man, Dawn of the Dead. Prod.: Diary of the Cannes Film Festival with Rex Reed, 1980. Prod.-dir. documentaries: Artists of the Old West, Remington & Russell, Buffalo Bill Cody (1988).

BAXTER, KEITH: Actor. b. Monmouthshire, Wales, April 29, 1933. e. Wales, entered Royal Acad. of Dramatic Art in 1951. 1952–55 in national service; returned to RADA. Did years of repertory work in Dublin, Croydon, Chichester, London's West End, and New York. Biggest stage hit in Sleuth, both London and N.Y. Later in Corpse (London, NY).
PICTURES: The Barretts of Wimpole Street, Peeping Tom, Chimes at Midnight, With Love in Mind, Ash Wednesday, Berlin Blues.
TELEVISION: For Tea on Sunday, Hold My Hand Soldier, Saint Joan.

BAXTER, MEREDITH: Actress. b. Los Angeles, CA, June 21, 1947. e. Interlochen Arts Academy. On stage in Guys and Dolls, Butterflies Are Free, Vanities, Country Wife, Talley's Folly, Love Letters, Diaries of Adam & Eve.
PICTURES: Ben, Stand Up and Be Counted, Bittersweet Love, All the President's Men, Jezebel's Kiss.
TELEVISION: Series: The Interns, Bridget Loves Bernie, Family, Family Ties. Movies: Cat Creature, The Stranger Who Looks Like Me, Target Risk, The Imposter, The Night That Panicked America, Little Women, The Family Man, Beulah Land, Two Lives of Carol Letner, Take Your Best Shot, The Rape of Richard Beck, Kate's Secret, The Long Journey Home (also co-exec. prod.), Winnie: My Life in the Institution, She Knows Too Much, The Kissing Place, Burning Bridges, Bump in the Night, A Mother's Justice, A Woman Scorned: The Betty Broderick Story, Her Final Fury: Betty Broderick - The Last Chapter, Darkness Before Dawn (also co-exec. prod.). Specials: The Diaries of Adam and Eve, Vanities.

BAXTER, STANLEY: Actor. b. Glasgow, Scotland, May, 1928. e. Hillhead H.S., Glasgow. Principal comedian in Howard & Wyndham pantomimes. Summer revues. Televised regularly on BBC-TV, and also frequent broadcaster. M.P. debut 1955 in Geordie.
STAGE: The Amorous Prawn, On the Brighter Side, Chase Me Comrade (Australia), Cinderella, What the Butler Saw,

Phil The Fluter, Mother Goose Pantomime seasons 1970–74. Jack & The Beanstalk, Cinderella, Mother Goose, Aladdin, Cinderella.
PICTURES: Geordie (debut, 1955), Very Important Person, Crooks Anonymous, The Fast Lady, Father Came Too, Joey Boy.
TELEVISION: Baxter on (series) 1964; The Confidence Course, The World of Stanley Baxter, Stanley Baxter Show, Time for Baxter, The Stanley Baxter Big Picture Show, The Stanley Baxter Moving Picture Show, Part III, The Stanley Baxter's Christmas Box, Bing Crosby's Merrie Olde Christmas, Stanley Baxter's Greatest Hits, Baxter on Television, Stanley Baxter Series, The Stanley Baxter Hour, Children's Royal, Stanley Baxter's Christmas Hamper, Stanley Baxter's Picture Annual, 1986; Mr. Majeika, (series, 1988–89), Fitby.

BEAL, JOHN: Actor, r.n. James Alexander Bliedung. b. Joplin, MO, Aug. 13, 1909. e. Wharton Sch., U. of Pennsylvania. Author-Illustrator: Actor Drawing. Served in U.S.A.A.F., W.W.II.
THEATRE: Bdwy: Another Language, She Loves Me Not, Voice of the Turtle, Teahouse of the August Moon, The Crucible, A Little Hotel on the Side, The Master Builder, The Seagull, Three Men on a Horse. Off Bdwy: Long Day's Journey into Night, Our Town.
PICTURES: Another Language (debut, 1933), Hat Coat and Glove, Little Minister, Les Miserables, Laddie, Break of Hearts, We Who Are About to Die, Man Who Found Himself, Double Wedding, Port of Seven Seas, I am the Law, Arkansas Traveler, Cat and the Canary, Great Commandment, Doctors Don't Tell, Atlantic Convoy, Edge of Darkness, Stand By, All Networks, Key Witness, Madame X, Double Wedding, Beg Borrow or Steal, Alimony, Song of Surrender, Chicago Deadline, My Six Convicts, Remains to Be Seen, The Vampire, That Night, The Sound and the Fury, Ten Who Dared, The House That Cried Murder, Amityville 3-D, The Firm.

BEALS, JENNIFER: Actress. b. Chicago, IL, Dec. 19, 1963. Fashion model. Made film debut in small role in My Bodyguard, 1980.
PICTURES: Flashdance, The Bride, Split Decisions, Vampire's Kiss, Layover, Rider in the Dark, The Lizard's Tale, Sons, Jackal's Run, A Reasonable Doubt, Dr. M, Blood and Concrete, In the Soup.
TELEVISION: Series: 2000 Malibu Road. Specials: The Picture of Dorian Grey, Cinderella (Faerie Tale Theatre). Movies: Terror Strikes the Class Reunion, Indecency.

BEAN, ORSON: Actor. b. Burlington, VT, July 22, 1928. r.n. Dallas Burrows. Performed in nightclubs as comic and on Broadway (Never Too Late, Will Success Spoil Rock Hunter?, Subways Are for Sleeping, Roar of the Grease Paint, the Smell of the Crowd, Ilya Darling.) Author: Me and the Orgone. Founder, administrator, dir. 15th St. School, NY.
PICTURES: How to Be Very Very Popular (debut, 1955), Anatomy of a Murder, Lola, Forty Deuce, Innerspace, Instant Karma.
TELEVISION: Series: The Blue Angel (host), I've Got a Secret (panelist), Keep Talking, To Tell the Truth (reg. panelist), Mary Hartman Mary Hartman, One Life to Live, Dr. Quinn: Medicine Woman. Special: Arsenic and Old Lace.

BEAN, SEAN: Actor. b. Sheffield, Yorkshire, England, Apr. 17, 1958.
PICTURES: Caravaggio, Stormy Monday, War Requeim, The Field, Patriot Games.
THEATRE: Romeo and Juliet, Fair Maid of the West, Midsummer Night's Dream, Who Knew Mackenzie and Gone, Deathwatch, Last Days of Mankind.
TELEVISION: Troubles, Small Zones, 15 Street, My Kingdom for a Horse, Winter Flight, Samson & Delilah, The True Bride, Prince, Tell Me That You Love Me, Clarissa.

BEART, EMMANUELLE: Actress. b. Gassin, France, 1965. Moved to Montreal at age 15. Returned to France and enrolled in drama school.
PICTURES: Premiers Desirs, L'Enfant Retrouve, L'Amour en Douce, Manon of the Spring, Date With an Angel, A Gauche en Sortant de L'Ascenseur, Les Enfants du Desorde, Capitaine Fracasse, La Belle Noiseuse, J'Embrasse Pas, Un Coeur en Hiver (A Heart in Winter), Ruptures.
TELEVISION: Zacharius, Raison Perdue.
THEATRE: La Repetition ou l'Amour Puni, La Double Inconstance.

BEATTY, NED: Actor. b. Lexington, KY, July 6, 1937. Worked at Barter Theatre in Virginia appearing in over 70 plays 1957–66 and with Arena Stage, Washington D.C. 1963–71. Broadway debut: The Great White Hope.
PICTURES: Deliverance (debut, 1972), The Life and Times of Judge Roy Bean, The Thief Who Came to Dinner, The Last American Hero, White Lightning, Nashville, W.W. and the Dixie Dance Kings, All the President's Men, The Big Bus, Network, Mikey and Nicky, Silver Streak, Exorcist II: The Heretic, Gray Lady Down, The Great Georgia Bank Hoax,

Superman, Alambrista!, Promises in the Dark, 1941, Wise Blood, American Success Company, Hopscotch, The Incredible Shrinking Woman, Superman II, The Toy, Touched, Stroker Ace, Back to School, The Big Easy, The Fourth Protocol, The Trouble With Spies, Switching Channels, Rolling Vengeance, The Unholy, Midnight Crossing, After the Rain, Purple People Eater, Physical Evidence, Time Trackers, Big Bad John, Chattahoochee, A Cry in the Wild, Repossessed, Going Under, Tennessee Waltz, Hear My Song, Prelude to a Kiss, Ed and His Dead Mother, Rudy. TELEVISION: *Series*: Szysznyk. *Special*: Our Town (1977). *Movies*: Footsteps, Marcus-Nelson Murders, Dying Room Only, The Execution of Private Slovik, Attack on Terror: The FBI vs. the Ku Klux Klan, The Deadly Tower, Tail Gunner Joe, Lucan, A Question of Love, Friendly Fire, Guyana Tragedy: The Story of Jim Jones, All God's Children, The Violation of Sarah McDavid, Splendor in the Grass, Pray TV, A Woman Called Golda, Kentucky Woman, Hostage Flight, Go Toward the Light, Spy, Last Train Home, Back to Hannibal, The Tragedy of Flight 103: The Inside Story, Trial: The Price of Passion, T Bone N Weasel. *Guest*: Murder She Wrote, M*A*S*H, Rockford Files, Alfred Hitchcock, B.L. Stryker, Roseanne. *Mini-Series*: Celebrity, The Last Days of Pompeii, Robert Kennedy and His Times.

BEATTY, WARREN: Actor., Producer, Director. r.n. Henry Warren Beaty. b. Richmond, VA, March 30, 1937. Brother of Shirley MacLaine. m. actress Annette Bening. e. Northwestern U. Studied with Stella Adler. Small roles on television; on stage in Compulsion (winter stock, North Jersey Playhouse); Broadway debut: A Loss of Roses (Theatre World Award). PICTURES: Splendor in the Grass (debut, 1961), The Roman Spring of Mrs. Stone, All Fall Down, Lilith, Mickey One, Promise Her Anything, Kaleidoscope, Bonnie and Clyde (also prod.), The Only Game in Town, McCabe and Mrs. Miller, $ (Dollars), The Parallax View, Shampoo (also prod., co-s.p.), The Fortune, Heaven Can Wait (also prod., co-dir., co-s.p.), Reds (also prod., dir., co-s.p.; Acad. Award for Best Director: 1981), Ishtar (also prod.), Dick Tracy (also prod., dir.), Bugsy (also co-prod.). TELEVISION: *Series*: The Many Loves of Dobie Gillis (1959–60). *Guest*: Kraft Television Theatre, Studio One, Suspicion, Alcoa Presents, One Step Beyond, Wagon Train.

BECK, ALEXANDER J.: Executive. b. Ung. Brod, Czechoslovakia, Nov. 5, 1924. e. Charles U., Prague, NYU. Owns 500 features and westerns for foreign distribution and library of 1400 shorts. Importer and exporter; Pres., chairman of bd. Alexander Beck Films, 1955; formed Albex Films and A.B. Enterprises, 1959; formed & pres., Beckman Film Corp., 1960; formed Alexander Beck Productions, 1964. In 1969 formed Screencom Int'l Corp., 1986, formed Beck Int'l Corp., 1987; formed Challenger Pictures Corp., 1988.

BECK, JACKSON: Actor-announcer-narrator. b. New York, NY. TV and radio commercials, children's records, comm. industrial films; Narrator.

BECK, JOHN: Actor. b. Chicago, IL. Jan. 28, 1943. Acted with midwestern theatre groups; in scores of TV series. PICTURES: Three in the Attic (debut, 1968), Mrs. Pollifax: Spy, Lawman, Pat Garrett and Billy the Kid, Paperback Hero, Nightmare Honeymoon, Sleeper, Rollerball, Sky Riders, The Big Bus, Audrey Rose, The Other Side of Midnight, Deadly Illusion. TELEVISION: *Series*: Nichols, Flamingo Road, Dallas. Guest star roles on Bonanza, Mannix, Hawaii Five-0, Love American Style, Lancer, Gunsmoke, Partners in Crime, What Really Happened to the Class of '65. *Movies*: The Silent Gun, Lock Stock and Barrel, Sidekicks, The Law, Attack on Terror The FBI vs the Ku Klux Klan, Flamingo Road (pilot), The Time Machine, The Call of the Wild, Gridlock, Peyton Place: The Next Generation, Perry Mason: The Case of the Lady in the Lake. *Mini-Series*: Wheels.

BECK, MICHAEL: Actor. b. Memphis, TN, Feb. 4, 1949. e. Millsaps Coll. on football scholarship (quarterback). Became active in college theatre. In 1971 attended Central Sch. of Speech and Drama, London; studied 3 years, following which toured England with repertory companies for 2 years. Returned to U.S.; cast as lead in independent film, Madman (shot in Israel in 1977). PICTURES: Madman, The Warriors, Xanadu, Megaforce, War Lords of the 21st Century, The Golden Seal, Triumphs of a Man Called Horse. TELEVISION: *Mini-Series*: Holocaust, Celebrity. *Movies*: Mayflower: the Pilgrim's Adventure, Alcatraz: The Whole Shocking Story, Fly Away Home, The Last Ninja, Rearview Mirror, Chiller, Blackout, Only One Survived, The Reckoning, Houston: Legend of Texas, Deadly Game, Deadly Aim, Stranger at My Door, Fade to Black. *Series*: Houston Knights.

BECKER, HAROLD: Director. Dir. documentaries, Eugene Atget, Interview with Bruce Gordon, Blind Gary Davis, Signet, Ivanhoe Donaldson. PICTURES: The Ragman's Daughter, The Onion Field,

The Black Marble, Taps, Vision Quest, The Boost, Sea of Love.

BEDELIA, BONNIE: Actress. b. New York, NY, March 25, 1946. e. Hunter Coll. THEATER: Enter Laughing, The Playroom, My Sweet Charlie (Theatre World Award). PICTURES: The Gypsy Moths (debut, 1969), They Shoot Horses Don't They?, Lovers and Other Strangers, The Strange Vengeance of Rosalie, The Big Fix, Heart Like a Wheel, Death of an Angel, Violets Are Blue, The Boy Who Could Fly, Die Hard, The Prince of Pennsylvania, Fat Man & Little Boy, Die Hard 2, Presumed Innocent, Needful Things. TELEVISION: *Series*: Love of Life (1961–7), The New Land. *Movies*: Then Came Bronson, Sandcastles, A Time for Love, Hawkins on Murder (Death and the Maiden), Message to My Daughter, Heatwave!, A Question of Love, Walking Through the Fire, Salem's Lot, Tourist, Fighting Back, Million Dollar Infield, Memorial Day, Alex: The Life of a Child, The Lady from Yesterday, Somebody Has to Shoot the Picture, Switched at Birth, A Mother's Right: The Elizabeth Morgan Story, The Fire Next Time. *Special*: The Gift. *Guest*: Fallen Angels (The Quiet Room).

BEERY, NOAH, JR.: Actor. b. New York, NY, Aug. 10, 1916. e. Urban and Harvard Mil. Acad. Son of Noah Beery, screen actor. Travelled with parents in stock company. Appeared as child in Mark of Zorro, 1920. PICTURES: Father and Son, Road Back, Only Angels Have Wings, Doolins of Oklahoma, Davy Crockett, Indian Scout, Last Outpost, Savage Horde, Rocketship XM, Two Flags West, Tropic Zone, Cimarron Kid, Wagons West, Story of Will Rogers, Wings of the Hawk, War Arrow, The Yellow Tomahawk, Black Dakotas, White Feather, Jubal, Fastest Gun Alive, Inherit the Wind, 7 Faces of Dr. Lao, Incident at Phantom Hill, Journey to Shiloh, Heaven With A Gun, Little Faus and Big Halsy, Walking Tall, The Spikes Gang, The Best Little Whorehouse in Texas. TELEVISION: *Series*: Circus Boy, Riverboat, Hondo, Doc Elliot, The Rockford Files, The Quest, Yellow Rose.

BEGLEY, ED, JR.: Actor. b. Los Angeles, CA, Sept. 16, 1949. Son of late actor Ed Begley. Debut in a guest appearance on My Three Sons at 17. PICTURES: The Computer Wore Tennis Shoes (debut, 1970), Now You See Him Now You Don't, Stay Hungry, Citizens Band (Handle With Care), Blue Collar, The One and Only, Goin' South, Hardcore, The Concorde: Airport '79, The In-Laws, Private Lessons, Cat People, Eating Raoul, Get Crazy, This Is Spinal Tap, Streets of Fire, Protocol, Transylvania 6-5000, Amazon Women on the Moon, The Accidental Tourist, Scenes From the Class Struggle in Beverly Hills, She-Devil, Meet the Applegates, Dark Horse, Greedy. TELEVISION: *Series*: Roll Out, St. Elsewhere (1982–88), Parenthood, Winnetka Road. *Guest*: Room 222, Love American Style, Happy Days, Columbo, M*A*S*H, Barnaby Jones, Doris Day Show, Mary Hartman Mary Hartman, Faerie Tale Theatre. *Movies*: Family Flight, Amateur Night at the Dixie Bar and Grill, Elvis, Hot Rod, A Shining Season, Rascals and Robbers—The Secret Adventures of Tom Sawyer and Huck Finn, Tales of the Apple Dumpling Gang, Voyagers, Not Just Another Affair, Still the Beaver, An Uncommon Love, Insight/The Clearing House, Roman Holiday, Spies Lies & Naked Thighs, Not a Penny More Not a Penny Less, In the Best Inerest of the Child, The Big One: The Great Los Angeles Earthquake, Chance of a Lifetime, The Story Lady, In the Line of Duty: Siege at Marion, Exclusive, Running Mates. Cooperstown. *Special*: Mastergate.

BELAFONTE, HARRY: Actor, Singer, Producer. b. New York, NY, March 1, 1927. Trained for stage at the Actors Studio, New Sch. for Social Research and American Negro Theatre. Professional debut, Royal Roost nightclub, N.Y., Village Vanguard, 1950. Broadway debut: John Murray Anderson's Almanac, 1953. Recording, concert artist. Emmy Award for Tonight With Harry Belafonte 1961. THEATER: Juno and the Paycock, John Murray Anderson's Almanac. (Tony Award, supp. actor, 1953), Three for Tonight, A Night With Belafonte, To Be Young Gifted and Black (prod.), Asinamali (co-prod.). PICTURES: Bright Road (debut, 1953), Carmen Jones, Island in the Sun, Odds Against Tomorrow, The World the Flesh and the Devil, The Angel Levine, Buck and the Preacher, Uptown Saturday Night (also prod.), Beat Street (prod. only), The Player. TELEVISION: *Series*: Sugar Hill Times. *Movie*: Grambling's White Tiger. Many variety specials.

BELAFONTE, SHARI: Actress. b. New York, NY, Sept. 22, 1954. Daughter of actor-singer Harry Belafonte. e. Carnegie-Mellon U., BFA, 1976. Worked as publicist's asst. at Hanna Barbera Prods. before becoming successful model (appearing on more than 200 magazine covers and in numerous TV commercials). PICTURES: If You Could See What I Hear, Time Walker, Murder One Murder Two, The Player.

TELEVISION: *Series*: Hotel (1983–88). *Pilot*: Velvet. *Guest*: Hart to Hart, Code Red, Trapper John M.D., Different Strokes, The Love Boat, Matt Houston. *Movies*: The Night the City Screamed, The Midnight Hour, Kate's Secret, Perry Mason: The Case of the All-Star Assassin. *Host*: Big Hex of Little Lulu, AM Los Angeles, Living the Dream: a Tribute to Dr. Martin Luther King, Jr.

BELFER, HAL B.: Executive producer, director, choreographer. b. Los Angeles, CA, Feb. 16. e. U. of Southern California (cinematography); U. of California (writing). Head of choreography dept. at 20th Century-Fox. Head of choreography dept. at Universal Studios. Dir. of entertainment, in Las Vegas, Riviera and Flamingo Hotels. Prod., musical shows for Mexico City, Aruba, Puerto Rico, Montreal, Las Vegas. Dir., TV commercials and industrials. H.R. Pufnstuf TV series. Theatricals: Over 150 features. Producer-director-choreographer, Premore, Inc. Develop TV specials and sitcom, tape and film. Exec. prod., Once Upon a Tour and Dora's World, Rose on Broadway, Secret Sleuth, Inn by the Side of the Road, Imagine That! Special staging "Tony The Pony" Series and prod., segment of What a Way to Run a Railroad; TV specials. Talent development programs, Universal Studios, 20th Century-Fox. Personal management and show packager; 1982, exec. prod., Enchanted Inn (TV Special), Cameo Music Hall I, Stage mgr.: Promises, Promises, A Chorus Line (Sahara Hotel, Las Vegas).

BEL GEDDES, BARBARA: Actress. r.n. Barbara Geddes Lewis. b. New York, NY, Oct 31, 1922. Father was Norman Bel Geddes, scenic designer. Bdwy debut in Out of the Frying Pan; toured USO camps in Junior Miss, 1941; Star of Tomorrow, 1949. Author-illustrator children's books: I Like to Be Me (1963), So Do I (1972). Also designer of greeting cards for George Caspari Co.
THEATER: Out of the Frying Pan, Deep Are the Roots, Burning Bright, The Moon Is Blue, Living Room, Cat on a Hot Tin Roof, The Sleeping Prince, Silent Night Holy Night, Mary Mary, Everything in the Garden, Finishing Touches.
PICTURES: The Long Night (debut, 1947), I Remember Mama (Acad Award nom.), Blood on the Moon, Caught, Panic in the Streets, Fourteen Hours, Vertigo, The Five Pennies, Five Branded Women, By Love Possessed, Summertree, The Todd Killings.
TELEVISION: Live TV in 1950s: Robert Montgomery Presents (The Philadelphia Story), Schlitz Playhouse of the Stars; several Alfred Hitchcock Presents episodes (incl. Lamb to the Slaughter), Our Town. *Series*: Dallas (Emmy Award, 1980).

BELL, TOM: Actor. b. Liverpool, England, 1932. Early career in repertory and on West End stage. First TV appearance in Promenade.
TELEVISION: No Trams to Lime Street, Love On the Dole, A Night Out, Cul de Sac, The Seekers, Long Distance Blue, The Virginian, The Rainbow, Prime Suspect.
PICTURES: Payroll, The Kitchen, H.M.S. Defiant, Prize of Arms, L-Shaped Room, Rebels Against the Light, Ballad in Blue, He Who Rides a Tiger, In Enemy Country, The Long Day's Dying, Lock Up Your Daughters, All the Right Noises, Quest for Love, The Spy's Wife, Wish You Were Here, Resurrected, The Magic Toy Shop, The Krays.

BELLAMY, EARL: Producer, Director. b. Minneapolis, MN, March 11, 1917. e. Los Angeles City Coll. Universal Studios. President, The Bellamy Productions Co.
PICTURES: Fluffy, Gun Point, Munsters Go Home, Sidewinder, Speedtrap.
TELEVISION: Bachelor Father, Wells Fargo, Lone Ranger, Alcoa Premiere, Arrest and Trial, The Virginian, The Crusaders, Schlitz Playhouse, Heinz, Rawhide, The Donna Reed Show, Andy Griffith Show, Wagon Train, Laramie, Laredo, I Spy, Mod Squad, Medical Center.

BELLFORT, JOSEPH: b. New York, NY, Sept. 20, 1912. e. NYU, Brooklyn Law Sch. Joined RKO Service Corp., Feb., 1930; trans. to RKO Radio Pictures, legal dept., May 1942; joined RKO Fgn. dept., Oct., 1944, handled Far Eastern division, Dec. 1946; then asst. to European gen. mgr.; gen. European mgr., 1949–1958; gen. sales mgr. National Screen Service, 1959; home office supv., Europe & Near East, 20th Century-Fox, 1963; home office intl. mgr., 20th Century-Fox, 1966. Ass't v.p. and foreign mgr. 20th Cent.-Fox, 1967; vice president 20th Century-Fox, Intl. Corp. & Inter-America, Inc. 1968; named sr. v.p., 1975. Resigned from Fox, 1977, to become v.p., Motion Picture Export Assn. of America in New York. Retired 1983.

BELLOCCHIO, MARCO: Director, writer. b. Piacenza, Italy, Nov. 9, 1939. e. Milan (letters and philosophy); Centro Sperimentale di Cinematografia, Rome; School of Fine Arts, London 1959–63. Collaborated on Paola and Viva il primo maggio rosso.
PICTURES: Fist in His Pocket, China Is Near, Leap into the Void, In the Name of the Father, Strike the Monster on Page One (co-dir., co-s.p.), Salo, Il Gabbiano, Vacations in Val

Trebbia, The Eyes the Mouth, Henry IV, Sabbeth, Devil in the Flesh, La Visione del Sabba.

BELMONDO, JEAN-PAUL: Actor. b. Neuilly-sur-Seine, France, April 9, 1933. e. private drama school of Raymond Girard, and the Conservatoire d'Art Dramatique. Formed a theater group with Annie Girardot and Guy Bedos.
THEATRE: Jean Marais' production of Caesar and Cleopatra, Treasure Party, Oscar.
PICTURES: A Pied a Cheval et En Voiture (By Foot Horse and Car), Look Pretty and Shut Up, Drole de Dimanche, Les Tricheurs, Les Copains du Dimanche, Charlotte et Son Jules, A Double Tour, Breathless, Classe Tous Risques, Moderato Cantabile, La Francaise et l'Amour, Les Distractions, Mademoiselle Ange, La Novice, Two Women, La Viaccia, Une Femme Est une Femme, Leon Morin, Pretre, Les Amours Celebres, Un Singe en Hiver, Le Doulos, L'Aine des Ferchaux, La Mer A Boire, Banana Peel, That Man From Rio, Cent Mille Dollars au Soleil, Echappement Libre, La Chasse a l'Homme, Dieu a Choisi Paris, Weekend a Zuydcocte, Par Un Beau Matin d'Ete, Up to His Ears, Is Paris Burning?, Casino Royale, The Thief of Paris, Pierrot le Fou, The Brain, Love Is a Funny Thing, Mississippi Mermaid, Borsalino, A Man I Like, The Burglars, Tender Scoundrel, Inheritor, Stavisky, Fear Over the City, L'Animal, The Professional, Ace of Aces, The Vultures, Happy Easter, Hold Up, Le Solitaire, Itinerary of a Spoiled Child (also prod.).

BELSON, JERRY: Producer, Director, Writer. With Garry Marshall, writer of The Dick Van Dyke Show (Emmy), and prod. of The Odd Couple (Emmy). Together team wrote and prod. feature films: How Sweet It Is (1968) and The Grasshopper as well as co-authoring the Broadway play The Roast (1980).
PICTURES: Smile (s.p.), Fun With Dick and Jane (s.p.), Smokey and the Bandit II (s.p.), Student Bodies (exec. prod.), The End (s.p.), Jekyll and Hyde Together Again (dir.), Surrender (dir., s.p.), For Keeps (prod.), Always (co-s.p.).
TELEVISION: The Dick Van Dyke Show, The Odd Couple, The Tracey Ullmann Show (co-creator, co-exec. prod.; 2 Emmy Awards).

BELUSHI, JAMES (Jim): Actor. b. Chicago, IL, June 15, 1954. e. DuPage Coll., Southern Illinois U. Brother, late John Belushi. Worked with Chicago's Second City Revue.
THEATER: Sexual Perversity in Chicago, The Pirates of Penzance, True West, Conversations With My Father.
PICTURES: Thief (debut, 1981), Trading Places, The Man with One Red Shoe, Salvador, About Last Night, Jumpin' Jack Flash, Little Shop of Horrors, Number One With a Bullet (co-s.p. only), The Principal, Real Men, Red Heat, Who's Harry Crumb? (cameo), K-9, Homer and Eddie, Wedding Band (cameo), Taking Care of Business, Mr. Destiny, The Palermo Connection, Only the Lonely, Masters of Menace, Curly Sue, Once Upon a Crime, Diary of a Hitman, Traces of Red, Last Action Hero (cameo).
TELEVISION: *Series*: Who's Watching the Kids?, Working Stiffs, Saturday Night Live. *Specials*: The Joseph Jefferson Awards, The Best Legs in the 8th Grade, Cinemax's Comedy Experiment's Birthday Boy (also prod., writer). *Mini-Series*: Wild Palms.

BENDICK, ROBERT: Indep. documentary prod., dir. b. New York, NY, Feb. 8, 1917. e. NYU, White School Photography. U.S. Air Force, W.W.II. Documentary and still cameraman before joining CBS Television as cameraman and dir.; 1940; rejoined CBS Television as dir. special events, 1946; promoted dir. news & special events; acting program dir. 1947; res. Oct. '51. Collab with Jeanne Bendick on Making the Movies, Electronics for Young People, Television Works Like This, Filming Works Like This, 1971; Prod. Peabody award-winning U.N. show The U.N. in Action; v.p., Cinerama Prod., co-prod. This Is Cinerama; co-dir., Cinerama Holiday; prod. Dave Garroway Show Today, prod., Wide Wide World 1955–56, NBC prod. dir. C.V. Whitney Pict., June, 1956; Merian C. Cooper Ent., 1957; prod. NBC, 1958. Prod.; Garroway Today Show, Bob Hope 25 Yrs. of Life Show, 1961; Bell Telephone Threshold Science Series, Groucho Marx, Merrily We Roll Along, US Steel Opening New York World's Fair, 1964. Prod. First Look Series 1965 (Ohio St. Award); prod. & dir. American Sportsman, ABC; prod., pilot, Great American Dream Machine (NET) (Emmy Award, 1971 and 1972); 1975, Co-exec. prod., Dick Cavett—Feeling Good. pres. Bendick Assoc. Inc.,; prod. of education audio-visual systems, Bd. of Governors, N.Y. Academy of TV Arts and Sciences. 1976, co-author with Jeanne Bendick, TV Reporting. Consultant, Warner Qube Cable Co.; 1978, produced/directed, Fight for Food (PBS). Program consultant to Times-Mirror Cable Co., L.A. Produced segment ABC 20/20. Member awards committee, National TV Acad. Arts & Science. Co-author with Jeanne Bendick of Eureka It's Television (1993).

BENEDICT, DIRK: Actor. r.n. Dirk Niewoehner. b. Helena, MT, March 1, 1945. e. Whitman Coll., Walla Walla, WA. Enrolled in John Fernald Academy of Dramatic Arts, Rochester, MI, after which had season with Seattle Repertory Theatre; also in summer stock at Ann Arbor, MI. Broadway debut, 1970,

Abelard and Heloise. Author: Confessions of a Kamikaze Cowboy.Film debut, Georgia, Georgia, 1972.
PICTURES: Ssssss, W, Battlestar Galactica, Scavenger Hunt, Ruckus, Underground Aces, Body Slam, Blue Tornado, Shadow Force, Cahoots.
TELEVISION: Guest: Love Boat, Murder She Wrote, Hawaii Five-O. Series: Chopper One, Battlestar Galactica, The A Team, Movies: Journey from Darkness, The Georgia Peaches, Scruples, Trenchcoat in Paradise.

BENEDICT, PAUL: Actor, Director. b. Silver City, NM, Sept. 17, 1938. Acted with the Theatre Company of Boston, Arena Stage, D.C.; Trinity Rep., Providence; Playhouse in the Park, Cincinnati; Center Stage, Baltimore; A.R.T., Cambridge.
PICTURES: They Might Be Giants, Taking Off, Up the Sandbox, Jeremiah Johnson, The Front Page, The Goodbye Girl, This is Spinal Tap, Arthur 2 on the Rocks, Cocktail, The Chair, The Freshman, Sibling Rivalry, The Addams Family.
TELEVISION: Series: Sesame Street (1969–74), The Jeffersons, Mama Malone. Movies: Hustling, Baby Cakes. Mini-Series: The Blue and the Gray. Guest: Kojak, Maude, All in the Family, Harry-O.
THEATRE: NY: Little Murders, The White House Murder Case, Bad Habits, It's Only a Play. LA: The Unvarnished Truth, It's Only a Play. Director: Frankie & Johnnie in the Clair de Lune, Bad Habits, The Kathy and Mo Show, Beyond Therapy, Geniuses.

BENING, ANNETTE: Actress. b. Topeka, KS, May 29, 1958. e. San Francisco St. Univ. m. actor Warren Beatty.
PICTURES: The Great Outdoors (debut, 1988), Valmont, Postcards from the Edge, The Grifters (Natl. Society of film Critics Award, Acad. Award nom., best supp. actress, 1990), Guilty by Suspicion, Regarding Henry, Bugsy.
THEATRE: Coastal Disturbances (Tony Award nom., Theatre World Award), Spoils of War.
TELEVISION: Guest: Miami Vice, Wiseguy. Pilot: It Had to Be You. Movies: Manhunt for Claude Dallas, Hostage.

BENJAMIN, RICHARD: Actor, Director. b. New York, NY, May 22, 1939. m. actress Paula Prentiss. e. Northwestern U.
THEATER: Central Park productions of The Taming of the Shrew, As You Like It; toured in Tchin Tchin, A Thousand Clowns, Barefoot in the Park, The Odd Couple. Broadway debut in Star Spangled Girl (Theatre World Award, 1966), also in The Little Black Book, The Norman Conquests. Directed London productions of Barefoot in the Park.
PICTURES: Actor: Thunder Over the Plains (debut, 1953), Crime Wave, Goodbye Columbus, Catch-22, Diary of a Mad Housewife, The Marriage of a Young Stockbroker, The Steagle, Portnoy's Complaint, The Last of Sheila, Westworld, The Sunshine Boys, House Calls, Love at First Bite, Scavenger Hunt, The Last Married Couple in America, Witches' Brew, How to Beat the High Cost of Living, First Family, Saturday the 14th. Director: My Favorite Year, Racing with the Moon, City Heat, The Money Pit, Little Nikita, My Stepmother Is an Alien, Downtown, Mermaids, Made in America, Milk Money.
TELEVISION: Series: He and She (with Paula Prentiss, 1967), Quark. Special: Arthur Miller's Fame. Movies: No Room to Run (Australia), Packin' It In.

BENNETT, ALAN: Author, Actor. b. Leeds, England, May 9, 1934. e. Oxford U. With Jonathan Miller, Dudley Moore and Peter Cook co-authored and starred in satirical revue Beyond the Fringe in London (1961) and on Bdwy (special Tony Award, 1963).
THEATER: Forty Years On (actor, author), Getting On, Habeas Corpus (also actor), The Old Country, Enjoy, Kafka's Dick, Single Spies (also dir.).
PICTURES: Actor: The Secret Policeman's Other Ball, Long Shot, Dream Child (voice), Little Dorrit. Writer: A Private Function, Prick Up Your Ears.
TELEVISION: Famous Gossips, On the Margin (also actor), An Evening With, A Day Out, Sunset Across the Bay, A Little Outing, A Visit from Miss Prothero, Me—I'm Afraid of Virginia Wood, Doris and Doreen, The Old Crowd, Afternoon Off, All Day on the Sands, The Insurance Man, Talking Heads (6 TV monologues), One Fine Day, Our Winnie, A Woman of No Importance, Rolling Home, Marks, An Englishman Abroad, Intensive Care (also appeared in), 102 Boulevard Haussmann, Poetry in Motion.

BENNETT, BRUCE: Actor. r.n. Herman Brix. b. Tacoma, WA, 1909; e. U. of Washington.
PICTURES: My Son Is Guilty, Lone Wolf Keeps a Date, Atlantic Convoy, Sabotage, Underground Agent, More the Merrier, Sahara, Man I Love, Stolen Life, Nora Prentiss, Cheyenne, Treasure of Sierra Madre, Dark Passage, Smart Girls Don't Talk, Second Face, Great Missouri Raid, Angels in the Outfield, Sudden Fear, Dream Wife, Dragonfly Squadron, Robbers Roost, Big Tipoff, Hidden Guns, Bottom of the Bottle, Strategic Air Command, Mildred Pierce, Danger Signal, Silver River, Younger Brothers, Task Force, Without Honor, Mystery Street, The Last Outpost, Three Violent People, The Outsider, etc.

BENNETT, CHARLES: Writer, Director. b. Shoreham, England, Aug. 2, 1899. British Army. Contract, Universal, 1937; wrote for British Ministry of Information, W.W.II; dir. s.p. over 50 TV shows, including Cavalcade of America, Schlitz Playhouse, The Christophers, Four Star.
PLAYS: Blackmail, The Last Hour, Sensation, The Danger Line, Page From a Diary, The Return, After Midnight.
PICTURES: Blackmail, The 39 Steps, Secret Agent, The Man Who Knew Too Much (orig.), Sabotage, The Girl Was Young, Balalaika, The Young in Heart, Foreign Correspondent, Reap the Wild Wind, Joan of Paris, They Dare Not Love, The Story of Dr. Wassell, Unconquered, Ivy, Sign of the Ram, Kind Lady, The Green Glove, Dangerous Assignment, Madness of the Heart (dir.), The Big Circus, The Lost World, Voyage to the Bottom of the Sea, Five Weeks in a Balloon.

BENNETT, HARVE: Producer. r.n. Harve Fischman. b. Chicago, IL, Aug. 17, 1930. e. UCLA. Quiz Kids radio show, 5 yrs.; newspaper columnist, drama critic; freelance writer; Assoc. prod., CBS-TV; freelance TV writer; prod. of special events. CBS-TV; dir., Television film commercials; program exec., ABC, vice pres., programs west coast—ABC-TV
TELEVISION: Pres., Bennett-Katleman. Productions at Columbia Studios. Series: Mod Squad. (prod., writer), The Young Rebels (creator-writer), Six Million Dollar Man (exec. prod.), Bionic Woman (exec. prod.), American Girls (exec. prod.). From Here to Eternity, Salvage 1, Time Trax (writer, exec. prod.). Mini-Series: Rich Man, Poor Man. Movies: A Woman Named Golda (exec. prod.; Emmy Award), The Jesse Owens Story (exec. prod.), Crash Landing: The Rescue of Flight 232 (writer).
PICTURES: Exec. prod. & co-story: Star Trek II: The Wrath of Khan; Star Trek IV: The Voyage Home (prod., co-s.p.), Star Trek V: The Final Frontier (prod., co-story). prod. & author of Star Trek III: The Search for Spock. 1984, entered long-term deal with Para.

BENNETT, HYWEL: Actor, Director. b. Garnant, South Wales, Apr. 8, 1944. Early career National Youth Theatre where he played many leading Shakespearean roles followed by extensive work in British theatre. 1971–81: directed numerous stage productions.
PICTURES: The Family Way (debut, 1967), Drop Dead My Love, Twisted Nerve, The Virgin Soldiers, The Buttercup Chain, Loot, Percy, Endless Night, Alice in Wonderland, Murder Elite, War Zone.
TELEVISION: Where The Buffalo Roam, Malice Aforethought, Tinker Tailor Soldier Spy, series, Artemis 81, Myself A Mandarin, Frankie and Johnnie, Check Point Chiswick, Twilight Zone, The Idiot, The Traveller, Death of a Teddy Bear, Three's One, Pennies From Heaven, Shelley (series), The Critic, The Consultant, Absent Friends, The Secret Agent, A Mind to Kill, Virtual Murder, The Other Side of Paradise.

BENSON, HUGH: Producer. Exec. Prod., Screen Gems; exec. prod., MGM Television. On staff Col.-TV, plots and long form.
PICTURES: Nightmare Honeymoon (prod.), Logan's Run (assoc. prod.), Billy Jack Goes to Washington (prod.).
TELEVISION: Producer: Contract On Cherry St., Child Stealers, Goldie and the Boxer, A Fire in the Sky, Shadow Riders, Confessions of a Lady Cop, The Dream Merchants, Goldie and the Boxer Go to Hollywood, Goliath Awaits, The Blue and the Gray, Hart to Hart, Master of Ballantrae, Anna Karenina, The Other Lover, I Dream of Jeannie 15 Yrs. Later, Miracle of the Heart: A Boy's Town Story, Crazy Like a Fox, In the Heat of the Night (pilot and series), Daughter of the Streets, Back to Hannibal: Tom and Huck Return, Danielle Steele's Fine Things, Danielle Steele's Changes, Shadow of a Stranger, Diana: Her True Story, Message From 'Nam.

BENSON, LEON: Producer, Director. b. Cincinnati, OH, Nov. 9. e. NYU, U. of Cincinnati. Advertising Dept. Paramount, 1938, head of Trailer Dept., 1940. U.S. Army Air Corps, 1942–46, Major. First head of TV Dept. L.A. office of J. Walter Thompson Co., 1946–51. Head of Story Dept. Ziv TV, 1951; prod. and dir. West Point, 1955–56; Sea Hunt, 1956–60; Ripcord, 1960–62. Prod.-Dir. Flipper TV series, 1963–64. Under contract, Universal, 1965–66, prod.-dir. episodes, Kraft Suspense Theatre, The Virginian. dir. episodes, Chrysler Theatre, Laredo. Prod. Tarzan TV series, 1966. Under contract, NBC Prods., 1967–70, as staff dir. Bonanza, High Chaparral. Prod. theatrical feature, Chosen Survivors, 1973. Also dir. Owen Marshall, Counsellor at Law, Mission Impossible, The Eleventh Hour, Ben Casey, Wild Wild West, Rat Patrol, The Lieutenant, Outer Limits, The Loner, Empire.

BENSON, ROBBY: Actor, Writer, Director. r.n. Robert Segal. b. Dallas, TX, Jan. 21, 1956. m. actress Karla DeVito. Father is Jerry Segal, novelist and screenwriter, mother is Ann Benson, veteran of Dallas stage and nat'l summer stock and nat'l spokesperson for Merrill Lynch. Appeared in commercials and summer stock at age 5. Bdwy debut at age 12 in Zelda. Dir. debut 1989, White Hot (a.k.a. Crack in the Mirror). Composed music for Diana Ross, Karla DeVito and soundtrack of film The Breakfast Club.
PICTURES: Jory (debut, 1973), Jeremy, Lucky Lady, Ode

to Billy Joe, One on One (also co-s.p. with father), The End, Ice Castles, Walk Proud (also co-s.p. & co-composer with father), Die Laughing (also prod., co-s.p., co-composer), Tribute, National Lampoon Goes to the Movies, The Chosen, Running Brave, Harry and Son, City Limits, Rent-a-Cop, White Hot (also dir.), Modern Love (also dir., s.p., composed songs), Beauty and the Beast (voice), Betrayal of the Dove (s.p. only), The Webbers.
TELEVISION: Movies: Death Be Not Proud, The Death of Richie, Remember When, Virginia Hill Story, All the Kind Strangers, Two of a Kind, California Girls, Invasion of Privacy, Homewrecker. Specials: Our Town, The Last of Mrs. Lincoln. Series: Search for Tomorrow, Tough Cookies. Guest: One Day at a Time, Alfred Hitchcock Presents (1985). Director: True Confessions (3 episodes).
STAGE: NY: Zelda, The Rothschilds, Dude, The Pirates of Penzance. Regional: Oliver!, Evita, The King and I, King of Hearts, Do Black Patent Leather Shoes Really Reflect Up?

BENTON, ROBERT: Writer, Director. b. Waxahachie, TX, 1932. e. U. of Texas, B.A. Was art director and later consulting ed. at Esquire Magazine where he met David Newman, a writer-editor, and formed writing partnership. Together wrote a monthly column for Mademoiselle (10 years). Benton made directorial debut with Bad Company, 1972.
PICTURES: With Newman wrote: Bonnie and Clyde, There Was a Crooked Man, What's Up, Doc? Co-s.p.: Superman (with Mario Puzo and Tom Mankiewicz). As dir-writer: Bad Company, The Late Show, Kramer vs. Kramer (Acad. Awards for best dir. & s.p.), Still of the Night, Places in the Heart (Acad. Award for best s.p.), Nadine, The House on Carroll Street (co-exec. prod. only), Billy Bathgate (dir. only).
STAGE: It's a Bird . . . It's a Plane . . . It's Superman (libretto), Oh! Calcutta (one sketch).

BERENGER, TOM: Actor. b. Chicago, IL, May 31, 1950. e. U. of Missouri (drama). Studied acting at H.B. Studios. Acted in regional theatres and off-off-Broadway. Plays include Death Story, The Country Girl, National Anthems, The Rose Tattoo, Electra, Streetcar Named Desire, End as a Man (Circle Rep.).
PICTURES: The Sentinel (debut, 1977), Looking for Mr. Goodbar, In Praise of Older Women, Butch and Sundance: The Early Days, The Dogs of War, Beyond the Door, The Big Chill, Eddie and the Cruisers, Fear City, Rustler's Rhapsody, Platoon, Someone to Watch Over Me, Shoot to Kill, Betrayed, Last Rites, Major League, Born on the Fourth of July, Love at Large, The Field, Shattered, At Play in the Fields of the Lord, Sniper, Sliver, Gettysburg, Chasers.
TELEVISION: Series: One Life to Live (1975–6). Movies: Johnny We Hardly Knew Ye. Mini-Series: Flesh and Blood, If Tomorrow Comes. Special: Dear America (reader).

BERENSON, MARISA: Actress. b. New York, NY, Feb. 15, 1947. Granddaughter of haute couture fashion designer Schiaparelli. Great niece of art critic and historian Bernard Berenson. Former model.
PICTURES: Death in Venice, Cabaret, Barry Lyndon, Killer Fish, S.O.B., The Secret Diary of Sigmund Freud, La Tete Dans le Sac, L'Arbalete, Desire, Quel Treno da Vienna, Il Giardino Dei Cigliegi, Winds of the South, White Hunter Black Heart, Night of the Cyclone, The Cherry Orchard, Flagrant Desire.
TELEVISION: Movies: Tourist, Playing for Time, Notorious. Mini-Series: Sins, Hemingway. Also: Lo Scialo, Blue Blood, Have a Nice Night, L'Enfant Des Loups, Oceano, Hollywood Detective, Bel Ami, Murder She Wrote (guest).

BERESFORD, BRUCE: Director. Writer. b. Sydney, Australia, Aug. 16, 1940. e. U. of Sydney, B.A. 1962. Worked as teacher in London, 1961. Film editor, East Nigerian Film Unit, 1966; sect. and head of prod., British Film Inst. Production Board, 1966–71.
PICTURES: Director: The Adventures of Barry McKenzie (also co-s.p.), Barry McKenzie Holds His Own (also prod., co-s.p.), Don's Party, The Getting of Wisdom, Money Movers, Breaker Morant (also s.p.), The Club, Puberty Blues, Tender Mercies, King David, The Fringe Dwellers (also s.p.), Crimes of the Heart, Aria (sequence), Her Alibi, Driving Miss Daisy, Mister Johnson (also co-s.p.), Black Robe, Rich in Love, A Good Man in Africa.

BERG, DICK: Writer, Producer. b. New York, NY. e. Lehigh U. 1942; Harvard Business Sch. 1943. Prior to 1960 writer for TV shows Playhouse 90 Studio One, Robert Montgomery Presents, Kraft Television Playhouse. 1961–69 prod., writer for Universal Studios; exec. prod. The Chrysler Theatre, Alcoa Premiere, Checkmate. Created and wrote Staccato (series). 1971–85: prod., writer of over 50 TV movies via his Stonehenge Prods. TV films won 15 Emmies, 23 nominations. Twice elected pres. National Acad. of Television Arts and Sciences.
PICTURES: Prod.: Counterpoint, House of Cards, Banning Shoot (also s.p.), Fresh Horses.
TELEVISION: Prod. &/or writer: Mini-series: A Rumor of War, The Martian Chronicles, The Word, Space, Wallenberg: A Hero's Story. Movies: Rape and Marriage: The Rideout Case, An Invasion of Privacy, Thief, Footsteps, Firehouse,

American Geisha, Class of '63, Louis Armstrong, Chicago Style, Everybody's Baby: The Rescue of Jessica McClure (exec. prod.)

BERG, JEFF: Executive. b. Los Angeles, CA, May 26, 1947. e. U of California, Berkeley, B.A., 1969. V.P., head lit. div., Creative Mgt. Associates, Los Angeles, 1969–75; v.p., m.p. dept., International Creative Associates, 1975–80; pres., 1980–. Dir., Joseph Intl. Industries.

BERGEN, CANDICE: Actress. b. Beverly Hills, CA, May 9, 1946. m. dir. Louis Malle. Daughter of late ventriloquist Edgar Bergen. e. U. of Pennsylvania. Modeled during college; freelance photo-journalist. Autobiography: Knock Wood (1984). Bdwy debut in Hurlyburly.
PICTURES: The Group (debut, 1966), The Sand Pebbles, The Day the Fish Came Out, Live for Life, The Magus, The Adventurers, Getting Straight, Soldier Blue, Carnal Knowledge, The Hunting Party, T. R. Baskin, 11 Harrowhouse, The Wind and the Lion, Bite the Bullet, The Domino Principle, A Night Full of Rain, Oliver's Story, Starting Over, Rich and Famous, Gandhi, Stick.
TELEVISION: Series: Murphy Brown (3 Emmy Awards). Mini-Series: Hollywood Wives. Movies: Arthur the King, Murder: By Reason of Insanity, Mayflower Madam. Specials: Woody Allen Special, Moving Day (Trying Times).

BERGEN, POLLY: Singer, Actress. r.n. Nellie Burgin b. Knoxville, TN, July 14, 1930. e. Compton Jr. Coll., CA. Prof. debut radio at 14; in light opera, summer stock; sang with orchestra and appeared in night clubs; Columbia recording star; on Bdwy stage, John Murray Anderson's Almanac, Champagne Complex, First Impressions. Bd. chmn. Polly Bergen Co.; chmn. Culinary Co., Inc.; co-chmn. Natl. Business Council for Equal Rights Amendment; Humanitarian Award: Asthmatic Research Inst. & Hosp., 1971; Outstanding Mother's Award, 1984.
PICTURES: At War With the Army (debut, 1950), That's My Boy, Warpath, The Stooge, Half a Hero, Cry of the Hunted, Arena, Fast Company, Escape from Ft. Bravo, Belle Sommers, Cape Fear, The Caretakers, Move Over Darling, Kisses for My President, A Guide for the Married Man, Making Mr. Right, Mother Mother, Cry-Baby.
TELEVISION: Series: Pepsi-Cola Playhouse (host 1954–55), To Tell the Truth (panelist), The Polly Bergen Show, Baby Talk. Guest: G.E. Theatre, Schlitz Playhouse, Playhouse 90, Studio One, Perry Como, Ed Sullivan Show, Bob Hope Show, Bell Telephone, Wonderful World of Entertainment, Dinah Shore Show, Dean Martin Show, Andy Williams Show, Red Skelton Show, Mike Douglas Show. Special: The Helen Morgan Story (Emmy Award, best actress, 1958). Movies: Death Cruise, Murder on Flight 502, Telethon, How to Pick Up Girls, The Million Dollar Face, Born Beautiful, Velvet, Addicted to His Love, She Was Marked For Murder, The Haunting of Sarah Hardy, My Brother's Wife, Lightning Field, Lady Against the Odds, Perry Mason: The Case of the Skin-Deep Scandal. Mini-Series: 79 Park Avenue, The Winds of War, War and Remembrance.

BERGER, HELMUT: Actor. b. Salzburg, Austria, May 29, 1943. e. Feldkirk College and U. of Perugia. First film, small role in Luchino Visconti's The Witches (Le Streghe) in 1966.
PICTURES: The Young Tigers, The Damned, Do You Know What Stalin Did To Women?, The Garden of the Finzi-Continis, Dorian Gray, A Butterfly with Bloody Wings, The Greedy Ones, The Strange Love Affair, Ludwig, Ash Wednesday, Conversation Piece, The Romantic Englishwoman, Orders to Kill, Madam Kitty, Merry-Go-Round, Code Name: Emerald, The Glass Heaven, Faceless, The Betrothed, The Godfather Part III.

BERGER, RICHARD L.: Executive. b., Tarrytown, NY, Oct. 25, 1939. e. Cornell U., UCLA 1963, B.S. In 1964 joined acct. dept., 20th Century-Fox; promoted to exec. position in Fox-TV. Was dir. of programming, then v.p. of programs. Appt. asst. v.p. prod. 20th-Fox. Left in 1975 to join CBS-TV as v.p. dramatic development. Returned to 20th-Fox in 1977 as v.p., domestic prod., 20th Century-Fox Pictures. Joined Disney as pres. Walt Disney Pictures; resigned 1984. Named sr. v.p., United Artists Corp., promoted to pres. MGM/UA Film Group, 1988.

BERGERAC, JACQUES: Actor. b. Biarritz, France, May 26, 1927. Career includes Five Minutes With Jacques Bergerac on radio; in the theatre, on tour in Once More with Feeling; on most major network TV shows.
PICTURES: Twist of Fate, The Time is Now, Strange Intruder, Come Away With Me, Les Girls, Gigi, Man and His Past, Thunder in the Sun, Hypnotic Eye, A Sunday in Summer, Fear No More, Achilles, A Global Affair, Taffy and the Jungle Hunter, The Emergency Operation, Lady Chaplin, The Last Party, One Plus One.

BERGMAN, ALAN: Songwriter. b. New York, NY. e. U. of North Carolina, UCLA. m. Marilyn Bergman with whom he collaborates.
PICTURES: In the Heat of the Night, The Thomas Crown Affair (Acad. Award for Best Song: The Windmills of Your Mind), John and Mary, Happy Ending, Gaily Gaily, Pieces of Dreams, Sometimes a Great Notion, Life and Times of Judge Roy Bean, The Way We Were (Acad. Award for title song), A Star Is Born, The One and Only, Same Time Next Year, And Justice for All, The Promise, A Change of Seasons, Yes Giorgio, Best Friends, Tootsie, Yentl, The January Man, Major League, Shirley Valentine, Switch.
TELEVISION: Queen of the Stardust Ballroom, Hollow Image, Sybil, and themes for Maude, Good Times, Alice, Nancy Walker Show, Brooklyn Bridge, etc.

BERGMAN, ANDREW: Writer, Director, Producer. b. Queens, NY, 1945. e. Harpur Coll., magna cum laude; U. of Wisconsin, Ph.D, history, 1970. Worked as publicist at United Artists. Author: We're in the Money, a study of Depression-era films, and the mysteries: The Big Kiss-Off of 1944 and Hollywood and Levine. Also wrote Broadway comedy, Social Security.
PICTURES: Writer: Blazing Saddles, The In Laws, So Fine (also dir.) Oh God You Devil, Fletch, Chances Are (exec. prod. only), The Freshman (also dir.), Soapdish, Honeymoon in Vegas (also dir.), Undercover Blues (co-exec. prod. only).

BERGMAN, INGMAR: Writer, Director. b. Uppsala, Sweden, July 14, 1918. e. Stockholm U. Directed university play prods.; wrote & dir. Death of Punch, 1940; first theatrical success, dir., Macbeth, 1940; writer-director, Svensk Film-industri, 1942–present; first s.p, Frenzy, 1943; first directorial assignment, Crisis, 1945; chief prod., Civic Malmo, 1956–60. Directed Swedish prod. Hamlet for stage at Brooklyn Acad. of Music, 1988.
PICTURES: Torment (s.p. only). Dir.-Writer: Crisis It Rains on Our Love, A Ship to India, Woman Without a Face (s.p. only), Night is My Future (dir. only), Eva (co-s.p. only), Port of Call, The Devil's Wanton, Three Strange Loves, To Joy, This Can't Happen Here (dir. only), Summer Interlude (Illicit Interlude), Secrets of Women, Summer With Monika, The Naked Night (Sawdust and Tinsel), A Lesson in Love, Dreams (Journey Into Autumn), Smiles of a Summer Night, The Last Couple Out (co-s.p. only), The Seventh Seal, Wild Strawberries, Brink of Life, The Magician, The Virgin Spring (dir. only), The Devil's Eye, Pleasure Garden (co-s.p. only), Through a Glass Darkly, Winter Light, The Silence, All These Women, Persona, Stimulantia (episode), Hour of the Wolf, Shame, The Ritual, The Passion of Anna, The Touch, Cries and Whispers, Scenes from a Marriage, The Magic Flute, Face to Face, The Serpent's Egg, Autumn Sonata, From the Life of the Marionettes, Fanny and Alexander, After the Rehearsal, Best Intentions (s.p. only).
AMERICAN TELEVISION: The Lie.

BERGMAN, MARILYN: Songwriter. b. New York, NY. e. NYU. m. Alan Bergman with whom she collaborates.
PICTURES: In the Heat of the Night, The Thomas Crown Affair (Acad. Award for Best Song: The Windmills of Your Mind), Happy Ending, John and Mary, Gaily Gaily, Pieces of Dreams, Sometimes a Great Notion, Life and Times of Judge Roy Bean, The Way We Were (Acad. Award for title song), A Star Is Born, The One and Only, Same Time Next Year, And Justice for All, The Promise, A Change of Seasons, Yes Giorgio, Best Friends, Tootsie, Yentl, The January Man, Major League, Shirley Valentine, Switch.
TELEVISION: Queen of the Stardust Ballroom, Hollow Image, Sybil, and themes for Maude, Good Times, Alice, Nancy Walker Show, Brooklyn Bridge, etc.

BERKOFF, STEVEN: Actor, Director, Writer. b. London, Eng., Aug. 3, 1937. e. studied drama in London and Paris. Founder of London Theatre Group. Author of plays, East, West, Greek Decadence, Sink the Belgrano, Kvetch (London, NY). Staged, adapted and toured with: Kafka's In the Penal Colony, The Trial and Metamorphosis; Agamemnon, The Fall of the House of Usher. Starred in Hamlet and Macbeth. NY theater: director: Kvetch (also writer, actor), Coriolanus, Metamorphosis (starring Baryshnikov). Also dir. Roman Polanski in Metamorphosis in Paris.
PICTURES: Actor: Nicholas and Alexandra, A Clockwork Orange, Barry Lyndon, The Passenger, Outland, McVicar, Octopussy, Beverly Hills Cop, Rambo: First Blood II, Revolution, Underworld, Absolute Beginners, Under the Cherry Moon, Streets of Yesterday, The Krays.
TELEVISION: Beloved Family, Knife Edge, War and Remembrance, A Season of Giants, Intruders.

BERLE, MILTON: Actor. r.n. Milton Berlinger. b. New York, NY, July 12, 1908. e. Professional Children's Sch., N.Y. Early appearances as child actor incl. film Tillie's Punctured Romance. In vaudeville; on N.Y. stage (Ziegfeld Follies 1936, Life Begins at 8:40, etc.): nightclubs; concurrently on radio & screen. Author: Out of My Trunk (1945), Earthquake (1959), Milton Berle: An Autobiography (1974).
TELEVISION: Series: Texaco Star Theatre (1948–54), Kraft Music Hall TV Show (1958–59), Jackpot Bowling (1960–61), Milton Berle Show (1966–7). Guest: Doyle Against the House, Dick Powell Show, Chrysler TV special, Lucy Show, F Troop, Batman, Love Boat, many others. Movies: Seven in Darkness, Evil Roy Slade, Legend of Valentino, Side By Side.
PICTURES: New Faces of 1937, Radio City Revels, Tall Dark and Handsome, Sun Valley Serenade, Rise and Shine, A Gentleman at Heart, Whispering Ghosts, Over My Dead Body, Margin for Error, Always Leave Them Laughing, Let's Make Love, The Bellboy (cameo), It's a Mad Mad Mad Mad World, The Loved One, The Oscar, Don't Worry We'll Think of a Title, The Happening, Who's Minding the Mint?, Where Angels Go . . . Trouble Follows, For Singles Only, Can Hieronymus Merkin Ever Forget Mercy Humppe and Find True Happiness?, Lepke, Won Ton Ton the Dog Who Saved Hollywood, The Muppet Movie, Cracking Up, Broadway Danny Rose, Driving Me Crazy.

BERLINGER, WARREN: Actor, b. Brooklyn, NY, Aug. 31, 1937. e. Columbia U.
STAGE: Annie Get Your Gun, The Happy Time, Bernardine, Take A Giant Step, Anniversary Waltz, Roomful of Roses, Blue Denim (Theatre World Award), Come Blow Your Horn, How To Succeed in Business Without Really Trying, (London) Who's Happy Now?, California Suite (1977–78 tour).
PICTURES: Teenage Rebel, Three Brave Men, Blue Denim, Because They're Young, Platinum High School, The Wackiest Ship in the Army, All Hands on Deck, Billie, Spinout, Thunder Alley, Lepke, The Four Deuces, I Will I Will . . . for Now, Harry and Walter Go to New York, The Shaggy D.A., The Magician of Lublin, The Cannonball Run, The World According to Garp, Going Bananas, Outlaw Force, Ten Little Indians, Hero.
TELEVISION: Series: Secret Storm (serial), The Joey Bishop Show, The Funny Side, A Touch of Grace, Operation Petticoat, Small & Frye, Shades of L.A. Guest: Alcoa, Goodyear, Armstrong, Matinee Theatre, The London Palladium, Kilroy, Bracken's World, Columbo. Movies: The Girl Most Likely To . . ., The Red Badge of Courage, Ellery Queen, Wanted: The Sundance Woman, Sex and the Single Parent, The Other Woman, Trial By Jury, Death Hits the Jackpot.

BERMAN, MONTY M.: Film and theatrical costumier. b. London, England, 1912. Personally costumed films and shows since 1931. Squad Leader RAF 1940–45; Bomber Command, M.B.E. Since war has costumed major films and shows and numerous TV prod.
PICTURES: Doctor Zhivago, Tom Jones, Longest Day, My Fair Lady, Oliver, Cromwell, Patton, Fiddler on the Roof, A Bridge Too Far, Julia, The Slipper and the Rose, A Little Night Music, Star Wars, Superman, James Bond Films, The Four Musketeers, Mommie Dearest, Raiders of the Lost Ark, Chariots of Fire, Superman II and III, Gandhi, Yentl, The Dresser, Indiana Jones and The Temple of Doom, Cotton Club, Out of Africa, The Living Daylights.

BERMAN, PANDRO S.: Producer. b. Pittsburgh, PA, March 28, 1905. Son of late Harry M. Berman, gen. mgr. Universal, FBO. Asst. dir. film ed., FBO; film & title ed. Columbia Studios; chief film ed. RKO, later asst. to William Le Baron & David Selznick; became prod. 1931 (RKO). A Champion of Champions Producer in Fame ratings. Joined MGM 1940.
PICTURES: What Price Hollywood, Symphony of Six Million, Bachelor Mother, The Gay Divorcee, Of Human Bondage, Morning Glory, Roberta, Alice Adams, Top Hat, Winterset, Stage Door, Vivacious Lady, Gunga Din, Hunchback of Notre Dame, Ziegfeld Girl, Honky Tonk, Seventh Cross, National Velvet, Dragon Seed, Portrait of Dorian Grey, Love Affair, Undercurrent, Sea of Grass, Three Musketeers, Madame Bovary, Father of the Bride, Father's Little Dividend, Prisoner of Zenda, Ivanhoe, All the Brothers Were Valiant, Knights of the Round Table, Long, Long Trailer, Blackboard Jungle, Bhowani Junction, Something of Value, Tea and Sympathy, Brothers Karamazov, Reluctant Debutante, Butterfield 8, Sweet Bird of Youth, The Prize, A Patch of Blue, Justine, Move.

BERMAN, STEVEN H: Executive. b. Middletown, OH, March 22, 1952. e. Ohio U., B.F.A. in playwriting, 1974; U. of Southern California, Annenberg Sch. of Communication studied management, 1977. m. Marcia Berman. Special research projects Paramount and ABC Television, 1977. Account exec., Gardner Advertising, 1978. Development exec., CBS Television, 1979–82. Dir. of comedy dev., CBS Television, 1982–84. Five years at CBS in series development, comedy and drama. Vice pres., dramatic dev., Columbia Pictures Television, 1984–85. Sr. v.p., Creative Affairs, Columbia Pictures Television, 1985–87. Exec. v.p., Columbia Television, div. of Columbia Entertainment Television, 1987–90. Indept. prod., Columbia Pictures TV, 1990–present.

BERNARD, MARVIN A.: Executive. b. New York, NY, Oct. 1, 1934. e. NYU. Lab technician to v.p. in charge of sales, Rapid Film Technique, Inc., 1949–63; developed technological advances in film rejuvenation and preservation, responsible for public underwriting; 1964–69; real estate sales & investments in Bahamas, then with Tishman Realty (commercial leasing div.); est. B-I-G Capital Properties; v.p. and operating head of International Filmtreat 1970–1973; authored Film Damaged Control Chart, a critical analysis of film care and repair—1971; founded Filmlife Inc. with latest chemical/mechanical and technical advancement in field of film rejuvenation and preservation. 1973–75 bd. chmn. and chief executive officer of Filmlife Inc., motion picture film rejuvenation, storage and distribution company. Feb. 1975 elected president in addition to remaining bd. chairman. 1979 consultant to National Archives of U.S. on m.p. preservation. 1981 dev. m.p. rejuvenation and preservation for 8mm and S8mm. 1986 introduced this technology to private home movie use before and after transfer to videotape. 1987, active mem. of awards comm. for tech. achievements, National Acad. TV Arts & Sciences. Recognition as leading authority and m.p. conservator from Intl. Communications Industries Assn. (ICIA), 1988.1989, Filmlife became 1st national film to video transfer lab in U.S.; elected to Princeton Film Preservation Group. Established Film/Video Hospital, repairing broken tapes & videocassettes, Aug. 1990.

BERNHARD, HARVEY: Producer. b. Seattle, WA, March 5, 1924. e. Stanford U. In real estate in Seattle, 1947–50; started live lounge entertainment at the Last Frontier Hotel, Las Vegas, 1950. Partner with Sandy Howard, 1958–60; v.p. in chg. prod., David L. Wolper Prods., dividing time between TV and feature films, 1961–68; with MPC, v.p., chg. prod., 1968–70. Now pres. of Harvey Bernhard Ent., Inc.
PICTURES: The Mack (1973), The Omen, Damien—Omen II, The Final Conflict, The Beast Within, Ladyhawke (exec. prod.), Goonies (prod.), Lost Boys.

BERNHARD, SANDRA: Actress, Comedian, Singer. b. Flint, MI, June 6, 1955. Moved to Scottsdale, AZ at 10. Began career in Los Angeles 1974 as stand-up comedian while supporting herself as manicurist in Beverly Hills. Has written articles for Vanity Fair, Interview, Spin, recorded and written lyrics for debut album I'm Your Woman (1985) and starred in one-woman off-Bdwy show Without You I'm Nothing (1988). Published collection of essays, short stories and memoirs, Confessions of a Pretty Lady (1988). Frequent guest on Late Night with David Letterman and Robin Byrd Show.
PICTURES: Cheech and Chong's Nice Dreams (debut, 1981), The King of Comedy, Sesame Street Presents: Follow that Bird, The Whoopee Boys, Casual Sex, Track 29, Heavy Petting, Without You I'm Nothing, Hudson Hawk, Inside Monkey Zetterland.
TELEVISION: Series: The Richard Pryor Show, Roseanne.

BERNSEN, CORBIN: Actor. b. North Hollywood, CA, Sept. 7, 1954. m. actress Amanda Pays. Son of actress Jeanne Cooper. e. UCLA, B.A. theater arts; M.F.A playwriting. Teaching asst. at UCLA while working on playwriting degree. 1981 studied acting in NY while supporting self as carpenter and model (Winston cigarettes). Built own theater in loft. Formed theatre co. Theatre of the Night.
PICTURES: Eat My Dust! (debut, 1976), King Kong, S.O.B., Hello Again, Bert Rigby You're a Fool, Major League, Disorganized Crime, Shattered, Frozen Assets, The Killing Box, The New Age.
TELEVISION: Series: Ryan's Hope, L.A. Law. Movies: Breaking Point, Line of Fire: The Morris Dees Story, Dead on the Money, Grass Roots, Love Can Be Murder. Guest: Anything But Love, Roc, The Larry Sanders Show.

BERNSTEIN, ARMYAN: Director-Writer.
PICTURES: Thank God It's Friday (s.p.), One From the Heart (co-s.p.), Windy City (dir. s.p.), Cross My Heart (dir., co-s.p.), Satisfaction (co-exec. prod.).

BERNSTEIN, BOB: Executive. Began public relations career 1952 at DuMont TV Network, followed by 2 yrs. as press agent for Liberace. With Billboard Magazine as review editor 3 yrs. Joined Westinghouse Bdg. Co. as p.r. director 1959. In 1963 named p.r. director for Triangle Publications, serving in various capacities to 1971. Joined Viacom Intl. as director of information services. In 1975 formed own co., March Five Inc., p.r. and promotion firm.

BERNSTEIN, ELMER: Composer, Conductor. b. New York, NY, April 4, 1922. Scholarship, Juilliard. e. Walden Sch., NYU., U.S. Army Air Force radio unit. After war 3 yrs. recitals, musical shows, United Nations radio dept; pres., Young Musicians Found.; 1st v.p. Academy of Motion Picture Arts & Sciences; co-chmn. music branch. Music dir. Valley Symphony. Recording artist, United Artists. More than 90 major films. Pres. of Composers & Lyricists Guild of America.
PICTURES: Never Wave at a WAC, Sudden Fear, Robot Monster, Cat Women of the Moon, It's a Dog's Life, Man With the Golden Arm, Storm Fear, The View From Pompey's Head, The Ten Commandments, Fear Strikes Out, Desire Under the Elms, Drango, The Naked Eye, Sweet Smell of Success, The Tin Star, Anna Lucasta, The Buccaneer, God's

Little Acre, Kings Go Forth, Some Came Running, The Miracle, The Story on Page One, From the Terrace, The Magnificent Seven, The Rat Race, By Love Possessed, The Commancheros, Summer and Smoke, The Young Doctors, Birdman of Alcatraz, Walk on the Wild Side, A Girl Named Tamiko, To Kill a Mockingbird, The Great Escape, The Cartetakers, Hud, Kings of the Sun, Rampage, Love With the Proper Stranger, The Carpetbaggers, Four Days in November, The World of Henry Orient, The Hallelujah Trail, The Reward, Seven Women, Cast a Giant Shadow, Hawaii, Thoroughly Modern Millie (Acad. Award, 1967), I Love You Alice B. Toklas, The Scalphunters, True Grit, The Gypsy Moths, Midas Run, Where's Jack?, Cannon for Cordoba, The Liberation of L.B. Jones, A Walk in the Spring Rain, Doctor's Wives, See Nov Evil, Big Jake, The Magnificent Seven Ride, Cahill U.S. Marshall, McQ., Gold, The Trial of Billy Jack, Report to the Commissioner, From Noon Till Three, The Incredible Sarah, The Shootist, Slap Shot, National Lampoon's Animal House, Bloodbrothers, Meatballs, The Great Santini, Saturn 3, The Blues Brothers, Airplane!, Zulu Dawn, Going Ape, Stripes, An American Werewolf in London, Honky Tonk Freeway, The Chosen, Five Days One Summer, Airplane II: The Sequel, Spacehunter, Class, Trading Places, Bolero, Ghostbusters, The Black Cauldron, Spies Like Us, Legal Eagles, Three Amigos, Amazing Grace and Chuck, Leonard Part 6, Da, Funny Farm, The Good Mother, Slipstream, My Left Foot, The Grifters, The Field, Oscar, A Rage in Harlem, Rambling Rose, Cape Fear (adapt.), The Babe, The Cemetery Club, Mad Dog and Glory, Lost in Yonkers, The Age of Innocence.
TELEVISION: Specials: Hollywood: The Golden Years, The Race for Space: Parts I & II, D-Day, The Making of the President—1960 (won Emmy Award), Hollywood and the Stars, Voyage of the Brigantine Yankee, Crucification of Jesus, NBC Best Sellers Theme (1976). Series: Julia, Owen Marshall, Ellery Queen, Serpico, The Chisholms. Movies: Gulag, Guyana Tragedy.

BERNSTEIN, JACK B.: Executive. b. New York, NY, May 6, 1937. e. City U. of New York, B.A., sociology. U.S. Army-Europe, 1956–58; research bacteriologist, 1959–61. Entered industry in 1962 with S.I.B. Prods., Paramount, as v.p. gen. mgr.; 1964–66, v.p. gen. mgr. C.P.I. Prods, 1966–73 prod. mgr. asst. dir., free lance. 1973–1982, assoc. prod. exec. prod. at several studios. 1983–86, v.p. worldwide prod., Walt Disney Pictures; 1987, sr. v.p., worldwide prod., United Artists Pictures; Oct., 1988–90, sr. v.p. worldwide prod., MGM Pictures. Member: DGA, Friars, Academy of MP Arts & Sciences; Academy of TV Arts & Sciences, AFI.
PICTURES: Asst. dir.: Hearts of the West. Prod. mngr.: Silver Streak. Assoc. Prod.: The Other Side of Midnight, The Fury, Butch and Sundance: The Early Days, Six Pack, Unfaithfully Yours. Exec. Prod.: North Dallas Forty, Monsignor, The Beast Within. Co-Prod.: The Mambo Kings, Under Siege.

BERNSTEIN, JAY: Producer, Personal manager. b. Oklahoma City, OK, June 7, 1937. e. Pomona Coll. 1963–76, pres. of Jay Bernstein Public Relations, representing over 600 clients. Formed Jay Bernstein Enterprises, acting as personal manager for Farrah Fawcett, Suzanne Somers, Kristy McNichol, Susan Hayward, Donald Sutherland, Bruce Boxleitner, Robert Conrad, Susan Saint James, Robert Blake, William Shatner, Linda Evans, Cicely Tyson, etc. Past pres., BernsteinThompson Entertainment Complex, entertainment and personal mgt. firm.
PICTURES: Exec. prod.: Sunburn, Nothing Personal.
TELEVISION: Exec. prod. Movies: The Return of Mike Hammer, Mickey Spillane's Margin for Murder; Wild, Wild, West, Revisited; More Wild, Wild West. Murder Me, Murder You, More Than Murder, The Diamond Trap. Series: Bring 'Em Back Alive, Mike Hammer, Houston Knights.

BERNSTEIN, WALTER: Director, Writer. b. New York, NY. Aug. 20, 1919. e. Dartmouth. Wrote for New Yorker Magazine; in W.W.II was roving correspondent for Yank Magazine. Returned to New Yorker after war. Wrote TV scripts; published book Keep Your Head Down (collection of articles).
PICTURES: Writer: Kiss the Blood Off My Hands (co-s.p.), That Kind of Woman, A Breath of Scandal (co-s.p.), Paris Blues, Heller in Pink Tights, The Magnificent Seven (uncredited), The Money Trap, Fail Safe, The Train, The Molly Maguires, The Front, Semi-Tough, The Betsy (co-s.p.), An Almost Perfect Affair, Yanks, Little Miss Marker (dir., debut), The House on Carroll Street.

BERNSTEIN, WILLIAM: Executive. b. New York, NY, August 30, 1933. e. Yale Law Sch., LL.B., 1959; NYU, B.A., 1954. Exec. vice pres.; Orion Pictures Corp. Asst. gen. counsel, then sr. v.p. United Artists 1959–78. Appointed pres. and CEO of Orion Pictures in 1991.

BERRI, CLAUDE: Actor, Director, Producer. b. Paris, July 1, 1934. r.n. Langmann. Began film career with short film Le Poulet, (prod. and dir.; won Acad. Award, short subject, 1966).
PICTURES: The Two of Us (dir.), Marry Me, Marry Me (dir.,

actor), Le Pistonne (dir.), Le Cinema de Papa (prod., dir.), Sex Shop (dir., s.p.), Male of the Century (dir., s.p., actor), The First Time (dir., s.p.), Tess (prod.), Inspecteur la Bavure (prod.), Je Vous Aime (prod., s.p.), Le Maitre d' Ecole (prod., dir., s.p.), A Quarter to Two Before Jesus Christ (prod.), L'Africain (prod.), Banzai (prod.), L'Homme Blesse (prod.), Garcon! Tchao Pantin (prod., s.p., dir.), Scemo Di Guerra, Jean la Florette (dir.), Manon of the Springs (dir.), The Bear (exec. prod.), Valmont (exec. prod.), The Door on the Left as You Leave the Elevator, Uranus (dir., s.p., prod.).

BERRY, JOHN: Director. b. New York, NY, 1917. Directed films in Hollywood mid and late '40s; went abroad during McCarthy era in U.S. where worked in French film industry. Later went to London to do stage work, acting as well as directing. Returned to U.S. to do stage work; returned to Hollywood to do TV.
PICTURES: Cross My Heart, From This Day Forward, Miss Susie Slagle's, Casbah, Tension, He Ran All the Way, Ça Va Barder, The Great Lover, Je Suis un Sentimental, Tamango, On Que Mambo, Claudine, Maya, The Bad News Bears Go to Japan, Thieves, Il y a maldonne, 'Round Midnight (actor only), A Man in Love (actor only), La Voyage a Paimpol (also prod.), Captive in the Land (also prod.).
TELEVISION: One Drink at a Time, Farewell Party, Mr. Broadway, Sister Sister (also prod.), Angel on My Shoulder, Honeyboy, Legitimate Defense.

BERRY, KEN: Actor. b. Moline, IL, Nov. 3, 1933.
PICTURES: Two for the Seesaw, Hello Down There, Herbie Rides Again, The Cat from Outer Space.
TELEVISION: Movies: Wake Me When the War Is Over, The Reluctant Heroes, Every Man Needs One, Letters from Three Lovers, Love Boat II. Series: The Ann Sothern Show, Bob Newhart Show (1962), F Troop, Mayberry RFD, Ken Berry Wow Show, Mama's Family. Guest: Dick Van Dyke Show, Hazel, Lucy Show, Carol Burnett, Sonny & Cher, etc.

BERTINELLI, VALERIE: Actress. b. Wilmington, DE, April 23, 1960. m. musician Eddie Van Halen. Dramatic training at Tami Lynn Academy of Artists in California. Made early TV appearances in the series, Apple's Way, in commercials, and in public service announcements. Started own prod. company to acquire properties for self.
TELEVISION: Movies: Young Love First Love, The Promise of Love, The Princess and the Cabbie, I Was a Mail Order Bride, The Seduction of Gina, Shattered Vows, Silent Witness, Rockabye, Pancho Barnes, In a Child's Name, What She Doesn't Know. Specials: The Secret of Charles Dickens, The Magic of David Copperfield. Series: One Day at a Time, Sydney, Cafe Americain. Mini-Series: I'll Take Manhattan.
PICTURE: Number One with a Bullet.

BERTOLUCCI, BERNARDO: Director, Writer, b. Parma, Italy, May 16, 1940. e. Rome U. Son of Attilio Bertolucci, poet and film critic. At age 20 worked as asst. dir. to Pier Paolo Pasolini on latter's first film, Accatone: in 1962 made debut film, The Grim Reaper, from script by Pasolini. 1962 published poetry book: In cerca del mistero. 1965–66: directed and wrote 3-part TV documentary: La vie del Petrolio for Ital. Oil co. in Iran. Collaborated on s.p. Ballata de un Milliardo, Sergio Leone's Once Upon a Time in the West, L'inchiesta. Produced films Sconcerto Rock, Io con te non ci sto piu, Lost and Found.
PICTURES: Director-Writer: The Grim Reaper, Before the Revolution, Love and Rage (episode: Agony), Partner, The Spider's Strategem, The Conformist, Last Tango in Paris, 1900, Luna, Tragedy of a Ridiculous Man, The Last Emperor (Acad. Awards for best dir. & s.p., 1987), The Sheltering Sky, Little Buddha.

BESCH, BIBI: Actress. b. Vienna, Austria, Feb. 1, 1942. Mother was actress Gusti Huber. Daughter is actress Samantha Mathis. Raised in Westchester County, NY. Appeared on soap daytime dramas as Secret Storm, Love is a Many-Splendored Thing, and Somerset.
TELEVISION: Series: Secrets of Midland Heights, The Hamptons. Movies: Victory at Entebbe, Peter Lundy and the Medicine Hat Stallion, Betrayal, Transplant, The Plutonium Incident, The Sophisticated Gents, Death of a Centerfold: The Dorothy Stratten Story, Secrets of a Mother and Daughter, The Day After, Lady Blue, Crazy From the Heart, Doing Time on Maple Drive. Mini-Series: Backstairs at the White House.
PICTURES: The Pack, Hardcore, The Promise, Meteor, The Beast Within, Star Trek II: The Wrath of Khan, The Lonely Lady, Date With an Angel, Kill Me Again, Tremors, Betsy's Wedding.
THEATRE: NY Stage: Fame, The Chinese Prime Minister, Here Lies Jeremy Troy, Once for the Asking.

BESSON, LUC: Director, Writer, Producer. b. Paris, France, March 18, 1959.
PICTURES: Le Dernier Combat (dir., prod., s.p.), Le Grand Carnaval (2nd unit dir.), Subway (dir., prod., s.p.), Kamikaze

(prod., s.p.), Taxi Boy (tech. advis.), The Big Blue (dir., s.p., lyrics, camera op.), La Femme Nikita (dir., s.p., song).

BEST, BARBARA: Publicist. b. San Diego, CA, Dec. 2, 1921. e. U. of Southern California, AB, 1943. Pub., 20th Century-Fox, 1943–49; reporter, San Diego Journal, 1950 Stanley Kramer Co. 1950–53; own agency, Barbara Best & Associates, 1953–66; 1966 exec. v.p. Jay Bernstein Public rel.; Freeman and Best, 1967–74; Barbara Best Inc. publ. rel. 1975–85; Barbara Best Personal Management, current.

BEST, JAMES: Actor. b. Corydon, IN, July 26, 1926. Magazine model; on stage; in European roadshow cast of My Sister Eileen; served as M.P. with U.S.A.A.F., W.W.II; m.p. debut in Comanche Territory, 1949.
PICTURES: Winchester 73, Air Cadet, Cimarron Kid, Steel Town, Ma & Pa Kettle at the Fair, Francis Goes to West Point, Seminole, The President's Lady, City of Bad Men, Column South, Riders to the Stars, The Raid, Caine Mutiny, Return from the Sea, The Left-Handed Gun, They Rode West, Seven Angry Men, Come Next Spring, Baby, The Rack, The Killer Shrews, The Mountain Road, Sounder, Ode to Billy Joe, The End, Hooper, Rolling Thunder.
TELEVISION: Series: Dukes of Hazzard. Movies: Run Simon Run, Savages, The Runaway Barge, The Savage Bees. Guest: Hawkins, Enos. Mini-Series: Centennial.

BETHUNE, ZINA: Actress, Dancer, Singer. b. New York, NY, Feb. 17, 1944. Broadway: Most Happy Fella, Grand Hotel. National tours: Sweet Charity, Carnival, Oklahoma!, Damn Yankees, Member of the Wedding, The Owl and The Pussycat, Nutcracker. New York City Ballet (Balanchine), Zina Bethune & Company Dance Theatre, Bethune Theatredanse. Special performance at the White House and Kennedy Center.
PICTURES: Sunrise At Campobello, Who's That Knocking at My Door, The Boost.
TELEVISION: Series: The Guiding Light, The Nurses, Love of Life. Guest: Lancer, Cains Hundred, Naked City, Route 66, Little Women, Santa Barbara, Judy Garland Show, Jackie Gleason Show, Gunsmoke, Dr. Kildare, Emergency, Planet of The Apes, Police Story, Chips, Hardy Boys, The Gymnast, Dirty Dancing. Movies: Nutcracker: Money Madness Murder (also choreographer). Specials: Little Women, Heart Dancing, From the Heart.

BETTGER, LYLE: Actor b. Philadelphia, PA, Feb. 13, 1915. e. Haverford School, Philadelphia, American Acad. of Dramatic Art, N.Y. m. Mary Rolfe, actress. Started in summer stock; in road cos. of Brother Rat, Man Who Came to Dinner.
STAGE: John Loves Mary, Love Life, Eve of St. Mark, The Male Animal, Sailor Beware, The Moon is Down.
PICTURES: No Man of Her Own, Union Station, First Legion, Greatest Show on Earth, The Denver & Rio Grande, Vanquished, Forbidden, The Great Sioux Uprising, All I Desire, Drums Across the River, Destry, Carnival Story, Sea Chase, Showdown at Abilene, Gunfight at OK Corral, Town Tamer, Johnny Reno, Nevada Smith, Return of The Gunfighter, Impasse, The Hawaiians, The Seven Minutes.
TELEVISION: Court of Last Resort, Grand Jury, Hawaii 5-0, Police Story, Bonanza, Combat, Gunsmoke, etc.

BETUEL, JONATHAN: Director.
PICTURES: My Science Project; Tripwire.

BEVILLE, HUGH M., JR.: Executive; b. April 18, 1908. e. Syracuse U., NYU (MBA). To NBC 1930 statistician, chief statistician; Research mgr., dir., research; U.S. Army 1942–46; dir. of research and planning for NBC, v.p., planning and research, 1956; v.p., planning, 1964; consultant, 1968; professor Business Admin., Southampton Coll., 1968. Exec. dir., Broadcast Rating Council, 1971–82, author-consultant, contributing editor, TV/Radio Age, 1982–85. Author, Audience Ratings; Radio, Television, Cable, 1985, Elected member, Research Hall of Fame, 1986.

BEY, TURHAN: Actor. b. Vienna, Austria, March 30, 1921. Made U.S. m.p. debut in 1941.
PICTURES: Footsteps in the Dark, Burma Convoy, Bombay Clipper, Drums of the Congo, Destination Unknown, Arabian Nights, The Unseen Enemy, Mummy's Tomb, White Savage, The Mad Ghoul, Follow the Boys, The Climax, Dragon Seed, Bowery to Broadway, Ali Baba and the 40 Thieves, Sudan, Night in Paradise, Out of the Blue, Amazing Mr. X, Parole, Inc., Adventures of Casanova, Song of India, Prisoners of the Casbah, Stolen Identity (prod. only).

BEYMER, RICHARD: Actor. r.n. George Richard Beymer, Jr., b. Avoca, IA, Feb. 21, 1939. e. N. Hollywood H.S., Actors Studio. Performer, KTLA, Sandy Dreams, Fantastic Studios, Inc., 1949, Playhouse 90.
PICTURES: Indiscretion of an American Wife, So Big, Johnny Tremain, The Diary of Anne Frank, High Time, West Side Story, Bachelor Flat, Five Finger Exercise, Hemingway's Adventures of a Young Man, The Longest Day, The Stripper, Grass (Scream Free), Cross Country, Silent Night Deadly Night 3: Better Watch Out.

TELEVISION: *Series*: Paper Dolls, Twin Peaks. *Movies*: Generation, With a Vengeance. *Guest*: The Virginian, Walt Disney (Boston Tea Party), Dr. Kildare, Man from U.N.C.L.E., Moonlighting, Murder She Wrote, The Bronx Zoo.

BIBAS, FRANK PERCY: Executive. b. New York, NY, 1917. e. Brown U., Columbia U. Capt., Army Air Corps, W.W.II. Entered m.p. ind. adv. dept., Donahue & Coe; later pub. dept. American Display, then to dist. dept., National Screen Service. In 1945 joined Casanave-Artlee Pictures Inc.; appt. v.p. in charge of sales 1946 (dist. Selznick reissues in U.S.); v.p. Casanave Pictures, Inc. & Sixteen M.M. Pictures Inc., from 1949 mgr. m.p. dept., McCann-Erickson ad agency; joined Roland Reed TV Inc., v.p., prod., 1955. Prod-dir. with Hal Roach Studios, 1957. 1961 to present N.Y.C. partner, Bibas-Redford Inc. Production Co. From 1986–, pres., Bibas Group Inc. and subsidiary, Spectrum Television Prod. (Miami, Fl). 1962 won Acad Award for Project Hope, documentary. Member: S.M.P.T.E., Acad. of TV Arts and Sciences, Directors Guild of America.

BICK, JERRY: Producer. b. New York, NY, April 26, 1923. e. Columbia U., Sorbonne. Taught English at U. of Georgia and was radio sports announcer in Savannah, GA, before entering film industry in pub. dept. of MGM, N.Y. Opened own literary agency in Hollywood after stint with MCA. Began career as producer in London; debut film, Michael Kohlhaas, 1969, made in Czechoslovakia. Oct. 1986–Jan. 1988, exec. v.p. worldwide prod., Heritage Entertainment.
PICTURES: The Long Goodbye, Thieves Like Us, Russian Roulette, Farewell My Lovely (exec. prod.), The Big Sleep, Against All Odds (exec. prod.), Swing Shift.

BIEHN, MICHAEL: Actor. b. Anniston, AL, 1957. At 18 years moved to Los Angeles and studied acting. First professional job in 1977 in TV pilot for Logan's Run.
PICTURES: Coach, Hog Wild, The Fan, The Lords of Discipline, The Terminator, Aliens, The Seventh Sign, Rampage, In a Shallow Grave, The Abyss, Navy Seals, Time Bomb, K2, DeadFall, Tombstone.
TELEVISION: *Series*: The Runaways. *Guest*: Logan's Run, Hill Street Blues, Police Story, Family. *Movies*: Zuma Beach, A Fire in the Sky, China Rose, Deadly Intentions, A Taste for Killing, Strapped. Pilots: James at 15, The Paradise Connection.

BIGELOW, KATHRYN: Director, Writer. b. 1951. e. SF Art Inst., Columbia. Studied to be painter before turning to film with short Set-Up, 1978.
PICTURES: The Loveless (feature debut, 1981; also s.p.), Near Dark (also s.p.), Blue Steel (also s.p.), Point Break.

BILBY, KENNETH W.: Executive. b. Salt Lake City, UT, Oct. 7, 1918. e. Columbia U., U. of Arizona, B.A. With N.Y. Herald-Tribune, 47–50; author, New Star in the Near East, 1950; pub. rel. rep. to RCA Victor, Camden, NJ, 1950–54; exec. v.p. National Broadcasting Co., N.Y., 1954–60; v.p. public affairs, RCA, 1960–62, exec. v.p., 1962–75; exec. v.p. corporate affairs, 1976–present.

BILL, TONY: Actor, Producer, Director. b. San Diego, CA, Aug. 23, 1940. e. Notre Dame U. Founded Bill/Phillips Prods. with Julia and Michael Phillips. 1971–73; Tony Bill Prods. 1973–, Acad. of M.P. Arts & Sciences, bd. of govs., bd of trustees, chmn. prods. branch.
PICTURES: *Actor*: Come Blow Your Horn (debut, 1963), Soldier in the Rain, Marriage on the Rocks, None But the Brave, You're a Big Boy Now, How to Steal the World, Ice Station Zebra, Never a Dull Moment, Castle Keep, Flap, Shampoo, Heartbeat, Little Dragons (also exec. prod.), Pee-wee's Big Adventure, Less Than Zero. *Co-producer*: Deadhead Miles, Steelyard Blues, The Sting (Acad. Award: Best Picture, 1973), Taxi Driver. *Prod.*: Hearts of the West (exec. prod.), Harry and Walter Go to New York, Boulevard Nights (exec. prod.), Going in Style, Little Dragons. *Director*: My Bodyguard, Six Weeks, Five Corners (also co-prod.), Crazy People, Untamed Heart (also co-prod.), A Home of Our Own.
TELEVISION: As actor: Microcops (pilot). *Special*: Lee Oswald Assassin (BBC, 1966). *Series*: What Really Happened to the Class of '65? *Movies*: Haunts of the Very Rich, Having Babies II, The Initiation of Sarah, With This Ring, Are You in the House Alone?, Portrait of an Escort, Freedom, Washington Mistress, Running Out, The Killing Mind. *Guest*: Alfred Hitchcock Presents (Night Caller, 1985). *Mini-Series*: Washington Behind Closed Doors. *Director*: Dirty Dancing (pilot), Love Thy Neighbor.

BILSON, BRUCE: Director. b. Brooklyn, NY, May 19, 1928. e. UCLA, BA, Theater Arts, 1950. m. actress Renne Jarrett. Father was prod. George Bilson, son is prod.-dir. Danny Bilson, daughter is prod. Julie Ahlberg. Asst. film ed. 1951–55; USAF photo unit 1952–53; asst. dir. 1955–65 including Andy Griffith Show, Route 66. Assoc. prod. The Baileys of Balboa. Dir. since 1965 of more than 350 TV shows. Emmy Award, Get Smart, DGA nom. The Odd Couple.

PICTURES: The North Avenue Irregulars, Chattanooga Choo Choo.
TELEVISION: *Series*: The Flash, Barney Miller, Get Smart (Emmy Award, 1968), Hogan's Heroes, House Calls, Alice, Private Benjamin, Life With Lucy, Spenser: For Hire, Hotel, Dallas, Hawaii Five-O, Dynasty, The Fall Guy, Nightingales, Dinosaurs. *Movies/pilots*: The Dallas Cowboys Cheerleaders, BJ and the Bear, The Misadventures of Sheriff Lobo, Half Nelson, Finder of Lost Loves, The Girl Who Came Gift Wrapped, The Ghosts of Buxley Hall, The New Gidget, Barefoot in the Park, The Bad News Bears, The Odd Couple, Harper Valley PTA.

BINDER, STEVE: Producer, Director, Writer. b. Los Angeles, CA, Dec. 12. e. Univ. of Southern California. 1960–61 announcer in Austria and Germany with AFN, Europe. Prof. of Cinema, Univ. Southern CA. Mem.: DGA, Producers Guild of America, Writers Guild of America, NARAS, ATAS.
TELEVISION: *Prod., Dir*: Steve Allen Show (1963–65, 1973), Elvis Presley Comeback Special, Barry Manilow Special (also writer, Emmy Award, 1977), Diana Ross in Central Park (dir., ACE Award), Diana Ross '81 (also writer), Ringling Bros & Barnum Bailey Circus (also writer), Pee-Wee's Playhouse, Big Fun on Swing Street, Barry Manilow, Pee-Wee's Playhouse Christmas Special (prod.), Diana's World Tour and over 200 major TV prods.
PICTURES: *Director*: The T.A.M.I. Show, Give 'Em Hell Harry.

BIONDI, JR. FRANK J.: Executive. b. Jan. 9, 1945. e. Princeton U.; Harvard U., MBA (1968). Various investment banking positions 1968–74; asst. treas. Children's TV Workshop 1974–78; v.p. programming HBO 1978–82; pres. HBO 1983, then chmn. & chief exec. off. 1984 joined Coca-Cola Co. as exec. v.p., entertainment business arm. Resigned 1987 to join Viacom International as pres. and CEO.

BIRKIN, JANE: Actress. b. London, England, Dec. 14, 1946. Mother of actress Charlotte Gainsbourg. Sister of director-writer Andrew Birkin. Was subject of Agnes Vardas' 1988 documentary Jane B. par Agnes V.
PICTURES: Blow-Up, Kaleidoscope, Wonderwall, Les Chemins de Katmandou, La Piscine, Cannabis, Romance of a Horse Thief, Trop jolies pour etre honnetes, Dark Places, Projection Privee, La Moutarde me monte au nex, Le Mouton Enrage, 7 Morts sur Ordonnance, Catherine et Cie, La Course a l'echalote, Je T'Aime Moi Non Plus, Seriex comme let plaisir, Le Diable au Coeur, L'Animal, Death on the Nile, Au bout du bout du banc, Melancolie Baby, La Miel, La Fille Prodigue, Evil Under the Sun, L'Ami de Vincent, Circulez u'a rien a voir, Love on the Ground, le Garde du Corps, The Pirate, Beethoven's Nephew, Dust, Leave All Fair, la Femme de ma vie, Comedie!, Kung Fu Master, Soigne ta droite, Daddy Nostalgia.

BIRMINGHAM, PAUL A.: Executive. b. Burbank, CA, Feb. 12, 1937. e. U. of California, U. of Southern California. Sr. v.p. studio operations and admin., Paramount Pictures.

BIRNEY, DAVID: Actor. b. Washington, DC, April 23, 1940. e. Dartmouth Coll., B.A., UCLA, M.A. Phd. Southern Utah St. (hon.). Following grad. sch. and the Army spent 2 yrs. in regional theatre, Amer. Shakespeare Festival, Hartford Stage Co., Barter Theatre, to N.Y. where appeared in Lincoln Center prod. of Summertree (Theatre World Award). Appeared for two yrs. on TV daytime series, Love Is a Many Splendored Thing, doing other stage roles in same period.
THEATER: NY debut NY Shakespeare Fest (Comedy of Errors); 3 seasons Lincoln Center Rep. Many NY and regional credits incl: Amadeus, Benefactors, Man and Superman, Hamlet, Richard II, III, Romeo & Juliet, King John, Titus Andronicus, Major Barbara, Biko Inquest, Playboy of the Western World, The Miser, Antigone, My Fair Lady, Camelot, Love Letters.
PICTURES: Caravan to Vaccares, Trial by Combat, Oh God Book II, Prettykill, Midnight.
TELEVISION: *Series*: Bridget Loves Bernie, Serpico, St. Elsewhere, Glitter, Beyond 2000 (host), Raising Kids (host), Great American TV Poll (host). *Mini-series*: Night of the Fox, Seal Morning, Adam's Chronicles, Testimony of Two Men, Master of the Game, Valley of the Dolls, The Bible. *Movies*: Murder or Mercy, Bronk, Serpico: The Deadly Game, Someone's Watching Me!, High Midnight, Only With Married Men, OHMS, Mom The Wolfman & Me, The Five of Me, The Long Journey Home (also co-exec. prod.), Love and Betrayal, Always Remember I Love You, Touch and Die, Keeping Secrets. *Specials*: Missing: Have You Seen This Person? Drop Everything and Read, 15 and Getting Straight, Diaries of Adam and Eve (co-prod.). Guest appearances in series & anthology shows.

BIROC, JOSEPH F.: Cinematographer. b. Union City, NJ, Feb. 12, 1900. e. Emerson H.S., Union City, NJ. At 18 worked at Paragon Studios film lab in Ft. Lee NJ. In 1920s became asst. cameraman and camera operator. During WW II, army capt. heading one of first crews to film liberation of Paris. 1989,

Amer. Soc. of Cinematographers' Lifetime Achievement Award.
PICTURES: It's a Wonderful Life, Bwana Devil, Glass Wall, Tall Texan, Vice Squad, Donovan's Brain, Appointment in Honduras, Down Three Dark Streets, Lone Wolf, T-Men in Action, Man Behind the Badge, Dear Phoebe, Nightmare, Tension at Table Rock, Attack, Black Whip, Run of the Arrow, Ride Back, Garment Jungle, China Gate, Ice Palace, FBI Story, 13 Ghosts, Home Before Dark, Operation Eichmann, Devil at 4 O'clock, Gold of the Seven Saints, Reprieve, Opium Eaters, Hitler, Sail a Crooked Ship, Bye Bye Birdie, Toys in the Attic, Promises-Promises, Under the Yum-Yum Tree, Viva Las Vegas, Kitten With a Whip, Ride the Wild Surf, Renegade Posse, Gunfight at Commanche Pass, Hush . . . Hush, Sweet Charlotte, I Saw What You Did, Flight of the Phoenix, The Russians Are Coming The Russians Are Coming, The Swinger, Warning Shot, Enter Laughing, Who Is Minding the Mint, Garden of Cucumbers, The Killing of Sister George, What Ever Happened to Aunt Alice?, Too Late the Hero, Mrs. Polifax Spy, Escape from the Planet of the Apes, The Organization, The Grissom Gang, Cahill, U.S. Marshall, The Longest Yard, The Towering Inferno (shared Acad. Award, 1974), Hustle, The Duchess and the Dirtwater Fox, The Choirboys, Beyond the Poseidon Adventure, Airplane!, Hammet, All the Marbles, Airplane II: The Sequel.
TELEVISION: The Honeymoon is Over (1951, one of 1st series prod. on film), Four Star Theatre, Readers Digest, Superman, Richard Diamond, Alcoa Theatre, Grindl, Solo, Ghost Breakers, Take Her She's Mine, Heaven Help Us, Hardy Boys, Brian's Song (Emmy Award, 1971), Gidget Gets Married, Ghost Story, Thursdays Game, Lonely Hearts, 555, Family Upside Down, S.S.T. Death Flight, Little Women, Scruples, The Gambler, A Death in California, A Winner Never Quits, Outrage.
TV PILOTS: Wonder Woman, Honky Tonk, The Money-changers, Washington, D.C., Clone Master, Desperate Lives, Casablanca, Another Jerk, House Detective, Hell Town U.S.A., Flag, Time Out for Dad.

BISSET, JACQUELINE: Actress. b. Weybridge, England, September 13, 1944. e. French Lycée, London. After photographic modeling made film debut in The Knack, 1965.
PICTURES: The Knack (debut, 1965), Cul de Sac, Two For The Road, Casino Royale, The Cape Town Affair, The Sweet Ride, The Detective, Bullitt, The First Time, Secret World, Airport, The Grasshopper, The Mephisto Waltz, Believe in Me, Stand Up and Be Counted, The Life & Times of Judge Roy Bean, The Thief Who Came to Dinner, Day for Night, Le Manifique, Murder on the Orient Express, End of the Game, The Spiral Staircase, St. Ives, Sunday Woman, The Deep, The Greek Tycoon, Secrets, Who Is Killing the Great Chefs of Europe?, Together? (I Love You I Love You Not), When Time Ran Out, Rich and Famous, Inchon, Class, Under the Volcano, High Season, Scenes From the Class Struggle in Beverly Hills, La Maison de Jade, Wild Orchid, The Maid.
TELEVISION: Movies: Forbidden, Anna Karenina, Choices. Mini-Series: Napoleon and Josephine: A Love Story.

BIXBY, BILL: Actor, Director. b. San Francisco, CA, Jan. 22, 1934. e. U. of California, Berkeley. Worked in indust. films. Gen. Motors, Chrysler.
TELEVISION: Series: Joey Bishop Show, My Favorite Martian, The Courtship of Eddie's Father, The Magician, Masquerade Party (panelist), Once Upon a Classic (host), The Incredible Hulk, The Book of Lists (host), Goodnight Beantown, True Confessions (host), Exploring Psychic Powers . . . Live (host) . Movies: Congratulations It's a Boy!, The Couple Takes a Wife, The Magician (pilot), Shirts/Skins, Barbary Coast (also dir.), The Invasion of Johnson Country, The Great Houdini, Fantasy Island (pilot), Black Market Baby, The Incredible Hulk (pilot), Agatha Christie's Murder Is Easy, Three on a Date (dir. only), I Had 3 Wives (dir. only), The Incredible Hulk Returns (also exec. prod.), The Trial of the Incredible Hulk (also exec. prod., dir.), The Death of the Incredible Hulk (also dir.), Another Pair of Aces (dir. only), Baby of the Bride (dir. only), Diagnosis of Murder, The Woman Who Loved Elvis (dir. only). Guest: The Many Loves of Dobie Gillis, Danny Thomas Show, Andy Griffith Show, J.J. Starbuck.
STAGE: Fantasticks (nat'l company), Under the Yum Yum Tree.
PICTURES: Lonely Are the Brave, Irma La Douce, Under the Yum Yum Tree, Ride Beyond Vengeance, Clambake, Doctor You've Got to Be Kidding, Speedway, The Apple Dumpling Gang, The Kentucky Fried Movie.

BLACK, ALEXANDER F.: Publicist. b. New Rochelle, NY, Dec. 27, 1918. e. Brown U., BA, 1940. Joined Universal 1941. U.S. Navy 1942–45, Lt. Sr. Grade. Rejoined Universal 1946 serving in various capacities in Foreign Department, becoming director of foreign publicity for Universal International Films, Inc. in 1967; 1974, named exec. in chg. intl. promotion for MCA-TV.

BLACK, KAREN: Actress. b. Park Ridge, IL, July 1, 1942. r.n. Karen Ziegler. e. Northwestern U. Left school for NY to join the Hecscher House, appearing in several Shakespearean plays. In 1965 starred in Playroom, which ran only 1 month but won her NY Drama Critic nom. as best actress.
PICTURES: You're a Big Boy Now (debut, 1966), Hard Contact, Easy Rider, Five Easy Pieces, Drive He Said, A Gunfight, Born To Win, Cisco Pike, Portnoy's Complaint, The Pyx, Little Laura and Big John, Rhinoceros, The Outfit, The Great Gatsby, Airport 1975, Law and Disorder, Day of the Locust, Nashville, Family Plot, Crime and Passion, Burnt Offerings, Capricorn One, Killer Fish, In Praise of Older Women, The Squeeze, The Last Word, Chanel Solitaire, Come Back to the Five and Dime Jimmy Dean Jimmy Dean, Killing Heat (The Grass is Singing), Can She Bake a Cherry Pie?, Martin's Day, Invaders from Mars, It's Alive III, Hostage, Eternal Evil, The Invisible Kid, Out of the Dark, Homer and Eddie, Night Angel, Deadly Intent, Judgment, Miss Right, Dead Girls Don't Dance, Zapped Again, Twisted Justice, The Children, Mirror Mirror, Children of the Night, Hotel Oklahoma, Killer's Edge, Club Fed, Evil Spirits, The Player, Rubin & Ed, The Trust.
STAGE: Happily Never After, Keep It in the Family, Come Back to the Five and Dime Jimmy Dean Jimmy Dean.
TELEVISION: Movies: Trilogy of Terror, The Strange Possession of Mrs. Oliver, Mr. Horn, Power, Where the Ladies Go, Because He's My Friend, Full Circle Again (Canadian TV). Guest: In the Heat of the Night.

BLACK, NOEL: Director. b. Chicago, IL, June 30, 1940. e. UCLA, B.A., 1959; M.A. 1964.
PICTURES: Skaterdater (short), Pretty Poison, Mirrors, A Man a Woman and a Bank, Private School, Mischief (s.p.,' exec. prod.).
TELEVISION: Trilogy, The American Boy, The World Beyond, I'm a Fool, The Golden Honeymoon, The Electric Grandmother, The Doctors Wilde, Meet the Munceys, Eyes of the Panther, The Hollow Boy. Movies: Mulligan's Stew, The Other Victim, Prime Suspect, Happy Endings, Quarterback Princess, Deadly Intentions, Promises to Keep, A Time to Triumph, My Two Loves, Conspiracy of Love, Too Young the Hero, The Town Bully.

BLACK, STANLEY: Composer, conductor, musical director. OBE. b. London, Eng. Resident conductor, BBC, 1944–52. Musical director 105 feature films and Pathe Newsreel music: Music dir. Associated British Film Studios 1958–64. Guest conductor, Royal Philharmonic Orchestra and London Symphony. Orchestra; many overseas conducting engagements including (1977) Boston Pops and Winnipeg Symphony. Associated conductor Osaka Philharmonic Orchestra. Exclusive recording contract with Decca Record Co. since 1944.
PICTURES: Crossplot, The Long, The Short and The Tall, Rattle of a Simple Man, The Young Ones, Hell Is a City, Top Secret, Valentino.

BLACK, THEODORE R.: Attorney. b. New Jersey, Aug. 11, 1906. e. Harvard U., B.A., 1927, LL.B., 1930 (Sigma Alpha Mu fraternity). Formerly General Counsel, bd. member, Republic Pictures Corp. Former member: Nat'l Panel of Arbitrators, American Arbit. Assn., Bd. N.Y. Ethical Culture Society.

BLACKMAN, HONOR: Actress. b. London, England, 1926. Stage debut. The Gleam 1946. Screen debut, Fame Is the Spur.
TELEVISION: African Patrol, The Witness, Four Just Men, Probation Officer series, Top Secret, Ghost Squad, Invisible Man, The Saint, The Avengers series, Voice of the Heart, The Upper Hand.
PICTURES: Fame is the Spur (debut, 1947), Quartet, Daughter of Darkness, A Boy A Girl and a Bike, Diamond City, Conspirator, So Long at the Fair, Set a Murderer, Green Grow the Rushes, Come Die My Love, Rainbow Jacket, Outsiders, Delavine Affair, Three Musketeers, Breakaway, Homecoming, Suspended Alibi, Dangerous Drugs, A Night to Remember, The Square Peg, A Matter of Who, Present Laughter, The Recount, Serena, Jason & the Golden Fleece, Goldfinger, The Secret of My Success, Moment to Moment, Life at the Top, A Twist of Sand, Shalako, Struggle for Rome, Twinky, The Last Grenade, The Virgin and the Gypsy, Fright, Something Big, Out Damned Spot, Summer, Cat and the Canary.

BLADES, RUBÉN: Actor, Composer, Singer, Writer. b. Panama City, Panama, July 16, 1948. e. U. of Panama (law and political science, 1974), Harvard U., L.L.M., 1985. Has recorded more than 14 albums, winning 2 Grammy Awards (1986, 1988). With his band Seis del Solar has toured U.S., Central America and Europe. President of Panama's Papa Egoro political party.
PICTURES: Actor: The Last Fight (debut, 1982), Crossover Dreams (also co-s.p.), Critical Condition, The Milagro Beanfield War, Fatal Beauty, Homeboy, Disorganized Crime, The Lemon Sisters, Mo' Better Blues, The Two Jakes, Predator 2, Homeboy, The Super, Life With Mikey, Color of Night. Music: Beat Street, Oliver & Company, Caminos Verdes (Venezuela), Q&A.

TELEVISION: *Guest*: Sesame Street. *Movies*: Dead Man Out (ACE Award), One Man's War, The Josephine Baker Story (Emmy nom.), Crazy from the Heart (Emmy nom.), The Heart of the Deal, Miracle on I-880.

BLAIN, GERARD: Actor, Director. b. Paris, Oct. 23, 1930. Began his professional career in 1943 as an extra in Marcel Carne's The Children of Paradise. Appeared on stage in Marcel Pagnol's Topaze (1944). Military service in a parachute regiment. In 1955 Julien Duvivier gave him his first major role in Voici le Temps des Assassins (Murder a la Carte). By 1969 had appeared in more than 30 stage and film roles before becoming a director and co-author.
PICTURES: Les Mistons (1957), Le Beau Serge, Les Cousins. In Italy: The Hunchback of Rome, L'Ora di Roma, I Defini, Run with the Devil, Young Husbands. In Germany: The American Friend, L'Enfant de l'Hiver. As director and author or co-author: Les Amis, Le Pelican (also actor), Un Enfant dans la Foule, Un Second Souffle, Le Rebelle, Portrait sur Michel Tournier, Pierre et Djemila.

BLAINE, VIVIAN: Actress. r.n. Vivian S. Stapleton. b. Newark, NJ, Nov. 21, 1921. e. South Side H.S., Newark. Singer with various bands in New Jersey 1937–39, thereafter nightclubs; 20th-Fox personal appearance on British stage from 1947; created role of Adelaide in Guys and Dolls on Broadway, London and film; N.Y. stage in Hatful of Rain, Company. Member: Academy of M.P. Arts & Sciences, AFTRA, Equity, S.A.G., A.G.V.A.
PICTURES: Through Different Eyes (debut, 1942), Girl Trouble, He Hired the Boss, Jitterbugs, Greenwich Village, Something for the Boys, Nob Hill, State Fair, Doll Face, Three Little Girls in Blue, If I'm Lucky, Skirts Ahoy, Main Street to Broadway, Guys and Dolls, Public Pigeon No. 1, The Dark, Parasite, I'm Going to Be Famous.
TELEVISION: *Series*: Those Two. *Guest*: Mary Hartman Mary Hartman, Amanda's, Murder She Wrote. *Movies*: A Year at the Top, The Cracker Factory, Fast Friends, Katie—Portrait of a Centerfold, Sooner or Later.

BLAIR, BETSY: Actress. r.n. Betsy Boger. b. New York, NY, Dec. 11, 1923. m. director Karel Reisz.
THEATRE: Panama Hattie Beautiful People, Richard II, Face of a Hero, actress in little theatre groups. *London*: Trial of Mary Dugan, Spoon River Anthology, Danger Memory.
PICTURES: The Guilt of Janet Ames (debut, 1947), A Double Life, Another Part of the Forest, Snake Pit, Kind Lady, Mystery Street, Marty, Halliday Brand, A Delicate Balance, Betrayed.
TELEVISION: Appearances on U.S. Steel Hour, Ford Theatre, Philco, Kraft, Suspicion (PBS) thirtysomething. *Movie*: Marcus Welby, M.D.—A Holiday Affair. *In England*: Wings of a Dove, Rainmaker, Death of a Salesman.

BLAIR, JANET: Actress. b. Blair, PA, April 23, 1921. r.n. Martha Janet Lafferty. With Hal Kemp's Orchestra; toured in South Pacific, 1950–52.
PICTURES: Three Girls About Town (debut, 1941), Blondie Goes to College, Two Yanks in Trinidad, Broadway, My Sister Eileen, Something to Shout About, Once Upon a Time, Tonight and Every Night, Tars and Spars, Gallant Journey, The Fabulous Dorseys, I Love Trouble, The Black Arrow, Fuller Brush Man, Public Pigeon No. 1, Boys Night Out, Burn Witch Burn, The One and Only Genuine Original Family Band.
TELEVISION: *Series*: Leave it to the Girls (panelist), Caesar's Hour, The Chevy Show, The Smith Family.

BLAIR, LINDA: Actress. b. St. Louis, MO, Jan. 22, 1959. Model and actress on TV commercials before going into films.
PICTURES: The Sporting Club (debut, 1971), The Exorcist, Airport '75, Exorcist II: The Heretic, Roller Boogie, Wild Horse Hank, Hell Night, Ruckus, Chained Heat, Savage Streets, Savage Island, Red Heat, Night Patrol, Night Force, Silent Assassins, Grotesque, Witchery, The Chilling, Bad Blood, Moving Target, Up Your Alley, Repossessed, Aunt Millie's Will, Zapped Again, Dead Sleep.
TELEVISION: *Movies*: Born Innocent, Sarah T.—Portrait of a Teenage Alcoholic, Sweet Hostage, Victory at Entebbe, Stranger in Our House, Calendar Girl Cop Killer? The Bambi Bembenek Story, Perry Mason: The Case of the Heartbroken Bride. *Guest*: Fantasy Island, Murder She Wrote.

BLAKE, DAVID M.: Producers' representative. b. Trincomalee, Ceylon, April 19, 1948. Ent. m.p. ind. 1968 British Lion Films, London. Lion Int'l. Films, O'Seas Division. Appointed 1970 U.S. representative. New York. British Lion Films, Shepperton Studios, Lion TV.

BLAKE, ROBERT: Actor. b. Nutley, NJ, Sept. 18, 1933. r.n. Michael Gubitosi.Started as a child actor in Our Gang comedies as Mickey Gubitosi, also appeared as Little Beaver in Red Ryder series. Later was Hollywood stunt man in Rumble on the Docks and The Tijuana Story. First adult acting job was at the Gallery Theater in Hatful of Rain.

PICTURES: I Love You Again (debut, 1940, as Bobby Blake), Andy Hardy's Double Life, China Girl, Mokey, Salute to the Marines, Slightly Dangerous, The Big Noise, Lost Angel, Red Ryder series (as Little Beaver), Meet the People, Dakota, The Horn Blows at Midnight, Pillow to Post, The Woman in the Window, A Guy Could Change, Home on the Range, Humoresque, In Old Sacramento, Out California Way, The Last Round-Up, Treasure of the Sierra Madre, The Black Rose, Blackout (also co-prod.), Apache War Smoke, Treasure of the Golden Condor, Veils of Bagdad, The Rack, Screaming Eagles, Three Violent People, Beast of Budapest, Revolt in the Big House, Pork Chop Hill, The Purple Gang, Town Without Pity, PT 109, The Greatest Story Ever Told, The Connection, This Property Is Condemned, In Cold Blood, Tell Them Willie Boy is Here, Ripped-Off, Corky, Electra Glide in Blue, Busting, Coast to Coast, Second-Hand Hearts.
TELEVISION: *Series*: The Richard Boone Show, Baretta (Emmy Award, 1975), Hell Town (also exec. prod.). *Movies*: The Big Black Pill (also creator & exec. prod.), The Monkey Mission (also creator & exec. prod.), Of Mice and Men (also exec. prod.), Blood Feud, Murder 1 - Dancer 3 (also exec. prod.), Heart of a Champion: The Ray Mancini Story, Judgment Day: The John List Story. *Guest*: One Step Beyond, Have Gun Will Travel, Bat Masterson.

BLAKELY, SUSAN: Actress. b. Frankfurt, Germany, Sept. 7, 1950, where father was stationed in Army. Studied at U. of Texas. m. prod. Steve Jaffe. Became top magazine and TV commercial model in N.Y.
PICTURES: Savages (debut, 1972), The Way We Were, The Lords of Flatbush, The Towering Inferno, Report to the Commissioner, Shampoo, Capone, Dreamer, The Concorde—Airport '79, Over the Top, Dream a Little Dream, My Mom's a Werewolf, Russian Holiday.
TELEVISION: *Series*: Falcon Crest. *Mini-Series*: Rich Man Poor Man. *Movies*: Secrets, Make Me an Offer, A Cry For Love, The Bunker, The Oklahoma City Dolls, The Heart of a Champion, Will There Really Be A Morning?, The Ted Kennedy Jr. Story, Blood & Orchids, April Morning, Fatal Confession: A Father Dowling Mystery, Broken Angel, Hiroshima Maiden, Ladykillers, Sight Unseen, The Incident, End Run, Dead Reckoning, Murder Times Seven, And the Sea Will Tell, Sight Unseen, Blackmail, Wildflower, Against Her Will: An Incident in Baltimore, Intruders. *Special*: Torn Between Two Fathers.

BLANCO, RICHARD M.: Executive. b. Brooklyn, NY. e. electrical engineering, Wentworth Institute. J.C., 1925–27; bus. admin., U. of California, 1939–40; U.S. Govt. Coll., 1942. Superv. Technicolor Corp., 1931–56; organ. and oper. Consumer Products, Kodachrome film process., Technicolor, 1956–62; dir. of MP Govt. and theatr. sales, N.Y. and Washington, DC, 1963–65; gen. mgr. of Technicolor Florida photo. operations at Kennedy Space Center., prod. document. and educ. films for NASA, 1965; VP of TV division, Technicolor Corp. of America; 1967 elected corporate v.p. Technicolor, Inc.; 1971 pres., Technicolor Graphic Services, Inc.; 1974, elected chmn. of bd. of Technicolor Graphic Services; 1977, elected to bd. of dirs. of Technicolor Inc.

BLANE, RALPH: Composer. b. Broken Arrow, OK, July 26, 1914. e. Northwestern U. Started as singer, then vocal arranger for Broadway shows; appeared on NBC radio. Formed partnership with Hugh Martin, wrote Best Foot Forward; m.p. composer since 1939.
PICTURES: Best Foot Forward, Meet Me in St. Louis, My Dream Is Yours, One Sunday Afternoon, My Blue Heaven, Friendly Island, Skirts Ahoy, French Line, Athena, Girl Rush, The Girl Most Likely, Who is Sylvia?, Ziegfeld Follies, Broadway Rhythm, Abbott and Costello in Hollywood, Easy to Wed.
TELEVISION: The Great Quillow. 1961; same in color for NBC, 1963.
BROADWAY: Three Wishes for Jamie, Tattered Tom, Something About Anne, Don't Flash Tonight, Meet Me in St. Louis.

BLANK, MYRON: Circuit executive. b. Des Moines, IA, Aug. 30, 1911. e. U. of Michigan. Son of A. H. Blank, circuit operator. On leaving coll. joined father in operating Tri-States and Central States circuits. On leave 1943–46 in U.S. Navy, officer in charge visual educ. Now pres. Central States Theatre Corp.; pres. TOA, 1955; chmn. bd. TOA Inc. 1956–57; exec. chmn. of NATO. Pres. of Greater Des Moines Comm.; treas., Iowa Methodist Medical Center; board, Iowa Des Moines Natl. Bank.; pres., Iowa Phoenix Corp., recipient of Brotherhood Award of National Conference of Christians & Jews; board, Simpson College; chmn., Blank Park Zoo. Built Anne Blank Child Guidance Center-Raymond Blank Hospital for Children. Endowed chair for gifted and talented children at Univ. of Iowa; permanent scholarship at Wertzman Inst., Israel. Sturdevant Award from NATO, Humanitarian Award from Variety Club in 1980.

BLATT, DANIEL: Producer. e. Philips Andover Acad., Duke U., Northwestern U. Sch. of Law. Independent producer since

1976; prior posts: resident counsel, ABC Pictures; exec. v.p. Palomar Pictures.
PICTURES: I Never Promised You a Rose Garden, Winter Kills, The American Success Company, The Howling, Independence Day, Cujo, Restless, The Boost.
TELEVISION: *Movies*: Circle of Children, Zuma Beach, The Children Nobody Wanted, Sadat, V—The Final Battle, Badge of the Assassin, Raid on Entebbe, Sacred Vows, A Winner Never Quits, Sworn to Silence, Common Ground. *Series*: V, Against the Law.

BLATTNER, ROBERT: Executive. b. Dover, DE, March 5, 1952. e. Harvard Coll., B.A., 1974; Harvard Business Sch., M.B.A., 1976. 1980–81, dir. sls., Columbia Pictures Home Entertainment; 1981–82, promoted to v.p. & gen. mgr.; 1982–83, v.p., gen. mgr., RCA/Columbia Pictures Home Video; named pres., 1983. Appt. pres., MCA Home Video, 1989.

BLATTY, WILLIAM PETER: Writer, Producer, Director. b. 1928. Novels include John Goldfarb Please Come Home, Twinkle Twinkle Killer Kane, The Exorcist, Legion (filmed as Exorcist III).
PICTURES: Writer: The Man From the Diner's Club, A Shot in the Dark, John Goldfarb Please Come Home, Promise Her Anything, What Did You Do in the War Daddy?, Gunn (co-s.p.), The Great Bank Robbery, Darling Lili (co-s.p.), The Exorcist (also prod.; Acad. Award for best adapt. s.p., 1973), Twinkle Twinkle Killer Kane (a.k.a. The Ninth Configuration; also dir., prod.); The Exorcist III (also dir.).

BLAU, MARTIN: Executive. b. New York, NY, June 6, 1924. e. Ohio U., 1948. Employed on newspapers in OH, TX, WV. Pub. dept., Columbia Pictures, 1951; asst. pub. mgr. 1959; pub. mgr., Columbia Internat'l, 1961; admin. asst. to v.p. of adv. & pub. Columbia Pictures, 1966. Dir. adv. and publicity, Columbia Pictures International, 1970; v.p., 1971; sr. v.p., 1985. Retired, 1988.

BLAUSTEIN, JULIAN: Producer. b. New York, NY, May 30, 1913. e. Harvard U., 1933. Ent. m.p. ind. as reader for Universal 1935; asst. story ed. 1935–36; story ed. 1936–38; in chg. story dept. Music Corp. of America 1938–39; story ed. Paramount 1939–41; Signal Corps Photo. Center 1941–46; edit. supervisor of Selznick 1946–48; to 20th-Fox as prod. 1949; apptd. exec. prod. 20th Cent.-Fox, 1951–Dec. 1952. Independent 1955–75.
PICTURES: Broken Arrow, Mister 880, Half Angel, The Guy Who Came Back, Take Care of My Little Girl, Day the Earth Stood Still, Outcasts of Poker Flat, Don't Bother to Knock, Desiree, The Racers, Storm Center, Cowboy, Bell, Book and Candle, The Wreck of the Mary Deare, Two Loves, The Four Horsemen of the Apocalypse, Khartoum, Three into Two Won't Go.

BLAY, ANDRE: Executive. In 1979, sold Magnetic Video to 20th Century Fox, named pres., CEO, 20th Century Fox Home Video; 1981, formed The Blay Corporation; 1982, joined with Norman Lear and Jerry Perenchio, founders of Embassy Communications, as chairman and CEO of Embassy Home Entertainment; 1986, when Embassy sold to Nelson Group, left to form Palisades Entertainment Group with Elliott Kastner.
PICTURES: Exec. Prod.: Prince of Darkness, They Live, Homeboy, The Blob, A Chorus of Disapproval.

BLECKNER, JEFF: Director, Producer. b. Brooklyn, NY, Aug. 12, 1943. e. Amherst College, BA., 1965; Yale Sch. of Drama, MFA 1968. Taught drama at Yale, also participated in the theater co. 1965–68. 1968–75 theater dir. NY Shakespeare Fest. Public Theatre (2 Drama Desk Awards, 1 Tony nom. for Sticks and Bones); Basic Training of Pavlo Hummel (Obie Award, 1971), The Unseen Hand (Obie Award). Began TV career directing The Guiding Light, 1975.
TELEVISION: Hill Street Blues (Emmy Award, DGA Award, 1983), Concealed Enemies (Emmy Award, 1984), Daddy, I'm Their Momma Now (Emmy nom.), Do You Remember Love (Christopher, Humanitas, Peabody Awards, Emmy nom.), Fresno, Terrorist on Trial, Brotherly Love, My Father, My Son; Favorite Son; Mancuso F.B.I. (exec. prod.), Lifestories (exec. prod.), Last Wish, In Sickness and In Health, The Round Table (pilot).

BLEES, ROBERT: Writer, Producer. e. Dartmouth, Phi Beta Kappa. Writer/photographer, Time and Life Magazines. Fiction: Cosmopolitan, etc. Exec. boards of Writers Guild, Producers Guild. Executive consultant, QM Prods.; BBC (England). Trustee, Motion Picture & TV Fund.
PICTURES: Magnificent Obsession, Autumn Leaves, The Glass Web.
TELEVISION: *Producer:* Combat!, Bonanza, Bus Stop, Kraft Theater. *Writer also:* Alfred Hitchcock, Cannon, Barnaby Jones, Harry O, Columbo. *Co-creator:* The New Gidget.

BLEIER, EDWARD: Executive. b. New York, NY, October 16, 1929. e. Syracuse U., 1951, C.U.N.Y., grad. courses. Reporter/sports caster: Syracuse and NY newspapers/stations: 1947–50. Prog. service mgr., DuMont Television Network,

1951; v.p., radio-television-film, Tex McCrary, Inc. 1958. American Broadcasting Company, 1952–57; 1959–68. v.p. in chg. pub. relations (marketing, advertising, publicity), & planning, broadcast div.; v.p. in chg. of daytime sales & programming; vice pres./gen. sales mgr., ABC-TV Network. U.S. Army Psy. War School; Ex-chmn., TV Committee, NASL; Trustee, NATAS; founder-director & vice-chmn., International TV Council (NATAS); past-pres., IRTS; trustee, Keystone Center for Scientific & Environmental Policy; Council on Foreign Relations; ATAS; AMPAS; guest lecturer at universities. Chmn., Steering comm., Aspen B'dcaster's Conference. 1969–present: Warner Bros. Inc.: Pres, pay-TV, cable & network features.

BLIER, BERTRAND: Director. b. Paris, France, 1939. Son of late actor Bernard Blier. Served as asst. dir. to Georges Lautner, John Berry, Christian-Jaque, Denys de la Paatelliere and Jean Delannoy for two years before dir. debut with Hitler Connais Pas.
PICTURES: Hitler Connais Pas (1963), Breakdown, Laisse Aller C'Est une Valse (s.p. only), Going Places, Calmos, Get Out Your Handkerchiefs; Acad. Award best foreign film, 1978), Buffet Froid, Beau-pere, My Best Friend's Girl, Notre Historie, Menage, Too Beautiful for You.

BLOCH, ROBERT: Writer. b. Chicago, IL, April 5, 1917. Novelist, short-story writer; 55 published books, incl. Psycho, Psycho II, The Night of the Ripper, Lori, Psycho House. Wrote radio series, Stay Tuned for Terror, adapting own stories; national pres., Mystery Writers of Amer., 1970–71; entered films, 1960.
PICTURES: The Couch, Cabinet of Caligari, Straitjacket, The Night-Walker, The Psychopath, The Deadly Bees (co-s.p.), Torture Garden, The House that Dripped Blood, Asylum. (Films adapted from published work): Psycho, The Skull.
TELEVISION: *Features:* The Cat Creature, The Dead Don't Die. Approx. 70 credits on Hitchcock, Thriller, Star Trek, Tales from the Dark Side, Monsters.

BLOCK, WILLARD: Executive. b. New York, NY, March 18, 1930.; e. Columbia Coll., Columbia U. Law Sch., 1952. Counter-Intelligence Corps., U.S. Army, 1952–54, account exec., Plus Marketing, Inc. 1954–55; joined sales staff, NBC Television Network, 1955–57; sales staff, CBS Enterprises, Inc., 1957; international sales mgr, 1960; dir., international sales, 1965; v.p.; 1967; v.p., Viacom Enterprises, 1971; pres., 1972; v.p. MCA-TV, 1973; v.p., gen. mgr., Taft, H-B International, Inc.; pres. Willard Block, Ltd.; 1979, named pres., Viacom Enterprises; 1982–1989, pres. Viacom Worldwide Ltd. Currently consultant to Sumitomo Corp., TCI, Insight Telecast; member bd. dirs. Insight Telecast.

BLOODSWORTH-THOMASON, LINDA: Producer. Writer. b. Poplar Bluff, MO, 1947. With husband Harry Thomason co-owner of Mozark Productions.
TELEVISION: Series: M·A·S·H (writer), Rhoda (writer), Filthy Rich (prod.), Lime Street (co-exec. prod., creator), Designing Women (co-exec. prod., creator, writer), Evening Shade (co-exec. prod., creator, writer). Pilots: Dribble (prod.), Over and Out (writer), London and Davis in New York (prod.).

BLOOM, CLAIRE: Actress. b. London, England, Feb. 15, 1931. e. Guildhall Sc. of Music & Drama, Central Sch. Stage debut with Oxford Rep 1946 in It Depends What You Mean. Other Stage work: The White Devil (London debut), The Lady's Not for Burning, Ring Round the Moon, A Streetcar Named Desire; at Stratford-on-Avon, Old Vic seasons, etc. Bdwy: Rashomon, A Doll's House, Hedda Gabler, Vivat Vivat Regina. Author: Limelight and After.
PICTURES: The Blind Goddess (debut, 1948), Limelight, Innocents in Paris, The Man Between, Richard III, Alexander the Great, The Brothers Karamazov, The Buccaneer, Look Back in Anger, The Royal Game (Schachnovelle), The Wonderful World of the Brothers Grimm, The Chapman Report, The Haunting, 80000 Suspects, Alta Inedelta, Il Maestro di Vigevano, The Outrage, The Spy Who Came In From the Cold, Charly, The Illustrated Man, Three into Two Won't Go, A Severed Head, Red Sky at Morning, A Doll's House, The Going Up of David Lev, Islands in the Stream, Clash of the Titans, Sammy and Rosie Get Laid, Crimes and Misdemeanors.
TELEVISION: Cyrano de Bergerac, Caesar and Cleopatra, Misalliance (Playhouse 90), Anna Karenina, Wuthering Heights, Ivanov, Wessex Tales, An Imaginative Woman, A Legacy, In Praise of Love, The Orestaia, Henry VIII, Backstairs at the White House, Brideshead Revisited, Hamlet, Cymbeline, King John, Ann and Debbie, Ellis Island, Separate Tables, Florence Nightingale, The Ghost Writer, Time and the Conways, Shadowlands, Liberty, Promises to Keep, The Belle of Amherst, Hold the Dream, Anastasia, Queenie, Intimate Contact, Beryl Markham: A Shadow on the Sun, Oedipus the King, The Lady and the Highwayman, The Camomile Lawn, The Mirror Crack'd from Side to Side, It's Nothing Personal.

BLOOM, VERNA: Actress. b. Lynn, MA, Aug. 7, 1939. e. Boston U. Studied drama at Uta Hagen-Herbert Berghof School.

Performed with small theatre groups all over country; then started repertory theatre in Denver. Appeared on Broadway in Marat/Sade (played Charlotte Corday).

PICTURES: Medium Cool (debut, 1969), The Hired Hand, High Plains Drifter, Badge 373, National Lampoon's Animal House, Honkytonk Man, After Hours, The Last Temptation of Christ.

TELEVISION: Movies: Where Have All the People Gone?, Sarah T.—Portrait of a Teenage Alcoholic, The Blue Knight, Contact on Cherry Street, Playing for Time, Rivkin—Bounty Hunter.

BLOOMER STEPHEN J.: Exhibitor. b. Belleville, IL, Nov. 12, 1947. e. Northern Illinois U., B.S. in education, 1969. Elementary school band director, 1969–75; insurance sales, New York Life Insurance Co., 1975–77; asst. mgr., New York Life, 1977–79; joined BAC Theatres Jan., 1979 as warehouse mgr.; Nov. 1979, named gen. mgr.

BLOUNT, LISA: Actress. b. Fayetteville, AK, July 1. e. Univ. of AK. Auditioned for role as extra in film September 30, 1955 and was chosen as the female lead.

PICTURES: September 30, 1955, Dead and Buried, An Officer and a Gentleman, Cease Fire, What Waits Below, Radioactive Dreams, Prince of Darkness, Nightflyers, South of Reno, Out Cold, Great Balls of Fire, Blind Fury, Femme Fatale, Cut and Run.

TELEVISION: Series: Sons and Daughters. Pilot: Off Duty. Movies: Murder Me Murder You, Stormin' Home, The Annihilator, Unholy Matrimony, In Sickness and in Health, An American Story. Guest: Moonlighting, Magnum P.I., Starman, Murder She Wrote, Hitchhiker, Picket Fences.

BLUM, HARRY N.: Executive. b. Cleveland, OH, Oct. 3, 1932. e. U. of Michigan, B.B.A., LL.B. Attorney memb. Ohio Bar Assoc.; toy & hobby industry executive, gen. mngr. Lionel division of General Mills, management consultant, and venture capital and investment manager before entering industry. Now heads The Blum Group, entertainment financing, packaging, production and worldwide distrib.

PICTURES: Executive Action (assoc. prod.), The Land That Time Forgot (assoc. prod.), At the Earth's Core (exec. prod.), Drive-In (assoc. prod.), Diamonds (exec. prod.), The Bluebird (assoc. prod.), Obsession (prod.), Skateboard (prod.), The Magician of Lublin (exec. prod.), Duran Duran—Arena (exec. prod.), Young Lady Chatterly II (exec. prod.), Eminent Domain (exec. prod.).

BLUM, MARK: Actor. b. Newark, NJ, May 14, 1950. Studied drama at U. of Minnesota and U. of Pennsylvania. Also studied acting with Andre Gregory, Aaron Frankel and Daniel Seltzer. Extensive Off-B'way work after debut in The Cherry Orchard (1976).

THEATER: NY stage: Green Julia, Say Goodnight Gracie, Table Settings, Key Exchange, Loving Reno, Messiah, It's Only a Play, Little Footsteps, Cave of Life, Gus & Al (Obie Award), Lost in Yonkers (Broadway). Regional: Brothers (New Brunswick, NJ), Close Ties (Long Wharf), The Cherry Orchard (Long Wharf), Iago in Othello (Dallas). At the Mark Taper Forum: An American Clock, Wild Oats, Moby Dick Rehearsed and An American Comedy.

PICTURES: Desperately Seeking Susan, Just Between Friends, Crocodile Dundee, Blind Date, The Presidio, Worth Winning.

TELEVISION: Series: Sweet Surrender, Capitol News. Pilot: Critical Condition. Guest: Miami Vice, St. Elsewhere, Roseanne. Movie: Condition: Critical.

BLUMOFE, ROBERT F.: Producer. b. New York, NY. e. Columbia Coll., AB, Columbia U. Sch. of Law, JD. v.p., West Coast oper., U.A., 1953–66; independent prod., pres. RFB Enterprises, Inc; American Film Institute, director, AFI-West, Sept. 1, 1977–81. Now indep. prod.

BLUTH, DON: Animator, Director, Producer, Writer. b. El Paso, TX, Sept. 13, 1938. e. Brigham Young U. Animator with Walt Disney Studios 1956 and 1971–79; animator with Filmation 1967; Co-founder and director with Gary Goldman and John Pomery, Don Bluth Productions, 1979–85; animator, Sullivan Studios, 1986–.

PICTURES: Animation director: Robin Hood, The Rescuers, Pete's Dragon, Xanadu, The Secret of Nimh (also prod., dir., s.p.), An American Tail (also co-prod., dir.), The Land Before Time (also co-prod., designer), All Dogs Go to Heaven (also co-prod., co-story), Rock-a-Doodle (also co-prod.).

TELEVISION: Banjo the Woodpile Cat (prod., dir., story, music and lyrics).

BLYTH, ANN: Actress. b. Mt. Kisco, NY, Aug. 16, 1928. e. New Wayburn's Dramatic Sch. On radio in childhood; with San Carlos Opera Co. 3 years; Broadway debut in Watch on the Rhine.

PICTURES: Chip Off the Old Block (debut, 1944), Merry Monahans, Babes on Swing Street, Bowery to Broadway, Mildred Pierce (acad. award nom.), Swell Guy, Brute Force,

Killer McCoy, A Woman's Vengeance, Another Part of the Forest, Mr. Peabody and the Mermaid, Red Canyon, Once More My Darling, Free for All, Top o' the Morning, Our Very Own, The Great Caruso, Katie Did It, Thunder on the Hill, I'll Never Forget You, Golden Horde, One Minute to Zero, The World in His Arms, Sally and Saint Anne, All the Brothers Were Valiant, Rose Marie, The Student Prince, King's Thief, Kismet, Slander, The Buster Keaton Story, The Helen Morgan Story.

TELEVISION: Guest: Lux Video Theatre (A Place in the Sun).

BOCHCO, STEVEN: Producer, Writer. b. New York, NY, Dec. 16, 1943. m. actress Barbara Bosson. e. Carnegie Tech, MFA. Won MCA fellowship in college, joined U-TV as apprentice. His shows typically feature several interwoven plots and characters, deal with social issues, and shift from comedy to drama within an episode.

PICTURES: The Counterfeit Killer (co-s.p.), Silent Running (co-s.p.).

TELEVISION: Writer and story ed.: Name of the Game, Columbo, McMillan and Wife; Delvecchio (writer-prod.), Paris (exec. prod.), Richie Brockelman (co-creator), Turnabout (writer), Invisible Man (writer), Vampire (writer), Hill St. Blues (creator, prod., writer; Emmys 1981, 1982, 1983, 1984), Every Stray Dog and Kid (exec. prod.), Bay City Blues (exec. prod., writer, creator), L.A. Law (Emmy Awards: 1987, 1989), Hooperman, Cop Rock, N.Y.P.D. Blue.

AWARDS: 6 Emmys, Humanitas, NAACP Image Award, Writers Guild, George Foster Peabody, Edgar Allen Poe.

BOCHNER, HART: Actor. b. Toronto, Ontario, Oct. 3, 1956. Son of actor Lloyd Bochner. e. U. of San Diego. Wrote, prod., dir. short film The Buzz (1992) starring Jon Lovitz. Director: film P.C.U. (1993).

PICTURES: Islands in the Stream (debut, 1977), Breaking Away, Terror Train, Rich and Famous, The Wild Life, Supergirl, Making Mr. Right, Die Hard, Apartment Zero, Mr. Destiny, Mad at the Moon, The Innocent.

TELEVISION: Movies: Haywire, Having It All, The Sun Also Rises, Fellow Traveller, And the Sea Will Tell, Complex of Fear. Mini-Series: East of Eden, War and Remembrance. Special: Teach 109.

BOCHNER, LLOYD: Actor. b. Toronto, Canada, July 29, 1924. Father of actor Hart Bochner.

PICTURES: Drums of Africa, The Night Walker, Sylvia, Tony Rome, Point Blank, The Detective, The Horse in the Gray Flannel Suit, Tiger by the Tail, Ulzana's Raid, The Man in the Glass Booth, The Lonely Lady, Millenium, The Naked Gun 2½.

TELEVISION: Series: One Man's Family, Hong Kong, The Richard Boone Show, Dynasty, Santa Barbara. Movies: Scalplock, Stranger on the Run, Crowhaven Farm, They Call It Murder, Satan's School for Girls, Richie Brockelman: Missing 24 Hours, Terraces, Immigrants, A Fire in the Sky, The Best Place to Be, The Golden Gate Murders, Mary and Joseph: A Story of Faith, Mazes & Monsters. Guest: Fantasy Island, Masquerade, The A-Team, Hotel, Crazy Like a Fox, Greatest Heroes of the Bible.

BODE, RALF: Cinematographer. b. Berlin, Germany. Attended Yale where was actor with drama school and acquired degree in directing. Received on-job training teaching combat photography and making films for Army at Ft. Monmouth. First professional job in films was gaffer on Harry, followed by long association with director John G. Avildsen, for whom served as gaffer and lighting designer on Guess What We Learned in School Today, Joe, and Cry Uncle. Later dir. of photography for Avildsen on Inaugural Ball and as East Coast dir. phot. for Rocky.

PICTURES: Saturday Night Fever, Slow Dancing in the Big City, Rich Kids, Coal Miner's Daughter, Dressed to Kill, Raggedy Man, A Little Sex, Gorky Park, First Born, Bring on the Night, Violets Are Blue, Critical Condition, The Big Town, The Accused, Distant Thunder, Cousins, Uncle Buck, One Good Cop, Love Field, Made in America.

TELEVISION: PBS Theatre in America, working as lighting designer and dir. of photo. Also many TV commercials.

BOETTICHER, BUDD: Producer, Director, Writer. r.n. Oscar Boetticher, Jr. b. Chicago, IL, July 29, 1916. e. Culver Military Acad., Ohio State U. bullfighter "Novillero"; then technical dir., Blood and Sand, 1941; asst. dir., Hal Roach studios and Columbia 1941–44; became feature director at Columbia in 1944; dir. Eagle Lion, 1946; dir., Universal; independ. prod., 1954. Autobiography: When in Disgrace—

PICTURES: Behind Locked Doors, Assigned to Danger, Black Midnight, Killer Shark, Wolf Hunters, Bullfighter and the Lady, The Cimarron Kid, Bronco Busters, Red Ball Express, Horizons West, City Beneath the Sea, Seminole, Man from the Alamo, Wings of the Hawk, East of Sumatra, The Magnificent Matador, Killer Is Loose, Seven Men From Now, Decision at Sundown, The Tall T, Buchanan Rides Alone, Ride Lonesome, Westbound, The Rise and Fall of Legs Diamond, Comanche Station, Arruza, A Time for Dying, My

Kingdom For—. Orig. s.p.: Bullfighter and the Lady, Magnificient Matador, Two Mules for Sister Sara, A Time For Dying, My Kingdom For . . . A Horse for Mister Barnum.

BOGARDE, SIR DIRK: Actor. b. Hampstead, London, March 28, 1921. r.n. Derek Van Den Bogaerd. e. Allen Glens Coll., Glasgow & University Coll., London. Knighted, Feb. 1992. Started theatrical career with Amersham Repertory Co., then London stage; in Army in W.W.II. Commandeur des arts et des Lettres, France, 1990. Hon. doc. litt., St. Andrews Univ., Sussex Univ. Top ten British star, 1953–54, 1956–64; number one British money-making star 1955, 1957, 1958, 1959; Variety Club Award—Best Performance 1961–64. Author of memoirs: A Postillion Struck by Lightning (1977), Snakes and Ladders (1978), An Orderly Man (1983), Backcloth, A Particular Friendship, Great Meadow, A Short Walk from Harrods. Novels: A Gentle Occupation, Voices in the Garden, West of Sunset, Jericho.
THEATER: (U.K.) Power With Glory (1947), Point of Departure, The Shaughraun, The Vortex, Summertime, Jezebel.
PICTURES: Dancing With Crime (1947), Esther Waters, Quartet, Once a Jolly Swagman, Dear Mr. Prohack, Boys in Brown, The Blue Lamp, So Long at the Fair, Blackmailed, Woman in Question, Hunted (Stranger in Between), Penny Princess, The Gentle Gunman, Appointment in London, Desperate Moment, They Who Dare, The Sleeping Tiger, Doctor in the House, For Better or Worse, The Sea Shall Not Have Them, Simba, Doctor at Sea, Cast a Dark Shadow, Spanish Gardener, Ill Met by Moonlight, Doctor at Large, Campbell's Kingdom, A Tale of Two Cities, The Wind Cannot Read, The Doctor's Dilemma, Libel, The Angel Wore Red, Song Without End, The Singer Not The Song, Victim, H.M.S. Defiant (Damn the Defiant), We Joined the Navy (cameo), The Password Is Courage, I Could Go on Singing, The Mind Benders, The Servant (Brit. Acad. Award, 1964), Hot Enough for June (Agent 8¾), Doctor in Distress, The High Bright Sun (McGuire Go Home), King and Country, Darling (Brit. Acad Award, 1965), Modesty Blaise, Accident, Our Mother's House, Sebastion, The Fixer, Justine, Oh What a Lovely War, The Damned, Death in Venice, The Serpent (Night Flight From Moscow), The Night Porter, Permission to Kill, Providence, A Bridge Too Far, Despair, Daddy Nostalgia.
TELEVISION: The Little Moon of Alban, Blithe Spirit, Upon This Rock, The Patricia Neal Story, May We Borrow Your Husband?, The Vision.

BOGART, PAUL: Director. b. New York, NY, Nov. 13, 1919. Puppeteer-actor with Berkeley Marionettes 1946–48; TV stage mgr., assoc. dir. NBC 1950–52; numerous Emmy Awards, Christopher Awards; recipient from French Festival Internationale Programmes Audiovisuelle, Cannes '91.
PICTURES: Marlowe, Halls of Anger, Skin Game, Class of '44, Mr. Ricco, Oh, God! You Devil, Torch Song Trilogy.
TELEVISION: U.S. Steel Hour, Kraft Theatre, Armstrong Circle Theatre, Goodyear Playhouse, The Defenders (Emmy Award, 1965), All in the Family (1975–9; Emmy Award, 1978), The Golden Girls (Emmy Award, 1986). Specials: Ages of Man, Mark Twain Tonight, The Final War of Ollie Winter, Dear Friends (Emmy Award, 1968). Secrets, Shadow Game (Emmy Award, 1970), The House Without a Christmas Tree, Look Homeward Angel, The Country Girl, Double Solitaire, The War Widow, The Thanksgiving Treasure; The Adams Chronicles, Natica Jackson. Movies: In Search of America, Tell Me Where It Hurts, Winner Take All, Nutcracker: Money, Madness and Murder, Broadway Bound.

BOGDANOVICH, PETER: Director, Producer, Writer, Actor. b. Kingston, NY, July 30, 1939. e. Collegiate Sch., Stella Adler Theatre Sch., N.Y. 1954–58. Stage debut, Amer. Shakespeare Festival, Stratford, CT, followed by N.Y. Shakespeare Festival, 1958. Off-Bway: dir.-co. prod. The Big Knife, 1959, Camino Real, Ten Little Indians, Rocket to the Moon, 1961, dir.-prod. Once in a Lifetime, 1964. Film critic and feature writer, Esquire, New York Times, Village Voice, Cahiers du Cinema, Los Angeles Times, New York Magazine, Vogue, Variety, etc. 1961–. Books: The Cinema of Orson Welles, 1961; The Cinema of Howard Hawks, 1962; The Cinema of Alfred Hitchcock, 1963; John Ford, 1968, enlarged 1978; Fritz Lang in America, 1969; Allan Dwan—The Last Pioneer, 1971; Pieces of Time, 1973, enlarged 1985; The Killing of the Unicorn: Dorothy Stratten (1960–1980), 1984; This is Orson Welles. Owner: The Holly Moon Co., Inc. (L.A.), 1992–present.
PICTURES: Voyage to the Planet of the Prehistoric Women (dir., s.p., narrator; billed as Derek Thomas), The Wild Angels (2nd unit dir., co-s.p., actor). Director: Targets (also prod., co-s.p., actor), The Last Picture Show (also co-s.p.), Directed by John Ford (also s.p., interviewer), What's Up Doc? (also prod., co-s.p.), Paper Moon (also prod.), Daisy Miller (also prod.), At Long Last Love (also prod., s.p.), Nickelodeon (also co-s.p.), Saint Jack (also co-s.p., actor), They All Laughed (also co-s.p.), Mask, Illegally Yours (also prod.), Texasville (also co-prod., s.p.), Noises Off (also co-exec. prod.), The Thing Called Love.

TELEVISION: The Great Professional (co-dir., writer, interviewer) BBC 1967; CBS This Morning (weekly commentary) 1987–89.
AWARDS: N.Y. Film Critics' Award, best s.p., British Academy Award, best s.p. (The Last Picture Show) 1971; Writer's Guild of America Award, best s.p. (What's Up Doc?) 1972; Silver Shell, Mar del Plata, Spain (Paper Moon, 1973); Best Director, Brussels Festival (Daisy Miller) 1974; Pasinetti Award, Critics Prize, Venice Festival (Saint Jack) 1979.

BOGOSIAN, ERIC: Actor, Writer. b. Woburn, MA, Apr. 24, 1953. e. studied 2 years at U. of Chicago, then Oberlin, theater degree, 1976. In high school, acted in plays with Fred Zollo (now prod.) and Nick Paleologus (now MA congressman). Moved to NY and worked briefly as gofer at Chelsea Westside Theater. Then joined downtown performance space, the Kitchen, first acting in others pieces, then creating his own incl. character Ricky Paul, a stand-up comedian in punk clubs. Theater pieces include: The New World, Men Inside, Voices of America, FunHouse, Drinking in America (Drama Desk and Obie Awards), Talk Radio, Sex Drugs Rock & Roll, Banging Nails Into the Floor With My Forehead.
PICTURES: Special Effects, Talk Radio (also s.p., winner Silver Bear 1988 Berlin Film Fest.), Sex Drugs Rock & Roll (also s.p.).
TELEVISION: Guest: Miami Vice, Twilight Zone. Movies: The Caine Mutiny Court Martial, Last Flight Out. Special: Drinking in America.

BOLAM, JAMES: Actor. b. Sunderland, England. Ent. ind. 1960.
PICTURES: The Kitchen, A Kind of Loving, Loneliness of the Long Distance Runner, HMS Defiant, Murder Most Foul, In Celebration.
TELEVISION: Likely Lads, When The Boat Comes In, Only When I Laugh, The Beiderbecke Affair, Father Matthews Daughter, Room at the Bottom, Andy Capp, The Beiderbecke Tapes, The Beiderbecke Connection, Second Thoughts.

BOLOGNA, JOSEPH: Actor, Writer. b. Brooklyn, NY., Dec. 30, 1938. e. Brown U. m. actress-writer Renee Taylor. Service in Marine Corps and on discharge joined ad agency, becoming director-producer of TV commercials. Collaborated with wife on short film, 2, shown at 1966 N.Y. Film Festival. Together they wrote Lovers and Other Strangers, Broadway play, in which both also acted. Wrote s.p. for film version. Both wrote and starred in Made for Each Other, and created and wrote TV series, Calucci's Dept.
PICTURES: Lovers and Other Strangers (co.-s.p. only), Made for Each Other (also co.-s.p.), Cops and Robbers, Mixed Company, The Big Bus , Chapter Two, My Favorite Year, Blame It on Rio , The Woman in Red, Transylvania 6-5000, It Had to Be You (also co-dir., co-s.p.), Coupe de Ville, Jersey Girl, Deadly Rivals.
TELEVISION: Series: Calucci's Dept. (creator, co-writer only), Rags to Riches, Top of the Heap. Movies: Honor Thy Father, Woman of the Year (also co-writer), Torn Between Two Lovers, One Cooks The Other Doesn't, Copacabana, A Time To Triumph, Prime Target, Thanksgiving Day, Citizen Cohn, The Danger of Love: The Carolyn Warmus Story. Special: Acts of Love and Other Comedies (Emmy, 1974). Mini-Series: Sins.

BOLT, ROBERT: Writer, b. Sale, England, Aug. 15, 1924. Ent. m.p. ind. 1961. m. actress Sarah Miles.
PICTURES: Lawrence of Arabia, Dr. Zhivago (Acad. Award, 1965), A Man For All Seasons (Acad. Award, 1966), Ryan's Daughter, Lady Caroline Lamb (also dir.), The Bounty, The Mission.
TELEVISION: Movie: Without Warning: The James Brady Story.

BONANNO, LOUIE: Actor. b. Somerville, MA, Dec. 17, 1961. e. Bentley Coll., Waltham, MA, BS-economics, finance; AS accountancy, 1983. Moved to NY, 1983 to study at Amer. Acad. of Dramatic Arts. Toured U.S. 1985–86 as Dangermouse for MTV/Nickelodeon. In L.A. appeared as stand-up comedian. Stage debut in The Head.
PICTURES: Sex Appeal (debut, 1986), Wimps, Student Affairs, Cool as Ice, Auntie Lee's Meat Pies.
TELEVISION: Eisenhower & Lutz (series), 227, Tour of Duty, TV 101, Santa Barbara, New York Story.

BOND, DEREK: Actor, Scriptwriter. b. Glasgow, Scotland, Jan. 26, 1920. e. Haberdasher Askes Sch., London. Stage debut in As Husbands Go, 1937; served in Grenadier Guards H.M. Forces 1939–46, awarded Military Cross; m.p. debut in Captive Heart, 1946; author of Unscheduled Stop, Two Young Samaritans, Ask Father Christmas, Packdrill, Double Strung, Order to Kill, The Riverdale Dam, Sentence Deferred, The Mavroletty Fund. Many TV appearances. Pres., British Actors Equity, 1984–86. Author: Steady Old Man.
PICTURES: Nicholas Nickleby, Joanna Godden, Uncle Silas, Scott of the Antarctic, Marry Me, Poets Pub, Weaker Sex, Broken Journey, Christopher Columbus, Tony Draws a Horse, Quiet Woman, Hour of Thirteen, Distant Trumpet, Love's a Luxury, Trouble in Store, Svengali, High Terrace,

Stormy Crossing, Rogues Yarn, Gideon's Day, The Hand, Saturday Night Out, Wonderful Life, Press For Time, When Eight Bells Toll, Intimate Reflections, Vanishing Army.

BONET, LISA: Actress. b. Los Angeles, CA, Nov. 16, 1967. First gained recognition on The Cosby Show as Denise Huxtable at the age of 15.
PICTURES: Angel Heart, Lights Out.
TELEVISION: Series: The Cosby Show, A Different World. Guest: Tales From the Dark Side. Special: Don't Touch.

BONET, NAI: Actress, Producer. Worked in entertainment field since age of 13, including opera, films, TV, stage, night clubs and records.
PICTURES: Actress: The Soul Hustlers, The Seventh Veil, Fairy Tales, The Soul of Nigger Charlie, The Spy with the Cold Nose, John Goldfarb Please Come Home, etc. Wrote and starred in Nocturna and Hoodlums.
TELEVISION: Johnny Carson Show, Merv Griffin Show, Joe Franklin Show, Beverly Hillbillies, Tom Snyder Show.

BONHAM-CARTER, HELENA: Actress. b. London, England, May 26, 1966. Great granddaughter of Liberal Prime Minister Lord Asquith. e. Westminster. Appeared on BBC in A Pattern of Roses; seen by director Trevor Nunn who cast her in Lady Jane, 1986, theatrical film debut. On London stage in Trelawny of the Wells.
PICTURES: Lady Jane, A Room with a View, Maurice (cameo), Francesco, The Mask, Getting It Right, Hamlet, Where Angles Fear to Tread, Howards End.
TELEVISION: Guest: Miami Vice. Movies: A Hazard of Hearts (U.S.), The Vision, Beatrix Potter, Marina's Story, Dancing Queen.

BONO, SONNY: Singer, Actor, Director, Writer. b. Detroit, MI, Feb. 16, 1935. r.n. Salvatore Bono. Started writing songs at age 16; entered record business as an apprentice prod. Became ass't. to Phil Spector, rock music prod. and did background singing. Recorded albums with former wife Cher, made two feature films and formed nightclub act with her. CBS comedy-variety series began as summer show in 1971 and made regular later that year. Elected Mayor, Palm Springs, CA 1988. Published autobiography in 1991.
PICTURES: Wild on the Beach, Good Times, Chastity (prod., s.p. only), Escape to Athena, Airplane II: The Sequel, Troll, Hairspray, Under the Boardwalk.
TELEVISION: Series: Sonny & Cher Comedy Hour, Sonny Comedy Revue. Movies: Murder on Flight 502, Murder in Music City, Top of the Hill. Guest: Shindig, Hullabaloo, Man from U.N.C.L.E., Love American Style, Murder She Wrote, Parker Lewis Can't Lose.

BOOKE, SORRELL: Actor. b. Buffalo, NY, Jan. 4, 1930. e. Columbia U. Joined summer stock company in Charleston, WV, and later in Provincetown, MA. After stint with armed forces returned to NY and off-Bdwy plays. Bdwy debut in The Sleeping Prince, followed by appearances in over 100 plays.
PICTURES: Gone Are the Days, Fail Safe, Black Like Me, Lady in a Cage, Up the Down Staircase, What's Up Doc?, The Iceman Cometh, The Take, Bank Shot, Freaky Friday, The Other Side of Midnight.
TELEVISION: Guest: Route 66, Soap, What's Happening!, Alice, Newhart. Series: Rich Man Poor Man—Book II, The Dukes of Hazard.

BOOKMAN, ROBERT: Executive. b. Los Angeles, CA, Jan. 29, 1947. e. U. of California, Yale Law Sch. Motion picture literary agent, IFA 1972–74, ICM 1974–79. 1979–84, ABC Motion Pictures v.p., worldwide production; 1984–6, Columbia Pictures, exec. v.p., world-wide prod. 1986, Creative Artists Agency, Inc., as motion picture literary and directors' agent.

BOONE, JR., ASHLEY A.: Executive. b. 1938. e. Brandeis U. Started career at United Artists in foreign adv./pub.; later with Cinema Center Films; adm. asst., Motown Records; assoc. prod. for Sidney Poitier's E & R Productions. Joined 20th-Fox in 1972 in sls. dept.; advanced to sr. sls. & mktg. positions in feature film operation. In 1979 appt. pres. of 20th-Fox Distribution & Marketing. Joined Ladd Co., v.p. in chg. dist. & mktg., 1983; Pres., Columbia Pictures Mktg. & Dist. Group, 1984. Resigned 1985 but remained special mkt. consultant. 1986, joined Lorimar Pictures as pres., mktg. & dist. 1990, joined Pathe Ent. as pres. of mktg. & distrib. Merged with MGM, 1991. Became pres. of Worldwide mktg. & distrib.

BOONE, PAT: Singer. b. Jacksonville, FL, June 1, 1934. e. David Lipscomb Coll., North Texas State Coll., grad. magna cum laude, Columbia U. Winner of Ted Mack's TV show; joined Arthur Godfrey TV show, 1955. m.p. debut in Bernadine. Most promising male movie star, Motion Picture Daily-Fame Poll 1957. One of top ten moneymaking stars, M.P. Herald-Fame Poll, 1957.
AUTHOR: Twixt Twelve and Twenty, Between You & Me and the Gatepost, The Real Christmas.
RECORDINGS: Ain't That a Shame, I Almost Lost My Mind, Friendly Persuasion, Love Letters in the Sand, April Love, Tutti Frutti.

PICTURES: Bernardine (debut, 1957), April Love, Mardi Gras, Journey to the Center of the Earth, All Hands on Deck, State Fair, The Main Attraction, The Yellow Canary, The Horror of It All, Never Put it in Writing, Goodbye Charlie, The Greatest Story Ever Told, The Perils of Pauline, The Cross and the Switchblade, Roger and Me.
TELEVISION: Series: Arthur Godfrey and His Friends, The Pat Boone-Chevy Showroom (1957–60), The Pat Boone Show (1966–8). Movie: The Pigeon.

BOORMAN, JOHN: Director, Producer, Writer. b. London, Eng., Jan. 18, 1933. Wrote film criticism at age of 17 for British publications incl. Manchester Guardian; founder TV Mag. Day By Day; served in National Service in Army; Broadcaster and BBC radio film critic 1950–54; film editor Independent Television News; prod. documentaries for Southern Television; joined BBC, headed BBC Documentary Film Unit 1960–64, indep. doc. about D.W. Griffith; chmn. Natl. Film Studios of Ireland 1975–85, governor Brit. Film Inst. 1985–.
PICTURES: Director: Catch Us If You Can (Having a Wild Weekend; debut, 1965), Point Blank, Hell in the Pacific, Leo The Last (also s.p.), Deliverance (also prod.; Acad. Award noms. for best picture & dir.), Zardoz (also prod., s.p.), Exorcist II: The Heretic (also prod.), Excalibur (also exec. prod., s.p.), The Emerald Forest (also prod.), Hope and Glory (also prod., s.p.; Acad. Award noms. for best picture & dir.; L.A. Film Critics Awards for best picture, dir. & s.p.; Natl. Society of Film Critics Awards for best dir.& s.p.), Where the Heart Is (also prod., co-s.p.), I Dreamt I Woke Up (also s.p., actor).
TELEVISION: Series: Citizen '63 (dir.), The Newcomers (dir.).

BOOTH, MARGARET: Film editor. b. Los Angeles, CA, 1898. Awarded honorary Oscar, 1977.
PICTURES: Why Men Leave Home, Husbands and Lovers, Bridge of San Luis Rey, New Moon, Susan Lenox, Strange Interlude, Smilin' Through, Romeo and Juliet, Barretts of Wimpole Street, Mutiny on the Bounty, Camille, etc. Supervising editor on Owl and the Pussycat, The Way We Were, Funny Lady, Murder by Death, The Goodbye Girl, California Suite, The Cheap Detective (also assoc. prod.), Chapter Two (also assoc. prod.); The Toy (assoc. prod.). Editor: Annie. Exec. Prod.: The Slugger's Wife.

BOOTH, SHIRLEY: Actress. b. New York, NY, Aug. 20, 1899. Joined Poli Stock Co., Hartford, CT, at 12; Broadway debut in Hell's Bells, 1925; on radio in Duffy's Tavern.
PLAYS: After Such Pleasures, 3 Men on a Horse, Philadelphia Story, My Sister Eileen, Tomorrow the World, Goodbye My Fancy (Tony Award, 1949), Come Back Little Sheba (Tony Award, 1950), A Tree Grows in Brooklyn, Time of the Cuckoo (Tony Award, 1953), The Desk Set, Look to the Lillies, Miss Isobel, Juno, Colettes Second String, The Glass Menagerie.
PICTURES: Come Back Little Sheba (debut, Acad. Award, best actress, 1952), Main Street to Broadway, About Mrs. Leslie, Hot Spell, The Matchmaker.
TELEVISION: Specials: Perle Mesta Story, The Glass Menagerie. Series: Hazel (1961–68; Emmy Awards, 1962 & 1963), A Touch of Grace.
(Died: Oct. 16, 1992)

BOOTHE, POWERS: Actor. b. Snyder, TX, 1949. e. Southern Methodist U. On Broadway in Lone Star.
TELEVISION: Series: Skag, Philip Marlowe. Movies: Skag, Plutonium Incident, Guyana Tragedy—The Story of Jim Jones (Emmy Award, 1980), A Cry for Love, Into the Homeland, Family of Spies, By Dawn's Early Light, Wild Card, Marked for Murder.
PICTURES: The Goodbye Girl, Cruising, Southern Comfort, A Breed Apart, Red Dawn, The Emerald Forest, Extreme Prejudice, Stalingrad, Rapid Fire, Blue Sky, Tombstone.

BORGE, VICTOR: Comedian, Pianist. b. Copenhagen, Denmark, Jan. 3, 1909. Child prodigy at age 8. Awarded scholarship to study in Berlin and Vienna. Later became humorous concert artist. Wrote and starred in musical plays and films in Denmark. Fled Nazis in 1940, came to America.
Appeared on Bing Crosby radio show. Concert and Nightclub tours. TV variety shows. One-man Broadway show Comedy in Music. 1953, three-year run. Second edition in 1965. Third edition 1977, Fourth edition in 1989. World tours. One-man TV shows. Guest conductor with major symphonies around the world. Recent recording, The Two Sides of Victor Borge. Author: My Favorite Intermissions and My Favorite Comedies in Music. Awarded Medal of Honor by Statue of Liberty Centennial Comm. Knighted by 5 Scandinavian countries, honored by U.S. Congress and U.N. Created Thanks to Scandinavia Scholarship Fund, Dana College, Univ. of Conn., SUNY—Purchase Scholarships. Recent video: Onstage with Victor Borge.

BORGNINE, ERNEST: Actor. b. Hamden, CT, Jan. 24, 1917. e. Randall Sch. of Dramatic Art, Hartford, CT. Joined Barter Theatre. Served in U.S. Navy; then little theatre work, stock companies; on Broadway in Harvey, Mrs. McThing; many TV appearances. Honors: 33rd Degree of the Masonic Order, Order of the Grand Cross, from same. Named honorary Mayor of Universal City Studios.

PICTURES: China Corsair (debut, 1951), The Mob, Whistle at Eaton Falls, From Here to Eternity, The Stranger Wore a Gun, Demetrius & the Gladiators, Johnny Guitar, Bounty Hunter, Vera Cruz, Bad Day at Black Rock, Marty (Acad. Award best actor 1955), Run for Cover, Violent Saturday, Last Command, Square Jungle, Catered Affair, Jubal, Best Things in Life are Free, Three Brave Men, The Vikings, Badlanders, Torpedo Run, Rabbit Trap, Season of Passion (Summer of the 17th Doll), Man on a String, Pay or Die, Go Naked in the World, Barabbas, McHale's Navy, Flight of the Phoenix, The Oscar, Chuka, The Dirty Dozen, Ice Station Zebra, Legend of Lylah Clare, The Split, The Wild Bunch, The Adventurers, Suppose They Gave a War and Nobody Came?, A Bullet for Sandoval, Bunny O'Hare, Willard, Rain for a Dusty Summer, Hannie Caulder, The Revengers, Ripped Off, The Poseidon Adventure, Emperor of the North Pole, The Neptune Factor, Man Hunt, Law and Disorder, Sunday in the Country, The Devil's Rain, Hustle, Shoot, Love By Appointment, The Greatest, Crossed Swords, Convoy, Strike Force, Diary of Madam X, The Black Hole, The Double McGuffin, Ravagers, When Time Ran Out, High Risk, Super Fuzz, Escape from New York, Deadly Blessing, Young Warriors, Codename: Wild Geese, Skeleton Coast, Spike of Bensonhurst, The Opponent, Any Man's Death, Laser Mission, Turnaround, Captain Henkel, Real Men Don't Eat Gummy Bears, Moving Target, The Last Match, Mistress.

TELEVISION: Series: McHale's Navy, Air Wolf. Movies: Sam Hill: Who Killed the Mysterious Mr. Foster?, The Trackers, Twice in a Lifetime, Future Cop, Jesus of Nazareth, Fire!, The Ghost of Flight 401, Cops and Robin, All Quiet on the Western Front, Blood Feud, Carpool, Love Leads the Way, Last Days of Pompeii, The Dirty Dozen: The Next Mission, Alice in Wonderland, The Dirty Dozen: The Deadly Mission, Treasure Island (Ital. TV), The Dirty Dozen: The Fatal Mission, Jake Spanner-Private Eye, Appearances, The Burning Shore, Mountain of Diamonds (Ital TV). Guest: Philco Playhouse, General Electric Theater, Wagon Train, Laramie, Zane Grey Theater, Alcoa Premiere, The Love Boat, Little House on the Prairie, Murder She Wrote, Home Improvement. Specials: Billy the Kid, Legend in Granite: The Vince Lombardi Story.

BORIS, ROBERT: Writer, Director. b. NY, NY, Oct. 12, 1945. Screenwriter before also turning to direction with Oxford Blues, 1984.

PICTURES: Electra Glide in Blue; Some Kind of Hero; Doctor Detroit; Oxford Blues (also dir.), Steele Justice (dir.); Buy and Cell (dir.)

TELEVISION: Birds of Prey; Blood Feud, Deadly Encounter, Izzy and Moe.

BORODINSKY, SAMUEL: Executive. b. Brooklyn, NY, Oct. 25, 1941. e. Industrial Sch. of Arts & Photography. Expert in film care and rejuvenation. Now exec. v.p., Filmtreat International Corp. Previously with Modern Film Corp. (technician) and Comprehensive Filmtreat, Inc. & International Filmtreat (service manager).

BOSCO, PHILIP: Actor. b. Jersey City, NJ, Sept. 26, 1930. e. Catholic U., Washington, DC, BA. drama, 1957. Studied for stage with James Marr, Josephine Callan and Leo Brady. Consummate stage actor (in over 100 plays, 61 in NY) whose career spans the classics (with NY Shakespeare Fest. and American Shakespeare Fest, CT.), 20 plays with Arena Stage 1957–60, to modern classics as a resident actor with Lincoln Center Rep. Co. in the 1960s, winning Tony and Drama Desk Awards for the farce Lend Me a Tenor, 1988.

THEATER: Auntie Mame (Bdwy debut, City Center revival, 1958), Measure for Measure, The Rape of the Belt (Tony nom.), Donnybrook, Richard III, The Alchemist, The East Wind, Galileo, Saint Joan, Tiger at the Gates, Cyrano de Bergerac, King Lear, The Miser, The Time of Your Life, Camino Real, Operation Sidewinder, Amphitryon, In the Matter of J. Robert Oppenheimer, The Good Woman of Setzuan, The Playboy of the Western World, An Enemy of the People, Antigone, Mary Stuart, The Crucible, Enemies, Mrs. Warren's Profession, Henry V, The Threepenny Opera, Streamers, Stages, The Biko Inquest, Whose Life Is It Anyway? A Month in the Country, Don Juan in Hell, Inadmissible Evidence, Ah! Wilderness, Come Back Little Sheba, Man and Superman, Major Barbara, The Caine Mutiny Court Martial, Heartbreak House, Come Back Little Sheba, Loves of Anatol, Be Happy for Me, Master Class, You Never Can Tell, A Man for All Seasons, Devil's Disciple, Lend Me a Tenor (Tony Award, 1989), The Miser, Breaking Legs.

PICTURES: Requiem for a Heavyweight, A Lovely Way to Die, Trading Places, The Pope of Greenwich Village, Walls of Glass, Heaven Help Us, Flanagan, The Money Pit, Children of a Lesser God, Suspect, Three Men and a Baby, Another Woman, Working Girl, The Luckiest Man in the World, Dream

Team, Blue Steel, Quick Change, True Colors, FX2, Shadows and Fog, Straight Talk, Angie I Says.

TELEVISION: Series: Tribeca. Specials: Prisoner of Zenda (1960), An Enemy of the People, A Nice Place to Visit, Read Between the Lines (Emmy Award). Guest: Nurses, Trials of O'Brien, Law and Order, Spenser: For Hire, The Equalizer, Against the Law, Janek. Movies: Echoes in the Darkness, Second Effort, Internal Affairs, Murder in Black and White, The Return of Eliot Ness.

BOSLEY, TOM: Actor. b. Chicago, IL, Oct. 1, 1927. e. DePaul U. Had roles on radio in Chicago and in stock productions before moving to New York. Appeared off-Broadway and on road before signed to play lead in Fiorello! for George Abbott on Broadway. First actor to win Tony, Drama Critics, ANTA and Newspaper Guild awards in one season for that role.

PICTURES: Love with the Proper Stranger, The World of Henry Orient, Divorce American Style, Yours Mine and Ours, The Secret War of Harry Frigg, To Find a Man, Mixed Company, Gus, O'Hara's Wife, Million Dollar Mystery, Wicked Stepmother.

TELEVISION: Specials: Alice in Wonderland (1953), Arsenic and Old Lace, The Drunkard, Profiles in Courage. Guest: Focus, Naked City, The Right Man, The Nurses, Route 66, The Perry Como Show. Series: That Was the Week That Was, Debbie Reynolds Show, The Dean Martin Show, Sandy Duncan Show, Wait Til Your Father Gets Home (voice), Happy Days, That's Hollywood (narrator), Murder She Wrote, Father Dowling Mysteries. Movies: Marcus Welby M.D.: A Matter of Humanities (pilot), Night Gallery, A Step Out of Line, Vanished, Congratulations It's a Boy!, Mr. & Mrs. Bo Jo Jones, Streets of San Francisco (pilot), No Place to Run, Miracle on 34th Street, The Girl Who Came Gift Wrapped, Death Cruise, Who Is the Black Dahlia?, Last Survivors, The Night That Panicked America, Love Boat, Testimony of 2 Men, Black Market Baby, With This Ring, The Bastard, The Triangle Factory Fire Scandal, The Castaways on Gilligan's Island, The Rebels, Return of the Mod Squad, For the Love of It, Jesse Owens Story, Fatal Confession: A Father Dowling Mystery, The Love Boat: A Valentine Voyage.

BOSTICK, ROBERT L.: b. Waynesboro, GA, Oct. 25, 1909. e. Georgia Inst. of Technology, M.E., eng., 1932. Started with National Theatre Supply, Atlanta, salesman, Memphis, 1933; br. mgr. 1937; br. mgr. Dallas, 1942; Vice Pres., Southern division mgr., 1952; retired 1968. Chief Barker Variety Club Tent 20, Memphis 1950–51. Since 1957, has served as International Rep., International Ambassador-at-Large, and International Vice Pres. for Variety Clubs International. Since 1968, owner & operator of theatres in Memphis and Charlotte areas.

BOSTWICK, BARRY: Actor. b. San Mateo, CA, Feb. 24, 1945. e. USIU Sch. of Performing Arts, San Diego, BFA in acting; NYU Grad. Sch. of the Arts. Made prof. stage debut while in coll. working with Walter Pidgeon in Take Her She's Mine, Joined APA Phoenix Rep. Co. making his Bdwy debut in Cock-A-Doodle Dandy.

THEATER: Salvation, House of Leather, Soon, The Screens, Colette, Grease (created role of Danny Zuko, 1972), They Knew What They Wanted, The Robber Bridegroom (Tony Award, 1977), She Loves Me, L'Historie du Soldat, Nick and Nora.

PICTURES: The Rocky Horror Picture Show, Movie Movie, Megaforce, Eight Hundred Leagues Down the Amazon, Weekend at Bernie's 2.

TELEVISION: Series: Foul Play, Dads. Movies: The Chadwick Family, The Quinns, Murder By Natural Causes, Once Upon a Family, Moviola—The Silent Lovers, Red Flag: The Ultimate Game, Summer Girl, An Uncommon Love, Deceptions, Betrayed by Innocence, Body of Evidence, Addicted to His Love, Parent Trap III, Till We Meet Again, Challenger, Captive, Between Love and Hate, Praying Mantis. Mini-Series: Scruples, George Washington, I'll Take Manhattan, War and Remembrance. Specials: A Woman of Substance, You Can't Take It With You, Working.

BOSUSTOW, NICK: Producer. b. Los Angeles, CA, March 28, 1940. e. Menlo Coll., CA, administration. MCA, intl. sales, 1963. Pres., Stephen Bosustow Productions, 1967; pres., ASIFA-West; Academy Award '70 best short, Is It Always Right to Be Right?; 1973 Acad. Award nom., The Legend of John Henry. TV specials: The Incredible Book Escape, Misunderstood Monsters, A Tale of Four Wishes, Wrong Way Kid (Emmy, 1984); The Hayley Mills Story Book (series). 1973, pres., Bosustow Entertainment, Inc.

BOSUSTOW, TED: Producer, Director, Editor. b. Hollywood, CA, Feb 18, 1938. e. UCLA cinema in Westwood; La Sorbonne, Paris.

PICTURES: Beware of Thin Ice, Big Boys Don't Cry, Avati and the Mezzotint. Edited short, Is It Always Right to Be Right? (AA, 1971).

TELEVISION: About a Week (community affairs series; Emmy award).

BOSWALL, JEFFERY: Producer, Director, Writer. b. Brighton, Eng., 1931. e. Taunton House School, Montpelier Coll., Brighton. Started career as an ornithologist for the Royal Society for the Protection of Birds. Joined BBC in 1958 as radio producer, moving to TV 1964 making films in diverse locations (Ethiopia and Antarctica). Contributed to 50 films as wildlife cameraman. Co-founder of British Library of Wildlife Sounds. 1987: returned to RSPB. Head of Film and Video Unit, 1987. 1992, sr. lecturer in Biological Film & Video, Derby Univ. Chairmanship BKSTS Intl Wildlife Filmmakers' Symposium.
TELEVISION: 18 films in the Private Lives series of which 4 (about the Kingfisher, Cuckoo, Starling and Jackass Penguin) won intl awards. Animal Olympians, Birds For All Seasons, Where the Parrots Speak Mandarin, Wildlife Safari to Ethiopia.
AUTHOR: Birds for All Seasons. Ed. Look and Private Lives. Contrib.: Times, Countryman, the Field, Wildlife and Countryside, BBC Wildlife, Scientific Film, Journal of the Society of Film and TV Arts, Image Technology. Has written for scientific journals and writes annual update for Encyclopedia Britannica on ornithology.

BOTTOMS, JOSEPH: Actor. b. Santa Barbara, CA, April 22, 1954. Brother of Sam and Timothy Bottoms. Did plays in jr. high school in Santa Barbara and then with community theatre.
PICTURES: The Dove (debut, 1974), Crime and Passion, The Black Hole, Cloud Dancer, King of the Mountain, Blind Date, Open House, Born to Race, Inner Sanctum.
TELEVISION: Movies: Trouble Comes to Town, Unwed Father, Stalk the Wild Child, The Intruder Within, Side By Side: The True Story of the Osmond Family, I Married Wyatt Earp, The Sins of Dorian Gray, Time Bomb, Braker, Island Sons, Cop Killer, Gunsmoke: To the Last Man, Treacherous Crossing, Liar's Edge. Mini-Series: Holocaust, Celebrity. Special: Winesburg Ohio. Guest: Owen Marshall, Murder She Wrote.

BOTTOMS, SAM: Actor. b. Santa Barbara, CA, Oct. 17, 1955. Brother of Timothy, Joseph and Ben Bottoms. Co-prod. documentary Picture This. Appeared in documentary Hearts of Darkness.
PICTURES: The Last Picture Show (debut, 1971), Class of '44, Zandy's Bride, The Outlaw Josey Wales, Apocalypse Now, Bronco Billy, Hunter's Blood, Gardens of Stone, After School, Ragin' Cajun, Dolly Dearest, In 'n Out, North of Chiang Mai, Prime Risk, The Trust.
TELEVISION: Series: Santa Barbara. Movies: Savages, Cage Without a Key, Desperate Lives, Island Sons. Mini-Series: East of Eden. Guest: Greatest Heroes of the Bible, Murder She Wrote, Doc Elliot, Eddie Capra, Lucas Tanner.

BOTTOMS, TIMOTHY: Actor. b. Santa Barbara, CA, Aug. 30, 1951. Brother of Joseph and Sam Bottoms. Early interest in acting; was member of S.B. Madrigal Society, touring Europe in 1967. Sang and danced in West Side Story local prod. With brother Sam co-prod. documentary Picture This about making of the Last Picture Show and Texasville.
PICTURES: Johnny Got His Gun (debut, 1971), The Last Picture Show, Love and Pain, The Paper Chase, The White Dawn, The Crazy World of Julius Vrooder, Operation Daybreak, A Small Town in Texas, Rollercoaster, The Other Side of the Mountain: Part 2, Hurricane, The High Country, Hambone and Hillie, In the Shadow of Kilimanjaro, The Sea Serpent, The Fantasist, Invaders from Mars, The Drifter, Mio in the Land of Faraway, Return to the River Kwai, A Case of Law, Texasville, Istanbul.
TELEVISION: Special: Look Homeward Angel. Mini-Series: The Money Changers, East of Eden. Movies: The Story of David, The Gift of Love, A Shining Season, Escape, Perry Mason: The Case of the Notorious Nun. Island Sons. Series: Land of the Lost.

BOUCHIER, CHILI: Actress. r.n. Dorothy Irene Boucher. b. Fulham, London, England, Sept. 12, 1909. m. Bluey Hill, Australian film director (d. 1986). British stage appearances include: Open Your Eyes, 1930; Lavender; Magnolia Street; Mother Goose; A Little Bit of Fluff; Rendezvous; Age of Consent; Tons of Money; The Mousetrap; Harvey; I Can't Imagine Tomorrow; Rookery Nook; French Dressing; Conduct Unbecoming; The Best of Dorothy Parker; Follies A Little Night Music (1987). Originally a model at Harrods, London. After her screen debut in 1927, she quickly became one of Britain's first international m.p. stars. Autobiography: For Dogs and Angels (1968).
PICTURES: A Woman in Pawn, Shooting Stars, Maria Marten, Dawn, Chick, You Know What Sailors Are, Warned Off, The Silver King, City of Play, Downstream, Enter the Queen, Call of the Sea, Kissing Cup's Race, Brown Sugar, Carnival, The Blue Danube, Ebb Tide, The King's Cup, Summer Lightning, Purse Strings, It's a Cop, To Be a Lady, The Office Wife, Death Drives Through, Royal Cavalcade, The Mad Hatters, Honours Easy, Lucky Days, Get Off My Foot, Mr. Cohen Takes a Walk, The Ghost Goes West, Faithful, Where's Sally?, Southern Roses, Gypsy, Mayfair

Melody, The Minstrel Boy, Change for a Sovereign, The Dark Stairway, Mr. Satan, The Singing Cop, The Return of Carol Deane, Everything Happens to Me, The Mind of Mr. Reeder, My Wife's Family, Facing the Music, Murder in Reverse, The Laughing Lady, Mrs. Fitzherbert, The Case of Charles Peace, Old Mother Riley's New Venture, The Wallet, The Counterfeit Plan, The Boy and the Bridge, Dead Lucky.
TELEVISION: Yesterday's Witness, Looks Familiar, Saturday Night at the Pictures, Catch a Fallen Star.

BOULTING, ROY: Producer, Director. b. Bray, Buckinghamshire, England, Nov. 21, 1913. e. McGill U., Montreal. Capt., Brit. Army, W.W.II. Dir. Charter Film, Charter Film Prod. Ltd. London; dir. British Lion Films, Ltd., 1958. 1977, co-author with Leo Marks of play, Favourites, Danny Travis, 1978.
PICTURES: Inquest, Trunk Crime, Pastor Hall, Thunder Rock, Desert Victory, Burma Victory, Fame is the Spur, Brighton Rock, Guinea Pig, Seven Days to Noon, Lucky Jim, High Treason, Singlehanded (Sailor of the King), Seagulls Over Sorrento (Crest of the Wave), Josephine and Men, Private's Progress, Run for the Sun, Brothers in Law, Happy Is the Bride, Carlton-Browne of the F.O., I'm All Right Jack, The Risk, The French Mistress, Heavens Above!, Rotten to The Core, The Family Way, Twisted Nerve, There's a Girl in My Soup, Soft Beds, Hard Battles, The Last Word, Agatha Christie's The Moving Finger (BBC).

BOWER, DALLAS: Producer, Director. b. London, 1907. Ent. film prod. 1927; film ed., writer, dir., prod. with BBC-TV 1936. Prod. and dir. opening program of BBC Television service, 1936. Commissioned in Royal Corps of Signals, 1939; supvr. film prod., Ministry of Inf., Films Div., 1942; prod. official and commercial documentaries; author, Plan for Cinema, 1936.
PICTURES AND TELEVISION: Aida, Tristan & Isolde, Master Peter's Puppet Show, Cinderella, Julius Caesar, The Tempest, The Taming of the Shrew, The Silver Box, The Mock Emperor, The Emperor Jones, Rope, Path of Glory, Victory over Space, Henry V, Alice in Wonderland, The Second Mrs. Tanquery, Fire One, Doorway to Suspicion, Adventures of Sir Lancelot.

BOWIE, DAVID: Singer, Actor. b. Brixton, South London, England, Jan. 8, 1947. r.n. David Robert Jones. m. model-actress Iman.Broadway debut: The Elephant Man (1980).
PICTURES: The Virgin Soldiers, Ziggy Stardust and the Spiders from Mars (1973, U.S. release 1983), The Man Who Fell to Earth, Just a Gigolo, Christiane F, The Hunger, Yellowbeard, Merry Christmas Mr. Lawrence, Into the Night, Absolute Beginners (also songs), Labyrinth (also songs), The Last Temptation of Christ, Imagine—John Lennon, The Linguini Incident, Twin Peaks: Fire Walk With Me.
TELEVISION: Specials: Christmas With Bing Crosby, The Midnight Special, Glass Spider Tour.

BOWSER, EILEEN: Curator, Film Archivist, Historian. b. Ohio, Jan. 18, 1928. e. Marietta Coll., B.A., 1950; U. of North Carolina, M.A., history of art, 1953. Joined Dept. of Film, Museum of Modern Art, 1954. Curator, Dept. of Film (1976–1993). Organized major exhib. of the films of D.W. Griffith, Carl-Theodor Dreyer, Art of the Twenties, recent acquisitions and touring shows. On exec. comm. of Federation Internationale des Archives du Film 1969–91, v.p. FIAF 1977–85; pres. FIAF Documentation Commission 1972–81. Film Archives Advisory Comm. since 1971. Assoc. of Univ. Seminars on Cinema and Interdisciplinary Interpretation. Publications: The Transformation of Cinema: 1907–15, Vol II, History of the American Film Series, The Movies, David Wark Griffith, Biograph Bulletins 1908–1912. A Handbook for Film Archives. Has written numerous articles on film history.

BOX, BETTY, OBE: Producer. b. Beckenham, Kent, England, 1920. Assisted Sydney Box in prod. 200 propaganda films in W.W.II. Assoc. prod. Upturned Glass.
PRODUCTIONS: Dear Murderer, When the Bough Breaks, Miranda, Blind Goddess, Huggett Family series. It's Not Cricket, Marry Me, Don't Ever Leave Me, So Long At the Fair, The Clouded Yellow, Appointment With Venus (Island Rescue). Venetian Bird (The Assassin), A Day to Remember, Doctor in the House, Mad About Men, Doctor at Sea, The Iron Petticoat, Checkpoint, Doctor at Large, Campbell's Kingdom, A Tale of Two Cities, The Wind Cannot Read, The 39 Steps, Upstairs and Downstairs, Conspiracy of Hearts, Doctor in Love, No Love for Johnnie, No, My Darling Daughter, A Pair of Briefs, The Wild and the Willing, Doctor in Distress, Hot Enough for June (Agent 8¾), The High Bright Sun, (McGuire Go Home), Doctor in Clover, Deadlier Than the Male, Nobody Runs Forever (The High Commissioner), Some Girls Do, Doctor in Trouble, Percy, The Love Ban, Percy's Progress (It's Not the Size That Counts).

BOXLEITNER, BRUCE: Actor. b. Elgin, IL, May 12, 1950. After high school enrolled in Chicago's Goodman Theatre, staging productions and working with lighting and set design in addition to acting.
TELEVISION: Series: How the West Was Won, Bring 'Em Back Alive, Scarecrow and Mrs. King. Movies: The Chadwick

Family, A Cry for Help, The Macahans, Kiss Me–Kill Me, Murder at the World Series, Happily Ever After, Wild Times, Kenny Rogers as The Gambler, Fly Away Home, Bare Essence, I Married Wyatt Earp, Kenny Rogers as The Gambler: The Adventure Continues, Passion Flower, Angel in Green, Kenny Rogers as the Gambler: The Legend Continues, Red River, The Town Bully, From the Dead of Night, The Road Raiders, Till We Meet Again, Murderous Vision, The Secret, Perfect Family, Double Jeopardy (also co-exec. prod.). *Mini-Series*: How the West Was Won, East of Eden, The Last Convertible.
PICTURES: Six-Pack Annie, The Baltimore Bullet, Tron, The Crystal Eye, Breakaway, Diplomatic Immunity, Kuffs, The Babe.

BOYARS, ALBERT: Executive. b. New York, NY, Aug. 11, 1924. e. NYU. U.S. Navy, 1942–45. David O. Alber Assoc., 1945–51: Greater N.Y. Fund, Robert S. Taplinger Assoc., Michael Myerberg· Prod., 1951–54: pub. rel. dir., Transfilm-Caravel Inc., and parent co. Buckeye Corp., 1954–63: director spec. projects in adv-pub-exploit. M-G-M, 1963–64; dir. of adv. & pub. Trans-Lux Corp., 1964; v.p. of adv. and pub. rel., Trans-Lux Multimedia Corp., 1976. Under his marketing aegis were the attractions The New York Experience, (in Rockefeller Center), and The Seaport Experience (at South Street Seaport, NY.).

BOYER, PHIL: TV Executive. b. Portland, OR, Dec. 13, 1940. e. Sacramento State U. Began broadcasting career as 12-year-old in Portland, establishing nation's first youth radio facility—a 5-watt facility in the basement of his home. At 16 began working at KPDQ, Portland; two years later joined KPTV, Portland, as announcer. In 1960 joined KEZI-TV, Eugene, OR, heading prod. and prog. depts. In 1965 named staff prod.-dir. for KCRA, TV, Sacramento, CA, becoming prod. mgr. in 1967 and prog. mgr. in 1969. In 1972 joined KNBC-TV, Los Angeles, as prog. dir. In 1974 named v.p., programming, of ABC Owned Television Stations; 1977, v.p.-gen. mgr., WLS-TV, Chicago; 1979, v.p.-gen. mgr. of WABC-TV, New York 1981; v.p., gen mgr., ABC-owned TV station div.; 1984, joined ABC Video Enterprises as v.p. intl. dev.; 1986 named sr. v.p., intl and prog. dev., CC/ABC Video Ent.

BOYETT, ROBERT LEE: Producer. e. Duke U., B.A.; Col. U., M.A., marketing. Began career in media and mkt. research at Grey Advertising, Inc. Was program development consultant for PBS. In 1973 joined ABC as dir. of prime time series TV, East Coast. In 1975 named ABC TV v.p. & asst. to v.p. programs for West Coast. In 1977 joined Paramount Pictures in newly created position of v.p., exec. asst. to pres. & chief operating officer. 1979, joined Miller-Milkis–Boyett Productions to produce for Paramount Television.
TELEVISION: Exec. prod.: Laverne and Shirley, Happy Days, Bosom Buddies, Mork and Mindy, Valerie, Perfect Strangers.

BOYLE, BARBARA D.: Executive. b. New York, NY, Aug. 11, 1935. e. U. of California, Berkeley, B.A., 1957; UCLA, J.D., 1960. Named to bar: California, 1961; New York, 1964; Supreme Court, 1964. Atty. in busn. affairs dept. & corp. asst. secty., American Intl. Pictures, Los Angeles, 1965–67; partner in entertainment law firm, Cohen & Boyle, L.A., 1967–74; exec. v.p. & gen. counsel, COO, New World Pictures, L.A., 1974–82. Sr. v.p. worldwide prod., Orion Pictures, L.A., 1982–86; exec. v.p., prod., RKO Pictures, L.A., 1986–87. President, Sovereign Pictures, L.A., 1988–92; Boyle-Taylor Prods., 1993 to present. Co-chmn. 1979–80, Entertainment Law Symposium Advisory Committee, UCLA Law Sch.
MEMBER: Academy of Motion Picture Arts & Sciences, Women in Film (pres., 1977–78, mem. of bd., chairperson 1981–84), Women Entertainment Lawyers Assn., California Bar Assn., N.Y. State Bar Assn., Beverly Hills Bar Assn., Hollywood Women's Political Committee, American Film Institute. Bd. mem.: Women Director's Workshop, Independent Feature Project/West, Los Angeles Women's Campaign Fund. Founding mem. UCLA Sch. of Law's Entertainment Advisory Council (& co-chairperson 1979 & 80).

BOYLE, LARA FLYNN: Actress. b. Davenport, IA, Mar. 24, 1970. e. Chicago Academy for the Visual and Performing Arts. First studied acting at the Piven Theatre.
TELEVISION: *Series*: Twin Peaks. *Mini-Series*: Amerika. *Movies*: Terror on Highway 91, Gang of Four, The Preppie Murders, The Hidden Room.
PICTURES: Poltergeist III, How I Got Into College, Dead Poets Society, May Wine, The Rookie, The Dark Backward, Mobsters, Wayne's World, Where the Day Takes You, The Temp, Eye of the Storm, Red Rock West, Equinox.

BOYLE, PETER: Actor. b. Philadelphia, PA, Oct. 18, 1933. e. LaSalle Coll. Was monk in Christian Bros. order before leaving in early 60s to come to N.Y. Acted in off-Broadway shows and joined The Second City in Chicago. Also did TV commercials.
PICTURES: The Virgin President (debut, 1968), The Monitors, Medium Cool, Joe, Diary of a Mad Housewife, T.R.

Baskin, The Candidate, Steelyard Blues, Slither, The Friends of Eddie Coyle, Kid Blue, Ghost in the Noonday Sun, Crazy Joe, Young Frankenstein, Taxi Driver, Swashbuckler, F.I.S.T., The Brink's Job, Hardcore, Beyond the Poseidon Adventure, Where the Buffalo Roam, In God We Trust, Outland, Hammett, Yellowbeard, Johnny Dangerously, Turk 182, Surrender, Walker, The In Crowd, Red Heat, The Dream Team, Speed Zone, Funny, Men of Respect, Solar Crisis, Kickboxer 2, Honeymoon in Vegas, Nervous Ticks, Malcolm X.
TELEVISION: *Series*: Comedy Tonight, Joe Bash. *Mini-Series*: From Here to Eternity. *Movies*: The Man Who Could Talk to Kids, Tail Gunner Joe, Echoes in the Darkness, Disaster at Silo 7, Guts and Glory: The Rise and Fall of Oliver North, Challenger, In the Line of Duty: Street War, Taking the Heat. *Specials*: 27 Wagons Full of Cotton, Conspiracy: The Trial of the Chicago Eight. *Guest*: Cagney & Lacey, Midnight Caller.
THEATER: *NY*: Shadow of Heroes, Paul Sills' Story Theatre, The Roast, True West, Snow Orchid.

BRABOURNE, LORD JOHN: Producer. b. London, England, Nov. 9, 1924.
PRODUCTIONS: Harry Black and the Tiger, Sink the Bismarck, H.M.S. Defiant, Othello, The Mikado, Up the Junction, Romeo and Juliet, Dance of Death, (Peter Rabbit and) Tales of Beatrix Potter, Murder on the Orient Express, Death On The Nile, Stories from a Flying Trunk, The Mirror Crack'd, Evil Under the Sun, A Passage to India, Little Dorrit.

BRACCO, LORRAINE: Actress. b. Brooklyn, NY, 1955. At 16 began modelling for Wilhelmina Agency appearing in Mademoiselle, Seventeen, Teen magazine. Moved to Paris where modelling career continued and led to TV commercials. After making her film debut in Duo sur Canape became a disc jockey on Radio Luxembourg, Paris. 1983 produced a TV special on fashion and music. In Lincoln Center workshop performance of David Rabe's Goose and Tom Tom, 1986.
PICTURES: Cormorra, The Pick-up Artist, Someone to Watch Over Me, Sing, The Dream Team, On a Moonlit Night, Good Fellas, Talent for the Game, Switch, Medicine Man, Radio Flyer, Traces of Red.
TELEVISION: Movie: Scam.

BRACKEN, EDDIE: Actor. b. New York, NY, Feb. 7, 1920. e. Prof. Children's Sch. for Actors, N.Y. m. Connie Nickerson, actress. Vaudeville & night club singer: stage debut in Lottery, 1930.
PLAYS: Lady Refuses, Iron Men, So Proudly We Hail, Brother Rat, What A Life, Too Many Girls, Seven Year Itch, Shinbone Alley, Teahouse of the August Moon, You Know I Can't Hear You When The Water's Running, The Odd Couple, Never Too Late, Sunshine Boys, Hotline to Heaven, Hello Dolly, Damn Yankees, Sugar Babies, Show Boat, The Wizard of Oz.
PICTURES: Too Many Girls (debut, 1940), Life With Henry, Reaching for the Sun, Caught in the Draft, The Fleet's In, Sweater Girl, Star Spangled Rhythm, Happy Go Lucky, Young and Willing, Miracle of Morgan's Creek, Hail the Conquering Hero, Rainbow Island, Bring on the Girls, Duffy's Tavern, Hold That Blonde, Out of This World, Ladies' Man, Fun on a Weekend, The Girl From Jones Beach, Summer Stock, Two Tickets to Broadway, About Face, We're Not Married, Slight Case of Larceny, Shinbone Alley (voice), National Lampoon's Vacation, Oscar, Home Alone 2: Lost in New York, Rookie of the Year.
TELEVISION: *Series*: I've Got a Secret (panelist), Make the Connection (panelist), Masquerade Party (host, 1957).*Guest*: Goodyear Playhouse, Studio One, Climax, Murder She Wrote, Blacke's Magic, Amazing Stories, Tales of the Dark Side, Golden Girls, Wise Guy, Empty Nest, Monsters. *Movie*: The American Clock.

BRADEN, WILLIAM: Executive, Producer. b. Alberta, Canada, 1939. e. Vancouver, B.C. Began career as stuntman in Hollywood, and has worked in all aspects of industry Worked for Elliott Kastner as prod. exec. and with Jeffrey Bloom, of Feature Films, Inc., as prod. and v.p. of prod. Also with Dunatai Corp., as head of film and TV prod. With Completion Bond Co. one yr. as prod. exec., Australia then with Filmaker Completion as pres. 4 years. Now indep. prod.
PICTURES: Pyramid (assoc. prod., prod. supvr.), Russian Roulette (prod. exec.) 92 in the Shade (prod. exec.), Breakheart Pass (prod. exec.), Dogpound Shuffle (asst. dir.), Dublin Murders (supvr. re-edit); He Wants Her Back (prod.); Goldengirl (prod. exec.); Running Scared (prod.); Death Valley (asst. dir.); The Seduction (prod. exec.); Slapstick (prod. exec.).
TELEVISION: Requiem for a Planet (series, prod./creator); Specials: Nothing Great is Easy (prod.); Russian King of the Channel (exec. prod.); I Believe (prod.); If My People . . . (prod.) America: Life in the Family (dir./prod.) Also various Movies of the Week for networks and many industrial and doc. films.

BRADLEY, BILL: Performer, r.n. William M. Silbert. b. Detroit, MI, Jan. 1, 1921. e. U. of Detroit, Southern Methodist U. Disc jockey, m.c., many radio-TV shows, Detroit; panelist, Songs for Sale, 1952; emcee, Bill Silbert show, Let's Go Bowling,

1952–53; Bill Silbert Show. WMGM radio; announcer, Red Buttons Show; Philco Phonorama Time; m.c., National Radio Fan Club; Magazine of the Air, Mutual #1 disc jockey, Billboard Magazine, 1955; KLAC Hollywood, Bill Bradley Show; KTLA, Hollywood, m.c. Crime Story, Greet the People, Ad Lib, Hollywood Diary. gen. sales mgr., A.E. KLOS, Los Angeles.
PICTURES: Bundle of Joy, Thunderjets, The Alligator People, Young Jesse James, Lost Missile, Breakfast at Tiffany's, Return to Peyton Place, Looking for Love, Goonies.
TELEVISION: Bronco, 77 Sunset Strip, Hawaiian Eye, Sugarfoot, Combat, Adventures in Paradise, Police Station, Michael Shayne, Roaring 20's, The Outlaws, Breaking Point, The Fugitive, Bill Dana Show, My Living Doll, Joey Bishop Show, Ben Casey, Bing Crosby Show. Many commercials, Mannix, Wild Wild West, Name of the Game.
RADIO: WXYZ, WWJ, Detroit; WMGM, Mutual Network, NBC, NY; KLAC, KABC-FM, KLOS, L.A.

BRADLEY, ED: Newscaster. b. Philadelphia, Pa., June 22, 1941. e. Cheyney State Coll., B.S. Worked way up through the ranks as local radio reporter in Philadelphia 1963–67 and NY 1967–71. Joined CBS News as stringer in Paris bureau, 1971; then Saigon bureau. Named CBS news correspondent, 1973. Became CBS News White House corr. and anchor of CBS Sunday Night News, 1976–81; principal corr. and anchor, CBS Reports, 1978–81; co-editor and reporter 60 Minutes since 1980.
TELEVISION: Special reports: What's Happened to Cambodia; The Boat People; The Boston Goes to China; Blacks in America—with all Deliberate Speed; Return of the CIA; Miami . . . The Trial That Sparked the Riot (Emmy); The Saudis; Too Little, Too Late (Emmy); Murder—Teenage Style (Emmy, 1981); In the Belly of the Beast (Emmy, 1982); Lena (Emmy, 1982).
AWARDS: Aside from numerous Emmys, has received Alfred I. duPont-Columbia University and Overseas Press Club Awards; George Foster Peabody and Ohio State Awards; and George Polk Award.

BRAEDEN, ERIC: Actor. b. Kiel, Germany, Apr. 3, r.n. Hans Gudegast. Awarded Federal Medal of Honor by pres. of Germany for promoting positive, realistic image of Germans in America.
PICTURES: Morituri, Dayton's Devils, 100 Rifles, Colossus: The Forbin Project, Escape from the Planet of the Apes, Lady Ice, The Adulteress, The Ultimate Thrill, Herbie Goes to Monte Carlo, The Ambulance.
TELEVISION: Series: The Rat Patrol, The Young and the Restless (People's Choice Award, Soap Opera Award, 2 Emmy noms.). Movies: Honeymoon With a Stranger, The Mask of Sheba, The Judge and Jake Wyler, Death Race, Death Scream, The New Original Wonder Woman (pilot), Code Name: Diamond Head, Happily Ever After, The Power Within, The Aliens Are Coming, Lucky.

BRAGA, SONIA: Actress. b. Maringa, Parana, Brazil, 1950. Began acting at 14 on live children's program on Brazilian TV, Gardin Encantado. Stage debut at 17 in Moliere's Jorge Dandin, then in Hair! Starred in many Brazilian soap operas including Gabriella, as well as a prod. of Sesame Street in Saõ Paulo.
PICTURES: The Main Road, A Moreninha, Captain Bandeira Vs. Dr. Moura Brasil, Mestica, The Indomitable Slave, The Couple, Dona Flor and Her Two Husbands, Gabriella, I Love You, A Lady in the Bus, Kiss of the Spider Woman, The Milagro Beanfield War, Moon Over Parador, The Rookie, Roosters.
TELEVISION: Movies: The Man Who Broke 1000 Chains, The Last Prostitute. Guest: The Cosby Show, Tales From the Crypt.

BRANAGH, KENNETH: Actor, Director, Producer, Author. b. Belfast, Northern Ireland, Dec. 10, 1960. m. actress Emma Thompson. Moved to Reading, England at 9. e. RADA. Went from drama school into West End hit Another Country, followed by Gamblers, The Madness, Francis. Royal Shakespeare Co.: Love Labors Lost, Hamlet, Henry V. Left Royal Shakespeare Company to form his own Renaissance Theater Co. with actor David Parfitt for which he wrote a play Public Enemy, wrote-directed Tell Me Honestly, directed Twelfth Night, produced-directed-starred in Romeo & Juliet, and played Hamlet, Benedick and Touchstone in a sold-out nationwide tour and London season. L.A.: King Lear, A Midsummer Night's Dream. Author: Beginning (1990). Received BAFTA's Michael Balcon Award for Outstanding Contribution to Cinema (1993). Made Oscar nominated short film Swan Song.
PICTURES: High Season (debut, 1987), A Month in the Country, Henry V (also dir., adapt.; BAFTA & Natl. Board of Review of Awards for Best Director, 1989), Dead Again (also dir.), Peter's Friends (also dir., prod.), Swing Kids, Much Ado About Nothing (also dir., adapt.).
TELEVISION: The Boy in the Bush (series), The Billy Plays, Maybury, To the Lighthouse, Coming Through, Ghosts,

The Lady's Not For Burning, Fortunes of War (mini-series) Thompson (series), Strange Interlude, Look Back in Anger.

BRANDAUER, KLAUS MARIA: Actor. b., Altaussee, Austria, June 22, 1944. m. film and TV dir.-screenwriter Karin Mueller. e. Acad. of Music and Dramatic Arts, Stuttgart, W. Germany. Was established in the German and Austrian theater before film debut.
PICTURES: The Salzburg Connection (debut, 1972), Mephisto (best actor, Cannes, 1981). Never Say Never Again, Colonel Redl, Out of Africa, The Lightship, Streets of Gold, Burning Secret, Hanussen, Hitlerjunge Salomon, Das Spinnennetz (The Spider's Web) The French Revolution, The Russia House, White Fang, The Resurrected, Seven Minutes (also dir.), Becoming Colette.
TELEVISION: Quo Vadis?

BRANDO, JOCELYN: Actress. b. San Francisco, CA, Nov. 18, 1919. Sister of actor Marlon Brando. e. Lake Forest Coll. Broadway in Mr. Roberts, Desire Under the Elms, Golden State.
PICTURES: The Big Heat (debut, 1953), China Venture, Ten Wanted Men, Nightfall, The Explosive Generation, The Ugly American, Bus Riley's Back in Town, The Chase, Movie Movie, Why Would I Lie?, Mommie Dearest.
TELEVISION: Movies: A Question of Love, Dark Night of the Scarecrow, Starflight—The Plane that Couldn't Land.

BRANDO, MARLON: Actor. b. Omaha, NB, April 3, 1924. Brother of actress Jocelyn Brando. e. Shattuck Military Acad., Faribault, MN. Studied Dramatic Workshop, NY; played stock Sayville, Long Island. Broadway debut: I Remember Mama, then Truckline Cafe, Candida, A Flag Is Born, A Streetcar Named Desire. One of top ten Money-Making Stars, M.P. Herald-Fame poll, 1954–55. Directed One-Eyed Jacks.
PICTURES: The Men (debut, 1950), A Streetcar Named Desire, Viva Zapata, Julius Caesar, Wild One, On the Waterfront (Acad. Award, best actor, 1954), Desiree, Guys and Dolls, Teahouse of the August Moon, Sayonara, The Young Lions, The Fugitive Kind, One-Eyed Jacks (also dir.), Mutiny on the Bounty, The Ugly American, Bedtime Story, The Saboteur-Code Name: Morituri, The Chase, Appaloosa, A Countess From Hong Kong, Reflections in a Golden Eye, Night of the Following Day, Candy, Burn!, The Nightcomers, The Godfather (Acad. Award, best actor, 1972), Last Tango in Paris, The Missouri Breaks, Superman, Apocalypse Now, The Formula, A Dry White Season, The Freshman, Christopher Columbus: The Discovery.
TELEVISION: Mini-Series: Roots: The Next Generations (Emmy Award, best supporting actor, 1979).

BRANDON, MICHAEL: Actor. b. Brooklyn, NY. e. AADA. Appeared on Bdwy in Does Tiger Wear a Necktie?
TELEVISION: Series: Emerald Point, Dempsey & Makepeace, Home Fires. Movies: The Impatient Heart, The Strangers in 7A, The Third Girl From the Left, Hitchhike!, The Red Badge of Courage, Queen of the Stardust Ballroom, Cage Without a Key, James Dean, Scott Free, Red Alert, The Comedy Company, A Vacation in Hell, A Perfect Match, Between Two Brothers, The Seduction of Gina, Deadly Messages, Rock 'n' Roll Mom, Dynasty: The Reunion, Not in My Family.
PICTURES: Lovers and Other Strangers, Jennifer on My Mind, Four Flies on Grey Velvet, Heavy Traffic (voice), FM, Promises in the Dark, A Change of Seasons, Rich and Famous.

BRANDT, RICHARD PAUL: Executive. b. New York, NY, Dec. 6, 1927. e. Yale U., BS, Phi Beta Kappa. Chmn. Trans Lux Corp.; chmn., Brandt Theatres; dir., Presidential Realty Corp.; chmn. emeritus & trustee, American Film Institute; trustee, American Theatre Wing; member, Tony Awards Management Comm.; vice-chmn. & trustee, College of Santa Fe.

BRAUNSTEIN, GEORGE GREGORY: Producer. b. New York, NY, May 23, 1947. e. Culver Military Acad., U. of California, B.A., biology, chemistry, 1970. U. W.L.A. Law School, J.D. 1987. Father is Jacques Braunstein (Screen Televideo Prods. At War with the Army, Young Lions, etc.).
PICTURES: Train Ride to Hollywood, Fade to Black, Surf II, And God Created Woman, Out Cold, Don't Tell Her It's Me.

BRAVERMAN, CHARLES: Producer, Director. b. Los Angeles, CA, March 3, 1944. e. Los Angeles City Coll., U. of Southern California, B.A. m. Kendall Carly Browne, actress. Child actor, 1950–57. Two time Emmy winner.
TELEVISION: An American Time Capsule, The Smothers Brothers Racing Team Special, How to Stay Alive, David Hartman . . . Birth and Babies, Breathe a Sigh of Relief, The Television Newsman, Getting Married, The Making of a Live TV Show, Televisionland, Nixon: Checkers to Watergate, Braverman's Condensed Cream of Beatles, Two Cops, Peanuts to the Presidency: The Jimmy Carter Campaign; The Making of Beatlemania, Willie Nelson Plays Lake Tahoe, Tony Bennett Sings, What's Up, America?, The Big Laff Off, Engelbert at the MGM Grand, Oscar's First 50 Years, Frankie

Valli Show, The Sixties, Showtime Looks at 1981, Roadshow, Kenny Rodger's America; St. Elsewhere; DTV (Disney Channel); Crazy Like a Fox; Dreams; The Richard Lewis Special; Prince of Bel Air, Brotherhood of Justice (both ABC movies); The Wizard; Heart of the City; Rags to Riches; The New Mike Hammer, Sledge Hammer!, Gabriel's Fire, Life Goes On, Beverly Hills 90210, FBI: Untold Stories, Final Shot: The Hank Gathers Story, Melrose Place, Northern Exposure (DGA nom.), Haunted Lives II.
PICTURES: Dillinger, Soylent Green, Same Time Next Year (all montages, titles), Can't Stop the Music (titles), Hit and Run (prod./dir.).

BRAZZI, ROSSANO: Actor. b. Bologna, Italy, Sept. 18, 1916. e. U. of Florence. Started career on Italian stage; has appeared in numerous Italian pictures.
PICTURES: (English Language): Little Women, Three Coins in the Fountain, Barefoot Contessa, Angela, Summertime, Loser Takes All, Interlude, The Story of Esther Costello, South Pacific, A Certain Smile, Count Your Blessings, Light in the Piazza, Rome Adventure, Dark Purpose, The Battle of the Villa Fiorita, The Christmas That Almost Wasn't, The Bobo, Woman Times Seven, Krakatoa East of Java, The Adventurers, Psychout for Murder, The Great Waltz, The Final Conflict, Fear City, Michelanglo and Me.
TELEVISION: (U.S.) Series: The Survivors. Guest: June Allyson Show, Run For Your Life, The Name of the Game, Hawaii Five-O, Fantasy Island, Charlie's Angels, Hart to Hart. Movies/Mini-Series: Honeymoon With a Stranger, The Far Pavillions, Christopher Columbus.

BRECHER, IRVING: Writer. b. New York, NY, Jan. 17, 1914. Yonkers Herald reporter; network programs writer for Milton Berle, Willie Howard, Al Jolson, etc., m.p. writer since 1937.
PICTURES: (collab. s.p.) Shadow of the Thin Man, Best Foot Forward, Meet Me in St. Louis; (collab. adapt.) Summer Holiday; (s.p.), Go West, At the Circus, Du Barry Was a Lady, Yolanda and the Thief, Life of Riley (dir.), Somebody Loves Me (dir.), Cry for Happy, Bye Bye Birdie, Sail a Crooked Ship (dir.).
TELEVISION: The People's Choice, The Life of Riley.

BREGMAN, MARTIN: Producer, Writer. b. New York, NY, May 18, 1931. m. actress Cornelia Sharpe. e. Indiana U., NYU. Began career as business and personal mgr. to Barbra Streisand, Faye Dunaway, Candice Bergen, Al Pacino, etc. Chairman NY Advisory Council for Motion Pictures, Radio and TV (co-founder, 1974).
PICTURES: Serpico, Dog Day Afternoon, The Next Man, The Seduction of Joe Tynan, Simon, The Four Seasons, Eddie Macon's Run, Venom, Scarface, Sweet Liberty, Real Men, A New Life, Sea of Love, Nesting, Betsy's Wedding, Whispers in the Dark, The Real McCoy, Carlito's Way.
TELEVISION: Prod.: S*H*E (movie), The Four Seasons (series).

BRENNAN, EILEEN: Actress. b. Los Angeles, CA, Sept. 3, 1935. e. Georgetown U., American Acad. of Dramatic Arts, N.Y. Daughter of silent film actress Jean Manahan. Big break came with lead in off-Broadway musical, Little Mary Sunshine (Obie & Theatre World Awards, 1960).
STAGE: The Miracle Worker (tour), Hello, Dolly! (Broadway), and revivals of The King and I, Guys and Dolls, Camelot, Bells Are Ringing, An Evening with Eileen Brennan, A Couple of White Chicks Sitting Around Talking.
PICTURES: Divorce American Style (debut, 1967), The Last Picture Show (BAFTA nom.), Scarecrow, The Sting, Daisy Miller, At Long Last Love, Hustle, Murder by Death, FM, The Cheap Detective, The Last of the Cowboys (a.k.a. The Great Smokey Roadblock), Private Benjamin (Acad. Award nom.), Pandemonium, The Funny Farm, Clue, Sticky Fingers, Rented Lips, The New Adventures of Pippi Longstocking, It Had to Be You, Stella, Texasville, White Palace, Joey Takes a Cab, I Don't Buy Kisses Anymore.
TELEVISION: Series: Rowan & Martin's Laugh-In, All My Children, 13 Queens Boulevard, A New Kind of Family, Private Benjamin (Emmy Award), Off the Rack. Special: Working. Movies: Playmates, My Father's House, The Night That Panicked America, The Death of Richie, When She Was Bad . . ., My Old Man, When the Circus Came to Town, Incident at Crestridge, Going to the Chapel, Deadly Intentions . . . Again?, Taking Back My Life: The Nancy Ziegenmeyer Story, Poisoned by Love: The Kern County Murders. Mini-Series: The Blue Knight, Black Beauty. Guest: Taxi, Magnum P.I., Newhart, All in the Family, Murder She Wrote.

BRENNER, JOSEPH: Executive. b. Brooklyn, NY, Oct. 27, 1918. e. Brooklyn Coll. Started as usher, 1935, becoming mgr., Rogers Theatre, 1936; salesman, Eagle Lion Films, 1946; Screen Guild Prods., 1948; sales mgr., Ellis Films, 1949; formed Joseph Brenner Associates, 1953.

BRESSON, ROBERT: Writer, director. b. France, Sept. 25, 1907. PICTURES: Les Anges du Peche, Les Dames du Bois de Boulogne, Le Journal d'un Cure de Campagne, Pickpocket, The Trial of Joan of Arc, Au Hazard Balthasar, Mouchette,

Une Femme Douce, Lancelot du Lac, Le Diable Probablement, De Weg Naar Bresson.

BREST, MARTIN: Director. b. Bronx, NY, Aug. 8, 1951. e. NYU Sch. of Film. m. producer Lisa Weinstein. Made award-winning short subject, Hot Dogs for Gauguin (featuring Danny DeVito). Accepted into fellowship program at American Film Institute, making first feature, Hot Tomorrows (dir., prod., s.p.), as AFI project. Appeared in Fast Times at Ridgemont High and Into the Night.
PICTURES: Going in Style (also s.p.), Beverly Hills Cop, Midnight Run (also prod.), Scent of a Woman (also prod.), Josh and S.A.M. (prod. only).

BRETT, JEREMY: Actor. b. Berkwell Grange, Warwickshire, Eng., Nov. 3, 1933. r.n. Jeremy Huggins. e. Eton, Central Sch. of Speech and Drama. London stage debut, Troilus and Cressida (Old Vic, 1956); NY stage debut, Richard II (1956).
THEATER: Selected London shows: Meet Me by Moonlight, Variations on a Theme, Mr. Fox of Venice, Marigold, The Edwardians, Johnny the Priest, The Kitchen, A Month in the Country, Macrune's Guevara, A Voyage Round My Father, Traveller Without Luggage, Design for Living. U.S.: With Old Vic in Amphytrion 38, Richard II, Macbeth, Romeo and Juliet, Troilus and Cressida, The Deputy, Robert and Elizabeth (L.A.), Dracula (L.A.), Aren't We All?
PICTURES: War and Peace, The Wild and the Willing, The Very Edge, My Fair Lady, The Medusa Touch.
TELEVISION: Romeo and Juliet (1957), Macbeth, Florence Nightingale, Deceptions, Jennie, Katherine Mansfield, The Merry Widow, Rebecca, The Adventures of Sherlock Holmes (1985–86), Picture of Dorian Gray, Dinner with Family, The School for Scandal, Hart to Hart.

BRIALY, JEAN-CLAUDE: Actor. b. Aumale, Algeria, March 30, 1933. e. Strasbourg U. (philosophy) also attended drama classes at Strasbourg Conservatoire. Made several short films with Jacques Rivette and Jean-Luc Godard. Popular actor in films of French New Wave directors.
PICTURES: Elena et les Hommes; Elevator to the Scaffold (1958); Les Cousins; Le Beau Serge; The 400 Blows; Tire au Flanc; La Chambre Ardente; A Woman is a Woman; The Devil and Ten Commandments; La Ronde; Un Homme de Trop; Lamiel; King of Hearts; Le Rouge et le Noir; The Bride Wore Black; Claire's Knee; A Murder is a Murder; The Phantom of Liberty; Catherine et Cie; The Accuser; L'Annee Sainte; Robert and Robert; Eglantine; Les Violets Clos; L'oiseau Rare; Un Amour De Pluie; Bobo Jacco; L'oeil Du Maitre; La Banquiere; La Nuit de Varennes; Cap Canaille; Le Demon Dan L'Isle; Edith and Marcel; Sarah; Stella; The Crime; Papy Fait de la Resistance; Pinot, Simple Flic, Comedie dété.

BRICKMAN, MARSHALL: Writer, Director. b. Rio de Janeiro, Brazil, Aug. 25, 1941. e. U. of Wisconsin. Banjoist, singer, writer with folk groups The Tarriers and The Journeymen before starting to write for TV. Appeared in films Funny and That's Adequate.
PICTURES: Writer (with Woody Allen): Sleeper, Annie Hall (Acad. Award, 1977), Manhattan, Manhattan Murder Mystery. Director-Writer: Simon, Lovesick, The Manhattan Project (also prod.). Co-Writer only: For the Boys, Intersection.
TELEVISION: Writer: Candid Camera 1966, The Tonight Show 1967–70. Specials: Johnny Carson's Repertory Co. in an Evening of Comedy (1969), Woody Allen Special. Prod.: Dick Cavett Show (1970–72, Emmy).

BRICKMAN, PAUL: Writer, Director. b. Chicago, IL. e. Claremont Men's Coll. Worked as camera asst., then story analyst at Paramount, Columbia, and Universal. Debut script: Citizen's Band (1977; also called Handle With Care). Debut as director with Risky Business (1983).
PICTURES: Handle With Care (assoc. prod., s.p.), The Bad News Bears in Breaking Training (s.p.), Risky Business, (dir., s.p.), Deal of the Century (s.p.), That's Adequate (interviewee), Men Don't Leave (dir., co-s.p.).

BRICUSSE, LESLIE: Composer. b. London, England, 1931. e. Cambridge Univ.
PICTURES: Wrote songs for: Goldfinger, In Like Flint, Gunn, A Guide for the Married Man, Dr. Dolittle (also s.p.; Acad. Award for song "Talk to the Animals" 1967), Goodbye Mr. Chips, Scrooge, Willy Wonka and the Chocolate Factory, Superman, Revenge of the Pink Panther, The Sea Wolves, Sunday Lovers, Victor/Victoria (Acad. Award), Santa Claus, That's Life, Home Alone, Hook, Tom & Jerry: The Movie.
TELEVISION: Theme songs for: Hart to Hart, I'm a Big Girl Now. Specials: Peter Pan, Babes in Toyland.
THEATRE: Book, music and lyrics (with Anthony Newley): Stop the World I Want to Get Off, The Roar of the Greasepaint—The Smell of the Crowd, The Good Old Bad Old Days, The Travelling Music Show. Also: Pickwick (lyrics), Over the Rainbow (lyrics), Sherlock Holmes (book, songs), Jekyll and Hyde (book, lyrics).

BRIDGES, ALAN: Director. b. England, Sept. 28, 1927.
PICTURES: An Act of Murder (1965), Invasion, Shelley, The Hireling, Out of Season, Summer Rain, The Return of the Soldier, The Shooting Party, Displaced Persons, Apt Pupil, Secret Places of the Heart, Fire Princess.
TELEVISION: The Father, Dial M For Murder, The Intrigue, The Ballade of Peckham Rye, The Initiation, Alarm Call: Z Cars, The Fontenay Murders, The Brothers Karamazov, The Idiot, Days to Come, Les Miserables, Born Victim, The Wild Duck, The Lie, Brief Encounter, Forget Me Not Lane, Double Echo, Saturday, Sunday Monday, Crown Matrimonial.

BRIDGES, BEAU: Actor. r.n. Lloyd Vernet Bridges III. b. Hollywood, CA, Dec. 9, 1941. e. UCLA, U. of Hawaii. f. Lloyd Bridges. Brother of Jeff Bridges.
PICTURES: Force of Evil (debut, 1948), No Minor Vices, The Red Pony, Zamba, The Explosive Generation, Village of the Giants, The Incident, For Love of Ivy, Gaily Gaily, The Landlord, Adam's Woman, The Christian Licorice Store, Hammersmith Is Out, Child's Play, Your Three Minutes Are Up, Lovin' Molly, The Other Side of the Mountain, Dragonfly, Swashbuckler, Two Minute Warning, Greased Lightning, Norma Rae, The Fifth Musketeer, The Runner Stumbles, Silver Dream Racer, Honky Tonk Freeway, Night Crossing, Love Child, Heart Like a Wheel, The Hotel New Hampshire, The Killing Time, The Wild Pair (also dir.), Seven Hours to Judgement (also dir.), The Iron Triangle, Signs of Life, The Fabulous Baker Boys, The Wizard, Daddy's Dyin', Married to It, Sidekicks.
TELEVISION: *Series:* Ensign O'Toole, United States, Harts of the West. *Guest:* Sea Hunt, Ben Casey, Dr. Kildare, Mr. Novak, Combat, Eleventh Hour, Cimarron Strip, Amazing Stories. *Movies:* The Man Without a Country, The Stranger Who Looks Like Me, Medical Story, The Four Feathers, Shimmering Light, The President's Mistress, The Child Stealer, The Kid from Nowhere (also dir.), Dangerous Company, Witness for the Prosecution, Red Light Sting, Alice in Wonderland, Outrage!, Fighting Choice, The Thanksgiving Promise (also dir., co-prod.), Everybody's Baby: The Rescue of Jessica McClure, Just Another Secret, Women & Men: Stories of Seduction (The Man in the Brooks Brothers Shirt), Guess Who's Coming for Christmas?, Without Warning: The James Brady Story (Emmy Award, 1992), Wildflower, Elvis and the Colonel, The Man With 3 Wives, The Positively True Adventures of the Alleged Texas Cheerleader-Murdering Mom.

BRIDGES, JEFF: Actor. b. Los Angeles, CA, Dec. 4, 1949. Appeared as infant in 1950 film The Company She Keeps. Made acting debut at eight in the TV series Sea Hunt starring his father, Lloyd Bridges. Studied acting at Herbert Berghof Studio, NY. Mil. service in Coast Guard reserves. Brother of actor-director Beau Bridges. Composed and performed song for film John and Mary. Named Male Star of the Year (1990) by NATO.
PICTURES: Halls of Anger (debut, 1970), The Yin and Yang of Mr. Go, The Last Picture Show (Acad. Award nom.), Fat City, Bad Company, The Iceman Cometh, The Last American Hero, Lolly-Madonna XXX, Thunderbolt and Lightfoot (Acad. Award nom.), Hearts of the West, Rancho Deluxe, Stay Hungry, King Kong, Somebody Killed Her Husband, The American Success Company, Winter Kills, Heaven's Gate, Cutter's Way (Cutter and Bone), Tron, The Last Unicorn (voice only), Kiss Me Goodbye, Against All Odds, Starman (Acad. Award nom.), Jagged Edge, 8 Million Ways to Die, The Morning After, Nadine, Tucker: The Man and His Dream, See You in the Morning, Cold Feet, The Fabulous Baker Boys, Texasville, The Fisher King, The Vanishing, American Heart (also co-prod.), Fearless.
TELEVISION: *Movies:* Silent Night, Lonely Night; In Search of America, The Thanksgiving Promise (cameo). *Special:* Faerie Tale Theatre (Rapunzel). *Guest:* Lloyd Bridges Show, The FBI, Most Deadly Game.

BRIDGES, LLOYD: Actor. b. San Leandro, CA, January 15, 1913. e. UCLA. Went into stock from college dramatics. Formed off-Bdwy theater, the Playroom Club. With wife taught drama at private sch. in Darien, CT when signed stock contract with Columbia. Bdwy. stage: Dead Pigeon, Oh Men! Oh Women!, Heart Song, Cactus Flower, Man of La Mancha.
PICTURES (include): Miss Susie Slage's, Abilene Town, Canyon Passage, Ramrod, Trouble with Women, Hideout, Home of the Brave, Calamity Jane and Sam Bass, Trapped, Rocketship XM, Try and Get Me (The Sound of Fury), The White Tower, Colt .45, Little Big Horn, Three Steps North, Whistle at Eaton Falls, Last of the Comanches, High Noon, Plymouth Adventure, Tall Texan, Kid from Left Field, City of Bad Men, Limping Man, Pride of the Blue Grass, Apache Woman, Wichita, Wetbacks, The Rainmaker, Ride Out for Revenge, The Goddess, Around the World Under the Sea, Attack on the Iron Coast, The Daring Game, The Happy Ending, To Find a Man, Running Wild, The Fifth Musketeer, Bear Island, Airplane!, Airplane II, Weekend Warriors, The Wild Pair, Tucker: The Man and His Dream, Cousins, Winter

People, Joe Versus the Volcano, Hot Shots!, Honey I Blew Up the Kid, Hot Shots Part Deux!.
TELEVISION: Early work on Bigelow Theatre (1950), Kraft Suspense Theatre, Robt. Montgomery Present, CBS Playhouse, Alcoa Hour, Philco Playhouse, U.S. Steel Hour, Climax Playhouse 90. *Series:* Police Story, Sea Hunt (1957–61), The Lloyd Bridges Show (1962–63), The Loner, San Francisco International Airport, Joe Forrester (1975–76), Paper Dolls, Capitol News, Harts of the West. *Movies:* Tragedy in a Temporary Town, The Fortress, The People Next Door, Paper Dolls, Silent Night, Lonley Night, The Thanksgiving Promise, She Was Marked For Murder, Cross of Fire, Leona Helmsley: The Queen of Mean, In the Nick of Time, Devlin. *Mini-series:* Roots, Disaster on the Coastliner, East of Eden, Movieola, The Blue and the Gray, George Washington, Dress Gray, North & South Book II.

BRIGHT, RICHARD: Actor. b. Brooklyn, NY, June 11. e. trained for stage with Frank Corsaro, John Lehne and Paul Mann.
THEATER: The Balcony (1959), The Beard, The Salvation of St. Joan, Gogol, The Basic Training of Pavlo Hummel, Richard III, Kid Twist, Short Eyes as well as regional theater.
PICTURES: Odds Against Tomorrow, Lion's Love, Panic in Needle Park, The Getaway, Pat Garrett and Billy the Kid, The Godfather, The Godfather II, Rancho Deluxe, Marathon Man, Citizens Band, Looking For Mr. Goodbar, On the Yard, Hair, The Idolmaker, Vigilante, Two of a Kind, Once Upon a Time in America, Crackers, Crimewave, Cut and Run, Brighton Beach Memoirs, 52-Pick-up, Time Out, Red Head, The Godfather Part III.
TELEVISION: Lamp Unto My Feet, Armstrong Circle Theater, The Verdict Is Yours, Kraft Television Theatre, Studio One, Cagney and Lacey, Beacon Hill, Hill Street Blues, From These Roots. Movies: A Death of Innocence, The Connection, The Gun, Cops and Robin, Sizzle, There Must Be A Pony, Penalty Phase. Mini-series: From Here to Eternity, Skag.

BRIGHT, RICHARD S.: Executive. b. New Rochelle, NY, Feb. 28, 1936. e. Hotchkiss Sch., 1953–54; Wharton Sch. of Finance, U. of Pennsylvania, 1954–58. With U.S. Army Finance Corp., 1959–60. Was corporate exec. prior to founding in 1973 Persky-Bright Organization, private investment group to finance films. Now bd. chmn., Persky-Bright Productions, Inc.
PICTURES: Last Detail, Golden Voyage of Sinbad, For Pete's Sake, California Split, The Man Who Would Be King, Funny Lady, The Front, and Equus. Financing/production services for: Hard Times, Taxi Driver, Missouri Breaks, Bound for Glory, Sinbad and the Eye of the Tiger, Hair, Body Heat, Still of the Night. Executive Producer: Tribute.
TELEVISION: The President's Mistress (co-producer), Dennis the Menace.
STAGE: A History of the American Film (1978); Album (Off-Broadway, co-prod.).

BRILLSTEIN, BERNIE: Producer, Talent Manager. b. New York, NY. 1931. e. NYU, B.S. advertising. Manager whose clients have incl. Lorne Michaels, John Belushi, Jim Henson and the Muppets. Chairman and chief exec. officer, Lorimar Film Entertainment. Founder, chmn., pres., The Brillstein Company.
PICTURES: Exec. prod.: The Blues Brothers, Up the Academy, Continental Divide, Neighbors, Doctor Detroit, Ghostbusters, Spies Like Us, Summer Rental, Armed and Dangerous, Dragnet, Ghostbusters II.
TELEVISION: Exec. prod.: Burns and Schreiber Comedy Hour, Buckshot, Open All Night, Show Business, Sitcom, Buffalo Bill, Jump, The Faculty, The Real Ghostbusters (exec. consultant), It's Garry Shandling's Show, The Days and Nights of Molly Dodd, The "Slap" Maxwell Show, The Boys (pilot), The Wickedest Witch, Normal Life.

BRIMLEY, WILFORD: Actor. b. Salt Lake City, UT, Sept. 27, 1934. Formerly a blacksmith, ranch hand and racehorse trainer, began in films as an extra and stuntman. Also acted as A. Wilford Brimley. Original mem. L.A. Actors Theatre.
PICTURES: True Grit (1969), Lawman, The China Syndrome, The Electric Horseman, Brubaker, Borderline, Absence of Malice, Death Valley, The Thing, Tender Mercies, Tough Enough, High Road to China, 10 to Midnight, Hotel New Hampshire, Harry and Son, The Stone Boy, The Natural, Country, Cocoon, Remo Williams: The Adventure Begins, American Justice, End of the Line, Cocoon: The Return, Eternity, The Firm, Hard Target.
TELEVISION: *Movies:* The Oregon Trail, The Wild Wild West Revisited, Amber Waves, Roughnecks, Rodeo Girl, The Big Black Pill, Ewoks: The Battle for Endor, Murder in Space, Thompson's Last Run, Act of Vengeance, Gore Vidal's Billy the Kid, Blood River. *Series:* Our House, Boys of Twilight. *Guest:* The Waltons.

BRINKLEY, DAVID: TV news correspondent. b. Wilmington, NC, July 10, 1920. e. U. of North Carolina, Vanderbilt U. Started writing for hometown newspaper. Joined United Press before entering Army, W.W.II. After discharge in 1943 joined NBC News in Washington as White House corr. Co-chmn. for many years with late Chet Huntley on NBC Nightly News. Then began David Brinkley's Journal. Moved to ABC to host This Week with David Brinkley.

BRISKIN, MORT: Producer, Writer. b. Oak Park, IL, 1919. e. U. of Southern California; attended Harvard and Northwestern law schools, being admitted to the bar at 20. Practiced law before entering m.p. industry in management with such stars as Mickey Rooney. Turned to production and also wrote screenplays for 16 of his 29 films. Created nine TV series and was prod. or exec. prod. of some 1,350 TV segments of which he wrote more than 300.
PICTURES: The River, The Magic Face, No Time for Flowers, The Second Woman, Quicksand, The Big Wheel, The Jackie Robinson Story, Ben, Willard, Walking Tall, Framed.
TELEVISION: Sheriff of Cochise, U.S. Marshal, The Texan, Grand Jury, The Walter Winchell File, Official Detective, Whirlybirds.

BRITTANY, MORGAN: Actress. r.n. Suzanne Cupito. b. Hollywood, CA, Dec. 5, 1951.
PICTURES: Gypsy, The Birds, Marnie, Yours Mine and Ours, Gable and Lombard, Sundown: The Vampire in Retreat.
TELEVISION: Series: Dallas, Glitter. Guest: B. L. Stryker. Movies: Amazing Howard Hughes, Delta County U.S.A., The Initiation of Sarah, Samurai, Stunt Seven, Death on the Freeway, The Dream Merchants, Moviola: The Scarlett O'Hara War, The Wild Women of Chastity Gulch, LBJ: The Early Years, Perry Mason: The Case of the Scandalous Scoundrel.

BRITTON, TONY: Actor. b. Birmingham, England, 1924. e. Thornbury Grammar Sch., Glos. Early career as clerk and in repertory; TV debut, 1952, The Six Proud Walkers (serial), m.p. debut, 1955 in Loser Takes All.
PLAYS: The Guv'nor, Romeo and Juliet, The Scarlet Pimpernel, The Other Man, The Dashing White Sergeant, Importance of Being Earnest, An Ideal Husband, School for Scandal, A Dream of Treason, That Lady, The Private Lives of Edward Whiteley, Affairs of State, The Night of The Ball, Gigi, The Seagull, Henry IV Part I, Kill Two Birds, Cactus Flower, A Woman of No Importance, The Boston Story, Lady Frederick, My Fair Lady, Move Over Mrs. Markham, No No Nanette, Dame of Sark, The Chairman, Murder Among Friends, The Seven Year Itch, St. Joan, The Tempest, King Lear, A Man for All Seasons.
PICTURES: Birthday Present, Behind the Mask, Operation Amsterdam, The Heart of a Man, The Rough and the Smooth, The Risk, The Horsemasters, Stork Talk, The Break, There's a Girl in My Soup, Forbush and The Penguins, Sunday Bloody Sunday, Night Watch, The Day of the Jackal.
TELEVISION: The Man Who Understood Women, Ooh La La, Call My Bluff, The Nearly Man, Friends and Brothers. Series: Melissa, Father Dear Father, Robins Nest, Don't Wait Up.

BROADNAX, DAVID: Producer, Writer, Actor. b. Columbus, GA, Dec. 16.
PICTURES: The Landlord (act.), Come Back Charleston Blue (act.), Sharpies (prod., co-s.p., act.), Zombie Island Massacre (prod., act., original story).
TELEVISION: As the World Turns, Another World, Edge of Night, Love Is a Many Splendored Thing, Search for Tomorrow, Saturday Night Live.

BROCCOLI, ALBERT: Producer. b. New York, NY, April 5, 1909. e. City Coll. of New York. Agriculturist in early years; entered m.p. ind. as asst. director, 20th Century-Fox, 1938. Worked with theatrical agent Charles Feldman 1948–51; producer, Warwick Films 1951–60; prod, Eon Prods., Ltd. since 1961. Thalberg Award, 1982.
PRODUCTIONS: Red Beret (Paratrooper), Hell Below Zero, Black Knight, Prize of Gold, Cockleshell Heroes, Safari, Zarak, April in Portugal, Pickup Alley, Fire Down Below, Arrivederci Roma, Interpol, How to Murder a Rich Uncle, Odongo, High Flight, No Time to Die, The Man Inside, Idle on Parade, Adamson of Africa, Bandit of Zhobe, Jazz Boat, Killers of Killimanjaro, In the Nick, Let's Get Married, The Trials of Oscar Wilde, Johnny Nobody, Carolina, Dr. No, Call Me Bwana, From Russia with Love, Goldfinger, Thunderball, You Only Live Twice, Chitty Chitty Bang Bang, On Her Majesty's Secret Service, Diamonds Are Forever, Live and Let Die, The Man with the Golden Gun, The Spy Who Loved Me, Moonraker, For Your Eyes Only, Octopussy, A View to a Kill, The Living Daylights, Licence to Kill.

BROCKMAN, JOHN J.: Executive. Vice pres. and gen. mgr. Microband Wireless Cable of New York, Inc. b. Sheboygan, WI, July 12, 1946. e. U. of Wisconsin, B.S., 1969; Bowling Green State U., M.S., 1971. Graduate asst., Bowling Green State U., 1970–70. 1972–75: system mgr. for Teltron Cable TV of The Milwaukee Journal Sch. 1975–77: gen. mgr. for Lynchburg Cablevision and American Cablevision of Amer. Television & Communications Corp., Englewood, CO. 1977–

78: gen. mgr. for Citizens Cable Communications, Inc., Ft. Wayne, IN. 1978–83: mid-east. and mid-central region mgr., Cox Cable Communications, Inc., Norfolk, VA and Ft. Wayne, IN. 1984–86: corp. v.p., corporate operating comm. member, pres. of operating cable co., Adams-Russell Co., Inc., Waltham, MA. 1986: consultant to Arthur D. Little, Inc., Cambridge, MA. 1974–75: co-chmn., technical comm., Wisc. Cable Communications Assn. 1975–76: advisor comm., Cable TV Curriculum, Indiana Vocational and Technical Coll. 1980: annual grad. school alumni lecturer, Today's Operating Communications Media, Bowling Green State U. 1981–82: founding comm. member and moderator for Great Lakes Cable Exposition. 1978–83: v.p. and dir., Illinois-Indiana Cable Assn.

BROCKMAN, MICHAEL: Executive. b. Brooklyn, NY, Nov. 19, 1938. e. Ithaca Coll. Became ABC v.p., daytime programming, ABC Entertainment, 1974; later v.p., tape prod. operations and admin. Left to become v.p., daytime programs, NBC Entertainment, 1977–1980. Became v.p. programs, Lorimar Prods. 1980–82; v.p. daytime and children's prog. CBS Entertainment, 1982–89. Added Late Night to title 1986. Became pres. ABC daytime, children's & late night entertainment 1989–90. Joined Mark Goodson Prods. as v.p. 1991.

BRODERICK, MATTHEW: Actor. b. New York, NY, Mar. 21, 1962. Son of late actor James Broderick and writer-dir./artist Patricia Broderick. Acted in a workshop prod. of Horton Foote's Valentine's Day with his father (1979).
STAGE: Torch Song Trilogy, Brighton Beach Memoirs (Tony & Theatre World Awards,1983), Biloxi Blues, The Widow Claire.
PICTURES: Max Dugan Returns (debut, 1983), War Games, Ladyhawke, 1918, On Valentine's Day, Ferris Bueller's Day Off, Project X, Biloxi Blues, Torch Song Trilogy, Glory, Family Business, The Freshman, Out on a Limb, The Night We Never Met, The Lion King (voice).
TELEVISION: Specials: Master Harold . . . and the Boys, Cinderella (Faerie Tale Theatre), The Year of the Generals (voice), A Simple Melody, A Life in the Theatre. Guest: Lou Grant.

BRODNEY, OSCAR: Writer, Producer. b. Boston, MA, 1906. e. Boston U., LL.B.; 1927; Harvard, LL.M., 1928. Atty., MA Bar, 1928–35.
PICTURES: She Wrote the Book, If You Knew Susie, Are You With It?, For the Love of Mary, Mexican Hayride, Arctic Manhunt, Yes Sir, That's My Baby, Double Crossbones, Gal Who Took the West, South Sea Sinner, Comanche Territory, Harvey; story, Frenchie, Francis Goes to the Races, Little Egypt, Francis Covers the Big Town, Willie and Joe Back at the Front, Scarlet Angel, Francis Goes to West Point, Walking My Baby Back Home, Sign of the Pagan, Glenn Miller Story, Black Shield of Falworth, Captain Lightfoot, The Spoilers, Purple Mask, Lady Godiva, Day of Fury, Star in the Dust, Tammy and the Bachelor, When Hell Broke Loose, Bobkins, Tammy Tell Me True, The Right Approach, All Hands on Deck, Tammy and the Doctor, The Brass Bottle, I'd Rather Be Rich.

BRODSKY, JACK: Producer. b. Brooklyn, NY, July 3, 1932. e. George Washington H.S. Writer for N.Y. Times; joined 20th-Fox publicity in N.Y. in 1956. Left in 1961 to head national ad-pub for Filmways. Joined Rastar Productions to work on Funny Girl; later named v.p. in charge of prod. In 1976 named v.p. in chg. film prod. prom., Rogers & Cowan; 1978, Columbia Pictures v.p., adv., pub., promo.; 1979, named exec. v.p. of Michael Douglas' Big Stick Productions; 1983; joined 20th-Fox as exec. v.p., worldwide adv., pub., exploit. Resigned 1985 to resume career as producer.
PICTURES: Little Murders, Everything You Always Wanted To Know About Sex (exec. prod.), Summer Wishes, Winter Dreams, Jewel of the Nile, Dancers (co-exec. prod., actor).
AUTHOR: The Cleopatra Papers, with Nat Weiss.

BROKAW, CARY: Executive, Producer. b. Los Angeles, CA, June 21, 1951. e. Univ. of CA/Berkeley, UCLA Grad. Sch. Worked at several positions at 20th Century Fox before serving as exec. v.p. for Cineplex Odeon Corp. 1983 became pres. of Island Alive; 1985, became co-chmn., pres. & CEO of Island Pictures. Formed Avenue Entertainment Pictures in 1987, becoming chmn. & CEO.
PICTURES: Executive Producer: Trouble in Mind, Down by Law, Nobody's Fool, Slamdance, Pascali's Island, Signs of Life, Cold Feet, Drugstore Cowboy, After Dark My Sweet, The Object of Beauty, Sex Drugs Rock & Roll, The Player, American Heart, Short Cuts (prod.).

BROKAW, NORMAN R.: Executive. b. New York, NY, April 21, 1927. Joined William Morris Agency as trainee, in 1943, junior agent, 1948; sr. agent, company exec. in m.p. and TV, 1951; 1974, v.p., William Morris Agency, World Wide all areas. 1981, named exec. v.p. & mem. of bd., William Morris Agency, worldwide; 1986, named co-chmn. of bd., WMA, worldwide. 1989, named pres. & CEO, William Morris Inc. worldwide. 1991, named Chmn. of Board of CEO. Member Acad. of TV

Arts & Sciences, Academy M.P. Arts & Sciences. Member bd. of dir. of Cedars-Sinai Medical Center, Los Angeles; pres., The Betty Ford Cancer Center. Clients include former President and Mrs. Gerald R. Ford, Bill Cosby, Gen. Alexander Haig, Priscilla Presley, and Andy Griffith.

BROKAW, TOM: TV Host, Anchorman. b. Yankton, S.D., Feb. 6, 1940, e. U. of South Dakota. Newscaster, weatherman, staff announcer KTIV, Sioux City, IA, 1960–62. Joined KMTV, NBC affiliate in Omaha, in 1962; 1965, joined WSB-TV, Atlanta. Worked in L.A. bureau of NBC News, anchored local news shows for KNBC, NBC station (1966–73). In 1973 named NBC News' White House correspondent; was anchor of NBC Saturday Night News. Named host of Today show in August, 1976. In 1982 co-anchor, NBC Nightly News. Co-anchor 1993 series NBC Newsmagazine. *Special:* Conversation with Mikhail S. Gorbachev.

BROLIN, JAMES: Actor, Director. b. Los Angeles, CA, July 18, 1940. r.n. James Bruderlin. e. UCLA. Father of actor Josh Brolin. Debut in Bus Stop (TV series); named most promising actor of 1970 by Fame and Photoplay magazines. Winner, Emmy and Golden Globe Awards. Also nominated for 3 additional Emmys and 2 Golden Globes.
 PICTURES: Take Her She's Mine (debut, 1963), John Goldfarb Please Come Home, Goodbye Charlie, Dear Brigette, Von Ryan's Express, Morituri, Fantastic Voyage, Way Way Out, The Cape Town Affair, Our Man Flint, The Boston Strangler, Skyjacked, Westworld, Gable and Lombard, The Car, Capricorn One, The Amityville Horror, Night of the Juggler, High Risk, Pee-wee's Big Adventure, Bad Jim, Super High Score, Ted & Venus, Gas Food Lodging, Cheatin' Hearts (also exec. prod.), Back Stab.
 TELEVISION: *Series:* Marcus Welby, M.D. (Emmy award), Hotel. *Movies:* Marcus Welby M.D. (A Matter of Humanities), Short Walk to Daylight, Class of '63, Trapped, Steel Cowboys, The Ambush Murders, Mae West, White Water Rebels, Cowboy, Beverly Hills Cowgirl Blues, Hold the Dream, Intimate Encounters, Voice of the Heart, Finish Line, Nightmare on the 13th Floor, And the Sea Will Tell, Deep Dark Secrets, The Sands of Time, Visions of Murder, Gunsmoke: The Long Ride, The Calling. *Special:* City Boy (PBS). *Director:* Hotel (12 episodes), The Young Riders.

BROMHEAD, DAVID M.: Executive. b. Teaneck, NJ, Jan. 7, 1960. e. Leighton Park Sch., Reading, England, 1973–78. Overseas sls. exec., Rank Film Dist., 1980; joined New World Pictures, 1984, dir. intl. dist.; named dir., TV dist., 1986.

BRON, ELEANOR: Actress. b. Stanmore, Middlesex, Eng., 1934. Started career in Establishment Club, London, and on American tour. Leading lady on British TV show Not So Much a Programme, More a Way of Life.
 PICTURES: Help, Alfie, Two for the Road, Bedazzled, Women in Love, The Millstone, Little Dorrit.
 THEATRE: The Doctor's Dilemma, Howard's End, The Prime of Miss Jean Brodie.
 TELEVISION: (U.S.) The Day Christ Died; The Attic: The Hiding of Anne Frank, Intrigue, Changing Step.

BRONDFIELD, JEROME: Writer. b. Cleveland, OH, Dec. 9, 1913. e. Ohio State U., 1936. Reporter, ed. on Columbus Dispatch, Associated Press, story ed., script head, RKO Pathe, Oct., 1944; writer, dir. & supvr. of many doc. shorts incl. This Is America series; TV writer; short story writer; collab. s.p., Below the Sahara; s.p. Louisiana Territory; doc. film writer; Author, Woody Hayes, The 100-Yard War, Knute Rockne, The Man and the Legend. Sr. editor, Scholastic, Inc.

BRONSON, CHARLES: Actor. b. Ehrenfeld, PA, Nov. 3, 1921. r.n. Charles Buchinsky. Worked as a coal miner. Served in Air Force (1943–6) as tail gunner on B29s in Pacific. Studied at Pasadena Playhouse.
 PICTURES: You're in the Navy Now (debut, 1951), The People Against O'Hara, The Mob, Red Skies of Montana, My Six Convicts, The Marrying Kind, Pat and Mike, Diplomatic Courier, Bloodhounds of Broadway, House of Wax, The Clown, Miss Sadie Thompson, Crime Wave, Tennessee Champ, Riding Shotgun, Apache, Drumbeat, Vera Cruz, Big House U.S.A., Target Zero, Jubal, Run of the Arrow, Machine Gun Kelly, Gang War, Showdown at Boot Hill, When Hell Broke Loose, Ten North Frederick, Never So Few, The Magnificent Seven, Master of the World, A Thunder of Drums, X-15, Kid Galahad, The Great Escape, Four for Texas, The Sandpiper, The Battle of the Bulge, This Property Is Condemned, The Dirty Dozen, Villa Rides, Guns for San Sebastian, Farewell Friend, Once Upon a Time in the West, Rider on the Rain, You Can't Win Em All, The Family, Cold Sweat, Twinky (Lola), Someone Behind the Door, Red Sun, Chato's Land, The Mechanic, The Valachi Papers, The Stone Killer, Chino, Mr. Majestyk, Death Wish, Breakout, Hard Times, Breakheart Pass, From Noon Till Three, St. Ives, The White Buffalo, Telefon, Love and Bullets, Caboblanco, Borderline, Death Hunt, Death Wish II, Ten to Midnight, The Evil That Men Do, Death Wish 3, Murphy's Law, Assassination,

Death Wish IV, Messenger of Death, Kinjite, The Indian Runner, Death Wish V.
 TELEVISION: *Series:* Man With a Camera, Empire, Travels of Jamie McPheeters. *Guest:* Philco Playhouse (Adventure in Java), Medic, A Bell for Adano, Gunsmoke, Have Gun Will Travel, Meet McGraw, The FBI, The Fugitive, The Virginian. *Movies:* Act of Vengeance, Raid on Entebbe, Yes Virginia There Is a Santa Claus, The Sea Wolf.

BRONSTON, SAMUEL: Producer. b. Bessarabia, Russia, March 26, 1908. e. Sorbonne, Paris. Film distributor, Paris; prod. exec. Columbia Studios, Hollywood; Martin Eden, City Without Men, Producer, Columbia Pictures; resigned to form Samuel Bronston Pict., Inc.; exec. prod. Jack London, A Walk in the Sun. color documentaries produced first time in Vatican; prod. John Paul Jones 1959; Received U.S. Navy Meritorious Pub. Serv. Citation; pres. Samuel Bronston Productions; 1960 prod. King of Kings, El Cid; 1962, 55 Days at Peking; 1963. The Fall of the Roman Empire; prod. Circus World, 1964, Condor Award, Society for Pan American Culture—for El Cid, 1962 (award shared with Stanford U.), The Hollywood Foreign Press Association Golden Globe for the achievement of his outstanding production of El Cid, 1962, Italian Order of Merit with Medal of Commendatore. Grand Cross of Merit by the Equestrian Order of the Knights of the Holy Sepulchre (the highest honor of the Catholic Church), the Encomienda of the Order of the Great Cross of Isabel la Catolica. President Samuel Bronston Studios, Madrid, Spain.

BROOK, PETER: Director. b. London, England, March 21, 1925. e. Magdalen Coll., Oxford. Gained fame as stage director before doing films. (Man and Superman, Marat/Sade, A Midsummer Night's Dream, etc.)
 PICTURES: The Beggar's Opera, Moderato Cantabile, Lord of the Flies (also s.p., edit), Marat/Sade, Tell Me Lies, King Lear (also s.p.), Meetings with Remarkable Men (also s.p.), The Tragedy of Carmen, Swann in Love (s.p. only), The Mahabharata.

BROOKS, ALBERT: Director, Writer, Actor. r.n. Albert Einstein. b. Los Angeles, CA, July 22, 1947. e. Carnegie Tech. Son of late comedian Harry Einstein (Parkyakarkus); brother, Bob Einstein. Sports writer KMPC, L.A. 1962–63. Recordings: Comedy Minus One, A Star is Bought (Grammy nom.).
 PICTURES: Actor: Taxi Driver, Real Life (also dir., co-s.p.), Private Benjamin, Modern Romance (also dir., co-s.p.), Twilight Zone—The Movie, Terms of Endearment (voice only), Unfaithfully Yours, Lost in America (also dir., co-s.p.), Broadcast News (Acad. nom. for best supp. actor), Defending Your Life (also dir., s.p.), I'll Do Anything.
 TELEVISION: *Series:* Dean Martin Presents the Golddiggers (1969), Saturday Night Live (prod., dir., short films 1975–6), Hot Wheels (voices), The Associates (wrote theme song). *Specials:* Milton Berle's Mad Mad Mad World of Comedy, General Electric's All-Star Anniversary. *Guest:* Love American Style, The Odd Couple, Ed Sullivan Show, Tonight Show, others.

BROOKS, DICK: Executive. b. New York, NY. e. U. of Georgia. Reporter, Atlanta (GA) Journal; sports ed. Gainesville Times; correspondent, Pacific Stars & Stripes; entered m.p. industry as staff writer, 20th Century-Fox pub. dept; nat'l pub. dir., Seven Arts Productions, Paramount pub. mgr.; nat'l pub. dir. 20th Century-Fox; adv-pub. dir, Rastar Prods; Warner Bros. pub. dir; formed Dick Brooks Unlimited, Beverly Hills entertainment p.r. and prod. company 1980.

BROOKS, JAMES L.: Director, Producer, Writer. b. North Bergen, NJ, May 9, 1940. e. NYU. Copyboy for CBS News, N.Y.; promoted to newswriter. 1965 moved to L.A. to work for David Wolper's documentary prod. co. 1969 conceived idea for series, Room 222; formed partnership with fellow writer Allan Burns. Together they created Mary Tyler Moore Show in 1970. 1977, established prod. co. on Paramount lot with other writers, producing and creating the series, The Associates and Taxi. Formed Gracie Films. Directed play Brooklyn Laundry in L.A.
 PICTURES: Real Life (actor), Starting Over (s.p., co-prod.), Modern Romance (actor), Terms of Endearment (dir., prod., s.p.; Academy Awards: best picture, dir., s.p., 1983), Broadcast News (dir., prod., s.p.), Big (co-prod.), Say Anything (exec. prod.), The War of the Roses (co-prod.), I'll Do Anything (dir., prod., s.p.).
 TELEVISION: *Movie:* Thursday's Game (writer, prod., 1971). *Series:* The Mary Tyler Moore Show (co-creator, writer, exec. prod.; won 5 Emmy Awards), Rhoda (writer, prod.), The New Lorenzo Music Show (writer), Lou Grant, (co-exec. prod.), *Co-creator, and/or exec. prod:* Taxi (3 Emmy Awards), Cindy, The Associates, Cheers, Tracey Ullman Show (Emmy Award), The Simpsons (2 Emmy Awards), Sibs, Phenom.

BROOKS, JOSEPH: Producer, Director, Writer, Composer, Conductor. Well-known for composing music for TV commercials before turning to producing, directing, writing and scoring theatrical feature, You Light Up My Life, in 1977. Winner of 21

Clio Awards (made by adv. industry), Grammy, Golden Globe, People's Choice, Amer. Music Awards; created music for 100 commercials. Has also composed for theatrical films. Winner of Cannes Film Festival Advertising Award.
PICTURES: *Scores*: The Garden of the Finzi-Continis, Marjoe, Jeremy, The Lords of Flatbush. *Prod.-Dir.-Writer-Composer*: You Light Up My Life (Acad. Award; Best Song), If Ever I See You Again (also actor).

BROOKS, MEL: Writer, Director, Actor. b. Brooklyn, NY, June 28, 1926. r.n. Melvin Kaminsky. m. actress Anne Bancroft. e. VA Military Inst. 1944. U.S. Army combat engineer 1944–46. As child did impressions and was·amateur drummer and pianist. First appearance as actor in Golden Boy in Red Bank, NJ. Was also director and social dir. of Grossingers in the Catskills. Became writer for Sid Caesar on TV's Broadway Review and Your Show of Shows, writing for latter for decade. Teamed with Carl Reiner for comedy record albums, 2000 Year Old Man and The 2000 and 13 Year Old Man. Founded Brooksfilms Ltd., 1980.
PICTURES: New Faces (co-s.p.), The Critic (short; dir., s.p., narrator; Acad. Award, 1963), The Producers (dir., s.p.; Acad. Award for best s.p., 1968), Putney Swope (actor), The Twelve Chairs (dir., s.p., actor), Blazing Saddles (dir., s.p., actor), Young Frankenstein (dir., co-s.p.), Silent Movie (dir., s.p., actor), High Anxiety (prod., dir., s.p., actor), The Muppet Movie (actor), History of the World—Part 1 (prod., dir., s.p., actor, composer), To Be or Not To Be (prod., actor), Spaceballs (dir., prod., co-s.p., actor), Look Who's Talking Too (voice), Life Stinks (dir., prod., co-s.p., actor), Robin Hood: Men in Tights (dir., prod., co-s.p., actor).
PICTURES AS EXEC. PROD.: The Elephant Man, The Doctor and the Devils, The Fly, 84 Charing Cross Road, Solarbabies, The Vagrant.
TELEVISION: *Special*: The Sid Caesar–Imogene Coca–Carl Reiner–Howard Morris Special (writer; Emmy Award, 1967). *Series*: Get Smart (co-creator, writer), When Things Were Rotten (creator, prod.), The Nutt House (prod.).
STAGE: New Faces of 1952 (sketches), Shinbone Alley (book), All-American (book).

BROSNAN, PIERCE: Actor. b. Navan, County Meath, Ireland, May 16, 1953. Left County Meath, Ireland for London at 11. Worked as commercial illustrator, then joined experimental theater workshop and studied at the Drama Center. On London stage (Wait Until Dark, The Red Devil Battery Sign, Filumena, etc.)
PICTURES: The Mirror Crack'd (debut, 1980), The Long Good Friday, Nomads, The Fourth Protocol, Taffin, The Deceivers, Mister Johnson, The Lawnmower Man, Mrs. Doubtfire.
TELEVISION: *Series*: Remington Steele. *Movies/Specials*:: Murphy's Stroke, The Manions of America, Nancy Astor, Noble House, Around the World in 80 Days, The Heist, Murder 101, Victim of Love, Live Wire, Death Train.

BROUGH, WALTER: Producer, Writer. b. Phila. PA, Dec. 19, 1935. e. La Salle U. (B.A.), USC (M.A.). Began career with Stage Society Theatre, LA. Currently CEO, Orb Enterprises, Inc.
PICTURES: Gabriella, A New Life, No Place to Hide, Run Wild, Run Free, The Desperadoes, Funeral for an Assassin (also prod.), On a Dead Man's Chest (also prod.), Jed and Sonny (also prod.).
TELEVISION: Doctor Kildare, The Fugitive, Branded, Name of the Game, Mannix, Mission Impossible, The Magician, Man From Atlantis, Police Story, Wildside, Heart of the City (also prod.), The Thunder Guys (pilot), Spencer for Hire (also prod.), Law & Harry McGraw, New Mission Impossible (also co-prod.), Over My Dead Body, Hunter, Tequila & Bonetti.

BROUGHTON, BRUCE: Composer. b. Los Angeles, CA , March 8, 1945. e. U. of Southern California, B.M., 1967. Music supvr., CBS-TV, 1967–77. Since then has been freelance composer for TV and films. Member: Academy of TV Arts & Sciences Society of Composers & Lyricists (past pres.), Academy of Motion Picture Arts & Sciences (governor). Nominated 15 times for Emmy; won Emmys for: Buck Rogers (1981), Dallas (1983, 1984), The First Olympics (1984), for Tiny Toon Adventures (1991), O Pioneers (1992). Nominated for Grammy for Young Sherlock Holmes.
PICTURES: The Prodigal, The Ice Pirates, Silverado (Acad. Award nom.), Young Sherlock Holmes, Sweet Liberty, The Boy Who Could Fly, Square Dance, Harry and the Hendersons, Monster Squad, Big Shots, Cross My Heart, The Rescue, The Presidio, Last Rites, Moonwalker, Jacknife, Betsy's Wedding, Narrow Margin, The Rescuers Down Under, All I Want for Christmas, Honey I Blew Up the Kid, Stay Tuned, Homeward Bound: The Incredible Journey, So I Married an Axe Murderer, For Love or Money.
TELEVISION: *Series*: Hawaii Five-0, Gunsmoke, Quincy, How the West Was Won, Logan's Run, The Oregon Trail, Buck Rogers, Dallas, Dinosaurs (theme), Capitol Critters (theme). *Movies*: The Paradise Connection, Desperate Voyage, The Return of Frank Cannon, Desperate Lives, Killjoy,

One Shoe Makes It Murder, The Master of Ballantrae, MADD, The Candy Lightner Story, Cowboy, A Thanksgiving Promise, The Old Man and the Sea, O Pioneers! *Mini-Series*: The Blue and the Gray, The First Olympics–Athens: 1896, George Washington II.

BROUMAS, JOHN G.: Executive. b. Youngstown, OH, Oct. 12, 1917. e. Youngstown. Usher, Altoona Publix Theatres, 1933, usher to asst. mgr., Warner Thea. 1934–39; mgr. Grand 1939–40; mgr. Orpheum 1940–41. W.W.II active, Officer Chemical Corps, commanding official 453rd Chem. Grp. (Reserve); Life member Reserve Officers Assoc.; Gen. mgr. Pitts & Roth Theatres 1946–54; President, Broumas Theatres; V.P. NATO, 1969; bd. of dir. of NATO of Va., Md., D.C.; pres., Broumas Theatre Service 1954–82; bd. chmn., Showcase Theatres 1965–82; mem. bd., Foundation of Religious Action (FRASCO). Mem. Nat'l Immigration Comm. Founder of John G. Broumas Scholarship for Drama at Youngstown State Univ.; past pres. & bd. chmn. Maryland Theatre Owners; v.p. & bd. of dir.—Virginia Theatre Owners bd. of dir. NATO of D.C.; pres. B.C. Theatres; Sponsor of Andre G. Broumas Memorial Award—West Point; sponsor, Broumas Scholastic and Athletic Scholarship for AHEPA Wash. D.C. area; director, McLean Bank, McLean, Va. 1972–86; mem., West Point Society, 1975; Past dir. and mem. Motion Picture Pioneers; Advisory Council: Will Rogers Memorial Hospital; Washington, D.C. Variety Club, Tent #11, bd. of gov. 1959, 1st asst. chief. barker, 1964 & 71, Chief barker 1965–66, 1972, and 1978–79, and bd. chmn., 1980; lecturer, Georgetown Univ., 1972–8; Life Patron, Variety Clubs Int'l, 1978 Life Liner, Variety Clubs Int'l.; AHEPA Humanitarian Award, 1981; Dept. of Army, Patriotic Civilian Service Medal, 1982; WOMPI "good guy" award, 1974; Gold Medal for distinguished service to m.p. industry, Chm. bd., McLean Bank; 1983–86; chmn. bd & pres. Madison Natl. Bank of VA. 1986–91; chmn. exec. comm., Mad. Natl. Bank of VA; dir. James Madison LT. Wash. D.C. 1987–91; order of St. Andrew; 1988 Bd. trustee, Leukemia Soc. of Amer.; 1989 bd. dir. Natl. Fdn. Coll., Football Hall of Fame (appreciation award Wash., D.C. 1989). Exec. committee, East Coast Div., Child Help U.S.A. 1989; received Distinguished Service Medal from Catholic U. Chmn. bd. Eagle Import Export Ltd. 1990–present. 1990, chmn. Hellenic Studies, Maryland Univ. Dir., Potamac Financial Group, 1991–92. Trustee: Education - Training Foundation, 1991–92. Dir., Potomac Financial Group 1991–92. Trustee: Education-Training Foundation, 1991–92.

BROWN, BLAIR: Actress. b. Washington, DC, 1948. e. National Theatre Sch. of Canada.
THEATER: The Threepenny Opera (NY Shakespeare Fest), Comedy of Errors, The Secret Rapture. Acted with Old Globe, San Diego, Stratford, Ont. Shakespeare Fest., Guthrie Theatre MN, Arena Stage, Wash.; Long Wharf, New Haven; Shaw Festival.
PICTURES: Paper Chase, The Choirboys, One-Trick Pony, Altered States, Continental Divide, Flash of Green. Stealing Home, Strapless, Passed Away.
TELEVISION: *Series*: The Days and Nights of Molly Dodd. *Mini-series*: Captains and the Kings, James Michener's Space, Arthur Hailey's Wheels, Kennedy. *Movies*: The 3,000 Mile Chase, The Quinns, And I Alone Survived, The Child Stealer, The Bad Seed, Hands of a Stranger, Eleanor and Franklin: The White House Years, Extreme Close-Up, Those Secrets, Majority Rule. *Specials*: School for Scandal, The Skin of Your Teeth, Lethal Innocence.

BROWN, BRYAN: Actor. b. Sydney, Australia, June 23, 1947. m. actress Rachel Ward. Began acting professionally in Sydney. Worked in repertory theatres in England with the National Theatre of Great Britain. Returned to Australia to work in films while continuing stage work with Theatre Australia. Theatrical film debut, Love Letters from Teralba Road, 1977.
PICTURES: The Irishman, Weekend of Shadows, Newsfront, Third Person Plural, Money Movers, Palm Beach, Cathy's Child, The Odd Angry Shot, Breaker Morant, Blood Money, Stir, Winter of Our Dreams, Far East, Give My Regards to Broad Street, Parker, The Empty Beach, F/X, Tai-Pan, Rebel, The Good Wife, Cocktail, Gorillas in the Mist, Shall We Dance, FX2 (also co-exec. prod.), Sweet Talker (also co-wrote story), Prisoners of the Sun, Blame it on the Bellboy.
TELEVISION: *Mini-series*: Against the Wind, A Town Like Alice, The Thorn Birds. *Movies*: The Shiralee (Aust.), Dead in the Water, Devlin, The Last Hit.

BROWN, CLANCY: Actor. b. Ohio. e. Northwestern Univ.
PICTURES: Bad Boys (debut, 1983), The Adventures of Buckaroo Banzai, The Bride, Highlander, Extreme Prejudice, Shoot to Kill, Season of Fear, Blue Steel, Waiting for the Light, Ambition, Past Midnight, Pet Sematary II, Thunder Alley, Rita Hayworth & Shawshank Redemption.
TELEVISION: *Movies*: Johnny Ryan, Love Lies & Murder, Cast a Deadly Spell, Desperate Rescue: The Cathy Mahone Story, Bloodlines, Last Light.

BROWN, DAVID: Executive, Producer. b. New York, NY, July 28, 1916. m. writer-editor Helen Gurley Brown. e. Stanford U., A.B., 1936; Columbia U. Sch. of Journalism, M.S., 1937. Apprentice reporter, copy-editing, San Francisco News & Wall Street Journal, 1936; night ed. asst. drama critic, Fairchild Publications, N.Y., 1937–39; edit. dir. Milk Research Council, N.Y., 1939–40; assoc. ed., Street & Smith Publ., N.Y., 1940–43; assoc. ed., exec. ed., then ed.-in-chief, Liberty Mag., N.Y., 1943–49; edit. dir., nat'l education campaign, Amer. Medical Assn., 1949; assoc. ed., man. ed., Cosmopolitan Mag., N.Y., 1949–52; contrib. stories & articles to many nat'l mags.; man. ed., story dept., 20th-Fox, L.A., Jan., 1952; story ed. & head of scenario dept., May, 1953–56; appt'd. member of exec. staff of Darryl F. Zanuck, 1956; mem. of exec. staff, 20th-Fox studios, and exec. studio story editor, 1956–1960; Prod. 20th-Fox Studios, Sept. 1960–62; Editorial v.p. New American Library of World Literature, Inc., 1963–64; exec. story opers., 20th Century-Fox, 1964–67; vp. dir. of story operations, 1967; exec. v.p., creative operations and mem. bd. of dir., 1969–71. Exec. v.p., mem. bd. of directors Warner Bros., 1971–1972; partner and director, The Zanuck/Brown Co., 1972–1988. Pres., Manhattan Project Ltd., 1988–; mem., bd. of trustees, American Film Institute, 1977–80. Recipient with Richard D. Zanuck of the Mo. Pic. Acad. of Arts & Sciences' Irving G. Thalberg Memorial Award. Books: Brown's Guide to Growing Gray, Delacorte, Let Me Entertain You, Morrow, The Rest of Your Life is the Best of Your Life, Barricade.
PICTURES: Sssssss, The Sting (Acad. Award, best picture: 1973), The Sugarland Express, The Black Windmill, Willie Dynamite, The Girl from Petrovka, The Eiger Sanction, Jaws, MacArthur, Jaws 2, The Island, Neighbors, The Verdict, Cocoon, Target, Cocoon: The Return, Driving Miss Daisy (exec. prod.), The Player, A Few Good Men, The Cemetery Club, Watch It.

BROWN, GEORG STANFORD: Actor, Director. b. Havana, Cuba, June 24, 1943. Acted on stage with the New York Shakespeare Fest., NY, in the 1960s. Gained fame as one of the rookie cops in the 1970s TV series The Rookies before turning to TV directing.
THEATER: All's Well That Ends Well, Measure for Measure, Macbeth, Murderous Angels, Hamlet, Detective Story.
PICTURES: The Comedians, Dayton's Devils, Bullitt, Colossus: The Forbin Project, The Man, Black Jack (Wild in the Sky), Stir Crazy, House Party 2.
TELEVISION: Series: The Rookies. Movies: The Young Lawyers, Ritual of Evil, The Rookies (pilot), Dawn: Portrait of a Teenage Runaway, The Night the City Screamed, The Kid With the Broken Halo, In Defense of Kids, The Jesse Owens Story, Murder Without Motive. Dir. of movies: Grambling's White Tiger, Kids Like These, Alone in the Neon Jungle, Stuck With Each Other, Father & Son: Dangerous Relations. Dir. of episodes: Charlie's Angels, Starsky and Hutch, Dynasty, Hill Street Blues, Great American Hero, Cagney & Lacey (Emmy Award, 1986).

BROWN, HIMAN: M.P. Producer, Director, b. New York, NY, July 21, 1910. e. City Coll. of New York, St. Lawrence U. Radio & TV package prod. since 1927 include: Inner Sanctum, Thin Man, Bulldog Drummond, Dick Tracy, Terry and the Pirates, Joyce Jordan MD, Grand Central Station, CBS Radio Mystery Theatre, pres. Production Center, Inc.
PICTURES: That Night, Violators, The Stars Salute, The Price of Silence, The Road Ahead.

BROWN, JIM: Actor. b. St. Simons Island, GA, Feb. 17, 1936. e. Manhasset H.S., Syracuse U. For nine years played football with Cleveland Browns; in 1964 won Hickock Belt as Professional Athlete of the year; founder, Black Economic Union.
PICTURES: Rio Conchos (debut, 1964), The Dirty Dozen, Ice Station Zebra, The Split, Riot, Dark Of The Sun, 100 Rifles, Kenner, El Condor, The Phynx, Tick . . . Tick . . . Tick, The Grasshopper, Slaughter, Black Gunn, I Escaped from Devil's Island, The Slams, Slaughter's Big Rip-Off, Three the Hard Way, Take a Hard Ride, Adios Amigo, Mean Johnny Barrows, Kid Vengeance, Fingers, One Down Two to Go (also exec. prod.), Richard Pryor: Here and Now (exec. prod. only), Pacific Inferno (also exec. prod.), Abducted, The Running Man, I'm Gonna Git You Sucka, L.A. Heat, Crack House, Twisted Justice, The Divine Enforcer.
TELEVISION: Movie: Lady Blue.

BROWN, WILLIAM: Executive. b. Ayr, Scotland, June 24, 1929. e. Ayr Acad., U. of Edinburgh, where graduated Bachelor of Commerce, 1950. Served to Lieutenant, Royal Artillery, 1950–52. Sales mgr. for Scotland Television Ltd. in London, 1958 to 1961, sales dir. 1961 to 1963. Deputy mng. dir. of Scottish Television Ltd. at Glasgow 1963–66, mng. dir. 1966–90. Deputy chmn. 1974–91. Chmn. from 1991. Chmn. Scottish Amicable Life Assurance Society Ltd. 1983–. Dir., Radio Clyde 1973–. Chmn., Scottish Arts Council, 1992–. Dir.: ITN, 1972–7, 1987–90; Channel 4 Co Ltd 1980–4; Scottish Opera Theatre Royal Ltd. 1974–90. Chmn.: Council, Indept. TV Cos. Assn. 1978–80. C.B.E., 1971. Ted Willis Award 1982. Gold

Medal, Royal TV Society 1984. Hon. Doctorates: Edinburgh U. (1990), Strathclyde U. (1992).

BROWNE, ROSCOE LEE: Actor, Director, Writer. b. Woodbury, NJ, May 2, 1925. e. Lincoln U., PA; postgraduate studies in comparative literature and French at Middlebury Coll., VT, Columbia U., N.Y. Taught French and Lit. at Lincoln U. until 1952. National sales rep. for Schenley Import Corp. 1946–56; United States' intl. track star and a member of ten A.A.U. teams. Twice American champion in the 1000-yard indoor competition, twice all-American and, in 1951 in Paris, ran the fastest 800 meters in the world for that year. Professional acting debut, 1956, in Julius Caesar at the NY Shakespeare Fest.; published poet and short story writer. Trustee: Millay Colony Arts, NY; Los Angeles Free Public Theatre.
NY STAGE: The Ballad of the Sad Cafe, The Cool World, General Seeger, Tiger Tiger Burning Bright!, The Old Glory, A Hand Is on the Gate (dir., actor), My One and Only. Off-Broadway: The Connection, The Blacks, Aria da Capo, Benito Cereno (Obie Award), Joe Turner's Come and Gone (L.A., S.F., Pittsburgh), Two Trains Running.
PICTURES: The Connection (debut, 1961), Black Like Me, The Comedians, Uptight, Topaz, The Liberation of L. B. Jones, Cisco Pike, The Cowboys, World's Greatest Athlete, Superfly T.N.T., The Ra Expeditions (narrator), Uptown Saturday Night, Logan's Run, Twilight's Last Gleaming, Nothing Personal, Legal Eagles, Jumpin' Jack Flash, Oliver & Company (voice), Moon 44, The Mambo Kings.
TELEVISION: Series: McCoy, Miss Winslow and Son, Soap, Falcon Crest. Movies: The Big Ripoff, Dr. Scorpion, Lady in a Corner, Columbo: Rest in Peace Mrs. Columbo, Meeting of Minds (Peabody Award), A Connecticut Yankee in King Arthur's Court (Peabody Award). Guest: All in the Family, Maude, Barney Miller, Soap, Head of the Class, The Cosby Show (Emmy Award), Falcon Crest. Mini-Series: King, Space.

BROWNING, KIRK: TV Director; b. New York, NY, March 28, 1921. e. Brooks School, Andover, MA, Avon Old Farms, Avon, CT., and Cornell U. 1940, reporter for News-Tribune in Waco, TX; with American Field Service, 1942–45; adv. copywriter for Franklin Spier, 1945–48; became floor mgr. NBC-TV 1949; app't asst. dir. NBC-TV Opera Theatre in 1951 directing NBC Opera Theatre, TV Recital Hall, and Toscanini Simulcasts.
TELEVISION: Trial of Mary Lincoln; Jascha Heifetz Special; Harry and Lena; NBC Opera Theatre; Producers Showcase; Evening with Toscanini; Bell Telephone; The Flood; Beauty and the Beast; Lizzie Borden; World of Carl Sandburg; La Gioconda (Emmy, 1980); Big Blonde; Working; Ian McKellan Acting Shakespeare; Fifth of July; Alice in Wonderland; Live From the Met—Centennial.

BROWNLOW, KEVIN: Film historian, Writer, Director, Film Editor. b. Crowborough, Eng., June 2, 1938. e. University College Sch. Asst. ed./editor, World Wide Pictures, London, 1955–61; film editor, Samaritan Films, 1961–65; film editor, Woodfall Films, 1965–68. Director, Thames Television 1975–90. Dir., Photoplay Productions 1990–present.
BOOKS: How It Happened Here (1968), The Parade's Gone By... (1968), Adventures with D.W. Griffith (editor, 1973), The War the West and the Wilderness (1979), Hollywood: The Pioneers (1980), Napoleon: Abel Gance's Classic Film (1983), Behind the Mask of Innocence (1990).
PICTURES: It Happened Here (dir. with Andrew Mollo) 1964, Charge of the Light Brigade (editor), Winstanley (with Andrew Mollo), Napoleon (restoration of 1927 film, re-released 1980).
TELEVISION: Charm of Dynamite (dir., ed.), All with David Gill: Hollywood (dir., s.p.), Unknown Chaplin (dir., prod.; Emmy Award), Buster Keaton: A Hard Act to Follow (prod.; 2 Emmy Awards), Harold Lloyd-The Third Genius, D.W. Griffith: Father of Film.

BRUBAKER, JAMES D.: Producer. b. Hollywood, CA, March 30, 1937. e. Eagle Rock H.S. Transportation coordinator 15 years before becoming unit prod. mgr., 1978–84. Then assoc. prod., exec. prod. & prod.
PICTURES: Assoc. Prod./Prod. Mgr.: True Confessions, Rocky III, Rhinestone. Exec. Prod.: The Right Stuff, Beer, Rocky IV, Cobra, Over the Top, Problem Child (also prod. mgr.), Brain Donors (also prod., prod. mgr.). Prod. mgr.: New York New York, Comes a Horseman, Uncle Joe Shannon, Rocky II, Raging Bull, Staying Alive, K-9, Mr. Baseball.
TELEVISION: Movie: Running Mates (prod.)

BRUCE, BRENDA: Actress. b. Manchester, England, 1922. e. privately. London stage debut, 1066 And All That; On screen 1944; Millions Like Us; TV Best Actress Award 1962.
PICTURES: Night Boat to Dublin, I See a Dark Stranger, They Came to a City, Carnival, Piccadilly Incident, While the Sun Shines, When the Bough Breaks, My Brother's Keeper, Don't Ever Leave Me, The Final Test, Law and Disorder, Behind the Mask, Peeping Tom, Nightmare, The Uncle.
BROADWAY: Gently Does It (1953), This Year Next Year, Happy Days, Woman in a Dressing Gown, Victor Eh!, Merry

Wives of Windsor, The Revenger's Tragedy, Little Murders, Winter's Tale, Pericles, Twelfth Night, Hamlet.
TELEVISION: Mary Britton series, Nearer to Heaven, Wrong Side of the Park, The Lodger, The Monkey and the Mohawk, Love Story, A Piece of Resistance, Give the Clown His Supper, Knock on Any Door, The Browning Version, Death of a Teddy Bear, Softly, Softly, The Girl, Happy, Family at War, Budgie.

BRUCKHEIMER, JERRY: Producer. b. Detroit, MI. e. U. of Arizona. Was adv. agency exec. in TV commercials before becoming producer of films. 1983, formed Don Simpson/Jerry Bruckheimer Prods. with Don Simpson and entered into deal with Paramount Pictures to produce.
PICTURES: Assoc. Prod.: Culpepper Cattle Company, Rafferty and the Gold Dust Twins. Producer: Farewell My Lovely, March or Die, Defiance, American Gigolo, Thief, Cat People (exec. prod.), Young Doctors in Love, Flashdance, Thief of Hearts, Beverly Hills Cop, Top Gun, Beverly Hills Cop II, Days of Thunder.

BRYAN, DORA: Actress. b. Southport, Lancashire, Eng., Feb. 7, 1924. e. Council Sch. Stage debut 1935. Screen debut The Fallen Idol, 1948.
PICTURES: No Room at the Inn, Once Upon a Dream, Blue Lamp, Cure for Love, Now Barabas, The Ringer, Women of Twilight, The Quiet Woman, The Intruder, You Know What Sailors Are, Mad About Men, See How They Run, Cockleshell Heroes, Child in the House, Green Man, Carry on Sergeant, Operation Bullshine, Desert Mice, The Night We Got the Bird, A Taste of Honey, Two a Penny, Apartment Zero.
TELEVISION: Virtual Murder, Casualty, Presenting Frank Subbs, Heartbeat.

BRYON, KATHLEEN: Actress. b. London, England, Jan. 11, 1922. e. London U., Old Vic. co. student, 1942. Screen debut in Young Mr. Pitt, 1943.
PICTURES: Silver Fleet, Black Narcissus, Matter of Life and Death, Small Back Room, Madness of the Heart, Reluctant Widow, Prelude to Fame, Scarlet Thread, Tom Brown's Schooldays, Four Days, Hell Is Sold Out, I'll Never Forget You, Gambler and the Lady, Young Bess, Night of the Silvery Moon, Profile, Secret Venture, Hand in Hand, Night of the Eagle, Hammerhead, Wolfshead, Private Road, Twins of Evil, Craze, Abdication, One of Our Dinosaurs Is Missing, The Elephant Man, From a Far Country.
TELEVISION: The Lonely World of Harry Braintree, All My Own Work, Emergency Ward 10, Probation Officer, Design for Murder, Sergeant Cork, Oxbridge 2000, The Navigators, The Worker; Hereward the Wake, Breaking Point, Vendetta, Play To Win, Who Is Sylvia, Portrait of a Lady, Callan, You're Wrecking My Marriage, Take Three Girls, The Confession of Mariona Evans, Paul Temple, The Worker, The Moonstone, The Challengers, The Golden Bowl, The Edwardians, The New Life, Menace, The Rivals of Sherlock Holmes, The Brontes, On Call, Edward VII, Sutherland's Law, Crown Court, Anne of Avonlea, Heidi, Notorious Woman, General Hospital, North & South, Angelo, Within these Walls, Jubilee, Z Cars, Tales from the Supernatural, Secret Army, An Englishman's Castle, The Professionals, Forty Weeks, Emmerdale Farm, Blake Seven, The Minders, Together, Hedda Gabler, Nancy Astor, God Speed Co-operation, Take Three Women, Reilly.

BUCHHOLZ, HORST: Actor. b. Berlin, Germany, Dec. 4, 1933. e. high school. In radio and stage plays. Film debut. Marianne (French), 1955.
PICTURES: Himmel Ohne Sterne (No Star in the Sky), Robinson Must Not Die, Non Petit, The Confessions of Felix Krull, Tiger Bay, The Magnificent Seven, Fanny, One Two Three, Nine Hours to Rama, The Empty Canvas, Marco the Magnificent, That Man in Istanbul, Cervantes, L'Astragale, The Great Waltz, The Catamount Killing, Avalanche Express, Sahara, Code Name: Emerald, And the Violins Stopped Playing, Aces: Iron Eagle III, Far Away So Close.
TELEVISION: Movies: The Savage Bees, Raid on Entebbe, Return to Fantasy Island, Berlin Tunnel 21, Family Affairs, The Lion of Granada, Come Back to Kampen. Mini-Series: The French Atlantic Affair.

BUCK, JULES: Producer. b. St. Louis, MO, July 30, 1917. Asst. to prod., The Killers; assoc. prod., Brute Force, Naked City, We Were Strangers; prod., Love Nest, Fixed Bayonets, Treasure of the Golden Condor, O.S.S., TV series; prod., The Day They Robbed the Bank of England, Great Catherine; formed Keep Films with Peter O'Toole. Co-prod., Under Milkwood. Prod., The Ruling Class. Exec. Prod., Man Friday. Prod., The Great Scout and Cathouse Thursday.
TELEVISION: (U.S.) Berlin Tunnel, The French Atlantic Affair, Raid on Entebbe, The Savage Bees.

BUCKLEY, BETTY: Actress. b. Fort Worth, TX, July 3, 1947. e. Texas Christian U., BA. Studied acting with Stella Adler. NY Stage debut: 1776 (1969); London debut: Promises Promises.
THEATER: Johnny Pott, What's a Nice Country Like You Doing in a State Like This?, Pippin, I'm Getting My Act

Together and Taking It on the Road, Cats (Tony Award, 1983), Juno's Swans, The Mystery of Edwin Drood, Song and Dance, Carrie.
PICTURES: Carrie, Tender Mercies, Frantic, Another Woman, Rain Without Thunder.
TELEVISION: Series: Eight is Enough (1978–81). Movies: The Ordeal of Bill Carney, Roses Are for the Rich, The Three Wishes of Billy Grier, Babycakes, Bonnie & Clyde: The True Story. Specials: Bobby and Sarah, Salute to Lady Liberty, Taking a Stand (Afterschool Special). Mini-Series: Evergreen. Guest: L.A. Law, Tribeca.

BUCKLEY, DONALD: Executive. b. New York, NY, June 28, 1955. e. C.W. Post Coll, NY, Sch. of Visual Arts. Ad. mgr., United Artists Theatres, 1975–78; acct. exec., Grey Advertising, 1978–80. Joined Warner Bros. in 1980 as NY adv. mgr.; 1986, promoted to east. dir. of adv./promo. for WB; 1988, named eastern dir. of adv. and publicity. 1991, promoted to v.p., East Coast Adv. & Publicity.

BUCKNER, ROBERT H.: Producer, Writer. b. Crewe, VA, May 28, 1906. e. U. of Virginia., U. of Edinburgh, Scotland. Newspaper corresp. New York World. 1926–27 in England: instructor, Belgian Mil. Acad. 1927–28: with Alfred A. Knopf, Inc., Doubleday, Doran, N.Y., pub., 1928–33; corresp. in Russia, Scandinavia, 1933–35; contrib. fiction, Amer. & Brit. mags., 1926–36. Author & collab. many s.p. a Champion of Champion Producer in Fame ratings.
PICTURES: Gold Is Where You Find It, Jezebel, Dodge City, Virginia City, Knute Rockne, Santa Fe Trial, Dive Bomber, Yankee Doodle Dandy, Desert Song. Gentleman Jim (prod.), Mission to Moscow, Desert Song, The Gang's All Here, Cheyenne, Life with Father. Rogue's Regiment (prod.), Sword in the Desert, Free For All, Deported, Bright Victory, The Man Behind the Gun, Safari.

BUJOLD, GENEVIEVE: Actress. b. Montreal, Canada, July 1, 1942. e. Montreal Conservatory of Drama. Worked in a Montreal cinema as an usher; American TV debut: St. Joan.
STAGE: The Barber of Seville, A Midsummer Night's Dream, A House . . . A Day.
PICTURES: La Guerre est Finie, La Fleur de L'Age, Entre La Mer et L'eau Douce, King of Hearts, The Thief of Paris, Isabel, Anne of the Thousand Days, Act of the Heart, The Trojan Women, The Journey, Kamouraska, Earthquake, Swashbuckler, Obsession, Alex and the Gypsy, Another Man Another Chance, Coma, Murder by Decree, Final Assignment, The Last Flight of Noah's Ark, Monsignor, Tightrope, Choose Me, Trouble in Mind, The Moderns, Dead Ringers, False Identity, Secret Places of the Heart, A Paper Wedding, An Ambush of Ghosts.
TELEVISION: Specials: Saint Joan, Antony and Cleopatra. Movies: Mistress of Paradise, Red Earth White Earth.

BURGHOFF, GARY: Actor. b. Bristol, CT, May 24, 1943.
TELEVISION: Series: The Don Knotts Show, M*A*S*H (Emmy Award, 1977). Guest: Good Guys, Name of the Game, Love American Style, Fernwood 2-Night, Sweepstakes, Love Boat, Fantasy Island. Movies: The Man in the Santa Claus Suit, Casino. Special: Twigs.
PICTURES: M*A*S*H, B.S. I Love You, Small Kill (also co-dir.).
THEATRE: NY: You're a Good Man Charlie Brown, The Nerd. Other: Finian's Rainbow, Bells Are Ringing, Sound of Music, The Boy Friend, Romanoff and Juliet, Whose Life Is It Anyway?.

BURKE, ALFRED: Actor. b. London, England, 1918. Ent. films 1954.
PICTURES: The Angry Silence, Moment of Danger, The Man Inside, The Man Upstairs, No Time To Die, Law and Disorder, Yangtse Incident, Interpol, Bitter Victory.
TELEVISION: The Crucible, Mock Auction, Parole, No Gun, No Guilt, The Big Knife, Parnell, The Strong Are Lonely, Home of the Brave, The Birthday Party, The Watching Eye, Public Eye series.

BURKE, DELTA: Actress. b. Orlando, FL, July 30, 1956. e. LAMDA. m. actor Gerald McRaney. Competed in Miss America contest as Miss Florida, prior to studying acting in England.
TELEVISION: Series: The Chisholms, Filthy Rich, 1st & Ten, Designing Women, Delta (also co-exec. prod.). Movies: Charleston, A Last Cry for Help, Mickey Spillane's Mike Hammer: Murder Me Murder You, A Bunny's Tale, Where the Hell's That Gold?!!? Love and Curses . . . And All That Jazz (also co-exec. prod.), Day-o.

BURKE, PAUL: Actor. b. New Orleans, LA, July 21, 1926. e. prep schools, New Orleans, Pasadena Playhouse.
TELEVISION: Series: Noah's Ark, Harbor Master, Five Fingers, Naked City, Twelve O'Clock High, Dynasty, Hot Shots. Guest: Playhouse 90, Studio One, Medic, Frontier, Men in Space, Man and the Challenge, Target, M-Squad, Black Saddle, Philip Marlowe, Martin Kane, Line Up, Dragnet, Man Without a Gun, Tightrope, Panic, Highway Patrol,

Magnum P.I., Hotel, T.J. Hooker, Finder of Lost Loves, Murder She Wrote. *Movies:* Crowhaven Farm, The Rookies, Lieutenant Schuster's Wife, Crime Club, Little Ladies of the Night, Wild and Wooly, Beach Patrol, Killing at Hell's Gate, Advice to the Lovelorn, The Red-Light Sting, Seduction of Gina.

PICTURES: South Sea Woman, Screaming Eagles, Valley of the Dolls, The Thomas Crown Affair, Once You Kiss a Stranger, Daddy's Gone A-Hunting, Psychic Killer.

BURNETT, CAROL: Actress, Comedienne, Singer. b. San Antonio, TX, April 26, 1933. Mother of actress Carrie Hamilton. e. Hollywood H.S., UCLA. Introduced comedy song, I Made a Fool of Myself Over John Foster Dulles, 1957; regular performer Garry Moore TV show, 1959–62; appeared several CBS-TV spls., 1962–63. Recipient outstanding commedienne award Am. Guild Variety Artists, 5 times; 5 Emmy awards for outstanding variety performance, Acad. TV Arts and Scis., TV Guide award for outstanding female performer 1961, 62, 63; Peabody Award, 1963; 5 Golden Globe awards for outstanding comedienne of year, Fgn. Press Assn.; Woman of Year award Acad. TV Arts and Scis. Voted one of the world's 20 most admired women in 1977 Gallup Poll. First Annual National Television Critics Award for Outstanding Performance, 1977. Inducted Acad. of Television Arts and Sciences Hall of Fame, 1985.

THEATER: *NY:* Once Upon a Mattress (debut, 1959; Theatre World Award), Fade Out-Fade In (1964). *Regional:* Calamity Jane, Plaza Suite (1970), I Do I Do, Same Time Next Year (1977).

PICTURES: Who's Been Sleeping in My Bed? (debut, 1963), Pete 'n' Tillie, The Front Page, A Wedding (Best Actress Award, San Sebastian Film Fest.), Health, The Four Seasons, Chu Chu and the Philly Flash, Annie, Noises Off.

TELEVISION: *Series:* Stanley, Pantomime Quiz, The Garry Moore Show (Emmy Award, 1962), The Entertainers, The Carol Burnett Show (in syndication as Carol Burnett & Friends), Carol & Company, Carol Burnett Show (1991). *Specials:* Julie & Carol at Carnegie Hall (Emmy Award, 1963), An Evening with Carol Burnett, Calamity Jane, Once Upon a Mattress, Carol + 2, Julie & Carol at Lincoln Center, 6 Rms Riv Vu, Twigs, Sills & Burnett at the Met, Dolly & Carol in Nashville, All-Star Party for Carol Burnett, Burnett Discovers Domingo, The Laundromat, Carol Carl Whoopi & Robin, Julie & Carol–Together Again, The Carol Burnett Show: A Reunion (also co-exec. prod.). *Movies:* The Grass Is Always Greener Over the Septic Tank, Friendly Fire, The Tenth Month, Life of the Party: The Story of Beatrice, Between Friends, Hostage. *Mini-Series:* Fresno. *Guest:* Twilight Zone, Jack Benny Program, Get Smart, The Lucy Show, Fame, Magnum P.I.

BURNS, GEORGE: Actor. r.n. Nathan Birnbaum. b. New York, NY, Jan. 20, 1896. In vaudeville as singer in children's quartet, later as roller skater, then comedian; formed team Burns & (Gracie) Allen, 1925; m. partner 1926. Team many years on Keith and Orpheum vaudeville circuits, then on screen in Paramount short subjects, on radio in England; in 1930 began long career Amer. radio. Feature picture debut 1932 in The Big Broadcast. Books: How to Live to Be 100: or More!; The Ultimate Diet, Sex and Exercise Book; Dr. Burns' Prescription for Happiness; Dear George: Advice and Answers from America's Leading Expert on Everything from A to Z; Gracie, Wisdom of the 90s.

PICTURES: The Big Broadcast (debut, 1932), International House, College Humor, Six of a Kind, We're Not Dressing, Many Happy Returns, Love in Bloom, Here Comes Cookie, College Holiday, A Damsel in Distress, College Swing, Honolulu, The Solid Gold Cadillac (narrator), The Sunshine Boys (Acad. Award, supp. actor, 1975), Oh God!, Sgt. Pepper's Lonely Hearts Club Band, Movie Movie, Just You and Me Kid, Oh God! Book II, Oh God! You Devil, 18 Again.

TELEVISION: *Series:* The George Burns & Gracie Allen show (1950–58, CBS-TV), George Burns Show, Wendy and Me, George Burns Comedy Week. *Movie:* Two of a Kind. *Specials:* Grandpa Will You Run With Me?, Disney's Magic in the Magic Kingdom (host); and numerous others.

BURNS, RALPH: Musical conductor, Composer. b. Newton, MA, June 29, 1922.

PICTURES: Lenny, Cabaret (Acad. Award, 1972), Lucky Lady, New York New York, Movie Movie, All That Jazz (Acad. Award, 1979), Urban Cowboy, Annie, My Favorite Year, Jinxed, Kiss Me Goodbye, Star 80, Perfect, National Lampoon's Vacation, Bert Rigby You're a Fool.

TELEVISION: Baryshnikov on Broadway, Liza and Goldie Special, Ernie Kovacs—Between the Laughter, After the Promise, Sweet Bird of Youth.

BURR, RAYMOND: Actor. b. New Westminster, B.C., Canada, May 21, 1917. e. Stanford U., U. of California, Columbia U.; U. of Chungking. Forestry svce.: appeared on stage in many countries in Night Must Fall, Mandarin, Crazy with the Heat, Duke in Darkness; dir., Pasadena Community Playhouse, 1943; on radio. Formed Royal Blue Ltd, TV prod. co. with business partner Robert Benevides, 1988.

PICTURES: Without Reservations, San Quentin, Code of the West, Desperate, I Love Trouble, Fighting Father Dunne, Pitfall, Raw Deal, Ruthless, Sleep My Love, Station West, Walk a Crooked Mile, Abandoned, Adventures of Don Juan, Black Magic, Bride of Vengeance, Love Happy, Red Light, Criss Cross, Borderline, Key to the City, Unmasked, Bride of the Gorilla, His Kind of Woman, M, The Magic Carpet, New Mexico, A Place in the Sun, The Whip Hand, Horizons West, Mara Maru, Meet Danny Wilson, Bandits of Corsica, The Blue Gardenia, Fort Algiers, Serpent of the Nile, Tarzan and the She-Devil, Casanova's Big Night, Gorilla at Large, Khyber Patrol, Passion, Rear Window, Thunder Pass, Count Three and Pray, A Man Alone, They Were So Young, You're Never Too Young, The Brass Legend, A Cry in the Night, Godzilla: King of the Monsters, Great Day in the Morning, Please Murder Me, Ride the High Iron, Secret of Treasure Mountain, Affair in Havana, Crime of Passion, Desire in the Dust, P.J., Tomorrow Never Comes, The Return, Out of the Blue, Airplane II: The Sequel, Godzilla 1985, Delirious.

TELEVISION: *Series:* Perry Mason (1957—66; Emmy Awards: 1959, 1961), Ironside (1967—75); Kingstone: Confidential (1977). *Mini-Series:* 79 Park Ave., Centennial. *Movies:* Ironside (pilot), Split Second to an Epitaph, The Priest Killer, Mallory: Circumstantial Evidence, Kingston: The Power Play (pilot), The Bastard (narrator), The Jordan Chance, Love's Strange Fury, Disaster on the Coastline, Curse of King Tut's Tomb, The Night the City Screamed, Peter and Paul, Perry Mason Returns, Grass Roots, The Return of Ironside; Perry Mason movies: The Case of the . . . Notorious Nun, Shooting Star, Lost Love, Murdered Madam, Scandalous Scoundrel, Sinister Spirit, Avenging Ace, Lady in the Lake, All-Star Assassin, Lethal Lesson, Musical Murder, Desperate Deception, Poisoned Pen, Silenced Singer, Maligned Mobster, Glass Coffin, Fatal Fashion, Fatal Framing, Reckless Romeo, Heartbroken Bride, Skin-Deep Scandal.

BURRILL, TIMOTHY: Producer, Executive. b. North Wales, June 8, 1931. e. Eton Coll., Sorbonne U. Paris. Grenadier Guards 2 yrs, then London Shipping Co. Ent. m.p. ind. as resident prod. Samaritan Films working on shorts, commercials, documentaries, 1954. Ass't. dir. on feature films: The Criminal, The Valiant Years (TV series), On The Fiddle, Reach for Glory, War Lover, Prod. mgr: The Cracksman, Night Must Fall, Lord Jim, Yellow Rolls Royce, The Heroes of Telemark, Resident prod. with World Film Services. 1970 prod. two films on pop music for Anglo-EMI. 1972 first prod. administrator National Film School in U.K. 1974 Post prod. administrator The Three Musketeers. Prod. TV Special The Canterville Ghost; assoc. prod, That Lucky Touch; UK Administrator, The Prince and the Pauper; North American Prod. controller, Superman 1; 1974–1983 council member of BAFTA; mng. dir., Allied Stars (Breaking Glass, Chariots of Fire); 1979–80 V. chmn. Film BAFTA; 1980–1983 chmn. BAFTA; 1981–92, Gov. National Film School, executive BFTPA mem. Cinematographer Films Council. 1982–1988 Gov Royal National Theatre; 1987–93, chmn., Film Asset Developments, Formed Burrill Prods, 1979–; Chmn. First Film Foundation. Exec. member PACT, 1991–.

PICTURES: *Prod.:* Privlege, Oedipus the King, A Severed Head, Three Sisters, Macbeth (assoc. prod.), Alpha Beta, Tess (co-prod.), Pirates of Penzance (co-prod.), Supergirl, The Fourth Protocol, To Kill a Priest (co-prod.), Return of the Musketeers, Valmont, The Rainbow Thief, The Lover, Bitter Moon, Sweet Killing.

BURROWS, JAMES: Director. b. Los Angeles, CA, Dec. 30, 1940. e. Oberlin, B.A.; Yale, M.F.A. Son of late Abe Burrows, composer, writer, director. Directed off-Bdwy.

PICTURE: Partners.

TELEVISION: *Series:* Mary Tyler Moore, Bob Newhart, Laverne and Shirley, Rhoda, Phyllis, Tony Randall Show, Betty White Show, Fay, Taxi (2 Emmy Awards), Lou Grant, Cheers (5 Emmy Awards), Dear John, Night Court, All is Forgiven (also exec. prod.), The Tortellinis (also exec. prod.), The Fanelli Boys, Flesh 'n' Blood (also exec. prod.). *Movie:* More Than Friends.

BURROWS, ROBERTA: Executive. e. Brandeis U; Academia, Florence, Italy. Career includes freelance writing for natl. magazines: GQ, Italian Bazar, US, Family Circle, and post as dir. of pub. for Howard Stein Enterprises and with Rogers & Cowan and Billings Associates. Joined Warner Bros. as sr. publicist 1979; named dir. east coast publicity, 1986. Resigned 1989 to dev. novelty products. Proj. co-ordinator at Orion Pictures in NY for The Silence of the Lambs, Little Man Tate, Married to It, Bill & Ted's Bogus Journey. Columnist, Max publication,

BURSTYN, ELLEN: Actress. b. Detroit, MI, Dec. 7, 1932. r.n. Edna Rae Gilhooley. Majored in art; was fashion model in Texas at 18. Moved to Montreal as dancer; then N.Y. to do TV commercials (under the name of Ellen McRae), appearing for a year on the Jackie Gleason show (1956–57). In 1957 turned to dramatics and won lead in Bdwy show, Fair Game. Then went to Hollywood to do TV and films. Returned to N.Y. to study acting with Lee Strasberg; worked in TV serial, The Doctors. Co-artistic dir. of Actor's Studio. 1982–8. Pres. Actors Equity Assn. 1982–85. On 2 panels of Natl. Endowment of the Arts and Theatre Advisory Council (NY).

THEATER: *NY*: Same Time Next Year (Tony Award, 1975), 84 Charing Cross Road, Shirley Valentine, Shimada. *L.A.*: Love Letters.

PICTURES: *As Ellen McRae*: For Those Who Think Young (debut, 1964), Goodbye Charlie, Pit Stop. *As Ellen Burstyn*: Tropic of Cancer, Alex in Wonderland, The Last Picture Show, The King of Marvin Gardens, The Exorcist, Harry and Tonto, Alice Doesn't Live Here Anymore (Acad. Award, 1974), Providence, A Dream of Passion, Same Time Next Year, Resurrection, Silence of the North, The Ambassador, In Our Hands (doc.), Twice in a Lifetime, Hanna's War, Dying Young, The Color of Evening, The Cemetery Club, Significant Other.

TELEVISION: *Movies*: Thursday's Game, The People Vs. Jean Harris, Surviving, Act of Vengeance, Into Thin Air, Something in Common, Pack of Lies, When You Remember Me, Mrs. Lambert Remembers Love, Taking Back My Life: The Nancy Ziegenmeyer Story, Grand Isle. *Special*: Dear America: Letters Home From Vietnam (reader). *Series*: The Doctors, The Ellen Burstyn Show. *Guest*: Cheyenne, Dr. Kildare, 77 Sunset Strip, Perry Mason, The Iron Horse.

BURTON, KATE: Actress. b. Geneva, Switzerland, Sept. 10, 1957. e. Brown Univ. (B.A.), Yale Drama Sch. D. of late Richard Burton. m. stage manager Michael Ritchie. Worked at Yale Repertory Theatre, Hartford, Stage Co., the Hartman, Huntington Theatre, Williamstown, Berkshire Theatre festivals, The O'Neil Playwright's Conference.

THEATER: Present Laughter (debut, 1982; Theatre World Award), Alice in Wonderland, Winners, The Accrington Pals, Doonesbury, The Playboy of the Western World, Wild Honey, Measure For Measure, Some Americans Abroad (Drama Desk nom.), Jake's Women.

TELEVISION: *Mini-Series*: Ellis Island, Evergreen. *Movies*: Alice in Wonderland, Uncle Tom's Cabin, Love Matters. *Series*: Home Fires. *Pilot*: Monty.

PICTURES: Big Trouble in Little China (debut, 1986), Life With Mikey.

BURTON, LEVAR: Actor. b. Landstuhl, Germany, Feb. 16, 1957. e. U. of Southern California. Signed to play role of Kunta Kinte in TV mini-series, Roots, while still in school. Has hosted Public TV children's shows, Rebop, and The Reading Rainbow.

PICTURES: Looking for Mr. Goodbar, The Hunter, The Supernaturals.

TELEVISION: *Mini-Series*: Roots. *Special*: Almos' a Man. *Movies*: Billy: Portrait of a Street Kid, Battered, One in a Million: The Ron Leflore Story, Dummy, Guyana Tragedy: The Story of Jim Jones, The Acorn People, Grambling's White Tiger, Emergency Room, The Jesse Owens Story, A Special Friendship, Roots: The Gift, Firestorm: 72 Hours in Oakland. *Series*: Star Trek: The Next Generation, Reading Rainbow (PBS; host).

BURTON, TIM: Director, Producer. b. Burbank, CA, 1958. Cartoonist since grade school in suburban Burbank. Won Disney fellowship to study animation at California Institute of the Arts. At 20 went to Burbank to work as apprentice animator on Disney lot where made Vincent, 6-minute animated short on his own which was released commercially in 1982 and won several film fest. awards. Also made Frankenweenie, 29 minute live-action film.

PICTURES: *Director*: Pee-wee's Big Adventure, Beetlejuice, Batman, Edward Scissorhands (also co-story), Batman Returns (also co-prod.), Singles (actor only), The Nightmare Before Christmas (co-prod. only), Cabin Boy (co-prod. only).

TELEVISION: *Dir*: Aladdin (Faerie Tale Theatre), Alfred Hitchcock Presents, Amazing Stories (Family Dog). *Exec. Prod.*: Beetlejuice (animated series), Family Dog (animated series).

BUSCEMI, STEVE: Actor. b. Brooklyn, NY, 1958. Started as standup comedian in New York City, also wrote and acted in several one-act plays; worked as fireman. Studied acting at Lee Strasberg Inst. in NY.

PICTURES: The Way It Is/Eurydice in the Avenue, No Picnic, Parting Glances, Sleepwalk, Heart, Kiss Daddy Good Night, Call Me, Force of Circumstance, Vibes, Heart of Midnight, Bloodhounds of Broadway, Borders, New York Stories (Life Lessons), Slaves of New York, Mystery Train, Tales from the Dark Side, Miller's Crossing, King of New York, Zandalee, Barton Fink, Billy Bathgate, Crisscross, In the Soup, Reservoir Dogs, Trusting Beatrice, Rising Sun, Airheads.

TELEVISION: *Mini-Series*: Lonesome Dove. *Guest*: Miami Vice, The Equalizer, L.A. Law.

BUSCH, H. DONALD: Exhibitor. b. Philadelphia, PA, Sept. 21, 1935. e. U. of Pennsylvania, physics, math, 1956; law school, 1959. 1960 to 1987 practiced law, anti-trust & entertainment. 1984, pres., Budco Theatres, Inc. 1975–1987, pres., Busch,

Grafman & Von Dreusche, P.C. 1987, pres. & CEO, AMC Philadelphia, Inc.

MEMBER: Former posts: Suburban General Hospital (dir.); Rainbow Fund (dir.); Society Hill Synagogue (dir.); Philadelphia All-Star Forum (dir.); Montgomery County Bar Assn. (dir.); Dir. & pres., Abington, PA school board (1974–77); dir., Sports Legends, Inc. (1972–84). Recent: NATO chmn (1990–1), chmn. emeritus, 1992; Showeast, gen. chmn., 1990–1; chmn. of W., 1992; Urban League (dir.), Will Rogers Memorial Fund (dir.). 1988, pres. of NATO, Pennsylvania.

BUSEY, GARY: Actor, Musician. b. Goose Creek, TX, June 29, 1944. e. Coffeyville Jr. Coll. A.B., 1963; attended Kansas State Coll, OK State U. Played drums with the Rubber Band 1963–70. Also drummer with Leon Russell, Willie Nelson as Teddy Jack Eddy.

PICTURES: Angels Hard as They Come (debut, 1971), Didn't You Hear?, Dirty Little Billy, The Magnificent Seven Ride, The Last American Hero, Lolly Madonna xxx, Hex, Thunderbolt and Lightfoot, You and Me, Gumball Rally, A Star Is Born, Straight Time, Big Wednesday, The Buddy Holly Story (Natl. Society of Film Critics Award, 1978), Foolin' Around, Carny, Barbarosa, D.C. Cab, The Bear, Insignificance, Silver Bullet, Let's Get Harry, Eye of the Tiger, Lethal Weapon, Bulletproof, Act of Piracy, Predator 2, My Heroes Have Always Been Cowboys, Hider in the House, Point Break, The Player, Under Siege, The Firm, Rookie of the Year.

TELEVISION: *Series*: The Texas Wheelers (1974–75). *Guest*: High Chaparral (debut, 1970), Gunsmoke, Saturday Night Live, The Hitchhiker (ACE Award). *Movies*: Bloodsport, The Execution of Private Slovik, The Law, Wild Texas Wind, Chrome Soldiers. *Mini-Series*: A Dangerous Life, The Neon Empire.

BUSFIELD, TIMOTHY: Actor. b. Lansing, MI, June 12, 1957. e. East Tennessee State U; Actor's Theatre of Louisville (as apprentice and resident). Founded Fantasy Theatre in Sacramento, 1986, a professional acting co., which performs in Northern CA schools, providing workshops on playwriting for children and sponsors annual Young Playwrights contest.

THEATER: Richard II, Young Playwrights Festival (Circle Rep.), A Tale Told, Getting Out (European tour), Green Mountain Guilds Children Theatre, Mass Appeal, The Tempest, A Few Good Men (Bdwy). Founded & co-prod. The "B" Theatre, 1992, prods. Mass Appeal, Hidden in This Picture.

PICTURES: Stripes, Revenge of the Nerds, Revenge of the Nerds II, Field of Dreams, Sneakers.

TELEVISION: *Series*: Reggie, Trapper John M.D., thirtysomething (Emmy Award, 1991; also dir. 3 episodes). *Guest*: Family Ties, Matlock, Paper Chase, Love American Style, After M.A.S.H., Hotel. *Movies*: Strays, Calendar Girl-Cop-Killer?: The Bambi Bembenek Story.

BUTTONS, RED: Performer. r.n. Aaron Chwatt. b. New York, NY, Feb. 5, 1919. Attended Evander Child H.S. in the Bronx. Singer at the age of 13; comic, Minsky's. U.S. Army, 1943; in Army and film version of Winged Victory. Received Golden Globe Award noms. for Harlow and They Shoot Horses Don't They?

TELEVISION: *Series*: The Red Buttons Show (1952–5; Best Comedian award 1953), Double Life of Henry Phyfe (1965); Knots Landing. *Movies*: Breakout, The New Original Wonder Woman, Louis Armstrong: Chicago Style, Telethon, Vega$, The Users, Power, The Dream Merchants, Leave 'Em Laughing, Reunion at Fairborough, Alice in Wonderland.

THEATER: Vickie, Wine Women and Song, Barefoot Boy With Cheek, Hold It The Admiral Had a Wife, Winged Victory, Tender Trap, Play It Again Sam, Teahouse of the August Moon.

PICTURES: Winged Victory (1944, debut), 13 Rue Madeleine, Footlight Varieties of 1951, Off Your Rocker, Sayonara (Acad. Award & Golden Globe Award, supp. actor, 1957), Imitation General, The Big Circus, One Two Three, The Longest Day, Gay Purr-ee (voice), Five Weeks in a Balloon, Hatari!, A Ticklish Affair, Your Cheatin' Heart, Harlow, Up From the Beach, Stagecoach, They Shoot Horses Don't They?, Who Killed Mary What's 'er Name?, The Poseidon Adventure, Gable and Lombard, Viva Knievel!, Pete's Dragon, Movie Movie, C.H.O.M.P.S., When Time Ran Out, 18 Again, The Ambulance.

BUZZI, RUTH: Actress. b. Westerly, RI, July 24, 1939. e. Pasadena Playhouse Col. of Theatre Arts. On Country Music charts with you Oughta Hear the Song.

PICTURES: Record City, Freaky Friday, The Apple Dumpling Gang Rides Again, The North Avenue Irregulars, The Villian, Surf Two, Skatetown USA, Chu Chu and the Philly Flash, The Being, The Bad Guys, Dixie Lanes, Up Your Alley, Diggin' Up Business, My Mom's a Werewolf, It's Your Life Michael Angelo, Wishful Thinking.

TELEVISION: *Series*: Rowan & Martin's Laugh-In, The Steve Allen Comedy Hour, The Donny & Marie Show, The Lost Saucer, Betsy Lee's Ghost Town Jamboree, Carol Burnett's The Entertainers; semi-regular on 12 other series including Flip, Tony Orlando & Dawn, That Girl, Glen Campbell's Goodtime Hour, Leslie Uggums Show, The Dean Martin Variety Hour; guest on 90 TV series and specials including Medical Center, Adam 12, Trapper John M.D., Love Boat. *Movie*: In Name Only. Nine cartoon voice-over series and over 150 on-camera commercials.

STAGE: Sweet Charity (Broadway), 4 off-Broadway shows incl. A Man's A Man, Little Mary Sunshine, 18 musical revues and Las Vegas club act.

AWARDS: 4 Emmy nominations; Golden Globe winner, AGVA Variety Artist of the Year, 1977, Rhode Island Hall of Fame, Presidential commendation for outstanding artist in the field of entertainment, 1980, NAACP Image Award.

BYGRAVES, MAX: Comedian, actor. b. London, England, October 16, 1922. e. St. Joseph's R.C. School, Rotherhithe. After RAF service, touring revues and London stage, M.P. debut 1949 in Skimpy in The Navy. TV debut in 1953, with own show. Autobiography, I Wanna Tell You A Story, pub. 1976. Received O.B.E., New Year's Honours 1983.

TELEVISION: Roamin' Holiday series.

PICTURES: Tom Brown's Schooldays, Charlie Moon, A Cry from the Streets, Boobikins, Spare the Rod.

NOVEL: The Milkman's on His Way, pub. 1977.

BYRD, CARUTH C.: Production executive. b. Dallas, TX, March 25, 1941. e. Trinity U, San Antonio. Multi-millionaire businessman, chmn. of Caruth C. Byrd Enterprises, Inc., who entered entertainment industry forming Communications Network Inc. in 1972, producer of TV commercials. Was principal investor in film Santee (1972) and in 1973 formed Caruth C. Byrd Prods. to make theatrical features. 1983, chrm., Lone Star Pictures, 1987, formed Caruth C. Byrd Television. Formed Caruth C. Byrd Entertainment Inc. May 1989. Concerts incl. Tom Jones, Natalie Cole, B.J. Thomas, Tammy Wynette, Seals & Croft, Eddie Rabbit, Helen Reddy, Jim Stafford, Tanya Tucker and many more.

PICTURES: Murph the Surf, The Monkeys of Bandapur (both exec. prod.), Santee, Sudden Death, Hollywood High II, Lone Star Country, Trick or Treats.

TELEVISION: Fishing Fever, Kids Are People Too, Tribute to Mom and Dad, Back to School, Texas 150: A Celebration Special.

BYRNE, DAVID: Actor, Singer, Director. b. Dumbarton, Scotland, May 14, 1952. Moved to Baltimore at 7. e. Rhode Island Sch. of Design studying photography, performance and video, and Maryland Inst. Coll. of Art 1971–72. Prod. and dir. music videos. Awarded MTV's Video Vanguard Award, 1985. Best known as the lead singer and chief songwriter of Talking Heads. Composed and performed original score for choreographer Twyla Tharp's The Catherine Wheel (Bdwy). Wrote music for Robert Wilson's The Knee Plays.

PICTURES: Stop Making Sense (conceived and stars in concert film), True Stories (director, s.p., narrator), The Last Emperor (music, Acad. Award), Married to the Mob (music), Heavy Petting.

CONTRIBUTED MUSIC: Times Square, The Animals' Film, King of Comedy, America is Waiting, Revenge of the Nerds, Down and Out in Beverly Hills, Dead End Kids, Cross My Heart.

TELEVISION: A Family Tree (Trying Times), Alive From Off-Center (also composed theme), Survival Guides; Rolling Stone Magazine's 20 Years of Rock and Roll.

BYRNE, GABRIEL: Actor. b. Dublin, Ireland, 1950. e. University Coll., Ireland. m. actress Ellen Barkin. Worked as archaeologist. then taught Spanish at girls' school. Participated in amateur theater before acting with Ireland's Focus Theatre, an experimental rep. co. and joining Dublin's Abbey Theatre Co. Cast in long-running TV series the Riordans. Also worked with National Theater in London.

PICTURES: On a Paving Stone Mounted, The Outsider, Excalibur, Wagner, Hanna K, The Keep, Defence of the Realm, Gothic, Lionheart, Siesta, Hello Again, Julia and Julia, A Soldier's Tale, The Courier, Miller's Crossing, Shipwrecked, Dark Obsession (Diamond Skulls), Cool World, Point of No Return, Into the West, In the Name of the Father (co-prod. only), A Dangerous Woman.

TELEVISION: *Series*: The Riordan's, Branken. *Movies*: Wagner, Mussolini, Christopher Columbus.

BYRNES, EDD: Actor. b. New York, NY, July 30, 1933. e. Harren H.S. Prof. debut, Joe E. Brown's Circus Show; appeared on stage in Tea and Sympathy, Picnic, Golden Boy, Bus Stop, Ready When You Are C.B., Storm in Summer.

PICTURES: Up Periscope, Marjorie Morningstar, Yellowstone Kelly, The Secret Invasion, Wicked Wicked, Grease, Stardust, Go Kill and Come Back, Payment in Blood, Troop Beverly Hills.

TELEVISION: *Series*: 77 Sunset Strip, Sweepstake $. Has appeared in over 300 TV shows incl.: Matinee Theatre, Crossroads, Jim Bowie, Wire Service, Navy Log, Oh Susanna!, Throb, Rags to Riches, Murder She Wrote. *Movies*: The Silent Gun, Mobile Tow, Telethon, Vegas, Twirl.

BYRUM, JOHN: Writer, Director. b. Winnetka, IL, March 14, 1947. e. New York U. Film School. First job as "go-fer" on industrial films and cutting dailies for underground filmmakers. Went to England where wrote 1st s.p., Comeback. From 1970–73 was in N.Y. writing and re-writing scripts for low-budget films.

PICTURES: Mahogany (s.p.), Inserts (s.p., dir.) Harry and Walter Go to New York (story, s.p.), Heart Beat (dir, s.p.), Sphinx (s.p.), Scandalous (co.-s.p.), The Razor's Edge (co-s.p., dir.), The Whoopee Boys (dir.), The War at Home (s.p.).

TELEVISION: Alfred Hitchcock Presents (1985).

C

CAAN, JAMES: Actor. b. Bronx, NY, March 26, 1940. e. Hofstra U. Studied with Sanford Meisner at the Neighborhood Playhouse. Appeared off-Broadway in La Ronde, 1961. Also on Broadway in Mandingo, Blood Sweat and Stanley Poole.

PICTURES: Irma La Douce (debut, 1963), Lady in a Cage, The Glory Guys, Red Line 7000, El Dorado, Games, Countdown, Journey to Shiloh, Submarine X-1, The Rain People, Rabbit Run, T.R. Baskin, The Godfather (Acad. Award nom.), Slither, Cinderella Liberty, The Gambler, Freebie and the Bean, Godfather II, Funny Lady, Rollerball, The Killer Elite, Harry and Walter Go To New York, Silent Movie, A Bridge Too Far, Another Man Another Chance, Comes a Horseman, Chapter Two, Hide in Plain Sight (also dir.), Thief, Bolero, Kiss Me Goodbye, Gardens of Stone, Alien Nation, Dick Tracy, Misery, The Dark Backward, For the Boys, Honeymoon in Vegas, The Program, Flesh & Bone.

TELEVISION: Much series guest work (Naked City, Route 66, Wagon Train, Ben Casey, Alfred Hitchcock Presents, etc.) 1962–69. *Movie*: Brian's Song (Emmy nom., 1971).

CACOYANNIS, MICHAEL: Producer, Director, Writer. b. Cyprus, June 11, 1922. Studied law in London, admitted to bar at age 21. Became a producer of BBC's wartime Greek programs while attending dramatic school. After acting on the stage in England, left in 1952 for Greece, where he made his first film, Windfall in Athens, with his own original script. While directing Greek classical plays, he continued making films.

PICTURES: Stella, The Girl in Black, A Matter of Dignity, Our Last Spring, The Wastrel, Electra, Zorba the Greek, The Day the Fish Came Out, The Trojan Women, Attila 74, Iphigenia, Sweet Country, Zoe.

CAESAR, IRVING: Author, Composer, Publisher. b. New York, NY, July 4, 1895. e. City Coll. of New York. Abroad with Henry Ford on Peace Ship, W.W.I; songwriter since then, songs with George Gershwin, Sigmund Romberg, Vincent Youmans, Rudolph Friml and others, songwriter for stage, screen and radio, including Swanee, Tea for Two, Sometimes I'm Happy, I Want to Be Happy, Lady Play Your Mandolin, Songs of Safety, Songs of Friendship, Songs of Health and Pledge of Allegiance to the Flag.

CAESAR, SID: Performer. b. Yonkers, NY, Sept. 8, 1922. Studied saxophone at Juilliard School; then appeared in service revue Tars and Spars. Cast by prod. Max Liebman in Bdwy revue Make Mine Manhattan in 1948. Voted best comedian in M.P. Daily's TV poll, 1951, 1952. Best Comedy Team (with Imogene Coca) in 1953. Recieved Sylvania Award, 1958. Formed Shelbrick Corp. TV, 1959. Appeared in Bdwy musical Little Me (1962), Off-Bdwy & Bdwy revue Sid Caesar & Company (1989). Author: Where Have I Been? (autobiography, 1982).

TELEVISION: *Series*: Admiral Broadway Revue, Your Show of Shows (1950–4; Emmy Award for Best Actor, 1952), Caesar's Hour (1954–7; Emmy Award for Best Comedian, 1956), Sid Caesar Invites You (1958), As Caesar Sees It (1962–3), The Sid Caesar Show (1963–4). *Movies*: Flight to Holocaust, Curse of the Black Widow, The Munsters' Revenge, Found Money, Love is Never Silent, Alice in Wonderland, Freedom Fighter, Side By Side. *Guest*: U.S. Steel Hour, G.E. Theatre, The Ed Sullivan Show, Carl Burnett Show, Lucy Show, That's Life, Love American Style, When Things Were Rotten, The Love Boat, Amazing Stories, others. *Specials*: Tiptoe Through TV, Variety - World of Show Biz, Sid Caesar and Edie Adams Together, The Sid Caesar Imogene Coca Carl Reiner Howard Morris Special, Christmas Snow.

PICTURES: Tars and Spars (debut, 1945), The Guilt of Janet Ames, It's a Mad Mad Mad Mad World, The Spirit is Willing, The Busy Body, A Guide for the Married Man, Airport 1975, Silent Movie, Fire Sale, Grease, The Cheap Detective, The Fiendish Plot of Dr. Fu Manchu, History of the World Part I, Grease 2, Over the Brooklyn Bridge, Cannonball Run II, Stoogemania, The Emperor's New Clothes.

CAGE, NICOLAS: Actor. b. Long Beach, CA, Jan. 7, 1964. r.n. Nicholas Coppola. Nephew of Francis Ford Coppola.

PICTURES: Fast Times at Ridgemont High (debut, 1982; billed as Nicholas Coppola), Valley Girl, Rumble Fish, Racing with the Moon, The Cotton Club, Birdy, The Boy in Blue,

Peggy Sue Got Married, Raising Arizona, Moonstruck, Vampire's Kiss, Fire Birds, Wild at Heart, Zandalee, Honeymoon in Vegas, Amos & Andrew, DeadFall, Guarding Tess.

CAHN, SAMMY: Lyricist, Producer. b. New York, NY, June 18, 1913. e. Seward Park H.S. Org. dance band with Saul Chaplin; collab. song writer for shows. m.p. 30 Acad. Award nominations, 4 Oscars for Three Coins in Fountain, All the Way, High Hopes, and Call Me Irresponsible! Only TV Emmy given a song, Love & Marriage, from the TV award winning Our Town. 1972, inducted into Songwriters' Hall of Fame. BDWY. MUSICALS: High Button Shoes, Skyscraper, Walking Happy, many songs.
PICTURES: Anchors Aweigh, Three Coins in Fountain, Romance on High Seas, Some Came Running, Robin & Seven Hoods, The Tender Trap, Pocketful of Miracles, Thoroughly Modern Millie.
(Died Jan. 15, 1993)

CAINE, MICHAEL: Actor. r.n. Maurice Micklewhite. b. London, England, March 14, 1933. Asst. stage mgr. Westminster Rep. (Sussex, UK 1953); Lowestoft Rep. 1953–55. London stage: The Room, The Dumbwaiter, Next Time I'll Sing For You (1963). Author: Michael Caine's Moving Picture Show or Not Many People Know This is the Movies, Acting on Film, What's It All About?. Awarded C.B.E., 1992. Video: Michael Caine Acting on Film.
TELEVISION: Series: Rickles (1975). In more than 100 British teleplays 1957–63 incl. The Compartment, The Playmates, Hobson's Choice, Funny Noises with Their Mouths, The Way with Reggie, Luck of the Draw, Hamlet, The Other Man. Movies: Jack the Ripper, Jekyll and Hyde, Blue Ice.
PICTURES: A Hill in Korea (debut, 1956; aka Hell in Korea), How to Murder A Rich Uncle, The Key, Two-Headed Spy, Blind Spot, Breakout (Danger Within), Foxhole in Cairo, Bulldog Breed, Day the Earth Caught Fire, Solo for Sparrow, Zulu, Ipcress File, Alfie (Acad. Award nom.), The Wrong Box, Gambit, Funeral in Berlin, Hurry Sundown, Woman Times Seven, Billion Dollar Brain, Deadfall, The Magus, Play Dirty, Italian Job, The Battle of Britain, Too Late the Hero, The Last Valley, Get Carter, Kidnapped, Zee and Company (X,Y & Zee), Pulp, Sleuth (Acad. Award nom.), The Black Windmill, The Destructors (The Marseille Contract), The Wilby Conspiracy, Peeper, The Romantic Englishwoman, The Man Who Would Be King, Harry and Walter Go to New York, The Eagle Has Landed, A Bridge Too Far, The Silver Bears, The Swarm, California Suite, Ashanti, Beyond the Poseidon Adventure, The Island, Dressed to Kill, The Hand, Victory, Deathtrap, Educating Rita (Acad. Award nom.), Beyond the Limit, Blame It on Rio, The Jigsaw Man, The Holcroft Covenant, Hannah and Her Sisters (Acad. Award, supp. actor, 1986), Water, Sweet Liberty, Mona Lisa, Half Moon Street, Jaws—The Revenge, The Whistle Blower, The Fourth Protocol (also exec. prod.), Surrender, Without a Clue, Dirty Rotten Scoundrels, A Shock to the System, Mr. Destiny, Bullseye!, Noises Off, The Muppet Christmas Carol, On Deadly Ground.

CALHOUN, RORY: Actor. r.n. Francis Timothy McCown. b. Los Angeles, CA, Aug. 8, 1922. e. Santa Cruz H.S. Worked as logger, miner, cowpuncher, firefighter; m.p. debut in Something for the Boys, 1944.
PICTURES: Something for the Boys (debut, 1944), The Bullfighters, Sunday Dinner for a Soldier, Nob Hill, The Great John L, Where Do We Go From Here?, Red House, Adventure Island, That Hagen Girl, Massacre River, Return of the Frontiersman, Sand, Ticket to Tomahawk, County Fair, Rogue River, I'd Climb the Highest Mountain, Miraculous Journey, Meet Me After the Show, With a Song in My Heart, Way of a Gaucho, The Silver Whip, Powder River, How to Marry a Millionaire, Yellow Tomahawk, River of No Return, Bullet Is Waiting, Dawn at Socorro, Four Guns to the Border, The Looters, Ain't Misbehavin', The Domino Kid, Treasure of Pancho Villa, The Spoilers, Red Sundown, Raw Edge, Flight to Hong Kong, Utah Blaine, Big Caper, Hired Gun, The Big Caper, Ride Out for Revenge, Apace Territory, Hemp Brown, Thunder Over Carolina, Adventures of Marco Polo, Treasure of Monte Cristo, Colossus of Rhodes, Gun Hawk, Young and the Brave, Face in the Rain, Call Me Bwana, Black Spurs, Young Fury, Finger on the Trigger, Our Man in Baghdad, Lady of the Nile, Apache Uprising, Dayton's Devils, Low Price of Fame, Night of the Lepus, Operation Cross Eagles, Won Ton Ton the Dog Who Saved Hollywood, Father Keno Story, Mule Feathers, Revenge of Bigfoot, Love and the Midnight Auto Supply, Motel Hell, Angel, Rollerblade Warriors, Avenging Angel, Hell Comes to Frogtown, Bad Jim, Fists of Steel, Pure Country.
TELEVISION: Series: U.S. Camera, The Texan, Capitol. Mini-Series: The Blue and the Gray, The Rebels. Movies: Flight to Holocaust, Flatbed Annie and Sweetie Pie: Lady Truckers. Guest: The Road Ahead, Day Is Done, Bet the Wild Queen, Zane Grey Theater, Killer Instinct, Land's End (pilot), Champion, Hart to Hart, Police Woman, Movin' On, Alias Smith & Jones.

CALLAN, MICHAEL: Actor, singer, dancer. b. Philadelphia, PA, Nov. 22, 1935. Singer, dancer, Philadelphia nightclubs; to New York in musicals, including The Boy Friend and West Side Story; dancer Copacabana; in short-run plays, Las Vegas: That Certain Girl. 1990s formed production company with James Darren and Tony Mordente.
PICTURES: They Came to Cordura, (debut) The Flying Fontaines, Because They're Young, Pepe, Mysterious Island, Gidget Goes Hawaiian, 13 West Street, Bon Voyage, The Interns, The Victors, The New Interns, Cat Ballou, Frasier, The Sensuous Lion, Lepke, The Photographer, The Cat and The Canary (1977), Record City, Double Exposure (also prod.), Freeway.
TELEVISION: Series: Occasional Wife, Superboy. Guest on major dramatic TV shows incl. Murder She Wrote, Superboy. Movies: In Name Only, Donner Pass: The Road to Survival, Last of the Great Survivors. Mini-Series: Blind Ambition, Scruples.

CALLOW, SIMON: Actor, Writer, Director. b. London, June 15, 1949. e. Queens, U. of Belfast, The Drama Centre. Originated role of Mozart in London premiere of Amadeus and Burgess/Chubb in Single Spies. Author: Being an Actor, Charles Laughton: A Difficult Actor, Shooting the Actor.
THEATER: London: Plumber's Progress, The Doctor's Dilemma, Soul of the White Ant, Blood Sports, The Resistible Rise of Arturo Ui, Amadeus, Restoration, The Beastly Beatitudes of Balthasar B, Titus Andronicus (Bristol Old Vic), Faust. Shakespeare's Sonnets. Director: The Infernal Machine (also translator), Jacques and His Master (also trans. L.A.), Single Spies, Shirley Valentine (London, NY), Carmen Jones.
PICTURES: Amadeus, A Room With a View, The Good Father, Maurice, Manifesto, Postcards from the Edge, Mr. and Mrs. Bridge, Ballad of the Sad Cafe (dir. only), Howards End.
TELEVISION: Man of Destiny, La Ronde, All the World's a Stage, Wings of Song, The Dybbuk, Instant Enlightenment, Chance of a Lifetime (series), David Copperfield, Honour, Profit and Pleasure, Old Flames, Revolutionary Witness: Palloy.

CALVET, CORINNE: Actress. r.n. Corinne Dibos. b. Paris, France, April 30, 1925. e. U. of Paris School of Fine Arts, Comedie Francaise. French stage and radio. Screen debut in France; La Part de L'Ombre, Nous Ne Sommes Pas Maries, Petrus. Author: Has Corinne Been a Good Little Girl?, The Kirlian Aura.
PICTURES: Rope of Sand (U.S. debut), When Willie Comes Marching Home, My Friend Irma Goes West, Quebec, On the Riviera, Peking Express, Thunder in the East, Sailor Beware, What Price Glory?, Powder River, Flight to Tangier, The Far Country, So This Is Paris, Bluebeard's Ten Honeymoons, Adventures of a Young Man, Apache Uprising, Too Hot to Handle, Dr. Heckle and Mr. Hype, Pound, Side Roads.
TELEVISION: Movies: The Phantom of Hollywood, She's Dressed to Kill, The French Atlantic Affair.

CAMERON, JAMES: Director, Writer. b. Kapuskasing, Ontario, Aug. 16, 1954. e. Fullerton Junior Col. (physics). 1990, formed Lightstorm Entertainment.
PICTURES: Piranha II—The Spawning (dir.), The Terminator (s.p., dir.), Rambo: First Blood Part II (co-s.p.), Aliens (dir., s.p.), The Abyss (dir., s.p.), Terminator 2: Judgment Day (co-s.p., dir., prod.), Point Break (exec. prod.).

CAMERON, JOANNA: Actress, director. r.n. Patricia Cameron. b. Aspen, CO, Sept. 20, 1951. e. U. of California, Sorbonne, Pasadena Playhouse, 1968. Guinness Record: Most network programmed TV commercials.
PICTURES: How To Commit Marriage (debut), B.S. I Love You, Pretty Maids All in a Row.
TELEVISION: Movies: The Great American Beauty Contest, Night Games, It Couldn't Happen to a Nicer Guy, High Risk, Swan Song. Series: Isis. Guest: The Survivors, Love American Style, Daniel Boone, Mission Impossible, The Partners, Search, Medical Center, Name of the Game, The Bold Ones, Marcus Welby, Petrocelli, Columbo, Switch, MacMillan, Spiderman. Specials: Bob Hope Special, Bob Hope 25th NBC Anniversary Special; numerous commercials. Director: Various commercials, CBS Preview Special, closed circuit program host U.S.N., all TV equipped ships—actress and dir. Documentaries: Razor Sharp (prod., dir.), El Camino Real (dir., prod.).

CAMERON, KIRK: Actor. b. Canoga Park, CA, Oct. 12, 1970. m. actress Chelsea Noble. Sister is actress Candace Cameron. Started doing TV commercials at age 9. Appeared in TV movies, series episodes, and Two Marriages (short-lived series).
PICTURES: The Best of Times, Like Father, Like Son, Listen to Me.
TELEVISION: Series: Two Marriages, Growning Pains. Movies: Goliath Awaits, Starflight: The Plane That Couldn't Land, A Little Piece of Heaven. Specials: The Woman Who Willed a Miracle, Andrea's Story. Ice Capades with Kirk Cameron.

CAMP, COLLEEN: Actress. b. San Francisco, CA, 1953. Spent 2 years as a bird trainer at Busch Gardens before being noticed by an agent and cast on TV. TV debut on The Dean Martin Show; feature film debut, Battle for the Planet of the Apes (1973). Assoc. prod. on Martha Coolidge's film The City Girl. Sang several songs in They All Laughed and made Billboard charts with song One Day Since Yesterday.
PICTURES: Battle for the Planet of the Apes, Swinging Cheerleaders, Funny Lady, Smile, Gumball Rally, Death Game, Cats in a Cage, Game of Death, Apocalypse Now, Cloud Dancer, They All Laughed, The Seduction, Valley Girl, Smokey and the Bandit III, Rosebud Beach Hotel, The Joy of Sex, Police Academy II, Doin' Time, D.A.R.Y.L., Clue, Walk Like a Man, Illegally Yours, Track 29, Wicked Stepmother, My Blue Heaven, Wayne's World, The Vagrant, Un-Becoming Age, Sliver, Last Action Hero, Greedy.
TELEVISION: Movies: Amelia Earhart, Lady of the House, Sisterhood, Addicted to His Love, Backfield in Motion, For Their Own Good. Mini-Series: Rich Man Poor Man Book II. Series: Dallas. Guest: Happy Days, Dukes of Hazzard, WKRP in Cincinnati, Magnum PI, Murder She Wrote, Tales from the Crypt. Specials: George Burns Comedy Week, Going Home Again.

CAMP, JOE: Producer, Director, Writer. b. St. Louis, MO, Apr. 20, 1939. e. U. of Mississippi, B.B.A. Acct. exec. McCann-Erickson Advt., Houston 1961–62; owner Joe Camp Real Estate 1962–64; acct. exec. Norsworthy-Mercer, Dallas 1964–69; dir. TV commercials; founder and pres. Mulberry Square Prods.
PICTURES: Benji, Hawmps, For the Love of Benji, The Double McGuffin, Oh Heavenly Dog, Benji the Hunted.
TELEVISION: The Phenomenon of Benji, Benji's Very Own Christmas Story, Benji at Work, Benji at Marineland.

CAMPANELLA, TOM: Executive. b. Houston, TX, 1944. e. City U. of NY. Joined Paramount Pictures 1968 as asst. business mgr.; later worked for corporate div. and Motion Picture Group. Named exec. dir., nat'l adv. 1979, made v.p., nat'l adv. 1982, appt. sr. v.p., adv., for M.P. Group of Paramount, 1984. Appointed exec. v.p., adv. & promo., 1990.

CAMPBELL, GLEN: Actor, Singer. b. Delight, AK, April 22, 1936. After forming local band became studio guitarist in Hollywood on records for such performers as Frank Sinatra and Elvis Presley. Won two Grammy awards for record By the Time I Get to Phoenix, 1967. Appeared frequently on Shindig on TV.
PICTURES: The Cool Ones, True Grit, Norwood, Any Which Way You Can, Rock a Doodle (voice).
TELEVISION: Series: The Smothers Brothers Comedy Hour, The Glen Campbell Goodtime Hour, The Glen Campbell Music show; many specials. Movie: Strange Homecoming.

CAMPBELL, WILLIAM: Actor. b. Newark, NJ, Oct. 30, 1926. e. Feagin Sch. of Drama. Appeared in summer stock. Broadway plays; m.p. debut in The Breaking Point (1950).
PICTURES: People Against O'Hara, Holiday for Sinners, Battle Circus, Code Two, Big Leaguer, Escape from Fort Bravo, High and the Mighty, Man Without a Star, Cell 2455 Death Row, Battle Cry, Running Wild, Backlash, Pretty Maids All in a Row, Black Gunn.
TELEVISION: Series: Cannonball, Dynasty, Crime Story. Pilot: The Heat: When You Lie Down With Dogs.

CANBY, VINCENT: Journalist, Critic. b. Chicago, IL, July 27, 1924. e. Dartmouth Coll. Navy officer during W.W.II. Worked on newspapers in Paris and Chicago. Joined Quigley Publications in 1951 in editorial posts on Motion Picture Herald. Reporter for Weekly Variety 1959–1965. Joined New York Times film news staff, 1965; named film critic, 1969. Author: Living Quarters (1975); End of the War (play, 1978); Unnatural Scenery (1979); After All (play, 1981); The Old Flag (1984).

CANDY, JOHN: Actor, Writer. b. Toronto, Ont., Oct. 31, 1950. Began acting in 11th grade and continued while studying journalism at Centennial Community Coll., Toronto. First professional job as member of children's theatre group; performed in satirical review, Creeps. Had roles in several low-budget Canadian films before joining Chicago's Second City Theatre in 1972 for two years. Returned to Toronto to join Second City group there, which evolved into SCTV television series. Contributed as performer and writer (1975–83), earning two Emmy Awards (writing) when show was picked up by NBC.
PICTURES: The Class of '44, It Seemed Like a Good Idea at the Time, Find the Lady, Tunnelvision, The Clown Murders, Faceoff, The Silent Partner, Lost and Found, 1941, The Blues Brothers, Stripes, Heavy Metal (voice), It Came From Hollywood, National Lampoon's Vacation, Going Berserk, Splash, Brewster's Millions, Volunteers, Sesame Street Presents Follow That Bird, Summer Rental, Armed and Dangerous, Little Shop of Horrors, Spaceballs, Planes Trains & Automobiles, The Great Outdoors, Hot to Trot (voice), Who's Harry Crumb? (also exec. prod.), Speed Zone, Uncle Buck, Home Alone, The Rescuers Down Under (voice), Nothing But Trouble, Masters of Menace, Career Opportunities, Only the Lonely, Delirious, JFK, Once Upon a Crime, Rookie of the Year, Cool Runnings.
TELEVISION: Specials: Comic Relief, The Last Polka, Young Comedians, Super Bowl 1989. Movie: Boris & Natasha (cameo).

CANNELL, STEPHEN J.: Writer, Producer. b. Los Angeles, CA, Feb. 5, 1942. e. U. of Oregon, B.A., 1964. After coll. worked at father's decorating firm for 4 years while writing scripts in evening. Sold 1st script for Adam 12, 1966. Asked to serve as head writer at Universal Studios. Chief exec. officer, Stephen J. Cannell Prods. TV prod. co. he formed 1979. Also formed The Cannell Studios, parent co. 1986. Natl. chmn., Orton Dyslexia Society. Received Mystery Writers award 1975; 4 Writers Guild Awards. Acted in films: Identity Crisis, Posse.
TELEVISION: Created or co-created over 20 series, has written more than 200 episodes and prod. or exec. prod. over 500 episodes. The Rockford Files (creator, writer, prod.; Emmy Award), The Jordan Chance, The Duke, Stone, 10 Speed and Brownshoe, Nightside, Midnight Offerings, The Greatest American Hero, The Quest, Prod.: The A-Team, Hardcastle and McCormick, The Rousters, Riptide, Brothers-in-Law, Creator, prod.: Baa, Baa Black Sheep, Richie Brockelman, Hunter, Wise Guy, 21 Jump Street, J.J. Starbuck, Sonny Spoon, Sirens (co-exec. prod.), Unsub (exec. prod., writer, pilot), Booker (exec. prod.), Top of the Hill (exec. prod.), Scene of the Crime (exec.-prod., creator), The Commish, The Hat Squad.

CANNON, DYAN: Actress. r.n. Samille Diane Friesen. b. Tacoma, WA, Jan. 4, 1937. e. U. of Washington. Studied with Sanford Meisner. Modelled. Directed, produced and wrote short film Number One (Acad. Award nom.).
TELEVISION: Mini-Series: Master of the Game. Movies: The Virginia Hill Story, Lady of the House, Having It All, Arthur the King, Jenny's War, Rock 'n' Roll Mom, Jailbirds, Christmas in Connecticut. Guest: Playhouse 90.
BROADWAY: The Fun Couple, Ninety-Day Mistress.
ROAD TOUR: How to Succeed in Business Without Really Trying.
PICTURES: The Rise and Fall of Legs Diamond (debut, 1960), This Rebel Breed, Bob & Carol & Ted & Alice (Acad. Award nom.), Doctors' Wives, The Anderson Tapes, The Love Machine, The Burglars, Such Good Friends, Shamus, The Last of Sheila, Child Under a Leaf, Heaven Can Wait (Acad. Award nom.), Revenge of the Pink Panther, Honeysuckle Rose, Coast To Coast, Deathtrap, Author Author, Caddyshack II, The End of Innocence (also dir., prod., s.p.), The Pickle.

CANNON, WILLIAM: Writer, Producer, Director. b. Toledo, OH, Feb. 11, 1937. e. Columbia Coll., B.A., 1959, M.B.A., 1962. Dir. Off-Broadway, Death of a Salesman, Pirates of Penzance, 1960. Wrote, prod., dir., Square Root of Zero, Locarno and San Francisco Film Festivals, 1963–65; Distrib., Doran Enterprises, Ltd.; author, Skidoo, (Par-Otto Preminger), 1968, Brewster McCloud, HEX, Knots Landing, Heaven on Earth, Author, Novel, The Veteran, 1974; Publisher, Highlife and Movie Digest, 1978; The Good Guys, 1987. Co-inventor: Cardz (TM), 1988.

CANOVA, DIANA: Actress. b. West Palm Beach, FL, June 1, 1952. Daughter of actress Judy Canova and musician Filberto Rivero. NY theater: They're Playing Our Song (1981). People's Choice award, favorite female performer, 1981.
PICTURE: The First Nudie Musical.
TELEVISION: Series: Dinah and Her New Best Friends, Soap, I'm a Big Girl Now, Foot in the Door, Throb, Home Free. Guest: Ozzie's Girls (debut), Happy Days, Love Boat, Fantasy Island, Hotel, Chico and the Man, Barney Miller, Murder She Wrote. Movies: The Love Boat II, With This Ring, Death of Ocean View Park, Night Partners.

CANTON, ARTHUR H.: Motion Picture Producer. b. New York, NY. e. N.Y.U, Columbia U. Capt. USAF. Pres., Canton-Weiner Films, indep. foreign films importers, 1947; Van Gogh (Acad. Award, short, 1949); MGM Pictures, eastern div. publicity mgr., executive liaison, advertising-publicity, Independent Productions; public relations executive, v.p.; pres., Blowitz, Thomas & Canton Inc., 1964; pres., Arthur H. Canton Co. Inc.; prod. exec., Warner Bros., 1968–70; advertising-publicity v.p., Columbia Pictures, 1971; exec. v.p. of advertising and publicity, Billy Jack Productions, 1974–76. Co-founder of Blowitz & Canton Co. Inc., 1976, chmn of bd. Now pres. of Arthur H. Canton Co. Member Academy of Motion Picture Arts and Sciences, Film Information Council.

CANTON, MARK: Executive. b. New York, NY, June 19, 1949. e. UCLA, 1978. v.p., m.p. dev., MGM; 1979, exec. v.p., JP Organization; 1980, v.p. prod., Warner Bros.; named sr. v.p., 1983 and pres. worldwide theatrical prod. div., 1985, v.p. worldwide m.p. production, 1989, appointed pres. of Columbia Pictures, 1991.

CAPRA, FRANK, JR: Executive. Son of famed director Frank Capra. Served in various creative capacities on TV series (Zane Grey Theatre, Gunsmoke, The Rifleman, etc.). Associate producer on theatrical films (Planet of the Apes, Play It Again Sam, Marooned, etc.). Joined Avco Embassy Pictures, 1981, as v.p., worldwide production. In July, 1981, became pres. of A-E. Resigned May, 1982 to become indep. producer. Now with Pinehurst Industry Studios, NC.
PICTURES: Producer: Born Again, The Black Marble, An Eye for an Eye, Vice Squad, Firestarter, Marie, Geronimo. Exec. prod.: Death Before Dishonor.

CAPSHAW, KATE: Actress. b. Ft. Worth, TX, 1953. r.n. Kathleen Sue Nail. e. U. of Missouri. m. director Steven Spielberg. Taught school before moving to New York to try acting. Success came on TV before theatrical debut in A Little Sex, 1982.
PICTURES: A Little Sex, Indiana Jones and the Temple of Doom, Best Defense, Dreamscape, Windy City, Power, SpaceCamp, Black Rain, Love at Large, My Heroes Have Always Been Cowboys.
TELEVISION: Series: The Edge of Night, Black Tie Affair. Movies: Missing Children: A Mother's Story, The Quick and the Dead, Her Secret Life, Internal Affairs.

CARA, IRENE: Singer, Actress. b. New York, NY, March 18, 1959. Off-Broadway shows include The Me Nobody Knows, Lotta. On Broadway in Maggie Flynn, Ain't Misbehavin', Via Galactica. Received Academy Award for co-writing theme song from Flashdance, 1983.
PICTURES: Aaron Loves Angela, Sparkle, Fame, D.C. Cab, City Heat, Certain Fury, Killing 'em Softly, Paradiso, Maximum Security, Happily Ever After (voice).
TELEVISION: Series: Love of Life, The Electric Company. Mini-Series: Roots—The Next Generation. Movies: Guyana Tragedy, Sister Sister, For Us the Living. Special: Tribute to Martin Luther King, Jr.

CARDIFF, JACK: Cinematographer, Director. b. Yarmouth, Eng., Sept. 18, 1914. Early career as child actor, later cinematographer on Stairway to Heaven, Black Narcissus, The Red Shoes, Scott of the Antarctic, Black Rose, Under Capricorn, Pandora and the Flying Dutchman, The African Queen, Magic Box, The Brave One, War and Peace, The Vikings, Ride A Wild Pony, The Prince and The Pauper, Behind the Iron Mask, Death on the Nile, Avalanche Express, The Fifth Musketeer, A Man, a Woman and a Bank; The Awakening, The Dogs of War, Ghost Story, The Wicked Lady, Scandalous, Conan the Destroyer, Cat's Eye, Rambo: First Blood II, Blue Velvet, Tai-Pan, Million Dollar Mystery; directorial debut 1958.
PICTURES: as director: Intent to Kill, Beyond This Place, Scent of Mystery, Sons and Lovers, Fanny, My Geisha, The Lion, The Long Ships, Young Cassidy, The Liquidator, Dark of the Sun, The Girl on the Motorcycle, Penny Gold, The Mutations, Wild Pony.
TELEVISION: As cinematographer: The Far Pavillions, The Last Days of Pompeii.

CARDINALE, CLAUDIA: Actress. b. Tunis, No. Africa, April 15, 1939.
PICTURES: Persons Unknown, 1958; Upstairs and Downstairs, Il Bell' Antonio, Rocco and His Brothers, Cartouche, The Leopard, 8½, The Pink Panther, Circus World, Time of Indifference, The Magnificent Cuckold, Sandra, Blindfold, Last Command, The Professionals, Don't Make Waves, The Queens, Day of the Owl, The Hell With Heroes, Once Upon a Time in the West, A Fine Pair, The Red Tent, Conversation Piece, Escape to Athena, The Salamander, French Bachelor, History, The French Revolution, Hiver '54, L'abbe Pierre, Mother, 588 Rue Paradis.
TELEVISION: Princess Daisy, Jesus of Nazareth.

CAREY, HARRY JR.: Actor. b. Saugus, CA, May 16, 1921. e. Newhall, CA, public school, Black Fox Military Acad., Hollywood. m. Marilyn Fix. Appeared in Railroads on Parade at 1939–40 NY World's Fair. Summer stock, Skowhegan, ME., with father; page boy, NBC, New York; U.S. Navy 1941–46.
PICTURES: Pursued (debut, 1948), Red River, Three Godfathers, She Wore a Yellow Ribbon, Wagonmaster, Rio Grande, Copper Canyon, Warpath, Wild Blue Yonder, Monkey Business, San Antone, Island in the Sky, Gentlemen Prefer Blondes, Beneath the 12-Mile Reef, Silver Lode, The Outcast, Long Gray Line, Mister Roberts, House of Bamboo, Great Locomotive Chase, The Searchers, The River's Edge, Rio Bravo, The Great Imposter, Two Rode Together, Alvarez Kelly, Bandolero, The Undefeated, Dirty Dingus Magee, Big Jake, Something Big, One More Train To Rob, Cahill: U.S. Marshall, Take a Hard Ride, Nickelodeon, The Long Riders, Endangered Species, Mask, Crossroads, The Whales of August, Cherry 2000, Illegally Yours, Breaking In, Bad Jim, Back to the Future Part III, Exorcist III.
TELEVISION: Movies: Black Beauty, The Shadow Riders, Wild Times, Once Upon a Texas Train. Guest: Gunsmoke, Rifleman, Laramie, Wagon Train, Have Gun Will Travel.

CAREY, MACDONALD: Actor. b. Sioux City, IA, March 15, 1913. e. Phillips Exeter Acad., U. of Wisconsin, U. of Iowa. On stage (stock); in radio serials. On Broadway in Anniversary Waltz; m.p. debut in 1942.
PICTURES: Dr. Broadway, Take a Letter Darling, Wake Island, Suddenly It's Spring, Variety Girl, Dream Girl, Hazzard, Streets of Laredo, Song of Surrender, South Sea Sinner, Copper Canyon, Great Missouri Raid, Mystery Submarine, Excuse My Dust, Meet Me After the Show, Let's Make It Legal, Cave of the Outlaws, My Wife's Best Friend, Count the Hours, Outlaw Territory, Fire Over Africa, Stranger At My Door, Tammy and the Doctor, Broken Sabre, End of the World, American Gigolo, It's Alive III.
TELEVISION: Series: Days of our Lives (since 1965). Mini-Series: Roots. Movies: Miracle on 34th Street, The Rebels, A Message from Holly.

CAREY, PHIL: Actor. b. Hackensack, NJ, July 15, 1925. e. Mohawk U., U. of Miami. U.S. Marines; New England stock; m.p. debut in Operation Pacific. TV: Laredo.
PICTURES: Inside the Walls of Folsom Prison, This Woman Is Dangerous, Springfield Rifle, Calamity Jane, Gun Fury, The Nebraskan, Massacre Canyon, Outlaw Stallion, They Rode West, Pushover, The Long Gray Line, Wyoming Renegades, Mister Roberts, Count Three and Pray, Three Stripes in the Sun, The Time Traveler, Once You Kiss a Stranger, Three Guns for Texas, The Seven Minutes.
TELEVISION: Series: Tales of the 77th Bengal Lancers, Philip Marlowe, Laredo, Untamed World (narrator). Movie: Scream of the Wolf.

CARIOU, LEN: Actor. b. St. Boniface, Manitoba, Canada, Sept. 30, 1939. e. St. Paul's Col.
THEATRE: NY stage: House of Atreus, Henry V, Applause (Theatre World Award), Night Watch, A Sorrow Beyond Dreams, Up from Paradise, A Little Night Music, Cold Storage, Sweeney Todd—The Demon Barber of Fleet Street (Tony Award), Master Class, Dance a Little Closer, Teddy & Alice, Measure for Measure, Mountain, The Speed of Darkness.
TELEVISION: Movies: Who'll Save Our Children?, Madame X, Surviving, Miracle on Interstate 880, Class of '61, The Sea Wolf. Specials: The Master Builder, Juno and the Paycock, Kurt Vonnegut's Monkey House (All the King's Men).
PICTURES: A Little Night Music, One Man, The Four Seasons, Lady in White.

CARISCH, GEORGE: Exhibitor. b. Minneapolis, MN, Dec. 12, 1935. e. Hamline U., B.S.; U. of Minnesota, B.E.E. Chmn., Carisch Theatres, Inc.

CARLIN, GEORGE: Actor, Comedian. b. New York, NY, May 12, 1937. Stand-up comedian and recording artist; received 1972 Grammy Award for Best Comedy Album: FM & AM. Has released 15 comedy albums between 1960–90. Has guested on many TV shows including Talent Scouts, On Broadway Tonight, Merv Griffin Show, Saturday Night Live. Author: Sometimes a Little Brain Damage Can Help (1984).
TELEVISION: Series: Kraft Summer Music Hall, That Girl, Away We Go, Tony Orlando and Dawn, Shining Time Station. Movies: Justin Case, Working Trash. Appeared in 8 HBO comedy specials.
PICTURES: With Six You Get Eggroll, Car Wash, Americathon (narrator), Outrageous Fortune, Bill & Ted's Excellent Adventure, Bill and Ted's Bogus Journey, Prince of Tides.

CARLINO, LEWIS JOHN: Writer, Director. b. New York, NY, Jan. 1, 1932. e. U. of Southern California. Early interest in theatre, specializing in writing 1-act plays. Winner of Obie award (off-Broadway play). Won Rockefeller Grant for Theatre, the Int'l. Playwriting Competition from British Drama League, Huntington Hartford Fellowship.
PICTURES: Writer: Seconds, The Brotherhood, The Fox (co-s.p.), A Reflection of Fear, The Mechanic (also prod.), Crazy Joe, The Sailor Who Fell From Grace With the Sea, (also dir.), I Never Promised You a Rose Garden (co-s.p.), The Great Santini (also dir.), Resurrection (s.p.), Class (dir. only), Haunted Summer.
PLAYS: Cages, Telemachus Clay, The Exercise, Double Talk, Objective Case, Used Car for Sale, Junk Yard.
TELEVISION: Honor Thy Father, In Search of America, Where Have All the People Gone?

CARLTON, RICHARD: Executive. b. New York, NY, Feb. 9, 1919. e. Columbia U., Pace Inst. Columbia Pictures 1935–41; U.S. Army 1941–45; National Screen Serv. 1945–51; Sterling Television 1951–54; U.M. & M. TV Corp. 1955; v.p. in charge of sales, Trans-Lux Television Corp., 1956; exec. v.p., Television Affiliates Corp., 1961; exec. v.p. Trans-Lux Television Corp.; v.p. Entertainment Div. Trans-Lux Corp., 1966. Pres., Schnur Appel, TV, Inc. 1970; Deputy Director, American Film Institute, 1973. Pres., Carlton Communications Corporation, 1982; exec. dir., International Council, National Academy of Television Arts and Sciences, 1983.

CARMICHAEL, IAN: Actor. b. Hull, England, June 18, 1920. e. Scarborough Coll., Bromsgrove Sch. Stage debut: R.U.R. 1939. Bdwy debut: Boeing-Boeing (1965). One of the top ten British money making stars Motion Picture Herald—Fame Poll 1957, 1958.
TELEVISION: New Faces, Twice Upon a Time, Passing Show, Tell Her The Truth, Lady Luck, Give My Regards to Leicester Square, Jill Darling, Don't Look Now, Regency Room, Globe Revue, Off the Record, Here and Now, The Girl at the Next Table, Gilt and Gingerbread, The Importance of Being Earnest, Simon and Laura, 90 Years On, The World of Wooster (series), The Last of the Big Spenders, The Coward Revue, Odd Man In, Bachelor Father (series), Lord Peter Wimsey (series), Alma Mater, Comedy Tonight, Song by Song, Country Calendar, Down at the Hydro, Obituaries, Strathblair.
PICTURES: Bond Street, Trottie True, Mr. Prohack, Time Gentlemen Please, Meet Mr. Lucifer, Betrayed, Colditz Story, Storm Over the Nile, Simon and Laura, Private's Progress, Brothers in Law, Lucky Jim, Happy Is the Bride, The Big Money, Right Left and Center, I'm Alright Jack, School for Scoundrels, Light Up the Sky, Double Bunk, The Amorous Prawn, Hide and Seek, Heavens Above, The Case of the 44's, Smashing Time, The Magnificent Seven Deadly Sins, From Beyond the Grave, The Lady Vanishes, Dark Obsession (Diamond Skulls).

CARNEY, ART: Performer. b. Mt. Vernon, NY, Nov. 4, 1918. Many radio shows. U.S. Army, 1944–45; played Ed Norton on Jackie Gleason's Honeymooners.
TELEVISION: Series: The Morey Amsterdam Show, Cavalcade of Stars, Henry Morgan's Great Talent Hunt, The Jackie Gleason Show (1951–55; 2 Emmy Awards), The Honeymooners (Emmy Award, 1955), The Jackie Gleason Show (1956–57), The Jackie Gleason Show (1966–70; 2 Emmy Awards), Lanigan's Rabbi. Guest: Studio One, Kraft Theatre, Playhouse 90, Alfred Hitchcock Presents (Safety for the Witness), Sid Caesar Show, Twilight Zone (Night of the Meek), Bob Hope Chrysler Theater (Timothy Heist), Danny Kaye Show, Men From Shiloh, Batman, Carol Burnett Show, Jonathan, Winters Show, Faerie Tale Theatre (The Emperor's New Clothes). Specials: Peter and the Wolf, Harvey, Our Town, Charley's Aunt, Art Carney Meets the Sorcerer's Apprentice, Very Important People, Jane Powell Special: Young at Heart, Man in the Dog Suit, The Great Santa Claus Switch. Movies: The Snoop Sisters, Death Scream, Katherine, Letters From Frank, Terrible Joe Moran (Emmy Award, 1984), The Night They Saved Christmas, A Doctor's Story, Izzy and Moe, Blue Yonder, Where Pigeons Go to Die.
PICTURES: Pot o'Gold (debut, 1941), The Yellow Rolls Royce, A Guide for the Married Man, Harry and Tonto (Acad. Award, Best Actor, 1974), W. W. and the Dixie Dancekings, Won Ton Ton the Dog Who Saved Hollywood, The Late Show, Scott Joplin, House Calls, Movie Movie, Ravagers, Sunburn, Going in Style, Defiance, Roadie, Steel, St. Helens, Take This Job and Shove It, Better Late Than Never, Firestarter, The Naked Face, The Muppets Take Manhattan, Night Friend, Last Action Hero.
STAGE: The Rope Dancers. Broadway: Take Her She's Mine, The Odd Couple, Lovers, The Prisoner of Second Avenue.

CARNEY, FRED: Producer, Director. b. Brooklyn, NY, June 10, 1914. e. Mt. Vernon H.S., 1932. Actor on Broadway & summer stock; prod. mgr. for radio show, Truth or Consequences; asst. to prod.-dir of Kraft TV Theatre, 3 yrs.; dir., Kraft, Pond's Show; creator-prod., Medical Horizons; dir., Lux Video Theatre; prod. commercials at Cunningham & Walsh. Assoc. Prod. Everybody's Talking for ABC-TV. Ass't. Exec. Dir., Hollywood Chpt., Nat'l Acad. TV; Assoc. prod. 40th Acad. Award show, ABC-TV Arts & Sciences.

CARON, LESLIE: Actress, Dancer. b. Paris, France, July 1, 1931. e. Convent of Assumption, Paris; Nat'l Conservatory of Dance, Paris 1947–50; Ballet de Paris 1954; joined Ballet des Champs Elysees. Stage: Orvet, Gigi (London).
THEATER: Orvet, Ondine, 13 Rue de l'Amour The Rehearsal, Women's Games, On Your Toes, One For the Tango.
PICTURES: An American in Paris (debut, 1951), The Man With a Cloak, Glory Alley, The Story of Three Loves, Lili (Acad. Award nom.; BFA Award), The Glass Slipper, Daddy Long Legs, Gaby, Gigi, The Doctor's Dilemma, The Man Who Understood Women, The Subterraneans, Austerlitz, Fanny, Guns of Darkness, Three Fables of Love, The L-Shaped Room (Acad. Award nom.; BFA Award), Father Goose, A Very Special Favor, Promise Her Anything, Is Paris Burning?, Head of the Family, The Beginners, Madron, Chandler, Purple Night, Valentino, The Man Who Loved Women, Golden Girl, Contract, Imperative, Unapproachable, Dangerous Moves, Warriors and Prisoners, Courage Mountain, Damage.
TELEVISION: Mini-Series: QB VIII, Master of the Game. Guest: Love Boat, Tales of the Unexpected, Carola, Falcon Crest. Movie: The Man Who Lived at the Ritz. Special: The Sealed Train.

CARPENTER, CARLETON: Actor. b. Bennington, VT, July 10, 1926 e. Bennington H.S., Northwestern U. (summer scholarship). Began career with magic act, clubs, camps, hospitals, New Eng.; then toured with carnival; first N.Y. stage appearance in Bright Boy. Appeared in nightclubs, radio; as magazine model. TV debut, Campus HoopLa show. Screen debut Lost Boundaries (also wrote song for film, I Wouldn't Mind). Member: SAG, AFTRA, AEA, ASCAP, Dramatists Guild, Mystery Writers of Amer. (ex.-treas., bd. mem.).
NY STAGE: Career Angel, Three To Make Ready, The Magic Touch, The Big People, Out of Dust, John Murray Anderson's Almanac, Hotel Paradiso, Box of Watercolors, A Stage Affair, Greatest Fairy Story Ever Told, Something for the Boys, Boys in the Band, Dylan, Hello Dolly!, Light Up the Sky, Murder at Rutherford House, Rocky Road, Apollo of Bellac, Sweet Adaline, Geo. White's Scandals, Life on the L.I.E. Miss Stanwyck is Still in Hiding, Good Ole Fashioned Revue, What is Turning Gilda So Grey?
PICTURES: Summer Stock, Father of the Bride, Three Little Words, Two Weeks With Love, Whistle at Eaton Falls, Fearless Fagan, Sky Full of Moon, Vengeance Valley, Up Periscope, Take the High Ground, Some of My Best Friends Are . . . , The Prowler, Simon, Byline, Cauliflower Cupids.
TELEVISION: Over 6,000 shows (live & filmed) since 1945.

CARPENTER, JOHN: Director, Writer. b. Carthage, NY, Jan. 16, 1948. e. U. of Southern California. At U.S.C. became involved in film short, Resurrection of Bronco Billy, which won Oscar as best live-action short of 1970. Also at U.S.C. began directing what ultimately became Dark Star, science fiction film that launched his career.
PICTURES: Director: Dark Star (also co-s.p., music), Assault on Precinct 13 (also s.p., music), Eyes of Laura Mars (co-s.p., co-story only), Halloween (also s.p., music), The Fog (also co-s.p., music), Escape from New York (also co-s.p., music), Halloween II (co-s.p., co-prod., co-music only), The Thing, Halloween III: Season of the Witch (co-prod., co-music only), Christine (also music), The Philadelphia Experiment (co-exec. prod. only), Starman, Black Moon Rising (co-s.p., story only), Big Trouble in Little China (also music), Prince of Darkness (also music, and as Martin Quatermass, s.p.), They Live (also music, and s.p. as Frank Armitage), Memoirs of an Invisible Man.
TELEVISION: Movies (director): Elvis, Someone is Watching Me (also writer), John Carpenter Presents Body Bags (also co-exec. prod., actor). Movies (writer): Zuma Beach, El Diablo, Blood River.

CARPENTER, ROBERT L.: Executive. b. Memphis, TN, March 20, 1927. Joined Universal Pictures in 1949 as booker in Memphis exchange; promoted to salesman there in 1952 and branch mgr. in 1958. In 1963 named Los Angeles branch mgr. In Dec. 1971 moved to New York to become asst. to general sales mgr. Named gen. sls. mgr. 1972, replacing Henry H. Martin when latter became pres. of Universal. Left in 1982 to become consultant and producer's rep. 1984, joined Cannon Releasing Corp. as east. div. mgr. Left in 1989 to become consultant and producers rep.

CARR, ALLAN: Producer, Personal Manager. b. Highland Park, IL, 1939. e. Lake Forest College, Northwestern U. First venture in show business as one of creators of Playboy Penthouse TV series in Chicago which subsequently inspired the Playboy Clubs for Hugh Hefner. Asst. to Nicholas Ray on King of Kings shot in Madrid. Became talent scout, launching Marlo Thomas in West Coast premiere of Sunday in New York. As personal manager guided careers of Ann-Margret, Peter Sellers, Tony Curtis, Marvin Hamlisch, Paul Anka, Herb Alpert and Melina Mercouri. Special marketing of The Deer Hunter, Tommy, The Natural.
PICTURES: Producer: The First Time, C.C. and Company, Survive, Grease (co-prod. and adapt.), Can't Stop the Music (co-prod. co. s.p.), Grease 2 (co-prod.), Where the Boys Are, Cloak and Dagger.

CARR, MARTIN: Producer, Director, Writer. b. New York, NY, Jan. 20, 1932. e. Williams Coll. Worked for all three networks.
TELEVISION: PBS Smithsonian World (exec. prod.). For CBS prod., wrote and dir. CBS Reports: Hunger in America, The Search for Ulysses, Gauguin in Tahiti, Five Faces of Tokyo, Dublin Through Different Eyes. For NBC prod., wrote and dir. NBC White Paper: Migrant, NBC White Paper: This Child is Rated X. Also directed drama, dance, music, opera specials and daytime serial for CBS-TV. ABC Close-Up. The Culture Thieves. PRS Global Paper: Waging Peace. ABC News 20/20; NBC, The Human Animal.
AWARDS: Winner of 5 Emmys; 3 Peabody awards; 2 DuPont Col. Journalism awards; Robert F. Kennedy award; Sidney Hillman award; Writers Guild Award.

CARRADINE, DAVID: Actor. b. Hollywood, CA, Dec. 8, 1936. e. San Francisco State U. Son of late actor John Carradine. Brother of actors Keith and Robert Carradine. Began career in local repertory; first TV on Armstrong Circle Theatre and East Side, West Side; later TV includes Shane series and

Kung Fu; N.Y. stage in The Deputy, Royal Hunt of The Sun (Theatre World Award).

PICTURES: Taggart, Bus Riley's Back in Town, Too Many Thieves, The Violent Ones, Heaven With a Gun, Young Billy Young, The Good Guys and the Bad Guys, The McMasters, Macho Callahan, Boxcar Bertha, Two Gypsies, You and Me (also dir.), A Country Mile (also prod.), Mean Streets, The Long Goodbye, Death Race 2000, Cannonball, Bound for Glory, Thunder and Lightning, The Serpent's Egg, Gray Lady Down, Deathsport, Circle of Iron, Fast Charlie: The Moon-beam Rider, The Long Riders, Cloud Dancer, Americana (also dir., prod.), Q, Trick or Treats, Safari 3000, Lone Wolf McQuade, Warrior and the Sorceress, On the Line, P.O.W. The Escape, Armed Response, The Misfit Brigade, Open Fire, Animal Protector, Warlords, Crime Zone, Night Children, Wizards of the Lost Kingdom 2, Sundown: The Vampire in Retreat, Nowhere to Run, Tropical Snow, Future Force, Think Big, Bird on a Wire, Sonny Boy, Project Eliminator, Evil Toons, Crime of Crimes, Dune Warriors, Try This One on For Size, Animal Instincts, Capital Punishment, First Force, Roadside Prophets, Double Trouble, Distant Justice, Waxworks II, Midnight Fear, Night Rhythms.

TELEVISION: Movies: Maybe I'll Come Home in the Spring, Kung Fu (1972 pilot), Mr. Horn, Gaugin the Savage, High Noon Part II, Jealousy, The Bad Seed, Kung Fu: The Movie, Oceans of Fire, Six Against the Rock, The Cover Girl & the Cop, I Saw What You Did, Brotherhood of the Gun, The Gambler Returns: Luck of the Draw. Mini-series: North & South Book II. Series: Shane, Kung Fu, Kung Fu: The Legend Continues. Guest: Darkroom, Amazing Stories.

CARRADINE, KEITH: Actor. b. San Mateo, CA, Aug. 8, 1949. e. Colorado State U. Father of actress Martha Plimpton. Son of late actor John Carradine, brother of David and Robert. First break in rock opera Hair. Composer: song I'm Easy from Nashville (Academy Award Best Song, 1975), music for Welcome to L.A. Theater: Wake Up It's Time to Go to Bed, Foxfire, Will Rogers Follies.

PICTURES: A Gunfight (debut, 1971), McCabe and Mrs. Miller, Hex, Emperor of the North Pole, Thieves Like Us, Antoine et Sebastien, Run Joe Run, Idaho Transfer, Nash-ville, You and Me, Lumiere, Welcome to L.A., The Duellists, Pretty Baby, Sgt. Pepper's Lonely Heart Club Band, Old Boyfriends, An Almost Perfect Affair, The Long Riders, Southern Comfort, Choose Me, Maria's Lovers, Trouble in Mind, The Inquiry, Backfire, The Moderns, Street of No Return, Cold Feet, Daddy's Dyin' . . . Who's Got the Will?, The Ballad of the Sad Cafe, Crisscross, The Bachelor.

TELEVISION: Movies: Man on a String, Kung Fu, The Godchild, A Rumor of War, Scorned and Swindled, A Winner Never Quits, Murder Ordained, Eye on the Sparrow, Blackout, Stones for Ibarra, My Father My Son, The Revenge of Al Capone, Judgment, Payoff. Mini-Series: Chiefs. Guest: Bo-nanza, Love American Style

CARRADINE, ROBERT: Actor. b. Hollywood, CA, March 24, 1954. Son of late actor John Carradine; brother of Keith and David Carradine.

PICTURES: The Cowboys (debut, 1972), Mean Streets, Aloha Bobby and Rose, Jackson County Jail, The Pom Pom Girls, Cannonball, Massacre at Central High, Joyride, Orca, Blackout, Coming Home, The Long Riders, The Big Red One, Heartaches, Wavelength, Revenge of the Nerds, Just the Way You Are, Number One with a Bullet, Revenge of the Nerds II, Buy and Cell, All's Fair, Rude Awakening, The Player.

TELEVISION: Series: The Cowboys. Movies: Footsteps, Rolling Man, Go Ask Alice, The Hatfields and the McCoys, The Survival of Dana, The Sun Also Rises, Monte Carlo, The Liberators, I Saw What You Did, The Incident, Clarence, Doublecrossed, Revenge of the Nerds III: The Next Genera-tion, Body Bags. Guest: Alfred Hitchcock Presents (1985), The Hitchhiker, Twilight Zone (1986). Specials: Disney's Totally Minnie, As Is.

CARRERA, BARBARA: Actress. b. Nicaragua, Dec. 31, 1951. Fashion model before film career.

PICTURES: Puzzle of a Downfall Child (debut, 1970), The Master Gunfighter, Embryo, The Island of Dr. Moreau, When Time Ran Out, Condorman, I the Jury, Lone Wolf McQuade, Never Say Never Again, Wild Geese II, The Underachievers, Love at Stake, Wicked Stepmother, Loverboy, Spanish Rose.

TELEVISION: Mini-Series: Centennial, Masada, Emma: Queen of the South Seas. Movies: Dallas. Movies: Sins of the Past, Murder in Paradise, Lakota Moon.

CARROLL, DIAHANN: Actress, Singer. b. New York, NY, July 17, 1935. r.n. Carol Diahann Johnson. m. singer Vic Damone. On Broadway in House of Flowers, No Strings (Tony Award, 1962), Agnes of God.

PICTURES: Carmen Jones (debut, 1954), Porgy and Bess, Goodbye Again, Paris Blues, Hurry Sundown, The Split, Claudine (Acad. Award nom.), The Five Heartbeats.

TELEVISION: Series: Julia, The Diahann Carroll Show, Dynasty. Movies: Death Scream, I Know Why the Caged Bird

Sings, Sister Sister, From the Dead of Night, Murder in Black and White. Mini-Series: Roots: The Next Generations; many specials; guest appearances incl. Andy Williams, Judy Gar-land, Dean Martin Shows.

CARROLL, GORDON: Producer. b. Baltimore, MD, Feb. 2, 1928. e. Princeton U. Advtg. exec., Foote, Cone & Belding, 1954–58; Ent. industry, Seven Arts Prods., 1958–61; v.p. staff prod., Jalem Prods., 1966–1969; independent producer to present.

PICTURES: How to Murder Your Wife, Luv, Cool Hand Luke, The April Fools, Pat Garrett and Billy the Kid, Alien, Blue Thunder, The Best of Times, Aliens, Red Heat.

CARROLL, PAT: Performer. b. Shreveport, LA, May 5, 1927. e. Immaculate Heart Coll., L.A, Catholic U., Washington, DC. Joined U.S. Army in capacity of Civilian Actress Technician. Night club entertainer in N.Y., 1950.

TELEVISION: Series: Red Buttons Show, Saturday Night Revue, Caesar's Hour, (Emmy, 1957), Masquerade Party (panelist), Keep Talking, You're in the Picture (panelist), Danny Thomas Show, Getting Together, Busting Loose, The Ted Knight Show, She's the Sheriff. Specials: Cinderella, Gertrude Stein. Guest: George Gobel Show, Jimmy Durante Show, many others. Movie: Second Chance.

STAGE: Catch a Star (debut, 1955), Gertrude Stein Ger-trude Stein (Drama Desk, Outer Critics Circle, Grammy Awards), Dancing in the End Zone, The Show Off. Shake-speare Theatre at the Folger: Romeo and Juliet (Helen Hayes Award), The Merry Wives of Windsors, A Quarrel of Spar-rows.

PICTURES: With Six You Get Eggroll, The Brothers O'Toole, The Last Resort, The Little Mermaid (voice).

CARSON, JEANNIE: Actress. b. Yorkshire, England, 1928. Amer. Citizen, 1966. In musicals Ace of Clubs, Love from Judy, Starlight Roof, Casino Reviews, Aladdin; Ent. motion pictures in 1954 in As Long as They're Happy, Alligator Named Daisy, Mad Little Island. 1979: founded Hyde Park Festival Theatre with husband William Biff McGuire. Has taught a musical drama class at U. of Washington. Awards: TV Radio Mirror, 1st Recipient of the Variety Club Theatre Award in England.

THEATER: U.S.: The Sound of Music, Blood Red Roses, Finian's Rainbow (revival). Tours of Camelot, 110 in the Shade, Cactus Flower, many others. Also extensive work with the Seattle Repertory Theatre as actress, and dir. with Seattle Bathhouse Theatre.

TELEVISION: Best Foot Forward, Little Women, Berkeley Square, The Rivals, Frank Sinatra Show, Heidi, What Every Woman Knows, Jimmy Durante Show, Pat Boone Show, A Kiss for Cinderella. Series: Hey Jeannie, Jeannie Carson Show.

PICTURES: A Date with a Dream, Love in Pawn, As Long as They're Happy, An Alligator Named Daisy, Mad Little Island, Seven Keys.

CARSON, JOHNNY: Comedian. b. Corning, IA, Oct. 23, 1925. e. U. of Nebraska, B.A. 1949. U.S. Navy service during WWII; announcer with station KFAB, Lincoln, Neb.; WOW radio-TV, Omaha, 1948; announcer, KNXT, Los Angeles, 1950; then program, Carson's Cellar (1951); quiz-master, Earn Your Vacation, 1954; head writer for Red Skelton Show; star of Johnny Carson Show, CBS-TV; Who Do You Trust, ABC-TV; The Tonight Show Starring Johnny Carson, NBC-TV (1962–92; 4 Emmy Awards). President Carson Productions. Author: Happiness is a Dry Martini (1965). Movies: Looking for Love, Cancel My Reservation.

CARTER, DIXIE: Actress. b. McLemoresville, TN, May 25, 1939. m. actor Hal Holbrook. e. U. of Tennessee, Knoxville, Rhodes Coll.; Memphis, Memphis State U. Off-Bdwy debut, A Win-ter's Tale with NY Shakespeare Fest (1963). London debut, Buried Inside Extra (1983). Lincoln Center musicals: The King & I, Carousel, The Merry Widow.

THEATER: Pal Joey (1976 revival), Jesse and the Bandit Queen (Theatre World Award), Fathers and Sons, Taken in Marriage, A Coupla White Chicks Sitting Around Talking, Buried Inside Extra, Sextet, Pal Joey.

PICTURE: Going Berserk.

TELEVISION: Series: The Edge of Night, On Our Own, Out of the Blue, Filthy Rich, Diff'rent Strokes, Designing Women. Movies: OHMS, The Killing of Randy Webster.

CARTER, JACK: Actor, r.n. Jack Chakrin. b. New York, NY, June 24, 1923. e. New Utrecht H.S., Brooklyn Coll., Feagin Sch. of Dramatic Arts. Worked as comm. artist for adv. agencies. Debut Bdwy. in Call Me Mister, 1947; starred in TV Jack Carter Show. Hosted first televised Tony Awards. Seen on most major variety, dram. programs, incl. Ed Sullivan Show. Emmy nom. 1962 for Dr. Kildare seg. Played most major nightclubs. On Broadway in Top Banana, Mr. Wonderful, Dir. several Lucy Shows. TV incl. specials, HA Comedy Special, Top Banana, Girl Who Couldn't Lose.

TELEVISION: Series: American Minstrels of 1949, Caval-cade of Stars, The Jack Carter Show. Movies: The Lonely Profession, The Family Rico, The Sex Symbol, The Great

Houdinis, The Last Hurrah, Human Feelings, Rainbow, The Gossip Columnist, The Hustler of Muscle Beach, For the Love of It. Guest: Blossom, Empty Nest, Nurses, Murder She Wrote.

PICTURES: The Horizontal Lieutenant, Viva Las Vegas, The Extraordinary Seaman, The Resurrection of Zachary Wheeler, Red Nights, Hustle, The Amazing Dobermans, Alligator, The Octagon, History of the World Part 1, Heartbeeps (voice), The Arena, Deadly Embrace, In the Heat of Passion, Social Suicide, The Opposite Sex, W.A.R.

CARTER, LYNDA: Actress. b. Phoenix, AZ, July 24. r.n. Lynda Jean Cordoba. Wrote songs and sang professionally in Ariz. from age of 15; later toured 4 yrs. with rock 'n roll band. Won beauty contests in Ariz. and became Miss World-USA 1973. Dramatic training with Milton Katselas, Greta Seacat, and Sandra Seacat.

TELEVISION: Series: Wonder Woman (3 yrs.). Specials: The New Original Wonder Woman Specials; 5 variety specials. Movies: The New Original Wonder Woman, A Matter of Wife . . . and Death, Baby Brokers, Last Song, Hotline, Rita Hayworth: The Love Goddess, Stillwatch (also exec. prod.), Mickey Spillane's Mike Hammer, Murder Takes All, Danielle Steel's Daddy, Posing: Inspired By 3 Real Stories.

PICTURE: Lightning in a Bottle.

CARTER, NELL: Actress. b. Birmingham, AL. Sept. 13, 1948.

THEATER: Hair, Dude, Don't Bother Me I Can't Cope, Jesus Christ Superstar, Ain't Misbehavin' (Tony & Theatre World Awards, 1978), Ain't Misbehaving (1988 revival), Hello Dolly! (L.A.).

TELEVISION: Series: Lobo, Gimme a Break, You Take the Kids, Hangin' With Mr. Cooper. Specials: Baryshnikov on Broadway, The Big Show, An NBC Family Christmas, Ain't Misbehavin' (Emmy Award), Christmas in Washington, Nell Carter, Never Too Old To Dream, Morton's By the Bay (pilot). Movies: Cindy, Maid for Each Other, Final Shot: The Hank Gathers Story.

PICTURES: Hair, Quartet, Back Roads, Modern Problems, Bebe's Kids (voice).

CARTLIDGE, WILLIAM: Director, Producer. b. England. b. June 16, 1942. e. Highgate Sch. Ent. m.p. ind. 1959. Early career in stills dept., Elstree Studio. Later worked as an asst. dir. on The Young Ones, Summer Holiday, The Punch & Judy Man, The Naked Edge. As 1st asst. dir., pictures included Born Free, Alfie, You Only Live Twice, The Adventurers, Young Winston, Friends. As assoc. prod., Paul and Michelle, Seven Nights in Japan, The Spy Who Loved Me, Moonraker. Prod.: Educating Rita, Not Quite Paradise, Consuming Passions, Dealers, The Playboys.

CARTWRIGHT, VERONICA: Actress. b. Bristol, Eng., 1949. m. writer-dir. Richard Compton. Sister is actress Angela Cartwright. Began career as child actress on TV series Daniel Boone, 1964–1966. Stage: The Hands of Its Enemies (Mark Taper Forum, LA 1984), The Triplet Connection (off-Bdwy).

PICTURES: In Love and War (debut, 1958), The Children's Hour, The Birds, Spencer's Mountain, One Man's Way, Inserts, Goin' South, Invasion of the Body Snatchers, Alien, Nightmares, The Right Stuff, My Man Adam, Flight of the Navigator, Wisdom, The Witches of Eastwick, Valentino Returns, False Identity, Man Trouble.

TELEVISION: Series: Daniel Boone. Guest: Leave It to Beaver, Twilight Zone. Mini-series: Robert Kennedy and His Times. Movies: Guyana Tragedy—The Story of Jim Jones, The Big Black Pill, Prime Suspect, Intimate Encounters, Desperate for Love, A Son's Promise, Hitler's Daughter, Dead in the Water, It's Nothing Personal. Specials: Who Has Seen the Wind?, Bernice Bobs Her Hair, Tell Me Not the Mournful Numbers (Emmy Award), Joe Dancer, Abby My Love.

CARUSO, DAVID: Actor. b. Queens, NY, Jan. 17, 1956.

PICTURES: An Officer and a Gentleman (debut, 1982), First Blood, Thief of Hearts, Blue City, China Girl, Twins, King of New York, Hudson Hawk, Mad Dog and Glory.

TELEVISION: Series: N.Y.P.D. Blue. Movies: Crazy Times, The First Olmypics - Athens 1896, Into the Homeland, Rainbow Drive, Mission of the Shark, Judgment Day: The John List Story. Guest: Crime Story.

CARVER, STEVE: Director. b. Brooklyn, NY, April 5, 1945. e. U. of Buffalo; Washington U., MFA. Directing, writing fellow, Film Inst. Center for Advanced Studies, 1970. (Writer, dir. films Patent and the Tell-Tale Heart). Florissant Valley Col., MO 1966–68. News photographer, UPI. Instructor, film and photography, Metropolitan Ed. Council in the Arts; St. Louis Mayor's Council on the Arts, Give a Damn (dir., prod.); asst. dir. Johnny Got His Gun; writer, editor with New World Pictures. Member: Sierra Club, Natl. Rifle Assn.

PICTURES: Arena, Big Bad Mama, Capone, Drum, Fast Charlie, The Moonbeam Rider, Steel, An Eye for an Eye, Lone Wolf McQuade (also prod.), Oceans of Fire, Jocks (also co-s.p.), Bulletproof (also co-s.p.), River of Death, Crazy Joe, The Wolves.

CARVEY, DANA: Actor. b. Missoula, MT, Apr. 2, 1955. e. San Francisco State Coll. As teenager created comic characters which later led to work as a stand-up comedian in local San Francisco comedy clubs. TV debut as Mickey Rooney's grandson on series, One of the Boys, 1982.

PICTURES: Halloween II, Racing With the Moon, This is Spinal Tap, Tough Guys, Moving, Opportunity Knocks, Wayne's World, Wayne's World 2, Clean Slate.

TELEVISION: Series: One of the Boys, Blue Thunder, Saturday Night Live. Special: Wayne & Garth's Saturday Night Live Music a Go-Go.

CASEY, BERNIE: Actor. b. Wyco, WV, June 8, 1939. e. Bowling Green U. Played pro-football with San Francisco 49ers and L.A. Rams.

PICTURES: Guns of the Magnificent Seven, Tick . . . Tick . . . Tick, Boxcar Bertha, Black Gunn, Hit Man, Cleopatra Jones, Maurie, Cornbread Earl and Me, Dr. Black/Mr. Hyde, Brothers, Sharky's Machine, Never Say Never Again, Revenge of the Nerds, Spies Like Us, Steele Justice, Rent-a-Cop, I'm Gonna Git You Sucka, Bill and Ted's Excellent Adventure, Another 48 HRS., Under Siege, The Cemetery Club, Street Knight.

TELEVISION: Series: Harris and Company, Bay City Blues. Movies: Brian's Song, Gargoyles, Panic on the 5:22, Mary Jane Harper Cried Last Night, It Happened at Lake Wood Manor, Ring of Passion, Love is Not Enough, Sophisticated Gents, Hear No Evil, The Fantastic World of D.C. Collins. Mini-Series: Roots—The Next Generations, The Martian Chronicles.

CASH, ROSALIND: Actress. b. Atlantic City, NJ, Dec. 31, 1938. e. CCNY. Theatre includes The Wayward Stork, Ceremonies in Dark Old Men, Fiorello!, Juneboug Graduates Tonight.

PICTURES: Klute, The Omega Man, Hickey and Boggs, The New Centurions, Melinda, Uptown Saturday Night, Amazing Grace, Cornbread Earl and Me, Dr. Black/Mr. Hyde, The Monkey Hustle, The Class of Miss MacMichael, Wrong is Right, The Adventures of Buckaroo Banzai Across the Eighth Dimension, The Offspring.

TELEVISION: Movies: A Killing Affair, Guyana Tragedy: The Story of Jim Jones, The Sophisticated Gents, Sister Sister, Special Bulletin, Go Tell It on the Mountain. Specials: Ceremonies in Dark Old Men, Angel Dust, The Joy That Kills.

CASS, PEGGY: Actress. b. Boston, MA, May 21, 1924. On Broadway in Burlesque, Bernardine, Auntie Mame (Tony & Theatre World Awards, 1957), A Thurber Carnival, Don't Drink the Water, Front Page, Plaza Suite, Last of the Red Hot Lovers, Once a Catholic, 42nd Street, The Octette Bridge Club.

PICTURES: The Marrying Kind, Auntie Mame, Gidget Goes Hawaiian, The Age of Consent, If It's Tuesday This Must Be Belgium, Paddy.

TELEVISION: Series: The Jack Paar Show, Keep Talking, The Hathaways, To Tell the Truth, The Doctors (1978–9), Women in Prison. Guest: Garry Moore Show, Barbara Stanwyck Show, Tales from the Darkside, Major Dad.

CASSEL, ALVIN I.: Executive. b. New York , NY, July 26. e. U. of Michigan, B.A., 1938. Capt. in U.S. Army European Theatre, 1941–45. Surveyed Central Africa for MGM, 1946–50, then assumed duties as asst. mgr. for MGM South Africa. Continued with MGM in West Indies, 1950–51 and Philippines, 1951–57. In 1957 joined Universal as mgr./supvr. for Southeast Asia; back to MGM in 1963 as supvr. S.E. Asia; 1967, with CBS Films as Far East supvr. In 1972 established Cassel Films to secure theatrical films for foreign distributors, principally in Far East, 1979, consultant to Toho-Towa co. of Japan and other Far East distributors.

CASSEL, JEAN-PIERRE: Actor. b. Paris, France, Oct. 27, 1932. Began as dancer, attracting attention of Gene Kelly in Left Bank nightspot, who gave him work. Appeared in plays before becoming established as leading French screen star.

PICTURES: Games of Love, The Gay Deceiver, Five Day Lover, The Vanishing Corporal, Cyrano and D'Artagnan, The Male Companion, A Woman Passed By, Is Paris Burning?, Those Magnificent Men in Their Flying Machines, The Killing Game, Oh! What a Lovely War, The Bear and The Doll, The Army of the Shadows, The Rupture, The Boat on the Grass, Baxter!, The Discreet Charm of the Bourgeoisie, The Three Musketeers, Le Mouton Enrage, Murder on the Orient Express, Who Is Killing the Great Chefs of Europe?, Chouans! Grandeson, From Hell to Victory, La Ville des Silence, The Green Jacket, Ehrengard, The Trout, Vive la Sociale! Tranches de Vie, Mangeclous, The Return of the Musketeers, Mr. Frost, Vincent & Theo, The Favor the Watch and the Very Big Fish, In Heaven As On Earth. Petain.

TELEVISION: Casanova (U.S.), The Burning Shore, Notorious, Warburg, Young Indiana Jones Chronicles.

CASSEL, SEYMOUR: Actor. b. Detroit, MI, Jan. 22, 1937. As a boy travelled with a troupe of burlesque performers including his mother. After high school appeared in summer stock in Michigan. Studied acting at American Theatre Wing and

Actor's Studio. After joining a workshop taught by John Cassavetes, began a long creative association with the director-actor. *Broadway*: The World of Suzy Wong, The Disenchanted.
PICTURES: Murder Inc., Shadows, Too Late Blues, Juke Box Racket, The Killers, The Sweet Ride, Coogan's Bluff, Faces (Acad. Award nom.), The Revolutionary, Minnie and Moskowitz, Black Oak Conspiracy, Death Game, The Killing of a Chinese Bookie, The Last Tycoon, Scott Joplin, Opening Night, Valentino, Convoy, California Dreaming, Ravagers, Sunburn, The Mountain Men, King of the Mountain, I'm Almost Not Crazy . . . John Cassavetes—The Man and His Work (doc.), Love Streams, Eye of the Tiger, Survival Game, Tin Men, Johnny Be Good, Plain Clothes, Colors, Track 29, Wicked Stepmother, Dick Tracy, White Fang, Cold Dog Soup, Mobsters, Diary of a Hitman, Honeymoon in Vegas, In the Soup, Indecent Proposal, Boiling Point, Chain of Desire, There Goes My Baby, Trouble Bound.
TELEVISION: *Movies*: The Hanged Man, Angel on My Shoulder, Blood Feud, I Want to Live, Beverly Hills Madame, Sweet Bird of Youth, My Shadow, Dead in the Water, Face of a Stranger, When Pigs Fly.

CASSIDY, DAVID: Singer, Actor. b. April 12, 1950. Son of late Jack Cassidy; brother of Shaun and Patrick.
THEATER: *Bdwy*: The Fig Leaves Are Falling (1968), Joseph and the Amazing Technicolor Dreamcoat, Blood Brothers. *London*: Time.
PICTURES: Instant Karma, The Spirit of '76.
TELEVISION: *Series*: The Partridge Family, Man Undercover. *Movie*: The Night the City Screamed. *Guest*: The Mod Squad, Bonanza, Adam-12, Ironside, Marcus Welby M.D., Police Story, The Love Boat, Alfred Hitchcock Presents, The Flash.

CASSIDY, JOANNA: Actress. b. Camden, NJ, Aug. 2, 1944. e. Syracuse U.
PICTURES: Bullitt (debut, 1968), Fools, The Laughing Policeman, The Outfit, Bank Shot, The Stepford Wives, Stay Hungry, The Late Show, Stunts, The Glove, Our Winning Season, Night Games, Blade Runner, Under Fire, Club Paradise, The Fourth Protocol, Who Framed Roger Rabbit, 1969, The Package, Where the Heart Is, Don't Tell Mom the Babysitter's Dead, All-American Murder, May Wine.
TELEVISION: *Series*: Shields and Yarnell, The Roller Girls. 240—Robert, Family Tree, Buffalo Bill, Code Name: Foxfire. *Movies*: She's Dressed to Kill, Reunion, Invitation to Hell, The Children of Times Square, Pleasures, A Father's Revenge, Nightmare at Bitter Creek, Wheels of Terror, Grass Roots, Taking Back My Life, Live! From Death Row, Perfect Family, Barbarians at the Gate, Stephen King's The Tommyknockers. *Mini-Series*: Hollywood Wives. *Special*: Roger Rabbit and the Secrets of Toontown (host). *Pilot*: Second Stage. *Guest*: Taxi, Love Boat, Hart to Hart, Charlie's Angels, Lou Grant.

CASSIDY, PATRICK: Actor. b. Los Angeles, CA, Jan. 4, 1961. Son of late actor Jack Cassidy and actress-singer Shirley Jones.
TELEVISION: *Series*: Bay City Blues, Dirty Dancing. *Movies*: Angel Dusted, Midnight Offerings, Choices of the Heart, Christmas Eve, Dress Gray, Something in Comon, Three on a Match. *Mini-Series*: Napoleon and Josephine: A Love Story. *Pilot*: The Six of Us.
PICTURES: Off the Wall, Just the Way You Are, Fever Pitch, Nickel Mountain, Love at Stake, Longtime Companion.
THEATRE: *NY*: The Pirates of Penzance, Leader of the Pack, Assassins. *Regional*: Conrack.

CASSIDY, SHAUN: Actor, Singer, Composer. b. Los Angeles, CA, Sept. 27, 1958. One of 3 sons of Shirley Jones and late Jack Cassidy. e. Beverly Hills H.S. Began recording in 1976 and toured Europe and Australia, appearing on numerous TV shows. Has had several hit records. *Bdwy*: Blood Brothers.
TELEVISION: *Series*: Hardy Boys Mysteries, Breaking Away. *Movies*: Like Normal People, Once Upon a Texas Train, Roots: The Gift, Strays (co-prod. & writer only). Numerous specials.
PICTURE: Born of Water (debut for Amer. Film Inst.).

CASTLE, NICK: Writer, Director. b. Los Angeles, CA, Sept. 21, 1947. e. Santa Monica Coll., U. of Southern California film sch. Son of late film and TV choreographer Nick Castle Sr. Appeared as child in films Anything Goes, Artists and Models. Worked with John Carpenter and other USC students on Acad. Award-winning short, The Resurrection of Bronco Billy.
PICTURES: Kiss Me Kill Me (dir.), Skatedown USA (s.p.), Tag: The Assassination Game (dir., s.p.), Escape from New York (co-s.p.), The Last Starfighter (dir.), The Boy Who Could Fly (dir., s.p.), Tap (dir., s.p.), Hook (co-story), Dennis the Menace (dir.).

CATES, GILBERT: Director, Producer. b. New York, NY, June 6, 1934. e. Syracuse U. Began TV career as guide at NBC studios in N.Y., working way up to prod. and dir. of game shows (Camouflage, Haggis Baggis, Mother's Day, etc.). Created Hootenanny and packaged and directed many TV

specials. Pres. Directors Guild of America 1983–87. Awarded DGA's Robert B. Aldrich award 1989.
PICTURES: The Painting (short), Rings Around the World, I Never Sang for My Father, Summer Wishes Winter Dreams (dir. only), One Summer Love, The Promise, The Last Married Couple in America, Oh God!—Book II, Backfire.
TELEVISION: *Specials*: International Showtime (1963–65 exec. prod.-dir.), Electric Showcase Specials (dir.-prod.) Academy Awards (prod.; Emmy Award, 1991), After the Fall (prod., dir.). *Movies*: To All My Friends on Shore (dir.-prod.), The Affair (dir.), Johnny, We Hardly Knew Ye (prod.-dir.), The Kid from Nowhere (prod.), Country Gold (dir.), Hobson's Choice (dir.), Burning Rage (dir., prod.), Consenting Adult (dir.), Fatal Judgement, My First Love (dir.), Do You Know the Muffin Man (dir.), Call Me Anna (dir., prod.), Absolute Strangers (dir., exec. prod.), In My Daughter's Name (co-exec. prod.).
STAGE: *Director*: Tricks of the Trade, Voices, The Price (Long Wharf Theatre). *Producer*: Solitaire/Double Solitaire, The Chinese and Mr. Fish, I Never Sang for My Father, You Know I Can't Hear You When the Water's Running.

CATES, JOSEPH: Producer, Director. b. 1924. e. NYU. Brother of Gilbert Cates. Father of actress Phoebe Cates. One of first producers and dirs. of live TV with Look Upon a Star, 1947. Prod., Jackie Gleason Cavalcade of Stars, game shows, ($64,000 Question, $64,000 Challenge, Stop the Music, Haggis Baggis), NBC Spectaculars (1955–60), High Button Shoes, The Bachelor, Accent on Love, Gene Kelly, Ethel Merman, Victor Borge, Yves Montand shows.
THEATER: *Prod. on B'way*: What Makes Sammy Run?, Joe Egg, Spoon River Anthology, Gantry, Her First Roman.
PICTURES: *Director*: Who Killed Teddy Bear, The Fat Spy, Girl of the Night.
TELEVISION: *Series*: International Showtime (Don Ameche Circuses). Prod.-dir. of spectaculars and special programs, 1955–1988: Johnny Cash, David Copperfield, Steve Martin; Anne Bancroft: The Woman in the Life of Man (Emmy Award), Jack Lemmon and Fred Astaire: S'Wonderful S'Marvelous S'Gershwin (Emmy Award), Annual Ford Theater Salutes to the President, Country Music Awards Show, Miss Teen Age America, Junior Miss pageants, Tony Awards 1992, International Emmies, The Ford Theatre Salute to the President, The 1993 Monte Carlo Circus Festival. *Movies*: Prod.: The Quick and the Dead, The Last Days of Frank and Jessie James, The Cradle Will Fall, Special People.

CATES, PHOEBE: Actress. b. New York, NY, July 16,1963. e. Juilliard. Daughter of prod-dir. Joseph Cates. m. actor Kevin Kline. Dance prodigy and fashion model before launching acting. NY stage debut The Nest of the Wood Grouse (1984).
PICTURES: Paradise (debut, 1982), Fast Times at Ridgemont High, Private School, Gremlins, Date With an Angel, Bright Lights Big City, Shag, Heart of Dixie, I Love You to Death (unbilled), Gremlins 2: The New Batch, Drop Dead Fred, Bodies Rest and Motion, My Life's in Turnaround.
TELEVISION: *Movies*: Baby Sister, Lace, Lace II. *Special*: Largo Desolato.

CATON-JONES, MICHAEL: Director. b. Broxburn, Scotland, 1958.
PICTURES: Scandal (debut, 1989), Memphis Belle, Doc Hollywood (also cameo), This Boy's Life.

CATTRALL, KIM: Actress. b. Liverpool, Eng., Aug. 21, 1956. e. American Acad. of Dramatic Arts, N.Y. Started stage career in Canada's Off-Bdwy. in Vancouver and Toronto; later performed in L.A. in A View from the Bridge, Agnes of God, Three Sisters, etc. On Bdwy in Wild Honey. Chicago Goodman Theatre in the Misanthrope. *Regional*: Miss Julie (Princeton).
PICTURES: Rosebud (debut 1975), The Other Side of the Mountain—Part II, Tribute, Ticket to Heaven, Porky's, Police Academy, Turk 182, City Limits, Hold-Up, Big Trouble in Little China, Mannequin, Masquerade, Midnight Crossing, Palais Royale, Honeymoon Academy, The Return of the Musketeers, Brown Bread Sandwiches, Bonfire of the Vanities, Star Trek VI: The Undiscovered Country, Split Second, Double Vision.
TELEVISION: *Movies*: Good Against Evil, The Bastard, The Night Rider, The Rebels, The Gossip Columnist, Sins of the Past, Miracle in the Wilderness, Running Delilah. *Mini-Series*: Scruples, Wild Palms.

CAULFIELD, MAXWELL: Actor. b. Glasgow, Scotland, Nov. 23, 1959. m. actress Juliet Mills. First worked as a dancer at a London nightclub. After coming to NY in 1978, ran the concession stand at the Truck and Warehouse Theatre. Won a Theatre World Award for Class Enemy.
THEATER: Entertaining Mr. Sloane, Salonika, Journey's End, Sleuth, The Elephant Man.
PICTURES: Grease 2, Electric Dreams, The Boys Next Door, The Supernaturals, Sundown: The Vampire in Retreat, Mind Games, Alien Intruder, Midnight Witness, Ipi/Tombi.
TELEVISION: *Series*: The Colbys. *Movies*: The Parade, Till We Meet Again, Blue Bayou.

CAVANAUGH, ANDREW: Executive. Held positions with Norton Simon, Inc. and Equitable Life Insurance Co. before joining Paramount Pictures in 1984 as v.p., human resources. 1985, appt. sr. v.p., administration, mng. personnel depts. on both coasts. Also oversees corp. admin. function for Paramount.

CAVANI, LILIANA: Director. b near Modena, in Emilia, Italy, January 12, 1937. e. U. of Bologna, diploma in classic literature, 1960; Ph.D. in linguistics. In 1960 took courses at Centro Sperimentale di Cinematografia in Rome where made short films Incontro Notturno and L'Evento. 1961 winner of RAI sponsored contest and started working for the new second Italian TV channel, 1962–66 directing progs. of serious political and social nature incl. History of 3rd Reich, Women in the Resistance, Age of Stalin, Philippe Petain—Trial at Vichy (Golden Lion Venice Fest.), Jesus My Brother, Day of Peace, Francis of Assisi. Has also directed operas Wozzeck, Iphigenia in Tauris and Medea on stage.
PICTURES: Galileo, I Cannibali, L'Ospite, Milarepa, Night Porter, Beyond Good and Evil, The Skin, Oltre la Porta, The Berlin Affair, Francesco.

CAVETT, DICK: Actor, Writer. b. Kearny, NE, Nov. 19, 1937. e. Yale U. Acted in TV dramas and Army training films. Was writer for Jack Paar and his successors on the Tonight Show. Also wrote comedy for Merv Griffin, Jerry Lewis, Johnny Carson. In 1967 began performing own comedy material in night clubs. On TV starred in Where It's At (special on ABC Stage 67) and What's In (special). Began daytime series for ABC-TV in 1968, three-weekly series summer of 1969. The Dick Cavett Show. 1989: The Dick Cavett Show (CNBC). Author: Cavett (with Christopher Porter) 1974.
THEATRE: Otherwise Engaged, Into the Woods.
PICTURES: Annie Hall, Power Play, Health, Simon, A Nightmare on Elm Street 3, Beetlejuice, Moon Over Parador, After School, Funny, Year of the Gun.

CAZENOVE, CHRISTOPHER: Actor. b. Winchester, Eng., Dec. 17, 1945. m. Angharad Rees. e. Eton, Oxford U., trained at Bristol Old Vic Theatre School. West End theater includes Hamlet (1969), The Lionel Touch, My Darling Daisy, The Winslow Boy, Joking Apart, In Praise of Rattigan, The Life and Poetry of T.S. Eliot. Bdwy. debut: Goodbye Fidel (1980).
PICTURES: There's a Girl in My Soup (1970), Royal Flash, East of Elephant Rock, The Girl in Blue Velvet, Zulu Dawn, Eye of the Needle, From a Far Country, Heat and Dust, Until September, Mata Hari, The Fantastist, Hold My Hand I'm Dying, Three Men and a Little Lady, Aces: Iron Eagle III.
TELEVISION: Series: The Regiment, The Duchess of Duke Street. Dynasty, A Fine Romance. Specials/movies: The Rivals of Sherlock Holmes (1971), Affairs of the Heart, Jennie: Lady Randolph Churchill, The Darkwater Hall Mystery, Ladykillers—A Smile Is Sometimes Worth a Million, The Red Signal, Lou Grant, The Letter, Jenny's War, Lace 2, Kane and Abel, Windmills of the Gods, Shades of Love, Souvenir, The Lady and the Highwayman, Tears in the Rain, Ticket to Ride (A Fine Romance), To Be the Best.

CELENTINO, LUCIANO: Producer, Director, Writer. b. Naples, Italy, 1940. e. Rome, Paris, London. Ent. ind. 1959. Wrote, prod., dir. many plays incl. Infamita di Questa Terra, Black Destiny, Honour, Stranger's Heart, Youth's Sin, Wanda Lontano Amore. Stage musicals such as Songs . . . Dots . . . And Fantasies, Night Club's Appointment, Filumena, Serenada, Mamma. Since 1964 film critic of Il Meridionale Italiano. From 1962 co-writer and first asst. director to Luigi Capuano and Vittorio De Sica. 1972: formed own company, Anglo-Fortunato Films. Co-wrote, prod., dir. Blood Money. Dir. Bandito (in Italy). Wrote and dir. Toujours, Parole, Jackpot; 1988: Panache (dir.), 1989: Was There a Way Out? (prod., wrote, dir.).

CELLAN-JONES, JAMES: Director. b. Swansea, Wales, July 13, 1931. e. St. John's Coll., Cambridge. Best known for his adaptations of classic novels for the BBC and PBS (shown on Masterpiece Theatre), he has been called "master of the mini-series."
PICTURE: The Nelson Affair.
TELEVISION: The Scarlet and the Black, The Forsyte Saga, Portrait of a Lady, The Way We Live Now, Solo, The Roads to Freedom, Eyeless In Gaza, The Golden Bowl, Jennie (DGA series award), Caesar and Cleopatra, The Adams Chronicles, The Day Christ Died, The Ambassadors, Unity Mitford, Oxbridge Blues (also prod.), Sleeps Six (also prod.), The Comedy of Errors, Fortunes of War, You Never Can Tell, Arms and the Man, A Little Piece of Sunshine, A Perfect Hero (also prod.), The Gravy Train Goes East, Maigret, Harnessing Peacocks, Brighton Belles.

CHABROL, CLAUDE: Director. b. Paris, France, June 24, 1930. A founding director of the French New Wave. Has starred his former wife Stephane Audran in numerous films.
PICTURES: Le Beau Serge, The Cousins, Leda, Les Bonnes Femmes, Les Godelureaux, The Third Lover, Seven Capital Sins, Ophelia, Landru, Le Tigre Aime la Chair Fraiche, Marie-Chantal Contre le Docteur Kah, Le Tigre Se

Parfume a la Dunamite, Paris vu par . . . Chabrol, La Ligne de Demarcation, The Champagne Murders, The Route to Corinth, Les Biches, Le Femme Infidele, This Man Must Die, Le Boucher, La Rapture, Ten Days' Wonder, Just Before Nightfall, Dr. Popaul, Les Noces Rouges, Nada, The Blood of Others (TV in U.S.), The Horse of Pride, Alouette, de te plumera; Poulet au Vinaigre, Inspector Lavadin, Masques, Le Cri du Hibou, Story of Women, Clichy Days, The Lark (actor only), Doctor M, Madame Bovary, Betty.

CHAKERES, MICHAEL H.: Executive. b. Ohio. e. Wittenberg U, 1935. Pres. and chmn. of bd. of Chakeres Theatres of Ohio and Kentucky. U.S. Army AF 1942–45. Bd. of Dir.: National NATO, NATO of Ohio, Will Rogers Hospital, Motion Picture Pioneers, Society National Bank, Wittenberg U., Springfield Foundation, Variety Club of Palm Beach, Tent No. 65. Member: Masonic Temple, Scottish Rite, I.O.O.F., AHEPA, Leadership 100, ARCHON-Order of St. Andrew, Rotary Club, City of Hope, University Club.

CHAKIRIS, GEORGE: Actor. b. Norwood, OH, Sept. 16, 1933. Entered m.p. industry as a dancer in films as Gentlemen Prefer Blondes, There's No Business Like Show Business, White Christmas, Brigadoon, The Girl Rush, Meet Me in Las Vegas.
PICTURES: Two and Two Make Six, West Side Story (Acad. Award, supp. actor, 1961), Diamond Head, Kings of the Sun, Flight From Ashiya, 633 Squadron, Bebo's Girl, McGuire Go Home!, Is Paris Burning?, The Young Girls of Rochefort, The Big Cube, The Day the Hot Line Got Hot, Why Not Stay for Breakfast?, Jerkyll and Hyde Together Again, Pale Blood.
TELEVISION: Series: Dallas (1985–6). Guest: Fantasy Island, Chips, Matt Houston, Scarecrow and Mrs. King, Hell Town, Murder She Wrote. Movie: Return to Fantasy Island. Special: Notorious Woman (PBS).

CHAMBERLAIN, RICHARD: Actor. b. Los Angeles, CA, March 31, 1935. Studied voice, LA Conservatory of Music 1958; acting with Jeff Corey. Founding mem. City of Angels, LA Theater Company. Became TV star in Dr. Kildare series, 1961–66. Founded prod. co. Cham Enterprises. Had hit record Three Stars Will Shine Tonight in 1962.
THEATER: Breakfast at Tiffany's, Night of the Iguana, Fathers & Sons, Blithe Spirit.
PICTURES: Secret of the Purple Reef (debut, 1960), A Thunder of Drums, Twilight of Honor, Joy in the Morning, Petulia, The Madwoman of Chaillot, Julius Caesar, The Music Lovers, Lady Caroline Lamb, The Three Musketeers, The Towering Inferno, The Four Musketeers, The Slipper and the Rose, The Swarm, The Last Wave, Murder by Phone, King Solomon's Mines, Alan Quartermain and the Lost City of Gold, The Return of the Musketeers.
TELEVISION: Specials: Hamlet (1970), Portrait of a Lady (BBC), The Woman I Love, The Lady's Not for Burning. Movies: F. Scott Fitzgerald and the Last of the Belles, The Count of Monte Cristo, The Man in the Iron Mask, Cook and Perry: The Race to the Pole, Wallenberg: A Hero's Story, Casanova, Aftermath: A Test of Love, The Night of the Hunter, Ordeal in the Arctic. Mini-Series: Centennial, Shogun, The Thorn Birds, Dream West, The Bourne Identity. Series: Dr. Kildare, Island Son (also co-exec. prod.) Host: The Astronomers.

CHAMBERS, EVERETT: Producer, Writer, Director. b. Montrose, CA; Aug. 19, 1926. e. New School For Social Research, Dramatic Workshop, N.Y. Entered industry as actor; worked with Fred Coe as casting dir. and dir., NBC, 1952–57; Author: Producing TV Movies.
PICTURES: Writer: Tess of the Storm Country, Run Across the River, The Kiss (dir., nom. best short film, Acad. Awards), The Lollipop Cover (also prod., dir.; best film award, Chicago Film Fest.), Private Duty Nurses, A Girl to Kill For.
TELEVISION: Producer. Series: Johnny Staccato (also writer), Target the Corrupters, The Dick Powell Theatre, The Lloyd Bridges Show (also writer), Peyton Place, Columbo, Future Cop, Timeslip (exec. prod., writer; 1985 Christopher & A.W.R.T. Awards), Lucan (also writer), Airwolf, Partners in Crime, Rin Tin Tin K-9 Cop (also creative consultant). Movies: Beverly Hills Madam, A Matter of Sex (exec. prod.), Will There Really Be a Morning?, Berlin Tunnel 21 (sprv. prod.), Night Slaves (also writer), Moon of the Wolf, Trouble Comes to Town, The Great American Beauty Contest, Can Ellen Be Saved? (also writer), Jigsaw John, Street Killing, Nero Wolfe, Twin Detectives (also writer), The Girl Most Likely to . . . , Sacrifice the Queen, Paris Conspiracy, Family Secret. Co-writer: Movies: The Perfect Town for Murder, Last Chance (pilot).

CHAMPION, JOHN C.: Director, Producer, Writer. b. Denver, CO, Oct. 13, 1923. e. Stanford U., Wittenberg Coll. p. Lee R. Champion, Supreme Court judge. Col. Entered m.p. in Fiesta; did some radio work; in stock at MGM briefly; co-pilot Western Air Lines, Inc., 1943; served in U.S. Army Air Force, air transport command pilot 1943–45; public relations officer AAF; writer & prod. for Allied Artists; v.p. prod. Commander Films Corp.; press. Champion Pictures, Inc.; prod., MGM,

Warner, Para., Universal, Member: SAG, SWG, SIMPP, SPG; TV Academy, Prod. Writer, Mirisch-U.A.; prod. TV Laramie series; created McHales Navy; author, novel, The Hawks of Noon, 1965; National Cowboy, Hall of Fame Award, 1976.
PICTURES: Panhandle, Stampede, Hellgate, Dragonfly Squadron, Shotgun, Zero Hour, The Texican, Attack on the Iron Coast, Submarine X-1, The Last Escape, Brother of the Wind, Mustang Country (dir-prod-writer).

CHAMPION, MARGE: Dancer, Actress. b. Los Angeles, CA, Sept. 2, 1923. r.n. Marjorie Celeste Belcher. e. Los Angeles public schools. p. Ernest Belcher, ballet master. Made debut with former husband Gower Champion as dancing team, played many nightclubs; m.p. Debut in Mr. Music; then signed by MGM; Star of Tomorrow, 1952.
STAGE: Blossom Time, Student Prince for Los Angeles Civic Opera; Dark of the Moon. Beggar's Holiday in N.Y.; 3 for Tonight, (Broadway 1955); toured, Invitation to A March, 1962. Director: Stepping Out, Lute Song (Berkshire Theatre Fest, 1989), She Loves Me, No No Nanette.
PICTURES: Mr. Music, Show Boat, Lovely to Look At, Everything I Have Is Yours, Give a Girl a Break, Three for the Show, Jupiter's Darling, The Swimmer, The Party, The Cock-eyed Cowboys of Calico County, Whose Life Is It Anyway? (choreographer only).
TELEVISION: Series: Admiral Broadway Revue, Marge and Gower Champion Show. Guest: GE Theatre, Chevy Show, Bell Telephone Hour, Ed Sullivan, Shower of Stars, Fame. Movie: Queen of the Stardust Ballroom (Emmy Award, choreography 1975).

CHANCELLOR, JOHN: TV Anchorman, News Reporter. b. Chicago, IL, 1927. e. U. of Illinois. After military service joined Chicago Sun-Times (1948) and after two years moved to NBC News as Midwest corr. In 1948 assigned to Vienna bureau. Subsequently reported from London; was chief of Moscow bureau before appt. as host of Today program for one year (1961). Left NBC 1965–67 to become dir. of Voice of America. In recent yrs. anchorman for special coverage of moon landings, political conventions, inaugurations etc. Anchorman, NBC Nightly News, 1970–82. Now sr. commentator, NBC News, delivering news commentaries on NBC Nightly News.

CHANNING, CAROL: Actress. b. Seattle, WA, Jan. 31, 1921. e. Bennington Coll. Long career on Broadway and road; most notably in Gentlemen Prefer Blondes, Lend an Ear (Theatre World Award), and Hello Dolly! (Tony Award, 1964), Lorelei, Legends (on tour with Mary Martin).
PICTURES: Paid in Full (debut, 1950), The First Traveling Saleslady, Thoroughly Modern Millie (Acad. Award nom.), Skidoo, Shinbone Alley (voice), Sgt. Pepper's Lonely Hearts Club Band (cameo), Happily Ever After (voice).
TELEVISION: Specials: Svengali and the Blonde, Three Men on a Horse, Crescendo, The Carol Channing Special; many guest appearances incl. Omnibus, George Burns Show, Lucy Show, Carol Burnett, Love Boat.

CHANNING, STOCKARD: Actress. r.n. Susan Stockard. b. New York, NY, Feb. 13, 1944. e. Radcliffe Coll., B.A., 1965. With Theater Co. of Boston, experimental drama company, 1967.
THEATER: Two Gentlemen of Verona, No Hard Feelings, Vanities (Mark Taper Forum, LA), They're Playing Our Song, The Lady and the Clarinet, Golden Age, The Rink, Joe Egg (Tony Award, 1985), Love Letters, Woman in Mind, House of Blue Leaves, Six Degrees of Separation, Four Baboons Adoring the Sun.
PICTURES: The Hospital (debut, 1971), The Fortune, The Big Bus, Sweet Revenge, Grease, The Cheap Detective, The Fish That Saved Pittsburgh, Safari 3000, Without a Trace, Heartburn, The Men's Club, A Time of Destiny, Staying Together, Meet the Applegates, Married to It, Six Degrees of Separation.
TELEVISION: Series: The Stockard Channing Show (1979–80). Movies: The Girl Most Likely To . . . , Lucan, Silent Victory: The Kitty O'Neil Story, Not My Kid, The Room Upstairs, Echoes in the Darkness, The Perfect Witness. Guest: Medical Center, Trying Times (The Sad Professor). Special: Tidy Endings.

CHAPIN, DOUG: Producer. Began career as actor; then switched to film production, making debut with When a Stranger Calls, 1979.
PICTURES: Pandemonium, American Dreamer.
TELEVISION: Movies: Belle Starr, Missing Pieces, Second Sight.

CHAPLIN, CHARLES S.: Executive. b. Toronto, Ont., Canada, June 24, 1911. Studied law. Entered m.p. ind. 1930 as office boy with United Artists; then office mgr. booker, St. John, N.B., 1933; br. mgr. 1935; to Montreal in same capacity, 1941; named Canadian gen. mgr., June 11, 1945; resigned 1962. Vice-pres. Canadian sls. mgr., Nat'l Screen Arts Prod., 1962; chief exec. off., v.p., dir. TV sls., Europe-Africa, Middle East-Socialist countries, 1968–70; v.p., WB-Seven Arts, 1970–72; exec. v.p. intl. film dist., NTA (Canada) Ltd., Toronto Intl. Film

Studios, 1972–80; pres., Charles Chaplin Enterprises, specializing in theatrical and TV sls. and prod. Pres.: B'nai Brith-, Toronto Bd. of Trade, various charitable org., many trade assns., past pres. Canadian M.P. Dist. Assn., Chmn. m.p. section Com. Chest, chmn. publ. rel. comm. & past-chmn., M.P. Industry Council; Natl. Board Council Christians & Jews, etc. Representing many indept. producers in Europe, Canada, Far East, South America, etc.

CHAPLIN, GERALDINE: Actress. b. Santa Monica, CA, July 3, 1944. e. Royal Ballet School, London. Daughter of Charles Chaplin. Starred in over 20 European productions, including seven with Spanish filmmaker, Carlos Saura. On NY stage in The Little Foxes.
PICTURES: Limelight (debut, 1952), Doctor Zhivago, A Countess from Hong Kong, Stranger in the House, I Killed Rasputin, The Hawaiians, Zero Population Growth, Innocent Bystanders, The Three Musketeers, The Four Musketeers, Nashville, Buffalo Bill and the Indians, Welcome to L.A., Cria, Roseland, Remember My Name, A Wedding, The Mirror Crack'd, Voyage en Douce, Bolero, Life is a Bed of Roses, Love on the Ground, The Moderns, White Mischief, The Return of the Musketeers, I Want to Go Home, The Children, Buster's Bedroom, Chaplin, The Age of Innocence.
TELEVISION: Specials: The Corsican Brothers, My Cousin Rachel, The House of Mirth. Mini-Series: The World. Movie: Duel of Hearts.

CHAPLIN, SAUL: Musical director, Producer. b. Brooklyn, NY, Feb. 19, 1912. e. NYU, 1929–34. Wrote vaudeville material, 1933–36; songwriter Vitaphone Corp.; other, 1934–40; Columbia, 1940–48; MGM, from 1948; songs include: Bei Mir Bist Du Schoen, Shoe Shine Boy, Anniversary Song.
PICTURES: Acad. Award, collab. best scoring of mus., American in Paris, 1951, 7 Brides for 7 Brothers, 1954; West Side Story, 1961; mus. dir., Lovely to Look At, Give A Girl a Break, Kiss Me Kate, Jupiter's Darling; mus. supv. Interrupted Melody, High Society; assoc. prod. Les Girls; music assoc. prod. Merry Andrew; assoc. prod. Can Can, West Side Story, The Sound of Music; prod. Star, assoc. prod., The Man of La Mancha; co-prod. That's Entertainment, Part Two.

CHAPMAN, MICHAEL: Cinematographer. b. New York, NY, Nov. 21, 1935. m. writer-dir. Amy Jones. Early career in N.Y. area working on documentaries before becoming camera operator for cinematographer Gordon Willis on The Godfather, Klute, End of the Road, The Landlord. Also camera operator Jaws.
PICTURES: The Last Detail, White Dawn, Taxi Driver, The Front, The Next Man, Fingers, The Last Waltz, Invasion of the Body Snatchers, Hard Core, The Wanderers, Raging Bull, Dead Men Don't Wear Plaid, Personal Best, The Man With Two Brains, All the Right Moves (dir.); The Clan of the Cave Bear (dir.); Shoot to Kill, Scrooged, Ghostbusters II, Quick Change, Kindergarten Cop.
TELEVISION: Death Be Not Proud, King, Gotham. Dir.: The Annihilator (pilot).

CHARISSE, CYD: Dancer, Actress. r.n. Tula Ellice Finklea. b. Amarillo, TX, March 8, 1921. e. Hollywood Prof. Sch. m. Tony Martin, singer. Toured U.S. & Europe with Ballet Russe. Named Star of Tomorrow 1948. Bdwy debut 1991 in Grand Hotel.
PICTURES: Something to Shout About (debut, 1943; billed as Lily Norwood), Mission to Moscow, Ziefeld Follies (first film billed as Cyd Charisse), The Harvey Girls, Three Wise Fools, Till the Clouds Roll By, Fiesta, Unfinished Dance, On an Island with You, Words and Music, Kissing Bandit, Tension, East Side West Side, Mark of the Renegade, Wild North, Singin' in the Rain, Sombrero, The Band Wagon, Brigadoon, Deep in my Heart, It's Always Fair Weather, Meet Me in Las Vegas, Silk Stockings, Twilight for the Gods, Party Girl, Five Golden Hours, Black Tights, Two Weeks in Another Town, The Silencers, Maroc 7, Won Ton Ton the Dog Who Saved Hollywood, Warlords of Atlantis.
TELEVISION: Movies: Portrait of an Escort, Swimsuit, Cinderalla Summer; many specials.

CHARLES, MARIA: Actress. b. London, England, Sept. 22, 1929. Trained at Royal Acad. of Dramatic Art. London Stage Debut 1946 in Pick Up Girl. Subseq.
STAGE (London): Women of Twilight, The Boy Friend, Divorce Me, Darling!, Enter A Free Man, They Don't Grow on Trees, Winnie the Pooh, Jack the Ripper, The Matchmaker, Measure for Measure, Annie (1979–80), Fiddler on the Roof, Steaming, Peer Gynt, The Lower Depths, When We Are Married, Follies. Dir.: Owl and the Pussycat.
PICTURES: Folly To Be Wise, The Deadly Affair, Eye of the Devil, Great Expectations, The Return of the Pink Panther, Cuba, Victor/Victoria.
TELEVISION: The Likes of 'Er, The Moon and the Yellow River, Down Our Street, Easter Passion, Nicholas Nickleby, The Voice of the Turtle, The Fourth Wall, The Good Old Days, Turn Out the Lights, Angel Pavement, The Ugliest Girl in Town, Other Peoples Houses, Rogues Gallery, The Prince and the Pauper, Crown Court, Bar Mitzvah Boy, Secret Army,

Agony, Never the Twain, La Ronde, Shine of Harvey Moon, Sheppey, La Ronde, Brideshead Revisited.

CHARTOFF, ROBERT: Producer. b. New York, NY., Aug. 26, 1933. e. Union College, A.B.; Columbia U., LL.B. Met Irwin Winkler through mutual client at William Morris Agency (N.M.) and established Chartoff-Winkler Prods. Currently pres., Chartoff Prods., Inc.
PICTURES: Double Trouble, Point Blank, The Split, They Shoot Horses Don't They?, The Strawberry Statement, Leo The Last, Believe in Me, The Gang That Couldn't Shoot Straight, The New Centurions, Up the Sandbox, The Mechanic, Busting, The Gambler, SPYs, Breakout, Nickelodeon, Rocky, New York New York, Valentino, Comes a Horseman, Uncle Joe Shannon, Rocky II, Raging Bull, True Confessions, Rocky III, The Right Stuff, Rocky IV, Beer, Rocky V, Straight Talk.

CHASE, BRANDON: Producer, Director. President MPA Feature Films, Inc.; newscaster-news director NBC-TV 1952–57. Executive director Mardi Gras Productions, Inc. and member of Board of Directors. Now pres., Group I Films, Ltd., and V.I. Prods., Ltd.
PICTURES: The Dead One, The Sinner and the Slave Girl, Bourbon Street Shadows, Verdict Homicide, Face of Fire, Four for the Morgue, Mission To Hell, The Wanton, Harlow, Girl In Trouble, Threesome, Wild Cargo, Alice in Wonderland, The Models, The Four Of Us, Against All Odds, The Giant Spider Invasion, House of 1,000 Pleasures, The Rogue, Eyes of Dr. Chaney, Alligator, Crash!, Take All of Me, The Psychic, UFOs Are Real, The Actresses, The Sword and the Sorcerer.
TELEVISION: Wild Cargo (series prod.-dir.); This Strange and Wondrous World (prod.-dir.), Linda Evans: Secrets to Stay Young Forever.

CHASE, CHEVY: Actor. r.n. Cornelius Crane Chase. b. New York, NY, Oct. 8, 1943. e. Bard Coll.; B.A. Studied audio research at CCS Institute. Worked as writer for Mad Magazine 1969. Teamed with Kenny Shapiro and Lane Sarasohn while still in school to collaborate on material for underground TV, which ultimately became off-off-Broadway show and later movie called Groove Tube. Co-wrote and starred in Saturday Night Live on TV, winning 2 Emmys as continuing single performance by a supporting actor and as writer for show. Wrote Paul Simon Special 1977 (Emmy Award).
PICTURES: The Groove Tube (debut, 1974), Tunnelvision, Foul Play, Caddyshack, Oh Heavenly Dog, Seems Like Old Times, Under the Rainbow, Modern Problems, National Lampoon's Vacation, Deal of the Century, Fletch, National Lampoon's European Vacation, Follow That Bird, Spies Like Us, Three Amigos, The Couch Trip (cameo), Funny Farm, Caddyshack II, Fletch Lives, National Lampoon's Christmas Vacation, L.A. Story (cameo), Nothing But Trouble, Memoirs of an Invisible Man, Hero (unbilled), Last Action Hero (cameo), Cops and Robbersons.
TELEVISION: Series: Saturday Night Live, The Chevy Chase Show.

CHASE, STANLEY: Producer. b. Brooklyn, NY, May 3. e. NYU, B.A.; Columbia U, postgraduate. m. actress/artist Dorothy Rice. Began career as assoc. prod. of TV show Star Time; story dept., CBS-TV; then produced plays Off-Broadway and on Broadway, winner Tony and Obie awards for The Threepenny Opera. Joined ABC-TV as dir. in chg. programming; prod., Universal Pictures & TV; exec. consultant, Metromedia Producers Org.; prod. & exec. Alan Landsburg Productions. Formed Stanley Chase Productions, Inc. in 1975, which heads as pres.
PICTURES: The Hell with Heroes, Colossus: The Forbin Project, Welcome to Blood City, High-Ballin', Fish Hawk, The Guardian, Mack the Knife.
TELEVISION: Inside Danny Baker (pilot); Al Capp special (prod., writer); Happily Ever After (pilot; prod., writer); Bob Hope Presents the Chrysler Theatre series; Jigsaw (pilot); Fear on Trial (Emmy nomination); Courage of Kavik: The Wolf Dog (exec. prod.); An American Christmas Carol, Grace Kelly.
STAGE: Producer of following Bdwy. plays: The Threepenny Opera, The Potting Shed, The Cave Dwellers, A Moon for the Misbegotten, European Tour: Free and Easy.

CHASMAN, DAVID: Executive. b. New York, NY, Sept. 28, 1925. e. Sch. of Industrial Art, 1940–43; Academie De La Grande-Chaumiere, 1949–50. Monroe Greenthal Co., Inc. 1950–53; Grey Advertising Agency, Inc., 1953–60. Freelance consultant to industry 1950–60; worked on pictures for UA, 20th-Fox, Columbia, Samuel Goldwyn, City Film; Adv. mgr. United Artists, 1960; exec. dir. adv., United Artists, 1962; exec. production, United Artists, London, 1964; v.p. in prod. United Artists, 1969; v.p. of west coast operations, U.A. 1970; Senior v.p. in charge of prod., U.A. 1972; president, Convivium Productions Inc., 1974. Joined Columbia 1977, named exec. v.p. worldwide theatrical prod. 1979. Joined MGM 1980; named exec. v.p.-worldwide theatrical prod.
PICTURES: Exec. prod.: Brighton Beach Memoirs, The Secret of My Success.

CHAUDHRI, AMIN QAMAR: Director, Producer, Cinematographer, Editor. b. Punjab, India, April 18, 1942. e. Hampstead Polytechnic, London, City U. of New York. Pres., Filmart Enterprises Ltd. & Filmart Int'l Ltd., Pres./CEO, Continental Film Group Ltd. Pres./CEO, Continental Entertainment Group, Ltd.
PICTURES: Director: Kashish, Khajuraho, Eternal, Urvasi, Konarak, The Land of Buddha. Producer: Night Visitors, Diary of a Hit Man. Producer/Director: Once Again, An Unremarkable Life, Tiger Warsaw, The Last Day of School, Gunga Din, Golden Chute, Wings of Grey, Call It Sleep .
CINEMATOGRAPHY: Right On, Sweet Vengeance, The Hopefuls, The Wicked Die Slow, Who Says I Can't Ride a Rainbow, Black Rodeo, Medium Is the Message, Death of a Dunbar Girl, Kashish, The Last Day of School.
TELEVISION: Reflections of India (prod.-dir.), Wild Wild East (edit.), Negrun (edit.), Medium is the Message (photog.).

CHER: Singer, Actress. r.n. Cherilyn Sarkisian. b. El Centro, CA, May 20, 1946. Began singing as backup singer for Crystals and Ronettes then, with then-husband Sonny Bono in 1965; first hit record I Got You Babe, sold 3 million. Made two films and then debuted nightclub musical-comedy act in 1969. CBS comedy-variety series started as summer show in 1971; became regular following December. NY stage debut: Come Back to the Five and Dime Jimmy Dean Jimmy Dean (1982).
PICTURES: Wild on the Beach (debut, 1965), Good Times, Chastity, Come Back to the Five and Dime Jimmy Dean Jimmy Dean, Silkwood, Mask, The Witches of Eastwick, Suspect, Moonstruck (Acad. Award, 1987), Mermaids, The Player.
TELEVISION: Series: Sonny & Cher Comedy Hour (1971–74), Cher, The Sonny and Cher Show (1976–77). Specials: Cher, Cher . . . Special, Cher and Other Fantasies, Cher: A Celebration at Caesar's Palace, Cher at the Mirage. Guest: Shindig, Hullabaloo, Hollywood Palace, The Man from U.N.C.L.E., Laugh-In, Glen Campbell, Love American Style.

CHERMAK, CY: Producer, Writer. b. Bayonne, NJ, Sept. 20, 1929. e. Brooklyn Coll., Ithaca Coll.
TELEVISION: Writer, prod., exec. prod.: Ironside, The Virginian, The New Doctors, Amy Prentiss, Kolchak: The Night Stalker, Barbary Coast, CHiPS. Movie: Murder at the World Series (prod., s.p.).

CHERTOK, JACK: Producer. b. Atlanta, GA, July 13, 1906. Began career as script clerk, MGM; later asst. cameraman, asst. dir., head of music dept., short subjects prod. (including Crime Does Not Pay, Robert Benchley, Pete Smith series.) Feature prod. MGM 1939–42 (The Penalty, Joe Smith, American, Kid Glove Killer, The Omaha Trail, Eyes in the Night, etc.). In 1942, apptd. Hollywood prod. chief, Co-Ord. Inter-Amer. Affairs, serving concurrently with regular studio work. Left MGM 1942 and prod. for Warner Bros. to late 1944; pres.: Produced The Corn is Green and Northern Pursuit for Warner Bros. Pres. Jack Chertok TV, Inc.
TELEVISION: Prod.: My Favorite Martian, Lone Ranger, Sky King, Cavalcade, Private Secretary, My Living Doll, Western Marshal, The Lawless Years.

CHETWYND, LIONEL: Executive, Writer, Director. b. London, England, 1940. m. actress Gloria Carlin. Emigrated to Canada, 1948. e. Sir George Williams U., Montreal, BA, economics; BCL-McGill U., Montreal. Graduate Work-Law—Trinity Coll. Oxford. Admitted to bar—Province of Quebec, 1968. C.B.C.—TV-Public Affairs and Talks, 1961–1965. CTV network 1965–67. Controller commercial TV and film rights, Expo '67. Freelance writer and consultant 1961–68. Asst. man. dir. Columbia Pictures (U.K.) Ltd. London 1968–72. Asst. man. dir. Columbia-Warner UK, 1971. Story and book for musical Maybe That's Your Problem, 1971–1973. Then Bleeding Great Orchids (staged London, and Off-Bdwy). Also wrote The American 1776, official U.S. Bi-centennial film and We the People/200 Constitutional Foundation. Former mem. of NYU grad. film sch. faculty, lecturer on screenwriting at Frederick Douglass Ctr. Harlem. Mem of Canadian Bar Assc. Served on bd. of gov., Commission on Battered Children, and the Little League.
PICTURES: The Apprenticeship of Duddy Kravitz (s.p.; Acad. Award nom.), Morning Comes (dir., s.p.), Two Solitudes (prod., dir., s.p., Grand Award Salonika), Quintet (s.p.), The Hanoi Hilton (dir., s.p.), Redline, (dir., s.p.).
TELEVISION: Johnny We Hardly Knew Ye (prod., s.p.; George Washington Honor Medal, Freedom Fdn.), It Happened One Christmas (s.p.), Goldenrod (prod., s.p.), A Whale for the Killing (s.p.), Miracle on Ice (s.p.; Christopher Award), Escape From Iran: The Canadian Caper (s.p.), Sadat (s.p.; NAACP Image Award), Children in the Crossfire (s.p.), To Heal a Nation (writer, exec. prod.), Evil in Clear River (exec. prod.; Christopher Award), So Proudly We Hail (exec. prod., dir., s.p.), The Godfather Wars (s.p.) Heroes of Desert Storm, Reverse Angle (PBS; exec. prod., writer).

CHINICH, JESSE: Executive. b. Hoboken, NJ, Dec. 17, 1921. e. NYU Law School, LLB, 1938. Lawyer with Hovell, Clarkson and Klupt, 1938–41; Capt., Air Force Intelligence, Pacific

Theatre, 1941–46; joined Paramount Theatres as film buyer, 1946–51; circuit supervisor, Rugoff & Becker, NYC, 1951–53; western div. sales mgr., Buena Vista Film Dist., Co., 1953–61; Ass't gen. sales mgr. co-ordinator Cinema V Dist.; ass't sales mgr., Allied Artists; sales executive, special projects, Warner Bros. Dist. Corp. Now Publisher of weekly newsletters.

CHINICH, MICHAEL: Producer. b. New York, NY. e. Boston U. Began career as casting agent in N.Y.; moved to L.A. to join MCA-Universal Pictures as executive in casting. Named head of feature film casting; then prod. v.p.
PICTURES: Casting dir.: Dog Day Afternoon, Coal Miner's Daughter, Animal House, Melvin and Howard, The Blues Brothers, Mask, Midnight Run, Twins, Ghostbusters II, Kindergarten Cop, Dave. Exec. Prod.: Pretty in Pink, Ferris Bueller's Day Off, Some Kind of Wonderful, Planes Trains and Automobiles (co-exec. prod.).

CHOMSKY, MARVIN J.: Director, Producer. b. Bronx, NY, May 23, 1929. e. Syracuse U., B.S.; Stanford U., M.A. Started in theatre business at early age as art dir. with such TV credits as U.S. Steel Hour, Playhouse 90, Studio One, etc. Later worked with Herbert Brodkin who advanced him to assoc. prod. with such TV shows as The Doctors and The Nurses. Brought to Hollywood in 1965 as assoc. prod. for Talent Associates, producing series of TV pilots. Art dir.: The Bubble.
PICTURES: Evel Knievel, Murph the Surf, Mackintosh and T.J., Good Luck Miss Wycoff, Tank.
TELEVISION: Series: The Wild Wild West, Gunsmoke, Star Trek, Then Came Bronson. Movies: Assault on the Wayne, Mongo's Back in Town, Family Flight, Fireball Forward, Female Artillery, The Magician, The F.B.I. Story: The F.B.I. Vs. Alvin Karpas, Mrs. Sundance, Attack on Terror: The F.B.I. Vs. the Ku Klux Klan, Kate McShane, Brink's: The Great Robbery, Law and Order, A Matter of Wife and Death, Victory at Entebbe, Little Ladies of the Night, Roots (co-dir.), Danger in Paradise, Holocaust (Emmy Award), Hollow Image, King Crab, Attica (Emmy Award), Inside the Third Reich (Emmy Award), My Body My Child, The Nairobi Affair, I Was a Mail Order Bride, Robert Kennedy and His Times, Evita Peron (also prod.), Peter the Great (also prod.; Emmy Award), The Deliberate Stranger (also prod.), Anastasia: The Mystery of Anna (also prod.), Billionaire Boys Club (also spv. prod.), Angel in Green, I'll Be Home for Christmas (also prod.), Brotherhood of the Rose (also prod.), Telling Secrets.

CHONG, RAE DAWN: Actress. b. Vancouver, 1962. Daughter of director-comedian Tommy Chong. Debut at 12 in The Whiz Kid of Riverton (TV). Bdwy debut 1991 in Oh Kay!
PICTURES: Quest for Fire (debut, 1982), Beat Street, The Corsican Brothers, Choose Me, Fear City, City Limits, American Flyers, Commando, The Color Purple, Soul Man, The Squeeze, The Principal, Walking After Midnight, Tales from the Darkside, Far Out Man, The Borrower, Amazon, Chaindance, Time Runner, When the Party's Over.
TELEVISION: Movies: The Top of the Hill, Badge of the Assassin, Curiosity Kills, Prison Stories: Women on the Inside, Father & Son: Dangerous Relations.

CHONG, TOMMY: Singer, Actor, Writer, Director. b. Edmonton, Alta., Canada, May 24, 1938. Father of actress Rae Dawn Chong. Was guitar player with various Canadian rhythm and blues combinations, teamed with Richard Marin (Cheech) in improvisational group. Has made comedy recordings.
PICTURES: Up in Smoke, Cheech and Chong's Next Movie (also dir., co-s.p.), Cheech and Chong's Nice Dreams (also dir., co-s.p.), Things Are Tough All Over, It Came from Hollywood, Still Smokin', Yellowbeard, The Corsican Brothers (also dir., s.p.), After Hours, Tripwire (cameo), Far Out Man (also dir., s.p.), The Spirit of 76, FernGully (voice).
TELEVISION: Trial and Error (co-exec. prod.).

CHOOLUCK, LEON: Producer, Director. b. New York, NY, March 19, 1920. e. City Coll. of New York, 1938. Production, distribution, editing with Consolidated Film Industries Ft. Lee 1936–40; staff sergeant, Army Pictorial Service as news photographer 1941–45; Indep. as asst. dir. and prod. mgr. 1946–56; prod. for Regal Films (Fox) Clover Prods. (Col.) Hugo Haas Prods. and Orbit Pro., (Col) 1957–58; dir. Highway Patrol, 1958. Various occupations on stage 1947–58; prod. mgr., Captain Sinbad, Daystar Prods., Stoney Burke (series), prod. mgr., assoc. prod., Daystar Prods., 1962–63 The Outer Limits, Lockup (dir.), prod. supv., Encyclopedia Britannica Films, in Spain, 1964; prod. supv., U.S. Pictures, Battle of the Bulge; loc. mgr., Three F Prods., assoc. prod. I Spy, TV Series, 1965–67. Vice Pres. Fouad Said Cinemobile Systems, 1969–70; ABC Pictures 1970–71 (Grissom Gang, Kotch).
PICTURES: Hell on Devil's Island, Plunder Road, Murder by Contract, City of Fear (prod.), The Fearmakers, Day of the Outlaw, Bramble Bush, Rise and Fall of Legs Diamond (assoc. prod.), Studs Lonigan, Three Blondes in His Life (dir.), El Cid, Midas Run (assoc. prod.), Payday; Three the Hard Way, Take a Hard Ride, Apocalypse Now, Loving Couples,

Square Dance. Wonders of China for Disney Circlevision Epcot (supv.).
TELEVISION: Prod. supv. 1974–76; Specials: Strange Homecoming, James Mitchener's Dynasty, Judge Horton and the Scottsboro Boys, Pearl, A Rumor of War, Murder in Texas, Love Boat, Dynasty, Breakdown (Alfred Hitchcock), On Wings of Eagles.

CHOW, RAYMOND: O.B.E. Producer. b. Hong Kong, 1927. e. St. John's U., Shanghai. Worked for Hong Kong Standard; then joined the Hong Kong office of the U.S. Information Service. In 1959 joined Shaw Brothers as head of publicity, became head of production before leaving in 1970 to start Golden Harvest to produce Chinese-language films in Hong Kong. Kung-fu films featuring Bruce Lee put Harvest into int'l market. Started English-language films in 1977, beginning with The Amsterdam Kill and The Boys in Company C. Named Showman of the Year 1984 by NATO. Awarded O.B.E. in 1988.
PICTURES: Armour of God, The Big Boss (and subsequent Bruce Lee films), The Cannonball Run (and Part II), High Road to China, Lassiter, Miracles, Mr. Boo (a.k.a. The Private Eyes; and many subsequent Michael Hui films), Painted Faces, Police Story (and Part II), Project A (and Part II), Rouge, Teenage Mutant Ninja Turtles (and Part II), The Reincarnation of Golden Lotus.

CHRISTIAN, LINDA: Actress. r.n. Blanca Rosa Welter. b. Tampico, Mexico, Nov. 13, 1924. e. Mexico, Venezuela, Palestine, South Africa, Holland, Italy; attended medical school in Palestine. Worked for British Censorship Bureau in Palestine; asst. to plastic surgeon; screen debut in Holiday in Mexico (1946).
PICTURES: Green Dolphin Street, Tarzan and the Mermaids, The Happy Time, Battle Zone, Slave of Babylon, Athena, Thunderstorm, The VIPs.

CHRISTIANSEN, ROBERT W.: Producer. b. Porterville, CA. e. Bakersfield Coll. Spent 3 years in Marine Corps. Worked on Hollywood Reporter in circulation and advertising. Joined Cinema Center Films; prod. asst. on Monte Walsh and Hail Hero. Co-produced first feature in 1970, Adam at Six A.M., with Rick Rosenberg, with whom co-produced all credits listed.
PICTURES: Adam at Six A.M., Hide in Plain Sight.
TELEVISION: Features: Suddenly Single, The Glass House, Gargoyles, A Brand New Life, The Man Who Could Talk to Kids, The Autobiography of Miss Jane Pittman, I Love You . . . Goodbye, Queen of the Stardust Ballroom, Born Innocent, A Death in Canaan, Strangers, Robert Kennedy and His Times, Kids Don't Tell, As Summers Die, Gore Vidal's Lincoln, Red Earth, White Earth, The Heist.

CHRISTIE, JULIE: Actress. b. Chukua, Assam, India, July 14, 1941. Father had tea plantation in India. e. in Britian, at 16 studied art in France, then attended Central Sch. of Music & Drama in London. 3 yrs. with Frinton-on-Sea Rep., before TV debut in A for Andromeda. Birmingham Rep.; Royal Shakespeare Co.; East European and American tour. NY stage: Uncle Vanya.
PICTURES: Crooks Anonymous (debut, 1962), Fast Lady, Billy Liar, Young Cassidy, Darling (Academy Award & BFA Award, 1965), Dr. Zhivago, Farenheit 451, Far From the Madding Crowd, Petulia, In Search of Gregory, The Go-Between, McCabe and Mrs. Miller, Don't Look Now, Shampoo, Nashville (cameo), Demon Seed, Heaven Can Wait, Memoirs of a Survivor, The Return of the Soldier, Heat and Dust, Golddiggers, Power, Miss Mary, La Memoire tatourée (Secret Obsession), Fools of Fortune.
TELEVISION: Debut: A is for Andromeda (UK series, 1962), Sins of the Fathers (Italian TV), Separate Tables, Dadah Is Death (Amer. TV debut, 1988), The Railway Station Man.

CHRISTINE, VIRGINIA: Actress. b. Stanton, IA, March 5, 1920. e. UCLA. Has appeared in more than 400 motion pictures and television productions.
PICTURES: Mission to Moscow, Counter Attack, The Killers, Cover Up, The Men, Cyrano De Bergerac, Cobweb, High Noon, Not as a Stranger, Spirit of St. Louis, Three Brave Men, Judgment At Nuremberg, The Prize, Four For Texas, Edge of Darkness, The Mummy's Curse, Girls of the Big House, Murder is My Business, The Wife of Monte Cristo, Dragnet, Flaming Star, Cattle King, A Rage to Live, Guess Who's Coming to Dinner, Hail Hero.
TELEVISION: Series: Tales of Wells Fargo. Movies: Daughter of the Mind, The Old Man Who Cried Wolf, Woman of the Year.

CHRISTOPHER, DENNIS: Actor. b. Philadelphia, PA, Dec. 2, 1955. e. Temple U. NY stage debut, Yentl the Yeshiva Boy (1974). Other NY theater: Dr. Needle and the Infectious Laughter Epidemic, The Little Foxes, Brothers, Exmass, A Pound on Demand, Advice from a Caterpillar. Regional theater incl. Balm in Gilead, American Buffalo. Appeared in 1991 short The Disco Years.

PICTURES: Blood and Lace, Didn't You Hear?, The Young Graduates, Fellini's Roma, Salome, 3 Women, September 30, 1955, A Wedding, California Dreaming, The Last Word, Breaking Away, Fade to Black, Chariots of Fire, Don't Cry It's Only Thunder, Alien Predator, Flight of the Spruce Goose, Jake Speed, Friends, A Sinful Life, Circuitry Man, Dead Women in Lingerie, Doppelganger.

TELEVISION: Movies: The Oregon Trail, Stephen King's IT, False Arrest, Willing to Kill: The Texas Cheerleader Story, Curacao. Specials: Bernice Bobs Her Hair, Jack and the Beanstalk (Faerie Tale Theatre), Cristabel. Guest: Trapper John M.D., Tales of the Unexpected, Stingray, Cagney & Lacey, Moonlighting, Hooperman, The Equalizer, Matlock, Murder She Wrote, Monsters, Civil Wars, Dark Justice.

CHRISTOPHER, JORDAN: Actor, Musician. b. Youngstown, OH. Oct. 23, 1941. e. Kent State U. Led rock 'n' roll group, The Wild Ones. Broadway debut, Black Comedy, 1967.
PICTURES: Return of the Seven, The Fat Spy, The Tree, Angel Angel Down We Go, Pigeons, Brainstorm, Star 80, That's Life!
TELEVISION: Series: Secrets of Midland Heights.

CHUNG, CONNIE: TV News Anchor. r.n. Constance Yu-Hwa Chung. m. anchor Maury Povich. b. Washington, D.C., Aug. 20, 1946. e. U. of Maryland, B.S. Entered field 1969 as copy person, writer then on-camera reporter for WTTG-TV, Washington; 1971, named Washington corr., CBS News; 1976, anchor KNXT, Los Angeles; 1983, anchor, NBC News at Sunrise; anchor, NBC Saturday Nightly News and news specials; 1989 moved to CBS as anchor, Sunday Night Evening News; anchor and reporter, Saturday Night with Connie Chung (later Face to Face With Connie Chung), 1989. Received Emmy Award for Shot in Hollywood (1987) and for Interview With Marlon Brando (1989). Became co-anchor, with Dan Rather, of CBS Evening News, 1993. Prime time series: Eye to Eye With Connie Chung, 1993.

CILENTO, DIANE: Actress. b. Queensland, Australia, April 2, 1934. e. Toowoomba. Went to New York and finished schooling and then American Acad. of Dramatic Art. First theatre job at 16; toured U.S. with Barter Co.; returned to London and joined Royal Acad. of Dramatic Art; several small parts and later repertory at Manchester's Library Theatre.
PICTURES: Wings of Danger (debut, 1952), The Angel Who Pawned Her Harp, Passing Stranger, Passage Home, Woman for Joe, Admirable Crichton, Truth About Women, Jet Storm, Stop Me Before I Kill!, I Thank a Fool, The Naked Edge, Tom Jones (Acad. Award nom.), Rattle of a Simple Man, The Third Secret, The Agony and the Ecstacy, Hombre, Negatives, Z.P.G. (Zero Population Growth), Hitler: The Last Ten Days, The Wicker Man, The Boy Who Had Everything, Duet for Four.
THEATRE: London stage: Tiger at the Gates (also NY: Theatre World Award), The Third Secret, The Four Seasons, The Bonne Soup, Heartbreak House. (NY): The Big Knife, Orpheus, Altona, Castle in Sweden, Naked, Marys, I've Seen You Cut Lemons.
TELEVISION: La Belle France (series), Court Martial, Blackmail, Dial M for Murder, Rogues Gallery, Rain, Lysistrata, The Kiss of Blood, For the Term of His Natural Life.

CIMINO, MICHAEL: Writer, Director. b. New York, NY, 1943. e. Yale U. BFA, MFA.
PICTURES: Silent Running (co-s.p.), Magnum Force (co-s.p.). Director: Thunderbolt and Lightfoot (also s.p.), The Deer Hunter (also co-wrote story, co-prod.; Acad. Awards for best picture & dir., 1978.), Heaven's Gate (also s.p.), Year of the Dragon (also co-s.p.), The Sicilian (also co-prod.), Desperate Hours (also co-prod.).

CIPES, ARIANNE ULMER: Executive. b. New York, NY, July 25, 1937. e. Royal Acad. of Dramatic Art, London, U. of London. Daughter of film director Edgar G. Ulmer. Actress, then production and dubbing, Paris; CDC, Rome; Titra, New York; 1975–77, v.p., Best International Films (international film distributor), Los Angeles; 1977 co-founder and sr. v.p./sales & services of Producers Sales Organization, 1981, named exec. v.p., American Film Marketing Assn. 1982, founded AUC Films, consulting and intl. and domestic sales-producers rep.

CIPES, JAY H.: Executive. b. Mt. Vernon, NY, Dec. 14, 1928. e. Cornell U. 1960–66, independent producer-packager-distributor European features for U.S. TV sales; 1967, producer, 20th Century-Fox TV; 1970, producer, Four Star TV; 1971, marketing exec. Technicolor, Inc.; 1973, v.p., marketing, Technicolor, Inc.; 1979 sr. v.p., director worldwide marketing, Technicolor, Inc. Professional Film Division. 1992, indept. consultant to prod. & post-prod. facilities.

CLARK, BOB: Director. b. New Orleans, LA, Aug. 5, 1941. e. Hillsdale Coll.
PICTURES: The Emperor's New Clothes, Children Shouldn't Play with Dead Things (as Benjamin Clark), Dead of Night, Black Christmas, Breaking Point, Murder by Decree, Tribute, Porky's (also prod., s.p.), Porky's II—The Next Day

(also prod., s.p.), A Christmas Story (also prod., s.p.), Rhinestone, Turk 182, From the Hip (also co-s.p.), Loose Cannons (also co-s.p.).

CLARK, CANDY: Actress. b. Norman, OK, June 20. Was successful model in N.Y. before landing role in Fat City, 1972. Off-Broadway debut 1981: A Couple of White Chicks Sitting Around Talking; followed by It's Raining on Hope Street. Appeared in short Blind Curve.
PICTURES: Fat City (debut, 1972), American Graffiti, I Will I Will . . . For Now, The Man Who Fell To Earth, Citizens Band (a.k.a. Handle With Care), The Big Sleep, When You Comin' Back Red Ryder, More American Graffiti, National Lampoon Goes to the Movies, Q, Blue Thunder, Amityville 3-D, Hambone and Hillie, Cat's Eye, At Close Range, The Blob, Original Intent, Deuce Coupe, Cool as Ice, Buffy the Vampire Slayer.
TELEVISION: Movies: James Dean, Amateur Night at the Dixie Bar and Grill, Where the Ladies Go, Rodeo Girl, Johnny Belinda, Cocaine and Blue Eyes, The Price She Paid.

CLARK, DANE: Actor. b. New York, NY, Feb. 18, 1915. e. Cornell U., St. John's. In radio series 2 yrs.; on N.Y. stage (Of Mice and Men, Dead End, The Country Girl, Brecht on Brecht, The Number, The Fragile Fox, A Thousand CLowns, Mike Downstairs, etc.). Natl. Co. of Two for the Seesaw.
PICTURES: The Glass Key (debut, 1942), Sunday Punch, Pride of the Yankees, Tennessee Johnson, Action in the North Atlantic, Destination Tokyo, The Very Thought of You, Hollywood Canteen, Pride of the Marines, God Is My Co-Pilot, Her Kind of Man, A Stolen Life, That Way With Women, Deep Valley, Embraceable You, Moonrise, Whiplash, Without Honor, Backfire, Barricade, Never Trust a Gambler, Fort Defiance, Highly Dangerous, Gambler and the Lady, Go Man Go, Blackout, Paid to Kill, Thunder Pass, Port of Hell, Toughest Man Alive, Massacre, The Man is Armed, Outlaw's Son, Blood Song, The Woman Inside, Last Rites.
TELEVISION: Series: Wire Service, Bold Venture, Perry Mason (1973–4). Specials: No Exit, The Closing Door, The French Atlantic Affair. Guest: Twilight Zone, I Spy, Mod Squad, Cannon, Hawaii 5-O, Murder She Wrote, Police Story, Highway to Heaven, The Rookies, many others. Movies: The Face of Fear, The Family Rico, Say Goodbye Maggie Cole, The Return of Joe Forrester, Murder on Flight 502, James Dean, Condominium. Mini-Series: Once an Eagle, The French Atlantic Affair.

CLARK, DICK: Performer; Chairman, CEO, dick clark prods., Inc. b. Mt. Vernon, NY, Nov. 30, 1929. e. Syracuse U. graduated 1951, summer announcer WRUN, Utica 1949, staff announcer WOLF, Syracuse 1950. After grad. 1951, took regular job with WOLF. Rejoined WRUN, Utica, then joined WKTV, Utica. Announcer WFIL Philadelphia 1952. Author: Your Happiest Years, 1959; Rock, Roll & Remember, 1976; To Goof or Not to Goof, 1963; Dick Clark's Easygoing Guide to Good Grooming, 1986; The History of American Bandstand, 1986. Formed dick clark productions 1956, TV and motion picture production with in-person concert division, cable TV programing dept.Host of two weekly synd. radio programs: Countdown American and Rock Roll & Remember. Founder and principal owner of Unistar Communications Group. Winner of 5 Emmys. Took company public in January, 1987 (NASDAQ: DCPI), serves as chmn. & CEO.
TELEVISION: Host of American Bandstand (ABC-TV nationwide), the Dick Clark Beechnut Show, Dick Clark's World of Talent, Record Years, Years of Rock. $25,000 Pyramid, $100,000 Pyramid, The Challengers.Producer: Where The Action Is, Swinging Country, Happening, Get It Together, Shebang, Record Years, Years of Rock. Executive Producer: American Music Awards, Academy of Country Music Awards, Dick Clark's New Year's Rockin' Eve, ACE Awards, Daytime Emmy Awards, Golden Globe Awards, Soap Opera Awards, Superstars and Their Moms, Caught in the Act (pilot). TV series: American Bandstand, TV's Bloopers & Practical Jokes, Puttin' on the Hits, Puttin' on the Kids, Dick Clark's Nitetime, Inside America, In Person From the Palace, Getting in Touch, Live! Dick Clark Presents! TV movies: Elvis, Man in the Santa Claus Suit, Murder in Texas, Reaching for the Stars, The Demon Murder Case, The Woman Who Willed a Miracle, Birth of the Beatles, Copacabana, Promised a Miracle, The Town Bully, Liberace, Backtrack, Death Dreams, Elvis and the Colonel. TV specials: Live Aid—An All-Star Concert for African Relief, Farm Aid III, Super Bloopers & New Practical Jokes, American Bandstand's 33⅓ Celebration, America Picks the #1 Songs, You Are the Jury, Thanks for Caring, Supermodel of the World, Freedom Festival '89, What About Me I'm Only Three, 1992 USA Music Challenge.
PICTURES: Actor: Because They're Young (debut, 1960), The Young Doctors, Killers Three. Producer: Psychout, The Savage Seven, Remo Williams: The Adventure Begins.

CLARK, DUNCAN C.: Executive. b. July, 1952, Sutton, Surrey, England. Entered industry in 1972. Appointed dir. of publicity and advertising, CIC, Jan. 1979, taking up similar post in 1981 for United Artists. On formation of U.I.P. in 1982, appt. dir., pub. and advertising, and deputy man. dir., July 1983. Feb., 1987 appt. v.p. advertising and pub., Columbia Pictures International (NY). In Aug. 1987, senior v.p. international marketing for Columbia (Burbank); appt. sr. v.p., Columbia Tri-Star Film Distributors, Inc., (NY). Relocated to corp. headquarters in Culver City, Nov. 1991.

CLARK, GREYDON: Producer, Director, Writer. b. Niles, MI, Feb. 7, 1943. e. Western Michigan U., B.A., theatre arts, 1963. Heads own company, World Amusement Corp., Sherman Oaks, CA.
PICTURES: Writer: Satan's Sadists, Psychic Killer. Dir.-writer: Mothers, Fathers, and Lovers, Bad Bunch. Prod.-writer-dir.: Satan's Cheerleaders, Hi-Riders, Angel's Brigade, Without Warning, Joysticks (prod., dir), Uninvited (dir.), Skin-heads (prod., dir, co-s.p.).

CLARK, HILARY J.: Executive. e. U. of Southern California, B.A., 1976. Began industry career 1978 as ad-pub admin. in co-op adv. dept., Buena Vista Dist. Co. Promoted to mgr. of natl. field pub & promo., 1980. Acted as unit publicist on numerous films (Explorers, Sylvester, Swing Shift, Twilight Zone, Cross-roads, etc.) before returning to BV 1986 as natl. pub. dir. for Walt Disney Pictures. Became exec. dir. of Natl. Publicity for Disney and Touchstone Pictures, 1988; v.p. Intl. Publicity for Buena Vista Intl., 1990.

CLARK, MATT: Actor, Director. b. Washington, DC, Nov. 25, 1936.
PICTURES: Black Like Me (debut, 1964), In the Heat of the Night, Will Penny, The Bridge at Remagen, Macho Callahan, Homer (co-s.p. only), Monte Walsh, The Beguiled, The Grissom Gang, The Cowboys, The Culpepper Cattle Company, The Great Northfield Minnesota Raid, Jeremiah Johnson, The Life and Times of Judge Roy Bean, Emperor of the North Pole, The Laughing Policeman, Pat Garrett and Billy the Kid, White Lightning, The Terminal Man, Hearts of the West, Outlaw Blues, Kid Vengeance, The Driver, Dreamer, Brubaker, An Eye for an Eye, Legend of the Lone Ranger, Ruckus, Some Kind of Hero, Honkytonk Man, Love Letters, The Adventures of Buckaroo Banzai, Country, Tuff Turf, Return to Oz, Let's Get Harry, Da (dir. only), The Horror Show, Back to the Future Part III, Cadence, Class Action, Frozen Assets, Fortunes of War, The Harvest.
TELEVISION: Series: Dog and Cat. Mini-Series: The Winds of War, War and Remembrance. Movies: The Execution of Private Slovik, The Great Ice Rip-Off, Melvin Purvis: G-Man, This is the West That Was, The Kansas City Massacre, Dog and Cat (pilot), Lacy and the Mississippi Queen, The Last Ride of the Dalton Gang, The Children Nobody Wanted, In the Custody of Strangers, Love Mary, Out of the Darkness, The Quick and the Dead, The Gambler III: The Legend Continues, Terror on Highway 91, Blind Witness, Deceptions, Dead Before Dawn, Barbarians at the Gate. Specials: Shadow of Fear, Andrea's Story. Pilots: The Big Easy, Highway Honeys, Traveling Man. Guest: Hardcastle and McCormick, Midnight Caller, Bodies of Evidence. Director: Midnight Caller, My Dissident Mom (Schoolbreak Special).
THEATRE: NY: A Portrait of the Artist as a Young Man, The Subject Was Roses, The Trial of the Catonsville Nine; Regional: One Flew Over the Cuckoo's Nest, Tonight We Improvise.

CLARK, PETULA: Actress, Vocalist. b. Ewell, Surrey, England, Nov. 15, 1932. On British stage in Sound of Music. Starred in own BBC TV series 1967–8. Winner of two Grammy Awards, 1964 (Best Rock and Roll Recording: Downtown), 1965 (Best Contemporary R & R Vocal Performance Female: I Know a Place).
PICTURES: Medal for the General (debut, 1944), The Huggets, Dance Hall, White Corridors, The Card, Made In Heaven, Gay Dog, Runaway Bus, Happiness of 3 Women, Track the Man Down, That Woman Opposite, Daggers Drawn, Finian's Rainbow, Goodbye Mr. Chips.

CLARK, SUSAN: Actress. r.n. Nora Golding. b. Sarnid, Ontario, Canada, March 8, 1940. Trained at Royal Acad. of Dramatic Art, London and Stella Adler Academy. Made m.p. debut in Banning, 1967.
PICTURES: Banning (debut, 1967), Coogan's Bluff, Mad-igan, Tell Them Willie Boy Is Here, Colossus: The Forbin Project, Skullduggery, Skin Game, Valdez Is Coming, Show-down, The Midnight Man, Airport 1975, Night Moves, The Apple Dumpling Gang, The North Avenue Irregulars, Murder by Decree, City on Fire, Promises in the Dark, Double Negative, Nobody's Perfekt, Porky's.
TELEVISION: Series: Webster. Movies: Something for a Lonely Man, The Challengers, The Astronaut, Trapped, Babe (Emmy Award, 1976), McNaughton's Daughter, Amelia Ear-hart, Jimmy B. and Andre (also co-prod.), The Choice, Maid in America (also co-prod.). Specials: Hedda Gabler, Double Solitaire.

CLARKE, LAURIE: Executive. b. Hampshire, Eng., 1934. Joined Rank Org. 1955. Controller of cinema operations in London's West End, Lisbon, Hamburg and Dublin in 1970's. Managing

dir. Rank's Top Rank Clubs subsidiary through 1980's. Appointed mng. dir. Rank's Odeon Cinemas, UK, 1990.

CLAYBOURNE, DOUG: Producer. b. Houston, TX, Jan. 19, 1947. e. Univ. of Tulsa, Art Center Col. of Design. Served in USMC, 1966–69. 1975, became asst. art dir. of City of San Francisco Magazine where he met Francis Ford Coppola. Worked on Apocalypse Now as prod. asst., asst. dir., post-prod. coordinator.
PICTURES: Producer: The Escape Artist, The Black Stallion Returns, Rumble Fish, The Serpent and the Rain-bow, Ernest Saves Christmas, Delirious. Exec. Prod.: Light of Day, The War of the Roses. Asst. Dir.: The Black Stallion (also post co-ord.), Legend of Billy Jean, Blue City, Peggy Sue Got Married.

CLAYBURGH, JILL: Actress. b. New York, NY, April 30, 1944. m. playwright David Rabe. e. Sarah Lawrence Coll. 1966. Former member of Charles Playhouse, Boston.
THEATER: The Nest (off-Broadway), The Rothschilds, Jumpers, Pippin, In the Boom Boom Room, Design For Living.
PICTURES: The Wedding Party (debut, 1969), The Tele-phone Book, Portnoy's Complaint, The Thief Who Came to Dinner, Terminal Man, Gable and Lombard, Silver Streak, Semi-Tough, An Unmarried Woman, Luna, Starting Over, It's My Turn, First Monday in October, I'm Dancing as Fast as I Can, Hannah K, Where Are The Children?, Shy People, Beyond the Ocean, Whispers in the Dark, Rich in Love.
TELEVISION: Series: Search For Tomorrow. Movies: The Snoop Sisters (Female Instinct), Miles To Go, Hustling, The Art of Crime, Griffin and Phoenix, Who Gets the Friends?, Fear Stalk, Unspeakable Acts, Reason for Living: The Jill Ireland Story, Trial: The Price of Passion, Firestorm: 72 Hours in Oakland. Guest: Medical Center, Rockford Files, Saturday Night Live.

CLAYTON, JACK: Producer, Director. b. 1921. Ent. m.p. 1935 as asst. dir. for London Films, Fox, Warner. Served H.M. Forces 1940–46; Naples is a Battlefield (dir., co-cine., s.p., 1944); prod. man. Ideal Husband; assoc. prod.: Queen of Spades, Flesh and Blood, Moulin Rouge, Beat the Devil, The Good Die Young, I Am a Camera.
PICTURES: Bespoke Overcoat (prod., dir. Oscar best short, 1956; Venice Festival prize-winning film); prod.: Sailors Beware, Dry Rot, Three Men in a Boat. Director: Room at the Top (BAFTA award best film 1958), The Innocents, The Pumpkin Eater, Our Mother's House (also prod.), The Great Gatsby, Something Wicked This Way Comes, The Lonely Passion of Judith Hearne.

CLEESE, JOHN: Actor, Writer. b. Weston-Super-Mare, England, Oct. 27, 1939. e. Clifton Coll., Cambridge U. Member Monty Python's Flying Circus. Co-author (with psychiatrist Robin Skynner) Families and How to Survive Them, Life and How to Survive It.
PICTURES: Interlude, The Best House in London, The Bliss of Mrs. Blossom, The Rise and Rise of Michael Rimmer (also co-s.p.), The Magic Christian (also co-s.p.), The Statue, And Now for Something Completely Different (also co-s.p.), Monty Python and the Holy Grail (also co-s.p.), The Life of Brian (also co-s.p.), The Great Muppet Caper, Time Bandits, The Secret Policeman's Other Ball, Monty Python Live at the Hollywood Bowl (also co-s.p.), Monty Python's The Meaning of Life (also co-s.p.), Yellowbeard, Privates on Parade, Silverado, Clockwise, A Fish Called Wanda (also co-s.p., exec. prod.), The Big Picture (cameo), Erik the Viking, Bullseye! (cameo), An American Tail: Fievel Goes West (voice), Splitting Heirs.
TELEVISION: Special: Taming of the Shrew. Series: The Frost Report, At Last the 1948 Show, Monty Python's Flying Circus, Fawlty Towers. Guest: Cheers (Emmy Award, 1987).

CLEMENS, BRIAN: Writer, Producer, Director. b. Croydon, Eng-land, 1931. Early career in advertising then wrote BBC TV play. Later TV filmed series as writer, script editor and features. Script editor "Danger Man"; Won Edgar Allen Poe Award for Best TV Thriller of 1962 (Scene of the Crime for U.S. Steel Hour). Various plays for Armchair Theatre; ATV Drama 70; Love Story. Winner two Edgar Allan Poe Awards, Cinema Fantastique Award for best s.p.
PICTURES: The Tell-Tale Heart, Station Six-Sahara, The Peking Medallion, And Soon The Darkness, The Major, When The Wind Blows, See No Evil, Dr. Jekyll and Sister Hyde, Golden Voyage of Sinbad, Watcher in the Woods, Stiff.
TELEVISION: Wrote and prod.: The Avengers (2 Emmy nom., Best Production, 1967 & 1968), The New Avengers, The Professionals, Escapade (in U.S. for Quinn Martin).

CLENNON, DAVID: Actor. b. Waukegan, IL. e. Univ. of Notre Dame, Yale Drama School.
PICTURES: The Paper Chase, Bound for Glory, The Greatest, Coming Home, Gray Lady Down, Go Tell the Spartans, On the Yard, Being There, Hide in Plain Sight, Missing, The Escape Artist, The Thing, Ladies and Gentle

men the Fabulous Stains, The Right Stuff, Hannah K., Star 80, Falling in Love, Sweet Dreams, Legal Eagles, He's My Girl, The Couch Trip, Betrayed, Downtown, Man Trouble, Light Sleeper, Matinee.
TELEVISION: *Series*: Rafferty, Park Place, thirtysomething. *Movies*: The Migrants, Crime Club, Helter Skelter, Gideon's Trumpet, Marriage is Alive and Well, Reward, Special Bulletin, Best Kept Secrets, Blood and Orchids, Conspiracy: The Trial of the Chicago 8. *Guest*: Alfred Hitchcock Presents, Murder She Wrote, Barney Miller. *Special*: The Seagull.
THEATRE: *NY*: Unseen Hand, Forensic and the Navigators, As You Like It, Little Eyolf, Medal of Honor Rag, The Cherry Orchard. *Regional*: Blood Knot, Loot, Marat/Sade, Beyond Therapy, others.

CLIFFORD, GRAEME: Director.
PICTURES: Frances, Burke & Wills, Gleaming the Cube.
TELEVISION: The Avengers, Barnaby Jones, Faerie Tale Theatre, The Turn of the Screw.

CLOSE, GLENN: Actress. b. Greenwich, CT, Mar. 19, 1947. e. Coll. of William and Mary. Began performing with a repertory group Fingernails, then toured country with folk-singing group Up With People. Professional debut at Phoenix Theatre, New York. Also accomplished musical performer (lyric soprano).
THEATER: *NY*: Love for Love, Rules of the Game, Member of the Wedding, Rex, Uncommon Women and Others, The Crucifer of Blood, Wine Untouched, The Winter Dancers, Barnum, Singular Life of Albert Nobbs (Obie Award), The Real Thing (Tony Award, 1984), Childhood, Joan of Arc at the Stake, Benefactors, Death and the Maiden (Tony Award, 1992). *Regional*: King Lear, Uncle Vanya, The Rose Tattoo, A Streetcar Named Desire, Brooklyn Laundry.
PICTURES: The World According to Garp (debut, 1982), The Big Chill, The Natural, The Stone Boy, Greystoke: The Legend of Tarzan Lord of the Apes (dubbed voice), Jagged Edge, Maxie, Fatal Attraction, Light Years (voice), Dangerous Liaisons, Immediate Family, Reversal of Fortune, Hamlet, Meeting Venus, Hook (cameo), House of the Spirits, The Paper.
TELEVISION: *Movies*: Too Far To Go, The Orphan Train, Something About Amelia, Stones for Ibarra, Sarah: Plain and Tall, Skylark (also co-exec. prod.). *Specials*: The Elephant Man, Broken Hearts Broken Homes (host, co-exec. prod.).

COATES, ANNE V.: Film editor, Producer. b. Reigate, Surrey, Eng. e. Bartrum Gables Coll. m. late dir. Douglas Hickox. Worked as nurse at East Grinstead Plastic Surgery Hospital.
PICTURES: Pickwick Papers, Grand National Night, Forbidden Cargo, To Paris With Love, Mongongo, The Truth About Women, The Horse's Mouth, Tunes of Glory, Don't Bother to Knock, Lawrence of Arabia (Acad. Award, ACE nom.), Becket (Acad. Award & ACE noms.), Young Cassidy, Those Magnificent Men in Their Flying Machines (co-ed.), Hotel Paridiso, Great Catherine, The Bofors Guns, The Adventurers, Friends, The Public Eye, The Nelson Affair, 11 Harrow House, Murder on the Orient Express (BAFTA nom.), Man Friday, Aces High, The Eagle Has Landed, The Medusa Touch (prod. & sprv. ed.), The Legacy, The Elephant Man (Acad. Award nom., BAFTA nom.), The Bushido Blade, Ragtime (co-ed.), The Pirates of Penzance, Greystoke: The Legend of Tarzan Lord of the Apes, Lady Jane, Raw Deal, Masters of the Universe, Farewell to the King (co-ed.), Listen to Me, I Love You to Death, What About Bob?, Chaplin, In the Line of Fire.

COBE, SANDY: Executive, Producer, Distributor. b. New York, NY, Nov. 30, 1928. e. Tulane U., B.A., fine arts. U.S. Army W.W.II & Korea, combat photographer; produced 11 features for Artmark Pictures, N.Y. General Studios, exec. v.p., distribution; First Cinema Releasing Corp., pres. Formed Sandy Cobe Productions, Inc., producer, packager, European features for U.S. theatrical & television. 1974 pres., Intercontinental Releasing Corporation, domestic and foreign distribution of theatrical features; 1989, named chmn. of bd. and CEO.
MEMBER: Dir. of bd., American Film Marketing Assn., Dir. of bd., Scitech Corp. USA, 14 year mem., Academy of Television Arts and Sciences, 32nd degree Mason, Shriner, Variety Club Int'l. Special commendations from: Mayor of Los Angeles, California State Senate, City and County of L.A., California Assembly and Senate, and Governor of CA.
PICTURES: Terror on Tour (prod.), Access Code (exec. prod.), A.R.C.A. D.E. (prod.), Terminal Entry (exec. prod.), Open House (prod.).

COBE, SHARYON REIS: Executive, Producer. b. Honolulu, HI, e. U. of Hawaii, Loyola Marymount U. Dancer Fitzgerald, & Sample, N.Y. United Air Lines, N.Y.; v.p., story editor, Gotham Publishing N.Y.; v.p., distribution-foreign sales, World Wide Film Distributors, L.A.; pres. and chief operating officer, Intercontinental Releasing Corp., L.A.
MEMBER: Variety Clubs Intl., Industry Rltns. Com., Amer. Film Mktg. Assoc., Indpt. Feature Projects West. (tent 25), Women in Film.

PICTURES: Home Sweet Home (prod. mgr.), To All a Good Night (assoc. prod.), Access Code (co-prod.), Terminal Entry (prod.), Open House (exec. in chg. of prod.).

COBLENZ, WALTER: Producer.
PICTURES: The Candidate, All the President's Men, The Onion Field, The Legend of the Lone Ranger, Strange Invaders, Sister Sister, 18 Again!, For Keeps, The Babe.

COBURN, JAMES: Actor. b. Laurel, NB, Aug. 31, 1928. e. Los Angeles City Coll., where he studied drama. Also studied with Stella Adler in NY for 5 years. Served in U.S. Army. First acting role in coast production of Billy Budd. Later to New York, where he worked on TV commercials, then in live teleplays on Studio One, GE Theatre, Robert Montgomery Presents. Summer stock in Detroit before returning to Hollywood. Commercial: Remington Rand.
PICTURES: Ride Lonesome (debut, 1959), Face of a Fugitive, The Magnificent Seven, Hell Is for Heroes, The Great Escape, Charade, The Americanization of Emily, The Loved One, Major Dundee, A High Wind in Jamaica, Our Man Flint, What Did You Do in the War Daddy?, Dead Heat on a Merry-Go-Round, In Like Flint, Waterhole No. 3, The President's Analyst, Duffy, Candy, Hard Contract, Last of the Mobile Hot Shots, The Carey Treatment, The Honkers, Duck You Sucker, Pat Garrett and Billy the Kid, The Last of Sheila, Harry in Your Pocket, A Reason to Live A Reason to Die, The Internecine Project, Bite the Bullet, Hard Times, Sky Riders, The Last Hard Men, Midway, Cross of Iron, California Suite (cameo), The Muppet Movie, Goldengirl, Firepower, The Baltimore Bullet, Loving Couples, Mr. Patman, High Risk, Looker, Martin's Day, Death of a Soldier, Phoenix Fire, Walking After Midnight, Train to Heaven, Young Guns II, Hudson Hawk, The Player, Hugh Hefner: Once Upon a Time (narrator), Deadfall, Sister Act 2.
TELEVISION: *Series*: Klondike, Acapulco, Darkroom (host), Hollywood Stuntmakers (host), Fifth Corner. *Movies*: Draw!, Sins of the Fathers, Malibu, The Dain Curse, Valley of the Dolls, Crash Landing: The Rescue of Flight 232, The Hit List. *Specials*: Pinocchio (Faerie Tale Theater), Mastergate. *Pilots*: Silver Fox, Greyhounds.

COCA, IMOGENE: Actress. b. Philadelphia, PA, Nov. 18, 1908. p. the late Joe Coca, orchestra leader, and Sadie Brady, vaudevillian. At 11, debut tap dancer in New York vaudeville; solo dancer Broadway musicals; as comedienne, in New Faces of 1934; with former husband, Bob Burton, in Straw Hat Revue in 1939, and others through 1942. New York night clubs, Cafe Society and Le Ruban Bleu, Palmer House, Chicago; Park Plaza, St. Louis, and at Tamiment resort. Seen on early experimental TV telecasts in 1939.1949 to TV via Broadway Revue, co-starring with Sid Caesar. Emmy Award, 1951. Returned to Broadway in Musical On the Twentieth Century.
PICTURES: Under the Yum Yum Tree, Promises! Promises!, Rabbit Test, National Lampoon's Vacation, Nothing Lasts Forever, Buy and Cell, Papa Was a Preacher.
TELEVISION: *Series*: Buzzy Wuzzy (host, 1948), Admiral Broadway Revue (1949), Your Show of Shows (1950–54). Imogene Coca Show (1954–5), Sid Caesar Invites You (1958), Grindl (1963–4), It's About Time (1966–7). *Special*: Ruggles of Red Gap. *Guest*: Fireside Theatre, Hollywood Palace, Love American Style, Moonlighting. *Movies*: Alice in Wonderland, Return of the Beverly Hillbillies.

COCCHI, JOHN: Writer, Critic. b. Brooklyn, NY, June 19, 1939. e. Fort Hamilton H.S., 1957; Brooklyn College, A.A.S., 1961. U.S. Army, 1963–65. Puritan Film Labs, manager, 1967–9. Independent-International Pictures, biographer-researcher, 1969. Boxoffice Magazine, critic, reporter, columnist, 1970–79. Co-author: The American Movies Reference Book (Prentice-Hall). Contributor: Screen Facts, Film Fan Monthly, Films in Review. Actor in: The Diabolical Dr. Ongo, Thick as Thieves, Captain Celluloid vs. the Film Pirates. Worked on dubbing: Dirtymouth, 1970. Author of film books incl. The Westerns: a Movie Quiz Book, Second Feature, Best of the B Films. Now free lance writer, researcher, agent. Recent credits: contributor to books, 500 Best American Films, 500 Best British and Foreign-Language Films. Consultant to Killiam Shows, Prof. Richard Brown, Photofest, Star Magazine; research chief for American Movie Classics channel, 1984–present.

COEN, ETHAN: Producer, Writer. b. St. Louis Park, MN, 1958. e. Princeton U. Co-wrote s.p. with brother, Joel, XYZ Murders (renamed Crime Wave).
PICTURES: *Producer/Co-Writer*: Blood Simple (also co-edited under pseudonym Roderick James), Raising Arizona, Miller's Crossing, Barton Fink, The Hudsucker Proxy.

COEN, GUIDO: Producer, Executive. In 1959 Became production exec. Twickenham Studios, 1963 Appt. a dir. there, then producer and executive prod. series pictures for Fortress Films and Kenilworth Films.
PICTURES: One Jump Ahead, Golden Link, The Hornet's Nest, Behind the Headlines, Murder Reported, There's

Always a Thursday, Date with Disaster, The End of the Line, The Man Without a Body, Woman Eater, Kill Her Gently, Naked Fury, Operation Cupid, Strictly Confidential, Dangerous Afternoon, Jungle Street, Strongroom, Penthouse, Baby Love, One Brief Summer, Burke and Hare, Au Pair Girls, Intimate Games.

COEN, JOEL: Director, Writer. b. St. Louis Park, MN, Nov. 29, 1954. e. Simon's Rock College, MA; studied film at NYU. Was asst. editor on Fear No Evil and Evil Dead. Co-wrote with brother, Ethan, s.p. for XYZ Murders (renamed Crime Wave.) Cameo role in film Spies Like Us, 1985.
PICTURES: *Director/Co-Writer*: Blood Simple (also co-editor, under pseudonym Roderick Jaynes), Raising Arizona, Miller's Crossing, Barton Fink (also co-editor, as Roderick Jaynes), The Hudsucker Proxy.

COHEN, ELLIS A.: Producer, Writer. b. Baltimore, MD, Sept. 15, 1945. e. Baltimore Jr. Coll., A.A. 1967, Univ. of W. LA, mini-law sch., 1992. Prod., Henry Jaffe Enterprises, Inc., 1963, talent coordinator, Cerebral Palsy Telethon, WBAL-TV, Baltimore; 1964, p.r. asst. Campbell-Ewald Adv. Agency, L.A.; 1966, and mgr., Hochschild Kohn Dept. Stores, Baltimore; 1968–69, asst. dir., p.r. entertainment, talent booking for Club Venus Night Club, Baltimore; 1968, created-edited The Forum Oracle, national entertainment mag. 1969–72, dir., p.r., Jewish Community Center of Baltimore; 1970, leave of absence to work as corr. in Israel, Denmark & London; 1972, dir., p.r.& adv., The Camera Mart, NY; 1972–74 creator & editor-in-chief, TV/New York Magazine, nationwide TV mag.; 1974–76 dir., worldwide pub./adv., William Morris Agency, Producer, New York Area Emmy Awards Telecast (1973 & 1974), WOR-TV (prod.), chmn., exec. prod. of TV Academy Celebrity drop-in luncheon series; 1972, talent coordinator Bob Hope's Celebrity Flood Relief Telethon. Executive producer, 1976 Democratic National Convention Gala. 1978, Account Exec., Solters & Roskin P.R. L.A. 1978 director of TV Network Boxing Events, Don King Productions, Inc., N.Y. 1980, prod.-writer, CBS Entertainment; pres. Ellis A. Cohen Prods. Since 1983, pres., Hennessey Entertainment, Ltd. First novel, Avenue of the Stars published 1990. First non-fiction book: Dangerous Evidence (1994).
MEMBER: Writers Guild of America, Producers Guild of America, World Affairs Council, Friars Club, Amer. Newspaper Guild, Intl. Press Corp., Israeli Press Corp., National Academy of TV Arts & Sciences, Academy of Television Arts & Sciences, Screen Actors Guild. Mayor Beame's Committee in the Public Interest for N.Y.C.; Natl. Writers Union.
TELEVISION: *Movies*: Aunt Mary (prod.-story); First Steps (prod.), Love Mary (prod.). *Specials*: NY Area Emmy Awards (prod. 1973 and 1974)

COHEN, IRWIN R.: Exhibition Executive. b. Baltimore, MD, Sept. 4, 1924. e. U. of Maryland, (LLB) 1948, admitted to Maryland and U.S. Bar same year. Active limited practice. R/C Theatres outgrowth of family business started in 1932. One of founders of Key Federal Bank, chairman of board Loan Comm., director and member of exec. comm. Pres. NATO of Virginia 1976–78, chairman 1978–80. Director, member of exec. comm., treasurer, chairman of finance comm. National NATO. Member of Motion Picture Pioneers, Variety Club, and various other orgs.

COHEN, LARRY: Director, Producer, Writer. b. New York, NY, Apr. 20, 1936. e. CCNY. Started as writer for TV series incl. Kraft Mystery Theatre, The Defenders, Arrest and Trial. Creator of series Branded, The Invaders.
PICTURES: Daddy's Gone A-Hunting (co-s.p.), El Condor (s.p.), Bone (Housewife; dir., prod., s.p.), Black Caesar (dir., prod., s.p.), It's Alive (dir., prod., s.p.), Demon (God Told Me To; dir., prod., s.p.), The Private Files of J. Edgar Hoover (dir., prod., s.p.), It Lives Again (dir., prod., s.p.), Success (American Success Company; story) Full Moon High (prod., dir., s.p.), Q (dir., prod., s.p.), I The Jury (s.p.), Perfect Strangers (Blind Alley; dir., prod., s.p.), The Man Who Wasn't There (story), Special Effects (dir., s.p.), Scandalous (story), The Stuff (exec. prod., dir., s.p.), Spies Like Us (actor), It's Alive III: Island of the Alive (exec. prod., dir., s.p.), Return to Salem's Lot (dir., exec. prod., s.p.), Best Seller (story), Deadly Illusion (s.p.), Maniac Cop (prod., s.p.), Wicked Stepmother (dir., exec. prod., s.p.), Maniac Cop II (prod., s.p.), The Ambulance (dir., s.p.), The Apparatus (dir., s.p.), Guilty As Sin (s.p.)
TELEVISION: *Movies*: Cool Million (Mask of Marcella; writer), Man on the Outside (writer), Shootout in a One Dog Town (co-writer, story) Desperado: Avalanche at Devil's Ridge (writer).

COHEN, ROB: Producer, Director. b. Cornwall-on-the-Hudson, NY, March 12, 1949. e. Harvard U. BA. Formerly exec. v.p. in chg of m.p. and TV for Motown. Started as dir. of m.p. for TV at 20th Century-Fox. Joined Motown at age of 24 to produce films. Headed own production co. 1985, appt. pres., Keith Barish Prods.
PICTURES: Mahogany (prod.), The Bingo Long Traveling All-Stars (prod.), Scott Joplin (prod.), Almost Summer (prod.),

Thank God It's Friday (prod.), The Wiz (prod.), A Small Circle of Friends (dir.), Scandalous (dir., co-s.p.), The Razor's Edge (prod.), The Legend of Billie Jean (prod.), Light of Day (co-prod.), The Witches of Eastwick (co-exec. prod.), The Monster Squad (co-exec. prod.), Ironweed (co-exec. prod.), The Running Man (co-exec. prod.), The Serpent and the Rainbow (exec. prod.), Disorganized Crime (exec. prod.), Bird on a Wire (prod.), The Hard Way (prod.), Dragon: The Bruce Lee Story (dir., co-s.p., actor).
TELEVISION: Miami Vice (dir.), Cuba and Claude (exec. prod.).

COHEN, ROBERT B.: Executive. e. George Washington U., B.A., Southern Texas Sch. of Law. 1980–84. Atty. for Greenberg, Glusker, Fields, Clamans and Machtinger (L.A.). Was asst. gen. counsel for Columbia Pictures. Joined Paramount 1985 as sr. atty. for M.P. Group. to oversee legal functions for assigned feature films; 1988 named v.p. in charge of legal affairs, Motion Picture Group of Paramount.

COHN, ROBERT: Producer. b. Avon, NJ, Sept. 6, 1920. e. U. of Michigan, B.A., 1941. p. Jack Cohn. Joined Columbia as asst. dir. In W.W.II as Signal Corps film cutter. Air Corps Training Lab. unit mgr., combat aerial m.p. camera man with 13th A.A.F. Awarded: DFC, Air Medal & 3 clusters, Purple Heart. Assoc. prod. Lone Wolf In London, 1947; prod. Adventures in Silverado, 1948, all Col. Headed Robert Cohn prod. unit at Columbia, pres. International Cinema Guild. Columbia European prod.: exec. Columbia Studios. Hollywood: formed Robert Cohn Prod.
PICTURES: Black Eagle, Rusty Leads the Way, Palomino, Kazan, Killer That Stalked New York, The Barefoot Mailman, Mission Over Korea, The Interns, The New Interns, The Young Americans.

COLBERT, CLAUDETTE: Actress: r.n. Lily Chauchoin. b. Paris, Sept. 13, 1905. e. public schools, Paris, New York; Art Students League, N.Y. On N.Y. stage (debut, Wild Wescotts; followed by Marionette Man, We've Got to Have Money, Cat Came Back, Kiss in a Taxi, Ghost Train, The Barker, Dynamo, etc.). First screen role in For the Love of Mike (silent); Academy Award best actress, 1934 (It Happened One Night); voted one of ten top Money Making Stars in Fame Poll, 1935, '36, '47.
PICTURES: The Hole in the Wall (talkie debut, 1929), The Lady Lies, The Big Pond, Young Man of Manhattan, Manslaughter, Honor Among Lovers, The Smiling Lieutenant, Secrets of a Secretary, His Woman, The Wiser Sex, Misleading Lady, The Man From Yesterday, Make Me a Star (cameo), The Phantom President, The Sign of the Cross, Tonight is Ours, I Cover the Waterfront, Three Cornered Moon, The Torch Singer, Four Frightened People, It Happened One Night (Acad. Award, 1934), Cleopatra, Imitation of Life, The Gilded Lily, Private Worlds, She Married Her Boss, The Bride Comes Home, Under Two Flags, Maid of Salem, I Met Him in Paris, Tovarich, Bluebeard's Eighth Wife, Zaza, Midnight, It's a Wonderful World, Drums Along the Mohawk, Boom Town, Arise My Love, Skylark, Remember the Day, The Palm Beach Story, No Time for Love, So Proudly We Hail, Practically Yours, Since You Went Away, Guest Wife, Tomorrow Is Forever, Without Reservations, The Secret Heart, The Egg and I, Sleep My Love, Family Honeymoon, Bride for Sale, Three Came Home, The Secret Fury, Thunder on the Hill, Let's Make It Legal, Outpost in Malaya (Planter's Wife), Daughters of Destiny, Si Versailles m'etait conte, Texas Lady, Parrish.
BROADWAY: Marriage Go Round, Irregular Verb to Love, The Kingfisher, Aren't We All?
TELEVISION: *Movie*: The Two Mrs. Grenvilles.

COLBY, RONALD: Producer, Director, Writer. b. New York, NY. e. Hofstra U., NYU. Began career as playwright at Cafe La Mama and Caffe Cino; performed in off-Bdwy shows; spent year as actor-writer in residence at Pittsburgh Playhouse. Served as dialogue coach and asst. to Francis Coppola; was v.p. of Zoetrope Studios. Directed several documentaries and short films.
PICTURES: Rain People (prod.), Hammett (prod.), Some Kind of Wonderful (exec. prod.), She's Having a Baby (exec. prod.).
TELEVISION: Margaret Bourke-White (co-prod.)

COLE, GARY: Actor. b. Park Ridge, IL, Sept. 20. e. Illinois State, theater major. Dropped out of coll. after 3 years and moved to Chicago where he tended bar, painted houses and worked with Steppenwolf Theatre group. In 1979 helped to form Remains Theatre, left in 1986 to become ensemble member of Steppenwolf.
TELEVISION: *Series*: Midnight Caller. *Movies*: Heart of Steel, Fatal Vision, Vital Signs, Those She Left Behind, The Old Man and the Sea, Son of the Morning Star, The Switch, When Love Kills: The Seduction of John Hearn. *Mini-series*: Echoes in the Darkness.
PICTURES: Lucas, In the Line of Fire.

COLE, GEORGE: Actor. b. London, Eng., Apr. 22, 1925. e. secondary sch. Surrey. Stage debut in White Horse Inn, 1939; m.p. debut in Cottage to Let, 1941.
PICTURES: Henry V, Quartet, My Brother's Keeper, Laughter in Paradise, Scrooge, Lady Godiva Rides Again, Who Goes There (Passionate Sentry), Morning Departure (Operation Disaster), Top Secret (Mr. Potts Goes to Moscow), Happy Family, Will Any Gentleman, Apes of the Rock, The Intruder, Happy Ever After (Tonight's the Night), Our Girl Friday (Adventures of Sadie), Belles of St. Trinian's, Prize of Gold, Where There's a Will, Constant Husband, Quentin Durward, The Weapon, It's a Wonderful Life, Green Man, Bridal Path, Too Many Crooks, Blue Murder at St. Trinians, Don't Panic Chaps, Dr. Syn, One Way Pendulum, Legend of Young Dick Turpin, The Great St. Trinian's Train Robbery, Cleopatra, The Green Shoes, Vampire Lovers, Fright, The Bluebird.
TELEVISION: Life of Bliss, A Man of Our Times, Don't Forget To Write, The Good Life, Minder (series), Root Into Europe (series).

COLEMAN, DABNEY: Actor. b. Austin, TX, Jan. 3, 1932. e. VA Military Inst. 1949–51; U. Texas 1951–57; Neighborhood Playhouse School Theater 1958–60.
PICTURES: The Slender Thread (debut, 1965), This Property Is Condemned, The Scalphunters, The Trouble With Girls, Downhill Racer, I Love My Wife, Cinderella Liberty, The Dove, The Towering Inferno, The Other Side of the Mountain, Bite the Bullet, The Black Streetfighter, Midway, Rolling Thunder, Viva Knievel, North Dallas Forty, Nothing Personal, How to Beat the High Cost of Living, Melvin and Howard, Nine to Five, On Golden Pond, Modern Problems, Young Doctors in Love, Tootsie, WarGames, The Muppets Take Manhattan, Cloak and Dagger, The Man with One Red Shoe, Dragnet, Hot to Trot, Where the Heart Is, Short Time, Meet the Applegates, There Goes the Neighborhood, Amos & Andrew, Clifford, The Beverly Hillbillies.
TELEVISION: Movies: Brotherhood of the Bell, Savage, Dying Room Only, The President's Plane is Missing, Bad Ronald, Attack on Terror: The FBI Versus the Ku Klux Klan, Returning Home, Kiss Me Kill Me, Maneaters Are Loose!, More Than Friends, Apple Pie, When She Was Bad, Murrow, Guilty of Innocence, Sworn To Silence (Emmy Award, 1987), Baby M, Maybe Baby, Never Forget, Columbo and the Murder of a Rock Star. Mini-Series: Fresno. Series: That Girl, Bright Promise, Mary Hartman Mary Hartman, Apple Pie, Forever Fernwood, Buffalo Bill, The Slap Maxwell Story, Drexell's Class. Special: Plaza Suite.

COLEMAN, GARY: Actor. b. Zion, IL, Feb. 8, 1968. Gained fame as star of TV's Diff'rent Strokes.
TELEVISION: Series: Diff'rent Strokes. Guest: America 2-Night, Good Times, The Jeffersons, Lucy Moves to NBC, The Big Show, etc. Movies: The Kid from Left Field, Scout's Honor, The Kid With the Broken Halo; The Kid with the 200 I.Q., Fantastic World of D.C. Collins, Playing With Fire.
PICTURES: On the Right Track, Jimmy the Kid.

COLEMAN, NANCY: Actress. b. Everett, WA, Dec. 30, 1917. e. U. of Washington. In radio serials; on New York stage in Susan and God, Liberty Jones, Desperate Hours, 1955; American Theatre Guild Rep. Co. tour of Europe and So. America, 1961. m.p. debut, 1941.
PICTURES: Kings Row, Dangerously They Live, Gay Sisters, Desperate Journey, Edge of Darkness, In Our Time, Devotion, Her Sister's Keeper, Violence, Mourning Becomes Electra, That Man from Tangier, Slaves.
TELEVISION: Valiant Lady, Producers Showcase, Kraft Theatre, Philco Playhouse, Robert Montgomery Presents, Lux Theatre, Alcoa Hour, Theatre Guild Playhouse, Play of the Week, Silver Theatre, Adams Chronicles.

COLEMAN, THOMAS J.: Executive. b. Connecticut, Apr. 13, 1950. e. Boston U. Pres., Twalzo Music Corp., 1973; v.p., natl. sls. mgr., United Intl. Pictures, 1973–74; founded Atlantic Releasing Corp., 1974; Atlantic Television, Inc., 1981. All Atlantic corps. consolidated into Atlantic Entertainment Group, 1986. Co. has distributed over 100 films and produced 30 features and TV movies. Sold Atlantic, March, 1989. Formed Independent Entertainment Group, named chmn. Feb., 1992 formed Rocket Pictures.
PICTURES: Producer or Exec. Prod.: Valley Girl, Alphabet City, Roadhouse, Night of the Comet, Starchaser, Teen Wolf, Extremities, The Men's Club, Modern Girls, Nutcracker, Teen Wolf Too (exec. prod.); Cop (exec. prod.); Patty Hearst (exec. prod.), 1969 (exec. prod.).

COLER, JOEL H.: Executive. b. Bronx, NY, July 27, 1931. e. Syracuse U., B.A. journalism. Worked as adv. asst. NBC; acct. exec. Grey advertising. Joined 20th Century-Fox 1964 as adv. coordinator Fox Intl.; 1967, named intl. adv./pub. mgr. 1974, named v.p. dir., intl. adv./pub. Nov. 1990, named v.p. publicity/promotions Fox Intl. 1991, v.p. Worldwide Distrib. Services. 1984, memb. L.A. Olympic Org. Com. Left Fox in 1992 to form Joel Coler & Friends intl. mktg. consultants.

COLIN, MARGARET: Actress. b. Brooklyn, NY, 1958. Raised on Long Island. Studied acting at Stella Adler Conservatory, Juilliard, Hofstra U. Left Hofstra to pursue acting career in Manhattan where she was cast in daytime TV series The Edge of Night. NY Theatre incl. work at Ensemble Studio, Geva Theatre and Manhattan Theatre Club (Aristocrats).
PICTURES: Pretty in Pink, Something Wild, Like Father Like Son, Three Men and a Baby, True Believer, Martians Go Home, The Butcher's Wife, Amos & Andrew.
TELEVISION: Series: The Edge of Night, As the World Turns, Foley Square, Leg Work, Sibs. Movies: Warm Hearts Cold Feet, The Return of Sherlock Holmes, The Traveling Man, Good Night Sweet Wife: A Murder in Boston.

COLLERAN, BILL: Producer, Director. b. Edgerton, WI, Nov. 6, 1922. Story department 20th Century-Fox 1945–46; Director Louis de Rochemont 1946–50; stage mgr. NBC 1951; assoc. dir. The Hit Parade 1952–53; Dir. The Hit Parade, various TV specs. 1954–56; Dir. Cinerama Windjammer 1956; TV Specs. Bing Crosby, Frank Sinatra, Debbie Reynolds 1957–60; various TV specs. 1960–65, Exec. Prod. Judy Garland Show, Dean Martin Show, 1965–66; Dir. Richard Burton's "Hamlet" film, Prod. "Popendipity" ABC-TV spec. various other TV specs. 1967–70; 1971–77 Various TV specials and series; 1978–83, prod., dir., writer for Hill-Eubanks Group and Little Joey, Inc.; 1984–86, dir. music video for Simba; developing film and TV projects for own production co. 1988, semi-retired.

COLLINS, GARY: Actor. b. Boston, MA, Apr. 30, 1938.
TELEVISION: Series: The Wackiest Ship in the Army, The Iron Horse, Sixth Sense, Born Free, Hour Magazine (host), Home. Movies: Quarantined, Getting Away from It All, Houston We've Got a Problem, The Night They Took Miss Beautiful, The Kid From Left Field, Jacqueline Susann's Valley of the Dolls, Danielle Steel's Secrets. Mini-Series: Roots.
PICTURES: The Pigeon That Took Rome, The Longest Day, Cleopatra, Stranded, Angel in My Pocket, Airport, Killer Fish, Hangar 18.

COLLINS, JOAN: Actress. b. London, Eng., May 23, 1933. e. Francis Holland Sch., London. Made stage debut in A Doll's House, Arts Theatre 1946. Autobiography: Past Imperfect (1978). Author: Katy, A Fight For Life, Joan Collins Beauty Book, Spare Time, Love & Desire & Hate. On London, LA and NY stage in Private Lives.
PICTURES: I Believe in You, Lady Godiva Rides Again, Judgment Deferred, Decameron Nights, Cosh Boy, The Square Ring, Turn the Key Softly, Our Girl Friday (Adventures of Sadie), The Good Die Young, Land of the Pharaohs, Virgin Queen, Girl in the Red Velvet Swing, Opposite Sex, Sea Wife, Island in the Sun, Wayward Bus, Stopover Tokyo, The Bravados, Rally Round the Flag Boys, Seven Thieves, Esther and the King, Road to Hong Kong, Warning Shot, Can Hieronymus Merkin Ever Forget Mercy Humppe and Find True Happiness?, If It's Tuesday This Must Be Belgium, Subterfuge, The Executioner, Up in the Cellar, Quest for Love, Inn of the Frightened People, Fear in the Night, Tales from the Crypt, Tales That Witness Madness, Dark Places, Alfie Darling, The Devil Within Her, The Bawdy Adventures of Tom Jones, Empire of the Ants, The Big Sleep, The Stud, Zero to Sixty, The Bitch, Game of Vultures, Sunburn, Homework, Nutcracker.
TELEVISION: Series: Dynasty. Movies: The Cartier Affair, The Making of a Male Model, Her Life as a Man, Paper Dolls, The Wild Women of Chastity Gulch, Drive Hard Drive Fast, Dynasty: The Reunion. Special: Hansel and Gretel (Faerie Tale Theater). Mini-Series: The Moneychangers, Sins, Monte Carlo (also exec. prod.).

COLLINS, PAULINE: Actress. b. Exmouth, Devon, Eng., Sept. 3, 1940. m. actor John Alderton (Thomas on Upstairs, Downstairs). e. Central School of Speech and Drama. Stage debut A Gazelle in Park Lane (Windsor, 1962). Best known to US audiences as Sarah in Upstairs, Downstairs.
THEATER: Passion Flower Hotel (London debut, 1965), The Erpingham Camp, The Happy Apple, The Importance of Being Earnest, The Night I Chased the Women with an Eel, Come as You Are, Judies, Engaged, Confusions, Romantic Comedy, Woman in Mind, Shirley Valentine (in London won Olivier Award as best actress, in NY won Tony, Drama Desk and Outer Critics Circle Awards.)
PICTURES: Secrets of a Windmill Girl, Shirley Valentine, City of Joy.
TELEVISION: Series: Upstairs Downstairs, Thomas and Sarah, Forever Green, No—Honestly (all with husband), Tales of the Unexpected, Knockback, Tropical Moon Over Dorking.

COLLINS, STEPHEN: Actor. b. Des Moines, IA, Oct. 1, 1947. Appeared off-Bdwy. in several Joseph Papp productions before Bdwy. debut in Moonchildren, followed by No Sex We're British, The Ritz, Moonchildren, Loves of Anatol, Censored Scenes from King Kong. Off-Bdwy: Twelfth Night, The Play's the Thing, Beyond Therapy, One of the Guys, The Old Boy, Putting It Together.

PICTURES: All the President's Men, Between the Lines, The Promise, Fedora, Star Trek: The Motion Picture, Loving Couples, Brewster's Millions, Jumpin' Jack Flash, Choke Canyon, The Big Picture, Stella, My New Gun.
TELEVISION: *Series*: Tales of the Gold Monkey, Tattinger's (revamped as Nick & Hillary), Working it Out. *Movies*: Brink's: The Great Robbery, The Henderson Monster, Dark Mirror, Threesome, Weekend War, A Woman Scorned: The Betty Broderick Story, The Disappearance of Nora. *Mini-Series*: The Rhinemann Exchange, Hold the Dream, Inside the Third Reich, The Two Mrs. Grenvilles, A Woman Named Jackie.

COLT, MARSHALL: Actor, Writer. b. New Orleans, LA, Oct. 26. e. Tulane U., B.S. physics; Pepperdine U., M.A. Clinical Psychology; Fielding Inst., phd. student, Clinical Pyschology. Combat tour in Southeast Asia during Vietnam War. Captain, U.S. Naval Reserve. Stage productions: (Hotel Universe, Who's Afraid of Virginia Woolf?, Zoo Story, Killer's Head, etc.).
PICTURES: Bimbo (short), North Dallas Forty, Those Lips, Those Eyes, Jagged Edge, Flowers in the Attic, Illegally Yours, Deceptions.
TELEVISION: *Guest*: Family, Paper Chase, Streets of San Francisco, Barnaby Jones, Murder She Wrote. *Series*: McClain's Law, Lottery! *Movies*: Colorado C-1, Sharon: Portrait of a Mistress, Once an Eagle, To Heal a Nation, Mercy or Murder, Guilty of Innocence.

COLTRANE, ROBBIE: Actor. b. Rutherglen, Scotland, 1950. Ent. ind. 1974. Early career at Traverse Theatre, Edinburgh. Work included John Byrn's Slab Boys Trilogy.
TELEVISION: Kick Up The Eighties, Alfresco, Laugh I Nearly Paid My Licence Fee, Comic Strip Presents Five Go Mad in Dorset, Beat Generation, Susie, Gino and Bullshitters, Miner's Strike, Tutti Frutti, Danny, the Champion of the World (Theatrical release in Europe), The Miners Strike, Robbie Coltrane Special, Mistero Buffo, Alive & Kicking, The Secret Ingredient, Jealousy (also dir., co-writer), The Bogie Man, Rednose of Courage, Coltrane in a Cadillac: A Tour of the Western Isles.
PICTURES: Flash Gordon, Subway Riders, Britannia Hospital, Scrubbers, Ghost Dance, Krull, National Lampoon's European Vacation, Caravaggio, Defence of the Realm, Chinese Boxes, Supergrass, Mona Lisa, Eat the Rich, Bert Rigby You're a Fool, Wonderland (a.k.a. The Fruit Machine), Let It Ride, Henry V, Nuns on the Run, Perfectly Normal, The Pope Must Die, Triple Bogey on a Par 5 Hole, Oh What a Night, The Adventures of Huck Finn.

COLUMBUS, CHRIS: Director, Writer: b. Spangler, PA, 1959. Grew up in Ohio. Started making short super 8 films in high school, studied screenwriting at New York U. Film Sch., graduated 1980. Sold first s.p., Jocks, while at college. Wrote for and developed TV cartoon series, Galaxy High School.
PICTURES: Writer: Reckless, Gremlins, The Goonies, Young Sherlock Holmes, Little Nemo: Adventures in Slumberland (co-s.p.). Director: Adventures in Babysitting (debut, 1987), Heartbreak Hotel (also s.p.), Home Alone, Only the Lonely (also s.p.), Home Alone 2: Lost in New York, Mrs. Doubtfire.
TELEVISION: Amazing Stories, Twilight Zone, Alfred Hitchcock Presents.

COMDEN, BETTY: Writer. b. Brooklyn, NY, May 3, 1919. e. Erasmus Hall, NYU sch. of ed., B.S. Nightclub performer and writer with The Revuers, 1939–44. NY City Mayor's Award Art and Culture, 1978. Named to Songwriters Hall of Fame, 1980. NYU Alumnae Assn.'s Woman of Achievement award, 1987. Kennedy Center Honors for Life Achievement, 1991.
THEATER: *With Adolph Green*: writer book, sketches & lyrics for Bway. shows. On the Town (book, lyrics, actress, 1944), Billion Dollar Baby (bk., Lyrics), Bonanza Bound! (bk., lyrics), Two on the Aisle (sketches and lyrics), Wonderful Town (lyrics, Tony Award, 1953), Peter Pan (lyrics), Bells Are Ringing (bk., lyrics), Say, Darling (lyrics), A Party With Comden and Green (bk., lyrics, star; 1959 and 1977); Do Re Mi (lyrics), Subways Are For Sleeping (bk., lyrics), Fade Out-Fade In (bk., lyrics), Leonard Bernstein's Theatre Songs, Hallelujah, Baby (lyrics, Tony Award, 1968), Applause (book, Tony Award), Lorelei (revision to book), By Bernstein (book and some lyrics), On the Twentieth Century (2 Tony Awards, book and lyrics); A Doll's Life (bk., lyrics), The Will Rogers Follies (Tony Award). *Actress only*: Isn't It Romantic.
PICTURES: *Writer with Adolph Green*: Good News, Take Me Out to the Ballgame (lyricst), On the Town, Barkleys of Broadway, Singin' in the Rain (also lyrics), The Band Wagon (also lyrics), It's Always Fair Weather (also lyrics), Auntie Mame, Bells Are Ringing (also lyrics), What a Way to Go, The Addams Family (lyrics). *Actress only*: Greenwich Village, Garbo Talks, Slaves of New York.

COMO, PERRY: Singer. b. Canonsburg, PA, May 18, 1912. e. Canonsburg local schools. p. Pietro and Lucille Travaglini Como. Barber at 15; joined Carlone Band, then Ted Weems in 1936; CBS sustaining show; played many night clubs, records for RCA Victor. Best Male vocalist M.P. Daily, TV poll,

1952–55; radio poll, 1954. Best Male vocalist M.P. Daily, TV Poll, 1956: best TV performer M.P.D.–Fame poll 1957. Interfaith Award, 1953; Emmy, Peabody, Christopher Awards, 1955–56. Knight Commander and Lady Com. (Mrs. Como) of Equestrian Order of Holy Sepulchre of Jerusalem; personality of the yr., Variety Club, 1956.
PICTURES: Something for the Boys (debut, 1944), Doll Face, If I'm Lucky, Words and Music.
TELEVISION: *Series*: The Chesterfield Supper Club, The Perry Como Show (1950–61; 4 Emmy Awards), The Kraft Music Hall, (1961–3); numerous annual holiday specials.

COMPTON, JOYCE: Actress. b. Lexington, KY, Jan. 27, 1907. e. Tulsa U. r.n. Olivia Joyce Compton. Screen debut in Ankles Preferred.
PICTURES: The Awful Truth, Spring Madness, Sky Murder, Turnabout, A Southern Yankee, If I Had a Million, Christmas in Connecticut, Artists and Models Abroad, Rustlers of Red Dog, The White Parade, Wild Party, Three Sisters, Sorry Wrong Number, Mighty Joe Young, Grand Canyon, Jet Pilot, The Persuader, Girl in the Woods, many others.

CONAWAY, JEFF: Actor. b. New York, NY, Oct. 5, 1950. Started in show business at the age of 10 when he appeared in Bdwy. production, All the Way Home. Later toured in Critics Choice before turning to fashion modeling. Toured with musical group, 3½, as lead singer and guitarist. Entered theatre arts program at NYU. Film debut at 19 in Jennifer on My Mind.
THEATER: Grease, The News.
PICTURES: Jennifer on My Mind (debut, 1971), The Eagle Has Landed, Pete's Dragon, I Never Promised You a Rose Garden, Grease, The Patriot, Elvira: Mistress of the Dark, Cover Girl, Tale of Two Sisters, The Sleeping Car, A Time to Die, Total Exposure, Almost Pregnant, Alien Intruder.
TELEVISION: *Series*: Taxi, Wizards and Warriors, Berrenger's, The Bold and the Beautiful. *Guest*: From Sea to Shining Sea (1974), Joe Forrester, The Mary Tyler Moore Show, Happy Days, Movin' On, Barnaby Jones, Kojak, Mickey Spillane's Mike Hammer. *Movies*: Having Babies, Delta County, U.S.A., Breaking Up Is Hard to Do, For the Love of It, Nashville Grab, The Making of a Male Model, Bay Coven, The Dirty Dozen: The Fatal Mission, Ghost Writer, Eye of the Storm.

CONDE, RITA: Actress. b. Cuba. r.n. Elizabeth Eleanor Conde Griffiths. Now American citizen. In numerous films and on TV in Hollywood and starred in Mexican film, El Ahijado de la Muerte.
PICTURES: Ride the Pink Horse, Two Roaming Champs, No Sad Songs for Me, Topaz, Change of Habit, Barquero, World's Greatest Lover, Love at First Bite.
TELEVISION: I Love Lucy, Zorro, I Spy, Thriller, Night Gallery, Ironside, Chico and the Man, Days of Our Lives, Capitol.

CONDON, CHRIS J.: Producer, Director, Motion Equipment Designer. b. Chicago, IL, Dec. 7, 1922. e. Davidson Inst., U. of Southern California. U.S. Air Force 1943–46. Founded Century Precision Optics, 1948. Designed Athenar telephoto lenses, Century Super wide-angle lenses and Duplikins. Cofounded StereoVision International, Inc. 1969 specializing in films produced in new 3-D process. Member SMPTE. Lecturer and consultant on motion picture optics and 3-D motion picture technology.
FILMS PRODUCED: The Wild Ride, The Surfer, Girls, Airline, The New Dimensions.

CONN, ROBERT A.: Executive. b. Philadelphia, PA, Jan. 16, 1926. e. Lehigh U. 1944; U. of Pennsylvania, 1948. 1st Lt. Days of EdenArmy Security Agency, 1944–46, 1951–52; furniture dist., Philadelphia, 1948–51; band & acct. dept., MCA, 1952–53; dir. of adv. & prom. Official Films N.Y. 1954; head of Official Films Philadelphia sales office serving PA, Baltimore, Washington, Cleveland and Detroit, 1956. Eastern Reg. Sls. Mgr. Flamingo Films, 1957; acct. exec. Dunnan and Jeffrey, Inc., 1961; v.p., Dunnan and Jeffrey, 1962; pres., adv. mgr., Suburban Knitwear Co., 1963; exec. v.p. Rogal Travel Service, 1964–68. pres. RAC Travel, Inc., Jenkintown, PA. and pres. Royal Palm Travel, Inc. Palm Beach, Florida, 1978; Rosenbluth Travel Service, 1979; v.p., natl. retail mktg., E.F. Hutton & Co. (N.Y.), 1983.

CONNELLY, PAUL V.: Executive. b. Boston, MA, June 11, 1923. e. Boston Coll., MA, 1951, B.S.B.A.; 1949; Fordham U., 1951–54; Asst. professor of Economics, Manhattan Coll., 1950–54; treas., America Corp. (formerly Chesapeake Industries), 1957–59; treas., dir., Pathe-America Dist. Co. Inc., Sutton Pictures Co.; v.p., dir., Pathe Labs., Inc.; pres., dir., Pathe-Deluxe of Canada, Ltd. 1959–65; pres. International Business Relations, 1965–67; v.p., treas., dir. Movielab, Inc., 1968; v.p.–finance, Tele-Tape Corp., 1970.

CONNERY, SEAN: Actor. b. Edinburgh, Scotland, Aug. 25, 1930. r.n. Thomas Connery. Worked as a lifeguard and a model before landing role in chorus of London prod. of South

Pacific, 1953. Prod. dir., The Bowler and the Bonnet (film doc.), I've Seen You Cut Lemons (London stage). Director of Tantallon Films Ltd. (First production: Something Like the Truth).

PICTURES: No Road Back (debut, 1957), Time Lock, Hell Drivers, Action of the Tiger, Another Time Another Place, Darby O'Gill and the Little People, Tarzan's Greatest Adventure, Frightened City, On the Fiddle (Operation Snafu), The Longest Day, Dr. No, From Russia With Love, Marnie, Woman of Straw, Goldfinger, The Hill, Thunderball, A Fine Madness, You Only Live Twice, Shalako, The Molly Maguires, The Red Tent, The Anderson Tapes, Diamonds Are Forever, The Offence, Zardoz, Murder on the Orient Express, The Terrorists, The Wind and The Lion, The Man Who Would Be King, Robin and Marian, The Next Man, A Bridge Too Far, The Great Train Robbery, Meteor, Cuba, Outland, Time Bandits, Wrong Is Right, Five Days One Summer, Sword of the Valiant, Never Say Never Again, Highlander, The Name of the Rose, The Untouchables (Acad. Award, supp. actor, 1987), The Presidio, Memories of Me (cameo), Indiana Jones and the Last Crusade, Family Business, The Hunt for Red October, Russia House, Robin Hood: Prince of Thieves (cameo), Highlander 2: The Quickening, Medicine Man (also exec. prod.), Rising Sun (also exec. prod.), A Good Man in Africa.

TELEVISION: Requiem for a Heavyweight, Anna Christie, Boy with the Meataxe, Women in Love, The Crucible, Riders to the Sea, Colombe, Adventure Story, Anna Karenina, Macbeth (Canadian TV).

CONNICK, HARRY, JR.: Musician, Actor. b. New Orleans, LA, Sept. 11, 1967. Began performing with Bourbon Street jazz combos at age 6. Studied classical piano. Albums: Harry Connick, Twenty, When Harry Met Sally . . . , Lofty's Roach Soufle, We Are in Love (Grammy Award, 1991), Blue Light Red Light, Twenty Five, Eleven. Acting debut in Memphis Belle (1990). Bdwy debut 1990 in An Evening with Harry Connick Jr.

PICTURES: When Harry Met Sally . . . (special musical performances and arrangements), Memphis Belle (actor), The Godfather Part III (performed theme song), Little Man Tate (actor).

TELEVISION: Special: Swinging Out With Harry. Guest: Cheers.

CONNOR, KENNETH: Actor. b. London, England, 1937. Ent. m.p. industry 1949 in The Lady Killers.

TELEVISION: Ted Ray Show, Show Called Fred, Charlie Farnabarn's Show, Alfred Marks Time, As You Like It, Dickie Valentine Show, Black and White Minstrel, Anne Shelton, Hi Summer, Don't Say a Word (series), Room at the Bottom, On the Houses, Frankie Howard Reveals All, Allo Allo, Hi de Hi, That's My Boy.

PICTURES: Carry on Sergeant, Carry on Nurse, Carry on Constable, Watch Your Stern, Carry on Regardless, Nearly a Nasty Accident, What a Carve Up, Call Me a Cab, Carry on Cleo, Captain Nemo, Carry On Up The Jungle, Carry On Matron, Carry On Abroad, Carry on England, Carry On Emanuelle.

CONNORS, MIKE: Actor. r.n. Krekor Ohanian. b. Fresno, CA, Aug. 15, 1925. e. UCLA. Film debut in Sudden Fear (1952) as Touch Connors.

PICTURES: Sky Commando, 49th Man, Island in the Sky, Day of Triumph, Five Guns West, The Twinkle in God's Eye, Oklahoma Woman, Swamp Woman, The Day the World Ended, The Ten Commandments, Flesh and Spur, Shake Rattle and Rock, Voodoo Woman, Live Fast Die Young, Suicide Battalion, Panic Button, Seed of Violence, Good Neighbor Sam, Where Love Has Gone, Harlow, Situation Hopeless—But Not Serious, Stagecoach, Kiss the Girls and Make Them Die, Avalanche Express, Nightkill, Too Scared to Scream, Fist Fighter, Friend to Friend.

TELEVISION: Series: Tightrope, Mannix (Golden Globe award), Today's FBI, Crimes of the Century (host). Movies: High Midnight, Beg Borrow or Steal, The Killer Who Wouldn't Die, Revenge for a Rape, Long Journey Back, The Death of Ocean View Park, Casino. Mini-series: War and Remembrance.

CONRAD, ROBERT: Actor, Singer. r.n. Conrad Robert Falk. b. Chicago, IL, March 1, 1935. e. public schools, Northwestern U. Prof. debut, nightclub singer. Formed Robert Conrad Productions, 1966. Later, A Shane Productions.

TELEVISION: Series: Hawaiian Eye, Wild Wild West, The D.A., Assignment Vienna, Baa Baa Black Sheep, The Duke, A Man Called Sloane, High Mountain Rangers, Jesse Hawkes. Guest: Lawman, Maverick, 77 Sunset Strip. Mini-Series: Centennial. Movies: Weekend of Terror, The D.A.: Conspiracy to Kill, Five Desperate Women, Adventures of Nick Carter, The Last Day, Smash-Up on Interstate 5, Wild Wild West Revisited, Breaking Up Is Hard To Do, More Wild Wild West, Coach of the Year, Will: G. Gordon Liddy, Confessions of a Married Man, Hard Knox, Two Fathers' Justice, Assassin, Charley Hannah, The Fifth Missile, One

Police Plaza, High Mountain Rangers (also dir., co-story), Glory Days (also dir.), Anything to Survive, Mario and the Mob. Sworn to Vengeance.

PICTURES: Thundering Jets, Palm Springs Weekend, Young Dillinger, Murph the Surf, The Lady in Red, Wrong Is Right, Moving Violations, Uncommon Courage.

CONRAD, WILLIAM: Actor, Producer, Director. b. Louisville, KY, Sept. 27, 1920. e. Fullerton Coll. Announcer-writer-director for L.A. radio station KMPC before becoming WWII fighter pilot in 1943; returned to radio drama as original Matt Dillon of Gunsmoke series.

PICTURES: The Killers (debut 1946), Body and Soul, To the Victor, Sorry Wrong Number, East Side West Side, One Way Street, Cry Danger, The Sword of Monte Cristo, The Racket, Cry of the Hunted, The Desert Song, The Naked Jungle, Five Against the House, Johnny Concho, The Conqueror, The Ride Back, —30—, Moonshine County Express. Producer for Warner Bros.: An American Dream, A Covenant with Death, First to Fight, The Cool Ones, The Assignment. Director: My Blood Runs Cold, Brainstorm, Two on a Guillotine.

TELEVISION: Klondike (prod. and dir.), 77 Sunset Strip (prod.), True (dir. 35 episodes). Actor: Movies: The Brotherhood of the Bell, The D.A., Conspiracy to Kill, O'Hara U.S. Treasury, Vengeance: The Story of Tony Cimo. Series: Cannon, Nero Wolfe, Jake and the Fatman. Narrator: Bullwinkle Show, Wild Wild World of Animal, Tales of the Unexpected, How the West Was Won (mini-series), Buck Rogers in the 25th Century.

CONTE, JOHN: Actor, Singer. b. Palmer, MA, Sept. 15, 1915. e. Lincoln H.S., Los Angeles. Actor, Pasadena Playhouse; radio anncr., m.c.; Armed Forces, W.W.II. Pres. KMIR-TV, Channel 36, Desert Empire Television Corp., Palm Springs, NBC Affiliate.

THEATRE: On Broadway in Windy City, Allegro, Carousel, Arms and the Girl.

TELEVISION: John Conte's Little Show (1950–52), Max Liebman Spectaculars and dramatic shows, host and star of NBC Matinee Theatre; (1955–58). TV Hour of Stars; Mantovani Welcomes You.

PICTURES: Thousands Cheer, Lost in a Harem, Trauma, Man With the Golden Arm, The Carpetbaggers.

CONTI, BILL: Composer. b. Providence, RI, April 13, 1942. Studied piano at age 7, forming first band at age 15. e. Louisiana State U., Juilliard School of Music. Moved to Italy with jazz trio where scored first film, Candidate for a Killing. Was: music supvr. on Blume in Love for Paul Mazursky.

PICTURES: Harry and Tonto, Next Stop Greenwich Village, Rocky, Handle With Care, Slow Dancing in the Big City, An Unmarried Woman, F.I.S.T., The Big Fix, Paradise Alley, Uncle Joe Shannon, Rocky II, A Man a Woman and A Bank, Goldengirl, The Seduction of Joe Tynan, The Formula, Gloria, Private Benjamin, Carbon Copy, Victory, For Your Eyes Only, I The Jury, Rocky III, Neighbors, Split Image, Bad Boys, That Championship Season, Unfaithfully Yours, The Right Stuff (Acad. Award, 1983), Mass Appeal, The Karate Kid, The Bear, Big Trouble, Gotcha, Beer, Nomads, F/X, The Karate Kid II, A Prayer for the Dying, Masters of the Universe, Baby Boom, Broadcast News, For Keeps, A Night in the Life of Jimmy Reardon, Betrayed, Cohen and Tate, Big Blue, Lean On Me, The Karate Kid Part III, Lock Up, The Fourth War, Backstreet Dreams, Rocky V, Necessary Roughness, Year of the Gun, A Captive in the Land, The Adventures of Huck Finn, Bound By Honor, By the Sword, Rookie of the Year.

TELEVISION: Kill Me If You Can, Stark, North and South, The Pirate, Smashup on Interstate 5, Papa & Me, Napoleon and Josephine, Murderers Among Us: The Simon Wiesenthal Story. Series themes: Cagney and Lacy, Dynasty, Falcon Crest, The Colbys, Kenya, Heartbeat, Lifestyles of the Rich and Famous, Emerald Point N.A.S., Dolphin Cove, The Elite, Instant Recall, Inside Edition.

CONTI, TOM: Actor. b. Paisley, Scotland, Nov. 22, 1941. Trained at Royal Scottish Academy of Music, Glasgow. Did repertory work in Scotland before London stage debut appearing with Paul Scofield in Savages, 1973.

THEATER: London: Devil's Disciple, Whose Life Is It Anyway?,They're Playing Your Song, Romantic Comedy, Two Into One, Italian Straw Hat, Jeffrey Bernard is Unwell. Director: Before the Party, The Housekeeper. NY: Whose Life Is It Anyway? (Tony Award, 1979), Last Licks (dir.).

PICTURES: Galileo (debut, 1975), Eclipse, The Duellists, The Haunting of Julia (Full Circle), Merry Christmas, Mr. Lawrence; Reuben, Reuben; American Dreamer, Miracles, Saving Grace, Beyond Therapy, Gospel According to Vic, That Summer of White Roses, Shirley Valentine.

TELEVISION: Mother of Men (1959), The Glittering Prizes, Madame Bovery, Treats, The Norman Conquests, The Wall, Nazi Hunter, The Quick and the Dead, Roman Holiday, The Dumb Waiter, Faerie Tale Theater, Fatal Judgement, Blade on the Feather, Voices Within: The Lives of Truddi Chase.

CONVERSE, FRANK: Actor. b. St. Louis, MO, May 22, 1938. e. Carnegie-Mellon. Early training on stage in New York. Active in repertory theatres. Two seasons with Amer. Shakespeare Fest.
PICTURES: Hurry Sundown, Hour of the Gun, The Rowdyman, The Pilot, The Bushido Blade, Spring Fever, Everybody Wins, Primary Motive.
TELEVISION: Guest: Mod Squad, Medical Center, Wonderworks, Guests of the Nation. Series: Coronet Blue, N.Y.P.D., Movin' On, The Family Tree, Dolphin Cove, One Life to Live. Movies: Dr. Cook's Garden, A Tattered Web, In Tandem, Killer on Board, Cruise Into Terror, Sgt. Matlovich Vs. the U.S. Air Force, Marilyn: The Untold Story, The Miracle of Kathy Miller, Anne of Green Gables—The Sequel, Alone in the Neon Jungle.
STAGE: The Seagull, Death of a Salesman, Night of the Iguana, A Man for All Seasons, The House of Blue Leaves, First One Asleep Whistle, Arturo Ui, The Philadelphia Story (80 revival), Brothers, A Streetcar Named Desire (1988 revival), Design for Living, The Crucible, Hobson's Choice, The Ride Down Mount Morgan, etc.

CONWAY, GARY: Actor. r.n. Gareth Carmody. b. Boston, MA, Feb. 4, 1936. e. U. of California at L.A. As college senior was chosen for title role in Teen-Age Frankenstein. After graduating served in military at Ford Ord, CA. In 1960 began contract with Warner Bros., appearing in films and TV. Has also appeared on stage. Has given several one-man shows as painter and is represented in public and private collections.
PICTURES: I Was a Teenage Frankenstein, Young Guns of Texas, Once Is Not Enough, The Farmer (also prod.), American Ninja (also s.p.), Over The Top (co-wrote story), American Ninja III: Blood Hunt (s.p.).
TELEVISION: Series: Burke's Law, Land of the Giants. Movie: The Judge and Jake Wyler. Guest: 77 Sunset Strip, Columbo, Police Story, Love Boat.

CONWAY, KEVIN: Actor. b. New York, NY, May 29, 1942.
THEATER: One Flew Over the Cuckoo's Nest, When You Comin' Back Red Ryder? (Obie and Drama Desk Awards), Of Mice and Men, Moonchildren, Life Class, Saved, The Elephant Man, Other Places, King John (NYSF), Other People's Money (Outer Critics Circle Award, best actor, 1989, also L.A. prod.), The Man Who Fell in Love with His Wife, Ten Below. Dir.: Mecca, Short Eyes (revival), One Act Play Fest (Lincoln Center), Milk Train Doesn't Stop Here Anymore (revival), The Elephant Man (tour), Other People's Money (Chicago, L.A. & S.F.).
PICTURES: Believe in Me, Portnoy's Complaint, Slaughterhouse Five, Shamus, F.I.S.T., Paradise Alley, The Fun House, Flashpoint, Homeboy, The Sun and the Moon (dir., prod.), Funny Farm, One Good Cop, Rambling Rose, Jennifer Eight.
TELEVISION: Series: All My Children. Movies: Johnny We Hardly Knew Ye, The Deadliest Season, Rage of Angels, The Lathe of Heaven, Attack on Fear, Something About Amelia, Jesse, When Will I Be Loved?, Breaking the Silence. Specials: The Scarlet Letter, The Elephant Man.

CONWAY, TIM: Actor. b. Willoughby, OH, Dec. 15, 1933. e. Bowling Green State U. After 2 yrs. Army service joined KYW-TV in Cleveland as writer-director and occasional performer. Comedienne Rose Marie discovered him and arranged audition for the Steve Allen Show on which he became regular. In 1962 signed for McHale's Navy, series. Also has done night club appearances.
PICTURES: McHale's Navy, McHale's Navy Joins the Air Force, The World's Greatest Athlete, The Apple Dumpling Gang, Gus, The Shaggy D.A., Billion Dollar Hobo, The Apple Dumpling Gang Rides Again, The Prize Fighter, The Private Eyes, Cannonball Run II, The Longshot (also s.p.), Cyclone.
TELEVISION: Series: The Steve Allen Show, McHale's Navy, Rango, The Tim Conway Show (1970), The Tim Conway Comedy Hour, The Carol Burnett Show (3 Emmy Awards), The Tim Conway Show (1980–81), Ace Crawford: Private Eye, Tim Conway's Funny America; guest appearances on Hollywood Palace and shows starring Garry Moore, Carol Burnett, Red Skelton, Danny Kaye, Dean Martin, Cher, Doris Day. Specials: Plaza Suite, many others. Movie: Roll Freddy Roll.

COOGAN, KEITH: Actor. b. Palm Springs, CA, Jan. 13, 1970. e. Santa Monica City Col. Grandson of late actor Jackie Coogan. Formerly acted as Keith Mitchell. Appeared in shorts All Summer in a Day and The Great O'Grady.
PICTURES: The Fox and the Hound (voice), Adventures in Babysitting, Hiding Out, Under the Boardwalk, Cousins, Cheetah, Book of Love, Toy Soldiers, Don't Tell Mom the Babysitter's Dead, Forever.
TELEVISION: Series: The MacKenzies of Paradise Cove, The Waltons, Gun Shy. Movies: A Question of Love, Million Dollar Infield, Kid With the Broken Halo, Battered, Memorial Day, Spooner. Specials: Wrong Way Kid, The Treasure of Alpheus T. Winterborn, Rascal, Over the Limit, A Town's Revenge. Guest: Growing Pains, Silver Spoons, Fame, CHips, The Love Boat, Mork and Mindy, 21 Jump Street, 8 is

Enough, Fantasy Island, Just the Ten of Us, Sibs, others. Pilots: Norma Rae, Apple Dumpling Gang, Wonderland Cove.

COOK, ELISHA, JR.: Actor. b. San Francisco, CA, Dec. 26, 1903. e. St. Albans, Chicago boarding school. Joined Frank Bacon in Lightnin' at the age of 14.
THEATRE: Appeared with Ethel Barrymore in Kingdom of God, Henry, Behave, Many a Slip, Three Cornered Moon, Coquette (London). Played in vaudeville and summer stock companies. Chrysalis, Ah, Wilderness (Theatre Guild).
PICTURES: Two in a Crowd (signed by Paramount, 1936), Pigskin Parade, The Maltese Falcon, Up in Arms, Casanova Brown, Cinderella Jones, Dillinger, The Big Sleep, The Long Night, Don't Bother to Knock, I the Jury, Shane, Thunder Over the Plains, Drum Beat, Outlaw's Daughter, Timberjack, Indian Fighter, The Killing, Voodoo Island, House on Haunted Hill, Platinum High School, High School Confidential, Johnny Cool, Welcome to Hard Times, Rosemary's Baby, The Great Bank Robbery, Blacula, The Great Northfield, Minnesota Raid, Emperor of the North, Electra-Glide in Blue, The Outfit, St. Ives, The Black Bird, The Champ, Carny, Hammett.
TELEVISION: Series: Magnum P.I. Movies: The Movie Murderer, Night Chase, Night Stalker, Mad Bull, Salem's Lot, Leave 'Em Laughing, Terror at Alcatraz, This Girl for Hire, Off Sides, It Came Upon the Midnight Clear, The Man Who Broke 1000 Chains, Trouble With Grandpa.

COOK, FIELDER: Director, Producer. b. Atlanta, GA, Mar. 9, 1923. e. Washington & Lee U., B.A., 1947; U. of Birmingham, Eng., post grad., 1948. Doctor of Fine Arts (Hon) (1973) (W & L). USNR, 1944; 7th Amphibious Force, 1944–45, J. Walter Thompson Co., 1947–56.
TELEVISION: Movies: Sam Hill: Who Killed the Mysterious Mr. Foster?, Goodbye Raggedy Ann (also exec. prod.), Homecoming, Miracle on 34th Street, This is the West That Was, Miles to Go Before I Sleep, Judge Horton and the Scottsboro Boys, Beauty and the Beast, A Love Affair: The Eleanor and Lou Gehrig Story, Too Far to Go (also released theatrically), I Know Why the Caged Bird Sings, Gaugin the Savage, Family Reunion, Will There Really Be a Morning?, Why Me?, A Special Friendship. Mini-Series: Evergreen. Specials: The Hands of Carmac Joyce, Teacher Teacher, The Rivalry, Valley Forge, The Price (Emmy Award), Harvey, Brigadoon (also prod.; 2 Emmy Awards), Seize the Day, Third and Oak: The Pool Hall.
PICTURES: Patterns, Home is the Hero, A Big Hand for the Little Lady, How to Save a Marriage and Ruin Your Life, Prudence and the Pill (co-dir.), Eagle in a Cage, From the Mixed Up Files of Mrs. Basil E. Frankweiler.

COOK, PETER: Actor. Writer. b. Torquay, Devonshire, Eng., Nov. 17, 1937. e. Cambridge U. Owner-producer of The Establishment Theatre Co. 1962–. Director, Private Eye magazine. With Dudley Moore, Alan Bennett and Jonathan Miller co-wrote and starred in Beyond the Fringe (London 1959, Broadway 1964). With Dudley Moore in revue Good Evening (Tony Award, 1974). Books with Dudley Moore: Dud and Pete, The Dagenham Dialogues. Contributor to satirical periodicals.
PICTURES: The Wrong Box, Bedazzled (also co-s.p.), A Dandy in Aspic, The Bed Sitting Room, Monte Carlo or Bust, The Rise and Rise of Michael Rimmer (also s.p.), Pleasure at Her Majesty's, The Adventures of Barry McKenzie, The Hound of the Baskervilles, Derek and Clive, The Secret Policeman's Other Ball (also co-s.p.), Yellowbeard, Supergirl, The Princess Bride, Whoops Apocalypse, Without a Clue, Getting It Right, Great Balls of Fire.
TELEVISION: On the Braden Beat, Royal Variety Performance, Eamonn Andrews Show, The New London Palladium Show, Alice in Wonderland. Series: own show with Dudley Moore, Not Only But Also (also s.p.), Soho, The Two of Us (U.S.), The Last Resort, Gone to Seed.

COOK, RICHARD: Executive. b. Bakersfield, CA, Aug. 20, 1950. e. USC. Began career 1971 as Disneyland sls. rep.; promoted 1974 to mgr. of sls. Moved to studio in 1977 as mgr., pay TV and non-theatrical releases. 1980, named asst. domestic sls. mgr., for Buena Vista; 1981 promoted to v.p. & asst. gen. sls. mgr.; 1984, promoted to v.p. & gen. sls. mgr., B.V.; 1985, appt. sr. v.p., domestic distribution. 1988: appt. pres. Buena Vista Pictures Distribution.

COOKE, ALISTAIR: Journalist, Broadcaster. b. Eng., Nov. 20, 1908. e. Jesus Coll., Cambridge U.; Yale U.; Harvard U. Film crit. of BBC 1934–37. London corr. NBC 1936–37. BBC commentator in U.S. since 1937. Chief Amer. corr., Manchester Guardian, 1948–72; English narrator, The March of Time, 1938–39; v.o. narrator, Sorrowful Jones, 1948; narrator, Three Faces of Eve, 1957; narrator, Hitler, 1973; Peabody award winner for International reporting, 1952, 1973–83; author, Douglas Fairbanks, Garbo & The Night Watchmen. A Generation on Trial, One Man's America, Christmas Eve, The Vintage Mencken, etc.; m.c. Omnibus, TV show, 1952–61; m.c. prod. U.N.'s International Zone (Emmy Award, 1958); m.c., Masterpiece Theatre since 1971. Writer & narrator,

America: A Personal History of The United States, TV series BBC, NBC, PBS, for which won 5 Emmy Awards, 1973; Franklin Medal, Royal Society of Arts, 1973; Hon. Knighthood, KBE, 1973.

BOOKS: America, 1973; Six Men, 1977; Talk About America, 1968; The Americans, 1979; Above London (with Robert Cameron), 1980; Masterpieces, 1981; The Patient Has the Floor, 1986, America Observed, 1988.

COOLIDGE, MARTHA: Director, Writer, Producer. b. New Haven, CT, Aug. 17, 1946. e. Rhode Island Sch. of Design. NYU Inst. of Film and TV grad. sch. m. writer Michael Backes. Dir. short films while in school. Wrote and prod. daily children's tv show Magic Tom in Canada Worked on commercials and political doc. film crews. Prod., dir. and writer of docs. which have won festival awards, including Passing Quietly Through; David: Off and On (American Film Fest.), Old Fashioned Woman (CINE Golden Eagle Award, Blue Ribbon Award, American film festival), Bimbo (short). Magic Tom in Canada. First feature film Not a Pretty Picture (won Blue Ribbon Award, Amer. Film Fest.) Helped start assn. of Indep. Video and Filmmakers, Inc. As an AFI/Academy Intern worked with Robert Wise on his film Audrey Rose, 1976. Wrote orig. story that was filmed as the The Omega Connection. DGA, member of bd. of dirs.; WIF, member bd. of. dirs.

PICTURES: The City Girl, Valley Girl, Joy of Sex, Real Genius, Plain Clothes, That's Adequate (interviewee), Rambling Rose (IFP Spirit Award, 1991), Lost in Yonkers, Angie I Says.

TELEVISION: The Twilight Zone; Sledge Hammer (pilot); House and Home (pilot). Movies: Trenchcoat in Paradise, Bare Essentials, Crazy in Love.

COONEY, JOAN GANZ: Executive, Producer. b. Phoenix, AZ, Nov. 30, 1929. e. U. of Arizona. After working as a reporter in Phoenix, moved to NY in 1953 where she wrote soap-opera summaries at NBC. Then was publicist for U.S. Steel Hour. Became producer of live weekly political TV show Court of Reason (Emmy Award) and documentaries (Poverty, Anti-Poverty and the Poor) before founding Children's Television Workshop and Sesame Street in 1969. Currently exec. dir. CTW.

COOPER, BEN: Actor. b. Hartford, CT, Sept. 30, 1933. e. Columbia U. On stage in Life with Father, (1942); numerous radio, TV appearances (500 shows), first show May 1945.

PICTURES: Woman They Almost Lynched, A Perilous Journey, Sea of Lost Ships, Flight Nurse, Fortune Hunter, Johnny Guitar, Hell's Outpost, Eternal Sea, Last Command, Fighting Chance, Headline Hunters, Rose Tattoo, Rebel in Town, The Fastest Gun Alive, Outlaw's Son, Chartroose Caboose, Gunfight at Comanche Creek, Arizona Raiders, Red Tomahawk, One More Train to Rob, Support Your Local Gunfighter.

COOPER, HAL: Director, Performer. b. New York, NY, Feb. 22, 1923. e. U. of Michigan. m. Marta Salcido; child actor in various radio prog. since 1932; featured Bob Emery's Rainbow House, Mutual, 1936–46; asst. dir. Dock St. Theatre, Charleston, SC, 1946–48.

TELEVISION: Your Sch. Reporter, TV Baby Sitter, The Magic Cottage (writer, prod.,) dir., Valiant Lady, Search for Tomorrow, Portia Faces Life; dir., assoc. prod. Kitty Foyle; prod. dir. Indictment; assoc. prod. dir. The Happy Time; prod. dir. For Better or Worse; dir., The Clear Horizon; Assoc., prod., dir., Surprise Package; dir. Dick Van Dyke Show; prod., dir., The Art Linkletter Show, The Object Is. Dir.: Death Valley Days, I Dream of Jeannie, That Girl, I Spy, Hazel, Gidget, Gilligan's Island, NYPD, Mayberry, Courtship of Eddie's Father, My World and Welcome to It, The Brady Bunch, The Odd Couple, Mary Tyler Moore, All in the Family. Exec. prod., dir. Maude, Phyl and Mikky, Love, Sidney, Gimme a Break, Empty Nest, Dear John, The Powers That Be.

COOPER, JACKIE: Actor, Director, Producer. b. Los Angeles, CA, Sept. 15, 1922. Began theatrical career at age of 3 as m.p. actor; was member of Our Gang comedies. First starring role in 1930 in Skippy. Worked at every major studio, always with star billing. At 20 enlisted in Navy. After three-yr. tour of duty went to N.Y. to work in live TV. Appeared on Broadway stage in Mr. Roberts and on natl. tour and in London. Directed as well as acted in films and filmed TV. Served as v.p. in chg. of TV prod., for Screen Gems, 1964–69, when resigned to return to acting, directing, producing. 2 Emmy Awards for directing M*A*S*H and The White Shadow. Retired 1989.

PICTURES: Actor—Movietone Follies, Sunny Side Up, Skippy, Young Donovan's Kid, Sooky, The Champ, When a Feller Needs a Friend, Divorce in the Family, Broadway to Hollywood, The Bowery, Lone Cowboy, Treasure Island, Peck's Bad Boy, Dinky, O'Shaughnessy's Boy, The Devil Is a Sissy, Boy of the Streets, White Banners, Gangster's Boy, That Certain Age, Newsboys' Home, Scouts to the Rescue (serial), Spirit of Culver, Streets of New York, What a Life, Two Bright Boys, The Big Guy, Return of Frank James, Seventeen, Gallant Sons, Life With Henry, Ziegfeld Girl, Glamour Boy, Her First Beau, Syncopation, Men of Texas, The Navy

Comes Through, Where Are Your Children?, Stork Bites Man, Kilroy Was Here, Everything's Ducky, The Love Machine, Chosen Survivors, Superman, Superman II, III & IV, Surrender. Director: Stand Up and Be Counted.

TELEVISION: Series: People's Choice (also directed 71 segments), Hennesey (also dir. 91 segments), Dean Martin Comedy World (host), Mobile One. Movies: Shadow on the Land, Maybe I'll Come Home in the Spring, The Astronaut, The Day the Earth Moved, The Invisible Man, Mobile Two, Operation Petticoat. Director: Having Babies III, Rainbow; White Mama, Rodeo Girl, Leave 'Em Laughing, Rosie (also prod.), Glitter; The Night They Saved Christmas, Izzy and Moe.

COOPER, SHELDON: Executive. e. Indiana U. Joined WGN Television, 1950 holding various positions in prod. including floor mgr., dir., prod.; 1961, named mgr. prod.; 1961 became exec. prod. for station; 1964, named asst. prog. mgr.; 1965, mgr. of dept.; 1966, v.p. prog. dev. with WGN Continental Productions Co.; elected to bd. of dir., Continental Broadcasting Co. and appointed station mgr., WGN TV, April 1974.; 1975, named v.p. and gen. mrg., WGN Continental Broadcasting.; 1977, dir., broadcasting; 1979, pres. and gen. mgr., WGN Television; 1982, chief exec. of newly formed Tribune Entertainment Co. and dir. of Tribune Co. Syndicate, Inc., 1982–present. One of founders of Operation Prime Time, consortium of independent stations. Awarded Emmys: 1960 as television's "man of the year behind the cameras" and 1964 for continuing excellence as writer, prod., executive, WGN TV. Chmn., Assoc. of Independent TV Stations, Inc. (INTV), 1980 and 1981; National v.p., Muscular Dystrophy Assoc.; 1980, on bd. National Assoc. of TV Prog. Executives (NATPE); first v.p., Chicago chap. Acad. of TV Arts and Sciences; v.p., trustee of national chap.

COOPERMAN, ALVIN: Producer. b. Brooklyn, NY. Started career with Lee & J. J. Shubert, 1939–51; color team, dev. color TV for FCC approval, 1953; prod. first color TV shows with mobile unit, 1954; developed & prod. first Wide Wide World, June 1955; mgr. program sls., NBC Network, 1955; exec. prod. Producers Showcase, Dodsworth, Rosalinda, 1956; prod. Jack and the Beanstalk, Festival of Music, 1957; dir. prog. NBC-TV, Apr. 1957; joined HJ Enterprises as prod. NBC-TV, The Shirley Temple Storybook, 1957; exec. prod. Screen Gems, 1958; prod. Du Pont Show, 1959; exec. prod. Roncom Prod. 1960; Prod., Untouchables, 1961–63; exec. dir., Shubert Thea. Ent. 1963; v.p., special programs, NBC, 1967–68; exec. v.p., Madison Square Garden Center, 1968–72; President, Madison Square Garden Center, Inc.; Founder, Madison Sq. Garden Prods. and Network. Chairman of the Board, Athena Communications Corporation. Pres., NY Television Academy, 1987–89.

TELEVISION: Producer: Romeo and Juliet, (Emmy nominee); Pele's Last Game; The Fourth King; Amahl and the Night Visitors; Live from Studio 8H—A Tribute to Toscanini, (Emmy Award); Live from Studio 8H—An Evening with Jerome Robbins and the New York City Ballet, (Emmy Award); Live from Studio 8H—Caruso Remembered; Ain't Misbehavin', (Emmy nominee), NAACP Image Award, Best TV Show of the Year); Pope John Paul II; My Two Loves, Safe Passage; Family Album, U.S.A. (26 half hours), Witness to Survival (26 half hrs.), Mobs and Mobsters.

COPPOLA, FRANCIS FORD: Writer, Producer, Director. b. Detroit, MI, April 7, 1939. Raise in NYC. Son of late composer Carmine Coppola. Brother of actress Talia Shire. e. Hofstra U, B.A., 1958; UCLA, 1958–68, M.F.A., cinema. While at UCLA was hired as asst. to Roger Corman as dialogue dir., sound man and assoc. prod. 1969; est. American Zoetrope, (later Zoetrope Studios), a prod. center in San Francisco. Publisher, City (magazine, 1975–6).

PICTURES: The Playgirls and the Bellboy (co-dir., co-s.p., 1962), Tonight For Sure (prod., dir.), The Premature Burial (asst. dir.), The Terror (assoc. prod., co-dir.), Dementia 13 (dir., s.p.), Is Paris Burning? (co-s.p.), This Property Is Condemned (co-s.p.), You're a Big Boy Now (dir., s.p.), Reflections in a Golden Eye (s.p.), Finian's Rainbow (dir.), The Rain People (dir., s.p.), Patton (co-s.p., Acad. Award), THX 1138 (exec. prod.), The Godfather (dir., co-s.p., prod.; Acad. Awards for best picture and s.p.), American Graffiti (exec. prod.), The Conversation (prod., dir., s.p.), The Godfather Part II (co-s.p., dir.; Acad. Awards for best dir., picture, s.p.), The Great Gatsby (s.p.), Apocalypse Now (prod., dir., co-s.p.), The Black Stallion (exec. prod.), One From the Heart (prod., dir., co-s.p.), Hammett (exec. prod.), The Escape Artist (prod.), The Black Stallion Returns (exec. prod.), The Outsiders (dir., prod.), Rumble Fish (prod., dir., s.p.), The Cotton Club, (dir., co-s.p.), Mishima (exec. prod.), Peggy Sue Got Married (dir.), Gardens of Stone (dir.), Tough Guys Don't Dance (co-exec. prod.), Lionheart (exec. prod.), Tucker: The Man and His Dream (dir.), New York Stories (Life Without Zoe; dir., co-s.p.), The Godfather Part III (dir., co-s.p., prod.), Wind (co-exec. prod.), Bram Stoker's Dracula (dir., co-prod.), The Secret Garden (exec. prod.).

TELEVISION: *Movie*: The People (exec. prod.). *Special*: Rip Van Winkle (Faerie Tale Theatre). *Series*: The Outsiders (exec. prod.).

CORBIN, BARRY: Actor. b. Dawson County, TX, Oct. 16, 1940. e. Texas Tech. Univ.
PICTURES: Urban Cowboy, Stir Crazy, Any Which Way You Can, Dead and Buried, The Night the Lights Went Out in Georgia, The Best Little Whorehouse in Texas, Six Pack, Honkytonk Man, The Ballad of Gregorio Cortez, WarGames, The Man Who Loved Women, Hard Traveling, My Science Project, Nothing in Common, Under Cover, Off the Mark, Permanent Record, Critters 2: The Main Course, It Takes Two, Who is Harry Crumb?, Short Time, Ghost Dad, The Hot Spot, Career Opportunities.
TELEVISION: *Series*: Boone, Spies, Northern Exposure. *Mini-Series*: The Thorn Birds, Lonesome Dove. *Movies*: Rage, This House Possessed, The Killing of Randy Webster, Murder in Texas, Bitter Harvest, A Few Days in Weasel Creek, Fantasies, Prime Suspect, Travis McGee, Flight #90: Disaster on the Potomac, The Jesse Owens Story, Fatal Vision, I Know My First Name is Steven, Last Flight Out, The Chase, Conagher, The Keys. *Guest*: Call to Glory, Murder She Wrote, Hill Street Blues, Matlock.

CORD, ALEX: Actor. r.n. Alexander Viespi. b. Floral Park, NY, May 3, 1933. Early career in rodeo; left to become actor. Studied at Shakespeare Academy (Stratford, Conn.) and Actor's Studio (N.Y.). Spent two yrs. in summer stock; in 1961 went on tour with Stratford Shakespeare Co. Author of novel Sandsong.
PICTURES: Synanon (debut, 1965), Stagecoach, A Minute to Pray A Second to Die, The Brotherhood, Stiletto, The Last Grenade, The Dead Are Alive, Chosen Survivors, Inn of the Damned, Sidewinder One, Grayeagle, Jungle Warriors, Street Asylum.
TELEVISION: *Series*: W.E.B., Cassie & Company, Airwolf. *Movies*: The Scorpio Letters, Hunter's Man; Genesis II, Fire !, Beggerman Thief, Goliath Awaits, The Dirty Dozen: The Fatal Mission.

CORDAY, BARBARA: Executive. b. New York, NY, Oct. 15, 1944. m. Barney Rosenzweig, TV producer. Began career as publicist in N.Y. and L.A. Turned to writing for TV; named v.p., ABC-TV, in chg. of comedy series development. 1982–84, headed own production co. in association with Columbia Pictures TV; June, 1984–1987 pres., Columbia Pictures TV. Aug., 1988: appointed CBS Entertainment, exec. v.p. primetime programs. Member: Caucus of Writers, Producers & Directors; Hollywood Women's Coalition.
TELEVISION: Writer: American Dream (pilot); and co-creator, Cagney and Lacey (series).

COREY, JEFF: Actor. b. New York, NY, Aug. 10, 1914. e. Feagin Sch. of Dram. Art. On stage in Leslie Howard prod. of Hamlet, 1936; Life and Death of an American, 1938, In the Matter of J. Robert Oppenheimer and Hamlet-Mark Taper Forum, L.A. King Lear, Beverly Music Center '73.
PICTURES: All That Money Can Buy, Syncopation, The Killers, Ramrod, Joan of Arc, Roughshod, Black Shadows, Bagdad, Outriders, The Devil and Daniel Webster, My Friend Flicka, Canyon City, Singing Guns, Seconds, In Cold Blood, Golden Bullet, Boston Strangler, True Grit, Butch Cassidy and The Sundance Kid, Beneath the Planet of the Apes, Getting Straight, Little Big Man, They Call Me Mister Tibbs, Clear and Present Danger, High Flying Lowe, Catlow, Something Evil, Premonition, Shine, Rooster, Oh God!, Butch and Sundance: The Early Days, Up River, Conan the Destroyer, Cognac, Messenger of Death, Bird on a Wire, The Judas Project, Ruby Cairo.
TELEVISION: The Untouchables, The Beachcomber, The Balcony, Yellow Canary, Lady in a Cage, Outer Limits, Channing, The Doctors and the Nurses, Perry Mason, Gomer Pyle, Wild, Wild West, Run for Your Life, Bonanza, Iron Horse, Judd for Defense, Garrisons Gorillas, Gunsmoke, Hawaii Five O, Star Trek, dir. The Psychiatrist, Night Gallery, Alias Smith and Jones, Sixth Sense, Hawkins, Owen Marshall, Police Story, Bob Newhart Show, Six Million Dollar Man, Doctors Hospital, Starsky and Hutch, Land of the Free (film), Kojak, McCloud, Captains Courageous (Bell Tel. Hr.), Bionic Woman, Barney Miller, One Day at a Time, The Pirate, Lou Grant, The Powers of Jonathan Starr, Cry for the Strangers, Today's FBI, Knots Landing, Archie Bunker's Place, Faerie Tale Theatre, Night Court, Helltown (series), Morning Star/Evening Star (series), New Love American Style, Starman, The A Team, A Deadly Silence (movie), Roseanne, Wolf, Jake and the Fatman, Rose and the Jackal, To My Daughter, Payoff, Sinatra.

CORMAN, GENE: Producer. r.n. Eugene H. Corman. b. Detroit, MI, Sept. 24, 1927. e. Stanford U. Went to work for MCA as agent 1950–57; left to produce his first feature film, Hot Car Girl. Partner with brother Roger in Corman Company and New World Distributors. Vice pres. 20th Century Fox Television, 1983–87; exec. v.p. worldwide production, 21st Century Film Corp.

PICTURES: Attack of the Giant Leaches, Not of This Earth, Blood and Steel, Valley of the Redwoods, Secret of the Purple Reef, Beast from Haunted Cave, Cat Burglar, The Intruder, Tobruk, You Can't Win Em All, Cool Breeze, Hit Man, The Slams, Von Richthofen and Brown, I Escaped from Devil's Island, Secret Invasion, Vigilante Force, F.I.S.T. (exec. prod.), The Big Red One, If You Could See What I Hear, Paradise, A Man Called Sarge.
TELEVISION: What's In It For Harry, A Woman Called Golda (won Emmy and Christopher Awards as prod.), Mary and Joseph, a Love Story, Blood Ties.

CORMAN, ROGER WILLIAM: Executive, Director, Producer, Writer, Distributor. b. Detroit, MI, April 5, 1926. e. Stanford U. 1947; Oxford U., England 1950. U.S. Navy 1944; 20th Century-Fox, production dept., 1948, story analyst 1948–49; Literary agent, 1951–52; story, s.p., assoc. prod. Highway Dragnet. Formed Roger Corman Prod. and Filmgroup. Prod. over 200 feature films and dir. over 60 of them. Formed production-releasing company, org., New World Pictures, Inc., 1970. Formed prod. co., New Horizons, 1984; distribution co., Concorde, 1985. On TV acted in film Body Bags.
PICTURES: Five Guns West (1955), House of Usher, Little Shop of Horrors, Pit and the Pendulum, The Intruder, Masque of the Red Death, Tomb of Ligeia, The Secret Invasion, The Wild Angels, The Trip, Bloody Mama, Von Richtofen and Brown, Gasss, St. Valentine's Day Massacre, Box Car Bertha, Big Bad Mama, Death Race 2000, Eat My Dust, Capone, Jackson County Jail, Fighting Mad, Thunder & Lightning, Grand Theft Auto, I Never Promised You A Rose Garden, Deathsport, Avalanche, Battle Beyond the Stars, St. Jack, Love Letters, Smokey Bites the Dust, Galaxy of Terror, Slumber Party Massacre Part II (prod.), Death Stalker, Barbarian Queen, Munchies, Stripped To Kill, Big Bad Mama II (prod.), Sweet Revenge (co-exec. prod.), The Drifter (exec. prod.), Daddy's Boys (prod.), Singles (exec. prod.), Crime Zone (exec. prod.), Watcher (exec. prod.), The Lawless Land (exec. prod.), Stripped to Kill 2 (exec. prod.), The Terror Within (prod.), Lords of the Deep (prod.), Two to Tango (prod.), Time Trackers (prod.), Heros Stand Alone (prod.), Bloodfist (prod.), Silk 2 (prod.), Edgar Allan Poe's The Masque of Red Death (prod.), Roger Corman's Frankenstein Unbound (prod., dir., s.p.), Hollywood Boulevard II (exec. prod.), Rock and Roll High School Forever (exec. prod.), The Silence of the Lambs (actor), Bloodfist II (prod.).

CORNELL, JOHN: Producer, Director, Writer. b. Kalgoorlie, Western Australia, 1941. m. actress Delvene Delancy. Grew up Bunbury. e. studied pharmacy for two years in Perth. Won internship at Western Australian Newspapers at 19, becoming columnist then London editor at 26. As Melbourne prod. of TV show, A Current Affair, discovered bridge rigger Paul Hogan. Put him on show, became his manager and formed JP Productions with him in 1972. Prod. and appeared on The Paul Hogan Show. Formed movie co. with Hogan, Rimfire Films.
PICTURES: Crocodile Dundee (prod., co-s.p.); Crocodile Dundee II (prod., dir., editor), Almost an Angel (dir., prod.).

CORNFELD, STUART: Producer. b. Los Angeles, CA. e. U. of California, Berkeley. Entered America Film Institute's Center for Advanced Film Studies as producing fellow, 1975. Joined Brooksfilm as asst. to Mel Brooks on High Anxiety. Assoc. prod., History of the World Part I.
PICTURES: Fatso (1980), The Elephant Man, (exec. prod.), National Lampoon's European Vacation (co-prod.), Girls Just Want to Have Fun (exec. prod.), The Fly, Moving, The Fly II (exec. prod.), Hider in the House (co-prod.).

CORRI, ADRIENNE: Actress. r.n. Adrienne Riccoboni. b. Glasgow, Scotland, Nov. 13, 1933. Ent. Royal Acad. of Dramatic Art at 13; parts in several stage plays including The Human Touch; m.p. debut in The River. Numerous TV appearances.
PICTURES: Quo Vadis, The River, The Kidnappers, Devil Girl From Mars, Lease of Life, Make Me An Offer, Feminine Touch, The Surgeon's Knife, The Big Chance, Corridors of Blood, The Rough and the Smooth, Hellfire Club, The Tell-Tale Heart, Dynamite Jack, A Study in Terror, Bunny Lake is Missing, Doctor Zhivago, Woman Times Seven, The Viking Queen, Africa - Texas Style!, The File of the Golden Goose, Moon Zero Two, Vampire Circus, A Clockwork Orange, Madhouse, Rosebud.

CORT, BUD: Actor. r.n. Walter Edward Cox. b. New Rochelle, NY, March 29, 1950. e. NYU. School of the Arts. Stage debut in Wise Child, Bdwy. L.A. theatre includes Forget-Me-Not Lane, August 11 1947, Endgame (Dramalogue Award), Demon Wine. Founding member of L.A. Classical Theatre. Theatrical film debut as extra in Up the Down Staircase 1967. Television debut in The Doctors.
PICTURES: Sweet Charity, M•A•S•H, Gas-s-s-s, The Traveling Executioner, Brewster McCloud, Harold and Maude, Die Laughing, Why Shoot the Teacher?, She Dances Alone, Hysterical, Electric Dreams (voice), Love Letters, The Secret Diary of Sigmund Freud, Maria's Lovers, Invaders from Mars,

Love at Stake, The Chocolate War, Out of the Dark, Brain Dead, Going Under, Ted and Venus (also dir., co-s.p.).
TELEVISION: *Special*: Bernice Bobs Her Hair. *Guest*: Faerie Tale Theatre (The Nightingale), The Hitchhiker: Made for Each Other (HBO), The New Twilight Zone, Midnight Caller. *Movies*: Brave New World, The Bates Motel.

CORT, ROBERT W.: Executive. e. U. of Pennsylvania (Phi Beta Kappa). Moved into feature prod. after having worked primarily in marketing/advertising. Joined Columbia Pictures as v.p., 1976; elevated to v.p., adv./pub./promo. Named exec. v.p. of mktg. for 20th-Fox, 1980. Moved into feature prod. as senior v.p., 1981. In 1983 named exec. v.p., prod., 20th-Fox Prods. 1985, joined Interscope Communications as pres.
PICTURES: Prod.: Critical Condition, Outrageous Fortune, Revenge of the Nerds II, Three Men and a Baby, The Seventh Sign, Cocktail, Bill & Ted's Excellent Adventure (exec. prod.), Renegades (exec. prod.), Blind Fury (exec. prod.), An Innocent Man, The First Power (exec. prod.), Bird on a Wire, Arachnophobia, Three Man and a Little Lady, Eve of Destruction, Class Action, Bill & Ted's Bogus Journey, Paradise, The Hand That Rocks the Cradle, The Cutting Edge, FernGully, The Gun in Betty Lou's Handbag, Out on a Limb, Jersey Girl.
TELEVISION: A Mother's Courage (co-exec. prod.; Emmy Award).

CORTESE, VALENTINA: Actress. b. Milan, Italy, Jan. 1, 1925. Started career at 15 in Orizzonte DiPinto while studying at Rome Acad. of Dramatic Art. Screen debut: La Cena Delle Beffe, 1941; brought to Hollywood by 20th Century-Fox, following picture, A Yank in Rome; experience on dramatic stage in variety of roles inc. Shakespeare, O'Neill, Shaw.
PICTURES: Cagliostro, Glass Mountain, Black Magic, Malaya, Thieves Highway, Shadow of the Eagle, House on Telegraph Hill, Les Miserables, Secret People, Lulu, The Barefoot Contessa, Le Amiche, Magic Fire, Calabuch, Barabbas, The Visit, Juliet of the Spirits, The Legend of Lylah Clare, The Secret of Santa Vittoria, The Assassination of Trotsky, Brother Sun Sister Moon, Day for Night, When Time Ran Out, The Adventures of Baron Munchausen, Young Toscanini, Buster's Bedroom.

CORTEZ, STANLEY: Dir. Photography. b. New York, NY, 1908. e. NYU. br. Ricardo Cortez, actor. Began working with portrait photographers (Steichen, Pirie MacDonald, Bachrach, etc.), N.Y. Entered film indust. with Paramount Pictures; to Hollywood as camera asst. and later second cameraman, various studios; pioneer in use of montage; Signal Corps W.W.II, Yalta, Quebec, etc. Received Film Critics of Amer. award for work on Magnificent Ambersons. Under personal contract to David O. Selznick, Orson Welles, Walter Wanger, David Wolper. Contributor, Encyclopedia Britannica.
PICTURES: Man on the Eiffel Tower, Shark River (A.A. nominee), Bad Lands of Dakota, Magnificent Ambersons, Eagle Squadron, Powers Girl, Since You Went Away (A.A. nominee) Smash Up, Flesh and Fantasy, Captain Kidd, Secret Beyond the Door, Fort Defiance, Riders to the Stars, Black Tuesday, Night of the Hunter, Man from Del Rio, Three Faces of Eve, Top Secret Affair, Angry Red Planet, Dinosaurus, Back Street, Shock Corridor, Nightmare in the Sun, The Naked Kiss, The Candidate, Blue, The Bridge of Remagen, The Date, Another Man, Another Chance. Special sequences on Damien, Omen II, Day the World Ended, Le Bon Vivant.

CORWIN, BRUCE CONRAD: Exhibitor. b. June 11, 1940, Los Angeles, CA. e. Wesleyan U. Pres., Metropolitan Theatres Corp.; chmn., Will Rogers Hospital area ind. campaigns; pres., Variety Boys Club; Board of Trustees American Film Institute; Board of Trustees U.C.L.A. Foundation; pres., Variety Club Tent 25; Pres., L.A. Children's Museum; 1989 voted exec. v.p. Foundation of Motion Picture Pioneers.

CORWIN, NORMAN: Writer, Producer, Director. b. Boston, MA, May 3, 1910. Sports ed. Greenfield, Mass. Daily Recorder, 1926–29; radio ed., news commentator, Springfield Republican & Daily News, 1929–36; prog. dir., CBS, 1938. Bok Medal "for distinguished services to radio," 1942; Peabody Medal, 1942; awarded grant by Amer. Acad. of Arts & Letters, 1942; Page One Award, 1944; Distinguished Merit Award, Nat'l Conf. of Christians & Jews, 1945; Unity Award, Interracial Film & Radio Guild, 1945; Wendell Willkie One World Flight Award, 1946; Met. Opera Award for modern opera in collab. Bernard Rogers, 1946; first award, Res. Comm. of U.N., 1950; Radio & TV first award, Nat'l Conf. of Christians & Jews, 1951; Honor Medal of Freedom Foundation for TV show, Between Americans, 1951; ent., Radio Hall of Fame, 1962. Hon. doctorate Columbia Col. of Comms., 1967; Lincoln U., 1990; Valentine Davies Award, WGA, 1972; P.E.N. Award, 1986; author of Thirteen by Corwin, More by Corwin, Untitled & Other Plays; The Plot to Overthrow Christmas, Dog in the Sky, Overkill and Megalove, Prayer for the 70s, Holes in a Stained Glass Window, Trivializing America; lectured at various colleges; taught courses UCLA, U.of Southern California, San Diego State U., regents lecturer, U.of California at

Santa Barbara; Chairman, Creative Writing, U.S.C.-Isomata; U. of Alberta, U.S.C., Witswatersrand U., Rand Afrikaans U., So. Africa, Cantatas, The Golden Door, 55; Yes Speak Out Yes (commissioned by U.N., 1968). Faculty, U.S.C. Sch. of Journalism, 1980–. Industry Achievement Award, Broadcast Promotion Assn. 1984; Stasheff lecturer, Univ. Michigan, 1984; sect'y., M.P. Academy Foundation, 1985. Int'l Radio Fest. Gold Medal, 1991; N.Y. Fest. Lifetime Achievement, 1991. First v.p., MoPic Acad., 1989. League of Women Voters Lifetime Achievement, 1993.
STAGE PLAYS: The Rivalry, The World of Carl Sandburg, The Hyphen, Overkill and Megalove, Cervantes. Together Tonight: Jefferson, Hamilton and Burr.
PICTURES: Once Upon a Time, Blue Veil, The Grand Design, Scandal in Scourie, Lust for Life (Acad. Award nom. best adapt. s.p.), The Story of Ruth.
TELEVISION: Inside the Movie Kingdom, The FDR series, The Plot to Overthrow Christmas, Norman Corwin Presents, The Court Martial of General Yamashita, Network at 50 (CBS). Writer-host Academy Leaders (PBS).
Chmn. Doc. Award Com., Motion Picture Acad. 1965–91; elected to bd. of gov., 1980; first v.p., 1988–89; Chmn., writers' exec. comm., M.P. Academy; co-chmn. scholarship com., m.p. Academy; mem.: Film Advisory Bd.; L.A. County Museum; Norman Corwin Presents series; bd. of trustees, Advisory Board, Filmex; bd. of dirs. WGA. Secretary, Academy Fdn. mem. bd. of dirs., Intl. Documentary Assoc.

COSBY, BILL: Actor, Comedian. b. Philadelphia, PA, July 12, 1938. e. Temple U., U. of Mass., Ed.D. Served in United States Navy Medical Corps. Started as night club entertainer. Has appeared on TV variety shows, in numerous one-nighters across the country, and concert tours. *Books*: Fatherhood, Time Flies.
TELEVISION: *Series*: I Spy (3 Emmy Awards for Best Actor), The Bill Cosby Show (1969–71), The New Bill Cosby Show (1972–3), Fat Albert and the Cosby Kids (1972–7), Cos (1976), The New Fat Albert Show (Emmy, 1981), The Cosby Show (1984–92), A Different World (exec. prod. only), You Bet Your Life, Here and Now (exec. prod. only). *Specials*: The Bill Cosby Special (Emmy Award, 1969), The Second Bill Cosby Special, Fat Albert Easter Special (voice), Cosby Salutes Alvin Ailey. *Movies*: To All My Friends on Shore (also exec. prod., story, music), Top Secret.
COMEDY ALBUMS: Bill Cosby Is A Very Funny Fellow . . . Right! (Grammy Award, 1964), I Started Out As a Child (Grammy Award, 1965), Why Is There Air? (Grammy Award, 1966), Wonderfulness, Revenge (Grammy Award for both, 1967), To Russell My Brother Whom I Slept With (Grammy Award, 1969), Bill Cosby is Not Himself These Days, Rat Own Rat Own Rat Own, My Father Confused Me ... What Must I Do? What Must I Do?, Disco Bill, Bill's Best Friend, Cosby and the Kids, It's True It's True, Bill Cosby - Himself, 200 MPH, Silverthroat, Hooray for the Salvation Army Band, 8:15 12:15, For Adults Only, Bill Cosby Talks to Kids About Drugs, Inside the Mind of Bill Cosby.
RADIO: The Bill Cosby Radio Program.
PICTURES: Hickey and Boggs, Man and Boy, Uptown Saturday Night, Let's Do It Again, Mother Jugs and Speed, A Piece of the Action, California Suite, The Devil and Max Devlin, Bill Cosby Himself, Leonard: Part VI (also co-prod., story), Ghost Dad, The Meteor Man.

COSELL, HOWARD: Sports Commentator. r.n. Howard Cohen. b. Winston-Salem, NC, March 25, 1920. e. NYU, 1940. Served with U.S. Army Transportation Corp. during WW II. Studied law and practiced 1946–56. Broadcasting career began in 1953 when hired to host program on which N.Y. area Little Leaguers were introduced to baseball stars. In 1956 ABC hired him for ten five-minute sports shows on weekends. He dropped legal work to concentrate on sports reporting. Has had wide variety of roles in TV: host of Sports Focus, commentator on ABC Monday Night Football, Monday Night Baseball, Sports Beat, and various sports specials. Has hosted the Howard Cosell Sports Magazine for 4 yrs. and hosts 14 shows each week on American Contemporary Radio Network. Has guested as himself on Laugh-In, Dean Martin Show, The Odd Couple and on numerous prime-time TV shows. Founder, Legend Prods. Columnist, Daily News 1986–; Faculty mem. Brown U. 1986–.
PICTURES: Bananas, The World's Greatest Athlete, Two Minute Warning, Broadway Danny Rose.

COSMATOS, GEORGE PAN: Director, Producer, Writer. b. Tuscany, Italy, Jan. 4. e. London U., London Film School. Asst. dir., Exodus and Zorba the Greek.
PICTURES: Restless (co.-prod., s.p., dir.); Massacre in Rome (co-s.p., dir.); The Cassandra Crossing (co.-s.p., dir.); Escape to Athena (co-s.p., dir.); Of Unknown Origin (dir.); Rambo: First Blood Part II (dir.), Cobra (dir.), Leviathan (dir.).

COSTA-GAVRAS: Director. r.n. Konstaninos Gavras. b. Athens, Greece, Feb. 13, 1933. French citizen. e. Studied at the Sorbonne; Hautes Etudes Cinematographique, (IDHEC). Was leading ballet dancer in Greece before the age of 20. Worked

as second, then first assistant to Marcel Ophuls, Rene Clair, Rene Clement and Jacques Demy. Pres. of the Cinematheque Francaise (1982–7).
PICTURES: The Sleeping Car Murders (dir., s.p.), Un Homme De Trop (won prize at the Moscow Fest., 1966), Z (dir., co-s.p., Acad. Award, Best Foreign Lang. Film), L'Aveu (The Confession), State of Siege, Special Section, Clair de Femme, Missing (also co-s.p.; Acad. Award for s.p.; Palm d'Or, Cannes Fest.), Hannah K. (also co.-s.p.), Family Business (also s.p.), Betrayed, Music Box (Golden Bear, Berlin Festival), The Little Apocalypse.

COSTNER, KEVIN: Actor. b. Lynwood, CA, Jan. 18, 1955. e. CA. State U, Fullerton majored in marketing. Acted with South Coast Actors' Co-op, community theater gp. while at coll. After grad. took marketing job which lasted 30 days. Early film work in low budget exploitation film, Sizzle Beach, 1974. Then one line as Luther Adler in Frances. Role in The Big Chill was edited from final print. 1989, set up own prod. co. TIG Prods. at Raleigh Studios.
PICTURES: Sizzle Beach U.S.A., Shadows Run Black, Night Shift, Chasing Dreams, Table for Five, Testament, Stacy's Knights, The Gunrunner, Fandango, Silverado, American Flyers, The Untouchables, No Way Out, Bull Durham, Field of Dreams, Revenge (also exec. prod.), Dances with Wolves (also dir., co-prod.; Acad. Awards for Best Picture & Director, 1990), Robin Hood: Prince of Thieves, JFK, The Bodyguard (also co-prod.), China Moon (exec. prod. only), A Perfect World, Rap Nui (co-prod. only), Wyatt Earp (also co-prod.).

COTTEN, JOSEPH: Actor. b. Petersburg, VA, May 13, 1905. m. actress Patricia Medina. Studied acting at Hickman Sch. of Expression (D.C.). In stock and on NY stage; also Orson Welles' Federal Theatre's productions and Mercury Theatre of the Air. Autobiography: Vanity Will Get You Nowhere (1988).
STAGE: Absent Father, Jezebel, Accent on Youth, Postman Always Rings Twice, The Philadelphia Story, Sabrina Fair, Once More With Feeling, Prescription: Murder, Calculated Risk.
TELEVISION: Series: The 20th Century Fox Hour (host), The Joseph Cotten Show, Hollywood and the Stars (host). Guest: Alfred Hitchcock Presents, On Trial, Desilu Playhouse. Movies: Some May Live, Split Second to an Epitaph, The Lonely Profession, Cutter's Trail, Assault on the Wayne, Do You Take This Stranger?, City Beneath the Sea, The Screaming Woman, The Devil's Daughter, The Lindbergh Kidnapping Case, Aspen, Return to Fantasy Island, Casino.
PICTURES: Citizen Kane (debut, 1941), Lydia, The Magnificent Ambersons, Journey Into Fear, Shadow of a Doubt, Hers to Hold, Gaslight, Since You Went Away, I'll Be Seeing You, Love Letters, Duel in the Sun, The Farmer's Daughter, Portrait of Jennie, Under Capricorn, Beyond the Forest, The Third Man, Two Flags West, September Affair, Walk Softly Stranger, Half Angel, Peking Express, Man With a Cloak, The Untamed Frontier, The Steel Trap, Niagara, Blueprint for Murder, Special Delivery, Bottom of the Bottle, Killer Is Loose, Halliday Brand, Touch of Evil (unbilled), From the Earth to the Moon, The Angel Wore Red, The Last Sunset, Hush Hush Sweet Charlotte, The Great Sioux Massacre, The Oscar, The Hellbenders, The Tramplers, The Money Trap, Brighty and the Grand Canyon, Jack of Diamonds, The White Comanche, Petulia, The Grasshopper, Tora! Tora! Tora!, Lady Frankenstein, Baron Blood, The Abominable Dr. Phibes, Soylent Green, A Delicate Balance, Twilight's Last Gleaming, Airport '77, Caravans, Guyana: Cult of the Damned, The Hearse, Heaven's Gate.

COURTENAY, TOM: Actor. b. Hull, England, Feb. 25, 1937 e. University Coll., London, Royal Acad. of Dramatic Art, 1960–61; Old Vic. Ent. TV 1961 in Private Potter and the Lads; I Heard the Owl Call My Name (U.S.).
STAGE: Billy Liar, Andorra, Hamlet, She Stoops to Conquer, Otherwise Engaged (N.Y. debut), The Dresser, Poison Pen.
PICTURES: The Loneliness of the Long Distance Runner (debut, 1962), Private Potter, Billy Liar, King and Country, Operation Crossbow, King Rat, Dr. Zhivago (Acad. Award nom.), Night of the Generals, The Day the Fish Came Out, A Dandy in Aspic, Otley, One Day in the Life of Ivan Denisovich, Catch Me a Spy, The Dresser (Acad. Award nom.), Happy New Year, Leonard Part VI, Let Him Have It, The Last Butterfly.
TELEVISION: Series: The Lads, Ghosts, Private Potter. Movies: I Heard the Owl Call My Name, Jesus of Nazareth, Absent Friends, Chekhov in Yalta.

COURTLAND, JEROME: Actor-Producer-Director. b. Knoxville, TN, Dec. 27, 1926. Began career in 40s as actor, then turned to directing and producing.
PICTURES: Actor: Kiss and Tell, Man from Colorado, Battleground, The Barefoot Mailman, The Bamboo Prison, Tonka, Black Spurs. Director: Run, Cougar, Run, Diamond on

Wheels. Producer: Escape to Witch Mountain, Ride a Wild Pony, Return from Witch Mountain, Pete's Dragon.
TELEVISION: Actor: The Saga of Andy Burnett, Tonka. Director: Hog Wild (also co-prod.), Harness Fever. Director: Knots Landing, Dynasty, Hotel, Love Boat, Fantasy Island.

COUSTEAU, JACQUES-YVES, CAPTAIN: Producer. b. St. Andre de Cubzac, Gironde, 1910. e. French Naval Acad. Trained as Navy flier, switched to Gunnery office and started diving experiments. 1943 with Emile Gagnan conceived and released Aqua-Lung, first regulated compressed air breathing device for deep sea diving. After WWII org. Experimental Diving Unit, performed oceanographic research. 1951 perfected first underwater camera equipment for TV. Founded environmental org. The Cousteau Society 1974. Awarded Chevalier de la Legion d Honneur for work in Resistance. Member National Acad. of Sciences. Elected to the Academic Francaise.
PICTURES: 20 short documentaries 1942–56; The Silent World (Acad. Award, 1957; Grand Prize Cannes, 1956); The Golden Fish (Acad. Award, short subject, 1959), World Without Sun (Acad. Award, 1965), Voyage to the Edge of the World.
TELEVISION: Nearly 100 TV films on his series: The World of Jacques-Yves Cousteau; The Undersea World of Jacques Cousteau (8 Emmys) Oasis in Space; The Cousteau Odyssey series; Cousteau/Amazon, Rediscovery of the World series (exec. prod.).

COUTARD, RAOUL: Cinematographer. b. Paris, France, 1924. Spent 4 years in Vietnam working for French Military Info. Service, later a civilian photographer for Time and Paris-Match. During WWII worked in photo labs. After war returned to France and formed prod. co. making documentaries. Joined Jean-Luc Godard as his cinematographer on Breathless (1960). His use of hand-held camera and natural light established him as a seminal cameraman of the French New Wave, working with Godard, Truffaut and later with Costa Gavras. Director: Hoa Binh (1971).
PICTURES: Breathless, Shoot the Piano Player, Lola, Jules and Jim, Bay of Angels, Les Carabiniers, Alphaville, The Soft Skin, Pierrot le Fou, La 317 eme Section, Weekend, Sailor From Gibralter, The Bride Wore Black, Z, The Confession, Le Crabe Tambour, Passion, First Name: Carmen, Dangerous Moves, Salt on the Skin, La Garce, Max My Love, Burning Beds, Let Sleeping Cops Lie, Bethune: The Making of a Hero.

COWAN, WARREN J.: Publicist. b. New York, NY, Mar. 13. e. Townsend Harris H.S., UCLA, graduated 1941. Entered public relations, 1941, with Alan Gordon & Associates; three yrs. Air Force; joined Henry C. Rogers office in 1945; became partner, 1949, and changed name to Rogers & Cowan, Public Relations; Advisor, Rogers & Cowan, Inc., 1960; pres., Rogers & Cowan, Inc., 1964; named bd. chmn., 1983. Active in various entertainment industry, civic and philanthropic orgs., including current post as national communications chmn. for the United Way of America. On advisory bd. of the National Association of Film Commissioners; serves on the Second Decade Council of the American Film Institute. On bd. L.A. County High School for the Arts.

COX, ALEX: Director, Writer. b. Liverpool, Eng., Dec. 15, 1954. Studied law at Oxford U. where he dir. and acted in plays for school drama society. Studied film prod. Bristol U. Received Fulbright Scholarship to study at UCLA film school, 1981.
PICTURES: Repo Man (also s.p.), Sid and Nancy (also co-s.p.), Straight to Hell (also co-s.p.), Walker (also co-editor), Highway Patrolman.

COX, COURTENEY: Actress. b. Birmingham, AL, June 15, 1964. Left AL to pursue modelling career in NY. Dir. Brian DePalma selected her to be the young woman who jumps out of audience and dances with Bruce Springsteen in his music video Dancing in the Dark. This break led to featured role in short-lived TV series Misfits of Science (1985–86).
PICTURES: Masters of the Universe, Down Twisted, Cocoon: The Return, Mr. Destiny, Blue Desert, Shaking the Tree, The Opposite Sex, Ace Ventura.
TELEVISION: Series: Misfits of Science, Family Ties. Movies: I'll Be Home for Christmas, Roxanne: The Prize Pulitzer, Till We Meet Again, Curiosity Kills, Battling for Baby, Topper.

COX, RONNY: Actor. b. Cloudcroft, NM, July 23, 1938. e. Eastern New Mexico Univ.
PICTURES: The Happiness Cage (debut, 1972), Deliverance, Hugo the Hippo (voice), Bound for Glory, The Car, Gray Lady Down, Harper Valley P.T.A., The Onion Field, Taps, The Beast Within, Some Kind of Hero, Courage, Beverly Hills Cop, Vision Quest, Hollywood Vice Squad, Steele Justice, Beverly Hills Cop II, Robocop, One Man Force, Loose Cannons, Martians Go Home!, Total Recall, Scissors, Captain America, Past Midnight.
TELEVISION: Series: Apple's Way, Spencer, St. Elsewhere, Cop Rock. Movies: The Connection, A Case of Rape,

Who Is the Black Dahlia?, Having Babies, Corey: For the People, The Girl Called Hatter Fox, Lovey: A Circle of Children Part II, Transplant, When Hell Was in Session, Fugitive Family, Courage of Kavik: The Wolf Dog, The Last Song, Alcatraz—The Whole Shocking Story, Fallen Angel, Two of a Kind, The Jesse Owens Story, The Abduction of Kari Swenson, Baby Girl Scott, In the Line of Duty: The FBI Murders, The Comeback, When We Were Young, With Murder in Mind, Perry Mason: The Case of the Heartbroken Bride. *Mini-Series*: Favorite Son. *Specials*: Our Town, Chicago 7 Trial.

COYOTE, PETER: Actor. r.n. Peter Cohon. b. New York, NY, 1942. Studied with San Francisco Actors Workshop. Theatre includes The Minstrel Show (dir.), Olive Pits (also co-writer), The Red Snake, True West, The Abduction of Kari Swenson, Baby Girl Scott.
PICTURES: Die Laughing (debut, 1980), Tell Me a Riddle, Southern Comfort, The Pursuit of D.B. Cooper, E.T.: The Extra Terrestrial, Endangered Species, Timerider, Cross Creek, Slayground, Stranger's Kiss, Heartbreakers, The Legend of Billie Jean, Jagged Edge, Outrageous Fortune, A Man in Love, Stacking, Heart of Midnight, The Man Inside, Crooked Hearts, Exposure, Bitter Moon.
TELEVISION: *Movies*: Alcatraz: The Whole Shocking Story, The People vs. Jean Harris, Isabel's Choice, Best Kept Secrets, Scorned and Swindled, The Blue Yonder, Child's Cry, Sworn to Silence, Echoes in the Darkness, Unconquered, A Seduction in Travis County, Living a Lie, Keeper of the City. *Special*: Abraham Lincoln: A New Birth of Freedom (voice).

CRAIG, MICHAEL: Actor. b. India, Jan. 27, 1929. At 16 joined Merchant Navy. 1949 returned to England and made stage debut in repertory. M.P. debut as crowd artist 1950.
PICTURES: Malta Story, The Love Lottery, Passage Home, The Black Tent, Yield to the Night, Eye-Witness, House of Secrets, High Tide At Noon, Sea of Sand, Sapphire, Upstairs and Downstairs, The Angry Silence, Cone of Silence, Doctor In Love, Mysterious Island, Payroll, No My Darling Daughter, A Pair of Briefs; A Life for Ruth, The Iron Maiden, Captive City, Summer Flight, Stolen Flight, Of a Thousand Delights, Life at the Top, Modesty Blaise, Star, The Royal Hunt of the Sun, Brotherly Love, A Town Called Hell, Vault of Horror, Inn of the Damned, Ride a Wild Pony, The Irishman, Turkey Shoot, Appointment with Death.

CRAIN, JEANNE: Actress. b. Barstow, CA, May 25, 1925. Model; crowned Miss Long Beach of 1941: Camera Girl of 1942.
PICTURES: The Gang's All Here (debut, 1943), Home in Indiana, In the Meantime Darling, Winged Victory, State Fair, Leave Her to Heaven, Margie, Centennial Summer, You Were Meant for Me, Apartment for Peggy, Letter to Three Wives, The Fan, Pinky, Cheaper by the Dozen, I'll Get By (cameo), Take Care of My Little Girl, People Will Talk, Model and the Marriage Broker, Belles on Their Toes, O. Henry's Full House, City of Bad Men, Dangerous Crossing, Vicki, Duel in the Jungle, Man Without a Star, The Second Greatest Sex, Gentlemen Marry Brunettes, Fastest Gun Alive, Tattered Dress, The Joker is Wild, Guns of the Timberland, Queen of the Nile, Twenty Plus Two, Madison Avenue, Pontius Pilate, Hot Rods to Hell, Skyjacked.

CRAMER, DOUGLAS S.: Executive. e. Northwestern U., Sorbonne, U. of Cincinnati, B.A.; Columbia U.M.F.A. m. Joyce Haber, columnist. Taught at Carnegie Inst. of Tech., 1954–55; Production asst. Radio City Music Hall 1950–51; MGM Script Dept. 1952; Manag. Dir. Cincinnati Summer Playhouse 1953–54. TV supvr. Procter and Gamble 1958–59; Broadcast supvr. Ogilvy, Benson and Mather, Adv. 1959–62; v.p. program dev. ABC-TV 1962–66; v.p. program dev. 20 Cent.-Fox TV 1966; Exec. v.p. in chg. of production, Paramount Television, 1968–71; exec. v.p. Aaron Spelling Prods. 1976–89; Pres. Douglas S. Cramer Co, 1989–.
PLAYS: Call of Duty, Love is a Smoke, Whose Baby Are You.
TELEVISION: Exec. prod.: Bridget Loves Bernie, QB VII, Dawn: Portrait of a Runaway, Danielle Steel's Fine Things, Kaleidoscope, Changes. Co-exec. prod.: Love Boat (1977–86), Vegas (1978–81), Wonder Woman, Dynasty, Matt Houston, Hotel, Colbys.

CRAVEN, GEMMA: Actress. b. Dublin, Ireland, June 1, 1950. e. Loretto Coll. Studied acting at Bush Davies School. London stage debut, Fiddler on the Roof (1970). Considerable work in theater throughout England and Ireland.
THEATER: London: Audrey, Trelawny, Dandy Dick, They're Playing Our Song, Song and Dance, Loot, A Chorus of Disapproval, Three Men on a Horse, South Pacific, Jacobowsky and the Colonel, The Magistrate, The London Vertigo.
PICTURES: Kingdom of Gifts; Why Not Stay for Breakfast; The Slipper and the Rose; Wagner, Double X: The Name of the Game.
TELEVISION: Pennies From Heaven, Must Wear Tights, She Loves Me, Song by Song by Noel Coward, Song by

Song by Alan Jay Lerner, East Lynne, Robin of Sherwood, Treasure Hunt, Gemma Girls and Gershwin, Boon, The Bill.

CRAVEN, WES: Director. Writer. b. Cleveland, OH, Aug. 2, 1939. e. Wheaton Coll., B.A.; Johns Hopkins, M.A. (philosophy). Worked as humanities prof. and synch-up asst. to dir. Sean Cunningham.
PICTURES: The Last House on the Left (also s.p., ed.), The Hills Have Eyes (also s.p., ed.), Deadly Blessing (also s.p.), Swamp Thing (also s.p.), A Nightmare on Elm Street (also s.p.), The Hills Have Eyes Part II (also s.p.), Deadly Friend, A Nightmare on Elm Street III: Dream Warriors (co-s.p., co-exec. prod. only), The Serpent and the Rainbow, Shocker (also exec. prod., s.p.), The People Under the Stairs (also s.p., co-exec. prod.).
TELEVISION: *Series*: Twilight Zone (1985, 7 episodes: Word Play, A Little Peace and Quiet, Shatterday, Chameleon, Dealer's Choice, The Road Less Traveled, Pilgrim Soul). The People Next Door (exec. prod.). *Movies*: A Stranger in Our House, Invitation to Hell, Chiller, Casebusters, Night Visions (also exec. prod., co-writer), Laurel Canyon (exec. prod. only), Body Bags (actor only).

CRAWFORD, MICHAEL: O.B.E. Actor. b. Salisbury, England, Jan. 19, 1942. r.n. Michael Dumble-Smith. Early career as boy actor in children's films, as a boy soprano in Benjamin Britten's Let's Make an Opera and on radio. Later star of TV's Not So Much a Programme, More a Way of Life. Solo albums incl. Songs from the Stage and Screen (1988).
STAGE: Come Blow Your Horn, Traveling Light, The Anniversary, White Lies and Black Comedy (N.Y.), No Sex Please We're British, Billy, Same Time Next Year, Flowers for Algernon, Barnum, The Phantom of the Opera (London: Laurence Olivier Award; New York; Tony, Drama Desk, Drama League and Outer Circle Critics Awards, 1988).
PICTURES: Soap Box Derby (1950), Blow Your Own Trumpet, A French Mistress, Two Living One Dead, Two Left Feet, The War Lover, The Knack and How to Get It, A Funny Thing Happened on the Way to the Forum, The Jokers, How I Won the War, Hello Dolly!, The Games, Hello-Goodbye, Alice's Adventures in Wonderland, Condorman, Once Upon a Forest (voice).
TELEVISION: Still Life, Destiny, Byron, Move After Checkmate, Three Barrelled Shotgun, Home Sweet Honeycomb, Some Mothers Do 'ave 'em, Chalk and Cheese, BBC Play for Today, Private View, Barnum.

CRENNA, RICHARD: Actor. b. Los Angeles, CA, Nov. 30, 1927. e. Belmont H.S., U. of Southern California.
RADIO: Boy Scout Jamboree, A Date With Judy, The Hardy Family, The Great Gildersleeve, Burns & Allen, Our Miss Brooks.
TELEVISION: *Series*: Our Miss Brooks, The Real McCoys, Slattery's People, All's Fair, It Takes Two, Pros & Cons. *Movies*: Footsteps, Thief, Passions, A Case of Deadly Force, The Day the Bubble Burst, Centennial, The Rape of Richard Beck (Emmy Award, 1985), Doubletake, The Price of Passion, Police Story: The Freeway Killings, Plaza Suite, Kids Like These, On Wings of Eagles, Internal Affairs, Blood Brothers: The Case of the Hillside Stranglers, Murder in Black and White, Stuck with Each Other, Montana, Last Flight Out, Murder Times Seven, And the Sea Will Tell, Intruders, Terror on Track 9, A Place to Be Loved.
PICTURES: Pride of St. Louis, It Grows on Trees, Red Skies of Montana, Over-Exposed, Our Miss Brooks, John Goldfarb Please Come Home, Made in Paris, The Sand Pebbles, Wait Until Dark, Star, Marooned, Midas Run, The Deserter, Doctor's Wives, Red Sky at Morning, Catlow, A Man Called Noon, Dirty Money, Breakheart Pass, The Evil, Wild Horse Hank, Death Ship, Stone Cold Dead, Body Heat, First Blood, Table for Five, The Flamingo Kid, Rambo: First Blood Part II, Summer Rental, Rambo III, Leviathan, Hot Shots! Part Deux.

CRICHTON, CHARLES: Director. b. Wallasey, Aug. 6, 1910. e. Oundle & Oxford. Collab. dir. Dead of Night.
PICTURES: Painted Boats, Hue and Cry, Against the Wind, Another Shore, Dance Hall, Lavender Hill Mob, Hunted (Stranger in Between), Titfield Thunderbolt, The Love Lottery, Divided Heart, Man in the Sky, Floods of Fear, Battle of the Sexes, The Third Secret, He Who Rides a Tiger, A Fish Called Wanda.
TELEVISION: The Wild Duck, Danger Man, The Avengers, Man in a Suitcase, The Strange Report, Shirley's World, Black Beauty, The Protectors, Space 1999, Return of the Saint, Dick Turpin 1 & 2 Series, Smuggler, Video Arts Shorts.

CRICHTON, MICHAEL: Writer, Director. r.n. John Michael Crichton. b. Chicago, IL, Oct. 28, 1942. e. Harvard U, 1969. Postdoctoral fellow, Salk Inst., La Jolla, 1969–70. Visiting writer, MIT, 1988. Has written books under different names, including A Case of Need (as Jeffry Hudson; filmed as The Carey Treatment), Binary. Other books incl. The Andromeda Strain, Five Patients, The Great Train Robbery, Jasper Johns, Congo, Sphere, Travels, Jurassic Park, Rising Son. Recipient Edgar Award, Mystery Writers Amer.: A Case of Need (1968),

The Great Train Robbery (1980). Named medical writer of year, Assn. of Amer. Med. Writers: Five Patients (1970). PICTURES: *Director-Writer*: Westworld, Coma, The Great Train Robbery, Looker, Runaway, Physical Evidence (dir. only). TELEVISION: *Movie*: Pursuit (dir.; script by Robert Dozier based on Crichton's book, Binary).

CRIST, JUDITH: Journalist, Critic. b. New York, NY, May 22, 1922. e. Hunter College, Columbia U. School of Journalism. Joined New York Herald Tribune, serving as reporter, arts editor, assoc. drama critic, film critic. Continued as film critic for New York World Journal Tribune, NBC-TV Today Show, New York Magazine, New York Post, Saturday Review, TV Guide, WWOR-TV. Now regular film critic for Coming Attractions. Teaches at Col. Grad. School of Journalism. AUTHOR: The Private Eye, The Cowboy and the Very Naked Girl; Judith Crist's TV Guide to the Movies; Take 22: Moviemakers on Moviemaking.

CRISTALDI, FRANCO: Producer. b. Turin, Italy, Oct. 3, 1924. Owner, prod. Vides Cinematografica; President of Italian Producer's Union. PICTURES: White Nights, The Strawman, The Challenge, Big Deal On Madonna Street, Kapo, The Dauphins, Salvatore Giuliano, The Assassin, Divorce Italian Style, The Organizer, Bebo's Girl, Seduced and Abandoned, Time of Indifference, Sandra, A Rose for Every-One, China Is Near, A Quiet Couple, The Red Tent, New Paradise Cinema. TELEVISION: Marco Polo.

CRONENBERG, DAVID: Writer, Director. b. Toronto, Ont., May 15, 1943. e. U. of Toronto. In college produced two short movies on 16mm. 1971, to Europe on a Canadian Council grant where shot in 1975 his first feature, Shivers (aka They Came From Within). PICTURES: They Came From Within (also s.p.), Rabid (also s.p.), Fast Company, The Brood (also s.p.), Scanners (also s.p.), Videodrome, The Dead Zone, Into the Night (cameo only), The Fly (also co-s.p., cameo), Dead Ringers (also co-prod., co-s.p.), Nightbreed (actor only), Naked Lunch (also s.p.), M. Butterfly.

CRONKITE, WALTER: Correspondent. b. St. Joseph, MO, Nov. 4, 1916. e. U. of Texas. Reporter and editor Scripps-Howard News Service, TX; radio reporter; U.P. correspondent. WW II corres. British Isles, N. Africa. Foreign Correspondent, France, Belgium, Netherlands, Soviet Union. Joined CBS as Washington news correspondent, 1950; anchorman and mng. editor, CBS Evening News, 1962–81; special correspondent, CBS News, 1981–present. Many TV shows including You Are There, Twentieth Century, Eyewitness to History: CBS Reports: 21st Century, Walter Cronkite's Universe. Past nat'l pres. & mem. bd. Trustees, Acad. TV Arts & Sciences. Mng. editor of CBS Evening News 1963–81; Special corres., Children of Apartheid, Walter Cronkite at Large.

CRONYN, HUME: Actor, Writer, Director. b. London, Ont., Canada, July 18, 1911. m. Jessica Tandy, actress. e. Ridley Coll., McGill U., Amer. Acad. of Dramatic Art. STAGE: (Actor N.Y. plays) High Tor, Escape This Night, Three Men on a Horse, Boy Meets Girl, Three Sisters, Mr. Big, The Survivors, Now I Lay Me Down to Sleep (dir.), Hilda Crane (dir.), The Fourposter (dir.), Madam Will You Walk, The Honeys, A Day by the Sea, The Man in the Dog Suit, The Egghead (dir.), Triple Play (dir. and toured with wife), Big Fish Little Fish (also in London), The Miser, The Three Sisters, Hamlet, The Physicists, Slow Dance on the Killing Ground (prod.), appeared at the White House, Hear America Speaking, Richard III, The Miser, A Delicate Balance (1966 and tour, 1967), The Miser, Hadrian VII (tour), Game Cuauty Court Martial, Promenade All, Krapp's Last Tape, Happy Days, Act Without Words, Coward In Two Keys, concert recital Many Faces Of Love, Noel Coward in Two Keys (National tour), Merchant of Venice and A Midsummer Night's Dream (Stratford Festival Theatre) Canada, The Gin Game (with Miss Tandy; Long Wharf Thea., New Haven, Bdwy, 1977, co-prod. with Mike Nichols; also toured U.S., Toronto, London, U.S.S.R., 1978–79). Foxfire (co-author, actor, at Stratford, Ont., 1980, Minneapolis, 1981 and N.Y., 1982–83); Traveler in the Dark (Amer. Repertory Theatre, Cambridge, MA), Foxfire (Ahmanson, LA 1985–86), The Petition (NY 1986). PICTURES: Shadow of a Doubt (debut, 1943), Phantom of the Opera, The Cross of Lorraine, Lifeboat, The Seventh Cross (Acad. Award nom.), Main Street After Dark, The Sailor Takes a Wife, A Letter for Evie, The Green Years, The Postman Always Rings Twice, Ziegfeld Follies, The Secret Heart (narrator), The Beginning or the End, Brute Force, Rope (adapt. only), The Bride Goes Wild, Top o' the Morning, Under Capricorn (adapt. only), People Will Talk, Crowded Paradise, Sunrise at Campobello, Cleopatra, Hamlet, Gaily Gaily, The Arrangement, There Was a Crooked Man, Conrack, The Parallax View, Honky Tonk Freeway, Rollover, The World According to Garp, Impulse, Brewster's Millions, Cocoon, Batteries Not Included, Cocoon: The Return, The Pelican Brief.

TELEVISION: *Series*: The Marriage. *Movies*: The Dollmaker (co-writer only), Foxfire (also co-writer), Day One, Age-old Friends, Christmas on Division Street, Broadway Bound (Emmy Award, 1992).

CROSBY, BOB: Band leader, Actor. r.n. George Robert C. b. Spokane, WA, Aug. 23, 1913. Brother of late singer-actor Bing Crosby. e. Gonzaga U. Began as singer; later featured vocalist Jimmie & Tommy Dorsey band. Org. own band (Bobcats); appeared with orch. on screen in Let's Make Music, 1940. PICTURES: Sis Hopkins, Reveille with Beverly, Thousands Cheer, Presenting Lily Mars, See Here Private Hargrove; Meet Miss Bobby Socks, Kansas City Kitty, My Gal Loves Music, Pardon My Rhythm, Singing Sheriff, Two Tickets to Broadway. TELEVISION: Bob Crosby Show.

CROSBY, CATHY LEE: Actress. b. Los Angeles, CA, Dec. 2. e. Grad. of U. of Southern California. Studied with Lee Strasberg. STAGE: Downside Risk, Almost Perfect (Off-Bdwy debut), Jellyroll Shoes, They Shoot Horses, Don't They? (wrote, dir. starred in 1st theatrical adapt. Hollywood Amer. Legion), Zoot Suit—The Real Story (writer, dir., actress, adapt., Beverly Hills). PICTURES: The Laughing Policeman (debut, 1973), Trackdown, The Dark, Coach, Training Camp (s.p.), San Sebastian (s.p.), Call Me By My Rightful Name, The Player. TELEVISION: *Movies*: Wonder Woman, Keefer, Roughnecks, World War III, Intimate Strangers, One Child. *Series*: That's Incredible, Fort Boyard. *Specials*: A Spectacular Evening in Egypt, Battle of the Network Stars, Circus of the Stars, Bob Hope Specials, Get High on Yourself.

CROSBY, KATHRYN: Actress. r.n. Kathryn Grandstaff. b. Houston, TX, Nov. 25, 1933. e. U. of Texas, UCLA. m. late actor-singer Bing Crosby. PICTURES: Forever Female, Rear Window, Living It Up, Arrowhead, Casanova's Big Night, Unchained, Cell 2455 Death Row, Tight Spot, Five Against the House, Reprisal, Guns of Fort Petticoat, Phenix City Story, Wild Party, Mister Cory, Night the World Exploded, Brothers Rico, Operation Mad Ball, The Big Circus. TELEVISION: *Guest*: Bob Hope Chrysler Theatre, Bing Crosby Christmas Specials, Suspense Theatre, Ben Casey, The Kathryn Crosby Show KPIX-TV, San Francisco. *Movie*: The Initiation of Sarah.

CROSBY, MARY: Actress. b. Los Angeles, CA, Sept. 14, 1959. e. U Tx. Daughter of performers Kathryn Crosby and the late Bing Crosby. Formerly acted as Mary Frances Crosby. Appeared from an early age in several TV variety specials with her parents. TELEVISION: *Series*: Brothers and Sisters, Dallas. *Movies*: With This Ring, A Guide for the Married Woman, Midnight Lace, Golden Gate, Confessions of a Married Man, Final Jeopardy, Stagecoach. *Mini-Series*: Pearl, Hollywood Wives, North and South Book II. PICTURES: The Last Plane Out, The Ice Pirates, Tapeheads, Body Chemistry, Corporate Affairs, Eating, The Berlin Conspiracy.

CROSS, BEN: Actor. r.n. Bernard Cross. b. London, England, Dec. 16, 1947. e. Royal Acad. of Dramatic Art. Worked as stagehand, prop-master, and master carpenter with Welsh Natl. Opera and as set builder, Wimbledon Theatre. THEATER: The Importance of Being Earnest (Lancaster, debut, 1972), I Love My Wife, Privates on Parade, Chicago, Lydie Breeze (NY debut, 1982), Caine Mutiny Court Martial. PICTURES: A Bridge Too Far (debut, 1977), Chariots of Fire, The Unholy, The Goldsmith's Shop, Paperhouse, The House of the Lord, Eye of the Widow, Cold Sweat. TELEVISION: *Movies/Specials*: Melancholy Hussar of the German Legion (1973, BBC), The Flame Trees of Thika, The Citadel, The Far Pavilions, Coming Out of the Ice, The Assisi Underground, Arthur Hailey's Strong Medicine, Steal the Sky, Pursuit, Twist of Fate, Nightlife, She Stood Alone, Diamond Fleece, Live Wire, Deep Trouble. *Series*: Dark Shadows (1991).

CROUSE, LINDSAY: Actress. b. New York, NY, May 12, 1948. Daughter of playwright Russel Crouse. e. Radcliffe. Began career as modern and jazz dancer; also flutist and pianist. THEATER: Was member of Circle Repertory Co. NY. The Shawl, The Cherry Orchard, Foursome, Present Laughter (Kennedy Center), Long Day's Journey Into Night, Hamlet (Circle Rep.), Twelfth Night (Circle Rep.), Reunion (Obie Award), Serenading Louie, The Stick Wife, The Homecoming (Bdwy debut; Theatre World Award). PICTURES: All the President's Men (debut, 1976), Slap Shot, Between the Lines, Prince of the City, The Verdict, Daniel, Iceman, Places in the Heart, House of Games, Communion, Desperate Hours. TELEVISION: *Movies*: Eleanor and Franklin, Lemon Sky, Chantilly Lace. *Pilot*: American Nuclear.

CROWE, CAMERON: Writer, Director. b. Palm Springs, CA, July 13, 1957. e. Calif. St. Univ., San Diego. Former Rolling Stone writer who went "undercover" to research book on high school life Fast Times at Ridgemont High which he later adapted into 1982 film.
PICTURES: American Hot Wax (actor), Fast · Times at Ridgement High (s.p.), The Wild Life (co-prod., s.p.), Say Anything (dir., s.p.), Singles (dir., s.p.).
TELEVISION: Series: Fast Times (creative consultant).

CROWTHER, LESLIE: Actor, Comedian. b. Nottingham, England, June 2, 1933. e. Ripmon Dance and Drama Sch. Ent. TV ind. 1960. Early career incl: Hi Summer revue, Crackerjack, Black and White Minstrel Show. Stage: Let Sleeping Wives Lie, and Pantomine. 1971–72; 1988–9. Own TV series (LWT). 1978–82 Hi Summer series (LWT). Starred in Bud 'n Ches (stage). Since 1985 presented The Price is Right (Central TV), 1990–2: Stars in Their Eyes. BBC radio series: Are You Sitting Comfortably?.

CRUEA, EDMOND D.: Executive. b. Jersey City, NJ, June 3. Joined Grand National Pictures, L.A., 1935; Monogram Pictures, 1938–41, L.A. & Seattle; U.S. Army Signal Corps, 1942–46; Monogram Pictures, Seattle, 1946–48; branch mgr., 1948–49; branch mgr. and district mgr. Allied Artists, 1950–65 (Seattle, Portland, San Francisco, and Los Angeles); v.p.-gen. sls. mgr., Allied Artists 1965–71; dir. distribution, Abkco Films div. of Abkco Industries, Inc.; 1971–73; pres. of Royal Dist. Corp., 1974; pres., Esco Film Corp., 1975; joined Film Ventures Intl. in 1976 as exec. v.p., succeeding to pres. and chief operating officer in 1976. Resigned 1977 to form Fil-Mark Inc. Co-founded New Image Releasing, Inc., 1982, as pres. & CEO 1985, v.p. theatrical, Cinetel Films; 1987 theatrical dist. consultant, Sony Pictures (NY) and Shining Armour Commun (London).

CRUISE, TOM: Actor. r.n. Thomas Cruise Mapother IV. b. Syracuse, NY, July 3, 1962. m. actress Nicole Kidman. Acted in high school plays; secured role in dinner theatre version of Godspell. Received American Cinema Award for Distinguished Achievement in Film, 1991.
PICTURES: Endless Love (debut, 1981), Taps, Losin' It, The Outsiders, Risky Business, All the Right Moves, Legend, Top Gun, The Color of Money, Cocktail, Rain Man, Born on the 4th of July (Golden Globe Award, Acad. Award nom., 1989), Days of Thunder (also co-wrote story), Far and Away, A Few Good Men, The Firm.
TELEVISION: Director: The Frightening Framis (episode of series Fallen Angels).

CRYER, JON: Actor. b. New York, NY, Apr. 16, 1965. Son of actor David Cryer and songwriter-actress Gretchen Cryer. On Bdwy. stage in Brighton Beach Memoirs.
PICTURES: No Small Affair (debut, 1984), Pretty in Pink, Morgan Stewart's Coming Home, O.C. and Stiggs, Superman IV, Hiding Out, Dudes, Penn and Teller Get Killed, Hot Shots!
TELEVISION: Series: The Famous Teddy Z. Special: Kurt Vonnegut's Monkey House.

CRYSTAL, BILLY: Actor. b. Long Island, NY, Mar. 14, 1947. e. Marshall U., Nassau Commun. Col., NYU (BFA in tv & film direction). Father, Jack, produced jazz concerts; family owned Commodore jazz record label. Worked with Alumni Theatre Group at Nassau Commun. College. Later teamed with two friends (billed as We the People, Comedy Jam, 3's Company) and toured coffee houses and colleges. Became stand-up comedian on own, appearing at Catch a Rising Star, The Comedy Story and on TV. Album: Mahvelous!. Book: Absolutely Mahvelous!
PICTURES: Rabbit Test (debut, 1978), Animalympics (voice), This is Spinal Tap, Running Scared, The Princess Bride, Throw Mama From the Train, Memories of Me (also co-prod., co-s.p.), When Harry Met Sally, City Slickers (also exec. prod.), Mr. Saturday Night (also dir., prod., co-s.p.).
TELEVISION: Series: Soap, The Billy Crystal Comedy Hour (also writer), Saturday Night Live (also writer), Sessions (creator, exec. prod. only). Guest: Saturday Night Live with Howard Cosell, Tonight Show, Dinah, Mike Douglas Show, That Was the Year That Was, All in the Family, Love Boat. Specials include: Battle of the Network Stars, Billy Crystal: A Comic's Line (also writer), A Comedy Salute to Baseball (also writer), On Location: Billy Crystal - Don't Get Me Started (also dir., writer), The Three Little Pigs (Faerie Tale Theatre), The Lost Minutes of Billy Crystal, Midnight Train to Moscow (also exec. prod., co-writer; Emmy Award 1990). Movies: SST—Death Flight, Human Feelings, Breaking Up Is Hard to Do, Enola Gay: The Men the Mission and the Atomic Bomb. Host: Grammy Awards (Emmy Awards for hosting, 1988, 1989), Academy Awards (Emmy Award for hosting, 1991; Emmy Award for co-writing, 1992).

CULBERG, PAUL S.: Executive. b. Chicago, IL, June 14, 1942. Began career in record industry, holding positions with Elektra Records & Wherehouse Record; 1977–80; v.p. sls. mktg., Cream Records.; 1980–82, dir. sls. Paramount Home Video; 1982, v.p. sls. mktg., Media Home Entertainment;

1984–9, pres., New World Video; 1989–present, COO, RCA Columbia/TriStar Home Video.

CULKIN, MACAULAY: Actor. b. New York, NY, Aug. 26, 1980. Acting debut at 4 yrs. old in Bach Babies at NY's Symphony Space. Appeared in several TV commercials. Studied ballet at George Ballanchine's School of American Ballet and danced in NY productions of H.M.S. Pinafore and The Nutcracker. Received Comedy Award and Youth in Film Award for role in Home Alone. Appeared in Michael Jackson video Black and White.
PICTURES: Rocket Gibraltar (debut, 1988), See You in the Morning, Uncle Buck, Jacob's Ladder, Home Alone, Only the Lonely, My Girl, Home Alone 2: Lost in New York, The Nutcracker, The Good Son, The Pagemaster, Getting Even With Dad.
TELEVISION: Guest: The Equalizer, Saturday Night Live, Bob Hope Christmas Special.
THEATRE: NY: Afterschool Special, Mr. Softee, Buster B. and Olivia.

CULLUM, JOHN: Actor. b. Knoxville, TN, Mar. 2, 1930. e. Univ. of TN. Father of actor John David Cullum.
TELEVISION: Series: Buck James, Northern Exposure. Guest: Quantum Leap (also dir.). Movies: The Man Without a Country, The Day After, Shoot Down, With a Vengeance.
PICTURES: All the Way Home, 1776, The Prodigal, Marie, Sweet Country.
THEATRE: NY: Camelot, On a Clear Day You Can See Forever (Theatre World Award, Tony nom.), Hamlet, Man of La Mancha, 1776, Shenandoah (Tony Award, Drama Desk & Outer Circle Critics Awards), The Trip Back Down, On the Twentieth Century (Tony Award), Deathtrap, Private Lives, Doubles, The Boys in Autumn, Aspects of Love.

CULP, ROBERT: Actor, Writer, Director. b. Berkeley, CA, Aug. 16, 1930. e. Stockton, College of the Pacific, Washington U., San Francisco State; to N.Y. to study with Herbert Berghof. Starred in off-Bwdy prod. He Who Gets Slapped. Best Actor of the Year in an off-Bwdy Play; motion picture debut, 1962; P.T. 109; television guest appearances in Rawhide, Wagon Train, Bob Hope Presents the Chrysler Theatre; wrote and acted in Rifleman, Cain's Hundred, The Dick Powell Show.
BROADWAY: The Prescott Proposals, A Clearing in the Woods.
TELEVISION: Series: Trackdown, I Spy (also wrote pilot and 7 shows), The Greatest American Hero (also wrote 2 shows). Movies: Sammy The Way Out Seal, The Hanged Man, See the Man Run, A Cold Night's Death, Outrage!, Houston We've Got a Problem, Strange Homecoming, A Cry for Help, Flood, Spectre, Last of the Good Guys, Women in White, Hot Rod, The Dream Merchants, The Night the City Screamed, Killjoy, Thou Shalt Not Kill, Her Life as a Man, The Calendar Girl Murders, Brothers-in-Law, The Blue Lightning, The Gladiator, The Key to Rebecca, Combat High, Voyage of Terror: The Achille Lauro Affair, Columbo Goes to College.
PICTURES: PT 109 (debut, 1963), The Raiders, Sunday in New York, Rhino, The Hanged Man, Bob & Carol & Ted & Alice, The Grove, A Name For Evil, Hannie Caulder, Hickey & Boggs (also dir. and uncredited co-s.p.), The Castaway Cowboy, Inside Out (Golden Heist), Sky Riders, Breaking Point, Great Scout and Cathouse Thursday, Golden Girl, National Lampoon Goes to the Movies, Turk 182, Big Bad Mama II, Silent Night Deadly Night 3: Better Watch Out, Pucker Up and Bark Like a Dog, Timebomb, The Pelican Brief.

CUMMINGS, CONSTANCE: C.B.E. Actress. b. Seattle, WA, May 15, 1910. r.n. Constance Cummings Halverstadt. p. D.V. Halverstadt, attorney, and Kate Cummings, concert soprano; m. Benn Levy, English playwright. Was chorus girl in The Little Show and also appeared in June Moon. Broadway debut: Treasure Girl, 1928; London debut: Sour Grapes, 1934. Joined National Theatre Co. 1971.
THEATER: Recent work: A Long Day's Journey into Night (with Laurence Olivier), The Cherry Orchard, Wings (Tony, Obie Awards 1979), The Chalk Garden, Téte a Tête.
PICTURES: The Criminal Code, The Love Parade, Lover Come Back, Guilty Generation, Traveling Husbands, The Big Timer, Behind the Mask, Movie Crazy, Night After Night, American Madness, The Last Man, Washington Merry-Go-Round, Attorney for the Defense, The Charming Deceiver, Channel Crossing, Broadway Through a Keyhole, The Mind Reader, Glamour, Looking for Trouble, This Man Is Mine, Remember Last Night?, Seven Sinners (Doomed Cargo), Strangers on a Honeymoon, Busman's Honeymoon, This England, The Foreman Went to France (Somewhere in France), Blithe Spirit, Into the Blue, The Scream, John and Julie, The Intimate Stranger, Battle of the Sexes, In the Cool of the Day, A Boy 10 Feet Tall.
TELEVISION: Touch of the Sun, Clutterbuck, The Last Tycoon, Ruth, Late Summer, Long Day's Journey Into Night, Jane Eyre, Wings, Agatha Christie's Dead Man's Folly.

CUMMINS, PEGGY: Actress. b. Prestatyn, North Wales, Dec. 18, 1925. e. Alexandra Sch., Dublin, Gate Theatre, Dublin.

Starred in Let's Pretend on London Stage 1938. In 1942; Salute John Citizen; Welcome Mr. Washington; On London Stage in Junior Miss, Alice in Wonderland, Peter Pan. From 1946 Hollywood, starred in Late George Apley. Returned to Eng. 1950.

PICTURES: Dr. O'Dowd, Her Man Gilbey, The Late George Apley, Moss Rose, Green Grass of Wyoming, Escape, That Dangerous Age, Gun Crazy, My Daughter Joy (Operation X), Who Goes There (Passionate Sentry), Street Corner (Both Sides of the Law), Meet Mr. Lucifer, Always a Bride, Love Lottery, Cash on Delivery, March Hare, Carry on Admiral, Night of the Demon, Hell Drivers, The Captain's Table, Your Money or Your Wife, Dentist in the Chair, In the Doghouse.

TELEVISION: The Human Jungle, Looks Familiar.

CUNNINGHAM, SEAN S.: Producer, Director. b. New York, NY, Dec. 31 1941. e. Franklin & Marshall, B.A.; Stanford U., M.F.A. Worked briefly as actor, moving into stage-managing. Became producer of Mineola Theatre (Long Island, NY) and took several productions to Broadway. Formed Sean S. Cunningham Films, Ltd., 1971. Produced commercials, industrial film, documentaries, features.

PICTURES: Together (prod.-dir.), Last House on the Left (prod.), The Case of the Full Moon Murders (prod.), Here Come the Tigers (prod.-dir.), Kick (prod.-dir.), Friday the 13th (prod.-dir.), A Stranger Is Watching (prod.-dir.), Spring Break (prod.-dir.), The New Kids (prod., dir.), House (prod.), House II (prod.), Deepstar Six (prod., dir.), The Horror Show (prod.), House III (prod.), House IV (prod.), Friday the 13th Part 9 (prod.).

CURRY, TIM: Actor. b. Cheshire, England, Apr. 19, 1946. e. Birmingham U. Albums: Read My Lips, Fearless, Simplicity.

PICTURES: The Rocky Horror Picture Show, The Shout, Times Square, Annie, The Ploughman's Lunch, Clue, Legend, Pass the Ammo, The Hunt for Red October, Oscar, FernGully ... The Last Rainforest (voice), Passed Away, Home Alone 2: Lost in New York, National Lampoon's Loaded Weapon 1, The Three Musketeers.

THEATRE: Hair, A Midsummer Night's Dream, The Rocky Horror Show, Travestities, Amadeus (Tony nom.), The Pirates of Penzance, Me and My Girl (U.S. tour), The Art of Success, My Favorite Year (Tony nom.).

TELEVISION: Movies: Oliver Twist, Stephen King's IT. Voice work - series: Peter Pan and the Pirates (Emmy Award, 1991), Captin Planet and the Planeteers, Fish Police. Specials: The Life of Shakespeare, Three Men in a Boat, Rock Follies, City Sugar.

CURTIN, JANE: Actress. b. Cambridge, MA, Sept. 6, 1947. e. Northeastern U. On stage in Proposition, Last of the Red Hot Lovers, Candida. Author, actress off-Bdwy musical revue Pretzel 1974–75.

PICTURES: Mr. Mike's Mondo Video, How to Beat the High Cost of Living, O.C. and Stiggs, Coneheads.

TELEVISION: Series: Saturday Night Live 1974–79; Kate & Allie (Emmy Awards: 1984, 1985), Working It Out. Movies: What Really Happened to the Class of '65, Divorce Wars—A Love Story, Suspicion, Maybe Baby, Common Ground. Special: Candida.

CURTIS, DAN: Producer, Director. b. Bridgeport, CT, Aug. 12, 1928. e. U. of Bridgeport, Syracuse U., B.A. Was sales exec. for NBC and MCA before forming own company, Dan Curtis Productions, which he now heads. Producer/owner of CBS Golf Classic (1963–73).

PICTURES: House of Dark Shadows (prod., dir.), Night of Dark Shadows (prod.-dir.), Burnt Offerings (prod., dir., co-s.p.).

TELEVISION: Producer: Series: Dark Shadows (ABC daytime series, 1966–71), Dark Shadows (prime time series, 1991). Movies: Director: The Night Stalker, Frankenstein, The Picture of Dorian Gray. Producer-Director: The Night Strangler, The Norliss Tapes, Scream of the Wolf, Dracula, Melvin Purvis: G-Man, The Turn of the Screw, The Great Ice-Rip Off, Trilogy of Terror, Kansas City Massacre, Curse of the Black Widow, When Every Day Was the Fourth of July (also co-story), The Winds of War, War and Remembrance (also co-s.p.). Director: The Last Ride of the Dalton Gang, The Long Days of Summer, Mrs. R's Daughter, Intruders (also co-exec. prod.).

CURTIS, JAMIE LEE: Actress. b. Los Angeles, CA, Nov. 22, 1958. m. actor, dir. Christopher Guest. Daughter of Janet Leigh and Tony Curtis.

PICTURES: Halloween (debut, 1978), The Fog, Prom Night, Terror Train, Halloween II, Road Games, Trading Places, Love Letters, Grandview USA, Perfect, Amazing Grace and Chuck, A Man in Love, Dominick and Eugene, A Fish Called Wanda, Blue Steel, Queens Logic, My Girl, Forever Young, My Girl 2.

TELEVISION: Special: Tall Tales (Annie Oakley). Series: Operation Petticoat (1977–78), Anything But Love. Movies: Operation Petticoat (pilot), She's in the Army Now, Death of a Centerfold: The Dorothy Stratten Story, Money on the Side, As Summers Die. Pilot: Callahan.

CURTIS, TONY: Actor. r.n. Bernard Schwartz. b. New York, NY, June 3, 1925. Father of Jamie Lee Curtis. e. Seward Park H.S. In U.S. Navy, amateur dramatics, N.Y., started Empire Players Theatre, Newark, NJ, with Dramatic Workshop, Cherry Lane Theatre, Jr. Drama workshop of Walt Whitman School; first prod. work with Stanley Woolf Players; m.p. debut unbilled in Criss-Cross; signed with U-I. Star of Tomorrow, 1953.

PICTURES: Criss Cross (debut, 1948), City Across the River, The Lady Gambles, Johnny Stool Pigeon, Francis, Sierra, I Was a Shoplifter, Winchester 73, Sierra, Kansas Raiders, Prince Who Was a Thief, Flesh and Fury, Son of Ali Baba, No Room for the Groom, Houdini, All American, Forbidden, Beachhead, Johnny Dark, Black Shield of Falworth, 6 Bridges to Cross, So This Is Paris, Purple Mask, Square Jungle, Rawhide Years, Trapeze, Mister Cory, Midnight Story, Sweet Smell of Success, The Vikings, Kings Go Forth, The Defiant Ones, The Perfect Furlough, Some Like It Hot, Operation Petticoat, Who Was That Lady?, The Rat Race, Spartacus, Pepe (cameo), The Great Impostor, The Outsider, Taras Bulba, 40 Pounds of Trouble, The List of Adrian Messenger, Captain Newman, M.D., Paris When it Sizzles, Wild and Wonderful, Sex and the Single Girl, Goodbye Charlie, The Great Race, Boeing-Boeing, Chamber of Horrors (cameo), Not With My Wife You Don't!, Arrivederci Baby!, Don't Make Waves, On My Way to the Crusades I Met a Girl Who—(a.k.a. The Chastity Belt), The Boston Strangler, Rosemary's Baby (voice), Those Daring Young Men in Their Jaunty Jalopies, Suppose They Gave a War and Nobody Came, You Can't Win 'Em All, Lepke, The Last Tycoon, Casanova & Co., The Manitou, Bad News Bears Go to Japan, Sextette, Little Miss Marker, The Mirror Crack'd, Brainwaves, King of the City, Insignificance, Club Life, The Last of Philip Banter, Balboa, Midnight, Lobster Man From Mars, The High-Flying Mermaid, Prime Target, Center of the Web.

TELEVISION: Series: The Persuaders, McCoy, Vega$. Movies: The Third Girl from the Left, The Count of Monte Cristo, Vega$, The Users, Moviola: The Scarlett O'Hara War, Inmates: A Love Story, Harry's Back, The Million Dollar Face, Mafia Princess, Murder in Three Acts, Portrait of a Showgirl, Tarzan in Manhattan, Thanksgiving Day, Christmas in Connecticut.

CUSACK, CYRIL: Actor. b. Durban, South Africa, Nov. 26, 1910. e. Newbridge, Co. Kildare; University Coll., Dublin, Eire. LL.D (Honoris Causa-National U. of Ireland); D. Litt (Hon. Causa-Dublin U.); Litt. D. (Hon. Causa-New U. of Ulster). Stage debut: Candida, Abbey Theatre, 1932. Screen debut: Odd Man Out, 1945.

PICTURES: Esther Waters, Escape, The Blue Lagoon, Once a Jolly Swagman, All Over the Town, Small Back Room, The Elusive Pimpernel, Soldiers Three, Blue Veil, Secret of Convict Lake, Gone to Earth (Wild Heart), Saadia, Passage Home, Man in the Road, Man Who Never Was, March Hare, Jacqueline, Spanish Gardener, Ill Met by Moonlight, Rising of the Moon, Miracle in Soho, Shake Hands with the Devil, Floods of Fear, Gideon's Day, A Terrible Beauty, Johnny Nobody, The Waltz of the Toreadors, I Thank a Fool, 80,000 Suspects, Passport to Oblivion, The Spy Who Came In from The Cold, Fahrenheit 451, Taming of the Shrew, I Was Happy Here, Oedipus Rex, Galileo, King Lear, Country Dance, David Copperfield, Harold and Maude, Sacco and Vanzetti, La La Polizia Ringrazia, The Day of the Jackal, Juggernaut, Homecoming, Galileo, Tristan and Iseult, True Confessions, Little Dorrit, My Left Foot, Far and Away, As You Like It.

TELEVISION: The Dummy, The Moon and Sixpence, What Every Woman Knows, The Enchanted, The Power and The Glory, The Chairs, Don Juan in Hell, The Lotus Eater, Krapp's Last Tape, Murder in the Cathedral, Six Characters in Search of An Author, The Big Toe, Workhouse Ward, In the Train, Purgatory, The Moon in the Yellow River, Passage to India, Deirdre, The Tower, Dial M for Murder, St. Francis, The Physicists, Trial of Marshal Petain, In the Bosom of the Country, Uncle Vanya, A Time of Wolves and Tigers, Them, Clochemerle, The Golden Bowl, The Reunion, I Stand Well With All Parties, Catholics, Crystal & Fox, Jesus of Nazareth, The Plough and The Stars, You Never Can Tell, Accidental Death, Oedipus the King (Theban plays), The Hitchhiker, Menace Unseen, The Small Assassin, Glenroe, The Tenth Man, Danny the Champion of the World.

CUSACK, JOAN: Actress. b. Evanston, IL, Oct. 11, 1962. Brother is actor John Cusack. e. U. of Wisconsin, Madison. Studied acting at Piven Theatre Workshop, Evanston, IL. While in coll. joined The Ark, local improvisational comedy group. Joined Saturday Night Live as regular for 1985–86 season.

THEATER: Road, Brilliant Traces (Theatre World Award for both), Cymbeline, The Celestial Alphabet Event, 'Tis Pity She's a Whore, A Midsummer Night's Dream.

PICTURES: My Bodyguard (debut, 1980), Class, Sixteen Candles, Grandview U.S.A., The Allnighter, Broadcast News, Stars and Bars, Married to the Mob, Working Girl (Acad. Award nom.), Say Anything, Men Don't Leave, My Blue

Heaven, The Cabinet of Dr. Ramirez, Hero, Toys, Addams Family Values.

CUSACK, JOHN: Actor. b. Chicago, IL, June 28, 1966. Sister is actress Joan Cusack. Member of Piven Theatre Workshop, IL. 10 years beginning when 8.
PICTURES: Class (debut, 1983), Sixteen Candles, Grandview U.S.A., The Sure Thing, The Journey of Natty Gann, Better Off Dead, Stand By Me, One Crazy Summer, Hot Pursuit, Eight Men Out, Tapeheads, Say Anything, Fat Man and Little Boy, The Grifters, True Colors, Shadows and Fog, Roadside Prophets, The Player, Bob Roberts, Map of the Human Heart, Money for Nothing.

CUSHING, PETER: O.B.E.: Actor. b. Kenley, Surrey, Eng., May 26, 1913. e. Purley Secondary Sch. Stage debut 1936 with Worthington Repertory Co. Daily Mail TV award actor, 1953–54; Guild of TV award, 1955; News Chronicle T.V. Top Ten award, 1956. Author: Peter Cushing: An Autobiography (1986), Past Forgetting: Memoirs of the Hammer Years (1988).
TELEVISION: Asmodee, Anastasia, 1984, Gaslight, Home at Seven, Tovarich, Beau Brummell, Epitaph for a Spy, Pride and Prejudice, The Moment of Truth, Uncle Harry, Eden End, Rookery Nook, The Creature, The Browning Version, Winslow Boy, Peace With Terror, Julius Caesar (Cassius), Monica. The Plan, Caves of Steel, Sherlock Holmes (series), Morecambe & Wise Show, Wild-life Spectacular, The Zoo Gang, Orson Welles Great Mysteries, Space 1999, The New Avengers, The Great Houdini, A Land Looking West, A Tale of Two Cities; The Vordal Blade, Tales of the Unexpected, Helen and Teacher, The Masks of Death, A One-way Ticket to Hollywood.
PICTURES: Vigil in the Night, Moulin Rouge, Hamlet, Black Knight, End of the Affair, Alexander the Great, Magic Fire, Time Without Pity, Curse of Frankenstein, Abominable Snowman, Dracula, John Paul Jones, The Hound of the Baskervilles, Violent Playground, The Mummy, Suspect, The Flesh and the Friends, The Revenge of Frankenstein, Cone of Silence, Bride of Dracula, Sword of Sherwood Forest, The Naked Edge, Cash on Demand, The Devil's Agent, Captain Clegg, Fury at Smuggler's Bay, Hell-Fire Club, The Man Who Finally Died, The Evil of Frankenstein, The Gorgon, Dr. Terror's House of Horrors, She, The Skull, Dr. Who and Daleks, The Frighten Bed Island, Daleks Invade Earth, Frankenstein Created Woman, Torture Garden, Some May Live, The Night of the Big Heat, Corruption, Death's Head Moth, One More Time, Frankenstein Must Be Destroyed, The Vampire Lovers, Scream and Scream Again, House That Dripped Blood, I Monster, Twins of Evil, Tales from the Crypt, Dracula A.D., Fear in the Night, Horror Express, The Creeping Flesh, Asylum, Nothing But the Night, And Now the Screaming Starts, Frankenstein and the Monster from Hell, The Satanic Rites of Dracula, The Revenge of Dr. Death, From Beyond the Grave, The Beast Must Die, Madhouse, Legend of the Seven Golden Vampires, Shatter, Tender Dracula, The Ghoul, Legend of the Werewolf, Land of the Minotaur, Death Corps, Trial by Combat, At The Earth's Core, Star Wars, Battleflag, The Uncanny, Hitler's Son, Touch of the Sun, Arabian Adventure, Black Jack, Monster Island, House of the Long Shadows, Sword of the Valiant, Top Secret!, Biggles.

D

DAFOE, WILLEM: Actor. b. Appleton, WI, July 22, 1955. Worked with experimental group Theatre X on the road before coming to New York. Built sets and debuted with the Wooster Group at the Performing Garage playing (literally) a chicken heart in Elizabeth Le Compte's Nayatt School. Current member of the Wooster Group, performing with them frequently in U.S. and Europe.
PICTURES: The Loveless (1983, debut), The Hunger, Streets of Fire, Roadhouse 66, To Live and Die in L.A., Platoon (Acad. Award nom.), Off Limits, The Last Temptation of Christ, Mississippi Burning, Triumph of the Spirit, Born on the Fourth of July, Cry-Baby, Wild at Heart, Flight of the Intruder, White Sands, Light Sleeper, Body of Evidence, Faraway So Close!

DAHL, ARLENE: Actress, Writer, Designer. b. Minneapolis, MN, Aug. 11, 1928. e. MN Business Coll.; U. of Minnesota, summers 1941–44; Minneapolis. Coll. of music. m. Marc A. Rosen. Mother of actor Lorenzo Lamas. At age 8, played heroine of children's adventure serials on radio. Internationally syndicated beauty columnist, Chgo. Tribune-N.Y. News Syndicate, 1951–71; Pres. Arlene Dahl Enterprises, (1951–75); Sleepwear Designer, A.N. Saab & Co., 1952–57; Natl. Beauty Advisor, Sears Roebuck & Co., 1970–75; v.p. Kenyon & Eckhart Advg. Co., pres., Women's World Div., Kenyon-Eckhart, 1967–72; Fashion Consultant, O.M.A. 1975–78, Int'l. Director of S.M.E.I., 1973–76, Designer, Vogue Patterns 1978–85. Pres., Dahlia Parfums Inc., 1975–80, pres., Dahlia Prods., 1978–81: pres. Dahlmark Prods.

1981–. Publs: Always Ask a Man, 1965, Your Beautyscope, 1969, Secrets of Hair Care, 1971, Secrets of Skin Care, 1973, Your Beautyscope 1977–78, Beyond Beauty, 1980, Lovescopes, 1983. Honrs. include: 8 Motion Picture Laurel Awards, 1948–63; Hds. of Fame Award, 1971, Woman of the Year, N.Y. Adv. Council, 1969. Mother of the Year, 1979; Coup de Chapeau, Deauville Film Fest 1983.
THEATER: Broadway: Mr. Strauss Goes to Boston (debut, 1946), Cyrano de Bergerac; Applause; major US tours include: Questionable Ladies, The King and I, One Touch of Venus, I Married an Angel, Mame, Pal Joey, Bell Book and Candle, The Camel Bell, Life With Father, A Little Night Music, Lilliom, Marriage Go Round, Blithe Spirit, Forty Carats, Dear Liar, Murder Among Friends.
PICTURES: My Wild Irish Rose (debut, 1947), The Bride Goes Wild, A Southern Yankee, Ambush, Reign of Terror (The Black Book), Scene of the Crime, The Outriders, Three Little Words, Watch the Birdie, Inside Straight, No Questions Asked, Caribbean, Jamaica Run, Desert Legion, Here Come the Girls, Sangaree, The Diamond Queen, Wicked as They Come, Fortune is a Woman, Bengal Brigade, Woman's World, Slightly Scarlet, She Played With Fire, Journey to the Center of the Earth, Kisses for My President, Les Ponyettes, DuBle en Liasse, Le Chemin du Katmandu. The Landraiders, A Place to Hide, Night of the Warrior.
TELEVISION: Max Factor Playhouse, Lux Television Theater, Pepsi Cola Playhouse, Opening Night, Arlene Dahl's Beauty Spot, Hostess, Model of the Year Show, Arlene Dahl's Starscope, Arlene Dahl's Lovescopes, One Life to Live (1981–84), Night of One Hundred Stars, Happy Birthday Hollywood, Who Killed Max Thorn?, Love Boat, Love American Style, Fantasy Island.

DALE, JIM: Actor. b. Rothwell, Northhamptonshire, England, Aug. 15, 1935. Debut as solo comedian at the Savoy, 1951. Joined National Theatre Co. in 1969 playing in Love's Labour's Lost, The Merchant of Venice, The National Health, The Card. U.S. theater: Mark Taper Forum: Comedians, Scapino. NY Theater: Taming of the Shrew, Scapino, Barnum (Tony and Drama Desk Awards, 1980), Joe Egg (Tony Award nom.), Me and My Girl, Privates on Parade. Has written songs and music for films: Twinky, Shalako, Joseph Andrews, Georgy Girl. Many tv appearances.
PICTURES: Raising the Wind, Carry on Spying, Carry On Cleo, The Big Job, Carry On Cowboy, Carry on Screaming, Lock Up Your Daughters, The National Health, Digby, Joseph Andrews, Pete's Dragon, Hot Lead Cold Feet, Unidentified Flying Oddball, Scandalous, Carry on Columbus.

DALEY, ROBERT: Producer. e. UCLA. Began career in pictures at Universal International and TV at Desilu.
PICTURES: Play Misty For Me, Dirty Harry, (exec. prod.), Joe Kidd, High Plains Drifter, Breezy, Magnum Force, Thunderbolt and Lightfoot, The Eiger Sanction, The Outlaw Josey Wales, The Enforcer, The Gauntlet, Every Which Way But Loose, Escape from Alcatraz (exec. prod.), Any Which Way You Can (exec. prod.), Bronco Billy (exec. prod.), Stick (exec. prod.), Real Genius (exec. prod.).
TELEVISION: The Untouchables, Ben Casey, The FBI, 12 O'Clock High, The Invaders, etc.

DALSIMER, SUSAN: Executive. Editor for E.P. Dutton before joining Lorimar Prods., as v.p. of east coast development. Left to become consultant for original programming at Home Box Office. 1987, named v.p., creative affairs, east coast, for Warner Bros.

DALTON, TIMOTHY: Actor. b. Colwyn Bay, No. Wales, March 21, 1944. Started acting at Natl. Youth Theatre; then studied at RADA. Prof. stage debut in Richard III and As You Like It at Birmingham Rep.
THEATER: Antony and Cleopatra, The Taming of the Shrew, Little Malcolm and His Struggle Against the Eunuchs, A Game Called Arthur, King Lear, Love's Labour's Lost, Henry IV, Henry V, Romeo and Juliet, The Vortex, The Romans, A Touch of the Poet.
PICTURES: The Lion in Winter (debut, 1968), Cromwell, The Voyeur, Wuthering Heights, Mary Queen of Scots, Permission to Kill, Sextette, Agatha, Flash Gordon, Chanel Solitaire, The Doctor and the Devils, The Living Daylights, Brenda Starr, Hawks, Licence to Kill, The King's Whore, The Rocketeer.
TELEVISION: Mini-Series: Centennial, Mistral's Daughter, Sins. Movie: The Master of Ballantrae. Specials: Florence Nightingale, Candida, Five Finger Exercise, Jane Eyre.

DALTREY, ROGER: Singer, Actor. b. London, England, March 1, 1944. Lead vocalist with The Who.
PICTURES: Woodstock, Tommy, Lisztomania, The Legacy, The Kids Are Alright, McVicar (also prod.), Mack the Knife, The Teddy Bear Habit, Father Jim, If Looks Could Kill, Buddy's Song.
TELEVISION: Movie: Forgotten Prisoners: The Amnesty Files.

DALY, JIM: Executive Director, Rank Organisation Plc. b. 1938. Managing director of Film and Television Services division which includes: Pinewood Studios, Rank Film Laboratories, Rank Film Distributors, Rank Advertising Films, Rank Theatres, Rank Video Services, Rank Video Services America, Film House Company, Canada. Appt. exec. dir., Rank Org. 1982.

DALY, JIM: Executive Director, Rank Organsation Pic. b. 1938. Mng. dir. of Film & tv services which includes Pinewood Studios, Rank's Film Lab.in U.K., Hollywood and Toronto, Rank Film Distribs., Odeon Cinemas, Rank Video Services Duplication business in Europe and U.S., Rank Retail Services U.S., Rank Precision Industries. Appt. exec. dir., Rank Org., 1982.

DALY, JOHN: Executive. b. London, England, July 16, 1937. After working in journalism joined Royal Navy. On leaving Service after three years, trained as underwriter with an Assurance Company. In 1966 became David Hemmings manager and in 1967 formed the Hemdale Company with Hemmings (who later sold interest) Chmn. Hemdale Holdings Ltd.
PICTURES: Images, Sunburn (co-prod., co-s.p.), High Risk, Going Ape, Deadly Force, Carbon Copy, Yellowbeard, Falcon and the Snowman, Terminator, Rivers Edge, At Close Range, Hoosiers, Platoon, Best Seller, Shag (exec. prod.), Vampire's Kiss (exec. prod.), Miracle Mile (prod.), Criminal Law (co-exec. prod.), War Party (prod.), The Boost, Out Cold (exec. prod.), Staying Together (exec. prod.).

DALY, ROBERT A.: Executive. b. New York, NY, Dec. 8, 1936. e. Brooklyn Coll., Hunter Coll. Joined CBS-TV in 1955; dir. of program acct.; dir. of research and cost planning; dir. of business affairs. Later named v.p., business affairs, NY; exec. v.p. of network on April, 1976. Named president, CBS Entertainment, Oct. 1977. In Oct. 1979 became responsible for CBS Theatrical Films as well as the TV operation. In 1980, appointed co-chmn. and co-chief exec. officer of Warner Bros. Sole title holder since Jan., 1982.

DALY, TIMOTHY: Actor. b. New York, NY, March 1, 1956. m. actress Amy Van Nostrand. Son of late actor James Daly, brother of actress Tyne Daly. e. Bennington Coll., B.A. Acted in summer stock while in college. Moved to NY where had own rock and roll band. Has performed in cabaret at Williamstown Theater Festival.
THEATER: Fables for Friends, Oliver Oliver, Mass Appeal, Bus Stop, Coastal Disturbances (Theatre World Award).
PICTURES: Diner, Just the Way You Are, Made in Heaven, Spellbinder, Love or Money, Year of the Comet.
TELEVISION: Special: The Rise and Rise of Daniel Rocket. Mini-series: I'll Take Manhattan, Queen. Series: Ryan's Four, Almost Grown, Wings. Movies: I Married a Centerfold, Mirrors, Red Earth White Earth, In the Line of Duty: Ambush in Waco. Guest: Midnight Caller, Hill Street Blues, Alfred Hitchcock Presents.

DALY, TYNE: Actress. r.n. Ellen Tyne Daly. b. Madison, WI, Feb. 21, 1946. Daughter of late actor James Daly and actress Hope Newell; sister of actor Timothy Daly.
THEATRE: The Butter and Egg Man (1966), That Summer That Fall, Skirmishes, The Black Angel, Rimers of Eldritch, Ashes, Three Sisters, Come Back Little Sheba (L.A., 1987), Gypsy (Tony Award, 1990-Best Actress), Queen of the Stardust Ballroom, The Seagull.
PICTURES: John and Mary, Angel Unchained, Play It As It Lays, The Adulterers, The Enforcer, Telefon, Speedtrap, Zoot Suit, The Aviator, Movers & Shakers.
TELEVISION: Series: Cagney & Lacey (4 Emmy Awards). Movies: In Search of America, A Howling in the Woods, Heat of Anger, The Man Who Could Talk to Kids, Larry, The Entertainer, Better Late Than Never, Intimate Strangers, The Women's Room, A Matter of Life or Death, Your Place or Mine, Kids Like These, Stuck With Each Other, The Last to Go, Face of a Stranger, Columbo: A Bird in the Hand. Guest: Medical Center, The Rookies, Columbo, Ray Bradbury Theatre, Wings.

DAMON, MARK: Executive. b. Chicago, IL, April 22, 1933. e. UCLA, B.A. literature, M.A. business administration. Actor: 1958 under contract to 20th Century Fox, 1960 winner Golden Globe Award—Newcomer of the Year; early career includes The Fall of The House of Usher, The Longest Day; 1961 moved to Italy, stayed 16 years appearing in leading roles in 50 films; 1974 head of foreign dept. for PAC, a leading film distributor in Italy; 1976 returned to the U.S. as exec. prod. of The Choirboys and in charge of its foreign distribution; 1977 founder and pres. of Producers Sales Organization, intl. distribution org. 1987: formed Vision Int'l.
PICTURES: The Arena (prod.), Exec. prod. or co-exec. prod.: The Choirboys, The Neverending Story, Das Boot, 9-1/2 Weeks (prod.), Short Circuit, Flight of the Navigator, Lost Boys, High Spirits, Bat 21 (co-prod.), Dark Angel, Wild Orchid (prod.), Wild Orchid II: Two Shades of Blue, Shadow of the Wolf.

DAMONE, VIC: Singer, Actor. r.n. Vito Farinola. b. Brooklyn, NY, June 12, 1928. m. actress-singer Diahann Carroll. e. Lafayette H.S., Brooklyn. Winner Arthur Godfrey talent show, 1947; then night clubs, radio, theatres. U.S. Army, 1951–53.
PICTURES: Rich Young and Pretty (debut, 1951), The Strip, Athena, Deep in My Heart, Hit the Deck, Kismet, Hell to Eternity.
TELEVISION: Series: Vic Damone Show, 1956–7, 1967; Lively Ones, 1962.

DAMSKI, MEL: Director. b. New York, NY, July 21, 1946. e. Colgate U., AFI. Worked as reporter, journalism professor. USC Cinema instructor.
PICTURES: Yellowbeard, Mischief, Happy Together.
TELEVISION: M*A*S*H, Lou Grant, Dolphin Cove. Movies: Long Journey Back, The Child Stealer, Word of Honor, The Legend of Walks Far Woman, American Dream, For Ladies Only, Making the Grade, An Invasion of Privacy, Badge of the Assassin, A Winner Never Quits, Attack on Fear, Hero in the Family, Murder by the Book, Hope Division, The Three Kings, Everybody's Baby: The Rescue of Jessica McClure, Back to the Streets of San Francisco.

DANA, BILL: Actor, Writer. b. Quincy, MA, Oct. 5, 1924. In night clubs and on TV.
PICTURES: Busy Body, The Barefoot Executive, The Nude Bomb (also s.p.).
TELEVISION: Series: The Steve Allen Show (performer, head writer, 1961), The Bill Dana Jose Jimenez Show (star, writer), Spike Jones Show (prod., writer, performer), Milton Berle Show (prod., writer, performer), No Soup Radio, Zorro and Son. Writer: All in the Family. Movies: The Snoop Sisters, Rosetti & Ryan: Men Who Love Women, A Guide for the Married Woman, Murder in Texas. Actor: Facts of Life, Too Close for Comfort, Golden Girls, Hollywood Palace, St. Elsewhere.

DANCE, CHARLES: Actor. b. Worcestershire, Eng., Oct. 10, 1946. e. Plymouth Coll. Art., Leicester Coll. of Art (graphic design degree). After first working as a West End theatre stagehand, made acting debut in 1970 in a touring company of It's a Two-Foot-Six-Inches-above-the Ground World. Worked in provincial repertory theaters. Joined the Royal Shakespeare Company 1975–80: Hamlet, Richard III, As You Like It. Lead in Henry V (1975, N.Y.), and Coriolanus (1979, Paris).
THEATER: revival of Irma La Douce (West End), Turning Over (London's Bush Theatre).
PICTURES: For Your Eyes Only, The McGuffin, Plenty, The Golden Child, Good Morning Babylon, White Mischief, The Hidden City, Pascali's Island, Alien³, China Moon, The Valley of Stone, Last Action Hero.
TELEVISION: The Jewel in the Crown, Edward VII, The Fatal Spring, Little Eyolf, Frost in May, Nancy Astor, Saigon - The Last Day, Out On a Limb, BBC's The Secret Servant, Rainy Day Woman, Out of the Shadows, First Born, Goldeneye, Phantom of the Opera (mini-series).

D'ANGELO, BEVERLY: Actress. b. Columbus, OH, Nov. 15, 1954. Studied visual arts and was exchange student in Italy before working as cartoonist for Hanna-Barbera Studios in Hollywood. Toured Canada's coffeehouse circuit as singer and appeared with rock band called Elephant. Joined Charlotte Town Festival Company. Bdwy. debut in rock musical, Rockabye Hamlet.
PICTURES: The Sentinel (debut 1977), Annie Hall, First Love, Every Which Way But Loose, Hair, Highpoint, Coal Miner's Daughter, Honky Tonk Freeway, Paternity, National Lampoon's Vacation, Finders Keepers, National Lampoon's European Vacation, Big Trouble, Maid to Order, In the Mood, Aria, Trading Hearts, High Spirits, National Lampoon's Christmas Vacation, Daddy's Dyin', Pacific Heights (unbilled), The Miracle, The Pope Must Die, Man Trouble, Lonely Hearts.
TELEVISION: Mini-Series: Captains and the Kings. Movies: A Streetcar Named Desire, Doubletake, Slow Burn, Hands of a Stranger, Trial: The Price of Passion, A Child Lost Forever, The Switch, Judgment Day: The John List Story. Special: Sleeping Beatuy (Faerie Tale Theatre).

DANGERFIELD, RODNEY: Actor, Comedian. r.n. Jacob Cohen. b. Babylon, NY, Nov. 22, 1921. Performer in nightclubs as Jack Roy 1941–51. Businessman 1951–63. Comedian 1963–pres-ent. Founder Dangerfields Nightclub 1969. Regular appearances on Dean Martin Show, 1972–3. Appeared in TV movie Benny and Barney: Las Vegas Undercover.
PICTURES: The Projectionist, Caddyshack, Easy Money (also co. s.p.), Back to School, Moving, Rover Dangerfield (voice, exec. prod., s.p., co-story, co-wrote songs), Ladybugs.

DANIEL, SEAN: Executive. b. Aug. 15, 1951. e. California Inst. of Arts film school. BFA, 1973. Was journalist for Village Voice before starting m.p. career as documentary filmmaker and asst. dir. for New World Pictures. In 1976 joined Universal Pictures as prod. exec.; 1979, named v.p., then pres., production. Resigned March, 1989 to become pres., The Geffen Co., film div.; resigned from Geffen, Nov. 1989. 1990, started own prod. co. in partnership with Universal Pictures. Co-produced films Pure Luck and American Me.

DANIELS, HAROLD: Director, Producer, Writer, b. Buffalo, NY. e. Carnegie Tech. Drama Dept. B.A., U. of Pittsburgh, PHG. Joined MGM in 1940, directed shorts and won award from M.P. Council; joined David Selznick as director, 1943–45; produced, directed and wrote Prince of Peace, won spec. award for dir.
STAGE: Director in Pittsburgh for Prof. Stage Guild Co., N.Y., Rhode Island and Boston Repertoire. Directed over 50 plays.
PICTURES: Woman from Tangier, Sword of Venus, Port Sinister, Roadblock, Daughter of the West Classics, Terror in the Haunted House, Date with Death, My World Dies Screaming, Bayou, Poor White Trash, Ten Girls Ago; directed, Night of the Beast, House of Black Death, Annabelle Lee, Moonfire. Pigmy, 1971.
TELEVISION: directed over 200 half-hour and hour films including My Hero, Readers Digest, Fury, Colt 45, Ellery Queen, Jim Backus Theatre, G.E. Theatre, etc. Wrote many original screenplays for both films and TV. The Phantom, On Guard, Death Valley Days, Hannibal Cobb.

DANIELS, JEFF: Actor. b. Georgia. Feb. 19, 1955. e. Central Michigan U. Apprentice with Circle Repertory Theatre, New York.
THEATRE: Brontosaurus, Short-Changed Review, The Farm, Fifth of July, Johnny Got His Gun (Obie Award), Lemon Sky, The Three Sisters, The Golden Age, Redwood Curtain.
PICTURES: Ragtime (debut, 1981), Terms of Endearment, The Purple Rose of Cairo, Marie, Heartburn, Something Wild, Radio Days, The House on Carroll Street, Sweet Hearts Dance, Checking Out, Arachnophobia, Welcome Home Roxy Carmichael, Love Hurts, The Butcher's Wife, There Goes the Neighborhood, Rain Without Thunder, Gettysburg.
TELEVISION: Movies: A Rumor of War, Invasion of Privacy, The Caine Mutiny Court Martial, No Place Like Home, Disaster in Time, Teamster Boss: The Jackie Presser Story. Specials: Fifth of July, The Visit (Trying Times). Guest: Breaking Away (pilot), Hawaii 5-0.

DANIELS, PAUL: TV performer, magician. b. South Bank, England, Apr. 6, 1938. Early career starring in British and overseas theatres. 1983, Magician Of The Year Award by Hollywood's Academy of Magical Arts. 1985, his BBC TV special awarded Golden Rose of Montreux trophy. Presenter of Every Second Counts and Paul Daniels Magic Show. Devised children's TV series, Wizbit and radio series Dealing With Daniels.

DANIELS, WILLIAM: Actor. b. Brooklyn, NY, Mar 31, 1927. m. actress Bonnie Bartlett. e. Northwestern U. Traveled around NY area as part of The Daniels Family song and dance troupe. Appeared with family on experimental TV in 1941. Stage debut in Life with Father. Brought to national attention in A Thousand Clowns in original Bdwy. play and film version.
PICTURES: Ladybug Ladybug, A Thousand Clowns, Two for the Road, The Graduate, The President's Analyst, Marlowe, 1776, The Parallax View, Black Sunday, Oh God, The One and Only, Sunburn, The Blue Lagoon, All Night Long, Reds, Blind Date, Her Alibi.
TELEVISION: Series: Captain Nice, The Nancy Walker Show, Freebie and the Bean, Knight Rider (voice), St. Elsewhere (Emmy Awards, 1985, 1986). Guest: East Side/West Side, For the People, Toma, The Rockford Files. Movies: Rooster, Rehearsal for a Murder, Murdock's Gang, A Case of Rape, Sarah T.—Portrait of a Teenage Alcoholic, One of Our Own, Francis Gary Powers, Killer on Board, The Bastard, Big Bob Johnson and His Fantastic Speed Circus, Sgt. Matlovich Vs. the U.S. Air Force, The Rebels, City in Fear, Damien: The Leper Priest, Million Dollar Face, Drop Out Father, The Little Match Girl, Knight Rider 2000 (voice), Back to the Streets of San Francisco. Mini-series: Blind Ambition, The Adams Chronicles.
STAGE: The Zoo Story, On a Clear Day You Can See Forever, 1776, Dear Me, The Sky Is Falling, A Little Night Music.

DANNER, BLYTHE: Actress. b. Philadelphia, PA, Feb. 3, 1943. e. Bard Coll. m. writer-producer Bruce Paltrow. Appeared in repertory cos. in U.S. before Lincoln Center (N.Y.) productions of Cyrano de Bergerac, Summertree, and The Miser (Theatre World Award for last).
THEATER: NY: Butterflies Are Free (Tony Award, 1971), Major Barbara, Twelfth Night, The Seagull, Ring Around The Moon, Betrayal, Blithe Spirit, A Streetcar Named Desire, Much Ado About Nothing. Williamstown: Picnic.
PICTURES: To Kill a Clown, 1776, Lovin' Molly, Hearts of the West, Futureworld, The Great Santini, Man Woman and Child, Brighton Beach Memoirs, Another Woman, Mr. and Mrs. Bridge, Alice, The Prince of Tides, Husbands and Wives.
TELEVISION: Movies: Dr. Cook's Garden, F. Scott Fitzgerald and The Last of the Belles, Sidekicks, A Love Affair: The Eleanor and Lou Gehrig Story, Too Far to Go, Eccentricities of a Nightingale, Are You in the House Alone?,

Inside the Third Reich, In Defense of Kids, Helen Keller: The Miracle Continues, Guilty Conscience, Money Power Murder, Judgment, Never Forget, Cruel Doubt, Getting Up and Going Home. Series: Adam's Rib, Tattingers (revamped as Nick & Hillary). Specials: To Confuse the Angel, George M, To Be Young Gifted and Black, The Scarecrow., Kiss Kiss Dahlings.

DANO, ROYAL: Actor. b. New York, NY, Nov. 16, 1922. On Broadway stage (Finian's Rainbow, That's the Ticket, Metropole, Mrs. Gibbins Boys, Three Wishes for Jaime, She Stoops to Conquer) before entering films.
PICTURES: Undercover Girl, Under the Gun, The Red Badge of Courage, Bend of the River, Johnny Guitar, The Far Country, The Trouble With Harry, Tribute to a Bad Man, Santiago, Moby Dick, Tension at Table Rock, Crime of Passion, Trooper Hook, All Mine to Give, Man in the Shadow, Saddle the Wind, Man of the West, Never Steal Anything Small, These Thousand Hills, Hound Dog Man, Face of Fire, Adventures of Huckleberry Finn, Cimarron, King of Kings, Savage Sam, 7 Faces of Dr. Lao, Welcome to Hard Times, Last Challenge, Day of the Evil Gun, If He Hollers Let Him Go, The Undefeated, The Great Northfield Minnesota Raid, The Culpepper Cattle Company, Ace Eli and Rodger of the Skies, Electra Glide in Blue, Big Bad Mama, The Wild Party, The Outlaw Josey Wales, The Killer Inside Me, In Search of the Historic Jesus, Take This Job and Shove It, Hammett, Something Wicked This Way Comes, The Right Stuff, Teachers, Red-Headed Stranger, Killer Klowns From Outer Space, Ghoulies II, Spaced Invaders.
TELEVISION: Movies: Backtrack, Simon Run, Moon of the Wolf, Huckleberry Finn, Manhunter, Murder at Peyton Place, Donner Pass, Strangers, From Here to Eternity, Once Upon a Texas Train.

DANSON, TED: Actor. b. San Diego, CA, Dec. 29, 1947. e. Kent Sch., Stanford U., Carnegie-Mellon U, 1972. Studied at Actors Inst. with Dan Fauci. New York stage debut, The Real Inspector Hound, 1972; 1978, mgr. and teacher, Actors Inst., L.A. Television debut, The Doctors. Founded Amer. Oceans Campaign; bd. mem. Futures for Children.
PICTURES: The Onion Field (debut, 1979), Body Heat, Creepshow, Little Treasure, Just Between Friends, A Fine Mess, Three Men and a Baby, Cousins, Dad, Three Men and a Little Lady, Made in America, Getting Even With Dad.
TELEVISION: Series: Somerset, Cheers (Emmy Award, 1990). Movies: The Women's Room, Once Upon a Spy, Our Family Business, Cowboy, Something about Amelia, When the Bough Breaks (also prod.), We Are the Children. Guest: Laverne & Shirley, Magnum P.I., Taxi, Saturday Night Live.

DANTE, JOE: Director. b. Morristown, NJ. Managing editor for Film Bulletin before going to Hollywood to work in advertising, creating campaigns for many films. Became protege of Roger Corman, co-directing Hollywood Boulevard. Appeared in Cannonball, Slumber Party Massacre, Eating Raoul, Sleepwalkers.
PICTURES: Piranha (also co-editor), Rock n' Roll High School (co-story only), Grand Theft Auto (editor only), The Howling (also co-editor), Twilight Zone—The Movie (dir. segment), Gremlins, Explorers, Innerspace, Amazon Women on the Moon (co-dir.), The 'Burbs, Gremlins II (also cameo), Matinee.
TELEVISION: Amazing Stories, Eerie Indiana.

D'ANTONI, PHILIP: Producer. Director. b. New York, NY, Feb. 19, 1929. e. Fordham U., business administration. Joined CBS in mailroom, advanced into prod., sales development, prog. analysis, mkt. rsrch. Became indep. radio-TV repr. in 1954 for two years; then joined Mutual Broadcasting as sales manager; later, exec. v.p. Resigned in 1962 to form own prod. co. Made theatrical film debut with Bullitt as producer; directing debut with The Seven Ups. Heads D'Antoni Prods.
PICTURES: Producer: Bullitt, The French Connection (Academy Award). Prod.-Dir: The Seven Ups.
TELEVISION: Movin' On (series, 1976) Elizabeth Taylor in London, Sophia Loren in Rome, Melina Mercouri in Greece, Jack Jones Special, This Proud Land, and 6 movies: Mr. Inside/Mr. Outside, The Connection, Strike Force, In Tandem, Rubber Gun Squad, Cabo.

DANZ, FREDRIC A.: Executive. b. Seattle, WA, Feb. 28, 1918. Is chairman of Sterling Recreation Organization Co., Seattle; member, Foundation of M.P. Pioneers; v.p., Variety Club Intl.

DANZA, TONY: Actor. b. Brooklyn, NY, Apr. 21, 1951. e. U. of Dubuque, IA on a wrestling scholarship. After grad. professional boxer before tested for role in TV pilot (Fast Lane Blues) which he won. Back to New York and fighting until called to coast to appear as Tony Banta in Taxi series. On L.A. & NY Stage: Wrong Turn at Lungfish.
PICTURES: Hollywood Knights, Going Ape, Cannonball Run II, She's Out of Control.
TELEVISION: Series: Taxi, Who's the Boss, Baby Talk (voice), George (co-exec. prod. only). Movies: Murder Can Hurt You!, Doing Life (also exec. prod.), Single Bars Single

Women, Freedom Fighter (also co-exec. prod.), The Whereabouts of Jenny (also co-exec. prod.), Dead and Alive.

D'ARBANVILLE, PATTI: Actress. b. New York, NY, 1951. Grew up in Greenwich Village. Landed first job as baby in Ivory Soap commercials. In early teens worked as disc jockey where discovered by Andy Warhol and cast in small role in film Flesh. Moved to Paris at 15 where she became successful model and was featured in book Scavullo on Beauty. Made film debut in Gerard Brach's 1969 film La Maison. Fluent in French, worked in French films until 1973 when moved to Los Angeles. Won Dramalogue Award for John Patrick Shanley's Italian-American Reconciliation (L.A. 1987).
PICTURES: La Maison, La Saigne, The Crazy American Girl, Rancho DeLuxe, Bilitis, Big Wednesday, The Main Event, Time After Time, The Fifth Floor, Hog Wild, Modern Problems, The Boys Next Door, Real Genius, Call Me, Fresh Horses, Wired.
TELEVISION: *Movies*: Crossing the Mob, Blind Spot. *Mini-Series*: Once an Eagle. *Guest*: Crime Story, R.E.L.A.X., Tough Cookies, Charlie's Angels, Barnaby Jones, Miami Vice, Murder She Wrote.

DARBY, KIM: Actress. r.n. Deborah Zerby. b. Hollywood, CA, July 8, 1948. e. Swanson's Ranch Sch., Van Nuys H.S. Studied at the Desilu Workshop in Hollywood. Professional debut on the Mr. Novak TV series.
TELEVISION: *Guest*: Eleventh Hour, Gunsmoke. *Special*: Flesh and Blood. *Movies*: Ironside (pilot), The People, Streets of San Francisco (pilot), Don't Be Afraid of the Dark, Story of Pretty Boy Floyd, This Was the West That Was, Flatbed Annie & Sweetiepie: Lady Truckers, Enola Gay, Embassy. *Mini-Series*: Rich Man Poor Man, The Last Convertible.
PICTURES: Bus Riley's Back in Town, True Grit, Generation, Norwood, The Strawberry Statement, The Grissom Gang, The One and Only, Better Off Dead, Teen Wolf Too.

DARK, JOHN: Producer. Pres. of J.D.Y.T. Producciones S.L., Coin Film City.
PICTURES: Light Up the Sky, Wind of Change, Loss of Innocence (Greengage Summer), The 7th Dawn, Casino Royale, Half a Sixpence, Bachelor of Arts, From Beyond the Grave, Madhouse, Land That Time Forgot, At the Earth's Core, People That Time Forgot, Warlords of Atlantis, Arabian Adventure, Slayground, Shirley Valentine, Stepping Out.

DARLEY, DICK: Director, Producer network TV series and specials. Over 180 TV film shows; over 1,370 TV live/tape shows. Numerous pilots and commercials. Credits in U.S. and 27 foreign countries include drama, musical-variety, comedy, sports and documentary.

DARREN, JAMES: Actor. b. Philadelphia, PA, June 8, 1936. Studied with Stella Adler group.
PICTURES: Rumble on the Docks (debut, 1956), The Brothers Rico, The Tijuana Story, Operation Mad Ball, Gunman's Walk, Gidget, The Gene Krupa Story, Because They're Young, All the Young Men, Let No Man Write My Epitaph, Guns of Navarone, Gidget Goes Hawaiian, Diamond Head, Gidget Goes to Rome, For Those Who Think Young, The Lively Set, Venus in Furs, The Boss' Son.
TELEVISION: *Series*: The Time Tunnel, T.J. Hooker. *Guest*: Police Story, Hawaii Five-0, Vega$, Baa Baa Blacksheep, One Day at a Time. *Movies*: City Beneath the Sea, The Lives of Jenny Dolan, Turnover Smith, Scruples. *Director of episodes*: T.J. Hooker, The A Team, Stingray, Werewolf, Hunter, Tequila and Bonetti, Raven, Police Story.

DARRIEUX, DANIELLE: Actress. b. Bordeaux, France, May 1, 1917. e. Lycée LaTour, Conservatoire de Musique.
PICTURES: Le Bal (debut, 1932), La Crise Est Finis, Mayerling, Tarass Boulba, Port Arthur, Un Mauvais Garcon, Club de Femmes, Abus de Confiance, Mademoiselle ma Mere, The Rage of Paris, Katia, Retour a l'Aube, Battlement de Coeur, Premier Rendezvous, Caprices, Adieu Cherie, Au Petit Bonbeur, Bethsabee, Ruy Blas, Jean de le Lune, Occupe-toi d'Amelie, La Ronde, Rich Young and Pretty, Five Fingers, Le Plaisir, La Verite sur Bebe Donge, Adorable Creatures, Le Bon Dieu sans Confession, The Earrings of Madame De, Le Rouge et le Noir, Bonnes a Tuer, Napoleon, Alexander the Great, A Friend of the Family, Loss of Innocence (Greengage Summer), Les Lions sont Laches, Les Bras de lat Nuit, Bluebeard (Landru), Patate, Le Coup de Grace, L'Or du Duc, Le Dimanche de la Vie, The Young Girls of Rochefort, La Maison de Campagne, Scene of the Crime, A Few Days With Me.
THEATRE: Coco, The Ambassador (Bdwy).

DARTNALL, GARY: Executive. b. Whitchurch, Eng., May 9, 1937. e. Kings Coll., Taunton. Overseas Div., Associated British Pathe; Eur. rep., 1958–60; Middle & Far East rep., Lion International Films; Amer. rep. 1962; pres., Lion International Inc., 1963; Amer. rep., Alliance International Films Distributors, Ltd., and London Independent Producers, Ltd.; pres., Alliance International Films Corp. & Dartnall Films Ltd., 1966; managing dir., Overseas Division, Walter Reade Organiza-

tion, 1969. pres., EMI Film Distributors, Inc., 1971; vice chmn., EMI Television Programs, Inc., 1976; pres., EMI Videograms, Inc., 1979; pres., VHD Programs, Inc. & VHD Disc Mfg. Co., 1980; chmn. & chief exec. officer, Thorn EMI Films, Ltd., & Thorn EMI Video, 1983. Also pres. & CEO, Thorn EMI Films, Inc.; chmn., Thorn EMI Cinemas; CEO, Thorn EMI Screen Entertainment Ltd. 1987: Acquired Southbrook Intl. Television and formed Palladium Inc., chmn. & CEO.

da SILVA, RAUL: Creative consultant, Writer, Director, Producer, b. New York, NY, June 12, 1933. e. Adelphi U., B.A. 1958, elected to Acad. of Distinction, Adelphi Alumni Assoc. 1978. Specializes in unusual conceptualization and plotting rework, stressing classic artistry and production values. Writer, dir. TV broadcast & cable advertising, exec. prod. adv. agencies; indep. writer, producer, dir., univ. lecturer (creative aspects of film prod. writing). Dir. & prod. of over 300 business and documentary films. Books incl. Motion Picture Production, World of Animation, Making Money in Film and Video (1st & 2nd editions).
PICTURES: Fear No Evil (creative consultant).
TELEVISION: Nat Hurst M.D., The Strangest Voyage (dir., prod.), Standing Tall (script consultant), Craftsmen in Concert (prod., dir.), Hidden Battlefield (dir., prod.). Video: The Rime of the Ancient Mariner.

Da SILVA, RAY: Director and designer of animated films, Animator, Illustrator, Character designer. b. New York, NY, July 13, 1934. e. School of Visual Arts, N.Y., also instructor there. Specializes in animation direction, character design. Numerous national and intl. TV spots for the advertising industry.
PICTURES: Raggedy Ann & Andy; Heavy Metal.
TELEVISION: The Strangest Voyage, Noah's Animals, The Little Brown Burro, Ichabod Crane.

DASSIN, JULES: Director. b. Middletown, CT, Dec. 18, 1911. m. actress Melina Mercouri. Actor on dramatic stage several years; radio writer. Joined MGM, 1940, as dir. short subjects; later dir. features.
PICTURES: Canterville Ghost, Brute Force, Naked City, Thieves' Highway, Night and the City, Rififi, He Who Must Die, T he Law, Never on Sunday (also actor), Topkapi, Phaedra, 10:30 p.m. Summer, Uptight, Promise at Dawn, The Rehearsal, A Dream of Passion, Circle of Two.
PLAYS: Ilya Darling, Medicine Show, Magdalena, Joy to the World, Isle of Children, Two's Company, Heartbreak House, Threepenny Opera, Sweet Bird of Youth, A Month in the Country, Who's Afraid of Virginia Woolf?, The Road to Mecca.

DAVEE, LAWRENCE W.: Engineer. b. Foxcroft, ME, March 28, 1900. e. U. of Maine.; B.S., elec. eng. Research eng. Bell Telephone Lab.; Fox Case Corp.; studio mgr. Fox Hearst Corp.; Bronx Studio. Elec. Research Prods., Inc.; Century Projector Corp., N.Y.; engineer & sales mgr.; pres. 1959. Member: 25–30 Club (Honorary). Lifemember, N.Y. State Projectionists. Samuel L. Warner Award 1968 SMPTE.

DAVENPORT, NIGEL: Actor. b. Cambridge, May 23, 1928. e. Trinity Coll., Oxford. Began acting after stint in British military at 18 years. First 10 years of professional career in theatre. Majority of screen work in British films in 1960s and 70s.
PICTURES: Look Back in Anger, Peeping Tom, In the Cool of the Day, The Third Secret, Sands of the Kalahari, A High Wind in Jamaica, Where the Spies Are,Life at the Top, A Man for All Seasons, Sebastian, The Strange Affair, Sinful Davey, Play Dirty, Virgin Soldiers, Royal Hunt of the Sun, The Mind of Mr. Soames, The Last Valley, No Blade of Grass, Villain, Mary Queen of Scots, Living Free, Charley-One-Eye, Phase IV, Island of Dr. Moreau, Zulu Dawn, Nighthawks, Chariots of Fire, Greystoke, Caravaggio, Without a Clue.
TELEVISION: A Christmas Carol (1984), Dracula, The Picture of Dorian Gray, The Ordeal of Dr. Mudd, Masada.

DAVIAU, ALLEN: Cinematographer. b. New Orleans, LA, June 14, 1942.
PICTURES: Close Encounters of the Third Kind (addtl. photog.), Harry Tracy, E.T.: The Extra-Terrestrial, Twilight Zone: The Movie (co-photog.), Indiana Jones and the Temple of Doom, The Falcon and the Snowman, The Color Purple, Harry and the Hendersons, Empire of the Sun, Avalon, Defending Your Life, Bugsy.
TELEVISION: *Movies*: Rage, Legs. *Special*: The Boy Who Drank Too Much. *Series*: Amazing Stories.

DAVID, KEITH: Actor. b. New York, NY, June 4, 1954. e. Juilliard.
PICTURES: The Thing, Platoon, Hot Pursuit, Braddock: Missing in Action III, Off Limits, Stars and Bars, Bird, They Live, Road House, Always, Men at Work, Marked for Death, Final Analysis, Article 99.
THEATRE: NY: The Pirates of Penzance, A Midsummer Night's Dream, Waiting for Godot, Miss Waters to You, La Boheme, Coriolanus, Titus Andronicus, A Map of the World, The Haggadah, Alec Wilder: Clues to a Life, Boesman & Lena, Jelly's Last Jam.

TELEVISION: *Movies*: Ladykillers, Murder in Black and White. *Mini-Series*: Roots: The Next Generations. *Guest*: The Equalizer, A Man Called Hawk.

DAVID, PIERRE: Executive, Producer. b. Montreal, Canada, May 17, 1944. e. U. of Montreal. Joined radio sta. CJMS 1966 as pub. rel. & spec. events dir., 1969, while running Mutual Broadcasting Network of Canada's live entertainment div., created new film dist. co. Mutual Films. 1972 added prod. unit and as prod. or exec. prod., prod. and dist. 19 French-lang. Canadian films. With filmmaker Roger Corman est. Mutual Pictures of Canada, Ltd to dist. films in English Canada; 1978 teamed Mutual Films with Victor Solnicki and Claude Heroux to prod. Eng.-lang. m.p. Pioneered 3-picture concept for Canadian m.p. investors. Moved to L.A. 1983 where became pres., Film Packages Intl. where prod. exec. on Platoon. Then joined Larry Thompson Org. as partner involved in dev. and/or prod. of m.p., Jan., 1987, named chmn. of bd. and chief exec. officer, Image Org., Inc. intl. dist. co. formed by David and Rene Malo. Also pres. Lance Entertainment, prod. co.
PICTURES: Prod.: The Brood, Hog Wild, Scanners, Dirty Tricks, Gas, The Funny Farm, Visiting Hours, Videodrome, Going Berserk, Of Unknown Origin, Covergirl, Breaking All the Rules, For Those I Loved, Blind-Fear (co-prod.), The Perfect Bride, Hot Pursuit, The Perfect Weapon, Bounty Tracker, Distant Cousins, Deep Cover, Marital Outlaw. *Exec. Prod.*: Quiet Cool, Scanners II: The New Order, Desire and Hell at Sunset Motel, Martial Law, Scanners III, Dolly Dearest, Mission of Justice, Deadbolt, Internal Affairs, Twin Sisters, Pin. *Prod.-Dir.*: Scanner Cop.

DAVID, SAUL: Producer. b. Springfield, MA., June 27, 1921. e. Classical H.S., Springfield; Rhode Island Sch. of Design. Started in radio, newspaper work and as editorial director for Bantam Books. Worked for Columbia Pictures, 1960–62; Warner Bros., 1962–63; 20th Century-Fox, 1963–67, and Universal, 1968–69; Executive story editor at MGM, 1972. Author: The Industry.
PICTURES: Von Ryan's Express, Our Man Flint, Fantastic Voyage, In Like Flint, Skullduggery, Logan's Run, Ravagers (exec. prod.).

DAVIDOVICH, LOLITA: Actress. b. Ontario, Canada, 1961. Also acted under the name Lolita David.
PICTURES: Class, Adventures in Babysitting, The Big Town, Blaze, The Object of Beauty, JFK, The Inner Circle, Raising Cain, Leap of Faith, Boiling Point, Younger and Younger.
TELEVISION: *Movies*: Two Fathers' Justice, Prison Stories: Women on the Inside (Parole Board), Keep the Change.

DAVIDSON, JOHN: Actor, Singer. b. Pittsburgh, PA, Dec. 13, 1941. e. Denison U. In numerous school stage prods. before coming to N.Y. in 1964 to co-star with Bert Lahr in Bdwy. show, Foxy. Signed as regular on The Entertainers with Carol Burnett.
PICTURES: The Happiest Millionaire, The One and Only Genuine Original Family Band, The Concorde—Airport '79, The Squeeze, Edward Scissorhands.
TELEVISION: *Special*: The Fantasticks. *Guest*: The FBI, The Interns, Owen Marshall, The Tonight Show, (also frequent guest host). *Series*: The Entertainers, Kraft Summer Music Hall, The John Davidson Show (1969), The Girl With Something Extra, The John Davidson Show (1976), The John Davidson Talk Show (1980), That's Incredible, New Hollywood Squares, Time Machine (game show), The $100,000 Pyramid. *Movies*: Coffee Tea or Me?, Shell Game, Roger & Harry: The Mitera Target, Dallas Cowboys Cheerleaders II.

DAVIDSON, MARTIN: Director, Writer. b. New York, NY, Nov. 7, 1939.
PICTURES: The Lords of Flatbush, Almost Summer, Hero at Large, Eddie and the Cruisers, Heart of Dixie (also exec. prod.), Hard Promises.
TELEVISION: *Series*: Family Honor, Call to Glory, Law and Order, Picket Fences. *Movies*: Long Gone, My Life and Times, A Murderous Affair: The Carolyn Warmus Story.

DAVIES, JOHN HOWARD: Producer, Director. b. London, England, March 9, 1939. e. Haileybory, IS.C. and Grenoble Univ. Former child actor played leading roles in Oliver Twist, The Rocking Horse Winner, Tom Brown's Schooldays.
TELEVISION: Prod./Dir.: Monty Python's Flying Circus, Steptoe and Son, Fawlty Towers, The Good Life, The Goodies, The Other One, No Job for a Lady, Mr. Bean.

DAVIS, ANDREW: Director. b. Chicago, IL. e. Univ. of IL. Former journalist and photographer before landing job as asst. cameraman on 1969 film Medium Cool. Was dir. of photog. on several tv commercials and documentaries.
PICTURES: Lepke (dir. of photog.), Stony Island (dir., prod., co-s.p.), Over the Edge (dir. of photog.), The Final Terror (dir.), Angel (dir. of photog.), Beat Street (dir.), Code of Silence (dir.), Above the Law (dir., co-prod., co-story), The Package (dir.), Under Siege (dir.), The Fugitive (dir.).

DAVIS, CARL: Composer. b. New York, NY, Oct. 28, 1936. e. Queens Coll., Bard Coll. and New England Coll. of Music. Worked as pianist with Robert Shaw Chorale and wrote music for revue Diversions (1958) and Twists (London). Moved to England 1961 writing incidental music for Joan Littlewood's Theatre Workshop Co., Royal Shakespeare Co. and National Theatre. Other theater music includes Jonathan Miller's Tempest, Forty Years On, and the musical The Vackees. Best known for composing new scores for silent classics (Napoleon, The Crowd, Greed, Intolerance, etc.) for screenings at which he conducts and for Thames TV The Silents series. Concert work: Paul McCartney's Liverpool Oratorio.
PICTURES: The Bofors Gun, Up Pompeii, Rentadick, Man Friday, The Sailor's Return, Birth of the Beatles, The French Lieutenant's Woman, Praying Mantis, The Aerodrome, Champions, Weather in the Streets, George Stevens: A Filmmaker's Journey, King David, The Rainbow, Scandal, Girl in a Swing, Fragments of Isabella, Frankenstein Unbound, Diary of a Madman, Raft of the Medusa, The Voyage.
TELEVISION: That Was the Week That Was, Hollywood, the Pioneers, World at War, Mayor of Casterbridge, Lorna Doone, Unknown Chaplin, Buster Keaton—A Hard Act to Follow, Treasure Island, The Snow Goose, Our Mutual Friend, Naked Civil Servant, Silas Marner, The Accountant, Secret Life of Ian Fleming, Why Lockerbie?, Buried Mirro, A Christmas Carol, Royal Collection, Hotel du Lac, Black Velvet Gown.

DAVIS, COLIN: Executive. Held executive positions in Canada in adv., bdcst., & p.r. with several companies, including Procter & Gamble, Young & Rubicam. Joined MCA TV Canada as v.p. & gen. mgr., 1977. Named dir. intl. sls., 1978. In 1986 appt. pres., MCA TV Int'l.

DAVIS, FRANK I.: Executive. b. Poolesville, MD, Feb. 18, 1919. e. U. of Maryland, A.B., 1941; Harvard Law School, LL.B., 1948. Law firm, Donovan, Leisure, Newton, Lombard and Irvine, 1948–50; v.p., gen. counsel, Vanguard Films, 1951; v.p., gen. counsel, Selznick Releasing Org., 1951–53; pres., The Selznick Company, 1953–55; v.p., Famous Artists Corp., 1956–62; v.p. George Stevens Productions Inc., 1962–65; exec. prod., The Greatest Story Ever Told; v.p. in charge of m.p. affairs, Seven Arts, 1966; exec. in chg. talent and exec. asst. to v.p. in chg. prod., MGM, 1967; dir. m.p. business affairs, MGM, 1970; v.p., business affairs, MGM, 1972; sr. v.p., motion picture business affairs, MGM/UA, 1983, exec. v.p., business affairs, MGM Pictures, 1986–88; sr. exec. v.p., business affairs, Pathe Entertainment Inc., 1989–90; sr. exec. v.p. of bus. affairs, MGM, 1990.

DAVIS, GEENA: Actress. b. Wareham, MA, Jan. 21, 1957. e. Boston U. Acted with Mount Washington Repertory Theatre Co., NH. Model before debut in Tootsie, 1982.
PICTURES: Tootsie, Fletch, Transylvania 6-5000, The Fly, Beetlejuice, The Accidental Tourist (Acad. Award, supp. actress, 1988), Earth Girls Are Easy, Quick Change, Thelma & Louise, A League of Their Own, Hero, Angie I Says.
TELEVISION: *Series*: Buffalo Bill (also wrote one episode), Sara. *Movie*: Secret Weapons. *Guest*: Family Ties, Riptide, Remington Steele, Saturday Night Live, Trying Times (The Hit List).

DAVIS, GEORGE W.: Art director. b. Kokomo, IN, Apr. 17, 1914. e. U. of Southern California.
PICTURES: All About Eve, David and Bathsheba, The Robe (Acad. Award, 1953), Love Is A Many Splendored Thing, Funny Face, The Diary of Anne Frank (Acad. Award, 1959), Cimarron, Period of Adjustment, Mutiny on the Bounty, The Wonderful World of the Brothers Grimm, Twilight of Honor, How the West Was Won, The Americanization of Emily, The Unsinkable Molly Brown, A Patch of Blue, Mr. Buddwing, The Shoes of the Fisherman, etc.

DAVIS, JUDY: Actress. b. Perth, Australia, 1956. m. actor Colin Friels. Left convent school as teenager to become a singer in a rock band. Studied at West Australia Inst. of Technology and National Inst. of Dramatic Art, Sydney. Worked with theatre companies in Adelaide and Sydney and at Royal Court Theatre, London. Los Angeles stage debut Hapgood.
PICTURES: High Rolling (debut, 1977), My Brilliant Career, Hoodwink, Heatwave, Winter of Our Dreams, The Final Option, A Passage to India (Acad. Award nom.), Kangaroo, High Tide, Georgia, Alice, Impromtu, Barton Fink, Naked Lunch, Where Angels Fear to Tread, Husbands and Wives (Acad. Award nom.), The New Age.
TELEVISION: Rocket to the Moon, A Woman Called Golda, One Against the Wind.

DAVIS, LUTHER.: Writer, Producer. b. New York, Aug. 29, 1921. Collab. book B'way musical Kismet (Tony Award), collab. s.p.; author, prod., Lady In A Cage. Prod. and wrote book for Bdwy musical, Timbuktu!, 1978–79. Wrote book for Bdwy musical Grand Hotel, 1989 (Tony Award nom.). Co-

prod., Eden Court and Not About Heroes (off-Bdwy. plays, 1985 and 1986).
PICTURES: Writer: The Hucksters, B.F.'s Daughter, Black Hand, A Lion Is in the Streets, The Gift of Love, Holiday for Lovers, The Wonders of Aladdin, Lady in a Cage (also prod.), Across 110th Street.
TELEVISION: Wrote, prod., Kraft Suspense Theatre and many pilots for series (Run for Your Life, Combat, The Silent Force, Eastside, Westside, etc.). Wrote, prod. Arsenic and Old Lace (TV special). Prod.: The People Trap (TV special). Wrote teleplays for MOW's Daughter of the Mind, The Old Man Who Cried Wolf, Colombo.

DAVIS, MAC: Singer, Songwriter, Actor. b. Lubbock, TX, Jan 21, 1942. e. Emory U., Georgia State Coll. Employed as ditch digger, service station attendant, laborer, probation officer and record company salesman before gaining fame as entertainer-singer in 1969. Recording artist and composer of many popular songs. On Bdwy 1992 in The Will Rogers Follies.
PICTURES: North Dallas Forty, Cheaper to Keep Her, The Sting II.
TELEVISION: Series: The Mac Davis Show. Movies: Brothers-In-Law, What Price Victory?, Blackmail.

DAVIS, MARTIN S.: Executive. b. New York, NY, Feb. 5, 1927. U.S. Army, 1943–46; joined Samuel Goldwyn Prod., Inc., 1944; with pub. dept. Allied Artists, 1955; Paramount Pictures, 1958. as dir. sales and marketing then dir. adv., pub. expl. 1960; v.p. in chg. of home office and asst. to pres.; 1963; exec. v.p., 1966; exec. comm. & bd. of dir. Member of Bd., Gulf & Western, 1967, named sr. v.p. 1969; elected Exec. v.p. and mem. exec. comm. Gulf & Western, 1974; elected CEO and chmn. of bd. and chmn. exec. comm. 1983. Member: bd. trustees, Museum of TV & Radio, Montefiore Medical Center, and Economic Club of NY; Chmn,. NYC Chap, Natl. Multiple Sclerosis Society; bd. of trustees Carnegie Hall. (Gulf & Western renamed Paramount Communications 1989). Co-chmn. of Corp. Advisory Committee of the Barbara Bush Foundation for Family Literacy.

DAVIS, OSSIE: Actor, Writer, Director. b. Cogdell, GA, Dec. 18, 1917. e. Howard U., Washington, DC. m. actress Ruby Dee. Studied acting in N.Y. with Rose McLendon Players, leading to Broadway debut in 1946 in Jeb. For years thereafter was one of best-known black actors on Broadway stage (Anna Lucasta, Jamaica, The Green Pastures, Wisteria Tree, A Raisin in the Sun, I'm Not Rappaport.) Wrote and starred in Purlie Victorious, repeating role for film version. Directed and appeared with Ms. Dee in her musical Take It From the Top. Co-hosted Ossie Davis and Ruby Dee Story Hour on radio (3 years). Published plays: Purlie Victorious, Langston, Escape to Freedom, Curtain Call, Mr. Aldredge, Sir.
PICTURES: Actor: No Way Out, Fourteen Hours, The Joe Louis Story, Gone Are the Days, The Cardinal, Shock Treatment, The Hill, Man Called Adam, The Scalphunters, Sam Whiskey, Slaves, Let's Do It Again, Hot Stuff, House of God, Harry and Son, Avenging Angel, School Daze, Do the Right Thing, Joe Versus the Volcano, Jungle Fever, Gladiator, Malcolm X (voice), Grumpy Old Men. Director: Cotton Comes to Harlem (also co-s.p.), Black Girl, Gordon's War, Countdown at Kusini (also star, prod.).
TELEVISION: Writer: Eastside/West Side, The Eleventh Hour. Acted in many top dramatic series (Name of the Game, Night Gallery, Bonanza, etc.), Martin Luther King: The Dream and the Drum; Co-host and co-prod. With Ossie and Ruby; Today is Ours (writer, dir.). Movies: All God's Children, Don't Look Back, Roots: The Next Generations, King, Teacher Teacher, The Ernest Green Story. Series: B.L. Stryker, Evening Shade. Mini-Series: Queen.

DAVIS, PETER: Author, Filmmaker. b. Santa Monica, CA, Jan. 2, 1937. e. Harvard Coll., 1953–57. Parents were screenwriter Frank Davis, and novelist-screenwriter Tess Slesinger. Writer-interviewer, Sextant Prods., FDR Series, 1964–65. Host, The Comers, PBS 1964–65. Author: Hometown (1982), Where Is Nicaragua? (1987), articles for Esquire, NY Times Mag., The Nation, NY Woman, TV Guide.
PICTURE: Hearts and Minds (prod., dir.; Acad. Award, best documentary, 1975; Prix Sadoul, 1974).
TELEVISION: Writer-prod.: Hunger in America (assoc. prod., WGA Award, 1968), The Heritage of Slavery, The Battle of East St. Louis, (Saturday Review Award, 1970; 2 Emmy nom.), The Selling of the Pentagon (WGA, Emmy, Peabody, George Polk, Ohio State, Sat. Review Awards, 1971), 60 Minutes (segment prod.), Middletown (series, prod., Dupont Citation, Emmy noms. 1983), The Best Hotel on Skidrow (ACE Award noms., 1992).

DAVIS-VOSS, SAMMI: Actress. b. Kidderminster, Worcestershire, Eng., June 21, 1964. Convent-educated before taking drama course. Performed in stage prods. with local drama society in Midlands, then Birmingham Rep. and Big

Brum Theatre Co. Plays include The Home Front, The Apple Club, Nine Days, Databased, Choosey Susie. London stage debut: A Collier's Friday.
PICTURES: Mona Lisa, Lionheart, Hope and Glory, A Prayer for the Dying, Consuming Passions, The Lair of the White Worm, The Rainbow, The Horseplayer, Shadow of China.
TELEVISION: Auf Wiedersehn Pet, The Day After the Fair, Pack of Lies, Chernobyl: The Final Warning, The Perfect Bride, Indecency. Series: Homefront.

DAVISON, BRUCE: Actor. b. Philadelphia, PA, June 28, 1946. e. Pennsylvania State U., NYU. debut, Lincoln Center Repertory.
THEATER: NY: King Lear (Lincoln Center), The Elephant Man, Richard III (NY Shakespeare Fest.), The Glass Menagerie. Regional: The Front Page (Long Wharf), Streamers (Westwood Playhouse; LA Critics Award), The Caine Mutiny Court Martial (Ahmanson), The Normal Heart (Las Palmas Theatre), Downside (Long Wharf).
PICTURES: Last Summer (debut, 1969), The Strawberry Statement, Willard, Been Down So Long It Looks Like Up To Me, The Jerusalem File, Ulzana's Raid, Mame, Mother Jugs and Speed, Grand Jury, Short Eyes, Brass Target, French Quarter, High Risk, A Texas Legend, Lies, Crimes of Passion, Spies Like Us, The Ladies Club, The Misfit Brigade, Longtime Companion (NY Film Critics, Natl. Society of Film Critics, & Golden Globe Awards, 1990), Steel and Lace, Short Cuts, An Ambush of Ghosts, Six Degrees of Separation.
TELEVISION: Movies: Owen Marshall: Counsellor at Law (A Pattern of Morality), The Affair, The Last Survivors, Deadman's Curve, Summer of My German Soldier, Mind Over Murder, The Gathering, Tomorrow's Child, Ghost Dancing, Poor Little Rich Girl: The Barbara Hutton Story, Lady in a Corner, Stolen: One Husband, Live! From Death Row, Desperate Choices: To Save My Child. Specials: Taming of the Shrew, The Lathe of Heaven, The Wave. Guest: Medical Center, Marcus Welby, Love American Style, Police Story, Lou Grant, Murder She Wrote, Alfred Hitchcok Presents (1985), Amazing Stories. Series: Hunter, Harry and the Hendersons.

DAVISON, DALE: Executive. b. North Hollywood, CA, March 21, 1955. e. U.C.L.A., B.A., 1978. Entered the motion picture industry in 1973 working for Pacific Theatres. Employed with Great Western Theatres 1974–77 as manager, dir. of concessions, and asst. vice pres. Partner with Great Western Theatres, 1978–1984. Founder and CEO, Cinema-Cal Enterprises, Inc., 1985–present.

DAVISON, JON: Producer. b. Haddonfield, NJ, July 21, 1949. e. NYU Film School. 1972, joined New World Pictures as natl. dir. of publ./adv.; 1972, named in charge of prod.; 1980, became indep. prod.
PICTURES: Hollywood Boulevard, Grand Theft Auto, Piranha, Airplane!, White Dog, Twilight Zone—The Movie (episode), Top Secret! Robocop, Robocop 2.

DAWBER, PAM: Actress, Singer. b. Detroit, MI, Oct. 18, 1954. m. actor Mark Harmon. e. Farmington H.S., Oakland Community Coll. Worked as model and did commercials. First professional performance as singer in Sweet Adeleine at Goodspeed Opera House, East Haddam, CT.
STAGE: Regional: My Fair Lady, The Pirates of Penzance, The Music Man, She Loves Me, Love Letters.
PICTURES: A Wedding, Stay Tuned.
TELEVISION: Series: Mork and Mindy, My Sister Sam. Movies: The Girl the Gold Watch and Everything, Remembrance of Love, Through Naked Eyes, Last of the Great Survivors, This Wife For Hire, Wild Horses, Quiet Victory: The Charlie Wedemeyer Story, Do You Know the Muffin Man, The Face of Fear, The Man With 3 Wives. Specials: Kennedy Center Honors, Salute to Andy Gibb, Night of the 100 Stars, 3rd Annual TV Guide Special.

DAY, DORIS: Singer, Actress. r.n. Doris Kappelhoff. b. Cincinnati, OH, Apr. 3, 1924. e. dancing, singing. Toured as dancer; radio and band singer; screen debut in Romance on the High Seas, 1948. Voted one of Top Ten Money-Making Stars in Motion Picture Herald-Fame poll, 1951–52. Best female vocalist. M. P. Daily radio poll, 1952.
PICTURES: Romance on the High Seas (debut, 1948), My Dream is Yours, It's a Great Feeling, Young Man With a Horn, Tea for Two, Storm Warning, West Point Story, Lullaby of Broadway, On Moonlight Bay, I'll See You in My Dreams, Starlift, The Winning Team, April in Paris, By the Light of the Silvery Moon, Calamity Jane, Lucky Me, Young at Heart, Love Me or Leave Me, The Man Who Knew Too Much, Julie, The Pajama Game, Teacher's Pet, Tunnel of Love, It Happened to Jane, Pillow Talk (Acad. Award nom.), Please Don't Eat the Daisies, Midnight Lace, Lover Come Back, That Touch of Mink, Bill Rose's Jumbo, The Thrill of It All, Move Over Darling, Send Me No Flowers, Do Not Disturb, Glass Bottom Boat, Caprice, The Ballad of Josie,

Where Were You When the Lights Went Out?, With Six You Get Eggroll.
TELEVISION: *Series*: The Doris Day Show (1968–73); Cable show: Doris Day's Best Friends (educational; 1985–86).

DAY, LARAINE: Actress. r.n. Laraine Johnson. b. Roosevelt, UT, Oct. 13, 1920. In school dramatics; with Players Guild, Long Beach, Calif.; toured in church prod. Conflict; Professionally on stage in Lost Horizon, The Women, Time of the Cuckoo, Angel Street.
PICTURES: Stella Dallas (debut, 1937 as Laraine Johnson), Scandal Street, Border G-Men, Young Dr. Kildare (and subsequent series), And One Was Beautiful, My Son My Son, Foreign Correspondent, The Trial of Mary Dugan, The Bad Man, Unholy Partners, Fingers at the Window, Journey for Margaret, Mr. Lucky, The Story of Dr. Wassell, Bride by Mistake, Those Endearing Young Charms, Keep Your Powder Dry, The Locket, Tycoon, My Dear Secretary, I Married a Communist (Woman on Pier 13), Without Honor, The High and the Mighty, Toy Tiger, Three for Jamie Dawn, The Third Voice.
TELEVISION: Appearances include Climax, Playhouse 90, Alfred Hitchcock, Wagon Train, Let Freedom Ring, Name of the Game, FBI, Sixth Sense, Medical Center, Murder on Flight 504 (movie), Fantasy Island, Love Boat, Lou Grant, Airwolf, Hotel, Murder She Wrote.

DAY, ROBERT: Director. b. England, Sept. 11, 1922. Started as cinematographer before turning to direction.
PICTURES: Director: The Green Man, Grip of the Stranger, First Man into Space, Corridors of Blood, Bobbikins, Two-Way Stretch, The Rebel, Operation Snatch, Tarzan's Three Challenges, She, Tarzan and the Valley of Gold, Tarzan and the Green River, Logan's Run, The Man with Bogart's Face.
TELEVISION: Pilots include: Banion, Kodiak, Dan August, Sunshine, Switch, Kingston, Dallas. Movies include: Ritual of Evil, The House of Greenapple Road, In Broad Daylight, Having Babies, The Grass Is Always Greener over the Septic Tank, Peter and Paul, Running Out, Scruples, Cook and Peary—The Race to the Pole, Hollywood Wives, The Lady from Yesterday, Diary of a Perfect Murder, Celebration, Family, Higher Ground.

DAY-LEWIS, DANIEL: Actor. b. London, England, Apr. 29, 1957. Son of late C. Day-Lewis, poet laureate of Eng., and actress Jill Balcon. Grandson of late Sir Malcolm Balcon who prod. Hitchcock's Brit. films. e. Bristol Old Vic. Theatre School. First professional job at 12 as ruffian scratching cars with broken bottle in film, Sunday Bloody Sunday. Then acted with Bristol Old Vic and Royal Shakespeare Co. Appeared in West End in, among others, Dracula, Another Country, Romeo and Juliet, A Midsummer Night's Dream, Hamlet (Natl Theater, 1989).
PICTURES: Gandhi, The Bounty, A Room With a View, My Beautiful Laundrette, The Unbearable Lightness of Being, Stars and Bars, Nanou, Eversmile New Jersey, My Left Foot (BAFTA, NY Film Critics, L.A. Film Critics, Natl. Society of Film Critics, & Acad. Award, 1989), The Last of the Mohicans, The Age of Innocence, In the Name of the Father.
TELEVISION: BBC Movies/Specials:A Frost in May, How Many Miles to Babylon?, My Brother Jonathan, The Insurance Man, History of Hamlet (host).

DAYTON, LYMAN D.: Producer. b. Salt Lake City, UT. Aug. 17, 1941. e. Brigham Young U.. m. Elizabeth Doty Dayton. After college worked in film lab at MGM, 1967–68; joined Screen Gems and General DeLuxe, 1968–69; became indep. prod. 1969. Heads Doty-Dayton Productions.
PICTURES: Where the Red Fern Grows, Seven Alone, Against A Crooked Sky, Pony Express Rider, Baker's Hawk, Young Rivals, Powder Keg.

DEAKINS, ROGER: Cinematographer. b. Devon, England, May 24, 1949. Accepted into National Film School in 1972 where he made documentary films: Around the World With Ridgeway, Zimbabwe, Eritrea—Behind the Lines, When the World Changed. Photographed first feature, Another Time Another Place in 1982.
PICTURES: 1984, The Innocent, Sid & Nancy, Shadey, Defense of the Realm, White Mischief, Stormy Monday, Pascali's Island, The Kitchen Toto, Mountains of the Moon, Air America, The Long Walk Home, Barton Fink, Homicide, Thunderheart, Passion Fish, The Secret Garden, Rita Hayworth and Shawshank Redemption.

DEAN, EDDIE: Actor. r.n. Edgar D. Glosup. b. Posey, TX, July 9, 1907. 1930–33 in radio throughout middle west; 1934 National Barn Dance, Station WLS; 1935 on CBS & NBC with same program. Featured male singer on TV KTLA Western Varieties 1944–55. Came to Hollywood in 1936; since then has starred in many westerns. Featured performer in western series for PRC in 1945. Voted one of the ten best money making Western Stars in Motion Picture Herald-Fame Poll 1936–47; recording artists, personal appearances, rodeos, fairs, etc.; 1966 V.P. Academy of Country & Western Music; 1967–68 on Bd. of Dir. of Academy of Western Music, Calif.

Winner, Pioneer Award of Academy of Country Music, 1978. In 1983 named ACM v.p.; also v.p. in 1985. Recorded video cassette 1986, A Tribute to Eddie Dean.

DEAN, JIMMY: Performer. b. Plainview, TX, Aug. 10, 1928. Joined armed forces, 1946–49; first appeared in various clubs in Wash., 1949; then app. on Town and Country Jamboree; toured Caribbean and Europe with his troupe; appeared in Las Vegas. TNN/Music City News Country Music Awards, Song-writer of the Year Awards.
SONGS: *Composer*: Big Bad John, Little Black Book, I.O.U., To a Sleeping Beauty, PT–109, Dear Ivan.
PICTURES: Diamonds Are Forever, Big Bad John.
TELEVISION: *Series*: The Jimmy Dean Show (1957; 1963–6), Daniel Boone, J.J. Starbuck. *Specials*: Sunday Night at the Palladium (London), Celebrities Offstage. *Movies*: The Ballad of Andy Crocker, Rolling Man, The City.

DEAN, MORTON: Television Newsman. b. Fall River, MA, Aug. 22, 1935. e. Emerson Coll. News dir., N.Y. Herald Tribune Net, 1957; corr. WBZ, 1960, corr. WCBS-TV, 1964; anchor, WCBW-TV News, 1967; corr., CBS News, 1967; anchor, CBS Sunday Night News, 1975; anchor, Sunday edition CBS Evening News, 1976; co-anchor, Independent Network News, 1985.

DEARDEN, JAMES: Writer, Director. b. London, Eng. Sept. 14, 1949. Son of late British director Basil Dearden. e. New Coll., Oxford U. Entered film industry in 1967 as production runner. After editing commercials and documentaries, and working as asst. dir., wrote, prod. and dir. first short film, The Contraption (Silver Bear Award, 1978 Berlin Film Fest.). 1978, began dir. commercials and made short, Panic (Cert. of Merit, 1980 Chicago Film Fest.). 1979, made 45-min film Diversion, which became basis for Fatal Attraction (Gold Plaque, best short drama, 1980 Chicago Film Fest.).
PICTURES: Fatal Attraction (s.p.), Pascali's Island (dir., s.p.), A Kiss Before Dying (dir., s.p.).
TELEVISION: The Cold Room (dir., writer, Special Jury Prize, dir., 1985 Fest. Intl. d'Avoriaz du Film Fantastique).

DE BROCA, PHILIPPE: Director. b. 1933.
PICTURES: Les Jeux de l'Amour, L'Amant, de Cinq Jours, Cartouche, That Man from Rio, Un Monsieur de Compagnie, Tribulations, Chinoise and King of Hearts, Devil by the Tail, Give Her the Moon, Chere Louise, Le Magnifique, Dear Inspector (and s.p.), The Skirt Chaser, Someone's Stolen the Thigh of Jupiter, The African, Louisiana (TV in U.S.), The Gypsy, Chouans! (dir., co-s.p.), Scheherazade..

DE CAMP, ROSEMARY: Actress. b. Prescott AZ, Nov. 14, 1913.
TELEVISION: *Series*: The Life of Reilly (with Jackie Gleason), Robert Cummings Show, That Girl. *Guest*: Death Valley Days, Partridge Family, Love American Style, Police Story, Rockford Files, Days of Our Lives, Misadventures of Sheriff Lobo, Love Boat, B.J. & the Bear. *Mini-Series*: Blind Ambition. *Movie*: The Time Machine.
PICTURES: Cheers for Miss Bishop (debut, 1941), Hold Back the Dawn, Jungle Book, Yankee Doodle Dandy, Eyes in the Night, THe Commandos Strike at Dawn, Smith of Minnesota, Without Men, This is the Army, The Merry Monahans, Bowery to Broadway, Blood on the Sun, Practically Yours, Rhapsody in Blue, Pride of the Marines, Danger Signal, Too Young to Know, From This Day Forward, Nora Prentiss, Night Unto Night, The Life of Riley, Look for the Silver Lining, Story of Seabiscuit, The Big Hangover, Night Into Morning, On Moonlight Bay, Scandal Sheet, Treasure of Lost Canyon, By the Light of the Silvery Moon, Main Street to Broadway, So This Is Love, Many Rivers to Cross, Strategic Air Command, 13 Ghosts, Saturday the 14th.

DE CAPRIO, AL: Producer-director. e. Brooklyn Tech., NYU. Started as radio engineer, cameraman, tech. dir., prod. & dir. CBS; dir. Sgt. Bilko, Car 54 Where Are You?, Musical specials for ABC, CBS, NBC; v.p. exec. prod. dir., MPO Videotronics, Pres. World Wide Videotape; retired.

DE CARLO, YVONNE: Actress. b. Vancouver, B.C., Sept. 1, 1922. e. Vancouver School of Drama, Fanchon & Marco, Hollywood. Specialty dancing at Florentine Gardens, Earl Carroll's; m.p. debut in This Gun for Hire, 1942. One-woman club act and 7-person club act. Autobiography, Yvonne (1987).
PICTURES: This Gun for Hire (debut, 1942), Harvard Here I Come, Youth on Parade, Road to Morocco, Let's Face It, The Crystal Ball, Salute for Three, For Whom the Bell Tolls, True to Life, So Proudly We Hail, The Deerslayer, Practically Yours, Story of Dr. Wassell, Standing Room Only, Here Come the Waves, Kismet, Salome Where She Danced, Frontier Gal, Brute Force, Song of Scheherazade, Slave Girl, Black Bart, Casbah, River Lady, Criss Cross, Gal Who Took the West, Calamity Jane and Sam Bass, Buccaneer's Girl, The Desert Hawk, Tomahawk, Hotel Sahara, Silver City, Scarlet Angel, San Francisco Story, Hurricane Smith, Sombrero, Sea Devils, Fort Algiers, Captain's Paradise, Border River, Passion, Tonight's the Night, Shotgun, Magic Fire, Flame of the Islands, Ten Commandments, Raw Edge, Death of a Scoun-

drel, Band of Angels, Timbuktu, McLintock!, A Global Affair, Law of the Lawless, Munster Go Home, Hostile Guns, The Power, Arizona Bushwhackers, The Seven Minutes, Play Dead, It Seemed Like a Good Idea at the Time, Won Ton Ton the Dog Who Saved Hollywood, Satan's Cheerleaders, Nocturna, Silent Scream, Guyana Cult of the Damned, The Man With Bogart's Face, Liar's Moon, American Gothic, Cellar Dweller, Mirror Mirror, Oscar.
BROADWAY STAGE: Follies.
TELEVISION: *Series*: The Munsters. *Movies*: The Girl on the Late Late Show, The Mark of Zorro, The Munsters' Revenge, A Masterpiece of Murder. *Guest*: Bonanza, Man From U.N.C.L.E., Murder She Wrote, Hollywood Sign (special), Johnny Carson, Merv Griffin, Steve Allen, David Frost, Perry Como.

DE CORDOVA, FREDERICK: Director. b. New York, NY, Oct. 27, 1910. e. Northwestern U., B.S. 1931. Gen. stage dir. Shubert enterprises, N.Y., 1938–41; same for Alfred Bloomingdale Prods., N.Y., and prod. Louisville (Ky.) Amphitheatre 1942–43; m.p. dir. Author: Johnny Came Lately, 1988.
PICTURES: (dial. dir.) San Antonio, Janie, Between Two Worlds; (dir.) Too Young to Know, Her Kind of Man, That Way with Women, Always Together, Wallflower, For the Love of Mary, Countess of Monte Cristo, Illegal Entry, Girl Who Took the West, Buccaneer's Girl, Peggy, Desert Hawk, Bedtime for Bonzo, Katie Did It, Little Egypt, Finders Keepers, Here Come the Nelsons, Yankee Buccaneer, Bonzo Goes to College, Column South.
TELEVISION: prod., dir. Burns and Allen, 1955–56; prod., December Bride, 1954–55; prod. and dir., Mr. Adams and Eve, prod. dir. December Bride; prod. dir. George Gobel Show; prod. dir., Jack Benny Program, 1960–63; dir., program planning, Screen Gems, 1964; prod. dir., Smothers Bros. Show, 1965–66; 1965 dir. I'll Take Sweden and Frankie & Johnny; 1966–70 dir. My Three Sons; 1971–present, prod., Tonight Show (4 Emmy Awards).

DeCUIR, JR., JOHN F.: Art Director, Production Designer. b. Burbank, CA, Aug. 4, 1941. e. U. of Southern California, bachelor of architecture. 1963. Son of John F. De Cuir, Sr. 1966–68, U.S. Coast Guard (holds commission with rank of Lt. Commander, USCGR). 1968–72, project designer, Walt Disney World, Walt Disney Prods. 1972–74, dir. of design, Six Flags Corp. 1974–9, project designer, EPCOT, Walt Disney Prods. 1980–86, pres., John F. De Cuir, Jr. Design Consultants, Inc.; 1987–pres., Cinematix Inc.
PICTURES: *Illustrator*: Cleopatra, The Honey Pot. *Design Concepts*: The Agony and the Ecstasy. *Art Director*: Raise the Titanic, Ghostbusters. *Special Effects Consultant*: Dead Men Don't Wear Plaid, Monsignor. *Producer*: Jazz Club, The Baltimore Clipper, The Building Puzzle. *Production Designer*: Fright Night, Top Gun, Apt Pupil, Elvira, Mistress of the Dark, Turner & Hooch, True Identity, Sleepwalkers, Sister Act 2.
TELEVISION: *Art Director*: Frank Sinatra Special—Old Blue Eyes Is Back, Annual Academy Awards Presentation 1971, Double Agent. *Production Design*: Double Switch, Earth * Star Voyager.

DEE, RUBY: Actress. b. Cleveland, OH, Oct. 27, 1924. r.n. Ruby Ann Wallace. e. Hunter Coll. m. actor-dir.-writer Ossie Davis. Worked as apprentice at Amer. Negro Theatre, 1941–44, studied at Actor's Workshop. Stage appearances include Jeb, Anna Lucasta, The World of Sholom Aleichem, A Raisin in the Sun, Purlie Victorious, Wedding Band, Boseman and Lena, Hamlet, Checkmates.
PICTURES: No Way Out, Jackie Robinson Story, Tall Target, Go Man Go, Edge of the City, St. Louis Blues, Take a Giant Step, Virgin Island, A Raisin in the Sun, Gone Are the Days, The Balcony, The Incident, Uptight, Buck and the Preacher, Black Girl, Countdown at Kusini, Cat People, Do the Right Thing, Love at Large, Jungle Fever, Cop and a Half.
TELEVISION: *Movies*: Deadlock, The Sheriff, It's Good to Be Alive, I Know Why the Caged Bird Sings, All God's Children, The Atlanta Child Murders, Go Tell it on the Mountain, Windmills of the Gods, The Court-Martial of Jackie Robinson, Decoration Day (Emmy Award, 1991), The Ernest Green Story. *Specials*: Actor's Choice, Seven Times Monday, Go Down Moses, Twin-Bit Gardens, Wedding Band, To Be Young Gifted and Black, Long Day's Journey into Night. *Mini-Series*: Roots: The Next Generation, Gore Vidal's Lincoln. *Series*: Peyton Place, With Ossie and Ruby, Middle Ages.

DEE, SANDRA: Actress. r.n. Alexandra Zuck. b. Bayonne, NJ, April 23, 1942. Modeled, Harry Conover and Huntington Hartford Agencies, N.Y., 1954–56; signed long term exclusive contract, U-I, 1957.
PICTURES: Until They Sail (debut, 1957), The Reluctant Debutante, The Restless Years, Stranger in My Arms, Imitation of Life, Gidget, The Wild and the Innocent, A Summer Place, The Snow Queen (voice), Portrait in Black, Romanoff and Juliet, Come September, Tammy Tell Me True, If a Man Answers, Tammy and the Doctor, Take Her She's Mine, I'd Rather Be Rich, That Funny Feeling, A Man Could

Get Killed, Doctor You've Got to Be Kidding!, Rosie, The Dunwich Horror.
TELEVISION: *Movies*: The Daughters of Joshua Cabe, Houston We've Got a Problem, The Manhunter, Fantasy Island (pilot). *Guest*: Steve Allen Show, Night Gallery, Love American Style, Police Woman.

DEELEY, MICHAEL: Producer. b. London, Eng. August 6, 1932. Ent. m.p. ind. 1951 and TV, 1967, as alt. dir. Harlech Television Ltd. Film editor, 1951–58. MCA-TV 1958–61, later with Woodfall as prod. and assoc. prod. Assoc. prod. The Knack, The White Bus, Ride of the Valkyrie. Great Western Investments Ltd.; 1972; Great Western Festivals Ltd.; 1973, man. dir. British Lion Films Ltd. 1975, purchased BLF, Ltd. Appt. Jnt. man. dir. EMI Films Ltd., 1977; pres., EMI Films, 1978, Member Film Industry Interim Action Committee, 1977–82; Deputy Chairman, British Screen Advisory Council, 1985. Appt. Chief Executive Officer, Consolidated Television Production & Distribution Inc., 1984.
PICTURES: Prod. One Way Pendulum, Robbery, The Italian Job, Long Days Dying (exec. prod.), Where's Jack, Sleep Is Lovely, Murphy's War, The Great Western Express, Conduct Unbecoming, The Man Who Fell to Earth, Convoy, The Deer Hunter (Acad. Award), Blade Runner, A Gathering of Old Men (TV; exec. prod.).

DE FINA, BARBARA: Producer. Started as prod. asst. before working at various jobs for such filmmakers as Woody Allen and Sidney Lumet. Became assoc. prod. of development for King/Hitzig Prods., working on Happy Birthday Gemini, Cattle Annie and Little Britches. Was unit mgr./assoc. prod. on Prince of the City. First worked with Martin Scorsese on The King of Comedy as unit mgr. Produced music video Bad.
PICTURES: Producer: The Color of Money, The Last Temptation of Christ, New York Stories (segment: Life Lessons), GoodFellas (exec. prod.), The Grifters (exec. prod.), Cape Fear, Mad Dog and Glory, The Age of Innocence.

DE HAVILLAND, OLIVIA: Actress. b. Tokyo, Japan, July 1, 1916. e. California schools and Notre Dame Convent, Belmont. Acting debut, Max Reinhardt's stage prod., A Midsummer Night's Dream; film debut in m.p. version, 1935; received 5 Academy Award nominations; won Academy Award as best actress for To Each His Own, 1946, and The Heiress, 1949; N.Y. Film Critics award twice, 1948–49; Women's Natl. Press Club Award, 1949; Look award, best perf. 3 times, 1941–48–49. Autobiography: Every Frenchman Has One (1962).
PICTURES: A Midsummer Night's Dream (debut, 1935), Alibi Ike, The Irish in Us, Captain Blood, Anthony Adverse, The Charge of the Light Brigade, Call It a Day, It's Love I'm After, The Great Garrick, Gold is Where You Find It, The Adventures of Robin Hood, Four's a Crowd, Hard to Get, Wings of the Navy, Dodge City, The Private Lives of Elizabeth and Essex, Gone With the Wind, Raffles, My Love Came Back, Santa Fe Trail, Strawberry Blonde, Hold Back the Dawn, They Died With Their Boots On, The Male Animal, In This Our Life, Princess O'Rourke, Thank Your Lucky Stars, Government Girl, The Well Groomed Bride, To Each His Own (Acad. Award), Devotion, Dark Mirror, The Snake Pit, The Heiress (Acad. Award, 1949), My Cousin Rachel, That Lady, Not as a Stranger, Ambassador's Daughter, Proud Rebel, Libel, Light in the Piazza, Lady in a Cage, Hush . . . Hush Sweet Charlotte, The Adventurers, Pope Joan, Airport '77, The Swarm, The Fifth Musketeer.
STAGE: Romeo and Juliet, 1951; U.S. tour Candida, 1951–52, N.Y., 1952; A Gift of Time, Bdwy. 1962.
TELEVISION: Special: Noon Wine (Stage 67). *Movies & Mini-series*: The Screaming Woman, Roots: The Next Generations, Murder is Easy, Charles & Diana: A Royal Romance, North & South Book II, Anastasia, The Woman He Loved.

DE LANNOY, JEAN: Director. b. Noisy-le-Sec, France, Jan. 12, 1908. e. Université de Paris, Lycée Montaigne, Lycée Louis le Grand, La Sorbonne; actor, 1927–29; film ed., 1929–37; dir., 1937–92.
PICTURES: Black Diamond, The Eternal Return, Symphonie Pastorale, The Chips Are Down, Souvenir, The Secret of Mayerling, Savage Triangle, Moment of Truth, Daughter of Destiny, The Bed, Action Man, La Peau de Torpedo, Das folle la guêpe, Bernadette, The Hunchback of Notre Dame, God Needs Men, Special Friendship.

DELANY, DANA: Actress. b. New York, NY, Mar. 13, 1956. e. Phillips Acad., Wesleyan U.
TELEVISION: *Series*: Love of Life, As the World Turns, Sweet Surrender, China Beach (2 Emmy Awards: 1989, 1992). *Guest*: Moonlighting, Magnum P.I. *Movies*: Threesome, Donato and Daughter. *Mini-Series*: Wild Palms.
PICTURES: Almost You, Where the River Runs Black, Masquerade, Moon Over Parador, Patty Hearst, Housesitter, Light Sleeper, Tombstone.

DE LAURENTIIS, DINO: Producer, Executive. b. Torre Annunziata, Italy, Aug. 8, 1919. Took part in Rome Experimental Film Center; dir., prod. chmn. of the bd. and CEO, De Laurentiis

Entertainment Group Inc.; founded in 1984 the DEG Film Studios in Wilmington, NC. Resigned 1988. Started Dino De Laurentiis Communications, 1990.

PICTURES: L'amore Canta, Il Bandito, La Figlia del Capitano, Riso Amaro, La Lupa, Anna, Ulysses, Mambo, La Strada, Gold of Naples, War and Peace, Nights of Cabiria, The Tempest, La Grande Guerra, Five Branded Women, Under Ten Flags, The Unfaithfuls, Barabbas, The Bible, Operation Paradise, The Witches, The Stranger, Diabolik, Anzio, Barbarella, Waterloo, Valachi Papers, Stone Killers, Serpico, Death Wish, Mandingo, Three Days of the Condor, Drum, Face to Face, Buffalo Bill and the Indians, King Kong, The Shootist, Orca, White Buffalo, Serpent's Egg, King of the Gypsies, The Brink's Job, Hurricane, Flash Gordon, Halloween II, Ragtime, Conan the Barbarian, Fighting Back, Amityville II: The Possession, Halloween III, The Dead Zone, Amityville 3-D, Firestarter, The Bounty, Conan the Destroyer, Stephen King's Cat's Eye, Red Sonja, Year of the Dragon, Marie, Silver Bullett, Raw Deal, Maximum Overdrive, Tai-Pan, Blue Velvet, The Bedroom Window, Crimes of the Heart, King Kong Lives, Million Dollar Mystery, Weeds, Desperate Hours, Kuffs, Once Upon a Crime, Body of Evidence, Army of Darkness.

DE LAURENTIIS, RAFFAELLA: Producer. Daughter of Dino De Laurentiis. Began career as prod. asst. on father's film Hurricane.Independent producer.

PICTURES: Beyond the Reef, Conan the Barbarian, Conan the Destroyer, Dune, Tai-Pan, Prancer, Dragon: The Bruce Lee Story.

DE LA VARRE, ANDRE, JR.: Producer, Director. b. Vienna, Austria, Oct. 26, 1934. Prod. Grand Tour travelogues; producer of promotion films for KLM, Swissair, tourist offices, recent productions: Bicentennial films for state of Virginia, city of Charleston, NY state; winner, Atlanta Film Festival, Sunset Travel Film Festival; Burton Holmes Travelogue subjects; Corporate Incentive Videos, V-P-R Educational Films; producer, director, lecturer, narrator.

DEL BELSO, RICHARD: Marketing Executive. b. Albany, NY, Aug. 9, 1939. e. Fordham U, 1961, NYU, 1965. Began career in adv./research dept. at Benton & Bowles Advertising, NY. Served as research dept. group head for Kenyon and Eckhart; group head for Grudin/Appell/Haley Research Co. (now known as A/H/F/ Marketing Research, Inc.). Two years as assoc. dir. of mktg., research for Grey Advertising (N.Y.). Joined MCA/Universal in 1976 as assoc. dir., mktg. research. In 1980 named v.p. & dir. of mktg. research for Warner Bros; became worldwide v.p. of mktg. research, 1984; named sr. v.p. worldwide theatrical film market research, 1990.

DELFONT, LORD BERNARD: President, First Leisure Corporation PLC. b. Tokmak, Russia, September 5, 1909. Brother of Lord Lew Grade. e. London, England. Entered theatrical management 1941. Since presented over 250 shows in London; pantomimes in provinces and seaside shows; presented annual Royal Variety Performance. Director of Delfont Mackintosh Theatres Ltd. 1969: Chief Barker (Pres.) Variety Club of Great Britain; Companion of the Grand Order of Water Rats, President of Entertainment. Artistes' Benevolent Fund, member of Saints and Sinners organisation. Appointed Pres., First Leisure Corp., Oct. 1992.

DELON, ALAIN: Actor. b. Sceaux, France, Nov. 8, 1935. Discovered by Yves Allegret. Served in French Navy as a Marine. Worked as cafe waiter, heavy-load carrier.

PICTURES: When a Woman Gets Involved (debut, 1957), Be Beautiful and Keep Quiet, 3 Murderesses, Christine, Le Chemin Des Ecoliers, Plein Soleil (Purple Noon), Quelle Joie de Vivre!, Rocco and His Brothers, Famous Loves, Eclipse, The Leopard, The Devil and the 10 Commandments, Any Number Can Win, The Black Tulip, The Felines (Joy House), L'Insoumis (also prod., co-s.p.), The Yellow Rolls Royce, Once a Thief, Lost Command, Is Paris Burning?, Texas Across the River, The Adventurers, Spirits of the Dead, Samaurai, Diabolically Yours, Girl on a Motorcycle, Goodbye Friend, The Swimming Pool, Jeff (also prod.), The Sicilian Clan, Borsalino, The Red Circle, Madly (also prod.), Doucement Les Basses, Red Sun, The Widow Cuderc, Assassination of Trotsky, Dirty Money, The Teacher, Scorpio, Shock Treatment, The Burning Barn, Big Guns, Two Men in the City, La Race des Seigneurs, Les Seins de Glace, Borsalino & Company (also prod.), Zorro, Police Story, The Gypsy, Mr. Klein (also prod.), Like a Boomerang (also prod., s.p.), The Gang (also exec. prod.), Armaggedon, L'Homme Presse, Mort d'un Pourri (also s.p.), Attention Les Enfants Regardent, The Concorde - Airport 79, The Doctor, Teheran 43, Three Men to Destroy (also dir, s.p.), For a Cop's Honor (also dir, s.p., prod.), The Shock (also s.p.), The Cache (also prod., dir., s.p.), Swann in Love, Our Story, Military Police (also exec. prod., s.p.), The Passage (also prod.), Let Sleeping Cops Lie (also prod., co-s.p.), New Wave, Dancing Machine, The Return of Casanova.

Del ROSSI, PAUL R.: Executive. b. Winchester, MA, Oct. 19, 1942. e. Harvard Coll, 1964; Harvard Business Sch., 1967. Sr. v.p., The Boston Co., 1977–1980; sr. consultant, Arthur D. Little, Inc.; presently pres., General Cinema Theatres.

DE LUISE, DOM: Comedian, Actor. b. Brooklyn, NY, Aug. 1, 1933. e. Tufts Coll. m. actress Carol Arthur. Sons: Peter, Michael, David. Spent two seasons with Cleveland Playhouse. Launched TV career on The Garry Moore Show with character, Dominick the Great, a bumbling magician.

PICTURES: Fail Safe (debut, 1964), Diary of a Bachelor, The Glass Bottom Boat, The Busybody, What's So Bad About Feeling Good?, Norwood, 12 Chairs, Who Is Harry Kellerman?, Every Little Crook and Nanny, Blazing Saddles, The Adventures of Sherlock Holmes' Smarter Brother, Silent Movie, The World's Greatest Lover, The End, The Cheap Detective, Sextette, The Muppet Movie, Hot Stuff (also dir.), The Last Married Couple in America, Fatso, Wholly Moses, Smokey and the Bandit II, History of the World—Part I, The Cannonball Run, The Best Little Whorehouse in Texas, The Secret of NIMH (voice), Cannonball Run II, Johnny Dangerously, Haunted Honeymoon, An American Tail (voice), Spaceballs (voice), A Taxi Driver in New York, Going Bananas, Oliver & Company (voice), All Dogs Go To Heaven (voice), Loose Cannons, Driving Me Crazy, Fievel Goes West (voice), Munchie (voice), Happily Ever After (voice), Robin Hood: Men in Tights.

TELEVISION: Series: The Entertainers, The Dean Martin Summer Show, Dom DeLuise Show, The Barrum-Bump Show, The Glenn Campbell Goodtime Hour, The Dean Martin Show, Lotsa Luck, Dom DeLuise Show (synd.), The New Candid Camera, Fievel's American Tails (voice). Movies: Evil Roy Slade, Only With Married Men, Happy (also exec. prod.). Guest: The Munsters, Please Don't Eat the Daises, Ghost and Mrs. Muir, Medical Center, Amazing Stories, Easy Street, B.L. Stryker.

STAGE: Little Mary Sunshine, Another Evening With Harry Stoones, All in Love, Half-Past Wednesday, Too Much Johnson, The Student Gypsy, Last of the Red Hot Lovers, Here's Love, Little Shop of Horrors, Die Fledermus (NY Met. Opera: 2 seasons).

del VALLE, JOHN: Publicist. b. San Francisco, CA, Mar. 23, 1904. e. U. of California. Adv., edit. staff various newspapers including asst. drama ed. S.F. Call-Bulletin, L.A. Mirror; adv.-publicity dir. San Francisco Fox Theatre 1933–36; publicist, Paramount Studio, 1936–42; pub. pub., adv. Arnold Prod. 1946; Chaplin Studios, 1947; Nat Holt Prod., 1948–52; Editor, TV Family mag., N.Y., 1952–53; adv. pub. dir. Century Films, 1954; pub. rel. Academy M.P. Arts & Sciences, 1965; publicist, various U.A. indep. film prod., 1955–56; unit publicist, Para., 1956; TC-F 1957–62, Para., 1962–63; Universal 1964–65; Mirisch Corp.—UA Filming, Hawaii, 1965; pub. rel. and editor, Atomics Int'l Div. North American Rockwell, 1966–71; present, freelance writer. NY Times Op. Ed. (1985), Gourmet Mag. (1989), others.

DEMBY, EMANUEL H.: Producer, Writer. b. New York, NY, Dec. 12, 1919. e. City Coll. of New York, New School, Chung Ang U., Ph.D. Pioneered new programs for radio, 1936–47; story dept., Universal Pictures, 1937; writer, Gangbusters, Crime of the Week, Thrill of the Week (NBC, CBS); TV shows; What's Playing, 1950–52; Hollywood to Broadway, How To Be a Cowboy; The Shadow; prod., theatrical features, filmed commercials; pub. rel. consultant. Author: My Forty Year Fight for Korea; Indonesia; King of the Hill; Hot Tip on Wall St.; prod. Cavalcade of Music (TV); The World in Space (TV, theatrical); The Edge of Violence (stage); Man Into Space; Year III-Space Age (TV); The Communications Gap, The Creative Consumer, (P.R. films). Book: Who's Alienated, Youth or Society? Research Consultant, NBC TV News; consultant, Radio Advertising Bureau, TV Info. Office, TV Luxembourg; Smash, Crash, Pow! (feature).

DEMME, JONATHAN: Director, Writer, Producer. b. Rockville Centre, NY, Feb. 22, 1944. e. U. of Florida. First job in industry as usher; was film critic for college paper, The Florida Alligator and the Coral Gable Times. Did publicity work for United Artists, Avco Embassy; sold films for Pathe Contemporary Films; wrote for trade paper, Film Daily, 1966–68. Moved to England in 1969; musical co-ordinator on Irving Allen's EyeWitness in 1970. In 1972 co-prod and co-wrote first film, Angels, Hard As They Come. Appeared in film Into the Night.

PICTURES: Hot Box (prod., co-s.p.), Black Mama White Mama (story). Director: Caged Heat (also s.p.), Crazy Mama (also s.p.), Fighting Mad (also s.p.), Citizen's Band (aka Handle With Care), Last Embrace, Melvin and Howard, Swing Shift, Stop Making Sense, Something Wild (also co-prod.), Swimming to Cambodia, Married to the Mob, Miami Blues (prod. only), The Silence of the Lambs (Acad. Award, 1991), Cousin Bobby, Philadelphia.

TELEVISION: Who Am I This Time (dir.), Accumation with Talking plus Water Motor (doc. on choreographer Trisha Brown), Survival Guides; numerous music videos (for UB40,

Chrissie Hynde, Sun City Video of Artists United Against Apartheid), A Family Tree (Trying Times series, PBS), Haiti: Dreams of Democracy, Women & Men 2 (A Domestic Dilemma; prod. only).
VIDEO: Suzanne Vega's Solitude Standing.

DE MORNAY, REBECCA: Actress. b. Santa Rosa, CA, Aug. 29, 1962. Spent childhood in Europe, graduating from high school in Austria. Returned to America, enrolling at Lee Strasberg's Los Angeles Institute; apprenticed at Zoetrope Studios.
THEATER: Born Yesterday (Pasadena Playhouse), Marat/Sade (Williamstown Fest.).
PICTURES: Risky Business, Testament, The Slugger's Wife, Runaway Train, The Trip to Bountiful, Beauty and the Beast, And God Created Woman, Feds, Dealers, Backdraft, The Hand That Rocks the Cradle, Guilty as Sin, The Three Musketeers.
TELEVISION: Movies: The Murders in the Rue Morgue, By Dawn's Early Light, An Inconvenient Woman, Blindside.

DEMPSEY, PATRICK: Actor. b. Lewiston, ME, Jan. 13, 1966. In high school became State downhill skiing champion. Juggling, magic and puppetry led to performances before Elks clubs and community org. Cast by Maine Acting Co. in On Golden Pond. In 1983 acted in Torch Song Trilogy in San Francisco and toured in Brighton Beach Memoirs. NY Theatre debut, 1991 in The Subject Was Roses.
PICTURES: Heaven Help Us, Meatballs III, Can't Buy Me Love, In the Mood, In a Shallow Grave, Some Girls, Loverboy, Coupe de Ville, Happy Together, Run, Mobsters, For Better and For Worse, Face the Music, With Honors.
TELEVISION: Movie: A Fighting Choice (debut). Series: Fast Times at Ridgemont High. Special: Merry Christmas Baby.

DE MUNN, JEFFREY: Actor. b. Buffalo, NY, Apr. 25, 1947. e. Union Col. Studied acting at Old Vic Theatre in Bristol, Eng.
PICTURES: You Better Watch Out (Christmas Evil), The First Deadly Sin, Resurrection, Ragtime, I'm Dancing as Fast as I Can, Frances, Windy City, Enormous Changes at the Last Minute, Warning Sign, The Hitcher, The Blob, Betrayed, Blaze, Newsies, The Tender, The New World.
THEATRE: NY: Comedians, A Prayer for My Daughter, Modigliani, Augusta, Hands of Its Enemy, Chekhov Sketchbook, A Midsummer Night's Dream, Total Abandon, Country Girl, Bent, K-2, Sleight of Hand, Spoils of War, One Shoe Off.
TELEVISION: Movies: The Last Tenant, Sanctuary of Fear, King Crab, Word of Honor, I Married Wyatt Earp, The Face of Rage, Sessions, When She Says No, Windmills of the Gods, Lincoln, Doubletake, A Time to Live, Who Is Julia?, Young Harry Houdini, The Haunted, Treacherous Crossing, Jonathan: The Boy Nobody Wanted, Barbarians at the Gate, Crash: The Fate of Flight 1502, Settle the Score. Specials: Mourning Becomes Electra, Peacemaker (Triple Play II), Sensiblity and Sense, The Joy That Kills, Teacher, Pigeon Feathers, Many Mansions, Wild Jackasses.

DENCH, JUDI, D.B.E.: Actress. b. York, England, Dec. 9, 1934. Studied for stage at Central Sch. of Speech and Drama. Theatre debut Old Vic, 1957. Created a Dame in 1988 Honours List. Recent Theatre: Cymbeline, Juno and the Paycock, A Kind of Alaska, The Cherry Orchard, The Plough and the Stars, Importance of Being Earnest, Pack of Lies, Mr. and Mrs. Nobody, Antony and Cleopatra, The Sea, Coriolanus, The Gift of the Gorgon. Director: Much Ado About Nothing, Look Back in Anger, Boys from Syracuse, Romeo and Juliet.
TELEVISION: Major Barbara, Pink String and Sealing Wax, Talking to a Stranger, The Funambulists, Age of Kings, Jackanory, Hilda Lessways, Luther, Neighbours, Parade's End, Marching Song, On Approval, Days to Come, Emilie, The Comedy of Errors, Macbeth (both RSC productions), Langrishe Go Down, On Giant's Shoulders, Love in a Cold Climate, Village Wooing, A Fine Romance (series), The Cherry Orchard, Going Gently, Saigon, Year of the Cat, Ghosts, Behaving Badly, Torch, Can You Hear Me Thinking?, Absolute Hell, As Time Goes By.
PICTURES: The Third Secret, He Who Rides a Tiger, A Study in Terror, Four in the Morning, A Midsummer Night's Dream (RSC Prod.), Dead Cert, Wetherby, A Room With a View, 84 Charing Cross Road, A Handful of Dust, Henry V.

DENEAU, SIDNEY, G.: Sales executive. Head film buyer Fabian Theatres; U.S. Army 1942–46; gen. mgr. Schine Theatres 1947; v.p., gen. sales mgr., Selznick Releasing Orgn., 1949; 1956; v.p. asst. gen. sales. mgr., Para. Film Dist., 1958; exec. v.p., Rugoff Theatres, 1964. Resigned, September, 1969 to engage in own theatre consultant business.

DENEUVE, CATHERINE: Actress. r.n. Catherine Dorleac. b. Paris, France, Oct. 22, 1943. Sister was the late Françoise Dorleac.
PICTURES: Les Collegiennes, Wild Roots of Love, The Doors Slam, Vice and Virtue, Satan Leads the Dance, Umbrellas of Cherbourg, (Cannes Film Fest. Award), Male

Hunt (La Chasse a l'Homme), Repulsion, Le Chant du Monde, La Vie de Chateau (A Matter of Resistance), Les Creatures, The Young Girls of Rochefort, Belle de Jour (Venice Film Fest. Award), Benjamin, Manon 70, Mayerling, La Chamade (Heartbeat), April Fools, Mississippi Mermaid, Tristana, Donkey Skin, Langolis, Liza, It Only Happens to Others, Dirty Money, The Slightly Pregnant Man, Zig-Zag, Hustle, Lovers Like Us, Act of Agression, The Beach Hut, Coupe de Foudre, March or Die, La Grande Bourgeoise, Courage - Let's Run, The Last Metro, I Love You, A Second Chance, Hotel of the Americas, Reporters, The Hunger, Fort Saganne, Scene of the Crime, Trouble Agent, Listening in the Dark, A Strange Place to Be (also prod.), Helmut Newton: Frames From the Edge (doc.), The White Queen, Indochine (Acad. Award nom.), Ma Saison Preferee (My Favorite Season).

DENHAM, MAURICE: Actor. b. Beckenham, Kent, England, Dec. 23, 1909. e. Tonbridge Sch. Started theatrical career with repertory com. 1934. Served in W.W.II. Played in numerous plays, films & radio shows.
PICTURES: Blanche Fury, London Belongs To Me, It's Not Cricket, Traveller's Joy, Landfall, Spider and the Fly, No Highway in the Sky, The Net, Time Bomb, Street Corner (Both Sides of the Law), Million Pound Note (Man With a Million), Eight O'Clock Walk, Purple Plain, Simon and Laura, 23 Paces to Baker Street, Checkpoint, Carrington V.C. (Court Martial), Doctor at Sea, Night of the Demon, Man With a Dog, Barnacle Bill, The Captain's Table, Our Man in Havana, Sink the Bismark, Two-Way Stretch, Greengage Summer, Invasion, Quartette, The Mark, HMS Defiant, The Very Edge, Paranoiac, The Set Up, Penang, The King's Breakfast, Downfall, Hysteria, The Uncle, Operation Crossbow, Legend of Dick Turpin, The Alphabet Murders, The Night Callers, The Nanny, Those Magnificent Men in Their Flying Machines, Heroes of Telemark, After the Fox, The Torture Garden, The Long Duel, The Eliminator, Danger Route, Attack on the Iron Coast, The Best House in London, Negatives, The Midas Run, Some Girls Do, The Touch of Love, The Virgin and the Gypsy, Bloody Sunday, Countess Dracula, Nicholas and Alexandra, The Day of the Jackal, Luther, Shout at the Devil, Julia, The Recluse, From a Far Country, Mr. Love, The Chain, Monsignor Quixote, Murder on the Orient Express, 84 Charing Cross Road.
TELEVISION: Uncle Harry, Day of the Monkey, Miss Mabel, Angel Pavement, The Paraguayan Harp, The Wild Bird, Soldier Soldier, Changing Values, Maigret, The Assassins, Saturday Spectacular, Vanishing Act, A Chance in Life, Virtue, Somerset Maugham, Three of a Kind, Sapper, Pig in the Middle, Their Obedient Servants, Long Past Glory, Devil in The Wind, Any Other Business, The Retired Colourman, Sherlock Holmes (series), Blackmail, Knock on Any Door, Danger Man, Dr. Finley's Casebook, How to Get Rid of Your Husband, Talking to a Stranger, A Slight Ache, From Chekhov with Love, Home Sweet Honeycomb, St. Joan, Julius Caesar, Golden Days, Marshall Petain, The Lotus Eaters, Fall of Eagles, Carnforth Practice. The Unofficial Rose, Omnibus, Balzac, Loves Labour Lost, Angels, Huggy Bear, The Portrait, The Crumbles Murder, A Chink In The Wall, Porridge, For God's Sake, Bosch, Marie Curie, Upchat Line, Secret Army, My Son, My Son, Edward and Mrs. Simpson, Gate of Eden, Potting Shed, Double Dealer, Minder, Agatha Christie Hour, Chinese Detective, The Old Men at the Zoo, The Hope and the Glory, Luther, Love Song, Mr. Palfrey, The Black Tower, Boon, Rumpole, All Passions Spent, Trial of Klaus Barbie, Miss Marple, Tears in the Rain, Behaving Badly, Seeing in the Dark, Inspector Morse: Fat Chance, La Nonna, Lovejoy, Memento Mori, Sherlock Holmes, The Last Vampire, Peak Pratice.

DE NIRO, ROBERT: Actor. b. New York, NY, Aug. 17, 1943. Studied acting with Stella Adler and Lee Strasberg; 1988, formed Tribeca Film Center in NY.
THEATER: One Night Stand of a Noisy Passenger (off-Bdwy); Cuba and His Teddy Bear (Public Theater and Bdwy., 1986; Theatre World Award).
PICTURES: The Wedding Party (debut, 1969), Greetings, Sam's Song (The Swap), Bloody Mama, Hi Mom, Born to Win, Jennifer on My Mind, The Gang That Couldn't Shoot Straight, Bang the Drum Slowly, Mean Streets, The Godfather Part II (Acad. Award, supp. actor, 1974), Taxi Driver, The Last Tycoon, New York New York, 1900, The Deer Hunter, Raging Bull (Acad. Award, 1980), True Confessions, The King of Comedy, Once Upon a Time in America, Falling in Love, Brazil, The Mission, Angel Heart, The Untouchables, Midnight Run, Jacknife, We're No Angels, Stanley and Iris, GoodFellas, Awakenings, Guilty by Suspicion, Backdraft, Cape Fear, Thunderheart (co-prod. only), Mistress (also co-prod.), Night and the City, Mad Dog and Glory, This Boy's Life, A Bronx Tale (also dir., co-prod.).
TELEVISION: Special: Dear America: Letters Home From Vietnam (reader).

DENISON, MICHAEL: C.B.E., Actor. b. Doncaster, York, Eng., Nov. 1, 1915. e. Harrow, Magdalen Coll., Oxford and Webber

Douglas Sch. m. Dulcie Gray, actress. Served overseas, Capt. Intelligence Corps, 1940–46. On stage first, 1938, Charlie's Aunt. Screen debut 1940, Tilly of Bloomsbury.

THEATRE: 50 London plays including Ever Since Paradise, Rain on the Just, Queen Elizabeth Slept Here, Fourposter, Dragon's Mouth, Bad Samaritan; Shakespeare Season Stratford-on-Avon; Edinburgh Festival. Meet Me By Moonlight, Let Them Eat Cake, Candida, Heartbreak House, My Fair Lady (Australia), Where Angels Fear to Tread, Hostile Witness, An Ideal Husband, On Approval, Happy Family, No. 10, Out of the Question, Trio, The Wild Duck, The Clandestine Marriage, The Dragon Variation, At the End of the Day, The Sack Race, Peter Pan, The Black Mikado, The First Mrs. Fraser, The Earl and the Pussycat, Robert and Elizabeth, The Cabinet Minister, Old Vic Season: Twelfth Night, Lady's Not for Burning, Ivanov, Bedroom Farce, The Kingfisher, Relatively Speaking, Coat of Varnish, Capt. Brassbound's Conversion, School for Scandal, Song at Twilight, See How They Run, The Tempest, Ring Round the Moon, The Apple Cart, Court in the Act, You Never Can Tell, The Chalk Garden, Joy, Dear Charles, Best of Friends, The Importance of Being Earnest.

PICTURES: Hungry Hill, My Brother Jonathan, The Blind Goddess, The Glass Mountain, Landfall, The Franchise Affair, Angels One Five, Tall Headlines, Importance of Being Earnest, There Was a Young Lady, Contraband Spain, The Truth About Women, Faces in the Dark.

TELEVISION: Boyd QC Series, Funeral Games, Unexpectedly Vacant, Tale of Piccadilly, The Twelve Pound Look, The Provincial Lady, Subject: This Is Your Life, Bedroom Farce, Private Schultz, Blood Money, The Critic, Scorpion, Cold Warrior, Good Behavior, Howard's Way.

DENNEHY, BRIAN: Actor. b. Bridgeport, CT, July 9, 1939. e. Columbia U. In Marine Corps five years, including Vietnam. After discharge in 1965 studied with acting coaches in N.Y., while working at part time jobs as a salesman, bartender, truck driver.

THEATER: Streamers, Galileo (Goodman Theatre), The Cherry Orchard.

PICTURES: Looking for Mr. Goodbar, Semi-Tough, F.I.S.T., Foul Play, 10, Butch and Sundance: The Early Days, Little Miss Marker, Split Image, First Blood, Never Cry Wolf, Gorky Park, Finders Keepers, River Rat, Cocoon, Silverado, Twice in a Lifetime, F/X, Legal Eagles, The Check is in the Mail, Best Seller, The Belly of an Architect, Return to Snowy River Part II, Miles From Home, Cocoon: The Return, The Last of the Finest, Presumed Innocent, FX2, Gladiator, Seven Minutes.

TELEVISION: *Movies*: Johnny We Hardly Knew Ye, It Happened at Lake Wood Manor, Ruby and Oswald, A Death in Canaan, A Real American Hero, Silent Victory: The Kitty O'Neil Story, The Jericho Mile, Dummy, The Seduction of Miss Leona, A Rumor of War, Fly Away Home, Skokie, I Take These Men, Blood Feud, Off Sides, Acceptable Risks, Private Sessions, The Lion of Africa, A Father's Revenge, Day One, Perfect Witness, Pride and Extreme Prejudice, Rising Son, A Killing in a Small Town, In Broad Daylight, The Burden of Proof, To Catch a Killer, Diamond Fleece, Teamster: The Jackie Presser Story, Deadly Matrimony, Foreign Affairs, Murder in the Heartland, Prophet of Evil: The Ervil LeBaron Story. *Mini-Series*: Evergreen. *Series*: Big Shamus, Little Shamus, Star of the Family. *Guest*: M*A*S*H, Lou Grant, Cagney and Lacey, Hunter, Tall Tales (Annie Oakley). *Special*: Dear America: Letter Home From Vietnam (reader).

DENVER, BOB: Actor. b. New Rochelle, NY, Jan. 9, 1935. e. Loyola U.

PICTURES: A Private's Affair, Take Her She's Mine, For Those Who Think Young, Who's Minding the Mint? The Sweet Ride, Did You Hear the One About the Travelling Saleslady?, Back to the Beach.

TELEVISION: *Series*: The Many Loves of Dobie Gillis, Gilligan's Island, The Good Guys, Dusty's Trail. *Movies*: Rescue from Gilligan's Island, The Castaways on Gilligan's Island, The Harlem Globetrotters on Gilligans Island, The Invisible Woman, High School USA, Bring Me the Head of Dobie Gillis. Also: Far Out Space Nuts, Scamps.

DENVER, JOHN: Singer, Actor. r.n. Henry John Deutschendorf. b. Roswell, NM, Dec. 31, 1943. Records, concerts, nightclubs.

PICTURES: Oh, God!, Fire and Ice (narrator).

TELEVISION: *Specials*: An Evening with John Denver (Emmy Award for Outstanding Special, 1975), Rocky Mountain Christmas, John Denver and the Muppets, Rocky Mountain Holiday, Salute to Lady Liberty, Jacques Cousteau—The First 75 Years, Julie Andrews . . . The Sound of Christmas, John Denver's Christmas in Aspen. *Movies*: The Christmas Gift, Foxfire, Higher Ground (co-exec. prod., co-music, actor).

De PALMA, BRIAN: Director, Writer, Producer. b. Newark, NJ, Sept. 11, 1940. e. Columbia U.,B.A.; Sarah Lawrence, M.A. While in college made series of shorts, including Wotan's Wake, winner of Rosenthal Foundation Award for best film

made by American under 25. Also judged most popular film of Midwest Film Festival (1963); later shown at San Francisco Film Festival. Dir.: The Responsive Eye (doc., 1966).

PICTURES: *Director*: Murder a La Mod (also s.p., edit.), Greetings (also co-s.p. ed.), The Wedding Party (also co-s.p., co-prod., ed.), Hi Mom (also co-story, s.p.), Dionysus in '69 (also co-prod., co-photog., co-ed.), Get To Know Your Rabbit, Sisters (also co-s.p.), Phantom of the Paradise (also co-s.p.), Obsession (also co-story), Carrie, The Fury, Home Movies (also s.p., co-prod.), Dressed to Kill (also s.p.), Blow Out (also s.p.), Scarface, Body Double (also prod., s.p.), Wiseguys, The Untouchables, Casualties of War, The Bonfire of the Vanities (also prod.), Raising Cain (also s.p.), Carlito's Way.

DEPARDIEU, GÉRARD: Actor. b. Chateauroux, France, Dec. 27, 1948. Studied acting at Theatre National Populaire in Paris. Made film debut at 16 in short by Roger Leenhardt (Le Beatnik et Le Minet). Acted in feature film by Agnes Varda (uncompleted).

PICTURES: Le Cri du Cormoran le Soir au-dessis des Jonques, Nathalie Granger, A Little Sun in Cold Water, Le Tueur, L'Affaire Dominici, Au Renedez-vous de la mort joyeuse, La Scoumone, Rude Journee our la Reine, Deux Hommes dans la Ville, The Holes, Going Places, Stavisky, Woman of the Granges, Vincent Francois Paul and the Others, The Wonderful Crook, 7 Morts sur ordonnance, Maitresse, Je t'Aime Moi Non Plus, The Last Woman, 1900, Barocco, Rene la Canne, Baxter Vera Baxter, The Truck, Tell Him I Love Him, At Night All Cats Are Gray, Get Out Your Handkerchiefs, The Left-Handed Woman, Bye Bye Monkey, Violanta, Le Sucre, Les Chiens, L'Ingorgo, Buffet Froid, Temporale Rosy, Mon Oncle d'Amerique, Loulou, The Last Metro, Inspector Blunder, I Love You, Choice of Arms, The Woman Next Door, Le Chevre. The Return of Martin Guerre, The Big Brother, Danton, The Moon in the Gutter, Les Comperes (also co-prod.), Fort Saganne, Le Tartuffe (also dir., co-s.p), Rive Droie Rive Gauche, Police, One Woman or Two, Menage, Ru du depart, Jean De Florette (also co-prod.), Under Satan's Sun (also co-prod.), A Strange Place for an Enounter (also co-prod.), Camille Claudel (also co-prod.), Dreux, Too Beautiful for You (also co-prod.), I Want to Go Home, Cyrano de Bergerac (also co-prod), Green Card, Uranus, Thanks for Life, My Father the Hero, 1492: Conquest of Paradise, Tous les Matins du Monde (All the Mornings of the World), My Father the Hero.

DEPEW, RICHARD H.: Executive. b. New York, NY, Jan. 16, 1925. e. Princeton U. U.S. Navy; American Broadcasting Co. 1947; TV dir., 1950; assistant, Eastern TV network program dir., 1953; mgr. of TV network program oper., 1954–57; Cunningham & Walsh; Radio & TV acct. supv. & programming coordinator, 1961–65 v.p. & dir. of TV programming; 1965 Broadcast supr., Ogilvy and Mather; 1967, v.p. dir. TV programing Fuller & Smith & Ross. V.P. Media and Programming 1969, FSR.; 1973, dir. of Corporate Underwriting Dept. WNET/13, Educational Broadcasting Corp. 1977 mgmt. supv., J. Walter Thompson, N.Y.; 1978, v.p.; Account Director, 1980, Marsteller, Inc., mgt. supvr., v.p., corporate adv.; Doremus & Co., 1983; exec. v.p., Knox Minisk & Harwood, Stowe, VT.

DEPP, JOHNNY: Actor. b. Owensboro, KY, June 9, 1963. Raised in Miramar, FL. At 13 started own rock group and has since performed with 15 different groups. Played lead guitar with band The Kids, with whom he moved to L.A. In 1983. With no prior acting experience made film debut in A Nightmare on Elm Street.

PICTURES: A Nightmare on Elm Street, Private Resort, Platoon, Cry-Baby, Edward Scissorhands, Freddy's Dead (cameo), Arizona Dreamers, Benny & Joon, Gilbert Grape.

TELEVISION: *Series*: 21 Jump Street. *Movie*: Slow Burn. *Guest*: Lady Blue.

DEREK, BO: Actress. r.n. Cathleen Collins. b. Torrance, CA., Nov. 20, 1956. Discovered by John Derek, actor turned filmmaker. Now married to him.

PICTURES: Orca (debut, 1977), 10, Change of Seasons, Fantasies (And Once Upon a Time), Tarzan the Ape Man (also prod.), Bolero (also prod.), Ghosts Can't Do It (also prod.), Hot Chocolate, Sognando la California (California Dreaming).

DEREK, JOHN: Actor, Producer, Director. b. Hollywood, CA, August 12, 1926. m. actress Bo Derek. Acting debut in 1945 in I'll Be Seeing You; appeared in numerous films throughout 1950s. In 1963, Nightmare in the Sun (debut as prod.), followed by Once Before I Die (debut as director, 1965).

PICTURES: *Actor*: I'll Be Seeing You (debut, 1945), Knock on Any Door, All the King's Men, Rogues of Sherwood Forest, Saturday's Hero, Mask of the Avenger, Scandal Sheet, The Family Secret, Thunderbirds, Mission Over Korea, The Last Posse, Prince of Pirates, Ambush at Tomahawk Gap, Sea of Lost Ships, The Outcast, The Adventures of Hajji Baba, Prince of Players, Run for Cover, An Annapolis Story, The Leather Saint, The Ten Commandments, Omar Khayyam, Fury at Showdown, High Hell, Prisoner of the Volga, Exodus. Nightmare in the Sun (also prod.), Once Before I Die (also

dir., prod.), A Boy . . . a Girl, Childish Things (also dir.). Director-Cinematographer: Fantasies (And Once Upon a Time), Tarzan The Ape Man, Bolero (also s.p.), Ghosts Can't Do It.
TELEVISION: Series: Frontier Circus.

DERN, BRUCE: Actor. b. Chicago, IL, June 4, 1936. e. U. of Pennsylvania. Father of actress Laura Dern. Studied acting with Gordon Phillips, member, Actor's Studio, 1959 after N.Y. debut in Shadow of a Gunman. Broadway: Sweet Bird of Youth, Orpheus Descending, Strangers. Film Awards: Natl. Soc. of Film Critics (Drive He Said, 1971), People's Choice (Coming Home, 1978), Genie (Middle Age Crazy, 1980), Silver Bear (That Championship Season, 1982).
PICTURES: Wild River (debut, 1960), Marnie, Hush Hush Sweet Charlotte, The Wild Angels, The St. Valentine's Day Massacre, Waterhole #3, The Trip, The War Wagon, Psych-Out, Rebel Rousers, Hang 'Em High, Will Penny, Number One, Castle Keep, Support Your Local Sheriff, They Shoot Horses Don't They?, Cycle Savages, Bloody Mama, The Incredible Two-Headed Transplant, Drive He Said, Silent Running, Thumb Tripping, The Cowboys, The King of Marvin Gardens, The Laughing Policeman, The Great Gatsby, Smile, Posse, Family Plot, Won Ton Ton the Dog Who Saved Hollywood, The Twist (Folies Bourgeoises), Black Sunday, Coming Home (Acad. Award nom.), The Driver, Middle Age Crazy, Tattoo, Harry Tracy: Desperado, That Championship Season, On the Edge, The Big Town, World Gone Wild, 1969, The 'Burbs, After Dark My Sweet, Diggstown.
TELEVISION: Series: Stoney Burke. Mini-Series: Space. Movies: Sam Hill: Who Killed the Mysterious Mr. Foster?, Toughlove, Roses Are for the Rich, Uncle Tom's Cabin, Trenchcoat in Paradise, The Court-Martial of Jackie Robinson, Into the Badlands, Carolina Skeletons, It's Nothing Personal. Guest: Naked City, Ben Casey, The Virginian, Twelve O'Clock High, The Big Valley, Gunsmoke, The FBI, Land of the Giants, Saturday Night Live, Fallen Angels (Murder Obliquely).

DERN, LAURA: Actress. b. Los Angeles, CA, Feb. 10, 1967. Daughter of actors Diane Ladd and Bruce Dern. Was an extra in several of her father's films and her mother's Alice Doesn't Live Here Anymore. Acting debut at age 13 in Foxes (1980).
PICTURES: Foxes, Ladies and Gentlemen: The Fabulous Stains, Teachers, Mask, Smooth Talk, Blue Velvet, Haunted Summer, Fat Man and Little Boy, Wild at Heart, Rambling Rose (Acad. Award nom.), Jurassic Park, A Perfect World.
TELEVISION: Movies: Happy Endings, Three Wishes of Billy Greer, Afterburn (Golden Globe Award). Special: The Gift (dir., co-writer only). Guest: Fallen Angels (Murder Obliquely).
THEATRE: NY: The Palace of Amateurs. L.A.: Brooklyn Laundry.

DE SANTIS, GREGORY JOSEPH: Producer, Writer, Director. b. Los Angeles, CA, July 12, 1947. e. U.S.C., Canaan Coll, Franklin Pierce Coll, Durham U (UK), Hatfield Coll. 1970–74 writer, prod., dir. radio and TV commercials; 1971–74 pres., Beverly Hills marketing group. 1975–present, chmn. Beverly Hills Org. Entertainment Group; 1988–present, pres. & CEO California Republic Pictures.
PICTURES: Prod.: Marlowe, Legal Tender, Car Trouble EMI-Warner, Pass the Buck, The Companion, Our Musical (also writer), Die Sister Die!, Zioux (writer), Beverly Hills Beat, Diary of a Surfing Film.
TELEVISION: Prod.: Antoinette of France, Trauma (series), Volleyball: A Sport Come of Age, The Nature Series, etc.

DESCHANEL, CALEB: Cinematographer, Director. b. Philadelphia, PA, Sept. 21, 1944. m. actress Mary Jo Deschanel. e. Johns Hopkins U., U. of Southern California Film Sch. Studied at Amer. Film Inst., interned under Gordon Willis then started making commercials, short subjects, docs.
PICTURES: Cinematographer: More American Graffiti, Being There, The Black Stallion, Apocalypse Now (2nd unit photog.), The Right Stuff, Let's Spend the Night Together (co-cinematographer), The Natural, The Slugger's Wife. Director: The Escape Artist, Crusoe.

DE TOTH, ANDRE: Writer, Director, Producer. b. Hungary. Dir.-writer European films, 1931–39; U.S. assoc. Alexander Korda prod., 1940; dir. Columbia, 1943; assoc. David Selznick, 1943; assoc. Hunt Stromberg-UA, 1944–45; staff dir., Enterprise 1946–47; dir., 20th-Fox, 1948–49; collab. story, The Gunfighter; dir., Columbia & Warner Bros., 1951; contract dir., Warner Bros., 1952; U.A. Columbia, W.B., 1953–55; Palladiums U.A., Denmark, 1956; Col. U.A. 1957; Columbia, 1960; assoc., Sam Spiegel, Horizon Pictures, Columbia, 1962; Harry Saltzman, Lowndes Prod., U.A. 1966–68; National General, 1969–70.
PICTURES: Passport to Suez, None Shall Escape, Since You Went Away, Pitfall, Springfield Rifle, Thunder Over the Plains, House of Wax, Bounty Hunter, Tanganyika, Indian Fighter, Monkey on My Back, Two Headed Spy, Man on a String, Morgan The Pirate, The Mongols, Gold for the

Caesars, Billion Dollar Brain, Play Dirty, El Condor, The Dangerous Game.

DEUTH, HOWARD: Director. b. New York, NY. e. Ohio State U. m. actress Lea Thompson. Son of music publisher Murray Deutch. Spent almost 10 yrs. working in various film media, including music videos and film trailer advertising, before feature directorial debut with Pretty in Pink, 1986.
PICTURES: Pretty in Pink, Some Kind of Wonderful, The Great Outdoors, Article 99, Getting Even With Dad.
TELEVISION: Tales from the Crypt (2 episodes; ACE Award for Dead Right).

DEUTCHMAN, IRA J.: Executive. b. Cherry Point, NC, Mar. 24, 1953. e. Northwestern U., B.S., majoring in film. Began career with Cinema 5, Ltd. serving, 1975–79, as non-theatrical sls. mgr.; dir. theatrical adv./pub./dir. acquisitions. Joined United Artists Classics, 1981 as dir. of adv./pub. 1982, left to become one of the founding partners in Cinecom Intl. Films, where headed mktg./dist. div. from inception. Resigned, Jan: 1989 to form the Deutchman Company, Inc., a production company and marketing consultancy firm. Currently pres. of Fine Line Features, a division of New Line Cinema, and sr. v.p. of parent corp. Adjunct prof. Columbia U. film dept. Serves on board of Independent Feature Project-West. On advisory bds. U.S. Film Festival and the Sundance Institute.
PICTURES: Exec. Prod.: Swimming to Cambodia, Matewan (assoc. prod.), Miles From Home (co-exec. prod.), Scenes from the Class Struggle in Beverly Hills, Straight Out of Brooklyn.

DEUTCHMAN, LAWRENCE SCOT: Executive. b. Bronx, NY, Dec. 10, 1960. e. Rutgers U. Wrote, prod. & dir. Mythbusters, award-winning public service campaign. 1986–89, various positions: Entertainment Industries Council, Inc.; wrote, prod., co-dir. That's a Wrap award-winning public service campaign; 1986–88, board member, Public Interest Radio & Television Educational Society; 1987–88, wrote, exec. prod., post-prod. sprv., Buckle Up award-winning educational & music video (CINE Golden Eagle); 1989: EIC: An Industry in Action (writer, prod., dir.); Campaigns: Natl. Red Ribbon Campaign, Office for Substance Abuse Prevention (writer, dir., exec. prod.), Stop the Madness (co-writer, prod.; award winner); 1990–92, dir. Prog. Develop. & Creative Affairs, EIC. Developed: Vince & Larry: The Amazing Crash Test Dummies (series, NBC), Drug Proofing Your Kids (tv special). Campaigns: Alcoholism Runs in Families, Texas Prevention Partnership (dir., exec. prod.), They Do as You Do (writer, exec. prod.). 1991: The Inhalant Problem in Texas docum. (co-exec. prod.), Inhalants: The Silent Epidemic award-winning drama (writer, co-exec. prod.), KBVO Fox Kids Club, segments (writer, prod., set designer), The Incredible Crash Dummies toy property (co-inventor), Ollie Odorfree property (creator). 1992–present: Pres., Dynamic Commun. Intl. Inc., v.p. & prod. mktg., EIC.

DEUTSCH, STEPHEN: Producer. b. Los Angeles, CA, June 30, 1946. e. UCLA, B.A.; Loyola Law Sch., 1974. Son of late S. Sylvan Simon. Stepson of Armand Deutsch. Private law practice before joining Rastar 1976 as asst. to Ray Stark; 1977, sr. v.p., Rastar; prod. head for SLM Inc. Film Co. entered independent prod. 1978.
PICTURES: Somewhere in Time, All the Right Moves, Russkies (co-exec. prod.), She's Out of Control, Bill & Ted's Excellent Adventure (exec. prod.), Lucky Stiff.

DEVANE, WILLIAM: Actor. b. Albany, NY, Sept. 5, 1939. Appeared in some 15 productions with N.Y. Shakespeare Festival, also Bdwy. & off-Bdwy. shows before heading to California for films and TV.
PICTURES: The Pursuit of Happiness, The 300 Hundred Year Weekend, Lady Liberty, McCabe and Mrs. Miller, Glory Boy (My Old Man's Place), Irish Whiskey Rebellion, Report to the Commissioner, Family Plot, Marathon Man, Bad News Bears in Breaking Training, Rolling Thunder, The Dark, Yanks, Honky Tonk Freeway, Testament, Hadley's Rebellion, Vital Signs.
TELEVISION: Series: From Here to Eternity, Knots Landing. Movies: Crime Club, The Bait, Fear on Trial, Red Alert, Black Beauty, Red Flag: The Ultimate Game, The Other Victim, Jane Doe, With Intent to Kill, Timestalker, Murder C.O.D., Nightmare in Columbia County, Obsessed, The President's Child. Prophet of Evil: The Ervil LeBaron Story. Special: The Missiles of October. Mini-Series: A Woman Named Jackie.

DE VITO, DANNY: Actor, Director. b. Asbury Park, NJ, Nov. 17, 1944. m. actress Rhea Perlman. e. Oratory Prep Sch. Studied at American Acad. of Dramatic Arts. Wilfred Acad. of Hair and Beauty Culture. At 18 worked as hair dresser for 1 yr. at his sister's shop. NY stage in The Man With a Flower in His Mouth (debut, 1969), Down the Morning Line, The Line of Least Existence, The Shrinking Bride, Call Me Charlie, Comedy of Errors, Merry Wives of Windsor (NYSF). Three By Pirandello. Performance in One Flew Over the Cuckoo's Nest led to casting in the film version. Prod. short films: The Sound Sleeper (1973), Minestrone (1975).

PICTURES: Lady Liberty (debut, 1971), Hurry Up or I'll Be 30, Scalawag, One Flew Over the Cuckoo's Nest, Deadly Hero, The Van, The World's Greatest Lover, Goin' South, Going Ape, Terms of Endearment, Romancing the Stone, Johnny Dangerously, The Jewel of the Nile, Head Office, Wiseguys, Ruthless People, My Little Pony (voice), Tin Men, Throw Momma from the Train (also dir.), Twins, The War of the Roses (also dir.), Other People's Money, Batman Returns, Hoffa (also dir., co-prod.), Jack the Bear, Last Action Hero (voice).

TELEVISION: Series: Taxi (Emmy & Golden Globe Awards; also dir. episodes), Mary (dir. only). Movies: Valentine, The Ratings Game (also dir.). Specials: All the Kids Do It (Afterschool Special), A Very Special Christmas Party, Two Daddies? (voice), What a Lovely Way to Spend an Evening (dir.), The Selling of Vince DeAngelo (dir.). Guest: Police Woman, Saturday Night Live, Amazing Stories (also dir.), The Simpsons (voice).

De WITT, JOYCE: Actress. b. Wheeling, WV, April 23, 1949. e. Ball State U., B.A., theatre; UCLA, MFA in acting. Classically trained, worked in theater since 13 as actress and dir. Has staged and/or starred in numerous musical revues.
TELEVISION: Series: Three's Company. Guest: musical specials, children's specials, telethon co-host and series incl. Baretta, The Tony Randall Show, Most Wanted, Risko, Finder of Lost Loves. Movie: With This Ring.

DEY, SUSAN: Actress. b. Pekin, IL, Dec. 10, 1952. Signed as magazine teen model at age 15. Made professional TV debut at 17, appearing in The Partridge Family, 1970–74.
TELEVISION: Series: The Partridge Family, Loves Me Loves Me Not, Emerald Point N.A.S., L.A. Law, Love and War. Movies: Terror on the Beach, Cage Without a Key, Mary Jane Harper Cried Last Night, Little Women, The Comeback Kid, The Gift of Life, Malibu, Sunset Limousine, I Love You Perfect, Bed of Lies, Lies and Lullabies (also co-prod.).
PICTURES: Skyjacked, First Love, Looker, Echo Park, That's Adequate.

DE YOUNG, CLIFF: Actor. b. Inglewood, CA, Feb. 12, 1947. e. California State Coll., Illinois State U. On stage in Hair, Sticks and Bones, Two By South, The Three Sisters, The Orphan.
PICTURES: Harry and Tonto, Blue Collar, Shock Treatment, Independence Day, The Hunger, Reckless, Protocol, Secret Admirer, F/X, Flight of the Navigator, Fear, Pulse, Rude Awakening, Glory, Flashback, Crackdown, Dr. Giggles.
TELEVISION: Series: Sunshine. Special: Sticks and Bones. Mini-Series: Centennial, Master of the Game, Captains and the Kings, King, Robert Kennedy and His Times. Movies: Sunshine, The 3000 Mile Chase, The Lindbergh Kidnapping Case, Scared Straight: Another Story, The Night That Panicked America, This Girl for Hire, The Awakening of Candra, Deadly Intentions, Sunshine Christmas, Fun and Games, Where Pigeons Go to Die, Fourth Story, Criminal Behavior, Love Can Be Murder, The Tommyknockers.

DIAMANT, LINCOLN: Executive. Biographer. Historian. b. New York, NY, Jan. 25, 1923. e. Columbia Coll., A.B. cum laude 1943. Cofounder, Columbia U. radio station. WKCR-FM; served in Wash. as prod., Blue Network (NBC), then in NY as CBS newswriter; 1949 joined World Pub. Co. as adv. and promo. dir.; 1952–69 worked in creative/TV dept. McCann-Erickson, Grey, then Ogilvy & Mather ad agencies (winning 6 Clio Awards). Prod. Lend Us Your Ears (Met. Museum Art broadcast series); founder, pres., Spots Alive, Inc., broadcast adv. consultants, 1969; Author, The Broadcast Communications Dictionary, Anatomy of a Television Commercial, Television's Classic Commercials, biography of Bernard Romans, Chaining the Hudson (Sons of Revolution Book Award), Stamping Our History. Contrib., to Effective Advertising, to Messages and Meaning; New Routes to English; columnist Back Stage/Shoot. Member, Broadcast Pioneers, Acad. TV Arts & Sciences; v.p. Broadcast Advertising Producer's Society of America. Adjunct faculty member, Pace U., Hofstra U. Fellow, Royal Society of Arts.

DIAMOND, BERNARD: Theatre Executive. b. Chicago, IL, Jan. 24, 1918. e. U. of Indiana, U. of Minnesota. Except for military service was with Schine Theatre chain from 1940 to 1963, working up from ass't. mng., booker, buyer, dir. of personnel to gen. mgr. Then joined Loews Theatres; last position, exec. v.p. Retired, 1985.

DIAMOND, NEIL: Singer, Songwriter. b. Brooklyn, NY, Jan. 24, 1941. Many concert tours.
PICTURES: Jonathan Livingston Seagull (music), Every Which Way But Loose (music), The Last Waltz (actor), The Jazz Singer (actor, music).
TELEVISION: Specials: Neil Diamond . . . Hello Again, I Never Cared for the Sound of Being Alone, I'm Glad You're Here With Me Tonight, Greatest Hits Live, Neil Diamond's Christmas Special.

DICKERSON, ERNEST (A.S.C.): Cinematographer. b. Newark, NJ, 1952. e. Howard U., architecture, NYU, grad. film school. First job, filming surgical procedures for Howard U. medical school. At NYU film school shot classmate Spike Lee's student films Sarah, and Joe's Bed Stuy Barbershop: We Cut Heads. Also shot Nike commercial and several music videos including Bruce Springsteen's Born in the U.S.A., Patti LaBelle's Stir It Up and Miles Davis' Tutu; and Branford Marsalis' Royal Garden Blues directed by Spike Lee. Admitted into Amer. Soc. of Cinematographers in 1989.
PICTURES: Brother From Another Planet, She's Gotta Have It (also cameo), Krush Groove, School Daze, Raw, Do the Right Thing, Def By Temptation, The Laser Man, Mo' Better Blues, Jungle Fever, Sex Drugs Rock & Roll, Juice (dir., co-s.p., story only), Cousin Bobby (co-photog.), Malcolm X.
TELEVISION: Do it Acapella (dir.; PBS).

DICKINSON, ANGIE: Actress. r.n. Angeline Brown. b. Kulm, ND, Sept. 30, 1931. e. Immaculate Heart Coll., Glendale Coll., secretarial course. Beauty contest winner.
PICTURES: Lucky Me (small part, 1954), Man With the Gun, The Return of Jack Slade, Tennessee's Partner, The Black Whip, Hidden Guns, Tension at Table Rock, Gun the Man Down, Calypso Joe, China Gate, Shoot Out at Medicine Bend, Cry Terror, I Married a Woman, Rio Bravo, Bramble Bush, Ocean's 11, A Fever in the Blood, The Sins of Rachel Cade, Jessica, Rome Adventure, Capt. Newman M.D., The Killers, The Art of Love, Cast a Giant Shadow, The Chase, The Poppy is Also a Flower, The Last Challenge, Point Blank, Sam Whiskey, Some Kind of a Nut, Young Billy Young, Pretty Maids All in a Row, The Resurrection of Zachary Wheeler, The Outside Man, Big Bad Mama, Klondike Fever, Dressed to Kill, Charlie Chan and the Curse of the Dragon Queen, Death Hunt, Big Bad Mama II, Even Cowgirls Get the Blues.
TELEVISION: Movies: The Love War, Thief, See the Man Run, The Norliss Tapes, Pray for the Wildcats, A Sensitive Passionate Man, Overboard, The Suicide's Wife, Dial M for Murder, One Shoe Makes It Murder, Jealousy, A Touch of Scandal, Stillwatch, Police Story: The Freeway Killings, Once Upon A Texas Train, Prime Target, Treacherous Crossing. Series: Police Woman, Cassie & Co. Guest: The Jimmy Durante Show (debut, 1956), Mike Hammer. Mini-Series: Pearl, Hollywood Wives, Wild Palms.

DILLER, BARRY: Executive. b. San Francisco, CA, Feb. 2, 1942. Joined ABC in April, 1966, as asst. to v.p. in chg. programming. In 1968, made exec. asst. to v.p. in chg. programming and dir. of feature films. In 1969, named v.p., feature films and program dev., east coast. In 1971, made v.p., Feature Films and Circle Entertainment, a unit of ABC Entertainment, responsible for selecting, producing and scheduling The Tuesday Movie of the Week, The Wednesday Movie of the Week, and Circle Film original features for airing on ABC-TV, as well as for acquisition and scheduling of theatrical features for telecasting on ABC Sunday Night Movie and ABC Monday Night Movie. In 1973, named v.p. in chg. of prime time TV for ABC Entertainment. In 1974 joined Paramount Pictures as bd. chmn. and chief exec. officer. 1983, named pres. of Gulf & Western Entertainment and Communications Group, while retaining Paramount titles. Resigned from Paramount in 1984 to join 20th Century-Fox as bd. chmn. and chief. exec. officer. Named chmn. & CEO of Fox, Inc. (comprising 20th Fox Film Corp., Fox TV Stations & Fox Bdcstg. Co.), Oct., 1985. Named to bd., News Corp. Ltd., June, 1987. Resigned from Fox in Feb., 1992. Named CEO of QVC Network Inc. TV shopping concern.

DILLER, PHYLLIS: Comedienne. b. Lima, OH, July 17, 1917. r.n. Phyllis Ada Driver. e. Sherwood Music Sch., 1935–37; Bluffton Coll., OH, 1938–39. Started as publicist at San Francisco radio station before becoming nightclub comic at the age of 37. Recordings: Phyllis Diller Laughs, Are You Ready for Phyllis Diller?, Great Moments of Comedy, Born to Sing.
THEATER: Hello Dolly! (Bdwy), Everybody Loves Opal, Happy Birthday, The Dark at the Top of the Stairs, Subject to Change, The Wizard of Oz, Nunsense.
PICTURES: Splendor in the Grass (debut, 1961), Boy Did I Get a Wrong Number!, The Fat Spy, Mad Monster Party (voice), Eight on the Lam, Did You Hear the One About the Traveling Saleslady?, The Private Navy of Sgt. O'Farrell, The Adding Machine, The Sunshine Boys (cameo), A Pleasure Doing Business, Pink Motel, Pucker Up and Bark Like a Dog, Dr. Hackenstein, Friend to Friend, The Nutcracker Prince (voice), The Boneyard, The Perfect Man, Wisecracks, Happily Ever After (voice).
TELEVISION: Series: Showstreet, The Pruitts of Southampton, The Beautiful Phyllis Diller Show. Specials: The Phyllis Diller Special (1963), An Evening With Phyllis Diller, Phyllis Diller's 102nd Birthday Party. Guest spots on many series including Laugh In, Love American Style, The Muppet Show, The Love Boat, CHiPs, , etc.
BOOKS: Phyllis Diller's Housekeeping Hints, Phyllis Diller's Marriage Manual, Phyllis Diller's The Complete Mother, The Joys of Aging and How to Avoid Them.

DILLMAN, BRADFORD: Actor. b. San Francisco, CA, April 14, 1930. m. actress-model Suzy Parker. e. Yale U., 1951.
THEATER: The Scarecrow (1953), Third Person, Long Day's Journey into Night (premiere; Theatre World Award), The Fun Couple.
PICTURES: A Certain Smile (debut, 1958), In Love and War, Compulsion, Crack in the Mirror, Circle of Deception, Sanctuary, Francis of Assisi, A Rage to Live, The Plainsman, Sergeant Ryker, Helicopter Spies, Jigsaw, The Bridge at Remagen, Suppose They Gave a War and Nobody Came, Brother John, The Mephisto Waltz, Escape from the Planet of the Apes, The Resurrection of Zachary Wheeler, The Iceman Cometh, The Way We Were, Chosen Survivors, 99 and 44/100% Dead, Gold, Bug, Mastermind, The Enforcer, The Lincoln Conspiracy, Amsterdam Kill, The Swarm, Piranha, Love and Bullets, Guyana: Cult of the Damned, Sudden Impact, Treasure of the Amazon, Man Outside, Lords of the Deep, Heroes Stand Alone.
TELEVISION: Series: Court-Martial, King's Crossing, Dynasty. Movies: Fear No Evil, Black Water Gold, Longstreet, Five Desperate Women, Revenge, Eyes of Charles Sand, The Delphi Bureau, Moon of the Wolf, Deliver Us From Evil, Murder or Mercy, Disappearance of Flight 412, Adventures of the Queen, Force Five, Widow, Street Killing, Kingston: The Power Play, The Hostage Heart, Jennifer: A Woman's Story, Before and After, The Memory of Eva Ryker, Tourist, The Legend of Walks Far Woman, Covenant, Heart of Justice.

DILLON, KEVIN: Actor. b. Mamaroneck, NY, Aug. 19, 1965. Younger brother of actor Matt Dillon. Stage work includes Dark at the Top of the Stairs, The Indian Wants the Bronx.
PICTURES: No Big Deal, Heaven Help Us, Platoon, Remote Control, The Rescue, The Blob, War Party, Immediate Family, The Doors, A Midnight Clear, The Penal Colony.
TELEVISION: Movie: When He's Not a Stranger. Special: Dear America: Letters Home from Vietnam (reader).

DILLON, MATT: Actor. b. New Rochelle, NY, Feb. 18, 1964. Discovered at age 14 in junior high school by casting dir who cast him in Over the Edge, 1978. Theater debut: Boys of Winter (Bdwy. 1985).
PICTURES: Over the Edge (debut, 1979), Little Darlings, My Bodyguard, Liar's Moon, Tex, The Outsiders, Rumble Fish, The Flamingo Kid, Target, Rebel, Native Son, The Big Town, Kansas, Bloodhounds of Broadway, Drugstore Cowboy, A Kiss Before Dying, Singles, The Saint of Fort Washington, Mr. Wonderful.
TELEVISION: Movie: Women & Men 2. Special: Dear America: Letters Home From Vietnam (reader).

DILLON, MELINDA: Actress. b. Hope, AR, Oct. 13, 1939. e. Chicago Sch. of Drama, Art Inst., Goodman Theatre. Launched career on Broadway in original prod. of Who's Afraid of Virginia Woolf? (Theatre World Award, Tony Award nom.).
PICTURES: The April Fools (debut, 1969), Bound for Glory, Slap Shot, Close Encounters of the Third Kind (Acad. Award nom.), F.I.S.T., Absence of Malice (Acad. Award nom.), A Christmas Story, Songwriter, Harry and the Hendersons, Staying Together, Spontaneous Combustion, Capt. America, The Prince of Tides, Demolition Man.
TELEVISION: Series: Paul Sills Story Theatre. Guest: Twilight Zone, The Defenders, Bonanza, East Side West Side, The Paul Sand Show, The Jeffersons, Good Morning America, The Today Show, Dick Cavett Show, Dinah Shore Show. Mini-Series: Space. Movies: Critical List, Transplant, Marriage is Alive and Well, The Shadow Box, Fallen Angel, Hellinger's Law, Right of Way, Shattered Spirits, Shattered Innocence, Nightbreaker, Judgment Day: The John List Story, Slow Bleed.

DILLOW, JEAN CARMEN: Producer, Writer, Actress, Director. In private life is Jean, Countess de l'Eau. At age 5 on stage, screen as last star of the Wampas Baby Stars. Film work in Eng., Germany, Switzerland, Mexico, Italy. Play writing with George S. Kaufman; screenplay-writing with Andrew Solt. Wrote and prod. with John Croydon. Wrote prod. dir., starred in TV feature The Pawn. Stage: There Is No Other Prince but Aly (London), Stage Door, The Man Who Came to Dinner, What a Life. Scripts: Spirit-Doll, The Resurrection. Starred in series of westerns for Republic, Monogram First National, Universal. Sang and danced in musicals and nightclubs. 1979, non-fiction books on phenomena: Do You Hear the Voices? and The Kidnapping of Aldo Moro. 1983 book Western Bullets are Blank, Mommy Angel, Dear Mr. Trump; screenplay The Shoe of the Ghost; teleplays: Jikoku-ten, The Ghost of Palazzo Palladio, Give the Highest Award to Mommy Angel; The House in Athens. 1986, prod., dir., co-starred in film with Rossano Brazzi. Co-starred and prod. with late son Guy. Author of three volume book Dear Mr. Trump.
(Died: Aug. 26, 1993)

DIMMOCK, PETER: C.V.O., O.B.E. b. Dec. 6, 1920. e. Dulwich Coll. & in France. R.A.F. pilot & staff officer during war. TV as prod. commentator BBC Outside Broadcasts Dept., 1946. Prod. more than 500 TV relays including telecast from Windsor Castle of King George VI's funeral, 1952. Coronation telecast Westminster Abbey; State Opening Parliament. Commentator, introduced BBC-TV weekly Sportsview, 1954–64. Head of BBC-TV Outside Broadcasts 1954–72. Head of BBC Enterprises 1973, v.p. ABC Cos., Inc., 1977. Vice President-Managing Director, ABC Sports Worldwide Enterprises Ltd. & ABC Sports Intl., Inc., Director Screensport. Fellow Royal TV Society.

DI PIETRA, ROSEMARY: Executive. Joined Paramount Pictures in 1976, rising through ranks to become director-corporate administration. 1985, promoted to exec. dir.-corporate administration.

DISHY, BOB: Actor. b. Brooklyn, NY. e. Syracuse U.
THEATER: Damn Yankees, From A to Z, Second City, Flora the Red Menace, By Jupiter, Something Different, The Goodbye People, The Good Doctor, The Creation of the World and Other Business, An American Millionaire, Sly Fox, Murder at Howard Johnsons, Grown Ups, Cafe Crown.
PICTURES: The Tiger Makes Out, Lovers and Other Strangers, The Big Bus, I Wonder Who's Killing Her Now?, The Last Married Couple in America, First Family, Author! Author!, Brighton Beach Memoirs, Critical Condition, Stay Tuned, Used People.
TELEVISION: Series: That Was the Week That Was, (1964–65). Specials: Story Theatre (dir.), The Cafeteria. Guest: The Comedy Zone. Movie: It Couldn't Happen to a Nicer Guy.

DISNEY, ROY E.: Producer, Director. Writer, Cameraman, Film editor. b. Los Angeles, CA, Jan. 10, 1930. e. Pomona Coll., CA. 1951 started as page, NBC-TV. Asst. film editor Dragnet TV series. 1952–78, Walt Disney Prods., Burbank, Calif., various capacities; vice chmn. of the board, The Walt Disney Co.; bd. chmn., Shamrock Holdings, Inc., bd. dir., Walt Disney Co.
PICTURES: Perri, Mysteries of the Deep, Pacific High.
TELEVISION: Walt Disney's Wonderful World of Color; The Hound That Thought He Was A Raccoon, Sancho, The Homing Steer, The Silver Fox and Sam Davenport, Wonders of the Water World, Legend of Two Gypsy Dogs, Adventure in Wildwood Heart. Also, The Postponed Wedding, (Zorro series), (Wonder World of Color); An Otter in the Family, My Family is a Menagerie, Legend of El Blanco, Pancho, The Fastest Paw in the West, The Owl That Didn't Give A Hoot, Varda the Peregrine Falcon, Cristobalito, The Calypso Colt, Three Without Fear, Hamade and the Pirates, Chango, Guardian of the Mayan Treasure, Nosey, the Sweetest Skunk in the World, Mustang!, Call It Courage, Ringo, the Refugee Raccoon, Shokee, the Everglades Panther, Deacon, the High-Noon Dog, Wise One, Whale's Tooth, Track of African Bongo, Dorsey, the Mail-Carrying Dog.

DiTOLLA, ALFRED W.: Executive. b. New York, NY, Sept. 21, 1926. e. NY Law School. Served in U.S. Naval Air Force during WWII. Member of I.A.T.S.E; appointed Intl. Rep., 1974; asst. to pres. 1978; pres., 1986. Member, Amer. Theatre Wing, Catholic Interracial Council, NY Variety Clubs, Acad. of TV Arts & Sciences, Theatrical Mutual Assn., Acad. of Motion Picture Arts & Sciences. Dir.: Will Roger Memorial Fund, Foundation of Motion Picture Pioneers. Named Entertainment Industry Man of the Year of the Theatrical Mutual Assn.; 1987, received Democratic Heritage Award from the Amer. Jewish Council. Trustee: IATSE Natl. Pension, Health & Welfare, Annuity and Vacation Funds, Actors Fund of America.

DIXON, BARBARA: Executive. b. Pasadena CA. e. U. of Southern California, grad. degree from Johns Hopkins U. Served as staff member of Senate Judiciary Committee and was dir. of legislation for Sen. Birch Bayh, 1974–79. Left to become dir. of Office of Government & Public Affairs of Natl. Transportation Safety Board. Named v.p., Fratelli Group, p.r. firm in Washington; took leave of absence in 1984 to serve as deputy press secty. to Democratic V.P. candidate, Geraldine Ferraro. In 1985 joined Motion Picture Assn. of America as v.p. for public affairs.

DIXON, DONNA: Actress. b. Alexandria, VA, July 20, 1957. m. actor, writer Dan Aykroyd. e. Studied anthropology and medicine, Mary Washington U. Left to become a model, both on magazine covers and in TV commercials (Vitalis, Max Factor, Gillette).
PICTURES: Dr. Detroit, Twilight Zone—The Movie, Spies Like Us, The Couch Trip, It Had To Be You, Speed Zone, Lucky Stiff.
TELEVISION: Series: Bosom Buddies, Berengers. Movies: Mickey Spillane's Margin for Murder, No Man's Land, Beverly Hills Madam. Specials: Women Who Rate a "10," The Shape of Things, The Rodney Dangerfield Show: I Can't Take it No More.

DIXON, WHEELER WINSTON: Educator, Writer, Filmmaker. b. New Brunswick, NJ, March 12, 1950. e. Rutgers U. In 1960s asst. writer for Time/Life publications; also writer for Interview magazine. 1976, directed TV commercials in NY. One season with TVTV, Los Angeles, as post-prod. suprv. 1978, formed Deliniator Films, Inc., serving as exec. prod./dir. Since 1984 has directed film prod. program at Univ. of Nebraska, where holds rank of tenured full prof. 1988, made chair, Film Studies Prog.; received Rockefeller Foundation grant. Author: The 'B' Directors, 1985; The Cinematic Vision of F. Scott Fitzgerald, 1986; PRC: A History of Producer's Releasing Corp., 1986; books on Freddie Francis, Terence Fisher, Reginald Le Borg, 1992–93. Prod., dir. with Gwendolyn Audrey-Foster: Women Who Made the Movies (video). Book: The Early Film Criticism of Francois Truffaut. Prod/Dir: What Can I Do? (feature film). 1992, Guest programmer at the British Film Inst./Natl. Film Theatre. 1993, Distinguished Teaching Award.

DMYTRYK, EDWARD: Director. b. Grand Forks, B.C., Canada, Sept. 4, 1908. Entered employ Paramount 1923, working as messenger after school. Film editor 1930–1939; dir. from 1939. One of the "Hollywood Ten" who was held in contempt by the House UnAmerican Activities Comm. 1947. The only one to recant. Autobiography: It's a Hell of a Life But Not a Bad Living (1979).
   PICTURES: The Hawk, Television Spy, Emergency Squad, Golden Gloves, Mystery Sea Raider, Her First Romance, The Devil Commands, Under Age, Sweethearts of the Campus, Blonde From Singapore, Confessions of Boston Blackie, Secrets of the Lone Wolf, Counter Espionage, Seven Miles from Alcatraz, Hitler's Children, The Falcon Strikes Back, Behind the Rising Sun, Captive Wild Woman Tender Comrade, Murder My Sweet, Back to Bataan, Cornered, Crossfire (Acad. Award nom.), So Well Remembered, Till the End of Time, Obsession, Give Us This Day, Mutiny, The Sniper, Eight Iron Men, The Juggler, The Caine Mutiny, Broken Lance, End of the Affair, Left Hand of God, Soldier of Fortune, The Mountain (also prod.), Raintree County, The Young Lions, Warlock, The Blue Angel, The Reluctant Saint (It.), A Walk on the Wild Side, The Carpetbaggers, Where Love Has Gone, Mirage, Alvarez Kelly, Shalako, Anzio, Bluebeard, The Human Factor, He is My Brother.

DOBSON, KEVIN: Actor. b. New York, NY, Mar. 18, 1943.
   TELEVISION: Series: Kojak, Shannon, Knots Landing (also dir. 9 episodes). Movies: The Immigrants, Transplant, Orphan Train, Hardhat and Legs, Reunion, Mark I Love You, Mickey Splillane's Margin for Murder, Money Power Murder (also prod.), Casey's Gift: For Love of a Child, Sweet Revenge, Fatal Friendship, Dirty Work, House of Secrets and Lies. Guest: The Nurses, The Doctors, Greatest Heroes of the Bible.
   PICTURES: Love Story, Bananas, Klute, The Anderson Tapes, The French Connection, Carnal Knowledge, Midway, All Night Long.

DOHERTY, SHANNEN: Actress. b. Memphis, TN, April 12, 1971. On stage in The Mound Builders.
   TELEVISION: Series: Little House on the Prairie, Our House, Beverly Hills 90210. Movies: The Other Lover, Obsessed. Mini-Series: Robert Kennedy and His Times. Pilot: His and Hers. Guest: 21 Jump Street.
   PICTURES: Night Shift, The Secret of NIMH (voice), Girls Just Want to Have Fun, Heathers, Freeze Frame, Blindfold.

DOLGEN, JONATHAN L.: Executive. e. Cornell U., NYU Sch. of Law. Began career with Wall Street law firm, Fried, Frank, Harris, Shriver & Jacobson. In 1976 joined Columbia Pictures Industries as asst. gen. counsel and deputy gen. counsel. 1979, named sr. v.p. in chg. of worldwide business affairs; 1980, named exec. v.p. Joined Columbia m.p. div., 1981; named pres. of Columbia Pay-Cable & Home Entertainment Group. Also pres. Columbia Pictures domestic operations, overseeing Music Group. 1985, joined 20th-Fox in newly created position of sr. exec. v.p. for telecommunications.

DOLLINGER, IRVING: Exhibitor. Columbia Amusement Co. b. New York, NY, Sept. 20, 1905. e. U. of Pennsylvania. Stanley-Fabian mgr., 1926. Then with Warner Theatres in New Jersey. Owner and operator of theatre since 1929. Past pres. Allied Theat. Owners of N.J. Pres., Assoc. Theats. of N.J., booking org. 1938–44; v.p. & buyer, Independent Theatre Service Eastern regional v.p. Allied States Assoc., 1949–54; treas., Nat'l Allied, 1955–56; partner, Triangle Theatre Service, 1957; chief barker, N.Y. Tent 35, Variety Club, 1966.

DOMINGUEZ, MARINE: Filmmaker. b. El Paso, TX, Oct. 6, 1952. e. Western New Mexico U., 1970–72; Michigan State U., 1972–74; U. of San Francisco, B.P.A., 1980. Educational counselor and director for non-profit community service org., assisting Hispanic youth with admission into academic or technical progs. and univs. Taught photography and Spanish to adults in recreational prog. Since 1982 has developed Hearts on Fire, fictional film about the prod. of the 1954 labor film Salt of the Earth. Produces television progs. and industrial videos. President, Saldeterre Productions, Inc.

DONAHUE, ELINOR: Actress. b. Tacoma, WA, Apr. 19, 1937.
   TELEVISION: Series: Father Knows Best, The Andy Griffith Show, Many Happy Returns, The Odd Couple, Mulligan's Stew, Please Stand By, Days of Our Lives, The New Adventures of Beans Baxter, Get a Life. Pilot: The Grady Nutt Show. Guest: One Day at a Time, Sweepstakes$, The Golden Girls. Movies: In Name Only, Gidget Gets Married, Mulligan's Stew (pilot), Doctors' Private Lives, Condominium, High School U.S.A. Special: Father Knows Best Reunion.
   PICTURES: Mr.Big, Tenth Avenue Angel, Unfinished Dance, Three Daring Daughters, Love is Better Than Ever, Girls Town, Pretty Woman, Freddy's Dead.

DONAHUE, PHIL: Television Personality. b. Cleveland, OH, Dec. 21, 1935. e. Notre Dame, BBA. m. actress Marlo Thomas. Worked as check sorter, Albuquerque Natl. Bank, 1957, then as announcer at KYW-TV & AM, Cleveland; news dir. WABJ radio, Adrian, MI; morning newscaster WHIO-TV. Interviews with Jimmy Hoffa and Billy Sol Estes picked up nationally by CBS. Host of Conversation Piece, phone-in talk show. Debuted The Phil Donahue Show, daytime talk show in Dayton, Ohio, 1967. Syndicated 2 years later. Moved to Chicago, 1974. Host, Donahue, now in 165 outlets in U.S. In 1979 a mini-version of show became 3-times-a-week segment on NBC's Today Show. Winner of several Emmys. Books: Donahue: My Own Story (1980), The Human Animal (1985).

DONAHUE, TROY: Actor. r.n. Merle Johnson, Jr. b. New York, NY, Jan. 27, 1937. e. Bayport H.S., N.Y. Military Acad. Columbia U., Journalism. Directed, wrote, acted in school plays. Summer stock, Bucks County Playhouse, Sayville Playhouse; contract, Warner Brothers, 1959.
   PICTURES: Man Afraid (debut, 1957), The Tarnished Angels, This Happy Feeling, The Voice in the Mirror, Live Fast Die Young, Monster on the Campus, Summer Love, Wild Heritage, The Perfect Furlough, Imitation of Life, A Summer Place, The Crowded Sky, Parrish, Susan Slade, Rome Adventure, Palm Springs Weekend, A Distant Trumpet, My Blood Runs Cold, Blast-Off (a.k.a. Those Fantastic Flying Fools), Come Spy With Me, Sweet Savior, Cockfighter, Seizure, Godfather Part II, Tin Man, Grandview, U.S.A., Low Blow, Cyclone, Deadly Prey, American Revenge, Dr. Alien (aka I Was a Teenage Sex Mutant), Sexpot, Hard Rock Nightmare, Bad Blood, John Travis, Solar Survivor, The Chilling, The Housewarming, Deadly Spy Games, Assault of the Party Nerds, Deadly Diamonds, Deadly Embrace, Cry-Baby, Double Trouble.
   TELEVISION: Series: Hawaiian Eye (1959–60), Surfside 6. Guest: Matt Houston. Movies: Split Second to an Epitaph, The Loneliest Profession, Malibu.

DONALDSON, ROGER: Director. b. Ballarat, Australia, Nov. 15, 1945. Emigrated to New Zealand at 19. Established still photography business; then began making documentaries. Directed Winners and Losers, a series of short dramas for NZ-TV.
   PICTURES: Sleeping Dogs (also prod.), Smash Palace (also s.p. prod.), The Bounty, Marie, No Way Out, Cocktail, Cadillac Man (also prod.), White Sands, The Getaway.

DONEN, STANLEY: Producer, Director. b. Columbia, SC, April 13, 1924. e. U. of South Carolina. Former dancer who co-dir. classic Amer. musicals with Gene Kelly.
   PICTURES: Director: On the Town (co-dir.), Royal Wedding, Fearless Fagan, Love is Better Than Ever, Singin' in the Rain (co-dir., co-choreog.), Give a Girl a Break (also choreog.), Seven Brides for Seven Brothers, Deep in My Heart (also co-choreog.), It's Always Fair Weather (co-dir.), Funny Face. Dir.-Prod.: Pajama Game, Kiss Them for Me, Indiscreet, Damn Yankees, Once More with Feeling, Surprise Package, The Grass Is Greener, Charade, Arabesque, Two for the Road, Bedazzled, Staircase, The Little Prince, Lucky Lady (dir. only), Movie Movie, Saturn 3, Blame It on Rio.

DONIGER, WALTER: Writer, Director, Producer. b. New York NY. e. Valley Forge Military Academy, Duke U., Harvard U. Graduate Business Sch. Entered m.p. business as writer later writer-prod-dir. Wrote documentaries in Army Air Forces M.P. Unit in W.W.II. WGA award nominee and other awards.
   PICTURES: Rope of Sand, Desperate Search, Cease Fire, Safe At Home, House of Women, Duffy of San Quentin, Along the Great Divide, Tokyo Joe, Alaska Seas, Steel Cage, Steel Jungle, Hold Back the Night, Guns of Fort Petticoat, Unwed Mother, Jive Junction (s.p.), Stone Cold (exec. prod.).
   TELEVISION: Movies: Kentucky Woman, Mad Bull, The Outlaws. Over 600 episodes on 50 different series including: Delvecchio, Mad Bull, Switch, Moving On, Baa, Baa, Blacksheep, McCloud, The Man and the City, Sarge, Owen Marshall, Peyton Place (200 episodes), Mr. Novak, The Greatest Show on Earth, Travels of Jaimie McPheeters, Outlaws, Hong Kong, Checkmate, Bat Masterson, The Web, Bold Venture, Tombstone Territory, Maverick, Rough Riders, Captain Grief, Lockup, Dick Powell, The Survivors, Bracken's World, Bold Ones, Kung Fu, Barnaby Jones, Marcus Welby, Lucas Tanner, etc.

DONNELLY, DONAL: Actor. b. Bradford, Eng. July 6, 1931. Studied for theatre at the Dublin Gate Theatre. Broadway debut: Philadelphia, Here I Come (1966). Other NY theater includes: Joe Egg, Sleuth (NY and U.S. tour), The Elephant Man, The Faith-Healer, The Chalk Garden, My Astonishing Self, Big Maggie, Execution of Justice, Sherlock's Last Case, Ghetto, Dancing at Lughnasa.
PICTURES: Rising of the Moon (1957), Gideon's Day, Shake Hands With the Devil, Young Cassidy, The Knack, Up Jumped a Swagman, The Mind of Mr. Soames, Waterloo, The Dead, The Godfather Part III, Indian Warrior.
TELEVISION: Juno and the Paycock (BBC, 1958); Home Is the Hero, The Venetian Twins; The Plough and the Stars; Playboy of the Western World; Sergeant Musgrave's Dance; Yes-Honestly (series).

DONNELLY, RALPH E.: Executive. b. Lynbrook, NY, Jan. 20, 1932. e. Bellmore, NY public school; W. C. Mepham H.S., 1949. Worked for Variety (publication) as writer, 1950; Long Island Press as daily columnist, 1951; joined Associated Independent Theatres, 1953, as gen. mgr.; later film buyer; in 1973 left to become independent buyer and booker for Creative Films; film buyer and v.p., RKO/Stanley Warner Theatres, 1976–79; v.p. & gen. mgr. for Cinema 5 Ltd. circuit, N.Y., 1980–87; 1987–93, exec. v.p. City Cinemas, N.Y. Now co-pres. of Cinema Connections.

DONNER, CLIVE: Director. b. London, Eng., Jan 21, 1926. Ent. m.p. ind. 1942. Asst. film ed. Denham Studios, 1942. Dir. London stage: The Formation Dancers, The Front Room Boys, Kennedy's Children (also NY). Film ed.: A Christmas Carol (Scrooge; 1951), The Card (The Promoter), Genevieve, Man With a Million (The Million Pound Note), The Purple Plain, I Am a Camera.
PICTURES: Director: The Secret Place, Heart of a Child, Marriage of Convenience, Some People, The Caretaker, Nothing But the Best, The Sinister Man, What's New Pussycat, Luv, Here We Go Round the Mulberry Bush, Alfred the Great, Vampira, Spectre, Rogue Male, Three Hostages, She Fell Among Thieves, The Nude Bomb, Charlie Chan and the Curse of the Dragon Queen, Stealing Heaven.
TELEVISION: Danger Man, Documentaries, Sir Francis Drake, Mighty and Mystical, British Institutions, Tempo. Movies: Spectre, The Thief of Baghdad, Oliver Twist, The Scarlet Pimpernel, Arthur the King, To Catch a King, A Christmas Carol, Dead Man's Folly, Babes in Toyland, Not a Penny More Not a Penny Less, Coup de Foudre (Love at First Sight), Terror Strikes the Class Reunion.

DONNER, RICHARD: Director. b. New York, NY, 1939. Began career as actor off-Bdwy. Worked with director Martin Ritt on TV production of Maugham's Of Human Bondage. Moved to California 1958, directing commercials, industrial films and documentaries. First TV drama: Wanted: Dead or Alive.
PICTURES: X-15, Salt and Pepper, Twinky (Lola), The Omen, Superman, Inside Moves, The Final Conflict (exec. prod. only), The Toy (also exec. prod.), Ladyhawke (also prod.), The Goonies (also prod.), Lethal Weapon (also prod.), The Lost Boys (exec. prod. only), Scrooged (also prod.), Lethal Weapon 2 (also prod.), Delirious (exec. prod. only), Radio Flyer, Lethal Weapon 3 (also prod.), Free Willy (co-exec. prod. only).
TELEVISION: Series episodes of Have Gun Will Travel, Perry Mason, Cannon, Get Smart, The Fugitive, Kojak, Bronk, Lucas Tanner, Gilligan's Island, Man From U.N.C.L.E., Wild Wild West, Tales From the Crypt, Two Fisted Tales, Twilight Zone, The Banana Splits, Combat. Movies: Portrait of a Teen-Age Alcoholic, Senior Year, A Shadow in the Streets, Tales From the Crypt (exec. prod.; also dir. episode: Dig That Cat . . . He's Real Gone).

D'ONOFRIO, VINCENT PHILLIP: Actor. b. Brooklyn, NY, 1960. Studied acting with the American Stanislavsky Theatre in NY, appearing in Of Mice and Men, The Petrified Forest, Sexual Perversity in Chicago, and The Indian Wants the Bronx.
PICTURES: The First Turn On!, Full Metal Jacket, Adventures in Babysitting, Mystic Pizza, Signs of Life, The Blood of Heros, Crooked Hearts, Dying Young, Fires Within, Naked Tango, JFK, The Player, Salt on Our Skin, Household Saints, Being Human.
THEATRE: Bdwy: Open Admissions.

DONOVAN, ARLENE: Producer. b. Kentucky. e. Stratford Coll., VA. Worked in publishing before entering industry as asst. to late dir. Robert Rosen on Cocoa Beach, uncompleted at his death. Worked as story editor, Columbia Pictures. 1969–82, literary head of m.p. dept. for ICM; involved in book publishing as well as stage and screen projects.
PICTURES: Still of the Night, Places in the Heart, Nadine, The House on Carroll Street (co-exec. prod.).

DONOVAN, HENRY B.: Executive, Producer. b. Boston, MA. Entered m.p. ind. for RKO Pathe Studios, property master, special effects dir., unit mgr., asst. dir., prod. mgr.; worked on over 310 pictures; Harry Sherman, Hopalong Cassidy features. 10 yrs., U.S. Army Signal Corps, as head of dept. of

California studios prod. training m.p.; pres.: Telemount Pictures, Inc. Prod., dir., writer Cowboy G Men (TV series). Wrote novel, Corkscrewed, Live Television.
PICTURES: Hopalong Cassidy Features, Gone with the Wind, Becky Sharp, Our Flag (dir.), Magic Lady (13 one-reel features), others. Cowboy G Men (prod., writer; 39 films).
TELEVISION: programming, finance, distribution. Global Scope; International TV; Dist., Financing, programming; sls. consultant, Intl. TV & motion pictures. Cable TV & distribution & program development, collector of movie memorabilia; DBS TV programming & financing: production software. Worldwide TV consultant. Producer of live action tv show Magic Lady. Creator, designer, writer for Silicon Valley.

DONOVAN, TATE: Actor. b. New York, NY, 1964. Raised in New Jersey. Studied acting at USC. Worked as still photographer for two Mutual of Omaha documentaries.
PICTURES: SpaceCamp, Clean and Sober, Dead Bang, Memphis Belle, Love Potion No. 9, Ethan Frome, Equinox.
TELEVISION: Movies: Not My Kid, Into Thin Air, A Case of Deadly Force, Nutcracker: Money Madness Murder. Special: Vietnam War Stories.
THEATRE: Rufian on the Stair, The American Plan, The Rhythm of Torn Stars, Bent.

DOOHAN, JAMES: Actor. b. Vancouver, B.C., Mar. 3, 1920. W.W.II capt. in Royal Canadian Artillery. 1946 won scholarship to Neighborhood Playhouse in N.Y. and taught there later. 1953, returned to Canada to live in Toronto, becoming engaged in acting career on radio, TV and in film. Then to Hollywood and chief fame as Chief Engineer Scott in TV series, Star Trek.
PICTURES: The Wheeler Dealers, The Satan Bug, Bus Riley's Back in Town, Pretty Maids All in a Row, Star Trek—The Motion Picture, Star Trek II: The Wrath of Khan, Star Trek III: The Search for Spock, Star Trek IV: The Voyage Home, Star Trek V: The Final Frontier, Star Trek VI: The Undiscovered Country, Double Trouble, National Lampoon's Loaded Weapon 1.
TELEVISION: Series: Star Trek. Guest: Hazel, Bonanza, The Virginia, Gunsmoke, Peyton Place, The Fugitive, Marcus Welby MD, Ben Casey, Bewitched, Fantasy Island, etc. Movie: Scalplock.

DOOLEY, PAUL: Actor. b. Parkersburg, WV, Feb. 22, 1928. Began career on N.Y. stage in Threepenny Opera. Later member of Second City. Bdwy. credits include The Odd Couple, Adaptation/Next, The White House Murder Case, Hold Me, etc. Co-creator and writer for The Electric Company on PBS. Owns co. called All Over Creation, which produces original industrial films and shows and has created over 1,000 radio commercials.
PICTURES: What's So Bad About Feeling Good?, The Out-of-Towners, Death Wish, The Gravy Train, Slap Shot, A Wedding, A Perfect Couple, Breaking Away, Rich Kids, Popeye, Health, Paternity, Endangered Species, Kiss Me Goodbye, Strange Brew, Going Berserk, 16 Candles, Big Trouble, O.C. and Stiggs, Monster in the Closet, Last Rites, Flashback, Shakes the Clown, The Player, My Boyfriend's Back.
TELEVISION: Specials: Faerie Tale Theater, The Firm, Traveler's Rest. Movies: The Murder of Mary Phagan, Lip Service, Guts and Glory: The Rise and Fall of Oliver North, When He's Not a Stranger, The Court Martial of Jackie Robinson, Guess Who's Coming for Christmas?, White Hot: The Mysterious Murder of Thelma Todd, Cooperstown, Mother of the Bride. Series: The Dom DeLuise Show, Coming of Age.

DORAN, LINDSAY: Executive. b. Los Angeles, CA. e. U. of California at Santa Cruz. Moved to London where was contributing author to The Oxford Companion to Film and the World Encyclopedia of Film. Returned to U.S. to write and produce documentaries and children's programs for Pennsylvania public affairs station WPSX-TV. Career in m.p. industry began in story dept. at Embassy Pictures which she joined in 1979; 1982 promoted to dir. of development; then v.p., creative affairs. 1985, joined Paramount Pictures as v.p., production, for M.P. Group. 1987, promoted to senior v.p., production.

DORTORT, DAVID: Executive Producer. b. New York, NY, Oct. 23, 1916. e. City Coll. of New York. Served U.S. Army, 1943–46. Novelist and short story writer, 1943–49. Also TV writer. Now pres. of Xanadu Prods., Aurora Enterprises, Inc., and Bonanza Ventures, Inc. & Pres. TV branch, WGA, West, 1954–55; TV-radio branch, 1955–57; v.p. PGA, 1967; pres. 1968. Chairman of The Caucus for Producers, Writers and Directors, 1973–75. Pres., PGA, 1980–81; campaign dir., Permanent Charities Comm., 1980–81; chmn., Interguild Council 1980–81.
AUTHOR: Novels include Burial of the Fruit and The Post of Honor.
PICTURES: The Lusty Men, Reprisal, The Big Land, Cry in the Night, Clash by Night, Going Bananas (exec. prod.).
TELEVISION: Creator and exec. prod., Bonanza; High Chaparral, The Chisholms, Hunter's Moon, Bonanza: Legends of the Ponderosa. Producer: The Restless Gun, The

Cowboys. Creator, story and exec. prod. Bonanza: The Next Generation.

DOUGHERTY, MARION: Executive. e. Penn St. U. Gained fame as casting director. Casting dir. on series Naked City, Route 66. Formed own co. in 1965. Acted as co-executive producer on Smile, 1975. In 1977 named v.p. in chg. talent for Paramount Pictures. In 1979 joined Warner Bros. as sr. v.p. in chg. talent to work with production dept. and producers and directors.

CASTING: A Little Romance (co-casting), Urban Cowboy (co-), Honky Tonk Freeway, Reds (co-), Firefox, Honkytonk Man, The World According to Garp, Sudden Impact, The Man With Two Brains (co-), The Killing Fields (co-), Swing Shift, The Little Drummer Girl, Lethal Weapon (also 2 & 3), Batman, Batman Returns, Forever Young, Falling Down.

DOUGLAS, GORDON: Director, b. New York, NY, Dec. 15, 1907. Actor with Hal Roach stock company; writer; collab. Topper series, Housekeeper's Daughter; dir., 30 Our Gang shorts, Laurel & Hardy shorts.

PICTURES: Saps at Sea, Broadway Limited, Devil with Hitler, First Yank into Tokyo, San Quentin, If You Knew Suzie, Black Arrow, Walk a Crooked Mile, Doolins of Oklahoma, Mr. Soft Touch, The Nevadan, Between Midnight and Dawn, Kiss Tomorrow Goodbye, Great Missouri Raid, Only the Valiant, I Was a Communist for the FBI, Come Fill the Cup, Mara Maru, Iron Mistress, She's Back on Broadway, So This Is Love, The Charge at Feather River, Them, Young at Heart, McConnell Story, Sincerely Yours, Santiago, The Big Land, Bombers B-52, Fort Dobbs, Yellowstone Kelly, Rachel Cade, Gold of 7 Saints, Follow That Dream, Call Me Bwana, Rio Conchos, Robin and the Seven Hoods, Sylvia, Harlow, Stagecoach, Way Way Out, In Like Flint, Chuka, Tony Rome, The Detective, Lady in Cement, Barquero, They Call Me Mr. Tibbs, Slaughter's Big Rip Off.

TELEVISION: Nevada Smith.

DOUGLAS, KIRK: Actor, Producer, Director. r.n. Issur Danielovitch (changed to Demsky). b. Amsterdam, NY, Dec. 9, 1918. m. Anne Buydens, pres. of Bryna Prod. Co. Father of Michael, Joel, Peter, Eric. e. St. Lawrence U, B.A, AADA. Stage debut in New York: Spring Again. U.S. Navy during W.W.II; resumed stage work. Did radio soap operas. Signed by Hal B. Wallis. Screen debut: The Strange Love of Martha Ivers. Autobiography: The Ragman's Son (1988).Recipient of U.S. Presidential Medal of Freedom, 1981. Career achievement award, National Board of Review, 1989. Received AFI Lifetime Achievement Award, 1991.

THEATER: Spring Again, Three Sisters, Kiss and Tell, Trio, The Wind is Ninety, Star in the Window, Man Bites Dog, One Flew Over the Cuckoo's Nest, The Boys of Autumn.

TELEVISION: Movies: Mousey, The Money Changers, Draw! (HBO), Victory at Entebbe, Remembrance of Love, Amos, Queenie, Inherit the Wind, The Secret. Guest: The Lucy Show, Tales From the Crypt (Yellow). Specials: Legend of Silent Night, Dr. Jekyll & Mr. Hyde.

PICTURES: Strange Love of Martha Ivers (debut, 1946), Out of the Past, I Walk Alone, Mourning Becomes Electra, The Walls of Jericho, My Dear Secretary, Letter to Three Wives, Champion, Young Man with a Horn, The Glass Menagerie, The Big Carnival (a.k.a. Ace in the Hole), Along the Great Divide, Detective Story, The Big Trees, The Big Sky, Bad and the Beautiful, Story of Three Loves, The Juggler, Act of Love, 20,000 Leagues Under the Sea, Ulysses, Man Without a Star, The Racers, The Indian Fighter (also prod.), Lust for Life, Top Secret Affair, Gunfight at the OK Corral, Paths of Glory, The Vikings (also prod.), Last Train from Gun Hill, The Devil's Disciple, Strangers When We Meet, Spartacus (also prod.), The Last Sunset, Town Without Pity, Lonely Are the Brave (also prod.), Two Weeks in Another Town, The Hook, List of Adrian Messenger (also prod.), For Love or Money, Seven Days in May (also prod.), In Harm's Way, The Heroes of Telemark, Cast a Giant Shadow, Is Paris Burning?, The Way West, The War Wagon, A Lovely Way to Die, The Brotherhood (also prod.), The Arrangement, There Was a Crooked Man, A Gunfight, Summertree (prod. only), The Light at the Edge of the World (also prod.), Catch Me a Spy, Scalawag (also dir., prod.), Master Touch, Once is Not Enough, Posse (also dir., prod.), The Chosen, The Fury, The Villain, Saturn III, Home Movies, The Final Countdown, The Man from Snowy River, Eddie Macon's Run, Tough Guys, Oscar, Welcome to Veraz, Greedy.

DOUGLAS, MICHAEL: Actor, Producer. b. New Brunswick, NJ, Sept 25, 1944. p. Kirk Douglas and Diana Dill. e. Black Fox Military Acad., Choate, U. of California. Worked as asst. director on Lonely Are the Brave, Heroes of Telemark, Cast a Giant Shadow; after TV debut in The Experiment (CBS Playhouse), appeared off-Broadway in City Scene, Pinkville (Theatre World Award). Produced 1993 Off-Bdwy show The Best of Friends.

PICTURES: Hail Hero (debut, 1969), Adam at 6 A.M., Summertree, Napoleon and Samantha, One Flew Over the Cuckoo's Nest (co-prod. only; Acad. Award for Best Picture,

1975), Coma, The China Syndrome (also prod.), Running (also exec. prod.), It's My Turn, The Star Chamber, Romancing the Stone (also prod.), Starman (exec. prod. only), A Chorus Line, The Jewel of the Nile (also prod.), Fatal Attraction, Wall Street (Acad. Award, Natl. Board of Review Award, 1987), Black Rain, The War of the Roses, Flatliners (co-exec. prod. only), Shining Through, Radio Flyer (co-exec. prod. only), Basic Instinct, Falling Down, Made in America (co-exec. prod. only).

TELEVISION: Series: Streets of San Francisco. Guest: The FBI, Medical Center. Movies: Streets of San Francisco (pilot), When Michael Calls.

DOUGLAS, MIKE: TV host, Commentator. r.n. Michael Delaney Dowd, Jr. b. Chicago, IL, Aug. 11, 1925. Started career singing with bands in and around Chicago. 1950–54 featured singer with Kay Kyser's band. In 1953 became host of WGN-TV's Hi Ladies in Chicago; also featured on WMAQ-TV, NBC, Chicago, as singer and host. Moved to Hollywood in late '50s, working as piano bar singer. In 1961 hired as host for new show on station KYW-TV in Cleveland, owned by Westinghouse Bdg. Co., featuring celebrity guests. This became the Mike Douglas Show which was later nationally syndicated and moved base of operations to Philadelphia, then Los Angeles. Ran 21 years til Mid-1982. Books: The Mike Douglas Cookbook (1969), Mike Douglas My Story (1978), When the Going Gets Tough.

PICTURES: Gator, Nasty Habits, The Incredible Shrinking Woman.

DOUGLAS, VALERIE: Executive. b. Hollywood, CA, Dec. 3. e. UCLA, journalism. Uncle was actor Elmo Lincoln (first Tarzan). 1945–46, publicist, Vic Shapiro Public Relations; 1946–49, sub-agent, Manning O'Conner Agency; 1949–51, TV coordinator, Bing Crosby Enterprises, Fireside Theatre Series; 1951–52, publicist, RKO Studios; 1952–59, personal mgr., Richard Burton, v.p. & dir. Denham Films, Ltd.; London; 1959–61, pub. coordinator, Hecht-Lancaster-Hill; 1961–64, dir. of pub. relations, IPAR Productions, France; 1964–67, v.p., Illustra Films, West Coast branch; 1967–75, asst. dir. pub., United Artists Corp., West Coast; 1975–78, exec. v.p., Guttman & Pam Public Relations; 1978, formed Suvarie, Inc., m.p. representation, of which is pres. 1978–84, personal mgr, the late actor Richard Burton. Executrix of the estate of Richard Burton, 1984–89. Consultant for Merrington Prods.

DOURIF, BRAD: Actor. b. Huntington, WV, Mar. 18, 1950. Studied with Stanford Meisner. Stage actor, three years with Circle Repertory Co., NY (When You Comin' Back Red Ryder?), before films and TV.

PICTURES: Split, One Flew Over the Cuckoo's Nest (Acad. Award nom., Golden Globe & BAFTA Awards, 1975), Group Portrait with Lady, Eyes of Laura Mars, Wise Blood, Heaven's Gate, Ragtime, Dune, Impure Thoughts, Istanbul, Blue Velvet, Fatal Beauty, Child's Play, Mississippi Burning, Medium Rare, The Exorcist: 1990, Spontaneous Combustion, Grim Prairie Tales, Sonny Boy, Graveyard Shift, Child's Play II, Hidden Agenda, Jungle Fever, The Horseplayer, Body Parts, Child's Play 3, Common Bonds, Scream of Stone, London Kills Me, Diary of the Hurdy Gurdy Man, Murder Blues, Final Judgment, Dead Certain, Amos & Andrew, Trauma, Color of Night.

TELEVISION: Movies: Sgt. Matlovitch vs. the U.S. Air Force, Guyana Tragedy—The Story of Jim Jones, I Desire, Vengeance: The Story of Tony Cimo, Rage of Angels: The Story Continues, Desperado: The Outlaw Wars, Class of '61. Mini-Series: Studs Lonigan, Wild Palms.Specials: Mound Builders, The Gardener's Son.Guest: Miami Vice, The Hitchhiker, Spencer for Hire, Tales of the Unexpected, Moonlighting, The Equalizer, Murder She Wrote.

DOWN, LESLEY-ANNE: Actress. b. London, England, March 17, 1954. At age of 10 modeled for TV and film commercials, leading to roles in features. Stage debut at 14 in All the Right Noises.

PICTURES: In the Devil's Garden, Countess Dracula, Pope Joan, Scalawag, From Beyond the Grave, Brannigan, The Pink Panther Strikes Again, The Betsy, A Little Night Music, The Great Train Robbery, Hanover Street, Rough Cut, Sphinx, Nomads, Scenes from the Goldmine, Night Trap (Mardi Gras for the Devil), Death Wish V.

TELEVISION: Series: Upstairs, Downstairs, Dallas. Movies: Agatha Christie's Murder is Easy, Hunchback of Notre Dame, The One and Only Phyllis Dixey, Arch of Triumph, Indiscreet, Lady Killers, Night Walk. Mini-Series: North and South Books I & II, Last Days of Pompeii. Specials: Unity Mitford. Heartbreak House. Pilots: Shivers, 1775.

STAGE: Great Expectations, Hamlet, etc.

DOWNEY, ROBERT, JR.: Actor. b. New York, NY, April 4, 1965. Son of indep. filmmaker Robert Downey. Film debut in his father's film Pound (1970). Named Rolling Stone's Hottest Actor for 1988.

PICTURES: Pound (debut, 1970), Greaser's Palace, Up the Academy, Baby Its You, Firstborn, Tuff Turf, Weird Science, To Live and Die in L.A., Back to School, America, The Pick-

Up Artist, Less Than Zero, Johnny B. Good, Rented Lips, 1969, True Believer, Chances Are, That's Adequate, Air America, Too Much Sun, Soapdish, Chaplin (Acad. Award nom., BAFTA Award), Heart and Souls, Short Cuts, The Last Party, Natural Born Killers.
TELEVISION: *Series*: Saturday Night Live. *Mini-Series*: Mussolini: The Untold Story.

DOWNS, HUGH: Broadcaster. b. Akron, OH, Feb. 14, 1921. e. Bluffton Coll., 1938. Wayne U., 1941. Col. U., N.Y., 1955; Supervisor of Science Programming, NBC's Science Dept. one yr.; science consultant for Westinghouse Labs., Ford Foundation, etc.; chmn. of bd., Raylin Prods., Inc. Today, Chairman, U.S. Committee for UNICEF. Chm., National Space Institute.
TELEVISION: Hawkins Falls, Kukla, Fran & Ollie, Short Story Playhouse, American Inventory, Home, Sid Caesar Show, Tonight (Jack Paar Show), Concentration, Today. *Host*: 20/20, Over-Easy.
RADIO: NBC's Monitor.

DOYLE, KEVIN: Executive. b. Sydney, Australia, June 21, 1933. e. N. Sydney Tech. HS., Aust. Jr. exec., asst. adv. & pub. div., 20th Century-Fox, Aust.; 1947–59; adv. & pub. dir., Columbia Pictures Aust., 1960–66; international ad/pub. mgr.; Columbia Pictures Int'l, N.Y. 1966; intl. pub./promo. mgr., 1980; 1987, Columbia Int'l. rep., Coca-Cola promotions/mktg. sub-committee; int'l pub./promo. mgr. Columbia Tri-Star Film Distributors Inc., 1988; int'l pub./promo. dir. Columbia/Tri-Star Film distrib. Inc. 1990. Retired from MoPic industry, 1992.

DOYLE-MURRAY, BRIAN: Actor, Writer. b. Chicago, IL., Oct. 31. Brother of comedian Bill Murray. Started as member of Chicago's Second City improv. troupe, before joining the Organic Theatre of Chicago and the Boston Shakespeare Co. Appeared Off-Bdwy in The National Lampoon Show and on radio on weekly National Lampoon Show.
PICTURES: Caddyshack (also co-s.p.), Modern Problems, National Lampoon's Vacation, Sixteen Candles, The Razor's Edge, Legal Eagles, Club Paradise (also co-s.p.), Scrooged, The Experts, How I Got Into College, Ghostbusters II, National Lampoon's Christmas Vacation, Nothing But Trouble, JFK, Wayne's World, Groundhog Day, Cabin Boy.
TELEVISION: *Series*: Saturday Night Live (also writer), Get a Life, Good Sports. *Movie*: Babe Ruth.

DRAGOTI, STAN: Director. b. New York, NY, Oct. 4, 1932. e. Cooper Union and Sch. of Visual Arts. 1959 hired as sketch at ad agency, promoted to sr. art dir., later TV dept. and art dir. of Young & Rubicam. Studied acting HB Studios. Directed Clio awarding-winning TV commercials (including I Love New York campaign).
PICTURES: Dirty Little Billy (1972), Love at First Bite, Mr. Mom, The Man with One Red Shoe, She's Out of Control, Necessary Roughness.

DRAI, VICTOR: Producer. b. Casablanca, Morocco, July 25, 1947. e. Lycée de Port Lyautey, 1957–63. In real estate in Los Angeles 1976–82; clothing designer/mfg. in Paris, France, 1969–76. Began producing features in 1984, The Woman in Red.
PICTURES: The Man with One Red Shoe, The Bride, Weekend at Bernie's, Folks!, Weekend at Bernie's 2.

DRAKE, CHARLES: Actor. r.n. Charles Ruppert; b. New York, NY, Oct. 2, 1914. e. Nicholas Coll., 1937. With Electric Boat Co., Groton, CT; adv. salesman; in little theatres.
PICTURES: I Wanted Wings, Man Who Came to Dinner, Now, Voyager, Air Force, Mr. Skeffington, Whistle Stop, Pretender, You Came Along, Tender Years, Bowie Knife, Comanche Territory, Air Cadet, Winchester '73, Harvey, Little Egypt, You Never Can Tell, Treasure of Lost Canyon, Red Ball Express, Bonzo Goes to College, Gunsmoke, Lone Hand, It Came from Outer Space, War Arrow, Glenn Miller Story, Tobor the Great, Four Guns to the Border, Female on the Beach, All That Heaven Allows, Price of Fear, The Arrangement.

DRAKLICH, NICK: Executive. b. Bakersfield, CA, Oct. 16, 1926. e. Fresno State Coll., Stanford U., Claremont Graduate Sch. Sr. v.p.—home entertainment for Republic Pictures Corp.

DRAZEN, LORI: Executive. Began career as asst. to dir. of adv. for Orion Pictures; creative dept. mgr., Kenyon & Eckhardt; gen. mgr., Seiniger Advertising; joined Warner Bros. 1985 as v.p., world-wide adv. & pub. services.

DREIFUSS, ARTHUR: Producer, Director, Writer. b. Frankfurt on Main, Germany, March 25, 1908. e. U. of Frankfurt on Main, Conservatory of Music, Columbia U. Choreographer for films Devil on Horseback, Hats Off; legit. producer: Allure, Baby Pompadour; producer many night club shows; associate producer Fanchon & Marco, Hollywood; dir. over 50 features and 53 TV shows for Columbia, RKO, Universal, Allied Artists, other majors; director Paul Muni debut Screen Gems–Ford Theatre, TV 1953; 1973, director, Wildlife in Crisis, Viacom TV series.

PICTURES: Director: Secret File (also prod.), Assignment Abroad (also prod.), The Last Blitzkrieg, Life Begins at Seventeen, Juke Box Rhythm, The Quare Fellow (also s.p.; voted Best Film 1962 by British Producers Assoc.), Riot on Sunset Strip, The Love-Ins, For Singles Only, The Young Runaways, A Time to Sing.

DREYFUSS, RICHARD: Actor. b. Brooklyn, NY, Oct. 29, 1947. e. Beverly Hills H.S.; San Fernando Valley State Coll. 1965–67. Prof. career began at Gallery Theatre (L.A.) in In Mama's House.
PICTURES: The Graduate, Valley of the Dolls, The Young Runaways, Hello Down There, Dillinger, American Graffiti, The Second Coming of Suzanne, The Apprenticeship of Duddy Kravitz, Jaws, Inserts, Close Encounters of the Third Kind, The Goodbye Girl (Acad. Award, 1977), The Big Fix (also co-prod.) The Competition, Whose Life Is It Anyway?, The Buddy System, Down and Out in Beverly Hills, Stand by Me, Tin Men, Stakeout, Nuts, Moon Over Parador, Let It Ride, Always, Postcards from the Edge, Once Around, Rosencrantz and Guildenstern Are Dead, What About Bob?, Lost in Yonkers, Another Stakeout.
TELEVISION: *Series*: Karen (1964–5). *Host*: American Chronicles. *Guest*: Love on a Rooftop, Occasional Wife, The Big Valley, Room 222, Judd for the Defense, Mod Squad, The Bold Ones. *Special*: Funny You Don't Look 200 (host, co-prod., co-writer). *Movies*: Two for the Money, Victory at Entebbe, Prisoner of Honor (also prod.).
STAGE: Journey to the Day, Incident at Vichy, People Next Door, Enemy Line, Whose Little Boy Are You, But Seriously, Major Barbara, The Time of Your Life, The Hands of Its Enemy (Mark Taper Forum, L.A.), The Normal Heart, Death and the Maiden, others.

DROMGOOLE, PATRICK: Film director, Stage prod., Executive. b. Iqueque, Chile, Aug. 30, 1930; e. Dulwich Coll., University Coll., Oxford. Joined BBC Radio as dir. 1954, later directing TV plays for BBC and ABC, incl. Armchair Theatre, Frontier, Dracula, Mystery Imagination. Joined HTV as West Country Programme Controller, 1968; dir. award-winning dramas; Thick as Thieves, Machinegunner. Developed Company's drama output and promoted policy of international pre-sales with such dramas as Jamaica Inn, Separate Tables, Catholics, Kidnapped, Robin of Sherwood, Arch of Triumph, Mr. Halpern and Mr. Johnson, Jenny's War, Codename Kyril, Wall of Tyranny, Strange Interlude, The Woman He Loved, Grand Larceny, Maigret. Made Fellow of RTS, 1978; chief exec. HTV Group since 1988. Fellow of RSA, 1989.
THEATER: *Director*: incl. first plays of Charles Wood, Joe Orton, David Halliwell, Colin Welland; Peter O'Toole in Man and Superman.
PICTURES: Two Vale South, Hidden Face, Dead Man's Chest, Anthony Purdy Esq., Point of Dissent, The Actors, King of the Wind (exec. prod.), Visage du Passé (dir.), Meutres en Douce.
TELEVISION: Outpost (sprv. exec. prod.).

DRU, JOANNE: Actress. r.n. Joanne La Cock. b. Logan, WV, Jan. 31, 1923. Sister of Peter Marshall. John Robert Powers model: on stage as showgirl in Hold on to Your Hats; a Samba Siren at Ritz Carlton & Paramount; with theatrical group under Batami Schneider.
PICTURES: Abie's Irish Rose (debut, 1946), Red River, She Wore a Yellow Ribbon, All the King's Men, Wagonmaster, 711 Ocean Drive, Vengeance Valley, Mr. Belvedere Rings the Bell, My Pal Gus, Return of the Texan, Pride of St. Louis, Thunder Bay, Outlaw Territory, Forbidden, Siege at Red River, Duffy of San Quentin, Southwest Passage, Three Ring Circus, Day of Triumph, Hell on Frisco Bay, The Warriors, Sincerely Yours, Drango, Light in the Forest, Wild and the Innocent, September Storm, Sylvia, Super Fuzz.
TELEVISION: *Series*: Guestward Ho. *Guest*: Ford Theatre, Schlitz Playhouse, Playhouse 90, Climax, Lux Video Theatre, David Niven Show, The Green Hornet, Marcus Welby M.D.

DRURY, JAMES: Actor. b. New York, NY, 1934. e. New York U. Acting debut at age 8 in biblical play for children at Greenwich Settlement Playhouse. Performed on stage while youngster. Signed by MGM in 1955, working one day in each of seven movies that year, including Blackboard Jungle. Then got two-year contract at 20th-Fox. Gained fame as hero of TV series, The Virginian, which had nine-year run.
PICTURES: Forbidden Planet, Love Me Tender, Bernardine, Toby Tyler, Pollyana, Ten Who Dared, Ride the High Country, The Young Warriors.
TELEVISION: *Series*: The Virginian (1962–71), Firehouse. *Movies*: Breakout, Alias Smith and Jones, The Devil and Miss Sarah, The Gambler Returns: Luck of the Draw.

DUBAND, WAYNE: Executive. b. Sydney, Australia, Feb. 13, 1947. Joined Warner Bros. 1969 as mgr. trainee in Australia. 1973, transferred to South Africa as mgr. dir.; 1977 gen. mgr. of CIC/Warner Bros. joint venture, also managing the CIC theatre operation there. 1980, named exec. asst. to Myron D. Karlin, pres. WB Intl., in Burbank. 1981, mgr. dir. of Warner/Columbia joint venture in France. 1985, appt. v.p. of sls. for WB Intl.

division. 1987, appt. senior v.p. for Warner Bros. Intl. division. 1992, appt. pres. Intl. Theatrical div., WB Intl.

DUBS, ARTHUR R.: Executive, Producer, Director, Writer, President and Owner of Pacific International Enterprises, b. Medford, OR, Feb. 26, 1930. e. Southern Oregon State Coll. Founded Pacific International Enterprises, 1969.
PICTURES: Producer-Director: American Wilderness, Vanishing Wilderness, Wonder of It All. Exec. Prod.: Challenge to Be Free. Prod.: Adventures of the Wilderness Family, Wilderness Family Part 2 (also s.p.), Mountain Family Robinson (also s.p.), Across the Great Divide, Sacred Ground, Mystery Mansion, Dream Chasers (also co-dir.). Co-Prod.: Windwalker.

DUDELHEIM, HANS RUDOLF: Communications Executive. b. Berlin, Germany, June 17, 1927. e. Sch. of Photography Berlin, New School of NY. Film editor, ABC, 1951–66. Prod/Dir/Edit.: Cinema Arts Assn. 1966–present; served as pres. 1987–present. Founder, 1961, Cinema Arts Film Soc. Editor of documentaries: Saga of Western Man, Comrade Student, Sublimated Birth (also prod.), Kent State, Sigmund Freud, IBM Motivation Project, The Forgotten Pioneers of Hollywood, Painting With Love.

DUDIKOFF, MICHAEL: Actor. b. Torrance, CA, Oct. 8, 1954.
PICTURES: Making Love, I Ought to Be in Pictures, Tron, Bachelor Party, Bloody Birthday, American Ninja, Radioactive Dreams, Avenging Force, American Ninja II: The Confrontation, Platoon Leader, River of Death, American Ninja 4: The Annihilation, Midnight Ride, Human Shield, Rescue Me.
TELEVISION: Mini-Series: North and South Book II. Movie: The Woman Who Sinned. Series: Star of the Family. Pilot: Sawyer and Finn. Guest: Happy Days, Dallas.

DUFFY, JAMES E.: Executive. b. Decatur, IL, April 2, 1926. e. Beloit Coll. Radio announcer, then reporter; joined publicity dept., ABC in 1949; named director of adv. & promo., then account exec. for Central division of ABC Radio Network; director of sales ABC Radio, 1957; central division account exec., ABC Television Network, 1955; natl. director of sales, ABC Radio central division, 1960; vice president, ABC Radio Network, 1961; exec. v.p. & natl. director of sales, 1962; vice president in charge of sales, ABC Television Network, 1963; president, ABC Television Network, 1970–85; pres., communications, 1985–86; v.p. Capital Cities/ABC, Inc.; pres., communications, ABC Network & Bdgst. Divisions.

DUFFY, PATRICK: Actor. b. Townsend, MT, March 17, 1949. e. U. of Washington. Became actor-in-residence in state of Washington, where performed with various statefunded groups. Acted off-Bdwy. Taught mime and movement classes in summer camp in Seattle. Moved to L.A. and began TV acting career.
TELEVISION: Specials: The Last of Mrs. Lincoln, Freedom Festival '89 (host). Movies: The Stranger Who Looks Like Me, Hurricane, Man From Atlantis, Enola Gay, Cry for the Strangers, Too Good to Be True, Alice in Wonderland, Unholy Matrimony, Murder C.O.D., Children of the Bride, Danielle Steel's Daddy. Series: Man from Atlantis, Dallas, Step By Step. Guest: Switch, George Burns' Comedy Week.

DUGAN, DENNIS: Actor, Director. b. Wheaton, IL, Sept. 5, 1946. m. actress Joyce Van Patten. Studied acting at Goodman Theatre School.
PICTURES: Night Call Nurses, The Day of the Locust, Night Moves, Smile, Harry and Walter Go to New York, Norman . . . Is That You?, Unidentified Flying Oddball, The Howling, Water, Can't Buy Me Love, She's Having a Baby, The New Adventures of Pippi Longstocking, Parenthood, Problem Child (also dir.), Brain Donors (dir. only).
TELEVISION: Series: Richie Brockelman: Private Eye, Empire, Shadow Chasers. Movies: Death Race, The Girl Most Likely To . . . , Last of the Good Guys, Country Gold, The Toughest Man in the World. Mini-Series: Rich man Poor Man. Guest: Hooperman, Moonlighting, M*A*S*H, The Rockford Files, Scene of the Crime, Making a Living, Hill Street Blues. Pilots: Alice, Father O Father, Did You Hear About Josh and Kelly?, Full House, Channel 99. Director: Hunter, Sonny Spoon, Wiseguy, Moonlighting.
THEATRE: NY: A Man's Man, The House of Blue Leaves. L.A.: Once in a Lifetime, Rainbows for Sales, Estonia, The Dining Room, The Kitchen.

DUIGAN, JOHN: Director, Writer. Lived in England and Malaya before moving to Sydney, Australia. e. Univ. of Melbourne, philosophy, M.A. Taught for several years at Univ. of Melbourne and Latrobe U. before entering films. Directed and wrote experimental short, The Firm Man (1974). Novels: Badge, Players, Room to Move.
PICTURES: Dir.-Writer: Trespassers, Mouth to Mouth, Winter of Our Dreams (Australian Writers Guild Award), Far East, The Year My Voice Broke (Australian Acad. Award for best dir., s.p.) Romero (dir. only), Flirting, Wide Sargasso Sea.
TELEVISION: Mini-Series: Vietnam (co-dir.). Movie: Fragments of War: The Story of Damien Parer.

DUKAKIS, OLYMPIA: Actress. b. Lowell, MA, June 20, 1931. m. actor Louis Zorich. e. Boston U., B.A., M.F.A. Founding mem. of The Charles Playhouse, Boston, establishing summer theatre 1957–60. Taught acting at NYU 1967–70 as instructor, 1974–83 as master teacher, and at Yale U. 1976. With husband conceived and guided artistic dev. of Whole Theatre Monclair, NJ, 1977–1990; producing artistic dir. Adapted plays for her co. and dir. theater there, at Williamstown Theatre Fest. and Delaware Summer Fest. Appeared in more than 100 plays on Bdwy, Off-Bdwy and in regional and summer theater.
THEATER: Who's Who in Hell, The Aspern Papers, Night of the Iguana, The Breaking Wall, Curse of the Starving Class, Snow Orchid, The Marriage of Bette and Boo (Obie Award), Social Security.
PICTURES: Lilith, Twice a Man, John and Mary, Made for Each Other, Death Wish, Rich Kids, The Wanderers, The Idolmaker, National Lampoon Goes to the Movies, Flanagan, Moonstruck (Acad. Award, supp. actress, 1987), Working Girl, Look Who's Talking, Steel Magnolias, Dad, In the Spirit, Look Who's Talking Too, The Cemetery Club, Digger, Over the Hill.
TELEVISION: Specials: The Rehearsal, Sisters, Last Act is a Solo. Series: Search for Tomorrow, One of the Boys. Movies: Nicky's World, The Neighborhood, FDR-The Last Year, King of America, Lucky Day, Fire in the Dark, Sinatra.

DUKE, BILL: Actor, Director. b. Poughkeepsie, NY, Feb. 26, 1943. e. Boston Univ., NY Univ. Sch. of the Arts. Recieved AFI Best Young Director Award for short The Hero (Gold Award, Houston Film Festival). Has written poetry, short stories for children. Member bd. of dirs. American Film Institute.
PICTURES: Actor: Car Wash, American Gigolo, Commando, Predator, No Man's Land, Action Jackson, Bird on a Wire, Street of No Return, Menace II Society. Director: A Rage in Harlem, Deep Cover, The Cemetery Club, Sister Act 2.
TELEVISION: Actor: Movies: Love is Not Enough, Sgt. Matlovich Vs. the U.S. Air Force. Series: Palmerstown U.S.A. Director: Series: A Man Called Hawk, Cagney & Lacey, Hill Street Blues, Miami Vice, Dallas. Specials: The Killing Floor, A Raisin in the Sun, The Meeting. Movie: Johnnie Mae Gibson.

DUKE, PATTY: Actress. r.n. Anna Marie Duke. b. New York, NY, Dec. 14, 1946. e. Quintano Sch. for Young Professionals. Mother of actors Sean and MacKenzie Astin. Pres., Screen Actors Guild, 1985–88. Author: Surviving Sexual Assault (1983), Call Me Anna (1987).
THEATRE: The Miracle Worker (Theatre World Award), Isle of Children.
PICTURES: I'll Cry Tomorrow (debut as extra 1955), The Goddess, Happy Anniversary, The 4-D Man, The Miracle Worker (Acad. Award, best supp. actress, 1962), Billie, Valley of the Dolls, Me Natalie, The Swarm, Something Special, Prelude to a Kiss.
TELEVISION: Series regular: The Brighter Day (1957), Patty Duke Show (1963–66), It Takes Two (1982–83), Hail to the Chief (1985), Karen's Song. Episodes: Armstrong Circle Theatre (1955), The SS Andrea Doria, U.S. Steel Hour (1959), All's Fair (1982). Specials: The Prince and the Pauper, Wuthering Heights, Swiss Family Robinson, Meet Me in St. Louis, The Power and the Glory. Movies: My Sweet Charlie (Emmy Award, 1970), Two on a Bench, If Tomorrow Comes, She Waits, Deadly Harvest, Nightmare, Look What's Happened to Rosemary's Baby, Fire!, Rosetti & Ryan: Men Who Love Women, Curse of the Black Widow, Killer on Board, The Storyteller, Having Babies III, A Family Upside Down, Women in White, Hanging by a Thread, Before and After, The Miracle Worker (Emmy Award, 1980), The Women's Room, Mom The Wolfman and Me, The Babysitter, Violation of Sarah McDavid, Something So Right, September Gun, Best Kept Secrets, Fight for Life, Perry Mason: The Case of the Avenging Angel, A Time to Triumph, Fatal Judgment, Everybody's Baby: The Rescue of Jessica McClure, Amityville: The Evil Escapes, Call Me Anna, Always Remember I Love You, Absolute Strangers, Last Wish, Grave Secrets: The Legacy of Hilltop Drive, A Killer Among Friends, Family of Strangers. Mini-Series: Captains and the Kings (Emmy Award, 1977), George Washington. Host: Fatal Passions.

DUKES, DAVID: Actor. b. San Francisco, CA, June 6, 1945. On Bdwy. in Don Juan, The Great God Brown, Chemin de Fer, The Visit, Holiday, School for Wives, The Play's the Thing, Love for Love, Rules of the Game, Dracula, Travesties, Frankenstein, Bent, Amadeus, M. Butterfly, Love Letters. Someone Who'll Watch Over Me.
PICTURES: The Strawberry Statement, The Wild Party, A Little Romance, The First Deadly Sin, Only When I Laugh, Without a Trace, The Men's Club, Catch the Heat, Rawhead Rex, Date With an Angel, Deadly Intent, See You in the Morning, The Handmaid's Tale.
TELEVISION: Series: Beacon Hill, All That Glitters, Sisters. Mini-Series: 79 Park Avenue, Space, George Washington, The Winds of War, War and Remembrance, Kane & Abel. Specials: Strange Interlude, Cat on a Hot Tin Roof. Movies: Go West Yound Girl, A Fire in the Sky, Some Kind of Miracle,

The Triangle Factory Fire Scandal, Mayflower—The Pilgrim Adventure, Margaret Sanger—Portrait of a Rebel, Miss All-American Beauty, Sentimental Journey, Turn Back the Clock, Held Hostage: The Sis and Jerry Levin Story, The Josephine Baker Story, Wife Mother Murderer, She Woke Up, Look at It This Way, Spies. *Guest*: All in the Family.

DULLEA, KEIR: Actor. b. Cleveland, OH, May 30, 1936. e. Rutgers Univ., San Francisco State Coll., Sanford Meisner's Neighborhood Playhouse. Worked as ice cream vendor, carpenter with a construction co. Acted as resident juvenile at the Totem Pole Playhouse in PA. N.Y. theatre debut in the revue Sticks and Stones, 1956; appeared in stock co. prods. at the Berkshire Playhouse and Philadelphia's Hedgerow Theatre, 1959, off-Broadway debut in Season of Choice, 1969.
THEATER: Dr. Cook's Garden, Butterflies Are Free, Cat on a Hot Tin Roof, P.S. Your Cat is Dead, The Other Side of Paradise.
TELEVISION: *Movies*: Black Water Gold, Law and Order, Legend of the Golden Gun, Brave New World, The Hostage Tower, No Place to Hide.
PICTURES: The Hoodlum Priest (debut, 1961), David and Lisa (Best Actor Award, S.F. Int'l Film Fest.), The Thin Red Line, Mail Order Bride, Bunny Lake Is Missing, Madame X, The Fox, 2001: A Space Odyssey, de Sade, Pope Joan, The Paperback Hero, Paul and Michelle, Black Christmas, Leopard in the Snow, Welcome to Blood City, The Haunting of Julia, The Next One, Brainwaves, Blind Date, 2010.

DUNAWAY, FAYE: Actress. b. Bascom, FL, Jan. 14, 1941. e. Texas, Arkansas, Utah, Germany, U. of Florida. Awarded a Fulbright scholarship in theatre. Boston U. of Fine Applied Arts. Appeared on N.Y. stage in: A Man for All Seasons, After the Fall (with Lincoln Center Repertory Co., three years), Hogan's Goat (Theatre World Award).
PICTURES: Hurry Sundown (debut, 1967), The Happening, Bonnie and Clyde, The Thomas Crown Affair, The Extraordinary Seaman, A Place for Lovers, The Arrangement, Puzzle of a Downfall Child, Little Big Man, The Deadly Trap, Doc, Oklahoma Crude, The Three Musketeers, Chinatown, The Towering Inferno, The Four Musketeers, Three Days of the Condor, Network (Acad. Award, 1976), Voyage of the Damned, Eyes of Laura Mars, The Champ, The First Deadly Sin, Mommie Dearest, The Wicked Lady, Ordeal by Innocence, Supergirl, Barfly, Midnight Crossing, Burning Secret, The Handmaid's Tale, Wait Until Spring Bandini, The Gamble, On a Moonlit Night, Scorchers, Double Edge, Arizona Dream, The Temp, Even Cowgirls Get the Blues.
TELEVISION: *Movies*: The Woman I Love, The Disappearance of Aimee, Evita, Peron, 13 at Dinner, Beverly Hills Madam, The Country Girl, Casanova, The Raspberry Ripple, Cold Sassy Tree, Silhouette. *Mini-Series*: Ellis Island, Christopher Columbus. *Specials*: Hogan's Goat, After the Fall. Series: It Had to Be You.

DUNCAN, LINDSAY: Actress. Stage actress with National Theatre, Royal Shakespeare Company.
THEATRE: Plenty, The Provok'd Wife, The Prince of Homburg, Top Girls, Progress, The Merry Wives of Windsor, Les Liaisons Dangereuses (RSC, West End, Broadway; Theatre World Award).
PICTURES: Loose Connections, Samson & Delilah, Prick Up Your Ears, Muck and Brass, Manifesto, The Reflecting Skin, Body Parts.
TELEVISION: Reilly, Ace of Spies, Dead Head (serial), Traffik, A Year in Provence.

DUNCAN, SANDY: Actress. b. Henderson, TX, Feb. 20, 1946. m. singer-dancer Don Correia. e. Len Morris Coll.
THEATER: The Music Man (NY debut, 1965); The Boyfriend, Ceremony of Innocence (Theatre World Award), Your Own Thing, Canterbury Tales, Peter Pan, Five Six Seven Eight Dance!, My One and Only.
PICTURES: $1,000,000 Duck, Star Spangled Girl, The Cat from Outer Space, Rock a Doodle (voice).
TELEVISION: *Series*: Funny Face (1971), The Sandy Duncan Show, Valerie's Family (later called Hogan Family). *Movies*: My Boyfriend's Back, Miracle on Interstate 880. *Mini-Series*: Roots. *Specials*: Pinocchio, Sandy in Disneyland, The Sandy Duncan Special.

DUNING, GEORGE: Composer, Conductor, Arranger. b. Richmond, IN, Feb. 25, 1908. e. Cincinnati Conservatory of Music, U. of Cincinnati. Musical director; music scores for many m.p. including: Jolson Sings Again, Eddy Duchin Story, From Here to Eternity, Picnic, World of Susie Wong, Devil at 4 O'Clock, Toys in the Attic, Any Wednesday, The Man with Bogart's Face. TV: No Time for Sergeants, Wendy and Me, The Farmer's Daughter, Big Valley, The Long Hot Summer, The Second Hundred Years, Star Trek, Mannix, Then Came Bronson; music dir. Aaron Spelling Prods., 1970–71, Bobby Sherman Show, Movies of the Week. Board of Directors, ASCAP.

DUNLAP, RICHARD D.: Producer, Director. b. Pomona, CA, Jan. 30, 1923. e. Yale U., B.A., 1944; M.F.A., 1948. U.S. Navy 1943–46; Instructor, English dept., Yale U., 1947–48; Prod.-dir., Kraft TV Theatre, 3 years; Dir, Assoc. Prod., Omnibus, 3 seasons; Dir., 25 half-hr. Dramatic Film Shows. Frank Sinatra Specials, Prod.-Dir., 11 Academy Award Shows, 4 Emmy Award Shows.

DUNNE, DOMINICK: Producer. Writer. Father of actor-prod. Griffin Dunne. Began career as stage manager at NBC-TV; then produced shows for CBS Studio One. Later exec. prod. at 20th-Fox TV, v.p. at Four Star. Novels: The Winners, The Two Mrs. Grenvilles, People Like Us, An Inconvenient Woman. Also: Fatal Charms, The Mansions of Limbo.
PICTURES: Boys in the Band (exec. prod.), The Panic in Needle Park, Play It as It Lays, Ash Wednesday.

DUNNE, GRIFFIN: Actor, Producer. b. New York, NY, June 8, 1955. Son of prod.-writer Dominick Dunne. m. actress Carey Lowell. Formed Double Play Prods. with Amy Robinson. Studied at Neighborhood Playhouse and with Uta Hagen. On Stage in Album, Marie and Bruce, Coming Attractions, Hotel Play, Search and Destroy (Theatre World Award).
PICTURES: *Actor*: The Other Side of the Mountain (debut, 1975), Head Over Heels (also prod.), The Fan, American Werewolf in London, Cold Feet, Almost You, Johnny Dangerously, After Hours (also co-prod.), Who's That Girl, Amazon Women on the Moon, Big Blue, Me and Him, Once Around (also co-prod.), My Girl, Straight Talk, Big Girls Don't Cry . . . They Get Even, The Pickle. *Producer only*: Baby It's You, Running on Empty, White Palace.
TELEVISION: *Movies*: The Wall, Secret Weapon. *Specials*: Lip Service, Trying Times: Hunger Chic. *Pilot*: Graham.

DURNING, CHARLES: Actor. b. Highland Falls, NY, Feb. 28, 1933.
PICTURES: Harvey Middleman–Fireman (debut, 1965), I Walk the Line, Hi Mom!, Pursuit of Happiness, Dealing, Deadhead Miles, Sisters, The Sting, The Front Page, Dog Day Afternoon, The Hindenburg, Breakheart Pass, Harry and Walter Go to New York, Twilight's Last Gleaming, The Choirboys, Enemy of the People, The Fury, The Greek Tycoon, Tilt, The Muppet Movie, North Dallas Forty, Starting Over, When a Stranger Calls, Die Laughing, The Final Countdown, True Confessions, Sharky's Machine, The Best Little Whorehouse in Texas (Acad. Award nom.), Tootsie, To Be or Not to Be (Acad. Award nom.), Two of a Kind, Hadley's Rebellion, Mass Appeal, Stick, The Man with One Red Shoe, Big Trouble, Stand Alone, Tough Guys, Where the River Runs Black, Solarbabies, Happy New Year, The Rosary Murders, A Tiger's Tail, Cop, Far North, Dick Tracy, V. I. Warshawski, Brenda Starr, Etolie, Cat Chaser, Fatal Sky, The Music of Chance, The Hudsucker Proxy.
TELEVISION: *Series*: Another World (1972), Cop and the Kid, Evening Shade. *Mini-Series*: Captains and the Kings, The Kennedys of Massachusetts. *Specials*: The Rivalry, The Dancing Bear, Working, Mr. Roberts, Side by Side (pilot), P.O.P. (pilot), Eye to Eye, Tales from Hollywood. *Movies*: The Connection, The Trial of Chaplain Jensen, Queen of the Stardust Ballroom, Switch, Special Olympics, Attica, Perfect Match, Crisis at Central High, Best Little Girl in the World, Dark Night of the Scarecrow, Death of a Salesman, Kenny Rogers as The Gambler III—The Legend Continues, The Man Who Broke 1000 Chains, Case Closed, Unholy Matrimony, Pime Target, It Nearly Wasn't Christmas, Dinner at Eight, The Return of Eliot Ness, The Story Lady, The Water Engine.
THEATRE: That Championship Season, Knock Knock, Au Pair Man, In the Boom Boom Room, The Happy Time, Indians, Cat on a Hot Tin Roof (Tony Award), Queen of the Stardust Ballroom.

DURSTON, DAVID E.: Writer, Director. b. Newcastle, PA, Sept. 10, 1925. e. Evanston Township H.S. Served as TV-radio director, Lynn Baker Adv. Agency, 1952–57; assoc. producer, Your Hit Parade, 1957–58. Acting credits include Winged Victory (Bdwy, film), Young Man's Fancy (B'way); Radio includes The Woolworth Hour (prod.), CBS Workshop (writer).
PICTURES: Felicia, Love Statue, Reflections, Blue Sextet (also edited), I Drink Your Blood, Stigma, Molokai, Savages Apprentice.
TELEVISION: as writer: Tales of Tomorrow, Navy Log, Hart to Hart, Ladies Man, The New Adventures of Flipper (story editor), Tournament of Roses Parade (exec. prod., 1954 & 55).

DURWOOD, RICHARD M.: Executive. b. Kansas City, MO, Aug. 18, 1929. e. Brown U., A.B. Pres. Crown Cinema Corp.
MEMBER: Motion Picture Assn. of Kansas City (pres.); United Motion Pictures Assn. (pres. 1972–73); Young NATO (chmn., 1968–69); Past Chief Barker, Tent #8; Past mem., exec. comm., National NATO.

DURWOOD, STANLEY H.: Chairman of the Board, American Multi-Cinema, Inc. b. 1920; e. Harvard Coll., B.S. (football, wrestling). Air Force navigator 3 years. Member: Harvard

Club of Kansas City; Harvard Club of New York. On board of United Missouri Bankshares.

DUSSAULT, NANCY: Actress. b. Pensacola, FL, Jun. 30, 1936. e. Northwestern U. On Bdwy. in Street Scene, The Mikado, The Cradle Will Rock, Do Re Mi (Theatre World Award), Sound of Music, Carousel, Fiorello, The Gershwin Years, Into the Woods. *L.A. stage*: Next in Line.
 PICTURE: The In-Laws.
 TELEVISION: *Special*: The Beggars Opera. *Host*: Good Morning America. *Series*: The New Dick Van Dyke Show, Too Close for Comfort (The Ted Knight Show).

DUTFIELD, RAY: Executive. b. March 18, 1924. Early career as chief accountant in Hawker Siddeley Group. Ent. m.p. ind. 1957, as exec. accountant with Rank Film Laboratories, gen. man., 1967; Appt. to board of dir., 1969; Appt. man. dir., 1970. Appt. man. dir., Rank Leisure Services, 1976 and vice-chmn., Rank Film Laboratories. 1979 January appt. chmn. and chief executive officer, Technicolor Limited, Fellow Member of Inst. Chartered Accounts, SMPTE, BKSTS, Member Institute of Directors, Institute of Marketing. Chairman, Technicolor U.K.

DUTTON, CHARLES S.: Actor. b. Baltimore, MD, Jan. 30, 1951. e. Towson St., Yale Sch. of Drama.
 TELEVISION: *Series*: Miami Vice, The Equalizer, Cagney and Lacey. *Movies*: Apology, The Murder of Mary Phagan. *Special*: Runaway.
 PICTURES: No Mercy, Crocodile Dundee II, Jacknife, An Unremarkable Life, Q & A, Mississippi Masala, Alien³, The Distinguished Gentleman, Menace II Society.
 THEATRE: *Yale Rep*: The Works, Beef No Chicken, Astopovo, Othello. *NY*: Ma Rainey's Black Bottom (Theatre World Award, 1983), Joe Turner's Come and Gone, The Piano Lesson.

DUVALL, ROBERT: Actor. b. San Diego, CA, Jan. 5, 1931. e. Principia College, IL. Studied at the Neighborhood Playhouse, NY.
 THEATER: *Off-Bdwy*: The Days and Nights of Bee Bee Fenstermaker, Call Me By My Rightful Name, A View From the Bridge (Obie Award, 1965). *Bdwy*: Wait Until Dark, American Buffalo.
 PICTURES: To Kill a Mockingbird (debut, 1962), Captain Newman M.D., Nightmare in the Sun, The Chase, Countdown, The Detective, Bullitt, True Grit, The Rain People, M·A·S·H, The Revolutionary, THX-1138, Lawman, The Godfather, Tomorrow, The Great Northfield Minnesota Raid, Joe Kidd, Lady Ice, Badge 373, The Outfit, The Conversation, Godfather Part II, Breakout, The Killer Elite, The Seven Percent Solution, Network, We're Not the Jet Set (dir., co-prod. only), The Eagle Has Landed, The Greatest, The Betsy, Invasion of the Body Snatchers (cameo), Apocalypse Now, The Great Santini, True Confessions, The Pursuit of D.B. Cooper, Tender Mercies (Acad. Award, 1983; also co-prod., songwriter), Angelo, My Love (dir., prod., s.p. only), The Stone Boy, The Natural, Bellizaire the Cajun (cameo; also creative consultant), The Lightship, Let's Get Harry, Hotel Colonial, Colors, The Handmaid's Tale, A Show of Force, Days of Thunder, Rambling Rose, Convicts, Newsies, Falling Down, The Plague, Wrestling Ernest Hemingway, Geronimo, The Paper.
 TELEVISION: *Movies*: Fame is the Name of the Game, The Terry Fox Story, Stalin. *Mini-Series*: Ike, Lonesome Dove. *Guest*: Great Ghost Tales, The Outer Limits, Naked City, Route 66, The Defenders, Alfred Hitchcock Presents, Twilight Zone, Combat, Wild Wild West, The FBI, Mod Squad.

DUVALL, SHELLEY: Actress, Producer. b. Houston, TX, July 7, 1949. Founded Think Entertainment, TV prod. co. Appeared in 1984 short film Frankenweenie.
 PICTURES: Brewster McCloud (debut, 1970), McCabe and Mrs. Miller, Thieves Like Us, Nashville, Buffalo Bill and the Indians, Three Women (best actress, Cannes Fest., 1977), Annie Hall, The Shining, Popeye, Time Bandits, Roxanne, Suburban Commando.
 TELEVISION: *Actress*: Bernice Bobs Her Hair, Lily, Twilight Zone, Mother Goose Rock 'n' Rhyme, Faerie Tale Theatre (Rumpelstiltskin, Rapunzel), Tall Tales and Legends (Darlin' Clementine). *Exec. Producer*: Faerie Tale Theatre, Tall Tales and Legends, Nightmare Classics, Dinner at Eight (movie), Mother Goose Rock 'n' Rhyme, Stories from Growing Up, Backfield in Motion (movie), Bedtime Stories.

DYSART, RICHARD A.: Actor. b. Brighton, MA, Mar. 30, 1929. e. Emerson Coll., B.S., M.S. Off-Bdwy. in The Quare Fellow, Our Town, Epitaph for George Dillon, Six Characters in Search of an Author, on Bdwy in A Man for All Seasons, All in Good Time, The Little Foxes, A Place without Doors, That Championship Season, Another Part of the Forest.
 PICTURES: Petulia, The Lost Man, The Sporting Club, The Hospital, The Terminal Man, The Crazy World of Julius Vrooder, The Day of the Locust, The Hindenberg, Prophecy, Meteor, Being There, An Enemy of the People, The Thing, The Falcon and the Snowman, Mask, Warning Signs, Pale Rider, Riding with Death, Wall Street, Back to the Future Part III.

TELEVISION: *Movies*: The Autobiography of Miss Jane Pittman, Gemini Man, It Happened One Christmas, First You Cry, Bogie, The Ordeal of Dr. Mudd, Churchill and the Generals (BBC), People Vs. Jean Harris, Bitter Harvest, Missing Last Days of Patton, Children—A Mother's Story, Malice in Wonderland, Day One, Bobby and Marilyn: Her Final Affair. *Special*: Sandburg's Lincoln, Jay Leno's Family Comedy Hour, Concealed Enemies (PBS), Charlie Smith and the Fritter Tree (PBS), Moving Target. *Mini-Series*: War and Remembrance. *Series*: L.A. Law (Emmy Award, 1992).

DZUNDZA, GEORGE: Actor. b. Rosenheim, Germany, 1945. Spent part of childhood in displaced-persons camps before he was moved to Amsterdam in 1949. Came to NY in 1956 where he attended St. John's U. as speech and theater major.
 THEATER: King Lear (NY Shakespeare Fest., debut, 1973), That Championship Season (tour, 1973), Mert and Phil, The Ritz, Legend, A Prayer for My Daughter.
 PICTURES: The Happy Hooker (1975), The Deer Hunter, Honky Tonk Freeway, Streamers, Best Defense, No Mercy, No Way Out, The Beast, Impulse, White Hunter Black Heart, The Butcher's Wife, Basic Instinct.
 TELEVISION: *Guest*: Starsky and Hutch, The Waltons. *Series*: Open All Night, Law and Order. *Movies*: The Defection of Simas Kudirka, Salem's Lot, Skokie, A Long Way Home, The Face of Rage, The Last Honor of Kathryn Beck, When She Says No, The Rape of Richard Beck, Brotherly Love, The Execution of Raymond Graham, Something is Out There, The Ryan White Story, Terror on Highway 91, What She Doesn't Know.

E

EASTWOOD, CLINT: Actor, Producer, Director. b. San Francisco, CA, May 31, 1930; e. Oakland Technical H.S., Los Angeles City Coll. Worked as a lumberjack in Oregon before being drafted into the Army, Special Services 1950–54. Then contract player at Universal Studios. Starred in TV series Rawhide, 1958–65. Formed Malpaso Productions, 1969. Made á Chevalier des Lettres by French gov., 1985. Mayor, Carmel, CA 1986–88. Best Director for Bird: Hollywood Foreign Press Assoc., Orson Award.
 PICTURES: Revenge of the Creature (debut, 1955), Francis in the Navy, Lady Godiva, Tarantula, Never Say Goodbye, Away All Boats, The First Traveling Saleslady, Star in the Dust, Escapade in Japan, Ambush at Cimarron Pass, Lafayette Escadrille, A Fistful of Dollars, For a Few Dollars More, The Witches, The Good The Bad and The Ugly, Hang 'Em High, Coogan's Bluff, Where Eagles Dare, Paint Your Wagon, Kelly's Heroes, Two Mules For Sister Sara, Beguiled, Play Misty For Me (also dir.), Dirty Harry, Joe Kidd, Breezy (dir. only), High Plains Drifter (also dir.), Magnum Force, Thunderbolt & Lightfoot, The Eiger Sanction (also dir.), The Outlaw Josey Wales (also dir.), The Enforcer, The Gauntlet (also dir.), Every Which Way But Loose, Escape from Alcatraz, Bronco Billy (also dir.), Any Which Way You Can, Firefox (also dir., prod.), Honky Tonk Man (also dir., prod.), Sudden Impact (also dir., prod.), Tightrope (also prod.), City Heat, Pale Rider (also dir., prod.), Heartbreak Ridge (also dir., prod.), The Dead Pool (also dir., prod.), Bird (dir. only), Thelonius Monk: Straight, No Chaser (exec. prod. only), Pink Cadillac, White Hunter Black Heart (also dir., prod.), The Rookie (also dir.), Unforgiven (also dir., prod.; Acad. Awards for Best Picture & Director; L.A. Film Critics Awards for Best Actor, Director & Picture; Natl. Society of Film Critics Awards for Best Director & Picture; Golden Globe Award for Best Director; DGA Award, 1992), In the Line of Fire, A Perfect World (also dir.).
 TELEVISION: *Series*: Rawhide. *Specials*: Fame Fortune and Romance, Happy Birthday Hollywood, Clint Eastwood: The Man From Malpaso. *Dir.*: Amazing Stories (Vanessa in the Garden). *Guest*: Navy Log, Maverick, Mr. Ed, Danny Kaye Show.

EBERTS, JOHN DAVID (JAKE): Producer, Financier. b. Montreal, Canada, July 10, 1941. e. McGill Univ., Harvard. President Goldcrest, founder & CEO 1976–83, 85–6; 1984 joined Embassy Communications Intl. 1985 founded and chief exec. of Allied Filmmakers. Film Prods. Award of Merit 1986; Evening Standard Special Award 1987. Publication: My Indecision is Final (1990).
 PICTURES: Chariots of Fire, Gandhi, Another Country, Local Hero, The Dresser, Cal, The Emerald Forest, The Name of the Rose, Hope and Glory, Cry Freedom, The Adventures of Baron Munchausen, Driving Miss Daisy, Dances With Wolves, Black Robe, Get Back, City of Joy, A River Runs Through It, Super Mario Bros., The Penal Colony.

EBSEN, BUDDY: Actor. r.n. Christian Ebsen, Jr. b. Belleville, IL, April 2, 1908. e. U. of Florida, Rollins Coll. Won first Broadway role as dancer in Ziegfeld's Whoopee in 1928. Sister, Vilma, became dancing partner and they played nightclubs and did road tours. Went to Hollywood and appeared in Broadway Melody of 1936 with Vilma then in many musicals as single. Later became dramatic actor and appeared on TV.

PICTURES: Broadway Melody of 1936, Born to Dance, Captain January, Banjo on My Knee, Yellow Jack, Girl of the Golden West, My Lucky Star, Broadway Melody of 1938, Four Girls in White, Parachute Battalion, They Met in Argentina, Sing Your Worries Away, Thunder in God's Country, Night People, Red Garters, Davy Crockett, Between Heaven and Hell, Attack, Breakfast at Tiffany's, The Interns, Mail Order Bride, The One and Only Genuine Original Family Band.

TELEVISION: Series: Davy Crockett, Northwest Passage, The Beverly Hillbillies, Barnaby Jones, Matt Houston. Guest: Hawaii Five-O, Gunsmoke. Movies: Stone Fox, The Daughters of Joshua Cabe, Horror at 37000 Feet, Smash-Up on Interstate 5, The President's Plane is Missing, Leave Yesterday Behind, The Paradise Connection, Fire on the Mountain, The Return of the Beverly Hillbillies, The Bastard, Tom Sawyer, Stone Fox, Working Trash. Special: The Legend of the Beverly Hillbillies.

STAGE: Flying Colors, Yokel Boy, The Male Animal, Ziegfeld Follies, Take Her She's Mine, Our Town, The Best Man.

EBY, GEORGE W.: Executive. b. Pittsburgh, PA, Jan. 2, 1914. e. Carnegie Tech., Pennsylvania State U., B.A. 1934. pres., Ice Capades, Inc., 1963–76, chmn., Jan. 1, 1979; Int. Chief Barker Variety Clubs, 1958–60. Retired, 1983.

ECKERT, JOHN M.: Producer, Production Executive. b. Chatham, Ontario, Canada, e. Ryerson Polytechnical Inst., 1968–71 (film major). 12 features as unit prod. mgr. or asst. dir. Member: DGA, DGC.

PICTURES: Power Play (assoc. prod.), Running (co-prod.), Middle Age Crazy (co-prod.), Dead Zone (unit prod. mgr.), Cats Eye (exec. in charge of prod.), Silver Bullet (assoc. prod.), Home Is Where the Heart Is (prod.), Millenium (suprv. prod.), Deep Sleep (prod.), Car 54 Where Are You? (s.p. prod.).

TELEVISION: Terry Fox Story (assoc. prod.), Special People (prod., Christopher Award), Danger Bay (series supv. prod., 1985–87).

EDDINGTON, PAUL: C.B.E., 1987. Actor. b. London, Eng., June 18, 1927. Since 1944 extensive career on stage. Ent. TV ind. 1955. Numerous television plays and series incl: Quartet, Blithe Spirit, Outside Edge, Murder at the Vicarage, The Adventures of Robin Hood, Fall of Eagles, The Rivals of Sherlock Holmes, Danger Man, The Prisoner, The Avengers, Van der Valk, Frontier, Special Branch, The Good Life, Yes Minister, Yes Prime Minister, The Camomile Lawn.

PICTURES: The Man Who Was Nobody, Jet Storm, The Devil's Brigade, Baxter.

EDELMAN, HERB: Actor. b. Brooklyn, NY, Nov. 5, 1930.

PICTURES: In Like Flint, Barefoot in the Park, The Odd Couple, I Love You Alice B. Toklas, P.J., The War Between Men and Women, The Way We Were, The Front Page, The Yakuza, Goin' Coconuts, California Suite, On the Right Track, Smorgasbord.

TELEVISION: Series: The Good Guys, Ladies' Man, Strike Force, 9 to 5, The Golden Girls, Knots Landing. Movies: In Name Only, The Feminist and the Fuzz, The Neon Ceiling, Banyon (pilot), Once Upon a Dead Man, The Strange and Deadly Occurance, Crossfire, Picking Up the Pieces, Marathon. Guest: Flying Nun, That Girl, Love American Style, Bewitched, Ironside, Partridge Family, Mission Impossible, Maude, Barney Miller, Kojak, Cagney and Lacey, Love Boat, St. Elsewhere, thirtysomething.

EDEN, BARBARA: Actress. b. Tucson, AZ, Aug. 23, 1934. r.n. Barbara Jean Huffman. e. San Francisco Conservatory of Music. Pres. Mi-Bar Productions. Dir. Security National Bank of Chicago.

PICTURES: Back from Eternity (debut, 1956), The Wayward Girl, A Private's Affair, From the Terrace, Twelve Hours to Kill, Flaming Star, All Hands on Deck, Voyage to the Bottom of the Sea, Five Weeks in a Balloon, The Interns, Swingin' Along (Double Trouble), The Wonderful World of the Brothers Grimm, The Yellow Canary, The Brass Bottle, The New Interns, Ride the Wild Surf, 7 Faces of Dr. Lao, Quick Let's Get Married, The Amazing Dobermans, Harper Valley PTA, Chattanooga Choo Choo.

TELEVISION: Series: How to Marry a Millionaire, I Dream of Jeannie, Harper Valley P.T.A., A Brand New Life, Dallas. Movies: The Feminist and the Fuzz, A Howling in the Woods, The Woman Hunter, Guess Who's Sleeping in My Bed, The Stranger Within, Let's Switch, How to Break Up a Happy Divorce, Stonestreet: Who Killed the Centerfold Model?, The Girls in the Office, Condominium, Return of the Rebels, I Dream of Jeannie: 15 Years Later, The Stepford Children, The Secret Life of Kathy McCormick (also co-prod.), Your Mother Wears Combat Boots, Opposites Attract, Her Wicked Ways, Hell Hath No Fury, I Still Dream of Jeannie, Visions of Murder.

EDWARDS, ANTHONY: Actor. b. Santa Barbara, CA, July 19, 1962. Grandfather designed Walt Disney Studios in the 1930s and worked for Cecil B. De Mille as conceptual artist. Acted in 30 plays from age 12 to 17. At 16 worked professionally in TV commercials. 1980 attended Royal Acad. of Arts, London. and studied drama at USC. On NY stage 1993 in Ten Below.

PICTURES: Fast Times at Ridgemont High (debut, 1982), Heart Like a Wheel, Revenge of the Nerds, The Sure Thing, Gotcha, Top Gun, Summer Heat, Revenge of the Nerds II (cameo), Mr. North, Miracle Mile, How I Got Into College, Hawks, Downtown, Delta Heat, Pet Sematary II.

TELEVISION: Series: It Takes Two, Northern Exposure. Movies: The Killing of Randy Webster, High School U.S.A., The Bill Johnson Story, El Diablo, Hometown Boy Makes Good. Specials: Unpublished Letters, Sexual Healing.

EDWARDS, BLAKE: Writer, Director, Producer. r.n. William Blake McEdwards. b. Tulsa, OK, July 26, 1922. m. actress Julie Andrews. e. Beverly Hills H.S. Coast Guard during war. Film acting debut, Ten Gentlemen from West Point (1942).

RADIO: Johnny Dollar, Line-up; writer-creator: Richard Diamond.

PICTURES: Writer only: Panhandle, Stampede, Sound Off, All Ashore, Cruising Down the River, Rainbow Round My Shoulder, Drive a Crooked Road, The Atomic Kid (story), My Sister Eileen, Operation Mad Ball, Notorious Landlady, Soldier in the Rain. Producer only: Waterhole #3. Director: Bring Your Smile Along (also s.p.), He Laughed Last (also s.p.), Mister Cory (also s.p.), This Happy Feeling (also s.p.), The Perfect Furlough (also s.p.), Operation Petticoat, High Time, Breakfast at Tiffany's, Experiment in Terror, Days of Wine and Roses, The Pink Panther (also s.p.), A Shot in the Dark (also s.p., prod.), The Great Race (also s.p., prod.), What Did You Do in the War Daddy? (also s.p., prod.), Gunn (also prod.), The Party (also s.p., prod.), Darling Lili (also s.p., prod.), Wild Rovers (also s.p., prod.), The Carey Treatment (also s.p., prod.), The Tamarind Seed (also s.p.), The Return of the Pink Panther (also s.p., prod.), The Pink Panther Strikes Again (also s.p., prod.), Revenge of the Pink Panther (also s.p., prod.), "10" (also co-prod., s.p.), S.O.B. (also co-prod., s.p.), Victor/Victoria (also co-prod., s.p.), Trail of the Pink Panther (also co-prod., co-s.p.), The Curse of the Pink Panther (also co-prod., s.p.), The Man Who Loved Women (also prod., co-s.p.), Micki and Maude, A Fine Mess (also s.p.), That's Life (also co-prod.), Blind Date, Sunset (also s.p.), Skin Deep (also s.p.), Switch (also s.p.), Son of the Pink Panther (also s.p.).

TELEVISION: City Detective (prod., 1953), The Dick Powell Show (dir.), Creator: Dante's Inferno, Mr. Lucky, Justin Case (exec. prod., dir., writer), Peter Gunn (exec. prod., dir., writer), Julie (exec. prod., dir.). Specials: Julie! (prod., dir.), Julie on Sesame St. (exec. prod.), Julie and Dick in Covent Garden (dir.).

EDWARDS, JAMES H.: Executive. President, Storey Theatres, Inc. b. Cedartown, GA, Aug. 14, 1927. e. Georgia State. U.S. Navy, 1948–50. With Ga. Theatre Co., 1950–1952; Storey Theatres, 1952–present. Formerly pres. & chmn., NATO of Ga; formerly pres., Variety Club of Atlanta. Former dir. at large, Nat'l. NATO. Director, numerous theatre cos.

EDWARDS, RALPH: Producer, Emcee. b. Merino, CO, June 13, 1913. e. U. of California, Berkeley. Began career in radio in 1929 as writer-actor-producer-announcer at station KROW, Oakland. Later joined CBS & NBC Radio in New York as announcer. 1940, originated, produced & emceed Truth or Consequences for both radio & TV. Also has produced and hosted This Is Your Life, The Ralph Edwards Show, Name That Tune, Cross Wits, The People's Court, This Is Your Life (special edition, 1987).

EDWARDS, VINCE: Actor. b. New York, NY, July 9, 1928. r.n. Vincent Edward Zoino. e. Ohio State U., U. of Hawaii, American Acad. of Dramatic Arts. N.Y. stage. High Button Shoes.

TELEVISION: Series: Ben Casey, Matt Lincoln. Guest: Studio One, Philco, Kraft, The Untouchables, General Electric Theatre, Hitchcock, The Deputy. Movies: Sole Survivor, Dial Hot Line, Do Not Fold Spindle or Mutilate, Firehouse, Maneater (dir. only), Death Stalk, Cover Girls, Courage and the Passion, Evening in Byzantium, The Dirty Dozen: The Deadly Mission, The Return of Ben Casey, Dilinger. MiniSeries: The Rhinemann Exchange.

PICTURES: Mr. Universe, Sailor Beware, Hiawatha, Rogue Cop, Cell 2455 Death Row, The Night Holds Terror, Serenade, The Killing, Hit and Run, The Scavengers, The Three Faces of Eve, The Hired Gun, Ride Out for Revenge, Island Woman, Murder by Contract, City of Fear, Too Late Blues, The Victors, Devil's Brigade, Hammerhead, The Desperados, The Mad Bomber, The Seduction, Space Raiders, Deal of the Century, Sno-Line, The Fix, Return to Horror High, Cellar Dweller, The Gumshoe Kid, Motorama.

EGGAR, SAMANTHA: Actress. b. London, Eng., March 5, 1939. e. student Webber-Douglas Dramatic Sch., London; Slade Sch. of Art.

PICTURES: The Wild and the Willing, Dr. Crippen, Doctor in Distress, Psyche 59, The Collector, Return From the Ashes, Walk Don't Run, Doctor Dolittle, The Molly Maguires, The Lady in the Car, Walking Stick, The Grove, Light at the Edge of the World, The Dead Are Alive, 7% Solution, The Uncanny, Welcome to Blood City, The Brood, The Exterminator, Demonoid, Why Shoot the Teacher, Curtains, Hot Touch, Loner, Ragin' Cajun, Dark Horse.

TELEVISION: Series: Anna and the King. Movies: Man of Destiny, Double Indemnity, All The Kind Strangers, The Killer Who Wouldn't Die, Ziegfeld: the Man and His Women, The Hope Diamond, Love Among Thieves, A Ghost in Monte Carlo. A Case for Murder. Guest: Columbo, Baretta, The Hemingway Play, Love Story, Kojak, McMillan & Wife, Streets of San Francisco, Starsky and Hutch, Hart to Hart, Murder She Wrote, Finder of Lost Loves, George Burns Comedy Week, Lucas Tanner, Hotel, Fantasy Island, Magnum, Stingray, Tales of the Unexpected, Heartbeat, Love Boat, 1st & Ten, Outlaws.

EICHHORN, LISA: Actress. b. Reading, PA, Feb. 4, 1952. e. Queen's U. Kingston, Canada and Eng. for literature studies at Oxford. Studied at Royal Acad. of Dramatic Art.
THEATER: The Hasty Heart (debut, L.A.). NY: The Common Pursuit, The Summer Winds, The Speed of Darkness, Down the Road.
PICTURES: Yanks, The Europeans, Why Would I Lie?, Cutter and Bone, Weather in the Streets, Wild Rose; Opposing Force, Moon 44, Grim Prairie Tales, The Vanishing, King of the Hill.
TELEVISION: Series: All My Children (1987). Movies: The Wall, Blind Justice, Devlin. Mini-Series: A Woman Named Jackie.

EIKENBERRY, JILL: Actress. b. New Haven, CT, Jan. 21, 1947. e. Yale U. Drama Sch. m. actor Michael Tucker.
THEATER: Broadway: All Over Town, Watch on the Rhine, Onward Victoria, Summer Brave, Moonchildren. Off-Bdwy: Lemon Sky, Life Under Water, Uncommon Women and Others, Porch, The Primary English Class.
PICTURES: Between the Lines, The End of the World in Our Usual Bed in a Night Full of Rain, An Unmarried Woman, Butch and Sundance: The Early Days, Rich Kids, Hide in Plain Sight, Arthur, The Manhattan Project.
TELEVISION: Movies: The Deadliest Season, Orphan Train, Swan Song, Sessions, Kane & Abel, Assault and Matrimony, Family Sins, A Stoning in Fulham County, My Boyfriend's Back, The Diane Martin Story, The Secret Life of Archie's Wife, An Inconvenient Woman, Living a Lie, A Town Torn Apart, Chantilly Lace. Series: L.A. Law, The Best of Families (PBS). Specials: Uncommon Women & Others, Destined to Live (prod., host), A Family Again.

EILBACHER, LISA: Actress. b. Saudi Arabia, May 5. Moved to California at age 7; acted on TV as child.
PICTURES: War Between Men and Women (1972), Run for the Roses (aka Thoroughbred), On the Right Track, An Officer and a Gentleman, Ten to Midnight, Beverly Hills Cop, Deadly Intent, Leviathan, Never Say Die.
TELEVISION: Guest: Wagon Train, Laredo, My Three Sons, Gunsmoke, Combat. Series: The Texas Wheelers, The Hardy Boys Mysteries, Ryan's Four, Me and Mom. Movies: Bad Ronald, Panache, Spider Man, The Ordeal of Patty Hearst, Love for Rent, To Race the Wind, This House Possessed, Monte Carlo, Deadly Deception, Joshua's Heart, Blind Man's Bluff, Deadly Matrimony. Mini-Series: Wheels, The Winds of War.

EISNER, MICHAEL D.: Executive. b. Mt. Kisco, NY, March 7, 1942. e. Denison U., B.A. Started career with programming dept. of CBS TV network. Joined ABC in 1966 as mgr. talent and specials. Dec., 1968 became dir. of program dev., east coast. 1971 named v.p., daytime programming, ABC-TV. 1975 made v.p., prog. planning and dev. 1976 named sr. v.p., prime time production and dev., ABC Entertainment. 1976, left ABC to join Paramount Pictures as pres. & chief operating officer. 1984, joined Walt Disney Prods. as chmn. & CEO.

EKBERG, ANITA: Actress. b. Malmö, Sweden, Sept. 29, 1931. Started career as a model.
PICTURES: Blood Alley, Artists and Models, Man in the Vault, War and Peace, Back from Eternity, Zarak, Pickup Alley, Valerie, Paris Holiday, The Man Inside, Screaming Mimi, Sign of the Gladiator, The Mongols, La Dolce Vita, Boccaccio '70, Call Me Bwana, 4 for Texas, The Alphabet Murders, Way Way Out, Woman Times Seven, The Glass Sphinx, The Cobra, If It's Tuesday This Must Be Belgium, The Clowns, Intervista.
TELEVISION: Movies: Gold of the Amazon Women, S*H*E.

EKLAND, BRITT: Actress. b. Stockholm, Sweden, Sept. 29, 1942.
TELEVISION: England: A Cold Peace. U.S.A.: Guest: Trials of O'Brien, McCloud, Six Million Dollar Man. Movies: Ring of Passion, The Great Wallendas, Valley of the Dolls 1981.

PICTURES: Too Many Thieves, After the Fox, Double Man, The Bobo, Night They Raided Minsky's, At Any Price, Stiletto, Cannibals, Machine Gun McCain, Tintomara, Percy, Get Carter, A Time for Loving, Endless Night, Baxter, Asylum, Ultimate Thrill, Man With the Golden Gun, Wicker Man, Royal Flash, Casanova & Co., High Velocity, Slavers, King Solomon's Treasure, The Monster Club, Fraternity Vacation, Moon in Scorpio, Scandal, Beverly Hills Vamp, The Children.

ELAM, JACK: Actor. b. Miami, AZ, Nov. 13, 1916. e. Santa Monica Jr. Coll., Modesto Jr. Coll. Worked in Los Angeles as bookkeeper and theatre mgr.; civilian employee of Navy in W.W.II; Introduction to show business was as bookkeeper for Sam Goldwyn. Later worked as controller for other film producers. Given first acting job by producer George Templeton in 1948; has since appeared in over 100 films.
PICTURES: Wild Weed (debut, 1949), Rawhide, Kansas City Confidential, The Moonlighter, Vera Cruz, Moonfleet, Kiss Me Deadly, Gunfight at OK Corral, Baby Face Nelson, Edge of Eternity, The Comancheros, The Rare Breed, The Way West, Firecreek, Once Upon a Time in the West, Support Your Local Sheriff, Rio Lobo, Dirty Dingus Magee, Support Your Local Gunfighter, The Wild Country, Hannie Caulder, Last Rebel, Pat Garrett and Billy the Kid, Hawmps, Grayeagle, Hot Lead Cold Feet, The Norsemen, The Villain, Apple Dumpling Gang Rides Again, The Cannonball Run, Jinxed, Cannonball Run II, Big Bad John, Suburban Commando.
TELEVISION: Series: The Dakotas, Temple Houston, The Texas Wheelers, Struck by Lightning, Detective in the House, Easy Street. Movies: The Over-the-Hill Gang, The Daughters of Joshua Cabe, Black Beauty, Once Upon a Texas Train, Where the Hell's That Gold!!!?.

ELEFANTE, TOM: Executive. Began career as usher at Loews Riviera in Coral Gables, FL; progressed through ranks to asst. mgr., mgr. & Florida division mgr. 1972, joined Wometco Theatres as gen. mgr. 1975, returned to Loews Theatres as southeast div. mgr.; 1979, named natl. dir. of concessions, moving to h.o. in New York. 1987, appt. sr. v.p. & gen. mgr., Loews. Served as pres. and chmn. of NATO of Florida. 1990, then pres. of N.A.T.O. of NY.

ELFAND, MARTIN: Executive. b. Los Angeles, CA, 1937. Was talent agent for ten years with top agencies; joined Artists Entertainment Complex in 1972. First film project as producer: Kansas City Bomber, first venture of AEC, of which he was sr. v.p. In 1977 joined Warner Bros. as production chief. 1980.
PICTURES: Prod.: Dog Day Afternoon, It's My Turn, An Officer and a Gentleman, King David, Clara's Heart. Exec. prod.: Her Alibi.

ELFMAN, DANNY: Composer. b. Los Angeles, CA, May 29, 1953. Member of rock band Oingo Boingo, recorded songs for such films as The Tempest, Fast Times at Ridgemont High, 16 Candles, Beverly Hills Cop, Weird Science, Texas Chainsaw Massacre 2, Something Wild. Appeared in Hot Tomorrows, Back to School.
PICTURES: Forbidden Zone, Pee-wee's Big Adventure, Back to School, Wisdom, Summer School, Beetlejuice, Midnight Run, Big-Top Pee-wee, Hot to Trot, Scrooged, Batman, Nightbreed, Dick Tracy, Darkman, Edward Scissorhands, Pure Luck, Article 99, Batman Returns, Sommersby.
TELEVISION: Series: Pee-wee's Playhouse, Sledgehammer, Fast Times, Tales from the Crypt; The Simpsons, The Flash, Beetlejuice, segments of Amazing Stories (Mummy Dearest, Family Dog), Alfred Hitchcock Presents (The Jar).

ELG, TAINA: Actress, Dancer. b. Helsinki, Finland, March 9, 1930. Trained and performed with Natl. Opera of Finland. Attended Sadler's Wells Ballet Sch. Toured with Swedish Dance Theatre, then Marquis de Cuevas Ballet.
PICTURES: The Prodigal (debut, 1955), Diane, Gaby, Les Girls, Watusi, Imitation General, The 39 Steps, The Bacchae, Liebestraum.
TELEVISION: Movie: The Great Wallendas. Mini-Series: Blood and Honor: Youth Under Hitler (narrator). Special: O! Pioneers.
THEATRE: Look to the Lilies, Where's Charley?, The Utter Glory of Morrissey Hall, Strider, Nine.

ELIAS, HAL: Executive. b. Brooklyn, NY, Dec. 23, 1899. Publicity dir., State Theatre, Denver; western exploitation mgr., MGM; adv. dept., pub. dept., MGM, Culver City studios; Head, MGM cartoon studio (Tom and Jerry); UPA Pictures, Inc., vice-pres. studio mgr.: Hollywood Museum; bd. dir., Academy of Motion Picture Arts & Sciences, 35 years; treasurer, AMPAS 1976–1979. Academy Oscar, 1979, for dedicated and distinguished service to AMPAS.

ELIZONDO, HECTOR: Actor. b. New York, NY, Dec. 22, 1936. m. actress Carolee Campbell. Studied with Ballet Arts Co. of

Carnegie Hall and Actors Studio. Many stage credits in N.Y. and Boston.
STAGE: Drums in the Night, The Prisoner of Second Avenue, Dance of Death, Steambath (Obie Award), The Great White Hope, Sly Fox, The Price.
PICTURES: Valdez Is Coming, Born to Win, Pocket Money, Deadhead Miles, Stand Up and Be Counted, The Taking of Pelham One Two Three, Report to the Commissioner, Thieves, Cuba, American Gigolo, The Fan, Young Doctors in Love, The Flamingo Kid, Private Resort, Nothing in Common, Overboard, Beaches, Leviathan, Pretty Woman (Golden Globe nom.), Taking Care of Business, Necessary Roughness, Frankie and Johnny, Final Approach, Samantha, There Goes the Neighborhood.
TELEVISION: Series: Popi (1976), Casablanca, Freebie and the Bean; A.K.A. Pablo (also dir.), Foley Sq, Down and Out in Bevery Hills, Fish Police (voice).Guest: The Wendie Barrie Show (1947), The Impatient Heart, Kojack, the Jackie Gleason Show, All in the Family, The Pirates of Dark Water (voice). Movies: The Impatient Heart, Wanted: The Sundance Woman, Honeyboy, Women of San Quentin, Courage, Out of the Darkness, Addicted to His Love, Your Mother Wears Combat Boots, Forgotten Prisoners: The Amnesty Files, Finding the Way Home, Chains of Gold, The Burden of Proof. Mini-Series: The Dain Curse. Specials: Medal of Honor Rag, Mrs. Cage.

ELKINS, HILLARD: Producer. b. New York, NY, Oct. 18, 1929. e. NYU, B.A., 1951. Exec.; William Morris Agy., 1949–51; exec. v.p., Gen. Artists Corp., 1952–53; pres., Hillard Elkins Mgmt., 1953–60; Elkins Prods. Intl. Corp., 1960–71; Elkins Prods. Ltd., 1972–; Hillard Elkins Entertainment Corp., 1974; Media Mix Prods., Inc., 1979–82.
MEMBER: Academy of Motion Picture Arts & Sciences, Acad. of TV Arts & Sciences, Dramatists Guild, League of New York Theatres, American Fed. of TV & Radio Artists.
PICTURES: Alice's Restaurant, A New Leaf, Oh Calcutta!, A Doll's House, Richard Pryor Live in Concert, Sellers on Sellers.
THEATRE: Come On Strong, Golden Boy, Oh Calcutta!, The Rothschilds, A Doll's House, An Evening with Richard Nixon, Sizwe Banzi Is Dead, etc.
TELEVISION: The Importance of Being Earnest, The Deadly Game, Princess Daisy, The Meeting (exec. prod.), Father & Son: Dangerous Relations.

ELKINS, SAUL: Producer. b. New York, NY, June 22, 1907. e. City Coll. of New York, B.S., 1927. Radio writer, dir., prod. 1930–2; dir., prod. stock co. touring Latin America 1932–4; writer Fox Films, 20th Century-Fox; writer RKO, Columbia 1937–42; writer, dial-dir., dir. Warner Bros. 1943–7; prod. Warner Bros. since 1947. Member: AMPAS, Screen Writer's Guild. Exec. prod., Comprenetics, Inc. Dir., Pioneer Prods., 1982.
PICTURES: Younger Brothers, One Last Fling, Homicide, House Across the Street, Flaxy Martin, Barricade, Return of the Frontiersmen, This Side of the Law, Colt 45, Sugarfoot, Raton Pass, The Big Punch, Smart Girls Don't Talk, Embraceable You.

ELLIOTT, LANG: Producer, Director. b. Los Angeles, CA, Oct. 18, 1949. Began acting in films at an early age, influenced by his uncle, the late actor William Elliott (known as Wild Bill Elliott). Employed by, among others the McGowan Brothers. Turned to film production; co-founded distribution co., The International Picture Show Co., serving as exec. v.p. in chg. of financing, production & distribution. In 1976 formed TriStar Pictures, Inc. to finance and distribute product. In 1980 sold TriStar to Columbia, HBO and CBS. 1982, formed Lang Elliott Productions, Inc. Co-founded Longshot Enterprises with actor Tim Conway to prod. films and home videos, 1985. Videos include Dorf on Golf, 'Scuse Me!, Dorf and the First Olympic Games. Formed Performance Pictures, Inc., in 1989, a prod. & distrib. company.
PICTURES: Prod: Ride the Hot Wind, Where Time Began, The Farmer, The Billion Dollar Hobo, They Went That-a-Way & That-a-Way, The Prize Fighter. Prod.-dir. The Private Eyes, Cage.
TELEVISION: Experiment in Love (prod.), Boys Will Be Boys (writer).

ELLIOTT, SAM: Actor. b. Sacramento, CA, Aug. 9, 1944; m. actress Katharine Ross. e. U. of Oregon.
PICTURES: (Debut, as card player in) Butch Cassidy and the Sundance Kid, The Games, Frogs, Molly and Lawless John, Lifeguard, The Legacy, Mask, Fatal Beauty, Shakedown, Road House, Prancer, Sibling Rivalry, Rush, Gettysburg, Tombstone.
TELEVISION: Movies: The Challenge, Assault on the Wayne, The Blue Knight, I Will Fight No More Forever, The Sacketts, Wild Times, Murder in Texas, Shadow Riders, Travis McGee, A Death in California, The Blue Lightning, Houston: The Legend of Texas, The Quick and the Dead, Conagher (also co-writer). Series: Mission: Impossible (1970–71), The Yellow Rose. Mini-Series: Once and Eagle,

Aspen. Guest: Lancer, The FBI, Gunsmoke, Streets of San Francisco, Hawaii 5-0, Police Woman.

ELWES, CARY: Actor. b. London, England, Oct. 26, 1962. e. Harrow. Studied for stage with Julie Bovasso at Sarah Lawrence, Bronxville, NY.
PICTURES: Another Country (debut 1984), Oxford Blues, The Bride, Lady Jane, The Princess Bride, Glory, Days of Thunder, Leather Jackets, Hot Shots!, Bram Stoker's Dracula, The Crush, Robin Hood: Men in Tights.

ENDERS, ROBERT: Producer, Writer. Began in television, being responsible for 64 hrs. of live programming weekly for industry and govt. as pres. of Robert J. Enders, Inc. In 1961 turned to theatrical prod. and writing. 1973: formed Bowden Prods. with partner Glenda Jackson. Made countless award-winning documentaries for govt. and industry including Dept. of Defense, U.S. Air Force, Civil Defense, Ford Motor Co.
PICTURES: A Thunder of Drums (prod.), The Maltese Bippy (prod.), How Do I Love Thee (prod.), Zig Zag (story), Voices (prod., s.p.), The Maids, (also s.p.), Hedda (prod.), Out of Season (exec. prod.), Conduct Unbecoming (s.p. and prod.), Nasty Habits (prod., s.p.), Stevie (prod., dir.), How to Score a Movie (dir., prod., s.p.), Seeing the Unseen (doc.), The Visit.
TELEVISION: The Best of the Post (prod. of series), Ben Franklin, High Noon (prod., special), Co-prod. of Acad. Award Show, 1968, The Princess and the Goblin (dir., writer, prod.), They Went That-Away (prod.), Strange Interlude (exec. prod., writer).

ENGEL, CHARLES F.: Executive. b. Los Angeles, CA, Aug. 30, 1937. e. Michigan State U., UCLA. Son of writer-producer Samuel G. Engel. Pgm. devel., ABC-TV, 1964–68; v.p. Univ.-TV, 1972; sr. v.p., 1977; exec. v.p., 1980; pres., MCA Pay-TV New Programming, 1981. ACE Award, 1988 for outstanding contribution to cable; v.p. Universal TV, exec. in chg. ABC Mystery Movie, 1989. Sr. v.p. 1992 in chg. Columbo, Murder She Wrote, Seaquest.
TELEVISION: Run a Crooked Mile (exec. prod.), Road Raiders (prod.), ABC Mystery Movie (exec. in chg. of prod.).

ENGELBERG, MORT: Producer. b. Memphis, TN. e. U. of Illinois, U. of Missouri. Taught journalism; worked as reporter for UPI, AP. Worked for US government, including USIA, Peace Corps., Office of Economic Opportunity; President's Task Force on War on Poverty. Left gov. service in 1967 to become film unit publicist, working on three films in Europe: Dirty Dozen, Far From the Madding Crowd, The Comedians. Returned to U.S.; appt. pub. mgr. for United Artists. Sent to Hollywood as asst. to Herb Jaffe, UA head of west coast prod., which post he assumed when Jaffe left. Left to join indep. prod., Ray Stark.
PICTURES: Smokey and the Bandit, Hot Stuff, The Villain, The Hunter, Smokey and the Bandit II, Smokey and the Bandit III, Nobody's Perfekt, The Heavenly Kid, The Big Easy, Maid to Order, Dudes, Three For the Road, Russkies, Pass the Ammo, Trading Hearts, Fright Night Part 2, Rented Lips, Remote Control.

ENGLANDER, MORRIS K.: Executive. b. New York, NY, July 5, 1934. e. Wharton Sch., U. of Pennsylvania. With General Cinema Corp. circuit before joining RKO Century Warner Theatres 1984 as exec. v.p., develp.; later co-vice chmn. of circuit. 1986, sr. real estate advisor, American Multi-Cinema. 1988: v.p. real estate Hoyts Cinemas Corp.; 1990 COO of Hoyts. Pres. & COO of Hoyts. 1991.

ENGLUND, ROBERT: Actor. b. Glendale, CA, June 6, 1949. e. UCLA, RADA. First significant role was in the Cleveland stage production of Godspell, 1971.
PICTURES: Buster and Billie, Hustle, Stay Hungry, Death Trap (Eaten Alive), The Last of the Cowboys, St. Ives, A Star is Born, Big Wednesday, Bloodbrothers, The Fifth Floor, Dead and Buried, Galaxy of Terror, Don't Cry It's Only Thunder, A Nightmare on Elm Street (& Parts II, III, IV, V, VI), Never Too Young to Die, 976-EVIL (dir. only), Phantom of the Opera, The Adventures of Ford Fairlane, Danse Macabre, Eugenie.
TELEVISION: Series: Downtown, V, Freddy's Nightmares, Nightmare Cafe. Specials and Movies: Hobson's Choice, Young Joe: the Forgotten Kennedy, The Ordeal of Patty Hearst, The Courage and the Passion, Mind Over Murder, Thou Shalt Not Kill, The Fighter, Journey's End, Starflight: The Plane That Couldn't Land, I Want to Live, Infidelity. Mini-Series: V, North and South Book II. Host: Horror Hall of Fame.

EPHRON, NORA: Writer, Director. b. New York, NY, May 19, 1941. e. Wellesley Col. Daughter of writers Henry and Phoebe Ephron. m. writer Nicholas Pileggi. Author: Heartburn, Crazy Salad, Scribble Scribble. Appeared in films Crimes and Misdemeanors, Husbands and Wives.
PICTURES: Writer: Silkwood, Heartburn, When Harry Met Sally . . . (also assoc. prod.), Cookie (also exec. prod.), My

Blue Heaven (also exec. prod.), This is My Life (also dir.), Sleepless in Seattle (also dir.).
TELEVISION: *Movie (writer)*: Perfect Gentlemen.

EPSTEIN, JULIUS J: Screenwriter. b. New York, NY, Aug. 22, 1909. e. Pennsylvania State U. Worked as publicist before going to Hollywood where began writing. Had long collaboration with twin brother, Philip G. Epstein. Under contract with Warner Bros. over 17 years.
PICTURES: Casablanca (Acad. Award, 1943), Arsenic and Old Lace, The Man Who Came to Dinner, Four Daughters, Saturday's Children, Mr. Skeffington, My Foolish Heart, Pete n' Tillie, Reuben Reuben (also co-prod.).

EPSTEIN, MEL: Producer. b. Dayton, OH, Mar. 25, 1910; e. Ohio State U. Adv. & edit. depts. on newspapers; entered m.p. ind. as player in 1931; then asst. dir., unit prod. mgr., second unit & shorts dir.; U.S. Army Signal Corps (1st Lt.); apptd Para. prod., 1946. Now retired.
PICTURES: Whispering Smith, Hazard, Copper Canyon, Dear Brat, Branded, The Savage, Alaska Seas, Secret of the Incas.
TELEVISION: Broken Arrow, Men into Space, The Islanders, Asphalt Jungle, Rawhide, Long Hot Summer, The Monroes, Custer, Lancer (pilot), unit mgr. Lancer (series), Medical Center (series).

ERDMAN, RICHARD: Actor, Director. b. Enid, OK, June 1, 1925. e. Hollywood H.S.
PICTURES: *Actor*: Janie, Objective Burma, Time of Your Life, Four Days Leave, The Men, Cry Danger, Jumping Jacks, Happy Time, The Stooge, Stalag 17, The Power and the Prize, Saddle the Wind, Namu The Killer Whale. *Director*: Bleep, The Brothers O'Toole. *Writer-Prod.*: The Hillerman Project.
TELEVISION: Ray Bolger Show, Perry Mason, Police Story, Tab Hunter Show, Alice, Bionic Woman, One Day at a Time, Playhouse of Stars, Twilight Zone, The Lucy Show, Lou Grant, Cheers, Wings. Movie: Jesse. *Director*: The Dick Van Dyke Show, Mooch (special). *Writer-Prod.*: More Than a Scarecrow.

ERICSON, JOHN: Actor. b. Detroit, MI, Sept. 25, 1926. e. American Acad. of Dramatic Arts. Appeared in summer stock; then Stalag 17 on Broadway.
PICTURES: Teresa (debut, 1951), Rhapsody, Student Prince, Green Fire, Bad Day at Black Rock, Treasure of Pancho Villa, The Cruel Tower, Return of Jack Slade, Oregon Passage, Forty Guns, Day of the Bad Man, Pretty Boy Floyd, Under Ten Flags, 7 Faces of Dr. Lao, The Money Jungle, The Destructors, The Bamboo Saucer, Bedknobs and Broomsticks, Crash, The Final Mission, Alien Zone, Slave Queen of Babylon, Project Saucer, Head or Tails, Golden Triangle, Queens Are Wild, Hustler Squad, $10,000 Caper, Operation Atlantis.
TELEVISION: *Series*: Honey West. *Movies*: The Bounty Man, Hog Wild, Hunter's Moon, House on the Rue Riviera, Tenafly. *Mini-Series*: Robert Kennedy and His Times, Space. *Guest*: Marcus Welby, Mannix, Streets of San Francisco, Fantasy Island, Bonanza, Medical Center, Route 66, Murder She Wrote, Police Story, General Hospital, Air Wolf, Gunsmoke, Police Woman, The FBI, One Day at a Time, Magnum P.I.

ERMAN, JOHN: Director. b. Chicago, IL, Aug. 3, 1935. e. U. of California. Debut as TV director, Stoney Burke, 1962.
TELEVISION: *Movies*: Letters From Three Lovers, Green Eyes, Alexander the Other Side of Dawn, Just Me and You, My Old Man, Moviola (This Year's Blonde; Scarlett O'Hara War; The Silent Lovers), The Letter, Eleanor: First Lady of the World, Who Will Love My Children? (Emmy Award, 1983), Another Woman's Child, A Streetcar Named Desire, Right to Kill?, The Atlanta Child Murders, An Early Frost, The Two Mrs. Grenvilles (also sprv. prod.), When the Time Comes, The Attic: The Hiding of Anne Frank (also prod.), David (also sprv. prod.), The Last Best Year (also sprv. prod.), The Last to Go (also prod.), Our Sons, Carolina Skeletons. *Mini-Series*: Roots: The Next Generations (co-dir.), Queen (also co-prod.).
PICTURES: Making It, Ace Eli and Rodger of the Skies, Stella.

ESBIN, JERRY: Executive. b. Brooklyn, NY, 1931. Started in mailroom at Columbia at 17 and worked for co. nearly 25 years. Then joined American Multi Cinema. Joined Paramount Pictures in 1975 as mgr. of branch operations; later named v.p., asst. sls. mgr. In 1980 named v.p., gen. sls. mgr. 1981, sr. v.p., domestic sls. & mktg. 1981, joined United Artists as sr. v.p., mktg. & dist.; 1982, named pres., MGM/UA m.p. dist. & mktg. div; 1983, sr. v.p., domestic dist., Tri-Star Pictures; 1985, promoted to exec. v.p.; 1989, joined Loews Theaters as sr. exec. v.p. and chief oper. officer, also in 1989 named pres. as well as chief operating officer, Loews Theater Management Corp.

ESMOND, CARL: Actor. b. Vienna, Austria, June 14, 1906. e. U. of Vienna. On stage Vienna, Berlin, London (Shakespeare,

Shaw, German modern classics). Acted in many European films under the name Willy Eichberger. Originated part of Prince Albert in Victoria Regina (London). On screen in Brit. prod. incl. Blossom Time, Even Song, Invitation to the Waltz. To U.S. in 1938. Guest star on many live and filmed TV shows. US stage incl. The Woman I Love, Four Winds. Appeared in Oscar nom. docum. Resisting Enemy Interrogation.
PICTURES: Dawn Patrol, First Comes Courage, Little Men, Sergeant York, Panama Hattie, Seven Sweethearts, Address Unknown, Margin for Error, Master Race, Ministry of Fear, Experiment Perilous, Story of Dr. Wassell, The Catman of Paris, Smash-up, Story of a Woman, Slave Girl, Walk a Crooked Mile, The Navy Comes Through, Sundown, Lover Come Back, This Love of Ours, Without Love, Mystery Submarine, The Desert Hawk, The World in His Arms, Thunder in the Sun, From the Earth to the Moon, Brushfire, Kiss of Evil, Agent for H.A.R.M., Morituri.

ESPOSITO, GIANCARLO: Actor. b. Copenhagen, Denmark, April 26, 1958. Made Bdwy debut as child in 1968 musical Maggie Flynn.
PICTURES: Running, Taps, Trading Places, The Cotton Club, Desperately Seeking Susan, Maximum Overdrive, Sweet Lorraine, School Daze, Do the Right Thing, Mo'Better Blues, King of New York, Harley Davidson and the Marlboro Man, Night on Earth, Bob Roberts, Malcolm X, Amos & Andrew.
TELEVISION: *Movies*: The Gentleman Bandit, Go Tell It on the Mountain, Relentless: Mind of a Killer. *Special*: Roanok. *Guest*: Miami Vice, Spencer: For Hire, Legwork.
THEATRE: *Bdwy*: Maggie Flynn, The Me Nobody Knows, Lost in the Stars, Seesaw, Merrily We Roll Along, Don't Get God Started. *Off-Bdwy*: Zooman and the Sign (Theatre World Award, Obie Award), Keyboard, Who Loves the Dancer, House of Ramon Igleslas, Do Lord Remember Me, Balm in Gilead, Anchorman, Distant Fires.

ESSEX, DAVID: Actor, Singer, Composer. b. Plaistow, London, Eng. July 23, 1947. e. Shipman Sch., Custom House. Started as a singer-drummer in East London band. 1967: Joined touring Repertory Co. in The Fantasticks, Oh, Kay, etc. 1970: West End debut in Ten Years Hard, 1972: Jesus Christ in Godspell, Che in Evita; Lord Byron in Childe Byron, 1983/4: Fletcher Christian in own musical Mutiny! on album and stage. International recording artist. Variety Club of Great Britain show business personality of 1978. Many gold & silver disc intl. awards. 1989, Royal Variety performance. World concerts since 1974.
TELEVISION: Top of the Pops, Own Specials, The River (also composed music), BBC series. Appearances on TV: France, Japan, Germany, Spain, Denmark, Australia. U.S.: Merv Griffin, Johnny Carson, Dinah Shore, American Bandstand, Midnight Special, Grammy Awards, Salute To The Beatles, Don Kirshner's Rock Concert, A.M. America, Phil Everly in Session, Paul Ryan Show.
PICTURES: Assault, All Coppers Are . . . , That'll Be the Day, Stardust, Silver Dream Racer (also wrote score), Shogun Mayeda.

ESSEX, HARRY J: Writer. b. New York, NY, Nov. 29, 1915. e. St. John's U., Brooklyn, B.A. With Dept. Welfare. Wrote orig. story, Man Made Monster, for Universal. During W.W.II in U.S. Army Signal Corps; scenarist; training films on combat methods, censorship.
PICTURES: Boston Blackie and the Law (orig. s.p.), Dangerous Business, Desperate, Bodyguard, He Walked by Night, Dragnet, Killer That Stalked New York, Wyoming Mail, The Fat Man, Undercover Girl, Las Vegas Story, Models, Inc., Kansas City Confidential, The 49th Man, It Came From Outer Space; I the Jury (dir., s.p.); Creature from the Black Lagoon; Southwest Passage (co-s.p., story), Devil's Canyon (adapt.); Mad at the World (dir., s.p.); Teen-age Crime Wave (collab. s.p.); Raw Edge; Lonely Man (story, s.p.); Sons of Katie Elder (co-s.p.), Man and Boy (co-s.p.), Octman (co-s.p.), The Cremators (prod., dir., s.p.), The Amigos (story and s.p.). Collaboration with Oscar Saul; Chrysalis, in collaboration with Ray Bradbury.
TELEVISION: Untouchables, The Racers, Alcoa Hour, Westinghouse, Desilu; story consultant and head writer: Target, The Corruptors, The Dick Powell Show, Bewitched, I Dream of Jeannie, Kraft Suspense Theatre, Hostage Flight.
NOVELIST: I Put My Right Foot In (Little Brown); Man and Boy, (Dell), 1971, Marina (Playboy Press), 1981.
PLAYS: Something for Nothing, Stronger Than Brass, Neighborhood Affair, One for the Dame, Fatty, Twilight, When the Bough Breaks, Dark Passion, Casa D'Amor, I Remember It Well.

ESTEVEZ, EMILIO: Actor. b. New York, NY, May 12, 1962. Oldest son of actor Martin Sheen; brother of actor Charlie Sheen. m. singer Paula Abdul.
PICTURES: Tex (debut, 1982), The Outsiders, Nightmares, Repo Man, The Breakfast Club, St. Elmo's Fire, That Was Then This is Now (also s.p.), Never on Tuesday, Maximum

Overdrive, Wisdom (also dir., s.p.), Stakeout, Young Guns. Men at Work (also dir., s.p.), Young Guns II, Freejack, The Mighty Ducks, National Lampoon's Loaded Weapon 1, Another Stakeout, Judgment Night.
TELEVISION: *Movies*: In the Custody of Strangers. Nightbreaker.

ESTRADA, ERIK: Actor. r.n. Enrique Estrada. m. actress Peggy Rowe. b. New York, NY, Mar. 16, 1949. Began professional career in Mayor John Lindsay's Cultural Program, performing in public parks. Joined American Musical Dramatic Acad. for training. Feature film debut in The Cross and the Switchblade (1970).
PICTURES: The New Centurions, Airport '75, Midway, Trackdown, Where Is Parsifal?, Lightblast, The Repentant, Hour of the Assassin, The Lost Idol, A Show of Force, Night of the Wilding, Twisted Justice, Caged Fury, Guns, Spirito, Do or Die, The Divine Enforcer, National Lampoon's Loaded Weapon 1.
TELEVISION: *Series*: CHiPS. *Guest*: on Hawaii Five-0, Six Million Dollar Man, Police Woman, Kojak, Medical Center, Hunter, Alfred Hitchcock Presents (1988). *Movies*: Fire!, Honeyboy, The Dirty Dozen: The Fatal Mission, She Knows Too Much, Earth Angel.

ESZTERHAS, JOE: Writer. Author of novel Charlie Simpson's Apocalypse (nom. National Book Award, 1974).
PICTURES: F.I.S.T., Flashdance, Jagged Edge, Big Shots, Betrayed, Checking Out, Music Box (also co-exec. prod.), Basic Instinct, Nowhere to Run (co-sp., co-exec. prod.), Sliver (also co-exec. prod.).

ETTINGER, EDWIN D.: Publicist. b. New York, NY, 1921. Entered m.p. ind. as office boy, MGM; pub. rel. and publ. for industrial, comm. clients, 1946–52; joined Ettinger Co., pub. rel., 1952; pub. rel. dir., Disneyland, 1955; marketing dir., Disneyland, 1955–65; v.p., M.C.A. Enterprises, Inc., 1965–66; Board chmn. & CEO, Recreation Environments, Inc., 1967–70; Board chmn. & CEO Recreations Inc., 1967–70; Pres., Ettinger, Inc., 1975–85; semi-retired in 1985.

ETTLINGER, JOHN A.: Producer, Director, Distributor. b. Chicago, IL, Oct. 14, 1924. e. Peddie Inst., Cheshire Acad. Signal Corps Photog. Center, 1942–45; with Paramount Theatres Corp., 1945–47; dir., KTLA, Paramount TV Prod., Inc., Los Angeles, 1948–50; radio-TV dir., Nat. C. Goldstone Agency, 1950–53; pres. Medallion TV Enterprises, Inc.; TV prod., View the Clue, Greenwich Village, High Road to Danger, Sur Demande, Star Route, Las Vegas Fights, Celebrity Billiards; Pres., KUDO-FM, Las Vegas.

EVANS, ANDREW C.: Executive. Joined Paramount Pictures 1977 as dir. of financial reporting. Named v.p., corporate controller, 1980; sr. v.p., 1984. Same year named exec. v.p., finance, for Motion Picture Group of co. 1985, promoted to sr. v.p., finance.

EVANS, BARRY: Actor, Director. b. Guildford, England, 1943. Trained Central School. Repertory: Barrow, Nottingham, Chester, Royal Court, Nat. Theatre, Hampstead Th. Club, Chips with Everything, London and Bdwy. Young Vic. Theatre Clwyd Mold.
TELEVISION: Redcap, Undermined, The Baron, The Class, Armchair Theatre, Love Story, Doctor in the House, Doctor at Large, Short Story, Crossroads, Mind Your Language, Dick Emery Show.
PICTURES: The White Bus, Here We Go 'Round the Mulberry Bush, Alfred the Great, Die Screaming, Marriane, The Adventures of a Taxi-Driver, Under the Doctor.

EVANS, GENE: Actor. b. Holbrook, AR, July 11, 1924. e. Colton H.S. Started career in summer stock, Penthouse Theatre, Altadena, CA. Screen debut: Under Colorado Skies, 1947.
PICTURES: Crisscross, Larceny, Berlin Express, Assigned to Danger, Mother Was a Freshman, Sugarfoot, Armored Car Robbery, Steel Helmet, I Was an American Spy, Force of Arms, Jet Pilot, Fixed Bayonets, Mutiny, Park Row, Thunderbirds, Donovan's Brain, Golden Blade, Hell and High Water, Long Wait, Cattle Queen of Montana, Wyoming Renegades, Crashout, Helen Morgan Story, Bravados, Sad Sack, The Hangman, Operation Petticoat, Support Your Local Sheriff, War Wagon, Nevada Smith, Young and Wild, Ballad of Cable Hogue, There Was a Crooked Man, Support Your Local Gunfighter, Camper John, Walking Tall, People Toys, Pat Garrett and Billy the Kid, Magic of Lassie, Blame It on the Night.
TELEVISION: *Series*: My Friend Flicka, Matt Helm, Spencer's Pilots. *Movies*: Kate Bliss & Ticker Tape Kid, Fire, The Sacketts, Shadow Riders, Travis McGee, The Alamo: 13 Days to Glory, Once Upon a Texas Train.

EVANS, LINDA: Actress. b. Hartford, CT, Nov. 18, 1942. e. Hollywood H.S., L.A. TV commercials led to contract with MGM.
PICTURES: Twilight of Honor (debut, 1963), Those Calloways, Beach Blanket Bingo, The Klansman, Mitchell, Avalanche Express, Tom Horn.

TELEVISION: *Series*: The Big Valley, Hunter, Dynasty. *Movies*: Nakia, The Big Ripoff, Nowhere to Run, Standing Tall, Gambler: The Adventure Continues, Bare Essence, The Last Frontier, I'll Take Romance, Dynasty: The Reunion, The Gambler Returns: Luck of the Draw. *Mini-Series*: North & South Book II.

EVANS, RAY: Songwriter. b. Salamanca, NY, Feb. 4, 1915. e. Wharton Sch. of U. of Pennsylvania. Musician on cruise ships, radio writer spec. material. Hellzapoppin', Sons o' Fun. Member: exec. bd. Songwriters Guild of America, Dramatists Guild, West Coast advisory bd. ASCAP, bd., Myasthenia Gravis Fdn. CA chap., Songwriters Hall of Fame, Motion Picture Acad.
SONGS: To Each His Own, Golden Earrings, Buttons and Bows (Academy Award, 1948), Mona Lisa (Academy Award, 1950), Whatever Will Be Will Be (Academy Award, 1956), A Thousand Violins, I'll Always Love You, Dreamsville, Love Song from Houseboat, Tammy, Silver Bells, Dear Heart, Angel, Never Let Me Go, Almost in Your Arms, As I Love You, In the Arms of Love, Wish Me a Rainbow.
PICTURES: Paleface, Sorrowful Jones, Fancy Pants, My Friend Irma, Aaron Slick From Punkin Crick, Son of the Paleface, My Friend Irma Goes West, The Night of Grizzly, Saddle the Wind, Isn't It Romantic, Capt. Carey U.S.A., Off Limits, Here Come the Girls, Red Garters, Man Who Knew Too Much, Stars Are Singing, Tammy, Houseboat, Blue Angel, A Private's Affair, All Hands on Deck, Dear Heart, The Third Day, What Did You Do in the War Daddy?, This Property Is Condemned.
BROADWAY MUSICALS: Oh Captain! Let It Ride!, Sugar Babies.
TELEVISION THEMES: Bonanza, Mr. Ed, Mr. Lucky, To Rome With Love.

EVANS, ROBERT: Producer. b. New York, NY, June 29, 1930. Father of actor Josh Evans. Radio actor at age 11; went on to appear in more than 300 radio prog. (incl. Let's Pretend, Archie Andrews, The Aldrich Family, Gangbusters) on major networks. Also appeared on early TV. At 20 joined brother, Charles, and Joseph Picone, as partner in women's clothing firm of Evan-Picone, Inc., 1952–67. In 1957 signed by Universal to play Irving Thalberg in The Man of a Thousand Faces after recommendation by Norma Shearer, Thalberg's widow. Guest columnist NY Journal American, 1958. Independent prod. at 20th Century-Fox. August, 1966–76, joined Paramount Pictures as head of prod., then exec. v.p. worldwide prod. (supervising Barefoot in the Park, Rosemary's Baby, Barbarella, Goodbye, Columbus, Love Story, The Godfather I & II, The Great Gatsby, etc.). Resigned to become indep. prod. again; with exclusive contract with Paramount.
PICTURES: *Actor*: Man of 1000 Faces, The Sun Also Rises, The Fiend Who Walked the West, The Best of Everything. *Independent Producer*: Chinatown, Marathon Man, Black Sunday, Players, Urban Cowboy, Popeye, The Cotton Club, The Two Jakes, Sliver.
TELEVISION: *Actor*: Elizabeth and Essex (1947), Young Widow Brown, The Right to Happiness. *Prod.*: Get High on Yourself.

EVERETT, CHAD: Actor. r.n. Raymond Lee Cramton. b. South Bend, IN, June 11, 1937. e. Wayne State U., Detroit. Signed by William T. Orr, head of TV prod. for Warner Bros. to 7-year contract. Appeared in many TV series as well as films. Next became contract player at MGM (1963–67). Received star on Hollywood Walk of Fame.
PICTURES: Claudelle Inglish (debut, 1961), The Chapman Report, Rome Adventure, Get Yourself a College Girl, The Singing Nun, Made in Paris, Johnny Tiger, The Last Challenge, First to Fight, The Impossible Years, Firechasers, Airplane II: The Sequel, Fever Pitch, Jigsaw, Heroes Stand Alone.
TELEVISION: *Series*: The Dakotas (1963), Medical Center (1969–76), Hagen, The Rousters. *Guest*: Hawaiian Eye, 77 Sunset Strip, Surfside Six, Lawman, Bronco, The Lieutenant, Redigo, Route 66, Ironside, Hotel, Murder She Wrote, Shades of L.A. *Movies*: Return of the Gunfighter, Intruder, The Love Boat, Police Story, Thunderboat Row, Malibu, The French Atlantic Affair, Mistress in Paradise, Journey to the Unknown, In the Glitter Palace. *Mini-Series*: Centennial.

EVERETT, RUPERT: Actor. b. Norfolk, England, 1959. e. Ampleforth Central School for Speech & Drama. Apprenticed with Glasgow's Citizen's Theatre. Originated role of Guy Bennett in Another Country on London stage in 1982 and made feature film debut in screen version in 1984.
PICTURES: Another Country, Real Life, Dance with a Stranger, Duet for One, Chronicle of a Death Foretold, The Right Hand Man, Hearts of Fire, The Gold-Rimmed Glasses, Jigsaw, The Comfort of Strangers, Inside Monkey Zetterland.
TELEVISION: Arthur the King, The Far Pavilions, Princess Daisy.

EVERSON, WILLIAM K.: Writer. b. Yeovil, Eng., April 8, 1929. Pub. dir., Renown Pictures Corp., Ltd., London, 1944; film critic; m.p. journalist; in armed forces, 1947–49; thea. mgr., pub. & booking consultant, Monseigneur News Theatres, London, 1949; pub. dir., Allied Artists Inc. Corp., 1951; prod., writer Paul Killiam Dorg., 1956. Writer-editor-researcher on TV series Movie Museum and Silents Please, also on TV specials and theatrical features Hollywood the Golden Years, The Valentino Legend, The Love Goddesses and The Great Director. Lecturer, archival consultant, American Film Institute representative. Film History instructor at NYU, The New School and Sch. of Visual Arts, all in NY. Also, Harvard U.

AUTHOR: Several books on movie history, including The Western, The Bad Guys, The American Movie, The Films of Laurel & Hardy, The Art of W. C. Fields, Hal Roach. The Detective in Film, Classics of the Horror Film, Claudette Colbert.

EVIGAN, GREG: Actor. b. South Amboy, NJ, Oct. 14, 1953. Appeared on NY stage in Jesus Christ Superstar and Grease.
TELEVISION: Series: A Year at the Top, B.J. and the Bear, Masquerade, My Two Dads, P.S. I Luv U. Movies: B.J. and the Bear (pilot), Private Sessions, The Lady Forgets, Lies Before Kisses. Guest: One Day at a Time, Barnaby Jones, Murder She Wrote, New Mike Hammer, Matlock.
PICTURES: Stripped to Kill, DeepStar Six.

EWELL, TOM: Actor. r.n. Yewell Tompkins. b. Owensboro, KY, April 29, 1909. e. U. of Wisconsin. Active in coll. dramatics; salesman at Macy's. NY stage debut: They Shall Not Die, 1934; thereafter many unsuccessful plays. U.S. Navy 1942–46. Returned to stage in John Loves Mary.
THEATRE: John Loves Mary, Small Wonder, Stage Door, Tobacco Road, Roberta, Key Largo, The Seven Year Itch (Tony Award, 1953), Tunnel of Love, Thurber Carnival (also in London), Patate (in Paris).
PICTURES: They Knew What They Wanted, Desert Bandit, Adam's Rib, Mr. Music, A Life of Her Own, American Guerilla in the Philippines, Up Front, Finders Keepers, Lost in Alaska, Willie & Joe Back at the Front, The Seven Year Itch, Lieutenant Wore Skirts, Girl Can't Help It, The Great American Pastime, A Nice Little Bank That Should Be Robbed, Tender Is the Night, State Fair, Suppose They Gave a War and Nobody Came?, To Find a Man, They Only Kill Their Masters, The Great Gatsby, Easy Money.
TELEVISION: Series: The Tom Ewell Show, Best of the West, Baretta. Movies: Promise Him Anything, The Return of Mod Squad, Terror at Alcatraz.

F

FABARES, SHELLEY: Actress. b. Los Angeles, CA, Jan. 19, 1944. r.n. Michele Marie Fabares. m. actor Mike Farrell. Earned gold record for 1962 single Johnny Angel.
TELEVISION: Series: Annie Oakley, The Donna Reed Show, The Little People (The Brian Keith Show), The Practice, Mary Hartman Mary Hartman, Highcliffe Manor, One Day at a Time, Coach. Guest: Twilight Zone, Mr. Novak, Love American Style, The Rookies, Marcus Welby, Hello Larry. Movies: U.M.C., Brian's Song, Two for the Money, Sky Hei$t, Pleasure Cove, Friendships Secrets & Lies, Gridlock, Memorial Day, Class Cruise, Deadly Relations.
PICTURES: Never Say Goodbye, Rock Pretty Baby, Marjorie Morningstar, Summer Love, Ride the Wild Surf, Girl Happy, Hold On!, Spinout, Clambake, A Time to Sing, Hot Pursuit, Love or Money.

FABRAY, NANETTE: Actress. b. San Diego, CA, Oct. 27, 1920. e. Los Angeles City Coll. d. Raoul Fabares and Lillian (McGovern) Fabares. m. Ranald MacDougall 1957, deceased 1973. First prof. stage appearance at age of three in vaudeville as Baby Nan. Leading lady in Charlie Chan radio series. Member of the cast, Showboat. 1938, won two-year scholarship to Max Reinhardt school in Hollywood, and starred in his CA productions of The Miracle, Six Characters in Search of an Author, and Servant With Two Masters.
PICTURES: Elizabeth and Essex, A Child is Born, The Bandwagon, The Happy Ending, Cockeyed Cowboys, Amy, Personal Exemptions.
TELEVISION: Series: Caesar's Hour (2 Emmy Awards), Westinghouse Playhouse, One Day at a Time. Specials: George M!, High Button Shoes, Alice Through the Looking Glass. Movies: Fame is the Name of the Game, But I Don't Want to Get Married!, Magic Carpet, The Couple Takes a Wife, The Man in the Santa Claus Suit.
BROADWAY SHOWS: Meet the People, By Jupiter, Jackpot, My Dear Public, Let's Face It, Bloomer Girl, Arms and the Girl, High Button Shoes, Make a Wish, Love Life (Tony Award, 1949), Mr. President, No Hard Feelings, Yes-Yes-Yes Nanette! (one-woman show by Danny Daniels).
AWARDS: Two Donaldson Awards for High Button Shoes and Love Life; Three Emmy Awards for Caesar's Hour as best comedienne, 1955, 1956, best supporting actress 1955; Woman of the Year, 1955, Radio and TV Editors of America;

Hollywood Women's Press Club, 1960; Honorary Mayor of Pacific Palisades 1967–68; One of Ten Best Dressed Women in America, Fashion Academy Award, 1950. President's Distinguished Service Award, 1970; Eleanor Roosevelt Humanitarian Award; Public Service Award; Amer. Acad. of Otolaryngology, 1977; Woman of the Year, CA Museum, Science and Industry 1975; Award of Merit, Amer. Heart Assoc. 1975; Screen Actors Guild Humanitarian Award, 1986.

FAHEY, JEFF: Actor. b. Buffalo, NY. Was member of Joffrey Ballet for 3 years. Appeared on Bdwy in Brigadoon (1980), tour of Oklahoma!, Paris prod. of West Side Story, and London prod. of Orphans.
PICTURES: Silverado (debut, 1985), Split Decisions, Backfire, Outback, True Blood, Out of Time, Last of the Finest, Impulse, White Hunter Black Heart, Body Parts, Iron Maze, The Lawnmower Man, Wyatt Earp.
TELEVISION: Series: One Life to Live. Movies: Execution of Raymond Graham, Parker Kane, Curiosity Kills, Iran: Days of Crisis, Sketch Artist, In the Company of Darkness, The Hit List, Blindsided, Quick.

FAIMAN, PETER: Director. b. Australia. Entered entertainment business through TV, involved early in production-direction of major variety series in Australia. Assoc. prod.-dir. of over 20 programs for The Paul Hogan Show and two Hogan specials filmed in England (1983). Developed Australia's most popular and longest-running national variety program, The Don Lane Show. Responsible for creative development of the TV Week Logie Awards on the Nine Network. For 4 years headed Special Projects Division of the Nine Network Australia. Resigned to establish own prod. co., Peter Faiman Prods. Pty Ltd. 1984. Made m.p. theatrical film debut as director of Crocodile Dundee, followed by Dutch.

FAIRBANKS, DOUGLAS, JR.: K.B.E., D.S.C., (Hon.) M.A., (OXON), (Hon.) D.F.I., Westminster (Fulton, MO), (Hon.) LL.D (Denver). Actor, Producer, Business executive. b. New York, NY, Dec. 9, 1909. e. Pasadena (CA) Polytech. Sch.; Harvard Mil. Acad., Los Angeles; Bovee and Collegiate Sch., N.Y.; was also tutored in Paris, London. Son of late Douglas Fairbanks. Began as screen actor 1923 in Stephen Steps Out; thereafter in more than 80 pictures. On U.S. stage from 1926. Formed own prod. co. 1935; commissioned Lieut. (j.g.) USNR Navy, 1940; Appt. Presidential envoy to certain South Amer. nations by Pres. Roosevelt. Helped org. British War Relief and was natl. chmn., committee for CARE. Capt., USNR (ret.) Awarded U.S. Silver Star, Combat Legion of Merit; Knight of Order of British Empire, 1949. Distinguished Service Cross, Knight of Justice of Order of St. John of Jerusalem; French Legion of Honor, Croix de Guerre with Palm, etc. Entered TV film prod., 1952. Autobiographies: The Salad Days (1988), A Hell of a War (1993).
THEATER: U.S.: Young Woodley, Saturday's Children, Present Laughter, Out on a Limb, Sleuth, The Pleasure of His Company (also U.K., Ireland, Australia, Hong Kong). U.K.: The Winding Journey, Moonlight in Silver, My Fair Lady, The Secretary Bird, The Pleasure of His Company.
PICTURES: (since sound): Forward Pass, The Careless Age, The Show of Shows, Party Girl, Loose Ankles, Little Accident, The Dawn Patrol, Little Caesar, Outward Bound, One Night at Susie's, Chances, I Like Your Nerve, Union Depot, It's Tough to Be Famous, Love is a Racket, Parachute Jumper, Morning Glory, Life of Jimmy Dolan, The Narrow Corner, Captured, Catherine the Great, Success at Any Price, Mimi, The Amateur Gentleman (also prod.), Man of the Moment, Accused, When Thief Meets Thief, The Prisoner of Zenda, Joy of Living, Having Wonderful Time, The Rage of Paris, Young in Heart, Gunga Din, The Sun Never Sets, Rulers of the Sea, Green Hell, Safari, Angels Over Broadway, The Corsican Brothers, Sinbad the Sailor, That Lady in Ermine, The Exile, Fighting O'Flynn, State Secret, Mr. Drake's Duck, Another Man's Poison (prod. only), Chase a Crooked Shadow (prod. only), Ghost Story.
TELEVISION: Series: Douglas Fairbanks Presents (also prod.). Guest: The Rheingold Theatre (also prod.), The Chevy Show, Route 66, Dr. Kildare, The Love Boat, B.L. Stryker. Special: The Canterville Ghost (ABC Stage '67). Movies: The Crooked Hearts, The Hostage Tower.

FAIRBANKS, JERRY: Executive Producer. b. San Francisco, CA, Nov. 1, 1904. Cameraman, 1924–29; prod., shorts, Universal, 1929–34; prod., Popular Science, Unusual Occupations, Speaking of Animals Series, Para., 1935–49; Winner two Acad. Awards; set up film div., NBC, 1948; formed NBC Newsreel, 1949; devel. Zoomar Lens and Multicam System; formed Jerry Fairbanks Prods., 1950.
TELEVISION: Public Prosecutor (first film series for TV); other series: Silver Theatre, Front Page Detective. Jackson and Jill, Hollywood Theatre, Crusader Rabbit.
PICTURES: The Last Wilderness, Down Liberty Road, With This Ring, Counterattack, Collision Course, Land of the Sea, Brink of Disaster, The Legend of Amaluk, North of the Yukon, Damage Report, The Boundless Seas.

FAIRCHILD, MORGAN: Actress. b. Dallas, TX, Feb. 3, 1950. e. Southern Methodist U.
PICTURES: Bullet for Pretty Boy, The Seduction, Pee-wee's Big Adventure, Red-Headed Stranger, Campus Man, Sleeping Beauty, Midnight Cop, Deadly Illusion, Phantom of the Mall.
TELEVISION: Series: Search for Tomorrow, Flamingo Road, Paper Dolls, Falcon Crest, Roseanne. Movies: The Initiation of Sarah, Murder in Music City, Concrete Cowboys, The Memory of Eva Ryker, Flamingo Road (pilot), The Dream Merchants, The Girl the Gold Watch and Dynamite, Honeyboy, The Zany Adventures of Robin Hood, Time Bomb, Street of Dreams, The Haunting of Sarah Harding, How to Murder a Millionare, Menu for Murder, Writer's Block. Perry Mason: The Case of the Skin-Deep Scandal. Mini-Series: 79 Park Avenue, North and South Book II.

FAIRCHILD, WILLIAM: Writer, Director. b. Cornwall, England, 1918. e. Royal Naval Coll., Dartmouth. Early career Royal Navy.
PICTURES: Screenplays: Morning Departure, Outcast of the Islands, The Gift Horse, The Net, Newspaper Story, Malta Story, The Seekers, Passage Home, Value For Money, John and Julie, The Extra Day, The Silent Enemy, Star!, Embassy, The Darwin Adventure, Invitation to the Wedding, Bruno Rising, The Promise, Statues in the Graden. Director: The Horsemasters.
TELEVISION PLAYS: The Man with the Gun, No Man's Land, The Signal, Four Just Men, Some Other Love, Cunningham 5101, The Break, The Zoo Gang, Lady with a Past.
STAGE: Sound of Murder, Breaking Point, Poor Horace, The Pay-Off, The Flight of the Bumble B.
BOOKS: A Matter of Duty, The Swiss Arrangement, Astrology for Dogs, Astrology for Cats, Catsigns (U.S.), The Poppy Factory, No Man's Land (U.S.).

FALK, PETER: Actor. b. New York, NY, Sept. 16, 1927. e. New Sch. for Social Research, B.A., 1951; Syracuse U. M.F.A. Studied with Eva Le Galliene and Sanford Meisner. Worked as efficiency expert for Budget Bureau State of CT.
THEATRE: Off-Broadway: Don Juan (debut, 1956), The Iceman Cometh, Comic Strip, Purple Dust, Bonds of Interest, The Lady's Not for Burning, Diary of a Scoundrel. On Broadway: Saint Joan, The Passion of Josef D., The Prisoner of Second Avenue. Regional: Light Up the Sky (L.A.), Glengarry Glen Ross (tour).
TELEVISION: Series: The Trials of O'Brien, Columbo (1971–77; Emmy Awards: 1972, 1975, 1976), Columbo (1989, also co-exec. prod., Emmy Award, 1990).Guest: Studio One, Kraft Theatre, Alcoa Theatre, N.T.A. Play of the Week, Armstrong Circle Theatre, Omnibus, Robert Montgomery Presents, Brenner, Deadline, Kraft Mystery Theatre, Rendezvous, Sunday Showcase, The Untouchables, Dick Powell Show (The Price of Tomatoes; Emmy Award, 1962), Danny Kaye Show, Edie Adams Show, Bob Hope Chrysler Theatre. Movies: Prescription: Murder, A Step Out of Line, Ransom for a Dead Man, Griffin and Phoenix: A Love Story, Columbo Goes to College, Caution: Murder Can Be Hazardous to Your Health, Columbo and the Murder of a Rock Star, Death Hits the Jackpot, Columbo: No Time to Die, Columbo: A Bird in the Hand (also exec. prod.). Specials: The Sacco–Vanzetti Story, The Million Dollar Incident, Brigadoon, A Hatful of Rain, Clue: Movies Murder and Mystery.
PICTURES: Wind Across the Everglades (debut, 1958), The Bloody Brood, Pretty Boy Floyd, The Secret of the Purple Reef, Murder Inc. (Acad. Award nom.), Pocketful of Miracles (Acad. Award nom.), Pressure Point, The Balcony, It's a Mad Mad Mad Mad World, Robin and the 7 Hoods, Italiano Brava Gente (Attack and Retreat), The Great Race, Penelope, Luv, Anzio, Castle Keep, Machine Gun McCann, Operation Snafu, Husbands, A Woman Under the Influence, Murder by Death, Mikey and Nicky, The Cheap Detective, The Brink's Job, Opening Night, The In-Laws, The Great Muppet Caper, All the Marbles, Big Trouble, Happy New Year, The Princess Bride, Wings of Desire, Vibes, Cookie, In the Spirit, Tune in Tomorrow, The Player, Faraway So Close!

FANTOZZI TONY: Theatrical Agent. b. New Britain, CT, May 1, 1933. William Morris Agency.

FARBER, BART: Executive. Joined United Artists Corp. in early 1960s when UA acquired ZIV TV Programs. Served as v.p. United Artists Television and United Artists Broadcasting. In 1971 named v.p. in charge of legal affairs of the cos. In January 1978, named sr. v.p.—TV, video and special markets; indep. consultant, TV, Pay TV, home video. 1982, joined Cable Health Network as v.p., legal & business affairs; 1984, v.p., business & legal affairs, Lifetime Network; 1986, independent communications consultant.

FARENTINO, JAMES: b. Brooklyn, NY, Feb. 24, 1938. e. American Acad. of Dramatic Arts.
THEATRE: Broadway: Death of a Salesman, A Streetcar Named Desire (revival, 1973; Theatre World Award). Off-Bdwy: The Days and Nights of Bebe Fenstermaker, In the

Summerhouse. Regional: One Flew Over the Cuckoo's Nest (Jos. Jefferson, Chas. MacArthur & Chicago Drama Critics League Awards), California Suite, The Best Man, Love Letters.
TELEVISION: Series: The Lawyers (The Bold Ones), Cool Million, Dynasty, Blue Thunder, Mary, Julie. Guest: Naked City, daytime soap operas, Laredo, Route 66, The Alfred Hitchcock Hour, Ben Casey, Twelve O'Clock High. Special: Death of a Salesman, DOS Pasos USA. Mini-Series: Sins, Jesus of Nazareth (Emmy Award nom.). Movies: Wings of Fire, Sound of Anger, The Whole World is Watching, Vanished, Longest Night, Family Rico, Cool Million, The Elevator, Crossfire, Possessed, Silent Victory: The Kitty O'Neil Story, Son Rise: A Miracle of Love, Evita Peron, That Secret Sunday, Something So Right (Emmy Award nom.), The Cradle Will Fall, License to Kill, A Summer to Remember, That Secret Sunday, Family Sins, The Red Spider, Who Gets the Friends?, Common Ground, In the Line of Duty: A Cop for the Killing, Miles From Nowhere, When No One Would Listen, Secrets of the Sahara (Ital. TV).Pilot: American Nuclear.
PICTURES: Psychomania (Violent Midnight), Ensign Pulver, The War Lord, The Pad... And How to Use It (Golden Globe Award, 1966), The Ride to Hangman's Tree, Banning, Rosie!, Me Natalie, The Story of a Woman, The Final Countdown, Dead and Buried, Her Alibi.

FARGAS, ANTONIO: Actor. b. Bronx, NY, Aug. 14, 1946. Studied acting at Negro Ensemble Co. and Actor's Studio.
PICTURES: The Cool World (debut, 1964), Putney Swope, Pound, Believe in Me, Shaft, Cisco Pike, Across 110th Street, Cleopatra Jones, Busting, Foxy Brown, Conrack, The Gambler, Cornbread Earl and Me, Next Stop Greenwich Village, Car Wash, Pretty Baby, Up the Academy, Firestarter, Streetwalkin', Night of the Sharks, Shakedown, I'm Gonna Git You Sucka, The Borrower, Howling VI: The Freaks, Whore.
TELEVISION: Series: Starsky and Hutch, All My Children. Movies: Starsky and Hutch (pilot), Huckleberry Finn, Escape, Nurse, The Ambush Murders, A Good Sport, Florida Straits, Maid for Each Other. Guest: Ironside, The Bill Cosby Show, Sanford and Son, Police Story, Kolchak The Night Stalker, Miami Vice, Kojak.
THEATRE: The Great White Hope, The Glass Menagerie, Mod Hamlet, Romeo and Juliet, The Slave, Toilet, The Amen Corner.

FARGO, JAMES: Director. b. Republic, WA, Aug. 14, 1938. e. U. of Washington, B.A.
PICTURES: The Enforcer, Caravans, Every Which Way But Loose, Forced Vengeance, Born to Race, Voyage of the Rock Aliens, Riding the Edge (also actor).
TELEVISION: Tales of the Gold Monkey, Gus Brown and Midnight Brewster, The Last Electric Knight, Hunter, Snoops, Sky High.

FARINA, DENNIS: Actor. b. Chicago, IL, 1944. Served 18 years with Chicago police before being introduced to producer-director Michael Mann who cast him in film Thief. Celebrity Chmn. of Natl. Law Enforcement Officers Memorial in Washington, D.C. On Chicago stage in A Prayer for My Daughter.
PICTURES: Thief (debut, 1981), Jo Jo Dancer Your Life is Calling, Manhunter, Midnight Run, Men of Respect, We're Talkin' Serious Money, Mac, Another Stakeout.
TELEVISION: Series: Crime Story. Mini-Series: Drug Wars: Columbia. Movies: Open Admissions, The Hillside Stranglers, People Like Us, Blind Faith, Cruel Doubt, The Disappearnce of Nora. Guest: Miami Vice, Hunter.

FARNSWORTH, RICHARD: Actor. b. Los Angeles, CA, Sept. 1, 1920. Active as stuntman for 40 years before turning to acting.
PICTURES: Comes a Horseman, Tom Horn, Resurrection, The Legend of the Lone Ranger, Ruckus, Waltz Across Texas, The Grey Fox, The Natural, Rhinestone, Into the Night, Sylvester, Space Rage, The Two Jakes, Misery, Highway to Hell.
TELEVISION: Series: Boys of Twilight. Movies: Strange New World, A Few Days in Weasel Creek, Travis McGee, Ghost Dancing, Anne of Green Gables, Chase, Wild Horses, Red Earth White Earth, Good Old Boy, The Fire Next Time.

FARR, FELICIA: Actress. b. Westchester, NY, Oct. 4, 1932. e. Pennsylvania State Coll. m. Jack Lemmon. Stage debut: Picnic (Players Ring Theatre).
PICTURES: Timetable, Jubal, Reprisal, The First Texan, The Last Wagon, 3:10 to Yuma, Onionhead, Hell Bent for Leather, Kiss Me Stupid, The Venetian Affair, Kotch, Charley Varrick, That's Life!, The Player.

FARR, JAMIE: Actor. r.n. Jameel Joseph Farah. b. Toledo, OH, July 1, 1934. e. Columbia Coll. Trained for stage at Pasadena Playhouse. Film debut in Blackboard Jungle, 1955. Gained fame as Klinger in TV series, M*A*S*H.
PICTURES: Blackboard Jungle (debut, 1955), The Greatest Story Ever Told, Ride Beyond Vengeance, Who's Minding

the Mint?, With Six You Get Eggroll, Cannonball Run, Cannonball Run II, Scrooged, Speed Zone, Curse II: The Bite.

TELEVISION: *Series*: The Chicago Teddy Bears, M*A*S*H (also dir.), The Gong Show (panelist), The $1.98 Beauty Show (panelist), After M*A*S*H (also dir.). *Guest*: Dear Phoebe, The Red Skelton Show, The Dick Van Dyke Show, The Danny Kaye Show, The Love Boat, The New Love American Style, Murder She Wrote. *Movies*: The Blue Knight, Amateur Night at the Dixie Bar and Grill, Murder Can Hurt You!, Return of the Rebels, For Love or Money, Run Till You Fall.

FARRELL, HENRY: Author of novels and screenplays
SCREENPLAYS: Whatever Happened to Baby Jane? Hush . . . Hush Sweet Charlotte, What's the Matter with Helen?
TELEVISION: How Awful About Allan, The House That Would Not Die, The Eyes of Charles Sand.

FARRELL, MIKE: Actor. b. St. Paul, MN, Feb. 6, 1939. m. actress Shelley Fabares.
TELEVISION: *Series*: Days of Our Lives, The Interns, The Man and the City, M*A*S*H. *Specials*: JFK: One Man Show (PBS), The Best of Natl. Geographic Specials (host/narrator). *Movies*: The Longest Night, She Cried Murder!, The Questor Tapes, Live Again Die Again, McNaughton's Daughter, Battered, Sex and the Single Parent, Letters from Frank, Damien: The Leper Priest, Prime Suspect, Memorial Day, Choices of the Heart, Private Sessions, Vanishing Act, A Deadly Silence, Price of the Bride, The Whereabouts of Jenny, Memorial Day (also prod.), Incident at Dark River (also prod.), Silent Motive (also prod.) *Director*: Run Till You Fall.
PICTURES: Captain Newman M.D., The Americanization of Emily, The Graduate, Targets. *Prod*: Dominick and Eugene.

FARROW, MIA: Actress. b. Los Angeles, CA, Feb. 9. 1945. r.n. Maria de Lourdes Villiers Farrow. d. of actress Maureen O'Sullivan and late dir. John Farrow. e. Marymount, Los Angeles, Cygnet House, London.
PICTURES: Guns at Batasi (debut, 1964), A Dandy in Aspic, Rosemary's Baby, Secret Ceremony, John and Mary, See No Evil, The Public Eye, Dr. Popaul (High Heels), The Great Gatsby, Full Circle (The Haunting of Julia), Avalanche, A Wedding, Death on the Nile, Hurricane, A Midsummer Night's Sex Comedy, The Last Unicorn (voice), Zelig, Broadway Danny Rose, Supergirl, The Purple Rose of Cairo, Hannah and Her Sisters, Radio Days, September, Another Woman, New York Stories (Oedipus Wrecks), Crimes and Misdemeanors, Alice (Natl. Board of Review Award, 1990), Shadows and Fog, Husbands and Wives, Widow's Peak.
TELEVISION: *Series*: Peyton Place. *Specials*: Johnny Belinda, Peter Pan. *Movie*: Goodbye Raggedy Ann.
THEATRE: *Debut*: Importance of Being Earnest (Madison Ave. Playhouse, NY, 1963); Royal Shakespeare Co. (Twelfth Night, A Midsummer Night's Dream, Ivanov, Three Sisters, The Seagull, A Doll's House), Mary Rose (London). *Bdwy debut*: Romantic Comedy (1979).

FASS, M. MONROE: Theatre Broker. b. New York, NY, Feb. 26, 1901. e. City Coll. of New York, M.E., engineering. Firm: Fass & Wolper. Entered real estate business in 1925, making first deal with Marcus Loew for land on which Paradise Theatre, Bronx, NY, was built. Thereafter made theatre deals (sale or lease of land or building) in most major cities in the U.S. and in major land or shopping centers. Member: Real Estate Board of N.Y.; Natl. Institute of Real Estate Brokers, Natl. Assoc. of Real Estate Board; Amer. Society of Real Estate Appraisers, Natl. Assoc. of Theatre Owners.

FAWCETT, FARRAH: Actress. b. Corpus Christi, TX, Feb. 2, 1947. e. U. of Texas. Picked as one of the ten most beautiful girls while a freshman; went to Hollywood and signed by Screen Gems. Did films, TV shows, and made over 100 TV commercials. Off Bdwy debut: Extremities (1983).
PICTURES: Love Is a Funny Thing, Myra Breckinridge, Logan's Run, Somebody Killed Her Husband, Sunburn, Saturn 3, Cannonball Run, Extremities, See You in the Morning.
TELEVISION: *Series*: Charlie's Angels, Good Sports. *Guest*: Owen Marshall Counselor at Law, The Six Million Dollar Man, Rockford Files, Harry-O. *Movies*: Three's a Crowd, The Feminist and the Fuzz, The Great American Beauty Contest, The Girl Who Came Gift-Wrapped, Murder on Flight 502, Murder in Texas, The Burning Bed, Red Light Sting, Between Two Women, Nazi Hunter: The Beate Klarsfeld Story, Poor Little Rich Girl: The Barbara Hutton Story, Margaret Bourke-White, Small Sacrifices, Criminal Behavior.

FAY, PATRICK J.: Director, Producer. b. June 7, 1916. e. Carnegie Tech. Dumont TV Network, 10 years. Director of over 100 Army training films.
TELEVISION: Bishop Sheen, Broadway to Hollywood, Cavalcade of Stars, Manhattan Spotlight, Life is Worth Living, Front Row Center, Ilona Massey Show, Alec Templeton Show, Maggi McNellis Show, Key to Missing Persons, Kids and Company; co-prod., dir., Confession; dir., TV film series,

Confession; dir. IBM Industrials, IBM World Trade, Europe Industrial, The Big Picture.
AUTHOR: Melba, The Toast of Pithole, The Last Family Portrait in Oil, Coal Oil Johnny, French Kate, No Pardon in Heaven, An Ill Wind, Tighten Your G-String, As It Was in the Beginning (Television 50 Yrs. Ago).
FILMS: Director for RCA, General Electric H.G. Peters Company, Bransby Films. Screenplays: Sanctuary, The Burning of New York City, Johnson's Island.

FEHR, RUDI: Executive. b. Berlin, Germany, July 6, 1911. m. Maris Wrixon, actress. Started career with Tobis-Klangfilm, Berlin. Joined Warner Bros. editorial department, 1936. Became producer, 1952; promoted to executive, 1956; Post Production Exec. Warner Bros.; WB title changed to dir. of editorial & post-prod. operations. Now retired; is consultant to industry.
PICTURES: *Editor*: Invisible Enemies, Honeymoon for Three, Desperate Journey, Watch on the Rhine, The Conspirators, Humoresque, Possessed, Key Largo, The Inspector General, House of Wax, Dial M for Murder. Co-edited One From the Heart. Nominated for Oscar as co-editor of Prizzi's Honor.

FEINSTEIN, ALAN: Actor. b. New York, NY, Sept. 8, 1941.
TELEVISION: *Series*: Edge of Night, Love Of Life, Search for Tomorrow, Jigsaw John, The Runaways, The Family Tree, Berrenger's. *Movies*: Alexander: The Other Side of Dawn, Visions, The Hunted Lady, The Users, The Two Worlds of Jenny Logan, On Fire. *Mini-Series*: Masada.
PICTURE: Looking for Mr. Goodbar.
NY STAGE: Malcolm, Zelda, A View from the Bridge (NY Drama Desk award), As Is, A Streetcar Named Desire.

FEITSHANS, BUZZ: Executive. Worked for 10 years at American-International as supvr. of prod. In 1975 formed A-Team Productions with John Milius. With Carolco Pictures: producer, 1981–6; exec. v.p. for mo. pic. production, member bd. dir. 1986–90. 1990–present, v.p. for Cinergi Prods.
PICTURES: Producer: Dillinger, Act of Vengeance, Foxy Brown, Big Wednesday, Hardcore, 1941, Extreme Prejudice (exec. prod.). Conan the Barbarian, First Blood, Uncommon Valor, Rambo II, Red Dawn, Rambo III, Total Recall.

FELD, FRITZ: Actor. b. Berlin, Germany, Oct. 15, 1900. e. U. of Berlin; Max Reinhardt Sch. of Drama, Berlin. Actor, prod. asst. dir. for Reinhardt in Berlin 7 yrs.; on screen 1918 in The Golem, UFA. Since found variously assoc. U.S. m.p. prod., as writer, director, actor: has appeared in more than 410 pictures. 1971; nat'l bd. dir., Screen Actors Guild. 1968 chairman of the American National Theatre Comm., Southern California Chapter. 1976 chairman Hollywood Museum Project committee—Screen Actors Guild, 20th Century-Fox Film corp. staged A Tribute to Fritz Feld—60 Years in the Movies and the Los Angeles City named a theater in Brentwood the Fritz Feld Community Theatre. In April 1979, elected honorary Mayor of Brentwood by the Chamber of Commerce.
TELEVISION: Dangerous Assignment, Racket Squad, Mr. & Mrs. North, Jimmy Durante Show, Jack Paar, Thin Man, Chevy Show, Red Skelton, Milton Berle, Colonel Flack, Accused, Peter Gunn, General Electric Thea., Kraft Music Hall, Danny Thomas, Bachelor Father, Adventures in Paradise, Follow the Sun, The Donna Reed Show, Valentine Day, No Time for Sergeants, The Farmer's Daughter, The Bing Crosby Show, Batman, Lost in Space, The Man From U.N.C.L.E., Laredo, Please Don't Eat the Daisies, Girl From U.N.C.L.E., The Smothers Bros., The Wild, Wild, West, Bewitched, Donald O'Connor Show, The Beverly Hillbillies, Land of the Giants, Arnie, Love, American Style, The Merv Griffin Show, The New Bill Cosby Show, The Julie Andrews Hour, Fire House, The Odd Couple, The Night Couple, The Night Stalker, Only with Married Men, The Mike Douglas Show, The Tonight Show, Tabitha, The Hardy Boys, Flying High, Over Easy, Hizzonner, General Hospital, Heidi, Supertrain, Love, Sidney, No Soap, Radio, Magnum P.I., Simon & Simon, Amazing Stories, George Burns Comedy Week, Shell Game, Last of the Great Survivors, Get Smart Again, B-Men (pilot).
STAGE: The Miracle, Once More With Feeling, Would Be Gentleman, Midsummer Night's Dream, Arsenic and Old Lace, You Can't Take It With You.
PICTURES: Wives and Lovers, Promises, Promises, Who's Minding the Store?, Four for Texas, The Patsy, Harlow, Made in Paris, Three on a Couch, Way . . . Way Out, The Comic, Hello Dolly!, The Computer Wore Tennis Shoes, The Phynx, Which Way to the Front? Herbie Rides Again, The Strongest Man in the World, Hoyt Axton's Country Western Rock 'Roll Show, The Sunshine Boys, Won Ton Ton the Dog Who Saved Hollywood, Broadway Rose, Silent Movie, Pennsylvania Lynch, Freaky Friday, The World's Greatest Lover, Herbie Goes Bananas, History of the World, All the Marbles, A Fine Mess, Barfly, Homer & Eddie.

FELDMAN, COREY: Actor. b. Reseda, CA, July 16, 1971. Has been performing since the age of 3 in over 100 commercials, television (Love Boat, Father Murphy, Foul Play, Mork and Mindy, Eight Is Enough, Alice, Gloria) and films.

PICTURES: Time After Time, The Fox and the Hound (voice), Friday the 13th—The Final Chapter, Gremlins, Friday the 13th—A New Beginning, The Goonies, Stand by Me, Lost Boys, License to Drive, The 'Burbs, Dream a Little Dream, Teenage Mutant Ninja Turtles (voice only), Rock 'n' Roll High School Forever, Edge of Honor, Meatballs 4, National Lampoon's Loaded Weapon 1, National Lampoon's Scuba School.

TELEVISION: Series: The Bad News Bears (1979–80); Madame's Place. Movies: Willa, Father Figure, Kid with a Broken Halo, Still the Beaver, Out of the Blue, When the Whistle Blows, I'm a Big Girl Now, Exile. Specials: 15 & Getting Straight, How to Eat Like a Child.

FELDMAN, EDWARD S.: Producer. b. New York, NY, Sept. 5, 1929. e. Michigan State U. Trade press contact, newspaper and mag. contact, 20th Century Fox 1950; dir. info. services, Dover Air Force Base. 1954–56; publicity coordinator, The World of Suzie Wong, Para., 1959; joined Embassy, dir. of publicity, 1969; vice pres. in chg., adv. & pub, Seven Arts Prods., 1962; v.p. exec. asst. to head prod. Warner-7 Arts Studio 1967, pres., m.p. dept., Filmways, 1970; Formed Edward S. Feldman Co., 1978.

PICTURES: What's the Matter With Helen? (exec. prod.), Fuzz (exec. prod.), Save the Tiger (prod.), The Other Side of the Mountain (prod.), Two-Minute Warning (prod.), The Other Side of the Mountain Part 2 (prod.), The Last Married Couple in America (co-prod.), Six Pack (co-exec. prod.), The Sender (prod.), Hot Dog . . . The Movie! (co-prod.), Witness (prod.), Explorers (co-prod.), The Golden Child (co-prod.), The Hitcher (exec. prod.), Near Dark (exec. prod.), Wired (prod.), Green Card (exec. prod.), The Doctor (exec. prod.), Honey I Blew Up the Kid (prod.), Forever Young (exec. prod.), My Father the Hero (exec. prod.).

TELEVISION: Exec. Prod.: Moon of the Wolf, My Father's House, Valentine, 300 Miles for Stephanie, Charles and Diana: A Royal Love Story, 21 Hours at Munich, King, Not in Front of the Children, Obsessed with a Married Woman.

FELDON, BARBARA: Actress. b. Pittsburgh, PA, Mar. 12, 1941. e. Carnegie Tech. Former fashion model, also appeared in many commercials. On NY stage in Past Tense, Cut the Ribbons.

TELEVISION: Series: Get Smart, The Marty Feldman Comedy Machine, The Dean Martin Comedy Hour (host), Special Edition (host), The 80's Woman (synd.; host). Movies: Getting Away From It All, Playmates, What Are Best Friends For?, Let's Switch, A Guide for the Married Woman, Sooner or Later, A Vacation in Hell, Before and After, Children of Divorce, Get Smart Again!

PICTURES: Fitzwilly, Smile, No Deposit No Return.

FELDSHUH, TOVAH: Actress. b. New York, NY, Dec. 27, 1953. e. Sarah Lawrence Col., Univ. of MN. For humanitarian work received the Israel Peace Medal and the Eleanor Roosevelt Humanitarian Award.

TELEVISION: Series: Mariah. Movies: Scream Pretty Peggy, The Amazing Howard Hughes, Terror Out of the Sky, The Triangle Factory Fire Scandal, Beggarman Thief, The Women's Room, Citizen Cohn, Sexual Considerations. Special: Saying Kaddish. Mini-Series: Holocaust.

THEATRE: NY: Cyrano, Straws in the Wind, Three Sisters, Rodgers and Hart, Yentl (Theatre World Award), Sarava, The Mistress of the Inn, Springtime for Henry, She Stoops to Conquer, Lend Me a Tenor, A Fierce Attachment, Sarah and Abraham, Six Wives, Hello Muddah Hello Fadduh.

PICTURES: Nunzio, The Idolmaker, Cheaper to Keep Her, Daniel, Brewster's Millions, The Blue Iguana, A Day in October.

FELL, NORMAN: Actor. b. Philadelphia, PA, March 24, 1924. e. Temple U. Studied acting with Stella Adler. Member, Actors Studio. Professional debut at Circle-in-the-Square Theatre in N.Y. in Bonds of Interest. Summer Stock; appearances on TV; moved to Hollywood in 1958 to begin theatrical film career.

PICTURES: Pork Chop Hill, Ocean's 11, Rat Race, Inherit the Wind, It's a Mad Mad Mad Mad World, The Graduate, Bullitt, If It's Tuesday This Must Be Belgium, Catch-22, The Stone Killer, Rabbit Test, The End, On the Right Track, Paternity, Stripped to Kill, C.H.U.D.II: Bud the Chud, The Boneyard, For the Boys, Hexed.

TELEVISION: Over 150 live plays from NY and some 200 shows filmed in Hollywood. Series: Joe and Mabel, 87th Precinct, Dan August, Needles and Pins, Three's Company, The Ropers, Teachers Only. Guest: Matt Houston, Crazy Like a Fox, Simon and Simon, It's Garry Shandling's Show, The Boys (pilot). Mini-Series: Rich Man Poor Man, Roots: The Next Generations. Movies: The Hanged Man, Three's a Crowd, The Heist, Thursday's Game, Death Stalk, Richie

Brockelman, Moviola: This Year's Blonde, For the Love of It, Uncommon Valor, The Jessie Owens Story.

FELLINI, FEDERICO: Director. b. Rimini, Italy. Jan. 20, 1920. m. actress Giulietta Masina. e. U. Rome. Journalist 1937–39; writer of radio dramas 1939–42, also cartoonist, caricaturist; then m.p. writer, actor, s.p., dir. Appeared as himself in Alex in Wonderland, We All Loved Each Other So Much. Recipient of honorary Academy Award (1993).

PICTURES: Writer: Open City, Paisan, Ways of Love, Senza Pieta, Fortunella, others. Director-Writer: Variety Lights (also prod.), The White Sheik, I Vitelloni, Love in the City (segment: The Matrimonial Agency), La Strada, Il Bidone (The Swindle), Nights of Cabiria, La Dolce Vita, Boccaccio '70 (segment: The Temptation of Dr. Antonio), 8-1/2, Juliet of the Spirits, Spirits of the Dead (segment: Toby Dammit), Fellini Satyricon, The Clowns (also actor), Fellini's Roma (also actor), Amarcord, Fellini's Casanova (also prod.), Orchestra Rehearsal (also actor), City of Women, And The Ship Sails On, Ginger and Fred, Intervista (also actor), Voice of the Moon.

FELLMAN, DANIEL R.: Executive. b. Cleveland, OH, March 14, 1943. e. Rider Coll., B.S., 1964. Joined Paramount N.Y. 1964; later sales mgr. Washington DC, Dallas. Next branch mgr. Cleveland; then Chicago. In 1969 joined Loews Theatres as film buyer. In 1971 joined Cinema National Theatres, division of Carrols Development Corp., as v.p./chief film buyer. In 1973 named v.p./dir., Cinema National Theatres. 1977, pres., American Theatre Mgt. Joined Warner Bros. in 1978 as eastern sales mgr. 1979 named v.p./ass't. gen. sales mgr. 1982, v.p., sls. mgr., WB. 1985, named v.p. & gen. sls. mgr.; sr. v.p., gen sales mgr., 1987. President Variety Club Tent 35, 1977–78. V.p. Motion Picture Pioneers; v.p., Will Rogers Fund bd. member. Named exec. v.p. WB domestic distrib., Jan. 1993.

FELLMAN, NAT D.: Executive. b. New York, NY, Feb. 19, 1910. Started as office boy, Warner Bros. Pictures, 1928; transferred to Warner Bros. Theatres, asst. to chief booker; handled pool, partnership operations; head buyer, booker for Ohio zone, 1941; asst. to chief film buyer in New York, 1943; apptd. chief film buyer, 1952; exec. asst. to v.p. and gen. mgr., Stanley Warner Theatres, 1955; asst. gen. mgr., Stanley Warner Theatres, 1962; acting gen. mgr., Stanley Warner Theatres, July, 1964; Stanley Warner Theatres, v.p. and gen. mgr., 1965; v.p., NGC Theatre Corp. and division mgr. Fox Eastern Theatres, 1968; v.p. National General Corp., and pres., National General Theatres, 1969; 1974, formed Exhibitor Relations Co., operations consultant; sold it and retired in 1982. Served as vice pres., Variety Clubs International and NATO, Chrm., presidents' advisory comm. Currently on bd. of dir., Motion Picture Pioneers and Will Rogers Inst.

FENADY, ANDREW J.: Producer, Writer. b. Toledo, OH, Oct. 4, 1928. e. U. of Toledo, 1946–50. Radio-prod.-actor-writer. Novels: The Man With Bogart's Face, The Secret of Sam Marlow, The Claws of the Eagle, The Summer of Jack London, Mulligan.

PICTURES: Stakeout on Dope Street, The Young Captives, Ride Beyond Vengeance, Chisum, Terror in the Wax Museum, Arnold, The Man with Bogart's Face.

TELEVISION: Series: Confidential File, The Rebel, Branded, Hondo. Movies: The Woman Hunter, Voyage of the Yes, The Stranger, The Hanged Man, Black Noon, Sky Heist, Mayday 40,000 Ft., The Hostage Heart, Mask of Alexander, Masterpiece of Murder, Who Is Julia?, Jake Spanner-Private Eye, The Love She Sought, Yes Virginia There is a Santa Claus, The Sea Wolf.

FENN, SHERILYNN: Actress. b. Detroit, MI, Feb. 1, 1965. PICTURES: The Wild Life (debut, 1984), Just One of the Guys, Out of Control, Thrashin', The Wraith, Zombie High, Two Moon Junction, Crime Zone, True Blood, Meridian: Kiss of the Beast, Wild at Heart, Backstreet Dreams, Ruby, Desire and Hell at Sunset Motel, Diary of a Hit Man, Of Mice and Men, Three of Hearts, Boxing Helena, Fatal Instinct.

TELEVISION: Series: Twin Peaks. Movies: Silence of the Heart, Dillinger. Guest: Cheers, 21 Jump Street, Heart of the City. Specials: Tales From the Hollywood Hills (A Table at Ciro's), Divided We Stand, A Family Again.

FENNELLY, VINCENT M.: Producer. b. Brooklyn, July 6, 1920. e. Holy Cross, 1938–42. U.S. Navy, 1942–46; salesman, Monogram, Des Moines, 1947; entered prod. field, 1949; indep. prod. for Monogram, 1950; Ent. TV field, 1957; prod. Transwestern Films, Inc., Frontier Pictures, Silvermine Productions Co., Allied Artists; Malcolm Enterprises, Hilgarde Enter.

PICTURES: Kansas Territory, Wagons West, Fargo, Marksman, Star of Texas, Topeka, Texas Bad Man, Bitter Creek, The Desperado, Seven Angry Men, Dial Red O, Bobby Ware Is Missing, At Gunpoint, Crime in the Streets, Last of the Badmen.

TELEVISION: Four Star Films, Alcoa-Goodyear, Trackdown, Wanted Dead or Alive, David Niven Show, Richard Diamond, Stagecoach West, The Dick Powell Theatre, Target, The Corruptors, Rawhide; A Man Called Shenandoah.

Fen-Fie

FENNEMAN, GEORGE: M.C., Announcer. b. Peking, China, Nov. 10, 1919. e. San Francisco State U. Appeared in 1951 film The Thing.
CREDITS: Groucho Marx Show, You Bet Your Life, M.C. Host: Surprise Package, Funny Funny Films, Talk About Pictures, On Campus, Donny & Marie, Spokesman for Home Savings of America/Savings of America.

FERRARA, ABEL: Director, Writer. b. Bronx, NY, 1951. Moved to Peekskill, NY, as teenager where he made short films with future writer Nicholas St. John. Traveled to England, worked for the BBC. Returned to U.S. to attended SUNY/Purchase, making short Could This Be Love, which received some theatrical distribution. Has used the pseudonymn Jimmy Laine.
PICTURES: *Director*: Driller Killer (also actor, s.p. songs), Ms. 45 (also actor), Fear City, China Girl (also songs), Cat Chaser, King of New York, Bad Lieutenant (also co-s.p.), Body Snatchers.

FERRAZZA, CARL J.: Executive. b. Cleveland, OH, Aug. 29, 1920. e. Catholic U. of America, Washington, DC. Started career 1945: as asst. mgr. & mgr. for Loews Theatres. 1952, joined Cincinnati Theatre Co., first as mgr. for Keith's Theatre, Cincinnati, and after prom. dir. for circuit. 1963, field rep. for United Artists, covering midwest. 1968, UA prom. mgr., N.Y. 1975–83, dir. of field activities, MGM/UA; 1984, joined Orion Pictures Distributing Corp. as v.p. promotional and field activities.

FERRELL, CONCHATA: Actress. b. Charleston, WV, Mar. 28, 1943. e. Marshall Univ.
TELEVISION: *Series*: Hot L Baltimore, B.J. and the Bear, McClain's Law, E/R, Peaceable Kingdom, L. A. Law, Hearts Afire. *Movies*: The Girl Called Hatter Fox, A Death in Canaan, Who'll Save My Children?, Before and After, The Seduction of Miss Leona, Reunion, Rape and Marriage: The Rideout Case, Life of the Party: The Story of Beatrice, Emergency Room, Nadia, The Three Wishes of Billy Grier, North Beach and Rawhide, Samaritan: The Mitch Snyder Story, Eye on the Sparrow, Your Mother Wears Combat Boots, Goodbye Miss 4th of July, Opposites Attract, Deadly Intentions . . . Again?, Backfield in Motion. *Guest*: Good Times, Love Boat, Lou Grant, St. Elsewhere, Frank's Place, Murder She Wrote, Who's the Boss?, Matlock. *Specials*: Portrait of a White Marriage, Picnic.
PICTURES: Deadly Hero, Network, Heartland, Where the River Runs Black, For Keeps?, Mystic Pizza, Edward Scissorhands, Family Prayers, True Romance, Samuari Cowboy, Heaven and Earth.
THEATRE: NY: The Three Sisters, Hot L Baltimore, Battle of Angels, The Sea Horse (Theatre World, Obie & Vernon Rice Drama Desk Awards), Wine Untouched. LA: Getting Out, Picnic.

FERRER, MEL: Producer, Director, Actor. b. Elberon, NJ, Aug. 25, 1917. e. Princeton U. During coll. and early career spent summers at Cape Cod Playhouse, Dennis, MA; then writer in Mexico, authored juvenile book, Tito's Hats; later ed. Stephen Daye Press, VT. Left publishing upon reaching leading-man status at Dennis; on Bdwy as dancer in You'll Never Know, Everywhere I Roam; others. Kind Lady, Cue For Passion; then to radio, serving apprenticeship in small towns; prod.-dir., NBC: dir. Land of the Free, The Hit Parade, and Hildegarde program. Entered m.p. ind., 1945, when signed by Columbia, dial. dir.: The Girl of the Limberlost; later, returned to Broadway, leading role, Strange Fruit; signed by David Selznick as producer-actor, on loan to John Ford as prod. asst. on The Fugitive; then to RKO for Vendetta. Stage: Ondine on Bway., 1954. The Best Man (L.A., 1987).
THEATER: Kind Lady, Cue for Passion, Strange Fruit, Ondine, The Best Man (L.A., 1987).
PICTURES: Lost Boundaries, Born to Be Bad, Vendetta (dir. only), The Secret Fury (dir. only), The Brave Bulls, Rancho Notorious, Scaramouche, Lili, Knights of the Round Table, Saadia, Oh Rosalinda, War and Peace, Paris Does Strange Things, The Sun Also Rises, The Vintage, Fraulein, The World The Flesh and the Devil, Green Mansions (dir. only), Blood and Roses, The Hands of Orlac, Devil and the 10 Commandments, The Longest Day, Fall of the Roman Empire, Paris When It Sizzles, Sex and the Single Girl, El Greco (also prod.), Every Day is a Holiday (dir.), Wait Until Dark (prod. only), A Time For Loving (prod.), Embassy (prod. only), "W." (prod., only), Brannigan, Death Trap (Eaten Alive), The Norsemen, The Tempter, Lili Marleen, The Visitor, The Fifth Floor, Mad Dog Anderson.
TELEVISION: *Series*: Behind the Screen, Falcon Crest. *Movies*: One Shoe Makes It Murder, Seduced, Outrages, Dream West, Peter the Great, Christine Cromwell, A Thanksgiving Promise (prod.).

FERRER, MIGUEL: Actor. b. Santa Monica, CA, Feb. 7, 1954. Son of actor Jose Ferrer and singer Rosemary Clooney. Began performing as a drummer. With actor Bill Mumy created comic book The Comet Man.

TELEVISION: *Series*: Twin Peaks, Broken Badges, On the Air. *Guest*: Miami Vice, Hill Street Blues, Cagney & Lacey, Shannon's Deal. *Pilot*: Badlands 2005. *Mini-Series*: Drug Wars: The Camarena Story. *Movies*: Downpayment on Murder, C.A.T. Squad, Guts & Glory: The Rise and Fall of Oliver North, Murder in High Places, In the Shadow of a Killer, Cruel Doubt, Scam.
PICTURES: Heartbreaker (debut, 1983), Lovelines, Star Trek III: The Search for Spock, Flashpoint, Robocop, Deepstar Six, Valentino Returns, Revenge, The Guardian, Twin Peaks: Fire Walk With Me, The Harvest, Point of No Return, Hot Shots! Part Deux, Another Stakeout.

FETZER, JOHN E.: Executive. b. Decatur, IN, March 25, 1901. e. Purdue U., U. of Michigan, A.B., Andrews U. Hon LL.D., Western Michigan U. 1958. Chairman, owner Fetzer Broadcasting Co., Kalamazoo, MI; chmn., Detroit Baseball Club; pres., owner Fetzer Communications, Inc., Kalamazoo; chairman, dir., Cornhusker TV Corp.; Mem., former bd. dir., Amer. Nat'l Bank and Trust Co., former mem. Bd. of Trustees, Kalamazoo Coll. Radio research Europe, 1925; asst. dir., U.S. Censorship in charge of radio. 1944–46; served as war corr. in ETO, 1945; spl. assignment radio, TV, newspaper mission to Europe and Middle East, 1952. chmn., TV code review bd., NARTB, 1952–55. Pres., Pro Am Sports System, 1983; Member, bd., Domino's Pizza, 1983. Fellow, Royal Society of Arts, London; mem., Acad. of Polit. Science. Clubs: Park, Kalamazoo Country, Kalamazoo; Radio and Television Execs. Soc. (Assoc.); Broadcast Pioneers, N.Y.

FIEDLER, JOHN: Executive. Launched m.p. career in 1975 working in commercials and industrial and ed. films. Joined Technicolor as sr. exec. in prod. svcs. in mktg. Joined Rastar 1980 as v.p., prod. dev. and asst. to Guy McElwaine, pres. & CEO. Joined Paramount as v.p. in prod.; then to Tri-Star Pictures in same post. Resigned to join Columbia Pictures as exec. v.p., worldwide prod., 1984, then pres. of prod. 1986. 1987, left to become independent prod. 1989 named pres. of prod., Rastar IndieProd.
PICTURES: The Beast, Tune in Tomorrow (prod.).

FIELD, DAVID M.: Executive. b. Kansas City, MO. e. Princeton U. Worked as reporter on city desk at Hartford (CT) Courant. In 1968 with NBC News in N.Y. and Washington, DC. Entered film school at U. of Southern California (L.A.) after which joined Columbia Pictures as west coast story editor. In 1973 went to ABC-TV Network as mgr., movies of the week. 1975, moved to 20th-Fox as v.p., creative affairs. Joined United Artists in 1978; named sr. v.p.—west coast production. Left in 1980 to become 20th-Fox exec. v.p. in chg. of worldwide production 1983, resigned to enter independent production deal with 20th-Fox, Consultant, Tri-Star Pictures. Wrote and produced Amazing Grace and Chuck, 1987.

FIELD, SALLY: Actress. b. Pasadena, CA, Nov. 6, 1946. m. prod. Alan Greisman. Daughter of Paramount contract actress Maggie Field Mahoney. Stepdaughter of actor Jock Mahoney. e. Actor's Studio 1973–75. Acting classes at Columbia studios. Picked over 150 finalists to star as lead in TV series, Gidget, 1965.
PICTURES: The Way West (debut, 1967), Stay Hungry, Smokey and the Bandit, Heroes, The End, Hooper, Norma Rae (Acad. Award, 1979), Beyond the Poseidon Adventure, Smokey and the Bandit II, Back Roads, Absence of Malice, Kiss Me Goodbye, Places in the Heart (Acad. Award, 1984), Murphy's Romance (also exec. prod.), Surrender, Punchline, Steel Magnolias, Not Without My Daughter, Soapdish, Dying Young (co-prod. only), Homeward Bound: The Incredible Journey (voice), Mrs. Doubtfire.
TELEVISION: *Series*: Gidget, The Flying Nun, Alias Smith and Jones, The Girl With Something Extra. *Movies*: Maybe I'll Come Home in the Spring, Marriage Year One, Mongo's Back in Town, Home for the Holidays, Hitched, Bridger, Sybil (Emmy Award, 1977). *Host*: Barbara Stanwyck: Fire and Desire. *Guest*: Hey Landlord, Marcus Welby M.D., Bracken's World. *Special*: All the Way Home.

FIELD, SHIRLEY-ANNE: Actress. b. London, June 27, 1938. Ent. films after repertory experience. Under contract to Ealing-M.G.M. 1958.
THEATRE: The Lily White Boys, Kennedy's Children, Wait Until Dark, The Life and Death of Marilyn Monroe, How the Other Half Loves.
PICTURES: It's Never Too Late, The Silen Affair, The Good Companions, Horrors of the Black Museum, Upstairs and Downstairs, Beat Girl, The Entertainer, Man in the Moon, Once More With Feeling, Peeping Tom, Saturday Night and Sunday Morning, These Are the Damned, The War Lover, Kings of the Sun, Alfie, Doctor in Clover, Hell is Empty, With Love in Mind, House of the Living Dead (Doctor Maniac), My Beautiful Laundrette, Getting It Right, The Rachel Papers, Shag, Hear My Song.
TELEVISION: Risking It, Buccaneer, U.S. Santa Barbara, Anna Lees, Lady Chatterly.

112

FIELD, TED: Producer. r.n. Frederick W. Field. e. U. of Chicago, Pomona Coll. Started career as one of owners of Field Enterprises of Chicago; transferred to west coast, concentrating on real estate. Founded Interscope Communications, diversified co., which develops and produces theatrical films, TV series and movies-of-the-week.
PICTURES: Revenge of the Nerds, Turk 182, Critical Condition, Outrageous Fortune, Three Men and a Baby, The Seventh Sign, Cocktail, Bill & Ted's Excellent Adventure (exec. prod.), Renegades (exec. prod), Innocent Man, The First Power (exec. prod.), Bird on a Wire, Three Men and a Little Lady, Paradise, The Hand That Rocks the Cradle, The Cutting Edge, FernGully, The Gun in Betty Lou's Handbag, Out on a Limb, Jersey Girl.
TELEVISION: The Father Clements Story (co-exec. prod.). Everybody's Baby: The Rescue of Jessica McClure (co-exec. prod.), My Boyfriend's Back, A Mother's Courage: The Mary Thomas Story (co-exec. prod.), Crossing the Mob, Murder Ordained, Foreign Affairs (co-exec. prod.).

FIELDS, ALAN: Executive. Spent five years with Madison Square Garden before joining Paramount Pictures. Career there included various positions: v.p. for pay-TV and Home Video TV. Spent two years at studio lot in L.A. as part of network TV organization. 1981, named bd. director for Paramount Pictures (U.K.) in London, serving as liaison to United Intl. Pictures and Cinema Intl. Corp., serving on operating committees of both. 1985, appt. v.p., Entertainment & Communications Group of Gulf & Western Industries, Inc., parent co. of Paramount; C.O.O., exec. v.p. Madison Square Garden Corp.

FIELDS, FREDDIE: Executive. b. Ferndale, NY, July 12, 1923. Vice-pres., member of bd. of directors, MCA-TV, MCA Canada Ltd., MCA Corp.; mem., Pres. Club, Wash., D.C.; pres., Freddie Fields Associates Ltd., 1960; Founder pres., chief exec. officer Creative Management Assoc. Ltd. Agency, Chicago, Las Vegas, Miami, Paris, Los Angeles, N.Y., London, Rome, 1961. Was exclusive agent of Henry Fonda, Phil Silvers, Judy Garland, Paul Newman, Peter Sellers, Barbra Streisand, Steve McQueen, Woody Allen, Robert Redford, Ryan O'Neal, Liza Minnelli and others. In 1975 sold interest in CMA (now International Creative Mgt.) but continued as consultant. Produced for Paramount Pictures. 1977: Looking for Mr. Goodbar. American Gigolo, Citizen's Band; Victory. In 1983 named pres. and COO, MGM Film Co. Resigned 1985 to become independent producer for MGM/UA. Fever Pitch. Poltergeist II, Crimes of the Heart, Millenium, Glory. Exec. Prod. of The Montel Williams Show.

FIERSTEIN, HARVEY: Actor, Writer. b. New York, NY, June 6, 1954. e. Pratt Inst.
THEATRE: Actor: Andy Warhol's Pork, The Haunted Host, Pouf Positive. Actor-Writer: Torch Song Trilogy (NY & London; Tony Awards: best actor, play; Theatre World Award), Safe Sex. Writer: Spookhouse, La Cage Aux Folles (Tony Award), Legs Diamond.
PICTURES: Garbo Talks, The Times of Harvey Milk (narrator), Torch Song Triology (also s.p.), The Harvest.
TELEVISION: Movies: The Demon Murder Case (voice), Apology. Guest: Miami Vice, The Simpsons (voice), Cheers, Murder She Wrote. Specials: Tidy Endings, In the Shadow of Love.

FINCH, JON: Actor. b. London, England, 1942. Came to acting via backstage activities, working for five years as company manager and director.
PICTURES: Vampire Lovers, Horror of Frankenstein, Sunday Bloody Sunday, Macbeth, L'affaire Martine Desclos, Frenzy, Lady Caroline Lamb, The Final Programme, Diagnosis Murder, Une Femme Fidele, The Man of the Green Cross, Battleflag, El Mister, Death on the Nile, La Sabina, Gary Cooper Which Art in Heaven, Breaking Glass, Power Play, Doktor Faustus, Giro City, Plaza Real, Streets of Yesterday, The Voice, Beautiful in the Kingdom, Mirror Mirror.
TELEVISION: The Martian Chronicles (U.S.), Peter and Paul, The Rainbow, Unexplained Laughter, Dangerous Curves, Maigret, Beautiful Lies, Make or Break.

FINESHRIBER, WILLIAM H., JR.: Executive. b. Davenport, IA, Nov. 4, 1909. e. Princeton U., B.A., 1931. Pub., CBS, 1931–34; mgr. Carnegie Hall, N.Y., 1934–37; script writer, dir., music comm., dir. of music dept., CBS, 1937–40; dir. of short wave programs, CBS, 1940–43; gen. mgr. CBS program dept. 1943–49; v.p. in charge of programs MBS, 1949–51; exec. v.p. & dir., MBS, 1951–53; v.p. & gen. mgr. of networks, NBC, 1953–54; v.p. in charge of Radio Network, NBC, 1955; v.p. Television Programs of America, 1956; director International operations, Screen Gems, 1957; v.p., Motion Picture Assoc. of America and Motion Picture Export Assoc. of America, 1960; bd. of dir., NARTB: exec. comm., bd. of dir., R.A.B; v.p. Radio Pioneers.

FINKELMAN, KEN: Director.
PICTURES: Airplane II: The Sequel; Head Office.

FINLAY, FRANK: Actor. C.B.E. b. Farnworth, Eng., Aug. 6, 1926. Rep. in Troon, 1951, Halifax and Sunderland, 1952–3, before winning Sir James Knott Scholarship to RADA. e. Studied acting at RADA. Appeared with Guildford Repertory Theatre Co. 1957. London stage debut: The Queen and the Welshman, 1957. Broadway debut, Epitaph for George Dillon, 1958. Extensive stage career, especially with the Royal Court, Chichester Fest., and National Theatre includes: Sergeant Musgrave's Dance; Chicken Soup with Barley; Roots; Platonov; Chips with Everything; Saint Joan; Hamlet; Othello (Iago to Olivier's Othello), Saturday, Sunday, Monday; Plunder; Watch It Come Down; Weapons of Happiness; Tribute to a Lady; Filumena (and N.Y.), Amadeus; The Cherry Orchard, Mutiny, Beyond Reasonable Doubt, Black Angel, A Slight Hangover.
PICTURES: The Longest Day, The Loneliness of the Long Distance Runner, Agent 8 3/4, Doctor in the Wilderness, Private Potter, The Comedy Man, Underworld Informers, A Study in Terror, Othello, The Jokers, The Deadly Bees, Robbery, I'll Never Forget What's 'is Name, The Shoes of the Fisherman, Inspector Clouseau, Twisted Nerve, Cromwell, The Molly Maguires, Assault, Gumshoe, Sitting Target, Shaft in Africa, The Three Musketeers, The Four Musketeers, The Wild Geese, Murder by Decree, Enigma, The Ploughman's Lunch, Return of the Soldier, The Key, 1919, Return of the Soldier, Lifeforce, The Return of the Musketeers, King of the Wind, Cthulhu Mansion.
TELEVISION: The Adventures of Don Quixote, Casanova, Candide, Julius Caesar, Les Miserables, This Happy Breed, The Lie, The Death of Adolph Hitler, Voltaire, The Merchant of Venice; Bouquet of Barbed Wire, 84 Charing Cross Road, Saturday Sunday Monday, Count Dracula, The Last Campaign, Thief of Bagdad, Betzi, Sakharov, A Christmas Carol, Arch of Triumph, The Burning Shore, In the Secret State, Verdict of Erebus, Mountain of Diamonds, Encounter, Stalin.

FINNEY, ALBERT: Actor. b. Salford, England, May 9, 1936. Studied for stage at Royal Acad. Dramatic Art making his West End debut 1958 in The Party.
THEATER: Appeared at Stratford-on-Avon, 1959, playing title role in Coriolanus, etc. Starting in 1960 on West End stage in The Lily White Boys, Billy Liar, Luther (NY, National Theatre), Much Ado About Nothing, Armstrong's Last Goodnight, Love for Love, Miss Julie, Black Comedy, A Flea in Her Ear, Joe Egg (NY), Alpha Beta, Krapp's Last Tape, Cromwell, Chez Nous, Hamlet, Tamburlaine, Uncle Vanya, Present Laughter. National Theatre, The Country Wife, The Cherry Orchard, Macbeth, The Biko Inquest, Sergeant Musgrave's Dance (also dir.), Orphans, Another Time (also Chicago), Reflected Glory.
PICTURES: The Entertainer (debut, 1960), Saturday Night and Sunday Morning, Tom Jones, The Victors, Night Must Fall, Two for the Road, Charlie Bubbles (also dir.), The Picasso Summer (TV in U.K.), Scrooge, Gumshoe, Alpha Beta (TV in U.K.), Murder on the Orient Express, The Adventure of Sherlock Holmes' Smarter Brother (cameo), The Duellists, Wolfen, Looker, Loophole, Shoot the Moon, Annie, The Dresser, Under the Volcano, Orphans, Miller's Crossing, The Playboys, Rich in Love, The Browning Version.
TELEVISION: The Claverdon Road Job, The Miser, Pope John Paul II, Endless Game, The Image, The Green Man.

FIRTH, COLIN: Actor. b. Grayshott, Hampshire, Eng., Sept. 10, 1960. Studied acting at the Drama Centre at Chalk Farm. On stage in Doctor's Dilemma, Another Country, Desire Under the Elms.
PICTURES: Another Country, 1919, A Month in the Country, Apartment Zero, Valmont, Wings of Fame, The Pleasure Principle, Femme Fatale.
TELEVISION: Series: Lost Empires. Movies: Camille, Dutch Girls, Tumbledown, Hostages. Special: Tales from the Hollywood Hills (Pat Hobby Teamed With Genius).

FIRTH, PETER: Actor. b. Bradford, Yorkshire, Oct. 27, 1953. Appeared in local TV children's show where casting director spotted him and got him role in series, The Flaxton Boys. Moved to London and worked in TV, first in children's show, later on dramas for BBC. Breakthrough role in Equus at National Theatre, 1973 which he repeated in film.
PICTURES: Brother Sun Sister Moon, Daniel and Maria, Diamonds on Wheels, Equus (Acad. Award nom.), Joseph Andrews, Aces High, When You Comin' Back Red Ryder, Tess, Lifeforce, Letter to Brezhnev, Trouble in Paradise, White Elephant, A State of Emergency, Born of Fire, The Tree of Hands, Prisoner of Rio, Burndown, The Hunt for Red October, The Rescuers Down Under (voice), The Perfect Husband, White Angel, Shadowlands.
STAGE: Equus (Theatre World Award), Romeo and Juliet, Spring Awakening, Amadeus.
TELEVISION: Series: The Flaxon Boys, Home and Away, Country Matters. Movies and specials: Here Comes the Doubledeckers, Castlehaven, The Sullen Sisters, The Simple Life, The Magistrate, The Protectors, Black Beauty, Arthur, Her Majesty's Pleasure, the Picture of Dorian Gray, Lady of the Camillias, The Flip Side of Domenic Hide, Blood Royal,

Northanger Abbey, The Way, The Truth: the Video, The Incident, Children Crossing, Prisoner of Honor, Married to Murder, The Laughter of God, Murder in Eden.

FISHBURNE, LAURENCE (LARRY): Actor. b. Augusta, GA, July 30, 1961. Raised in Brooklyn. Landed role on daytime serial One Life to Live at age 11. On NY stage in Short Eyes, Two Trains Running (Tony and Theatre World Awards).
PICTURES: Cornbread Earl and Me (debut, 1975), Fast Break, Apocalypse Now, Willie and Phil, Death Wish II, Rumble Fish, The Cotton Club, The Color Purple, Quicksilver, Band of the Hand, A Nightmare on Elm Street 3: Dream Warriors, Gardens of Stone, School Daze, Red Heat, King of New York, Cadence, Class Action, Boyz N the Hood, Deep Cover, What's Love Got to Do With It, Searching for Bobby Fischer.
TELEVISION: *Series*: One Life to Live, Pee-wee's Playhouse. *Guest*: M*A*S*H, Trapper John, M.D., Spenser: For Hire.*Movies*: A Rumor of War, I Take These Men, Father Clements Story, Decoration Day.

FISHER, AL: Executive. b. Brooklyn, NY. Entered m.p. industry as office boy, Fox Metropolitan Theatres; U.S. Army Provost Marshal General's Office, 1942–46; Universal Pictures, mgr., Park Avenue Theatre, N.Y. & Copley Plaza Theatre, Boston, 1946; Eagle Lion Film Co., mgr., Red Shoe's Bijou Theatre, N.Y., 1947; Stanley Kramer Prods., exploitation, Cyrano de Bergerac, 1951; press agent, 1951; prod., Bway show, Daphine, 1952; joined United Artists Corporation, 1952, named dir. of exploitation; now freelancing as producer's repr.

FISHER, CARRIE: b. Beverly Hills, CA, Oct. 21, 1956. e. London Central Sch. of Speech & Drama. Daughter of Debbie Reynolds and Eddie Fisher. On Broadway in the chorus of revival of Irene (1972) and Censored Scenes from King Kong. Author: Postcards From the Edge (1987), Surrender the Pink (1990).
PICTURES: Shampoo (debut, 1975), Star Wars, Mr. Mike's Mondo Video, The Empire Strikes Back, The Blues Brothers, Under the Rainbow, Return of the Jedi, Garbo Talks, The Man with One Red Shoe, Hannah and Her Sisters, Hollywood Vice Squad, Amazon Women on the Moon, Appointment with Death, The 'Burbs, Loverboy, She's Back, When Harry Met Sally, The Time Guardian, Postcards From the Edge (s.p. only), Sibling Rivalry, Drop Dead Fred, Soapdish, This is My Life.
TELEVISION: *Movies*: Leave Yesterday Behind, Liberty, Sunday Drive, Sweet Revenge. *Specials*: Come Back Little Sheba, Classic Creatures: Return of the Jedi, Thumbelina (Faerie Tale Theatre), Paul Reiser: Out on a Whim, Two Daddies? (voice), Trying Times (Hunger Chic). *Guest*: Laverne and Shirley, George Burns' Comedy Week.

FISHER, EDDIE: Singer. b. Philadelphia, PA, Aug. 10, 1928. Father of actress Carrie Fisher. Band, nightclub, hotel singer; discovered by Eddie Cantor. Army 1951–53; many hit records include; Wish You Were Here, Lady of Spain; radio & TV shows, NBC. *Series*: Coke Time With Eddie Fisher (1953–7), The Eddie Fisher Show (1957–9).
PICTURES: Bundle of Joy, Butterfield 8, Nothing Lasts Forever.

FISHER, LUCY: Executive. b. Oct. 2, 1949. e. Harvard U., B.A. Exec. chg. creative affairs, MGM; v.p., creative affairs, 20th Century Fox; v.p., prod., Fox. 1980, head of prod., Zoetrope Studios; 1980–82, v.p., sr. prod. exec., Warner Bros.; 1983, sr. v.p. prod., WB.

FISK, JACK: Director. b. Ipava, IL, Dec. 19. e. Cooper Union-Pa. Acad. of the Fine Arts. m. actress Sissy Spacek. Career in films as designer turning to direction with Raggedy Man (1981).
PICTURES: Director: Raggedy Man, Violets Are Blue, Daddy's Dyin', ... Who's Got the Will? Art Director: Badlands, Phantom of the Paradise, Carrie, Days of Heaven, Heart Beat.

FITELSON, H. WILLIAM: Attorney, counsel to Fitelson, Lasky and Aslan, law firm, New York, specializing in the field of communications (publishing, motion pictures, theatre, television, radio); b. New York, NY, Jan. 21, 1905. e. Columbia U. (extension), New York Law School. Newspaper and editorial work, librarian and tutor New York Law School, Story Department Tiffany-Stahl Productions 1929, counsel Tiffany-Stahl Productions 1929–32, United States counsel to British and foreign motion picture and theatrical producers, counsel to The Theatre Guild and numerous members motion picture industry, theatre industry, newspaper and publishing, television and radio interests, managing director Theatre Guild Television and radio divisions, including U.S. Steel Hour. Non-legal consultant on communications projects to Allen & Co., and Columbia Pictures Industries.

FITZGERALD, GERALDINE: Actress. b. Dublin, Ireland, Nov. 24, 1914. e. Dublin Art Sch. Mother of director Michael Lindsay-Hogg. On stage Gate Theat., Dublin; then in number of Brit. screen prod. including Turn of the Tide, Mill on the Floss. On N.Y. stage in Heartbreak House. Founded Everyman Street Theatre with brother Jonathan Ringkamp.
PICTURES: Blind Justice, Radio Parade of 1935, Department Store, The Turn of the Screw, 3 Witnesses, The Mill on the Floss, Wuthering Heights (U.S. debut, 1939), Dark Victory, A Child is Born, Till We Meet Again, Flight from Destiny, Shining Victory, Gay Sisters, Watch on the Rhine, Ladies Courageous, Wilson, The Strange Affair of Uncle Harry, Three Strangers, O.S.S., Nobody Lives Forever, So Evil My Love, The Obsessed, Ten North Frederick, The Fiercest Heart, The Pawnbroker, Rachel Rachel, Believe in Me, The Last American Hero, Harry and Tonto, Echoes of a Summer, The Mango Tree, Bye Bye Monkey, Lovespell, Arthur, Easy Money, Poltergeist II, Arthur 2: On the Rocks.
STAGE: Sons and Soldiers, Portrait in Black, The Doctor's Dilemma, King Lear, Hide and Seek, A Long Day's Journey Into Night, (1971), Ah, Wilderness, The Shadow Box, A Touch of the Poet, Songs of the Streets (one woman show), Mass Appeal (dir. only), The Lunch Girls (dir.).
TELEVISION: *Series*: Our Private World, The Best of Everything. *Movies*: Yesterday's Child, The Quinns, Dixie: Changing Habits, Do You Remember Love?, Circle of Violence, Night of Courage, Bump in the Night. Mini-Series: Kennedy. *Special*: Street Songs.

FLATTERY, THOMAS L.: Executive-Lawyer b. Detroit, MI, Nov. 14, 1922. e. U.S. Military Acad., West Point, B.S., 1944–47; UCLA, J.D., 1952–55; U. of Southern California, LL.M. 1955–65. Radioplane Company, staff counsel and asst. contract admin. 1955–7. Gen'l counsel and asst. sec'y, McCulloch Corp., CA, 1957–64; sec'y and corporate counsel, Technicolor, Inc., 1964–70; Vice President, Secretary & General Counsel, Amcord, Inc. (formerly American Cement Corporation) 1970–72; Vice President, Secretary & General Counsel, Schick Incorporated, 1972–75; counsel asst. secretary, C.F. Braun & Co., 1975–76; sr. vice pres., secretary & general counsel PCC Technical Industries, Inc. 1976–86 (a unit of The Peru Control Corporation); V.P. & gen counsel and secretary, G & H Technology, Inc. (a unit of The Penn Central Corp.), 1986–93. Attorney at law, 1993.

FLAXMAN, JOHN P.: Producer. b. New York, NY, March 3, 1934. e. Dartmouth U., B.A. 1956. 1st Lt. U.S. Army, 1956–58. Ent. m.p. industry in executive training program, Columbia Pictures Corp., 1958–63; exec. story consultant, Profiles in Courage, 1964–65; head of Eastern Literary Dept., Universal Pictures, 1965; writer's agent, William Morris Agency, 1966; partner with Harold Prince in Media Productions, Inc. 1967; prod. m.p. Something for Everyone. Founded Flaxman Film Corp., 1975 Prod. Jacob Two-Two Meets the Hooded Fang, 1976. President-Tricorn Productions 1977; pres. Filmworks Capital Corp., 1979–83; Becker/Flaxman & Associates, 1979–83; pres., Cine Communications, 1983–present. Producer Off-Broadway, Yours, Anne (1985).
TELEVISION: The Caine Mutiny Court-Martial (prod.).

FLEISCHER, RICHARD O.: Director. b. Brooklyn, NY, Dec. 8, 1916. e. Brown U., B.A.; Yale U., M.F.A. Son of animator Max Fleischer. Stage dir.; joined RKO Pathe 1942. Author: Just Tell Me When to Cry.
PICTURES: Flicker Flashbacks (s.p., prod.), This Is America (dir., s.p.), Design for Death (co-prod.; Acad. Award. Best Feature-Length Documentary). Director: Child of Divorce, Banjo, So This Is New York, Bodyguard, Follow Me Quietly, Make Mine Laughs, The Clay Pigeon, Trapped, Armored Car Robbery, The Narrow Margin, The Happy Time, Arena, 20000 Leagues Under the Sea, Violent Saturday, Girl in the Red Velvet Swing, Bandido, Between Heaven and Hell, The Vikings, These Thousand Hills, Compulsion, Crack in the Mirror, The Big Gamble, Barabbas, Fantastic Voyage, Doctor Dolittle, The Boston Strangler, Che!, Tora! Tora! Tora!, 10 Rillington Place, The Last Run, See No Evil, The New Centurions, Soylent Green, The Don Is Dead, The Spikes Gang, Mr. Majestyk, Mandingo, The Incredible Sarah, Crossed Swords, Ashanti, The Jazz Singer, Tough Enough, Amityville 3-D, Conan the Destroyer, Red Sonja, Million Dollar Mystery, Call From Space.

FLEMING, JANET BLAIR: Executive. b. Ottawa, Canada, November 29, 1944. e. Carlton U., Ottawa, Canada, B.A. Secretary to Canada's Federal Minister of Transport 1967–72; 1973–77, asst. to Sandy Howard—business affairs; 1977, co-founder and v.p./sales & admin. of Producers Sales Organization; 1981, named sr. v.p.; 1982, sr. v.p., acquisitions; 1983, exec. v.p., Skouras Pictures; 1985 promoted to pres., intl. div.; 1987–88 mgr. Lift Haven Inn, Sun Valley, ID; 1989–present, owner/partner Premiere Properties (prop. management, Sun Valley, ID).

FLEMING, RHONDA: Actress. r.n. Marilyn Louis. b. Los Angeles, CA, Aug. 10. m. Ted Mann (Mann Theatres). e. Beverly Hills H.S. p. Harold and Effie Graham Louis. Member, several charity orgs. Bd. of Dir. trustee of World Opportunities Intl. (Help the Children). Alzheiner Rsch., etc. L.A. Civic Light Opera in Kismet revival, 1976. Broadway debut, 1973: The Women (revival). Opened Rhonda Fleming Mann Clinic for

Women's Comprehensive Care at U.C.L.A. Medical Center, 1991. Many awards incl. Woman of the Year Award from City of Hope 1986 & 1991.

PICTURES: In Old Oklahoma, Since You Went Away, When Strangers Marry, Spellbound, Abiline Town, Spiral Staircase, Adventure Island, Out of the Past, A Connecticut Yankee in King Arthur's Court, The Great Lover, The Eagle and the Hawk, The Redhead and the Cowboy, The Last Outpost, Cry Danger, Crosswinds, Little Egypt, Hong Kong, Golden Hawk, Tropic Zone, Pony Express, Serpent of the Nile, Inferno, Those Redheads from Seattle, Jivaro, Yankee Pasha, Tennessee's Partner, While the City Sleeps, Killer Is Loose, Slightly Scarlet, Odongo, Queen of Babylon, Gunfight at the OK Corral, Buster Keaton Story, Gun Glory, Bullwhip, Home Before Dark, Alias Jesse James, The Big Circus, The Crowded Sky, The Patsy (cameo), Won Ton Ton The Dog Who Saved Hollywood, The Nude Bomb.

TELEVISION: Guest: Wagon Train, Police Woman, Love Boat, McMillian and Wife, Legends of the Screen, Road to Hollywood, Wildest West Show of Stars. Movies: The Last Hours Before Morning, Love for Rent, Waiting for the Wind.

FLEMYNG, ROBERT: Actor. b. Liverpool, England, Jan. 3, 1912. e. Halleybury Coll. Stage debut: Rope, 1931. Screen debut: Head Over Heels, 1937.

PICTURES: Bond Street, The Guinea Pig, The Conspirators, The Blue Lamp, Blackmailed, The Magic Box, The Holly and the Ivy, Cast a Dark Shadow, Man Who Never Was, Funny Face, Let's Be Happy, Wisdom's Way, Blind Date, A Touch of Larceny, Radtus (Italian), The King's Breakfast, The Deadly Affair, The Spy with the Cold Nose, The Quiller Memorandum, Deathhead Avenger, Oh! What a Lovely War, Battle of Britain, Cause for Alarm, Young Winston, The Darwin Adventure, Travels with My Aunt, Golden Rendezvous, The Medusa Touch, The Four Feathers, The Thirty-Nine Steps, Paris By Night, Kafka.

TELEVISION: appearances in England, U.S. inc.: Rainy Day, Playhouse 90, Wuthering Heights, Browning Version, After the Party, Boyd Q.C., They Made History, Somerset Maugham Show, Woman in White, The Datchet Diamonds, Probation Officer, Family Solicitor (series), Man of the World, Zero One, Compact, (serial), Day by the Sea, The Living Room, Hawks and Doves, Vanity Fair, The Inside Man, The Doctor's Dilemma, The Persuaders, Major Lavender, Public Eye, Florence Nightingale, Edward VIII, Spy Trap, The Venturers' Loyalties, The Avengers, Crown Court, Enemy at the Door, Rebecca, Edward and Mrs. Simpson, The Ladykiller, Professionals, Fame Is the Spur, Crown Court, Spider's Webb, Executive Suite, Small World, Perfect Scoundrels, Short Story.

FLETCHER, LOUISE: Actress. b. Birmingham, AL, July 22, 1934. e. U. of North Carolina, B.A. Came to Hollywood at age 21; studied with Jeff Corey. Worked on TV shows (including Playhouse 90, Maverick). Gave up career to be a mother for 10 yrs.; returned to acting in 1973. Board of Directors: Deafness Research Foundation, 1980—.Honorary Degrees: Doctor of Humane Letters from Gallaudet U. and West Maryland Col.

PICTURES: Thieves Like Us, Russian Roulette, One Flew Over the Cuckoo's Nest (Acad. Award, 1975), Exorcist II: The Heretic, The Cheap Detective, Natural Enemies, The Magician of Lublin, The Lucky Star, The Lady in Red, Strange Behavior, Mamma Dracula, Brainstorm, Strange Invaders, Firestarter, Once Upon a Time in America, Overnight Sensation, Invaders from Mars, The Boy Who Could Fly, Nobody's Fool, Flowers in the Attic, Two Moon Junction, Best of the Best, Shadow Zone, Blue Steel, Blind Vision, The Player, Georgino.

TELEVISION: Series: Boys of Twilight. Movies: Can Ellen Be Saved?, Thou Shalt Not Commit Adultery, A Summer to Remember, Island, Second Serve, J. Edgar Hoover, The Karen Carpenter Story, Final Notice, Nightmare on the 13th Floor, In a Child's Name, The Fire Next Time. Guest: Twilight Zone, Tales from the Crypt, Civil Wars.

FLINN, JOHN C.: Publicist. b. Yonkers, NY, May 4, 1917. e. U. of California. p. late John C. Flinn, pioneer m.p. executive. In pub. dept. David O. Selznick, 1936–39; until publicist, then head planter, Warner, 1936–46; joined Monogram as asst. to nat'l adv. & pub. head & pub. mgr. Aug. 5, 1946; apptd. nat'l dir. of pub. & adv. of Allied Artists Pictures Corp., March, 1951, appt'd studio dir. adv. & pub., Columbia, March, 1959; v.p., Jim Mahoney & Associates (pub. rel. firm) in 1971. Joined MGM West Coast publicity department as publicity coordinator, January, 1974; Rejoined Columbia Pictures in Feb., 1974 as studio pub. dir.; 1979, promoted to dir. industry relations. Joined MGM/UA pub. staff, 1988 to work on m.p. academy campaign for Moonstruck. Engaged by Paramount 1988–89 to assist in Acad. Award campaigns. Retired.

FLOREA, JOHN: Producer, Director, Writer. b. Alliance, OH, May 28, 1916. Served as photo journalist with Life magazine, 1940–50; assoc. editor Colliers magazine, 1950–53. Prod.-dir. with David Gerber 1979–84.

TELEVISION: Dir. several episodes: Sea Hunt series, 1957–60; Bonanza, Outlaws, Outpost (pilot), The Virginian, Honey West, Daktari, Gentle Ben, Cowboy in Africa, High Chapparal, Destry Rides Again, Not For Hire, Ironside, Highway Patrol, Target, Everglades, (also prod.), CHIPS, MacGyver. Prod.-dir. of film Islands of the Lost. With Ivon Tors Films. Nominated as one of the Top 10 directors in America by DGA for 1968 Mission Impossible episode. Dir. several Ironside episodes. Doc: Kammikazi, Attack Hawaiian Hospitality, Million Dollar Question, Marineland, Brink of Disaster. (Valley Freedom Award), Dangerous Report, (for CIA), The Runaways (Emmy Award), Down the Long Hills, Dark Canyon.

PICTURES: A Time to Every Purpose, The Astral Factor, The Invisible Strangler, Hot Child in the City.

FLYNN, JOHN: Director-Writer. b. Chicago IL. e. George Washington U, Stanford, UCLA, B.A. (Eng.). Worked in mailroom at MCA then with p.r. firm. Began career as trainee script supvr. for dir. Robert Wise on West Side Story. Soon working as ass't. dir. on MGM-TV shows. Made dir. debut with The Sergeant, 1969.

PICTURES: The Jerusalem File, The Outfit (also s.p.), Rolling Thunder, Defiance, Touched, Best Seller, Lock Up.

TELEVISION: Marilyn—The Untold Story (dir.)

FOCH, NINA: Actress. b. Leyden, Holland, April 20, 1924; daughter of Consuelo Flowerton, actress, & Dirk Foch, symphony orch. conductor. Many stage, radio, television appearances. Adjunct Prof., U. of Southern California, 1966–67; 1978–80, Adjunct professor, USC Cinema-TV grad. sch. 1986–; sr. faculty, American Film Inst., 1974–77; Board of Governors, Hollywood Acad. of Television Arts & Sciences, 1976–77; Exec. Comm. Foreign Language Film Award, Acad. of Motion Picture Arts & Sciences, 1970–. Co-chmn., exec. comm. Foreign Language Film Award 1983–.

PICTURES: The Return of the Vampire (debut, 1943), Nine Girls, Cry of the Werewolf, She's a Soldier Too, She's a Sweetheart, Shadows in the Night, I Love a Mystery, Prison Ship, Song to Remember, My Name is Julia Ross, Boston Blackie's Rendezvous, Escape in the Fog, The Guilt of Jane Ames, Johnny O'Clock, The Dark Past, Johnny Allegro, Undercover Man, St. Benny the Dip, An American in Paris, Young Man With Ideas, Scaramouche, Sombrero, Fast Company, Executive Suite, Four Guns to the Border, Ten Commandments, Illegal, You're Never Too Young, Three Brave Men, Cash McCall, Spartacus, Such Good Friends, Salty, Mahogany, Jennifer, Rich and Famous, Skin Deep, Sliver.

TELEVISION: Series: Q.E.D. (panelist), It's News to Me (panelist), Shadow Chasers. Movies: Outback Bound, In the Arms of a Killer, The Sands of Time. Mini-series: War and Remembrance, Tales of the City. Guest star, most major series incl. L.A. Law, Dear John, Hunter; talk shows, specials.

FOGARTY, JACK V.: Executive, Producer, Writer. b. Los Angeles, CA. e. UCLA. Management, MGM, 1960–62; exec. prod. mgr., Cinerama, Inc., 1962–64; assoc. prod., The Best of Cinerama, 1963; est. own p.r. firm, 1965; pres., AstroScope, Inc., 1969–74.

TELEVISION: (writer/prod.) The Rookies, S.W.A.T., Charlie's Angels, Most Wanted, Barnaby Jones, A Man Called Sloane, Trapper John, T.J. Hooker, Crazy Like a Fox, The Equalizer, Jake and the Fatman, Murder She Wrote, Charlie's Angels (story edit.); exec. story consultant: Most Wanted, A Man Called Sloane, Sheriff Lobo, T.J. Hooker. Producer: T.J. Hooker, Jessie.

FOGELSON, ANDREW: Executive. b. New Rochelle, NY, August 5, 1942. e. Union Coll., 1960–64. First entered m.p. industry in 1968 with Warner Bros., starting as copywriter and soon made exec. asst. to v.p. of adv.-pub. In 1973 apptd. v.p., marketing services. Joined Columbia Pictures in Dec. 1973, as v.p. in chg. world-wide adv.-pub. In 1977 went to Warner Bros. as exec. v.p. in chg. worldwide adv.-pub. 1979 left to become pres. of Rastar Prods. Resigned 1981 to become indep. prod. under Summa Entertainment Group banner. Formed AFA co., a marketing co., 1988.

PICTURES: Wrong Is Right (exec. prod.), Blue Thunder (exec. prod.), Spring Break (exec. prod.), Just One of the Guys (prod.)

FOLEY, JAMES: Director. b. New York, NY. E. NYU, USC. While at USC directed two short films, Silent Night and November which brought him attention. Directed two Madonna videos: Live to Tell and Papa Don't Preach.

PICTURES: Reckless, At Close Range, Who's That Girl, After Dark My Sweet, Glengarry Glen Ross.

FOLSEY, GEORGE, JR: Producer, Editor. b. Los Angeles, CA, Jan. 17, 1939. Son of late cinematographer George Folsey Sr. e. Pomona Coll., B.A., 1961.

PICTURES: Editor: Glass Houses (1970), Bone, Hammer, Black Caesar, Schlock, Trader Horn, Bucktown, J.D.'s Revenge, Norman . . . Is That You?, Tracks, The Chicken Chronicles, The Kentucky Fried Movie, National Lampoon's

Animal House, Freedom Road, The Great Santini (addt'l editing), The Blues Brothers (also assoc. prod.). Producer: An American Werewolf in London, Twilight Zone—The Movie (assoc. prod.); Trading Places (exec. prod. & 2nd unit dir.), Into the Night (co-prod.), Spies Like Us (co-prod.), Clue (co-exec. prod.), Three Amigos, Coming to America (co-prod., co-editor), Greed (co-exec. prod.).

VIDEO: Michael Jackson's Thriller (co-prod., editor).

FONDA, BRIDGET: Actress. b. Los Angeles, CA, Jan. 27, 1964. Daughter of actor Peter Fonda. Grew up in Los Angeles and Montana. e. NYU theater prog. Studied acting at Lee Strasberg Inst., and with Harold Guskin. Starred in grad. student film PPT. Workshop stage performances include Confession and Pastels.

PICTURES: Aria (Tristan and Isolode sequence; debut), You Can't Hurry Love, Light Years (voice), Scandal, Shag, Strapless, Frankenstein Unbound, The Godfather Part III, Drop Dead Fred (unbilled), Doc Hollywood, Leather Jackets, Out of the Rain, Iron Maze, Single White Female, Singles, Army of Darkness, Point of No Return, Bodies Rest and Motion, Little Buddha, Camilla, Cop Gives Waitress 2 Million Dollar Tip.

TELEVISION: Specials: Jacob Have I Loved (Wonderworks), The Edge (The Professional Man). Guest: 21 Jump Street.

FONDA, JANE: Actress. b. New York, NY, Dec. 21, 1937. e. Emma Willard Sch., Troy, NY. Active in dramatics, Vassar. Father, late actor Henry Fonda. Brother is actor-dir. Peter Fonda. m. executive Ted Turner. Appeared with father in summer stock production, The Country Girl, Omaha, NB. Studied painting, languages, Paris. Art Students League, N.Y. Appeared in The Male Animal, Dennis, MA. Modeled, appeared on covers, Esquire, Vogue, The Ladies Home Journal, Glamour, and McCall's, 1959. Appeared in documentaries Introduction to the Enemy and No Nukes.

PICTURES: Tall Story (debut, 1960), Walk on the Wild Side, The Chapman Report, Period of Adjustment, In the Cool of The Day, Sunday in New York, The Love Cage (Joy House), La Ronde (Circle of Love), Cat Ballou, The Chase, La Curee (The Game is Over), Any Wednesday, Hurry Sundown, Barefoot in the Park, Barbarella, Spirits of the Dead, They Shoot Horses Don't They?, Klute (Acad. Award, 1971), F.T.A. (also prod.), Tout va Bien, Steelyard Blues, A Doll's House, The Bluebird, Fun with Dick and Jane, Julia, Coming Home (Acad. Award, 1978), Comes a Horseman, California Suite, The China Syndrome, The Electric Horseman, Nine To Five, On Golden Pond, Roll-Over, Agnes of God, The Morning After, Leonard Part 6 (cameo), Old Gringo, Stanley and Iris.

STAGE: There Was A Little Girl (Theatre World Award), Invitation to a March, The Fun Couple, Strange Interlude.

TELEVISION: Specials: Lily—Sold Out, Tell Them I'm a Mermaid, Fonda on Fonda (host). Movie: The Dollmaker (Emmy, 1984). Series: 9 to 5 (exec. prod.).

FONDA, PETER: Actor, Director. b. New York, NY, Feb. 23, 1939. e. studied at U. of Omaha. Son of late actor Henry Fonda. Brother of Jane Fonda and father of actress Bridget Fonda.

PICTURES: Tammy and the Doctor (debut, 1963), The Victors, Lilith, The Young Lovers, The Wild Angels, The Trip, Spirits of the Dead, Easy Rider (also co-s.p., co-prod.), Idaho Transfer (dir.), The Last Movie, The Hired Hand (also dir.), Two People, Dirty Mary Crazy Larry, Open Season, Race with the Devil, 92 In the Shade, Killer Force, Fighting Mad, Futureworld, Outlaw Blues, High Ballin'!, Wanda Nevada (also dir.), Cannonball Run (cameo), Split Image, Certain Fury, Dance of the Dwarfs, Mercenary Fighters, Jungle Heat, Diajobu My Friend, Peppermint Frieden, Spasm, The Rose Garden, Fatal Mission, Family Spirit, Reckless, Bodies Rest & Motion, DeadFall.

TELEVISION: A Reason to Live, The Hostage Tower, A Time of Indifference, Sound, Certain Honorable Men, Montana.

FONTAINE, JOAN: Actress. b. Tokyo, Oct. 22, 1917. r.n. Joan de Havilland. e. American School in Japan. Sister of Olivia de Havilland, actress. Mother remarried man named Fontaine in 1925. Joan began acting with theatre group in San Diego as Joan Burfield, then as Joan Fontaine in Call it a Day (L.A.), where she was spotted and signed to contract by prod. Jesse Lasky. Sold contract to RKO. On B'way in Tea and Sympathy (1954); won Academy Award for best actress, 1941, for Suspicion. Acad. Award nom. for Rebecca and The Constant Nymph. Author: No Bed of Roses (1978) Appeared in The Lion in Winter at Vienna's English Speaking Theatre 1979.

PICTURES: No More Ladies (debut, 1935), Quality Street, You Can't Beat Love, Music for Madame, Maid's Night Out, A Damsel in Distress, Blonde Cheat, The Man Who Found Himself, The Duke of West Point, Sky Giant, Gunga Din, Man of Conquest, The Women, Rebecca, Suspicion, This Above All, The Constant Nymph, Jane Eyre, Frenchman's Creek, Affairs of Susan, From This Day Forward, Ivy, The Emperor Waltz, Letter from an Unknown Woman, Kiss the Blood Off My Hands, You Gotta Stay Happy, Born to Be Bad, Septem-

ber Affair, Darling How Could You?, Something to Live For, Ivanhoe, Decameron Nights, Flight to Tangier, The Bigamist, Casanova's Big Night, Serenade, Beyond a Reasonable Doubt, Island in the Sun, Until They Sail, A Certain Smile, Voyage to the Bottom of the Sea, Tender is the Night, The Devil's Own.

TELEVISION: Numerous guest appearances from 1950s through 1987; also: Crossings, Dark Mansions, Cannon, The Users, Bare Essence.

FOOTE, HORTON: Writer. b. Wharton, TX, March 14, 1916. Actor before becoming playwright. Plays include Only the Heart, The Chase, Trip to Bountiful, Traveling Lady, Courtship, 1918, The Widow Claire, Habitation of Dragons, Lily Dale, Valentine's Day, Dividing the Estate, Talking Pictures, The Roads to Home, Night Seasons.

PICTURES: Storm Fear, To Kill a Mockingbird (Oscar, 1962), Baby The Rain Must Fall, Hurry Sundown, Tomorrow, Tender Mercies (Oscar, 1983), 1918, The Trip to Bountiful, On Valentine's Day, Convicts, Of Mice and Men.

TELEVISION: Only the Heart, Ludie Brooks, The Travelers, The Old Beginning, Trip to Bountiful, Young Lady of Property, Death of the Old Man, Flight, The Night of the Storm, The Roads to Home, Drugstore: Sunday Night, Member of the Family, Traveling Lady, Old Man, Tomorrow, The Shape of the River, The Displaced Person, Barn Burning, The Habitation of Dragons.

FORBES, BRYAN: Actor, Writer, Producer, Director. m. actress Nanette Newman. Former head of prod., man. dir., Associated British Prods. (EMI). b. Stratford (London), July 22, 1926. Stage debut, The Corn Is Green (London), 1942; screen debut, The Small Back Room, 1948. Pres.: National Youth Theatre of Great Britain, 1985–; Pres.: Writers Guild of Great Britain, 1988–

THEATRE: Director: Macbeth, Star Quality, Killing Jessica, The Living Room.

PICTURES: Actor: Tired Men, The Small Back Room All Over the Town, Dear Mr. Prohack, Green Grow The Rushes, The Million Pound Note (Man With a Million), An Inspector Calls, The Colditz Story, Passage Home, Appointment in London, Sea Devils, The Extra Day, Quatermass II, It's Great To be Young, Satellite In The Sky, The Baby and The Battleship, Yesterday's Enemy, The Guns of Navarone, A Shot in The Dark, Of Human Bondage, Restless Natives. Writer: The Cockleshell Heroes, The Black Tent, Danger Within, I Was Monty's Double (also actor), The League of Gentlemen (also actor), The Angry Silence (also prod., actor), Man in the Moon, Only Two Can Play, Station Six Sahara, Of Human Bondage (also actor), Hopscotch, Chaplin. Director-Writer: Whistle Down the Wind (dir. only), The L-Shaped Room (also actor), Seance on a Wet Afternoon (also prod.), King Rat, The Wrong Box, The Whisperers, Deadfall, The Madwoman of Chaillot (dir. only), The Raging Moon (Long Ago Tomorrow; also actor), The Stepford Wives (dir., actor), The Slipper and the Rose (also actor), International Velvet (also actor), Sunday Lovers (co-dir. only), Better Late Than Never (Menage a Trois), The Naked Face. Exec. Prod.: Hoffman, Forbush and the Penguins, The Railway Children, Peter Rabbit and the Tales of Beatrix Potter, The Go-Between, And Soon The Darkness, On The Buses, Dulcima.

TELEVISION: Actor: Johnnie Was a Hero, The Breadwinner, French Without Tears, Journey's End, The Gift, The Road, The Heiress, December Flower, First Amongst Equals. Writer/Dir.: I Caught Acting Like The Measles (documentary on the life of Dame Edith Evans) Goodbye Norma Jean and Other Things (documentary on the life of Elton John) Jessie, The Endless Game.

PUBLICATIONS: Short stories: Truth Lies Sleeping. Novels: The Distant Laughter, Familiar Strangers (U.S.: Stranger), The Rewrite Man, The Endless Game, A Song at Twilight (U.S.: A Spy at Twlight), The Twisted Playground. Novelizations: The Slipper and the Rose, International Velvet. Non-Fiction: Ned's Girl (bio. of Dame Edith Evans) That Despicable Race (history of the British acting tradition). Autobiographies: Notes for a Life, A Divided Life.

FORBES, DAVID: Executive. b. Omaha, NE, Nov. 9, 1945. e. U. of Nebraska. Began career with MGM in 1968 as field man in Detroit; later named asst. natl. field coordinator at studio. Director, Metrovision, 1973. Director special projects for 20th-Fox, 1974; made natl. dir. marketing services, 1976. In 1977 left to join Rastar Prods. as marketing dir. Named v.p. & asst. to pres., Columbia Pictures, 1980; 1982, joined Almi Distributing Corp. as vice chmn. Joined MGM/UA, 1987. Pres. MGM/UA Distribution and pres. worldwide marketing, MGM Film Group; 1989 UA Film Group pres. marketing and dist. 1990, became pres. Orion Pictures.

FORD, GLENN: Actor. r.n. Gwylin Ford; b. Quebec, Canada, May 1, 1916. On stage in western co. Children's Hour 1935; on Broadway in: Broom for a Bride, Soliloquy; served in U.S. Marine Corps 1942–45.

PICTURES: Heaven With a Barbed Wire Fence (debut, 1940), My Son is Guilty, Convicted Women, Men Without

Souls, Babies for Sale, Blondie Play Cupid, Lady in Question, So Ends Our Night, Texas, Go West Yound Lady, Adventures of Martin Eden, Flight Lieutenant, Destroyer, Desperadoes, Stolen Life, Gilda, Gallant Journey, Framed, Mating of Millie, Return of October, Loves of Carmen, Man from Colorado, Mr. Soft Touch, Undercover Man, Lust for Gold, Doctor and the Girl, The White Tower, Convicted, Flying Missile, The Redhead and the Cowboy, Follow the Sun, The Secret of Convict Lake, Green Glove, Young Man with Ideas, Affair in Trinidad, Time Bomb (Terror on a Train), Man from the Alamo, Plunder of the Sun, Big Heat, Appointment in Honduras, Human Desire, The Americano, Violent Men, Blackboard Jungle, Interrupted Melody, Trial, Ransom, Fastest Gun Alive, Jubal, Teahouse of the August Moon, 3:10 to Yuma, Don't Go Near the Water, Cowboy, The Sheepman, Imitation General, Torpedo Run, It Started with a Kiss, The Gazebo, Cimarron, Cry for Happy, Pocketful or Miracles, The Four Horsemen of The Apocalypse, Experiment in Terror, Love Is a Ball, The Courtship of Eddie's Father, Advance to the Rear, Fate Is the Hunter, Dear Heart, The Rounders, The Money Trap, Is Paris Burning?, Rage, A Time for Killing, The Last Challenge, Day of the Evil Gun, Heaven with a Gun, Smith!, Santee, Midway, Superman, The Visitor, Virus, Happy Birthday to Me, Border Shootout, Raw Nerve.
TELEVISION: *Series*: Cade's County, Friends of Man (narrator), The Family Holvak, When Havoc Struck (narrator). *Movies*: Brotherhood of the Bell, The Greatest Gift, Punch and Jody, The 3000 Mile Chase, Evening in Byzantium, The Sacketts, Beggarman Thief, The Gift, Final Verdict. Mini-Series: Once an Eagle.

FORD, HARRISON: Actor. b. Chicago, IL, July 13, 1942. e. Ripon Coll. Started acting in summer stock at Williams Bay, WI, in Damn Yankees, Little Mary Sunshine. Moved to L.A. where he acted in John Brown's Body. Signed by Columbia Studios under seven-year contract. Took break from acting to undertake carpentry work which included building Sergio Mendes' recording studio. Returned to acting winning notice in American Graffiti.
PICTURES: Dead Heat on a Merry-Go-Round (debut, 1966), Luv, A Time for Killing, Journey to Shiloh, Zabriskie Point, Getting Straight, American Graffiti, The Conversation, Star Wars, Heroes, Force 10 from Navarone, Hanover Street, The Frisco Kid, More American Graffiti (cameo), Apocalypse Now, The Empire Strikes Back, Raiders of the Lost Ark, Blade Runner, Return of the Jedi, Indiana Jones and the Temple of Doom, Witness (Acad. Award nom.), The Mosquito Coast, Frantic, Working Girl, Indiana Jones and the Last Crusade, Presumed Innocent, Regarding Henry, Patriot Games, The Fugitive.
TELEVISION: *Movies*: The Intruders, James A. Michener's Dynasty, The Possessed. *Guest*: The Virginian, Ironside, The FBI, Love American Style, Gunsmoke, The Young Indiana Jones Chronicles. *Special*: Trial of Lt. Calley.

FORMAN, SIR DENIS, O.B.E., M.A.: Executive. b. Moffat, Dumfriesshire, Scot., Oct. 13, 1917. e. Loretto Sch., Musselburgh, Pembroke Coll., Cambridge. Served in Argyll & Sutherland Highlanders, W.W.II. Entered film business May, 1946, production staff Central Office of Information, 1947; Chief Production Officer C.O.I. 1948; appointed dir. of the British Film Inst., 1949; joined Granada Television Ltd., 1955. Jnt. Mng. Dir., 1965 chmn., British Film Inst., Bd. of Gov., 1971–73. Chmn. Granada T.V. 1975–1987. Chmn. Novello & Co. 1972. Fellow, British Acad. Film & TV Arts, 1976. Dep. chmn. Granada Group, 1984–90, now consultant.

FORMAN, JEROME A.: Executive. b. Hood River, Oregon, June 20, 1934. e. U Arizona. Became gen. mgr. Forman and United Theatres of the Northwest in 1966. 1971, joined Pacific Theatres; 1972, appointed v.p. and gen. mgr.; 1978–87, exec. v.p.; 1987–present, president. One of the original founders of the ShoWest Convention. Currently chmn. emeritus, NATO of Calif. Presently 1991 chmn. NATO. 1991 elected chmn. bd. of Will Rogers Memorial Fund.

FORMAN, MILOS: Director. b. Caslav, Czechoslovakia, Feb. 18, 1932. Trained as writer at Czech Film Sch. and as director at Laterna Magika. Won Int'l. attention with first film Black Peter, 1963. Emigrated to U.S. after collapse of Dubcek govt. in Czechoslovakia.
PICTURES: Competition, Firemen and Pavla (a.k.a. Black Peter; Czech Film Critics Award, 1963; Grand Prix Locarno, 1964.), Loves of a Blonde, Firemen's Ball, Taking Off, Visions of Eight (Decathlon segment), One Flew Over the Cuckoo's Nest (Acad. Award, 1975), Hair, Ragtime, Amadeus (Acad. Award, 1984), Heartburn (actor only), Valmont, New Year's Day (actor only).

FORREST, FREDERIC: Actor. b. Waxahachie, TX, Dec. 23, 1936. e. Texas Christian U., U. of Oklahoma, B.A. Studied with Sanford Meisner and Lee Strasberg. Began career off-off Bdwy at Caffe Cino in The Madness of Lady Bright then off-Bdwy in Futz, Massachusetts Trust and Tom Paine, all with La Mama Troupe under direction of Tom O'Horgan. Moved to Hollywood in 1970.

PICTURES: When the Legends Die (debut, 1972), The Don is Dead, The Conversation, The Gravy Train, Permission to Kill, The Missouri Breaks, It Lives Again, Apocalypse Now, The Rose, One from the Heart, Hammett, Valley Girl, The Stone Boy, Return, Where Are the Children?, Stacking, Tucker: The Man and His Dream, Valentino Returns, Music Box, The Two Jakes, Cat Chaser, Rain Without Thunder, Falling Down, Trauma.
TELEVISION: *Movies*: Larry, Promise Him Anything, Ruby and Oswald, Calamity Jane, Right to Kill?, The Deliberate Stranger, Quo Vadis, Little Girl Lost, Saigon: Year of the Cat (U.K.), Best Kept Secrets, Who Will Love My Children? A Shadow on the Sun, Margaret Bourke-White, Citizen Cohn, The Habitation of Dragons. *Mini-Series*: Die Kinder.

FORREST, STEVE: Actor. b. Huntsville, TX, Sept. 29, 1925. r.n. William Forrest Andrews. Brother of late actor Dana Andrews. e. UCLA, 1950. Acted at La Jolla Playhouse; appeared on radio, TV; m.p. debut in Geisha Girl.
PICTURES: Bad and the Beautiful, Battle Circus, The Clown, Band Wagon, Dream Wife, So Big, Take t' High Ground, Phantom of the Rue Morgue, Prisoner of Wa Rogue Cop, Bedeviled, It Happened to Jane, Heller in Pi Fights, Five Branded Women, Flaming Star, The Secoi Time Around, The Longest Day, The Yellow Canary, Rascal, The Wild Country, The Late Liz, North Dallas Forty, Mommie Dearest, Sahara, Spies Like Us, Amazon Women on the Moon.
TELEVISION: *Movies*: The Hatfields and the McCoys, Wanted: The Sundance Women, The Last of the Mohicans, Testimony of Two Men, Maneaters are Loose, Hollywood Wives, Gunsmoke: Return to Dodge, Columbo: A Bird in the Hand. *Series*: The Baron, S.W.A.T., Dallas.

FORSTATER, MARK: Producer. b. Philadelphia, PA, 1943. e. City Coll. of New York, Temple U. In 1967 moved to England; studied at U. of Manchester and London Intl. Film School. First job in industry with Anglia TV on program, Survival. Began producing in 1970 with British Film Institute. Set up Chippenham Films to make documentaries. Moved into features in 1974 with Monty Python and the Holy Grail.
PICTURES: The Odd Job, Marigolds in August, The Grass Is Singing, Xtro, Paint It Black, Wherever She Is, The Wolves of Willoughby Chase, Death of a Schoolboy, Streets of Yesterday, Wherever You Are (exec. prod.). Shorts: The Glitterball, Wish You Were Here.
TELEVISION: The Cold Room, Forbidden.

FORSTER, ROBERT: Actor. b. Rochester, NY, July 13, 1941. e. Heidelberg Coll., Alfred U., Rochester U., B.S.
THEATRE: Mrs. Dally Has a Lover, A Streetcar Named Desire, The Glass Menagerie, 12 Angry Men, The Sea Horse, One Flew Over the Cuckoo's Nest.
PICTURES: Reflections in a Golden Eye (debut, 1967), The Stalking Moon, Medium Cool, Justine, Cover Me Babe, Pieces of Dreams, Journey Through Rosebud, The Don is Dead, Stunts, Avalanche, The Black Hole, Lady in Red (unbilled), Crunch, Alligator, Vigilante, Walking the Edge, Hollywood Harry (also prod., dir.), The Delta Force, Committed, Esmeralda Bay, Heat from Another Sun, The Banker, Peacemaker, Diplomatic Immunity, 29th Street, Badge of Silence, South Beach.
TELEVISION: *Series*: Banyon, Nakia, Once a Hero. *Movies*: Banyon, The Death Squad, Nakia, The City, Standing Tall, The Darker Side of Terror, Goliath Awaits, In the Shadow of a Killer, Sex Love and Cold Hard Cash. *Pilots*: Checkered Flag, Mickie & Frankie.

FORSYTH, BILL: Director. Writer. b. Glasgow, Scotland, July 29, 1946. At 16 joined film co. For next 10 years made industrial films, then documentaries. Joined Glasgow Youth Theater.
PICTURES: *Director-Writer*: That Sinking Feeling (also prod.), Gregory's Girl, Local Hero, Comfort and Joy, Housekeeping, Breaking In, Rebecca's Daughters, Being Human.
TELEVISION: Andrina.

FORSYTHE, JOHN: Actor. b. Penn's Grove, NJ, Jan. 29, 1918. r.n. John Freund. Former commentator for Brooklyn Dodgers, prior to becoming actor.
STAGE: Mr. Roberts, All My Sons, Yellow Jack, Teahouse of the August Moon, and others.
TELEVISION: Started in 1947; appeared on Studio One, Kraft Theatre, Robert Montgomery Presents, and others. *Series*: Bachelor Father, The John Forsythe Show, To Rome with Love, Charlie's Angels (voice only), Dynasty, Powers That Be. *Movies*: See How They Run, Shadow on the Land, Murder Once Removed, The Letters, Lisa—Bright and Dark, Cry Panic, Healers, Terror on the 40th Floor, The Deadly Tower, Amelia Earhart, Tail Gunner Joe, Never Con a Killer, Cruise Into Terror, With This Ring, The Users, A Time for Miracles, Sizzle, The Mysterious Two, On Fire, Opposites Attract, Dynasty: The Reunion.
PICTURES: Destination Tokyo (debut, 1943), Captive City, It Happens Every Thursday, The Glass Web, Escape from Fort Bravo, Trouble with Harry, Ambassador's Daughter, Everything But the Truth, Kitten with a Whip, Madame X, In

Cold Blood, The Happy Ending, Topaz, And Justice for All, Scrooged.

FORSYTHE, WILLIAM: Actor. b. Brooklyn, NY.
PICTURES: King of the Mountain, Once Upon a Time in America, Cloak and Dagger, The Lightship, Raising Arizona, Extreme Prejudice, Weeds, Patty Hearst, Dead Bang, Torrents of Spring, Dick Tracy, Career Opportunities, Out for Justice, Stone Cold, Sons, American Me, The Waterdance, The Gun in Betty Lou's Handbag.
TELEVISION: Series: The Untouchables (1993). Movies: The Miracle of Kathy Miller, The Long Hot Summer, Cruel Doubt, Willing to Kill: The Texas Cheerleader Story. Guest: CHiPs, Fame, Hill Street Blues. Mini-Series: Blind Faith.
THEATRE: A Streetcar Named Desire, A Hatful of Rain, Othello, Julius Caesar, 1776, Hair, Godspell.

FORTE, FABIAN: Singer, Actor. b. Philadelphia, PA, Feb. 6, 1943. e. South Philadelphia H.S. At 14, signed contract with Chancellor Records. Studied with Carlo Menotti.
RECORDS: Turn Me Loose, Tiger, I'm a Man, Hound Dog Man (debut, 1959), The Fabulous Fabian (gold album).
PICTURES: Hound Dog Man (debut, 1959), High Time, North To Alaska, Love in a Goldfish Bowl, Five Weeks in a Balloon, Mr. Hobbs Takes a Vacation, Longest Day, Ride the Wild Surf, Dear Brigette, 10 Little Indians, Fireball 500, Dr. Goldfoot and the Girl Bombs, Thunder Alley, Maryjane, The Wild Racers, Devil's Eight, A Bullet for Pretty Boy, Little Laura and Big John, Get Crazy.
TELEVISION: Movies: Getting Married, Katie: Portrait of a Centerfold, Crisis in Mid-Air. Guest: Bus Stop, Love American Style, Laverne & Shirley, The Love Boat.

FOSSEY, BRIGITTE: Actress. b. Tourcoing, France, 1947. After a remarkable debut at the age of 5 in Rene Clement's Forbidden Games (1952) returned to school, studying philosophy and translating. Rediscovered by director Jean-Gabriel Albicocco and cast in Le Grand Meaulnes (1967).
PICTURES: Forbidden Games, The Happy Road, Le Grand Meaulnes, Adieu l'Ami, M Comme Matheiu, Making It, The Blue Country, The Man Who Loved Women, The Good and the Bad, The Swiss Affair, Quintet, Mais ou et donc Orincar, The Triple Death of the Third Character, A Bad Son, The Party, Chanel Solitaire, A Bite of Living, Imperativ, The Party-2, Enigma, Au nom de tous les Meins, Scarlet Fever, A Strange Passion, A Case of Irresponsibility, The Future of Emily, The False Confidences, Cinema Paradiso.

FOSTER, CHRISTINE: Executive. r.n. Mary Christine Foster. b. Los Angeles, CA, March 19, 1943. e. Immaculate Heart Coll, B.A. 1967. UCLA MJ, 1968. Teacher while member of Immaculate Heart Community, 1962–65. Teacher, Pacific U., Tokyo, 1968; dir., research and dev. Metromedia Producers Corp., 1968–71; dir., dev. and prod. services, The Wolper Org. 1971–76; manager, film progs. NBC Television Network 1976–77; v.p. movies for TV & mini-series, Columbia Pictures TV, 1977–81; v.p. series programs, Columbia Pictures TV 1981; v.p. prog. dev., Group W. Prods. 1981–87; Partner, The Agency, 1988–90; Agent, Shapiro-Lichtman Talent Agency, 1990–; Member: exec. comm. Humanitas Awards, 1986–; Member, Activities Committee, Acad. of TV Arts & Sciences, 1989–91; L.A. Roman Catholic Archiodean Communications Comm., 1986–89; Immaculate Heart H.S. bd of trustees, 1981–88, 1989–present; Women in Film, bd of dirs., 1977–78; Teacher UCLA Extension, 1987–; Lecturer, Univ. of Siegen, Germany, 1990–. Foreign and domestic University and public group lecturer and speaker.

FOSTER, DAVID: Producer. b. New York, NY, Nov. 25, 1929. e. Dorsey H.S., U. of Southern California Sch. of Journalism. U.S. Army, 1952–54; entered public relations field in 1952 with Rogers, Cowan & Brenner; Jim Mahoney, 1956; Allen, Foster, Ingersoll & Weber, 1958; left field in 1968 to enter independent m.p. production. Partner in Turman-Foster Co.
PICTURES: Co-produced (with Mitchell Brower): McCabe and Mrs. Miller, The Getaway. Co-produced (with Lawrence Turman): The Nickel Ride (exec. prod.), The Drowning Pool, The Legacy, Tribute (exec. prod.), Caveman, The Thing, Second Thoughts, Mass Appeal, The Mean Season (prod.), Short Circuit, Running Scared (co-prod.), Full Moon in Blue Water, Short Circuit II, Gleaming the Cube, The Getaway (1993).
TELEVISION: Jesse (co-exec. prod), Between Two Brothers, Surrogate Mother.

FOSTER, JODIE: Actress. r.n. Alicia Christian Foster. b. Los Angeles, CA, Nov. 19, 1962. e. Yale U. Started acting in commercials including famous Coppertone ad. Acting debut on Mayberry, R.F.D. TV series (1968). Followed with many TV appearances, from series to movies of the week.
PICTURES: Napoleon and Samantha (debut, 1972), Kansas City Bomber, Tom Sawyer, One Little Indian, Alice Doesn't Live Here Anymore, Taxi Driver, Echoes of a Summer, Bugsy Malone, Freaky Friday, The Little Girl Who Lives Down the Lane, Il Casotto Moi fleur bleue, Candleshoe, Foxes, Carny, O'Hara's Wife, The Hotel New Hampshire,

Mesmerized (also co-prod.), Siesta, Five Corners, Stealing Home, The Accused (Acad. Award, 1988), The Silence of the Lambs (Acad. Award, 1991), Little Man Tate (also dir.), Shadows and Fog, Sommersby.
TELEVISION: Series: Bob & Carol & Ted & Alice, Paper Moon. Guest: The Courtship of Eddie's Father, Gunsmoke, Julia, Mayberry R.F.D., Ironside, My Three Sons. Specials: The Secret Life of T.K. Dearing, Rookie of the Year, The Fisherman's Wife. Movies: Smile Jenny You're Dead, The Blood of Others, Svengali, Backtrack.

FOSTER, JULIA: Actress. b. Lewes, Sussex, England, 1944. First acted with the Brighton Repertory Company, then two years with the Worthing, Harrogate and Richmond companies. 1956, TV debut as Ann Carson in Emergency Ward 10.
PICTURES: Term of Trial, The Loneliness of the Long Distance Runner, The Small World of Sammy Lee, The System (The Gir Getters), The Bargee, One Way Pendulum, Alfie, Half a Sixpence.
TELEVISION: A Cosy Little Arrangement, The Planemakers, Love Story, Taxi, Consequences, They Throw It at You, Crime and Punishment, The Image.
STAGE: The Country Wife, What the Butler Saw.

FOSTER, MAURICE DAVID: Producer, Writer. e. St. Paul's. Ent. m.p. ind. 1943 as asst. to gen. man. and prod. sup. Easling Studios. From 1950–61, prod. sup. and dir. Film Finances, 1961–63, dir. and gen. man. MGM British Studios.
PICTURES: The Jokers, Assignment K, The Osterman Weekend.

FOSTER, MEG: Actress. b. Reading, PA, May 14, 1948. e. N.Y. Neighborhood Playhouse.
PICTURES: Adam at 6 A.M., A Different Story, Once in Paris, Carny, Ticket to Heaven, The Osterman Weekend, The Emerald Forest, The Wind, Dead On, They Live, Leviathan, Relentless, Stepfather 2, Blind Fury, Tripwire, Diplomatic Immunity, Project Shadowchaser.
TELEVISION: Movies: The Death of Me Yet, Sunshine, Things In This Season, Promise Him Anything, James Dean, Sunshine Christmas, Guyana Tragedy, Legend of Sleepy Hollow, Desperate Intruder, Best Kept Secrets, Desperate, Back Stab, To Catch a Killer. Series: Sunshine, Cagney & Lacey. Guest: Here Come the Brides, Mod Squad, Men at Law, Hawaii Five-O, Murder She Wrote, Miami Vice. Mini-Series: Washington: Behind Closed Doors. Special: The Scarlet Letter.

FOWKES, RICHARD O.: Executive. b. Yonkers, NY, April 15, 1946. e. NYU, Geo. Washington U. Staff attorney for The Dramatists Guild, 1973–77; joined Paramount Pictures as assoc. counsel, 1977–80; moved to UA (NYC) as prod. attorney from 1980–82; returned to Paramount in 1982 as v.p., legal & bus. affairs.; MoPic division (LA) in 1983; promoted to sr. v.p., bus. affairs & acquisitions, 1989.

FOWLER, HARRY: Actor. b. Lambeth Walk, London, Dec. 10, 1926. e. West Central Sch., London. Stage debut, Nothing Up My Sleeve (London) 1950; Screen debut, 1941.
PICTURES: Demi-Paradise, Don't Take It to Heart, Champaigne Charlie, Painted Boats, Hue and Cry, Now Barabbas, The Dark Man, She Shall Have Murder, The Scarlet Thread, High Treason, The Last Page, I Believe in You, Pickwick Papers, Top of the Form, Angels One Five, Conflict of Wings (Fuss Over Feathers), A Day to Remember, Blue Peter, Home and Away, Booby Trap, Town on Trial, Lucky Jim, Birthday Present, Idle on Parade, Don't Panic Chaps, Heart of a Man, Crooks Anonymous, The Longest Day, Lawrence of Arabia, Flight from Singapore, The Golliwog, Ladies Who Do, Clash By Night, The Nanny, Life at the Top, Start the Revolution Without Me, The Prince and The Pauper, Fanny Hill, Chicago Joe and the Showgirl.
TELEVISION: Stalingrad, I Remember the Battle, Gideon's Way, That's for Me, Our Man at St. Mark's, Dixon of Dock Green, Dr. Finlay's Case Book, I Was There, Cruffs Dog Show, The Londoners, Jackanory, Get This, Movie Quiz, Get This (series), Going a Bundle, Ask a Silly Answer, London Scene, Flockton Flyer, Sun Trap, The Little World of Don Camillo, World's End, Minder, Dead Ernest, Morecambe Wise Show, Gossip, Entertainment Express, Fresh Fields, Supergram, A Roller Next Year, Harry's Kingdom, Body Contact, Davro's Sketch Pad, The Bill, In Sickness and in Health, Casualty, Leaves on the Line, Young Indiana Jones Chronicles.

FOWLEY, DOUGLAS: Actor. b. New York, NY, May 30, 1911. e. St. Francis Xavier's Mil. Acad., N.Y. In stock; operated dramatic sch. N.Y.; on screen in bit parts. From 1934 in regular roles.
PICTURES: Battleground, Just This Once, This Woman Is Dangerous, Singin' in the Rain, Man Behind the Gun, Slight Case of Larceny, Naked Jungle, Casanova's Big Night, Lone Gun, The High and the Mighty, Three Ring Circus, Texas Lady, Broken Star, Girl Rush, Bandido, Nightmare in the Sun, The North Avenue Irregulars, From Noon Till Three, The White Buffalo.

TELEVISION: The Moneychangers, Starsky and Hutch, Sunshine Christmas, Oregon Trail. Series: The Life and Legend of Wyatt Earp, Pistols and Petticoats, Gunsmoke.

FOX, EDWARD: Actor. b. London, England, April 13, 1937. Comes from theatrical family; father was agent for leading London actors; brother of actor James Fox.
PICTURES: The Mind Benders, Morgan, The Frozen Dead, The Long Duel, The Naked Runner, The Jokers, I'll Never Forget What's 'is Name, The Battle of Britain, Oh! What a Lovely War, Skullduggery, The Go-Between, The Day of The Jackal, A Doll's House, Galileo, The Squeeze, A Bridge Too Far, The Duellists, The Big Sleep, Force 10 from Navarone, The Cat and the Canary, Soldier of Orange, The Mirror Crack'd, Gandhi, Never Say Never Again, The Dresser, The Bounty, Wild Geese II, The Shooting Party, Return From the River Kwai.
TELEVISION: Edward and Mrs. Simpson, A Hazard of Hearts, Anastasia: The Mystery of Anna, Shaka Zulu, Robin Hood, The Crucifer of Blood.

FOX, JAMES: Actor. b. London, England, May 19, 1939. Brother of actor Edward Fox. Ent. films as child actor in 1950 as William Fox in The Magnet, The Miniver Story, One Wild Oat, Lavender Hill Mob, Serenade and others. Left acting in 1973 to lead religious life. Returned to films 1982.
TELEVISION: The Door, Espionage, Love Is Old, Love Is New, Nancy Astor, Country, New World, Beryl Markham: A Shadow on the Sun, Sun Child, She's Been Away (BBC; shown theatrically in U.S.), Never Come Back, Slowly Slowly in the Wind, Patricia Highsmith Series, As You Like It, A Question of Attribution.
PICTURES: The Secret Partner, What Every Woman Wants, The Loneliness of the Long-Distance Runner, Tam-ahiné, The Servant, Those Magnificent Men in their Flying Machines, King Rat, The Chase, Thoroughly Modern Millie, Arabella, Duffy, Loves of Isadora, Performance, Anna Pavlova, Runners, Greystoke: The Legend of Tarzan, A Passage to India, Absolute Beginners, The Whistle Blower, Comrades, High Season, The Mighty Quinn, Farewell to the King, The Boys in the Island, The Russia House, Patriot Games, Afraid of the Dark, Hostage, Remains of the Day.

FOX, MICHAEL J.: Actor. b. Edmonton, Alberta, Canada, June 9, 1961. r.n. Michael Andrew Fox. m. actress Tracy Pollan. Appeared in Vancouver TV series Leo and Me, and on stage there in The Shadow Box. Moved to Los Angeles at age 18.
PICTURES: Midnight Madness (debut, 1980), The Class of 1984, Back to the Future, Teen Wolf, Light of Day, The Secret of My Success, Bright Lights Big City, Casualties of War, Back to the Future Part II, Back to the Future Part III, The Hard Way, Doc Hollywood, Homeward Bound: The Incredible Journey (voice), Life With Mikey, For Love or Money, Where the Rivers Flow North, Greedy.
TELEVISION: Series: Palmerstown, U.S.A., Family Ties (3 Emmy Awards). Guest: Lou Grant, The Love Boat, Night Court, Trapper John M.D., Tales from the Crypt (The Trap; also dir.). Specials: Teachers Only, Time Travel: Fact Fiction and Fantasy, Dear America: Letters Home From Vietnam, James Cagney: Top of the World (host). Movies: Letters from Frank, High School USA, Poison Ivy, Family Ties Vacation. Director: Brooklyn Bridge (episode).

FOX, RICHARD: Executive. b. New York, NY, Feb. 24, 1947. Joined Warner Bros. Intl. as mgt. trainee in October 1975, working in Australia and Japan. 1977, named gen. mgr. of Columbia-Warner Dist., New Zealand. Served as gen. mgr. of WB in Tokyo, 1978–1981. Joined WB in L.A. as exec. asst. to Myron D. Karlin, pres. of WB Intl., 1981; appt. v.p., sls. 1982; 1983, promoted to exec. v.p. of intl. arm; 1985, named pres. of WB Intl., assuming post vacated by Karlin. March 1992, promoted to exec. v.p., Intl. Theatrical Enterprises, WB.

FOX, RICHARD A.: Executive. b. Buffalo, NY, Jan 5, 1929. e. U. of Buffalo, 1950. Chmn., Fox Theatres Management Corp. Pres., Nat'l NATO 1984–86; chmn., Nat'l NATO 1986–1988.

FOXWELL, IVAN: Producer. b. London, Eng., Feb. 22, 1914. Entered m.p. ind. 1933 as technician with British & Dominions Film Corp., subsequently with Paramount British & London Films; Assoc. with Curtis Bernhardt in Paris 1937 becoming producer & collaborating on story, s.p. of Carefour, Le Train pour Venise, De Mayerling á Sarajevo, others. In W.W.II with BEF and AEF 1939–46. Returned to British films 1947 as producer, co-author screen adapt., No Room at the Inn; prod., collab. s.p., Guilt Is My Shadow; prod., Twenty-Four Hours of a Woman's Life; co-author s.p. and prod. The Intruder, The Colditz Story (TV series adapt. 1972), Manuela, A Touch of Larceny, Tiara Tahiti, The Quiller Memorandum; s.p. and prod. Decline and Fall. Director, Foxwell Film Prods. Ltd.

FOXWORTH, ROBERT: Actor. b. Houston, TX, Nov. 1, 1941. e. Carnegie-Mellon U. Began acting at age 10 at Houston Alley Theatre and stayed with stage part-time while completing formal education. Returned to theatre on full-time basis after graduation. Made TV debut in Sadbird, 1969.
TELEVISION: Series: The Storefront Lawyers, Falcon Crest. Movies: The Devil's Daughter, Frankenstein, Mrs. Sundance, The Questor Tapes (pilot), The FBI Story: The FBI Vs. Alvin Karpis, James Dean, It Happened at Lakewood Manor, Death Moon, The Memory of Eva Ryker, Act of Love, Peter and Paul, The Return of the Desperado, Double Standard, Face to Face, The Price of the Bride, With Murder in Mind. Specials: Hogan's Goat, Another Part of the Forest.
PICTURES: Treasure of Matecumbe (debut, 1976), The Astral Factor, Airport '77, Damien: Omen II, Prophecy, The Black Marble, Beyond the Stars.
STAGE: NY: Henry V, Terra Nova, The Crucible (Theatre World Award), Love Letters, Candida. Regional: Antony & Cleopatra, Uncle Vanya, Cyrano de Bergerac, Who's Afraid of Virginia Woolf?

FRAKER, WILLIAM A.: Cinematographer, Director. b. Los Angeles, CA, 1923. e. U. of Southern California Film Sch. Worked as camera operator with Conrad Hall; moved to TV before feature films.
PICTURES: Cinematographer: Games, The Fox, President's Analyst, Fade In, Rosemary's Baby, Bullitt, Paint Your Wagon, Dusty and Sweets McGee, Day of the Dolphin, Rancho Deluxe, Aloha Bobby and Rose, Lipstick, The Killer Inside Me, Gator, Exorcist II, Looking for Mr. Goodbar, American Hot Wax, Heaven Can Wait, Old Boyfriends, 1941, The Hollywood Knights, Divine Madness, Sharky's Machine, The Best Little Whorehouse in Texas, WarGames, Irreconcilable Differences, Protocol, Fever Pitch, Murphy's Romance, SpaceCamp, Burglar, Baby Boom, Chances Are, An Innocent Man, The Freshman, Memoirs of an Invisible Man, Honeymoon in Vegas, Tombstone. Director: Monte Walsh, Reflection of Fear, Legend of the Lone Ranger.
TELEVISION: Stony Burke, Outer Limits, Ozzie and Harriet, Daktari, B.L. Stryker: The Dancer's Touch (dir.).

FRANCIOSA, ANTHONY: Actor. b. New York, NY, Oct. 25, 1928. e. Ben Franklin h.s. in NY. Erwin Piscator's Dramatic Workshop (4-year scholarship). First stage part in YWCA play; joined Off-Broadway stage group; stock at Lake Tahoe, CA, Chicago and Boston.
THEATRE: Broadway: End as a Man, The Wedding Breakfast, A Hatful of Rain (Theatre World Award), Rocket to the Moon, Grand Hotel.
PICTURES: A Face in the Crowd, This Could Be The Night, A Hatful of Rain, Wild Is The Wind, The Long Hot Summer, The Naked Maja, Career, Story On Page One, Go Naked in the World, Period of Adjustment, Rio Conchos, The Pleasure Seekers, A Man Could Get Killed, Assault on a Queen, The Swinger, Fathom, In Enemy Country, The Sweet Ride, A Man Called Gannon, Ghost in the Noonday Sun, Across 110th Street, The Drowning Pool, Firepower, The World is Full of Married Men, Death Wish II, Julie Darling, Ghost in the Noonday Sun, Death Is in Fashion, Tenebrae, Help Me Dream, The Cricket, Senelith, A Texas Legend, Backstreet Dreams, Death House, Brothers in Arms, Double Threat.
TELEVISION: Series: Valentine's Day, The Name of the Game, Search, Matt Helm, Finder of Lost Loves. Movies: Fame is the Name of the Game, Deadly Hunt, Earth II, The Catcher, This is the West That Was, Matt Helm, Curse of the Black Widow, Side Show, Till Death Do Us Part, Ghost Writer. Mini-series: Aspen, Wheels. Guest: Kraft Theatre, Philco Playhouse, Danger, Naked City, Arrest & Trial, Playhouse 90, etc.

FRANCIS, ANNE: Actress b. Ossining, NY, Sept. 16, 1932. Child model; radio TV shows as child & adult; on Bdwy in Lady in the Dark.
PICTURES: Summer Holiday (debut, 1948), So Young So Bad, Whistle at Eaton Falls, Elopement, Lydia Bailey, Dream Boat, A Lion Is in the Streets, Rocket Man, Susan Slept Here, Rogue Cop, Bad Day at Black Rock, Battle Cry, Blackboard Jungle, Scarlet Coat, Forbidden Planet, The Rack, Great American Pastime, The Hired Gun, Don't Go Near the Water, Crowded Sky, Girl of the Night, Santa Bug, Brainstorm, Funny Girl, Hook Line and Sinker, More Dead Than Alive, The Love God?, Impasse, Pancho Villa, Survival, Born Again, The High Fashion Murders, The Return, Little Vegas.
TELEVISION: Series: Honey West, My Three Sons, Dallas, Riptide. Guest: Partners in Crime, Crazy Like a Fox, Jake and the Fatman, Twilight Zone, Finder of Lost Loves, Golden Girls, Matlock, Murder She Wrote. Movies: Wild Women, The Intruders, The Forgotten Man, Mongo's Back in Town, Fireball Forward, Haunts of the Very Rich, Cry Panic, FBI Vs. Alvin Karpis, The Last Survivors, A Girl Named Sooner, Banjo Hackett, Little Mo, The Rebels, Beggarman Thief, Detour to Terror, Rona Jaffe's Mazes and Monsters, Poor Little Rich Girl: The Barbara Hutton Story, Laguna Heat, My First Love, Love Can Be Murder.

FRANCIS, ARLENE: Actress. r.n. Arlene Francis Kazanjian; b. Boston, MA, Oct. 20, 1908. e. Convent of Mount St. Vincent Acad., Riverdale, NY, Finch Finishing Sch., Theatre Guild

Sch., NY. m. Martin Gabel, late actor. Author: That Certain Something (1960); Arlene Francis—A Memoir (1978).

STAGE: The Women (1937), Horse Eats Hat (Mercury Theater), Danton's Death, All That Glitters, Doughgirls, The Overtons, Once More With Feeling, Tchin-Tchin, Beekman Place, Mrs. Dally, Dinner at Eight, Kind Sir, Lion in Winter, Pal Joey, Who Killed Santa Claus?, Gigi, Social Security.

TELEVISION: Soldier Parade 1949–55, Blind Date, What's My Line; Home, Arlene Francis Show, Talent Patrol, etc.

RADIO: Arlene Francis Show, Emphasis, Monitor, Luncheon at Sardis.

PICTURES: Stage Door Canteen, All My Sons, One Two Three, The Thrill of It All, Fedora.

FRANCIS, CONNIE: Singer. r.n. Constance Franconero. b. Newark, NJ, Dec. 12, 1938. Appeared, Star Time when 12 years old; won Arthur Godfrey's Talent Scout Show, 12 years old. Autobiography: Who's Sorry Now (1984). Regular on series The Jimmie Rodgers Show, 1959.

GOLD RECORDS: Who's Sorry Now, My Happiness. Numerous vocalist awards.

PICTURES: Where the Boys Are, Follow the Boys, Looking For Love.

FRANCIS, FREDDIE: Producer, Director, Cameraman. b. London, 1917. Joined Gaumont British Studios as apprentice to stills photographer; then clapper boy at B.I.P. Studios, Elstree; camera asst. at British Dominion. After W.W.II returned to Shepperton Studios to work for Korda and with Powell and Pressburger as cameraman.

PICTURES: Director: Two and Two Make Six, Paranoiac, Vengeance, Evil of Frankenstein, Nightmare, Hysteria, Dr. Terror's House of Horrors, The Skull, Traitor's Gate, The Psychopath, The Deadly Bees, They Came from Beyond Space, Torture Garden, Dracula Has Risen from the Grave, Mumsy Nanny Sonny and Girly, Trog, Tales from the Crypt, The Creeping Flesh, Countdown, Tales That Witness Madness, The Ghoul, Legend of The Werewolf, The Doctor and the Devils, Dark Tower. Cameraman: Moby Dick (second unit photo., special effects), Room at the Top, Saturday Night and Sunday Morning, Sons and Lovers (Oscar), The Innocents, The Elephant Man, The French Lieutenant's Woman, Dune, Clara's Heart, Her Alibi, Brenda Starr, Glory (Acad. Award), Man in the Moon, Cape Fear, School Ties.

TELEVISION: A Life in the Theatre.

FRANCIS, KEVIN: Producer, Executive. b. London, England, 1949. 1967–70, production mgr., assoc. producer. 1970–72, produced It's Life, Passport, Trouble with Canada; 1972, founder, Tyburn Productions Limited; 1973, produced Persecution; 1974, produced The Ghoul and Legend of the Werewolf; 1975, founder, Tyburn Productions Inc.; 1976, prod. Film Techniques Educ. Course for BFI. Since 1977 exec. prod., Master of the Shell, The Masks of Death, Courier, Murder Elite, The Abbot's Cry, A One-Way Ticket to Hollywood, The Moorgate Legacy, etc.

FRANKENHEIMER, JOHN: Director. b. Malba, NY, Feb. 19, 1930. e. Williams Coll. Actor, dir., summer stock; radio-TV actor, dir., Washington, DC; then joined CBS network in 1953. Theater: The Midnight Sun (dir., 1959).

TELEVISION: I Remember Mama, You Are There, Danger, Climax (Emmy Award for best dramatic series), Studio One, Playhouse 90 (Emmy Award for best dramatic series), Du Pont Show of the Month; Ford Startime, Sunday Showcase; The Comedian, For Whom the Bell Tolls, The Days of Wine and Roses, Old Man, The Turn of the Screw, The Browning Version, The Rainmaker (1982).

PICTURES: The Young Stranger, The Young Savages, Birdman of Alcatraz, All Fall Down, The Manchurian Candidate (also co-prod.), Seven Days in May, The Train, Seconds, Grand Prix, The Fixer, The Extraordinary Seaman, The Gypsy Moths, I Walk the Line, The Horsemen, The Impossible Object (Story of a Love Story), The Iceman Cometh, 99 and 44/100% Dead, French Connection II, Black Sunday, Prophecy, The Challenge, The Holcroft Covenant, 52 Pick-Up, Dead-Bang, The Fourth War, Year of the Gun.

FRANKLIN, BONNIE: Actress. b. Santa Monica, CA, Jan. 6, 1944. e. UCLA. On Bdwy. in Dames at Sea, Your Own Thing, Applause (Theatre World Award). Off-Bdwy. in Frankie and Johnny in the Claire de Lune.

TELEVISION: Series: One Day at a Time. Movies: The Law, A Guide for the Married Woman, Breaking Up Is Hard to Do, Portrait of a Rebel: Margaret Sanger, Your Place or Mine, Sister Margaret and Saturday Night Ladies, Shalom Sesame.

FRANKLIN, MICHAEL HAROLD: Executive. b. Los Angeles, CA, Dec. 25, 1923. e. U. of California, A.B., U. of Southern California, LL.B. Admitted to CA bar, 1951; pvt. practice in L.A. 1951–52; atty. CBS, 1952–54; atty. Paramount Pictures, 1954–58; exec. dir. Writers Guild Am. West, Inc. 1958–78; national exec. dir., Directors Guild of America 1978–. Mem. Am. Civil Liberties Union, Los Angeles Copyright Soc., Order of Coif.

FRANKLIN, PAMELA: Actress. b. Tokyo, Japan, Feb. 4, 1950. Attended Elmshurst Ballet Sch., Camberley, Surrey.

PICTURES: The Innocents (debut, 1961), The Lion, The Third Secret, Flipper's New Adventure, The Nanny, Our Mother's House, The Prime of Miss Jean Brodie, The Night of the Following Day, And Soon the Darkness, Necromancy, Ace Eli and Rodger of the Skies, The Legend of Hell House, Food of the Gods.

TELEVISION: Movies: The Horse Without a Head (theatrical in U.K.), See How They Run, David Copperfield (theatrical in U.K.), The Letters, Satan's School for Girls, Crossfire, Eleanor and Franklin.

FRANKLIN, RICHARD: Director. b. Melbourne, Australia, July 15, 1948. e. USC (Cinema, 1967).

PICTURES: The True Story of Eskimo Nell (also co-prod.), Patrick (also co-prod.), The Blue Lagoon (co-prod. only), Road Games (also prod.), Psycho II, Cloak and Dagger, Into the Night (act. only), Link (also prod.), FX2.

TELEVISION: Beauty and the Beast (pilot), A Fine Romance (pilot).

FRANKLIN, ROBERT A.: Executive. b. New York, NY, April 15. e. U. of Miami, B.B.A., 1958; Columbia Pacific U., M.B.A., 1979; Ph.D., 1980 majoring in marketing. Before entering film industry worked with House of Seagram (1959–64); Canada Dry Corp. (1964–66); J. M. Mathes Adv. (1966–67). In 1967 joined 20th Century-Fox as dir. of mkt. planning. Formed RP Marketing Intl. (entertainment consulting firm) in 1976 and World Research Systems (computer software marketer). In 1981 joined MPAA; 1983, named v.p., administration and information services. In 1986, named v.p. worldwide market research. Chmn., MPAA research comm.; member, AMA and ESOMAR.

FRANZ, ARTHUR: Actor. b. Perth Amboy, NJ, Feb. 29, 1920. e. Blue Ridge Coll., MD. U.S. Air Force. Radio, TV shows.

THEATRE: Streetcar Named Desire, Second Threshold.

PICTURES: Jungle Patrol, Roseanna McCoy, Red Light, Doctor and the Girl, Sands of Iwo Jima, Strictly Dishonorable, Submarine Command, Member of the Wedding, Flight Nurse, Bad for Each Other, Eddie Cantor Story, Caine Mutiny, Steel Cage, Battle Taxi, New Orleans Uncensored, Bobby Ware Is Missing, Atomic Submarine, The Human Factor, That Championship Season.

FRAWLEY, JAMES: Director. b. Houston, TX, 1937. Studied drama at Carnegie Tech. and Actors Studio, where later taught and ran the directors unit. Was charter member of comedy group, The Premise; has acted in plays on and off Bdwy. Won Emmy Award for Monkees series, where staged two musical numbers a week for two seasons.

PICTURES: Kid Blue, The Big Bus, The Muppet Movie, Fraternity Vacation.

TELEVISION: Episodes: The Monkees (Emmy Award, 1967), Columbo, Cagney and Lacey, Law and Order, Trials of Rosie O'Neill. Movies: Delancy Street, Gridlock, The Outlaws, Assault and Matrimony, Spies Lies and Naked Thighs, The Secret Life of Archie's Wife.

FRAZIER, SHEILA E.: Actress. b. Bronx, NY, Nov. 13, 1948. e. Englewood, NJ. Was exec. sect'y. and high-fashion model. Steered to acting career by friend Richard Roundtree. Studied drama with N.Y. Negro Ensemble Co. and New Federal Theatre, N.Y.

PICTURES: Super Fly (debut), Superfly T.N.T., The Super Cops, California Suite, What Does It Take?, Three the Hard Way, The Hitter, I'm Gonna Git You Sucker.

TELEVISION: Movie: Firehouse. Mini-Series: King. Series: The Lazarus Syndrome.

FREARS, STEPHEN: Director. b. Leicester, Eng., June 20, 1941. e. Cambridge, B.A in law. Joined Royal Court Theatre, working with Lindsay Anderson on plays. Later assisted Karel Reisz on Morgan: A Suitable Case for Treatment, Albert Finney on Charlie Bubbles, and Lindsay Anderson on If . . . Worked afterwards mostly in TV, directing and producing. First directorial credit was 30-minute film The Burning, 1967.

PICTURES: Gumshoe (dir. debut 1971), Bloody Kids, The Hit, My Beautiful Laundrette, Prick Up Your Ears, Sammy and Rosie Get Laid, Dangerous Liaisons, The Grifters, Hero (GB: Accidental Hero).

TELEVISION: A Day Out (1971), England Their England, Match of the Day, Sunset Across the Bay, Three Men in a Boat, Daft as a Brush, Playthings, Early Struggles, Last Summer, 18 Months to Balcomb Street, A Visit from Miss Protheroe, Abel's Will, Cold Harbour, The Snapper, Song of Experience; series of six Alan Bennett plays; Long Distance Information, Going Gently, Loving Walter, Saigon: Year of the Cat, December Flower.

FREDERICKSON, H. GRAY, JR.: Producer. b. Oklahoma City, OK, July 21, 1937. e. U. of Lausanne, Switzerland, 1958–59; U. of Oklahoma. B.A., 1960. Worked one yr. with Panero, Weidlinger & Salvatori Engineering Co., Rome Italy. In 1979 named v.p. of feature films, Lorimar Films.

PICTURES: Candy, Inspector Sterling, Gospel 70, An Italian in America, The Man Who Wouldn't Die, The Good, the Bad and the Ugly, Intrigue in Suez, How to Learn to Love Women, God's Own Country, Wedding March, An American Wife, Natika, Echo in the Village, Little Fauss and Big Halsey, Making It, The Godfather, The Godfather Part II (co-prod; Acad. Award for Best Picture, 1974), Hit (exec. prod.), Apocalypse Now (co.-prod.; Acad. Award nom.), One From the Heart, The Outsiders, UHF, The Godfather Part III (co-prod.), Ladybugs (exec. prod.).
TELEVISION: Producer: The Return of Mickey Spillane's Mike Hammer, Houston Nights.

FREEDMAN, JERROLD: Director, Writer. b. Philadelphia, PA, Oct. 29, 1942. e. Univ. of PA. Novel: Against the Wind.
PICTURES: Kansas City Bomber, Borderline, Native Son.
TELEVISION: Director-Writer: Blood Sport, Betrayal, Some Kind of Miracle, Legs, This Man Stands Alone. Director: The Streets of L.A., The Boy Who Drank Too Much, Victims, The Seduction of Gina, Best Kept Secrets, Seduced, Family Sins, Unholy Matrimony, The Comeback, Night Walk, A Cold Night's Death, The Last Angry Man, Goodnight Sweet Wife: A Murder in Boston, Condition: Critical.

FREEMAN, AL, JR.: Actor. b. San Antonio, TX, March 21, 1934. e. LA City Coll.
THEATER: The Long Dream (1960), Kicks and Co., Tiger Tiger Burning Bright, Trumpets of the Lord, Blues for Mister Charlie, Conversation at Midnight, Look to the Lilies, Are You Now or Have You Ever Been?, The Poison Tree.
PICTURES: Torpedo Run, Black Like Me, Dutchman, Finian's Rainbow, The Detective, Castle Keep, The Lost Man, A Fable (also dir.), Seven Hours to Judgement, Malcolm X.
TELEVISION: Movie: My Sweet Charlie. Mini-Series: Roots: The Next Generations, King. Series: Hot L Baltimore, One Life to Live (Emmy, 1979).

FREEMAN, JOEL: Producer. b. Newark, NJ, June 12, 1922. e. Upsala Coll. Began career at MGM studios in 1941. In Air Force Mot. Pic. Unit 1942–46. Became assist. dir. at RKO in 1946. In 1948 returned to MGM as asst. dir.; later assoc. prod. In 1956 entered indep. field as prod. supv. on various features and TV series. In 1960 to Warner Bros., assoc. producing Sunrise at Campobello, The Music Man and Act One. After such films as Camelot and Finian's Rainbow, became studio exec. at Warners. Presently senior v.p. prod., New Century Entertainment Corp.
PICTURES: Producer: The Heart Is a Lonely Hunter, Shaft, Trouble Man, Love at First Bite, Octagon, The Kindred.

FREEMAN, MORGAN: Actor. b. Memphis, TN, June 1, 1937. e. LA City Coll. Served in Air Force 1955–59 before studying acting. Broadway debut in Hello Dolly! with Pearl Bailey. Took over lead role in Purlie. Became known nationally when he played Easy Reader on TV's The Electric Company (1971–76).
THEATER: NY: Ostrich Feathers, The Nigger Lovers (1967), Hello Dolly!, Scuba Duba, Purlie, Cockfight, The Last Street Play, The Mighty Gents (Drama Desk, Clarence Derwent Awards), Coriolanus (Obie Award), Julius Caesar, Mother Courage, Buck, Driving Miss Daisy (Obie Award), The Gospel at Colonus (Obie Award), Taming of the Shrew.
PICTURES: Who Says I Can't Ride a Rainbow? (debut, 1972), Brubaker, Eyewitness, Harry and Son, Teachers, Marie, That Was Then...This Is Now, Street Smart (Acad. Award nom.; NY & LA Film Critics & Natl. Board of Review Awards, supp. actor, 1987), Clean and Sober, Lean on Me, Johnny Handsome, Glory, Driving Miss Daisy (Natl. Board of Review & Golden Globe Awards; Acad. Award nom., 1989), The Bonfire of the Vanities, Robin Hood: Prince of Thieves, The Power of One, Unforgiven, Bopha (dir. only), Rita Hayworth and Shawshank Redemption.
TELEVISION: Movies: Hollow Image, Attica, The Marva Collins Story, The Atlanta Child Murders, Resting Place, Flight For Life, Roll of Thunder Hear My Cry, Charlie Smith and the Fritter Tree, Clinton and Nadine. Series: The Electric Company, Another World (1982–4). Specials: The Civil War (narrator), Follow the Drinking Gourd (narrator).

FRELENG, FRIZ: Writer, Producer. b. Kansas City, MO, Aug. 21, 1906. Animator, Walt Disney Studio, 1928–29; Charles Mintz Studio, 1929–30, prod.-dir., Warner Bros. 1930–63. Formed partnership with David DePatie in 1963. Five Academy Awards, 3 Emmy Awards.
CARTOON FILMS: Bugs Bunny series, Daffy Duck, Sylvester, Yosemite Sam, Porky Pig, Tweetie Pie, Speedy Gonzales, Halloween Is Grinch Night, Pink Panther in Olympinks, Dr. Seuss' Pontoffel Pock. Recent compilations: The Looney, Looney Bugs Bunny Movie, Bugs Bunny's 3rd Movie: 1001 Rabbit Tales. Numerous series of television shows.

FRESCO, ROBERT M.: Writer. b. Burbank, CA, Oct. 18, 1928. e. Los Angeles City Coll. Newspaperman. Los Angeles, 1946–47; U.S. Army, 1948–49; staff writer, Hakim Prod., 1950–51; various screenplays, 1951–56.

PICTURES: Tarantula, They Came to Destroy the Earth, Monolith.
TELEVISION: Scripts for Science Fiction Theatre, Highway Patrol.

FREWER, MATT: Actor. b. Washington, D. C., Jan. 4, 1958. Raised in Victoria, British Columbia. Studied drama at the Bristol Old Vic Theatre, appearing in Romeo and Juliet, Macbeth, Waiting for Godot, Deathtrap.
TELEVISION: BBC: Tender is the Night, Robin of Sherwood, U.S. Series: Max Headroom, Doctor Doctor, Shaky Ground. Movie: The Positively True Adventures of the Alleged Texas Cheerleader-Murdering Mom. Guest: Miami Vice.
PICTURES: The Lords of Discipline (debut, 1983), Supergirl, Spies Like Us, Ishtar, The Fourth Protocol, Far From Home, Speed Zone, Honey I Shrunk the Kids, Short Time, The Taking of Beverly Hills.

FRICKER, BRENDA: Actress. b. Dublin, Ireland, Feb. 17, 1945. Appeared in short film The Woman Who Married Clark Gable. Theatre work includes appearances with the RSC, Royal Court Theatre, and The National Theatre.
PICTURES: Quatermass Conclusion, Bloody Kids, Our Exploits at West Poley, My Left Foot (Acad. Award, supp., 1989), The Field, Utz, Home Alone 2: Lost in New York, So I Married an Axe Murderer.
TELEVISION: Series: Casualty. Specials: Licking Hitler, The House of Bernarda Alba, The Ballroom Romance. Mini-Series: Brides of Christ, The Sound and the Silence.

FRIEDBERG, A. ALAN: Executive. b. New York, NY, Apr. 13, 1932. e. Columbia Coll., B.A. 1952, Junior Phi Beta Kappa, Summa Cum Laude; Harvard Law School 1955. Past pres. and chmn. of bd. NATO, currently memb. of exec. committee. V.P. Foundation of Motion Picture Pioneers. 1990, named chmn. Loews Theatre Mgmt. Co.

FRIEDKIN, JOHN: Executive. b. New York, NY, Dec. 9, 1926. e. Columbia Univ. Entered industry in New York as publicist for Columbia Pictures; spent eight years at Young & Rubicam adv. agency. Formed Sumner & Friedkin with Gabe Sumner as partner; left to join Rogers & Cowan, where named v.p. in 1967 resigned to join 20th-Fox, moving to California in 1972 when home offices were transferred. Appointed Fox v.p. worldwide publ. & promo. In 1979 joined Warner Bros. as v.p., adv. pub. for intl. div; 1988, joined Odyssey Distributors Ltd. as sr. v.p., intl. marketing. 1990, formed indept. marketing firm.

FRIEDKIN, WILLIAM: Director. b. Chicago, IL, Aug. 29, 1939. m. producer Sherry Lansing. Joined WGN-TV, 1957, worked for National Education TV, did TV documentaries before feature films. Dir. Bdwy play Duet for One.
PICTURES: Good Times (debut, 1967), The Night They Raided Minsky's, The Birthday Party, The Boys in the Band, The French Connection (Academy Award, 1971), The Exorcist, Sorcerer (also prod.), The Brink's Job, Cruising (also s.p.), Deal of the Century, To Live and Die in L.A. (also co-s.p.), Rampage (also s.p.), The Guardian (also co-s.p.), Blue Chips.
TELEVISION: Movies: C.A.T. Squad (also exec. prod.), C.A.T. Squad: Python Wolf. Special: Barbra Streisand: Putting It Together. Series: Tales From the Crypt (On a Dead Man's Chest).

FRIEDMAN, ARNOLD J.: Executive b. New York, NY. Entered m.p. industry as exploiteer for Columbia Pictures Corp. 1957–60; advng dept. United Artists Corp. 1960–62; adv. mgr., Embassy Pictures Corp. and later director of adv., publ., prom. for Embassy Pictures Television, 1962–67; pres. Arnold Friedman's Company, 1967–70; dir. of ad./pub./promo for Metromedia Producers Corp., 1970–72; creative dir., ITC, 1973–76; vice pres. of theatrical & TV adv./pub./promo. for Cinema Shares International. Ltd., 1976–79; pres., Arcady Communications, 1980–present.

FRIEDMAN, JOSEPH: Executive. b. New York, NY. e. City Coll. of New York, 1940–42, NYU, 1946–47. U.S. Navy 3 yrs. Asst. to nat'l dir. field exploitation, Warner Bros. Pictures, 1946–58; nat'l exploitation mgr., Paramount Pictures, 1958–60; exec. asst. to dir. of adv., publicity & exploitation, Para., 1961; dir. adv. & pub., Paramount 1964; a v.p., Para., 1966; v.p. in charge of marketing, 1968; v.p., adv., and p.r., Avco Embassy Pictures, 1969; v.p., p.r. American Film Theatre 1973; v.p., adv. and p.r., ITC, motion picture div, 1976, pres., Joseph Friedman Marketing and Advertising, Inc., 1977. Exec. dir. New Jersey M.P. & T.V. Commission, 1978; v.p. worldwide adv./pub./promo., Edie & Ely Landau, Inc., 1980; exec. dir., New Jersey Motion Picture & Television Commission, 1981.

FRIEDMAN, ROBERT L.: Executive. b. Bronx, NY, March 1, 1930. e. DeWitt Clinton H.S, Bronx. Started as radio announcer and commentator with Armed Forces Radio Service in Europe and U.S. sr. v.p., distrib. & marketing, United Artists Corp.; pres. domestic distribution, Columbia Pictures. 1984, named pres., AMC Entertainment Int'l Inc. 1992, named pres. of

AMC Entertainment - the Motion Picture Group. On Century City bd. of dirs.; chmn. of Entertainment Industry Council. MEMBER: M.P. Associates Foundation, Phila., pres. 2 yrs.; Variety Club (on board) M.P. Pioneers; (on board) area chmn. Distrib., chmn., Will Rogers Hospital Foundation, American Film Inst., Academy of M.P. Arts & Sciences.

FRIEDMAN, SEYMOUR MARK: Director. b. Detroit, MI, Aug. 17, 1917. e. Magdalene Coll., Cambridge, B.S. 1936; St. Mary's Hospital Medical Sch., London. Entered m.p. ind. as asst. film ed. 1937; 2nd asst. dir. 1938; 1st asst. dir. 1939, on budget pictures; entered U.S. Army 1942; returned to ind. 1946; dir. Columbia Pictures 1947. Vice president & executive production for Columbia Pictures Television, division of Columbia Pictures Industries, 1955.
MEMBER: Screen Directors Guild.
PICTURES: To the Ends of the Earth, Rusty's Birthday, Prison Warden, Her First Romance, Rookie Fireman, Son of Dr. Jekyll, Loan Shark, Flame of Calcutta, I'll Get You, Saint's Girl Friday, Khyber Patrol, African Manhunt, Secret of Treasure Mountain.

FRIEDMAN, STEPHEN: Writer, Producer. b. March 15, 1937. e. U. of Pennsylvania, Harvard Law School. Worked as lawyer for Columbia Pictures (1960–63) and Ashley-Famous Agency. 1963–67: Paramount Pictures. Formed and heads Kings Road Productions.
PICTURES: Producer: The Last Picture Show, Lovin' Molly (also s.p.), Slap Shot, Bloodbrothers, Fast Break, Hero at Large, Little Darlings, Eye of the Needle, All of Me, Creator, Enemy Mine.

FRIELS, COLIN: Actor. b. Scotland. e. Australia Natl. Inst. of Dramatic Art. m. actress Judy Davis. First began acting with the State Theatre Co. of So. Australia and the Sydney Theatre Co. Theatre includes Sweet Bird of Youth and Hedda Gabler. TV includes special Stark.
PICTURES: Buddies, Monkey Grip, For the Term of His Natural Life, Kangaroo, Malcolm, High Tide, Ground Zero, Grievous Bodily Harm, Warm Nights on a Slow Moving Train, Darkman, Class Action, Dingo, A Good Man in Africa.

FRIENDLY, FRED W.: Producer, Journalist, Writer, Educator. r.n. Fred Wachenheimer. b. New York, NY, October 30, 1915. e. Cheshire Acad., Nichols Junior Coll. U.S. Army, Information and Education Section 1941–45. Editor and correspondent for China, Burma and India for CBI Roundup 1941–45. President, CBS News 1964–66; Edward R. Murrow Professor of Broadcast Journalism, Columbia U., 1966–present; advisor on TV, Ford Foundation, 1966–; member: Mayor's Task Force on CATV and Telecommunications, NYC, 1968; teacher and director: Television Workshop, Columbia U. Sch. of Journalism.
RADIO: Producer-writer-narrator, Foodprints in the Sand of Time, 1938; co-prod. Hear It Now, 1951.
BOOKS: See It Now (1955); Due to Circumstances Beyond Our Control (1967); The Good Guys, the Bad Guys and the First Amendment: Free Speech vs. Fairness in Broadcasting (1976), Minnesota Rag: The Dramatic Story of the Landmark Supreme Court Case that Gave New Meaning to Freedom of the Press (1981); The Constitution: That Delicate Balance (1984); The Presidency and the Constitution (1987).
AWARDS: Ten George Foster Peabody Awards; DeWitt Carter Reddick Award, 1980; See It Now (35 major awards incl. Overseas Press Club, Page One Award, New York Newspaper Guild, National Headliners Club Award, 1954); CBS Reports (40 major awards). Honorary L.H.D. degrees: U. of Rhode Island, Grinnell U., Iowa U. Military: Legion of Merit medal, Soldier's Medal for heroism, 4 Battle Stars.

FRIES, CHARLES W.: Executive. b. Cincinnati, OH, Sept. 30, 1928. e. Ohio State U., B.S. Exec.-prod., Ziv Television; v.p., prod., Screen Gems; v.p., prod., Columbia Pictures; exec. v.p., prod. and exec. prod., Metromedia Prod. Corp., 1970–74; pres., exec. prod., Alpine Prods. and Charles Fries Prods. 1974–83; chmn. & pres., Fries Entertainment, 1984. Nat'l. treas., TV Academy; pres., Alliance TV Film Producers; exec. comm., MPPA. Chmn., Caucus of Producers, Writers and Directors, board of governors and exec. comm. of Academy of TV Arts and Sciences. Bd. trustees, secretary & chmn., Exec. committee & vice-chmn., American Film Institute. Director of the Center Theatre Group.
PICTURES: Exec. Prod.: Cat People, Flowers in the Attic, Troop Beverly Hills.
TELEVISION: Movies: Toughlove, The Right of the People, Intimate Strangers, Bitter Harvest, A Rumor of War, Blood Vows: The Story of a Mafia Wife, The Alamo: 3 Days to Glory, Intimate Betrayal, Two Women, Drop Out Mother, LBJ: The White House Years, The Crucible, The Rose Kennedy Story, It's Howdy Doody Time: A 40 Year Celebration, Crash Course, Supercarrier, Bridge to Silence, The Case of the Hillside Stranglers.

FRONTIERE, DOMINIC: Executive, Composer. b. New Haven, CT, June 17, 1931. e. Yale School of Music. Studied composing, arranging and conducting; concert accordionist, World's

Champion Accordionist, 1943; An Hour with Dominic Frontiere, WNHC-TV, New Haven, 3 years, 1947; exec. vice-pres., musical dir., Daystar Prods. Composer or arranger over 75 films.
PICTURES: Giant, Gentlemen Prefer Blondes, Let's Make Love, High Noon, Meet Me in Las Vegas, 10,000 Bedrooms, Hit the Deck, Marriage-Go-Round, The Right Approach, One Foot in Hell, Hero's Island, Hang 'Em High, Popi, Barquero, Chisum, A for Alpha, Cancel My Reservation, Hammersmith is Out, Freebie and the Bean, Brannigan, The Gumball Rally, Cleopatra Jones and the Casino of Gold, The Stunt Man, Modern Problems, The Aviator.
TELEVISION: Composer-conductor: The New Breed, Stoney Burke, Bankamericard commercials (Venice Film Fest. Award for best use of original classical music for filmed TV commercials), Outer Limits, Branded, Iron Horse, Rat Patrol, Flying Nun, The Invaders, Name of the Game, That Girl, Twelve O'Clock High, Zig Zag, The Young Rebel, The Immortal, Fugitive, The Love War. Movie: Washington Behind Closed Doors.

FROST, LINDA SMITH: Executive. b. Louisville, KY, March 13, 1956. e. Wellesley College. Dir. of marketing, South Coast Plaza. dir. of marketing Rouse Company; dir. special events and marketing, Broadway Dept. Stores. V.P. marketing Media Home Entertainment.

FRUCHTMAN, MILTON A.: Producer, Director. b. New York, NY, e. Columbia U. B.S.; Columbia U., M.S. Worked for Columbia and independent producers in various production capacities, set up first worldwide TV network, Eichmann Trial. Received numerous Peabody, Emmy, and Gabriel awards, Gold Hugo Awards (Chicago Film and TV Festival), Martin Luther King Festival Award, DGA Award.
TELEVISION: High Adventure Series, Every Man's Dream, Verdict for Tomorrow (Peabody Award, 1962), Assignment Southeast Asia, It Happened in Naples; Son of Sulan, The Secret of Michaelangelo, Every Man's Dream (Peabody), Dance Theatre of Harlem, Those Who Sing Together, The Makebelievers.

FRYE, WILLIAM: Producer. Was agency exec. before beginning prod. career as associate prod. of Four Star Playhouse in assoc. with late Dick Powell, David Niven and Charles Boyer. Later joined Revue Prods., which became Universal TV; he produced General Electric Theatre and other series. Has produced many Movie of the Week entries for ABC-TV.
PICTURES: The Trouble with Angels, Where Angels Go, Trouble Follows, Airport 1975, Airport 1977, Raise the Titanic, Apt Pupil.

FUCHS, LEO L.: Independent producer. b. Vienna, June 14, 1929. Moved to U.S., 1939. e. Vienna and New York. U.S. Army cameraman 1951–53; int'l. mag. photographer until entered motion pictures as producer with Universal in Hollywood in 1961.
PICTURES: Gambit, A Fine Pair; Jo (French version of The Gazebo), Sunday Lovers, Just the Way You Are.

FUCHS, MICHAEL: Executive. b. New York, NY, March 9, 1946. e. Union Coll., NYU Law School (J.D. degree). Show business lawyer before joining Home Box Office in 1976, developing original and sports programming. Named chmn. and CEO of HBO in 1984 till present.

FUEST, ROBERT: Director. b. London, 1927. Early career as painter, graphic designer. Ent. TV industry as designer with ABC-TV, 1958. 1962: directing doc., commercials. 1966: Wrote and dir. Just Like a Woman, 1967–68; dir. 7 episodes of The Avengers, 1969: wrote and directed 6 episodes of The Optimists.
PICTURES: And Soon the Darkness, Wuthering Heights, Doctor Phibes, Doctor Phibes Rides Again (also .p.); The Final Programme (also s.p., design), The Devil's Rain, The Geller Effect (s.p. only), The New Avengers, The Gold Bug, Revenge of the Stepford Wives, The Big Stuffed Dog, Mystery on Fire Island, Aphrodite, Worlds Beyond, Cat's Eyes.

FULLER, SAMUEL: Director, Writer, Producer. b. Worcester, MA, Aug. 12, 1912. m. actress Christa Lang. Copy boy, N.Y. Journal; reporter, rewrite man, N.Y. Graphic, N.Y Journal, San Diego Sun; journeyman reported many papers. Writer of many orig. s.p.; in U.S. Army, 16th Inf. 1st U.S. Inf. Div. 1942–45.
PICTURES: Director-Writer: I Shot Jesse James, Baron of Arizona, The Steel Helmet (also prod.), Fixed Bayonets, Park Row (also prod.), Pickup On South Street, Hell and High Water, House of Bamboo, Run of the Arrow (also prod.), China Gate (also prod.), Forty Guns, Verboten!, The Crimson Kimono (also prod.), Underworld U.S.A. (also prod.), Merrill's Marauders, Shock Corridor (also prod.), The Naked Kiss (also prod.), Dead Pigeon on Beethoven Street, The Big Red One, White Dog (also actor), Thieves After Dark, Street of No Return (also actor, edit.), Tini Kling. Actor only: The Last Movie, The American Friend, Scott Joplin, 1941, Hammett,

State of Things, Slapstick of Another Kind, Return to Salem's Lot, Helsinki Napoli All Night Long, Sons.

AUTHOR: Crown of India, 144 Piccadilly Street, Dead Pigeon on Beethoven Street, The Rifle, The Big Red One, The Dark Page, La Grande Melee (Battle Royal), Pecos Bill and the Soho Kid, Once Upon Samuel Fuller (Stories of America; interview book).

FUNT, ALLEN: Producer, Performer. b. New York, NY, Sept. 16, 1914. Best known as producer and creator of Candid Camera series which originated on radio in 1947 as Candid Microphone which inspired theatrical film shorts. TV version began in 1948 as Candid Mike, changed in 1949 to Candid Camera which played off and on until 1960 when became regular series on CBS, lasting until 1967. Revived briefly in early '70s and again in mid '80s in new format; then syndicated as The New Candid Camera. Candid Camera Christmas Special, 1987, Candid Camera: Eat! Eat!, Eat!, Candid Camera on Wheels. Produced and starred in film, What Do You Say to a Naked Lady?

FURIE, SIDNEY J.: Director, Writer, Producer. b. Toronto, Canada, Feb. 28, 1933. Ent. TV and films 1954. Canadian features include: Dangerous Age, A Cool Sound from Hell. Also dir. many Hudson Bay TV series. To England 1960. Films since include Dr. Blood's Coffin, During One Night, Brewster's Millions, The Young Ones, The Boys. 1961 appt. exec. dir. Galaworldfilm Productions, Ltd.

PICTURES: The Leather Boys, Wonderful Life, The Ipcress File, The Appaloosa, The Naked Runner, The Lawyer, Little Fauss and Big Halsy, Lady Sings the Blues, Hit!, Sheila Levine is Dead and Living in New York, Gable and Lombard, The Boys in Company C, The Entity, Purple Hearts (also prod., s.p.), Iron Eagle, Superman IV: The Quest For Peace, Iron Eagle II (also co-s.p.), The Taking of Beverly Hills, Ladybugs.

FURNESS, BETTY: Actress, TV Correspondent. b. New York, NY, Jan. 3, 1916. Stage and screen actress in the '30s & '40s; TV commercial spokeswoman for Westinghouse in '50s, leading consumer advocate in '70s. Host on both local TV and radio shows in New York (Dimension in a Woman's World, At Your Beck and Call, Ask Betty Furness, etc.). Named President Johnson's asst. for consumer affairs in 1967. 1970, chmn, exec. dir. of New York state's consumer protection board. Commissioner NY City Dept. of Consumer Affairs in 1943. Joined WNBC-TV in 1974 as consumer reporter and weekly contributor to Today Show. 1988: Betty's Attic. Left NBC in 1992.

PICTURES: Professional Sweetheart, Emergency Call, Lucky Devils, Beggars in Ermine, Keeper of the Bees, Magnificent Obsession, Swing Time, The President's Mystery, Mama Steps Out, North of Shanghai.

FURST, AUSTIN O.: Executive. e. Lehigh U., B.S. in economics/marketing. Began career in marketing dept., Proctor and Gamble; 1972 joined Time Inc. as dir., new subscription sales for Time magazine; later joined Time Inc.'s new magazine dev. staff for People magazine; named circulation mgr., People magazine, 1974; 1975 named pres., Time Inc.'s Computer Television Inc., a pay-per-view hotel operation and was responsible for successful turnaround and sale of co.; 1976, vice pres., programming, Home Box Office; named exec. v.p. HBO, 1979; appointed pres. and CEO, Time-Life Films, Inc., 1980; 1981 established Vestron after acquiring home video rights to Time/Life Video Library; chmn. and CEO, Vestron, Inc.

G

GABOR, ZSA ZSA: Actress. r.n. Sari Gabor. b. Hungary, Feb. 6, 1918. e. Lausanne, Switzerland. Stage debut in Europe. Author: Zsa Zsa's Complete Guide to Men (1969), How to Get a Man How to Keep a Man and How to Get Rid of a Man (1971), One Lifetime is Not Enough (1991). As accomplished horsewoman has won many prizes in various intl. horse shows. Stage work incl. 40 Carats, Blithe Spirit.

PICTURES: Lovely to Look At, We're Not Married, Moulin Rouge, The Story of Three Loves, Lili, Three Ring Circus, Death of a Scoundrel, Girl in the Kremlin, The Man Who Wouldn't Talk, Touch of Evil, Queen of Outer Space, Country Music Holiday, For the First Time, Pepe, Boys' Night Out, Picture Mommy Dead, Arrivederci Baby, Jack of Diamonds, Won Ton Ton the Dog Who Saved Hollywood, Frankenstein's Great Aunt Tillie, A Nightmare on Elm Street 3, The Naked Gun 2½, Happily Ever After (voice).

GAFFNEY, ROBERT: Producer. Director. b. New York, NY, Oct. 8, 1931. e. Iona Coll., 1949–51. Staff, Louis de Rochemont; prod., Rooftops of New York, in assoc. with Robert Associates, prod. staff, Cinerama Holiday, Man on a String; camera technical consultant, Cinemiracle prod., Windjam-McCarty, 1960; prod. industrial films, Seneca Prods., Prod., Light

Fantastic; prod., Troublemaker; assoc. prod., Harvey Middleman Fireman; dir., Frankenstein Meets the Space Monster.

GAIL, MAX: Actor. b. Grosse Point, MI, Apr. 5, 1943. e. Univ. of Mich.

TELEVISION: Series: Barney Miller, Whiz Kids, Normal Life. Mini-Series: Pearl. Movies: The Priest Killer, Like Mom Like Me, Desperate Women, The 11th Victim, The Aliens Are Coming, Fun and Games, Letting Go, The Other Lover, Killer in the Mirror, Intimate Strangers, Can You Feel Me Dancing?, Tonight's the Night, Man Against the Mob, The Outside Woman.

PICTURES: The Organization, Dirty Harry, D.C. Cab, Heartbreakers.

THEATER: NY: The Babe.

GALE, BOB: Writer, Producer. b. St. Louis, MO, May 25, 1951. e. U. of Southern California Sch. of Cinema. Joined with friend Robert Zemeckis to write screenplays, starting with episode for TV series, McCloud. Also co-wrote story for The Night-stalker series. Turned to feature films, co-writing with Zemeckis script for I Wanna Hold Your Hand, on which Gale also acted as associate producer. Exec. prod. of CBS animated series Back to the Future.

PICTURES: I Wanna Hold Your Hand (co-s.p., co-assoc. prod.), 1941 (co-s.p.), Used Cars (prod., co-s.p.), Back to the Future (co.-prod., s.p.), Back to the Future Part II (prod., co-s.p.), Back to the Future Part III (prod., s.p.), Trespass (co-exec. prod., co-s.p.).

GALE, GEORGE: Executive. b. Budapest, Hungary, May 26, 1919. e. Sorbonne U., Paris, France. Feature editor, Budapest Ed., U.S. Army Pictorial Service. Feature and TV editor MGM, Hal Roach, Disney Studios; prod. and prod. exec. Ivan Tors; American National Enterprises, Inc. Producer and director. Supervised the production of over 30 features for television syndication and numerous theatrical and TV features. Member ACE and Academy of Motion Picture Arts and Sciences. Formed George Gale Productions, Inc. in 1976.

GALLAGHER, PETER: Actor. b. New York, NY, Aug. 19, 1955. e. Tufts Univ.

PICTURES: The Idolmaker (debut, 1980), Summer Lovers, Dream Child, My Little Girl, High Spirits, Sex Lies and Videotape, Tune in Tomorrow, Late for Dinner, The Cabinet of Dr. Ramirez, The Player, Bob Roberts, Watch It, Short Cuts, Mother's Boys, Malice, The Hudsucker Proxy.

TELEVISION: Series: Skag. Movies: Skag, Terrible Joe Moran, The Caine Mutiny Court-Martial, The Murder of Mary Phagan, I'll Be Home for Christmas, Love and Lies, An Inconvenient Woman. Specials: The Big Knife, Long Day's Journey Into Night, Private Contentment, Guys & Dolls: Off the Record.

THEATER: NY: Hair (1977 revival), Grease, A Doll's Life (Theatre World Award), The Corn is Green, The Real Thing (Clarence Derwent Award), Long Day's Journey Into Night (Tony Award nom.; also London), Guys & Dolls. Also: Another Country, Pride & Prejudice (both Long Wharf).

GALLIGAN, ZACH: Actor. b. New York, NY, Feb. 14, 1964. e. Columbia U.

PICTURES: Gremlins, Nothing Lasts Forever, Waxwork, Mortal Passions, Rising Storm, Gremlins II, Zandalee, Lost in Time, Round Trip to Heaven, All Tied Up, Waxwork II.

TELEVISION: Movies: Jocobo Timerman: Prisoner Without a Name Cell Without a Number, Surviving, Psychic, Elysian Fields. Specials: The Prodigious Hickey, The Return of Hickey, The Beginning of the Firm, A Very Delicate Matter, The Hitchhiker: Toxic Shock. Mini-Series: Crossings. Pilot: Interns in Heat. Guest: Tales From the Crypt (Strung Along), Melrose Place.

GAMBON, MICHAEL: Actor. b. Dublin, Ireland, Oct. 19, 1940. Ent. Ind. 1966. Early experience in theatre. 1985–87 Acting at National Theatre and London's West End. 1988: in Harold Pinter's Mountain Language.

PICTURES: Othello, The Beast Must Die, Turtle Diary, Paris By Night, The Rachel Papers, A Dry White Season, The Cook the Thief His Wife and Her Lover, Mobsters, Toys, Clean Slate, Indian Warrior.

TELEVISION: Uncle Vanya, Ghosts, Oscar Wilde, The Holy Experiment, Absurd Person Singular, The Singing Detective (serial), The Heat of the Day, The Storyteller, Maigret Sets a Trap.

GAMMON, JAMES: Actor. b. Newman, IL, Apr. 20. e. Boone H.S., Orlando, FL. Former television cameraman. First acting role was small part on Gunsmoke. Head of Los Angeles' Met Theatre for 10 years.

PICTURES: Cool Hand Luke (debut, 1967), Journey to Shiloh, Macho Callahan, A Man Called Horse, Macon County Line, Black Oak Conspiracy, Urban Cowboy, Any Which Way You Can, Smithereens, Vision Quest, Sylvester, Silverado, Silver Bullet, Made in Heaven, Ironweed, The Milagro Beanfield War, Major League, Revenge, Coupe de Ville, I Love You to Death, Leaving Normal, Crisscross, The Painted Desert, Cabin Boy.

TELEVISION: *Series*: Bagdad Cafe. *Guest*: Bonanza, The Wild Wild West, Cagney & Lacey, The Equalizer, Crime Story, Midnight Caller. *Movies*: Kansas City Massacre, Rage, Women of San Quentin, M.A.D.D.: Mothers Against Drunk Drivers, Hell Town, The Long Hot Summer, Roe vs. Wade, Dead Aim, Conagher, Stranger at My Door, Men Don't Tell. *Mini-Series*: Lincoln.

THEATRE: The Dark at the Top of the Stairs (L.A. Critics Circle Award, best actor), Bus Stop (L.A. Drama Critics award, best director), Curse of the Starving Class (NY, L.A.), A Lie of the Mind (NY, L.A.).

GANIS, SIDNEY M.: Executive. b. New York, NY, Jan. 8, 1940. e. Brooklyn Coll. Staff writer, newspaper and wire service contact, 20th Century-Fox 1961–62; radio, TV contact and special projects, Columbia Pictures 1963–64. Joined Seven Arts Prod. 1965 as publicity mgr.; 1967, appt. prod. publicity mgr. Warner-7 Arts, Ass't prod., There Was a Crooked Man, 1969. Studio publicity dir., Cinema Center Films, 1970. Director of Ad-Pub for Mame, Warner Bros., 1973; Director of Advertising, Warner Bros., 1974; named WB v.p., worldwide adv. & pub., 1977; 1979, sr. v.p., Lucasfilm, Ltd.; 1982 Emmy winner, exec. prod., best documentary, The Making of Raiders of the Lost Ark. 1986, joined Paramount Pictures as pres., worldwide mktg; 1986, named pres., Paramount Motion Picture Group. 1988, elected trustee University Art Museum, Berkeley, CA. 1991, appointed exec. v.p., Sony Pictures Ent. Exec. v.p., pres. mktg. & distrib., Columbia Pictures, 1992. Elected to bd. of govs. Acad. of MoPic Arts & Sciences, 1992.

GANZ, BRUNO: Actor. b. Zurich, Switzerland, March 22, 1941.

THEATER: Member of the Berlin Theater troupe, Schaubuhne. Hamlet (1967), Dans La Jungle Des Villes, Torquato Tasso, La Chevauchee Sur Le Lac de Constance, Peer Gynt, Hamlet (1984).

PICTURES: Der Sanfte Lauf (1967), Sommergaste (1975), The Marquise of O, Lumiere, The Wild Duck, The American Friend, The Lefthanded Woman, The Boys from Brazil, Black and White Like Day and Night, Knife in the Head, Nosferatu the Vampyre, Return of a Good Friend, 5% Risk, An Italian Woman, Polenta, La Provinciale, La Dame Aux Camelias, Der Erfinder, Etwas Wird Sichtbar, Circle of Deceit, Hande Hoch, Logik Der Gerfuhls, War and Peace, In the White City, System Ohne Schatten, Der Pendler, Wings of Desire, Bankomatt, Strapless, The Last Days of Chez Nous, Especially on Sunday, Faraway So Close!

TELEVISION: Father and Son (Italian TV).

GANZ, LOWELL: Writer. b. 1948. Worked as staff writer on tv series The Odd Couple. Met writing partner Babaloo Mandel at The Comedy Store in the early 1970s. Was co-creator Laverne & Shirley, prod. of Happy Days. First teamed with Mandel on script for 1982 comedy Night Shift.

PICTURES: Night Shift, Splash (Acad. Award nom.), Spies Likes Us, Gung Ho, Vibes, Parenthood, City Slickers, A League of Their Own, Mr. Saturday Night (also cameo), Greedy.

GANZ, TONY: Producer. b. New York, NY. e. studied film at Harvard U. Produced documentaries for PBS in N.Y. Moved to L.A. 1973 where in charge of dev., Charles Fries Productions. Then joined Ron Howard Productions 1980. Left to form own prod. co. with Deborah Blum.

PICTURES: Gung Ho, Clean and Sober, Vibes.

TELEVISION: Series: American Dream Machine, Maximum Security (exec. prod.). Movies: Bitter Harvest, Into Thin Air.

GARCIA, ANDY: Actor. b. Havana, Cuba, Apr. 12, 1956. e. Florida International U, Miami. Family moved to Miami Beach in 1961. Spent several years acting with regional theaters in Florida.

PICTURES: Blue Skies Again (debut, 1983), A Night in Heaven, The Mean Season, 8 Million Ways to Die, The Untouchables, Stand and Deliver, American Roulette, Black Rain, Internal Affairs, A Show of Force, The Godfather Part III (Acad. Award nom.), Dead Again, Hero, Jennifer Eight, Significant Other.

TELEVISION: Guest: Alfred Hitchcock Presents, Archie Bunker's Place, From Here to Eternity, Hill Street Blues, Brothers, Foley Square. Movie: Clinton and Nadine.

GARDINER, PETER R.: Executive. b. Santa Monica, CA, Apr. 25, 1949. Independent still photographer and industrial filmmaker before joining Paramount, 1973, in feature post-prod. 1979, joined Warner Bros. as asst. dir., corporate services. 1987, promoted to v.p., opns., WB corporate film-video services.

GARFIELD, ALLEN: Actor. b. Newark, NJ, Nov. 22, 1939. r.n. Allen Goorwitz. e. Actors Studio. Worked as journalist for Newark Star Ledger and Sunday Morning Herald (Australia) prior to becoming an actor. Has also acted as Allen Goorwitz.

PICTURES: Greetings, Putney Swope, Hi Mom!, The Owl and the Pussycat, Bananas, Believe in Me, Roommates, The Organization, Taking Off, Cry Uncle!, You've Got to Walk it Like You Talk It or You'll Lose That Beat, Get to Know Your Rabbit, The Candidate, Top of the Heap, Deadhead Miles, Slither, Busting, The Conversation, The Front Page, Nashville, Gable and Lombard, Mother Jugs & Speed, The Brink's Job, Skateboard, One-Trick Pony, The Stunt Man, Continental Divide, One from the Heart, State of Things, The Black Stallion Returns, Get Crazy, Irreconcilable Differences, Teachers, The Cotton Club, Desert Bloom, Beverly Hills Cop II, Chief Zabu, Let it Ride, Night Visitor, Dick Tracy, Club Fed, Until the End of the World, Jack and His Friends, Family Prayers.

TELEVISION: Movies: Footsteps, The Marcus-Nelson Murders, The Virginia Hill Story, Serpico: The Deadly Game, The Million Dollar Rip-Off, Nowhere to Run, Ring of Passion, Leave 'Em Laughing, Citizen Cohn.

GARFINKLE, LOUIS: Writer, Director, Producer. b. Seattle, WA, February 11, 1928. e. U. of California, U. of Washington, U. of Southern California (B.A., 1948). Writer KOMO, Seattle, 1945; Executive Research, Inc., 1948; Writer, educ. doc. screenplays, Emerson Films, EBF. 1948–50; s.p. You Can Beat the A-Bomb (RKO), 1950; Writer-dir. training films, info. films, Signal Photo, 1950–53; Copy, Weinberg Adv., 1953; Head of Doc. Research in TV, U. of California, Berkeley, 1954–55; staff, Sheilah Graham Show, 1956; formed Maxim Prod. Inc. with Albert Band, 1956. Co-creator Collaborator Interactive Computer Software to asst. in writing stories for screen & TV, 1990; formed Collaborator Systems Inc. with Cary Brown and Francis X. Feighan, 1991. Received Best Screenwriting Tool Award from Screen Writers Forum, 1991. Member: AMPAS, WGA West, ATAS, Dramatists Guild, Board of Advisers Filmic Writing Major, USC School of Cinema & TV.

PICTURES: Screenplay: The Young Guns (also story), I Bury the Living (also story, co-prod.), Face of Fire (also co-prod.), Hellbenders, A Minute to Pray A Second to Die, The Love Doctors (also story, prod.), Beautiful People, The Models (also story), The Doberman Gang (also story), Little Cigars (also story), The Deer Hunter (story collab.; Acad. Award nom.)

TELEVISION: Writer: 712 teleplays for Day in Court, Morning Court, Accused, 1959–66. Co-writer-creator: Direct Line (pilot), June Allyson Show, Threat of Evil, Death Valley Days, Crullers At Sundown, Captain Dick Mine, No. 3 Peanut Place (pilot).

GARFUNKEL, ART: Singer, Actor. b. New York, NY, Nov. 5, 1942. e. Columbia Coll. Began singing at age 4. Long partnership with Paul Simon began in grade school at 13 in Queens, NY; first big success in 1965 with hit single, Sound of Silence. Partnership dissolved in 1970. Film debut in Catch 22 (1970). Winner of 4 Grammy Awards.

PICTURES: Catch-22 (debut, 1970), Carnal Knowledge, Bad Timing/A Sensual Obsession, Good to Go, Boxing Helena.

GARLAND, BEVERLY: Actress. b. Santa Cruz, CA, Oct. 17, 1930. r.n. Beverly Fessenden. e. Glendale Coll., 1945–47.

TELEVISION: Series: Mama Rosa, Pantomime Quiz, The Bing Crosby Show, My Three Sons, Scarecrow & Mrs. King. Guest: Decoy, Twilight Zone, Dr. Kildare, Medic (Emmy nom. 1954), Magnum P.I., Remington Steele. Movies: Cutter's Trail, Say Goodbye Maggie Cole, Weekend Nun, Voyage of the Yes, Unwed Father, Healers, Day the Earth Moved, This Girl for Hire, The World's Oldest Living Bridesmaid, Finding the Way Home.

PICTURES: D.O.A., The Glass Web, Miami Story, Bittercreek, Two Guns and a Badge, Killer Leopard, The Rocket Man, Sudden Danger, Desperate Hours, Curucu: Beast of the Amazon, Gunslinger, Swamp Woman, The Steel Jungle, It Conquered the World, Not of This Earth, Naked Paradise, The Joker is Wild, Chicago Confidential, Badlands of Montana, The Saga of Hemp Brown, Alligator People, Stark Fever, Twice Told Tales, Pretty Poison, The Mad Room, Where the Red Fern Grows, Airport 1975, Roller Boogie, It's My Turn, Death Falls.

GARNER, JAMES: Actor. r.n. James Baumgarner. b. Norman, OK, April 7, 1928. e. Norman H.S. Joined Merchant Marine, U.S. Army, served in Korean War. Prod. Paul Gregory suggested acting career. Studied drama at N.Y. Berghof School. Toured with road companies; Warner Bros. studio contract followed.

PICTURES: Toward the Unknown (debut, 1956), The Girl He Left Behind, Shoot Out at Medicine Bend, Sayonara, Darby's Rangers, Up Periscope, Cash McCall, The Children's Hour, Boys' Night Out, The Great Escape, The Thrill of It All, The Wheeler Dealers, Move Over Darling, The Americanization of Emily, 36 Hours, The Art of Love, Mister Buddwing, A Man Could Get Killed, Duel at Diablo, Grand Prix, Hour of the Gun, The Pink Jungle, How Sweet It Is, Support Your Local Sheriff, Marlowe, A Man Called Sledge, Support Your Local Gunfighter, Skin Game, They Only Kill Their Masters, One Little Indian, The Castaway Cowboy, Health, The Fan, Victor/Victoria, Tank, Murphy's Romance (Acad. Award nom.), Sunset, The Distinguished Gentleman, Fire in the Sky.

TELEVISION: *Series*: Maverick, Nichols, Rockford Files, Bret Maverick, Man of the People. *Movies*: The Rockford Files (pilot), The New Maverick (pilot), The Long Summer of George Adams, The Glitter Dome, Heartsounds, Promise (also exec. prod.), Obsessive Love, My Name is Bill W. (also exec. prod.), Decoration Day, Barbarians at the Gate. *Mini-Series*: Space.

GARR, TERI: Actress. b. Lakewood, OH, Dec. 11, 1949. Began career as dancer, performing S.F. Ballet at 13. Later appeared with L.S. Ballet and in original road show co. of West Side Story. Several film appearances as a dancer incl. Fun in Acapulco, Viva Las Vegas, What a Way to Go, Roustabout, etc. Did commercials; appeared in film Head written by a fellow acting student, Jack Nicholson. Career boosted by appearance on TV as semi-regular on The Sonny and Cher Show.
PICTURES: Maryjane, Head, The Moonshine War, The Conversation, Young Frankenstein, Won Ton Ton the Dog Who Saved Hollywood, Oh God!, Close Encounters of the Third Kind, Mr. Mike's Mondo Video, The Black Stallion, Witches' Brew, Honky Tonk Freeway, The Escape Artist, Tootsie (Acad. Award nom.), The Sting II, The Black Stallion Returns, Mr. Mom, Firstborn, Miracles, After Hours, Full Moon in Blue Water, Out Cold, Let It Ride, Short Time, Waiting for the Light, The Player, Mom and Dad Save the World.
TELEVISION: *Series regular*: Shindig, The Ken Berry "Wow" Show, (1972), Burns and Schreiber Comedy Hour, Girl With Something Extra, The Sonny and Cher Comedy Hour, The Sonny Comedy Revue, Good and Evil.*Movies*: Law and Order, Doctor Franken, Prime Suspect, Winter of Our Discontent, To Catch a King, Intimate Strangers, Pack of Lies, A Quiet Little Neighborhood A Perfect Little Murder, Stranger in the Family, Deliver Them From Evil: The Taking of Alta View. *Specials*: The Frog Prince (Faerie Tale Theatre), Drive She Said (Trying Times), Paul Reiser: Out on a Whim, Mother Goose Rock 'n' Rhyme, The Whole Shebang. *Mini-Series*: Fresno. *Guest*: Tales from the Crypt (The Trap), The Larry Sanders Show.

GARRETT, BETTY: Singer, Actress. b. St. Joseph, MO, May 23, 1919. e. scholarships; Annie Wright Seminary, Tacoma, WA; Neighborhood Playhouse, N.Y. Sang in night clubs, hotels, Broadway shows: Call Me Mister (Donaldson Award, 1946), Spoon River Anthology, A Girl Could Get Lucky, Meet Me in St. Louis (1989). Motion Picture Herald, Star of Tomorrow, 1949. Starred in one woman show, Betty Garrett and Other Songs, beginning in 1974 and touring through 1990 (Bay Area Critics Award); also in autobiographical show, No Dogs or Actors Allowed (Pasadena Playhouse, 1989).
PICTURES: The Big City (debut, 1948), Words and Music, Take Me Out to the Ball Game, Neptune's Daughter, On the Town, My Sister Eileen, Shadow on the Window.
TELEVISION: *Series*: All in the Family, Laverne and Shirley. *Guest*: Love Boat, Black's Magic, Somerset Gardens, Murder She Wrote. *Movies*: All the Way Home, Who's Happy Now.

GARRETT, LAWRENCE G. JR.: Executive. b. San Francisco, Nov. 5, 1942. e. U. of California; Thunderbird Graduate Sch. 1967, joined Columbia Pictures Intl., Panama, Mexico; 1969, Paramount Pictures, mgr., Venezuela; 1973, MCA-TV asst. mgr., Mexico; 1973–76, Shearson Hayden Stone Institutional investment; 1977, United Artists, Argentina, Austral-Asia mgr. dir.; 1980, Avco Embassy, sls. supvr. Latin American-Far East; 1981, head intl. sls., Shapiro Entertainment; 1982, head intl. sls., Goldfarb Distributors; 1983–86, dir./intl. sls. & acquisitions, Arista Films; 1987, v.p. intl. theatrical & video sls., ITC Entertainment.

GARSON, GREER: Actress. b. County Down, Northern Ireland, Sept. 29, 1908. e. London U., B.A. cum laude; post grad. studies, Grenoble U. France. After early career in art research and editing for Encyclopaedia Britannica and market research with Lever's Ltd. Advertising Service became actress with Birmingham Rep. Co. starring in 13 West End prods. before lured to Hollywood by MGM, 1938. Screen debut 1939 in Goodbye, Mr. Chips. Academy Award best actress, 1942 Mrs. Miniver. Voted one of the ten best Money-Making Stars in Motion Picture Herald-Fame Poll 1942–46 inclusive. Photoplay Mag. Gold Medal 1944–45 and top British Award 1942, 1943, 1944. Numerous other awards incl. L.A. Times Woman of the Year, Woman of the World Award from Intl. Orphans, Inc. 1987 Gov. Award for contrib. to arts NM, 1988 USA Film Fest. Master Screen Artist. Active in civic and benevolent activities. With late husband Col. E.E. (Buddy) Fogelson, awarded Dept. of Interior's citation for environmental preservation efforts. Founded Fogelson Museum NM 1987. Established The Greer Garson Theatre and Fogelson Library Center at the College of Santa Fe; founding donor for Fogelson Forum at Dallas Presbyterian Hospital, Garson Communications Center at Col. of Santa Fe, Fogelson Pavillion in Dallas. Opened The Greer Garson Theatre at Southern Methodist Univ., Dallas.

THEATER: Stage debut Birmingham (England) Rep. theat. 1932 in Street Scene; London debut 1935 in Golden Arrow opposite Laurence Olivier; continued London stage to 1938 (Vintage Wine, Mademoiselle, Accent on Youth, Page from a Diary, Old Music, etc.).
PICTURES: Goodbye Mr. Chips (debut, 1939), Remember?, Pride and Prejudice, Blossoms in the Dust, When Ladies Meet, Mrs. Miniver (Acad. Award, 1942), Random Harvest, Madame Curie, The Youngest Profession (cameo), Mrs. Parkington, Valley of Decision, Adventure, Desire Me, Julia Misbehaves, That Forsyte Woman, The Miniver Story, The Law and the Lady, Scandal at Scourie, Julius Caesar, Her Twelve Men, Strange Lady in Town, Sunrise at Campobello, Pepe, The Singing Nun, The Happiest Millionaire.
TELEVISION: *Specials*: The Little Foxes, Crown Matrimonial, My Father Gave Me America, The Little Drummer Boy, Holiday Tribute to Radio City, Perry Como's Christmas in New Mexico, A Gift of Music (host), Bicentennial Tribute to Los Angeles. *Movie*: Little Women.

GARTNER, MICHAEL G.: Executive. b. Des Moines, IA, Oct. 25, 1938. e. Carleton Coll., Northfield, MN; NYU Sch. of Law. Began newspaper career at 15 with The Des Moines Register in Iowa. Became the paper's editor, later pres., COO and editorial chmn. of the parent Des Moines Register and Tribune Co. Worked for 14 years at the Wall Street Journal in various positions. Served as editor of Gannett-owned Louisville Courier-Journal and Louisville Times, and owner of the Daily Tribune of Ames, IA. Appointed president of NBC News, August 1988.

GARY, LORRAINE: Actress. b. New York, NY, Aug. 16, 1937. r.n. Lorraine Gottfried. m. executive Sidney J. Scheinberg. e. Columbia Univ.
PICTURES: Jaws, Car Wash, I Never Promised You a Rose Garden, Jaws 2, Just You and Me Kid, 1941, Jaws—The Revenge.
TELEVISION: *Movies*: The City, The Marcus-Nelson Murders, Partners in Crime, Pray for the Wildcats, Man on the Outside, Lanigan's Rabbi, Crash.

GASSMAN, VITTORIO: Actor. b. Genoa, Italy, Sept. 1, 1922. e. Acad. of Dramatic Art, Rome. Stage actor, 1943; m.p. debut, 1946.
PICTURES: Daniele Cortis, Mysterious Rider, Bitter Rice, Lure of Sila, The Outlaws, Anna, Streets of Sorrow; to U.S., Cry of the Hunted, Sombrero, The Glass Wall, Rhapsody, Girls Marked Danger, Mambo, War and Peace, World's Most Beautiful Woman, Tempest, The Love Specialist, The Great War, Let's Talk About Women, Il Successo, The Tiger, Woman Times Seven, Ghosts—Italian Style, Scent of a Woman, Viva Italia!, A Wedding, Quintet, Immortal Bachelor, The Nude Bomb, Sharky's Machine, Tempest, I Picari, The Family, The Sleazy Uncle, The House of the Lord, The Hateful Dead, To Forget Palermo, Los Alegres Picaro, Scheherzade, The Long Winter.

GATWARD, JAMES: Executive. b. London, England. Ent. Ind. 1957. Early career as freelance drama prod. dir. in Canada, USA, UK (with ITV & BBC). Prod. dir. various intern. co-productions in UK, Ceylond, Australia, Germany. Currently chief executive and Dep. chmn. TVS Television Ltd., chmn. Telso Communications Ltd., dir. of ITN, Channel Four, Super Channel, Oracle Teletext.

GAVIN, JOHN: Executive, Former Actor. b. Los Angeles, CA, April 8, 1932. m. actress Constance Towers. e. St. John's Military Acad., Villanova Prep at Ojai, Stanford Univ., Naval service: air intelligence officer in Korean War. Broadway stage debut: Seesaw, 1973. 1961–73 public service experience as spec. advisor to Secretary Gen. of OAS, performed gp. task work for Dept. of State and Exec. Office of the President. Pres. Screen Actors Guild, 1971–73. Named U.S. Ambassador to Mexico, 1981–86. Chmn. Century Council; partner in Gavin & Dailey, a venture capital firm; Pres., Gamma Services Corp. (Intl. Consultants); dir., Atlantic Richfield Co., Dresser Industries. Consultant to Dept. of State and serves pro-bono on many boards.
PICTURES: Behind the High Wall, Four Girls in Town, Quantez, A Time to Love and a Time to Die, Imitation of Life, Psycho, Midnight Lace, Spartacus, A Breath of Scandal, Romanoff and Juliet, Tammy Tell Me True, Back Street, Thoroughly Modern Millie, Mad Woman of Chaillot, Jennifer.
TELEVISION: *Movies*: Cutler's Trail, The New Adventures of Heidi, Sophia Loren: Her Own Story. *Series*: Destry, Convoy. *Mini-Series*: Doctors' Private Lives.

GAY, JOHN: Writer. b. Whittier, CA, April 1, 1924. e. LA City Coll.
PICTURES: Run Silent, Run Deep, Separate Tables, The Happy Thieves, Four Horsemen, The Courtship of Eddie's Father, The Hallelujah Trail, The Last Safari, The Power, No Way to Treat a Lady, Soldier Blue, Sometimes a Great Notion, Hennessey, A Matter of Time.
TELEVISION: Amazing Howard Hughes, Kill Me If You Can, Captains Courageous, Red Badge of Courage, All My Darling Daughters, Les Miserables, Transplant, A Private

Battle, A Tale of Two Cities, The Bunker, Berlin Tunnel 21, Stand By Your Man, Dial "M" For Murder, The Long Summer of George Adams, A Piano for Mrs. Cimino, The Hunchback of Notre Dame, Ivanhoe, Witness for the Prosecution, Samson and Delilah, Fatal Vision, Doubletake, Uncle Tom's Cabin, Outlaw, Six Against the Rock, Around the World in 80 Days, Blind Faith, Cruel Doubt.

GAYNOR, MITZI: Actress. r.n. Francisca Mitzi Von Gerber. b. Chicago, IL, Sept. 4, 1931. e. Powers Professional H.S., Hollywood. Studied ballet since age four; was in L.A. Light Opera prod. Roberta. Stage: Anything Goes (natl. co., 1989).
OPERA: Fortune Teller, Song of Norway, Louisiana Purchase, Naughty Marietta, The Great Waltz.
PICTURES: My Blue Heaven (debut, 1950), Take Care of My Little Girl, Golden Girl, We're Not Married, Bloodhounds of Broadway, The I Don't Care Girl, Down Among the Sheltering Palms, There's No Business Like Show Business, Three Young Texans, Anything Goes, The Birds and the Bees, The Joker is Wild, Les Girls, South Pacific, Happy Anniversary, Surprise Package, For Love or Money.

GAZZARA, BEN: Actor. b. New York, NY, Aug. 28, 1930. e. Studied at CCNY 1947–49. Won scholarship to study with Erwin Piscator; joined Actor's Studio, where students improvised a play, End as a Man, which then was performed on Broadway with him in lead. Screen debut (1957) in film version of that play retitled The Strange One.
PICTURES: The Strange One (debut, 1957), Anatomy of a Murder, The Passionate Thief, The Young Doctors, Convicts Four, Conquered City, A Rage to Live, The Bridge at Remagen, Husbands, The Neptune Factor, Capone, Killing of a Chinese Bookie, Voyage of the Damned, High Velocity, Opening Night, Saint Jack, Bloodline, They All Laughed, Inchon, Tales of Ordinary Madness, Road House, Quicker Than the Eye, Don Bosco, A Lovely Scandal, Girl from Trieste, Il Camorrista, Tatooed Memory, Beyond the Ocean (also dir., s.p.), Forever.
TELEVISION: Series: Arrest and Trial, Run for Your Life. Movies: When Michael Calls, Maneater, QB VII, The Death of Ritchie, A Question of Honor, An Early Frost, A Letter to Three Wives, Police Story: The Freeway Killings, Downpayment on Murder, People Like Us, Lies Before Kisses, Blindsided, Love Honor & Obey; The Last Mafia Marriage.
THEATER: Jezebel's Husband, End as a Man, Cat on a Hot Tin Roof, A Hatful of Rain, The Night Circus, Epitaph for George Dillon, Two for the Seesaw, Strange Interlude, Traveler Without Luggage, Hughie, Who's Afraid of Virginia Woolf, Dance of Death, Thornhill, Shimada.

GEARY, ANTHONY: Actor. b. Coalville, UT, May 29, 1947. e. U. of Utah.
TELEVISION: Series: Bright Promise, General Hospital (1978–83; 1990–). Guest: The Young and the Restless, Osmond Family Holiday Special, Sunset Beat, Murder She Wrote, Hotel, All in the Family, Streets of San Francisco. Movies: Intimate Agony, Sins of the Past, The Imposter, Kicks, Perry Mason: The Case of the Murdered Madam, Do You Know the Muffin Man?
PICTURES: Blood Sabbath (debut, 1969), Johnny Got His Gun, Private Investigations, Disorderlies, Penitentiary III, You Can't Hurry Love, Pass the Ammo, Dangerous Love, It Takes Two, UHF, Night Life, Crack House, Night of the Warrior, Scorchers.

GEBHARDT, FRED: Producer, Writer, Exhibitor. b. Vienna, Austria, Mar. 16, 1925. e. Schotten Gymnasium, Vienna, UCLA, 1939. Usher Boyd Theatre, Bethlehem, PA; Mgr., Rivoli Thea. L.A., 1944; 18 yrs. mgr. many theatres. Fox West Coast, then Fine Arts Theatre. Writer, prod.: 12 To the Moon, The Phantom Planet; prod., Assignment Outer Space, Operation M; s.p., All But Glory, The Starmaker, Shed No Blood, Fortress in Heaven, Eternal Woman.
BOOKS: Mental Disarmament, All But Glory, Starmaker, Shed No Blood, The Last of the Templars.
Pres., Four Crown Prods., Inc.; recipient of Medal of Americanism, D.A.R., 1963; Honorary Lifetime Member, P.T.A., Young Man of The Year Award, 1956, 24 Showmanship Awards; Mem. Acad. M.P. Arts and Sciences, Ind. M.P. Prod. Assoc.

GEE, CHARLOTTE: Executive. Served for 6 years as adv.-pub. mgr. for Village Roadshow Corp., Warner Bros. Australian dist. 1986, joined WB as dir. project pub. 1987, named WB v.p., pub. 1989, named v.p. pub. & promo.

GEESON, JUDY: Actress. b. Arundel, Sussex, England, Sept. 10, 1948. e. Corona Stage Sch. Began professional career on British TV, 1960.
PICTURES: To Sir with Love, Berserk, Here We Go Round the Mulberry Bush, Prudence and the Pill, Hammerhead, Three into Two Won't Go, The Oblong Box, Two Gentlemen Sharing, The Executioner, Nightmare Hotel, 10 Rillington Place, Doomwatch, Fear in the Night, It's Not the Size That Counts, Brannigan, Diagnosis Murder, The Eagle Has

Landed, Carry On England, Dominique, Horror Planet, The Plague Dogs (voice).
TELEVISION: Dance of Death, Lady Windermere's Fan, Room with a View, The Skin Game, Star Maidens, Poldark, She, The Coronation, Murder She Wrote, Astronomy (Triple Play II). Movie: The Secret Life of Kathy McCormick.
THEATRE: Othello, Titus Andronicus, Two Gentlemen of Verona, Section Nine, An Ideal Husband.

GEFFEN, DAVID: Executive, Producer. b. Brooklyn, NY, Feb. 21, 1943. Began in mailroom of William Morris Agency before becoming agent there and later at Ashley Famous. With Elliott Roberts founded own talent management co. for musicians. Founded Asylum Records, 1970. Pres. then chmn. Elektra-Asylum Records 1973–76. Sold co. to Warner Communications for whom he headed film prod. unit. Vice-chmn. Warner Bros. Pictures, 1975; exec. asst. to chmn., Warner Communications, 1977; Member music faculty Yale U., 1978. Formed Geffen Records 1980 and Geffen Film Co. Producer of Broadway shows Master Harold . . . and the Boys, Cats, Good, Dreamgirls, Social Security, Chess. 1990, sold record co. to MCA, Inc.
PICTURES: Personal Best, Risky Business, Lost in America, After Hours, Little Shop of Horrors, Beetlejuice (exec. prod.), Men Don't Leave, Defending Your Life.

GELBART, LARRY: Writer. b. Chicago, IL, Feb. 25, 1925. Began at 16 writing material for Danny Thomas on Fanny Brice Show. Followed by Duffy's Tavern, Bob Hope and Jack Paar radio shows, Sid Caesar's Caesar's Hour.
THEATER: The Conquering Hero, A Funny Thing Happened on the Way to the Forum (with Burt Shevlove; Tony Award), Sly Fox, Mastergate, City of Angels (Tony Award), Power Failure.
PICTURES: The Notorious Landlady, The Thrill of It All, The Wrong Box (also assoc. prod.), Not With My Wife You Don't, The Chastity Belt, A Fine Pair, Oh God!, Movie Movie, Neighbors, Tootsie, Blame It on Rio (also exec. prod.).
TELEVISION: Series: Caesar's Hour, M*A*S*H (Emmy, 1974, also co-prod.), United States. Movie: Barbarians at the Gate. Special: Mastergate.

GELFAN, GREGORY: Executive. b. Los Angeles, CA, Aug. 7, 1950. Was entertainment atty. with Kaplan, Livingston et. al., and Weissmann, Wolff et. al. before joining Paramount Pictures in 1983 as dir. of business affairs. 1985, named v.p., business affairs, for M.P. Group of Paramount; 1989 promoted to sr. v.p. in chg. of business affairs.

GELLER, BRIAN L.: Executive. b. New York, NY, Feb. 3, 1948. e. Queens Coll. Entered industry with Columbia Pictures as sls. trainee in 1966, leaving in 1968 to go with American Intl. Pictures as asst. branch mgr. In 1969 joined Cinemation Industries as eastern div. sls. mgr.; 1978, left to become gen. sls. mr. of NMD Film Distributing Co. 1982, named dir. of dist., Mature Pictures Corp. 1983, gen. sls. mgr., Export Pix.; with Cinema Group as east. sls. mgr.; joined Scotti Brothers Pictures as national sales, mgr.
MEMBER: Motion Picture Bookers Club of N.Y.; Variety Tent 35, Motion Picture Pioneers.

GENDECE, BRIAN: Producer, Executive. b. St. Louis, MO, Dec. 3, 1956. e. Drury Coll., Springfield, MO. 1981–85, Director of Business Affairs, Weinstein/Skyfield Productions and Skyfield Management. 1986–87, dir. of business affairs,Cannon Films; 1987–89, dir. creative affairs, Cannon Films; 1989 co-pres., Sheer Entertainment; indie first look Epic Prods.; 1991 owner The Gendece Film Co.; 1991–93, prod./dir., 21st Century Film.
PICTURES: Runaway Train, Salsa, Rope Dancin', The Hunters, The American Samurai.
STAGE: Jack Klugman as Lyndon.
VIDEO: Bad Habits, Shape Up with Arnold, Laura Branigan's Your Love, How to Become a Teenage Ninja, L.A. Raiders' Wild Wild West, The Making of Crime and Punishment.

GEOFFREYS, STEPHEN: Actor. b. Cincinnati, OH, Nov. 22, 1959. e. NYU. Bdwy debut 1984 in The Human Comedy (Tony nom., Theatre World Award).
PICTURES: Heaven Help Us (debut, 1985), Fraternity Vacation, Fright Night, At Close Range, 976-EVIL, The Chair, Moon 44.
THEATRE: NY: The Human Comedy, Maggie Magalita, Songs on a Shipwrecked Sofa.
TELEVISION: Guest: Amazing Stories (Moving Day), Twilight Zone (The Elevator). Movie: The Road Raiders.

GEORGE, GEORGE W.: Writer, Producer. b. New York, NY, Feb. 8, 1920. e. Williams Coll. U.S. Navy, 1941–44; screenwriter since 1948. President, Jengo Enterprises, dev. theatrical and m.p. projects.
PICTURES: Writer: Bodyguard, The Nevadan, Woman on Pier 13, Peggy, Mystery Submarine, Red Mountain Experiment, Alcatraz, Fight Town, Smoke Signal, Desert Sands, Uranium Boom, Halliday Brand, Doc, The James Dean Story, The Two Little Bears. Prod.: The James Dean Story, A Matter

of Innocence, Twisted Nerve, Hello-Goodbye, Night Watch, Rich Kids, My Dinner with Andre.
STAGE: *Prod.:* Dylan, Any Wednesday, Ben Franklin in Paris, The Great Indoors, Happily Never After, Night Watch, Via Galactica, Bedroom Farce, Program for Muder (also co-author).
TELEVISION: Climax, Screen Gems, Loretta Young Show, The Rifleman, Peter Gunn, The Real McCoys, Adventures in Paradise, Hong Kong, Follow the Sun.

GEORGE, LOUIS: Executive. b. Karavas, Kyrenia, Cyprus, June 7, 1935. e. Kyrenia Business Acad., Cyprus (honored 1951). Emigrated to U.S. in 1952. After brief stint in Foreign Exchange Dept. of City National Bank, New York, served in U.S. Army, 1953–55. Entered industry in 1956 as theatre manager with Loew's Theatres in N.Y. metro area, managing Metropolitan, Triboro, New Rochelle, between 1958–66. In 1966 joined MGM as dir. of intl. theatre dept. In 1969 promoted to dir. of world-wide non-theatrical sales. From 1972 to 1974 served as regional dir. of MGM Far East operations. In 1974 left MGM to establish Arista Films, Inc., an indep. prod./dist. co. Pres. & chief executive officer, Arista Films, Inc. Also bd. member, American Film Marketing Assn., chmn. Copyright and Film Security Committee of the Assn.
PICTURES: Slaughterhouse Rock, Buying Time, Violent Zone (exec. prod.), Angels Brigade, Final Justice, Surf II, Crackdown.

GEORGE, SUSAN: Actress, Producer. b. Surrey, England, July 26, 1950. m. actor-prod. Simon MacCorkindale. e. Corona Acad.
PICTURES: Billion Dollar Brain, The Sorcerers, Up the Junction, The Strange Affair, The Looking Glass War, All Neat in Black Stockings, Twinky (Lola), Spring and Port Wine, Eye Witness (Sudden Terror), Die Screaming Marianne, Fright, Straw Dogs, Sonny and Jed, Dirty Mary Crazy Larry, Mandingo, Out of Season, A Small Town in Texas, Tintorera, Tomorrow Never Comes, Enter the Ninja, Venom, House Where Evil Dwells, Jigsaw Man, Lightning: The White Stallion, Stealing Heaven (exec. prod. only), That Summer of White Roses (also exec. prod.).
TELEVISION: Swallows and Amazons, Adam's Apple, Weaver's Green, Compensation Alice, The Right Attitude, Dracula, Lamb to the Slaughter, Royal Jelly, Masquerade, Czechmate, Hotel, Blacke's Magic, Jack the Ripper, Castle of Adventure.

GERALD, HELEN: Actress. b. New York, NY, Aug. 13. e. U. of Southern California, 1948. Stage: Italian Teatro D'Arte, Les Miserables, The Civil Death, Feudalism.
PICTURES: The Gay Cavalier, The Trap, Tarzan and the Leopard Woman, Cigarette Girl, Meet Miss Bobby Socks, G.I. War Brides, Gentleman's Agreement, A Bell for Adano, Tomorrow Is Forever, Janie, Grand Prix, The Sandpiper, Make Mine Mink, Best of Everything.
TELEVISION: Robert Montgomery Presents, Frontiers of Faith, Valiant Lady, Kraft Theatre, Gangbusters, Adventures of The Falcon, Schlitz Playhouse of Stars, This Is the Answer, Man from U.N.C.L.E., Run for Your Life, Perry Mason.

GERARD, GIL: Actor. b. Little Rock, AK, Jan. 23, 1943. e. Arkansas State Teachers Coll. Appeared in over 400 TV commercials. On stage in I Do! I Do!, Music Man, Stalag 17, Applause, etc.
PICTURES: Some of My Best Friends Are (1971), Man on a Swing, Hooch (also co-prod.), Airport '77, Buck Rogers in the 25th Century, Soldier's Fortune.
TELEVISION: Series: The Doctors, Buck Rogers in the 25th Century, Nightingales, Sidekicks, E.A.R.T.H. Force, Code 3 (host). Movies: Ransom for Alice, Killing Stone, Help Wanted: Male, Not Just Another Affair, Hear No Evil, Johnny Blue (pilot), For Love or Money, Stormin' Home, International Airport, Final Notice, The Elite, Last Electric Knight.

GERARD, LILLIAN: Publicist, Writer b. New York, NY, Nov. 25, 1914. e. Baruch, CCNY, Columbia U. Publicity, Rialto Theatre, 1936; publicity-adv. Filmarte Theatre, 1938, Gerard Associates, 1938–47; V.P. and managing dir. of Paris Theatre, 1948–62; publicity-adv. dir., Rugoff Theatres, 1962. Film consultant to Times Films, Lopert Films, Landau Co., 1962–65. Adjunct Professor, Film, 1968–70, Columbia U., Sch. of the Arts, Special Projects Co-Ordinator, Museum of Modern Art, 1968–80. Now associated with Philip Gerard in Gerard Associates.

GERARD, PHILIP R.: Executive. b. New York, NY, Aug. 23, 1913. e. City Coll. of New York, B.B.A. 1935; Columbia U.. Publicity dir. Mayer-Burstyn 1936–39; Gerard Associates, 1939–41; in public relations U.S. War Dept. 1942–44; with MGM 1944–48; with Universal Pictures since 1948; Eastern pub. mgr., 1950–59; Eastern ad. and pub. dir., Dec. 1959–68; N.Y. Production Exec., 1968–76. As of Jan. 1, 1977 formed Gerard Associates, film consultants on marketing, production and acquisitions. N.Y.C. Board member of CSS/RSVP (Retired Seniors Volunteer Program); Community Service Society. Member: Visitor's Day Comm., New York Hospital; volunteer at the International Center.

GERBER, DAVID: Executive. b. Brooklyn, NY. e. U. of the Pacific. m. actress Laraine Stephens. Joined Batten, Barton, Durstine and Osborn ad agency in N.Y. as TV supvr. Left to become sr. v.p. of TV at General Artists Corp. In 1956, named v.p. in chg. sales at 20th-Fox TV where sold and packaged over 50 prime-time series and specials. Entered indep. prod. with The Ghost and Mrs. Muir, followed by Nanny and the Professor. In 1970 was exec. prod. of The Double Deckers, children's series made in England. In 1972 he joined Columbia Pictures Television as an indep. prod., 1974 was named exec. v.p. worldwide prod. for CPT. 1976 returned to indep. prod. 1985, joined MGM/UA TV broadcasting group in chg. world-wide prod. 1986 named president, MGM/UA Television. Nov., 1988, appt. chmn and CEO, MGM/UA Television Prods. group.
TELEVISION: exec. prod.: Cade's County, Police Story (Emmy, best dramatic series), Police Woman, The Lindbergh Kidnapping Case, Joe Forrester, The Quest and Gibbsville, To Kill a Cop, Power, Medical Story, Born Free, Beulah Land, The Night the City Screamed, Follow the North Star.

GERBER, MICHAEL H.: Executive. b. New York, NY, Feb. 6, 1944. e. St. Johns U., B.A., 1969; St. Johns U. School of Law, J.D., 1969. Atty. for Screen Gems, 1969–71; asst. secy. & asst. to gen. counsel, Columbia Pictures Industries, 1971–74; corporate counsel and secretary, Allied Artists Pictures, 1974, v.p. corporate affairs, Allied Artists, 1978; v.p., business affairs, Viacom Intl. 1980, pres., first run, intl. distrib. & acquisitions, Viacom Enterprises.

GERE, RICHARD: Actor. b. Philadelphia, PA, Aug. 29, 1949. e. U. of Massachusetts. Started acting in college; later joined Provincetown Playhouse and Seattle Repertory Theatre. Composed music for productions of these groups. Appeared on Broadway in Grease, Soon, Habeas Corpus, Bent (Theatre World Award), A Midsummer Night's Dream (Lincoln Center); and in London in Taming of the Shrew with Young Vic. Off-Bdwy in Killer's Head.
PICTURES: Report to the Commissioner (debut, 1975), Baby Blue Marine, Looking for Mr. Goodbar, Days of Heaven, Bloodbrothers, Yanks, American Gigolo, An Officer and a Gentleman, Breathless, Beyond the Limit, The Cotton Club, King David, Power, No Mercy, Miles From Home, Internal Affairs, Pretty Woman, Rhapsody in August, Final Analysis (also co-exec. prod.), Sommersby (also co-exec. prod.), Mr. Jones (also co-exec. prod.), Intersection.
TELEVISION: Guest: Kojak. Movies: Strike Force, And the Band Played On. Pilot: D.H.P.

GERTZ, IRVING: Composer, Musical director. b. Providence, RI, May 19, 1915. e. Providence Coll. of Music, 1934–37. Assoc. with Providence Symph. Orch., comp. choral works for Catholic Choral Soc.; music dept., Columbia, 1939–41; U.S. Army, 1941–46; then comp. arranger, mus. dir. for many cos. incl. Columbia, U-I, NBC, 20th Century Fox.
PICTURES: Bandits of Corsica, Gun Belt, Long Wait, The Fiercest Heart, First Travelling Saleslady, Fluffy, Nobody's Perfect, Marines Let's Go!, It Came from Outer Space, The Man from Bitter Ridge, Posse from Hell, The Creature Walks Among Us, The Incredible Shrinking Man, Hell Bent for Leather, Seven Ways from Sundown, Francis Joins the WACS, Raw Edge, East of Sumatra, A Day of Fury, To Hell and Back, Cult of the Cobra, Plunder Road, Top Gun, Tombstone Express, The Alligator People, Khyber Patrol, The Wizard of Baghdad.
Record album (Dot Records) Leaves of Grass; published works for mixed voices; Fluffy, feature, Universal. Marines, Let's Go! feature, 20th Century Fox Serenata for String Quartet, Divertimento for String Orchestra, Tableau for Orchestra.
TELEVISION: Orig. theme & scores: America, The Golden Voyage, Across the Seven Seas, The Legend of Jesse James, Daniel Boone, Voyage to the Bottom of the Sea, Peyton Place, Land of the Giants, Lancer, Medical Center, Boutade for Wood-Wind Quartet, Salute to All Nations, A Village Fair, Liberty! Liberte! (for symphony orchestra).

GERTZ, JAMI: Actress. b. Chicago, IL, Oct. 28, 1965. e. NYU. Won a nationwide talent search competition headed by Norman Lear to cast TV comedy series Square Pegs. Following series studied at NYU drama school. Los Angeles theater includes Out of Gas on Lovers' Leap and Come Back Little Sheba. On NY stage in Wrong Turn at Lungfish. Also appeared in the Julian Lennon music video Stick Around.
PICTURES: Endless Love (debut, 1981), Alphabet City, Sixteen Candles, Mischief, Quicksilver, Crossroads, Solar-babies, The Lost Boys, Less Than Zero, Listen to Me, Renegades, Silence Like Glass, Don't Tell Her It's Me, Sibling Rivalry, Jersey Girls.
TELEVISION: Series: Square Pegs, Dreams, Sibs. Guest: The Facts of Life.

GETTY, ESTELLE: Actress. b. New York, NY, July 25, 1923. e. attended New School for Social Research. Trained for stage with Gerald Russak and at Herbert Berghof Studios. Worked as comedienne on Borscht Belt circuit and as actress with Yiddish theatre. Founder Fresh Meadows Community theater.

Also worked as acting teacher and coach and secretary. Author, If I Knew What I Know Now . . . So What? (1988).

THEATER: The Divorce of Judy and Jane (off-Bdwy debut, 1971), Widows and Children First, Table Settings, Demolition of Hannah Fay, Never Too Old, A Box of Tears, Hidden Corners, I Don't Know Why I'm Screaming, Under the Bridge There's a Lonely Place, Light Up the Sky, Pocketful of Posies, Fits and Starts, Torch Song Trilogy (off-Bdwy, Bdwy and tour, Drama Desk nom.), 1982, Helen Hayes Award, best supp. performer in a touring show).

PICTURES: The Chosen, Tootsie, Protocol, Mask, Mannequin, Stop Or My Mom Will Shoot.

TELEVISION: Series: The Golden Girls (Golden Globe Award, Emmy Award), The Golden Palace. Movies: No Man's Land, Victims for Victims: the Teresa Saldana Story, Copacabana. Guest: Cagney and Lacey, Nurse, Baker's Dozen, One of the Boys, Fantasy Island.

GETZ, DON: Executive. b. Chicago, IL. March 28, 1920. Early career in radio until 1952. 1952: Ent. dist. with GBD Int. Releasing handling US and foreign dist. for Mr. Hulot's Holiday, Jour de Fete, Diabolique, Holiday for Henrietta, Ali Baba. 1957: formed Getz-Buck Productions and prod. number of films in UK and France. 1961: formed Playpoint Films Ltd., for prod. and dist. of TV and theatrical films in UK and Continent. 1963: formed Artxo Films with Artie Shaw to dist. imported films in the USA. 1964: joined Official Films Inc. as vice-pres. Int. 1968: consultant to Humphries Group. 1971: reactivated Playpoint Films as sales agent for foreign producers handling The Great Catherine, Foxtrot, Caligula, One Away, Disappearance, The Illusionist, The Pointsman, Turkish Delight, The Lift, Chain Reaction, Year of the Quiet Sun, Shadow of Victory, Istanbul, Iris, Good Hope, One Month Later, Great Rock 'n Roll Swindle, Enemy, Who Do I Gotta Kill?

GETZ, JOHN: Actor. e. Univ Iowa, Amer. Conservatory Theatre (SF). Appeared on Bdwy in They're Playing Our Song, M. Butterfly. LA stage: Money & Friends.

TELEVISION: Series: Rafferty, Suzanne Pleshette is Maggie Briggs, MacGruder & Loud, Mariah. Movies: Killer Bees, A Woman Called Moses, Kent State, Rivkin: Bounty Hunter, Muggable Mary: Street Cop, Not in Front of the Children, Concrete Beat, The Execution, In My Daughter's Name. Mini-Series: Loose Change.

PICTURES: Tattoo, Thief of Hearts, Blood Simple, The Fly, The Fly II, Born on the Fourth of July, Men at Work, Don't Tell Mom the Babysitter's Dead, Curly Sue.

GHOSTLEY, ALICE: Actress. b. Eve, MO, Aug. 14, 1926. e. Univ. of OK.

TELEVISION: Series: The Jackie Gleason Show (1962–4), Captain Nice, The Jonathan Winters Show, Bewitched, Mayberry R.F.D., Nichols, The Julie Andrews Hour, Temperatures Rising, Designing Women. Movie: Two on a Bench. Specials: Cinderella, Twelfth Night, Shangri-La, Everybody's Doin' It. Guest: Please Don't Eat the Daisies, Get Smart, Love American Style, Hogan's Heroes, The Odd Couple, What's Happening!, Good Times, Gimme a Break, The Golden Girls, etc.

PICTURES: New Faces (debut, 1954), To Kill a Mockingbird, My Six Loves, Ace Eli and Rodger of the Skies, Gator, Rabbit Test, Grease, Not for Publication.

THEATRE: New Faces of 1952, Sandhog, Trouble in Tahiti, Maybe Tuesday, A Thurber Carnival, The Sign in Sidney Brustein's Window (Tony Award, 1965), Stop Thief Stop, Annie.

GIANNINI, GIANCARLO: Actor. b. Spezia, Italy, Aug. 1, 1942. Acquired degree in electronics but immediately after school enrolled at Acad. for Drama in Rome. Cast by Franco Zeffirelli as Romeo at age of 20. Subsequently appeared in a play also directed by Zeffirelli, Two Plus Two No Longer Make Four, written by Lina Wertmuller.

PICTURES: Rita la Zanzara, Arabella, Anzio, Fraulein Doktor, The Secret of Santa Vittoria, Love and Anarchy, The Seduction of Mimi, Swept Away by an Unusual Destiny in the Blue Sea of August, Seven Beauties, How Funny Can Sex Be?, A Night Full of Rain, The Innocent, Buone Notizie (also prod.), Revenge, Travels with Anita, Lili Marleen, Lovers and Liars, La Vita e Bella, Picone Sent Me, Immortal Bachelor, American Dreamer, Fever Pitch, Saving Grace, New York Stories (Life Without Zoe), I Picari, The Sleazy, Uncle, Snack Bar Budapest, Oh King, Blood Red, Brown Bread Sandwiches, Killing Time, Short Cut, Once Upon a Crime.

TELEVISION: Sins.

GIBBS, DAVID: Executive. b. 1944. Ent. motion picture industry 1961, Kodak research, worked as a photographer for Kodak 1963–66. Lectured at Harrow College of Technology and Kodak Photographic School until 1972. Left Kodak, 1975, after three years as a market specialist to join Filmatic Laboratories. Appt. asst. man. director, 1977, becoming chmn. and man. director, 1989. Member of RTS, SMPTE and IVCA. Past Chmn. BISFA 1988–90. President of the British Kinematograph, Sound and Television Society.

GIBBS, MARLA: Actress. b. Chicago, IL, June 14, 1931. e. Cortez Peters Business School, Chicago. Worked as receptionist, switchboard operator, travel consultant (1963–74) before co-starring as Florence Johnston on the Jeffersons (1974–85). Formed Marla Gibbs Enterprises, Los Angeles, 1978. Member of CA State Assembly, 1980. Image Award NAACP, 1979–83.

TELEVISION: Series: The Jeffersons, Checking In, 227. Movies: The Missing Are Deadly, Tell Me Where It Hurts, Nobody's Child. Mini-Series: The Moneychangers. Special: You Can't Take It With You.

PICTURES: Black Belt Jones, Sweet Jesus, Preacher Man.

GIBSON, DEREK: Executive. b. Huyton, England, July 7, 1945. e. Wigan Col. Head of Prod. at Astral Bellevue Pathe, 1979–80; v.p. Sandy Howard Prods.; Pres. Hemdale Film Group., 1982–present.

PICTURES: Prod./Exec. Prod. incld.: The Terminator, Hoosiers, Salvador, Platoon (Acad. Award winner for Best Picture, 1986), River's Edge, Best Seller, Criminal Law.

GIBSON, HENRY: Actor. b. Germantown, PA, Sept. 21, 1935. e. Catholic U. of America. Appeared as child actor with stock companies, 1943–57; Bdwy. debut in My Mother My Father and Me, 1962.

PICTURES: The Nutty Professor, Kiss Me Stupid, The Outlaws Is Coming, Charlotte's Web (voice), The Long Goodbye, Nashville (best supp. actor, Nat'l Soc. Film Critics, 1975), The Last Remake of Beau Geste, Kentucky Fried Movie, A Perfect Couple, The Blues Brothers, Tulips, Health, The Incredible Shrinking Woman, Monster in the Closet, Brenda Starr, Inner Space, Switching Channels, The 'Burbs, Night Visitor, Gremlins II, Tune in Tomorrow, Tom and Jerry: The Movie (voice).

TELEVISION: Series: Laugh-In (1968–72). Movies: Evil Roy Slade, Every Man Needs One, The New Original Wonder Woman (pilot), Escape from Bogen County, The Night They Took Miss Beautiful, Amateur Night at the Dixie Bar & Grill, For the Love of It, Nashville Grab, Long Gone, Slow Burn, Return to Green Acres. Mini-Series: Around the World in 80 Days.

GIBSON, MEL: Actor. b. Peekskill, NY, Jan. 3, 1956. Emigrated in 1968 to Australia with family. Attended Nat'l Inst. of Dramatic Art in Sydney; in 2nd yr. was cast in his first film, Summer City (1977). Graduated from NIDA, 1977. Joined South Australian Theatre Co. in 1978, appearing in Oedipus, Henry IV, Cedoona. Other plays include Romeo and Juliet, No Names No Pack Drill, On Our Selection, Waiting for Godot, Death of a Salesman.

PICTURES: Summer City (debut, 1977; a.k.a. Coast of Terror), Mad Max, Tim, Chain Reaction (unbilled), Attack Force Z, Gallipoli, The Road Warrior (Mad Max II), The Year of Living Dangerously, The Bounty, The River, Mrs. Soffel, Mad Max Beyond Thunderdome, Lethal Weapon, Tequila Sunrise, Lethal Weapon 2, Bird on a Wire, Air America, Hamlet, Lethal Weapon 3, Forever Young, The Man Without a Face (also dir.).

TELEVISION: Series: The Sullivans, The Oracle (Aust.) Special: The Ultimate Stuntman: A Tribute to Dar Robinson. Guest host: Saturday Night Live.

GIELGUD, SIR JOHN: Actor. b. London, England, Apr. 14, 1904. e. Westminster Sch., Lady Benson's Sch. (dram.); London; Royal Acad. of Dramatic Art. Knighted, 1953. Autobiography: Early Stages (1983).

THEATRE: Began stage career in Shakespearean roles; on London stage also in the Constant Nymph, The Good Companions, Dear Octopus, The Importance of Being Earnest, Dear Brutus, etc., various Shakespearean seasons, London & N.Y. 1988: The Best of Friends.

PICTURES: Who is the Man? (1924), The Clue of the New Pin, Insult (sound film debut, 1932); later (f.) films: The Good Companions, Secret Agent, The Prime Minister, Julius Caesar, Romeo and Juliet, Richard III, Around the World in 80 Days, Barretts of Wimpole Street, Saint Joan, Hamlet, Becket, To Die in Madrid (narrator), The Loved One, Chimes at Midnight, Sebastian, Assignment to Kill, Charge of the Light Brigade, The Shoes of the Fisherman, Oh What a Lovely War, Julius Caesar, Eagle in a Cage, Lost Horizon, Galileo, 11 Harrowhouse, Gold, Murder on the Orient Express, Aces High, Providence, Portrait of the Artist as a Young Man, Joseph Andrews, Murder by Decree, Caligula, The Human Factor, The Elephant Man, The Formula, Sphinx, Lion of the Desert, Arthur (Acad. Award, supp. actor, 1981), Chariots of Fire, Priest of Love, Gandhi, The Wicked Lady, Invitation to the Wedding, Scandalous, The Shooting Party, Plenty, Time After Time (1985), Whistle Blower, Appointment with Death, Bluebeard Bluebeard, Arthur 2 on the Rocks, Getting It Right, Strike It Rich, Prospero's Books, Shining Through, The Power of One.

TELEVISION: A Day by the Sea, The Browning Version (U.S.), The Rehearsal, Great Acting, Ages of Man, Mayfly and th Frog, Cherry Orchard, Ivanov, From Chekhov With Love, St. Joan, Good King Charles' Golden Days, Conversation at Night, Hassan, Deliver Us from Evil, Heartbreak House,

Brideshead Revisited, The Canterville Ghost, The Hunchback of Notre Dame, Inside the Third Reich, Marco Polo, The Scarlet and the Black, The Master of Ballantrae, Wagner. The Far Pavillions, Camille, Romance on the Orient Express, Funny You Don't Look Now 200, Oedipus the King, A Man For All Seasons, War and Remembrance, Summer Lease (Emmy Award, 1991), The Best of Friends. Special: John Gielgud: An Actor's Life.

GILBERT, ARTHUR N.: Producer. b. Detroit, MI, Oct. 17, 1920. Lt., U.S.M.C., 1941–45. e. U. of Chicago, 1946. Special Agent, FBI, 1946–53; world sales dir., Gen. Motors, Cadillac Div., 1953–59; investments in mot. pictures and hotel chains, 1959–64; exec. prod., Mondo Hollywood, 1965; exec. prod. Jeannie-Wife Child, 1966; assoc. prod., The Golden Breed, 1967; commissioned rank of Colonel U.S.M.C., 1968; 1970–80, exec. prod. Jaguar Pictures Corp; Columbia, 1981–86; Indi Pic. Corp. Also account exec. and v.p. Pacific Western Tours. v.p., Great Basion Corp. Bev. Hills 1987–9; v.p., Lawrence 3-D TV 1990–present; v.p. Cougar Prods. Co. 1990–91. Producer in development at Jonte Prods. of Paris/London, 1992–93.
PICTURES: The Glory Stompers, Fire Grass, Cycle Savages, Bigfoot, Incredible Transplant, Balance of Evil.

GILBERT, BRUCE: Producer. b. Los Angeles, CA, March 28, 1947. e. U. of California. Pursued film interests at Berkeley's Pacific Film Archive; in summer involved in production in film dept. of San Francisco State U. Founded progressive preschool in Bay Area. Became story editor in feature film division of Cine-Artists; involved in several projects, including Aloha, Bobby and Rose. Formally partnered with Jane Fonda in IPC Films, Inc. Currently president, American Filmworks, 1980–.
PICTURES: Coming Home (assoc. prod.); The China Syndrome (exec. prod.); Nine to Five (prod.); On Golden Pond (prod.); Rollover (prod.); The Morning After (prod.); Man Trouble (prod.), Jack the Bear (prod.).
TELEVISION: Nine to Five (series-exec. prod.); The Dollmaker (movie-exec. prod.), By Dawn's Early Light (writer, exec. prod.).

GILBERT, LEWIS: Producer, Writer, Director, Former Actor. b. London, England, Mar. 6, 1920. In RAF, W.W.II. Screen debut, 1932; asst. dir. (1930–39) with London Films, Assoc. British, Mayflower, RKO-Radio; from 1939–44 attached U.S. Air Corps Film Unit (asst. dir., Target for Today). In 1944 joined G.B.I. as writer and dir. In 1948, Gainsborough Pictures as writer, dir., 1949; Argyle Prod. 1950; under contract Nettlefold Films, Ltd. as dir.
PICTURES: Under One Roof, I Want to Get Married, Haunting Melody. Director: The Little Ballerina, Marry Me (s.p. only), Once a Sinner, Scarlet Thread, There Is Another Sun, Time Gentlemen Please, Emergency Call, Cosh Boy, Johnny on the Run, Albert R.N., The Good Die Young, The Sea Shall Not Have Them, Reach for the Sky, Cast a Dark Shadow, The Admirable Crichton, Carve Her Name with Pride, A Cry from the Street, Ferry to Hong Kong, Sink the Bismarck, Light Up the Sky, The Greengage Summer, H.M.S. Defiant, The Patriots, Spare the Rod, The Seventh Dawn, Alfie, You Only Live Twice, The Adventurers, Friends (also prod., story), Paul & Michelle (also prod., story), Operation Daybreak, Seven Nights in Japan, The Spy Who Loved Me, Moonraker, Educating Rita (also prod.), Not Quite Paradise, Shirley Valentine (also prod.), Stepping Out (also co-prod.).

GILBERT, MELISSA: Actress. b. Los Angeles, May 8, 1964. Made debut at age of 3 in TV commercial. Comes from show business family: father, late comedian Paul Gilbert; mother, former dancer-actress Barbara Crane. Grandfather, Harry Crane created The Honeymooners. NY Off-Bdwy debut A Shayna Madel (1987; Outer Critics Circle & Theatre World Awards).
TELEVISION: Series: Little House on the Prairie, Stand By Your Man. Guest: Gunsmoke, Emergency, Tenafly, The Hanna-Barbera Happy Hour, Love Boat. Movies: Christmas Miracle in Caulfield U.S.A., The Miracle Worker, Splendor in the Grass, Choices of the Heart, Choices, Penalty Phase, Family Secrets, Killer Instincts, Without Her Consent, Forbidden Nights, Blood Vows: The Story of a Mafia Wife, Joshua's Heart, Donor, The Lookalike, With a Vengeance, Family of Strangers, With Hostile Intent, Don't Look Back, Conspiracy of Silence: The Shari Karney Story, Conspiracy of Terror.
PICTURES: Sylvester (debut, 1985), Ice House.

GILER, DAVID: Producer, Writer, Director. b. New York, NY. Son of Bernie Giler, screen and TV writer. Began writing in teens; first work an episode for ABC series, The Gallant Men. Feature film career began as writer on Myra Breckenridge (1970).
PICTURES: Writer: The Parallax View, Fun with Dick and Jane, The Blackbird (also dir.), Southern Comfort (also prod.). Prod.: Alien, Rustlers' Rhapsody, Let It Ride, Alien³.
TELEVISION: Writer: The Kraft Theatre, Burke's Law, The Man from U.N.C.L.E., The Girl from U.N.C.L.E., Tales From the Crypt (exec. prod.).

GILLIAM, TERRY: Writer, Director, Actor, Animator. b. Minneapolis, MN, Nov. 22, 1940. e. Occidental Coll. Freelance writer and illustrator for various magazines and ad agencies before moving to London. Member, Monty Python's Flying Circus (1969–76). Books incl. numerous Monty Python publications. Honorary degrees: DFA Occidental Col. 1987, DFA Royal Col. of Art 1989.
PICTURES: And Now for Something Completely Different (animator, co-s.p., actor), Monty Python and the Holy Grail (co-dir., co-s.p., actor), Jabberwocky (dir., co-s.p.); Life of Brian (actor, co-s.p.), Time Bandits (prod., dir., co-s.p.), Monty Python Live at the Hollywood Bowl (actor, co-s.p.), The Miracle of Flight (animator, writer), Monty Python's The Meaning of Life (co-s.p., act.), Spies Like Us (actor), Brazil (co-s.p., dir.), The Adventures of Baron Munchausen (dir., co-s.p.), The Fisher King (dir.).

GILLIAT, LESLIE: Producer. b. New Malden, England, 1917. e. Epsom Coll. Ent. m.p. ind. 1935.
PICTURES: Only Two Can Play, The Amorous Prawn, Joey Boy, The Great St. Trinians Train Robbery, A Dandy in Aspic, The Virgin Soldiers, The Buttercup Chain, Endless Night, Priest of Love (prod. supvr.), The Zany Adventures of Robin Hood (assoc. prod.).

GILLIS, ANN: Actress. r.n. Alma Mabel Connor. b. Little Rock, AK, Feb. 12, 1927. Screen debut 1936 in The Great Ziegfeld; thereafter in 36 child and adolescent roles.
PICTURES: Singing Cowboy, The Garden of Allah, Adventures of Tom Sawyer, Peck Bad Boy at the Circus, Little Orphan Annie, The Underpup, Edison the Man, All This and Heaven Too, My Love Came Back, Little Men, Nice Girl?, Mr. Dynamite, Janie, The Cheaters, In Society, The Time of Their Lives, Sweetheart of Sigma Chi, 2001: A Space Odyssey.

GILMORE, WILLIAM S.: Producer. b. Los Angeles, CA, March 10, 1934. e. U. of California at Berkeley. Started career in film editing before becoming asst. dir. and prod. mgr. at Universal Studios, where worked on 20 feature films. Headed prod. for Mirisch Co. in Europe; then to Zanuck/Brown Co. as exec. in chg. prod. Sr. v.p./prod. of Filmways Pictures, supervising literary development, prod. and post-prod.
PICTURES: Jaws (prod. exec.), The Last Remake of Beau Geste, Defiance, Deadly Blessing, Tough Enough, Against All Odds, White Nights, Little Shop of Horrors, The Man in the Moon, The Player, A Few Good Men, Watch It, The Sandlot.
TELEVISION: Just You and Me, One in a Million—The Ron Leflore Story, The Legend of Walks Far Woman, S.O.S. Titanic, Another Woman's Child, Women and Men, Women and Men 2.

GILROY, FRANK: Writer, Director. b. New York, NY, Oct. 13, 1925. e. Dartmouth; postgrad. Yale School of Drama. TV writer: Playhouse 90, US Steel Hour, Omnibus, Kraft Theatre, Lux Video Theater, Studio One. Bdwy. playwright; won Pulitzer Prize & Tony for The Subject Was Roses, 1965. Other plays: Who'll Save the Plowboy?, The Only Game in Town, Present Tense, The Housekeeper, Last Licks. Novels: Private, Little Ego (with Ruth Gilroy), From Noon to 3. Book: I Wake Up Screening!: Everything You Need to Know About Making Independent Films Including a Thousand Reasons Not To (1993).
PICTURES: Writer: The Fastest Gun Alive, The Gallant Hours, The Subject Was Roses, The Only Game in Town. Dir.-writer: Desperate Characters (also prod.), From Noon Till Three, Once in Paris, The Gig, The Luckiest Man in the World.
TELEVISION: Writer-Dir.: Nero Wolfe, Turning Point of Jim Malloy.

GIMBEL, ROGER: Producer. b. March 11, 1925. e. Yale. Began television prod. career as copy and creative chief of RCA Victor TV, then became assoc. prod. of the Tonight Show for NBC; named head of prog. dev. of NBC daytime programming; then prod. of the 90-minute NBC Tonight Specials, including the Jack Paar Show and the Ernie Kovacs Show. Became prod. and co-packager of the Glen Campbell Goodtime Hour for CBS, 1969; v.p. in chg. of prod. for Tomorrow Entertainment, 1971. Formed his own prod. co., Roger Gimbel's Tomorrow Enterprises, Inc., 1975; prod. Minstrel Man. Became U.S. pres. of EMI-TV, 1976. Received special personal Emmy as exec. prod. of War of the Children, 1975. Produced 33 movies for TV under the EMI banner and won 18 Emmys. In 1984, EMI-TV became The Peregrine Producers Group, Inc., of which he was pres. & COO. 1987, spun off Roger Gimbel Prods. as an independent film co; 1988–89, president-exec. prod., Carolco/Gimbel Productions, Inc.
TELEVISION: The Autobiography of Miss Jane Pittman, Born Innocent, Birds of Prey, Brand New Life, Gargoyles, Glass House, In This House of Brede, I Heard the Owl Call My Name, I Love You, Good-Bye, Larry, Miles to Go, Queen of the Stardust Ballroom, Tell Me Where It Hurts, Things in Their Season, War of the Children (Emmy award, Outstanding Single Program, Drama or Comedy), Aurora, Rockabye, Blackout, Apology, Montana, Shattered Dreams, Chernobyl:

The Final Warning, Desperate Rescue: The Cathy Mahone Story.

GINGOLD, DAN: Freelance Executive Producer, Producer, Director. Credits include all types live and film prod. Specialist in Special Events, Documentary and non-fiction television. Awards include Emmy, Ohio State U., DuPont/Columbia U., Ed Murrow, Assoc. Press, San Francisco State, Cine Golden Eagle, NY Int'l. Film Fest. Asst prof., School of Journalism, U. of Southern California.

GINNA, ROBERT EMMETT, JR.: Producer, Writer. b. New York, NY, Dec. 3, 1925. e. U. of Rochester, Harvard U., M.A. In U.S. Navy, W.W.II. Journalist for Life, Scientific American, Horizon, 1950—55; 1958—61, contributor to many magazines. Staff writer, producer, director NBC-TV, 1955—58; v.p., Sextant, Inc., dir., Sextant Films Ltd., 1961—64; Founded Windward Productions, Inc., Windward Film Productions, Ltd., 1965. Active in publishing 1974—82; sr. ed. People; ed. in chief, Little Brown; asst. mging., Life. Resumed pres., Windward Prods., Inc., 1982; publishing consultant.
PICTURES: Young Cassidy (co-prod.); The Last Challenge (co-s.p.); Before Winter Comes (prod.); Brotherly Love (prod.).

GINSBERG, SIDNEY: Executive. b. New York, NY, Oct. 26, 1920. e. City Coll. of New York, 1938. Entered m.p. ind., as asst. mgr., Loew's Theatres; joined Trans-Lux 1943, as thea. mgr.; film booker; helped form Trans-Lux Distributing Corp., 1956; asst. to pres., Trans-Lux Dist. Corp.; asst. vice-pres., Trans-Lux Picture, Distributing and TV Corp., 1961, V.P. Trans-Lux Dist. Corp., 1967, V.P. in charge of worldwide sales, 1969. Haven International Pictures, Inc., Haven Int'l 1970; IFIDA gov., 1970, v.p. sales, Scotia International Films, Inc., 1971; exec. v.p., Scotia American Prods; 1977, pres., Rob-Rich Films Inc.; 1979, exec. v.p., A Major Studio, Inc.; 1980, exec. v.p., The Health and Entertainment Corp. of America; 1982, sr. acct. rep., 3M-Photogard; 1984, pres., Rob-Rich Films.

GINSBURG, LEWIS S.: Distributor, Importer, Prod. b. New York, NY, May 16, 1914. e. City Coll. of New York, 1931—32. Columbia U., 1932—33. Ent. film industry, tabulating dept., United Artists, Sept. 1933; sls. contract dept. 1934; asst. to eastern district mgr., 1938; slsmn., New Haven exch., 1939. Army, 1943. Ret. to U.S., then formed first buying & booking service in Connecticut, 1945—55; in chg., New England Screen Guild Exchanges, 1955; TV film distr., 1955; Formed & org. International Film Assoc., Vid-EX Film Distr. Corp., 1961. Prod., TV half-hour series; vice-pres. in chg., dist., Desilu Film Dist. C., 1962; organized Carl Releasing Co., 1963; Walter Reade-Sterling Inc., 1964—65; formed L.G. Films Corp.; contract and playdate mgr., 20th Fox, 1965—68. Cinerama Releasing Corp. Adm. Ass't to sales mgr., 1968—69; 20th Cent.-Fox. Nat'l sales coordinator, 1969—present. 1970, 20th Century-Fox, Asst. to the Sales Mgr. 1971, Transnational Pictures Corp., v.p. in chg. of dist., pres., Stellar IV Film Corp., 1972.

GIRARDOT, ANNIE: Actress. b. Paris, France, Oct. 25, 1931. Studied nursing. Studied acting at the Paris Conservatory, made her acting debut with the Comedie Française. Has acted on the French stage and in reviews in the Latin Quarter.
PICTURES: Rocco and His Brothers, The Organizer, Les Galoises Bleues, Live For Life, Trois Chambres A Manhattan (Best Actress Award at the Venice Film Festival), Story of a Woman, Love Is a Funny Thing, The Slap, No Time for Breakfast, Traffic Jam, Five Days in June, Prisonniers, Comedie D'Amour.

GISH, ANNABETH: Actress. b. Albuquerque, NM. Started acting at age 8; appeared in several TV commercials in Iowa.
PICTURES: Desert Bloom, Hiding Out, Mystic Pizza, Shag, Coupe de Ville.
TELEVISION: Movies: Hero in the Family, When He's Not a Stranger, The Last to Go, Lady Against the Odds, Silent Cries.

GISH, LILLIAN: Actress. b. Springfield, OH, Oct. 14, 1896. Sister of late Dorothy Gish, actress. At 5 appeared in In Convict's Stripes, at Rising Sun, OH; following year danced in Sarah Bernhardt prod. in N.Y. In 1913 appeared with Mary Pickford in A Good Little Devil, N.Y. Began screen career 1912 with Biograph, beginning assn. with D. W. Griffith, dir., for whom she made 40 films including The Birth of a Nation, Intolerance, Hearts of the World, The Great Love, Broken Blossoms, Way Down East and Orphans of the Storm. One of the first women to dir. film (Remodeling Her Husband, 1920), and one of first actors to gain artistic control of projects (La Boheme, The Scarlet Letter). Continued in films: White Sister, Romola, The Wind, La Boheme, Scarlet Letter. From 1930 on N.Y. stage in number orig. prods. & classics 1969—71, one woman int'l concert tour, Lillian Gish and the Movies. Received honorary Oscar, 1971. International touring with illustrated lecture on the art of film and TV, 1974. Lecture tour on Queen Elizabeth 2, 1975. Campaigned for film preservation and lobbied for D. W. Griffith commemorative stamp.

Honoree Kennedy Center Honors, 1982; 1983, AFI Life Achievement Award, Commander of Arts & Letters from French govt.
THEATER: Uncle Vanya, Camille, 9 Pine Street, Within the Gates, Hamlet, Star Wagon, Old Maid, Dear Octopus, Life With Father, Mr. Sycamore, The Marquise, Legend of Leonora, Crime and Punishment, Miss Mable, Curious Savage, A Passage to India, Too True to be Good, Romeo and Juliet (Stratford Shakespeare Theatre, 1965), The Trip to Bountiful (Theatre Guild 1954); Chalk Garden, The Family Reunion, Portrait of a Madonna, Wreck of the 5:25, Uncle Vanya, All The Way Home, Anya, I Never Sang for My Father, A Musical Jubilee (1976).
PICTURES: Sound films: One Romantic Night, His Double Life, Commandos Strike at Dawn, Top Man, Miss Susie Slagle's, Duel in the Sun, Portrait of Jennie, Night of the Hunter, The Cobweb, Orders to Kill, The Unforgiven, Follow Me Boys!, Warning Shot, The Comedians, A Wedding (her 100th film), Hambone and Hillie, Sweet Liberty, The Whales of August.
TELEVISION: I Mrs. Bibbs, Sound and the Fury, Ladies in Retirement, Detour, The Joyous Season, The Trip to Bountiful, Grandma Moses, The Quality of Mercy, The Corner Drugstore, Day Lincoln Was Shot, Mornings at Seven, The Grass Harp, Grandma T.N.T., Mr. Novak, Alfred Hitchcock Hour, Breaking Point, The Spiral Staircase, Arsenic and Old Lace, A Gift of Music, Kennedy Center Honors (1982), AFI Salute to Lillian Gish, The Silent Years (hostess). Movies: Twin Detectives; Thin Ice; Hobson's Choice.
AUTHOR: The Movies, Mr. Griffith and Me (1969), Dorothy and Lillian Gish (1973), An Actor's Life For Me (1987).
(Died: Feb. 27, 1993)

GIVENS, ROBIN: Actress. b. New York, NY, Nov. 27, 1964. e. Sarah Lawrence Col., Harvard Univ. Graduate Sch. of Arts & Sciences. While at college became model, made appearances on daytime dramas The Guiding Light and Loving.
TELEVISION: Series: Head of the Class, Angel Street. Movies: Beverly Hills Madam, The Women of Brewster Place, The Penthouse.
PICTURES: A Rage in Harlem (debut, 1991), Boomerang.

GLASER, PAUL MICHAEL: Actor, Director. b. Cambridge, MA, March 25, 1943. e. Tulane U., Boston U., M.A. Did five seasons in summer stock before starting career in New York, making stage debut in Rockabye Hamlet in 1968. Appeared in numerous off-Bdwy. plays and got early TV training as regular in daytime series, Love of Life and Love Is a Many Splendored Thing.
PICTURES: Actor: Fiddler on the Roof, Butterflies Are Free, Phobia. Director: Band of the Hand, The Running Man, The Cutting Edge.
TELEVISION: Series: Starsky and Hutch. Guest: Kojak, Toma, The Streets of San Francisco, The Rockford Files, The Sixth Sense, The Waltons. Movies: Trapped Beneath the Sea, The Great Houdinis, Wait Till You Mother Gets Home!, Princess Daisy, Jealousy, Attack on Fear, Single Bars Single Women, Amazons (dir. only).

GLAZER, WILLIAM: Executive b. Cambridge, MA. e. State U. of New York, Entered m.p. ind. with Ralph Snider Theatres 1967—69; General Cinema Corp. 1969—71; Loews Theatres 1971—73; Joined Sack Theatres 1973 as Dist. mgr.; 1974 Exec. Asst. to Pres.; 1976 Gen. Mgr.; 1980 V.P. Gen. Mgr.; 1982 Exec. V.P. Member of SMPTE; NATO (Bd of Dir); Theatre Owners of New England Bd of Dir, also pres.; 1982—1985.

GLEASON, LARRY: Executive. b. Boston, MA, Apr. 30, 1938. e. Boston Coll., M.A., 1960. Held various positions, western div., mgr., General Cinema Corp.; 1963—73; gen. mgr., Gulf States Theatres, New Orleans, 1973—74; pres., Mann Theatres, 1974—85; joined DeLaurentiis Entertainment Group as pres., mktg./dist., Dec., 1985. Named sr. v.p., Paramount Pictures Corp, theatrical exhibition group, Jan. 1989. Named pres. Paramount Pictures Corp. theatrical exhib. group, Jan. 1991. Foundation of Motion Picture Pioneers v.p. Member, Variety Club, Will Rogers Foundation.

GLEN, JOHN: Director. b. Sunbury on Thames, Eng., May 15, 1932. Entered industry in 1947. Second unit dir.: On Her Majesty's Secret Service, The Spy Who Loved Me, Wild Geese, Moonraker (also editor). Editor: The Sea Wolves.
PICTURES: For Your Eyes Only (dir. debut, 1981), Octopussy, A View to a Kill, The Living Daylights, Licence to Kill, Aces: Iron Eagle III, Christopher Columbus: The Discovery.

GLENN, CHARLES OWEN: Executive. b. Binghamton, NY, March 27, 1938. e. Syracuse U., B.A., U. of Pennsylvania. Capt., U.S. Army, 1961—63. Asst. to dir. of adv., 20th Cent. Fox, 1966—67; asst. adv. mgr., Paramount, 1967—68; acct. spvsr. & exec., MGM record & m.p. div., 1968—69; nat'l adv. mgr., Paramount, 1969—70; nat'l. dir. of adv., Paramount, 1970—71; v.p. adv.-pub.-prom., 1971—73; v.p. marketing, 1974; v.p. prod. mktg., 1975; joined American Intl. Pictures as v.p. in chg. of adv./creative affairs, 1979. 1980, when Filmways took AIP

over he was named their v.p. in chg. worldwide adv./pub./promo.; joined MCA/Universal in 1982 as exec. v.p., adv.-promo.; 1984, appt., Orion Pictures adv.-pub.-promo. exec. v.p.; 1987, appt. Orion mktg. exec. v.p. 1989 recipient Outstanding Performance Award Leukemia Society of Amer. for completing NYC Marathon. 1993, pres. mktg., Bregman/Baer Prods. Featured in 1993 film Philadelphia.
MEMBER: Exec. comm. public relations branch, Academy of M.P. Arts & Sciences. Holder of NATO mktg. exec. of year (1983) award, Clio Award for U.S. adv. of Platoon; Variety Club, Motion Picture Pioneers.

GLENN, SCOTT: Actor. b. Pittsburgh, PA, Jan. 26, 1942. e. William & Mary Coll. Worked as U.S. Marine, newspaper reporter before going to New York to study drama. Off-Bdwy. productions included Fortune in Men's Eyes, Long Day's Journey into Night. On Bdwy in Burn This. Member of Actors Studio.
PICTURES: The Baby Maker (debut, 1970), Angels Hard as They Come, Hex, Nashville, Fighting Mad, More American Graffiti, Apocalypse Now, Urban Cowboy, Cattle Annie and Little Britches, Personal Best, The Challenge, The Right Stuff, The Keep, The River, Wild Geese II, Silverado, Verne Miller, Man on Fire, Off Limits, Miss Firecracker, The Hunt for Red October, The Silence of the Lambs, My Heroes Have Always Been Cowboys, Backdraft, The Player, Slaughter of the Innocent.
TELEVISION: Movies: Gargoyles, As Summers Die, Intrigue, The Outside Woman, Women & Men 2, Shadowhunter.

GLENNON, JAMES M.: Cinematographer. b. Burbank, CA, Aug. 29, 1942. e. UCLA. m. actress Charmaine Glennon. Focus Awards judge 1985–; bd. of dirs., UCLA Theatre Arts Alumni Assoc. 1985–. TV work includes Lemon Sky for American Playhouse.
PICTURES: Return of the Jedi, El Norte, The Wild Life, Smooth Talk, Flight of the Navigator, Time of Destiny, A Show of Force.

GLESS, SHARON: Actress. b. Los Angeles, CA, May 31, 1943. m. producer Barney Rosenzweig. London stage: Misery.
TELEVISION: Mini-series: Centennial, The Immigrants, The Last Convertible. Movies: The Longest Night, All My Darling Daughters, My Darling Daughters' Anniversary, Richie Brockelman: Missing 24 Hours, The Flying Misfits, The Islander, Crash, Whisper in the Gloom (Disney), Hardhat and Legs, Moviola: The Scarlett O'Hara War, Revenge of the Stepford Wives, The Miracle of Kathy Miller, Hobson's Choice, The Sky's No Limit, Letting Go, The Outside Woman, Honor Thy Mother. Series: Marcus Welby, M.D., Faraday and Co., Switch, Turnabout, House Calls, Cagney and Lacey (2 Emmy Awards, Golden Globe Award), The Trials of Rosie O'Neill (Golden Globe Award).
PICTURES: Airport 1975, The Star Chamber.

GLICK, HYMAN J.: Executive. b. Russia, Dec. 15, 1904. e. NYU, B.C.S., 1926. C.P.A. (N.Y.); with public accounting firm, N.Y., 1923–29; own public accounting business, 1929–32. Became assoc. m.p. ind. as member comptrollers' com., repr. Republic; 1932–36, tax & financial counsel Mascot Pictures Corp. Joined Republic 1936 as comptroller; apptd. asst. secy.-asst. treas. Jan., 1945. Retired, 1985.
MEMBER: B'nai Brith Lodge 1325; NY State Society of CPAs, Acad. of Mo. Pic. Arts and Sciences, State Soc. of Certified Public Accountants, Am. Inst. of Accountants. Resigned Republic, 1959; CPA (Calif.), member, Calif. Soc. of CPA; Own Accounting and Tax Practice.

GLICK, PHYLLIS: Executive. b. New York, NY. e. Queens Coll. of C.U.N.Y. Began career with Otto-Windsor Associates, as casting director; left to be independent. 1979, joined ABC-TV as mgr. of comedy series development; promoted 1980 to director, involved with all comedy series developed for network. 1985, joined Paramount Pictures as exec. dir., production, for M.P. Group; 1989, co-exec. prod., Living Dolls.

GLOBUS, YORAM: Producer. b. Israel. Came to U.S. 1979. Has co-produced many films with cousin and former partner Menahem Golan. Sr. exec. v.p., Cannon Group; Pres. and CEO Cannon ENtertainment and Cannon Films; 1989 named chmn. and C.E.O Cannon Entertainment and officer of Cannon Group Inc.; then co-pres. Pathe Communications Corp. and chmn. and C.E.O. Pathe Intl. Left MGM/Pathe in 1991.
PICTURES: All as producer or exec. prod. with Menahem Golan: Sallah; Trunk to Cairo; My Margo; What's Good for the Goose; Escape to the Sun; I Love You, Rosa; The House on Chelouch Street; The Four Deuces; Kazablan; Diamonds; God's Gun; Kid Vengeance, Operation Thunderbolt, The Uranium Conspiracy, Savage Weekend, The Magician of Lublin, The Apple, The Happy Hooker Goes to Hollywood, Dr. Heckyl and Mr. Hype, The Godsend, New Year's Evil, Schizoid, Seed of Innocence, Body and Soul, Death Wish II, Enter the Ninja, Hospital Massacre, The Last American Virgin, Championship Season, Treasure of Four Crowns, 10

to Midnight, Nana, I'm Almost Not Crazy...John Cassavetes: The Man and His Work, The House of Long Shadows, Revenge of the Ninja, Hercules, The Wicked Lady, Sahara, The Ambassador, Bolero, Exterminator 2, The Naked Face, Missing in Action, Hot Resort, Love Streams, Breakin', Grace Quigley, Making the Grade, Ninja III—The Domination, Breakin' 2: Electric Boogaloo, Over the Brooklyn Bridge, The Delta Force, The Assisi Underground, Hot Chili, The Berlin Affair, Missing in Action 2—The Beginning, Rappin', Thunder Alley, American Ninja, Mata Hari, Death Wish 3, King Solomon's Mines, Runaway Train, Fool for Love, Invasion U.S.A., Maria's Lovers, Murphy's Law, The Naked Cage, P.O.W.: The Escape, The Texas Chainsaw Massacre, Part 2, Invaders from Mars, 52 Pick-Up, Link, Firewalker, Dumb Dicks, The Nutcracker: The Motion Picture, Avenging Force, Hashigaon Hagadol, Journey to the Center of the Earth, Prom Queen, Salome, Otello, Cobra, America 3000, American Ninja 2: The Confrontation, Allan Quartermain and the Lost City of Gold, Assassination, Beauty and the Beast, Down Twisted, Duet for One, The Emperor's New Clothes, The Hanoi Hilton, The Barbarians, Dutch Treat, Masters of the Universe, Number One with a Bullet, Rumpelstiltskin, Street Smart, UnderCover, The Assault, Hansel and Gretel, Going Bananas, Snow White, Sleeping Beauty, Tough Guys Don't Dance, Shy People, Dancers, Red Riding Hood, King Lear, Braddock: Missing in Action III, Too Much, Die Papierene Brucke, Field of Honor, Barfly (exec. prod.), Surrender (exec. prod.), Death Wish 4: The Crackdown (exec. prod.), Gor (exec. prod.), Business as Usual (exec. prod.), Over the Top, Superman IV: The Quest for Peace, prod.: Delta Force, Operation Crackdown, Manifesto, Stranglehold, Delta Force II, Cyborg, Step By Step. exec. prod.: The Kitchen Toto, Doin' Time on Planet Earth, Kickboxer, Kinjite, A Man Called Sarge, The Rose Garden, The Secret of the Ice Cave.

GLOVER, CRISPIN: Actor. b. New York, NY 1964. e. Mirman School. Trained for stage with Dan Mason and Peggy Feury. Stage debut, as Friedrich Von Trapp, The Sound of Music, Los Angeles, 1977. Wrote books, Rat Catching (1987), Oak Mot (1990), Concrete Inspection (1992). Recorded album The Big Problem Does Not Equal the Solution - The Solution Equals Let it Be.
PICTURES: Private Lessons, My Tutor, Racing with the Moon, Friday the 13th—The Final Chapter, Teachers, Back to the Future, At Close Range, River's Edge, Twister, Where the Heart Is, Wild at Heart, The Doors, Little Noises, Rubin and Ed, Thirty Door Key, Even Cowgirls Get the Blues, Gilbert Grape, Crime and Punishment, Chasers.
TELEVISION: Movie: High School U.S.A. Special: Hotel Room (Blackout).

GLOVER, DANNY: Actor. b. San Francisco, CA, July 22, 1947. e. San Francisco State U. Trained at Black Actors Workshop of American Conservatory Theatre. Appeared in many stage productions (Island, Macbeth, Sizwe Banzi Is Dead, etc.). On N.Y. stage in Suicide in B Flat, The Blood Knot, Master Harold . . . and the Boys (Theatre World Award).
PICTURES: Escape from Alcatraz, Chu Chu and the Philly Flash, Out, Iceman, Places in the Heart, Witness, Silverado, The Color Purple, Lethal Weapon, Bat-21, Lethal Weapon 2, To Sleep with Anger (also exec. prod.), Predator 2, Flight of the Intruder, A Rage in Harlem, Pure Luck, Grand Canyon, Lethal Weapon 3, The Saint of Fort Washington, Bopha.
TELEVISION: Mini-Series: Chiefs, Lonesome Dove, Queen. Movies: Face of Rage, Mandela, Dead Man Out. Specials: A Place at the Table, A Raisin in the Sun. Guest: Lou Grant, Palmerstown U.S.A., Gimme a Break; Hill Street Blues, Many Mansions.

GLOVER, JOHN: Actor. b. Kingston, NY, Aug. 7, 1944. e. Towson State Coll., Baltimore. On regional theatre circuit; in plays off-Bdwy (A Scent of Flowers, Subject to Fits, The House of Blue Leaves, The Selling of the President). With APA Phoenix Co. in Great God Brown (Drama Desk Award), The Visit, Don Juan, Chermin de Fer, Holiday. Other NY stage: The Importance of Being Earnest, Hamlet, Frankenstein, Whodunnit, Digby, L.A.: The Traveler (L.A. Drama Critics Award).
PICTURES: Shamus, Annie Hall, Julia, Somebody Killed Her Husband, Last Embrace, Success, Brubaker, Melvin and Howard, The Mountain Men, The Incredible Shrinking Woman, A Little Sex, The Evil That Men Do, A Flash of Green, 52 Pick-Up, White Nights, Something Special, Masquerade, A Killing Affair, Rocket Gibraltar, The Chocolate War, Scrooged, Meet the Hollowheads, Gremlins 2, Robocop 2, Ed and His Dead Mother.
TELEVISION: Movies: A Rage of Angels, The Face of Rage, Ernie Kovacs—Between the Laughter, An Early Frost (Emmy nom.), Apology, Moving Target, Hot Paint, Nutcracker: Money Madness and Murder (Emmy nom.), David, The Traveling Man, Twist of Fate, Breaking Point, El Diablo, What Ever Happened to Baby Jane?, Dead on the Money, Drug Wars: The Cocaine Cartel, Grass Roots, Majority Rule. Special: An Enemy of the People, Paul Reiser: Out on a

Whim. Mini-Series: Kennedy, George Washington. *Series:* South Beach. *Guest:* L.A. Law (Emmy nom.)

GLYNN, CARLIN: Actress. b. Cleveland, OH, Feb. 19, 1940. m. actor-writer-dir. Peter Masterson. Daughter is actress Mary Stuart Masterson. e. Sophie Newcomb College, 1957–58. Studied acting with Stella Adler, Wynn Handman and Lee Strasberg in NY. Debut, Gigi, Alley Theatre, Houston, TX 1959. NY stage debut Waltz of The Toreadors, 1960. On stage in The Best Little Whorehouse in Texas (Tony, Eleanora Duse & Olivier Awards), Winterplay, Alterations, Pal Joey (Chicago; Jos. Jefferson Award). Adjunct professor at Columbia U film sch. Resource advisor at the Sundance Inst.
PICTURES: Three Days of the Condor, Continental Divide, Sixteen Candles, The Trip to Bountiful, Gardens of Stone, Blood Red, Night Game, Convicts.
TELEVISION: *Series:* Mr. President. *Mini-Series:* A Woman Named Jackie.

GODARD, JEAN-LUC: Writer, Director. b. Paris, France, Dec. 3, 1930. e. Lycee Buffon, Paris. Journalist, film critic Cahiers du Cinema. Acted in and financed experimental film Quadrille by Jacques Rivette, 1951. 1954: dir. first short, Operation Beton. 1956, was film editor. 1957: worked in publicity dept. 20th Century Fox.
PICTURES: Breathless (feature debut, 1960), Le Petit Soldat, A Woman is a Woman, My Life to Live, Les Carabiniers, Contempt, Band of Outsiders, The Married Woman, Alphaville, Pierrot le Fou, Masculine-Feminine, Two or Three Things I Know About Her, La Chinoise, Weekend, Sympathy for the Devil, Le Gai Savoir, Tout a Bien (co-dir.), Numero Deux, Every Man For Himself, First Name Carmen, Hail Mary, Aria, King Lear, Keep Up Your Right (dir., edit, s.p., actor), Nouvelle Vogue.

GODBOLD, GEOFF: Executive. b. London, England, 1935. Ent. ind. 1959. Specialized in supply of location requirements for film and TV prods. Formed Prop Workshops Ltd., co-promoted Television Recordings Ltd. Man. dir. Facilities (Screen & Television) Ltd. Dir. TV Recordings, Investments, Ltd.; Centrepoint Screen Prod. Ltd.; Tape Commercials, Ltd. Council Mem. Film and TV Contractors Assoc. Dir. Lancair Export Services Ltd.; 1968 Freelance production buyer, Screen Gems and Tigon. 1969. Feature Prod. Rep. Film Div. N.A.T.T.K.E. Man. dir. Setpieces Ltd. Film & TV Prop. Hire. 1984: Carlton Communication. 1985: mng. dir., Set Pieces Ltd. 1990, freelance "prop stock" consultant.
PICTURES: Dubious Patriot, Every Home Should Have One, Melody, Up Pompeii. Morocco location, Young Winston. The Asphyx, Our Miss Fred, Death of a Snow Queen, Man in the Iron Mask. TV: The Professionals.

GODUNOV, ALEXANDER: Dancer, Actor. b. Ujno-Sakalin, Soviet Union, Nov. 28, 1949. e. Riga Music Sch. 1958–67; trained for dance at Riga Choreography Sch. and for stage at Stella Adler Acting Sch. Dancer with Moiseyev's Ballet Co. 1958–66; principal dancer Bolshoi Dance Co. 1967–79; American Ballet Theatre, NY 1979–82.
PICTURES: Witness (debut, 1985), The Money Pit, Die Hard, The Runestone, Waxworks II.
TELEVISION: Godunov: The World to Dance In (1983).

GOLAN, MENAHEM: Producer, Director, Writer. b. Israel, 1929. e. NYU. Studied theater dir. at Old Vic Theatre London, m.p. prod. at City Coll, NY. Co-founder and prod. with cousin Yoram Globus, Golan-Globus Prods., Israel, then L.A., 1962. Later Noah Films, Israel, 1963, Ameri-Euro Pictures Corp, before buying controlling share in Cannon Films, 1979. Sr. exec. v.p., Cannon Group; chmn. of bd., Cannon Entertainment and Cannon Films. 1988, dir. and sr. exec. v.p. Cannon Group, chmn. and head of creative affairs, Cannon Entertainment when it became div. of Giancarlo Parretti's Pathe Communications Corp. Resigned March, 1989 to form 21st Century Film Corp as chmn. and CEO.
PICTURES: Director/co-writer: Kasablan, Diamonds, Entebbe (Operation Thunderbolt), Teyve and His Seven Daughters, What's Good for the Goose? Lepke, The Magician of Lublin, The Goodsend, Happy Hooker Goes to Hollywood, Enter the Ninja. Producer-Writer-Director: Mack the Knife, Hanna's War. Producer-Director: The Uranium Conspiracy, Delta Force, Over the Brooklyn Bridge, Over the Top. Producer/Exec. prod.: Sallah, Runaway Train, Sallah, Fool For Love, Maria's Lovers, Cobra, Evil Angels, I Love You Rosa, Body and Soul, also: Deathwish II, The Last American Virgin, That Championship Season, House of Long Shadows, Revenge of the Ninja, Hercules, The Movie Tales (12 children's fairy tales films), The Wicked Lady, Cobra, Barfly (exec. prod.), Breakin', Missing in Action, Dancers (prod.), Surrender (exec. prod.), Death Wish 4: The Crackdown (exec. prod.), King Lear (prod.), Too Much (prod.), Powaqquatsi (exec. prod.), Mercenary Fighters (prod.), Doin' Time on Planet Earth (prod.), Manifesto (prod.), Kinjite (exec. prod.), Messenger of Death (exec. prod.), Alien From L.A. (prod.), Hero and the Terror (exec. prod.), Haunted Summer (exec. prod.), A Cry in the Dark (exec. prod.), Delta Force—Operation Crackdown (prod.), A Man Called Sarge (exec.

prod.), Stranglehold: Delta Force II (prod.), Cyborg (prod.), The Rose Garden (exec. prod.), Rope Dancing (exec. prod.), The Phantom of the Opera.

GOLCHAN, FREDERIC: Director, Producer. b. Neuilly sur Seine, France. e. UCLA, NYU, HEC in Paris, NYU Bus.Sch. Journalist/photographer for various European magazines. Worked for American Express, 1979–80. Started indept. investment banking firm, 1980–84. Started own production co., 1985.
PICTURES: Flagrant Desire, Quick Change, Intersection.
TELEVISION: Freedom Fighter, Home by Midnight.

GOLD, ERNEST: Composer, Conductor. b. Vienna, Austria, July 13, 1921. e. State Acad. for Music and Performing Arts, Austria 1937–38; private study, 1939–49 in U.S. Worked as song writer 1939–42 and taught in private schools, 1942. Composed 1st score for Columbia Pictures, 1945. Musical dir., Santa Barbara Symphony, 1958–59. Taught at UCLA, 1973 and 1983–90 (adult ed.). Gold record for soundtrack of Exodus, 1968.. Acad. Award nom., On the Beach (1959), It's a Mad Mad Mad Mad World (song and score 1963), The Secret of Santa Vittoria (1968). Won Acad. Award for Exodus (1961). Received star on Walk of Fame on Hollywood Blvd., 1975. Elected to bd. of govs., Acad. of Motion Picture Arts and Sciences, 1984.
PICTURES: include: Too Much Too Soon, On the Beach, Exodus, Inherit the Wind, Judgment at Nuremberg, A Child Is Waiting, Pressure Point, It's a Mad Mad Mad Mad World, Ship of Fools, The Secret of Santa Vittoria, Cross of Iron, Fun With Dick and Jane, Good Luck Miss Wyckoff, The Runner Stumbles, Tom Horn.
TELEVISION: Small Miracle, Wallenberg: a Hero's Story, Gore Vidal's Lincoln.

GOLDBERG, FRED: Publicist. b. New York, NY, Aug. 26, 1921. e. Pace Col., Sch. of Marketing & Adveristing. Expl. Paramount, 1946; asst. mgr. trade contact, syndicate contact, NY newspaper contact promotion mgr., 1946–52; asst. publ. mgr. RKO, 1952; natl. publ. mgr., IFE, 1953; v.p. Norton and Condon, pub., 1953; returned to IFE Sept. 1954 as natl. pub. mgr.; head of NY office, Arthur Jacobs, then Blowitz-Maskel, 1956; exec. asst. to dir. pub., adv. UA Corp., 1958; exec. dir., adv., pub. exploitation, UA Corp., 1961; named v.p., 1962; sr. v.p., 1972; sr. v.p., dir. of mrkt., 1977. Left in 1978 to be consultant with Piener, Hauser & Bates Agency. In 1979 joined Columbia Pics. as sr. v.p. in chg. of adv./pub. Left in 1981 to form new company. Became teacher of M.P. Marketing & Distrib. at Univ. of Miami's Sch. of Communications. Author: Motion Picture Marketing & Distribution.

GOLDBERG, LEONARD: Executive, Producer. b. Brooklyn, NY, Jan. 24, 1934. e. Wharton Sch., U. of Pennsylvania. Began career in ABC-TV research dept.; moved to NBC-TV research div.; 1961 joined Batten, Barton, Durstine & Osborn ad agency in chg. of daytime TV shows and overall bdcst. coordinator. In 1963 rejoined ABC-TV as mgr. of program devel. In 1966 named VP in chg of network TV programming. Resigned in 1969 to join Screen Gems as VP in chg. of prod. Left for partnership with Aaron Spelling in Spelling/Goldberg Prods.; later produced TV and theatrical films under own banner, Mandy Prods. 1986, named pres., COO, 20th Century Fox. Resigned, 1989. Elected to the board of Spectradyne Inc.
TELEVISION: *Series:* The Rookies (1972–76), Starsky and Hutch, Charlie's Angels, Family, Hart to Hart, T.J. Hooker, Fantasy Island, Paper Dolls, The Cavanaughs, Class of '96. *Movies:* Brian's Song, Little Ladies of the Night, The Legend of Valentino, The Boy in the Plastic Bubble, Something About Amelia, Alex: The Life of a Child, She Woke Up.
PICTURES: Prod.: All Night Long, WarGames, Space Camp, Sleeping With the Enemy, The Distinguished Gentleman, Aspen Extreme.

GOLDBERG, WHOOPI: Actress. b. New York, NY, Nov. 13, 1949. r.n. Caryn Johnson. e. Sch. for the Performing Arts. Began performing at age 8 in N.Y. with children's program at Hudson Guild and Helena Rubenstein Children's Theatre. Moved to San Diego, CA, 1974, and helped found San Diego Rep. Theatre appearing in Mother Courage, Getting Out. Member: Spontaneous Combustion (improv. group). Joined Blake St. Hawkeyes Theatre in Berkeley, partnering with David Schein. Went solo to create The Spook Show, working in San Francisco and later touring U.S. & Europe. 1983 performance caught attention of Mike Nichols which led to Bdwy. show (for which she received a Theatre World Award) based on it and directed by him. Founding member of Comic Relief benefits. Theatrical film debut in The Color Purple (1985; Image Award NAACP, Golden Globe).
THEATER: small roles in B'way prods. of Pippin, Hair, Jesus Christ Superstar. 1988: toured in Living on the Edge of Chaos.
PICTURES: The Color Purple (debut, 1985; Acad. Award nom.), Jumpin' Jack Flash, Burglar, Fatal Beauty, The Telephone, Clara's Heart, Beverly Hills Brats (cameo), Homer and Eddie, Ghost (Acad. Award, supp. actress, 1990), The Long

Walk Home, Soapdish, House Party 2 (cameo), The Player, Sister Act, Wisecracks, Sarafina!, The Magic World of Chuck Jones, National Lampoon's Loaded Weapon 1, Made in America, The Lion King (voice), Sister Act 2.
TELEVISION: Series: Star Trek: The Next Generation, Bagdad Cafe, The Whoopi Goldberg Show (synd. talk show). Specials: Whoopi Goldberg Direct From Broadway, Comic Relief, Carol Carl Whoopi and Robin, Scared Straight: 10 Years Later, Funny You Don't Look 200, Comedy Tonight (host), My Past is My Own (Schoolbreak Special), Free to Be . . . a Family, The Debbie Allen Special. Guest: Moonlighting (Emmy nom.), A Different World. Movie: Kiss Shot.

GOLDBLUM, JEFF: Actor. b. Pittsburgh, PA, Oct. 22, 1952. Studied at Sanford Meisner's Neighborhood Playhouse in New York. On Bdwy. in Two Gentlemen of Verona, The Moony Shapiro Songbook. Off-Bdwy: El Grande de Coca Cola, City Sugar, Twelfth Night.
PICTURES: Death Wish (debut, 1974), California Split, Nashville, Next Stop Greenwich Village, St. Ives, Special Delivery, The Sentinel, Annie Hall, Between the Lines, Remember My Name, Thank God It's Friday, Invasion of the Body Snatchers, Threshold, The Big Chill, The Right Stuff, The Adventures of Buckaroo Banzai, Into the Night, Silverado, Transylvania 6-5000, The Fly, Beyond Therapy, Vibes, Earth Girls Are Easy, Twisted Obsession, The Tall Guy, Mr. Frost, The Player, Deep Cover, The Favor the Watch and the Very Big Fish, Fathers and Sons, Jurassic Park.
TELEVISION: Movies: The Legend of Sleepy Hollow, Rehearsal for Murder, Ernie Kovacs: Between the Laughter, The Double Helix (BBC), Framed. Series: Tenspeed and Brownshoe. Guest: The Blue Knight, It's Garry Shandling's Show.

GOLDEN, HERBERT L.: b. Philadelphia, PA, Feb. 12. e. Temple U., 1936, B.S. Reporter, rewrite man. asst. city ed., Philadelphia Record, 1933–38; joined Variety, 1938; on leave of absence, 1942–43, when asst. to John Hay Whitney and Francis Alstock, directors, M.P. Division, Coordinator of Inter-American Affairs (U.S.); commissioned in U.S. Navy, 1943, served on destroyer to 1946; then returned to Variety. m.p. ed. Consultant on motion pictures, Good Housekeeping magazine McGraw-Hill Publications, American Yearbook. Ent. Ind. Div. Bankers Trust Co., N.Y., 1952; named v.p. 1954–56; treas., Children's Asthma Research Institute, 1956; v.p. & mem. of bd. United Artists Corp., 1958; member of board, MPAA, 1959; pres., Lexington Int., Inc. investments, 1962; mem. bd., chmn. exec. com., Perfect Photo Inc., 1962; 1965 sect. & mem. bd. Century Broadcasting Group; chmn. G & G Thea. Corp.; pres. Diversifax Corp., 1966; consult. Pathe Lab, 1967; Mem. bd. Childhood Prod. Inc., 1967. Member bd. Music Makers Group, Inc., 1962. Mem. bd. Cinecom Corp., 1968; pres., Vere/Swiss Corp., 1977; mem. bd., Coral Reef Publications, Inc., 1977. Returned to Bankers Trust, 1979, to head its Media Group (service to film and TV industries).

GOLDEN, JEROME B.: Executive, Attorney. b. New York, NY, Nov. 26, 1917. e. St. Lawrence U., LL.B., 1942. Member legal dept., Paramount Pictures, Inc., 1942–50; United Paramount Theatres, Inc., 1950–53; American Broadcasting Companies, Inc., 1953; secy., ABC, 1958–86; vice-pres., ABC, 1959–86. Consultant.

GOLDEN, PAT: Casting Director. b. Pittsburgh, PA, July 21, 1951. e. U Pittsburgh, Carnegie-Mellon U. Has directed plays for theatre incl. Homeboy at Perry St. Th. in NY. Was in casting dept. of NY Shakespeare Festival Public Th., 1971–75. Served as assoc. prod. on PBS series The Negro Ensemble Company's 20th Anniversary.
PICTURES: Rich Kids, Ragtime, Beat Street, Krush Groove, The Killing Fields, Blue Velvet, Platoon (Awarded Casting Society of America Award), Dear America, The Handmaid's Tale, House Party 2 (assoc. prod.), Voyager.

GOLDENSON, LEONARD H.: Executive. b. Scottsdale, PA, December 7, 1905. e. Harvard Coll., B.A., Harvard Law School, LL.B. Practiced law, New York; counsel in reorg. Paramount theats. in New England, 1933–37; in 1937 apptd. asst. to vice-pres. Paramount in charge theat. operations; became head of theat. operations, 1938; elected pres. Paramount Theat. Service Corp., vice-pres. Paramount Pictures, Inc., 1938; dir. Paramount Pictures, 1942 (also pres. various Paramount theat. subsids) Pres., chief exec. off. and director United Paramount Theatres, Inc., 1950, and of American Broadcasting-Paramount Theatres, Inc., 1953, result of merger of ABC and United Paramount Theatres, Inc.; name changed to American Broadcasting Companies, Inc. 1965; Chairman of the Board and Chief Executive Officer; of American Broadcasting Companies, Inc. to 1986. Presently Chmn. of Exec. Comm. & Dir. Capital Cities/ABC, Inc. 1972; mem., board chmn. of United Cerebral Palsy Assns.; trustee, John F. Kennedy Center for the Performing Arts; dir., Daughters of Jacob Geriatric Center; mem., International Radio and Television Society; Founder Member of Hollywood Museum; Trustee of Children's Cancer Research Foundation of the Children's Medical Center, Boston, MA; Director of

Allied Stores Corporation; Trustee of Highway Users Federation for Safety and Mobility; Member of National Academy of Television Arts and Sciences; Member of Uptown Advisory Committee of Bankers Trust Company; Graduate Director of The Advertising Council, Inc.; Associate Trustee and Member of Advisory Council for the Performing Arts of University of Pennsylvania; Member of Broadcast Pioneers; Member of Inter Lochen Arts Academy-National Advisory Board; Member of Motion Picture Pioneers; Member of National Citizens' Advisory Committee on Vocational Rehabilitation; Member of United Negro College Fund-National Corporations Committee; Director of World Rehabilitation Fund, Inc. Director Research America; Trustee Emeritus Museum of Broadcasting; Hon. Chmn. Acad. of TV Arts & Sciences.

GOLDMAN, BO: Writer. b. New York, NY, Sept. 10, 1932. e. Princeton U., B.A., 1953. Wrote lyrics for Bdwy musical version of Pride and Prejudice entitled First Impressions (1959). Assoc. prod. & script editor for Playhouse 90 1958–60; writer-prod., NET Playhouse 1970–71, Theater in America 1972–74.
PICTURES: One Flew Over the Cuckoo's Nest (co-s.p.; WGA & Acad. Awards, 1975), The Rose (co-s.p.), Melvin and Howard (NY Film Critics, WGA & Acad. Awards, 1980), Shoot the Moon, Swing Shift (uncredited), Little Nikita (co-s.p.), Dick Tracy (uncredited), Scent of a Woman (Golden Globe Award).

GOLDMAN, EDMUND: Executive-Producer. b. Shanghai, China, Nov. 12, 1906. e. in Shanghai and San Francisco. Entered ind. as asst. mgr., for Universal in Shanghai, 1935–36; named mgr. Columbia Pictures' Philippine office, 1937. In 1951 named Far East. supvr. for Columbia, headquartering in Tokyo. From 1953 to 1991 indep. m.p. dist., specializing in foreign marketing, representing indep. producers and distributors. Retired, 1991.
PICTURES: Surrender Hell (prod.), The Quick and the Dead (exec. prod.).

GOLDMAN, JANE: Executive. e. Barnard Coll., NYU School of Law. Represented Warner Bros. in special assignments while in general law practice; joined Warner Communications Inc. in N.Y. as full-time attorney, counselling dist. div. in copyright and anti-trust matters. 1985, named v.p., gen. counsel for WB Dist. Corp., at Warner Studio.

GOLDMAN, MICHAEL F.: Executive. b. Manila, Philippines, Sept. 28, 1939. e. UCLA, B.S. in acct., 1962 California C.P.A. certificate issued June, 1972. In 1962 incorporated Manson International, which was sold in 1986. Incorporated Quixote Prods., 1979. Also owner and sole proprietor Taurus Film co. of Hollywood, founded 1964. Co-founder and first chief financial officer of American Film Marketing Association, sponsor of First American Film Market in Los Angeles in 1981; v.p. of AFMA 1982 and 1983, President AFMA 1984 and 1985. Chmn. AFMA, 1992–3. AFMA bd. mbr., 1981–87, 1988–present; Co-founder, Cinema Consultants Group, 1988. Produced feature, Jessi's Girls in 1975.

GOLDMAN, SHEPARD: Writer. b. Brooklyn, NY; e. Hofstra U, NYU: Comedy/dramas. Varied genres; novels and songs made into films.
PICTURES: An Unfinished Victory, Our Tender Hearts, Queens, Salsa (co-s.p.), Spiderman, The Merry Wives of Beverly Hills, The China.
STAGE: The Last Salt of Summer.
TELEVISION: Chumbles Story Hour; Sensations.
AWARDS: Gold Medal—best adaptation, 15th Houston Int'l Film Festival; Gold Medal—best original comedy, 17th Houston Int'l Film Festival.

GOLDMAN, WILLIAM: Writer. b. Chicago, IL, Aug. 12, 1931. e. Oberlin College, B.A., Columbia U., M.A. Novels include The Temple of Gold, Your Turn to Curtsy, My Turn to Bow, Soldier in the Rain (filmed), Boys and Girls Together, The Thing of It Is, No Way to Treat a Lady (filmed), Father's Day, The Princess Bride (filmed), Marathon Man (filmed), Magic (filmed), Tinsel, Control, Heat (filmed), The Silent Gondoliers, The Color of Light, Brothers. Non-fiction: The Season, Adventures in the Screen Trade, Wait Until Next Year (w/Mike Lupica), Hype and Glory.
PICTURES: Harper, Butch Cassidy and the Sundance Kid (Acad. Award, 1969), The Hot Rock, The Stepford Wives, The Great Waldo Pepper, All the President's Men (Acad. Award, 1976), Marathon Man (based on his novel), A Bridge Too Far, Magic (based on his novel), Heat (based on his novel), The Princess Bride (based on his novel), Misery, Memoirs of an Invisible Man (co-s.p.), Year of the Comet, Chaplin (co-s.p.).

GOLDSMITH, JERRY: Composer. b. Los Angeles, CA, Feb. 10, 1929. e. Los Angeles City Coll. Studied piano with Jacob Gimpel and music composition, harmony, theory with Mario Castelnuovo-Tedesco. With CBS radio first with own show (Romance) and then moved on to others (Suspense). Began scoring for TV, including Climax, Playhouse 90, Studio One, Gunsmoke, etc. Emmy Awards for QB VIII, Masada, Babe, The Red Pony.

PICTURES INCLUDE: Black Patch (debut), Lonely Are the Brave, Freud (AA nom.), The Stripper, The Prize, Seven Days in May, Lilies of the Field, In Harm's Way, Von Ryan's Express, Our Man Flint, A Patch of Blue (AA nom.), The Blue Max, Seconds, Stagecoach, The Sand Pebbles (AA nom.), In Like Flint, Planet of the Apes (AA nom.), The Ballad of Cable Hogue, Tora! Tora! Tora!, Patton (AA nom.), The Wild Rovers, The Other, Papillon (AA nom.), The Reincarnation of Peter Proud, Chinatown (AA nom.), Logan's Run, The Wind and the Lion (AA nom.), The Omen (Acad. Award), Islands in the Stream, MacArthur, Coma, Damien: Omen II, The Boys From Brazil (AA nom.), The Great Train Robbery, Alien, Star Trek—The Motion Picture (AA nom.), The Final Conflict, Outland, Raggedy Man, Mrs. Brisby: The Secret of Nimh, Poltergeist (AA nom.), First Blood, Twilight Zone—The Movie, Psycho II, Under Fire (AA nom.), Gremlins, Legend (European ver.), Explorers, Rambo: First Blood II, Poltergeist II: The Other Side, Hoosiers (AA nom.), Extreme Prejudice, Innerspace, Lionheart, Rent-a-Cop, Rambo III, Criminal Law, The 'Burbs, Leviathan, Star Trek V: The Final Frontier, Total Recall, Gremlins 2: The New Batch (also cameo), The Russia House, Not Without My Daughter, Sleeping With the Enemy, Medicine Man, Basic Instinct, Mom and Dad Save the World, Mr. Baseball, The Public Eye, Love Field, Forever Young, Matinee, The Vanishing.

GOLDSMITH, MARTIN M.: Writer. b. New York, NY, Nov. 6, 1913. Bush pilot, playwright, novelist, screenwriter.
AUTHOR: Novels include: Double Jeopardy, Detour, Shadows at Noon, Miraculous Fish of Domingo Gonzales. Play: Night Shift.
PICTURES: Detour, Blind Spot, Narrow Margin, Mission Over Korea, Overland Pacific, Hell's Island, Fort Massacre, Bat Masterson, It Happens Every Thursday, Shakedown.
TELEVISION: Playhouse 90, Goodyear Playhouse, Twilight Zone.

GOLDSTEIN, MILTON: Executive. b. New York, NY, Aug. 1, 1926. e. NYU, 1949. In exec. capac., Paramount; foreign sales coord., The Ten Commandments, Psycho; v.p. foreign sales, Samuel Bronston org.; asst. to Pres., Paramount Int'l, special prods., 1964; Foreign sales mgr., 1966; v.p., world wide sales, 1967, Cinerama; Sr. v.p. Cinema Center Films, 1969; pres., Cinema Center Films, 1971; v.p. Theatrical Mktg. & Sales, Metromedia Producers Corp., 1973; in March, 1974, formed Boasberg-Goldstein, Inc., consultants in prod. and dist. of m.p.; 1975, named exec. vice pres., Avco Embassy Pictures; 1978, named exec. v.p. & chief operating officer, Melvin Simon Prods. 1980, named pres.; 1985, pres. Milt Goldstein Enterprises, Inc.; 1990, chairman and ceo, HKM Films. 1991, pres., Introvision movies.

GOLDSTONE, JAMES: Director. b. Los Angeles, CA. June 8, 1931. e. Dartmouth Coll., B.A., Bennington Coll., M.A. Film editor from 1950. Writer, story editor from 1957. TV dir. starting from 1958.
TELEVISION: Pilots of Star Trek, Ironside, Iron Horse, The Senator, etc. Specials-Movies: A Clear and Present Danger (Emmy nom.), Eric (Virgin Islands Int'l. Film Fest. Gold Medal). Journey from Darkness (Christopher Award). Studs Lonigan (miniseries 1978), Kent State, (Emmy, best dir., special), Things in Their Season, Calamity Jane, The Sun Also Rises, Dreams of Gold, Earthstar Voyager, The Bride in Black.
PICTURES: Jigsaw, Man Called Gannon, Winning, Brother John, Red Sky at Morning, The Gang That Couldn't Shoot Straight, They Only Kill Their Masters, Swashbuckler, Rollercoaster, When Time Ran Out.

GOLDTHWAIT, BOBCAT (BOB): Comedian, Actor. b. Syracuse, NY, 1962. Performed with comedy troupe The Generic Comics in early 1980's. Album: Meat Bob.
PICTURES: Police Academy 2: Their First Assignment (debut, 1985), One Crazy Summer, Police Academy 3: Back in Training, Burglar, Police Academy 4: Citizens on Patrol, Hot to Trot, Scrooged, Shakes the Clown (also dir., s.p.)
TELEVISION: Series: Capitol Critters (voice). Specials: Bob Godthwait: Don't Watch This Show, Share the Warmth, Is He Like That All the Time? (also dir., writer), Bob Saget: In the Dream Suite, Comic Relief, Medusa: Dare to Be Truthful. Guest: Tales From the Crypt, Married... With Children, The Larry Sanders Show.

GOLDWYN, SAMUEL, JR.: Producer, Director. b. Los Angeles, CA, Sept. 7, 1926. e. U. of Virginia. Father of actor Tony Goldwyn. U.S. Army, 1944; following war writer, assoc. prod., J. Arthur Rank Org.; prod. Gathering Storm on London stage; returned to U.S., 1948; assoc. prod., Universal; recalled to Army service, 1951; prod., dir., Army documentary films including Alliance for Peace (Edinburgh Film Festival prize); prod. TV shows, Adventure series for CBS, 1952–53; prod. TV series, The Unexpected, 1954; pres., The Samuel Goldwyn Company, 1955–. Also established Samuel Goldwyn Home Entertainment, and Goldwyn Pavilion Cinemas.
PICTURES: Prod.: Man With the Gun, The Sharkfighters, The Proud Rebel, The Adventures of Huckleberry Finn, The

Young Lovers (also dir.), Cotton Comes to Harlem, Come Back Charleston Blue, The Golden Seal, Mystic Pizza (exec. prod.), Stella.
TELEVISION: The Academy Awards, 1987; April Morning (co-exec. prod.); Acad. Awards, 1988 (prod.).

GOLIGER, NANCY: Executive. b. Brooklyn, NY, July 7, 1948. Began career in entertainment industry at Bill Gold Adv. & B.G. Charles. Joined Warner Bros. as natl. adv. mgr.; promoted to dir., creative adv. With Universal as dir. adv.; PolyGram Pictures, v.p., domestic & foreign adv./pub.; Seiniger Advertising, exec. v.p. & gen. mgr. 1985, joined Paramount Pictures as sr. v.p., prod./mktg. for M.P. Group.

GOLINO, VALERIA: Actress. b. Naples, Italy, Oct. 22, 1966.
PICTURES: A Joke of Destiny (debut, 1983), Blind Date, My Dearest Son, Little Fires, Dumb Dicks, Love Story (Storia d'Amore), Last Summer in Tangiers, The Gold-Rimmed Glasses, Three Sisters, Big Top Pee-wee, Rain Man, Torrents of Spring, The King's Whore, Traces of an Amorous Life, Hot Shots!, The Indian Runner, Hot Shots! Part Deux.

GONZALEZ-GONZALEZ, PEDRO: Actor. b. Aguilares, TX, May 24, 1925. Comedian in San Antonio Mexican theatres.
PICTURES: Wing of the Hawk, Ring of Fear, Ricochet Romance, High and the Mighty, Strange Lady in Town, Bengazi, I Died a Thousand Times, Bottom of the Bottle, Gun the Man Down, Wetbacks, The Love Bug, Hellfighters, Support Your Local Gunfighter, Dreamer, Lust in the Dust.
TELEVISION: O'Henry Stories, Felix, the Fourth, Hostile Guns.

GOOD, CHARLES E.: Executive. b. 1922. Joined Buena Vista in 1957 in Chicago office; progressed from salesman to branch mgr. and then district mgr. Later moved to Burbank as domestic sales mgr. in 1975; 1978, named v.p. & general sales mgr.; 1980, appointed pres., BV Distribution Co. Resigned presidency 1984; became BV consultant until retirement, April, 1987.

GOODMAN, DAVID Z.: Writer. e. Queens Coll., Yale School of Drama.
PICTURES: Lovers and Other Strangers, Straw Dogs, Farewell My Lovely, Logan's Run, Eyes of Laura Mars, Man Woman and Child (co.-s.p.).

GOODMAN, JOHN: Actor. b. Afton, MO, June 20, 1952. e. Southwest Missouri State U. Moved to NY in 1975 where he appeared on stage (incl. A Midsummer Night's Dream) and in commercials. On Broadway in Loose Ends, Big River. L.A. stage in Antony and Cleopatra.
PICTURES: Eddie Macon's Run (1983, debut), The Survivors, Revenge of the Nerds, C.H.U.D., Maria's Lovers, Sweet Dreams, True Stories, Raising Arizona, Burglar, The Big Easy, The Wrong Guys, Punchline, Everybody's All-American, Sea of Love, Always, Stella, Arachnophobia, King Ralph, Barton Fink, The Babe, Matinee, Born Yesterday, The Flintstones.
TELEVISION: Series: Roseanne. Movies: The Face of Rage, Heart of Steel, The Mystery of Moro Castle, Murder Ordained. Mini-Series: Chiefs. Guest: The Equalizer, Moonlighting.

GOODRICH, ROBERT EMMETT: Executive. b. Grand Rapids, MI, June 27, 1940. e. U. of Michigan, B.A., 1962; J.D., 1964; NYU. LL.M, 1966. Pres. & Secty. Goodrich Quality Theaters, Inc. 1967–present, developed circuit from father's one theater to 119 screens at 17 locations in 9 Mich. cities, 3 Indiana cities, 2 Illinois cities. Owns and operates 6 FM/3 AM radio stations in Grand Rapids, MI, Lansing, MI, Muskegon, MI, and Davenport, IA.
MEMBER: NATO; Will Rogers Inst. advisory comm; bd., Mich. Millers Mutual Insurance Co.; State of MI Bar Assn.

GOODWIN, RICHARD: Producer. b. Bombay, India, Sept. 13, 1934. e. Rugby. Entered film world by chance: while waiting to go to Cambridge U. took temporary job as tea boy at studio which led to 20-year-long association with producer Lord Brabourne.
PICTURES: Prod. Mgr.: The Sheriff of Fractured Jaw, Carve Her Name with Pride, The Grass Is Greener, Sink the Bismarck, HMS Defiant. Prod.: The Tales of Beatrix Potter. Co-Prod.: Murder on the Orient Express, Death on the Nile, The Mirror Crack'd, Evil Under the Sun, A Passage to India, Little Dorrit.

GOODWIN, RONALD: Composer, Arranger, Conductor. b. Plymouth, Eng., 1925. e. Pinner County Grammar Sch. Early career: arranger for BBC dance orchestra; mus. dir., Parlophone Records; orchestra leader for radio, TV and records. Fut. m.p. ind., 1958. Many major film scores. Guest cond. R.P.O., B.S.O., Toronto Symph. Orch. New Zealand Symphony Orch., Sydney Symphony Orch. Royal Scottish Orch., BBC Scottish Symphony Orch., BBC Welsh Symphony Orch., BBC Radio Orch., BBC Concert Orch., London Philharmonic Orch., Gothenberg Symphony Orch., Norwegian Opera Orch. & Chorus, Halle Orchestra, Singapore Symphony Orch.,

Australian Pops Orch, Detroit Symphony Orchestra, Danish Radio Orchestra, Odense Symphony Orch.

PICTURES: Whirlpool, I'm All Right Jack, The Trials of Oscar Wilde, Johnny Nobody, Village of the Damned, Murder She Said, Follow the Boys, Murder at the Gallop, Children of the Damned, 633 Squadron, Murder Most Foul, Murder Ahoy, Operation Crossbow, The ABC Murders, Of Human Bondage, Those Magnificent Men in Their Flying Machines, The Trap, Mrs. Brown, You've Got a Lovely Daughter; Submarine X-1, Decline and Fall, Where Eagles Dare, Monte Carlo or Bust, Battle of Britain, The Executioner, The Selfish Giant, Frenzy, Diamonds on Wheels, The Little Mermaid, The Happy Prince, One of Our Dinosaurs Is Missing, Escape From the Dark, Born to Run, Beauty and the Beast, Candleshce, Force Ten from Navarone, Spaceman and King Arthur, Clash of Loyalties, Valhalla.

GORDON, ALEX: Producer. b. London, Eng., Sept. 8, 1922. e. Canford Coll., Dorset, 1939. Writer, m.p. fan magazines, 1939–41; British Army, 1942–45; pub. dir. Renown Pictures Corp., 1946–47; P.R. and pub. rep. for Gene Autry, 1948–53; v.p. and prod. Golden State Productions, 1954–58; prod. Alex Gordon Prods., 1958–66; producer Twentieth Century-Fox Television, 1974–76; film archivist/preservationist, 1976–84; v.p., Gene Autry's Flying A Pictures, 1985.

PICTURES: Lawless Rider, Bride of the Monster, Apache Woman, Day the World Ended, Oklahoma Woman, Girls in Prison, The She-Creature, Runaway Daughters, Shake Rattle and Rock, Flesh and the Spur, Voodoo Woman, Dragstrip Girl, Motorcycle Gang, Jet Attack, Submarine Seahawk, Atomic Submarine, The Underwater City, The Bounty Killer, Requiem for a Gunfighter.

TELEVISION: Movie of the Year, Golden Century, Great Moments in Motion Pictures.

GORDON, BERT I.: Producer, Director, Writer. b. Kenosha, WI; U. of Wisconsin.

PICTURES: Beginning of the End, The Amazing Colossal Man, The Fantastic Puppet People, The Cyclops, The Spider, Tormented, Boy and the Pirates, The Magic Sword, Village of the Giants, Picture Mommy Dead, How to Succeed With the Opposite Sex, Necromancy, Geronimo, The Mad Bomber, The Police Connection, The Food of the Gods, The Coming, The Big Bet, Malediction, Satan's Princess.

GORDON, BRUCE: Executive. b. Sidney, Australia, Feb. 4, 1929. Began career in Australian entertainment industry 1952 with Tivoli Circuit, live theatre chain; acted as advance man, front-of-house mgr., adv. dir.; promoted to busn. mgr., 1958. Named Tivoli membr. bd. of management, 1960–62. Joined Desilu Studios in 1962, developing Far East territories; promoted 1968 when Paramount acquired Desilu to mng. dir. Para. Far East opns. Named to bd. of TV Corp., 1969, operator of Channel 9 TV stns. & co.'s theatres in Sydney, Melbourne. Dir. on bd. of Academy Investments, operator of Perth theatre chain; responsible for building Perth Entertainment Centre. Named pres., Paramount TV Intl. Services, Ltd., 1974, in New York office. Based in Bermuda since 1985.

GORDON, CHARLES: Executive, Producer. b. Belzoni, MS. Began career as a talent agent with William Morris Agency. Left to write and develop television programming creating and producing 5 pilots and 3 series. Left TV to enter motion picture production in partnership with brother Lawrence Gordon. President and chief operating officer, The Gordon Company.

PICTURES: Exec. prod.: Die Hard, Leviathan. Co-prod.: Night of the Creeps, The Wrong Guys, Field of Dreams, K-9, Lock Up, The Rocketeer, The Super, Unlawful Entry.

TELEVISION: Writer-creator: When the Whistle Blows. Exec. prod.: The Renegades. Exec. prod.-creator: Just Our Luck, Our Family Honor.

GORDON, DON: Actor. b. Los Angeles, CA, Nov. 13, 1926. r.n. Donald Walter Guadagno. Served, U.S. Navy, 1941–45. Studied acting with Michael Chekhov. e. Columbia U. Theatre includes On an Open Roof, Stockade.

TELEVISION: Series: The Blue Angels, Lucan, The Contender. Guest: The Defenders, Remington Steele, Charlie's Angels, Twilight Zone, Simon & Simon, Outer Limits, MacGyver, etc. Movies: Happiness is a Warm Clue, Street Killing, Confessions of a Married Man.

PICTURES: Bullitt, The Lollipop Cover (best actor, Chicago Film Fest.), W.U.S.A., The Last Movie, Papillon, The Gambler, Out of the Blue, The Final Conflict, The Beast Within, Lethal Weapon, Skin Deep, The Exorcist III, The Borrower.

GORDON, GALE: Actor. r.n. Charles T. Aldrich, Jr. b. New York, NY, Feb. 2, 1906. Son of vaudeville performer Charles Aldrich and actress Gloria Gordon. Was radio performer in 1930s (Received award from Radio Hall of Fame). Stage debut in The Dancers; m.p. debut in The Pilgrimage Play, 1929.

PICTURES: Rally 'Round the Flag Boys, All in a Night's Work, Don't Give Up the Ship, Visit to a Small Planet, All Hands on Deck, Speedway, The 'Burbs.

TELEVISION: Series: My Favorite Husband, Our Miss

Brooks, The Brothers, Dennis The Menace, The Lucy Show, Here's Lucy, Life With Lucy.

GORDON, KEITH: Actor, Director, Writer. b. Bronx, NY, Feb. 3, 1961.

PICTURES: Actor: Jaws 2, All That Jazz, Home Movies, Dressed to Kill, Christine, The Legend of Billie Jean, Static (also co-s.p., co-prod.), Back to School. Director-Writer: The Chocolate War, A Midnight Clear.

TELEVISION: Mini-Series: Studs Lonigan, Wild Palms (co-dir.). Movies: Kent State, Single Bars Single Women, Combat High. Special: My Palikari (Amer. Playhouse).

THEATRE: A Traveling Companion, Richard III, Album, Back to Back The Buddy System, Third Street.

GORDON, LAWRENCE: Producer, Executive. b. Belzoni, MS, March 25, 1936. e. Tulane U. (business admin.). Assist. to prod. Aaron Spelling at Four Star Television, 1964. Writer and assoc. prod. on several Spelling shows. 1965, joined ABC-TV as head of west coast talent dev; 1966, TV and motion pictures exec. with Bob Banner Associates; 1968 joined AIP as v.p. in charge of project dev.; 1971 named v.p., Screen Gems (TV div. of Columbia Pictures) where he helped dev. Brian's Song and QB VII. Returned to AIP as v.p. worldwide prod. Formed Lawrence Gordon Prods. at Columbia Pictures; 1984–86, pres. and COO 20th Century Fox. Currently indep. prod. with 20th Century Fox. Producer of Bdwy. musical Smile.

PICTURES: Dillinger (1973), Hard Times, Rolling Thunder, The Driver, The End, Hooper, The Warriors, Xanadu, Paternity, Jekyll and Hyde, Together Again, 48 Hours, Streets of Fire, Brewster's Millions, Lucas, Jumpin' Jack Flash, Predator, The Couch Trip, The Wrong Guys, Die Hard, Leviathan (exec. prod.), K-9, Field of Dreams, Lock Up, Family Business, Another 48 HRS, Die Hard 2, Predator 2, The Rocketeer, Used People.

TELEVISION: (Co-creator and co-exec. prod.) Dog and Cat, Matt Houston, Renegades, Just Our Luck, Our Family Honor.

GORDON, RICHARD: Producer. b. London, Eng., Dec. 31, 1925. e. U. of London, 1943. Served in Brit. Royal Navy, 1944–46; ed. & writer on fan magazines & repr. independent American cos. 1946, with publicity dept. Assoc. Brit. Pathe 1947; org. export-import business for independent, British and American product; formed Gordon Films, Inc., 1949; formed Amalgamated prod., 1956; formed Grenadier Films, Ltd. 1971. 1992, prod. of A Tribute to Orson Welles.

PICTURES: The Counterfeit Plan, The Haunted Strangler, Fiend Without a Face, The Secret Man, First Man into Space, Corridors of Blood, Devil Doll, Curse of Simba, The Projected Man, Naked Evil, Island of Terror; Tales of the Bizarre, Tower of Evil, Horror Hospital, The Cat and the Canary, Inseminoid.

GORDY, BERRY: Executive. b. Detroit, MI, Nov. 28, 1929. Was working on auto assembly line in Detroit when decided to launch record co., Motown. In 1961 wrote song, Shop Around; recording by Smokey Robinson made it his first million dollar record. Expanded into music publishing, personal mgt., recording studios, film and TV, also backing stage shows. Former bd. chmn., Motown Industries. Chmn. The Gordy Co. Received Business Achievement Award, Interracial Council for Business Opportunity, 1967; Whitney M. Young Jr. Award, L.A. Urban League, 1980; Inducted into Rock and Roll Hall of Fame, 1988.

PICTURES: Lady Sings the Blues (prod.), Bingo Long Traveling All-Stars and Motor Kings (exec. prod.), Mahogany (dir.), Almost Summer, The Last Dragon (exec. prod.).

GORE, MICHAEL: Composer/record producer. b. New York City, New York, March 5, 1951. e. Yale University and studied in Paris with composer Max Deustch. Began writing pop songs for his sister singer Lesley Gore; as a staff songwriter for Screen Gems-Columbia; and as a producer of classical recordings for CBS Records.

PICTURES: Fame (Acad. Awards 1981 Best Score and Best Song); Terms of Endearment; Footloose; Pretty in Pink; Broadcast News; Defending Your Life, The Butcher's Wife.

TELEVISION: Generations (theme); Fame (theme).

GORING, SIR MARIUS: Actor. b. Newport, Isle of Wight, May 23, 1912. e. Cambridge U., Universities of Frankfurt-on-Main, Munich, Vienna, Paris. Early career with Old Vic; stage debut 1927, Jean Sterling Rackinlay's Children's Matinees. 1940–46 served with H. M. Forces and Foreign Office.

PICTURES: Rembrandt, Dead Men Tell No Tales, Flying 55, Consider Your Verdict, Spy in Black, Pastor Hall, The Case of the Frightened Lady, The Big Blockade, The Night Raider, Lilli Marlene, Stairway to Heaven, Night Boat to Dublin, Take My Life, Red Shoes, Mr. Perrin and Mr. Traill, Odette, Pandora and the Flying Dutchman, Circle of Danger, Highly Dangerous, So Little Time, The Man Who Watched Trains Go By, Rough Shoot, The Barefoot Contessa, Break in the Circle, Quentin Durward, Ill Met by Moonlight, The Moonraker, Family Doctor, Angry Hills, Whirlpool, Treasure of St. Teresa, Monty's Double, Beyond the Curtain, Desert

Mice, The Inspector, Girl on a Motorcycle, Subterfuge, Zeppelin.

TELEVISION: Numerous appearances, Sleeping Dog, Man in a Suitcase, Scarlet Pimpernel, The Expert.

GOROG, LASZLO: Writer. b. Hungary, Sept. 30, 1903. e. U. of Sciences, Budapest. Playwright, short story writer, asst. editor, Budapest, 1928–39.

PICTURES: Tales of Manhattan, The Affairs of Susan, She Wouldn't Say Yes, The Land Unknown, Mole People.

TELEVISION: 4 Star, Dupont, The Roaring Twenties, 77 Sunset Strip, Maverick, etc.

GORTNER, MARJOE: Actor, Producer. b. Long Beach, CA, Jan. 14, 1944. Was child evangelist, whose career as such was basis for Oscar-winning documentary film, Marjoe. Acted in films and TV; turned producer in 1978 for When You Comin' Back Red Ryder?

PICTURES: Earthquake, Bobbie Joe and the Outlaw, The Food of the Gods, Viva Knievel, Sidewinder One, Acapulco Gold, Starcrash, When You Comin' Back Red Ryder?, Mausoleum, Jungle Warriors, Hellhole, American Ninja III: Blood Hunt.

TELEVISION: Movies: The Marcus-Nelson Murders, Pray for the Wildcats, The Gun and the Pulpit, Mayday at 40000 Feet. Guest: Police Story, Barnaby Jones, The A-Team. Series: Falcon Crest.

GOSSETT, LOUIS, JR.: Actor. b. Brooklyn, NY, May 27, 1936. e. NYU, B.S. Also nightclub singer during 1960s. On stage in Take a Giant Step (debut, 1953), The Desk Set, Lost in the Stars, A Raisin in the Sun, Golden Boy, The Blacks, Blood Knot, The Zulu and the Zayda, My Sweet Charlie, Carry Me Back to Morningside Heights, Murderous Angels (L.A. Drama Critics Award).

PICTURES: A Raisin in the Sun (debut, 1961), The Bushbaby, The Landlord, Skin Game, Travels With My Aunt, The Laughing Policeman, The White Dawn, River Niger, J.D.'s Revenge, The Deep, Choirboys, An Officer and a Gentleman (Acad. Award, supp. actor, 1982), Jaws 3-D, Finders Keepers, Enemy Mine, Iron Eagle, Firewalker, The Principal, Iron Eagle II, Toy Soldiers, The Punisher, Aces: Iron Eagle III, Diggstown, Monolith, A Good Man in Africa.

TELEVISION: Series: The Young Rebels, The Lazarus Syndrome, The Powers of Matthew Star, Gideon Oliver. Movies: Companions in Nightmare, It's Good to Be Alive, Sidekicks, Delancey Street, The Crisis Within, Don't Look Back, Little Ladies of the Night, To Kill a Cop, The Critical List, This Man Stands Alone, Sadat, The Guardian, A Gathering of Old Men, The Father Clements Story, Roots: The Gift, El Diablo, Sudie and Simpson, The Josephine Baker Story, Carolina Skeletons, Father & Son: Dangerous Relations (also co-exec. prod.). Mini-Series: Roots (Emmy Award), Backstairs at the White House. Specials: Welcome Home, A Triple Play: Sam Found Out, Zora is My Name, The Century Collection Presents Ben Vereen: His Roots. Guest: The Mod Squad, Bill Cosby Show, Partridge Family, The Rookies, Love American Style, Police Story, Rockford Files, many others.

GOTTESMAN, STUART: Executive. b. New York, NY, June 11, 1949. Started career in mailroom of Warner Bros., 1972; later named promo. asst. to southwestern regional fieldman; promoted to that post which held for 10 years. 1987, named WB dir. field activities; 1990, appointed v.p. WB national field operations.

GOTTLIEB, CARL: Writer, Director, Actor. b. New York, NY, March 18, 1938. e. Syracuse U., B.S., 1960.

PICTURES: Actor: Maryjane (1968), M.A.S.H., Up the Sandbox, Cannonball, The Jerk, The Sting II, Johnny Dangerous, The Committee, Into the Night Director: The Absent-Minded Waiter (short), Caveman (also co-s.p.), Amazon Women on the Moon (co-dir.). Co-Writer: Jaws, Which Way Is Up?, Jaws II, The Jerk, Doctor Detroit, Jaws 3-D.

TELEVISION: Writer: Smothers Bros. Comedy Hour (Emmy), The Odd Couple, Flip Wilson, Bob Newhart Show, The Super, Crisis at Sun Valley, The Deadly Triangle. Director: Paul Reiser: Out on a Whim. Director-Co-creator: Leo & Liz in Beverly Hills. Co-creator: George Burns' Comedy Week.

GOUGH, MICHAEL: Actor. b. Malaya, Nov. 23, 1917. e. Rose Hill Sch., in Kent, England, and at Durham School. Studied at Old Vic School in London; first stage appearance in 1936 at Old Vic Theatre. N.Y. stage debut 1937 in Love of Women. London debut in 1938 in The Zeal of Thy House. M.P. debut in 1948 in Blanche Fury; since in over 50 films. Won 1979 Tony Award for Bedroom Farce.

PICTURES: Anna Karenina, The Man in the White Suit, Rob Roy, The Sword and the Rose, Richard III, Reach for the Sky, Horror of Dracula, The Horse's Mouth, Konga, Mr. Topaze, The Phantom of the Opera, Black Zoo, Dr. Terror's House of Horrors, The Skull, Berserk, Walk with Love and Death, Women in Love, They Came From Beyond Space, Trog, Julius Caesar, The Go-Between, Henry VIII and His Six Wives, Savage Messiah, The Legend of Hell House, Galileo,

The Boys from Brazil, The Dresser, Top Secret!, Oxford Blues, Caravaggio, Memed My Hawk, The Fourth Protocol, Out of Africa, The Serpent and the Rainbow, Batman, Strapless, Let Him Have It, Blackeyes, Batman Returns, Little Nemo (voice), Wittgenstein.

TELEVISION: The Search for the Nile, QB VII, Shoulder to Shoulder, The Citadel, Smiley's People, Brideshead Revisited, Mistral's Daughter, Lace II, Inside the Third Reich, To the Lighthouse, The Citadel, Suez, Vincent the Dutchman, Heart Attack Hotel, After the War, The Shell Seekers, Children of the North, Dr. Who, Sleepers.

GOULD, ELLIOTT: Actor. r.n. Elliott Goldstein. b. Brooklyn, NY, August 29, 1938. e. Professional Children's Sch., NY 1955. Vaudeville: appeared at Palace Theater, 1950. Broadway debut in Rumple (1957).

STAGE: Say Darling, Irma La Douce, I Can Get It for You Wholesale, On the Town (London), Fantasticks (tour), Drat the Cat, Little Murders, Luv (tour), Hit the Deck (Jones Beach), Rumors, Breakfast With Les & Bess.

TELEVISION: Specials: Once Upon A Mattress, Come Blow Your Horn, Jack and the Beanstalk (Faerie Tale Theater), Paul Reiser: Out on a Whim, Prime Time, Out to Lunch, Casey at the Bat (Tall Tales & Legends), Guest: Twilight Zone, Electric Company, Saturday Night Live, George Burns Comedy Week, Ray Bradbury Theatre, The Hitchhiker. Movies: The Rules of Marriage, Vanishing Act, Conspiracy: The Trial of the Chicago 8, Stolen: One Husband, Somebody's Daughter, Bloodlines: Murder in the Family. Series: E/R, Together We Stand, Sessions (HBO).

PICTURES: Quick Let's Get Married (debut, 1965), The Night They Raided Minsky's, Bob & Carol & Ted & Alice (Acad. Award nom.), M*A*S*H, Getting Straight, Move, I Love My Wife, Little Murders (also prod.), The Touch, The Long Goodbye, Busting, S*P*Y*S!, California Split, Who?, Nashville (guest), Whiffs, I Will I Will . . . For Now, Harry and Walter Go to New York, Mean Johnny Barrows, A Bridge Too Far, Capricorn One, Matilda, The Silent Partner, Escape to Athena, The Muppet Movie, The Last Flight of Noah's Ark, The Lady Vanishes, Falling in Love Again, The Devil and Max Devlin, Dirty Tricks, The Naked Face, Over the Brooklyn Bridge, The Muppets Take Manhattan, Inside Out, My First 40 Years, Lethal Obsession (Der Joker), The Telephone, The Big Picture, Dangerous Love, Night Visitor, The Wounded King, The Lemon Sisters, Judgment, Dead Men Don't Die, Bugsy, Strawanser, The Player, Exchange Lifeguards, Wet and Wild Summer.

GOULD, HAROLD: Actor. b. Schenectady, NY, Dec. 10, 1923. e. SUNY, Albany, B.A. Cornell U., MA., Ph.D. Instructor of theatre and speech, 1953–56, Randolph Macon's Woman's Col., Lynchburg, VA. Asst. prof. drama and speech, 1956–60, Univ. of Calif., Riverside. Acted with Ashland, OR Shakespeare Fest. in 1958 and Mark Taper Forum (The Miser, Once in a Lifetime). Won Obie Award for Off-Bdwy debut in The Increased Difficulty of Concentration, 1969. ACE Award for Ray Bradbury Theatre.

THEATER: The House of Blue Leaves, Fools, Grown Ups, Artist Descending a Staircase, I Never Sang for My Father, Freud (one man show), Love Letters, Incommunicado, King Lear (Utah Shakespearean Fest.).

PICTURES: Two for the Seesaw, The Couch, Harper, Inside Daisy Clover, Marnie, An American Dream, The Arrangement, The Lawyer, Mrs. Pollifax: Spy, Where Does It Hurt?, The Sting, The Front Page, Love and Death, The Big Bus, Silent Movie, The One and Only, Seems Like Old Times, Playing for Keeps, Romero.

TELEVISION: Series: Rhoda (Emmy nom.), Park Place, Foot in the Door, Under One Roof, Singer and Sons, Golden Girls, Feather and Father Gang. Movies: To Catch a Star, Moviola (Emmy nom.), Washington Behind Closed Doors, Aunt Mary, Better Late Than Never, King Crab, Have I Got a Christmas for You, Man in the Santa Claus Suit, I Never Sang For My Father, Get Smart Again!, Mrs. Delafield Wants to Marry (Emmy nom.). Special: The Sunset Gang. Guest: Police Story (Emmy nom.), Tales from the Hollywood Hills: The Closed Set, Ray Bradbury Theater (Emmy nom.).

GOULET, ROBERT: Singer, Actor. b. Lawrence, MA., Nov. 26, 1933. e. school, Edmonton; scholarship, Royal Conservatory of Music. Sang in choirs, appeared with numerous orchestras; disk jockey, CKUA, Edmonton; pub. rel., Rogo & Rove, Inc.

STAGE: NY: Camelot (as Lancelot; Theatre World Award), The Happy Time (Tony Award, 1968), Camelot (as King Arthur; 1993 revival). Regional: numerous tours including I Do I Do, Carousel, On a Clear Day You Can See Forever, Kiss Me Kate, South Pacific, The Fantasticks, Camelot (as King Arthur).

TELEVISION: Series: Robert Goulet Show, Blue Light. Guest: The Ed Sullivan Show, Garry Moore, The Enchanted Nutcracker, Omnibus, The Broadway of Lerner and Loewe, Rainbow of Stars, Judy Garland Show, Bob Hope Show, The Bell Telephone Hour, Granada—TV special (U.K.), Jack Benny, Dean Martin, Andy Williams, Jack Paar, Red Skelton,

Hollywood Palace, Patty Duke Show, The Big Valley, Mission Impossible, Police Woman, Cannon, Murder She Wrote, Mr. Belvedere, Fantasy Island, Matt Houston, Glitter, WKRP in Cincinnati. *Pilot:* Make My Day. *Specials:* Brigadoon, Carousel, Kiss Me Kate.
  PICTURES: Gay Purr-ee (voice), Honeymoon Hotel, I'd Rather Be Rich, I Deal in Danger, Atlantic City, Beetlejuice, Scrooged, The Naked Gun 2½: The Smell of Fear.

GOWDY, CURT: Sportscaster. b. Green River, WY, July 31, 1919. Basketball star at U. of Wyoming. All-Conference member; graduated U. of Wyoming. 1942. Officer in U.S. Air Force WWII, then became sportscaster. Voted Sportscaster of the Year, 1967, Nat'l Assn. of Sportswriters Broadcasters. Best Sportscaster, Fame, 1967. Did play-by-play telecasts for 16 World Series, 7 Super Bowls, 12 Rose Bowls, 8 Orange Bowls, 18 NCAA Final 4 college basketball championships. In 1970 was the first individual from the field of sports to receive the George Foster Peabody Award. Hosted the American Sportsman outdoor TV show on ABC for 20 years. (Received 8 Emmy Awards). Inducted into the Sportscasters Hall of Fame in 1981, the Fishing Hall of Fame in 1982, and the Baseball Hall of Fame in 1984.

GRADE, LORD LEW: Executive. r.n. Louis Winogradsky. b. Tokmak, Russia, Dec. 25, 1906. Brother of Lord Bernard Delfont. Came to Eng. 1912. Was first a music hall dancer until 1934 when he became an agent with Joe Collins, founding Collins and Grade Co. Joint managing dir. Lew & Leslie Grade Ltd. theatrical agency until 1955; Chmn. & mng. dir., ITC Entertainment Ltd. 1958–82; chmn. & chief exec., Associated Communications Corp. Ltd., 1973–82; pres. ATV Network Ltd., 1977–82; chmn., Stoll Moss Theatres Ltd., 1969–82; chmn. & chief exec., Embassy Communications International Ltd., 1982–85; chmn. & chief exec., The Grade Co. 1985–; Dir. Euro Disney S.C.A. Paris 1988, v.p. British Olympic Assn. Fellow BAFTA, 1979, KCSS 1979. Autobiography: Still Dancing (1988).
  NY THEATER: Prod.: Merrily We Roll Along, Starlight Express.

GRADE, MICHAEL: Executive. b. London, England, March 8, 1943. e. Stowe. Entered industry 1966. Early career as newspaper columnist, became an executive at London Weekend Television then Embassy Television in Hollywood. Joined BBC Television, 1983 as controller of BBC 1 and director of Programmes (TV), 1986. Joined Channel 4 as chief executive, 1988.

GRAF, BILLY: Executive. b. 1945. Entered industry 1965. Was asst. dir.; unit/location mgr./production mgr. for American, British and European companies. Now line producer, production mgr., asst. director. Has worked on numerous music videos & commercials.
  PICTURES: Alfie, A Man for All Seasons, Billion Dollar Brain, Scrooge, Run Wild Run Free, The Best House in London, Chitty Chitty Bang Bang, Galaxina, Khartoum, You Only Live Twice, Women in Love, Song of Norway, Prudence and the Pill, Hammerhead, Underground Aces, Purple Rain, Teen Wolf, Housesitter, The Spoiler, Wiretrap, Satan's Princess.
  TELEVISION: Secret Agent, The Saint, "Q" Branch, Private Eye Public Ear, The Avengers, Department "S," The Dave Cash Radio Show, Meanwhile in Santa Monica.

GRAF, WILLIAM N.: Executive. b. New York, NY, Oct. 11, 1912. Entered industry in 1934. 1937–42, exec. secty./asst. to Mark Hellinger at Warner Bros. & 20th-Fox. 1942–45, writer of armed forces training films. First m.p. unit, AAF Combat Cameraman 1946–50, exec. secty./asst. to Harry Cohn, pres., Columbia Pictures; 1951, prod. asst. to Jack Fier, prod. head, Columbia. 1952–65, Amer. repr. for British productions, Columbia Pictures; 1965–66, exec. asst. to M. J. Frankovich, Columbia Pictures, London; 1965–66, v.p., Columbia Pictures Intl., London; 1969–70, indep. prod., Cinema Center Films; 1980, v.p. in chg. of prod., Legion Films, Inc., Beverly Hills; 1984, pres., Billy Graf Prods. 1984, 1st v.p., Interguild Federal Credit Union, Writers, Dirs, Prods, & Cameramen; 1988, appt. bd. of dirs., Permanent Charities Comm.; 1987, exec. comm., Foreign Films Acad. of M.P. Arts & Sciences. Also comm. mem., Short and Feature Documentaries.
  PICTURES: (Producer) The Red Beret, A Man for All Seasons, Sinful Davey, The African Elephant. (Exec.): The Bridge on the River Kwai, Lawrence of Arabia, The Guns of Navarone, Born Free.

GRAFF, RICHARD B.: Executive. b. Milwaukee, WI, Nov. 9, 1924. e. U. of Illinois. Served U.S. Air Force; Universal Pictures 1946 to 1964 in Chicago, Detroit, Chicago and NY home office as asst. to genl. sales mgr.; 1964 joined National General in Los Angeles. In 1967 became v.p. and general sales mgr. of National General Pictures, formed and operated company. 1968, exec. v.p. in charge of world-wide sales and marketing. 1968 made v.p. of parent company; v.p. general sales mgr. AIP in 1971; 1975, pres. Cine Artists Pictures; 1977, pres. The Richard Graff Company Inc; 1983, pres. of

domestic distribution, MGM/UA. 1987, pres., worldwide distribution, Weintraub Entertainment Group. 1990, pres. The Richard Graff Company, Inc.

GRAFF, TODD: Actor, Writer. b. New York, NY, Oct. 22, 1959. e. SUNY/Purchase.
  PICTURES: *Actor:* Sweet Lorraine (also composed songs), Five Corners, Dominick & Eugene, The Abyss, An Innocent Man, Opportunity Knocks, City of Hope. *Writer:* Used People, The Vanishing (also co-prod.), Fly by Night (also actor), Angie I Says.
  TELEVISION: *Special:* Vietnam War Story.
  THEATRE: *NY:* Baby (Tony nom., Theatre World Award), Birds of Paradise. *Author:* The Grandma Plays, Sheila Levine.

GRANET, BERT: Producer, Writer. b. New York, NY, July 10, 1910. e. Yale U. Sch. of Fine Arts (47 workshop). From 1936 author s.p. orig. & adapt. numerous pictures. Exec. prod.: Universal, 1967–69, CBS, Desilu Studios.
  PICTURES: Quick Money, The Affairs of Annabel, Mr. Doodle Kicks Off, Laddie, A Girl a Guy and a Gob, My Favorite Wife, Bride by Mistake, Sing Your Way Home, Those Endearing Young Charms, The Locket, Do You Love Me?, The Marrying Kind, Berlin Express, The Torch, Scarface Mob.
  TELEVISION: Desilu (1957–61), Twilight Zone (pilot), The Untouchables (pilot), Scarface Mob; Loretta Young Show (1955–56), Walter Winchell File 1956–57, Lucille Ball-Desi Arnaz Show 1957–60, Westinghouse Desilu Playhouse, The Great Adventure.

GRANGER, FARLEY: Actor. b. San Jose, CA, July 1, 1925. e. Hollywood. U.S. Armed Forces 1944–46. Joined Eva Le Gallienne's National Rep. Co. in 1960s (The Sea Gull).
  PICTURES: The North Star (debut, 1943), The Purple Heart, Rope, Enchantment, They Live By Night, Roseanna McCoy, Side Street, Our Very Own, Edge of Doom, Strangers on a Train, Behave Yourself, I Want You, O. Henry's Full House, Hans Christian Andersen, Story of Three Loves, Small Town Girl, Senso, Naked Street, Girl in the Red Velvet Swing, Rogue's Gallery, Something Creeping in the Dark, They Call Me Trinity, Replica of a Crime, Amuk, The Slasher, The Redhead with the Translucent Skin, Kill Me My Love, Planet Venus, Night Flight From Moscow, Man Called Neon, Arnold, Savage Lady, The Co-ed Murders, The Prowler, The Imagemaker.
  TELEVISION: *Series:* One Life to Live (1976–7), As the World Turns (1986–8). *Movies:* The Challengers, The Lives of Jenny Dolan, Widow, Black Beauty. *Guest:* Playhouse of Stars, U.S. Steel Hour, Producer's Showcase, Climax, Ford Theatre, Playhouse 90, 20th Century Fox Hour, Robert Montgomery Presents, Arthur Murray Dance Party, Wagon Train, Masquerade Party, Kojak, 6 Million Dollar Man, Ellery Queen.

GRANGER, STEWART: Actor. r.n. James Stewart. b. May 6, 1913. e. Webber-Douglas Sch. of Acting, London. In Brit. Army, W.W.II. On stage from 1935, Hull Repertory theat.; Birmingham Repertory; Malvern Festivals (1936–37); Old Vic Co. Film debut. A Southern Maid (1933). Voted one of Brit. top ten money-making stars in M.P. Herald-Fame Poll, 1943, 1944, 1945, 1946, 1947, 1949.
  PICTURES: In Great Britain: So This Is London, Convoy, Secret Mission, Thursday's Child, Man in Grey, The Lamp Still Burns, Fanny by Gaslight, Love Story, Waterloo-Road, Madonna of the Seven Moons, Caesar and Cleopatra, Caravan, Magic Bow, Captain Boycott, Blanche Fury, Saraband for Dead Lovers, Woman Hater, Adam and Evalyn. In U.S.: King Solomon's Mines, Soldiers Three, Light Touch, Wild North, Scaramouche, Prisoner of Zenda, Salome, Young Bess, All the Brothers Were Valiant, Beau Brummell, Green Fire, Moonfleet, Footsteps in the Fog, Bhowani Junction, Last Hunt, The Little Hut, Gun Glory, The Whole Truth, Harry Black, North to Alaska, The Secret Partner, Sodom and Gomorrah, Swordsman of Siena, The Secret Invasion, The Crooked Road, Requeim for a Secret Agent, Frontier Hellcat, Rampage at Apache Wells, Red Dragon, Target for Killing, The Last Safari, The Trygon Factor, The Wild Geese, Hell Hunters.
  TELEVISION: *Series:* The Men from Shiloh. *Movies:* The Hound of the Baskervilles, Crossings, A Hazard of Hearts, Royal Romance of Charles and Diana, Chameleons.
  THEATRE: Bdwy: The Circle.
  (Died Aug. 16, 1993)

GRANT, DAVID MARSHALL: Actor. b. New Haven, CT, June 21, 1955. e. Juilliard, Yale School of Drama.
  PICTURES: French Postcards (debut, 1979), Happy Birthday Gemini, The End of August, American Flyers, The Big Town, Bat 21, Air America, Strictly Business, Forever Young.
  THEATRE: *NY:* Sganarelle, Table Settings, The Tempest, Bent, The Survivor, Making Movies, Angels in America: Millenium Approaches. *Regional:* Bent (also dir.), Lake Boat, Free and Clear, True West, The Wager, Rat in the Skull, Snakebite (author).

TELEVISION: *Series*: thirtysomething. *Movies*: Kent State, Legs, Sessions, Dallas: The Early Years, What She Doesn't Know, Citizen Cohn, Through the Eyes of a Killer. *Special*: A Doonesbury Special (voice). *Pilot*: Graham.

GRANT, HUGH: Actor. b. London, Eng., Sept. 9, 1960. e. New Coll., Oxford U. Acted with OUDS before landing role in Oxford Film Foundation's Privileged (1982) that began career. Acted at Nottingham Playhouse and formed revue group, The Jockeys of Norfolk.
PICTURES: Privileged, Maurice, White Mischief, The Lair of the White Worm, The Dawning, Remando al Viento, Impromptu, Crossing the Line, Bitter Moon, Remains of the Day, Night Train to Venice.
TELEVISION: The Last Place on Earth (mini-series), The Demon Lover, The Detective, Handel: Honour, Profit and Pleasure, Ladies in Charge, The Lady and the Highwayman, Champagne Charlie, Till We Meet Again, Our Sons.

GRANT, LEE: Actress. r.n. Lyova Rosenthal. b. New York, NY, Oct. 31, 1931. m. producer Joseph Feury. Mother of actress Dinah Manoff. At 4 was member of Metropolitan Opera Company; played princess in L'Orocolo. Member of the American Ballet at 11. e. Juilliard Sch. of Music, studied voice, violin and dance. At 18 with road co. Oklahoma as understudy. Acting debut: Joy to the World.
THEATRE: acted in a series of one-acters at ANTA with Henry Fonda. Detective Story (won Critics Circle Award 1949), Lo and Behold, A Hole in the Head, Wedding Breakfast; road co. Two for the Seesaw, The Captains and the Kings; toured with Electra, Silk Stockings, St. Joan, Arms and the Man, The Maids (Obie Award), Prisoner of Second Avenue.
TELEVISION: *Series*: Search for Tomorrow (1953–4), Peyton Place (Emmy Award, 1965), Fay. *Guest*: Studio One, The Kraft Theatre, Slattery's People, The Fugitive, Ben Casey, The Nurses, The Defenders, East Side/West Side, One Day at a Time, Bob Hope Show (Emmy nom.). *Movies*: Night Slaves, The Love Song of Bernard Kempenski, BBC's The Respectful Prostitute, The Neon Ceiling (Emmy Award), Ransom for a Dead Man, Lt. Schuster's Wife, Partners in Crime, What Are Best Friends For?, Perilous Voyage, The Spell, Million Dollar Face, For Ladies Only, Thou Shalt Not Kill, Bare Essence, Will There Really Be A Morning?, The Hijacking of the Achille Lauro, She Said No, Something to Live For: The Alison Gertz Story, In My Daughter's Name, Citizen Cohn. *Mini-Series*: Backstairs at the White House, Mussolini—The Untold Story. *Special*: Plaza Suite. *Director*: Nobody's Child, Shape of Things, When Women Kill, A Matter of Sex, Down and Out in America, No Place Like Home.
PICTURES: Detective Story (debut, 1951), Storm Fear, Middle of the Night, Affair of the Skin, The Balcony, Terror in the City, Divorce American Style, In the Heat of the Night, Valley of the Dolls, Buona Sera Mrs. Campbell, The Big Bounce, Marooned, The Landlord, There Was a Crooked Man, Plaza Suite, Portnoy's Complaint, The Internecine Project, Shampoo (Acad. Award, supp. actress, 1975), Voyage of the Damned, Airport '77, Damien: Omen II, The Swarm, The Mafu Cage, When You Comin' Back Red Ryder, Little Miss Marker, Charlie Chan and the Curse of the Dragon Queen, Visiting Hours, Teachers, The Big Town, Defending Your Life. *Dir.*: Tell Me a Riddle, Willmar Eight, Staying Together.

GRANT, RICHARD E.: Actor. b. Mbabane, Swaziland, May 5, 1957. e. Cape Town U., South Africa (combined English and drama course). Co-founded multi-racial Troupe Theatre Company with fellow former students and members of Athol Fugard and Yvonne Bryceland's Space Theatre, acting in and directing contemporary and classic plays. Moved to London 1982 where performed in fringe and rep. theater. Nominated most promising newcomer in Plays and Players, 1985, for Tramway Road.
PICTURES: Withnail and I, Hidden City, How to Get Ahead in Advertising, Killing Dad, Mountains of the Moon, Henry and June, Warlock, L.A. Story, Hudson Hawk, The Player, Bram Stoker's Dracula, The Age of Innocence.
TELEVISION: *Series*: Sweet Sixteen. *Movies/Specials*: Honest Decent and True, Lizzie's Pictures, Codename Kyril, Thieves in the Night (also released theatrically), Here Is the News, Suddenly Last Summer.

GRASGREEN, MARTIN: Executive. b. New York, NY, July 1, 1925. Entered m.p. ind. Jan., 1944, Columbia Pictures h.o. in contract dept. Promoted to travelling auditor April, 1946. Appt. office mgr. Omaha branch Dec., 1948; salesman Omaha, Dec., 1950. Transferred to Indianapolis, 1952, as city salesman; transferred to Cleveland as sales mgr., 1953. Left Columbia in 1960 to become 20th-Fox branch mgr. in Cleveland. Transferred to Philadelphia in 1965 as branch mgr.; transferred to N.Y. in 1967 as Eastern dist. mgr. Resigned in 1970 to form Paragon Pictures, prod.-dist. co. In Jan., 1975, formed Lanira Corp., representing producers for U.S. sales and dist. of films in U.S. Retired to Sanibel, FL, 1980.

GRASSHOFF, ALEX: Director. b. Boston, MA, Dec. 10, 1930. e. USC. 3 Acad. Award nominations for feature documentaries; Really Big Family; Journey to the Outer Limits; Young Americans (Acad. Award, 1968).
PICTURES: A Billion For Boris, J.D. and the Salt Flat Kid, The Last Dinosaur, The Jailbreakers.
TELEVISION: Series: The Rockford Files, Toma, Chips, Night Stalker, Barbary Coast, Movin' On. Specials: The Wave (Emmy), Future Shock (honored 1973 Cannes Film Fest.), Frank Sinatra, Family and Friends.

GRASSO, MARY ANN: Executive. b. Rome, NY, Nov. 3, 1952. e. U. of Calif., Riverside, B.A. art history, 1973; U. of Oregon, Eugene, Master of Library Science, 1984. Dir., Warner Research Collection, 1975–85; mgr., CBS-TV, docu-drama, 1985–88; Instructor 1980–88 UCLA Extension, American Film Institute. exec. dir. National Association of Theater Owners, 1988–present. Member: Acad. Motion Picture Arts & Sciences, American Society of Association Executives , Phi Beta Happa. Woman of Achievement, BPOA Awarded 1984.
TV credits: The Sacrlet O'Hara Wars, This Year's Blonde, The Silent Lovers, A Bunnies Tale, Embassy.

GRAVES, PETER: Actor. b. London, Oct. 21, 1911. e. Harrow. With Knight, Frank & Rutley, then Lloyds prior to theat. career. First stage appearance 1934 in Charles B. Cochran's Streamline.
THEATRE: Novello musicals at Drury Lane; repertory at Windsor, Old Chelsea, The Merry Widow, The Sound of Music, Private Lives. Recent: The Reluctant Peer, The Last of Mrs. Cheyney, Dear Charles, An Ideal Husband (S. Africa), A Boston Story (tour), His, Hers, and Theirs, The Great Waltz, No Sex Please We're British.
PICTURES: Mrs. Fitzherbert, Spring in Park Lane, Maytime in Mayfair, Lady With a Lamp, Encore, Derby Day (Four Against Fate), Lilacs in the Spring (Let's Make Up), Admirable Crichton, Alfie, The Wrong Box, The Jokers, I'll Never Forget What's Is Name, How I Won the War, Assassination Bureau, The Adventurers, The Slipper and the Rose.
TELEVISION: Those Wonderful Snows, Chelsea at 9, One O'Clock Show, Lunch Box, 2 Cars, Dickie Henderson Show, Ivor Novello Series, East Lynne, Ninety Years On, The Sleeping Doe, The Frobisher Game, The Jazz Age series, Kate series, Crown Court, Softly, Softly, 10 from the 20s, Quiller, Duchess of Duke Street, Looks Familiar, Bulman, Shades of Darkness, God Knows Where's Port Talbot, Campaign, The Woman He Loved, Shadow on the Sun, Sherlock Holmes, Prime Time.

GRAVES, PETER: Actor. r.n. Peter Aurness. b. Minneapolis, MN, March 18, 1926. e. U. of Minnesota. Brother of actor James Arness. Played with bands, radio announcer, while at school; U.S. Air Force 2 yrs.; summer stock appearances.
PICTURES: Rogue River (debut, 1950), Fort Defiance, Red Planet Mars, Stalag 17, East of Sumatra, Beneath the 12-Mile Reef, Killers From Space, The Raid, Black Tuesday, Wichita, Long Gray Line, Night of the Hunter, Naked Street, Fort Yuma, Court Martial of Billy Mitchell, It Conquered the World, The Beginning of the End, Death in Small Doses, Poor White Trash (Bayou), Wolf Larsen, A Rage to Live, Texas Across the River, Valley of Mystery, The Ballad of Josie, Sergeant Ryker, The Five Man Army, Sidecar Racers, Parts: The Clonus Horror, Survival Run, Airplane!, Savannah Smiles, Airplane II: The Sequel, Number One With a Bullet.
TELEVISION: *Series*: Fury, Whiplash, Court-Martial, Mission Impossible, New Mission: Impossible. *Movies*: A Call to Danger, The President's Plane is Missing, Scream of the Wolf, The Underground Man, Where Have All the People Gone?, Dead Man on the Run, SST-Death Flight, The Rebels, Death on the Freeway, The Memory of Eva Ryker, 300 Miles for Stephanie, If It's Tuesday It Still Must Be Belgium. *Mini-Series*: Winds of War, War and Remembrance. *Host/narrator*: Discover! The World of Science, Biography.

GRAVES, RUPERT: Actor. b. Weston-Super-Mare, England, June 30, 1963. Before film debut worked as a clown with the Delta travelling circus in England.
THEATER: The Killing of Mr. Toad, 'Tis Pity She's a Whore, St. Ursula's in Danger, Sufficient Carbohydrates, Amadeus, Torch Song Trilogy, A Madhouse in Goa, A Midsummer Night's Dream.
PICTURES: A Room with a View, Maurice, A Handful of Dust, The Children, Where Angels Fear to Tread, Damage.
TELEVISION: British: Vice Versa (1980–81), All for Love, A Life of Puccini, Fortunes of War, Good and Bad at Games, Inspector Morse.

GRAY, COLEEN: Actress. r.n. Doris Jensen. b. Staplehurst, NB, Oct. 23, 1922. e. Hamline U., B.A. summa cum laude, 1943, Actor's Lab. m. Fritz Zeiser. Member: Nat'l Collegiate Players, Kappa Phi, a capella choir, little theatres, 1943–44.
PICTURES: State Fair (debut, 1945), Kiss of Death, Nightmare Alley, Fury at Furnace Creek, Red River, Sleeping City, Riding High, Father Is a Bachelor, Apache Drums, Lucky Nick Cain, Models Inc., Kansas City Confidential, Sabre Jet, Arrow in the Dust, The Fake, The Vanquished, Las Vegas Shakedown, Twinkle in God's Eye, Tennessee's Partner, The

Killing, Wild Dakotas, Death of a Scoundrel, Frontier Gambler, Black Whip, Star in the Dust, The Vampire, Hell's Five Hours, Copper Sky, Johnny Rocco, The Leech Woman, The Phantom Planet, Town Tamer, P.J., The Late Liz, Cry from the Mountain.
TELEVISION: *Series*: Window on Main Street, Days of Our Lives, (1966–67), Bright Promise (1968–72). *Guest*: Family Affair, Ironside, Bonanza, Judd for the Defense, Name of the Game, The FBI, The Bold Ones, World Premiere, Mannix, Sixth Sense, McCloud, Tales from the Dark Side. *Movies*: Ellery Queen: Don't Look Behind You, The Best Place to Be.

GRAY, DULCIE: C.B.E. Actress b. Malaya, Nov. 20, 1919. e. Webber Douglas Sch. Stage debut 1939, Aberdeen, Hay Fever, Author: Love Affair (play), 18 detective novels, book of short stories. 8 radio plays; co-author with husband Michael Denison, An Actor and His World; Butterflies on My Mind, The Glanville Women, Anna Starr; Mirror Image, Looking Forward Looking Back.
STAGE: 40 West End plays including Little Foxes, Brighton Rock, Dear Ruth, Rain on the Just, Candida, An Ideal Husband, Where Angels Fear to Tread, Heartbreak House, On Approval, Happy Family, No. 10, Out of the Question, Village Wooing, Wild Duck, At The End of the Day, The Pay Off, A Murder Has Been Announced, Bedroom Farce, A Coat of Varnish, School for Scandal, The Living Room.
PICTURES: Two Thousand Women, A Man About the House, Mine Own Executioner, My Brother Jonathan, The Glass Mountain, They Were Sisters Wanted for Murder, The Franchise Affair, Angels One Five, There Was a Young Lady, A Man Could Get Killed, The Trail of the Pink Panther, The Curse of the Pink Panther.
TELEVISION: Milestones, The Will, Crime Passionel, Art and Opportunity, Fish in the Family, The Governess, What the Public Wants, Lesson in Love, The Happy McBaines, Winter Cruise, The Letter, Tribute to Maugham, Virtue, Beautiful Forever, East Lynne, Unexpectedly Vacant, The Importance of Being Earnest, This Is Your Life, Crown Court, Making Faces, Read All About It, The Voysey Inheritance, Life After Death, The Pink Pearl, Britain in the Thirties, Rumpole (The Old Boy Net.), Cold Warrior, Hook, Line and Sinker, Howard's Way (series), Three Up and Two Down.

GRAY, GORDON: Broadcast Management Consultant. b. Albert Lea, MN, Nov. 16, 1905. e. U. of Missouri. Entered broadcasting ind. 1932, v.p., gen. mgr., WOR, WOR TV; pres. WKTV, Utica, N.Y., KAUZ, Wichita Falls, Tex. Founded Central N.Y. Cable, Utica, N.Y. Chmn., Board of Governors, WFTV, Orlando, Fla. and management consultant, presently.

GRAY, LINDA: Actress. b. Santa Monica, CA, Sept. 12, 1940.
TELEVISION: *Series*: Dallas. *Movies*: The Big Ripoff, Murder in Peyton Place, The Grass is Always Greener Over the Septic Tank, Two Worlds of Jennie Logan, Haywire, The Wild and the Fire, Not In Front of the Children, The Entertainers, Highway Heartbreaker, Moment of Truth: Why My Daughter?
PICTURES: Under the Yum Yum Tree, Palm Springs Weekend, Dogs, Fun With Dick and Jane, Oscar.

GRAY, SPALDING: Performance artist, Actor, Writer. b. Barrington, RI, June 5, 1941. Began career as actor in 1965 at Alley Theater, Housten, then off-Bdwy in Tom Paine at LaMama Co. In 1969 joined the Wooster Group, experimental performance group. Has written and performed autobiographical monologues (Three Places in Rhode Island, Sex and Death to the Age 14, Swimming to Cambodia, Monster in a Box) throughout U.S, Europe and Australia. Taught theater workshops for adults and children and is recipient of Guggenheim fellowship. Artist in resident Mark Taper Forum, 1986–87. Bdwy debut: Our Town (1988).
PICTURES: *Actor*: Hard Choices, The Killing Fields, True Stories, Swimming to Cambodia (also s.p.), Stars and Bars, Clara's Heart, Beaches, Heavy Petting, Straight Talk, Monster in a Box (also s.p.), The Pickle, King of the Hill.
TELEVISION: Terrors of Pleasure (HBO Special). *Movies*: The Image, To Save a Child.

GRAY, THOMAS K.: Executive, producer. b. New York City, N. Y., July 1, 1945. e. U. of Arizona, B. A., post grad work at American Graduate School of Inter'l Management, Phoenix. Began career as management trainee with United Atists film exchange in Spain, 1970, and year later became managing director, UA, Chile. Also managing director for UA, New Zealand, 1972; Columbia, 1973; South and East Africa, 1974. Joined Cinema Inter'l Corp., London, as exec. assist. to co-chairman, 1974, and moved up to managing director of CIC/ Warner, South Africa, 1976. Returned to UA as vice pres. Far East, Latin America, Africa and Australia, 1977. Joined Golden Communications Overseas Ltd., London, as vice pres. foreign sales, 1980. With Golden Harvest Films, Inc. since 1984 as sr. vice pres., production. Executive in charge of prod. for Golden Harvest features: Flying, The Protector, China O'Brien, China O'Brien II, A Show of Force, Teenage Mutant Ninja Turtles, Best of Martial Arts (prod.), Teenage Mutant Ninja Turtles II: Secret of the Ooze (prod.), Teenage Mutant Ninja Turtles III.

GRAYSON, KATHRYN: Actress, Singer. r.n. Zelma Hedrick. b. Winston-Salem, NC, Feb. 9, 1923. e. St. Louis schools.
PICTURES: Andy Hardy's Private Secretary (debut, 1941), The Vanishing Virginian, Rio Rita, Seven Sweethearts, Thousands Cheer; Anchors Aweigh, Ziegfeld Follies, Two Sisters from Boston, Till the Clouds Roll By, It Happened in Brooklyn, The Kissing Bandit, That Midnight Kiss, The Toast of New Orleans, Grounds for Marriage, Show Boat, Lovely to Look At, Desert Song, So This Is Love, Kiss Me Kate, Vagabond King.
TELEVISION: GE Theatre (Emmy nomination), 1960; Die Fledermaus, ABC, 1966; Murder, She Wrote.
STAGE: Debut in N.Y. and tour, Camelot, 1963; Rosalinda, Merry Widow, Kiss Me Kate, Showboat (N.Y. and U.S. tour).

GRAZER, BRIAN: Producer. b. Los Angeles, CA, July 12, 1951. e. U. of Southern California. Started as legal intern at Warner Bros.; later script reader (for Brut/Faberge) & talent agent. Joined Edgar J. Scherick-Daniel Blatt Co.; then with Ron Howard as partner in Imagine Films Entertainment. Received NATO/ShoWest Producer of the Year Award, 1992.
PICTURES: Night Shift, Splash (also co-story), Real Genius, Spies Like Us, Armed and Dangerous (also co-story), Like Father Like Son, Vibes, The 'Burbs, Parenthood, Cry-Baby (co-exec. prod.), Kindergarten Cop, The Doors (co-exec. prod.), Closet Land (co-exec. prod.), Backdraft (exec. prod.), My Girl, Far and Away, Housesitter, Boomerang, CB4 (co-exec. prod.), Cop and a Half, For Love or Money, My Girl 2, The Paper.
TELEVISION: *Movies*: Zuma Beach, Thou Shalt Not Commit Adultery, Splash Too. *Series* (executive prod.): Shadow Chasers, Take Five, Ohara, Parenthood. *Special*: Poison (prod.)

GREEN, ADOLPH: Writer, Actor. b. New York, NY, Dec. 2, 1915. m. actress-singer Phyllis Newman. Began career in the cabaret act The Revuers with partner Betty Comden and Judy Holliday (1944).
THEATER: Wrote book, sketches and/or lyrics for many Broadway shows including: On the Town (also actor), Billion Dollar Baby, Bonanza Bound! (also actor), Two on the Aisle, Wonderful Town (Tony Award, lyrics), Peter Pan (Mary Martin), Say Darling, Bells Are Ringing, A Party with Comden and Green (1959 & 1977), Do Re Mi, Subways Are For Sleeping, Fade Out Fade In, Halleuljah Baby (Tony Awards, lyrics & best musical), Applause (Tony Award, book), Lorelei: Or Gentlemen Still Prefer Blondes (new lyrics), by Bernstein (book), On the Twentieth Century (Tony Awards, best book & lyrics, 1978), A Doll's Life, The Will Rogers Follies (Tony Award, best lyrics).
PICTURES: *Writer With Betty Comden*: Good News, On the Town, Barkleys of Broadway, Take Me Out to the Ball Game, Singin' in the Rain, Bandwagon, It's Always Fair Weather, Auntie Mame; What a Way to Go. As *actor*: Greenwich Village, Simon, My Favorite Year, Lily in Love, Garbo Talks, I Want to Go Home.

GREEN, GUY: Director. b. Somerset, Eng. Nov. 5, 1913. Joined Film Advertising Co. as projectionist & camera asst. 1933; camera asst., Elstree Studios (BIP) 1935; started as camera operator on films including One of Our Aircraft Is Missing, In Which We Serve, This Happy Breed. 1944: Director of Photography; Dir of Allied Film Makers Ltd.
PICTURES: *Dir. of Photography*: The Way Ahead, Great Expectations (Acad. Award), Oliver Twist, Captain Horatio Hornblower, I Am A Camera.*Director*: River Beat, Tears For Simon, House of Secrets, Sea of Sand, The Angry Silence, The Mark, Light In The Piazza, Diamond Head, A Patch of Blue (also writer), Pretty Polly, A Matter of Innocence, The Magus, A Walk in the Spring Rain, Luther, Once Is Not Enough, The Devil's Advocate.
TELEVISION: (U.S.) Incredible Journey of Dr. Meg Laurel; Isabel's Choice; Jennifer: A Woman's Story; Arthur Hailey's Strong Medicine, Jimmy B. and Andre, Inmates.

GREEN, JACK: Cinematographer. Started as camera operator for Bruce Surtees.
PICTURES: *Camera operator*: Firefox, Honky Tonk Man, Risky Business, Syudden Impact, Tightrope, Beverly Hills Cop, City Heat, Pale Rider, Ratboy. *Cinematographer*: Heartbreak Ridge, Like Father Like Son, The Dead Pool, Bird, Pink Cadillac, Race for Glory, White Hunter Black Heart, The Rookie, Deceived, Unforgiven, Rookie of the Year, A Perfect World.

GREEN, JOSEPH: Executive. b. Warsaw, Poland, Apr. 23, 1905. e. high school, prep school. Industry, legitimate theatre prod. Foreign film dist. since 1933; headed Green Film Co., Warsaw, Poland; head of Sphinx Film Dist. Co., N.Y., until 1940. co-owner, Art Theatre Circuit, N.Y., 1940–52; pres., Globe Dist. Co. of Foreign Films; formed President Films, Inc., 1954, now Globe Pictures, Inc. Beginning in 1979 a renaissance of Joseph Green's Yiddish film Classics produced in Poland in pre-W.W.II days, including Yiddle with He's Fiddle, Abriele der Mamen, Der Purinspieler, Mamele.

GREEN, JOSEPH. Executive, Producer, Director. b. Baltimore, MD, Jan. 28, 1938. e. U. of Maryland, B.A. Since 1970 has headed own distribution co. Joseph Green Pictures and released its library of 150 features to theatres, TV and cable.
PICTURES: The Brain that Wouldn't Die (dir., s.p.), The Perils of P.K. (assoc. prod., dir.), Psychedelic Generation (prod., dir.).

GREEN, MALCOLM C.: Theatre Executive. b. Boston, MA, Mar. 1, 1925. e. Harvard Coll. Began career as asst. mgr., Translux Theatre, Boston & Revere Theatre, Revere, MA. Treas., Interstate Theatres, 1959–64. Film Buyer, Interstate, 1959–72. Formed Theatre Management Services in 1972 with H. Rifkin and P. Lowe and Cinema Centers Corp. with Rifkin and Lowe families in 1973. Treas., Cinema Center, & pres., Theatre Mgmt. Services. Cinema Center grew to 116 theatres in 6 Northeast states, sold to Hoyts Cinemas Corp. 1986. Sr. v.p., Hoyts Cinemas Corp. 1986–89. Pres., Theatre Owners of New England, 1964–65; chmn bd., 1965–69; treas., 1970–84. Pres., NATO, 1986–88, Chmn Bd, 1988–90. Dir., Natl. Assoc. Theatre Owners. Chmn., NATO of New York State. Director, Vision Foundation. Dir., The Lyric Stage, Boston 1990–3; dir. & v.p., New Hampshire Music Festival.

GREENAWAY, PETER: Director. Writer. b. Newport, Wales, Apr. 5, 1942. Trained as a painter, first exhibition was at Lord's Gallery in 1964. Started making short films and documentaries in 1966, including: A Walk Through H, The Falls, Act of God, Vertical Features Remake. Directorial feature debut in 1982. For television made Death in the Seine, and a series of 9 Cantos from Dante's Inferno in collaboration with painter Tom Phillips.
PICTURES: The Draughtsman's Contract, A Zed and Two Noughts, The Belly of an Architect, Drowning By Numbers, The Cook The Thief His Wife and Her Lover, Prospero's Books, The Baby of Macon.

GREENE, CLARENCE: Producer, Writer. b. New York, NY, 1918. e. St. John's U., L.L.B. Author of play Need a Lawyer. Formed Greene-Rouse prods. with Russell Rouse; Acad. Oscar co-orig. story Pillow Talk. Acad. award nom. co-orig. s.p. The Well. Two Writers Guild nominations. Writers Guild award outstanding teleplay, One Day in the Life of Ivan Denisovitch. Co-prod., writer TV series Tightrope.
PICTURES: Prod., collab. s.p. The Town Went Wild, D.O.A., The Well, The Thief, Wicked Woman, New York Confidential, A House Is Not a Home, The Oscar. Prod.: Unidentified Flying Objects, The Gun Runners, Fastest Gun Alive, Thunder in the Sun, The Caper of the Golden Bulls, D.O.A. (story, 1988).

GREENE, DAVID: Director, Writer. b. Manchester, Eng., Feb. 22, 1921. Early career as actor. To U.S. with Shakespeare company early 1950's; remained to direct TV in Canada, New York and Hollywood.
TELEVISION: The Defenders. Movies: The People Next Door, Mdame Sin, Count of Monte Cristo, Friendly Fire, The Trial of Lee Harvey Oswald, A Vacation in Hell, The Choice, World War III, Rehearsal For Murder, Take Your Best Shot, Ghost Dancing, Prototype, Sweet Revenge, The Guardian, Fatal Vision (Emmy nom.), Guilty Conscience, This Child Is Mine, Vanishing Act, Miles to Go, Circle of Violence, The Betty Ford Story, After the Promise; Inherit the Wind, Liberace: Behind the Music, Red Earth, White Earth; The Penthouse (dir., exec. prod.), Small Sacrifices (Peabody Award), Honor Thy Mother.
PICTURES: The Shuttered Room, Sebastian, The Strange Affair, I Start Counting, Godspell, Gray Lady Down, Hard Country (prod., dir.).

GREENE, ELLEN: Actress, Singer. b. Brooklyn, NY, Feb. 22. e. Ryder Coll. After coll. joined musical road show. Appeared in cabaret act at The Brothers & the Sisters Club and Reno Sweeney's, NY. Off-Bdwy debut, Rachel Lily Rosenbloom. Bdwy in the The Little Prince and The Aviator. With NY Shakespeare Fest. in In the Boom Boom Room, The Sorrows of Steven, The Threepenny Opera (Tony nom.). Film debut Next Stop, Greenwich Village (1976). Off Bdwy. co-starred in musical Little Shop of Horrors 1982, repeated role in film. Also Off-Bdwy in Weird Romance. L.A. stage: David's Mother.
PICTURES: Next Stop Greenwich Village (debut, 1976), I'm Dancing as Fast as I Can, Little Shop of Horrors, Me and Him, Talk Radio, Pump Up the Volume, Stepping Out, Rock a Doodle (voice), Fathers and Sons.
TELEVISION: Special: Rock Follies. Movie: Glory Glory. Mini-Series: Seventh Avenue. Pilot: Road Show.

GREENE, GRAHAM: Actor. b. Six Nations Reserve, Ontario, Canada. Member of the Oneida tribe. First show business job as audio technician for several rock bands. Began acting in theatre in England.

PICTURES: Running Brave, Revolution, Powwow Highway, Dances With Wolves (Acad. Award nom.), Thunderheart, Clearcut, Rain Without Thunder, Benefit of the Doubt.
TELEVISION: U.S.: Movies: Unnatural Causes, The Last of His Tribe, Cooperstown. Guest: Adderly, L.A. Law. Canada: Series: 9B, Spirit Bay. Movies: Murder Sees the Light, The Great Detective, Street Legal.
THEATRE: Diary of a Crazy Boy, Coming Through Slaughter, Crackwalker, Jessica, Dry Lips Oughta Move to Kapuskasing.

GREENFIELD, LEO: Executive. b. New York, NY, April 26, 1916. e. St. John's U, Coll. of Arts & Sciences. v.p., gen. sales mgr. Buena Vista, 1962; Columbia road show sales mgr. 1966; v.p.-gen. sales mgr., Cinerama Rel. Corp. 1966; pres.-gen. sales mgr., Warners, 1969; sr. v.p. worldwide distribution, MGM 1975; v.p. distribution & marketing, Marble Arch Productions, 1978; exec. v.p. Associated Film Distribution, 1979; pres., distribution, F/M, 1986; pres., dist., Kings Road Entertainment, 1987; pres., Greenlee Assoc., 1988.

GREENHUT, ROBERT: Producer. b. New York, NY. Began career as prod. asst. on Arthur Hiller's The Tiger Makes Out, 1967. Worked in various capacities on such films as Pretty Poison, The Night They Raided Minsky's, Where's Poppa?, The Owl and the Pussycat, Husbands, etc. Received Crystal Apple from city of NY and Eastman Kodak Award for lifetime achievement.
PICTURES: Huckleberry Finn (assoc. prod.), Lenny (assoc. prod.), Dog Day Afternoon (assoc. prod.), The Front (assoc. prod.), Annie Hall (exec. prod.), Interiors (exec. prod.), Hair (assoc. prod.), Manhattan (exec. prod.), Stardust Memories (prod.), Arthur (prod.), A Midsummer Night's Sex Comedy (exec. prod.), The King of Comedy (exec. prod.), Zelig (prod.), Broadway Danny Rose (prod.), The Purple Rose of Cairo (prod.), Hannah and Her Sisters (prod.), Heartburn (co-prod.), Radio Days (prod.), September (prod.), Big (co-exec. prod.), Another Woman (prod.), Working Girl (co-exec. prod.), New York Stories (prod.), Crimes and Misdemeanors (prod.), Quick Change (co-prod.), Postcards From the Edge (co-exec. prod.), Alice (prod.), Regarding Henry (exec. prod.), Shadows and Fog (prod.), A League of Their Own (prod.), Husbands and Wives (prod.), Manhattan Murder Mystery (prod.), Wolf (co-exec. prod.).

GREENWALD, ROBERT: Director, Producer, Teacher. b. New York, NY, Aug. 28, 1948. e. Antioch Coll., New School for Social Research. Teaches film and theatre at NYU, New Lincoln, New School. Formed Robert Greenwald Prods.
PICTURES: Director: Xanadu, Sweet Hearts Dance (also exec. prod.), Hear No Evil.
TELEVISION: Prod: The Desperate Miles, 21 Hours at Munich, Delta Country USA, Escape From Bogen County, Getting Married, Portrait of a Stripper, Miracle on Ice, The Texas Rangers, The First Time, Exec. prod.: My Brother's Wife. Director: Sharon: Portrait of a Mistress, In the Custody of Strangers, The Burning Bed, Katie: Portrait of a Centerfold, Flatbed Annie and Sweetpie: Lady Truckers, Shattered Spirits (also exec. prod.), Forgotten Prisoners, The Portrait, Daddy, Murder in New Hampshire.
STAGE: A Sense of Humor, I Have a Dream, Me and Bessie.

GREER, JANE: Actress. b. Washington, DC, Sept. 9, 1924. r.n. Bettyjane Greer. Orchestra singer; photograph as WAC on Life Magazine cover won screen debut in Pan-Americana 1945 (as Bettejane Greer).
PICTURES: Pan American, Two O'Clock Courage, George White's Scandals, Dick Tracy (first film as Jane Greer), Falcon's Alibi, Bamboo Blonde, Sunset Pass, Sinbad the Sailor, They Won't Believe Me, Out of the Past, Station West, Big Steal, You're in the Navy Now, The Company She Keeps, You For Me, Prisoner of Zenda, Desperate Search, The Clown, Down Among the Sheltering Palms, Run for the Sun, Man of a Thousand Faces, Where Love Has Gone, Billie, The Outfit, Against All Odds, Just Between Friends, Immediate Family.
TELEVISION: Movie: Louis L'Amour's The Shadow Riders. Guest: Murder She Wrote, Twin Peaks.

GREGORY, JOHN R.: Executive, Producer, Writer. b. Brooklyn, NY, Nov. 19, 1918. e. Grover Cleveland H.S., 1935, New Inst. of M.P. & Telev., 1952; Sls., adv. dept. Fotoshop, Inc., N.Y., 1938–42; Spec. Serv., Photo. instructor, chief projectionist, supv., war dept. theatres, U.S. Army, 1942–46; sls. mgr., J. L. Galef & Son, N.Y.; 1948–49, gen. mgr., Camera Corner Co.; 1949–58, pres.; City Film Center, Inc., 1957; exec. v.p., Talent Guild of New York, 1958; pres., Teleview Prods., Inc., 1961; executive producer, City Film Productions, 1970. Executive post-production supervisor, Jerry Liotta Films, 1977.
AUTHOR: many articles in nat'l publications dealing with m.p. practices and techniques; tech. editor, Better Movie-Making magazine, 1962; editor, pub., National Directory of Movie-Making Information, 1963; assoc. ed., Photographic Product News, 1964; contrib. editor, U.S. Camera. M.P. columnist, contributing ed. Travel and Camera magazine,

1969; Advisory panelist, Photo-methods (N.Y.), 1975. Consultant, Photographic Guidance Council, 1957, assoc. Society of M.P. & Television-Engineers, 1952.

GREIST, KIM: Actress. b. Stamford, CT, May 12, 1958. e. New Sch. for Social Research.
THEATER: Second Prize: Two Months in Leningrad, Twelfth Night (NY Shakespeare Fest.).
PICTURES: C.H.U.D. (debut, 1984), Brazil, Manhunter, Throw Momma from the Train, Punchline, Why Me?, Homeward Bound: The Incredible Journey.
TELEVISION: *Guest*: Miami Vice, Tales From the Darkside. *Movies*: Payoff, Duplicates.

GREY, JENNIFER: Actress. b. New York, NY, Mar. 26, 1960. Daughter of actor Joel Grey. Appeared as dancer in Dr. Pepper commercial before making NY stage debut in Off-Bdwy play Album.
PICTURES: Reckless (debut, 1984), Red Dawn, The Cotton Club, American Flyers, Ferris Bueller's Day Off, Dirty Dancing, Bloodhounds of Broadway, Stroke of Midnight (If the Shoe Fits), Wind.
TELEVISION: *Movies*: Murder in Mississippi, Criminal Justice, Eyes of a Witness, A Case for Murder.

GREY, JOEL: Actor, Singer. b. Cleveland, OH, April 11, 1932. r.n. Joel Katz. Son of performer Mickey Katz; father of actress Jennifer Grey. e. Alexander Hamilton H.S., L.A. Acting debut at 9 years in On Borrowed Time at Cleveland Playhouse. Extensive nightclub appearances before returning to theatre and TV.
PICTURES: About Face (debut, 1952), Calypso Heat Wave, Come September, Cabaret (Acad. Award, supp. actor, 1972), Man on a Swing, Buffalo Bill and the Indians, The 7 Percent Solution, Remo Williams: The Adventure Begins, Kafka, The Player, The Music of Chance.
TELEVISION: *Specials*: Jack and the Beanstalk, George M! *Guest*: Maverick, December Bride, Ironside, Night Gallery, The Burt Bacharach Show, The Tom Jones Show, The Englebert Humperdinck Show, The Carol Burnett Show, The Julie Andrews Hour, Brooklyn Bridge. *Movies*: Man on a String, Queenie.
STAGE: Come Blow Your Horn, Stop the World—I Want to Get Off, Half a Sixpence, Harry: Noon and Night, Littlest Revue, Cabaret (Tony Award, 1967), George M!, Goodtime Charley, The Grand Tour, Cabaret (1987, Bdwy revival), Herringbone.

GREY, VIRGINIA: Actress. b. Los Angeles, CA, March 22, 1917. Screen career started 1927 with Uncle Tom's Cabin.
PICTURES: Misbehaving Ladies, Secrets, Dames, The Firebird, The Great Ziegfeld, Rosalie, Test Pilot, The Hardys Ride High, Hullaballoo, Blonde Inspiration, The Big Store, Grand Central Murder, Idaho, Strangers in the Night, Blonde Ranson, Unconquered, Who Killed Doc Robbin, Bullfighter and the Lady, Highway 301, Slaughter Trail, Desert Pursuit, Perilous Journey, Jeanne Eagles, The Restless Years, No Name on the Bullet, Portrait in Black, Tammy Tell Me True, Back Street, Bachelor In Paradise, Black Zoo, The Naked Kiss, Love Has Many Faces, Madame X, Rosie, Airport.

GRIEM, HELMUT: Actor. b. Hamburg, Germany, 1940; e. Hamburg U.
PICTURES: The Damned, The Mackenzie Break, Cabaret, Ludwig, Voyage of the Damned, Sergeant Steiner, Breakthrough, The Glass Cell, Berlin Alexanderplatz, Malou, La Passante, The Second Victory.
TELEVISION: Peter the Great.

GRIER, DAVID ALAN: Actor. b. Detroit, MI, June 30, 1955. e. Univ. of MI, Yale.
PICTURES: Streamers, A Soldier's Story, From the Hip, Amazon Women on the Moon, Off Limits, I'm Gonna Git You Sucka, Me and Him, Loose Cannons, Almost an Angel, The Player, Boomerang.
TELEVISION: *Series*: All is Forgiven, In Living Color.
THEATRE: A Soldier's Play, The First (Theatre World Award).

GRIER, PAM: Actress. b. Winston-Salem, NC, 1949.
PICTURES: The Big Doll House, Big Bird Cage, Black Mama White Mama, Cool Breeze, Hit Man, Women in Cages, Coffy, Scream Blacula Scream, Twilight People, The Arena, Foxy Brown, Bucktown, Friday Foster, Sheba Baby, Drum, Greased Lightning, Fort Apache The Bronx, Tough Enough, Something Wicked This Way Comes, The Vindicator, On the Edge, Stand Alone, The Allnighter, Above the Law, The Package, Class of 1999, Bill & Ted's Bogus Journey, Posse.
TELEVISION: *Mini-Series*: Roots: The Next Generations. *Movie*: A Mother's Right: The Elizabeth Morgan Story. *Guest*: Miami Vice, Crime Story, Pacific Station, Frank's Place, The Cosby Show, Night Court.

GRIFFIN, MERV: Executive, Singer, M.C. b. San Mateo, CA, July 6, 1925. e. U. of San Francisco, Stanford U. The Merv

Griffin Show, KFRC-Radio, 1945–48; vocalist, Freddy Martin's orch., 1948–52; recorded hit song I've Got a Lovely Bunch of Coconuts; Contract Warner Bros., 1952–54; toured Niteclubs, 1954–55; Prod. Finian's Rainbow, City Center, N.Y., 1955. Chairman, Merv Griffin Prods.
TELEVISION: *Series*: The Freddy Martin Show (vocalist), Summer Holiday, Morning Show, The Robert Q. Lewis Show, Keep Talking (emcee), Play Your Hunch (emcee), Saturday Prom, The Merv Griffin Show (1962–3), Talent Scouts, Word for Word, Merv Griffin Show (1965–86; Emmy Award for writing, 2 Emmy Awards for hosting), Secrets Women Never Share (exec. prod., host, 1987). *Creator*: Jeopardy, Wheel of Fortune.
PICTURES: By the Light of the Silvery Moon, So This is Love, Boy From Oklahoma, Phantom of the Rue Morgue, Hello Down There, Two Minute Warning, Seduction of Joe Tynan, The Man With Two Brains, The Lonely Guy, Slapstick of Another Kind.

GRIFFITH, ANDY: Actor. b. Mount Airy, NC, June 1, 1926. e. U. of North Carolina. Began career as standup comedian, monologist, recording artist (What It Was Was Football, 1954). TV acting debut in U.S. Steel Hour production of No Time for Sergeants, which he later played on Broadway and film.
THEATRE: *Broadway*: No Time for Sergeants (Theatre World Award), Destry Rides Again.
TELEVISION: *Series*: The Andy Griffith Show, The Headmaster, The New Andy Griffith Show (1971), Salvage One, Matlock. *Movies*: Strangers in 7A, Go Ask Alice, Pray for the Wildcats, Winter Kill, Savages, Street Killing, Girl in the Empty Grave, Deadly Games, Salvage, Murder in Texas, For Lovers Only, Murder in Coweta County, The Demon Murder Case, Fatal Vision, Crime of Innocence, Diary of a Perfect Murder, Return to Mayberry, Under the Influence, Matlock: The Vacation (also co-exec. prod.). *Mini-Series*: Washington Behind Closed Doors, Centennial, From Here to Eternity, Roots: The Next Generations.
PICTURES: A Face in the Crowd (debut, 1957), No Time for Sergeants, Onionhead, The Second Time Around, Angel in My Pocket, Hearts of the West, Rustler's Rhapsody.

GRIFFITH, MELANIE: Actress. b. New York, NY, Aug. 9, 1957. m. actor Don Johnson. Daughter of actress Tippi Hedren. Moved to Los Angeles at 4. e. Catholic academies until Hollywood Prof. Sch., 1974. Did some modeling before being cast in Night Moves at 16. Studied acting with Stella Adler, Harry Mastrogeorge and Sandra Seacat.
PICTURES: Smile, Night Moves, The Drowning Pool, One on One, Joyride, Roar, Fear City, Body Double, Something Wild, Cherry 2000, The Milagro Beanfield War, Stormy Monday, Working Girl (Acad. Award nom.), In the Spirit, Pacific Heights, The Bonfire of the Vanities, Paradise, Shining Through, A Stranger Among Us, Born Yesterday, Milk Money.
TELEVISION: *Series*: Carter Country. *Mini-series*: Once an Eagle. *Movies*: Daddy I Don't Like It Like This, Steel Cowboy, The Star Maker, She's in the Army Now, Golden Gate, Women & Men: Stories of Seduction (Hills Like White Elephants). *Guest*: Vega$, Miami Vice, Alfred Hitchcock Presents.

GRILLO, BASIL F.: Executive. b. Angel's Camp, CA, Oct. 8, 1910. e. U. of California, Berkeley, A.B. Certified public accountant, exec. vice-pres., dir., Bing Crosby Ent., Inc., 1948–57; bus. mgr., Bing Crosby, 1945; co-organizer, dir., 3rd pres., & treas., Alliance of T.V. Film Producers, 1950–54; exec. prod., BCE, Inc., shows incl. Fireside Thea., Rebound, Royal Playhouse, The Chimps; dir., KCOP, Inc., 1957–60; dir KFOX, Inc., 1958–62; pres., dir., Bing Crosby Prods., 1955–72; dir., Seven Leagues Ent., Inc., 1958; dir. Electrovision Prods., 1970, chief exec. off., Bing Crosby Enterprises.

GRIMALDI, ALBERTO: Producer. b. Naples, Italy, Mar. 28, 1925. Studied law, serving as counsel to Italian film companies, before turning to production with Italian westerns starring Clint Eastwood and Lee Van Cleef. Is pres. of P.E.A. (Produzioni Europee Associate, S.A.S.).
PICTURES: For a Few Dollars more, The Good the Bad and the Ugly, The Big Gundown, Three Steps in Delirium, A Quiet Place in the Country, The Mercenary, Satyricon, Burn!, The Decameron, Man of the East, The Canterbury Tales, Last Tango in Paris, Bawdy Tales, Arabian Nights, Salo or the 100 Days of Sodom, Fellini's Casanova, 1900, Illustrious Corpses, Lovers and Liars, Hurricane Rosy, Ginger and Fred.

GRIMES, GARY: Actor. b. San Francisco, CA, June 2, 1955. Family moved to L.A. when he was nine. Made film debut at 15 in Summer of '42, 1971. Voted Star of Tomorrow in QP poll, 1971.
PICTURES: Summer of '42, The Culpepper Cattle Company, Cahill: United States Marshall, Class of '44, The Spikes Gang, Gus.
TELEVISION: *Mini-Series*: Once an Eagle.

GRIMES, TAMMY: Actress. b. Lynn, MA, Jan. 30, 1934. Mother of actress Amanda Plummer. e. Stephens Coll, The Neighborhood Playhouse. Recipient: Woman of Achievment Award

(ADL), Mother of the Year Award, Mayor's Outstanding Contribution to the Arts Award (NYC). Member: bd. dirs., Upper East-Side Historic Preservation District (NYC).

THEATER: Look After Lulu (Theatre World Award, 1959), Littlest Revue, Stratford (Ont.) Shakespeare Fest., Bus Stop, Cradle Will Rock, Unsinkable Molly Brown (Tony Award, 1961), High Spirits, Finian's Rainbow, Only Game in Town, Private Lives (Tony Award, 1970), California Suite, 42nd Street, Tartuffe, A Month in the Country, The Importance of Being Earnest, Mademoiselle Columbe, Blythe Spirit, Waltz of the Toreadors, Taming of the Shrew, Orpheus Descending, Tammy Grimes: A Concert in Words and Music.

PICTURES: Three Bites of the Apple (debut, 1967), Play It as It Lays, Somebody Killed Her Husband, The Runner Stumbles, Can't Stop the Music, The Last Unicorn (voice), The Stuff, No Big Deal, America, Mr. North, Slaves of New York.

TELEVISION: Specials: Omnibus, Hollywood Sings, Hour of Great Mysteries, Four Poster. Guest: St. Elsewhere, The Young Riders. Series: The Tammy Grimes Show. Movies: The Other Man, The Horror at 37,000 Feet, The Borrowers, You Can't Go Home Again, An Invasion of Privacy.

GRISSMER, JOHN: Executive, Producer, Director. b. Houston, TX, Aug. 28, 1933. e. Xavier U., B.S., 1955; Catholic U., M.F.A., dramatic writing, 1959. Taught drama courses, directed student productions at U. of Connecticut & American U., Washington, DC. Produced and co-wrote House That Cried Murder, 1973; co-produced, wrote and directed Scalpel; directed Nightmare at Shadow Woods. Partner in P.J. Productions Co. & North Salem Prods., Inc.

GRIZZARD, GEORGE: Actor. b. Roanoke Rapids, NC, April 1, 1928. e. U. of North Carolina, B.A., 1949. Has been member of Arena Stage, Washington, D.C., APA repertory company and Tyrone Guthrie resident company in Minneapolis.

THEATER: The Desperate Hours. (Bdwy debut, 1955), The Happiest Millionaire (Theatre World Award), The Disenchanted, Face of a Hero, Big Fish, Little Fish, Who's Afraid of Virginia Woolf?, The Glass Menagerie, You Know I Can't Hear You When the Water's Running, The Gingham Dog, Inquest, The Country Girl, The Creation of the World and Other Business, Crown Matrimonial, The Royal Family, California Suite, Man and Superman, Another Antigone.

PICTURES: From the Terrace, Advise and Consent, Warning Shot, Happy Birthday Wanda June, Comes a Horseman, Firepower, Seems Like Old Times, Wrong Is Right, Bachelor Party.

TELEVISION: Mini-series: The Adams Chronicles, Queen. Movies: Travis Logan D.A., Indict & Convict, The Stranger Within, Attack on Terror: The FBI vs. the Ku Klux Klan, The Lives of Jenny Dolan, The Night Rider, Attica, Not In Front of the Children, The Deliberate Stranger, Underseige, That Secret Sunday, International Airport, Embassy, The Shady Hill Kidnapping, Oldest Living Graduate (Emmy Award), Perry Mason: The Case of the Scandalous Scoundrel, David, Caroline?, Iran: Days of Crisis, Not in My Family, Triumph Over Disaster: The Hurricane Andrew Story. Special: Enemy of the People. Mini-Series: Robert Kennedy and His Times, Queen.

GRODIN, CHARLES: Actor, Director, Writer. b. Pittsburgh, PA, April 21, 1935. e. U. of Miami. After time with Pittsburgh Playhouse studied acting with Uta Hagen and Lee Strasberg; began directing career in New York 1965 as asst. to Gene Saks. Has appeared in some 75 plays all over country. Has also written scripts, produced plays. Author of books It Would Be So Nice If You Weren't Here, and How I Get Through Life.

THEATER: Tchin-Tchin (Bdwy debut, 1962), Absence of a Cello, Same Time Next Year, It's a Glorious Day . . . And All That (dir., co-author), Lovers and Other Strangers (dir.), Thieves (prod., dir.), Unexpected Guests (prod.,dir.), Price of Fame (also author), One of the All-Time Greats (author).

PICTURES: Actor: Sex and the College Girl (1964), Rosemary's Baby, Catch-22, The Heartbreak Kid, 11 Harrowhouse (also adapt.), King Kong, Thieves, Heaven Can Wait, Real Life, Sunburn, It's My Turn, Seems Like Old Times, The Incredible Shrinking Woman, The Great Muppet Caper, The Lonely Guy, The Woman in Red, Movers and Shakers (also co-prod., s.p.), Last Resort, Ishtar, The Couch Trip, You Can't Hurry Love, Midnight Run, Taking Care of Business, Clifford, Beethoven, Dave, So I Married an Axe Murderer, Heart and Souls, Beethoven's 2nd.

TELEVISION: Candid Camera (writer, dir.), The Simon & Garfunkel Special (writer), Paul Simon Special (writer, dir.; Emmy Award, 1978), Acts of Love and Other Comedies (dir.), Paradise (prod., dir.). Actor: Guest: The Defenders, My Mother the Car, The FBI, Guns of Will Sonnett, The Big Valley. Specials: Grown Ups, Love Sex and Marriage (also writer), Charley's Aunt. Movies: Just Me and You, The Grass is Always Greener Over the Septic Tank. Mini-Series: Fresno.

GROSBARD, ULU: Director. b. Antwerp, Belgium. Jan. 9, 1929. e. U. of Chicago, B.A. 1950, M.A. 1952. Trained at Yale Sch. of Drama 1952–53. Asst. dir. to Eliza Kazan on Splendor in the

Grass, 1961; asst. dir.: West Side Story, The Hustler, The Miracle Worker. Unit mgr.: The Pawnbroker.

THEATER: The Days and Nights of Beebee Fenstermaker, The Subject Was Roses, A View From the Bridge, The Investigation, That Summer—That Fall, The Price, American Buffalo, The Woods, The Wake of Jamie Foster, The Tenth Man.

PICTURES: The Subject Was Roses, Who Is Harry Kellerman?, Straight Time, True Confessions, Falling in Love.

GROSS, KENNETH H.: Executive. b. Columbus, OH, Feb. 12, 1949. e. New School for Social Research, U. of London. Conducted film seminars at New School and active in several indep. film projects. Published film criticism in various journals and magazines. Joined ABC Entertainment 1971. Named supvr. of feature films for ABC-TV. Appt. mgr. of feature films, 1974. Promoted in Nov, 1975 to program executive, ABC Entertainment Prime Time/West Coast. Moved to L.A. offices, 1975, promoted to exec. producer, movies for TV, ABC Ent. 1976; 1978, with literary agency F.C.A. as partner in Los Angeles; 1979 producer for Lorimar; then with Intl. Creative Mgt; 1982, formed own literary talent agency, The Literary Group; 1985, merged agency with Robinson-Weintraub & Assoc. to become Robinson-Weintraub-Gross & Assoc. 1993, founding partner of Paradigm, a talent and literary agency.

GROSS, MARY: Actress. b. Chicago, IL, March 25, 1953. Sister of actor Michael Gross. e. Loyola U. Is also student of the harp. In 1980 discovered by John Belushi who saw her perform as resident member of Chicago's Second City comedy troupe, where she won Chicago's Joseph Jefferson Award as best actress for the revue, Well, I'm Off to the Thirty Years War. First came to national attention as regular on Saturday Night Live, 1981–85.

PICTURES: Club Paradise, Couch Trip, Casual Sex, Big Business, Feds, Troop Beverly Hills.

TELEVISION: Series: Saturday Night Live, The People Next Door. Specials: Comic Relief I, The Second City 25th Anniversary Reunion.

GROSS, MICHAEL: Actor. b. Chicago, IL, June 21, 1947. m. casting dir. Elza Bergeron. Brother of actress-comedienne Mary Gross. e. U. Illinois, B.A., Yale School of Drama, M.F.A. Worked NY Shakespeare Fest. (Sganarelle, An Evening of Moliere Farces, Othello). Off-Bdwy in Endgame, No End of Blame (Obie Award), Put Them All Together, Geniuses, Territorial Rites. Broadway: Bent, The Philadelphia Story. L.A. stage: Hedda Gabler, The Real Thing, Love Letters, Money & Friends.

PICTURES: Just Tell Me What You Want, Big Business, Tremors, Cool as Ice, Alan & Naomi.

TELEVISION: Series: Family Ties. Movies: A Girl Named Sooner, FDR: The Last Year, Dream House, The Neighborhood, Little Gloria Happy at Last, Cook and Peary—The Race to the Pole, Summer Fantasy, Family Ties Vacation, A Letter to Three Wives, Right to Die, In the Line of Duty: The FBI Murders, A Connecticut Yankee in King Arthur's Court, Vestige of Honor, In the Line of Duty: Manhunt in the Dakotas, With a Vengeance.

GROSSBERG, JACK: Producer, Executive. b. Brooklyn, NY, June 5, 1927. Member: Academy of Motion Picture Arts & Sciences. Directors Guild of America.

PICTURES: Requiem For A Heavyweight, Pretty Poison, The Producers, Don't Drink the Water, Take the Money and Run, Bananas, Everything You Always Wanted To Know About Sex, Sleeper, A Delicate Balance, Luther, Rhinoceros, Leadbelly, King Kong, The Betsy, Fast Break, A Stranger is Watching, Brainstorm, Strange Brew, Touch and Go, The Experts, Little Monsters.

GROSSMAN, ERNIE: Executive. b. New York, NY, Sept. 19, 1924. Still dept., pressbook edit., asst. field mgr., Warner Bros., 1940–58; Studio publicist, 1958–60; exploitation, promo. mgr. field dept., 1960–64; nat'l mgr., pub., exploit., promo.; 1964–67 exec. co-ord. advt., pub. & promo., Warner-7 Arts, 1967; WB nat'l supv. ad.-pub., 1970. exec. assist. to Richard Lederer, 1971–72; 1973 nat'l dir. of Pub. & Promotion, Warner Bros. Inc.; 1977, natl. dir. of adv.-pub.; 1980–85, natl. dir. promo. 1987, named south-west special events dir.

GROSSMAN, HOWARD K.: Producer. b. York, PA, June 12, 1950. e. Emerson Col. Started in mail room at Burbank Studios; Became asst. story edit. WB-TV, 1974; asst. dir. At Long Last Love, 1975; asst. to Orson Welles.

TELEVISION: The Beach Boys: A Celebration Concert, Beach Boys 20th Anniversary Special, Billy Joel Live from Long Island (assoc. prod.), American Rock, Culture Club: A Kiss Across the Ocean, The Thompson Twins Album Flash, Tru West, The Dining Room, Heartbreak House.

PICTURES: Apprentice to Murder.

GRUEN, ROBERT: Executive. b. New York, NY, Apr. 2, 1913, e. Carnegie Mellon U., B.A. Stage designer, 1934–35; designer, 20th-Fox, 1936; prod. exec., National Screen Service Corp.,

1936; head, Robert Gruen Associates, ind. design org., 1940; nat. pres. Industrial Designers Inst., 1954–55; dir. and v.p., National Screen Service Corp. since 1951; senior v.p. 1975–78; dir., NSS Corp., Continental Lithograph and NSS, Ltd., 1978–85. Retired 1985.

GRUENBERG, LEONARD S.: Executive. b. Minneapolis, MN, Sept. 10, 1913, e. U. of Minnesota. Began as salesman Republic Pictures, Minneapolis, 1935; with RKO in same capacity, 1936; promoted to city sales mgr., St. Louis, 1937, then branch mgr., Salt Lake City, 1941; later that year apptd. Rocky Mt. Dist. Mgr., Denver, CO); 1946 Metropolitan, div. mgr., v.p. NTA, v.p. Cinemiracle Prods.; Pres., Chmn. of bd., Sigma III Corp., 1962. Chmn. of bd., Filmways, 1967. Chmn. of bd. Gamma III Dist. Co. & Chmn of bd. and Pres. Great Owl Corp., 1976. Member Variety Club, Sigma Alpha Mu Fraternity; Lieut. Civil Air Patrol, Lieut. Comdr., U.S.N.R.

GRUSIN, DAVID: Composer, Conductor, Performer. b. Littleton, CO, June 26, 1934. Directed music for the Andy Williams Show on TV for 7 yrs in the 1960s, where met Norman Lear and Bud Yorkin, producers of the series, who signed him to score their first feature film, Divorce, American Style (1967).
PICTURES: Waterhole No. 3, The Graduate, Candy, The Heart Is a Lonely Hunter, Winning, Where Were You When the Lights Went Out?, Generation, A Man Called Gannon, Tell Them Willie Boy Is Here, Adam at 6 A.M., Halls of Anger, The Gang That Couldn't Shoot Straight, The Pursuit of Happiness, Shoot Out, Fuzz, The Great Northfield Minnesota Raid, The Friends of Eddie Coyle, The Midnight Ride, W.W. and the Dixie Dancekings, The Yakuza, Three Days of the Condor, Murder By Death, The Front, Fire Sale, Mr. Billion, Bobby Deerfield, The Goodbye Girl, Heaven Can Wait, And Justice for All, The Champ, The Electric Horseman, My Bodyguard, Absence of Malice, On Golden Pond, Reds, Author! Author!, Tootsie, Scandalous, Racing with the Moon, The Pope of Greenwich Village, The Little Drummer Girl, Falling in Love, Goonies, The Milagro Beanfield War (Acad. Award, 1988), Clara's Heart, Tequila Sunrise, A Dry White Season, Havana, The Bonfire of the Vanities, For the Boys, The Firm.
TELEVISION: Movies: Deadly Dream, Prescription: Murder, Scorpio Letters, Eric, The Family Rico, The Death Squad; themes to many series.

GUARDINO, HARRY: Actor. b. Brooklyn, NY, Dec. 23. 1925, e. Haaren H.S.
STAGE: Bdwy: End as a Man, A Hatful of Rain, Anyone Can Whistle, One More River, Natural Affection, The Rose Tattoo (revival), Seven Descents of Myrtle, Woman of the Year.
TELEVISION: Series: The Reporter, Monty Nash, New Adventures of Perry Mason. Guest: Studio One, Playhouse 90, The Alcoa Theatre, Naked City, Dr. Kildare, The Untouchables, The Dick Powell Show. Movies: The Lonely Profession, The Last Child, Police Story, Partners in Crime, Indict and Convict, Get Christie Love!, Street Killing, Having Babies, Contract on Cherry Street, Evening in Byzantium, Pleasure Cove, Sophisticated Gents, The Neon Empire.
PICTURES: Sirocco, Flesh and Fury, Big Tip-Off, Hold Back Tomorrow, Houseboat, Pork Chop Hill, The Five Pennies, Five Branded Women, King of Kings, Hell is for Heroes, The Pigeon That Took Rome, Rhino!, Treasure of San Grennaro, Adventures of Bullwhip Griffin, Madigan, Valley of Mystery, Jigsaw, The Hell With Heroes, Lovers and Other Strangers, Red Sky at Morning, Dirty Harry, They Only Kill Their Masters, Capone, Whiffs, St. Ives, The Enforcer, Rollercoaster, Matilda, Goldengirl, Any Which Way You Can.

GUBER, PETER: Producer. b. 1942. e. Syracuse U., B.A.; U. at Florence (Italy), S.S.P.; Sch. of Law, J.D., L.L.M. Recruited by Columbia Pictures as exec. asst. in 1968 while at NYU. Graduate Sch. of Business Adm. With Col. seven yrs. in key prod. exec. capacities, serving last three as studio chief. Formed own company, Peter Guber's Filmworks, which in 1976 was merged with his Casablanca Records to become Casablanca Record and Filmworks where he was co-owner & chmn. bd. 1980 formed Polygram Pictures later bringing in Jon Peters as partner. 1983 sold Polygram and formed Guber-Peters. 1988 merged co. with Burt Sugarman's Barris Industries to form Guber-Peters-Barris Entertainment Co. Co-chmn. & man. dir. 1989 took full control of co. with Sugarman's exit and addition of Australia's Frank Lowy as new partner. 1989 became co-chairman of Columbia Pictures. Awards: Producer of Year, NATO, 1979; NYU Albert Gallatin Fellowship; Syracuse U Ardent Award. Visiting prof., & chmn. producer's dept., UCLA Sch. of Theatre Arts. Member of NY, CA and Wash. DC Bars. Books: Inside the Deep, Above the Title.
PICTURES: The Deep (first under own banner), Midnight Express (6 Golden Globes, 2 Oscars), Co Prod. with Jon Peters: An American Werewolf in London, Missing, Flashdance (exec. prod.), D.C. Cab (exec. prod.), Endless Love, Vision Quest (exec. prod.), The Legend of Billie Jean, Head

Office, Clan of the Cave Bear, Six Weeks (exec. prod.), The Pursuit of D.B. Cooper (exec. prod.), Clue (exec. prod.), The Color Purple (exec. prod.), The Witches of Eastwick; Innerspace (exec. prod.), Who's That Girl (exec. prod.); Gorillas in the Mist (exec. prod.); Caddyshack II, Rain Man (exec. prod.), 4 Golden Globes, 4 Oscars), Batman, Johnny Handsome, Tango and Cash, Batman Returns, This Boy's Life.
TELEVISION: Mysteries of the Sea (doc. Emmy Award), Exec. prod.: Television and the Presidency, Double Platinum, Dreams (series), Movies: Stand By Your Man, The Toughest Man in the World (exec. prod.), Bay Coven, Oceanquest, Brotherhood of Justice, Nightmare at Bitter Creek, Finish Line.

GUEST, CHRISTOPHER: Actor, Writer, Composer. b. New York, NY, Feb. 5, 1948. m. actress Jamie Lee Curtis. Brother of actor Nicholas Guest. Wrote the musical score and acted in National Lampoon's Lemmings off-Bdwy. On Bdwy in Room Service, Moonchildren. Cast member Saturday Night Live 1984–85.
PICTURES: The Hot Rock, Death Wish, The Fortune, Girlfriends, The Last Word, The Long Riders, Heartbeeps, This is Spinal Tap (also co-s.p.), Little Shop of Horrors, Beyond Therapy, The Princess Bride, Sticky Fingers, The Big Picture (dir. co-s.p., story), A Few Good Men.
TELEVISION: Series: Saturday Night Live (1984–5). Movies: It Happened One Christmas, Haywire, Million Dollar Infield, A Piano for Mrs. Cimino. Specials: The TV Show, The Chevy Chase Special (also writer), The Billion Dollar Bubble, Lily Tomlin (also writer, Emmy Award, 1976), A Nice Place to Visit (writer only), Spinal Tap Reunion (also co-writer). Mini-Series: Blind Ambition.

GUEST, LANCE: Actor. b. Saratoga, CA, July 21, 1960. e. UCLA.
PICTURES: Halloween II, I Ought To Be in Pictures, The Last Starfighter, Jaws—The Revenge, The Wizard of Loneliness.
TELEVISION: Series: Lou Grant, Knots Landing. Guest: St. Elsewhere. Movies: Confessions of a Married Man. Specials: One Too Many, My Father My Rival, The Roommate. Mini-Series: Favorite Son.

GUEST, VAL: Writer, Director, Producer. b. London, England. e. England and America. Journalist with Hollywood Reporter, Zit's Los Angeles Examiner and Walter Winchell.
PICTURES: Murder at the Windmill, Miss Pilgrim's Progress, The Body Said No, Mr. Drake's Duck, Happy Go Lovely, Another Man's Poison, Penny Princess, The Runaway Bus, Life With the Lyons, Dance Little Lady, Men of Sherwood Forest, Lyons in Paris, Break in the Circle, It's A Great Life, Quatermass Experiment, They Can't Hang Me, The Weapon, The Abominable Snowman, Carry on Admiral, It's a Wonderful World, Camp on Blood Island, Up the Creek, Further Up the Creek, Life Is a Circus, Yesterday's Enemy, Expresso Bongo, Hell Is a City, Full Treatment, The Day the Earth Caught Fire, Jigsaw, 80,000 Suspects, The Beauty Jungle, Where the Spies Are, Casino Royale (co-dir.), Assignment K, When Dinosaurs Ruled the Earth, Tomorrow, The Persuaders, Au Pair Girls, The Adventurer, Confessions of a Window Cleaner, Killer Force, Diamond Mercenaries, The Boys in Blue.
TELEVISION: Space 1999, The Persuaders, The Adventurer, The Shillingbury Blowers, The Band Played On, Sherlock Holmes & Dr. Watson, Shillingbury Tales, Dangerous Davies, The Last Detective, In Possession, Mark of the Devil, Child's Play, Scent of Fear.

GUILLAUME, ROBERT: Actor. b. St. Louis, MO, Nov. 30, 1937. e. St. Louis U., Washington U. Scholarship for musical fest. in Aspen, CO. Then apprenticed with Karamu Theatre where performed in operas and musicals. Bdwy. plays and musicals include Fly Blackbird, Kwamina, Guys and Dolls, Purlie, Jacques Brel is Alive and Well and Living in Paris. In L.A. in Phantom of the Opera.
TELEVISION: Series: Soap (Emmy Award, 1979), Benson (Emmy Award, 1985), The Robert Guillaume Show, Saturdays, Pacific Station, Fish Police (voice). Guest: Dinah, Mel and Susan Together, Rich Little's Washington Follies, Jim Nabors, All in the Family, Sanford and Son, The Jeffersons, Marcus Welby, M.D., Carol & Company, Sister Kate, A Different World. Mini-Series: North and South. Movies: The Kid From Left Field, The Kid with the Broken Halo, You Must Remember This, The Kid with the 100 I.Q. (also exec. prod.); Perry Mason: The Case of the Scandalous Scoundrel, The Penthouse, Fire and Rain. Specials: Purlie, 'S Wonderful 'S Marvellous 'S Gershwin, John Grin's Christmas, Martin Luther King: A Look Back A Look Forward, Living the Dream: A Tribute to Dr. Martin Luther King Jr. (host), The Debbie Allen Special, Carol & Company, Sister Kate, Story of a People (host), Mastergate. Pilot: Driving Miss Daisy.
PICTURES: Super Fly T.N.T. (debut, 1973), Seems Like Old Times, Prince Jack, They Still Call Me Bruce, Wanted Dead or Alive, Lean On Me, Death Warrant, The Meteor Man, The Lion King (voice).

GUILLERMIN, JOHN: Director. b. London, England, Nov. 11, 1925. e. City of London Sch., Cambridge U. RAF pilot prior to entering film industry.
PICTURES: The Waltz of the Torreadors, Guns at Batasi, Rapture, The Blue Max, House of Cards, The Bridge of Remagen, El Condor, Skyjacked, Shaft in Africa, The Towering Inferno, King Kong, Death on the Nile, Mr. Patman, Sheena, King Kong Lives, The Favorite.
TELEVISION: Movie: The Tracker.

GUINNESS, SIR ALEC: Actor. b. London, Eng., April 2, 1914; e. Pembroke Lodge, Southbourne & Roborough Sch., Eastbourne. Created C.B.E. 1955; Knighted 1959. Stage debut: London, 1934. Theatre appearances in London, New York & Continent. Special Acad. Award, 1979, for services to film.
THEATER: includes: Libel! (walk-on debut, 1934), with John Gielgud's Co. (1937–38), Hamlet with Old Vic (1938–39), Great Expectations (own adapt.), Cousin Murial, The Tempest, Thunder Rock, Flare Path (NY), The Brothers Karamozov, Vicious Circle, The Cocktail Party (NY), The Prisoner, Hotel Paradiso, Ross, Exit the King, Dylan (NY, Tony Award), A Voyage Round My Father, Habeas Corpus, Yahoo, The Old Country, The Merchant of Venice, A Walk in the Woods.
PICTURES: Great Expectations (debut, 1946), Oliver Twist, Kind Hearts & Coronets, Run For Your Money, Last Holiday, The Mudlark, Lavender Hill Mob (Acad. Award nom.), The Man in the White Suit, The Card (The Promoter), Malta Story, Captain's Paradise, Father Brown (The Detective), To Paris with Love, The Prisoner, The Ladykillers, The Swan, The Bridge on the River Kwai (Academy Award, 1957), Barnacle Bill (All at Sea), The Horse's Mouth (also s.p.; Acad. Award nom. for s.p.), The Scapegoat, Our Man in Havana, Tunes of Glory, A Majority of One, H.M.S. Defiant (Damn the Defiant!), Lawrence of Arabia, The Fall of the Roman Empire, Situation Hopeless But Not Serious, Doctor Zhivago, Hotel Paradiso, The Quiller Memorandum, The Comedians, Cromwell, Scrooge, Brother Sun Sister Moon, Hitler: The Last Ten Days, Murder by Death, Star Wars (Acad. Award nom.), The Empire Strikes Back, Raise the Titanic!, Lovesick, Return of the Jedi, A Passage to India, A Handful of Dust, Little Dorrit (Acad. Award nom.), Kafka.
TELEVISION: The Wicked Scheme of Jebel Deeks (National Acad. nom.), Twelfth Night, Conversation at Night, Solo, E.E. Cummings, Little Gidding, The Gift of Friendship, Caesar and Cleopatra, Little Lord Fauntleroy, Tinker Tailor Soldier Spy (7-part series; BAFTA Award), Smiley's People (mini-series; BAFTA Award), Edwin, Monsignor Quixote, Tales From Hollywood.

GULAGER, CLU: Actor. b. Holdenville, OK, Nov. 16, 1928. Father, John Gulager, cowboy entertainer. e. Baylor U. Starred at school in original play, A Different Drummer, where spotted by prod. of TV's Omnibus; invited to New York to recreate role on TV.
PICTURES: The Killers, Winning, The Last Picture Show, Company of Killers, McQ, The Other Side of Midnight, A Force of One, Touched by Love, The Initiation, Lies, Into the Night, Prime Risk, The Return of the Living Dead, Hunter's Blood, The Hidden, Tapeheads, Uninvited, I'm Gonna Git You Sucka, Teen Vamp, My Heroes Have Always Been Cowboys.
TELEVISION: Series: The Tall Man, The Virginian, The Survivors, San Francisco International Airport, MacKenzies of Paradise Cove. Movies: San Francisco International, Glass House, Footsteps, Smile Jenny You're Dead, Houston We've Got a Problem, Hit Lady, Killer Who Wouldn't Die, Charlie Cobb: Nice Night for a Hanging, Ski Lift to Death, Sticking Together, A Question of Love, Willa, This Man Stands Alone, Kenny Rogers The Gambler, Skyward, Living Proof: The Hank Williams Jr. Story, Bridge Across Time. Mini-Series: Once an Eagle, Black Beauty, King, North and South II, Space.

GUMBEL, BRYANT: Announcer, News Show Host. b. New Orleans, LA, Sept. 29, 1948. e. Bates Coll. Started as writer for Black Sports Magazine, NY, 1971; sportscaster, then sports dir., KNBC, Los Angeles. Sports host NBC Sports NY 1975–82. Now host on Today Show, New York (Emmy Awards, 1976, 1977).
TELEVISION: Super Bowl games, '88 Olympics, Games People Play, The R.A.C.E.

GUMPERT, JON: Executive. e. Cornell U. Law Sch. Sr. v.p., business affairs, MGM/UA Entertainment; pres., World Film Services, Inc., indep. prod. co. in N.Y. 1985, named v.p., business affairs, Warner Bros; 1989 sr. v.p. Vista Films. Named sr. v.p. legal bus. affairs, Universal Pictures 1990.

GUNN, MOSES: Actor. b. St. Louis, MO, Oct. 2, 1929. e. Tennessee State U. Taught speech and drama at Grambling Coll. Came to N.Y. and first cast in off-Bdwy. prod. of Genet's The Blacks. Later joined Negro Ensemble Company.
PICTURES: What's So Bad About Feeling Good?, The Great White Hope, WUSA, Wild Rovers, Shaft, The Hot Rock, Shaft's Big Score, Eagle in a Cage, The Iceman Cometh, Amazing Grace, Rollerball, Aaron Loves Angela,

Cornbread Earl & Me, Remember My Name, Twinkle Twinkle Killer Kane, Ragtime, Amityville II: The Possession, Firestarter, The Never Ending Story, Certain Fury, Heartbreak Ridge, Leonard Part 6, The Luckiest Man in the World, Dixie Lanes.
STAGE: In White America, Day of Absence, Song of the Lusitanian Bogey, Summer of the 17th Doll, Daddy Goodness, Harvest, Titus Andronicus, Measure for Measure, Romeo and Juliet, The Tempest, As You Like It, Macbeth, Othello, A Hand Is on the Gate, Sty of the Blind Pig, The Poison Tree, First Breeze of Summer, King John.
TELEVISION: Series: The Cowboys, Good Times, The Contender, Father Murphy. Movies: Carter's Army, The Sheriff, Of Mice and Men, Haunts of the Very Rich, Law of the Land, Women of Brewster Place, Memphis. Mini-Series: Roots. Specials: First Breeze of Summer. Guest: Tales From the Crypt (Fitting Punishment), Hawaii Five-O, The FBI, Kung Fu.

GUNSBERG, SHELDON: Executive. b. Jersey City, NJ, Aug. 10, 1920. e. St. Peters Coll., New Jersey State Normal, NYU. With Night of Stars, Madison Sq. Garden, 1942; for. pub., 20th-Fox 1942; United Artists, 1945–47; Universal, roadshows. Rank product, asst. adv., pub. dir., 1947–54; v. pres., Walter Reade Theatres; exec. v.p. & dir., Walter Reade Org. 1962; Made chief operating officer, 1971; president, and Chief Executive Officer, 1973; chmn. & CEO, 1984. Member: Film Society of Lincoln Center: bd. of dirs. (1955–present), chmn., bldg. committee, Walter Reade Theatre (1986–92), exec. v.p (1987–90).

GURIAN, PAUL R.: Executive, Producer. b. New Haven, CT, Oct. 18, 1946. e. Lake Forest Coll., U. of Vienna, NYU. Started producing films in 1971 with Cats and Dogs, a dramatic short which won prizes at Chicago Int. Film Fest and Edinburgh Fest. In 1977 formed Gurian Entertainment Corp., to acquire film properties for production.
PICTURES: The Garden Party (PBS program), Profile Ricardo Alegria (short), Bernice Bobs Her Hair (shown at 1977 N.Y. Film Festival); Cutter and Bone; Peggy Sue Got Married, The Seventh Sign (exec. prod.).

GUTTENBERG, STEVE: Actor. b. Brooklyn, NY, Aug. 24, 1958. e. Sch. of Performing Arts, N.Y. Off-Bdwy. in The Lion in Winter; studied under John Houseman at Juilliard; classes with Lee Strasberg and Uta Hagen. Moved to West Coast in 1976; landed first TV role in movie, Something for Joey. Bdwy debut 1991 in Prelude to a Kiss.
PICTURES: Rollercoaster, The Chicken Chronicles, The Boys from Brazil, Players, Can't Stop the Music, Diner, The Man Who Wasn't There, Police Academy, Police Academy 2, Cocoon, Bad Medicine, Police Academy 3, Short Circuit, The Bedroom Window, Police Academy 4: Citizens on Patrol (also prod. assoc.), Amazon Women on the Moon, Surrender, Three Men and a Baby, High Spirits, Cocoon: The Return, Don't Tell Her It's Me, Three Men and a Little Lady.
TELEVISION: Guest: Police Story, Doc. Series: Billy, No Soap Radio. Movies: Something for Joey, To Race the Wind, Miracle on Ice, The Day After. Specials: Gangs (co-prod.), Pecos Bill: King of the Cowboys.

GWYNNE, FRED: Actor. b. New York, NY, July 10, 1926. e. Harvard U. Copywriter J. Walter Thompson 1955–60. On stage in Mrs. McThing, Irma La Douce, Twelfth Night, Texas Trilogy, The Lincoln Mask, Cat on a Hot Tin Roof, Winter's Tale, Arsenic and Old Lace, Whodunnit.
PICTURES: On the Waterfront (debut, 1954), Munster Go Home, Luna, Simon, So Fine, The Cotton Club, Off Beat, Water, The Boy Who Could Fly, The Secret of My Success, Fatal Attraction, Ironweed, Disorganized Crime, Pet Sematary, My Cousin Vinny, Shadows and Fog.
TELEVISION: Series: Car 54 Where Are You? (1961–63), The Munsters (1964–66). Specials: Harvey, The Hasty Heart, Arsenic and Old Lace, The Lesson, Dames at Sea, The Littlest Angel. Movies: Captains Courageous, Sanctuary of Fear, The Munsters' Revenge, Vanishing Act, The Christmas Star, Murder by the Book, Murder in Black and White. Mini-Series: Kane & Abel.
(Died: July 2, 1993)

H

HAAS, LUKAS: Actor. b. West Hollywood, CA, Apr. 16, 1976. Kindergarten school principal told casting dir. about him which resulted in film debut in Testament. NY stage debut in Mike Nichols' Lincoln Center production of Waiting for Godot (1988). Appeared in AFI film The Doctor.
PICTURES: Testament (debut, 1983), Witness, Solarbabies, Lady in White, The Wizard of Loneliness, See You in the Morning, Music Box, Rambling Rose, Convicts, Alan and Naomi, Leap of Faith.
TELEVISION: Movies: Love Thy Neighbor, Shattered Spirits, The Ryan White Story, The Perfect Tribute. Guest: Amazing Stories (Ghost Train), Twilight Zone, The Young

Indiana Jones Chronicles. *Pilot*: Brothers-in-Law. *Specials*: A Place at the Table, My Dissident Mom, Peacemaker (Triple Play II).

HABER, JOYCE: Writer, syndicated Hollywood columnist. r.n. Mrs. Joyce Haber Cramer. b. New York, NY, Dec. 28, 1932. e. Brearley Sch., N.Y., class of 1948; Bryn Mawr Coll., 1949–50, cum laude list; Barnard Coll., B.A., 1953. Researcher, Time magazine, 1953–63; Hollywood Reporter, L.A. Bureau Time, 1963–66; Columnist, Los Angeles Times, 1966–75; contributing editor, Los Angeles Magazine, 1977–80. Published Caroline's Doll Book, illus. by R. Taylor, 1962. freelance writing: Esquire, Herald Tribune's New York Magazine, Harper's Bazaar, New York Magazine, Town and Country. Published The Users, a novel, 1976.

HACK, SHELLEY: Actress. b. Greenwich, CT, July 6, 1952. e. Smith Coll. and U. of Sydney, Australia. Made modeling debut at 14 on cover of Glamour Magazine. Gained fame as Revlon's Charlie Girl on TV commercials.
PICTURES: Annie Hall, If Ever I See You Again, Time After Time, The King of Comedy, Troll, The Stepfather, Blind Fear, Me Myself and I, The Finishing Touch.
TELEVISION: *Series*: Charlie's Angels, Cutter to Houston, Jack and Mike, Seaquest. *Movies*: Death on the Freeway, Trackdown: Finding the Goodbar Killer, Found Money, Single Bars Single Women, Bridesmaids, Casualty of War, Taking Back My Life: The Nancy Ziegenmeyer Story, Not in My Family.

HACKER, CHARLES R.: Executive. b. Milwaukee, WI, Oct. 8, 1920. e. U. of Wisconsin. Thea. mgr., Fox Wisc. Amuse. Corp., 1940; served in U.S.A.F., 1943–45; rejoined Fox Wisconsin Amusement Corp.; joined Standard Theatres Management Corp. 1947, on special assignments; apptd. district mgr. of Milwaukee & Waukesha theatres 1948; joined Radio City Music Hall Corp. as administrative asst. July, 1948; mgr. of oper., 1952; asst. to the pres., Feb. 1957; v.p., Radio City Music Hall Corp., 1964; appointed executive vice president and chief operating officer, February 1, 1973. Pres., Landmark Pictures, May, 1979. Elected treas. Will Rogers Memorial Fund, 1978. Award: Quigley Silver Grand Award for Showmanship, 1947. Member: U.S. Small Business Admin. Region 1, Hartford Advisory Council since 1983.

HACKETT, BUDDY: Actor, Comedian. r.n. Leonard Hacker. b. Brooklyn, NY, Aug. 31, 1924. Prof. debut, borscht circuit.
TELEVISION: *Series*: School House, Stanley, Jackie Gleason Show, Jack Paar Show, You Bet Your Life (1980), Fish Police (voice). *Movie*: Bud and Lou.
THEATRE: *Bdwy*: Call Mr. Mister, Lunatics and Lovers, I Had a Ball.
PICTURES: Walking My Baby Back Home, Fireman Save My Child, God's Little Acre, Everything's Ducky, All Hands on Deck, The Music Man, The Wonderful World of Brothers Grimm, It's a Mad Mad Mad Mad World, Muscle Beach Party, The Good Guys and the Bad Guys (cameo), The Love Bug, Loose Shoes, Scrooged, The Little Mermaid (voice).

HACKFORD, TAYLOR: Director, Producer. b. Santa Barbara, CA, Dec. 31, 1944. e. USC, B.A. (international relations). Was Peace Corps volunteer in Bolivia 1968–69. Began career with KCET in Los Angeles 1970–77. As prod.-dir. won Oscar for short, Teenage Father, 1978. Theatrical film debut as director with The Idolmaker (1980).
PICTURES: *Director*: The Idolmaker, An Officer and a Gentleman, Against All Odds (also co-prod.), White Nights (also co-prod.), Chuck Berry: Hail! Hail! Rock 'n' Roll, Everyone's All-American (also co-prod.), Bound By Honor (also prod.). *Prod.*: La Bamba, Exec. Prod.: Rooftops, The Long Walk Home, Sweet Talker, Queens Logic, Defenseless, Mortal Thoughts.

HACKMAN, GENE: Actor. b. San Bernardino, CA, Jan. 30, 1930. First major broadway role in Any Wednesday. Other stage productions include: Poor Richard, Children from Their Games, A Rainy Day in Newark, The Natural Look, Death and the Maiden. Formed own production co., Chelly Ltd.
PICTURES: Mad Dog Coll (debut, 1961), Lilith, Hawaii, A Covenant With Death, Bonnie and Clyde (Acad. Award nom.), First to Fight, Banning, The Split, Riot, The Gypsy Moths, Downhill Racer, Marooned, I Never Sang for My Father (Acad. Award nom.), Doctors' Wives, The Hunting Party, The French Connection (Acad. Award, 1971), Cisco Pike, Prime Cut, The Poseidon Adventure, Scarecrow, The Conversation, Zandy's Bride, Young Frankenstein, Night Moves, Bite the Bullet, French Connection II, Lucky Lady, The Domino Principle, A Bridge Too Far, March or Die, Superman, All Night Long, Superman II, Reds, Eureka, Under Fire, Uncommon Valor, Misunderstood, Target, Twice in a Lifetime, Power, Hoosiers, Superman IV, No Way Out, Another Woman, Bat-21, Split Decisions, Full Moon in Blue Water, Mississippi Burning (Acad. Award nom.), The Package, Loose Cannons, Postcards From the Edge, Narrow Margin, Class Action, Company Business, Unforgiven (Acad. Award, Natl. Soc. of Film Critics, NY Film Critics, BAFTA, LA Film Critics &

Golden Globe Awards for best supp. actor, 1992), The Firm, Geronimo.
TELEVISION: *Guest*: U.S. Steel Hour, The Defenders, Trials of O'Brien, Hawk, CBS Playhouse's My Father My Mother, The F.B.I., The Invaders, The Iron Horse. *Movie*: Shadow on the Land.

HADLOCK, CHANNING M.: Marketing. TV Executive. b. Mason City, IA. e. Duke U., U. of North Carolina. Newspaperman, Durham, NC Herald, war corr., Yank; NBC, Hollywood; television prod.-writer, Cunningham & Walsh Adv.; v.p. account supr. Chirug & Cairns Adv.; v.p. Marketing Innovations; dir. mktg. Paramount Pictures; mktg. svcs, Ogilvy & Mather; mktg, Time Life Books.

HAGERTY, JULIE: Actress. b. Cincinnati, OH, June 15, 1955. Studied drama for six years before leaving for NY where studied with William Hickey. Made acting debut in her brother Michael's theatre group in Greenwich Village called the Production Company.
THEATER: The Front Page (Lincoln Center), The House of Blue Leaves (Theatre World Award, 1986), Wild Life, Born Yesterday (Phil. Drama Guild), The Years, Three Men on a Horse.
PICTURES: Airplane! (debut, 1980), A Midsummer Night's Sex Comedy, Airplane II: The Sequel, Lost in America, Goodbye New York, Bad Medicine, Beyond Therapy, Aria, Bloodhounds of Broadway, Rude Awakening, Reversal of Fortune, What About Bob?, Noises Off.
TELEVISION: *Series*: Princesses. *Specials*: The Visit (Trying Times). House of Blue Leaves, Necessary Parties. *Movie*: The Day the Women Got Even.

HAGGAR, PAUL: Executive. Veteran of over 40 yrs. with Paramount Pictures, working way up from studio mail room to become apprentice editor in 1953; promoted to asst. editor 1955; music editor, 1957. In 1968 named head of post-prod. for all films and TV made by Paramount. 1985, named sr. v.p., post-prod. for Studio Group.

HAGGARD, PIERS: Director. b. Scotland, 1939. e. U. of Edinburgh. Son of actor Stephen Haggard; great grandnephew of author Rider Haggard. Began career in theatre in 1960 as asst. to artistic dir. at London's Royal Court. Named director of Glasgow Citizens' Theatre. 1963–65 worked with the National Theatre, where co-directed Hobson's Choice and The Dutch Courtesan. Has directed many prize winning TV commercials.
PICTURES: Wedding Night, Blood on Satan's Claw, Quatermass Conclusion, The Fiendish Plot of Dr. Fu Manchu, Venom, A Summer Story.
TELEVISION: Pennies from Heaven, Quatermass, A Triple Play: Sam Found Out, The Fulfillment of Mary Gray, Back Home, Chester Cycle of Mystery Plays, Mrs. Reinhardt, Knockback, Return to Treasure Island, Visitors, Centrepoint, I'll Take Romance, Four Eyes and Six-Guns.

HAGMAN, LARRY: Actor. b. Fort Worth, TX, Sept. 21, 1931. e. Bard Coll. Son of late actress Mary Martin. First stage experience with Margo Jones Theatre in the Round in Dallas. Appeared in N.Y. in Taming of the Shrew; one year with London production of South Pacific. 1952–56 was in London with US Air Force where produced and directed show for servicemen. Returned to N.Y. for plays on and off Bdwy: God and Kate Murphy (Theatre World Award), The Nervous Set, The Warm Peninsula, The Beauty Part. Starred in daytime serial, Edge of Night, for over 2 years.
PICTURES: Ensign Pulver, Fail Safe, In Harm's Way, The Group, The Cavern, Up in the Cellar, Beware! The Blob (also dir.), Harry and Tonto, Stardust, Mother Jugs and Speed, The Big Bus, The Eagle Has Landed, Checkered Flag or Crash, Superman, S.O.B.
TELEVISION: *Series*: The Edge of Night, I Dream of Jeannie, The Good Life, Here We Go Again, Dallas, Staying Afloat. *Movies*: Three's a Crowd, Vanished, A Howling in the Woods, Getting Away from It All, No Place to Run, The Alpha Caper, Blood Sport, What Are Best Friends For?, Sidekicks, Hurricane, Sarah T.—Portrait of a Teenage Alcoholic, The Big Rip-Off, Return of the World's Greatest Detective, Intimate Strangers, The President's Mistress, Last of the Good Guys, Deadly Encounter. *Special*: Applause.

HAHN, HELENE: Executive. b. New York, NY. e. Loyola U. Instructor of entertainment law at Loyola. Attorney for ABC before joining Paramount in 1977 in studio legal dept. 1979, moved to business affairs; promoted to dir. 1980, v.p., 1981; sr. v.p., 1983. Left in 1985 to join Walt Disney Pictures as sr. v.p., business & legal affairs for m.p. division. 1987, promoted to exec. v.p., Walt Disney Studios.

HAID, CHARLES: Actor, Director, Producer. b. San Francisco, CA, June 2, 1943. e. Carnegie Tech. Appeared on NY stage in Elizabeth the First. Co-produced Godspell. Prod. & dir. short film The Last Supper.
TELEVISION: *Series*: Kate McShane, Delvecchio, Hill Street Blues, Cop Rock (prod. only). *Movies*: The Execution

of Private Slovik, Remember When, Things in Their Season, Kate McShane (pilot), Foster and Laurie, A Death in Canaan, The Bastard, Death Moon, Twirl, Divorce Wars, Children in the Crossfire (also co-prod.), Code of Vengeance, Six Against the Rock, Weekend War, The Great Escape II: The Untold Story, A Deadly Silence, Fire and Rain, Man Against the Mob: The Chinatown Murders, In the Line of Duty: A Cop for the Killing (also co-prod.), In the Line of Duty: Siege at Marion (dir. only), The Nightman (dir., prod. only), Cooperstown (also dir.), For Their Own Good, The Fire Next Time.
PICTURES: The Choirboys, Who'll Stop the Rain, Oliver's Story, House of God, Altered States, Square Dance (co-exec. prod. only), Cop, The Rescue, Nightbreed, Storyville.

HAIM, COREY: Actor. b. Toronto, Canada, Dec. 23, 1972. Performed in TV commercials at 10; signed as regular on children's show, The Edison Twins.
PICTURES: Firstborn (debut, 1984), Secret Admirer, Silver Bullet, Murphy's Romance, Lucas, The Lost Boys, License to Drive, Watchers, Dream a Little Dream, Fast Getaway, Prayer of the Roller Boys, The Dream Machine, Oh What a Night, Blown Away, The Double-O Kid, National Lampoon's Scuba School.
TELEVISION: Movie: A Time to Live. Series: Roomies.

HAIMOVITZ, JULES: Executive. b. New York, NY, 1951. e. Brooklyn Coll., B.A., M.A., theoretical mathematics. Worked at ABC-TV in operations and audience research before joining Viacom International for 11 years finally as pres. of Viacom Networks Group with responsibility for Showtime/The Movie Channel, MTV and other pay TV networks. Sept. 1987, named pres. and COO, Aaron Spelling Productions, Inc.

HALE, BARBARA: Actress. b. DeKalb, IL, April 18, 1922. Was married to late actor Bill Williams. Son is actor William Katt. e. Chicago Acad. of Fine Arts. Beauty contest winner, Little Theatre actress. Screen debut, 1943.
PICTURES: Gildersleeve's Bad Day, The Seventh Victim, Higher and Higher, Belle of the Yukon, The Falcon Out West, Falcon in Hollywood, Heavenly Days, West of the Pecos, First Yank in Tokyo, Lady Luck, A Likely Story, Boy with Green Hair, The Clay Pigeon, Window, Jolson Sings Again, And Baby Makes Three, Emergency Wedding, Jackpot, Lorna Doone, First Time, Last of the Comanches, Seminole, Lone Hand, A Lion Is in the Streets, Unchained, Far Horizons, Houston Story, 7th Cavalry, Oklahoman, Slim Carter, Desert Hell, Buckskin, Airport, Soul Soldier, Giant Spider Invasion, Big Wednesday.
TELEVISION: Series: Perry Mason (Emmy Award, 1959). Movies: Perry Mason Returns (1985) and other Perry Mason's incl. The Case of the . . . Murdered Madam, Avenging Ace, Lady in the Lake, Scandalous Scoundrel, Lethal Lesson, Poisoned Pen, Fatal Fashion, Reckless Romeo.

HALEY, JR., JACK: Executive, Director. b. Los Angeles, CA, Oct. 25, 1933. e. Loyola U. Son of late actor Jack Haley. 1959–67 Wolper Prods., 1967–73. sr. v.p. at Wolper before joining MGM. Named dir. of creative affairs. Left in 1974, to join 20th Century-Fox as pres. of TV div. and v.p., TV for 20th-Fox Film Corp. Winner of 2 Peabody Awards, best prod. at Int'l. TV Festival at Monte Carlo and 3 Silver Lion Awards at Venice Film Festival. Won Emmy for best dir. in music or variety shows for Movin' On with Nancy. Directed M.P. Academy Awards Show in 1970; prod. it in 1974 and 1979. Left Fox 1976 to be indep. prod.
PICTURES: Director: Norwood, The Love Machine, That's Entertainment (also prod, s.p.), Better Late Than Never (prod. only), That's Dancing (also co-prod., s.p.).
TELEVISION: The Incredible World of James Bond, The Legend of Marilyn Monroe, The Supremes, The Hidden World, Movin' with Nancy (Emmy, dir., 1968), With Love Sophia, Monte Carlo, Life Goes to War: Hollywood and the Homefront; Heroes of Rock n' Roll (exec. prod.), 51st Academy Awards (Emmy, 1979), Hollywood, the Golden Years (with David Wolper), Ripley's Believe It or Not, The Night They Saved Christmas, Cary Grant: A Celebration (exec. prod.).

HALL, ANTHONY MICHAEL: Actor. b. Boston, MA, Apr. 14, 1968.
PICTURES: Six Pack (debut, 1982), National Lampoon's Vacation, Sixteen Candles, The Breakfast Club, Weird Science, Out of Bounds, Johnny Be Good, Edward Scissorhands, A Gnome Named Norm, Into the Sun, Six Degrees of Separation.
TELEVISION: Series: Saturday Night Live (1985–6). Movies: Rascals and Robbers: The Secret Adventures of Tom Sawyer and Huck Finn, Running Out.

HALL, ARSENIO: Actor, Comedian. b. Cleveland, OH. Feb. 12, 1959. e. Kent State U. Became interested in magic at 7, which later led to own local TV special, The Magic of Christmas. Switched from advertising career to stand-up comedy, 1979. Discovered at Chicago nightclub by singer Nancy Wilson.
PICTURES: Amazon Women on the Moon (debut, 1987), Coming to America, Harlem Nights.

TELEVISION: Series: The 1/2 Hour Comedy Hour (1983, co-host), Thicke of the Night, Motown Revue, The Late Show (1987, host), The Arsenio Hall Show, The Party Machine With Nia Peeples (prod. only).

HALL, CONRAD: Cinematographer. b. Tahiti, June 21, 1926. Worked as camera operator with Robert Surtees, Ted McCord, Ernest Haller; moved to TV as director of photography before feature films.
PICTURES: Wild Seed, The Saboteur—Code Name Morituri, Harper, The Professionals, Rogue's Gallery, Incubus, Divorce American Style, In Cold Blood, Cool Hand Luke, Hell in the Pacific, Butch Cassidy and the Sundance Kid (Acad. Award), Tell Them Willie Boy Is Here, The Happy Ending, Fat City, Electra-Glide in Blue, The Day of the Locust, Smile, Marathon Man, Black Widow, Tequila Sunrise, Class Action, Jennifer Eight, Searching for Bobby Fischer.
TELEVISION: It Happened One Christmas.

HALL, HUNTZ (HENRY): Actor. b. Boston, MA, 1920. In 1937 appeared in stage and screen production Dead End.
PICTURES: Crime School, Angels with Dirty Faces, They Made Me a Criminal, Hell's Kitchen, Muggs Rides Again, Live Wires, A Walk in the Sun, Jinx Money, Smuggler's Cove, Fighting Fools, Blues Busters, Bowery Battalion, Ghost Chasers, Crazy Over Horses, Let's Go Navy, Here Come the Marines, Hold That Line, Feudin' Fools, No Holds Barred, Private Eyes, Paris Playboys, Bowery Boys Meet the Monsters, Clipped Wings, Jungle Gents, Bowery to Bagdad, High Society, Spy Chasers, Jail Busters, Dig That Uranium, Up in Smoke, Second Fiddle to a Steel Guitar, Gentle Giant, The Phynx, Herbie Rides Again, The Manchu Eagle Murder Caper Mystery, Won Ton Ton the Dog Who Saved Hollywood, Valentino, Gas Pump Girls, Cyclone.
TELEVISION: Series: The Chicago Teddy Bears. Movie: Escape. Guest: Barefoot in the Park, Diff'rent Strokes, Night Heat.

HALMI, ROBERT SR.: Producer: b. Budapest, Hungary, Jan 22, 1924. Originally writer-photographer under contract to Life Magazine.
PICTURES: Documentaries for U.N. Features include: Hugo the Hippo, Visit to a Chief's Son, The One and Only, Brady's Escape, Cheetah, Mr. and Mrs. Bridge.
TELEVISION: Bold Journey (dir.-cin.), American Sportsman, The Oriental Sportsman, The Flying Doctor, The Outdoorsman, Julius Boros Series, Rexford, Who Needs Elephants, Calloway's Climb, Oberndorf Revisited, True Position, Wilson's Reward, Nurse, Buckley Sails, A Private Battle, My Old Man, Mr. Griffin and Me, When the Circus Came to Town, Best of Friends, Bush Doctor, Peking Encounter, Svengali, China Rose, Cook and Peary—The Race to the Pole, Terrible Joe Moran, Nairobi Affair, The Night They Saved Christmas, Spies, Lies and Naked Thighs, exec. prod.: The Prize Pulitzer, Paradise, Bridesmaids, Face to Face, Margaret Bourke-White, The Incident, Josephine Baker Story, The Secret, An American Story, Call of the Wild, Blind Spot.

HALSTROM, LASSE: Director. b. Sweden, 1946. Began career filming and editing inserts for Swedish TV. Directed program Shall We Dance? for Danish TV.
PICTURES: A Love and His Lass, ABBA: The Movie, Father-to-Be, The Rooster, Happy We, The Children of Bullerby Village, More About the Children, My Life as a Dog, Once Around (U.S. debut, 1991).

HAMADY, RON: Producer. b. Flint, MI, June 16, 1947. e. U. of California, B.A. 1971. Co-founder of The Crystal Jukebox, record productions, music management and music publishing co. Produced 12 hit albums for Decca Records of England and London Records, U.S. Entered m.p. industry in 1975–76, producing Train Ride to Hollywood for Taylor-Laughlin dist. Co.
PICTURES: Fade to Black, Surf II, And God Created Woman (1987), Out Cold, Don't Tell Her It's Me.

HAMEL, VERONICA: Actress. b. Philadelphia, PA, Nov. 20, 1943. e. Temple U. Moved to NY and began a modelling career with Eileen Ford Agency. Off B'way debut: The Big Knife. Acted in dinner theater prods. Moved to L.A. 1975.
PICTURES: Cannonball, Beyond the Poseidon Adventure, When Time Ran Out, A New Life, Taking Care of Business.
TELEVISION: Movies: The Gathering, Ski Lift to Death, The Gathering II, The Hustler of Muscle Beach, Valley of the Dolls, Sessions, Twist of Fate, She Said No, Stop at Nothing, Deadly Medicine (also co-exec. prod.), Baby Snatcher (also co-exec. prod.), The Disappearance of Nora. Mini-Series: 79 Park Avenue, Kane & Abel. Series: Hill Street Blues. Guest: Kojak, Rockford Files, Bob Newhart Show, Switch.

HAMILL, MARK: Actor. b. Oakland, CA, Sept. 25, 1952.
PICTURES: Star Wars (debut, 1977), Wizards (voice), Corvette Summer, The Empire Strikes Back, The Big Red One, The Night the Lights Went Out in Georgia, Britannia Hospital, Return of the Jedi, Slipstream, Midnight Ride, Black

Magic Woman, Time Runner, The Guyver, Sleepwalkers (cameo).
TELEVISION: Series: General Hospital, The Texas Wheelers, Batman (voice). Movies: Sarah T.—Portrait of a Teenage Alcoholic, Eric, Delancey Street: The Crisis Within, Mallory: Circumstantial Evidence, The City, Earth Angel, Body Bags. Guest: Room 222, The Partridge Family, Headmaster, Medical Center, Owen Marshall, The FBI, Streets of San Francisco, One Day at a Time, Manhunter, Hooperman, Alfred Hitchcock Presents, Amazing Stories, The Flash.
THEATRE: NY: The Elephant Man (Bdwy debut), Amadeus (also Natl. tour), Harrigan 'n' Hart, Room Service (off-Bdwy), The Nerd.

HAMILL, PETE: Journalist, Writer. b. Brooklyn, NY, June 24, 1935. Worked as ad designer, NBC page boy and sheet metal worker before joining staff of New York Post. In 1962 won Mike Berger Award of Columbia U. Graduate Sch. of Journalism for N.Y.'s worst slum. Received citation from Newspaper Reporters' Assn. for series on N.Y. Police Dept.
PICTURES: Doc, Death at an Early Age, Badge 373.
TELEVISION: Laguna Heat, The Neon Empire. Adaptations of his novels Flesh and Blood, The Gift.
BOOKS: A Killing for Christ (novel), Irrational Ravings (collection of N.Y. Post columns), The Seventeenth Christmas (novel), The Invisible City: A NY Sketchbook.

HAMILTON, GEORGE: Actor. b. Memphis, TN, Aug. 12, 1939. e. grammar, Hawthorne, CA; military sch., Gulfport, MS, N.Y. Hackley Prep Sch., FL, Palm Beach H.S. Won Best Actor Award for the state of Florida, high sch. contest.
TELEVISION: Guest: Rin Tin Tin, The Donna Reed Show. Special: The Veil. Mini-Series: Roots. Movies: Two Fathers' Justice, Monte Carlo, Poker Alice, Caution: Murder Can Be Hazardous to Your Health, The House on Sycamore Street. Series: The Survivors, Paris 7000, Dynasty, Spies.
PICTURES: Crime and Punishment USA (debut, 1959), Home from the Hill, All The Fine Young Cannibals, Where the Boys Are, Angel Baby, By Love Possessed, A Thunder of Drums, Light in the Piazza, Two Weeks in Another Town, Act One, The Victors, Looking for Love, Your Cheatin' Heart, Viva Maria, That Man George, Doctor You've Got to Be Kidding!, Jack of Diamonds, A Time for Killing, The Power, Togetherness, Evel Knievel, The Man Who Loved Cat Dancing, Once Is Not Enough, The Happy Hooker Goes to Washington, Love at First Bite (also exec. prod.), Sextette, From Hell to Victory, Zorro the Gay Blade (also co-prod.), The Godfather Part III, Doc Hollywood, Once Upon a Crime.

HAMILTON, GUY: Director. b. Paris, France, Sept. 24, 1922. Ent. m.p. industry 1939 as apprentice at Victorine Studio, Nice; Royal Navy, 1940–45, in England asst. dir., Fallen Idol, Third Man, Outcast of the Islands, African Queen.
PICTURES: The Ringer, The Intruder, An Inspector Calls, Colditz Story, Manuela, The Devil's Disciple, A Touch of Larceny, The Best of Enemies, The Party's Over, Man in the Middle, Goldfinger, Funeral in Berlin, Battle of Britain, Diamonds Are Forever, Live and Let Die, The Man with the Golden Gun, Force Ten from Navarone, The Mirror Crack'd, Evil Under the Sun, Remo Williams.

HAMILTON, LINDA: Actress. b. Salisbury, MD, Sept. 26, 1956. Appeared on NY stage in Looice and Richard III.
TELEVISION: Series: Secrets of Midland Heights, King's Crossing, Beauty and the Beast. Movies: Reunion, Rape and Marriage—The Rideout Case, Country Gold, Secrets of a Mother and Daughter, Secret Weapons, Club Med, Go Toward the Light. Guest: Hill Street Blues, Murder She Wrote.
PICTURES: Tag: The Assassination Game, Children of the Corn, The Stone Boy, The Terminator, Black Moon Rising, King Kong Lives!, Mr. Destiny, Terminator 2: Judgment Day.

HAMLIN, HARRY: Actor. b. Pasadena, CA, Oct. 30, 1951. e. U. of California, Yale U., 1974 in theatre, psychology. Awarded IT&T Fulbright Grant, 1977. Joined American Conservatory Theatre, San Francisco, for two years' study before joining McCarter Theatre, Princeton (Hamlet, Faustus in Hell.) Bdwy debut Awake and Sing! (1984).
PICTURES: Movie Movie (debut, 1978), King of the Mountain, Clash of the Titans, Making Love, Blue Skies Again, Maxie.
TELEVISION: Mini-series: Studs Lonigan, Master of the Game, Space, Favorite Son. Movies: Laguna Heat, Deceptions, Deadly Intentions . . . Again?, Deliver Them From Evil: The Taking of Alta View, Poisoned By Love: The Kern County Murders. Series: L.A. Law.

HAMLISCH, MARVIN: Composer. b. New York, NY, June 2, 1944. e. Juilliard. Accompanist and straight man on tour with Groucho Marx 1974–75; debut as concert pianist 1975 with Minn. Orch. Scores of Broadway shows: A Chorus Line (Tony Award); They're Playing Our Song, Smile, The Goodbye Girl. Winner 4 Grammy Awards.
PICTURES: The Swimmer (1968), Take the Money and Run, Bananas, Save the Tiger, Kotch, The Way We Were (2 Acad. Awards for orig. score and title song, 1973), The Sting

(Acad. Award for music adapt., 1973), The Spy Who Loved Me, Same Time Next Year, Ice Castles, Chapter Two, Seems Like Old Times, Starting Over, Ordinary People, The Fan, Sophie's Choice, I Ought to Be in Pictures, Romantic Comedy, D.A.R.Y.L., Three Men and a Baby, Little Nikita, The January Man, The Experts, Frankie and Johnny.
TELEVISION: Series: Good Morning, America (theme), Brooklyn Bridge. Movies: The Entertainer (also prod.), A Streetcar Named Desire, The Two Mrs. Grenvilles, Women & Men: Stories of Seduction, Switched at Birth.

HAMMOND, PETER: Actor, Writer, Director. b. London, Eng., Nov. 15, 1923. e. Harrow Sch. of Art. Stage debut: Landslide, Westminster Theatre. Screen debut: Holiday Camp.
PICTURES: The Huggetts, Helter Skelter, Fools Rush In, The Reluctant Widow, Fly Away Peter, The Adventurers, Operation Disaster, Come Back, Peter, Little Lambs Eat Ivy, Its Never Too Late, The Unknown, Morning Departure. Confession, dir.: Spring and Port Wine.
TELEVISION: William Tell, Robin Hood, The Buccaneers series. 1959–61. writ., dir. TV plays. Dir.: Avengers, 4 Armchair Theatres, Theatre 625, BBC classic serials Count of Monte Cristo, Three Musketeers, Hereward the Wake, Treasure Island, Lord Raingo, Cold Comfort Farm, The White Rabbit, Out of the Unknown, Follyfoot; Lukes Kingdom, Time to Think, Franklin's Farm, Sea Song, Shades of Greene, Our Mutual Friend, The House that Jack Built, The King of the Castle, The Black Knight, Kilvert's Diary, Turgenev's Liza, Wuthering Heights, Funnyman, Little World of Don Camillo, Rumpole of the Bailey, Bring on the Girls, Hallelujah Mary Plum, Aubrey Beardsley, The Happy Autumn Fields, The Combination, Tales of the Unexpected, The Glory Hole, The Hard Word, Shades of Darkness—The Maze, The Blue Dress.

HAMNER, EARL: Producer, Writer. b. Schuyler, VA, July 10, 1923. e. U. of Richmond 1940–43, Northwestern U.; U of Cincinnati, Coll. Conservatory of Music, B.F.A., 1958. With WLW, Cincinnati, as radio writer-producer; joined NBC 1949 as writer; (The Georgia Gibbs Show, The Helen O'Connell Show); freelance 1961–71; writer, prod. Lorimar Prods. 1971–86; writer prod. Taft Ent. 1986–; Pres. Amanda Prods.
PICTURES: Palm Springs Weekend, Spencer's Mountain, Chitty Chitty Bang Bang, The Tamarind Seed, Charlotte's Web (adaptor), Where the Lilies Bloom.
TELEVISION: Exec. prod.: Series: The Waltons (creator, co-prod., narrator), Apple's Way (creator), The Young Pioneers (creator); Joshua's World, Falcon Crest; Boone (also creator), Morning Star/Evening Star (also narrator), Movies: The Homecoming: A Christmas Story (s.p. only), You Can't Get There From Here (s.p. only), A Wedding on Walton's Mountain; Mother's Day on Walton's Mountain, A Day of Thanks on Walton's Mountain (exec. prod. actor), The Gift of Love—A Christmas Story (exec. prod., s.p.).

HAMPSHIRE, SUSAN: Actress. b. London, Eng., May 12, 1941.
STAGE: Expresso Bongo, Follow That Girl, Fairy Tales of New York, Ginger Man, Past Imperfect, She Stoops to Conquer, On Approval, The Sleeping Prince, A Doll's House, Taming of the Shrew, Peter Pan, Romeo & Jeanette, As You Like It, Miss Julie, The Circle, Arms and the Man, Man and Superman, Tribades, An Audience Called Edward, The Crucifer of Blood, Night and Day, The Revolt, House Guest, Blithe Spirit, Married Love, A Little Night Music, The King and I, Noel & Gertie, Relative Values.
TELEVISION: Andromeda, The Forsyte Saga, Vanity Fair, Katy, The First Churchills; An Ideal Husband, The Lady Is a Liar, The Improbable Mr. Clayville, musical version of Dr. Jekyll and Mr. Hyde, The Pallisers, Barchester Chronicles, Leaving, Leaving II, Going to Pot (I, II, and III), Don't Tell Father.
PICTURES: The Three Lives of Thomasina, Night Must Fall, Wonderful Life, Paris Au Mois d'Aout, The Fighting Prince of Donegal, The Trygon Factor, Monte Carlo or Bust, Rogan, David Copperfield, A Room in Paris, Living Free, Time for Loving, Malpertius, Baffled, Neither the Sea nor the Sand, Roses and Green Peppers, David the King, Bang.

HAMPTON, JAMES: Actor. b. Oklahoma City, OK, July 9, 1936. e. N. Tx. St. Univ.
TELEVISION: Series: F Troop, The Doris Day Show, Love—American Style, Mary, Maggie. Movies: Attack on Terror: The FBI Versus the Ku Klux Klan, Force Five, The Amazing Howard Hughes, Three on a Date, Thaddeus Rose and Eddie, Stand By Your Man, Through the Magic Pyramid, World War III, The Burning Bed. Mini-Series: Centennial.
PICTURES: Fade In, Soldier Blue, The Man Who Loved Cat Dancing, The Longest Yard, W.W. & The Dixie Dancekings, Hustle, Hawmps!, The Cat from Outer Space, Mackintosh & T.J., The China Syndrome, Hangar 18, Condorman, Teen Wolf, Teen Wolf Too, Police Academy 5, Pump Up the Volume, The Giant of Thunder Mountain.

HANCOCK, JOHN: Director. b. Kansas City, MO, Feb. 12, 1939. e. Harvard. Was musician and theatre director before turning to films. Dir. play A Man's a Man, NY 1962. Artistic dir. San

Francisco Actors Workshop 1965–66, Pittsburgh Playhouse 1966–67. Obie for dir. Midsummer Night's Dream, NY 1968. Nominated for AA for short, Sticky My Fingers, Fleet My Feet.
PICTURES: Let's Scare Jessica to Death, Bang the Drum Slowly, Baby Blue Marine, California Dreaming, Weeds (also co-s.p.), Prancer.
TELEVISION: The Twilight Zone (1986), Hill Street Blues.

HAND, BETHLYN J.: Executive. b. Alton, IL. e. U. of Texas. Entered motion picture industry in 1966 as administrative assistant to president of Motion Picture Association of America, Inc. In 1975 became associate director of advertising administration of MPAA. In 1976 became director of advertising administration; in 1979 became; v.p.—west coast activities, board of directors, Los Angeles. S.P.C.A. 1981, appointed by Governor to Calif. Motion Picture Council 1983, elected vice chmn., California Motion Picture Council. 1990, named sr. v.p. MPAA.

HANDEL, LEO A.: Producer. b. Vienna, Austria, Mar. 7, 1924. e.Univ. of Vienna (phd. economics). Dir. audience research, MGM, 1942–51; organized Meteor Prod., 1951; organized Leo A. Handel Prod., for TV films, 1953; author, Hollywood Looks at Its Audience, also TV plays; pres., Handel Film Corp. Exec. prod. & v.p., Four Crown Prods., Inc. Prod.-writer-dir., feature film, The Case of Patty Smith, 1961; book, A Dog Named Duke, 1965.
TELEVISION: prod. TV series including Everyday Adventures, Magic of the Atom. exec. prod., Phantom Planet, Americana Series, Specials, Age of the Atom; Sweden-Vikings Now Style, Benjamin Franklin, The Mexican American Heritage and Destiny, The American Indian, Police Dog, Art in America (10 half-hour films), Stress-Distress, Computer and You, Thailand, The Philippines, Germ Wars, Measuring Things, Safety for Seniors, The Dropouts; Singapore—Crossroad of the Orient, Black American Odyssey, Puerto Rico—Progress in the Caribbean, Nuclear Power Production (1988), Trees and Our Environment, Trees and Their Anatomy, Water: The Eternal Cycle, Food Safety, Malaysia, Food Safety, Recycle Me!, The Five Food Groups.

HANKS, TOM: Actor. b. Concord, CA, July 9, 1956. m. actress Rita Wilson. Traveled around Northern CA. with family before settling in Oakland, CA. e. Chabot Jr. Col., California State U. Began career with Great Lakes Shakespeare Festival, Cleveland (3 seasons) and NY's Riverside Theater (Taming of the Shrew).
PICTURES: He Knows You're Alone (debut, 1980), Splash, Bachelor Party, The Man with One Red Shoe, Volunteers, The Money Pit, Nothing in Common, Every Time We Say Goodbye, Dragnet, Big (Acad. Award nom.), Punchline, The 'Burbs, Turner and Hooch, Joe Versus the Volcano, The Bonfire of the Vanities, Radio Flyer (unbilled), A League of Their Own, Sleepless in Seattle, Philadelphia.
TELEVISION: Series: Bosom Buddies. Guest: The Love Boat, Taxi, Happy Days, Family Ties, Saturday Night Live, Tales From the Crypt (None but the Lonely Heart; also dir.), Fallen Angels (I'll Be Waiting; also dir.). Movie: Rona Jaffe's Mazes and Monsters. Episode Dir:. A League of Their Own.

HANNA, WILLIAM: Executive. b. Melrose, NM, July 14, 1911. e. Compton Coll. Studied engineering and journalism. Joined firm in CA as structural engineer; turned to cartooning with Leon Schlessinger's company in Hollywood. In 1937 hired by MGM as director and story man in cartoon dept. There met Joseph R. Barbera and created famous cartoon series Tom & Jerry, continuing to produce it from 1938 to 1957. Left MGM in 1957 to form Hanna-Barbera Productions to make cartoons for TV. These series have included Yogi Bear, Huckleberry Hound, The Flintstones, The Jetsons. Hanna-Barbera became a subsidiary of Taft Broadcasting Co. in 1968 with both men operating studio under long-term agreements with Taft (which became Great American Broadcasting, 1987). Hanna is sr. v.p. of Hanna-Barbera Productions. Co-exec. prod. & dir. of 1993 tv movie I Yabba Dabba Do! Company entered theatrical production with Loopy De Loop in 1960, followed by Hey There It's Yogi Bear, Man Called Flintstone, Charlotte's Web, C.H.O.M.P.S., Heidi's Song, Once Upon a Forest. Co-Exec. Prod. on live-action film of The Flintstones.

HANNAH, DARYL: Actress. b. Chicago, IL, 1960. Niece of cinematographer Haskell Wexler. e. UCLA. Studied ballet with Maria Tallchief. Studied with Stella Adler.
PICTURES: The Fury (debut, 1978), The Final Terror, Hard Country, Blade Runner, Summer Lovers, Reckless, Splash, The Pope of Greenwich Village, Clan of the Cave Bear, Legal Eagles, Roxanne, Wall Street, High Spirits, Crimes and Misdemeanors, Steel Magnolias, Crazy People, At Play in the Fields of the Lord, Memoirs of an Invisible Man, Grumpy Old Men.
TELEVISION: Movies: Paper Dolls, Attack of the 50 Ft. Woman.

HANNEMANN, WALTER A.: Film editor. b. Atlanta, GA, May 2, 1914. e. U. of Southern California, 1935. Editorial training, RKO 1936–40; edit. supvr., Universal, 1941–42; consultant

1970–75 national educational media. Bd. of Govs., TV Academy (2 terms, 1960 & 1970); bd. of govs., Acad of M.P. Arts and Sciences. 1983–86; board of dir., m.p. film editors, 1944–48, 1981–88.
PICTURES: Interval, The Revengers, Dream of Kings, Guns of the Magnificent Seven, Krakatoa: East of Java, The Bob Mathias Story, Pay or Die, Al Capone, (Amer. Cinema Editor's Award, 1959), Hell's Five Hours, Armoured Command, Only the Valiant, Time of Your Life, Kiss Tomorrow Goodbye, Blood on the Sun, Guest in the House, Texas Masquerade, Cannon for Cardoba, El Condor, Maurie, Lost in the Stars, Mad Mad Movie Making, Big Mo, Two Minute Warning (Oscar nominee) The Peter Hill Puzzle, Smokey and the Bandit (Oscar nominee), Other Side of the Mountain—Part II, The Visitor, The Villain, Return of Maxwell Smart, Charlie Chan and the Curse of the Dragon Woman.
TELEVISION: Death Valley Days, Reader's Digest, Rosemary Clooney Show, The New Breed, The Fugitive, Twelve O'Clock High, The Invaders, Hawaii Five-O, Streets of San Francisco, Cannon, Barnaby Jones, Caribe. Movies: The Man Who Broke a 1000 Chains, Intimate Strangers, The Abduction of Saint Anne, The Day the Loving Stopped.

HANSON, CURTIS: Director, Writer. b. Los Angeles, CA. Editor of Cinema magazine before becoming screenwriter.
PICTURES: Writer: The Silent Partner, White Dog, Never Cry Wolf. Director: The Arousers (Sweet Kill), Little Dragons, The Bedroom Window (also s.p.), Bad Influence, The Hand That Rocks the Cradle.
TELEVISION: Movie: The Children of Times Square.

HARBACH, WILLIAM O.: Producer. b. Yonkers, NY, Oct. 12, 1919. e. Brown U. p. Otto Harbach, lyricist, author. U.S. Coast Guard, 1940–45; actor, MGM, 1945–47; broadcast co-ordinator. NBC, 1947–49; stage mgr., 1949–50; dir., NBC, 1950–53; prod., Tonight, 1954; prod. Steve Allen Show, 1960–61 prod., dir., Bing Crosby shows; prod., Milton Berle Special, 1962; prod., Hollywood Palace Shows, 1963–69.; co-produced Julie Andrews Show, 1972–73. Emmy for Shirley MacLaine's Gypsy in My Soul, 1976; Bob Hope Special, 1981 and 1982.

HARE, DAVID: Writer, Director. b. Hastings, Sussex, England, 1947. e. Lancing Coll., Jesus Coll., Cambridge. After leaving univ. in 1968 formed Portable Theatre Company, experimental touring group. Hired by Royal Court Theater as literary manager, 1969. 1970, first full-length play, Slag, prod. at Hampstead Theatre Club. Resident dramatist, Royal Court (1970–71), and Nottingham Playhouse (1973). Assoc. dir., National Theatre. West End debut, Knuckle.
THEATER: Slag, The Great Exhibition, Brassneck, Knuckle, Fanshen, Teeth 'n' Smiles, Plenty, A Map of the World, Pravda, The Bay at Nice, Secret Rapture, Racing Demon, Murmuring Judges, Rules of the Game (new version of Pirandello Play).
PICTURES: Writer: Plenty, Wetherby (also dir.), Paris by Night (also dir.), Strapless (also dir.), Damage.
TELEVISION: Dir.-Writer: Licking Hitler (1979); Dreams of Leaving; Saigon: Year of the Cat (writer only), Knuckle (writer only), Heading Home.

HAREWOOD, DORIAN: Actor. b. Dayton, OH, Aug. 6, 1950. m. actress Ann McCurry. e. U. of Cincinnati.
THEATER: Jesus Christ Superstar (road co.), Two Gentlemen of Verona, Miss Moffat, Streamers, Over Here, Don't Call Back (Theatre World Award), The Mighty Gents.
PICTURES: Sparkle, Gray Lady Down, Looker, Tank, Against All Odds, The Falcon and the Snowman, Full Metal Jacket, Pacific Heights, Solar Crisis, Shattered Image.
TELEVISION: Series: Strike Force, Trauma Center, Glitter, The Trials of Rosie O'Neill, Viper. Mini-Series: Roots: The Next Generations, Amerika. Movies: Foster and Laurie, Panic in Echo Park, Siege, An American Christmas Carol, High Ice, Beulah Land, The Ambush Murders, I Desire, The Jesse Owens Story, Guilty of Innocence, God Bless the Child, Kiss Shot, Polly, Polly—Comin' Home!, Getting Up and Going Home. Pilot: Half 'n' Half.

HARGREAVES, JOHN: Executive. b. Freckleton, Lancashire, Eng., July 1921. Joined Gainsborough Pictures 1945. Transferred to Denham Studios 1946 and later Pinewood Studios. Joined Allied Film Makers 1960, then Salamander Film Productions as Bryan Forbes' financial controller and asst. prod. 1965. Joined EMI Film Prods. Ltd. as asst. man. dir. and prod. controller May 1969–May 1972. Produced Don Quixote (with Rudolf Nureyev, in Australia), 1973. Asst. prod. The Slipper and the Rose 1975, man. dir; Cinderella Promotions Ltd, 1978: assoc. prod., International Velvet. Orion repr., 1979, The Awakening; post prod. exec., Fiendish Plot of Dr. Fu Manchu, 1980; Orion rep. for Excalibur, 1981, MGM rep., Year of Living Dangerously, Australia, 1982. 1983–, U.K. dir. and production executive for Completion Bond Company, Inc. Cal. USA.

HARLIN, RENNY: Director. b. Finland. e. Univ. of Helsinki film school. Formed prod. co. Midnight Sun Pictures.

PICTURES: Born American (debut, 1986), Prison, A Nightmare on Elm Street IV: The Dream Master, Die Hard 2, The Adventures of Ford Fairlane, Rambling Rose (prod. only), Cliffhanger.

HARMON, MARK: Actor. b. Burbank, CA, Sept. 2, 1951. Son of actress Elyse Knox and football star Tom Harmon. m. actress Pam Dawber. Brother of actresses Kelly and Kristin Harmon. On stage in Wrestlers, The Wager (both L.A.), Key Exchange (Toronto).
PICTURES: Comes a Horseman, Beyond the Poseidon Adventure, Let's Get Harry, Summer School, The Presidio, Stealing Home, Worth Winning, Till There Was You, Cold Heaven.
TELEVISION: Series: Sam, 240-Robert, Flamingo Road, St. Elsewhere, Reasonable Doubts. Movies: Eleanor and Franklin: The White House Years, Getting Married, Little Mo, Flamingo Road (pilot), The Dream Merchants, Goliath Awaits, Intimate Agony, The Deliberate Stranger, Prince of Bel Air, Sweet Bird of Youth, Dillinger, Fourth Story, Long Road Home, Shadow of a Doubt. Guest: Adam-12, Laverne & Shirley, Nancy Drew, Police Story, Moonlighting. Mini-Series: Centennial.

HARNELL, STEWART D.: Executive. b. New York, NY, Aug. 18, 1938. e. U. of Miami, UCLA, New School for Social Research. Entertainer with Youth Parade in Coral Gables, FL, 1948–55, performing for handicapped children, Variety Club, etc. Singer, dancer, musician. Had own bands, Teen Aces & Rhythm Rascals, 1950–56; performed on Cactus Jim TV show and Wood & Ivory, 1953–54, WTVJ, Miami. Catskills, Sand Lake, NY, 1954–55. Joined National Screen Service as exec. trainee in 1960 in Chicago; worked as booker & salesman. Transferred to N.Y. home office, 1963; worked in special trailer production. Promoted to asst. gen. sls. mgr., 1964–66; New Orleans branch mgr., 1966–67; Atlanta division mgr., 1967–70. Formed own independent distribution co., 1970–77 Harnell Independent Productions. Resumed post as gen. sls. mgr. of NSS, New York, 1977–78; resigned to become pres. of Cinema Concepts Theatre Service, Atlanta, in 1978 to present. Chief barker of Variety Club of Atlanta, Tent 21, 1972, 1976, 1979, 1988, 1989. In 1986 formed Cinema Concepts Communications, film-video animation studio in Atlanta. Motion Picture Pioneers Bd. of Director (1990–2)

HARPER, JESSICA: Actress. b. Chicago, IL, Oct. 10, 1949. m. prod. exec. Thomas E. Rothman. e. Sarah Lawrence Coll. Understudied on Broadway for Hair for one year. Appeared in summer stock and off-Bdwy shows (Richard Farina: Long Time Coming Longtime Gone, Doctor Selavy's Magic Theatre.)
PICTURES: Taking Off, Phantom of the Paradise, Love and Death, Inserts, Suspiria, The Evictors, Stardust Memories, Shock Treatment, Pennies from Heaven, My Favorite Year, The Imagemaker, Once Again, The Blue Iguana, Big Man on Campus.
TELEVISION: Series: Little Women, It's Garry Shandling's Show. Mini-series: Studs Lonigan, Aspen (The Innocent and the Damned). When Dreams Come True. Special: The Garden Party. Guest: Tales From the Darkside, The Equalizer, Trying Times (Bedtime Story), Wiseguy.

HARPER, TESS: Actress. b. Mammoth Springs, AR, 1952. e. Southwest Missouri State Coll., Springfield. Worked in Houston, then Dallas in children's theater, dinner theater, and commercials.
PICTURES: Tender Mercies (debut, 1983), Amityville 3-D, Silkwood, Flashpoint, Crimes of the Heart (Acad. Award nom.), Ishtar, Far North, Her Alibi, Criminal Law, Daddy's Dyin', My Heroes Have Always Been Cowboys, Man in the Moon, My New Gun.
TELEVISION: Mini-Series: Chiefs, Celebrity. Movies: Kentucky Woman, Starflight: The Plane That Couldn't Land, A Summer to Remember, Promises to Keep, Little Girl Lost, Unconquered, In the Line of Duty: Siege at Marion, Willing to Kill: The Texas Cheerleader Story.

HARPER, VALERIE: Actress. b. Suffern, NY. Aug. 22, 1940. e. Hunter Coll, New Sch. for Social Research. Started as dancer in stage shows at Radio City Music Hall. First professional acting in summer stock in Conn.; actress with Second City Chicago 1964–69; Appeared on Bdwy. in Take Me Along, Wildcat, Subways Are for Sleeping, Something Different, Story Theatre, Metamorphoses. Won 3 Emmys for best performance in supporting role in comedy for portrayal of Rhoda on The Mary Tyler Moore Show and 1 for best leading actress on Rhoda.
PICTURES: Freebie and the Bean, Chapter Two, The Last Married Couple in America, Blame It on Rio.
TELEVISION: Series: The Mary Tyler Moore Show, Rhoda, Valerie, City. Movies: Thursday's Game, Night Terror, Fun and Games, The Shadow Box, The Day the Loving Stopped, Farrell for the People (pilot), Don't Go to Sleep, An Invasion of Privacy, Execution, Strange Voices, Drop Out Mother, The People Across the Lake, Stolen: One Husband.

HARRELSON, WOODY: Actor. b. Midland, TX, July 23, 1961. e. Hanover Col. First professional acting job as understudy for Bdwy production of Biloxi Blues.
TELEVISION: Series: Cheers (Emmy Award, 1989). Movies: Bay Coven, Killer Instinct. Special: Mother Goose Rock 'n' Rhyme.
PICTURES: Wildcats (debut, 1986), Cool Blue, L.A. Story, Doc Hollywood, Ted and Venus, White Men Can't Jump, Indecent Proposal, I'll Do Anything, Natural Born Killers.
THEATRE: NY: The Boys Next Door. L.A.: 2 on 2 (also wrote & prod.), The Zoo Story (also prod.), Brooklyn Laundry.

HARRINGTON, CURTIS: Director, Writer. b. Los Angeles, CA, Sept. 17, 1928. e. U. of Southern California, B.A. Exec. asst. to Jerry Wald, 1955–61 Associate producer at 20th Cent. Fox.
PICTURES: Assoc. Prod.-Writer: Night Tide, Return to Peyton Place, The Stripper. Director-Writer: Night Tide, Queen of Blood, Games, What's the Matter with Helen? Who Slew Auntie Roo?, The Killing Kind, Mata Hari.
TELEVISION: Series: Hotel, Dynasty, The Colby's, Twilight Zone, Baretta, Vegas. Movies: How Awful About Alan, The Cat Creature, Killer Bees, The Dead Don't Die, Devil Dog.

HARRINGTON, PAT: Actor. b. New York, NY, Aug. 13, 1929. e. Fordham U. Served USAF as 1st Lt., 1952–54. Time salesman for NBC, 1954–58.
TELEVISION: Series: The Steve Allen Show, The Danny Thomas Show, The Jack Paar Show, Stump the Stars (host), Mr. Deeds Goes to Town, One Day at a Time (Emmy Award, 1984).
PICTURES: The Wheeler Dealers, Move Over Darling, Easy Come Easy Go, The President's Analyst, 2000 Years Later, The Candidate.

HARRIS, BARBARA: Actress. b. Evanston, IL, July 25, 1935. r.n. Sandra Markowitz. e. Wright Junior Coll., Chicago; Goodman Sch. of the Theatre; U. of Chicago. Joined acting troup, The Compass. Founding member, Second City Players, 1960. Came to N.Y. where first role was in Oh Dad Poor Dad Mamma's Hung You in the Closet and I'm Feeling So Sad (Theatre World Award), repeating in m.p.
THEATER: Mother Courage and Her Children, Dynamite Tonight, On a Clear Day You Can See Forever, The Apple Tree (Tony Award, 1967), Mahogany.
PICTURES: A Thousand Clowns (debut, 1965), Oh Dad Poor Dad, Plaza Suite, Who Is Harry Kellerman?, The War Between Men and Women, The Manchu Eagle Murder Caper Mystery, Mixed Company, Nashville, Family Plot, Freaky Friday, Movie Movie, The North Avenue Irregulars, The Seduction of Joe Tynan, Second Hand Hearts, Peggy Sue Got Married, Nice Girls Don't Explode, Dirty Rotten Scoundrels.
TELEVISION: Guest: Alfred Hitchcock Presents, Naked City, The Defenders.

HARRIS, BURTT: Producer, Actor. Began career as actor; later worked with Elia Kazan as prod. asst. and asst. dir. on America America, Splendor in the Grass, and The Arrangement. Worked as second unit dir. and asst. dir. on many films as well as producer and actor.
PICTURES: Associate Producer: Little Murders, The Wiz, Cruising, Gilda Live. Executive Producer: The Verdict, Just Tell Me What You Want, See No Evil, Hear No Evil, Family Business. Producer: Prince of the City, Daniel, Deathtrap, Garbo Talks, The Glass Menagerie, Q & A. Co-Producer: D.A.R.Y.L. Actor: Splendor in the Grass, Fail Safe, The Taking of Pelham 1–2–3, The Wanderers, The Verdict, Daniel, Garbo Talks, D.A.R.Y.L., Running on Empty, Hudson Hawk, Undertow, A Stranger Among Us.

HARRIS, ED: Actor. b. Tenafly, NJ, Nov. 28, 1950. m. actress Amy Madigan. Played football 2 years at Columbia U. prior to enrolling in acting classes at OK State U. Summer stock. Grad. CA Institute of the Arts, B.F.A. 1975. Worked in West Coast Theater.
THEATER: NY: Fool For Love (off-Bdwy debut, Obie Award), Precious Sons (Theatre World Award). LA: Scar.
PICTURES: Coma (debut, 1978), Borderline, Knightriders, Dream On, Creepshow, The Right Stuff, Under Fire, Swing Shift, Places in the Heart, Alamo Bay, A Flash of Green, Sweet Dreams, Code Name: Emerald, Walker, To Kill a Priest, Jacknife, The Abyss, State of Grace, Glengarry Glen Ross, China Moon, The Firm, Needful Things.
TELEVISION: Movies: The Amazing Howard Hughes, The Seekers, The Aliens Are Coming (Alien Force), The Last Innocent Man, Paris Trout, Running Mates.

HARRIS, JAMES B.: Producer, Director, Writer. b. New York, NY, Aug. 3, 1928. e. Juilliard Sch. U.S. film export, 1947; Realart Pictures, 1948; formed Flamingo Films, 1949; formed Harris-Kubrick Productions, 1954. formed James B. Harris Prods., Inc., 1963.
PICTURES: Producer: The Killing, Paths of Glory, Lolita, The Bedford Incident (also dir.), Some Call It Loving (also dir., s.p.), Telefon, Fast-Walking (also dir., s.p.), Cop (also dir., s.p.), Boiling Point (dir., s.p.).

HARRIS, JULIE: Designer. b. London, England. e. Chelsea Arts Sch. Entered industry in 1945 designing for Gainsborough Studios. First film, Holiday Camp.
PICTURES: Greengage Summer, Naked Edge, The War Lover, Fast Lady, Chalk Garden, Psyche 59, A Hard Day's Night, Darling, Help, The Wrong Box, Casino Royale, Deadfall, Prudence and the Pill, Decline and Fall, Goodbye Mr. Chips, Sherlock Holmes, Follow Me!, Live and Let Die, Rollerball, Slipper and The Rose, Dracula.
TELEVISION: Laura (with Lee Radziwill), Candleshoe, The Sailor's Return, Lost and Found, The Kingfisher, Arch of Triumph, Sign of Four, Hound of the Baskervilles, A Hazard of Hearts, A Perfect Hero.

HARRIS, JULIE: Actress. b. Grosse Pointe, MI, Dec. 2, 1925. e. Yale Drama Sch.
THEATER: Sundown Beach, Playboy of the Western World, Macbeth, Young and the Fair, Magnolia Alley, Monserrat, Member of the Wedding, I Am a Camera (Tony Award, 1952), Colombe, The Lark (Tony Award, 1956), A Shot in the Dark, Marathon 33, Ready When You Are, C.B., Break a Leg, Skyscraper, Voices, And Miss Reardon Drinks a Little, 40 Carats (Tony Award, 1969), The Last of Mrs. Lincoln (Tony Award, 1973), In Praise of Love, The Belle of Amherst (Tony Award, 1973), Driving Miss Daisy (Natl. co.), Lucifer's Child, Lettice & Lovage (tour).
PICTURES: The Member of the Wedding (debut, 1952; Acad. Award nom.), East of Eden, I Am a Camera, The Truth About Women, The Poacher's Daughter, Requeim for a Heavyweight, The Haunting, Harper, You're a Big Boy Now, Reflections in a Golden Eye, The Split, The People Next Door, The Hiding Place, Voyage of the Damned, The Bell Jar, Nutcracker: The Motion Picture (voice), Gorillas in the Mist, Housesitter, The Dark Half.
TELEVISION: Specials: Little Moon of Alban (Emmy Award, 1959), Johnny Belinda, A Doll's House, Ethan Frome, The Good Fairy, The Lark, He Who Gets Slapped, The Heiress, Victoria Regina (Emmy Award, 1962), Pygmalion, Anastasia, The Holy Terror, The Power and The Glory, The Woman He Loved. Movies: The House on Greenapple Road, How Awful About Alan, Home for the Holidays, The Greatest Gift, The Gift, Too Good To Be True, The Christmas Wife, They've Taken Our Children: The Chowchilla Kidnapping, When Love Kills: The Seduction of John Hearn. Series: Thicker Than Water, The Family Holvak, Knots Landing. Mini-Series: Backstairs at the White House.

HARRIS, MEL: Actress. b. Bethlehem, PA, July 12, 1957. r.n. Mary Ellen Harris. e. Columbia. Career as successful model before turning to acting in 1984. NY theatre debut in Empty Hearts, 1992 (Theatre World Award).
TELEVISION: Series: thirtysomething. Guest: M*A*S*H, Alfred Hitchcock Presents, Rags to Riches, Heart of the City, The Wizard. Movies: Seduced, Harry's Hong Kong, Cross of Fire, My Brother's Wife, The Burden of Proof, Grass Roots, Child of Rage, With Hostile Intent.
PICTURES: Wanted: Dead or Alive, Cameron's Closet, K-9, Raising Cain, Desperate Motive.

HARRIS, NEIL PATRICK: Actor. b. Albuquerque, NM, June 15, 1973. While attending week-long theatre camp at New Mexico St. Univ. met writer Mark Medoff who suggested him for co-starring role in Clara's Heart.
TELEVISION: Series: Doogie Howser, M.D., Capitol Critters (voice). Movies: Too Good to Be True, Home Fires Burning, Cold Sassy Tree, Stranger in the Family, Sudden Fury. Guest: B. J. Stryker, Carol & Company, Roseanne, Quantum Leap, Murder She Wrote.
PICTURES: Clara's Heart (debut, 1988), Purple People Eater.

HARRIS, PHIL: Orchestra leader. b. Linton, IN, June 24, 1906. m. Alice Faye, actress. Co-starred with Faye in weekly radio show; on NBC; 16 yrs. with Jack Benny Show; many TV appearances. In 1933: with orchestra in Melody Cruise. In 1936: Vitaphone short prod. In 1937: Turn Off the Moon. In 1939: Man About Town. In 1940: Buck Benny Rides Again, Dreaming Out Loud.
PICTURES: I Love a Bandleader, Wabash Avenue, Wild Blue Yonder, Starlift, High and the Mighty, Anything Goes, Good-Bye My Lady, The Jungle Book (voice), The Aristocats (voice of Scat Cat), Rock a Doodle (voice).

HARRIS, RICHARD: Actor. b. Limerick, Ireland, Oct. 1, 1930. Attended London Acad. of Music and Dramatic Arts. Prod.-dir. Winter Journey 1956. Prof. acting debut in Joan Littlewood's prod. of The Quare Fellow, Royal Stratford, 1956. Recorded hit song MacArthur's Park, 1968. Author of novel Honor Bound (1982) and poetry compilation: I in the Membership of My Days (1973).
THEATER: London: A View from the Bridge, Man Beast and Virtue, The Ginger Man. (U.S.): Camelot.
PICTURES: Alive and Kicking (debut, 1958), Shake Hands With the Devil, The Wreck of the Mary Deare, A Terrible Beauty, The Long The Short and The Tall, Guns of Navarone, Mutiny on the Bounty, This Sporting Life (Acad. Award nom.),

The Red Desert, Major Dundee, The Heroes of Telemark, The Bible, Hawaii, Caprice, Camelot, The Molly Maguires, A Man Called Horse, Cromwell, Man in the Wilderness, The Hero (a.k.a. Bloomfield; also dir., s.p.), The Deadly Trackers, 99 and 44/100% Dead, Juggernaut, Echoes of a Summer (also co-exec. prod.), Robin and Marian, Return of a Man Called Horse (also co-exec. prod.), The Cassandra Crossing, Gulliver's Travels, Orca, Golden Rendezvous, The Wild Geese, The Ravagers, The Last Word, Game for Vultures, High Point, Your Ticket Is No Longer Valid, Tarzan the Ape Man, Martin's Day, Triumphs of a Man Called Horse, Mack the Knife, The Field (Acad. Award nom.), Patriot Games, Unforgiven, Silent Tongue, Wrestling Ernest Hemingway.
TELEVISION: Specials: Ricardo, The Iron Harp, The Snow Goose, Camelot. Movie: Maigret, The Return.

HARRIS, ROBERT A: Archivist, Producer. b. New York, NY, Dec. 27, 1945. e. NYU, Sch. of Commerce and Sch. of Arts, 1968. Worked as exec. trainee with 7 Arts assoc., NY while in school, 1960–68; worked in corp. communications, Pepsico, 1970–71; formed Center for Instructional Resources, SUNY Purchase, 1971–73; organized Images Film Archive, dist. of classic theatrical and non theat. films, 1974; pres., Images Video and Film Archive, 1985; formed Davnor Prods., president 1986–present; formed The Film Preserve, Ltd. pres. 1989–.
PICTURES: 1975–80: restored Abel Gance films Beethoven, J'Accuse, Lucetia Borgia; 1974–79: worked with Kevin Brownlow to complete restoration of Abel Gance's Napoleon. Partnered with Francis Coppola/Zoetrope Studios to present Napoleon at Radio City Music, Jan. 1981 and worldwide tour; 1986–89; reconstruction and restoration of David Lean's Lawrence of Arabia for Columbia Pictures, released Feb., 1989; The Grifters (prod.); restoration and reconstruction of Stanley Kubrick's Spartacus for Univ. Pictures, released April, 1991.

HARRIS, ROSEMARY: Actress. b. Ashby, Suffolk, Sept. 19, 1930. e. India and England. Early career, nursing; studied Royal Acad. of Dramatic Art, 1951–52. Screen debut in Beau Brummell (1954).
PLAYS: Climate of Eden (NY debut 1952), Seven Year Itch, Confidential Clerk (Paris Festival), and with Bristol Old Vic in The Crucible, Much Ado About Nothing, Merchant of Venice; also in The Tale of Two Cities, Dial M for Murder, etc. With Old Vic, 1955–56; U.S. tour, 1956–57; U.S. stage, 1958–63. Chichester Festivals 1962 and 63; Nat'l Theatre 1963–64; You Can't Take It With You, 1965; The Lion in Winter (Tony Award, 1966), 1967, APA Repertory Co., Heartbreak House, The Royal Family, The New York Idea (Obie Award), A Pack of Lies, Hay Fever.
TELEVISION: Series: The Chisholms. Specials: Cradle of Willow (debut, 1951); Othello, The Prince and the Pauper, Twelfth Night; Wuthering Heights, Notorious Woman (Emmy, 1976), Blithe Spirit, Profiles in Courage, To the Lighthouse, Strange Interlude, Tales From the Hollywood Hills: The Old Reliable. Mini-Series: Holocaust, The Chisholms.
PICTURES: Beau Brummell, The Shiralee, A Flea in Her Ear, The Boys from Brazil, The Ploughman's Lunch, Crossing Delancey.

HARRIS, TIMOTHY: Writer, (Producer). b. Los Angeles, CA, July 21, 1946. e. Charterhouse, 1963–65; Peterhouse Coll., Cambridge, 1966–69, M.A. Honors Degree, Eng. lit. Author of novels, Kronski/McSmash, Kyd For Hire, Goodnight and Goodbye; author of novelizations, Steelyard Blues, Hit, Heatwave, American Gigolo.
PICTURES: Co-writer with Herschel Weingrod: Cheaper to Keep Her, Trading Places (BAFTA nom., orig. s.p.; NAACP Image Awards, best m.p. 1983), Brewster's Millions, My Stepmother is an Alien, Paint It Black, Twins (People's Choice Award, best comedy, 1988), Kindergarten Cop, Pure Luck. Co-Prod.: Falling Down.
TELEVISION: Street of Dreams (based on his novel Goodnight and Goodbye; also exec. prod.).

HARRISON, GEORGE: Singer, Composer, Producer. b. Liverpool, England, Feb. 25, 1943. Former member, The Beatles. Winner of 2 Grammys on own in addition to Beatles' group awards.
PICTURES: Appeared with Beatles in A Hard Day's Night, Help!, Yellow Submarine (cameo), Let It Be. Appeared in and prod. The Concert for Bangladesh. Exec. Prod.: Little Malcolm. Exec. Prod. for Handmade Films: Life of Brian (also cameo), Time Bandits, Monty Python Live at the Hollywood Bowl, The Missionary, Privates on Parade, Scrubbers, Bullshot, A Private Function, Water (also cameo), Mona Lisa, Shanghai Surprise (also songs, cameo), Withnail and I, Five Corners, Bellman and True, The Lonely Passion of Judith Hearne, Track 29, How to Get Ahead in Advertising, Powwow Highway, Checking Out, Cold Dog Soup, Nuns on the Run, The Raggedy Rawney.

HARRISON, GREGORY: Actor, Producer, Director. b. Avalon, Catalina Island, CA, May 31, 1952. Started acting in school plays; then joined Army (1969–71). Studied at Estelle

Harman Actors Workshop; later with Lee Strasberg and Stella Adler. Film debut in Jim, the World's Greatest (1976). Formed Catalina Productions with Franklin Levy, 1981.
THEATER: Child's Play, Carnal Knowledge, Picnic, The Hasty Heart, Love Letters, Festival, Billy Budd, The Subject Was Roses, The Promise.
PICTURES: Jim: the World's Greatest, Fraternity Row, Razorback, North Shore (also 2nd unit dir.), Voice of a Stranger (also 2nd unit dir.), Cadillac Girls.
TELEVISION: Series: Logan's Run, Trapper John M.D. (also dir. 6 episodes), Falcon Crest, The Family Man, True Detectives. Guest: M*A*S*H, Barnaby Jones. Pilot: The Gregory Harrison Show. Movies: The Gathering, Enola Gay, Trilogy in Terror, The Best Place To Be, The Women's Room, For Ladies Only (also co-prod.), Thursday's Child (co-exec. prod. only), The Fighter, Legs (co-exec. prod. only), Samson & Delilah (exec. prod. only), Seduced (also exec. prod.), Oceans of Fire, Hot Paint, Red River, Dangerous Pursuit, Angel of Death, Bare Essentials, Breaking the Silence, Duplicates, Split Images, Caught in the Act. Mini-series: Centennial, Fresno.

HARROLD, KATHRYN: Actress. b. Tazewell, VA, Aug. 2, 1950. e. Mills Coll. Studied acting at Neighborhood Playhouse in N.Y., also with Uta Hagen. Appeared in Off-Bdwy. plays for year; then joined experimental theatre group, Section Ten, touring East, performing and teaching at Connecticut Coll. and NYU. Cast in TV daytime serial, The Doctors.
PICTURES: Nightwing (debut, 1979), The Hunter, Modern Romance, The Pursuit of D.B. Cooper, Yes Gorgio, The Sender, Into the Night, Raw Deal, Someone to Love.
TELEVISION: Movies: Son-Rise: A Miracle of Love, Vampire, Bogie, An Uncommon Love, Women in White, Man Against the Mob, Dead Solid Perfect, Capital News, Rainbow Drive, Deadly Desire. Series: The Doctors (1976–8), MacGruder and Loud, Bronx Zoo, I'll Fly Away, The Larry Sanders Show.

HARRYHAUSEN, RAY: Producer, Writer, Special Effects Expert. b. Los Angeles, CA, June 29, 1920. e. Los Angeles City Coll. While at coll. made 16mm animated film, Evolution, which got him job as model animator for George Pal's Puppetoons in early '40s. Served in U.S. Signal Corps; then made series of filmed fairy tales with animated puppets for schools and churches. In 1946 worked on Mighty Joe Young as ass't. to Willis O'Brien. Designed and created special visual effects for The Beast from 20,000 Fathoms; then began evolving own model animation system called Dynarama. In 1952 joined forces with prod. Charles H. Schneer, using new process for first time in It Came from Beneath the Sea. Subsequently made many films with Schneer in Dynarama. Received Gordon E. Sawyer Award for Acad. of Motion Picture Arts & Sciences, 1992.
PICTURES: Mighty Joe Young, Beast From 20000 Fathoms, It Came From Beneath the Sea, Earth Vs. the Flying Saucers, Animal World, Twenty Million Miles to Earth, 7th Voyage of Sinbad, The Three Worlds of Gulliver, Mysterious Island, Jason and the Argonauts, First Men in the Moon, One Million Years B.C., The Valley of Gwangi, The Golden Voyage of Sinbad, Sinbad and the Eye of the Tiger, Clash of the Titans (co. prod., special effects).

HART, HARVEY: Director. b. Canada, Mar. 19, 1928. Began career on TV in native country then went to Hollywood.
PICTURES: Dark Intruder, Bus Riley's Back in Town, Sullivan's Empire, The Sweet Ride, Fortune and Men's Eyes, The Pyx, Aliens Are Coming, The High Country, Utilities.
TELEVISION: East of Eden, This Is Kate Bennett, Maserati and the Brain, Born Beautiful, Master of the Game (co-dir.), Reckless Disregard, Beverly Hills Madam, Stone Fox, Passion and Paradise (mini-series).

HARTLEY, MARIETTE: Actress. b. New York, NY, June 21, 1940. Student Carnegie Tech. Inst. 1956–57; studied with Eva Le Gallienne. Appeared in Shakespeare Festival, Stratford 1957–60. Co-host Today Show, 1980. Co-host on CBS Morning Show, 1987. Returned to stage in King John (NYSF in Central Park), 1989. Nominated for 6 Emmys for Best Actress. Received 3 Clio Awards, 1979, 1980, and 1981, for acting in commercials. Autobiography: Breaking the Silence.
PICTURES: Ride the High Country, Marnie, Marooned, Barquero, Skyjacked, Improper Channels, O'Hara's Wife, 1969, Encino Man.
TELEVISION: Series: Peyton Place, The Hero, Good Night Beantown, WIOU. Guest: The Rockford Files, The Incredible Hulk (Emmy Award, 1979), Stone. Movies: Earth II, Sandcastles, Genesis II, Killer Who Wouldn't Die, Last Hurrah, M.A.D.D.: Mothers Against Drunk Drivers, Drop-Out Father, One Terrific Guy, Silence of the Heart, My Two Loves, Murder C.O.D., Diagnosis of Murder, The House on Sycamore Street, Child of Rage. Mini-series: Passion and Paradise.

HARTMAN, DAVID: Actor. b. Pawtucket, RI, May 19, 1935. e. Duke U., 1956. Was 2nd Lt. in Air Force; entered American Acad. of Dramatic Arts, N.Y. Appeared in off-Bdwy. musicals and

summer stock; toured with Belafonte singers. Bdwy. debut in Hello, Dolly!
PICTURES: The Ballad of Josie, Nobody's Perfect, Ice Station Zebra, The Island at the Top of the World.
TELEVISION: Series: The Virginian, The Bold Ones, Lucas Tanner, Berth and Babies (prod.). Host ABC's Good Morning, America, The Shooters (writer, exec. prod.; narrator), David Hartman—The Future Is Now (also exec. prod.; writer). Movies: San Francisco International, The Feminist and the Fuzz, I Love a Mystery, You'll Never See Me Again, Miracle on 34th Street, Lucas Tanner (pilot).

HARTMAN, LISA: Actress. Houston, TX, June 1, 1956. Attended NYC's H.S. of Performing Arts prior to becoming a nightclub performer.
TELEVISION: Series: Tabitha, Knots Landing, High Performance, 2000 Malibu Road. Movies: Murder at the World Series, Valentine Magic on Love Island, Where the Ladies Go, Gridlock, Jacqueline Susann's Valley of the Dolls 1981, Beverly Hills Cowgirl Blues, Full Exposure: The Sex Tapes Scandal, The Operation, The Take, Bare Essentials, Fire: Trapped on the 39th Floor, Not of This World, Red Wind, The Return of Eliot Ness, Without a Kiss Goodbye.
PICTURES: Deadly Blessing, Where the Boys Are.

HARTZ, JIM: TV Newsman, Panelist. b. Feb. 3, 1940, Tulsa, OK. Pre-med student at U. of Tulsa, where worked in spare time as reporter for radio station KRMG. In 1963 left studies for career as newsman and joined KOTV in Tulsa. In 1964 moved to NBC News in New York, acting as reporter and anchorman. In 1974 became co-host of Today Show, joined Barbara Walters.

HARVEY, ANTHONY: Director. b. London, Eng., June 3, 1931. Royal Acad. of Dramatic Art. Two yrs. as actor. Ent. m.p. ind. 1949 with Crown Film Unit.
PICTURES: Editor: Private's Progress, Brothers-in-Law, Man in the Cocked Hat, Carlton Brown of the F.O., I'm Alright Jack, The Angry Silence, The Millionairess, Lolita, The L-Shaped Room, Dr. Strangelove, Spy Who Came In From the Cold, The Whisperers. Director: Dutchman, The Lion in Winter, They Might Be Giants, Eagles' Wing, Players, The Abdication, Richard's Things, Grace Quigley.
TELEVISION: The Disappearance of Aimee, Svengali, The Patricia Neal Story, The Glass Menagerie.

HARWOOD, RONALD: Writer. b. Cape Town, South Africa, 1934. e. Royal Acad. of Dramatic Art.
THEATER: The Dresser, Interpreters, Another Time, Reflected Glory.
TELEVISION: The Barber of Stamford Hill, Private Potter, Take a Fellow Like Me, The Lads, Convalescence, Guests of Honor, The Guests. Adapted several of the Tales of the Unexpected, Mandela, Breakthrough at Rykjavik, Countdown to War, All the World's a Stage (series).
PICTURES: Barber of Stamford Hill, Private Potter (written with Casper Wrede), subsequently High Wind in Jamaica, Eye Witness, One Day in the Life of Ivan Denisovich, Operation Daybreak, The Dresser, The Doctor and the Devils.

HASSANEIN, RICHARD C.: Executive. b. New York, NY, Aug. 13, 1951; e. Staunton Military Acad., 1966–70; American U., 1970–74. Booker/real estate dept. opns., United Artists Theater Circuit, 1974–77; joined United Film Distribution Co., 1977; named pres. 1978. Resigned as pres. Feb. 1988. 1988–91 served as pres., producers' rep., foreign & U.S. sls., of Myriad Enterprises. Joined Todd-AO Glen Glenn Studios in June 1991 as v.p. of new bus. ventures. Nov. 1991 appointed exec. v.p. of Todd-AO Studios East, NY.

HASSANEIN, SALAH M.: Executive. b. Suez, Egypt, May 31, 1921. e. British Sch., Alexandria, Egypt. Nat'l Bank of Egypt, Cairo, 1939–42. Asst. division mgr. Middle East, 20th-Fox, Cairo, Egypt, 1942–44; U.S. armed forces, 1945–47; usher, asst. mgr., Rivoli Theatre, N.Y., 1947–48. Film buyer, booker, oper. v.p. U.A. Eastern Theas., 1948–59; pres. 1960; exec. v.p. U.A. Communications, Inc. 1960; v.p. United Artists Cable Corp., 1963. Exec. v.p., Todd-AO Corp., 1980. President, Warner Bros. International Theaters, 1988.
PICTURES: Exec. prod.: Knightriders; Creepshow; Hello Again; Love or Money.

HASSELHOFF, DAVID: Actor. b. Baltimore, MD, July 17, 1952.
PICTURES: Starcrash, Witchery, W.B., Blue and the Bean.
TELEVISION: Series: The Young and the Restless, Knight Rider, Baywatch. Movies: Griffin and Phoenix, Semi Tough, After Hours—Getting to Know Us, The Cartier Affair, Bridge Across Time, Perry Mason: The Case of the Lady in the Lake, Baywatch: Panic at Malibu Pier, Knight Rider 2000.

HASTINGS, DON: Performer; b. Brooklyn, NY, Apr. 1, 1934. e. Professional Children's Sch., Lodge H.S. On Bdwy in Life With Father, I Remember Mama, Summer and Smoke, etc.; on various radio shows, Video Ranger on Capt. Video 1949–55; The Edge of Night, 1956–60; As the World Turns since

1960. Author of scripts for As the World Turns, The Guiding Light.

HATFIELD, HURD: Actor. b. New York, NY, Dec. 7, 1918. e. Morristown prep, Horace Mann H.S., Riverdale Acad., Columbia U., Chekhov Drama Sch., Devonshire, Eng. On dramatic stage, Lower Depths, Twelfth Night, Cricket on the Hearth, King Lear. N.Y. stage 1952, Venus Observed.
PICTURES: Dragon Seed (debut, 1944), The Picture of Dorian Gray, Diary of a Chambermaid, The Beginning or the End, The Unsuspected, The Checkered Coat, Joan of Arc, Chinatown at Midnight, Destination Murder, Tarzan and Slave Girl, Left-Handed Gun, King of Kings, El Cid, Harlow, Mickey One, The Boston Strangler, Von Richtofen and Brown, King David, Crimes of the Heart, Her Alibi.
TELEVISION: Movies: Thief, The Norliss Tapes, You Can't Go Home Again, Lies of the Twins. Mini-Series: The Word.

HATFIELD, TED: Executive. b. Wilton Junction, IA, Aug. 26, 1936. e. Hot Springs, AR. U.S. Army-NCO Academy, 1954. 1949–67 ABC Paramount Theatres, advanced from usher to district mgr. 1967–70 MGM asst. exploitation dir.; 1970–83, MGM national advertising coordinator; 1983–87, MGM/UA v.p., field operations. 1987–91, MGM/UA v.p., exhibitor relations. 1991–, TriStar, v.p., exhib. rltns.
MEMBER: Motion Picture Pioneers; Western LA Council, Boy Scout Commissioner; Culver City Chamber of Commerce, past v.p./presidents award; Jaycees, Past State v.p.; Advertising Federation, past state pres., Culver City Commissioner.

HAUER, RUTGER: Actor. b. Breukelen, Netherlands, Jan. 23, 1944. Stage actor in Amsterdam for six years.
PICTURES: Repelsteeltje (debut, 1973), Turkish Delight, Pusteblume, The Wilby Conspiracy, Keetje Tippel, Het Jaar van de Kreeft, Max Havelaar, Griechische Feigen, Soldier of Orange, Pastorale 1943, Femme Entre Chien et Loup, Mysteries (also co-prod.), Gripsta en de Gier, Spetters, Nighthawks, Chanel Solitaire, Blade Runner, Eureka, The Osterman Weekend, A Breed Apart, Ladyhawke, Flesh and Blood, The Hitcher, Wanted: Dead or Alive, The Legend of the Holy Drinker, Bloodhounds of Broadway, The Blood of Heroes, Blind Fury, Ocean Point, On a Moonlit Night, Past Midnight, Split Second, Buffy the Vampire Slayer.
TELEVISION: Movies: Escape from Sobibor, Inside The Third Reich, Deadlock, Blind Side, Voyage. Series: Floris (Netherlands TV). Mini-Series: Maketub: The Law of the Desert (Italy).

HAUSER, WINGS: Actor. b. Hollywood, CA. Nickname derived from playing wing back on h.s. football team. Began studying acting in 1975.
PICTURES: First to Fight, Who'll Stop the Rain, Homework, Vice Squad, Deadly Force, Uncommon Valor (assoc. prod., story only), Mutant (Night Shadows), A Soldier's Story, Jo Jo Dancer Your Life is Calling, 3:15, Tough Guys Don't Dance, Nightmare at Noon, The Wind, Hostage, Dead Man Walking, The Carpenter, The Siege of Firebase Gloria, No Safe Haven (also co-s.p.), L.A. Bounty, Bedroom Eyes II, Beastmaster 2.
TELEVISION: Series: The Young and the Restless, The Last Precinct, Lightning Force, Command 5, Roseanne. Movies: Hear No Evil, Ghost Dancing, The Long Hot Summer, Perry Mason: The Case of the Scandalous Scoundrel, Highway Man.

HAUSMAN, MICHAEL: Producer. Former stockbroker and still photographer. Entered film industry as assoc. prod. and prod. mgr. on The Heartbreak Kid and Taking Off. Worked as head of prod. for Robert Stigwood on Saturday Night Fever.
PICTURES: I Never Promised You A Rose Garden; Alambrista!; Heartland; Rich Kids; One-Trick Pony; Ragtime (exec. prod., 1st asst. dir.); The Ballad of Gregorio Cortez; Silkwood; Amadeus (exec. prod.); Places in the Heart (exec. prod.); Desert Bloom; Flight of the Spruce Goose; No Mercy; House of Games; Things Change; Valmont, Homicide, State of Grace.
TELEVISION: Lip Service (exec. prod.).

HAVERS, NIGEL: Actor. b. London, Eng., Nov. 6, 1949. e. Leicester U., trained for stage at Arts Educational Trust. Father, Sir Michael Havers, was Attorney General of Britain. As child played Billy Owen on British radio series, Mrs. Dale's Diary. Records voice overs and books for the blind.
THEATER: Conduct Unbecoming, Richard II, Man and Superman (RSC), Family Voices, Season's Greetings, The Importance of Being Earnest.
PICTURES: Pope Joan (debut, 1972), Full Circle, Who is Killing the Great Chefs of Europe?, Chariots of Fire, A Passage to India, Burke and Wills, The Whistle Blower, Empire of the Sun, Farewell to the King, Clichy Days.
TELEVISION: Series: A Horseman Riding By, Don't Wait Up. Mini-series: The Glittering Prizes, Nicholas Nickleby, Pennies From Heaven, Winston Churchill: The Wilderness Years, Nancy Astor, The Little Princess, Death of the Heart, Naked Under Capricorn, Sleepers. Movies: The Charmer,

Private War of Lucina Smith. Guest: Thriller, Star Quality: Noel Coward Stories (Bon Voyage), A Question of Guilt, Aspects of Love, Upstairs Downstairs, Edward VII.

HAVOC, JUNE: Actress. r.n. Hovick. b. Seattle, WA, Nov. 8, 1916. Sister of late Gypsy Rose Lee, actress. Made film bow at 2 yrs. old in Hal Roach prod. Danced with Anna Pavlova troupe, then entered vaudeville in own act. Later, joined Municipal Opera Company, St. Louis, and appeared in Shubert shows. Musical comedy debut: Forbidden Melody (1936). To Hollywood, 1942. Author: Early Havoc (1959), More Havoc (1980).
PICTURES: Four Jacks and a Jill, My Sister Eileen, Sing Your Worries Away, Hi Diddle Diddle, Hello Frisco, Hello, No Time for Love, Timber Queen, Casanova Burlesque, Sweet and Low Down, Brewster's Millions, Intrigue, Gentleman's Agreement, When My Baby Smiles at Me, The Story of Molly X, Red Hot and Blue, Chicago Deadline, Mother Didn't Tell Me, Once a Thief, Follow the Sun, Lady Possessed, Three for Jamie Dawn, The Private Files of J. Edgar Hoover, Can't Stop the Music, Return to Salem's Lot.
PLAYS: Pal Joey, Sadie Thompson, Mexican Hayride, Dunnigan's Daughter, Dream Girl, Affairs of State, The Skin of Our Teeth, A Midsummer Night's Dream (Stratford, CT. American Shakespeare Fest., 1958), Tour for U.S. Dept. of St., 1961; wrote Marathon 33. The Ryan Girl, The Infernal Machine, The Beaux Strategem, A Warm Peninsula, Dinner at Eight, Habeas Corpus. An Unexpected Evening with June Havoc (one woman show, London 1985). Toured England in The Gift, 1987. Appeared in Eleemosynary, 1991.
TELEVISION: Anna Christie, The Bear, Cakes and Ale, Daisy Mayme, The Untouchables; co-owner, Willy, MacMillan & Wife, The Paper Chase, Murder She Wrote. Series: More Havoc (1964–65), Search for Tomorrow, General Hospital.

HAWKE, ETHAN: Actor. b. Austin, TX, Nov. 6, 1970. Attended NYU. Studied acting at McCarter Theatre in Princeton, NJ, the British Theatre Assn., Carnegie Mellon U. Co-founder of Malaparte Theatre Co.
PICTURES: Explorers (debut, 1985), Dead Poets Society, Dad, White Fang, Mystery Date, A Midnight Clear, Waterland, Alive, Rich in Love, Reality Bites.
THEATRE: NY: Casanova (Off-Bdwy debut, 1991), A Joke, The Seagull (Bdwy debut, 1992), Sophistry.

HAWN, GOLDIE: Actress. b. Washington, DC, November 21, 1945. Was a professional dancer (performed in Can-Can at the N.Y. World's Fair, 1964), and made TV debut dancing on an Andy Griffith Special.
PICTURES: The One and Only Genuine Original Family Band (debut, 1968), Cactus Flower (Acad. Award, supp. actress, 1969), There's a Girl in My Soup, $ (Dollars), Butterflies Are Free, The Sugarland Express, The Girl From Petrovka, Shampoo, The Duchess and the Dirtwater Fox, Foul Play, Private Benjamin (Acad. Award nom.; also exec. prod.), Seems Like Old Times, Lovers and Liars (Travels With Anita), Best Friends, Swing Shift, Protocol (also exec. prod.), Wildcats (also exec. prod.), Overboard (also exec. prod.), Bird on a Wire, My Blue Heaven (co-exec. prod. only), Deceived, Crisscross (also co-exec. prod.), Housesitter, Death Becomes Her.
TELEVISION: Series: Good Morning World, Rowan & Martin's Laugh-In (1968–70). Specials: Goldie, Goldie & Liza, Goldie and the Kids: Listen to Us.

HAWTHORNE, NIGEL: Actor. b. Coventry, England, Apr. 5, 1929. Extensive career on stage. Ent. TV ind. 1953. Films, 1957. Won 1991 Tony Award for best actor for Shadowlands, Olivier Award for The Madness of George III (Natl. Th.).
TELEVISION: Mapp and Lucia, The Knowledge, The Miser, The Critic, Barchester Chronicles, Marie Curie, Edward and Mrs. Simpson, Yes Minister, Yes Prime Minister (series), The Oz Trials, Flea-Bites. The Shawl, Relatively Speaking.
PICTURES: Young Winston, The Hiding Place, Watership Down (voice), History of the World Part 1, Plague Dogs (voice), Firefox, Gandhi, The Black Cauldron (voice), The Chain, Turtle Diary, Freddie as F.R.O.7 (voice), Demolition Man.

HAYES, HELEN: Actress. r.n. Helen H. Brown. b. Washington, DC, Oct. 10, 1900. e. Sacred Heart Convent, Wash. Wife of the late writer, Charles MacArthur. Started film career in 1931. Dubbed "The First Lady of the American Stage."
PLAYS: What Every Woman Knows, Coquette, Petticoat Influence, The Good Fairy, Mary of Scotland, Victoria Regina, Harriet, Happy Birthday, Wisteria Trees, Mrs. McThing, Skin of Our Teeth, Glass Menagerie, The Show Off, Front Page (revivals).
PICTURES: Arrowsmith, The Sin of Madelon Claudet (Acad. Award 1931–32), A Farewell to Arms, The Son Daughter, The White Sister, Another Language, Night Flight, What Every Woman Knows, Crime Without Passion (cameo), Vanessa: Her Love Story, Stage Door Canteen, My Son John, Main Street to Broadway, Anastasia, Third Man on the Mountain (cameo), Airport (Acad. Award, supp. actress, 1970), Herbie Rides Again, One of Our Dinosaurs Is Missing, Candleshoe.

TELEVISION: *Specials*: Twelve Pound Look, Mary of Scotland, Dear Brutus, Skin of Our Teeth, Christmas Tie, Drugstore on a Sunday Afternoon, Omnibus. *Movies*: Do Not Fold Spindle or Mutilate, The Snoop Sisters, Victory at Entebbe, A Family Upside Down, Murder is Easy, A Caribbean Mystery, Murder with Mirrors. *Mini-Series*: The Moneychangers. *Series*: The Snoop Sisters.
(Died: March 17, 1993)

HAYES, JOHN MICHAEL: Writer. b. Worcester, MA, May 11, 1919. e. U. of Massachusetts, 1941.
PICTURES: Red Ball Express, Thunder Bay, Torch Song, War Arrow, Rear Window, To Catch a Thief, Trouble with Harry, It's A Dog's Life, Man Who Knew Too Much, The Matchmaker, Peyton Place, But Not for Me, Butterfield 8, The Children's Hour, Where Love Has Gone, The Chalk Garden, Judith, Nevada Smith.
TELEVISION: Pancho Barnes.

HAYES, PETER LIND: Actor: b. San Francisco, CA, June 25, 1915. m. Mary Healy. Was radio singer, actor, vaudeville, night clubs. Producer, Grace Hayes Lodge Review: on TV show with Mary Healy.
PICTURES: Million Dollar Legs, All Women Have Secrets, These Glamour Girls, Seventeen, Dancing on a Dime, Playmates, Seven Days Leave, 5000 Fingers of Dr. T, Once You Kiss a Stranger.

HAYNES, TIGER: Actor. b. St. Croix, V.I., Dec. 13, 1914. Organized singing group The Three Flames, whose hit record Open the Door, Richard led to a vaudeville career, 39 weeks on radio and nightclub and TV dates.
THEATER: introduced in New Faces of 1956, Finian's Rainbow, Kiss Me Kate (City Center revival), Fade Out-Fade In, Two Gentlemen of Verona, The Great White Hope (National Company), The Wiz (Tin Woodsman), A Broadway Musical, Comin' Uptown, My One and Only. Off-Bdwy: Bags, Louis, Taking My Turn.
PICTURES: Times Square, Moscow on the Hudson, All that Jazz, Trading Places, Ratboy, The Mosquito Coast, The Long Lost Friend, Enemy Territory, A Gathering of Old Men, Dead Bang.
TELEVISION: In the Heat of the Night, The Cosby Show, On the 5:48, Benny's Place.

HAYS, ROBERT: Actor. b. Bethesda, MD, July 24, 1947. e. Grossmont Coll., San Diego State U. Left school to join San Diego's Old Globe Theatre five years, appearing in such plays as The Glass Menagerie, The Man in the Glass Booth, Richard III.
PICTURES: Airplane! (debut, 1980), Take This Job and Shove It!, Utilities, Airplane II: The Sequel, Trenchcoat, Touched, Scandalous, Cat's Eye, Honeymoon Academy, Hot Chocolate, Homeward Bound: The Incredible Journey, Fifty Fifty.
TELEVISION: *Series*: Angie, Starman, FM, Cutters. *Movies*: Young Pioneers, Young Pioneers' Christmas, Delta County U.S.A., The Initiation of Sarah, The Girl The Gold Watch and Everything, California Gold Rush, The Fall of the House of Usher, The Day the Bubble Burst, Murder by the Book, Running Against Time. *Mini-series*: Will Rogers: Champion of the American People. *Special*: Mr. Roberts. *Guest*: Love Boat, Harry O, Laverne and Shirley.

HEADLY, GLENNE: Actress. b. New London, CT, March 13, 1957. e. High Sch. of Performing Arts. Studied at HB Studios then American Coll. of Switzerland. In Chicago joined St. Nicholas New Works Ensemble. Won 3 Joseph Jefferson awards for work with Steppenwolf Ensemble in Say Goodnight Gracie, Miss Firecracker Contest, Balm in Gilead, Coyote Ugly, Loose Ends. Directed Canadian Gothic.
THEATER: Balm in Gilead, Arms and the Man, Extremities, The Philanthropist (Theatre World Award).
PICTURES: Four Friends (debut, 1981), Dr. Detroit, Fandango, The Purple Rose of Cairo, Eleni, Making Mr. Right, Nadine, Stars and Bars, Dirty Rotten Scoundrels, Paperhouse, Dick Tracy, Mortal Thoughts, Getting Even With Dad.
TELEVISION: *Movies*: Seize the Day, Grand Isle, And the Band Played On. *Mini-Series*: Lonesome Dove (Emmy nom.). *Special*: Hotel Room (Tricks).

HEALD, ANTHONY: Actor. b. New Rochelle, NY, Aug. 25, 1944. e. Michigan St. Univ.
PICTURES: Silkwood (debut, 1983), Teachers, Outrageous Fortune, Happy New Year, Orphans, Postcards From the Edge, The Silence of the Lambs, The Super, Whispers in the Dark, Searching for Bobby Fisher, Ballad of Little Jo.
TELEVISION: *Movie*: A Case of Deadly Force. *Mini-Series*: Fresno. *Pilot*: After Midnight. *Guest*: Hard Copy, Crime Story, Spenser for Hire, Miami Vice, Tales From the Darkside, Against the Law, Law and Order, Class of '96, Cheers.
THEATRE: *Bdwy*: The Wake of Jamey Foster, The Marriage of Figaro, Anything Goes, A Small Family Business. *Off-Bdwy*: The Glass Menagerie, The Electra Myth, Inadmissible Evidence, Misalliance (Theatre World Award), The Caretaker, The Fox, The Philanthropist, Henry V, The Foreigner, Digby,

Principia Scriptoriae, The Lisbon Traviata, Elliot Loves, Lips Together Teeth Apart, Pygmalion, Later Life. *Regional*: Quartermaine's Terms, J.B., Look Back in Anger, The Rose Tattoo, Bonjour la Bonjour, The Matchmaker.

HEALY, JOHN T.: Executive. e. Brooklyn Coll. Taught economics and was associated with Lehigh Valley Industries and General Food Corp. before joining ABC, Inc. in 1970 as assoc. dir. of corp. planning. Named dir. of planning and develop. June, 1972. Elected v.p., planning and admin. of ABC Leisure Group, March, 1974; elected vice pres. of corporate planning, 1976.

HEARD, JOHN: Actor. b. Washington, D.C., Mar. 7, 1946. e. Catholic U. Career began at Organic Theatre, starring in Chicago & N.Y. productions of Warp. Other stage roles include Streamers, G.R. Point (Theatre World Award), Othello, Split, The Glass Menagerie, Total Abandon, The Last Yankee.
PICTURES: Between the Lines (debut, 1977), First Love, On the Yard, Head Over Heels (Chilly Scenes of Winter), Heart Beat, Cutter and Bone (Cutter's Way), Cat People, Best Revenge, Violated, Heaven Help Us, Lies, C.H.U.D., Too Scared to Scream, After Hours, The Trip to Bountiful, The Telephone, The Milagro Beanfield War, The Seventh Sign, Big, Betrayed, Beaches, The Package, Home Alone, End of Innocence, Awakenings, Rambling Rose, Deceived, Mindwalk, Radio Flyer, Gladiator, Waterland, Home Alone 2: Lost in New York, In the Line of Fire, Me and Veronica, The Pelican Brief.
TELEVISION: *Special*: The Scarlet Letter. *Mini-Series*: Tender Is the Night. *Movies*: Will There Really Be a Morning?, Legs, Out on a Limb, Necessity, Cross of Fire, Dead Ahead: The Exxon Valdez Disaster, There Was a Little Boy.

HEATHERTON, JOEY: Actress. b. Rockville Centre, NY, Sept. 14, 1944. Daughter of singer & TV's "Merry Mailman" Ray Heatherton, Cry-Baby.
PICTURES: Twilight of Honor, Where Love Has Gone, My Blood Runs Cold, Bluebeard, The Happy Hooker Goes to Washington, Cry-Baby.
TELEVISION: *Series*: Dean Martin Presents The Golddiggers, Joey and Dad. *Movie*: The Ballad of Andy Crocker.

HECKART, EILEEN: Actress. b. Columbia, OH, Mar. 29, 1919. e. Ohio State U., American Theatre Wing. m. Jack Yankee.
THEATER: Voice of the Turtle, Brighten the Corner, They Knew What They Wanted, Hilda Crane, Picnic, The Bad Seed, A View From the Bridge, Family Affair, Pal Joey, Invitation to a March, Everybody Loves Opal, Dark at the Top of the Stairs, And Things That Go Bump in the Night, You Know I Can't Hear You When the Water's Running, Too True to Be Good, Barefoot in the Park, Butterflies Are Free, Veronica's Room, The Effect of Gamma Rays on Man in the Moon Marigolds, Eleemosynary, The Cemetery Club, Love Letters, Driving Miss Daisy.
PICTURES: Miracle in the Rain (debut, 1956), Somebody Up There Likes Me, The Bad Seed, Bus Stop, Hot Spell, Heller in Pink Tights, My Six Loves, Up the Down Staircase, No Way to Treat a Lady, The Tree, Butterflies Are Free (Acad. Award, supp., 1972), Zandy's Bride, The Hiding Place, Burnt Offerings, Heartbreak Ridge.
TELEVISION: *Guest*: Kraft, Suspense, Philco Playhouse, The Web, Mary Tyler Moore, Annie McGuire. *Movies*: The Victim, FBI Story: The FBI Versus Alvin Karpis, Sunshine Christmas, Suddenly Love, White Mama, FDR: The Last Year, The Big Black Pill, Games Mother Never Taught You, Seize the Day. *Mini-Series*: Backstairs at the Whitehouse.
AWARDS: Daniel Blum and Outer Circle (Picnic), Foreign Press, and Donaldson, Oscar nom. and Film Daily Citation, (Bad Seed), TV Sylvania for the Haven, Variety Poll of N.Y. and Drama Critics (Dark at The Top of the Stairs); Emmy (Save Me a Place at Forest Lawn). Also 5 Tony noms., 5 Emmy noms. Honorary Doctorates from: Ohio St. Univ., Sacred Heart, Niagara Univ.

HECKERLING, AMY: Director. b. New York, NY, May 7, 1954. e. Art & Design H.S., NYU, (film and TV), American Film Institute. Made shorts (Modern Times, High Finance, Getting It Over With), before turning to features.
PICTURES: Fast Times at Ridgemont High, Johnny Dangerously, Into the Night (actor only), National Lampoon's European Vacation, Look Who's Talking, Look Who's Talking Too, Look Who's Talking 3 (co-exec. prod. only).
TELEVISION: George Burns Comedy Hour, Fast Times, They Came From Queens.

HEDLUND, DENNIS: Executive. b. Hedley, TX, Sept. 3, 1946. e. U. of Texas, Austin, B.A., business admin., 1968. Captain U.S. Marine Corp Services, 1966–72. 1970–74, newscaster and disc jockey, KGNC, Amarillo, TX; KOMA, Oklahoma City, OK; WTIX, New Orleans, LA; WFLA, Tampa, FL; 1974–77, national sales mgr., Ampex Corp., NY; 1977–80, vice pres., Allied Artists Video Corp., NY; 1980–present, founder and president, Kultur Video.

HEDREN, TIPPI: Actress. r.n. Nathalie Hedren. b. Lafayette, MN, Jan. 18, 1935. Mother of actress Melanie Griffith. Was hired by Alfred Hitchcock for leading role in The Birds after being spotted on a commercial on the Today Show.
PICTURES: The Birds (debut, 1963), Marnie, A Countess From Hong Kong, Satan's Harvest, Tiger By the Tail, Mr. Kingstreet's War, The Harrad Experiment, Roar (also prod.), Deadly Spygames, Foxfire Light, In the Cold of the Night, Pacific Heights, Inevitable Grace.
TELEVISION: Series: The Bold and the Beautiful. Guest: Run for Your Life, The Courtship of Eddie's Father, Alfred Hitchcock Presents (1985), Baby Boom, Hart to Hart, In the Heat of the Night, Hotel, Improv (guest host), Tales From the Darkside. Movies: Through the Eyes of a Killer, Shadow of a Doubt, Perry Mason: The Case of the Skin-Deep Scandal.

HEFFNER, RICHARD D.: Executive. b. New York, NY, Aug. 5, 1925. e. Columbia U. Instrumental in acquisition of Channel 13 (WNET) as New York's educational tv station; served as its first general manager. Previously had produced and moderated Man of the Year, The Open Mind, etc. for commercial and public TV. Served as dir. of public affairs programs for WNBC-TV in N.Y. Was also dir. of special projects for CBS TV Network and editorial consultant to CBS, Inc. Editorial Board. Was radio newsman for ABC. Exec. editor of From The Editor's Desk on WPIX-TV in New York. Taught history at U. of California at Berkeley, Sarah Lawrence Coll., Columbia U. and New School for Social Research, N.Y. Served as American specialist in communications for U.S. Dept. of State in Japan, Soviet Union, Germany, Yugoslavia, Israel, etc. Prof. of Communications and Public Policy at Rutgers U. In July, 1974 appt. chmn. of classification and rating admin. rating board.

HEFFRON, RICHARD T.: Director. b. Chicago, Oct. 6, 1930.
PICTURES: Fillmore, Newman's Law, Trackdown, Futureworld, Outlaw Blues, I, the Jury, The French Revolution.
TELEVISION: The Morning After, Dick Van Dyke Special, I Will Fight No More Forever, Toma (pilot), Rockford Files (pilot), North and South (mini-series). Movies: The California Kid, Young Joe Kennedy, A Rumor of War, A Whale for the Killing, The Mystic Warrior, V: The Final Battle, Anatomy of an Illness, Convicted: A Mother's Story, Guilty of Innocence, Samaritan, Napoleon and Josephine: A Love Story, Broken Angel, Pancho Barnes.

HEIDER, FREDERICK: Producer. b. Milwaukee, WI, Apr. 9, 1917. e. Notre Dame U., Goodman Theatre, Chicago. Actor in Globe Theatre, Orson Welles' Mercury Theatre.
TELEVISION & RADIO: Chesterfield Supper Club, Sammy Kaye's So You Want to Lead a Band, Frankie Carle Show, Jo Stafford Show, prod., writer, Paul Whiteman Goodyear Revue, Billy Daniels Show, Martha Wright Show, Earl Wrightson Show, Club Seven, Mindy Carson Show; prod., ABC, Ted Mack Family Hour, Dr. I.Q., Miss America Pageant, Bishop Sheen's Life Is Worth Living, Voice of Firestone, Music for a Summer Night. Music for a Spring Night, The Bell Telephone Hour. Publisher, Television Quarterly, National Academy of Television Arts and Sciences. Currently columnist, The Desert Sun, Palm Springs, CA.

HELD, DAVID: Executive. Entered industry as atty. in United Artists' legal dept. 1976, joined Paramount as sr. atty. in legal dept.; transferred to business affairs 1977; promoted to v.p.; business affairs, 1979. Left for sabbatical 1983; re-entered industry with Samuel Goldwyn Co. as v.p., business affairs. 1984, returned to Paramount as sr. v.p. in chg. business affairs.

HELLER, FRANKLIN: Producer, Director. b. Dover, NJ, Sept. 15, 1911. e. Carnegie Inst. of Technology, B.A., 1934. Actor, 1934–36; stage mgr., Sam Harris-Max Gordon Prods., 1936–44; exec. prod., USO shows N.Y., 1944–45; prod. & dir., Paramount, 1945–47; dir., summer stock, 1947–48; prod. & dir., CBS TV, 1949–54; exec., prod. and dir. Goodson-Todman Prods., 1954–69; exec. prod. Protocol Prods., 1969–72 Literary Representative 1972. Dirs. Guild of America, Nat'l bd. 1965–77; Treas. 1965–69; Sec. 1970–73; Chr. Publications 1966–76.
TELEVISION SHOWS: What's My Line?, Beat the Clock, The Front Page, The Web, Danger, To Tell the Truth, I've Got a Secret.

HELLER, PAUL M.: Producer. b. New York, NY, Sept. 25, 1927. e. Hunter Coll., Drexel Inst. of Technology. President, Intrepid Productions. Studied engineering until entry into U.S. Army as member of security agency, special branch of signal corps. Worked as set designer (Westport, East Hampton, Palm Beach) and in live TV and then on theatrical films. Produced the NY Experience and South Street Venture. Debut as film producer, David and Lisa, 1963. From 1964 to 1969 was president of MPO Pictures Inc. Joined Warner Bros. as prod. exec., 1970. Founded the Community Film Workshop Council for the American Film Institute. In 1972 founded Sequoia Pictures, Inc. with Fred Weintraub. Pres. of Paul Heller Prods.

Inc. formed in 1978. Founded the Audrey Skirball-Kenis Theatre.
PICTURES: David and Lisa, The Eavesdropper, Secret Ceremony, Enter the Dragon, Truck Turner, Golden Needles, Dirty Knight's Work, Outlaw Blues, The Pack, The Promise, Pygmalion (cable), First Monday in October, Withnail and I, My Left Foot (exec. prod.), The Lunatic.

HELLMAN, JEROME: Producer. b. New York, NY, Sept. 4, 1928. e. NYU. Joined ad dept. of New York Times then went to William Morris Agency as apprentice. Made asst. in TV dept. Worked as agent for Jaffe Agency. After hiatus in Europe joined Ashley-Steiner Agency (later IFA) where clients included Franklin Schaffner, Sidney Lumet, George Roy Hill, John Frankenheimer. Functioned as TV prod., including Kaiser Aluminum Hour. Left to form own agency, Ziegler, Hellman and Ross. Switched to feature prod. with The World of Henry Orient in 1964.
PICTURES: A Fine Madness, Midnight Cowboy (Acad. Award), The Day of the Locust, Coming Home, Promises in the Dark (also dir.), The Mosquito Coast.

HELLMAN, MONTE: Director, Editor. b. New York, NY, 1932. e. Stanford Univ., UCLA. Started by working for Roger Corman's company as director, editor, 2nd Unit director. Acted in The Christian Licorice Story.
PICTURES: Director: Beast from Haunted Cave, Creature from the Haunted Sea, Back Door to Hell, Flight to Fury, Ride in the Whirlwind (also edit., prod.), The Shooting (also edit., prod.), Two-Lake Blacktop (also edit.), Cockfighter, China 9 Liberty 37 (also prod., s.p.), Iguana (also s.p., edit.), Silent Night Deadly Night 3 (also story). Editor: Bus Riley's Back in Town, The Wild Angels, The Long Ride Home, How to Make It, The Killer Elite. Second Unit Director: The Last Woman on Earth, Ski Troop Attack, The Terror. Exec. Prod.: Reservoir Dogs.

HELMOND, KATHERINE: Actress. b. Galveston, TX, July 5, 1934. Initial stage work with Houston Playhouse and Margo Jones Theatre, Dallas. Joined APA Theatre, NY, and Trinity Square Rep. Co., RI, Hartford Stage, CT and Phoenix Rep. NY. In 1950s opened summer stock theatre in the Catskills. Taught acting at American Musical and Dramatic Acad., Brown U. and Carnegie-Mellon U. 1983, accepted into AFI's Directing Workshop for Women. Directed Bankrupt.
THEATER: The Great God Brown, House of Blue Leaves (Clarence Derwent, NY and LA Drama Critics Awards, 1972).
PICTURES: The Hindenberg, Baby Blue Marine, Family Plot, Time Bandits, Brazil, Shadey, Overboard, Lady in White, Inside Monkey Zetterland.
TELEVISION: Series: Soap, Who's The Boss? (also dir), Benson (dir. only). Movies: Dr. Max, Larry, Locusts, The Autobiography of Miss Jane Pittman, The Legend of Lizzie Borden, The Family Nobody Wanted, Cage Without a Key, The First 36 Hours of Dr. Durant, James Dean, Wanted: The Sundance Woman, Little Ladies of the Night, Getting Married, Diary of a Teenage Hitchhiker, Scout's Honor, World War III, For Lovers Only, Rosie: The Rosemary Clooney Story, Meeting of the Minds, When Will I Be Loved?, The Perfect Tribute, Deception: A Mother's Secret, Grass Roots. Special: Christmas Snow.

HEMINGWAY, MARGOT: formerly Margaux Hemingway. Actress, Model. b. Portland, OR, Feb. 1955. Granddaughter of writer Ernest Hemingway. Sister of Mariel Hemingway.
PICTURES: Lipstick, Killer Fish, They Call Me Bruce?, Over the Brooklyn Bridge, Killing Machine, Porta Mi La Luna, Mass in C Minor, Inner Sanctum, Deadly Rivals.

HEMINGWAY, MARIEL: Actress. b. Ketchum, ID, Nov. 22, 1961. Granddaughter of writer Ernest Hemingway. Sister of Margot Hemingway, model and actress.
PICTURES: Lipstick (debut, 1976), Manhattan (Acad. Award nom.), Personal Best, Star 80, The Mean Season, Creator, Superman IV: The Quest for Peace, Sunset, The Suicide Club (also co-prod.), Delirious, Falling From Grace.
TELEVISION: Series: Civil Wars. Movies: I Want to Keep My Baby, Steal the Sky, Into the Badlands, Desperate Rescue: The Cathy Mahone Story. Mini-Series: Amerika. Guest: Tales From the Crypt.

HEMMINGS, DAVID: Actor, Director. b. Guildford, England, Nov. 18, 1941. Early career in opera. Ent. m.p. ind. 1956. Former co-partner in Hemdale Company.
THEATER: Adventures in the Skin Trade, Jeeves.
TELEVISION: Auto Stop, Big Toe, Out of the Unknown, Beverly Hills Cowgirl Blues, Clouds of Glory, Davy Crockett: Rainbow in the Thunder (also dir.). Director only: Hardball, Magnum PI, A-Team, Airwolf, Murder She Wrote, In the Heat of the Night, Quantum Leap, The Turn of the Screw, Tales From the Crypt, Passport to Murder (movie). Guest: Northern Exposure, The Raven, Ned Blessing.
PICTURES: Some People, Two Left Feet, The System (The Girl-Getters), The Eye of the Devil, Blow Up, Camelot, Charge of the Light Brigade, Only When I Larf, Barbarella, The Best House in London, Alfred the Great, The Walking

Stick, Fragment of Fear, The Love Machine, Unman Wittering and Zigo, Voices, Juggernaut, Running Scared (director), The 14, Mr. Quilp, Deep Red, Islands in the Stream, The Squeeze, The Disappearance, Blood Relatives, Crossed Swords, Power Play, Murder by Decree, Just a Gigolo (also dir.), Thirst, Beyond Reasonable Doubt, Harlequin, Race to the Yankee Zephyr (dir., prod. only), Man Woman and Child, Prisoners (also exec. prod.), Coup D'Grat (also prod.), The Rainbow, Dark Horse (dir. only).

HEMSLEY, SHERMAN: Actor. b. Philadelphia, PA, Feb. 1, 1938. TELEVISION: Series. All in the Family, The Jeffersons, Amen, Dinosaurs (voice). Guest: The Rich Little Show, Love Boat, E/R, 227.
PICTURES: Love at First Bite, Stewardess School, Ghost Fever, Mr. Nanny.
THEATRE: NY: Purlie.

HENDERSON, SKITCH: Music Director. r.n. Lyle Cedric Henderson. b. Birmingham, England, Jan. 27, 1918. e. U. of California. Began as pianist in dance bands, then theatre orchestras, films and radio on West Coast. Accompanist to Judy Garland on tour. Served, USAF, WW II. Music director radio, Bing Crosby. Toured with own dance band, 47–49. Music Director, NBC Network. Music Director "Street Scene," [New York Opera]. Guest conductor, symphony orchestras including New York Philharmonic, London Philharmonic. Founder and Music Director, New York Pops Orchestra. Music Director, Florida Orchestra Pops, Virginia Symphony Pops, Louisville Orchestra Pops. Made many records; Grammy Award for RCA album [New York Philharmonic with Leontyne Price and William Warfield, highlights from PORGY AND BESS]. Instrumental works: Skitch's Blues; Minuet on the Rocks; Skitch in Time; Come Thursday; Curacao. Scores: TV background; American Fantasy; Film background: Act One.
TELEVISION: former Music Director, NBC Network, inc. Steve Allen Show, Tonight Show, Today Show.

HENKIN, HOWARD, H.: Executive writer, Producer, Director. b. New York, NY, Sept. 13, 1926. e. U. of Delaware, 1944. U.S. Army, 1944–46, TV dept.; Newell Emmett Agency, 1947–48; gen. mgr., TelePrompter, 1950–54; eastern sales mgr., Shamus Culhane Prod. 1955–57; Academy Pictures 1957–58; pres. HFH Productions, 1958; pres., Henkin Prods. Inc. & Henkin-Faillace Prods. Inc., 1962–68; ch. of bd., Trio Prods., Inc., 1968–80; author The Dot System.

HENNER, MARILU: Actress. b. Chicago, IL, Apr. 6, 1952. e. U. of Chicago. Studied singing and dancing, appearing in musicals in Chicago and on Broadway in Over Here and Pal Joey. Gained fame as Elaine in TV series, Taxi.
PICTURES: Between the Lines (debut, 1977), Blood Brothers, Hammett, The Man Who Loved Women, Cannonball Run II, Johnny Dangerously, Rustler's Rhapsody, Perfect, L.A. Story, Noises Off.
TELEVISION: Series: Taxi, Evening Shade. Movies: Dream House, Stark, Love with a Perfect Stranger, Ladykillers, Chains of Gold.

HENNING, LINDA KAYE: Actress, Singer. b. Toluca Lake, CA, Sept. 16, 1944. Daughter of prod. Paul Henning. e. Cal State Northridge, UCLA.
STAGE: Gypsy, Applause, Damn Yankees, I Do, I Do, Pajama Game, Sugar, Wonderful Town, Fiddler on the Roof, Sound of Music, Vanities, Born Yesterday, Mary, Mary, Bus Stop, etc.
PICTURE: Bye Bye Birdie.
TELEVISION: Series: Petticoat Junction. Guest: Beverly Hillbillies, Happy Days, Mork & Mindy, Double Trouble, Barnaby Jones, The New Gidget, Hunter. Pilots: Kudzu, The Circle, Family. Movie: The Return of the Beverly Hillbillies.

HENNING, PAUL: TV Producer, Writer. b. Independence, MO, Sept. 16, 1911. e. Kansas City Sch. of Law, grad. 1932. Radio singer and disc jockey. Also acted, ran sound effects, sang, wrote scripts. To Chicago 1937–38, to write Fibber McGee and Molly. To Hollywood as writer for Rudy Vallee, 1939. Wrote scripts for Burns and Allen 10 years, including transition radio to TV. In 1953 wrote, produced live and film shows for Dennis Day. Created, wrote, produced Bob Cummings Show, 1954–59. The Beverly Hillbillies, 1962–71, Petticoat Junction, 1963–70. Exec. prod. Green Acres series. Wrote motion pictures, Lover Come Back, Bedtime Story. Co-writer, Dirty Rotten Scoundrels.

HENRIKSEN, LANCE: Actor. b. New York, NY, May 5, 1943. Appeared on Bdwy in The Basic Training of Pavo Hummel, Richard III.
PICTURES: It Ain't Easy (debut, 1972), Dog Day Afternoon, The Next Man, Mansion of the Doomed, Close Encounters of the Third Kind, Damien: Omen II, The Visitor, The Dark End of the Street, Prince of the City, Piranha II: The Spawning, Nightmares, The Right Stuff, Savage Dawn, The Terminator, Jagged Edge, Choke Canyon, Aliens, Near Dark, Deadly Intent, Pumpkinhead, Hit List, The Horror Show,

Johnny Handsome, Survival Quest, Stone Cold, Comrades in Arms, Delta Heat, Alien 3, Jennifer Eight, Excessive Force, Super Mario Bros., Hard Target, Man's Best Friend, Color of Night, The Penal Colony.
TELEVISION: Movies: Return to Earth, Question of Honor, Blood Feud, Reason for Living: The Jill Ireland Story. Guest: Scene of the Crime, Paul Reiser: Out on a Whim, Tales From the Crypt (Cutting Cards).

HENRY, BUCK: Actor, Writer. b. New York, NY, Dec. 9, 1930. r.n. Henry Zuckerman. e. Dartmouth Coll. Acted in Life with Father, (tour, 1948); Fortress of Glass, Bernardine, Bdwy; 1952–54, U.S. Army; No Time for Sergeants (Nat'l. Co.), The Premise, improvisational theatre, off-Bdwy.
TELEVISION: Series: Garry Moore Show (writer), Steve Allen Show (writer, performer), The Bean Show (writer), That Was the Week That Was (writer, performer), Get Smart (co-creator, story editor), Captain Nice (writer, exec. prod.), Alfred Hitchcock Presents (1985, actor, writer), Quark (writer), The New Show (performer, writer), Falcon Crest (actor), Trying Times: Hunger Chic (dir.). Guest: Saturday Night Live, Murphy Brown. Movie: Keep the Change. Special: Mastergate.
PICTURES: Actor: The Secret War of Harry Frigg, Is There Sex After Death?, Taking Off, The Man Who Fell to Earth, Old Boyfriends, Gloria, Eating Raoul, Aria, Dark Before Dawn, Rude Awakening, Tune in Tomorrow, Defending Your Life, The Player, The Linguini Incident, Short Cuts, Grumpy Old Men. Writer: Candy, The Owl and the Pussycat, What's Up Doc?, The Day of the Dolphin, Protocol. Actor-Writer: The Troublemaker, The Graduate, Catch-22. Actor-Writer-Director: Heaven Can Wait (co-dir.), First Family.

HENRY, JUSTIN: Actor. b. Rye, NY, May 25, 1971. Debut at 8 in Kramer vs. Kramer, 1979 for which he received an Academy Award nomination.
PICTURES: Kramer Vs Kramer, Sixteen Candles, Martin's Day, Sweet Hearts Dance.
TELEVISION: Movie: Tiger Town.

HENSON, LISA: Executive. e. Harvard U. Joined Warner Bros., 1983, as exec. asst. to head of prod. 1985, named dir. of creative affairs. 1985, promoted to v.p., prod. 1992, became exec. v.p., production.

HEPBURN, AUDREY: Actress. b. Brussels, Belgium, May 4, 1929. Trained as ballet dancer. Appeared on London stage; on Bdwy in Gigi (Theatre World Award), Ondine (Tony Award, 1954). Named Star of Tomorrow, 1954. 1988 appointed goodwill ambassador for UNICEF. Recipient: Cecil B. DeMille Award (1990), special BAFTA Award (1991), posthumous Jean Hersholt Humanitarian Award for her work with UNICEF, 1993. Academy Award nominations for Best Actress: Sabrina (1954), The Nun's Story (1959), Breakfast at Tiffany's (1961), Wait Until Dark (1967).
PICTURES: Dutch in 7 Lessons (debut, 1948), One Wild Oat, Young Wives' Tale, Laughter in Paradise, The Lavender Hill Mob, Secret People, Monte Carlo Baby, Roman Holiday (Academy Award, 1953), Sabrina, War and Peace, Funny Face, Love in the Afternoon, Green Mansions, The Nun's Story, The Unforgiven, Breakfast at Tiffany's, The Children's Hour, Charade, Paris When It Sizzles, My Fair Lady, How to Steal a Million, Two for the Road, Wait Until Dark, Robin and Marian, Sidney Sheldon's Bloodline, They All Laughed, Always.
TELEVISION: Specials: Rainy Day in Paradise Junction (CBS TV Workshop), Mayerling (Producers Showcase). Movie: Love Among Thieves. Host: Gardens of the World. (Died: Jan. 20, 1993)

HEPBURN, KATHARINE: Actress. b. Hartford, CT, May 12, 1907. Author: The Making of the African Queen (1987), Me: Stories of My Life (1991).
PICTURES: A Bill of Divorcement, Christopher Strong, Morning Glory (Acad. Award, 1933), Little Women, Spitfire, The Little Minister, Break of Hearts, Alice Adams, Sylvia Scarlett, Mary of Scotland, A Woman Rebels, Quality Street, Stage Door, Bringing Up Baby, Holiday, The Philadelphia Story, Woman of the Year, Keeper of the Flame, Stage Door Canteen, Dragon Seed, Without Love, Undercurrent, The Sea of Grass, Song of Love, State of the Union, Adam's Rib, The African Queen, Pat and Mike, Summertime, Iron Petticoat, The Rainmaker, Desk Set, Suddenly Last Summer, Long Day's Journey Into Night, Guess Who's Coming to Dinner (Acad. Award, 1967), The Lion in Winter (Acad. Award, 1968), The Madwoman of Chaillot, The Trojan Women, A Delicate Balance, Rooster Cogburn, Olly Olly Oxen Free, On Golden Pond (Acad. Award, 1981), Grace Quigley.
TELEVISION: Movies: The Glass Menagerie, Love Among the Ruins (Emmy Award), The Corn Is Green, Mrs. Delafield Wants To Marry, Laura Lansing Slept Here, The Man Upstairs. Special: Katharine Hepburn: All About Me (host, co-writer).
THEATRE: Death Takes a Holiday, Warrior's Husband, The Lake, The Philadelphia Story, As You Like It, Millionairess,

Merchant of Venice, Taming of the Shrew, Measure for Measure, Coco, A Matter of Gravity, West Side Waltz.

HEPPEL, ALAN: Executive. e. Harvard U., B.A., Yale U., Stanford Law Sch. With Haldeman and Peckerman as associate, practicing entertainment law. 1985, joined Paramount Pictures as atty. for M.P. Group. Member, California Bar Assn.

HERALD, PETER: Executive. b. Berlin, Germany, Dec. 20, 1930. e. UCLA, B.A. US Gov't. film officer in Europe 8 years. In charge of continental European prod. operation for Walt Disney Prods., 6 years. Supervisory prod. manager, Columbia Pictures, 3 years. Corporate Prod. mgr. Universal 3 years.
PICTURES: Executive-, Co-, Assoc.-, Line Producer and/or Production Mgr.: Almost Angels, Magnificent Rebel, Miracle of the White Stallions, Emil and the Detectives, There Was a Crooked Man, Outrageous Fortune, National Lampoon's Class Reunion, Doctor Detroit, D. C. Cab; The Great Waltz, Foul Play, Nightwing. W. W. and the Dixie Dancekings, Mandingo, W. C. Fields and Me, Alex and the Gypsy, Silver Streak, Star Wars, Stick, Married to It, many others.

HERMAN, NORMAN: Producer, Director. b. Newark, NJ, Feb. 10, 1924. e. Rutgers U., NYU. Was accountant in California; in 1955 switched to film ind., joining American Int'l Pictures. Headed AIP prod. dept. 4 years, incl. prod., post-prod., labor negotiations, supervising story dept., etc. Pres. of Century Plaza Prods. for 9 yrs. Sr. v.p./staff writer DEG, 1986–9; Pres. No. Carolina Studios, 1989–90.
PICTURES: Prod. except as noted: Sierra Stranger, Hot Rod Girl, Hot Rod Rumble, Crime Beneath Seas, Look in any Window (exec. prod. mgr.), Tokyo After Dark (also dir., s.p.), Everybody Loves It (dir.), Mondy Teeno (also dir. co-s.p.), Glory Stompers, Three in the Attic (assoc. prod.), Pretty Boy Floyd, Dunwich Horror, Three in the Cellar, Angel Unchained, Psych-Out, Sadismo (s.p.), Bloody Mama, Bunny O'Hare, Killers Three, Frogs (exec. prod.), Planet of Life (s.p.), Blacula, Dillinger (s.p.), Legend of Hell House, Dirty Mary Crazy Larry, Rolling Thunder, In God We Trust (exec. prod.), Blue Velvet (consultant).
TELEVISION: Writer: Robert Taylor Detective, Iron Horse, Invaders, Adam 12, Lancer. Director-Producer: Hannibal Cobb, You Are the Judge.

HERMAN, PEE-WEE: Actor, Writer. r.n. Paul Rubenfeld. Professional name Paul Reubens. b. Peekskill, NY, Aug. 27, 1952. Raised in Sarasota, FL. e. Boston U., California Inst. of the Arts (1976). Pee-wee character made debut, 1978 at Groundlings, improvisational theater, Los Angeles followed by The Pee-wee Herman Show, a live show which gave 5 months of sold-out performances at the L.A. rock club, Roxy and was later taped for HBO special. Guest appearances on Late Night With David Letterman, The Gong Show, 227, Tonight Show, Mork & Mindy, Joan Rivers' The Late Show, and The Dating Game.
PICTURES: Midnight Madness, The Blues Brothers, Cheech & Chong's Next Movie, Cheech and Chong's Nice Dreams, Pandemonium, Meatballs Part II, Pee-wee's Big Adventure (also co-s.p.), Flight of the Navigator (voice), Back to the Beach, Big Top Pee-wee (also co-s.p., co-prod.), Batman Returns, Buffy the Vampire Slayer.
TELEVISION: Series: Pee-wee's Playhouse (creator, co-dir., co-writer, exec. prod., 12 Emmy Awards). Specials: Pinocchio (as Paul Reubens, Faerie Tale Theatre), Pee-wee Herman Show, Pee-wee's Playhouse Christmas Special (star, exec. prod., co-dir. co-writer).

HERMAN, PINKY: Journalist, Songwriter. b. New York, NY, Dec. 23, 1905. e. NYU. Song writer; member, ASCAP. Counsel member, S.P.A.; writer, M.P. News, 1930; 1934; charter member, Songwriters Protective Assoc.; writer, M.P. Daily, 1935–43; columnist, Radio Daily, 1943–50; TV columnist for M.P. Daily. Retired, 1973. Councilman; The Lambs. Exec. prod., Lambs Club Productions (1960–69). Former TV editor, Quigley Publications. Bicentennial Chmn. Lauderdale Lakes, FL, 1975–6. Voted Man of the Year 1976 by Lauderdale Lakes Junior Chamber of Commerce.
SONGS: include: (collab.) Face the Sun, All Around the Town, Boom Ta Ra Ra, It Must Be LUV, Piano Teacher Song, Manhattan Merry Go Round (performed on NBC 1931–49), Lucky, I'm Still in Love With You, Havin' A Wonderful Time, Where Can You Be, Seven Days a Week, Texas Lullaby, Lighthouse in the Harbor, I'm Cuckoo Over Your, It's a Coincidence, If I Had a Million Dollars, I'd Like to Kiss Susie Again, Face the Sun, If You're Mine (Say You're Mine), The Boss of Santa Claus, The Declaration of Independence, We're Americans All, Right Around the Corner from My House, My Fav'rite Initials Are U.S.A., With You, Lauderdale Lakes What a Town (Official song for city of Lauderdale Lakes, FL).

HEROUX, CLAUDE: Producer. b. Montreal, Canada, Jan. 26, 1942. e. U. of Montreal. 1979, prod. v.p., Film Plan Intl., Montreal.
PICTURES: Valerie, L'Initiation, L'Amour Humain, Je t'aime, Echoes of a Summer, Jacques Brel Is Alive and Well and Living in Paris, Breaking Point, Born for Hell, Hog Wild, City of Fire, Dirty Tricks, Gas, Visiting Hours, Videodrome, The Funny Farm, Going Berserk, Of Unknown Origin, Covergirl.
TELEVISION: The Park is Mine, Popeye Doyle.

HERRMANN, EDWARD: Actor. b. Washington, DC, July 21, 1943. e. Bucknell U. Postgrad. Fulbright scholar, London Acad. Music and Dramatic Art 1968–69. Acted with Dallas Theater Center 4 years.
THEATER: NYC: The Basic Training of Pavlo Hummel, Moonchildren, Mrs. Warren's Profession (Tony Award, 1976), Journey's End, The Beach House, The Philadelphia Story, Plenty, Tom and Viv, Julius Caesar, Not About Heroes. London: A Walk in the Woods. Regional: many prods. with Williamstown Playhouse; Harvey, Twelfth Night, Love Letters, Three Sisters.
PICTURES: Lady Liberty, The Paper Chase, The Day of the Dolphin, The Great Gatsby, The Great Waldo Pepper, The Betsy, Brass Target, Take Down, The North Avenue Irregulars, Harry's War, Reds, Death Valley, A Little Sex, Annie, Mrs. Soffel, The Purple Rose of Cairo, The Man With One Red Shoe, Compromising Positions, The Lost Boys, Overboard, Big Business, Hero (unbilled), Born Yesterday, My Boyfriend's Back.
TELEVISION: Series: Beacon Hill, Our Century (host). Guest: M*A*S*H, St. Elsewhere. Mini-Series: Freedom Road. Movies: Eleanor and Franklin, Eleanor and Franklin: The White House Years, A Love Affair: The Eleanor and Lou Gehrig Story, Portrait of a Stripper, The Gift of Life, Memorial Day, So Proudly We Hail, Sweet Poison, Fire in the Dark. Specials: Sorrows of Gin, The Private History of The Campaign That Failed, Murrow, Dear Liar, Concealed Enemies, The Return of Hickey, The Beginning of the Firm, Last Act is a Solo, The End of a Sentence.

HERSHEY, BARBARA: Actress. r.n. Barbara Herzstein. b. Los Angeles, CA, Feb. 5, 1948. e. Hollywood H.S. Briefly in the mid-1970s acted under the name Barbara Seagull.
PICTURES: With Six You Get Eggroll (debut, 1968), Heaven With a Gun, Last Summer, The Liberation of L.B. Jones, The Baby Maker, The Pursuit of Happiness, Dealing, Boxcar Bertha, Angela (Love Comes Quietly), The Crazy World of Julius Vrooder, Diamonds, You and Me, The Last Hard Men, Dirty Knights' Work, The Stunt Man, Americana, Take This Job and Shove It, The Entity, The Right Stuff, The Natural, Hannah and Her Sisters, Hoosiers, Tin Men, Shy People (Cannes Film Fest. Award, 1987), A World Apart (Cannes Film Fest. Award, 1988), The Last Temptation of Christ, Beaches, Tune in Tomorrow, Defenseless, The Public Eye, Falling Down, Swing Kids, Splitting Heirs, A Dangerous Woman.
TELEVISION: Series: The Monroes, From Here to Eternity. Guest: Gidget, The Farmer's Daughter, Run for Your Life, The Invaders, Daniel Boone, CBS Playhouse, Chrysler Theatre, Kung Fu, Alfred Hitchcock Presents (1985). Movies: Flood, In the Glitter Palace, Just a Little Inconvenience, Sunshine Christmas, Angel on My Shoulder, My Wicked Wicked Ways . . . The Legend of Errol Flynn, Passion Flower, A Killing in a Small Town (Emmy & Golden Globe Awards, 1990), Paris Trout, Stay the Night. Mini-Series: A Man Called Intrepid. Special: Working.

HERSKOVITZ, MARSHALL: Producer, Director, Writer. b. Philadelphia, PA, Feb. 23, 1952. e. Brandeis U., BA, 1973; American Film Inst., MFA. 1975. Worked as freelance writer, dir., and prod. on several TV shows. Received Humanitas Award, 1983 and Writers Guild award, 1984.
TELEVISION: Family (writer, dir.), White Shadow (writer), Special Bulletin (prod., writer, 2 Emmys for writing and dramatic special), thirtysomething (exec. prod., co-writer, dir; 2 Emmy awards for writing and dramatic series, 1988; Also Humanitas Award and Directors Guild Award, 1988 & 1989, Peabody Award, 1989.).
PICTURE: Jack the Bear (dir.).

HERTZ, WILLIAM: Executive. b. Wishek, ND, Dec. 5, 1923. Began theatre career in 1939 with Minnesota Amusement in Minneapolis; 1946 joined Fox West Coast Theatres; theatre mgr., booking dept.; 1965 appointed Los Angeles first-run district mgr.; promoted to Pacific Coast Division Mgr., National General Corp., 1967; v.p. Southern Pacific Div. Mgr., National General Theatres, Inc. 1971. Now with Mann Theatres as dir. of marketing, public relations.

HERZOG, WERNER: Producer, Director. r.n. Werner Stipetic. b. Sachrang, Germany, September 5, 1942. e. U. of Munich, Duquesne U., Pittsburgh. Wrote first s.p. 1957; 1961 worked nights in steel factory to raise money for films; 1966, worked for U.S. National Aeronautics and Space Admin.
PICTURES: Signs of Life, Even Dwarfs Started Small, Fata Morgana, The Land of Silence and Darkness; Aguirre—Wrath of God, The Great Ecstasy of the Sculptor Steiner, Every Man for Himself and God Against All, Soufriere, Heart of Glass, Stroszek, Kaspar Hauser, Nosferatu, Woyzeck (also

s.p.), Fitzcarraldo, Where the Green Ants Dream, Slave Coast (dir., s.p.), Echoes of a Somber Empire.

HESSEMAN, HOWARD: Actor. b. Salem, OR, Feb. 27, 1940. Started with the San Francisco group, The Committee and worked as a disc jockey in San Francisco in the late 1960s.
PICTURES: Petulia, Billy Jack, Steelyard Blues, Shampoo, The Sunshine Boys, Jackson County Jail, The Big Bus, The Other Side of Midnight, Silent Movie, Honky Tonk Freeway, Private Lessons, Loose Shoes, Doctor Detroit, This is Spinal Tap, Police Academy 2: Their First Assignment, Clue, My Chauffeur, Flight of the Navigator, Heat, Amazon Women on the Moon, Rubin and Ed.
TELEVISION: Series: WKRP in Cincinnati, One Day at a Time, Head of the Class. Guest: Mary Hartman Mary Hartman, Fernwood 2night, George Burns Comedy Week.Movies: Hustling, The Blue Knight (pilot), Tail Gunner Joe, The Amazing Howard Hughes, Tarantulas: The Deadly Cargo, The Ghost on Flight 401, The Comedy Company, More Than Friends, Outside Chance, The Great American Traffic Jam, Victims, One Shoe Makes It Murder, Best Kept Secrets, The Diamond Trap, Call Me Anna, Murder in New Hampshire: The Pamela Smart Story, Quiet Killer, Lethal Exposure.

HESSLER, GORDON: Producer, Director. b. Berlin, Germany, 1930. e. Reading U., England. Dir., vice pres., Fordel Films, Inc., 1950–58; dir., St. John's Story (Edinborough Film Festival), March of Medicine Series; Dr. Albert Lasker Award; story edit., Alfred Hitchcock Presents 1960–62; assoc. prod., dir., Alfred Hitchcock Hour, 1962; prod., Alfred Hitchcock Hour; prod., dir., Universal TV 1964–66.
PICTURES: The Woman Who Wouldn't Die, The Last Shot You Hear, The Oblong Box, Scream and Scream Again, Cry of the Banshee, Murders of the Rue Morgue, Sinbad's Golden Voyage, Medusa, Embassy, Puzzle, Pray for Death, Rage of Honour, The Misfit Brigade, The Girl in a Swing (also s.p.), Out on Bail, Mayeda.
TELEVISION: Alfred Hitchcock Presents, 1960–62; Alfred Hitchcock Hour, 1962–65; Run For Your Life, Convoy, Bob Hope Chrysler Show, 1964–66; ABC Suspense Movies of the Week, ABC Movies of the Week, 1973. Lucas Tanner, Night Stalker, Amy Prentiss, Switch; Kung Fu, Sara, Hawaii Five-O; Blue Knight; Wonder Woman, Master, Chips, Tales of the Unexpected, Equilizer.
Pilots: Tender Warriors.

HESTON, CHARLTON: Actor. b. Evanston, IL, Oct. 4, 1924. e. Northwestern U. Sch. of Speech. Radio, stage, TV experience. Following coll. served 8 yrs. 11th Air Force, Aleutians. After war, dir. and co-starred with wife at Thomas Wolfe Memorial Theatre, Asheville, NC in State of the Union, Glass Menagerie; member, Katharine Cornell's Co., during first year on Broadway; Anthony and Cleopatra, other Bway. plays, Leaf and Bough, Cockadoodle Doo; Studio One (TV): Macbeth, Taming of the Shrew, Of Human Bondage, Julius Caesar. Pres. Screen Actors Guild 1966–71; Member, Natl. Council on the Arts, 1967–72; Trustee: Los Angeles Center Theater Group, American Film Inst. 1971–; chmn. 1981–; Received Jean Hersholt Humanitarian award from Amer. Acad. M.P. Arts and Sciences, 1978.
RECENT THEATER: A Man for All Seasons, The Caine Mutiny (dir., in China).
PICTURES: Dark City (debut, 1950), The Greatest Show on Earth, The Savage, Ruby Gentry, The President's Lady, Pony Express, Arrowhead, Bad for Each Other, The Naked Jungle, The Secret of the Incas, The Far Horizons, Lucy Gallant, The Private War of Major Benson, The Ten Commandments, Three Violent People, Touch of Evil, The Big Country, The Buccaneer, Ben-Hur (Acad. Award, 1959), The Wreck of the Mary Deare, El Cid, The Pigeon That Took Rome, 55 Days at Peking, Major Dundee, The Agony and the Ecstasy, The War Lord, The Greatest Story Ever Told, Khartoum, Counterpoint, Planet of the Apes, Will Penny, Number One, Beneath the Planet of the Apes, Julius Caesar, The Hawaiians, The Omega Man, Antony and Cleopatra (also dir.), Skyjacked, Soylent Green, The Three Musketeers, Airport 1975, Earthquake, The Four Musketeers, The Last Hard Men, Midway, Two Minute Warning, Crossed Swords (The Prince and the Pauper), Gray Lady Down, Mountain Men, The Awakening, Mother Lode (also dir.), Almost an Angel (cameo), Solar Crisis, Tombstone.
TELEVISION: The Colbys. Mini-Series: Chiefs. Movies: The Nairobi Affair, The Proud Men, A Man For All Seasons (also dir.), Original Sin, Treasure Island, The Little Kidnappers, The Crucifer of Blood, Crash Landing: The Rescue of Flight 232. Special: Charlton Heston Presents the Bible (also writer).

HETZEL, RALPH D.: Executive. b. Corvallis, OR, August 18, 1912. e. Pennsylvania State U., A.B., 1933; U. of London, 1935–36. Private secy. to Gov. Pinchot of PA, 1933–35; did research & study, 1936–39; exec. secty. natl. hdqts., CIO, 1937–40; economic dir., 1938–40; in service, 1942–45. Consultant on labor, Natl. Selective Service hdqts., 1942; manpower consul-

tant War Prod. Bd., 1942–43; dept. vice chmn., manpower requirements, W.P.B., 1943–45; acting vice-chmn., 1945; dir. Office of Labor Requirements, Civilian Prod. Admin., 1945–46; asst. to Secy. of Commerce, U.S. Dept. of Comm., 1946–48; asst. to secty. & dir. Office of Program Planning, 1948–51; asst. admin., Economic Stabilization Agency, 1951; exec. v.p. Motion Picture Association, MP Export Assn., 1951–71; Past president, International Federation of Film Producers Assns.; member of Board of Trustees, California Institute of the Arts and of Pennsylvania State U.; member of Film Advisory Committee of Museum of Modern Art, and of Advisory Council of Edward R. Murrow Center of Public Diplomacy at Tufts U. Dean, Coll. of Fine and Professional Arts, Professor of Art, Kent State U., 1971–76; provost and vice president, academic affairs, California Inst. of the Arts 1976–80; faculty member, 1976–.

HEYMAN, JOHN: Producer. b. England, 1933. e. Oxford U. Started with British TV, creating writing and producing entertainment and documentary programs; expanded into field of personal management, forming International Artists, largest independent p.r. agency in Europe. 1963, formed World Film Services, Ltd. to produce, package and finance films. 1973, formed Genesis Project, educational film co. whose first venture was to translate the Bible onto film.
PICTURES: Privilege, Boom!, Secret Ceremony, Twinky, Bloomfield, The Go-Between, Daniel, Beyond the Limit, The Dresser, A Passage to India (co-prod.), Martin's Day, Steaming, D.A.R.Y.L.

HEYWOOD, ANNE: Actress. b. Birmingham, England, Dec. 11, 1931. m. late producer Raymond Stross. Family tree dates back to Shakespearean actor Thomas Heywood (1570–1641). e. scholarship London Acad. of Dramatic Art and Music. Joined Highbury Theater Players and Birmingham Rep. Starred as Peter Pan, Shakespeare Memorial Theatre, Stratford on Avon.
PICTURES: Checkpoint, Doctor at Large, Dangerous Exile, The Depraved, Violent Playground, Floods of Fear, Heart of a Man, Upstairs and Downstairs, A Terrible Beauty, Carthage in Flames, Petticoat Pirates, Stork Talk, Vengeance (The Brain), Over My Dead Body, The Very Edge, 90 Degrees in the Shade, The Fox, Midas Run, The Chairman, The Nun of Monza, I Want What I Want, Trader Horn, Good Luck Miss Wyckoff, What Waits Below.
TELEVISION: The Equalizer.

HICKMAN, DARRYL: Actor. b. Hollywood, CA, July 28, 1930. Brother of actor Dwayne Hickman. Started screen career 1938 with The Starmaker. Was with CBS as exec. prod., daytime programming. Returned to acting with Network in 1976.
PICTURES: Grapes of Wrath, Young People, Jackass Mail, Northwest Rangers, Keeper of the Flame, And Now Tomorrow, Salty O'Rourke, Captain Eddie, Kiss and Tell, Leave Her to Heaven, Black Gold, Happy Years, Submarine Command, Destination Gobi, Island in the Sky, Sea of Lost Ships, Southwest Passage, The Human Comedy, Men of Boys Town, Fighting Father Dunn, Tea and Sympathy, Network, Looker, Sharky's Machine.
TELEVISION: Series: The Many Loves of Dobie Gills, The Americans. Movie: High School U.S.A.

HICKS, CATHERINE: Actress. b. New York NY, Aug. 6, 1951. e. St. Mary's Notre Dame; Cornell U. (2 year classical acting prog.). On Bdwy. in Tribute, Present Laughter.
PICTURES: Death Valley, Better Late Than Never, Garbo Talks, The Razor's Edge, Fever Pitch, Peggy Sue Got Married, Star Trek IV: The Voyage Home, Like Father Like Son, Child's Play, She's Out of Control, Cognac, Liebestraum.
TELEVISION: Series: Ryan's Hope (1976–8), The Bad News Bears, Tucker's Witch. Movies: Love for Rent, To Race the Wind, Marilyn—the Untold Story, Valley of the Dolls 1981, Happy Endings, Laguna Heat, Spy, Hi Honey I'm Dead. Pilot: The Circle Game.

HIFT, FRED: Executive. b. Vienna, Nov. 27, 1924. e. Vienna, London, Chicago. Early career reporter Chicago Sun and radio work with CBS News, New York; radio desk of NY Times. 1946 joined Boxoffice magazine; 1947 Quigley Publications; 1950 Variety. 1960 began career as publicist on Exodus. 1961 dir. pub., The Longest Day for Darryl Zanuck. 1962 joined Fox in Paris as ad-pub. dir. for Europe. 1964 became dir. European prod. pub. with headquarters London. Formed own pub., p.r. co., Fred Hift Associates, 1970. 1979, joined Columbia Pictures as dir. of eastern ad-pub operations in N.Y.; 1980, to United Artists as intl. adv./pub. v.p. Left to establish Fred Hift Associates, intl. mktg. consultant in New York. 1983, joined Almi Pictures as v.p., mktg. 1985, reactivated F.H.A. 1986, returned to freelance journalism. Currently contributes to a variety of magazines and newspapers and also does reports on radio.

HILL, ARTHUR: Actor. b. Melfort, Saskatchewan, Canada, Aug. 1, 1922. e. U. of British Columbia. Moved to England in 1948, spending ten years in varied stage & screen pursuits; starred on Broadway in The Matchmaker, Home of the Brave, The Male Animal, Look Homeward Angel, All the Way Home, Who's Afraid of Virginia Woolf? (Tony Award, 1963), More Stately Mansions. Film debut in Miss Pilgrim's Progress; other British work includes The Body Said No, Raising A Riot, The Deep Blue Sea.

PICTURES: The Young Doctors, The Ugly American, In the Cool of the Day, Moment to Moment, Harper, Petulia, The Chairman, Rabbit Run, The Pursuit of Happiness, The Andromeda Strain, The Killer Elite, Futureworld, A Bridge Too Far, A Little Romance, Butch and Sundance: The Early Days, The Champ, Dirty Tricks, Making Love, The Amateur, Something Wicked This Way Comes (narrator), One Magic Christmas.

TELEVISION: Series: Owen Marshall: Counselor-At-Law, Hagen, Glitter. Movies: The Other Man, Vanished, Ordeal, Owen Marshall: Counselor at Law (pilot; a.k.a. A Pattern of Morality), Death Be Not Proud, Judge Horton and the Scottsboro Boys, Tell Me My Name, The Ordeal of Dr. Mudd, Revenge of the Stepford Wives, The Return of Frank Cannon, Angel Dusted, Tomorrow's Child, Intimate Agony, Prototype, Love Leads the Way, Murder in Space, Churchill and the Generals, The Guardian, Perry Mason: The Case of the Notorious Nun.

HILL, BERNARD: Actor. b. Manchester, Eng., December 17, 1944. Joined amateur dramatic society in Manchester then studied drama at Manchester Art Coll. Joined Liverpool Everyman rep. co. West End debut as John Lennon in John, Paul, George, Ringo . . . and Burt. Also in Normal Service, Shortlist, Twelfth Night, Macbeth, Cherry Orchard, Gasping.

PICTURES: Dirty Knight's Work, Gandhi, The Bounty, The Chain, Restless Natives, No Surrender, Bellman and True, Drowning by Numbers, Shirley Valentine, Mountains of the Moon, Double X: The Name of the Game.

TELEVISION: I Claudius, Squaring the Circle, John Lennon: A Journey in the Life, New World, St. Luke's Gospel, Boys from the Blackstuff, Burston Rebellion.

HILL, DEBRA: Producer, Director, Writer. b. Philadelphia, PA. Career on feature films started with work as script supvr., asst. dir. and 2nd unit dir. of 13 pictures. Producer's debut with Halloween, 1980, for which also co-wrote script with director John Carpenter.

PICTURES: Halloween (also co-s.p.), The Fog (and co-s.p.), Escape from New York, Halloween II (and co-s.p.), Halloween III: Season of the Witch, The Dead Zone, Clue, Head Office, Adventures in Babysitting, Big Top Pee-wee, Heartbreak Hotel, Gross Anatomy, The Fisher King.

TELEVISION: Adventures in Babysitting (pilot, exec. prod.), El Diablo (exec. prod.), Monsters (dir. episodes), Dream On (dir. episodes), Attack of the 50 Ft. Woman.

HILL, GEORGE ROY: Director. b. Minneapolis, MN, Dec. 20, 1921. e. Yale U., Trinity Coll., Dublin. Started as actor, Irish theatres and U. St. Margaret Webster's Shakespeare Repertory Co., also off-Bdwy. Served as Marine pilot in W.W.II and Korean War. Wrote TV play, My Brother's Keeper, for Kraft Theatre, later rose to director with show. TV assignments as writer-dir. included A Night to Remember, The Helen Morgan Story, Judgment at Nuremberg, Child of Our Time. Directed first Broadway play in 1957, Look Homeward Angel, followed by The Gang's All Here, Greenwillow, Period of Adjustment, Moon on a Rainbow Shawl (also prod.), Henry, Sweet, Henry.

PICTURES: Period of Adjustment (debut, 1962), Toys in the Attic, The World of Henry Orient, Hawaii, Thoroughly Modern Millie, Butch Cassidy and the Sundance Kid, Slaughterhouse Five, The Sting (Acad. Award, 1973), The Great Waldo Pepper (also prod., s.p.), Slap Shot, A Little Romance, The World According to Garp (also prod., cameo), The Little Drummer Girl, Funny Farm.

HILL, JAMES: Producer, Director, Writer. b. Yorkshire, England. Ent. ind. 1938. Early career as asst. dir. and asst. editor. Wrote and dir. many documentaries incl. Giuseppina (Oscar), The Home-Made Car, several children's features. Dir. The Kitchen, Born Free, The Dock Brief, Lunch Hour, Black Beauty, The Belstone Fox, A Study in Terror, Cuba Si (TV series), A Sunday in September, The Saint TV series, The Avengers, The Wild and the Free, Worzel Gummidge (TV series.) Prod. dir. The Young Visitors (Channel 4).

HILL, TERENCE: Actor. r.n. Mario Girotti. b. Venice, March 29, 1941. First attracted attention as actor in Visconti's The Leopard, 1963. Gained fame in European-made westerns. Formed Paloma Films.

PICTURES: God Forgives, I Don't, Boot Hill, Ace High, Barbagia, Anger of the Wind, They Call Me Trinity, Trinity Is Still My Name, My Name Is Nobody, Mr. Billion, March or Die, Super Fuzz, Don Camillo (also dir.), Renegade Luke (also exec. prod.).

HILL, WALTER: Director, Writer, Producer. b. Long Beach, CA, Jan. 10, 1942. e. Michigan State U.

PICTURES: Hickey and Boggs (s.p.), The Getaway (s.p.), Thief Who Came to Dinner (s.p.), The Mackintosh Man (s.p.),

The Drowning Pool (s.p.), Hard Times (dir., s.p.), The Driver (dir., s.p.), The Warriors (dir., s.p.), Alien (prod.), The Long Riders (dir.), Southern Comfort (dir., s.p.), 48 HRS (dir., s.p.), Streets of Fire (dir., s.p.), Brewster's Millions (dir.), Crossroads (dir.), Blue City (prod., s.p.), Aliens (exec. prod., story), Extreme Prejudice (dir.), Red Heart (dir., prod.), Johnny Handsome (dir.), Another 48 HRS (dir.), Alien (s.p., prod.), Trespass (dir.), The Getaway (1993, co-s.p.), Geronimo (dir., co-prod.).

TELEVISION: Series: Tales From the Crypt (exec. prod.; also dir. & writer of episodes: The Man Who Was Death, Cutting Cards, Deadline: ACE Award).

HILLER, ARTHUR: Director. b. Edmonton, Alberta, Can., Nov. 22, 1923. e. U. of Alberta, U. of Toronto, U. of British Columbia. Worked for Canadian Broadcasting Corp. before moving to L.A. Pres. of Directors Guild of America.

TELEVISION: Matinee Theatre, Playhouse 90, Climax, Alfred Hitchcock Presents, Gunsmoke, Ben Casey, Rte. 66, Naked City, The Dick Powell Show.

PICTURES: The Careless Years, Miracle of the White Stallions, The Wheeler Dealers, Americanization of Emily, Promise Her Anything, Penelope, Tobruk, The Tiger Makes Out, Popi, The Out-of-Towners, Love Story, Plaza Suite, The Hospital, Man of La Mancha, The Crazy World of Julius Vrooder, The Man in the Glass Booth, W. C. Fields and Me, Silver Streak, Nightwing, The In-Laws (also co-prod.), Making Love, Author Author, Romantic Comedy, Lonely Guy (also prod.), Teachers, Outrageous Fortune, See No Evil Hear No Evil, Taking Care of Business, Married to It, The Babe.

HILLER, DAME WENDY: D.B.E., 1975, O.B.E., 1971, Hon. LLD, Manchester, 1984. Actress. b. Bramhall, Cheshire, Eng., Aug. 15, 1912. e. Winceby House Sch., Bexhill. On stage 1930, Manchester Repertory Theatre, England; then on British tour. London debut 1935 in Love On the Dole; to N.Y., same role 1936. m.p. debut in Lancashire Luck, 1937.

PLAYS: First Gentleman, Cradle Song, Tess of the D'Urbervilles, Heiress (NY & London), Ann Veronica, Waters of the Moon, Night of the Ball, Old Vic Theatre, Wings of the Dove, Sacred Flame, Battle of Shrivings, Crown Matrimonial, John Gabriel Borkman, Waters of the Moon (revival), Aspern Papers (revival), The Importance of Being Earnest, Driving Miss Daisy.

PICTURES: Lancashire Luck (debut, 1937), Pygmalion, Major Barbara, I Know Where I'm Going, Outcast of the Islands, Single Handed (Sailor of the King), Something of Value, How to Murder a Rich Uncle, Separate Tables (Acad. Award, supp. actress, 1958) Sons and Lovers, Toys in the Attic, A Man For All Seasons, Murder on the Orient Express, Voyage of the Damned, The Cat and the Canary, The Elephant Man, Making Love, The Lonely Passion of Judith Hearne.

TELEVISION: The Curse of King Tut's Tomb, David Copperfield (theatrical in U.K.), Witness for the Prosecution, Anne of Green Gables—The Sequel, Peer Gynt, The Kingfisher, All Passion Spent, A Taste for Death, Ending Up, The Best of Friends, The Countess Alice.

HILLERMAN, JOHN: Actor. b. Denison, TX, Dec. 20, 1932. e. U. of Texas. While in U.S. Air Force joined community theatre group and went to New York after completing military service. Studied at American Theatre Wing, leading to summer stock and off-Bdwy.

PICTURES: The Last Picture Show, Lawman, The Carey Treatment, What's Up Doc?, Skyjacked, High Plains Drifter, The Outside Man, The Thief Who Came to Dinner, Paper Moon, Blazing Saddles, Chinatown, At Long Last Love, The Nickel Ride, The Day of the Locust, Lucky Lady, Audrey Rose, Sunburn, History of the World Part I, Up the Creek.

TELEVISION: Series: Ellery Queen, The Betty White Show, Magnum P.I. (Emmy Award), The Hogan Family. Movies: Sweet Sweet Rachel, The Great Man's Whiskers, The Law, Ellery Queen, The Invasion of Johnson County, Relentless, Kill Me If You Can, A Guide for the Married Woman, Betrayal, Marathon, The Murder That Wouldn't Die, Little Gloria . . . Happy at Last, Assault and Matrimony, Street of Dreams, Hands of a Murderer. Mini-Series: Around the World in 80 Days.

HILLMAN, WILLIAM BRYON: Writer, Director, Producer. b. Chicago, IL, Feb. 3, 1951. e. Oklahoma Military Acad., UCLA. Head of production at Intro-Media Productions; Fairchild Entertainment; Spectro Productions; Double Eagle Entertainment Corp; Excellent Films Inc.; Creative consultant for The Hit 'Em Corp. Presently head of SpectroMedia Entertainment.

PICTURES: Dir.-Writer: His Name is Janey (also exec. prod.), Tis the Season (also co-prod.), Strangers (also co-prod.), Back on the Street (also co-prod.), Loner (also co-prod.), Fast & Furious, The Master, Lovelines (s.p. only), Double Exposure (also co-prod.), The Passage, Campus, The Photographer (also prod.), The Man From Clover Grove (also co-prod.), Thetus, The Trail Ride (also co-prod.), Betta Betta (also prod.), Ragin' Cajun (also co-prod.).

TELEVISION: Working Together (pilot writer), Disco-Theque Pilot (dir., writer), Everything Will Be Alright (writer), Money (dir., writer), RIPA (writer).
NOVELS: Silent Changes, The Combination, The Liar, Additives The Perfect Crime, Why Me, The Loner.

HINES, GREGORY: Actor, Dancer. b. NY, Feb. 14, 1946. Early career as junior member of family dancing act starting at age 2. Nightclub debut at 5 as Hines Kids with brother Maurice (later renamed Hines Brothers as teenagers) and joined by father as Hines, Hines and Dad. Bdwy debut at 8 in The Girl in Pink Tights. Continued dancing with brother until 1973. Formed and performed with jazz-rock band, Severance. Solo album, Gregory Hines (1988).
THEATER: The Last Minstral Show (closed out of town), Eubie (Theatre World Award), Comin' Uptown (Tony Award nom.), Sophisticated Ladies (Tony Award nom.), Twelfth Night, Jelly's Last Jam (Tony Award, 1992).
PICTURES: History of the World—Part I (debut, 1981), Wolfen, Deal of the Century, The Muppets Take Manhattan, The Cotton Club (also choreographer), White Nights, Running Scared, Off Limits, Tap (also choreographer), Eve of Destruction, A Rage in Harlem.
TELEVISION: Guest: The Tonight Show, Motown Returns to the Apollo, Saturday Night Live. Movies: White Lie, T Bone N Weasel.

HINGLE, PAT: Actor. b. Miami, FL, July 19, 1924. e. U. of Texas, 1949. Studied at Herbert Berghof Studio, American Theatre Wing, Actor's Studio.
THEATRE: End as a Man (N.Y. debut, 1953), The Rainmaker, Festival, Cat on a Hot Tin Roof, Girls of Summer, Dark at the Top of the Stairs, J.B., The Deadly Game, Macbeth and Troilus and Cresida (with American Shakespeare Festival, Stratford, CT), Strange Interlude, Blues for Mr. Charlie, A Girl Could Get Lucky, The Glass Menagerie, The Odd Couple, Johnny No-Trump, The Price, Child's Play, The Selling of the President, That Championship Season, The Lady from the Sea, A Life, Thomas Edison: Reflections of a Genius (one man show).
RADIO: Voice of America.
PICTURES: On the Waterfront (debut, 1954), The Strange One, No Down Payment, Splendor in the Grass, All the Way Home, The Ugly American, Invitation to a Gunfighter, Nevada Smith, Sol Madrid, Hang 'em High, Jigsaw, Norwood, Bloody Mama, WUSA, The Carey Treatment, One Little Indian, Running Wild, Nightmare Honeymoon, The Super Cops, The Gauntlet, When You Comin' Back Red Ryder?, Norma Rae, Sudden Impact, Running Brave, Going Berserk, The Falcon and the Snowman, Brewster's Millions, Maximum Overdrive, Baby Boom, The Land Before Time (voice), Batman, The Grifters, Batman Returns.
TELEVISION: Series: Stone. Guest: Gunsmoke, MASH, Blue Skies, Matlock, Twilight Zone, The Untouchables, Trapper John M.D., Murder She Wrote, In the Heat of the Night, Cheers. Movies: The Ballad of Andy Crocker, A Clear and Present Danger, The City, Sweet Sweet Rachel, If Tomorrow Comes, Trouble Comes to Town, The Last Angry Man, The Secret Life of John Chapman, Escape from Bogen County, Sunshine Christmas, Tarantulas, Elvis, Stone (pilot), Disaster at the Coastliner, Wild Times, Of Mice and Men, Washington Mistress, The Fighter, Stranger on My Land, The Town Bully, Everybody's Baby: The Rescue of Jessica McClure, Not of This World, Gunsmoke: To the Last Man, Citizen Cohn, The Habitation of Dragons, Simple Justice. Mini-Series: War and Remembrance, The Kennedy's of Massachusetts.

HINKLE, ROBERT: Actor, Producer, Director. b. Brownfield, TX, July 25, 1930. e. Texas Tech. U. Joined Rodeo Cowboys Association, 1950 and rodeoed professionally until 1953 when began acting career in Outlaw Treasure. Pres. Cinema Pictures, Inc.
PICTURES: Giant, All the Fine Young Cannibals, Hud, The First Texan, Dakota Incident, Gun the Man Down, The Oklahoman, First Traveling Saleslady, No Place to Land, Under Fire, Speed Crazy, The Gunfight at Dodge City, Broken Land, Law in Silver City, Producer-director: Ole Rex (award for Family Entertainment), Born Hunter, Trauma, Something Can Be Done, Mr. Chat, Stuntman, Hud, Jumping Frog Jubilee, Mr. Chat-Mexico Safari, Trail Ride, Virginia City Cent., Texas Today, Texas Long Horns, Kentucky Thoroughbred Racing, Country Music, Guns of a Stranger.
TELEVISION: Prod. & Dir.: Test Pilot, Dial 111, Juvenile Squad, X13 Vertijet, Cellist Extraordinary, Sunday Challenge, The Drifter, Country Music Tribute, World of Horses, Country Music Videos.

HIRD, THORA: Actress. b. Morecambe, Lancashire, Eng., May 28, 1914. e. The Nelson Sch., Morecambe.
PICTURES: (Screen debut, 1940) The Black Sheep of Whitehall; Street Corner, Turn the Key Softly, Personal Affair, The Great Game, Storks Don't Talk, Shop Soiled, For Better or Worse; Love Match, One Good Turn, Quatermass Experiment, Simon and Laura, Lost, Sailor Beware, Home and Away, Good Companions, The Entertainer, A Kind of Loving,

Term of Trial, Bitter Harvest, Rattle of a Simple Man, Some Will Some Won't, The Nightcomers, Consuming Passions.
TELEVISION: The Winslow Boy, The Bachelor, What Happens to Love, The Witching Hour, So Many Children, The Queen Came By, Albert Hope, All Things Bright and Beautiful, Say Nothing, Meet the Wife, Who's a Good Boy Then? I AM! Dixon of Dock Green, Romeo and Juliet, The First Lady, Ours Is a Nice House, The Foxtrot, Seasons, She Stoops to Conquer, Villa Maroc, When We Are Married, In Loving Memory, Flesh and Blood, Your Songs of Praise Choice, Hallelujah, Happiness, That's the Main Thing, Intensive Care, In Loving Memory, Praise Be, Last of the Summer Wine, The Fall, Cream Cracker Under the Settee (Talking Heads), Perfect Scoundrels.

HIRSCH, JUDD: Actor. b. New York, NY, March 15, 1935. e. City Coll. of New York. Studied physics but turned to acting; first acting job in 1962 performing with stock co. in Colorado. Returned to N.Y. to work on stage and since has also done films and TV. Won Emmy as best actor in a comedy 1981 and 1983 for Taxi.
THEATER: Barefoot in the Park, Scuba Duba, Mystery Play, Hot L Baltimore, King of the United States, Knock Knock, Chapter Two; Talley's Folly (Obie Award), I'm Not Rappaport (Tony Award), Conversations With My Father (Tony Award).
PICTURES: Serpico, King of the Gypsies, Ordinary People, Without a Trace, The Goodbye People, Teachers, Running on Empty.
TELEVISION: Series: Delvecchio, Taxi (1978–83), Detective in the House, Dear John. Movies: The Law, Fear on Trial, Legend of Valentino, The Keegans, Sooner or Later, Marriage is Alive and Well, Brotherly Love, First Steps, The Great Escape: The Untold Story, She Said No.

HIRSCHFIELD, ALAN J.: Executive. b. Oklahoma City, OK; Oct. 10, 1935. e. U. of Oklahoma, B.A.; Harvard Business School, M.B.A. V.P., Allen & Co., 1959–66; Financial v.p. & dir. Warner/7 Arts, 1967–68; v.p. & dir., American Diversified Enterprises, 1969–73; pres. & chief exec. officer, Columbia Pictures Industries, 1973–78; consultant, Warner Communications, 1979, 1980–85, chmn. and chief exec. officer, 20th Century-Fox. Current: Co-CEO Data Broadcasting Corp.
Vice Chairman: Cancer Research Institute. Pres. of Jackson Hole Land Trust, Dir. of Ameriscribe Inc., Cantel Inc., CPP Belwin, Conservation Intl.

HIRSHAN, LEONARD: Theatrical Agent. b. New York, NY, Dec. 27, 1927. e. NYU. Joined William Morris Agency as agent trainee, New York, 1951. Agent legit theatre & TV dept. 1952–54. Sr. exec. agent M.P. dept., California office, 1955; sr. v.p., 1983; head of m.p. dept., west coast, 1986; named exec. v.p. and mem. bd. of dir., William Morris Agency, 1989; mem. bd. of dir., Center Theater Group, 1988; bd. governors Cedars-Sinai Hospital in L.A. 1987.

HIRT, AL: Musician. b. New Orleans, LA, Nov. 7, 1922. e. Cincinnati Conservatory of Music. Military service four years. Played with Tommy and Jimmy Dorsey bands, Ray McKinley and Horace Heidt; appeared, Dunes Hotel, Harrah's Club, Basin Street East, Cloisters, Palmer House, Eden Roc Hotel, Greek Theatre. European tour concerts. Inaugural Ball, President John F. Kennedy, Jan. 1961. Grammy Award 1964 for single Java. Voted best trumpter, Playboy Jazz Poll 1962–77.
TELEVISION: Dinah Shore Show, Jack Paar Show, Ed Sullivan, NBC Special Home For the Holidays, Bell Telephone Hour Rainbow of Stars, Andy Williams Show, Tonight Show, Today Show, Perry Como Show, Lively Ones, Jerry Lewis Show, Fanfare.
PICTURES: World By Night, Rome Adventure.
RECORDINGS: RCA: The Greatest Horn in the World, Al—He's the King—Hirt, Horn-A-Plenty, Al Hirt at the Mardi Gras, Trumpet & Strings, Our Man in New Orleans, Honey in the Horn, Beauty and the Beard, Pop Goes the Trumpet, Boston Pops, many others.

HITZIG, RUPERT: Producer, Director. New York, NY, Aug. 15, 1942. e. Harvard. At CBS as doc. writer-producer-director; later moved into dramas and comedy. Alan King's partner in King-Hitzig Prods.
TELEVISION: Much Ado About Nothing; The Wonderful World of Jonathan Winters; Playboy After Dark; How to Pick Up Girls; Return to Earth, Saturday Night Live, Birds of Prey, annual comedy awards, television series and numerous specials.
PICTURES: Prod.: Electra Glide in Blue, Happy Birthday Gemini, Cattle Annie and Little Britches, Wolfen (also 2nd unit dir.), Jaws 3-D, The Last Dragon, The Squeeze. Dir.: Night Visitor, Backstreet Dreams.

HOBERMAN, DAVID: Executive. Started career as prod. exec. with TAT Communications for five years. 1982–85, worked as m.p. agent with Writers and Artists Agency and later at Ziegler Associates and ICM. 1985, named v.p. of prod. for Walt Disney Pictures based at studio. 1987, promoted to sr.

v.p., prod. 1988, named president, production. 1989, pres. Touchstone Pictures.

HOBIN, BILL: TV Producer, Director. r.n. Charles W. Hobin; b. Evanston, IL, Nov. 12, 1923. e. U. of Southern California. Prod. mgr., Coronet Instructional Films, Glenview, IL; dir., Garroway at Large, Wayne King Show from Chic., 1949–51; dir., Assignment Manhunt; Nothing But the Best; Les Paul and Mary Ford; Your Show of Shows, 1951–54; assoc. prod.-dir., Max Liebman Presents (Spectaculars), prod. dir. Fred Waring Show, Andy Williams Show, Pat Boone, Timex All-Star Jazz Show. dir. Your Hit Parade. Prod.-dir. The Golden Circle, 1959; The Bell Telephone Hour, 1959–60; The American Cowboy; Sing Along with Mitch, 1960–63; dir., Judy Garland Show; prod., dir., Victor Borge at Carnegie Hall; dir., m.p. Chrysler Show-Go-Round, N.Y. World's Fair. Dir.: Meredith Willson Special; Jack Jones on the Move Special; Red Skelton Hour, 1964–68; prod.; Red Skelton Hour, 1968–70; prod. and dir. The Bill Cosby Special I, 1968; prod., dir., The Tim Conway Comedy Hour; prod., dir. The CBS Newcomers series; dir. An Evening With My Three Sons special, prod., dir. Michel Legrand Special; prod., dir. Fred Astaire special; director, Maude; director, A Touch of Grace; prod.-dir.: Dinah, Won't You Please Come Home!; Bobby Goldsboro Show (syn); Your Hit Parade; prod.-dir. Flip Wilson Special; Dionne Warwick Special, Wayne Newton Special, all 1975; 1976— dir., Welcome (Back), Kotter, Prod.-dir., Monty Hall's Variety Special. Dir., Bert Convy Show; dir., George Burns Special; McLean Stevenson Show; dir., Three's Company. Producer-director Bob Hope Specials, (1978–79); director Celebrity Challenge of the Sexes, 1979; director, Steve Allen Special; director, No Soap Radio, 1982.

HOCK, MORT: Executive. Blaine-Thompson Agency; A. E. Warner Bros., 1948; David Merrick B'way Prod., 1958; asst. adv. mgr., Paramount Pictures Corp., 1960; adv. mgr., United Artists Corp., 1962; dir. adv., United Artists Corp., July 1964; adv. dir., Para., 1965; v.p. advertising and public relations, Paramount Pict. Corp., 1968–71; v.p., marketing, Rastar Prods., 1971; exec. v.p., Charles Schlaifer & Co., 1974; sr. v.p. entertainment div., DDB Needham Worldwide, 1983.

HODGE, PATRICIA: Actress. b. Cleethorpes, Lincolnshire, England, Sept. 29, 1946. Studied at London Acad. of Music and Dramatic Arts.
THEATER: Popkiss, Two Gentlemen of Verona, Pippin, The Mitford Girls, Benefactors, Noel and Gertie.
PICTURES: The Elephant Man, Betrayal, Sunset, Thieves in the Night, Diamond's Edge.
TELEVISION: The Naked Civil Servant, Rumpole of the Bailey, Edward and Mrs. Simpson, Holding the Fort, Jemima Shore Investigates, Hay Fever, Hotel Du Lac, The Life and Loves of a She-Devil, Exclusive Yarns, Let's Face the Music of . . . , Inspector Morse, The Shell Seekers, The Secret Life of Ian Fleming, The Heat of the Day, Rich Tea and Sympathy, The Cloning of Joanna May.

HOFFMAN, DUSTIN: b. Los Angeles, CA, Aug. 8, 1937. m. Lisa Hoffman. e. Los Angeles Conservatory of Music, Santa Monica Coll., Pasadena Playhouse, 1958. Worked as an attendant at a psychiatric institution, a demonstrator in Macy's toy dept., and a waiter. First stage role 1960 in Yes Is for a Very Young Man, at Sarah Lawrence Coll. Acted in summer stock, television and dir. at community theatre. Asst. dir. Off-Bdwy A View From the Bridge. Broadway and Off Broadway plays include: A Cook for Mr. General (bit part, Bdwy debut), Harry Noon and Night, Journey of the Fifth Horse (Obie Award), Eh? (Vernon Rice & Theatre World Awards), Jimmy Shine, All Over Town (dir. only), Death of a Salesman (Drama Desk Award), The Merchant of Venice (also London).
TELEVISION: Specials: Journey of the Fifth Horse, The Star Wagons, Free to Be You and Me, Bette Midler: Old Red Hair is Back, Common Threads: Stories from the Quilt (narrator), The Earth Day Special. Movies: The Point (narrator), Death of a Salesman (Emmy Award). Guest: Naked City, The Defenders.
PICTURES: The Tiger Makes Out (debut, 1967), Madigan's Millions, The Graduate (Acad. Award nom.), Midnight Cowboy (Acad. Award nom.), John and Mary, Little Big Man, Who Is Harry Kellerman?, Straw Dogs, Alfredo Alfredo, Papillon, Lenny (Acad. Award nom), All the President's Men, Marathon Man, Straight Time, Agatha, Kramer vs. Kramer (Acad. Award, 1979), Tootsie (Acad. Award nom.), Ishtar, Rain Man (Acad, Award, 1988), Family Business, Dick Tracy, Billy Bathgate, Hook, Hero.

HOFFMAN, JOSEPH: Writer. b. New York, NY, Feb. 20, 1909. e. UCLA. Newspaperman, screen writer, magazine writer. TV prod. Now TV and screen freelance writer.
PICTURES: China Sky, Don't Trust Your Husband, Gung-Ho, And Baby Makes Three, Weekend with Father, Duel at Silver Creek, At Sword's Point, Has Anybody Seen My Gal?, Against All Flags, No Room for the Groom, Lone Hand, Yankee Pasha, Rails into Laramie, Tall Man Riding, Chicago

Syndicate, Live a Little, How to Make Love and Like It, Sex and the Single Girl.
TELEVISION: Producer: Ford Theatre, Colt 45. Writer: Leave It to Beaver, My Three Sons, The Virginian, Love American Style, Bonanza, Patty Duke Show, Family Affair, etc.

HOGAN, PAUL: Actor, Writer. b. Lightning Ridge, Australia, Oct. 8, 1939. m. actress Linda Kozlowski. Worked as rigger before gaining fame on Australian TV as host of nightly current affairs show (A Current Affair) and The Paul Hogan Show. Shows now syndicated in 26 countries. In U.S. gained attention with commercials for Australian Tourist Commission. 1985, starred in dramatic role on Australian TV in series, Anzacs. Live one-man show, Paul Hogan's America, 1991.
PICTURES: Fatty Finn (debut, 1980), Crocodile Dundee (also co-s.p.), Crocodile Dundee II (also exec. prod., co-s.p.), Almost an Angel (also exec. prod., s.p.).
TELEVISION: Anzacs: The War Down Under.

HOGARTH, JOHN M.: Executive. b. Hampstead, London, England, 1931. Man. Dir. Mayfair Entertainment Ltd.

HOLBROOK, HAL: Actor. b. Cleveland, OH, Feb. 17, 1925. m. actress Dixie Carter. e. Denison U., 1948. Summer stock 1947–53. Gained fame and several awards for performance as Mark Twain on stage in Mark Twain Tonight over a period of years throughout the US and abroad.
THEATER: Mark Twain Tonight (Tony Award, 1966), Do You Know the Milky Way?, Abe Lincoln in Illinois, American Shakespeare Fest., Lincoln Center Repertory (After the Fall, Marco Millions, Incident at Vichy, Tartuffe), The Glass Menagerie, The Apple Tree, I Never Sang For My Father, Man of La Mancha, Does a Tiger Wear a Necktie?, Lake of the Woods, Buried Inside Extra, The Country Girl, King Lear. Regional: Our Town, The Merchant of Venice, Uncle Vanya.
PICTURES: The Group (debut, 1966), Wild in the Streets, The People Next Door, The Great White Hope, They Only Kill Their Masters, Magnum Force, The Girl from Petrovka. All the President's Men, Midway, Julia, Rituals, Capricorn One, Natural Enemies, The Fog, The Kidnapping of the President, Creepshow, Star Chamber, Wall Street, The Unholy, Fletch Lives, The Firm.
TELEVISION: Series: The Senator (Emmy Award), Designing Women, Portrait of America (4 annual ACE Awards, Emmy Award), Evening Shade. Movies: Coronet Blue, The Whole World is Watching, A Clear and Present Danger, Travis Logan, Suddenly Single, Goodbye Raggedy Ann, That Certain Summer, Murder by Natural Causes, Legend of the Golden Gun, When Hell Was in Session, Off the Minnesota Strip, The Killing of Randy Webster, Under Siege, Behind Enemy Lines, Dress Gray, The Fortunate Pilgrim, Three Wishes for Billy Grier, Emma, Queen of the South Seas, Day One, Sorry Wrong Number, A Killing in a Small Town, Bonds of Love. Specials: Mark Twain Tonight, Pueblo (Emmy Award), Sandburg's Lincoln (Emmy Award), Our Town, Plaza Suite, The Glass Menagerie, The Awakening Land, The Oath: 33 Hours in the Life of God, Omnibus. Mini-Series: North and South Books I & II, Celebrity, George Washington, Rockport Christmas.

HOLDRIDGE, LEE: Composer. b. Port-au-Prince, Haiti, March 3, 1944. e. Manhattan School of Music. Music arranger for Neil Diamond, 1969–73, with whom he collaborated on the score for Jonathan Livingston Seagull. Wrote score for Bdwy musical Into the Light (1986). With Alan Raph wrote score for the Joffrey Ballet's Trinity.
PICTURES: Jeremy, Jonathan Livingston Seagull, Forever Young Forever Free, Mustang Country, The Other Side of the Mountain-Part 2, The Pack, Moment By Moment, Oliver's Story, French Postcards, Tilt, American Pop, The Beastmaster, Mr. Mom, Micki and Maude, Splash, Sylvester, 16 Days of Glory, Transylvania 6-5000, The Men's Club, Big Business, Old Gringo, Pastime.
TELEVISION: Series: One Life to Live, Hec Ramsey, Moonlighting, Beauty and the Beast, Bob. Movies: East of Eden, Fly Away Home, The Day the Loving Stopped, For Ladies Only, The Sharks, The Story Lady, One Against the Wind, In Love With an Older Woman, Running Out, Thursday's Child, Wizards and Warriors, The Mississippi, Legs, I Want to Live, Letting Go, Fatal Judgment, The Tenth Man, I'll Take Manhattan, Do You Know the Muffin Man?, Incident at Dark River, A Mother's Courage, In the Arms of a Killer, Face of a Stranger, Day-O, Deadly Matrimony, Killer Rules, One Against the Wind, Call of the Wild, Torch Song.

HOLLAND, AGNIESZKA: Director, Writer. b. Warsaw, Poland, Nov. 28, 1948. e. FAMU, Prague. m. director Laco Adamik. Studied filmmaking in Czechoslovakia with Milos Forman and Ivan Passer. Moved to Paris in 1981.
PICTURES: Screen Tests (dir., s.p. episode), Provincial Actors (dir., s.p.), Bez Znieczulenia (s.p.), Goraczka (dir.), A Woman Alone (dir., s.p.), Danton (s.p.), Przesluchanie (actor), Love in Germany (s.p.), Angry Harvest (dir., s.p.), Anna (s.p., story), Les Possedes (s.p.), La Amiga (s.p.), To Kill a Priest (dir., s.p.), Korczak (s.p.), Europa Europa (dir., s.p.), Olivier Olivier (dir., s.p.), The Secret Garden.

TELEVISION: Evening With Abdon, The Children of Sunday, Something for Something.

HOLLAND, TOM: Director, Writer. b. Highland, NY. e. Northwestern U. Started as actor, working at Bucks County Playhouse in PA and HB Studios in NY. Appeared on daytime serials Love of Life, Love is a Many-Splendored Thing. Turned to commercial prod. while attended UCLA law school, then took up screenwriting.
PICTURES: Writer: The Beast Within, The Class of 1984, Pyscho II, Cloak and Dagger. Director: Fright Night (also s.p.), Fatal Beauty, Child's Play (also co-s.p.), The Temp.
TELEVISION: Movie: The Stranger Within. Series: Tales From the Crypt (dir. 3 episodes: Love Come Hack to Me - also co-writer, Four-Sided Triangle - also co-writer, King of the Road).

HOLLENDER, ALFRED L.: Advertising executive. b. Chicago, IL. e. U. of Illinois. Was associated with Radio Stations WIND-WJJD, Chicago as continuity ed., program dir. & asst. to pres.; entered military service in 1943; exec. v.p. & partner of Louis G. Cowan, Inc., exec. v.p. and dir. radio-TV dept., Grey Adv. Agency; pres., Grey Int'l.

HOLLIMAN, EARL: Actor. b. Delhi, LA, Sept. 11, 1928. e. U. of Southern California, Pasadena Playhouse. Pres., Actors and Others for Animals. Golden Globe winner.
STAGE: Camino Real (Mark Taper Forum), A Streetcar Named Desire (Ahmanson).
PICTURES: Scared Stiff, Girls of Pleasure Island, Destination Gobi, East of Sumatra, Devil's Canyon, Tennessee Champ, The Bridges at Toko-Ri, Broken Lance, Big Combo, I Died a Thousand Times, Forbidden Planet, Giant, Burning Hills, The Rainmaker, Gunfight at the OK Corral, Trooper Hook, Don't Go Near the Water, Hot Spell, The Trap, Last Train From Gun Hill, Visit to a Small Planet, Armored Command, Summer and Smoke, The Sons of Katie Elder, A Covenant with Death, The Power, Anzio, The Biscuit Eater, Good Luck Miss Wyckoff, Sharky's Machine.
TELEVISION: Series: Hotel de Paree (1959–60); Wide Country (1962–63); Police Woman (1974–78), P.S. I Luv You (1991), Delta (1992). Pilot: Twilight Zone. Movies: Tribes, Alias Smith and Jones, Cannon, The Desperate Mission, Trapped, Cry Panic, I Love You . . . Goodbye, Alexander: The Other Side of Down, The Solitary Man, Where the Ladies Go, Country Gold, Gunsmoke: Return to Dodge, American Harvest, P.S. I Luv You (pilot). Mini-Series: The Thorn Birds.

HOLM, CELESTE: Actress. b. New York, NY, Apr. 29, 1919. e. Univ. Sch. for Girls, Chicago, Francis W. Parker, Chicago, Lycée Victor Durui (Paris), U. of Chicago, UCLA. p. Theodor Holm and Jean Parke Holm. m. actor Wesley Addy.
THEATRE: On Bdwy incl. Gloriana, The Time of Your Life, 8 O'Clock Tuesday, Another Sun, Return of the Vagabond, My Fair Ladies, Papa Is All, All the Comforts of Home, The Damask Cheek, Oklahoma!, Bloomer Girl, She Stoops to Conquer, Affairs of State, Anna Christie, The King and I, Interlock, Third Best Sport, Invitation to a March, Mame, Candida, Habeas Corpus, The Utter Glory of Morrissey Hall, I Hate Hamlet. Off-Bdwy: A Month in the Country. Theatre-in-Concert for the U.S. State Department in 8 countries May–July 1966. Also: Janet Flanner's Paris Was Yesterday; Natl. Tour: Mame (Sarah Sidons Award), Hay Fever, Road to Mecca, Cocktail Hour.
PICTURES: Three Little Girls in Blue (debut, 1946), Carnival in Costa Rica, Gentleman's Agreement (Acad. Award, supp. actress, 1947), Road House, The Snake Pit, Chicken Every Sunday, Come to the Stable (Acad. Award nom.), A Letter to Three Wives (voice), Everybody Does It, Champagne for Caesar, All About Eve (Acad. Award nom.), The Tender Trap, High Society, Bachelor Flat, Doctor You've Got To Be Kidding, Tom Sawyer, Bittersweet Love, The Private Files of J. Edgar Hoover, Three Men and a Baby.
TELEVISION: Specials: A Clearing in the Wood, Play of the Week, Cinderella, Nora's Christmas Gift. Mini-Series: Backstairs at the White House (Emmy nom.). Movies: Underground Man, Death Cruise, Love Boat II, Midnight Lace, The Shady Hill Kidnapping, This Girl for Hire, Murder by the Book, Polly, Polly—Comin' Home! Pilot: Road Show. Series: Honestly Celeste, Who Pays, Nancy, Jessie, Falcon Crest, Christine Cromwell, Loving. Guest: Love Boat, Trapper John M.D., Magnum P.I.
RADIO: People at the U.N., Theatre Guild on the Air, Mystery Theatre.

HOLM, IAN: C.B.E. Actor. b. Ilford, Essex, England, Sept. 12, 1931. r.n. Ian Holm Cuthbert. e. Royal Acad. of Dramatic Art. On British stage—Love Affair, Titus Andronicus, Henry IV, Ondine, Becket, The Homecoming (Tony Award, 1967), Henry V, Richard III, Romeo and Juliet, The Sea, etc.—before entering films.
PICTURES: The Bofors Gun (debut, 1968), A Midsummer Night's Dream, The Fixer, Oh! What a Lovely War, A Severed Head, Nicholas and Alexandra, Mary Queen of Scots, Young Winston, The Homecoming, Juggernaut, Robin and Marian, Shout at the Devil, March or Die, Alien, Chariots of Fire

(Acad. Award nom.), Time Bandits, Return of the Soldier, Greystoke: The Legend of Tarzan Lord of the Apes, Dance With a Stranger, Wetherby, Dreamchild, Brazil, Laughterhouse, Another Woman, Henry V, Hamlet, Kafka, Naked Lunch, The Hour of the Pig.
TELEVISION: Mini-Series/Movies: Les Miserables, S.O.S. Titanic, Napoleon, We the Accused, All Quiet on the Western Front, Holocaust, Man in the Iron Mask, Jesus of Nazareth, Thief of Bagdad, Game Set and Match, A Season of Giants. Specials: The Browning Version, Murder By the Book, Uncle Vanya, Tailor of Gloucester, The Lost Boys, The Last Romantics.

HOMEIER, SKIP: Actor. r.n. George Vincent Homeier. b. Chicago, IL, Oct. 5, 1930. e. UCLA. Started in radio, 1936–43; on B'way stage, Tomorrow the World, 1943–44.
PICTURES: Tomorrow the World, Boy's Ranch, Mickey, Arthur Takes Over, The Big Cat, The Gunfighter, Halls of Montezuma, Has Anybody Seem My Gal?, Beachhead, The Black Widow, Ten Wanted Men, The Road to Denver, The Burning Hills, Between Heaven and Hell, Cry Vengeance, Dakota Incident, No Road Back, Stranger at My Door, Thunder Over Arizona, The Tall T, Decision at Durango, The Punderers of Painted Flats, Commanche Station, Showdown, Bullet for a Badman, The Ghost and Mr. Chicken, Tiger By the Tail.
TELEVISION: Series: Dan Raven, The Interns. Guest: Playhouse 90, Alcoa Hour, Kraft Theatre, Studio 1, Armstrong Circle Theatre, Alfred Hitchcock. Movies: The Challenge, Two for the Money, Voyage of the Yes, Helter Skelter, Overboard, The Wild Wild West Revisited Mini-Series: Washington: Behind Closed Doors.

HONG, WILSON S.: Cinematographer. b. Butte, MT, Dec. 18, 1934. e. Montana State U., Brooks Inst. of Photography. 1965, Freelance photographer for national magazine and world-wide newspaper syndication; 1966, Photographic Director of US Forest Service Fire & Research Division; 1967, first cameraman on various documentaries, industrials, commercials, sports specials.
PICTURES: Bigfoot, Operation North Slope, John Wayne's No Substitute for Victory', The Hellcats, Dear Dead Delilah, Zodiac Killer, Velvet Vampire, Mrs. McGrudy, The Day the Adults Died, Sundown in Watts, Parallax View, 1776, Don't Go West, Drum, White Buffalo, MacArthur, An Enemy of the People, Sergeant Pepper's Lonely Hearts Club Band, Mulefeathers, Winter Kills, Mission to Glory, The Unfinished, They Only Kill Their Masters, The Fearless Five.
TELEVISION: Snowmobile Grand Prix, Indianapolis International Drag Races, The Great Outdoors (23 episodes), Thank you America (spec.), The Unser Story, Gun Hawks (pilot), Keep it Up (pilot), Where are they Now? (pilot), Hunting and Fishing the North American Continent (spec.), The Blue Knight, A Dream for Christmas, The Toy Game, Moose (pilot), The Jerry Show, Apple's Way, The Moneychangers, Young Maverick, Rudi Gernreich/Future, Ours, Max Factor and Pepsi-Cola commercials, The Groovy Seven (pilot).

HOOKS, KEVIN: Actor, Director. b. Philadelphia, PA, Sept. 19, 1958. Son of actor-director Robert Hooks.
PICTURES: Sounder, Aaron Loves Angela; A Hero Ain't Nothin' But a Sandwich; Take Down, Innerspace, Strictly Business (also dir.), Passenger 57 (dir. only).
TELEVISION: Series: The White Shadow, He's the Mayor. Movies: Just an Old Sweet Song, The Greatest Thing That Almost Happened, Friendly Fire, Can You Hear the Laughter?—The Story of Freddie Prinze, Roots: The Gift (dir.), Murder Without Motive: The Edmund Perry Story (dir.). Mini-Series: Backstairs at the White House. Special: Home Sweet Homeless (dir.).

HOOKS, ROBERT: Actor, Director, Producer. b. Washington, D.C., April 18, 1937. Father of actor-director Kevin Hooks. Co-founder and exec. dir. Negro Ensemble Co. NY 1968–present. Founder DC Black Theatre, Washington, D.C. 1973–77. Co-star of TV series: NYPD, 1967–69.
THEATER: Tiger Tiger Burning Bright (Bdwy. debut, 1962), Ballad for Bimshire, The Blacks, Dutchman, Henry V, Happy Ending, Day of Absence, Where's Daddy? (Theatre World Award for last two), Hallelujah, Baby?, Kongi's Harvest, A Soldier's Play (Mark Taper Forum, LA). Co-prod.: with Gerald S. Krone: Song of the Lusitanian Bogey, Daddy Goodness, Ceremonies in Dark Old Men, Day of Absence, The Sty of the Blind Pig, The River Niger, The First Breeze of Summer.
PICTURES: Sweet Love Bitter, Hurry Sundown, The Last of the Mobile Hot-Shots, Trouble Man, Aaron Loves Angela, Airport '77, Fast-Walking, Star Trek III: The Search For Spock, Passenger 57, Posse.
TELEVISION: Series: N.Y.P.D., Supercarrier. Pilots: The Cliff Dweller, Two for the Money, Down Home. Movies: Carter's Army, Vanished, The Cable Car Murder, Crosscurrent, Trapped, Ceremonies in Dark Old Men, Just an Old Sweet Song, The Killer Who Wouldn't Die, The Courage and the Passion, To Kill a Cop, A Woman Called Moses, Hollow Image, Madame X, The Oklahoma City Dolls, The Sophisti-

cated Gents, Cassie and Co., Starflight—The Plane that Couldn't Land, Feel the Heat, Sister, Sister, The Execution.

HOOL, LANCE: Producer, Director. b. Mexico City, Mex., May 11, 1948. e. Univ. of the Americas.
PICTURES: *Producer:* Cabo Blanco, Ten to Midnight, The Evil That Men Do, Missing in Action (also s.p.), Missing in Action 2 (dir.), Steel Dawn (also dir.), Options, Damned River.
TELEVISION: The Tracker.

HOOPER, TOBE: Director. b. Austin, Texas, Jan. 25. e. Univ. of TX. Began film career making documentary and industrial films and commercials in Texas. Was asst. dir. of U. of Texas film program, continuing filmmaking while working with students. First feature film: documentary Peter Paul & Mary, followed by Eggshells. Directed Billy Idol video Dancing With Myself.
PICTURES: The Texas Chainsaw Massacre, Eaten Alive, Funhouse, Poltergeist, Lifeforce, Invaders from Mars, The Texas Chainsaw Massacre Part 2, Spontaneous Combustion, Sleepwalkers (actor only).
TELEVISION: *Movies:* Salem's Lot, I'm Dangerous Tonight. *Series episodes:* Amazing Stories, A Nightmare on Elm Street-Freddy's Nightmare: The Series. (No More Mr. Nice Guy-1st episode), Equalizer (No Place Like Home), Tales from the Crypt (Dead Wait). *Pilot:* Haunted Lives.

HOPE, BOB: Actor. b. Eltham, England, May 29, 1903. Started in vaudeville; plays include: Roberta, Ziegfeld Follies, Red, Hot & Blue; author, They Got Me Covered, I Never Left Home, So This Is Peace. Voted one of ten best Money-Making Stars in M.P. Herald-Fame Poll, 1941–47, 49–53. On radio and TV with numerous specials U.S.O shows and guest appearances. Emmy Governors Award, 1984.
PICTURES: Big Broadcast of 1938, College Swing, Give Me a Sailor, Thanks for the Memory, Never Say Die, Some Like It Hot, Cat and Canary, Road to Singapore, Ghost Breakers, Road to Zanzibar, Caught in the Draft, Louisiana Purchase, My Favorite Blonde, Road to Morocco, Nothing But the Truth, They Got Me Covered, Star Spangled Rhythm, Let's Face It, Road to Utopia, Princess and Pirate, Monsieur Beaucaire, My Favorite Brunette, Where There's Life, Road to Rio, Paleface, Sorrowful Jones, Great Lover, Fancy Pants, Lemon Drop Kid, My Favorite Spy, Son of Paleface, Road to Bali, Off Limits, Scared Stiff (cameo), Here Come the Girls, Casanova's Big Night, Seven Little Foys, That Certain Feeling, Iron Petticoat, Beau James, Paris Holiday, Alias Jesse James, The Five Pennies (cameo), Facts of Life, Bachelor in Paradise, Road to Hong Kong, Call Me Bwana, A Global Affair, I'll Take Sweden, Boy Did I Get a Wrong Number, Eight on the Lam, The Private Navy of Sgt. O'Farrell, How to Commit Marriage, Cancel My Reservation, The Muppet Movie, Spies Like Us (cameo).

HOPE, HARRY: Producer, Director, Writer. b. May 26, 1926. e. UCLA, Etudes Universitaires Internationales, Ph.D. Entered m.p. industry as special effects man, Republic Studios, 1944; associate producer Star Productions; formed Blue Bird Film Co. Has since produced, directed and written 33 feature films, including Like the Gull, 1967, which won creative classical film award at Asian Film Festival. Founded Western International and directed First Leisure Corp. as exec. v.p. until 1972. From then until present, pres. of Harry Hope Production. Among recent film credits: Smokey and the Judge, Sunset Cove, Doomsday Machine, Death Dimension, Thunderfist, Tarzana, The Mad Butcher, Death Blow, Pop's Oasis.

HOPKINS, SIR ANTHONY, C.B.E.: Actor. b. Port Talbot, South Wales, Dec. 31, 1937. Trained at Royal Acad. of Dramatic Art; Welsh Coll. of Music & Drama. Joined National Theatre, gaining fame on stage in England, then TV and films. Appeared in short The White Bus.
THEATER: Julius Caesar (debut, 1964), Juno and the Paycock, A Flea in Her Ear, The Dance of Death, Three Sisters, As You Like It, The Architect and the Emperor of Assyria, Equus (NY and Los Angeles). Pravda, Old Times, The Lonely Road, King Lear, Anthony and Cleopatra, M. Butterfly, An Evening With Dylan Thomas.
PICTURES: The Lion in Winter (debut, 1968), Hamlet, The Looking Glass War, When Eight Bells Toll, Young Winston, A Doll's House, The Girl from Petrovka, Juggernaut, Audrey Rose, A Bridge Too Far, International Velvet, Magic, The Elephant Man, A Change of Seasons, The Bounty, 84 Charing Cross Road, The Good Father, A Chorus of Disapproval, Desperate Hours, The Silence of the Lambs (Acad. Award, Natl. Board of Review, NY Film Critics & BAFTA Awards, 1991), Freejack, Howards End, The Efficiency Expert (Spotswood), Bram Stoker's Dracula, Chaplin, The Trial, Remains of the Day, The Innocent, Shadowlands, Legends of the Fall.
TELEVISION: *Mini-Series:* War and Peace, QB VII, Hollywood Wives. *Movies:* Dark Victory, The Lindbergh Kidnapping Case (Emmy Award, 1976), Victory at Entebbe, All Creatures Great and Small, Mayflower: The Pilgrim's Adventure, The Bunker (Emmy Award, 1981), Peter and Paul, The

Hunchback of Notre Dame, A Married Man, Guilty Conscience, Arch of Triumph, Mussolini: The Rise and Fall of Il Duce, Blunt, The Dawning, The Tenth Man, Across the Lake, Heartland, Great Expectations, One Man's War, To Be the Best, Selected Exits. *Special:* Dylan Thomas: A Return Journey (host & dir.)

HOPKINS, BO: Actor. b. Greenwood, SC, Feb. 2, 1942. Studied with Uta Hagen in N.Y. then with Desilu Playhouse training school in Hollywood. Parts in several prods. for that group won him an agent, an audition with director Sam Peckinpah and his first role in latter's The Wild Bunch.
PICTURES: The Wild Bunch (debut, 1969), Monte Walsh, The Moonshine War, The Culpepper Cattle Co., The Getaway, White Lightning, The Man Who Loved Cat Dancing, American Graffiti, The Nickel Ride, The Day of the Locust, Posse, The Killer Elite, A Small Town in Texas, Tentacles, Midnight Express, More American Graffiti, The Fifth Floor, Sweet Sixteen, Night Shadows, Trapper Country, War, The Bounty Hunter, The Stalker, Nightmare at Noon, The Tenth Man, Big Bad John, Center of the Web, Inside Monkey Zetterland, The Ballad of Little Jo.
TELEVISION: *Series:* Doc Elliott, The Rockford Files, Dynasty. *Movies:* The Runaway Barge, Kansas City Massacre, Charlie's Angels (pilot), The Invasion of Johnson County, Dawn: Portrait of a Teenage Runaway, Thaddeus Rose and Eddie, Crisis in Sun Valley, Plutonium Incident, A Smoky Mountain Christmas, Beggerman Thief, Down the Long Hills, Last Ride of the Dalton Gang, Casino, Rodeo Girl, Ghost Dancing, Blood Ties.

HOPPER, DENNIS: Actor. b. Dodge City, KS, May 17, 1936. e. San Diego, CA, public schools. Author: Out of the Sixties (1988), book of his photographs.
TELEVISION: *Movies:* Wild Times, Stark, Paris Trout, Doublecrossed, Backtrack (also dir.), Nails, The Heart of Justice.*Guest:* Pursuit, Espionage, Medic, Loretta Young Show.
PICTURES: Rebel Without a Cause, I Died a Thousand Times, Giant, The Steel Jungle, The Story of Mankind, Gunfight at the OK Corral, From Hell to Texas, The Young Land, Key Witness, Night Tide, Tarzan and Jane Regained Sort Of, The Sons of Katie Elder, Queen of Blood, Cool Hand Luke, Glory Stompers, The Trip, Panic in the City, Hang 'Em High, True Grit, Easy Rider (also dir., co-s.p.), The Last Movie (also dir., s.p.), Kid Blue, James Dean—The First American Teenager, Mad Dog Morgan, Tracks, The American Friend, Couleur Chair, The Sorcerer's Apprentices, L'Ordre et la Securite du Monde, Resurrection, Apocalypse Now, Out of the Blue (also dir.), King of the Mountain, Renacida, White Star, Human Highway, Rumble Fish, The Osterman Weekend, My Science Project, The Texas Chainsaw Massacre Part 2, Hoosiers (Acad. Award nom.), Blue Velvet, Black Widow, River's Edge, Straight to Hell, The Pick Up Artist, O.C. and Stiggs, Riders of the Storm, Blood Red, Colors (dir. only), Flashback, Chattachoochee, The Hot Spot (dir. only), Superstar: The Life and Times of Andy Warhol, The Indian Runner, Hearts of Darkness: A Filmmaker's Apocalypse, Midnight Heat, Eye of the Storm, Boiling Point, Super Mario Bros., True Romance, Chasers (dir. only).

HORDERN, SIR MICHAEL: Actor. b. Berkhampstead, Eng. Oct. 3, 1911. e. Brighton Col. Early career in business before stage appearance, 1937. M.P. debut The Girl in the News, 1939. TV debut 1946. 1939–45 Naval Service. Knighted 1983.
PICTURES: School for Secrets, Passport to Pimlico, The Astonished Heart, Trio, A Christmas Carol, Tom Brown's School Days, The Heart of the Matter, The Constant Husband, The Night My Number Came Up, Alexander the Great, The Black Prince, Storm Over The Nile, Pacific Destiny, The Baby and the Battleship, The Spanish Gardener, No Time for Tears, Windom's Way, I Was Monty's Double, Girls at Sea, Moment of Danger, Sink the Bismarck, Man in the Moon, El Cid, Cleopatra, The V.I.P.s, Dr. Syn Alias the Scarecrow (tv in U.S.), The Yellow Rolls Royce, Genghis Khan, The Spy Who Came in From the Cold, Khartoum, Cast a Giant Shadow, A Funny Thing Happened on the Way to the Forum, The Taming of the Shrew, The Jokers, How I Won the War, I'll Never Forget What's 'is Name, Where Eagles Dare, The Bed-Sitting Room, Anne of the Thousand Days, Futtocks End, Some Will Some Won't, Demons of the Mind, Up Pompeii, The Possession of Joel Delaney, Girl Stroke Boy, The Pied Piper, Alice's Adventures in Wonderland, England Made Me, Theatre of Blood, The Mackintosh Man, Juggernaut, Mr. Quilp, Barry Lyndon (narrator), Lucky Lady, Royal Flash, The Slipper and the Rose, Joseph Andrews, The Medusa Touch, Watership Down (voice), Wildcats of St. Trinian's, The Missionary, Gandhi, Yellowbeard, Young Sherlock Holmes (voice), Lady Jane, Labyrinth (voice), The Trouble With Spies, Comrades, Dark Obsession (Diamond Skulls), Freddie as F.R.O. 7 (voice).
TELEVISION: Doctor's Dilemma, The Great Adventure, The Witness, The Indifferent Shepherd, Dock Brief, Mr. Kettle and Mrs. Moon, Guinea Pig, The Gathering Dusk, Farewell My City, Flowering Cherry, I Have Been Here Before, Without

the Grail, The Outstation, The Square, Any Other Business, The Stone Dance, The Quails, A Waltz on the Water, August for the People, Land of My Dreams, Condemned to Acquittal, Nelson, The Browning Version, Whistle and I'll Come to You, The Man Who Murdered in Public, A Crack in the Ice, Sir Jocelyn the Minister Would Like a Word, Six Dates with Barker, Don Juan in Hell, Tartoffe, Tall Stories, The Magistrate, Edward VII, King Lear, Cakes and Ale, Chester Mystery Cycle, Paddington Bear (story teller), The Saints Go Marching In, Mrs. Bixby and the Colonel's Coat, Romeo and Juliet, Oliver Twist, The Tempest, All's Well That Ends Well, You're Alright: How Am I?, King Lear, Rod and Line, Cymbeline, Trelawney of the Wells, Paradise Postponed, The Secret Garden, Suspicion, Danny the Champion of the World, Ending Up, The Green Man, Memento Mori.

HORN, ALAN: Executive. b. New York, NY, Feb. 28, 1943. e. Union Coll., Harvard Business Sch. 1971, joined Tandem Prods., 1972; named v.p., business affairs, and of sister co., T.A.T. Communications, 1973; 1977, exec. v.p. & COO; pres., 1978. In 1983 named chmn. Embassy Communications. 1986 joined 20th Century Fox as pres. COO. Left Fox Sept. 1986. Co-founded Castle Rock Entertainment 1987.

HORNE, LENA: Vocalist, Actress. b. Brooklyn, NY, June 30, 1917. Radio with Noble Sissle, Charlie Barnet, other bands. Floor shows at Cotton Club, Cafe Society, Little Troc, etc. Started screen career 1942. Appeared in short subjects Harlem Hotshots, Boogie Woogie Dream. Autobiographies: In Person (1950), Lena (1965) Recipient Kennedy Center Honors for Lifetime contribution to the Arts, 1984. Spingarn Award, NAACP, 1983; Paul Robeson Award, Actors Equity Assn., 1985.
THEATRE: Blackbirds, Dance With Your Gods, Jamaica, Pal Joey (L.A. Music Center), Lena Horne: The Lady and Her Music (Tony Award).
PICTURES: The Duke is Tops (debut, 1938), Panama Hattie, Cabin in the Sky, Stormy Weather, I Dood It, Thousands Cheer, Broadway Rhythm, Swing Fever, Two Girls and a Sailor, Ziegfeld Follies, Till the Clouds Roll By, Words and Music, Duchess of Idaho, Meet Me in Las Vegas, Death of a Gunfighter, The Wiz.
TELEVISION: Guest: Music '55, Perry Como Show, Here's to the Ladies, The Cosby Show. Specials: The Lena Horne Show (1959), The Frank Sinatra Timex Show, Lena in Concert, Harry and Lena, Lena Horne: The Lady and Her Music.

HORNER, HARRY: Art director, Director. b. Holic, Czechoslovakia, July 24, 1910. e. U. of Vienna, Dept. of Architecture, 1928–33; Acad. of the Theatre, Vienna, 1930–32, Max Reinhardt's Seminary. Joined Max Reinhardt Thea. Co., Vienna and Salzburg Festivals; to U.S. as asst. to Reinhardt on pageant, The Eternal Road. Stage designer, N.Y. theatre 10 yrs. (Lady in the Dark, Family Portrait, others). Designer and dir. at San Francisco Opera, Metropolitan Opera, Vancouver Festivals, Hollywood Bowl. First m.p. as prod. designer, 1938, Our Town (co-credit, Wm. Cameron Menzies). later Little Foxes, Stage Door Canteen. Army service, 1942–45; designed Winged Victory for Air Force.
PICTURES: Designer: The Heiress (Acad. Award), Born Yesterday, Separate Tables, The Hustler (Acad. Award), They Shoot Horses Don't They?, Who is Harry Kellerman?, Up the Sandbox, The Black Bird, Harry and Walter Go to New York, Audrey Rose, The Driver, Moment by Moment, The Jazz Singer. Co-Prod.: Fahrenheit 451. Director: Beware My Lovely, Red Planet Mars. Vicki, New Faces, Life in the Balance, Step Down to Terror, Lonesome Gun, Wild Party, Man From Del Rio.
TELEVISION: Omnibus, Cavalcade, Reader's Digest, Author's Playhouse, Four Star Theatre, Gunsmoke, Revue Productions, Dupont Theatre. Since 1959 prod., dir., TV series, The Royal Canadian Mounted Police.

HORNER, JAMES: Composer. b. Los Angeles, CA. e. Royal Col. of Music: London, USC, UCLA. Received Grammy Awards for the song Somewhere Out There (from the film An American Tail), and for instrumental composition from Glory.
PICTURES: The Lady in Red, Battle Beyond the Stars, Humanoids from the Deep, Deadly Blessing, The Hand, Wolfen, The Pursuit of D.B. Cooper, 48 HRS, Star Trek II: The Wrath of Khan, Something Wicked This Way Comes, Krull, Brainstorm, Testament, Gorky Park, The Dresser, Uncommon Valor, The Stone Boy, Star Trek III: The Search for Spock, Heaven Help Us, Cocoon, Volunteers, Journey of Natty Gann, Commando, Aliens, Where the River Runs Black, The Name of the Rose, An American Tail, P.K. and the Kid, Project X, Batteries Not Included, Willow, Red Heat, Vibes, Cocoon: The Return, The Land Before Time, Field of Dreams, Honey I Shrunk the Kids, Dad, Glory, I Love You to Death, Another 48 HRS., Once Around, My Heroes Have Always Been Cowboys, Class Action, The Rocketeer, An American Tail: Fievel Goes West, Thunderheart, Patriot Games, Unlawful Entry, Sneakers, Swing Kids, A Far Off

Place, Jack the Bear, Once Upon a Forest, Searching for Bobby Fischer, Man Without a Face.

HORSLEY, LEE: Actor. b. Muleshoe, TX, May 15, 1955. e. U. of No. Colorado. On stage in Mack and Mabel, West Side Story, Sound of Music, Oklahoma!, Forty Carats.
PICTURE: The Sword and the Sorcerer.
TELEVISION: Series: Nero Wolfe, Matt Houston, Guns of Paradise, Bodies of Evidence. Mini-series: Crossings, North and South Book II. Movies: The Wild Women of Chastity Gulch, Infidelity, When Dreams Come True, Thirteen at Dinner, Single Women Married Men, The Face of Fear, Danielle Steel's Palomino.

HORTON, PETER: Actor. b. Bellevue, WA, Aug. 20. e. Univ. of CA, Santa Barbara. Stage work includes appearances with Lobero Rep. Co. Theatre in Santa Barbara, Butterflies Are Free in L.A.
TELEVISION: Series: Seven Brides for Seven Brothers, thirtysomething (also dir., episodes), Class of '96 (consultant, dir., actor). Pilot: Sawyer and Finn. Movies: She's Dressed to Kill, Miracle on Ice, Freedom, Choices of the Heart. Guest: The White Shadow, St. Elsewhere. Director: The Wonder Years, One Too Many (Afterschool Special).
PICTURES: Serial, Fade to Black, Split Image, Children of the Corn, Where the River Runs Black, Amazon Women on the Moon (also co-dir.), Sideout, Singles.

HORTON, ROBERT: Actor. b. Los Angeles, CA, July 29, 1924. e. U. of Miami, UCLA, Yale. Coast Guard; many legit. plays; many radio & TV appearances. Star of Broadway musical 110 in the Shade.
PICTURES: A Walk in the Sun, The Tanks Are Coming, Return of the Texan, Pony Soldier, Apache War Smoke, Bright Road, The Story of Three Loves, Code Two, Arena, Prisoner of War, Men of the Fighting Lady, The Green Slime, The Dangerous Days of Kiowa Jones, The Spy Killer, Foreign Exchange.
TELEVISION: Series: Kings Row, Wagon Train, A Man Called Shenandoah, As the World Turns. Movie: Red River. Guest: Alfred Hitchcock Presents, Suspense, Houston Knights, Murder She Wrote.

HORWITZ, SOL: Executive. b. Chicago, IL, April 2, 1920. e. U. of Chicago. U.S. Navy, 1942–45. Film booker and buyer for Balaban and Katz and Allied Theatres of Illinois, in Chicago before moving to New York where served in same capacity for Walter Reade Org., Cinema 5, Loews, Inc. In sls. divisions of EDP Films, Screenvision, and Castle Hill Prods. Now project administrator for Short Film Showcase and v.p. development, Angelika Films.

HOSKINS, BOB: Actor. b. Bury St. Edmunds, Suffolk, England, Oct. 26, 1942. Porter and steeplejack before becoming actor at 25. Veteran of Royal Shakespeare Co. Appeared with Britain's National Theatre (Man Is Man, King Lear, Guys and Dolls, etc.)
PICTURES: National Health (debut, 1973), Royal Flash, Inserts, Zulu Dawn, The Long Good Friday, Pink Floyd: The Wall, Beyond the Limit, Lassiter, The Cotton Club, Brazil, Sweet Liberty, Mona Lisa (Acad. Award nom.), A Prayer for the Dying, The Lonely Passion of Judith Hearne, Who Framed Roger Rabbit, The Raggedy Rawney (also dir., co-s.p.), Heart Condition, Mermaids, Shattered, Hook, The Inner Circle, The Favor the Watch and the Very Big Fish, Passed Away, Super Mario Bros.
TELEVISION: Villians on the High Road (debut, 1972), New Scotland Yard, On the Move, Rock Follies, In the Looking Glass, Napoleon, Flickers, Pennies from Heaven, Othello, Mussolini, The Dunera Boys.

HOUGH, JOHN: Director. b. London, Eng., Nov. 21, 1941. Worked in British film. prod. in various capacities; impressed execs. at EMI-MGM Studios, Elstree, London, so was given chance to direct The Avengers series for TV. Began theatrical films with Sudden Terror for prod. Irving Allen, 1971.
PICTURES: Twins of Evil, Treasure Island, The Legend of Hell House, Dirty Mary Crazy Larry, Escape to Witch Mountain, Return to Witch Mountain, Brass Target, Watcher in the Woods, Biggles—Adventures in Time, Howling IV—The Original Nightmare.
TELEVISION: A Hazard of Hearts (also co-prod.), The Lady and the Highwayman (also prod.), A Ghost in Monte Carlo (also prod.), Duel of Hearts (also prod.), Distant Scream, Black Carrion, Check-Mate.

HOWARD, ARLISS: Actor. b. Independence, MO, 1955. e. Columbia Col.
PICTURES: Sylvester, The Lightship, Full Metal Jacket, Plain Clothes, Tequila Sunrise, Men Don't Leave, For the Boys, Ruby, Crisscross, The Sandlot, Wilder Napalm, Natural Born Killers.
TELEVISION: Movies: Hands of a Stranger, I Know My First Name is Steven, Somebody Has to Shoot the Picture, Iran: Days of Crisis, Till Death Us Do Part, Those Secrets.
THEATRE: American Buffalo, Lie of the Mind.

HOWARD, JAMES NEWTON: Composer. Started as keyboard player for Elton John, before composing and producing for such artists as Cher, Diana Ross, Barbra Streisand, Chaka Khan, Randy Newman.
PICTURES: 8 Millions Ways to Die, Some Girls, Everybody's All-American, Promised Land, Major League, The Package, Pretty Woman, Coupe de Ville, Flatliners, Three Men and a Little Lady, Dying Young, The Man in the Moon, My Girl, The Prince of Tides, Grand Canyon, Glengarry Glen Ross, Night and the City, Alive, Falling Down, Dave, The Saint of Fort Washington.

HOWARD, KEN: Actor. b. El Centro, CA, March 28, 1944. e. Yale Drama Sch. Left studies to do walk-on in Bdwy. musical, Promises Promises. Starred as Thomas Jefferson in 1776 on Bdwy. (Theatre World Award) and in film version.
PICTURES: Tell Me That You Love Me Junie Moon (debut, 1970), Such Good Friends, The Strange Vengeance of Rosalie, 1776, Second Thoughts, Oscar.
TELEVISION: Series: Adam's Rib, The Manhunter, The White Shadow, It's Not Easy, The Colbys, Dynasty, Dream Girl U.S.A., What Happened? (host). Guest: Bonanza, Medical Center. Movies: Manhunter, Superdome, Critical List, A Real American Hero, Damien: The Leper Priest, Victims, Rage of Angels, The Trial of George Armstrong Custer, He's Not Your Son, Rage of Angels: The Story Continues, Murder in New Hampshire: The Pamela Smart Story, Memories of Midnight. Specials: Strange Interlude, The Man in the Brown Suit, Mastergate. Mini-Series: The Thorn Birds.
STAGE: Promises Promises, Child's Play (Tony Award, 1970) , Seesaw, 1600 Pennsylvania Avenue, The Norman Conquests, Equus, Rumors.

HOWARD, RON: Actor, Director, Producer. b. Duncan, OK, March 1, 1954. e. Univ. of So. Calif. Acting debut as Ronny Howard at age of 2 with parents, Rance and Jean Howard, in The Seven Year Itch at Baltimore's Hilltop Theatre. Two years later traveled to Vienna to appear in first film, The Journey. Brother is actor Clint Howard, also former child actor. Co-Chairman of Imagine Films Entertainment.
PICTURES: Actor: The Journey (debut, 1959), Five Minutes to Live (a.k.a. Door-to-Door Maniac), The Music Man, The Courtship of Eddie's Father, Village of the Giants, Wild Country, American Graffiti, Happy Mother's Day . . . Love George (a.k.a. Run Stranger Run), The Spikes Gang, Eat My Dust!, The Shootist, The First Nudie Musical (cameo), Grand Theft Auto (also dir.), More American Graffiti. Director: Grand Theft Auto (dir. debut, 1977; also actor, co-s.p.), Night Shift, Splash, Cocoon, Gung Ho (also exec. prod.), Willow, Parenthood (also co-story), Backdraft, Far and Away (also co-prod., co-story), The Paper. Exec. Prod.: Leo & Loree, No Man's Land, Vibes, Clean and Sober, Closet Land.
TELEVISION: Series: The Andy Griffith Show, The Smith Family, Happy Days. Guest: Red Skelton Hour, Playhouse 90, Dennis the Menace, Many Loves of Dobie Gillis, Five Fingers, Twilight Zone, Dinah Shore Show, The Fugitive, Dr. Kildare, The Big Valley, I Spy, Danny Kaye Show, Gomer Pyle USMC, The Monroes, Love American Style, Gentle Ben, Gunsmoke; Disney TV films (incl. A Boy Called Nuthin', Smoke). Movies: The Migrants, Locusts, Huckleberry Finn, Act of Love, Bitter Harvest, Fire on the Mountain, Return to Mayberry. Director (Movies): Cotton Candy (also co-writer), Skyward (also co-exec. prod.), Through the Magic Pyramid (also exec. prod.). Co-Exec. Prod. (Movie): When Your Lover Leaves.

HOWARD, SANDY: Producer. b. Aug. 1, 1927. e. Florida So. Coll. Ent. m.p. ind. 1946.
PICTURES: Perils of the Deep, One Step to Hell, Jack of Diamonds, Tarzan and the Trappers, A Man Called Horse, Man in the Wilderness, Together Brothers, Neptune Factor, The Devil's Rain, Sky Riders, The Last Castle, Embryo, Magna I—Beyond the Barrier Reef, The Battle, Island of Dr. Moreau, City on Fire, Death Ship (exec. prod.), Avenging Angel, The Boys Next Door, Street Justice (exec. prod.), Nightstick, Dark Tower (exec. prod.), Truk Lagoon (exec. prod.).
TELEVISION: Over 50 TV series.

HOWELL, C. THOMAS: Actor. b. Los Angeles, CA, Dec. 7, 1966. m. actress Rae Dawn Chong. Former junior rodeo circuit champion.
PICTURES: E.T.: The Extra Terrestrial, The Outsiders, Tank, Grandview U.S.A., Red Dawn, Secret Admirer, The Hitcher, Soul Man, A Tiger's Tale, Side Out, Far Out Man, Young Toscanini, The Return of the Musketeers, Kid, Nickel and Dime, Breaking the Rules, First Force, Gettysburg, That Night.
TELEVISION: Series: Little People (only 4 yrs. old), Two Marriages. Movies: Into the Homeland, Curiosity Kills, Acting on Impulse. Guest: Nightmare Classics (Eye of the Panther).

HOWELLS, URSULA: Actress. b. Sept. 17, 1922. e. St. Paul's Sch., London. Stage debut, 1939, at Dundee Repertory with Bird in Hand followed by several plays inc. Springtime for Henry in N.Y., 1951; m.p. debut in Flesh and Blood, 1950; TV debut in Case of the Frightened Lady for BBC, 1948.

TELEVISION: Many appearances including The Small Back Room, A Woman Comes Home, For Services Rendered, Mine Own Executioner, The Cocktail Party.
PICTURES: The Oracle (Horse's Mouth), Track the Man Down, They Can't Hang Me, Keep It Clean, Long Arm (Third Key), Death and The Sky Above, Mumsy Nanny Sonny and Girly, Crossplot.

HUBLEY, SEASON: Actress. b. New York, NY, May 14, 1951. Former model. Studied acting with Herbert Berghoff.
PICTURES: Lolly Madonna XXX, Catch My Soul, Hardcore, Escape from New York, Vice Squad, Prettykill.
TELEVISION: Series: Kung Fu, Family, All My Children. Movies: She Lives, The Healers, SST-Death Flight, Loose Change, Elvis, Mrs. R's Daughter, Three Wishes of Billy Grier, Under the Influence, Christmas Eve, Shakedown on Sunset Strip, Unspeakable Acts, Child of the Night, Steel Justice. Guest: The Partridge Family, The Rookies, Kojak, Twilight Zone, Alfred Hitchcock Presents.

HUDDLESTON, DAVID: Actor, Producer. b. Vinton, VA, Sept. 17, 1930. e. American Acad. of Dramatic Arts. Father of actor Michael Huddleston. On stage in A Man for All Seasons, Front Page, Everybody Loves Opal, Ten Little Indians, Silk Stockings, Fanny, Guys and Dolls, The Music Man, Desert Song, Mame. Broadway: The First, Death of a Salesman.
PICTURES: All the Way Home (debut, 1963), A Lovely Way to Die, Slaves, Norwood, Rio Lobo, Fools, Parade, Bad Company, Blazing Saddles, McQ, Capricorn One, World's Greatest Lover, Gorp, Smokey and the Bandit II, Santa Claus, Frantic, Life With Mikey.
TELEVISION: Series: Tenafly, Petrocelli, The Kallikaks, Hizzoner. Movies: Sarge: The Badge or the Cross, The Priest Killer, Suddenly Single, The Homecoming, Brian's Song, Tenafly (pilot), Brock's Last Case, Hawkins on Murder, Heatwave, The Gun and the Pulpit, The Oregon Trail, Shark Kill, Sherlock Holmes in New York, Kate Bliss and the Ticker Tape Kid, Oklahoma City Dolls, Family Reunion, Computerside, M.A.D.D.: Mothers Against Drunk Drivers, Finnegan Begin Again, Family Reunion, Spot Marks the X, The Tracker, Margaret Bourke-White, In a Child's Name. Mini-Series: Once an Eagle.

HUDSON, ERNIE: Actor. b. Benton Harbor, MI, Dec. 17, 1945. e. Wayne St. Univ., Yale Sch. of Drama. Former Actors Ensemble Theater while in Detroit. Professional stage debut in L.A. production of Daddy Goodness.
PICTURES: Leadbelly (debut, 1976), The Main Event, The Jazz Singer, Penitentiary II, Ghostbusters, The Joy of Sex, Weeds, Leviathan, Ghostbusters II, The Hand That Rocks the Cradle, The Crow, The Penal Colony, Airheads.
TELEVISION: Series: Highcliffe Manor, The Last Precinct, Broken Badges. Mini-Series: Roots: The Next Generations, Wild Palms. Movies: White Mama, Dirty Dozen: The Fatal Mission, Love on the Run. Guest: Fantasy Island, Little House on the Praire, One Day at a Time, Diff'rent Strokes, St. Elsewhere.

HUDSON, HUGH: Producer, Director. b. England. e. Eton. Began career as head of casting dept. with ad agency in London; left for Paris to work as editor for small film co. Returned to London to form Cammell-Hudson-Brownjohn Film Co., production house., turning out award-winning documentaries (Tortoise and Hare, A is for Apple). 1970, joined Ridley Scott to make TV commercials. 1975, formed Hudson Films to produce. Debut as director of theatrical features with Chariots of Fire, 1981.
PICTURES: Director: Fangio, Chariots of Fire, Greystoke: The Legend of Tarzan Lord of the Apes (also prod.), Revolution, Lost Angels.

HUGGINS, ROY: Writer, Producer. b. Litelle, WA, July 18, 1914. e. U. of California 1935–39; U. of California Graduate School, 1939–41. m. Adele Mara, actress. Spec. rep., U.S. Civil Service Comm., 1941–43; industrial eng.. 1943–46; writer 3 novels and many stories for Sat. Eve. Post; pres., Public Arts, Inc., 1968. V.P., 20th Century-Fox TV, 1961.
PICTURES: Writer: I Love Trouble, Too Late for Tears, Lady Gambles, Fuller Brush Man (story), Good Humor Man (story), Woman in Hiding (adapt.), Sealed Cargo (co-s.p.), Hangman's Knot (also dir.), Gun Fury (co-s.p.), Three Hours to Kill, Pushover, A Fever in the Blood (prod.).
TELEVISION: Series Prod.: Cheyenne, Conflict, Maverick (Emmy Award, 1959). Prod. of pilots: Colt .45, 77 Sunset Strip. Series Creator: The Fugitive, The Rockford Files (also pilot), City of Angels. Exec. prod. of series: Run for Your Life, The Outsiders, The Bold Ones, Alias Smith and Jones, Toma. Movie: Pretty Boy Floyd. Mini-Series: Captains and the Kings, Aspen, Wheels.

HUGHES, BARNARD: Actor. b. Bedford Hills, NY, July 16, 1915. Winner of Emmy for role as Judge in Lou Grant series (1978) and Tony Award for Da (1978).
PICTURES: Midnight Cowboy, Where's Poppa?, Cold Turkey, Pursuit of Happiness, The Hospital, Rage, Sisters, Deadhead Miles, Oh God!, First Monday in October, Tron,

Best Friends, Maxie, Where Are the Children?, The Lost Boys, Da, Doc Hollywood, Sister Act 2. TELEVISION: *Series*: Doc, Mr. Merlin, The Cavanaughs, Blossom. *Movies*: Guilty or Innocent, The Sam Sheppard Murder Case, See How She Runs, The Caryl Chessman Story, Tell Me My Name, Look Homeward, Angel, Father Brown: Detective, Nova, Homeward Bound, The Sky's No Limit, A Caribbean Mystery, Night of Courage, A Hobo's Christmas, Day One, Home Fires Burning, Guts and Glory: The Rise and Fall of Oliver North, The Incident, Miracle Child.

HUGHES, JOHN: Writer, Director, Producer. b. Detroit, MI. Editor of National Lampoon before writing film script of National Lampoon's Class Reunion (1982). Made directorial debut with Sixteen Candles in 1984 which also wrote. In 1985 entered into deal with Paramount Pictures to write, direct and produce films with his own production unit, The John Hughes Co.
PICTURES: National Lampoon's Class Reunion (s.p.), National Lampoon's Vacation (s.p.), Mr. Mom (s.p.), Nate and Hayes (co- s.p.), Sixteen Candles (dir., s.p.), The Breakfast Club (co-prod., s.p., dir.), National Lampoon's European Vacation (co-s.p.), Weird Science (s.p., dir.), Pretty in Pink (s.p.), Ferris Bueller's Day Off (dir., s.p., co-prod.), Some Kind of Wonderful (prod., s.p.), Planes, Trains & Automobiles (s.p., dir., prod.), She's Having a Baby (prod., dir., s.p.), The Great Outdoors (s.p., exec. prod.), Uncle Buck (dir, co-prod., s.p.), National Lampoon's Christmas Vacation (co-prod., s.p.), Home Alone (s.p., prod.), Career Opportunities (prod., s.p.), Only the Lonely (co-prod.), Dutch (prod., s.p.), Curly Sue (dir, s.p., prod.), Home Alone 2: Lost in New York (prod., s.p.), Dennis the Menace (prod., s.p.).

HUGHES, KATHLEEN: Actress. r.n. Betty von Gerkan; b. Hollywood, CA, Nov. 14, 1928. e. Los Angeles City Coll., UCLA. m. Stanley Rubin, producer, mother of 4, Michael played Baby Matthew on Peyton Place. Studied drama; under contract, 20th-Fox, 1948–51; starred in Seven Year Itch 1954, La Jolla Playhouse; signed by UI, 1952. Theatre includes You Can't Take It With You, An Evening With Tennessee Williams, The Bar Off Melrose.
PICTURES: Road House, Mother is a Freshman, Mr. Belvedere Goes to College, Take Care of My Little Girl, It Happens Every Spring, When Willie Comes Marching Home, My Blue Heaven, Mister 880, No Way Out, I'll See You in My Dreams, Thy Neighbor's Wife, For Men Only (The Tall Lie), Sally and Saint Anne, Golden Blade, It Came From Outer Space, Dawn at Socorro, Glass Web, Cult of the Cobra, Three Bad Sisters, Promise Her Anything, The President's Analyst, The Take, Pete and Tillie, Ironweed, The Couch Trip, Revenge.
TELEVISION: *Guest*: Bob Cummings Show, Hitchcock, 77 Sunset Strip, G.E. Theatre, Bachelor Father, Frank Sinatra Show, Ed Wynn Show, Alan Young Show, The Tall Man, Dante, Tightrope, Markham, I Dream of Jeannie, Peyton Place, Gomer Pyle, Kismet, Ghost and Mrs. Muir, Bracken's World, The Survivors, Julia, Here's Lucy, To Rome with Love, The Interns, The Man and the City, Mission Impossible, The Bold Ones, Lucas Tanner, Marcus Welby, Barnaby Jones, Medical Center, M.A.S.H., General Hospital, Quincy, Finder of Lost Loves, The Young and the Restless. *Movies*: Babe, Forbidden Love, The Spell, Portrait of an Escort, Capitol, Mirror, Mirror, And Your Name is Jonah.

HUGHES, KEN: Writer, Director. b. Liverpool, Eng., 1922. Ent. ind. as sound engineer with BBC, 1940; Doc. films, Army training films. Novels: High Wray, The Long Echo, An Enemy of the State. Scripts: The Matarese Circle, Tussy is Me, The Queen's Own, RatsHallo Berlin. Wrote book and lyrics for stage musical Oscar. Member: Assn. Cone Technicians, Writers' Guild of Great Britain.
PICTURES: Joe Macbeth, Confession, The Trials of Oscar Wilde, The Small World of Sammy Lee, Arrivederci Baby, Casino Royale (co-dir.), Chitty Chitty Bang Bang, Cromwell, Internecine Project, Sextette.
TELEVISION: Eddie (Emmy Award for writing, 1959), Sammy (Brit. Acad. Award). Serials: Solo for Canary, Enemy of the State. Series: Lenin 1917 (The Fall of Eagles), The Haunting, The Voice, Oil Strike North, Colditz, Churchill (BBC).
AWARDS: Golden Globe, Emmy, British TV Acad. Award (Script Writer of Year), Avorias Festival Merit Award, British Writer's Guild Award, British Critics Award (best serial).

HUKE, BOB, B.S.C.: Cinematographer. b. London, Eng., May 31, 1920. e. St. John's Leatherhead, Birmingham Univ. Ent. m.p. ind. 1937, Asst. cameraman Pygmalion, French Without Tears, etc.; 1939–44 Royal Navy. 1945–9 camera operator Great Expectations, Uncle Silas, Seven Days to Noon and others. 1950–56 Brazil. Contract dir. of photo. for Cia Cinematographica Vera Cruz, 1957–59 dir. own company, Zenith, 1960. dir. photo, 3 Dinah Shore Shows, Spain, Paris, Copenhagen. NBC 1961. Dir. photo. Reach For Glory, The War Lover, The Very Edge, 1962; The Brain, 8 Danny Thomas Shows in Europe. 1963 Sandres of the River. 1964, Ballad in Blue, License to Share. TV & cinema commercials,

1955. 1966, 2nd Unit You Only Live Twice; 1968, 2nd Unit, Battle of Britain, 1969; 2nd unit: Ryan's Daughter, Saturn 3. Dir. of Photo: The Virgin and the Gypsy. Under Milk Wood, Conduct Unbecoming, Porridge. Six features for Shaw Bros., Golden Harvest, etc. 2nd unit on To Be the Best.

HULCE, TOM: Actor. b. White Water, WI, Dec. 6, 1953. e. NC School of the Arts. Understudied and then co-starred in Equus on Broadway. Directorial stage debut Sleep Around Town.
THEATER: Memory of Two Mondays, Julius Caesar, Candida, The Sea Gull, The Rise and Rise of Daniel Rocket, Eastern Standard, A Few Good Men.
PICTURES: September 30, 1955 (debut, 1978), National Lampoon's Animal House, Those Lips Those Eyes, Amadeus (Acad. Award nom.), Echo Park, Slamdance, Dominick and Eugene, Parenthood, Shadowman, The Inner Circle, Fearless.
TELEVISION: *Specials*: Emily Emily, The Rise and Rise of Daniel Rocket, Song of Myself, Forget-Me-Not Lane, Tall Tales and Legends (John Henry). *Mini-Series*: The Adams Chronicles. *Movies*: Murder in Mississippi, Black Rainbow.

HUNNICUT, GAYLE: Actress. b. Fort Worth, TX, February 6, 1943. e. UCLA, B.A., with honors, theater arts & English major. Early career, community theatres in Los Angeles.
PICTURES: The Wild Angels (debut, 1966), P.J., Eye of the Cat, Marlowe, Fragment of Fear, The Freelance, Voices, Running Scared, Legend of Hell House, Scorpio, L'Homme Sans Visage, The Spiral Staircase, The Sell Out, Strange Shadows in an Empty Room, Once in Paris, One Take Two, Fantomas, Privilege, Sherlock Holmes, Target, Dream Lover, Turnaround, Silence Like Glass.
TELEVISION: *Series*: Dallas (1989–91). *Movies*: The Smugglers, The Million Dollar Face, The Return of the Man From U.N.C.L.E., The First Olympics: Athens 1896. *Specials*: Man and Boy, The Golden Bowl, The Ambassadors, The Ripening Seed, Fall of Eagles, The Switch, Humboldt's Gift, The Life and Death of Dylan Thomas, Return of the Saint, The Lady Killers, Savage in the Orient, Strong Medicine. *Mini-Series*: A Man Called Intrepid, The Martian Chronicles, Dream West. *Guest*: Taxi.
THEATER: The Ride Across Lake Constance, Twelfth Night, The Tempest, Dog Days, The Admirable Crichton, A Woman of No Importance, Hedda Gabler, Peter Pan, Macbeth, Uncle Vanya, The Philadelphia Story, Miss Firecracker Contest, Exit The King, The Doctor's Dilemma, So Long on Lonely Street, The Big Knife.

HUNT, HELEN: Actress. b. Los Angeles, CA, June 15, 1963. Daughter of director Gordon Hunt.
PICTURES: Rollercoaster, Girls Just Want to Have Fun, Peggy Sue Got Married, Project X, Miles From Home, Trancers, Stealing Home, Next of Kin, The Waterdance, Only You, Bob Roberts, Mr. Saturday Night.
TELEVISION: *Series*: Swiss Family Robinson, Amy Prentiss, The Fitzpatricks, It Takes Two, Mad About You. *Movies*: Pioneer Woman, All Together Now, Death Scream, The Spell, Transplant, Angel Dusted, Child Bride of Short Creek, The Miracle of Kathy Miller, Quarterback Princess, Choices of the Heart, Bill: On His Own, Sweet Revenge, Incident at Dark River, Into the Badlands, Murder in New Hampshire: The Pamela Smart Story, In the Company of Darkness. *Specials*: Weekend, Land of Little Rain. *Special*: Sexual Healing. *Guest*: St. Elsewhere, Family, Mary Tyler Moore Show, The Hitchhiker.
THEATRE: Been Taken, Our Town, The Taming of the Shrew.

HUNT, LINDA: Actress. b. Morristown, NJ, Apr. 2, 1945. e. Interlochen Arts Acad., MI, and Chicago's Goodman Theatre & Sch. of Drama.
PICTURES: Popeye (debut, 1980) The Year of Living Dangerously (Acad. Award, supp. actress, 1983), The Bostonians, Dune, Silverado, Eleni, Waiting for the Moon, She-Devil, Kindergarten Cop, If Looks Could Kill, Rain Without Thunder, Twenty Bucks, Younger and Younger.
THEATRE: Long Wharf Theatre, New Haven: (Hamlet, The Rose Tattoo, Ah, Wilderness). *NY*: Mother Courage, End of the World (Tony nom.), A Metamorphosis in Miniature (Obie Award), Top Girls (Obie Award), Aunt Dan and Lemon, The Cherry Orchard.
TELEVISION: *Series*: Space Rangers. *Movie*: The Room Upstairs. *Specials*: Ah Wilderness, The Room. *Guest*: Fame.

HUNT, MARSHA: Actress. b. Chicago, IL, Oct. 17, 1917. Screen debut 1935.
BROADWAY PLAYS: Joy to the World, Devils Disciple, Legend of Sarah, Borned in Texas, Tunnel of Love, The Paisley Convertible.
PICTURES: (61 including) Virginia Judge, College Holiday, Easy to Take, Blossoms in the Dust, Panama Hattie, Joe Smith American, These Glamour Girls, Winter Carnival, Irene, Pride and Prejudice, Flight Command, The Affairs of Martha, Kid Glove Killer, Seven Sweethearts, Cheers for Miss Bishop, Trial of Mary Dugan, Thousands Cheer, The Human

Comedy, None Shall Escape, Lost Angel, Cry Havoc, Bride by Mistake, Music for Millions, Valley of Decision, A Letter for Evie, Smash-Up, Carnegie Hall, The Inside Story, Raw Deal, Jigsaw, Take One False Step, Actors and Sin, Happy Time, No Place to Hide, Back from the Dead, Bombers B-52, Blue Denim, The Plunderers, Johnny Got His Gun.

TELEVISION: Series: Peck's Bad Girl. Guest: Philco, Studio One, Ford Theatre, Show of Shows, G.E. Theatre, Climax, Hitchcock, The Defenders, Twilight Zone, Cains Hundred, Gunsmoke, The Breaking Point, Outer Limits, Profiles in Courage, Ben Casey, Accidental Family, Run For Your Life, My Three Sons, The Outsiders, Name of the Game, Univ.'s 120, Ironside, Marcus Welby, M.D., Police Story, The Young Lawyers, Harry-O, The Mississippi, Hot Pursuit, Shadow Chaser, Matlock, Murder She Wrote, Star Trek: The Next Generation.

HUNT, PETER: Director, Editor. b. London, Eng., March 11, 1928. e. Romford, England and Rome, Italy, London Sch. of Music. Actor English Rep. Entered film as camera asst. Documentary, later asst film editor documentary, then asst editor features. London Films then editor—credits incl. Hill in Korea, Admirable Crichton, Cry From the Streets, Greengage Summer (Loss of Innocence), Ferry To Hong Kong, H.M.S. Defiant (Damn the Defiant). Supervising editor/2nd Unit Director: Dr. No, Call Me Bwana, From Russia With Love, Goldfinger, Ipcress File, Thunderball, You Only Live Twice. Associate producer: Chitty Chitty Bang Bang. Director: On Her Majesty's Secret Service, Gullivers Travels, Gold, Shout at the Devil, Death Hunt, Wild Geese II, Hyper Sapien, Assassination.

TELEVISION: Director: Series: The Persuaders, Shirley's World, The Pencil, Smart Alec Kill (Philip Marlowe). Movies: The Beasts Are in the Streets, Eye of a Witness. Mini-Series: Last Days of Pompeii.

HUNT, PETER H.: Director. b. Pasadena, CA, Dec. 16, 1938. e. Hotchkiss, Yale U., Yale Drama Sch. m. actress Barbette Tweed. Director for Williamston Theatre since 1957. Lighting designer on Bdwy. (1963–69)

PICTURES: 1776, Give 'Em Hell Harry.

TELEVISION: Specials: Adventures of Huckleberry Finn, Life on the Mississippi, A Private History of a Campaign That Failed, A New Start, Mysterious Stranger, Sherlock Holmes (cable), Bus Stop (cable). Movies: Flying High, Rendezvous Motel, When She Was Bad, Skeezer, The Parade, Sins of the Past, It Came Upon the Midnight Clear, Charley Hannah, Danielle Steel's Secrets, Sworn to Vengeance. Pilots: Adam's Rib, Hello Mother Goodbye, Ivan the Terrible, Quark, Mixed Nuts, Wilder and Wilder, The Main Event, Nuts and Bolts, The Good Witch of Laurel Canyon, Masquerade, Stir Crazy, The Wizard of Elm Street, Travelling Man, My Africa.

STAGE: 1776 (London & Bdwy.), Georgy (Bdwy.), Scratch (Bdwy.), Goodtime Charley (Bdwy.), Give 'Em Hell Harry, Magnificent Yankee (Kennedy Center). Tours: Bully, Three Penny Opera, Sherlock Holmes, Bus Stop.

AWARDS: Tony, Ace, Peabody (Bdwy.), N.Y. Drama Critics, London Drama Critics, Edgar Allan Poe, Christopher.

HUNT, WILLIE: Executive Producer. b. Van Nuys, CA, Oct. 1, 1941. e. Utah State U., B.A., 1963. m. writer Tim Considine. Started in industry as secretary at Warner Bros., 1965; named exec. secty. to Ted Ashley, WB, 1969; story analyst, WB, 1974; story editor, WB, 1975; named West Coast story editor for WB, 1978; joined MGM in 1979 as v.p., motion picture development. Moved to United Artists as v.p.-prod., 1982. In 1983 sr., v.p. of prod. at Rastar Prods.; 1984, indep. prod., Tri-Star Pictures; 1986, sr. v.p., Freddie Fields Prods. 1988: Loverboy (co-prod.) 1989, sr. v.p. Considine Prods.

HUNTER, HOLLY: Actress. b. Conyers, GA. March 20, 1958. e. studied acting Carnegie Mellon. Appeared Off-Broadway in Battery (1981) and Weekend Near Madison. Appeared in five Beth Henley plays: The Miss Firecracker Contest (Off-Bdwy), as a replacement in Crimes of the Heart (Bdwy) The Wake of Jamey Foster (Bdwy), Lucky Spot (Williamstown Theater Festival), and Control Freaks (also co-prod., L.A.). Also: A Lie of the Mind (L.A.).

PICTURES: The Burning (debut, 1981), Swing Shift, Raising Arizona, Broadcast News (Acad. Award nom.), End of the Line, Miss Firecracker, Animal Behavior, Always, Once Around, The Firm, The Piano (Cannes Film Fest. Award, 1993).

TELEVISION: Movies: Svengali, An Uncommon Love, With Intent to Kill, A Gathering of Old Men, Roe vs. Wade (Emmy Award), Crazy in Love, The Positively True Adventures of the Alleged Texas Cheerleader-Murdering Mom. Guest: Fame (pilot).

HUNTER, KIM: Actress. r.n. Janet Cole. b. Detroit, MI, Nov. 12, 1922. e. public schools. d. Donald and Grace Mabel (Lind) Cole. Studied acting with Charmine Lantaff Camine, 1938–40, Actors Studio; First stage appearance, 1939; played in stock, 1940–42; Broadway debut in A Streetcar Named Desire, 1947; frequent appearances summer stock and repertory theater, 1940–; appeared Am. Shakespeare Festi-val, Stratford, CT, 1961. Autobiography-cookbook: Loose in the Kitchen (1975).

STAGE: NY: Darkness at Noon, The Chase, The Children's Hour (revival), The Tender Trap, Write Me a Murder, Weekend, The Penny Wars, The Women, The Cherry Orchard, To Grandmother's House We Go, When We Dead Awaken, Territorial Rites, Cat on a Hot Tin Roof, Man and Superman, A Murder of Crows. Tours: Two Blind Mice, They Knew What They Wanted, And Miss Reardon Drinks a Little, In Praise of Love. Regional: The Glass Menagerie, The Lion in Winter, The Chalk Garden, Elizabeth the Queen, Semmelweiss, The Belle of Amherst, The Little Foxes, Another Part of the Forest, Ghosts, Death of a Salesman, Life With Father, Sabrina Fair, Faulkner's Bicycle, Antique Pink, The Belle of Amherst, Painting Churches, A Delicate Balance, Jokers, Remembrance, The Gin Game, A Murder of Crows, Watch on the Rhine, Suddenly Last Summer, A Smaller Place, Open Window, The Cocktail Hour, The Belle of Amherst, Love Letters.

PICTURES: The Seventh Victim (debut, 1943), Tender Comrade, When Strangers Marry (Betrayed), You Came Along, Stairway to Heaven (A Matter of Life and Death), A Canterbury Tale, A Streetcar Named Desire (Acad. Award, supp. actress, 1951), Anything Can Happen, Deadline: U.S.A., The Young Stranger, Bermuda Affair, Storm Center, Money Women and Guns, Lilith, Planet of the Apes, The Swimmer, Beneath the Planet of the Apes, Escape from the Planet of the Apes, Dark August, The Kindred, Two Evil Eyes.

TELEVISION: Made TV debut on Actors Studio Program, 1948. Series: The Edge of Night (1979–80). Specials: Requiem for a Heavyweight, The Comedian (both on Playhouse 90); Give Us Barabbas, Stubby Pringle's Christmas, Project: U.F.O., Three Sovereigns for Sarah, Vivien Leigh: Scarlett and Beyond, Martin Luther King: The Dream and the Drum, Hurricane Andrew Project. Guest: Love American Style, Columbo, Cannon, Night Gallery, Mission Impossible, Marcus Welby, Hec Ramsey, Griff, Police Story, Ironside, Medical Center, Baretta, Gibbsville, The Oregon Trail, Scene of the Crime, Hunter, Murder She Wrote, Class of '96. Movies: Dial Hot Line, In Search of America, The Magician (pilot), Unwed Father, Born Innocent, Bad Ronald, Ellery Queen (Too Many Suspects), The Dark Side of Innocence, The Golden Gate Murders, F.D.R.: The Last Year, Skokie, Private Sessions, Drop-Out Mother, Cross of Fire, Bloodlines: Murder in the Family. Mini-Series: Once an Eagle, Backstairs at the White House.

HUNTER, ROSS: Producer. r.n. Martin Fuss. b. Cleveland, OH, May 6, 1916. e. Western Reserve U., M.A. School teacher, 1942–43; actor, Columbia Pictures, 1944–46; returned to school teaching; stage prod. & dir.; m.p. dialogue dir.; assoc. prod. U-I, 1950–51; prod., U-I, 1951. Moved production Co. from Universal to Columbia, 1971. Moved to Paramount, 1974. Moved to NBC, 1978–82.

PICTURES: As actor: Louisiana Hayride, Ever Since Venus, She's a Sweetheart, Out of the Depths, Submarine Below, Hit the Hay, Eve Knew Her Apples, Bandit of Sherwood Forest, Groom Wore Spurs. As producer: Take Me to Town, All I Desire, Tumbleweed, Taza Son of Cochise, Magnificent Obsession, Naked Alibi, Yellow Mountain, Captain Lightfoot, One Desire, The Spoilers, All That Heaven Allows, There's Always Tomorrow, Battle Hymn, Tammy and the Bachelor, Interlude, My Man Godfrey, The Restless Years, This Happy Feeling, Stranger in My Arms, Imitation of Life, Pillow Talk, Portrait in Black, Midnight Lace, Back Street, Flower Drum Song, Tammy Tell Me True, If a Man Answers, Tammy and the Doctor, The Thrill of It All, The Chalk Garden, I'd Rather Be Rich, The Art of Love, Madame X, The Pad, Thoroughly Modern Millie, Rosie, Airport, Lost Horizon.

TELEVISION: Lives of Jenny Dolan, The Moneychangers, The Best Place to Be, A Family Upside Down, Suddenly Love.

HUNTER, TAB: Actor. r.n. Arthur Gelien. b. New York, NY, July 11, 1931. U.S. Coast Guard; odd jobs. Entered industry in 1948.

PICTURES: The Lawless (debut, 1950), Island of Desire, Gun Belt, Steel Lady, Return to Treasure Island, Track of the Cat, Battle Cry, Sea Chase, The Burning Hills, The Girl He Left Behind, Lafayette Escadrille, Gunman's Walk, Damn Yankees, That Kind of Woman, They Came to Cordura, The Pleasure of His Company, Operation Bikini, The Golden Arrow, Ride the Wild Surf, The Loved One, War Gods of the Deep, Birds Do It, Fickle Finger of Fate, Hostile Guns, The Arousers (Sweet Kill), Life and Times of Judge Roy Bean, Timber Tramp, Won Ton Ton the Dog Who Saved Hollywood, Polyester, Pandemonium, Grease 2, Lust in the Dust (also co-prod.), Cameron's Closet, Grotesque, Out of the Dark, Dark Horse (also story).

TELEVISION: Movies: San Francisco International , Katie: Portrait of a Centerfold. Series: The Tab Hunter Show, Mary Hartman Mary Hartman.

HUNTER, TIM: Director. e. Harvard, AFI.

PICTURES: Over the Edge (co-s.p.). Dir.: Tex (also s.p.),

Sylvester, River's Edge, Paint It Black, The Saint of Fort Washington.
TELEVISION: *Movie*: Lies of the Twins.

HUPPERT, ISABELLE: Actress. b. Paris, France, March 16, 1955. e. Conservatoire National d'Art Dramatique.
PICTURES: Faustine and the Beautiful Summer (debut, 1971), Cesar and Rosalie, Going Places, Rosebud, The Rape of Innocence, The Judge and the Assassin, The Lacemaker, Violette (Cannes Fest. Award, 1977), The Bronte Sisters, Loulou, Heaven's Gate, Coup de Torchon, Every Man for Himself, The True Story of Camille, Wings of the Dove, Deep Water, Entre Nous, The Trout, Cactus, Signed Charlotte, The Bedroom Window, The Possessed, Story of Women (Venice Fest Award, 1988), Milan Noir, Madame Bovary, Revenge of a Woman, Malina, Apres l'Amour (After Love).

HURD, GALE ANNE: Producer. b. Los Angeles, CA, Oct. 25, 1955. e. Stanford U., Phi Beta Kappa, 1977. m. director Brian DePalma. Joined New World Pictures in 1977 as exec. asst. to pres. Roger Corman, then named dir. of advertising and pub. and moved into prod. management capacities on several New World films. Left in 1982 to form own co., Pacific Western Productions. Honored by NATO with special merit award for Aliens. Served as juror, U.S. Film Fest., Utah, 1988 and for 1989 Focus Student Film Awards. Member, Hollywood Women's Political Committee. Board of Trustees, AFI; Board of Dir., Women in Film. The Amer. Film Inst. created Gale Anne Hurd production grants for Institute's Directing Workshop for Women.
PICTURES: Smokey Bites the Dust (co-prod. with Roger Corman, 1981), The Terminator (Grand Prix, Avoriaz Film Fest., France), Aliens (Hugo Award) Alien Nation (Saturn nom.), The Abyss, Downtown (exec. prod.), Tremors (exec. prod.), Terminator 2 (exec. prod.), The Waterdance, Raising Cain, The Penal Colony.

HURLOCK, ROGER W.: Pres. Hurlock Cine-World. b. Cambridge, MD, May 30, 1912. e. Baltimore City Coll. Ent. m.p. ind. as publicist, Hippodrome Theatre, Balt.; asst. mgr., Lessor-operator Imperial and Majestic Theatres, Balt., 1931–35; real estate, bldg., farming, Maryland and Alaska, 1936–58; elected bd. mem., Allied Artists, 1958; asst. to pres., 1961–63; chmn. budget comm., 1963; chmn. policy comm., 1964; c.p. exec. comm. member, 1964; v.p., chf. operating officer 1965; chmn. exec. comm., 1966; pres., 1967. pres., Hurlock Cine-World, 1969.

HURT, JOHN: Actor. b. Shirebrook, Derbyshire, Jan. 22, 1940. e. St. Martin's Sch. for Art, London, RADA.
PICTURES: The Wild and the Willing (debut, 1962), This is My Street, A Man for All Seasons, The Sailor from Gibraltar, Before Winter Comes, Sinful Davey, In Search of Gregory, 10 Rillington Place, Mr. Forbush and the Penguins, The Pied Piper, Little Malcolm, The Ghoul, East of Elephant Rock, Disappearance, Midnight Express (Acad. Award nom.) Watership Down (voice), The Lord of the Rings (voice), The Shout, Alien, The Elephant Man (Acad. Award nom.), Heaven's Gate, History of the World Part I, Night Crossing, Partners, The Plague Dogs (voice), The Osterman Weekend, Champions, The Hit, Success is the Best Revenge, 1984, The Black Cauldron (voice), Jake Speed, From the Hip, Spaceballs, Aria, Vincent (voice), White Mischief, Little Sweetheart, Scandal, Frankenstein Unbound, The Field, King Ralph, Romeo-Juliet, Resident Alien, I Dreamt I Woke Up, Lapse of Memory, Dark at Noon, Monolith, Even Cowgirls Get the Blues, Crime and Punishment.
TELEVISION: Playboy of the Western World, A Tragedy of Two Ambitions, Green Julia, Nijinsky, Shades of Green, Ten from the Twenties, The Peddler, The Naked Civil Servant, I Claudius, Spectre, Crime and Punishment, The Storyteller (series host), Deadline, The Jim Henson Hour, The Investigation: Inside a Terrorist Bombing, Six Characters in Search of an Author.
STAGE: The Dwarfs, Little Malcolm and His Struggle Against the Eunuchs, Man and Superman, Belcher's Luck, Ride a Cock Horse, The Caretaker, Romeo and Juliet, Ruffian on the Streets, The Dumb Waiter, Travesties, The Arrest, The Seagull, The London Vertigo.

HURT, MARY BETH: Actress. b. Marshalltown, IA, Sept. 26, 1948. m. writer-director Paul Schrader. e. U. of Iowa, NYU Sch. of Arts. Stage debut in 1973 with N.Y. Shakespeare Fest. (More Than You Deserve, Dream, The Cherry Orchard).
THEATER: As You Like It (Central Park), 2 seasons with Phoenix Theater, Love For Love, Tralawny of the Wells, Secret Service, Boy Meets Girl, Father's Day, Crimes of the Heart, The Misanthrope, Benefactors, The Nest of the Wood Grouse, The Day Room, Othello.
PICTURES: Interiors (debut, 1978), Head Over Heels (Chilly Scenes of Winter), A Change of Seasons, The World According to Garp, D.A.R.Y.L., Compromising Positions, Parents, Slaves of New York, Defenseless, Light Sleeper, My Boyfriend's Back, The Age of Innocence, Six Degrees of Separation.
TELEVISION: *Series*: Nick and Hillary. *Movie*: Baby Girl

Scott. *Specials*: Forty Eight, Secret Service (NET Theatre). *Guest*: Kojak.

HURT, WILLIAM: Actor. b. Washington, DC, Mar. 20, 1950. Lived as child in South Pacific when father was dir. of Trust Territories for U.S. State Dept. e. Tufts as theology major, switched to drama in jr. year, Juilliard. Oregon Shakespearean Fest. Leading actor with New York's Circle Repertory Company (Theatre World Award), since 1976, appearing in The Fifth of July, My Life (Obie Award), Ulysses in Traction, The Runner Stumbles, Hamlet, Childe Byron, Beside Herself. Also appeared with the New York Shakespeare Festival— Henry V (1976) and Midsummer's Night's Dream (1982), and in Hurlyburly off-Bdwy and on Bdwy. Regional: Good (S.F.), Ivanov (Yale).
PICTURES: Altered States (debut, 1980), Eyewitness, Body Heat, The Big Chill, Gorky Park, Kiss of the Spider Woman (Academy Award, 1985), Children of a Lesser God, Broadcast News, A Time of Destiny, The Accidental Tourist, I Love You to Death, Alice, The Doctor, Until the End of the World, The Plague.
TELEVISION: *Specials*: Verna: USO Girl, Best of Families, All The Way Home.

HUSSEIN, WARIS: Director. b. Lucknow, UP India, Dec. 9, 1938.
TELEVISION: *British*: Sleeping Dog, Death of a Teddy Bear, Toggle, Spoiled, Days In the Trees, A Passage to India, Girls in Uniform, St. Joan, A Casual Affair, The Six Wives of Henry VIII (also re-edited and shown theatrically), Divorce His/Divorce Hers, Shoulder to Shoulder, Georges Sand, Chips With Everything, The Glittering Prizes, Love Letters on Blue Paper, Sarah Bernhardt, Blind Love, Romance, Daphne Laureola, Waiting for Sheila, Armchair Thriller, Edward and Mrs. Simpson, The Clothes in the Wardrobe. *U.S.*: Death Penalty, And Baby Makes Six, The Henderson Monster, Baby Comes Home, Callie and Son, Coming Out of the Ice, Little Gloria: Happy at Last, Princess Daisy, Winter of Our Discontent, Arch of Triumph, Copacabana, Surviving, When the Bough Breaks, Intimate Contact, Downpayment on Murder, Onassis: The Richest Man in the World, Killer Instinct, Those She Left Behind, The Shell Seekers, Forbidden Nights, Switched at Birth, She Woke Up, For the Love of My Child: The Anissa Ayala Story, Murder Between Friends.
PICTURES: A Touch of Love, Quacker Fortune Has a Cousin in The Bronx, Melody, The Possession of Joel Delaney.

HUSSEY, OLIVIA: Actress. b. Buenos Aires, Apr. 17, 1951. Attended Italia Conti Stage School, London. Began acting at age 8.
PICTURES: The Battle of the Villa Fiorita, Cup Fever, All the Right Noises, Romeo and Juliet, Summertime Killer, Lost Horizon, Black Christmas, Death on the Nile, The Cat and the Canary, Virus, The Man With Bogart's Face, Distortions, The Jeweler's Shop, Undeclared War.
TELEVISION: *Movies/Mini-Series*: Jesus of Nazareth, The Pirate, The Bastard, Ivanhoe, Last Days of Pompeii, The Corsican Brothers, Psycho IV: The Beginning, Stephen King's IT, Save Me, Quest of the Delta Knights, H-Bomb. *Guest*: Murder She Wrote.

HUSTON, ANJELICA: Actress. b. Santa Monica, CA, July 8, 1951. Daughter of late writer-dir.-actor John Huston. Granddaughter of actor Walter Huston. Sister of director Danny Huston. Raised in St. Clerans, Ireland. Appeared in 3-D Disney short Captain Eo.
PICTURES: A Walk With Love and Death (debut, 1969), Sinful Davey, Swashbuckler, The Last Tycoon, The Postman Always Rings Twice, The Ice Pirates, This is Spinal Tap, Prizzi's Honor (Acad. Award, supp. actress, 1985), Gardens of Stone, The Dead, A Handful of Dust, Mr. North, Crimes and Misdemeanors, Enemies a Love Story, The Witches, The Grifters, The Addams Family, The Player, Manhattan Murder Mystery, Addams Family Values.
TELEVISION: *Movies*: The Cowboy and the Ballerina, Family Pictures, And the Band Played On. *Specials*: Faerie Tale Theatre, A Rose for Miss Emily. Mini-Series: Lonesome Dove.

HUSTON, DANNY: Director. b. Rome, Italy, May 14, 1962. Youngest son of director-actor John Huston and actress Zoe Sallis. Brother of actress Anjelica and screenwriter Tony Huston. e. Overseas School, Rome; Intl branch of Milfield School in Exeter, London Film School. A constant visitor to his father's sets throughout the world, he began working on his father's films, beginning in Cuernavaca, Mexico as second-unit dir. on Under the Volcano. Directed TV doc. on Peru and on making of Santa Claus: The Movie, and TV features Bigfoot and Mr. Corbett's Ghost. Feature film debut, Mr. North (1988), followed by Becoming Colette.

HUTTE, ROBERT E.: Exhibitor. b. Escanaba, MI, Oct. 22, 1917. e. Wisc. Inst. of Technology. Mgr. insp. lab. Iowa Ord. Plant 1940–42, Army Artil. 1942, Entered business as exhibitor in Southern Iowa 1943, Owned & managed theatres in Southern Iowa. Elected board of directors, Allied Theatre Owners of Iowa, Nebraska & Missouri 1948, 50, 52. Democratic candidate Iowa State Auditor 1960; Pres. Insurance Advisors, Des Moines, IA; pres Leisure Homes, Nursing Homes; pres., Leisure Homes of Texas; pres. Wodon & Romar Prods., Austin, TX 1970–75. Real estate broker & pres Leisure Mor, theatres in West TX; elected board of dir. National Independent Theatre Exhibitors 1979; Pres. Southwestern Indep. Theatre Exhibitors Assn. of TX, OK, AR, LA & NM; 1979 elected pres. Natl. Independent Theatre Exhibitors Assn. 1980–present. Lifetime member, Foundation of Motion Picture Pioneers.

HUTTON, BETTY: Actress. b. Battle Creek, MI, Feb. 26, 1921. Appeared on Bdwy in Panama Hattie, Annie.
PICTURES: The Fleet's In (debut, 1942), Star Spangled Rhythm, Happy Go Lucky, Let's Face It, Miracle of Morgan's Creek, And the Angels Sing, Here Come the Waves, Incendiary Blonde, Duffy's Tavern, The Stork Club, Cross My Heart, Perils of Pauline, Dream Girl, Red Hot and Blue, Annie Get Your Gun, Let's Dance, Sailor Beware (cameo), The Greatest Show on Earth, Somebody Loves Me, Spring Reunion.
TELEVISION: Series: The Betty Hutton Show (1959–60).

HUTTON, BRIAN, G.: Director. b. New York, NY, 1935.
PICTURES: The Wild Seed, The Pad, Sol Madrid, Where Eagles Dare, Kelly's Heroes, X Y and Zee, Night Watch, The First Deadly Sin, High Road to China, Hostile Takeover.
TELEVISION: Someone is Watching Me, Institute For Revenge.

HUTTON, LAUREN: Actress. r.n. Mary Hutton. b. Charleston, SC, Nov. 17, 1943. e. U. of South Florida, Sophie Newcombe Coll. As model featured on more covers than any other American.
Stage: Extremities.
PICTURES: Paper Lion (debut, 1968), Little Fauss and Big Halsy, Rocco Papaleo, The Gambler, Gator, Welcome to L.A., Viva Knievel, A Wedding, American Gigolo, Paternity, Zorro the Gay Blade, Tout Feu, Tout Flamme, Hecate, Lassiter, Once Bitten, Flagrant Desire, Malone, Blue Blood, Bulldance, Run For Your Life, Billions, Guilty as Charged, Missing Pieces.
TELEVISION: Mini-Series: The Rhinemann Exchange, Sins. Movies: Someone is Watching Me, Institute for Revenge, Starflight, The Cradle Will Fall, Scandal Sheet, The Return of Mike Hammer, Time Stalker, Monte Carlo, Perfect People, Fear. Series: Paper Dolls, Falcon Crest.

HUTTON, ROBERT: Actor. r.n. R. Winne. b. Kingston, NY, June 11, 1920. e. Blair Acad., NJ. In summer stock prior to screen career, 1943.
PICTURES: Destination Tokyo, Janie, Roughly Speaking, Hollywood Canteen, Too Young to Know, Love and Learn, Always Together, Steel Helmet, New Mexico, Racket, Slaughter Trail, Casanova's Big Night, The Slime People (also co-prod., dir.), Now It Can Be Told (assoc. prod.), The Vulture, You Only Live Twice, They Came From Beyond Space, Torture Garden, Tales from the Crypt.

HUTTON, TIMOTHY: Actor. b. Malibu, CA, Aug. 16, 1960. Son of late actor Jim Hutton. In high school plays; toured with father in Harvey during vacation. NY stage debut, Love Letters (1989), followed by Prelude to a Kiss, Babylon Gardens. Directed Cars video, Drive (1984).
TELEVISION: Movies: Zuma Beach, Friendly Fire, The Best Place to Be, And Baby Makes Six, Young Love First Love, Father Figure, A Long Way Home, Zelda. Director: Amazing Stories (Grandpa's Ghost).
PICTURES: Ordinary People (Acad. Award, supp. actor, 1980), Taps, Daniel, Iceman, The Falcon and The Snowman, Turk 182, Made in Heaven, A Time of Destiny, Betrayed (cameo), Everybody's All American, Torrents of Spring, Q&A, The Temp, The Dark Half.

HUYCK, WILLARD: Writer, Director. e. U. of Southern California. Worked as reader for Larry Gordon, executive at American-International Pictures; named Gordon's asst., working on scene rewrites for AIP films. First screen credit on The Devil's Eight as co-writer with John Milius, also U.S.C. graduate. Left AIP to write original scripts, with Gloria Katz. Both signed by Francis Ford Coppola to write and direct films for his America Zoetrope but projects never materialized. Co-wrote American Graffiti with Katz (1973) and Lucky Lady (1975). Huyck made directorial debut in 1979 with French Postcards, co-written with Katz, who also produced.
PICTURES: French Postcards (dir., co-s.p.), Indiana Jones and the Temple of Doom (co.-s.p.), Best Defense (dir., co.-s.p.), Howard the Duck (dir., co.-s.p.).
TELEVISION: A Father's Homecoming (co-exec. prod., co-s.p.), American River (co-exec. prod., co-s.p.).

HYAMS, JOSEPH: Advertising & Publicity Executive. b. New York, NY, Sept. 21, 1926. e. NYU Ent. industry, 1947. Various publicity posts, 20th Century-Fox, Columbia Pictures, 1947–55; eastern pub. mgr., Figaro Prods., 1955–56; West Coast pub. mgr., Hecht-Hill-Lancaster, 1955–58; pub. adv. dir.,

Batjac Prods. 1959–60 national adv. & pub. dir., Warner Bros., Seven Arts, 1960. v.p., world-wide pub., Warner Bros., Inc., 1970–1987; appointed sr. v.p., special projects, Dec., 1987.

HYAMS, PETER: Director, Writer, Cinematographer. b. New York, NY, July 26, 1943. e. Hunter Coll., Syracuse U. Joined CBS news staff N.Y. and made anchor man. Filmed documentary on Vietnam in 1966. Left CBS in 1970 and joined Paramount in Hollywood as writer. Hired by ABC to direct TV features.
PICTURES: T.R. Baskin (s.p., prod.), Busting (s.p., dir.), Our Time (dir.), Peeper (dir.), Telefon (co-s.p.), Capricorn One (s.p., dir.), Hanover Street (dir., s.p.), The Hunter (co-s.p.), Outland (dir., s.p.), Star Chamber (s.p., dir.), 2010 (prod., dir., s.p., photog.), Running Scared (exec. prod., dir., photog.), The Monster Squad (co-exec. prod.), The Presidio (dir., photog.), Narrow Margin (dir., s.p., photog.), Stay Tuned (dir., photog.).
TELEVISION: The Rolling Man, Goodnight My Love (s.p., dir.).

HYDE, TOMMY: Executive. r.n. Thomas L. b. Meridian, MS, June 29, 1916. e. Lakeland H.S., grad., 1935. Worked E.J. Sparks Theatres, 1932–41. Florida State Theatres, 1941–42. U.S. Navy, 1942–46. Florida State Theatres, 1946–47; city mgr. (Tallahassee). Talgar Theatres, 1947–58; v.p. and gen. mgr. Kent Theatres, 1958–86; vice-pres. Motion Picture Films, Inc.; pres., NATO of Florida, 1961–62; chmn. bd. 1963–70; 1987–93, theatre consultant.

HYER, MARTHA: Actress. b. Fort Worth, TX, Aug. 10, 1924. e. Northwestern U., Pasadena Playhouse.
PICTURES: Thunder Mountain, The Velvet Touch, The Clay Pigeon, Roughshod, The Lawless, Outcast of Black Mesa, Salt Lake Raiders, Frisco Tornado, Wild Stallion, Abbott and Costello Go to Mars, Riders to the Stars, Scarlet Spear, So Big, Battle of Rogue River, Lucky Me, Down Three Dark Streets, Sabrina, Cry Vengeance, Wyoming Renegades, Kiss of Fire, Paris Follies of 1956, Francis in the Navy, Red Sundown, Showdown at Abilene, Battle Hymn, Kelly and Me, Mister Cory, The Delicate Delinquent, My Man Godfrey, Paris Holiday, Once Upon a Horse, Houseboat, Some Came Running, Big Fisherman, Best of Everything, Ice Palace, Desire in the Dust, The Right Approach, The Last Time I Saw Archie, Girl Named Tamiko, Man from the Diner's Club, Wives and Lovers, Pyro, The Carpetbaggers, First Men in the Moon, Blood on the Arrow, Bikini Beach, Sons of Katie Elder, The Chase, Night of the Grizzly, Picture Mommy Dead, The Happening, Some May Live, War Italian Style, House of a Thousand Dolls, Once You Kiss a Stranger, Crossplot.

HYSON, KEVIN: Executive. b. Duxford, U.K., Jan. 7, 1951. e. Kings' School, Ely, U.K. 1960–1969. Joined Universal Pictures Ltd., London, 1969 in print and technical dept. Joined Cinema International Corp. London, 1970; gen. mgr., Cinema International Corp., Dominican Republic, 1974–76; gen. mgr., Cinema International Corp., Panama and Central America, 1976–79; mng. dir., CIC/Warner, South Africa, 1979–81; v.p., YK Cinema International Corp., Japan, 1981–83. Joined Columbia Pictures International, 1983; v.p., Latin America and Pacific for Columbia Pictures Int'l, 1984; v.p., advertising and publicity, 1985; exec. v.p., theatrical distribution and marketing, Columbia Pictures Int'l., 1986. Joined Walt Disney Pictures as v.p. int'l marketing, 1988; appt. sr. v.p., theatrical distribution and marketing, Buena Vista Intl., 1989.

I

IANNUCCI, SALVATORE J.: Executive. b. Brooklyn, NY, Sept. 24, 1927. e. NYU, B.A., 1949; Harvard Law School, J.D., 1952. 2 yrs. legal departments RCA and American Broadcasting Companies, Inc.; 14 yrs. with CBS Television Network: asst. dir. of bus. affairs, dir. of bus. affairs, v.p. of bus. affairs; 2 yrs. v.p. admin. National General Corp.; 2-1/2 yrs. pres. of Capital Records; 4-1/2 yrs. Corp. v.p. and dir. of Entertainment Div. of Playboy Enterprises, Inc.; 4 yrs. partner with Jones, Day, Reavis & Pogue in Los Angeles office, handling entertainment legal work; Pres., Filmways Entertainment, and sr. v.p., Filmways, Inc.; exec. v.p., Embassy Communications; COO, Aaron Spelling Prods.; sr. partner Bushkin, Gaims, Gaines, & Jonas; now pres. and chief operating officer, Brad Marks International.

IBBETSON, ARTHUR: Cinematographer. b. England, Sept. 8, 1922.
PICTURES: The Horse's Mouth, The Angry Silence, The League of Gentlemen, Tunes of Glory, Whistle Down the Wind, Nine Hours to Rama, I Could Go on Singing, The Chalk Garden, A Countess from Hong Kong, Inspector Clouseau, Where Eagles Dare, The Walking Stick, Anne of the Thousand Days (Oscar nominee), The Railway Children, Willy Wonka and the Chocolate Factory, A Doll's House, 11 Harrow House, A Little Night Music, The Medusa Touch, The Prisoner of Zenda, Hopscotch, Nothing Personal (co-cin.), The Bounty, Santa Claus: The Movie.
TELEVISION: Frankenstein: the True Story, Little Lord

Fauntleroy (Emmy), Brief Encounter, Babes in Toyland, Witness for the Prosecution, Master of the Game.

IBERT, LLOYD: Executive. Began career as mgng. editor, Independent Film Journal. 1973, joined Paramount Pictures pub. dept.; named sr. publicist. 1985, appointed dir., natl. pub. for M.P. Group.

IDLE, ERIC: Actor, Writer. b. South Shields, Co. Durham, Eng., March 29, 1943. e. Pembroke Coll., Cambridge, 1962–65. Pres. Cambridge's Footlights appearing at Edinburgh Fest. 1963–64. Member Monty Python's Flying Circus appearing on BBC, 1969–74.
STAGE: Oh What a Lovely War, Monty Python Live at the Hollywood Bowl (1978), Monty Python Live (NY, 1976), The Mikado (English Natl. Opera, 1986). Author: Pass the Butler (1982).
BOOKS: Hello Sailor, The Rutland Dirty Weekend Book, as well as co-author of Monty Python books: Monty Python's Big Red Book, The Brand New Monty Python Book, Monty Python and the Holy Grail, The Complete Works of Shakespeare and Monty Python.
PICTURES: And Now for Something Completely Different (also co-s.p.), Monty Python and the Holy Grail (also co-s.p.), Monty Python's Life of Brian (also co-s.p.), Monty Python Live at the Hollywood Bowl (also co-s.p.), Monty Python's The Meaning of Life (also co-s.p.), Yellowbeard, National Lampoon's European Vacation, Transformers (voice), The Adventures of Baron Munchausen, Nuns on the Run, Too Much Sun, Missing Pieces, Mom & Dad Save the World, Splitting Heirs (also s.p., exec. prod.).
TELEVISION: Isadora (debut, 1965), The Frost Report (writer), Do Not Adjust Your Set, Monty Python's Flying Circus, Rutland Weekend Television (series), All You Need is Cash (The Rutles), Faerie Tale Theater (The Frog Prince; dir. writer ACE Award, 1982; The Pied Piper), Saturday Night Live, The Mikado, Around the World in 80 Days, Nearly Departed (series).

IGER, ROBERT: Executive. b. 1951. Joined ABC in 1974 as studio supervisor. In 1976 moved to ABC Sports where in 1985 was named v.p. in charge of program planning and dev. as well as scheduling and rights acquisitions for all ABC Sports properties. In 1987, named v.p. programming for ABC Sports and mgr. & dir. for ABC's Wide World of Sports; 1988, appt. exec. v.p., ABC Network Group. April, 1989 named pres., ABC Entertainment.

IMAMURA, SHOHEI: Director, Producer, Writer. b. Tokyo, Japan, Sept. 15, 1926. e. Waseda U. Joined Shochiku Ofuna Studio 1951 asst. dir., transferred Nikkatsu in 1954 as asst. dir., director Stolen Desire 1958 then 4 more films before refusing to work on any film distasteful to him; and wrote play later made into film directed by him in 1968; later turned to documentaries and from 1976 onward as independent; Ballad of Narayamá awarded Golden Palm Prize, Cannes Festival, 1983.
PICTURES: Stolen Carnal Desire, Big Brother, Hogs and Warships, Insect Woman, God's Profound Desire, The Pornographers, A Man Vanishes, Human Evaporation, History of Postwar Japan, Vengeance Is Mine, Eijanaika, The Ballad of Narayama, Zegen, Black Rain.

IMI, TONY: Cinematographer. b. London, March 27, 1937. Ent. ind. 1959. Has worked primarily in England, Germany and US.
PICTURES: The Raging Moon, Dulcima, The Slipper and the Rose, International Velvet, Brass Target, Ffolkes, The Sea Wolves, Night Crossing, Nate and Hayes, Not Quite Jerusalem, Enemy Mine, Empire State, American Roulette, Buster, Options, Wired, Fire Birds, Pretty Hattie's Baby, Shopping.
TELEVISION: Queenie, The Return of Sherlock Holmes, Oceans of Fire, The Last Days of Frank and Jesse James, Reunion at Fairborough, A Christmas Carol, Sakharov, Princess Daisy, John Paul II, Little Gloria Happy at Last, Inside the Third Reich, Dreams Don't Die, For Ladies Only, Nicholas Nickleby, A Tale of Two Cities, Babycakes, Old Man and the Sea, Fourth Story, The Last to Go, Our Sons, Carolina Skeletons, Child of Rage, Queen, Cobb's Law, For the Love of My Child: The Anissa Ayala Story, Blind Angel.

IMMERMAN, WILLIAM J.: Producer, Attorney, Executive. b. New York, NY, Dec. 29, 1937. e. Univ. Wisconsin, BS, 1959; Stanford Law, 1963. 1963–65, served as deputy district attorney, LA County. 1965–72, assoc. counsel, v.p.- bus. affairs, American Intl. Pictures. Joined 20th Century-Fox in 1972 as v.p., business affairs. 1977–1979, producer at Warner Bros. 1979, founder and chmn. of bd. of Cinema Group Inc. 1978–present, pres. Salem Productions. 1988–present, pres. Distribution Expense Co. and ImmKirk Financial Corp. 1988–89, spec. consultant to office of pres., Pathe Communications. 1989–90, vice chmn. Cannon Pictures. 1986–90, dir. Heritage Ent., Inc. 1991–present, v.p. The Crime Channel. Stage Productions: Berlin to Broadway (LA), The Knife Thrower's Assistant (LA, tour), The Wiz (Bdwy).

PICTURES: Exec. prod.: Highpoint, Southern Comfort, Hysterical, Mind Games, Take this Job and Shove It, Where the Red Ferns Grows Part II. Prod.: Primal Rage, Nightmare Beach.

INGALLS, DON: Producer, Writer. b. Humboldt, NB, July 29, 1928. e. George Washington U., 1948. Columnist, Washington Post; producer-writer, ATV England and Australia; writer-prod., Have Gun Will Travel, also prod. for TV: The Travels of Jamie McPheeters, The Virginian, Honey West, Serpico, Kingston: Confidential. Exec. story consultant The Sixth Sense; prod.: Fantasy Island, T.J. Hooker, Duel at Shiloh, Smile of the Dragon, In Preparation: Watchers on the Mountain, Hearts & Diamonds.
TELEVISION: Writer: Gunsmoke, Have Gun Will Travel, The Bold Ones, Marcus Welby M.D., Mod Squad, Star Trek, Honey West, Bonanza, The Sixth Sense, Then Came Bronson, Police Story, World Premier Movie, Shamus, Flood, Capt. America, The Initiation of Sarah, Blood Sport, and others.
PICTURES: Airport-1975, Who's Got the Body?

INGELS, MARTY: Actor, Former Comedian, Executive. b. Brooklyn, NY, Mar. 9, 1936. m actress-singer Shirley Jones. U.S. Infantry 1954–58. Ent. show business representing Army, Name That Tune. Stage: Sketchbook revue, Las Vegas. Pres., Celebrity Brokerage, packaging celebrity events and endorsements. Active in community affairs and charity funding.
TELEVISION: Series: I'm Dickens . . . He's Fenster, The Phyllis Diller Show. Guest: Phil Silvers Show, Steve Allen, Jack Paar, Playboy Penthouse, Bell Telephone Hour, Manhunt, Ann Sothern Show, Peter Loves Mary, The Detectives, Joey Bishop Show, Hennessey, Dick Van Dyke Show, Burke's Law, Hollywood Palace, Family, Murder She Wrote.
PICTURES: The Ladies Man, Armored Command, The Horizontal Lieutenant, The Busy Body, Wild and Wonderful, A Guide for the Married Man, If It's Tuesday It Must be Belgium, For Singles Only, Instant Karma.

INGSTER, BORIS: Writer, Director. b. 1913. In 1935: collaborated on adaptation, The Last Days of Pompeii, RKO. In 1936: Dancing Pirate, RKO. In 1937: collaborated on screen play Thin Ice, 20th-Fox. In 1938: Happy Landing.
PICTURES: Judge Steps Out, Southside 1–1000; Something for the Birds, Abdullah's Harem, California-story, Cloak & Dagger, The Amazing Mrs. Holliday.
TELEVISION: Wagon Train, The Alaskans, The Roaring 20's, Travels of Jaimie McPheeters, The Man From U.N.C.L.E.

INSDORF, ANNETTE: Film professor, critic, translator, and television host. b. Paris, France, July 27, 1950. e. 1963–68 studied voice, Julliard Sch. of Music and performed as singer; Queens Coll. (summa cum laude), B.A. 1972; Yale U., M.A., 1973; Yale U., Ph.D., 1975. 1973: soloist in Leonard Bernstein's Mass (European premiere in Vienna and BBC/WNET TV). 1975–87: professor of film, Yale U. Author of François Truffaut (1979; updated 1989), Indelible Shadows: Film and the Holocaust (1983, updated 1989). Since 1979: frequent contributor to NY Times (Arts and Leisure), Los Angeles Times, San Francisco Chronicle, Elle, and Premiere. Named Chevalier dans l'ordre des arts et lettres by French Ministry of Culture, 1986. Since 1987, dir. of Undergrad. Film Studies, Columbia U., and prof. Graduate Film Div. 1990 named chmn. of Film Div. 1987: exec.-prod. Shoeshine (short film nom. for Oscar). 1989: exec. prod., Abrams' Performance Pieces (named best fiction short, Cannes Fest).

IRONS, JEREMY: Actor. b. Isle of Wight, Sept. 19, 1948. m. actress Sinead Cusack. e. Sherborne Sch., Dorset. Stage career began at Marlowe Theatre, Canterbury, where he was student asst. stage manager. Accepted at Bristol Old Vic Theatre Sch. for two-yr. course; then joined Bristol Old Vic Co. In London played in Godspell, Much Ado About Nothing, The Caretaker, Taming of the Shrew, Wild Oats, Rear Column, An Audience Called Edouard, etc. N.Y. stage debut, The Real Thing (Tony Award, 1984).
PICTURES: Nijinsky (debut, 1980), The French Lieutenant's Woman, Moonlighting, Betrayal, The Wild Duck, Swann in Love, The Mission, Dead Ringers, A Chorus of Disapproval, Danny the Champion of the World (tv in U.S.), Australia, Reversal of Fortune (Acad. Award, 1990), Kafka, Waterland, Damage, M. Butterfly, The House of the Spirits.
TELEVISION: The Pallisers, Notorious Woman, Love for Lydia, Langrishe Go Down, Brideshead Revisited, The Captain's Doll, Autogeddon, Tales From Hollywood, The Dream of a Ridiculous Man.

IRVIN, JOHN: Director. b. Newcastle, England, May 7, 1940. In cutting rooms at Rank Organisation before making first film—documentary Gala Day on grant from British Film Inst. Other documentaries before turning to features.
PICTURES: The Dogs of War, Ghost Story, Champions, Turtle Diary, Raw Deal, Hamburger Hill, Next of Kin, Eminent Domain, Widow's Peak.

TELEVISION: The Nearly Man, Hard Times, Tinker Tailor Soldier Spy, Robin Hood.

IRVING, AMY: Actress. b. Palo Alto, CA, Sept. 10, 1953. e. American Conservatory Theatre, London Acad. of Dramatic Art. Daughter of late Jules Irving and actress Priscilla Pointer.
THEATER: NY: Amadeus, Heartbreak House, Road to Mecca. LA: The Heidi Chronicles.
PICTURES: Carrie (debut, 1976), The Fury, Voices, Honeysuckle Rose, The Competition, Yentl (Acad. Award nom.), Micki and Maude, Rumpelstiltskin, Who Framed Roger Rabbit (voice), Crossing Delancey, Show of Force, An American Tail: Fievel Goes West (voice), Benefit of the Doubt, Kleptomania.
TELEVISION: Movies: James Dean, James A. Michener's Dynasty, Panache, Anastasia: The Mystery of Anna. Mini-Series: Once an Eagle. Special: Turn of the Screw.

IRWIN, BILL: Actor. b. Santa Monica, CA, April 11, 1950.
PICTURES: Popeye (debut, 1980), A New Life, Eight Men Out, My Blue Heaven, Scenes From a Mall, Hot Shots, Stepping Out, Silent Tongue.
THEATRE: Bdwy: Accidental Death of an Anarchist, 5-6-7-8- Dance, Largely New York, Fool Moon. Off-Bdwy: The Regard of Flight, The Courtroom, Not Quite New York, Waiting for Godot.
TELEVISION: Specials: The Regard of Flight, Bette Midler - Mondo Beyondo, The Paul Daniels Magic Show (BBC), The Last Mile. Guest: Saturday Night Live, Tonight Show, Cosby Show, Northern Exposure.

IRWIN, CHRISTOPHER: Producer, Executive. b. England 1948. e. U. of Sussex, Eng., B.A., social studies. From 1967 to 1969 worked as freelance producer-presenter for BBC Radio Brighton. Was with the Federal Trust (the institute concerned with European affairs) 1969 to 1975, during which time worked for the Secretariat of the North Atlantic Assembly. Joined the BBC's External Services as talks producer in 1975, moving in 1977 to the BBC's central Secretariat. From 1977 to 1978 was seconded to the International Institute for Strategic Studies. In 1978 went to Scotland as Secretary, BBC Scotland, and was closely associated with early stages of Radio Scotland. Member of BBC's Future Policy Group, the "think tank" of the Corporation. Appointed Head of Radio Scotland May 1980.

ISAACS, CHERYL BOONE: Executive. b. Springfield, MA. Entered m.p. industry 1977 as staff publicist for Columbia Pictures. Worked five years after that for Melvin Simon Prods., named v.p. Left to become dir. of adv./pub. for The Ladd Co. 1984, named dir., pub. & promo., West Coast, for Paramount Pictures. Promoted vice pres., publicity, Paramount Pictures in 1986. Promoted to sr. v.p., Worldwide Publicity, Paramount in 1991. Member A.M.P.A.S. Board of Governors since 1988.

ISAACS, PHIL: Executive. b. New York, NY, May 20, 1922. e. City Coll. of New York. In U.S. Navy, 1943-46. Joined Paramount Pictures in 1946 as bookers asst., N.Y. exch. Branch mgr. in Washington; then mgr. Rocky Mt. div. In 1966 was Eastern-Southern sls. mgr.; 1967 joined Cinema Center Films as v.p. domestic dist. In 1972 named v.p., marketing, for Tomorrow Entertainment; Joined Avco-Embassy 1975 as v.p., gen. sls. mgr., named exec. v.p., 1977. 1978 joined General Cinema Corp. as v.p. 1980 v.p., gen. sls. mgr., Orion Pictures. 1983, formed Phil Isaacs Co; 1988, v.p., general sales mgr., TWE Theatrical; 1989, appointed pres. Became pres. South Gate Entertainment 1989.

ISRAEL, NEAL: Writer, Director. m. director Amy Heckerling.
PICTURES: Tunnelvision (exec. prod., s.p., actor), Cracking Up (s.p., actor), Americathon (dir., s.p.), Police Academy (s.p.), Bachelor Party (dir., s.p.), Johnny Dangerously (actor), Moving Violations (dir., s.p.), Real Genius (s.p.), It's Alive III (s.p.), Buy and Cell (co-s.p.), Look Who's Talking Too (co-prod., actor), Spurting Blood (exec. prod., s.p.), All I Want for Christmas (co-s.p.), Breaking the Rules (dir.).
TELEVISION: Lola Falana Special (s.p.), Mac Davis Show, Ringo, Marie (prod.), Twilight Theatre (writer, prod.). Movies: The Cover Girl and the Cop (dir.), Woman With a Past (co-exec. prod.), Taking the Heat (co-prod.).

ITAMI, JUZO: Director, Actor. b. Kyoto, Japan, 1933. m. actress Nobuko Miyamoto. Son of Mansaku Itami, pioneering Japanese film director. After successful stint as commercial artist, became an actor as well as essayist (Listen, Women, a collection of his work). Directing debut The Funeral (1984).
PICTURES: Actor: 55 Days at Peking, Lord Jim, I Am a Cat, The Makioka Sisters, The Family Game. Director: The Funeral (5 Japanese Acad. Awards), Tampopo, A Taxing Woman (8 Japanese Acad. Awards), A Taxing Woman's Return (dir., s.p.), Sweet Home (exec. prod. only).

IVANEK, ZELJKO: Actor. b. Ljubljana, Yugoslavia, Aug. 15, 1957. Came to U.S. with family in 1960 and returned to homeland before settling in Palo Alto, CA, in 1967. Studied at Yale, majoring in theatre studies: graduated in 1978. Also graduate

of London Acad. of Music and Dramatic Arts. Regular member of Williamstown Theatre Festival, appearing in Hay Fever, Charley's Aunt, Front Page. Bdwy. debut in The Survivor.
THEATER: Bdwy: Brighton Beach Memoirs, Loot, Two Shakespearean Actors. Regional: Master Harold . . . and the Boys (Yale Rep. premiere prod.), Hamlet (Guthrie), Ivanov (Yale Rep.). Off Bdwy: Cloud 9, A Map of the World, The Cherry Orchard.
PICTURES: Tex, The Sender, The Soldier, Mass Appeal, Rachel River, School Ties.
TELEVISION: Movies: The Sun Also Rises, Echoes in the Darkness, Aftermath: A Test of Love, Our Sons. Special: All My Sons. Guest: Homicide - Life on the Street.

IVERS, IRVING N.: Executive. b. Montreal, Canada, Feb. 23, 1939. e. Sir George Williams U. Worked for 10 years in radio and TV in variety of executive capacities in station management before entering film business. Joined Columbia Pictures in 1973, serving as director of mktg. and dir. of adv. 1973–77; named Canadian sls. mgr. 1977–78; v.p. of adv./ pub. 1978–80. In 1980 joined 20th Century-Fox as sr. v.p. of adv./pub./promo.; exec. v.p., worldwide adv., pub., promo. 1980–83; pres., worldwide mkt., MGM/UA/Entertainment Co. 1983–86. In 1986 to Warner Bros. as v.p., intl. adv./pub. Oct. 1991 to Astral Commun., Toronto as pres. of Astral Films and Astral Video.

IVES, BURL: Ballad singer, Actor. r.n. Burl Icle Ivanhoe b. Hunt Township, IL, June 14, 1909. e. Teacher's Coll., Charleston, IL. Professional football player, itinerant worker, radio singer, specializing ballads.
STAGE: On Bdwy in Cat on a Hot Tin Roof.
PICTURES: Smoky (debut, 1946), Green Grass of Wyoming, Station West, So Dear to My Heart, Sierra, East of Eden, The Power and the Prize, A Face in the Crowd, Wind Across the Everglades, Desire Under the Elms, The Big Country (Acad. Award, supp. actor, 1958), Cat on a Hot Tin Roof, Day of the Outlaw, Our Man in Havana, Let No Man Write My Epitaph, The Spiral Road, Summer Magic, The Brass Bottle, Ensign Pulver, The Daydreamer (voice), Blast-Off, The McMasters, Baker's Hawk, Hugo the Hippo (voice), Just You and Me Kid, Earthbound, White Dog, Uphill All the Way, Two Moon Junction.
TELEVISION: Special: Rudolph the Red-Nosed Reindeer (narrator). Movies: The Sound of Anger, The Whole World is Watching, The Man Who Wanted to Live Forever, The Bermuda Depths, New Adventures of Heidi, Poor Little Rich Girl, The Ewok Adventure. Series: O.K. Crackerby, The Bold Ones (The Lawyers). Mini-Series: Captains and the Kinds, Roots.

IVEY, JUDITH: Actress. b. El Paso, TX, Sept. 4, 1951. m. ind. prod., Tim Braine. e. Illinois State U. Stage debut in The Sea in Chicago, 1974.
STAGE: Bedroom Farce, The Goodbye People, Oh Coward!, Design for Living, Piaf, Romeo and Juliet, Pastorale, Two Small Bodies, Steaming (Tony & Drama Desk Awards), Second Lady (off-Bdwy work she helped develop), Hurlyburly (Tony & Drama Desk Awards), Precious Sons (Drama Desk nom.), Blithe Spirit, Mrs. Dally Has a Lover, Park Your Car in Harvard Yard, many others.
PICTURES: Harry and Son (debut, 1984), The Lonely Guy, The Woman in Red, Compromising Positions, Brighton Beach Memoirs, Hello Again, Sister Sister, Miles from Home, In Country, Everybody Wins, Alice, Love Hurts, There Goes the Neighborhood.
TELEVISION: Movies: The Shady Hill Kidnapping, Dixie: Changing Habits, We Are the Children, The Long Hot Summer, Jesse and the Bandit Queen, Decoration Day, Her Final Fury: Betty Broderick - The Last Chapter. Series: Down Home, Designing Women.

IVORY, JAMES: Director. b. Berkeley, CA, June 7, 1928. e. U. of Oregon, B.F.A., 1951; U. of Southern California, M.A. (cinema) 1956. First film Venice: Theme and Variations (doc. made as M.A. thesis, 1957). Early work: The Sword and the Flute, The Delhi Way. Formed Merchant Ivory Productions with prod. Ismail Merchant and long-time script writer Ruth Prawer Jhabvala.
PICTURES: The Householder, Shakespeare Wallah (also co-s.p.), The Guru (also co-s.p.), Bombay Talkie (also co-s.p.), Savages, The Wild Party, Roseland, The Europeans (also cameo), Quartet, Heat and Dust, The Bostonians, A Room with a View, Maurice (also co-s.p.), Slaves of New York, Mr. and Mrs. Bridge, Howards End, Remains of the Day.
TELEVISION: Noon Wine (exec. prod.). Dir: Adventures of a Brown Man in Search of Civilization, Autobiography of a Princess (also released theatrically), Hullabaloo Over George and Bonnie's Pictures, Jane Austen in Manhattan (also released theatrically), The Five Forty Eight.

J

JACKSON, ANNE: Actress. b. Allegheny, PA, Sept. 3, 1926. e. Neighborhood Playhouse, Actors Studio. Married to actor Eli Wallach. Stage debut in The Cherry Orchard, 1944. Autobiography: Early Stages.
THEATER: Major Barbara, Middle of the Night, Typist and the Tiger, Luv, Waltz of the Toredors, Twice Around the Park, Summer and Smoke, Nest of the Woodgrouse, Marco Polo Sings a Solo, The Mad Woman of Chaillot, Cafe Crown, Lost in Yonkers.
PICTURES: So Young So Bad (debut, 1950), The Journey, Tall Story, The Tiger Makes Out, How to Save a Marriage and Ruin Your Life, The Secret Life of an American Wife, The Angel Levine, Zig Zag, Lovers and Other Strangers, Dirty Dingus Magee, Nasty Habits, The Bell Jar, The Shining, Sam's Son, Funny About Love, Folks!.
TELEVISION: Series: Everything's Relative. Special: 84 Charing Cross Road. Movies: The Family Man, A Woman Called Golda, Private Battle, Blinded By the Light, Leave 'em Laughing, Baby M.

JACKSON, BRIAN: Actor, Film/Stage Producer. b. Bolton, England, 1931. Early career in photography then numerous stage performances incl. Old Vic, Royal Shakespeare. Ent. film/TV industry 1958. Formed Quintus Plays, 1965; formed Brian Jackson Productions 1966; formed Hampden Gurney Studios Ltd. 1970. Co-produced The Others 1967; presented The Button, 1969; co-produced the documentary film Village in Mayfair, 1970; 1971: Formed Brian Jackson Films Ltd.; produced Yesterday, The Red Deer, The Story of Tutankhamen.
TELEVISION: Moon Fleet, Private Investigator, Life of Lord Lister, Z Cars, Vendetta, Sherlock Holmes, Mr. Rose, Hardy Heating International, Nearest & Dearest, The Persuaders, The Paradise Makers, The New Avengers, Smugglers Bay, The Tomorrow People, Secret Army, Last Visitor for Hugh Peters, Six Men of Dorset, Commercials: featured as the man from Delmonte for 5 years.
PICTURES: Incident in Karandi, Carry On Sergeant, Gorgo, Jack the Ripper, Taste of Fear, Heroes of Telemark, Only the Lonely, The Deadly Females, The Revenge of the Pink Panther, Deceptions, Shadow Chasers.
STAGE: Mame, Drury Lane, Fallen Angels, In Praise of Love.

JACKSON, GLENDA: Actress. b. Birkenhead, England, May 9, 1936. Stage debut: Separate Tables (Worthing, Eng. 1957). Ent. m.p. ind. 1955. Became member of Parliament, 1992.
THEATER: (Eng.): All Kinds of Men, Hammersmith, The Idiot, Alfie. Joined Royal Shakespeare Co in experimental Theatre of Cruelty season. Marat Sade (London, N.Y.), Three Sisters, The Maids, Hedda Gabler, The White Devil, Rose, Strange Interlude (N.Y.), Macbeth (N.Y.), Who's Afraid of Virginia Woolf? (L.A.).
PICTURES: Marat-Sade (debut, 1967), Tell Me Lies, Negatives, Women in Love (Acad. Award, 1970), The Music Lovers, Sunday Bloody Sunday, Mary Queen of Scots, The Boy Friend, Triple Echo, The Nelson Affair, A Touch of Class (Acad. Award, 1973), The Maids, The Temptress, The Romantic Englishwoman, The Devil is a Woman, Hedda, The Incredible Sarah, Nasty Habits, House Calls, Stevie, The Class of Miss McMichael, Lost and Found, Health, Hopscotch, Giro City, The Return of the Soldier, Turtle Diary, Beyond Therapy, Business as Usual, Salome's Last Dance, The Rainbow, The Visit.
TELEVISION: Movies: The Patricia Neal Story, Sakharov. Mini-Series: Elizabeth R (2 Emmy Awards, 1972). Special: Strange Interlude, A Murder of Quality, The House of Bernarda Alba.

JACKSON, JOHN HENRY: Executive. b. New York, NY, April 27, 1916. e. Holy Cross Acad., 1930; Professional Children's Sch., 1934; Georgia Tech, 1936. Performed as vaudeville artist touring Europe, 1928–29; Fair dates and indoor circus, 1929–34; Billy Rosie's Jumbo, 1935; Texas Centennial, 1936; George Abbott's Too Many Girls, 1938. Joined Radio City Music Hall, 1943 with Glee Club; stage manager, 1944–51; director of stage operations, 1958; v.p., 1970; prod., 1971; pres., Tri-Marquee Productions, Ltd., 1979. Retired 1980. Produced p.r. events W.R. Grace Co. 1980–86.

JACKSON, KATE: Actress. b. Birmingham, AL, Oct. 29, 1949. e. U. of Mississippi, Birmingham Southern U. Did summer stock before going to N.Y. to enter American Acad. of Dramatic Arts, appearing in Night Must Fall, The Constant Wife, Little Moon of Alban. Worked as model and became tour guide at NBC. First role on TV in Dark Shadows (series).
PICTURES: Night of Dark Shadows, Limbo, Thunder and Lightning, Dirty Tricks, Making Love, Loverboy.
TELEVISION: Movies: Satan's School for Girls, Killer Bees, Death Cruise, Death Scream, Charlie's Angels (pilot), Death at Love House, James at 15 (pilot), Topper, Inmates: A Love Story, Thin Ice, Listen to Your Heart, The Stranger Within, Quiet Killer, Homewrecker (voice), Adrift. Series: Dark Shadows, The Rookies, Charlie's Angels, Scarecrow and Mrs. King, Baby Boom. Guest: The Jimmy Stewart Show.

JACKSON, MICHAEL: Singer, Composer. b. Gary, IN, Aug. 29, 1958. Musical recording artist with family group known as Jackson 5: all brothers, Jackie, Jermaine, Tito, Marlon, and Michael. Sister is singer Janet Jackson.
PICTURES: Save the Children, The Wiz, Moonwalker (also exec. prod., story).
TELEVISION: Series: The Jacksons (1976–7). Specials: Free to Be You and Me, Sandy in Disneyland, Motown on Showtime: Michael Jackson.

JACKSON, MICK: Director. b. Grays, England. e. Bristol Univ. Joined BBC as film editor, following post-grad work in film & tv. Produced and directed many documentaries for the BBC.
PICTURES: Chattahoochee, L.A. Story, The Bodyguard, Clean Slate.
TELEVISION: Documentaries: The Ascent of Man, Connections, The Age of Uncertainty. Movies/Specials: Threads, The Race for the Double Helix, Yuri Nosenko KGB (HBO). Mini-Series: A Very British Coup.

JACKSON, SAMUEL L.: Actor. b. 1949. e. Morehouse Col. m. actress LaTanya Richardson. Co-founder, member of the Just Us Theatre Co. in Atlanta.
MOVIES: Ragtime, Eddie Murphy Raw, School Daze, Do the Right Thing, Sea of Love, Def by Temptation, Mo' Better Blues, GoodFellas, Jungle Fever (Cannes Film Fest. & NY Film Critics Awards, 1991), Strictly Business, Juice, White Sands, Patriot Games, Johnny Suede, Jumpin at the Boneyard, Fathers and Sons, National Lampoon's Loaded Weapon 1, Amos & Andrew, Menace II Society, Jurassic Park, True Romance, The New Age.
THEATRE: Negro Ensemble Company: Home, A Soldier's Story, Sally/Prince, Colored People's Time. NY Shakespeare Fest: Mother Courage, Spell #7, The Mighty Gents. Yale Rep: The Piano Lesson, Two Trains Running. Seattle Rep: Fences.

JACOBI, DEREK: Actor. b. London, England, Oct. 22, 1938. e. Cambridge. On stage in Pericles, The Hollow Crown, Hobson's Choice, The Suicide, Breaking the Code (London, NY).
PICTURES: Othello (debut, 1965), The Three Sisters, The Day of the Jackal, Blue Blood, The Odessa File, The Medusa Touch, The Human Factor, Enigma, Secret of NIMH (voice), Little Dorrit, Henry V, Dead Again.
TELEVISION: She Stoops to Conquer, Man of Straw, The Pallisers, I, Claudius, Philby, Burgess and MacLean, Hamlet. Movies: Othello, Three Sisters, Interlude, Charlotte, The Man Who Went Up in Smoke, The Hunchback of Notre Dame, Inside the Third Reich, The Secret Garden, The Tenth Man (Emmy Award). Series: Minder, Tales of the Unexpected, Mr. Pye.

JACOBS, BARRY: Executive. b. London, England, 1924. Ent. m.p. ind. 1938. Served in RAF 1943–46. Circuit rep. Warner Bros. 1938–59. Overseas sales rep. independent producers 1960–62. Formed Eagle Films Ltd. dist. organization UK 1962. Entered prod. 1969. Exec. prod. The Wife Swappers, Groupie Girl, Bread, Naughty, The Love Box, Sex and The Other Woman, On the Game, Eskimo Nell. Formed Elephant Entertainment Ltd. & Elephant Video Ltd., 1986; exhibitor: Tivoli Birmingham and Theatre One Coventry.

JACOBS, JOHN: Executive. b. New York, NY. e. Syracuse U.'s Newhouse Communications Sch. Full-service agency background, including 13 years with Grey Advertising agency, where handled Warner Bros. & Warner Home Video accts. Supvr. media on RCA, ABC-TV, Murdoch Publishing, Radio City Music Hall, etc. Named v.p. & group media dir. for Grey. 1986, left to join Warner Bros. as v.p., media.

JACOBY, FRANK DAVID: Director, Producer. b. New York, NY, July 15, 1925. e. Hunter Coll., Brooklyn Coll. m. Doris Storm, producer/director educational films, actress. 1949–52: NBC network TV director; 1952–56: B.B.D.O., Biow Co., TV producer/director; 1956–58 Metropolitan Educational TV Association, Director of Production; 1958–65: United Nation, film producer/director; 1965 to present: President, Jacoby/Storm Productions, Inc., Westport, Conn., documentary, industrial, educational films and filmstrips. Clients include Xerox Corp., Random House, Publ., Lippincott Co., IBM, Heublein, G.E., and Pitney Bowes. Winner, Sherwood Award, Peabody Award. Member, Director's Guild of America; winner, Int'l TV & Film Festival, National Educational Film Festival, American Film Festival.

JACOBY, JOSEPH: Producer, Director, Writer. b. Brooklyn, NY, Sept. 22, 1942. e. NYU. Sch. of Arts and Sciences, majoring in m.p. As undergraduate worked part-time as prod. asst. on daytime network TV shows and as puppeteer for Bunin Puppets. In 1964 joined Bil Baird Marionettes as full-time puppeteer, working also on Baird film commercials. Made feature m.p. debut as prod.-dir of Shame, Shame Everybody Knows Her Name, 1968. Contributing essayist, NY Woman Magazine.

PICTURES: Hurry Up, or I'll Be 30 (dir., writer, prod.), The Great Bank Hoax (co-prod., dir., s.p.).

JACOBY, SCOTT: Actor. b. Chicago, IL, Nov. 19, 1956.
PICTURES: The Little Girl Who Lives Down the Lane, Love and the Midnight Auto Supply, Our Winning Season, Return to Horror High, To Die For, To Die For II.
TELEVISION: Movies: No Place to Run, That Certain Summer (Emmy Award, supp. 1973), The Man Who Could Talk to Kids, Bad Ronald, Smash-Up on Interstate 5, No Other Love, The Diary of Anne Frank. Mini-Series: 79 Park Avenue. Series: One Life to Live (1973–4). Guest: Medical Center, Marcus Welby M.D., The Golden Girls.

JACON, BERNARD: Executive. b. Louisiana. Manager, promotion, Small & Strausberg Theatres, New York; buyer & gen. mgr., Mantell Theatres N.Y., gen. mgr. & assoc., Rockaway Beach Theatres, Universal Pictures, home office & field, br. operations & sales. Mgr., sales & dist. (Continental Films) Superfilms Distribution Corp., New York 1946–49; vice-pres. in chg. of sales & dist., Lux Film Distributing Corp., N.Y., 1949–52; v.p. sales, dist. IFE Releasing, 1952–55; org. nat'l distrib. co., Jacon Film Distributors, Inc., as pres., 1956; nat'l consultant to independent distributors, producers & exhibitors, member of the Pioneers & Variety; 1979, formed Bernie Jacon, Inc., natl. co-ordinator for producers and distributors.

JACQUEMIN, ROBERT: Executive. Began career as media buyer; later in station representation as v.p. of regional sls. for Telerep, Inc. Entered syndication as pres. of Television Marketing Services, St. Louis. Joined Paramount Domestic Television and Video Programming as midwest div. mgr. in St. Louis; later sr. v.p., sls. in N.Y. 1981, named exec. v.p., sls. & mktg. 1985, joined Walt Disney Pictures as sr. v.p., domestic TV dist., a new syndication div. formed by the co.; promoted to president, Oct. 1988.

JACQUES, ROBERT C.: Film editor. b. Cincinnati, OH, Feb. 24, 1919. e. U. of Michigan, U. of Southern California. Asst. film ed., RKO Radio 1939–42; film ed., Pathe News, 1942–44; chief film ed., NBC Television, 1944–48; prod. chief, Ziv TV film dept. 1948–51; free lance m.p. film ed., 1951–52; supervising film ed., prod. mgr., American Film Prod., 1952–53; prod. supvr., ed., Telenews and Screen Gems 1953; film ed., RKO Radio, 1953–55; supervising film ed., George Blake Enterprises, 1955–57; v.p. Peter Elgar Productions 1957–60; supv. film editor, Transfilm-Caravel Inc. 1960–62; v.p. in chg. of completion, Filmex, Inc., 1962. V.P. in charge of completion, Filmex Inc. 1962–69. Free lance film editor, May–Nov. 1969. V.P. of own co., Double Image Inc., film and videotape editorial service, Nov. 1969–1983. Freelance post-prod. consultant, 1983. Retired 1983.

JAECKEL, RICHARD: Actor. b. Long Beach, NY, Oct. 10, 1926. e. Hollywood H.S., 1943. Performed odd jobs upon graduation, with plans toward entering Merchant Marine when of age; worked as delivery boy in mail room, 20th Century-Fox.
PICTURES: Guadalcanal Diary (debut, 1943), Wing and a Prayer, Jungle Patrol, City Across the River, Battleground, Sands of Iwo Jima, The Gunfighter, Sea Hornet, Hoodlum Empire, My Son John, Come Back Little Sheba, Big Leaguer, Sea of Lost Ships, Shanghai Story, Violent Men, Apache Ambush, Attack!, 3:10 to Yuma, The Naked and the Dead, The Gallant Hours, Town Without Pity, Four for Texas, Town Tamer, The Dirty Dozen, The Devil's Brigade, The Green Slime, Chisum, Sometimes a Great Notion, Ulzana's Raid, Pat Garrett and Billy the Kid, The Outfit, Chosen Survivors, The Drowning Pool, Part II—Walking Tall, Grizzly, Mako: The Jaws of Death, Day of the Animals, Twilight's Last Gleaming, Delta Fox, Speedtrap, The Dark, Herbie Goes Bananas, All the Marbles, Cold River, Killing Machine, Starman, Black Moon Rising, Delta Force II, Ghetto Blasters.
TELEVISION: Guest: U.S. Steel Hour, Elgin Hour, Goodyear Playhouse, Kraft, Producer's Showcase. Special: The Petrified Forest. Movies: The Deadly Dream, Firehouse, The Red Pony, Partners in Crime, Born Innocent, The Last Day Go West Young Girl, Champions: A Love Story, Salvage, The $5.20 an Hour Dream, Reward, The Awakening of Candra, Dirty Dozen: The Next Mission, Baywatch: Panic at Malibu Pier. Series: Frontier Circus, Banyon, Firehouse, Salvage One, At Ease, Spenser for Hire, Supercarrier, Baywatch.

JAFFE, LEO: Executive. b. April 23, 1909. e. NYU. Started at Columbia, 1930; v.p., Columbia Pictures, January, 1954; 1st v.p., treas., member of board, 1956; v.p. & treas., 1958; exec. v.p., Columbia Pictures, 1962; Pres. Columbia Pictures, 1968; pres., Columbia Pictures Industries, Inc, 1970, president & chief executive officer, Columbia Pictures Industries, Inc., Chairman of board of directors to Aug., 1978. Currently chmn. emeritus. Industry honors: Motion Picture Pioneer of the Year, 1972; Acad. of Motion Picture Arts and Sciences Jean Hersholt Humanitarian Award, 1979; NATO Award-Knight of Malta.

JAFFE, STANLEY R.: Producer. b. New Rochelle, NY, July, 31, 1940. Graduate of U. of Pennsylvania Wharton Sch. of Finance. Joined Seven Arts Associates, 1962; named exec. ass't to president, 1964; later, head of East Coast TV programming. Produced Goodbye, Columbus, in 1968 for Paramount; then joined that company as exec. v.p., 1969. Produced A New Leaf, 1969. Named pres. of Paramount in 1970; resigned 1971 to form own prod. unit. Joined Columbia as exec. v.p. of global prod. in 1976, but resigned to be independent producer. Named pres. & CEO of Paramount Communications in 1991.
PICTURES: Goodbye Columbus, A New Leaf, Bad Company, Man on a Swing, Bad News Bears, Kramer vs. Kramer, Taps, Without a Trace (prod.-dir.). Co-prod. with Sherry Lansing: Racing with the Moon, Firstborn, Fatal Attraction, The Accused, Black Rain, School Ties.

JAFFE, STEVEN-CHARLES: Producer. b. Brooklyn, NY, 1954. e. U. of Southern California, cinema. First professional job as documentary prod. on John Huston's Fat City. Served as prod. asst. on The Wind and the Lion in Spain. Assoc. prod. on Demon Seed (written by brother Robert); served as location mgr. on Who'll Stop the Rain; assoc. prod. on Time After Time. On tv worked as 2nd unit dir. on The Day After.
PICTURES: Those Lips Those Eyes, Motel Hell (also co-s.p.), Scarab (dir.), Flesh + Blood (2nd unit. dir.), Near Dark, Plain Clothes (exec. prod.), The Fly II, Ghost (exec. prod., 2nd unit dir.), Company Business, Star Trek VI: The Undiscovered Country.

JAGGER, MICK: Singer, Composer, Actor. b. Dartford, Kent, England, July 26, 1943. Lead singer with Rolling Stones.
PICTURES: Performance, Ned Kelly, Gimme Shelter, Sympathy for the Devil, Ladies and Gentlemen: The Rolling Stones, The London Rock 'n' Roll Show, Let's Spend the Night Together, At the Max, Freejack.
TELEVISION: Special: The Nightingale (Faerie Tale Theatre).

JAGGS, STEVE: Executive. b. London, England, June 29, 1946. Ent. motion picture industry, 1964. Gained experience in the film production and laboratory areas with Colour Film Service and Universal Laboratories. Joined Agfa-Gevaert Ltd., Motion Picture Division, 1976. Appt. sales manager, 1979; divisional manager, 1989. Joined Pinewood Studios, 1992, as managing director. Joined Rank Org., Nov. 1992. Appoint. mng. dir. of Pinewood Studios, Jan. 1993.

JAGLOM, HENRY: Director, Writer, Editor. b. London, Eng., Jan. 26, 1943. Studied acting, writing and directing with Lee Strasberg and at Actors Studio. Did off-Bdwy. shows; went to West Coast where guest-starred in TV series (Gidget, The Flying Nun, etc.). Shot documentary film in Israel during Six Day War. Hired as edit consultant for Easy Rider by producer Bert Schneider. Acted in Psych Out, Drive He Said, The Last Movie, Thousand Plane Raid, Lili Aime Moi, The Other Side of the Wind (Orson Welles' unreleased last film). Wrote and dir. first feature, A Safe Place, in 1971. Created The Women's Film Co. (to prod. and distrib. motion pictures by women filmmakers), and International Rainbow Pictures. Presented Academy Award winning documentary Hearts and Minds.
PICTURES: Dir.-Writer: A Safe Place, Tracks, Sitting Ducks (also actor), National Lampoon Goes to the Movies (co-dir.), Can She Bake A Cherry Pie?, Always (also actor, prod.), Someone To Love (also actor, prod., edit.), New Year's Day (also actor, prod., edit.), Eating (also edit.), Venice Venice (also actor), Lucky Ducks, Baby Fever.

JALBERT, JOE JAY: Executive. e. U. of Washington. Was ski captain in school and began film career as technical director on Downhill Racer, 1969, also cinematographer and double for Robert Redford. 1970, produced Impressions of Utah, documentary, with Redford. Won Emmy for cinematography on TV's Peggy Fleming Special. In 1970 formed Jalbert Productions, Inc., to make feature films, TV sports, specials, commercials, etc. Co. has produced Winter Sports cast and 9 official films at Innsbruck Winter Olympics (1976), Lake Placid (1980), Sarajevo (1984). Awarded official film contract for 1992 Albertville Winter Olympic Games.

JAMES, BRION: Actor. b. Beaumont, CA, 1945.
PICTURES: Bound for Glory, Blue Sunshine, Black Sunday, Corvette Summer, The Postman Always Rings Twice, Southern Comfort, The Ballad of Gregorio Cortez, Blade Runner, 48 HRS, Silverado, Crimewave, Flesh + Blood, Enemy Mine, Armed and Dangerous, Steel Dawn, Dead Man Walking, Cherry 2000, Nightmare at Noon, The Wrong Guys, Red Heat, Red Scorpion, The Horror Show, Mom, Time of the Beast, Tango & Cash, Street Asylum, Another 48 HRS, The Player, Nemesis, Wishman.
TELEVISION: Movies: Flying High, Mrs. Sundance, Kiss Meets the Phantom of the Park, Trouble in High Timber Country, Killing at Hell's Gate, Hear No Evil, Family Ties as The Gambler: The Adventure Continues, Overkill: The Aileen Wuornos Story. Guest: Rockford Files, Hunter, The Young Riders, Cagney & Lacey, Quincy, Little House on the Prairie, Dynasty, etc.
THEATRE: Long Day's Journey Into Night, Picnic, Basic

Training Pavlo Hummell, Mother Courage, George Washington Slept Here.

JAMES, CLIFTON: Actor. b. Portland, OR, May 29, 1925. e. U. of Oregon. Studied at Actors Studio. Made numerous appearances on stage and TV, as well as theatrical films.
PICTURES: On The Waterfront, David and Lisa, Cool Hand Luke, The Reivers, Tick Tick Tick, The New Centurions, Live and Let Die, The Last Detail, Bank Shot, Juggernaut, The Man with the Golden Gun, Rancho DeLuxe, Silver Streak, The Bad News Bears in Breaking Training, Superman II, Whoops Apocalypse, Eight Men Out, The Bonfire of the Vanities.
TELEVISION: *Series*: City of Angels, Lewis and Clark. *Movies*: Runaway Barge, Friendly Persuasion, The Deadly Tower, Hart to Hart (pilot), Undercover With the KKK, Guyana Tragedy: The Story of Jim Jones, Carolina Skeletons. *Mini-Series*: Captains and the Kings.
THEATRE: *NY: Bdwy*: J.B., All the Way Home, The Shadow Box, American Buffalo; *Off-Bdwy*: All the King's Men.

JAMES, DENNIS: Performer. b. Jersey City, NJ, Aug. 24, 1917. e. St. Peter's Coll., Jersey City. Received Doctorate in 1988. Formerly M.C., actor, sports commentator on radio; award winning sports commentator for wrestling. 25 TV first to credit; currently pres., Dennis James Prod. For past 42 years host of Cerebral Palsy Telethon, having helped raised over 500 million dollars. Given star on Hollywood Walk of Fame.
TELEVISION: *Series*: Cash and Carry, Prime Time Boxing, The Original Amateur Hour (1948–60), Chance of a Lifetime (host), Two for the Money, Judge for Yourself, The Name's the Same, High Finance, Haggis Baggis, Your First Impression, People Will Talk, The Price Is Right, PDQ, Your All-American College Show, New Price Is Right, Name That Tune. *Actor*: Kraft Theatre, Dick Powell Theatre, Tycoon, Batman, 77 Sunset Strip.
PICTURES: The One and Only, Rocky III, Mr. Universe.

JAMES, POLLY: Writer. b. Ancon, Canal Zone. e. Smith Coll. Newspaper work, Panama; with trade mag., N.Y.; screenwriter since 1942.
PICTURES: Mrs. Parkington, The Raiders, Redhead from Wyoming, Quantrill's Raiders.

JAMESON, JERRY: Director. b. Hollywood, CA. Started as editorial asst.; then editor and supv. editor for Danny Thomas Prods. Turned to directing.
PICTURES: Dirt Gang, The Bat People, Brute Core, Airport '77, Raise the Titanic.
TELEVISION: *Movies*: Heatwave!, The Elevator, Hurricane, Terror on the 40th Floor, The Secret Night Caller, The Deadly Tower, The Lives of Jenny Dolan, The Call of the Wild, The Invasion of Johnson County, Superdome, A Fire in the Sky, High Noon—Part II, The Return of Will Kane, Stand By Your Man, Killing at Hell's Gate, Hotline, Starflight: The Plane That Couldn't Land, Cowboy, This Girl for Hire, Last of the Great Survivors, The Cowboy and the Ballerina, Stormin' Home, One Police Plaza, The Red Spider, Terror on Highway 91, Fire and Rain, Gunsmoke: The Last Ride.

JANKOWSKI, GENE F.: Executive. b. Buffalo, NY, May 21, 1934. e. Canisius Coll., B.S., Michigan State U., M.A. in radio, TV and film. Joined CBS radio network sls, 1961 as acct. exec.; eastern sls. mgr., 1966; moved to CBS-TV as acct. exec. 1969; gen. sls. mgr. WCBS-TV, 1970; dir. sls, 1971; v.p. sls., CBS-TV Stations Divisions, 1973; v.p., finance & planning, 1974; v.p., controller, CBS Inc. 1976; v.p. adm., 1977; exec. v.p. CBS/Broadcast Group, 1977; pres., CBS/Broadcast Group, 1977; chmn. CBS/Broadcast Group, 1988–89; chmn. Jankowski Communications System, Inc. Aug., 1989–. Member: pres., Intl. Council of National Acad. of Television Arts & Sciences; chmn. & trustee Amer. Film Institute; trustee, Catholic U. of Amer.; director, Georgetown U.; bd. of gov. American Red Cross; vice chmn., business comm. Metropolitan Museum of Art. Member, Library of Congress Film Preservation Board; adjunct prof. telecommunications, Michigan St. U.
AWARDS: Received Distinguished Communications Medal from South Baptist Radio & Television Commission; honorary Doctorate of Humanities, Michigan State U.; Humanitarian Award, National Conference of Christians and Jews, etc.

JARMAN, CLAUDE, JR.: Actor. b. Nashville, TN, Sept. 27, 1934. e. MGM Sch. Received special Oscar for The Yearling.
PICTURES: The Yearling (debut, 1946), High Barbaree, Sun Comes Up, Intruder in the Dust, Roughshod, Outriders, Inside Straight, Rio Grande, Hangman's Knot, Fair Wind to Java, Great Locomotive Chase.
TELEVISION: *Mini-Series*: Centennial.

JARMUSCH, JIM: Director, Writer, Composer, Actor. b. Akron, OH, 1953. e. attended Columbia U., went to Paris in senior year. NYU Film Sch., studied with Nicholas Ray and became his teaching asst. Appeared as an actor in Red Italy and Fraulein Berlin. Composed scores for The State of Things and Reverse Angle. Directorial debut Permanent Vacation (also

prod., s.p., music, ed. 1980). Wrote and directed New World using 30 minutes of leftover, unused film from another director. (Won International Critics Prize, Rotterdam Film Festival.) Expanded it into Stranger Than Paradise.
PICTURES: *Dir.-Writer*: Stranger Than Paradise (also ed., Best Film Award, National Society of Film Critics; Golden Leopard, Locarno Film Festival; Camera d'Or best new director, Cannes), Down by Law, Straight to Hell (actor only), Candy Mountain (actor only), Mystery Train (also s.p.), Leningrad Cowboys Go America (actor only), Night on Earth, In the Soup (actor only).

JARRE, MAURICE: Composer. b. Lyon, France, 1924. Studied at Paris Cons. Was orchestra conductor for Jean Louis Barrault's theatre company four years. In 1951 joined Jean Vilar's nat'l theatre co., composing for plays by Shakespeare, Moliere, O'Neill, Eliot, and Victor Hugo. Musical.dir., French National Theatre for 12 years before starting to compose film scores in 1952. Also written ballets (Masques de Femmes, Facheuse Rencontre, The Murdered Poet, Maldroros, The Hunchback of Notre Dame) and served as cond. with Royal Phil. Orch, London, Japan Phil. Orch, Osaka Symph. Orch., Quebec Symp. Orch, Central Orchestra of People's Republic of China.
PICTURES: Hotel des Invalides, La Tete contre les Murs, Eyes Without a Face, Crack in the Mirror, Sundays and Cybele, The Longest Day, Lawrence of Arabia (Acad. Award, 1962), The Collector, Is Paris Burning?, Weekend at Dunkirk, Dr. Zhivago (Acad. Award, 1965), Night of the Generals, The Professionals, Grand Prix, Five Card Stud, Isadora, The Damned, Ash Wednesday, The Life and Times of Judge Roy Bean, The Mackintosh Man, The Effect of Gamma Rays on Man-in-the-Moon Marigolds, Island at the Top of the World, Mandingo, Posse, The Man Who Would Be King, Winter Kills, The Magician of Lublin, Resurrection, The American Success Company, The Black Marble, Taps, Firefox, Young Doctors in Love, Don't Cry It's Only Thunder, The Year of Living Dangerously, Dreamscape, A Passage to India (Acad. Award, 1984), Top Secret!, Witness (BAFTA, 1985), Mad Max Beyond Thunderdome, Solarbabies, The Mosquito Coast, Tai-Pan, No Way Out, Fatal Attraction, Gaby—A True Story, Julia and Julia, Moon Over Parador, Gorillas in the Mist, Wildfire, Distant Thunder, Chances Are, Dead Poets Society (BAFTA, 1989), Prancer, Enemies a Love Story, Ghost, After Dark My Sweet, Jacob's Ladder, Almost an Angel, Only the Lonely, Fires Within, Shadow of the Wolf.

JARRICO, PAUL. Writer, Producer. b. Los Angeles, CA, Jan. 12, 1915. e. USC, 1936.
PICTURES: *Prod.*: Salt of the Earth. *Writer*: Tom, Dick and Harry (Academy nomination), Thousands Cheer, Song of Russia, The Search, The White Tower, Not Wanted, The Girl Most Likely, Messenger of Death.
TELEVISION: Call to Glory, Fortune Dane, Seaway, The Defenders.

JARROTT, CHARLES: Director. b. London, England, June 16, 1927. Son of British businessman and former singer-dancer at Gaiety Theatre. Joined British Navy; wartime service in Far East. After military service turned to theatre as asst. stage mgr. with Arts Council touring co. In 1949 joined Nottingham Repertory Theatre as stage dir. and juvenile acting lead. In 1953 joined new co. formed to tour Canada; was leading man and became resident leading actor for Ottawa Theatre. In 1955 moved to Toronto and made TV acting debut opposite Katharine Blake whom he later wed. 1957 dir. debut in TV for Canadian Bdcstg. Co. Became CBC resident dir. Moved to London to direct for Armchair Theatre for ABC-TV. Then became freelance dir., doing stage work, films, TV.
PICTURES: Anne of the Thousand Days, Mary Queen of Scots, Lost Horizon, The Dove, The Littlest Horse Thieves, The Other Side of Midnight, The Last Flight of Noah's Ark, Condorman, The Amateur, The Boy in Blue.
TELEVISION: The Hot Potato Boys, Roll On, Bloodin' Death, Girl in a Birdcage, The Picture of Dorian Gray, Rain, The Rose Affair, Roman Gesture, Silent Song, The Male of the Species, The Young Elizabeth, A Case of Libel, Dr. Jekyll and Mr. Hyde. *U.S. Movies/Mini-Series*: A Married Man, Poor Little Rich Girl: The Barbara Hutton Story, The Woman He Loved, Till We Meet Again (mini-series), Night of the Fox (mini-series), Lucy & Desi: Before the Laughter, Changes, Yes Virginia There is a Santa Claus, Stranger in the Mirror, Jackie Collins' Lady Boss.
STAGE: The Duel, Galileo, The Basement, Tea Party, The Dutchman, etc.

JASON, RICK: Actor. b. New York, NY, May 21, 1926. e. American Acad. of Dramatic Arts.
THEATRE: Broadway debut: Now I Lay Me Down To Sleep (Theatre World Award).
PICTURES: Sombrero, Saracen Blade, This Is My Love, Lieutenant Wore Skirts, Wayward Bus, Partners, Illegally Yours. and approx. 35 others.
TELEVISION: *Series*: The Case of the Dangerous Robin, Combat. *Mini-Series*: Around the World in 80 Days. *Movies*:

The Monk, Who is the Black Dahlia?, The Best Place to Be; approx. 200 other appearances.

JAYSTON, MICHAEL: Actor. b. Nottingham, England, Oct. 28, 1935. Member of Old Vic theatre Co. & Bristol Old Vic.
PICTURES: A Midsummer Night's Dream, Cromwell, Nicholas and Alexandra, The Public Eye, The Nelson Affair, Dominique.
TELEVISION: She Fell Among Thieves, Tinker Tailor Soldier Spy.

JEFFREYS, ANNE: Actress. b. Goldsboro, NC, Jan. 26, 1923. m. actor Robert Sterling. Named by Theatre Arts Magazine as "one of the 10 outstanding beauties of the stage." Trained for operatic career. Sang with NY's Municipal Opera Co. while supplementing income as a Powers model. Appeared as Tess Trueheart in Dick Tracy features.
PICTURES: I Married an Angel, Billy the Kid Trapped, Joan of Ozark, The Old Homestead, Tarzan's New York Adventure, X Marks the Spot, Yokel Boy, Catterbox, Man from Thunder River, Nevada, Step Lively, Dillinger, Sing Your Way Home, Those Endearing Young Charms, Zombies on Broadway, Dick Tracy Vs. Cueball, Genius at Work, Step By Step, Vacation in Reno, Trail Street, Riffraff, Return of the Bad Men, Boys' Night Out, Panic in the City, Southern Double Cross, Clifford.
THEATER: On Bway. in Street Scene, Kiss Me Kate, Romance, Three Wishes for Jamie, Kismet.
TELEVISION: Series: Topper, Love That Jill, Bright Promise, Delphi Bureau, General Hospital, Finder of Lost Loves. Guest: Falcon Crest, Hotel, Murder She Wrote, L.A. Law. Movies: Beggarman Thief, A Message from Holly.
STOCK: Camelot, King & I, Kismet, Song of Norway, Bells Are Ringing, Marriage Go Round, No Sex Please, We're British, Take Me Along, Carousel, Anniversary Waltz, Do I Hear a Waltz, Ninotchka, Pal Joey, Name of the Game, Destry Rides Again, The Merry Widow, Bitter Sweet, Desert Song, High Button Shoes, Sound of Music.

JEFFRIES, LIONEL: Actor, Director. b. Forest Hill, London, England, 1926. e. Queens Elizabeth's Grammar Sch, Wimbone Dorset. Ent. m.p. ind. 1952.
THEATER: Hello, Dolly!, See How They Run, Two Into One, Pygmalion (U.S.), The Wild Duck.
PICTURES: The Black Rider, The Volditz Story, No Smoking, Will Any Gentleman?, Windfall, All for Mary, Bhowani Junction, Eyewitness, Jumping for Joy, Lust for Life, Creeping Unknown (Quatermass Experiment), Baby and the Battleship, Decision Against Time, Doctor at Large, High Terrace, Hour of Decision, Up in the World, Behind the Mask, Blue Murder at St. Trinian's, Dunkirk, Girls at Sea, Law and Disorder, Orders to Kill, Revenge of Frankenstein, Up the Creek, Bobbikins, The Circle (The Vicious Circle), Idol on Parade, Nowhere to Go, The Nun's Story, Jazzboat, Let's Get Married, Trials of Oscar Wilde, Please Turn Over, Tarzan the Magnificent, Two-Way Stretch, Fanny, The Hellions, Life is a Circus, Kill or Cure, Mrs. Gibbons' Boys, Operation Snatch, The Notorious Landlady, The Wrong Arm of the Law, Call Me Bwana, The Crimson Blade, First Men in the Moon, The Long Ships, Murder Ahoy, The Secret of My Success, The Truth About Spring, You Must Be Joking!, Arrivederci Baby!, The Spy With a Cold Nose, Oh Dad Poor Dad, Blast Off! (Rocket to the Moon), Camelot, Chitty Chitty Bang Bang, Sudden Terror, The Railway Children (dir., s.p. only), Lola (Twinky), Who Slew Auntie Roo?, The Amazing Mr. Blunden (dir., s.p. only), Baxter (dir. only), Royal Flash, Wombling Free (voice, also dir., s.p.), The Water Babies (dir. only), The Prisoner of Zenda, Better Late Than Never, A Chorus of Disapproval.
TELEVISION: Father Charlie, Tom Dick and Harriet, Cream in My Coffee, Minder, Danny: the Champion of the World, Jekyll and Hyde, Boon Morse, Ending Up, Look at It This Way.

JENKINS, CHARLES: Animation producer. b. Yorkshire, England, 1941. Ent. m.p. ind. 1957. Joined T.V.C. as gen. ass't 1958. Animated and prod. various prods. Joined Dick Williams, pioneered use of Oxberry Camera for animation, 1966. Esta. Trickfilm Ltd., prod. optical effects for Yellow Submarine, 1967.

JENKINS, DAN: Public Relations Consultant. b. Montclair, NJ, Dec. 5, 1916. e. U. of Virginia. 1938. U.S. Army, 1940–45; major, infantry. P.R. officer, Hq. Eighth Army. Mng. ed., Motion Picture Magazine, 1946–48; editor, Tele-Views Magazine, 1949–50; TV editor, columnist, Hollywood Reporter, 1950–53; Hollywood bureau chief, TV Guide, 1953–63; v.p., exec. dir. TV dept., Rogers, Cowan & Brenner, Inc. 1969. Formed Dan Jenkins Public Relations, Inc. 1971. Joined Charles A. Pomerantz Public Relations, Ltd. as v.p., 1975, while retaining own firm. Sr. associate, Porter, Novelli, Assocs., 1981. Mem. bd. trustees, Natl. Academy of TV Arts & Sciences; bd. gov., Hollywood chapter, Natl. Academy of TV Arts & Sciences, 1967–71. Rejoined Rogers & Cowan, 1983, v.p., TV dept. Retired, 1988.

JENKINS, GEORGE: Art dir. b. Baltimore, MD, Nov. 19, 1908. e. U. of Pennsylvania. Hollywood-New York art dir. since 1946; TV pictures for Four Star Playhouse and revue productions; NBC-TV opera, Carmen; color dir., CBS-TV, 1954; NBC color spec. Annie Get Your Gun, 1957; TV music with Mary Martin, 1959. Professor, Motion Picture Design, UCLA, 1985–88.
STAGE: Mexican Hayride, I Remember Mama, Dark of the Moon, Lost in the Stars, Bell, Book and Candle, Bad Seed, Happiest Millionaire, Two for the Seesaw, Ice Capades, Jones Beach spec., Song of Norway, Paradise Island, Around the World in 80 Days, Mardi Gras, Miracle Worker, Critics Choice, A Thousand Clowns, Jennie, Generation, Wait Until Dark, Only Game in Town, Night Watch, Sly Fox.
PICTURES: Best Years of Our Lives, Secret Life of Walter Mitty, Miracle Worker, Mickey One, Up the Down Staircase, Wait Until Dark, Subject Was Roses, Klute, 1776, Paper Chase, Parallax View, Night Moves, Funny Lady, All the President's Men (Acad. Award), Comes a Horseman, China Syndrome, Starting Over, The Postman Always Rings Twice, Rollover, Sophie's Choice, Orphans, See You in the Morning, Presumed Innocent.
TELEVISION: The Dollmaker.

JENNINGS, PETER. TV News Anchor. b. Toronto, Canada, July 29, 1938. Son of Canadian broadcaster Charles Jennings. e. Carleton U.; Rider Coll. Worked as a bank teller and late night radio host in Canada. Started career as host of Club Thirteen, a Canadian American Bandstand-like dance prog., then as a newsman on CFJR (radio), Ottawa; then with CJOH-TV and CBS before becoming co-anchor of first national news program on Canadian commercial network, CTV. Joined ABC in 1964 as NY corr.; 1965, anchor, Peter Jennings with the News; 1968, natl. corr., ABC News; 1969, overseas assignments; 1975, Washington corr. and anchor for AM America; 1977, chief foreign corr.; 1978, foreign desk anchor, World News Tonight; 1983, anchor, sr. editor, World News Tonight.

JENS, SALOME: Actress. b. Milwaukee, WI, May 8, 1935. e. Northwestern U. Member Actors Studio. On stage in The Disenchanted, Far Country, Night Life, Winter's Tale, Mary Stuart, Antony and Cleopatra, After the Fall, Moon For the Misbegotten, The Balcony.
PICTURES: Angel Baby, The Fool Killer, Seconds, Me Natalie, Cloud Dancer, Harry's War, Just Between Friends.
TELEVISION: Movies: In the Glitter Palace, Sharon: Portrait of a Mistress, The Golden Moment: An Olympic Love Story, A Killer in the Family, Playing with Fire, Uncommon Valor. Guest: Mary Hartman, Mary Hartman. Series: Falcon Crest. Mini-Series: From Here to Eternity.

JEPHCOTT, SAMUEL C.: Executive. b. Southampton, England. July 23, 1944. e. Arts Educational Sch., London. Entered industry as child actor The Grove Family BBC TV, 1956. Eight years in advertising producing TV commercials. Emigrated to Toronto, Canada in 1968. Exec. secty., Directors Guild of Canada, 1969–72. Film prod. management, 1972–75. Joined Compass Film Sales Ltd., 1975–77. Joined Nielsen-Ferns Intl. Ltd. in chg. of distribution and prod., 1977–81. Mgr. distribution, CBC Enterprises, 1982–84. Mako Films, 1985–87. 1984–92, dir., gen. mgr., Canadian Film & TV Production Assn., pres., Cyclops Communications Corp.
PICTURES: The Hard Part Begins (prod. mgr.); Sunday In The Country (2nd a.d.); Me (prod. mgr.); Lions For Breakfast (prod. mgr.); It Seemed Like a Good Idea at the Time, (2nd A.D.); Love at First Sight, (prod. accountant); Find the Lady (stills); The Water Babies, TV, (prod. mgr.); The Wars (prod. supvr.); (TV) The Last Frontier (TV prod.).

JERGENS, ADELE: Actress. b. Brooklyn, NY, Nov. 26, 1917. Began career in musical shows during summer vacation at 15; won contest, New York's World Fair, as model; appeared on New York stage; night clubs, U.S. and abroad.
PICTURES: Edge of Doom, Side Street, Abbott and Costello Meet the Invisible Man, Sugarfoot, Try and Get Me, Show Boat, Somebody Loves Me, Aaron Slick from Punkin' Crick, Overland Pacific, Miami Story, Fireman Save My Child, Big Chase, Strange Lady in Town, The Cobweb, Girls in Prison, The Lonesome Trail, Treasure of Monte Cristo.

JESSEL, IAN: Executive. b. London, England, Apr. 16, 1939. e. Oxford. Joined Rank Organisation in 1962 as graduate trainee and became responsible for acquisition of indep. product. Formed Target International Pictures in 1968. In 1970 joined World Film Sales becoming man. dir. 1972. World Film Sales merged with ITC in 1974. Elected to board 1975. Appointed dir. Classic Cinemas and ITC Film Distributors (UK), 1979. Appt. man. dir. ITC Films Int., 1980. Joined CBS Theatrical Films, Sept. 1981, as vice-pres. int. distribution, now based in Los Angeles.

JETER, MICHAEL: Actor. b. Lawrenceberg, TN, Aug. 20, 1952.
TELEVISION: Series: One Life to Live, Hothouse, Evening Shade (Emmy Award, 1992). Movies: My Old Man, Sentimental Journey, When Love Kills: The Seduction of John Hearn.

Mini-Series: From Here to Eternity. *Guest*: Lou Grant, Designing Women.
PICTURES: Hair, Soup for One, Zelig, Dead Bang, Tango & Cash, Just Like in the Movies, Miller's Crossing, The Fisher King, Sister Act 2.
THEATRE: Alice, G.R. Point (Theatre World Award), Cloud 9, Greater Tuna, Once in a Lifetime, Zoo Story, Waiting for Godot, Only Kidding, The Boys Next Door, Grand Hotel (Tony Award).

JEWISON, NORMAN P.: Producer, Director. b. Toronto, Canada, July 21, 1926. e. Malvern Collegiate Inst., Toronto, 1940–44; Stage and TV actor 1950–52. Director, Canadian Broadcasting Corp 1953–58. Victoria Coll., U. of Toronto, 1946–50, B.A. Awarded 1988 Acad. of Canadian Cinema and Television Special Achievement Award.
TELEVISION: Exec. prod. of 8 Judy Garland shows. *Prod.-Dir.*: Judy Garland specials, The Andy Williams Show. *Dir. of Specials*: Tonight with Harry Belafonte, The Broadway of Lerner and Loewe.
PICTURES: *Director*: 40 Pounds of Trouble, The Thrill of It All, Send Me No Flowers, Art of Love, The Cincinnati Kid, The Russians Are Coming The Russians Are Coming. *Prod.-Director*: In The Heat of the Night (Acad. Award, best picture, 1967), The Thomas Crown Affair, Gaily Gaily, The Landlord (prod. only), Fiddler on the Roof, Jesus Christ Superstar (also co-s.p.), Billy Two Hats (prod. only), Rollerball, F.I.S.T., And Justice for All, The Dogs of War (exec. prod. only), Best Friends, Iceman (prod. only), A Soldier's Story, Agnes of God, Moonstruck, The January Man (prod. only), In Country, Other People's Money.

JHABVALA, RUTH PRAWER: Writer. b. Cologne, Germany, May 7, 1927. Emigrated with her family to England, 1939. e. Hendon County Sch., Queen Mary Coll., London U. (degree in English). m. architect C.S.H. Jhabvala, 1951 and moved to Delhi. Novels published in England and U.S.: 1955–87: To Whom She Will, Esmond in India, The Nature of Passion, The Householder; Get Ready for Battle; Heat and Dust, In Search of Love and Beauty, Three Continents. Has written most of the screenplays for the films of Ismail Merchant and James Ivory.
PICTURES: The Householder (1963, wrote s.p. based on her novel), Shakespeare Wallah (with Ivory), The Guru (with Ivory), Bombay Talkie (with Ivory), Autobiography of a Princess, Roseland, Hullabaloo Over Georgie and Bonnie's Pictures (TV), The Europeans, Jane Austen in Manhattan, Quartet, Heat and Dust (based on her own novel; BAFTA Award), The Bostonians, A Room with a View (Acad. Award, 1986), Madame Sousatzka (co.-s.p. with John Schlesinger), Mr. and Mrs. Bridge (NY Film Critics Award), Howards End (Acad. Award, 1992).

JILLIAN, ANN: Actress. b. Cambridge, MA, Jan. 29, 1951. Began career at age 10 in Disney's Babes in Toyland; in film version of Gypsy at age 12. Broadway debut in musical, Sugar Babies, 1979. Formed own company: 9-J Productions, developing TV movies and series.
PICTURES: Babes in Toyland, Gypsy, Mr. Mom.
TELEVISION: *Series*: Hazel, It's a Living, Jennifer Slept Here, Ann Jillian. Many appearances on series (Love Boat, Fantasy Island, Twilight Zone, Ben Casey). *Mini-series*: Ellis Island (Emmy nom.), Alice in Wonderland, Malibu. *Movies*: Mae West (Emmy nom.), Death Ride to Osaka, Killer in the Mirror, Convicted: A Mother's Story, Perry Mason: The Case of the Murdered Madam, The Ann Jillian Story (Golden Globe Award; Emmy nom.), Original Sin, First Impressions, This Wife for Hire, Little White Lies, Mario and the Mob, Labor of Love: The Arlette Schweitzer Story.

JOANOU, PHIL: Director. b. 1962. e. USC. Student film The Last Chance Dance won him first professional job directing 2 episodes of tv's Amazing Stories (Santa 85, The Doll).
PICTURES: Three O'Clock High, U2: Rattle and Hum, State of Grace, Final Analysis.
TELEVISION: *Mini-Series*: Wild Palms (co-dir.). *Series*: Fallen Angels (Dead-End for Delia).

JOFFE, CHARLES H.: Executive. b. Brooklyn, NY, July 16, 1929. e. Syracuse U. Joined with Jack Rollins to set up management-production org., clients including Woody Allen, Ted Bessell, Billy Crystal, David Letterman, Tom Poston, Robin Williams.
PICTURES: *Produced*: Don't Drink the Water, Take the Money and Run, Everything You Always Wanted to Know About Sex but Were Afraid To Ask, Love and Death, Annie Hall, House of God. *Exec. prod.*: Play It Again Sam, Bananas, Sleeper, Manhattan, Interiors, Stardust Memories, Arthur, A Midsummer Nights' Sex Comedy, Zelig, Broadway Danny Rose, The Purple Rose of Cairo, Hannah and Her Sisters, Radio Days, September, Another Woman, New York Stories (Oedipus Wrecks), Crimes and Misdemeanors, Alice, Shadows and Fog, Husbands and Wives, Manhattan Murder Mystery.
TELEVISION: Woody Allen specials. Star of the Family, Good Time Harry.

JOFFE, EDWARD: Producer, Director, Writer. Worked in m.p., theatre, commercial radio and as journalist before ent. TV ind. in Britain as writer/prod with ATV. Has prod. & dir. over 4000 progs. 1959–61 staff prod. Granada TV. 1962, dir., Traitor's Gate & Traveling Light for Robt Stigwood, prod. & numerous series for Grampian TV; 1967, dir. film The Price of a Record—Emmy finalist, Special Mention Salerno Film Fest shown in over 70 countries; 1967–8 films, Columba's Folk & So Many Partings ITV entries in Golden Harp Fest.; 1968, prod., dir. Tony Hancock's Down Under in Australia, prod. dir. Up At The Cross; prod. dir. ind. film, Will Ye No' Come Back Again; dir., This Is . . . Tom Jones; prod. dir., The Golden Shot; 1971, senior production lecturer, Thomson TV College; dir., films for U.S. for London Television Service; Evening Standard Commercials for Thames TV. Co. prod. dir.,ind. film Sound Scene, 1972–8, Contract prod. dir. Thames TV various series: Magpie, Today, Opportunity Knocks. The David Nixon Show, Seven Ages of Man, Problems, Finding Out; 1980; production consultant, CBC-TV; 1978–82, prod. dir. series Writers' Workshop, About Books; 1978, film, Places & Things (British Academy Award nom.) film, Who Do You Think You Are? (British Academy Award nom., ITV's Japan Prize entry, Special Jury Award San Francisco Intl. Film Fest), 1981, Film Images, (British Academy Award nom.; Gold Plaque Chicago Intl. Film Fest.); The Protectors (medal winner Intl. Film & TV Festival, N.Y.). 1982–86: Film Rainbow Coloured Disco Dancer. Various Series: Taste of China, Jobs Ltd. Spin-Offs, The Buzz. Doc.: War Games in Italy. 1989–93, devised, prod., dir. Video View for ITV Network; Co-prod. & dir. 2 series Sprockets; dir. Challenge; dir. Travellers Checks. Dir. Screen Scene Prods, String of Pearls, PLC, String of Pearls 2 PLC. Companies produced mopics Double X (line prod.), Littel Devils - The Birth, To Catch a Yeti, The Paper Man.

JOFFÉ, ROLAND: Director, Producer. b. London, Eng., Nov. 17, 1945. e. Lycee Francaise, Carmel Col. Manchester U., England. Worked in British theatre with the Young Vic, the National Theatre and the Old Vic. 1973 became youngest director at National Theatre. 1978, moved into directing TV for Granada TV, then Thames and B.B.C. before feature debut in 1984 with The Killing Fields.
TELEVISION: *Documentaries*: Rope, Ann, No Mama No. Plays: The Spongers, Tis Pity She's a Whore, The Legion Hall Bombing, United Kingdom (also co-wrote). *Series*: Coronation Street, Bill Brand, The Stars Look Down.
PICTURES: *Director*: The Killing Fields (Cannes Film Festv. best picture award, 1984), The Mission, Fat Man and Little Boy (also co-s.p.), Made in Bangkok (prod. only), City of Joy (also co-prod.), Super Mario Bros. (prod. only).

JOHNS, GLYNIS: Actress. b. Durban, South Africa, Oct. 5, 1923. e. in England. Daughter of Mervyn Johns, actor, and Alys Steele, pianist. On London stage from 1935 (Buckie's Bears, The Children's Hour, A Kiss for Cinderella, Quiet Week-End; Gertie, N.Y. stage, 1952; Major Barbara, N.Y., 1956–57.) Voted one of top ten British Money-making stars in Motion Picture Herald-Pathe poll, 1951–54.
STAGE: Too Good to Be True (NY, 1964), The King's Mare (London, 1967), Come as You Are (1970), The Marquise (Tour, 1971–72), A Little Night Music, NY 1973 (Tony Award), Cause Celebre (London, 1977,) Harold and Maude (Canada, 1977), Hay Fever (U.K. tour, 1978), The Boy Friend (Toronto, 1984), The Circle (NY 1989).
PICTURES: South Riding (debut, 1938), Murder in the Family, Prison Without Bars, On the Night of the Fire, Mr. Brigg's Family, Under Your Hat, The Prime Minister, 49th Parallel, Adventures of Tartu, Half-Way House, Perfect Strangers, This Man Is Mine, Frieda, An Ideal Husband, Miranda, Third Time Lucky, Dear Mr. Proback, State Secret, Flesh and Blood, No Highway in the Sky, Appointment With Venus (Island Rescue), Encore, The Magic Box, The Card (The Promoter), The Sword and the Rose, Rob Roy, Personal Affair, The Weak and the Wicked, The Seekers (Land of Fury), The Beachcomber, Mad About Men, Court Jester, Josephine and Men, Loser Takes All, All Mine to Give, Around the World in 80 Days, Another Time Another Place, Shake Hands with the Devil, The Sundowners, The Spider's Web, The Cabinet of Caligari, The Chapman Report, Papa's Delicate Condition, Mary Poppins, Dear Brigette, Don't Just Stand There, Lock Up Your Daughters, Under Milk Wood, Vault of Horror, Zelly and Me, Nuckie.
TELEVISION: *Series*: Glynis, Coming of Age. *Episodes of*: Dr. Kildare, Roaring Twenties, Naked City, The Defenders, Danny Kaye Show. *Also*: Noel Coward's Star Quality, Mrs. Amworth, All You Need Is Love, Across a Crowded Room, Little Gloria, . . . Happy at Last, Skagg.

JOHNSON, ARTE: Actor. b. Chicago, IL, Jan. 20, 1934. Gained fame on Rowan and Martin's Laugh-In.
PICTURES: Miracle in the Rain, The Subterraneans, The Third Day, The President's Analyst, Love at First Bite, A Night at the Magic Castle, Tax Season, Evil Spirits, Munchie.
TELEVISION: *Series*: It's Always Jan, Sally, Hennesey, Don't Call Me Charlie, Rowan & Martin's Laugh-In (Emmy

Award, 1969), Ben Vereen . . . Comin' at Ya!, The Gong Show (panelist), Games People Play, Glitter, General Hospital. *Movies*: Twice in a Lifetime, Blood and Lou, If Things Were Different, Detour to Terror, The Love Tapes, Condominium, Making of a Male Model, Alice in Wonderland, Dan Turner—Hollywood Detective.

JOHNSON, BEN: Actor. b. Pawhuska, OK, June 13, 1918. Stunt rider & performer in rodeos, touring country; did stunt work in many films before acting debut.
PICTURES: Three Godfathers, Mighty Joe Young, She Wore a Yellow Ribbon, Wagonmaster, Rio Grande, Wild Stallion, Fort Defiance, Shane, Rebel in Town, War Drums, Slim Carter, Fort Bowie, Ten Who Dared, Tomboy and the Champ, One-Eyed Jacks, Cheyenne Autumn, Major Dundee, The Rare Breed, Will Penny, Hang 'Em High, The Wild Bunch, The Undefeated, Chisum, Something Big, The Last Picture Show (Academy Award, best supp. actor, 1971), Corky, Junior Bonner, The Getaway, Dillinger, The Train Robbers, Kid Blue, The Sugarland Express, Bite The Bullet, Hustle, Breakheart Pass, The Town That Dreaded Sundown, The Greatest, Grayeagle, The Swarm, The Hunter, Terror Train, Soggy Bottom U.S.A., Ruckus, Tex, Champions, Red Dawn, Let's Get Harry, Trespasses, Dark Before Dawn, Cherry 2000, Back to Back, My Heroes Have Always Been Cowboys, Radio Flyer.
TELEVISION: *Series*: The Monroes. *Movies*: Runaway!, Blood Sport, Dream West, Locusts, The Shadow Riders, Red Pony, The Sacketts, Wild Horses, Wild Times, Stranger on My Land, The Chase. *Guest*: Alfred Hitchcock Presents (1958), Laramie, Have Gun Will Travel, Bonanza, The Virginian.

JOHNSON, DON: Actor. b. Flatt Creek, MO, Dec. 15, 1949. m. actress Melanie Griffith. Worked at ACT (Amer. Conservatory Th.), San Francisco. On stage there in Your Own Thing. In L.A. in Fortune and Men's Eyes. Recording: Heartbeat (1986).
PICTURES: The Magic Garden of Stanley Sweetheart (debut, 1970), Zachariah, The Harrad Experiment, A Boy and His Dog, Return to Macon County, Soggy Bottom USA, Cease Fire, Sweet Hearts Dance, Dead-Bang, The Hot Spot, Harley Davidson and the Marlboro Man, Paradise, Born Yesterday, Guilty as Sin.
TELEVISION: *Series*: From Here to Eternity, Miami Vice. *Mini-Series*: The Rebels, Beulah Land, The Long Hot Summer. *Movies*: First You Cry, Ski Lift to Death, Katie: Portrait of a Centerfold, Revenge of the Stepford Wives, Amateur Night at the Dixie Bar and Grill, Elvis and the Beauty Queen, The Two Lives of Carol Letner. *Special*: Don Johnson's Heartbeat (music video, also exec. prod.). Guest: Kung Fu, The Bold Ones, Police Story.

JOHNSON, G. GRIFFITH: Executive. b. New York, NY, Aug. 15, 1912. e. Harvard U., 1934, A.M. 1936, Ph.D. 1938. U.S. Treasury Dept. 1936–39; Dept. of Comm., 1939–40; O.P.A. & predecessor agencies, 1940–46; consulting economist, 1946–47; dir., Econ. Stab. Div., Nat'l. Security Resources Bd., 1948–49; chief econ., U.S. Bur. of Budget, 1949–50; econ. advisor to Econ. Stab. Admin. 1950–52; Exec. v.p. MPEAA, 1965, MPAA, 1971; Asst. Sec'y of State for Economic Affairs, 1962–65; v.p. MPAA, 1953–62; Author of several books & articles.

JOHNSON, J. BOND: Producer, Executive. b. Fort Worth, TX, June 18, 1926. e. Texas Wesleyan Univ., B.S., 1947; Texas Christian U., M.Ed., 1948; Southern Methodist U., B.D., 1952; U. of Southern California, Ph.D., 1967. Army Air Forces, W.W.II; public information officer, captain, U.S. Marine Corps. Korean War. Formerly member Marine Corps Reserve, Motion Picture Production Unit, Hollywood. Was Colonel, U.S. Army; now retired. Newspaper reporter, Fort Worth Star-Telegram, 1942–48; pres., West Coast News Service, 1960; pres., exec. prod., Bonjo Prods., Inc., 1960, President, chief executive officer, Cine-Media International, 1975 managing partner, Capra-Johnson Productions, Ltd., 1978.
PICTURES: Sands of Iwo Jima, Retreat Hell, Flying Leathernecks; photographed aerial portions, Jamboree 53, Norfleet, Devil at My Heels, Kingdom of the Spiders, Ordeal at Donner Pass, Place of the Dawn, Lies I Told Myself, Backstretch, Airs Above The Ground, The Jerusalem Concert, The Berkshire Terror, The Seventh Gate.
TELEVISION: Series: Creator, story consultant, tech. advisor, Whirlpool. Exec. producer, creator: On The Go (TV News-Sports), Coasties, Desert Rangers. Producer: Fandango.

JOHNSON, LAMONT: Director, Producer, Actor. b. Stockton, CA, Sept. 30, 1922. e. UCLA. 4 time winner of Director's Guild Award for TV work.
TELEVISION: *Series*: The Defenders, Profiles in Courage, Twilight Zone. *Movies*: Deadlock, My Sweet Charlie, That Certain Summer, The Execution of Pvt. Slovik, Fear on Trial, Off the Minnesota Strip, Crisis at Central High, Escape from Iran, Dangerous Company, Life of the Party: The Story of Beatrice, Ernie Kovacs: Between the Laughter, Wallenberg: A Hero's Story (also co-prod.; Emmy Award), Unnatural

Causes, Gore Vidal's Lincoln (Emmy Award), The Kennedys of Massachusetts, Voices Within: The Lives of Truddi Chase, Crash Landing: The Rescue of Flight 232.
PLAYS: The Egg, Yes is For a Very Young Man; dir., two operas, L.A. Philharmonic, 1964; founder, dir., UCLA Professional Theatre Group.
PICTURES: A Covenant With Death, McKenzie Break, A Gunfight, The Groundstar Conspiracy, You'll Like My Mother, The Last American Hero, Lipstick, One on One, Somebody Killed Her Husband, Cattle Annie and Little Britches, Spacehunter.

JOHNSON, LAURIE: Music Composer, Director. b. Feb. 7, 1927. Studied Royal Coll. of Music.
STAGE: Lock Up Your Daughters, Pieces of Eight, The Four Musketeers.
PICTURES: Good Companions, Moonraker, Girls at Sea, Operation Bullshine, Tiger Bay, I Aim at the Stars, Spare The Road, What a Whopper, Bitter Harvest, Seige of the Saxons, Dr. Strangelove, The First Men in the Moon, Beauty Jungle, East of Sudan, Hot Millions, And Soon the Darkness, Mister Jerico, Cause for Alarm, The Beltstone Fox, Hedda, It Lives Again.
TELEVISION: All Things Bright and Beautiful, The Lady and the Highwayman (exec. prod., music).

JOHNSON, MARK: Producer. b. Washington, DC. Moved to Spain at age 7, lived there for eleven years before returning to America. e. Univ. of VA, Univ. of IA. Joined Directors Guild training program receiving first credit on Next Stop Greenwich Village. Worked as prod. asst., then asst. dir. on High Anxiety, Movie Movie, The Brink's Job, and Escape From Alcatraz. Starting with Diner in 1982 served as executive prod. or prod. on all Barry Levinson films. With Levinson formed Baltimore Pictures in 1989.
PICTURES: Diner (exec. prod.). Producer: The Natural, Young Sherlock Holmes, Tin Men, Good Morning Vietnam, Rain Man (Acad. Award for Best Picture of 1988), Avalon, Kafka (co-exec. prod.), Bugsy (L.A. Film Critics & Golden Globe Awards for Best Picture of 1991), Toys, Sniper, Wilder Naplam.

JOHNSON, RICHARD: Actor. b. Essex, England, July 30, 1927. Studied at Royal Acad. of Dramatic Art. First stage appearance Opera House, Manchester, then with John Gielgud's repertory season, 1944. Served in Royal Navy 1945–48. Subsequent stage appearances incl. The Madwoman of Chaillot, The Lark. Visited Moscow with Peter Brook's production of Hamlet. Royal Shakespeare Thea.: Stratford, London, 1957–62. Royal Shakespeare Co. 1972–73. National Theatre, 1976–77. Founded United British Artists, 1983.
PICTURES: Saadia, Never So Few, Cairo, The Haunting, 80,000 Suspects, The Pumpkin Eater, The Amorous Adventures of Moll Flanders, Operation Crossbow, Khartoum, La Strega in Amore, Deadlier Than the Male, The Rover, Danger Route, Twist of Sand, Oedipus the King, Trajan's Column, Lady Hamilton, Some Girls Do, Julius Caesar, The Deserters, The Beloved, Hennessy, Aces High, The Comeback, Zombie, A Nightingale Sang in Berkeley Square, The Monster Club, What Waits Below, Lady Jane, Turtle Diary. *Producer*: Turtle Diary, Castaway, The Lonely Passion of Judith Hearne.
TELEVISION: The Flame is Love, Haywire, The Four Feathers, Portrait of a Rebel: Margaret Sanger, A Man For All Seasons, Voice of the Heart, The Crucifer of Blood, Duel of Hearts. *Guest*: Wagon Train, Lou Grant, Ironside, Knots Landing, That Girl, MacGyver, Police Story, Route 66, many others. Live TV incl. Lux Video Theatre, Front Row Center, Hallmark Hall of Fame.

JOHNSON, RUSSELL: Actor. b. Ashley, PA, Nov. 10, 1924. e. Girard Coll, Actors Laboratory, L.A. W.W.II, Army Air Corps. Author: Here on Gilligan's Isle (1993).
PICTURES: A Town of the 80's, Stand at Apache Landing, A Distant Trumpet, Ma & Pa Kettle at Waikiki, Rogue Cop, Loan Shark, Seminole, Tumbleweed, Blue Movies, It Came From Outer Space, Many Rivers to Cross, Law and Order, Black Tuesday, This Island Earth, Rock All Night, Attack of the Crab Monsters, The Space Children, For Men Only, The Greatest Story Ever Told, MacArthur.
TELEVISION: *Series*: Black Saddle, Gilligan's Island. *Guest*: Studio One, Front Row Center, Playhouse 90, Lux Video Theatre, Mobile One, The Great Adventure Jane Powell Show, Climax, You Are There, Rawhide, Twilight Zone, Gunsmoke, Outer Limits, Cannon, Marcus Welby, That Girl, The FBI, Dallas, Fame, Dynasty, My Two Dads, Bosom Buddies, Buffalo Bill, Vanished, Harry Truman Biography, Truman vs. MacArthur, Knots Landing, Santa Barbara, many others. Movie: With a Vengeance.

JOHNSON, VAN: Actor. b. Newport, RI, Aug. 25, 1916. Began in vaudeville; then on N.Y. stage New Faces of 1937, Eight Men of Manhattan, Too Many Girls, Pal Joey. Voted one of the top ten Money Making Stars in Motion Picture Herald-Fame Poll 1945–46. Stage includes The Music Man (London), La Cage aux Folles (NY) and numerous tours.

PICTURES: Too Many Girls (debut, 1940), Murder in the Big House, Somewhere I'll Find You, War Against Mrs. Hadley, Dr. Gillespie's New Assistant, The Human Comedy, Pilot No. 5, Dr. Gillespies's Criminal Case, Guy Named Joe, White Cliffs of Dover, Three Men in White, Two Girls and a Sailor, Thirty Seconds Over Tokyo, Between Two Women, Thrill of Romance, Weekend at the Waldorf, Easy to Wed, No Leave No Love, Till the Clouds Roll By, High Barbaree, Romance of Rosy Ridge, Bride Goes Wild, State of the Union, Command Decision, Mother is a Freshman, In the Good Old Summertime, Scene of the Crime, Battleground, Big Hangover, Duchess of Idaho, Three Guys Named Mike, Grounds for Marriage, Go For Broke, Too Young to Kiss, It's a Big Country, Invitation, When in Rome, Washington Story, Plymouth Adventure, Confidentially Connie, Remains to Be Seen, Easy to Love, Caine Mutiny, Siege at Red River, Men of the Fighting Lady, Brigadoon, Last Time I Saw Paris, End of the Affair, Bottom of the Bottle, Miracle in the Rain, 23 Paces to Baker Street, Slander, Kelly and Me, Action of the Tiger, The Last Blitzkreig, Subway in the Sky, Beyond This Place, Enemy General, Wives and Lovers, Divorce American Style, Yours Mine and Ours, Where Angels Go . . . Trouble Follows, Company of Killers, Eagles Over London, The Kidnapping of the President, The Purple Rose of Cairo.
TELEVISION: Special: Pied Piper of Hamelin. Mini-Series: Rich Man Poor Man, Black Beauty. Movies: Doomsday Flight, San Francisco International, Call Her Mom, The Girl on the Late Late Show, Superdome. Guest: I Love Lucy, G.E. Theatre, Batman, Love American Style, The Love Boat, Murder She Wrote.

JOHNSTON, MARGARET: Actress. e. Sydney U., Australia. London stage debut: Murder Without Crime. Screen debut: Rake's Progress, 1945.
TELEVISION: Always Juliet, Taming of the Shrew, Man with a Load of Mischief, Light of Heart, Autumn Crocus, Androcles and the Lion, Sulky Five, Windmill Near a Frontier, The Shrike, The Out of Towners, Looking for Garrow, The Typewriter, The Glass Menagerie, That's Where the Town's Going, The Vortex.
PICTURES: A Man about the House, Portrait of Clare, The Magic Box, Knave of Hearts, Touch and Go, Night of the Eagle, The Nose on My Face, Life at the Top, Schizo, Mr. Sebastian.
THEATRE: Ring of Truth, The Masterpiece, Lady Macbeth, Merchant of Venice, Measure for Measure, Othello.

JOLLEY, STAN: Producer, Director, Production Designer, Art Director. b. New York, NY, May 17, 1926. e. U. of Southern California, col. of architecture. Son of actor I. Stanford Jolley. In Navy in W.W.II. Has acted in capacities listed for many feature films and TV series. One of orig. designers of Disneyland. Nominated for AA, Witness.
PICTURES: Producer and Production Designer: Knife For the Ladies. Assoc. Producer and Prod. Designer: The Good Guys and the Bad Guys; 2nd Unit director: Superman. Production Designer: Dutch, The Good Mother, Witness, Taps, Caddyshack, Cattle Annie and Little Britches, Americathon (also second unit director), Swarm, Drum, Framed, Dion Brothers, Mixed Company, Walking Tall, Terror in the Wax Museum, Night of the Lepus (also second unit director), War Between Men and Women, Law Man, The Phynx. Art Director: Young Billy Young, Ride Beyond Vengeance, Broken Saber, The Restless Ones, Mail Order Bride, Toby Tyler, Nine Lives of Elfego Baca. Assoc. producer & prod. designer & 2nd unit director, Happily Ever After.
TELEVISION FEATURES: 2nd Unit Director and Production Designer: Swiss Family Robinson, Adventures of the Queen, Woman Hunter, Production Designer: Abduction of Carrie Swenson, Eagle One, No Man's Land, Last of the Great Survivors, Like Normal People, Rescue From Gilligan's Island, Flood, Voyage of the Yes, The Stranger, Punch & Jody, City Beneath the Sea, Women of San Quentin, Miniseries: Howard, the Amazing Mr. Hughes.
TELEVISION SERIES: Assoc. Prod. & Prod. Designer: Jessie; Art Director: Walt Disney Presents, Pete and Gladys, Gunsmoke, Mr. Ed., Branded, Voyage to the Bottom of the Sea, Land of the Giants, O'Hara, Shane, Acapulco, The Racers. Production Designer: Walking Tall, Today's F.B.I., For Love and Honor, Macgyver. Pilots: 8, including Get Smart. Docudrama: Under Fire. Cartoon: Disney's Donald in Mathmagic Land. Documentary: Crisis in the Wetlands (prod./dir.).

JONES, AMY HOLDEN: Director, Writer. b. Philadelphia, PA, Sept. 17, 1953. m. cinematographer, Michael Chapman. e. Wellesley Coll., B.A., 1974; film and photography courses, Massachusetts Inst. of Technology. Winner, first place, Washington National Student Film Festival, 1973.
PICTURES: Editor: Hollywood Boulevard (debut, 1976), American Boy, Corvette Summer, Second Hand Hearts. Director: Slumber Party Massacre, Love Letters (also s.p.), Mystic Pizza (s.p. only), Maid to Order (also co-s.p.), It Had to Be Steve (also co-s.p.).

JONES, CHUCK: Prod., Dir., Writer, Animator. b. Spokane, WA, Sept. 21, 1912. e. Chouinard Art Inst. Dir., Warner Bros. Animation until 1962 where he created and directed Roadrunner & Coyote, Pepe le Pew; directed and helped create Bugs Bunny, Porky Pig, Daffy Duck etc. Created Snafu character, U.S. Armed Service. Co-prod., wrote, dir., Bugs Bunny Show, ABC-TV. Headed MGM Animation Dept. Dir.: How the Grinch Stole Christmas, Horton Hears a Who, The Dot and the Line, Pogo, The Phantom Tollbooth. Lecturer and teacher at many universities. Currently independent, Chuck Jones Enterprises, Producer, Director, Writer (for ABC-TV) The Cricket in Times Square; A Very Merry Cricket; Yankee Doodle Cricket and (for CBS-TV) Rudyard Kipling's Rikki-Tikki-Tavi; The White Seal; Mowgli's Brothers, Saint-Saens' The Carnival of the Animals, Ogden Nash lyrics, with Daffy Duck & Bugs Bunny; A Connecticut Rabbit in King Arthur's Court, based on Mark Twain's original story, with Bugs Bunny, Daffy Duck, Porky Pig, Elmer Fudd, etc., two specials featuring Raggedy Ann and and How in The Great Santa Claus Caper and The Pumpkin Who Couldn't Smile; plus a feature compilation of past work: Chuck Jones' Bugs Bunny/Road Runner Movie. Most recently: Daffy Duck's Thanks-for-Giving Special and Bugs Bunny's Bustin' Out All Over. Recipient Academy Award for best animated cartoons for Scenti-Mental Reasons, 1950, The Dot and The Line, 1965; best documentary short subject for So Much for So Little, 1950. 1989, published Chuck Amuck: The Life and Times of an Animated Cartoonist. 1990, chmn. Chuck Jones Prods.; consultant to Warner Bros. Cartoons. Created animated sequence for 1992 live action feature Stay Tuned.

JONES, CHUCK: Public Relations Executive. b. Detroit, MI, Dec. 6, 1943. e. Michigan St. U., B.A. advertising. Entered m.p. industry in 1969. Publicist, Harold Rand & Co., Public Rltns., 1970–71. Publicist, AIP, 1971, Radio/tv, newspaper, magazine & syndicate contract UA Corp., 1972–73. Eastern adv./pub. dir., Embassy Pictures, 1981–82. Established Chuck Jones Public Relations, 1973 and has been pres. since then.

JONES, DAVID: Director, Producer. b. Poole, Eng., Feb. 19, 1934. e. Christ's Coll., Cambridge U., B.A., 1954, M.A., 1957. Immigrated to U.S. in 1979. Artistic controller, then assoc. dir., Royal Shakespeare Co., 1964–75; artistic dir, RSC at Aldwych Theatre 1975–78; artistic dir, Brooklyn Acad. of Music Theatre Co., NY 1979–81; prof. Yale Sch. of Drama, 1981.
THEATER: Sweeney Agonistes (debut, 1961); U.S.: Summerfolk, Loves Labour's Lost, Winter's Tale, Barbarians, Jungle of Cities.
PICTURES: Betrayal, Jacknife, The Trial.
TELEVISION: Prod.: Monitor 1958–64 (BBC series), Play of the Month,The Beaux' Stratagem, Langrishe Go Down, Ice Age. Dir.: Shakespeare series, BBC 1982–83, Devil's Disciple, The Christmas Wife, Sensibility and Sense.

JONES, DEAN: Actor. b. Decatur, AL, Jan. 25, 1931. e. Asbury Coll., Wilmore, KY. Prof. debut as blues singer, New Orleans; U.S. Navy, 1950–4. Author: Under Running Laughter.
STAGE: There Was a Little Girl, Under the Yum-Yum Tree, Company, Into the Light.
PICTURES: Tea and Sympathy, The Rack, The Opposite Sex, These Wilder Years, The Great American Pastime, Designing Woman, Ten Thousand Bedrooms, Jailhouse Rock, Until They Sail, Imitation General, Torpedo Run, Handle with Care, Night of the Quarter Moon, Never So Few, Under the Yum-Yum Tree, The New Interns, That Darn Cat, Two on a Guillotine, Any Wednesday, The Ugly Dachshund, Monkeys Go Home, Blackbeard's Ghost, The Horse in the Grey Flannel Suit, The Love Bug, $1,000,000 Duck, Snowball Express, Mr. Super Invisible, The Shaggy D.A., Herbie Goes to Monte Carlo, Born Again, Other People's Money, Beethoven.
TELEVISION: Series: Ensign O'Toole, The Chicago Teddy Bears, What's It All About World?, Herbie the Love Bug. Movies: Guess Who's Sleeping in My Bed?, When Every Day Was the 4th of July, Long Days of Summer, Fire and Rain, The Great Man's Whiskers, Saved By the Bell: Hawaiian Style.

JONES, GEMMA: Actress. b. London, Eng., Dec. 4, 1942. e. Royal Acad. of Dramatic Art.
THEATER: Baal, Alfie, The Cavern, The Pastime of M Robert, Portrait of a Queen, Next of Kin, The Marriage of Figaro, And A Nightingale, Breaking the Silence.
PICTURES: The Devils, Paperhouse, On the Black Hill.
TELEVISION: The Lie, The Way of the World, The Merchant of Venice, The Duchess of Duke Street (series), The Jim Henson Hour.

JONES, GRACE: Singer, Actress. b. Spanishtown, Jamaica, May 19, 1952. e. Syracuse U. Modelled and appeared in several Italian pictures before career as singer.
PICTURES: Conan the Destroyer, A View to a Kill, Vamp, Straight to Hell, Siesta, Boomerang.

JONES, GRIFFITH: Actor. b. London, England, 1910. e. University College, London; Royal Acad. of Dramatic Art (gold medal

1932). In H.M. Forces, W.W.II. Stage debut, London, 1930, in Carpet Slippers; N.Y. debut 1935 in Escape Me Never. Many stage successes. In many Brit. pictures from 1932.

PICTURES: Escape Me Never, The Faithful Heart, Catherine the Great, The Mill on the Floss, A Yank at Oxford, Four Just Men, Atlantic Ferry, This Was Paris, The Day Will Dawn, Uncensored, Henry V. Rake's Progress, Wicked Lady, They Made Me a Fugitive, Good Time Girl, Miranda, Look Before You Love, Once Upon a Dream, Honeymoon Deferred, Star of My Night, Scarlet Web, The Sea Shall Not Have Them, Face in the Night, Wanted on Voyage, The High Wall, Hidden Homicide, Strangler's Web, Decline and Fall.

PLAYS: The Moonraker, Quadrille, Alice Thro' the Looking Glass, Love Machine, Dead on Nine, The Entertainer, Expresso, The Sound of Murder, Treasure Island, Two Accounts Rendered, The Cavern, The Doctor's Dilemma, Jockey Club Stakes. 1973, Nottingham P'House, 1974 Crucible, Sheffield. Member of Royal Shakespeare Co. 1975–80, 1981–86, 1987–91.

TELEVISION: The Breaking Point, The Ware Case, When in Rome, A Moment in the Sun, Hell Hath No Fury, Margret, No Hiding Place, The Collection, By Invitation Only, A Woman of No Importance, Freedom in September, Blythe Spirit, Treasure Island, The Three Sisters, Emergency Ward, Vendetta, The Cabinet Papers, Man in a Suitcase, Boy Meets Girl, Troubleshooters, Strange Report, Avengers, Inside Man, A Matter of Principle, Doom Watch, Warm Feet, Warm Heart, Paul Temple, The Persuaders, The Lotus Eaters, The Black Arrow, Arrow, Spy Trap, Crown Court, Fallen Eagles, The Apple Cart, Comedy of Errors, Macbeth, The Three Sisters, Nicholas Nickleby.

JONES, HENRY: Actor. b. Philadelphia, PA, Aug. 1, 1912. e. St. Joseph's Coll. On stage in Hamlet, Henry IV, Time of Your Life, My Sister Eileen, The Solid Gold Cadillac, Bad Seed, Sunrise at Campobello (Tony Award, 1958), Advise and Consent.

PICTURES: This is the Army, Lady Says No, Taxi, The Bad Seed, The Girl He Left Behind, The Girl Can't Help It, Will Success Spoil Rock Hunter?, 3:10 to Yuma, Vertigo, Cash McCall, The Bramble Bush, Angel Baby, Never Too Late, The Champagne Murders, Stay Away Joe, Project X, Support Your Local Sheriff, Rascal, Angel in My Pocket, Butch Cassidy and the Sundance Kid, Rabbit Run, Dirty Dingus Magee, Skin Game, Support Your Local Gunfighter, Napoleon and Samantha, Pete 'n' Tillie, Tom Sawyer, The Outfit, Nine to Five, Deathtrap, Balboa, Caddo Lake, Nowhere to Run, Dick Tracy, Arachnophobia, The Grifters.

TELEVISION: Series: Honestly Celeste! (1954), Channing, The Girl With Something Extra, Phyllis, Kate Loves a Mystery, Gun Shy, Code Name: Foxfire, I Married Dora. Movies: The Crucible, Something for a Lonely Man, The Movie Murderer, Love Hate Love, Who is the Black Dahlia?, Tail Gunner Joe, CaliforniaGold Rush, The Leftovers, Grass Roots. Guest: Lost in Space, We'll Get By, B.J. and the Bear, Falcon Crest.

JONES, JAMES EARL: Actor. b. Arkabutla, MS, Jan. 17, 1931. e. U. of Michigan. Son of actor Robert Earl Jones. Awarded Hon. Doctor of Fine Arts (Yale, Princeton); Medal for Spoken Language (Amer. Acad. and Inst. of Arts and Letter; Hon. Doctor of Humane Letters (Columbia Coll. & U. of Mich.).

THEATER: Moon on a Rainbow Shawl (Theatre World Award), The Cool World, Othello, Paul Robeson, Les Blancs, The Great White Hope (Tony Award, 1969), The Iceman Cometh, Of Mice and Men, A Lesson from Aloes, Master Harold . . . and the Boys, Fences (Tony Award, 1986).

PICTURES: Dr. Strangelove (debut, 1964), The Comedians, King: A Filmed Record . . . Montgomery to Memphis (narrator), The End of the Road, The Great White Hope, Malcolm X (narrator), The Man, Claudine, Deadly Hero, Swashbuckler, The Bingo Long Travelling All-Stars and Motor Kings, The River Niger, The Greatest, Star Wars (voice), Exorcist II: The Heretic, The Last Remake of Beau Geste, A Piece of the Action, The Bushido Blade, Blood Tide, Return of the Jedi (voice), Conan the Barbarian, City Limits, My Little Girl, Soul Man, Alan Quartermain and the Lost City of Gold, Gardens of Stone, Matewan, Pinocchio and the Emperor of the Night (voice), Coming to America, Three Fugitives, Field of Dreams, Best of the Best, The Hunt for Red October, Grim Prairie Tales, The Ambulance, True Identity, Convicts, Patriot Games, Sneakers, Sommersby, The Sandlot, Meteor Man, Clean Slate, The Lion King (voice).

TELEVISION: Series: Paris, Me and Mom, Gabriel's Fire (Emmy Award, 1991), Pros & Cons. Movies: The UFO Incident, Jesus of Nazareth, The Greatest Thing That Almost Happened, Guyana Tragedy—The Story of Jim Jones, Golden Moment: An Olympic Love Story, Philby, Burgess and MacLean, The Atlanta Child Murders, The Vegas Strip War, By Dawn's Early Light, Heat Wave (Emmy Award, 1991), Last Flight Out, The Last Elephant. Specials: King Lear, Soldier Boy, Mathnet, Bailey's Bridge, Third and Oak: The Pool Hall, Teach 109.

JONES, JEFFREY: Actor. b. Buffalo, NY, Sept. 28, 1947. e. Lawrence U., Wisconsin. While pre-med student, performed in 1967 prod. of Hobson's Choice and was invited by Sir Tyrone Guthrie to join Guthrie Theatre in Minneapolis. After short time in South America, studied on full scholarship at London Acad. of Music and Dramatic Arts before joining Stratford Theater in Ontario. 1973–74 worked with Vancouver touring children's theater co. Playhouse Holiday. Moved to N.Y. where performed on stage.

THEATER: The Elephant Man (Bdwy debut), Trelawney of the Wells, Secret Service, Boy Meets Girl, Cloud Nine, Comedy of Errors, The Tempest, The Death of Von Richtoven.

PICTURES: The Revolutionary, The Soldier, Easy Money, Amadeus, Transylvania 6-5000, Ferris Bueller's Day Off, Howard the Duck, The Hanoi Hilton, Beetlejuice, Without a Clue, Who Is Harry Crumb?, Valmont, The Hunt for Red October, Over Her Dead Body, Mom and Dad Save the World, Stay Tuned, Out on a Limb.

TELEVISION: Mini-series: George Washington: The Forging of a Nation, Fresno. Movie: Kenny Rogers as "The Gambler" III—The Legend Continues. Guest: Amazing Stories, Twilight Zone, Remington Steele. Series: The People Next Door.

JONES, JENNIFER: Actress. r.n. Phyllis Isley. b. Tulsa, OK, Mar. 2, 1919. e. Northwestern U., American Acad. of Dramatic Arts. Daughter of Phil R., Flora Mae (Suber) Isley, exhib. m. industrialist Norton Simon. Toured with parents stock company as child; in summer stock in East; little theat. East & West. Began screen career as Phyllis Isley. First major role The Song of Bernadette (Acad. Award, 1943). Pres., Norton Simon Museum.

PICTURES: Dick Tracy's G-Men (debut, 1939), The New Frontier, The Song of Bernadette (Acad. Award, 1943; first film as Jennifer Jones), Since You Went Away, Love Letters, Cluny Brown, Duel in the Sun, Portrait of Jennie, We Were Strangers, Madame Bovary, Carrie, Wild Heart (Gone to Earth), Ruby Gentry, Indiscretion of an American Wife, Beat the Devil, Love Is a Many-Splendored Thing, Good Morning Miss Dove, Man in the Gray Flannel Suit, Barretts of Wimpole Street, Farewell to Arms, Tender Is the Night, The Idol, Angel Angel Down We Go, The Towering Inferno.

JONES, KATHY: Executive. b. Aug. 27, 1949. Began career as acct. exec. for m.p. clients, Stan Levinson assoc., Dallas. Joined Paramount Pictures in 1977 as sr. publicist in field marketing then exec. dir., field mktg. Left to join Time-Life Films as v.p., domestic mktg., for m.p. div. Returned to Paramount 1981 as v.p., domestic pub. & promo. 1984, appt. sr. v.p., domestic pub. & promo. for Motion Picture Group, Paramount. Formed m.p. consultancy with Buffy Shutt, 1987. 1989, appt. exec. v.p., marketing, Columbia Pictures. 1991, appt. exec. v.p. marketing, TriStar Pictures.

JONES, QUINCY: Producer, Composer, Arranger, Recording Artist. b. Chicago, IL, March 14, 1933. e. Seattle U., Berklee Sch. Music, Boston Conservatory, Trumpeter and arranger for Lionel Hampton's orch. 1950–53, played with Dizzy Gillespie, Count Basie and arranged for orchs., singers-Frank Sinatra, Sarah Vaughn, Peggy Lee, Dinah Washington and led own orch. for European tours, and recordings. Prod. recordings for Michael Jackson, Tevin Campbell, Barbra Streisand, Donna Summer. Music dir. and v.p., Mercury Records 1961–64 before scoring films. Prod. & arranged We Are the World recording. Owns own Qwest Records record company.

PICTURES: The Pawnbroker, Mirage, The Slender Thread, Made in Paris, Walk Don't Run, Banning, The Deadly Affair, In the heat of the Night, In Cold Blood (Acad. Award nom.), Enter Laughing, A Dandy in Aspic, For Love of Ivy, The Hell With Heroes, The Split, Up Your Teddy Bear, Jocelyn, McKenna's Gold, The Italian Job, Bob & Carol & Ted & Alice, The Lost Man, Cactus Flower, John and Mary, The Last of the Mobile Hotshots, The Out-of-Towners, They Call Me Mister Tibbs, Brother John, Dollars, The Anderson Tapes, Yao of the Jungle, The Hot Rock, The New Centurions, Come Back Charleston Blue, The Getaway, The Wiz (also cameo), The Color Purple (also co-prod.; Acad. Award nom.), Listen Up.

TELEVISION: Mini-Series: Roots (Emmy, 1977). Special: An American Reunion (exec. prod.). Series: Fresh Prince of Bel Air.

JONES, SAM J.: Actor. b. Chicago, IL, Aug. 12, 1954.
PICTURES: "10," Flash Gordon, My Chauffeur, Silent Assassins, White Fire, One Man Force, Double Trouble, Driving Force.

TELEVISION: Series: Code Red, The Highwayman. Movies: The Incredible Journey of Dr. Meg Laurel, Stunts Unlimited, Code Red (pilot), No Man's Land.

JONES, SHIRLEY: Actress. b. Smithton, PA, March 31, 1934. m. actor-prod. Marty Ingels. Former Miss Pittsburgh. Natl. chair, Leukemia Foundation. Book: Shirley & Marty: An Unlikely Love Story, (Wm. Morrow, 1990). Received hom. Doctor of Humane Letters degree from Point Park Col. 1991.

THEATRE: Appeared with Pittsburgh Civic Light Opera in Lady in the Dark, Call Me Madam. Broadway: South Pacific, Me and Juliet, Maggie Flynn.
PICTURES: Oklahoma! (debut, 1955), Carousel, April Love, Never Steal Anything Small, Bobbikins, Elmer Gantry (Acad. Award, supp., actress, 1960), Pepe, Two Rode Together, The Music Man, A Ticklish Affair, Bedtime Story, Fluffy, The Secret of My Success, The Happy Ending, The Cheyenne Social Club, Beyond the Poseidon Adventure, Tank.
TELEVISION: Movies: Silent Night Lonely Night, But I Don't Want to Get Married, The Girls of Huntington House, The Family Nobody Wanted, Winner Take All, The Lives of Jenny Dolan, Yesterday's Child, Evening in Byzantium, Who'll Save Our Children, A Last Cry For Help, Children of An Lac, Intimates: A Love Story, There Were Times Dear, Widow. Series: The Partridge Family, Shirley, The Slap Maxwell Story. Guest: McMillan, The Love Boat, Hotel, Murder She Wrote, Empty Nest.

JONES, TERRY: Writer, Actor, Director. b. Colwyn Bay, North Wales, Feb. 1, 1942. Worked with various rep. groups before joining BBC script dept. Was member of Monty Python's Flying Circus.
PICTURES: Actor: And Now for Something Completely Different (also co-s.p.), Monty Python.and the Holy Grail (also co-dir., co-s.p.), Monty Python's Life of Brian (also dir., co-s.p.), Monty Python's The Meaning of Life (also co-s.p., dir., music), Labyrinth (s.p. only), Personal Services (dir. only), Erik the Viking (also dir., s.p.).
TELEVISION: Late Night Lineup, The Late Show, A Series of Birds, Do Not Adjust Your Set, The Complete and Utter History of Britain, Monty Python's Flying Circus, Secrets.

JONES, TOMMY LEE: Actor. b. San Saba, TX, Sept. 15, 1946. Worked in oil fields; graduated Harvard, where earned a degree, cum laude, in English. Broadway debut in A Patriot for Me; appeared on stage in Four in a Garden, Ulysses in Nighttown, Fortune and Men's Eyes.
PICTURES: Love Story (debut, 1970), Eliza's Horoscope, Jackson County Jail, Rolling Thunder, The Betsy, Eyes of Laura Mars, Coal Miner's Daughter, Back Roads, Nate and Hayes, River Rat, Black Moon Rising, The Big Town, Stormy Monday, The Package, Firebirds, JFK (Acad. Award nom.), Under Siege, House of Cards, The Fugitive, Blue Sky, Heaven and Earth, Natural Born Killers, The Client.
TELEVISION: Movies: Charlie's Angels (pilot), Smash-Up on Interstate 5, The Amazing Howard Hughes, The Executioner's Song (Emmy Award), Broken Vows, The Park is Mine; Yuri Nosenko: KGB, Gotham, Stranger on My Land, April Morning. Mini-Series: Lonesome Dove. Specials: The Rainmaker, Cat on a Hot Tin Roof.

JORDAN, GLENN: Director, Producer. b. San Antonio, TX, April 5, 1936. e. Harvard, B.A.; Yale Drama Sch. Directed plays off-Bdwy. and on tour.
PICTURES: Director: Only When I Laugh, The Buddy System, Mass Appeal.
TELEVISION: Specials: Hogan's Goat, Paradise Lost, Benjamin Franklin (prod.; Emmy Award), Eccentricities of a Nightingale, The Oath, The Court Martial of Gen. George Armstrong Custer. Movies: Frankenstein, The Picture of Dorian Gray, Shell Game, One of My Wives is Missing, Delta County U.S.A., In the Matter of Karen Ann Quinlan, Sunshine Christmas, Les Miserables, Son Rise: A Miracle of Love, The Family Man, The Women's Room (also prod.), The Princess and the Cabbie, Lois Gibbs and the Love Canal, Heartsounds, Dress Grey, Promise (also prod.; 2 Emmy Awards), Something in Common (also prod.), Echoes in the Darkness (also prod.), Jesse (also prod.), Home Fires Burning (also prod.), Challenger (also prod.), Sarah: Plain and Tall (also prod.), Aftermath: A Test of Love (also prod.), The Boys (also prod.), O Pioneers! (also prod.), Barbarians at the Gate (also co-exec. prod.).

JORDAN, HENRIETTA: Executive. b. New York, NY, Feb. 26, 1917. Ent. m.p. ind. as ass't to exec. v.p., UPA Pictures, 1950; v.p. in charge of sales, Format Prods, Inc. v.p. and assoc. prod., 1962–71. Assoc. prod. Levitow-Hanson Films, Inc., 1972–74; Producer, Image West, Ltd., 1975–84; dir. sls., Cause & EFX, 1984–85; dir. sls., Modern Videofilm Graphics, 1986–88; Personal Communications, Hank Jordan Enterprises, 1988–.

JORDAN, NEIL: Director. Writer. b. Sligo, Ireland, Feb. 25, 1950. e. University Coll, Dublin, B.A., 1972. Novels: The Past, Night in Tunisia, Dream of a Beast.
PICTURES: Traveller (s.p.), The Courier (co-exec. prod.). Dir.-Writer: Angel, The Company of Wolves, Mona Lisa (LA Film Critics Award for best screenplay, 1986), High Spirits, We're No Angels (dir. only), The Miracle, The Crying Game (Acad. Award, WGA & NY Film Critics Awards for best original screenplay, 1992).
TELEVISION: Mr. Solomon Wept (BBC), RTE (Ireland), Seduction, Tree, Miracles and Miss Langan.

JORDAN, RICHARD: Actor. b. New York, NY, July 19, 1937. e. Harvard U.
PICTURES: Lawman (debut, 1970), Valdez Is Coming, Chato's Land, Trial of the Catonsville Nine, The Friends of Eddie Coyle, The Yakuza, Rooster Cogburn, Logan's Run, Interiors, Old Boyfriends, A Nightingale Sang in Berkeley Square, Raise the Titanic, A Flash of Green (also prod.), Dune, The Mean Season, The Men's Club, Solarbabies, The Secret of My Success, Romero, The Hunt for Red October, Timebomb, Shout, Heaven is a Playground, Primary Motive, Posse, Gettysburg.
TELEVISION: Mini-Series: Captains and the Kings, The French Atlantic Affair. Movies: The Defection of Simas Kudirka, Les Miserables, The Bunker, Washington Mistress, The Murder of Mary Phagan. Special: Three Hotels.
(Died August 30, 1993)

JOSEPHSON, ERLAND: Actor, Director, Writer. b. Stockholm, Sweden, June 15, 1923. Acted in over 100 plays in Sweden. Joined Sweden's Royal Dramatic Theatre in 1956 replacing Ingmar Bergman as head of the theater, 1966–76. Closely associated with Bergman, with whom he staged plays in his late teens. Co-authored s.p. The Pleasure Garden and Now About These Women. Also has pub. poetry, six novels, and scripts for stage, screen and radio. American stage debut: The Cherry Orchard, 1988.
PICTURES: It Rains on Our Love, To Joy, Brink of Life, The Magician, Hour of the Wolf, The Passion of Anna, Cries and Whispers, Scenes from a Marriage, Face to Face, Beyond Good and Evil, I'm Afraid, Autumn Sonata, To Forget Venice, One and One (also dir.), The Marmalade Revolution (also dir., s.p.), Montenegro, Sezona Mira u Parizu, Fanny and Alexander, After the Rehearsal, Angela's War, Behind the Shutters, A Case of Irresponsibility, Dirty Story, Amarosa, The Flying Devils, Garibaldi, The General, The Last Mazurka, The Sacrifice, Saving Grace, Unbearable Lightness of Being, Hanussen, Meeting Venus, The Ox, Sofie.

JOSEPHSON, MARVIN A: Executive. b. Atlantic City, NJ, March 6, 1927. e. Cornell U., B.A., 1949; L.L.B. NYU, 1952. Lawyer at CBS Television 1952–55; founded Broadcast Management Inc. which became Josephson International Inc. in 1955. Josephson International Inc. is the parent co. of International Creative Management, Inc. and ICM Artists Ltd.

JOSIAH, JR., WALTER J.: Executive. b. New York, NY, Nov. 9, 1933. e. Fordham U., B.S.:SS, 1955: Harvard Law School, LL.B., 1962. U.S. Air Force, 1955–58, First Lt. and Pilot. Associate, Simpson Thacher & Bartlett, 1962–67. Legal staff, Paramount Pictures, 1967–69. Asst. resident counsel, 1969; chief resident counsel, 1970 and v.p. & chief resident counsel, 1971–82. ex.-v.p. & general counsel, Motion Picture Association of America, Inc., 1983.
Professional Associations: Chmn., Committee 307, Authors Rights, 1981–82, Patent, Trademark & Copyright Law Section of the American Bar Assn.; Association of the Bar of the City of NY (Committee on Copyright and Literary Property, 1976–79, 1982–85, chmn. 1986–89); Copyright Society of the U.S.A.—Member of the Board of Trustees commencing June, 1981; v.p.; from June 1988; pres. beginning June 1990; member, Motion Picture Academy of Arts and Sciences; Copyright Office Advisory Committee, 1981–82; National Sculpture Society—advisor to the president; Advisory Board, Publication: Communications and the Law; Member, President's Club Executive Committee and Annual Fund Council, Fordham U.

JOURDAN, LOUIS: Actor, r.n. Louis Gendre. b. Marseille, France, June 19, 1920. Stage actor prior to m.p. On radio as regular on Connie Boswell Presents, 1944. On Bdwy in The Immoralist, Tonight in Samarkand, On a Clear Day You Can See Forever (Boston, previews), 13 Rue de l'Amour.
PICTURES: Le Corsaire (debut, 1940), Her First Affair, La Boheme, L'Arlesienne, La Belle, Adventure, Felicie Nanteuil, The Paradine Case, Letter from an Unknown Woman, No Minor Vices, Madame Bovary, Bird of Paradise, Anne of the Indies, The Happy Time, Decameron Nights, Three Coins in the Fountain, The Swan, Julie, The Bride is Much Too Beautiful, Dangerous Exile, Gigi, The Best of Everything, Can-Can, Leviathan, Streets of Montmartre, Story of the Count of Monte Cristo, Mathias Sandorf, The VIPs, Made in Paris, To Commit a Murder, A Flea in Her Ear, Young Rebel (Cervantes), Silver Bears, Double Deal, Swamp Thing, Octopussy, The Return of Swamp Thing, Counterforce, Year of the Comet.
TELEVISION: Series: Paris Precinct (1954–55), Host: Romance Theatre. Mini-series: The French Atlantic Affair, Dracula. Movies: Run a Crooked Mile, Fear No Evil, Ritual of Evil, The Great American Beauty Contest, The Count of Monte Cristo, The Man in the Iron Mask, The First Olympics-Athens, Beverly Hills Madam. Guest: Ford Theatre, The FBI, Name of the Game, Charlie's Angels.

JOY, ROBERT: Actor. b. Montreal, Canada, Aug. 17, 1951. e. Memorial Univ. of Newfoundland Rhodes Scholar. Acted in

179

regional and off-Broadway theatre. Off-Bdwy debut The Diary of Anne Frank (1978). Has composed music for stage, radio and film.

THEATER: NY Shakespeare Fest. (Found a Peanut, Lenny and the Heartbreakers, The Death of von Richtofen), Life and Limb, Fables for Friends, Welcome to the Moon, What I Did Last Summer, Lydie Breeze, Romeo and Juliet (La Jolla Playhouse; Drama-Logue Award), Hay Fever (Bdwy debut), Big River (premiere), The Nerd, Hyde in Hollywood, The Taming of the Shrew, Shimada, Goodnight Desdemona (Good Morning Juliet).

PICTURES: Atlantic City, Ragtime, Ticket to Heaven, Threshold, Terminal Choice, Amityville 3-D, Desperately Seeking Susan, Joshua Then and Now, Adventure of Faustus Bidgood (also co-prod. music), Radio Days, Big Shots, The Suicide Club, She's Back!, Millenium, Longtime Companion, Shadows and Fog, The Dark Half, I'll Do Anything.

TELEVISION: Series: One Life to Live. Guest: The Equalizer, Moonlighting. Specials: The Prodigious Hickey, The Return of Hickey, The Beginning of the Firm, Hyde in Hollywood. Movies: Escape from Iran: The Canadian Caper, Gregory K, Woman on the Run: The Lawrencia Bembenek Story.

JUDD, EDWARD: Actor. b. Shanghai, 1934. e. Far East. Stage: The Long and the Short and the Tall, The Tinker. Numerous TV appearances.

PICTURES: The Day the Earth Caught Fire, Stolen Hours, The World Ten Times Over, Mystery Submarine, The Long Ships, First Men in the Moon, Strange Bedfellows, Invasion, Island of Terror, The Vengeance of She, Vault of Horror, Assassin, Shakedown, The Kitchen Toto.

JULIA, RAUL: Actor. b. San Juan, PR, Mar. 9, 1944. e. U. of Puerto Rico; studied for theatre with Wynn Handman. New York stage debut in La Vida Es Sueño, 1964.

THEATER: The Marriage Proposal (1966), Macduff in Macbeth (first assgn. with NY Shakespeare Fest., 1966), The Ox Cart, Titus Andronicus, No Exit, The Memorandum, Your Own Thing, The Cuban Thing (Bdwy debut), Paradise Gardens East, Conercio Was Here to Stay, City Way, The Castro Complex, Pinkville, Two Gentlemen of Verona, Hamlet (Delacorte Theater), As You Like It, King Lear, The Robber Bridegroom, Via Galactica, Where's Charley, Threepenny Opera (Lincoln Center), Dracula, The Taming of the Shrew, Betrayal, Othello, Nine, The Tempest, Design for Living, Arms and the Man, Macbeth, Othello, Man of La Mancha.

PICTURES: Stiletto (debut, 1969), Panic in Needle Park, The Organization, Been Down So Long It Looks Like Up to Me, Gumball Rally, Eyes of Laura Mars, Strong Medicine, One From the Heart, The Escape Artist, Tempest, Kiss of the Spider Woman, Compromising Positions, The Morning After, La Gran Fiesta, The Penitent, Moon Over Parador, Trading Hearts, Tequila Sunrise, Tango Bar, Romero, Mack the Knife, Presumed Innocent, Frankenstein Unbound, The Rookie, Havana, The Addams Family, The Plague, Addams Family Values.

TELEVISION: Series: Sesame Street (recurring role). Specials: King Lear, The National Health. Guest: Love of Life, Aces Up. Movies: McCloud: Who Killed Miss U.S.A.?, Death Scream, Florida Straits, Mussolini: The Untold Story, Onassis: The Richest Man in the World.

JURADO, KATY: Actress. r.n. Maria Christina Jurado Garcia. b. Guadalajara, Mexico, Jan. 16, 1927. Numerous Mexican films. Also m.p. columnist for Mexican publications.

PICTURES: Bullfighter and the Lady (U.S. debut, 1951), High Noon, San Antone, Arrowhead, Broken Lance (Acad. Award nom.), The Racers, Trial, Trapeze, Man from Del Rio, The Badlanders, One Eyed Jacks, Barabbas, Smoky, A Covenant with Death, Stay Away Joe, Pat Garrett and Billy the Kid, Under the Volcano.

TELEVISION: Movies: Any Second Now, A Little Game, Evita Peron, Lady Blue. Series: A.K.A. Pablo.

JUROW, MARTIN: Producer. b. New York, NY. Dec. 14, 1911. e. William and Mary, Harvard Law Sch. Associated with MCA, William Morris, pres., Famous Artists; prod., G & E Productions; co-prod. with Richard Shepherd Jurow-Shepherd Productions. Distinguished visiting professor Southern Methodist Univ.

PICTURES: The Hanging Tree, The Fugitive Kind, Love in a Goldfish Bowl, Breakfast at Tiffany's, The Pink Panther, The Great Race, Soldier in the Rain, Sylvester, Papa Was a Preacher, Waltz Across Texas, The End of August, Terms of Endearment (co-prod.).

K

KAGAN, JEREMY: Director, Writer. b. Mt. Vernon, NY, Dec. 14, 1945. e. Harvard; NYU, MFA; student Amer. Film Inst. 1971.

Film animator, 1968; multi-media show designer White House Conf. on Youth and Ed. Previously credited as Jeremy Paul Kagan.

PICTURES: Scott Joplin, Heroes, The Big Fix, The Chosen (1st prize, Montreal World Film Fest., 1981), The Sting II, The Journey of Natty Gann (Gold Prize, Moscow Film Fest., 1987), Big Man on Campus, By the Sword.

TELEVISION: Series: Columbo, The Bold Ones. Movies: Unwed Father, Judge Dee and the Monastery Murders, Katherine (also writer), Courage. Specials: My Dad Lives in a Downtown Hotel, Conspiracy: The Trial of the Chicago 8 (also writer). ACE Award, 1988).

KAHN, JUDITH: Executive. Background in mktg., including graphic design, adv./promo. Creative dir. at Intralink Film Graphic Design; returned to New York as consultant to corporate clients, including cable, TV, and m.p. accts. 1985, joined Paramount Pictures as v.p., creative svcs. of M.P. Group.

KAHN, MADELINE: Actress, Singer. b. Boston, MA., Sept. 29. e. Hofstra U. Broadway bow in New Faces of '68. Trained as opera singer and appeared in La Boheme, Showboat, Two by Two, Candide. Appeared in short film The Dove.

PICTURES: What's Up Doc? (debut, 1972), Paper Moon (Acad. Award nom.), From the Mixed-Up Files of Mrs. Basil E. Frankweiler, Blazing Saddles (Acad. Award nom.), Young Frankenstein, At Long Last Love, The Adventures of Sherlock Holmes' Smarter Brother, Won Ton Ton the Dog Who Saved Hollywood, High Anxiety, The Cheap Detective, The Muppet Movie, Simon, Happy Birthday Gemini, Wholly Moses, First Family, History of the World—Part I, Yellowbeard, Slapstick of Another Kind, City Heat, Clue, My Little Pony (voice), An American Tail (voice), Betsy's Wedding.

THEATER: Promenade, Two by Two, In the Boom Boom Room, On the Twentieth Century, Born Yesterday, The Sisters Rosensweig (Tony Award, 1993).

TELEVISION: Series: Comedy Tonight, Oh Madeline!, Mr. President. Specials: Harvey, The Perfect Guy (afterschool special), Celebrating Gershwin: The Jazz Age, Irving Berlin Gala, Stephen Sondheim Gala. Movie: For Richer For Poorer.

KAHN, MILTON: Publicist. b. Brooklyn, NY, May 3, 1934. e. Syracuse U., Ohio U., B.S.J. 1957. Formed Milton Kahn Associates, Inc. in 1958. Represented: Gregory Peck, Joan Crawford, Steve Allen, Glenn Ford, Lee Grant, Herb Alpert, Roger Corman, Robert Aldrich, Arthur Hiller, Chuck Norris, Bob Cousy, Michael Landon, Dean Hargrove, Bill Conti, etc. and New World Pictures (1970–83), Avco-Embassy, Vista Films, Roger Corman's Concorde (1983–), Electric Shadow Prods.

KAHN, RICHARD: Executive. b. New Rochelle. NY, Aug. 29, 1929. e. Wharton Sch. of Finance and Commerce, U. of Pennsylvania, B.S., 1951; U.S. Navy, 3 yrs.; joined Buchanan & Co., 1954; ent. m.p. ind., pressbook writer, Columbia Pictures, 1955; exploitation mgr.; 1958; natl. coord. adv. and pub., 1963; natl. dir. of adv., pub. and exploitation, 1968; v.p., 1969; 1974 v.p. in chg. of special marketing projects; 1975; moved to MGM as v.p. in chg. of worldwide advertising, publicity and exploitation; 1978, named v.p. in chg. worldwide mktg. & pres., MGM Intl. 1980, elected bd. of govs. Academy of M.P. Arts & Sciences. 1982, named exec. v.p. of adv., pub., promo. for MGM/UA; 1983, formed the Richard Kahn Co., dist. & mktg. consultancy, 1984–88. Faculty mem. Peter Stark m.p. producing prog., USC Sch. of Cinema & TV. Exec. chmn. Film Industry Council. 1982 elected sect. Acad. of Motion Picture Arts & Sciences; elected v.p. 1983–7; elected pres. 1988.

KALB, MARVIN: TV news reporter. e. City Coll. of New York; Harvard, M.A., 1953, Russian Language Sch., Middlebury Coll. Worked for U.S. State Dept., American Embassy, Moscow; CBS News, 1957; writer, reporter-researcher. Where We Stand: reporter-assignment editor; Moscow Bureau Chief, 1960–63; first dip. corres., Washington Bureau, 1963. Chief diplomatic corr. CBS News and NBC News, moderator Meet the Press; Teacher and lecturer; first dir. Joan Shorenstein Barone Center on the Press, Politics and Public Policy at John F. Kennedy Sch. of Govt. of Harvard U., since June, 1987. Host of PBS series, Candidates '88.

BOOKS: Eastern Exposure, Kissinger, Dragon in the Kremlin, Roots of Involvement, The U.S. in Asia, 1784–1971, Candidates '88 (with Hendrik Hertzberg).

KALISH, EDDIE: Executive. b. New York, NY, Apr. 27, 1939. Reporter/reviewer, Variety, 1959–64; sr. publicist, Paramount Pictures, 1964–65; adv./pub./promo dir., Ken Greengras Personal Management, 1965–66; pub. dir., Harold Rand & Co., 1966–67; independent publicist overseas, 1967–75; rejoined Paramount Pictures in 1975 as dir. of intl. mktg.; later named v.p.; 1978, named v.p., worldwide pub. & promo. In 1979 appt. senior v.p., worldwide mktg. In 1980 joined United Artists as v.p.—domestic mktg.; sr. v.p., adv., pub., promo, for MGM/UA 1981–82; became sr. v.p., worldwide mkt., PSO, 1982–1986. Now pres., Kalish/Davidson Marketing, Inc.

KAMBER, BERNARD M.: Executive. e. U. of Pennsylvania. New England exploitation rep. U.A. 1940; Army service 1941–43; dir. special events dept. U.A., 1943; asst. to Gradwell L. Sears, nat'l distrib. chmn. 6th War Loan Drive; dir. pub. 7th War Loan Drive, 1943–47; dir. pub. & prom. Eagle Lion Classics, 1951; org. Kamber Org., pub. rel. rep. for ind. prod. v.p. sales, adv. pub. Ivan Tors Prod. Greene-Rouse Prods.; June 1953; exec. asst. Hecht-Hill-Lancaster, chg. of N.Y. off., 1957; v.p. Hecht-Hill-Lancaster Companies, 1958; formed Cinex Distr. Corp., 1962; Pres. Cinex and Posfilm, Inc.; 1967 v.p. in chg. sls. Du Art Film Lab. Inc; 1975 joined Technicolor, Inc.

KAMEY, PAUL: b. New York, NY, Aug. 25, 1912. Worked on newspapers including NY Journal American. Ent. m.p. industry 1938; worked for MGM and 20th Century Fox; during ware, writer, Office of War information; joined Universal, 1949; eastern pub. mgr., Universal Pictures. 1968. Freelance publicist.

KANE, CAROL: Actress. b. Cleveland, OH, June 18, 1952. e. Professional Children's Sch., NY. Began professional acting career at age 14, touring, then on Bdwy. in The Prime of Miss Jean Brodie. Other stage credits include, The Tempest, The Effect of Gamma Rays on Man-in-the-Moon Marigolds, Are You Now or Have You Ever Been? Arturo Ui, The Enchanted, The Tempest, Macbeth, Tales of the Vienna Woods, Frankie and Johnny in the Claire de Lune, Control Freaks.
PICTURES: Carnal Knowledge (debut, 1971), Desperate Characters, Wedding in White, The Last Detail, Dog Day Afternoon, Hester Street, Harry and Walter Go to New York, Annie Hall, Valentino, The World's Greatest Lover, The Mafu Cage, The Muppet Movie, When a Stranger Calls, Pandemonium, Norman Loves Rose, Over the Brooklyn Bridge, Racing with the Moon, The Secret Diary of Sigmund Freud, Transylvania 6-5000, Jumpin' Jack Flash, Ishtar, The Princess Bride, Sticky Fingers, License to Drive, Scrooged, Flashback, Joe Vs. the Volcano, My Blue Heaven, The Lemon Sisters, Ted and Venus, In the Soup, Addams Family Values.
TELEVISION: Series: Taxi (2 Emmy Awards), All is Forgiven, American Dreamer. Movies: An Invasion of Privacy, Burning Rage, Drop Out Mother. Specials: Faerie Tale Theatre, Paul Reiser: Out on a Whim, Tales From the Crypt (Judy, You're Not Yourself Today).

KANE, JOHN: Publicity Manager. b. New York, NY. e. Rutgers, B.A.; NYU, M.A. Publicist, Solters & Roskin, 1976–80. Unit publicist: Fame, Tender Mercies, Prince of the City, 1980–82. 1982–90, Home Box Office, unit publicist, manager. 1991, unit publ. for Ricochet, Arrowtooth Waltz.

KANE, STANLEY D.: Judge. b. Minneapolis, MN, Dec. 21, 1907. e. U. of Minnesota, B.A. (magna cum laude), 1930; M.A., 1931; Minnesota Coll. of Law, LL.B., 1940. Instructor, U. of Minnesota, 1930–33. Exec. sec. Allied Theatre Owners of the Northwest, 1933–37; city attorney, Golden Valley, MN, 1940–63; City Atty., Champlin, MN, 1955–60; on faculty, Minnesota Coll. of Law, 1940–44; trial attorney & trial examiner, National Labor Relations Board, Minneapolis, New Orleans, N.Y., 1943–46; special, gen. counsel, Puerto Rico Labor Relations Bd., 1946; exec. vice-pres. & gen. counsel, North Central Allied Independent Theatre Owners, 1946–63; recording sec. Allied States Assn., 1947 to 1956; Dist. Court Judge, Hennepin County, 1963; elected to 6-yr. term, 1964; re-elected, 1970; serving full-time as sr. judge since 1978. Retired in 1990.

KANEW, JEFF: Director.
PICTURES: Black Rodeo, Natural Enemies, Eddie Macon's Run, Revenge of the Nerds, Gotcha, Tough Guys, Troop Beverly Hills, V. I. Warshawski.
TELEVISION: Alfred Hitchcock Presents (1985).

KANIN, FAY: Writer. b. New York, NY. e. Elmira Coll., U. of Southern California, 1937. m. Michael Kanin, writer. Contrib. fiction to mags., Writers Guild of Amer. pres. 1971–73; Acad. Motion Picture Arts & Sciences 1983–88. also bd. mem. of latter. Co-chair, National Center for Film and Video Preservation; Bd. of trustees, Amer. Film Institute; Chair, Natl. Film Preservation Board.
PICTURES: My Pal Gus, Rhapsody, The Opposite Sex, Teacher's Pet, Swordsman of Siena, The Right Approach.
BROADWAY: Goodbye My Fancy, His and Hers, Rashomon, The Gay Life, Grind (1985).
TELEVISION: Heat of Anger, Tell Me Where It Hurts (Emmy Award, 1974), Hustling, Friendly Fire (also co-prod., Emmy Award, San Francisco Film Fest. Award, Peabody Award), Heartsounds (Peabody Award).

KANIN, GARSON: Director, Writer. b. Rochester, NY, Nov. 24, 1912. e. American Acad. of Dramatic Arts. Was married to actress Ruth Gordon. (d. 8/28/81). m. actress Marian Seldes. Musician, actor, appearing in Spring Song, Little Ol' Boy, and others. Prod. assist. George Abbott on Three Men on a Horse, Brother Rat, Room Service; dir. Hitch Your Wagon,

Too Many Heroes, Broadway plays; In June, 1937, Samuel Goldwyn's prod. staff, 1938, joined RKO, prod.-dir. contract. In 1942: prod. for U.S. Office of Emergency Management. Joined armed forces, W.W.II; co-dir. True Glory (Acad. Award, 1945). 1989, received Writers Guild Valentine Davies Award with brother Michael. Pres., Authors League of America.
PICTURES: Dir.: A Man to Remember, Next Time I Marry, The Great Man Votes, Bachelor Mother, Tom Dick & Harry, My Favorite Wife, They Knew What They Wanted. Dir.-Writer: Where It's At, Some Kind of a Nut. Writer: From This Day Forward, A Double Life, Adam's Rib, Born Yesterday, The Marrying Kind, Pat and Mike, It Should Happen To You, The Rat Race, High Time.
THEATRE: Writer/Dir.: Born Yesterday, The Smile of the World, The Rat Race, The Live Wire, A Gift of Time, Do Re Mi, Come on Strong, Small War on Murray Hill, The Amazing Adele, The Good Soup, Dreyfus in Rehearsal, Happy Ending, Peccadillo. (writer and/or dir.) Dir.: The Rugged Path, Years Ago, How I Wonder, The Leading Lady, The Diary of Anne Frank, Into Thin Air, Hole in the Head, Sunday in New York, Funny Girl, I Was Dancing, A Very Rich Woman, We Have Always Lived in the Castle, Idiot's Delight, Ho! Ho! Ho!.
BOOKS: Remembering Mr. Maugham, Cast of Characters, Tracy and Hepburn, Hollywood, Blow Up a Storm, The Rat Race, A Thousand Summer,; One Hell of an Actor, It Takes a Long Time to Become Young, Moviola, Smash, Together Again!, Cordelia.
TELEVISION: Movie: Hardhat and Legs (co-writer). Series: Mr. Broadway.

KANTER, HAL: Writer, Director, Producer. b. Savannah, GA, Dec. 18, 1918. On Bdwy. contributor to Hellzapoppin. Then began writing radio dramas before mil. service, WW II. Served as combat corresp. Armed Forces Radio; writer, Paramount, 1951–54; dir., RKO, 1956; writer, prod. for Lucille Ball Prods. (1979–80). Savannah Prods., 1982–86. Received Writers Guild Paddy Chayefsky Laurel Award, 1989.
TELEVISION: Writer: Danny Kaye Show, Amos 'n Andy, Bing Crosby Show, Jack Paar, Beulah, Ed Wynn Show, George Gobel Show (also creator, prod.), Kraft Music Hall (also dir., prod.; 1958–59), Chrysler Theatre (also prod., dir.; 1966–67), Julia (also dir., prod., creator), Jimmy Stewart Show (also prod., dir., creator), All In The Family (exec. prod.: 1975–76), Chico & The Man (spv. prod., 1976–77), You Can't Take It With You. Specials (writer): AFI Life Achievement Awards for Henry Fonda & Alfred Hitchcock, 25 Annual Academy Awards. Member: bd. of dir., WGAW; bd. of govs. AMPAS; v.p. Writers Guild Foundation.
PICTURES: Writer: My Favorite Spy, Off Limits, Road to Bali, Casanova's Big Night, About Mrs. Leslie, Money from Home, Artists and Models, The Rose Tattoo, I Married a Woman (dir.), Loving You (dir.), Mardi Gras, Once Upon a Horse (dir.), Blue Hawaii, Pocketful of Miracles, Bachelor in Paradise, Move Over Darling, Dear Brigitte, others.

KANTER, JAY: Executive. b. Dec. 12, 1926. Entered industry with MCA, Inc., where was v.p. Left after more than 20 yrs. to become indep. prod., then pres. of First Artists Production Co., Ltd. In 1975 joined 20th-Fox as v.p. prod.; 1976, named sr. v.p., worldwide prod. Named v.p., The Ladd Co., 1979. Joined MGM/UA Entertainment Co. as pres., worldwide prod., Motion Picture Division, 1984. In 1985, named pres., worldwide prod. UA Corp.; then pres., production MGM Pictures Inc.; 1989, named chmn. of prod. of Pathé Entertainment Co. 1991, became COO & chmn. of prod., MGM-Pathe Commun. Co. (MGM Communications, May 1992).

KANTOR, IGO: Producer, Film Editor. b. Vienna, Austria, Aug. 18, 1930. e. UCLA, A.A. 1950; B.S., 1952; M.S., 1954. Foreign corres., Portugal magazine, FLAMA, 1949–57, music supvr., Screen Gems, Columbia 1954–63; post-prod. supvr., film ed., features, TV; assoc. prod., 1963–64; prod., exec., International Entertainment Corp., 1965. pres., Synchrofilm, Inc., post-production co. and Duque Films, Inc., production co. 1968–74. 1975–present, produced and edited films. 1982, pres., Laurelwood Prods; 1988, pres. Major Arts Corp.
PICTURES: Assoc. Producer: Bye Bye Birdie, Under the Yum Yum Tree, Gidget Goes to Rome, A House Is Not a Home, Pattern for Murder, Willy. Producer: Assault on Agathon (also edit.), FTA, Dixie Dynamite (assoc. prod., edit.), Kingdom of the Spiders (also edit., music supvr.), The Dark (assoc. prod.), Good Luck Miss Wyckoff (prod. spvr.), Hardly Working, Kill and Kill Again, Mutant, Shaker Run, Act of Piracy, They Call Me Bruce Levy.
TELEVISION: From Hawaii with Love (1984), The Grand Tour, It's a Wonderful World (prod.-dir.), Nosotros Golden Eagle Awards (prod.), United We Stand (pre-Olympic special), Legends of the West With Jack Palance, Mom U.S.A.

KAPLAN, GABRIEL: Actor, Comedian. b. Brooklyn, NY, March 31, 1945. After high school worked as bellboy at Lakewood, NJ hotel, spending free time studying comedians doing routines. Put together a comedy act, landing engagements in small clubs and coffee houses all over U.S. Made several appear-

ances on Tonight Show, Merv Griffin Show, Mike Douglas Show, etc. Has played Las Vegas clubs.
TELEVISION: *Series*: Welcome Back, Kotter, Gabriel Kaplan Presents the Future Stars, Lewis and Clark. *Movie*: Love Boat (pilot).
PICTURES: Fast Break, Tulips, Nobody's Perfekt.

KAPLAN, JONATHAN: Director, Writer. b. Paris, Nov. 25, 1947. Son of composer Sol Kaplan. e. U. of Chicago, B.A.; NYU, M.F.A. Made short film Stanley Stanley. Member of tech. staff Fillmore East, NY 1969–71. New World Pictures' Roger Corman post-grad. sch. of filmmaking, Hollywood, 1971–73. As actor on Bdwy in Dark at the Top of the Stairs. Appeared in films: Cannonball, Hollywood Boulevard.
PICTURES: *Director*: Night Call Nurses, Student Teachers, The Slams, Truck Turner, White Line Fever (also co-s.p.), Mr. Billion, Over the Edge, Heart Like a Wheel, Project X, The Accused, Immediate Family, Unlawful Entry, Love Field.
TELEVISION: *Movies*: The 11th Victim, The Hustler of Muscle Beach, The Gentleman Bandit, Girls of the White Orchid.

KAPOOR, SHASHI: Actor. b. Calcutta, India, Mar. 18, 1938. Son of late Prithviraj Kapoor, Indian film and stage actor. As child worked in Prithvi Theatre and in brother, Raj's films. Toured with father's co. at 18 and joined the Kendals' Shakespeareana Co. in India. Starred in over 200 Indian films as well as several Merchant-Ivory Prods.
PICTURES: Pretty Polly, Siddhartha, The Householder, Bombay Talkie, Shakespeare Wallah, Heat and Dust, USTAV (Festival of Love, also prod.), The New Delhi Times, Sammy and Rosie Get Laid, The Deceivers, Nomads, Ajuba.

KARDISH, LAURENCE: Curator, Dept. of Film, Museum of Modern Art. b. Ottawa, Ontario, Canada, Jan. 5, 1945. e. Carlton U. Ottawa, Canada, 1966, Honors B.A. in philosophy; Columbia U., Sch. of the Arts, 1968, M.F.A. in film, radio, and television. 1965–66: Canadian Film Inst., programmer for National Film Theatre, Ottawa; researched a history of Canadian filmmaking. 1965: founded first film society in Canada to exhibit Amer. avant-garde films (Carleton U. Cine Club); directed summer seminar on film, Carleton U., 1966. 1966–68: New American Cinema Group, Inc., NY, worked for the Film-Makers' Distribution Center. 1968: joined Dept. of Film, MOMA; made curator 1984. Since 1968 involved with Cineprobe prog., since 1972 participated in selection of films for New Directors/New Films series; dir. exhibitions of surveys of national cinemas (Senegal, Scandinavia, French-speaking Canada) and retrospectives of indep. Amer. filmmakers (includ. Rudolph Burkhardt, Stan Brakhage, Shirley Clarke), The Lubitsch Touch, Columbia Pictures, Warner Bros., MGM, Universal, RKO, and directors. 1980: toured Europe with prog. of indep. Amer. films. Author of: Reel Plastic Magic (1972); as well as essays and monographs–Mark Rappaport and the Scenic Route; Senegal: 15 Years of an African Cinema; New Cinema from Iceland; Of Light and Texture; Andrew Noren and James Herbert; Michael Balcon and the Idea of a National Cinema; Intl. Avant-Garde: Scattered Pieces; Berlin and Film. Directed feature film Slow Run (1968). On jury for Channel 13's Indep. Focus series and on Board of Advisors, Collective for Living Cinema, NY. 1982–82: bd. of dirs. of National Alliance of Media Arts Centers; 1987–89: on Jerome Foundation panel. 1986 on Camera d'Or jury, Cannes Film Fest.

KARINA, ANNA: Actress. b. Copenhagen, Denmark, 1940. r.n. Hanna Karin Bayer. Had appeared in Danish shorts before going to Paris at 17 and working in commercials. Gained international renown in the 7 films she made with former husband Jean-Luc Godard.
PICTURES: Celo From Five to Seven, Three Fables of Love, My Life to Live, A Woman is a Woman, Sweet and Sour, Circle of Love, She'll Have to Go, Le Petit Soldat, Band of Outsiders, Pierrot le Fou, Alphaville, Made in U.S.A., The Stranger, La Religieuse, The Oldest Profession, The Magus, Before Winter Comes, Laughter in the Dark, Justine, Rendevous a Bray, Willie and the Chinese Cat, Vivre Ensemble (also dir.), Story of a Mother, L'Ami de Vincent, Ave Maria.

KARLIN, FRED: Composer, Conductor. b. Chicago, IL, June 16, 1936. e. Amherst Coll., B.A. Composer and arranger for Benny Goodman. Won Academy Award for Best Song for For All We Know (from Lovers and Other Strangers) and Emmy for original music in The Autobiography of Miss Jane Pittman. 4 Acad. Award noms., 10 Emmy Award noms.; Image Award for score to Minstrel Man.Co-author (with Rayburn Wright) of On the Track: A Guide to Contemporary Film Scoring (Schirmer).
PICTURES: Up the Down Staircase, Yours, Mine and Ours, The Sterile Cuckoo (including music for song, Come Saturday Morning), Westworld, Futureworld, Lovers and Other Strangers, Gravy Train, Mixed Company, Leadbelly, Loving Couples.
TELEVISION: More than 100 movies and mini-series, including The Autobiography of Miss Jane Pittman, The Awakening Land, The Plutonium Incident, Minstrel Man,

Sophia Loren—Her Own Story, Green Eyes, Strangers: The Story of a Mother and Daughter, Calamity Jane, Ike: the War Years, Inside the Third Reich, Hollywood—The Gift of Laughter, Not in Front of the Children, Dream West, Hostage Flight, A Place to Call Home, Robert Kennedy and His Times, Dadah Is Death, Bridge to Silence, The Secret.

KARLIN, MYRON D.: Executive. b. Revere, MA, Sept. 21, 1918. e. UCLA. Joined m.p. business in 1946 as gen. mgr. for MGM in Ecuador. Two yrs. later assigned same spot for MGM in Venezuela. In 1952–53 was gen. sales mgr. for MGM in Germany, after which managing dir. in Argentina, returning to Germany as mgr. dir. in 1956. Named mgn. dir. for United Artists in Italy. 1960–68 was pres. of Brunswick Int'l., while also serving as advisor to World Health Organization and UNESCO. In 1969 was European mgr. for MGM and mgn. dir. in Italy. Joined Warner Bros. Int'l. in May, 1970 as v.p. of European dist. In March, 1972 appt. v.p. in chg. of int'l. operations for WB; 1977, appt. pres., WB Int'l. & exec. v.p., Warner Bros., Inc; 1985, named exec. v.p., intl. affairs, WB, Inc. Now pres. & COO, Motion Picture Export Assn.

KARRAS, ALEX: Actor. b. Gary, IN, July 15, 1935. e. Univ. of Iowa. As football player with Iowa State U., picked for All Amer. team. Received Outland Trophy, 1957. Former professional football player with Detroit Lions, 1958–62, and 1964–71. Sportswriter, Detroit Free Press, 1972–73. Also worked as prof. wrestler, salesman, steel worker and lecturer. m. actress Susan Clark. With her formed Georgian Bay Prods., 1979. Autobiographies: Even Big Guys Cry (with Herb Gluck, 1977), Alex Karras: My Life in Football Television and Movies (1979), Tuesday Night Football (1991).
PICTURES: Paper Lion (as himself; debut, 1968), Blazing Saddles, FM, Win Place or Steal, Jacob Two-Two Meets the Hooded Fang, When Time Ran Out, Nobody's Perfekt, Porky's, Victor Victoria, Against All Odds.
TELEVISION: *Commentator and host*: Monday Night Football (1974–76). *Mini-series*: Centennial. *Movies*: Hardcase, The 500-Pound Jerk, Babe, Mulligan's Stew, Mad Bull, Jimmy B. & Andre, Alcatraz: The Whole Shocking Story, Word of Honor (also exec. prod.), Maid in America. *Series*: Webster (also co-prod.).

KARTOZIAN, WILLIAM F.: Executive. b. San Francisco, CA, July 27, 1938. e. Stanford U., 1960; Harvard Law Sch., 1963. Deputy Attorney General State of CA, 1963–64; assoc. in law firm of Lillick, McHose, Wheat, Adams & Charles, San Francisco, 1964–65; corp. counsel and dir., Natl. Convenience Stores, Houston, 1965–67; v.p. and corp. counsel, United Artists Theatre Circuit, 1967–75; owner, Festival Enterprises, Inc., 1970–86; chmn. San Francisco Theatre Employers Assoc., 1973–76; Theatre Assoc. of CA, Inc., dir. 1972–86, v.p. 1974–75, pres. 1975–79, chmn. of bd. 1979–81; member, State of CA Industrial Welfare Comm. Amusement and Recreation Industries Wage Board, 1975–76; National Assoc. of Theatre Owners: dir. 1976–86, v.p. 1980–86, president 1988–present. Owner, Regency Enterprises, Inc., 1986–present; chmn. of bd., Lakeside Inn & Casino, Stateline, NV 1985–present. Member: Calif. Film Commission, 1988–present.
MEMBER: Stanford U. Alumni Assoc. dir. 1968–72, pres. 1971–72; dir. Stanford U. Athletic Board 1987–present, chmn. 1992–present; chmn. bd. of trustees, James T. Watkins IV Fund 1973–79; dir. Frontier Village, Inc. 1972–73; dir., Stanford Daily Publishing Corp. 1974–78; Variety Club Blind Babies Fdn.: trustee 1979–present, v.p. 1980–82, pres. 1982–85, pres. 1991–93; member: CA and TX bar assocs., American Judicature Society, Commonwealth Club of CA, Blackhawk Country Club.

KASDAN, LAWRENCE: Writer, Director. b. West Virginia, Jan. 14, 1949. e. U. of Michigan. Clio award-winning advertising copywriter, Detroit and LA before becoming screen writer. Became director with Body Heat (1981).
PICTURES: The Empire Strikes Back (co-s.p.), Raiders of the Lost Ark (co-s.p.), Continental Divide (s.p.), Body Heat (dir., s.p.), Return of the Jedi (co-s.p.), The Big Chill (co-exec. prod., dir., co-s.p.), Into the Night (actor), Silverado (prod., dir., co-s.p.), Cross My Heart (prod.), The Accidental Tourist (dir., co-prod., co-s.p.), Immediate Family (exec. prod.), I Love You to Death (dir., actor), Grand Canyon (dir., co-s.p.), Jumpin at the Boneyard (exec. prod.), The Bodyguard (s.p., co-prod.), Wyatt Earp (dir., co-prod., co-s.p.).

KASLOFF, STEVE: Writer. b. New York, NY, Nov. 13, 1952. e. Pratt Institute, 1974, cum laude. Writer/supvr., Young & Rubicam, 1974–76; writer/sprv., Ally & Gargano, 1976; writer/supvr., Marsteller Inc., 1976–79; writer/creative supvr., Scali, McCabe, Sloves, 1979–82. hired as youngest v.p., Columbia Pictures, 1982; promoted to sr. v.p., creative dir., Columbia, 1983. Exclusive screenwriting deal at Columbia, 1988–90. Sr. v.p. creative dir., 20th Century Fox, screenwriting deal, 1991–present. Member, WGA.
AWARDS: Winner of numerous Clio Awards and over 200 other awards & medals for creative work (trailers, TV commercials, radio commercials, posters, etc.) on such films

as Tootsie, Ghostbusters, Total Recall, Home Alone, Dances With Wolves, Terminator 2, Home Alone 2, Last Action Hero, etc. Has directed stage productions, commercials & special teaser trailers.

KASSAR, MARIO: Executive, Producer. b. Lebanon, Oct. 10, 1951. At age of 18 formed own foreign distribution co. Kassar Films International, specializing in sale, dist. and exhibition of films in Asia and Europe. In 1976 became partners with Andrew Vajna who had own dist. co., forming Carolco. First prod. First Blood, followed by Rambo: First Blood Part II. Became sole chmn. of Carolco in 1989.
PICTURES: *Exec. Prod.:* Angel Heart, Extreme Prejudice, Rambo III, Red Heat, Iron Eagle II, Deep Star Six, Johnny Handsome, Mountains of the Moon, Total Recall, Air America, Jacob's Ladder, L.A. Story, The Doors, Terminator 2: Judgment Day, Rambling Rose, Basic Instinct, Universal Soldier, Light Sleeper, Chaplin, Cliffhanger.

KASTNER, ELLIOTT: Producer. b. New York, NY, Jan. 7, 1933. e. U. of Miami, Columbia U. Was agent then v.p. with MCA, before becoming indep. prod., financing and personally producing 65 feature films in 25 yrs. Based in London, NY & LA.
PICTURES: Harper, Kaleidoscope, The Bobo, Sweet November, Sol Madrid, Michael Kohlaas, Laughter in the Dark, Night of the Following Day, Where Eagles Dare, A Severed Head, Tam Lin, The Walking Stick, X Y and Zee, The Nightcomers, Big Truck and Poor Clare, Face to the Wind, Fear Is the Key, The Long Goodbye, Cops and Robbers, Jeremy, 11 Harrowhouse, Spot, Rancho Deluxe, 92 in the Shade, Farewell My Lovely, Russian Roulette, Breakheart Pass, The Missouri Breaks, Swashbuckler, Equus, A Little Night Music, Black Joy, The Stick Up, The Medusa Touch, The Big Sleep, Absolution, Goldengirl, Yesterday's Hero, ffolkes, The First Deadly Sin, Death Valley, Man Woman and Child, Garbo Talks, Oxford Blues, Nomads, Heat, Angel Heart, Jack's Back, The Blob, White of the Eye, Zombie High, Never on Tuesday, Homeboy, A Chorus of Disapproval, The Last Party.

KATLEMAN, HARRIS L.: Executive. b. Omaha, NB, Aug. 19, 1928. e. UCLA. Joined MCA in 1949; in 1952 transferred to N.Y. as head of TV Packaging Dept. Left to join Goodson-Todman Prods. in 1955, where named v.p., 1956; exec. v.p., 1958; sr. exec. v.p., 1968. Was directly responsible for all programs prod. in L.A., including The Rebel, Branded, The Richard Boone Show (Emmy noms., Fame Award of Year), and Don Rickles Show, on which was exec. prod. Joined Metro-Goldwyn-Mayer in 1972 as v.p. of MGM-TV; promoted following year to pres. MGM-TV and sr. v.p. of MGM, Inc. Resigned as pres., MGM-TV September, 1977. Formed Bennett/Katleman Productions under contract to Columbia Pictures. Exec. prod.: From Here to Eternity, Salvage 1; 1980, named bd. chmn. 20th-Fox Television. Appointed pres. & CEO, Twentieth TV, 1982. Oversaw prod. of final years of M*A*S*H, as well as Mr. Belvedere, The Fall Guy, Trapper John M.D., L.A. Law, Hooperman, Anything But Love, Tracey Ullman Show, Alien Nation, The Simpsons, In Living Color. Resigned, May 1992. Formed Shadow Hill Prods. under contract to Twentieth.

KATSELAS, MILTON GEORGE: Director, Writer, Teacher, Painter. b. Pittsburgh, PA, Feb. 22, 1933. e. drama dept., Carnegie Inst. of Technology (now Carnegie-Mellon U.). Acting teacher owner, Beverly Hills Playhouse. Has exhibited paintings in 4 major exhibitions.
STAGE: Has directed more than 30 stage prod., including on Broadway The Rose Tattoo, Butterflies are Free, and Camino Real. Off-Broadway: Call Me By My Rightful Name, The Zoo Story. Awards: Recipient of the L.A. Drama Critics Circle Award, Drama Logue Best Director Award, NAACP and Tony Nominations for Best Director.
PICTURES: Butterflies Are Free, 40 Carats, Report to the Commissioner, When You Comin' Back Red Ryder?
TELEVISION: *Movies:* The Rules of Marriage, Strangers—The Story of a Mother and Daughter.

KATT, WILLIAM: Actor. b. Los Angeles, CA, Feb. 16, 1955. Son of actors Barbara Hale and Bill Williams. e. Orange Coast Coll. Majored in music, playing piano and guitar. Acted with South Coast Repertory Theatre, later working in productions at the Ahmanson and Mark Taper Theatres in L.A. Phoenix Rep (N.Y.): Bonjour La Bonjour. Regional: Sarah and Abraham, Days of Wine and Roses.
PICTURES: Carrie (debut, 1976), First Love, Big Wednesday, Butch and Sundance: The Early Days, Baby, Rising Storm, House, White Ghost, Wedding Band, Naked Obsession, Double X: The Name of the Game, House IV: Home Deadly Home, Desperate Motive.
TELEVISION: *Series:* The Greatest American Hero, Top of the Hill, Good Sports. *Movies:* Night Chase, The Daughters of Joshua Cabe, Can Ellen Be Saved?, Perry Mason Returns and several Perry Mason follow-ups (Murdered Madam, Avenging Ace, Scandalous Scoundrel, Lady in the Lake,

Notorious Nun, Shooting Star, Lost Love, Sinister Spirit), Swim Suit. *Specials:* Pippin, The Rainmaker.

KATZ, GLORIA: Producer, Writer. e. UCLA. Film Sch. Joined Universal Pictures as editor, cutting educational films. Later joined forces with Willard Huyck, whom she had met at U.C.L.A. Pair signed by Francis Ford Coppola to write and direct for his newly created company, American Zoetrope. Projects didn't materialize but Katz and Huyck teamed to write script for America Graffiti for director George Lucas.
PICTURES: American Graffiti (co-s.p.), Luk Lady (co-s.p.), French Postcards (co-s.p., prod.), Indiana Jones and the Temple of Doom (co.-s.p.), Best Defense (prod., co.-s.p.), Howard the Duck (prod., co.-s.p.).
TELEVISION: *Co-Producer, Co-Writer:* A Father's Homecoming, Mothers Daughters and Lovers.

KATZ, MARTY: Producer. b. Landsburg, West Germany, Sept. 2, 1947. e. UCLA, U. of Maryland. Served in Vietnam War as U.S. Army first lieut.; awarded Bronze Star as combat pictorial unit director. 1971, dir. of film prod., ABC Circle Films; 1976, exec. v.p., prod., Quinn Martin Prods; 1978–80, producer and consultant, Paramount Pictures' 1981–85, independent producer (Lost in America, Heart Like a Wheel). 1985, joined Walt Disney Prods. as sr. v.p., motion picture & TV prod. Named exec. v.p. motion picture and TV production, 1988–92. 1992–present, prod. Marty Katz Prods./Walt Disney Studios.

KATZ, NORMAN B.: Executive. b. Scranton, PA, Aug. 23, 1919. e. Columbia U. In U.S. Army 1941–46 as intelligence officer, airborne forces. Entered m.p. industry in 1947 with Discina Films, Paris, France, as prod. asst. Named exec. asst. to head of prod. in 1948. In 1950 named v.p. Discina Int'l. Films and in 1952 exec. v.p. In 1954 joined Associated Artists Prods. as foreign mgr.; named dir. of foreign operation in 1958. In 1959 became dir. of foreign operations for United Artists Associated. 1961 joined Seven Arts Associated Corp. of v.p. in chg. of foreign operations; named exec. v.p., Seven Arts Prods. Int'l. in 1964. Named exec. v.p. Warner Bros.—Seven Arts Int'l. in 1967. In 1969 appt. exec. v.p. and chief exec. off. Warner Bros. International and bd. mem. of Warner Bros. Inc. In 1974 named sr. v.p. int'l. div. of American Film Theatre. Pres. of Cinema Arts Associated Corp. 1979, exec. v.p. and bd. member, American Communications Industries and pres., chief exec. off. of ACI subsidiary, American Cinema; 1983, pres., The NORKAT Co., Also, bd. chmn., CEO, American Film Mktg. Assoc., 1985–87; chmn. Amer. Film Export Assn. 1988–92.

KATZENBERG, JEFFREY: Executive. b. 1950. Entered motion picture industry in 1975 as asst. to Paramount Pictures chmn. and CEO Barry Diller in NY. In 1977, became exec. dir. of mktg.; later same year moved to west coast as v.p. of programming for Paramount TV. Promoted to v.p., feature production for Paramount Pictures 1978; 2 years later assumed role of sr. v.p. prod. of m.p. div; 1982, pres. of prod., m.p. and TV, Paramount Pictures. Left to join The Walt Disney Company, 1984; chairman of The Walt Disney Studios since 1984.

KAUFMAN, HAL: Creative director, TV Writer, Producer. b. New York, NY, Dec. 16, 1924; e. U. of Texas, 1943–44; U. of Michigan, 1944–47. Started career as petroleum geologist, Western Geophysical Co., 1947–48; TV writer-prod-dir., KDYL-TV, Salt Lake City, 1948–49; prog. dir., WLAV-TV, Grand Rapids, 1949–51; prod. mgr., WOOD-TV, Grand Rapids, 1951–54; TV writer-prod., Leo Burnett Company, Chicago, 1954–56; TV writer-prod., Gordon Best Company, Chicago, 1957–58; sr. writer, TV/Radio creative dept., Needham, Louis & Brorby, Inc., 1959; vice-pres., asst. copy dir., Needham, Louis & Brorby, Inc., 1962; dir., TV, Radio prod., Needham, Louis & Brorby, Inc., 1963; dir., broadcast design, production, Needham, Louis & Brorby, Inc., 1964; assoc. creat. dir., asst. Exec. v.p., Needham, Harper & Steers, Inc., 1965; Creat. dir. L.A., 1966; Sr. v.p. and mem. bd. of dir., 1966. 1969, creative & marketing consultant in Beverly Hills. 1970 Exec. v.p., principle, Kaufman, Lansky Inc., Beverly Hills and San Diego; 1974 editor and publisher Z Magazine; program dir., Z Channel, Theta Cable TV. 1979, sr. v.p./adv. & p.r. & asst. to pres. & bd. chmn., World Airways, Inc. 1982-v.p., Creative director, Admarketing, Inc., Los Angeles. 1985, mktg. & adv. consultant copy dir., Teleflora, Inc.; pres. Hal Kaufman Inc., mktg. & adv. consultant; pres. Brochures on Video, library division, creators and prods. of promotional videos, distribs. religious videos to libraries; pres. Pious Publications, prods. and distribs. of religious videos. Member, Directors Guild of America, SAG, AFTRA. 1974.

KAUFMAN, LEONARD B.: Producer, Writer, Director. b. Newark, NJ, Aug. 31, 1927. e. NYU. In W.W.II served with Army Special Services writing and directing camp shows. Nat'l magazine writer, 1945–48; radio writer, including Errol Flynn Show, 1948–50; radio and TV writer, 1950–52. Headed own public relations firm: Kaufman, Schwartz, and Associates,

1952–64. Joined Ivan Tors Films as writer-prod., 1964. Films Corp., 1958.
PICTURES: Clarence the Cross-eyed Lion, Birds Do It (story).
TELEVISION: Daktari, Ivan Tors' Jambo, O'Hara U.S. Treasury (pilot feature and series). Producer: Hawaii-Five O, The New Sea Hunt, Scruples (mini-series), The Hawaiian (pilot), Writer: Knightrider, Dukes of Hazzard, Hawaii-Five O, Wet Heat (pilot), Hawaiian Heat, Island Sons (movie).

KAUFMAN, LLOYD: e. Yale Univ., 1969. From 1974–present, pres. of Troma, Inc.
PICTURES: The Girl Who Returned (prod., dir., s.p.), Cry Uncle (prod. mgr.), Joe (prod. asst.), Sugar Cookie (exec. prod., s.p.), Silent Night Bloody Night (assoc. prod.), Battle of Love's Return (dir., prod.), Sweet Savior (prod. mgr.), Mother's Day (assoc. prod.), Rocky (pre-prod. spvr.), Slow Dancing in the Big City (prod. spvr.), The Final Countdown (assoc. prod.), Squeeze Play (dir., prod.), Waitress (Co- dir., prod.), Stuck on You (co-dir., co-prod., co-s.p.), The First Turn-On (co-dir., co-prod.), Screamplay (exec. prod.), When Nature Calls (assoc. prod.), The Toxic Avenger (co-dir., co-prod., co-s.p., story), Blood Hook (exec. prod.), Girl School Screams (exec. prod.), Class of Nuke 'Em High (co-dir., co-prod.), Lust for Freedom (exec. prod.), Monster in the Closet (exec. prod.), Troma's War (Co-dir., co-prod., co-s.p., story), Toxic Avenger Part II (co-dir., co-prod., co-s.p., story), Fortress of Amerikkka (prod.), Toxic Avenger III: The Last Temptation of Toxie (co-dir., co-s.p., prod.), Class of Nuke 'Em High Part II: Subhumanoid Meltdown (co-s.p., co-prod., story), Sgt. Kabukiman N.Y.P.D. (co-dir., co-prod., co-s.p.), The Good the Bad and the Subhumanoid (co-s.p., co-prod., co-story).

KAUFMAN, PHILIP: Writer, Director, Producer. b. Chicago, IL, Oct. 23, 1936. e. U. of Chicago, Harvard Law Sch. Was teacher in Italy and Greece before turning to film medium.
PICTURES: Co-Writer only: The Outlaw Josey Wales, Raiders of the Lost Ark. Director: Goldstein (co-dir., co-s.p., co-prod.), Fearless Frank (also s.p., prod.), The Great North-field Minnesota Raid (also s.p., prod.), The White Dawn, Invasion of the Body Snatchers, The Wanderers (also co-s.p.), The Right Stuff (also s.p.), The Unbearable Lightness of Being (also co-s.p.), Henry & June (also co-s.p.), Rising Sun (also co-s.p.).

KAUFMAN, VICTOR: Executive. b. New York, NY, June 21, 1943. e. Queens Coll.; NYU Sch. of Law, J.D., 1967. Taught criminal law at UCLA before joining Wall St. law firm, Simpson Thacher & Bartlett. Joined Columbia Pictures as asst. general counsel, 1974. Named chief counsel, 1975; then made vice chmn. Columbia Pictures. Later exec. v.p. Columbia Pictures Industries and vice chmn. Columbia Pictures motion picture div. when conceived a new studio as a joint venture between Coca-Cola, Time Inc.'s Home Box Office and CBS, Inc. forming Tri-Star Pictures. Named chmn. and CEO Tri-Star, 1983. When Columbia Pictures and Tri-Star merged in late 1987, became pres. and CEO of new entity, Columbia Pictures Entertainment. In June 1988, dropped title of chmn. of Tri-Star.

KAUFMANN, CHRISTINE: Actress. b. Lansdorf, Graz, Austria, Jan. 11, 1945. e. school in Munich, Germany. Film debut as a dancer. Salto Mortale at 7 yrs of age.
PICTURES: Rosenrosli (Little Rosie), Schweigende Engel (Silent Angel), Maedchen in Uniform, Winter Vacation, The Last Days of Pompeii, Red Lips, Taras Bulba (U.S debut), Twon Without Pity, Murder in the Rue Morgue, Bagdad Cafe, Der Geschichtenerzahler.

KAURISMAKI, AKI: Director, Writer. b. Finland, April 4, 1957. Brother is filmmaker Mika Kaurismaki. First film credit was acting and writing his brother's The Liar in 1980. Directed short subjects: Rocky VI, Thru the Wire, Those Were the Days. Served as writer on brother's features: Jackpot 2, The Worthless (also actor), The Clan: The Tale of the Frogs, Rosso.
PICTURES: Director: The Saimaa Gesture (co-dir., with Mika), Crime and Punishment, Calimari Union, Shadows in Paradise, Hamlet Goes Business, Ariel, Leningrad Cowboys Go America, The Match Factory Girl, I Hired a Contract Killer, La Vie de Boheme (The Bohemian Life).

KAVNER, JULIE: Actress. b. Los Angeles, Sept. 7, 1951. e. San Diego State U. Professional debut as Brenda Morgenstern on TV's Rhoda, 1974–78.
TELEVISION: Series: Rhoda (Emmy Award, 1978), The Tracey Ullman Show, The Simpsons (voice). Special: The Girl Who Couldn't Lose (Afternoon Playbreak). Movies: Katherine, No Other Love, The Revenge of the Stepford Wives. Pilot: A Fine Romance. Guest: Lou Grant, Petrocelli, Taxi.
PICTURES: National Lampoon Goes to the Movies, Bad Medicine, Hannah and Her Sisters, Radio Days, Surrender, New York Stories (Oedipus Wrecks), Awakenings, Alice, This is My Life, Shadows and Fog.

STAGE: Particular Friendships (Off-Bdwy), Two for the Seesaw (Burt Reynolds' dinner theater, FL), It Had to Be You (Canada).

KAY, GILBERT LEE: Director, Writer. b. Chicago, IL, June 28. e. Los Angeles City Coll. Was asst. dir. at various studios from 1942–53; started directing on own in 1954. Formed Pearly Gate Productions, London.
PICTURES: Writer: Three Bad Sisters, The Tower, Ocean's 11, Comeback, Take Five, Fame!, Anything for Money, The Wrong Mrs. Wright, Now It Can Be Told, It Happened in Lisbon, The Secret Door, A Harvest of Evil (also dir.), Sometimes I Love You, White Comanche, Ragan, Devil May Care, Maybe September, The Oedipus Vendetta, The Lotus Affair, Candle in the Wind, Royal Flush.
TELEVISION: Directed: Treasury Men in Action, Man Behind the Badge, Reader's Digest, Passport to Danger, Hollywood Profile, Highway Patrol, Arabian Nights, Telephone Time, Silent Service, The Grey Ghost, Man with a Camera, Adventures in Paradise, Shotgun Slade, Perry Mason, Follow the Sun, Frontier Circus. Wrote: The Uncivil Engineer, 8:46 to Southampton.
PLAYS: Directed: Two Faced Coin, Some Call It Love, French Without Tears, Burlesque, London by Night, The Man from Madrid, Paris, With Love. Wrote and Directed: West End, Please Omit Flowers, The Girl from Soho.

KAY, GORDON: Producer. b. Montreal, Canada, Sept. 6, 1916; e. Williams Coll., M.A. Asst. prod. Republic 1946, assoc. prod., 1947. apptd. secy.-treas.; exec. asst. to head of prod. at Republic, Feb., 1951; prod., Univ. 1955; pres. Gordon Kay & Assoc., 1958.
PICTURES: Wild Frontier, Bandits of Dark Canyon, Oklahoma Badlands, Bold Frontiersman, He Rides Tall, Fluffy, Taggart, Gunpoint, Beardless Warriors.

KAYLOR, ROBERT: Director. b. Plains, MT, Aug. 1, 1934. e. Art Center Sch. of Design. Received awards at Cannes, San Francisco and Dallas Film Festivals, Guggenheim Fellow, Amer. Film Inst.
PICTURES: Derby, Carny, Nobody's Perfect.

KAZAN, ELIA: Director. b. Constantinople, Turkey, Sept. 7, 1909. e. Williams Coll., Yale Dramatic Sch. With Group Theatre as apprentice & stage mgr.; on stage, 1934–41; plays include: Waiting for Lefty, Golden Boy, Gentle People, Five-Alarm, Lilliom. Author (novels): The Arrangement, The Assassins, The Understudy, Acts of Love, The Anatolian, A Life (auto-biography, 1988).
THEATER: Director: Skin of Our Teeth, All My Sons, Streetcar Named Desire, Death of a Salesman, Cat on a Hot Tin Roof (co-dir.), One Touch of Venus, Harriet, Jocobowsky and the Colonel, Tea and Sympathy, Dark at the Top of the Stairs, J.B., Sweet Bird of Youth, Lincoln Center Repertory Theatre (co-dir., prod.), After The Fall, But For Whom Charlie.
PICTURES: Actor: City for Conquest, Blues in the Night. Director: A Tree Grows in Brooklyn, Boomerang, Sea of Grass, Gentleman's Agreement (Acad. Award, 1947), Pinky, Panic in the Streets, A Streetcar Named Desire, Viva Zapata, Man on a Tightrope, On the Waterfront (Acad. Award, 1954). Prod.-Dir.: East of Eden, Baby Doll, Face in the Crowd, Wild River, Splendor in the Grass, America America (also s.p.), The Arrangement (also s.p.), The Visitors, The Last Tycoon.

KAZAN, LAINIE: Singer, Actress. b. New York, NY, May 15, 1942. e. Hofstra U. On stage and performed in niteries.
PICTURES: Dayton's Devils, Lady in Cement, Romance of a Horse Thief, One from the Heart, My Favorite Year, Lust in the Dust, The Delta Force, The Journey of Natty Gann, Harry and the Hendersons, Beaches, Eternity, 29th Street, I Don't Buy Kisses Anymore, The Cemetery Club.
TELEVISION: Series: The Dean Martin Summer Show, Tough Cookies, Karen's Song. Pilot: Family Business, The Lainie Kazan Show. Movies: A Love Affair: The Eleanor and Lou Gehrig Story, A Cry for Love, Sunset Limousine, The Jerk Too, Obsessive Love. Guest: Too Close for Comfort, Dick Van Dyke Show, Beverly Hills 90210, Tales From the Crypt, Faerie Tale Theatre (Pinocchio), Hotel, Johnny Carson Show, Dean Martin, Merv Griffin, Joan Rivers, Amazing Stories, Pat Sajak Show, The Famous Teddy Z.

KAZANJIAN, HOWARD G.: Producer. b. Pasadena, CA, July 26, 1943. e. U. of Southern California Film Sch.; DGA Training Program. Exec. Prod.: The Making of Raiders of the Lost Ark.
PICTURES: Asst. Dir.: Camelot, Finian's Rainbow, The Wild Bunch, The Arrangement, The Front Page, The Hindenberg, Family Plot. Assoc. Prod.: Rollercoaster. Producer: More American Graffiti, Raiders of the Lost Ark, Return of the Jedi, Demolition Man.

KAZURINSKY, TIM: Actor, Writer. b. Johnstown, PA, March 3, 1950. Raised in Australia. Worked as copywriter for Chicago ad agency. Took acting class at Second City and quit job to become actor and head writer for Second City Comedy Troupe. Co-starred with John Candy in CTV/NBC's series Big

City Comedy, 1980. Joined cast of Saturday Night Live as writer-actor 1981–84.

PICTURES: *Actor*: My Bodyguard, Somewhere in Time, Continental Divide, Neighbors, Police Academy II: Their First Assignment, Police Academy III: Back in Training, About Last Night (also co-s.p.), Police Academy IV: Citizens on Patrol, For Keeps (s.p. only), Road to Ruin (also s.p.), Hot to Trot, Wedding Band, A Billion for Boris, Shakes the Clown.

TELEVISION: *Movies*: This Wife for Hire, Dinner at Eight.

KEACH, STACY: Actor, Director, Producer. b. Savannah, GA, June 2, 1942. Brother of actor James Keach. Began professional acting career in Joseph Papp's 1964 prod. of Hamlet in Central Park. Has won three Obie Awards, Vernon Rice Drama Desk Award for Macbird, Drama Desk Award, Tony Nomination for Indians.

PICTURES: The Heart Is a Lonely Hunter (debut, 1968), End of the Road, The Traveling Executioner, Brewster McCloud, Doc, The New Centurions, Fat City, Watched!, Life and Times of Judge Roy Bean, Luther, The Gravy Train, The Killer Inside Me, Conduct Unbecoming, Street People, The Squeeze, Slave of the Cannibal God, The Great Battle, Gray Lady Down, Up in Smoke, The Ninth Configuration (a.k.a. Twinkle Twinkle Killer Kane), The Long Riders (also exec. prod., co-s.p.), Nice Dreams, Road Games, Butterfly, That Championship Season, Class of 1999, False Identity, Milena.

TELEVISION: *Series*: Caribe, Mickey Spillane's Mike Hammer. *Movies*: All the Kind Strangers, Caribe, The Blue and the Gray, Princess Daisy, Murder Me Murder You, More Than Murder, Wait Until Dark, Mistral's Daughter, Hemingway, Mickey Spillane's Mike Hammer: Murder Takes All, The Forgotten, Mission of the Shark, Revenge on the Highway, Rio Diablo, Body Bags. *Director*: Incident at Vichy, Six Characters in Search of an Author.

STAGE: Long Day's Journey into Night, Macbird, Indians, Hamlet, Deathtrap, Hughie, Barnum, Cyrano de Bergerac, Peer Gynt, Henry IV Parts I & II, Idiot's Delight, Solitary Confinement.

KEACH, SR., STACY: Executive. b. Chicago, IL, May 29, 1914. Father of actors, Stacy and James. e. Northwestern U., B.S. & M.A. Was instructor in theatre arts at Northwestern and Armstrong Coll. and dir. at Pasadena Playhouse before entering industry. For 4½ yrs. was under contract at Universal Pictures; 3 yrs. at RKO; had own prod. on NBC, CBS. In 1946 began producing and directing industrial stage presentations for Union Oil Co. and from then on became full-time prod. of m.p. and stage industrial shows. In 1946 formed Stacy Keach Productions, of which he is pres. In addition to directing, producing and writing he occasionally appears as actor in films. Played Clarence Birds Eye on TV commercials as well as other commercials. Voiceovers/spokesman for many major American Cos.

KEATON, DIANE: Actress. b. Santa Ana, CA, Jan. 5, 1946. e. Santa Ana Coll. Appeared in summer stock and studied at Neighborhood Playhouse in N.Y. Made prof. debut in Bdwy. prod. of Hair (1968); then co-starred with Woody Allen in Play It Again, Sam, repeating role for film version. Off-B'way: The Primary English Class. Author: photography books: Reservations (co-ed.), Still Life. Directed 1982 short What Does Dorrie Want?

PICTURES: Lovers and Other Strangers (debut, 1970), The Godfather, Play It Again Sam, Sleeper, The Godfather Part II, Love and Death, I Will I Will . . . for Now, Harry and Walter Go to New York, Annie Hall (Acad. Award, 1977), Looking for Mr. Goodbar, Interiors, Manhattan, Reds, Shoot the Moon, The Little Drummer Girl, Mrs. Soffel, Crimes of the Heart, Radio Days, Heaven (dir. only), Baby Boom, The Good Mother, The Lemon Sisters (also prod.), The Godfather Part III, Father of the Bride, Manhattan Murder Mystery.

TELEVISION: *Movie*: Running Mates. *Guest*: Love American Style, The FBI, Mannix. *Director*: The Girl With the Crazy Brother, Twin Peaks, Wildflower (movie).

KEATON, MICHAEL: Actor. r.n. Michael Douglas. b. Coraopolis, PA, Sept. 5, 1951. Speech major, Kent State U. 2 years. Drove cab and ice-cream truck, worked for PBS station in Pittsburgh and appeared in regional theatre prods., while performing in local coffeehouses. Became mem. of improvisational troup Jerry Vale. Moved to L.A. where honed craft at Comedy Store and Second City Improv. Workshops as stand-up comic.

PICTURES: Night Shift (debut, 1982), Mr. Mom, Johnny Dangerously, Gung Ho, Touch and Go, The Squeeze, Beetlejuice, Clean and Sober, The Dream Team, Batman, Pacific Heights, One Good Cop, Batman Returns, Much Ado About Nothing, My Life, The Paper.

TELEVISION: *Series*: All's Fair, Mary, The Mary Tyler Moore Hour, Working Stiffs, Report to Murphy. *Movie*: Roosevelt and Truman.

KEEL, HOWARD: Actor. r.n. Harold Keel. b. Gillespie, IL, April 13, 1919. e. high school, Fallbrook, CA. Began career following George Walker scholarship award for singing, L.A.; appeared in plays, Pasadena Auditorium, concerts; won awards, Mis-

sissippi Valley and Chicago Musical Festivals. Stage debut: Carousel, 1945; principal role (Oklahoma).

PICTURES: The Small Voice (debut, 1948), Annie Get Your Gun, Pagan Love Song, Three Guys Named Mike, Show Boat, Texas Carnival, Callaway Went Thataway, Lovely to Look At, Desperate Search, I Love Melvin (cameo), Ride Vaquero, Fast Company, Kiss Me Kate, Calamity Jane, Rose Marie, Seven Brides for Seven Brothers, Deep in My Heart, Jupiter's Darling, Kismet, Floods of Fear, Big Fisherman, Armored Command, Day of the Triffids, The Man from Button Willow (voice), Waco, Red Tomahawk, The War Wagon, Arizona Bushwhackers.

PLAYS: Saratoga, No Strings, The Ambassador, Man of La Mancha.

TELEVISION: Series: Dallas. Guest: Zane Grey Theatre, Bell Telephone Hour, Tales of Wells Fargo, Death Valley Days, Here's Lucy, Sonny and Cher, The Love Boat, etc. Specials: A Toast to Jerome Kern, Roberta, Music of Richard Rodgers.

KEESHAN, BOB: Performer. b. Lynbrook, NY, June 27, 1927. e. Fordham U. As network page boy became assistant to Howdy Doody's Bob Smith and originated role of Clarabelle the Clown; created children's programs Time for Fun, Tinker's Workshop, Mister Mayor, Captain Kangaroo (1955–85).

KEITEL, HARVEY: Actor. b. Brooklyn, NY, May 13, 1939. Served in U.S. Marine Corps. Over 10 yrs. experience in summer stock repertory and little theatre after studying at Actors Studio with Lee Strasberg and Frank Corsaro. Starred in Martin Scorsese's student film Who's That Knocking at My Door?

THEATER: *NY*: Up to Thursday, Death of a Salesman, Hurlyburly, A Lie of the Mind.

PICTURES: Who's That Knocking at My Door? (debut, 1968), Mean Streets, Alice Doesn't Live Here Anymore, That's the Way of the World, Taxi Driver, Mother Jugs and Speed, Buffalo Bill and the Indians, Welcome to L.A., The Duellists, Fingers, Blue Collar, Eagle's Wing, Deathwatch, Saturn 3, Bad Timing, The Border, Exposed, La Nuit de Varennes, Corrupt, Falling in Love, Knight of the Dragon (Star Knight), Camorra, Off Beat, Wise Guys, The Men's Club, The Investigation (The Inquiry), The Pick-Up Artist, The Last Temptation of Christ, The January Man, The Two Jakes, Mortal Thoughts, Thelma & Louise, Two Evil Eyes (The Black Cat), Bugsy (Acad. Award nom.), Sister Act, Reservoir Dogs (also co-prod.), Bad Lieutenant, Point of No Return, Rising Sun, The Piano, Snake Eyes.

TELEVISION: *Movie*: The Virginia Hill Story. *Special*: This Ain't Bebop (Amer. Playhouse).

KEITH, BRIAN: Actor. b. Bayonne, NJ, Nov. 14, 1921. p. Robert Keith, actor. U.S. Marines, 1942–45; worked in stock co., radio shows, comm. films for TV; on Bdwy in Mr. Roberts, Darkness at Noon.

PICTURES: Arrowhead (debut, 1953), Jivaro, Alaska Seas, Bamboo Prison, Violent Men, Tight Spot, Five Against the House, Nightfall, Storm Center, Run of the Arrow, Chicago Confidential, Hell Canyon Outlaws, Dino, Appointment With a Shadow, Desert Hell, Fort Dobbs, Sierra Baron, Villa!, Violent Road, The Young Philadelphians, Ten Who Dared, The Deadly Companions, The Parent Trap, Moon Pilot, Savage Sam, The Pleasure Seekers, The Raiders, A Tiger Walks, Those Calloways, The Hallelujah Trail, The Rare Breed, Nevada Smith, The Russians Are Coming the Russians Are Coming, Way Way Out, Reflections in a Golden Eye, With Six You Get Egg Roll, Krakatoa: East of Java, Gaily Gaily, Suppose They Gave a War and Nobody Came, The McKenzie Break, Scandalous John, Something Big, The Yakuza, The Wind and the Lion, Joe Panther, Nickelodeon, Hooper, Meteor, Mountain Men, Charlie Chan and the Curse of the Dragon Queen, Sharky's Machine, Death Before Dishonor, Young Guns, Welcome Home.

TELEVISION: Numerous dramas on Studio One, Suspense, Philco Playhouse, etc. Series: Crusader, The Westerner, Family Affair, The Little People (The Brian Keith Show), Archer, Hardcastle and McCormick, Pursuit of Happiness, Heartland, Walter & Emily. Mini-Series: Centennial, The Chisholms. Movies: Second Chance, The Quest, The Loneliest Runner, In the Matter of Karen Ann Quinlan, The Seekers, Moviola: The Silent Lovers, World War III, Cry for the Strangers, 13 Days at the Alamo, Perry Mason: The Case of the Lethal Lesson, Lady in a Corner, The Gambler Returns: Luck of the Draw.

KEITH, DAVID: Actor, Director. b. Knoxville, TN, May 8, 1954. e. U. of Tennessee, B.A., speech and theater. Appearance at Goodspeed Opera House in musical led to role in CBS sitcom pilot, Co-Ed Fever.

PICTURES: The Rose, The Great Santini, Brubaker, Back Roads, Take This Job and Shove It, An Officer and a Gentleman, Independence Day, The Lords of Discipline, Firestarter, The Curse (dir. only), White of the Eye, The Further Adventures of Tennessee Buck (also dir.), Heartbreak

Hotel, The Two Jakes, Off and Running, Desperate Motive, Caged Fear, Distant Cousins.
TELEVISION: *Series:* Co-ed Fever, Flesh 'N' Blood, Local Heroes.*Movies:* Are You in the House Alone?, Friendly Fire, Gulag, Golden Moment—An Olympic Love Story, Guts and Glory: The Rise and Fall of Oliver North, Liar's Edge. *Mini-Series:* If Tomorrow Comes. Guest: Happy Days, Runaways.

KEITH, PENELOPE: O.B.E. Actress. b. Sutton, Surrey, Eng., 1939. London stage debut, The Wars of the Roses (RSC, 1964). Extensive theater work including The Norman Conquests, Donkey's Years, The Apple Cart, Hobson's Choice, Captain Brassbound's Conversion, Hay Fever. Film debut, Think Dirty, 1970.
PICTURES: Take a Girl Like You, Every Home Should Have One, Penny Gold, Priest of Love.
TELEVISION: *Series:* Kate, The Good Life, To the Manor Born, Executive Stress; *Movies-Specials:* Private Lives, The Norman Conquests, Donkey's Years.

KELLER, MARTHE: Actress. b. Basel, Switzerland, 1946. e. Stanislavsky Sch. Munich. Joined a Heidelberg repertory group and Schiller Rep. in Berlin. Started acting in France and attracted attention of U.S. directors after appearing in Claude Lelouch's And Now My Love. Has acted in over 50 plays in French, German, Eng. & Italian.
PICTURES: Funeral in Berlin, The Devil by the Tail, Give Her the Moon, Old Maid, Elle Court, Le Chute d'un corps, And Now My Love, Down the Ancient Staircase, Marathon Man, Black Sunday, Bobby Deerfield, Fedora, The Formula, The Amateur, Wagner, Femmes de Personne, Joan Luiu: But One Day in the Country, I Come on Monday Dark Eyes, Rouge Basier, The Artisan, Lapse of Memory.
TELEVISION: The Charthouse of Parma, The Nightmare Years.

KELLERMAN, SALLY: Actress. b. Long Beach, CA, June 2, 1936. m. Jonathan Krane. e. Hollywood H.S. Studied acting in N.Y. at the Actors Studio and in Hollywood with Jeff Corey. Recorded album Roll With the Feeling. Has done voice-overs for many commercials.
TELEVISION: *Guest:* Mannix, It Takes a Thief, Chrysler Theatre. *Mini-Series:* Centennial. *Movies:* For Lovers Only, Dempsey, Secret Weapons, September Gun, Drop Dead Gorgeous, Boris and Natasha (also assoc. prod.). *Specials:* Big Blonde, Verna: USO Girl, Elena, Faerie Tale Theatre, Dr. Paradise.
PICTURES: Reform School Girl (debut, 1959), Hands of a Stranger, The Third Day, The Boston Strangler, The April Fools, M*A*S*H (Acad. Award nom.), Brewster McCloud, Last of the Red Hot Lovers, Lost Horizon, Slither, Reflection of Fear, Rafferty and the Gold Dust Twins, The Big Bus, Welcome to L.A., The Mouse and His Child (voice), Magee and the Lady, A Little Romance, Serial, Head On (Fatal Attraction), Foxes, Loving Couples, Moving Violations, Lethal (KGB: The Secret War), Back to School, That's Life!, Meatballs III, Three For the Road, Someone to Love, You Can't Hurry Love, Paramedics (voice), All's Fair, Limit Up, The Secret of the Ice Cave, The Player, Doppelganger, Happily Ever After (voice), Younger and Younger.
THEATRE: Women Behind Bars, Holiday.

KELLEY, DeFOREST: Actor. b. Atlanta, GA, Jan. 20, 1920. e. Decatur Boys' H.S.
PICTURES: Fear in the Night, Variety Girl, Canon City, The Men, House of Bamboo, Man in the Gray Flannel Suit, Tension at Table Rock, Gunfight at the O.K. Corral, Raintree County, The Law and Jake Wade, Warlock, Where Love Has Gone, Marriage on the Rocks, Night of the Lepus, Star Trek: The Motion Picture, Star Trek II: The Wrath of Khan, Star Trek III: The Search for Spock, Star Trek IV: The Voyage Home, Star Trek V: The Final Frontier, Star Trek VI: The Undiscovered Country.
TELEVISION: Star Trek (series).

KELLEY PATRICK: Executive. Joined MCA in 1950 as agent; with them for 20 years; named v.p. in chg. of talent for Universal's theatrical and TV project in 1964. Left MCA in 1970 to form First Artists with star partners Barbra Streisand, Sidney Poitier, Paul Newman (later joined by Steve McQueen and Dustin Hoffman). Resigned 1975 as F.A. bd. chmn. to head Pan Arts Corp., prod. co. of which George Roy Hill is bd. chmn.
PICTURES: A Little Romance (exec. prod.), The Little Drummer Girl (exec. prod.), The World According to Garp (exec. prod.), Funny Farm (exec. prod.), Deadly Friend (exec. prod.).

KELLOGG, PHILIP M.: Executive. b. March 17, 1912, Provo, WA. e. UCLA. Special feature writer for Hearst papers and magazines, 1933–34; MGM story dept., production dept., Irving Thalberg unit, 1934–35; Warner Bros. Film editor, 1935–41; Berg-Allenberg Agency, 1941–50; U.S. Naval Reserve officer, 1941–46; William Morris Agency, 1950–present, co-head of m.p. dept., dir. WMA, Ltd., London.

KELLY, GENE: Actor, Director, Dancer. b. Pittsburgh, PA, Aug. 23, 1912. e. Pennsylvania State U., U. of Pittsburgh. Bricklayer, concrete mixer, soda clerk, dance instructor before going on stage, in N.Y. prods. (Leave It to Me, One for the Money, The Time of Your Life, Pal Joey). Special Academy Award for advancing dance films, 1951. Received American Film Institute Life Achievement Award, 1985.
THEATER: *Choreographer:* The Time of Your Life, Best Foot Forward, Billy Rose's Diamond Horsehoe. *Director:* Flower Drum Song.
PICTURES: For Me and My Gal (debut, 1942), Pilot No. 5, Du Barry Was a Lady, Thousands Cheer, The Cross of Lorraine, Cover Girl, Christmas Holiday, Anchors Aweigh (Acad. Award nom.), Ziegfeld Follies, Living in a Big Way, The Pirate, The Three Musketeers, Words and Music, Take Me Out to the Ball Game, On the Town (also co-dir.), Black Hand, Summer Stock, An American in Paris, Singin' in the Rain (also co-dir.), It's A Big Country, The Devil Makes Three, Love is Better Than Ever (cameo), Brigadoon, Crest of the Wave, Deep in My Heart, Invitation to the Dance (also dir.), It's Always Fair Weather (also co-dir.), The Happy Road (also dir., prod.), Les Girls, Marjorie Morningstar, The Tunnel of Love (dir. only), Inherit the Wind, Let's Make Love, Gigot (dir. only), What a Way to Go, A Guide for the Married Man (dir. only), The Young Girls of Rochefort, Hello Dolly! (dir. only), The Cheyenne Social Club (dir., prod. only), 40 Carats, That's Entertainment, That's Entertainment Part 2 (also dir.), Viva Knievel!, Xanadu, That's Dancing.
TELEVISION: *Series:* Going My Way, The Funny Side. *Specials:* Jack and the Beanstalk (also prod.; Emmy Award), The Gene Kelly Show, Gene Kelly in New York New York, Woman of the Year (dir. only), many others. *Mini-Series:* North and South, Sins.

KELLY, JIM: Actor. b. Paris, KY. e. U. of Louisville. Studied karate at univ., winning trophies and int'l. middleweight championship. Opened school for karate in L.A. Did modelling and TV commercials. Was technical advisor for fight scenes on Melinda and played role in it.
PICTURES: Enter the Dragon (debut), Black Belt Jones, Three the Hard Way.

KELLY, NANCY: Actress. b. Lowell, MA, March 25, 1921. e. Immaculate Conception Acad., N.Y.; St. Lawrence Acad., L.I.; Bentley Sch. for Girls. In number of pictures as child, and on stage in Susan and God (N.Y. prod. 1937). Returned to screen in Submarine Patrol (1938).
PICTURES: Tailspin, Jesse James, Stanley and Livingstone, Frontier Marshal, He Married His Wife, One Night in the Tropics, Sailor's Lady, Parachute Batallion, Fly By Night, To the Shores of Tripoli, Friendly Enemies, Tornado, Tarzan's Desert Mystery, Women in Bondage, Gamblers Choice, Show Business, Double Exposure, Song of the Sarong, Betrayal From the East, Follow That Woman, Woman Who Came Back, Murder in the Music Hall, Crowded Paradise, The Bad Seed.
STAGE: The Big Knife, Season in the Sun, 1950–51; Bad Seed, 1954–55 (Tony Award); The Gingerbread Lady (Nat'l tour); Remote Asylum.
TELEVISION: *Movies:* The Imposter (debut 1974), Murder at the World Series. *Guest:* Medical Center.

KELSEY, LINDA: Actress. b. Minneapolis, MN, July 28, 1946. e. U. of Minnesota, B.A.
TELEVISION: *Series:* Lou Grant (1977–81), Day by Day. *Movies:* The Picture of Dorian Gray, Something for Joey; Eleanor and Franklin: The White House Years, The Last of Mrs. Lincoln, A Perfect Match, Attack on Fear, His Mistress, Nutcracker, Baby Girl Scott. *Special:* Home Sweet Homeless. *Mini-Series:* Captains and the Kings.

KEMENY, JOHN: Producer. b. Budapest, Hungary. Producer for National Film Board of Canada, 1957–69. Formed International Cinemedia Center, Ltd. in 1969 in Montreal, as partner.
PICTURES: The Apprenticeship of Duddy Kravitz, White Line Fever, Shadow of the Hawk, Ice Castles, Atlantic City, Bay Boy, The Wraith, Quest for Fire (co-prod.), Nowhere to Hide (exec. prod.), Iron Eagle II.
TELEVISION: Murderers Among Us: The Simon Wiesenthal Story (co-prod.), Josephine Baker.

KEMP, JEREMY: Actor. b. Chesterfield, England, Feb. 3, 1935. e. Abbottsholme Sch., Central Sch. of Speech and Drama. Service with Gordon Highlanders. Early career on stage incl. Old Vic Theatre Company, 1959–61. Recent theatre: Celebration, Incident at Vichy, Spoiled, The Caretaker. National Theatre, 1979–80.
TELEVISION: Z Cars, The Lovers of Florence, The Last Reunion, Colditz, Brassneck, Rhinemann Exchange, Lisa, Goodbye, Henry VIII, St. Joan, The Winter's Tale, Unity, The Contract, Sadat, King Lear, Sherlock Holmes, George Washington, Peter the Great, The Winds of War, War and Remembrance, Slip-Up (The Great Paper Chase), Cop-out, Summers Lease, Prisoner of Honor, Duel of Hearts, Star Trek: The Next Generation (guest).
PICTURES: Dr. Terror's House of Horrors, Cast a Giant

Shadow, Operation Crossbow, The Blue Max, Assignment K, Twist of Sand, Strange Affair, Darling Lilli, The Games, Sudden Terror, The Blockhouse, Pope Joan, The Bellstone Fox, 7% Solution, A Bridge Too Far, East of Elephant Rock, Leopard in the Snow, Caravans, The Prisoner of Zenda, The Return of the Soldier, Top Secret!, When the Whales Came.

KEMPER, VICTOR J.: Cinematographer. b. Newark, NJ, April 14, 1927. e. Seton Hall, B.S. Engineer Channel 13, Newark 1949–54; Tech. supervisor EUE Screen Gems NY 1954–56; v.p. engineering General TV Network. Pres. VJK Prods.
  PICTURES: Husbands, The Magic Garden of Stanley Sweetheart, They Might Be Giants, Who is Harry Kellerman?, The Hospital, The Candidate, Last of the Red Hot Lovers, Shamus, The Friends of Eddie Coyle, Gordon's War, The Hideaways, The Gambler, The Reincarnation of Peter Proud, Dog Day Afternoon, Stay Hungry, The Last Tycoon, Mikey and Nicky, Slapshot, Audrey Rose, Oh God!, The One and Only, Coma, Eyes of Laura Mars, Magic, Night of the Juggler, And Justice for All, The Jerk, The Final Countdown, Xanadu, The Four Seasons, Chu Chu and the Philly Flash, Partner, Author! Author! National Lampoon's Vacation, Mr. Mom, The Lonely Guy, Cloak and Dagger, Secret Admirer, Pee Wee's Big Adventure, Clue, Bobo, Hot to Trot, Cohen and Tate, See No Evil, Hear Evil, Crazy People, FX2, Another You, Married to It, Beethoven.

KEMP-WELCH, JOAN: Freelance, TV Director, Producer, Actress. b. Wimbleton, Eng., 1906. First appearance on stage 1927. Subsequently many stage parts and stage directorial assignments. First appeared in films 1938. Films included 60 Glorious Years, They Flew Alone, The Citadel, Busman's Honeymoon. Over 200 repertory and touring productions. West End theatre prods. include: Dead on Nine, Vicious Circle, Our Town, Desire Under the Elms. Since 1954 TV dir. Received TV Oscar for Light Entert., 1958. Desmond Davis Award for services to TV 1963. Silver Dove Monte Carlo Award, 1961 for Electra. The Lover, awarded Prix Italia 1963. Many other productions, incl. musicals, ballet, dramas, series, outside broadcasts. Notably Galla, with Maria Callas, A Midsummer Night's Dream, Laudes Evangelli (Massine's ballet).

KENNEDY, BURT: Director. b. Muskegon, MI, Sept. 3, 1922. e. Ravenna H.S. U.S. Army 1942–46; awarded Silver Star, Bronze Star and Purple Heart with Oak Leaf Cluster. Began as writer of TV and film scripts, and was writer, producer and director of Combat series and many TV and theatrical westerns.
  PICTURES: The Canadians (also s.p.), Mail Order Bride (also s.p.), The Rounders (also s.p.), The Money Trap, Return of the Seven, The War Wagon, Welcome to Hard Times (also s.p.), Support Your Local Sheriff, The Good Guys and the Bad Guys, Young Billy Young (also s.p.), The Devil's Backbone, Dirty Dingus Magee, Support Your Local Gunfighter, Hannie Caulder, The Train Robbers (also s.p.), The Killer Inside Me, Wolf Lake (also s.p.), The Trouble with Spies (also prod., s.p.), Big Bad John (also s.p.), Suburban Commando.
  TELEVISION: Series: Combat (prod., writer) The Rounders (also writer), How the West Was Won, The Yellow Rose, Simon & Simon, Magnum P.I. Mini-Series: The Rhinemann Exchange. Movies: Shoot out in a One-Dog Town, Side kicks (also prod.), All the Kind Strangers, Kate Bliss and the Ticker Tape Kid, The Wild Wild West Revisited, The Concrete Cowboys, More Wild Wild West, The Alamo-Thirteen Days to Glory, Down the Long Hills, Once Upon a Texas Train (also prod., writer), Where the Hell's That Gold?!!? (also prod., writer).

KENNEDY, GEORGE: Actor. b. New York, NY, Feb. 18, 1925. f. orchestra leader at N.Y. Proctor Theatre, m. dancer with Le Ballet Classique in vaudeville. At 2 acted in touring co. of Bringing Up Father. At 7, disc jockey with his own radio show for children. Joined W.W.II Army at 17, earned two Bronze Stars and combat and service ribbons. In Army 16 years, became Capt. and Armed Forces Radio and TV officer. 1957, opened first Army Information Office, N.Y. Served as technical advisor to Phil Silvers's Sergeant Bilko TV series. Began acting in 1959 when discharged from Army.
  TELEVISION: Guest: Sugarfoot, Cheyenne. Series: Blue Knight, Sarge, Counterattack: Crime in America, Dallas. Movies: See How They Run, Sarge: The Badge or the Cross, Priest Killer, A Great American Tragedy, Deliver Us From Evil, A Cry in the Wilderness, The Blue Knight, The Archer: Fugitive from the Empire, Jesse Owens Story, Liberty, International Airport, Kenny Rogers as the Gambler III, The Gunfighters, What Price Victory, Good Cops Bad Cops, Final Shot: The Hank Gathers Story. Mini-Series: Backstairs at the White House.
  PICTURES: Little Shepard of Kingdom Come (debut, 1961), Lonely Are the Brave, The Man From the Diner's Club, Charade, Strait Jacket, Island of the Blue Dolphins, McHale's Navy, Mirage, In Harm's Way, The Sons of Katie Elder, Flight of the Phoenix, Shenandoah, Hush . . . Hush Sweet Charlotte, Hurry Sundown, The Dirty Dozen, Cool Hand Luke

(Acad. Award, supp. actor, 1967), The Ballad of Josie, Pink Jungle, Bandolero!, The Boston Strangler, Guns of the Magnificent Seven, The Good Guys and the Bad Guys, Airport, . . . tick . . . tick . . . tick, Zig Zag, Dirty Dingus Magee, Fool's Parade, Lost Horizon, Cahill: U.S. Marshal, Thunderbolt and Lightfoot, Airport 1975, Earthquake, The Human Factor, The Eiger Sanction, Airport '77, Mean Dog Blues, Death on the Nile, Brass Target, The Concorde—Airport 79, Death Ship, The Double McGuffin, Steel, Virus, Modern Romance, A Rare Breed, Search and Destroy, Wacko, Bolero, Chattanooga Choo Choo, The Delta Force, Radioactive Dreams, Creepshow 2, Born to Race, Demon Warp, Counterforce, Nightmare at Noon, Private Roads, Uninvited, The Terror Within, The Naked Gun, Esmeralda Bay, Ministry of Vengeance, Brain Dead, Hangfire, The Naked Gun 2-1/2, Driving Me Crazy, Distant Justice.

KENNEDY, KATHLEEN: Producer. Raised in Weaverville and Redding in No. Calif. e. San Diego State U. Early TV experience on KCST, San Diego, working as camera operator, video editor, floor director and news production coordinator. Produced talk show, You're On. Left to enter m.p. industry as prod. asst. on Steven Spielberg's 1941. Founding member and pres. of Amblin Entertainment.
  PICTURES: Raiders of the Lost Ark (prod. assoc.), Poltergeist (assoc. prod.), E.T.: The Extra-Terrestrial (prod.), Twilight Zone: The Movie (co-assoc. prod.), Indiana Jones and the Temple of Doom (assoc. prod.), Exec. prod. (with Frank Marshall): Gremlins, The Goonies, Back to the Future, The Color Purple (prod.), Young Sherlock Holmes (co-prod.), An American Tail, Innerspace, Empire of the Sun, Batteries Not Included, Who Framed Roger Rabbit, The Land Before Time, Indiana Jones and the Last Crusade, (prod. exec.), Dad, Always (prod.), Joe Versus the Volcano, Gremlins II, Hook (co-prod.), Noises Off, Alive, A Far Off Place, Jurassic Park. Exec. Prod: Schindler's List, A Dangerous Woman, The Flintstones.
  TELEVISION: Amazing Stories (spv. prod.), You're On (prod.), Roger Rabbit & the Secrets of Toontown (exec. prod.).

KENNEDY, SCOTT: Executive. r.n. Joseph W. Kennedy. b. New York, NY, Feb. 11, 1934. e. La Salle, NYU. Started as office boy at NBC in 1950, before studying acting in NY. Appeared on TV in The Defenders and The Naked City, in film Advise and Consent. Host of Scott Kennedy Luncheon radio show in 1964. Joined United Artists in Boston in 1967 as salesman. Named UA Chicago sls. mgr. (1969–72), Jacksonville branch mgr. (1972–8), southern div. mgr. (1978–9). 1980 named v.p. & asst. gen. sls. mgr. responsible for UA eastern sls. territories. 1983 joined Tri-Star Pictures as v.p. southern div. mgr. Dallas.

KENNEY, H. WESLEY: Producer, Director, stage, TV, film. b. Dayton, OH, Jan. 3, 1926. grad. Carnegie Inst. of Technology. 13 Emmy noms. Six-time Emmy winner; 1974–75 dir., All in the Family, dir. pilot for the Jeffersons; exec. prod. Days of Our Lives; 1979–81, dir., Ladies Man, Filthy Rich, Flo, 1981. Exec. prod. Young and Restless, 1981–86; exec. prod., General Hospital, 1986–89. Guest Instructor, UCLA; guest lecturer, Televisia: Mexico City. Dir: Ten Little Indians (Advent Th., L.A.).

KENSIT, PATSY: Actress. b. London, England, Mar. 4, 1968. Made film debut at the age of 4 in The Great Gatsby. Later appeared in commercials directed by Tony Scott and Adrian Lyne.
  PICTURES: The Great Gatsby (debut, 1974), Alfie Darling, The Blue Bird, Hanover Street, Absolute Beginners, Lethal Weapon 2, A Chorus of Disapproval, Chicago Joe and the Showgirl, Timebomb, Twenty-One, Blame It on the Bellboy, Beltenebros, Bitter Harvest.
  TELEVISION: BBC: Great Expectations, Silas Marner, Tycoon: The Story of a Woman, Adam Bede. U.S.: The Corsican Brothers.

KENT, JEAN: Actress. b. London, England, June 29, 1921. e. Marist Coll., Peekham, London; p. prof. Fields & Norrie. First stage appearance at 3 and at 10 played in parents' act; chorus girl at Windmill Theatre, London, 1935; 2 yrs. repertory; Screen debut: It's That Man Again, 1941.
  PICTURES: Trottie True, Her Favorite Husband, The Reluctant Widow, The Woman in Question, The Browning Version, Big Frame, Before I Wake, Shadow of Fear, Prince and the Showgirl, Bon Jour Tristesse, Grip of the Strangler, Beyond This Place, Please Turn Over, Bluebeard's Ten Honeymoons, Shout at the Devil, The Saving of Aunt Esther.
  TELEVISION: A Call on the Widow, The Lovebird, The Morning Star, November Voyage, Love Her to Death, The Lion and the Mouse, The Web, Sir Francis Drake series, Yvette, Emergency Ward 10, County Policy, Coach 7, Smile on the Face of the Tiger, No Hiding Place, Kipling, This Man Craig, The Killers, Vanity Fair, A Night with Mrs. Da Tanka, United serial. The Family of Fred, After Dark, Thicker than Water series, The Young Doctors, Brother and Sister, Up Pompei, Steptoe and Son, Doctor at Large, Family at War, K

is for Killing, Night School, Tycoon series, Crossroads (series), Lyttons Diary, Lovejoy (series), Missing Persons, After Henry (series), Shrinks (series).

KENT, JOHN B.: Theatre executive, Attorney. b. Jacksonville, FL, Sept. 5, 1939. e. Yale U., U. of Florida, Law Sch., NYU grad. sch. of law (L.L.M. in taxation, 1964). Partner in Kent, Ridge & Crawford, P.A.; Pres. & dir, Kent Investments, Inc. (1977 to present); dir. and off. Kent Theatres, Inc.; dir. & v.p. Kent Enterprises, Inc. (1961–present); v.p. and gen. counsel (1970 to present). Was pres. 1967–70 when resigned to devote full time to law practice. NATO dir. (1972) and Presidents' Advisory Cabinet, (1979 to present) v.p./dir. NATO of Fla., 1968 to present. Member of Rotary Club of Jacksonville, Fla. Bar Ass'n., American Bar Ass'n..

KENYON, CURTIS: Writer. b. New York, NY, March 12, 1914.
TV PLAYS: Cavalcade of America, Fireside Theatre, Schlitz Playhouse, U.S. Steel Hour, 20th Century-Fox Hour. Series: Hawaii 5-0.
PICTURES: Woman Who Dared, Lloyds of London, Wake Up and Live, Love and Hisses, She Knew All the Answers, Twin Beds, Seven Days' Leave, Thanks for Everything, Princess and the Pirate, Bathing Beauty, Fabulous Dorseys, Tulsa, Two Flags West, Mr. Ricco.

KERASOTES, GEORGE G.: Exhibitor. b. Springfield, IL. e. U. of Illinois, 1929–33; Lincoln Coll. of Law 1935–37. Past pres. Theatre Owners of Illinois. Past pres. Kerasotes Theatres, 1935–85. Past pres., Theatre Owners of America, 1959–60. Chmn. of board of TOA 1960–62; chmn. ACE Toll TV com.; bd. mem. NATO; treas., bd. of dir., mem. exec. comm., chmn. insurance comm. chmn., George Kerasotes Corp., GKC Theatres. Director St. Anthony's Hellenic Church—Hellenic Golf Classic. Director, Will Rogers Hospitals; Director, Pioneers. Robert W. Selig ShoWester of the Year, NATO, Las Vegas, 1992.

KERKORIAN, KIRK: Executive. b. Fresno, CA, June 6, 1917. e. Los Angeles public schools. Served as capt., transport command, RAF, 1942–44. Commercial air line pilot from 1940; founder Los Angeles Air Service (later Trans Intl. Airlines Corp.), 1948; Intl. Leisure Corp., 1968; controlling stockholder, Western Airlines, 1970; chief exec. officer, MGM, Inc., 1973–74; chmn. exec. comm., vice-chmn. bd., 1974–1978. Stepped down from exec. positions while retaining financial interest in MGM/UA.

KERNS, JOANNA: Actress. b. San Francisco, CA, Feb. 12, 1953. r.n. Joanna de Varona. Former gymnast, became dancer, appeared on tv commercials. Sister is olympic swimmer and tv commentator Donna de Varona. NY stage: Ulysses in Nighttown.
TELEVISION: Series: The Four Seasons, Growing Pains (also wrote one episode). Guest: Three's Company, Magnum P.I., Hill Street Blues, Hunter, etc. Movies: The Million Dollar Rip-Off, Marriage Is Alive and Well, Mother's Day on Walton's Mountain, A Wedding on Walton's Mountain, A Day of Thanks on Walton's Mountain, The Return of Marcus Welby M.D., A Bunny's Tale, The Rape of Richard Beck, Stormin' Home, Mistress, Those She Left Behind, Like Mother Like Daughter, The Preppie Murder, Blind Faith, Captive, The Nightman, Not in My Family, The Man With 3 Wives.
PICTURES: Coma, Cross My Heart, Street Justice.

KERR, DEBORAH: Actress. b. Helensburgh, Scotland, Sept. 30, 1921; e. Phyllis Smale Ballet Sch. m. Anthony Bartley. On stage 1939 in repertory. Began Brit. screen career 1940 in Major Barbara; voted "Star of Tomorrow" Motion Picture Herald-Fame Poll, 1942. Voted one of top ten British money-making stars in Motion Picture Herald-Fame Poll, 1947. Bdwy debut in Tea and Sympathy, 1953.
PICTURES: Major Barbara, Love on the Dole, Penn of Pennsylvania, Hatter's Castle, The Day Will Dawn (The Avengers), The Life and Death of Colonel Blimp, Perfect Strangers (Vacation From Marriage), I See a Dark Stranger (The Adventuress), Black Narcissus (Acad. Award nom.), The Hucksters (U.S. debut), If Winter Comes, Edward My Son, Please Believe Me, King Solomon's Mines, Quo Vadis, The Prisoner of Zenda, Thunder in the East, Dream Wife, Julius Caesar, Young Bess, From Here to Eternity (Acad. Award nom.), End of the Affair, The King and I (Acad. Award nom.), The Proud and the Profane, Tea and Sympathy, Heaven Knows Mr. Allison (Acad. Award nom.), An Affair to Remember, Bonjour Tristesse, Separate Tables (Acad. Award nom.), The Journey, Count Your Blessings, Beloved Infidel, The Sundowners (Acad. Award nom.), The Grass Is Greener, The Innocents, The Naked Edge, The Chalk Garden, The Night of the Iguana, Marriage On the Rocks, Casino Royale, Eye of the Devil, Prudence and the Pill, The Gypsy Moths, The Arrangement, The Assam Garden.
TELEVISION: Movies: A Woman of Substance, Reunion at Fairborough, Hold the Dream, Witness for the Prosecution.

KERR, FRASER: Actor. b. Glasgow, Scotland, Feb. 25, 1931. Early career in repertory. Tours of Canada and America. Ent.

TV 1956. Series incl. Emergency Ward 10, Dixon of Deck Green, Murder Bag. Many Shakespeare plays. Radio: BBC Drama Rep. Co., 39 Steps, The Ringer, The Bible, What Every Woman Knows, The Ruling Class.
STAGE & TELEVISION: Night Must Fall, Never a Cross Word, The Inside Man, On the Buses, Dr. Finlay's Casebook, Wicked Woman, Madelaine July, Doctor in the House, Counterstrike, Waggoner's Walk, Juno and the Paycock, Aquarius, Erv, Upstairs and Downstairs, Cover to Cover, Janine, Robert the Bruce, Caliph of Bagdad, Watch it, Sailor!, The Fosters, Weekend World, Doctor at Sea, Dads Army, Algernon Blackwood, Waiting for Sheila, Weekend Show, Mind Your Language, Yes, Minister, Dick Emery Show, Bottle Boys, The Hard Man, Brigadoon, Hair of the Dog.
PICTURES: What a Whopper, Carry on Regardless, Way of McEagle, Thomasina, Theatre of Death, Tom, Dick and Harriet, Granny Gets the Point, Nothing but the Night, The Lord of the Rings, Kidnapped, The Derelict, Bloomfield, Ace of Diamonds, Andy Robson, It's a Deal!, Howard's Way, One Step Beyond, The Trawler.
RECORD PRODUCER: Tales of Shakespeare Series, The Casket Letters of Mary Queen of Scots.

KERR, JOHN: Actor. b. New York, NY, Nov. 15, 1931. p. Geoffrey Kerr, actor, and June Walker, actress. e. Harvard U., B.A., Columbia U., M.A. Actor in summer stock, TV; on Broadway in Bernardine, Tea and Sympathy (Tony Award, 1954), All Summer Long. Left show business in 1970 to become attorney.
PICTURES: The Cobweb, Gaby, Tea and Sympathy, The Vintage, South Pacific, Girl of the Night, Pit and the Pendulum, Seven Women from Hell.
TELEVISION: Series: Arrest and Trial, Peyton Place. Mini-Series: Washington: Behind Closed Doors. Movies: Yuma, The Longest Night, Incident on a Dark Street.

KERSHNER, IRVIN: Director. b. Philadelphia, PA, April 29, 1923. e. Tyler Sch. of Fine Arts of Temple U., 1946; Art Center Sch., U. of Southern California. Designer, photography, adv., documentary, architectural; doc. filmmaker, U.S.I.S., Middle East, 1950–52; dir., cameraman, TV doc., Confidential File, 1953–55; dir.-prod.-writer, Ophite Prod.
PICTURES: Stakeout on Dope Street, The Young Captives, The Hoodlum Priest, A Face in the Rain, The Luck of Ginger Coffey, A Fine Madness, The Flim Flam Man, Loving, Up the Sandbox, S*P*Y*S, Return of a Man Called Horse, Eyes of Laura Mars, The Empire Strikes Back, Never Say Never Again, Wildfire (exec. prod. only), The Last Temptation of Christ (actor only), Orders, Robocop 2.
TELEVISION: Series: The Rebel, Naked City, numerous pilots and other nat'l. shows. Movies: Raid on Entebbe (theatrical in Europe), The Traveling Man. Pilot: Seaquest.

KERWIN, BRIAN: Actor. b. Chicago, IL, Oct. 25, 1949. e. USC.
PICTURES: Hometown USA (debut, 1979), Nickel Mountain, Murphy's Romance, King Kong Lives, Torch Song Trilogy, S.P.O.O.K.S., Hard Promises, Love Field.
TELEVISION: Series: The Young and the Restless (76–77), The Misadventures of Sheriff Lobo. Mini-Series: The Chisholms, The Blue and the Gray, Bluegrass. Movies: A Real American Hero, Power, Miss All-American Beauty, Intimate Agony, Wet Gold, The Greatest Thing That Almost Happened, Challenger, Switched at Birth, Against Her Will: An Incident in Baltimore. Special: Natica Jackson (Tales of the Hollywood Hills). Guest: St. Elsewhere, The Love Boat, B.J. and the Bear, Roseanne, Murder She Wrote, Simon & Simon, Highway to Heaven.
THEATRE: NY: Emily (Theatre World Award), Lips Together Teeth Apart. LA: Strange Snow (LA Drama Critics Award), Who's Afraid of Virginia Woolf?, A Loss of Roses, Torch Song Trilogy.

KEYES, EVELYN: Actress. b. Port Arthur, TX, Nov. 20, 1919. e. high school. Began career as a dancer in night clubs. Autobiography: Scarlett O'Hara's Younger Sister (1977).
PICTURES: The Buccaneer, Union Pacific, Gone with the Wind, Slightly Honorable, Before I Hang, The Face Behind the Mask, Here Comes Mr. Jordan, Ladies in Retirement, The Adventures of Martin Eden, Flight Lieutenant, The Desperadoes, Nine Girls, A Thousand and One Nights, The Jolson Story, The Thrill of Brazil, The Mating of Millie, Johnny O'Clock, Enchantment, Mrs. Mike, Mr. Soft Touch, The Prowler, The Killer That Stalked New York, Smuggler's Island, The Iron Man, One Big Affair, Shoot First, 99 River Street, Hell's Half Acre, Top of the World, Seven Year Itch, Around the World in 80 Days, Return to Salem's Lot, Wicked Stepmother.
TELEVISION: Murder She Wrote.

KEYLOUN, MARK: Actor. b. Dec. 20, 1960. e. Georgetown U. Worked in New York theatre.
PICTURES: Those Lips Those Eyes, Sudden Impact, Forty-Deuce, Mike's Murder.
TELEVISION: Evergreen, War Stories: The Mine.

KIDDER, MARGOT: Actress. b. Yellowknife, Canada, Oct. 17, 1948.
PICTURES: Gaily Gaily (debut, 1969), Quackser Fortune Has a Cousin in the Bronx, Sisters, The Gravy Train, Black Christmas, The Great Waldo Pepper, 92 in the Shade, The Reincarnation of Peter Proud, Superman, Mr. Mike's Mondo Video, The Amityville Horror, Willie and Phil, Superman II, Heartaches, Shoot the Sun Down, Some Kind of Hero, Trenchcoat, Superman III, Little Treasure, GoBots (voice), Superman IV: The Quest for Peace, Miss Right, Mob Story, White Room, A Quiet Day in Belfast, Crime and Punishment.
TELEVISION: Series: Nichols (1971–72), Shell Game. Movies: Suddenly Single, The Bounty Man, Honky Tonk, Louisiana, The Glitter Dome, Picking Up the Pieces, Vanishing Act, Body of Evidence, To Catch a Killer. Specials: Bus Stop, Pygmalion. Guest: Murder She Wrote. Director: White People, Love 40.

KIDMAN, NICOLE: Actress. b. Hawaii, 1967. m. actor Tom Cruise. Raised in Australia. Made acting debut at 14 in Australian film Bush Christmas.
PICTURES: Dead Calm, Days of Thunder, Billy Bathgate, Far and Away, Flirting, Malice, My Life.
TELEVISION: Mini-Series: Vietnam, Bangkok Hilton.

KIEL, RICHARD: Actor. b. Detroit, MI, Sept. 13, 1939.
PICTURES: The Phantom Planet, Eegah!, The Magic Sword, Roustabout, The Human Duplicators, Las Vegas Hillbillies, A Man Called Dagger, Skidoo, The Longest Yard, Flash and the Firecat, Silver Streak, The Spy Who Loved Me, Force 10 from Navarone, They Went Thataway and Thataway, Moonraker, The Humanoid, So Fine, Hysterical, Cannonball Run II, Pale Rider, Think Big, The Giant of Thunder Mountain (also co-s.p., co-exec. prod.).
TELEVISION: Series: The Barbary Coast, Van Dyke & Company. Movies: Now You See It Now You Don't, The Barbary Coast (pilot).

KILEY, RICHARD: Actor. b. Chicago, IL, Mar. 31, 1922. e. Loyola U. Started prof. career radio, Jack Armstrong, Tom Mix, Ma Perkins, etc.
STAGE: Streetcar Named Desire (touring co.), Misalliance, Kismet, Time Limit, Redhead (Tony Award), No Strings, Man of LaMancha (Tony Award), Her First Roman, The Incomparable Max, Voices, Absurd Person Singular, All My Sons.
PICTURES: The Mob, The Sniper, Eight Iron Men, Pick-Up on South Street, Blackboard Jungle, Phenix City Story, Spanish Affair, Pendulum, The Little Prince, Looking for Mr. Goodbar, Endless Love, Jurassic Park (voice).
TELEVISION: Series: A Year in the Life (Emmy Award, 1988). Mini-series: The Thorn Birds (Emmy Award, 1983), George Washington, If Tomorrow Comes, A.D. Movies: Night Gallery, Incident in San Francisco, Murder Once Removed, Jigsaw, Friendly Persuasion, The Macahans, Angel on My Shoulder, Golden Gate, Isabel's Choice, Pray TV, The Bad Seed, Do You Remember Love, My First Love, The Final Days, Gunsmoke: The Last Apache, Separate But Equal, Absolute Strangers. Special: Mastergate.

KILLIAM, PAUL: Producer, Performer. b. Mass., Sept. 12, 1916. e. Harvard U. News supervisor, WOR-Mutual; prod.-performer TV Hometown. Matinee in N.Y. units for CBS-TV Morning Show, NBC-TV Home Show; ind. prod. cartoons, shorts, comedies: prod. film series, Paul Killiam Show, Movie Museum, Silents Please.

KILMER, VAL: Actor. b. Los Angeles, CA, Dec. 31, 1959. m. actress Joanne Whalley. e. Hollywood's Professional's Sch., Juilliard, NY. NY stage: Electra and Orestes. Co-wrote and starred in How It All Began (later presented at Public Theatre), Henry IV Part One, 'Tis Pity She's a Whore. Broadway debut, Slab Boys. Also: As You Like It (Gutherie MN), Hamlet (Colorado Shakespeare Fest.).
PICTURES: Top Secret! (debut, 1984), Real Genius, Top Gun, Willow, Kill Me Again, The Doors, Thunderheart, True Romance, The Real McCoy, Tombstone.
TELEVISION: Movies: The Murders in the Rue Morgue, The Man Who Broke 1000 Chains, Gore Vidal's Billy the Kid.

KIMBLEY, DENNIS: Executive. Early career in Kodak Testing Dept. responsible for quality control motion picture films. Joined Marketing Division 1966. Chairman BKSTS FILM 75 and FILM 79 Conference Committee. President BKSTS 1976–78. Governor, London International Film School, 1983. Bd. member, British Board of Film Classification; dir. of Children's Film Unit.

KING, ALAN: Actor, Producer. b. New York, NY, Dec. 26, 1927. Stars semi-annually at Sands Hotel, Las Vegas. Author, Anybody Who Owns His Own Home Deserves It, Help I'm a Prisoner in a Chinese Bakery.
TELEVISION: Guest/Host: The Tonight Show, Kraft Music Hall. Prod-star NBC-TV specials: Comedy is King, On Location: An Evening With Alan King at Carnegie Hall, etc. Mini-Series: Seventh Avenue. Movies: Return to Earth (co-exec. prod. only), How to Pick Up Girls (also exec. prod.), Pleasure Place.

STAGE: The Impossible Years, The Investigation, Dinner at Eight, The Lion in Winter, Something Different. Host: Alan King: Inside the Comic Mind (Comedy Central).
PICTURES: Actor: Hit the Deck, Miracle in the Rain, The Girl He Left Behind, The Helen Morgan Story, On the Fiddle, Bye Bye Braverman, The Anderson Tapes, Just Tell Me What You Want, Prince of the City (cameo), Author! Author!, I the Jury, Lovesick, Cat's Eye, You Talkin' To Me?, Memories of Me (also co-prod.), Enemies a Love Story, The Bonfire of the Vanities, Night and the City. Producer: Happy Birthday Gemini, Cattle Annie and Little Britches (co-prod.), Wolfen (exec. prod.).

KING, ANDREA: Actress. r.n. Georgette Barry; b. Paris, France, Feb. 1,1919. e. Edgewood H.S., Greenwich, CT. m. N.H. Willis, attorney. Started career on N.Y. stage, following high school; in Growing Pains & Fly Away Home, Boy Meets Girl, Angel Street (Boston); Life with Father (Chicago); signed by Warner, 1943. Screen debut as Georgette McKee in The Ramparts We Watch, 1940.
PICTURES: Hotel Berlin, God is My Co-Pilot, The Very Thought of You, The Man I Love, The Beast With Five Fingers, Shadow of a Woman, Roughly Speaking, My Wild Irish Rose, Ride the Pink Horse, Mr. Peabody and the Mermaid, Song of Surrender, Southside 1-10001, I Was a Shoplifter, Dial 1119, Lemon Drop Kid, Mark of the Renegade, World in His Arms, Red Planet Mars, Darby's Rangers, Band of Angels, Daddy's Gone A-Hunting, The Linguini Incident, The Color of Evening.
TELEVISION: Movie: Prescription Murder. Specials: Dream Girl, Officer and the Lady, Witness for the Prosecution. Guest: Fireside Theatre, many others.
TELEVISION: Maya series, King International Corp.

KING, LARRY: Talk Show Host, Writer. b. Brooklyn, NY, Nov. 19, 1933. Started as disc jockey on various Miami radio stations from 1958–64. Became host of radio talk show, broadcast from Miami before moving to Arlington, VA, in 1978. Show has run since then on Mutual Broadcasting System. Host of CNN tv talk show since 1985, Larry King Live. Starred in tv special Larry King Extra. Author: Larry King by Larry King, Tell It to the King, Mr. King You're Having a Heart Attack, Tell Me More. Columnist for Miami Beach Sun-Reporter, Sporting News, USA Today. Appeared in films Ghostbusters, Eddie and the Cruisers II: Eddie Lives, The Exorcist III.

KING, PERRY: Actor. b. Alliance, OH, Apr. 30, 1948. e. Yale. Studied with John Houseman at Juilliard. Bdwy debut 1990 in A Few Good Men.
PICTURES: Slaughterhouse-Five, The Possession of Joel Delaney, The Lords of Flatbush, Mandingo, The Wild Party, Lipstick, Andy Warhol's Bad, The Choirboys, A Different Story, Search and Destroy, Class of 1984, Killing Hour, The Clairvoyant, Switch.
TELEVISION: Guest: Medical Center, Hawaii Five-O, Apple's Way, Cannon. Series: The Quest, Riptide, Almost Home. Mini-Series: Aspen, The Last Convertible, Captain and the Kings. Movies: Foster and Laurie, The Cracker Factory, Love's Savage Fury, City in Fear, Inmates: A Love Story, Golden Gate, Helen Keller: The Miracle Continues, Stranded, Perfect People, Shakedown on Sunset Strip, The Man Who Lived at the Ritz, Disaster at Silo 7, The Prize Pulitzer, Danielle Steel's Kaleidoscope, Only One Survived, Something to Live For. Pilot: Half 'n' Half.

KING, PETER: Executive, Barrister-at-law. b. London, England, Mar. 22, 1928. e. Marlborough, Oxford U. (MA - honors). Bd., Shipman & King Cinemas Ltd., 1956; borough councillor, 1959–61; chmn., London & Home counties branch, CEA, 1962–63; pres., CEA, 1964; mang. dir. Shipman & King Cinemas Ltd., 1959–68. Chmn. & mang. dir. Paramount Pictures (U.K.) Ltd. Britain, 1968–70; mang. dir., EMI Cinemas and Leisure Ltd., 1970–74. Chmn. & mang. dir. King Publications/pub. Screen Intl., 1974–89; pres., Screen Intl., 1989–90; chmn. & mang. dir., Rex Publications Ltd., 1990–; pub., Majesty, 1990–; pub. Preview.

KING, STEPHEN: Writer. b. Portland, ME, Sept. 21, 1947. e. Univ. of Maine at Orono (B.S.). Best-selling novelist specializing in thrillers many of which have been adapted to film by others: Carrie, The Shining, The Dead Zone, Christine, Cujo, Children of the Corn, Firestarter, Cat's Eye, Stand By Me (The Body), The Running Man, Pet Sematary, Misery, Apt Pupil, The Lawnmower Man, The Dark Half, Needful Things. TV adaptations: Salem's Lot, IT, Sometimes They Come Back, The Tommyknockers.
PICTURES: Knightriders (actor), Creepshow (s.p., actor), Children of the Corn (s.p.), Silver Bullet (s.p.), Maximum Overdrive (dir., s.p., actor), Creepshow II (actor), Pet Sematary (s.p., actor), Sleepwalkers (s.p., actor).
TELEVISION: Series: Golden Years (creator, writer).

KING, ZALMAN: Actor, Director, Writer. b. Trenton, NJ, 1941. r.n. Zalman King Lefkowitz. m. writer Patricia Knop.
PICTURES: Actor: The Ski Bum, You've Got to Walk It Like You Talk It or You'll Lose the Beat, Neither by Day Nor Night,

Some Call It Loving, Trip with the Teacher, Sammy Somebody, The Passover Plot, Blue Sunshine, Tell Me a Riddle, Galaxy of Terror. *Exec. Prod.*: Roadie (also co-story), Endangered Species, Siesta. *Prod./Writer*: Nine-1/2 Weeks. Director-Writer: Wildfire, Two Moon Junction, Wild Orchid, Wild Orchid II: Two Shades of Blue.

TELEVISION: *Series*: The Young Lawyers, Red Shoe Diaries (dir. episodes). *Guest*: Alfred Hitchcock Presents, Land of the Giants, Gunsmoke, Adam 12, Charlie's Angels, etc. *Movies*: The Dangerous Days of Kiowa Jones, Stranger on the Run, The Young Lawyers (pilot), The Intruders, Smile Jenny You're Dead, Like Normal People, Red Shoe Diaries (exec. prod., dir., co-writer), Lake Consequence (co-prod., co-writer).

KINGMAN, DONG: Fine Artist. b. Oakland, CA, Mar. 31, 1911. e. Hong Kong 1916–1920. 1928, mem. motion picture co., Hong Kong branch; 1935; began to exhibit as fine artist in San Francisco; promotional, advertising or main title artwork for following films: World of Suzie Wong, Flower Drum Song, 55 Days of Peking, Circus World, King Rat, The Desperados, The Sand Pebbles, Lost Horizon-1973. 1966–7, created 12 paintings for Universal Studio Tour for posters and promotion; 1968, cover painting for souvenir program for Ringling Bros.-Barnum and Bailey Circus; treasurer for Living Artist Production since 1954; Exec. V.P. 22nd-Century Films, Inc. since 1968, Prod. & dir. short, Hongkong Dong. Also short subject film Dong Kingman, filmed and directed by James Wong Howe.

KINGSLEY, BEN: Actor. b. Yorkshire, England, Dec. 31, 1943. r.n. Krishna Banji. Started career with Salford Players, amateur co. in Manchester. Turned pro in 1966 and appeared on London stage at a Chichester Festival Theatre. 1967, joined Royal Shakespeare Co., where starred in A Midsummer Night's Dream, Tempest, Measure for Measure, Merry Wives of Windsor, Volpone, Cherry Orchard, Hamlet, Othello, Judgement, Kean (NY). Played Squeers in Nicholas Nickleby in 1980 in London.

PICTURES: Fear is the Key (debut, 1972), Gandhi (Acad. Award, 1982), Betrayal, Turtle Diary, Harem, Maurice, Testimony, Pascali's Island, Without a Clue, Slipstream, The 5th Monkey, The Children, Necessary Love, Romeo-Juliet (voice), Bugsy (Acad. Award nom.), Freddie as F.R.O. 7 (voice), Sneakers, Dave, Searching for Bobby Fisher, Schindler's List.

TELEVISION: Silas Marner, Kean, Oxbridge Blues, Camille, The Sealed, Train, Sahara Secret, Murderers Among Us: The Simon Wiesenthal Story.

KINGSLEY, DOROTHY: Writer. (Mrs. William W. Durney). b. New York, NY, Oct. 14, 1909. e. Detroit Arts and Crafts Acad. Radio writer for Bob Hope, 1938; Edgar Bergen, 1939–43.

PICTURES: The Skipper Surprised His Wife, Bathing Beauty, Easy to Wed, On an Island With You, Broadway Rhythm, Here We Go Again, Look Who's Laughing, Date With Judy, Neptune's Daughter, Two Weeks with Love, Angels in the Outfield, Texas Carnival, It's a Big Country, When in Rome, Small Town Girl, Dangerous When Wet, Kiss Me Kate, Seven Brides for Seven Brothers, Jupiter's Darling, Don't Go Near the Water, Pal Joey, Green Mansions, Can-Can, Pepe, Half a Sixpence, Valley of the Dolls.

TELEVISION: Created series, Bracken's World.

KINGSLEY, WALTER: Executive. b New York, NY, Oct. 20, 1923. e. Phillips Acad., Andover; Amherst Coll., B.A., 1947. Charter member Big Brothers of Los Angeles. WCOP, Boston, 1948–50; Ziv Television Programs, Inc., 1950–58; President, Independent Television Corp. (ITC), 1958–62. Member bd. dir Big Brothers of Amer.; pres. Kingsley Co., 1962–66; exec. v.p. Wolper Prods. Metromedia Prods. Corp., 1966–72; faculty, Inter-Racial Council of Business Opportunity, N.Y.; 1972–82, pres., Kingsley Company, Commercial Real Estate; 1983–present, special consultant, American Film Inst.; bd. mem.: Big Brothers/Big Sisters of America; Big Brothers of Greater Los Angeles.

KINOY, ERNEST: Writer. Started career in radio writing sci. fic. programs (X Minus One, Dimension X). Wrote for nearly all early dramatic shows, including Studio One, Philco Playhouse, Playhouse 90.

PICTURES: Brother John, Buck and the Preacher, Leadbelly, White Water Summer (co-s.p.).

TELEVISION: The Defenders (Emmy Award, 1964), Naked City, Dr. Kildare, Jacob and Joseph (special), David, the King (special), Roots I & II, Victory at Entebbe, Skokie, Murrow, The President's Plane is Missing, Stones for Ibarra, Gore Vidal's Lincoln, The Fatal Shore.

KINSKI, NASTASSJA: Actress. r.n. Nastassja Nakszynski. b. Berlin, Germany, Jan. 24, 1960. m. prod and talent agent, Ibrahim Moussa. Daughter of late actor Klaus Kinski.

PICTURE: Falsche Bewegung (1975), To the Devil a Daughter, Passion Flower Hotel, Stay as You Are, Tess, One From the Heart, Cat People, For Your Love Only, Exposed, The Moon in the Gutter, Unfaithfully Yours, The Hotel New

Hampshire, Maria's Lovers, Paris Texas, Revolution, Symphony of Love, Harem, Malady of Love, Silent Night, Torrents of Spring, On a Moonlit Night, Magdalene, The Secret, Night Sun, Faraway So Close!

KIRBY, BRUNO: Actor. b. New York, NY, Apr. 28, 1949. Also acted as B. Kirby Jr., and Bruce Kirby Jr. On Bdwy. 1991 in Lost in Yonkers.

PICTURES: The Harrad Experiment, Cinderella Liberty, The Godfather Part 2, Baby Blue Marine, Between the Lines, Almost Summer, Where the Buffalo Roam, Borderline, Modern Romance, This is Spinal Tap, Birdy, Flesh and Blood, Tin Men, Good Morning Vietnam, Bert Rigby You're a Fool, When Harry Met Sally . . ., We're No Angels, The Freshman, City Slickers, Hoffa (unbilled), Golden Gate.

TELEVISION: *Series*: The Super. *Movies*: All My Darling Daughters, A Summer Without Boys, Some Kind of Miracle, Million Dollar Infield. *Special*: Mastergate. *Guest*: Room 222, Columbo, Kojak, Emergency, It's Garry Shandling's Show, Tales From the Crypt, Fallen Angels (I'll Be Waiting).

KIRK (BUSH), PHYLLIS: Actress. b. Syracuse, NY, Sept. 18, 1926. Perfume repr. model, Conover Agcy.; Bdwy play debut in My Name Is Aquilon; actress, summer stock; screen debut in Our Very Own; B'way production of Point of No Return. Worked as interviewer-host on all three major networks Executive with ICPR and Stone Associates. Joined CBS News in Los Angeles, 1978; 1988 named v.p. media relations Stone/Hallinan Associates.

TELEVISION: *Series*: The Red Buttons Show, The Thin Man.

PICTURES: Our Very Own, A Life of Her Own, Two Weeks with Love, Mrs. O'Malley and Mr. Malone, Three Guys Named Mike, About Face, Iron Mistress, Thunder Over the Plains, House of Wax, Crime Wave, River Beat, Canyon Crossroads, Johnny Concho, Back From Eternity, City After Midnight, The Sad Sack.

KIRKLAND, SALLY: Actress. b. NY, NY, Oct. 31, 1944. e. Actors Studio, studied acting with Uta Hagen and Lee Strasberg. Achieved notoriety in the 1960s for on-stage nudity (Sweet Eros, Futz), for work in experimental off-off Bdwy theater and as part of Andy Warhol's inner circle. Appeared as featured actress in over 25 films and countless avant-garde shows, before winning acclaim (and Acad. Award nom.) as the star of Anna (1987). 1983 founded Sally Kirkland Acting Workshop, a traveling transcendental meditation, yoga and theatrical seminar. Formed Artists Alliance Prods. with Mark and David Buntzman, 1988.

THEATER: The Love Nest, Futz, Tom Paine, Sweet Eros, Witness, One Night Stand of a Noisy Passenger, The Justice Box, Where Has Tommy Flowers Gone?, In the Boom Boom Room (L.A., Drama-Logue's best actress award, 1981), Largo Desolato.

PICTURES: The Thirteen Most Beautiful Woman (1964), Blue, Futz!, Coming Apart, Going Home, The Young Nurses, The Way We Were, Cinderella Liberty, The Sting, Candy Stripe Nurses, Big Bad Mama, Bite the Bullet, Crazy Mama, Breakheart Pass, A Star is Born, Pipe Dreams, Hometown U.S.A., Private Benjamin, The Incredible Shrinking Woman, Human Highway, Love Letters, Fatal Games, Talking Walls, Anna, Melanie Rose (High Stakes), Crack in the Mirror (White Hot), Paint It Black, Cold Feet, Best of the Best, Revenge, Bullseye, Two Evil Eyes, JFK, In the Heat of Passion, The Player, Blast 'Em, Primary Motive, Double Threat, Forever, Cheatin' Hearts (also co-exec. prod.).

TELEVISION: *Movies*: Kansas City Massacre, Death Scream, Stonestreet: Who Killed the Centerfold Model?, Georgia Peaches, Heat Wave, The Haunted. Double Jeopardy, The Woman Who Loved Elvis, Double Deception. *Specials*: Willow B—Women in Prison, Summer, Largo Desolato. *Series*: Falcon Crest. *Guest*: Roseanne

KIRKWOOD, GENE: Producer. Company: Kanter-Kirkwood Entertainment.

PICTURES: Rocky (Acad. Award, picture, 1976), New York New York (assoc. prod.), Comes a Horseman, Uncle Joe Shannon, The Idolmaker, A Night in Heaven, Gorky Park, The Keep, The Pope of Greenwich Village, Legs Diamond, Ironweed, UHF (co-prod.).

KITT, EARTHA: Actress, Singer. b. Columbia, SC, Jan. 26, 1928. Professional career started as dancer in Katherine Dunham group; toured U.S., Mexico & Europe with group, then opened night club in Paris; in Orson Welles stage prod. of Faust for European tour; N.Y. night clubs; stage in U.S., New Faces of 1952; at Macambo Hollywood, 1953. Author: Thursday's Child, A Tart Is Not a Sweet, Alone with Me, Confessions of a Sex Kitten.

PICTURES: New Faces (debut, 1954), The Mark of the Hawk (a.k.a. Accused), St. Louis Blues, Anna Lucasta, Synanon, Friday Foster, Erik the Viking, Ernest Scared Stupid, Boomerang.

TELEVISION: *Guest*: Batman (as Catwoman), I Spy, Miami Vice. *Movies*: Lt. Schuster's Wife, To Kill a Cop. *Special*: THEATRE: NY: New Faces of 1952, Shinbone Alley, Mrs.

Patterson, The Skin of Our Teeth, The Owl and the Pussycat, Timbuktu.

KLEES, ROBERT E.: Executive. b. New York, NY, Feb. 21, 1927. e. Duke U., 1947–51; U. of California Graduate Sch. of Management, 1973–75. U.S. Navy, 1944–46; Union Carbide Corp., 1951–57; director of communications, Beckman Instruments, Inc., 1957–69; co-founder and v.p. mktg., International Biophysics Corp., 1969–73; sr. v.p., mktg., Deluxe Laboratories, Inc., div. of 20th Century-Fox Film Corp, 1975–83. Member: Navy League of U.S., U.S. Naval Institute, Sons of American Revolution.

KLEIN, ALLEN: Producer. b. New Jersey, Dec. 18, 1931. e. Upsala. Pres. ABKCO Films, a division of ABKCO Music & Records, Inc.
PICTURES: Force of Impulse, Pity Me Not, Charlie is My Darling, Stranger in Town, Sympathy for the Devil, Mrs. Brown You've Got A Lovely Daughter, The Stranger Returns, The Silent Stranger, Come Together, Pearl & The Pole, Let It Be, Gimme Shelter, El Topo, Blind Man, The Concert for Bangladesh, The Holy Mountain, The Greek Tycoon, Personal Best, It Had to Be You, The Rolling Stones Rock and Roll Circus.

KLEIN, HAROLD J.: Executive. b. New York, NY, e. U. of West Virginia, New York Law Sch. Reviewer, sales staff. Showman's Trade Review; booker, Brandt Theatres; booker, later vice-pres., gen. mgr., JJ Theatres, 1941–59; account exec., exec. v.p., dir. of world-wide sales, ABC Films, Inc., N.Y., Pres., Klein Film Assn.; exec. v.p., Plitt Theatres, Inc. to Nov., 1985; pres., H.J.K. Film Associates, also acting consultant to P.E.G. (Plitt Entertainment Gp.). Retired.

KLEIN, MALCOLM C.: Executive. b. Los Angeles, CA, Nov. 22, 1927. e. UCLA, grad., 1948; U. of Denver. Prod. dir. management, KLAC-TV (KCOP), L.A., 1948–52; acct. exec., KABC-TV, 1952–56; asst. gen. sales mgr., KABC-TV, 1956–59; exec. vice-pres. gen. mgr., NTA Broadcasting, N.Y., 1959; v.p., gen. mgr., RKO-General-KHJ-TV, 1960; joined National General Corp. 1968, vice-pres. Creative Services and Marketing. Pres. National General Television Productions, Inc., Pres. NGC Broadcasting Corp.; 1971, pres. Filmways TV Presentations; 1972, pres. Malcolm C. Klein & Assoc. mgmt. & mktg. consultants; 1973 gen'l. exec. Sterling Recreation Organization & Gen'l Mgr. Broadcast Division; pres., American Song Festival 1976; memb. of faculty, UCLA, USC. Exec. v.p., Telease Inc. & American Subscription Television; 1981, sr. v.p., mng. dir., STAR-TV (subscription TV); 1982, sr. v.p., InterAmerican Satellite TV Network. 1983: Pres. Malcolm C. Klein & Assoc., management consultant. exec. dir. programming, Interactive Network.

KLEIN, ROBERT: Actor, Comedian. b. New York, NY, Feb. 8, 1942. e. Alfred U, Yale Drama School. Was member of Chicago's Second City comedy group. Comedy albums: Child of the '50s (Grammy nom.), Mind Over Matter, New Teeth, Let's Not Make Love.
TELEVISION: Series: Comedy Tonight, Robert Klein Time, TV's Bloopers and Practical Jokes. Movies: Your Place or Mine, Poison Ivy, This Wife for Hire. Guest: The Tonight Show, ABC Comedy Special, George Burns Comedy Week, Twilight Zone, Late Night With David Letterman. Also appeared in HBO comedy specials.
THEATRE: NY: The Apple Tree, Morning Noon and Night, New Faces of 1968, They're Playing Our Song (Tony Award nom.), The Sisters Rosensweig.
PICTURES: The Landlord, The Owl and the Pussycat, Rivals, The Bell Jar, Hooper, Nobody's Perfekt, The Last Unicorn (voice), Tales from the Darkside—The Movie.

KLEINER, HARRY: Writer, Producer. b. Philadelphia, PA, 1916. e. Temple U., B.S.; Yale U., M.F.A.
PICTURES: Screenplay: Miss Sadie Thompson, Salome, Carmen Jones, Garment Jungle (also prod.), Fantastic Voyage, Bullitt (co-s.p.), Le Mans, Extreme Prejudice, Red Heat (co-s.p.).
TELEVISION: Writer: Rosenberg Trial.

KLEISER, RANDAL: Director, Producer. b. Lebanon, PA, July 20, 1946. e. U. of Southern California.
PICTURES: Street People (s.p.). Director: Grease, The Blue Lagoon, Summer Lovers (also s.p.), Grandview U.S.A., Flight of the Navigator, North Shore (exec. prod., story only), Big Top Pee-Wee, Getting it Right (also prod.), White Fang, Return to the Blue Lagoon (exec. prod. only), Honey I Blew Up the Kid.
TELEVISION: Movies: All Together Now, Dawn: Portrait of a Teenage Runaway, The Boy in the Plastic Bubble, The Gathering. Series: Marcus Welby, M.D., The Rookies, Starsky and Hutch, Family.

KLINE, FRED W.: Publicist. b. Oakland, CA, May 17, 1918. e. U. of California, Berkeley. M.P. pub. rel. since 1934; pres. The Fred Kline Agency; pres. Kline Communications Corporation; Owner, Fred Kline Agency, Inc.; Kline Communications Corp.; Fred W. Kline Prod., Inc.; Capitol News Service, Sacramento;

L.A. News Bureau; Capitol Radio News Service, Inc.; Advisor, Calif. Film Commission. Member, Regional Filming Task Force Committee, Los Angeles City Council.

KLINE, KEVIN: Actor. b. St. Louis, MO, Oct. 24, 1947. m. actress Phoebe Cates. e. Indiana U. Studied at Juilliard Theater Center (1968–72), and became founding member of John Houseman's The Acting Company, touring in classics, including The School for Scandal, She Stoops to Conquer, The Three Sisters, and modern works. Bdwy. debut in musical, The Robber Bridegroom (1977).
THEATER: Understudied Raul Julia in Lincoln Center's The Threepenny Opera; On the Twentieth Century (Tony Award, 1978), Loose Ends, The Pirates of Penzance (Tony Award, 1981), Richard III, Henry V (Central Park), Arms and the Man, Hamlet, Much Ado About Nothing, Hamlet (1990, also dir.), Measure for Measure.
PICTURES: Sophie's Choice (debut, 1982), The Pirates of Penzance, The Big Chill, Silverado, Violets Are Blue, Cry Freedom, A Fish Called Wanda (Acad. Award, supp. 1988), The January Man, I Love You to Death, Soapdish, Grand Canyon, Consenting Adults, Chaplin, Dave.
TELEVISION: Series: Search For Tomorrow (1976–77). Specials: The Time of Your Life, Hamlet (also co-dir.).

KLINGER, TONY: Producer, Director, Writer. Pres. Avton Communications & Entertainment Inc. b. London, 1950. Ent. m.p. industry, 1966.
PICTURES: The Kids are Alright, Extremes, The Butterfly Ball, Mr. J, The Festival Game, Rock of Ages, Promo Man, Rachel's Man, Gold, Shout at the Devil (assoc. prod.), Electric Sound Sandwich, Deep Purple Rises Over Japan, Riding High (co-prod.).
TELEVISION: Series: You Can, Starsigns, Make the Grade (exec. prod.).

KLUGMAN, JACK: Actor. b. Philadelphia, PA, April 27, 1922. e. Carnegie Tech. Appeared on Broadway in Saint Joan, Stevedore; later understudied in Mister Roberts, taking over the doctor role; recent stage work includes Gypsy, The Odd Couple (on tour and stock), I'm Not Rappaport, Three Men on a Horse.
PICTURES: Timetable (debut, 1956), Twelve Angry Men, Cry Terror, The Scarface Mob, Days of Wine and Roses, I Could Go on Singing, The Yellow Canary, Act One, Hail Mafia, The Detective, The Split, Goodbye Columbus, Who Says I Can't Ride a Rainbow?, Two Minute Warning.
TELEVISION: Guest: The Defenders (Emmy Award for role in Blacklist segment), The FBI, Ben Casey, 90 Bristol Court. Series: Harris Against the World, The Odd Couple (Emmy Awards, 1971, 1973), Quincy M.E., You Again?. Movies: Fame is the Name of the Game, Poor Devil, The Underground Man, One of My Wives is Missing. Mini-Series: Around the World in 80 Days.

KNIGHT, SHIRLEY: Actress. b. Goessell, KS, July 5, 1936. e. Lake Forest Coll., D.F.A., 1978. Won 1976 Tony Award for Kennedy's Children.
PICTURES: Five Gates to Hell (debut, 1959), Ice Palace, The Dark at the Top of the Stairs (Acad. Award nom.) The Couch, Sweet Bird of Youth (Acad. Award nom.), House of Women, Flight from Ashiya, The Group, Dutchman (Best Actress, Venice Film Fest.), Petulia, The Counterfeit Killer, The Rain People, Juggernaut, Secrets, Beyond the Poseidon Adventure, Endless Love, The Sender, Prisoners, Panther Squad.
TELEVISION: Movies: The Outsider, Shadow Over Elveron, Friendly Persuasion, Medical Story, Return to Earth, 21 Hours at Munich, The Defection of Simas Kudirka, Champions: A Love Story, Playing for Time (Emmy nom.), Billionaire Boys Club, Bump in the Night, Shadow of a Doubt, To Save a Child, When Love Kills: The Seduction of John Hearn. Specials: The Country Girl, The Lie. Guest: The Equalizer (Emmy nom.), thirtysomething (Emmy Award).

KNOTTS, DON: Actor. b. Morgantown, WV, July 21, 1924. e. U. of West Virginia, U. of Arizona. Drafted into U.S. Army where became part of show called Stars and Gripes, teamed with comedian Mickey Shaughnessy. After schooling resumed, was offered teaching fellowship but went to New York to try acting instead. Started out in radio show Bobby Benson and the B Bar B's. Appeared on TV, leading to role in No Time for Sergeants on Bdwy.; appeared in film version.
PICTURES: No Time for Sergeants (debut, 1958), Wake Me When It's Over, The Last Time I Saw Archie, It's a Mad Mad Mad Mad World, Move Over Darling, The Incredible Mr. Limpet, The Ghost and Mr. Chicken, The Reluctant Astronaut, The Shakiest Gun in the West, The Love God?, How to Frame a Figg (also co-story), The Apple Dumpling Gang, No Deposit No Return, Gus, Herbie Goes to Monte Carlo, Hot Lead and Cold Feet, The Apple Dumpling Gang Rides Again, The Prize Fighter, Ther Private Eyes, Cannonball Run II, Pinocchio and the Emperor of Night (voice).
TELEVISION: Series: Search for Tomorrow (1953–5), Steve Allen Show, Andy Griffith Show (played Barney Fife; won 5 Emmy Awards), The Don Knotts Show, Three's

Kno-Koe

Company, What a Country, Matlock. *Movies*: I Love a Mystery, Return to Mayberry.

KNOWLES, PATRIC: Actor. r.n. Reginald Lawrence Knowles. b. Horsforth, Yorkshire, England, Nov. 11, 1911. Joined Abby Repertory Theatre, 1930; Oxford Playhouse Repertory, 1932–33. Film debut (Ireland) in Irish Hearts, 1934; on London stage in By Appointment; U.S. m.p. debut in Charge of the Light Brigade, 1936; served in Canadian RAF & as civilian instructor USAF, W.W.II.
PICTURES: Honours Easy, Mister Hobo, Two's Company, Give Me Your Heart, It's Love I'm After, Expensive Husbands, Adventures of Robin Hood, How Green Was My Valley, Forever and a Day, Of Human Bondage, Bride Wore Boots, Ivy, Kitty, Monsieur Beaucaire, Dream Girl, Big Steal, Quebec, Three Came Home, Mutiny, Tarzan's Savage Fury, Jamaica Run, Flame of Calcutta, World Ransom, Khyber Patrol, No Man's Woman, Band of Angels, Auntie Mame, The Way West, In Enemy Country, The Devil's Brigade, Chisum, The Man, Terror in the Wax Museum, Arnold.

KNOX, ALEXANDER: Actor. b. Strathroy, Ont., Jan. 16, 1907. e. Western Ontario U. Author, novels: Bride of Quietness, Night of the White Bear, The Enemy I Kill, Raider's Moon, The Kidnapped Surgeon; plays, Old Master, The Closing Door, Red On White. Screenplays: collaboration credit on The Judge Steps Out, Sister Kenny.
TELEVISION: Potsdam, Tinker Tailor Soldier Spy, Suez, Churchill And The Generals, Helen and Teacher, Empire, Darwin, Oppenheimer, The Last Place on Earth, Lovejoy.
STAGE: (N.Y.) Romeo and Juliet, The Three Sisters, Jupiter Laughs, Jason, The Closing Door; (London) King of Nowhere, Geneva, In Good King Charles' Golden Days, The Jealous God, Winter Journey, Henry VIII, Return to Tyassi, Burnt Flower Bed, When We Dead Awaken.
PICTURES: The Sea Wolf, This Above All, Commandos Strike at Dawn, None Shall Escape, Over 21, Wilson, Sign of the Ram, Judge Steps Out, Sister Kenny, Tokyo Joe, I'd Climb the Highest Mountain, Two of a Kind, Man in the Saddle, Son of Dr. Jekyll, The Greatest Love, Saturday's Hero, Paula, Sleeping Tiger, Divided Heart, The Night My Number Came Up, Reach for the Sky, High Tide at Noon, Davy, Hidden Fear, Chase a Crooked Shadow, The Vikings, Two-Headed Spy, Operation Amsterdam, Intent to Kill, Wreck of the Mary Deare, Oscar Wilde, These Are the Damned, The Share Out, The Longest Day, Man in the Middle, Woman of Straw, Mr. Moses, Crack in the World, Modesty Blaise, Khartoum, Accident, How I Won the War, Villa Rides, Shalako, Fraulein Doktor, Skullduggery, Puppet on a Chain, Nicholas and Alexandra, Holocaust 2000 (The Chosen), Gorky Park, Joshua Then and Now.

KNOX, GORDON: Producer. b. Greenville, TX. e. U. of Missouri. In addition to making documentary films for several years has been employed by Warner Bros., and Walter Wanger Prods. Joined Princeton Film Center in 1940; Pres. SKS Prod. Inc., Santa Fe, NM Pres., PFC Productions, Inc., Princeton, NJ.

KOCH, HOWARD: Writer. b. New York, NY, Dec. 12, 1902. e. St. Stephen's Coll., 1922, B.A.; Columbia Law Sch., 1925. LL.B. Hon. degree Doctor of Human Letters, Bard Coll., 1972. Playwright (Give Us This Day, In Time to Come, Straitjacket). Began screen career collab. s.p. The Sea Hawk. Radio: wrote War of the Worlds play for Orson Welles' broadcast. book: The Panic Broadcast (Little, Brown & Co.); Academy Award best s.p. (Casablanca). As Time Goes By, Memoirs of a Writer in Hollywood, New York and Europe published by Harcourt, Brace and Jovanovich.
PICTURES: The Letter, Shining Victory, In This Our Life, Casablanca, Mission to Moscow, Letter From an Unknown Woman, The Thirteenth Letter, The War Lover, The Fox, Loss of Innocence, No Sad Songs for Me, Sergeant York, Three Strangers, The Intimate Stranger.

KOCH, HOWARD W.: Producer, Director. b. New York, NY, Apr. 11, 1916. Runner on Wall St. Began film career in Universal's contracts and playdate dept. in NY; asst. cutter, 20th-Fox; asst. dir., 20th-Fox, Eagle Lion, MGM; 2nd unit dir., freelance; In 1953, joined Aubrey Schenck Prod. forming Bel Air Prods., made films for U.A.; 1961–64, prod. Frank Sinatra Enterprises; v.p., chg. prod., Paramount Pictures Corp., 1964–66, Past pres. of the Academy of Motion Picture Arts and Sciences, 1977–79. On June 11, 1977, elected to the National Board of Directors Guild of America for two year term. 1980 honored by NATO as prod. of year. 1985 Silver Medallion Award of Honor, Motion Picture Television Fund. Produced eight Academy Award shows, 1972–1983. Has had a 24 year relationship with Paramount as exec., prod., and dir. 1990, received Jean hersholt Humanitarian Award, honored by Amer. Society of Cinematographers.
TELEVISION: *Director*: Miami Undercover, The Untouchables, Maverick, Cheyenne, Hawaiian Eye. *Movies*: The Pirate (prod.), Hollywood Wives (1985 mini-series), Crossings (1986 mini-series). Specials: Ol' Blue Eyes Is Back (prod.), Oscar's Best Actors (prod., dir.), Oscar's Best Movies (prod., dir.), Who Loves Ya Baby (prod.), On the Road with Bing (prod., dir.), The Stars Salute the Olympics (prod.).
PICTURES: Executive Producer: Come Blow Your Horn, Sergeants Three, Manchurian Candidate, X-15, Robin and the 7 Hoods, None But the Brave, The President's Analyst, For Those Who Think Young, Dragonslayer. Producer: War Paint, Beachhead, Yellow Tomahawk, Desert Sands, Fort Yuma, Frontier Scout, Ghost Town, Broken Star, Crimes Against Joe, Three Bad Sisters, Emergency Hospital, Rebel in Town, The Black Sheep, Pharaoh's Curse, Tomahawk Train, Revolt at Fort Laramie, War Drums, Voodoo Island, Hellbound, The Dalton Girls, The Odd Couple, On a Clear Day You Can See Forever, Plaza Suite, Star Spangled Girl, Last of the Red Hot Lovers, Jacqueline Susann's Once Is Not Enough, Some Kind of Hero, Airplane II: The Sequel, Collision Course. A Howard W. Koch Production: A New Leaf, Airplane!, Ghost. Producer/Director: Badge 373. Director: Jungle Heat, Shield for Murder, Big House USA, Fort Bowie, Violent Road, Untamed Youth, Born Reckless, Frankenstein 1970, Andy Hardy Comes Home, The Last Mile, Girl in Black Stockings.

KOCH, HOWARD W., JR.: Producer. b. Los Angeles, CA, Dec. 14, 1945. Was asst. dir. and in other industry posts before turning to production. Pres. & chief exec. off., Rastar (Peggy Sue Got Married, The Secret of My Success, Nothing in Common, Violets Are Blue, Amazing Chuck and Grace prod. under presidency); 1987, set up own prod. co. at De Laurentiis Entertainment Group. Oct. 1987: named president of the De Laurentiis Entertainment Group, Resigned April 1988 to produce independently.
PICTURES: Heaven Can Wait, The Other Side of Midnight, The Frisco Kid (exec. prod.). Co-prod./prod.: The Idolmaker, Gorky Park, Honky Tonk Freeway, The Keep, A Night in Heaven, The Pope of Greenwich Village, Rooftops, The Long Walk Home, Necessary Roughness, Wayne's World, The Temp, Sliver, Wayne's World 2.

KOCH, JOANNE: Executive Director, The Film Society of Lincoln Center. b. NY, NY, Oct. 7, 1929. e. Goddard College, B.A. political science, 1950. Dept. of Film, Museum of Modern Art, as circulation asst., film researcher, motion picture stills archivist, 1950. Early 1960s, technical dir., film dept. MOMA, supervised the implementation of MOMA's film preservation program. 1967, asst. to publisher of Grove Press, active in preparation of Grove's case in I Am Curious Yellow censorship trial. Joined film div., Grove, first in distribution then as tech. dir. and prod. coord. 1971 joined Film Society of Lincoln Center as prog. dir. of Movies-in-the-Parks. June, 1971 made admin. dir. Exec. dir. of N.Y. Film Festival, Film Comment magazine, Film-in-Education, New Directors/New Films, annual Film Society Tribute and Walter Reade Theater at Lincoln Center.

KOENEKAMP, FRED J.: Cinematographer. b. Los Angeles, CA, Nov. 11, 1922. Member of American Society of Cinematographers.
PICTURES: Heaven With a Gun, The Great Bank Robbery, Patton, Beyond the Valley of the Dolls, Flap, Skin Game, Billy Jack, Kansas City Bomber, The Magnificent Seven Ride, Rage, Harry in Your Pocket, Papillon, Uptown Saturday Night, The Towering Inferno (Acad. Award), The Wild McCullochs, Doc Savage, Posse, Embryo, The Other Side of Midnight, Fun With Dick and Jane, Islands in the Streams, Bad News Bears in Breaking Training, The Dominic Principle, White Line Fever, The Swarm, The Champ, Amityville Horror, Love and Bullets, When Time Ran Out, The Hunter, First Family, When Time Ran Out, First Monday in October, Carbon Copy, Yes Giorgio, Two of a Kind, Adventures of Buckaroo Banzai: Across the 8th Dimension, Mismatch, Listen to Me, Welcome Home, Flight of the Intruder.
TELEVISION: Nearly 30 TV movies including Disaster on the Coastline, Tales of the Gold Monkey, Money on the Side, Return of the Man from U.N.C.L.E., Summer Fantasies, Whiz Kids, Flight 90, —Disaster on the Potomac, Obsessive Love, City Killer, Las Vegas Strip War, A Touch of Scandal, Not My Kid, Hard Time on Planet Earth (pilot), Return of the Shaggy Dog, Foreign Exchange, Splash Too, Hard Times, many others.

KOENIG, WALTER: Actor, Writer, Director , Producer. b. Chicago, IL, Sept. 14, 1936. e. Grinnell Coll. (IA), U. of California. Performed in summer stock; after college enrolled at Neighborhood Playhouse, N.Y.; first acting job in TV's Day in Court. Books: Chekov's Enterprise, Buck Alice and the Actor Robot.
PICTURES: The Deadly Honeymoon, Star Trek—The Motion Picture, Star Trek II: The Wrath of Khan, Star Trek III: The Search for Spock, Star Trek IV: the Voyage Home, Star Trek V: the Final Frontier, Moontrap, Star Trek VI: The Undiscovered Country.
TELEVISION: *Guest*: Colombo, Medical Center, Ironside, Mannix, Alfred Hitchcock Presents, Mr. Novak, Ben Casey, The Untouchables, Combat. *Movies*: The Questor Tapes, Goodbye Raggedy Ann. *Writer*: Family, The Class of '65, The Powers of Matthew Star.

KOHN, HOWARD EDWARD, II: Executive. b. McKeesport, PA, Oct. 25, 1920. e. NYU. National dir. of adv., publicity, roadshow dept., United Artists; indep. prod., Hidden Fear, 1957; pres. Lioni-Warren-Kohn, Inc., 1958; national roadshow dir., Columbia Pictures, Porgy and Bess, 1959; World wide co-ordinator, national co-ordinator adv. & pub. for El Cid, June 1961; named world wide co-ordinator adv., pub. all Samuel Bronston Productions, April 1962; pres., Starpower Inc., 1968; exec. v.p., Avanti Films 1970; v.p. Avariac Prods., 1971; pres., Blossom Films, 1973. Elected member of ASCAP, 1975. Pres., Avanti Associates, 1976. Pres. Channel Television Prods., Inc., 1985; pres. Search Television Prods. 1988. Pres. Avanti Music Co. 1991. Exec. v.p., Petard TV and Video Prods.

KOHNER, PANCHO: Producer. b. Los Angeles, CA, Jan. 7, 1939. e. U. of Southern California, U. of Mexico, Sorbonne.
PICTURES: The Bridge in the Jungle (also dir-s.p.), The Lie, Victoria (also s.p.), Mr. Sycamore (also dir., s.p.), St. Ives, The White Buffalo, Love and Bullets, Why Would I Lie?, 10 to Midnight, The Evil That Men Do, Murphy's Law, Assassination, Death Wish IV, Messenger of Death, Kinjite, Madeline.

KOHNER, SUSAN: Actress. b. Los Angeles, CA. Nov. 11, 1936. m. designer & author John Weitz. Sons Paul (playwright) and Christopher Weitz (journalist). Mother, Lupita Tovar, was one of Mexico's leading film actresses. Father was talent rep. Paul Kohner. e. U. of California, 1954–55. Received Acad. Award nom. for Imitation of Life 1959, and Golden Globe Awards, 1959 and 1960. On bd. of associates, Juilliard Sch. NY.
STAGE: Love Me Little, He Who Gets Slapped, A Quiet Place, Rose Tatoo, Bus Stop, St. Joan, Sunday in New York, Take Her She's Mine, Pullman Car, Hiawatha, as well as summer stock.
PICTURES: To Hell and Back, The Last Wagon, Trooper Hook, Dino, Imitation of Life, The Big Fisherman, The Gene Krupa Story, All the Fine Young Cannibals, By Love Possessed, Freud.
TELEVISION: Alcoa Hour, Schlitz Playhouse, Four Star Theatre, Matinee Theatre, Climax, Suspicion, Playhouse 90, Route 66, Dick Powell Theatre.

KONCHALOVSKY, ANDREI: (also known as Mikhalkov Koncha-lovski) Director, Writer. b. Moscow, Soviet Union, Aug. 20, 1937. Great grandfather: painter Sourikov; grandfather: painter Konchalovski; father is a writer; mother poet Natalia Konchalovskaia; brother is director Nikita Mikhalkov. e. as pianist Moscow Conservatoire, 1947–57; State Film Sch. (VGIK) under Mikhail Romm (1964). Worked as scriptwriter during 1960s especially with Andrei Tarkovsky. 1962: asst. to Tarkovsky on Ivan's Childhood. In Milan and Paris directed operas Eugene Onegin, La Pique Dame. 1980: moved to US.
PICTURES: The Boy and the Pigeon (1961, short film, dir.), The Steamroller and the Violin (s.p.), Andrey Rublev (s.p.), The First Teacher (dir.), The Story of Asya Klyachina, Who Loved But Did Not Marry (dir.), A Nest of Gentlefolk (dir., s.p.), Tashkent City of Bread (s.p.), The Song of Manshuk (s.p.), Uncle Vanya (dir.), The End of Chieftain (s.p.), Romance for Lovers (dir.), Siberiade (Jury prize, Cannes, 1979), Split Cherry Tree (short for U.S., cable TV, 1982). Director: Maria's Lovers, Runaway Train, Duet for One, Shy People (also co-s.p.), Tango and Cash, Homer and Eddie, The Inner Circle (also co-s.p.).
THEATRE: The Seagull, Theatre de L'Odeon (Paris).

KONIGSBERG, FRANK: Executive. b. Kew Gardens, NY, March 10, 1933. e. Yale, Yale Law Sch. Worked as lawyer at CBS for six years; moved to NBC 1960–65 in legal dept. as dir. prog. and talent administration. Left to package TV special for Artists Agency Rep. (later AFA) in Los Angeles; sr. v.p. of West Coast office seven years. Executive producer of many TV series, pilots, variety specials and made-for-TV movies. Formed own Konigsberg Company. Theatrical film debut as prod., Joy of Sex (1984).
TELEVISION: Movies (all exec. prod.): Pearl, Ellis Island, Bing Crosby: His Life and Legend, Dummy, Before and After, Guyana Tragedy, A Christmas Without Snow, The Pride of Jesse Hallam, Hard Case, Divorce Wars, Coming Out of the Ice, Onassis: The Richest Man in the World (exec. prod.), Where the Hell's That Gold?!!?, Senior Prom, Babycakes. Series (exec. prod.): It's Not Easy, Breaking Away, Dorothy.

KOPELSON, ARNOLD: Producer, Financier, Intl. Distributor. b. New York, NY, Feb. 14, 1935. e. New York Law Sch., J.D., 1959; NYU, B.S. 1956. Has executive-produced, produced, packaged, developed or distributed with partner, Anne Kopelson over 100 films. Handled intl. dist. of Twice in a Lifetime, Salvador, Warlock, Triumph of the Spirit and prod. Platoon. Chmn. Arnold Kopelson Prods., Co-chmn. Inter-Ocean Film Sales, Ltd.
PICTURES: Foolin' Around (prod.), The Legacy (exec. prod.), Lost and Found (exec. prod.), Night of the Juggler (exec. prod.), Dirty Tricks (exec. prod.), Final Assignment (exec. prod.), Jungle Warriors (prod.), Gimme an "F" (exec. prod.), Platoon (prod.; Acad. Award, best picture, 1986), Hot Pursuit (prod.), Warlock (exec. prod.), Triumph of the Spirit

(prod.), Fire Birds (exec. prod.), Out for Justice (prod.), Falling Down (prod.), The Fugitive (prod.).

KORBAN, BERNARD: Executive. b. New York, NY, Nov. 28, 1923; e. RCA Inst. of Technology, NYU. U.S. Army 1942–46; 1951–58, public relations and promotions for Davega Stores; 1959–62, exploitation fieldman for Universal Pictures; 1962–66, supvr. of fieldmen and exploitation activities; 1966–68, exec. in chg. field activities; exec. assist. to v.p., adv. pub. and promotion; 1972 dir. of exploitation, National General Pictures; 1973, dir. of marketing, promotion and worldwide dist. for Brut Prods; 1974, dir. of mkt., Avco Embassy Pictures, 1975, v.p., of advertising/publicity/promotion, Cine Artists Pictures Corp.; advertising/publicity, United Artists Corp. West Coast ad. mgr.; then UA v.p., West Coast adv.; v.p. West Coast adv./promo., MGM/UA; 1983, v.p., gen. mgr., AC&R/ DHB & BESS, San Diego.

KORMAN, HARVEY: Actor, Director. b. Chicago, IL, Feb. 15, 1927. e. Wright Junior Coll. Began dramatic studies at Chicago's Goodman Sch. of Drama at the Arts Inst. Acted in small roles in Broadway plays and did TV commercials until break came as comedian for Danny Kaye Show on TV. Staged comedy sketches for Steve Allen variety series in 1967. Became Carol Burnett's leading man on her show 1967 to 1977. Directed two episodes of The New Dick Van Dyke Show.
PICTURES: Lord Love a Duck, Last of the Secret Agents, Three Bites of the Apple, Don't Just Stand There, The April Fools, Blazing Saddles, Huckleberry Finn, High Anxiety, Americathon, Herbie Goes Bananas, First Family, History of the World—Part I, Trail of the Pink Panther, Curse of the Pink Panther, The Longshot, Munchie.
TELEVISION: Series: The Danny Kaye Show, The Carol Burnett Show (4 Emmy Awards), The Tim Conway Show (1980–1), Mama's Family, Leo and Liz in Beverly Hills, The Nutt House. Movies: Three's a Crowd, Suddenly Single, The Love Boat (pilot), Bud and Lou, The Invisible Woman, Carpool, Crash Course. Special: The Carol Burnett Show: A Reunion (also co-exec. prod.).

KORMAN, LEWIS J.: Executive. b. 1945. Partner, Kaye, Scholer, Fierman, Hays & Handler 1978; founding partner, Gelberg & Abrams where pioneered dev. of public limited partnerships, Delphi Partners, to help finance Columbia Pictures' and Tri-Star Pictures' films. 1986, became consultant to Tri-Star involved in negotiations that led to acquisition of Loews Theatre Corp. that year. Joined Tri-Star, 1987, as sr. exec. v.p. In 1988 appt. to additional post of chief operating officer and named dir. of Columbia Pictures Entertainment Inc.; 1989 also became chmn., Motion Picture Group. 1990, resigned his positions after Columbia sale to Sony. Co-founder, pres. & COO of Savoy Pictures Ent., Inc., 1992.

KORTY, JOHN: Director, Producer, Writer, Animator. b. Lafayette, IN, June 22, 1936. e. Antioch Coll, B.A. 1959. President, Korty Films. Documentary: Who Are the DeBolts? And Where Did They Get Nineteen Kids? (Acad. Award: 1977; Emmy & DGA Awards: 1978–9). Short Films: The Language of Faces (AFSC, 1961), Imogen Cunningham: Photographer (AFI grant, 1970), The Music School. Animation: Breaking the Habit (Oscar nom.), Twice Upon a Time.
PICTURES: Crazy Quilt (1966), Funnyman, Riverrun, Alex and the Gypsy, Oliver's Story.
TELEVISION: Movies: The People, Go Ask Alice, Class of '63, The Autobiography of Miss Jane Pittman (Emmy & DGA Awards, 1974), Farewell to Manzanar (Huminatas, Christopher Awards), Forever, A Christmas Without Snow (also writer, prod.), The Haunting Passion, Second Sight: A Love Story, The Ewok's Adventure, Resting Place, Baby Girl Scott, Eye on the Sparrow, Winnie, Cast the First Stone, A Son's Promise, Line of Fire: The Morris Dees Story, Long Road Home, Deadly Matrimony.

KOSCINA, SYLVA: Actress. b. Yugoslavia, Aug. 22, 1933. Grew up in Italy; as model placed under contract for films by Carlo Ponti.
PICTURES: The Railroad Man (debut), Hercules, Hercules Unchained, Swordsman of Siena, Jessica, Cyrano and D'Artagnan, Agent 8 3/4, The Little Nuns, Let's Talk About Women, Juliet of the Spirits, That Man in Istanbul, Three Bites of the Apple, Made in Italy, Deadlier Than the Male, The Secret War of Harry Frigg, A Lovely Way to Die, The Hornet's Nest, Battle of Neretva, The Student Connection, Lisa and the Devil, Casanova & Co., Sunday Lovers.

KOTCHEFF, TED: Director. r.n. William Theodore Kotcheff. b. Toronto, Canada, Apr. 7, 1931. Ent. TV ind. 1952. After five years with Canadian Broadcasting Corp. joined ABC-TV in London, 1957.
TELEVISION: Specials: Of Mice and Men, Desperate Hours, The Human Voice.
LONDON STAGE: Progress the Park, Play with a Tiger, Luv, Maggie May, The Au Pair Man, Have You Any Dirty Washing, Mother Dear?
PICTURES: Tiara Tahiti (debut, 1963), Life at the Top, Two Gentlemen Sharing, Outback, Billy Two Hats, The Appren-

ticeship of Duddy Kravitz, Fun with Dick and Jane, Who Is Killing The Great Chefs of Europe?, North Dallas Forty (also co-s.p.), First Blood, Split Image (also prod.), Uncommon Valor (also exec. prod.), Joshua Then and Now, The Check is in the Mail (prod. only), Switching Channels, Winter People, Weekend at Bernie's (also actor), Folks!

KOTTO, YAPHET: Actor. b. New York, NY, Nov. 15, 1937. Has many stage credits, including starring roles on Broadway in The Great White Hope, The Zulu and the Zayda. Off-Bdwy.: Blood Knot, Black Monday, In White America, A Good Place To Raise a Boy.
PICTURES: The Limit (also prod.), Nothing But a Man, 5 Card Stud, Thomas Crown Affair, The Liberation of L. B. Jones, Man and Boy, Across 110th Street, Bone, Live and Let Die, Truck Turner, Report to the Commissioner, Sharks' Treasure, Friday Foster, Drum, Monkey Hustle, Blue Collar, Alien, Brubaker, Fighting Back, Star Chamber, Eye of the Tiger, Warning Sign, Prettykill, The Running Man, Midnight Run, Nightmare of the Devil (also prod., dir.), Terminal Entry, Jigsaw, A Whisper to a Scream, Tripwire, Ministry of Vengeance, Hangfire, Freddy's Dead, Almost Blue, Intent to Kill.
TELEVISION: Series: Homicide. Movies: Night Chase, Raid on Entebbe, Rage, Playing With Fire, The Park Is Mine, Women of San Quentin, Badge of the Assassin, Harem, Desperado, Perry Mason: The Case of the Scandalous Scoundrel, Prime Target, After the Shock, Chrome Soldiers, It's Nothing Personal, Extreme Justice, The American Clock. Guest: Alfred Hitchcock Presents.

KOVACS, LASZLO: Cinematographer. b. Hungary, May 14, 1933. Came to U.S. 1957; naturalized 1963. e. Acad. Drama and M.P. Arts, Budapest, MA 1956.
PICTURES: Hell's Angels on Wheels, Hell's Bloody Devils, Psych Out, The Savage Seven, Targets, A Man Called Dagger, Single Room Furnished, Easy Rider, That Cold Day in the Park, Getting Straight, Alex in Wonderland, Five Easy Pieces, The Last Movie, Marriage of a Young Stockbroker, The King of Marvin Gardens, Pocket Money, What's Up, Doc?, Steelyard Blues, Paper Moon, Slither, A Reflection of Fear, Huckleberry Finn, For Pete's Sake, Freebie and the Bean, Shampoo, At Long Last Love, Baby Blue Marine, Nickelodeon, Close Encounters of the Third Kind (addl. photo. only), Harry and Walter Go to New York, New York New York, F.I.S.T., The Last Waltz, Paradise Alley, Butch and Sundance: The Early Days, The Runner Stumbles, Heart Beat, Inside Moves, The Legend of the Lone Ranger, Frances, The Toy, Crackers, Ghostbusters, Mask, Legal Eagles, Little Nikita, Say Anything, Shattered, Radio Flyer, Life With Mikey, The Next Karate Kid.

KOZAK, HARLEY JANE: Actress. b. Wilkes-Barre, PA, Jan. 28, 1957. e. NYU's School of the Arts. Member of Nebraska Repertory Theatre.
PICTURES: House on Sorority Row, Clean and Sober, When Harry Met Sally . . ., Parenthood, Sideout, Arachnophobia, Necessary Roughness, The Taking of Beverly Hills, All I Want for Christmas, The Favor.
TELEVISION: Series: The Guiding Light, Santa Barbara, Texas. Guest: L.A. Law, Highway to Heaven. Movies: So Proudly We Hail, The Amy Fisher Story.

KOZLOWSKI, LINDA: Actress. b. 1956. m. actor Paul Hogan. Began professional acting career soon after graduating from Juilliard Sch., N.Y., 1981. Stage debut in How It All Began at the Public Theatre. In regional theatre appeared in Requiem, Translations, Make and Break, as well as on Broadway and on tour with Dustin Hoffman in Death of a Salesman and the TV adaptation.
PICTURES: Crocodile Dundee, Crocodile Dundee II, Helena, Almost an Angel.
TELEVISION: Mini-Series: Favorite Son.

KRABBE, JEROEN: Actor. b. Amsterdam, The Netherlands, Dec. 5, 1944. Trained for stage at De Toneelschool, Acad. of Dramatic Art, Amsterdam, 1965. Also studied at Acad. of Fine Arts, grad. 1981. Founded touring theater co. in the Netherlands and translated plays into Dutch. Also costume designer. As a painter, work has been widely exhibited. Author: The Economy Cookbook. Dir. debut, new stage adaptation of The Diary of Anne Frank, 1985 in Amsterdam.
PICTURES: Soldier of Orange, A Flight of Rainbirds, Spetters, The Fourth Man, Turtle Diary, Jumpin' Jack Flash, No Mercy, The Living Daylights, Shadow of Victory, A World Apart, Crossing Delancey, Shadowman, Scandal, The Punisher, Melancholia, Till There Was You, Kafka, The Prince of Tides, For a Lost Soldier, King of the Hill, The Fugitive.
TELEVISION: Danton's Death (debut, 1966), William of Orange, World War Three. Movies: One for the Dance, Family of Spies, After the War, Secret Weapon, Robin Hood (theatrical in Europe), Murder East Murder West, Dynasty: The Reunion, Stalin.

KRAMER, LARRY: Writer, Producer. b. Bridgeport, CT, 1935. e. Yale U., B.A. 1957. Ent. m.p. ind. 1958. Story edit. Columbia Pictures, N.Y. London 1960–65. Asst. to David Picker and

Herb Jaffe, UA, 1965. Assoc. prod. and additional dialogue Here We Go Round the Mulberry Bush, 1968. Writ. prod. Women in Love (Acad. Award nom. for best s.p., 1970). Lost Horizon, 1973 (s.p.). Novel: Faggots (1978). Theater: The Normal Heart (NY Shakespeare Festival and throughout the world), Just Say No, The Destiny of Me. Cofounder: Gay Men's Health Crisis, Inc. (community AIDS org.). Founder: ACT UP: AIDS Coalition to Unleash Power (AIDS activist and protest org.). Book of Essays: Reports from the Holocaust: The Making of an AIDS Activist (St. Martin's Press, 1988).

KRAMER, SIDNEY: Sales executive. b. New York, NY, Oct. 25, 1911. e. New York Law Sch., LL.B., City Coll. of New York. Gen. sales mgr., RKO Pathe, June 1953; dir. and v.p. Cellofilm Corp. 1941–56; foreign sales mgr., RKO Radio, 1954–59; v.p. Cinemiracle Intl. 1960–61; v.p. T.P.E.A., 1960–61; foreign sls. mgr., Cinerama, Inc., 1962–65; Exec. Commonwealth Theatres, Puerto Rico, Inc., 1965–68; Exec. v.p. Cobian Jr. Enterprises Inc. 1968. M.P. consultant-exhibition, dist., foreign and Caribbean area, Oct., 1968–70. Pres. Coqui Internat'l. Inc.; 1970–80; vice. pres. of UAPR, Inc., Puerto Rico, U.A. Communications, Inc. 1981–91. Currently, consultant in Florida, various theatre circuits.

KRAMER, STANLEY E.: Executive producer, Director. b. New York, NY, Sept. 29, 1913; e. NYU, B.Sc., 1933. Entered m.p. ind. via back lot jobs; with MGM research dept.; film cutter 3 yrs.; film ed.; m.p. & radio writer; served in U.S Signal Corps, 1st Lt.
PICTURES: Producer: So This is New York, Champion, Home of the Brave, The Men, Cyrano de Bergerac, Death of a Salesman, High Noon, My Six Convicts, The Sniper, The Four Poster, The Happy Time, Eight Iron Men, 5,000 Fingers of Dr. T, Wild One, The Juggler, Caine Mutiny, Pressure Point, A Child is Waiting, Invitation to a Gunfighter. Dir.-Prod.: Not as a Stranger, Pride and the Passion, The Defiant Ones, On the Beach, Inherit the Wind, Judgment at Nuremberg, It's a Mad Mad Mad Mad World, Ship of Fools, Guess Who's Coming to Dinner, The Secret of Santa Vittoria, R.P.M.*, Bless the Beasts and Children, Oklahoma Crude, The Domino Principle, The Runner Stumbles.
TELEVISION: Guess Who's Coming to Dinner? (pilot).

KRANE, JONATHAN: Executive. b. 1952. m. actress Sally Kellerman. e. St. Johns Coll. grad. with honors, 1972; Yale Law Sch., 1976. Joined Blake Edwards Entertainment in 1981, becoming pres. Formed talent management co. Management Company Entertainment Group representing clients such as John Travolta, Sally Kellerman, Kathryn Harrold, Sandra Bernhard, Howie Mandel, Drew Barrymore, others. Began producing vehicles for clients and transformed co. into production, distribution, management and finance co. Chairman and chief exec. officer, Management Company Entertainment Group (MCEG).
PICTURES: Exec. prod./prod.: Boardwalk, Honeymoon, Fly Away Home, The Man Who Loved Women, Micki & Maude, A Fine Mess, That's Life, The Chocolate War, The Experts, Fatal Charm, Boris and Natasha, Look Who's Talking, Chud II: Bud the Chud, With You I'm Nothing (prod.), Look Who's Talking Too, Convicts, Cold Heaven, Breaking the Rules, Look Who's Talking 3.
TELEVISION: Prod.: Howie Mandel Life at Carnegie Hall, Howie Mandel: The North American Watusi Tour.

KRANTZ, STEVE: Executive. b. New York, NY, May 20, 1923. m. novelist Judith Krantz. e. Columbia U., B.A. Dir. progs., NBC, New York, 1953; dir. prog. dev., Screen Gems, N.Y., 1955; v.p., gen. mgr. Screen Gems, Canada, 1958; dir. int. sls., 1960; formed Steve Krantz Productions, Inc. 1964.
TELEVISION: Series: Steve Allen Show, Kate Smith Show, Hazel, Dennis the Menace, Winston Churchill—The Valiant Years, Marvel Super Heroes, Rocket Robin Hood. Mini-series: Princess Daisy, Sins, Mistral's Daughter, I'll Take Manhattan. Movies: Dadah is Death (exec. prod.), Till We Meet Again, Deadly Medicine, Deadly Matrimony, Torch Song.
PICTURES: Fritz the Cat, Heavy Traffic (prod.), Cooley High, Ruby, Which Way Is Up?

KREIMAN, ROBERT T.: Executive. b. Kenosha, WI, Sept. 16, 1924. Served W.W.II Capt Army Corps of Engineers-ETO. e. Stanford U., 1943; U. of Wisconsin, 1942–1946–49. Dir., sales training, mgr., audio visual sales, Bell & Howell Co. 1949–58; V.P., Argus Cameras, Inc., 1958–61; V.P., gen. mgr., Commercial & Educ. Div., Technicolor 1961–69, v.p. gen. mgr., The Suburban Companies; 1969–71: pres. and chief exec. officer, Deluxe General, Inc. pres. and director of Movietonews, Inc. Bd. chmn. Keith Cole Photograph, Inc. 1972–78. bd. chmn., pres. and chief exec. officer, Pace International Corp., 1969 to present. past pres. of U.C.L.A. Executive Program Ass'n. Fellow SMPTE, Member M.P. Academy; TV Academy; assoc. mem., American Society of Cinematographers.

KRESS, HAROLD F.: Film Editor, Director. b. Pittsburgh, PA, June 26, 1913. e. UCLA. Film ed., Command Decision, Madame Curie, Mrs. Miniver, The Yearling; crime shorts; 5-reel Army documentary short, Ward Care for Psychotic Patients. Member: Acad. of M.P. Arts and Sciences, Screen Directors Guild, Film Editors Guild.

PICTURES: Director: Painted Hills, No Questions Asked, Apache War Smoke. Editor: Ride Vaquero, Saadia, Rose Marie, Valley of the Kings, The Cobweb, The Prodigal, I'll Cry Tomorrow, Teahouse of the August Moon, Silk Stockings, Until They Sail, Merry Andrew, Imitation General, The World the Flesh and the Devil, Count Your Blessings, Home from the Hill, How the West Was Won (Acad. Award), The Greatest Story Ever Told, Walk Don't Run, Alvarez Kelly, The Poseidon Adventure, The Iceman Cometh, 99 and 44/100% Dead, The Towering Inferno (Acad. Award).

KREUGER, KURT: Actor. b. St. Moritz, Switzerland, July 23, 1917. e. U. of Lausanne, Polytechnic. London. Came to U.S. 1937, partner in travel bureau: acted in Wharf Theat. group. Cape Cod, 1939; Broadway debut in Candle in the Wind with Helen Hayes, 1941.

PICTURES: Sahara, Mademoiselle Fifi, None Shall Escape, Escape in the Desert, Hotel Berlin, Paris Underground, The Spider Dark Corner, Unfaithfully Yours, Spy Hunt, Fear, Enemy Below, What Did You Do in the War Daddy?, The St. Valentine's Day Massacre.

KRIER, JOHN N.: Executive. b. Rock Island, IL. e. Augustana Coll. Joined A. H. Blank Theatres, Grad. Publix Theatres Manager Training Sch., 1930: managed theatres in Illinois, Iowa, Nebraska; joined Intermountain Theatres, Salt Lake City, 1937: appointed Purchasing Head, 1946: buyer-booker, 1952: v.p., gen. mgr., 1955: appt. v.p. gen mgr. ABC Theas., Arizona, 1968: appt. v.p. gen'l mgr. director Film Buying ABC Theatres of California & ABC Intermountain Theatres, Feb. 1972. Became consultant ABC Southern Theatres, 1974. Joined Exhibitors Relations Inc. as partner, 1978. Elected pres., 1982. Became owner, 1988.

KRIGE, ALICE: Actress. b. Upington, South Africa, June 28, 1954. Moved to London at 22 and studied at School of Speech and Drama. Professional debut on British TV: The Happy Autumn Fields. In London prod. of Forever Yours, Maylou. West End debut, Arms and the Man, 1981. Two seasons with Royal Shakespeare Co. at Stratford and London (The Tempest, King Lear, The Taming of the Shrew, Cyrano de Bergerac.)

PICTURES: Chariots of Fire, Ghost Story, King David, Barfly, Haunted Summer, See You in the Morning, S.P.O.O.K.S., Sleepwalkers.

TELEVISION: *Movies:* Wallenberg: A Hero's Story, Dream West, A Tale of Two Cities, Second Serve, Baja Oklahoma, Max and Helen, Iran: Days of Crisis, Ladykiller, Judgment Day: The John List Story, Double Deception. *Mini-Series:* Ellis Island.

KRIM, ARTHUR B.: Attorney. b. New York, NY, 1910. e. Columbia U., B.A., 1930; J.D. 1932; L.L.D (hon.) 1982. 1932 became member law firm Philips, Nizer, Benjamin, Krim & Ballon; sr. partner 1935–78; of counsel 1978–. Pres. Eagle Lion films 1946–49. N.Y. elected pres. United Artists Feb. 20, 1951; chairman of bd., 1969 to January 1978; Chmn. of Board, Orion Pictures Company, March, 1978–.

Special cons. to Pres. U.S. 1968–69; mem. President's Gen. Adv. Com. Arms Control 1977–80; chmn. Democratic Natl. Finance Comm. 1966–68. Bd. of dirs: Weizmann Inst. Science, 1948–; UN Association 1961–; Lyndon Baines Johnson Foundation 1969–; John F. Kennedy Foundation 1964–; Arms Control Assn. 1985–; chmn. bd. trustee Columbia U. 1977–82, chmn. emeritus 1982–. Received Jean Hersholt Humanitarian Award from Acad. M.P. Arts & Sciences 1975.

KRISEL, GARY: Executive. b. California. Pres., TV animation, Walt Disney Television.

KRISTOFFERSON, KRIS: Actor, Singer. b. Brownsville, TX, June 22, 1936. e. Pomona Coll., Oxford U. (Rhodes Scholar). Joined U.S. Army briefly and taught English literature at West Point. Started writing songs (country music), hits have included Me and Bobby McGee, Why Me, Lord, Sunday Mornin' Comin' Down, etc.

PICTURES: The Last Movie (debut, 1971), Cisco Pike, Pat Garrett and Billy the Kid, Blume in Love, Bring Me the Head of Alfredo Garcia, Alice Doesn't Live Here Anymore, Vigilante Force, The Sailor Who Fell from Grace with the Sea, A Star Is Born, Semi-Tough, Convoy, Heaven's Gate, Rollover, Flashpoint, Songwriter, Trouble in Mind, Big Top Pee-wee, Millennium, Welcome Home, Original Intent, Night of the Cyclone, Sandino, No Place to Hide, Cheatin' Hearts.

TELEVISION: *Movies/Mini-Series:* Freedom Road, The Lost Honor of Kathryn Beck, The Last Days of Frank and Jesse James, Blood and Orchids, Stagecoach, The Tracker, Dead or Alive, Pair of Aces, Another Pair of Aces, Miracle in the Wilderness, Christmas in Connecticut. Mini-Series: Amerika.

KRONICK, WILLIAM: Writer, Director. b. Amsterdam, NY. e. Columbia Coll., A.B. U.S. Navy photography; wrote, dir. featurette, A Bowl of Cherries.

TV DOCS: Wrote, dir., prod.: The Ultimate Stuntman: a Tribute to Dar Robinson, To the Ends of the Earth, Mysteries of the Great Pyramid; George Plimpton Specials; National Geographic, Ripley's Believe It or Not, The World's Greatest Stunts. Prod.: In Search of. . . Series. Dir. movie The 500 Pound Jerk.

PICTURES: Nights in White Satin (s.p.); Horowitz in Dublin (dir., s.p.); Flash Gordon and King Kong (2nd unit dir.).

KRUEGER, RONALD P.: Executive. b. St. Louis, MO, Oct. 19, 1940. e. Westminister Coll., 1961. Began working in theatres as a teenager. Assumed presidency Wehrenberg Theatres, 1963.

MEMBER: NATO, bd. member, regional v.p.; American Film Inst.; advisory bd. mbr., Salvation Army; Motion Picture Pioneers; Demolay Legion of Honor; bd. trustees, Westminster Col. at Fulton, MO; Divan mbr. Moolah Temple Shrine; past Master Tuscan Lodge 360 AF & AM; Scottish Rite 32 KCCH.

KRUGER, HARDY: Actor. b. Berlin, Germany, April 12, 1928. Ent. m.p. ind. 1943; on stage since 1945. Filmed in U.S., Britain, USSR, Australia, Italy, Yugoslavia, France, Israel, and Germany (starred in approx. 25 German films). Has published 8 books, novels, travelogues, etc.

PICTURES: The One That Got Away, Bachelor of Hearts (German version of The Moon Is Blue), The Rest Is Silence (German film of Hamlet), Cry Double Cross, Blind Date, Taxi Pour Tobrouk, Sundays and Cybele, Three Fables of Love, Hatari! (U.S. debut, 1963), Le Gros Coup, Les Pianos Mecaniques (The Uninhibited), Le Chant du Monde, Flight of the Phoenix, The Defector, La Grande Sauterelle, Le Franciscain de Bourges, The Nun of Monza, The Secret of Santa Vittoria, The Battle of Neretva, The Red Tent, Night Hair Child, Le Moine, Death of a Stranger, Barry Lyndon, Paper Tiger, Un Solitarire, Potato Fritz, A Bridge Too Far, L'Autopsie d'un Monstre, The Wild Geese, Society Limited, Wrong Is Right, The Inside Man.

TELEVISION: *Mini-Series:* War and Remembrance. *Series:* Globetrotter (also prod; 1986).

KRUGER, JEFFREY S.: Producer, Concert impresario, Record and music publisher, Film distribution executive. b. April 19, 1931, London, England. Chmn., of TKO Entertainment Group Ltd. Bulldog Records, Ember Records, Kruger Leisure Organisation. Produced feature films Rock You Sinners; Sweet Beat; The Amorous Sex. Distributor of Jack Nicholson's The Shooting, Love Child, Dial Rat For Terror, Starcrash, Kill the Shogun, Red Light In the Whitehouse, Enforcer from Death Row; A Whale of A Tale, Vengeance of the Barbarians, From Nashville with Music, Togetherness, Forbidden Love, Search for the Evil One, Gallery of Horrors, Grave of the Vampire, Tomb of the Undead, Sex and the Lonely Woman, House of Terror, Smoke in the Wind, Ten Fingers of Steel, Psychopath, Choppers, Deadwood 76, Good Time Outlaws, Ground Zero, Journey to the Centre of Time, and others. Produced (in association with B.B.C.-TV): 20 musical specials starring Glen Campbell, Marvin Gaye, Jacksons, Charley Pride, George Burns, Charlie Rich, Anne Murray, Helen Reddy, Dionne Warwick, Blood Sweat and Tears, War, David Soul, Frankie Laine, Jerry Lee Lewis, others. Concert presentations include Julio Iglesias, Placido Domingo, Rudolf Nureyev, Anne Murray, George Burns, etc. Music publ. through Songs For Today and TKO Publising Ltd. Own record prod. and dist. via Bulldog Records and TKO Music Ltd. Director TKO Entertainment Group Ltd. (Concerts) Ltd. Songs For Today Ltd. TKO Video Ltd.: TKO Film & TV Ltd., TKO Music Ltd., TKO Publishing Ltd., The Kruger Organization Inc. Recipient, certificate of merit from city of Beverly Hills & commendation from city of Los Angeles.

KUBRICK, STANLEY: Director, Producer, Writer. b. Bronx, NY, July 26, 1928. e. Taft H.S. Staff photog. Look magazine; dir., edit., cinematog. of short documentaries Day of the Fight, Flying Padre; dir., cinematog. of docum. The Seafarers. Received Luchino Visconti Award in Italy for contribution to the cinema, 1988.

PICTURES: *Director:* Fear and Desire (also prod., co-s.p., photog., edit.), Killer's Kiss (also co-prod., co-s.p., story, photog., edit.), The Killing (also s.p.), Paths of Glory (also co-s.p.), Spartacus, Lolita. *Dir.-Prod.-Writer:* Dr. Strangelove, 2001: A Space Odyssey (also special photog. effects design. & dir.; Acad. Award for special effects, 1968), A Clockwork Orange, Barry Lyndon, The Shining, Full Metal Jacket.

KUHN, THOMAS G.: Executive/Executive Producer. b. Chicago, IL, Nov. 10, 1935. e. Northwestern U., B.A.; U. of Southern California, M.B.A. KNBC-TV sales; NBC business affairs, ; dir. live night time progs. Warner Bros. TV, v.p. prod.; exec. prod., TV, Alice; The Awakening Land; Torn Between Two Lovers; The Jayne Mansfield Story; Long Way Home. Staff, v.p., west coast, for RCA Video Discs. Pres., RCA Video Prods.; pres., Lightyear Ent., 1987. Exec. prod.: Aria, The Return of Swamp Thing, Heaven, The Lemon Sisters, Stories to Remember, The JFK Assassination: The Jim Garrison Tapes, Trouble Bound.

KULIK, SEYMOUR (BUZZ): Producer, Director. b. New York, NY, 1923. Joined CBS-TV as prod.-dir., 1956; 1964: v.p. chg. West Coast Prods., Bob Banner Associates Inc., 1965; 1967 Prod-Dir. with Paramount Studios.
TELEVISION: *Series*: Lux Video Theatre, Kraft Theatre, You Are There, Climax, Playhouse 90, The Defenders, Dr. Kildare, Twilight Zone, Dick Powell Playhouse, Kentucky Jones (exec. prod.). *Movies*: Vanished, Owen Marshall—Counsellor at Law (A Pattern of Morality), Brian's Song (DGA Award), Incident on a Dark Street, Pioneer Woman, Remember When, Bad Ronald, Cage Without a Key, Matt Helm, Babe, The Lindbergh Kidnapping Case, Never Con a Killer, Kill Me If You Can, Ziegfeld: The Man and His Women, From Here to Eternity, Rage of Angels, George Washington (also sprv. prod.), Kane and Abel, Her Secret Life, Women of Valor, Too Young the Hero, Around the World in 80 Days, Jackie Collins' Lucky/Chances, Miles From Nowhere.
PICTURES: The Explosive Generation, The Yellow Canary, Warning Shot (also prod.), Villa Rides, Riot, To Find a Man, Shamus, The Hunter.

KURALT, CHARLES: TV News Correspondent. b. Wilmington, NC, Sept. 10, 1934. e. U. of North Carolina. Reporter-columnist for Charlotte News until joining CBS News as writer in 1957. Promoted to news assignment desk in 1958. Became first host of CBS News series, Eyewitness, in 1960. Named CBS News chief Latin American correspondent (based in Rio de Janeiro) in 1961 Appt. CBS News chief west coast correspondent in 1963; transferred to New York, 1964. Has worked on CBS Reports, CBS News Specials, and On the Road series for CBS Evening News (Emmy Award, 1969). Now host of CBS News Sunday Morning. Author: To the Top of the World (1968), Dateline America (1979), On the Road with Charles Kuralt (1985), A Life on the Road (1990).

KUREISHI, HANIF: Writer. b. South London, Eng., Dec. 5, 1956. e. King's Coll. (philosophy). At 18, first play presented at Royal Court Theatre where he ushered before becoming writer in residence. Early in career, wrote pornography as Antonia French. Stage and TV plays include: The Mother Country, Outskirts, Borderline and adaptations (Mother Courage). The Rainbow Sign, With Your Tongue Down My Throat (novella) and short stories have been pub. Anglo-Pakistani writer's first s.p. My Beautiful Laundrette earned Acad. Award nom., 1986 and began creative relationship with dir. Stephen Frears.
PICTURES: My Beautiful Laundrette, Sammy and Rosie Get Laid, London Kills Me (also dir.).

KURI, EMILE: Set decorator. b. Cuernavaca, Mex., June 11, 1907. e. Chaminade Coll., 1924–27. Career began with 50 Hopalong Cassidy episodes for Harry Sherman. Under contract to Selznick Intl., Liberty Films, and Walt Disney Prods., supv. all film and tv sets, and all decor for both Disneyland and Disney World.
PICTURES: 71 films incl. The Silver Queen (Oscar nom.), I'll Be Seeing You, Spellbound, It's a Wonderful Life, Duel in the Sun, Paradine Case, The Heiress (Academy Award, 1949), Fancy Pants, A Place in the Sun, Carrie (Oscar nom.), The War of the Worlds, Shane, The Actress, Executive Suite (Oscar nom.), 20,000 Leagues Under the Sea (Academy Award, 1954), Old Yeller, The Absent-Minded Professor (Oscar nom.), The Parent Trap, Mary Poppins (Oscar nom.), Bedknobs & Broomsticks (Oscar nom.).
TELEVISION: 15 seasons of The Wonderful World of Disney (Emmy Award, 1963), The Academy Awards (1960–70).

KURI, JOHN A.: Producer, Writer. b. Los Angeles, CA, Feb. 16, 1945. Son of set decorator and Disneyland co-designer, Emile Kuri. Began 13 yr. employment with Disney at age 16 in construction and maintenance at Disneyland. Progressed through mgmt. in Park Operations. 1969 transferred to Disney Studios in set decorating. 1973 became art director. 1975 at 20th Cent. Fox exec. asst. to prod. Irwin Allen. Formed own co., 1976. Wrote, prod., and dir. TV special on city of Las Vegas.
PICTURES: Captive Hearts (prod., co.s.p. 2nd unit dir., co-lyrics.) Set decorator: Apple Dumpling Gang, Leadbelly, Report to the Commissioner, Castaway Cowboy, Superdad, Mad Mad Movie Makers.
TELEVISION: Conagher (prod.), Through the Magic Pyramid (assoc. prod., art dir.), Skyward (prod., 2nd unit dir.), Skyward Christmas (prod., 2nd unit dir.), Airwolf (2nd unit prod., dir.); O'Hara (co-creator, series). Art dir: The Plutonium Incident, Scared Straight Another Story, Young Love First Love, Marriage is Alive and Well, Little Shots, The Red Pony (and set decorator, Emmy nom., 1973). Set decorator: Michael O'Hara IV, The Mouse Factory (22 episodes).

KUROSAWA, AKIRA: Director, Writer. b. Japan. March 23, 1910. e. Attended Tokyo Acad. of Fine Arts, 1928. Asst. dir. to Kajiro Yamamoto, Photo-Chemical Laboratories (PCL Studios, later renamed Toho Films), 1936–43. Became dir., 1943. Founded Kurosawa Prods., 1960; Dir. Yonki Kai Prods., 1971. Autobiography: Something Like An Autobiography (1982).
PICTURES: Sanshiro Sugata, The Most Beautiful, Those Who Tread on The Tiger's Tail, Sanshiro Sugata—Part 2, No Regrets for Our Youth, Those Who Make Tomorrow, One Wonderful Sunday, Drunken Angel, The Quiet Duel, Stray Dog, Scandal, Rashomon, The Idiot, Ikiru, The Seven Samurai, I Live in Fear, The Lower Depths, Throne of Blood, The Bad Sleep Well, The Hidden Fortress (also prod.), Yojimbo, Sanjuro, High and Low, Red Beard, Dodes'kaden (also prod.), Dersu Uzala, Kagemusha, Ran, Runaway Train (orig. s.p. only), Dreams.

KURTIS, BILL: News Correspondent, Anchor. b. Pensacola, FL, Sept. 21, 1940. e. U. of Kansas, Washington U. Sch. of Law, Topeka. Member, American Bar Assn. Career in broadcast journalism began at WIBW Radio in Topeka. Joined CBS News as reporter-producer at Los Angeles bureau in 1970; named CBS news correspondent in 1971. Joined WBBM-TV, Chicago, in 1973 as co-anchor of news broadcasts. In 1982 returned to CBS News as correspondent and co-anchor of CBS Morning News. Left in 1985 to return to Chicago.

KURTZ, GARY: Producer, Director. b. Los Angeles, CA, July 27, 1940. e. U. of Southern California Cinema Sch. Began prof. career during college. Has worked as cameraman, soundman, editor, prod. supervisor and asst. dir. on documentaries and features. Worked on many low budget features for Roger Corman including: The Terror, Beach Ball, Track of the Vampire, Planet of Blood, The Shooting, Ride in the Whirlwind. Drafted into Marines. Spent 2 yrs. in Photo Field as cameraman, editor and still photo.
PICTURES: The Hostage (prod. spvr., ed.), Two-Lane Blacktop (line prod.), Chandler (line prod.), American Graffiti (co.-prod.); Star Wars (prod.), The Empire Strikes Back (prod.), The Dark Crystal (prod., 2nd unit dir.), Return to Oz (exec. prod.), Slipstream (prod.).

KURTZ, SWOOSIE: Actress. b. Omaha, NE, Sept. 6, 1944. e. Studied at U. Southern Calif., London Acad. of Music and Dramatic Art.
THEATER: Who's Afraid of Virginia Woolf? (with Mike Nichols and Elaine May), The Effect of Gamma Rays on Man-in-the-Moon Marigolds, Fifth of July (Tony Award), House of Blue Leaves (Tony and Obie Awards), Uncommon Women and Others, Six Degrees of Separation, Lips Together Teeth Apart.
PICTURES: Slap Shot, First Love, Oliver's Story, The World According to Garp, Against All Odds, Wildcats, True Stories, Vice Versa, Bright Lights Big City, Dangerous Liaisons, Stanley and Iris, A Shock to the System, Reality Bites.
TELEVISION: *Series*: As the World Turns (1971), Mary, Love Sidney, Sisters. *Movies*: Walking Through the Fire, Marriage Is Alive and Well, Mating Season, A Caribbean Mystery, Guilty Conscience, A Time to Live, The Image, Terror on Track 9, The Positively True Adventures of the Alleged Texas Cheerleader-Murdering Mom, And the Band Played On. *Specials*: Uncommon Women, Fifth of July, House of Blue Leaves, Baja Oklahoma, The Visit (Trying Times). *Guest*: Kojak, Carol & Company (Emmy Award, 1990).

KURYS, DIANE: Director. b. France, 1948. In 1970 joined Jean-Louis Barrault's theatre group, acted for 8 years on stage, television and film. Adapted and translated staged plays. 1977, wrote screenplay for Dibolo Menthe (Peppermint Soda) which she also directed and co-prod. Film won Prix Louis Deluc, Best Picture. Co-prod. Alexandre Arcady's Coup de Sirocco and Le Grand Pardon.
PICTURES: Peppermint Soda (dir., co-prod., s.p.), Cocktail Molotov (s.p., dir.), Entre Nous (s.p., dir.), A Man in Love (s.p., dir.), C'est la vie.

KUTNER, MARTIN: Executive. Joined Paramount Pictures in 1971 as eastern div. mgr.; has held various positions in sls. dept. Named v.p., gen. sls. mgr.; in 1980 appt. sr. v.p., domestic distribution; 1983, exec. v.p., distribution; 1984, exec. v.p., intl. mkt. & dist.

KWIT, NATHANIEL TROY, JR.: Executive. b. New York, NY, May 29, 1941. e. Cornell U., B.A.; NYU, M.B.A. 1964–68, American Broadcasting Co., Inc., exec. asst. to pres. of ABC Films. 1968–71, National Screen Service Corp., New York branch mgr., asst. genl. sls. mgr. 1971, founder, CEO Audience Marketing, Inc., later acquired by Viacom International as operating subsidiary. 1974 named v.p. marketing services, Warner Bros., Inc. 1979, named v.p. in charge video and special markets division, United Artists Corp.; 1981, named sr. v.p. in chg. UA television, video, special market div. Following acquisition of UA Corp. by MGM in 1981 promoted to pres., dist. & mktg. for MGM/UA Entertainment Co. 1983, pres. & CEO, United Satellite Communications, direct broadcast TV co. 1986, founder, pres. Palladium Entertainment, Inc.

L

LACHMAN, ED: Cinematographer. b. 1948. Son of a Morristown, NJ movie theater owner. e. Ohio U., BFA. Filmed documentaries Ornette: Made in America, Strippers, Huie's Sermon. Assisted Sven Nykvist on King of the Gypsies, Hurricane; Vittorio Storaro on Luna; Robby Muller on The American Friend and They All Laughed. Co-director of photography on Werner Herzog's La Soufriere and Stroszek and Wim Wenders' Lightning Over Water and A Tokyo Story.
PICTURES: Scalpel, Union City, Say Amen Somebody, Little Wars, Split Cherry Tree, Strippers, The Little Sister, Insignificance (American sequences) Desperately Seeking Susan, True Stories, Making Mr. Right, Chuck Berry: Hail Hail Rock and Roll, Less Than Zero, El Dia Que Me Quieras.
TELEVISION: Get Your Kicks on Route 66 (dir., cinematography, American Playhouse.), A Gathering of Old Men, Backtrack.

LADD, JR., ALAN: Executive. b. Los Angeles, CA, Oct. 22, 1937. Son of late actor Alan Ladd. Motion picture agent, Creative Management Associates, 1963–69. M.p. producer, 1969–73; produced 9 films in 4 yrs. Joined 20th Century-Fox in 1973 in chg. of creative affairs in feature div. Promoted to v.p., production, 1974. In 1975 named sr. v.p. for worldwide prod.; 1976, promoted to pres. of 20th Century-Fox Pictures. Resigned & formed The Ladd Co., 1979. In 1985 appt. pres. & COO, MGM/UA Entertainment Film Corp; appointed chairman of board, CEO Metro-Goldwyn-Mayer Pictures Inc., 1986; resigned Sept., 1988; 1989 named co-chmn. Pathe Communications Corp. and chmn., CEO, Pathe Entertainment. Chmn., & CEO, MGM-Pathe Ent., 1989–92. Chmn & CEO MGM-Pathe Commun. Co., 1991–2. Co-chmn. & Co-CEO, MGM, 1992–93.
PICTURES: Prod.: Walking Stick, A Severed Head, Tam Lin, Villian, Zee and Co. Exec. prod.: Fear is the Key, Nightcomers, Vice Versa.

LADD, CHERYL: Actress. r.n. Cheryl Stoppelmoor. b. Huron, S.D., July 12, 1951. Joined professional Music Shop Band while in high school; after graduation toured with group ending up in Los Angeles. Cast as voice of Melody character in animated Josie and the Pussycats. Studied acting with Milton Katselas. Did TV commercials, small parts in TV. Film debut 1972 in Jamaica Reef (aka Evil in the Deep, unreleased).
TELEVISION: Series: The Ken Berry "Wow" Show, Charlie's Angels. Specials: Ben Vereen . . . His Roots, General Electric's All-Star Anniversary, John Denver and the Ladies; 3 of her own specials. Guest: Police Woman, Happy Days, Switch, etc. Movies: Satan's School for Girls, When She Was Bad, Grace Kelly Story, Romance on the Orient Express, A Death in California, Crossings, Deadly Care, Bluegrass, Kentucky Woman, Jekyll & Hyde, The Fulfillment of Mary Gray, The Girl Who Came Between Them, Crash: The Mystery of Flight 1501, Danielle Steel's Changes, Locked Up: A Mother's Rage, Dead Before Dawn.
PICTURES: Purple Hearts, Now and Forever, Millennium, Lisa, Poison Ivy.

LADD, DAVID ALAN: Actor, Producer. b. Los Angeles, CA, Feb. 5, 1947. Son of late actor Alan Ladd. On stage in The Glass Menagerie and Alpha Beta. Exec. v.p. feature film prod. at Pathe Entertainment.
PICTURES: Actor: The Lone Ranger, The Big Land, The Proud Rebel, The Sad Horse, A Dog of Flanders, Raymie, Misty, R.P.M., Catlow, Deathline (Raw Meat), The Klansman, The Day of the Locust, Wild Geese. Producer: The Serpent and the Rainbow.
TELEVISION: Guest: Zane Gray Theatre, Wagon Train, Playhouse 90, Pursuit, Ben Casey, Gunsmoke, Love American Style, Kojak, Emergency, Tom Sawyer, Bonanza, etc. Producer: When She Was Bad, ABC Variety specials.

LADD, DIANE: Actress. b. Meridian, MS, Nov. 29. r.n. Diane Rose Lanier. Mother of actress Laura Dern. e. St. Aloysius Acad.; trained for stage at Actors Studio with Frank Corsaro in N.Y. Worked as model and as Copacabana nightclub dancer. At 18 in touring co. of Hatful of Rain. NY debut: Orpheus Descending.
THEATER: Carry Me Back to Morningside Heights, One Night Stands of a Noisy Passenger, The Wall, The Goddess, The Fantastiks, Women Speak, Texas Trilogy; Lu Ann Hampton Laverty, Love Letters.
PICTURES: Wild Angels (debut, 1966), Rebel Rousers, The Reivers, Macho Calahan, WUSA, White Lightning, Chinatown, Alice Doesn't Live Here Anymore (Acad. Award nom.), Embryo, All Night Long, Sweetwater, Something Wicked This Way Comes, Black Widow, Plain Clothes, National Lampoon's Christmas Vacation, Wild at Heart (Acad. Award nom.), A Kiss Before Dying, Rambling Rose (Acad. Award nom.), The Cemetery Club, Forever, Carnosaur, Hold Me Thrill Me Kiss Me, Father Hood.
TELEVISION: Movies: The Devil's Daughter, Black Beauty, Thaddeus Rose and Eddie, Willa, Guyana Tragedy, Desperate Lives, Grace Kelly, Crime of Innocence, Bluegrass, Rock Hudson, The Lookalike, Shadow of a Doubt. Guest: Hazel,

Gunsmoke, City of Angels, The Love Boat, Dr. Quinn Medicine Woman (pilot). Series: The Secret Storm, Alice (Golden Globe Award).

LAFFERTY, PERRY: Executive. b. Davenport, IA, Oct. 3, 1920. e. Yale U. With CBS-TV as v.p., programs, Hollywood, 1965–76. Sr. v.p., programs and talent, west coast, for NBC Entertainment. 1985. resigned. Currently TV Consultant, AT&T.
TELEVISION: Maybe Baby (exec. prod.).

LAFONT, BERNADETTE: Actress. b. Oct. 28, Nimes, France. Made her debut in 1957 in Truffaut's first film Les Mistons. Has worked with such international directors as Chabrol, Szabo, Eustache.
PICTURES: Le Beau Serge, Leda, Male Hunt, Les Bonnes Femmes, The Thief of Paris, Such a Gorgeous Kid Like Me, The Mother and the Whore, Zig-Zag, Violette, Like a Turtle on Its Back, Il Ladrone (The Thief), Waiting for the Moon, The Seasons of Pleasure, Prisonnieres, City for Sale.

LAHTI, CHRISTINE: Actress. b. Birmingham, MI, April 4, 1950. m. dir. Thomas Schlamme. e. U. of Michigan. Trained for stage at Herbert Berghof Studios with Uta Hagen. TV commercials. As a mime, performed with Edinburgh Scotland's Travis Theatre. N.Y. stage debut in The Woods, 1978.
THEATER: The Zinger, Hooter (Playwrights Horizon), Loose Ends, Division St., The Woods (Theatre World Award), Scenes and Revelations, Present Laughter, The Lucky Spot, Summer and Smoke (LA), The Heidi Chronicles, Three Hotels.
PICTURES: And Justice For All (debut, 1979), Whose Life Is It Anyway?, Ladies and Gentlemen the Fabulous Stains, Swing Shift (Acad. Award nom.), Just Between Friends, Housekeeping, Stacking, Running on Empty, Miss Firecracker (cameo), Gross Anatomy, Funny About Love, The Doctor, Leaving Normal.
TELEVISION: Movies: Dr. Scorpion, The Last Tenant, The Henderson Monster, The Executioner's Song, Love Lives On, Single Bars Single Women, No Place Like Home, Crazy From the Heart, The Fear Inside, The Good Fight. Mini-Series: Amerika.

LAI, FRANCIS: Composer. b. France, April 26, 1932.
PICTURES: A Man and a Woman, I'll Never Forget What's 'is Name, The Bobo, Three Into Two Won't Go, Hello Goodbye, Hannibal Brooks, The Games, Mayerling, House of Cards, Rider on the Rain, Love Story (Oscar), Le Petit Matin, Another Man, Another Chance, Wanted: Babysitter, Bilitis, The Good and the Bad, Widow's Nest, Cat and Mouse, The Body of My Enemy, Emmanuelle 2; The Forbidden Room, International Velvet, Oliver's Story, Passion Flower Hotel, Robert and Robert, The Small Timers, By the Blood Brothers, Beyond the Reef, Bolero, A Second Chance, Edith and Marcel, My New Partner, Marie, A Man and a Woman: 20 Years Later, Bernadette, Itinerary of a Spoiled Child., Der Aten (The Spirit), La Belle Histoire.
TELEVISION: The Berlin Affair, The Sex Symbol, Sins.

LAKE, RICKI: Actress. b. New York, NY, Sept. 21, 1968. e. Manhattan's Professional Children's School. Won role in Hairspray while attending Ithaca Col. Theatre work incl. Off-Bdwy appearances in The Early Show, Youngsters; in LA: A Girl's Guide to Chaos.
PICTURES: Hairspray (debut, 1988), Working Girl, Cookie, Cry-Baby, Last Exit to Brooklyn, Where the Day Takes You, Inside Monkey Zetterland, Skinner, Serial Mom.
TELEVISION: Series: China Beach. Movies: Babycakes, The Chase, Based on an Untrue Story. Specials: A Family Again, Starting Now. Guest: Kate and Allie, Fame.

LAMARR, HEDY: Actress. r.n. Hedwig Kiesler. b. Vienna, Nov. 9, 1915. At 17 starred in Ecstasy (awarded top Italian film-prize). Autobiography: Ecstasy and Me (1966).
PICTURES: Algiers, Lady of the Tropics, I Take This Woman, Boom Town, Comrade X, Come Live with Me, Ziegfeld Girl, H. M. Pulham Esq., Tortilla Flat, Crossroads, White Cargo, The Heavenly Body, The Conspirators, Experiment Perilous, Her Highness and the Bellboy, The Strange Woman, Dishonored Lady, Let's Live a Little, Samson and Delilah, A Lady Without a Passport, Copper Canyon, My Favorite Spy, Loves of 3 Queens, The Story of Mankind, The Female Animal.

LAMAS, LORENZO: Actor. b. Los Angeles, CA, Jan. 20, 1958. e. Santa Monica City Coll. Son of the late actor Fernando Lamas and actress Arlene Dahl. Studied at Tony Barr's Film Actors Workshop (Burbank Studios). Appeared on commercials for Diet Coke, BVD, Coors (Hispanic).
PICTURES: Grease, Tilt, Take Down, Body Rock, Snakeater, Night of the Warrior, Snakeater II, Final Impact, Snakeater III, Killing Streets, CIA Code Name: Alexa, CIA: Target Alexa, The Swordsman, Bounty Tracker.
TELEVISION: Series: California Fever, Secrets of Midland Heights, Falcon Crest, Dancin' to the Hits (host), Renegade.Guest: The Love Boat, Switch, Sword of Justice, The

Hitchhiker, Dear John. *Movies*: Detour to Terror, CIA: Code Name Alexa.

LAMBERT, CHRISTOPHER (also CHRISTOPHE): Actor. b. New York , NY, Mar. 29, 1957; reared in Geneva. Parents French. m. actress Diane Lane. Studied at Paris Conservatoire Drama Academy. Won role in small French film, Le Bar du Telephone.
PICTURES: La Dame de Coeur, Legitime Violence, Greystoke: The Legend of Tarzan Lord of the Apes, Subway (Cesar Award), Highlander, The Sicilian, To Kill a Priest, After the Rain, Why Me?, Highlander 2: The Quickening, Priceless Beauty, Knight Moves, Fortress, Gunmen, Roadflower.

LAMBERT, MARY: Director. b. Arkansas. e. attended U. of Denver, Rhode Island Sch. of Design where began making short films. Worked in variety of prod. jobs before moving to Los Angeles and directing TV commercials and music videos (includ. Madonna's Material Girl, Like a Virgin, Like a Prayer, others for Sting, Janet Jackson and Mick Jagger).
PICTURES: Siesta, Pet Sematary, Pet Sematary 2.

LAMBERT, VERITY: Producer. b. London, England, Nov. 27. Ent. TV 1961; prod. Dr. Who, Adam Adamant Lives, Detective, Somerset Maugham (all BBC series). Since 1971: (series), Budgie, Between The Wars. 1974: Appt. controller of Drama, Thames Television. 1979: Chief exec. Euston Films. 1983: Director of Production Thorn EMI Films Ltd. Relinquished her position as controller of Drama Thames Television and retaining pos. as chief exec., Euston Films. Became indep. prod. developing projects for film and TV incl. BBC. Founded own company, Cinema Verity Ltd., 1985.
PICTURES: Link, Morons from Outer Space, Restless Natives, Dreamchild, Not for Publication, Clockwise, A Cry in the Dark.
TELEVISION: May to December, The Boys from the Bush, Sleepers, GBH, So Haunt Me, Comics, Coasting, Sam Saturday, Running Late.

LAMOUR, DOROTHY: Actress. b. New Orleans, LA, Dec. 10, 1914. e. Spencer's Business Sch. Miss New Orleans 1931; sang on radio programs.
PICTURES: Jungle Princess (debut, 1936), Swing High Swing Low, High Wide and Handsome, Last Train From Madrid, Thrill of a Lifetime, The Hurricane, Big Broadcast of 1938, Her Jungle Love, Tropic Holiday, Spawn of the North, St. Louis Blues, Man About Town, Disputed Passage, Johnny Apollo, Typhoon, Road to Singapore, Moon Over Burma, Chad Hanna, Road to Zanzibar, Caught in the Draft, Aloma of the South Seas, The Fleet's In, Beyond the Blue Horizon, Road to Morocco, Star Spangled Rhythm, They Got Me Covered, Dixie, Riding High, And the Angels Sing, Rainbow Island, Medal for Benny, Duffy's Tavern, Road to Utopia, Masquerade in Mexico, My Favorite Brunette, Road to Rio, Wild Harvest, Variety Girl, On Our Merry Way, Lulu Belle, Girl from Manhattan, Lucky Stiff, Slightly French, Manhandled, Here Comes the Groom, The Greatest Show on Earth, Road to Bali, Road to Hong Kong, Donovan's Reef, Pajama Party, The Phynx, Won Ton Ton the Dog Who Saved Hollywood, Creepshow 2.
TELEVISION: *Movie*: Death at Love House. *Guest*: Murder She Wrote, I Spy, Marcus Welby, Love Boat, Crazy Like a Fox, Remington Steele, Damon Runyon Theatre, Hart to Hart. *Specials*: Bob Hope Specials, Entertaining the Troops, Remembering Bing, many others.

LANCASTER, BURT: Actor. b. New York, NY, Nov. 2, 1913. e. NYU. Performed as acrobat with Ringling Bros., in carnivals and vaudeville as part of Lang and Cravat, acrobatic team with Nick Cravat, 1932–39. Floor walker, dept. store salesman Chicago, 1939–42. Also fireman and engineer in meat packing plant. Served in U.S. Army Special Service in Italy & N. Africa, W.W.II; NY stage debut: A Sound of Hunting (1945); screen debut in The Killers, 1946. Formed Hecht-Lancaster Orgn. in partnership with Harold Hecht; 1954–57 became Hecht-Hill-Lancaster (with James Hill).
PICTURES: The Killer (debut, 1946), Desert Fury, I Walk Alone, Brute Force, Variety Girl, Sorry Wrong Number, Kiss the Blood Off My Hands, Criss Cross, All My Sons, Rope of Sand, Mister 880, The Flame and the Arrow, Vengeance Valley, Ten Tall Men, Jim Thorpe—All American, The Crimson Pirate (also co-prod.), Come Back Little Sheba, South Sea Woman, From Here to Eternity, His Majesty O'Keefe, Three Sailors and a Girl (cameo), Apache, Vera Cruz, The Kentuckian (also dir.), The Rose Tattoo, Trapeze, The Rainmaker, Gunfight at the OK Corral, Sweet Smell of Success, Run Silent Run Deep (also co-prod.), Separate Tables, The Devil's Disciple, The Unforgiven, Elmer Gantry (Acad. Award, 1960), The Young Savages, Judgment at Nuremberg, Birdman of Alcatraz, The Leopard, A Child is Waiting, The List of Adrian Messenger, Seven Days in May, The Hallelujah Trail, The Train, The Professionals, The Swimmer, The Scalphunters, The Gypsy Moths, Castle Keep, Airport, King: A Filmed Record ... Montgomery to Memphis, Valdez Is Coming, Lawman, Ulzana's Raid, Scorpio, Executive Action, The Midnight Man (also prod., co-dir., co-s.p.), Conversation

Piece, Buffalo Bill and the Indians, The Cassandra Crossing, Twilight's Last Gleaming, The Island of Dr. Moreau, 1900, Go Tell the Spartans, Zulu Dawn, Cattle Annie and Little Britches, Atlantic City, La Pelle, Local Hero, The Osterman Weekend, Little Treasure, Tough Guys, Rocket Gibraltar, The Jeweller's Shop, Field of Dreams.
TELEVISION: *Movies*: Victory at Entebbe, Scandal Sheet, On Wings of Eagles, Barnum, Scandal Sheet, Sins of the Fathers (German), Phantom of the Opera, Voyage of Terror: The Achille Lauro Affair, Separate But Equal. Mini-Series: Moses the Lawgiver, Marco Polo. *Special*: Legacy of the Hollywood Backlist (narrator).

LANDAU, ELY A.: Executive. b. New York, NY, Jan. 20, 1920. Formed National Telefilm Associates, Inc., 1954; org. NTA Film Network, 1956; pres., chmn. of bd., National Telefilm Associates, Inc., 1957; resigned, 1961; formed Ely Landau Company, Inc., 1963; dist. The Servant, King and Country, Umbrellas of Cherbourg; prod. Long Day's Journey into Night, The Fool Killer, The Pawnbroker, A Face of War, The Madwoman of Chaillot. Prod. King—A Filmed Record—Montgomery to Memphis, 1968; organized, directed one-night simultaneous charity showing 633 theatres U.S., 1970; 1972 Formed American Film Theatre, and the Ely Landau Organization, Inc. 1972–74 produced Iceman Cometh, Rhinoceros, The Homecoming, A Delicate Balance, Luther, Lost in the Stars, Butley, Galileo, In Celebration, The Man in the Glass Booth. Also prod.: The Greek Tycoon, Hopscotch, The Chosen, Beatlemania—The Movie, The Deadly Game, Separate Tables (TV), Mr. Halpern and Mr. Johnson (TV), The Holcroft Covenant.
THEATER: Off-B'way: The Chosen (co-prod.) (1987).

LANDAU, MARTIN: Actor. b. Brooklyn, NY, June 20, 1931. e. Pratt Inst., Art Students League, Cartoon and staff artist on N.Y. Daily News; studied 3 yrs. at Actors Studio. Represented by William Morris Agency.
PICTURES: Pork Chop Hill, North by Northwest, The Gazebo, Stagecoach to Dancer's Rock, Cleopatra, The Hallelujah Trail, The Greatest Story Ever Told, Decision at Midnight, Alien Attack, Nevada Smith, They Call Me Mister Tibbs, Operation Snafu, A Town Called Hell, Black Gunn, Strange Shadows in an Empty Room, Meteor, Destination Moonbase Alpha, Without Warning, Trial By Terror, Cosmic Princess, Journey Through the Black Sun, The Last Word, The Return, Alone in the Dark, The Being, Access Code, Treasure Island, Run if You Can, W.A.R., Sweet Revenge, Cyclone, Real Bullets, Empire State, Delta Fever, Tucker: The Man and His Dream (Acad. Award nom.), Crimes and Misdemeanors (Golde Globe Award, Acad. Award nom.), Paint It Black, Firehead, Tipperary, The Color of Evening, Mistress, Eye of the Stranger, Time is Money, Sliver, Intersection.
TELEVISION: *Series*: Mission Impossible (1966–69; 3 Emmy noms., Golden Globe Award), Space 1999. *Movies*: Welcome Home Johnny Bristol, Savage, The Death of Ocean View Park, Harlem Globetrotters on Gilligan's Island, Fall of the House of Usher, Max and Helen (ACE Award nom.), The Neon Empire, By Dawn's Early Light (ACE Award nom.), Something to Live For: The Alison Gertz Story, Legacy of Lies (ACE Award nom.), 12:01. Numerous guest appearances.
STAGE: Middle of the Night, Uncle Vanya, Stalag 17, Wedding Breakfast, First Love, The Goat Song.

LANDAU, RICHARD H.: Writer. b. New York, NY, Feb. 21, 1914. e. U. of Arizona, Yale U. With Small-Landau agency handling writers and stories; shorts dept. writer MGM 1939; writer for RKO Radio since 1942; wrote documentaries and training films for U.S. Army.
PICTURES: Gun in His Hand, Strange Confession, Challenge in the Night, Back to Bataan, Little Iodine, Christmas Eve, Crooked Way, Johnny One Eye, Roadblock, Lost Continent, F.B.I. Girl, Stolen Face, Bad Blonde, Spaceways, Sins of Jezebel, Blackout, Deadly Game, A Race for Life, Pearl of the South Pacific, Creeping Unknown.

LANDERS, HAL: Producer. b. Chicago, IL, June 26, 1928. Company: The Hal Landers Co.
PICTURES: Joy Ride; Damnation Alley; Gypsy Moths; Monte Walsh; The Hot Rock; Bank Shot; Death Wish; Death Wish II (exec. prod.).

LANDES, MICHAEL: Executive. b. Bronx, NY, Feb. 4, 1939. e. Fairleigh Dickinson, B.A., 1961; Rutgers, J.D., 1964; NYU, L.L.M., 1965. 17 years of corporate law and financing experience as sr. partner in law firm of Hahn and Hessen. Co-chairman of The ALMI Group formed, 1978. Co-chmn. & CEO of Almi Pictures Inc. formed, 1982. In July 1986, Almi sold its 97-screen RKO Century Warner Theatre chain to Cineplex Odeon. Nov. 1986, purchased Video Shack Inc. assets and formed RKO Warner Video, Inc.; Chmn since inception. May 1988, became chairman, Damon Creations, Inc. which merged with Enro Holding Corp. and Enro Shirt Co. into Damon Creations. Sold Damon, 1988. Chmn./CEO, RKO Warner Intl. Ltd. a video franchisor and chmn./CEO of The Lexington Group Ltd., org. 1990. Member: World Business Council (WBC). Chief Executives Organization (CEO); Association for a Better New York; bd. of dirs. Motion Picture Pioneers; Academy of Motion Picture Arts and Sciences; bd. of dirs. Periwinkle Theatre Productions.

LANDIS, JOHN: Director. b. Chicago, IL, Aug. 3, 1950.
PICTURES: Battle for the Planet of the Apes (actor only), Schlock (also actor, writer), Death Race 2000 (actor only), Kentucky Fried Movie (also actor), National Lampoon's Animal House, 1941 (actor only), The Blues Brothers (also co-s.p.), An American Werewolf in London (also s.p.), Trading Places, Twilight Zone—The Movie (sequence dir. & writer; co-prod.), The Muppets Take Manhattan (actor only), Into the Night (also actor), Spies Like Us, Three Amigos, Amazon Women on the Moon (sequence dir.; co-exec. prod.), Coming to America, Spontaneous Combustion (actor only), Darkman (actor only), Oscar, Diva Las Vegas (actor only) Sleepwalkers (actor only), Innocent Blood, Venice/Venice (actor only).
TELEVISION: *Series*: Dream On (exec. prod. and dir.), Topper (exec. prod. & dir.). *Movie*: Psycho IV (actor only).
Videos: Thriller, Black or White (both for Michael Jackson).

LANDRES, PAUL: Director. b. New York, NY, Aug. 21, 1912. e. UCLA. Started as asst. film editor at Universal 1931. Editor 1937 to 1949 of many feature films. Director of feature films and TV since 1949. Under directorial contract to Warner Bros. 1961–62. Director of 22 feature films for theatrical release.
PICTURES: Oregon Passage, A Modern Marriage, Mark of the Vampire, Navy Bound, The Curse of Dracula, Miracle of the Hills, 54 Washington Street and Son of a Gunfighter.
TELEVISION: 91 hour films and over 300 half hour shows including among many others, multiple episodes of Bonanza, Daktari, The Rifleman, 77 Sunset Strip, Maverick Hawaiian Eye, The Plainsman, Readers Digest, Topper, Wyatt Earp, Blondie, etc.

LANDSBURG, ALAN: Executive, Producer, Writer. b. New York, NY, May 10, 1933. e. NYU. Producer for NBC News Dept., 1951–59; producer-writer, CBS, 1959–60; exec. prod., Wolper Productions/Metromedia Producers Corp., 1961–70; chairman, The Alan Landsburg Company, 1970–present. Co-exec. prod.: Jaws 3-D, Porky's II: The Next Day.
TELEVISION: *Exec. prod.*: Biography, National Geographic Specials (1965–70): The Undersea World of Jacques Cousteau; In Search of. . ., That's Incredible. Movies: Adam, Fear on Trial, Parent Trap II, Adam: His Song Continues, The George McKenna Story, Long Gone, Strange Voices, Bluegrass, A Place at the Table, Too Young the Hero, A Stoning in Fulham County, High Risk, Destined to Live, Quiet Victory: The Charlie Wedemeyer Story, The Ryan White Story, Unspeakable Acts (co-exec. prod., writer), A Mother's Right: The Elizabeth Morgan Story (writer), The Hunter (writer).

LANE, DIANE: Actress. b. New York, NY, Jan. 2, 1965. m. actor Christopher Lambert. Acted in stage classics (Medea, Electra, As You Like It) at La Mama Experimental Theatre Club, NY.
PICTURES: A Little Romance (debut, 1979), Touched by Love, National Lampoon Goes to the Movies, Cattle Annie and the Little Britches, Six Pack, Ladies and Gentlemen: The Fabulous Stains, The Outsiders, Rumble Fish, Streets of Fire, The Cotton Club, The Big Town, Lady Beware, Priceless Beauty, Vital Signs, My New Gun, Chaplin, Knight Moves, Indian Summer.
STAGE: The Cherry Orchard, Agamemnon, Runaways.
TELEVISION: *Movies*: Child Bride of Short Creek, Miss All-American Beauty, Descending Angel. *Mini-Series*: Lonesome Dove.

LANE, NATHAN: Actor. r.n. Joseph Lane. b. Jersey City, NJ, Feb. 3, 1956.
PICTURES: Ironweed (debut, 1987), Joe Vs. the Volcano, The Lemon Sisters, He Said She Said, Frankie and Johnny, Life With Mikey, Addams Family Values, The Lion King (voice).
TELEVISION: *Series*: One of the Boys. *Guest*: Days and Nights of Molly Dodd, Miami Vice. *Movie*: Jacqueline Susann's Valley of the Dolls. *Specials*: Alice in Wonderland, The Last Mile.
THEATRE: *Bdwy*: Present Laughter, Merlin, Wind in the Willows, Some Americans Abroad, On Borrowed Time, Guys & Dolls (Drama Desk & Outer Critics Circle Awards), Laughter on the 23rd Floor. *Off-Bdwy*: A Midsummer Night's Dream, Measure for Measure, Claptrap, The Common Pursuit, In a Pig's Valise, Uncounted Blessings, The Film Society, The Lisbon Traviata (also L.A.; Drama Desk & LA Drama Critics Circle Awards), Bad Habits, Lips Together Teeth Apart (also L.A.).

LANG, CHARLES: Cinematographer. b. Bluff, UT, March 27, 1902. e. Lincoln H.S., Los Angeles; U. of Southern California. Entered m.p. ind. with Paramount Film Laboratory, then asst. cameraman; dir. of photography, Paramount, 1929–52; then freelance.
PICTURES: A Farewell to Arms (Academy Award for best photography, 1933), The Uninvited, Ghost and Mrs. Muir, A Foreign Affair, September Affair, Ace in the Hole, Sudden Fear, Sabrina, Queen Bee, Man from Laramie, The Rainmaker, Some Like It Hot, The Magnificent Seven, Facts of Life, One-Eyed Jacks, Summer and Smoke, Charade, Father Goose, Wait Until Dark, Inside Daisy Clover, Hotel, Flim Flam Man, The Stalking Moon, Cactus Flower, Bob & Carol & Ted & Alice, The Love Machine, Doctors' Wives, Butterflies Are Free.

LANG, DAVID: Writer. b. New York, NY, Nov. 30, 1913. Was in Merchant Marine three years. Joined Charles Mintz Studio (Columbia) as cartoonist. Moved to MGM cartoon dept. 1938–40. Radio writer, Calling All Cars, KNX, Los Angeles, 1941. Contract writer at MGM, 1941–43. Yank on the Burma Road, Gambler's Choice, Hired Gun, North West Mounted Police, Midnight Manhunt, People Are Funny, Caged Fury, One Exciting Night, Flaxy Martin, Smart Money, Chain of Circumstance, Ambush at Tomahawk, The Nebraskan, Black Horse Canyon, Screaming Eagles, Hellcats of the Navy, Buckskin Lady, Queen of Burlesque.
TELEVISION: Cheyenne, 87th Precinct, Ford Theatre, Gallant Men, Westinghouse Theatre, Adventures in Paradise, Bonanza, Trackdown, Wanted Dead or Alive, Rifleman, Rawhide, Have Gun Will Travel. At least two hundred credits in above series. Novelist. Oedipus Burning.

LANG, JENNINGS: Executive. b. New York, NY, May 28, 1915. e. St. John's U. Law Sch. m. actress-singer Monica Lewis. Went into law practice in 1937 with Seligsburg and Lewis, m.p. law specialists. 1938 to Hollywood as 2nd asst. dir. at Grand National Studios. Opened own office as actor's agent; first client, comedian Hugh Herbert. In 1940 joined Jaffe Agency; made partner and v.p. in 1942. Was pres. from 1948 to May, 1950, when resigned to join MCA. Worked in all phases of MCA operations; in 1952 made v.p. of MCA TV Ltd., and bd. mem. Involved with prod. and sales of TV prods. from inception of Revue (now Universal City Studios) in 1950. Organized Revue's New Projects Dept., creator and exec. in chg. of prog. dev. Involved with creation and sales of such series as Wagon Train, The Robert Cummings Show, Bachelor Father, Wells Fargo, Mike Hammer. Supvr. of Universal's World Premiere films. Made exec. prod. at MCA (Universal) for motion pictures.
PICTURES: *Exec. prod.*: Coogan's Bluff, Winning, They Might Be Giants, Puzzle of a Downfall Child, The Beguiled, Act of the Heart, Tell Them Willie Boy Is Here, Play Misty for Me, Pete 'n Tillie, High Plains Drifter, Slaughterhouse Five, Charley Varrick, Breezy, The Great Waldo Pepper, Airport '75, Earthquake, Joe Kidd, The Great Northfield Minnesota Raid, The Eiger Sanction, Airport 1977, The Front Page, The Hindenburg. *Producer*: Swashbuckler, Roller Coaster, House Calls, Nunzio, Airport '79—The Concorde, Little Miss Marker, The Nude Bomb, The Sting II, Stick.

LANG, OTTO: Producer, Director, Four Academy Award nominations for Cinemascope Specials, Twentieth Century-Fox Film Corp. Saga of Western Man; ABC-TV Specials—The Legend of Cortez; Beethoven: Ordeal and Triumph.
TELEVISION: Man from U.N.C.L.E., Daktari, Iron Horse, Cheyenne, Dick Powell Show, Zane Gray Theatre, Ann Sothern Show, Rifleman, Bat Masterson, Seahunt, The Deputy, Surfside 6, Hawaiian Eye. Prod. Twentieth Century Fox Hour. Dir.: Man and the Challenge, Aquanauts, World of Giants. Dir. feature for Cinerama: Search for Paradise.
PICTURES: *Prod.*: Call Northside 777, Five Fingers, White Witch Doctor. Specialist for foreign locations. Many segments for This World of Ours; Wide, Wide World. 1969. *Assoc. prod*: Tora! Tora! Tora!

LANG, STEPHEN: Actor. b. Queens, NY, July 11, 1952. e. Swarthmore Col. Professional debut 1976 at Washington D.C.'s Folger Theatre.
PICTURES: Twice in a Lifetime, Band of the Hand, Manhunter, Project X, Last Exit to Brooklyn, The Hard Way, Another You, Guilty As Sin, Gettysburg, Tombstone.
TELEVISION: *Series*: Crime Story. *Movies*: King of America, Death of a Salesman, Stone Pillow, Babe Ruth, Taking Back My Life: The Nancy Ziegenmeyer Story, Darkness Before Dawn, Murder Between Friends. *Special*: Anyone for Tennyson? *Guest*: Tribeca.
THEATRE: NY: Rosencrantz and Guildenstern Are Dead, Henry V, Bloomsday on Broadway, The Shadow of a Gun, Saint Joan, Hamlet, Johnny on the Spot, Death of a Salesman, Barbarians, The Winter's Tale, A Few Good Men, The Speed of Darkness.

LANGE, HOPE: Actress. b. Redding Ridge, CT, Nov. 28, 1931. e. Reed Col., Portland, OR; Barmore Jr. Coll., N.Y. Parents: John Lange, musician (Arr. music for stage shows, including Show Boat); Minnette Buddecke Lange, actress. Prof. stage debut at in The Patriots on Broadway; then understudy The Hot Corner.
PICTURES: Bus Stop (debut, 1956), The True Story of Jesse James, Peyton Place (Acad. Award nom.),The Young Lions, In Love and War, The Best of Everything, Wild in the Country, Pocketful of Miracles, Love Is a Ball, Jigsaw, Death

Wish, I Am the Cheese, The Prodigal, A Nightmare on Elm Street Part 2, Blue Velvet, Tune in Tomorrow.
TELEVISION: *Series*: The Ghost and Mrs. Muir (2 Emmy Awards), The New Dick Van Dyke Show, Knight and Dave. *Movies*: Crowhaven Farm, That Certain Summer, The 500 Pound Jerk, I Love You—Goodbye, Fer-de-Lance, The Secret Night Caller, Love Boat II, Like Normal People, The Day Christ Died, Beulah Land, Pleasure Palace, Private Sessions, Dead Before Dawn, Cooperstown. *Special*: A Family Tree (Trying Times). *Mini-Series*: The Henry Ford Story: Man and the Machine.

LANGE, JESSICA: Actress. b. Cloquet, MN, Apr. 20, 1949. e. U. of Minnesota. Left to study mime 2 years under Etienne Decroux in Paris. Dancer, Opera Comique, Paris; model with Wilhelmina agy, NY. Worked in experimental theatre in New York. Broadway debut 1992 in A Streetcar Named Desire (Theatre World Award).
PICTURES: King Kong (debut, 1976), All That Jazz, How to Beat the High Cost of Living, The Postman Always Rings Twice, Frances, Tootsie (Acad. Award, supp., 1982), Country (also co-prod.), Sweet Dreams, Crimes of the Heart, Far North, Everybody's All American, Music Box, Men Don't Leave, Cape Fear, Blue Sky, Night and the City.
TELEVISION: *Special*: Cat on a Hot Tin Roof. *Movie*: O Pioneers!

LANGELLA, FRANK: Actor. b. Bayonne, NJ, Jan. 1, 1938. Studied acting at Syracuse U., later in regional repertory, summer stock, and on and off Bdwy. Bdwy debut: Seascape (1975, Tony Award).
THEATER: member Lincoln Ctr. Rep. co. 1963. The Immoralist (Off-Bdwy debut, 1963), Benito Cereno, The Old Glory (Obie Award), Good Day (Obie Award), The White Devil (Obie Award), Long Day's Journey Into Night, Yerma, The Devils (L.A.), Dracula, A Cry of Players, Cyrano de Bergerac, The Tooth of the Crime, Ring Around the Moon, Amadeus, Passion, Design for Living, Sherlock's Last Case, Les Liaisons Dangereuses (Ahmanson, L.A.), The Tempest, My Fair Lady, Scenes From an Execution (L.A.).
PICTURES: Diary of a Mad Housewife (debut, 1970), The Twelve Chairs, The Deadly Trap, The Wrath of God, Dracula, Those Lips Those Eyes, Sphinx, The Men's Club, Masters of the Universe, And God Created Woman, True Identity, 1492: Conquest of Paradise, Body of Evidence, Dave.
TELEVISION: *Specials*: Benito Cereno (1965), The Good Day, The Ambassador, The Sea Gull, The American Woman: Portrait in Courage, Eccentricities of a Nightingale, Sherlock Holmes, Fortitude (Kurt Vonnegut's Monkey House). *Movies*: The Mark of Zorro, Liberty.

LANGFORD, FRANCES: Singer, Actress. b. Lakeland, FL, April 4, 1913. e. Southern Coll. Stage experience in vaudeville, nightclubs, national radio programs. In 1935: collab. on lyrics and appeared in Every Night at Eight, Collegiate Broadway Melody of 1936, Palm Springs, Born to Dance, The Hit Parade, Hollywood Hotel, Dreaming Out Loud, Too Many Girls, The Hit Parade of 1941, All-American Coed, Swing It Soldier, Mississippi Gambler, Yankee Doodle Dandy, This Is the Army, Career Girl, The Girl Rush, Dixie Jamboree, Radio Stars on Parade, People Are Funny, Deputy Marshall, Purple Heart Diary, Glenn Miller Story; TV appearances with Don Ameche.

LANGNER, PHILIP: Producer, b. New York, NY, Aug. 24, 1926. e. Yale U. President of The Theatre Guild and Theatre Guild Films, Inc. Producer the Westport Country Playhouse 1947—53. Joined The Theatre Guild 1954. Produced 28 plays on Broadway at the Theatre Guild including the Matchmaker, Bells Are Ringing, The Tunnel of Love, Sunrise at Campobello, A Majority of One, The Unsinkable Molly Brown, A Passage to India, Seidman and Son, The Royal Hunt of the Sun, The Homecoming, Absurd Person Singular and Golda.
FILMS: Producer: The Pawnbroker, Slaves, Born to Win. Associate Prod.: Judgment at Nuremberg, A Child Is Waiting.

LANSBURY, ANGELA: Actress. b. London, England, Oct. 16, 1925. Sister of Bruce and Edgar Lansbury. e. South Hampstead Sch. for Girls, England; Acad. of Music, London; Feagin Dramatic Sch., N.Y. p. Moyna Macgill, actress; also rel. to Robert B. Mantell, actor, Rt. Hon. George Lansbury, gov't. official. Screen debut in Gaslight, 1944, which won Hollywood Foreign Correspondents' Assoc. award. Exercise and lifestyle video: Positive Moves, 1988.
PICTURES: Gaslight (debut, 1944; Acad. Award nom.), National Velvet, Picture of Dorian Gray (Acad. Award nom.), Harvey Girls, Hoodlum Saint, The Private Affairs of Bel Ami, Till the Clouds Roll By, If Winter Comes, Tenth Avenue Angel, State of the Union, Three Musketeers, Red Danube, Samson and Delilah, Kind Lady, Mutiny, Remains to Be Seen, Purple Mask, A Lawless Street, Court Jester, Please Murder Me, Key Man (A Life at Stake), The Long Hot Summer, The Reluctant Debutante, The Summer of the 17th Doll (Season of Passion), Dark at the Top of the Stairs, A Breath of Scandal, Blue Hawaii, All Fall Down, In the Cool of the Day, The Manchurian Candidate (Acad. Award nom.), The World

of Henry Orient, Dear Heart, The Greatest Story Ever Told, Harlow, The Amorous Adventures of Moll Flanders, Mr. Buddwing, Something for Everyone, Bedknobs and Broomsticks, Death on the Nile, The Lady Vanishes, The Mirror Crack'd, The Last Unicorn (voice), The Pirates of Penzance, The Company of Wolves, Beauty and the Beast (voice).
BROADWAY: Hotel Paradiso (NY debut, 1957), A Taste of Honey, Anyone Can Whistle, Mame (Tony Award, 1966), Dear World (Tony Award, 1969), Gypsy (Tony Award, 1975), The King and I, Sweeney Todd (Tony Award, 1979), A Little Family Business, Mame (1983 revival).
TELEVISION: *Special*: Sweeney Todd. *Movies*: Little Gloria . . . Happy at Last, The Gift of Love: A Christmas Story, The First Olympics: Athens 1896, Lace, Rage of Angels: The Story Continues, Shootdown, The Shell Seekers, The Love She Sought, Mrs. 'arris Goes to Paris. *Series*: Pantomime Quiz, Murder She Wrote.

LANSBURY, BRUCE: Executive. b. London, England, Jan. 12, 1930. Brother of Angela and twin Edgar. e. UCLA. m. actress Moyna Macgill. Writer, prod. KABC-TV, Los Angeles, 1957—59; joined CBS-TV, 1959, was ass't. dir., program dev., Hollywood, director for daytime and nighttime programs, and v.p., programs, New York; 1964—66, indep. prod., Broadway stage; 1966—69 producer, Wild Wild West, CBS series; 1969—72, prod. Mission: Impossible, Paramount Movies of Week; now v.p., creative affairs, Paramount TV.
TELEVISION: Great Adventure (series; prod.), Wings of the Water (exec. prod.), Murder She Wrote.

LANSBURY, EDGAR: Producer, Director, Designer. b. London, England, Jan. 12, 1930. e. UCLA. Brother of Angela and Bruce Lansbury. Started career as scenic designer and art director. 1955—60, art dir., CBS; 1962—63, exec. art dir. prod. for WNDT-TV, educational sta.; On Bdwy. produced such shows as The Subject Was Roses, Promenade, Waiting for Godot, Long Day's Journey into Night, Gypsy, The Night That Made America Famous, American Buffalo, Amphigorey: The Musical, etc. Director on stage: Without Apologies, Advice From a Caterpillar, The Country Club.
PICTURES: *Producer*: The Subject Was Roses, Godspell, The Wild Party, Squirm, Blue Sunshine, He Knows You're Alone, The Clairvoyant.
TELEVISION: The Defenders (art. dir.), Summer Girl (exec. prod.), Wings of the Water (exec. prod.), A Stranger Waits.

LANSING, SHERRY: Executive. b. Chicago, IL, July 31, 1944. e. Northwestern U. m. director William Friedkin. Taught math, English and drama in L.A. city high schools, 1966—69. Acted in films (Loving, Rio Lobo) and numerous TV shows. Story editor for Wagner Intl. Prod. Co., 1972—74. Talent Associates, in chg. West Coast development (all projects), 1974—75. Appt. MGM story editor, 1975. In 1977 named MGM v.p. of creative affairs, Nov., 1977, appointed vice pres., production, at Columbia Pictures. January, 1980, appointed pres., Twentieth Century-Fox Productions. Resigned 1982 to form new production co. with Stanley R. Jaffee: Jaffee—Lansing Prods.
PICTURES: Co-prod.: Racing with the Moon, Firstborn, Fatal Attraction, The Accused, Black Rain, School Ties, Indecent Proposal.
TELEVISION: When the Time Comes (exec. prod.), Mistress.

LANTZ, WALTER: Animated cartoon producer. b. New Rochelle NY, April 27, 1900. Producer and creator of Woody Woodpecker, Andy Panda, Chilly Willy. Started with Gregory La Cava, 1916 with Katzenjammer Kids, Happy Hooligan and Krazy Kat. Joined J. R. Bray in 1922, producing Col. Heeza Liar, Dinky Doodle. Started with Universal Pictures in 1928. Produced first Technicolor cartoon for Paul Whiteman's King of Jazz. Produced Oswald Rabbit. Created Woody Woodpecker in 1941. Produced the first Woody Woodpecker TV show in 1957. Toured the Pacific War Zone on a handshake tour for the USO, with wife Gracie, the voice of Woody Woodpecker. Has been awarded the Golden Globe Award, the ASIFA Award, and in 1979 the Oscar for achievement in the field of animation. Now producing the Woody Woodpecker TV show. 1986, awarded a star on Hollywood Walk of Fame.

LaPAGLIA, ANTHONY: Actor. b. Adelaide, Australia, 1959. Former teacher, moved to U.S. in 1984. Made Off-Bdwy debut in Bouncers, followed by On the Open Road.
PICTURES: Slaves of New York (debut, 1989), Betsy's Wedding, He Said/She Said, One Good Cop, 29th Street, Whispers in the Dark, Innocent Blood, So I Married an Axe Murderer, The Client.
TELEVISION: *Movies*: Criminal Justice, Keeper of the City, Black Magic.

LARDNER, RING W., JR.: Writer. b. Chicago, IL, Aug. 19, 1915. p. writer-humorist Ring W. and Ellis A. e. Phillips Andover Acad, Princeton U. Was reporter on New York Daily Mirror. Publ. writer, Selznick International. Shared orig. screenplay Academy Award with Michael Kanin for Woman of the Year, 1942. 1947, mem. of "Hollywood 10." In collab. with Ian Hunter conceived and wrote under pseudonyms many episodes in 5

TV series while blacklisted. M*A*S*H (Acad. Award, s.p. based on material from another medium, 1970). 1989, received Writers Guild Laurel Award. Author of novels: The Ecstacy of Owen Muir, All For Love, and memoir, The Lardners My Family Remembered. Also collab. on Bdwy musical Foxy. 1992, WGA Ian McLellan Hunter Memorial Award for Lifetime Achievement.
PICTURES: Woman of the Year, The Cross of Lorraine, Tomorrow the World, Forever Amber, Forbidden Street, Four Days Leave, Cloak and Dagger, The Cincinnati Kid, M*A*S*H, The Greatest.

LARKIN, JAMES J.: Executive. b. Brooklyn, NY, Nov. 2, 1925. e. Columbia U., 1947–52. U.S. Air Force, 1943–46; BOAC rep. to entertainment ind., 1948–60; pres., Transportation Counselors Inc., 1960–62; pres., Larkin Associates, Inc., 1962–65; exec. Radio N.Y. Worldwide, 1965–68, V.P. Grolier Educational Corp., 1968–69; V.P. Visual Informational Systems, 1969–73. Pres., Business Television Services, Inc., 1973; exec. prod., Madhouse Brigade, 1977–79; prod.-writer, All Those Beautiful Girls, 1979–80.

LARROQUETTE, JOHN: Actor. b. New Orleans, LA., Nov. 25, 1947. Disc jockey on FM radio during 1960s and early 70s. Acted on L.A. stage from 1973 (The Crucible, Enter Laughing, Endgame). Prof. debut, TV series Doctor's Hospital, 1976–78. Was narrator for film Texas Chainsaw Massacre.
PICTURES: Altered States, Heart Beat, Green Ice, Stripes, Cat People, Hysterical, Twilight Zone—the Movie, Choose Me, Meatballs Part II, Star Trek III: The Search for Spock, Summer Rental, Blind Date, Second Sight, Madhouse, Tune in Tomorrow.
TELEVISION: Series: Doctor's Hospital, Baa Baa Black Sheep, Night Court (4 Emmys, 1985–88), The John Larroquette Show. Movies: Bare Essence, The Last Ninja, Hot Paint, Convicted, One Special Victory (also co-exec. prod.).

LARSON, BOB: Producer. e. UCLA. First job while in high school as prod. asst. on Sol Lesser's The Red House (1947). Worked way up after schooling thru film ranks; prod. mgr., Forty Pounds of Trouble, Freud, etc., for Universal Pictures. Joined Bryna Prods. as exec. in chg. prod. (Spartacus, The Vikings). Assoc. prod., asst. dir. for Clint Eastwood on Play Misty for Me. Rejoined Universal for decade; then went to David Wolper Prods. Became independent, producing TV pilot, Strange New World, at Warner Bros.; two films at Universal: Now partner with director Michael Apted, collaborating on Coal Miner's Daughter, Continental Divide, Bring on the Night, 28 Up, River Rat, Critical Condition, Fletch Lives.

LASSALLY, WALTER: Cinematographer. b. Berlin, Germany, Dec. 18, 1926. Entered indust. as clapper-boy at Riverside Studios. During 1950s allied himself with Britain's Free Cinema filmmakers working for Lindsay Anderson, Gavin Lambert, Tony Richardson and Karel Reisz.
PICTURES: A Girl in Black (1956), Beat Girl, A Taste of Honey, Electra, The Loneliness of the Long Distance Runner, Tom Jones, Zorba the Greek (Acad. Award, 1964), The Day the Fish Came Out, Joanna, Oedipus the King, The Adding Machine, Three Into Two Won't Go, Something for Everyone, Twinky (Lola), Savages, Happy Mother's Day ... Love George, To Kill a Clown, The Wild Party, Pleasantville, The Great Bank Hoax, Woman Across the Way, Hullabaloo Over George and Bonnie's Pictures, Something Short of Paradise, The Blood of Hussain, Angels of Iron, Memoirs of a Survivor, Too Far to Go, Heat and Dust, Private School, The Bostonians, The Deceivers, Fragments of Isabella, The Perfect Murder, One Good Cop, Ballad of the Sad Cafe, Switch, Father of the Bride.
TELEVISION: Mrs. Delafield Wants to Marry, My Africa.

LASSER, LOUISE: Actress. b. New York, NY, April 11, 1939. e. Brandeis U., New School for Social Research. Appeared on stage before theatrical film debut in 1965 with What's New, Pussycat?
THEATER: I Can Get It For You Wholesale, The Third Ear, Henry Sweet Henry, Lime Green/Khaki Blue, The Chinese, Marie & Bruce, A Coupla White Chicks Sitting Around Talking.
PICTURES: What's Up Tiger Lily? (voice), Take the Money and Run, Bananas, Such Good Friends, Everything You Always Wanted to Know About Sex, Slither, In God We Trust, Stardust Memories, Crimewave, Nightmare at Shadow Woods (Blood Rage), Surrender, Sing, Rude Awakening, Modern Love, Frankenhooker.
TELEVISION: Series: Mary Hartman Mary Hartman, It's a Living. Movies: Coffee Tea or Me?, Isn't It Shocking?, Just Me and You (also writer), For Ladies Only. Guest: Bob Newhart Show, Mary Tyler Moor Show, Taxi, St. Elsewhere, Empty Nest.

LASZLO, ANDREW: Cinematographer. b. Hungary, Jan. 12, 1926.
PICTURES: One Potato Two Potato, You're a Big Boy Now, The Night They Raided Minskys, Popi, The Out of Towners, Lovers and Other Strangers, The Owl and the Pussycat,

Jennifer on My Mind, To Find a Man, Class of 44, Countdown at Kussini, Thieves, Angesa, Somebody Killed Her Husband, The Warriors, The Funhouse, Southern Comfort, I the Jury, First Blood, Streets of Fire, Thief of Hearts, Remo Williams: The Adventure Begins, Poltergeist II, Innerspace, Star Trek V: The Final Frontier, Ghost Dad, Newsies.
TELEVISION: Documentaries: High Adventure with Lowell Thomas, The Twentieth Century. Series: The Phil Silvers Show, Joe and Mabel, Mama, Brenner, Naked City, The Nurses, Doctors and Nurses, Coronet Blue. Specials: New York New York, The Beatles at Shea Stadium, Ed Sullivan Specials. Movies and feature pilots: The Happeners, The Cliffdwellers, Daphne, Teacher Teacher, Blue Water Gold, The Man Without a Country, The Unwanted, Spanner's Key, Thin Ice, Love is Forever. Mini-series: Washington Behind Closed Doors, The Dain Curse, Top of the Hill, Shogun, and numerous commericals.

LATHROP, PHILIP: Cinematographer. b. Oct. 22, 1916.
PICTURES: Experiment in Terror, Days of Wine and Roses, The Pink Panther, Lonely Are the Brave, Soldier in the Rain, Thirty Six Hours, The Americanization of Emily, The Cincinnati Kid, Never Too Late, What Did You Do in the War Daddy? The Happening, The Russians Are Coming, Point Blank, Finian's Rainbow, I Love You Alice B. Toklas, The Illustrated Man, The Gypsy Moths, Rabbit Run, The Hawaiians, The Traveling Executioner, They Shoot Horses Don't They?, The Wild Rovers, The Thief Who Came to Dinner, Mame, The Prisoner of Second Avenue, Earthquake, Airport '75, The Blackbird, Hard Times, Killer Elite, The Swashbuckler, Airport 1977, The Driver, A Different Story, Moment By Moment, Foolin' Around, The Concorde-Airport '79, Little Miss Marker, Loving Couples, A Change of Seasons, All Night Long, Jekyll and Hyde Together Again, National Lampoon's Class Reunion, Deadly Friend.
TELEVISION: Captains Courageous, Celebrity, Malice in Wonderland (Emmy Award), Picking Up the Pieces, Love on the Run, Christmas Snow (Emmy Award, 1987), Little Girl Lost.

LATSIS, PETER C.: Publicist. b. Chicago, IL, Mar. 9, 1919. e. Wright Jr. Coll., Chicago. Newspaper reporter, Chicago Herald-American, 1942–45; Army, 1943; joined Fox West Coast Theatres, Los Angeles, in theatre operations 1945; adv.-pub. dept. 1946; asst. dir. adv.-pub. 1955; press rep. National Theatres, 1958; press relations dir., National General Corp., 1963; home office special field pub. repr., American International Pictures, 1973; Filmways Pictures, 1980–82; Recipient of Publicists Guild's Robert Yeager Award, 1983. Member, Motion Picture Pioneers.

LATTANZI, MATT: Actor. m. actress-singer Olivia Newton-John.
PICTURES: Xanadu (1980), Rich and Famous, Grease 2, My Tutor, That's Life!, Roxanne, Blueberry Hill, Catch Me If You Can, Diving In.
TELEVISION: Series: Paradise Beach.

LATTUADA, ALBERTO: Director. b. Milan, Italy, 1914. Son of Felice Lattuada, musician, opera composer, and writer of scores of many of son's films, Studied architecture; founded the periodical Cominare. Later founded Italian Film Library of which he still pres. Also, pres., Cinema D'Essay, First screen work as scriptwriter and asst. dir. of two films, 1940.
PICTURES: Mill on the Po, Anna, The Overcoat, La Lupa, Love in the City, White Sister, Flesh Will Surrender, Without Pity, The She Wolf, Tempest, The Unexpected, Mafioso, The Mandrake, Matchless, The Betrayal, The Steppe, Oh, Serafina, Stay as You Are.

LAUGHLIN, TOM: Actor, Producer, Director, Writer. b. Minneapolis, MN, 1938. e. U. of Indiana, U. of Minnesota where had athletic scholarships. m. actress Delores Taylor. Travelled around world, studying in Italy with Dr. Maria Montessori. Established, ran a Montessori school in Santa Monica for several yrs. Worked his way to Hollwood, where acted in bit parts until stardom came in Born Losers in 1967. Produced and starred in Billy Jack and The Trial of Billy Jack, also writing s.p. with wife under pseudonym Frank Christina. Heads own prod. co., Billy Jack Enterprises.
PICTURES: Actor: Tea and Sympathy, South Pacific, Gidget, Tall Story. Actor-Dir.-Prod.-Writer: The Proper Time, The Young Sinner, Born Losers, Billy Jack, The Trial of Billy Jack, The Master Gunfighter, Billy Jack Goes to Washington.

LAUNER, DALE: Writer. b. Cleveland, OH. E. Cal State Northridge. Son of actor John S. Launer.
PICTURES: Ruthless People, Blind Date, Dirty Rotten Scoundrels, My Cousin Vinny, Love Potion #9 (also dir.).

LAURENTS, ARTHUR: Writer, Director. b. New York, NY, July 14, 1917. e. Cornell U., B.A., 1937. First Professional writing as radio script writer in 1939. In Army 1941–45. Member of the Council of the Dramatists Guild; Theatre Hall of Fame.
STAGE PLAYS: Author: Home of the Brave (Sidney Howard Award), Heartsong, The Bird Cage, The Time of the Cuckoo, A Clearing in the Woods, Invitation to a March, West

Side Story, Gypsy, Hallelujah, Baby! (Tony Award), Scream, The Enclave, Running Time. *Director*: Invitation to a March, I Can Get It for You Wholesale, La Cage aux Folles (Tony Award). Author-Director: Anyone Can Whistle, Do I Hear a Waltz?, The Madwoman of Central Park West, Birds of Paradise, Gypsy (revival), Nick and Nora.

SCREENPLAYS: The Snake Pit, Rope, Caught, Anna Lucasta, Anastasia, Bonjour Tristesse, The Way We Were (from his own novel), The Turning Point (also co-prod.; Golden Glove, Writer's Guild Award).

LAURIA, DAN: Actor. b. Brooklyn, NY, April 12, 1947. e. So Conn. St. Col., Univ. of Conn. Served in U.S. Marine Corps., 1970–73.
TELEVISION: *Series*: One Life to Live, Hooperman, The Wonder Years. *Movies*: Johnny Brass, Johnny Bull, Doing Life, At Mother's Request, Angel in Green, David, Howard Beach: Making the Case for Murder, The Big One: The Great Los Angeles Earthquake, Overexposed, Dead and Alive, From the Files of Joseph Wambaugh: A Jury of One, In the Line of Duty: Ambush in Waco. Guest: Growing Pains, Mike Hammer, Moonlighting, Hill Street Blues.
PICTURES: Without a Trace, Stakeout, Another Stakeout.

LAURIE, PIPER: Actress. r.n. Rosetta Jacobs. b. Detroit, MI, Jan. 22, 1932. e. Los Angeles H.S. Acted in school plays, signed by U.I. in 1949.
THEATRE: The Glass Menagerie (revival), Marco Polo Sings a Solo, The Innocents, Biography, Rosemary, The Alligators, The Last Flapper (tour), The Destiny of Me.
PICTURES: Louisa (debut, 1950), The Milkman, Francis Goes to the Races, The Prince Who Was a Thief, Son of Ali Baba, Has Anybody Seen My Gal, No Room for the Groom, Mississippi Gambler, Golden Blade, Dangerous Mission, Johnny Dark, Dawn at Socorro, Smoke Signal, Ain't Misbehavin', Kelly and Me, Until They Sail, The Hustler (Acad. Award nom.), Carrie (Acad. Award nom.), Ruby, The Boss' Son, Tim, Return to Oz, Children of a Lesser God (Acad. Award nom.), Distortions, Appointment with Death, Tiger Warsaw, Dream a Little Dream, Mother Mother, Other People's Money, Storyville, Rich in Love, Trauma, Wrestling Ernest Hemingway.
TELEVISION: *Specials*: Days of Wine and Roses (Emmy nom.), The Road That Led Afar (Emmy nom.), The Deaf Heart (Emmy nom.), The Secret Life of Margaret Sanger. *Movies*: In the Matter of Karen Ann Quinlan, Rainbow, Skag, The Bunker (Emmy nom.), Mae West, Love Mary, Toughlove, Promise (Emmy Award, 1987), Go To the Light, Rising Son, Poisoned By Love: The Kern County Murders, Lies and Lullabies. *Series*: Skag, Twin Peaks (Golden Globe Award, Emmy nom.). *Mini-Series*: The Thorn Birds (Emmy nom.), Tender is the Night. Guest: St. Elsewhere (Emmy nom.)

LAUTER, ED: Actor. b. Long Beach, NY, Oct. 30, 1940.
PICTURES: The New Centurions, The Last American Hero, Executive Action, Lolly Madonna XXX, The Longest Yard, French Connection II, Breakheart Pass, Family Plot, King Kong, The Chicken Chronicles, Magic, The Amateur, Death Hunt, Timerider, The Big Score, Eureka, Lassiter, Cujo, Finders Keepers, Death Wish 3, Girls Just Want to Have Fun, Youngblood, 3:15, Raw Deal, Chief Zabu, Revenge of the Nerds II, Gleaming the Cube, Fat Man and Little Boy, Tennessee Waltz, School Ties.
TELEVISION: *Series*: B.J. and the Bear. *Movies*: Class of '63, The Migrants, The Godchild, Satan's Triangle, A Shadow in the Streets, Last Hours Before Morning, The Clone Master, The Jericho Mile, Love's Savage Fury, Undercover with the KKK, The Boy Who Drank Too Much, Guyana Tragedy—The Story of Jim Jones, Alcatraz—The Whole Shocking Story, In the Custody of Strangers, Rooster, The Seduction of Gina, Three Wishes of Billy Grier, The Last Days of Patton, The Thanksgiving Promise, Calendar Girl Cop Killer?: The Bambi Bembenek Story, Extreme Justice.

LAVEN, ARNOLD: Director, Producer. b. Chicago, IL, 1922.
PICTURES: Without Warning, Vice Squad, Down Three Dark Streets, The Rack, Slaughter on Tenth Ave., Anna Lucasta, The Glory Guys, Rough Night, Jericho, Sam Whiskey.
TELEVISION: Part creator and director TV pilots: The Rifleman, Robert Taylor's Detectives, The Plainsmen. Many TV films.

LAVIN, LINDA: Actress. b. Portland, ME, Oct. 15, 1937. e. Coll. of William & Mary. First professional job in chorus of Camden County (N.J.) Music Circus. Worked in plays both off and on Broadway before turning to TV, where guest-starred on such series as Family, Rhoda, Phyllis and Harry O.
THEATER: Oh Kay! (Off-Bdwy debut, 1960), A Family Affair (Bdwy. debut), Revues: Wet Paint (Theatre World Award), The Game Is Up, The Mad Show, member acting co.: Eugene O'Neil Playwright's Unit, 1968; It's a Bird It's a Plane . . . It's Superman, Something Different, Little Murders (Outer Critics Circle & Sat. Review Awards), Cop Out, The Last of the Red Hot Lovers (Tony nom.), Story Theatre, Dynamite Tonight, Broadway Bound (Tony, Drama Desk, Outer Critics Circle & Helen Hayes Awards), Gypsy.

PICTURES: The Muppets Take Manhattan, See You in the Morning, I Want to Go Home.
TELEVISION: *Series*: Barney Miller, Alice (2 Golden Globe Awards; 2 Emmy noms.), Room for Two (also co-exec. prod.). *Movies*: The Morning After, Like Mom and Me, The $5.20 an Hour Dream, A Matter of Life and Death (also exec. prod. & developed), Another Woman's Child, A Place to Call Home (also exec. prod. & developed), Lena: My Hundred Children.

LAW, JOHN PHILLIP: Actor. b. Hollywood, CA, Sept. 7, 1937. e. Neighborhood Playhouse. Bdwy debut in Coming on Strong. Appeared at Lincoln Center in After the Fall, Marco Millions, The Changeling, and Tartuffe. Has made more than 50 films in more than 20 countries world wide.
PICTURES: High Infidelity, Three Nights of Love, The Russians Are Coming The Russians Are Coming the Russians Are Coming (U.S. debut), Hurry Sundown, Barbarella, Danger Diabolik, The Sergeant, Death Rides a Horse, Skidoo, Diary of a Telephone Operator, Von Richtofen and Brown, The Hawaiians, Michael Strogoff, The Love Machine, The Last Movie, The Golden Voyage of Sinbad, Stardust, Open Season, Your God My Hell, The Spiral Staircase, Dr. Justice, African Rage, Whispers in the Dark, Portrait of an Assassin, The Crystal Man, Death in November, Ring of Darkness, The Cassandra Crossing, She-Wolf of Devil's Moor, Attack Force Z, Tarzan the Ape Man, The Tin Man, Night Train to Terror, Rainy Day Friends (L.A. Bad), No Time to Die, American Commando (Mr. Salvage), Johann Straus, Moon in Scorpio, Stryker (Combat Force), The Overthrow, Space Mutiny, Rage to Kill, Thunder Warrior III, A Case of Honor, Blood Delirium, Alienator, L.A. Heat, Gorilla, The Guest, Cold Heat, Alaska Story, Angel Eyes.
TELEVISION: *Series*: The Young and the Restless (1989). *Movie*: The Best Place to Be, A Great Love Story (It.), Experiences (It.), The Fourth Man (Austrian). Guest: The Love Boat, Murder She Wrote.

LAW, LINDSAY, Producer. e. NYU School of the Arts. Producer of specials for Warner Bros. Television, head of drama for WNET/New York and prod. for Theatre in America before becoming exec. prod. of American Playhouse. Advisory Board of Independent Feature Project/West, Sundance Film Festival.
PICTURES: *Exec. prod.*: On Valentine's Day, Smooth Talk, Native Son, In a Shallow Grave, Stand and Deliver, The Thin Blue Line, El Norte, The Wizard of Loneliness, Signs of Life, Bloodhounds of Broadway, Big Time, Eat a Bowl of Tea, Longtime Companion, Thousand Pieces of Gold, Straight Out of Brooklyn, Daughters of the Dust, Thank You and Goodnight, All the Vermeers in New York, Brother's Keeper, Ethan Frome, The Music of Chance.
TELEVISION: *Prod.*: The Girls in Their Summer Dresses, The Time of Your Life, You Can't Take It With You, The Good Doctor, The Most Happy Fella, The Eccentricities of a Nightingale, Cyrano de Bergerac (assoc. prod.). *Prod. for American Playhouse*: Working, for Colored Girls Who Have Considered Suicide/When the Rainbow Is Enuf, Private Contentment, *Exec. prod.*: Concealed Enemies (Emmy Award, 1984), Land of Little Rain, Ask Me Again, The Diaries of Adam and Eve, A Walk in the Woods, Fires in the Mirror.

LAWRENCE, BARBARA: Actress. b. Carnegie, OK, Feb. 24, 1930. e. UCLA. Mother Berenice Lawrence. Child model; successful screen try-out, 1944; screen debut in Billy Rose Diamond Horse Shoe (1945).
PICTURES: Margie, Captain from Castile, You Were Meant for Me, Give My Regards to Broadway, Street with No Name, Unfaithfully Yours, Letter to Three Wives, Mother Is a Freshman, Thieves Highway, Two Tickets to Broadway, Here Come the Nelsons, The Star, Arena, Paris Model, Her 12 Men, Oklahoma, Man with a Gun, Pay the Devil, Joe Dakota.

LAWRENCE, MARC: Actor. r.n. Max Goldsmith. b. New York, NY, Feb. 17, 1914. e. City Coll. of New York. On stage in The Tree (Eva La Galliene Rep. Theatre.). Sour Mountain, Waiting for Lefty, Golden Boy, View From the Bridge.
PICTURES: White Woman, Little Big Shot, Dr. Socrates, Road Gang, San Quentin, The Ox Bow Incident, I Am the Law, While New York Sleeps, Dillinger, Flame of Barbary Coast, Club Havana, Don't Fence Me In, The Virginian, Life with Blondie, Yankee Fakir, Captain from Castile, I Walk Alone, Calamity Jane and Sam Bass, The Asphalt Jungle, Hurricane Island, My Favorite Spy, Girls Marked Danger, Helen of Troy, Johnny Cool, Nightmare in the Sun, Savage Pampas, Johnny Tiger, Custer of the West, Nightmare in the Sun, Krakatoa East of Java, The Kremlin Letter, Fraser: The Sensuous Lion, The Man With the Golden Gun, Marathon Man, A Piece of the Action, Foul Play, Goin' Cocoanuts, Hot Stuff, Night Train to Terror, The Big Easy, Ruby, Newsies, Marilyn I Love You.

LAWRENCE, STEVE: Actor. b. New York, NY, July 8, 1935. m. singer Eydie Gorme. Singer in nightclubs and on TV.
PICTURES: Stand Up and Be Counted, The Blues Brothers, The Lonely Guy.

TELEVISION: *Specials*: Steve and Eydie Celebrate Irving Berlin (also co-exec. prod.; Emmy Award, 1979). many specials; *Series*: Tonight, The Steve Lawrence-Eydie Gorme Show (1958), Foul-Ups Bleeps and Blunders (host). *Guest*: Police Story, Murder, She Wrote. *Movie*: Alice in Wonderland. THEATRE: What Makes Sammy Run?, Golden Rainbow.

LAWRENCE, VICKI: Actress. b. Inglewood, CA, March 26, 1949. Singer and recording artist appearing with Young Americans (1965–7). Gained fame on The Carol Burnett Show as comedienne (1967–78), winning Emmy Award in 1976. Gold record for The Night the Lights Went Out in Georgia (1972). TELEVISION: *Movie*: Having Babies. *Series*: Carol Burnett Show, Jimmie Rodgers Show, Mama's Family. *Host*: Win Lose or Draw (1987–88), Vicki! (synd. talk show).

LAWSON, SARAH: Actress. b. London, Eng., Aug. 6, 1928. e. Heron's Ghyll Sch., Sussex. Stage debut in Everyman (Edinburgh Festival) 1947; screen debut in The Browning Version, 1953; TV debut in Face to Face, 1949.
PICTURES: Street Corner, You Know What Sailors Are, Blue Peter, It's Never Too Late, Links of Justice, Three Crooked Men, Man with a Dog, Night Without Pity, The World Ten Times Over, Island of the Burning Doomed, The Devil's Bride, The Stud, The Dawning (prod.).
TELEVISION: Face to Face, River Line, Whole Truth, Lady From the Sea, Mrs. Moonlight, Silver Card, An Ideal Husband, Love and Money, Rendezvous, Invisible Man, Saber Buccaneers, White Hunter, Flying Doctor, On the Night of the Murder, Haven in Sunset, The Odd Man, Zero 1 (series), The Innocent Ceremony, Department S, The Marrying Kind, The Expert, The Persuaders, Trial, Starcast, The Midsummer of Colonel Blossum, Callen, Crime of Passion, Full House, Father Brown, Within These Walls These Walls Series, The Standard, The Purple Twlight, The Professionals, Bergerac, Cuffy, Lovejoy.

LAZARUS, PAUL N.: Executive. b. Brooklyn, NY, March 31, 1913. e. Cornell U., B.A., 1933. In U.S. Army, W.W. II. Entered m.p. ind. 1933 as gen. asst., press book dept., Warner Bros.; pres., AMPA, 1939–40. Joined Buchanan & Co., 1942 as m.p. account exec. To United Artists 1943 as dir. adv. & pub. Named asst. to pres., July 1948; joined Columbia exec. staff, New York, Aug. 1950; elected v.p. Columbia, Jan. 1954–62; exec. vice-pres. Samuel Bronston Prods., 1962–64; v.p., chg. Motion Pictures, Subscription Television Inc., 1964; exec. officer and partner, Landau Releasing Organization, 1964–65, exec. v.p., member bd. of dir., Nat'l Screen Serv. Corp., 1965–75. Lecturer and consultant, Film Studies Program, U. of California at Santa Barbara. 1975 to present. Consultant to Kenya Film Corp., Nairobi, 1983. Director, Santa Barbara Intl. Film Festival, 1986–87. Chief of Staff, Santa Barbara Writers' Conference, 1976–. Vice-chmn. Santa Barbara County Film Council, 1989–92.

LAZARUS, PAUL N. III: Executive. b. New York, NY, May 25, 1938. e. Williams Coll., BA.; Yale Law Sch., L.L.B. Third generation film exec. Began career with Palomar Pictures Int'l. as exec. v.p.; joined ABC Pictures Corp. as v.p. in chg. of creative affairs. Mng. dir., CRM Productions, maker of educational films; v.p. for motion pictures. Marble Arch Productions; 1983, v.p. in chg. of prod., Home Box Office. 1985, Film Commissioner, New Mexico; 1987, Dir. of Film Program, U of Miami.
PICTURES: Prod.: Extreme Close-Up, Westworld, Futureworld, Capricorn One, Hanover Street, Barbarosa, Doubles.

LAZARUS, THEODORE R.: Executive. b. Brooklyn, NY, Aug. 5, 1919. e. Yale U., B.A., 1940. Adv. mgr., Eagle Lion Classics, 1951; adv., sales prom. mgr., WMGM, New York, 1951; then with Donahue and Coe adv. agency; secy., treas., George Blake Enterprises, TV film prod. firm, 1955; v.p. Gommi-TV, 1956; Charles Schlaifer and Co., Inc., 1957; adv. mgr., Paramount Pictures Corp., 1964; pres., Cinema Lodge, B'nai B'rith, 1968–71. Member, bd. of directors, NY chapter, Variety, The Children's Charity. Retired Jan. 1991.

LEACHMAN, CLORIS: Actress. b. Des Moines, IA, April 30, 1930. e. Northwestern U. Broadway stage, television, motion pictures.
TELEVISION: *Series*: Hold It Please, Charlie Wild: Private Detective, Bob and Ray, Lassie, Mary Tyler Moore Show (Emmy Awards 1974, 1975), Phyllis (Golden Globe Award), The Facts of Life, The Nutt House, Walter & Emily. *Movies*: Silent Night Lonely Night, Suddenly Single, Haunts of the Very Rich, A Brand New Life (Emmy Award), Crime Club, Dying Room Only, The Migrants, Hitchhike!, Thursday's Game, Death Sentence, Someone I Touched, A Girl Named Sooner, Death Scream, The New Original Wonder Woman, The Love Boat (pilot), It Happened One Christmas, Long Journey Back, Willa, Mrs. R's Daughter, S.O.S. Titanic, The Acorn People, Advice to the Lovelorn, Miss All-American Beauty, Dixie: Changing Habits, Demon Murder Case, Ernie Kovacs: Between the Laughter, Deadly Intentions, Love Is Never Silent, Wedding Bell Blues, Danielle Steel's Fine Things, In Broad Daylight, A Little Piece of Heaven, Fade to

Black, Without a Kiss Goodbye, Miracle Child. *Specials*: Oldest Living Graduate, Of Thee I Sing, Breakfast With Les and Bess, Screen Actors Guild 50th Anniversary Celebration (Emmy Award, 1984). *Guest*: Twilight Zone, Untouchables, Big Valley, That Girl, Marcus Welby, Night Gallery, Cher (Emmy Award, 1975), Love Boat.
PICTURES: Kiss Me Deadly (debut, 1955), The Rack, The Chapman Report, Butch Cassidy and the Sundance Kid, Lovers and Other Strangers, The People Next Door, W.U.S.A., The Steagle, The Last Picture Show (Acad. Award, supp. actress, 1971), Dillinger, Charlie and the Angel, Happy Mother's Day . . . Love George, Daisy Miller, Young Frankenstein, Crazy Mama, High Anxiety, The Mouse and His Child (voice), The North Avenue Irregulars, The Muppet Movie, Scavenger Hunt, Foolin' Around, Yesterday, Herbie Goes Bananas, History of the World—Part I, My Little Pony (voice), Shadow Play, Walk Like a Man, Hansel and Gretel, Prancer, Texasville, Love Hurts, My Boyfriend's Back, The Beverly Hillbillies.

LEAR, NORMAN: Producer, Director, Writer. b. New Haven, CT, July 27, 1922. e. Emerson Coll. In public relations 1945–49. Began in TV as co-writer of weekly one-hour variety show, The Ford Star Revue in 1950. Followed as writer for Dean Martin and Jerry Lewis on the Colgate Comedy Hour and for the Martha Raye and George Gobel TV shows. With partner, Bud Yorkin, created and produced such specials as Another Evening with Fred Astaire, Henry Fonda and the Family, An Evening with Carol Channing, and The Many Sides of Don Rickles. In 1965 their company, Tandem Productions, also produced the original Andy Williams Show. Moved into motion pictures in 1963, writing and producing Come Blow Your Horn. Formed Act III Communications, 1987.
PICTURES: Never Too Late (prod.), Divorce-American Style (prod., s.p.), The Night They Raided Minsky's (co.-prod., co-s.p.), Start the Revolution Without Me (exec.-prod.), Cold Turkey, (s.p., prod., dir.), The Princess Bride (exec. prod.), Breaking In (exec. prod.), Fried Green Tomatoes (co-exec. prod.).
TELEVISION: *Creator-dir.*: TV Guide Award Show (1962), Henry Fonda and the Family (1963), Andy Williams Specials, Robert Young and the Family. *Exec. prod. and creator or developer*: All in the Family (3 Emmy Awards), Maude, Good Times, Sanford and Son, The Jeffersons, Mary Hartman Mary Hartman, One Day at a Time, All's Fair, A Year at the Top, All that Glitters, Fernwood 2 Night, The Baxters, Palmerstown, I Love Liberty, Heartsounds, Sunday Dinner.

LEARNED, MICHAEL: Actress. b. Washington, DC, Apr. 9, 1939. Studied ballet and dramatics in school. Many stage credits include Under Milkwood, The Three Sisters, A God Slept Here, etc.; resident performances with Shakespeare festivals in Canada, Stratford, CT, and San Diego, CA. Gained fame on hit TV series, The Waltons, as the mother, Olivia.
PICTURES: Touched by Love, Power, Dragon: The Bruce Lee Story.
TELEVISION: *Series*: The Waltons (3 Emmy Awards: 1973, 1974, 1976), Nurse (Emmy Award, 1982), Hothouse, Living Dolls. *Guest*: Gunsmoke, Police Story, St. Elsewhere, Murder She Wrote, Who's the Boss?. *Movies*: Hurricane, It Couldn't Happen to a Nicer Guy, Widow, Little Mo, Nurse (pilot), Off the Minnesota Strip, A Christmas Without Snow, Mother's Day on Walton Mountain, The Parade, A Deadly Business, Mercy or Murder?, Roots: The Gift, Gunsmoke: The Last Apache, Aftermath: A Test of Love, Keeping Secrets. *Specials*: All My Sons, Picnic.

LEAUD, JEAN-PIERRE: Actor. b. Paris, France, May 5, 1944. Parents were screenwriter Pierre Leaud and actress Jacqueline Pierreux. At 14 chosen to play Antoine Doinel in Truffaut's The 400 Blows and subsequent autobiographical films Love at 20, Stolen Kisses, Bed and Board, Love on the Run. Also closely identified with major films by Jean-Luc Godard.
PICTURES: The 400 Blows, The Testament of Orpheus, Love at Twenty, Masculine-Feminine, Made in USA, Le Depart, La Chinoise, Weekend, Stolen Kisses, Le Gai Savoir, Pigsty, The Oldest Profession, Bed and Board, Last Tango in Paris, Day for Night, Lola's Lolos, Love on the Run, Rebelote, Detective, Just a Movie, Seen by...20 Years After, Treasure Island, The Grandeur and Decadence of a Small-Time Filmmaker, With All Hands, Time to Aim, Jane B, por Agnes V.; 36 Fillete, La Femme de Paille (The Straw Woman), The Color of the Wind, Femme de Papier, Bunker Palace Hotel, I Hired a Contract Killer.

LEDER, HERBERT JAY: Writer, Director, Producer, b. New York, NY, Aug. 15, 1922. e. B.A., Ph.D. Play Doctor on Broadway; Director TV dept., Benton and Bowles Adv. chg. all T.V. & Film production, 13 yrs.; Features: writer, Fiend Without a Face; writer-director co-prod., Pretty Boy Floyd; writer-director, co-producer, Nine Miles to Noon; writer, Aquarius Mission, Love Keeps No Score of Wrongs; writer, prod-dir., The Frozen Dead, It; Mia, writer-dir., Candyman, writer-director; writer,

The Winners, The Way It Is, The Cool Crazies. Sponsored Films: Child Molester, Bank Robber, Shoplifter, Untouchables.

LEDERER, RICHARD: Executive. b. New York, NY, Sept. 22, 1916. e. U. of Virginia, B.S., 1938. Freelance writer, 1939–41; U.S. Army. Cryptanalyst, Signal Intell. Serv 1941–45; Adv. copywriter, Columbia Pictures, 1946–50; Adv. copywriter, Warner Bros., 1950–53; copy chief, Warner Bros., 1950–53; copy chief, Warner Bros., 1953–57; Asst. Nat'l Adv. mgr., Warner Bros. studios, 1957–59; Prod., theatrical, TV. Warner Bros. studios, 1959–60; Dir. of adv., publicity, Warner Bros. Pictures, 1960; v.p. Warner Bros. Pictures, 1963. V.P. production, Warner Bros. Studio, 1969–70; indep. prod. to May, 1971, when returned to WB as adv.-pub., v.p. Independent producer. 1980: Hollywood Knights. Joined Orion Pictures as v.p., adv. Resigned, 1984.

LEE, ANNA: Actress. M.B.E. r.n. Joan Boniface Winnifrith. b. Jan. 2, 1913, Kent, England. e. Central School of Speech Training and Dramatic Art, Royal Albert Hall. With London Repertory Theatre; toured in the Constant Nymph and Jane Eyre. In 1930s known as Britain's Glamour Girl. 1939 came to US to star in My Life With Caroline. Entertained troops with U.S.O. during WWII. 1950 moved to N.Y. to appear in live TV.
PICTURES: British: The Camels Are Coming, Non Stop New York, King Solomon's Mines, You're in the Army Now, Passing of the Third Floor Back, Return to Yesterday, Young Man's Fancy, The Four Just Men. Hollywood: My Life With Caroline, Flying Tigers, How Green Was My Valley, This Earth is Mine, Flesh and Fantasy, Bedlam, Fort Apache, Horse Soldiers, Gideon of Scotland Yard, The Last Hurrah, Commandos Strike at Dawn, Hangmen Also Die, Seven Women, The Sound of Music, In Like Flint.
TELEVISION: Guest star on all major television shows from 1950 to 1977. Eleanor and Franklin, The Night Rider, The Beasts are Loose, Scruples, General Hospital (continuing role as Lila Quartermaine, 1978–present).

LEE, CHRISTOPHER: Actor. b. London, England, May 27, 1922. e. Wellington Coll. Served RAF 1940–46. Ent. m.p. ind. 1947. Autobiography: Tall, Dark and Gruesome (1977).
PICTURES: include: Corridor of Mirrors (debut, 1947), One Night With You, A Song for Tomorrow, Scott of the Antarctic, Hamlet, The Gay Lady, Capt. Horatio Hornblower, Valley of the Eagles, The Crimson Pirate, Babes in Bagdad, Moulin Rouge, Innocents of Paris, That Lady, The Warriors, Cockleshell Heroes, Storm Over the Nile, Port Afrique, Private's Progress, Beyond Mombasa, Battle of the River Plate, Night Ambush, She Played With Fire, The Traitors, Curse of Frankenstein, Bitter Victory, Truth About Women, Tale of Two Cities, Dracula, Man Who Could Cheat Death, The Mummy, Too Hot to Handle, Beat Girl, City of the Dead (Horror Hotel), Two Faces of Dr. Jekyll, The Terror of the Tongs, The Hands of Orlac, Taste of Fear, The Devil's Daffodil, Pirates of Blood River, Devil's Agent, Red Orchid, Valley of Fear, Katharsis, Faust '63, The Virgin of Nuremberg, The Whip and the Body, Carmilla, The Devil Ship Pirates, The Gorgon, The Sign of Satan, The House of Blood, Dr. Terror's House of Horrors, She, The Skull, The Mask of Fu Manchu, Dracula, Prince of Darkness, Rasputin, Theatre of Death, Circus of Fear, The Brides of Fu Manchu, Five Golden Dragons, Vengeance of Fu Manchu, Night of the Big Heat, The Pendulum, The Face of Eve, The Devil Rides Out, The Blood of Fu Manchu, The Crimson Altar, Dracula Has Risen from the Grave, The Oblong Box, De Sade 70, Scream and Scream Again, The Magic Christian, Julius Caesar, One More Time, Count Dracula, Bloody Judge, Taste the Blood of Dracula, Private Life of Sherlock Holmes, El Umbragolo, Scars of Dracula, House That Dripped Blood, I Monster, Hannie Caulder, Dracula 72, Horror Express, Creeping Flesh, Death Line, Nothing but the Night, The Wicker Man, Poor Devil, Dark Places, Dracula Is Dead?, Eulalie Quitte les champs, The Three Musketeers, Earthbound, Man with the Golden Gun, The Four Musketeers, Killer Force, Diagnosis—Murder, Whispering Death, The Keeper, To the Devil a Daughter, Pere et Fils, Airport 77, Alien Encounter, The End of the World, Return from Witch Mountain, Caravans, The Silent Flute, The Passage, 1941, Bear Island, Serial, The Pirates, Jaguar Lives, Arabian Adventure, An Eye for an Eye, House of Long Shadows, Howling II, The Return of Captain Invincible, Roadtrip, Dark Mission, Olympus Force, Murder Story, Mio In the Land of Faraway, The Girl, The Return of the Musketeers, Honeymoon Academy, The French Revolution, Gremlins 2, The Rainbow Thief, L'Avaro, Jackpot, Double Vision, Shogun Mayeda, Special Class, Death Train, Journey of Honor, Cybereden.
TELEVISION: The Disputation, Metier du Seigneur, Movies: Poor Devil, Harold Robbins' The Pirate, Captain America II, Once a Spy, Charles and Diana: A Royal Love Story, Far Pavilions, Shaka Zulu, Goliath Awaits, Massarati and the Brain, Around the World in 80 Days, Treasure Island, Sherlock Holmes and the Leading Lady, Sherlock Holmes and the Incident at Victoria Falls, Young Indiana Jones (pilot), The Care of Time.

LEE, MICHELE: Actress. b. Los Angeles, CA, June 24, 1942. On Broadway in How to Succeed in Business Without Really Trying, Seesaw.
PICTURES: How To Succeed in Business Without Really Trying, The Love Bug, The Comic.
TELEVISION: Series: Knots Landing (also dir. several episodes). Movies: Only With Married Men, Dark Victory, Bud and Lou, Letter to Three Wives, Single Women Married Men (also exec. prod.), The Fatal Image, My Son Johnny, Broadway Bound, When No One Would Listen (also exec. prod.).

LEE, PEGGY: Singer, Actress. r.n. Norma Egstrom; b. Jamestown, ND, May 26, 1920. Began career as night club vocalist in Fargo & radio singer, WDAY, then with Sev Olsen, bandleader, Minneapolis, Will Osborne; Benny Goodman; collab. (with Dave Barbour) popular songs, Manana, It's a Good Day, What More Can a Woman Do?, Fever, Johnny Guitar, So What's New. Leading song stylist-composer. TV & records; screen debut in Mr. Music (Bing Crosby) (1950); singer on Bing Crosby program, many TV specials.
PICTURES: Mr. Music, The Jazz Singer, Pete Kelly's Blues (Acad. Award nom.), Lady and the Tramp (voices, song collab.).
TELEVISION: Series: TV's Top Tunes, Songs for Sale. Guest: The Jimmy Durante Show.

LEE, SPIKE: Director, Producer, Writer, Actor. b. Atlanta, GA, Mar. 20, 1957. r.n. Shelton Jackson Lee. Son of jazz bass musician, composer Bill Lee. e. Morehouse Coll B.A.(Mass communications), MFA NYU Film Sch. Completed 2 student features and hour-long thesis: Joe's Bed-Stuy Barbershop: We Cut Heads which won student Acad. Award from Acad. M.P. Arts & Sciences. Wrote, prod., dir., co-starred in indep. feature, She's Gotta Have It, budgeted at $175,000. Appeared as actor in 1991 film Lonely in America.
PICTURES: Joe's Bed-Stuy Barbershop: We Cut Heads (co-prod., dir., s.p., editor). Dir.-Prod.-S.P.-Actor: She's Gotta Have It (LA Film Critics Award for best new director, 1986), School Daze, Do the Right Thing (LA Film Critics Awards for best picture & director, 1989), Mo' Better Blues, Jungle Fever, Malcolm X, Crooklyn.
TELEVISION: Guest: The Debbie Allen's Special, Spike & Co. Do It A Capella.

LEEDS, MARTIN N.: Film-TV Executive. b. New York, NY, Apr. 6, 1916. e. NYU, B.S., 1936; J.D., 1938. Admitted N.Y. Bar, 1938, Calif. Bar, 1948; dir. indsl. relations Wabash Appliance Corp., 1943–44 indsl. bus. relations cons. Davis & Gilbert. 1944–45; dir. indsl. relations Flying Tiger Lines, 1947; dir. bus. affairs CBS. TV div., 1947–53; exec. v.p. Desilu Productions, Inc., 1953–60; v.p. Motion Picture Center Studios, Inc.: mem. Industry comm. War Manpower Comm., 1943; chmn. Com. to form Television Code of Ethics: U.S. Army 1941. Mem. Los Angeles Bar Assn.; exec. v.p. in chg. of West Coast oper. & member of bd. of dir. Talent Associates—Paramount Ltd., Hollywood, 1962; TV production consultant; exec. v.p., Electronovision Prods. Inc., 1964; TV prod. & MP prod. consultant, 1965. Pres., chief exec. officer member of bd., Beverly Hills Studios, Inc., 1969, sr. v.p., American Film Theatre, 1973; 1975, motion picture and TV attorney & consultant.

LEEWOOD, JACK: Producer. b. New York, NY. May 20, 1913. e. Upsala Coll., Newark U., NYU. 1926–31 with Gottesman-Stern circuit as usher, asst. and relief mgr.; 1931–43 Stanley-Warner, mgr. of Ritz, Capitol and Hollywood theatres 1943–47. Joined Warner Bros. field forces in Denver-Salt Lake; Seattle-Portland, 1947–48. Dir. pub. & adv. Screen Guild Prod.; 1948–52 Lippert Productions; prod. exec.; 1953–56 Allied Artists; 1957–62 prod. 20th Cent. Fox; 1965–68 prod., Universal; 1976–78. Affiliated Theatre S.F. & HTN.; 1978–83. Hamner Prod.
PICTURES: Holiday Rhythm, Gunfire, Hi-Jacked, Roaring City, Danger Zone, Lost Continent, F.B.I. Girl, Pier 23, Train to Tombstone, I Shot Billy the Kid, Bandit Queen, Motor Patrol, Savage Drums, Three Desperate Men, Border Rangers, Western Pacific Agent, Thundering Jets, Lone Texan, Little Savage, Alligator People, 13 Fighting Men, Young Jesse James, Swingin' Along, We'll Bury You, 20,000 Eyes, Thunder Island, The Plainsman, Longest 100 Miles, Escape to Mindanao, Dallas Cowboys Cheerleaders, When Hell Was in Session, Fugitive Family, Dallas Cowboys Cheerleaders II, Million Dollar Face, Portrait of a Showgirl, Margin For Murder, Anatomy of an Illness, Malibu.

LEFFERTS, GEORGE: Producer, Writer, Director. b. Paterson, NJ. e. Univ. of MI. Dir. numerous award-winning TV series, films. Exec. prod.-Time-Life films prod./writer, Movie of the Week (NBC) Biog: Who's Who in America, Who's Who in the World. Exec. prod., Bing Crosby Productions, prod., NBC 10 yrs, Independent.
TELEVISION: Emmy Award, prod. Hallmark Hall of Fame Teacher Teacher; Benjamin Franklin (Emmy Award, 1975); Wrote, prod., directed Purex Specials for Women; Producer's Guild Award. Exec. prod. Breaking Point series. 1987, writer, Our Group; 1989 the Jean Seberg Story. Other shows: The Bill Cosby Show, Studio One, Kraft Theatre, Chrysler Thea-

tre, Sinatra Show, Lights Out, Alcoa, The Harness (Movie of the Week), The Bold Ones, She's Dressed to Kill, The Night They Took Miss Beautiful, One Life to Live (writer), Ryan's Hope (prod.).
PICTURES: The Stake, Mean Dog Blues, The Living End, The Boat, The Teenager.
BROADWAY: The Boat, 1968, Hey Everybody, 1970.

LEFKO, MORRIS E.: b. March 30, 1907. Entered m.p. ind. as poster clerk; booker, salesman, br. mgr., Indianapolis, RKO, June 1941; br. mgr., Pittsburgh, July 1944; East Central dist. mgr., July, 1948; appt. sales exec. of Ten Commandments Unit. Para. Film Dist. Corp., N.Y., 1956; v.p. in chg. sls., Michael Todd Co., 1958. Joined MGM, Inc., July 1960 sls. mgr., of road shows, Ben-Hur, King of Kings, Mutiny on the Bounty; vice pres., gen. sales mgr., MGM, 1963. Exec. consultant to Pres., Cinema 5 Ltd., Jan. 1970. v.p., Network Cinema Corp., 1972; American Film Theatre, Ely Landau Co., Nov., 1972; v.p., sls. mgr. Brut Prods., 1976.

LEGRAND, MICHEL JEAN: Composer, Conductor. b. France, 1932. Son of well-known arranger, composer and pianist, Raymond Legrand. At 11 Michel, a child prodigy, entered Paris Cons. and graduated nine years later with top honors in composition and as solo pianist. In late fifties turned to composing for films and has composed, orchestrated and conducted scores of more than 140 films.
PICTURES: Lola, Eva, Vivre Sa Vie, La Baie des Anges, The Umbrellas of Cherbourg, Banda a Part, Un Femme Mariee, Un Femme est une Femme, The Young Girls of Rochefort, Ice Station Zebra, The Thomas Crown Affair (Acad. Award for best song: The Windmills of Your Mind, 1968), Pieces of Dreams, The Happy Ending, Picasso Summer, Wuthering Heights, The Go-Between, Summer of '42 (Acad. Award, 1971), The Nelson Affair, Breezy, The Three Musketeers, Sheila Levine, Gable and Lombard, Ode to Billy Joe, The Savage, The Other Side of Midnight, The Fabulous Adventures of the Legendary Baron Munchausen, The Roads of the South, The Hunter, The Mountain Men, Atlantic City, Falling in Love Again, Best Friends, A Love in Germany, Never Say Never Again, Yentl (Acad. Award, 1983), Hell Train, Micki and Maude, Secret Places, Spirale, Parking, Switching Channels, Three Seats for the 26th Cinq jours en juin (dir. debut, s.p., music), Dingo, The Pickle.
TELEVISION: Brian's Song, The Jesse Owens Story, A Woman Called Golda, As Summers Die, Crossings, Sins, Promises to Keep, Not a Penny More Not a Penny Less, The Burning Shore.

LEGUIZAMO, JOHN: Actor. b. Bogota, Colombia, July 22, 1965. Moved to Queens, NY at age 5. e. NYU. Appeared in award-winning student film Five Out of Six, while in school. Made professional debut on Miami Vice on tv.
PICTURES: Casualties of War, Revenge, Die Hard 2, Street Hunter, Out for Justice, Hangin' With the Homeboys, Regarding Henry, Whispers in the Dark, Super Mario Bros., Night Owl, Carlito's Way.
TELEVISION: Specials: Mambo Mouth (also writer), Spic-O-Rama (also writer).
THEATRE: A Midsummer Night's Dream, La Pura Vida, Mambo Mouth (also writer; Obie & Outer Critics Circle Awards), Spic-O-Rama (also writer; Theatre World Award).

LEHMAN, ERNEST: Writer, Producer, Director. b. NY, NY, 1923. e. City Coll. of New York. Began career as free-lance journalist and magazine fiction writer. First pub. books, The Comedian, The Sweet Smell of Success. First hardcover novel, The French Atlantic Affair followed by Farewell Performance, and first non-fiction book, Screening Sickness. 1987, 1988, 1990: Acad. Awards show (co-writer). The Ernest Lehman Collection is archived at the Humanities Research Center , Univ. of TX at Austin.
PICTURES: Writer: Executive Suite, Sabrina (co-s.p.), The King and I, Somebody Up There Likes Me, Sweet Smell of Success (co-s.p.; based on his own novelette), North By Northwest, From the Terrace, West Side Story, The Prize, The Sound of Music, Who's Afraid of Virginia Woolf? (also prod.), Hello Dolly! (also prod.), Portnoy's Complaint (also dir., prod.), Family Plot, Black Sunday (co-s.p.).

LEIBMAN, RON: Actor. b. New York, NY, Oct. 11, 1937. m. actress Jessica Walter. e. Ohio Wesleyan U. Joined Actor's Studio in N.Y.; first professional appearance in summer theatre production of A View from the Bridge.
STAGE: The Premise, Dear Me, The Sky is Falling, We Bombed in New Haven (Theatre World Award), Cop Out, Room Service, I Oughta Be in Pictures, The Deputy, Bicycle Ride to Nevada, Doubles, Rumors, Angels in America: Millenium Approaches (Tony & Drama Desk Awards).
PICTURES: Where's Poppa (debut, 1970), The Hot Rock, Slaughterhouse Five, Your Three Minutes Are Up, Super Cops, Won Ton Ton the Dog Who Saved Hollywood, Norma Rae, Up the Academy, Zorro the Gay Blade, Romantic Comedy, Phar Lap, Rhinestone, Seven Hours to Judgement, Door to Door.

TELEVISION: Series: Kaz (Emmy Award, 1979), Pacific Station. Movies: The Art of Crime, A Question of Guilt, Rivkin: Bounty Hunter, Many Happy Returns, Christmas Eve, Terrorist on Trial: The United States vs. Salim Ajami.

LEIDER, GERALD J.: Producer, Executive. b. Camden, NJ, May 28, 1931. e. Syracuse U., 1953; Bristol U., Eng., 1954, Fulbright Fellowship in drama. m. Susan Trustman. 1955 joined MCA, Inc., N.Y.; 1956–59 theatre producer in N.Y., London; Shinbone Alley, Garden District, and Sir John Gielgud's Ages of Man. 1960–61; director of special programs, CBS/TV; 1961–62, dir. of program sales, CBS-TV; 1962–69, vice pres., television operation, Ashley Famous Agency, Inc. Sept. 1969–Dec. 1974, pres. Warner Bros. Television, Burbank. Jan. 1975–Dec. 1976, exec. vice pres. foreign production Warner Bros. Pictures, Rome. Jan. 1977–1982, independent producer under Jerry Leider Productions; 1982–87, pres., ITC Prods., Inc. Named pres. and CEO, ITC Entertainment Group, 1987–present.
PICTURES: Wild Horse Hank, The Jazz Singer (1980), Trenchcoat.
TELEVISION: And I Alone Survived, Willa, The Hostage Tower, The Scarlet and the Black, Secrets of a Married Man, The Haunting Passion, Letting Go, A Time to Live, The Girl Who Spelled Freedom, Unnatural Causes, Poor Little Rich Girl.

LEIGH, JANET: Actress. r.n. Jeanette Helen Morrison. b. Merced, CA, July 6, 1927. Mother of actresses Jamie Lee Curtis and Kelly Curtis. e. Coll. of Pacific, music. Autobiography: There Really Was a Hollywood. (1984). Theatre includes Murder Among Friends, Love Letters (with Van Johnson).
PICTURES: The Romance of Rosy Ridge (debut, 1947), If Winter Comes, Hills of Home, Words and Music, Act of Violence, Little Women, That Forsyte Woman, Red Danube, Doctor and the Girl, Holiday Affair, Two Tickets to Broadway, Strictly Dishonorable, Angels in the Outfield, It's a Big Country, Just This Once, Scaramouche, Fearless Fagan, Naked Spur, Confidentially Connie, Houdini, Walking My Baby Back Home, Prince Valiant, Living It Up, Black Shield of Falworth, Rogue Cop, My Sister Eileen, Pete Kelly's Blues, Safari, Jet Pilot, Touch of Evil, The Vikings, The Perfect Furlough, Who Was That Lady?, Psycho (Acad. Award nom.), Pepe, The Manchurian Candidate, Bye Bye Birdie, Wives and Lovers, Three on a Couch, Harper, An American Dream, Kid Rodelo, Grand Slam, Hello Down There, One Is a Lonely Number, Night of the Lepus, Boardwalk, The Fog.
TELEVISION: Movies: Honeymoon With a Stranger, House on Green Apple Road, The Monk, Deadly Dream, Mirror, Mirror; Telethon; Murder at the World Series. Guest: Matt Houston, Starman, Murder She Wrote.

LEIGH, JENNIFER JASON: Actress. b. Los Angeles, CA, Feb. 5, 1962. r.n. Jennifer Leigh Morrow. Daughter of late actor Vic Morrow and TV writer Barbara Turner. Won L.A. Valley Coll. best actress award for The Shadow Box on stage (1979).
PICTURES: Eyes of a Stranger (debut, 1981), Wrong is Right, Fast Times at Ridgemont High, Easy Money, Grandview U.S.A., The Hitcher, Flesh + Blood, The Men's Club, Undercover, Sister Sister, Heart of Midnight, The Big Picture, Miami Blues, Last Exit to Brooklyn, Backdraft, Crooked Hearts, Rush, Single White Female, Short Cuts, The Hudsucker Proxy, Mrs. Parker and the Round Table.
TELEVISION: Movies: Angel City, The Killing of Randy Webster, The Best Little Girl in the World, The First Time, Girls of the White Orchid, Buried Alive.

LEIGH, MIKE: Director, Writer. b. Salford, England, Feb. 20, 1943. e. RADA, Camberwell Art Sch., Central Sch. of Arts & Crafts, London Film Sch. m. actress Alison Steadman. Directed 1977 TV drama Abigail's Party. 1987 short: Short and Curlies.
PICTURES: Bleak Moments, Hard Labour, Nuts in May, The Kiss of Death, Who's Who, Grown-Up, Home Sweet Home, Meantime, Four Days in July, High Hopes, Life is Sweet, Naked.

LEIGH, SUZANNA: Actress. b. England, 1945. Studied at the Arts Educational Sch. and Webber Douglas Sch. Film debut in Oscar Wilde (1961). 1964: TV series made in France, Three Stars. 1965–66: Under contract to Hal Wallis and Paramount, TV film series in West Indies, One On An Island. 1969: TV play, The Plastic People. 1970.
PICTURES: Bomb in High Street, To Love a Vampire, Boeing Boeing, Paradise Hawaiian Style, The Deadly Bees, Deadlier Than the Male, The Lost Continent, Subterfuge, Beware My Brethren, Son of Dracula.
TELEVISION: The Persuaders.

LEITCH, DONOVAN: Actor. Son of folksinger Donovan. Brother of actress Ione Skye. Acted in jr. high sch. musical then had bit part in PBS. show K.I.D.S.
PICTURES: And God Created Women (1988), The Blob, The In Crowd, Cutting Class, Glory, Gas Food Lodging, Dark Horse.
TELEVISION: Movie: For the Very First Time. Guest: Life Goes On.

LELAND, DAVID: Director, Writer, Actor. b. Cambridge, Eng., April 20, 1947. Began as actor at Nottingham Playhouse. Then joined newly formed company at Royal Court Theatre, London. Also appeared in films Time Bandits, The Missionary, and his own Personal Services and on TV in The Jewel in the Crown. As stage director specialized in complete seasons of new works at the Crucible in Sheffield and London venues. Wrote play Psy-Warriors.
PICTURES: Mona Lisa (co-s.p.), Personal Services (s.p.), Wish You Were Here (dir., s.p.), Checking Out (dir.), The Big Man (dir.; a.k.a. Crossing the Line).
TELEVISION: Wrote Birth of a Nation, Flying Into the Wind, Rhino, Made in Britain, Beloved Enemy, Ligmalion, Psy-Warriors.

LELOUCH, CLAUDE: Director, Cinematographer. b. Paris, France, Oct. 30, 1937. Began m.p. career with short subjects, 1956; French military service, motion picture department, 1957–60; formed Films 13, 1960; publicity Films and Scopitones, 1961–62.
PICTURES: Le Propre de L'homme (Man's Own), L'amour avec des Si (Love With Ifs), Une fille et des Fusils (Guns and a Girl), To Be a Crook, A Man and A Woman, Live for Life, Challenge in the Snow, Far From Vietnam, A Man I Like, Life, Love, and Death, Love Is a Funny Thing (dir., photog. s.p.); The Crook (dir., photog., s.p.), Simon the Swiss, Adventure Is Adventure (prod., dir., s.p.), Smic, Smac, Smoc, La Bonne Annee, And Now My Love, Seven Suspects For Murder, Another Man, Another Chance, Edith and Marcel (prod., s.p.); A Man and a Woman: 20 Years Later, Bandits, Itinerary of a Spoiled Child (prod., dir., s.p.).

LeMASTERS, KIM: Executive. e. U.C.L.A., B.A., 1971. Joined CBS in July, 1979 as director, dramatic program dev. Named vice pres., dramatic program dev., 1979; vice pres., comedy program dev., 1980; vice pres., program dev., Nov. 1981; and vice pres. program dev. and production, 1982. Left CBS to serve as vice pres., motion picture production for Walt Disney Productions 1984–85; returned to CBS, 1985 as vice pres., mini-series, CBS Entertainment; appointed vice pres., programs, 1986. Named president, CBS Entertainment, 1987.

LE MAT, PAUL: Actor. b. Rahway, NJ, Sept. 22, 1945. Studied with Milton Katselas, Herbert Berghof Studio, A.C.T., San Francisco, Mitchel Ryan-Actor's Studio.
PICTURES: American Graffiti, Aloha Bobby and Rose, Citizens Band (a.k.a. Handle With Care), More American Graffiti, Melvin and Howard, Death Valley, Jimmy the Kid, Strange Invaders, P.K. and the Kid, Rock & Rule (voice), The Hanoi Hilton, Private Investigations, Puppet Master, Easy Wheels, Deuce Coupe, Grave Secrets, Veiled Threat, Wishman, Caroline at Midnight.
TELEVISION: Movies: Firehouse, The Gift of Life, The Night They Saved Christmas, The Burning Bed, Long Time Gone, Secret Witness, On Wings of Eagles, Into the Homeland, In the Line of Duty: Siege at Marion, Woman With a Past, Blind Witness.

LEMMON, JACK: Actor. b. Boston, MA. Feb. 8, 1925. r.n. John Uhler Lemmon III. e. Harvard U. m. actress Felicia Farr. Father of actor Chris Lemmon. Stage debut as a child; radio actor on soap operas; stock companies; U.S. Navy, W.W.II; many TV shows. Narrated film Stowaway in the Sky. Appeared in AFI short Wednesday. Albums: A Twist of Lemmon, Jack Lemmon Plays and Sings Music From Some Like It Hot. Recipient: American Film Institute Life Achievement Award (1988), Lincoln Center Tribute (1993).
THEATER: Broadway: Room Service (debut, 1953), Face of a Hero (1960), Tribute (1978), Long Day's Journey into Night (1986). Off-Bdwy: Power of Darkness. Regional: Idiot's Delight (1970, L.A.), Juno and the Paycock (1975, L.A.), Tribute (1979, Denver and L.A.), A Sense of Humor (Denver, L.A., S.F., 1983–84), Long Day's Journey into Night (Durham NC, Washington DC, London, Israel), Veterans Day (London, 1989).
PICTURES: It Should Happen to You (debut, 1953), Phffft, Three for the Show, Mr. Roberts (Acad. Award, supp. actor, 1955), My Sister Eileen, You Can't Run Away from It, Fire Down Below, Operation Mad Ball, Cowboy, Bell Book and Candle, Some Like It Hot (Acad. Award nom.), It Happened to Jane, The Apartment (Acad. Award nom.), Pepe, The Wackiest Ship in the Army, The Notorious Landlady, Days of Wine and Roses (Acad. Award nom.), Irma La Douce, Under the Yum Yum Tree, Good Neighbor Sam, How to Murder Your Wife, The Great Race, The Fortune Cookie, Luv, The Odd Couple, The April Fools, The Out-of-Towners, Kotch (dir. debut; also cameo), The War Between Men and Women, Avanti!, Save the Tiger (Acad. Award, 1973), The Front Page, The Prisoner of Second Avenue, Alex and the Gypsy, Airport '77, The China Syndrome (Cannes Film Fest. Award; Acad. Award nom., 1979), Tribute (Acad. Award nom.), Buddy Buddy, Missing (Cannes Film Fest. Award; Acad. Award nom., 1982), Mass Appeal, Macaroni, That's Life, Dad, JFK, The Player, Glengarry Glen Ross, Short Cuts, Grumpy Old Men.
TELEVISION: Series: That Wonderful Guy (1949–50), Toni

Twin Time (host), Ad Libbers, Heaven For Betsy (1952), Alcoa Theatre: A Turn of Fate (1957–8). Radio Soap Operas: The Brighter Day, Road of Life. Guest on numerous dramatic shows: Studio One, Playhouse 90 (Face of a Hero), Kraft Theatre, The Web, Suspense, etc. Specials: The Day Lincoln Was Shot, 'S Wonderful 'S Marvelous 'S Gershwin, Get Happy, The Entertainer, Long Day's Journey into Night, The Wild West (narrator), A Life in the Theatre. Movies: The Murder of Mary Phagan, For Richer For Poorer.

LENO, JAY: Comedian, Actor. r.n. James Leno. b. New Rochelle, NY, April 28, 1950. e. Emerson College, B.A. speech therapy, 1973. Raised in Andover, MA. Worked as Rolls Royce auto mechanic and deliveryman while seeking work as stand-up comedian. Performed in comedy clubs throughout the U.S. and as opening act for Perry Como, Johnny Mathis, John Denver and Tom Jones. Guest on numerous talk shows and specials.
PICTURES: Fun With Dick and Jane, The Silver Bears, American Hot Wax, Americathon, Collision Course, Dave.
TELEVISION: Series: The Marilyn McCoo & Billy Davis Jr. Show (1977), The Tonight Show (guest host: 1987–92; host: 1992.). Specials: Jay Leno and the American Dream (also prod.), The Jay Leno Show, Our Planet Tonight, Jay Leno's Family Comedy Hour.

LENZ, KAY: Actress. b. Los Angeles, CA, March 4, 1953.
PICTURES: Breezy, White Line Fever, The Great Scout and Cathouse Thursday, Moving Violation, Mean Dog Blues, The Passage, Fast Walking, House, Stripped to Kill, Death Wish IV, Headhunter, Physical Evidence, Fear, Streets, Falling From Grace.
TELEVISION: Series: Reasonable Doubts. Movies: The Weekend Nun, Lisa, Bright and Dark, A Summer Without Boys, Unwed Father, The Underground Man, The FBI Story: The FBI Versus Alvin Karpis, Journey from Darkness, Rich Man, Poor Man, The Initiation of Sarah, The Seeding of Sarah Burns, Sanctuary of Fear, The Hustler of Muscle Beach, Murder by Night, Heart in Hiding, How the West Was Won, Traveling Man, Escape, Hitler's Daughter. Guest: Midnight Caller (Emmy Award, 1989), Moonlighting, Hill St. Blues, Hotel, Cannon, McGyver, Cagney & Lacey, McCloud, Riptide, many others. Mini-Series: Rich Man Poor Man—Book II.

LEON, SOL: Executive. b. New York, NY, July 2, 1913. e. NYU, City Coll. of New York, Brooklyn Law Sch., B.B.L., master of law. Exec. v.p., William Morris Agency, L.A.

LEONARD, ROBERT SEAN: Actor. b. Westwood, NJ, Feb. 28, 1969. Raised in Ridgewood, NJ. Started acting at age 12 in local summer stock. Joined NY Shakespeare Festival at 15.
PICTURES: The Manhattan Project (debut, 1986), My Best Friend is a Vampire, Dead Poets Society, Mr. & Mrs. Bridge, Swing Kids, Married to It, Much Ado About Nothing, The Age of Innocence.
THEATRE: Off-Bdwy: Coming of Age in Soho, Sally's Gone—She Left Her Name, The Beach House, When She Danced, Romeo and Juliet. Bdwy: Brighton Beach Memoirs, Breaking the Code, The Speed of Darkness, Candida (Tony nom.). Regional: Biloxi Blues (tour), Rocky and Diego, Long Day's Journey Into Night, King Lear.
TELEVISION: Movies: My Two Loves, Bluffing It. Pilot: The Robert Klein Show.

LEONARD, SHELDON: Actor. r.n. Sheldon Leonard Bershad. b. New York, NY, Feb. 22, 1907. e. Syracuse U., B.A. Theatre mgr., Publix; N.Y. stage, 10 yrs.; sec., Directors Guild of America. 3 Emmy awards, Sylvania award, 4 TV Director of the Year nominations by D.G.A, Cinematographers Governors Award, D.G.A. Aldrich Award. Inducted into TV Hall of Fame.
PICTURES: Another Thin Man, Tall, Dark and Handsome, Tortilla Flat, Rise and Shine, Lucky Jordan, Somewhere in the Night, Her Kind of Man, It's a Wonderful Life, The Gansters, If You Knew Susie, Sinbad the Sailor, My Dream Is Yours, Take One False Step, Iroquois Trail, Here Come the Nelsons, Young Man with Ideas, Stop You're Killing Me, Diamond Queen, Money from Home, Guys and Dolls, Pocketful of Miracles.
TELEVISION: dir. Make Room for Daddy, 1953–56 (2 Emmys); Damon Runyon, G.E. Theatre, Electric Theatre, Jewelers' Showcase, Jimmy Durante Show; prod.-dir. Danny Thomas Show; package & exec. prod., Andy Griffith Show, Dick Van Dyke Show; exec. prod., Gomer Pyle, U.S.M.C., I Spy, My World and Welcome To It (Emmy Award). In 1975 starred in Big Eddie (series), 1977, exec. prod. and co-star in Top Secret.

LERNER, JOSEPH: Producer, Director, Writer. m. Geraldine Lerner, actor on Broadway, radio actor & dir.; with RKO, Columbia and Republic as dir., dial. dir., writer, 2nd unit dir., test dir., dir.-writer & head of special productions U.S. Army Signal Corps Photographic Center; writer of commercial and educational films 1946–47; vice-pres. in chg. of prod. Visual Arts Productions 1947; vice-pres. in chg. prod. Laurel Films 1949; prod.-dir., TV Gangbusters series, Grand Tour series;

Girl on the Run, com. ind. films, Three Musketeers series TV, dir.-prod, 1961; Director, producer, writer, many TV commercials, documentaries 1967–73. President, The Place for Film Making, Inc.; pres., Astracor Associates Ltd. in production: The Ditch Digger's Daughter, The Little Hat, The Mapmakers, Trip the Light Fantastic. Writer & line prod. for Gold Shield Prods. Final Connection. Also lecturer and instructor at NYU, Wm. Patterson Coll., Broward Community Coll. (FL), College at Boca Raton. Member: Eastern Council of the Directors Guild of America.
  CREDITS: (writer-dir.) Fight Never Ends; (prod.-writer) Kings of the Olympics, Olympics Cavalcade; (prod.-dir.-writer) United Nations Case Book (for CBS-TV), C-Man; (prod.-dir.) Guilty Bystander, Mr. Universe, writer, director co-producer, The Dark of Day. Has done many rewrites for various production companies in U.S. and abroad.

LERNER, MICHAEL: Actor. b. Brooklyn, NY, June 22, 1941. Prior to acting was professor of dramatic literature at San Francisco St. Col. (1968–9). Studied acting in London on Fullbright Scholarship. Was member of San Francisco's American Conservatory Theatre. Appeared in L.A. prod. of Hurlyburly.
  PICTURES: Alex in Wonderland, The Candidate, Busting, Newman's Law, Hangup, St. Ives, The Other Side of Midnight, Outlaw Blues, Goldengirl, Borderline, Coast to Coast, The Baltimore Bullet, The Postman Always Rings Twice, Threshold, Strange Invaders, Movers and Shakers, Anguish, Vibes, Eight Men Out, Harlem Nights, Barton Fink (Acad. Award nom.), Newsies, Amos & Andrew, The Penal Colony.
  TELEVISION: Movies: Firehouse, Sarah T: Portrait of a Teenage Alcoholic, Vega$ (pilot), Ruby & Oswald, Hart to Hart (pilot), Moviola: This Year's Blonde, Blood Feud, Rita Hayworth: Love Goddess, The Execution, This Child is Mine, Betrayal of Trust, Hands of a Stranger, King of Love, Framed, Omen IV: The Awakening, Comrades of Summer. Special: The Missiles of October. Guest: Amazing Stories, Macgyver. Pilots: Grandpa Max, The Boys, I Gave at the Office.

LESLIE, ALEEN: Writer. b. Pittsburgh, PA, Feb. 5, 1908. e. Ohio State U. Contributor to magazines; columnist Pittsburgh Press; orig. & wrote radio series A Date with Judy 1941–50. Bdwy play Slightly Married, 1943; wrote, prod. Date with Judy, TV series; author, The Scent of the Roses, The Windfall.
  PICTURES: Doctor Takes a Wife, Affectionately Yours, Henry Aldrich Plays Cupid, Stork Pays Off, Henry Aldrich Gets Glamour, It Comes Up Love, Rosie the Riveter, Father Was a Fullback, Father Is a Bachelor.

LESLIE, JOAN: Actress. r.n. Joan Brodell; b. Detroit, MI, January 26, 1925. p. Agnes and John Brodell. e. St. Benedicts, Detroit; Our Lady of Lourdes, Toronto; St. Mary's Montreal; Immaculate Heart. H.S., L.A. Star of Tomorrow, 1946. Now on bd. of dir., St. Anne's Maternity Home, Damon Runyon Foundation.
  PICTURES:(as Joan Brodel): Camille, Men with Wings, Foreign Correspondent; (as Joan Leslie): Thieves Fall Out, The Wagons Roll at Night, High Sierra, Sergeant York, The Hard Way, The Male Animal, Yankee Doodle Dandy, The Sky's the Limit, This Is the Army, Thank Your Lucky Stars, Hollywood Canteen, Rhapsody in Blue, Where Do We Go From Here?, Too Young to Know, Janie Gets Married, Cinderella Jones, Two Guys From Milwaukee, Repeat Performance, Northwest Stampede, Born To Be Bad, Skipper Surprised His Wife, Man in the Saddle, Hellgate, Toughest Man in Arizona, The Woman They Almost Lynched, Flight Nurse, Hell's Outpost, Jubilee Trail, Revolt of Mamie Stover.
  TELEVISION: Guest: Ford Theatre, G.E. Theatre, Queen for a Day, Simon and Simon, Murder, She Wrote. Movies: Charley Hannah, The Keegans, Turn Back the Clock. Various commercials.

LESTER, MARK: Actor. b. Oxford, England, July 11, 1958. Ent. m.p. ind. 1963.
  PICTURES: Allez France (The Counterfeit Constable), Fahrenheit 451, Our Mother's House, Oliver!, Run Wild Run Free, Sudden Terror, Melody, Black Beauty, Who Slew Auntie Roo?, Redneck, Scalawag, Crossed Swords (The Prince and the Pauper).
  TELEVISION: The Boy Who Stole the Elephants, Graduation Trip, Danza Alla Porto Gli Olmi (Italian Entry Berlin '75), Seen Dimly Before Dawn.
  STAGE: The Murder Game, The Prince and the Pauper 1976.

LESTER, MARK LESLIE: Director. b. Cleveland, OH, Nov. 26, 1946. e. U. of California, Northridge, B.A.
  PICTURES: Steel Arena, Truck Stop Women, The Way He Was, Bobbi Jo and the Outlaw, Stunts, Roller Boogie, The Class of 1984, The Funhouse (exec. prod. only), Firestarter, Commando, Armed and Dangerous, Class of 1999, Showdown in Little Tokyo.
  TELEVISION: Gold of the Amazon Women, Extreme Justice.

LESTER, RICHARD: Director, Composer. b. Philadelphia, PA, Jan. 19, 1932. Early career: dir. and mus. dir. TV, CBS, Phila., CBC-TV, Toronto. Ent. m.p. ind. 1957. TV: dir. TV Goon Shows. Composed (with Reg. Owen) Sea War Series. Short Film: composed and dir., Running Jumping and Standing Still.
  PICTURES: It's Trad Dad, The Mouse on the Moon, A Hard Day's Night, The Knack, Help! A Funny Thing Happened on the Way to the Forum, How I Won the War, Petulia, The Bed Sitting Room, The Three Musketeers, Juggernaut, The Four Musketeers, Royal Flash, Robin & Marian, The Ritz, Superman (uncredited sequence dir. only), Butch and Sundance: The Early Days, Cuba, Superman II, Superman III, Finders Keepers (also exec. prod.), The Return of the Musketeers, Get Back.

LESTZ, EARL: Executive. b. Philadelphia, PA, Aug. 23, 1938. Affiliated for 18 years with Federated Department Stores, of which was sr. v.p. of operations for its Bullock's chain before joining Paramount Pictures in April, 1983, as sr. v.p. of studio operations. 1985, named pres., operations for Paramount Studio Group.

LETTER, LOUIS N.: Executive, b. New York, NY, August, 1937. e. Brooklyn Coll., business administration. v.p. and dir. of operations, Century Theatres, New Hyde Park, N.Y. Exec. v.p., RKO Century Warner Theatres, New York. Regional dir., Edward T. De Bartolo Corp., Youngstown, OH.

LETTERMAN, DAVID: Performer, Writer. b. Indianapolis, IN, Apr. 12, 1947. e. Ball State U. Began career as weatherman and talk show host on Indianapolis TV before going to Hollywood.
  TELEVISION: Writer: Good Times, Paul Lynde Comedy Hour, John Denver Special, Bob Hope Special. Performer: The Starland Vocal Band (also writer), Mary (1978), Tonight Show (guest host 1978–82), the David Letterman Show (Daytime Emmy Award for writing: 1981), Late Night with David Letterman (1982–93, on NBC; 4 Emmy Awards for Writing), An NBC Family Christmas, The Larry Sanders Show (guest), Late Show With David Letterman (1993–, on CBS).

LE VIEN, JACK: Producer, Director. b. New York, NY, 1918. Film ed., reporter, Pathe News; military service, 1941–46; news ed., gen. mgr., v.p., Pathe News; chmn, American Newsreel Assoc., 1956–59; dir. of prod., Hearst Metrotone News; prod. in assoc., ABC-TV, The Valiant Years; exec. prod., Black Fox; prod. The Finest Hours, A King's Story; chmn., exec. prod., Le Vien Films Ltd.; prod.; Other World of Winston Churchill, The Gathering Storm, Walk With Destiny, The Amazing Voyage of Daffodil and Daisy, The Queens Drum Horse, Where the Lotus Fell, Churchill and the Generals, The Glittering Crowd, A Question of Choice.

LEVIN, GERALD M. Executive. b. Philadelphia, PA, May 6, 1939. e. Harvard U., Univ. of PA Law Sch. Attorney, 1963–7. Gen. mgr. & COO of Development Sources Corp., 1969. IBEC rep. in Tehran, Iran, 1971. Joined HBO in 1972 as v.p. of programming, then pres. & CEO, 1973–76; promoted to chmn, 1976. Became Time Inc. group v.p., video, 1979. Elected v.p. Time Inc., 1975; exec. v.p. in 1974; on bd. of dirs., 1983–87. Named vice-chmn, Time Warner, 1989; COO, 1991; pres. & co-CEO of Time Warner, Inc., Feb. 1992.

LEVIN, ROBERT B.: Executive. b. Chicago, IL. e. U. of Illinois. Operated own adv. firm for five years. 1982, named sr. v.p., Needham Harper World Wide Advertising Agency, Chicago. 1985, joined Walt Disney Pictures as sr. v.p., mktg. 1988: Named pres. Buena Vista Pictures marketing.

LEVINSON, ART: Producer. Began film career as office boy at Universal Studios where he entered training program and rapidly rose from asst. director to production manager on Harry and Tonto. Assoc. prod.: Breaking Away, Mr. Mom, Teachers.
  PICTURES: My Favorite Year, Racing with the Moon, The Money Pit, Mannequin, Little Nikita, My Stepmother Is an Alien (exec. prod.).
  TELEVISION: Billionaire Boys Club (assoc. prod.), Curacao (prod.).

LEVINSON, BARRY: Director, Producer, Writer, Actor. b. Baltimore, MD, Apr. 6, 1942. e. American Univ. Wrote and acted in L.A. comedy show leading to work on network tv incl. writing and performing on The Carol Burnett Show. Co-wrote film scripts with Mel Brooks, and then-wife Valerie Curtin.
  PICTURES: First Love (prod.), The Internecine Project (prod., s.p.), Who? (prod.), Silent Movie (co-s.p., actor), High Anxiety (co-s.p., actor), . . . And Justice for All (co-s.p.), Inside Moves (co-s.p.), History of the World Part I (actor), Diner (dir., s.p.), Best Friends (co-s.p.), Unfaithfully Yours (co-s.p.), The Natural (dir.), Young Sherlock Holmes (dir., s.p.), Tin Men (dir., s.p.), Good Morning Vietnam (dir.), Rain Man (dir., actor; Acad. Award for Best Director, 1988), Avalon (dir., s.p.; WGA Award), Bugsy (dir.), Toys (dir., co-s.p.).
  TELEVISION: Movies: Catholics (prod.), Suspicion (prod., co-writer). Series: The Tim Conway Comedy Hour (writer), The Marty Feldman Comedy Machine (writer), The Carol Burnett Show (writer; Emmy Awards: 1974, 1975), Harry

(exec. prod.), Homicide: Life on the Streets (dir., co-exec. prod.). *Pilot*: Diner (exec. prod., dir.). *Specials*: Stopwatch 30 Minutes of Investigative Ticking (exec. prod.), Displaced Person (prod.; Emmy Award: 1985).

LEVINSON, NORM: Executive. b. New Haven, CT. Started theatre business as usher for Loew's Theatres, 1940. U.S. Army, 1943–46. Returned Loew's Theatres managerial positions New Haven and Hartford, CT. MGM press representative, Minneapolis, Jacksonville, Atlanta, Dallas. General Manager, Trans-Texas Theatres, Dallas. President, Academy Theatres, Inc., Dallas. Promoted World Championship Boxing, Dallas and Johannesburg, South Africa. Executive Vice President, Cobb Theatres, Birmingham, Alabama; v.p., world-wide mktg., Artists Releasing Corp., Encino, CA.; head film buyer, Chakeres Theatres, Ohio & Kentucky.

LEVY, BERNARD: Executive. b. Boca Raton, FL. e. Brooklyn Law Sch., L.L.B. Legal staff of Superintendent of Insurance of the state of New York in the rehabilitation and liquidation of guaranteed title and mortgage companies, 1934–36; private practice of law, 1936–46; legal staff, Paramount Pictures, Inc., 1946–50; legal staff, United Paramount Theatres, 1950–51; exec. asst. to Edward L. Hyman, vice-pres., American Broadcasting Companies, Inc., in chg. of theatre administration, north, 1951–62; apptd. exec. liaison officer for southern motion picture theatres, ABC, Inc., 1962–64; exec. liaison officer, m.p. theas., ABC, Inc., 1965–72; vice pres., ABC Theatre Division, 1973. Retired, 1976.

LEVY, BUD: Executive. b. Jackson Heights, NY, April 3, 1928. e. NYU. Member: Variety Clubs Int'l., M.P. Pioneers, President's Advisory Board-NATO; director: NATO, TOP, CATO. Elected pres., Trans-Lux Corp., 1980. Pres. Trans Lux Theatres, (a subsidiary of Cinamerica Theatres, later Crown Theatres). Will Rogers Memorial Fund, Chmn., Cara Committee for NATO; chmn. ShowEast; v.p. NATO; dir. Motion Picture Pioneers.

LEVY, DAVID: Executive. b. Philadelphia, PA, Jan. 2. e. Wharton Sch., U. of Pennsylvania, B.S. in Eco., M.B.A., As v.p. & assoc. dir., Young & Rubicam. Inc., 1938–59, acquisitions for clients include: People's Choice, Kate Smith Hour, Wagon Train, Four Star Playhouse, What's My Line, Father Knows Best, Goodyear Playhouse, Life of Riley, Gunsmoke, Arthur Godfrey's Talent Scouts, I Married Joan, The Web, Treasury Men in Action, Person to Person, Maverick, etc. Prod. We the People, Manhattan at Midnight. Writer: Kate Smith radio series. With War Finance div. of U.S. Treasury Dept. on detached duty from U.S. Navy, 1944–46. Was v.p. in chg. of network TV progs. & talent, NBC, 1959–61. Acquisitions for network include: Sing-a-Long With Mitch, Peter Pan, Bonanza, Dr. Kildare, Bob Newhart Show, Thriller, Car 54-Where Are You?, Loretta Young Show, Sunday Showcase, Alfred Hitchcock Presents, Dick Powell Show, Saturday Night at the Movies, Hazel, Klondike, Victory at Sea, Joey Bishop Show, Shirley Temple Show, etc. *Created*: Bat Masterson, The Addams Family, Americans, Outlaws, Pruitts of Southampton, Sarge, Hollywood Screen Test, Face the Music, etc. *Developed*: Double Life of Henry Phyffe, Name That Tune, You Asked for It. Assigned as writer, training film section, photographic div., Bureau of Aeronautics, U.S. Navy. Novels: The Chameleons, The Gods of Foxcroft, Network Jungle, Potomac Jungle, as well as numerous TV plays and short stories. Currently creative consultant to Mark Goodson Prods. Pres., Wilshire Prods. Exec. dir., Caucus for Prods., Writers and Dirs.

LEVY, EUGENE: Actor, Writer. b. Hamilton, Canada, Dec. 17, 1946. e. McMaster U. Acted with coll. ensemble theater. Film debut in Ivan Reitman's Cannibal Girls, 1970, before joining Toronto's Second City troupe which eventually led to his work as writer-performer on Second City Television's various programs (Second City TV, SCTV Network 90, SCTV Network) 1977–83. Won Emmy Award 1983 for writer of SCTV Network. Appeared in tv movie Partners in Love. Canadian theater: Godspell (1971), The Owl and the Pussycat, Love Times Four.
PICTURES: Cannibal Girls, Running, Strange Brew, Heavy Metal (voice), Going Berserk, National Lampoon's Vacation, Splash, Armed and Dangerous, The Canadian Conspiracy, Club Paradise, Speed Zone, Father of the Bride, Once Upon a Crime (also dir.), Stay Tuned.

LEVY, HERMAN M.: Attorney. Hamden, CT. b. New Haven, CT, Sept. 27, 1904. e. Yale, B.A., 1927, Yale Law Sch., LL.B., 1929; Phi Beta Kappa, was in legal dept. RCA Photophone; newspaper reporter; admitted to Connecticut bar, 1929. In 1939 elected exec. secy. of MPTO of Connecticut. In 1943: Elected general counsel MPTOA. Elected gen. counsel, Theatre Owners of America, 1947–63. Pres., New Haven County Bar Assn., 1964; legislative agent, Conn. Assn. of Theatre Owners. Retired, legislative agent, 1981.
AUTHOR: More Sinned Against . . . Natl. Bd. of Review Magazine, 1941. Proving the Death of a Non-Resident Alien, Conn. Bar Journal, 1950; Need for a System of Arbitration

M.P. Ind., Arbitration Journal, 1950; reprint of Industry Case Digest, 20th Century-Fox vs. Boehm in the Journal (Screen Producers Guild); Book Review of Antitrust in the Motion Picture Industry, by Michael Conant (Univ. of Calif. Law Review).

LEVY, JULES V.: Producer. b. Los Angeles, CA, Feb. 12, 1923. e. U. of Southern California. Property dept., W.B., 1941; First motion picture unit, Army Air Force, Culver City, CA.
PICTURES: The Vampire, Return of Dracula, Vice Squad, Without Warning, Down Three Dark Streets, Geronimo, Glory Guys, Clambake, Scalphunters, Sam Whiskey, Underground, McKenzie Break, The Hunting Party, The Honkers, McQ, Brannigan, White Lightning, Gator, Kansas City Bomber, Safari 3000.
TELEVISION: Rifleman, Robert Taylor's Detectives, Law of the Plainsman, The Big Valley.

LEVY, MICHAEL: Executive. b. Brooklyn, NY. e. Brown U. Started in industry in editorial dept. of trade-paper Variety; held posts in New York with ABC Motion Pictures and with Diener/Hauser/Bates Advertising. Worked for Lawrence Gordon Productions as exec. asst. to Gordon and as story editor. Joined 20th Century Fox in January, 1985, as dir. of creative affairs for studio. 1986, named v.p., production, m.p. div., Fox; appointed sr. v.p. production, 20th Century Fox, 1988; named pres., Silver Pictures, 1989.

LEVY, NORMAN: Executive. b. Bronx, NY, Jan. 3, 1935. e. City Coll. of New York. In 1957 joined Universal Pictures, holding various sales positions; 1967, went to National General Pictures, ultimately being named v.p. and exec. asst. to pres.; 1974, Columbia Pictures, v.p., gen. sls. mgr. In 1975 named Columbia exec. v.p. in chg. of domestic sls.; 1977, exec. v.p., mktg; 1978. pres., Columbia Pictures Domestic Distribution. In 1980 joined 20th-Fox as pres. of Entertainment Group; 1981, vice-chmn., 20th Century-Fox Film Corp. Resigned 1985 to become chmn, ceo, New Century/Vista Film Co. 1991, chmn. and CEO, Creative Film Enterprises.

LEWELLEN, A. WAYNE: Executive. b. Feb. 16, 1944. e. U. of Texas. Joined Paramount Pictures 1973 as brch. mgr., Dallas-Oklahoma City territory; 1974, named South. dist. mgr.; 1978, South. div. mgr. July, 1984, named v.p., domestic dist., South. div.; 1985, appt. exec. v.p., gen. sls. mgr. (New York). 1986, named pres., domestic dist.

LEWINE, ROBERT F.: Executive. b. New York, NY, Apr. 16, 1913. e. Swarthmore Coll. Worked for restaurant chain, in real estate; U.S. Navy, 1942; creative staff, Cine-Television Studios, Inc.; v.p. in charge of oper., 1946; formed own co., 1947, for prod. of TV comm., industrial m.p.; also eastern rep., Dudley Films; radio-TV dir., Hirshon-Garfield, Inc., 1953; eastern prog. dir., ABC, 1953; dir., ABC-TV network prog. dept., 1954; v.p. in charge of programming and talent ABC-TV network, 1956; v.p., NBC, prog. dept. chg. nighttime programming, 1957; v.p. network programs, 1958: v.p Figaro, Inc., 1958; v.p. programs, CBS Films, 1959; v.p. programs, Hollywood CBS Television Network, Apr., 1962; officer Acad. TV Arts & Sciences from 1954, Exec. comm., dir., Acad. TV Arts & Sciences. Pres., N.Y. Chapter 1959; nat'l. pres., 1961; nat'l. trustee, 1961–63; National pres., Academy TV Arts & Sciences, 1961–63; first vice pres., dir., Academy TV Arts & Sciences Foundation; pres., 1964; exec. v.p., Creative Management Associates Ltd.; v.p., Warner Bros., TV Pres. Nat'l Acad. of Television Arts and Sciences; trustee, Columbia College, L.A., Calif.; trustee, American Women in Radio and Television Foundation. 1977-NBC Television Network, exec. prod. dir.; chmn. PAW Society (Preservation of Animal Wildlife); Member Int'l Advisory Council, Population Institute; Chmn. of the bd., Riverside Broadcasting Company. Since 1978 guest lecturer at UCLA and U. of Southern California. Recipient of NATVAS Founder's Award, 1992.

LEWIS, ARTHUR: Producer, Director, Writer. b. New York, NY, Sept. 15, 1918. e. USC, Yale U. Began career as writer and assoc. prod. on the Jones Family TV series. Five years in U.S. Army; returned to screenwriting before producing Three Wishes for Jamie on Broadway and producing and directing Guys and Dolls in London's West End. In mid-60s and 70s produced over 25 plays with Bernard Delfont in the West End of London.
PICTURES: Producer: Loot, Baxter, The Killer Elite, Brass Target.
TELEVISION: Brenner, The Asphalt Jungle (prod. writer), The Nurses. *Movies*: The Diary of Anne Frank, Splendor in the Grass.

LEWIS, EDWARD: Producer. b. Camden, NJ, Dec. 16, 1922. e. Bucknell U. Began entertainment career as script writer, then co-produced The Admiral Was a Lady and teamed with Marion Parsonnet to bring the Faye Emerson Show to TV. Subsequently prod. first Schlitz Playhouse and China Smith series. Was v.p. of Kirk Douglas' indep. prod. co., where was assoc. prod. and writer-prod. Collaborated with John Frankenheimer on 8 films.

PICTURES: Lizzie (assoc. prod.), The Careless Years (prod., s.p.), Spartacus, The Last Sunset, Lonely Are the Brave, The List of Adrian Messenger, Seconds, Grand Prix, The Fixer (exec. prod.), The Gypsy Moths (exec.), I Walk the Line (exec.), The Horsemen, The Iceman Cometh (exec.), Rhinoceros, Lost in the Stars, Missing (co-prod.), Crackers, The River, Executive Action, Brothers (prod., s.p.).
TELEVISION: Islai: The Last of His Tribe (exec. prod.), The Thorn Birds (exec. prod.).

LEWIS, EMMANUEL: Actor. b. Brooklyn, NY, March 9, 1971. Began in TV commercials and has done TV and radio voice-overs. Singer and dancer and, following personal appearance tours in Japan, became recording star there. Theatrical debut in A Midsummer Night's Dream at N.Y. Shakespeare Festival (1982).
TELEVISION: Tonight Show, The Phil Donahue Show, Webster (series). Movie: Lost in London.

LEWIS, GEOFFREY: Actor. b. San Diego, CA, 1935. Father of actress Juliette Lewis, actors Lightfield & Peter Lewis.
PICTURES: Welcome Home Soldier Boys, The Culpepper Cattle Company, Bad Company, High Plains Drifter, Dillinger, Thunderbolt and Lightfoot, Macon County Line, The Great Waldo Pepper, Smile, The Wind and the Lion, Lucky Lady, The Return of a Man Called Horse, Every Which Way But Loose, Tilt, Human Experiments, Tom Horn, Broncho Billy, Heaven's Gate, Any Which Way You Can, Shoot the Sun Down, I the Jury, Ten to Midnight, Night of the Comet, Lust in the Dust, Stitches, Fletch Lives, Out of the Dark, Pink Cadillac, Catch Me If You Can, Disturbed, Double Impact, The Lawnmower Man, Point of No Return, Wishman, The Man Without a Face, Only the Strong.
TELEVISION: Series: Flo, Gun Shy. Movies: Moon of the Wolf, Honky Tonk, The Great Ice Rip-Off, Attack on Terror: The FBI Versus the Ku Klux Klan, The New Daughters of Joshua Cabe, The Great Houndinis, The Deadly Triangle, The Hunted Lady, When Every Day Was the Fourth of July, The Jericho Mile, Samurai, Salem's Lot, Belle Starr, The Shadow Riders, Life of the Party: The Story of Beatrice, The Return of the Man From U.N.C.L.E., Travis McGee, September Gun, Stormin' Home, Dallas: The Early Years. Guest: Mannix, Barnaby Jones, Starsky and Hutch, Streets of San Francisco, Police Woman, Little House on the Prairie, Laverne & Shirley, Lou Grant, Magnum P.I., Amazing Stories, Murder She Wrote, Paradise.

LEWIS, HAROLD G.: Executive. b. New York, NY, Sept. 18, 1938. e. Union Coll., 1960, electrical engineer. Joined ATA Trading Corp. in 1960 and has been pres. since 1977. Producer of feature animation. Importer and exporter for theatrical and TV features, documentaries, series, classics. Pres., ATA Trading Corp., and Favorite TV, Inc.

LEWIS, JERRY: Actor, Director, Writer. r.n. Joseph Levitch. b. Newark, NJ, Mar. 16, 1926. e. Irvington H.S. Parents Danny and Rae Lewis, prof. entertainers. Debut at 5 at a NY Borscht Circuit hotel singing Brother Can You Spare a Dime? 1946 formed comedy-team with Dean Martin at 500 Club, Atlantic City, NJ; then appeared on NBC tv, performed many m.p. theatres before being signed by Hal Wallis; for m.p. debut in My Friend Irma 1949. Voted Most Promising Male Star in Television in m.p. Daily's 2nd annual TV poll, 1950. Voted (as team) one of top ten money making stars in m.p. Herald-Fame poll, 1951, 1953–54–57. Number 1, 1952; best comedy team in m.p. Daily's 16th annual radio poll, 1951, 1952, 1953; 1956 formed Jerry Lewis Prods. Inc., functioning as prod., dir., writer & star. Full professor USC, taught grad. film dir. Book: The Total Filmmaker (1971) based on classroom lectures. National Chairman & bd. memeber, Muscular Dystrophy Association. Autobiography: Jerry Lewis In Person (1982).
PICTURES: My Friend Irma (debut, 1949), My Friend Irma Goes West, At War with the Army, That's My Boy, Sailor Beware, Jumping Jacks, Scared Stiff, The Stooge, Road to Bali (cameo), The Caddy, Money from Home, Living It Up, Three Ring Circus, You're Never Too Young, Artists and Models, Pardners, Hollywood or Bust, The Delicate Delinquent (also prod.), The Sad Sack, Rock-a-Bye Baby, The Geisha Boy (also prod.), Don't Give Up the Ship, Li'l Abner (cameo), Visit to a Small Planet, Cinderfella (also prod.), The Bellboy (also dir., prod., s.p.), The Ladies Man (also dir., prod., co-s.p.), The Errand Boy (also dir., co-s.p.), It's Only Money, The Nutty Professor (also dir., co-s.p.), Who's Minding the Store?, It's a Mad Mad Mad Mad World (cameo), The Patsy (also dir., co-s.p.), The Disorderly Orderly, Boeing-Boeing, The Family Jewels (also dir., prod., co-s.p.), Three on a Couch (also dir., prod.), Way . . . Way Out, The Big Mouth (also dir., prod., co-s.p.), Don't Raise the Bridge Lower the River, Hook Line and Sinker (also prod.), Which Way to the Front? (also dir., prod.), One More Time (dir. only), The Day the Clown Cried (also dir., co-s.p.), Hardly Working (also dir., co-s.p.), The King of Comedy, Smorgasbord (Cracking Up; also dir., co-s.p.), Slapstick of Another Kind, Cookie, Mr. Saturday Night (cameo), Arizona Dream.
TELEVISION: Movie: Fight for Life. Series: Colgate Comedy Hour, The Jerry Lewis Show (1963), Jerry Lewis Show (1967–9).Guest: Wiseguy (5 episodes).

LEWIS, JOSEPH H.: Director. b. New York, NY, Apr. 6, 1907. e. DeWitt Clinton H.S. Camera boy, MGM; then asst. film ed. in chge. film ed., Republic; dir. in chge. 2nd units; dir. Universal; U.S. Signal Corps., WW II; dir. RKO, Columbia, W.B.
PICTURES: My Name is Julia Ross, So Dark the Night, Jolson Story, The Swordsman, Return of October, Undercover Man, Gun Crazy, Lady Without Passport, Retreat Hell!, Desperate Search, Cry of the Hunted, Big Combo, A Lawless Street.
TELEVISION: Rifleman series, Barbara Stanwyck Show: The Big Valley.

LEWIS, MICHAEL J.: Composer. b. Wales, 1939. First film score 1969, The Mad Woman of Chaillot, won Ivor Novello Award for best film score. 1973: first Broadway musical, Cyrano, Grammy nomination '74, Caesar and Cleopatra (T.V. '76), The Lion the Witch and the Wardrobe (Emmy, 1979).
PICTURES: The Man Who Haunted Himself, Julius Caesar. Upon This Rock, Unman Wittering and Zigo, Running Scared, Baxter, Theatre of Blood, 11 Harrowhouse, 92 in the Shade, Russian Roulette, The Stick-Up, The Medusa Touch, The Legacy, The Passage, The Unseen, ffolkes, Sphinx, Yes Giorgio, The Hound of the Baskervilles, On the Third Day, The Naked Face.

LEWIS, MONICA: Singer, Actress. b. Chicago, IL, May 5, 1925. e. Hunter Coll., N.Y. p. Leon Lewis, concert pianist, former medical dir. CBS; Jessica Lewis, child star with Nazimova; member Ben Greet's Shakespearean players, sang leading roles. Chicago Opera Co.; later vocal teacher. Started career as radio singer, own show, WMCA, N.Y.; on Beat the Band, 1946; co-star Chesterfield program; sang leading role, Girl Crazy, Ford Sunday Evening Hour, Own program, Monica Makes Music; co-star Revere Camera show. Among first ten female singers in country on recording polls. Vocalist: Stork Club, Astor Roof, Copacabana, Persian Room.
PICTURES: Inside Straight, Excuse My Dust, The Strip, Everything I Have Is Yours, Affair With a Stranger, Charlie Varrick, Earthquake, Roller Coaster, Airport '77, Nunzio, Concorde-Airport '79.

LIBERMAN, FRANK P.: Publicist. b. New York, NY, May 29, 1917. e. Cheshire Acad., CT, 1934; Lafayette Coll., Easton, PA, B.A. 1938. m. Patricia Harris, casting dir. Worked as copy boy, N.Y. Daily News, 1938–39. Began career as publicist at Warner Bros., home office as messenger, 1939, promoted to press-books dept., transferred to Warner's Chicago office as field exploitation man. U.S. Signal Corps, 1941, public relations officer, Army Pictorial Service, on temporary duty with War Dept., Bureau of Public Relations in Pentagon. Discharged as Capt., 1946. Rejoined Warner Bros. on coast 2 years, 1947, est. own public relations office, 1947. Owner, Frank Liberman and Associates, Inc.

LIBERTINI, RICHARD: Actor. b. Cambridge, MA, May 21. Original member of Second City troupe in Chicago. With MacIntyre Dixon appeared as the Stewed Prunes in cabaret performances.
THEATER: Three by Three (1961), Plays for Bleecker Street, The Cat's Pajamas, The Mad Show, Bad Habits. Solo: The White House Murder Case, Don't Drink the Water, Paul Sill's Story Theatre, Ovid's Metamorphoses, The Primary English Class, Neopolitan Ghosts, Love's Labor's Lost.
PICTURES: The Night They Raided Minsky's, Don't Drink the Water, Catch-22, The Out-of-Towners, Lovers and Other Strangers, Lady Liberty, Fire Sale, Days of Heaven, The In-Laws, Popeye, Sharky's Machine, Soup for One, Best Friends, Deal of the Century, Going Berserk, Unfaithfully Yours, All of Me, Fletch, Big Trouble, Betrayed, Fletch Lives, Animal Behavior. Duck Tales: The Movie (voice), Lemon Sisters, Awakenings, Bonfire of the Vanities.
TELEVISION: Series: The Melba Moore-Clifton Davis Show, Soap, Family Man, The Fanelli Boys, Pacific Station. Guest: George Burns Comedy Week, Barney Miller, Bob Newhart. Pilots: Calling Dr. Storm, M.D., Fair Game. Movies: Three on a Date, Extreme Close-Up. Specials: Let's Celebrate, The Fourth Wise Man, Fame (Hallmark Hall of Fame), The Trial of Bernhard Goetz, Equal Justice.

LICCARDI, VINCENT G.: Executive. b. Brooklyn, NY. Started as messenger at Universal Pictures, asst. adv. mgr. on Around the World in 80 Days, asst. to exec. coord. of sales & Adv. on Spartacus; National Dir. of Adv. & Publ., Continental; Nat. Dir. Adv. & Publ., Braintree Prod., adv. pub. mgr. Allied Artists, ad. mgr. Paramount, National Dir. Adv.-Publ., UMC Pictures, Screenwriter, Playboy to Priest, The Rivals, The Rivals-Part II, The Greatest Disaster of All Time, The Lady on the 9:40, All That Heaven Allows, All Mine to Love, Twice Over, Lightly!, Mr. Jim.

LIDER, EDWARD W. Executive. b. New Bedford, MA, March 13, 1922. e. Dartmouth, Harvard Law Sch. Served as attorney-at-law, 1948–50. President & treasurer, Fall River Theatres

Corp. & Nathan Yamins Enterprises, 1950 to present; member of bd., Theatre Owners of New England; past pres., Theatre Owners of New England; past member of bd. & past treas., Allied States Assoc. of M.P. Exhibitors; general manager of Sonny & Eddy's Theatres in Boston: Exeter St., Academy, Harvard Square, Central Square, Allston C1nema-C2nema and Galeria Theatres.

LIEBERFARB, WARREN: Executive. e. Wharton Sch. of Commerce and Finance, U. of Pennsylvania, B.S., economics; U. of Michigan, M.B.A. Started career in industry at Paramount Pictures as dir. of mktg. and exec. asst. to Stanley Jaffe, then pres. Later joined 20th-Fox as v.p.—special market dist. (cable, pay-TV, non-theatrical). Joined Warner Bros. as v.p., exec. asst. to Ted Ashley, bd. chmn.; later named v.p., intl. adv.-pub. In 1979 joined Lorimar as v.p., of Lorimar Productions, Inc., the parent company, based in New York, Promoted to sr. v.p. 1982, named v.p. mktg., Warner Home Video; named pres., 1985.

LIEBERMAN, ROBERT: Director. b. Buffalo, NY, July 16, 1947. e. Univ. of Buffalo. m. actress Marilu Henner. Dir. short films incl. Pear Facts. Moved to LA, became editor for Desort-Fisher commercial production house, which led to dir. tv ad spots.
PICTURES: Table for Five, All I Want for Christmas, Fire in the Sky.
TELEVISION: Movies: Fighting Back—The Story of Rocky Blier, Will—G. Gordon Liddy, To Save a Child (also exec. prod.). Series: thirtysomething, Dream Street (pilot), The Young Riders (pilot), Gabriel's Fire (also exec. prod.), Pros and Cons (exec. consultant).

LIEBERSON, SANFORD: Producer. b. Los Angeles, CA, 1936. Early career with William Morris Agency. 1961–62, agent in Rome for Grade Org. Returned to LA as Founding Member CMA agency then exec. in charge of European opeations. 1979, named pres. of 20th-Fox Productions, which company he joined in 1977 as v.p.—European production. Previously an independent producer forming Good Times. With David Putnam formed Visual Programming Systems to produce, acquire and consult in the Home VIdeo area for CBS, Phillips, Time/Life, etc. VPS. As v.p. intl. prod. at Fox, spv. intl. release of such films as Star Wars, 1900, Alien, Chariots of Fire, Nine to Five, Quest for Fire. V.P. Intl. prod. for The Ladd Company spv. Outland, Body Heat, Blade Runner, The Right Stuff, Police Academy, etc. Chief of prod. at Goldcrest Harvest: Dance With a Stranger, Room With a View, Absolute Beginners, etc. Pres. intl. prod. MGM spv. Russia House, Thelma & Louise, Liebestraum, Not Without My Daughter, Criss Cross, etc.
PICTURES: Producer: Melody, Pied Piper, Radio Wonderful, James Dean : First American Teenager, Bugsy Malone, Slade in Flame, Final Programme, Stardust, That'll Be the Day, Brother Can You Spare a Dime, Swastika, Double Headed Eagle, All This and World War II, Mahler, Lisztomania, Jabberwocky, Chariots of Fire, Rita Sue and Bob Too, Stars and Bars, The Mighty Quinn.

LIGHT, JUDITH: Actress. b. Trenton, NJ, Feb. 9, 1949. e. Carnegie-Mellon Univ. (BFA). Toured with USO in prod. of Guys and Dolls during college. Acted with Milwaukee and Seattle rep. companies. Made Bdwy. debut in 1975 prod. of A Doll's House with Liv Ullmann. Other stage work: A Streetcar Named Desire, As You Like It, Richard III. Landed role of Karen Wolek on daytime serial One Life to Live in 1977.
TELEVISION: Series: One Life to Live (2 Emmy Awards), Who's the Boss? Movies: Intimate Agony, Dangerous Affection, The Ryan White Story, My Boyfriend's Back, In Defense of a Married Man, Wife Mother Murderer, Men Don't Tell. Guest: St. Elsewhere, Family Ties, Remington Steele.

LIGHTMAN, M. A.: Exhibitor. b. Nashville, TN, Apr. 21, 1915. e. Southwestern U., Vanderbilt U., 1936, B.A. Bd. chmn. Malco Theatres, Inc., Memphis, Tenn.

LINDBLOM, GUNNEL: Actress, Director. b. Gothenburg, Sweden, 1931. Discovered by Ingmar Bergman while studying at drama school of Gothenburg Municipal Theatre (1950–53); she moved to Malmo, where he was director of the local Municipal Theatre. Under Bergman's direction she played in Easter, Peer Gynt, Faust, etc. between 1954–59. Later appeared in many Bergman films. Since 1968 has been on staff of Stockholm's Royal Dramatic Theatre, assisting Bergman and then beginning to direct on her own. Made film debut as director with Summer Paradise in 1977.
PICTURES: Actress: The Seventh Seal, Wild Strawberries, The Virgin Spring, Winter Light, The Silence, Rapture, Loving Couples. Director: Summer Paradise, Sally and Freedom, Summer Nights on Planet Earth.

LINDEN, HAL: Actor. b. Bronx, NY, March 20, 1931. e. City Coll. of New York. Began career as saxophone player and singer, playing with bands of Sammy Kaye, Bobby Sherwood, etc. Drafted and performed in revues for Special Services. After discharge enrolled at N.Y.'s American Theatre Wing; ap-

peared on Bdwy. in Bells Are Ringing, replacing Sydney Chaplin.
THEATRE: On a Clear Day, Wildcat, Something More, Subways Are for Sleeping, Ilya Darling, The Apple Tree, Wildcat, The Education of HYMAN KAPLAN, Three Men on a Horse, Pajama Game, The Rothschilds (Tony Award, 1971), I'm Not Rappaport, Sisters Rosensweig.
TELEVISION: Series: Animals Animals Animals (host), Barney Miller, Blacke's Magic, Jack's Place. Specials: I Do! I Do!, The Best of Everything. Movies: Mr. Inside/Mr. Outside, The Love Boat (pilot), How to Break Up a Happy Divorce, Father Figure, Starflight: The Plane That Couldn't Land, The Other Woman, My Wicked Wicked Ways, The O'Connors, Dream Breakers.
PICTURES: Bells Are Ringing, When You Comin' Back Red Ryder?, A New Life.

LINDFORS, VIVECA: Actress. b. Uppsala, Sweden, Dec. 29, 1920. e. Royal Dramatic Sch., Stockholm. Stage debut in Ann-Scofi Hedvig school prod. Screen debut in The Crazy Family, 1941; reached stardom in If I Should Marry the Minister. Autobiography: Viveka . . . Viveka.
PICTURES: To the Victor (U.S. debut), Adventures of Don Juan, Night Unto Night, Backfire, No Sad Songs for Me, This Side of the Law, Dark City, Flying Missile, Gypsy Fury, Journey into Light, Four in a Jeep, The Raiders, No Time for Flowers, Run for Cover, Moonfleet, Halliday Brand, I Accuse!, Tempest, Weddings and Babies, Story of Ruth, King of Kings, These Are the Damned, No Exit, An Affair of the Skin, Sylvia, Brainstorm, Cauldron of Blood, Dark Dreams of August, Coming Apart, Puzzle of a Downfall Child, The Way We Were, A Bell from Hell, Tabu, Welcome to L.A., Girl Friends, A Wedding, Voices, Natural Enemies, Linus, The Hand, Creepshow, Silent Madness, The Sure Thing, Unfinished Business (prod. & dir.), Lady Beware, Going Undercover, Rachel River, Forced March, The Exorcist III, Misplaced, Zandalee, Goin' to Chicago, Adios, Luba, North of Pittsburgh, The Linguini Incident.
TELEVISION: Movies: A Question of Guilt, Marilyn: The Untold Story, Playing for Time, Mom The Wolfman and Me, The Best Little Girl in the World, For Ladies Only, Divorce Wars, Inside the Third Reich, A Doctor's Story, Passions, The Three Wishes of Billy Grier; Secret Weapons; The Ann Jillian Story, Child of Darkness Child of Light. Guest: Playhouse 90, Alcoa Hour, Climax, Naked City, Bonanza, The FBI, Hotel, Life Goes On (Emmy Award, 1990), many others.

LINDSAY, ROBERT: Actor. b. Ilkeston, Derbyshire, Eng., Dec. 12, 1949. e. Royal Acad. of Dramatic Art. With Manchester's Royal Exchange Theatre Co. (Hamlet, The Cherry Orchard, The Lower Depths). Also in Godspell, The Three Musketeers, Me and My Girl, (London—Olivier Award, NY—Tony, Theatre World and Drama Desk Awards, 1987), Cyrando de Bergerac.
PICTURES: That'll Be the Day (debut, 1974), Bert Rigby, You're a Fool, Strike It Rich.
TELEVISION: Series: Citizen Smith, Give Us A Break. Mini-series: Confessional. Specials: King Lear, G.B.H. (BAFTA Award).

LINK, WILLIAM: Writer, Producer. b. Philadelphia, PA, Dec. 15, 1933. e. U. of Pennsylvania, B.S., 1956. With partner, late Richard Levinson, wrote and created numerous TV series and movies, specializing in detective-mystery genre. Books: Fineman, Stay Tuned: An Inside Look at the Making of Prime-Time Television, Off Camera. Stage incl.: Prescription Murder, Guilty Conscience, Merlin.
PICTURES: The Hindenberg, Rollercoaster.
TELEVISION: Series writer-creator: Mannix, Ellery Queen, Tenafly, Columbo (Emmy, 1972), Murder She Wrote. Movies, writer-prod.: That Certain Summer, My Sweet Charlie (Emmy, 1970), The Judge and Jake Wyler, Savage (exec. prod., s.p.), The Execution of Private Slovik, The Gun, A Cry for Help (prod. only), The Storyteller, Murder by Natural Causes, Stone, Crisis at Central High, Rehearsal For Murder (also exec. prod.), Take Your Best Shot, Prototype (also exec. prod.), The Guardian (also exec. prod.), Guilty Conscience (also exec. prod.), Vanishing Act (also exec. prod.), The United States Vs. Salim Ajami, The Boys (also co-exec. prod.).

LINKLETTER, ART: Emcee, Producer. b. Moose Jaw, Saskatchewan, Canada, July 17, 1912. e. San Diego State Coll. Radio prg. mgr., San Diego Exposition, 1935; radio pgm. mgr. S.F. World's Fair, 1937–39; freelance radio ann. and m.c. 1939–42; m.c. People are Funny since 1942. Starred Inside Beverly Hills, NBC-TV, 1955; exec. prod. host, NBC-TV spec. Salute to Baseball, 1956; host, Art Linkletter's Secret World of Kids, NBC-TV's Ford Startime, 1959; 1969 House Party series became the Linkletter Show. Author of: The Secret World of Kids, 1959, Kids Say the Darndest Things, 1957, Linkletter Down Under, 1969, Yes, You Can, 1979; Old Age is Not For Sissies, 1988.
PICTURES: People Are Funny, Champagne for Caesar, The Snow Queen.

LINN-BAKER, MARK: Actor, Director. b. St. Louis, MO, June 17, 1954. e. Yale Univ., Yale Sch. of Drama (M.F.A., 1979). Founding memb. American Repertory Th. in Cambridge, MA; founding prod./dir. NY Stage & Film Co. in NYC & Poughkeepsie.
TELEVISION: *Series*: Comedy Zone, Perfect Strangers. *Movies*: Wedding Bell Blues, Bare Essentials. *Specials*: Doonesbury (voice of Kirby), The Ghost Writer (Amer. Playhouse), The Whole Shebang. *Director*: episodes of Family Matters, Family Man, Going Places.
PICTURES: Manhattan (bit), The End of August, My Favorite Year, Me and Him (voice only), Noises Off.
THEATRE: *Bdwy*: Doonesbury.

LINSON, ART: Producer, Director. b. Chicago, IL, 1942. e. UCLA; LLD. UCLA, 1967. Was rock music manager with record prod. Lou Adler and ran own record co., Spin Dizzy records before turning to film production. Debuted as director also with Where the Buffalo Roam.
PICTURES: Rafferty and the Gold Dust Twins (co.-prod.), Car Wash, American Hot Wax (also co-s.p.), Where the Buffalo Roam (also dir.), Melvin and Howard, Fast Times at Ridgemont High (co-prod.), The Wild Life (also dir.), The Untouchables (prod.), Scrooged (co-prod.), Casualties of War (prod.), We're No Angels (prod.), Dick Tracy (exec. prod.), Singles, Point of No Return, This Boy's Life.

LIOTTA, RAY: Actor. b. Newark, NJ, Dec. 18, 1955. e. Univ. of Miami.
PICTURES: The Lonely Lady (debut, 1983), Something Wild, Dominick and Eugene, Field of Dreams, GoodFellas, Article 99, Unlawful Entry, The Penal Colony.
TELEVISION: *Series*: Another World, Casablanca, Our Family Honor. *Movies*: Harhat and Legs, Crazy Times, Women and Men 2.

LIPPERT, ROBERT J., JR.: Producer, Director, Film editor. b. Alameda, CA, Feb. 28, 1928. e. St Mary's Coll., 1946; all conference football 1947. Film editor of 65 motion pictures. Produced and directed nine pictures for Lippert Pictures and 20th Century Fox. Present position is president, for Lippert Theatres headquartered in Pebble Beach, CA.

LIPSTONE, HOWARD H.: Executive, Producer. b. Chicago, IL, Apr. 28, 1928. e. UCLA, U. of Southern California. Ass't to gen. mgr. at KLTA, 1950–55; program dir. at KABC-TV, 1955–65; exec. ass't to pres. at Selmur Prods., ABC subsidiary, 1965–69. Ivan Tors Films & Studios as exec. v.p., 1969–70; pres.; pres., Alan Landsburg Prods., 1970–1985; The Landsburg Co., 1985 to present. Co-exec. prod.: The Outer Space Connection, The Bermuda Triangle, Mysteries, The White Lions, Jaws 3-D.
TELEVISION: exec. in charge of prod.: The Savage Bees, Ruby and Oswald, The Triangle Factory Fire Scandal, Strange Voices, A Place at the Table, Kate & Allie, Gimme a Break, A Stoning in Fulham County, The Ryan White Story, Quiet Victory, Unspeakable Acts, In Defense of a Married Man, Triumph of the Heart.

LIPTON, PEGGY: Actress. b. New York, NY, Aug. 30, 1947. Former model. Co-wrote song L.A. is My Lady (recorded by Frank Sinatra). Recorded album Peggy Lipton.
TELEVISION: *Series*: The John Forsythe Show, The Mod Squad (Golden Globe Award, 1971), Twin Peaks. *Movies*: The Return of the Mod Squad, Addicted to His Love, Fatal Charm.
PICTURES: The Purple People Eater, Kinjite (Forbidden Subjects), Twin Peaks: Fire Walk With Me.

LISI, VIRNA: Actress. b. Ancona, Italy, Nov. 8, 1937.
PICTURES: Duel of the Titans, Eva, How To Murder Your Wife, Casanova 70, Not with My Wife You Don't, Assault on a Queen, The Birds Bees and the Italians, Made in Italy, The 25th Hour, The Girl and the General, Arabella, Better a Widow, The Christmas Tree, The Secret of Santa Vittoria, The Statue, Bluebeard, The Serpent, Ernesto, I Love N.Y., I Ragazzi di Via Panisperna, Merry Christmas Happy New Year, Miss Right.
TELEVISION: (U.S.) Christopher Columbus.

LISTER, MOIRA: Actress. b. Capetown, South Africa, b. Aug. 6, 1923. e. Holy Family Convent, Johannesburg. Stage debut at 6 yrs. of age in Vikings of Heligoland; screen debut in Shipbuilders, 1943. Numerous TV appearances.
PICTURES: Love Story, Wanted for Murder, Don Chicago, Uneasy Terms, So Evil My Love, Another Shore, Once a Jolly Swagman, Run for Your Money, Pool of London, White Corridors, Something Money Can't Buy, Cruel Sea, Grand National Night, Limping Man, Trouble in Store, John and Julie, Deep Blue Sea, Seven Waves Away (Abandon Ship), The Yellow Rolls Royce, Joey Boy, Double Man, Stranger in the House, The Choice, Ten Little Indians.

LITHGOW, JOHN: Actor. b. Rochester, NY, Oct. 19, 1945. Father was prod. of Shakespeare Fests. in midwest. e. Harvard. Fulbright fellowship to study at London Acad. of Music and Dramatic Art. Acted and directed in London with Royal Shakespeare Co. and Royal Court Theatre.
THEATER: The Changing Room (Tony Award, 1973), My Fat Friend, The Comedians, A Memory of Two Mondays, Anna Christie, Once in a Lifetime, Requiem for a Heavyweight, Beyond Therapy, Kaufman at Large, The Front Page, M Butterfly, Who's Afraid of Virginia Woolf? (LA).
PICTURES: Dealing (debut, 1972), Obsession, The Big Fix, Rich Kids, All That Jazz, Blow Out, I'm Dancing as Fast as I Can, The World According to Garp (Acad. Award nom.), Twilight Zone—The Movie, Terms of Endearment (Acad. Award nom.), Footloose, The Adventures of Buckaroo Banzai, 2010, Santa Claus, The Manhattan Project, Mesmerized, Harry and the Hendersons, Distant Thunder, Out Cold, Memphis Belle, Ricochet, At Play in the Fields of the Lord, Raising Cain, Cliffhanger, The Pelican Brief, A Good Man in Africa.
TELEVISION: *Guest*: Amazing Stories (Emmy Award, 1987), *Movies*: Mom The Wolfman and Me, Not in Front of the Children, The Day After, The Glitter Dome, Resting Place, Baby Girl Scott, The Traveling Man, The Last Elephant, The Boys.

LITTLE, RICH: Actor. b. Ottawa, Canada, Nov. 26, 1938. Impersonator in night clubs.
TELEVISION: *Series*: Love on a Rooftop, The John Davidson Show, ABC Comedy Hour (The Kopycats), The Julie Andrews Hour, The Rich Little Show, The New You Asked For It (host). *Specials*: Rich Little's Christmas Carol, Rich Little's Washington Follies, Parade of Stars, The Christmas Raccoons, Rich Little and Friends in New Orleans, etc.
PICTURES: Dirty Tricks, Happy Hour.

LITTMAN, LYNNE: Director, Producer. b. New York, NY, June 26. e. Sarah Lawrence. B.A., 1962; Student the Sorbonne 1960–61. Researcher for CBS News 1965; assoc. prod. Natl. Educational TV 1964–68; dir. NIMH film series on drug abuse UCLA Media Center 1970; prod., dir. documentary films, news and pub. affairs series KCET Community TV, So. Calif. 1971–77; dir. WNET non-fiction tv series. 1979; exec. v.p., movies-for-TV, ABC, 1980–81; Received Ford Fdn. Grant 1978 and numerous awards. Acad. Award film tribute to women, 1993.
PICTURES: In the Matter of Kenneth (doc.); Wanted-Operadoras (doc.); Till Death Do Us Part (doc.); Number Our Days (doc. short; Acad Award 1977); Testament (co-prod., dir.), In Her Own Time.

LITTO, GEORGE: Producer. b. Philadelphia, PA. e. Temple U. Joined William Morris Agency in New York and then became indep. literary agent. Opened own office in Hollywood, 1965. Packaged film and TV productions, including M*A*S*H for Robert Altman, Hang 'Em High. Hawaii Five-O for TV prior to entering indep. prod.; 1981–82, chmn. bd. & CEO, Filmways; 1983–85 indep. prod. 20th Century Fox.
PICTURES: Thieves Like Us (exec. prod.), Drive-In (exec. prod.), Obsession (prod.), Over the Edge (prod.), Dressed To Kill (prod.). Blow Out (prod.), Kansas (prod.), Night Game (prod.).

LITVINOFF, SI: Producer, Executive. b. New York, NY, April 5, 1929. e. Adelphi Coll., A.B.; NYU Sch. of Law, LL.B. Theatrical lawyer, personal and business manager in New York until 1967 when left firm of Barovick, Konecky & Litvinoff to produce plays and films. June, 1987: sr. v.p. for production and dev., Hawkeye Entertainment, Inc.
STAGE: Leonard Bernstein's Theatre Songs, Cry of the Raindrop, Girl of the Golden West, Little Malcolm and His Struggle Against the Eunuchs, I and Albert (London).
PICTURES: The Queen, All the Right Noises, Walkabout, A Clockwork Orange (exec. prod.), Glastonbury Fayre (exec. in chg. prod.); The Man Who Fell to Earth (exec. prod.)
TELEVISION: Exec. prod.: 15th Annual Saturn Awards, Doobie Brothers Retrospective, Listen to the Music 1989.

LIVINGSTON, JAY: Composer, Lyricist. b. McDonald, PA, March 28, 1915; e. U. of Pennsylvania, 1937, UCLA, 1964–65. Army, W.W.II. Accompanist and arranger for various NBC singers and singing groups 1940–42, N.Y.; author music and special material for Olsen & Johnson, including various editions of Hellzapoppin', and Sons O'Fun: began composing m.p. songs, 1944. Under contract to Paramount, 1945–55; then freelance. Cameo appearance in Sunset Boulevard. Composed songs for over 100 films. Writer of songs and special material for Bob Hope, 1945–present. Collab. music and lyrics for Bdwy show Oh Captain! 1958; Let It Ride, 1961. Two songs for Sugar Babies, 1980.
SONG HITS: G'bye Now, Stuff Like That There, To Each His Own, Golden Earrings, Silver Bells, Buttons and Bows (Acad. Award, 1949), Mona Lisa (Acad. Award, 1951), Que Sera Sera (Acad. Award, 1957), Tammy (Acad. nom.), Almost In Your Arms (Acad. nom.), Bonanza (TV Theme), Mister Ed (TV Theme), Dear Heart, (Acad. nom.), Wish Me a Rainbow, In the Arms of Love, Never Let Me Go, As I Love You, All the Time, Maybe September.
PICTURES: Monsieur Beaucaire, The Paleface, My Friend Irma Goes West, Streets of Laredo, Isn't It Romantic?, My

Favorite Brunette, Fancy Pants, The Lemon-Drop Kid, Son of Paleface, The Stars Are Singing, Here Come the Girls, Somebody Loves Me, Aaron Slick from Punkin' Crick, Houseboat, Tammy and the Bachelor, The Man Who Knew Too Much, Dear Heart, Here Comes the Groom, My Friend Irma, The Night of the Grizzly, This Property Is Condemned, The Oscar, Never Too Late, Harlow, What Did You Do in the War Daddy?, Wait Until Dark, Red Garters, Sorrowful Jones.

LLOYD, CHRISTOPHER: Actor. b. Stamford, CT, Oct. 22, 1938. Studied at Neighborhood Playhouse, NY. Starred off-Bdwy. in Kaspar, winning Drama Desk and Obie Awards, 1973.
PICTURES: One Flew Over the Cuckoo's Nest (debut, 1975), Goin' South, Butch and Sundance: The Early Days, The Onion Field, The Lady in Red, Schizoid, The Black Marble, The Postman Always Rings Twice, The Legend of the Lone Ranger, National Lampoon Goes to the Movies, Mr. Mom, To Be or Not to Be, Star Trek III: The Search for Spock, Adventures of Buckaroo Banzai, Joy of Sex, Back to the Future, Clue, Miracles, Walk Like a Man, Who Framed Roger Rabbit?, Track 29, Eight Men Out, The Dream Team, Back to the Future Part II, Why Me?, Back to the Future Part III, Duck Tales the Movie (voice), Suburban Commando, The Addams Family, Twenty Bucks, Dennis the Menace, Addams Family Values, The Pagemaster.
TELEVISION: Series: Taxi (Emmy Awards: 1982, 1983), Back to the Future. Specials: Pilgrim Farewell, Tales From Hollywood Hills: Pat Hobby—Teamed With Genius. Movies: Lacy and the Mississippi Queen, September Gun, The Word, Stunt Seven, The Cowboy and the Ballerina, Money on the Side, T Bone N Weasel, Dead Ahead: The Exxon Valdez Disaster. Guest: Barney Miller, Best of the West, Cheers, Amazing Stories, Avonlea (Emmy Award, 1992).

LLOYD, EMILY: Actress. b. North London, Eng., Sept. 29, 1970. Father is stage actor Roger Lloyd Pack, mother worked as Harold Pinter's secretary. Father's agent recommended that she audition for screenwriter David Leland's directorial debut Wish You Were Here when she was 15.
PICTURES: Wish You Were Here (Natl. Society of Film Critics Award, 1987), Cookie, In Country, Chicago Joe and the Showgirl, Scorchers, A River Runs Through It.

LLOYD, EUAN: Producer. b. Rugby, Warwick, England, Dec. 6, 1923. e. Rugby. Entered m.p. ind. in 1939 as theatre manager, then pub. dir.; dir. of Publ. Rank, 1946; joined Associated British-Pathe, Ltd. in same capacity; 1952 asst. to prod., Warwick Film Prod. Ltd. v.p. Highroad Productions, 1962–64. Rep. Europe Goldwyn's Porgy & Bess 1959.
PICTURES: April in Portugal, Heart of Variety, Invitation to Monte Carlo, The Secret Ways, Genghis Khan, Poppy Is Also a Flower, Murderer's Row, Shalako, Catlow, The Man Called Noon, Paper Tiger, The Wild Geese, The Sea Wolves, Who Dares Wins, Wild Geese II, The Final Option, Centrifuge.

LLOYD, NORMAN: Actor, Producer, Director. b. Jersey City, NJ, Nov. 8, 1914. e. NYU, 1932. Acted on Bdwy in: Noah, Liberty Jones, Everywhere I Roam, 1935–44; in various stock companies. Founder with Orson Welles and John Houseman of Mercury Theatre, NY.
PICTURES: Actor: Saboteur, Spellbound, The Southerner, A Walk in the Sun, A Letter for Evie, The Unseen, Green Years, The Beginning or The End, Limelight. Prod. asst. on Arch of Triumph and The Red Pony, 1946, Young Widow, No Minor Vices, The Black Book, Scene of the Crime, Calamity Jane and Sam Bass, Buccaneer's Girl, The Flame and the Arrow, He Ran All the Way, The Light Touch, Audrey Rose, FM, The Nude Bomb, Jaws of Satan, Dead Poets Society, Journey of Honor (Shogun Mayeda), The Age of Innocence. Producer: Up Above the World.
STAGE: Village Green, King Lear, The Cocktail Party, The Lady's Not for Burning, Madame Will You Walk, The Golden Apple, Major Barbara, The Will & Bart Show.
TELEVISION: Assoc. prod.: The Alfred Hitchcock Show, 1957 and exec. prod. 1963. Prod.-Dir.: The Alfred Hitchcock Hour, The Name of the Game, Hollywood Television Theater, Tales of the Unexpected. Actor: St. Elsewhere (series). Movies: Prod.-Dir.: The Smugglers, Companions in Nightmare, What's a Nice Girl Like You (prod.), The Bravos (prod.), Amityville: The Evil Escapes.

LOBELL, MICHAEL: Producer. b. Brooklyn, NY, May 7, 1941. e. Michigan State U. on athletic baseball scholarship. Worked briefly in garment indust. Entered film industry in 1974 by buying Danish distribution rights to The Apprenticeship of Duddy Kravitz. Formed Lobell/Bergman Prods. with Andrew Bergman.
PICTURES: Dreamer, Windows, So Fine, The Journey of Natty Gann, Chances Are, The Freshman, White Fang, Honeymoon in Vegas.

LO BIANCO, TONY: Actor. b. New York, NY. Oct. 19, 1936. Performed on N.Y. stage as well as in films and TV. Former artistic dir. Triangle Theatre, NY. Won Obie Award for performance in Yanks 3, Detroit 0, Top of the Seventh. Also

acted on stage in The Office, The Rose Tattoo, The View From the Bridge, The Royal Hunt of the Sun, Hizzoner.
PICTURES: The Honeymoon Killers, The French Connection, The 7-Ups, Demon, F.I.S.T., Bloodbrothers, Separate Ways, City Heat, Too Scared to Scream (dir. only), La Romana, City of Hope, Boiling Point.
TELEVISION: Series: Jessie, Palace Guard. Guest: Police Story. Movies: Mr. Inside Mr. Outside, The Story of Joseph and Jacob, Hidden Faces, Legend of Black Hand, Lady Blue, Marco Polo, Welcome Home Bobby, Blood Ties, Madigan, A Last Cry for Help, Mr. Inside Mr. Outside, Marciano, Another Woman's Child, The Last Tenant, Goldenrod, Shadow in the Streets, Eugene O'Neill's A Glory of Ghosts, Police Story: The Freeway Killings, The Ann Jillian Story, Body of Evidence, Hizzoner (Emmy Award), Off Duty, True Blue, Perry Mason: The Case of the Poisoned Pen, Malcolm Takes a Shot, In the Shadow of a Killer, Stormy Weathers, Teamster Boss: The Jackie Presser Story. Director: Police Story, Kaz, Cliffhangers.

LOCKE, SONDRA: Actress. b. Shelbyville, TN, May 28, 1947.
PICTURES: The Heart is a Lonely Hunter (debut, 1968), Cover Me Babe, Willard, A Reflection of Fear, The Second Coming of Suzanne, The Outlaw Josey Wales, Death Game, The Gauntlet, Every Which Way But Loose, Bronco Billy, Any Which Way You Can, Sudden Impact. Director: Ratboy (dir. debut, 1986; also star), Impulse.
TELEVISION: Movies: Friendships, Secrets and Lies, Rosie: The Rosemary Clooney Story. Guest: Amazing Stories.

LOCKHART, JUNE: Actress. b. New York, NY, June 25, 1925. p. actors, Gene and Kathleen Lockhart. Bdwy debut For Love or Money, 1947.
PICTURES: A Christmas Carol (1938), All This and Heaven Too, Adam Had Four Sons, Sergeant York, Miss Annie Rooney, Forever and a Day, White Cliffs of Dover, Meet Me in St. Louis, Son of Lassie, Keep Your Powder Dry, Easy to Wed, She-Wolf of London, Bury Me Dead, The Yearling, T-Men, It's a Joke Son, Time Limit, Butterfly, Deadly Games, Strange Invaders, Troll, Rented Lips, The Big Picture, Dead Women in Lingerie.
TELEVISION: Series: Who Said That? (panelist), Lassie, Lost in Space, Petticoat Junction, General Hospital. Movies: But I Don't Want to Get Married, The Bait, Who is the Black Dahlia?, Curse of the Black Widow, The Gift of Love, Walking Through the Fire, The Night They Saved Christmas, Perfect People, A Whisper Kills, Danger Island. Mini-Series: Loose Change.

LOCKWOOD, GARY: Actor. r.n. John Gary Yusolfsky. b. Van Nuys, CA, Feb. 21, 1937. Began in Hollywood as stuntman.
PICTURES: Tall Story, Splendor in the Grass, Wild in the Country, The Magic Sword, It Happened at the World's Fair, Firecreek, 2001: A Space Odyssey, They Came to Rob Las Vegas, Model Shop, The Body, R.P.M., Stand Up and Be Counted, The Wild Pair.
TELEVISION: Series: Follow the Sun, The Lieutenant. Movies: Earth II, Manhunter, The FBI Story: The FBI Versus Alvin Karpus—Public Enemy, The Ghost of Flight 401, The Incredible Journey of Dr. Meg Laurel, Top of the Hill, The Girl The Gold Watch & Dynamite, Emergency Room.

LOCKWOOD, ROGER: Executive. b. Middletown, CT, June 7, 1936. e. Ohio Wesleyan U. Sports writer for Akron Beacon Journal, 1960–62. On executive staff of Lockwood & Gordon Theatres; exec. v.p. SBC Theatres, 1969–73. In 1974 asst. to exec. v.p., General Cinema Corp. In 1975 formed Lockwood/Friedman Theatres, buying-booking and exhibition organization. Pres., Theatre Owners of New England, 1971–72; pres., Young NATO 1965–67; bd. of dir. NATO, 1962–1968. Board of dir. Tone, 1968–present; pres., Jimmy Fund, present; 1979–80, Variety Club of New England, pres. Director, Dana-Farber Cancer Institute, 1983–present. 1988, formed Lockwood/McKinnon Company Inc. operating theatres and Taco Bell Restaurants.

LOGGIA, ROBERT: Actor. b. New York, NY, Jan. 3, 1930. e. U. of Missouri, B.A. journalism, 1951. Studied with Stella Adler and at The Actors Studio. Broadway debut, The Man with the Golden Arm, 1955.
THEATER: Toys in the Attic, The Three Sisters, In the Boom Boom Room, Wedding Band.
PICTURES: Somebody Up There Likes Me (debut, 1956), The Garment Jungle, Cop Hater, The Lost Missile, Cattle King, The Greatest Story Ever Told, Che, First Love, Speed Trap, Revenge of the Pink Panther, The Ninth Configuration (a.k.a. Twinkle Twinkle Killer Kane), S.O.B., An Officer and a Gentleman, Trail of the Pink Panther, Psycho II, Curse of the Pink Panther, Scarface, Prizzi's Honor, Jagged Edge, Armed and Dangerous, That's Life, Over the Top, Hot Pursuit, The Believers, Gaby: A True Story, Big, Oliver & Company (voice), Relentless, S.P.O.O.K.S., Triumph of the Spirit, Opportunity Knocks, The Marrying Man, Necessary Roughness, Gladiator, Innocent Blood.
TELEVISION: Series: T.H.E. Cat, Emerald Point N.A.S.,

Mancuso, Sunday Dinner. *Play of the Week*: Miss Julie. *Specials*: The Nine Lives of Elfego Baca (1958), Conspiracy: The Trial of the Chicago 8, Merry Christmas Baby. *Movies*: Mallory, Circumstantial Evidence, Street Killing, Scott Free, Raid on Entebbe, No Other Love, Casino, A Woman Called Golda, A Touch of Scandal, Intrigue, The O'Connors, Dream Breakers, Afterburn, Lifepod. *Mini-Series*: Arthur Hailey's The Moneychangers, Echoes in the Darkness, Favorite Son, Wild Palms.

LOLLOBRIGIDA, GINA: Actress. b. Subiaco, Italy, July 4, 1927. e. Acad. of Fine Arts, Rome. Film debut (Italy) L'aguila nera, 1946.
PICTURES: Pagliacci, The City Defends Itself, The White Line, Fanfan the Tulip, Times Gone By, Beat the Devil, Crossed Swords, The Great Game, Beauties of the Night, Wayward Wife, Bread Love and Dreams, Bread Love and Jealousy, Young Caruso, World's Most Beautiful Woman, Trapeze, Hunchback of Notre Dame, Solomon and Sheba, Never So Few, The Unfaithfuls, Fast and Sexy, Where the Hot Wind Blows, Go Naked in the World, Come September, Imperial Venus, Woman of Straw, That Splendid November, Hotel Paradiso, Buona Sera Mrs. Campbell, Plucked, The Private Navy of Sgt. O'Farrell, Bad Man's River, King Queen Knave, The Lonely Woman, Bambole.
TELEVISION: *Movie*: Deceptions. *Series*: Falcon Crest.

LOM, HERBERT: Actor. r.n. Herbert Charles Angelo Kuchacevich ze Schluderpacheru. b. Prague, Sept. 11, 1917. e. Prague U. Stage training London Embassy, Old Vic—Sadlers Wells and Westminster Schools. British film debut (Mein Kampf—My Crimes) (1941); on TV, The Human Jungle Series.
PICTURES: Tomorrow We Live, Secret Mission, Young Mr. Pitt, Dark Tower, Hotel Reserve, The Seventh Veil, Night Boat to Dublin, Dual Alibi, Good Time Girl, The Golden Salamander, State Secret, The Black Rose, Whispering Smith vs. Scotland Yard, Two on the Tiles, Mr. Denning Drives North, Hell Is Sold Out, Gaunt Stranger, Rough Shoot, The Net, The Love Lottery, Star of India, Beautiful Stranger, The Lady-killers, War and Peace, Fire Down Below, Hell's Drivers, Chase a Crooked Shadow, Passport to Shame, Roots of Heaven, The Big Fisherman, Northwest Frontier (Flame Over India), I Aim at the Stars, Spartacus, Mysterious Island, Mr. Topaz, The Frightened City, El Cid, Tiara Tahiti, The Phantom of the Opera, Horse Without a Head, A Shot in the Dark, Uncle Tom's Cabin, Return from the Ashes, Gambit, The Assignment, Villa Rides, Doppelganger, Mr. Jericho, Dorian, Mark of the Devil, Count Dracula, Murders in the Rue Morgue, Asylum, And Now the Screaming Starts, Dark Places, Death in Persepolis, Return of the Pink Panther, Ten Little Indians (1975), The Pink Panther Strikes Again, Charleston, Revenge of the Pink Panther, The Lady Vanishes, The Man with Bogart's Face, Hopscotch, The Acts of Peter and Paul, The Trail of the Pink Panther, The Curse of the Pink Panther, Memed My Hawk, Dead Zone, King Solomon's Mines, Whoops Apocalypse, Coast of Skeletons, Master of Dragonard Hill, Going Bananas, Skeleton Coast, Ten Little Indians (1989), River of Death, The Masque of the Red Death, The Sect, The Pope Must Die, Son of the Pink Panther.

LOMITA, SOLOMON: Executive. b. New York, NY, April 23, 1937. Started industry career with United Artists Corp. as follows: adm., intl. dept., 1962; asst., intl. sales, same year. 1963, asst. intl. print mgr.; 1965, intl., print mgr. In 1973 appt. dir. of film services. 1981, v.p., film services. In 1985 named v.p., post-prod., Orion Pictures; in March, 1989 promoted to sr. v.p.

LONDON, BARRY: Executive. Joined Paramount Pictures 1971 in L.A. branch office as booker; later salesman. 1973, sls. mgr., Kansas City-St. Louis; 1974, branch mgr. Transferred to San Francisco, first as branch mgr.; later as district mgr. 1977, eastern div. mgr. in Washington, DC, 1978–81, western div. mgr. In March, 1981, named v.p., gen. sls. mgr. June, 1983, advanced to sr. v.p., domestic distribution. 1984, named pres., domestic div., for Motion Picture Group of Paramount; 1985, named president, marketing and domestic distribution; 1988, named pres. Motion Picture Group.

LONDON, JERRY: Director. b. Los Angeles, CA, Jan 21, 1937. Apprentice film editor, Desilu Prods., 1955; film ed., Daniel Boone, 1962; staged plays in local theater workshops; editor, assoc. prod., then dir. Hogan's Heroes. Formed Jerry London Prods., 1984.
PICTURE: Rent-a-Cop (feature debut, 1988).
TELEVISION: *Series*: Mary Tyler Moore Show, Love American Style, The Bob Newhart Show, Marcus Welby, M.D., Kojak, The Six Million Dollar Man, Police Story, Rockford Files. *Mini-series*: Wheels, Shogun (DGA, best dir., special award), Chiefs (also sprv. prod.), Ellis Island (also sprv. prod.), If Tomorrow Comes, A Long Way From Home. *Movies*: Killdozer, McNaughton's Daughter, Cover Girls, Evening in Byzantium, Women in White, Father Figure, The Chicago Story, The Ordeal of Bill Carney (also prod.), The Gift of Life (also prod.), The Scarlet and the Black, Arthur Hailey's Hotel (also prod.), With Intent to Kill (exec. prod. only), Dark

Mansions, Manhunt For Claude Dallas, Harry's Hong Kong, Family Sins (exec. prod. only), Macgruder and Loud (also prod.), Dadah Is Death (also prod.), Kiss Shot (also exec. prod.), The Haunting of Sarah Hardy (also exec. prod.), Vestige of Honor, A Season of Giants, Victim of Love, Grass Roots, Calendar Girl Cop Killer?: The Bambi Bembenek Story (also prod.), A Twist of the Knife, Labor of Love: The Arlette Schweitzer Story.

LONDON, JULIE: Singer, Actress. r.n. Julie Peck. b. Santa Rosa, CA, Sept. 26, 1926. Launched as actress by agent Sue Carol (wife of Alan Ladd) who arranged screen test, followed by contract for 6 films. As singer has appeared in nightclubs and recorded.
PICTURES: The Red House, Tap Roots, Task Force, Return of the Frontiersman, The Fat Man, Fighting Chance, The Great Man, The Girl Can't Help It, Crime Against Joe, Drango, Saddle the Wind, Man of the West, Voice in the Mirror, A Question of Adultery, The Wonderful Country, Night of the Quarter Moon, The Third Voice, The George Raft Story.
TELEVISION: *Series*: Emergency. *Guest*: Perry Como Show, Steve Allen Show, Ed Sullivan Show. *Movie*: Emergency (pilot).

LONDON, MILTON H.: Executive. b. Detroit, MI, Jan. 12, 1916. e. U. of Michigan, B.A., 1937. Wayne U. Law Sch., 1938. U.S. Army 1943–46. Invented Ticograph system of positive admissions control for theatres, 1950; pres. Theatre Control Corp., 1950–62; secy-treas. Co-op. Theas. of Michigan Inc., 1956–63; exec. comm., Council of M.P. Organizations, 1957–66; dir. M.P. Investors, 1960–67; exec. dir. Allied States Assoc. of M.P. Exhib., 1961–66; exec. dir. National Assoc. of Theatre Owners, 1966–69 pres.; NATO of Michigan, 1954–74; Mich. State Fire Safety Bd., Chief Barker, Variety Club of Detroit, Tent No. 5. 1975–76; Life Patron and Lifeliner, Variety Clubs International; trustee, Variety Club Charity for Children; chmn., Variety Club Myoelectric Center; dir., Motion Picture Pioneers; advisory comm., Will Rogers Inst.; trustee, Detroit Inst. for Children; pres., Metropolitan Adv. Co.; intl. ambassador, Variety Clubs Int'l; Detroit News 1991 Michiganian of the Year.

LONE, JOHN: Actor. b. Hong Kong. Studied at Chin Ciu Academy of the Peking Opera in Hong Kong, Moved to LA where he studied acting at Pasadena's American Acad. of Dramatic Art, becoming member of the East-West Players.
PICTURES: Iceman (debut, 1984), Year of the Dragon, The Last Emperor, The Moderns, Echoes of Paradise, Shadow of China, Shanghai 1920, M. Butterfly.
TELEVISION: The Dance and the Railroad, Paper Angels (dir.).
THEATRE: NY: F.O.B., The Dance and the Railroad (Obie Awards for both plays), Paper Angels (dir.), Sound and Beauty (also dir.).

LONG, SHELLEY: Actress. b. Ft. Wayne, IN, Aug. 23, 1949. e. Northwestern U. Was co-host, assoc. prod. of local tv show Sorting It Out.
PICTURES: A Small Circle of Friends (debut, 1980), Caveman, Night Shift, Losin' It, Irreconcilable Differences, The Money Pit, Outrageous Fortune, Hello Again, Troop Beverly Hills, Don't Tell Her It's Me, Frozen Assets.
TELEVISION: *Series*: Cheers (Emmy Award, 1983), Good Advice. *Movies*: The Cracker Factory, Princess and the Cabbie, Promise of Love, Voices Within: The Lives of Truddi Chase, Fatal Memories, A Message From Holly. *Special*: Basic Values: Sex Shock & Censorship in the '90's.

LONGSTREET, STEPHEN: Writer, Painter. b. New York, NY, April 18, 1907; e. Rutgers U.; Parsons Coll.; Rand Sch., London, B.A. Humorist, cartoonist (New Yorker, Collier's, etc.) 1930–37; ed. Free World Theat., radio plays; ed. film critic, Saturday Review of Literature, 1940, U.S. at War, Time 1942–43; writer for screen from 1942. On staff UCLA. Elected pres. Los Angeles Art Assoc. 1970. 1974: appointed Prof. English Dep., U. of Southern California. Modern Writing Course. Writers Guild, Comm. of Public Relations. Film and book critic for Readers' Syndicate since 1970. Professor performing arts dept. U. of Southern California since 1973, where in 1979, presented 12 great silent films, The Art & Entertainment of Silent Films. Rutgers U., lecturer, 1986, on Griffith, Hawks, Hitchcock, Ford, Welles. L.A. Art Assoc. lecture series 1988 The Dreams That Swallowed the World: The Hollywood Scene 1940–88. Art show Movie Faces.
WRITINGS: Decade, The Golden Touch, The Gay Sisters, Last Man Around the World, Chico Goes to the Wars, Pedlocks, Lion at Morning, Promoters, Boy in the Model T, Sometimes I Wonder (with Hoagy Carmichael), Wind at My Back (with Pat O'Brien), Goodness Had Nothing to Do With It (with Mae West), The Young Men of Paris, The Wilder Shore, War Cries on Horseback, Yoshiwara, Geishas and Courtesans, Canvas Falcons, Men and Planes of World War I, We All Went to Paris. Chicago 1860–1919, (show business & society), Divorcing (a novel); The General (novel, 1974), All Star Cast (Hollywood), 1977; The Queen Bees (1979), Our

Father's House (1985), Storyville to Harlem (Jazz 1988), Dictionary of Jazz, (1989); Dreams that Swallowed the World (The Movies, 1989), Jazz Solos (poems & images).

STAGE: High Button Shoes (book, revived in Jerome Robbins' Broadway, 1989).

PICTURES: The Gay Sisters, Golden Touch, Stallion Road, Jolson Story, Silver River, Helen Morgan Story, First Traveling Saleslady, Untamed Youth, Duel in the Sun, Greatest Show on Earth, The Crime, Uncle Harry, Rider on a Dead Horse, The Imposter.

TELEVISION: Casey Jones (series), Clipper Ship (Playhouse 90), Man Called X, m.c. author of The Sea; m.c. Press & Clergy, 1960–63; Viewpoint; series Boy in the Model T, Young Man From Boston, 1967, Blue and the Grey. Appeared on Early Hollywood.

LONSDALE, PAMELA: Producer and Executive Producer for Children's drama, Thames TV for 15 years. Now freelance. Prod. short feature film, Exploits at West Poley (for CFTF). Prod.: Writer to Twelve (Central TV comedy series). Exec. prod. for E.B.U.'s world drama exchange for 2 years. Winner British Acad. Award for Rainbow, 1975.

LOOS, MARY: Writer. b. San Diego, CA, May 6, 1914. e. Stanford U., 1933. Actress m.p.; in public relations field N.Y. 1938; jewelry designer for Paul Flato; author of novel Return in the Vineyard, 1945. secy. Voyager Films, Inc., literary exec. M. J. Frankovich Prod. Novel: The Beggars Are Coming, 1974, Belinda, 1976; The Barstow Legend, 1978; A Pride of Lovers, 1981.

PICTURES: Rose Marie, Maytime, Crusades, Cleopatra, Mr. Belvedere Goes to College, Mother Was a Freshman, Ticket to Tomahawk, When Willie Comes Marching Home, Father Was a Fullback, I'll Get By, Meet Me After the Show, Let's Do It Again, The French Line, Gentlemen Marry Brunettes, Over-Exposed, Woman's World.

LORD, JACK: Actor, Writer, Artist, Director, Producer. b. New York, NY, Dec. 30, 1930. r.n. John Ryan. e. NYU. (Chancellor Chase scholarship), B.S., Fine Arts, 1954. Studied at Sanford Meisner's Neighborhood Playhouse and with Lee Strasberg at the Actors Studio. Artist, represented in various museums incl. Metropolitan Museum of Art, Museum of Modern Art, Brooklyn Museum, in NY, Bibliotheque National, Paris; British Museum; Fogg Museum, Harvard U. St. Gaudens Plaque for Fine Arts; On Bway in Traveling Lady (Theatre World Award, 1959), Cat on a Hot Tin Roof. Fame Award, new male star, 1963, Named to Cowboy Fall of Fame, 1963. mem. of Directors Guild of America. Awards: St. Gauden's Artist Award, 1948; G. Washington Honor Medal from Freedom Foundation at Valley Forge, 1984; Veterans Admin., Administrator's Award, 1980; Salute to Hospitalized Veterans, Tripler Army Medical Center, 1985; East-West Center Distinguished Service Award, 1981. Author: Jack Lord's Hawaii. . . A Trip Through the Last Eden, 1971. Pres., Lord and Lady Enterprises, Inc. Appeared in Williamsburg documentary Story of a Patriot.

PICTURES: The Court Martial of Billy Mitchell, Tip On a Dead Jockey, God's Little Acre, Man of the West, The Hangman, True Story of Lynn Stuart, Walk Like a Dragon, Doctor No, Ride to Hangman's Tree, Counterfeit Killer.

TELEVISION: Series: Stoney Burke (1962–3), Hawaii Five-O (1968–79; 250 episodes), creator of Tramp Ship, McAdoo, Yankee Trader, The Hunter TV series. Guest: Man Against Crime (debut), Playhouse 90, Goodyear Playhouse, Studio One, U.S. Steel. Have Gun Will Travel (pilot), Untouchables, Naked City, Rawhide, Bonanza, The Americans, Route 66, Gunsmoke, Stagecoach West, Dr. Kildare, Greatest Show on Earth, Combat, Chrysler Theatre, 12 O'Clock High, The Loner, Laredo, The FBI, The Invaders, The Fugitive, The Virginian, Man from U.N.C.L.E., High Chaparral, Ironside. Movie: Doomsday Flight. Director: Death with Father, How to Steal a Masterpiece, Honor Is an Unmarked Grave, The Bells Toll at Noon, Top of the World, Why Won't Linda Die, Who Says Cops Don't Cry; episodes of Hawaii Five-O. Creator, director, and exec. producer of M Station: Hawaii (2-hr special, 1979).

LOREN, SOPHIA: Actress. b. Rome, Italy, Sept. 20, 1934. e. Naples. In films since 1950. m. producer Carlo Ponti. Autobiography: Sophia: Living and Loving (with A.E. Hotchner, 1979).

PICTURES: Africa Beneath the Seas, Village of the Bells, Good People's Sunday, Neapolitan Carousel, Day in the District Court, Pilgrim of Love, Aida, Two Nights with Cleopatra, Our Times, Attila, Scourge of God, Gold of Naples, Too Bad She's Bad, Scandal in Sorrento, Miller's Beautiful Wife, Lucky to Be a Woman, Boy on a Dolphin (U.S. debut, 1957), The Pride and the Passion, Legend of the Lost, Desire Under the Elms, The Key, Houseboat, The Black Orchid, That Kind of Woman, Heller in Pink Tights, It Started in Naples, A Breath of Scandal, The Millionairess, Two Women (Acad. Award, 1961), El Cid, Boccaccio 70, Madame Sans-Gene, Five Miles to Midnight, The Condemned of Altona, Yesterday Today and Tomorrow, The Fall of the

Roman Empire, Marriage Italian Style, Operation Crossbow, Lady L, Judith, Arabesque, A Countess from Hong Kong, More than a Miracle, Ghosts—Italian Style, Sunflower, The Priest's Wife, Lady Liberty, White Sister, Man of La Mancha, The Voyage, The Verdict (Jury of One), The Cassandra Crossing, A Special Day, Angela, Brass Target, Firepower, Blood Feud.

TELEVISION: Movies/Specials: Brief Encounter, Sophia Loren—Her Own Story, Softly Softly, Rivals of Sherlock Holmes, Fantasy Island, Aurora, Courage, Mario Puzo's The Fortunate Pilgrim.

LOUDON, DOROTHY: Actress. b. Boston, MA, Sept. 17, 1933.

TELEVISION: Series: It's a Business?, Laugh Line, The Garry Moore Show, Dorothy, The Thorns (sang opening song). Specials: Many appearances on the Tony Awards; also Carnegie Hall Salutes Stephen Sondheim.

THEATRE: Bdwy: Nowhere to Go But Up (Theatre World Award), The Fig Leaves Are Falling, Sweet Potato, Three Men on a Horse, The Women, Annie (Tony Award, 1977), Ballroom, Sweeney Todd, West Side Waltz, Noises Off, Jerry's Girls. Off-Bdwy: The Matchmaker. Regional: Driving Miss Daisy, Love Letters.

PICTURE: Garbo Talks.

LOUGHLIN, LORI: Actress. b. Long Island, NY, July 28, 1964. Started modeling at age 7 for catalogues, then tv commercials. First professional acting job at 18 as regular on daytime serial The Edge of Night.

PICTURES: Amityville 3-D (debut, 1983), The New Kids, Secret Admirer, Back to the Beach, The Night Before.

TELEVISION: Series: The Edge of Night, Full House. Movies: North Beach and Rawhide, Brotherhood of Justice, A Place to Call Home, Doing Time on Maple Drive, A Stranger in the Mirror.

THEATRE: Grease.

LOUIS, JEAN: Designer. b. Paris, France, Oct. 5, 1907. Head designer, Hattie Carnegie, 7 yrs., before accepting post as Chief Designer Columbia Pictures. Later Universal Studios. Free lance in m.p. & TV. Pres. Jean-Louis, Inc.

LOUISE, TINA: Actress. b. New York, NY, Feb. 11. e. Miami U., N.Y. Neighborhood Playhouse, Actors Studio, Bdwy.

STAGE: Two's Company, The Fifth Season, John Murray Anderson's Almanac, Li'l Abner, Fade Out Fade In, Come Back to the 5 and Dime Jimmy Dean Jimmy Dean.

PICTURES: God's Little Acre, The Trap, The Hangman, Day of the Outlaw, Armored Command, The Warrior Empress, Siege of Syracuse, For Those Who Think Young, The Wrecking Crew, The Good Guys and the Bad Guys, How to Commit Marriage, The Happy Ending, The Stepford Wives, Mean Dog Blues, Dog Day, Hell Riders, Evils of the Night, O.C. and the Stiggs, Dixie Lanes, The Pool, Johnny Suede, Miloha.

TELEVISION: Series: Jan Murray Time, Gilligan's Island, Dallas, Rituals. Guest: Mannix, Ironside, Kung Fu, Police Story, Kojak. Movies: But I Don't Want to Get Married, A Call to Danger, Death Scream, Look What's Happened to Rosemary's Baby, Nightmare in Badham County, SST—Death Flight, Friendships Secrets and Lies, The Day the Women Got Even, Advice to the Lovelorn, The Woman Who Cried Murder.

LOVITZ, JON: Actor, Comedian. b. Tarzana, CA, July 21, 1957. e. U. of California at Irvine. Studied acting at Film Actors Workshop. Took classes at the Groundlings, L.A. comedy improvisation studio, 1982. Performed with Groundling's Sunday Company, before joining main company in Chick Hazzard: Olympic Trials. Developed comedy character of pathological liar which he later performed when he became regular member of Saturday Night Live in 1985.

PICTURES: The Last Resort, Ratboy, Jumpin' Jack Flash, Three Amigos, Big, My Stepmother Is an Alien, Brave Little Toaster (voice), Mr. Destiny, An American Tail: Fievel Goes West (voice), A League of Their Own, Mom and Dad Save the World, National Lampoon's Loaded Weapon 1, Coneheads, North.

TELEVISION: Guest: The Paper Chase. Series: Foley Square, Saturday Night Live, The Critic (voice). Special: The Please Watch the Jon Lovitz Special.

LOWE, CHAD: Actor. b. Dayton, OH, Jan. 15, 1968. Brother of actor Rob Lowe. Stage debut in L.A. production of Blue Denim. On NY stage in Grotesque Love Songs.

PICTURES: Oxford Blues, Apprentice to Murder, True Blood, Nobody's Perfect, Highway to Hell.

TELEVISION: Movies: Silence of the Heart, There Must Be a Pony, April Morning, So Proudly We Hail, An Inconvenient Woman, Captive. Series: Spencer, Life Goes On. Special: No Means No (Emmy nom.).

LOWE, PHILIP L.: Executive. b. Brookline, MA, Apr. 17, 1917. e. Harvard. Army 1943–46. Checker, Loew's 1937–39; treasurer, Theatre Candy Co., 1941–58; Pres., ITT Sheraton Corp., 1969–70; Principal, Philip L. Lowe and Assoc.

LOWE, PHILIP M.: Executive. b. New Rochelle, NY, May 9, 1944. e. Deerfield Acad., Harvard Coll., cum laude in psychology, 1966; Columbia Business Sch., 1968. Work experience includes major marketing positions at General Foods, Gillette, Gray Advertising, and Estee Lauder Cosmetics before co-founding Cinema Centers Corp. and Theatre Management Services in Boston. Pres. of Lowe Group of Companies (cable television, broadcasting, hotels, real estate and management consulting). Past pres. and chmn. of the bd; National Association of Concessionaires (NAC); past director, National Association of Theater Owners (NATO). Professor of Marketing, Bentley Coll., Waltham, MA.; Contributing Editor; The Movie Business Book, Prentice-Hall, Inc. 1983.

LOWE, ROB: Actor. b. Charlottesville, VA, Mar. 17, 1964. Brother of actor Chad Lowe. Made Bdwy. debut 1992 in A Little Hotel on the Side.
PICTURES: The Outsiders (debut, 1983), Class, The Hotel New Hampshire, Oxford Blues, St. Elmo's Fire, Youngblood, About Last Night . . ., Square Dance, Masquerade, Illegally Yours, Bad Influence, Stroke of Midnight (If the Shoe Fits), The Dark Backward, Wayne's World, The Finest Hour.
TELEVISION: Series: A New Kind of Family. Movie: Thursday's Child. Specials: A Matter of Time, Schoolboy Father, Suddenly Last Summer.

LOWRY, DICK: Director. b. Oklahoma City, OK. e. U. of Oklahoma. Commercial photographer before being accepted by AFI.
PICTURES: The Drought (short); Smokey and the Bandit—Part 3.
TELEVISION: Mini-Series: Dream West. Movies: OHMS, Kenny Rogers as the Gambler, Jayne Mansfield Story, Angel Dusted, Coward of the County, A Few Days in Weasel Creek, Rascals and Robbers: The Secret Adventures of Tom Sawyer and Huck Finn, Missing Children—A Mother's Story, Living Proof: The Hank Williams Jr. Story, Kenny Rogers as the Gambler—The Adventure Continues (also prod.), Off Sides (Pigs Vs. Freaks), Wet Gold, The Toughest Man in the World, Murder with Mirrors, American Harvest, Kenny Rogers as The Gambler III (also co-exec. prod.), Case Closed, In the Line of Duty: The FBI Murders, Unconquered (also prod.), Howard Beach: Making the Case For Murder, Miracle Landing (also prod.), Archie: To Riverdale and Back, In the Line of Duty: A Cop for the Killing (also prod.), In the Line of Duty: Manhunt in the Dakotas (also prod.), A Woman Scorned: The Betty Broderick Story (also co-prod.), In the Line of Duty: Ambush in Waco (also prod.).

LOWRY, HUNT: Producer. b. Oklahoma City, OK, Aug. 21, 1954. e. Rollins Coll., & Wake Forest. Abandoned plans to study medicine to enter film-making industry; first job for New World Pictures where he met Jon Davison, with whom was later to co-produce. Next made TV commercials as prod. asst. and then producer. Left to go freelance as commercials producer. 1980, appt. assoc. prod. to Davison on Airplane!
PICTURES: Humanoids from the Deep, Get Crazy, Top Secret!, Revenge (co-prod.), Career Opportunities, Only the Lonely, Last of the Mohicans, Striking Distance, My Life.
TELEVISION: Movies (exec. prod.): Rascals and Robbers: The Secret Adventures of Tom Sawyer and Huckleberry Finn, Baja Oklahoma. Movies (prod.): His Mistress, Surviving, Wild Horses. Mini-Series: Dream West (prod.).

LOY, MYRNA: Actress. r.n. Myrna Williams; b. Helena MT, Aug. 2, 1905. e. Westlake Sch. for Girls. Appeared in stage presentations, Grauman's Chinese theatre, then Hollywood. Film debut Pretty Ladies, 1925; thereafter in more than 100 pictures. Voted one of the ten best Money-Making Stars in Motion Picture Herald-Fame Poll, 1937, 38. Organizer Hollywood Film com. U.S. Natl Comm. for UNESCO, 1949; mem. eomm, 1950–54; asst. head welfare activities ARC, NY 1941–45; mem. Amer. Assn. UN, Natl Comm. Against Discrimination in Housing. Recipient Kennedy Center Honor, 1988.
STAGE: Marriage-Go-Round, There Must Be a Pony, Good Housekeeping, Barefoot in the Park, Dear Love, The Women, Don Juan in Hell, Relatively Speaking.
PICTURES: The Jazz Singer, The Desert Song, Last of the Duanes, Body and Soul, A Connecticut Yankee, Hush Money, Transatlantic, Rebound, Consolation Marriage, The Devil to Pay, Arrowsmith, Emma, The Wet Parade, Vanity Fair, New Morals for Old, Woman in Room 13, 13 Women, Love Me Tonight, The Mask of Fu Manchu, Animal Kingdom, Topaze, The Barbarian, The Prizefighter and the Lady, When Ladies Meet, Penthouse, Night Flight, Men in White, Manhattan Melodrama, The Thin Man, Stamboul Quest, Evelyn Prentice, Broadway Bill, Wings in the Dark, Whipsaw, Wife Versus Secretary, The Great Ziegfeld, To Mary With Love, Libeled Lady, After the Thin Man, Parnell, Double Wedding, Manproof, Test Pilot, Too Hot to Handle, Lucky Night, The Rains Came, Another Thin Man, I Love You Again, Third Finger Left Hand, Love Crazy, Shadow of the Thin Man, The Thin Man Goes Home, So Goes My Love, The Best Years of Our Lives, The Bachelor and the Bobby Soxer, Song of the Thin Man, Mr. Blandings Builds His Dream House, The Red Pony, If This Be Sin (That Dangerous Age), Cheaper by the Dozen,

Belles on Their Toes, Ambassador's Daughter, Lonely Hearts, From the Terrace, Midnight Lace, The April Fools, Airport 1975, The End, Just Tell Me What You Want.
TELEVISION: Meet Me in St. Louis, Minerva, George Gobel, Perry Como, Happy Birthday—June Allyson Show, Family Affair, The Virginians, Movies: Death Takes a Holiday (1970), Do Not Fold Spindle or Mutilate, The Couple Takes a Wife, The Elevator, It Happened at Lakewood Manor, Summer Solstice.

LUBCKE, HARRY R.: Registered Patent Agent. b. Alameda, CA, Aug. 25, 1905. e. U. of California, B.S., 1929. Holds numerous U.S. and foreign patents on television. In 1931: station W6XAO went on air on what is now television Channel No. 2 to become first station of kind in nation. New Mt. Lee studios built at cost of $250,000 in 1941, housing then largest TV stage 100x60x30 ft. Pioneered present television standard of 525 line (Aug., 1940). In 1942, television programs to promote war bond sale. 1942–46 dir. war research for which certificates of commendation were received from Army & Navy.
MEMBER: Pres., Acad. TV Arts & Sciences, 1949. Dir. TV Don Lee Broadcasting System to Dec. 31, 1950; cons. TV engineer, 1951; registered patent agent, 1952. Life Fellow, 1951, IEEE, AAAS, SMPTE, 1967. Board of Governors, Patent Law Association of Los Angeles, 1974. Life Member National Academy of Television Arts & Sciences, member engineering Emmy Awards Committee. Member Blue Ribbon panel Emmy Awards Committee; 1978; Diamond Circle, of Pacific Pioneer Broadcasters, 1980; American Bar Assn., 1982.

LUBIN, ARTHUR: Director. b. Los Angeles, CA, 1901. Since 1935 has directed numerous pictures, including John Wayne's first four films at Universal: Hell on Ice, California Straight Ahead, Adventure's End, I Covered the War.
PICTURES: Buck Privates in the Navy, Hold That Ghost, Keep 'em Flying, Ride 'em Cowboy, Eagle Squadron, Phantom of the Opera, White Savage, Ali Baba and the Forty Thieves, Delightfully Dangerous, Francis, Queen for a Day, Francis Goes to the Races, Rhubarb, Francis Covers the Big Town, Francis Goes to West Point, It Grows on Trees, South Sea Woman, Star of India, Lady Godiva, Francis in the Navy, Footsteps in the Fog, First Traveling Saleslady, Escapade in Japan, The Thief of Baghdad, The Incredible Mr. Limpett, Rain for a Dusty Summer, Night in Paradise, The Spider Woman Strikes Back, New Orleans, Impact, Queen for a Day, Star of India, Hold On!
TELEVISION: Maverick (Henry Fonda episodes), 77 Sunset Strip, Bonanza, the entire Mister Ed series (prod.-dir.).

LUCAS, GEORGE: Producer, Director, Writer. b. Modesto, CA, May 14, 1944. e. U. of Southern California, cinema. Made short film called THX-1138 and won National Student Film Festival Grand Prize, 1967. Signed contract with WB. Ass't. to Francis Ford Coppola on The Rain People, during which Lucas made 2-hr. documentary on filming of that feature entitled Filmmaker.
PICTURES: THX-1138 (dir., co-s.p.), American Graffiti (dir., co-s.p.), Star Wars (dir., s.p.), More American Graffiti (exec. prod.), The Empire Strikes Back (exec. prod., story), Raiders of the Lost Ark (exec. prod., co-s.p., story), Return of the Jedi (exec. prod., co-s.p., story), Indiana Jones and the Temple of Doom (exec. prod., story), Mishima (exec. prod.), Labyrinth (exec. prod.), Howard the Duck (exec. prod.), Willow (exec. prod., story), Tucker: The Man and His Dream (exec. prod.), The Land Before Time (co-exec. prod.), Indiana Jones and the Last Crusade (co-exec. prod., co-story).
TELEVISION: Exec. Prod.: The Ewok Adventure (movie), Ewoks: the Battle for Endor (movie); The Young Indiana Jones Chronicles (series).

LUCCHESI, GARY: Executive. b. San Francisco, CA, 1955. Entered industry as a trainee with the William Morris Agency, 1977. Joined Tri-Star, 1983, as vice pres. of production, became sr. vice pres., 1985. Joined Paramount Pictures as exec. vice pres., April 1987; pres. of motion picture production division, 1987–92. Producer: Jennifer Eight.

LUCCI, SUSAN: Actress. b. Scarsdale, NY, Feb. 23, 1948. e. Marymount Col. Was semifinalist in NY State Miss Universe Pageant. First professional job as "color girl" for CBS, sitting for cameras as new lighting system for color tv was developed. Had bit parts in films Me Natalie and Goodbye Columbus. Performed on 1983 album Love in the Afternoon.
TELEVISION: Series: All My Children (1970–). Movies: Invitation to Hell, Mafia Princess, Anastasia: The Story of Anna, Haunted By Her Past, Lady Mobster, The Bride in Black, The Woman Who Sinned, Double Edge, Between Love and Hate.
PICTURES: Daddy You Kill Me, Young Doctors in Love (cameo).

LUCKINBILL, LAURENCE: Actor. b. Fort Smith, AR, Nov. 21, 1934. m. actress Lucie Arnaz. e. U. of Arkansas, Catholic U. of America. On Bdwy. in A Man for All Seasons, Arms and the Man, The Boys. in the Band, Alpha Beta, The Shadow Box, Poor Murderer, Chapter Two, Past Tense.

PICTURES: The Boys in the Band, Such Good Friends, The Promise, Not for Publication, Cocktail, Messenger of Death, Star Trek V: The Final Frontier.

TELEVISION: *Series:* The Secret Storm, Where the Heart Is, The Delphi Bureau. *Movies:* The Delphi Bureau (pilot), Death Sentence, Panic on the 5:22, Winner Take All, The Lindbergh Kidnapping Case, The Mating Season, To Heal a Nation. *Mini-Series:* Ike. *Specials:* Lyndon Johnson (one-man show), Voices and Visions (narrator), The 5:48, Lucy & Desi: A Home Movie (co-exec. prod., co-dir., writer).

LUDDY, TOM: Producer. e. U. of California at Berkeley where he operated student film societies and rep. cinemas. Entered industry via Brandon Films. 1972, prog. dir. and curator of Pacific Film Archives. 1979, joined Zoetrope Studios as dir. of special projects where dev. and supervised revival of Gance's Napoleon and Our Hitler—A Film From Germany. Coordinated Koyaanisqatsi, Every Man For Himself, Passion. A founder, Telluride Film Fest. Served on selection comm., N.Y. and pres. San Francisco Film Fest.

PICTURES: Mishima (co-prod.), Tough Guys Don't Dance (co-exec. prod.), Barfly, King Lear (assoc. prod.), Manifesto (exec. prod.), Powwaqatsi (assoc. prod.), Wait Until Spring Bandini, Wind, The Secret Garden (co-prod.).

LUDWIG, IRVING H.: Executive. b. Nov. 3. Rivoli Theatre, N.Y., mgr., theatre oper., Rugoff and Becker, 1938–39; opened first modern art type theatre, Greenwich Village, 1940. With Walt Disney Prod. in charge of theatre oper. on Fantasia, 1940–41; buyer-booker, Rugoff and Becker, 1942–45; film sales admin., Walt Disney Prod. home office, 1945–53; v.p. and domestic sales mgr., Buena Vista Dist. Co., 1953; pres. gen. sales mgr., 1959–80.

MEMBER: Bd. of dir., Will Rogers Memorial Fund, Foundation of M.P. Pioneers; M.P. Bookers of NY; Academy of M.P. Arts & Sciences.

LUEDTKE, KURT: Writer. b. Grand Rapids, MI, Sept. 29, 1938. e. Brown U., B.A., 1961. Reporter Grand Rapids Press 1961–62. Miami Herald, 1963–65; Detroit Free Press (reporter, asst. photography dir., asst. mgr. ed., asst. exec. ed., exec. ed. 1965–78.).

PICTURES: Absence of Malice, Out of Africa (Acad. Award, 1985), Walls.

LUFKIN, DAN W.: Executive. Chairman of Exec. Comm., Columbia Pictures Industries (appt. July, 1978). Co-founder of Donaldson, Lufkin & Jenrette Securities Corp., investment banking and brokerage firm. Served as first commissioner of Dept. of Environmental Protection for state of Connecticut. Joined Columbia board in November, 1977.

LUFT, LORNA: Actress, Singer. b. Hollywood, CA, Nov. 21, 1952. Daughter of actress-singer Judy Garland and producer Sid Luft. Has sung in nightclubs. Appeared on 1990 recording of Girl Crazy.

PICTURES: I Could Go on Singing (extra, unbilled), Grease 2, Where the Boys Are.

TELEVISION: *Series:* Trapper John. *Movie:* Fear Stalk. *Guest:* Twilight Zone, Hooperman, Murder She Wrote, Tales from the Dark Side, The Cosby Show.

THEATRE: *NY:* Judy Garland at Home at the Palace, Promises Promises, Snoopy, Extremities. *Tours:* They're Playing Our Song, Grease, Little Shop of Horrors, Jerry Herman's Broadway, The Unsinkable Molly Brown, Guys and Dolls.

LUKE, PETER: Playwright, Director. b. England, Aug. 12, 1919. Author of plays for TV: Small Fish Are Sweet, 1958; Pigs Ear with Flowers, 1960; Roll on Bloomin' Death, 1961; A Man on Her Back (with William Sansom), 1965; Devil a Monk Won't Be, 1966. wrote and directed films for BBC-TV: Anach 'Cuan (about the late Sean O Riada) 1967; Black Sound—Deep Song (about Federico Garcia Lorca) 1968; Author of Stage play, Hadrian VII, first produced at Birmingham Rep in 1967 and has been staged around the world. Stage Play, Bloomsbury. Author of autobiography, Sisyphus & Reilly, publ., 1972, Prod. Phoenix Theatre 1974.

LUMET, SIDNEY: Director. b. Philadelphia, PA, June 15, 1924. e. Professional Children's Sch.; Columbia U. Child actor in plays: Dead End, George Washington Slept Here, My Heart's in the Highlands, and films: The 400 Million, One Third of a Nation. U.S. Armed Forces, W.W.II, 1942–46; dir. summer stock 1947–49; taught acting, H.S. of Prof. Arts. Assoc. dir. CBS, 1950, dir. 1951.

PICTURES: 12 Angry Men, Stage Struck, That Kind of Woman, The Fugitive Kind, A View From the Bridge, Long Day's Journey into Night, Fail Safe, The Pawnbroker, The Hill, The Group, The Deadly Affair (also prod.), Bye Bye Braverman (also prod.), The Sea Gull (also prod.), The Appointment, Last of the Mobile Hot-Shots (also prod.), King: A Filmed Record . . . Montgomery to Memphis (co-dir., prod.), The Anderson Tapes, Child's Play, The Offence, Serpico,

Lovin' Molly, Murder on the Orient Express, Dog Day Afternoon, Network, Equus, The Wiz, Just Tell Me What You Want (also co-prod.), Prince of the City (also co-s.p.), Deathtrap, The Verdict, Daniel (also co-exec. prod.), Garbo Talks, Power, The Morning After, Running on Empty, Family Business, Q & A. (also s.p.), A Stranger Among Us, Guilty As Sin.

TELEVISION: Mama, Danger, You Are There, Omnibus, Best of Broadway, Alcoa, Goodyear Playhouse, Kraft Television Theatre (Mooney's Kid Don't Cry, The Last of My Gold Watches, This Property is Condemned), Playhouse 90, Play of the Week (The Dybbuk, Rashomon, The Iceman Cometh—Emmy Award). *Specials:* The Sacco and Vanzetti Story, John Brown's Raid, Cry Vengeance.

LUNDGREN DOLPH: Actor. b. Stockholm, Sweden, Nov. 3, 1959. e. Washington State U., won Fulbright to Massachusetts Inst. of Technology, Royal Inst. of Technology, Stockholm, M.S.C. Was doorman at Limelight disco in NY while studying acting. Full Contact Karate champion. Made workout video, Maximum Potential.

PICTURES: A View to a Kill, Rocky IV, Masters of the Universe, Red Scorpion, The Punisher, I Come in Peace, Cover-Up, Showdown in Little Tokyo, Universal Soldier.

LUPINO, IDA: Actress, Director. b. London, England, Feb. 4, 1918. e. Royal Acad. of Dramatic Art, London. Daughter of Stanley Lupino, English stage and screen comedian. Brit. m.p. debut in Her First Affair, 1933; in U.S. m.p. 1934! ent. independent prod., becoming one of the first major women director-screenwriters beginning with Not Wanted (also writer, prod.). Also maintained acting career at same time.

PICTURES: Her First Affair, Money for Speed, High Finance, The Ghost Camera, I Lived with You, Prince of Arcadia, Search for Beauty, Come on Marines, Ready for Love, Paris in Spring, Smart Girl, Peter Ibbetson, Anything Goes, One Rainy Afternoon, Yours for the Asking, The Gay Desperado, Sea Devils, Let's Get Married, Artists and Models, Fight for Your Lady, The Lone Wolf Spy Hunt, The Lady and the Mob, The Adventures of Sherlock Holmes, The Light That Failed, They Drive By Night, High Sierra, The Sea Wolf, Out of the Fog, Ladies in Retirement, Moontide, The Hard Way, Life Begins at 8:30, Forever and a Day, Thank Your Lucky Stars, In Our Time, Hollywood Canteen, Pillow to Post, Devotion, The Man I Love, Escape Me Never, Deep Valley, Road House, Lust for Gold, Woman in Hiding, Not Wanted (co-s.p., prod.), Never Fear (dir.), Outrage (dir., s.p.), Hard Fast & Beautiful (dir.), On Dangerous Ground, Beware My Lovely, The Hitch-Hiker (dir., s.p.), Jennifer, The Bigamist (also dir.), Private Hell 36 (also co-prod., s.p.), Women's Prison, The Big Knife, While the City Sleeps, Strange Intruder, The Trouble With Angels (dir.), Junior Bonner, Deadhead Miles, The Devil's Rain, The Food of the Gods, My Boys Are Good Boys.

TELEVISION: *Series:* Four Star Playhouse (also dir. several episodes), Mr. Adams and Eve. *Specials:* No. 5 Checked Out, the Trial of Mary Surrat. *Guest:* Honey West, Virginian, Batman, Wild Wild West, Sam Benedict, Untouchables, G. E. Theater, Have Gun Will Travel, Thriller, Mr. Novak, Hong Kong, The Rogues, Chrysler Theatre, Kraft Theatre, Gilligan's Island, The Ghost and Mrs. Muir, The Bill Cosby Show, To Catch a Thief, Mod Squad, Family Affair. *Movies:* Women in Chains, The Strangers in 7A, I Love a Mystery, Female Artillery, The Letters. *Dir. of episodes:* Have Gun Will Travel, The Donna Reed Show, Hong Kong, Thriller, G.E. Theatre, Mr. Kovak, Dr. Kildare.

LUPONE, PATTI: Actress. b. Northport, NY, Apr. 21, 1949. e. Julliard.

PICTURES: 1941, Fighting Back, Witness, Wise Guys, Driving Miss Daisy, Family Prayers.

THEATRE: School for Scandal, Three Sisters, The Beggars Opera, The Robber Bridegroom, Meaure for Measure, Edward II, The Water Engine, Working, Evita (Tony Award, 1980), Oliver!, Anything Goes, Les Miserables (London), Sunset Boulevard (London).

TELEVISION: *Series:* Life Goes On. *Movies:* LBJ: The Early Years, The Water Engine.

LURASCHI, LUIGI G.: Exec. b. London, Jan 7, 1906. e. U. of Zurich. Long Island Studio, Paramount, 1929; home officer mgr. For. dept. hd, For. & dom. Censorship; Hollywood to 1960. Asst. Prod., Dino De Laurentiis Prod. 1960–65; asst. to pres. for prod. activities, Paramount, 1965. 1967 continental prod. exec. Paramount-Rome. 1976–present, v.p., intl. prod., London.

LYDON, JAMES: Actor. b. Harrington Park, NJ, May 30, 1923; e. St. Johns Mil. Sch. On N.Y. stage in Prologue to Glory, Sing Out the News. On screen 1939, Back Door to Heaven.

PICTURES: *Actor:* Thoroughbreds, Naval Academy, Henry Aldrich series, Twice Blessed, Life With Father, Out of the Storm, Joan of Arc, Miss Mink of 1949, Tucson, Gasoline Alley, Island in the Sky, The Desperado, Battle Stations, My Blood Runs Cold (assoc. prod.), Brainstorm, Scandalous John, Vigilante Force. *Studio Prod.:* An American Dream, A

Covenant With Death, First to Fight, The Cool Ones, Chubasco, Countdown, Assignment to Kill. *Assoc. Prod.*: The Learning Tree.
TELEVISION: *Guest*: Frontier Circus (assoc. prod.). *Co-ordin. Prod.*: Wagon Train, Alfred Hitchcock Hour. *Assoc.*: McHale's Navy, 77 Sunset Strip, Mr. Roberts. *Series*: So This Is Hollywood, The First Hundred Years, Love That Jill. *Movies*: Ellery Queen, The New Daughters of Joshua Cabe, Peter Lundy and the Medicine Hat Stallion.

LYLES, A. C.: Producer. b. Jacksonville, FL. May 17, 1918. e. Andrew Jackson H.S. Paramount Publix's Florida Theatre, 1928; interviewed Hollywood celebrities, Jacksonville Journal, 1932; mail boy, Paramount Studios, Hollywood, 1937; publicity dept., 1938; hd. of adv., publ. dept., Pine-Thomas unit at Paramount, 1940; assoc. prod., The Mountain; prod., Short Cut to Hell; assoc. prod., Rawhide (TV series). President, A. C. Lyles Productions, Inc. (Paramount Pictures).
PICTURES: Short Cut to Hell, Raymie, The Young and the Brave, Law of the Lawless, Stage to Thunder Rock, Young Fury, Black Spurs, Hostile Guns, Arizona Bushwackers, Town Tamer, Apache Uprising, Johnny Reno, Waco, Red Tomahawk, Fort Utah, Buckskin, Rogue's Gallery, Night of the Lepus, The Last Day, Flight to Holocaust.
TELEVISION: A Christmas for Boomer, Here's Boomer (series), Dear Mr. President, Conversations With the Presidents.

LYNCH, DAVID: Director, Writer. b. Missoula, Montana, Jan. 20, 1946. e. Pennsylvania Acad. of Fine Arts, where received an independent filmmaker grant from America Film Institute. Made 16mm film, The Grandmother. Accepted by Center for Advanced Film Studies in Los Angeles, 1970. Wrote and directed Eraserhead (with partial AFI financing) which became cult movie. Acted in film Zelly & Me.
PICTURES: *Director-Writer*: Eraserhead (also prod., edit., prod.-design, f/x), The Elephant Man, Dune, Blue Velvet, Wild at Heart, Twin Peaks: Fire Walk With Me (also co-exec. prod., actor).
TELEVISION: *Series*: Twin Peaks (dir., exec. prod., writer), On the Air (exec. prod., dir., writer). *Special*: Hotel Room (co-dir., co-exec. prod.).

LYNCH, KELLY: Actress. b. Minneapolis, MN, 1959. Former model.
PICTURES: Osa, Bright Lights Big City, Cocktail, Road House, Warm Summer Rain, Drugstore Cowboy, Desperate Hours, Curly Sue, For Better and For Worse, Three of Hearts.
TELEVISION: *Guest*: Miami Vice, The Equalizer, Spenser for Hire, The Hitcher, The Edge (Black Pudding). *Movie*: Something in Common.

LYNCH, PAUL M.: Director.
PICTURES: Hard Part Begins; Blood and Guts; Prom Night; Cross Country; Flying, Blindside, Bullies.
TELEVISION: *Series*: Voyagers, Blacke's Magic, Murder She Wrote, In the Heat of the Night, Tour of Duty, Beauty and the Beast, Twilight Zone (1987), Moonlighting, Star Trek: The Next Generation, Dark Shadows, Tour of Duty, Top Cops, Mike Hammer, Hooerman, Bronx Zoo. *Movies*: Cameo By Night, Going to the Chapel, She Knows Too Much, Murder by Night, Drop Dead Gorgeous.

LYNCH, RICHARD: Actor. b. Brooklyn, NY, Feb. 12. Made Bdwy. debut in The Devils, both on and off Bdwy. Also in Live Like Pigs, The Orphan, The Basic Training of Pavlo Hummel, The Lady From the Sea, Arthuro-U, Lion in Winter.
PICTURES: Scarecrow (debut, 1973), The Seven Ups, The Delta Fox, The Premonition, Steel, The Formula, The Sword and the Sorcerer, Savage Dawn, Invasion U.S.A., Cut and Run, Night Force, The Barbarians, Little Nikita, Bad Dreams, Melanie Rose (High Stakes), Spirit, Aftershock, Return to Justice, One Man Force, The Forbidden Dance, October 32nd, Double Threat, H.P. Lovecraft's Necromonicon, Crime & Punishment.
TELEVISION: *Series*: Battlestar Gallactica, The Phoenix. *Movies*: Starsky and Hutch (pilot), Roger & Harry: The Mitera Target, Good Against Evil, Dog and Cat, Vampire, Alcatraz—The Whole Shocking Story, Sizzle, White Water Rebels, The Last Ninja.

LYNDON, VICTOR: Producer, Writer. b. London. e. St. Paul's. Ent. m.p. ind. 1942 as asst. dir., Gainsborough Pictures. Novel: Bermuda Blue (1984).
PICTURES: as prod. mgr. The African Queen, As assoc. prod., Dr. Strangelove, Darling, 2001 A Space Odyssey. As prod., Spare The Rod, Station Six—Sahara, The Optimists.

LYNE, ADRIAN: Director. b. Peterborough, England, March 4, 1941. Started as director of commercials.
PICTURES: Foxes, Flashdance, 9½ Weeks, Fatal Attraction, Jacob's Ladder, Indecent Proposal.

LYNLEY, CAROL: Actress. b. New York, NY, Feb. 13, 1942.
PICTURES: The Light in the Forest (debut, 1958), Holiday for Lovers, Blue Denim, Hound-Dog Man, Return to Peyton Place, The Last Sunset, The Stripper, Under the Yum-Yum

Tree, The Cardinal, The Pleasure Seekers, Shock Treatment, Harlow, Bunny Lake Is Missing, The Shuttered Room, Danger Route, Once You Kiss a Stranger, The Maltese Bippy, Norwood, Beware the Blob!, The Poseidon Adventure, Cotter, The Four Deuces, The Washington Affair, The Cat and the Canary, The Shape of Things to Come, Vigilante, Dark Tower, Blackout, Howling VI: The Freaks.
TELEVISION: *Series*: The Immortal. *Movies*: Shadow on the Land, The Smugglers, The Immortal, Weekend of Terror, The Cable Car Murder, The Night Stalker, The Elevator, Death Stalk, Willow B, Women in Prison, Flood, Fantasy Island, Having Babies II, Cops and Robin, The Beasts Are on the Streets.

LYNN, ANN: Actress. b. London, England, 1934. Ent. films and TV, 1958.
PICTURES: Naked Fury, Piccadilly Third Stop, The Wind of Change, Strongroom, Flame in the Streets, Black Torment, Four in the Morning, Baby Love, Hitler—The Last Ten Days, Screamtime.
TELEVISION: After The Show, All Summer Long, Trump Card, Man at the Top, The Expert, Hine, The Intruders, Too Far, King Lear, The Zoo Gang. *Movies*: The Uncle, Morning Tide, Shot In the Dark, Estuary, Who Pays the Ferryman, The Professionals, Zeticula, Westway. The Perfect House, Minder, To the Sound of Guns, Crown Court, Just Good Friends, Starting Out, Paradise Park. *Series*: The Cheaters, The Other Side of the Underneath.

LYNN, JEFFREY: Actor. r.n. Ragnar Godfrey Lind. b. Auburn, MA, Feb. 16, 1909; e. Bates Coll. m.p. debut in 1938.
PICTURES: Four Daughters, Yes My Darling Daughter, Daughters Courageous, Espionage Agent, Roaring Twenties, Four Wives, Child Is Born, Fighting 69th, It all Came True, All This and Heaven, Too; My Love Came Back, Four Mothers, Million Dollar Baby, Law of the Tropics, Body Disappears, For the Love of Mary, Black Bart, Letter to Three Wives, Strange Bargain, Home Town Story, Up Front, Captain China, Lost Lagoon, Butterfield 8, Tony Rome.
BROADWAY: (Revival) Dinner at Eight.

LYNN, JONATHAN: Director, Writer, Actor. b. Bath, England, Apr. 3, 1943. Was artistic dir. of Cambridge Theatre Company, 1976—81, Company Director of Natl. Theatre, 1987. Play: Pig of the Month. Books: Doctor in Charge, A Proper Man, The Complete Yes Prime Minister, Mayday.
PICTURES: The Internecine Project (s.p.), Into the Night (actor), Clue (dir., s.p.), Nuns on the Run (dir., s.p.), Three Men and a Little Lady (actor), My Cousin Vinny (dir.), The Distinguished Gentleman (dir.), Greedy (dir.).
TELEVISION: Doctor on the Go, My Name is Harry Worth, My Brother's Keeper, Yes Minister, Yes Prime Minister.

LYON, FRANCIS D. "PETE": Director, Editor. b. Bowbells, ND, July 29, 1905. e. Hollywood H.S., UCLA. WWII: writer, prod., dir., OWI; assoc. with training, exploitation and information films. Maj. U.S. Army Signal Corps.
PICTURES: *As film editor*: Shape of Things to Come (parts), Knight Without Armour, Rembrandt, Intermezzo, Adam Had Four Sons, The Great Profile, Four Sons, Daytime Wife, Body and Soul (Acad. Award, 1947), He Ran All the Way. *As director*: Crazylegs, The Bob Mathias Story (Christopher Award), The Great Locomotive Chase, Cult of the Cobra, The Oklahoman, Gunsight Ridge, Bailout at 43,000, Escort West, Cinerama South Seas Adventure (co-dir.), The Young and the Brave, Destination Inner Space, The Destructors, The Money Jungle, The Girl Who Knew Too Much. *Producer*: Tiger by the Tail.
TELEVISION: *Series*: Laramie, Perry Mason, Zane Grey Theatre, Bus Stop, M. Squad, Wells Fargo, Kraft Suspense Theatre, Death Valley Days, Follow the Sun, etc.

LYON, SUE: Actress. b. Davenport, IA, July 10, 1946. e. Hollywood Prof. Sch.
PICTURES: Lolita, Night of the Iguana, Seven Women, Tony Rome, The Flim Flam Man, Evel Knievel, Crash, End of the World.
TELEVISION: *Movies*: But I Don't Want to Get Married!, Smash-Up on Interstate 5, Don't Push—I'll Charge When I'm Ready.

LYONS, STUART: Producer. b. Manchester, England, Dec. 27, 1928. e. Manchester U. Ent. m.p. ind. 1955. Asst. dir. TV series 1955—56. Casting dir. Associated British, 1956/60. Freelance cast. dir., 1960/63. Joined 20th Century-Fox Productions as cast. dir., 1963. Appt. director 20th Century-Fox Productions Ltd., 1967, man. dir. 1968. 1971: left Fox on closure Europe prod., to resume indep. prod. London Prod. Rep. for Neue Constantin Film, Munich: Salt on Our Skin, House of the Spirits.
PICTURES: *As casting director*: Over fifty films including Those Magnificent Men in Their Flying Machines, Cleopatra, The Long Ships, Guns at Batasi, High Wind in Jamaica, The Blue Max. *As indep. producer*: The Slipper and the Rose, Meetings with Remarkable Men, Danses Sacrees, Turnaround. As prod. consultant: Eleni; The Witches, A Dan-

gerous Life, Delta Force II, State of Grace, Captive in the Land (as rep. of Completion Bond Co.). *Prod. Spvr.*: Death Train.

M

MAC ARTHUR JAMES: Actor. b. Los Angeles, CA, Dec. 8, 1937. e. Harvard. p. Helen Hayes, Charles MacArthur. Stage debut, summer stock; The Corn Is Green, 1945; Life with Father, 1953.
PICTURES: The Young Stranger, The Light in the Forest, Third Man on the Mountain, Kidnapped, Swiss Family Robinson, The Interns, Spencer's Mountain, Cry of Battle, The Truth About Spring, The Bedford Incident, Ride Beyond Vengeance, The Love-Ins, Hang 'em High, Angry Breed.
TELEVISION: *Series*: Hawaii Five-0. *Movies*: Alcatraz—The Whole Shocking Story, The Night the Bridge Fell Down.

MACCHIO, RALPH: Actor. b. Long Island, NY, Nov. 4, 1962. Started with TV commercials. On Broadway in Cuba and His Teddy Bear, 1986; Off-Bdwy in Only Kidding.
PICTURES: Up the Academy (debut, 1980), The Outsiders, The Karate Kid, Teachers, Crossroads, The Karate Kid Part II, Distant Thunder, The Karate Kid Part III, Too Much Sun, My Cousin Vinny.
TELEVISION: *Series*: Eight is Enough (1980–81). *Movies*: Journey to Survival, Dangerous Company, The Three Wishes of Billy Grier, The Last P.O.W.?: The Bobby Garwood Story.

MAC CORKINDALE, SIMON: Actor, Producer, Screenwriter. b. Isle-of-Ely, England, Feb. 2, 1952. m. actress Susan George. On stage in Dark Lady of the Sonnets, Pygmalion, French Without Tears, etc.
PICTURES: Death on the Nile, Quatermass Conclusion, Caboblanco, Robbers of the Sacred Mountain, The Sword and the Sorcerer, Jaws 3-D, Riddle of the Sands, Sincerely Violet, Stealing Heaven (prod. only), That Summer of White Roses (co-prod., co-s.p. only).
TELEVISION: *Specials*: I Claudius, Romeo and Juliet, Quatermass. *Movies*: The Manions of America, Falcon's Gold, Jesus of Nazareth, Twist of Fate, Obsessive Love. *Miniseries*: Pursuit. *Series*: Manimal, Falcon Crest, Counterstrike.

MAC DONALD, PHILIP: Writer. b. Scotland; e. St. Paul's Sch. London. Novelist, playwright. Began screen career 1933.
PICTURES: Sahara, Action in Arabia, The Body Snatcher, Strangers in the Night, Dangerous Intruder, Man Who Cheated Himself, Circle of Danger, Mask of the Avenger, Ring of Fear, Tobor the Great.

MacDOWELL, ANDIE: Actress. b. Gaffney, SC, Apr. 21, 1958. r.n. Rose Anderson MacDowell. Former model.
PICTURES: Greystoke: The Legend of Tarzan Lord of the Apes (debut, 1984), St. Elmo's Fire, Sex Lies and Videotape (Best Actress Award, L.A. Film Critics), Green Card, The Object of Beauty, Hudson Hawk, The Player, Groundhog Day, Ruby Cairo, Bad Girls.
TELEVISION: *Movies*: Domestic Dilemma, Women and Men 2. *Mini-Series*: Sahara's Secret (Italy).

MAC GRAW, ALI: Actress. b. Pound Ridge, NY, Apr. 1, 1939. e. Wellesley Coll. Mother of actor Josh Evans. Editorial asst. Harper's Bazaar Mag.; asst. to photographer Melvin Sokolsky. Was top fashion model. Published autobiography Moving Pictures in 1991.
PICTURES: A Lovely Way to Die (debut, 1968), Goodbye Columbus, Love Story, The Getaway, Convoy, Players, Just Tell Me What You Want.
TELEVISION: *Mini-Series*: The Winds of War. *Movies*: China Rose, Survive the Savage Sea, Gunsmoke: The Long Ride. *Series*: Dynasty.

MAC LACHLAN, KYLE: Actor. b. Yakima, WA, Feb. 22, 1959. e. Univ. of WA. Acted in high school and college, then in summer stock. Cast as lead in Dune by director David Lynch in a nationwide search.
PICTURES: Dune, Blue Velvet, The Hidden, Don't Tell Her It's Me, The Doors, Twin Peaks: Fire Walk With Me, Where the Day Takes You, Rich in Love, The Trial, The Flintstones.
TELEVISION: *Series*: Twin Peaks. *Guest*: Tales From the Crypt (Carrion Death). *Movie*: Dream Breakers.

MAC LAINE, SHIRLEY: Actress. b. Richmond, VA, April 24, 1934. Sister of actor-prod. Warren Beatty. e. Washington and Lee H.S., Arlington, VA. Dancer, singer; signed by Hal Wallis. Producer of film documentary on China, The Other Half of The Sky. Star of video: Relaxing Within.
PICTURES: The Trouble with Harry (debut, 1955), Artists and Models, Around the World in 80 Days, Hot Spell, The Matchmaker, The Sheepman, Some Came Running, Ask Any Girl, Career, Can-Can, The Apartment, Ocean's 11 (cameo), All in a Night's Work, Two Loves, My Geisha, The Children's Hour, Two for the Seesaw, Irma La Douce, What A Way To Go, John Goldfarb Please Come Home, The Yellow Rolls

Royce, Gambit, Woman Times Seven, The Bliss of Mrs. Blossom, Sweet Charity, Two Mules for Sister Sara, Desperate Characters, The Possession of Joel Delaney, The Turning Point, Being There, Loving Couples, Change of Seasons, Terms of Endearment (Acad. Award, 1983), Cannonball Run II, Madame Sousatzka, Steel Magnolias, Postcards From the Edge, Waiting for the Light, Defending Your Life (cameo), Used People, Wrestling Ernest Hemingway, Guarding Tess.
TELEVISION: *Series*: Shirley's World. Variety Specials (Won 1980 Emmy Award for co-writing Every Little Movement). *Movie*: Out on a Limb (also co-s.p.).
AUTHOR: Don't Fall off the Mountain, You Can Get There from Here, Out on a Limb, Dancing in the Light, It's All In the Playing, Going Within, Dance While You Can. Editor: McGovern: The Man and His Beliefs (1972).

MACLEOD, GAVIN: Actor. b. Mt. Kisco, NY, Feb. 28, 1931. e. Ithaca Coll.
PICTURES: I Want to Live, Compulsion, Operation Petticoat, McHale's Navy, McHale's Navy Joins the Air Force, The Sand Pebbles, Deathwatch, The Party, Kelly's Heroes.
TELEVISION: *Series*: McHale's Navy, Mary Tyler Moore Show, The Love Boat. *Movies*: The Intruders, Only with Married Men, Ransom for Alice, Murder Can Hurt You, Student Exchange, The Love Boat: The Valentine Voyage. *Mini-Series*: Scruples. *Special*: Last Act is a Solo.

MAC NAUGHTON, ROBERT: Actor. b. New York, NY, Dec. 19, 1966. Entered entertainment industry in 1979. Member Circle Rep. Co., N.Y.
TELEVISION: *Movies*: Angel City, A Place to Call Home. *Specials*: Big Bend Country, The Electric Grandmother, Hear My Cry.
PICTURES: E.T.: The Extra-Terrestrial, I Am the Cheese.
STAGE: Critic's Choice, A Thousand Clowns, Camelot, The Diviners, The Adventures of Huckleberry Finn, Henry V, Tobacco Road, Master Harold . . . and the Boys, Tomorrow's Monday, Talley and Son.

MAC NICOL PETER: Actor. b. Dallas, TX. e. U. of Minnesota.
THEATER: *Manhattan Theatre Club*: Crimes of the Heart. *NY Shakespeare Fest*: Found a Peanut, Rum and Coke, Twelfth Night, Richard II, Romeo & Juliet. Regional theatre includes Guthrie, Alaska Rep., Long Wharf, Dallas Theatre Center, Trinity Rep. Bdwy: Crimes of the Heart (Theatre World Award), The Nerd.
PICTURES: Dragonslayer (debut, 1981), Sophie's Choice, Heat, Ghostbusters II, American Blue Note, Hard Promises, Housesitter, Addams Family Values.
TELEVISION: *Movies*: Johnny Bull, By Dawn's Early Light. *Guest*: Faerie Tale Theatre, Days and Nights of Molly Dodd. *Series*: Powers That Be.

MADDEN, BILL: Executive. b. New York, NY, March 1, 1915. e. Boston U. Joined Metro-Goldwyn-Mayer as office boy, 1930; student salesman, 1938; asst. Eastern div. sales mgr., 1939; U.S. Navy, 1942–46; Boston sales rep., M.G.M., 1947–53; Philadelphia branch mgr., 1954–59; Midwest div. sales mgr., 1960–68; roadshow sales mgr., 1969; v.p., general sales mgr., 1969–74, M.G.M.; corp., v.p. & gen. sls. mgr., MGM, 1974; retired from MGM, 1975; 1976–present, exec. consultant to motion picture industry; lecturer and instructor at UCLA. Member: Academy M.P. Arts & Sciences, Motion Picture Associates, American Film Institute. Motion Picture Pioneers.

MADDEN, DAVID: Executive. e. Harvard U., 1976; UCLA, M.A., 1978. Joined 20th Century-Fox in Nov., 1978 as story analyst. Named story editor, 1980; exec. story editor, 1982. Appt. v.p., creative affairs for 20th-Fox Prods., 1983; v.p., prod., 20th Century-Fox Prods; 1980, v.p., production, Paramount Pictures.
PICTURES: Renegades (prod.), Blind Fury (exec. prod.), Eve of Destruction (prod.).

MADIGAN, AMY: Actress. b. Chicago, IL, Sept. 11, 1951. m. actor Ed Harris. For 10 years traveled country performing in bars and clubs with band. Then studied at Lee Strasberg Inst., L.A. NY Stage: The Lucky Spot (Theatre World Award), A Streetcar Named Desire.
PICTURES: Love Child (debut, 1982), Love Letters, Streets of Fire, Places in the Heart, Alamo Bay, Twice in a Lifetime (Acad. Award nom.), Nowhere To Hide, The Prince of Pennsylvania, Field of Dreams, Uncle Buck, The Dark Half.
TELEVISION: *Special*: The Laundromat. *Movies*: Crazy Times, The Ambush Murders, Victims, Travis McGee, The Day After, Roe vs. Wade, Lucky Day.

MADISON, GUY: Actor. r.n. Robert Moseley. b. Bakersfield, CA, Jan. 19, 1922. e. Bakersfield Jr. Coll. U.S. Navy; Wild Bill Hickok radio and TV shows, Star of Tomorrow, 1954.
PICTURES: Since You Went Away (debut, 1944), Till the End of Time, Honeymoon, Texas, Brooklyn and Heaven, Massacre River, Drums in the Deep South, Red Snow, Charge at Feather River, The Command, The Hard Man, Five Against the House, Beast of Hollow Mountain, Last Frontier, On the Threshold of Space, Hilda Crane, Bullwhip, Gunmen

of The Rio Grande, Sandokan Fights Back, Sandokan Against the Leopard of Sarawak, Mystery of Thug Island, Shatterhand, Payment in Blood. 1960–75 starred in 45 foreign films; Pacific Connection, Cross Bow, River River.
TELEVISION: Red River.

MADONNA: Singer, Actress. r.n. Madonna Louise Veronica Ciccone. b. Pontiac, MI, Aug. 16, 1958. e. U. of Michigan. Gained fame as rock & recording star before professional acting debut in Desperately Seeking Susan, 1985. NY stage debut: Speed-the-Plow, 1988.
PICTURES: A Certain Sacrifice, Vision Quest, Desperately Seeking Susan, Shanghai Surprise, Who's That Girl?, Bloodhounds of Broadway, Dick Tracy, Truth or Dare (also exec. prod.), Shadows and Fog, A League of Their Own, Body of Evidence, Snake Eyes.

MADSEN, MICHAEL: Actor. b. Chicago, IL, 1958. Sister is actress Virginia Madsen. Started acting with Chicago's Steppenwolf Theatre appearing in such plays as Of Mice and Men, A Streetcar Named Desire. On Bdwy in A Streetcar Named Desire (1992).
PICTURES: WarGames, Racing With the Moon, The Natural, Blood Red, Kill Me Again, The Doors, Thelma & Louise, Straight Talk, Reservoir Dogs, Trouble Bound, House in the Hills, Free Willy, Money for Nothing, Fixing the Shadow, The Getaway, Lights Out, Wyatt Earp.
TELEVISION: Movies: Our Family Honor, Baby Snatcher. Pilot: Diner.

MADSEN, VIRGINIA: Actress. b. Winnetka, IL, Sept. 11, 1963. Mother is Emmy-winning Chicago filmmaker, brother is actor Michael Madsen. Studied with Chicago acting coach Ted Liss. Prof. debut, PBS, A Matter of Principle.
PICTURES: Class (debut, 1983), Electric Dreams, Dune, Creator, Fire With Fire, Modern Girls, Zombie High, Slam Dance, Mr. North, Hot to Trot, Heart of Dixie, The Hot Spot, Highlander 2: The Quickening, Candyman, Becoming Colette.
TELEVISION: Movies: Mussolini: The Untold Story, The Hearst and Davies Affair, Long Gone, Gotham, Third Degree Burn, Ironclads, Victim of Love, Love Kills. Guest: The Hitchhiker.

MAGNOLI, ALBERT: Director, Writer, Editor.
PICTURES: Jazz (dir.), Reckless (edit.). Director: Purple Rain (also s.p.), American Anthem, Street Knight.
TELEVISION: Movie: Born to Run.

MAGNUSON, ANN: Actress, Writer, Performance Artist. b. Charleston, WV, Jan. 4, 1956. e. Denison U. Intern at Ensemble Studio Theatre when she came to NY in 1978. Ran Club 57, an East Village club, 1979. Has performed in East Village clubs, downtown art spaces & on college campuses since 1980 and at Whitney Museum, Soguestu Hall (Tokyo), Walker Art Ctr. (Minn.), Lincoln Center, Serious Fun Festival. Also performs with band Bongwater (Shimmy Disc Records).
PICTURES: Vortex, The Hunger, Perfect Strangers, Desperately Seeking Susan, Making Mr. Right, A Night in the Life of Jimmy Reardon, Sleepwalk, Mondo New York, Tequila Sunrise, Checking Out, Heavy Petting, Love at Large, Cabin Boy.
TELVISION: Night Flight, Made for TV, Alive from Off Center (co-host), Vandemonium (Cinemax), Table at Ciro's (Tales From the Hollywood Hills). Series: Anything but Love.

MAHARIS, GEORGE: Actor. b. Astoria, NY, Sept. 1, 1928.
PICTURES: Exodus, Sylvia, Quick Before It Melts, The Satan Bug, A Covenant with Death, The Happening, The Desperadoes, Sword and the Sorcerer, Last Day of the War, The Land Raiders, Doppelganger.
TELEVISION: Series: Route 66, Most Deadly Game. Guest: Naked City. Movies: Escape to Mindanao, The Monk, The Victim, Murder on Flight 502, Look What's Happened to Rosemary's Baby, SST-Death Flight, Return to Fantasy Island, Crash, A Small Rebellion. Mini-Series: Rich Man Poor Man.

MAHONEY, JOHN: Actor. b. Manchester, Eng., June 20, 1940. Mem. of Stratford Children's Theatre from age 10–13. Moved to U.S. at 19, taught Eng. at Western Illinois U. Then freelance ed. of medical manuscripts; assoc. ed., Quality Review Bulletin. At 35 quit medical book editing to become an actor. Studied acting, Chicago's St. Nicholas Theatre. Prof. debut, The Water Engine, 1977. Joined Steppenwolf Theatre Co., 1979. (The Hothouse, Taking Steps, Death of a Salesman).
THEATER: Orphans (Theatre World Award), The House of Blue Leaves (Tony and Clarence Derwent Awards), The Subject Was Roses.
PICTURES: Mission Hill, Code of Silence, The Manhattan Project, Streets of Gold, Tin Men, Suspect, Moonstruck, Frantic, Betrayed, Eight Men Out, Say Anything, Love Hurts, The Russia House, Barton Fink, Article 99, In the Line of Fire.

TELEVISION: Series: Lady Blue, H.E.L.P., The Human Factor. Movies: The Killing Floor, Chicago Story, First Steps, Listen to Your Heart, Dance of the Phoenix, First Steps, Trapped in Silence, Favorite Son, The Image, Dinner at Eight, The 10 Million Dollar Getaway, The Secret Passion of Robert Clayton. Special: The House of Blue Leaves.

MAIN, DAVID: Writer, Producer. b. Essex, Eng., 1929. Extensive television experience in Britain producing and directing for A.T.V., Granada, A.B.C. and B.B.C. Emigrated to Canada in 1960. Directed Moment of Truth for N.B.C., and Quentin Durgens M.P. for C.B.C., Famous Jury Trials for 20th Century Fox. In 1977–78 directed King of Kensington, Le Club, A Gift to Last for CBC. President of Velvet Screen Plays Ltd. a subsidiary of Quadrant Films Ltd.
PICTURES: Sunday in the Country (story & co-writer), It Seemed Like a Good Idea at the Time (co-writer), Find the Lady (story, co-writer, co-producer), Double Negative (co-prod.), Nothing Personal (co-prod.).

MAJORS, LEE: Actor. b. Wyandotte, MI, April 23, 1939. Star athlete in high school; turned down offer from St. Louis Cardinals in final year at Eastern Kentucky State Coll. to pursue acting career. In L.A. got job as playground supervisor for park dept. while studying acting at MGM Studio.
PICTURES: Will Penny (debut, 1968), The Liberation of L. B. Jones, Norsemen, Killer Fish, Steel, Agency, The Last Chase, Scrooged, Keaton's Cop.
TELEVISION: Series: The Big Valley, The Men From Shiloh, Owen Marshall-Counselor at Law, The Six Million Dollar Man, The Fall Guy, Tour of Duty, Raven. Pilot: Road Show (also exec. prod.). Movies: The Ballad of Andy Crocker, Weekend of Terror, The Gary Francis Powers Story, The Cowboy and the Ballerina, A Rocky Mountain Christmas, The Return of the Six Million Dollar Man and the Bionic Woman, Danger Down Under (exec. prod., actor), The Bionic Showdown: the Six Million Dollar Man and the Bionic Woman, Fire!, Trapped on the 37th Floor.

MAKEPEACE, CHRIS: Actor. b. Montreal, Canada, April 22, 1964. e. Jarvis Collegiate Institute. Trained for stage at Second City Workshop.
PICTURES: Meatballs (debut, 1979), My Bodyguard, The Last Chase, The Oasis, The Falcon and the Snowman, Vamp, Captive Hearts, Aloha Summer.
TELEVISION: Movies: The Terry Fox Story, The Mysterious Stranger, Mazes and Monsters, The Undergrads. Series: Going Great (host, 1982–84), Why On Earth?

MAKO: Actor. r.n. Makoto Iwamatsu. b. Kobe, Japan, Dec. 10, 1933. e. Pratt Inst.
PICTURES: The Ugly Dachshund, The Sand Pebbles (Acad. Award nom.), The Private Navy of Sgt. O'Farrell, The Great Bank Robbery, The Hawaiians, The Island at the Top of the World, Prisoners, The Killer Elite, The Big Brawl, The Bushido Blade, Under the Rainbow, An Eye for an Eye, Conan the Barbarian, The House Where Evil Dwells, Testament, Conan the Destroyer, Armed Response, P.O.W. The Escape, Silent Assassins, The Wash, Tucker: The Man and His Dream, An Unremarkable Life, Taking Care of Business, Pacific Heights, The Perfect Weapon, Sidekicks, Robocop 3, Rising Sun.
TELEVISION: Series: Hawaiian Heat. Movies: The Challenge, If Tomorrow Comes, The Streets of San Francisco (pilot), Judge Dee and the Monastery Murders, Farewell to Manzanar, When Hell Was in Session, The Last Ninja, Girls of the White Orchid. Guest: McHale's Navy, Ensign O'Toole, 77 Sunset Strip, I Spy, F Troop, Hawaii Five-O.
THEATRE: NY: Pacific Overtures (Tony Award nom.), Shimada. Regional: Rashomon.

MALDEN, KARL: Actor. r.n. Mladen Sekulovich. b. Gary, IN, Mar. 22, 1914. e. Art Inst. of Chicago 1933–36; Goodman Theatre Sch. Elected pres., Acad. of Motion Picture Arts & Sciences, 1989.
BWAY PLAYS: Golden Boy, Key Largo, Flight to West, Missouri Legend, Uncle Harry, Counterattack, Truckline Cafe, All My Sons, Streetcar Named Desire, Desperate Hours, Desire Under the Elms, The Egghead.
PICTURES: They Knew What They Wanted (debut, 1940), Winged Victory, 13 Rue Madeleine, Boomerang, Kiss of Death, The Gunfighter, Where the Sidewalk Ends, Halls of Montezuma, Streetcar Named Desire (Acad. Award, supp. actor, 1951), The Sellout, Diplomatic Courier, Operation Secret, Ruby Gentry, I Confess, Take the High Ground, Phantom of the Rue Morgue, On the Waterfront, Baby Doll, Bombers B-52, Time Limit (dir. only), Fear Strikes Out, The Hanging Tree, One Eyed Jacks, Pollyanna, Parrish, All Fall Down, Birdman of Alcatraz, Gypsy, How the West Was Won, Come Fly With Me, Cheyenne Autumn, Dead Ringer, The Cincinnati Kid, Nevada Smith, Murderer's Row, Hotel, Blue, Adventures of Bullwhip Griffin, Billion Dollar Brain, Hot Millions, Patton, Cat O'Nine Tails, Wild Rovers, Summertime Killer, Beyond the Poseidon Adventure, Meteor, The Sting II, Twilight Time, Billy Galvin, Nuts.

TELEVISION: *Series*: Streets of San Francisco, Skag. *Movies*: Captains Courageous, Word of Honor, With Intent to Kill, Alice in Wonderland, Fatal Vision (Emmy Award), My Father My Son, The Hijacking of the Achille Lauro, Call Me Anna, Absolute Strangers, Back to the Streets of San Francisco.

MALICK, TERENCE: Producer, Writer, Director. b. Waco, Texas, Nov. 30, 1943. e. Harvard U. Attended Oxford U. on Rhodes scholarship. Worked for Newsweek, Life and The New Yorker; lectured on philosophy at M.I.T. Studied at American Film Inst. in Beverly Hills and made short funded by AFI.
PICTURES: Pocket Money (co-s.p. only), The Gravy Train (co-s.p. under pseudonym David Whitney), Deadhead Miles (co-s.p.), Badlands (prod., dir., s.p.), Days of Heaven (s.p., dir.).

MALIN, AMIR JACOB: Executive. b. Tel-Aviv, Israel, Mar. 22, 1954. e. Brandeis U., 1972–76; Boston U. Sch. of Law, 1976–79. Staff atty., WGBH-TV, Boston, 1979–81; pres. and co-CEO, Cinecom Entertainment Group, Inc, 1982–92. Films acquired and distributed include Come Back to the Five and Dime, Jimmy Dean, Jimmy Dean; Metropolis; The Brother from Another Planet; Stop Making Sense; Coca-Cola Kid; A Room with a View; Swimming to Cambodia; Matewan; A Man in Love; Maurice, Miles From Home. Partner, October Films, Inc. Films acquired and distrib., Life is Sweet, Adam's Rib, The Living End, Tous les Matins du Monde (All the Mornings of the World), Ruby in Paradise, A Heart in Winter, Bad Behavior.
PICTURES: Exec. prod.: Swimming to Cambodia, Matewan, Miles From Home, Scenes from the Class Struggle in Beverly Hills, The Handmaid's Tale, Tune in Tomorrow.

MALKOVICH, JOHN: Actor, Producer, Director. b. Christopher, IL, Dec. 9, 1953. e. Illinois State U. Founding member Steppenwolf Ensemble in Chicago with group of college friends, 1976. Starred in Say Goodnight Gracie and True West (Obie Award) which then was brought to New York. NY Stage work includes Death of Salesman, Burn This, States of Shock. Director: Balm in Gilead, Arms and the Man, The Caretaker.
PICTURES: Places in the Heart (Acad. Award nom.), The Killing Fields, Eleni, Making Mr. Right, The Glass Menagerie, Empire of the Sun, Miles From Home, Dangerous Liaisons, The Accidental Tourist (co-exec. prod. only), The Sheltering Sky, Queens Logic, The Object of Beauty, Shadows and Fog, Of Mice and Men, Jennifer Eight, Alive, In the Line of Fire.
TELEVISION: *Special*: Rocket to the Moon. *Movies*: Word of Honor, American Dream, Death of a Salesman (Emmy Award, 1986).

MALLE, LOUIS: Director, Producer, Writer. b. Thumeries, France, Oct. 30, 1932. m. actress Candice Bergen. e. Sorbonne (Pol. Science). Studied filmmaking at Institut des Hautes Etudes Cinematographiques 1951–53. Started in film industry as assistant to Robert Bresson and cameraman to oceanographer Jacques Cousteau, 1954–55 then corres. for French TV in Algeria, Vietnam and Thailand 1962–64. Began career somewhat ahead of most young French directors referred to as the Nouvelle Vougue (New Wave). Became internationally known with Les Amants (The Lovers) in 1958. Has also acted in films (A Very Private Affair, A Very Curious Girl, Milky Way).
PICTURES: Silent World (co-dir., photog. with J. Y. Cousteau), A Condemned Man Escapes (prod. asst. to Bresson), Mon Oncle (photog. only). *Director*: Elevator to the Gallows (also s.p.), The Lovers (also s.p.), Calcutta (doc.; also s.p., photog., actor), Zazie in the Metro (also s.p.), A Very Private Affair (also s.p., actor), Vive Le Tour (doc.; also s.p., photog., actor), The Fire Within (also s.p.), Viva Maria (also prod., s.p.), The Thief of Paris (also prod., s.p.), Spirits of the Dead (co-dir.), Phantom India (doc.; also photog.), Murmur of the Heart (also s.p.; Acad. Award nom. for best s.p.), Humain Trop Humain (doc.; also prod., photog.), Place de la Republique (doc.; also prod., photog.), Lacombe Lucien (also prod., s.p.), Black Moon (also s.p.), Pretty Baby (also prod., story), Atlantic City (Acad. Award nom.), My Dinner With Andre, Crackers, Alamo Bay (also prod.), Au Revoir Les Enfants (Goodbye Children; also s.p., prod.; Golden Lion Award, Venice Film Fest., 1987), May Fools (Milou en Mai; also co-s.p.), Damage (also prod.).
TELEVISION: *Documentaries*: God's Country, And the Pursuit of Happiness.

MALLERS, ANTHONY: Theatre Owner. b. Portland, IN, Oct. 4, 1933. e. Indiana U., B.S., business admin. Entered industry in 1957. Now pres. of Mallers Theatres, headquartered in Muncie, Ind.

MALMUTH, BRUCE: Director, Actor. b. Brooklyn, NY, Feb. 4, 1937. e. City Coll. of New York, Brooklyn Coll. Grad. studies in film, Columbia U. and U. of Southern California. Acted in and dir. college productions. Moved to California and obtained job as page at NBC. In Army assigned to special services as director; reassigned to New York. Upon release began 10-year Clio-winning career as dir. of TV commercials. Debut as director of features with Nighthawks, 1981. Founder, Los Angeles Aspiring Actors and Directors Workshop Thea-

tre incl.: Two Guys Second Wind (writer, dir., prod.), Thanksgiving Blood (writer, dir.).
PICTURES: *Director*: Nighthawks, The Man Who Wasn't There, Where Are the Children? (also actor), Hard to Kill. *Actor*: The Karate Kid (also Part II), For Keeps?, Happy New Year, Lean on Me.
TELEVISION: Baseballs or Switchblades? (prod., writer, dir., Emmy Award-winning doc.), A Boy's Dream, Twilight Zone, Beauty and the Beast (Heartbreak winner).

MALONE, DOROTHY: Actress. b. Chicago, IL, Jan. 30, 1925. e. Southern Methodist U.
PICTURES: Falcon and the Co-eds (debut, 1943), The Big Sleep, Night and Day, One Sunday Afternoon, Two Guys From Texas, The Nevadan, The Bushwackers, Jack Slade, The Killer That Stalked New York, Scared Stiff, Torpedo Alley, The Lone Gun, Pushover, Security Risk, Private Hell 36, The Fast and the Furious, Young at Heart, Battle Cry, Sincerely Yours, Artists and Models, At Gunpoint, Five Guns West, Tall Man Riding, Pillars of the Sky, Tension at Table Rock, Written on the Wind (Acad. Award, supp. actress, 1956), Man of a Thousand Faces, Quantez, The Tarnished Angels, Tip on a Dead Jockey, Too Much Toon Soon, Warlock, The Last Voyage, The Last Sunset, Beach Party, Fate is the Hunter (unbilled), Abduction, Golden Rendezvous, Good Luck Miss Wyckoff, Winter Kills, The Day Time Ended, The Being, Basic Instinct.
TELEVISION: *Series*: Peyton Place. *Guest*: Dick Powell Theatre, Loretta Young Show, Philip Morris Playhouse, Dr. Kildare, Bob Hope Show, Jack Benny Show, The Untouchables, Phyllis Diller Show, The Greatest Show On Earth, Ken Murray's Blackouts, Death Valley Days. *Movies*: The Pigeon, Little Ladies of the Night, Murder in Peyton Place, Katie: Portrait of a Centerfold, Condominium, Peyton Place: The Next Generation. *Mini-Series*: Rich Man Poor Man. *Specials*: Gertrude Stein Story, The Family That Prays Together.

MAMET, DAVID: Writer. b. Chicago, IL, Nov. 30, 1947. e. Goddard Coll. Artist-in-residence, Goddard Coll. 1971–73. Artistic dir. St. Nicholas Theatre Co., Chicago, 1973–75. Co-founder Dinglefest Theatre; assoc. artistic dir., Goodman Theatre, Chicago. Plays include Lakefront, The Woods, American Buffalo, Sexual Perversity in Chicago, Duck Variations, Edmond, A Life in the Theatre, The Water Engine, Prairie du Chien, Glengarry Glen Ross (Pulitzer Prize 1984 & 4 Tony Awards), Speed-the-Plow, Sketches of War (benefit for homeless Vietnam Veterans).
PICTURES: The Postman Always Rings Twice, The Verdict, The Untouchables, House of Games (also dir.), Things Change (dir., co-s.p), We're No Angels, Homicide (also dir.), Hoffa.
TELEVISION: Lip Service (exec. prod.), Hill Street Blues, A Life in the Theatre.

MANASSE, GEORGE: Producer. b. Florence, Italy, Jan. 1, 1938. e. U. of North Carolina.
PICTURES: *Prod.*: Who Killed Mary What's 'er Name? Squirm, Blue Sunshine, He Knows You're Alone. *Prod. Mgr.*: Greetings, Joe, Fury on Wheels, Slow Dancing in the Big City, Tribute, Porky's II: The Next Day, Neighbors, Death Wish III, Torch Song Trilogy, Indecent Proposal, Coneheads.
TELEVISION: *Line Prod.*: Series: American Playwright's Theatre (Arts & Ent.) The Saint in Manhattan (pilot), Movie: The Killing Floor, Vengeance: The Story of Tony Cimo. *Prod. Mgr.*: Series: St. Elsewhere, Annie McGuire. Movies: Sanctuary of Fear, Mr. Griffith and Me, Peking Encounter, When the Circus Came to Town, Murder, Inc. Muggable Mary, Running Out, Dropout Father, He's Fired, She's Fired, Intimate Strangers, Drop Out Mother, Vengeance: The Story of Tony Cimo, The Saint in Manhattan, The Diamond Trap, The Prize Pulitzer. (also suprv. prod.), Orpheus Descending (also suprv. prod.). John and Yoko, Marilyn and Me, The Woman Who Sinned.

MANCIA, ADRIENNE: Curator, Dept. of Film, Museum of Modern Art. b. New York, NY. e. U. of Wisconsin. B.A.; Columbia U., M.A. Worked in film distribution industry in New York prior to joining Dept. of Film, Museum of Modern Art, 1964; responsible for film exhibition since 1965. In 1977, appointed curator. Restructured Museums' Auditorium Exhibition Prog., creating a balance between classic cinema and contemporary work. Initiated innovative programs such as Cineprobe and What's Happening? Served on numerous int'l film juries. Co-founder New Directors/New Films. Chevalier de l'ordre des arts et des lettres (Republic of France), 1985). Ufficiale dell Ordine al Merito della Repubblica Italiana, 1988.

MANCINI, HENRY: Composer. b., Cleveland, OH, April 16, 1924. Arranged music for the Glenn Miller Story, The Benny Goodman Story, then began composing scores. Winner of 4 Academy Awards (18 noms.) and 20 Grammys (72 noms.). Author: Sounds and Scores: A Practical Guide to Professional Orchestration, and autobiography: Did They Mention the Music? Honorary Doctorate Degrees from Duquesne U, Mt. St. Mary's Col., Washington & Jefferson Col., Calif. Inst. for the Arts in Valencia.

220

PICTURES: Touch of Evil, High Time, Breakfast at Tiffany's (2 Acad. Awards, best score and song, 1961), Bachelor in Paradise, Days of Wine and Roses (Acad. Award, best song, 1962), The Second Time Around, Experiment in Terror, Mr. Hobbs Takes a Vacation, Hatari!, The Pink Panther, Charade, A Shot in the Dark, Dear Heart, The Great Race, Arabesque, What Did You Do in the War Daddy?, Gunn, Two for the Road, Wait Until Dark, The Party, Gaily Gaily, The Hawaiians, The Molly Maguires, Darling Lili, Visions of Eight, Oklahoma Crude, 99 44/100% Dead, The White Dawn, The Girl from Petrovka, The Great Waldo Pepper, W. C. Fields and Me, The Pink Panther Strikes Again, Silver Streak, Revenge of the Pink Panther, Who Is Killing the Great Chefs of Europe?, Prisoner of Zenda, Nightwing, "10," Little Miss Marker, Change of Seasons, Back Roads, S.O.B., Mommie Dearest, Victor/Victoria (Acad. Award, best song score, 1982), Trail of the Pink Panther, Curse of the Pink Panther, The Man Who Loved Women, Harry and Son, That's Dancing, Life Force, Santa Claus: The Movie, A Fine Mess, The Great Mouse Detective, That's Life!, Blind Date, The Glass Menagerie, Sunset, Without a Clue, Physical Evidence, Welcome Home, Ghost Dad, Switch, Married to It, Tom and Jerry: The Movie.
TELEVISION: Peter Gunn, Mr. Lucky, Newhart, Hotel, A Family Upside Down, The Moneychangers, The Shadow Box, Thorn Birds, Blue Knight, Best Place to Be, Remington Steele, Peter Gunn (1989), Never Forget.

MANCUSO, FRANK G.: Executive. b. Buffalo, NY, July 25, 1933. e. State U. of New York. Film buyer and operations supvr. for Basil Enterprises, theatre circuit, from 1958 to 1962. Joined Paramount as booker in Buffalo branch, 1962. Named sls. repr. for branch in 1964 and branch mgr. in 1967. In 1970 appt. v.p./gen. sls. mgr., Paramount Pictures Canada, Ltd., becoming pres. in 1972. In 1976 relocated with Paramount in U.S. as western div. mgr. in L.A. In Jan., 1977, appt. gen. sls. mgr. of N.Y., office; two months later promoted to v.p.—domestic distribution; 1979, named exec. v.p., distribution & mktg. In 1983 made pres. of entire Paramount Motion Picture Group. 1984, appointed chmn. and chief exec. officer, Paramount Pictures; resigned 1991. Motion Picture Pioneers Man of the Year, 1987. Member of Board: Acad. of M.P. Arts and Sciences, M.P. Association of America, Will Rogers Memorial Fund, Variety Clubs Intl., Sundance Institute, Amer. Film Institute, Museum of Broadcasting, Motion Picture Pioneers. Appointed Chmn. & CEO of MGM, 1993.

MANCUSO, FRANK, JR.: Producer. b. Buffalo, NY, Oct. 9, 1958. Son of Frank G. Mancuso. e. Upsala Coll. Began with industry at age 14, booking short subjects in Canadian theatres. Worked in gross receipts dept. in Paramount corporate offices in New York and later with paralegal div. Initial prod. work as location asst. for Urban Cowboy in Houston, TX. Served as assoc. prod. of Friday the 13th Part II and prod. of Friday the 13th Part III in 3-D.
PICTURES: Off the Wall, The Man Who Wasn't There, April Fool's Day, Friday the 13th, Part IV: The Final Chapter; Friday the 13th—A New Beginning (exec. prod.), Friday the 13th, Part VII (exec. prod.); Back to the Beach; Permanent Record, Internal Affairs, He Said/She Said.
TELEVISION: Friday the 13th: The Series (exec. prod.).

MANDEL, BABALOO: Writer. r.n. Marc Mandel. b. 1949. Started as comedy writer for Joan Rivers, among others. First teamed with Lowell Ganz on script for 1982 film Night Shift.
PICTURES: Night Shift, Splash (Acad. Award nom.), Spies Like Us, Gung Ho, Vibes, Parenthood, City Slickers, A League of Their Own, Mr. Saturday Night (also cameo), Greedy.

MANDEL, LORING: Writer. b. Chicago, IL, May 5, 1928. e. U. of Wisconsin, B.S. 1949. Long career writing scripts for TV, dating back to 1955 when penned Shakedown Cruise. Governor, Natl. Acad. of TV Arts & Sciences 1964–68; Pres. Writers Guild of America East 1975–77; Natl. Chmn. 1977–79.
PICTURES: Countdown, Promises in the Dark, The Little Drummer Girl, etc.
TELEVISION: Do Not Go Gentle Into That Good Night (Emmy, 1967), Breaking Up, Project Immortality (Sylvania Award, 1959), A House His Own, Trial of Chaplain Jensen, The Raider, etc.

MANDEL, ROBERT: Director. e. Columbia Univ.
PICTURES: Night at O'Rears (also prod.), Independence Day, F/X, Touch and Go, Big Shots, School Ties.
TELEVISION: Hard Time on Planet Earth.

MANDELL, ABE: Executive. b. Oct. 4, 1922. e. U. of Cincinnati. Entered broadcasting as actor on Cincinnati radio station prior to W.W.II. Served U.S. Army in Southwest Pacific, 1942–45. Formed indep. motion picture distribution co. in the Far East. Company, which became the largest indep. motion picture dist. in the Far East, also operated and owned motion picture theaters throughout the Phillipines and Indonesia, 1946–56; network-regional sales exec., Ziv Television, 1956–58; dir. foreign operations, Independent Television Corporation, 1958; v.p.-foreign oper., 1960; v.p.-sales and adm., 1961;

exec. v.p., 1962; pres. 1965. 1976 corporate name changed from Independent Television Corp. to ITC Entertainment, Inc. President to 1983 of ITC Entertainment, with Robert Mandell heads New Frontier Prods.

MANES, FRITZ: Producer. b. Oakland, CA, Apr. 22, 1936. e. U Calif., Berkeley, B.A. UCLA, 1956. Armed Service: 1951–4. U.S. Marines, Korea, Purple Heart. TV ad exec. and stunt-man before becoming exec. prod. on films for Clint Eastwood. Has formed own production co., Sundancer Prods. Membership, DGA, SAG.
PICTURES: in various capacities: The Outlaw Josey Wales, The Enforcer. Assoc. prod.: The Gauntlet, Every Which Way But Loose, Escape From Alcatraz, Bronco Billy. Prod.: Any Which Way You Can (also 2nd asst. dir.), Firefox (exec. prod.), Honky Tonk Man (exec. prod.), Tightrope (prod.), Sudden Impact (exec. prod.), City Heat (prod.), Pale Rider (exec. prod.), Ratboy (exec. prod.), Heartbreak Ridge (exec. prod., prod. mgr.).

MANKIEWICZ, DON M.: Writer. b. Berlin, Germany, Jan. 20, 1922. p. Herman J. Mankiewicz. e. Columbia, B.A., 1942; Columbia Law Sch. Served in U.S. Army, 1942–46; reporter, New Yorker magazine, 1946–48; author of novels See How They Run, Trial, It Only Hurts a Minute; magazine articles, short stories. President, Producers Guild of America (1987).
TELEVISION: Studio One, On Trial, One Step Beyond, Playhouse 90, Profiles in Courage. Exec. story consultant: Hart to Hart, Simon & Simon, Crazy Like a Fox, Adderly.
PICTURES: Trial, I Want to Live, (Acad. Award nom.), The Chapman Report, The Black Bird.
TV PILOTS: Ironside, Marcus Welby, M.D., Sarge; Lanigan's Rabbi (collab.); Rosetti and Ryan (collab.)

MANKIEWICZ, JOSEPH L.: Writer, Director. b. Wilkes-Barre, PA, Feb. 11, 1909. e. Columbia U. Asst. corr. in Berlin, Chicago Tribune; Ufa studio, translating subtitles into Eng. for release in Eng. & U.S.; returned to U.S. 1929 to join brother, Herman, on Paramount writing staff; MGM, 1933; Fox, 1943–51; dir., La Boheme, Metropolitan Opera House, 1953. Founding member & secretary Screen Writers Guild 1933. President Dir. Guild of Amer., 1950. Academy Awards: 1949, Letter to Three Wives, best s.p., dir.; 1950, All About Eve, best s.p., dir. D.W. Griffith Award for Lifetime Achievement, Directors Guild of Amer., 1986; Golden Lion Award, lifetime achievement, Venice Film Fest. 1987. Chevalier de la Legion d'Honneur—France 1988; Akira Kurosawa Award for Lifetime Achievement, San Francisco 1989. Life Member, Academy of Motion Picture Arts and Sciences (1991).
PICTURES: Writer: Skippy, Million Dollar Legs, If I Had a Million, Alice in Wonderland. Producer: Fury, Gorgeous Hussy, Mannequin, Three Comrades, Shopworn Angel, Philadelphia Story, Woman of the Year, Keys of the Kingdom (also s.p.). Director-Writer: Dragonwyck, Somewhere in the Night, Late George Apley, Ghost and Mrs. Muir, Escape, House of Strangers (dir. only), Letter to Three Wives, All About Eve, People Will Talk, 5 Fingers (dir. only), Julius Caesar, Barefoot Contessa, Guys and Dolls, Quiet American (also prod.), Suddenly Last Summer (dir. only), Cleopatra, The Honey Pot, There Was a Crooked Man, Sleuth.
(Died: Feb. 5, 1993)

MANKIEWICZ, TOM: Writer, Director. b. Los Angeles, CA, June 1, 1942.
PICTURES: Writer: The Sweet Ride (debut), Diamonds Are Forever, Live and Let Die, The Man with the Golden Gun, Mother Jugs and Speed (also prod.), The Cassandra Crossing, The Eagle Has Landed, Ladyhawke. Exec. Prod.: Hot Pursuit. Creative consultant: Superman, Superman II. Director: Dragnet (also s.p.), Delirious.
TELEVISION: Pilot: Hart to Hart (writer, dir.). Movie: Taking the Heat (dir.)

MANKOWITZ, WOLF: Author, Playwright, Producer, Impresario. b. London, 1924. Journalist. Ent. m.p. in 1952. Musical play based on his story Expresso Bongo. Musical play, Make Me An Offer; Belle; Pickwick; Passion Flower Hotel.
PICTURES: Make Me An Offer, Kid For Two Farthings, The Bespoke Overcoat, Trapeze, Expresso Bongo, The Millionaires, The Long and Short and Tall, The Day The Earth Caught Fire, Where the Spies Are, Assassination Bureau, Bloomfield: Black Beauty, Treasure Island, The Hireling, Almonds and Raisins.
TELEVISION: The Killing Stones, A Cure for Tin Ear, The Battersea Miracle. Series: Conflict, Dickens of London.

MANN, ABBY: Writer. b. Philadelphia, PA, 1927. e. NYU. First gained fame on TV writing for Robert Montgomery Theatre, Playhouse 90, Studio One, Alcoa, Goodyear Theatre. Acad. Award for film adaptation of own teleplay Judgment at Nuremberg into theatrical film.
PICTURES: Judgment at Nuremberg, A Child Is Waiting, The Condemned of Altona, Ship of Fools, The Detective, Report to the Commissioner.
TELEVISION: Series: Kojak (creator). Movies: The Marcus-Nelson Murders (Emmy Award; also exec. prod.), Medical

Story (also exec. prod.), This Man Stands Alone (exec. prod. only), Skag (also co-exec. prod.), The Atlanta Child Murders, King, Murderers Among Us, The Simon Wiesenthal Story (co-s.p., co-exec. prod.; Emmy Award), Teamster Boss: The Jackie Presser Story (also co-exec. prod.). *Special*: War and Love.

MANN, DELBERT: Director, Producer. b. Lawrence, KS, Jan. 30, 1920. e. Vanderbilt U., Yale U. U.S. Air Force, 1942–45; stage mgr., summer stock, dir. Columbia, S.C. Town Theatre, 1947–49; asst. dir., NBC-TV, 1949; dir., NBC-TV, 1949–55. Past pres. Directors Guild of America.
STAGE: A Quiet Place, Speaking of Murder, Zelda, opera: Wuthering Heights; New York City Center.
PICTURES: *Director*: Marty (Acad. Award, 1955), The Bachelor Party, Desire Under the Elms, Separate Tables, Middle of the Night, The Dark at the Top of the Stairs, The Outsider, Lover Come Back, That Touch of Mink, A Gathering of Eagles, Dear Heart, Quick Before It Melts (also prod.), Mister Buddwing (also prod.), Fitzwilly, The Pink Jungle, Kidnapped, Birch Interval, Night Crossing.
TELEVISION: Philco-Goodyear TV Playhouse, Producer's Showcase, Omnibus, Playwrights '56, Playhouse 90, Ford Star Jubilee, Lights Out, Mary Kay and Johnny, The Little Show, Masterpiece Theatre, Ford Startime. *Movies/Specials*: Heidi, David Copperfield, No Place to Run, She Waits (also prod.), Jane Eyre, The Man Without a Country, A Girl Named Sooner, Francis Gary Powers: The True Story of the U-2 Spy Incident, Tell Me My Name, Breaking Up, Home to Stay, Love's Dark Ride, Thou Shalt Not Commit Adultery, All Quiet on the Western Front, Torn Between Two Lovers, To Find My Son, All the Way Home, The Member of the Wedding, The Gift of Love, Bronte, Love Leads the Way, A Death in California, The Last Days of Patton, The Ted Kennedy, Jr. Story, April Morning (also co-prod.), Ironclads, Against Her Will: An Incident in Baltimore (also prod.).

MANN, MICHAEL: Director, Writer, Producer. b. Chicago, IL, Feb. 5, 1943. e. U. of Wisconsin, London Film Sch. Directed commercials and documentaries in England. Returned to U.S. in 1972. Wrote for prime-time TV (episodes of Starsky and Hutch, Police Story, Vegas).
PICTURES: *Exec. Prod. only*: Band of the Hand. *Director-Writer*: Thief (also exec. prod.), The Keep, Manhunter, The Last of the Mohicans (also co-prod.).
TELEVISION: The Jericho Mile (s.p., dir.; DGA, 1980 best director award, Emmy Award for writing). Miami Vice (exec. prod.), Crime Story (exec. prod.), L.A. Takedown (dir., s.p., exec. prod.). *Mini-Series*: Drug Wars: The Camarena Story (co-exec. prod.; Emmy Award), Drug Wars: The Cocaine Cartel (exec. prod.).

MANNE, S. ANTHONY: Executive. b. New York, NY, July 19, 1940. e. Wharton Sch., U. of Pennsylvania, B.S., economics. Joined Columbia Pictures 1963; international dept. 1964; asst. mgr., Brazil, 1968; mgr., Brazil, 1969–72. Joined JAD Films, 1976; United Artists, v.p., Latin American supervisor, 1980; Columbia Pictures Intl., v.p., continental mgr., 1981; appointed sr. v.p., sales manager, 1984; exec. v.p., Tri-Star Intl, 1987; appointed exec. v.p., foreign mgr. Columbia Tri-Star Film Distributors, 1988.

MANNIX, DAVID K.: Executive. b. Brooklyn, NY, 1952. e. Fordham U., B.S.; Pepperdine U., M.B.A. Joined Paramount Pictures in 1973 as supervisor, TV accounting; 1976, Mgr. financial analysis; 1978, asst. studio controller; 1979, director, production operations; 1981, executive director, studio operations; 1984, promoted to v.p. 1988; promoted to sr. v.p. studio operations.

MANOFF, DINAH: Actress. b. New York, NY, January 25, 1958. e. CalArts. Daughter of actress-director Lee Grant and late writer Arnold Manoff. Prof. debut PBS prod. The Great Cherub Knitwear Strike. Guest starred on Welcome Back Kotter.
THEATER: I Ought to Be in Pictures (Tony & Theatre World Awards, 1980), Gifted Children, Leader of the Pack, Alfred and Victoria: A Life (L.A. Theatre Center), Kingdom of Earth (TheatreWest).
PICTURES: Grease (debut, 1978), Ordinary People, I Ought to Be in Pictures, Child's Play, Staying Together, Bloodhounds of Broadway, Welcome Home Roxy Carmichael.
TELEVISION: *Series*: Soap (1978–79), Empty Nest. *Movies*: Raid on Entebbe, Night Terror, The Possessed, For Ladies Only, A Matter of Sex, The Seduction of Gina, Flight #90: Disaster on the Potomac, Classified Love, Crossing the Mob, Backfire, Babies, Maid for Each Other (also co-exec. prod., co-story). *Mini-Series*: Celebrity.

MANSON, ARTHUR: Executive. b. Brooklyn, NY, Feb. 21, 1928. e. City Coll. of New York, grad. Inst. Film Technique, 1945; editor, American Traveler; U.S. Army, 1946; Advance agent, co. mgr., Henry V, U.S., 1948–50; producer's publ. rep., Stanley Kramer Distributing Corp., Samuel Goldwyn Produc-

tions, 1951–52, dir. of adv. and publ., MGM Pictures of Canada, Ltd., 1952–53; publ. and adv. rep., Cinerama widescreen process, 1953–58; dir. worldwide ad-pub Cinerama 1958–60; adv. mgr., Columbia Pictures, 1961–62; nat'l dir. of adv., publ., Dino De Laurentiis, 1962–64; exec. asst. to v.p. adv. & pub., 20th Century-Fox, 1964–67; v.p., adv. & pub. Cinerama. Inc., and Cinerama Releasing Corp.; 1967–74; exec. v.p., sales & marketing, BCP, service of Cox Broadcasting Corp., 1974–75; v.p. worldwide marketing Warner Bros., 1976. In 1977 formed own company, Cinemax Mkt. & Dist. Corp. and is pres. Chmn. NY screen committee, Acad. of Mo. Pic. Arts & Sciences.

MANTEGNA, JOE: Actor. b. Chicago, IL, Nov. 13, 1947. e. Morton Jr. Coll., Goodman Sch. of Drama, 1967–69. Member: The Organic Theatre Company, Chicago (The Wonderful Ice Cream Suit, Cops, and 2 European tours with ensemble). Later mem. of Goodman Theater where he began long creative assoc. with playwright-dir. David Mamet (A Life in Theatre, The Disappearance of the Jews). In national co. of Hair, Godspell, Lenny. Broadway debut: Working. Narrated documentaries Crack U.S.A. and Death on the Job.
THEATER: Bleacher Bums (also conceived and co-author), Leonardo (L.A., co-author), Glengarry Glen Ross (Tony Award), Speed-the-Plow.
PICTURES: Who Stole My Wheels? (Towing), Second Thoughts, Compromising Positions, The Money Pit, Off Beat, Three Amigos, Critical Condition, House of Games, Weeds, Suspect, Things Change (Venice Film Fest. best actor award, 1988), Wait Until Spring Bandini, Alice, The Godfather III, Queens Logic, Homicide, Bugsy, Body of Evidence, Family Prayers, Searching for Bobby Fisher, Airheads.
TELEVISION: *Series*: Comedy Zone. *Guest*: Soap, Bosom Buddies, Archie Bunker's Place, Magnum P.I., Open All Night, Fallen Angels (The Quiet Room). *Special*: Bleacher Bums (Emmy Award). *Movies*: Elvis, Comrades of Summer, The Water Engine.

MANULIS, MARTIN: Producer, Director. b. New York, NY, May 30, 1915. e. Columbia Col., B.A. 1935. Head of prod. John C. Wilson, 1941–49; mgr. dir., Westport Country Playhouse, 1945–50; dir. Bdwy plays; staff prod. & dir. CBS-TV, 1951–58; head prod. 20th-Fox Television. Now pres. Martin Manulis Prods. Ltd. 1987, artistic dir., Ahmanson Theatre, L.A.
BROADWAY: (and on tour): Private Lives, Made in Heaven, The Philadelphia Story, Pride's Crossing, Laura, The Men We Marry, The Hasty Heart, The Show Off.
TELEVISION: Suspense, Studio One, Climax, Best of Broadway, Playhouse 90. Mini-Series: Chiefs, Space, The Day Christ Died, Grass Roots.
PICTURES: Days of Wine and Roses, Luv, Duffy, The Out-of-Towners.

MARA, ADELE: Actress. r.n. Adelaida Delgado; b. Dearborn, MI, April 28, 1923. m. Roy Huggins. Singer, dancer with Xavier Cugat orchestra.
PICTURES: Shut My Big Mouth, Blondie Goes to College, Alias Boston Blackie, You Were Never Lovelier, Riders of the Northwest Mounted, Magnificent Rogue, Passkey to Danger, Traffic in Crime, Exposed, The Trespasser, Blackmail, Campus Honeymoon, Sands of Iwo Jima, Wake of the Red Witch, Sea Hornet, Count The Hours, Back from Eternity, Curse of the Faceless Man, The Big Circus.
TELEVISION: *Series*: Cool Million. *Mini-Series*: Wheels.

MARAIS, JEAN: Actor. b. Cherbourg, France, Dec. 11, 1913. e. Coll. St. Germain, Lycée Janson de Sailly, Lycée Condorcet. Painter; photog; stage actor; French Air Army; m.p. debut in Pavillon Brule.
PICTURES: Carmen, Eternal Return, Beauty and the Beast, Ruy Blas, Les Parents Terribles, Secret of Mayerling, Souvenir, Orpheus, Eagle with Two Heads, Inside a Girl's Dormitory, Royal Affairs in Versailles, Paris Does Strange Things, Le Capitan, Le Bossu, La Princesse de Cleves, Le Capitaine Fracasse, Honorable Stanilleu, Agent Secret, Patute, Fantomas, Le Gentleman de Cocody.

MARANS, MARDI: Executive. e. U. of California. Worked in L.A. office of Doyle Dane Bernbach ad agency. Joined Warner Bros. in March, 1975, as asst. to media director. In 1979 appt. v.p. and director of media for WB, responsible for worldwide planning and placement of all film advertising. 1986, exec. v.p., worldwide mktg., Paramount Pictures.

MARCH, DONALD: Production Executive. b. New York, NY, July 26, 1942. Held sr. programming positions with ABC-TV network and Robert Stigwood Org. before joining CBS in 1977 as director, special projects, motion pictures for TV and mini-series. Later promoted to v.p., motion pictures for TV. Left CBS to serve as pres. of Filmways' theatrical div. in early 1979; later that year rejoined CBS as v.p., theatrical films, with responsibility for selection, dev. and prod. of pictures for theatrical release. 1984, sr. v.p., HBO Premiere Films. Independent prod., 1987 with ITC.

TELEVISION: Billionaire Boys Club (exec. prod.), Clinton and Nadine (prod.), David (prod.).

MARCHAND, NANCY: Actress. b. Buffalo, NY, June 19, 1928. m. actor-dir. Paul Sparer. e. Carnegie Tech. Stage debut The Late George Apley (In ME, 1946), Bwdy debut Taming of the Shrew (1951). Also in The Balcony (Obie Award, 1960), Morning's at Seven (Drama Desk & Outer Critics Circle Awards), Sister Mary Ignatius Explains It All to You, Taken in Marriage, The Plough and the Stars, Awake and Sing, The Cocktail Hour (Obie Award, 1990), The End of the Day. Was an original mem of APA-Phoenix Theater.
PICTURES: The Bachelor Party (debut, 1957), Ladybug Ladybug, Me Natalie, Tell Me That You Love Me Junie Moon, The Hospital, The Bostonians, From the Hip, The Naked Gun.
TELEVISION: Specials: Little Women (1951), numerous live prods. (incl. Marty), Kiss Kiss Dahlings. Series: Beacon Hill, Adams Chronicles, Love of Life, Search for Tomorrow, Lou Grant (4 Emmy Awards). Movies: Some Kind of Miracle, Willa, Once Upon a Family, Killjoy, The Golden Moment—An Olympic Love Story, Sparkling Cyanide. Mini-Series: North and South Book II.

MARCOVICCI, ANDREA: Actress, Singer. b. New York, NY, Nov. 18, 1948. Acted on NY stage in The Wedding of Iphigenia, The Ambassadors, Nefertiti, Hamlet. Frequent performer in night clubs.
PICTURES: The Front, The Concorde: Airport 1979, The Hand, Spacehunter: Adventures in the Forbidden Zone, Kings and Desperate Men, The Stuff, Someone to Love, Jack the Bear.
TELEVISION: Series: Love is a Many-Splendored Thing, Berrenger's, Trapper John M.D. Movies: Cry Rape!, Smile Jenny You're Dead, Some Kind of Miracle, A Vacation in Hell, Packin' It In, Spraggue, Velvet, The Water Engine.

MARCUS, LOUIS: Producer, Director, Writer. b. Cork, Ireland, 1936. e. National U. of Ireland, B.A., 1959. Based in Dublin since 1959, where has made nearly 30 theatrical documentary films. Produces and directs for Louis Marcus Documentary Film Production of Dublin and Louis Marcus Films Ltd. of London. In 1964 appt. by Irish govt. as bd. mem. of Dublin's Abbey Theatre. In 1972 appt. by govt. as mem. of Cultural Relations Comm. of Dept. of Foreign Affairs. Elected mem. of Academy of M.P. Arts & Sciences (short subject branch) 1974.
PICTURES: Fleadh Cheoil, Horse Laughs, Woes of Golf, Children at Work, Conquest of Light.
AUTHOR: The Irish Film Industry (1968).

MARENSTEIN, HAROLD: exec. b. New York, NY, Nov. 30, 1916. e. City Coll. of New York, 1937. Shipping, picture checking service, Warner Bros., 1935–45; Booking, Loew's Inc., 1945–48; Booking, contracts, Selznick Rel. Org., 1948–51; contracts, Paramount, 1951–52; asst. sls. gr., International Rel. Org., 1952; asst. sls. mgr., Janus Films, 1961–64; sls. exec., Rizzoli Films, 1965; 1967, nat'l. sales dir., Continental Dist.; gen. sales mgr., Cinemation Industries, 1968. v.p.-sales, dir., Cinemation Industries, 1971; 1976, gen. sls. mgr., General National Films; 1980, gen. sls. mgr., Lima Productions. Now retired.

MARGOLIN, JANET: Actress. b. New York, NY, July 25, 1943. e. N.Y.H.S. of Performing Arts. While playing in Bdwy. show, Daughter of Silence (Theatre World Award), discovered by dir. Frank Perry and hired for lead in his David and Lisa.
PICTURES: David and Lisa (debut, 1963), The Greatest Story Ever Told, Bus Riley's Back in Town, Morituri, Nevada Smith, The Eavesdropper (Argentina), Enter Laughing, Buona Sera Mrs. Campbell, Take the Money and Run, Your Three Minutes Are Up, Annie Hall, Last Embrace, Distant Thunder, Ghostbusters II.
TELEVISION: Series: Lanigan's Rabbi. Movies: Planet Earth, Pray for the Wildcats, The Last Child, Lanigan's Rabbi, The Triangle Factory Fire Scandal, Plutonium Incident, Murder in Peyton Place, Murder C.O.D.

MARGOLIN, STUART: Actor, Director, Writer. b. Davenport, IA, Jan. 31, 1940. Wrote play Sad Choices which was produced Off-Bdwy when he was only 20.
TELEVISION: Series: Occasional Wife, Love American Style, Nichols, The Rockford Files (Emmy Awards, 1979, 1980), Bret Maverick, Mr. Smith. Guest: Hey Landlord, He & She, The Monkees, M*A*S*H, Gunsmoke, The Mary Tyler Moore Show (also dir.), Rhoda, Magnum P.I., Hill Street Blues. Movies: The Intruders, The Ballad of Andy Crocker (writer, associate prod. only), A Summer Without Boys (voice), The Rockford Files (pilot), The California Kid, This is the West That Was, Lanigan's Rabbi, Perilous Voyage, A Killer in the Family, Three of a Kind, To Grandmother's House We Go. Director: Suddenly Love, A Shining Season, The Long Summer of George Adams.
PICTURES: The Gamblers, Kelly's Heroes, Limbo, Death Wish, The Big Bus, Futureworld, Days of Heaven, S.O.B.,

Class, Running Hot, A Fine Mess, Paramedics (dir. only), Iron Eagle II, Bye Bye Blues, Guilty By Suspicion.

MARGULIES, STAN: Producer. b. New York, NY, Dec. 14, 1920. e. De Witt Clinton H.S., NYU, B.S., June, 1940. Army Air Force, May, 1942; pub. rels. Air Force and the Infantry, wrote service magazines, newspapers including Yank; spec. feature writer & asst. Sunday editor, Salt Lake City Tribune; publicist, RKO Studios, Hollywood, March, 1947; continued publicity work at CBS-Radio, 20th Century-Fox, Walt Disney Productions. Bryna Films, 1955; became vice-pres., 1958; also served exec. prod., TV series, Tales of the Vikings; prod. aide. Spartacus.
PICTURES: 40 Pounds of Trouble, Those Magnificent Men in Their Flying Machines, Don't Just Stand There, The Pink Jungle, If It's Tuesday This Must Be Belgium, I Love My Wife, Willy Wonka and the Chocolate Factory, One Is a Lonely Number, Visions of Eight.
TELEVISION: Movies: The 500 Pound Jerk, She Lives, The Morning After, Unwed Father, Men of the Dragon, I Will Fight No More Forever, Roots (Emmy Award), Roots: The Next Generations (Emmy Award), Moviola, Agatha Christie's Murder Is Easy, The Thorn Birds, Agatha Christie's A Caribbean Mystery, A Killer in the Family, Sparkling Cyanide, The Mystic Warrior, A Bunny's Tale, Out on a Limb, Broken Angel, Crossing to Freedom, Separate But Equal (Emmy Award).

MARILL, ALVIN H.: Executive Editor. b. Brockton, MA, Jan. 10, 1934. e. Boston U., 1955. Director music programming, writer/prod., WNAC, Boston 1961–65; dir. music prog., WRFM, NY 1966–67; publicity writer, RCA Records 1967–72; sr. writer/editor, RCA Direct Marketing 1972–80; partner, TLK Direct Marketing 1977–80; mgr., A & R Administration, RCA Direct Marketing 1980–83; Exec. editor, CBS TV (1984–88); editor, Carol Publ. Group (1988–); Television editor, Films in Review 1973–84; Author: Samuel Goldwyn Presents; Robert Mitchum on the Screen; The Films of Anthony Quinn; The Films of Sidney Poitier; Katharine Hepburn; A Pictorial Study; Boris Karloff—A Pictorial Biography; Errol Flynn—A Pictorial Biography; The Complete Films of Edward G. Robinson, More Theatre: Stage to Screen to Television, Movies Made for Television 1984–89. Co-author: The Films of Tyrone Power. Editor: Moe Howard & The 3 Stooges. Assoc. editor: Leonard Maltin's TV Movies; Writer/researcher: The Great Singers (record/tape collections). Jury member: 1983 Locarno Film Fest.

MARIN, RICHARD (CHEECH): Actor, Writer. b. Los Angeles, CA, July 13, 1946. e. California State U, B.S. Teamed with Tommy Chong in improvisational group, City Works (Vancouver). Their comedy recordings include Sleeping Beauty, Cheech and Chong Big Bama, Los Cochinos, The Wedding Album (Grammy Award), Get Out of My Room.
PICTURES: Up in Smoke (also co-s.p.), Cheech and Chong's Next Movie (also co-s.p.), Cheech and Chong's Nice Dreams (also co-s.p.), Things Are Tough All Over (also co-s.p.), It Came from Hollywood, Still Smokin' (also co-s.p.), Yellowbeard, Cheech and Chong's The Corsican Brothers (also co-s.p.), After Hours, Echo Park, Born in East L.A. (also s.p., dir.), Fatal Beauty, Oliver & Company (voice), Troop Beverly Hills, Ghostbusters II, Rude Awakening, Far Out Man, The Shrimp on the Barbie, FernGully (voice).
TELEVISION: Series: The Golden Palace. Specials: Get Out of My Room (also dir., songs), Charlie Barnett—Terms of Enrollment.

MARK, LAURENCE M.: Producer, Executive. b. New York, NY. e. Wesleyan U., B.A.; & NYU, M.A. Started career as trainee and publicist for United Artists; also asst. to producer on Lenny, Smile, etc. Joined Paramount Pictures as mktg./prod. liaison dir. and then exec. dir., pub. for m.p. division in New York. Named v.p., prod./mktg. at Paramount Studio; 1980, v.p., west coast mktg.; 1982 promoted to post as v.p., prod. 1984 (projects incl. Trading Places, Terms of Endearment, Lady Jane); joined 20th Century-Fox as exec. v.p., prod. (projects incl. The Fly, Broadcast News); 1986, established Laurence Mark Productions at Fox; 1989 moved headquarters to Walt Disney Studios.
PICTURES: Black Widow (exec. prod.), Working Girl (exec. prod.), My Stepmother is an Alien (exec. prod.), Cookie (prod.), Mr. Destiny (exec. prod.), True Colors (prod.), One Good Cop (prod.), The Adventures of Huck Finn (prod.), Gunmen (prod.).
TELEVISION: Sweet Bird of Youth (exec. prod.).
THEATRE: Brooklyn Laundry (L.A.).

MARKHAM, MONTE: Actor. b. Manatee, FL, June 21, 1938. e. U. of Georgia. Military service in Coast Guard after which joined resident theatre co. at Stephens College, MO, where also taught acting. Joined Actor's Workshop Theatre, San Francisco, for three years. Made TV debut in Mission: Impossible episode. June, 1992 formed Perpetual Motion Films with Adam Friedman.
PICTURES: Hour of the Gun, Guns of the Magnificent Seven, One Is a Lonely Number, Midway, Airport '77, Ginger

in the Morning, Off the Wall, Jake Speed, Hot Pursuit, Defense Play (also dir.), Neon City (also dir.).
TELEVISION: *Series*: The Second Hundred Years, Mr. Deeds Goes to Town, The New Perry Mason, Dallas, Rituals, Baywatch (also dir. episodes). *Movies*: Death Takes a Holiday, The Astronaut, Visions, Hustling, Ellery Queen, Relentless, Drop-Out Father, Hotline, Baywatch: Panic at Malibu Pier. *Host-narrator-prod.-dir.*: Air Combat, Combat at Sea.
BROADWAY: Irene (Theatre World Award), Same Time Next Year.

MARKLE, PETER: Director.
PICTURES: The Personals (also photog.), Hot Dog . . . The Movie, Youngblood, Bat-21.
TELEVISION: *Movies*: Desperate, Nightbreaker, Breaking Point, El Diablo, Through the Eyes of a Killer.

MARKOWITZ, ROBERT: Director. Irvington, NJ, b. Feb. 7, 1935. e. Boston Univ. Mostly on TV before theatrical debut with Voices, 1979.
TELEVISION: *Movies*: Children of the Night, Phantom of the Opera, The Deadliest Season, The Storyteller, Kojak: The Belarus File, My Mother's Secret Life, Pray TV, A Long Way Home, Alex: The Life of a Child, Adam: His Song Continues, The Wall, A Cry for Help: The Tracey Thurman Story, Too Young to Die, Decoration Day, Love Lies and Murder, Afterburn.

MARKS, ALFRED: O.B.E. Actor-Comedian. b. London, 1921. TV, own series, Alfred Marks Time with wife, comedienne Paddie O'Neil.
PICTURES: Desert Mice, There Was a Crooked Man, Weekend with Lulu, The Frightened City, She'll Have to Go, Scream and Scream Again, Our Miss Fred, Valentino, Sleeps Six.
TELEVISION: Blanding's Castle, Hobson's Choice, Paris 1900, The Memorandum.

MARKS, ARTHUR: Producer, Director, Writer, Film Executive. b. Los Angeles, CA, Aug. 2, 1927. At 19 began work at MGM Studios as production messenger. Became asst. dir. in 1950, youngest dir. member of Directors Guild of Amer., 1957. President and board member of Arthur Prod., Inc.
PICTURES: Togetherness (prod., dir., s.p.), Class of '74 (dir., s.p.), Bonnie's Kids (dir., s.p.), Roommates (dir., s.p.), A Detroit 9000 (prod., dir.), The Centerfold Girls (prod., dir.), A Woman For All Men (dir.), Wonder Woman (exec. prod.), The Candy Snatchers (exec. prod.), Bucktown (dir.), Friday Foster (prod., dir.), J.D.'s Revenge (prod., dir.), Monkey Hustle (prod., dir.). Writer: Empress of the China Seas, Gold Stars, Mean Intentions, Hot Times, Starfire.
TELEVISION: Prod. of Perry Mason series, 1961–66; dir. of over 100 Perry Mason episodes; writer-dir. of numerous TV shows including I Spy, Mannix, Starsky & Hutch, Dukes of Hazzard, Young Daniel Boone, My Friend Tony.

MARKS, RICHARD E.: Executive. e. UCLA; UCLA Sch. of Law. 1978–82, v.p., legal & business affairs for Ziegler/Diskant Literary Agency. Joined Paramount Pictures 1984 as sr. atty. for Network TV Div., as project atty. for Family Ties, Cheers, etc. 1985, named sr. atty. for M.P. Group for The Golden Child, Beverly Hills Cop II, etc.; 1987 joined Weintraub Entertainment Group as v.p. business affairs, m.p. div. 1990, counsel for Disney projects such as The Rocketeer, Beauty and the Beast. 1991, joined Media Home Entertainment as sr. v.p. in charge of all business and legal affairs.

MARS, KENNETH: Actor. b. Chicago, IL, 1936.
TELEVISION: *Series*: He & She, The Don Knotts Show, Sha Na Na, The Carol Burnett Show (1979). *Guest*: The Facts of Life. *Movies*: Second Chance, Guess Who's Sleeping in My Bed?, Someone I Touched, The New Original Wonder Woman, Before and After, The Rules of Marriage, Get Smart Again.
PICTURES: The Producers, Butch Cassidy and the Sundance Kid, Desperate Characters, What's Up Doc?, The Parallax View, Young Frankenstein, Night Moves, The Apple Dumpling Gang Rides Again, Full Moon High, Yellowbeard, Protocol, Prince Jack, Fletch, Radio Days, For Keeps?, Illegally Yours, Rented Lips, Police Academy 6: City Under Siege, The Little Mermaid (voice), Shadows and Fog.

MARSH, JEAN: Actress, Writer. b. London, Eng., July 1, 1934. NY stage debut Much Ado About Nothing, 1959. As a child appeared in films: Tales of Hoffman; as principal dancer in Where's Charley. Co-creator, co-author and starred as Rose, Upstairs, Downstairs.
THEATER: *Broadway*: Travesties, The Importance of Being Earnest, Too True to Be Good, My Fat Friend, Whose Life Is It Anyway?, Blithe Spirit.
PICTURES: Cleopatra, The Limbo Line, Frenzy, Dark Places, The Eagle Has Landed, The Changeling, Return to Oz, Willow.
TELEVISION: Upstairs Downstairs (Emmy Award, 1975), Nine to Five, The Grover Monster, A State Dinner with Queen Elizabeth II, Mad About the Boy: Noel Coward—A Celebra-

tion, Habeas Corpus, Uncle Vanya, Twelfth Night, Pygmalion, On the Rocks Theatre, The Corsican Brothers, Master of the Game, Danny, the Champion of the World, Act of Will, A Connecticut Yankee in King Arthur's Court.

MARSHALL, ALAN: Producer. b. London, Eng., Aug. 12, 1938. Co-founder Alan Parker Film Company, 1970. Formerly film editor. Received Michael Balcon Award, British Acad., Outstanding Contribution to Cinema, 1985.
PICTURES: Bugsy Malone, Midnight Express, Fame, Shoot the Moon, Pink Floyd: The Wall, Another Country (Cannes Film Fest, best artistic contribution award, 1984), Birdy (Special Jury Award, Cannes Film Fest., 1985), Angel Heart, Homeboy, Jacob's Ladder, Basic Instinct, Cliffhanger.
TELEVISION: No Hard Feelings, Our Cissy, Footsteps.

MARSHALL, E. G.: Actor. r.n. Everett Marshall. b. Minnesota, June 18, 1910. Acting debut with Oxford Players, 1933. Numerous TV appearances on all networks.
BROADWAY: Jason, Jacobowsky and the Colonel, Skin of Our Teeth, Iceman Cometh, Woman Bites Dog, The Survivors, The Gambler, The Crucible, The Little Foxes.
PICTURES: House on 92nd Street (debut, 1945), 13 Rue Madeleine, Call Northside 77, The Caine Mutiny, Pushover, Bamboo Prison, Broken Lance, The Silver Chalice, The Left Hand of God, The Scarlet Hour, The Mountain, 12 Angry Men, The Bachelor Party, Man on Fire, The Buccaneer, The Journey, Compulsion, Cash McCall, Town Without Pity, The Chase, The Bridge at Remagen, Tora Tora Tora, The Pursuit of Happiness, Billy Jack Goes to Washington, Interiors, Superman II, Creepshow, Power, My Chauffeur, La Gran Fiesta, National Lampoon's Christmas Vacation, Two Evil Eyes (The Black Cat), Consenting Adults.
TELEVISION: *Series*: The Defenders (2 Emmy Awards), The Bold Ones (The New Doctors). *Movies*: Collision Course, The Winter of Our Discontent, Under Siege, At Mother's Request, Emma, Queen of the South Seas, The Hijacking of the Achille Lauro, Ironclads, Stephen King's The Tommyknockers.

MARSHALL, FRANK: Producer, Director. Raised in Newport Beach, CA. Worked on first feature film in 1967 while still a student at UCLA. Protege of Peter Bogdanovich, working on his production crew and serving as asst. on Targets, location manager The Last Picture Show, What's Up Doc?, assoc. prod. on Paper Moon, Daisy Miller, Nickelodeon, etc. Line producer on Orson Welles' The Other Side of the Wind (unreleased) and Martin Scorsese's The Last Waltz. Worked with Walter Hill on The Driver (assoc. prod.) and The Warriors (exec. prod.). Began collaboration with Steven Spielberg as prod. for Raiders of the Lost Ark.
PICTURES: Raiders of the Lost Ark (prod.), Poltergeist (prod.), E.T.: The Extra-Terrestrial (prod. supvr.). *Exec. Producer*: Twilight Zone—The Movie, Indiana Jones and the Temple of Doom, Fandango, Gremlins, The Goonies, Back to the Future (also 2nd unit dir.), The Color Purple (prod.), Young Sherlock Holmes, An American Tail, Innerspace, The Money Pit (prod.), Empire of the Sun (prod.), Who Framed Roger Rabbit (prod., 2nd unit dir.), The Land Before Time, Indiana Jones and the Last Crusade, Dad, Back to the Future Part II, Always (prod.), Joe Versus the Volcano, Back to the Future Part III, Gremlins II, Arachnophobia (also dir.), Cape Fear, An American Tail: Fievel Goes West, Hook (co-prod.), Noises Off (prod.), Alive (also dir.), Swing Kids, A Far Off Place, We're Back.
TELEVISION: Amazing Stories (series exec. prod.), Roger Rabbit and the Secrets of Toontown (exec. prod.), Alive: The Miracle of the Andes (exec. prod.).

MARSHALL, GARRY: Producer, Director, Writer. b. New York, NY, Nov. 13, 1934. Sister is director-actress Penny Marshall. e. Northwestern U. Copy boy and reporter for N.Y. Daily News while writing comedy material for Phil Foster, Joey Bishop. Was drummer in his own jazz band and successful stand-up comedian and playwright. Turned Neil Simon's play The Odd Couple into long running TV series (1970). Partner with Jerry Belson many years. Wrote Bdwy play, The Roost (with Belson, 1980), also Wrong Turn at Lungfish (with Lowell Ganz, 1992; also dir., actor).
PICTURES: *Writer-Producer*: How Sweet It Is, The Grasshopper. *Director*: Young Doctors in Love (also exec. prod.), The Flamingo Kid (also s.p.), Nothing in Common, Overboard, Beaches, Pretty Woman, Frankie and Johnny. *Actor*: Psych-Out, Lost in America, Soapdish, A League of Their Own, Hocus Pocus.
TELEVISION: Writer for Jack Paar Show, Joey Bishop Show, Danny Thomas Show, Lucy, Dick Van Dyke Show, I Spy. *Dir.-writer*: Hey Landlord, The Odd Couple, The Little People (Brian Keith Show). *Creator and exec. prod.*: Happy Days, Laverne and Shirley, Blansky's Beauties, Who's Watching the Kids? Mork and Mindy, Angie, Joanie Loves Chachi. *Movie*: Evil Roy Slade (co-prod., co-writer).

MARSHALL, PENNY: Actress, Director. b. New York, NY, Oct. 15, 1943. Father: industrial filmmaker and Laverne and Shirley prod., Tony Marscharelli. Brother is prod.-dir. Garry Marshall.

Daughter is actress Tracy Reiner. Dropped out of U. of New Mexico to teach dancing. Acted in summer stock and competed on The Original Amateur Hour before going to Hollywood to make TV debut in The Danny Thomas Hour (1967–68). Debut as theatrical director 1986: Jumpin' Jack Flash.
PICTURES: Actress: How Sweet It Is, The Savage Seven, The Grasshopper, 1941, Movers and Shakers, The Hard Way, Hocus Pocus. Director: Jumpin' Jack Flash, Big, Awakenings, A League of Their Own. Exec. Prod.: Calendar Girl.
TELEVISION: Series: The Bob Newhart Show, The Odd Couple, Friends and Lovers, Laverne and Shirley. Guest: Danny Thomas Hour, The Super, Happy Days, Saturday Night Live, Comedy Zone, Chico and the Man. Movies: The Feminist and the Fuzz, Evil Roy Slade, The Couple Takes a Wife, The Crooked Hearts, Love Thy Neighbor, Let's Switch, More Than Friends, Challenge of a Lifetime. Specials: Lily for President. Director: Laverne and Shirley, Working Shifts, Tracey Ullman Show, A League of Their Own.

MARSHALL, PETER: Actor, TV Show Host. r.n. Pierre La Cock. b. Clarksburg, WV, March 30. Brother of actress Joanne Dru. Began career as NBC page in N.Y. Teamed with the late Tommy Noonan in comedy act for nightclubs, guesting on Ed Sullivan Show and other variety shows. In 1950 made Las Vegas stage debut and since has been headliner there and in Reno and Lake Tahoe. New York stage, in Bdwy musical Skyscraper. On London stage in H.M.S. Pinafore; Bye, Bye Birdie. In La Cage aux Folles (national company and Bdwy), 42nd St. (Atlantic City), Rumors (natl. co.).
PICTURES: The Rookie, Swingin' Along, Ensign Pulver, The Cavern, Americathon, Annie.
TELEVISION: Host: Two of the Most (local N.Y. show), The Hollywood Squares, NBC Action Playhouse, The Peter Marshall Variety Show, Mrs. America Pagent, Mrs. World; many guest appearances.

MARSHALL, ZENA: Actress. b. Kenya, Africa, 1926. e. France, finishing school in Ascot, Eng., RADA. Made her stage debut in repertory. Many TV appearance U.S. and England including Bob Hope show, Harpers W.I., Ghost Squad.
PICTURES: Caesar and Cleopatra (debut, 1945), Good Time Girl, Miranda, Sleeping Car to Trieste, Marry Me, Dark Interval, Blind Man's Bluff, Love's a Luxury, Deadly Nightshade, My Wife's Family, Bermuda Affair, Let's Be Happy, Crosstrap, Dr. No, The Guilty Party, Those Magnificent Men in Their Flying Machines, The Terrornauts.
TELEVISION: International Detective, Invisible Man, Dial 999, Danger Man, Sir Francis Drake, Man of the World, Human Jungle, Sentimental Agent, Court Martial.

MARTEL, GENE: Producer, director. b. New York, NY, June 19, 1906. e. City Coll. of New York , U. of Alabama, Sorbonne, Paris. Newspaperman, New York and Birmingham, AL; dancer, actor, choreographer, director Broadway; prod. dir., many documentaries; films for State Dept., others; dir. for Paramount Pictures. Joined Princess Pictures 1952 to make films in Europe; formed own co., Martel Productions Inc., 1956.
PICTURES: Check-mate, Double-barrelled Miracle, The Lie, Double Profile, Sergeant and the Spy, Black Forest, Eight Witnesses, Fire One, Phantom Caravan, Doorway to Suspicion, Diplomatic Passport, Immediate Disaster.

MARTENS, RALPH R.: Executive b. New York, NY, Apr. 12, 1943. e. State U. of New York at Albany. USMC-USMCR 1962–present, 1970–73 Tampax Inc. 1973–79 Pannell Kerr Forster and Co., CPA's 1979–84, asst. treas. Motion Picture Association of America, MPEAA, AMPECA, AFRAM FILMS, 1984 Treas., MPAA, MPEAA, AMPECA and AFRAM. In 1988, named vice president. Member ASAE, IMA, AMA.

MARTIN, DEAN: Actor, Singer. r.n. Dino Crocetti. b. Steubenville, OH, June 7, 1917. e. Steubenville H.S. Was amateur prizefighter; worked at odd jobs, mill hand, gasoline attendant, prior to acting career. Joined comedian Jerry Lewis at 500 Club, Atlantic City, NJ, as straight man-singer, 1946; as team played many theatres, night clubs until 1956. Voted (with Jerry Lewis) one of the top ten Money-Making Stars in Motion Picture Herald-Fame poll, 1951, 1953–55; Number One, 1952.
PICTURES: My Friend Irma (debut, 1949), My Friend Irma Goes West, At War with the Army, That's My Boy, Sailor Beware, Jumping Jacks, The Stooge, The Caddy, Road to Bali (cameo), Scared Stiff, Money from Home, Living It Up, Three Ring Circus, You're Never Too Young, Artists and Models, Pardners, Hollywood or Bust, 10,000 Bedrooms, The Young Lions, Some Came Running, Rio Bravo, Career, Who Was That Lady?, Bells Are Ringing, Ocean's 11, Pepe, All in a Night's Work, Ada, The Road to Hong Kong (cameo), Sergeants 3, Who's Got the Action?, Toys in the Attic, Come Blow Your Horn (cameo), Who's Been Sleeping in My Bed, Four for Texas, What a Way to Go!, Robin and the Seven Hoods, Kiss Me Stupid, The Sons of Katie Elder, Marriage on the Rocks, The Silencers, Texas Across the River, Murderers' Row, The Ambushers, Rough Night in Jericho, Bandolero, Five Card Stud, How to Save a Marriage, The Wrecking

Crew, Airport, Something Big, Showdown, Mr. Ricco, The Cannonball Run, Cannonball Run II.
TELEVISION: Series: The Colgate Comedy Hour, Dean Martin Show (1965–74), Half Nelson. Guest: Club Oasis, Danny Thomas Show, Rawhide, Lucy Show, Carol Burnett, Sheriff Lobo, many others.

MARTIN, DEWEY: Actor. b. Katemcy, TX, Dec. 8, 1923. e. U. of Georgia. U.S. Navy, W.W.II; actor, little theatres & stock; film debut in Knock on Any Door (1949).
PICTURES: Kansas Raiders, The Thing, Big Sky, Tennessee Champ, Prisoner of War, Men of the Fighting Lady, Land of the Pharaohs, Desperate Hours, Proud and Profane, 10,000 Bedrooms, Battle Ground, The Longest Day, Savage Sam, Seven Alone.
TELEVISION: Live: G.E. Theatre, U.S. Steel, Playhouse 90, Playwrights 56, Daniel Boone (mini-series), Doc Holliday (series), Wheeler and Murdoch, Outer Limits, Twilight Zone.

MARTIN, EDWIN DENNIS: Executive. b. Columbus, GA, Jan. 30, 1920. e. U. of Georgia, B.S., 1940. Past pres., Martin Theatre Cos.; past pres. TOA, International, past pres., Variety. Retired.

MARTIN, MILLICENT: Actress, Singer. b. Romford, Eng., June 8, 1934. Toured U.S. in The Boy Friend, 1954–57.
STAGE: Expresso Bongo, The Crooked Mile, Our Man Crichton, Tonight at 8:30, The Beggar's Opera, Puss 'n Boots, Aladdin, Peter Pan, The Card, Absurd Person Singular, Aladdin, Side by Side by Sondheim, King of Hearts, Move Over Mrs. Markham, Noises Off, One Into Two, 42nd Street (N.Y. & L.A.), The Cemetery Club, Shirley Valentine, The Boyfriend, Noel, Follies.
TELEVISION: Series: The Picadilly Palace, From a Bird's Eye View, Mainly Millicent, Millie, Dowtown. Also: Harry Moorings, Kiss Me Kate, London Palladium Color Show, Tom Jones, Englebert Humperdinck show, That Was the Week That Was, LA Law, Max Headroom, Newhart, Murphy Brown.
PICTURES: The Horsemaster, The Girl on the Boat, Nothing But the Best, Those Magnificent Men in Their Flying Machines, Alfie, Stop the World I Want To Get Off, Invasion Quartet.

MARTIN, PAMELA SUE: Actress. b. Westport, CT, Jan. 15, 1953. Did modelling and TV commercials before entering films.
PICTURES: To Find a Man, The Poseidon Adventure, Buster and Billie, Our Time, The Lady in Red, Torchlight (also assoc. prod. & s.p.), Flicks, A Cry in the Wild.
TELEVISION: Series: Nancy Drew Mysteries, Hardy Boys Mysteries, Dynasty, The Star Games (host). Movies: The Girls of Huntington House, The Gun and the Pulpit, Human Feelings, Bay Coven.

MARTIN, STEVE: Actor, Writer. b. Waco, TX, Aug. 14, 1945. e. Long Beach Col., UCLA. Grew up in Southern California. Worked at Disneyland, teaching himself juggling, magic and the banjo. Became writer for various TV comedy shows, incl. Smothers Brothers Comedy Hour (Emmy Award for writing, 1968–9), Glen Campbell Show, Sonny & Cher. Wrote and starred in Acad. Award nominated short The Absent-Minded Waiter. Author: Cruel Shoes (1980). Albums: Let's Get Small (Grammy Award, 1977), A Wild and Crazy Guy (Grammy Award, 1978), Comedy is Not Pretty, The Steve Martin Brothers. Gold Record for single King Tut. Off-Bdwy. debut 1988 in Waiting for Godot (with Robin Williams).
PICTURES: Sgt. Pepper's Lonely Hearts Club Band (debut, 1978), The Kids Are Alright, The Muppet Movie, The Jerk (also co-s.p.), Pennies From Heaven, Dead Men Don't Wear Plaid (also co-s.p.), The Man With Two Brains (also co-s.p.), The Lonely Guy, All of Me (NY Film Critics & Natl. Board of Review Awards for Best Actor, 1984), Movers and Shakers, Three Amigos (also co-s.p., exec. prod.), Little Shop of Horrors, Roxanne (also s.p., exec. prod.; Natl. Society of Film Critics & L.A. Film Critics Awards for Best Actor, WGA Award for Best Adapted Screenplay, 1987), Planes Trains & Automobiles, Dirty Rotten Scoundrels, Parenthood, My Blue Heaven, L.A. Story (also s.p., co-exec. prod.), Father of the Bride, Grand Canyon, Housesitter, Leap of Faith.
TELEVISION: Series: Andy Williams Presents Ray Stevens, The Ken Berry "WOW" Show, Half the George Kirby Comedy Hour, The Sonny and Cher Comedy Hour, The Smothers Brothers Show (1975), The Johnny Cash Show. Guest: The Tonight Show, Cher, The Carol Burnett Show, Saturday Night Live, The Muppet Show, Steve Allen Comedy Hour. Specials: HBO On Location: Steve Martin, Steve Martin—A Wild and Crazy Guy, Comedy is Not Pretty, Steve Martin's Best Show Ever, Smothers Brothers Comedy Hour 20th Reunion. Producer: Domestic Life (series). Pilot: Leo & Liz in Beverly Hills (writer, creator, co-prod., dir.).Movies: The Jerk Too (exec. prod. only), And the Band Played On.

MARTIN, TONY: Singer, Musician, Actor. b. Oakland, CA, Dec. 25, 1913. r.n. Alvin Morris. e. Oakland H.S., St. Mary's Coll. m. Cyd Charisse, actress-dancer. Sang, played saxophone & clarinet in high school band, engaged by nearby theatres for vaudeville; with Five Red Peppers, jazz group at 14 yrs.; two yrs. later with band, Palace Hotel, San Francisco; radio debut Walter Winchell program, 1932; joined Tom Gerund's band, World's Fair Chicago, 1933; played night clubs. First starring radio show, Tune Up Time (singer & emcee); on Burns and Allen program; own show for Texaco, Carnation Contented Hour.

RECORDINGS: Begin the Beguine, Intermezzo, The Last Time I Saw Paris, I'll See You in My Dreams, Domino, September Song, For Every Man There's a Woman.

PICTURES: Banjo on My Knee, Sing Baby Sing, Follow The Fleet, You Can't Have Everything, Life Begins in College, Ali Baba Goes To Town, Sally Irene and Mary, Knetucky Moonshine, Music in My Heart, Ziegfeld Girl, The Big Store, Till The Clouds Roll By, Cabash, Two Tickets to Broadway, Here Come the Girls, Easy to Love, Deep in My Heart, Hit the Deck, Quincannon Frontier Scout, Let's Be Happy, Dear Mr. Wonderful.

MASEFIELD, JOSEPH R.: Executive, Producer, Director, Writer. b. New York, NY, June 20, 1933. e. American Acad. of Dramatic Arts, 1950. Writer-performer, club work (as Steve Parker). Later, actor in stock; formed EEF Film Productions, 1956; prod. A Story Like Two (short), A City Eats (doc.). In m.p. as unit mgr., asst. dir. and prod. mgr. Later writer and film editor: Montage (Time-Life); Ages of Man (IBM); Festival of Two Worlds (Bell Telephone Hour) and special, The New Face of Israel. Asst. dir., prod. mgr., Mitgebracht Aus New York (German TV), The Devils Doubloon, (feature); Writer-director, Citizen Smith, feature documentary. Co-director and assoc. prod. Hear My Song, (Cavalier Films), 1969 producer The Spy. 1969, vice pres. in charge of prod. PCI, Inc. Pub. rel. director, The Max Steiner Music Society; pres., Joseph R. Masefield & Associates. In 1974, formed Majer Prods. with Steve Jerro.

PICTURES: A New Life, The Vanquished, Trio, Living Planet, The Burning Man.

MASINA, GIULIETTA: Actress. b. Giorgio di Piano, Italy, Feb. 22, 1921. m. director Federico Fellini. e. U. of Rome. Was a school teacher before acting on stage and on radio in Rome. Met Fellini when he asked her to audition for radio soap opera, 1942. Film debut: Rossallini's Paisan, 1946.

PICTURES: Without Pity, Variety Lights, The White Sheik, Behind Closed Shutters, The Greatest Love, La Strada, Forbidden Women, The Swindlers, Nights of Cabiria, Fortunella, Juliet of the Spirits, Non Stuzzicate la Zanazara, The Madwoman of Chaillot, Ginger and Fred.

MASLANSKY, PAUL: Producer. b. New York, NY, Nov. 23, 1933. e. Washington and Lee U., 1954. Moved to Europe performing as jazz musician in Paris, 1959–60. Entered film business with documentary Letter from Paris. Asst. to prods. Charles Shneer and Irving Allan in England, Italy and Yugoslavia, 1961–2. In Charge of physical prod. in Europe for UA, 1965–7.

PICTURES: Castle of the Living Dead, Revenge of the Blood Beast, Sister of Satan, Eyewitness, Big Truck, Poor Claire, Deathline, Sugar Hill (also dir.), Race With the Devil, Hard Times, The Blue Bird, Circle of Iron, Damnation Alley (co-prod.), When You Comin' Back Red Ryder (co-prod.), Hot Stuff, The Villain, Scavenger Hunt, The Salamander, Ruckus, Love Child, Police Academy, Police Academy 2: Their First Assignment, Return to Oz, Police Academy 3: Back in Training, Police Academy 4: Citizens on Patrol, Police Academy 5: Assignment Miami Beach, For Better or Worse (exec. prod.), Police Academy 6: City Under Siege (prod.), Ski Patrol (exec. prod.), Honeymoon Academy (exec. prod.). The Russia House (prod.), Cop and a Half (prod.).

TELEVISION: Movie: The Gun and the Pulpit. Mini-Series: King.

MASON, JACKIE: Comedian, Actor. b. Sheboygan, WI June 9, 1934. e. City College. Was a rabbi before becoming stand-up comedian. Records include The World According to Me! Has lectureship in his name at Oxford Univ. in England.

THEATER: Enter Solly Gold (1965), A Teaspoon Every Four Hours (Amer. National Theatre & Academy Theatre), Sex-a-Poppin (revue, prod. only), The World According to Me! (one-man show, special Tony Award, 1987), Jackie Mason: Brand New.

PICTURES: Operation Delilah (debut, 1966), The Stoolie (also prod.), The Jerk, History of the World Part I, Caddyshack II.

TELEVISION: Guest: Steve Allen, Ed Sullivan, Jack Paar, Garry Moore, Perry Como and Merv Griffin Shows. Johnny Carson, Arsenio Hall, Evening at the Improv, Late Night with David Letterman. Series: Chicken Soup, Jackie Mason (synd.). Specials: Jack Paar is Alive and Well!, The World According to Me! (ACE Award), Jackie Mason on Broadway (Emmy Award for Writing).

MASON, JOHN DUDLEY: Executive. b. Ashland, KY, Oct 29, 1949. e. Amherst Coll., B.A., cum laude, 1971; Claremont Graduate Sch. and University Center, M.A., 1973; Amos Tuck Sch. of Business Administration, Dartmouth Coll., M.B.A.,

1978. Program officer, National Endowment for the Humanities, 1972–76; analyst (1978–79), asst. mgr. (1979–80), mgr. (1980) strategic planning, Consolidated Rail Corp.; Consultant, Frito-Lay, Division, PepsiCo (1980–82); mgr, corporate planning, The Dun & Bradstreet Corp. (1982–86); finance director, anti-piracy (1986–90), v.p. Finance, anti-piracy (1990–92), Motion Picture Association of America, Inc. Chmn, New Century Artists' Mgmt., 1990-present. Chmn., Finance Comm. and mem., bd. of dir. Association de Gestion Int'l. Collective des Oeuvres Audiovisuelles (AGICOA) 1987–88. Director, Instituto Venezolano de Representacion Cinematografica (INVERECI), Caracas, Venezuela (1988–92). Director: Foundation for the Protection of Film & Video Works (FVWP), Taipei, Taiwan (1987–92). Dir. sec. Korean Federation Against Copyright Theft, 1990–92; Dir., Japan & Intl. M.P. Copyright Assn., Tokyo, 1990–92; Trustee and Treasurer, Design Industries Foundation for AIDS, 1990–present.

MASON, KENNETH M.: Executive. b. Rochester, NY; Sept. 21, 1917. e. Washington and Jefferson Coll. (BA, 1938); U. of Rochester, graduate work; Dr. of Laws (H), Washington & Jefferson Coll., 1989. Began career with Eastman Kodak Co. in Kodak Park cine processing dept. in 1935; transferred following year to film dev. dept., Kodak Research Lab. Returned to coll. in 1938, 1939 returned to Kodak same dept. Later joined film planning dept., remaining there until entering U.S. Navy in 1943. Returned to Kodak in 1946 as staff engineer in Kodak Office motion picture film dept. In 1950 appt. mgr. of Midwest Division, of M.P. Film Dept.; became gen. mgr., Midwest Division, m.p. products sales dept. in 1963; named sls. mgr. of NYC region in 1965; appt. regional sls. mgr., Pacific Southern Region, Hollywood, in 1970; 1974 appt. mgr., product programs and research, Motion Picture and Audiovisual Markets Division, Kodak Office; 1974 named gen. mgr. of that division. Elected asst. v.p. of co. on March 28, 1974, v.p., Dec. 11, 1978. Retired Oct. 1, 1982. Former chmn., Inter-Society Committee for the Enhancement of Theatrical Presentation.

MEMBER: Trustee emeritus, Board of Trustees of Washington and Jefferson Coll. (and former chmn); past pres. of Society of Motion Picture & Television Engineers and honorary member; honorary fellow of British Kinematograph Sound & Television Society; mem. of University Film & Video Assn., Motion Picture Academy, American Society of Cinematographers, Variety Club. Board of dir.: Will Rogers Institute, Allied Film & Video, Univ. Film & Video Fdn.

MASON, MARSHA: Actress. b. St. Louis. April 3, 1942. e. Webster Coll. Came to N.Y. to continue dramatic studies and embark on theatre career. Member of American Conservatory Theatre, San Francisco.

THEATER: The Deer Park, Cactus Flower, The Indian Wants the Bronx, Happy Birthday Wanda June, Private Lives, You Can't Take It With You, Cyrano de Gerberac, A Doll's House, The Crucible, The Good Doctor, Old Times, The Big Love. Dir.: Juno's Swans.

PICTURES: Blume in Love (debut, 1973), Cinderella Liberty, Audrey Rose, The Goodbye Girl, The Cheap Detective, Promises in the Dark, Chapter Two, Only When I Laugh, Max Dugan Returns, Heartbreak Ridge, Stella, Drop Dead Fred.

TELEVISION: Series: Love of Life, Sibs. Specials: Brewsie and Willie, The Good Doctor, Cyrano de Bergerac. Movies: Lois Gibbs and the Love Canal, Surviving, Trapped in Silence, The Image, Dinner at Eight. Dir.: Little Miss Perfect.

MASON, PAMELA: Actress, Writer. b. Westgate. England. Mar. 10, 1918. Stage debut, 1936, The Luck of the Devil, London; also playwright (in collab. James Mason, Flying Blind, Made in Heaven), Author novels This Little Hand, A Lady Possessed, The Blinds Are Down, Ignoramus, Began Brit. screen career 1938, I Met a Murderer (orig. story & s.p.; cast); also in They Were Sisters, 1944. In 1946 (s.p. & cast) The Upturned Glass; (acted) Pandora and the Flying Dutchman; acted, collab. s.p. Lady Possessed, Syndicated TV, Pamela Mason Show, author Marriage Is the First Step Toward Divorce. syndicated TV The Weaker Sex?; author, The Female Pleasure Hunt; lectures at women's clubs countrywide. Columnist for Movieine Magazine. Appeared in film Everything You Always Wanted to Know About Sex.

MASSEN, OSA: Actress. b. Denmark, Copenhagen. Jan. 13, 1916.

PICTURES: Honeymoon in Bali, Honeymoon for Three, A Woman's Face, Accent on Love, You'll Never Get Rich, The Devil Pays Off, Ireland, Strange Journey, Night Unto Night, Deadline at Dawn, Gentleman Misbehaves, Rocketship XM.

MASSEY, ANNA: Actress. b. Sussex, England, Aug. 11, 1937. Daughter of late actor Raymond Massey. Sister of actor Daniel Massey. On London stage in The Reluctant Debutante (debut, 1958), The Prime of Jean Brodie, Slag, The Importance of Being Earnest, Spoiled, Doctor's Delimma, School for Scandal, With National Theatre.

PICTURES: Gideon of Scotland Yard, Peeping Tom, Bunny Lake Is Missing, DeSade, The Looking Glass War, David Copperfield (TV in U.S.), Frenzy, A Doll's House, Vault of

Horror, A Little Romance, Sweet William, Another Country, The Chain, Five Days One Summer, Foreign Body, Mountains of the Moon, La Couleur du Vent, The Tall Guy, Killing Dad, Impromptu.
TELEVISION: Remember the Germans, Wicked Woman, The Corn Is Green, Sakharov, Hotel Du Lac (BAFTA Award), A Hazard of Hearts, Around the World in 80 Days, Tears in the Rain, The Man from the Pru.

MASSEY, DANIEL: Actor. b. London, Eng., Oct. 10, 1933. e. Eaton and King's Colleges. e. Cambridge U. Son of late actor Raymond Massey. Brother of actress Anna Massey. Active on stage and TV. On Broadway in She Loves Me, Gigi (musical).
PICTURES: In Which We Serve (1942), Girls at Sea, Upstairs and Downstairs, The Queen's Guard, Go to Blazes, The Entertainer, Operation Bullshine, The Amorous Adventures of Moll Flanders, The Jokers, Star! (Acad. Award nom.), Fragment of Fear, Mary Queen of Scots, Vault of Horror, The Incredible Sarah, The Devil's Advocate, Warlords of Atlantis, Bad Timing: A Sensual Obsession, The Cat and the Canary, Victory, Scandal.
TELEVISION: Aren't We All (debut, 1958). Series: The Roads to Freedom. Mini-series: The Golden Bowl. Movies: Love with a Perfect Stranger, Intimate Contact, Inspector Morse, Look of Love, Bye Bye Columbus, Stalin.

MASTERS, BEN: Actor. b. Corvallis, OR, May 6, 1947. e. Univ. of Oregon.
THEATER: The Cherry Orchard, Waltz of the Toreadors, Plenty, Captain Brassbound's Conversion, The Boys in the Band, Eden Court, What the Butler Saw, The White Whore and the Bit Player, Key Exchange.
PICTURES: Mandingo (1975), All That Jazz, Key Exchange, Dream Lover, Making Mr. Right.
TELEVISION: Series: Heartbeat. Guest: Barnaby Jones, Kojack. Movies: One of Our Own, The Shadow Box, The Neighborhood, Illusions, The Deliberate Stranger, Street of Dreams, Cruel Doubt, Running Mates, A Twist of the Knife. Mini-Series: Loose Change, Celebrity, Noble House.

MASTERSON, MARY STUART: Actress. b. Los Angeles, CA, June 28, 1966. Daughter of writer-director-actor Peter Masterson and actress Carlin Glynn. e. Goddard Col. Made film debut at age 8 in The Stepford Wives (1975). Spent summer at Stage Door Manor in Catskills; two summers at Sundance Inst. Studied acting with Gary Swanson. Member of the Actor's Studio. Off-Bdwy debut in Been Taken. Off-Bdwy debut in Lily Dale followed by The Lucky Spot (Manhattan Theatre Club). Regional: Moonlight and Valentines, Three Sisters.
PICTURES: The Stepford Wives (debut, 1975), Heaven Help Us, At Close Range, My Little Girl, Some Kind of Wonderful, Gardens of Stone, Mr. North, Chances Are, Immediate Family (Natl. Board of Review Award, 1989), Funny About Love, Fried Green Tomatoes, Married to It, Benny & Joon, Bad Girls.
TELEVISION: Movie: Love Lives On. Guest: Amazing Stories (Go to the Head of the Class).

MASTERSON, PETER: Actor, Writer, Director. r.n. Carlos Bee Masterson, Jr. b. Houston, TX, June 1, 1934. m. actress Carlin Glynn. Father of actress Mary Stuart Masterson. e. Rice U., Houston, BA. 1957. NY stage debut, Call Me By My Rightful Name, 1961. Film debut Ambush Bay, 1965.
THEATER: Marathon '33, Blues for Mr. Charlie, The Trial of Lee Harvey Oswald, The Great White Hope, That Championship Season, The Poison Tree, The Best Little Whorehouse in Texas (co-author, dir.), The Last of the Knucklemen (dir.).
PICTURES: Actor: Counterpoint, In the Heat of the Night, Tomorrow, The Exorcist, Man on a Swing, The Stepford Wives, Gardens of Stone. Writer: The Best Little Whore House in Texas. Director: The Trip to Bountiful, Full Moon in Blue Water, Blood Red, Night Game, Convicts.
TELEVISION: Camera Three, Pueblo; The Quinns; A Question of Guilt.

MASTORAKIS, NICO: Writer, Director, Producer. b. Athens, Greece, 1941. Writer of novels and screenplays, including Fire Below Zero, and Keepers of the Secret (co-author). Pres. Omega Entertainment Ltd. since Jan. 1978.
PICTURES: Writer/dir./prod.: The Time Traveller, Blind Date, Sky High, The Zero Boys, The Wind, Terminal Exposure, Nightmare at Noon, Glitch, Ninja Academy, Hired to Kill, In the Cool of the Night, At Random. Prod.: The Greek Tycoon, Red Tide, Grandmother's House, Darkroom, Bloodstone (prod., co-s.p.).

MASTRANTONIO, MARY ELIZABETH: Actress. b. Oak Park, IL, Nov. 17, 1958. e. U. of Illinois 1976–78 where trained for opera. m. director Pat O'Connor. Worked as singer & dancer for summer at Opryland Theme Park in Nashville. Came to NY as understudy and vacation replacement as Maria in West Side Story revival. NY stage appearances: Copperfield (1981), Oh Brother, Amadeus, Sunday in the Park With George (Playwright's Horizons), The Human Comedy, Henry V, Figaro, Measure For Measure, The Knife, Twelfth Night.

PICTURES: Scarface (debut, 1983), The Color of Money (Acad. Award nom.), Slam Dance, The January Man, The Abyss, Fools of Fortune, Class Action, Robin Hood: Prince of Thieves, Consenting Adults.
TELEVISION: Mini-Series: Mussolini: The Untold Story. Special: Uncle Vanya.

MASTROIANNI, MARCELLO: Actor. b. Fontana Liri, Italy, Sept. 28, 1924. e. U. of Rome theatrical company. Draftsman in Rome, 1940–43. WWII, drew military maps until captured by Nazis and escaped. Theatrical debut in Rome in Angelica, 1948. Film debut in I Mizrabili (1948). Formed indep. prod. co., Master Films, 1966.
PLAYS: Death of a Salesman, Streetcar Named Desire, Ciao Rudy.
PICTURES: Too Bad She's Bad, A Dog's Life, Three Girls from Rome, The Miller's Beautiful Wife, Fever to Live, The Ladykillers of Rome, Love a La Carte, Days of Love, White Nights, Big Deal on Madonna Street, Where the Hot Wind Blows, The Tailor's Maid, Most Wonderful Moment, Bell Antonio, LaDolce Vita, Divorce Italian Style, Ghosts of Rome, La Notte, A Very Private Affair, The Organizer, 8½, Yesterday Today and Tomorrow, Marriage Italian Style, Casanova '70, The 10th Victim, The Poppy Is Also a Flower, Shoot Loud Louder . . . I Don't Understand, The Stranger, Ghosts Italian Style (cameo), Kiss the Other Shiek, The Man With the Balloons, A Place for Lovers, Leo the Last, Diamonds for Breakfast, Sunflower, The Pizza Triangle, The Priest's Wife, Fellini's Roma (cameo), It Only Happens to Others, What?, The Grande Bouffe, Massacre in Rome, Down the Ancient Stairs, The Sunday Woman, A Special Day, Wifemistress, Bye Bye Monkey, Stay as You Are, Blood Feud, City of Women, La Pelle, Gabriella, La Nuit de Varennes, Henry IV, The Last Horror Film (cameo), Macaroni, Ginger and Fred, Federico Fellini's Intervista, Dark Eyes, Miss Arizona, Traffic Jam, The Two Lives of Martia Pascal, Splendor, Everybody's Fine, The Suspended Step of the Stork, A Fine Romance, Used People, The Beekeeper, The Children Thief.

MASUR, RICHARD: Actor. b. New York, NY, Nov. 20, 1948.
TELEVISION: Series: Hot L Baltimore, One Day at a Time, Empire. Mini-Series: East of Eden. Movies: Having Babies, Betrayal, Mr. Horn, Walking Through the Fire, Fallen Angel, Money on the Side, An Invasion of Privacy, The Demon Murder Case, Adam, John Steinbeck's The Winter of Our Discontent, Fight #90: Disaster on the Potomac, The Burning Bed, Obsessed With a Married Woman, Wild Horses, Embassy, Adam: His Song Continues, Roses Are for the Rich, Cast the First Stone, When the Bough Breaks, Settle the Score, Always Remember I Love You, Stephen King's IT, The Story Lady, And the Band Played On. Director: Torn Between Two Fathers (After School Special).
PICTURES: Whiffs, Bittersweet Love, Semi-Tough, Who'll Stop the Rain, Hanover Street, Scavenger Hunt, Heaven's Gate, I'm Dancing As Fast As I Can, The Thing, Timerider, Risky Business, Under Fire, Nightmares, The Mean Season, My Science Project, Head Office, Heartburn, The Believers, Walker, Rent-a-Cop, Shoot to Kill, License to Drive, Far from Home, Flashback, Going Under, My Girl, Encino Man, The Man Without a Face, My Girl 2.
THEATRE: Bdwy: The Changing Room.

MATHESON, TIM: Actor. b. Los Angeles, CA, Dec. 31, 1947. e. California State U. Debut on TV at age 12 in Window on Main Street. At 19 contract player for Universal. 1985, turned to direction: St. Elsewhere episode and music videos. Formed own productions co. at Burbank Studios 1985, acted off-Bdwy. in True West. With partner Daniel Grodnick bought National Lampoon from founder Matty Simons, becoming exec. officer and chmn. 1989; resigned in 1991.
PICTURES: Divorce American Style (debut, 1967), Yours Mine and Ours, How to Commit Marriage, Magnum Force, Almost Summer, National Lampoon's Animal House, Dreamer, The Apple Dumpling Gang Rides Again, 1941, House of God, A Little Sex, To Be or Not To Be, Up the Creek, Impulse, Fletch, Speed Zone, Blind Fury (co-prod. only), Drop Dead Fred, Solar Crisis.
TELEVISION: Movies: Owen Marshall: Counselor-at-Law, Lock Stock and Barrel, Hitched, Remember When, The Last Day, The Runaway Barge, The Quest, Mary White, Listen to Your Heart, Obsessed with a Married Woman, Blind Justice, Warm Hearts Cold Feet, Bay Coven, The Littlest Victims, Little White Lies, Buried Alive, Joshua's Heart, Stephen King's Sometimes They Come Back, The Woman Who Sinned, Quicksand: No Escape, Relentless: Mind of a Killer, Trial & Error, Dying to Love You. Series: Window on Main Street, Jonny Quest (voice), The Virginian, Bonanza, The Quest, Tucker's Witch, Just in Time (also co-exec. prod.), Charlie Hoover. Pilot: Nikki & Alexander. Special: Bus Stop.

MATHEWS, CAROLE: Actress. b. Montgomery, IL, Sept. 13, 1920. e. Aurora, IL H.S. Started as night club, radio entertainer; to Hollywood, 1944.
PICTURES: Massacre River, Great Gatsby, Special Agent, The Man With My Face, Meet Me At the Fair, Port of Hell,

Shark River, Treasure of Ruby Hills, Betrayed Women, Requirement for a Redhead, Swamp Women, Showdown at Boot Hill, Female Fiends, 13 Fighting Men, Look In Any Window, Tender Is the Night.

TELEVISION: *Series*: The Californians. *Guest*: Steel Hour, Kraft Theatre, Lux Video, Hitchcock Presents, Studio One, Texan, 77 Sunset Strip, Perry Mason, Four Star Theatre, M-Squad, Death Valley Days, Guestward Ho, Two Faces West, Johnny Midnight, Pete & Gladys, 87th Precinct, Ben Casey.

MATLIN, MARLEE: Actress. b. Morton Grove, IL, Aug. 24, 1965. e. John Hersey H.S., Chicago, public school with special education program for deaf. e. William Rainey Harper Coll., majoring in criminal justice. Performed at Children's Theatre of the Deaf in Des Plaines at age 8, playing many leading roles. As adult appeared in only one stage show. Theatrical film debut in Children of a Lesser God.

PICTURES: Children of a Lesser God (debut, 1986; Acad. Award, Golden Globe), Walker, The Player, The Linguini Incident, Hear No Evil.

TELEVISION: *Series*: Reasonable Doubts. *Movie*: Bridge to Silence. *Specials*: Face the Hate, Meaning of Life, Free to Laugh, Creative Spirit. *Guest*: Sesame Street, Adventures in Wonderland.

MATTHAU, CHARLES: Director. b. New York, NY, Dec. 10, 1964. Son of actor Walter Matthau. e. U. of Southern California Film School. While at USC wrote and dir. The Duck Film, a silent comedy short (Golden Seal Award, London Amateur Film Fest. and C.I.N.E. Eagle Award.) Also dir. short, I Was a Teenage Fundraiser. President, The Matthau Company organized 1989.

PICTURES: Doin' Time on Planet Earth. (nom. Saturn Award, best dir., Acad. of Science Fiction.)

TELEVISION: *Movie*: Mrs. Lambert Remembers Love (dir., prod.; Golden Eagle, Golden Medal & Houston Fest. Grand Awards).

MATTHAU, WALTER: Actor. b. New York, NY, Oct. 1, 1920. Served in Air Force W.W.II. Studied journalism at Columbia U. and acting at New Sch. for Social Research's dramatic workshop, 1946, then acted in summer stock. First Broadway role, 1948, in Anne of a Thousand Days.

THEATRE: *Bdwy*: Will Success Spoil Rock Hunter?, Once More With Feeling, Once There Was a Russian, A Shot in the Dark (Tony Award, 1962), The Odd Couple (Tony Award, 1965). L.A.: Juno and the Paycock.

PICTURES: The Kentuckian (debut, 1955), The Indian Fighter, Bigger Than Life, A Face in the Crowd, Slaughter on Tenth Avenue, King Creole, Voice in the Mirror, Ride a Crooked Trial, Onionhead, Strangers When We Meet, The Gangster Story (also dir.), Lonely Are the Brave, Who's Got the Action?, Island of Love, Charade, Ensign Pulver, Fail Safe, Goodbye Charlie, Mirage, The Fortune Cookie (Acad. Award, supp. actor, 1966), A Guide for the Married Man, The Odd Couple, The Secret Life of an American Wife, Candy, Cactus Flower, Hello Dolly!, A New Leaf, Plaza Suite, Kotch (Acad. Award nom.), Pete n' Tillie, Charley Varrick, The Laughing Policeman, Earthquake, The Taking of Pelham One Two Three, The Front Page, The Sunshine Boys (Acad. Award nom.), The Bad News Bears, Casey's Shadow, House Calls, California Suite, Little Miss Marker (also exec. prod.), Hopscotch, First Monday in October, Buddy Buddy, I Ought to Be in Pictures, The Survivors, Movers and Shakers, Pirates, The Couch Trip, Il Piccolo Diavolo (The Little Devil), JFK, Dennis the Menace.

TELEVISION: Many appearances 1952–65 on Philco-Goodyear Playhouse, Studio One, Playhouse 90, Kraft Theatre, Awake and Sing, Insight, Muni. *Series*: Tallahassee 7000 (1961). *Movies*: The Incident, Mrs. Lambert Remembers Love, Against Her Will: An Incident in Baltimore. *Special*: The Stingiest Man in Town (voice).

MATURE, VICTOR: Actor. b. Louisville, KY, Jan. 29, 1913. On Bdwy in Lady in the Dark; U.S. Coast Guard, W.W.II.

PICTURES: The Housekeeper's Daughter (debut, 1939), One Million B.C., Captain Caution, No No Nanette, I Wake Up Screaming, Shanghai Gesture, Song of the Islands, My Gal Sal, Footlight Serenade, Seven Days Leave, My Darling Clementine, Moss Rose, Kiss of Death, Fury at Furnace Creek, Cry of the City, Red Hot and Blue, Easy Living, Samson and Delilah, Wabash Avenue, I'll Get By (cameo), Stella, Gambling House, Las Vegas Story, Androcles and the Lion, Million Dollar Mermaid, Something for the Birds, Glory Brigade, Affair with a Stranger, The Robe, Veils of Bagdad, Dangerous Mission, Betrayed, Demetrius & the Gladiators, The Egyptian, Chief Crazy Horse, Violent Saturday, Last Frontier, The Sharkfighters, Safari, Zarak, The Long Haul, Pickup Alley, China Doll, Tank Force, The Bandit of Zhobe, Escort West, Big Circus, Timbuktu, Hannibal, The Tartars, After the Fox, Head, Every Little Crook and Nanny, Won Ton Ton the Dog Who Saved Hollywood, Firepower, The Screamer.

TELEVISION: *Movie*: Samson and Delilah.

MAURA, CARMEN: Actress. b. Madrid, Spain, Sept. 15, 1945. e. Madrid's Catholic Inst. Daughter of ophthalmologist faced family disapproval and custody battle when she became an actress. After working as cabaret entertainer, translator (has degree in French), and occasional voiceover dubber, met aspiring director Pedro Almodovar when they were cast in stage prod. of Sartre's Dirty Hands and starred in several of his films. Hosted weekly Spanish tv talk show Esta Noche.

PICTURES: El Hombre Oculto (debut, 1970), El Love Feroz, The Petition, Paper Tigers, Que Hace una Chica Como tu en un Sitio Como Este?, Pepi Luci Bom . . . And Other Girls on the Heap (1980), El Cid Cabreador, Dark Habits, What Have I Done to Deserve This?, Extramuros, Se Infiel y No Mires Con Quien, Matador, Law of Desire, Women on the Verge of a Nervous Breakdown, Baton Rouge, Ay Carmela!, In Heaven As on Earth, The Anonymous Queen, Shadows in a Conflict, Louis the Child King.

MAUREY, NICOLE: Actress. b. France, Dec. 20, 1926. Studied dancing; French films include Blondine, Pamela, Le Cavalier Noir, Journal D'Un Cure De Campagne, Les Compagnes de la Nuit; many television and stage appearances in France; U.S. film debut in Little Boy Lost (1953).

PICTURES: Secret of the Incas, Bold and the Brave, The Weapon, The Constant Husband, Scapegoat, Me and the Colonel, Jayhawkers, House of the Seven Hawks, High Time, Day of the Triffids, Why Bother to Knock?, The Very Edge.

TELEVISION: U.S. and U.K.: Tomorrow We Will Love, Casablanca, The Billion Franc Mystery, Champion House, I Thought They Died Years Ago.

MAXWELL, RONALD F.: Director, Writer. b. Jan. 5, 1947. e. NYU Coll. of Arts & Sciences; NYU Sch. of the Arts, Inst. of Film & Television Graduate Sch., M.F.A., 1970. Producer-Director for PBS Theater-in-America (1974–8).

PICTURES: The Guest, Little Darlings; The Night the Lights Went Out in Georgia; Kidco; Gettysburg (also co-s.p.).

TELEVISION: Sea Marks (prod., dir.); Verna: USO Girl (prod., dir.), Parent Trap II (dir.).

MAY, ELAINE: Actress, Director, Screenwriter. b. Philadelphia, PA, April 21, 1932. Mother of actress Jeannie Berlin. Father was prod.-dir. Jack Berlin whose travelling theater she acted with from age 6 to 10. Repertory theatre in Chicago, 1954; comedy team with Mike Nichols, 1955. Appeared with improvisational theater group, The Compass, Chicago. Co-starred in An Evening with Mike Nichols and Elaine May. Author of plays: A Matter of Position, Not Enough Rope, Hot Line, Better Point of Valour, Mr. Gogol & Mr. Preen.

PICTURES: *Actress*: Luv, Enter Laughing, A New Leaf (also dir., s.p.), California Suite, In the Spirit. *Director*: The Heartbreak Kid, Mikey and Nicky (also s.p.), Ishtar (also s.p.). *Writer*: Such Good Friends, Heaven Can Wait.

TELEVISION: *Guest*: Jack Paar, Omnibus, Dinah Shore Show, Perry Como, Laugh Lines (panelist, 1959). *Series regular*: Keep Talking (1958–9).

MAYER, GERALD: Producer, Director. b. Montreal, Canada; p. both deceased: Jerry G., mgr. MGM studio, and Rheba G Mayer (later Mrs. Hal Elias). e. Stanford U., journalism; corr. for San Francisco Examiner; pres. Sigma Delta Chi, prof. journalism soc. Navy lieut. amphibious forces, W.W.II. Entered m.p. ind. in prod. dept. MGM studios; first dir. assignment Dial 1119 (1950).

PICTURES: Inside Straight, Sellout, Holiday for Sinners, Bright Road (Christopher Award for direction), The Marauders, African Drumbeat, and The Man Inside (Canadian).

TELEVISION: Canadian Broadcasting Corp. (prod./dir., TV drama), prod. The Swiss Family Robinson (British-Canadian-West German TV series). Director for U.S. TV: One Last Ride (mini-series), Airwolf, Night Heat, Lou Grant, Eight Is Enough, Quincy, Logan's Run, Mannix, Mission Impossible, Police Surgeon, Cimarron Strip, Peyton Place, Judd for the Defense, Bonanza, The Fugitive, Chrysler Thea., Ben Casey, Slattery's People, Profiles in Courage, The Defenders, Gunsmoke, etc.

MAYER, MICHAEL F.: Attorney, Executive. b. White Plains, NY, Sept. 8, 1917. e. Harvard Coll., B.S., 1939; Yale Law Sch., L.L.B., 1942. Armed Forces 1942–46, Air Medal (1945); vice-pres. Kingsley International Pictures Corp., 1954–62. Exec. Dir. and general counsel, Independent Film Importers and Distributors of America Inc. (IFIDA), 1959–67. Special Counsel, French Society of Authors, Composers and Publishers, 1961–72; British Performing Rights Society, 1962–67. Author: Foreign Films on American Screens (1966); Divorce and Annulment (1967); What You Should Know About Libel and Slander (1968); Rights of Privacy (1972); The Film Industries (1973–revised ed. pub. in 1978). Lecturer on motion picture problems at NYU, Stanford U., U. of Pennsylvania, Dartmouth Coll., State U. of New York, Albany. Teacher of courses on Business Problems in Film, New School (1971–82). Secty. of Film Society of Lincoln Center, Inc. (1972–88).

MAYER, ROGER LAURANCE: Executive. b. New York, NY, Apr. 21, 1926. e. Yale U., B.A. 1948; Yale Law Sch., L.L.B. and J.D.

1951. In 1952 was practicing attorney; joined Columbia Pictures that year as atty. and named general studio exec., 1957. Left in 1961 to join MGM Studio as asst. gen. mgr. Since with MGM as follows: v.p., operations, 1964; v.p., administration, 1975–84. Also exec. v.p., MGM Laboratories, 1974–83. Named pres., MGM Laboratories and sr. v.p., studio admin.; MGM Entertainment Co. 1983–86; joined Turner Entertainment Co. as pres. and chief operating officer 1986–present.

MEMBER: Los Angeles County Bar Assn., Calif. Bar Assn., Los Angeles Copyright Society, Acad. of Motion Picture Arts & Sciences. Trustee, Motion Picture & TV Relief Fund and asst. v.p., Permanent Charities Fund.

MAYER, SEYMOUR R.: Executive. b. New York, NY, July 30, 1912. e. N.Y. schools. Div. mgr., Loew's in-town theatres, 1933; Armed Forces, W.W.II, as Major in charge of overseas m.p. service; with Loew's International: 1946, 1st v.p.; MGM Int'l.: 1963–69; pres., MGM Int'l.; worldwide sales, 1970; pres., MSD Int'l. worldwide sales.

MAYO, VIRGINIA: Actress. r.n. Virginia Jones. b. St. Louis, MO, Nov. 30, 1920. e. St. Louis dramatic school. With Billy Rose's Diamond Horseshoe; then N.Y. stage, Banjo Eyes.

PICTURES: Jack London (debut, 1943), Up in Arms, The Princess and the Pirate, Wonder Man, Kid from Brooklyn, Best Years of Our Lives, Secret Life of Walter Mitty, Out of the Blue, A Song is Born, Smart Girls Don't Talk, The Girl from Jones Beach, Flaxy Martin, Colorado Territory, Always Leave Them Laughing, White Heat, Red Light, Backfire, The Flame and the Arrow, West Point Story, Along the Great Divide, Captain Horatio Hornblower, Painting the Clouds with Sunshine, Starlift, She's Working Her Way Through College, Iron Mistress, She's Back on Broadway, South Sea Woman, Devil's Canyon, King Richard & the Crusaders, Silver Chalice, Pearl of the South Pacific, Great Day in the Morning, Proud Ones, Congo Crossing, Big Land, The Story of Mankind, The Tall Stranger, Fort Dobbs, Westbound, Jet Over the Atlantic, Young Fury, Fort Utah, Castle of Evil, Won Ton Ton the Dog Who Saved Hollywood, French Quarter, Evil Spirits, Seven Days Ashore.

MAYRON, MELANIE: Actress. b. Philadelphia, PA, Oct. 20, 1952. e. American Academy of Dramatic Arts, 1972. Debut Godspell (tour), NY stage debut: The Goodbye People, 1979. Gethsemane Springs, (Mark Taper Forum, 1976), Crossing Delancey, (1986, Jewish Rep. Theatre, NY). With Catlin Adams, co-prod., co-wrote short, Little Shiny Shoes.

PICTURES: Harry and Tonto (debut, 1974), Gable and Lombard, Car Wash, The Great Smokey Roadblock, You Light Up My Life, Girl Friends (Best actress award, Locarno Film Festival) Heartbeeps, Missing, The Boss' Wife, Sticky Fingers (also co-s.p., co-prod. with Catlin Adams), Checking Out, My Blue Heaven.

TELEVISION: Series: thirtysomething (Emmy, 1989). Movies: Playing For Time, Will There Really Be a Morning?, Hustling, The Best Little Girl in the World, Wallenberg: A Hero's Story, Ordeal in the Arctic. Guest: Rhoda. Specials: Lily Tomlin: Sold Out, Cinder Ella: A Modern Fairy Tale, Wanted: The Perfect Guy.

MAYSLES, ALBERT: Director, Cinematographer. b. Boston, MA, Nov. 1926. e. Syracuse (B.A.), Boston U., M.A. Taught psychology there for 3 years. With late brother David (1932–87) pioneered in "direct cinema" documentary filmmaking, using hand-held cameras synchronous sound, no narration, to capture the drama of daily life, as is without need to invent stories. Entered filmmaking photographing Primary with D.A. Pennebaker, Richard Leacock and Robert Drew, 1960. Formed Maysles Films, Inc. 1962, making non-fiction feature films, commercials and corp. films.

PICTURES: Showman (1962), Salesman, What's Happening! The Beatles in the U.S.A., Meet Marlon Brando, Gimme Shelter, Christo's Valley Curtain, Grey Gardens, Running Fence, Vladimir Horowitz: The Last Romantic, Ozawa, Islands, Horowitz Plays Mozart, The Umbrellas, Heart, Fellow Passengers, Christo in Paris, Soldiers of Music: Rostvopovitch Returns to Russia, Baroque Duet.

TELEVISION: Vladimir Horowitz: The Last Romantic (Emmy Award), Soldiers of Music: Rostopovich Returns to Russia (Emmy Award). Sports Illustrated: The Making of the Swimsuit Issue (co-dir.), Abortion: Desperate Choices.

MAZURSKY, PAUL: Producer, Director, Writer, Actor. b. Brooklyn, NY, April 25, 1930. e. Brooklyn Coll. Started acting in 1951 Off-Bdwy (Hello Out There, The Seagull, Major Barbara, Death of a Salesman, He Who Gets Slapped), TV and films. Was nightclub comic 1954–1960 and directed plays. Began association with Larry Tucker for producing, directing, writing and performing in Second City, semi-improvisational revue. For four years they wrote the Danny Kaye TV show and created and wrote the Monkees series. First theatrical film I Love You Alice B. Toklas, 1969, which he wrote and exec. produced with Tucker.

PICTURES: Prod.-Dir.-Co-Writer-Actor: Bob and Carol and Ted and Alice (prod.-dir.-co-s.p.), Alex in Wonderland, Blume

in Love, Harry and Tonto, Next Stop Greenwich Village (prod.-dir.-s.p.), An Unmarried Woman, Willie and Phil, Tempest, Moscow on the Hudson, Down and Out in Beverly Hills, Moon Over Parador, Enemies A Love Story, Scenes From a Mall, The Pickle.

PICTURES: As actor only: Fear and Desire, Blackboard Jungle, Deathwatch, A Star is Born, A Man a Woman and a Bank, Into the Night, Punchline, Scenes From the Class Struggle in Beverly Hills, Man Trouble.

McBRIDE, JIM: Writer, Director. b. New York, NY, Sept. 16, 1941. m. costume designer Tracy Tynan. Began in underground film scene in New York. First film: David Holzman's Diary, 1967, which won grand prize at Mannheim and Pesaro Film Festivals, and was named to the Library of Congress' list of important American films designated for preservation in 1991.

PICTURES: My Girlfriend's Wedding (actor, s.p., dir.), Glen and Randa (s.p., dir.), Pictures from Life's Other Side (dir.), Hot Times (dir., s.p., actor), Last Embrace (actor only), Breathless (co.-s.p., dir.), The Big Easy (dir.), Great Balls of Fire (dir., co-s.p.).

TELEVISION: The Wonder Years (2 episodes), Blood Ties, Twilight Zone (The Once and Future King, 1986).

McCALL, JOAN: Writer, Actress. b. Grahn, KY. e. Berea Coll. Staff writer for The Days of Our Lives, Another World, As the World Turns, under the pen name Joan Pommer; Search for Tomorrow, Capitol, Santa Barbara, Divorce Court. Starred on Broadway in Barefoot in the Park, The Star Spangled Girl, A Race of Hairy Men, and road companies of Barefoot in the Park, Star Spangled Girl, and Don't Drink the Water, Los Angeles co. of Jimmy Shine.

PICTURES: Grizzly, Act of Vengeance, The Devil Times Five. Screenwriter: The Predator, Between Two Worlds, Timelapse.

McCALLUM, DAVID: Actor. b. Glasgow, Scotland, Sept. 19, 1933. Early career in rep. theatres and dir. plays for Army. Ent. m.p. Ind. 1953.

PICTURES: The Secret Place, Hell Drivers, Robbery Under Arms, Violent Playground, A Night to Remember, The Long and the Short and the Tall, Jungle Street, Billy Budd, Freud, The Great Escape, The Greatest Story Ever Told, To Trap a Spy, The Spy With My Face, Around the World Under the Sea, One Spy Too Many, Three Bites of the Apple, Sol Madrid, Mosquito Squadron, The Kingfisher Caper, Dogs, King Solomon's Treasure, Watcher in the Woods, Terminal Choice, The Wind, The Haunting of Morella, Hear My Song, Dirty Weekend, Shattered Image.

TELEVISION: Series: The Man From U.N.C.L.E., Colditz (BBC, 1972–4), The Invisible Man, Sapphire and Steel (BBC), Trainer (BBC). Guest: Hitchcock, Murder She Wrote. Movies: Teacher, Teacher, Hauser's Memory, Frankenstein: The True Story, Behind Enemy Lines, Freedom Fighters, She Waits, The Man Who Lived at the Ritz, The Return of Sam McCloud, Mother Love (BBC).

McCALLUM, JOHN: Actor, Producer, Director. b. Brisbane, Australia, CBE. Mar. 14, 1918. e. Royal Acad. of Dramatic Art. Served in Australian Imperial Forces, W.W.II. Appeared in repertory with Old Vic & Stratford-on-Avon. On stage, 1937 in Judgment Day, Australian tour, 1955–56; on screen first 1944, Australia is Like This. Asst. man. dir. J. C. Williamson Theatres, Ltd., Australia, 1958; man. dir., 1960–66. Resigned chmn. Williamson-Powell Int. Films, 1965; chmn. Fauna Prod.; dir.: Relatively Speaking; Plaza Suite, My Fair Lady (Australia). Prod. TV Series, Skippy, Barrier Reef, Boney, Shannons Mob; London Stage Constant Wife. 1974 Comedy Theatre, Melbourne. 1976 Chichester Fest. 1976–77 The Circle. Exec. prod. Bailey's Bird, TV series. The Chalk Garden. The Kingfisher (tour, Far and Middle East), 1988, Hayfever, The Royal Baccarat Scandal Chichester Fest, and Haymarket Theatre London; The Cocktail Hour (U.K., Australia tour).

PICTURES: A Son Is Born, Joe Goes Back, Root of All Evil, The Loves of Joanna Godden, It Always Rains on Sunday, Miranda, The Calendar, A Boy, a Girl and a Bike, Traveler's Joy, The Woman in Question, Valley of the Eagles, Lady Godiva Rides Again, Derby Day (Four Against Fate), Trent's Last Case, The Long Memory, Melba, Devil on Horseback, Trouble in the Glen, Smiley (in Australia), Safe Harbour, Nickel Queen (dir.); The Z Men (prod.); The Highest Honor (exec. prod.).

McCAMBRIDGE, MERCEDES: Actress. b. Joliet, IL, March 17, 1918. e. Mundelein Coll., Chicago, B.A. Did some radio work while in college; opposite Orson Welles two seasons, on Ford Theatre, other air shows; New York stage in: Hope for the Best, (1945); Place of Our Own, Twilight Bar, Woman Bites Dog, The Young and Fair, Lost in Yonkers. Starred on own radio show, 1952. Member: National Inst. Alcohol Abuse and Alcoholism, Washington. Autobiography: The Two of Us.

PICTURES: All the King's Men (debut, 1949; Acad. Award, supp. actress), Lightning Strikes Twice, Inside Straight, The Scarf, Johnny Guitar, Giant, A Farewell to Arms, Touch of Evil (unbilled), Suddenly Last Summer, Cimarron, Angel Baby, 99

Women, Like a Crow on a June Bug (Sixteen), The Exorcist (voice), Thieves, The Concorde—Airport '79, Echoes.
TELEVISION: *Series:* One Man's Family, Wire Service; also numerous guest appearances. *Movies:* Killer By Night, Two For the Money, The Girls of Huntington House, The President's Plane is Missing, Who is the Black Dahlia?, The Sacketts.

McCARTHY, ANDREW: Actor. b. Westfield, NJ, Nov. 29, 1962. e. NYU. Studied acting at Circle-in-the-Square. Bdwy: The Boys of Winter. Off Bdwy: Bodies Rest and Motion, Life Under Water, Neptune's Hips, Mariens Kammer.
PICTURES: Class (debut, 1983), Heaven Help Us, St. Elmo's Fire, Pretty in Pink, Mannequin, Waiting for the Moon, Less Than Zero, Kansas, Fresh Horses, Weekend at Bernie's, Quiet Days in Clichy, Dr. M (Club Extinction), Year of the Gun, Only You, Weekend at Bernie's 2, Mrs. Parker & the Round Table.
TELEVISION: *Specials:* Dear Lola, Common Pursuit. *Guest:* Amazing Stories (Grandpa's Ghost), Tales From the Crypt (Loved to Death).

McCARTHY, KEVIN: Actor. b. Seattle, WA, Feb. 15, 1914. Brother of late author Mary McCarthy. e. U. of Minnesota. Acted in sch. plays, stock; Bdwy debut in Abe Lincoln in Illinois. In U.S. Army; On London stage in Death of a Salesman (1949–50).
BROADWAY THEATER: Flight to West, Winged Victory, Truckline Cafe, Joan of Lorraine, Death of a Salesman, Anna Christie, Red Roses For Me, Love's Labour's Lost, Advise and Consent, The Day The Money Stopped, Two For the Seesaw, Cactus Flower, Alone Together, The Three Sisters, Happy Birthday Wanda June.
PICTURES: Death of a Salesman (debut, 1951), Drive a Crooked Road, Gambler from Natchez, Stranger on Horseback, Annapolis Story, Nightmare, Invasion of the Body Snatchers, The Misfits, 40 Pounds of Trouble, A Gathering of Eagles, The Prize, The Best Man, Mirage, A Big Hand for the Little Lady, Three Sisters, Hotel, The Hell With Heroes, If He Hollers Let Him Go, Ace High, Kansas City Bomber, Alien Thunder, Buffalo Bill and the Indians, Piranha, Invasion of the Body Snatchers (1978, cameo), Hero at Large, Those Lips Those Eyes, The Howling, My Tutor, Twilight Zone—The Movie, Hostage, Innerspace, UHF, Fast Food, Dark Tower, Love or Money, The Sleeping Car, Eve of Destruction, Final Approach, The Distinguished Gentleman, Matinee.
TELEVISION: Active on TV since 1949. *Pilot:* Second Stage. *Movies:* The Making of a Male Model, Deadly Intentions, The Midnight Hour, A Masterpiece of Murder, Poor Little Rich Girl: The Barbara Hutton Story; The Long Journey Home; Once Upon a Texas Train; In the Heat of the Night, Channel 99, The Rose and the Jackal, Dead on the Money, Duplicates. *Mini-series:* Passion and Paradise. *Series:* The Colbys, The Survivors, Flamingo Road, Amanda's, Second Start.

McCARTNEY PAUL: Singer, Musician. b. Liverpool, England, June 18, 1942. As member of The Beatles co-starred in A Hard Day's Night, Help!, Yellow Submarine (cameo), and Let It Be. Wrote songs for several films on own, including Live and Let Die (title), Oh Heavenly Dog, Spies Like Us. Wrote scores for The Family Way, Beyond the Limit. Wrote script, music and acted in Give My Regards to Broad Street, cameo in Eat the Rich. Concert films: Rockshow, Get Back.

McCLANAHAN, RUE: Actress. b. Healdton, OK, Feb. 21. e. U. of Tulsa (B.A. cum laude). On Bdwy. in Sticks and Bones, Jimmy Shine, California Suite. Obie Award for Who's Happy Now? (1970). Member: Actors Studio, NYC.
PICTURES: They Might Be Giants, The People Next Door, The Pursuit of Happiness, Modern Love.
TELEVISION: *Series:* Maude, Mama's Family, The Golden Girls (Emmy Award, 1987), The Golden Palace. *Movies:* Having Babies III, Sgt. Matlovich Vs. the U.S. Air Force, Rainbow, Topper, The Great American Traffic Jam, Word of Honor, The Day the Bubble Burst, The Little Match Girl, Liberace, Take My Daughters Please, Let Me Hear You Whisper, To the Heroes, After the Shock, Children of the Bride, To My Daughter, The Dreamer of Oz, Baby of the Bride, Mother of the Bride (also co-exec. prod.). *Specials:* The Wickedest Witch, The Man in the Brown Suit.

McCLORY, SEAN: Actor. b. Dublin, Ireland, March 8, 1924. e. Jesuit Coll., Natl. U. at Galway (medical sch.). With Gaelic Theatre, Galway; Abbey Theatre. Dublin. Brought to U.S., in 1946 under contract to RKO Pictures, then Warners, then Batjac (John Wayne's co.). Prod. and dir. numerous plays, member of the Directors Guild of America and author of drama, Moment of Truth; Pax: The Benedictions in China. Editor: The Jester: The Masques Club 50th Anniv. Mng. Editor: A.N.T.A. News (2 yrs). For past 3 years starred in 30 ninety-minute radio dramas for California Artists Radio Theatre.
PLAYS: Shining Hour, Juno and the Paycock, Anna Christie, Escape to Autumn, King of Friday's Men, Lady's Not for Burning, Billy Budd, Dial M for Murder, The Winslow Boy,

Shadow of a Gunman (Dramalogue Award for Best Actor), Saint Joan, many others.
PICTURES: Film debut: Dick Tracy vs. Cueball, Roughshod, Beyond Glory, Daughter of Rosie O'Grady, Storm Warning, Lorna Doone, What Price Glory, The Quiet Man, Diane, Island in the Sky, Ring of Fear, Them, Long Grey Line, Cheyenne Autumn, Plunder of the Sun, Anne of the Indies, I Cover the Underworld, Man in the Attic, Guns of Fort Petticoat, King's Thief, Moonfleet, Bandolero, Day of the Wolves, Valley of the Dragons, Follow Me Boys, Rogue's March, The Gnome-Mobile, Well of the Saints, In Search of Historic Jesus, Roller Boogie, My Chauffeur, The Dead.
TELEVISION: Matinee Theatre, Climax, Lost in Space, My Three Sons, Suspense, The Untouchables, Hitchcock, Thriller, Beverly Hillbillies, Bonanza, Gunsmoke, Mannix, Little House on the Prairie, Perry Mason, S.W.A.T., The New Daughters of Joshua Cabe, The Captains And the Kings, Once an Eagle, Fish, Columbo, How the West Was Won, Fantasy Island, Battlestar Galactica, Trapper John, Blue Knight. Falcon Crest, Simon and Simon, Murder She Wrote, Young Houdini. Series: The Californians (also dir.), Kate McShane; Bring 'Em Back Alive, General Hospital (continuing guest role).

McCLURE, DOUG: Actor. b. Glendale, CA, May 11, 1935. e. UCLA.
PICTURES: The Enemy Below, South Pacific, Gidget, Because They're Young, The Unforgiven, The Lively Set, Shenandoah, Beau Geste, The King's Pirate, Nobody's Perfect, Backtrack, What Changed Charley Farthing?, The Land That Time Forgot, At the Earth's Core, The People That Time Forgot, Warlords of Atlantis, Humanoids from the Deep, Firebird 2015 A.D., House Where Evil Dwells, Cannonball Run II, 52 Pick-Up, Omega Syndrome, Tapeheads, Dark Before Dawn.
TELEVISION: *Mini-Series:* Roots. *Movies:* The Longest Hundred Miles, Terror in the Sky, The Birdmen, The Death of Me Yet, Playmates, The Judge and Jake Wyler, Shirts/Skins, Death Race, Satan's Triangle, SST-Death Flight, Wild and Woolly, The Rebels, Nightside, The Gambler Returns: Luck of the Draw, Battling for Baby. *Series:* Overland Trail, Checkmate, The Virginian (The Men From Shiloh), Search, The Barbary Coast, Out of This World.

McCLURE, MARC: Actor. b. San Mateo, CA, Mar. 31, 1957.
PICTURES: Freaky Friday, Coming Home, I Wanna Hold Your Hand, Superman, Superman II, Superman III, Supergirl, Back to the Future, Superman IV: The Quest for Peace, Amazon Women on the Moon, Perfect Match, Chances Are, After Midnight, Back to the Future Part III, Grim Prairie Tales, The Vagrant.
TELEVISION: *Series:* California Fever. *Movies:* James at 15, Little White Lies.

McCLURG, EDIE: Actress. b. Kansas City, MO, July 23, 1951. e. Syracuse Univ. Newswriter and documentary producer for National Public Radio affiliate, KCUR-FM. Joined the Pitschel Players in LA 1975; then became member of the Groundlings Improv Comedy Revue.
PICTURES: Carrie (debut, 1976), Cheech and Chong's Next Movie, Oh God Book II, Secret of NIMH (voice), Pandemonium, Cracking Up, Eating Raoul, Mr. Mom, The Corsican Brothers, Ferris Bueller's Day Off, Back to School, The Longshot, Planes Trains and Automobiles, She's Having a Baby, Elvira: Mistress of the Dark, The Little Mermaid (voice), Curly Sue, A River Runs Through It.
TELEVISION: *Series:* Tony Orlando and Dawn, The Kallikaks, The Big Show, Harper Valley PTA, No Soap Radio, Madame's Place, Small Wonder, Toegther We Stand, Valerie (The Hogan Family), Drexell's Class. *Specials:* Cinderella (Faerie Tale Theatre), The Pee-wee Herman Show, Martin Mull's History of White People in America, Once Upon a Brothers Grimm, The Chevy Chase Show, A Home Run for Love. *Guest:* WKRP in Cincinnati, The Richard Pryor Show, The Jeffersons, Trapper John M.D., Alice, Diff'rent Strokes, The Incredible Hulk, Madame's Place. *Movies:* Bill on His Own, Crash Course, Senior Prom, Menu for Murder. *Voice Characterizations:* The Snorks, The 13 Ghosts of Scooby Doo, The New Jetsons.

McCORMICK, PAT: Writer, Actor. b. July 17, 1934. Served as comedy writer for such performers as Jonathan Winters, Phyllis Diller.
TELEVISION: *Series (as writer):* Jack Paar Show, Tonight Show, etc. *Series (as actor):* The Don Rickles Show, The New Bill Cosby Show, Gun Shy. *Movies (as actor):* Mr. Horn, Rooster, The Jerk Too.
PICTURES: (as actor): Buffalo Bill and the Indians, Smokey and the Bandit, A Wedding, Hot Stuff, Scavenger Hunt, Smokey and the Bandit 2, History of the World Part 1, Under the Rainbow (also co-s.p.), Smokey and the Bandit 3, Rented Lips, Scrooged.

McCOWEN, ALEC: Actor. b. Tunbridge Wells, England, May 26, 1925. e. Royal Acad. of Dramatic Art. On stage in London in Hadrian the Seventh, etc. On Bdwy. in Antony and Cleopatra,

After the Rain, The Philanthropist, The Misanthrope, Equus, Someone Who'll Watch Over Me, etc.
PICTURES: The Cruel Sea, Time Without Pity, Town on Trial, The Doctor's Dilemma, A Night to Remember, The One That Got Away, Silent Enemy, The Loneliness of the Long Distance Runner, The Agony and the Ecstasy, The Devil's Own, The Hawaiians, Frenzy, Travels with My Aunt, Stevie, Hanover Street, Never Say Never Again, Forever Young, The Assam Garden, Personal Services, Cry Freedom, Henry V, The Age of Innocence.

McDONNELL, MARY: Actress. b. Ithaca, NY, 1952.
PICTURES: Matewan, Tiger Warsaw, Dances With Wolves (Acad. Award nom., Golden Globe Award), Grand Canyon, Sneakers, Passion Fish (Acad. Award nom.), Blue Chips .
TELEVISION: Series: E/R. Movies: Money on the Side, Courage, The American Clock. Special: O Pioneers!
THEATRE: NY: Buried Child, Savage in Limbo, All Night Long, Black Angel, A Weekend Near Madison, Three Ways Home, Still Life, The Heidi Chronicles. Regional: National Athems, A Doll's House, A Midsummer Night's Dream, The Three Sisters.

McDORMAND, FRANCES: Actress. b. Illinois, 1958. Daughter of a Disciples of Christ preacher traveled Bible Belt with family, settling in PA at 8. e. Yale Drama School. Regional theater includes Twelfth Night, Mrs. Warren's Profession, The Three Sisters, All My Sons. Two seasons with O'Neill Playwrights Conference.
THEATER: Awake and Sing, Painting Churches, On the Verge, A Streetcar Named Desire (Tony nom.), The Sisters Rosensweig.
PICTURES: Blood Simple, Raising Arizona, Mississippi Burning (Acad. award nom.), Chattahoochee, Dark Man, Miller's Crossing (unbilled), Hidden Agenda, The Butcher's Wife, Passed Away, Short Cuts.
TELEVISION: Guest: Twilight Zone, Spenser: For Hire, Hill St. Blues. Series: Leg Work. Movie: Crazy in Love.

McDOWALL, BETTY: Actress. b. Sydney, Australia. e. Mt. Bernard Convent, N. Sydney. Early career radio, stage in Australia; ent. BBC TV, 1952; since in West End plays, many TV and radio plays and films.
STAGE: Age of Consent, Ghost Train, The Kidders, The Dark Halo, Period of Adjustment, Rule of Three, Signpost to Murder, Hippolytus, The Winslow Boy, Woman in a Dressing Gown, As Long as It's Warm, Caprice—in a Pink Palazzo, Sweet Bird of Youth, There Was an Old Woman, What the Butler Saw, Two Dozen Red Roses, A Boston Story, The Man Most Likely To . . . , Sleeping Partner.
TELEVISION: Mid-Level and Glorification of Al Toolum, The Black Judge, Phone Call for Matthew Quade, Thunder on the Snowy, Shadow of Guilt, Traveling Lady, Torment, Biography, Notes for a Love Song, Esther's Altar, The Corridor People, The Braden Beat, The Douglas Fairbanks, Ivanhoe, The Foreign Legion, Fabian of the Yard, Four Just Men, Flying Doctor, No Hiding Place, Z' Cars, Days of Vengeance, Flower of Evil, Outbreak of Murder, Call Me Sam, The Prisoner, Public Eye, The Forgotten Door, All Out for Kangaroo Valley, Barry Humphries Scandals, Castle Haven, Albert and Victoria, Follyfoot, The Man Who Came to Dinner, Anne of Avonlea, Little Lord Fauntleroy, The Bass Player and the Blond (4 plays), The Gingerbread Lady. Series: Boyd Q.C.
PICTURES: First lead in England, Timelock, She Didn't Say No, Jack the Ripper, The Shiralee, Jackpot, Dead Lucky, Spare the Rod, Golliwog, Echo of Diana, First Men in the Moon, Ballad in Blue, The Liquidators, Willy Wagtails by Moonlight, The Omen.
RADIO: Anna Christie, The Little Foxes, Another Part of the Forest, The Archers.

McDOWALL, RODDY: Actor. b. London, England, Sept. 17, 1928. e. St. Joseph's, London. First appeared in British film Murder in the Family at age of 9. In 1940 signed by 20th Century-Fox. Star of Tomorrow, 1944. Named Screen Actors Guild representative on National Film Preservation Bd., 1989. Published two volumes of his photography: Double Exposure (1966), and Double Exposure II (1989).
PICTURES: Murder in the Family (debut, 1938), I See Ice, John Halifax Gentleman, Convict 99, Scruffy, Yellow Sands, Hey Hey USA, Poison Pen, The Outsider, Dead Man's Shoes, Just Williams, His Brother's Keeper, Saloon Bar, You Will Remember, This England, Man Hunt (U.S. debut, 1941), How Green Was My Valley, Confirm or Deny, Son of Fury, On the Sunny Side, The Pied Piper, My Friend Flicka, Lassie Come Home, White Cliffs of Dover, The Keys of the Kingdom, Thunderhead Son of Flicka, Molly and Me, Holiday in Mexico, Macbeth, Rocky, Kidnapped, Tuna Clipper, Black Midnight, Killer Shark, Everybody's Dancin', Big Timber, Steel Fist, The Subterraneans, Midnight Lace, The Longest Day, Cleopatra, Shock Treatment, The Greatest Story Ever Told, That Darn Cat, The Loved One, The Third Day, Inside Daisy Clover, Lord Love A Duck, The Defector, It, Adventures of Bullwhip Griffin, The Cool Ones, Planet of the Apes, 5 Card Stud,

Hello Down There, Midas Run, Angel Angel Down We Go, Pretty Maids All in a Row, Escape from the Planet of the Apes, Bedknobs and Broomsticks, Corky (unbilled), Conquest of the Planet of the Apes, The Devil's Widow (dir. only), Life and Times of Judge Roy Bean, The Poseidon Adventure, The Legend of Hellhouse, Arnold, Battle for the Planet of the Apes, Dirty Mary Crazy Larry, Funny Lady, Mean Johnny Barrows, Embryo, Sixth and Main, Rabbit Test, Laserblast, The Cat from Outer Space, Circle of Iron, Scavenger Hunt, The Black Hole (voice), Charlie Chan and the Curse of the Dragon Queen, Evil Under the Sun, Class of 1984, Fright Night, GoBots (voice), Dead of Winter, Overboard (also exec. prod.), Doin' Time on Planet Earth, The Big Picture, Destroyer, Fright Night Part 2, Cutting Class, Shakma, Going Under, The Color of Evening, Double Trouble, The Naked Target.
THEATRE: On B'way in Misalliance, Escapade, Doctor's Dilemma, No Time for Sergeants, Good as Gold, Compulsion, Handful of Fire, Look After Lulu, The Fighting Cock (Tony Award, 1960), Camelot, The Astrakhan Coat.
TELEVISION: Specials: Stratford Shakespeare Festival, He's for Me, Not Without Honor (Emmy Award, 1961), Camilla (Nightmare Classics). Movies: Night Gallery, Terror in the Sky, A Taste of Evil, What's a Nice Girl Like You . . . ?, Miracle on 34th Street, The Elevator, Flood, Thief of Baghdad, The Immigrants, The Martian Chronicles, Hart to Hart (pilot), Memory of Eva Ryker, Million Dollar Face, Mae West, This Girl for Hire, The Zany Adventures of Robin Hood, Alice in Wonderland, Earth Angel, An Inconvenient Woman, Deadly Game, The Sands of Time. Mini-Series: The Rhinemann Exchange, Hollywood Wives, Around the World in 80 Days. Series: Planet of the Apes, Fantastic Journey, Tales of the Gold Monkey, Bridges to Cross. Guest: Goodyear TV Playhouse, Ponds Theatre, Oldsmobile Music Theatre, Campbell Soundstage, Batman, The Invaders, Love American Style, Carol Burnett Show, George Burns Comedy Week, Love Boat, Matlock, Murder She Wrote, many others.

McDOWELL, MALCOLM: Actor. b. Leeds, England, June 13, 1943. Was spearholder for the Royal Shakespeare Co. in season of 1965–66 when turned to TV and then to films. NY stage: Look Back in Anger (also on video), In Celebration, Another Time. Made screen debut in small role in Poor Cow, 1967. LA stage: Hunting Cockroaches.
PICTURES: If . . . , Figures in a Landscape, The Raging Moon (US title: Long Ago Tomorrow), A Clockwork Orange, O Lucky Man!, Royal Flash, Voyage of the Damned, Aces High, The Passage, Time After Time, Caligula, Cat People, Britannia Hospital, Blue Thunder, Cross Creek, Get Crazy, Sunset, Buy and Cell, The Caller, Class of 1999, Disturbed, In the Eye of the Snake, Moon 44, The Maestro, Schweitzer, Assassin of the Tsar, The Player, Happily Ever After (voice), Chain of Desire, East Wind, Night Train to Venice.
TELEVISION: Movies: Arthur the King, Gulag, Monte Carlo. Guest: Faerie Tale Theatre (Little Red Riding Hood), Tales fromt the Crypt (Reluctant Vampire).

McELWAINE, GUY: Executive. b. Culver City, CA, June 29, 1936. Started career in pub. dept. of MGM, 1955; 1959, joined m.p. div. of Rogers and Cowen. 1964, formed own public relations firm; then joined CMA. Left to become sr. exec. v.p. in chg. worldwide m.p. production, Warner Bros., 1975. In 1977 became sr. exec. v.p. in chg. worldwide m.p. activities and pres. of intl. film mktg. at Intl. Creative Management (ICM), formerly CMA. 1981, named pres. and chief exec. officer Rastar Films. Left in 1982 to become pres., Columbia Pictures; given additional title of chief exec. officer, 1983. In 1985 named chmn. and on board of Columbia Pictures Industries. Resigned, 1986. Joined Weintraub Entertainment Group as exec. v.p. and chmn., m.p. div. 1987–89; returned to Intl. Creative Management, Aug. 1989 as vice chmn.

McEVEETY, BERNARD: Director. Comes from film family; father was pioneer as unit mgr. at New York's Edison Studios; brothers Vincent, also a dir., and Joseph, writer are at Disney Studios. Bernard's career began in 1953 at Paramount where was asst. dir. for 6 yrs. Earned full dir. responsibility on The Rebel, TV series.
PICTURES: Napoleon and Samantha, One Little Indian, The Bears and I.
TELEVISION: Numerous episodes on Bonanza, Gunsmoke, Combat and Cimarron Strip (also prod.), Centennial, Roughnecks, The Machans.

McEVEETY, VINCENT: Director. Joined Hal Roach Studios in 1954 as second asst. dir. Then to Republic for The Last Command. First Disney assignments: Davy Crockett shows and Mickey Mouse Club. Moved to Desilu as first asst. dir. on The Untouchables; made assoc. prod. with option to direct. Did segments of many series, including 34 Gunsmoke episodes. First theatrical film: Firecreek, 1968.
PICTURES: $1,000,000 Duck, The Biscuit Eater, Charley and the Angel, Superdad, The Strongest Man in the World, Gus, Treasure of Matecumbe, Herbie Goes to Monte Carlo, Apple Dumpling Gang Rides Again, Herbie Goes Bananas, Amy.

TELEVISION: Blood Sport, Wonder Woman, High Flying Spy, Ask Max, Gunsmoke: Return to Dodge, Murder She Wrote, Simon and Simon (26 episodes), Columbo: Rest in Peace Mrs. Columbo.

McGAVIN, DARREN: Actor. b. Spokane, WA, May 7, 1922. e. Coll. of the Pacific.
PLAYS: Death of a Salesman, My Three Angels, The Rainmaker, The Lovers, The King and I, Dinner at Eight (revival), Captain Brassbound's Conversion (LA), The Night Hank Williams Died.
PICTURES: Summertime, The Man with the Golden Arm, Court Martial of Billy Mitchell, Beau James, Delicate Delinquent, The Case Against Brooklyn, Bullet for Badman, The Great Sioux Massacre, Mission Mars, Mrs. Polifax-Spy, Happy Mother's Day . . . Love George (dir. only), No Deposit No Return, Airport 77, Hot Lead and Cold Feet, Zero to Sixty, Hangar 18, Firebird 2015 A.D., A Christmas Story, The Natural, Turk 182, Raw Deal, From the Hip, Dead Heat, Blood and Concrete.
TELEVISION: Series: Crime Photographer, Mike Hammer, Riverboat, The Outsider, Kolchak: The Night Stalker, Small & Frye. Movies: The Outsider (pilot), The Challenge, The Challengers, Berlin Affair, Tribes, Banyon, The Death of Me Yet, Night Stalker, Something Evil, The Rookies, Say Goodbye Maggie Cole, The Night Strangler, The Six Million Dollar Man (pilot), Brink's: The Great Robbery, Law and Order, The Users, Love for Rent, Waikiki, Return of Marcus Welby M.D., My Wicked Wicked Ways, Inherit the Wind, The Diamond Trap, By Dawn's Early Light, The American Clock. Specials: Unclaimed Fortunes (host), Clara (ACE Award), Mastergate, Miracles and Ohter Wonders (host), The Secret Discovery of Noah's Ark (host). Mini-Series: Ike, The Martian Chronicles, Around the World in 80 Days. Guest: Goodyear TV Playhouse, Alfred Hitchcock Presents, Route 66, U.S. Steel Hour, The Defenders, Love American Style, The Name of the Game, Owen Marshall, Police Story, The Love Boat, Murphy Brown (Emmy Award, 1990), many others.

McGILLIS, KELLY: Actress. b. Newport Beach, CA, July 9, 1957. e. Juilliard. D.C. Stage: The Merchant of Venice, Twelfth Night, Measure for Measure, Much Ado About Nothing.
PICTURES: Reuben Reuben (debut, 1983), Witness, Top Gun, Made in Heaven, Promised Land, The House on Carroll Street, The Accused, Winter People, Cat Chaser, Before and After Death, The Babe.
TELEVISION: Movies: Sweet Revenge, Private Sessions, Grand Isle (also prod.), Bonds of Love.

McGINLEY, JOHN C.: Actor. b. New York, NY, Aug. 3, 1959 e. NYU.
PICTURES: Sweet Liberty, Platoon, Wall Street, Shakedown, Talk Radio, Lost Angels, Fat Man and Little Boy, Born on the Fourth of July, Point Break, Highlander 2: The Quickening, Article 99, Little Noises, A Midnight Clear, Fathers and Sons, Hear No Evil, Watch It (also co-prod.), Car 54 Where Are You?, The New Age.
TELEVISION: Movies: Clinton & Nadine, Cruel Doubt.
THEATRE: NY: Danny and the Deep Blue Sea, The Ballad of Soapy Smith, Jesse and the Games, Requiem for a Heavyweight, Love as We Know It, Talk Radio, Florida Crackers.

McGOOHAN, PATRICK: Actor. b. New York, Mar. 19, 1928. Early career in repertory in Britain. London stage work 1954 in Serious Charge; 1955 Orson Welles' Moby Dick. Ent. films 1954. On Broadway in Pack of Lies (1987).
PICTURES: The Dam Busters (debut, 1954), I Am a Camera, The Dark Avenger (The Warrior), Passage Home, High Tide at Noon, Zarak, Hell Drivers, The Gypsy and the Gentleman, Nor the Moon by Night, Two Living One Dead, All Night Long, Life for Ruth (Walk in the Shadow), The Three Lives of Thomasina, Dr. Syn: Alias the Scarecrow (first shown on tv in U.S. as The Scarecrow of Romney Marsh), The Quare Fellow, Ice Station Zebra, The Moonshine War, Mary Queen of Scots, Catch My Soul (dir. only), Silver Streak, Kings and Desperate Men, Brass Target, Escape From Alcatraz, Scanners, Trespasses, Baby: Secret of the Lost Legend.
TELEVISION: Series: Danger Man (also dir. episodes), Secret Agent, The Prisoner. Movies: Jamaica Inn; Of Pure Blood, Man in the Iron Mask. Guest: Columbo (Emmy Awards: 1975, 1990).

McGOVERN, ELIZABETH: Actress. b. Evanston, IL, July 18, 1961. Acted in high school in California; studied at American Conservatory Theatre, San Francisco and Juilliard Sch. of Dramatic Art.
THEATER: NY: To Be Young Gifted and Black (1981, debut), My Sister in This House (Theatre World, Obie Awards), Painting Churches, The Hitch-Hiker, A Map of the World, Aunt Dan and Lemon (L.A.), Two Gentlemen of Verona, A Midsummer Night's Dream (NY Shakespeare Fest.), Love Letters, Twelfth Night (Boston), Major Barbara (Alaska), Ring Around the Moon (D.C.), Maids of Honor, The Three Sisters, As You Like It.

PICTURES: Ordinary People (debut, 1980), Ragtime (Acad. Award nom.), Lovesick, Racing with the Moon, Once Upon a Time in America, Native Son, The Bedroom Window, She's Having a Baby, Johnny Handsome, The Handmaid's Tale, A Shock to the System, Tune in Tomorrow, King of the Hill, The Favor, Me and Veronica.
TELEVISION: Movie: Women and Men: Stories of Seduction (The Man in the Brooks Brothers Shirt). Specials: Ashenden, Tales From Hollywood.

McGRATH, THOMAS J.: Producer. b. New York, NY, Oct. 8, 1932. e. Washington Square Coll. of NYU, B.A., 1956; NYU Sch. of Law, LL.B., 1960. Has practiced law in N.Y. from 1960 to date. Became indep. prod. with Deadly Hero in 1976; Author, Carryover Basis Under The 1976 Tax Reform Act, published in 1977.

McGREGOR, CHARLES: Executive. b. Jersey City, NJ, April 1, 1927. e. NYU. 1958–1969, co-founder, pres. and chief exec. officer, Banner Films, Inc. (World Wide TV Distribution), 1955–58, salesman and div. mgr., Flamingo Films (domestic TV Dist.). 1953–55; Professional mgr. ABC Music Publishing. 1951–53: Prod. and partner Telco Prods. and GM Productions (prods. of network and local shows). 1969–77: exec. v.p. in chg. of w-w dist., WB-TV; 1977–89, pres. WB-TV Distribution; 1989–present, exec. v.p., corp. projects, WB.

McGUIRE, DON: Writer, Director. b. Chicago, IL, Feb. 28, 1919. U.S. Army, 4 yrs.; press agent, Chicago and Hollywood; newsman, Hearst papers, Chicago; then actor, writer.
PICTURES: Double Deal, Dial 1119, Meet Danny Wilson, Back at the Front, Walking My Baby Back Home, Three Ring Circus, Bad Day at Black Rock, Artists and Models, Johnny Concho (dir.), Delicate Delinquent (dir.), Suppose They Gave a War and Nobody Came, Tootsie (co-story), Hear Me Good.
TELEVISION: Henessey (dir., writer, co-prod., series) Not for Hire (series creator), Don't Call Me Charlie (series creator, writer, prod.), From Here to Eternity, Berlin Air Lift.
AUTHOR: Novels: The Day Television Died, 1600 Flobgle Street, The Hell with Walter Cronkite.

McGUIRE, DOROTHY: Actress. b. Omaha, NE, June 14, 1919. e. Ladywood convent, Indianapolis; Pine Manor, Wellesley, MA.
STAGE: Our Town, My Dear Children, Swinging the Dream, Claudia, Legend of Lovers, Winesberg Ohio, Night of the Iguana (1976), Cause Celebre, Another Part of the Forest, I Never Sang for My Father.
PICTURES: Claudia (debut, 1943), A Tree Grows in Brooklyn, The Enchanted Cottage, The Spiral Staircase, Claudia and David, Till the End of Time, Gentleman's Agreement (Acad. Award nom.), Mother Didn't Tell Me, Mister 880, Callaway Went Thataway, I Want You, Invitation, Make Haste to Live, 3 Coins in the Fountain, Trial, Friendly Persuasion, Old Yeller, The Remarkable Mr. Pennypacker, This Earth is Mine, A Summer Place, The Dark at the Top of the Stairs, Swiss Family Robinson, Susan Slade, Summer Magic, The Greatest Story Ever Told, Flight of the Doves, Jonathan Livingston Seagull (voice).
TELEVISION: Series: Little Women. Movies: She Waits, The Runaways, Little Women, The Incredible Journey of Dr. Meg Laurel, Ghost Dancing, Amos, Between the Darkness and the Dawn, Caroline? Mini-Series: Rich Man Poor Man. Specials: The Philadelphia Story, To Each His Own, Another Part of the Forest, I Never Sang for My Father. Guest on: Love Boat, The Young & the Restless, Highway to Heaven, Fantasy Island, St. Elsewhere.

McHATTIE, STEPHEN: Actor. b. Antigonish, Nova Scotia, Canada, Feb. 3. e. Acadia U. Trained for stage at American Acad. of Dramatic Arts.
THEATER: (NY): The American Dream (debut, 1968), Pictures in the Hallway, Twelfth Night, Mourning Becomes Electra, The Iceman Cometh, Alive and Well in Argentina, The Winter Dancers, Casualties, The Three Sisters, The Misanthrope, Heartbreak House, Mensch Meier, Haven, Search and Destroy.
PICTURES: Von Richthofen and Brown (debut, 1970), The People Next Door, The Ultimate Warrior, Moving Violation, Tomorrow Never Comes, Death Valley, Best Revenge, Belizaire the Cajun, Salvation!, Call Me, Sticky Fingers, Caribe, Bloodhounds on Broadway, Erik.
TELEVISION: Series: Highcliffe Manor, Mariah, Scene of the Crime. Mini-series: Centennial. Movies: Search for the Gods, James Dean, Look What's Happened to Rosemary's Baby, Mary and Joseph: A Story of Faith, Roughnecks, Terror on Track 9.

McHUGH, JAMES: Agent, Manager. b. Boston, MA, Oct. 21, 1915. e. Holy Cross Coll. Joined MCA 1939. U.S. Army Signal Corps, 1944–46. MCA-British and European, 1945–50. Post grad. studies, Boston Coll. Formed James McHugh, Talent Agency 1953. Pres., Artists Mgr. Corp., pres., Irenadele Publishing Co. pres.

McKEAN, MICHAEL: Actor, Writer. b. NYC, Oct. 17, 1947. e. NYU. Featured on L.A. radio show The Credibility Gap.

McK-McN

PICTURES: 1941, Used Cars, Young Doctors in Love, This is Spinal Tap (also co-s.p., co-wrote songs), D.A.R.Y.L., Clue, Jumpin' Jack Flash, Light of Day, Planes Trains and Automobiles, Short Circuit 2, Earth Girls Are Easy, The Big Picture (also co-s.p.), Hider in the House, Flashback, Book of Love, True Identity, Memoirs of an Invisible Man, Man Trouble, Coneheads, Airheads.
TELEVISION: *Series*: Laverne & Shirley, Grand, Sessions. *Movies*: More Than Friends, Classified Love, Murder in High Places. *Special*: Spinal Tap Reunion.
THEATRE: Accomplice (Theatre World Award).

McKELLEN, SIR IAN: Actor. b. Burnley, England, May 25, 1939. e. Cambridge. C.B.E. 1979, Knighted 1991.
THEATRE: *London stage*: Much Ado About Nothing, Trelawny of the Wells, A Lily in Little India, The Man of Destiny, Black Comedy, Dr. Faustus, King John, Henceforward, Uncle Vanya, Richard III. *On Bdwy*: The Promise, Amadeus (Tony Award, 1981), Ian McKellen Acting Shakespeare, Wild Honey (also London), Richard III (Brooklyn). Assoc. Dir. Nat'l Theatre, 1991, Cameron Mackintosh Prof. of Contemporary Theatre, Oxford Univ.
PICTURES: Alfred the Great, The Promise, A Touch of Love, Priest of Love, The Keep, Plenty, Zina, Scandal, Last Action Hero, The Ballad of Little Jo, I'll Do Anything, Six Degrees of Separation.
TELEVISION: Hamlet, David Copperfield, The Scarlet Pimpernel, Hedda Gabler, Ian McKellen Acting Shakespeare, Every Good Boy Deserves Favor, Loving Walter, Windmills of the Gods, Macbeth, Othello, Countdown to War, And the Band Played On, Mister Shaw's Missing Millions.

McKEON, DOUG: Actor. b. Pompton Plains, NJ, June 10, 1966.
THEATRE: Dandelion Wine, Truckload, Brighton Beach Memoirs, Death of a Buick, The Big Day.
PICTURES: Uncle Joe Shannon, On Golden Pond, Night Crossing, Mischief, Turnaround, Where the Red Fern Grows Part 2.
TELEVISION: *Series*: Edge of Night, Big Shamus Little Shamus, Little Niagra. *Mini-Series*: Centennial. *Movies*: Tell Me My Name, Daddy I Don't Like It Like This, The Comeback Kid, An Innocent Love, Desperate Lives, At Mother's Request, Silent Eye, Heart of a Champion: The Ray Mancini Story, Breaking Home Ties.

McKERN, LEO: Actor. r.n. Reginald McKern. b. Sydney, New South Wales, Australia, Mar. 16, 1920. On stage in She Stoops to Conquer, Hamlet, Merry Wives of Windsor, Cat on a Hot Tin Roof, A Man for All Seasons, Boswell for the Defence.
PICTURES: All For Mary (1955), X the Unknown, Time Without Pity, The Mouse That Roared, Yesterday's Enemy, Scent of Mystery, Jazz Boat, Mr. Topaze, The Day the Earth Caught Fire, A Jolly Bad Fellow, King and Country, Agent 8-3/4 (Hot Enough for June), Help!, The Amorous Adventures of Moll Flanders, A Man for All Seasons, Assignment K, Decline and Fall of a Bird Watcher, The Shoes of the Fisherman, Ryan's Daughter, Massacre in Rome, The Adventure of Sherlock Holmes' Smarter Brother, The Omen, Candleshoe, Damien: Omen II, The Last Tasmanian, The Blue Lagoon, The French Lieutenant's Woman, Ladyhawke, The Chain, Traveling North.
TELEVISION: King Lear, Murder with Mirrors, House on Garibaldi Street, Reilly: Ace of Spies, Rumpole of the Bailey, The Master Builder, The Last Romantics, A Foreign Field.

McLAGLEN, ANDREW V.: Director. b. London, Eng., July 28, 1920. Son of late actor Victor McLaglen. e. U. of Virginia, 1939–40. Asst. m.p. dir., 1944–54; dir., 1955–present.
PICTURES: Man in the Vault, Gun the Man Down, Seven Men from Now, The Abductors, Freckles, The Little Shepherd of Kingdom Come, McLintock!, Shenandoah, The Rare Breed, The Way West, The Ballad of Josie, Monkeys Go Home, Devil's Brigade, Bandolero, The Undefeated, Chisum, Fool's Parade, Something Big, One More Train to Rob, Cahill: U.S. Marshal, Mitchell, The Last Hard Men, The Wild Geese, ffolkes, The Sea Wolves, Sahara (also exec. prod.), Return from the River Kwai, Eye of the Widow.
TELEVISION: *Series*: Gunsmoke, Have Gun—Will Travel, Perry Mason, Rawhide, The Lineup, The Lieutenant. *Movies*: Log of the Black Pearl, Stowaway to the Moon, Banjo Hackett: Roamin' Free, Murder at the World Series, Louis L'Amour's The Shadow Riders, Travis McGee, The Dirty Dozen: The Next Mission, On Wings of Eagles. *Mini-Series*: The Blue and the Gray.

McLERIE, ALLYN ANN: Actress. b. Grand Mere, Quebec, Canada, Dec. 1, 1926. m. actor-singer George Gaynes. e. high school, N.Y. Dancer since 15 in many Bdwy shows.
THEATER: One Touch of Venus, On the Town, Finian's Rainbow, Where's Charley, Miss Liberty, Time Limit, South Pacific (revival).
PICTURES: Words and Music (debut 1948), Where's Charley, Desert Song, Calamity Jane, Phantom of the Rue Morgue, Battle Cry, They Shoot Horses, Don't They?, The

Cowboys, Jeremiah Johnson, The Magnificent Seven Ride, Cinderella Liberty, All the President's Men.
TELEVISION: *Series*: Tony Randall Show, Punky Brewster, Days and Nights of Molly Dodd. *Mini-Series*: The Thorn Birds, Beulah Land. *Specials*: Oldest Living Graduate, The Entertainer, Return Engagement.

McMAHON, ED: Performer. b. Detroit, MI, March 6, 1923. e. Boston Coll.; Catholic U. of America, B.A., 1949. U.S. Marines, 1942–53. First job on TV was as the clown on Big Top, 1950–51. First joined Johnny Carson as his sidekick on daytime quiz show Who Do You Trust? in 1958.
TELEVISION: *Series*: Big Top, Who Do You Trust?, The Tonight Show (1962–92), Missing Links (emcee), Snap Judgment (emcee), The Kraft Music Hall (host, 1968), Concentration (emcee), NBC Adventure Theatre (host), Whodunnit? (emcee), Star Search (host), TV's Bloopers and Practical Jokes (host). *Movies*: Star Marker, The Great American Traffic Jam (Gridlock), The Kid From Left Field. *Specials*: Macy's Thanksgiving Day Parade (host), Jerry Lewis Labor Day Telethon (co-host).
THEATRE: Stock; Bdwy.: Impossible Years.
PICTURES: The Incident, Slaughter's Big Rip-Off, Fun with Dick and Jane, The Last Remake of Beau Geste (cameo), Butterfly, Full Moon High.

McMAHON, JOHN J.: Executive. b. Chicago, IL, 1932. e. Northwestern U. Served with U.S. Army in Korea, beginning career on WGN-TV, Chicago; associated with ZIV-United Artists TV Productions during 1950s; joined ABC in 1958: v.p. & gen. mgr., WXYTZ-TV, Detroit, then KABC-TV, Los Angeles, 1968; v.p., ABC, 1968–72; joined NBC in 1972 as v.p., programs, west coast, NBC-TV; president, Hollywood Radio & Television Society; board member, Permanent Charities Committee. June, 1980, named pres. of Carson Prods. (Johnny Carson's prod. co.).
TELEVISION: If It's Tuesday It Still Must Be Belgium (exec. prod.), My Father My Son (exec. prod.).

McMARTIN, JOHN: Actor. Warsaw, IN, e. Columbia U. Off-Broadway debut: Little Mary Sunshine (1959: Theatre World Award).
THEATER: The Conquering Hero, Blood Sweat and Stanley Poole, Children from Their Games, A Rainy Day in Newark, Pleasures and Palaces (Detroit), Sweet Charity, Follies, The Great God Brown, Sondheim: A Musical Tribute, Forget-Me-Not-Lane (Mark Taper Forum), The Visit, Chemin de Fer, The Rules of the Game, A Little Family Business, Passion (Mark Taper), Solomon's Child, Julius Caesar, A Little Night Music (Ahmanson), Love for Love, Happy New Year, Don Juan, Artist Descending a Staircase, Henry IV (Kennedy Ctr.), Custer (Kennedy Ctr.), Money & Friends (L.A.).
PICTURES: A Thousand Clowns, What's So Bad About Feeling Good?, Sweet Charity, All The President's Men, Thieves, Brubaker, Blow Out, Pennies From Heaven, Dream Lover, Legal Eagles, Native Son, Who's That Girl, A Shock to the System.
TELEVISION: *Series*: Falcon Crest, Beauty and the Beast. *Guest*: Cheers, Mary Tyler Moore Show, Murder She Wrote, Magnum P.I., The Golden Girls, Empty Nest, Law and Order, others. *American Playhouse Specials*: Edith Wharton Story, Rules of the Game, The Greatest Man in the World, Private Contentment, The Fatal Weakness, Concealed Enemies. *Movies*: Ritual of Evil, Fear on Trial, The Defection of Simas Kudirka, The Last Ninja, Murrow, Day One, Roots: The Gift, Separate But Equal, Citizen Cohn.

McNALLY, STEPHEN: Actor r.n. Horace McNally. b. New York, NY, July 29, 1913. e. Fordham U., LL.B. In school dramatics; practiced law 2 yrs., N.Y.; stage, films, 1942.
PICTURES: Thirty Seconds Over Tokyo, The Harvey Girls, Johnny Belinda, Rogues' Regiment, Winchester 73, Wyoming Mail, No Way Out, Air Cadet, Apache Drums, Raging Tide, Lady Pays Off, Devil's Canyon, Make Haste to Live, A Bullet Is Waiting, Man from Bitter Ridge, Tribute to a Bad Man, Hell's Five Hours, The Fiend Who Walked the West, Hell Bent for Leather, Requiem for a Gunfighter, Once You Kiss a Stranger, Black Gunn.

McNAMARA, WILLIAM: Actor. b. Dallas, TX, 1965. e. Columbia U. Joined Act I theatre group at Williamstown Theatre Festival, 1986; studied acting at Lee Strasberg Institute.
PICTURES: The Beat (debut, 1988), Stealing Home, Dream a Little Dream, Stella, Texasville, Terror at the Opera, Aspen Extreme, Chasers.
TELEVISION: *Series*: Island Son. *Specials*: Soldier Boys (Afterschool Special), Secret of the Sahara, The Edge (Indian Poker), It's Only Rock 'n' Roll (Afterschool Special). *Movies*: Wildflower (ACE Award nom.), Doing Time on Maple Drive, Honor Thy Mother, Sworn to Vengeance.

McNAUGHTON, JOHN: Director. b. Chicago, IL, Jan. 13, 1950.
PICTURES: Henry: Portrait of a Serial Killer, The Borrower, Sex Drugs Rock & Roll, Mad Dog and Glory.

233

McNICHOL, KRISTY: Actress. b. Los Angeles, CA, Sept. 11, 1962. Brother is actor Jimmy McNichol. Made debut at age of 7 performing in commercials. Given regular role in Apple's Way; began appearing on such series as Love American Style and The Bionic Woman. Attracted attention of Spelling-Goldberg Productions, who cast her as Buddy Lawrence in Family series, 1976–80.

PICTURES: The End (debut, 1978), Little Darlings, The Night the Lights Went Out in Georgia, Only When I Laugh, White Dog, The Pirate Movie, Just the Way You Are, Dream Lover, You Can't Hurry Love, Two Moon Junction, The Forgotten One.

TELEVISION: Series: Apple's Way, Family (Emmy Awards: 1977, 1979), Empty Nest. Movies: The Love Boat II, Like Mom Like Me, Summer of My German Soldier, My Old Man, Blinded by the Light, Love Mary, Women of Valor, Children of the Bride, Mother of the Bride (also co-exec. prod.).

McRANEY, GERALD: Actor. b. Collins, MS, Aug. 19, 1948. m. actress Delta Burke. e. U. of Mississippi. Left school to become surveyor in oil fields after which joined acting company in New Orleans. Studied acting with Jeff Corey; landed guest role on TV series, Night Gallery.

TELEVISION: Series: Simon & Simon, Major Dad (also exec. prod.). Guest: The Incredible Hulk, The Rockford Files, The Dukes of Hazzard, Eight Is Enough, How the West Was Won, Hawaii Five-O, Barnaby Jones, Gunsmoke, Designing Women. Movies: Roots II, The Jordan Chance, Women in White, Trial of Chaplain Jenson, The Law, The Haunting Passion, A Hobo's Christmas, Where the Hell's That Gold?!!?, The People Across the Lake, Dark of the Moon, Murder By Moonlight, Blind Vengeance, Vestige of Honor, Love and Curses . . . And All That Jazz (also dir., co-exec. prod.), Fatal Friendship.

PICTURES: Night of Bloody Horror, Keep Off My Grass, The Neverending Story, American Justice.

McSHANE, IAN: Actor. b. Blackburn, England, Sept. 29, 1942. e. Royal Acad. of Dramatic Art. Stage work includes The House of Fred Ginger, The Easter Man, The Glass Menagerie (England). NY: The Promise. LA: Inadmissible Evidence, Betrayal.

PICTURES: The Wild and the Willing (debut, 1962), The Pleasure Girls, Gypsy Girl (Sky West and Crooked), The Battle of Britain, If It's Tuesday This Must Be Belgium, Pussycat Pussycat I Love You, Villain, The Devil's Widow (Tam-Lin), Sitting Target, The Last of Sheila, Journey Into Fear, The Fifth Musketeer, Cheaper to Keep Her, Exposed, Ordeal By Innocence, Torchlight, Too Scared to Scream.

TELEVISION: Wuthering Heights, The Pirate, Disraeli, The Letter, Marco Polo, Bare Essence, Grace Kelly, Evergreen, A.D., The Murders in the Rue Morgue, Grand Larceny, War and Remembrance, Chain Letter (pilot), The Great Escape II: the Untold Story, The Young Charlie Chaplin, Lovejoy (also II), Sauce For Goose, Dick Francis Mysteries (Blood Sport), Perry Mason: The Case of the Desperate Deception, Columbo: Rest in Peace Mrs. Columbo.

McTIERNAN, JOHN: Director. b. Albany, NY, Jan. 8, 1951. e. Juilliard (acting), SUNY/Old Westbury (filmmaking). m. prod. Donna Dubrow. First effort was film The Demon's Daughter, unreleased to date.

PICTURES: Nomads (also s.p.), Predator, Die Hard, The Hunt for Red October, Medicine Man, Last Action Hero (also co-prod.).

MEADOWS, AUDREY: Actress. b. Wu Chang, China, Feb. 8, 1926. e. Miss Hill's School for Girls. Sister of actress Jayne Meadows. Parents were Episcopal missionaries. Arrived in U.S. in early 1930s, making singing debut at Carnegie Hall. Appeared on Bdwy. in 1952 in Top Banana.

TELEVISION: Series: Bob and Ray, Club Embassy, The Jackie Gleason Show (Emmy Award, 1954), What's in a Word (panelist), What's Going On? (panelist), The Name's the Same (panelist), The Honeymooners, The Jackie Gleason Show (1956–7), Keep Talking (panelist), Masquerade Party (panelist), Too Close for Comfort, Uncle Buck. Guest: Steve Allen Show, Alfred Hitchcock Presents, Please Don't Eat the Daisies, Carol Burnett Show, Love American Style, The Love Boat, Murder She Wrote, many others.

PICTURES: That Touch of Mink, Take Her She's Mine, Rosie!

MEADOWS, JAYNE: Actress. b. Wu Chang, China, Sept. 27, 1924. m. performer Steve Allen. Sister of actress Audrey Meadows. Parents were Episcopal missionaries. Came to U.S. in early 1930s. Made her Bdwy. debut in 1941 in Spring Again.

TELEVISION: Series: I've Got a Secret, The Steve Allen Show, Art Linkletter Show, Steve Allen Comedy Hour, Medical Center, Steve Allen's Laugh Back, Meeting of Minds, It's Not Easy. Movies: Now You See It Now You Don't, James Dean, Sex and the Married Woman, The Gossip Columnist, Miss All-American Beauty, Alice in Wonderland, A Masterpiece of Murder, Parent Trap Hawaiian Honeymoon. Guest: Robert Montgomery Presents, The Web, Ann Southern

Show, Love American Style, Here's Lucy, The Love Boat, St. Elsewhere, many others.

PICTURES: Undercurrent (debut, 1946), Dark Delusion, Lady in the Lake, Song of the Thin Man, Luck of the Irish, Enchantment, David and Bathsheba, The Fat Man, College Confidential, Da Capa (Finland), Norman Is That You?, City Slickers (voice), The Player.

THEATRE: NY: Spring Again, Another Love Story, Kiss Them for Me, The Gazebo, Once in a Lifetime (revival), Many Happy Returns, etc. Regional: Love Letters, Lost in Yonkers, The Fourposter, Cinderella, Tonight at 8:30, Powerful Women in History (1 woman show).

MEANEY, DONALD V.: Executive. b. Newark, NJ. e. Rutgers U. Sch. of Journalism. Worked as reporter for Plainfield (NJ) Courier-News, Newark Evening News. Became news director of radio station WCTC in New Brunswick, NJ; later for WNJR, Newark. Joined NBC in 1952 as news writer; two years later became nat'l. TV news editor. Promoted to mgr., national news, 1960 and mrg., special news programs, 1961. Appt. dir. of news programs 1962 and gen. mgr., NBC News, 1965; v.p., news programming, NBC, 1967; v.p. news, Washington, 1974; mrg. dir., affiliate & intl. liaison, 1979; sr. mng. editor, intl. liaison, 1984; retired from NBC, 1985. Now on faculty of American U. Sch. of Communications.

MEARA, ANNE: Actress, Writer. b. Brooklyn, NY Sept. 20, 1929. m. actor-writer Jerry Stiller. e. Herbert Berghof Studio, 1953–54. Apprenticed in summer stock on Long Island and Woodstock NY, 1950–53. Acted with NY Shakespeare Fest. 1957 and 1988 (Romeo and Juliet). With husband joined St. Louis improv. theater The Compass, 1959 and Chicago's Medium Rare. They formed comedy act in 1962 appearing (34 times) on The Ed Sullivan Show and making the nightclub and comedy club circuit incl. The Village Gate, The Blue Angel, The Establishment. Formed own prod. company, writing, prod. and recording award-winning radio and TV commercials.

THEATER: A Month in the Country, Maedchen in Uniform, Ulysses in Nightown, The House of Blue Leaves, Spookhouse, Bosoms and Neglect, Eastern Standard, Anna Christie.

PICTURES: The Out-of-Towners, Lovers and Other Strangers, Nasty Habits, The Boys From Brazil, Fame, The Perils of P.K., The Longshot, My Little Girl, Awakenings, Highway to Hell.

TELEVISION: Guest on numerous TV game and talk shows and variety shows. Series: The Greatest Gift (1954 soap opera), The Paul Lynde Show, The Corner Bar, Take Five with Stiller and Meara (1977–78; synd.), Kate McShane, Rhoda, Archie Bunker's Place, ALF (also writer), All My Children. Movies: Kate McShane (pilot), The Other Woman. Specials: The Sunset Gang, Avenue Z Afternoon.

MECHANIC, BILL: Executive. b. Detroit, MI. e. Michigan State U., B.A.; U. of Southern California, Ph.D. in film pending. Entered industry 1978 as dir. of programming for SelecTV; promoted to v.p., 1980. Joined Paramount 1982; 1984, to Disney as v.p., pay TV sls. 1985, named sr. v.p., video, of new Walt Disney video div.; 1987, named president, int'l theatrical distribution and worldwide video, Walt Disney.

MEDAK, PETER: Director. b. Budapest, Hungary, Dec. 23, 1940. Dir. Miss Julie on stage. Dir. operas Salome, La Voix Humaine.

PICTURES: Negatives, Day in the Death of Joe Egg, Ruling Class, Ghost in the Noonday Sun, Odd Job, The Changeling, Zorro the Gay Blade, Men's Club, The Krays, Let Him Have It. Romeo Is Bleeding.

TELEVISION: Third Girl from the Left, The Babysitter, The Dark Secret of Black Bayou, Mistress of Paradise, Cry for the Stranger, Faerie Tale Theatre, Twilight Zone, Nabokov, Crime Story, Mount Royal, La Voix Humaine, Tales From the Crypt.

MEDAVOY, MIKE: Executive. b. Shanghai, China, Jan. 21, 1941. Lived in China until 1947 when family moved to Chile. Came to U.S. in 1957. e. UCLA, grad. 1963 with honors, history. Started working in mail room at Universal Studios and became a casting director, then went to work for Bill Robinson as an agent trainee. Two years later joined GAC and CMA where he was a v.p. in the motion picture dept.. In 1971 joined IFA as v.p. in charge of motion picture dept. Represented American and foreign creative talents, incl. Jane Fonda, Donald Sutherland, Michelangelo Antonioni, Jean-Louis Trintignant, Karel Reisz, Steven Spielberg, Robert Aldrich, George Cukor, John Milius, Terry Malick, Raquel Welch, Gene Wilder and Jeanne Moreau. While at IFA was involved in packaging The Sting, Young Frankenstein, Jaws and others, before joining United Artists Corp. in May, 1974, as sr. v.p. in chg. of West Coast prod. In 1978 named exec. v.p., Orion Pictures Co. (In 1982 Orion team took over Filmways, Inc.) While prod. head received 7 Oscars for best picture: One Flew Over the Cuckoo's Nest, Rocky, Annie Hall, Amadeus, Platoon, Dances With Wolves, The Silence of the

Lambs. 1990, appointed chairman Tri-Star Pictures, & member Columbia Pictures Board of Directors.

MEMBER: Filmex board; board of trustees, U.C.L.A. Foundation; advisory board, College for Intl. Strategic Affairs at U.C.L.A.; steering committee of Royce 270, U.C.L.A.; visiting committee, Boston Museum of Fine Arts; advisory bd., Tel Aviv U.; bd., Museum of Science & Industry; Co-Chmn.: Olympic Sports Federation, Music Center Unified Fund Campaign; bd. of governors, Sundance Inst.

MEDFORD, DON: Director. b. Detroit, MI, 1917. e. Purdue U., U. of North Carolina, B.A., Yale U., M.F.A. Actor, stage mgr., summer theatres; producer, Bdwy stage, Christopher Award.

TELEVISION: Incident in San Francisco, Coach of the Year, Kraft Theatre, General Electric Theatre, Alfred Hitchcock Presents, Climax, Twilight Zone, U.S. Steel Hour, Dick Powell, Eleventh Hour, Dr. Kildare, Fugitive, 12 O'clock High, The FBI, Man From U.N.C.L.E., Cimarron Strip, Baretta, Police Story, Kaz, Streets of San Francisco, Dynasty, Sizzle, Helltown.

FILMS: To Trap a Spy, Cosa Nostra, The Hunting Party, The Organization, The November Plan.

MEDINA, PATRICIA: Actress. b. London, Eng. July 9, 1921. m. actor Joseph Cotten. In many British films.

PICTURES: Secret Journey, Hotel Reserve, Don't Take It to Heart, Waltz Time, Secret Heart (U.S. debut, 1946), Moss Rose, Foxes of Harrow, Fighting O'Flynn, Francis, Fortunes of Captain Blood, Abbott & Costello in Foreign Legion, The Lady and the Bandit, The Magic Carpet, Valentino, Aladdin and His Lamp, Captain Pirate, Lady in the Iron Mask, Desperate Search, Siren of Bagdad, Plunder of the Sun, Botany Bay, Sangaree, Drums of Tahiti, Phantom of the Rue Morgue, Black Knight, Pirates of Tripoli, Duel on the Mississippi, Mr. Arkadin, Uranium Boom, Stranger at My Door, Miami Expose, The Beast from Hollow Mountain, Missiles from Hell, Count Your Blessings, Snow White and the Three Stooges, The Killing of Sister George, Latitude Zero.

MEDMAN, EDWARD A: Executive. b. Philadelphia, PA, Nov. 11, 1937. e. U. of Pennsylvania Wharton Sch., 1955–58; U. of Pennsylvania Law Sch., 1958–61, J.D.S. General Counsel's staff, National Labor Relations Board, Washington, DC, 1962–66; Trial Attorney NLRB, New York 1966–69; joined law firm of Poletti, Freidin, Prashker, Feldman & Gartner, 1969; sr. labor attorney, National Broadcasting Company 1970–72; joined The Burbank Studios, Dec. 1972, v.p., legal/business affairs.

MEDOFF, MARK: Writer. e. Univ. of Miami, Stanford U. Honorary doctor of humane letters, Gallaudet Univ. Prof. & dramatist in residence, New Mexico St. Univ. Novel: Dreams of Long Lasting.

PICTURES: Off Beat, Children of a Lesser God, Clara's Heart, City of Joy.

THEATRE: When You Comin' Back Red Ryder? (Obie Award), Children of a Lesser God (Tony Award), The Wager, Kringle's Window.

TELEVISION: Movie: Apology.

MEDWIN, MICHAEL: Actor, Writer, Producer. b. London, England, 1923. e. Institut Fischer. Switzerland. Stage debut 1940; m.p. acting debut in Root of All Evil, 1946. Acted with National Theatre 1977–78.

PICTURES: My Sister and I, Mrs. Christopher, Gay One, Children of Chance, Operation Diamond, Black Memory, Just William's Luck, Ideal Husband, Picadilly Incident, Night Beat, Courtney's of Curzon Street, Call of the Blood, Anna Karenina, William Comes to Town, Woman Hater, Look Before You Love, Forbidden, For Them That Trespass, Queen of Spades, Trottie True, Boys in Brown, Trio, Long Dark Hall, Curtain Up, Street Corner (Both Sides of the Law), I Only Asked, Carry on Nurse, Wind Cannot Read, Heart of a Man, Crooks Anonymous, It's All Happening, Night Must Fall, I've Gotta Horse, 24 Hours To Kill, Scrooge. Prod: Charlie Bubbles, If. . ., Spring and Port Wine, O Lucky Man! Gumshoe, Law and Disorder, Memoirs of a Survivor, Diamond's Edge.

TELEVISION: Granada's Army Game, Shoestring, The Love of Mike, Three Live Wires, Memorial Films Ltd.

THEATRE: Spring and Port Wine, Joe Egg, Forget-me-not Lane, Chez Nous, Alpha Beta, Another Country, Crystal Clear, Interpreters, Orpheus, Noises Off.

MEEKER, CHARLES R.: Producer. b. June 17. e. U. of Texas Sch. of Law. 1967–84, associated with Melveny & Myers, law firm specializing in entertainment industry. 1976, named active partner. Now pres., Feldman Meeker Co.; partnered with Edward S. Feldman.

PICTURES: Exec. Prod.: The Hitcher, Children of a Lesser God, Near Dark, Wired (prod.).

MELCHIOR, IB: Director, Writer. b. Copenhagen, Denmark, Sept. 17, 1917. Son of late singer Lauritz Melchior. e. Coll., Stenhus, Denmark, 1936; U. of Copenhagen, 1937. Actor. stage mgr., English Players, 1937–38; co-dir. 1938; actor in 21 stage

prod. in Europe and U.S. on radio; set designer; stage man. dept., Radio City Music Hall, 1941–42; U.S. Military Intelligence, 1942–45; writer, dir., m.p. shorts for TV, 1947–48; TV actor, 1949–50; assoc. dir., CBS-TV, July, 1950; assoc. prod., G-L Enterprises, 1952–53; dir., Perry Como Show, 1951–54; dir. March of Medicine, 1955–56; writer, dir. of M.P. & TV films. 1957. Documentary writ. & dir. awarded Top Award by Nat'l. Comm. for Films for Safety. 1960. Golden Scroll Award, Acad. of Science Fiction, Best Writing, 1976; Hamlet Award, Shakespeare Society of America, excellence in playwriting, Hour of Vengeance, 1982.

PICTURES: When Hell Broke Loose, Live Fast Die Young, The Angry Red Planet, Reptilicus, Journey to the Seventh Planet, The Case of Patty Smith, Robinson Crusoe on Mars, The Time Travellers, Ambush Bay, Planet of the Vampires, Death Race 2000.

AUTHOR: Novel, Order of Battle, 1972; Sleeper Agent, 1975; The Haigerloch Project, 1977; The Watchdogs of Abaddon, 1979; The Marcus Device, 1980; The Tombstone Cipher, 1982; Eva, 1984; V—3, 1985; Code Name: Grand Guignol, 1987, Steps & Stairways, 1989, Quest, 1990, Order of Battle: Hitler's Werewolves, 1991; Case by Case, 1993.

MELNICK, DANIEL: Executive. b. New York, NY, April 21, 1934. e. NYU. 1952–54, prod. The Children's Theatre at Circle in the Sq., NY. In 1954 was (youngest) staff prod. for CBS-TV; then exec. prod., East Side West Side and N.Y.P.D. Joined ABC-TV as v.p. in chg. of programming. Partner in Talent Associates. Joined MGM as v.p. in chg. of prod.; in 1974 named sr. v.p. & worldwide head of prod.; 1977 in charge of worldwide production, Columbia Pictures; named pres., 1978. Resigned to form independent production co., IndieProd. Company.

PICTURES: Prod.: Straw Dogs, That's Entertainment (exec. prod.), That's Entertainment Part 2, All That Jazz (exec. prod.), Altered States (exec. prod.), First Family, Making Love, Unfaithfully Yours (exec. prod.), Footloose (exec. prod.), Quicksilver; Roxanne, Punchline (co-prod.), Mountains of the Moon, Total Recall, Air America, L.A. Story.

TELEVISION: Death of a Salesman (prod., Emmy Award), The Ages of Man (prod., Emmy Award, 1966); exec. prod. with David Susskind: East Side/West Side, N.Y.P.D., Get Smart, Chain Letter (pilot, exec. prod.). Movie: Get Smart Again! (exec. prod.).

MELNICK, SAUL: Executive. With a background in the video industry at CBS Video Enterprises, Pacifica Manufacturing Co. and Arista Records, joined MGM/UA Home Video in 1982 as national sales manager, rising to sales v.p. in 1983, and v.p. sales and marketing in 1984. Joined Tri-Star as pres. of home video unit; 1987; June 1988, appointed exec. v.p. Loews Theater Management; resigned 1990.

MELNIKER, BENJAMIN: Motion Picture Producer, Attorney; b. Bayonne, NJ. e. Brooklyn Coll.; LL.B., Fordham Law Sch. Loew's Theatres usher, private law practice employed Legal Department Metro-Goldwyn-Mayer, vice president and general counsel, 1954–69, executive vice president, 1968–70, resigned from MGM December 1971; also member MGM bd. dir. and mem. MGM exec. com.; Adjunct associate professor, New York Law Sch., 1976–77; prod. & exec. prod. motion pictures, 1974–86; former motion picture chmn. Anti-Defamation League, B'nai B'rith; Mem. Am., N.Y. State bar assns., Bar Assn. City N.Y., Acad. of Motion Picture Arts and Scis.

PICTURES: Mitchell, Shoot, Winter Kills, Swamp Thing, Batman (exec. prod.), The Return of the Swamp Thing (prod.), Batman Returns.

TELEVISION: Three Sovereigns for Sarah, Television's Greatest Bets.

MENGES, CHRIS: Cinematographer, Director. b. Kington, Eng., Sept. 15, 1940.

PICTURES: Cinematographer: Kes, The Empire Strikes Back (second unit), Local Hero, Comfort and Joy, The Killing Fields (Acad. Award, 1984), Marie, The Mission (Acad. Award, 1986), Singing the Blues in Red, Shy People, High Season. Director: A World Apart, Crisscross.

TELEVISION: World in Action, Opium Warlords, Opium Trail, East 103rd Street, etc.

MENKEN, ALAN: Composer. b. 1950. Raised in New Rochelle, NY. e. NYU. Began composing and performing at Lehman Engel Musical Theatre Workshop at BMI, where he met future partner, lyricist Howard Ashman. With Ashman made Off-Bdwy debut in 1979 with score of God Bless You Mr. Rosewater. Wrote music for workshop Battle of the Giants, and music and lyrics for Manhattan Theatre Club Prod. of Real Life Funkies. With Ashman wrote 1982 Off-Bdwy hit Little Shop of Horrors. Other theatre credits incl. Kicks, The Apprenticeship of Duddy Kravitz, Diamonds, Personals, Let Freedom Sing, Weird Romance. Score for TV special: Lincoln.

PICTURES: Little Shop of Horrors (Acad. Award nom. for Best Song), The Little Mermaid (2 Acad. Awards: Best Song, Music Score, 1989), Rocky V (song), Beauty and the Beast (2 Acad. Awards: Best Song, Music Score, 1991), Newsies,

Aladdin (2 Acad. Awards: Best Song, Music Score), Home Alone 2: Lost in New York (song), Life With Mikey.

MERCHANT, ISMAIL: Producer, Director. b. Bombay, India, Dec. 25, 1936. e. St. Xavier's Coll., Bombay; NYU, M.A. business admin. Formed Merchant Ivory Prods., 1961 with James Ivory. First film, The Creation of Women (theatrical short, 1961, nom. for Acad. Award). Published cookbook, Ismail Merchant's Indian Cuisine; and book Hullabaloo in Old Jeypore: The Making of "The Deceivers" (1989).
PICTURES: *Producer:* The Householder, Shakespeare Wallah, The Guru, Bombay Talkie, Savages, Autobiography of a Princess, The Wild Party, Roseland, Hullabaloo Over Georgie and Bonnie's Pictures, The Europeans, Jane Austen in Manhattan, Quartet, Heat and Dust, The Bostonians, A Room With a View, Maurice, My Little Girl (exec. prod.), The Deceivers, Slaves of New York, The Perfect Murder (exec. prod.), Mr. and Mrs. Bridge, Ballad of the Sad Cafe, Howards End (BAFTA Award), In Custody (dir. debut), Remains of the Day.
TELEVISION: *Director:* Mahatma and the Mad Boy, Courtesans of Bombay.

MERCOURI, MELINA: Actress. b. Athens, Greece, Oct. 18, 1925. m. dir.-prod. Jules Dassin. Schooling and training in Athens, fluent in French, German and English. Stage debut on Athens stage in avant-garde work; early stage career in Paris. Also made vocal recordings. Mem. of Greek Parliament for Port of Piraeus, 1977–89; Minister of Culture and Sciences for Greek Gov't. 1981–85; Minister of Culture, Youth and Sports, 1985–89.
PLAYS: Mourning Becomes Electra, La Nuit de Samaracande, Les Compagnons de la Marjolaine, Il Etait une Gare, Le Moulin de la Galette; to Greece 1954, in Stella. Also: A Streetcar Named Desire, Helen or the Joy of Living, The Queen of Clubs, The Seven Year Itch, Sweet Bird of Youth, Ilya Darling (Bdwy).
PICTURES: Stella, He Who Must Die, The Gypsy and the Gentleman, The Law, Never on Sunday (Acad. Award nom.), Viva Henry IV Viva Love, Il Giudizio Universale, Phaedra, The Victors, Topkapi, The Player Pianos, 10:30 P.M. Summer, A Man Could Get Killed, Gaily Gaily, Promise at Dawn, The Rehearsal, Once Is Not Enough, Nasty Habits, Maya and Brenda, A Dream of Passion, Not By Coincidence.

MEREDITH, BURGESS: Actor. b. Cleveland, OH, Nov. 16, 1909. e. Amherst Coll., M.A. (hon.). m: Kaja Sundsten. Capt. U.S. Army Air Corps, W.W.II. On stage, 1929, Civic Repertory Co., N.Y.
STAGE PLAYS: Little Ol' Boy, She Loves Me Not, The Star Wagon, Winterset, High Tor, Remarkable Mr. Pennypacker, etc.
PICTURES: Winterset (debut, 1936), There Goes the Groom, Spring Madness, Idiot's Delight, Of Mice and Men, Castle on the Hudson, Second Chorus, San Francisco Docks, That Uncertain Feeling, Tom Dick and Harry, Street of Chance, Story of G.I. Joe, Diary of a Chambermaid (also s.p., co-prod.), Magnificent Doll, On Our Merry Way (also prod.), Mine Own Executioner, Jigsaw, Man on the Eiffel Tower (also dir.), Gay Adventure, Joe Butterfly, Advise and Consent, The Cardinal, In Harm's Way, A Big Hand for the Little Lady, Madame X, Batman, Crazy Quilt (narrator), Hurry Sundown, Torture Garden, Stay Away Joe, Skidoo, McKenna's Gold, Hard Contract, The Reivers (narrator), There Was a Crooked Man, Clay Pigeon, Such Good Friends, A Fan's Notes, The Man, Golden Needles, The Day of the Locust (Acad. Award nom.), 92 in the Shade, The Hindenburg, Burnt Offerings, Rocky (Acad. Award nom.), The Sentinel, Golden Rendezvous, The Manitou, Foul Play, Magic, The Great Bank Hoax, Rocky II, Final Assignment, When Time Ran Out, Clash of the Titans, True Confessions, The Last Chase, Rocky III, Twilight Zone: The Movie (narrator), Broken Rainbow (voice), Santa Claus, King Lear, Full Moon in Blue Water, State of Grace, Rocky V, Odd Ball Hall, Grumpy Old Men.
TELEVISION: *Movies:* Lock Stock and Barrel, Getting Away From It All, The Last Hurrah, Johnny We Hardly Knew Ye, Tail Gunner Joe (Emmy Award, 1977), Probe, Outrage!, Wet Gold, Night of the Hunter. *Series:* Mr. Novak, Batman (frequent guest), Search, Those Amazing Animals (host), Gloria. *Special:* Mastergate.

MERRICK, DAVID: Producer. r.n. David Margulois. b. Hong Kong, Nov. 27, 1912. e. Washington U.; St. Louis U. LL.B. Famed Broadway stage impresario with long record of hits, including Fanny, The Matchmaker, Look Back in Anger, The Entertainer, Jamaica, World of Suzie Wong, La Plume de Ma Tante, Epitaph for George Dillon, Destry Rides Again, Gypsy, Take Me Along, Irma La Douce, A Taste of Honey, Becket (Tony Award), Do Re Mi, Carnival, Sunday in New York, Ross, Subways Are For Sleeping, I Can Get It for You Wholesale, Stop the World. . .I Want to Get Off, Tchin Tchin, Oliver!, Luther, 110 in the Shade, Arturo Ui, Hello Dolly! (Tony Award), Oh What a Lovely War, Pickwick, The Roar of the Greasepaint . . ., Inadmissible Evidence, Cactus Flower, Marat/Sade (Tony Award), Philadelphia Here I Come, Don't Drink the Water, I Do! I Do!, How Now Dow Jones, The Happy Time,

Rosencrantz and Guildenstern Are Dead (Tony Award), 40 Carats, Promises, Promises, Play It Again Sam, Child's Play, Four in a Garden, A Midsummer Night's Dream, Sugar, Out Cry, Mack and Mabel, Travesties, Very Good Eddie, Private Lives, 42nd Street (Tony Award), Oh Kay!.
PICTURES: Child's Play (debut), The Great Gatsby, Semi-Tough, Rough Cut.

MERRILL, DINA: Actress. r.n. Nedenia Hutton; b. New York, NY, Dec. 29, 1928. Fashion model, 1944–46. A Co-owner and vice-chmn. RKO Pictures, m.p. and TV prod. co.
PLAYS: Regional theatre: My Sister Eileen, Major Barbara, Misalliance, Othello, Twelfth Night, Loved, Surprise. Off-Broadway: Importance of Being Earnest, Smile of the Cardboard Man, Suddenly Last Summer. Broadway: Angel Street, On Your Toes.
PICTURES: Desk Set (debut, 1957), A Nice Little Bank That Should Be Robbed, Don't Give Up the Ship, Operation Petticoat, The Sundowners, Butterfield 8, Twenty Plus Two, The Young Savages, The Courtship of Eddie's Father, I'll Take Sweden, Running Wild, The Meal (Deadly Encounter), The Greatest, A Wedding, Just Tell Me What You Want, Twisted, Caddyshack II, True Colors, The Player.
TELEVISION: *Debut:* Kate Smith Show 1956. *Guest:* Four Star Theatre, Playwrights '56, Climax!, Playhouse 90, Westinghouse Presents, The Investigators, Checkmate, The Rogues, Bob Hope Presents, To Tell the Truth, Hotel, Hawaii Five-O, Murder She Wrote. *Series:* Hot Pursuit. *Mini-Series:* Roots: The Next Generations. *Movies:* The Sunshine Patroit, Seven in Darkness, The Lonely Profession, Mr. & Mrs. Bo Jo Jones, Family Flight, The Letters, Kingston: The Power Play, The Tenth Month, Repeat Performance, Turn Back the Clock, Fear, Brass Ring, Anne to the Tenth Power, Not in My Family.

MERSON, MARC: Producer. b. New York, NY, Sept. 9, 1931. e. Swarthmore Coll. Entered Navy in 1953; assigned as publicist to Admiral's Staff of Sixth Fleet Command in the Mediterranean. Upon discharge joined trade paper Show Business as feature editor. Joined CBS-TV as asst. to casting director. Left after 3 yrs. to work for Ely Landau as casting dir., packager and sometime producer of The Play of the Week on TV. Returned to CBS for 3-yr. stint doing specials and live programs. Left to organize Brownstone Productions as indep. prod. Now partner with Alan Alda in Helix Productions to package and produce TV shows.
PICTURES: The Heart Is a Lonely Hunter, People Soup (short), Leadbelly, Doc Hollywood (exec. prod.).
TELEVISION: Kaz, We'll Get By, Off the Rack, Jessica Novak, Waverly Wonders, Stage 67, Androcles and the Lion, Dummler and Son (pilot), The David Frost Revue (synd. series), We'll Get By. *Movie:* Rules of Marriage (spr. prod.).

MESSICK, DON: Actor. b. Buffalo, NY, Sept. 7, 1926. e. Ramsay Streett, Sch. of Acting, Baltimore; American Theatre Wing, NY. Began performing as ventriloquist at age 13 in rural Maryland. Own radio show at 15 in Salisbury, MD (WBOC) for two years, writing and portraying all the characters in a one-man weekly comedy show. Worked in Hanna-Barbera cartoons since company began in 1957, voicing Ruff in their first series on NBC, 1958. *Voices:* Boo Boo Bear and Ranger Smith on Yogi Bear Show, Astro on The Jetsons, Scooby Doo and Scrappy Doo on Scooby Doo series, Papa Smurf and Azrael on Smurfs, Droopy on Droopy & Dripple, Dr. Benton Quest on Jonny Quest (all Hanna-Barbera Prods.); Hamton J. Pig on Tiny Toon Adventures (WB). Has done numerous national commercials.

MESTRES, RICARDO: Executive. b. New York, NY, Jan. 23, 1958. e. Harvard U. Gained filmmaking experience during summers as prod. asst. on TV features. Joined Paramount Pictures as creative exec. 1981. Promoted to exec. dir. of production, 1982 and to v.p., prod. in 1984. Named v.p. of prod., Walt Disney Pictures, 1985. Promoted to sr. v.p., prod.,1986. Named president, production, Touchstone Pictures, 1988. In 1989, appt. pres., Hollywood Pictures, a new m.p. company created by The Walt Disney Company.

METCALF, LAURIE: Actress. b. Edwardsville, IL, June 16, 1955. e. Illinois St. Univ. One of the original members of the Steppenwolf Theatre Company.
PICTURES: Desperately Seeking Susan (debut, 1985), Making Mr. Right, Candy Mountain, Stars and Bars, Miles From Home, Uncle Buck, Internal Affairs, Pacific Heights, JFK, Mistress.
TELEVISION: *Series:* Roseanne (Emmy Award, 1992). *Movie:* The Execution of Raymond Graham.
THEATRE: *Chicago:* True West, Fifth of July. *NY:* Balm in Gilead (Obie & Theatre World Awards). *L.A.:* Wrong Turn at Lungfish.

METZLER, JIM: Actor. b. Oneonta, NY, June 23. e. Dartmouth Coll.
PICTURES: Four Friends, Tex, River's Edge, Hot to Trot, Sundown: The Vampire in Retreat, 976—EVIL, Old Gringo, Circuitry Man, Delusion, One False Move, Waxwork II: Lost in Time, A Weekend with Barbara und Ingrid.

TELEVISION: *Series*: Cutter to Houston, The Best Times. *Mini-Series*: North and South, North and South Book II, On Wings of Eagles. *Movies*: Do You Remember Love, Princess Daisy, Christmas Star, The Alamo: 13 Days to Glory, The Little Match Girl, Murder By Night, Crash: The Mystery of Flight 1501, Love Kills.

MEYER, BARRY M: Executive. With ABC-TV in legal and business affairs depts. before joining Warner Bros. TV in 1971 as dir. of business affairs. 1972, named v.p. of business affairs for Warner TV arm; promoted to exec. v.p. of div. 1978. 1984, named exec. v.p. of Warner Bros., Inc.

MEYER, NICHOLAS: Director, Writer. b. New York, NY, Dec. 24, 1945. e. U. of Iowa. Was unit publicist for Love Story, 1969. Story ed. Warner Bros. 1970–71. Author: The Love Story Story, The Seven Percent Solution, Target Practice, The West End Horror, Black Orchid, Confession of a Homing Pigeon.
PICTURES: The Seven Percent Solution (s.p.), Time After Time (s.p., dir.), Star Trek II: The Wrath of Khan (dir.), Volunteers (dir.), The Deceivers (dir.), Company Business (dir., s.p.) Star Trek VI: The Undiscovered Country (dir., co-s.p.), Sommersby (co-s.p.).
TELEVISION: *Movies*: Judge Dee (writer), The Night That Panicked America (writer), The Day After (dir.).

MEYER, RUSS: Producer, Director. b. Oakland, CA, March 21, 1922. In 1942 joined Army Signal Corps, learned m.p. photography and shot combat newsreels. Worked as photographer for Playboy Magazine. Pres., RM Films Intl. Inc. 3 vol. autobiography: A Clean Breast: The Life and Loves of Russ Meyer, 1992.
PICTURES: The Immoral Mr. Teas, Eve and the Handyman, Erotica, Wild Gals of the Naked West, Heavenly Bodies, Lorna, Motor Psycho, Fanny Hill, Mudhoney, Mondo Topless, Faster Pussycat Kill Kill, Finders Keepers Lovers Weepers, Goodmorning and Goodbye, Common Law Cabin, Vixen, Cherry Harry & Raquel, Beyond the Valley of the Dolls, The Seven Minutes, Black Snake, The Supervixens, Up, Beneath the Valley of the Ultra Vixens, The Breast of Russ Meyer (series of videos), Amazon Women on the Moon (actor).

MEYERS, ROBERT: Executive. b. Mount Vernon, NY, Oct. 3, 1934. e. NYU. Entered m.p. industry as exec. trainee in domestic div. of Columbia Pictures, 1956. Sales and adv. 1956–60; transferred to sales dept. Columbia Pictures International, N.Y., posts there included supervisor of intl. road-shows and exec. ass't. to continental mgr. Joined National General Pictures as v.p.-foreign sales, 1969. Created JAD Films International Inc. in Feb. 1974 for independent selling and packaging of films around the world. September, 1977, joined Lorimar Productions Inc. as sr. v.p. of Lorimar Distribution Intl. Became pres. in April, 1978. Joined Filmways Pictures in 1980, named pres. & COO. Pres. of American Film Mktg. Assn.; 1982, formed new co., R.M. Films International. Rejoined Lorimar 1985. as pres., Lorimar Motion Pictures, intl. distribution. Nov., 1988 joined Orion as pres., Orion Pictures Intl.

MICHAELS, JOEL B.: Producer. b. Buffalo, NY, Oct. 24, 1938. Studied acting with Stella Adler. Many co-prods. with Garth Drabinsky, Cineplex Corp. Pres. of Cineplex Odeon, 1986–90.
PICTURES: The Peace Killers, Your Three Minutes Are Up (prod. spvr.), Student Teachers (prod. spvr.), The Prisoners (assoc. prod.), Lepke (assoc. prod.), The Four Deuces (asso. prod.), Bittersweet Love, The Silent Partner, The Changeling, Tribute, The Amateur, Losin' It (exec. prod.), The Philadelphia Experiment, Three of Hearts (exec. prod.).

MICHAELS, LORNE: Writer, Producer. b. Toronto, Canada, Nov. 17, 1944. e. U. of Toronto, 1966. CEO, Broadway Video, since 1979.
TELEVISION: Rowan and Martin's Laugh-In (writer, 1968–69), CBC comedy specials (writer, prod., 1969–72), Lily Tomlin Specials (writer, prod., 1972–75, 2 Emmy Awards), Perry Como (writer, prod., 1974), Flip Wilson (writer, prod.), Saturday Night Live (creator, prod., writer 1975–80, 4 Emmys; exec. prod., 1985–.), Beach Boys (writer, prod.), Paul Simon (writer, prod., Emmy Award, 1978), The Rutles: All You Need Is Cash (writer, prod.), Steve Martin's Best Show Ever (prod.), Simon and Garfunkel: The Concert in the Park (exec. prod.), The Coneheads (exec. prod.), The New Show (prod.), 1988 Emmy Awards (prod.), Coca-Cola Presents Live: The Hard Rock, On Location: Kids in the Hall (exec. prod.), The Rolling Stones: Steel Wheels Concert (exec. prod.), Paul Simon: Born at the Right Time in Central Park (exec. prod.), The Kids in the Hall (series co-prod.).
PICTURES: *Producer*: Gilda Live (also writer), Nothing Lasts Forever, Three Amigos (also co-s.p.), Wayne's World, Coneheads, Wayne's World 2.
THEATRE: Gilda Radner Live From New York (prod., dir.).

MICHAELS, RICHARD: Director. b. Brooklyn, NY, Feb. 15, 1936. e. Cornell U. Script supervisor 1955–64 and associate

producer before starting directing career in 1968 with Bewitched (54 episodes), of which was also assoc. prod.
TELEVISION: Series: episodes of Love, American Style, The Odd Couple, Delvecchio, Ellery Queen, Room 222. Movies: Once an Eagle (mini-series), Charlie Cobb, Having Babies II, Leave Yesterday Behind, My Husband Is Missing, . . . And Your Name Is Jonah (winner, Christopher Award), Once Upon a Family, The Plutonium Incident, Scared Straight, Another Story (winner, Scott Newman Drug Abuse Prevention Award), Homeward Bound (winner, Banff Intl. TV Festival Special Jury Award & Christopher Award), Berlin Tunnel 21, The Children Nobody Wanted, One Cooks, The Other Doesn't, Sadat (mini-series), Jessie (pilot), Silence of the Heart, Heart of a Champion: The Ray Mancini Story, Rockabye, Kay O'Brien (pilot), I'll Take Manhattan (mini-series); Leg Work (pilot), Red River (movie), Indiscreet, Love and Betrayal, Her Wicked Ways, Leona Helmsley: The Queen of Mean, Triumph of the Heart: The Ricky Bell Story, Backfield in Motion, Miss America: Behind the Crown.
PICTURES: How Come Nobody's On Our Side?, Blue Skies Again.

MICHEL, WERNER: Executive. e. U. of Berlin, U. of Paris, Ph.D. Radio writer, dir., co-author two Broadway revues, 1938, 1940; dir. French feature films; dir. Broadcast Div., Voice of America, 1942–46; prod., dir., CBS, 1946–48; asst. prog. dir., CBS, 1948–50; dir. of Kenyon and Eckhart TV dept., 1950–52; prod., DuMont TV network, 1952–55; dir., Electronicam TV-Film Prod., 1955–56; prod., Benton and Bowles; Procter and Gamble, 1956–57; v.p. & dir. TV-radio dept., Reach, McClinton Advertising, Inc., 1957–62; consultant, TV Programming & Comm'l-Prod., N. W. Ayer & Son, Inc.; v.p., dir., TV dept., SSCB Advertising, 1963, pgm. exec., ABC-TV Hollywood, 1975; director, dramatic programs, 1976; sr. v.p., creative affairs, MGM-TV, 1977; exec. v.p., Wrather Entertainment Intl., 1979; sr. v.p., creative affairs, MGM-TV, 1980–82; COO, Guber-Peters TV, 1982–84; sr. v.p., creative TV dept., Kenyon & Eckhart, & NY, 1984–86; sr. v.p. corp. TV dept. Bozell, Inc. NY, 1986–.

MICHELET, MICHEL: Composer. b. Kiev, Russia, June 27, 1899. Prof., Kiev & Vienna Conserv. Composed concert compositions, ballets, stage music; ent. m.p. industry, composed scores 105 films, in France, Italy and Germany; to U.S. 1941; author many concert compositions. Recent works incl. Requiem, Oratorio, 7 Visions of Judea (1989), Sonata for Cello and Piano (Rastropovich). Member: French Soc. of Composers (SACEM).
PICTURES: Voice in the Wind (AA nom.), Hairy Ape (AA nom.), Music for Millions, The Chase, Lured, Siren of Atlantis, Man on the Eiffel Tower, The Journey, Once a Thief, Tarzan's Peril, Fort Algiers, Un Missionaire, Le Secret de Soeur Angele, Petersburger, Nachte, Challenge (Tribute to Modern Art). Also did scores for many U.S. Information Service documentaries; arr. of Russian music Anastasia; Afrodife (score).

MICHELL, KEITH: Actor. b. Adelaide, Australia, Dec. 1, 1926. Early career as art teacher, radio actor; toured Australia with Stratford Shakespearean Co. 1952–53; Stratford Memorial Theatre 1954–55, Old Vic Theatre 1956–57. Irma la Douce, Chichester, Art of Seduction, The First 400 Years, Robert & Elizabeth, Kain, The King's Mare, 1969: Man of La Mancha (London, N.Y.): Abelard & Heloise (London); (NY and LA), Hamlet, (London). Artistic Director, Chichester Festival Theatre. Toured Australia with Chichester Festival Co., London: Crucifer of Blood, (London): On the Twentieth Century, (Melbourne Theatre Co.): Pete McGynty, (London): Captain Beaky Christmas Show. (Chichester): On the Rocks (Brisbane): The Tempest, (UK tour 1983): Amadeus (San Francisco). 1984–85: La Cage aux Folles (USA and Australia), Portraits, The Bacarat Scandal (Chichester, 1988).
TELEVISION: *Great Britain*: Pygmalion, Act of Violence, Mayerling Affair, Wuthering Heights, The Bergonzi Hands, Ring Round The Moon, Spread of the Eagle, The Shifting Heart, Loyalties, Julius Caesar, Antony and Cleopatra, Kain, The Ideal Husband, The Six Wives of Henry VIII (series). Keith Michell at various London theatres, Dear Love. Selections from Keith Michell in Concert at Chichester, Captain Beaky & his Band, Captain Beaky, Volume 2, The Gondoliers, The Pirates of Penzance, Ruddigore. *U.S.*: Story of the Marlboroughs, Jacob and Joseph, Story of David, The Tenth Month, The Day Christ Died, The Miracle, Murder She Wrote. *Australia*: *Series*: My Brother Tom, Captain James Cook.
PICTURES: True as a Turtle, Dangerous Exile, Gypsy and the Gentleman, The Hellfire Club, All Night Long, Seven Seas to Calais, Prudence and the Pill, House of Cards, Henry VIII and his Six Wives, Moments, The Deceivers.

MIDLER, BETTE: Actress, Singer. b. Honolulu, HI, Dec. 1, 1945. e. U. of Hawaii. Appeared on Bdwy. in Fiddler on the Roof, Salvation; also in Tommy with Seattle Opera Co., 1971. Gained fame as singer-comic in nightclubs and cabarets. Has toured extensively with own stage shows: The Divine Miss M, Clams on the Half-Shell, Divine Madness, Art of Bust,

Experience the Divine. Won 3 Grammy Awards: The Divine Miss M, The Rose, Blueberry Pie (from In Harmony). Author: A View From a Broad, The Saga of Baby Divine. Special Tony Award, 1973.

PICTURES: Hawaii (debut, 1966), The Rose (Acad. Award nom.; 2 Golden Globe Awards), Divine Madness, Jinxed, Down and Out in Beverly Hills, Ruthless People, Outrageous Fortune, Big Business, Oliver & Company (voice), Beaches (also prod.), Stella, Scenes from a Mall, For the Boys (Acad. Award nom., Golden Globe Award; also co-prod.), Hocus Pocus.

TELEVISION: Specials: The Fabulous Bette Milder Show, Ol' Red Hair is Back (Emmy Award, 1978), Bette Midler's Mondo Beyondo, Mud Will Be Flung Tonight. Movie: Gypsy. Guest: The Tonight Show (Emmy Award, 1992).

MIFUNE, TOSHIRO: Actor. b. Tsingtao, China, April 1, 1920. e. Japanese schools. Served five years Japanese army. Joined Toho Studio 1946.

PICTURES: Snow Trail, Drunken Angel, Eagle of Pacific, Seven Samurai, I Live in Fear, Legend of Musashi, Throne of Blood, Riksha Man, Three Treasures, Last Gunfight, I Bombed Pearl Harbor, Rose in Mud, Rashomon, Yojimbo, Animus Trujano (Mexican), Kiska, Red Beard, High and Low, Judo Sag, The Lost World of Sinbad, Hell in the Pacific, Paper Tiger, Midway, Winter Kills, 1941, The Challenge, Inchon, The Bushido Blade, Princess from the Moon, The Death of a Master, Journey of Honor, Shadow of the Wolf.

TELEVISION: (U.S.) Shogun.

MIGDEN, CHESTER L.: Executive. b. New York, NY, May 21, 1921; e. City Coll. of New York, B.A., 1941, Columbia U., LL.B, 1947. Member New York Bar. Attorney for National Labor Relations Board 1947–51. Currently exec. dir., Assn. of Talent Agents. Was exec of Screen Actors Guild 1952–81; nat'l. exec. secty., 1973–81.

MIKELL, GEORGE: Actor. b. Lithuania. In Australia 1950–56 acting with Old Vic Co. Ent. films 1955. TV 1957. To England 1957; since appeared in numerous film and TV prod.

TELEVISION: Counsel at Law, Six Eyes on a Stranger, The Mask of a Clown, Green Grows the Grass, Opportunity Taken, OSS Series, Espinage, The Danger Man, Strange Report, The Survivors, The Adventurer, Colditz, The Hanged Man, Quiller, Martin Hartwell, Flambards, Sweeney, The Secret Army, Sherlock Holmes, When the Boat Comes In, Brack Report, Bergerac, The Brief, Glass Babies (Australia), Hannay, Night of the Fox (mini-series), Secrets (Australia).

PICTURES: The Guns of Navarone, The Password Is Courage, The Great Escape, Deadline for Diamonds, Where The Spies Are, The Spy Who Came in From the Cold, I Predoni Del Sahara (Italy), Sabina (Israel), The Double Man, Attack on the Iron Coast, Zeppelin, Young Winston, Scorpio, The Tamarind Seed, Sweeney Two, The Sea Wolves, Victory, Emerald, Kommissar Zufall (Germany).

STAGE: Five Finger Exercise, Altona, The Millionairess, Love from a Stranger, Portrait of a Queen, Farewell, Judas, Flare Path.

MILCHAN, ARNON: Producer. b. Israel, Dec. 6, 1944. Began producing and financing films in Israel. Also producer of stage plays incl. Ipi Tombi, It's So Nice to be Civilized, and Amadeus in Paris starring Roman Polanski.

PICTURES: Black Joy, The Medusa Touch, Dizengoff, The King of Comedy, Once Upon a Time in America (also actor), Brazil, Stripper, Legend, Man on Fire, Who's Harry Crumb?, The War of the Roses, Big Man on Campus, Pretty Woman, Q & A, Guilty by Suspicion, JFK, The Mambo Kings, Memoirs of an Invisible Man, The Power of One, Under Siege, Sommersby, Falling Down, Made in America, Free Willy, That Night, Heaven and Earth, The New Age, Striking Distance, Six Degrees of Separation, Second Best, Boys on the Side, The Client.

TELEVISION: Masada.

MILES, CHRISTOPHER: Director. b. London, England, April 19, 1939. e. I.D., H.E.C., 1962. Sister is actress Sarah Miles. Studied film in Paris at the Institut des Hautes Etudes Cinematographiques.

PICTURES: The Six-Sided Triangle, Up Jumped a Swagman, The Virgin and the Gypsy, Time for Loving, The Maids (also co-s.p.), That Lucky Touch, Priest of Love (also prod.), The Marathon (also co-s.p.), Aphrodisias (also co-s.p.), Some Stones of No Value (also co-s.p.).

MILES, SARAH: Actress. b. Ingatestone, Eng., Dec. 31, 1941. m. writer Robert Bolt. e. Royal Acad. of Dramatic Art. Brother is actor Christopher Miles.

PICTURES: Term of Trial (debut, 1962), The Servant, The Ceremony, Those Magnificent Men in Their Flying Machines, I Was Happy Here, Blowup, Ryan's Daughter, Lady Caroline Lamb, The Man Who Loved Cat Dancing, The Hireling, The Sailor Who Fell from Grace with the Sea, The Big Sleep, Priest of Love, Venom, Loving Walter, Ordeal by Innocence, Steaming, Hope and Glory, White Mischief.

THEATRE: Vivat! Vivat Regina!

TELEVISION: James Michener's Dynasty, Great Expectations, Harem, Queenie, A Ghost in Monte Carlo.

MILES, SYLVIA: Actress. b. New York, NY, Sept. 9, 1934. Attended Pratt Inst., NYC. e. Actors Studio, Dramatic Workshop of the New School.

PICTURES: Murder Inc. (debut, 1960), Parrish, Pie in the Sky, Violent Midnight, Terror in the City, Midnight Cowboy (Acad. Award nom.), The Last Movie, Who Killed Mary Whats'ername?, Heat, 92 in the Shade, Farewell My Lovely (Acad. Award nom.), The Great Scout and Cathouse Thursday, The Sentinel, Shalimar (Deadly Thief), Zero to Sixty, The Funhouse, Evil Under the Sun, No Big Deal, Critical Condition, Sleeping Beauty, Wall Street, Crossing Delancey, Spike of Bensonhurst, She-Devil.

THEATRE: Rosebloom, The Iceman Cometh, The Balcony, The Riot Act, Vieux Carre, The Night of the Iguana, Tea with Mommy and Jack, Ruthless.

TELEVISION: Series: All My Children. Guest: Miami Vice, The Equalizer, Tonight Show, etc.

MILES, VERA: Actress. r.n. Vera Ralston. b. Boise City, OK, Aug. 23, 1929. e. public schools, Pratt and Wichita, KS.

TELEVISION: Guest: Climax, Pepsi Cola Playhouse, Schlitz Playhouse, Ford Theatre. Movies: The Hanged Man, In Search of America, Cannon (pilot), Owen Marshall: Counselor at Law (pilot), A Howling in the Woods, Jigsaw, A Great American Tragedy, Baffled!, Runaway!, Live Again Die Again, Underground Man, The Strange and Deadly Occurence, NcNaughton's Daughter, Judge Horton and the Scottsboro Boys, Smash-up on Interstate 5, Fire!, And I Alone Survived, Roughnecks, Our Family Business, Rona Jaffe's Mazes and Monsters, Travis McGee, Helen Keller—The Miracle Continues, The Hijacking of the Achille Lauro.

PICTURES: Two Tickets to Broadway, For Men Only, Rose Bowl Story, Charge at Feather River, So Big, Pride of the Blue Grass, Tarzan's Hidden Jungle, Wichita, The Searchers, 23 Paces to Baker Street, Autumn Leaves, Wrong Man, Beau James, Web of Evidence, FBI Story, Touch of Larceny, Five Branded Women, Psycho, Back Street, The Man Who Shot Liberty Valance, A Tiger Walks, Those Calloways, Follow Me Boys!, The Spirit Is Willing, Gentle Giant, Sergeant Ryker, Kona Coast, It Takes All Kinds, Hellfighters, Mission Batangas, The Wild Country, Molly and Lawless John, One Little Indian, The Castaway Cowboy, Twilight's Last Gleaming, Thoroughbred, Brainwaves, Psycho II, The Initiation, Into the Night.

MILGRAM, HANK: Theatre Executive. b. Philadelphia, PA, April 20, 1926. e. U. of Pennsylvania, Wharton Sch. In industry 47 years; now exec. v.p. Milgram Theatres. Variety Club Board member for past 43 years, past president and chairman of the board of Variety Club of Phila.; presently Variety Club Intl. v.p.

MILIUS, JOHN: Writer, Director. b. St. Louis, MO. April 11, 1944. e. Los Angeles City Coll., U. of Southern California (cinema course). While at latter won National Student Film Festival Award. Started career as ass't. to Lawrence Gordon at AIP. Began writing screenplays, then became director with Dillinger (1973).

PICTURES: Devil's 8 (s.p.), Evel Knievel (s.p.), The Life and Times of Judge Roy Bean (s.p.), Jeremiah Johnson (co-s.p.), Dillinger (dir., s.p.), Magnum Force (co-s.p.), The Wind and the Lion (dir., s.p.), Big Wednesday (dir., co-s.p., actor), Apocalypse Now (s.p.), Hardcore (exec. prod.), 1941 (exec. prod., co-s.p.), Used Cars (co-exec. prod.), Conan the Barbarian (dir., co-s.p.), Uncommon Valor (co-prod.), Red Dawn (dir., co-s.p.), Extreme Prejudice (story), Farewell to the King (dir., s.p.), Flight of the Intruder (dir., co-s.p), Geronimo.

MILKIS, EDWARD: Producer: b. Los Angeles, CA, July 16, 1931. e. U. of Southern California. Began career as asst. editor, ABC-TV, 1952; Disney, 1954; MGM, 1957; editor, MGM, 1960–65; assoc. prod., Star Trek, 1966–69; exec. in chg. post-prod., Paramount, 1969–72; formed Miller-Milkis Prods., 1972; Miller-Milkis-Boyett, 1979. Now heads Edward K. Milkis Prods.

PICTURES: Silver Streak; Foul Play; The Best Little Whorehouse in Texas.

TELEVISION: Petrocelli; Bosom Buddies (exec. prod.); Happy Days; Laverne and Shirley; Feel the Heat.

MILLAR, STUART: Producer, Director. b. New York, NY, 1929. e. Stanford U.; Sorbonne, Paris. Ent. industry working for Motion Picture Branch, State Dept., Germany. documentaries, Army Signal Corps, Long Island, Germany; journalist, International News Service, San Francisco; assoc. prod.-dir., The Desperate Hours; assoc. prod.-dir., Friendly Persuasion.

PICTURES: Producer: The Young Stranger; Stage Struck; Birdman of Alcatraz. I Could Go On Singing, The Young Doctors, Stolen Hours, The Best Man, Paper Lion, Little Big Man, When The Legends Die (also dir.), Rooster Cogburn (dir. only), Shoot the Moon (co-exec. prod.).

TELEVISION: Isabel's Choice (prod.), Vital Signs (prod.,

dir.), Killer Instinct (prod.), Dream Breaker (prod., dir.), Lady in a Corner (prod.).

MILLER, ANN: Actress. r.n. Lucille Ann Collier. b. Houston, TX, Apr. 12, 1919. e. Albert Sidney Johnson H.S., Houston; Lawler Prof. Sch., Hollywood. Studied dance as child; played West Coast vaudeville theatres. Autobiography, Miller's High Life (1974).
STAGE: George White's Scandals (1940), Mame (1969), Sugar Babies.
PICTURES: Anne of Green Gables (debut, 1934), The Good Fairy, Devil on Horseback, New Faces of 1937, Life of the Party, Stage Door, Radio City Revels, Having Wonderful Time, Room Service, You Can't Take It with You, Tarnished Angel, Too Many Girls, Hit Parade of 1941, Melody Ranch, Time Out for Rhythm, Go West Young Lady, True to the Army, Priorities on Parade, Reveille with Beverly, What's Buzzin' Cousin?, Jam Session, Hey Rookie, Carolina Blues, Eadie Was a Lady, Eve Knew Her Apples, Thrill of Brazil, Easter Parade, The Kissing Bandit, On the Town, Watch the Birdie, Texas Carnival, Two Tickets to Broadway, Lovely To Look At, Small Town Girl, Kiss Me Kate, Deep in My Heart, Hit the Deck, Opposite Sex, Great American Pastime, Won Ton Ton the Dog Who Saved Hollywood.
TELEVISION: *Special*: Dames at Sea. *Guest*: Love American Style, The Love Boat.

MILLER, ARTHUR: Writer. b. New York, NY, Oct. 17, 1915. e. U. of Michigan. Plays include Situation Normal; All My Sons, Death of a Salesman (Pulitzer Prize, 1949), The Crucible (Tony Award), A View from the Bridge, After the Fall, Incident at Vichy, The Price, Up From Paradise, Situation Normal, The American Clock. Novel: *Focus*. Autobiography: Timebends (1987).
PICTURES: *Film versions of plays*: All My Sons, Death of a Salesman, The Crucible, A View From the Bridge. *Original s.p.*: The Misfits, Everybody Wins.
TELEVISION: Death of a Salesman (Emmy Award, 1967), Fame, After The Fall, Playing for Time (Emmy Award, 1981).

MILLER, BARRY: Actor. b. Los Angeles, CA, Feb. 6, 1958. New York stage debut, My Mother My Father and Me, 1980.
THEATER: Forty Deuce, The Tempest, Biloxi Blues (Tony, Theatre World, Outer Critics Circle and Drama Desk Awards, 1985), Crazy He Calls Me.
PICTURES: Lepke (debut, 1975), Saturday Night Fever, Voices, Fame, The Chosen, The Journey of Natty Gann, Peggy Sue Got Married, The Sicilian, The Last Temptation of Christ, Love at Large, The Pickle.
TELEVISION: *Specials*: The Roommate, Conspiracy: The Trial of the Chicago Eight. *Series*: Joe and Sons, Szysznyk, Equal Justice. *Guest*: The Bill Cosby Show. *Movies*: Brock's Last Case, Having Babies, The Death of Richie.

MILLER, CHERYL: Actress. b. Sherman Oaks, CA, Feb. 4, 1943. e. UCLA, Los Angeles Conservatory of Music.
PICTURES: First film, Casanova Brown, age 19 days. Appeared in over 100 films as child, more recently in the Monkey's Uncle, Clarence the Cross-Eyed Lion, The Initiation, Doctor Death.
TELEVISION: *Series*: Daktari. *Guest*: Perry Mason, Bachelor Father, Flipper, Donna Reed, Leave It to Beaver, Farmer's Daughter, Wonderful World of Color, Dobie Gillis, Bright Promise, Love American Style, Emergency, Cade's County. *Movie*: Gemini Man.

MILLER, DICK (RICHARD): Actor, Writer. b. New York, NY, Dec. 25, 1928. e. City Coll. of New York, Columbia U. Grad. NYU. Theater Sch. of Dramatic Arts. Commercial artist, psychologist (Bellevue Mental Hygiene Clinic, Queens General Hosp. Psychiatric dept.) Served in U.S. Navy, W.W.II. Boxing champ, U.S. Navy. Semi-pro football. Broadway stage, radio disc jockey, The Dick Miller Show, WMCA, WOR-TV. Over 500 live shows. Did first live night talk show with Bobby Sherwood, Midnight Snack, CBS, 1950. Wrote, produced and directed radio and TV shows in NY in early 1950s. Wrote screenplays; T.N.T. Jackson, Which Way to the Front, Four Rode Out and others. Has appeared on all major TV series and regular on The Flame (3 years) and The Flash.
PICTURES: Has appeared in over 135 features, including: Apache Woman, Oklahoma Woman, It Conquered the World, The Undead, Not of This Earth, The Gunslinger, War of the Satellites, Naked Paradise, Rock All Night, Sorority Girl, Carnival Rock, A Bucket of Blood, Little Shop of Horrors, Atlas, Capture That Capsule, Premature Burial, X—The Man With the X Ray Eyes, The Terror, Beach Ball, Ski Party, Wild Wild Winter, Wild Angels, Hell's Angels on Wheels, The Trip, St. Valentine's Day Masacre, A Time for Killing, The Dirty Dozen, Targets, The Legend of Lilah Clare, Wild Racers, Target Harry, Which Way to the Front (also co-s.p.), Night Call Nurses, The Grissom Gang, Ulzana's Raid, Executive Action, The Slams, Student Nurses, Big Bad Mama, Truck Turner, Capone, T.N.T. Jackson, The Fortune, White Line Fever, Crazy Mama, Moving Violation, Hustle, Cannonball, Vigilante Force, New York New York, Mr. Billion, Hollywood Boulevard, Grand Theft Auto, I Wanna Hold Your Hand, Piranha,

Corvette Summer, Rock 'n' Roll High School, Lady in Red, Dr. Heckle and Mr. Hype, The Happy Hooker Goes Hollywood, Used Cars, The Howling, Heartbeeps, White Dog, Get Crazy, Lies, Heart Like a Wheel, All the Right Moves, Twilight Zone: The Movie, National Lampoon Goes to the Movies, Space Raiders, Swing Shift, Gremlins, The Terminator, Explorers, After Hours, Night of the Creeps, Project X, Armed Response, Chopping Mall, Amazon Women on the Moon, Innerspace, Angel III, The Burbs, Under the Boardwalk, Far From Home, Mob Boss, Gremlins 2: The New Batch, Unlawful Entry, Amityville 1992: It's About Time, Motorama, Matinee.

MILLER, (DR.) GEORGE: Director, Producer. b. Chinchilla, Queensland, Australia, 1945. Practiced medicine in Sydney; quit to work on films with Byron Kennedy, who became longtime partner until his death in 1983. Early work: Violence in the Cinema Part One (short, dir., s.p.), Frieze—An Underground Film (doc., editor only), Devil in Evening Dress (doc., dir., s.p.). First worldwide success with Mad Max.
PICTURES: Mad Max (dir., s.p.), Chain Reaction (assoc. prod.), The Road Warrior (dir., co-s.p.), Twilight Zone—The Movie (dir. segment), Mad Max Beyond Thunderdome (co-dir., prod., co-s.p.), The Witches of Eastwick (dir.), The Year My Voice Broke (exec. prod.), Dead Calm (exec. prod.), Flirting (exec. prod.), Lorenzo's Oil (dir., co-s.p., co-prod.).
TELEVISION: The Dismissal (mini-series; exec. prod., co-writer & dir. of first episode). *Prod.*: Bodyline, The Cowra Breakout. Exec. *Prod.*: Vietnam (mini-series), Dirtwater Dynasty, Sports Crazy.

MILLER, GEORGE: Director. b. Australia.
PICTURES: In Search of Anna (asst. dir.), The Man from Snowy River, The Aviator, The Never Ending Story II, Over the Hill, Frozen Assets, Gross Misconduct.
TELEVISION: Cash and Company, Against the Wind, The Last Outlaw, All the Rivers Run.

MILLER, JAMES R.: Executive. Began m.p. industry career in 1971 in legal dept. of United Artists (N.Y.). Left to go with Paramount Pictures in legal dept.; then moved to Columbia in 1977 as sr. counsel; later assoc. gen. counsel. In 1979 named Warner Bros. v.p.—studio business affairs; 1984, v.p. chg. world-wide business affairs; 1987, sr. v.p.; 1989, exec. v.p. business and acquisition.

MILLER, JP: Writer. b. San Antonio, TX, Dec. 18, 1919. e. Rice U., 1937–41; Yale Drama Sch., 1946–47. U.S. Navy, Lieut., 1941–46; pub. poetry, short stories.
ORIGINAL DRAMAS: Philco TV Playhouse: Hide and Seek, Old Tasslefoot, The Rabbit Trap, The Pardon-me Boy; Playhouse 90, Days of Wine and Roses, CBS Playhouse, The People Next Door (Emmy Award, 1969), The Unwanted, The Lindbergh Kidnapping Case, Helter Skelter, Gauguin the Savage, I Know My First Name is Steven (story, co-s.p.).
PICTURES: The Rabbit Trap, (story, s.p.) Days of Wine and Roses (story s.p.) The Young Savages (co-author, s.p.) Behold A Pale Horse, (s.p.) The People Next Door (story, s.p.).
NOVELS: The Race for Home, Liv, The Skook.
PLAYS: Days of Wine and Roses, The People Next Door, Privacy.

MILLER, JASON: Writer, Actor. b. Scranton, PA, April 22, 1939. Entered regional playwriting contest during high school in Scranton, PA and since has moved back and forth between acting and writing. Wrote That Championship Season, winner of N.Y. Drama Critics Best Play award, 1972, Tony Award, 1973, and Pulitzer Prize for Drama.
PICTURES: *Actor*: The Exorcist, The Nickel Ride, The Ninth Configuration (Twinkle Twinkle Killer Kane), Monsignor, Toy Soldiers, Light of Day, The Exorcist III. *Director-Writer*: That Championship Season.
TELEVISION: *Movies*: A Home of Our Own, F. Scott Fitzgerald in Hollywood, Vampire, Henderson Monster, Marilyn: The Untold Story, Best Little Girl in the World, Deadly Care, A Mother's Courage: The Mary Thomas Story. *Mini-Series*: The Dain Curse.

MILLER, MAX B.: Executive. b. Los Angeles, Feb. 23, 1937. Father, Max Otto Miller, producer silent features and shorts. Great grandfather was Brigham Young. e. Los Angeles Valley Coll., UCLA, Sherwood Oaks Coll. Writer of articles on cinema for American Cinematographer and other publications. Owns and manages Fotos Intl., entertainment photo agency with offices in 46 countries. Recipient of Golden Globe Award in 1976 for Youthquake, documentary feature. Also director of Films International (prod., Shoot Los Angeles) and pres. of MBM Prod., Inc. Active member of Hollywood Foreign Press Assn. (from 1974–82 bd member; twice chmn.), Independent Feature Project, Acad. of TV Arts & Sciences, L.A. Int'l, Film Exhibition, Soc. of M.P. & TV Engineers, Film Forum, Amer. Cinemateque.

MILLER, PENELOPE ANN: Actress. b. Los Angeles, CA, Jan. 13, 1964. Daughter of actor-filmmaker Mark Miller and journalist Bea Miller. e. studied acting with Herbert Berghof.

THEATER: *NY*: The People From Work (1984), Biloxi Blues (Bdwy and L.A.), Moonchildren, Our Town (Tony nom.).

PICTURES: Adventures in Babysitting (1987, debut), Biloxi Blues, Big Top Pee-Wee, Miles From Home, Dead-Bang, Downtown, The Freshman, Awakenings, Kindergarten Cop, Other People's Money, Year of the Comet, The Gun in Betty Lou's Handbag, Chaplin, Carlito's Way.

TELEVISION: *Series*: The Guiding Light, As the World Turns, The Popcorn Kid. *Guest*: Tales From the Darkside, Miami Vice, St. Elsewhere, Family Ties, The Facts of Life. *Specials*: Tales From the Hollywood Hills: The Closed Set, Our Town.

MILLER, ROBERT ELLIS: Director. b. New York, NY, July 18, 1932. e. Harvard U. Worked on Broadway and TV before feature film debut with Any Wednesday (1966).

PICTURES: Any Wednesday (debut, 1966), Sweet November, The Heart Is a Lonely Hunter, The Buttercup Chain, The Big Truck, The Girl from Petrovka, The Baltimore Bullet, Reuben Reuben, Brenda Starr, Hawks, Bed and Breakfast.

TELEVISION: The Voice of Charlie Pont, The Other Lover, Madame X, Just an Old Sweet Song, Her Life as a Man, Ishi: Last of His Tribe, Intimate Strangers, Killer Rules.

MILLER, RONALD W.: Producer. b. Los Angeles, CA, April 17, 1933. e. U. of Southern California. Football player with Los Angeles Rams. Two years U.S. Army. 1957 joined Walt Disney Productions as 2nd asst.` dir. Old Yeller. Assoc. prod. TV series Walt Disney Presents; assoc. or co-prod. additional 37 episodes Disney TV. Exec. prod. Walt Disney's Wonderful World of Color. Assisted Walt Disney, Pageant Direct 1960 U.S. Olympics. By 1968, v.p., exec. prod. mem. bd. of dir. Walt Disney Productions. 1980, named pres. & chief operating off.; 1983, pres. & chief executive off., Disney Productions. Resigned in 1984.

PICTURES: Bon Voyage, Summer Magic, Son of Flubber, Moon Pilot, The Misadventures of Merlin Jones, A Tiger Walks, The Monkey's Uncle, That Darn Cat, Robin Crusoe, U.S.N., Monkey's Go Home, Prod. of: Never a Dull Moment, The Boatniks, The Wild Country, No Deposit, No Return, Treasure of Matecumbe, Freaky Friday, The Littlest Horse Thieves, Herbie Goes to Monte Carlo, Pete's Dragon, Candleshoe, Return from Witch Mountain, Cat from Outer Space, The North Avenue Irregulars, Herbie Goes Bananas, The Black Hole, Midnight Madness, Watcher in the Woods, The Last Flight of Noah's Ark. *Exec. prod.*: Condorman; The Devil and Max Devlin, Tex, Never Cry Wolf, Night Crossing, Tron.

MILLS, DONNA: Actress. b. Chicago, IL, Dec. 11, 1945. e. U. of Illinois. Left school to pursue career in theatre, beginning as dancer with stage companies around Chicago and touring. In NY became regular on soap opera, The Secret Storm. On Bdwy in Don't Drink the Water.

TELEVISION: *Series*: Love Is a Many Splendored Thing, The Good Life, Knots Landing. *Guest*: Lancer, Dan August. *Movies*: Haunts of the Very Rich, Rolling Man, Night of Terror, The Bait, Live Again Die Again, Who is the Black Dahlia?, Beyond the Bermuda Triangle, Look What's Happened to Rosemary's Baby, Smash-Up on Interstate 5, Fire!, Curse of the Black Widow, The Hunted Lady, Superdome, Doctors' Private Lives, Hanging by a Thread, Waikiki, Bare Essence, He's Not Your Son, Woman on the Run, Outback Bound, The Lady Forgets, Intimate Encounters, The World's Oldest Living Bridesmaid, Runaway Father, False Arrest, In My Daughter's Name (also co-exec. prod.), The President's Child.

PICTURES: The Incident (debut, 1968), Play Misty for Me.

MILLS, HAYLEY: Actress. b. London, Eng., April 18, 1946. Father is actor John Mills. Sister is actress Juliet Mills. e. Elmhurst Boarding Sch., Surrey, and Institute Alpine Vidamanette, Switz. Made m.p. debut in Tiger Bay 1959 with father; then signed Disney contract 1960. Received special Academy Award for her role in Pollyana.

PICTURES: Tiger Bay (debut, 1959), Pollyanna, The Parent Trap, Whistle Down the Wind, In Search of the Castaways, Summer Magic, The Chalk Garden, The Moonspinners, That Darn Cat, The Truth About Spring, Sky West and Crooked (Gypsy Girl), Trouble with Angels, The Family Way, A Matter of Innocence (Pretty Polly), Twisted Nerve, Take a Girl Like You, Mr. Forbush and the Penguins, Endless Night, Deadly Strangers, Silhouettes, What Changed Charley Farthing, The Kingfisher Caper, Appointment with Death, After Midnight, The Last Straw.

TELEVISION: The Flame Trees of Thika (mini-series), Parent Trap (Parts II, III, IV, V), Amazing Stories, Illusion of Life, Good Morning Miss Bliss (series), Murder She Wrote, Back Home (series), Tales of the Unexpected.

THEATRE: The King and I (Australian tour), Fallen Angels (U.K., Australia, New Zealand).

MILLS, SIR JOHN: Actor, Producer. b. Suffolk, England, February 22, 1908. m. Mary Hayley Bell. Father of actresses Hayley and Juliet. Previously clerk. Film actor since 1933. One of top ten money-making Brit. stars in Motion Picture Herald-Fame Poll, 1945, 1947, 1949–50, 1954, 1956–58. Oscar for Ryan's

Daughter. Recipient special award 1988, British Academy of Film and Television Arts.

PICTURES: We Dive at Dawn, The Young Mr. Pitt, In Which We Serve, This Happy Breed, Blue for Waterloo, Cottage To Let, Way to the Stars, Waterloo Road, Great Expectations, So Well Remembered, October Man, Scott of the Antarctic, Operation Disaster, Mr. Denning Drives North, Gentle Gunman, Long Memory, Hobson's Choice, End of the Affair, Colditz Story, Above Us the Waves, Escapade, It's Great to be Young, Around the World in 80 Days, War and Peace, Baby and the Battleship, Town on Trial, Monty's Double, Dunkirk, Summer of the 17th Doll, Tiger Bay, Swiss Family Robinson, Tunes of Glory, The Singer Not the Song, Flame in the Streets, Tiara Tahiti, The Valiant, The Chalk Garden, The Truth about Spring, The Great Spy Mission, King Rat, The Wrong Box, Sky West and Crooked (dir.), The Family Way, Cowboy in Africa, Chukka, A Black Veil For Lisa, Oh! What a Lovely War, Run Wild Run Free, Ryan's Daughter (Acad. Award, supp. actor, 1970), Adam's Woman, Dulcima, Oklahoma Crude, Young Winston, Lady Caroline Lamb, The Human Factor, Trial By Combat, The Big Sleep, 39 Steps, Gandhi, Sahara, Who's That Girl.

STAGE: Good Companions, 1975; Great Expectations, 1976; Separate Tables, 1977; Goodbye, Mr. Chips, 1982; Little Lies, 1983; Little Lies (Toronto, 1984), The Petition, Pygmalion (NY).

TELEVISION: Masks of Death, Murder with Mirrors, Woman of Substance, Hold the Dream, Edge of the Wind, When the Wind Blows, Around the World in 80 Days, The Lady and the Highwayman, The True Story of Spit MacPhee, A Tale of Two Cities, Ending Up, Frankenstein.

MILLS, JULIET: Actress. b. London, England, Nov. 21, 1941. m. actor, Maxwell Caulfield. Father is actor John Mills. Sister is actress Hayley Mills. Made stage debut at 14 in Alice Through the Looking Glass.

PICTURES: So Well Remembered, The History of Mr. Polly, No, My Darling Daughter, Twice Around the Daffodils, Nurse on Wheels, Carry on Jack, The Rare Breed, Oh What a Lovely War!, Avanti!, Beyond the Door, The Man With the Green Cross, Barnaby and Me.

TELEVISION: *Series*: Nanny and the Professor. *Movies*: Wings of Fire, The Challengers, Letters from Three Lovers, Alexander: The Other Side of Dawn, The Cracker Factory, Columbo: No Time to Die. *Mini-Series*: QB VII (Emmy Award, 1975), Once an Eagle. *Guest*: Hotel, Dynasty, The Love Boat. *Special*: She Stoops to Conquer.

MILNER, JACK: Executive Producer. b. Jersey City, NJ, Nov. 2, 1910. e. Roosevelt H.S., L.A., CA. M.P. industry 1927. Worked many phases from laboratory-camera-editorial dept. to financing and co-producing feature pictures; formed Milner Bros. Productions with brother Dan Milner, 1955; prod. Phantom from 10,000 Leagues, From Hell It Came, Jail Break, etc.

TELEVISION: prod. My Dog Sheppy, From Here to Now, Come as You Are.

MILNER, MARTIN: Actor. b. Detroit, MI, Dec. 28, 1931. e. U. of Southern California. Army 1952–54, directed 20 training films.

PICTURES: Life With Father (debut, 1947), Sands of Iwo Jima, The Halls of Montezuma, Our Very Own, Operation Pacific, I Want You, The Captive City, Battle Zone, Mr. Roberts, Pete Kelly's Blues, On the Threshold of Space, Gunfight at the O.K. Corral, Sweet Smell of Success, Marjorie Morningstar, Too Much Too Soon, Compulsion, 13 Ghosts, Valley of the Dolls.

TELEVISION: *Series*: The Stu Erwin Show (1954–55), The Life of Riley (1957–8), Route 66 (1960–64), Adam-12 (1968–75), Swiss Family Robinson (1975–76). *Movies*: Emergency!, Runaway!, Hurricane, Swiss Family Robinson (pilot), Flood, SST—Death Flight, Black Beauty, Little Mo, Crisis in Mid-Air, The Seekers, The Ordeal of Bill Carney. *Mini-Series*: The Last Convertible.

MIMIEUX, YVETTE: Actress. b. Los Angeles, CA, Jan. 8, 1939. e. Vine Street Sch., Le Conte Jr. H.S., Los Angeles, Los Ninos Heroes de Chapultepec, Mexico City, Hollywood H.S., CA. Appeared with a theatrical group, Theatre Events; Sympn. Concert: Persephone, Oakland Orchestra, 1965, N.Y. Philharmonic, Lincoln Center, L.A. Philharmonic, Hollywood Bowl.

PICTURES: Platinum High School (debut, 1960), Time Machine, Where the Boys Are, The Four Horsemen of the Apocalypse, Light in the Piazza, The Wonderful World of the Brothers Grimm, Diamond Head, Toys in the Attic, Joy in the Morning, Reward, Monkeys Go Home, Dark of the Sun, Caper of the Golden Bulls, Picasso Summer, Three in the Attic, The Delta Factor, Skyjacked, The Neptune Factor, Journey Into Fear, Jackson County Jail, The Black Hole, Mystique (Circle of Power), Lady Boss.

TELEVISION: *Series*: Most Deadly Game, Berrenger's. *Movies*: Death Takes A Holiday, Black Noon, Hit Lady, The Legend of Valentino, Snowbeast, Ransom for Alice, Devil Dog: The Hound of Hell, Outside Chance, Disaster on the

Coastliner, Forbidden Love, Night Partners, Obsessive Love (also co-prod., co-writer), Perry Mason: The Case of the Desperate Deception.

STAGE: I Am a Camera, 1963; Owl and the Pussycat, 1966.

CONCERTS: Persephone—Houston Symphony, London Royal Philharmonic.

MINER, STEVE: Director. b. Chicago, IL, June 18, 1951. e. Dean Junior Col. Began career as prod. asst. on Last House on the Left (1970). Launched a NY-based editorial service, and dir., Prod., edited sport, educational and indust. films.

PICTURES: Here Come the Tigers! (co-prod.), Manny's Orphans (co-prod., s.p.), Friday the 13th (assoc. prod.). Director: Friday the 13th Part 2 (also prod.), Friday the 13th Part 3, Soul Man, House, Warlock (also prod.), Wild Hearts Can't Be Broken, Forever Young, My Father the Hero.

TELEVISION: The Wonder Years (sprv. prod., dir., DGA Award for pilot). Pilots: B-Men, Elvis, Laurie Hill, Against the Grain.

MINNELLI, LIZA: Actress, Singer. b. Los Angeles, CA, Mar. 12, 1946. p. actress-singer Judy Garland & dir. Vincente Minnelli. e. attended sch. in CA, Switzerland, and the Sorbonne. Left to tour as lead in The Diary of Anne Frank, The Fantastiks, Carnival and The Pajama Game. In concert with mother, London Palladium 1964. In concert Carnegie Hall, 1979, 1987. 1993. Film debut as child in mother's film In the Good Old Summertime (1949).

THEATER: Best Foot Forward (off-Bdwy debut, 1963, Theatre World Award), Flora The Red Menace (Tony award, 1965), Liza at the Winter Garden (Special Tony, 1974), Chicago, The Act (Tony Award, 1978), Are You Now or Have You Ever Been?, The Rink (Tony nom., 1984).

PICTURES: In the Good Old Summertime, Journey Back to Oz (voice; 1964, released in U.S. in 1974), Charlie Bubbles, The Sterile Cuckoo (Acad. Award nom.), Tell Me That You Love Me Junie Moon, Cabaret (Acad. Award, 1972), That's Entertainment!, Lucky Lady, Silent Movie, A Matter of Time, New York New York, Arthur, The Muppets Take Manhattan, That's Dancing!, Rent-a-Cop, Arthur 2 On The Rocks, Stepping Out.

TELEVISION: Specials: Judy and Liza at the London Palladium, The Dangerous Christmas of Red Riding Hood, Liza, Liza with a Z (Emmy Award, 1972). Goldie and Liza Together, Baryshnikov on Broadway, Liza in London, Faerie Tale Theater (Princess and the Pea), A Triple Play: Sam Found Out, Frank Sammy and Liza: The Ultimate Event. Movie: A Time to Live.

MIOU MIOU: Actress r.n. Sylvette Hery. b. Paris, France, Feb. 22, 1950. Worked as child with mother unloading fruits and vegetables at Les Halles market. First job as apprentice in upholstery workshop. In 1968 helped created Montparnasse cafe-theatre, Cafe de la Gare with comedian Coluche. Returned to stage in Marguerite Duras' La Musica, 1985.

PICTURES: La cavale (debut, 1971), Themroc, Quelques messieurs trop tranquilles, elle court, la banlieue, Les granges brulees, The Adventures of Rabbi Jacob, Going Places, La grand trouille, Lily aime-moi, The Genius, No Problem!, Victory March, F comme Fairbanks, Jonah Who Will Be 25 in the Year 2000, Al piacere di rivederla, Dites-lui que je l'aime, Les routes du Sud, L'ingorgo una storia impossibile, Au revoir...a lundi, Le Derobade, La femme flic, Est-ce raisonnable?, La guerule du loup, Josepha, Guy De Maupassant, Entre Nous, Attention, une femme peut en chacher une autre!, Canicule, Flight of the Phoenix, Blanche et Marie, Menage, Les portes tournates, La lectrice, Milou in May, Netchaiev is Back, The Jackpot, Le Bal des Casse-Pieds.

MIRISCH, DAVID: Executive. b. Gettysburg, PA, July 24, 1935. e. Ripon Coll. United Artists Corp., 1960–63; former exec. with Braverman-Mirisch adv. public rel. firm.

MIRISCH, MARVIN E.: Executive. b. New York, NY, March 19, 1918. e. City Coll. of New York, B.A., 1940. Print dept., contract dept., asst. booker, N.Y. exch.; head booker, Grand National Pictures, Inc., 1936–40; officer, gen. mgr. vending concession operation 800 theatres, Midwest, Theatres Candy Co., Inc., Milwaukee, Wisc., 1941–52; exec., corporate officer in chg., indep. producer negotiations, other management functions, Allied Artists Pictures, Inc., 1953–57; Chmn. of Bd., chief exec. officer in chg. of all business affairs, admin. & financing, distr. liaison, The Mirisch Company, Inc., 1957 to present. Member of Board of Governors and former vice-president of Academy of Motion Picture Arts & Sciences. Member Motion Pictures Pioneers. Past president of Academy of MPAS Foundation.

PICTURES: Exec. prod.: Dracula, Romantic Comedy.

MIRISCH, WALTER: Producer. b. New York, NY, Nov. 8, 1921. e. U. of Wisconsin, BA, 1942; Harvard Grad. Sch. of Business Admin., 1943. In m.p. indust. with Skouras Theatres Corp., 1938–40; Oriental Theatre Corp., 1940–42. 1945 with Mono-

gram, A.A.: apptd. exec. prod. Allied Artists, July, 1951; pres. and exec. head of prod. The Mirisch Corporation 1969; 1960–61 pres. Screen Prod. Guild; 1962, mem. bd. dir., MPAA; bd. Gvnrs., Academy of Motion Pictures Arts and Sciences, 1964; 1967, pres., Center Thea. Group of L.A.; bd. dir., Wisconsin Alum. Assn.; bd. of dir. Cedars-Sinai Medical Center, Bd. of Advisors, California State U.—Northridge, Board of Governors, Acad. of Motion Picture Arts & Sciences. President, Permanent Charities Committee 1962–63; President, Acad. of Motion Picture Arts & Sciences, 1973–77. Recipient Thalberg Award 1978, Hersholt Award, 1984.

PICTURES: The Magnificent Seven, By Love Possessed, Two for the Seesaw, Toys in the Attic, Hawaii, Fitzwilly, In the Heat of the Night, They Call Me Mister Tibbs, The Organization, Mr. Majestyk, Midway, Gray Lady Down, Same Time, Next Year, Prisoner of Zenda, Dracula, Romantic Comedy.

MIRREN, HELEN: Actress. b. London, England, 1946.

THEATRE: Troilus and Cressida, 2 Gentlemen of Verona, Hamlet, Miss Julie, Macbeth, Teeth 'n' Smiles, The Seagull, Bed Before Yesterday, Henry VI, Measure for Measure, The Duchess of Malfi, Faith Healer, Antony and Cleopatra, Roaring Girl, Extremities, Madame Bovary, Two Way Mirror, Sex Please We're Italian!, Woman in Mind (LA).

PICTURES: A Midsummer's Night Dream (debut, 1968), Age of Consent, Savage Messiah, O! Lucky Man, Hamlet, Caligula, Hussy, The Long Good Friday, The Fiendish Plot of Dr. Fu Manchu, Excalibur, Cal, 2010, White Nights, Heavenly Pursuits, The Mosquito Coast, Pascali's Island, When the Whales Came, The Cook The Thief His Wife and Her Lover, The Comfort of Strangers, Where Angels Fear to Tread, Dr. Bethune, The Gift.

TELEVISION: Miss Julie, The Applecart, The Little Minister, The Changeling, Blue Remembered Hills, As You Like It, A Midsummer Night's Dream, Mrs. Reinhart, After the Party, Cymbeline, Coming Through, Cause Celebre, Red King White Knight, Prime Suspect (BAFTA Award), Prime Suspect 2.

MISCHER, DON: Producer, Director. b. San Antonio, TX, March 5, 1941. e. U. of Texas, B.A. 1963, M.A. 1965. Pres., Don Mischer Productions, recipient 9 Emmy Awards, 8 Directors Guild Awards, 2 NAACP Image Awards, and a Peabody. Producer: Michael Jackson's Super Bowl XXVII Halftime Show, The Kennedy Center Honors, Tony Awards (3 yrs), Carnegie Hall 100th Anniversary, Gregory Hines Tap Dance in America, Opening of EuroDisney, The Muppets Celebrate Jim Henson, AFI Salutes to Billy Wilder and Gene Kelly, Irving Berlin's 100th Birthday, Baryshnikov by Tharp, Motown 25, Motown Apollo, Grand Reopening of Carnegie Hall, specials with Goldie Hawn, Liza Minnelli, Bob Hope, Robin Williams, Pointer Sisters. Also: The Great American Dream Machine, Donohue and Kids, The Presidential Inaugural, 6 Barbara Walters Specials, Ain't Misbehavin', It's Garry Shandling's Show. Founded Don Mischer Productions, 1978.

MITCHELL, CAMERON: Actor. b. Dallastown, PA, Nov. 4, 1918. e. Theatre Sch., N.Y.; New York Theatre Guild, 1938–40. On stage with Lunt & Fontanne, Taming of the Shrew. Radio announcer, sportscaster before joining U.S. Army Air Forces 1942–44. Star of Tomorrow, 1954.

PICTURES: Mighty McGurk, High Barbaree, Cass Timberlane, Leather Gloves, The Sellout, Death of a Salesman, Japanese War Bride, Flight to Mars, Man in the Saddle, Outcasts of Poker Flat, Okinawa, Les Miserables, Pony Soldier, Powder River, Man on a Tightrope, How to Marry a Millionaire, Hell & High Water, Gorilla at Large, Garden of Evil, Desiree, Strange Lady in Town, Love Me Or Leave Me, House of Bamboo, Tall Men, View from Pompey's Head, Carousel, Monkey on My Back, Face of Fire, Inside The Mafia, The Unstoppable Man, The Last of the Vikings, Three Came to Kill, Blood and Black Lace, Dog Eat Dog, Ride in the Whirlwind, Hombre, Island of the Doomed, Nightmare in Wax, Buck and the Preacher, Slaughter, The Midnight Man, The Klansman, Viva Knievel!, The Swarm, Frankenstein Island, Without Warning, Texas Lightning, Raw Force, Kill Squad, Blood Link, My Favorite Year, Blood Link, Killpoint, Prince Jack, Night Train to Terror, Low Blow, The Tomb, Night Force, Deadly Prey, Mission to Kill, The Offspring, Hollywood Cop, The Messenger, Rage to Kill, No Justice, Terror in Beverly Hills, Final Curtain, Space Mutiny, Code Name Vengeance, Action U.S.A., Easy Kill.

TELEVISION: Series: High Chapparal, Swiss Family Robinson. Movies: Andersonville Trial, The Bastard, Black Beauty, How the West Was Won, Partners in Crime, Wild Times.

MITCHUM, JIM: Actor. b. Los Angeles, CA, May 8, 1941. m. actress Wendy Wagner. Son of Robert Mitchum. e. Univ. H.S., L.A. Went directly from school to Hollywood Professional Sch. On-job prof. training at Barter Theatre in Virginia.

PICTURES: Thunder Road (debut), The Last Time I Saw Archie, The Victors, Ride the Wild Surf, In Harm's Way, Ambush Bay, Tramplers, Invisible Six, Moonrunners, Beat

Generation, Ride the Wild Surf, Trackdown, Code Name Zebra, Mercenary Fighters, Hollywood Cop.
TELEVISION: Jake Spanner: Private Eye.

MITCHUM, ROBERT: Actor. b. Bridgeport, CT, Aug. 6, 1917. Odd jobs; to California; joined Long Beach Players Guild; appeared in Hopalong Cassidy series with William Boyd; in Westerns 8 yrs. RKO. Biography: It Sure Beats Working (1975, by Mike Tomkies).
PICTURES: Hoppy Serves a Writ (debut, 1943), The Leather Burners, Border Patrol, Follow the Band, Colt Comrades, The Human Comedy, We've Never Been Licked, Beyond the Last Frontier, Bar 20, Doughboys in Ireland, Corvette K-225, Aerial Gunner, The Lone Star Trail, False Colors, The Dancing Masters, Riders of the Deadline, Cry Havoc, Gung Ho, Johnny Doesn't Live Here Anymore, When Strangers Marry, The Girl Rush, Thirty Seconds Over Tokyo, Nevada, West of the Pecos (All made 1943–44) Gained recognition: Story of G.I. Joe, Undercurrent, Locket, Til' the End of Time, Pursued, Desire Me, Crossfire, Out of the Past, Rachel and the Stranger, Blood on the Moon, Red Pony, Big Steal, Holiday Affair, Where Danger Lives, My Forbidden Past, His Kind of Woman, Racket, Macao, One Minute to Zero, Lusty Men, Angel Face, White Witch Doctor, Second Chance, She Couldn't Say No, River of No Return, Track of the Cat, Night of the Hunter, Not as a Stranger, Man with the Gun, Foreign Intrigue, Bandido, Heaven Knows Mr. Allison, Fire Down Below, The Enemy Below, Thunder Road, The Hunters, The Angry Hills, Wonderful Country, Home from the Hill, A Terrible Beauty, The Grass is Greener, Sundowners, The Last Time I Saw Archie, Cape Fear, The Longest Day, List of Adrian Messenger, Two for the Seesaw, Rampage, Man in the Middle, What a Way to Go!, Mr. Moses, The Way West, El Dorado, Anzio, Villa Rides, Five Card Stud, Secret Ceremony, Young Billy Young, Good Guys and the Bad Guys, Ryan's Daughter, Going Home, Wrath of God, Friends of Eddie Coyle, The Yakuza, Farewell My Lovely, Midway, The Last Tycoon, Amsterdam Kill, The Big Sleep, Breakthrough, Matilda, Nightkill, Agency, That Championship Season, Maria's Lovers, The Ambassador, Mr. North, Scrooged, Midnight Ride, Presumed Dangerous, Cape Fear (1991), Tombstone.
TELEVISION: Series: A Family for Joe, African Skies. Mini-Series: The Winds of War, North and South, War and Remembrance. Movies: One Shoe Makes it Murder, A Killer in the Family, The Hearst and Davies Affair, Reunion at Fairborough, Promises to Keep, Thompson's Last Run, Brotherhood of the Rose, Jake Spanner: Private Eye, A Family for Joe.

MOCIUK, YAR W.: Executive. b. Ukraine, Jan. 26, 1927. e. City Coll. of New York; World U.; Peoples U. of Americas, Puerto Rico. Expert in field of m.p. care and repair; holds U.S. patent for method and apparatus for treating m.p. film. Has also been film producer and director. Founder and pres. of CM Films Service, Inc. until 1973. Now chmn. of bd. and pres. of Filmtreat International Corp. Member: M.P. & TV Engineers; Univ. Film Assn. Pres., Ukrainian Cinema Assn. of America.

MODINE, MATTHEW: Actor. b. Loma Linda, CA, March 22, 1959. Raised in Utah. Studied with Stella Adler.
PICTURES: Baby It's You (debut, 1983), Private School, Streamers, Hotel New Hampshire, Mrs. Soffel, Birdy, Vision Quest, Full Metal Jacket, Orphans, Married to the Mob, The Gamble, Gross Anatomy, Pacific Heights, Memphis Belle, Wind, Equinox, Short Cuts, The Browning Version.
TELEVISION: Movie: And the Band Played On. Specials: Eugene O'Neill: Journey Into Greatness, Texas, Amy and the Angel.

MOFFAT, DONALD: Actor. b. Plymouth, England, Dec. 26, 1930. Studied acting Royal Academy of Dramatic Art, 1952–54. London stage debut Macbeth, 1954. With Old Vic before Broadway debut in Under Milkwood, 1957. Worked with APA-Phoenix Theatre Co. and as actor and dir. of numerous Bdwy and regional productions.
THEATER: The Bald Soprano, Jack, Ivanov, Much Ado About Nothing, The Tumbler, Duel of Angels, A Passage to India, The Affair, The Taming of the Shrew, The Caretaker, Man and Superman, War and Peace, You Can't Take It With You, Right You Are . . . If You Think You Are, School for Scandal, The Wild Duck, The Cherry Orchard, Cock-A-Doodle Dandy, Hamlet, Chemin de Fer, Father's Day, Forget-Me-Not-Lane, Terra Nova, The Kitchen, Waiting for Godot, Painting Churches, Play Memory, Passion Play, The Iceman Cometh, Uncommon Ground, Love Letters, As You Like It.
PICTURES: Pursuit of the Graf Spee (debut, 1957), Rachel Rachel, The Trial of the Catonsville Nine, R.P.M., Great Northfield Minnesota Raid, Showdown, The Terminal Man, Earthquake, Land of No Return, Promises in the Dark, Health, On the Nickel, Popeye, The Thing, The Right Stuff, Alamo Bay, The Best of Times, Monster in the Closet, The Unbearable Lightness of Being, Far North, Music Box, The Bonfire of the Vanities, Class Action, Regarding Henry, Housesitter.

TELEVISION: Guest: Camera Three (1958), You Can't Have Everything (U.S. Steel Hour), Murder, She Wrote, Dallas. Specials: Forget-Me-Not Lane, Tartuffe, Waiting for Godot. Series: The New Land (1974), Logan's Run. Movies: Devil and Miss Sarah, Call of the Wild, Eleanor and Franklin: The White House Years, Exo-Man, Mary White, Sergeant Matlovich vs. the U.S. Air Force, The Word, The Gift of Love, Strangers: The Story of a Mother and Daughter, Ebony Ivory and Jade, Mrs. R's Daughter, The Long Days of Summer, Jacqueline Bouvier Kennedy, Who Will Love My Children?, Through Naked Eyes, License to Kill, Cross of Fire, A Son's Promise, Kaleidoscope, The Great Pretender, Babe Ruth, Columbo: No Time to Die, Teamster Boss: The Jackie Presser Story, Majority Rule.

MOGER, STANLEY H.: Executive. Pres., SFM Entertainment, Exec. Vice Pres., SFM Media Corp. b. Boston, MA, Nov. 13, 1936. e. Colby Coll., Waterville, ME, B.A., 1958. Announcer/TV personality/WVDA and WORL (Boston) 1953–54; WGHM (Skowhegan) 1955–56; WTWO-TV (Bangor) 1955; WMHB (Waterville) 1956–57; WTVL (Waterville) 1957–58; unit pub. dir., Jaguar Prods., 1958–59; US Army reserve, 1958–64, with calls to active duty in 1958–59 and 1961–62; account exec., NBC Films/California National Productions, Chicago 1959–60; asst. sales mgr., Midwest, RCA/NBC Medical Radio System, 1960; acct. exec. Hollingbery Co., Chicago, 1960–63; and NY 1963–66; acct. exec., Storer TV Sales, 1966–69; co-founded SFM, Sept. 29, 1969. In 1978, named pres., SFM Entertainment which was responsible for the revival of Walt Disney's Mickey Mouse Club, The Adventures of Rin-Tin-Tin; Mobil Showcase Network; SFM Holiday Network. Exec. prod.: Television-Annual 1978–79: Your New Day with Vidal Sassoon, The Origins Game; Believe You Can and You Can, Walt Disney Presents Sport Goofy (series); The World of Tomorrow. March of Time . . . on the March (England), Sports Pros and Cons, Unclaimed Fortunes; Sea World Summer Night Magic; America's Dance Honors, Allen & Rossi's 25th Anniversary Special, Paris '89 Celebration; U.S. Sports Academy Awards, K-Nite Color Radio, Into the Night With Brad Garrett (ABC-TV).
PROPERTIES: SFM Holiday Network, Car Care Central, March of Time series, Co-Packager Superstars; Adventures of the Wilderness Family; Across the Great Divide; Mysteries from Beyond Earth; To the Ends of the Earth; Challenge To Be Free; Wonder of It All; Great American Cowboy; Deal; Dayan; Sports Illustrated; General Foods Golden Showcase Network—Shock Trauma; 1983 official film of the America's Cup Challenge: Countdown to the Cup; Pinocchio in Outer Space; Rudyard Kipling's Jungle Book; The Heisman Trophy Annual Award Specials; Walt Disney World's Very Merry Xmas Parade; The Indomitable Teddy Roosevelt; Crusade in the Pacific; Rosepetal Place; Hugga-Bunch; Jayce and the Wheeled Warriors; Time Travel: Fact, Fiction and Fantasy; Zoobilee Zoo; Photon; Just the Facts (Dragnet special); Willie Nelson's Summer Picnic; Crusade in Europe; King Kong: The Living Legend; SFM Children's Theatre; Ghost Dance; Sea World's All-Star, Lonestar Celebration; George Stevens: A Filmmaker's Journey; Gorillas in the Mist Special; Tappin'; Care Bears (series); Crystal Light National Aerobics Championships (1986 & 87); U.S. Man of the Year Pageant; The Digital Discovery. Series: The Infinite Voyage, Sea World's Miracle Babies & Friends; Think Fast (racing series); So Power Passes; Pillar of Fire; A Celebration of Country at Ford's Theatre, In Our Image; Command Performance at Ford's Theatre, Witness to Survival (series); Sea World Mother Earth Celebration; The Kitchen Fairy (series), Sea World Star Spangled Summer, Ford's Theatre Celebrates Hispanic America, Circus Circus Circus, Wichita Town, Mayday for Mother, Presidential Portraits, Tribute to the Singing Cowboy, many others.

MOKAE, ZAKES: Actor. b. Johannesburg, South Africa, Aug. 5, 1935. e. RADA. Came to US in 1969. Has appeared in many plays written by Athol Fugard incl. Master Harold . . . and the Boys, Blood Knot.
PICTURES: The Island, Roar, Cry Freedom, The Serpent and the Rainbow, A Dry White Season, Gross Anatomy, Dad, A Rage in Harlem, The Doctor, Body Parts, Dust Devil.
TELEVISION: Special: Master Harold . . . and the Boys. Movies: One in a Million: The Ron LeFlore Story, Parker Kane.

MOLINA, ALFRED: Actor. b. London, Eng., May 24, 1953. e. Guildhall Sch. of Music and Drama. Began acting with the National Youth Theatre. Worked as stand-up comic for street theatre group. Joined Royal Shakespeare Co., 1977 (Frozen Assets, The Steve Biko Inquest, Dingo, Bandits, Taming of the Shrew, Happy End), Also in Serious Money, Speed-the-Plow, Accidental Death of an Anarchist (Plays and Players' Most Promising New Actor Award), The Night of the Iguana.
PICTURES: Raiders of the Lost Ark (debut, 1981), Meantime, Number One, Ladyhawke, Eleni, Water, Letter to Brezhnev, Prick Up Your Ears, Manifesto, Not Without My Daughter, Enchanted April, American Friends, The Trial, Myth of the White Wolf.

TELEVISION: The Losers, Anyone for Dennis, Joni Jones, Cats' Eyes, Blat, Casualty, Virtuoso, Apocolyptic Butterflies, The Accountant, Drowning in the Shallow End, El C.I.D., Ashenden, Hancock, A Polish Practice, Year in Provence.

MOLINARO, EDOUARD: Director. b. Bordeaux, France, May 13, 1928. Made amateur films at university and launched professional career via award-winning technical shorts. First feature film, Le Dos au Mur, 1957.
PICTURES: Girls for the Summer, A Ravishing Idiot, Gentle Art of Seduction, La Cage aux Folles (also Part II), Sunday Lovers, Just the Way You Are, The Door on the Left as You Leave the Elevator.

MOLL, RICHARD: Actor. b. Pasadena, CA, Jan. 13, 1943.
TELEVISION: Series: Night Court. Movies: The Jericho Mile, The Archer: Fugitive from the Empire, Combat High, Dream Date, Class Cruise. Specials: Reach for the Sun, The Last Halloween, Words Up! Guest: Remington Steele, Facts of Life, Sledge Hammer, My Two Dads, Highlander.
PICTURES: Caveman, The Sword and the Sorcerer, Metalstorm: The Destruction of Jared-Syn, The Dungeonmaster, House, Wicked Stepmother, Think Big, Driving Me Crazy, National Lampoon's Loaded Weapon 1, Sidekicks, The Flintstones.

MONASH, PAUL: Producer, Writer. b. New York, NY, June 14, 1917. e. U. of Wisconsin, Columbia U. Was in U.S. Army Signal Corps and Merchant Marine; newspaper reporter; high school teacher; and civilian employee of U.S. gov't. in Europe. Wrote two novels: How Brave We Live, The Ambassadors. Entered industry writing TV scripts for Playhouse 90, Studio One, Theatre Guild of the Air, Climax, etc. Authored two-part teleplay which launched The Untouchables. In 1958 won Emmy award for The Lonely Wizard (Schlitz Playhouse of Stars), dramatization of life of German-born electrical inventor Charles Steinmetz. Made m.p. debut as exec. prod. of Butch Cassidy and the Sundance Kid, 1969.
PICTURES: Slaughterhouse-Five (prod.), The Friends of Eddie Coyle (prod., s.p.), The Front Page (prod.), Carrie (prod.), Big Trouble in Little China (prod.).
TELEVISION: Child Bride of Short Creek, The Day the Loving Stopped, Trial of Chaplain Jensen, Killer Rules (writer).

MONICELLI, MARIO: Director. b. Rome, Italy, May 15, 1915. Ent. m.p. industry in production; later co-authored, collab., comedies. Dir.: Big Deal on Madonna Street, The Great War, Tears of Joy, Boccaccio '70, The Organizer, Casanova, Girl With a Pistol, Amici Mie, Viva Italia!, Travels With Anita, Lovers and Liars (also, s.p.), Il Marchese de Grillo (also s.p.), Amici, Miei, Atto (All My Friends 2, also s.p.), Bertoldo, Bertoldino, E Cacasenna (also, s.p.), The Two Lives of Mattia Pascal, I Picari (dir., co-s.p.).

MONKHOUSE, BOB: TV-radio-cabaret Comedian, Comedy writer. b. Beckenham, Kent, June 1, 1928. e. Dulwich Coll. Debut 1948 while serving in RAF, own radio comedy series 1949–83 (winters), own TV series, BBC 1952–56; ITV 1956–83; BBC 1983–90, ITV 1990–. Several West End revues, Boys from Syracuse; Come Blow Your Horn; The Gulls; others. Films include: Carry On, Sergeant; Weekend with Lulu; Dentist in the Chair; She'll Have to Go; Bliss of Mrs. Blossom; others. Major cabaret attraction U.K., Australia, Hong Kong. British star of numerous TV series including: What's My Line?; Who Do You Trust?; Mad Movies; Quick on the Draw; Bob Monkhouse Comedy Hour; The Golden Shot (8 years); Celebrity Squares (4 yrs); I'm Bob, He's Dickie! (1978–81); Family Fortunes (1979–83); Bob Monkhouse Tonight (1983–86), Bob's Full House (1984–90), Bob Says Opportunity Knocks (1987–89), $64,000 Question (1990–ongoing). Regular dramatic guest spots ITV & BBC-TV, was under exclusive contract to Central TV to host $64,000 Question & live Saturday night people show. Comedian of the Year, 1987. After-Dinner Speaker of the Year, 1989.

MONKS, JOHN, JR.: Writer, Actor, Producer, Director. b. Brooklyn, NY, June 25, 1910. e. Virginia Military Inst., A.B. Actor, stock, Bdwy, radio, m.p. U.S. Marines, 1942; commissioned Major, 1945. Playwright Co-author Brother Rat. Wrote book A Ribbon and a Star.
PICTURES: Brother Rat, Co-author, Brother Rat and a Baby, Strike Up the Band, The House on 92nd Street, 13 Rue Madeleine, Wild Harvest, Dial 1119., The West Point Story, People Against O'Hara. Where's Charley. So This Is Love, Knock on Any Door, No Man Is an Island.
TELEVISION: Climax: The Gioconda Smile, A Box of Chocolates; 20th Century-Fox Hour: Miracle on 34th St.; Gen. Electric Theatre: Emily; CBS Special: High Tor; SWAT; Creator serial: Paradise Bay.

MONTAGNE, EDWARD J.: Producer, Director. b. Brooklyn, NY, May 20, 1912. e. Loyola U., of Notre Dame. RKO Pathe, 1942; U.S. Army, 1942–46; prod. many cos. after army.

PICTURES: Tattooed Stranger, The Man with My Face, McHale's Navy, McHale's Navy Joins the Air Force, P.J., The Reluctant Astronaut.
TELEVISION: Man Against Crime, Cavalier Theatre, The Vaughn Monroe Show, The Hunter, I Spy, McHale's Navy; exec. prod. of film-CBS-N.Y., Phil Silvers Show. Prod. & head of programming, Wm. Esty Adv. Co., 1950; Program consultant, William Esty Co.; v.p. Universal TV prod. & dir.: 5 Don Knotts features; prod.: Andy Griffith, Angel in My Pocket, Ellery Queen, A Very Missing Person, Short Walk to Daylight, Hurricane, Terror on the 40th Floor, Francis Gary Powers, Million Dollar Ripoff, Crash of Flight 401, High Noon—Part 2, Harper Valley PTA.

MONTALBAN, RICARDO: Actor. b. Mexico City, Mex., Nov. 25, 1920. Appeared in Mexican pictures 1941–45; to U.S. On Bdwy in Her Cardboard Lover with Tallulah Bankhead. Later in Jamaica, The King and I, Don Juan in Hell. Autobiography: Reflections: A Life in Two Worlds (1980).
PICTURES: Fiesta (U.S. debut, 1947), On an Island With You, Kissing Bandit, Neptune's Daughter, Battleground, Border Incident, Mystery Street, Right Cross, Two Weeks with Love, Across the Wide Missouri, Mark of Renegade, My Man and I, Sombrero, Latin Lovers, Saracen Blade, Life in The Balance, Three for Jamie Dawn, Sayonara, Let No Man Write My Epitaph, Hemingway's Adventures of a Young Man, The Reluctant Saint, Love Is a Ball, Cheyenne Autumn, The Money Trap, Madame X, The Singing Nun, Sol Madrid, Blue, Sweet Charity, The Deserter, Escape From the Planet of the Apes, Conquest of the Planet of the Apes, The Train Robbers, Joe Panther, Won Ton Ton the Dog Who Saved Hollywood, Star Trek II: The Wrath of Khan, Cannonball Run II, The Naked Gun.
TELEVISION: Series: Fantasy Island, The Colbys. Guest: How the West Was Won Part II (Emmy Award). Movies: Longest Hundred Miles, The Pigeon, Black Water Gold, The Aquarians, Sarge: The Badge or the Cross, Face of Fear, Desperate Mission, Fireball Foreward, Wonder Woman, The Mark of Zorro, McNaughton's Daughter, Fantasy Island, Captains Courageous, Return to Fantasy Island.

MONTGOMERY, ELIZABETH: Actress. b. Los Angeles, CA, April 15, 1933. e. Amer. Acad. of Dramatic Arts. Daughter of the late actor Robert Montgomery. Bdwy debut: Late Love. Narrated theatrical documentaries Cover Up: Behind the Iran Contra Affair, and The Panama Deception.
PICTURES: The Court-Martial of Billy Mitchell (debut, 1955), Johnny Cool, Who's Been Sleeping in My Bed?
TELEVISION: Series: Robert Montgomery Presents, Bewitched. Movies: The Victim, Mrs. Sundance, A Case of Rape, The Legend of Lizzie Borden, Dark Victory, A Killing Affair, The Awakening Land, Jennifer: A Woman's Story, Missing Pieces, Second Sight: A Love Story, Amos, Between the Darkness and the Dawn, Face to Face, Sins of the Mother, With Murder in Mind, Black Widow Murders: The Blanche Taylor Moore Story. Guest: Studio One, Alcoa Premiere, Playhouse 90, Climax, Burke's Law, many others.

MONTGOMERY, GEORGE: Actor. r.n. George Montgomery Letz; b. Brady, MT, Aug. 29, 1916. e. U. of Montana. Armed Services, W.W.II.
PICTURES: Cisco Kid and the Lady (1939), Star Dust, Young People, Charter Pilot, Jennie, Cowboy and the Blonde, Accent on Love, Riders of the Purple Sage, Last of the Duanes, Cadet Girl, Roxie Hart, Ten Gentlemen from West Point, Orchestra Wives, China Girl, Brasher Doubloon, Three Little Girls in Blue, Lulu Belle, Belle Starr's Daughter, Girl From Manhattan, Sword of Monte Cristo, Texas Rangers, Indian Uprising, Cripple Creek, Pathfinder, Jack McCall Desperado, Fort Ti, Gun Belt, Battle of Rogue River, Lone Gun, Masterson of Kansas, Seminole Uprising, Robbers' Roost, Too Many Crooks, Stallion Trail, The Steel Claw, Watusi, Samar, Hallucination Generation, Hostile Guns, Ransom in Blood.

MOONJEAN, HANK: Producer, Director. Began as asst. dir. at MGM. Later turned to producing.
PICTURES: Assoc. Prod.: The Great Gatsby, WUSA, The Secret Life of An American Wife, Child's Play, Welcome to Hard Times, The Singing Nun. Exec. Prod.: The Fortune, The End. Producer: Hooper, Smokey and the Bandit II, The Incredible Shrinking Woman, Paternity, Sharky's Machine, Stroker Ace, Dangerous Liaisons, Beauty and the Beast, Stealing Home.

MOORE, CONSTANCE: Actress. b. Sioux City, IA, Jan. 18, 1922. Sang on radio; Lockheed prog., 2 yrs; Jurgen's Show, 2 yrs. Screen debut 1938. TV shows, nightclubs. N.Y. Stage: The Boys from Syracuse, By Jupiter, Annie Get Your Gun, Bells Are Ringing, Affairs of State.
PICTURES: Prison Break, A Letter of Introduction, I Wanted Wings, Take A Letter Darling, Show Business, Delightfully Dangerous, Earl Carroll Vanities and Sketchbook, In Old Sacramento, Hit Parade of 1947, Spree.

MOORE, DEMI: Actress. b. Roswell, NM, Nov. 11, 1962. r.n. Demi Guynes. m. actor Bruce Willis. Began modeling at age 16. Off B'way debut: The Early Girl, 1987 (Theatre World Award).
PICTURES: Choices (debut, 1981), Parasite, Young Doctors in Love, Blame It on Rio, No Small Affair, St. Elmo's Fire, About Last Night, One Crazy Summer, Wisdom, The Seventh Sign, We're No Angels, Ghost, Nothing But Trouble, Mortal Thoughts (also co-prod.), The Butcher's Wife, A Few Good Men, Indecent Proposal.
TELEVISION: Series: General Hospital. Guest: Kaz, Vega$, Moonlighting, Tales from the Crypt (Dead Right). Specials: Bedrooms, The New Homeowner's Guide to Happiness.

MOORE, DICKIE: Actor. b. Los Angeles, CA, Sept. 12, 1925. m. actress Jane Powell. Began picture career when only 11 months old, appearing with John Barrymore in The Beloved Rogue. Appeared in numerous radio, television and stage prods. in NY and L.A. and over 100 films. Co-author and star, RKO short subject, The Boy and the Eagle (nom. Acad. Award). Author: Opportunities in Acting, Twinkle Twinkle Little Star (But Don't Have Sex or Take the Car), 1984. Now public relations executive.
PICTURES: Blonde Venus, The Squaw Man, So Big, Oliver Twist, Story of Louis Pasteur, Peter Ibbetson, Sergeant York, Heaven Can Wait, Out of the Past, Eight Iron Men, Member of the Wedding.

MOORE, DUDLEY: Actor, Writer, Musician. b. Dagenham, Essex, Eng., April 19, 1935. e. Oxford, graduating in 1958. Toured British Isles with jazz group before joining Peter Cook, Jonathan Miller and Alan Bennett in creating hit revue, Beyond the Fringe, in U.K. and N.Y. Appeared later with Peter Cook on Bdwy. in Good Evening. Composed film scores: 30 is a Dangerous Age Cynthia, Inadmissible Evidence, Staircase, Six Weeks.
PICTURES: The Wrong Box, Bedazzled, 30 is a Dangerous Age Cynthia (also co-s.p., music), Monte Carlo or Bust (Those Daring Young Men in Their Jaunty Jalopies), The Bed Sitting Room, Alice's Adventures in Wonderland, The Hound of the Baskervilles, Foul Play, "10", Wholly Moses, Arthur (Acad. Award nom.), Six Weeks, Lovesick, Romantic Comedy, Unfaithfully Yours, Best Defense, Micki and Maude, Santa Claus, Like Father Like Son, Arthur 2 On the Rocks (also exec. prod.), The Adventures of Milo and Otis (narrator), Crazy People, Blame it on the Bellboy, The Pickle.
TELEVISION: Series: Dudley.

MOORE, ELLIS: Consultant. b. New York, NY, May 12, 1924. e. Washington and Lee U., 1941–43. Newspaperman in AK, TN, 1946–52. Joined NBC 1952; mgr. of bus. pub., 1953; dir., press dept., 1954; dir., press & publicity, Dec. 22, 1959; vice-pres., 1961; pub. rel. dept., Standard Oil Co. (N.J.), 1963–66; v.p. press relations, ABC-TV Network, 1966–68; v.p. public relations ABC-TV Network, 1968–70; v.p. public relations, ABC, 1970, v.p. public relations, ABC, Inc., 1972; v.p. corporate relations, ABC, Inc., 1979; v.p., public affairs, ABC, Inc., 1982–85. P.R. consultant, 1985. Retired, 1992.

MOORE, GARRY: Performer. r.n. Thomas Garrison Morfit; b. Baltimore, MD, Jan. 31, 1915. Continuity writer, WBAL; announcer, sports commentator, KWK, St. Louis; comedian, writer, Club Matinee show, Chicago; Everything Goes, N.Y.; teamed with Jimmy Durante on radio to 1947; m.c., Take It or Leave It, Breakfast in Hollywood. Elected to TV Academy Hall of Fame.
TELEVISION: Star of Garry Moore Show, I've Got A Secret. Best TV daytime show: Fame Poll, 1958; To Tell The Truth (Best Primetime Variety Show, Emmy Award, 1962; Peabody Award).

MOORE, KIERON: Actor. b. Skibereen, Co. Cork, Eire, 1925. e. St. Mary's Coll., Dublin. Stage debut, 1945 in Desert Rats; appeared in Red Roses For Me. Film debut 1947 in A Man About the House.
PICTURES: Anna Karenina, Mine Own Executioner, Ten Tall Men, David and Bathsheba, Saints and Sinners, Naked Heart, Honeymoon Deferred, Man Trap (Man in Hiding), Conflict of Wings (Fuss Over Feathers), Green Scarf, Blue Peter, Satellite in the Sky, Three Sundays to Live, The Key, The Angry Hills, The Day They Robbed the Bank of England, League of Gentlemen, The Siege of Sidney Street, Faces of Evil, Lion of Sparta, Steel Bayonet, I Thank a Fool, Double Twist, The Day of the Triffids, The Thin Red Line, The Main Attraction, Crack in the World, Son of a Gunfighter, Never Love a Savage, Run Like a Thief, Custer of the West. Director: The Progress of Peoples, The Parched Land.

MOORE, MARY TYLER: Actress. b. Brooklyn. NY, Dec. 29, 1936. Began as professional dancer and got first break as teenager in commercials (notably the role in Hotpoint appliance ads); then small roles in series Bachelor Father, Steve Canyon, and finally as the switchboard oper. in Richard Diamond (though only her legs were seen). Broadway: Breakfast at Tiffany's (debut), Whose Life Is It Anyway? (special Tony Award, 1980), Sweet Sue. Chairman of Bd., MTM Enter-prises, Inc, which she founded with then-husband Grant Tinker.
TELEVISION: Series: Richard Diamond Private Detective (1959), The Dick Van Dyke Show (1961–66; 2 Emmy Awards), The Mary Tyler Moore Show (1970–77; 3 Emmy Awards), Mary (1978), The Mary Tyler Moore Hour (1979), Mary (1985–86), Annie McGuire (1988). Guest: Bachelor Father, Steve Canyon, 77 Sunset Strip, Hawaiian Eye, Love American Style. Movies: Run a Crooked Mile, First You Cry, Heartsounds, Finnegan Begin Again, Gore Vidal's Lincoln, The Last Best Year, Thanksgiving Day, Stolen Babies. Special: How to Survive the 70's, How to Raise a Drugfree Child.
PICTURES: X-15 (debut, 1961), Thoroughly Modern Millie, Don't Just Stand There, What's So Bad About Feeling Good?, Change of Habit, Ordinary People (Acad. Award nom.), Six Weeks, Just Between Friends.

MOORE, ROGER: Actor, Director. b. London, England, Oct. 14, 1927. e. art school, London; Royal Acad. of Dramatic Art. Appointed Special Ambassador for UNICEF, 1991.
PLAYS: Mr. Roberts, I Capture the Castle, Little Hut, others. Bdwy: A Pin to See the Peepshow.
TELEVISION: Series: The Alaskans, Maverick, The Saint, The Persuaders. Movies: Sherlock Holmes in New York, The Man Who Wouldn't Die.
PICTURES: Last Time I Saw Paris, Interrupted Melody, The King's Thief, Diane, The Miracle, Gold of the Seven Saints, The Sins of Rachel Cade, Rape of the Sabines, No Man's Land, Crossplot, The Man Who Haunted Himself, Live and Let Die, Gold, The Man with the Golden Gun, That Lucky Touch, Street People, Shout at the Devil, The Spy Who Loved Me, The Wild Geese, Escape To Athena, Moonraker, ffolkes, The Sea Wolves, Sunday Lovers, For Your Eyes Only, The Cannonball Run, Octopussy, The Curse of the Pink Panther, The Naked Face, A View to a Kill, The Magic Snowman (voice), Bed and Breakfast, Bullseye!, Fire Ice and Dynamite.

MOORE, TERRY: Actress. r.n. Helen Koford; b. Los Angeles, CA, Jan. 7, 1929. mother Luella Bickmore, actress. Photographer's model as a child; on radio; with Pasadena Playhouse 1940; in m.p. 1933. Star of Tomorrow: 1958. Formed Moore/Rivers Productions, 1988 with partner-manager Jerry Rivers. Has also acted as Helen Koford, Judy Ford, and Jan Ford.
PICTURES: The Howards of Virginia, Gaslight, Son of Lassie, Sweet and Low Down, Shadowed, Devil on Wheels, Return of October, Mighty Joe Young, The Great Ruppert, He's a Cockeyed Wonder, Gambling House, The Barefoot Mailman, Two of a Kind, Come Back Little Sheba, Sunny Side of the Street, Man on a Tightrope, Beneath the 12-mile Reef, King of the Khyber Rifles, Daddy Long Legs, Shack Out on 101, Postmark for Danger, Between Heaven and Hell, Peyton Place, Bernardine, A Private's Affair, Cast a Long Shadow, Why Must I Die?, Platinum High School, City of Fear, Black Spurs, Town Tamer, Waco, A Man Called Dagger, The Daredevil, Death Dimension (Black Eliminator), Double Exposure, Hellhole, Beverly Hills Brats (also co-prod., co-story).
TELEVISION: Series: Empire. Movies: Quarantined, Smash-Up on Interstate 5, Jake Spanner: Private Eye.

MOORE, THOMAS W.: Executive. e. U. of Missouri. Naval aviator, USNR, 1940–45. Adv. dept., Star, Meridian, MS; v.p., adv. mgr., Forest Lawn Memorial Park; account exec., CBS-TV Film Sales, Los Angeles; gen. sales mgr., CBS-TV Film Sales, 1956; v.p. in chg. programming & talent, 1958; pres., ABC-TV Network, 1962; chmn. bd., Ticketron, 1968; pres., Tomorrow Entertainment, Inc. 1971; chmn., 1981.

MORANIS, RICK: Actor, Writer. b. Toronto, Canada, Apr. 18, 1954. Began career as part-time radio engineer while still in high school. Hosted own comedy show on radio then performed in Toronto cabarets and nightclubs and on TV. Joined satirical TV series SCTV during its 3rd season on CBC, for which he won Emmy for writing when broadcast in U.S. Created characters of the McKenzie Brothers with Dave Thomas and won Grammy nom. for McKenzie Brothers album. With Thomas co-wrote, co-directed and starred in film debut Strange Brew, 1983. Supplied voice for cartoon series Rick Moranis in Gravedale High.
PICTURES: Strange Brew (debut, 1983; also co-dir., co-s.p.), Streets of Fire, Ghostbusters, The Wild Life, Brewster's Millions, Head Office, Club Paradise, Little Shop of Horrors, Spaceballs, Ghostbusters II, Honey I Shrunk the Kids, Parenthood, My Blue Heaven, L.A. Story, Honey I Blew Up the Kid, Splitting Heirs, The Flintstones.

MOREAU, JEANNE: Actress. b. Paris, France, Jan. 23, 1928. e. Nat'l Conservatory of Dramatic Art. Stage debut with Comedie Française, acting there until 1952 when she joined the Theatre Nationale Populaire. Directorial debut: La Lumière (film), 1976.
PLAYS: A Month in the Country, La Machine Infernale, Pygmalion, Cat on a Hot Tin Roof.
PICTURES: The She-wolves, Elevator to the Scaffold, The Lovers, Le Dialogue Des Carmelites, Les Liaisons Dangereuses, Moderato Cantabile, La Notte, Jules and Jim, A Woman Is a Woman, Eva, The Trial, Bay of Angels, The

Victors, Le Feu Follet, Diary of a Chambermaid, The Yellow Rolls-Royce, The Train, Mata Hari, Viva Maria, Mademoiselle, Chimes at Midnight, Sailor From Gibraltar, The Bride Wore Black, The Immortal Story, Great Catherine, Monte Walsh, Alex in Wonderland, The Little Theatre of Jean Renoir, The Last Tycoon, French Provincial, La Lumière (also dir., s.p.), Mr. Klein, The Adolescent (dir., s.p. only), Plein Sud, Querelle, The Trout, La Femme Nikita, The Suspended Step of the Stork, La Femme Farde, Until the End of the World, Alberto Express, The Lover (voice), Map of the Human Heart, The Old Lady Who Wades in the Sea, Anna Karamazova, See You Tomorrow, My Name is Victor.

MORENO, RITA: Actress. r.n. Rosa Dolores Alvario. b. Humacao, Puerto Rico, Dec. 11, 1931. Spanish dancer since childhood; night club entertainer. Has won all 4 major show business awards: Oscar, Tony, 2 Emmys and Grammy (for Best Recording for Children: The Electric Company, 1972).
  THEATER: Skydrift (debut, 1945), Sign in Sidney Brustein's Window, Gantry, Last of the Red Hot Lovers, The National Health (Long Wharf, CT), The Ritz (Tony Award, 1975), Wally's Cafe, The Odd Couple (female version).
  PICTURES: So Young So Bad (debut, 1950 as Rosita Moreno), Pagan Love Song, Toast of New Orleans, Singin' in the Rain, The Ring, Cattle Town, Ma and Pa Kettle on Vacation, Latin Lovers, Fort Vengeance, Jivaro, El Alamein, Yellow Tomahawk, Garden of Evil, Untamed, Seven Cities of Gold, Lieutenant Wore Skirts, The King and I, The Vagabond King, The Deerslayer, This Rebel Breed, Summer and Smoke, West Side Story (Acad. Award, supp. actress, 1961), Cry of Battle, The Night of the Following Day, Marlowe, Popi, Carnal Knowledge, The Ritz, The Boss' Son, Happy Birthday Gemini, The Four Seasons, Life in the Food Chain (Age Isn't Everything), The Italian Movie.
  TELEVISION: Series: The Electric Company, Nine to Five, B.L. Styker, Top of the Heap. Movies: Evita Peron, Anatomy of a Seduction, Portrait of a Showgirl. Guest: The Muppet Show (Emmy, 1977), The Rockford Files (Emmy, 1978). Special: Tales From the Hollywood Hills: The Golden Land.

MORGAN, ANDRE: Producer. b. Morocco, 1952. e. U. of Kansas. Golden Harvest Films 1972–84. Producer. Exec. v.p., Golden Communications 1976–84. Formed Ruddy-Morgan Productions with Albert S. Ruddy, 1984.
  PICTURES: Enter the Dragon, The Amsterdam Kill, The Boys in Company C, Cannonball Run II, High Road to China, Lassiter, Farewell to the King, Speed Zone, Impulse, Miracle in the Wilderness, Ladybugs.

MORGAN, DENNIS: Actor. r.n. Stanley Morner; b. Prentice, WI, Dec. 10, 1910. e. Carroll Coll. Started with State Lake Theat., Chicago. Toured midwest in Faust, sang in Empire Room of Palmer House, Chicago, appeared on NBC programs and sang lead in Xerxes. Screen debut, 1936. Star of Tomorrow (1941).
  PICTURES: Suzy (debut, 1936), The Great Ziegfeld, The Return of Dr. X, Kitty Foyle, The Fighting 69th, Three Cheers for the Irish, Affectionately Yours, Bad Men of Missouri, Wings for the Eagle, Captains of the Clouds, In This Our Life, The Hard Way, Thank Your Lucky Stars, The Desert Song, Hollywood Canteen, Shine on Harvest Moon, The Very Thought of You, God is My Co-Pilot, Christmas in Connecticut, The Time the Place and the Girl, One More Tomorrow, My Wild Irish Rose, Two Guys from Milwaukee, Two Guys from Texas, Cheyenne, Perfect Strangers, To the Victor, One Sunday Afternoon, It's a Great Feeling, The Lady Takes a Sailor, Raton Pass, Pretty Baby, Painting the Clouds with Sunshine, This Woman Is Dangerous, Cattle Town, Gun That Won the West, Pearl of the South Pacific, Uranium Boom, Rogues' Gallery, Won Ton Ton The Dog Who Saved Hollywood.
  TELEVISION: Series: Beacon Street.

MORGAN, HARRY: Actor. r.n. Harry Bratsburg. b. Detroit, MI, Apr. 10, 1915. e. U. of Chicago. Screen debut 1942. Previously acted as Henry Morgan.
  TELEVISION: Series: December Bride, Pete and Gladys, The Richard Boone Show, Kentucky Jones, Dragnet, The D.A., Hec Ramsey, M*A*S*H (Emmy Award, 1980), After M*A*S*H, Blacke's Magic, You Can't Take It With You. Movies: Dragnet (pilot), But I Don't Want to Get Married!, The Feminist and the Fuzz, Ellery Queen: Don't Look Behind You, Hec Ramsey (pilot), Sidekicks, The Last Day (narrator), Exo-Man, The Magnificent Magnet of Santa Mesa, Maneaters Are Loose!, Murder at the Mardi Gras, The Bastard, Kate Bliss and the Ticker Tape Kid, The Wild Wild West Revisited, Better Late Than Never, Roughnecks, Scout's Honor, More Wild Wild West, Rivkin: Bounty Hunter, Agatha Christie's Sparkling Cyanide, The Incident, Against Her Will: An Incident in Baltimore. Mini-Series: Backstairs at the White House, Roots: The Next Generations.
  PLAYS: Gentle People, My Heart's in the Highlands, Thunder Rock, Night Music, Night Before Christmas.
  PICTURES: To the Shores of Tripoli, Loves of Edgar Allen Poe, Orchestra Wives, The Ox-Bow Incident, Happy Land,

Wing and a Prayer, A Bell for Adano, Dragonwyck, From This Day Forward, The Gangster, All My Sons, The Big Clock, Moonrise, Yellow Sky, Madame Bovary, The Saxon Charm, Dark City, Appointment with Danger, The Highwayman, When I Grow Up, The Well, Blue Veil, Bend of the River, Scandal Sheet, My Six Convicts, Boots Malone, High Noon, What Price Glory, Stop You're Killing Me, Arena, Torch Song, Thunder Bay, Glenn Miller Story, About Mrs. Leslie, Forty-Niners, Far Country, Not As a Stranger, Backlash, Strategic Air Command, Teahouse of the August Moon, Inherit the Wind, The Mountain Road, How the West Was Won, John Goldfarb Please Come Home, What Did You Do in the War Daddy?, Frankie and Johnny, The Flim Flam Man, Support Your Local Sheriff, Viva Max!, The Barefoot Executive, Support Your Local Gunfighter, Scandalous John, Snowball Express, Charlie and the Angel, The Apple Dumpling Gang, The Greatest, The Shootist, Cat from Outer Space, The Apple Dumpling Gang Rides Again, Dragnet.

MORGAN, MICHELE: Actress. r.n. Simone Roussel; b. Paris, France, Feb. 29, 1920. e. Dieppe, dramatic school, Paris. Decided on acting career at 15 yrs., won role at 17 opposite Charles Boyer in Gribouille. (later filmed as The Lady in Question, Hollywood). Made several pictures abroad; to U.S. 1940. First Amer. film Joan of Paris, 1942. Recent theatre includes Les Monstres Sacres.
  PICTURES: Higher and Higher, Passage to Marseilles, The Chase, Symphonie Pastorale, Fallen Idol, Fabiola, 7 Deadly Sins, Moment of Truth, Daughters of Destiny, Naked Heart, Proud and the Beautiful, Grand Maneuver, Marguerite de la Nuit, The Mirror Has Two Faces, Landru, Oasis, Lost Command, Benjamin, Cat and Mouse, Seven Steps to Murder, Robert et Robert.

MORIARTY, CATHY: Actress. b. Bronx, NY, Nov. 29, 1960. Raised in Yonkers, NY.
  PICTURES: Raging Bull (debut, 1980; Acad. Award nom.), Neighbors, White of the Eye, Burndown, Kindergarten Cop, Soapdish, The Mambo Kings, The Gun in Betty Lou's Handbag, Matinee, Another Stakeout.
  TELEVISION: Guest: Tales from the Crypt.

MORIARTY, MICHAEL: Actor. b. Detroit, MI, April 5, 1941. e. Dartmouth. Studied at London Acad. of Music and Dramatic Arts. Appeared with New York Shakespeare Festival, Charles Street Playhouse (Boston), Alley Theatre (Houston) and Tyrone Guthrie Theatre (Minneapolis). Broadway debut in The Trial of the Catonsville Nine.
  THEATER: Find Your Way Home (Tony & Theatre World Awards, 1974), Richard III, Long Day's Journey Into Night, Henry V, GR Point, Whose Life Is It Anyway (Kennedy Center), The Ballad of Dexter Creed, Uncle Vanya, Caine Mutiny Court Martial.
  PICTURES: Glory Boy (debut, 1971), Hickey and Boggs, Bang the Drum Slowly, The Last Detail, Shoot It Black Shoot It Blue, Report to the Commissioner, Who'll Stop the Rain, Too Far To Go, Q, Blood Link, Odd Birds, Pale Rider, The Stuff, Troll, The Hanoi Hilton, It's Alive III: Island of the Alive, Return to Salem's Lot, Dark Tower, Full Fathom Five, The Secret of the Ice Cave.
  TELEVISION: Series: Law and Order. Movies: A Summer Without Boys, The Glass Menagerie (Emmy Award, 1974), The Deadliest Season, The Winds of Kitty Hawk, Too Far to Go (also distributed theatrically), Windmills of the Gods, Frank Nitti: The Enforcer, Tailspin: Behind the Korean Airline Tragedy, Born Too Soon. Mini-Series: Holocaust (Emmy Award, 1978). Guest: The Equalizer.

MORITA, NORIYUKI "PAT": Entertainer. Actor. b. Isleton, CA, June 28, 1932. Began show business career as comedian in nightclubs for such stars as Ella Fitzgerald, Johnny Mathis, Diana Ross and the Supremes, Glen Campbell, etc. Worked in saloons, coffee houses, and dinner theatres before becoming headliner in Las Vegas showrooms, Playboy Clubs, Carnegie Hall, etc. Guest on most TV talk, variety shows and series: M*A*S*H, Love Boat, Magnum, P.I. etc.
  PICTURES: Thoroughly Modern Millie, Every Little Crook and Nanny, Cancel My Reservation, Where Does It Hurt?, Midway, When Time Ran Out, Full Moon High, Savannah Smiles, Jimmy the Kid, The Karate Kid (Acad. Award nom.), Night Patrol, Slapstick of Another Kind, The Karate Kid Part II, Captive Hearts, Collision Course, The Karate Kid Part III, Do Or Die, Lena's Holiday, Honeymoon in Vegas, Even Cowgirls Get the Blues, The Next Karate Kid.
  TELEVISION: Series: The Queen and I, Sanford and Son, Happy Days, Mr. T and Tina, Blansky's Beauties, Ohara, The Karate Kid (voice for animated series). Movies: Evil Roy Slade, A Very Missing Person, Brock's Last Case, Punch and Jody, Farewell to Manzanar, Human Feelings, For the Love of It, The Vegas Strip Wars, Amos, Babes in Toyland, Hiroshima: Out of the Ashes.

MORITZ, MILTON I: Executive. b. Pittsburgh, PA, Apr. 27, 1933. e. Woodbury Coll., grad. 1955. Owned, operated theatres in L.A., 1953–55; U.S. Navy 1955–57; American International Pictures asst. gen. sls. mgr., 1957; nat'l. dir. of adv. and publ.

1958; v.p. and bd. mem. of American International Pictures, 1967; 1975, named ˙sr. v.p.; in 1980 formed own co., The Milton I. Moritz Co., Inc., Inc., mktg. & dist. consultant. 1987, joined Pacific Theatres as v.p. in chg. of adv., p.r. & promotions. Pres. of Variety Club of Southern California Tent 25, 1975–76.

MORRICONE, ENNIO: Composer, Arranger. b. Rome, Nov. 10, 1928. Studied with Goffredo Petrassi at the Acad. of Santa Cecilia in Rome. Began career composing chamber music and symphonies as well as music for radio, TV and theater. Wrote for popular performers incl. Gianni Morandi. Early film scores for light comedies. Gained reknown for assoc. with Ital. westerns of Sergio Leone (under name of Dan Davio).
PICTURES: IL Federal (1961, debut), A Fistful of Dollars, The Good the Bad and the Ugly, El Greco, Fists in the Pocket, Battle of Algiers, Matcheless, Theorem, Once Upon a Time in the West, Investigation of a Citizen, Fraulein Doktor, Burn, The Bird with the Crystal Plumage, Cat O'Nine Tails, The Red Tent, Four Flies in Grey Velvet, The Decameron, The Black Belly of the Tarantula, Bluebeard, The Serpent, Blood in the Streets, Eye of the Cat, The Human Factor, Murder on the Bridge, Sunday Woman, The Inheritance, Partner, Orca, The Heretic, Exorcist II, 1900, La Cage aux Folles, Days of Heaven, Bloodline, Stay as You Are, The Humanoid, The Meadow, A Time to Die, Travels With Anita, When You Comin' Back Red Ryder?, Almost Human, La Cage aux Folles II, The Island, Tragedy of a Ridiculous Man, Windows, Butterfly, So Fine, White Dog, Copkiller, Nana, The Thing, Treasure of the Four Crowns, Sahara, Once Upon a Time in America, Thieves After Dark, The Cage, La Cage aux Folles III, The Forester's Sons, The Red Sonja, Repentier, The Mission, The Venetian Woman, The Untouchables, Quartiere (Neighborhood), Rampage, Frantic, A Time of Destiny, Casualties of War, Cinema Paradiso, State of Grace, Hamlet, Bugsy, City of Joy, The Bachelor, In the Line of Fire.
TELEVISION: (U.S.): Marco Polo, Moses—The Lawgiver, Scarlet and the Black, C.A.T. Squad, The Endless Game, Octopus 4.

MORRIS, ANITA: Actress. b. Durham, NC, March 14, 1943. e. AADA.
PICTURES: The Happy Hooker, So Fine, The Hotel New Hampshire, Maria's Lovers, Absolute Beginners, Blue City, Ruthless People, Aria, 18 Again!, A Sinful Life, Bloodhounds of Broadway, Martians Go Home.
TELEVISION: Series: Berrenger's, Down and Out in Beverly Hills. Movies: A Masterpiece of Murder, A Smoky Mountain Christmas. Guest: Miami Vice, Cheers, Who's the Boss?, Matlock, Murder She Wrote.
THEATRE: NY: Jesus Christ—Superstar, Seesaw, Rachel Lily Rosenbloom, The Magic Show, Unsung Cole, Sugar Babies, Nine.

MORRIS, GARRETT: Actor. b. New Orleans, LA, Feb. 1, 1937. e. Dillard Univ., Julliard Sch. of Music, Manhattan Sch. of Music. Was singer and arranger for Harry Belafonte Folk Singers and Broadway actor before achieving fame as original cast member of Saturday Night Live.
TELEVISION: Series: Roll Out, Saturday Night Live (1975–80), It's Your Move, Hunter, Martin. Movies: The Invisible Woman, Maid for Each Other. Guest: Scarecrow and Mrs. King, Love Boat, Married With Children, Murder She Wrote, The Jeffersons.
PICTURES: Where's Poppa? (debut, 1970), The Anderson Tapes, Cooley High, Car Wash, How to Beat the High Cost of Living, The Census Taker, The Stuff, Critical Condition, The Underachievers, Dance to Win.
THEATRE: Porgy and Bess, I'm Solomon, Show Boat, Hallelujah Baby!, The Basic Training of Pavlo Hummel, Finian's Rainbow, The Great White Hope, Ain't Supposed to Die a Natural Death, The Unvarnished Truth.

MORRIS, HOWARD: Actor, Director. b. New York, NY, Sept. 4, 1919. e. NYU. U.S. Army, 4 yrs.
PICTURES: Director: Who's Minding the Mint?, With Six You Get Egg Roll, Don't Drink the Water. Actor: The Nutty Professor, High Anxiety, History of the World Part I, Splash, Life Stinks.
BROADWAY: Hamlet, Call Me Mister, John Loves Mary, Gentlemen Prefer Blondes, Finian's Rainbow.
TELEVISION: Series: Your Show of Shows, Caesar's Hour. Movies: The Munster's Revenge, Portrait of a Showgirl, Return to Mayberry. Voices: Jetsons, Flintstones, Mr. Magoo. Producer: The Corner Bar. Director: Dick Van Dyke Show, Get Smart, Andy Griffith Show (also frequent guest); also many commericals.

MORRIS, JOHN: Composer, Conductor, Arranger. b. Elizabeth, NJ. e. student Juilliard Sch. Music 1946–48, U. of Washington. 1947, New Sch. Social Research 1946–49. Member: ASCAP, Acad. of M.P. Arts & Sciences, American Federation of Musicians.
STAGE: Composer: Broadway: My Mother, My Father and Me, Doll's House, Camino Real, A Time For Singing (musical), Take One Step, Young Andy Jackson, 15 Shakespeare

plays for NY Shakespeare Fest. & Amer. Shakespeare Fest, Stratford CT. Musical supervisor, conductor, arranger: Mack and Mabel, Much Ado About Nothing, Bells Are Ringing and 24 other Bdwy musicals. Off-Bdwy: Hair.
RECORDS: Wildcat, All-American, Bells Are Ringing, First Impressions, Bye Bye Birdie, Kwamina, Baker Street, Rodgers and Hart, George Gershwin Vols. 1 & 2, Jerome Kern, Lyrics of Ira Gershwin, Cole Porter, others.
PICTURES: The Producers, The Twelve Chairs, The Gambler, Blazing Saddles (Acad. Award nom.), Bank Shot, Young Frankenstein, Sherlock Holmes' Smarter Brother, Silent Movie, The Last Remake of Beau Geste, The In-Laws, The World's Greatest Lover, In God We Trust, High Anxiety, The Elephant Man (Acad. Award nom.), Table for Five, History of the World, Part One, Yellowbeard, The Doctor and the Devils Clue, To Be or Not to Be, The Woman in Red, Johnny Dangerously, Haunted Honeymoon, Dirty Dancing, Spaceballs, Ironweed, The Wash, Second Sight, Stella, Life Stinks.
TELEVISION: Composer: Fresno, Katherine Anne Porter, Ghost Dancing, The Firm, The Mating Season, Splendor in the Grass, The Electric Grandmother, The Scarlet Letter, Georgia O'Keeffe, The Adams Chronicles, The Franken Project, The Tap Dance Kid (Emmy, 1986), Make Believe Marriage, The Desperate Hours, The Skirts of Happy Chance, Infancy and Childhood, The Fig Tree, The Little Match Girl, Favorite Son, The Last Best Year, The Last to Go, The Sunset Gang, Our Sons. Themes: ABC After School Special, Making Things Grow, The French Chef, Coach. Musical sprv., conductor, arranger Specials: Anne Bancroft Special #1 (Emmy Award), S'Wonderful S'Marvelous S'Gershwin (Emmy Award), Hallmark Christmas specials.

MORRIS, OSWALD: Cinematographer. b. London, Eng., Nov. 22, 1915. Left school at 16 to work for two years as camera dept. helper at studios. Was lensman for cameraman Ronald Neame who gave Morris first job as cameraman; in 1949 when Neame directed The Golden Salamander he made Morris dir. of photography.
PICTURES: The Golden Salamander, The Card, The Man Who Never Was, Moulin Rouge, Beat the Devil, Moby Dick, Heaven Knows Mr. Allison, A Farewell to Arms, The Roots of Heaven, The Key, The Guns of Navarone, Lolita, Term of Trial, The Pumpkin Eater, Mister Moses, The Hill, The Spy Who Came in from the Cold, Reflections in a Golden Eye, Oliver!, Gooodbye Mr. Chips, Scrooge, Fiddler on the Roof (Acad. Award), Sleuth, Lady Caroline Lamb, The Mackintosh Man, The Odessa File, The Man Who Would Be King, The Seven Per Cent Solution, Equus, The Wiz, Just Tell Me What You Want, The Great Muppet Caper, The Dark Crystal.
TELEVISION: Dracula (1974).

MORRIS, RICHARD: Director, Writer. b. San Francisco, CA, May 14, 1924. e. Burlingame H.S., 1939–42; Chouinard Art Inst., 1946–47; Neighborhood Playhouse, 1947–48. U.S. Army special services, writing shows, Victory Bond; Universal-Int., talent dept., writing directing skits, writing music for acting class and Korean War entertainment troups; s.p. Take Me to Town, Finders Keepers.
AUTHOR, STAGE: The Unsinkable Molly Brown.
PICTURES: If a Man Answers, Thoroughly Modern Millie, Change of Habit.
TELEVISION: Wrote & dir. teleplays, Loretta Young Show, wrote & dir. The Pearl (Loretta Young Show), wrote teleplays, Private Secretary, Ford Theatre, Kraft Television Theatre, dir., The Wild Swans (Shirley Temple Show-Christopher Award).

MORRISSEY, PAUL: Writer, Director, Photographer. b. New York, NY, 1939. e. Fordham U. Service in Army. Was involved in indep. film prod. prior to joining Andy Warhol for whom he produced such films as Chelsea Girls, Four Stars, Bike Boy, Nude Restaurant, Lonesome Cowboys, Blue Movie.
PICTURES: Flesh, Trash, Heat, Women in Revolt, L'Amour, Andy Warhol's Frankenstein (a.k.a. Flesh for Frankenstein), Andy Warhol's Dracula (a.k.a. Blood of Dracula), Hound of the Baskervilles, Forty Deuce, Madame Wang's, Mixed Blood, Beethoven's Nephew, Spike of Bensonhurst.

MORROW, JEFF: Actor. b. New York, NY, Jan. 13, 1907. e. Pratt Inst. Starred 2 years as radio's Dick Tracy, star of TV series Union Pacific, U.S. Steel, Wagon Train, etc.
BROADWAY: Romeo and Juliet, St. Joan, Billy Budd, Lace On Her Petticoat, Three Wishes For Jamie. In Los Angeles Lincoln in Norman Corwin's Lincoln-Douglas Debates.
PICTURES: The Robe, Flight to Tangiers, Tanganyika, Siege at Red River, Sign of the Pagan, Captain Lightfoot, This Island Earth, The World in My Corner, Pardners, Kronos, Story of Ruth, Dino Risi's Giovane Normale (Italy) Hour of Decision.

MORROW, ROB: Actor. b. New Rochelle, NY, Sept. 21, 1962.
TELEVISION: Series: Tattinger's, Northern Exposure. Guest: Spenser: For Hire, Everything's Relative, Fame.
PICTURES: Private Resort, Quiz Show.
THEATRE: NY: The Chosen, Scandal (workshop), Soulful

Scream of a Chosen Son, The Boys of Winter, Slam, Third Secret.

MORSE, DAVID: Actor. b. Beverly, MA, Oct. 11, 1953.
TELEVISION: *Series*: St. Elsewhere. *Movies*: Shattered Vows, When Dreams Come True, Prototype, Downpayment on Murder, Six Against the Rock, Winnie, Brotherhood of the Rose, Cross of Fire, Dead Ahead: The Exxon Valdez Disaster, Miracle on Interstate 880. *Guest*: Nurse. *Special*: A Place at the Table.
PICTURES: Inside Moves, Desperate Hours, The Indian Runner, The Good Son, The Getaway.

MORSE, ROBERT: Actor. b. Newton, MA, May 18, 1931. Served U.S. Navy. Studied with American Theatre Wing, New York. Following radio work, appeared on Broadway stage in The Matchmaker, 1956.
BROADWAY: The Matchmaker, Say Darling (Theatre World Award), Take Me Along, How to Succeed in Business Without Really Trying (Tony Award, 1962), Sugar, So Long 174th Street, Tru (Tony Award, 1990).
PICTURES: The Proud and the Profane (debut, 1956), The Matchmaker, The Cardinal, Honeymoon Hotel, Quick Before It Melts, The Loved One, Oh Dad Poor Dad Mama's Hung You in the Closet and I'm Feeling So Sad, How to Succeed in Business Without Really Trying, A Guide for the Married Man, Where Were You When the Lights Went Out?, The Boatniks, Hunk, The Emperor's New Clothes.
TELEVISION: *Series*: The Secret Storm (1954), That's Life. *Specials*: The Stingiest Man in Town (voice), Kennedy Center Tonight—Broadway to Washington, Tru. *Movie*: The Calendar Girl Murders. *Mini-Series*: Wild Palms. *Guest*: Masquerade, Alfred Hitchcock Presents, Naked City, Love American Style, Twilight Zone, Murder She Wrote.

MORTON, ARTHUR: Composer, Arranger. b. Duluth, MN, Aug. 8, 1908. e. U. of Minnesota, 1929. Composer for various film cos. including Universal, RKO, United Artists; with Columbia since 1948.
PICTURES: Night Life of the Gods, Princess O'Hara, Riding on Air, Fit for a King, Turnabout, Walking Hills, The Nevadan, Rogues of Sherwood Forest, Father is a Bachelor, Never Trust a Gambler, Harlem Globetrotters, Big Heat, Pushover, He Laughed Last.
ORCH. ARRANGEMENTS: Laura, Smokey, From Here to Eternity, Jolson Story, Salome, Phfft, No Sad Songs For Me, Born Yesterday, Long Gray Line, Man from Laramine, My Sister Eileen, Queen Bee, Picnic, Jubal, Autumn Leaves, Johnny Concho, Harder They Fall, 3:10 to Yuma, Full of Life, Garment Jungle, They Came to Cordura, Strangers When We Meet, Touch of Mink, Critics Choice, Diamond Head, Toys in the Attic, Man from the Diners' Club, Von Ryan's Express, The Saboteur, Code Name—Morituri, In Harm's Way, What a Way to Go, The New Interns, Rio Conchos, Dear Brigitte, Our Man Flint, Planet of the Apes, Flim Flam Man, Justine, Patton, Tora Tora Tora, Mephisto Waltz, Ballad of Cable Hogue, Traveling Executioner, Escape from the Planet of the Apes, Cold Turkey, Wild Rovers, The Other, Ace Eli, One Little Indian, The Don is Dead, Papillon, Chinatown, Breakout, The Wind and the Lion, Logan's Run, The Omen, Islands in the Stream, Passover Plot, Twilight's Last Gleaming, Damnation Alley, MacArthur, Capricorn One, Coma, The Swarm, Omen II (Damien), Boys from Brazil, Magic, Superman, Alien, Players, Meteor, Star Trek, Inchon, Masada, The Final Conflict, Outland, Raggedy Man, Night Crossing, Poltergeist, The Secret of NIMH, First Blood, Psycho II, Twilight Zone, Under Fire, The Lonely Guy, Gremlins, Supergirl, Rambo: First Blood Part II, Explorers, King Solomon's Mines, Link, Poltergeist II, Hoosiers, Lionheart, Extreme Prejudice, Innerspace, Rent a Cop, Rambo III, Warlock, The 'Burbs, Leviathan, Star Trek V: The Final Frontier, Total Recall, Gremlins II, Russia House, Not Without My Daughter, Medicine Man, Gladiator, Mr. Baseball, Forever Young, The Vanishing.
TELEVISION: Black Saddle, Laramie, Bus Stop, Follow the Sun, My Three Sons, Peyton Place, Medical Center, Daniel Boone, Lancers, National Geographic, Say Goodbye, How to Stay Alive, Hooray For Hollywood, The Waltons, Apple's Way, Medical Story.

MORTON, JOE: Actor. b. New York, NY, Oct. 18, 1947. e. Hofstra U.
PICTURES: ... And Justice for All, The Brother From Another Planet, Trouble in Mind, Zelly and Me, The Good Mother, Tap, Terminator 2: Judgment Day, City of Hope, Of Mice and Men, Forever Young.
TELEVISION: *Series*: Grady, Equal Justice, Tribeca. Movies: The Challenger, Terrorist on Trial: The United States Vs. Salim Ajami, Howard Beach: Making a Case for Murder, Death Penalty, Legacy of Lies. *Special*: The File of Jill Hatch. *Guest*: A Different World, Hawk.
THEATRE: *NY*: Hair, Raisin (Theatre World Award), Oh Brother, Honky Tonk Nights, A Midsummer Night's Dream, King John, Cheapside, Electra, A Winter's Tale, Oedipus Rex, Julius Caesar, The Tempest.

MOSES, CHARLES ALEXANDER: Executive, Writer, Producer. b. Chicago, CA, March 1, 1923. e. Aeronautical U., Northwestern U., Englewood Eve. Jr. Coll., Antioch U. Pub. rel. dir., Goldblatt Bros. dept. store chain, Chicago; field adv-promo exec., United Artists, unit publicist for over 30 films, exec., Screen Gems; European adv-pub superv., Paris, United Artists; adv-pub dir., Bel Air Prod., V.P. adv-pub dir., Associates & Aldrich Co., adv-pub dir., Sinatra Enterprises, assoc. studio pub. dir., Universal Studios, adv-pub rep., Universal Studios from Paris for Europe, exec-in-chg New York domestic & foreign adv-pub dept., Universal, adv-pub superv., Orion Pictures Co. Own firm, Charles A. Moses Co., adv-marketing-pub. rel., acc'ts included United Artists, Columbia Picts., 20th Century-Fox, UA-TV, Brut Prod., Michael Klinger Ltd., ITT, Cinecom, Cinemation Industries, Hemdale Leisure Corp., Faberge, Stein & Day Publishers; Information, Inc., Automated Learning, Darrell Waters Ltd., Ebefilms, Phoenix Films, Valley Cable TV, Jensen Farley Picts., Taft Internat'l Picts, auto shows, TV shows, art galleries, events, guilds, Cinevent Prod., Dimitri Tiomkin, Dale Wasserman, American Internat'l Picts., Filmways. Orig. stories, Frankenstein 1970 (Allied Artists), Store (Brut Prod.); Prod., Radio Free Europe, Munich, Goldblatt radio, TV shows (WGN); Writer-prod-dir., documentaries, Carson Prod., Mason City; Screenplays, Abigail, The Callers; Musical book, Daddy. Past pres., The Publicists Guild of America (IATSE, Local 818).

MOSES, GILBERT: Producer, Director. b. Cleveland, OH, Aug. 20, 1942. Staff mem. Free Press, Jackson, MS 1963–64; editor, 1964; co-founder artistic dir. Free Southern Theatre; member Second City, Chicago, 1967. New York Stage director; m.p. debut Willie Dynamite (also score and lyrics), 1973; The Fish That Saved Pittsburgh, 1979.
STAGE: Ain't Supposed to Die a Natural Death (Tony nom.), Slave Ship (Obie award), The Taking of Miss Janie (Obie & NY Drama Critics Awards), Dreaming Emmett, Buried Child.
TELEVISION: Roots (Emmy nom.), A Fight for Jenny, The Greatest Thing That Almost Happened, The Day They Came to Arrest the Book (Schoolbreak), Runaway (Wonderworks), Snoops. Afterschool Specials: Daddy Can't Read (prod. & dir.), Over the Limit (prod.), A Question About Sex (co-prod.).

MOSLEY, ROGER E.: Actor. b. Los Angeles, CA. Planned career in broadcasting but turned to acting, first appearing in small roles on TV in: Night Gallery, Baretta, Kojak, Cannon, Switch.
PICTURES: The New Centurions (debut, 1972), Hit Man, Terminal Island, Stay Hungry, Leadbelly, The Greatest, Semi-Tough, Heart Condition, Unlawful Entry.
TELEVISION: *Series*: Magnum P.I., You Take the Kids. *Guest*: Baretta, Kojak, Cannon, Switch. *Movies*: Cruise Into Terror, I Know Why the Caged Bird Sings, The Jericho Mile, Attica. *Mini-Series*: Roots: The Next Generations.

MOSS, FRANK L.: Writer, Producer. b. New York, NY, Aug. 25, 1913. e. Duke U., Columbia U. Reporter, drama & film critic, N.Y.: U.S. Army Air Force, 1942–46, Instructor, UCLA, 1985–86 on advanced screenplay writing. 1987–88 private tutoring on screenplay and TV writing. For military made 22 Air Force training films, 17 documentaries. Author: The Hack.
PLAYS: Author: Glamour Girl, Call To Arms (collab), So Goes the Nation (collab), Some People's Children, American Pastoral, City on a Hill.
PICTURES: To Have and Have Not, The Unvanquished, Whiphand, Caribbean, Sangaree, Papago Wells, The Half Breed, Sweetheart of Sigma Chi.
TELEVISION: *Writer*: Telephone Hour, Four Star Playhouse, Winston Churchill's Valiant Years, Route 66, Wagon Train, Laramie, Wild Wild West, The Texan, G.E. Theater, Wire Service, U.S. Marshall, M-Squad, Stoney Burke, Tales of the Texas Rangers, T.V. Reader's Digest, Sheriff of Cochise, Whirlybirds, Line-Up, Wyatt Earp, Rin Tin Tin, Walter Winchell File, Daniel Boone, Man Who Never Was, Felony Squad, Richard Diamond, Lassie, Like the Rich People, Hired Mother, Shenandoah, Counterspy, White Hunter, Hondo, Northwest Mounted Police, Casey Jones, Cowboy in Africa. Pilots: Outer Limits, Grand Jury, The Texan, Bush Pilot, Lafitte, Cortez. *Prod.-Story Ed.*: Screen Televideo, Sovereign Prod., Wire Service, T.V. Reader's Digest, Wyatt Earp.

MOSS, IRWIN: Executive. e. Syracuse U., Harvard Law Sch. Member NY State Bar. Began industry career as director of package negotiations for CBS-TV; 1970–80, exec. v.p. & natl. head of business affairs for I.C.M.; 1978–80, sr. v.p., NBC Entertainment; 1980, pres., Marble Arch TV. 1982, joined Paramount Pictures as sr. v.p. for motion picture div. 1984, exec. v.p., L. Taffner Ltd.

MOSTEL, JOSH: Actor. b. New York, NY, Dec. 21, 1946. Son of late Zero Mostel. m. producer Peggy Rajski. e. Brandeis U., B.A. 1970. Part of The Proposition, a Boston improvisational comedy group. Stage debut The Homecoming (Provincetown Playhouse, MA).
STAGE: Unlikely Heroes, The Proposition, An American Millionaire, A Texas Trilogy, Gemini, Ferocious Kisses (dir.), Men in the Kitchen (Long Wharf, New Haven.), The Dog Play,

The Boys Next Door, Love As We Know It (dir.), A Perfect Diamond, Threepenny Opera, Misconceptions (dir.), Red Diaper Baby (dir.).

PICTURES: Going Home (debut, 1971), The King of Marvin Gardens, Jesus Christ Superstar, Harry and Tonto, Deadly Hero, Fighting Back, Sophie's Choice, Star 80, Almost You, The Brother from Another Planet, Windy City, Compromising Positions, The Money Pit, Stoogemania, Radio Days, Matewan, Wall Street, Heavy Petting, Animal Behavior, City Slickers, Naked Tango, Little Man Tate, City of Hope, Searching for Bobby Fischer.

TELEVISION: *Series*: Delta House, At Ease, Murphy's Law. *Mini-Series*: Seventh Avenue. *Special*: The Boy Who Loved Trolls (PBS). Co-wrote Media Probes: The Language Show.

MOUND, FRED: Executive. b. St. Louis, MO, April 10, 1932. e. St. Louis U., Quincy Coll. 1946–52, assoc. with father, Charles Mound, at Park Theatre in Valley Park, Mo.; 1952–53, Universal Pictures (St. Louis); 1953, booker, UA, St. Louis; 1955 promoted to salesman in Kansas City; 1957, salesman, St. Louis; 1962, Indianapolis branch mgr. In 1967 named UA regional mgr., Dallas and in 1970 became S.W. Div. mgr; 1976–77, asst. gen. sls. mgr. for Southern, N.W. and S.W. Division operating out of Dallas. In June, 1977 appt. v.p., asst. gen. sls. mgr. of UA; Nov. 1978, appt. v.p. gen sls. mgr. for A.F.D. Pictures in Los Angeles; April, 1981, v.p. asst. gen. sls. mgr. for Universal Pictures; Jan., 1984, sr. v.p., gen. sls. mgr., Universal Pictures Distribution; named exec. v.p. Sept., 1988. Foundation of Motion Picture Pioneers v.p., 1989. Appointed pres. Universal distrib., 1990.

MOUNT, THOM: Executive. b. Durham, NC, May 26, 1948. e. Bard Coll.; CA Institute of the Arts, MFA. Started career with Roger Corman and as asst. to prod., Danny Selznick at MGM. Moved to Universal under former div. exec. Ned Tanen. At 26, named pres. and head of prod. at Universal. During 8-year tenure was responsible for dev. and prod. of more than 140 films (including Smokey and the Bandit, Animal House, others).

PICTURES: Pirates (exec. prod.), My Man Adam, Can't Buy Me Love, Frantic, Bull Durham (co-prod.), Stealing Home, Tequila Sunrise, Roger Corman's Frankenstein Unbound, The Indian Runner (exec. prod.).

TELEVISION: Son of the Morning Star, Open Admissions.

THEATRE: Open Admissions (co-prod.), Death and the Maiden.

MOYERS, BILL: TV Correspondent. b. Hugo, OK, June 5, 1934. e. U. of Texas; Southwestern Baptist Theological Sem. Aide to Lyndon B. Johnson; assoc. dir., Peace Corps, 1961–2, and deputy dir., 1963. Spec. asst. to Pres. Johnson, 1963–65 and press secty. 1965–67. Editor and chief corr., CBS Reports. Bill Moyers Journal on PBS. Established Public Affairs TV, Inc., 1986.

MUDD, ROGER: Newscaster. b. Washington, DC, Feb. 9, 1928. e. Washington & Lee U., U. of North Carolina. Reporter for Richmond News-Leader, 1953; news. dr., WRNL, 1954; WTOP, Washington, 1956; joined CBS News 1961 as congressional correspondent (2 Emmy Awards). 1977, Natl. Aff. corr.; 1978, corr., CBS Reports; 1980–87: NBC News as chief Washington corr., chief political corr., co-anchor; 1987 joined The MacNeil/Lehrer News Hour as special correspondent; essayist, and chief congressional corr. 1992 became contributing correspondent.

MUHL, EDWARD E.: Executive, Producer. b. Richmond, IN, Feb. 17, 1907. Gen. mgr., Universal 1948–53; v.p., studio in charge of prod. 1953–68. Consultant, Alcor Prods., Ft. Smith, AR, 1985–90. Co-author, consultant, s.p., Soldier: Other Side of Glory, 1991–2.

MUIR, E. ROGER: Producer. b. Canada, Dec. 16, 1918. e. U. of Minnesota. Partner Minn. Advertising Services Co.; Photographer, Great Northern Railway; motion picture producer Army Signal corps; NBC TV producer, Howdy Doody, exec. producer, Concentration. Now pres. Nicholson-Muir Prods, TV program packager, U.S. Spin-Off, Pay Cards, Canada Pay Cards, Headline Hunters, Definition, Celebrity Dominoes; co-creator Newlywed Game, exec. prod. I Am Joe's Heart, I Am Joe's Lung, I Am Joe's Spine, I Am Joe's Stomach, The New Howdy Doody Show, Supermates, Second Honeymoon, Groaner, Generation Jury, Shopping Game, Guess What, I Am Joe's Kidney, I Am Joe's Liver, It's Howdy Doody Time: A 40 Year Celebration. Retired 1993.

MULDAUR, DIANA: Actress. b. New York, NY, Aug. 19, 1938. e. Sweet Briar Coll. Began on New York stage the turned to films and TV, appearing on numerous major network shows.

PICTURES: The Swimmer, Number One, The Lawyer, One More Train to Rob, The Other, Chosen Survivors, McQ, Beyond Reason.

TELEVISION: *Series*: The Secret Storm, The Survivors, McCloud, Born Free, The Tony Randall Show, Hizzoner, Fitz and Bones, A Year in the Life, Star Trek: The Next Generation, L.A. Law. *Movies*: McCloud: Who Killed Miss U.S.A.?,

Call to Danger, Ordeal, Planet Earth, Charlie's Angels (pilot), Pine Canyon is Burning, Deadly Triangle, Black Beauty, To Kill a Cop, Maneaters Are Loose!, The Word, The Miracle Worker, The Return of Frank Cannon, Terror at Alcatraz, The Return of Sam McCloud.

MULGREW, KATE: Actress. b. Dubuque, IA, April 29, 1955. e. NYU. Stage work includes stints with American Shakespeare Festival, O'Neill Festival and at Hartman Theatre, Stamford.

PICTURES: Lovespell, A Stranger Is Watching, Remo Williams: The Adventure Begins, Throw Momma from the Train.

TELEVISION: *Series*: Ryan's Hope (1975–77), Kate Columbo (Kate Loves a Mystery), Heartbeat, Man of the People. *Movies*: The Word, Jennifer: A Woman's Story, A Time for Miracles, The Manions of America, Roses Are for the Rich, Roots: The Gift, Danielle Steel's Daddy, Fatal Friendship.

MULHERN, MATT: Actor. b. Philadelphia, PA, July 21, 1960. e. Rutgers Univ.

PICTURES: One Crazy Summer, Extreme Prejudice, Biloxi Blues.

TELEVISION: *Series*: Major Dad. *Movie*: Gunsmoke: To the Last Man.

THEATRE: *NY*: Biloxi Blues, Wasted, The Night Hank Williams Died.

MULHOLLAND, ROBERT E.: Executive. b. 1933. e. Northwestern U. Joined NBC News as newswriter in Chicago in 1962. In 1964 made midwestern field producer for Huntley-Brinkley Report. In 1964 moved to London as European producer for NBC News; 1965, named Washington producer of Huntley-Brinkley Report. Transferred to L.A. in 1967 to be director of news, west coast. Named exec. prod. of NBC Nightly News. In 1973 appt. v.p., NBC news.; 1974 exec. v.p. of NBC News. In 1977 appt. pres. of NBC Television Network; also elected to board of directors; 1981, pres. & CEO. Resigned, 1984. Dir. Television Info. Office, NYC 1985–7. Prof. Northwestern U. 1988–.

MULL, MARTIN: Actor. b. Chicago, IL, Aug. 18, 1943. e. Rhode Island Sch. of Design. Started as humorist, making recordings for Warner Bros., Capricorn, ABC Records, etc.

PICTURES: FM (debut, 1978), My Bodyguard, Serial, Take This Job and Shove It, Flicks, Mr. Mom, Clue, O.C. and Stiggs, Home is Where the Hart Is, Rented Lips (also s.p., exec. prod.), Cutting Class, Ski Patrol, Far Out Man, Think Big, Ted and Venus, The Player.

TELEVISION: *Series*: Mary Hartman Mary Hartman, Fernwood 2-Night, America 2-Night, Domestic Life, His and Hers, Roseanne, The Jackie Thomas Show, Family Dog (voice). *Specials*: The History of White People in America (also prod.), Candid Camera Christmas Special (1987), Portrait of a White Marriage, The Whole Shebang. *Movies*: Sunset Limousine, California Girls.

MULLER, PETER: Executive, Producer, Attorney. b. Teplitz-Sanov, Czechoslovakia, March 4, 1947. e. NYU, NYU Law Sch. Served as entertainment editor, Ambience and Women's Life magazines. Former CEO, Producers Releasing Corp., Pres. of PRC's entertainment div. Consultant to German TV show Am Laifen Band. Has worked with French and Eng. communication cos. Co-organizer; album and video of theater artists to fight world hunger, Broadway Feeds the World. Pres. and founder of The Muller Entertainment Group, Inc. Member: bd. of dirs. NYU Alumni Assoc., NYU's nominating comm.; American Bar Assoc.; ABA Forum on the Entertainment and Sports Industries; and ABA Forum on Patent, Trademark, Copyright Law; NY State Bar Assoc.; former pres. and CEO of ACA Joe Inc. Author: Show Business Law. Member: NYSBA Entertainment Arts and Sports Law Section, The President's Assoc. of the American Mgmt. Assoc. Lawyers for the Arts. Expert with Technical Advisory Services for Attorneys. Frequent lecturer on Entertainment Law and Entertainment Business. Member NYU Alumni Council. Author: The Music Business - A Legal Perspective, Show Business Law.

MÜLLER, ROBBY: Cinematographer. b. Netherlands, April 4, 1940. e. Dutch Film Acad. Asst. cameraman in Holland before moving to Germany where he shot 9 films for Wim Wenders.

PICTURES: Kings of the Roads, Alice of the Cities, Saint Jack, Honeysuckle Rose, They All Laughed, Body Rock, Repo Man, Paris, Texas, The Longshot, To Live and Die in L.A., Down By Law, Tricheurs, Barfly, Il Piccolo Diavolo, Mystery Train, Until the End of the World.

MULLIGAN, RICHARD: Actor. b. New York, NY, Nov. 13, 1932. On stage in All the Way Home, Never Too Late, Mating Dance, Hogan's Goat, Thieves, etc.

PICTURES: One Potato Two Potato, The Group, Little Big Man, Irish Whiskey Rebellion, From the Mixed-Up Files of Mrs. Basil E. Frankweiler, The Big Bus, Scavenger Hunt, S.O.B., Trail of the Pink Panther, Meatballs Part II, Teachers,

Micki and Maude, Doin' Time, The Heavenly Kid, A Fine Mess, Quicksilver, Oliver & Company (voice).
TELEVISION: *Movies:* Having Babies III, Malibu, Jealousy, Poker Alice, Gore Vidal's Lincoln, Guess Who's Coming to Christmas? *Series:* The Hero, Diana, Soap (Emmy Award, 1980), Reggie, Empty Nest (Emmy Award, 1989).

MULLIGAN, ROBERT: Director. b. Bronx, NY. Aug. 23, 1925. e. Fordham U.
PICTURES: Fear Strikes Out (1957), The Rat Race, The Great Imposter, Come September, The Spiral Road, To Kill a Mockingbird, Love with the Proper Stranger, Baby the Rain Must Fall, Inside Daisy Clover, Up the Down Staircase, The Stalking Moon, Pursuit of Happiness, Summer of '42, The Other (also prod.), The Nickel Ride (also prod.), Blood Brothers, Same Time Next Year (also prod.), Kiss Me Goodbye (also prod.), Clara's Heart, Man in the Moon.
TELEVISION: The Moon and the Sixpence (Emmy Award, 1960), Billy Budd, Ah Wilderness, A Tale of Two Cities, The Bridge of San Luis Rey, Playhouse 90, Alcoa—Goodyear Studio One, Hallmark Hall of Fame.

MULRONEY, DERMOT: Actor. b. Alexandria, VA, Oct. 31, 1963. e. Northwestern Univ.
PICTURES: Sunset, Young Guns, Survival Quest, Staying Together, Longtime Companion, Career Opportunities, Bright Angel, There Goes My Baby, Where the Day Takes You, Samantha, Point of No Return, Silent Tongue, The Thing Called Love, Bad Girls.
TELEVISION: *Movies:* Sin of Innocence, Daddy, Unconquered, Long Gone, The Heart of Justice, Family Pictures. *Special:* Toma: The Drug Knot.

MUMY, BILL: Actor. r.n. Charles William Mumy Jr. b. El Centro, CA, Feb. 1, 1954. Began acting as Billy Mumy at age 6. Played with band America in 1970's, also with bands Bill Mumy & The Igloos, and The Jenerators. Has made 8 albums with Barnes & Barnes. With actor Miguel Ferrer wrote comic books Comet Man and Trip to the Acid Dog. Has also written stories for Star Trek, The Hulk, and Spiderman comic books, and Lost in Space comic published by Innovation. Wrote music for Disney's Adventures in Wonderland series (Emmy nom.)
TELEVISION: *Series:* Lost in Space, Sunshine. *Movies:* Sunshine, The Rockford Files (pilot), Sunshine Christmas. *Guest:* The Twilight Zone, Alfred Hitchcock Presents, Bewitched, The Virginian, I Dream of Jeannie, The Adventures of Ozzie and Harriet, Ben Casey, The Red Skelton Show, Lancer, Here Come the Brides, Riverboat, Have Gun Will Travel, Matlock, Me and Mom, The Flash, Superboy. *Pilots:* The Two of Us, Archie, Space Family Robinson. *Host:* Inside Space (SciFi Channel).
PICTURES: Tammy Tell Me True, Palm Springs Weekend, A Ticklish Affair, A Child is Waiting, Dear Brigitte, Rascal, Bless the Beasts and Children, Papillon, Twilight Zone—The Movie, Hard to Hold, Captain America, Double Trouble.

MURDOCH, RUPERT: Executive. b. Australia, March 11, 1931. Son of Sir Keith Murdoch, head of The Melbourne Herald and leading figure in Australian journalism. e. Oxford U., England. Spent two years on Fleet St. before returning home to take over family paper, The Adelaide News. Acquired more Australian papers and in 1969 expanded to Britain, buying The News of the World. Moved to U.S. in 1973, buying San Antonio Express and News. Conglomerate in 1985 included New York Post, New York Magazine, The Star, The Times of London, The Boston Herald, The Chicago Sun-Times along with TV stations, book publishing companies, airline, oil and gas companies, etc. 1985, made deal to buy 20th Century-Fox Film Corp. from owner Martin Davis. Sold the NY Post, 1988 to conform with FCC regulations. Purchased Triangle Publications 1988 (including TV Guide).

MURPHY, BEN: Actor. b. Jonesboro, AR, March 6, 1942. e. U. of Illinois. Degree in drama from Pasadena Playhouse. Acted in campus productions and toured in summer stock. Film debut with small role in The Graduate, 1967.
PICTURES: Yours Mine and Ours, The Thousand Plane Raid, Sidecar Racer, Time Walker.
TELEVISION: *Series:* The Name of the Game, Alias Smith and Jones, Griff, Gemini Man, The Chisholms, Lottery!, Berrenger's, The Dirty Dozen. *Movies:* The Letters, Wild Bill Hickock, Bridger, Heat Wave, Runaway, This Is the West That Was, Gemini Man, Hospital Fire, The Cradle Will Fall, Stark: Mirror Image. *Mini-Series:* The Winds of War.

MURPHY, EDDIE: Actor. b. Brooklyn, NY, Apr. 3, 1961. e. Roosevelt High Sch. Wrote and performed own comedy routines at youth centers and local bars at age 15. Worked on comedy club circuit; at 19 joined TV's Saturday Night Live as writer and performer. Recordings: Eddie Murphy, Eddie Murphy: Comedian, How Could It Be?, Love's Alright. Voted Top-Money Making Star of 1988 on Quigley Poll, NATO/ShoWest Star of the Decade, for 1980's.
PICTURES: 48 HRS. (debut, 1982), Trading Places, Best Defense, Beverly Hills Cop, The Golden Child, Beverly Hills

Cop II, Eddie Murphy Raw (also s.p., exec. prod.), Coming to America (also story), Harlem Nights (also dir., s.p, exec. prod.), Another 48 HRS., Boomerang (also story), The Distinguished Gentleman.
TELEVISION: *Series:* Saturday Night Live (1981–4). *Pilots:* What's Alan Watching? (exec. prod., also cameo), Coming to America (exec. prod.). *Movie:* The Kid Who Loved Christmas (exec. prod.).

MURPHY, JOHN F.: Theatre Executive. b. Brooklyn, NY, Mar. 25, 1905. e. City Coll. of New York. Entire career with Loew's Theatres; started as asst. mgr. Hillside & Valencia Theatres, Jamaica, NY; apptd. gen. mgr. in chg. of out-of-town Theatres, 1942–54; v.p. Loew's Theatres, Aug., 1954; dir., Loew's Theatres, Oct., 1956; exec. v.p., Loew's Theatre, 1959; ret. July 1963; continues on bd. as advisor and director emeritus.

MURPHY, MICHAEL: Actor. b. Los Angeles, CA, May 5, 1938. e. U. of Arizona. Taught English and Drama in L.A. city school system, 1962–64. N.Y. stage debut as director of Rat's Nest, 1978.
PICTURES: Double Trouble (debut, 1967), Countdown, The Legend of Lylah Clare, The Arrangement, That Cold Day in the Park, MASH, Count Yorga: Vampire, Brewster McCloud, McCabe and Mrs. Miller, What's Up Doc?, The Thief Who Came to Dinner, Phase IV, Nashville, The Front, An Unmarried Woman, The Great Bank Hoax, The Class of Miss Mac Michael, Manhattan, The Year of Living Dangerously, Strange Behavior, Cloak and Dagger, Salvador, Mesmerized, Shocker, Folks, Batman Returns, Clean Slate.
TELEVISION: *Series:* Two Marriages, Hard Copy. *Guest:* Saints and Sinners, Ben Casey, Dr. Kildare, Bonanza, Combat. *Movies:* Autobiography of Miss Jane Pittman, John Cheever's Oh Youth and Beauty, The Caine Mutiny Court-Martial, Tailspin: Behind the Korean Airlines Tragedy. *Special:* Tanner '88.

MURRAY, BARBARA: Actress. b. London, England, Sept. 27, 1929. Stage debut in Variety, 1946; screen debut in Badger's Green, 1948. Various TV appearances.
PICTURES: Passport to Pimlico, Don't Ever Leave Me, Boys in Brown, Poets Pub, Tony Draws a Horse, Dark Man, Frightened Man, Mystery Junction, Another Man's Poison, Hot Ice, Street Corner (Both Sides of the Law), Meet Mr. Lucifer, Doctor at Large, Campbell's Kingdom, A Cry from the Streets, Girls in Arms.

MURRAY, BILL: Actor. b. Wilmette, IL, Sept. 21, 1950. e. attended Regis Coll. Was pre-med student; left to join brother, Brian Doyle-Murray, in Second City, the Chicago improvisational troupe. Appeared with brother on radio in National Lampoon Radio Hour, and in off-Bdwy. revue, National Lampoon Show. Also on radio provided voice of Johnny Storm, the Human Torch, on Marvel Comics' Fantastic Four. Hired by ABC for Saturday Night Live with Howard Cosell; then by NBC for Saturday Night Live, 1977.
PICTURES: Jungle Burger (debut, 1975), Meatballs, Mr. Mike's Mondo Video, Where the Buffalo Roam, Loose Shoes (aka Coming Attractions), Caddyshack, Stripes, Tootsie, Ghostbusters, The Razor's Edge (also co-s.p.), Nothing Lasts Forever, Little Shop of Horrors, Scrooged, Ghostbusters II, Quick Change (also co-prod., co-dir.), What About Bob?, Mad Dog and Glory, Groundhog Day.
TELEVISION: *Series:* Saturday Night Live (1977–80) also writer; Emmy Award for writing 1977). *Pilot:* The TV TV Show (1977). *Movie:* All You Need Is Cash. *Specials:* It's Not Easy Being Me—The Rodney Dangerfield Show, Steve Martin's Best Show Ever, Second City—25 Years in Revue.

MURRAY, DON: Actor, Director, Writer. b. Hollywood, CA, July 31, 1929. Mother was a Ziegeld Girl, father was dance dir. for Fox Studio.
PLAYS: *Broadway:* Insect Comedy, Rose Tattoo, The Skin of Our Teeth, The Hot Corner, Smith (a musical), The Norman Conquests; Same Time, Next Year. *National tours:* California Suite, Chicago.
PICTURES: Bus Stop (debut, 1956), The Bachelor Party, Hatful of Rain, From Hell to Texas, These Thousand Hills, Shake Hands With the Devil, One Foot in Hell, The Hoodlum Priest (also co-prod., co-s.p.), Advise and Consent, Escape From East Berlin, One Man's Way, Baby the Rain Must Fall, Kid Rodelo, The Plainsman, Sweet Love Bitter, The Viking Queen, Childish Things (Confession of Tom Harris; also prod., co-s.p.), The Cross and the Switchblade (dir., s.p. only), Happy Birthday Wanda June, Conquest of the Planet of the Apes, Call Me by My Rightful Name (also prod., co-s.p.), Deadly Hero, Endless Love, I Am the Cheese, Damien (dir., s.p. only), Radioactive Dreams, Peggy Sue Got Married, Scorpion, Made in Heaven, Ghosts Can't Do It.
TELEVISION: *Series:* Made in America (panelist), The Outcasts, Knots Landing, Brand New Life, Sons and Daughters. *Movies:* The Borgia Stick, Daughter of the Mind, The Intruders, The Girl on the Late Late Show, The Sex Symbol, A Girl Named Sooner, Rainbow, Crisis in Mid-Air, License to Kill, A Touch of Scandal, Something in Common, Stillwatch, The Stepford Children, Return of the Rebels, The Boy Who

Drank Too Much. Quarterback Princess, Mistress. *Specials*: For I Have Loved Strangers (also writer), Hasty Heart, Billy Budd, Winterset, Alas Babylon, My Dad Isn't Crazy Is He?

MURRAY, JAN: Comedian, Actor. b. Bronx, NY, Oct. 4, 1917. Performed in nightclubs, vaudeville, Bdwy, radio, TV, films.
TELEVISION: *Series* (emcee/host): Songs for Sale, Go Lucky, Sing It Again, Blind Date, Dollar a Second (also creator, prod.), Jan Murray Time, Treasure Hunt (also creator, prod.), Charge Account (also creator, prod.), Chain Letter. *Guest*: Zane Grey Theatre, Dr., Kildare, Burke's Law, The Lucy Show, Love American Style, Mannix, Ellery Queen, Hardcastle and McCormick. *Movies*: Roll Freddy Roll, Banjo Hackett: Roamin' Free, The Dream Merchants.
PLAYS: A Funny Thing Happened on the Way to the Forum, Guys and Dolls, Silk Stockings, Bye Bye Birdie, A Thousand Clowns, Come Blow Your Horn, The Odd Couple, Make a Million, Don't Drink the Water, Critic's Choice, You Know I Can't Hear You When the Water Is Running.
PICTURES: Who Killed Teddy Bear?, Tarzan and the Great River, A Man Called Dagger, Which Way to the Front?, History of the World Part I, Fear City.

MUSANTE, TONY: Actor. b. Bridgeport, CT, June 30. e. Oberlin Coll. B.A. Directed local theatre, then appeared off-Broadway, in regional theater, and on Dupont Show of the Month (Ride With Terror).
THEATER: *Bdwy*: The Lady From Dubuque, P.S. Your Cat Is Dead, 27 Wagons Full of Cotton, Memory of Two Mondays. *Off-bdwy*: Grand Magic, Cassatt, A Gun Play, Benito Cereno, L'Histoire du Soldat, Match-Play, The Zoo Story, The Pinter Plays (The Collection), Kiss Mama, The Balcony, Snow Orchid, Frankie and Johnny in the Claire de Lune. *Regional*: The Big Knife, A Streetcar Named Desire, The Taming of the Shrew, Widows, The Archbishop's Ceiling, Dancing in the Endzone, Two Brothers, Souvenir. APA Shakespeare Rep., Wait Until Dark, Anthony Rose, Mount Allegro, Double Play, Falling Man, others.
PICTURES: Once a Thief, The Incident, The Detective, The Mercenary, The Bird with the Crystal Plumage, The Grissom Gang, The Last Run, Anonymous Venetian, Collector's Item, The Repenter, The Pisciotta Case, Goodbye and Amen, Break Up, Nocturne, The Pope of Greenwich Village, One Night at Dinner, Appointment in Trieste, Devil's Hill.
TELEVISION: *Series*: Toma. *Guest*: Chrysler Theatre, Alfred Hitchcock Hour, N.Y.P.D., The Fugitive, Trials of O'Brien, Police Story, Medical Story. *Movies*: Rearview Mirror, The Court Martial of Lt. William Calley, Desperate Miles, The Quality of Mercy, Nowhere to Hide, My Husband Is Missing, The Story of Esther, High Ice, Last Waltz on a Tightrope, Weekend (Amer. Playhouse), Nutcracker: Money Madness & Murder, Breaking Up Is Hard To Do, The Baron.

MUSTO, MICHAEL J.: Producer, Writer. b. New York, NY. e. S. Niagara U. Apprentice for J. J. Shubert. Comedy Workshop, N.Y. W-Co. Hellzapoppin, Wrote, Prod. Dir. Burlesque shows and stage revues. Prod. Industrial Films, Commercials, Operas, Fund Raising Shows. Prod. Films: The Glass House, Phenomena 7-7, Down Tin Pan Alley, Single Room Furnished, Educated Heart, Agnes, Spring Fancy, The Atheist, Man Who Cried Wolf, Several Robert Montgomery Presents, Hallmark Hall of Fame, TV Specials, The Bold Ones, Strange Is the Wind. Wrote: Due-Bill Marriage, Spring Fancy, Who's On First, Pratt's Fall, Charlie Daniels Band, Special Break, Heads-Feed Cats, Seymour, Granada, Seppi and His Brothers, Amato and the Yenta, The Cliffdwellers, Other. Owner. Empire Films and Cinema City Studios, dinner theatres.

MYERS, JULIAN F.: Public Relations. b. Detroit, MI, Feb. 22, 1918. e. Wayne U., 1935–37, U. of Southern California, 1937–39. Distribution, Loew's Detroit, 1941–42; asst. story editor, idea man, Columbia, 1942–46; publicist, 20th Century-Fox, 1948–62; public relations, Julian F. Myers, Inc., 1962; pres., Myers Studios, Inc., 1966; pres., New Horizons Broadcasting Corp., 1968–69; sr. publicist American Intl. Pictures, 1970–80. Pres., Hollywood Press Club; former member Variety Club; Academy of Motion Pictures Arts & Sciences; Board of Governors Film Industry Workshops, Inc. 1977, western vice-pres., The Publicists Guild; Recipient of Publicists Guild's Robert Yeager Award; 1979, re-elected western v.p., Publicists Guild. First male member Hollywood Women's Press Club. Co-founder HANDS (Hollywood Answering Needs of Disaster Survivors). Member, M.P. Pioneers. Winner, 1980 Publicists Guild Les Mason Award. Instructor in publicity, UCLA, 1979 to present, and at Loyola Marymount U, 1991–present. Filmways Pictures, pub. dept., 1980–81. Exec. v.p., worldwide m.p. and TV pub./mktg., Hanson & Schwam Public Relations 1981 to 1991. Author of Myersystem and Myerscope guides. Member: USC Cinema & TV Alumni Assn., West Coast P.R. Will Rogers Inst., Acad. TV Arts Sciences; bd. of dir., Show Biz Expo., p.r. co-ord. committee AMPAS. Columnist, California Press Bureau. Bd. of Dirs., Show Biz Expo. Publicist, Prods. Guild of America. Pres. Julian Myers Public Rltns., nominated MoPic Showmanship of the Year, Publicists Guild of America, 1993.

MYERS, PETER S.: Executive. b. Toronto, Ont., Canada, May 13, 1923. e. U. of Toronto. Toronto br. mgr., 20th Century-Fox, 1948; man. dir. Canada, 1951; gen. sales mgr. in chg. of dom. distrib., US & Canada, 1968; sr. v.p., 20th-Fox Ent.; pres., 20th-Fox Classics, 1983; pres., Hemdale Releasing Corp., 1986; pres. & CEO, Four Seasons Entertainment, 1989.

MYERS, STANLEY: Composer. Since 1966 has composed scores for over 60 British, American, German and French films including:
PICTURES: Kaleidoscope (1966), Ulysses, No Way to Treat a Lady, Michael Kohlhaas, Otley, Two Gentlemen Sharing, Take a Girl Like You, Tropic of Cancer, The Walking Stick, Long Ago Tomorrow, A Severed Head, Tam Lin, King, Queen, Knave; Sitting Target, Summer Lightning, X,Y, Zee; The Blockhouse, The Apprenticeship of Duddy Kravitz, Caravan to Vaccares, Little Malcolm, The Wilby Conspiracy, Coup de Grace, The Class of Miss MacMichael, The Deerhunter, The Greek Tycoon, The Martian Chronicles, A Portrait of the Artist as a Young Man, The Secret Policeman's Other Ball, Yesterday's Hero, Watcher in the Woods, Absolution, The Incubus, Lady Chatterly's Lover, Eureka, Moonlighting, Blind Date, Beyond the Limit, The Next One, Success is the Best Revenge, The Chain, Dreamchild, Insignificance, The Lightship, The Wind, Castaway, My Beautiful Laundrette, Prick Up Your Ears, Wish You Were Here, The Second Victory, Taffin, Track 29, Stars and Bars, Trading Hearts, Sammy and Rosie Get Laid, Scenes From the Class Struggle in Beverly Hills, Torrents of Spring.
TELEVISION: Series (U.K.): Widows (parts 1 & 2), Nancy Astor, Diana. Series (U.S.): The Martian Chronicles, Florence Nightingale. Movies: Strong Medicine, Smart Money, Baja Oklahoma, Monte Carlo.

MYERSON, BERNARD: Executive. b. New York, NY, March 25, 1918. Entered m.p. ind. with Fabian Theatres, 1938–63; last position as exec. v.p.; joined Loew's Theatres as v.p., 1963; exec. v.p. and board member, Loew's Corp.; pres. Loew's Theatres, 1971. Chmn. & pres., Loews Theatre Management Corp., 1985, presently chmn. of board Emeritus; Vice chmn. & mem. of Executive Committee Greater N.Y. Chapter, National Foundation of March of Dimes; Honorary chmn., bd. mem., & former pres., Will Rogers Memorial Fund; Mem. exec. comm., bd., National Assn. Theatre Owners; bd. mem., & former pres., Motion Picture Pioneers. treas. Variety Intl.; mem., Board of Directors Burke Rehabilitation Center; mem. N.Y.S. Governor's Council on M.P. & T.V. Development; mem. M.P. & T.V. Com. USIA, vice-chmn., adv. bd. of Tisch Sch. of Arts, NYU.

N

NABORS, JIM: Actor. b. Sylacauga, AL, June 12, 1932. Discovered performing in an L.A. nightclub in early 1960's by Andy Griffith, who asked him to appear on his series. Developed a second career as a singer. Between 1966–72 had 12 albums on best selling charts.
PICTURES: The Best Little Whorehouse in Texas, Stroker Ace, Cannonball Run II.
TELEVISION: Series: Andy Griffith Show, Gomer Pyle USMC, The Jim Nabors Hour, The Lost Saucer, The Jim Nabors Show (synd. talk show). Movie: Return to Mayberry.

NADER, GEORGE: Actor. b. Pasadena, CA, Oct. 19, 1921. e. Occidental Coll., B.A.; Pasadena Playhouse, B.T.A. Served in U.S. Navy. Many TV appearances, film debut in Monsoon (1953). First novel, Chrome, (Putnam).
PICTURES: Robot Monster, Carnival Story, Miss Robin Crusoe, Sins of Jezebel, Fours Guns to the Border, Six Bridges to Cross, Lady Godiva, Second Greatest Sex, Away All Boats, Appointment With a Shadow, Congo Crossing, Unguarded Moment, Four Girls in Town, Man Afraid, Joe Butterfly, Nowhere to Go, The Secret Mark of D'Artagnan, The Great Space Adventure, Zigzag, The Human Duplicators, House of a Thousand Dolls, Alarm on 83rd Street, Murder at Midnight, Count-Down for Manhattan, Dynamite in Green Silk, The Check and Icy Smile, The Murder Club From Bklyn, Death in a Red Jaguar, End Station of the Damned, Bullets on Broadway, Beyond Atlantis.
TELEVISION: Guest: Letter to Loretta, Fireside Theatre, Chevron Theatre. Series: Ellery Queen, Man and the Challenge, Shannon. Movie: Nakia.

NAIFY, MARSHALL: Executive. b. Sacramento, CA, March 23, 1920. e. U. of Southern California. U.S.A.F. Chmn. exec. comm. & bd. chmn., United Artists Communications, Inc.; pres., Magna Pictures Corp.

NAIFY, ROBERT: Executive. b. Sacramento, CA. e. Attended Stanford U. Worked for United California Theatres since 1946 in various capacities: theatre manager, purchasing agent, film buyer, general manager and president. 1963 became exec. vice president, United Artists Communications; and in 1971 became president and CEO until 1987. Currently president Todd-AO Corporation.

NAIR, MIA: Director, Producer. b. Bhubaneswar, India, 1957. e. Irish Catholic Missionary School in India, Delhi U., Harvard U. A course in documentary filmmaking at Harvard led to directing 4 non-fiction films includ. India Cabaret (1985) and Children of Desired Sex. Feature debut as producer-director, Salaam Bombay! in 1988 won Camera d'Or for best first feature, and Prix du Publique at Cannes Fest. as well as Acad. Award nomination for best foreign film.

NALLE, BILLY: Theatre concert organist, popular field, ASCAP Composer. b. Fort Myers, FL, Apr. 24, 1921; graduate, The Juilliard Sch. Over 5000 major TV shows from New York; now artist-in-residence, Wichita Theatre Organ, Inc. Reader's Digest, Telarc & WTO Records Artist. Public Relations: Billy Nalle Music, Wichita.

NAMATH, JOE: Actor. b. Beaver Falls, PA, May 31, 1943. e. U. of Alabama. Former professional football star.
PICTURES: Norwood, C.C. & Co., The Last Rebel, Avalanche Express, Chattanooga Choo-Choo, Going Under.
TELEVISION: Series: The Waverly Wonders. Host: Monday Night Football (1985). Movie: Marriage Is Alive and Well. Guest: Here's Lucy, The Brady Bunch, The Love Boat, Kate and Allie.

NARDINO, GARY: Executive. b. Garfield, NJ, Aug. 26, 1935. e. Seton Hall U. Awarded honorary degree of Doctor of Laws. Entered industry in 1959 as agent, representing Lorimar Prods. and Talent Associates, among others. Named sr. v.p. of ICM's New York TV dept; then v.p. of William Morris Agency, heading N.Y. TV dept. Pres. of Paramount TV Production Division, 1977–83. Pres., of Gary Nardino Prods., Inc., formed 1983, to dev. and produce theatrical features and TV programming; 1988, named chmn. & CEO, Orion Television Entertainment.
PICTURES: Star Trek III: the Search for Spock (exec. prod.), Fire with Fire (prod.).
TELEVISION: Exec. prod.: Brothers, At Your Service, Joanna.

NARIZZANO, SILVIO: Producer, Director. b. Montreal, Canada, Feb. 8, 1927. e. U. of Bishop's, Lennoxville, Quebec, B.A. Was active as actor-director in Canadian theatre before going to England for TV and theatrical film work.
PICTURES: Director: Under Ten Flags (co-dir.), Die! Die! My Darling!, Georgy Girl, Blue, The Man Who Had Power Over Women, Loot, Redneck, The Sky Is Falling, Why Shoot the Teacher?, The Class of Miss MacMichael, Choices, Double Play. Producer: Negatives, Fadeout, Redneck.
TELEVISION: Come Back Little Sheba, Staying On, Young Shoulders, Miss Marple (series).

NASH, N. RICHARD: Writer. b. Philadelphia, PA, June 8, 1913.
BROADWAY: Second Best Bed, The Young and Fair, See the Jaguar, The Rainmaker, Girls of Summer, Handful of Fire, Wildcat, 110 in the Shade, The Happy Time, Echoes, Wildfire, The Torch, Magic, The Bluebird of Happiness, Breaking the Tie, Come As You Are.
PICTURES: Nora Prentiss, The Vicious Years, The Rainmaker, Porgy and Bess, Sainted Sisters, Dear Wife, Welcome Stranger, Dragonfly.
TV: Many TV plays for Television Playhouse, U.S. Steel, General Electric.
NOVELS: Cry Macho, East Wind, Rain, The Last Magic, Aphrodite's Cave, Radiance, Behold the Man, The Wildwood.

NATWICK, MILDRED: Actress. b. Baltimore, Md, June 19, 1908. e. Bryn Mawr Sch., Baltimore, Bennett Sch., Millbrook. Prof. stage debut in Carry Nation, 1932; London debut in Day I Forget.
PLAYS: Wind and the Rain, Distaff Side, End of Summer, Love from a Stranger, Candida, Missouri Legend, Stars in Your Eyes, Grass Harp, Blithe Spirit, (Barter Theatre award), Waltz of the Toreadors (Tony nom.), The Firstborn, The Good Soup, Critic's Choice, Barefoot in the Park, Our Town, Landscape, 70, Girls 70, (Tony noms.), Bedroom Farce.
PICTURES: The Long Voyage Home, The Enchanted Cottage, Yolanda and the Thief, The Late George Apley, A Woman's Vengeance, Three Godfathers, The Kissing Bandit, She Wore a Yellow Ribbon, Cheaper by the Dozen, The Quiet Man, Against All Flags, The Trouble with Harry, The Court Jester, Teenage Rebel, Tammy and the Bachelor, Barefoot in the Park (Acad. Award nom.), If It's Tuesday This Must Be Belgium, Trilogy, The Maltese Bippy, Daisy Miller, At Long Last Love, Kiss Me Goodbye, Dangerous Liaisons.
TELEVISION: Blithe Spirit (Emmy nom.), House Without a Xmas Tree, Thanksgiving Treasure, Money to Burn, Do Not Fold Spindle or Mutilate, The Snoop Sisters (Emmy Award), The Easter Promise, Little Women, McMillan and Wife, Hawaii Five-O, Love Boat, You Can't Take It With You, Alice— Maid in America, Deadly Deception.

NAUGHTON, DAVID: Actor, Singer. b. Hartford, CT, Feb. 13, 1951. Brother of actor James Naughton. e. U. of Pennsylvania, B.A.

Studied at London Acad. of Music and Dramatic Arts. Numerous TV commercials, including music for Dr. Pepper. On Bdwy. in Hamlet, Da, Poor Little Lambs.
PICTURES: Midnight Madness, An American Werewolf in London, Separate Ways, Hot Dog—The Movie, Not for Publication, The Boy in Blue, Separate Vacations, Kidnapped, Ti Presento un' Amica. Quite By Chance, The Sleeping Car, Overexposed.
TELEVISION: Series: Making It, At Ease, My Sister Sam. Movies: I Desire, Getting Physical, Goddess of Love, Body Bags. Guest: Twilight Zone, Murder She Wrote.

NAUGHTON, JAMES: Actor. b. Middletown, CT, Dec. 6, 1945. Father of actor Greg Naughton. e. Brown U., A.B., 1967; Yale U., M.F.A., drama, 1970.
THEATER: I Love My Wife (Bdwy debut, 1977), Long Day's Journey Into Night (Theatre World, Drama Desk and New York Critics Circle Award, 1971), Whose Life Is It, Anyway?, Who's Afraid of Virginia Woolf? (Long Wharf), The Glass Menagerie (Long Wharf), Losing Time, Drinks Before Dinner, Hamlet (Long Wharf), Julius Caesar (Amer. Shakespeare Festival), 8 seasons at Williamstown Theatre Festival, City of Angels (Tony & Drama Desk Awards), Four Baboons Adoring the Sun.
PICTURES: The Paper Chase (debut, 1972), Second Wind, A Stranger is Watching, Cat's Eye, The Glass Menagerie, The Good Mother.
TELEVISION: Special: Look Homeward Angel (1972). Series: Faraday and Company (1973–74), Planet of the Apes, Making the Grade, Trauma Center, Raising Miranda. Movies: F. Scott Fitzgerald and the Last of the Belles, The Last 36 Hours of Dr. Durant, The Bunker, My Body My Child, Parole, The Last of the Great Survivors, Between Darkness and the Dawn, Sin of Innocence, Traveling Man, Antigone.

NEAL, PATRICIA: Actress. b. Packard, KY, Jan. 20, 1926. e. Northwestern U. Doctor's asst., cashier, hostess, model, jewelry store clerk. In summer stock; Broadway debut in Voice of the Turtle, 1946. Autobiography: As I Am (with Richard DeNeut, 1988).
THEATRE: Voice of the Turtle, Another Part of the Forest (Tony, Donaldson & Drama Critic Awards), The Children's Hour, Roomful of Roses, The Miracle Worker. England: Suddenly Last Summer.
TELEVISION: Movies: The Homecoming, Things in Their Season, Eric, Tail Gunner Joe, A Love Affair: The Eleanor and Lou Gehrig Story, The Bastard, All Quiet on the Western Front, Shattered Vows, Love Leads the Way, Caroline?, A Mother's Right: The Elizabeth Morgan Story, Heidi. Guest: Little House on the Prairie, Murder She Wrote. BBC: Days & Nights of Beebee Finstermaker, The Country Girl, Clash By Night, The Royal Family.
PICTURES: John Loves Mary (debut 1949), The Fountainhead, It's a Great Feeling, The Hasty Heart, Bright Leaf, Three Secrets, The Breaking Point, Raton Pass, Operation Pacific, The Day the Earth Stood Still, Weekend With Father, Diplomatic Courier, Washington Story, Something for the Birds, Stranger From Venus, Your Woman, A Face in the Crowd, Breakfast at Tiffany's, Hud (Academy Award, 1963), Psyche '59, In Harm's Way, The Subject Was Roses (Acad. Award nom.), The Night Digger, Baxter, Happy Mother's Day . . . Love George, "B" Must Die, The Passage, Ghost Story, An Unremarkable Life.

NEAME, RONALD: Cinematographer, Producer, Director. b. Hendon, Eng. April 23, 1911. e. U. Coll. Sch., London. p. Elwin Neame, London photog., & Ivy Close, m.p. actress. Entered m.p. ind. 1928; asst. cameraman on first full-length Brit. sound film Blackmail, dir. by Alfred Hitchcock, 1929; became chief cameraman & lighting expert, 1934; in 1945 joint assoc. prod., Noel Coward Prods.
PICTURES: Cinematographer: Girls Will Be Boys (co-c), Happy (co-c), Elizabeth of England, Honours Easy (co-c), Invitation to the Waltz (co-c), Joy Ride, Music Hath Charms, The Crimes of Stephen Hawke, The Improper Dutchess, A Star Fell From Heaven, Against the Tide, Brief Ecstasy, Feather Your Nest, Keep Fit, Weekend Millionaire, Gaunt Stranger, The Phantom Strikes, The Crime of Peter Frame, Dangerous Secrets, I See Ice (co-c), Penny Paradise, Who Goes Next? Cheers Boys Cheer, Sweeney Todd: The Demon Barber of Fleet Street, Let's Be Famous, Trouble Brewing, The Ware Case, It's In the Air (co-c), Let George Do It, Return to Yesterday, Saloon Bar, Four Just Men, Major Barbara, A Yank in the R.A.F. (Brit. flying sequence), One of Our Aircraft is Missing, In Which We Serve, This Happy Breed, Blithe Spirit, Brief Encounter, Great Expectations (also co-s.p.), Oliver Twist (also co-s.p.), A Young Man's Fancy, Passionate Friends, Take My Life. Director: Golden Salamander (also cos.p.), The Card (The Promoter), Million Pound Note (Man With a Million), Man Who Never Was, Seventh Sin, Windom's Way, The Horse's Mouth, Tunes of Glory, Escape from Zahrain, I Could Go on Singing, The Chalk Garden, Mister Moses, Gambit, A Man Could Get Killed (co-dir.), Prudence and the Pill (co-dir.), The Prime of Miss Jean Brodie, Scrooge, The

Poseidon Adventure, The Odessa File, Meteor, Hopscotch, First Monday in October, Foreign Body, The Magic Balloon.

NEEDHAM, HAL: Director, Writer. b. Memphis, TN, March 6, 1931. e. Student public schools. Served with Paratroopers U.S. Army 1951–54. Founder Stunts Unlimited, Los Angeles, 1970; stuntman Stunts Unltd. 1956–65; dir. and stunt coordinator second unit, 1965–75; dir. writer, 1976–present. Chmn. of bd., Camera Platforms International, Inc. 1985. Owner Budweiser Rocket Car (fastest car in the world). Member Screen Actors Guild, AFTRA, Writers Guild of America, Directors Guild of America.
PICTURES: Dir.: Smokey and the Bandit (debut, 1977; also co-story), Hooper, The Villain, Smokey and the Bandit II, The Cannonball Run, Megaforce (also co-s.p.), Stroker Ace (also co-s.p.), Cannonball Run II (also co-s.p.), RAD, Body Slam.
TELEVISION: Hal Needham's Wild World of Stunts (syndicated series he wrote, directed and starred in). Directed Death Car on the Freeway (movie), Stunts Unlimited (pilot), B.L. Stryker (episode).

NEESON, LIAM: Actor. b. Ballymena, Northern Ireland, June 7, 1952. Former amateur boxer. Was driving a fork lift truck for a brewery when he joined the Lyric Player's Theatre in Belfast. Made prof. debut in The Risen (1976) and stayed with rep. co. 2 years. Moved to Dublin as freelance actor before joining the Abbey Theatre. Stage includes The Informer (Dublin Theatre Fest.), Translations (National Theatre, London). NY theatre debut 1992 in Anna Christie.
PICTURES: Excalibur (debut, 1981), Krull, The Bounty, Lamb, The Innocent, The Mission, Duet For One, A Prayer for the Dying, Suspect, Satisfaction, The Dead Pool, The Good Mother, High Spirits, Next of Kin, Dark Man, Crossing the Line (The Big Man), Shining Through, Under Suspicion, Husbands and Wives, Leap of Faith, Ethan Frome, Ruby Cairo, Schindler's List.
TELEVISION: Merlin and the Sword, Across the Water (BBC), Ellis Island, A Woman of Substance, Sweet As You Are.

NEFF, HILDEGARDE: Actress, author. r.n. Hildegard Knef. b. Ulm, Germany, Dec. 28, 1925. e. Art Acad., Berlin. Film cartoonist for UFA, Berlin; on Berlin stage after war; appeared in German films: Murderers Are Among Us, Between Yesterday and Tomorrow, Film Without Title, The Sinner. On B'way in: Silk Stockings. U.S. m.p. debut in Decision Before Dawn. Author of best-selling autobiography, The Gift Horse, 1971.
PICTURES: Diplomatic Courier, Night Without Sleep, Snows of Kilimanjaro, Holiday for Henrietta, Man Between, Svengali, The Girl From Hamburg, Subway in the Sky, And So to Bed, Mozambique, The Lost Continent, Witchery, Fedora.

NEGULESCO, JEAN: Director. b. Craiova, Rumania , Feb. 29, 1900. e. Liceul Carol U., Rumania. Stage dir., artist, painter. Came to U.S. in 1927. Memoirs: Things I Did and Things I Think I Did (1983).
PICTURES: The Mask of Dimitrios, The Conspirators, Nobody Lives Forever, Three Strangers, Humoresque, Deep Valley, Johnny Belinda, Road House, Forbidden Street, Three Came Home, Under My Skin, Mudlark, Take Care of My Little Girl, The Full House, Phone Call From a Stranger, Lydia Bailey, Lure of the Wilderness, Titanic, Scandal at Scourie, How to Marry a Millionaire, The Rains of Ranchipur, Woman's World, Three Coins in the Fountain, Daddy Long Legs, Boy on a Dolphin, The Gift of Love, A Certain Smile, Count Your Blessings, The Best of Everything, Jessica, The Pleasure Seekers, Hello Goodbye.
(Died: July 18, 1993)

NEILL, SAM: Actor. b. N. Ireland, Sept. 14, 1947. Raised in New Zealand. e. U. of Canterbury. In repertory before joining N.Z. National Film Unit, acting and directing documentaries and shorts.
PICTURES: Sleeping Dogs (debut, 1977), The Journalist, My Brilliant Career, Just Out of Reach, Attack Force Z, The Final Conflict, Possession, Enigma, Le Sang des Autres, Robbery Under Arms, Plenty, For Love Alone, The Good Wife, A Cry in the Dark (Australian Film Inst. Award), Dead Calm, The French Revolution, The Hunt for Red October, Until the End of the World, Hostage, Memoirs of an Invisible Man, Death in Brunswick, Jurassic Park, The Piano.
TELEVISION: The Sullivans, Young Ramsay, Lucinda Brayford, The Country Girls. Mini-Series: Kane and Abel, Reilly Ace of Spies, Amerika. Movies: From a Far Country: Pope John Paul II, Ivanhoe, The Blood of Others, Arthur Hailey's Strong Medicine, Leap of Faith, Fever, One Against the Wind, The Sinking of the Rainbow Warrior, Family Pictures.

NELLIGAN, KATE: Actress. b. London, Ontario, Canada, March 16, 1951. On stage in Barefoot in the Park, A Streetcar Named Desire, Playboy of the Western World, Private Lives, Plenty, Serious Money, Spoils of War, Bad Habits.
PICTURES: The Romantic Englishwoman (debut, 1975), Dracula, Mr. Patman, Eye of the Needle, Without a Trace, The Mystery of Henry Moore, Eleni, Frankie and Johnny (BAFTA Award), The Prince of Tides (Acad. Award nom.), Shadows and Fog, Fatal Instinct, Wolf.
TELEVISION: The Onedin Line, The Lady of the Camelias, Therese Raquin, Count of Monte Cristo, Victims, Kojak: The Price of Justice, Love and Hate: The Story of Colin and Joann Thatcher, Three Hotels, Terror Strikes the Class Reunion, Diamond Fleece, Liar Liar.

NELSON, BARRY: Actor. r.n. Robert Neilson. b. Oakland, CA, Apr. 16, 1923. e. U. of California. London stage: No Time for Sergeants, 1957.
PICTURES: A Guy Named Joe, Winged Victory, Man with My Face, First Traveling Saleslady, Mary Mary, Airport, Pete 'n' Tillie, The Shining, Island Claws.
BROADWAY: Light Up the Sky, Rat Race, Moon Is Blue, Mary Mary, Cactus Flower, Everything in the Garden, Seascape, The Norman Conquests, The Act, 42nd Street.
TELEVISION: Series: The Hunter, My Favorite Husband. Mini-Series: Washington: Behind Closed Doors. Movies: The Borgia Stick, Seven in Darkness, Climb an Angry Mountain. Guest: Murder She Wrote.

NELSON, CRAIG T.: Actor. b. Spokane, WA, April 4, 1946. Began career as writer/performer on Lohman and Barkley Show in Los Angeles. Teamed with Barry Levinson as a comedy writer. Wrote for Tim Conway Show, Alan King TV special; guest appearances on talk shows and Mary Tyler Moore Show. Produced series of 52 half-hour films on American artists, American Still. Returned to L.A. in 1978 and acting career.
PICTURES: And Justice for All (debut, 1979), Where the Buffalo Roam, Private Benjamin, Stir Crazy, The Formula, Poltergeist, Man Woman and Child, All the Right Moves, The Osterman Weekend, Silkwood, The Killing Fields, Poltergeist II, Red Riding Hood, Action Jackson, Rachel River, Me and Him, Troop Beverly Hills, Turner & Hooch.
TELEVISION: Series: Call to Glory, Coach. Guest: Wonder Woman, Charlie's Angels, How the West Was Won. Movies: Diary of a Teenage Hitchhiker, Rage, Promise of Love, Inmates: A Love Story, Chicago Story, Paper Dolls, Alex: The Life of a Child, The Ted Kennedy Jr. Story, Murderers Among Us: The Simon Wiesenthal Story, Extreme Close-Up, The Josephine Baker Story, The Switch, The Fire Next Time. Mini-Series: Drug Wars: The Camarena Story.

NELSON, DAVID: Actor. b. New York, NY, Oct. 24, 1936. e. Hollywood High., U. of Southern California. Son of Ozzie Nelson, Harriet Hilliard, brother of late Rick Nelson.
PICTURES: Here Comes the Nelsons, Peyton Place, The Remarkable Mr. Pennypacker, Day of the Outlaw, The Big Circus, "30," The Big Show, No Drums No Bugles, Cry-Baby. Director: A Rare Breed, The Last Plane Out.
TELEVISION: Series: Adventures of Ozzie and Harriet. Movies: Smash-Up on Interstate 5, High School U.S.A. Dir.: Easy To Be Free (special), OK Crackerby (series).

NELSON, GENE: Dancer, actor, director, choreographer. r.n. Gene Berg. b. Seattle, WA, March 24, 1920. e. Santa Monica, CA H.S. Began dancing and ice skating in school; joined Sonja Henie Hollywood Ice Revue, featured in It Happens on Ice, Center Theatre, NY; played in This Is the Army, W.W.II; after discharge. To Hollywood for I Wonder Who's Kissing Her Now; joined Hollywood group prod. stage musical, Lend an Ear; to Warner for Daughter of Rosie O'Grady (1950). Prof. of Theatre Arts at San Francisco State Univ. School of Creative Arts, 1989–90.
PICTURES: Actor: I Wonder Who's Kissing Her Now, Gentleman's Agreement, Apartment For Peggy, The Daughter of Rosie O'Grady, Tea for Two, Starlift, West Point Story, Lullaby of Broadway, Painting the Clouds With Sunshine, She's Working Her Way Through College, She's Back on Broadway, Three Sailors and a Girl, Crime Wave, So This Is Paris, Oklahoma, The Way Out, Atomic Man, 20,000 Eyes, The Purple Hills, Thunder Island, S.O.B. Director: The Hand of Death, Hootenany Hoot, Your Cheatin' Heart, Kissin' Cousins, Harum Scarum, The Cool Ones (also s.p.).
TELEVISION: Series Director: Mod Squad, I Dream of Jeannie, FBI, 12 O'Clock High, Hawaii Five-O, Farmer's Daughter, Donna Reed Show, Burke's Law, Felony Squad, Laredo, The Rifleman, The Wackiest Ship, Iron Horse, FBI, The Rookies, Quincy, Operation Petticoat. Movies (Director): Wake Me When the War is Over (also co-prod.), The Letters. Movies (Actor): Family Flight, A Brand New Life.
BROADWAY: Lend an Ear, Follies, Music Music, Good News.

NELSON, HARRIET: Singer, actress. r.n. Harriet Hilliard. b. Des Moines, IA, July 18, 1914. e. H.S., Kansas City. m. late Ozzie Nelson. Mother of late actor David Nelson and late actor-singer Rick Nelson. Appeared in dramatic & musical roles in shows; singer with Ozzie Nelson band; on radio shows: Believe It or Not, Seeing Stars, Red Skelton, Adventures of Ozzie & Harriet. Appeared in films: Follow the Fleet, She's My Everything, Sweetheart of the Campus, Here Come the Nelsons.

TELEVISION: Adventures of Ozzie and Harriet, (1952–66). STAGE: Marriage-Go-Round; rec.: Ozzie and Harriet. PLAYS: Impossible Years, State Fair.

NELSON, JUDD: Actor. b. Portland, ME, Nov. 28, 1959. e. Haverford/Bryn Mawr Coll. Studied acting at Stella Adler Conservatory. NY theatre includes Carnal Knowledge.
PICTURES: Making the Grade (debut, 1984), Fandango, The Breakfast Club, St. Elmo's Fire, Blue City, Transformers (voice), From the Hip, Relentless, Far Out Man, New Jack City, The Dark Backward, Every Breath, Blindfold.
TELEVISION: Guest: Moonlighting. Movies: Billionaire Boys Club, Hiroshima: Out of the Ashes.

NELSON, LORI: Actress. r.n. Dixie Kay Nelson. b. Santa Fe, NM, Aug. 15, 1933. e. Canoga Park H.S. Child actress; photographer's model; film debut in Ma and Pa Kettle at the Fair (1952).
PICTURES: Bend of the River, Francis Goes to West Point, All I Desire, All-American, Walking My Baby Back Home, Tumbleweed, Underwater, Destry, Revenge of the Creature, I Died a Thousand Times, Sincerely Yours, Mohawk, Day the World Ended, Pardners, Hot Rod Girl, Ma and Pa Kettle at Waikiki, Gambling Man, Untamed Youth.
TELEVISION: Series: How to Marry a Millionaire. Guest: Wagon Train, Laramie, Family Affair, The Texan, Wanted Dead or Alive, Sam Spade, G.E. Theatre, Riverboat, Sugarfoot, The Young and the Restless, Climax, The Millionaire, Wells Fargo, etc. Special: The Pied Piper of Hamelin.
THEATRE: The Pleasure of His Company, Who Was That Lady I Saw You With, Affairs of Mildred Wilde, Sweet Bird of Youth, Picnic, 'night Mother.

NELSON, TRACY: Actress. b. Santa Monica, CA, Oct. 25, 1963. e. Bard Col. Daughter of late singer-actor Rick Nelson. Sister of singers Matthew & Gunnar Nelson. m. actor William Moses. Studied acting in England.
TELEVISION: Series: Square Pegs, Glitter, Father Dowling Mysteries. Movies: Kate's Secret, Tonight's the Night, If It's Tuesday It Still Must Be Belgium, Fatal Confession: A Father Dowling Mystery, Highway Heartbreaker. Guest: The Adventures of Ozzie and Harriet, Hotel, Family Ties, The Love Boat.
PICTURES: Yours Mine and Ours (debut, 1968), Maria's Lovers, Down and Out in Beverly Hills.

NELSON, WILLIE: Composer, Singer, Actor. b. Abbott, TX, April 30, 1933. Worked as salesman, announcer, host of country music shows on local Texas stations; bass player with Ray Price's band. Started writing songs in the 60s; performing in the 70s.
PICTURES: The Electric Horseman (debut, 1979), Honeysuckle Rose, Thief, Barbarosa, Hell's Angels Forever, Songwriter, Red-Headed Stranger (also prod.), Walking After Midnight.
TELEVISION: Movies: The Last Days of Frank and Jesse James, Stagecoach, Coming Out of the Ice, Baja Oklahoma, Once Upon a Texas Train, Where the Hell's That Gold?!!?, Pair of Aces, Another Pair of Aces, Wild Texas Wind. Special: Willie Nelson—Texas Style (also prod.).

NEMEC, CORIN: Actor. r.n. Joseph Charles Nemec IV. b. Little Rock, AR, Nov. 5, 1971. Began acting in commercials at age 13.
TELEVISION: Series: Parker Lewis Can't Lose. Movies: I Know My First Name is Steven (Emmy nom.), For the Very First Time, My Son Johnny. Pilot: What's Alan Watching? Guest: Webster, Sidekicks.
PICTURES: Tucker: The Man and His Dream, Solar Crisis.

NERO, FRANCO: Actor. r.n. Franceso Sparanero. b. Parma, Italy, 1941.
PICTURES: The Bible—The Beginning (debut, 1966), Django, Camelot, The Hired Killer, The Wild Wild Planet, The Brute and the Beast, The Day of the Owl, Sardinia, Mafia, Vendetta, Companeros, Detective Belli, The Mercenary, A Quiet Place in the Country, Tristana, The Virgin and the Gypsy, Battle of the Neretva, Confessions of a Police Captain, The Vacation, Pope Joan, Deaf Smith and Johnny Ears, The Last Days of Mussolini, Force Ten from Navarone, The Roses of the Danzig, Mimi, The Man With Bogart's Face, Enter the Ninja, Mexico in Flames, Querelle, Kamikaze '89, The Salamander, Wagner, Victory March, Day of the Cobra, Ten Days That Shook the World, Der Falke, The Repenter, The Forester's Sons, Garibaldi the General, The Girl, Sweet Country, Die Hard 2, Brothers and Sisters, A Breath of Life.
TELEVISION: Mini-series: The Last Days of Pompeii. Movies: The Legend of Valentino, 21 Hours at Munich, The Pirate, Young Catherine.

NESMITH, MICHAEL: Musician, Producer. b. Houston, TX, Dec. 30, 1942. Original member of The Monkees, later became producer of videos and films. Chmn. & CEO Pacific Arts Corp. video company, distrib. of PBS Home Video. Won Grammy award for music video Elephant Parts. Exec. prod. & performer in video Dr. Duck's Super Secret All-Purpose Sauce.
TELEVISION: Series: The Monkees, Michael Nesmith in

Television Parts (also prod.). Special: 33⅓ Revolutions Per Monkee.
PICTURES: Actor: Head, Burglar (cameo). Exec. Prod.: Timerider (also co-s.p.), Repo Man, Square Dance, Tapeheads.

NETTER, DOUGLAS: Executive, Producer. b. Seattle, WA. 1955–57, gen. mgr. Todd A.O.; 1958–60, Sam Goldwyn Productions; 1961–67, Formed own co. representing producers; 1968–69, Jalem Productions; 1969–75, exec. v.p. MGM; 1976, prod., Mr. Ricco. 1977, American co-prod., The Wild Geese.
TELEVISION: prod., Louis L'Amour's The Sacketts, (miniseries). exec. prod., The Buffalo Soldiers (pilot); prod., Wild Times, (mini-series); exec. prod. Roughnecks, (mini-series); exec. prod. Cherokee Trail; exec. prod., Five Mile Creek (Australian based TV series for Disney Channel); prod., Captain Power and the Soldiers of the Future (pilot); exec. prod., Captain Power and the Soldiers of the Future (syn. series); exec. prod., Stealth F22 (film for Lockheed Aeronautical Systems); exec. prod.: Babylon 5 (syn. series).

NETTLETON, LOIS: Actress. b. Oak Park, IL, 1931. e. Studied at Goodman Theatre, Chicago and Actors Studio. Replaced Kim Hunter in Darkness at Noon on Broadway. Emmy Award: Performer Best Daytime Drama Spec., The American Woman: Portraits in Courage (1977). Also Emmy: Religious Program, Insight (1983).
PLAYS: Cat on a Hot Tin Roof, Silent Night, Lonely Night, God and Kate Murphy, The Wayward Stork, The Rainmaker, A Streetcar Named Desire.
PICTURES: A Face in the Crowd (debut, 1957), Period of Adjustment, Come Fly with Me, Mail Order Bride, Valley of Mystery, Bamboo Saucer, The Good Guys and the Bad Guys, Dirty Dingus Magee, The Sidelong Glances of a Pigeon Kicker, The Honkers, Echoes of a Summer, Deadly Blessing, Butterfly, Soggy Bottom U.S.A., The Best Little Whorehouse in Texas.
TELEVISION: Series: Accidental Family, You Can't Take It With You. Guest: Medical Center, Barnaby Jones, Alfred Hitchcock, All That Glitters, In the Heat of the Night. Movies: Any Second Now, Weekend of Terror, The Forgotten Man, Terror in the Sky, Women in Chains, Fear on Trial, Tourist, Manhunt for Claude Dallas. Mini-Series: Washington: Behind Closed Doors, Centennial. Special: Traveler's Rest.

NEUFELD, MACE: Producer. b. New York, NY, July 13, 1928. e. Yale Col. Started as professional photographer, before becoming prod. asst. at Dumont Television Network. Wrote musical material for performers incl. Sammy Davis Jr., Dorothy Loudon, Ritz Brothers, etc. and theme for Heckle and Jeckle animated series. 1951 formed indept. TV prod. and personal mgmt. co. For TV produced programs for Dick Van Dyke, Elaine May and Mike Nichols. Formed indept. production co. with Nichols and Buck Henry. 1980 created Neufeld-Davis Prods. with Marvin Davis. Formed Neufeld/Rehme Prods. with Robert G. Rehme in 1989. On Bdwy prod. Flying Karamazov Brothers show.
PICTURES: The Omen, Damien: Omen II, The Frisco Kid, The Funhouse, The Aviator, Transylvania 6-5000, No Way Out, The Hunt for Red October, Flight of the Intruder, Necessary Roughness, Patriot Games.
TELEVISION: Movies/Miniseries: East of Eden, Angel on My Shoulder, American Dream, Cagney and Lacey (pilot), A Death in California. Specials: The Magic Planet, The Flying Karamazov Brothers.

NEWBROOK, PETER: Producer, Director of photography. b. Chester Castle, England, June 29, 1920. e. Ewell Castle, Surrey. Entered m.p. ind. Warner Bros. Studios, Teddington. Chmn. Titan Int'l. Productions, Ltd. Esquire Music Co. Past Pres., British Society of Cinematographers.
PICTURES: After working on such pictures as The Sound Barrier, The Captain's Paradise, Hobson's Choice, Summer Madness, The Deep Blue Sea, Anastasia, The Bridge on the River Kwai; became dir. photog.: Lawrence of Arabia (2nd unit), 1961. Dir. of Photog.: In The Cool of the Day, That Kind of Girl, The Yellow Teddybears, Saturday Night Out, The Black Torment (also prod.), Gonks Go Beat (also prod.), The Sandwich Man, Press For Time, Corruption, The Smashing Bird I Used to Know, Bloodsuckers, She'll Follow You Anywhere, Crucible of Terror, The Asphyx, The Wonderful World of Greece, Bosom Friends, Where's Your Sense of Humor?, Last of the Midnight Gardeners.
TELEVISION: Tales of the Unexpected, Coronation Street, Emmerdale Farm.

NEWELL, MIKE: Director. b. 1942.
PICTURES: The Awakening, Bad Blood, Dance With a Stranger, Amazing Grace and Chuck, Soursweet, Enchanted April, Into the West.
TELEVISION: Series: Budgie, Eleventh Hour. Movies: Big Soft Nelly, Mrs. House, The Man in the Iron Mask, The Gift of Friendship, Blood Feud.

NEWHART, BOB: Actor, Comedian. b. Chicago, IL, Sept. 5, 1929. e. Loyola U. In Army 2 yrs., then law school; left to become copywriter and accountant. Acted with theatrical stock co. in Oak Park; hired for TV man-in-street show in Chicago. Recorded hit comedy album for Warner Bros. Records: The Button Down Mind of Bob Newhart, followed by two more successful albums. Did series of nightclub engagements and then acquired own TV variety series in 1961. Frequently appears in Las Vegas and headlines college concerts. Has guested on most major TV variety and comedy series. Grand Marshall: Tournament of Roses Parde, 1991. Inducted into TV Hall of Fame, 1993.
PICTURES: Hell is for Heroes (debut, 1962), Hot Millions, Catch-22, On a Clear Day You Can See Forever, Cold Turkey, The Rescuers (voice), Little Miss Marker, First Family, The Rescuers Down Under (voice).
TELEVISION: Series: The Bob Newhart Show (1961–2, variety), The Entertainers, The Bob Newhart Show (1972–8, sit-com), Newhart, Bob. Movies: Thursday's Game, Marathon, The Entertainers.

NEWLAND, JOHN: Director, Actor. b. Cincinnati, OH, Nov. 23, 1917. Began as a singer-dancer in vaudeville and on Bdwy; many TV appearances, especially as host of One Step Beyond. Actor, dir., Robert Montgomery Show, My Lover, My Son. Turned to full-time dir. and prod. in the 1960's.
PICTURES: Bulldog Drummond, That Night, The Violators, The Spy With My Face, Hush-a-Bye Murder, Purgatory.
TELEVISION: Producer: A Sensitive, Passionate Man, Overboard, Angel City, The Five of Me, Timestalker, The Next Step Beyond, The Suicide's Wife, Arch of Triumph, Too Good to be True.

NEWLEY, ANTHONY: Actor, Writer, Composer, Singer. b. Hackney, Eng., Sept. 24, 1931.
PICTURES: Adventures of Dusty Bates (debut, 1946), Little Ballerina, The Guinea Pig, Vice Versa, Oliver Twist, Vote for Huggett, Don't Ever Leave Me, A Boy a Girl and a Bike, Golden Salamander, Madeleine, Highly Dangerous, Those People Next Door, Top of the Form, The Weak and the Wicked, Up to His Neck, Blue Peter, The Cockleshell Heroes, Battle of the River Plate, Above Us the Waves, Port Afrique, The Last Man to Hang, Fire Down Below, How to Murder a Rich Uncle, Good Companions, X the Unknown, High Flight, No Time to Die (Tank Force), The Man Inside, The Bandit of Zhobe, The Lady Is a Square, Idle on Parade, Killers of Kilimanjaro, Let's Get Married, Jazz Boat, In the Nick, The Small World of Sammy Lee, Play It Cool, Stop the World I Want to Get Off (songs only), Dr. Dolittle, Sweet November, Can Hieronymus Merkin Ever Forget Mercy Humppe and Find True Happiness? (also dir., s.p., songs), Willie Wonka and the Chocolate Factory (songs only), Summertree (dir. only), Mr. Quilp (also music), It Seemed Like a Good Idea at the Time, The Garbage Pail Kids Movie.
TELEVISION: Specials: Sunday Night Palladium, Saturday Spectaculars, Anthony Newley Special (London). Guest: The Johnny Darling Show, Hollywood Squares, Merv Griffin Show, The Tonight Show, Limited Partners, Fame, Magnum P.I., Alfred Hitchcock Theatre, Murder She Wrote, Simon & Simon. Movies: Malibu, Alice in Wonderland, Blade in Hong Kong, Stagecoach, Coins in a Fountain, Polly Comin' Home, Boris and Natasha. Series (BBC): Sammy, The Strange World of Gurney Slade, The Anthony Newley Show (1972).
PLAYS: West End stage: Cranks (also dir., writer), Stop The World—I Want to Get Off (also composer with Leslie Bricusse, dir., writer; also NY), The Roar of the Greasepaint - The Smell of the Crowd (also composer with Bricusse, writer, dir.; also NY), The Good Old Bad Old Days (also composer with Bricusse, writer, dir.), Royalty Follies (also dir., writer), The World's Not Entirely to Blame, It's a Funny Old World We Live In. Regional: Chaplin, Once Upon a Song. British tour: Scrooge (1992–3).
AWARDS: Male Singer of the Year Award, Las Vegas, 1972; Elected to Songwriters Hall of Fame, 1989. Gold records for composing Goldfinger, Candy Man, What Kind of Fool Am I?

NEWMAN, ALFRED S.: Executive. b. Brooklyn, NY, Nov. 16. e. NYU. Public relations work for Equitable Life Insurance, Trans World Airlines prior to joining Columbia Pictures in 1968 as writer in publicity dept.; named New York publicity mgr., 1970; national publicity mgr., 1972; joined MGM as East adv't-pub. dir., 1972; named director of adv't. pub. and promotion, 1974; named v.p., worldwide adv., pub., promo., 1978; v.p., pub./ promo., MGM/UA, 1981. With 20th Century-Fox as v.p. adv./ pub./promo. for TV & corporate, 1984–85; joined Rogers & Cowan as sr. v.p. & head of corporate entertainment, 1985; named exec. v.p., 1987; Oct. 1988 named pres. and CEO. Sterling Entertainment Co. and exec. v.p. worldwide marketing of parent co. MCEG; formed Newman & Associates, 1989; joined Hill and Knowl Entertainment as founding mng. dir., 1990. Re-opened Newman and Assocs., 1991.

NEWMAN, BARRY: Actor. b. Boston, MA, Nov. 7, 1938. e. Brandeis U.

TELEVISION: Series: Petrocelli, Nightingales. Movies: Night Games, Sex and the Married Woman, King Crab, Fantasies, Having It All, Second Sight: A Love Story, Fatal Vision, My Two Loves, The Mirror Crack'd (BBC).
PICTURES: Pretty Boy Floyd, The Lawyer, Vanishing Point, The Salzburg Connection, Fear is the Key, City on Fire, Amy.

NEWMAN, DAVID: Composer. b. Los Angeles, CA. e. USC. Son of late composer Alfred Newman. Cousin of composer Randy Newman. Music director at Robert Redford's Sundance Institute.
PICTURES: Critters, Vendetta, The Kindred, My Demon Lover, Malone, Dragnet, Throw Momma from the Train, Pass the Ammo, Bill & Ted's Excellent Adventure, Disorganized Crime, The Brave Little Toaster, Heathers, Little Monsters, Gross Anatomy, The War of the Roses, Madhouse, Fire Birds, The Freshman, DuckTales: The Movie, Mr. Destiny, Meet the Applegates, The Marrying Man, Talent for the Game, Don't Tell Mom the Babysitter's Dead, Bill & Ted's Bogus Journey, Rover Dangerfield, Paradise, Other People's Money, The Mighty Ducks, Hoffa, The Sandlot.

NEWMAN, DAVID: Writer. b. New York, NY, Feb. 4, 1937. e. U. of Michigan, M.S., 1959. Was writer-editor at Esquire Magazine where he met Robert Benton, an art director, and formed writing partnership. All early credits co-written with Benton; later ones with Leslie Newman and others.
PICTURES: Bonnie and Clyde, There Was a Crooked Man, Floreana, What's Up Doc?, Money's Tight, Bad Company, The Crazy American Girl, Superman (co-s.p.), Superman II (co-s.p.), Jinxed (co-s.p.), Superman III (co-s.p.), Sheena (co-s.p.), Still of the Night, Santa Claus—The Movie, Moonwalker.
STAGE: It's a Bird . . . It's a Plane . . . It's Superman (libretto), Oh! Calcutta (one sketch).

NEWMAN, EDWIN: News Correspondent. b. New York, NY, Jan. 25, 1919. Joined NBC News in 1952, based in N.Y. since 1961. Reports news on NBC-TV and often assigned to anchor instant specials. Has been substitute host on Today, appeared on Meet the Press and has reported NBC News documentaries. Host of interview series, Speaking Freely, on WNBC-TV, N.Y.; Television (PBS series, host).

NEWMAN, JOSEPH M.: Producer, Director, Writer. b. Logan, UT, Aug. 7, 1909. Started as office boy MGM, 1925; jobs in production dept. to 1931; asst. to George Hill, Ernst Lubitsch, etc., 1931–37; asstd. in organization of MGM British studios 1937; dir. short subjects 1938; dir. Crime Does Not Pay series 1938–42; Major in U.S. Army Signal Corps 1942–46; dir. 32 Army Pictorial Service Pictures. TV work includes Alfred Hitchcock Presents, Twilight Zone. Member: AMPAS, SDG Masons.
PICTURES: Northwest Rangers, Abandoned, Jungle Patrol, Great Dan Pitch, 711 Ocean Drive, Lucky Nick Cain, Guy Who Came Back, Love Nest, Red Skies of Montana, Outcasts of Poker Flat, Pony Soldier, Dangerous Crossing, Human Jungle, Kiss of Fire, This Island Earth, Flight to Hong Kong, Fort Massacre, Big Circus, Tarzan The Ape Man, King of the Roaring Twenties, Twenty Plus Two, The George Raft Story, Thunder of Drums.

NEWMAN, LARAINE: Actress. b. Los Angeles, CA, Mar. 2, 1952. Founding member of the Groundlings.
TELEVISION: Series: Manhattan Transfer, Saturday Night Live. Guest: George Burns Comedy Week, St. Elsewhere, Laverne & Shirley, Alfred Hitchcock Presents, Amazing Stories, Faerie Tale Theatre (The Little Mermaid), Twilight Zone, Dream On, Likely Suspects. Specials: Steve Martin's Best Show Ever, The Lily Tomlin Special, Bob Ray Jane Laraine & Gilda. Movies: Her Life as a Man, This Wife for Hire.
PICTURES: Tunnelvision (debut, 1976), American Hot Wax, Wholly Moses!, Stardust Memories (unbilled), Perfect, Sesame Street Presents Follow That Bird (voice), Invaders from Mars, Problem Child 2, Witchboard II, Coneheads.
THEATRE: Bdwy: Fifth of July.

NEWMAN, NANETTE: Actress, Writer. b. Northampton, Eng., 1934. m. to prod.-dir.-writer Bryan Forbes. Ent. films in 1946 and TV in 1951. Author: God Bless Love, That Dog, Reflections, The Root Children, Amy Rainbow, Pigalev, Archie, Christmas Cookbook, Summer Cookbook, Small Beginnings, Bad Baby, Entertaining with Nanette Newman and Her Daughters, Charlie the Noisy Caterpillar, Sharing, The Pig Who Never Was, ABC, 123, Cooking for Friends.
TELEVISION: The Glorious Days, The Wedding Veil, Broken Honeymoon, At Home, Trial by Candlelight, Diary of Samuel Pepys, Faces in the Dark, Balzac (BBC), Fun Food Factory, TV series, Stay with Me Till Morning, Let There Be Love (series), West Country Tales, Jessie, Late Expectations (series).
FILMS: The Personal Affair, The League of Gentlemen, The Rebel, Twice Around the Daffodils, The L-Shaped Room, Wrong Arm of the Law, Of Human Bondage, Seance on a Wet Afternoon, The Wrong Box, The Whisperers, Deadfall, The Madwoman of Chaillot, Captain Nemo and the Under-

water City, The Raging Moon (Long Ago Tomorrow), The Stepford Wives, It's a 2'2" Above the Ground World (The Love Ban), Man at the Top, International Velvet, The Endless Game.

NEWMAN, PAUL: Actor, Director. b. Cleveland, OH, Jan. 26, 1925. m. actress Joanne Woodward. e. Kenyon Coll., Yale Sch. of Drama, The Actors Studio. Summer stock; on Broadway in Picnic, The Desperate Hours, Sweet Bird of Youth, Baby Want a Kiss. Formed First Artists Prod. Co. Ltd. 1969 with Sidney Poitier, Steve McQueen and Barbra Streisand. Appeared in documentaries King: A Filmed Record . . . Memphis to Montgomery and Hello Actors Studio.
TELEVISION: Philco, U.S. Steel, Playhouse 90, The Web. Dir.: The Shadow Box.
PICTURES: The Silver Chalice (debut, 1954), The Rack, Somebody Up There Likes Me, The Helen Morgan Story, Until They Sail, The Long Hot Summer, The Left-Handed Gun, Cat on a Hot Tin Roof, Rally 'Round the Flag Boys, The Young Philadelphians, From the Terrace, Exodus, The Hustler, Paris Blues, Sweet Bird of Youth, Hemingway's Adventures of a Young Man, Hud, A New Kind of Love, The Prize, What a Way to Go!, The Outrage, Harper, Lady L, Torn Curtain, Hombre, Cool Hand Luke, The Secret War of Harry Frigg, Rachel Rachel (dir. only), Winning, Butch Cassidy and the Sundance Kid, WUSA, Sometimes a Great Notion (also dir.), Pocket Money, The Life and Times of Judge Roy Bean, The Effect of Gamma Rays on Man-in-the-Moon Marigolds (dir. only), The Mackintosh Man, The Sting, The Towering Inferno, The Drowning Pool, Buffalo Bill and the Indians or Sitting Bull's History Lesson, Silent Movie, Slap Shot, Quintet, When Time Ran Out..., Fort Apache The Bronx, Absence of Malice, The Verdict, Harry and Son (also dir., co-s.p., co-prod.), The Color of Money (Acad. Award, 1986), The Glass Menagerie (dir. only), Fat Man & Little Boy, Blaze, Mr. and Mrs. Bridge, The Hudsucker Proxy.

NEWMAN, RANDY: Composer, Singer. b. Los Angeles, CA, Nov. 28, 1943. Nephew of musicians Lionel and Alfred Newman. Studied music at UCLA. Debut album: Randy Newman Creates Something New Under the Sun. Songs include Short People. I Think It's Gonna Rain Today, I Love L.A. Began writing songs and scores for films in 1971 with The Pursuit of Happiness.
PICTURES: Pursuit of Happiness, Cold Turkey, Ragtime, The Natural, Three Amigos (also co-wrote s.p.), Parenthood, Avalon, Awakenings.

NEWMAN, SYDNEY: O. C., F.R.S.A., F.R.T.S. for Canadian Film Development Corp. b. Toronto, Canada. Studied painting, drawing, commercial art at Central Techn. Sch. To Hollywood in 1938. Joined National Film Board of Canada under John Grierson. Prod. over 300 shorts. Later became exec. prod. all Canadian government cinema films, 1947–52; Canadian Broadcasting Corp., 1952, as dir. outside broadcasts, features and documentaries. Later became drama sup. and prod. General Motors Theatre. Joined ABC-TV in England, 1958. as sup. of drama and prod. of Armchair Theatre: Head of Drama Group, TV, BBC, 1963. Commissioned and prod. first TV plays by Arthur Hailey, Harold Pinter, Mordecai Richler, Alun Owen, Angus Wilson, Peter Luke. Devised, created Dr. Who (1962) and The Avengers (1959). Fellow Society of Film & TV Arts, 1968; Fellow Royal Television Society, 1990. Prod. Associated British Pictures. SFTA award 1968; Zeta award, Writers Guild, Gt. Btn., 1970. 1970: Special advisor, ch. dir., Broadcast Programmes branch, Canadian Radio & TV Commission, Ottawa. Aug., 1970: Appt. Canadian Govt. Film Commissioner and chmn., National Film Board of Canada; Trustee, National Arts Centre, Ottawa; bd. mem., Canadian Broadcasting Corporation, Canadian Film Development Corp. Recognition Award from S.M.P.T.E. (USA), Canadian Picture Pioneers Special Award. Special Advisor on Film to the Secretary of State for Canada, 1975–77; pres., Sydney Newman Enterprises. 1981: Made Officer of the Order of Canada. Left Canadian Film Develop. Corp. 1983. At present Creative Consultant to film & tv producers.

NEWMAN, WALTER BROWN: Writer. b. 1920.
PICTURES: Ace in the Hole (co-s.p.), Underwater, The Man with the Golden Arm (co-s.p.), The True Story of Jesse James, Crime and Punishment, USA, The Interns (co-s.p.), Cat Ballou (co-s.p.), Bloodbrothers, The Champ.

NEWMAR, JULIE: Actress. r.n. Julie Newmeyer. b. Hollywood, CA, Aug. 16, 1933. e. UCLA. Studied acting with Lee Strasberg at the Actor's Studio. Holds patent for special panty hose design. Appeared in George Michael video Too Funky.
TELEVISION: Series: My Living Doll, Batman (frequent guest; as Catwoman). Movies: McCloud: Who Killed Miss U.S.A.?, The Feminist and the Fuzz, A Very Missing Person, Terraces. Guest: Omnibus, Route 66, Jonathan Winters Show, Beverly Hillbillies, The Monkees, Love American Style, Love Boat, Half Nelson, Fantasy Island, Hart to Hart, Buck Rogers.
PICTURES: Just for You (debut, 1952), Seven Brides for

Seven Brothers, The Rookie, Li'l Abner, The Marriage-Go-Round, For Love or Money, McKenna's Gold, The Maltese Bippy, Hysterical, Streetwalkin', Body Beat, Nudity Required, Ghosts Can't Do It.
THEATRE: NY: Silk Stockings, Li'l Abner, The Marriage-Go-Round (Tony Award, 1959). Other: In the Boom Boom Room (L.A.), Damn Yankees, Irma La Douce, Guys and Dolls, Dames at Sea, Stop the World, The Women.

NEWTON-JOHN, OLIVIA: Actress, Singer. b. Cambridge, Eng. Sept. 26, 1948. m. actor Matt Lattanzi. Brought up in Melbourne, Australia, where won first talent contest at 15, with prize trip to England. Stayed there 2 yrs. performing as part of duo with Australian girl singer, Pat Carroll (Farrar), in cabarets and on TV. Started recording; several hit records. Became a regular guest on TV series, It's Cliff Richard. Gained world-wide prominence as singer, winning several Grammys and other music awards. 1983 opened Koala Blue, U.S. Clothing Stores featuring Australian style clothes and goods.
PICTURES: Toomorow, Grease, Xanadu, Two of a Kind.
TELEVISION: Specials: Olivia Newton-John—Let's Get Physical, Standing Room Only—Olivia Newton-John, Olivia Newton-John in Australia, Christmas in Washington. Movie: A Mom for Christmas.

NEY, RICHARD: Actor, Writer, Producer, Financier. b. New York, NY, Nov. 12, 1917. e. Columbia U., B.A., 1940. Acted in RCA TV demonstration, New York World's Fair; on stage in Life with Father. In armed services, W.W.II. Many TV shows. Financial advisor consultant, Richard Ney and Associates; financial advisor, lecturer; author, The Wall Street Jungle, The Wall Street Gang, Making it in the Market.
PICTURES: Mrs. Miniver, War Against Mrs. Hadley, Late George Apley, Ivy, Joan of Arc, The Fan, Secret of St. Ives, Lovable Cheat, Babes in Bagdad, Miss Italia, Sergeant and The Spy, Midnight Lace, The Premature Burial.

NGOR, HAING S.: Actor. b. Cambodia, 1950. Started as doctor in Cambodia. Escaped to Thailand following four years under Khmer Rouge; then immigrated to U.S. resuming career as doctor before being picked for debut role in The Killing Fields. Autobiography: A Cambodia Odyssey.
PICTURES: The Killing Fields (debut, 1984; Acad. Award, best supp. actor), Iron Triangle, Vietnam Texas, Ambition, Heaven and Earth.
TELEVISION: Movies: In Love and War, Last Flight Out. Guest: Hotel, China Beach, Miami Vice, Highway to Heaven.

NICHOLAS, DENISE: Actress. b. Detroit, MI, July 12, 1945. e. Univ. of MI.
TELEVISION: Series: Room 222, Baby I'm Back, In the Heat of the Night. Movies: Five Desperate Women, The Sophisticated Gents, Jacqueline Susann's Valley of the Dolls, Mother's Day. Guest: NYPD, The FBI, Love American Style, Police Story, The Love Boat, The Cosby Show.
PICTURES: Blacula, The Soul of Nigger Charley, Mr. Ricco, Let's Do It Again, A Piece of the Action, Capricorn One, Marvin and Tighe, Ghost Dad.
THEATRE: Daddy Goodness, Ceremonies in Dark Old Men, Dame Lorraine, Summer of the 17th Doll, Poetry Show, Their Eyes Were Watching God.

NICHOLS, MIKE: Director, Producer, Actor. b. Berlin, Germany, Nov. 6, 1931. m. news correspondent Diane Sawyer. e. U. of Chicago. Compass Players, teamed with Elaine May; night clubs.
STAGE: Barefoot in the Park (Tony Award), The Knack, Luv (Tony Award), The Odd Couple, The Apple Tree, The Little Foxes, Plaza Suite (Tony Award), Uncle Vanya, The Prisoner of 2nd Avenue (Tony Award), Streamers, Comedians, The Gin Game, Drinks Before Dinner. Annie (prod. only; Tony Award), The Real Thing (2 Tony Awards), Hurlyburly, Social Security, Elliot Loves, Death and the Maiden.
PICTURES: Who's Afraid of Virginia Woolf? (debut, 1966), The Graduate (Acad. Award, 1967), Catch-22, Carnal Knowledge, The Day of the Dolphin, The Fortune, Gilda Live, Silkwood (also co-prod.), The Longshot (exec. prod. only), Heartburn, Biloxi Blues, Working Girl, Postcards From the Edge, Regarding Henry, Wolf.
TELEVISION: Broadway, An Evening with Mike Nichols and Elaine May. Exec. prod.: Family, The Thorns.

NICHOLS, NICHELLE: Actress. b. Robbins, IL, 1936. Started singing and dancing with Duke Ellington and his band at age 16. Was appointee to the bd. of dirs. of the National Space Institute in the 1970s recruiting women and minority astronauts for Space Shuttle Program. Received NASA's distinguished Public Service Award. Member of the bd. of govs. of the National Space Society. One of the original founders of KWANZA Foundation. Awarded star on Hollywood Walk of Fame (1992).
TELEVISION: Series: Star Trek. Guest: The Lieutenant, Tarzan. Special: Antony and Cleopatra.
PICTURES: Porgy and Bess, Mr. Buddwing, Made in Paris,

Truck Turner, Star Trek: The Motion Picture, Star Trek II: The Wrath of Khan, Star Trek III: The Search for Spock, Star Trek IV: The Voyage Home, The Supernaturals, Star Trek V: The Final Frontier, Star Trek VI: The Undiscovered Country.
STAGE: Horowitz and Mrs. Washington, Reflections (one woman show). Nominated for Sarah Siddons Award for performances in Kicks and Company, The Blacks.

NICHOLSON, JACK: Actor, Producer, Director, Writer. b. Neptune, NJ, April 22, 1937. Began career in cartoon department of MGM. Made acting debut in Hollywood stage production of Tea and Sympathy. Made directing debut with Drive, He Said (1971). Has received 9 Academy Award nominations for acting.
PICTURES: Cry Baby Killer (debut, 1958), Too Soon to Love, Little Shop of Horrors, Studs Lonigan, The Wild Ride, The Broken Land, The Raven, The Terror, Thunder Island (co-s.p. only), Back Door to Hell, Flight to Fury (also s.p.), Ensign Pulver, Ride in the Whirlwind (also co-prod., s.p.), The Shooting (also co-prod.), The St. Valentine's Day Massacre, Rebel Rousers, Hell's Angels on Wheels, The Trip (s.p. only), Head (also co-prod., co-s.p.), Psych-Out, Easy Rider, On a Clear Day You Can See Forever, Five Easy Pieces, Carnal Knowledge, Drive He Said (dir., co-prod., co-s.p. only), A Safe Place, The King of Marvin Gardens, The Last Detail, Chinatown, Tommy, The Passenger, The Fortune, One Flew Over the Cuckoo's Nest (Acad. Award, 1975), The Missouri Breaks, The Last Tycoon, Goin' South (also dir.), The Shining, The Postman Always Rings Twice, Reds, The Border, Terms of Endearment (Acad. Award, supp. actor, 1983), Prizzi's Honor, Heartburn, The Witches of Eastwick, Broadcast News, Ironweed, Batman, The Two Jakes (also dir.), Man Trouble, A Few Good Men, Hoffa, Wolf.
TELEVISION: Guest: Tales of Wells Fargo, Cheyenne, Hawaiian Eye, Dr. Kildare, Andy Griffith Show, Guns of Will Sonneth.

NICKELL, PAUL: Director. e. Morehead, KY, State Teachers Coll., U. of North Carolina. English instructor, North Carolina State Coll.; then cameraman, asst. dir., dir. WPTZ, Philadelphia; dir. CBS-TV 1948.
TELEVISION: Studio One, Best of Broadway, Climax, Playhouse 90.

NICKSAY, DAVID: Executive., Producer. e. Mass., Hampshire Coll. Entered industry thru Directors Guild of America's training program, apprenticing on Rich Man Poor Man and rising to second asst. dir. on Oh, God. Producer of many TV projects and theatrical films with Edgar Scherick prod. co. 1986, joined Paramount Pictures as v.p., prod., for M.P. Group. Assoc. prod., prod. mgr.: I'm Dancing as Fast as I Can. Became sr. v.p., prod. Paramount, M.P. Group, 1987; resigned 1989 to become pres. and head of prod. at Morgan Creek Prods. Mem. of bd.
PICTURES: Prod.: Mrs. Soffel, Lucas Sprv. prod.: Big Top Pee-Wee, Summer School, Coming to America, The Untouchables, Scrooged, Star Trek V: The Final Frontier, Major League, Were No Angels, Harlem Nights, The Two Jakes, White Sands, Stay Tuned.
TELEVISION: Call to Glory (pilot), Little Gloria Happy at Last, etc.

NICOL, ALEX: Actor, Director. b. Ossining, NY, Jan. 20, 1919; e. Fagin Sch. of Dramatic Arts, Actor's Studio. U.S. Cavalry.
THEATRE: Forward the Heart, Sundown Beach, Hamlet, Richard II, South Pacific, Mr. Roberts, Cat on a Hot Tin Roof.
PICTURES: Sleeping City, Target Unknown, Air Cadet, Raging Tide, Meet Danny Wilson, Red Ball Express, Because of You, Tomahawk, Redhead From Wyoming, Lone Hand, Law and Order, Champ for a Day, Black Glove, Heat Wave, About Mrs. Leslie, Dawn at Socorro, Strategic Air Command, Man from Laramie, Great Day in the Morning, Sincerely Yours, Five Branded Women, Via Margutta, Under 10 Flags, Gunfighters at Casa Grande, Sleeping Skull (dir.), Then There Were Three (dir.), The Brutal Land, Bloody Mama, Homer, The Gilded Cage, Point of Terror (dir.), Hells Black Night, Screaming Skull (dir.).

NIELSEN, LESLIE: Actor. b. Regina, Sask., Canada, Feb. 11, 1926. e. Victoria H.S., Edmonton. Disc jockey, announcer for Canadian radio station; studied at Lorne Greene's Acad. of Radio Arts, Toronto and at Neighborhood Playhouse; N.Y. radio actor summer stock. Toured country in one-man show, Darrow, 1979. Author: The Naked Truth (1993).
TELEVISION: Guest: Studio One, Kraft, Philco Playhouse, Robert Montgomery Presents, Pulitzer Prize Playhouse, Suspense, Danger, Justice, Man Behind the Badge, Ben Casey, Walt Disney (Swamp Fox), Wild Wild West, The Virginian, The Loner. Series: The New Breed, Peyton Place, The Protectors, Bracken's World, The Explorers (host), Police Squad, Shaping Up. Special: Death of a Salesman. Movies: See How They Run, Shadow Over Elveron, Hawaii Five-O (pilot), Companions in Nightmare, Trial Run, Deadlock, Night Slaves, The Aquarians, Hauser's Memory, Incident in San Francisco, They Call It Murder, Snatched, The Letters, Happiness is a Warm Clue, Can Ellen Be Saved?, Brink's:

The Great Robbery, Little Mo, Institute for Revenge, OHMS, The Night the Bridge Fell Down, Cave-In!, Reckless Disregard, Blade in Hong Kong, Fatal Confession: A Father Dowling Mystery, Chance of a Lifetime. Mini-series: Backstairs at the White House.
PICTURES: Ransom, Vagabond King, Forbidden Planet, Opposite Sex, Hot Summer Night, Tammy and the Bachelor, The Sheepman, Night Train To Paris, Harlow, Dark Intruder, Beau Geste, The Plainsman, Gunfight in Abilene, The Reluctant Astronaut, Counterpoint, Rosie, Dayton's Devils, How to Commit Marriage, Change of Mind, Four Rode Out, The Resurrection of Zachary Wheeler, The Poseidon Adventure, And Millions Will Die, Day of the Animals, Viva Knievel!, The Amsterdam Kill, City on Fire, Airplane!, Prom Night, The Creature Wasn't Nice, Wrong Is Right, Creepshow, The Patriot, Soul Man, Nightstick, Nuts, Home is Where the Hart Is, The Naked Gun, Dangerous Curves, Repossessed, The Naked Gun 2-1/2: The Smell of Fear, All I Want for Christmas, Surf Ninjas.

NIMOY, LEONARD: Actor, Director. b. Boston, MA, Mar. 26, 1931. e. Boston Col. Joined Pasadena Playhouse. Along with active career in films, TV and stage, has been writer and photographer. Author of three books on photography and poetry, as well as autobiography, I Am Not Spock. Has also been speaker on college lecture circuit.
PICTURES: Queen for a Day, Francis Goes to West Point, Rhubarb, Them!, The Brain Eaters, The Balcony, Catlow, Invasion of the Body Snatchers, Star Trek—The Movie, Star Trek II: The Wrath of Khan, Star Trek III: The Search for Spock (also dir.), Transformers: The Movie (voice), Star Trek IV: The Voyage Home (also. dir., co-story), Three Men and a Baby (dir. only), The Good Mother (dir. only), Star Trek V: The Final Frontier, Funny About Love (dir. only), Star Trek VI: The Undiscovered Country (also exec. prod., co-story).
TELEVISION: Series: Star Trek, Mission: Impossible, In Search Of . . . (host). Movies: Assault on the Wayne, Baffled, The Alpha Caper, The Missing Are Deadly, The Sun Also Rises, A Woman Called Golda, Never Forget (also co-prod.). Mini-Series: Marco Polo. Guest: Bonanza, Twilight Zone, Wagon Train, The Virginian, Night Gallery, Columbo, T.J. Hooker, Star Trek: The Next Generation.
STAGE: Full Circle, Equus, Sherlock Holmes, Vincent (also dir., writer; one-man show), Love Letters.

NIVEN, DAVID, JR.: Executive. b. London, England, Dec. 15, 1942. e. Univ. of Grenoble, London Sch. of Economics. Joined William Morris Agency in Beverly Hills in 1963. Transferred same yr. to New York; over next five yrs. worked for agency's European offices in Rome, Madrid and London. In 1968–72, Columbia Pictures' U.K. office as v.p. of production; 1972–76, mg. dir. and v.p. of Paramount Pictures in U.K. In 1976 became indep. prod. West Coast corresp. & interviewer for Inside Edition. Appeared as actor in 1962 film Lisa, and on tv series America's Most Wanted.
PICTURES: Producer: The Eagle Has Landed, Escape to Athena, Monsignor, Better Late Than Never, Kidco, That's Dancing!, Pyscho Cop II, Girl With the Hungry Eyes, Cool Surface (also actor), Blue Flame.
TELEVISION: The Night They Saved Christmas (exec. prod., s.p.), Cary Grant: A Celebration, Minnelli on Minnelli, The Wonderful Wizard of Oz. Panelist: To Tell the Truth (1991–2).

NIX, WILLIAM PATTERSON: Executive. b. Philadelphia, PA, April 10, 1948. e. Georgetown U., A.B., 1970; Antioch, M.A., 1971; Hofstra U. Sch. of Law, J.D., 1976; NYU Sch. of Law, LL.M., 1979. Pres.; IP Assocs. Ltd., NY, NY. Firm handles mo. pic., tv, satellite, cable and other clients' licensing, marketing and production clients. Was Sr. v.p. of both the Motion Picture Association of America and Motion Picture Export Assoc. of America. Chmn. of MPAA committee on copyright and literary property matters, and worldwide director of film industry's anti-piracy programs (1976–91). Member, Acad. of M.P. Arts & Sciences.

NIXON, AGNES: Writer, Producer. b. Nashville, TN, Dec. 10, 1927. e. Northwestern Sch. of Speech, Catholic U. Landed 1st job writing radio serial dialogue (Woman in White, 1948–51), three days after graduating from college. Became a freelance writer for TV dramatic series Studio One, Philco Playhouse, Robert Montgomery Presents, Somerset Maugham Theatre, Armstrong Circle Theatre, Hallmark Hall of Fame, My True Story, Cameo Theatre. Then wrote for daytime series Search For Tomorrow, As The World Turns, Guiding Light and Another World before creating her first soap opera. As creator-producer: One Life to Live, All My Children, Loving. Also evening mini-series The Manions of America. Credited with bringing social issues (Vietnam War, abortion, drug addiction, child abuse, AIDS) to daytime TV. Guest writer, the New York Times 1968–72, and TV Guide. Appeared on Good Morning America and other interview and news programs. Trustee, Television Conference Inst., 1979–82. Received National Acad. of Television Arts & Sciences' Trustee Award, 1981; Junior Diabetic Assn. Super Achiever Award, 1982;

Communicator Award for American Women in Radio and Television, 1984. Intl. Radio & TV Society; Natl. Acad. of TV Arts & Sciences; bd. of Harvard Foundation; The Friars Club.

NIXON, CYNTHIA: Actress. b. New York, NY, April 9, 1966. e. Barnard Coll. Started stage career at 12. *Broadway:* The Philadelphia Story (Theatre World Award), Hurlyburly, The Real Thing, The Heidi Chronicles. *Off-Broadway:* Moonchildren, Romeo and Juliet, The Balcony Scene, Servy N Bernice 4-Ever, On the Bum.
PICTURES: Little Darlings (1980), Tattoo, Prince of the City, I Am the Cheese, Amadeus, The Manhattan Project, Let It Ride.
TELEVISION: *Movies:* The Murder of Mary Phagan, The Love She Sought, Love Lies and Murder, Face of a Stranger. *Specials:* The Fifth of July, Kiss Kiss Dahlings, Tanner '88. *Guest:* The Equalizer, Gideon Oliver, Murder She Wrote.

NIZER, LOUIS: Author, Attorney. b. London, Eng., Feb. 6, 1902. e. Columbia Coll., B.A., 1922; Columbia U. Law Sch., LL.B., 1924. Recipient of Columbia U. Curtis Oratorical Prize two times. Sr. partner of law firm, Phillips, Nizer, Benjamin, Krim & Ballon & special counsel to the Motion Picture Assn. of America. Writer of numerous books and articles in leading periodicals and newspapers; lecturer on legal subjects at many universities and bar associations. Also painter and writer of musical compositions.
BOOKS: Reflections without Mirrors, The Implosion Conspiracy, The Jury Returns, My Life in Court, What to Do With Germany, Thinking on Your Feet, Between You and Me, New Courts of Industry, Legal Essays. Excerpt from My Life in Court adapted to Bdwy. play, A Case of Libel, and also for TV movie. Chapter of The Jury Returns adapted for TV movie.

NOBLE, PETER: Writer, Producer, Actor, TV personality. b. London, Eng., June 18; e. Hugh Myddelton Sch., Latymer Sch. Author several books on m.p. ind.; writer & conducts movie radio prog. for B.B.C. & Luxembourg (Film Time, Movie-Go-Round, Peter Noble's Picture Parade). Formed Peter Noble Productions, 1953; Acted in many pictures; Ed. Screen International, 1975. Editor Screen International Film & TV Yearbook, 1974. London Columnist, Hollywood Reporter, 1967–75. Radio Show, 1989–90.
PICTURES: Production assoc., Runaway Bus; asst. prod., To Dorothy a Son; co-prod., s.p. at St. Fanny's; s.p.; Three Girls in Paris; assoc. prod., Lost; s.p., Captain Banner; prod., Strange Inheritance.
AUTHOR: Editor, British Film Year Book; author of biographies of Bette Davis, Erich Von Stroheim, Ivor Novello, Orson Welles. Author books, I Know That Face, The Negro in Films. Wrote screen plays, The King of Soho, Love in the Limelight, The Story of Ivor Novello.
TELEVISION: Find the Link, Other Screen, Film Fanfare, Movie Memories, Yakity Yak, Startime, Thank Your Lucky Stars, Juke Box, Jury, Simon Dee Show, Star Parade, Who's Whose, Movie Magazine, The Big Noise, The Name Game, Line Up, Tea Break, Today. Prod. consult. On The Braden Beat, The Frost Program, Dee Time. 1969–70 Prod. Cons. Simon Dee Show. Appeared on Anything You Can Do, Looks Familiar, Password; prod. consultant Movie Quiz (series). Appears frequently on Today TV series, Two's Company, Sounds Familiar. Prod. con. Musical Time Machine BBC2 series, Talking about films on radio, including BBC Star Sound, Radio Luxembourg, Film Focus, Newsnight, Looks Familiar Nationwide, Hotel TV Network, The Time of Your Life, Channel 4 News, Nationwide. TV series: Show Business, This Is Britain. TV appearances: Looks Familiar, Electric Picture Show, Gossip, Entertainment Tonight (USA), This Is Britain (TV cable series), Cannes Film Festival (Premiere TV Cable), Kilroy. Radio includes The Colour Supplement (series); Good Afternoon New York (WOR weekly show U.S.); Loose Ends (BBC), The Pete Murray Show (LBC), Cinema 2 (BBC), Where Are They Now? (LBC). TV includes The Golden Gong (TV film). 1988–89: Elstree—The British Hollywood; Saturday Night at the Movies (series).

NOIRET, PHILIPPE: Actor. b. Lille, France, Oct. 1, 1930. e. Centre Dramatique de l'Ouest. Company mem. Theatre National Populaire 1951–63, and worked as nightclub entertainer before film debut in Agnes Varda's short, La Pointe Court. Bdwy debut Lorenzaccio (1958). Has played character roles in numerous international films.
PICTURES: Gigi (debut, 1948), Olivia, Agence Matrimoniale, La Pointe Courte, Ravissante, Zazie dans le Metro, The Billionaire, Crime Does Not Pay, Therese Desqueyroux, Cyrano and D'Artagnan, None But the Lonely Spy, Death Where Is Thy Victory?, Monsieur, Les Copains, Lady I, La Vie de Chateau, Tender Scoundrel, The Night of the Generals, Woman Times Seven, The Assassination Bureau, Mr. Freedom, Justine, Topaz, Clerambard, Give Her the Moon, A Room in Paris, Murphy's War, A Time for Loving, Five-Leaf Clover, The Assassination, Sweet Deception, Poil de Carotte, The French Conspiracy, The Serpent, The Day of the Jackel, La Grande Bouffe, Let Joy Reign Supreme, The Old Gun, The Judge and the Assassin, A Woman at Her Window,

Purple Taxi, Dear Inspector, Due Pezzi di Pane, Who Is Killing the Great Chefs of Europe?, Death Watch, Street of the Crane's Foot, A Week's Vacation, Heads or Tails, Three Brothers, Kill Birgitt Haas, Coup de Torchon, L'Etoile du Nord, Amici, Miei, Atto 2, L'Africain, A Friend of Vincents, Le Grand Carnival, Fort Saganne, Les Ripoux, Souvenirs, Next Summer, The Gold-Rimmed Glasses, No Downing Allowed, My New Partner, 'Round Midnight, Let's Hope It's a Girl, The 4th Power, The Thrill of Genius, The Secret Wife, Twist Again in Moscow, Masks, The Family Chouans!, IL Frullo del Passero, Young Toscanini, The Return of the Musketeers, Moments of Love, Cinema Paradiso, Life and Nothing But, Palermo Connection, My New Partner 2, Uranus, I Don't Kiss, The Two of Us, Especially on Sunday.

NOLTE, C. ELMER, JR.: Executive v.p. b. Baltimore, Md., Oct. 19, 1905. Managing dir., F. H. Durkee Enterprises, Baltimore. Pres., NATO of Md., 1955–56; treas., 1957–59; pres., 1952–66, 67–69. Now v.p. & gen. mgr.

NOLTE, NICK: Actor. b. Omaha, NB, Feb. 8, 1941. Attended 5 colleges in 4 yrs. on football scholarships, including Pasadena City Coll. and Phoenix City Coll. Joined Actors Inner Circle at Phoenix and appeared in Orpheus Descending, After the Fall, Requiem For a Nun. Did stock in Colorado. In 1968 joined Old Log Theatre in Minneapolis and after 3 yrs. left for New York, appearing at Cafe La Mama. Went to L.A. and did plays The Last Pad and Picnic, as well as several guest spots on TV series before big break in mini-series Rich Man Poor Man as Tom Jordache.
PICTURES: Return to Macon County (debut, 1975), The Deep, Who'll Stop the Rain, North Dallas Forty, Heart Beat, Cannery Row, 48 HRS., Under Fire, Teachers, Grace Quigley, Down and Out in Beverly Hills, Extreme Prejudice, Weeds, Three Fugitives, New York Stories (Life Lessons), Farewell to the King, Everybody Wins, Q&A, Another 48 HRS, Cape Fear, The Prince of Tides (Golden Globe Award, Acad. Award nom., 1991), The Player, Lorenzo's Oil, I'll Do Anything, Blue Chips.
TELEVISION: *Mini-series:* Rich Man Poor Man. *Movies:* Winter Kill (pilot), The California Kid, Death Sentence, The Runaway Barge. *Guest:* Medical Center, Streets of San Francisco, The Rookies.

NORMAN, BARRY: Writer/presenter. b. London. Early career as show business editor London Daily Mail; humorous columnist The Guardian. Entered TV as writer, presenter FILM 72–81 and 83–93. 1982: presenter Omnibus. Writer/host: The Hollywood Greats and Talking Pictures. Radio work incl.: Going Places, The News Quiz, Breakaway, The Chip Shop. Books incl.: The Hollywood Greats, Movie Greats, Film Greats, Talking Pictures, 100 Best Films of the Century (all non-fiction). Seven novels incl.: A Series of Defeats, Have a Nice Day, Sticky Wicket, The Bird Dog Tapes.

NORRIS, CHUCK: Actor. r.n. Carlos Ray. b. Ryan, OK, Mar. 10, 1940. World middleweight karate champion 1968–74. Owner of karate schools.
PICTURES: The Wrecking Crew (debut, 1969), Slaughter in San Francisco, Return of the Dragon, The Student Teachers, Breaker! Breaker!, Good Guys Wear Black, Game of Death, A Force of One, The Octagon, An Eye for an Eye, Silent Rage, Forced Vengeance, Lone Wolf McQuade, Missing in Action, Missing in Action 2, Code of Silence, Invasion U.S.A. (also co-s.p.), Delta Force, Firewalker, Braddock: Missing in Action III (also co-s.p.), Hero and the Terror, Delta Force II, The Hitman, Sidekicks (also co-exec. prod.).
TELEVISION: *Series:* Chuck Norris's Karate Kommandos (animated series, voice), Walker: Texas Ranger. *Special:* The Ultimate Stuntman: A Tribute to Dar Robinson (host).

NORTH, SHEREE: Actress. r.n. Dawn Bethel. b. Los Angeles, CA, Jan. 17, 1933. e. Hollywood H.S. Amateur dancer with USO at 11; prof. debut at 13; many TV appearances; on Broadway in Hazel Flagg, I Can Get It For You Wholesale.
PICTURES: Excuse My Dust, Here Come the Girls, Living It Up, How To Be Very Very Popular, Lieutenant Wore Skirts, Best Things in Life Are Free, No Down Payment, Way to the Gold, In Love and War, Mardi Gras, Destination Inner Space, Madigan, The Gypsy Moths, The Trouble With Girls, Lawman, The Organization, Charley Varick, The Outfit, Breakout, Survival, The Shootist, Telefon, Rabbit Test, Maniac Cop, Cold Dog Soup, Defenseless.
TELEVISION: *Series:* Big Eddie, I'm a Big Girl Now, Bay City Blues, *Guest:* Archie Bunker's Place. *Movies:* Then Came Bronson (pilot), Vanished, Rolling Man, Trouble Comes to Town, Snatched, Maneater, Key West, Winter Kill, A Shadow in the Streets, Most Wanted, The Night They Took Miss Beautiful, A Real American Hero, Amateur Night at the Dixie Bar and Grill, Women in White, Portrait of a Stripper, Marilyn: The Untold Story, Legs, Scorned and Swindled, Jake Spanner - Private Eye, Dead on the Money.

NOSSECK, NOEL: Director, Producer. b. Los Angeles, CA, Dec. 10, 1943. Began as editor with David Wolper Prods; made documentaries; turned to features.

PICTURES: *Director*: Best Friends (also prod.), Youngblood, Dreamer, King of the Mountain.
TELEVISION: Movies: Return of the Rebels, The First Time, Night Partners, Summer Fantasies, Different Affair, Stark, A Mirror Image, Roman Holiday, Full Exposure: The Sex Tapes Scandal, Follow Your Heart, Opposites Attract, A Mother's Justice, Without a Kiss Goodbye, Born Too Soon. *Pilots*: Aaron's Way, Half 'n Half, Fair Game.

NOURI, MICHAEL: Actor. b. Washington, DC, Dec. 9, 1945. e. Avon Old Farms, Rollins Coll., Emerson Coll. Studied for theatre with Larry Moss and Lee Strasberg. New York stage debut in Forty Carats, 1969.
PICTURES: Goodbye Columbus (debut, 1969), Flashdance, Gobots (voice), The Imagemaker, The Hidden, Chameleon, Fatal Sky, Total Exposure, Black Ice.
TELEVISION: *Series*: Beacon Hill, Search for Tomorrow, The Curse of Dracula, The Gangster Chronicles, Bay City Blues, Downtown, Love and War. *Movies*: Contract on Cherry Street, Fun and Games, Secrets of a Mother and Daughter, Sprague, Between Two Women, Rage of Angels: The Story Continues, Quiet Victory: the Charlie Wedemeyer Story, Shattered Dreams, Danielle Steel's Changes, In the Arms of a Killer, Psychic, Exclusive, The Sands of Time. *Mini-Series*: The Last Convertible.

NOVAK, KIM: Actress. r.n. Marilyn Novak. b. Chicago, IL, Feb, 13, 1933. e. Wright Junior Coll., Los Angeles City Coll. Started as model, named World's Favorite Actress, Brussels World Fair.
PICTURES: The French Line (debut, 1954), Pushover, Phffft!, Five Against the House, Son of Sinbad, Picnic, Man with the Golden Arm, Eddy Duchin Story, Jeanne Eagels, Pal Joey, Vertigo, Bell Book and Candle, Middle of the Night, Pepe, Strangers When We Meet, The Notorious Landlady, Boys' Night Out, Of Human Bondage, Kiss Me Stupid, The Amorous Adventures of Moll Flanders, The Legend of Lylah Clare, The Great Bank Robbery, Tales That Witness Madness, The White Buffalo, The Mirror Crack'd, Just a Gigolo, The Children, Liebestraum.
TELEVISION: *Series*: Falcon Crest. *Guest*: Alfred Hitchcock Presents (1985). *Movies*: Third Girl From the Left, Satan's Triangle, Malibu.

NOVELLO, DON: Writer, Comedian, Actor. b. Ashtabula, OH, Jan. 1, 1943. e. U. of Dayton, B.A., 1964. Best known as Father Guido Sarducci on Saturday Night Live. Was advertising copy writer before writing and performing on The Smothers Brothers Comedy Hour (1975). Writer for Van Dyke and Company, and writer-performer on Saturday Night Live 1978–80. Producer: SCTV Comedy Network (1982) and performer-writer on Broadway in Gilda Radner—Live From New York (1979) as well as filmed version (Gilda Live!). Recordings: Live at St. Douglas Convent, Breakfast in Heaven. Author: The Lazlo Letters: The Amazing Real-Life Actual Correspondence of Lazlo Toth, American!, The Blade, Citizen Lazlo.
PICTURES: Gilda Live!, Head Office, Tucker: The Man and His Dream, New York Stories (Life Without Zoe), The Godfather Part III.
TELEVISION: Cable specials: Fr. Guido Sarducci Goes to College, The Vatican Inquirer—The Pope Tour.

NOYCE, PHILIP: Director. b. Griffith, New South Wales, Australia, Apr. 27, 1950. Began making films at school and university. Made first short film at age 15: Better to Reign in Hell. 1980 became part-time mgr., Sydney Filmmaker's Co-operative and in 1973 was selected for Australian Natl. Film School in Sydney, for year-long training prog. which resulted shorts Good Afternoon, Carvan Park, Castor and Pollux, God Knows Why But It Works, and 60-minute film Backroads.
PICTURES: Backroads (also prod., s.p.), Newsfront (also s.p.; Australian Academy Awards for Best Director & Screenplay, 1978), Heatwave (also co-s.p.), Echoes of Paradise, Dead Calm, Blind Fury, Patriot Games, Sliver (also cameo).
TELEVISION: *Mini-Series*: Dismissal, Cowra Breakout. *Episodes*: The Hitchhiker, Nightmare Cafe.

NUREYEV, RUDOLF: Dancer, Actor. b. Razdolnaia, Russia, Mar. 17, 1938. e. Leningrad Ballet Sch. Mem. Kirov Ballet 1955–61. Naturalized Austrian. Asked for and granted political asylum in 1961 in Paris while performing with Kirov Ballet. Joined Marquis de Cuevas Ballet Co., 1961. Debut Feb. 1962 with Royal Ballet, Covent Garden with Margot Fonteyn. Artistic dir. Paris Opera Ballet, 1983–. Has appeared as guest artist with 25 major cos. incl. ABT, Australian Ballet, Deutsche Opera Ballet, Dutch Natl. ballet, Natl. Ballet of Canada, etc. Received Capezio Dance Award, 1987.
PICTURES: An Evening with the Royal Ballet, Swan Lake, Romeo and Juliet, The Sleeping Beauty, Don Quixote, Valentino, Exposed.
TELEVISION: Julie Andrews Invitation to the Dance with Rudolf Nureyev.
(Died: Jan. 6, 1993)

NYKVIST, SVEN: Cinematographer. b. Moheda, Sweden, Dec. 3, 1922. e. Stockholm Photog. Sch. Asst. cameraman 1941–44.

Became internationally known through photographing most of Ingmar Bergman's pictures.
PICTURES: Sawdust and Tinsel, The Virgin Spring, Winter Light, Karin Mansdotter, The Silence, Loving Couples, Persona, Hour of the Wolf, Cries and Whispers (Acad. Award), The Dove, Black Moon, Scenes from a Marriage, The Magic Flute, Face to Face, One Day in the Life of Ivan Denisovich, The Tenant, The Serpents' Egg, Pretty Baby, Autumn Sonata, King of the Gypsies, Hurricane, Starting Over, Willie and Phil, From the Life of the Marionettes, The Postman Always Rings Twice, Cannery Row, Fanny and Alexander (Acad. Award), Swann in Love, The Tragedy of Carmen, After the Rehearsal, Agnes of God, Dream Lover, The Sacrifice, The Unbearable Lightness of Being, Katinka, Another Woman, New York Stories (Oedipus Wrecks), Crimes and Misdemeanors, The Ox (dir., co-s.p. only), Chaplin, Sleepless in Seattle, With Honors.
TELEVISION: Nobody's Child.

O

O'BRIAN, HUGH: Actor. r.n. Hugh C. Krampe. b. Rochester, NY, Apr. 19, 1930; U. of Cincinnati, UCLA. U.S. Marine Corps, where at age 18 he served as youngest drill instructor in Marine Corps history. Actor, stock cos.; actor with many m.p. cos. Founder, chmn. and C.E.O.: Hugh O'Brian Youth Foundation, 1958; Nat'l Chmn., Cystic Fibrosis Research Foundation 1969–74; Co-founder and pres. Thalians 1955–58; Founder Hugh O'Brian Annual Acting Awards at UCLA, 1962.
PICTURES: Rocketship X-M, The Return of Jesse James, Never Fear, Vengeance Valley, Fighting Coast Guard, Little Big Horn, On the Loose, The Cimarron Kid, Red Ball Express, The Battle of Apache Pass, Sally and Saint Anne, Son of Ali Baba, The Raiders, The Lawless Breed, Meet Me at the Fair, Seminole, Man from the Alamo, Back to God's Country, The Stand at Apache River, Saskatchewan, Fireman Save My Child, Drums Across the River, Broken Lance, There's No Business Like Show Business, White Feather, The Twinkle in God's Eye, Brass Legend, The Fiend Who Walked the West, Alias Jesse James (cameo), Come Fly with Me, Love Has Many Faces, In Harm's Way, Ten Little Indians, Ambush Bay, Africa—Texas Style!, Killer Force, The Shootist, Game of Death, Doin' Time on Planet Earth, Twins.
TELEVISION: *Series*: The Life and Legend of Wyatt Earp, Search. *Specials*: Hallmark Hall of Fame, Dial M for Murder, A Punt a Pass and a Prayer, Playhouse 90, G.E. Theatre, Fireside Theatre, It's a Man's World. *Movies*: Wild Women, Harpy, Probe (a.k.a. Search), Murder on Flight 502, Benny & Barney: Las Vegas Undercover, Fantasy Island, Murder at the World Series, Cruise Into Terror, The Seekers, Gunsmoke: The Last Apache, The Gambler Returns: Luck of the Draw.
THEATER: Bdwy Plays: Destry Rides Again, First Love, Guys and Dolls. National co. of Cactus Flower, Music Man, Rainmaker, Plaza Suite.

O'BRIEN, LIAM: Writer. b. New York, NY, March, 1913. e. Fordham U., Manhattan Coll., A.B., 1935. Author B'way play Remarkable Mr. Pennypacker, 1953.
PICTURES: Chain Lightning, Redhead and the Cowboy, Of Men and Music, Diplomatic Courier, Here Comes the Groom, The Stars Are Singing, Young at Heart.

O'BRIEN, MARGARET: Actress. r.n. Angela Maxine O'Brien. Los Angeles, CA, Jan. 15, 1938. Screen debut at 3 in Babes on Broadway (1941). Awarded special Acad. Award as best child actress, 1944. Voted one of ten best money-making stars in Motion Picture Herald-Fame Poll 1945–46.
PICTURES: Babes on Broadway (debut, 1941), Journey for Margaret, Dr. Gillespie's Criminal Case, Lost Angel, Thousands Cheer, Madame Curie, Jane Eyre, The Canterville Ghost, Meet Me in St. Louis, Music for Millions, Our Vines Have Tender Grapes, Bad Bascomb, Three Wise Fools, Unfinished Dance, Tenth Avenue Angel, The Big City, The Secret Garden, Little Women, Her First Romance, Two Persons Eyes (Jap.), Agente S3S Operazione Uranio (It.), Glory, Heller in Pink Tights, Anabelle Lee, Diabolic Wedding, Amy.
TELEVISION: *Guest*: Marcus Welby (1972). *Movies*: Death in Space, Split Second to an Epitaph, Testimony of Two Men.

O'BRIEN, VIRGINIA: Actress. b. Los Angeles, CA, Apr. 18, 1919. Singer, comedienne with a distinctive dead-pan delivery. On stage in Meet the People. 1990, performed at London Palladium.
PICTURES: Hullabaloo (debut, 1940), The Big Store, Lady Be Good, Ringside Maisie, Ship Ahoy, Panama Hattie, DuBarry Was a Lady, Thousands Cheer, Meet the People, Two Girls and a Sailor, The Harvey Girls, Ziegfeld Follies, Till Clouds Roll By, The Showoff, Merton of the Movies, Francis in the Navy, Gus.

O'CONNELL, JACK: Producer, Director, Writer, Lyricist. b. Boston, MA. B.A. Princeton U., M.B.A. Harvard Business Sch. After

being a creative group head in all media and doing 500 TV commercials working with Fellini on La Dolce Vita, then asst. director to Antonioni on L'Avventura.
PICTURES: Writer-producer-director Greenwich Village Story, Revolution, Christa (aka Swedish Flygirls), Up the Girls Means Three Cheers for Them All. Our 20th Century Revolution. Features have represented U.S. by invitation at Cannes, Locarno, Berlin, Venice and Leningrad Film Festivals.

O'CONNOR, CARROLL: Actor. b. New York, NY, Aug. 2, 1924. e. University Coll., Dublin; U. of Montana. Three years with Dublin's Gate Theatre, then N.Y. where stage credits include Ulysses in Nighttown, Playboy of the Western World, The Big Knife, Brothers, Home Front.
PICTURES: Fever in the Blood (debut, 1960), Parrish, By Love Possessed, Lad: A Dog, Belle Sommers, Lonely Are the Brave, Cleopatra, In Harm's Way, What Did You Do in the War Daddy?, Hawaii, Not With My Wife You Don't, Warning Shot, Point Blank, Waterhole No. 3, The Devil's Brigade, For Love of Ivy, Death of a Gunfighter, Marlowe, Kelly's Heroes, Doctors' Wives, Law and Disorder.
TELEVISION: Series: All in the Family (4 Emmy Awards; later retitled Archie Bunker's Place), In the Heat of the Night (Emmy Award, 1989). Guest: US Steel Hour, Armstrong Circle Theatre, Kraft Theatre. Special: Of Thee I Sing. Movies: Fear No Evil, The Last Hurrah (also writer), Brass, Convicted, The Father Clements Story.
AUTHOR: Ladies of Hanover Tower (play).

O'CONNOR, DONALD: Actor. b. Chicago, IL, Aug. 28, 1925. In vaudeville with family and Sons o' Fun (Syracuse, N.Y.) before screen debut 1938 in Sing You Sinners; return to vaudeville 1940–41, then resumed screen career with What's Cookin'?, 1942. Entered armed services, 1943. Star of Tomorrow, 1943.
PICTURES: Sing You Sinners (debut, 1938), Sons of the Legion, Men With Wings, Tom Sawyer Private Detective, Unmarried, Death of a Champion, Million Dollar Legs, Night Work, On Your Toes, Beau Geste, Private Buckaroo, Give Out Sisters, Get Hep to Love, When Johnny Comes Marching Home, Strictly in the Groove, It Comes Up Love, Mr. Big, Top Man, Chip Off the Old Block, Patrick the Great, Follow the Boys, The Merry Monahans, Bowery to Broadway, This Is the Life, Something in the Wind, Are You With It?, Feudin' Fussin' and a-Fightin'. Yes Sir That's My Baby, Francis, Curtain Call at Cactus Creek, The Milkman, Double Crossbones, Francis Goes to the Races, Singin' in the Rain, Francis Goes to West Point, I Love Melvin, Call Me Madam, Francis Covers the Big Town, Walking My Baby Back Home, Francis Joins the WACS, There's No Business Like Show Business, Francis in the Navy, Anything Goes, The Buster Keaton Story, Cry for Happy, The Wonders of Aladdin, That Funny Feeling, That's Entertainment, Ragtime, Pandemonium, A Time to Remember, Toys.
TELEVISION: Series: Colgate Comedy Hour, 1951–54 (Emmy Award 1954; also Voted best TV performer, M.P. Daily poll, 1953), The Donald O'Connor Texaco Show, The Donald O'Connor Show (synd.). Movie: Alice in Wonderland.

O'CONNOR, GLYNNIS: Actress. b. New York, NY, Nov. 19, 1955. Daughter of ABC News prod. Daniel O'Connor and actress Lenka Peterson. e. State U., NY at Purchase. Stage includes Domestic Issues (Circle Rep., NY, 1983), The Taming of the Shrew (Great Lakes Shakespeare Fest.), The Seagull (Mirror Rep.).
PICTURES: Jeremy (debut, 1973), Baby Blue Marine, Ode to Billy Joe, Kid Vengeance, California Dreaming, Those Lips Those Eyes, Night Crossing, Melanie, Johnny Dangerously.
TELEVISION: Series: Sons and Daughters. Mini-series: Black Beauty. Movies: The Chisholms, Someone I Touched, All Together Now, The Boy in the Plastic Bubble, Little Mo, My Kidnapper, My Love, The Fighter, Love Leads the Way, Why Me?, Sins of the Father, The Deliberate Stranger, To Heal a Nation.

O'CONNOR, PAT: Director. b. Ardmore, Ireland, 1943. After working in London at odd jobs (putting corks in wine bottles, paving roads), came to U.S. e. UCLA, B.A. Studied film and TV at Ryerson Institute in Toronto. 1970, trainee prod., dir. with Radio Telefis Eireann. 1970–78 prod. and dir. over 45 TV features and current affairs documentaries. (The Four Roads, The Shankhill, Kiltyclogher, One of Ourselves, Night in Ginitia). A Ballroom of Romance won British Acad. Award (1981).
PICTURES: Cal, (1984), A Month in the Country, Stars and Bars, The January Man, Fools of Fortune.

O'DONNELL, CHRIS: Actor. b. Winetka, IL, 1970.
PICTURES: Men Don't Leave (debut, 1990), Fried Green Tomatoes, Blue Sky, School Ties, Scent of a Woman, The Three Musketeers.

O'HARA, CATHERINE: Actress, Writer, Director. b. Toronto, Canada, Mar. 4, 1954. Professional debut in 1974 with

Toronto's Second City. Co-founder of SCTV in 1976 (Emmy and Canadian Nellie Awards for writing).
PICTURES: Nothing Personal, Rock & Rule (voice), After Hours, Heartburn, Beetlejuice, Dick Tracy, Betsy's Wedding, Home Alone, Little Vegas, There Goes the Neighborhood, Home Alone 2: Lost in New York.
TELEVISION: Series: SCTV, Steve Allen Comedy Hour, SCTV Network 90. Guest: Trying Times (Get a Job), Comic Relief, Dream On (also dir.).

O'HARA, GERRY: Director. b. Boston-Lincs., England 1924. e. St. Mary's Catholic Sch., Boston. Junior Reporter Boston Guardian. Entered industry in 1942 with documentaries and propaganda subjects. Dir. debut 1963 That Kind of Girl.
PICTURES: Game for Three Lovers, Pleasure Girls (also s.p.), Maroc 7, Love in Amsterdam, All the Right Noises (also s.p.), Leopard in the Snow, The Bitch, Fanny Hill, The Mummy Lives (also co-s.p.). Writer: Ten Little Indians, Havoc in Chase County, Phantom of the Opera, De Sade's Nightmare.
TELEVISION: The Avengers, Man in a Suitcase, Journey into the Unknown, The Professionals (story editor, writer), Special Squad (story consultant), Cats Eyes (exec. story editor), Operation Julie (writer; mini-series), Sherlock Holmes & The Leading Lady, Sherlock Holmes & The Incident at Victoria Falls (co-writer).

O'HARA, MAUREEN: Actress. r.n., Maureen FitzSimons. b. Dublin. Aug. 17, 1921. Abbey Sch. of Acting. Won numerous prizes for elocution. Under contract to Erich Pommer-Charles Laughton. Co-starred, Abbey & Repertory Theatre: U.S. film debut in Jamaica Inn (1939).
PICTURES: Kicking the Moon Around (debut, 1938), My Irish Molly, Jamaica Inn, Hunchback of Notre Dame, A Bill of Divorcement, Dance Girl Dance, They Met in Argentina, How Green Was My Valley, To the Shores of Tripoli, Ten Gentlemen from West Point, The Black Swan, The Immortal Sergeant, This Land is Mine, The Fallen Sparrow, Buffalo Bill, The Spanish Main, Sentimental Journey, Do You Love Me?, Miracle on 34th Street, Sinbad the Sailor, Foxes of Harrow, Sitting Pretty, Woman's Secret, Forbidden Street, Father Was a Fullback, Bagdad, Comanche Territory, Tripoli, Rio Grande, At Sword's Point, Flame of Araby, Quiet Man, Kangaroo, Against All Flags, Redhead from Wyoming, War Arrow, Fire over Africa, Magnificent Matador, Lady Godiva, Long Gray Line, Lisbon, Everything But the Truth, Wings of Eagles, Our Man in Havana, The Parent Trap, The Deadly Companions, Mr. Hobbs Takes a Vacation, McLintock, Spencer's Mountain, The Battle of the Villa Fiorita, The Rare Breed, How Do I Love Thee, Big Jake, Only the Lonely.
TELEVISION: Movie: The Red Pony. Specials: Mrs. Miniver, Scarlet Pimpernel, Spellbound, High Button Shoes, Who's Afraid of Mother Goose.

O'HERLIHY, DAN: Actor. b. Wexford, Ireland, May 1, 1919. e. National U. of Ireland (Bachelor of Architecture). Actor with Abbey Theatre, Dublin Gate, Longford Prod.; announcer on Radio Eireann; on Broadway in The Ivy Green. Extensive TV from 1952. Nom. Acad. Award, Best Actor, 1954.
PICTURES: Odd Man Out, Kidnapped, Larceny, Macbeth, The Iroquois Trail, The Blue Veil, The Desert Fox, The Highwayman, Soldiers Three, At Swords Point, Invasion U.S.A., Operation Secret, Actors and Sin, Sword of Venus, Adventures of Robinson Crusoe, Black Shield of Falworth, Bengal Brigade, The Purple Mask, Virgin Queen, City After Midnight, Home Before Dark, Imitation of Life, The Young Land, The Night Fighters, One Foot in Hell, King of the Roaring 20s, The Cabinet of Caligari, Fail Safe, The Big Cube, 100 Rifles, Waterloo, The Carey Treatment, The Tamarind Seed, MacArthur, Halloween III: The Season of the Witch, Last Starfighter, The Whoopee Boys, Robocop, The Dead, Robocop 2.
TELEVISION: Series: The Travels of Jamie McPheeters (1953–54), The Long Hot Summer, Hunter's Moon, The Whiz Kids, Man Called Sloane, Twin Peaks. Mini-series: QB VII, Jennie: Lady Randolph Churchill, Nancy Astor. Movies: The People, Deadly Game, Woman on the Run, Good Against Evil. BBC: Colditz, The Secret Servant, Artemis, The Last Day, Jennie, Nancy Astor. Guest: The Equalizer, L.A. Law, Murder She Wrote, Ray Bradbury Theatre, Father Dowling.

OHLMEYER, DONALD W. JR.: Executive, Producer, Director. b. New Orleans, LA, Feb. 3, 1945. e. U. of Notre Dame, B.A. (Communications), 1967. Producer and director at both ABC and NBC. Formed Ohlmeyer Communications Company, 1982 (diversified prod. and dist. of entertainment and sports prog.). Assoc. dir., ABC Sports, NY 1967–70; director, ABC Sports, 1971–72 (dir. 1972 Olympic Games); prod.: ABC Sports, NY 1972–77 (prod. and dir. 1976 Winter and Summer Olympics; prod. ABC's Monday Night Football, 1972–76); exec. prod.: NBC Sports, NY 1977–82 (exec. prod., 1980 Olympics, The World Series, The Super Bowl). Special Bulletin (exec. prod.), John Denver's Christmas in Aspen (exec. prod.). Chmn. and CEO, Ohlmeyer Communications Co., LA, 1982–present. Recipient of 14 Emmy Awards,

Humanitas Prize, Award for Excellence, National Film Board. Member, Directors Guild of America.

TELEVISION: Heroes of Desert Storm (dir.), Disney's Christmas on Ice (dir.). *Series*: Lifestories (dir./exec. prod.). *Movies*: Cold Sassy Tree (exec. prod.), Crazy in Love (exec. prod.).

O'HORGAN, TOM: Director. b. Chicago, IL, May 3, 1926. e. DePaul U. At age 12 wrote opera, Doom on the Earth. Is also musician, singer, actor. Responsible for developing many revolutionary off-off Bdwy. artistic innovations in such productions as The Maids, Tom Paine, Futz.

PICTURES: Futz, Rhinoceros.

STAGE: Broadway: Hair, Lenny, Jesus Christ, Superstar, Inner City, Dude.

O'KEEFE, MICHAEL: Actor. b. Larchmont, NY, April 24, 1955. e. NYU. Amer. Acad of Dramatic Arts. m. singer Bonnie Raitt. Co-founder, Colonnades Theatre Lab, NY. On Bdwy. stage in Streamers, Mass Appeal (Theatre World Award) and Fifth of July. Off-Bdwy: Killdeer (NYSF), Moliere in Spite of Himself, Christmas on Mars, Short Eyes.

PICTURES: Gray Lady Down (debut, 1978), The Great Santini (Acad. Award nom.), Caddyshack, Split Image, Nate and Hayes, Finders Keepers, The Slugger's Wife, The Whoopee Boys, Ironweed, Out of the Rain, Me and Veronica.

TELEVISION: *Series*: Against the Law. *Movies*: The Lindbergh Kidnapping Case, Friendly Persuasion, Panache, The Dark Secret of Harvest Home, A Rumor of War, Unholy Matrimony, Bridge to Silence, Disaster at Silo 7, Too Young to Die?, In the Best Interest of the Child, Fear.

OLDMAN, GARY: Actor. b. New Cross, South London, Eng., March 21, 1958. Won scholarship to Rose Bruford Drama College, (B.A. Theatre Arts) after studying with Greenwich Young People's Theatre. Acted with Theatre Royal, York and joined touring theatre co. Then in 1980 appeared with Glasgow Citizens Theatre in Massacre at Paris, Chinchilla, Desperado Corner, A Waste of Time (also touring Europe and South America). London stage: Minnesota Moon, Summit Conference, Rat in the Skull, Women Beware Women, The War Plays, Real Dreams, The Desert Air, Serious Money (Royal Shakespeare Co.), The Pope's Wedding (Time Out's Fringe Award, best newcomer 1985–86; British Theatre Assc. Drama Mag. Award, Best Actor 1985).

PICTURES: Sid and Nancy (Evening Standard Film Award for best newcomer), Prick Up Your Ears, Track 29, We Think The World of You, Criminal Law, Chattahoochee, State of Grace, Rosencrantz and Guildenstern Are Dead, Exile, Before and After Death, JFK, Bram Stoker's Dracula, True Romance, Romeo is Bleeding.

TELEVISION: Remembrance, Meantime, Honest Decent and True, Rat in the Skull, The Firm, Heading Home., Fallen Angels.

OLIN, KEN: Actor, Director. b. Chicago, IL, July 30, 1954. e. Univ. of PA. m. actress Patricia Wettig. Studied acting with Warren Robertson and Stella Adler. Made Off-Bdwy deput in Taxi Tales, 1978.

TELEVISION: *Series*: The Bay City Blues, Hill Street Blues, Falcon Crest, thirtysomething (also dir.). *Movies*: Women at West Point, Flight 90: Disaster on the Potomac, There Must Be a Pony, Tonight's the Night, Cop Killer, A Stoning in Fulham County, Goodnight Sweet Wife: A Murder in Boston, The Broken Cord (dir. only), Doing Time on Maple Drive (dir. only), Telling Secrets. *Guest*: Murder She Wrote, Hotel, The Hitchhiker.

PICTURES: Ghost Story, Queen's Logic, Myth of the White Wolf (dir.).

OLIN, LENA: Actress. b. Stockholm, Sweden, 1955. Member of the Royal Dramatic Theatre in Stockholm. Daughter of actor-director Stig Olin.

PICTURES: The Adventures of Picasso, Karleken, Fanny and Alexander, Grasanklingar, After the Rehearsal, Pa live och dod, Friends, The Unbearable Lightness of Being, S/Y Gladjen, Enemies a Love Story (Acad. Award nom.), Havana, Mr. Jones, Romeo is Bleeding.

THEATRE: NY: Miss Julie.

OLMI, ERMANNO: Director. b. Bergamo, Italy, July 24, 1931. e. Accademia d'Arte Drammatica, Milan. Worked as a clerk for an electric company Edisonvolta 1949–52, until 1952 when he began directing theatrical and cinematic activities sponsored by co. 1952–61, directed or supervised over 40 short 16mm and 35mm documentary films. 1959 first feature film, semi-doc. Time Stood Still. With other friends and Tullio Kezich formed prod. co. 22 December S.P.A., 1961. 1982, Helped found Hypothesis Cinema, a sch. for aspiring dirs.

PICTURES: The Sound of Trumpets (Ge Posto), The Fiances, A Man Named John, One Fine Day, During the Summer, The Circumstance, The Tree of the Wood Clogs (Palm d'or, Cannes, 1978), Camminacammina, Lunga Vita Alla Signora, La Leggenda Del Santo Bevitore, Il Segreto Del

Bosco Vecchio. Documenatries: Artigiani Veneti, Lungo II Fiume.

TELEVISION: The Scavenger.

OLMOS, EDWARD JAMES: Actor. b. East Los Angeles, CA, February 24, 1947. e. East Los Angeles City Coll., CA State U. Started as rock singer with group Eddie James and the Pacific Ocean. By the early 1970s acted in small roles on Kojak and Hawaii Five-O. 1978 starred in Luis Valdez's musical drama Zoot Suit at Mark Taper Forum (L.A. Drama Critics Circle Award, 1978), later on Bdwy (Theatre World Award, Tony nom.), and in film version. Formed YOY Productions with director Robert Young. Numerous awards for humanitarian work.

PICTURES: Aloha Bobby and Rose (debut, 1975), Alambrista!, Virus, Wolfen, Zoot Suit, Blade Runner, The Ballad of Gregorio Cortez (also assoc. prod., composer and musical adaptor), Saving Grace, Stand and Deliver (also co-prod.; Acad. Award nom., Golden Globe nom., for best actor), Triumph of the Spirit, Talent for the Game, American Me (also dir., co-prod.), Roosters.

TELEVISION: *Movies*: Evening in Byzantium, 300 Miles for Stephanie. *Specials*: Sequin, Y.E.S. Inc. *Series*: Miami Vice (Golden Globe & Emmy Awards, supp. actor; also dir. episodes). *Mini-series*: Mario Puzo's The Fortunate Pilgrim.

O'LOUGHLIN, GERALD STUART: Actor. b. New York, NY, Dec. 23, 1921. e. Blair Acad., Lafayette Coll., U. of Rochester, Neighborhood Playhouse. U.S. Marine, W.W.II.

THEATRE: Broadway: Streetcar, Shadow of a Gunman, Dark at the Top of the Stairs, A Touch of the Poet, Cook for Mr. General, One Flew Over the Cuckoo's Nest, Calculated Risk, Lovers and Other Strangers. Off Broadway: Who'll Save the Plowboy (Obie Award), Harry Noon and Night, Machinal.

PICTURES: Lovers and Lollipops, Cop Hater, A Hatful of Rain, Ensign Pulver, A Fine Madness, In Cold Blood, Ice Station Zebra, Desperate Characters, The Organization, The Valachi Papers, Twilight's Last Gleaming, Frances, Crimes of Passion, City Heat, Quicksilver.

TELEVISION: *Movies*: Murder At The World Series, Something For Joey, Wheels, Blind Ambition, Women In White, Wilson's Reward, A Matter of Life & Death, Under Siege, Perry Mason: The Case of the Notorious Nun, Child's Cry (aka Who'll Hear The Child Cry), Crash (of Flight 401), Detour, Pleasure Palace, In the Arms of a Killer. *Mini-Series*: Wheels, Roots: The Next Generations, The Blue and the Gray. *Series*: Men At Law (aka Storefront Lawyers), The Rookies, Automan, Our House. *Guest*: Alcoa Premiere, Armstrong Circle Theatre, Philco-Goodyear, Danger, Suspense, The Defenders, For the People, Ben Casey, Dr. Kildare, 12 O'Clock High, Going My Way, Naked City, Quincy M.E., Gunsmoke, FBI, Green Hornet, The Senator, Medical Center, Ironsides, Mission Impossible, Mannix, Judd For The Defense, Hawaii 5 O, Cades County, Cannon, Room 222, Charlie's Angels, Quincy, M*A*S*H, Trapper John, Fame, Matt Houston, T.J. Hooker, Too Close for Comfort, Riptide, Murder She Wrote, Highway to Heaven, Dirty Dancing, Equal Justice, many others. Special: My Luke and I.

OLSON, DALE C: Executive. b. Fargo, ND, Feb. 20, 1934. e. Portland State Coll., OR. Owner, Dale C. Olson & Associates; formerly sn. v.p & pres., m.p. div., Rogers & Cowan public relations. Journalist on Oregonian newspaper, West Coast editor, Boxoffice Magazine, 1958–1960; critic and reporter, Daily Variety, 1960–1966; director of publicity, Mirisch Corporation, 1966–1968; Rogers & Cowan, 1968–1985. Past pres., Hollywood Press Club, awarded Bob Yaeger and Les Mason award by Publicists Guild; v.p. Diamond Circle, City of Hope; delegate for U.S. to Manila International Film Festival. Chmn. public rltns. coordin. committee & member natl. bd. of trustees, Acad. of Mo. Pic Arts & Sciences, 1989–91. Chmn. Western Council, Actors Fund of America, 1991.

OLSON, JAMES: Actor. b. Evanston, IL, Oct. 8, 1930. e. Northwestern U.

THEATRE: NY: The Young and the Beautiful, Romulus, The Cinese Prime Minister, J.B., Slapstick Tragedy, Three Sisters, Sin of Pat Muldoon, Winter's Tale, Of Love Remembered, Twelve Dreams.

PICTURES: The Sharkfighters, The Strange One, Rachel Rachel, Moon Zero Two, The Andromeda Strain, The Groundstar Conspiracy, The Mafu Cage, Ragtime, Amityville II: The Possession, Commando, Rachel River.

TELEVISION: *Movies*: Paper Man, Incident on a Dark Street, Manhunter, A Tree Grows in Brooklyn, The Sex Symbol, The Family Nobody Wanted, Someone I Touched, Man on the Outside, Strange New World, Law and Order, The Spell, Moviola: The Silent Years, Cave-In!, The Parade. *Specials*: Missiles of October, Vince Lombardi Story, Court-Martial of Geoge Armstrong Custer.

OLSON, NANCY: Actress. b. Milwaukee, WI, July 14, 1929. e. U. of Wisconsin, UCLA. No prof. experience prior to films.

PICTURES: Canadian Pacific (debut, 1949), Sunset Boulevard (Acad. Award nom.), Union Station, Mr. Music, Submarine Command, Force of Arms, Big Jim McLain, So Big, Boy

from Oklahoma, Battle Cry, Pollyanna, The Absent-Minded Professor, Son of Flubber, Smith!, Snowball Express, Airport 1975, Making Love.
TELEVISION: Series: Kingston: Confidential, Paper Dolls. Special: High Tor.

O'NEAL, PATRICK: Actor. b. Ocala, FL, Sept. 26, 1927. e. U. of Florida; Neighborhood Playhouse. In stock cos. before N.Y. TV, 1951. Has appeared in over 300 television shows (live and film).
PICTURES: The Mad Magician, The Black Shield of Falworth, From the Terrace, A Matter of Morals, The Cardinal, In Harm's Way, King Rat, Chamber of Horrors, A Fine Madness, Alvarez Kelly, Matchless, Assignment to Kill, Where Were You When the Lights Went Out?, The Secret Life of an American Wife, Castle Keep, The Kremlin Letter, Stiletto, El Condor, Corky, The Way We Were, Silent Night Bloody Night, The Stepford Wives, Like Father Like Son, New York Stories (Life Lessons), Q & A, Alice, For the Boys, Under Siege.
TELEVISION: Movies: Companions in Nightmare, Cool Million, Crossfire, Killer Who Wouldn't Die, Twin Detectives, Deadliest Season, Sharon: Portrait of a Mistress, The Last Hurrah, To Kill a Cop, Like Mom Like Me, Make Me an Offer, Fantasies, Sprague, Perry Mason Returns, Perry Mason: The Case of the Skin-Deep Scandal. Series: Dick and the Duchess, Diagnosis: Unknown, Kaz, Emerald Point NAS. Mini-Series: The Moneychangers, War Chronicles, Maigret.

O'NEAL, RON: Actor. b. Utica, NY, Sept. 1, 1937. e. Ohio State U. Spent 9 yrs. at Karamu House in Cleveland (inter-racial theatre) from 1957 to 1966, acting in 40 plays. 1967–68 spent in N.Y. teaching acting in Harlem. Appeared in all-black revue 1968, The Best of Broadway, then in summer stock. Acted off-Bdwy in American Pastorale and The Mummer's Play. 1970 joined the Public Theatre. Break came with No Place To be Somebody, which won him the Obie, Clarence Derwent, Drama Desk and Theatre World Awards.
PICTURES: Move, The Organization, Super Fly, Super Fly TNT (also dir., story), The Master Gunfighter, Brothers, The Master Gunfighter, Brothers, A Force of One, When a Stranger Calls, The Final Countdown, St. Helens, Red Dawn, Mercenary Fighters, Hero and the Terror, Up Against the Wall (also dir.).
TELEVISION: Series: Bring 'em Back Alive, The Equalizer. Mini-Series: North and South. Movies: Freedom Road, Brave New World, Guyana Tragedy: The Story of Jim Jones, Sophisticated Gents, Playing with Fire, North Beach and Rawhide, As Summers Die.
STAGE: Tiny Alice, The Dream of Monkey Mountain.

O'NEAL, RYAN: Actor. r.n. Patrick Ryan O'Neal. b. Los Angeles, CA, April 20, 1941. Parents, screenwriter-novelist, Charles O'Neal, and actress Patricia Callaghan. Father of actress Tatum O'Neal and actor Griffin O'Neal. Boxer, L.A. Golden Gloves, 1956 & 57. Began as stand-in, then stunt man, then actor in Tales of the Vikings series, in Germany, 1959; freelanced in Hollywood; Screen Gems Pilots, Donny Dru, Our Man Higgins.
PICTURES: The Big Bounce (debut, 1969), The Games, Love Story (Acad. Award nom.), Wild Rovers, What's Up Doc?, Paper Moon, The Thief Who Came to Dinner, Barry Lyndon, Nickelodeon, A Bridge Too Far, The Driver, Oliver's Story, The Main Event, So Fine, Green Ice, Partners, Irreconcilable Differences, Fever Pitch, Tough Guys Don't Dance, Chances Are.
TELEVISION: Series: Empire (1962–63), Peyton Place (1964–69), Good Sports. Movies: Love Hate Love, Small Sacrifices, The Man Upstairs. Special: Liza Minnelli: A Triple Play. Guest: Dobie Gillis, Leave It to Beaver, My Three Sons, Perry Mason. Pilot: 1775.

O'NEAL, TATUM: Actress. b. Los Angeles, CA, Nov. 5, 1963. Daughter of Ryan O'Neal and Joanna Moore. NY stage debut 1992 in A Terrible Beauty.
PICTURES: Paper Moon (debut, 1973; Acad. Award, supp. actress), The Bad News Bears, Nickelodeon, International Velvet, Little Darlings, Circle of Two, Certain Fury, Little Noises.
TELEVISION: Movie: Woman on the Run: The Lawrencia Bembenek Story. Special: 15 and Getting Straight. Guest: Cher, Faerie Tale Theatre (Goldilocks and the Three Bears).

O'NEIL, THOMAS F.: Executive. b. Kansas City, MO, Apr. 18, 1915. e. Holy Cross Coll., 1933–37. Employed by General Tire and Rubber Co., 1937–41; U.S. Coast Guard, 1941–46; v.p., dir., Yankee Network, Boston, 1948–51; pres. chmn. of bd. RKO General, Inc., since 1952. Arranged purchase RKO Radio by General Teleradio, Inc. from Howard Hughes, July, 1955; chairman of the Board, RKO General, Inc., dir., General Tire & Rubber Co.

O'NEILL, ED: Actor. b. Youngstown, OH, Apr. 12, 1946. e. Ohio Univ., Youngstown State. Taught social studies in Youngstown prior to becoming an actor. Made NY stage debut Off-Off-

Bdwy in Requeim for a Heavyweight at SoHo Rep. Theatre. Bdwy debut in Knockout.
TELEVISION: Series: Married . . . With Children. Pilot: Farrell for the People. Movies: The Day the Women Got Even, Popeye Doyle, Right to Die, The Whereabouts of Jenny.
PICTURES: Deliverance, Cruising, The Dogs of War, Disorganized Crime, K-9, The Adventures of Ford Fairlane, Sibling Rivalry, Dutch, Wayne's World, Blue Chips.

O'NEILL, JENNIFER: Actress. b. Rio de Janeiro, Brazil, Feb. 20, 1949. e. Dalton Sch. Model before entering films. Spokeswoman: CoverGirl cosmetics. Pres., Point of View Productions and Management.
PICTURES: Rio Lobo, Summer of '42, Such Good Friends, The Carey Treatment, Glass Houses, Lady Ice, The Reincarnation of Peter Proud, Whiffs, Caravans, The Psychic, The Innocent, A Force of One, Cloud Dancer, Steel, Scanners, Committed, I Love N.Y., Love is Like That, Invasion of Privacy, The Gentle People.
TELEVISION: Series: Bare Essence, Cover Up. Movies: Love's Savage Fury, The Other Victim, Chase, Perry Mason: The Case of the Shooting Star, The Red Spider, Glory Days, Full Exposure: the Sex Tapes Scandal, Personals, Perfect Family. Mini-series: A.D.

ONTKEAN, MICHAEL: Actor. b. Vancouver, British Columbia, Canada, Jan. 24, 1950. e. U. of New Hampshire. Son of Leonard and Muriel Cooper Ontkean, actors. Acting debut at 4 with father's rep. theater. Child actor with Stratford Shakespeare Fest., CBC and Natl Film Bd. Attended coll. 2 years on hockey scholarship. Theater: Public Theatre, NY, Williamstown Theatre Fest., Mark Taper Lab, The Kitchen, Soho.
PICTURES: The Peace Killers, Pick Up on 101, Necromancy, Hot Summer Weekend, Slap Shot, Voices, Willie and Phil, Making Love, Just the Way You Are, The Allnighter, Maid to Order, Clara's Heart, Street Justice, Cold Front, Bye Bye Blues, Postcards from the Edge.
TELEVISION: Series: The Rookies, Twin Peaks. Movies: The Rookies (pilot), The Blood of Others, Kids Don't Tell, The Right of the People, In Defense of a Married Man, In a Child's Name, Legacy of Lies.

OPATOSHU, DAVID: Actor. b. New York, NY, Jan. 30, 1918. e. Morris H.S. U.S. Army, 1942–46; played character roles with The Group Theatre at 21; appeared on Broadway.
THEATRE: Me and Molly, Once More With Feeling, Silk Stockings, The Reclining Figure, The Wall, Bravo Giovanni, Does a Tiger Wear a Neck-Tie?
PICTURES: Cimmarron, Naked City, The Brothers Karamazov, Exodus, Act of Mercy, Best of Enemies, Torn Curtain, Enter Laughing, The Fixer, Romance of a Horse Thief, Public Enemy No. 1, The Light Ahead, Forty Days of Musa Dagh, Beyond Evil, In Search of Historic Jesus.
TELEVISION: Studio One, Playhouse 90, Philco Playhouse, U.S. Steel Hour, Alfred Hitchcock Presents. Movies: Conspiracy of Terror, Masada, Raid on Entebbe, Under Siege, Francis Gary Powers, The Smugglers, Conspiracy "Chicago 8." Guest: Gabriel's Fire (Emmy Award, 1991).

OPHULS, MARCEL: Director, Writer. b. Frankfurt-am-Main, Germany, Nov. 1, 1927. Born Hans Marcel Oppenheim. Son of German director Max Ophuls. e. Occidental Coll., U. of California, Berkeley, Sorbonne (philosophy). Family moved to France, 1932, then to Hollywood, 1941. Military service with Occupation forces in Japan, 1946; performed with theater unit, Tokyo. 1951 began working in French film industry as asst. dir., using name Marcel Wall. 1956–59, radio and TV story ed., West Germany. Later worked for French TV as reporter and dir. news mag. features. 1968 doc. dir. for German TV. 1975–78 staff prod. CBS News, then ABC News.
PICTURES AND DOCUMENTARIES: Asst. dir.: Moulin Rouge (1953); Act of Love, Marianne de ma jeunesse, Lola Montes (dir. by Max Ophuls). Director and writer: Matisse; Love at 20 (German sketch); Banana Peel (co-s.p.); Munich, or Peace in Our Time (TV); The Sorrow and the Pity (Awards include: Prix de Dinard, National Society of Film Critics, New York Film Critics.) Clavigo; The Harvest of My Lai (TV); America Revisited (TV); Two Whole Days (TV); A Sense of Loss; The Memory of Justice; Hotel Terminus—the Life and Times of Klaus Barbie (Awards include: Intl. Jury Prize, Cannes; Peace prize, Berlin; Acad. Award, best documentary, 1988); November Days (TV, 1990; Brit. TV Acad. Award; German TV Award), MacArthur Fellowship 1991. Member of American Acad. of MoPic Arts & Sciences.

OPOTOWSKY, STAN: Executive. b. New Orleans, LA, Apr. 13, 1923. e. Tulane U. Served in U.S. Marine Corps as combat corr. and later joined United Press, working in New Orleans, Denver, and New York. Published own weekly newspaper in Mississippi before returning to N.Y. to join New York Post as mgr. editor and traveling natl. corr. Is also cinematographer and film editor. Joined ABC News as TV assignment editor; named asst. assignment mgr. In 1974 named dir. of opera-

261

tions for ABC News TV Documentaries. In 1975 named dir. of TV News Coverage, ABC News.
AUTHOR: TV: The Big Picture, The Longs of Louisiana, The Kennedy Government, Men Behind Bars.

O'QUINN, TERRY: Actor. b. Michigan.
PICTURES: Heaven's Gate, Without a Trace, All the Right Moves, Places in the Heart, Mrs. Soffel, Mischief, Silver Bullet, SpaceCamp, The Stepfather, Black Widow, Young Guns, Pin, Stepfather 2, Blind Fury, The Rocketeer, Prisoners of the Sun, Company Business, The Cutting Edge.
TELEVISION: Movies: FDR: The Final Year, Prisoner Without a Name Cell Without a Number, Right to Kill, Unfinished Business, An Early Frost, Stranger on My Land, Women of Valor, When the Time Comes, Perry Mason: The Case of the Desperate Deception, Son of the Morning Star, The Last to Go, Deliver Them From Evil: The Taking of Alta View, Trial: The Price of Passion, Sexual Advances, Wild Card, The Good Fight, Born Too Soon, Visions of Murder.
THEATRE: Bdwy: Foxfire, Curse of an Aching Heart. Off-Bdwy: Richard III, Groves of Academy, Total Abandon.

ORBACH, JERRY: Actor. b. Bronx, NY, Oct. 20, 1935. e. U. of Illinois, Northwestern U. Trained for stage with Herbert Berghof and Lee Strasberg. N.Y. stage debut in Threepenny Opera, 1955.
THEATER: The Fantasticks (original cast, 1960), Carnival, The Cradle Will Rock, Guys and Dolls, Scuba Duba, Promises Promises (Tony Award, 1969), 6 Rms Riv Vu, Chicago, 42nd Street.
PICTURES: Cop Hater, Mad Dog Coll, John Goldfarb Please Come Home, The Gang That Couldn't Shoot Straight, A Fan's Notes, Sentinel, Prince of the City, Brewster's Millions, F/X, The Imagemaker, Dirty Dancing, Someone to Watch Over Me, Crimes and Misdemeanors, Last Exit to Brooklyn, I Love N.Y., A Gnome Named Norm, California Casanova, Dead Women in Lingerie, Out for Justice, Toy Soldiers, Delusion, Delirious, Beauty and the Beast (voice), Straight Talk, Universal Soldier, Mr. Saturday Night, The Cemetery Club.
TELEVISION: Series: The Law and Harry McGraw. Guest: Shari Lewis Show, Jack Paar, Bob Hope Presents, Love American Style, Murder She Wrote, Kojak, Golden Girls, Hunter. Movies: An Invasion of Privacy, Out on a Limb, Love Among Thieves, In Defense of a Married Man, Broadway Bound, Quiet Killer. Mini-Series: Dream West.

ORKIN, AD: Executive. b. Jackson, MS, Dec. 7, 1922. e. U. of Mississippi. With Trans World Airlines as flt. eng. 1945–50. Previously co-owner of Orkin Amusements in Jackson. Now owner, Pike Triple Cinema in Troy, Alabama area. Operates Orkin Badge Co. & Orkin Computers Co.

O'ROURKE, JOHN J.: Executive. b. New York, NY, July 3, 1922. e. City Coll. of New York, 1950. Entered the industry 1939 Music Hall/New York. 20th Century Fox Film Corp. 1941–59, asst. to dir. of exploitation, MGM, 1960–62; asst. exploitation mgr. Astor Pictures 1962–63; exploitation mgr. 1963–67; National dir. of exploitation Avco Embassy Pictures, 1967; national co-ordinator roadshows, United Artists, 1968; asst. roadshow mgr. Universal Pictures. 1969 joined Cinemation Industries as dir. advertising, publicity and exploitation. 1974, v.p., Harry K. McWilliams Assoc. Advertising, 1977, vice pres., Benjamin Philip Associates, Inc., Advertising.

ORTEGA, KENNY: Director, Choreographer. b. Palo Alto, CA. e. American Conserv. Theatre, Canada Col. Started acting at age 13. Earned several scholarships to dance academies in San Francisco Bay area. Regional theatre roles in Oliver, Hair, The Last Sweet Days of Isaac, before staging shows for rock band The Tubes. First major tv job choreographing Cher special. Directed/choreographed concerts and/or music videos for such performers as Michael Jackson, Kiss, Elton John, Cher, Rod Stewart, Diana Ross, Madonna, Billy Joel, Oingo Boingo, Miami Sound Machine, Pointer Sisters, Toto.
PICTURES: Director/Choreographer: Newsies, Hocus Pocus. Choreographer: The Rose (asst. to Toni Basil), Xanadu, One From the Heart, St. Elmo's Fire, Pretty in Pink, Ferris Bueller's Day Off, Dirty Dancing, Salsa (also assoc. prod.), Shag.
TELEVISION: Series: Dirty Dancing (dir., choreog.), Hull High (dir., co-exec. prod., choreog.). Choreographed many specials incl. American Music Awards, Academy Awards, NAACP Awards, music specials starring Cher, Olivia Newton-John, Neil Diamond, Smokey Robinson, etc.

OSBORNE, JOHN: Dramatist. b. London, England, Dec. 12, 1929.
AUTHOR: Plays include 1956: Look Back in Anger. 1957: Epitaph for George Dillon. 1958: The Entertainer. 1959: The World of Paul Slickey. 1961: Luther. 1963: Plays for England. 1964: Inadmissible Evidence, A Patriot for Me, A Bond Honoured, Time Present, The Hotel in Amsterdam, West of Suez, Hedda Gabler (adaptn.), The Father (adaptn.).
PICTURES: Films of his plays include Look Back in Anger, The Entertainer. Film scripts: Tom Jones (Oscar, 1963), The Charge of the Light Brigade.

TELEVISION: The Right Prospectus, Very Like A Whale, A Subject of Scandal and Concern, The Gift of Friendship, Jack and Jill, You're Not Watching Me Mummy, Try a Little Tenderness.

O'SHEA, MILO: Actor. b. Dublin, Ireland, June 2, 1926. Member of Dublin Gate Theatre Co., 1944. before screen career. On Bdwy. in Staircase, Dear World, The Comedians, A Touch of the Poet, Waiting For Godot (Brooklyn Acad. of Music). Mass Appeal, My Fair Lady, Corpse!, Meet Me in St. Louis, Remembrance. London Theatre: Treasure Hunt, Glory Be, Hans Andersen, Corpse, Can-Can.
PICTURES: Carry on Cabby, Never Put It in Writing, Ulysses, Romeo and Juliet, Barbarella, The Adding Machine, The Angel Levine, Paddy, Sacco and Vanzetti, Loot, Digby: The Biggest Dog in the World, Theatre of Blood, It's Not the Size That Counts, Arabian Adventure, The Pilot, The Verdict, The Purple Rose of Cairo, The Dream Team, Opportunity Knocks, Only the Lonely, The Playboys.
TELEVISION: Series: Once a Hero. Mini-Series: QB VII, Ellis Island, The Best of Families. Movies: Two By Forsythe, Peter Lundy and the Medicine Hat Stallion, Portrait of a Rebel: Margaret Sanger, And No One Could Save Her, A Times for Miracles, Broken Vows, Angel in Green, Murder in the Heartland, The Golden Girls, Cheers, Who's the Boss, Beauty and the Beast, St. Elsewhere.

OSHIMA, NAGISA: Director, Writer. b. Kyoto, Japan, March 31, 1932. e. U. of Kyoto (law), 1954. Joined Shochiku Ofuna Studios in 1954 as asst. dir.; 1956 wrote film criticism and became editor-in-chief of film revue Eiga hihyo; 1959 promoted to director. 1962–65 worked exclusively in TV; 1962–64 made documentaries in Korea and Vietnam; 1975 formed Oshima Prods. 1976, his book of Realm of the Senses seized by police. With editor, prosecuted for obscenity, acquitted. Pres. of Directors Guild of Japan, 1980–present.
PICTURES: A Town of Love and Hope (1959); Cruel Story of Youth, The Sun's Burial; Night and Fog in Japan; The Catch, The Rebel; A Child's First Adventure; The Pleasures of the Flesh; Violence at Noon; Ban on Ninja; Death By Hanging; He Died After the War; The Ceremony; Dear Summer Sister; In the Realm of the Senses; Phantom Love; Empire of Passion; Merry Christmas, Mr. Lawrence (also s.p.); Max Mon Amour; Cruel Story of Youth.

OSMOND, DONNY: Singer, TV Host. b. Ogden, UT, Dec. 9, 1957. Seventh of 9 children, he was fifth member of family to become professional singer. (Four brothers, Alan, Wayne, Merrill and Jay, are original and present members of Osmond Bros., who originally sang barbershop quartet.) Made debut at 4 on Andy Williams Show. Has had 12 gold albums. Was co-host with sister of Donny & Marie on TV.
PICTURE: Goin' Cocoanuts (with Marie).
TELEVISION: Series: The Andy Williams Show, Donny and Marie. Movie: Wild Women of Chastity Gulch.

OSMOND, MARIE: Singer, TV Host. b. Ogden, UT, Oct. 13, 1959. Began career at age of 7 while touring with her brothers. Her first album, Paper Roses, became a gold one. Appeared as co-host with brother Donny on TV's Donny & Marie and in feature film Goin' Cocoanuts.
TELEVISION: Series: Donny and Marie, Marie, Ripley's Believe It or Not (co-host). Movies: Gift of Love, I Married Wyatt Earp, Side By Side.

O'STEEN, SAM: Editor, Director. b. Nov. 6, 1923. Entered m.p. industry 1956 as asst. to editor George Tomassini on The Wrong Man. Became full editor in 1963 on Youngblood Hawke. Directorial debut with TV film A Brand New Life, 1972.
PICTURES: Editor: Kisses for My President; Robin and the 7 Hoods; Youngblood Hawke; Marriage on the Rocks; None But the Brave; Who's Afraid of Virginia Woolf?; Cool Hand Luke; The Graduate; Rosemary's Baby; The Sterile Cuckoo (supr. ed.); Catch-22; Carnal Knowledge; Portnoy's Complaint; Day of the Dolphin; Chinatown; Straight Time; Sparkle (dir); Hurricane; Amityville II: The Possession, Silkwood; Heartburn; Nadine; Biloxi Blues; Frantic; Working Girl; A Dry White Season (co-ed.), Postcards from the Edge, Regarding Henry.
TELEVISION: Director: A Brand New Life, I Love You Goodbye, Queen of the Stardust Ballroom (DGA Award), High Risk, Look What's Happened to Rosemary's Baby, The Best Little Girl in the World, Kids Don't Tell.

O'SULLIVAN, KEVIN P.: Executive. b. New York, NY, April 13, 1928. e. Queens Coll., Flushing, NY. Associated with television 40 yrs., initially as a talent; later as businessman. Won first prize in Arthur Godfrey Talent Scouts competition in 1948. 1950–55 professional singer, actor on TV, in theatre, night clubs. 1955–57 on radio-TV promotion staff, Ronson Corp. 1958–61 salesman, Television Programs of America. 1961–67 director of program services, Harrington, Righter and Parsons. In 1967 joined ABC Films, domestic sales div. as v.p. & gen. sales mgr. In Jan., 1969 named v.p., gen. mgr., ABC Films, Inc.; in April same yr. named pres. In July 1970 made pres., ABC Int'l. TV, while retaining position as pres., ABC Films. In April, 1973 became pres., chief operating officer, Worldvision Enterprises, Inc., co. formed to succeed ABC Films when FCC stopped networks from TV program dist. Elected chmn. & chief exec. officer Worldvision, 1982. Named pres., Great American Broadcasting Group, 1987. Resigned, 1988. Named pres., Kenmare Prods. Inc., April, 1988.

O'SULLIVAN, MAUREEN: Actress. b. Boyle, Eire, May 17, 1911; mother of actress Mia Farrow. e. convents in Dublin, London; finishing sch., Paris. Film debut: Song O' My Heart (1930).
PICTURES: Just Imagine, A Connecticut Yankee, The Big Shot, MGM Tarzan series (6 films), Skyscraper Souls, Strange Interlude, Payment Deferred, Tugboat Annie, Stage Mother, The Barretts of Wimpole Street, The Thin Man, Hide-Out, David Copperfield, West Point of the Air, The Flame Within, Woman Wanted, Anna Karenina, Cardinal Richelieu, The Bishop Misbehaves, The Voice of Bugle Ann, The Devil Doll, A Day at the Races, Emperor's Candlesticks, Between Two Women, My Dear Miss Aldrich, A Yank at Oxford, Hold That Kiss, Port of Seven Seas, The Crowd Roars, Spring Madness, Let Us Live, Sporting Blood, Pride and Prejudice, Maisie Was a Lady, Big Clock, Where Danger Lives, Bonzo Goes to College, All I Desire, Mission Over Korea, Duffy of San Quentin, Steel Cage, The Tall T, Wild Heritage, Never Too Late, The Phynx, Too Scared to Scream, Hannah and Her Sisters, Peggy Sue Got Married, Stranded.
STAGE: Never Too Late, The Front Page, No Sex Please, We're British, Mornings at Seven; regional theatre.
TELEVISION: *Movies*: The Crooked Hearts, The Great Houdinis, With Murder in Mind, The Habitation of Dragons. Guest: Pros & Cons; many others. *Special*: Good Old Boy (Wonderworks)

O'TOOLE, ANNETTE: Actress. b. Houston, TX, April 1, 1953. e. UCLA.
PICTURES: Smile, One on One, King of the Gypsies, Foolin' Around, Cat People, 48 HRS, Superman III, Cross My Heart, Love at Large.
TELEVISION: *Movies*: The Girl Most Likely To. . ., The Entertainer, The War Between the Tates, Love For Rent, Stand By Your Man, Copacabana, Arthur Hailey's Strong Medicine, Broken Vows, Stephen King's IT, The Dreamer of Oz, White Lies, Kiss of a Killer. *Mini-Series*: The Kennedys of Massachusetts. *Specials*: Vanities, Best Legs in the Eighth Grade, Secret World of the Very Young, Unpublished Letters.

O'TOOLE, PETER: Actor. b. Connemara, Ireland, Aug. 2, 1932. Studied at Royal Acad. of Dramatic Art. Early career with Bristol Old Vic. Partner with Jules Buck, Keep Films, Ltd. Autobiography: Loitering With Intent (1993).
THEATRE: On London Stage in Major Barbara, Oh My Papa, The Long the Short and the Tall, Baal, Hamlet, Ride a Cock Horse, Macbeth, Man and Superman, Jeffrey Bernard is Unwell, Our Song. 1960, with the Stratford-on-Avon Company (The Taming of the Shrew, Merchant of Venice, etc). Dublin: Arms and the Man, Waiting for Godot. Toronto: Present Laughter, Uncle Vanya. Bdwy debut 1987 in Pygmalion.
PICTURES: Kidnapped (debut, 1959), The Savage Innocents, The Day They Robbed the Bank of England, Lawrence of Arabia, Becket, Lord Jim, What's New Pussycat?, The Bible, How to Steal a Million, The Night of the Generals, Casino Royale (cameo), Great Catherine, The Lion in Winter, Goodbye Mr. Chips, Brotherly Love (Country Dance), Murphy's War, Under Milk Wood, The Ruling Class, Man of La Mancha, Rosebud, Man Friday, Foxtrot, Caligula, Power Play, Zulu Dawn, The Stunt Man, My Favorite Year, Supergirl, Creator, Club Paradise, The Last Emperor, High Spirits, On a Moonlit Night, Helena, Wings of Fame, The Nutcracker Prince (voice), The Rainbow Thief, Isabelle Eberhardt, King Ralph, Rebecca's Daughters, The Seventh Coin.
TELEVISION: *Movies*: Rogue Male (BBC), Svengali, Kim, Crossing to Freedom. *Specials*: Present Laughter, Pygmalion, The Dark Angel. *Series*: Strumpet City (BBC). *Mini-Series*: Masada.

O'TOOLE, STANLEY: Producer. Earliest experience with production costs; worked on Cleopatra, Singer, Not the Song, No Love for Johnny, Victim, etc. In 1966 named chief cost acct. for Paramount in U.K.; 1967, promoted to prod. exec. Worked on Downhill Racer, Running Scared, etc. Produced The Last of Sheila in 1972; 1974–75 was in Prague working on Operation Daybreak. Produced The Seven-Per-Cent Solution. Formed own Martinat Co. and produced The Squeeze, The Boys from Brazil, Nijinsky, Sphinx, Outland, Enemy Mine, Lionheart, The Last Emperor, Quigley Down Under, Dead Sleep.

OTWELL, RONNIE RAY: Theatre Executive. b. Carrollton, GA, Aug. 13, 1929. e. Georgia Inst. of Technology. Entered industry as mgr., Bremen Theatre (GA), 1950; dir. pub., adv., Martin Theatres, Columbus (GA), 1950–63; v.p.; dir. Martin Theatres of Ga., Inc., 1963, Martin Theatres of Ala., Inc., 1963; dir. Martin Theatres of Columbus, 1963; sr. v.p., Martin

Theatres Companies, 1971. Member: NATO, GA, NATO, Columbus C of C; Columbus Mus. Arts & Crafts; Assn. U.S. Army.

OVITZ, MICHAEL: Talent Agent, Executive. b. Encino, CA, Dec. 14, 1946. e. UCLA, 1968. Attended law school for short period. Started as trainee at William Morris Agency before becoming agent, 1969–75. Co-founder of Creative Artists Agency, 1975. Currently president and chief stock holder.

OWEN, ALUN: Writer. b. Liverpool, Eng., Nov. 25, 1925.
STAGE: A Little Winter Love, Maggie May, Progress to the Park, The Rough and Ready Lot, There'll Be Some Changes Made, Norma (Mixed Doubles), Shelter, Fashion of Your Time, The Ladies, Lucia.
TELEVISION: The Ruffian, No Trams to Lime Street, After the Funeral, Lena O My Lena (for ITV's Armchair Theatre); The Rose Affair (two awards, 1961), Ways of Love, You Can't Win 'Em All, A Hard Knock, Dare to be a Daniel, The Stag, The Strain, A Local Boy, Ruth, Funny, Pal, Giants and Ogres, The Piano Player, The Web Flight, Buttons, Lucky, Left. Ronnie Barker and Forget-me-not series, Lady of the Lake, The Look, Passing Through, The Runner, Sea Link, Kisch-Kisch, Colleagues, Francis.
PICTURES: The Criminal, A Hard Day's Night, Minding the Shop, Park People, You'll Be the Death of Me, McNeil, Cornelius, Emlyn, Caribbean Idyll, Ned Kelly.

OWEN, BILL: Actor. r.n. Bill Rowbotham. b. Acton, Eng., Mar. 14, 1914. Screen debut in Way to the Stars (1945). Numerous TV appearances.
PICTURES: School for Secrets, Daybreak, Dancing With Crime, Easy Money, When the Bough Breaks, My Brother's Keeper, Martha, Parlor Trick, The Roundabout, Trottie True, Once a Jolly Swagman, A Day to Remember, You See What I Mean, Square Ring, Rainbow Jacket, Ship That Died of Shame, Not so Dusty, Davy, Carve Her Name with Pride, Carry on Sergeant, Carry on Nurse, Night Apart, Shakedown, Hell Fire Club, Carry on Regardless, Carry on Cabby!, Secret of Blood Island, Georgy Girl, Headline Hunters, O Lucky Man!, Kadoyng, In Celebration, When The Screaming Stopped, Comeback, Laughter House.
TELEVISION: Last of the Summer Wine (series).

OWENSBY, EARL: Producer, Actor. b. North Carolina, 1935. Set up his own studio in Shelby, NC. Built new studio in Gaffney, SC, 1985.
PICTURES: Challenge, Dark Sunday, Buckstone County Prison, Frank Challenge—Manhunter, Death Driver, Wolfman, Seabo, Day of Judgment, Living Legend, Lady Grey, Rottweiler, Last Game, Hyperspace, Hit the Road Running, Rutherford County Line.

OXENBERG, CATHERINE: Actress. b. NY, NY, Sept. 21, 1961. Daughter of the exiled Princess Elizabeth of Yugoslavia, raised among intl. jet set with Richard Burton acting as her tutor. Modeled before making TV debut in The Royal Romance of Charles and Diana (1982).
PICTURES: The Lair of the White Worm, The Return of the Musketeers.
TELEVISION: *Series*: Dynasty. *Movies*: The Royal Romance of Charles and Diana, Roman Holiday, Swimsuit, Trenchcoat in Paradise, Ring of Scorpio, K-9000, Charles & Diana: Unhappily Ever After.

OZ, FRANK: Puppeteer, Director. b. Hereford, Eng., May 25, 1944. r.n. Frank Oznowicz. Gained fame as creator and performer of various characters on Sesame Street and the Muppet Show (Fozzie Bear, Miss Piggy, Animal, Cookie Monster, Grover and Bert) 1976–81, winning 4 Emmy Awards. Vice president Jim Henson Prods.
PICTURES: *Performer*: The Muppet Movie, The Blues Brothers, The Empire Strikes Back, The Great Muppet Caper (also prod.), American Werewolf in London, The Dark Crystal (also co-dir.), Return of the Jedi, Trading Places, The Muppets Take Manhattan (also dir., co-s.p.), Spies Like Us, Labyrinth, Innocent Blood, The Muppet Christmas Carol (also exec. prod.). *Director only*: Little Shop of Horrors, Dirty Rotten Scoundrels, What About Bob?, Housesitter.
TELEVISION: Sesame Street, The Muppet Show, Saturday Night Live, various variety shows.

P

PAAR, JACK: Actor. b. Canton, OH, May 1, 1918. Radio announcer in Cleveland, Buffalo; served in U.S. Armed Forces, W.W.II; entertained in Pacific zone with 28th Special Service Div. On radio with own show, then quiz show Take It or Leave It. First host of The Tonight Show; various specials.
TELEVISION: Series: Up to Paar (emcee, 1952), Bank on the Stars (emcee, 1953), The Jack Paar Show (1954), The Morning Show (1954), The Tonight Show (retitled The Jack Paar Show (1957–62), The Jack Paar Program (1962–5), ABC Late Night (1973). Specials: Jack Paar Diary, Jack Paar

Remembers, Jack Paar is Alive and Well (prod., 1987), He Kids You Not.

PICTURES: Variety Time (debut, 1948), Easy Living, Walk Softly Stranger, Footlight Varieties, Love Nest, Down Among the Sheltering Palms.

BOOKS: I Kid You Not (1960), My Sabre is Bent, Three on a Toothbrush, P.S. Jack Paar (1983).

PACINO, AL: Actor. b. New York, NY, Apr. 25, 1940. e. High Sch. for the Performing Arts, NY; Actors Studio, 1966; HB Studios, NY. Gained attention as stage actor initially at Charles Playhouse, Boston (Why Is a Crooked Letter, The Peace Creeps, Arturo Ui) Artistic dir. (with Ellen Burstyn), Actors Studio (1982–84).

STAGE: The Indian Wants the Bronx (Obie Award), Does a Tiger Wear a Necktie? (Tony & Theatre World Awards, 1969), The Local Stigmatic, Camino Real, The Connection, Hello Out There, Tiger at the Gates, The Basic Training of Pavlo Hummel (Tony Award, 1977), Richard III, American Buffalo, Julius Caesar, Chinese Coffee, Salome.

PICTURES: Me Natalie (debut, 1969), The Panic in Needle Park, The Godfather, Scarecrow, Serpico, The Godfather Part II, Dog Day Afternoon, Bobby Deerfield, And Justice for All, Cruising, Author! Author!, Scarface, Revolution, Sea of Love, Dick Tracy, The Godfather Part III, Frankie and Johnny, Glengarry Glen Ross, Scent of a Woman (Acad. Award, 1992), Carlito's Way.

PAGE, ANTHONY: Director. b. Bangalore, India, Sept. 21, 1935. e. Oxford. Stage work includes Inadmissible Evidence, Waiting for Godot, A Patriot for Me, Look Back in Anger, Uncle Vanya, Mrs. Warren's Profession, Alpha Beta, Heartbreak House, etc.

PICTURES: Inadmissible Evidence, Alpha Beta, I Never Promised You a Rose Garden, Absolution, The Lady Vanishes.

TELEVISION: Specials: Pueblo, The Missiles of October, The Parachute, Sheppey. Movies: F. Scott Fitzgerald in Hollywood, FDR—The Last Year, The Patricia Neal Story, Bill, Johnny Belinda, Grace Kelly, Bill—On His Own, Murder: By Reason of Insanity, Forbidden, Monte Carlo, Second Serve, Pack of Lies, Scandal in a Small Town, The Nightmare Years, Chernobyl: The Final Warning.

PAGE, PATTI: Performer, recording artist. r.n. Clara Ann Fowler. b. Claremore, OK, Nov. 8, 1927. e. U. of Tulsa. Staff performer, radio stat. KTUL, Tulsa; Top recording star of the 1950s and 60s (The Tennessee Waltz, How Much is That Doggie in the Window, etc.). Appeared on CBS radio show; star Patti Page Show, TV film series, The Big Record; author, Once Upon a Dream.

PICTURES: Elmer Gantry, Dondi, Boys Night Out.

TELEVISION: Series: Music Hall, Scott Music Hall, Patti Page Show, The Big Record (host), Patti Page Olds Show.

PAGET, DEBRA: Actress. r.n. Debralee Griffin. b. Denver, CO, Aug. 19, 1933; e. drama & dancing privately. Stage debut in 'Marry Wives of Windsor, 1946; in Jeanne D'Arc little theatre prod.

PICTURES: Cry of the City (debut, 1948), House of Strangers, Broken Arrow, Fourteen Hours, Bird of Paradise, Anne of the Indies, Belles on Their Toes, Les Miserables, Stars & Stripes Forever, Prince Valiant, Demetrius & the Gladiators, Princess of the Nile, Gambler from Natchez, White Feather, Seven Angry Men, Last Hunt, The Ten Commandments, Love Me Tender, The River's Edge, Omar Khayyam, From the Earth to the Moon, Why Must I Die?, Cleopatra's Daughter, Journey to the Lost City, The Most Dangerous Man Alive, Tales of Terror, The Haunted Palace.

PAGETT, NICOLA: Actress. b. Cairo, Egypt, June 15, 1945. r.n. Nicola Scott. e. Royal Acad. of Dramatic Art. Appeared with Citizen's Rep. Theatre, Glasgow.

THEATER: Cornelia (debut, 1964, Worthing, U.K.), A Boston Story (London debut, 1968), A Midsummer Night's Dream, Widowers' Houses, The Misanthrope, A Voyage 'Round My Father, The Ride Across Lake Constance, Ghosts, The Seagull, Hamlet, The Marriage of Figaro, A Family and a Fortune, Gaslight, Yahoo, Old Times (L.A.).

PICTURES: Anne of the Thousand Days (1969), There's a Girl in My Soup, Operation Daybreak, Oliver's Story, Privates on Parade.

TELEVISION: Series: Upstairs Downstairs (Elizabeth Bellamy). Movies: Frankenstein: The True Story, The Sweeney, Aren't We All, A Woman of Substance (mini-series), Anna Karenina.

PAIGE, JANIS: Actress r.n. Donna Mae Jaden. b. Tacoma, WA, Sept. 16, 1923. Sang with Tacoma Opera Co. m.p. debut, 1944, Hollywood Canteen. Star of Tomorrow, 1947. Album: Let's Fall in Love. Owns and operates Ipanema, Janeiro, Rio-Cali, and Dindi Music Cos.

STAGE: Pajama Game, Remains to Be Seen, Here's Love, Mame, Alone Together.

PICTURES: Hollywood Canteen (debut, 1944), Of Human Bondage, Two Gals and a Guy, The Time the Place and the

Girl, Two Guys from Milwaukee, Her Kind of Man, Cheyenne, Love and Learn, Always Together, Wallflower, Winter Meeting, One Sunday Afternoon, Romance on the High Seas, House Across the Street, Younger Brothers, Mr. Universe, Fugitive Lady, Two Guys and a Gal, Silk Stockings, Please Don't Eat the Daisies, Bachelor in Paradise, The Caretakers, Welcome to Hard Times, The Dark Road (It.), Follow the Boys (Fr.).

TELEVISION: Special: Roberta (1958 and 1969). Series: It's Always Jan, Lanigan's Rabbi, Gun Shy, Baby Makes Five, Trapper John M.D, Capitol, General Hospital, Santa Barbara. Guest: Plymouth Playhouse, Alcoa Premiere, Columbo, Banacek, Flamingo Road, St. Elsewhere. Movies: The Turning Point of Jim Malloy, Return of Joe Forrester, Lanigan's Rabbi (pilot), Valentine Magic on Love Island, Angel on My Shoulder, The Other Woman, No Man's Land.

PAINE, CHARLES F.: Executive. b. Cushing, TX, Dec. 23, 1920. e. Stephen F. Austin U. Pres. Tercar Theatre Company; pres., NATO of Texas, 1972–73. NATO board member, 1973 to present; Motion Picture Pioneers member; Variety Club of Texas member.

PAKULA, ALAN J.: Producer, Director. b. New York, NY, April 7, 1928. e. Yale U., B.A., 1948. Worked in Leland Hayward's office; asst. administrator, Warner Bros. cartoon dept, Prod. apprentice, MGM, 1950; prod. asst., Para. 1951; prod. Para., 1955. Own prod. co., Pakula-Mulligan Prod. Stage prod. and m.p. dir. prod. 1988 received Eastman Award for Continued Excellence in M.P.

STAGE: Comes a Day, Laurette, There Must Be a Pony.

PICTURES: Producer: Fear Strikes Out, To Kill a Mockingbird, Love With the Proper Stranger, Baby the Rain Must Fall, Inside Daisy Clover, Up the Down Staircase, The Stalking Moon. Director: The Sterile Cuckoo, Klute (also prod.), Love and Pain and the Whole Damn Thing (also prod.), The Parallax View (also prod.), All the President's Men, Comes a Horseman, Starting Over (also prod.), Rollover, Sophie's Choice (also prod., s.p.), Dream Lover (also prod.), Orphans (also prod.), See You in the Morning (also prod., s.p.), Presumed Innocent, Consenting Adults (also prod.), The Pelican Brief (also prod., co-s.p.).

AWARDS: N.Y. Film Critics for best director, All the President's Men (1976); London Film Critics for best director, Klute (1971).

PALANCE, JACK: Actor. b. Lattimer, PA, Feb. 18, 1920. e. U. of North Carolina. Professional fighter; U.S. Air Corps.

STAGE: The Big Two, Temporary Island, The Vigil, Streetcar Named Desire, Darkness at Head.

PICTURES: Panic in the Streets (debut, 1950), Halls of Montezuma, Sudden Fear, Shane, Flight to Tangier, Arrowhead, Second Chance, Man in the Attic, Sign of the Pagan, Silver Chalice, Kiss of Fire, Big Knife, I Died a Thousand Times, Attack!, Lonely Man, House of Numbers, The Man Inside, Ten Seconds to Hell, Battle of Austerliz, Sword of the Conqueror, The Mongols, Barabbas, Warriors Five, Contempt, Once a Thief, The Professionals, Torture Garden, Kill a Dragon, The Mercenary, Deadly Sanctuary, They Came to Rob Las Vegas, The Desperados, Che, Legion of the Damned, A Bullet for Rommel, The McMasters, Monte Walsh, Companeros, The Horsemen, Chato's Land, Oklahoma Crude, Craze, The Four Deuces, The Great Adventure, The Sensuous Nurse, Portrait of a Hitman, One Man Jury, Angel's Brigade, The Shape of Things to Come, Cocaine Cowboys, Hawk the Slayer, Without Warning, Alone in the Dark, Gor, Bagdad Cafe, Young Guns, Outlaw of Gor, Batman, Tango and Cash, City Slickers (Acad. Award, supp. actor, 1991), Solar Crisis, Cops and Robbersons.

TELEVISION: Specials: Requiem for a Heavyweight (Emmy Award, 1957), Dr. Jekyll and Mr. Hyde. Movies: Dracula, The Godchild, The Hatfields and the McCoys, Bronk (pilot), Last Ride of the Dalton Gang, The Ivory Ape, Golden Moment: An Olympic Love Story, Keep the Change. Series: The Greatest Show on Earth, Bronk, Ripley's Believe It or Not (host).

PALCY, EUZHAN: Director. b. Martinique, 1957. e. Earned a degree in French lit., Sorbonne and a film degree from Vaugirard School in Paris. Began career working as TV writer and dir. in Martinique. Also made 2 children's records. In Paris worked as film editor, screenwriter and dir. of shorts. She received grant from French gov. to make 1st feature Sugar Cane Alley which cost $800,000 and won Silver Lion Prize at Venice Film Fest., 1983.

PICTURES: Sugar Cane Alley, A Dry White Season (also co-s.p.).

PALIN, MICHAEL: Actor, Writer. b. Sheffield, Yorkshire, England, May 5, 1943. e. Oxford. Performed there in The Birthday Party and in revue Hang Your Head Down and Die (also in West End prod., 1964). At Oxford met Terry Jones, began writing comedy together, incl. TV series The Frost Report. Became member of Monty Python's Flying Circus. On stage with troupe both in London and on Bdwy.

PICTURES: And Now for Something Completely Different, Monty Python and the Holy Grail (also co-s.p.), Jabberwocky,

Life of Brian (also co-s.p.), Time Bandits, The Secret Policeman's Other Ball, Monty Python Live at the Hollywood Bowl (also co-s.p.), The Missionary (also co-prod., s.p.), Monty Python's The Meaning of Life (also co-music, co-s.p.), A Private Function, Brazil, A Fish Called Wanda, American Friends (also co-s.p.).
TELEVISION: Do Not Adjust Your Set, The Frost Report, Monty Python's Flying Circus, Marty Feldman Comedy Machine, How To Irritate People, Pythons in Deutschland, Secrets, Ripping Yarns, Around the World in 80 Days, GBH, Pole to Pole.

PALMER, BETSY: Actress. b. East Chicago, IN, Nov. 1, 1926. e. DePaul U. Studied at Neighborhood Playhouse, HB Studio with Uta Hagen. On Broadway in The Grand Prize, Affair of Honor, Cactus Flower, Roar Like a Dove, Eccentricities of a Nightingale, Same Time Next Year and many regional prods.
PICTURES: Mister Roberts, The Long Gray Line, Queen Bee, The Other Life of Lynn Stuart, The Tin Star, The Last Angry Man, Friday the 13th, Friday the 13th Part II.
TELEVISION: All major live shows such as Studio One, U.S. Steel Hour, Kraft Theatre. Series: Masquerade Party (panelist), What's It For? (panelist), I've Got a Secret (panelist, 10 years), No. 96 (series), Candid Camera (host), Wifeline (host). Guest: As the World Turns, Murder She Wrote, Out of This World, Charles in Charge, Knots Landing. Movies: Isabel's Choice, Windmills of the Gods, Goddess of Love, Death Hits the Jackpot, Still Not Quite Human.

PALMER, GREGG: Actor. r.n. Palmer Lee. b. San Francisco, CA, Jan. 25, 1927; e. U. of Utah. U.S. Air Force, 1945–46; radio announcer, disc jockey; then to Hollywood; over 800 TV appearances.
PICTURES: Cimarron Kid, Battle at Apache Pass, Son of Ali Baba, Red Ball Express, Francis Goes to West Point, Sally and St. Anne, The Raiders, Back at the Front, Redhead From Wyoming, Column South, Veils of Bagdad, Golden Blade, The All American, Taza Son of Cochise, Magnificent Obsession, Playgirl, To Hell and Back, Creature Walks Among Us, Hilda Crane, Zombies of Mora Tau, Revolt of Fort Laramie, Rebel Set, Thundering Jets, Forty Pounds of Trouble, Night Hunt, The Undefeated, Chisum, Rio Lobo, Big Jake, Providenza (Italy), Ci Risiamo Vero Providenza (Italy, Spain), The Shootist, The Man With Bogart's Face, Scream.
TELEVISION: Guest appearances incl: Wagon Train, Loretta Young, Wyatt Earp, Have Gun Will Travel, Sea Hunt, Roaring 20's, Mannix, The High Chaparral, Cannon, Baretta, Gunsmoke, etc. Movies: Go West Young Girl, Hostage Heart, How the West Was Won, True Grit, Beggarman, Thief; The Blue and the Gray (mini-series).

PALMER, PATRICK: Producer. b. Los Angeles, CA, Dec. 28, 1936. Began career with 10-year apprenticeship at Mirisch Company, involved in making of West Side Story, Seven Days in May, The Fortune Cookie, etc. 1966, associated with Norman Jewison, serving as assoc. prod. on The Landlord, Fiddler on the Roof, Jesus Christ Superstar, Rollerball, etc. 1972, prod. with Jewison Billy Two Hats; exec. prod. on The Dogs of War.
PICTURES: Co-prod.: And Justice for All, Best Friends, Iceman, A Soldier's Story, Agnes of God, Children of a Lesser God, Moonstruck, Stanley & Iris, Mermaids, Paradise.

PALTROW, BRUCE: Director, Producer, Writer. b. New York, NY, Nov. 26, 1943. e. Tulane U., B.F.A. m. actress Blythe Danner. Produced stage plays.
PICTURE: A Little Sex (co-prod., dir.).
TELEVISION: Shirts and Skins; You're Gonna Love It Here; Big City Boys; The White Shadow (creat. dir.); St. Elsewhere (exec. prod.-dir.), Tattinger's (exec. prod., dir., co-writer), Nick & Hillary (exec. prod.).

PAM, JERRY: Publicist. b. London, England, Oct. 17, 1926. e. Cambridge, London U. Reporter, Paris, London; freelance writing, Australia; 1950–53. To U.S. in 1953, on Hollywood Reporter, drama ed. Beverly Hills Citizen, 1953–54; publicist, Moulin Rouge, MGM studios; drama ed., Valley Times 1959–61; partner, Pam and Joseph pub. rel. counsellors; est. Jerry Pam & Associates, pub. rel., April 1965; formed Guttman & Pam, Ltd., 1971. Exec. prod., Highpoint, 1979. Prod., On the Film Scene (weekly series on Z Channel).

PAMPANINI, SILVANA: Actress. b. Rome, Italy, Sept. 25, 1925. e. Academy of St. Cecilia. Studied singing, several concert appearances. Elected Miss Italia of 1946–47; m.p. debut in Secret of Don Giovanni.
PICTURES: Second Ark, Twin Trouble, O.K. Nero, City Stands Trial, A Husband for Anna, Songs of Half a Century, Songs Songs Songs, Matrimony, Enchanting Enemy, A Day in District Court, Loves of Half a Century, Slave of Sin, Orient Express, Merry Squadron, Princess of the Canary Islands, Mademoiselle Gobette, Don Juan's Night of Love, Roman Tales.

PANAMA, CHARLES A. (CHUCK): Publicist, b. Chicago, IL, Feb. 2, 1925. e. Northwestern U., Beloit Coll., U. of California at L.A. Publicist, Los Angeles Jr. Chamber of Commerce; So.

Calif. sports ed., Los Angeles bureau, INS; publicist, 20th Century-Fox Studios; adv.-pub. dir., Arcola Pics.; opened L.A. office, John Springer Associates; v.p. Jerry Pam & Assoc.; Account exec., Rogers, Cowan & Brenner, Inc.; dir. m.p. div., Jim Mahoney & Assoc.; v.p. Guttman & Pam, Ltd.; asst. pub. dir., Twentieth TV. Owner, pres. Chuck Panama P.R.; winner 1990 Les Mason Award and Robert Yeafer Award 1993, Publicists Guild of America.

PANAMA, NORMAN: Writer, Producer, Director. Co-authored The Glass Bed (novel), and plays: A Talent for Murder & The Bats of Portobello.
PICTURES: Co-writer: Road to Utopia, My Favorite Blonde, Happy Go Lucky, Star-Spangled Rhythm, Thank Your Lucky Stars, And the Angels Sing, Duffy's Tavern, Our Hearts Were Growing Up, Monsieur Beaucaire, It Had to Be You, Mr. Blandings Builds His Dream House, Return of October, White Christmas, Li'l Abner, The Facts of Life. Co-dir./co-s.p. (with Melvin Frank): The Reformer and the Red-head, Strictly Dishonorable, Callaway Went Thataway, Above and Beyond, Knock on Wood, The Court Jester. Dir.-Writer: The Road to Hong Kong, Not With My Wife You Don't, How to Commit Marriage, I Will I Will . . . for Now.
TELEVISION: Dir.: Barnaby and Me, The Stewardesses, Li'l Abner, Mrs. Katz and Katz (TV pilot), How Come You Never See Dr. Jekyll and Mr. Hyde Together?, Coffee Tea or Me.

PANKIN, STUART: Actor. b. Philadelphia, PA, Apr. 8, 1946. e. Dickinson Col., Columbia U. Stage debut 1968 in The War of the Roses.
PICTURES: Scavenger Hunt, Hangar 18, The Hollywood Knights, An Eye for an Eye, Earthbound, Irreconcilable Differences, The Dirt Bike Kid, Fatal Attraction, Love at Stake, Second Sight, That's Adequate, Arachnophobia, Mannequin 2 on the Move, The Vagrant, Indian Warrior.
TELEVISION: Series: The San Pedro Beach Bums, No Soap Radio, Not Necessarily the News (ACE Award), Nearly Departed, Dinosaurs (voice). Movie: Valentine Magic on Love Island. Pilots: Car Wash, Wonderful World of Philip Malley. Guest: Night Court, Crazy Like a Fox, Golden Girls, Stingray, Family Ties, It's Garry Shandling's Show, Hooperman, Barney Miller. Special: Stuart Pankin (also co-exec. prod., co-writer).
THEATRE: NY: Timon of Athens, Tale of Cymbeline, Mary Stuart, The Crucible, Twelfth Night, Glorious Age, Wings, Gorky, Joseph and the Amazing Technicolor Dreamcoat, Three Sisters, The Inspector General.

PANTOLIANO, JOE: Actor. b. Jersey City, NJ, Sept. 12, 1954.
PICTURES: The Idolmaker, Monsignor, Risky Business, Eddie and the Cruisers, The Mean Season, The Goonies, Running Scared, La Bamba, The Squeeze, Amazon Women on the Move, Empire of the Sun, The In Crowd, Midnight Run, Downtown, The Last of the Finest, Short Time, Zanda-lee, Used People, Three of Hearts, The Fugitive, Calendar Girl, Goin' to Mexico.
TELEVISION: Series: Free Country, The Fanelli Boys. Mini-Series: Robert F. Kennedy: His Life and Times, From Here to Eternity. Guest: Tales from the Crypt (ACE Award nomination), Amazing Stories, L.A. Law, The Hitchhiker. Movies: More Than Friends, Alcatraz: The Whole Shocking Story, Nightbreaker, Destination America, El Diablo, One Special Victory, Through the Eyes of a Killer.
THEATRE: NY: The Kitchen, The Off Season, The Death Star, Visions of Kerouac. Regional: One Flew Over the Cuckoo's Nest, Skaters, Brothers, Italian American Reconciliation (Dramalogue Award), Orphans (Dramalogue Award, Drama Critic Circle nomination), Pvt. Wars.

PAPAS, IRENE: Actress. b. near Corinth, Greece, Sept. 3, 1926. Entered dramatic school at 12. At 16 sang and danced in variety shows. Film debut in 1951 Greek film, Lost Angels; 1958 Greek Popular theatre in Athens.
STAGE: The Idiot, Journey's End, The Merchant of Venice, Inherit the Wind, That Summer, That Fall, Iphigenia in Aulis.
PICTURES: Dead City, The Unfaithful, Attila the Hun, Theodora, Whirlpool, Tribute to a Bad Man, The Guns of Navarone, Antigone (Best Actress Award, Salonika Film Fest.), Electra (Best Actress Award, Salonika Film Fest.), Zorba the Greek, The Brotherhood, Anne of the Thousand Days, Z, A Dream of Kings, A Ciascuno il Suo, The Odyssey, The Trojan Women, Moses, Mohammed: Messenger of God, Iphigenia, Bloodline, Lion of the Desert, Erendira, Into the Night, The Assisi Underground, Sweet Country, High Season, Island, Drums of Fire, Banquet, Zoe.
TELEVISION: Moses the Lawgiver.

PARE, MICHAEL: Actor. b. Brooklyn, NY, Oct. 9, 1959. e. Culinary Inst. of America, Hyde Park, NY. Worked as chef, and model before being discovered by ABC talent agent.
PICTURES: Eddie and the Cruisers (debut, 1983), Streets of Fire, The Philadelphia Experiment, Under Cover (Aust.), Space Rage, Instant Justice, The Women's Club, World Gone Wild, Eddie and the Cruisers II: Eddie Lives, Moon 44, Concrete War, The Closer, Into the Sun, Midnight Heat, First Light.

TELEVISION: *Series*: The Greatest American Hero (1981–83), Houston Knights. *Movie*: Crazy Times.

PARISH, JAMES ROBERT: Film historian/marketing exec. b. Cambridge, MA, Apr. 21, 1944. e. U. of PA (BBA, Phi Beta Kappa); U. of PA Law School (LLB). Member of NY Bar. Founder Entertainment Copyright Research Co., Inc. 1968–69, film reporter, Motion Picture Daily, weekly Variety. 1969–70, entertainment publicist, Harold Rand & co (NY). Currently marketing consultant in direct marketing industry, contributor to arts sections of major national newspapers and entertainment trade papers, series editor of show business books and author of over 75 books on the entertainment industry including: Hollywood's Great Musicals, Prostitution in Hollywood Films, Ghosts & Angels in Hollywood Films, Hollywood Songsters, Prison Pictures from Hollywood, Hollywood Baby Boomers, The Great Detective Pictures, The Great Cop Pictures, The Great Science Fiction Pictures II, Complete Actors TV Credits (1948–88). The Great Combat Pictures, Black Action Pictures From Hollywood, The Great Detective Pictures, The Great Western Pictures II: The Great Gangster Pictures II: The Great Spy Pictures II, Actors TV Credits, The Best of MGM, The Forties Gals, The Great American Movies Book, Hollywood Happiness, The Funsters, Hollywood on Hollywood, The Hollywood Beauties, Elvis!, The Great Science Fiction Pictures, The Child Stars, The Jeannette MacDonald Story, Great Movie Heroes, Liza!, The RKO Gals, Vincent Price Unmasked, The George Raft File, The Emmy Awards, Hollywood Death Book, Gays & Lesbians in Mainstream Cinema, Hollywood Celebrity Death Book (updated), Let's Talk: America's Favorite TV Talk Show Hosts, Today's Country Music Stars.

PARKER, ALAN: Director, Writer. b. Islington, London, England, Feb. 14, 1944. Worked way up in advertising industry from mail room to top writer and director of nearly 500 TV commercials between 1969–78.
PICTURES: Melody (s.p., 1968). *Director*: No Hard Feelings (also s.p.), Our Cissy (also s.p.), Footsteps (also s.p.), Bugsy Malone (also s.p.; Brit. Acad. Award for best s.p.), Midnight Express (Brit. Acad. Award), Fame, Shoot the Moon, Pink Floyd—The Wall, Birdy, Angel Heart, Mississippi Burning, Come and See the Paradise (also s.p.), The Commitments (also cameo); BAFTA Award for best dir., 1991).
TELEVISION: The Evacuees (Brit. Acad. Award).

PARKER, ELEANOR: Actress. b. Cedarville, OH, June 26, 1922. In Cleveland play group; in summer stock Martha's Vineyard; at Pasadena Community Playhouse.
PICTURES: They Died With Their Boots On, Buses Roar, Mysterious Doctor, Mission to Moscow, Between Two Worlds, Very Thought of You, Crime By Night, Hollywood Canteen, Last Ride, Pride of the Marines, Never Say Goodbye, Of Human Bondage, Escape Me Never, Woman in White, Voice of the Turtle, It's a Great Feeling, Chain Lightning, Caged, Three Secrets, Valentino, Millionaire for Christy, Detective Story, Scaramouche, Above and Beyond, Escape from Fort Bravo, Naked Jungle, Valley of the Kings, Many Rivers to Cross, Interrupted Melody, Man with the Golden Arm, King and Four Queens, Lizzie, Seventh Sin, A Hole in the Head, Home from the Hill, Return to Peyton Place, Madison Avenue, Panic Button, The Sound of Music, The Oscar, An American Dream, Warning Shot, Tiger and the Pussycat, Eye of the Cat, Sunburn.
TELEVISION: *Series*: Bracken's World. *Movies*: Maybe I'll Come Home in the Spring, Vanished, Home for the Holidays, The Great American Beauty Contest, Fantasy Island (pilot), The Bastard, She's Dressed to Kill, Once Upon a Spy, Madame X, Dead on the Money. *Pilot*: Guess Who's Coming to Dinner. *Guest*: Murder She Wrote.

PARKER, FESS: Actor. b. Fort Worth, TX, Aug. 16, 1924. e. U. of Southern California. U.S. Navy, 1943–46; national co., Mr. Roberts, 1951.
PICTURES: Untamed Frontier (debut, 1952), No Room for the Groom, Springfield Rifle, Thunder Over the Plains, Island in the Sky, Kid from Left Field, Take Me to Town, Them, Battle Cry, Davy Crockett King of the Wild Frontier (from Disney TV show), Davy Crockett and the River Pirates (from TV show), The Great Locomotive Chase, Westward Ho the Wagons, Old Yeller, The Light in the Forest, The Hangman, The Jayhawkers, Hell Is for Heroes, Smoky.
TELEVISION: *Series*: Mr. Smith Goes to Washington, Daniel Boone. *Guest*: Jonathan Winters, Walt Disney presents (Davy Crockett), Playhouse 90 (Turn Left at Mt. Everest), Ed Sullivan, Danny Kaye Show, Phyllis Diller, Joey Bishop, Dean Martin, Red Skelton, Glen Campbell, Andy Williams. *Movie*: Climb an Angry Mountain.

PARKER, JAMESON: Actor. b. Baltimore, MD, Nov. 18, 1947. e. Beloit Coll. Professional stage debut in Washington Theatre Club production, Caligula. Acted with Arena Stage in DC; worked in dinner theatres and summer stock. Moved to N.Y., working in TV commercials and acted in play, Equus (Coconut Grove Playhouse).
PICTURES: The Bell Jar (debut, 1979), A Small Circle of Friends, White Dog, American Justice (also prod.), Prince of Darkness, The Crystal Eye.
TELEVISION: *Series*: Somerset, One Life to Live, Simon and Simon. *Movies*: Women at West Point, Anatomy of a Seduction, The Gathering Part II, The Promise of Love, Callie and Son, A Caribbean Mystery, Who Is Julia?, Spy, She Says She's Innocent, Dead Before Dawn.

PARKER, SARAH JESSICA: Actress. b. Nelsonville, OH, Mar. 25, 1965. Dancer with Cincinnati Ballet and American Ballet Theatre. Professional debut at age 8 in TV special The Little Match Girl.
PICTURES: Rich Kids (debut, 1979), Somewhere Tomorrow, Footloose, Firstborn, Girls Just Want to Have Fun, Flight of the Navigator, L.A. Story, Honeymoon in Vegas, Hocus Pocus, Striking Distance.
TELEVISION: *Series*: Square Pegs, A Year in the Life, Equal Justice. *Specials*: The Almost Royal Family, Life Under Water. *Movies*: My Body My Child, Going for the Gold: The Bill Johnson Story, A Year in the Life, The Room Upstairs, Dadah is Death, Twist of Fate, The Ryan White Story, In the Best Interest of the Children.
THEATRE: NY: The Innocents, By Strouse, Annie (title role for 2 yrs.), To Gillian on Her 37th Birthday, The Heidi Chronicles, The Substance of Fire.

PARKER, SUZY: Actress. r.n. Cecelia Parker. b. San Antonio, TX, Oct. 28, 1933. m. actor Bradford Dillman. e. schools in NY, FL. Began career at 17 as fashion model; becoming the highest paid fashion model and cover girl in U.S.; went to Paris under contract to fashion magazine; film debut as model in Funny Face (1957); signed by 20th-Fox prod. chief Buddy Adler for part opposite Cary Grant in Kiss Them for Me.
PICTURES: Kiss Them For Me, Ten North Frederick, The Best of Everything, Circle of Deception, The Interns, Chamber of Horrors.

PARKES, WALTER F.: Producer, Writer. b. Bakersfield, CA. e. Yale, Stanford Univ. 1978 prod. & dir. documentary The California Reich which was nominated for Acad. Award.
PICTURES: WarGames (s.p.; Acad. Award nom.). *Producer*: Volunteers, Project X, True Believer, Awakenings (Acad. Award nom.), Sneakers (also co-s.p.).
TELEVISION: *Series*: Eddie Dodd (prod., writer). *Pilot*: Birdland (prod., writer).

PARKINS, BARBARA: Actress. b. Vancouver, British Columbia, Canada, May 22, 1943.
PICTURES: Valley of the Dolls, The Kremlin Letter, Puppet on a Chain, The Mephisto Waltz, Bear Island, Breakfast in Paris.
TELEVISION: *Series*: Peyton Place, Scene of the Crime. *Mini-Series*: Captains and the Kings. *Movies*: A Taste of Evil, Snatched, Law of the Land, Testimony of Two Men, Young Joe: The Forgotten Kennedy, Ziegfield: The Man and His Women, The Critical List, The Manions of America, Uncommon Valor, To Catch a King, Calendar Girl Murders, Peyton Place: The Next Generation, Jennie: Lady Randolph Churchill. *Guest*: Murder She Wrote.

PARKS, GORDON: Director, Writer, Photographer, Composer, Poet, Photojournalist. b. Fort Scott, KS, Nov. 30, 1912. From the age of 15 worked as piano player, bus boy, dining car waiter and prof. basketball player in MN before taking up photog. in late 1930s. Awarded 1st Julius Rosenwald Fellowship in photog. 1942. Worked with Roy Stryker at Farm Security Admin., WWII Office of War Info. correspondent. Photo-journalist, Life Mag., 1949–68, editorial dir.: Essence Magazine 1970–73 (and founder). Film debut 1961 with doc. Flavio (dir. and writer), followed by Diary of a Harlem Family (doc.) (Emmy Award). Winner of numerous awards including NAACP's Spingarn Medal and Kansas Governor's Medal of Honor, Natl. Medal of Arts, 1988. Recipient of 23 honorary degrees in lit., fine arts, humane letters.
AUTHOR: The Learning Tree, A Choice of Weapons, A Poet and His Camera, Whispers of Intimate Things, In Love, Born Black, Moments Without Proper Names, Flavio, To Smile in Autumn, Shannon, Voices in the Mirror.
PICTURES: The Learning Tree (Library of Congress Natl. Film Registry Classics honor, 1989), Shaft, Shaft's Big Score, Super Cops, Leadbelly.
TELEVISION: The Odyssey of Solomon Northup, Moments Without Proper Names, Martin.

PARKS, MICHAEL: Actor. b. Corona, CA, April 4, 1938.
PICTURES: Wild Seed (debut, 1964), Bus Riley's Back in Town, The Bible, The Idol, The Happening, The Last Hard Men, Sidewinder One, ffolkes, Hard Country, Savannah Smiles, Spiker, Club Life, The Return of Josey Wales (also dir.), Spiker, Arizona Heat, Nightmare Beach, Prime Suspect, The Hitman, Storyville.
TELEVISION: *Series*: Then Came Bronson, The Colbys, Twin Peaks. *Movies*: Can Ellen Be Saved?, Savage Bees, Chase, Dangerous Affection, Gore Vidal's Billy the Kid, The China Lake Murders.

PARRETTI, GIANCARLO: Executive. b. Orvieto, Italy, Oct. 23, 1941. Hotelier in Sicily in the late 1970's. Managing dir. of Naples newspaper Diario, until 1981. 1987, purchased Cannon Group, renaming it Pathe Communications. 1990, company acquired MGM/UA, Communications. Resigned 1991.

PARRISH, ROBERT R.: Director, Producer. b. Columbus, GA, Jan. 4, 1916. Actor before joining RKO in 1933, first as assistant director, then film editor. With various companies since, including 20th Century-Fox, Universal, Columbia, United Artists, J. Arthur Rank, etc. Won Academy Award, best film editing, Body and Soul, 1947. U.S. Navy 1941–45; won documentary Academy Award, 1942 and 1943 for Battle of Midway and December 7th. Formed own independent production company, Trimark Productions, Inc., 1955. Autobiographies: Growing Up in Hollywood, 1976; Hollywood Doesn't Live Here Anymore.
PICTURES: *Actor*: City Lights, All Quiet on the Western Front, The Informer, The Divine Lady. *Editor*: Body and Soul, Caught, A Double Life, No Minor Vices, All the King's Men. *Director*: Cry Danger, The Mob, San Francisco Story, Assignment—Paris, My Pal Gus, Rough Shoot, The Purple Plain, Lucy Gallant, Fire Down Below, Saddle the Wind, The Wonderful Country, In the French Style, Up From the Beach, Casino Royale (co-dir.), The Bobo, Duffy, A Town Called Bastard, The Marseilles Contract, Mississippi Blues (doc., co-dir. with Bertrand Tavernier).

PARSONS, ESTELLE: Actress. b. Marblehead, MA, Nov. 20, 1927. e. Connecticut Coll. for Women, Bachelor's degree in political science. Attended Boston U. Law Sch. Helped harvest crops in England with the Women's Land Army. Was active in politics; worked for the Committee for the Nation's Health in Wash. and the Republican Finance Committee in Boston. Was elected to public office in Marblehead, Mass. Joined NBC-TV's Today Show as prod. asst.; then writer, feature producer and commentator. Appeared in two Julius Monk revues, Jerry Herman's Nightcap.
STAGE: Happy Hunting, Whoop Up, Beg Borrow or Steal, Mrs. Dally Has a Lover (Theater World Award), Next Time I'll Sing to You (Obie Award), In the Summer House (Obie Award), Ready When You Are C.B., Malcolm, The Seven Descents of Myrtle, And Miss Reardon Drinks a Little, The Norman Conquests, Ladies of the Alamo, Miss Margarida's Way, Pirates of Penzance, The Unguided Missile, Threepenny Opera, Lincoln Center Repertory Theatre, Mahagonny, Forgiving Typhoid Mary, Shimada.
PICTURES: Ladybug Ladybug (debut, 1963), Bonnie and Clyde (Acad. Award, supp. actress, 1967), Rachel Rachel, Don't Drink the Water, Watermelon Man, I Walk the Line, I Never Sang For My Father, Two People, For Pete's Sake, Foreplay, Dick Tracy, The Lemon Sisters.
TELEVISION: *Mini-Series*: Backstairs at the White House. *Special*: The Front Page. *Guest*: All in the Family, Roseanne. *Movies*: Terror on the Beach, The Gun and the Pulpit, The UFO Incident, The Gentleman Bandit, Open Admissions, A Private Matter, The American Clock.

PARSONS, LINDSLEY: Executive Vice Pres., Film Finances, Inc. Pres., Completion Service Co., Hollywood. Toronto. b. Tacoma, WA, Sept. 12, 1915. e. U. of California at L.A. On ed. staff City News Service, L.A.: Alhambra Post-Advocate; Calexico Chronicle; Santa Rosa Press Democrat; Humboldt Times; San Marino News (ed. & pub.). Joined Monogram 1931 as pub. dir. in 1933 author s.p. Sagebrush Trails; then wrote orig. s.p. Westerns for Monogram, Republic, Grand Nat'l. In 1939 assoc. prod. Tough Kid; from 1940 prod. numerous westerns; prod. Wayne Morris & James Oliver Curwood series for Allied Artists; prod. Motion Pictures Int'l, 1956–72. Exec. v.p., dir., Film Finances, Inc.
PICTURES: Rocky, Rhythm Inn, Casa Manana, Big Timber, Call of the Klondike, Sierra Passage, Yukon, Manhunt, Yellow Fin, Northwest Territory, Desert Pursuit, Torpedo Alley, Jack Slade, Loophole, Cry Vengeance, Finger Man, Return of Jack Slade, Come On, The Intruder, Cruel Tower, Dragon Wells Massacre, Portland Expose, Oregon Passage, Wolf Larsen, Crash Boat, The Purple Gang, Mara of the Wilderness, Good Times, The Big Cube.
TELEVISION: Gray Ghost (series); Files of Jeffrey Jones, The Whistler.

PARTON, DOLLY: Singer, Composer, Actress. b. Sevierville, TN, Jan. 19, 1946. Gained fame as country music singer, composer and radio and TV personality. Many awards for recordings. Co-partner with Sandy Gallin, Sandollar Prods.
PICTURES: Nine to Five (debut, 1980; also wrote & sang title song), The Best Little Whorehouse in Texas (also wrote additional songs), Rhinestone (also songs), Steel Magnolias, Straight Talk (also songs).
TELEVISION: *Guest*: Porter Wagoner Show, Cass Walker program, Bill Anderson Show, Wilbur Bros. Show. *Specials*: Kenny Dolly & Willie: Something Inside So Strong, A Tennessee Mountain Thanksgiving. *Series*: Dolly (1976), Dolly (1987–8). *Movies*: A Smoky Mountain Christmas (also songs), Wild Texas Wind (also co-writer, co-prod.).

PARTRIDGE, DEREK: TV talk and magazine show host, Interviewer, Newscaster, Presenter, Narrator, Writer. b. London, England, June 29, 1935. Ent. journalism on the Daily Express. Ent. industry 1959 as documentary scriptwriter with Film Producers' Guild. 1976–78: Rhodesian TV: Chief news anchor, live magazine programme Frankly Partridge, quizmaster The Kwhizz Kids. 1979 (Miami): newscaster, daily What's Happening South Florida, and Focus (WKAT/ABC). 1980 (New York): To the Point, and Special Edition. 1981–82: TV (Los Angeles): Newscaster/writer/interviewer for Financial News Network. 1982: The Romance of Words. The Guinness Book of Records Specials (announcer). Video Aktuell (Hollywood celebrities for German TV). Financial Inquiry (anchor/interviewer). 1984: Election Coverage '84. 1986: The Story of a News Story (Emmy winner), Travel Time. 1987: Information Power (Emmy winner). 1986–88: Music programmes host (Gulf Air, Saudia, Royal Jordanian). Interviewer: TV's Bloopers & Practical Jokes. Health Line '87; American Life Styles; Star du Siècle (French TV); Sexuality—Today's Decisions. 1988: Law in America; World Access TV; Over 50, City on the Line. 1989: Fine Art, Golf Video Magazine. 1990–93: TNT—The Naked Truth. 1990: Sky TV News. 1991: Bon Voyage, Sunsport Magazine. 1992: Prime Life Today.

PASETTA, MARTY: Producer-Director. b. June 16, 1932. e. U. Santa Clara.
TELEVISION: AFI Salutes to Fred Astaire, John Huston, Lillian Gish, Alfred Hitchcock and Jimmy Stewart; Gene Kelly Special; Elvis Aloha From Hawaii; Oscar (17), Emmy (2) and Grammy (8) Award Shows; A Country Christmas (1978–81); The Monte Carlo Show; Texaco Star Theatre-Opening Night; Burnett Discovers Domingo; Disneyland's 30th Anniversary Celebration; 15 Years of Cerebral Palsy Telethon; A Night at the Moulin Rouge; Soap Opera Awards; An All-Star Celebration Honoring Martin Luther King; Disneyland's Summer Vacation Party; Disney's "Captain EO" Grand Opening; 15th Anniversary of Disney World; Beach Boys. . . 25 Years Together; Super Night At the Superbowl; 20th Anniversary of Caesars Palace; Paris by Night with George Burns; "I Call You Friend" Papal Spacebridge '87; Walt Disney World's Celebrity Circus; Las Vegas—An All-Star 75th Anniversary; Julio Iglesias—Sold Out; The Ice Capades with Kirk Cameron; American All-Star Tribute Honoring Elizabeth Taylor.

PASSER, IVAN: Director, Writer. b. Prague, Czechoslovakia, July 10, 1933. e. Film Faculty of Acad. of Musical Arts, Prague. 1961, asst. dir. to Milos Forman on Audition which led to scripting for Forman. 1969, moved to U.S., worked in NY as longshoreman while studying Eng. U.S. dir. debut: Born to Win, 1971.
PICTURES: *Writer*: Loves of a Blonde, A Boring Afternoon, Fireman's Ball. *Director*: Intimate Lighting (also s.p.), Born to Win, Law and Disorder, Crime and Passion, The Silver Bears, Cutter and Bone, Creator, Haunted Summer.
TELEVISION: (U.S.) Faerie Tale Theatre. *Movies*: Fourth Story, Stalin.

PASTER, GARY M.: Executive. b. St. Louis, MO, July 4, 1943. e. U. of Missouri, B.A.; U. of California at L.A., U. of Southern California Graduate Sch. of Business. 1970, joined The Burbank Studios as asst. to the pres. and as treas. 1976 v.p.—admin. and chmn. of the exec. comm. September, 1977 pres. Board of Directors/Trustees: Permanent Charities Committee of Entertainment Industry, St. Joseph Medical Center Fdn. American Women in Radio & TV, William H. Parker L.A. Police Fdn. Member: Academy of Motion Picture Arts and Sciences, Los Angeles Film Dev. Council, Hollywood Radio and T.V. Society, Acad. of Television Arts and Sciences. Advisory bd., Kaufman Astoria Studios, N.Y.

PATINKIN, MANDY: Actor. b. Chicago, IL, Nov. 30, 1952. r.n. Mandel Patinkin. e. U. of Kansas, Juilliard Sch. (Drama Div.; 1972–74). m. actress Kathryn Grody. In regional theatre before coming to New York where played with Shakespeare Festival Public Theater (Trelawny of the Wells, Hamlet, Rebel Women). Recordings: Mandy Patinkin, Dress Casual.
THEATER: Savages, The Shadow Box (bdwy debut), Evita (Tony Award, 1980), Henry IV, Part I (Central Park), Sunday in the Park With George (Tony nom.), The Knife, Follies in Concert, A Winter's Tale, Dress Casual (solo concert), The Secret Garden, Falsettos.
PICTURES: The Big Fix (debut, 1978), Last Embrace, French Postcards, Night of the Juggler, Ragtime, Daniel, Yentl, Maxie, The Princess Bride, The House on Carroll Street, Alien Nation, Dick Tracy, True Colors, Impromptu, The Doctor, The Music of Chance, Life With Mikey, Indian Warrior.
TELEVISION: *Guest*: That Thing on ABC, That 2nd Thing on ABC, Taxi, Sparrow, Streets of Gold, Midnight Special. *Movie*: Charleston.

PATRIC, JASON: Actor. b. Queens, NY, 1966. Son of playwright-actor Jason Miller. Grandson of performer Jackie Gleason. Began professional career with Vermont's Champlain Shakespeare Festival.
PICTURES: Solarbabies (debut, 1986), The Lost Boys, The

Beast, Denial, After Dark My Sweet, Roger Corman's Frankenstein Unbound, Rush, Geronimo.
TELEVISION: *Movie*: Tough Love. *Special*: Teach 109.
THEATRE: *N.Y.*: Beirut. *L.A.*: Out of Gas on Lovers' Leap.

PATRICK, C.L.: Theatre Executive. b. Honaker, VA., Dec. 6, 1918. Former pres. of Fuqua Industries which owned Martin Theatres and Gulf States Theatres. Prior to this was pres. and chairman of Martin Theatres. Presently chairman of board Carmike Cinemas, Inc. v.p. Variety International; director, Will Rogers Institute; Motion Picture Pioneer of 1976; Recipient of: Sherrill Corwin Award, 1984; Salah Hassanein Humanitarian Award, ShowEast '88; Show South's Exhibitor of the Decade Award, 1990.

PATRICK, MATTHEW: Director, Writer. b. Ann Arbor, MI, Nov. 28, 1955. e. Hampshire Col., Amer. Film Inst. Prod., dir. of short film Triptych, winner of Acad. Award for student film, 1978.
PICTURES: Trapped (prod., dir., photog.), Graffiti (Acad. Award nom., best live action short film), The Lawless Land (co-s.p.), Hider in the House (dir.).

PATRICK, MICHAEL W.: Executive. b. Columbus, GA, May 17, 1950. e. Columbus Coll, B.S., 1972. Pres., CEO, Carmike Cinemas. 1989, assumed additional post of chief exec. Board of dir., Columbus Bank and Trust Co.
MEMBER: exec. comm., Will Rogers Institute; Variety Intl.; Motion Picture Pioneers.

PATTON, WILL: Actor. b. Charleston, SC, June 14, 1954. e. NC School of the Arts, 1975.
THEATER: Tourists and Refugees #2 (La Mama E.T.C., Obie Award, Best Actor), Fool For Love (1982 Obie Award, Best Actor), Goose and Tomtom (Public Theatre), A Lie of the Mind.
PICTURES: King Blank, Silkwood, Variety, Desperately Seeking Susan, After Hours, Chinese Boxes, Belizaire the Cajun, No Way Out, Stars and Bars, Wildfire, The Lizard's Tale, Signs of Life, Everybody Wins, Jackal's Run, A Shock to the System, The Rapture, Cold Heaven, In the Soup, The Paint Job.
TELEVISION: *Movies*: Kent State, Dillinger, The Deadly Desire, In the Deep Woods, A Child Lost Forever, Taking the Heat. *Series*: Ryan's Hope, Search For Tomorrow.

PAUL, M. B.: Cameraman, Director. r.n. Morrison Bloomfield Paul. b. Montreal, Canada. Sept. 30, 1909. e. De Paul U. Newsreel, publicity picture service; partner, Seymour Studios, 1930–33; film test biz. own studio. Hollywood, 1933–35; prod. adv. films, asst. in N.Y. E.W. Hammons, 1945–47; Acad. Award, one-piece color translucent background system, 1950. Dir. of photography, optical effects, Daystar, United Artists, Outer Limits, 1963; designed, patented, Scenoramic process, 1965. Camera, Paradise Road. Features, Film project supervision A/V consult. Sceno 360 surround system development. Mem. AMPAS, Friars, SMPTE.

PAUL, STEVEN: Director, Actor. b. New York, NY, May 16, 1958.
THEATER: Actor: Happy Birthday Wanda June, Burning.
PICTURES: Happy Birthday Wanda June (actor), Falling in Love Again (prod., dir., co-s.p., actor), Slapstick of Another Kind (dir., s.p., prod.), Never Too Young to Die (prod., co-s.p.), Fear (prod.), Eternity (prod., dir., actor), Emanon (exec. prod.), Illusions (prod.), Double O Kid (prod.).
TELEVISION: Actor: A Visiting Angel, Whatever Happened to Dobie Gillis?

PAULEY, JANE: TV host and journalist. b. Indianapolis, IN, Oct. 31, 1950. m. Doonesbury creator Garry Trudeau. e. Indiana U. Involved in Indiana state politics before joining WISH-TV, Indianapolis, as reporter. Co-anchored midday news reports and anchored weekend news reports. Co-anchor of nightly news at WMAQ-TV, NBC station in Chicago. Joined Today Show in October, 1976, as featured regular, prior to which had made guest appearances on that program; co-host until 1990. Began own series Real Life With Jane Pauley in 1991.

PAVAN, MARISA: Actress. r.n. Marisa Pierangeli. b. Cagliari, Sardinia, Italy, June 19, 1932. e. Torquato Tasso Coll. Twin sister of late Pier Angeli, actress. Came to U.S. 1950; m.p. debut in What Price Glory (1952).
PICTURES: Down Three Dark Streets, Drum Beat, Rose Tattoo, Diane, Man in the Gray Flannel Suit, John Paul Jones, Solomon and Sheba, Midnight Story.

PAVLIK, JOHN M.: Executive. b. Melrose, IA, Dec. 3, 1939. e. U. of Minnesota, B.A., 1963. Reporter, Racine (WI) Journal-Times, San Bernardino (CA) Sun-Telegram, 1963–66; Writer, News Bureau, Pacific Telephone, Los Angeles, 1966–68; asst. dir. of public relations, Association of Motion Picture and Television Producers, 1968–72; dir. of public relations, 1972–78; v.p., 1978–79; exec. administrator, Academy of Motion Picture Arts and Sciences, 1979–82; exec. dir., M.P. & TV Fund, 1982–88; consultant, 1988–89; dir. of endowment dev., Academy Foundation, 1989–present; member, board of dir., Permanent Charities Comm. of the Entertainment Industries, 1979–84; member, bd. of dir., Hollywood Chamber of Com-

merce, 1979–85; v.p., Los Angeles Film Dev. Committee, 1977–78, member, exec. council, 1974–85; special consultant, California Motion Picture Council, 1974–79; member, advisory board, Assn. of Film Commissioners Intl., 1988–present.

PAVLOW, MURIEL: Actress. b. June 27, 1921. e. England, Switzerland. Stage debut in Dear Octopus, 1938; screen debut in Romance in Flanders (1937). TV incl. Hamlet, Last Evensong, Boon.
PICTURES: Quiet Wedding, Night Boat to Dublin, Shop at Sly Corner, It Started in Paradise, The Net (Project M7), Malta Story, Conflict of Wings (Fuss Over Feathers), Doctor in the House, Simon and Laura, Reach for the Sky, Eye Witness, Tiger in the Smoke, Doctor at Large. Rooney, Whirlpool, Murder She Said.

PAXTON, BILL: Actor. b. Fort Worth, TX, May 17, 1955. e. NYU. Studied acting with Stella Adler. First professional job as set dresser for film Big Bad Mamma. Dir. short films Fish Heads, Scoop (also s.p.)
PICTURES: Stripes, The Lords of Discipline, Mortuary, Streets of Fire, Impulse, The Terminator, Weird Science, Commando, Aliens, Near Dark, Pass the Ammo, Next of Kin, Brain Dead, The Last of the Finest, Navy SEALS, Predator 2, The Dark Backward, One False Move, The Vagrant, Trespass, Indian Summer, Boxing Helena, Monolith, Tombstone.
TELEVISION: *Mini-Series*: Fresno. *Movies*: Deadly Lessons, The Atlanta Child Murders, An Early Frost. *Guest*: Miami Vice.

PAY, WILLIAM: UK Manager Quigley Publishing Co., Inc. b. London, England. Joined London office Quigley Publications. Served in RAF, 1941–46; rejoined Quigley; dir. Burnup Service Ltd., 1951; London news ed., Quigley Pub., 1955. Dir., Quigley Pub. Ltd., 1961; appt. mgr. dir., 1963; mgr. dir., Burnup Company. Appt. Sec. British Kinematograph Sound & TV Society. Conference Co-ordinator biennial Intern. Film & TV Technology Conferences in U.K., 1975–87.

PAYMER, DAVID: Actor. b. Long Island, NY, Aug. 30, 1954. e. Univ. of Mich. First professional job with natl. company of Grease, which he later appeared in on Bdwy. Has also taught acting at UCLA and the Film Actor's Workshop, performed stand-up comedy and served as staff writer on The New Leave It to Beaver Show.
PICTURES: The In-Laws (debut, 1979), Airplane II: The Sequel, Best Defense, Irreconcilable Differences, Perfect, Howard the Duck, No Way Out, Crazy People, City Slickers, Mr. Saturday Night (Acad. Award nom.), Searching for Bobby Fischer, Heart and Souls.
TELEVISION: *Series*: The Commish. *Movies*: Grace Kelly, Pleasure. *Guest*: Cagney & Lacy, The Paper Chase, Taxi, Cheers, L.A. Law, Hill Street Blues, Moonlighting, Murphy Brown.

PAYNE, NORMAN: Artists' and writers' manager. b. London, England. Ent. entertainment ind., 1939. Early career music, then formed talent agency, J.P. Productions, 1945. Later bought by MCA, 1951. Became dir. MCA and head of light ent. for theatres and TV throughout Europe. On MCA terminating reformed agency. TV offices also in Germany, Australia.

PAYNTER, ROBERT: Cinematographer. b. London, England, Mar. 12, 1928. e. Mercer Sch. First job in industry at 15 years as camera trainee with Government Film Dept.
PICTURES: Hannibal Brooks (debut, 1969), The Nightcomers, The Mechanic, Firepower, Superman, Superman II, Trading Places, An American Werewolf in London, The Final Conflict (co-cine.), Superman III, The Muppets Take Manhattan, Into the Night, Spies Like Us, Little Shop of Horrors, When the Whales Came.

PAYS, AMANDA: Actress. b. Berkshire, England, June 6, 1959. m. actor Corbin Bernsen. Began as a model. Studied French, art and pottery at Hammersmith Polytechnic. Acting debut: Cold Room (HBO).
PICTURES: Oxford Blues, The Kindred, Off Limits, Leviathan, Exposure.
TELEVISION: *Series*: Max Headroom, The Flash. *Mini-Series*: A.D. *Movies*: 13 at Dinner, The Pretenders, Parker Kane, Dead on the Money.

PAYSON, MARTIN D.: Executive. b. Brooklyn, NY, Jan. 4, 1936. e. Cornell U., NYU Sch. of Law, LLB, 1961. Practiced law privately before joining Warner Communications, Inc. as v.p. 1970. Later named exec. v.p.—gen. counsel. 1987, appt. to 3-member office of pres., WCI. Was vice chmn. Time Warner Inc., until Dec. 1992. Retired.

PEAKER, E. J.: Actress, Singer, Dancer. Edra Jeanne Peaker, b. Tulsa, OK, Feb. 22. e. U. of New Mexico, U. of Vienna, Austria. Stage debut Bye, Bye Birdie; film debut Hello Dolly (1969). Films include All American Boy, Private Roads, The Four Deuces, Graduation Day, Fire in the Night, I Can't Lose, Out of This World.

TELEVISION: *Series*: That's Life. *Guest*: The Flying Nun, That Girl, Love American Style, Odd Couple, Police Woman, Rockford Files, Get Christie Love, Houston Knights, Hunter, Quincy, Charlie's Angels, Six Million Dollar Man. *Movies*: Three's a Crowd, Getting Away From It All.

PEARCE, CHRISTOPHER: Producer. b. Dursley, Eng, Nov. 19, 1943. Entered industry as gen. mgr. American Zoetrope. From 1982 to 1985 served as exec. in chg. of prod. for Cannon Films Inc. overseeing prod. on 150 films incl. That Championship Season, Runaway Train, Fool For Love and Barfly. In 1987 became sr. v.p. and chief operating officer Cannon Group. Since pres., and chief exec. officer Cannon Pictures.
PICTURES: Prod. Coming Out of the Ice.

PEARCE, RICHARD: Director, Cinematographer. b. San Diego, CA, Jan. 25, 1943. e. Yale U., B.A. degree in Eng. lit., 1965. New School for Social Research, M.A., degree in political economics. Worked with Don Pennebaker and Richard Leacock on documentaries. Photographed Emile de Antonio's America Is Hard to See. In 1970 went to Chile where he dir., photographed and edited Campamento, an award-winning documentary.
PICTURES: *As photographer* (Acad. Award winning documentaries): Woodstock, Marjoe, Interviews With My Lai Veterans, Hearts and Minds. *As director*: Heartland, Threshold, Country, No Mercy, The Long Walk Home, Leap of Faith.
TELEVISION: The Gardener's Son, Siege, No Other Love, Sessions, Dead Man Out, The Final Days.

PECK, GREGORY: Actor, Producer. r.n. Eldred Gregory Peck. b. La Jolla, CA, April 5, 1916. e. U. of California; Neighborhood Playhouse Sch. of Dramatics. Father of actors Tony and Cecilia Peck. On dramatic stage (The Doctor's Dilemma, The Male Animal, Once in a Lifetime, The Play's the Thing, You Can't Take It With You, The Morning Star, The Willow and I, Sons and Soldiers, etc.). Voted one of ten best Money-Making Stars Motion Picture Herald-Fame Poll, 1947, 1952. Co-prod. and starred in Big Country, for his company, Anthony Productions; prod. the Trial of the Catonsville Nine, The Dove (St. George Productions). Pres., Acad. M.P. Arts and Sciences, 1967–70. Founding mem., bd. mem and chmn. American Film Inst. Recipient, Jean Hersholt Humanitarian Award, 1986. AFI Life Achievement Award, 1989. Voice of Florenz Ziegfeld in 1991 Bdwy musical The Will Rogers Follies.
PICTURES: Days of Glory (debut, 1944), Keys of the Kingdom, Valley of Decision, Spellbound, The Yearling, Duel in the Sun, Macomber Affair, Gentleman's Agreement, The Paradine Case, Yellow Sky, The Great Sinner, 12 O'Clock High, The Gunfighter, Only the Valiant, David and Bathsheba, Captain Horatio Hornblower, The World in His Arms, The Snows of Kilimanjaro, Roman Holiday, Night People, Man With a Million, Purple Plain, Man in the Gray Flannel Suit, Moby Dick, Designing Woman, The Bravados, The Big Country (also prod.), Pork Chop Hill (also prod.), Beloved Infidel, On the Beach, Guns of Navarone, To Kill a Mockingbird (Acad. Award, 1962), Cape Fear (also prod.), How the West Was Won, Captain Newman M.D., Behold a Pale Horse (also prod.), Mirage, Arabesque, MacKenna's Gold, Stalking Moon, The Chairman, Marooned, I Walk the Line, Shootout, Billy Two Hats, The Omen, MacArthur (also prod.), The Boys from Brazil (also prod.), The Sea Wolves (also prod.), Amazing Grace and Chuck, Old Gringo, Other People's Money, Cape Fear.
TELEVISION: *Mini-series*: The Blue and the Gray. *Movies*: The Scarlet and the Black (also prod.), The Portrait. *Special*: We the People 200: The Constitutional Gala.

PEDAS, JIM: Executive. b. Youngstown, OH. e. Thiel College. Opened Circle Theatre in Washington, D.C. in 1957 with brother Ted. 1984 formed Circle Releasing, serving as Secretary/Treasurer; Circle Films, serving as v.p. See Ted Pedas entry.

PEDAS, TED: Executive. b. Farrell, PA, May 6, 1931. e. Youngstown St. Univ., Wharton Sch. of Business at Univ. of Pa., Geo. Washington Univ. In 1957, with brother Jim, opened Circle Theatre in Washington D.C. one of the first repertory houses. Circle/Showcase group of m.p. theatres expanded to over 80 quality screens before being sold in 1988. 1973–78, served on board of Cinema 5 in NY. 1984, Circle Releasing formed to distribute films with Ted serving as president. Releases include Blood Simple, A Letter to Brezhnev, The Navigator, Bye Bye Blues. Circle Films has produced the Coen Brothers' Raising Arizona, Miller's Crossing, and Barton Fink.

PEERCE, LARRY: Director. b. Bronx, NY. Son of late singer Jan Peerce.
PICTURES: One Potato Two Potato, The Big T.N.T. Show, The Incident, Goodbye Columbus, The Sporting Club, A Separate Peace, Ash Wednesday, The Other Side of the Mountain, Two Minute Warning, The Other Side of the Mountain—Part II, The Bell Jar (also exec. prod.), Why Would I Lie?, Love Child, Hard to Hold, Wired.

TELEVISION: *Movies*: A Stranger Who Looks Like Me, Love Lives On, I Take These Men, The Fifth Missile, Prison for Children, Queenie, Elvis and Me, The Neon Empire, The Court—Martial of Jackie Robinson, Child of Rage, Poisoned by Love: The Kern County Murders.

PEÑA, ELIZABETH: Actress. b. Cuba, Sept. 23, 1961. Moved to New York City in 1969 where she attended NY High School for Performing Arts. Off-Bdwy in Blood Wedding, Antigone, Romeo & Juliet, Act One & Only, Italian American Reconciliation.
PICTURES: El Super, Times Square, They All Laughed, Fat Chance, Crossover Dreams, Down and Out in Beverly Hills, La Bamba, Batteries Not Included, Vibes, Blue Steel, Jacob's Ladder, The Waterdance.
TELEVISION: *Series*: Tough Cookies, I Married Dora, Shannon's Deal. *Movies*: Fugitive Among Us, Roommates.

PENDLETON, AUSTIN: Actor. b. Warren, OH, Mar. 27, 1940. e. Yale Univ.
PICTURES: Skidoo (debut, 1968), Catch-22, What's Up Doc?, Every Little Crook and Nanny, The Thief Who Came to Dinner, The Front Page, The Great Smokey Roadblock, The Muppet Movie, Starting Over, Simon, First Family, My Man Adam, Off Beat, Short Circuit, Hello Again, Mr. & Mrs. Bridge, The Ballad of the Sad Cafe, True Identity, My Cousin Vinny, Charlie's Ear, Rain Without Thunder, My Boyfriend's Back, Searching for Bobby Fischer, Mr. Nanny, Guarding Tess.
THEATRE: *Actor*: Oh Dad Poor Dad, Fiddler on the Roof, The Little Foxes, The Last Sweet Days of Isaac, The Runner Stumbles, Educating Rita, Doubles, The Sorrows of Frederick, Grand Hotel. *Director*: Say Goodnight Gracie, John Gabriel Borkman, The Little Foxes.

PENN, ARTHUR: Director. b. Philadelphia, PA, Sept. 27, 1922. e. Black Mountain Coll., Asheville, NC; U. of Perugia, U. of Florence in Italy. Began as TV dir. in 1953, twice winner of Sylvania Award. Dir. stage plays Two for the Seesaw, Miracle Worker (Tony Award), Toys in the Attic, All the Way Home, Golden Boy, Wait Until Dark, Sly Fox, Monday After the Miracle, Hunting Cockroaches.
PICTURES: The Left-Handed Gun (debut, 1958), The Miracle Worker, Mickey One (also prod.), The Chase, Bonnie and Clyde, Alice's Restaurant (also s.p.), Little Big Man, Visions of Eight (co-dir.), Night Moves, The Missouri Breaks, Four Friends (also co-prod.), Target, Dead of Winter, Penn and Teller Get Killed (also prod.).
TELEVISION: *Movies*: North Beach and Rawhide, The Portrait.

PENN, CHRISTOPHER: Actor. b. Malibu, CA. Son of director Leo Penn and actress Eileen Ryan. Brother of actor Sean Penn and musician Michael Penn. Studied acting with Peggy Feury.
PICTURES: Rumble Fish (debut, 1983), All the Right Moves, Footloose, The Wild Life, Pale Rider, At Close Range, Made in USA, Best of the Best, Mobsters, Leather Jackets, Reservoir Dogs, Best of the Best 2, The Pickle, The Music of Chance, Josh and S.A.M., Short Cuts, True Romance, Beethoven's 2nd.
TELEVISION: *Guest*: The Young Riders, North Beach and Rawhide.

PENN, SEAN: Actor. b. Burbank, CA, Aug. 17, 1960. Son of actor-director Leo Penn and actress Eileen Ryan. Brother of actor Christopher Penn and musician Michael Penn. e.Santa Monica H.S. Served as apprentice for two years at Group Repertory Theatre, L.A. Acted in Earthworms, Heartland, The Girl on the Via Flaminia, etc. First prof appearance as guest star on TV's Barnaby Jones. On Bdwy. in Heartland, then Slab Boys. Also Hurlyburly (Westwood Playhouse, LA).
PICTURES: *Actor*: Taps (debut, 1981), Fast Times at Ridgemont High, Bad Boys, Crackers, Racing with the Moon, The Falcon and the Snowman, At Close Range, Shanghai Surprise, Colors, Judgment in Berlin, Casualties of War, We're No Angels, State of Grace, Carlito's Way. *Dir./Writer*: The Indian Runner.
TELEVISION: *Movie*: The Killing of Randy Webster. *Guest*: Barnaby Jones. *Special*: Dear America (reader).

PENNEBAKER, D.A.: Director. b. Evanston, IL, 1926. r.n. Donn Alan Pennebaker. e. Yale U. Studied engineering, set up own electronics firm. Worked in advertising, before writing and directing documentaries, as well as experimental films. In 1958 joined Richard Leacock, Willard Van Dyke and Shirley Clarke in equipment-sharing film co-op, Filmakers. In 1960 joined Robert Drew operating out of Time Life with Leacock, Albert Maysles and others. Set up Leacock Pennebaker with Leacock and made several films that were blown up from 16mm to 35mm and released in theatres. Currently worksd with co-dir. Chris Hegedus and son Frazer Pennebaker, continuing to film unscripted dramas of real events in cinema verite style.
PICTURES: Daybreak Express (1956), Opening in Moscow, Primary, David, Jane, Crisis, The Chair, On the Pole, Mr. Pearson, Don't Look Back, Monterey Pop, Beyond the Law, One P.M., Sweet Toronto, Maidstone, Ziggy Stardust, From

the Pole to the Equator (ed. only), Wild, Town Bloody Hall, The Energy War, Dance Black America, Rockaby, Delorean, Happy Come Home, Depeche Mode, The Music Tells You, The War Room.

PEPLOE, CLARE: Writer, director. Sister of screenwriter Mark Peploe and wife of dir. Bernardo Bertolucci.
PICTURES: Couples and Robbers (s.p.); Zabriskie Point (asst. to Antonioni); 1900 (asst. to Bertolucci); High Season (dir., co-s.p.).

PEPPARD, GEORGE: Actor, b. Detroit, MI, Oct. 1, 1928. e. Dearborn H.S., Carnegie Mellon Inst., B.F.A., fine arts. U.S. Marine Corps. Legit. stage debut, Pittsburgh Playhouse, 1949. Worked as mason, construction laborer, fencing instructor, radio announcer, cab driver.
STAGE: Girls of Summer, The Pleasure of His Company, Papa: The Legendary Lives of Ernest Hemingway (one-man show), The Lion in Winter.
PICTURES: The Strange One (debut, 1957), Pork Chop Hill, Home from the Hill, The Subterraneans, Breakfast At Tiffany's, How the West Was Won, The Victors, The Carpetbaggers, The Third Day, Operation Crossbow, The Blue Max, Tobruk, Rough Night in Jericho, P.J., What's So Bad About Feeling Good?, House of Cards, Pendulum, Cannon for Cordoba, The Executioner, One More Train to Rob, The Groundstar Conspiracy, Newman's Law, Damnation Alley, Five Days From Home (also dir., prod., s.p.), Your Ticket Is No Longer Valid, From Hell to Victory, Battle Beyond the Stars, Race to the Yankee Zephyr, Target Eagle, Silence Like Glass, The Tigress.
TELEVISION: Series: Banacek, Doctors' Hospital, The A Team. Special: Little Moon of Alban. Guest: Suspicion, U.S. Steel Hour, Alfred Hitchcock Presents, Matinee Theatre, Alcoa-Goodyear Playhouse, Studio One, Hallmark Hall of Fame. Movies: The Bravos, Banacek (pilot), One of Our Own, Guilty or Innocent: The Sam Sheppard Murder Case, Crisis in Mid-Air, Torn Between Two Lovers, Man Against the Mob, Man Against the Mob II.

PERAKOS, SPERIE P.: Executive. b. New Britain, CT, Nov. 12, 1915. e. Cheshire Acad., Yale U., Harvard Law Sch. Student mgr., Stanley-Warner thtrs., 1939–40; Perakos Theatres 1940 to present; Capt., U.S.A. Intelligence with 35 inf. division. Fellow, Pierson Coll., Yale, 1946–present; Yale Alumni Bd., 1949 to present; Yale Alumni Film Bd. 1952 to present; member Alumni Council for Yale Drama Sch.; past pres. Yale Club of New Britain, Conn.; dir. of Films & Filmings Seminars, Pierson Coll., Yale; prod. Antigone, 1962; pres. Norma Film Prod., Inc., 1962 to present. Past pres. and chmn. Yale's Peabody Museum Associates. Pres., Perakos Theatres, Conn. Theatre Circuit, Inc. Member, Exec. Board of Natl' Assn. of Theatre Owners, C.A.R.A.

PERENCHIO, ANDREW J.: Executive. b. Fresno, CA, Dec. 20, 1930. e. U. of California. Vice pres., Music Corp. of America, 1958–62; General Artists Corp., 1962–64; pres., owner, Chartwell Artists, Ltd., theatrical agency, Los Angeles, 1964; pres. & CEO, Tandem Productions, Inc., and TAT Communications Co., 1973–83, then became principal with Norman Lear in Embassy Communications. Held post of pres. & CEO of Embassy Pictures.

PERKINS, ELIZABETH: Actress. b. Queens, NY, Nov. 18, 1961. Grew up in Vermont. After high school moved to Chicago to study at Goodman School of Drama. Two months after moving to NY in 1984, landed a role in the national touring co. of Brighton Beach Memoirs, later performing part on Broadway. Acted with Playwright's Horizon, NY Ensemble Theater, Shakespeare in the Park and Steppenwolf Theatre Co. Appeared in short Teach 109.
PICTURES: About Last Night...(debut, 1986), From the Hip, Big, Sweethearts Dance, Love at Large, Avalon, He Said She Said, Enid is Sleeping (Over Her Dead Body), The Doctor, Indian Summer, The Flintstones.
TELEVISION: Movie: For Their Own Good.

PERKINS, MILLIE: Actress. b. Passaic, NJ, May 12, 1938.
PICTURES: The Diary of Anne Frank (debut, 1959), Wild in the Country, Ensign Pulver, Ride in the Whirlwind, The Shooting, Wild in the Streets, Cockfighter, Table for Five, At Close Range, Jake Speed, Slam Dance, Wall Street, Two Moon Junction, The Pistol, Dulcinea, The Witch Who Came from the Sea.
TELEVISION: Series: Knots Landing, Elvis. Guest: thirtysomething, Murder She Wrote, Our House, Jessie, Hart to Hart, Glitter, Wagon Train. Movies: A.D., The Thanksgiving Promise, Penalty Phase, Anatomy of an Illness, Shattered Vows, License to Kill, Strange Voices, Broken Angel, Best Intentions, The Other Love, Haunting Passion, A Gun in the House, Model Mother, Macbeth (cable tv), Call Me Anna, 72 Hours. Guest: U.S. Steel Hour, Breaking Point.

PERLMAN, RHEA: Actress. b. Brooklyn, NY, March 31, 1948. e. Hunter Coll. m. actor-dir. Danny DeVito. Co-founder Colon-

nades Theatre Lab., NY and New Street prod. co with Danny DeVito.
TELEVISION: Specials: Funny You Don't Look 200, Two Daddies (voice), The Last Halloween. Series: Cheers (4 Emmy Awards, supp actress, 1984, 85, 86 and 89). Movies: I Want to Keep My Baby!, Stalk the Wild Child, Having Babies II, Intimate Strangers, Mary Jane Harper Cried Last Night, Like Normal People, Drop-out Father, The Ratings Game, Dangerous Affection, A Family Again, To Grandmother's House We Go, A Place to Be Loved.
PICTURES: Love Child, My Little Pony (voice), Enid is Sleeping (Over Her Dead Body), Ted & Venus, Class Act, There Goes the Neighborhood.

PERLMAN, RON: Actor. b. New York, NY, April 13, 1950. While in high school, part of comedy team that played clubs. e. City U. of NY, U. of Minnesota, M.F.A. Joined Classic Stage Company, NY, for 2 years.
THEATER: NY: The Architect and the Emperor of Assyria (also toured Europe), American Heroes, The Resistible Rise of Arturo Ui, Tiebele and Her Demon, La Tragedie de Carmen, A Few Good Men.
PICTURES: Quest for Fire, The Ice Pirates, The Name of the Rose, Sleepwalkers, The Adventures of Huck Finn, Crime and Punishment.
TELEVISION: Series: Beauty and the Beast. Movies: A Stoning in Fulham County, Blind Man's Bluff.

PERLMUTTER, DAVID M.: Producer. b. Toronto, Canada, 1934. e. U. of Toronto. Pres., Quadrant Films Ltd.
PICTURES: The Neptune Factor, Sunday in the Country, It Seemed Like a Good Idea at the Time, Love at First Sight, Find the Lady, Blood and Guts, The Third Walker, Two Solitudes, Fast Company, Double Negative, Nothing Personal, Misdeal, Love.

PERMUT, DAVID A.: Producer. b. New York, NY, 1952. In 1974, became pres., Diversified Artists Intl.; 1975, pres., Theatre Television Corp.; 1979, formed Permut Presentations, Inc., of which is pres. Production deals with Columbia Pictures (1979), Lorimar Productions (1981), Universal (1985), United Artists (1986), and New Line Cinema (1991).
PICTURES: Give 'Em Hell Harry, Fighting Back (exec. prod.), Blind Date, Richard Pryor—Live in Concert (exec. prod.), Dragnet, The Marrying Man, 29th Street, Captain Ron, Consenting Adults, The Temp, Three of Hearts.
TELEVISION: Mistress (sprv. prod.), Love Leads the Way (exec. prod.), Triumph of the Heart: The Ricky Bell Story (prod.), Breaking the Silence (prod.).

PERREAU, GIGI: Actress. r.n. Ghislaine Perreau; b. Los Angeles, CA, Feb. 6, 1941. Prof. m.p. debut in Madame Curie 1943; many stage and TV guest appearances. Now teaching and directing. Among first 50 stars to be honored with star on Hollywood Walk of Fame.
PICTURES: Yolanda and the Thief, Dark Waters, Abigail, Dear Heart, High Barbaree, Song of Love, Green Dolphin Street, Family Honeymoon, Roseanna McCoy, My Foolish Heart, Shadow on the Wall, For Heaven's Sake, Never a Dull Moment, Reunion in Reno, Lady Pays Off, Weekend with Father, Has Anybody Seen My Gal, Bonzo Goes to College, There's Always Tomorrow, Man in the Gray Flannel Suit, Dance With Me Henry, Wild Heritage, The Cool and the Crazy, Girls Town, Tammy Tell Me True, Look in Any Window, Journey to the Center of Time, Hell on Wheels.
TELEVISION: Series: The Betty Hutton Show, Follow the Sun.

PERRINE, VALERIE: Actress. b. Galveston, TX, Sept. 3 1943. e. U. of Arizona. Was showgirl in Las Vegas before discovered by agent Robert Walker who got her contract with Universal Pictures.
PICTURES: Slaughterhouse 5 (debut, 1972), The Last American Hero, Lenny (N.Y. Film Critics Award, Acad. Award nom., Cannes Fest.; Actress of the Year, United Motion Picture Assn.), W. C. Fields & Me, Mr. Billion, Superman, The Magician of Lublin, The Electric Horseman, Can't Stop the Music, Superman II, Agency, The Border, Water, Maid to Order, Bright Angel, Boiling Point.
TELEVISION: Movies: The Couple Takes a Wife, Ziegfeld: The Man and His Women, Marian Rose White, Malibu, When Your Lover Leaves, Sweet Bird of Youth, Un Casa a Roma The Burning Shore. Series: Leo and Liz in Beverly Hills. Special: Steambath.

PERRY, ANTHONY: Producer. b. London, England, 1929. Ent. m.p. ind. 1948 with Two Cities story dept. asst. story ed., Rank Prods. Wrote orig. story and prod. asst. Simba. Prod., The Secret Place in 1957. Created and prod. TV series, Interpol Calling, 1959; founded Eyeline Films, prod. many Brit. prize-winning commercials. Sold Eyeline Films, 1963; wrote, dir. Emma, 1964–65, res. prod. Keep Films/Embassy Prods., London, 1966–67; prod. Dare I Weep, Dare I Mourn, for ABC-TV, and Fernandel TV series. Admin. Yellow Submarine, joined Trickfilm as man. dir. Chmn. Film & TV Copyrights, Ltd.

PICTURES: The Impersonator, Girl on Approval, The Party's Over.

PERRY, FRANK: Executive, Director, Producer, Writer. b. 1930. Served as apprentice, Westport, CT Country Playhouse; spent nine years in theater as stage mgr., prod. mgr., and managing director. U.S. Army, 1952–54; director-observer, Actors Studio, 1955; also prod. for the Theatre Guild. Pres. & CEO Corsair Pictures.
PICTURES: Somersault, David and Lisa, Ladybug Ladybug, The Swimmer, Last Summer, Trilogy, Diary of a Mad Housewife, Doc, Play It As It Lays, Man on a Swing, Rancho Deluxe, Mommie Dearest (also co-s.p.), Monsignor, Compromising Positions, Hello Again.
TELEVISION: *Specials*: Truman Capote's A Christmas Memory, Thanksgiving Visitors, JFK—A One Man Show. *Movies*: Skag (pilot), Dummy.

PERRY, LUKE: Actor. b. Fredricktown, MO, Oct. 11, 1966. r.n. Coy Luther Perry III.
TELEVISION: *Series*: Loving, Another World, Beverly Hills 90210.
PICTURES: Terminal Bliss, Buffy the Vampire Slayer, The Webbers, 8 Seconds to Glory.

PERRY, SIMON: Producer, Writer. b. Farnham, Eng., Aug. 5, 1943. e. Cambridge Univ., 1965. Ent. ind. 1974. Early career in stage and television production. Prod. mini-budget feature Knots; prod. dir. Eclipse. Served on bureau staff of Variety. Ran the National Film Development Fund for two years. In 1982 set up Umbrella Films to produce Another Time Another Place, Loose Connections, Hotel Du Paradis, Nanou, White Mischief, The Playboys.

PERSCHY, MARIA: Actress. b. Eisenstadt, Austria, Sept. 23, 1940. e. Max Rheinhardt Seminar, Vienna. Widow of John Melson, writer. Started in 1958 with German film (Nasser Asphalt) and has appeared in over 50 European and U.S. features. Has also appeared on European TV. Recipient of Laurel Award in 1963.
PICTURES: Man's Favorite Sport, Squadron 633, Ride the High Wind, Murders in the Rue Morgue, Last Day of the War, The Desperate Ones, The Tall Woman, Witch Without a Broom, etc.
TELEVISION: General Hospital, Hawaii Five-O.

PERSKY, LESTER: Executive. b. New York, NY, July 6, 1927. e. Brooklyn Coll. Officer in U.S. Merchant Marine, 1946–48. Founder and pres. of own adv. agency, 1951–1964. Theatrical stage producer, 1966–69. Produced Fortune and Men's Eyes for MGM in 1971. In 1973 creative director and co-owner Persky Bright Org. (owner-financier of numerous motion pictures for private investment group). Films include Last Detail, Golden Voyage of Sinbad, For Pete's Sake, California Split, The Man Who Would Be King, The Front, Shampoo. Also Hard Times, Taxi Driver, Missouri Breaks, Funny Lady, Gator, Bound for Glory, Sinbad and the Eye of the Tiger. Lester Persky Productions, Inc.
PICTURES: Produced Equus, Hair, Yanks.
TELEVISION: *Mini-Series*: Poor Little Rich Girl (Golden Globe Award, 1987), A Woman Named Jackie (Emmy Award, 1992).

PERSOFF, NEHEMIAH: Actor. b. Jerusalem, Israel, Aug. 2, 1919. e. Hebrew Technical Inst., 1934–37. Electrician, 1937–39; signal maint., N.Y. subway, 1939–41. L.A. Critics Award 1971 for Sholem-Sholem Alecheim, and The Dybbuk.
STAGE: Sundown Beach, Galileo, Richard III, King Lear, Peter Pan, Peer Gynt, Tiger At the Gates, Colombe, Flahooly, Montserrat, Only in America. Tour: Fiddler on the Roof, Man of La Mancha, Oliver, Death of a Salesman (Stratford, Ont.), Peter Pan (Capt. Hook), I'm Not Rappaport, Sholem Aleichem (Drama Log & Bay Area Critics Circle Awards).
PICTURES: On the Waterfront, The Wild Party, The Wrong Man, Men in War, This Angry Age, The Badlanders, Never Steal Anything Small, Al Capone, Some Like It Hot, Green Mansions, The Big Show, The Commancheros, The Hook, Fate Is the Hunter, The Greatest Story Ever Told, The Power, The Money Jungle, Panic in the City, The People Next Door, Mrs. Pollifax—Spy, Red Sky at Morning, Psychic Killer, Voyage of the Damned, In Search of Historic Jesus, Yentl, An American Tail (voice), The Last Temptation of Christ, Testament, Twins, The Dispossessed, An American Tail: Fievel Goes West (voice).
TELEVISION: Philco-Goodyear Show, Kraft, For Whom the Bells Tolls (Sylvania Award, 1958), Producers Showcase, Danger, You Are There, Untouchables, Route 66, Naked City, Wagon Train, Rawhide, Gunsmoke, Thriller, Hitchcock, Bus Stop, Five Fingers, Mr. Lucky, The Wild, Wild West, I Spy, Columbo, Barney Miller, Sadat, Adderly, The French Atlantic Affair, The Big Knife, L.A. Law, Star Trek, Law and Order, Reasonable Doubts.

PERTWEE, JON: TV Performer. b. London, England, July 7, 1919. e. Sherborne, Royal Acad. of Dramatic Art. Early career, Arts League of Service Traveling Theatre, 5 yrs. repertory; regularly on radio, TV, music hall, theatre film, and pantomime.
PICTURES: Murder At the Windmill, Miss Pilgrim's Progress, Will Any Gentleman?, Gay Dog, It's A Wonderful Life, Mr. Drake's Duck, A Yank in Ermine, Ugly Duckling, Just Joe, Not a Hope in Hell, Nearly a Nasty Accident, Ladies Who Do, Carry on Cleo, I've Gotta Horse, Carry On Cowboy, Carry On Screaming, A Funny Thing Happened On the Way To The Forum, Up in the Air, The Hod, March of the Desert, One of our Dinosaurs Is Missing, The House that Dripped Blood, The Island of Young Tigers, The Boys in Blue.
TELEVISION: (BBC) Own series, Sunday Night at the London Palladium Compere Variety Show, Doctor Who series, Who Dunnit, Worzel Gummidge.
STAGE: See You Inside, A Funny Thing Happened On The Way To The Forum, There's A Girl In My Soup, Oh Clarence, My Dear Gilbert, The Bedwinner, Don't Just Lie There, Say Something, Irene, Touch It Light, Dr. Who-The Ultimate Adventure, Scrooge.

PESCI, JOE: Actor. b. Newark, NJ, Feb. 9, 1943. Raised in Belleville, NJ. First show business job as child on TV's Star Time Kids. Worked as mason's laborer, restaurant owner, prior to becoming actor.
PICTURES: Death Collector, Raging Bull, I'm Dancing as Fast as I Can, Dear Mr. Wonderful, Easy Money, Eureka, Once Upon a Time in America, Man on Fire, Moonwalker, Lethal Weapon 2, Betsy's Wedding, Goodfellas (Acad. Award, supp. actor, 1990), Home Alone, The Super, JFK, My Cousin Vinny, Tuti Dentro, Lethal Weapon 3, The Public Eye, Home Alone 2: Lost in New York, With Honors.
TELEVISION: *Series*: Half Nelson. *Movies*: Half Nelson (pilot), Backtrack. *Guest*: Tales From the Crypt (Split Personality).

PESCOW, DONNA: Actress. b. Brooklyn, NY, March 24, 1954. e. American Acad. of Dramatic Arts. Started career on summer tour in Ah Wilderness in 1975. Did bit in ABC daytime series, One Life to Live.
PICTURES: Saturday Night Fever, Jake Speed.
TELEVISION: *Series*: Angie, All My Children, Out of This World. *Movies*: Advice to the Lovelorn, The Day the Bubble Burst, Human Feelings, Rainbow, Policewoman Centerfold, Obsessed with a Married Woman.

PETERS, BERNADETTE: Actress. r.n. Bernadette Lazzara. b. New York, NY, Feb. 28, 1948. e. Quintano Sch. for Young Professionals, NY. Professional debut at age 5 on TV's Horn & Hardart Children's Hour, followed by Juvenile Jury and Name That Tune. Stage debut with N.Y. City Center production of The Most Happy Fella (1959).
THEATER: Gypsy (1961), This is Goggle, Riverwind, The Penny Friend, Curley McDimple, Johnny No-Trump, George M! (Theatre World Award), Dames at Sea (Drama Desk Award), La Strada, W.C. & Me, On the Town (1971 revival), Tartuffe, Mack and Mabel, Sally and Marsha, Sunday in the Park With George, Song and Dance (Tony, Drama Desk & Drama League Awards), Into the Woods, The Goodbye Girl.
PICTURES: Ace Eli and Rodger of the Skies (debut, 1973), The Longest Yard, W.C. Fields & Me, Vigilante Force, Silent Movie, The Jerk, Tulips, Pennies from Heaven, Heartbeeps, Annie, Slaves of New York, Pink Cadillac, Alice, Impromptu.
TELEVISION: *Series*: All's Fair (1976–77). *Mini-Series*: The Martian Chronicles. *Specials*: George M, They Said It with Music, Party at Annapolis, Rich Thin and Beautiful (host), Faerie Tale Theatre, The Last Mile. Pilot: The Owl and the Pussycat. *Movies*: The Islander, David, Fall from Grace, The Last Best Year.

PETERS, BROCK: Actor. r.n. Brock Fisher. b. Harlem, NY, July 2, 1927. e. CCNY, U. of Chicago. Had numerous featured roles on and off Bdwy. in road and stock cos., nightclubs, TV. Toured with DePaur Infantry Chorus as bass soloist, 1947–50. Appeared in short film From These Roots.
THEATER: Porgy and Bess (debut, 1943), Anna Lucasta, My Darlin' Aida, Mister Johnson, King of the Dark Chamber, Othello, Kwamina, The Great White Hope (tour), Lost in the Stars, Driving Miss Daisy (Natl. Co.).
PICTURES: Carmen Jones (debut, 1954), Porgy and Bess, To Kill a Mockingbird, Heavens Above, The L-Shaped Room, The Pawnbroker, Major Dundee, P.J., The Daring Game, The Incident, Ace High, The MacMasters, Black Girl, Soylent Green, Slaughter's Big Rip-off, Lost in the Stars, Million Dollar Dixie Deliverance, Framed, Two-Minute Warning, From These Roots (short), Star Trek IV: The Voyage Home, Star Trek VI: The Undiscovered Country.
TELEVISION: Arthur Godfrey's Talent Scouts (debut, 1953), *Series*: The Young and the Restless. *Guest*: Eleventh Hour, It Takes a Thief, Mannix, Mod Squad. *Mini-series*: Seventh Avenue, Black Beauty, Roots: the Next Generations. *Movies*: Welcome Home Johnny Bristol, SST: Death Flight, The Incredible Journey of Doctor Meg Laurel, The Adventures of Huckleberry Finn, Agatha Christie's Caribbean Mystery, To Heal a Nation, Broken Angel, The Big One: The Great Los Angeles Earthquake, Highway Heartbreakers, The

Secret. *Specials*: Challenge of the Go Bots (voice), Living the Dream: A Tribute to Dr. Martin Luther King. *Co-prod.*: This Far By Faith (1975).

PETERS, JON: Producer. b. Van Nuys, CA, 1947. Started hairstyling business; built it into multimillion-dollar firm before turning film producer. Formed Jon Peters Organization. 1980, joined with Peter Guber and Neil Bogart to form The Boardwalk Co. (dissolved 1981). Later Guber-Peters-Barris Company. 1989, became co-chairman of Columbia Pictures. Resigned, 1991.
PICTURES: A Star Is Born, Eyes of Laura Mars, The Main Event, Die Laughing, Caddyshack, Co-prod./co-exec. prod. with Peter Guber: An American Werewolf in London, Missing, Six Weeks, Flashdance, D.C. Cab, Vision Quest, Legend of Billie Jean, Clue, The Color Purple, Head Office, The Clan of the Cave Bear, Youngblood, The Witches of Eastwick, Innerspace, Who's That Girl, Gorillas in the Mist, Caddyshack II, Rain Man, Batman, Tango and Cash, The Bonfire of the Vanities, Batman Returns, This Boy's Life.
TELEVISION: Bay Coven (co-exec. prod.), Nightmare at Bitter Creek (exec. prod.).

PETERSEN, PAUL: Actor. b. Glendale, CA, Sept. 23, 1945. e. Valley Coll. Original Disney Mouseketeer (TV). Recorded hit songs She Can't Find Her Keys and My Dad in 1962. In the late 1960's turned to writing—beginning with a Marcus Welby script followed by paperback novels in 1970's. Author of book about Disney empire, Walt Mickey and Me (1977), and co-author of It's a Wonderful Life Trivia Book (1992).
PICTURES: Houseboat, This Could Be the Night, The Happiest Millionaire.
TELEVISION: *Series*: The Donna Reed Show. *Guest*: Playhouse 90, Lux Video Theatre, GE Theatre, The Virginian, Ford Theatre, Valentine's Day, Shindig. *Movies*: Something for a Lonely Man, Gidget Grows Up, Scout's Honor.

PETERSEN, WILLIAM: Actor. b. Chicago, IL, 1953. e. Idaho State U. Active in Chicago theatre; helped to found Ix, an ensemble acting group now called the Remains Theatre. Acted in Moby Dick, In the Belly of the Beast, A Streetcar Named Desire, etc. 1986, formed company with prod. Cynthia Chvatal called High Horse Prods.
PICTURES: To Live and Die in L.A., Manhunter, Amazing Grace and Chuck, Cousins, Young Guns II, Hard Promises (also co-prod.), Passed Away.
TELEVISION: *Movies*: Long Gone (HBO), Keep the Change (also co-prod.), Curacao. *Mini-Series*: The Kennedys of Massachusetts.

PETERSEN, WOLFGANG: Director, Writer. b. Emden, Germany, Mar. 14, 1941. Career as asst. stage director at Ernst Deutsch Theatre in Hamburg before entering 4 year program at the German Film & TV Academy where he directed for television and later theatrical films.
PICTURES: One of Us Two, Black and White Like Day (also s.p.), The Consequence (also s.p.), Das Boot (The Boat; also s.p.), The NeverEnding Story (also s.p.), Enemy Mine, Shattered (also s.p., co-prod.), In the Line of Fire (also co-exec.prod.).
TELEVISION: Smog (Prix Futura Award, 1975), For Your Love Only (also released theatrically), Scenes of the Crime (series).

PETERSON, S. DEAN: Executive. b. Toronto, Canada, December 18, 1923. e. Victoria Coll., U. of Toronto. W.W.II service RCNVR; 1946 TV newsreel cameraman NBC; founded own prod. co. in 1947; incorporated Dordean Realty Limited to acquire new studios 1959; formed Peterson Production Limited in 1957 to make TV commercials and sponsored theatrical shorts; has intl. awards as prod., dir., dir. of photography; formed Studio City Limited in 1965 to produce TV series and features acquiring an additional studio complex and backlot in Kleinberg, Ontario; 1972 formed SDP Communications Ltd. to package M.P. and TV; 1970 incorporated Intermedia Financial Services Limited to provide specialized financing and consultation to companies in M.P. and TV industries.
Past-President Canadian Film and Television Assn., mbr. Variety Club, Tent 28; Canadian Society of Cinematographers; Directors Guild of America, Directors Guild of Canada, SMPTE.

PETERSON, RICHARD W.: Executive. b. Denver, CO, June 15, 1949. e. Col. Sch. of Broadcasting, Harper Coll. Joined Kennedy Theatres, Chicago, 1966. In 1968 went with Great States Theatres (now Cineplex Odeon), Chicago. Was city mgr. of Crocker and Grove Theatres, Elgin, IL. In 1973 joined American Automated Theatres, Oklahoma City, as dir. of adv., pub. Promoted to dir. of U.S. theatre operations. Worked for American International Pictures, Dallas, TX. Then moved to Dal Art Film Exchange and B & B Theatres as general mgr.; 1987 took over 7 screens from McLendon and formed own co., Peterson Theatres, Inc, now operating 17 screens.

PETRIE, DANIEL: Director. b. Glace Bay, Nova Scotia, Nov. 26, 1920. e. St. Francis Xavier U., Nova Scotia; Columbia U., MA, 1945; postgrad. Northwestern U. Broadway actor 1945–46. TV director from 1950.
PICTURES: The Bramble Bush, A Raisin in the Sun, The Main Attraction, The Stolen Hours, The Idol, Spy With a Cold Nose, The Neptune Factor, Buster and Billie, Lifeguard, The Betsy, Resurrection, Fort Apache The Bronx, Six Pack, The Bay Boy (also s.p., Genie Award), Square Dance, Rocket Gibraltar, Cocoon: The Return.
THEATRE: Shadow of My Enemy, Who'll Save The Plowboy?, Mornin' Sun, Monopoly, The Cherry Orchard, Volpone, A Lesson from Aloes.
TV FILMS: *Movies*: Silent Night Lonely Night, A Howling in the Woods, A Stranger in Town, Moon of the Wolf, Trouble Comes to Town, Mousey, Returning Home, Eleanor and Franklin (Emmy Award, 1976), Sybil, Eleanor and Franklin: The White House Years (Emmy Award, 1977), Harry Truman, Plain Speaking (Emmy nom.), The Dollmaker (Emmy nom.), The Execution of Raymond Graham(Emmy nom.), Half a Lifetime, My Name is Bill W. (also prod.; Emmy nom.), Mark Twain and Me (also prod.), A Town Torn Apart (also prod.).

PETROU, DAVID MICHAEL: Writer, Producer, Public Relations Executive. b. Washington, DC, Nov. 3, 1949. e. U. of Maryland, B.A.; Georgetown U., M.A. Publicity assoc., Psychiatric Institutes of America, Washington, DC, 1971; assoc. dir. of publicity & film liaison, Random House, 1974; guest lecturer, screen writing & film production, The American University Consortium, Washington, DC, spring, 1980; Woodrow Wilson Fellowship, 1971. Entered industry in 1975. Joined Salkind Organization in chg. of literary projects. Worked in numerous production capacities on Crossed Swords, Superman, Superman II. 1977, exec. in chg. of literary development, Salkind. Wrote Crossed Swords (1978) and The Making of Superman. Co-authored screenplay, Shoot to Kill. 1978–79, promotional dev. on Time after Time for Warner Bros.; 1980–83, dir., special projects Joseph Kennedy Foundation. Organized U.S. premiere of Superman II and The Empire Strikes Back; 1983–84, sr. editor for entertainment, Regardie's Magazine; 1984, organized Washington, DC premiere of Indiana Jones and the Temple of Doom; 1984–86, sr. exec., p.r. div., Abramson Associates; 1986–88, sr. v.p., Eisner, Held & Petrou, Inc., p.r. agency; 1988–present, pres. & chief operating officer, Eisner, Petrou & Associates Inc. Baltimore-Wash., marketing communications agency. 1992, named chmn. of American Film Institute's Second Decade Council.

PEVERALL, JOHN: Producer. b. Islington, England. Started in entertainment industry in 1945 in mail room of J. Arthur Rank Prods. Promoted to asst. dir. Time out for military service in Royal Air Force Air-Sea Rescue Unit. Resumed career as asst. dir. and unit prod. mgr. on several films produced in Britain and throughout Europe. In 1969 became associated with newly-formed Cinema Center Films as prod. exec. in London. When firm suspended activities became freelance as asst. dir.
PICTURES: Conduct Unbecoming and The Man Who Fell to Earth (both assoc. prod.), The Deer Hunter (prod.).

PEVNEY, JOSEPH: Director, Actor. b. New York, NY, 1920. e. NYU. m. the late actress Mitzi Green. Began career in vaudeville at 13 as jr. mem. song & dance team; later on stage in Home of the Brave. US Army ETO W.W.II. Actor turned director.
STAGE: Counsellor at Law, Key Largo, Native Son; (dir.) Swan Song, Let Freedom Sing.
PICTURES: *Actor*: Nocturne, Outside The Wall, Body & Soul; Counsellor at Law (dir.), Key Largo, Native Son. *Director*: The Strange Door, Shakedown, Air Cadet, Lady from Texas, Meet Danny Wilson, Iron Man, Flesh and Fury, Just Across the Street, Because of You, Desert Legion, It Happens Every Thursday, Back to God's Country, Yankee Pasha, Playgirl, Three Ring Circus, Six Bridges to Cross, Foxfire, Female on the Beach, Away All Boats, Congo Crossing, Tammy and the Bachelor, The Midnight Man, Man of a Thousand Faces, Twilight for the Gods, Torpedo Run, Cash McCall, The Plunderers (also prod.), Crowded Sky, Portrait of a Mobster, Night of the Grizzly.
TELEVISION: Trapper John M.D., Contract for Life: The S.A.D.D. Story. Movies: Who is the Black Dahlia, My Darling Daughter's Anniversary, Mysterious Island of Beautiful Women.

PEYSER, JOHN: Producer, Director. b. New York, NY, Aug. 10, 1916. e. Colgate U., 1938. In TV ind. since 1939, with Psychological Warfare Div., ETO, W.W.II; pres. Peyser/Vance Productions, Woodland Hills, CA.
TELEVISION: Director: Hawaii Five-O, Mannix, Movin On, Swiss Family Robinson, Bronk, Combat, Untouchables, Rat Patrol, Honeymoon with a Stranger.
PICTURES: Spain, The Open Door; Kashmiri Run; Four Rode Out; Massacre Harbor.

272

PFEIFFER, MICHELLE: Actress. b. Santa Ana, CA, Apr. 29, 1957. While attending jr. coll. and working as supermarket checkout clerk, began taking acting classes in L.A. Stage debut in L.A. prod. of A Playground in the Fall. At 20, signed as regular in short lived TV series Delta House. NY Theatre debut 1989 in Twelfth Night (Central Park).
PICTURES: Hollywood Nights, Falling in Love Again, Charlie Chan and The Curse of the Dragon Queen, Grease 2, Scarface, Into the Night, Ladyhawke, Sweet Liberty, The Witches of Eastwick, Amazon Women on the Moon, Married to the Mob, Tequila Sunrise, Dangerous Liaisons (Acad. Award nom.), The Fabulous Baker Boys (NY Film Critics, L.A. Film Critics & Natl. Society of Film Critics Awards, Acad. Award nom., 1989), The Russia House, Frankie and Johnny, Batman Returns, Love Field (Acad. Award nom.), The Age of Innocence, Wolf.
TELEVISION: Series: Delta House, B.A.D. Cats. Movies: The Solitary Man, Callie and Son, Splendor in the Grass, The Children Nobody Wanted. Specials: One Too Many, Tales from the Hollywood Hills (Natica Jackson). Guest: Fantasy Island.

PHILLIPS, D. JOHN: Motion Picture Theatre Consultant. b. New York, NY, Feb. 6, 1909. Advertising and publicity mgr. Borden Co. Produce Sales Div., 1933–36; adv. & pub. mgr., Paul R. Dillon Co., Inc., 1936–41. Became field exploitation rep., United Artists Corp., 1941–42; Short Subjects & Paramount News adv. & pub. mgr. Paramount Pictures, 1942–47; exec. dir. Metropolitan Motion Pictures Theatres Assn., 1947–79, New York.

PHILLIPS, JULIA: Producer. b. Brooklyn, NY, April 7, 1944. e. Mt. Holyoke Coll. Production asst. at McCall's Magazine; later became textbook copywriter for Macmillan; story editor, Paramount; creative exec., First Artists Prods., NY. In 1970 with former husband, Michael Phillips and actor Tony Bill formed Bill/Phillips Productions to develop film projects. Author: You'll Never Eat Lunch in This Town Again (Random House, 1991).
PICTURES: Steelyard Blues, The Sting, Taxi Driver, The Big Bus, Close Encounters of the Third Kind, The Beat (co-prod.).

PHILLIPS, LESLIE: Actor, Producer. b. London, England, April 20, 1924. Early career as child actor. Ent. m.p. ind. 1935.
PICTURES: The Citadel (debut, 1938), Pool of London, Breaking the Sound Barrier, Train of Events, The Fake, The Limping Man, THe Gamma People, The Barretts of Wimpole Street, Brothers in Law, High Flight, Just My Luck, Les Girls, Smallest Show on Earth, Value for Money, I Was Monte's Double, The Angry Hills, Carry on Nurse, King Ferdinand of Naples, This Other Eden, The Navy Lark, Doctor in Love, Watch Your Stern, No Kidding, Week-End With Lulu, VIP, Carry on Constable, Inn for Trouble, Please Turn Over, Raising the Wind, In the Doghouse, Crooks Anonymous, Fast Lady, Father Came Too, Doctor in Clover, You Must Be Joking, Maroc 7, Some Will Some Won't, Doctor in Trouble, The Magnificent 7 & Deadly Sins, Not Now Darling, Don't Just Lie There, Spanish Fly, Not Now Comrade, Out of Africa, Empire of the Sun, Scandal, Mountains of the Moon, King Ralph, Carry on Columbus.
TELEVISION: Our Man at St. Marks, Impasse, The Gong Game, Time and Motion Man, Reluctant Debutante, A Very Fine Line, The Suit; The Culture Vultures (series), Edward Woodward Show, Casanova 74 (series), Redundant—or the Wife's Revenge. TV film: You'll Never See Me Again, Mr. Palfrey of Westminister, Monte Carlo, Rumpole, Summers Lease, Chancer, Comic Strip, Who Bombed Birmingham, Life After Life, Thacker, Chancer II, The Oz Trial, Lovejoy, Boon, The Changeling, Bermuda Grace.

PHILLIPS, LOU DIAMOND: Actor. b. Philippines, Feb. 17, 1962. Raised in Corpus Christi, TX. e. U. of Texas, Arlington (BFA. drama). Studied film technique with Adam Roarke, becoming asst. dir./instructor with the Film Actor's Lab, 1983–86. Regional theater includes: A Hatful of Rain, Whose Life Is It Anyway?, P.S. Your Cat Is Dead, The Lady's Not for Burning, Doctor Faustus, Hamlet.
PICTURES: Angel Alley, Interface, Trespasses (also co-s.p.), Harley, La Bamba, Stand and Deliver, Young Guns, Dakota (also assoc. prod.), Disorganized Crime, Renegades, The First Power, A Show of Force, Young Guns II, Ambition (also s.p.), The Dark Wind, Shadow of the Wolf.
TELEVISION: Movies: Time Bomb, The Three Kings, Extreme Justice. Special: Avenue Z Afternoon. Guest: Dallas, Miami Vice.

PHILLIPS, MICHAEL: Producer. b. Brooklyn, NY, June 29, 1943. e. Dartmouth Coll., B.A., 1965. NYU, Law Sch. J.D., 1968. Indep. m.p. prod. 1971. In 1970 formed prod. co. with former wife, Julia, and actor Tony Bill.
PICTURES: Steelyard Blues, The Sting (Acad. Award for Best Picture, 1973), Taxi Driver, The Big Bus, Close Encounters of the Third Kind, Heartbeeps, Cannery Row, The Flamingo Kid, Don't Tell Mom the Babysitter's Dead, Mom and Dad Save the World, Eyes of an Angel.

PHILLIPS, MICHELLE: Actress. b. Long Beach, CA, June 4, 1944. r.n. Holly Gilliam. Mother of actress-singer Chynna Phillips. Former member of The Mamas and the Papas. Co-wrote hit single California Dreamin'. Author: California Dreamin': The Story of The Mamas and The Papas (1986).
TELEVISION: Series: Hotel, Knots Landing. Mini-Series: Aspen, The French Atlantic Affair. Movies: The Death Squad, The California Kid, The Users, Moonlight, Mickey Spillane's Mike Hammer: Murder Me Murder You, Secrets of a Married Man, Stark: Mirror Image, Assault and Matrimony, Trenchcoat in Paradise. Guest: Hotel, Fantasy Island, Love Boat.
MOVIES: Monterey Pop, Dillinger, Valentino, Sidney Sheldon's Bloodline, The Man With Bogart's Face, Savage Harvest, American Anthem, Let It Ride, Scissors.

PHOENIX, RIVER: Actor. b. Madras, Oregon, August 23, 1970. Sisters Rainbow, Liberty and Summer and brother Leaf are also actors. Spent childhood traveling to Mexico, Puerto Rico, and Venezuela with parents who were then independent Christian missionaries with The Children of God. Returned to Florida at 7. First TV appearance, singing and playing guitar on Fantasy TV. Began acting career at 10 in Seven Brides for Seven Brothers on TV. Also plays guitar and records own original songs.
PICTURES: Explorers (debut, 1985), Stand By Me, Mosquito Coast, A Night in the Life of Jimmy Reardon, Little Nikita, Running on Empty (Acad. Award nom.), Indiana Jones and the Last Crusade, I Love You to Death, Dog Fight, My Own Private Idaho, Sneakers, The Thing Called Love, Silent Tongue.
TELEVISION: Guest: Hotel, It's Your Move, Family Ties. Mini-Series: Celebrity, Robert Kennedy and His Times. Movie: Surviving.

PIALAT, MAURICE: Director. b. Cunlhat, Puy de Dome, France, Aug. 21, 1925. Worked as a painter and sometime actor before turning to film in 1952. Made a number of short films including L'Amour Existe (award winner Venice Film Fest., 1960) Worked in television before feature debut in 1967. Television: Janine (1961), Maitre Galip (1962), La Maison des Bois (1971).
PICTURES: L'Enfance Nue (Prix Jean Vigo Award), Nous Ne Vieillirons pas Ensemble, La Gueule Ouverte, Passe Ton Bac D'Abord, Loulou, A Nos Amours (Prix Louis Delluc), Police, Under Satan's Sun (Golden Palm Award, Cannes Festival), Van Gogh.

PICCOLI, MICHEL: Actor. b. Paris, France, Dec. 27, 1925. r.n. Jacques Piccoli. Since his film debut in The Sorcerer in 1945 has had impressive career on the French stage and in films working for major French dirs. Renoir, Bunuel, Melville, Resnais, Clouzot, Godard as well as Hitchcock. Until 1957 was mgr. of Theatre Babylone in Paris. Formed prod. co. Films 66. Produced: Themroc (1972); La Faille; Les Enfants Gates.
PICTURES: The Sorcerer, Le Point du Jour, French Can Can, The Witches of Salem, Le Bal des Espiona, Gina, Le Doulos, Contempt, Diary of a Chambermaid, Lady L, La Guerre Est Finie, The Young Girls of Rochefort, Un Homme de Trop, Belle de Jour, La Chamade, Dillinger Is Dead, L'Invasion, The Milky Way, Topaz, The Things of Life, Ten Days' Wonder, The Discreet Charm of the Bourgeoisie, Themroc, Wedding in Blood, La Grande Bouffe, The Last Woman, Leonor, 7 Deaths by Prescription, The Weak Spot, F For Fairbanks, Mado, Todo Modo, Rene the Cane, Spoiled Children, Strauberg Is Here, The Fire's Share, Little Girl in Blue Velvet, The Savage State, The Sugar, The Bit Between the Teeth, La Divorcement, Leap into the Void, The Price for Survival, Atlantic City, The Prodigal Daughter, Beyond the Door, The Eyes The Mouth, Passion, A Room in Town, Will the High Salaried Workers Please Raise Their Hands!!!, The General of the Dead Army, La Passante, The Prize of Peril, Adieu Bonaparte, Dangerous Moves, Danger in the House, Long Live Life!, Success Is the Best Revenge, The Sailor 512, Departure, Return, Mon beau-frere a tue ma soeur, The Nonentity, The Prude, Bad Blood, Undiscovered Country, Blanc de Chine, Le Peuple Singe (narrator), The French Revolution, May Fools, La Belle Noiseuse, The Children Thief, Archipelago, Punctured Life, Martha and I.

PICERNI, PAUL: Actor. b. New York, NY, Dec. 1, 1922. e. Loyola U., Los Angeles. U.S. Air Force 1943–46; head of drama dept. Mt. St. Mary's Coll., 1949–50. TV credits include Untouchables (co-star).
TELEVISION: Philco Playhouse, Climax, Lux, Loretta Young Show, Desilu, Kojak, Mannix, Police Story, Lucy Special, Quincy, Alice, Trapper John, Vegas, Fall Guy, Capitol, Hardcastle and McCormick, Matt Houston, Simon and Simon.
PICTURES: Breakthrough, I Was a Communist for the FBI, Mara Maru, Desert Song, She's Back on Broadway, House of Wax, Shanghai Story, To Hell and Back, Miracle in the Rain, Bobby Ware Is Missing, Omar Khayyam, Brothers Rico, The Young Philadelphians, Strangers When We Meet, The Young

Marrieds, The Scalphunters, Airport, Kotch, Beyond the Poseidon Adventure.

PICKER, DAVID V.: Executive. b. New York, NY, May 14, 1931. e. Dartmouth Coll., B.A., 1953. Father Eugene Picker, exec. Loew's Theatres. Ent. industry in 1956 as adv. pub. & exploitation liaison with sls. dept., United Artists Corp.; exec. v.p. U.A. Records; asst. to Max Youngstein, v.p.; v.p. U.A.; first v.p. UA; pres. 1969 Resigned 1973 to form own production co. In 1976 joined Paramount Pictures as pres. of m.p. div.; v.p., Lorimar Productions; independent; 1987, pres. & COO, Columbia Pictures. Resigned.
   PICTURES: Juggernaut, Lenny, Smile, Royal Flash, Won Ton Ton, The One and Only, Oliver's Story, Bloodline (prod.), The Jerk (prod.), Dead Men Don't Wear Plaid (prod.), The Man with Two Brains, Beat Street (prod.), The Appointments of Dennis Jennings (short, prod.), Stella (exec. prod.), Traces of Red, Leap of Faith, Matinee, The Saint of Fort Washington.

PICKER, EUGENE D.: Executive b. New York, NY, Nov. 17, 1903. p. David V. and Celia C. Picker. e. NYU and Sch. of Business. Started with father in Bronx theatres; joined Loew's Inc., 1920; in charge circuit operations, New York area, 1945; v.p. Loew's Theatres, Sept. 1954; member bd. of dir., 1956, exec. v.p. Sept. 1958; pres. Loew's Theatres, March 1959. Res. 1961 as pres. Loew's Theatres; joined U.A. as v.p., July 1961. Joined Trans-Lux Corp. as exec. v.p., Jan. 1967; pres. & chief oper. Officer of Entertainment Division of Trans-Lux Corp. to 1984 then confirmed as member bd. of directors; Exec. consultant motion picture industry Jan. 1, 1974 and Pres. E.D.P. Films Inc. as of June 1974 to 1982; pres. NATO, 1969–71, ch. bd., 1971–72, Bd. dir., Will Rogers Hospital, bd. ch. At present mem. bd. of dirs., Trans Lux Corp. and Foundation of Motion Picture Pioneers and Broadway Association.

PICKMAN, JEROME: Executive. b. New York, NY, Aug. 24, 1916. e. St. John's U.; Brooklyn Law Sch. of St. Lawrence U., LL.B. Reporter N.Y. newspapers; U.S. Army World War II; Ad-pub exec. 20th-Fox, 1945–46; v.p., dir., adv. & pub., later v.p. domestic gen. sls. mgr., Paramount Pictures; sr. sls. exec. Columbia Pictures; pres. Motion Picture Div. of Walter Reade Org.; pres., Levitt-Pickman Film Corp.; sr. v.p., domestic distribution, Lorimar Productions; pres., Pickman Film Corp., Cineworld Enterprises Corp.; pres. Scotti Bros. Pictures Distribution, 1986. Consultant, various entertainment entities, legal and financial individuals and organizations.

PIERCE, FREDERICK S.: Executive. b. New York, NY, April 8, 1933. e. Bernard Baruch Sch. of B.A., City Coll. of New York. Served with U.S. Combat Engineers in Korean War. Associated with Benj. Harrow & Son, CAP, before joining ABC in 1956. Served as analyst in TV research dep.; prom. to supvr. of audience measurements, 1957, named mgr. next year. In 1961 made dir. of research; 1962 dir. of research, sales dev. Named dir. of sales planning, sales devel. April, 1962; elec. v.p., Feb. 1964 and made nat. dir. of sales for TV. In 1968 named v.p., planning; March. 1970 named asst. to pres. In July 1972, named v.p, in chg. ABC TV planning and devel. and asst. to pres. ABC TV, March, 1973. Named sr. v.p., ABC TV, Jan., 1974. Elected pres., ABC Television Division, October, 1974. Pres. & chief operating off., ABC, Inc., 1983. Formed Frederick Pierce Co. and also Pierce/Silverman Co. with Fred Silverman, 1989.

PIERSON, FRANK: Producer, Director, Writer. b. Chappaqua, NY, May 12, 1925. e. Harvard U. Was correspondent for Time magazine before entering show business as story editor of TV series, Have Gun, Will Travel. Later served as both producer and director for show. Developed a number of properties for Screen Gems before writing theatrical screenplays.
   PICTURES: Writer: Cat Ballou, Cool Hand Luke, The Anderson Tapes, Dog Day Afternoon (Acad. Award, 1975), In Country, Presumed Innocent. Director-Writer: The Looking Glass War, A Star Is Born, King of the Gypsies.
   TELEVISION: Series: Nichols (prod.), Alfred Hitchcock Presents (1985; dir.). Movies: The Neon Ceiling (dir.). Haywire (co-writer), Somebody Has to Shoot the Picture (dir.; ACE Award, 1990), Citizen Cohn.

PIGOTT-SMITH, TIM: Actor. b. Rugby, England, May 13, 1946. e. U. of Bristol, B.A., Bristol Old Vic Theatre Sch., 1969. Acted with Bristol Old Vic, Royal Shakespeare Co. On stage in As You Like It, Major Barbara, Hamlet, School for Scandal, Sherlock Holmes (Bdwy debut, 1974), Benefactors, Entertaining Strangers, The Winter's Tale, Antony and Cleopatra, Cymbaline, The Tempest.
   PICTURES: Aces High (debut, 1976), Man in a Fog, Sweet William, Richard's Things, Joseph Andrews, Clash of the Titans, Lucky Village, Victory, State of Emergency, Remains of the Day.
   TELEVISION: Dr. Who (debut, 1970), Mini-series: Winston Churchill: The Wilderness Years, The Jewel in the Crown. Movies: Eustace and Hilda, The Lost Boys, I Remember Nelson, Measure for Measure, Henry IV, Day Christ Died,

Hunchback of Notre Dame, Fame Is the Spur, Glittering Prizes, Dead Man's Folly, The Case of Sherlock Holmes (host), Life Story, Hannah, The True Adventures of Christopher Columbus, The Chief.

PIKE, CORNELIA M.: b. Holyoke, MA, 1933. e. Boston U. Sch. of Commun., BS Magna Cum Laude. Asst. Promotion & Publicity Dir. WNAC/WNAC-TV 1954–56, Boston, MA. Women's Director/On-air personality: WKNE Keene, NH 1957–60; WSMN Nashua, NH 1963–67; WHOB, Nashua, NH 1967–68. Mngr. Seattle Winters Interior Design, Boston, MA 1979–81. Sls. Mngr./VP Pike Productions, Inc. 1981 to present. Company produces and markets trailers to exhibitors in U.S., UK, Germany, Australia and New Zealand. Alpha Epsilon Rho, Natl. Bdcstg. Soc. 1st VP, Variety Club of New England. Bd. dirs., Variety Club of New England. Life Patron, Variety Clubs International.

PIKE, JOHN S.: Executive. b. Cleveland, OH, Oct. 26, 1946. e. Univ. of Miami. Joined Paramount Pictures as v.p., video programming; promoted to sr. v.p., video prog. 1984, named sr. v.p., current network programming; 1985, promoted to exec. v.p., Paramount Network TV. Appt. pres., Network TV and Intl. co-production, 1991.

PILCHER, TONY: Producer. b. Boston, England, 1936. e. Shrewsbury Sch. Ent. m.p. industry 1960 with Anglo-Scottish Pictures. Became prod. exec. 1961, German rep. and exec. 1963. Joined AB-Pathe as German rep., TV and Advertising Films division 1964. TV prod., Heumann Ogilvy & Mather, Frankfurt, 1966; prod. Chambers and Partners; Guild TV; Wace Film, Signal Films, Rayant TV, Filmshop, Europartners 1967 to date.

PINCHOT, BRONSON: Actor. b. New York, NY, May 20, 1959. e. Yale U. Grew up in Pasadena. Studied acting at Yale. On NY stage in Poor Little Lambs, Zoya's Apartment.
   PICTURES: Risky Business (debut, 1983), Beverly Hills Cop, The Flamingo Kid, Hot Resort, After Hours, Second Sight, Blame it on the Bellboy, True Romance.
   TELEVISION: Series: Sara (1985), Perfect Strangers, The Trouble With Larry. Movie: Jury Duty—The Comedy.

PINSKER, ALLEN: Executive. b. New York, NY, Jan. 23, 1930. e. NYU. Mgr., Hempstead Theatre, 1950. In 1954 joined Island Theatre Circuit as booker-buyer; named head buyer 1958. In 1968 joined United Artists Eastern Theatres as film buyer; head buyer, 1969, v.p., 1970. Named v.p. United Artists Theatre Circuit, 1972. In 1973 named UAET exec: v.p., member bd., 1974. Appt. pres. & COO, UA Communications, Inc., theatre division, 1987. March, 1987, named pres. and CEO, United Artists Theatre Circuit, Inc. and exec. v.p., United Artists Communications, Inc.; 1988, became member, bd. dir. United Artists Comm. Inc.

PINTER, HAROLD: Writer, Director, Actor. b. London, England, Oct. 10, 1930. Began career as actor then turned to writing and direction. Plays include The Dumb Waiter, Slight Ache, The Room, The Birthday Party, The Caretaker, The Homecoming, The Collection, Landscape, Silence, Old Times, No Man's Land, The Hothouse, Betrayal, One for the Road, Mountain Language, Party Time.
   PICTURES: The Caretaker, The Servant, The Pumpkin Eater, The Quiller Memorandum, Accident, The Go-Between, The Homecoming, The Last Tycoon, The French Lieutenant's Woman, Betrayal, Turtle Diary, The Handmaid's Tale, Reunion, The Comfort of Strangers, The Trial.
   TELEVISION: A Night Out, Night School, The Lover, Tea Party, The Basement, Langrishe Go Down, Heat of the Day.

PISCOPO, JOE: Actor, Comedian. b. Passaic, NJ, June 17, 1951. Stage appearances in regional and dinner theaters in South and Northeast. Worked as stand-up comic at the Improvisation and the Comic Strip clubs, NY 1976–80. Author: The Piscopo Tapes. Television debut as regular on Saturday Night Live, 1980–84.
   PICTURES: American Tickler or the Winner of 10 Academy Awards (1976), King Kong, Johnny Dangerously, Wise Guys, Dead Heat, Sidekicks.
   TELEVISION: Series: Saturday Night Live. Guest: Comic Relief (1986).

PISIER, MARIE-FRANCE: Actress. b. Indochina, May 10, 1944. First discovered by François Truffaut who cast her in Love at Twenty (1976). When film completed returned to school for degree in political science. Continued to work in films.
   PICTURES: French Provincial, Trans-Europe Express, Stolen Kisses, Celine et Julie Vont en Bateau, Cousin Cousine, Souvenirs d'en France, Barocco, The Other Side of Midnight, Serail, Love on the Run, Les Apprentis Sourciers, The Bronte Sisters, French Postcards, La Banquiere, Chanel Solitaire, Der Zauberberg (The Magic Mountain), Ace of Aces, Hot Touch, The Prize of Peril, Der Stille Ocean, L'Ami de Vincent, Miss Right.
   TELEVISION: (U.S.) French Atlantic Affair, Scruples.

PITT, BRAD: Actor. b. Shawnee, OK, Dec. 18, 1963. Raised in Springfield, MO. Studied journalism at Univ. of MO at Columbia. Moved to L.A. where he studied acting with Roy London. Appeared in short film Contact.
PICTURES: Cutting Class, Happy Together, Across the Tracks, Thelma & Louise, Cool World, Johnny Suede, The Favor, A River Runs Through It, Kalifornia, Legends of the Fall.
TELEVISION: Series: Glory Days. Movies: Too Young to Die, The Image. Guest: Head of the Class, Tales From the Crypt.

PLACE, MARY KAY: Actress, Writer. b. Tulsa, OK, Sept. 23, 1947. e. U. of Tulsa. Worked in production jobs and as Tim Conway's asst. for his TV show also as sect. for Norman Lear on Maude before starting to write for TV series (Mary Tyler Moore Show, Phyllis, Maude, M*A*S*H, etc.).
PICTURES: Bound For Glory (debut, 1976), New York New York, More American Graffiti, Starting Over, Private Benjamin, Modern Problems, Waltz Across Texas, The Big Chill, Smooth Talk, A New Life, Bright Angel, Captain Ron, Samantha.
TELEVISION: Series: Mary Hartman Mary Hartman (Emmy Award, 1977).Guest: All in the Family, Mary Tyler Moore Show, Fernwood 2-Night, Tonight Show, Saturday Night Live (host), thirtysomething.Movies: The Girl Who Spelled Freedom, Act of Love, For Love or Money, Out on the Edge, Just My Imagination, Telling Secrets. Specials: John Denver Special, Martin Mull's History of White People in America I & II, Portrait of a White Marriage, The Gift, 4 specials on religion, white crime, stress and politics.

PLATT, MILT: Executive. b. New York, NY, Feb. 25, 1912. e. City Coll. of New York, RCA Inst., Ohio State U. U.S. Army 1942–46; div. mgr., RKO Radio Pictures until 1957; gen. sls. mgr. Continental Dist., 1957–65; vice-pres. & gen. sls. mgr. Sherpix, 1965; v.p. & gen. sls. mgr., Comet Film Distributors, Inc., 1965; v.p. & sls. mgr., Times Film Corp., 1968. Pres. Eagle Amusement Co., 1970. Appointed member of the Appeals Board of the MPA rating system, 1971; pres. of Pisces Group, Ltd., 1972; v.p. & gen. sls. mgr., International Co-productions, inc., 1974. pres., Milton Platt Co., 1975. Member governing committee, IFIDA. Now retired.

PLEASENCE, DONALD: Actor. b. Worksop, England, Oct. 5, 1919. Repertory, first London appearance in Twelfth Night. RAF, WW II. Since London stage, N.Y. stage, ent. m.p, ind. 1953.
STAGE: Vicious Circle, Saint's Day, Hobson's Choice, The Rules of the Game, The Lark, Ebb Tide, The Caretaker, Poor Bitos, The Man in the Glass Booth, Wise Child (N.Y.); voted actor of the year, 1958.
PICTURES: The Beachcomber, Value for Money, 1984, Stowaway Girl (Manuela), The Man Inside, A Tale of Two Cities, The Two-Headed Spy, Look Back in Anger, Killers of Kilimanjaro, Battle of the Sexes, The Shakedown, The Wind Cannot Read, Mania, Circus of Horrors, Sons and Lovers, Hell is a City, The Horsemasters (TV in U.S.), Spare the Rod, No Love for Johnnie, The Risk, Hands or Orlac, The Inspector, Lisa, No Place Like Homicide! (What a Carve Up!), The Caretaker, The Great Escape, Dr. Crippen, The Greatest Story Every Told, The Hallelujah Trial, Fantastic Voyage, Cul-de-Sac, Eye of the Devil, Night of the Generals, You Only Live Twice, Matchless, Will Penny, The Madwoman of Chaillot, Mister Freedom, Soldier Blue, THX 1138, Outback, The Pied Piper, The Jerusalem File, Innocent Bystanders, Deadline (Raw Meat), Wedding in White, The Rainbow Boys, Tales That Witness Madness, The Black Windmill, The Mutations, Escape to Witch Mountain, Hearts of the West, From Beyond the Grave, Journey Into Fear, The Devil Within Her, Watch Out We're Mad, Dirty Knights' Work (Trial by Combat), The Last Tycoon, Goldenrod, The Passover Plot, The Eagle Has Landed, The Uncanny, Tomorrow Never Comes, Land of the Minotaur, Oh God!, Telefon, Power Play, Out of the Darkness (Night Creature), Sgt. Pepper's Lonely Hearts Club Band, Halloween, Good Luck Miss Wyckoff, Dracula, Jaguar Lives, The Monster Club, Escape From New York, Blood Relatives, Halloween II, Alone in the Dark, Devonsville Terror, Race to the Yankee Zephyr, A Breed Apart, Terror in the Aisles, The Ambassador, Barry McKenzie Holds His Own, Creepers, Warrior of the Lost World, Frankenstein's Great Aunt Tillie, To Kill a Stranger, Warrior Queen, Cobra Mission, Nosferatu in Venice, Prince of Darkness, Ground Zero, Halloween 4: The Return of Michael Myers, Hanna's War, Phantom of Death, River of Death, Halloween 5: The Revenge of Michael Myers, Paganini Horror, Ten Little Indians, Buried Alive, American Tiger, Billions, Shadows and Fog, Dien Bien Phu.
TELEVISION: Fate and Mr. Browne, Small Fish Are Sweet, The Silk Purse, A House of His Own, The Traitor, The Millionairess, The Cupboard Machinal, The Hatchet Man, The Bandstand, Ambrose, Thou Good and Faithful Servant, Call Me Daddy, Taste, The Fox Trot, Omnibus, Julius Caesar,

Occupations, The Joke, The Cafeteria, Hindle Wakes, Master of the Game, Arch of Triumph, The Great Escape: The Untold Story, Scoop, Punishment Without Crime, The Room.

PLESHETTE, EUGENE: Executive. b. Brooklyn, NY, Jan. 7. e. City Coll. of New York, LaSalle U., Paramount Pict. Acting Sch. Stage actor; assoc. prod. and dir. three off-Broadway plays; treas. and house mgr. N.Y. Paramount; v.p. Reid-Singer Music; exec. mgr. Brooklyn Paramount thea., 1945; mgn. dir. 1953; v.p. in chg. of ABC Merchandising Inc., AB-PT, Inc. and American Broadcasting Co., 1962; exec. v.p., MSG-ABC Prods., Inc. 1965; exec. v.p Don Reid TV Prod.; 1975, President, Pleshette Associates.

PLESHETTE, SUZANNE: Actress. b. New York, NY, Jan. 31, 1937. e. Performing Arts H.S., Finch Coll., Syracuse U. Broadway debut, Compulsion.
STAGE: The Cold Wind and the Warm, The Golden Fleecing, The Miracle Worker, Compulsion, Two for the Seesaw, Special Occasions.
PICTURES: The Geisha Boy (debut, 1958), Rome Adventure, 40 Pounds of Trouble, The Birds, Wall of Noise, A Distant Trumpet, Fate is the Hunter, Youngblood Hawke, A Rage to Live, The Ugly Dachshund, Nevada Smith, Mister Buddwing, The Adventures of Bullwhip Griffin, Blackbeard's Ghost, The Power, If It's Tuesday This Must Be Belgium, Suppose They Gave a War and Nobody Came, Target Harry, Support Your Local Gunfighter, The Shaggy D.A., Hot Stuff, Oh God! Book II.
TELEVISION: Series: The Bob Newhart Show, Suzanne Pleshette Is Maggie Briggs, Bridges to Cross, Nightingales. Movies: Wings of Fire, Along Came a Spider, Hunters Are for Killing, River of Gold, In Broad Daylight, Law and Order, Richie Brockelman: Missing 24 Hours, Kate Bliss and the Ticker Tape Kid, Flesh and Blood, For Love or Money, Fantasies, If Things Were Different, Help-Wanted-Male, Dixie Changing Habits, Starmaker, One Cooks, The Other Doesn't, Legend of Valentino, Kojak The Belarus File, A Stranger Waits, Alone in the Neon Jungle, Leona Helmsley: The Queen of Mean, Battling for Baby, A Twist of the Knife.

PLESKOW, ERIC: Executive. b., Vienna, Austria, April 24, 1924. Served as film officer, U.S. War dept., 1946–48; entered industry in 1948 as asst. gen. mgr., Motion Picture Export Association, Germany; 1950–51, continental rep. for Sol Lesser Prods.; joined United Artists in 1951 as Far East Sales Mgr.; named mgr., S. Africa, 1952; mgr., Germany, 1953–58; exec. asst. to continental mgr., 1958–59; asst. continental mgr., 1959–60; continental mgr., 1960–62; v.p. in charge of foreign distribution, 1962; exec. v.p. & chief operating off., Jan. 1, 1973; pres. & chief exec. off., Oct. 1, 1973. Resigned in 1978 to become pres. and chief exec. officer of Orion Pictures Co.; 1982, became pres. & chief exec. officer of Orion Pictures Corp; appointed chmn. of bd. 1991.

PLIMPTON, MARTHA: Actress. b. New York, NY, Nov. 16, 1970. Daughter of actors Shelley Plimpton and Keith Carradine. Acting debut in film workshop of Elizabeth Swados's musical Runaways. At 11 gained recognition as model in Richard Avedon's commercials for Calvin Klein jeans. Also on stage in The Hagadah, Pericles, The Heidi Chronicles, Robbers.
PICTURES: Rollover (debut 1981 in bit role), The River Rat, Goonies, The Mosquito Coast, Shy People, Stars and Bars, Running on Empty, Another Woman, Parenthood, Stanley and Iris, Silence Like Glass, Samantha, Inside Monkey Zetterland, Josh and S.A.M.. My Life's in Turnaround.
TELEVISION: Movies: Daybreak, Chantilly Lace.

PLOWRIGHT, JOAN: C.B.E. Actress. b. Scunthrope, Brigg, Lincolnshire, Eng., Oct. 28, 1929. m. late Lord Laurence Olivier. Trained for stage at Laban Art of Movement Studio, 1949–50; Old Vic Theatre Sch. 1950–52; with Michel St. Denis, Glen Byam Shaw and George Devine. London stage debut The Duenna, 1954. Broadway debut The Entertainer, 1958. Won Tony Award in 1961 for A Taste of Honey. With Bristol Old Vic Rep., Royal Court, National Theatre in numerous classics and contemporary plays.
RECENT THEATER: Saturday Sunday Monday, The Seagull, The Bed Before Yesterday, Filumena, Enjoy, Who's Afraid of Virginia Woolf?, Cavell, The Cherry Orchard, The Way of the World, Mrs. Warren's Profession, Time and the Conways.
PICTURES: Moby Dick (1956), Time Without Pity, The Entertainer, Three Sisters, Equus, Wagner, Brimstone and Treacle, Britannia Hospital, The Dressmaker, Drowning By Numbers, The Divider, Conquest of the South Pole, I Love You to Death, Avalon, Enchanted April, Last Action Hero, Dennis the Menace, A Place for Annie, A Pin for the Butterfly, Widow's Peak.
TELEVISION: Odd Man In, Secret Agent, School for Scandal, The Diary of Anne Frank, Twelfth Night, Merchant of Venice, Daphne Laureola, Saturday Sunday Monday, A Nightingale Sang, House of Bernarda Alba, Stalin, Clothes in the Wardrobe. Pilot: Driving Miss Daisy (U.S.).

PLUMMER, AMANDA: Actress. b. New York, NY, March 23, 1957. e. Middlebury Coll. Daughter of Christopher Plummer and Tammy Grimes.
THEATER: Artichokes, A Month in the Country, A Taste of Honey (Theatre World Award), Agnes of God (Tony Award, 1982), The Glass Menagerie, A Lie of the Mind, Life Under Water, You Never Can Tell, Pygmalion, The Milk Train Doesn't Stop Here Anymore.
PICTURES: Cattle Annie and Little Britches, The World According to Garp, Daniel, The Hotel New Hampshire, Static, The Courtship, Made in Heaven, Prisoners of Inertia, Joe Versus the Volcano, California Casanova, The Fisher King, Freejack, So I Married an Axe Murderer, Needful Things.
TELEVISION: Movies: The Dollmaker, The Unforgivable Secret, Riders to the Sea, Miss Rose White (Emmy Award, 1992), The Sands of Time. Specials: Gryphon, The Courtship. Pilot: True Blue.

PLUMMER, CHRISTOPHER: Actor. b. Toronto, Canada, Dec. 13, 1927. Father of actress Amanda Plummer. Stage & radio career began in Canada (French & English); toured U.S. in The Constant Wife; Bway debut in The Starcross Story, 1953. On Bdwy in The Dark is Light Enough;, Home is the Hero, J.B., The Lark, The Good Doctor, Cyrano (musical, Tony Award, 1974), Othello (Tony nom.), Macbeth. London: leading actor, Royal Shakespeare Theatre, 1961–2, Becket (Evening Standard Award), Natl. Theatre, 1969–70. Canada: leading actor, Stratford Festival (6 yrs.). Voice used in 1988 Oscar winning short The Man Who Painted Trees.
TELEVISION: Series: Counterstrike. Movies/Specials: Hamlet at Elsinore (Emmy nom.), Don Juan in Hell (BBC), Little Moon of Alban, Prince and the Pauper, Jesus of Nazareth, Steiglitz and O'Keefe, Oedipus Rex, Omnibus, After the Fall, The Moneychangers (Emmy Award, 1977), Desperate Voyage, The Shadow Box, When the Circus Came to Town, Dial M for Murder, Little Gloria—Happy at Last, The Scarlet and the Black, The Thorn Birds, The Velveteen Rabbit, Crossings, A Hazard of Hearts, A Ghost in Monte Carlo, Young Catherine, Danielle Steel's Secrets, Stranger in the Mirror, Liar's Edge.
PICTURES: Stage Struck, Wind Across the Everglades, Fall of the Roman Empire, The Sound of Music, Inside Daisy Clover, Night of the Generals, Triple Cross, Oedipus the King, High Commissioner (Nobody Runs Forever), The Battle of Britain, The Royal Hunt of the Sun, Lock Up Your Daughters, Waterloo, The Pyx, The Return of the Pink Panther, Conduct Unbecoming, The Man Who Would Be King, The Spiral Staircase, Aces High, The Day That Shook the World, The Assignment, The Disappearance, International Velvet, Murder by Decree, The Silent Partner, Hanover Street, Starcrash, Highpoint, Somewhere in Time, Eyewitness, The Amateur, Dreamscape, Ordeal by Innocence, Lily in Love, The Boy in Blue, The Boss' Wife, An American Tail (voice), Dragnet, Souvenir, Light Years (voice), Nosferatu in Venice, I Love N.Y., Shadow Dancing, Mindfield, Red Blooded American Girl, Where the Heart Is, Firehead, Star Trek VI: The Undiscovered Country, Rock-a-Doodle (voice), Money, Impolite, Malcolm X, Wolf.

PODELL, ALBERT N.: Attorney. b. New York, NY, Feb. 25, 1937. e. Cornell U., U. of Chicago, NYU Sch. of Law. Articles editor, Playboy magazine, 1959–60; dir. of photog. and m.p. reviewer Argosy magazine, 1961–64; Author: Who Needs a Road? (Bobbs-Merrill, 1967); mng. edit., The Players Magazine, 1965–6); account exec. on 20th Century-Fox at Diener, Hauser, Greenthal, 1966–68; national advertising mgr., Cinema Center Films, 1969; account supervisor and creative dir. on Columbia Pictures at Charles Schlaifer, 1969–72; creator & dir. of Annual Motion Picture Advertising Awards sponsored by Cinema Lodge, B'nai B'rith. Attorney specializing in litigation, matrimonial law, rep. of performers (1976–present). Pres., 1989–present, Jean Cocteau Rep. Th. Chmn. of Trustees, 1987–91, Assn. for Redevelopment of Dramatic Arts. Dir. & writer: A Class Above.

PODHORZER, MUNIO: Executive. b. Berlin, Germany, Sept. 18, 1911. e. Jahn-Realgymnasium, U. of Berlin Medical Sch. U.S. Army, 1943–47; pres. United Film Enterprises, Inc.; formerly secy.-treas. 86th St. Casino Theatre, N.Y.; former v.p. Atlantic Pictures Corp.; former pres. Casino Films, Inc.; former pres. Film Development Corp.; former rep. Export-Union of the German Film Ind.; former U.S. rep. Franco-London Film, Paris; former pres., Venus Productions Corp.; former U.S. rep. Atlas Int'l Film GmbH, Munich; former U.S. rep. Bavaria Atelier Gesellschaft U.S.; past rep. Israfilm U.S., Tel-Aviv; past rep. Tigon British Film Prod., London; past rep. Elias Quere-jeta, P.C., Madrid; past rep. Equiluz Films, Madrid; past rep. Airport Cine, Haiti; Les Films Du Capricorne, Paris; Schon-gerfilm, German; Profilmes, Spain; Ligno, Spain; Films D'Alma, France; Intra Films, Italy. Member: Variety Club, Cinema Lodge, B'nai B'rith, Past Board of Governors IFIDA; past pres. CID Agents Assoc. Former gen. foreign sales mgr., theatrical division of National Telefilm Associates; past rep. Barcino Films, S.A. Spain; Eagle Films Ltd., UK; Les Films Jacques Leitienne, France; Nero Film Classics, USA; Schon-

gerfilm, Germany; Profilmes, S.A. Spain; VIP Ltd., Israel. Presently representing Atlas Film & AV, Germany; KFM Films, Inc. U.S.A.; Compagnie France Film, Canada; Cia. Iberoamerican de TV, S.A. Spain; Israel. Co-chmn., entertainment div., United Jewish Appeal, Federation of Jewish Philanthropies, 1981–83.

PODHORZER, NATHAN: Executive. b. Brody, Poland, Nov. 27, 1919. e. City Coll. of New York, Rutgers U., U. of Southern California. U.S. Army, 1942–46; documentary film prod., Israel, 1946–57; vice pres., secy., United Film Enterprises, Inc.

POE, STEPHEN: Executive. Began career as lawyer with Rutan & Tucker; 1976, joined 20th Century-Fox as prod. counsel; later v.p., business affairs. Turned to producing in 1982, first in association with Frank Mancuso Jr. Productions. 1986, acted as consultant and indep. prod. counsel for United Artists Pictures. 1987, joined CBS/Fox Video as sr. v.p. of acquisitions and programming.

POITIER, SIDNEY: Actor, Director. b. Miami, FL, Feb. 20, 1927. m. actress Joanna Shimkus. e. Miami, FL. Appeared on stage with Amer. Negro Theatre in Days of Our Youth. Appeared in Army Signal Corps documentary From Whence Cometh My Help. Formed First Artists Prod. Co. Ltd., 1969, with Paul Newman and Barbra Streisand. Autobiography: This Life (1980). Recipient 1992 AFI Life Achievement Award.
STAGE: Strivers Road, You Can't Take It With You, Anna Lucasta (Bdwy debut, 1948), Lysistrata, Freight, A Raisin in the Sun.
PICTURES: No Way Out (debut 1950), Cry the Beloved Country, Red Ball Express, Go Man Go, Blackboard Jungle, Good-Bye My Lady, Edge of the City, Something of Value, Band of Angels, Mark of the Hawk, The Defiant Ones, Virgin Island, Porgy and Bess, All the Young Men, A Raisin in the Sun, Paris Blues, Pressure Point, Lilies of the Field (Acad. Award, 1963), The Long Ships, The Greatest Story Ever Told, The Bedford Incident, Slender Thread, A Patch of Blue, Duel at Diablo, To Sir With Love, In the Heat of the Night, Guess Who's Coming to Dinner, For Love of Ivy, The Lost Man, They Call Me Mister Tibbs, Brother John, The Organization, Buck and the Preacher (also dir.), A Warm December (also dir.), Uptown Saturday Night (also dir.), The Wilby Conspiracy, Let's Do It Again (also dir.), A Piece of the Action (also dir.), Stir Crazy (dir. only), Hanky Panky (dir. only), Fast Forward (dir. only), Shoot To Kill, Little Nikita, Ghost Dad (dir. only), Sneakers.
TELEVISION: Movie: Separate But Equal. Guest: Philco TV Playhouse, ABC Stage '67.

POLANSKI, ROMAN: Director, Writer. b. Paris, France, Aug. 18, 1933. Lived in Poland from age of three. Early career, art school in Cracow; Polish Natl. Film Acad., 1954–59. Radio Actor 1945–47; on stage 1947–53; asst. dir., Kamera film prod. group 1959–61. Co-founder Cadre Films, 1964. Wrote, dir. and acted in short films: Two Men and a Wardrobe, When Angels Fall, The Fat and the Lean, Mammals. On stage as actor in Amadeus (and dir., Warsaw & Paris), Metamorphosis (Paris, 1988). Acted in numerous Polish and intl. films (The Generation, The Magic Christian, Andy Warhol's Dracula, Back in the U.S.S.R.). Autobiography: Roman (1984).
PICTURES: Wrote & dir. features: Knife in the Water, Repulsion, Cul-De-Sac, The Fearless Vampire Killers (also actor), Rosemary's Baby, A Day at the Beach (s.p., prod. only), Weekend of a Champion (prod. only), Macbeth (also prod.), What? (a.k.a. Che?; also actor), Chinatown (dir. & actor only), The Tenant (also actor), Tess, Pirates, Frantic, Bitter Moon.

POLEDOURIS, BASIL: Composer. b. Kansas City, MO, Aug. 21, 1945. e. Long Beach St. Univ., USC. While at USC composed music for short films by John Milius and Randal Kleiser. Became first American Film Institute intern.
PICTURES: Big Wednesday, Tintorera, Dolphin, The Blue Lagoon, Conan the Barbarian, Summer Lovers, House of God, Conan the Destroyer, Making the Grade, Red Dawn, Protocol, Flesh and Blood, Iron Eagle, Robocop, No Man's Land, Cherry 2000, Spellbinder, Split Decisions, Farewell to the King, Wired, The Hunt for Red October, Quigley Down Under, Flight of the Intruder, White Fang, Return to the Blue Lagoon, Harley Davidson & the Marlboro Man, Wind, Hot Shots Part Deux, Free Willy, Robocop 3.
TELEVISION: Mini-Series: Amerika, Lonesome Dove (Emmy Award, 1989). Movies: Congratulations It's a Boy, A Whale for the Killing, Fire on the Mountain, Amazons, Single Women Single Bars, Prison for Children, Misfits of Science, Island Sons, Intrigue, L.A. Takedown, Nasty Boys, Ned Blessing, Lone Justice.

POLL, MARTIN H.: Producer. b. New York, NY, Nov. 24, 1926. e. Wharton Sch., U. of Pennsylvania. Pres Gold Medal Studios (1956–61).
PICTURES: prod. A Face in the Crowd, Middle of the Night, The Goddess, Butterfield 8, Love Is a Ball, Sylvia, The Lion in Winter, The Appointment, The Magic Garden of

Stanley Sweetheart, The Man Who Loved Cat Dancing, Night Watch, Love and Death (exec. prod.); The Sailor who Fell From Grace with the Sea, Somebody Killed Her Husband, Nighthawks, Gimme an F, Haunted Summer, My Heroes Have Always Been Cowboys.
TELEVISION: Series: Car 54 Where Are You? Movies: Arthur the King, Stunt Seven. Mini-Series: A Town Called Alice, The Dain Curse, Diana: Her True Story.

POLLACK, SYDNEY: Director, Producer. b. South Bend, IN, July 1, 1934. m. Claire Griswold. e. Neighborhood Playhouse. Assistant to Sanford Meisner at Neighborhood Playhouse. Appeared as actor on Bdwy in A Stone for Danny Fisher, The Dark is Light Enough. Dir. debut in 1960.Dir. play at UCLA, P.S. 193. Prepared the American version of The Leopard.
TELEVISION: As actor: Playhouse 90 (several segments), Shotgun Slade. Dir.: Ben Caseys (15 episodes), The Game (Bob Hope-Chrysler Theatre; Emmy Award), Two is the Number. Co-Prod. of TV movie A Private Matter. Exec. prod. (series): Fallen Angels.
PICTURES: Director: The Slender Thread, This Property is Condemned, The Scalphunters, Castle Keep, They Shoot Horses Don't They? (also prod.), Jeremiah Johnson, The Way We Were (also prod.), The Yakuza (also prod.), Three Days of the Condor, Bobby Deerfield (also prod.), The Electric Horseman, Absence of Malice (also prod.), Tootsie (also prod., actor), Out of Africa (also prod.; Acad. Awards for Best Picture & Director, 1985), Havana (also prod.), The Firm. Producer/Executive Producer: Honeysuckle Rose (exec. prod.), Songwriter (prod.), Bright Lights Big City (prod.), The Fabulous Baker Boys (prod.), Presumed Innocent (prod.), White Palace (exec. prod.), King Ralph (co-exec. prod.), Dead Again (exec. prod.), Leaving Normal (exec. prod.), Searching for Bobby Fischer (exec. prod.). Actor: The Player, Death Becomes Her, Husbands and Wives.

POLLAN, TRACY: Actress. b. New York, NY, June 22, 1960. m. actor Michael J. Fox.
TELEVISION: Series: Family Ties. Movies: For Lovers Only, Sessions, Trackdown: Finding the Goodbar Killer, A Good Sport, Dying to Love You.
PICTURES: Promised Land, Bright Lights Big City, A Stranger Among Us.
THEATRE: Bdwy: Jake's Women.

POLLARD, MICHAEL J.: Actor. b. Passaic, NJ, May 30, 1939. e. Montclair Academy, Actors Studio.
THEATER: Comes a Day, Loss of Roses, Enter Laughing, Bye Bye Birdie, Leda Had a Little Swan, Our Town.
PICTURES: Adventures of a Young Man (debut, 1962), The Stripper, Summer Magic, The Wild Angels, The Russians Are Coming The Russians Are Coming, Caprice, Enter Laughing, Bonnie and Clyde (Acad. Award nom.), Jigsaw, Hannibal Brooks, Little Fauss and Big Halsy, Dirty Little Billy, The Legend of Frenchie King, Between the Lines, Melvin and Howard, America, Heated Vengeance, The Patriot, The American Way (Riders of the Storm), Roxanne, Scrooged, Fast Food, Season of Fear, Next of Kin, Tango and Cash, Why Me?, Dick Tracy, I Come in Peace, Joey Takes a Cab, The Art of Dying, Another You, Enid Is Sleeping (Over Her Dead Body), Split Second, The Arrival, Heartstopper, Arizona Dream, Motorama.
TELEVISION: Guest: Alfred Hitchcock Presents (Anniversary Gift, 1959), Going My Way, Route 66, Here's Lucy, Mr. Novak, Honey West, I Spy, Lost in Space, Dobie Gillis, Get Christie Love, Star Trek, Simon & Simon, The Fall Guy, Gunsmoke, Guns of Paradise, The Young Riders, Nasty Boys. Movies: The Smugglers, Stuck With Each Other, Working Trash. Series: Leo and Liz in Beverly Hills.

POLLEXFEN, JACK: Producer, Director, Writer. b. San Diego, CA, June 10, 1918. e. Los Angeles City Coll. Newspaperman, magazine writer, playwright; prod. for RKO, United Artists, Columbia, Allied Artists.
PICTURES: Son of Sinbad, At Swords Point, Secret of Convict Lake, Desert Hawk, Lady in the Iron Mask, Dragon's Gold, Problem Girls, Captive Women, Captain Kidd and the Slave Girl, Neanderthal Man, Captain John Smith and Pocahontas, Return to Treasure Island, Sword of Venus, Daughter of Dr. Jekyll, Monstrosity, Son of Dr. Jekyll, Mr. Big, Man from Planet X, Indestructible Man, Port Sinister, Treasure of Monte Cristo, Bulldog Drummond, Grey City.

POLLOCK, DALE: Producer. b. Cleveland, OH, May 18, 1950. e. Brandeis U., B.A. anthropology, San Jose State U, M.A., mass communication. Began journalistic career in Santa Cruz in early '70s, serving as reporter and film critic for Daily Variety from 1977 to 1980. Then joined Los Angeles Times as film writer, winning paper's Award for Sustained Excellence in 1984. In 1985 left to take post with The Geffen Film Co. as executive in chg. creative development. Joined A&M Films as v.p. in chg. prod., Jan. 1986. Became pres., 1989. Author: Skywalking (about George Lucas).
PICTURES: The Beast (exec. prod.), The Mighty Quinn (exec. prod.). Producer: House of Cards, Worth Winning,

Blaze, Crooked Hearts, A Midnight Clear, A Home of Our Own.

POLLOCK, THOMAS: Executive. b. 1943. In 1971, after 3 years as business mgr. for American Film Institute's film marketing wing, formed law firm Pollock Bloom, and Dekom with young filmmakers such as George Lucas and Matthew Robbins as clients. Served as chmn. Filmex, 1973–81. 1986, named chmn. MCA's Universal motion picture group., also v.p., MCA, Inc.

POLONSKY, ABRAHAM: Director, Writer. b. New York, NY, Dec. 5, 1910. e. City Coll. of New York, B.A.; Columbia Law Sch. Taught at City Coll. 1932 until war. Wrote s.p. Golden Earrings, I Can Get it For You Wholesale. Wrote novels: The Enemy Sea, The Discoverers, The World Above, The Season of Fear, Zenia's Way. Blacklisted from 1951–66.
PICTURES: Writer: Golden Earrings, I Can Get It for You Wholesale, Body and Soul (also story), Force of Evil (also dir.), Odds Against Tomorrow, Madigan, Tell Them Willie Boy is Here (also dir.), Romance of a Horse Thief (dir.), Avalanche Express, Monsignor.

PONTECORVO, GILLO: Director. b. Pisa, Italy, Nov. 19, 1919. Younger brother of Prof. Bruno Pontecorvo, Harwell scientist who defected in 1950. Worked as asst. dir., directed documentary shorts before feature debut in 1957.
PICTURES: Die Windrose Giovanna; La Grande Strada Azzurra; Kapo; The Battle of Algiers; Queimada! (Burn); Ogro.

PONTI, CARLO: Producer. b. Milan, Italy, Dec. 11, 1913. m. actress Sophia Loren. e. U. of Milan, 1934. Prod. first picture in Milan, Little Old World; prod. Lux Film Rome; prod. first of a series of famous Toto pictures, Toto Househunting.
PICTURES: A Dog's Life, The Knight Has Arrived, Musolino, The Outlaw, Romanticism, Sensuality, The White Slave, Europe 1951, Toto in Color, The Three Corsairs, Ulysses, The Woman of the River, An American of Rome, Attila, War and Peace, The Last Lover, The Black Orchid, That Kind of Woman, Marriage Italian Style, The Great Spy Mission, Happily Ever After, The Girl and the General, Sunflower, Best House in London, Lady Liberty, White Sister, What?, Andy Warhol's Frankenstein, The Passenger, The Cassandra Crossing, A Special Day, Saturday Sunday Monday.
TELEVISION: Mario Puzo's The Fortunate Pilgrim (exec. prod.).

POOLE, FRANK S.: Executive. b. London, England, Oct. 11, 1913. e. Dulwich Coll., 1925–31. Ent. m.p. ind. 1931. Early career with Pathe Pictures, Twickenham Film Distributors, until joining 20th Century Fox as London branch office supervisor 1939. War service 1940–46. Rejoined Fox 1946–53; appt. Leed Branch mgr. 1954–59; supv. 1959–61; asst. sls. mgr. 1961 until joined Rank Film Distrib. as asst. sls. mgr. 1962. Appt. sls. mgr. July 1965, and to board as dir. of sls. Aug. 1965. Appt. gen. mgr. 1968; jnt. mng. dir. 1969; appt. mng. dir. July 1970; appt. dir. Rank Overseas Film Dist. Ltd., 1972; appt. co-chmn Fox-Rank Distributors Ltd., Dec. 1972; appt. vice-chairman Rank Film Distributors Ltd. 1977. 1975, elected to Committee of Cinema & TV Veterans. Oct., 1978, retired from Rank Organisation. Appt. chmn., Appeal Tribunal for the Film Industry. Appt. chmn., Grebelands Mgt. Committee & to exec. council of CTBF, 1979, assoc. Geoff Reeve & Associates. 1980, chmn. & mng. dir., Omandry Intl. Ltd. 1982 appointed film consultant U.K.-Europe to the Alberta Government. Pres., Cinema & TV Veterans 1990–2.

PORTER, DON: Actor. b. Miami, OK, Sept. 24, 1912. e. Oregon Inst. of Tech. Wide theatre work; then m.p. roles. U.S. Army, 3 yrs.
TELEVISION: Series: Private Secretary, Ann Sothern Show, Gidget. Guest: Bionic Woman, Hawaii Five-O, Switch, Love Boat, Three's Company, The President's Mistress, The Murder That Wouldn't Die, The Last Song, Dallas; Old Money.
STAGE: The Best Man, Any Wednesday, Generation, Plaza Suite, The Price, How To Succeed in Business Without Really Trying, Harvey.
PICTURES: The Racket, The Savage, 711 Ocean Drive, Because You're Mine, Our Miss Brooks, Bachelor in Paradise, Youngblood Hawke, The Candidate, 40 Carats, Mame, White Line Fever.

POST, TED: Producer, Director. b. Brooklyn, NY, March 31. Dir. many stage plays; dir. CBS-TV Repertoire Thea.; Producer-dir., NBC-TV Coney Island of the Mind. Directed Everyone Can Make Music.
TELEVISION: Series: Studio One, Ford Theatre, Playhouse of Stars, Alcoa Theatre, Gunsmoke, Rawhide, Twilight Zone, Wagon Train, Combat, Peyton Place, Alcoa, Defenders, Route 66, Baretta, Columbo. Movies: Night Slaves, Dr. Cook's Garden, Yuma, Five Desperate Women, Do Not Fold Spindle or Mutilate, The Bravos, Sandcastles, Girls in the Office, Diary of a Hitchhiker, Stagecoach. Pilots: Cagney & Lacey, Beyond Westworld, Steve Canyon, Perry Mason. Mini-series: Rich Man, Poor Man II (episode 3).

PICTURES: The Peacemaker (debut, 1956), The Legend of Tom Dooley, Hang 'em High, Beneath The Planet of the Apes, The Harrad Experiment, Magnum Force, Whiffs, Good Guys Wear Black, Go Tell the Spartans, Nightkill, The Human Shield.

POSTER, STEVEN: Cinematographer. A.S.C. b. Chicago, IL, Mar. 1, 1944. e. L.A. Art Center Coll. Started as commercial cinematographer before moving into feature films. 2nd unit worl incld. Close Encounters of the Third Kind, Blade Runner. Member, American Society of Cinematographers.
PICTURES: Blood Beach, Dead and Buried, Spring Break, Strange Brew, Testament, The New Kids, The Heavenly Kid, Blue City, The Boy Who Could Fly, Aloha Summer, Someone to Watch Over Me, Big Top Pee-wee, Next of Kin, Opportunity Knocks, Rocky V, Life Stinks, The Cemetery Club.
TELEVISION: Movies: The Grass is Always Greener, The Cradle Will Fall, I'll Take Manhattan, Class of '65.

POSTON, TOM: Actor. b. Columbus, OH, Oct. 17, 1927.
PICTURES: The City That Never Sleeps, Zotz, The Old Dark House, Soldier in the Rain, Cold Turkey, The Happy Hooker, Rabbit Test, Up the Academy, Carbon Copy.
TELEVISION: Movies: The Girl The Gold Watch and Everything, Save the Dog!, A Quiet Little Neighborhood A Perfect Little Murder. Series: The Steve Allen Show (Emmy Award, 1959), Pantomime Quiz, To Tell the Truth, On the Rocks, We've Got Each Other, Mork and Mindy, Newhart. Guest: Fame.

POTTER, DENNIS: Writer. b. Forest of Dean, Gloucester, Eng., May 17, 1935. e. New Coll., Oxford U.
THEATER: Vote Vote Vote for Nigel Barton (1968), Son of Man, Only Make Believe, Brimstone and Treacle, Sufficient Carbohydrate.
PICTURES: Writer: Pennies From Heaven, Brimstone and Treacle, Gorky Park, Dreamchild, Track 29, Secret Friends (also dir.), Blackeyes (also dir.).
TELEVISION: Series: Casanova. Mini-series: Pennies From Heaven, Blue Remembered Hills, Blade on the Feather, Rain on the Roof, Cream in My Coffee, Traitor, Paper Roses, The Singing Detective, Christabel (also exec. prod.). Tele-plays: The Confidence Courses, Stand Up Nigel Barton, Vote Vote Vote for Nigel Barton, Almost Cinderella, Son of Man, Lay Down Your Arms, Follow the Yellow Brick Road, Only Make Believe, Joe's Ark, Schmoedipus, Late Call, Double Dare, Where Adam Stood, Brimstone and Treacle.
NOVELS: The Glittering Coffin, The Changing Forest, Hide and Seek, Blackeyes.

POTTER, MADELEINE: Actress. b. Washington D.C. Daughter of diplomat, spent childhood traveling between Washington and Hong Kong and Tanzania. Stage debut at 15 in one-woman show as Sarah Bernhardt in Washington D.C.
THEATER: Lydie Breeze (NY debut), Plenty, Slab Boys, Coastal Disturbances, Hamlet (Folger Theater, Wash.), Rich-ard III (NY Shakespeare Fest.), Abingdon Square, The Daughters of Dionysius, Metamorphosis, Pygmalion, Getting Married, The Crucible, A Little Hotel on the Side.
PICTURES: The Bostonians (debut, 1984), Hello Again, The Suicide Club, Slaves of New York, Bloodhounds of Broadway, Two Evil Eyes (The Black Cat).
TELEVISION: Movie: Svengali.

POTTLE, HARRY: Production designer. b. London, England, 1925. e. Ealing Coll. of Arts. Fleet Air Arm, 1944–47. Ent. m.p. ind. 1947. Designed Blind Date, 1960. Human Jungle, Avengers (TV series). Art Director, You Only Live Twice, Chitty Chitty Bang Bang, The Adventurers. Production De-signer: The Wilby Conspiracy, The Tamarind Seed, 39 Steps, Murder by Decree, Bear Island, Matarese Circle, Desert King, Turk 182, Collision Course, Loose Cannons, Act of Will.

POTTS, ANNIE: Actress. b. Nashville, TN, Oct. 28, 1952. e. Stephens Coll., MO, BFA. Amateur stage debut at 12 in Heidi. Then in summer stock; on road in Charley's Aunt, 1976. Serves on auxilliary bd. of MADD (Mothers Against Drunk Driving). Ambassador for Women for the Amer. Arthritis Fdn.
PICTURES: Corvette Summer (debut, 1978), King of the Gypsies, Heartaches, Ghostbusters, Crimes of Passion, Pretty in Pink, Jumpin' Jack Flash, Pass the Ammo, Who's Harry Crumb?, Ghostbusters II, Texasville, Breaking the Rules.
TELEVISION: Movies: Black Market Baby, Flatbed Annie and Sweetie Pie, Cowboy, It Came Upon the Midnight Clear, Why Me?. Series: Goodtime Girls, Designing Women. Guest: Remington Steele, Magnum P.I., Twilight Zone.

POUND, LESLIE: Executive. b. London, Nov. 3, 1926. Entered industry in 1943 as reporter on British trade paper, Screen International. Following military service in India and Singa-pore returned to work for that publication until 1952 when joined Paramount pub. office in London on the The Greatest Show on Earth. Named dir. of adv./pub. in U.K. for Para-mount. 1958, retained Para. position when Cinema Intl. Corp. was formed. 1977, joined Lew Grade in ITC Entertainment as worldwide dir. of pub./adv. 1982, intl. pub. chief for Embassy Pictures in Los Angeles. 1982, named Paramount Pictures v.p., intl. mktg. for motion picture div., N.Y. Now relocated in L.A. with mktg. div. as sr. v.p.

POWELL, JANE: Actress, Singer. r.n. Suzanne Burce. b. Portland, OR, Apr. 1, 1929. m. pub. relations exec. Dick Moore. Had own radio program over KOIN, Portland; singer on natl. networks; Star of Tomorrow, 1948. Autobiography: The Girl Next Door . . . and How She Grew (1988). Video: Jane Powell's Fight Back With Fitness. President of Theatre Authority, Inc.
PICTURES: Song of the Open Road (debut, 1944), De-lightfully Dangerous, Holiday in Mexico, Three Daring Daugh-ters, Date With Judy, Luxury Liner, Nancy Goes to Rio, Two Weeks With Love, Royal Wedding, Rich Young and Pretty, Small Town Girl, Three Sailors and a Girl, Seven Brides for Seven Brothers, Athena, Deep in My Heart, Hit the Deck, The Girl Most Likely, The Female Animal, Enchanted Island.
STAGE: Irene (Broadway, 1974). Tour nationally with South Pacific, Peter Pan, My Fair Lady, The Unsinkable Molly Brown, I Do I Do, Same Time Next Year, Chapter Two.
TELEVISION: Specials: Ruggles of Red Gap, Give My Regards to Broadway, Meet Me in St. Louis, Jane Powell Show. Series: Alcoa Theatre (1957–8), Loving, As the World Turns. Guest: Growing Pains, others. Movies: The Letters, Mayday at 40,000 Feet. Host: The Movie Musicals (PBS).

POWERS, MALA: Actress. r.n. Mary Ellen Powers. b. San Francisco, CA, Dec. 20, 1931. p. George and Dell Powers, latter, dramatic coach. e. UCLA. Pasadena Playhouse in For Keeps, 1946; Distant Isle; Actor's Lab, Hollywood; did considerable radio, theatre and tv work. Writer, narrator Children's Story, and Dial A Story (1979). Author: Follow the Star (1980), Follow the Year (1984). Teaches Michael Chekhov technique of acting.
PICTURES: Outrage, Edge of Doom, Cyrano de Bergerac, Rose of Cimarron, City Beneath the Sea, City That Never Sleeps, Geraldine, Yellow Mountain, Rage at Dawn, Bengazi, Tammy and the Bachelor, Storm Rider, Death in Small Doses, The Colossus of New York, Sierra Baron, Unknown Terror, Flight of the Lost Balloon, Rogue's Gallery, Doomsday Plus Seven, Daddy's Gone-A-Hunting, Six Tickets to Hell.
TELEVISION: Series: Hazel, The Man and the City. Guest: Daniel Boone.

POWERS, C. F. (MIKE) JR: Executive. b. San Francisco, CA, March 6, 1923. e. Park Coll., MO, Columbia U., N.Y., graduated U. of Oregon. Entered film business with P.R.C. in Portland, 1950, and then United Artists. Moved to Seattle, WA as branch mgr. of 20th Century Fox, 1960. Was then western division mgr. for 20th Century Fox until 1967, then western division mgr. for Cinerama till 1973. Became exec. v.p., head film buyer for Robert L. Lippert Theatres, Transcontinental Theatres and Affiliated Theatres until 1978. Western div. mgr. Orion Pictures, 1982–4. Mike Powers Ent. (a buying and booking combine and indept. film distrib.). 1984–6 Western district mgr. Embassy Pictures. Became western division mgr. for Filmways Pictures. Past president of Catholic Entertain-ment Guild of Northern Calif.; past pres. of Variety Club Tent 32, San Francisco. Currently m.p. consultant to U.S. Federal Govt.

POWERS, STEFANIE: Actress. r.n. Stefanie Federkiewicz. b. Hollywood, CA, Nov. 2, 1942. Theatrical m.p. debut in Among the Thorns, 1961. TV debut in The Girl from U.N.C.L.E. series.
PICTURES: Tammy Tell Me True, Experiment in Terror, The Interns, If a Man Answers, McClintock, Palm Springs Week-end, The New Interns, Love Has Many Faces, Die Die My Darling (Fanatic), The Young Sinner, Stagecoach, Warning Shot, The Boatniks, Crescendo, The Magnificent 7 Ride, Herbie Rides Again, It Seemed Like a Good Idea at the Time, Escape to Athena, Nowhere to Run, Invisible Stranger (a.k.a. The Astral Factor).
TELEVISION: Series: The Girl From U.N.C.L.E., Feather and Father Gang, Hart to Hart. Mini-series: Washington: Behind Closed Doors, Hollywood Wives. Movies: Five Des-perate Women, Paper Man, Sweet Sweet Rachel, Hardcase, No Place to Run, Shootout in a One-Dog Town, Skyway to Death, Sky Heist, Return to Earth, Family Secrets (also prod.), A Death in Canaan, Mistral's Daughter, Deceptions, At Mother's Request, Beryl Markham: A Shadow on the Sun (also co-prod.), She Was Marked for Murder, Love and Betrayal, When Will I Be Loved?, The Burden of Proof, Survive the Night.

PRATLEY, GERALD: Commentator, b. and e. London, Eng. Joined Canadian Broadcasting Corp., 1946; writer, narrator and producer of The Movie Scene and Music from the Films; asst. member British Film Academy, dir. Canadian Film Institute 1953; chairman Toronto and District Film Council 1956; co-dir. & founder A.G.E. Film Society, Toronto; contribu-tor to U.S. and European film journals; film consult., Cana-dian Centennial Comm. Chmn., Canadian Film Awards;

director, Stratford Film Festival; director, Ontario Film Institute, Toronto. Prof. of film, York U., U. of Toronto. Seneca Coll., McMaster U. Author: Cinema of John Frankenheimer; Otto Preminger; David Lean; John Huston, Torn Sprockets. Mem., classification board, Ontario Theatre branch. 1984. Mem. Advisory boards film depts., Humber College, Ryerson Polytechnical Institute; Mem. TV Ontario Adult Programming Order of Canada, 1984, Can. Picture Pioneers Assn. Cultural Executives, St. George's Society, Arts and Letters Club.

PRENTISS, PAULA: Actress, r.n. Paula Ragusa. b. San Antonio, TX, March 4, 1939. m. actor-director Richard Benjamin. e. Northwestern U., Bachelor degree in drama, 1959. On TV in He & She; on stage in As You Like It, Arf!, The Norman Conquests, Love Letters.
PICTURES: Where the Boys Are (debut, 1960), The Honeymoon Machine, Bachelor in Paradise, The Horizontal Lieutenant, Follow the Boys, Man's Favorite Sport, The World of Henry Orient, Looking for Love, In Harm's Way, What's New Pussycat?, Catch 22, Move, Born to Win, Last of the Red Hot Lovers, Crazy Joe, The Parallax View, The Stepford Wives, The Black Marble, Saturday the 14th, Buddy Buddy.
TELEVISION: Series: He & She. Movies: The Couple Takes a Wife, Having Babies II, No Room to Run (Australian), Friendships Secrets and Lies, Top of the Hill, Packin' It In, M.A.D.D.: Mothers Against Drunk Drivers.

PRESLE, MICHELINE: Actress. r.n. Micheline Chassagne. b. Paris, France, Aug. 22, 1922. e. Raymond Rouleau Dram. Sch. m.p. debut in Je Chante; on stage in Colinette. Am. Stram Gram, Spectacle des Allies; to U.S., 1945; Flea in Her Ear, Magic Circus, Who's Afraid of Virginia Woolf? (tour), Gigi, Nuit de Valognes, Boomerang, Adriana Mont, etc.
PICTURES: Jeunes Filles en Detresse, L'Histoire de Rire, La Nuit Fantastique, Felicie Nanteuil, Seul Amour, Faibala, Boule de Suif, Jeux Sont Faix, Diable au Corps, Under My Skin, Some Kind of News, American Guerilla in the Philippines, Adventures of Captain Fabian, Sins of Pompeii, House of Ricordi, Archipelago of Love, Thieves After Dark, Le Chien, At the Top of the Stairs, Le Jour de Rois. Fine Weather, But Storms Due Towards Evening, Confidences, Alouette, je te plumerai, I Want to Go Home.
TELEVISION: The Blood of Others; many others.

PRESLEY, PRISCILLA: Actress. b. Brooklyn, NY, May 24, 1945. Raised in Connecticut. e. Wiesbaden, West Germany where met and married Elvis Presley (1967–73). Studied acting with Milton Katselas, dance at Steven Peck Theatre Art School and karate at Chuck Norris Karate School. Formed a business, Bis and Beau, marketing exclusive dress designs. Became TV spokesperson for beauty products.
PICTURES: The Naked Gun: From the Files of Police Squad! (debut, 1988), The Adventures of Ford Fairlane, The Naked Gun 2-1/2: The Smell of Fear.
TELEVISION: Series: Those Amazing Animals (host, 1980–81), Dallas. Movies: Love is Forever, Elvis and Me (prod. only).

PRESSMAN, EDWARD R.: Producer. b. New York, NY. e. Fieldston Sch.; grad., Stanford U.; studied at London Sch. of Economics. Began career with film short, Girl, in collaboration with director Paul Williams in London. They formed Pressman-Williams Enterprises.
PICTURES: Prod.: Out of It, The Revolutionary, Dealing: or the Berkeley to Boston Forty Brick, Lost Bag Blues, Sisters, Badlands (exec. prod.), Phantom of the Paradise; Paradise Alley (exec. prod.); Old Boyfriends; Heartbeat (exec. prod.); The Hand; Conan the Barbarian (exec. prod.); Das Boot (exec. prod.); The Pirates of Penzance (exec. prod.); Crimewave (exec. prod.); Plenty; Half Moon Street (exec. prod.); True Stories (exec. prod.); Good Morning Babylon; Masters of the Universe (exec. prod.); Walker (exec. prod.); Wall Street; Cherry 2000 (exec. prod.) Paris By Night (exec. prod.); Talk Radio; Martians Go Home (exec. prod.), Blue Steel., Reversal of Fortune, To Sleep with Anger (exec. prod.), Waiting for the Light (exec. prod.), Homicide, Year of the Gun, Iron Maze (co-exec. prod.), Storyville (prod.), Bad Lieutenant (prod.), Hoffa (co-prod.).

PRESSMAN, LAWRENCE: Actor. b. Cynthiana, KY, July 10, 1939. e. Kentucky Northwestern U. On Bdwy. in Man in the Glass Booth, Play It Again, Sam, etc.
PICTURES: Man in the Glass Booth, The Crazy World of Julius Vrooder, Hellstrom Chronicle, Shaft, Making It, Walk Proud, Nine to Five, Some Kind of Hero, The Hanoi Hilton, The Waterdance.
TELEVISION: Series: Mulligan's Stew, Doogie Howser M.D. Movies: Cannon, The Snoop Sisters, The Marcus-Nelson Murder, Winter Kill, The First 36 Hours of Dr. Durant, Rich Man, Poor Man, Man from Atlantis, The Trial of Lee Harvey Oswald, The Gathering, Like Mom, Like Me, Blind Ambition, Little Girl Lost, Breaking Point, White Hot: The Mysterious Murder of Thelma Todd.

PRESSMAN, MICHAEL: Director, Producer. b. New York, NY, July 1, 1950. e. California Inst. of Arts. Comes from show business family; was actor in college.
PICTURES: Director: The Great Texas Dynamite Chase, The Bad News Bears Breaking Training, Boulevard Nights, Those Lips Those Eyes (also prod.), Some Kind of Hero, Doctor Detroit, Teenage Mutant Ninja Turtles II: The Secret of the Ooze.
TELEVISION: Movies: Like Mom, Like Me, The Imposter, The Christmas Gift, Final Jeopardy, Private Sessions, Haunted by Her Past, To Heal a Nation, Shootdown, The Revenge of Al Capone, Incident at Dark River, Man Against the Mob (also co-prod.), Joshua's Heart, Quicksand: No Escape.

PRESTON, KELLY: Actress. b. Honolulu, HI, Oct. 13, 1962. e. UCLA, USC. m. actor John Travolta.
PICTURES: Metalstorm: The Destruction of Jared-Syn (debut, 1983), Christine, Mischief, Secret Admirer, Space-Camp, 52 Pick-Up, Amazon Women on the Moon, A Tiger's Tale, Love at Stake, Spellbinder, Twins, The Experts, Run, Only You.
TELEVISION: Series: For Love and Honor, Capitol. Movies: The Perfect Bride, The American Clock. Guest: Blue Thunder.

PREVIN, ANDRE: Composer, Conductor. b. Berlin, Germany, Apr. 6, 1929. Composed and conducted over 50 m.p. scores. Music director, Pittsburgh Symphony Orchestra, & conductor emeritus of London Symphony Orchestra. Music Director, Royal Philharmonic Orch., 1985–89. Guest conductor of most major symphony orchestras in U.S. and Europe.
PICTURES: Three Little Words, Cause for Alarm, It's Always Fair Weather, Bad Day at Black Rock, Invitation to the Dance, Catered Affair, Designing Woman, Silk Stockings, Gigi (Academy Award), Porgy and Bess (Academy Award), Subterraneans, Bells are Ringing, Pepe, Elmer Gantry, Four Horsemen of the Apocalypse, One Two Three, Two for the Seesaw, Long Day's Journey Into Night, Irma LaDouce (Academy Award), My Fair Lady (Academy Award), Goodbye Charlie, Inside Daisy Clover, Fortune Cookie, Thoroughly Modern Millie, Valley of the Dolls, Paint Your Wagon, The Music Lovers, Jesus Christ Superstar.

PRICE, FRANK: Executive. b. Decatur, IL, May 17, 1930. e. Michigan State U. following naval service. Joined CBS in N.Y. in 1951 as story editor and writer. Moved to Hollywood in 1953, serving as story editor first at Columbia and then NBC (Matinee Theatre). In 1958 joined Universal as an assoc. prod. and writer. In 1961 named exec. prod. of The Virginian TV series. Appt. exec. prod. of Ironside; later did It Takes a Thief and several World Premiere movies. In 1964 named v.p. of Universal TV; 1971, sr. v.p.; 1974, pres. Also v.p., MCA, Inc. In 1978 left to join Columbia as pres. of new company unit, Columbia Pictures Productions. In 1979 named chmn. & CEO of Columbia Pictures. In 1983 joined Universal: named chmn., motion picture group, pres. of Universal Pictures, and v.p. of MCA. In 1987 formed Price Entertainment Inc. as chmn. & CEO to produce movies and create TV shows for dist. through Columbia Pictures Entertainment. 1990, integrated Price Entertainment Inc., into Columbia and was named chairman. Resigned, 1991.

PRICE, VINCENT: Actor. b. St. Louis, MO, May 27, 1911. e. Yale U., U. of London, Nuremberg U. Autobiography: I Know What I Like (1959).
PICTURES: Service DeLuxe (debut, 1938), Private Lives of Elizabeth and Essex, Tower of London, Green Hell, The Invisible Man Returns, House of Seven Gables, Brigham Young, Hudson's Bay, The Song of Bernadette, The Eve of St. Mark, Wilson, Laura, The Keys of the Kingdom, A Royal Scandal, Leave Her to Heaven, Dragonwyck, Shock, Long Night, Moss Rose, The Web, Up in Central Park, Abbot & Costello Meet Frankenstein (voice), Three Musketeers, Rogue's Regiment, The Bribe, Bagdad, Baron of Arizona, Champagne for Caesar, Curtain Call at Cactus Creek, His Kind of Woman, Adventures of Captain Fabian, Las Vegas Story, House of Wax, Dangerous Mission, Casanova's Big Night, Mad Magician, Son of Sinbad, Serenade, The Vagabond King (narrator), While the City Sleeps, The Ten Commandments, The Story of Mankind, The Fly, House on Haunted Hill, The Big Circus, Return of the Fly, The Bat, The Tingler, House of Usher, Master of the World, Pit and the Pendulum, Queen of the Nile, Rage of the Buccaneers, Confessions of an Opium Eater, Convicts 4, Tower of London, Tales of Terror, The Raven, Twice Told Tales, Diary of a Madman, Comedy of Terrors, Beach Party, Last Man on Earth, The Haunted Palace, The Masque of the Red Death, Tomb of Ligeia, War Gods of the Deep, Dr. Goldfoot and the Bikini Machine, Dr. Goldfoot and the Girl Bombs, The House of 1,000 Dolls, Witchfinder General (The Conqueror Worm), The Jackals, Spirits of the Dead (narrator), More Dead Than Alive, The Trouble With Girls, The Oblong Box, Scream and Scream Again, Cry of the Banshee, Abominable Dr. Phibes, Dr. Phibes Rise Again!, Theatre of Blood, Madhouse, It's Not

the Size That Counts, Journey Into Fear, Scavenger Hunt, The Monster Club, House of the Long Shadows, Bloodbath at the House of Death, Escapes, The Great Mouse Detective (voice), The Offspring (From a Whisper to a Scream), The Whales of August, Dead Heat, Edward Scissorhands.
TELEVISION: *Movies*: What's a Nice Girl Like You. . ., Backtrack, The Heart of Justice. *Guest*: F Troop, Here's Lucy, Voyage to the Bottom of the Sea, Batman. *Series*: Time Express, Mystery! (host), many dramatic roles in 1950s and 60s as well as hosting E.S.P. and The Chevy Mystery Show and panelist on Pantomime Quiz (1950–52).

PRIES, RALPH W.: Executive. b. Atlanta, GA, August 31, 1919. Graduated Georgia Inst. of Technology. V.P., MEDIQ, Inc.; pres. MEDIQ/PRN Life Support Services, Inc.; past pres., Odgen Food Service Corp.; exec. comm. and bd., Firstrust Savings Bank and chmn. of audit comm.; Boards of St. Christopher's Hospital for Children, Moss Rehabilitation Hospital, United Hospital Corp., Philadelphia Heart Instil. Former intl pres., Variety Clubs Intl.; previously on bd. of Hahnemann U. and Hosp., chmn. of bd. Likoff Cardiovascular Instit., pres. Main Line Reform Temple, Wynnewood, PA.

PRIESTLEY, JASON: Actor. b. Vancouver, Canada, Aug. 28, 1969. First screen appearance was as baby in 1969 film That Cold Day in the Park, in which his mother had bit part. Child actor in many Canadian TV commercials. First major U.S. acting job in 1986 TV movie Nobody's Child. Moved to L.A. in 1987. Theatre includes The Addict, The Breakfast Club.
TELEVISION: *Series*: Sister Kate, Beverly Hills 90210. *Movies*: Stacie (Canada), Nobody's Child, Teen Angel & Teen Angel Returns (Disney TV). *Guest*: Danger Bay (Canada), MacGyver, 21 Jump Street, Adventures of Beans Baxter, Quantum Leap.
PICTURES: The Boy Who Could Fly, Nowhere to Run, Watchers, Calendar Girl, Tombstone.

PRIMUS, BARRY: Actor. b. New York, NY, Feb. 16, 1938. e. Bennington Coll., City Coll. of NY.
THEATER: The King and the Duke, The Nervous Set, Henry IV, Parts I and II, Creating the World, Teibele and the Demon, Lincoln Center Rep. (The Changling, After the Fall).
PICTURES: The Brotherhood, Puzzle of a Downfall Child, Been Down So Long It Looks Like Up to Me, Von Richtofen and Brown, Boxcar Bertha, The Gravy Train, New York New York, Avalanche, Autopsy, The Rose, Heartland, Night Games, Absence of Malice, The River, Down and Out in Beverly Hills, Jake Speed, Space Camp, Talking Walls, The Stranger, Big Business, Cannibal Women in the Avocado Jungle of Death, Torn Apart, Guilty by Suspicion, Mistress (dir., s.p.), Night and the City.
TELEVISION: *Series*: Cagney and Lacey. *Mini-Series*: Washington Behind Closed Doors. *Movies*: Big Rose, Roger & Harry: The Mitera Target, Portrait of a Showgirl, Paper Dolls, I Want to Live, Heart of Steel, Brotherly Love. *Guest*: Law and Order.

PRINCE: Singer, Actor. r.n. Prince Rogers Nelson. b. Minneapolis, MN, June 7, 1958. Famous as rock star and recording artist before film debut in Purple Rain (1984).
PICTURES: Purple Rain, Under the Cherry Moon (also dir., s.p.), Sign O' the Times (also dir., songs), Batman (songs only), Graffiti Bridge (also dir., s.p., songs).

PRINCE, HAROLD: Director, Producer. b. New York, NY, Jan. 30, 1928. e. U. of Pennsylvania. Worked as stage mgr. for George Abbott on three shows, later co-produced, produced and/or directed the following: The Pajama Game (Tony Award), Damn Yankees (Tony Award), New Girl In Town, West Side Story, A Swim in the Sea, Fiorello! (Tony/Pulitzer), Tenderloin, A Call on Kurpin, Take Her She's Mine, A Funny Thing Happened on the Way to the Forum (Tony Award), She Loves Me, The Matchmaker (revival), Fiddler On The Roof, Poor Bitos, Baker Street, Flora, The Red Menace, Superman, Cabaret (Tony Award), Zorba, Company, Follies, The Great God Brown, The Visit, Love for Love (the last three all revivals), A Little Night Music (Tony Award), Candide (Tony Award), Pacific Overtures, Side by Side by Sondheim, Some of My Best Friends, On the Twentieth Century, Evita (London, 1978, Bdwy. 1979, LA, Australia & Chicago, 1980; Vienna & Mexico City, 1981), Sweeney Todd (Bdwy., Tony Award 1979; London, 1980), Merrily We Roll Along, A Doll's Life, Play Memory, End of the World, Diamonds, Grind, Roza, Cabaret (revival), Phantom of the Opera (London, 1986; NY, 1988; Tony Award), Grandchild of Kings (dir. & adapt.), Kiss of the Spider Woman, Silverlake, Sweeney Todd, Candide and Don Giovanni for N.Y. City Opera, Girl of Golden West for Chicago Lyric Opera Co. and San Francisco Opera; Willie Stark for Houston Grand Opera; Madama Butterfly for Chicago Lyric Opera and Turandot for Vienna State Opera and Faust for Metropolitan Opera.
MOVIES: *Co-producer*: The Pajama Game (1957), Damn Yankees. *Director*: Something for Everyone, A Little Night Music.

AUTHOR: Contradictions, Notes on Twenty-Six Years in the Theatre (Dodd, Mead & Co., New York, 1974).

PRINCE, WILLIAM: Actor. b. Nichols, NY, Jan. 26, 1913. With Maurice Evans, actor, 2 yrs., radio announcer. On N.Y. stage, Ah, Wilderness; m.p. debut in 1943. Many TV credits.
STAGE: Guest in the House, Across the Board on Tomorrow Morning, The Eve of St. Mark, John Loves Mary, As You Like It, I Am a Camera, Forward the Heart, Affair of Honor, Third Best Sport, The Highest Tree, Venus at Large, Strange Interlude, The Ballad of the Sad Cafe, Mercy Street.
PICTURES: Destination Tokyo, Cinderella Jones, The Very Thought of You, Roughly Speaking, Objective Burma, Pillow to Post, Carnegie Hall, Dead Reckoning, Lust for Gold, Cyrano de Bergerac, Secret of Treasure Mountain, Macabre, Sacco and Vanzetti, The Heartbreak Kid, The Stepford Wives, Family Plot, Network, Rollercoaster, The Gauntlet, The Cat from Outer Space, The Promise, Bronco Billy, Love & Money, Kiss Me Goodbye, Movers and Shakers, Fever Pitch, Spies Like Us, Nuts, Vice Versa, Spontaneous Combustion, The Taking of Beverly Hills.
TELEVISION: *Mini-Series*: George Washington, War and Remembrance. *Movies*: Key West, Night Games, Murder 1 Dancer O, Found Money, The Portrait

PRINCIPAL, VICTORIA: Actress. b. Fukuoka, Japan, Jan 3, 1950. Went to New York to become model; studied acting privately with Jean Scott at Royal Acad. of Dramatic Art in London before moving to Hollywood.
PICTURES: The Life and Times of Judge Roy Bean (debut, 1972), The Naked Ape, Earthquake, I Will I Will . . . for Now, Vigilante Force.
TELEVISION: *Series*: Dallas. *Guest*: Fantasy Island (pilot), Love Story, Love American Style, Greatest Heroes of the Bible. *Movies*: The Night They Stole Miss Beautiful, The Pleasure Palace, Last Hours Before Morning, Not Just Another Affair, Mistress, Naked Lie (also exec. prod.), Blind Witness (also exec. prod.), Sparks: The Price of Passion (also exec. prod.), Don't Touch My Daughter (also exec. prod.), The Burden of Proof, Seduction: Three Tales From the Inner Sanctum (also co-exec. prod.), Midnight's Child (exec. prod. only), Beyond Obsession.

PRINE, ANDREW: Actor. b. Jennings, FL, Feb. 14, 1936. e. U. of Miami. m. actress Heather Lowe. Mem. Actors Studio. On stage in Look Homeward, Angel, A Distant Bell, Mrs. Patterson, Borak. Ahmanson Theatre, LA: Long Day's Journey into Night, The Caine Mutiny. South Coast Rep.: Goodbye Freddy.
PICTURES: The Miracle Worker, Advance to the Rear, Texas Across the River, Bandolero!, The Devil's Brigade, This Savage Land, Generation, Chisum, Riding Tall, Simon: King of the Witches, Barn of the Naked Dead (Terror Circus), One Little Indian, The Centerfold Girls, Grizzly, The Town That Dreaded Sundown, Winds of Autumn, High Flying Lowe, The Evil, Amityville II: The Possession, Playing with Fire, Eliminators, Chill Factor, The Big One, Life on the Edge, Double Exposure.
TELEVISION: *Series*: The Wide Country, The Road West, W.E.B., Dallas, Room for Two. *Movies*: And the Children Shall Lead, Roughing It, Callie & Son, The Deputies, Another Part of the Forest, Night Slaves, Split Second to an Epitaph, Along Came a Spider, Night Slaves, Wonder Woman, Law of the Land, Tail Gunner Joe, Last of the Mohicans, A Small Killing, Mind over Murder, M-Station Hawaii, Christmas Miracle in Caulfield, Young Abe Lincoln, U.S.A., Donner Pass: The Road to Survival, Mission the Shark. *Mini-Series*: V: The Final Battle.

PROSKY, ROBERT: Actor. b. Philadelphia, PA, Dec. 13, 1930. Won TV amateur talent search contest, leading to scholarship with American Theatre Wing. 23-year veteran with Washington's Arena stage. Taught acting and appeared in over 150 plays including Death of a Salesman, Galileo, The Caucasian Chalk Circle, You Can't Take It With You, Our Town. Broadway prods. include Moonchildren, A View from the Bridge, Pale Horse Pale Rider, Arms and the Man, Glengarry Glen Ross (Tony Award nom.), A Walk in the Woods (Tony Award nom.). Tours incl.: Our Town, Inherit the Wind, A Walk in the Woods (Soviet Union), You Can't Take It With You, After the Fall (Hong Kong).
PICTURES: Thief, Hanky Panky, Monsignor, The Lords of Discipline, Christine, The Keep, The Natural, Outrageous Fortune, Big Shots, Broadcast News, The Great Outdoors, Things Change, Loose Cannons, Gremlins II: The New Batch, Funny About Love, Green Card, Life in the Food Chain (Age Isn't Everything), Far and Away, Hoffa, Last Action Hero, Rudy, Mrs. Doubtfire.
TELEVISION: *Series*: Hill Street Blues, Lifestories (host). *Movies*: World War III, The Ordeal of Bill Carny, Lou Grant, The Adams Chronicles, Old Dogs, Into Thin Air, The Murder of Mary Phagan, Home Fires Burning, From the Dead of Night, Heist, Dangerous Pursuit, Johnny Ryan, Against the Mob, A Green Journey, The Love She Sought, Double Edge,

Life on the High Wire, Teamster Boss: The Jackie Presser Story. *Guest*: Coach.

PROVINE, DOROTHY: Actress. b. Deadwood, SD, Jan. 20, 1937. e. U. of Washington.
TELEVISION: *Series*: The Alaskans, The Roaring 20's. *Movie*: The Sound of Anger.
PICTURES: The Bonnie Parker Story, Riot in Juvenile Prison, The 30 Foot Bride of Candy Rock, Wall of Noise, It's A Mad Mad Mad Mad World, Good Neighbor Sam, The Great Race, That Darn Cat, One Spy Too Many, Kiss the Girls and Make Them Die, Who's Minding the Mint?, Never a Dull Moment.

PRYCE, JONATHAN: Actor. b. North Wales, June 1, 1947. e. Royal Acad. of Dramatic Art. Actor and artistic dir. of Liverpool Everyman Theatre Co. On London stage in Comedians, Taming of the Shrew, Antony and Cleopatra, Tally's Folly, Hamlet (Olivier Award), Macbeth, The Seagull, Uncle Vanya, Miss Saigon. *NY*: Comedians (Tony & Theatre World Awards, 1977), Accidental Death of an Anarchist, Miss Saigon (Tony Award, 1991).
PICTURES: Voyage of the Damned, Breaking Glass, Loophole, The Ploughman's Lunch, Something Wicked This Way Comes, Doctor and the Devils, Brazil, Haunted Honeymoon, Jumpin' Jack Flash, Man on Fire, Consuming Passions, The Adventures of Baron Munchausen, The Rachel Papers, Freddie as F.R.O. 7 (voice), Glengarry Glen Ross, The Age of Innocence.
TELEVISION: Comedians, Playthings, Partisans, For Tea on Sunday, Timon of Athens, Praying Mantis, Murder Is Easy, Daft as a Brush, Martin Luther Heretic, The Caretaker, Glad Day, The Man From the Pru, Roger Doesn't Live Here Anymore, Selling Hitler, Whose Line Is It Anyway?, Mr. Wroes Virgins, Barbarians at the Gate.

PRYOR, RICHARD: Actor. b. Peoria, IL, Dec. 1, 1940. At age 7 played drums with professionals. Made NY debut as standup comic in 1963, leading to appearances on TV (Johnny Carson, Merv Griffin, Ed Sullivan). Co-wrote TV scripts for Lily Tomlin (Emmy Award, 1974) and Flip Wilson; co-wrote film Blazing Saddles. Won Grammy Awards for albums That Nigger's Crazy, Is It Something I Said?, Bicentennial Nigger.
PICTURES: The Busy Body (debut, 1967), The Green Berets, Wild in the Streets, The Phynx, You've Got to Walk It Like You Talk It Or You'll Lose That Beat, Dynamite Chicken, Lady Sings the Blues, Hit!, Wattstax, The Mack, Some Call It Loving, Blazing Saddles (co-s.p. only), Uptown Saturday Night, Adios Amigo, The Bingo Long Traveling All-Stars and Motor Kings, Car Wash, Silver Streak, Greased Lightning, Which Way Is Up?, Blue Collar, The Wiz, California Suite, Richard Pryor—Live in Concert (also prod., s.p.), The Muppet Movie, Richard Pryor is Back Live in Concert (also s.p.), Wholly Moses, In God We Trust, Stir Crazy, Bustin' Loose (also co-prod., co-s.p.), Richard Pryor: Live on Sunset Strip (also prod., s.p.), Some Kind of Hero, The Toy, Superman III, Richard Pryor: Here and Now (also dir., s.p.), Brewster's Millions, Jo Jo Dancer Your Life Is Calling (also prod.-dir.-s.p.), Critical Condition, Moving, See No Evil Hear No Evil, Harlem Nights, Another You.
TELEVISION: *Series*: The Richard Pryor Show (1977), Pryor's Place. *Guest*: Wild Wild West, Partridge Family, The Mod Squad. *Movies*: The Young Lawyers, Carter's Army.

PRYOR, THOMAS M.: Journalist. b. New York, NY, May 22, 1912. Joined NY Times, 1929; m.p. dept. 1931 as reporter, added asst. film critic; Hollywood bureau chief, corres., NY Times, 1951–59; editor, Daily Variety, 1959–88; 1988– Consultant to Variety & Daily Variety. 1990, retired.

PTAK, JOHN: Agent. b. San Diego, CA. Graduated UCLA film department, 1968. Theatre mgr. and booker for Walter Reade Organization and Laemmle Theatres, 1966–1969. Admin. exec. at American Film Institute's Center for Advanced Studies, 1969–1971. International Famous Agency (ICM), 1971–1975. Vice Pres., William Morris Agency, 1976 to 1991. Currently Creative Artists Agency. Represents motion picture and television talent.

PULLMAN, BILL: Actor. b. Hornell, NY, 1954. e. SUNY at Oneonta, Univ. of Mass. at Amherst.
PICTURES: Ruthless People (debut, 1986), Spaceballs, The Serpent and the Rainbow, Rocket Gibraltar, The Accidental Tourist, Cold Feet, Brain Dead, Sibling Rivalry, Bright Angel, Going Under, Newsies, A League of Their Own, Singles, Nervous Ticks, The Favor, Sommersby, Sleepless in Seattle, Malice, Mr. Jones, Wyatt Earp.
TELEVISION: Movies: Home Fires Burning, Crazy in Love.
THEATRE: *NY*: Dramathon '84, Curse of the Starving Class. *LA*: All My Sons, Barabbas, Nanawatai, Demon Wine, Control Freaks.

PURCELL, PATRICK B.: Executive. b. Dublin, Ireland, Mar. 16, 1943. e. Fordham U., M.B.A., 1973. In pub. & acct., England, 1969–69; acct., Associated Hosp. Service, N.Y., 1968–70;

joined Paramount Pictures, 1970; v.p., fin., 1980–83; exec. v.p. fin. & admin. 1983–.

PURDOM, EDMUND: Actor. b. Welwyn Garden City, England, Dec. 19, 1924. e. St. Ignatius Coll., London. Played leads, character roles for Northampton Rep. Co., Kettering Rep., two seasons at Stratford-On-Avon; London stage in Way Things Go, Malade Imaginaire, Romeo and Juliet, played in Caesar and Cleopatra, Antony and Cleopatra, London and N.Y.; TV and radio appearances N.Y., London.
PICTURES: Titanic, Julius Caesar, Student Prince, The Egyptian, Athena, The Prodigal, King's Thief, Strange Intruder, The Cossacks, Herod the Great, Trapped in Tangiers, Malaga (Moment of Danger), The Last of the Vikings, Nights of Rasputin, The Loves of Salambo, Lafayette, White Slave Ship, Queen of the Nile, The Comedy Man, The Beauty Jungle, The Yellow Rolls Royce, Pieces, Don't Open Till Christmas (also dir.), After the Fall of New York.
TELEVISION: Mini-Series: The Winds of War, The Scarlet and the Black. Movie: Sophia Loren: Her Own Story.

PURL, LINDA: Actress. b. Greenwich, CT, Sept. 2, 1955. Moved to Japan at age 2. Appeared in Japanese theatre, TV. e. Toho Geino Academy. Back to US in 1971. On stage in The Baby Dance (New Haven, NYC), Hedda Gabler, The Real Thing (Mark Taper), The Merchant of Venice (Old Globe Theatre), Romeo & Juliet, Doll's House.
PICTURES: Jory, Crazy Mama, W.C. Fields & Me, Leo and Loree, The High Country, Visiting Hours, Viper, Natural Causes.
TELEVISION: *Series*: The Secret Storm, Beacon Hill, Happy Days, Matlock, Under Cover, Young Pioneers. *Movies*: Eleanor and Franklin, Little Ladies of the Night, Testimony of Two Men, A Last Cry for Help, Women at West Point, Like Normal People, The Flame is Love, The Night the City Screamed, The Adventures of Nellie Bly, The Last Days of Pompeii, The Manions of America, Addicted to His Love, Spies Lies and Naked Thighs, Before the Storm, Spy Games, Danielle Steel's Secrets, Body Language.

PUTTNAM, DAVID, CBE: Hon. LL.D Bristol 1983; Hon. D. Litt, Leicester 1986. Hon. Litt. D., Leeds 1992. Producer. b. London, England 1941. e. Michenden Sch. In advertising before joining VPS/Goodtimes Prod. Co. Dir. of Britain's National Film Finance Corp. (1980–5); Also served on Cinema Films Council and governing council of the British Acad. of Film & Television Arts. Officier dans L'Ordre des Arts et des Lettres, 1986. Chmn. National Film and Television Sch., 1988. Trustee, Tate Gallery. Past Pres., Council for the Protection of Rural England; Fellow, Royal Soc. of Arts; Fellow, Royal Geographical Soc., Hon. Fellow, The Chartered Society of Designers. appt. Chmn. & CEO, Columbia Pictures. Resigned 1987. Received Eastman 2nd Century Award, 1988. Sept., 1988 formed a joint venture for his Enigma Productions Ltd. with Warner Bros., Fujisankei Comm. Gp. of Japan, British Satellite Broadcasting & Country Nat West to prod. 4 films. Appt. chmn. ITEL intl. TV dist. agency, 1989. Dir., Anglia Television Group and Survival Anglia.
PICTURES: Melody, The Pied Piper, That'll Be The Day, Stardust, Mahler, Bugsy Malone, The Duellists, Midnight Express, Foxes, Chariots of Fire (Acad. Award, best picture, 1981), Local Hero, Cal, The Killing Fields, The Mission, Defence of the Realm, Memphis Belle, Meeting Venus, Being Human. Co-produced documentaries: Swastika, James Dean—The First American Teenager, Double-Headed Eagle, Brother Can You Spare a Dime?
TELEVISION: P'Tang Yang Kipperbang, Experience Preferred, Secrets, Those Glory Glory Days, Sharma and Beyond, Winter Flight, Josephine Baker, Without Warning: The James Brady Story, A Dangerous Man: Lawrence After Arabia.

Q

QUAID, DENNIS: Actor. b. Houston, TX Apr. 9, 1954. Brother of Randy Quaid. m. actress Meg Ryan. e. U. of Houston. Appeared in Houston stage productions before leaving for Hollywood. On N.Y. stage with his brother in True West, 1984. Performs with rock band The Electrics and wrote songs for films The Night the Lights Went Out in Georgia, Tough Enough, The Big Easy. Formed Summers/Quaid Productions with producer Cathleen Summers, 1989.
PICTURES: I Never Promised You a Rose Garden, September 30, 1955, Our Winning Season, Seniors, G.O.R.P., Breaking Away, The Long Riders, All Night Long, Caveman, The Night the Lights Went Out in Georgia (also wrote songs), Tough Enough, Jaws 3-D, The Right Stuff, Dreamscape, Enemy Mine, The Big Easy (also composed and sang song), Innerspace, Suspect, D.O.A., Everybody's All-American, Great Balls of Fire, Postcards From the Edge, Come See the Paradise, Wilder Napalm, Undercover Blues, Flesh & Bone.

TELEVISION: *Movies*: Are You in the House Alone?, Amateur Night at the Dixie Bar and Grill, Bill, Johnny Belinda, Bill: On His Own.

QUAID, RANDY: Actor. b. Houston, TX, Oct. 1, 1950. Brother of actor Dennis Quaid. Discovered by Peter Bogdanovich while still jr. at Drama Dept. at U. of Houston and cast in his Targets and The Last Picture Show, 1971. Off-B'way debut: True West (1983).
PICTURES: Targets, The Last Picture Show, What's Up Doc?, Paper Moon, Lolly-Madonna XXX, The Last Detail (Acad. Award nom.), The Apprenticeship of Duddy Kravitz, Breakout, The Missouri Breaks, Bound for Glory, The Choirboys, Midnight Express, Three Warriors, Foxes, The Long Riders, Heartbeeps, National Lampoon's Vacation, The Wild Life, The Slugger's Wife, Fool for Love, The Wraith, Sweet Country, No Man's Land, Moving, Caddyshack II, Parents, Bloodhounds of Broadway, Out Cold, National Lampoon's Christmas Vacation, Martians Go Home!, Days of Thunder, Quick Change, Cold Dog Soup, Texasville, The Paper.
TELEVISION: *Movies*: Getting Away From It All, The Great Niagara, The Last Ride of the Dalton Gang, To Race the Wind, Guyana Tragedy: The Story of Jim Jones, Of Mice and Men, Inside the Third Reich, Cowboy, A Streetcar Named Desire, LBJ: The Early Years, Dead Solid Perfect, Evil in Clear River, Frankenstein. *Series*: Saturday Night Live (1985–6), Davis Rules. *Special*: Dear America (reader).

QUIGLEY, MARTIN, JR.: Educator, Writer. b. Chicago, IL, Nov. 24, 1917. e. A.B. Georgetown U.; M.A., Ed. D, Columbia U. M.P. Herald, Oct. 1939; sprcl. ed. rep., M.P. Herald & M.P. Daily, May, 1941; wartime work in U.S., England, Eire & Italy, Dec. 1941–Oct. 1945; assoc. ed., Quigley Pub., Oct. 1945; ed. M.P. Herald, July, 1949; also edit. dir. of all Quigley Pub., 1956; pres. Quigley Pub. Co., 1964; author, Great Gaels, 1944, Roman Notes, 1946, Magic Shadows—the Story of the Origin of Motion Pictures, 1948, Govt. Relations of Five Universities, 1975; Peace Without Hiroshima, 1991. Editor, New Screen Techniques, 1953; m.p. tech. section, Encyclopaedia Brit., 1956; co-author, Catholic Action in Practice, 1963. Co-author: Films in America, 1929–69, 1970. Pres., QWS, Inc., educational consultants, 1975–81. Adjunct professor of higher education, Baruch College Univ. City of New York 1977–1989; Teachers College, Columbia Univ., 1990. Village of Larchmont, N.Y., trustee, 1977–79; mayor, 1980–84. Board of trustees, American Bible Society, 1984–; Religious Education Ass'n., treasurer, 1975–80 & chairperson, 1981–84; Laymen's Nat'l. Bible Association, chmn. education committee, 1983–; Will Rogers Institute, chmn. Health education committee, 1980–.

QUIGLEY, WILLIAM J.: Executive. b. New York, NY, July 6, 1951. e. Wesleyan U., B.A., 1973; Columbia U., M.S., 1983. From 1973 to 1974 was advt. circulation mgr. for Quigley Publishing Co. Taught school in Kenya in 1974; returned to U.S. to join Grey Advt. as media planner. In 1975 joined Walter Reade Organization as asst. film buyer; promoted to head film buyer in 1977. Named v.p., 1982. In 1986 joined Vestron, Inc. as sr. v.p. to establish Vestron Pictures. Named pres., Vestron Pictures, 1987–89. In 1990 joined Fair Lanes Entertainment, Inc. as v.p. mktg. 1993, joined United Artists Theatre as sr. v.p., marketing.
PICTURES: Exec. prod.: Steel Dawn, The Dead, Salome's Last Dance, The Unholy, Waxwork, Burning Secret, The Lair of the White Worm, Paint It Black, The Rainbow, Twister.

QUINLAN, KATHLEEN: Actress. b. Pasadena, CA, Nov. 19, 1954. Played small role in film, One Is a Lonely Number, while in high school. Stage: Taken in Marriage (NY Public Theatre; Theatre World Award), Uncommon Women and Others, Accent on Youth (Long Wharf, CT), Les Liaisons Dangereuses.
PICTURES: One is a Lonely Number (debut, 1972), American Graffiti, Lifeguard, Airport '77, I Never Promised You a Rose Garden, The Promise, The Runner Stumbles, Sunday Lovers, Hanky Panky, Independence Day, Twilight Zone—The Movie, Warning Sign, Wild Thing, Man Outside, Sunset, Clara's Heart, The Doors.
TELEVISION: *Movies*: Can Ellen Be Saved?, Lucas Tanner (pilot), Where Have All the People Gone?, The Missing Are Deadly, The Abduction of St. Anne, Turning Point of Jim Malloy, Little Ladies of the Night, She's in the Army Now, When She Says No, Blackout, Children of the Night, Dreams Lost Dreams Found, Trapped, The Operation, Strays, An American Story, Stolen Babies.

QUINN, AIDAN: Actor. b. Chicago, IL, March 8, 1959. Spent time in Ireland as a boy, following high sch. graduation. Returned to Chicago at 19, worked as tar roofer. Chicago stage: The Man in 605 (debut), Scheherazade, The Irish Hebrew Lesson, Hamlet.
THEATER: Fool for Love (off-Bdwy debut), A Lie of the Mind, A Streetcar Named Desire (Theatre World Award).
PICTURES: Reckless (debut, 1984), Desperately Seeking Susan, The Mission, Stakeout, Crusoe, The Handmaid's Tale, The Lemon Sisters, Avalon, At Play in the Fields of the Lord, The Playboys, Benny & Joon, Blink, Legends of the Fall.
TELEVISION: *Special*: All My Sons. *Movies*: An Early Frost, Perfect Witness, Lies of the Twins, A Private Matter.

QUINN, ANTHONY: Actor. b. Chihuahua, Mexico, Apr. 21, 1915. Began on screen, 1936.
PICTURES: Parole, Daughter of Shanghai, Last Train From Madrid, Partners in Crime, The Plainsman, Swing High Swing Low, Waikiki Wedding, The Buccaneer (1938), Bulldog Drummond in Africa, Dangerous to Know, Hunted Men, King of Alcatraz, Tip-Off Girls, Island of Lost Men, King of Chinatown, Television Spy, Union Pacific, City for Conquest, Emergency Squad, Ghost Breakers, Parole Fixer, Road to Singapore, Blood and Sand, Bullets for O'Hara, Knockout, Manpower, The Perfect Snob, Texas Rangers Ride Again, They Died With Their Boots On, Thieves Fall Out, The Black Swan, Larceny Inc., Road to Morocco, Guadalcanal Diary, The Ox-Bow Incident, Buffalo Bill, Irish Eyes Are Smiling, Roger Touhy Gangster, Ladies of Washington, China Sky, Back to Bataan, Where Do We Go From Here?, California, Imperfect Lady, Sinbad the Sailor, Black Gold, Tycoon, The Brave Bulls, Mask of the Avenger, Viva Zapata! (Acad. Award, supp. actor, 1952), The Brigand, World in His Arms, Against All Flags, Ride Vaquero, City Beneath the Sea, Seminole, Blowing Wild, East of Sumatra, Long Wait, Magnificent Matador, Ulysses, Naked Street, Seven Cities of Gold, La Strada, Attila the Hun, Lust for Life (Acad. Award, supp. actor, 1956), Wild Party, Man from Del Rio, Hunchback of Notre Dame, Ride Back, The River's Edge, Wild is the Wind, The Buccaneer (1958; dir. only), Hot Spell, Black Orchid, Last Train From Gun Hill, Warlock, Portrait in Black, Heller in Pink Tights, Savage Innocents, The Guns of Navarone, Barabbas, Requiem for a Heavyweight, Lawrence of Arabia, Behold a Pale Horse, The Visit, Zorba the Greek (also assoc. prod.), High Wind in Jamaica, Marco the Magnificent, Lost Command, The 25th Hour, The Happening, Guns for San Sebastian, The Rover, The Magus, Shoes of the Fisherman, The Secret of Santa Vittoria, A Dream of Kings, A Walk in the Spring Rain, R.P.M., Flap, Across 110th Street (also exec. prod.), Deaf Smith and Johnny Ears, The Don Is Dead, The Destructors, The Inheritance, The Con Artists, Mohammad: Messenger of God, The Greek Tycoon, Caravans, The Passage, Lion of the Desert, High Risk, The Salamander, A Man of Passion, Stradivarius, Revenge, Ghosts Can't Do It, A Star for Two, Only the Lonely, Jungle Fever, Mobsters, Last Action Hero.
TELEVISION: Much dramatic work in the early 1950s. *Series*: The City, American Playwrights Theater (host). *Movies*: Jesus of Nazareth, Treasure Island (Italian TV), Onassis: The Richest Man in the World, The Old Man and the Sea.

R

RABE, DAVID WILLIAM: Writer. b. Dubuque, IA, March 10, 1940. m. actress Jill Clayburgh. e. Loras Coll.
PLAYS: The Basic Training of Pavlo Hummel (Obie Award, 1971), Sticks and Bones (Tony Award, 1971), The Orphan, In the Boom Boom Room, Streamers, Hurlyburly.
PICTURES: *Writer*: I'm Dancing As Fast As I can (also exec. prod.), Streamers, Casualties of War, State of Grace.
TELEVISION: Sticks and Bones.

RABINOVITZ, JASON: Executive. b. Boston, MA, e. Harvard Coll., B.A. where elected to Phi Beta Kappa. Following W.W.II service as military intelligence captain with paratroops, took M.B.A. at Harvard Business Sch., 1948. Started in industry in 1949 as asst. to secty.-treas., United Paramount Theatres. Asst. controller, ABC, 1953; adm. v.p., ABC-TV, 1956; joined MGM as asst. treas., 1957; named MGM-TV gen. mgr., director of business & financial affairs, 1958; treas. & chief financial officer, MGM, Inc., 1963; financial v.p. & chief financial officer, 1967. In 1971 named exec. v.p. & dir. Encyclopedia Brittanica Education Corp.; sr. v.p., American Film Theatre, 1974–75. Rejoined MGM as v.p./exec. asst. to the pres., 1976. Elected v.p. finance, 1979; promoted to sr. v.p., finance & corporate admin., MGM Film Co. & UA Prods. Resigned, 1984. Now film & TV consultant and indep. producer.

RADIN, PAUL: Producer. b. New York, NY, Sept. 15, 1913. e. NYU. After college went in adv. Became v.p. in chg. of m.p. div. of Buchanan & Co. During WWII posted in Middle East as film chief for Office of War Information for that area. On return to U.S. assigned by Buchanan to ad campaign for Howard Hughes' The Outlaw. Turned to talent mgr., joining the Sam Jaffe Agency. Then joined Ashley-Famous Agency. Became exec. prod. for Yul Brynner's indep. prod. co. based in Switzerland, with whom made such films as The Journey, Once More with Feeling, Surprise Package.
PICTURES: Born Free, Living Free, Phase IV, The Blue Bird.

TELEVISION: The Incredible Journey of Dr. Meg Laurel, The Ordeal of Dr. Mudd, Crime of Innocence, Series: Born Free, The Wizard.

RADNITZ, ROBERT B.: Producer. b. Great Neck, NY, Aug. 9, 1924. e. U. of Virginia. Taught 2 years at U. of Virginia, then became reader for Harold Clurman; wrote several RKO This Is America scripts, then to Broadway where co-prod., The Frogs of Spring; prod. The Young and the Beautiful; to Hollywood working at United Artists, then as story consultant for 20th Century-Fox; prod. A Dog of Flanders (1960—first feature), first U.S. film to win Golden Lion Award at Venice Film Festival. Board of Directors, Producer Guild of America: v.p., last 3 years; bd. member, Producers Branch, Acad. of MoPic Arts & Sciences, last 4 yrs.; First producer with retrospective at Museum of Modern Art, and by joint resolution of both houses of Congress, 1973. Pres. Robert B. Radnitz Productions, Ltd. Vice pres., Producers Guild, 1982, 1984.
PICTURES: Misty, Island of the Blue Dolphins, And Now Miguel, My Side of the Mountain, The Little Ark, Sounder (Acad. Award nom.), Where the Lilies Bloom, Birch Interval, Sounder 2, A Hero Ain't Nothin' But a Sandwich, Cross Creek.
TELEVISION: Mary White (Emmy for teleplay-nominated for best film) Christopher Award for TV special; Never Forget (ACE Award nom. for Best Film).

RAFELSON, BOB: Producer, Director, Writer. b. New York, NY, 1933. e. Dartmouth, B.A. (philosophy). Left NY in teens to ride in rodeos in AZ. Worked on cruise ship, then played drums and bass with jazz combos in Acapulco. 1953 won Frost Natl. Playwriting competition. Dir. his award-winning play at Hanover Experimental Theatre, N.H. After Army Service did program promotion for a radio station, was advisor for Shochiku Films, Japan, then hired by David Susskind to read scripts for Talent Assocs. Writer-assoc. prod., DuPont Show of the Month and Play of the Week (also script sprv.). Joined Screen Gems in California, developing program idea for Jackie Cooper, then head of TV prod. arm of Columbia. Later formed BBS Productions with Burt Schneider and Steve Blauner; their first film, Head (1968).
PICTURES: Prod.-Dir.-Co-s.p.: Head, Five Easy Pieces, The King of Marvin Gardens, Stay Hungry, The Postman Always Rings Twice (prod., dir.), Black Widow (dir.), Mountains of the Moon (dir., co-s.p.), Man Trouble (dir.). Co-Prod. only: Easy Rider, The Last Picture Show, Drive He Said. Actor: Always (1985).
TELEVISION: The Monkees (1966–68, creator, writer, dir., Emmy Award, 1967). Adapted 34 prods., Play of the Week. Dir. music video: All Night Long, with Lionel Ritchie.

RAFFERTY, FRANCES: Actress. b. Sioux City, IA, June 26, 1922; e. U. of California, premedical student UCLA. TV series, December Bride, Pete and Gladys.
PICTURES: Seven Sweethearts, Private Miss Jones, Girl Crazy, War Against Mrs. Hadley, Thousands Cheer, Dragon Seed, Honest Thief, Mrs. Parkington, Barbary Coast Gent, Hidden Eye, Abbott and Costello in Hollywood, Adventures of Don Coyote, Money Madness, Lady at Midnight, Old Fashioned Girl, Rodeo, Shanghai Story.

RAFFIN, DEBORAH: Actress. b. Los Angeles, CA, March 13, 1953. m. producer Michael Viner. Mother is actress Trudy Marshall. e. Valley Coll. Was active fashion model before turning to acting when discovered by Ted Witzer. Author: Sharing Christmas (Vols. I & II). Debut in 40 Carats (1973). Publisher Dove Books On Tape. Head of Dove Films, prod. co.
PICTURES: 40 Carats (debut, 1973), The Dove, Once Is Not Enough, God Told Me To (Demon), Assault on Paradise (Maniac!), The Sentinel, Touched by Love, Dance of the Dwarfs (Jungle Heat), Death Wish 3, Claudia, Scanners II.
TELEVISION: Series: Foul Play. Movies: A Nightmare in Badham County, Ski Lift to Death, How to Pick Up Girls, Willa, Mind Over Murder, Haywire, For the Love of It, Killing at Hell's Gate, For Lovers Only, Running Out, Sparkling Cyanide, Threesome, The Sands of Time. Mini-Series: The Last Convertible, James Clavell's Noble House, Windmills of the Gods (also co-prod.). Guest: B.L. Stryker.

RAGLAND, ROBERT OLIVER: Composer. b. Chicago, IL, July 3, 1931. e. Northwestern U., American Conservatory of Music, Vienna Acad. of Music. Professional pianist at Chicago nightclubs. In U.S. Navy; on discharge joined Dorsey Bros. Orchestra as arranger. On sls. staff at NBC-TV, Chicago. 1970, moved to Hollywood to become composer for movies; has scored 62 feature films plus many TV movies and series segments. Has also written some 45 original songs.
PICTURES: The Touch of Melissa, The Yin and Yang of Mr. Go, The Thing with Two Heads, Prayer: Kill, Abby, Seven Alone, The Eyes of Dr. Chaney, Return to Macon County, The Daring Dobermans, Shark's Treasure, Grizzly, Pony Express Rider, Mansion of the Doomed, Mountain Family Robinson, Only Once in a Lifetime, Jaguar Lives, The Glove, Lovely But Deadly, "Q", The Day of the Assassin, A Time To Die, The

Winged Serpent, Trial by Terror, The Guardian, Ten to Midnight, Dirty Rebel, Hysterical, Brainwaves, Where's Willie?, The Supernaturals, Nightstick, Messenger of Death, The Fifth Monkey, No Place to Hide, Ice Runner, The Buffalo Soldiers, Raffles.
TELEVISION: Photoplay's Stars of Tomorrow, Wonder Woman, Barnaby Jones, Streets of San Francisco, High Ice, The Girl on the Edge of Town, The Guardian, etc.

RAILSBACK, STEVE: Actor. b. Dallas, TX, 1948. Studied with Lee Strasberg. On stage in Orpheus Descending, This Property Is Condemned, Cherry Orchard, Skin of Our Teeth, etc.
PICTURES: The Visitors, Cockfighter, Angela, The Stunt Man, Deadly Games, Turkey Shoot, The Golden Seal, Torchlight, Lifeforce, Armed and Dangerous, Blue Monkey, The Wind, Distortions, Deadly Intent, Alligator II, After-Shock, Forever.
TELEVISION: Movies: Helter Skelter, Good Cops Bad Cops, The Forgotten, Spearfield's Daughter, Sunstroke, Bonds of Love. Mini-Series: From Here to Eternity.

RAIMI, SAM: Director. b. Royal Oak, MI, Oct. 23, 1959. e. Michigan St. Univ. Formed Renaissance Pictures, Inc.
PICTURES: Dir.-Writer: The Evil Dead, Crimewave, Evil Dead II, Darkman, Army of Darkness. Co-Writer: The Hudsucker Proxy. Producer: Hard Target. Actor: Spies Like Us, Thou Shalt Not Kill . . . Except, Maniac Cop, Miller's Crossing, Innocent Blood, Indian Summer, Intruder.
TELEVISION: Movies: Journey to the Center of the Earth (actor), Mantis (prod., writer), Body Bags (actor), The Stand (actor).

RAJSKI, PEGGY: Producer. b. Stevens Point, WI. e. Univ. of Wisconsin. Began film career as prod. manager on John Sayles film Lianna, before becoming producer. Prod. of Bruce Springsteen music videos, incld. Glory Days which one American Video Award.
PICTURES: The Brother From Another Planet, Matewan, Eight Men Out, The Grifters, Little Man Tate, Used People.

RAKOFF, ALVIN: Producer, Director. b. Toronto, Canada, 1937. e. U. of Toronto. Early career as journalist. Dir. in French & U.S. T.V. England, Canada. Emmy Award winner, 1968 for Call Me Daddy. Emmy Award, 1982 for A Voyage Around My Father.
STAGE: Hamlet, Albert Hall Royal Charity, etc.
PICTURES: On Friday at 11, The Comedy Man, Crossplot, Hoffman, Say Hello to Yesterday, City on Fire, Death Ship, Dirty Tricks.
TELEVISION: The Caine Mutiny Court Martial, Requiem for a Heavyweight, Our Town, The Velvet Alley, A Town Has Turned to Dust, Jokers Justice, Call Me Back, Day Before Atlanta, Heart to Heart, The Seekers, Sweet War Man, The Move after Checkmate, The Stars in My Eyes, Call Me Daddy, Summer & Smoke, Don Quixote, Shadow of a Gunman, The Impeachment of Andrew Johnson, Cheap in August, In Praise of Love, Nicest Man in the World, Dame of Sark, The Kitchen, Romeo and Juliet, Voyage Round My Father, Mr. Halpern and Mr. Johnson, The First Olympics—Athens 1896, Paradise Postponed, Haunting Harmony, Gas & Candles, The Best of Friends, Sam Saturday.

RAKSIN, DAVID: Composer. b. Philadelphia, PA, Aug. 4, 1912. e. U. of Pennsylvania, studied music with Isadore Freed and Arnold Schoenberg. Composer for films, ballet, dramatic and musical comedy, stage, radio and TV, symphony orchestra and chamber ensembles. Arranger of music of Chaplin film, Modern Times; pres. Composers and Lyricists Guild of America, 1962–70; animated films include Madeline and The Unicorn in the Garden (UPA). Professor of Music and Urban Semester, U. of Southern California, and faculty, UCLA Sch. of Music. Coolidge Commission from the Library of Congress: Oedipus Memneitai (Oedipus Remembers) for bass/baritone, 6-part chorus and chamber orchestra premiered there under dir. of composer, Oct. 30, 1986. Pres., Society for the Preservation of Film Music, 1992. Recipient of ASCAP Golden Score Award for Career Achievement, 1992.
PICTURES: Laura, Secret Life of Walter Mitty, Smoky, Force of Evil, Across the Wide Missouri, Carrie, Bad and the Beautiful, Apache, Suddenly, Big Combo, Jubal, Hilda Crane, Separate Tables, Al Capone, Night Tide, Too-Late Blues, Best of the Bolshoi (music for visual interludes), Two Weeks in Another Town, The Redeemer, Invitation to a Gunfighter, Sylvia, A Big Hand for the Little Lady, Will Penny, Glass Houses, What's the Matter with Helen?
TELEVISION: Series: Wagon Train, Five Fingers, Life With Father, Father of the Bride, Ben Casey, Breaking Point, Medical Center. Specials: Journey, Tender is the Night, Prayer of the Ages, Report from America, The Olympics (CBC), The Day After, Lady in a Corner.

RAMIS, HAROLD: Writer, Director, Actor, Producer. b. Chicago, IL, Nov. 21, 1944. e. Washington U., St. Louis. Assoc. ed. Playboy Mag. 1968–70; writer, actor, Second City, Chicago 1970–73; National Lampoon Radio Show, Lampoon show 1974–75.

TELEVISION: Head writer and actor SCTV, 1976–78; prod., head writer Rodney Dangerfield Show 1982. *Exec. Prod.*: Will Rogers—Look Back and Laugh.

PICTURES: National Lampoon's Animal House (co-s.p.), Meatballs (co-s.p.), Caddyshack (co-s.p., dir.), Stripes (co-s.p., actor), Heavy Metal (voice), National Lampoon's Vacation (dir.), Ghostbusters (co-s.p., actor), Back to School (co-s.p., exec. prod.), Club Paradise (co-s.p., dir.), Armed and Dangerous (exec. prod., co-s.p.), Baby Boom (actor), Caddyshack II (co-s.p.), Stealing Home (actor), Ghostbusters II (co-s.p., actor), Rover Dangerfield (co-story), Groundhog Day (dir., co-s.p., co-prod., actor).

RAMPLING, CHARLOTTE: Actress. b. Sturmer, England, Feb. 5, 1946. e. Jeanne D'Arc Academie pour Jeune Filles, Versailles; St. Hilda's, Bushey, England. Ent. m.p. ind. 1966.

PICTURES: The Knack, Rotten to the Core, Georgy Girl, The Long Duel, The Damned, Target: Harry (How to Make It), Three, Ski Bum, Corky, Tis Pity She's a Whore, Asylum, The Night Porter, Giordano Bruno, Zardoz, Caravan to Vaccares, Yuppi Dui La Chair De L'orchidee, Farewell My Lovely, Foxtrot, Orca, Purple Taxi, Stardust Memories, The Verdict, Viva La Vie, Angel Heart, Mascara, D.O.A., Max My Love, He Died with His Eyes Open, Paris By Night, The Riddle, Ocean Point, Helmut Newton: Frames from the Edge (doc.), Hammers Over the Anvil.

TELEVISION: *BBC Series*: The Six Wives of Henry VIII, The Superlative Seven, The Avengers. *Movies*: Sherlock Holmes in New York, Mystery of Cader Iscom, The Fantasists, What's in it for Henry, Zinotchka, Infidelities, La Femme Abandonnee.

RAND, HAROLD: Executive. b. New York, NY, Aug. 25, 1928. e. Long Island U., B.S., 1948–50; City Coll. of New York, 1945–46. U.S. Army 1946–48; ent. m.p. ind. 1950, pub. dept. 20th-Fox; variety of posts incl. writer, trade press, newspaper contacts; joined Walt Disney's Buena Vista pub. mgr., 1957; pub. mgr. Paramount Pictures, 1959; formed own pub. rel. firm, 1961; dir. of pub. Embassy Picture Corp. 1962; dir. of world pub. 20th Century Fox 1962; resigned 1963; dir. of adv. & pub.; Landau Co., 1963; dir. world pub., Embassy Pictures, 1964; est. Harold Rand & Co., Inc., 1966, pres. of p.r. & mktg. firm. Appt. mktg., dir., Kaufman Astoria Studios, 1984; elected v.p., 1985.

RANDALL, STEPHEN F.: Executive. Held marketing posts with United Vintners and Clorox. Joined Columbia Pictures in 1978 as director of research; named v.p. in 1980 and sr. v.p. in 1982. 1983, joined Tri-Star Pictures as sr. v.p. of marketing; promoted to exec. v.p.; 1988 named sr. v.p. of prod., Tri-Star.

RANDALL, TONY: Actor. r.n. Leonard Rosenberg. b. Tulsa, OK, Feb. 26, 1920. e. Northwestern U. Prof. N.Y. debut as actor in Circle of Chalk; then in Candida and others; U.S. Army 1942–46; radio actor on many shows. Founder/Artistic Director of National Actors Theatre in NYC, 1991.

STAGE: The Corn is Green, Antony & Cleopatra, Caesar & Cleopatra, Inherit the Wind, Oh Men! Oh Women!, Oh Captain, The Sea Gull, The Master Builder, M. Butterfly, A Little Hotel on the Side, Three Men on a Horse.

PICTURES: Oh Men! Oh Women! (debut, 1957), Will Success Spoil Rock Hunter?, No Down Payment, The Mating Game, Pillow Talk, The Adventures of Huckleberry Finn, Let's Make Love, Lover Come Back, Boys' Night Out, Island of Love, The Brass Bottle, 7 Faces of Dr. Lao, Send Me No Flowers, Fluffy, The Alphabet Murders, Bang Bang You're Dead, Hello Down There, Everything You Always Wanted to Know About Sex*, Scavenger Hunt, Foolin' Around, The King of Comedy, My Little Pony (voice), It Had to Be You, That's Adequate, Gremlins 2: The New Batch (voice), Fatal Instinct.

TELEVISION: *Series*: One Man's Family, Mr. Peepers, The Odd Couple (Emmy Award, 1975), The Tony Randall Show, Love Sidney. *Guest*: TV Playhouse, Max Liebman Spectaculars, Sid Caesar, Dinah Shore, Playhouse 90, Walt Disney World Celebrity Circus. *Movies*: Kate Bliss and the Ticker Tape Kid, Sidney Shorr: A Girl's Best Friend, Off Sides, Hitler's SS: Portrait in Evil, Sunday Drive, Save the Dog!.

RANSOHOFF, MARTIN: Executive. b. New Orleans, LA, 1927. e. Colgate U., 1949. Adv., Young & Rubicam, 1948–49; slsmn, writer, dir., Gravel Films, 1951; formed own co., Filmways, 1952; industrial films, commercials; formed Filmways TV Prods., Filmways, Inc., Filmways of Calif. chmn., bd. Filmways, Inc., resigned from Filmways in 1972 and formed own independent motion picture and television production company.

TELEVISION: Mister Ed, The Beverly Hillbillies, Petticoat Junction, Green Acres, The Addams Family.

PICTURES: Boys' Night Out, The Wheeler Dealers, The Americanization of Emily, The Sandpiper, The Cincinnati Kid, The Fearless Vampire Killers, Don't Make Waves, Ice Station Zebra, Castle Keep, Hamlet (exec. prod.), Catch-22, The Moonshine War, See No Evil, 10 Rillington Place, Fuzz, Save The Tiger, The White Dawn, Silver Streak (exec. prod.), Nightwing, The Wanderers, A Change of Seasons, American

Pop, Hanky Panky, Class, Jagged Edge, The Big Town, Switching Channels, Physical Evidence, Welcome Home.

RAPHAEL, FREDERIC: Writer. b. Chicago, IL, Aug. 14, 1931. e. Charterhouse, St. John's Coll., Cambridge. Novels: The Earlsdon Way, The Limits of Love, A Wild Surmise, The Graduate Wife, The Trouble With England, Lindmann, Orchestra and Beginners, Like Men Betrayed, Who Were You With Last Night?, April June and November, Richard's Things, California Time, The Glittering Prizes, Sleeps Six & Other Stories, Oxbridge Blues & Other Stories, Heaven & Earth, Think of England, After the War, A Double Life. Biographies: Somerset Maugham and His World, Byron. Translations: (with Kenneth McLeish), Poems of Catullus The Oresteia. Essays: Bookmarks, Cracks in the Ice, Of Gods and Men. Ent. m.p. ind., 1956. Several plays for ATV, 1960–62.

PICTURES: Bachelor of Hearts, Don't Bother to Knock (1961), Nothing But the Best, Darling (Acad. Award, 1965), Two for the Road, Far from the Madding Crowd, A Severed Head, Daisy Miller, Richard's Things.

TELEVISION: The Glittering Prizes (Royal TV Society Writer Award 1978), Rogue Male, School Play, Something's Wrong, Best of Friends, Richard's Things, Oxbridge Blues (ACE Award, best s.p.), After the War, Byrow, The Man in the Brooks Brothers Shirt (also dir.; ACE Award best picture), Without Prejudice (BBC).

PLAYS: From the Greek (1979), An Early Life.

RAPHEL, DAVID: Executive. b. Boulogne-s/Seine, France, Jan. 9, 1925. e. university in France. Entered m.p. ind. as asst. to sales mgr. in France, 20th-Fox, 1950–51; asst. mgr. in Italy, 1951–54; mgr. in Holland, 1954–57; asst. to European mgr. in Paris, 1957–59; European mgr. for TV activities in Paris, 1959–61; Continental mgr. in Paris, 1961–64, transferred to N.Y. as vice-pres. in chg. of international sales, 1964; named pres., 20th Century-Fox International, 1973. In Feb., 1975, also appointed sr. vice-pres., worldwide marketing, feature film division, for 20th-Fox, (L.A.). In Nov. 1976, joined ICM, appointed dir. general of ICM (Europe) headquartered in Paris. In 1979 elected pres. ICM (L.A.) 1980, formed Cambridge Film Group Ltd.

RAPPER, IRVING: Director. b. London, Eng., 1904. Stage prod. London: Five Star Final, assoc. Gilbert Miller, Grand Hotel. NY: The Animal Kingdom, The Firebird, The Late Christopher Bean.

PICTURES: Shining Victory, One Foot in Heaven, The Gay Sisters, Now Voyager, The Adventures of Mark Twain, Rhapsody in Blue, The Corn Is Green, Deception, Voice of the Turtle, Anna Lucasta, The Glass Menagerie, Another Man's Poison, Forever Female, Bad For Each Other, The Brave One, Strange Intruder, Marjorie Morningstar, The Miracle, Joseph and His Brethren, Pontius Pilate, The Christine Jorgensen Story, Born Again, Justus.

RAPPOPORT, GERALD J.: Executive, Film Producer. b. New York, NY, Aug. 25, 1925. e. NYU. U.S. Marine Corps. 1954–1958, pres., Major Artists Representatives Corp.; dir. of Coast Sound Services, Hollywood; 1960 to 1991, pres., International Film Exchange Ltd. 1992, CEO of IFEX Intl.

RASHAD, PHYLICIA: Actress-singer. b. Houston, TX, June 19, 1948. m. sportscaster Ahmad Rashad. Sister of Debbie Allen. e. Howard U., B.F.A., magna cum laude, 1970. NY School of Ballet. Acted under maiden name of Phylicia Ayers-Allen. Recording, Josephine Superstar (1979). Conceived (with Michael Peters) and appeared in revue Phylicia Rashad & Co. in 1989 in Las Vegas.

THEATER: Ain't Supposed to Die a Natural Death, The Duplex, The Cherry Orchard, The Wiz, Weep Not For Me, Zooman and the Sign, In an Upstate Motel, Zora, Dreamgirls, Sons and Fathers of Sons, Puppetplay, A Raisin in the Sun, Into the Woods, Jelly's Last Jam.

TELEVISION: *Series*: One Life to Live, The Cosby Show (People's Choice Award, NAACP Image Award, Emmy nom.). *Movies*: Uncle Tom's Cabin, False Witness, Polly, Polly—Comin' Home!, Jailbirds. *Specials*: Nell Carter—Never Too Old to Dream, Superstars and Their Moms, Our Kids and the Best of Everything, The Debbie Allen Special.

RATHER, DAN: News Correspondent, Anchor. b. Wharton, TX, Oct. 31, 1931. e. Sam Houston State Coll., BA journalism. Instructor there for 1 year. Worked for UPI and Houston Chronicle. Joined radio staff KTRH, Houston. Joined CBS News in 1962 as chief of southwest bureau in Dallas. Transferred to overseas burs. (including chief of London Bureau 1965–66), then Vietnam before returning as White House corr. 1966. White House Correspondent, 1964 to 1974. Covered top news events, from Democratic and Republican national conventions to President Nixon's trip to Europe (1970) and to Peking and Moscow (1972). Anchored CBS Reports, 1974–75. Presently co-editor of 60 minutes (since 1975) and anchors Dan Rather Reporting on CBS Radio Network (since 1977). Anchor for 48 Hours, 1988. Winner of numerous awards, including 5 Emmys. Anchorman on CBS-

TV Evening News, 1981–. Autobiography: The Camera Never Blinks: Adventures of a TV Journalist (co-author, 1977).

RAUCHER, HERMAN: Writer. b. Apr. 13, 1928. e. NYU. Author of novels— Watermelon Man, Summer of '42 and Ode to Billy Joe—adapted to films by him.
PICTURES: Sweet November, Watermelon Man, Summer of '42, Class of '44, Ode to Billy Joe, The Other Side of Midnight.
TELEVISION: Studio One, Alcoa Hour, Goodyear Playhouse, Matinee Theatre, Remember When? (movie).

RAVETCH, IRVING: Writer, Producer. b. 1920. e. UCLA. m. Harriet Frank.
PICTURES: Writer: The Long Hot Summer, The Sound and the Fury, Home from the Hill,•The Dark at the Top of the Stairs, Hud, Hombre, The Reivers (also prod.), The Cowboys, Cohrack (co-s.p.), Norma Rae (co.-s.p.), Murphy's Romance (co-s.p.), Stanley and Iris (co-s.p.).

RAYBURN, GENE: Performer, b. Christopher, IL, Dec. 22, 1917. e. Knox Coll., Galesburg, IL. NBC guide; with many radio stations in Baltimore, Philadelphia, N.Y.; U.S. Army Air Force, 1942–45, Rayburn and Finch, show, WNEW, NY, 1945–52; Gene Rayburn Show, NBC radio; TV shows: Many appearances as host-humorist on game shows, variety shows, drama shows. Summer stock: leads in comedies.
BROADWAY: Bye Bye Birdie, Come Blow Your Horn.
TELEVISION: Series: The Name's the Same, Tonight (announcer), Make the Connection, The Steve Allen Show, The Steve Lawrence-Eydie Gorme Show (announcer), The Match Game, Dough Re Mi, The Sky's the Limit, Choose Up Sides, Tic Tac Dough, Play Your Hunch, Snap Judgment, Amateur's Guide to Love. Guest: The Love Boat, Fantasy Island.

RAYE, MARTHA: Actress. b. Butte, MT, Aug. 27, 1916. p. Reed and Hooper, professionals. On stage: sang and did comedy with Paul Ash's orchestra; was in Earl Carroll's Sketch Book; Lew Brown's Calling All Stars. Appeared in night clubs. Bdwy: Hang on to Your Hat.
PICTURES: Rhythm on the Range (debut, 1936), The Big Broadcast of 1937, College Holiday, Hideway Girl, Waikiki Wedding, Mountain Music, Artists and Models, Double or Nothing, The Big Broadcast of 1938, College Swing, Give Me a Sailor, Tropic Holiday, Never Say Die, $1000 a Touchdown, The Farmer's Daughter, The Boys from Syracuse, Navy Blues, Keep 'Em Flying, Hellzapoppin', Pin Up Girl, Four Jills in a Jeep, Monsieur Verdoux, Billy Rose's Jumbo, The Phynx, Pufnstuf, The Concorde—Airport '79.
TELEVISION: Series: All Star Revue, Martha Raye Show, The Bugaloos, McMillan and Wife, Alice. Movies: Gossip Columnist, Alice in Wonderland. Guest: Carol Burnett Show, Murder She Wrote.

RAYMOND, GENE: Actor, Director, Producer, Composer. r. n. Raymond Guion, b. New York, NY, Aug. 13, 1908. Began acting at age 5 in stock productions. Bdwy debut, The Piper, 1920. Air Force Reserve, W.W.II. Major, US Army Air Corps, 1942–45. Formed ind. prod. co., Masque Prod., 1949. Song composer. Vice-pres. Arthritis Found.; Past pres. Motion Pic. and TV Fund; Pres. LA Chapt., Air Force Assn.; trustee, Falcon Found; trustee SGA; Bd., Acad. TV Arts and Sciences; Mem. Players Club, NY Athletic Club, Army and Navy. Awarded Legion of Merit, USAF; Humanitarian Award, AF Assn.; Better World Award, VFW.
STAGE: Why Not?, The Potters, Cradle Snatchers, Take My Advice, Say When, Mirrors, Jonesy, Young Sinners, Shadow of My Enemy, 1957, National Co., The Best Man 1960, Write Me A Murder, Kiss Me Kate, Candida, Madly in Love.
PICTURES: Personal Maid, Ladies of the Big House, The Night of June 13th, Forgotten Commandments, If I Had A Million, Red Dust, Ex-Lady, Sadie McKee, Brief Moment, I am Suzanne, Flying Down to Rio, The Woman in Red, The House on 56th Street, Seven Keys to Baldpate, The Bride Walks Out, Hooray for Love, Zoo in Budapest, Behold My Wife, Mr. and Mrs. Smith, Smilin' Thru, The Locket, Sofia, Hit the Deck, Walking On Air, Coming Out Party, Life of the Party, She's Got Everything, Ann Carver's Profession, Transient Lady, The Best Man, I'd Rather Be Rich.
TELEVISION: Series: Fireside Theatre (host), What's Going On? (panelist), Hollywood Summer Theatre (host), TV Reader's Digest (host), Paris 7000. Guest: Lux Video Theatre, Robert Montgomery Presents, Climax, Playhouse 90, Kraft Theatre, Red Skelton, U.S. Steel Hour, The Defenders, Outer Limits, Matinee Theater (also dir.), The Man From U.N.C.L.E., Girl from U.N.C.L.E., Laredo, Ironsides, Julia, Judd For the Defense.

RAYMOND, PAULA: Actress. r.n. Paula Ramona Wright, b. San Francisco, CA., Nov. 23, 1925. e. San Francisco Jr. Coll. 1942. Started career in little theatre groups, San Francisco; leading roles Ah! Wilderness, Peter Pan, other plays; also sang lead coloratura roles in Madame Butterfly, Carmen, etc.; ballerina with S.F. Opera Ballet; classical pianist; model,

Meade-Maddick Photographers; also director, cinematographer, editor and writer.
PICTURES: Devil's Doorway, Inside Straight, Duchess of Idaho, Crisis, Grounds For Marriage, Tall Target, Texas Carnival, The Sellout, Bandits of Corsica, City That Never Sleeps, Beast from 20,000 Fathoms, The Human Jungle, King Richard & the Crusaders, Human Jungle, Gun That Won the West, The Flight That Disappeared, 5 Bloody Graves, Blood of Dracula's Castle.
TELEVISION: Guest: Perry Mason, 77 Sunset Strip, Wyatt Earp, Man from U.N.C.L.E., Maverick, The Untouchables, Bachelor Father, Bat Masterson, Temple Houston, Peter Gunn, many others.

RAYNOR, LYNN S.: Producer, Production Executive. b. 1940. Produced West Coast premiere of The Balcony by Genet, The Crawling Arnold Review by Feiffer. Joined Television Enterprises, 1965; Commonwealth United, 1968 as business affairs exec. later production spvr. 1972 opened London branch of the Vidtronics Co. 1974, formed Paragon Entertainment. 1976, producer, PBS. 1977, producer, James Flocker Enterprises. 1979, exec. in charge of prod., Lawrance Schiller Prods. 1981, prod., Polygram Pictures; 1984, producer, NewlandRaynor Prods.; 1985, Columbia Pictures TV.
TELEVISION: Waiting for Godot, Camp Wilderness (synd. series), Marilyn: The Untold Story (movie), The Execution, The Pete Gray Story, The Kennedys of Massachusetts, Common Ground.
PICTURES: Ghosts That Still Walk, Alien Encounters, Fanny Hill, Dangerously.

REA, STEPHEN: Actor. b. Northern Ireland, 1949. Formed the Field Day Theatre Co. in 1980, appearing in most of their productions. Other theatre incl. Playboy of the Western World, High Society, Someone Who'll Watch Over Me (also Bdwy; Theatre World Award). Acted with Royal Natl. Theatre.
PICTURES: Angel, The Company of Wolves, The Doctor and the Devils, Life Is Sweet, The Crying Game (Acad. Award nom.), Bad Behavior.
TELEVISION: Shadow of a Gunman, Fugitive, I Didn't Know You Cared, Professional Foul, The Seagull, Out of Town Boys, Calbe Williams, Joyce in June, The House, Four Days in July, Shergar, Scout, Lost Belongings, The Big Gamble, Not With a Bang, Saint Oscar, Hedda Gabler.

REAGAN, RONALD: Actor, Politician. b. Tampico, IL, Feb. 6, 1911. e. high school, Eureka Coll. m. Nancy Davis. Wrote weekly sports column for a Des Moines, IA newspaper; broadcast sporting events. Signed as actor by Warner Bros. in 1937. In W.W.II. 1942–45, capt., USAAF. Actor until 1966 on TV as well. Program supvr., General Electric Theatre, Death Valley Days. Gov., California, 1967–74. Businessman and rancher. Elected Pres. of U.S., 1980. Re-elected, 1984.
PICTURES: Love Is On the Air, Submarine D-1, Hollywood Hotel, Sergeant Murphy, Swing Your Lady, Brother Rat, Going Places, Accidents Will Happen, Cowboy from Brooklyn, Boy Meets Girl, Girls on Probation, Going Places, Dark Victory, Naughty but Nice, Hell's Kitchen, Code of the Secret Service, Smashing the Money Ring, Angels Wash Their Faces, Brother Rat and a Baby, Murder in the Air, Tugboat Annie Sails Again, Knute Rockne - All American, Santa Fe Trail, An Angel From Texas, Nine Lives Are Not Enough, The Bad Man, International Squadron, Million Dollar Baby, Kings Row, That Hagen Girl, Night Unto Night, Voice of the Turtle, John Loves Mary, Girl from Jones Beach, It's a Great Feeling, The Hasty Heart, Louisa, Last Outpost, Bedtime for Bonzo, Storm Warning, Hong Kong, She's Working Her Way Through College, The Winning Team, Tropic Zone, Law & Order, Prisoner of War, Cattle Queen of Montana, Tennessee's Partner, Hellcats of the Navy, The Killers.

REARDON, BARRY: Executive. b. Hartford, CT, Mar. 8, 1931. e. Holy Cross Col., Trinity Col. Began industry career with Paramount Pictures; named v.p.; left to join General Cinema Theatres Corp. as sr. v.p. Now with Warner Bros. as pres. of domestic distribution co.

REASON, REX: Actor. b. Berlin, Germany, Nov. 30, 1928. e. Hoover H.S., Glendale, CA. Worked at various jobs; studied dramatics at Pasadena Playhouse.
PICTURES: Storm Over Tibet, Salome, Mission Over Korea, Taza Son of Cochise, This Island Earth, Smoke Signal, Lady Godiva, Kiss of Fire, Creature Walks Among Us, Raw Edge, Miracle of The Hills, The Rawhide Trail, Under Fire, Thundering Jets, The Sad Horse, Yankee Pasha.
TELEVISION: Series: Man Without a Gun, Roaring Twenties.

REDDY, HELEN: Singer. b. Melbourne, Australia, Oct. 25, 1942. Parents were producer-writer-actor Max Reddy and actress Stella Lamond. e. in Australia. Began career at age four as singer and had appeared in hundreds of stage and radio roles with parents by age of 15. Came to New York in 1966, subsequently played nightclubs, appeared on TV. First single hit record: I Don't Know How To Love Him (Capitol). Grammy

Award, 1973, as best female singer of year for I Am Woman. Most Played Artist by the music operators of America: American Music Award 1974; Los Angeles Times Woman of the Year (1975); No. 1 Female Vocalist in 1975 and 1976; Record World, Cash Box and Billboard; named one of the Most Exciting Women in the World by International Bachelor's Society, 1976. Heads prod. co. Helen Reddy, Inc.

PICTURES: Airport 1975 (debut), Pete's Dragon.

TELEVISION: Series: The Helen Reddy Show (Summer, 1973), Permanent host of Midnight Special. Appearances on David Frost Show, Flip Wilson Show, Mike Douglas Show, Tonight Show, Mac Davis Show, Merv Griffin Show (guest host), Sesame Street, Live in Australia (host, 1988); Muppet Show.

REDFORD, ROBERT: Actor. b. Santa Monica, CA, Aug. 18, 1937. r.n. Charles Robert Redford. Attended U. of Colorado; left to travel in Europe, 1957. Attended Pratt Inst. and American Acad. of Dramatic Arts. Founded Sundance Film Institute.

BROADWAY: Tall Story (walk on), The Highest Tree, Sunday in New York (Theatre World Award), Barefoot in the Park.

PICTURES: War Hunt (debut, 1962), Situation Hopeless But Not Serious, Inside Daisy Clover, The Chase, This Property Is Condemned, Barefoot in the Park, Downhill Racer (also exec. prod.), Butch Cassidy and the Sundance Kid, Tell Them Willie Boy is Here, Little Fauss and Big Halsy, The Hot Rock, The Candidate (also co-exec. prod.), Jeremiah Johnson, The Way We Were, The Sting (Acad. Award nom.), The Great Gatsby, The Great Waldo Pepper, Three Days of the Condor, All The President's Men (also exec. prod.), A Bridge Too Far, The Electric Horseman, Brubaker, The Natural, Out of Africa, Legal Eagles, Havana, Sneakers, Indecent Proposal. Exec. Producer: Promised Land, Some Girls, Yosemite: The Fate of Heaven (also narrator), The Dark Wind, Incident at Oglala (also narrator). Director: Ordinary People (Acad. Award, 1980), The Milagro Beanfield War (also co-prod.), A River Runs Through It (also prod., narrator), Quiz Show.

TELEVISION: Guest: Maverick, Playhouse 90, Play of the Week (The Iceman Cometh), Alfred Hitchcock Presents, Route 66, Twilight Zone, Dr. Kildare, The Untouchables, The Virginian, The Defenders.

REDGRAVE, CORIN: Actor. b. London, England, July 16, 1939. e. Cambridge. p. late Sir Michael Redgrave and Rachel Kempson. Brother of Vanessa and Lynn Redgrave. On stage with England Stage Co.: A Midsummer Night's Dream, Chips with Everything. RSC: Lady Windermere's Fan, Julius Caesar, Comedy of Errors, Antony and Cleopatra. Young Vic: Rosmersholm.

PICTURES: A Man for All Seasons, The Deadly Affair, Charge of the Light Brigade, The Magus, Oh What a Lovely War, When Eight Bells Toll, Serail, Excalibur, Eureka, Between Wars, The Fool, In the Name of the Father.

TELEVISION: I Berlioz.

REDGRAVE, LYNN: Actress. b. London, England, Mar. 8, 1943. Sister of Vanessa and Corin Redgrave. p. late Sir Michael Redgrave and Rachel Kempson. m. dir., actor, manager John Clark. Ent. m.p. and TV, 1962. Broadway debut Black Comedy.

THEATER: NY: My Fat Friend (1974), Mrs. Warren's Profession, Knock Knock, Misalliance, St. Joan, Twelfth Night (Amer. Shakespeare Fest), Sister Mary Ignatius Explains It All For You, Aren't We All?, Sweet Sue, A Little Hotel on the Side, The Master Builder, Shakespeare for My Father (also writer). L.A.: Les Liaisons Dangereuses.

PICTURES: Tom Jones (debut, 1963), Girl With Green Eyes, Georgy Girl (Acad. Award nom.), The Deadly Affair, Smashing Time, The Virgin Soldiers, The Last of the Mobile Hot-Shots, Viva la Muerta Tua (Don't Turn the Other Cheek), Every Little Crook and Nanny, Everything You Always Wanted to Know About Sex*, The National Health, The Happy Hooker, The Big Bus, Sunday Lovers, Morgan Stewart's Coming Home, Midnight, Getting It Right.

TELEVISION: BBC: Pretty Polly, Ain't Afraid to Dance, The End of the Tunnel, I Am Osango, What's Wrong with Humpty Dumpty, Egg On the Face of the Tiger, Blank Pages, A Midsummer Night's Dream, Pygmalion, William, Vienna 1900, Daft as a Brush, Not For Women Only, Calling the Shots. United States: Co-host: A.M. America. Movies: Turn of the Screw, Sooner or Later, Beggarman Thief, Gauguin the Savage, Seduction of Miss Leona, Rehearsal for Murder, The Bad Seed, My Two Loves, Jury Duty: The Comedy, What Ever Happened to Baby Jane? Mini-Series: Centennial. Series: House Calls, Teachers Only, Chicken Soup. Guest: The Muppet Show, Walking on Air, Candid Camera Christmas Special, Woman Alone, Tales From the Hollywood Hills: The Old Reliable, Death of a Son.

REDGRAVE, VANESSA: O.B.E. Actress. b. London, England, Jan. 30, 1937. p. Sir Michael Redgrave and Rachel Kempson. Sister of Lynn and Corin Redgrave. Mother of actresses Joely and Natasha Richardson. Early career with Royal Shakespeare Company.

STAGE: Daniel Deronda, Cato Street, The Threepenny Opera, Twelfth Night, As You Like It, Taming of the Shrew, Cymbeline, The Sea Gull, The Prime of Miss Jean Brodie, Antony & Cleopatra, Design for Living, Macbeth, Lady from the Sea, The Aspern Papers, Ghosts, Anthony and Cleopatra, Taming of the Shrew, Tomorrow Was War, A Touch of the Poet, Orpheus Descending, Madhouse in Goa, The Three Sisters, When She Danced, Maybe, Heartbreak House.

PICTURES: Behind the Mask (debut, 1958), Morgan: A Suitable Case for Treatment (Acad. Award nom.), A Man for All Seasons, Blow-up, Sailor from Gibraltar, Red and Blue, Camelot, Charge of the Light Brigade, Isadora (Acad. Award nom.), Oh! What a Lovely War, The Sea Gull, Drop Out, Trojan Women, The Devils, La Vacanza, Mary Queen of Scots (Acad. Award nom.), Murder on the Orient Express, Out of Season, The Seven Percent Solution, Julia (Acad. Award, supp. actress, 1977), Agatha, Yanks, Bear Island, The Bostonians (Acad. Award nom.), Steaming, Wetherby, Prick Up Your Ears, Consuming Passions, Comrades, The Ballad of the Sad Cafe, Romeo-Juliet (voice), Howards End (Acad. Award nom.), Breath of Life, The Wall, Sparrow, They, House of the Spirits, Crime and Punishment, Mother's Boys, Great Moments in Aviation.

TELEVISION: Movies/Specials: A Farewell to Arms, Katherine Mansfield, Playing for Time (Emmy Award), My Body My Child, Wagner, Three Sovereigns for Sarah, Peter the Great, Second Serve, A Man For All Seasons, Orpheus Descending, Young Catherine, What Ever Happened to Baby Jane?. Guest: Faerie Tale Theatre (Snow White and the 7 Dwarfs).

REDSTONE, EDWARD S.: Exhib. b. Boston, MA, May 8, 1928. e. Colgate U., B.A., 1949; Harvard Grad. Sch. of Bus. Admin., M.B.A., 1952. v.p.; treas. Northeast Drive-In Theatre Corp.; v.p., Theatre Owners of New England, 1962; chmn., advis. coms., mem. bd. dirs., TOA; gen. conven. chmn., joint convention TOA & NAC, 1962; pres. National Assn. of Concessionaires, 1963; chief barker. Variety Club of New England, 1963; pres., Theatre Owners of New England; gen. chmn., 35th annual reg. convention.

REDSTONE, SUMNER MURRAY: Entertainment Corporation Executive, Lawyer; b. Boston, MA, May 27, 1923. e. Harvard, B.A., 1944, LLB., 1947. Served to 1st Lt. AUS, 1943–45. Admitted to MA Bar 1947; U.S. Ct. Appeals 1st Circuit 1948, 8th Circuit 1950, 9th Circuit 1948; D.C. 1951; U.S. Supreme Ct. 1952; law sec. U.S. Ct. Appeals for 9th Circuit 1947–48; instr. U. San Francisco Law Sch. and Labor Management Sch., 1947; special asst. to U.S. Atty. General, 1948–51; partner firm Ford, Bergson, Adams, Borkland & Redstone, Washington, D.C. 1951–54; exec. v.p. Northeast Drive-In Theatre Corp., 1954–68; pres. Northeast Theatre Corp.; Chmn. bd., president & chief exec. officer, National Amusements, Inc; chmn. bd., Viacom International, Inc.; Asst. pres. Theatre Owners of America, 1960–63; pres. 1964–65; Bd chmn National Assoc. of Theatre Owners, 1965–66; Member: Presidential Advisory Committee John F. Kennedy Center for the Performing Arts; chmn. Jimmy Fund, Boston 1960; met. div. Combined Jewish Philanthropies 1963; sponsor Boston Museum of Science; Trustee Children's Cancer Research Foundation; Art Lending Library; bd. dirs. Boston Arts Festival; v.p., exec. committee Will Rogers Memorial Fund; bd. overseers Dana Farber Cancer Institute; mem. corp. New England Medical Center; Motion Picture Pioneers; bd. mem. John F. Kennedy Library Foundation; 1984–85, 1985–86 State Crusade Chairman American Cancer Society; Board of Overseers Boston Museum of Fine Arts; Professor, Boston U. Law Sch. 1982–83, 1985–86. Acquired Viacom in 1987. Member: Boston Bar Assn., Massachusetts Bar Assn., Harvard Law Sch. Assn., American Judicature Soc.

AWARDS: Decorated Army Commendation medal. Named one of ten outstanding young men Greater Boston Chamber of Commerce 1958; William J. German Human Relations Award Entertainment and Communications Division American Jewish Committee, 1977; 1985 recipient, Boston U. Law Sch. Silver Shingle Award for Distinguished Public Service; Communicator of the Year B'nai B'rith Communications, Cinema Lodge 1980; named "Man of the Year," Entertainment Industries div., UJA-Federation, NY, 1988, Variety of New England Humanitarian Award, 1989; Motion Picture Pioneers Pioneer of the Year, 1991.

REED, OLIVER: Actor. b. Wimbledon, England, Feb. 13, 1938. Nephew of late British dir. Sir Carol Reed. Dropped out of school in teens and worked as a bouncer, a boxer, and a taxi driver before first break on BBC-TV series The Golden Spur. Film debut as extra in Beat Girl (1960).

PICTURES: Beat Girl (Wild for Kicks), League of Gentlemen, The Angry Silence, Two Faces of Dr. Jekyll, Sword of Sherwood Forest, Bulldog Breed, No Love for Johnnie, His and Hers, The Rebel, Curse of the Werewolf, Pirates of Blood

River, Captain Clegg (Night Creatures), The Damned, The Party's Over, Scarlet Blade (Crimson Blade), Paranoic, Shuttered Room, The System (The Girl-Getters), Brigand of Kandahar, The Trap, The Shuttered Room, I'll Never Forget What's 'is Name, The Jokers, Oliver, The Assassination Bureau, Hannibal Brooks, Women in Love, Take a Girl Like You, The Lady in the Car with Glasses and a Gun, Hunting Party, The Devils, Zero Population Growth, Sitting Target, Triple Echo, One Russian Summer, Dirty Weekend, Revolver (Blood in the Streets), Blue Blood, Three Musketeers, Tommy, The Four Musketeers, Lisztomania (cameo), Ten Little Indians, Royal Flash, Sell Out, Burnt Offerings, The Great Scout and Cathouse Thursday, Assault on Paradise (Ransom), Tomorrow Never Comes, Crossed Swords, The Big Sleep, The Class of Miss MacMichael, Dr. Heckyl & Mr. Hype, The Brood, Lion of the Desert, Condorman, Venom, The Great Question, Spasms, The Sting II, Two of a Kind, Black Arrow, Gor, Captive, Castaway, Dragonard, Fair Trade, The Return of the Musketeers, Hold My Hand I'm Dying, Fire With Fire, The Misfit Brigade, Rage to Kill, Skeleton Coast, Damnation Express, Captive Rage, The Adventures of Baron Munchausen, The Fall of the House of Usher, Master of Dragonard Hill, Outlaws, The Pit and the Pendulum, Panama, Severed Ties.
TELEVISION: The Lady and the Highwayman, Treasure Island, A Ghost in Monte Carlo, Prisoner of Honor, Army.

REED, PAMELA: Actress. b. Tacoma, WA, Apr. 2, 1953. Ran daycare center and worked with Head Start children before studying drama at U. of Washington. Worked on Trans-Alaska pipeline. Off-Broadway showcases.
THEATER: Curse of the Starving Class (Off-Bdwy debut, 1978), All's Well That Ends Well (Central Park), Getting Out (Drama Desk Award), Aunt Dan and Lemon, Fools, The November People (Broadway debut), Sorrows of Stephen, Mrs. Warren's Profession, Getting Through the Night, Best Little Whorehouse in Texas, Fen, Standing on My Knees, Elektra.
PICTURES: The Long Riders (debut, 1980), Melvin and Howard, Eyewitness, Young Doctors in Love, The Right Stuff, The Goodbye People, The Best of Times, Clan of the Cave Bear, Rachel River, Chattahoochee, Cadillac Man, Kindergarten Cop, Passed Away, Bob Roberts.
TELEVISION: Series: The Andros Targets (TV debut, 1977), Grand. Movies: Inmates—A Love Story, I Want To Live, Heart of Steel, Scandal Sheet, Caroline?, Woman With a Past, Born Too Soon. Special: Tanner '88. Mini-Series: Hemingway. Guest: L.A. Law, The Simpsons (voice).

REES, ROGER: Actor. b. Aberystwyth, Wales, May 5, 1944. e. Camberwell Sch. of Art, Slade Sch. of Fine Art. Stage debut Hindle Wakes (Wimbledon, U.K., 1964). With Royal Shakespeare Co. from 1967. Starred in the title role The Adventures of Nicholas Nickleby (London and NY, 1980–81, Tony Award). Hapgood (London, L.A.). Off-Bdwy. in The End of the Day. Assoc. dir. Bristol Old Vic Theatre Co., 1986–present. Playwright with Eric Elice of Double Double and Elephant Manse.
PICTURES: Star 80 (debut, 1983), Keine Storung Bitte, Mountains of the Moon, If Looks Could Kill, Stop! Or My Mom Will Shoot, Robin Hood: Men in Tights.
TELEVISION: Movies: A Christmas Carol (released theatrically in Europe), Place of Peace, Under Western Eyes, Bouquet of Barbed Wire, Saigon: The Year of the Cat. Imaginary Friends, The Adventures of Nicolas Nickleby, The Comedy of Errors, Macbeth, The Voysey Inheritance, The Ebony Tower, The Finding, The Return of Sam McCloud, Charles & Diana: Unhappily Ever After. Series: Cheers, Singles.

REESE, DELLA: Actress, Singer. b. Detroit, MI, July 6, 1932. r.n. Deloreese Patricia Early. e. Wayne St. Univ. As teen toured with Mahalia Jackson. Began recording in 1950's. Hit songs include Don't You Know.
TELEVISION: Series: The Della Reese Show, Chico and the Man, It Takes Two, Charlie & Company, The Royal Family. Guest: The Ed Sullivan Show, Sanford and Son, The Rookies, McCloud, Welcome Back Kotter, The Love Boat, Night Court, The A-Team. Movies: The Voyage of the Yes, Twice in a Lifetime, The Return of Joe Forrester, Nightmare in Badham County. Mini-Series: Roots: The Next Generations.
PICTURES: Let's Rock!, Psychic Killer, Harlem Nights, The Distinguished Gentleman.

REEVE, CHRISTOPHER: Actor. b. New York, NY, Sept. 25, 1952. e. Cornell U., B.A.; graduate work at Juilliard. Stage debut at McCarter Theatre in Princeton at age 9. Bdwy. debut with Katharine Hepburn in A Matter of Gravity.
THEATER: New York: A Matter of Gravity, My Life, Fifth of July, The Marriage of Figaro, The Winter's Tale, Love Letters. L.A.: Summer and Smoke. Williamstown: The Front Page, Mesmer, Richard Corey, Royal Family, The Seagull, The Greeks, Holiday, Camino Real, John Brown's Body, Death Takes a Holiday. Regional: The Irregular Verb to Love,

Beggar's Opera, Troilus and Cressida, The Love Cure. London debut: The Aspern Papers.
PICTURES: Gray Lady Down (debut, 1978), Superman, Somewhere in Time, Superman II, Deathtrap, Monsignor, Superman III, The Bostonians, The Aviator, Street Smart, Superman IV: The Quest for Peace (also co-story), Switching Channels, Noises Off, Morning Glory, The Remains of the Day.
TELEVISION: Series: Love of Life. Movies: Anna Karenina, The Great Escape II: The Untold Story, The Rose and the Jackal, Bump in the Night, Death Dreams, Mortal Sins, Nightmare in the Daylight, The Sea Wolf. Specials: Faerie Tale Theatre (Sleeping Beauty), The Last Ferry Home, Earth and the American Dream. Guest: Tales From the Crypt.

REEVES, KEANU: Actor. b. Beirut, Lebanon, Sept. 2, 1964. Lived in Australia and NY before family settled in Toronto. e. studied at Toronto's High School for the Performing Arts, then continued training at Second City Workshop. Made Coca-Cola commercial at 16. At 18 studied at Hedgerow Theatre in PA for summer. Professional debut on Hanging In, CBC local Toronto TV show. Toronto stage debut in Wolf Boy.
PICTURES: Prodigal, Flying (Canadian films); Youngblood, River's Edge, The Night Before, Permanent Record, The Prince of Pennsylvania, Dangerous Liaisons, Bill and Ted's Excellent Adventure, Parenthood, I Love You to Death, Tune in Tomorrow, Point Break, Bill and Ted's Bogus Journey, My Own Private Idaho, Bram Stoker's Dracula, Much Ado About Nothing, Even Cowgirls Get the Blues, Little Buddha.
TELEVISION: Movies: Act of Vengeance, Under the Influence, Babes In Toyland. Specials: I Wish I Were Eighteen Again, Life Under Water. Guest: the Tracey Ullman Show.

REEVES, STEVE: Actor. b. Glasgow, MT, Jan. 21, 1926. Delivered newspapers. Mr. Pacific, Mr. America, Mr. World, Mr. Universe. On stage in Kismet, The Vamp, Wish You Were Here.
PICTURES: Athena, Jail Bait, Hercules, Hercules Unchained, Goliath and the Barbarians, Giant of Marathon, Last Days of Pompeii, Duel of the Titans, White Warrior, Morgan the Pirate, The Thief of Baghdad, The Trojan Horse, The Slave, Sandokan the Great, A Long Ride From Hell.

REHME, ROBERT G.: Executive. b. Cincinnati, OH, May 5, 1935. e. U. of Cincinnati. 1953, mgr., RKO Theatres, Inc., Cincinnati; 1961, adv. mgr., Cincinnati Theatre Co.; 1966, dir. of field adv., United Artists Pictures; 1969, named dir. of pub. and field adv./promotion, Paramount Pictures; 1972, pres., BR Theatres and v.p., April Fools Films, gen. mgr. Tri-State Theatre Service; 1976, v.p. & gen. sls. mgr., New World Pictures; Feb. 1978, joined Avco Embassy Pictures as sr. v.p. & chief operating officer; Dec. 1978, named exec. v.p.; 1979, named pres., Avco Embassy Pictures, Inc,. 1981, joined Universal Pictures as pres. of distribution & marketing; 1982, named pres. of Universal Pictures; 1983, joined New World Pictures as co-chmn. & chief exec. officer. Elected pres., Academy Foundation, 1988, pres. Foundation of Motion Picture Pioneers, 1989. 1st v.p., AMPAS. 1989, partner, Neufeld/Rehme prods. at Paramount. 1992, pres. of Academy of Motion Picture Arts & Sciences.

REID, BERYL: O.B.E. Actress. b. Hereford, England, June 17, 1920. Career in radio before London stage debut in revue, After the Show, 1951. Also on stage in The Killing of Sister George (London, NY, Tony Award), Spring Awakening, Campiello, Born in the Gardens, etc.
PICTURES: The Belles of St. Trinian's, The Extra Day, Trial and Error, Two-Way Stretch, Inspector Clouseau, Star!, The Assassination Bureau, The Killing of Sister George, Entertaining Mr. Sloane, The Beast in the Cellar, Dr. Phibes Rises Again, Psychomania, Father Dear Father, No Sex Please We're British, Joseph Andrews, Carry on Emmanuelle, Yellowbeard, The Doctor and the Devils, Didn't You Kill My Brother?.
TELEVISION: Series: Educating Archie (BBC, 1952–56), Beryl Reid Says Good Evening, The Secret Diary of Adrian Mole. Mini-Series: Tinker Tailor Soldier Spy, Smiley's People. Movie: Duel of Hearts. Numerous specials.

REID, TIM: Actor. b. Norfolk, CA, Dec. 19, 1944. m. actress Daphne Maxwell. Started as half of comedy team of Tim and Tom in 1969, before becoming solo stand-up comedian. Published photo/poetry collection As I Find It, 1982.
TELEVISION: Series: Easy Does It . . . Starring Frankie Avalon, The Marilyn McCoo and Billy Davis Jr. Show, The Richard Pryor Show, WKRP in Cincinnati, Teachers Only, Simon and Simon, Frank's Place (also co-exec. prod.), Snoops (also co-exec. prod.). Guest: That's My Mama, Rhoda, What's Happening, Matlock. Movies: Perry Mason: The Case of the Silenced Singer, Stephen King's IT. Special: Mastergate.
PICTURES: Dead Bang, The Fourth War.

REILLY, CHARLES NELSON: Actor, Director. b. New York, NY, Jan. 13. 1931. e. U. of CT. On Broadway mostly in comedy roles before turning to TV and films. Recently directed stage plays.

THEATER: As actor: Bye Bye Birdie (debut), How to Succeed in Business (Tony Award, 1962), Hello Dolly!, Skyscraper, God's Favorite. Acted in 22 off-Bdwy plays. Founded musical comedy dept. HB Studios. Conceived and dir.: The Belle of Amherst, Paul Robeson, The Nerd (dir.). Resident dir.: Burt Reynolds' Jupiter Theatre.
PICTURES: A Face in the Crowd, Two Tickets to Paris, The Tiger Makes Out, Cannonball Run II, Body Slam, All Dogs Go to Heaven (voice), Rock-a-Doodle (voice).
TELEVISION: Series: The Steve Lawrence Show, The Ghost and Mrs. Muir, Dean Martin Presents The Golddiggers, Liddsville, Arnie, It Pays to Be Ignorant (1973–4), Match Game P.M., Sweethearts (game show host). Guest: Tonight Show (guest host), Dean Martin Show. Movies: Call Her Mom, The Three Kings.

REINAUER, RICHARD: Executive. b. Chicago, IL, April 28, 1926. e. U. of Illinois, grad. 1952. Prod., dir., freelance, 1952–59; bus. mgr., asst. prod., Showcase Theatre Evanston, 1952; prod., dir., NBC, Chicago, 1953–55; film dir., Kling Studios, 1956; broadcast supvis. Foote Cone & Belding, 1956–59; dir., radio, TV & m.p., American Medical Assoc., 1959–64; pres., Communications Counselors, 1963–64; exec. dir., TV Arts & Sciences Foundation, 1964; pres., Acad. of TV Arts & Sciences, Chicago Chapter, 1970–72. assoc. prod. & asst. dir. Wild Kingdom & asst. to pres., Don Meier Prods., 1965–1988. Member—Illinois Nature Preserve Commission. Lifetime member: Acad. of TV Arts & Sciences, Pres. Pinewood Prods. Film Co.

REINBERG, DEBORAH: Executive. Attorney in entertainment field for Manatt, Phelps, Rothenberg and Phillips before joining Elektra/Asylum Records as v.p., business affairs. July, 1984, joined Warner Bros. Inc. as dir. of music, business & legal affairs. 1985, promoted to newly created position of v.p., business affairs, music.

REINER, CARL: Performer, Director, Writer. b. New York, NY, March 20, 1923. Father of actor-director Rob Reiner. Comedian on Bdwy: Call Me Mr., Inside U.S.A., Alive and Kicking. Author (novels): Enter Laughing, All Kinds of Love.
TELEVISION: Series: The Fashion Story, The Fifty-Fourth Street Revue, Eddie Condon's Floor Show, Your Show of Shows (also writer), Droodles (panelist), Caesar's Hour (also writer; Emmy Award, 1957 for supp. actor), Sid Caesar Invites You, Keep Talking, Dinah Shore Chevy Show (writer), Take a Good Look (panelist), The Dick Van Dyke Show (also creator-prod.-dir.-writer; 6 Emmy Awards), Art Linkletter Show, The Celebrity Game (host), The New Dick Van Dyke Show (creator-prod.-writer), Good Heavens (also exec. prod.), Sunday Best (host). Movies: Medical Story, Skokie. Guest: Comedy Spot, Judy Garland Show, Burke's Law, That Girl, Night Gallery, Faerie Tale Theatre (Pinocchio), It's Garry Shandling's Show.
PICTURES: Actor only: Happy Anniversary, Gidget Goes Hawaiian, It's a Mad Mad Mad Mad World, The Russians Are Coming, Don't Worry We'll Think of a Title, A Guide for the Married Man, Generation, The End, The Spirit of '76. Writer-Actor: The Gazebo, The Thrill of It All (also co-prod.), The Art of Love. Director: Enter Laughing (also co-s.p.), The Comic (also s.p., actor), Where's Poppa?, Oh God! (also actor), The One and Only, The Jerk (also actor), Dead Men Don't Wear Plaid (also co-s.p., actor), The Man With Two Brains (also co-s.p.), All of Me, Summer Rental, Summer School (also actor), Bert Rigby You're a Fool (also s.p.), Sibling Rivalry, Fatal Instinct.
RECORDINGS: Carl Reiner and Mel Brooks, The 2000 Year Old Man, The 2001 Year Old Man, 2013 Year Old Man.
AUTHOR: Broadway plays: Enter Laughing, Something Different.

REINER, ROB: Actor, Director, Writer. b. New York, NY, March 6, 1947. Son of actor-writer-director Carl Reiner. Worked as actor with regional theatres and improvisational comedy troupes. Wrote for the Smothers Brothers Comedy Hour. Breakthrough as actor came in 1971 when signed by Norman Lear for All in the Family on TV, playing Mike Stivic (Meathead). Directorial debut with This Is Spinal Tap, 1984. Co-founder of Castle Rock Entertainment.
PICTURES: Actor only: Enter Laughing, Halls of Anger, Where's Poppa?, Summertree, Fire Sale, Throw Momma From the Train, Postcards From the Edge, The Spirit of '76, Sleepless in Seattle. Director: This is Spinal Tap (also actor, co-s.p.), The Sure Thing, Stand by Me, The Princess Bride. Dir./Co-Prod.: When Harry Met Sally . . . , Misery, A Few Good Men (Acad. Award nom. for best picture; DGA nom.), North.
TELEVISION: Series: All in the Family (1971–78; Emmy Awards: 1974, 1978), Free Country (also co-writer), Morton & Hayes (also co-creator, co-exec. prod.). Movies: Thursday's Game, More Than Friends (also co-writer, co-exec. prod.), Million Dollar Infield (also co-prod., co-writer). Guest: Gomer Pyle, Batman, Beverly Hillbillies, Room 222, Partridge Family, Odd Couple, It's Garry Shandling's Show.

REINHARDT, GOTTFRIED: Producer, Writer. b. Berlin, Germany, 1911. p. Max Reinhardt, noted theatrical prod.; Else Rein-

hardt, actress; brother, Wolfgang Reinhardt, prod. e. Berlin. Began career at 19 as asst. to prod. Ernst Lubitsch, father's friend, with m.p. Design For Living; asst. to Walter Wanger; later to Bernard H. Hyman (Saratoga; San Francisco). Wrote orig. story, I Live My Life, The Great Waltz; collab. Bridal Suite; book for NY musicals, Rosalinda, Helen of Troy. U.S. Army service, Signal Corps. 1942–46.
PICTURES: Comrade X, Rage in Heaven, Two-Faced Woman, (co-prod.) Homecoming, Command Decision, The Great Sinner, The Red Badge of Courage, Invitation, Young Man With Ideas, (dir. 2 seq.) Story of Three Loves, Betrayed, Town Without Pity (prod.), Situation Hopeless, But Not Serious (prod.), Hitler: The Last Ten Days (prod., co-s.p.).

REINHOLD, JUDGE: Actor. b. Wilmington, DE, 1957. r.n. Edward Ernest Reinhold Jr. e. Mary Washington Coll., North Carolina Sch. of Arts. Acted in regional theatres including Burt Reynolds dinner theater in FL. before signed to TV contract at Paramount. Theatrical film debut in Running Scared, 1979.
PICTURES: Stripes, Pandemonium, Fast Times at Ridgemont High, Lords of Discipline, Roadhouse 66, Gremlins, Beverly Hills Cop, Head Office, Off Beat, Ruthless People, Beverly Hills Cop II, Vice Versa, Rosalie Goes Shopping, Daddy's Dyin', Enid is Sleeping (Over Her Dead Body), Zandalee, Near Misses, Baby on Board.
TELEVISION: Movies: Survival of Dana, A Matter of Sex, Four Eyes, Promised a Miracle, Black Magic, Four Eyes and Six-Guns. Guest: Wonder Woman, Magnum P.I., Booker, Brothers and Sisters. Specials: A Step Too Slow, The Willmar Eight, The Parallax Garden.

REISENBACH, SANFORD E.: Executive. e. NYU. Associated with Grey Advertising for 20 years; exec. v.p. and pres. of Grey's leisure/entertainment division in N.Y. In August, 1979, joined Warner Bros. as exec. v.p. in chg. of worldwide adv. & pub.; named pres., worldwide adv. & pub., 1985. Appt. exec. v.p. of marketing and planning, Warner Bros. Inc., 1988.

REISER, PAUL: Actor. b. New York, NY, Mar. 30, 1957. e. SUNY/ Binghampton. Started performing as a stand-up comic in such clubs as Catch a Rising Star, the Improv, and the Comic Strip.
PICTURES: Diner (debut, 1982), Beverly Hills Cop, Aliens, Beverly Hills Cop II, Cross My Heart, Crazy People, The Marrying Man.
TELEVISION: Series: My Two Dads, Mad About You. Special: Paul Reiser—Out on a Whim. Guest: The Tonight Show, Late Night With David Letterman. Movie: Sunset Limousine. Pilots: Diner, Just Married.

REISNER, ALLEN: Director. b. New York, NY.
PICTURES: The Day They Gave Babies Away, St. Louis Blues, All Mine to Give.
TELEVISION: Movies/Specials: Captain and the Kings, Mary Jane Harper Cried Last Night, Your Money or Your Wife, To Die in Paris, The Clift, Skag, They're Playing Our Song, The Gentleman From Seventh Avenue, Escape of Pierre Mendes-France, Deliverance of Sister Cecelia, The Sound of Silence. Series: Murder She Wrote, Twilight Zone, Hardcastle & McCormick, Airwolf, The Mississippi, Hawaii Five-O, Blacke's Magic, Law and Harry McGraw, Playhouse 90, Studio One, Climax, United States Steel Hour, Suspense, Danger, etc.

REISS, JEFFREY C.: Executive. b. Brooklyn, NY, April 14, 1942. e. Washington U., St. Louis, B.A., 1963. Consultant at NYU and Manhattanville Coll. and instructor at Brooklyn Coll. before entering industry. Agt. in literary dept. for General Artists Corp., 1966. Supervised development in N.Y. of Tandem Prods. for Norman Lear, 1968. Produced off-Bdwy plays 1968–70. Dir. of progm. acquistion devel. for Cartridge TV, Inc. (mfg. of first hom video cassette players-recorders) 1970–73. Joined ABC Entertainment as director of network feature films, 1973–75. Founder and pres., Showtime Pay TV Network, 1976– 80. Co-founder, pres. & CEO, Cable Health Network, 1981– 83. 1983, named vice chmn. & CEO, Lifetime Cable Network following Cable Health Network merger with Daytime. Chmn. of the board, pres. & CEO, Reiss Media Enterprises, Inc. 1984. Founder & chmn. of board, Request Television (pay-per-view svc.), 1985–present.

REISS, STUART A.: Set decorator. b. Chicago, IL, July 15, 1921. e. L.A. High Sch., 1939. Property man, 20th-Fox, 1939–42; U.S. Army Air Corps, 1942–45; set decorator, 20th-Fox since 1945; 6 Acad. nom.; 2 Acad. Awards, Diary of Anne Frank, Fantastic Voyage. Worked on over 30 tv shows.
PICTURES: Titanic, How to Marry a Millionaire, Hell and High Water, There's No Business Like Show Business, Soldier of Fortune, The Seven Year Itch, Man in the Grey Flannel Suit, Teen Age Rebel, The Diary of Anne Frank (Acad. Award, 1959), What a Way to Go, Fantastic Voyage (Acad. Award, 1966), Doctor Doolittle, Oh God!, The Swarm, Beyond the Poseidon Adventure, Carbon Copy, All the Marbles, The Man Who Loved Women, Micki and Maude, A Fine Mess.

REISZ, KAREL: Director. b. Ostrava, Czechoslovakia, July 21, 1926. m. actress Betsy Blair. e. Britain. Wrote, Technique of Film Editing for British Film Academy. Worked with British Film Institute and National Film Library, 1954. Co-dir. short Momma Don't Allow (1956) with Tony Richardson.
PICTURES: Producer: Every Day Except Christmas, This Sporting Life. Director: We Are the Lambeth Boys, Saturday Night & Sunday Morning, Night Must Fall, Morgan, Isadora, The Gambler, Who'll Stop the Rain, The French Lieutenant's Woman (also co-prod.), Sweet Dreams, Everybody Wins.
TELEVISION: On the Road.

REITMAN, IVAN: Director, Producer. b. Komarmo, Czecho-slovakia, Oct. 26, 1946. e. McMaster U. Moved to Canada, 1951. Produced Canadian TV show in 1970s with Dan Aykroyd as announcer.
THEATER: The National Lampoon Show (prod.), The Magic Show (co-prod.), Merlin (dir., prod.).
PICTURES: Foxy Lady (dir., prod., edit.), Cannibal Girls (dir., exec. prod.), They Came From Within (Shivers; prod.), Death Weekend (The House By the Lake; prod.), Rabid (exec. prod.), Blackout (prod.), Animal House (prod.), Meat-balls (prod., dir.), Stripes (prod., dir.), Heavy Metal (prod.), Spacehunter (exec. prod.), Ghostbusters (prod., dir.), Legal Eagles (prod., dir.), Big Shots (exec. prod.), Casual Sex? (exec. prod.), Feds (exec. prod.), Twins (prod., dir.), Ghostbus-ters II (prod., dir.), Kindergarten Cop (prod., dir.), Stop! Or My Mom Will Shoot (prod.), Beethoven (exec. prod.), Dave (dir., prod.), Beethoven's 2nd (exec. prod.).
TELEVISION: Series: Delta House.

RELPH, MICHAEL: Producer, Director, Writer, Designer. 1942 art dir. Ealing Studios then assoc. prod. to Michael Balcon on The Captive Heart, Frieda, Kind Hearts and Coronets, Saraband (also designed: nominated Oscar). 1948 appt. producer and formed prod/dir. partnership Basil Dearden (until 1972). 1971–76 Governor Brit. Film Institute. Chairman B.F.I. Prod. Board. Chairman Film Prod. Assoc. of G.B., member Films Council.
PICTURES: (For Ealing) The Blue Lamp (Brit. Film Acad-emy: Best Brit. Film 1950), I Believe in You, The Gentle Gunman, The Square Ring, The Rainbow Jacket, Out of the Clouds, The Ship That Died of Shame, Davy (for Brit. Lion), The Smallest Show on Earth. (for Rank) Violent Playground, Rockets Galore (Island Fling U.S.), Sapphire (Brit. Film Academy: Best Brit. Film 1959), 1960 Founder Dir. Allied Film Makers: Prod. The League of Gentlemen, Man in the Moon (co-author s.p.), Victim, Life For Ruth (Walk in the Shadow U.S.). Also produced: Secret Partner, All Night Long, The Mind Benders, A Place To Go (author s.p.), Woman of Straw (co-author s.p.), Masquerade (co-author s.p.), The Assassina-tion Bureau (prod., s.p., designer), The Man Who Haunted Himself (prod., co-author s.p.) 1978, exec. in chg. prod., Kendon Films, Ltd. exec. prod., Scum, 1982, co-prod., An Unsuitable Job for a Woman. 1984, exec. prod.: Treasure Houses of Britain; TV series, prod., Heavenly Pursuits, 1985–86; Gospel According to Vic (U.S.). Prod. Consultant: Tor-rents of Spring.

RELPH, SIMON: Producer. b. London, Eng., April 13, 1940. Entered industry 1961.
PICTURES: Reds (exec. prod.), The Return of the Soldier (co-prod.), Privates on Parade, The Ploughman's Lunch, Secret Places (co-prod.), Laughterhouse (exec. prod.), Wetherby, Comrades.

RELYEA, ROBERT E.: Producer, Executive. b. Santa Monica, CA, May 3, 1930. e. UCLA, B.S., 1952. In Army 1953–55. Entered industry in 1955 as assoc. prod. and 2nd unit dir. on The Great Escape; asst. dir. on The Magnificent Seven and West Side Story. Partnered with Steve McQueen was exec. prod. on Bullitt and The Reivers. 1979–82, exec. v.p. with Melvin Simon Prods. Served as exec. v.p. in chg. world wide prod., Keith Barish Prods. 1983–85. Served as sr. v.p. prod., Lorimar Prods. 1985–80. Named sr. v.p. features prod. management, Paramount Pictures Motion Picture Gp., 1989.
PICTURES: Exec. Prod.: Bullitt, The Reivers, Day of the Dolphin. Prod: Love at First Bite, My Bodyguard, Porkys.

REMAR, JAMES: Actor. b. Boston, MA, Dec. 31, 1953. Studied acting at NY's Neighborhood Playhouse and with Stella Adler. Appeared on NY stage in Yo-Yo, Early Dark, Bent and California Dog Fight.
PICTURES: On the Yard (debut, 1979), The Warriors, Cruising, The Long Riders, Windwalker, Partners, 48 HRS, The Cotton Club, The Clan of the Cave Bear, Band of the Hand, Quiet Cool, Rent-a-Cop, The Dream Team, Drugstore Cowboy, Tales from the Darkside, Silence Like Glass, White Fang.
TELEVISION: Movies: The Mystic Warrior, Desperado, Deadlock, Brotherhood of the Gun, Fatal Charm, Indecency. Guest: Hill Street Blues, Miami Vice, The Equalizer, The Hitchhiker.

REMBUSCH, TRUEMAN T.: Exhibitor. b. Shelbyville, IN, July 27, 1909. f. Frank J. Rembusch, pioneer exhibitor. Inventor &

manufacturer Glass Mirror Screen. e. U. of Notre Dame Sch. of Commerce, 1928. m. Mary Agnes Finneran. Ent. m.p. ind., 1928, servicing sound equip., father's circuit; became mgr., 1932; elect. bd. of dir., Allied Theatre Owners of Ind., 1936–45, pres. 1945–51, 1952–53; dir. chmn. Allied TV Committee, 1945–50; pres. Allied States Assn., 1950–51; 1952, named by Allied as one of triumvirate heading COMPO; elected chmn. Joint Com. on Toll TV, 1954; Nov. 1953 named by Gov. of Indiana as dir. State Fair Board. Currently pres. Syndicate Thea., Inc., Franklin, Ind. member, In Notre Dame Club of Indianapolis (Man of Yr., 1950); BPOE, 4th Degree K of C, Meridian Hills Country Club, Marco Island Country Club. American Radio Relay League (amateur & commerce, li-censes); OX5 Aviation Pioneers; awarded patent, recording 7 counting device, 1951; dir. Theatre Owners of Indiana; dir. to NATO; dir. NATO member ad hoc comm; 1972 chair, NATO Statistical Committee; 1976–NITE Award service to Indepen-dent Exhibition.

REMSEN, BERT: Actor. b. Glen Cove, NY, Feb. 25, 1925. e. Ithaca Coll.
PICTURES: Pork Chop Hill, Kid Galahad, Moon Pilot, Brewster McCloud, Thieves Like us, Baby Blue Marine, McCabe and Mrs. Miller, Sweet Hostage, Nashville, California Split, Tarantulas, Buffalo Bill and the Indians, A Wedding, The Rose, Uncle Joe Shannon, Carny, Borderline, Second Hand Hearts, Joni, Inside Moves, Looking to Get Out, Sting II, Lies, Independence Day, Code of Silence, Stand Alone, Eye of the Tiger, South of Reno, Remote Control, Vietnam, Texas; Miss Firecracker, Daddy's Dyin' . . . Who's Got the Will?, Dick Tracy, Only the Lonely, Evil Spirits, The Player, The Body-guard, Jack the Bear.
TELEVISION: Series: Gibbsville, It's a Living, Dallas. Movies: Who Is Julia?, The Awakening Land, Burning Rage, Crazy Times, Hobson's Choice, If Tomorrow Comes, Love For Rent, Mothers Against Drunk Driving, Little Ladies of the Night, Memorial Day, Maid for Each Other, There Was a Little Boy. Guest: Matlock, Jake and the Fatman. Mini-Series: Space.

RESNAIS, ALAIN: Director. b. Cannes, France, June 3, 1922. Began career as asst. dir. to Nicole Vedres on compilation of film for Paris 1900. During '50s worked as assist. editor and editor; experimented with making his own 16mm films. Directed or co-dir. several short films: Van Gogh, Gauguin, Guernica, The Statues Also Die, Night and Fog, etc.
PICTURES: Hiroshima Mon Amour (feature debut, 1959), Last Year at Marienbad, Muriel, La Guerre Est Finie (The War is Over), Je t'Aime Je t'Aime, Stavisky, Providence, Mon Oncle d'Amerique, Life is a Bed of Roses, L'Amour a Mort, Melo (also s.p.), I Want to Go Home.

RESNICK, JOEL H.: Executive. b. New York, NY, April 28, 1936. e. U. of Pennsylvania, P.A., 1958; New York Law Sch. 1961, admitted to N.Y. State Bar. In 1962 received Masters of Law degree in taxation. 1961–66 served as associate with New York law firm, Phillips, Nizer, Benjamin, Krim & Ballon. Was in-house counsel to United Artists Corp. 1967, joined UA as spec. asst. to the sr. v.p. & gen. mgr. 1970, moved to American Multi-Cinema, Inc., Kansas City, as asst. to pres. 1972, named v.p. in chg. development; 1976, promoted to v.p. in chg. film development. 1977, named exec. v.p. 1983, elected exec. v.p. & dir., AMC Entertainment. 1984, appt. to office of pres. as chmn. & CEO, film mktg. 1986, resigned to join Orion Pictures Distribution Corp. as pres. Has served as co-chmn. NATO trade practices comm. since 1979. In 1982 elected pres., NATO; 1984, became chmn. NATO bd. 1989, v.p. Foundation of Motion Picture Pioneers. 1990, resigned from Orion, Pres., GKC Theatres, Springfield, IL, 1991–92.

RETTIG, TOM: Actor. b. Jackson Heights, NY, Dec. 10, 1941. On stage in Annie Get Your Gun.
PICTURES: Panic in the Streets, Two Weeks with Love, The Jackpot, For Heaven's Sake, The Strip, Elopement, Gobs and Gals, Paula, The Lady Wants Mink, 5000 Fingers of Dr. T, So Big, The Egyptian, River of No Return, The Raid, The Cobweb, At Gunpoint, The Last Wagon.
TELEVISION: Series: Lassie (1954–58). Guest: Studio One, Wagon Train, Mr. Novak, Matinee Theater, Lawman, U.S. Steel Hour, Burns and Allen Show, Peter Gunn, Death Valley Days, Allan Young Show, many others.

REVILL, CLIVE: Actor. r.n. Selsby. b. Wellington, New Zealand, Apr. 18, 1930. e. Rongotal Coll., Victoria U.
STAGE: Irma La Douce, The Mikado, Oliver, Marat/Sade, Jew of Malta, Sherry, Chichester Season, The Incomparable Max (N.Y.), Sherlock Holmes (N.Y.), Lolita (N.Y.), Pirates of Penzance (L.A.), Mystery of Edwin Drood, My Fair Lady.
PICTURES: The Headless Ghost, Bunny Lake Is Missing, Once Upon a Tractor, Modesty Blaise, A Fine Madness, Kaleidoscope, The Double Man, Fathom, Italian Secret Service, Nobody Runs Forever, Shoes of the Fisherman, Assassination Bureau, The Private Life of Sherlock Holmes, The Buttercup Chain, A Severed Head, Boulevard de Rhum, Avanti!, Escape to the Sun, Ghost in the Noonday Sun, The Legend of Hell House, The Little Prince, The Black Windmill,

One of Our Dinosaurs Is Missing, Galileo, Matilda, Zorro the Gay Blade, Transformers (voice), Rumpelstiltskin, The Emperor's New Clothes, Mack the Knife, CHUD II: Bud the Chud, Frog Prince, Let Him Have It, Robin Hood: Men in Tights, Crime and Punishment.
TELEVISION: Chicken Soup with Barley, Volpone, Bam Pow Zapp, Candida, Platonov, A Bit of Vision, Mill Hill, The Piano Player, Hopcroft in Europe, A Sprig of Broome, Ben Franklin in Paris, Pinocchio, The Great Houdini, Show Business Hall of Fame, Feather and Father, Winner Take All, The New Avengers, Licking Hitler, Columbo, Centennial, A Man Called Sloane, Nobody's Perfect, Marya, Moviola, Diary of Anne Frank, Mikado, The Sorcerer, Wizards & Warriors, George Washington, Murder She Wrote, Faerie Tale Theatre, Twilight Zone, Newhart, Hunter, Star Trek, The Sea Wolf.

REY, FERNANDO: Actor. r.n. Fernando Casado Arambillet. b. La Coruña, Spain, Sept. 20, 1917. e. Madrid Sch. of Architecture. Left to fight in Spanish Civil War with father for 3 years. Dubbed dialogue of foreign films into Spanish before beginning acting career. Has made over 150 films since 1939. Made Knight of Arts and Letters, Cannes, 1986.
PICTURES: Tierra Sedienta, Don Quixote, The Mad Queen, Don Juan, Welcome Mr. Marshall, Viridiana, Chimes at Midnight, The Return of the Seven, The Phantom of Liberty, Tristana, The Adventurers, The French Connection, The Discreet Charm of the Bourgeoisie, Seven Beauties, French Connection II, That Obscure Object of Desire, Voyage of the Damned, The Assignment, Quintet, Monsignor, The Stranger, The Hit, Rustler's Rhapsody, Padre Nuestro, Saving Grace, The Enchanted Forest, Traffic Jam, Pasodoble, El Tunel, Hard to Be a God, Moon Over Parador, Diario de Invierno, Drums of Fire, Esmeralda Bay, 1492.
TELEVISION: A.D., Black Arrow, Jesus of Nazareth, Captain James Cook (Aust. TV).

REYNOLDS, BURT: Actor, Director. b. Waycross, GA, Feb. 11, 1936. Former Florida State U. football star; TV and film stunt performer. Won fame as actor on TV in series Riverboat. Founded the Burt Reynolds Dinner Theater in Jupiter, FL, 1979.
THEATER: Mister Roberts (NY City Center), Look We've Come Through (Bdwy debut, 1956), The Rainmaker.
PICTURES: Angel Baby (debut, 1961), Armored Command, Operation CIA, Navajo Joe, Fade In, Impasse, Shark, Sam Whiskey, 100 Rifles, Skullduggery, Fuzz, Deliverance, Everything You Always Wanted To Know About Sex, Shamus, White Lightning, The Man Who Loved Cat Dancing, The Longest Yard, W.W. & The Dixie Dancekings, At Long Last Love, Hustle, Lucky Lady, Gator (also dir.), Silent Movie, Nickelodeon, Smokey and the Bandit, Semi-Tough, The End (also dir.), Hooper, Starting Over, Rough Cut, Smokey and the Bandit I, Cannonball Run, Paternity, Sharky's Machine (also dir.), The Best Little Whorehouse in Texas, Best Friends, Stroker Ace, Smokey and the Bandit III (cameo), The Man Who Loved Women, Cannonball Run II, City Heat, Stick (also dir.), Uphill All the Way (cameo), Heat, Malone, Rent-a-Cop, Switching Channels, Physical Evidence, Breaking In, All Dogs Go to Heaven (voice), Modern Love, The Player (cameo), Cop and a Half.
TELEVISION: Series: Riverboat, Gunsmoke, Hawk, Dan August, Out of This World (voice), B.L. Stryker (also co-exec. prod.), Evening Shade (Emmy Award, 1991). Movies: Hunters Are for Killing, Run Simon Run, The Man Upstairs (co-exec. prod. only). Host: The Story of Hollywood. Dir.: Alfred Hitchcock Presents (1985).

REYNOLDS, DEBBIE: Actress. r.n. Mary Frances Reynolds. b. El Paso, TX, April 1, 1932. Mother of actress Carrie Fisher. e. Burbank H.S., Burbank, CA. With Burbank Youth Symphony during h.s.; beauty contest winner (Miss Burbank) 1948; signed by Warner Bros.; on stage in Personal Appearances, Blis-Hayden Theater. Star of Tomorrow, 1952. Autobiography: Debbie: My Life (1988).
PICTURES: June Bride (debut, 1948), The Daughter of Rosie O'Grady, Three Little Words, Two Weeks With Love, Mr. Imperium, Singin' in the Rain, Skirts Ahoy, I Love Melvin, Give a Girl a Break, The Affairs of Dobie Gillis, Susan Slept Here, Athena, Hit the Deck, The Tender Trap, The Catered Affair, Bundle of Joy, Tammy and the Bachelor, This Happy Feeling, The Mating Game, Say One for Me, It Started with a Kiss, The Gazebo, The Rat Race, Pepe (cameo), The Pleasure of His Company, The Second Time Around, How the West Was Won, My Six Loves, Mary Mary, Goodbye Charlie, The Unsinkable Molly Brown (Acad. Award nom.), The Singing Nun, Divorce American Style, How Sweet It Is, What's the Matter with Helen?, Charlotte's Web (voice), That's Entertainment!, The Bodyguard (cameo), Heaven and Earth.
TELEVISION: Series: The Debbie Reynolds Show, Aloha Paradise. Movies: Sadie and Son, Perry Mason: The Case of the Musical Murders, Battling for Baby. Special: Jack Paar Is Alive and Well.
STAGE: Bdwy: Irene, Woman of the Year.

REYNOLDS, MARJORIE: Actress. b. Buhl, ID, Aug. 12, 1921. On screen as child 1923 (Scaramouche, Svengali, Revelation, etc.).
PICTURES: Murder in Greenwich Village (1937), College Humor, Holiday Inn, Star-Spangled Rhythm, Dixie, Ministry of Fear, Up in Mabel's Room, Three Is a Family, Duffy's Tavern, Bring on the Girls, Time of Their Lives, Meet Me on Broadway, Heaven Only Knows, Bad Men of Tombstone, Great Jewel Robber, Rookie Fireman, Home Town Story, No Holds Barred, Models Inc., Silent Witness, Juke Box Rhythm.
TELEVISION: Series: The Life of Riley.

REYNOLDS, SHELDON: Writer, Producer, Director. b. Philadelphia, PA, 1923. e. NYU. Radio-TV writer; programs include My Silent Partner, Robert Q. Lewis Show, We the People, Danger, Adventures of Sherlock Holmes (prod., dir., writer), Dick and the Duchess (prod., dir., writer), Foreign Intrigue (dir., prod., writer). TV Special: Sophia Loren's Rome (dir., writer). Movies: Foreign Intrigue (dir., prod., s.p.), Assignment to Kill (dir., s.p.).

REYNOLDS, STUART: Producer. b. Chicago, IL, March 22, 1907. e. Chicago law schools. Adv. exec., Lord and Thomas, BBDO. General Mills; sales exec. Don Lee-Mutual; formed Stuart Reynolds Prod., TV films. Now motion picture & TV program consultant.
TELEVISION: General Electric Theatre, Cavalcade of America, Your Jeweler's Showcase, Wild Bill Hickok. Producer and worldwide distributor of educational/training films; Eye of the Beholder.

RHODES, CYNTHIA: Actress, Dancer. b. Nashville, TN, Nov. 21, 1956. m. singer Richard Marx. Appeared on many TV specials, inc. Opryland USA, Music Hall America.
PICTURES: Xanadu, One From the Heart, Flashdance, Staying Alive, Runaway, Dirty Dancing.

RHYS-DAVIES, JOHN: Actor. b. Salisbury, England, 1944. Grew up in Wales and East Africa. Began acting at Truro School in Cornwall at 15. e. U. of East Angelia where he founded school's dramatic society. Worked as teacher before studying at Royal Academy of Dramatic Art, 1969. Appeared in 23 Shakespearean plays.
PICTURES: The Black Windmill, Sphinx, Raiders of the Lost Ark, Victor/Victoria, Sahara, Sword of the Valiant, Best Revenge, King Solomon's Mines, In the Shadow of Kilimanjaro, Firewalker, The Living Daylights, Waxwork, Rising Storm, Indiana Jones and the Last Crusade, Young Toscanini, Journey of Honor, The Seventh Coin.
TELEVISION: Mini-series: Shogun, James Clavell's Noble House, Riley, Ace of Spies, I, Claudius, War and Remembrance. Movies: The Little Match Girl, Sadat, Kim, The Naked Civil Servant, The Trial of the Incredible Hulk, Goddess of Love, The Gifted One, Great Expectations, Desperado, Secret Weapon, Before the Storm, Spy Games, Perry Mason: The Case of the Fatal Framing. Pilot: Company. Series: Under Cover, The Untouchables.

RICH, DAVID LOWELL: Director. b. New York, NY, Aug. 31, 1920. e. U. Michigan. Started career on live television in New York: Studio One, Playhouse, etc. Left for Hollywood to work on feature films for Columbia Pictures, as well as TV series, Naked City, Route 66, etc.
PICTURES: Senior Prom, Hey Boy Hey Girl, Have Rocket Will Travel, Madame X, The Plainsman, Rosie, A Lovely Way to Die, Eye of the Cat, Concorde—Airport '79, Chu Chu and the Philly Flash.
TELEVISION: Movies: See How They Run, Marcus Welby M.D., The Mask of Sheba, The Sheriff, All My Darling Daughters, The Judge and Jake Wyler, Brock's Last Case, Crime Club, Satan's School for Girls, Sex Symbol, The Daughters of Joshua Cabe Return, You Lie So Deep My Love, Ransom for Alice, Telethon, Little Women, The Hearst and Davies Affair, His Mistress, Scandal Sheet, Infidelity, Borgia Stick, Defection of Simas Kudirka (Emmy Award), Defiant Ones, Choices, I Want to Live, The Sky's No Limit, The Fighter, Thursday's Child, Enola Gay, Nurse, Convicted, A Family Upside Down, SST—Death Flight, Secret Life of John Chapman, Aloha Means Goodbye, Death Race, Lt. Schuster's Wife, Assignment Munich, Horror at 37,000 Feet, Berlin Affair, Runaway.

RICH, JOHN: Producer, Director. b. Rockaway Beach, NY, e. U. of Michigan, B.A., Phi Beta Kappa, 1948; M.A. 1949; Sesquicentennial Award, 1967. bd. of dir., Screen Dir. Guild of America, 1954–1960; v.p. 1958–1960 Founder-Trustee, Producers-Directors Pension Plan, chmn. of bd. 1965, 1968, 1970; treasurer, Directors Guild of America, 1966–67; v.p. 1967–72.
TELEVISION: Director: Academy Awards, The Dick Van Dyke Show, All in the Family (also prod.), Mr. Sunshine, Dear John, MacGyver.
AWARDS: Directors Guild Award, Most Outstanding Directorial Achievement, 1971. Christopher award: Henry Fonda as Clarence Darrow, 1975. NAACP Image Award, 1974; 2

Golden Globe Awards: All in the Family, 1972–73.; DGA Robert B. Aldrich Award for 1992.
PICTURES: Director: The New Interns, Wives and Lovers, Boeing-Boeing, Roustabout, Easy Come Easy Go.

RICH, LEE: Producer, Executive. b. Cleveland, OH, Dec. 10, 1926. e. Ohio U. Adv. exec.; resigned as sr. v.p., Benton & Bowles, to become producer for Mirisch-Rich TV, 1965 (Rat Patrol; Hey, Landlord). Resigned 1967 to join Leo Burnett Agency. Left to form Lorimar Productions in 1969 and served as pres. until 1986 when left to join MGM/UA Communications as chmn. & CEO. Resigned 1988; signed 3-year deal with Warner Bros. setting up Lee Rich Prods. there.
PICTURES: Producer: The Sporting Club. Executive Producer: The Man, The Choirboys, Who Is Killing the Great Chefs of Europe?, The Big Red One, Hard to Kill, Innocent Blood, Passenger 57.
TELEVISION: Exec. Prod.: Series: The Waltons (1972–81, Emmy, 1973), Dallas, Knots Landing. Mini-series: The Blue Knight, Helter Skelter, Studs Lonigan. Movies: Do Not Fold Spindle or Mutilate; The Homecoming: A Christmas Story, The Crooked Hearts, Pursuit, The Girls of Huntington House, Dying Room Only, Don't Be Afraid of the Dark, A Dream for Christmas, The Stranger Within, Bad Ronald, The Runaway Barge, Runaways, Returning Home, Eric, Conspiracy of Terror, Widow, Green Eyes, Killer on Board, Desperate Women, Long Journey Back, Mary and Joseph: A Story of Faith, Mr. Horn, Some Kind of Miracle, Young Love, First Love, A Man Called Intrepid, Flamingo Road, Marriage Is Alive and Well, A Perfect Match, Reward, Skag, Killjoy, A Matter of Life and Death, Our Family Business, Mother's Day on Walton's Mountain, This is Kate Bennett, Two of a Kind, A Wedding on Walton's Mountain, A Day of Thanks on Walton's Mountain, Secret of Midland Heights, Face of Fear, Killer Rules.
AWARDS: Honorary doctorate in communications, Ohio U., 1982; Distinguished Citizenship Award, Southwestern U. Sch. of Law, 1983; named Man of Year by Beverly Hills Lodge of B'nai B'rith, 1983. Has won 3 George Foster Peabody Awards, 4 Humanitas Awards, 2 Christopher Medals. Twice named Television Showman of the Year by Pub. Guild of Amer.

RICHARD, CLIFF: O.B.E. Singer, Actor. b. India, Oct. 14, 1940. r.n. Harold Webb. Ent. show business 1958 in TV series Oh Boy. Other TV includes Sunday Night at the London Palladium, several Cliff Richard Shows; film debut in Serious Charge, 1959; star, play Aladdin, London Palladium Theatre, 1964–65. Top British Singer, 1960–71. Voted top box-office star of Great Britain, 1962–63, 1963–64. Stageplays: Five Finger Exercise (1970), The Potting Shed (1971). Twice rep. U.K. in Eurovision Song Contest. 3 BBC TV series plus doc. series. Innumerable platinum, gold and silver discs. In 1989 became first UK artist to release 100 singles; voted top male vocalist of the 80's by UK Indept. TV viewers. Has made numerous videos. Starred in Time, rock musical, London 1986–87.
PICTURES: Expresso Bongo, The Young Ones, Summer Holiday, Wonderful Life, Finder's Keepers, Two a Penny, Take Me High.

RICHARDS, BEAH: Actress. b. Vicksburg, MS. e. Dillard U. On Bdwy. in The Miracle Worker, A Raisin in the Sun, The Amen Corner (Theatre World Award), etc.
PICTURES: Take a Giant Step, The Miracle Worker, Gone Are the Days, In the Heat of the Night, Hurry Sundown, Guess Who's Coming to Dinner, Great White Hope, Mahogany, Homer and Eddie, Drugstore Cowboy.
TELEVISION: Series: The Bill Cosby Show (1970), Sanford and Son, Frank's Place (Emmy Award, 1988), Hearts Afire. Movies: Footsteps, Outrage, A Dream for Christmas, Just an Old Sweet Song, Ring of Passion, Roots II—The Next Generation, A Christmas Without Snow, One Special Victory.

RICHARDS, DICK: Producer, Director, Writer. b. New York, NY, July 9, 1934. In U.S. Army as photo-journalist; work appeared in Life, Look, Time, Esquire, etc. as photographer. Won over 100 int'l. awards, for commercials and photographic art work.
PICTURES: The Culpepper Cattle Co. (prod., dir., s.p.), Rafferty and the Gold Dust Twins (dir.), Farewell, My Lovely (dir.), March or Die (prod., dir., s.p.), Tootsie (co-prod.); Death Valley (dir.); Man Woman and Child (dir.), Heat (dir.).

RICHARDSON, JOELY: Actress. b. London, Eng., January 9, 1965. Daughter of actress Vanessa Redgrave and director Tony Richardson, sister of actress Natasha Richardson. e. Lycee, St. Paul's Girl's School, London; Pinellas Park H.S. (Florida), The Thacher Sch. (Ojai, CA), Royal Acad. of Dramatic Art. London stage: Steel Magnolias, Beauty and the Beast (Old Vic); also at Liverpool Playhouse, RSC.
PICTURES: Wetherby (debut, 1985 with mother), Drowning By Numbers, About That Strange Girl, King Ralph, Shining Through, Rebecca's Daughters.
TELEVISION: Body Contact, Behaving Badly, Available Light, Heading Home, Lady Chatterly.

RICHARDSON, MIRANDA: Actress. b. Southport, England, 1958. Studied acting at the drama program at Bristol's Old Vic Theatre School. Began acting on stage, 1979. Appeared in Moving, at the Queen's Theatre and continued in All My Sons, Who's Afraid of Virginia Woolf?, The Life of Einstein in provincial theatres. Also A Lie of the Mind (London), The Changeling, Mountain Language.
PICTURES: Dance with a Stranger (debut, 1985), The Innocent, Empire of the Sun, Eat the Rich, Twisted Obsession, The Bachelor, Enchanted April, The Crying Game, Damage (BAFTA Award; Acad. Award nom.).
TELEVISION: The Hard Word, Sorrel and Son, A Woman of Substance, After Pilkington, Underworld, Death of the Heart, The Black Adder (series), Die Kinder (mini-series), Sweet as You Are (Royal TV Society's Best Actress Award).

RICHARDSON, NATASHA: Actress. b. London, Eng., May 11, 1963. Daughter of actress Vanessa Redgrave and director Tony Richardson. e. Central Sch. of Speech and Drama. Appeared at the Leeds Playhouse in On the Razzle, Top Girls, Charley's Aunt. Performed A Midsummer Night's Dream and Hamlet with the Young Vic. In 1985 starred with mother in The Seagull (London), also starred in the musical High Society. Won London Theatre Critics Most Promising Newcomer award, 1986. NY stage debut 1992 in Anna Christie.
PICTURES: Every Picture Tells a Story (debut, 1984). Gothic, A Month in the Country, Patty Hearst, Fat Man and Little Boy, The Handmaid's Tale, The Comfort of Strangers, The Favor the Watch and the Very Big Fish, Past Midnight, Widow's Peak.
TELEVISION: Ellis Island (mini-series), In a Secret State, The Copper Beeches (epis. of Sherlock Holmes), Ghosts, Suddenly Last Summer, Hostages, Zelda.

RICHE, ALAN: Executive. e. U. of Arizona. Began career as music agent with GAC, later moving into its TV dept. Joined CMA 1969 as m.p. & literary agent. With Guber-Peters Co. as v.p., creative affairs. 1987, named sr. v.p. of prod. for De Laurentiis Entertainment Group. Resigned Dec. 1987.

RICHMAN, PETER MARK: Actor. b. Philadelphia, PA, April 16, 1927. Previously acted as Mark Richman. Member of Actors Studio since 1954.
THEATRE: Credits incl.: End as a Man, Masquerade, A Hatful of Rain, The Zoo Story, Blithe Spirit, Night of the Iguana, 12 Angry Men, Babes in Toyland, Funny Girl, The Best Man.
PICTURES: Friendly Persuasion, The Strange One, The Black Orchid, Dark Intruder, Agent for H.A.R.M., For Singles Only, Friday 13th Part VIII—Jason Takes Manahattan, The Naked Gun 2-1/2.
TELEVISION: Series: Longstreet, Dynasty, Cain's Hundred, Mystery of the Keys. Movies: House on Greenapple Road, Yuma, Mallory: Circumstantial Evidence, The Islander, Dempsey, Blind Ambition, City Killer, Bonanza: The Next Generation. Guest: Three's Company, Murder She Wrote, Star Trek: The Next Generation, many others.

RICHMOND, TED: Producer. b. Norfolk, VA, June 10, 1912. e. Massachusetts Inst. of Technology. Ent. m.p. ind. as publicity dir., RKO Theats.; later mgr. Albany dist. Pub. dir. Palban circuit, N.Y.: Paramount upper N.Y. state theats.; Grand Nat'l Pictures. Author Grand Nat'l series Trigger Pal, Six Gun Rhythm. Formed T. H. Richmond Prods., Inc., 1941. Formed Copa Prod. with Tyrone Power, 1954. Reactivated Copa Prod. Ltd., England, 1960.
PICTURES: Hit the Hay, The Milkman, Kansas Raiders, Shakedown, Smuggler's Island, Strange Door, Cimarron Kid, Bronco Buster, Has Anybody Seen My Gal, No Room for the Groom, Weekend with Father, The Mississippi Gambler, Desert Legion, Column South, Bonzo Goes to College, Forbidden, Walking My Baby Back Home, Francis Joins the Wacs, Bengal Brigade, Count Three and Pray, Nightfall, Abandon Ship, Solomon and Sheba, Charlemagne. Formed Ted Richmond Prod. Inc. for MGM release, 1959. Bachelor in Paradise, Advance to the Rear; Pancho Villa; Return of the 7; Red Sun; Producer, Papillon, The Fifth Musketeer.

RICHTER, W. D.: Writer, Director. b. New Britain, CT, Dec. 7, 1945. e. Dartmouth Coll. B.A.; U. of Southern California Film Sch., grad. study.
PICTURES: Writer: Slither, Peeper, Nickelodeon, Invasion of the Body Snatchers, Dracula, Brubaker, All Night Long, Big Trouble in Little China, Needful Things. Prod.-Dir.: Adventures of Buckaroo Banzai, Late for Dinner.

RICKERT, JOHN F.: Executive. b. Kansas City, MO, Oct. 29, 1924. e. U. of Southern California. Joined Universal Pictures in 1951; left in 1957 to start independent productions. From 1960 to 1968 handled indep. roadshow distribution (4-walling). In 1969 formed Cineworld Corporation, natl. dist. co., of which he is pres. In 1975–76 did tax shelter financing for 13 films. Currently involved in distribution, production packaging and intl. co-production as pres. of Coproducers Corp.

RICKLES, DON: Actor, Comedian. b. New York, NY, May 8, 1926. e. AADA.
TELEVISION: *Series:* The Don Rickles Show (1968), The Don Rickles Show (1972), C.P.O. Sharkey, Foul-Ups Bleeps and Blunders, Daddy Dearest. *Movie:* For the Love of It. *Guest:* The Big Show, F Troop, Laugh-In, Kraft Music Hall, Dean Martin's Celebrity Roasts, Tales From the Crypt, many others.
PICTURES: Run Silent Run Deep, Rabbit Trap, The Rat Race, X: The Man With the X-Ray Eyes, Muscle Beach Party, Bikini Beach, Beach Blanket Bingo, Enter Laughing, The Money Jungle, Where It's At, Kelly's Heroes, Keaton's Cop, Innocent Blood.

RICKMAN, ALAN: Actor. b. London, England, 1946. Began as graphic designer before studying acting at RADA. Joined the Royal Shakespeare Co. where he starred in Les Liaisons Dangereuses; received Tony Award nomination for 1987 NY production.
PICTURES: Die Hard (debut, 1988), The January Man, Quigley Down Under, Closet Land, Truly Madly Deeply, Robin Hood: Prince of Thieves (BAFTA Award, 1991), Close My Eyes, Bob Roberts.
TELEVISION: *Series:* The Barchester Chronicles (BBC). *Specials:* Smiley's People, Romeo and Juliet, Bonnie Prince Charley, Girls on Top. *Guest:* Fallen Angels (Murder Obliquely).
THEATRE: Commitments, The Last Elephant, The Grass Widow, Lucky Chance, The Seagull, As You Like It, Troilus and Cressida.

RIEGERT, PETER: Actor. b. New York, NY, Apr. 11, 1947. e. U. of Buffalo, B.A. Brief stints as 8th grade English teacher, social worker, and aide de camp to politician Bella Abzug 1970, before turned actor, off-off Bdwy. Appeared with improvisational comedy group War Babies. Debuted on Bdwy. in Dance with Me. Then as Chico Marx in Minnie's Boys, followed by Sexual Perversity in Chicago, Isn't it Romantic?, La Brea Tarpits, A Rosen By Any Other Name, The Nerd, Mountain Language/The Birthday Party, The Road to Nirvana. Film debut in short, A Director Talks About His Film.
PICTURES: National Lampoon's Animal House, Americathon, Head Over Heels, National Lampoon Goes to the Movies, Local Hero, City Girl, A Man in Love, Le Grand Carnaval, The Stranger, Crossing Delancey, That's Adequate, The Passport, A Shock to the System, The Object of Beauty, Beyond the Ocean, Oscar, The Runestone, Passed Away, Utz.
TELEVISION: *Specials:* Concealed Enemies, The Hit List, W. Eugene Smith: Photography Made Difficult. *Mini-Series:* Ellis Island. *Movies:* News at Eleven, Barbarians at the Gate. *Series:* The Middle Ages.

RIFKIN, HARMON "BUD": Theatre Executive. b. Springfield, MA, Apr. 1, 1942. e. Clark U., A.B., 1964; Boston Coll. Graduate Sch. of Business Admin., M.B.A., 1967. Worked for Rifkin Theatres while student; upon graduation continued in film and equipment purchasing and financial management for circuit. 1972, co-founded Cinema Centers Corp. & Theatre Management Services; pres. and C.E.O. of Hoyts Cinema Corp. with responsibility for new theatre dev. and gen. operations through 1988. 1988–90, partner in develop. of Silver City Galleria Mall with the Pyramid Cos.; 1991–, partner in Natl. Develop. of New England; 1992–93, pres. of NATO.
MEMBER: Exec. Comm. and v.p. of Natl. Assoc. of Theatre Owners. Past program chmn., v.p., pres. & chmn. of Theatre Owners of New England.

RIFKIN, JULIAN: Exhibitor. b. Boston, MA, May 26, 1915. e. Massachusetts Inst. of Technology. Member bd. of dir. Allied States Assoc.of M.P. Exhibitors, and Theatre Owners of America. Pres. Theatre Owners of New England 1961–63. Chairman bd. Theatre Owners of New England. 1964–65. Past pres. Allied Artists Corp. of New England. Pres., 1968–69, chmn. of bd. Nat'l Assoc. of Theatre Owners, 1970. Pres. Rifkin Theatres. Pres. Cinema Centers Corp. Chmn. NATO Code and Rating Comm., 1968–79. Received Sherrill C. Corwin Memorial Award, 1985. Senior consultant, Hoyts Cinema Corp. 1986–9.

RIGG, DIANA: C.B.E. (1987). Actress. b. Doncaster, England, July 20, 1938. With the Royal Shakespeare Co. at Aldwych Theatre, 1962–64. Ent. TV in The Avengers series, 1965. Ent. films 1967. Recent London stage: Follies, Medea.
PICTURES: A Midsummer's Night Dream, The Assassination Bureau, On Her Majesty's Secret Service, Julius Caesar, The Hospital, Theatre of Blood, A Little Night Music, The Great Muppet Caper, Evil Under the Sun, Snow White, A Good Man in Africa.
TELEVISION: *Series:* The Avengers, Diana, Mystery (host). *Movies:* In This House of Brede, Witness for the Prosecution, A Hazard of Hearts, Mother Love, Mrs. 'arris Goes to Paris. *Specials:* King Lear, Bleak House.

RINGWALD, MOLLY: Actress. b. Sacramento, CA, Feb. 16, 1968. Daughter of jazz musician Bob Ringwald; began performing at age 4 with his Great Pacific Jazz Band at 6 and recorded album, Molly Sings. Professional debut at 5 in stage play, The Glass Harp. Appeared in TV's New Mickey Mouse Club, a West Coast stage production of Annie and in TV series, The Facts of Life. Off-Bdwy debut: Lily Dale (Theatre World Award, 1986).
PICTURES: Tempest (debut, 1982), P.K. and the Kid, Spacehunter: Adventures in the Forbidden Zone, Sixteen Candles, The Breakfast Club, Pretty in Pink, The Pick-Up Artist, For Keeps?, King Lear, Fresh Horses, Strike It Rich, Betsy's Wedding, Face the Music.
TELEVISION: *Series:* The Facts of Life. *Movies:* Packin' It In, Surviving, Women and Men: Stories of Seduction (Dust Before Fireworks), Something to Live For: The Alison Gertz Story.

RISSIEN, EDWARD L.: Executive. b. Des Moines, IA. e. Grinnell Coll., Stanford U., B.A., 1949. Army Air Force, W.W.II. Bdwy. stage, mgr., 1950–53; v.p., Mark Stevens. Prods., 1954–56; prod., v.p., Four Star, 1958–60; prog. exec., ABC-TV, 1960–62; v.p., Bing Crosby Prods., 1963–66; v.p., Filmways TV Prods.; assoc. producer, Columbia, 1968–69; indep. producer, 1970; prod., WB, 1971; exec. v.p., Playboy Prods., 1972–80; consultant & indep. prod., 1981–82; sr. consultant, cable, Playboy Prods., 1982–85; pres., Playboy Programs, 1985–8. Board of dirs.: Heritage Entertainment, Inc. 1985–8. Indept. prod., 1989–present. Theatre producer in London: The School of Night, Shattered.
PICTURES: Snow Job (prod.), Castle Keep (prod. exec.), The Crazy World of Julius Vrooder (prod.), Saint Jack (exec. prod.).
TELEVISION: *Movies* (exec. prod.): Minstrel Man, A Whale for the Killing, The Death of Ocean View Park, Big Bob Johnson, The Great Niagara, Third Girl from the Left, A Summer Without Boys.

RISSNER, DANTON: Executive. b. Brooklyn, NY, March 27, 1940. e. Florida So. Col. Began as agent with Ashley Famous (later Intl. Famous), 1967–69. In 1969 joined Warner Bros. as v.p., chg. European prod.; 1970, moved to United Artists as v.p., chg. European prod. 1973, named v.p. in chg. East Coast & European prod. for UA; 1975, v.p. in chg. of world-wide prod. Resigned 1978; 1981, exec. v.p., 20th Century-Fox. 1984, joined UA as sr. v.p., motion pictures.
PICTURES: *Prod.:* Up the Academy, A Summer Story.
TELEVISION: Backfire (prod.).

RITCHIE, MICHAEL: Director. b. Waukesha, WI, Nov. 28, 1938. e. Harvard U. where he directed first production of Arthur Kopit's play, Oh Dad Poor Dad Mama's Hung You in the Closet and I'm Feeling So Sad. Professional career began as ass't. to Robert Saudek on Ford Foundation's Omnibus TV series. Later became assoc. prod. and then dir. on Saudek's Profiles in Courage series. Then had dir. assignments on top series (Man from U.N.C.L.E., Dr. Kildare, The Big Valley, Felony Squad). Appeared as actor in film Innocent Blood.
PICTURES: Downhill Racer, Prime Cut, The Candidate, Smile (also prod., lyricist), The Bad News Bears, Semi-Tough, An Almost Perfect Affair (also co-s.p.), The Island, Divine Madness (also prod.), The Survivors, Fletch, Wildcats, The Golden Child, The Couch Trip, Fletch Lives, Diggstown, Cops and Robbersons.
TELEVISION: *Series:* Profiles in Courage (also prod.), Man from U.N.C.L.E., Run for Your Life, Dr. Kildare, The Big Valley, Felony Squad, The Outsider (pilot), The Sound of Anger. *Movie:* The Positively True Adventures of the Alleged Texas Cheerleader-Murdering Mom.

RITTER, JOHN: Actor. b. Burbank, CA, Sept. 17, 1948. Father was late Tex Ritter, country-western star. m. actress Nancy Morgan. Attended Hollywood H.S. Interest in acting began at U. of Southern California in 1968. Appeared with college cast at Edinburgh Festival; later with Eva Marie Saint in Desire Under the Elms. Gained fame as star of TV series, Three's Company.
PICTURES: The Barefoot Executive, Scandalous John, The Other, The Stone Killer, Nickelodeon, Americathon, Hero at Large, Wholly Moses, They All Laughed, Real Men, Skin Deep, Problem Child, Problem Child II, Noises Off, Stay Tuned.
TELEVISION: *Movies:* Evil Roy Slade, The Night That Panicked America, Leave Yesterday Behind, The Comeback Kid, Pray TV, In Love with an Older Woman, Sunset Limousine, Love Thy Neighbor, Letting Go, Unnatural Causes, A Smoky Mountain Christmas, The Last Fling, Prison for Children, Tricks of the Trade, My Brother's Wife, Stephen King's IT, The Dreamer of Oz, The Summer My Father Grew Up, Danielle Steel's Heartbeat. *Series:* The Waltons, Three's Company (Emmy Award, 1984), Three's a Crowd, Hooperman, Have Faith (exec. prod.), Anything But Love (exec. prod., also guest), Fish Police (voice), Hearts Afire.

RIVE, KENNETH: Executive. b. London, England, July 26, 1919. Early career as actor, radio compere, theatrical agent. Served in Intell. Corps. during W.W.II. After demob. theatre sup. and

gen. man. cinema co. promoted dir. 1947. Started in continental exhibition forming Gala Film Distrib. Ltd., 1950 of which he is mng. dir. & chief exec.
PICTURES: During One Night, The Boys, Devil Doll, Curse of Simba.

RIVERA, CHITA: Actress, Dancer. b. Washington, DC, Jan. 23, 1933. r.n. Concita del Rivero. Trained for stage at American School of Ballet.
THEATER: Call Me Madam (1952), Guys and Dolls, Can-Can, Shoestring Revue, Seventh Heaven, Mr. Wonderful, Shinbone Alley, West Side Story, Bye Bye Birdie, Bajour, Sondheim: A Musical Tribute, Chicago, Hey Look Me Over, Merlin, The Rink (Tony Award, 1984), Jerry's Girls, Kiss of the Spider Woman (Tony Award, 1993).
PICTURE: Sweet Charity (1969).
TELEVISION: Series: The New Dick Van Dyke Show. Specials: Kennedy Center Tonight—Broadway to Washington!, Pippin, Toller Cranston's Strawberry Ice, TV Academy Hall of Fame, 1985. Movies: The Marcus-Nelson Murders, Mayflower Madam.

RIVERA, GERALDO: TV Reporter. b. New York, NY, July 4, 1943. e. U. of Arizona, Brooklyn Law Sch., 1969, Columbia Sch. of Journalism. Started legal career 1st as clerk with Harlem Assertion of Rights Community Action for Legal Services 1968–70; chmn, One-to-One Foundation. Then practiced law. Switched to journalism, making several TV documentaries on such subjects as institutions for retarded, drug addiction, migrant workers, etc. Joined WABC-TV, New York, in 1970. Winner 3 national and local Emmys, George Peabody Award, 2 Robert F. Kennedy Awards. Appeared in film The Bonfire of the Vanities.
TELEVISION: Geraldo Rivera: Good Night America; Good Morning America (contributor); 20/20. Specials: The Mystery of Al Capone's Vault, American Vice: The Doping of a Nation; Innocence Lost: The Erosion of American Childhood; Sons of Scarface: The New Mafia; Murder: Live From Death Row, The Investigators (prods.), Devil Worship: Exposing Satan's Underground. Movie: Perry Mason: The Case of the Reckless Romeo.

RIVERS, JOAN: Actress, Writer, Director. r.n. Joan Molinsky. b. New York, NY, June 8, 1933. e. Barnard Coll. (Phi Beta Kappa). Formerly fashion coordinator Bond clothing stores. Most of career on TV and in nightclubs; with Second City 1961–62; TV debut: Johnny Carson Show, 1965; nat'l syndicated columnist, Chicago Tribune 1973–76; Hadassah Woman of the Year, 1983; Jimmy Award for Best Comedian 1981; Chair., National Cystic Fibrosis Foundation. 1978 created TV series Husbands Wives and Lovers. Author: Having a Baby Can Be a Scream (1974), Can We Talk? (1983), The Life and Hard Times of Heidi Abramowitz (1984), Enter Talking (1986). On Broadway in Fun City (also co-writer), Broadway Bound (1988).
PICTURES: The Swimmer, Rabbit Test (also dir., s.p.), The Muppets Take Manhattan, Spaceballs (voice).
TELEVISION: Series: The Tonight Show (regular substitute guest host: 1983–6), The Late Show (host), The New Hollywood Squares, The Joan Rivers Show (morning talk show). Movie: How to Murder a Millionaire.

ROBARDS, JASON: Actor. b. Chicago, IL, July 26, 1922. Served in Navy during W.W.II. Studied acting at Acad. of Dramatic Arts. Began with Children's World Theatre (1947), stock radio parts, asst. stage mgr. and actor in Stalag 17, The Chase, D'Oyle Carte Opera Co., Stratford Ontario Shakespeare Fest. American Gothic, Circle in the Square.
THEATER: The Iceman Cometh (Obie Award, 1956), Long Day's Journey into Night (Theatre World Award), The Disenchanted (Tony Award, 1959), Toys in the Attic, Big Fish Little Fish, A Thousand Clowns, After the Fall, But for Whom Charlie, Hughie, The Devils, We Bombed in New Haven, The Country Girl, A Moon for the Misbegotten, Long Day's Journey Into Night (Brooklyn Acad. of Music, 1975, Bdwy, 1988), A Touch of the Poet, O'Neill and Carlotta, You Can't Take It With You, Ah Wilderness, A Month of Sundays, Established Price (Long Wharf), Love Letters, Park Your Car in Harvard Yard.
PICTURES: The Journey (debut, 1959), By Love Possessed, Tender Is the Night, Long Day's Journey Into Night, Act One, A Thousand Clowns, A Big Hand for the Little Lady, Any Wednesday, Divorce American Style, The St. Valentine's Day Massacre, Hour of the Gun, The Night They Raided Minsky's, (Loves of) Isadora, Once Upon a Time in the West, Operation Snafu, The Ballad of Cable Hogue, Tora! Tora! Tora!, Fools, Julius Caesar, Johnny Got His Gun, Murders in the Rue Morgue, The War Between Men and Women, Pat Garrett and Billy the Kid, A Boy and His Dog, Mr. Sycamore, All the President's Men (Acad. Award, supp. actor, 1976), Julia (Acad. Award, supp. actor, 1977), Comes a Horseman, Hurricane, Raise the Titanic!, Caboblanco, Melvin and Howard, Legend of the Lone Ranger, Burden of Dreams, Max Dugan Returns, Something Wicked This Way Comes, Square

Dance, Bright Lights Big City, The Good Mother, Dream a Little Dream, Parenthood, Quick Change, Reunion, Storyville, The Adventures of Huck Finn, The Trial, Philadelphia.
TELEVISION: Specials: Abe Lincoln in Illinois, The Iceman Cometh, A Doll's House, Noon Wine, Belle of 14th Street, The House Without a Christmas Tree, For Whom the Bell Tolls, You Can't Take It With You, Hughie. Mini-Series: Washington: Behind Closed Doors. Movies: A Christmas to Remember, Haywire, F.D.R.: The Last Year, The Atlanta Child Murders, The Day After, Sakharov, Johnny Bull, The Long Hot Summer, Laguna Heat, Norman Rockwell's Breaking Home Ties, Inherit the Wind (Emmy Award, 1988), The Christmas Wife, The Perfect Tribute, Chernobyl: The Final Warning, An Inconvenient Woman, Black Rainbow, Mark Twain & Me, Heidi. Guest: Studio One, Philco Playhouse, Hallmark.

ROBARDS, SAM: Actor. b. New York, NY, December 16. m. actress Suzy Amis. Son of actors Jason Robards and Lauren Bacall. e. National Theater Institute and studied with Uta Hagen at H.B. Studios.
THEATER: Off-Bdwy: Album, Flux, Taking Steps, Moonchildren. Kennedy Center: Idiot's Delight and regional theater.
PICTURES: Tempest, Not Quite Paradise, Fandango, Bright Lights Big City, Bird, Casualties of War, The Ballad of Little Jo.
TELEVISION: Series: Movin' Right Along (PBS), TV 101, Get a Life! Movies: Jacobo Timerman: Prisoner Without a Name Cell Without a Number, Into Thin Air, Pancho Barnes.

ROBBINS, MATTHEW: Writer, Director. e. U. of Southern California Sch. of Cinema. Wrote early scripts in collaboration with Hal Barwood, Robbins branching out into directing also with Corvette Summer in 1978.
PICTURES: Writer: The Sugarland Express, The Bingo Long Traveling All-Stars and Motor Kings, Corvette Summer (also dir.), Dragonslayer (also dir.), Warning Sign, Batteries Not Included (also dir.), Bingo (dir. only).

ROBBINS, RICHARD: Composer. b. Boston, MA, Dec. 4, 1940. Bachelor of Music and Graduate Studies at New England Conservatory of Music. Received Frank Huntington Beebe Fellowship to Austria where he studied musicology, chamber music. Later became dir. of Mannes College of Music Preparatory School, N.Y. Has worked closely with James Ivory and Ismail Merchant. Also dir. doc. films Sweet Sounds, Street Musicians of Bombay. Awards: Best Score, Venice Film Festival for Maurice; Best Score, BFI Anthony Asquith Award for A Room with a View. Acad. Award nom. for Howards End.
PICTURES: The Europeans (supr. score), Jane Austen in Manhattan, Quartet, Heat and Dust, The Bostonians, A Room with a View, Maurice, Sweet Lorraine, My Little Girl, Slaves of New York, Mr. & Mrs. Bridge, The Ballad of the Sad Cafe, Howards End, Remains of the Day.
TELEVISION: Love and Other Sorrows.

ROBBINS, TIM: Actor. b. West Covina, CA, Oct. 16, 1958. Son of Greenwich Village folksinger, worked as actor while in high school. e. NYU. Transferred to UCLA theatre prog. Studied French with actor George Bigot of the Theatre du Soleil. 1981, co-founder and artistic dir., The Actors Gang, in L.A.; dir. them in and co-authored Alagazam: After the Dog Wars, Violence: The Misadventures of Spike Spangle - Farmer, Carnage: A Comedy (also prod. in NY).
PICTURES: No Small Affair, Toy Soldiers, The Sure Thing, Fraternity Vacation, Top Gun, Howard the Duck, Five Corners, Bull Durham, Tapeheads, Miss Firecracker, Twister, Erik the Viking, Cadillac Man, Jacob's Ladder, Jungle Fever, The Player (Cannes Film Fest. Award for best actor, 1992), Bob Roberts (also dir., s.p., co-wrote songs), Short Cuts, The Hudsucker Proxy, Rita Hayworth and Shawshank Redemption.
TELEVISION: Movies: Quarterback Princess, Malice in Wonderland. Guest: Hardcastle and McCormick, St. Elsewhere, Hill St. Blues.

ROBERT, PATRICIA HARRISON: Executive. b. Atlanta, GA, March 31, 1939. e. Manhattanville Coll. of the Sacred Heart, Ecole Française (Paris), U. of Virginia Graduate Sch. Dir. of pub. & pub. relations, Gerald Rafshoon Advertising, 1965–69; drama critic, Atlanta Magazine, 1965–68; drama critic, feature writer, The Atlanta Constitution, 1968–69; asst. to publicity dir., The Walter Reade Organization, 1969–70; dir. of publicity—public relations, Radio City Music Hall, 1970. Became dir. of advertising—public relations, 1973; appt. v.p., 1976. Named east coast pub. dir., Universal Pictures, 1983. In 1984 appt. v.p., pub., Orion Pictures Dist. Corp.

ROBERTS, CURTIS: Producer. b. Dover, England. e. Cambridge U. Child actor. Germany; numerous pictures for Rank Org.; prod. England, on Broadway in Gertie, Island Visit; co-prod. on Broadway, Horses in Midstream, Golden Apple, Tonight or Never; tour and N.Y. The Journey, Bdwy. Now pres., CGC Films, Munich.

TELEVISION: Rendezvous, Deadly Species, Top Secret, The Ilona Massey Show, When In Rome, Ethan Frome, Black Chiffon, Illusion in Java (mini-series).

PICTURES: An Actress in Love, La Die, Hypocrite, Jet Over the Atlantic, The Vixen, Farewell Party, Polly's Return, Rain Before Seven, Halloween, Malaga, My Dear Children, Bus Stop, Eve Arden Show, Norma, The Lion's Consort, Whispers.

BOOKS: History of Summer Theatre; The History of Vaudeville; Other Side of the Coin, 1969; History of Music (Popular) 1900–70, 1970; History of English Music Halls, 1972; Latta, 1972; Then There Were Some, 1979; I Live to Love, 1985; Gabor the Merrier, 1991.

TOURS: Blithe Spirit, Showboat, Kiss Me Kate, Generation, The Camel Bell, Farewell Party, Twentieth Century, Great Sebastians, Goodbye Charlie, Time of the Cuckoo, Under Papa's Picture, Everybody's Gal, Divorce Me Darling, Gingerbread Lady, September Song, Same Time Next Year, Funny Girl, Pal Joey, South Pacific, It Girl; Fanny, Breaking Up the Act (pre-Bdwy.), Good, Good Friends, Together (pre-Bdwy, 1992). Recipient: Lawrence J. Quirk Photoplay Award 1990.

ROBERTS, ERIC: Actor. b. Biloxi, MS, April 18, 1956. Father founded Actors and Writers Workshop in Atlanta, 1963. Sister is actress Julia Roberts. Began appearing in stage prods. at age 5. Studied in London at Royal Acad. of Dramatic Art, 1973–74. Returned to U.S. to study at American Acad. of Dramatic Arts. Stage debut in Rebel Women.

THEATER: Mass Appeal, The Glass Menagerie (Hartford Stage Co.), A Streetcar Named Desire (Princeton's McCarter Theater), Alms for the Middle Class (Long Wharf), Burn This (Broadway debut; Theatre World Award).

PICTURES: King of the Gypsies (debut, 1978), Raggedy Man, Star 80, The Pope of Greenwich Village, The Coca Cola Kid, Runaway Train (Acad. Award nom.), Nobody's Fool, Rude Awakening, Options (cameo), Blood Red, Best of the Best, The Ambulance, Lonely Hearts, Final Analysis, Best of the Best 2, By the Sword.

TELEVISION: Specials: Paul's Case, Miss Lonelyhearts, Dear America (reader). Movies: To Heal a Nation, The Lost Capone, Descending Angel, Vendetta: Secrets of a Mafia Bride, Fugitive Among Us, Love Honor & Obey: The Last Mafia Marriage, Voyage.

ROBERTS, JULIA: Actress. b. Smyrna, GA, Oct. 28, 1967. Brother is actor Eric Roberts. m. musician Lyle Lovett. Parents ran theater workshop in Atlanta.

PICTURES: Blood Red (debut, 1986), Satisfaction, Mystic Pizza, Steel Magnolias (Acad. Award nom.), Pretty Woman (Acad. Award nom.), Flatliners, Sleeping With the Enemy, Dying Young, Hook, The Player, The Pelican Brief.

TELEVISION: Movie: Baja Oklahoma.

ROBERTS, PERNELL: Actor. b. Waycross, GA, May 18, 1930. e. U. of Maryland. Left college to begin working with summer stock companies, joining Arena Stage in Washington, DC in 1950. In 1952 began appearing off-Bdwy. (where he won a Drama Desk Award for Macbeth, 1957); made Bdwy. debut in 1958 in Tonight in Samarkand.

PICTURES: Desire Under the Elms (debut, 1958), The Sheepman, Ride Lonesome, The Errand Boy (cameo), Four Rode Out, The Magic of Lassie.

TELEVISION: Series: Bonanza (1959–65), Trapper John M.D. (1979–86), FBI: The Untold Stories (host). Movies: The Silent Gun, San Francisco International, The Bravos, Adventures of Nick Carter, Assignment: Munich, Dead Man on the Run, The Deadly Tower, The Lives of Jenny Dolan, Charlie Cobb: Nice Night for a Hanging, The Immigrants, The Night Rider, Hot Rod, High Noon Part II: The Return of Will Kane, Incident at Crestridge, Desperado, Perry Mason: The Case of the Sudden Death Payoff, Perry Mason: The Case of the All-Star Assassin, Donor. Mini-Series: Captains and the Kings, Centennial, Around the World in 80 Days.

ROBERTS, TONY: Actor. b. New York, NY, Oct. 22, 1939. e. Northwestern U.

THEATRE: Bdwy: How Now Dow Jones, Don't Drink the Water, Play It Again Sam, Promises Promises, Barefoot in the Park, Absurd Person Singular, Sugar, Murder at the Howard Johnson's, They're Playing Our Song, Doubles, Arsenic and Old Lace, Jerome Robbins' Broadway, The Seagull. Off-Bdwy: The Cradle Will Rock, The Good Parts. NY City Opera: Brigadoon, South Pacific. Dir: One of the All-Time Greats (Off-Bdwy).

PICTURES: Million Dollar Duck, Star Spangled Girl, Play It Again Sam, Serpico, The Taking of Pelham One Two Three, Lovers Like Us (Le Sauvage), Annie Hall, Just Tell Me What You Want, Stardust Memories, A Midsummer Night's Sex Comedy, Amityville 3-D, Key Exchange, Hannah and Her Sisters, Radio Days, 18 Again, Popcorn, Switch.

TELEVISION: Series: Rosetti and Ryan, The Four Seasons, The Lucie Arnaz Show, The Thorns. Movies: The Lindbergh Kidnapping Case, Girls in the Office, If Things Were Different, Seize the Day, Messiah on Mott Street, A Question of Honor, A Different Affair, Our Sons, Not in My Family. Guest: The Defenders, Phyllis, Storefront Lawyers, MacMillan, Trapper John, Love American Style, Love Boat, Hotel.

ROBERTS, WILLIAM: Writer, Producer. b. Los Angeles, CA. e. U. of Southern California.

PICTURES: The Mating Game, The Magnificent Seven, Wonderful World of the Brothers Grimm, Come Fly With Me, The Devil's Brigade, The Bridge At Remagen, One More Train to Rob, Red Sun, The Last American Hero, Posse, Ten to Midnight.

TELEVISION: created Donna Reed Show.

ROBERTSON, CLIFF: Actor. b. La Jolla, CA, Sept. 9, 1925.

STAGE: Mr. Roberts, Late Love, The Lady and the Tiger, The Wisteria Tree, Orpheus Descending (Theatre World Award), Love Letters.

PICTURES: Picnic (debut, 1955), Autumn Leaves, The Girl Most Likely, The Naked and the Dead, Gidget, Battle of the Coral Sea, As the Sea Rages, All in a Night's Work, Underworld USA, The Big Show, The Interns, My Six Loves, PT 109, Sunday in New York, The Best Man, 633 Squadron, Love Has Many Faces, Masquerade, Up From the Beach, The Honey Pot, The Devil's Brigade, Charly (Academy Award, 1968), Too Late the Hero, J.W. Coop (also dir., s.p.), The Great Northfield Minnesota Raid, Ace Eli and Rodger of the Skies, Man on a Swing, Out of Season, Three Days of the Condor, Shoot, Obsession, Dominique, Fraternity Row (narrator), Class, Brainstorm, Star 80, Shaker Run, Malone, Wild Hearts Can't Be Broken, Wind.

TELEVISION: Series: Falcon Crest. Guest: Philco-Goodyear, Studio One, Robert Montgomery Presents, The Game (Emmy Award), Batman. Movies: Man Without a Country, My Father's House, Washington: Behind Closed Doors, Dreams of Gold, Key to Rebecca, Henry Ford—The Man and the Machine, Dead Reckoning. Also spokesman for AT&T.

ROBERTSON, DALE: Executive, Actor, Producer. r.n. Dayle; b. Harrah, OK, July 14, 1923. e. Oklahoma Military Coll. Prof. prizefighter; U.S. Army Sept. 1942–June 1945; Film debut in Fighting Man of the Plains (1949). Star of Tomorrow, M.P. Herald—Fame Poll, 1951.

PICTURES: Caribou Trail, Two Flags West, Call Me Mister, Take Care of My Little Girl, Golden Girl, Lydia Bailey, Return of the Texan, Outcasts of Poker Flat, O. Henry's Full House, Farmer Takes a Wife, Gambler from Natchez, Sitting Bull, Son of Sinbad, Day of Fury, Dakota Incident, Hell Canyon Outlaws, Fast and Sexy, Law of the Lawless, Blood on the Arrow, The Walking Major, Coast of Skeletons, The One-Eyed Soldier.

TELEVISION: Series: Tales of Wells Fargo, The Iron Horse, Death Valley Days, Dynasty, Dallas, J.J. Starbuck. Movies: Scalplock, Melvin Purvis: G-Man, Kansas City Massacre, Last Ride of the Dalton Gang. Guest: The Love Boat, Matt Houston, Murder She Wrote.

ROBIN, DANY: Actress. b. Paris, France, 1927. Dancer since child. Played at the opera; acted on stage in Paris, then m.p.

PICTURES: Thirst of Men, Naughty Martine (L'Eventail), American Language debut in Act of Love, 1954. Holiday for Henrietta, Topaz, The Best House in London.

ROBINSON, BRUCE: Actor, Director, Writer. b. Kent, England, 1946. e. Central School of Speech and Drama. As actor appeared in 12 films but began writing novels and screenplays long before he gave up acting in 1975.

PICTURES: Actor: Romeo and Juliet (debut), The Story of Adele H. (last film as actor). Writer: The Killing Fields (Acad. Award nom.), Fat Man and Little Boy. Director-Writer: Withnail and I, How to Get Ahead in Advertising, Jennifer Eight.

ROBINSON, JAMES G.: Executive, Producer. e. Univ. of Maryland. Was photographer and Baltimore businessman prior to entering m.p. industry. Producer of films The Stone Boy, Where the River Runs Black, and Streets of Gold. Founded Morgan Creek Prods. in 1987, Morgan Creek Intl. in 1989, and The Morgan Creek Music Group in 1990. Chairman and CEO of Morgan Creek.

PICTURES: Exec. Prod. for Morgan Creek: Young Guns, Skin Deep, Renegades, Enemies a Love Story, Coupe de Ville, Nightbreed, Young Guns II, The Exorcist III, Pacific Heights, Robin Hood: Prince of Thieves, Freejack, White Sands, The Crush, True Romance, Ace Ventura.

ROBINSON, PHIL ALDEN: Director, Writer. b. Long Beach, NY. e. Union Col., Schenectady. Write and directed training films for Air Force, before writing two episodes for series Trapper John M.D.

PICTURES: All of Me (s.p.). Dir.-Writer: In the Mood, Field of Dreams, Sneakers.

TELEVISION: Series: Trapper John M.D. (writer), The George Burns Comedy Week (dir.)

ROCCO, ALEX: Actor. b. Cambridge, MA, Feb. 29, 1936.

PICTURES: St. Valentine's Day Massacre, Blood Mania, The Godfather, Slither, Detroit 9000, Friends of Eddie Coyle,

The Outside Man, Stanley, Freebie and the Bean, Three the Hard Way, Rafferty and the Gold Dust Twins, Hearts of the West, Fire Sale, House Calls, Rabbit Test, Voices, Herbie Goes Bananas, The Stunt Man, Nobody's Perfekt, The Entity, Cannonball Run II, Stick, Gotcha!, P.K. and the Kid, Return to Horror High, Dream a Little Dream, Wired, The Pope Must Die.
TELEVISION: Series: Three for the Road, The Famous Teddy Z (Emmy Award, 1990), Sibs. Movies: Hustling, The Blue Knight, A Question of Guilt, The Grass is Always Greener Over the Septic Tank, Badge of the Assassin, Rock 'n' Roll Mom, The First Time, A Quiet Little Neighborhood A Perfect Little Murder, An Inconvenient Woman, Boris & Natasha, Love Honor & Obey: The Last Mafia Marriage. Mini-Series: 79 Park Avenue.

RODDAM, FRANC: Director. b. Stockton, England, Apr. 29, 1946. Studied at London Film Sch. Spent two years as adv. copywriter/prod. with Ogilvy, Benson, Mather before joining BBC as documentary filmmaker. Founder of Union Pictures 1991.
PICTURES: Quadrophenia, The Lords of Discipline, Rain Forest (s.p. only), The Bride, Aria (sequence), War Party (also co-exec. prod.), K2.
TELEVISION: Director: The Family, Mini, Dummy. Creator: Aufwiedersehen Pet, Making Out, Masterchief, Harry.

ROEG, NICOLAS: Director, Cameraman. b. London, England. Aug. 15, 1928. m. actress Theresa Russell. Entered film industry through cutting rooms of MGM's British Studios, dubbing French films into English. Moved into prod. as clapper boy and part of photographer Freddie Young's crew at Marylebone Studios London 1947. Next became camera operator (Trials of Oscar Wilde, The Sundowners). Had first experience as cameraman on TV series (Police Dog and Ghost Squad). Debut as director on Performance; co-directed with Donald Cammell. First solo dir. film, Walkabout.
PICTURES: Cameraman: The Miniver Story, The Trial of Oscar Wilde, The Sundowners, Lawrence of Arabia, Jazz Boat, Information Received, The Great Van Robbery. Dir. of Photography: The Caretaker, Dr. Crippen, Nothing But the Best, Masque of the Red Death, A Funny Thing Happened on the Way to the Forum, Fahrenheit 451, Far from the Madding Crowd, The Girl-Getters, Petulia. Director-Cameraman: Performance (co.-dir.), Walkabout. Director: Don't Look Now, The Man Who Fell To Earth, Bad Timing, Eureka, Insignificance, Castaway, Aria (sequence, also co-s.p.), Track 29, The Witches, Without You I'm Nothing (exec. prod. only), Cold Heaven.
TELEVISION: Movie: Sweet Bird of Youth.

ROEVES, MAURICE: Actor, Director, Writer. b. Sunderland, England, Mar. 19, 1937. Ent. industry, 1964. Played Macduff to Alec Guinness's Macbeth, London stage. Early films: Ulysses, Oh! What a Lovely War, Young Winston, The Eagle Has Landed, Who Dares Wins. Dir. many stage plays.
TELEVISION: In USA and UK incl.: Scobie (series), The Gambler, Allergy, Magnum P.I., Remington Steele, Escape to Victoria, Inside the Third Reich, Journal of Bridgitte Hitler, Tutti Fruitti, Unreported Incident, Bookie, North & South Part II.

ROGERS, CHARLES (BUDDY): Actor. b. Olathe, KS, Aug. 13, 1904. p. Maude & Bert Henry Rogers. e. U. of Kansas, and was trained for screen in Paramount Picture Sch. Appeared in Fascinating Youth and others. In armed services W.W.II. In 1945 named w.p. & treas. Comet Prods., Inc. Assoc. prod. Sleep My Love, 1950, pres. PRB, Inc., prod. radio, video shows.
PICTURES: Wings, My Best Girl, Get Your Man, Abie's Irish Rose, The Lawyer's Secret, Road to Reno, Working Girls, This Reckless Age, Best of Enemies. Fox: Take a Chance, Dance Band, Old Man Rhythm, One In a Million, Let's Make a Night of It, This Way Please, Golden Hoofs, Mexican Spitfire's Baby, Sing for Your Supper, Mexican Spitfire at Sea, Mexican Spitfire Sees a Ghost, Don't Trust Your Husband, many others.

ROGERS, FRED: Television Host, Producer. b. Latrobe, PA, March 20, 1928. e. Rollins Coll., B.A., music composition, 1951; Pittsburgh Theol. Seminary, M. Div. 1962. In 1951 served as asst. prod. of NBC-TV's The Voice of Firestone and NBC-TV Opera Theatre. Later promoted to network floor dir., supervising Your Lucky Strike Hit Parade, Kate Smith Hour, etc. In Nov., 1953, joined WQED-TV in Pittsburgh, educational TV station, to handle programming. In 1954 started Children's Corner series, writing, producing and performing; it ran 7 years. In 1963 was ordained minister of Presbyterian Church, dedicated to working with children and families through media. Same year introduced Mister Rogers on Canadian Bdctg. Corp. of 15-min. daily program. Ran for one year—was similar in content to present half-hour program, Mister Rogers' Neighborhood. In 1964 programs were incorporated into larger, half-hour format on ABC affiliate in Pittsburgh. In 1966, 100 programs acquired by Eastern Educational Network, broadcast in Pittsburgh, and seen for first time in other cities. Program now carried over 300 PBS stations. Author of numerous non-fiction books for children

and adults and albums and videos released by Family Communication. Also prod. 20 part PBS series Old Friends New Friends, interview/documentary format for adults, 1978–9. Recipient of 2 Emmy Awards and over 25 honorary degrees from colleges and universities.

ROGERS, GINGER: Actress. r.n. Virginia Katherine McMath. b. Independence, MO, July 16, 1911. On stage in vaudeville, m.p. theat. presentations & musical comedy (Girl Crazy). Film debut 1930. Voted among ten best Money-Making Stars in M.P. Herald-Fame Poll 1935, '37. Autobiography: Ginger - My Story (1991).
PICTURES: Young Man of Manhattan (debut, 1930), Queen High, The Sap From Syracuse, Follow the Leader, Honor Among Lovers, The Tip Off, Suicide Fleet, Carnival Boat, The Tenderfoot, The 13th Guest, Hat Check Girl, You Said a Mouthful, 42nd Street, Broadway Bad, Gold Diggers of 1933, Professional Sweetheart, A Shriek in the Night, Don't Bet on Love, Sitting Pretty, Flying Down to Rio, Chance at Heaven, Finishing School, Twenty Million Sweethearts, Upperworld, The Gay Divorcee, Romance in Manhattan, Roberta, Star of Midnight, In Person, Top Hat, Follow the Fleet, Swing Time, Stage Door, Shall We Dance, Carefree, Having Wonderful Time, Vivacious Lady, The Story of Irene & Vernon Castle, Bachelor Mother, Fifth Avenue Girl, Tom Dick & Harry, Primrose Path, Kitty Foyle (Acad. Award, 1940), Lucky Partners, Roxie Hart, Tales of Manhattan, The Major & the Minor, Once Upon a Honeymoon, Tender Comrade, Lady in the Dark, I'll Be Seeing You, Weekend at the Waldorf, Heartbeat, Magnificent Doll, It Had to Be You, The Barkleys of Broadway, Perfect Strangers, Groom Wore Spurs, Storm Warning, We're Not Married, Dream Boat, Monkey Business, Forever Female, Black Widow, Twist of Fate, Tight Spot, First Traveling Saleslady, Oh Men! Oh Women!, Teenage Rebel, Quick Let's Get Married, Harlow.
TELEVISION: Guest: Perry Como Show, Pontiac, Pat Boone, Dinah Shore, Bob Hope, Ed Sullivan, Hollywood Palace, Steve Allen, Jack Benny. Special: Cinderella.

ROGERS, HENRY C.: Chairman of the Executive Comm. b. Irvington, NJ, April 19, 1914. e. U. of Pennsylvania, 1934. Formed Rogers & Cowan, 1949, with Warren Cowan; 1969, bd. chmn., Rogers & Cowan, Inc.

ROGERS, KENNY: Singer, Actor, Songwriter. b. Crockett, TX, Aug. 21, 1938. Country and western singer. Member Bobby Doyle Trio, Christy Minstrels, 1966–67; The First Edition 1967–76. On screen in Six Pack (1982).
TELEVISION: Series: Rollin' on the River. Movies: The Dream Makers, Kenny Rogers as The Gambler, Coward of the County, The Gambler Part II—The Adventure Continues, Wild Horses; Kenny Rogers as The Gambler Part III—The Legend Continues, The Gambler Returns: Luck of the Draw, Rio Diablo. Specials: Kenny, Dolly & Willie: Something Inside So Strong, Christmas in America.

ROGERS, LAWRENCE H., II: Executive. b. Trenton, NJ, Sept. 6, 1921. e. Princeton U. 1942, U.S. Army, 1942–1946; WSAZ, Huntington, WV. Radio & TV. V.P. & gen. mgr., 1949–55; WSAZ, Inc., President, 1955–59; Taft Broadcasting Co., v.p., 1959–63; Taft Broadcasting Co., President, 1963–76. cert., Harvard Business Sch., 1963; Vice Chairman, Hanna-Barbera Productions, L.A., CA, and Cinemobile Systems, Hollywood. Director: Cine Artists International, Hollywood; Cincinnati Financial Corp.; Pres., Omega Commun., Orlando, FL, 1976–83. Inter-Ocean Insurance Co., Cinti.; Cardinal Fund, Ohio; Federal Reserve Bank of Cleveland, Cincinnati Branch; Theater Development Fund, New York; Greater Cincinnati Foundation. Author, 1990, Orlando Shoot-Out.

ROGERS, MIMI: Actress. b. Coral Gables, FL, Jan. 27, 1956.
PICTURES: Blue Skies Again (debut, 1983), Gung Ho, Street Smart, Someone to Watch Over Me, The Mighty Quinn, Hider in the House, Desperate Hours, The Doors, The Rapture, The Palermo Connection, The Player, White Sands, Dark Horse.
TELEVISION: Series: The Rousters, Paper Dolls. Episodes: Magnum, P.I., Hart to Hart, Quincy, M.E., Hill Street Blues, Tales From the Crypt. Movies: Divorce Wars, Hear No Evil, You Ruined My Life, Fourth Story, Deadlock, Ladykiller, Bloodlines: Murder in the Family.

ROGERS, PETER: Executive. b. Rochester, Eng., Feb. 20, 1916. e. Kings Sch., Rochester. Journalist and in theatre and BBC; joined G. W. H. Productions 1941 as script writer; with Gainsborough Studios; asst. scenario ed. to Muriel Box; assoc. prod.; personal asst. to Sydney Box 1949.
PICTURES: Dear Murderer, Holiday Camp, When the Bough Breaks, Here Come the Huggetts, Huggetts Abroad, Vote for Huggett, It's Not Cricket, Marry Me, Don't Ever Leave Me, Appointment with Venus (Island Rescue), The Clouded Yellow, The Dog and the Diamonds (Children's Film Found), Up to His Neck, You Know What Sailors Are, Cash on Delivery, To Dorothy A Son, Gay Dog, Circus Friends, Passionate Stranger, After the Ball, Time Lock, My Friend

Charles, Chain of Events, Carry on Sergeant, Flying Scott, Cat Girl, Solitary Child, Carry On Teacher, Carry On Nurse, Carry On Constable, Please Turn Over, Watch Your Stern, The Tommy Steele Story, The Duke Wore Jeans, No Kidding, Carry On Regardless, Raising the Wind, Twice Around the Daffodils, Carry on Cruising, The Iron Maiden, Nurse on Wheels, Carry on Cabby, This Is My Street, Carry On Jack, Carry on Spying, Carry on Cleo, The Big Job, Carry on Cowboy, Carry on Screaming, Don't Lose Your Head, Follow that Camel, Carry on Doctor, Carry on Up the Khyber, Carry on Camping, Carry on Assault, Carry on Henry, Quest, Revenge, Carry on At Your Convenience, All Coppers Are. . ., Carry on Matron, Carry on Abroad, Bless This House, Carry on Girls, Carry on Dick, Carry on Behind, Carry on England, The Best of Carry On, Carry on Emmanuelle, Carry on Columbus.
TELEVISION: Ivanhoe series, Carry on Laughing, Carry on Laughing (2), What a Carry On (2), Laugh With the Carry On's.

ROGERS, ROY: Actor. r.n. Leonard Slye. b. Cincinnati, OH Nov. 5, 1911. m. actress-singer Dale Evans. Radio singer; many m.p. from 1937. Voted No. 1 Money-Making Western Star in M.P. Herald-Fame, 1943–54 inclusive; also voted one of ten best money-making stars in 1945, '46. Acting & prod. TV films, 1952 with wife, Dale Evans; one-hour spectaculars, Chevy Show, 1959–60; contracted for several TV specials and for nationwide appearances with Roy Rogers touring show in Canada & U.S., 1962; state fairs, rodeos since 1962; TV series. Happy Trails with Roy and Dale (cable). Star of 86 feature films and 104 TV episodes.
PICTURES: Under Western Stars, The Old Barn Dance, Billy the Kid Returns, Come On Rangers, Rough Riders, Round-Up, Frontier, Pony Express, Southward Ho!, In Old Caliente, Wall Street Cowboy, Heart of the Golden West, Sunset Serenade, Son of Paleface, MacKintosh and T.J.

ROGERS, WAYNE: Actor. b. Birmingham, AL, April 7, 1933. e. Princeton U.
PICTURES: Odds Against Tomorrow (debut, 1959), The Glory Guys, Chamber of Horrors, Cool Hand Luke, WUSA, Pocket Money, Once in Paris, The Gig, The Killing Time.
TELEVISION: Series: Edge of Night, Stagecoach West, M*A*S*H, City of the Angels, House Calls, High Risk (host). Movies: Attack on Terror: The FBI Versus the Ku Klux Klan, Making Babies II, It Happened One Christmas, The Top of the Hill, Chiefs, He's Fired She's Hired, The Lady from Yesterday, American Harvest, Drop-Out Mother, One Terrific Guy, Bluegrass, Passion and Paradise, Miracle Landing. Mini-Series: Chiefs. Exec. prod.: Perfect Witness, Age-Old Friends.

ROHMER, ERIC: Director. Writer. r.n. Jean Maurice Scherer. b. Nancy, France, April 4, 1920. Professor of literature. Film critic for La Gazette du Cinema and its successor Cahiers du Cinema which he edited, 1957–63. With Claude Chabrol wrote book on Alfred Hitchcock as a Catholic moralist, 1957. 1959 directorial debut, Le Signe du Lion. In 1962 began a series of 6 Moral Tales; from 1980 with The Aviator's Wife began another series of 7 films called Comedies and Proverbs. Staged Catherine de Heilbronn in Nanterre, 1979.
PICTURES: Short films: Presentation ou Charlotte et Son Steack (1961), Veronique et Son Cancre, Nadja a Paris, Place de L'etoile, Une Etudiante d'aujourd'hui, Fermiere a Montfaucon. Feature films (dir. & s.p.): Le Signe du Lion, La Boulangere de Monceau, La Carriere de Suzanne, La Collectionneuse, My Night at Maude's, Claire's Knee, Chloe in the Afternoon, The Marquise of O, Perceval, The Aviator's Wife, Le Beau Mariage, Pauline at the Beach, Full Moon in Paris, Summer, Boyfriends and Girlfriends, Four Adventures of Reinette and Mirabelle (also prod.), A Tale of Springtime.
TELEVISION: Carl Dreyer, Le Celluloid et le Marbre, Ville Nouvelle, Catherine de Heilbronn. Between 1964–69 directed series of documentaries for French TV: Les Cabinets et Physique du XVIII siecle, Les Metamorphoses du Paysage Industriel, Don Quichotte, Edgar Poe, Pascal, Louis Lumiere, etc.

ROIZMAN, OWEN: Cinematographer. b. Brooklyn, NY, Sept. 22, 1936.
PICTURES: The French Connection, The Gang That Couldn't Shoot Straight, Play It Again Sam, The Heartbreak Kid, The Exorcist, The Taking of Pelham 1-2-3, The Stepford Wives, Independence, Three Days of the Condor, The Return of the Man Called Horse, Network, Straight Time, Sgt. Pepper's Lonely Hearts Club Band, The Electric Horseman, The Black Marble, True Confessions, Absence of Malice, Taps, Tootsie, Vision Quest, I Love You to Death, Havana, The Addams Family, Grand Canyon.

ROLAND, GILBERT: Actor. r.n. Luis Alonso. b. Juarez, Mexico, Dec. 11, 1905. p. Father Francisco Alonso, a bullfighter in Spain. e. private schools in Mexico.
PICTURES: Plastic Age (1925) Camille, New York Nights, Call Her Savage, No Living Witness, She Done Him Wrong, Our Betters, After Tonight, Ladies Love Danger, Mystery Woman, Midnight Taxi, Thunder Trail, Last Train From Madrid,

Juarez, The Sea Hawk, My Life With Caroline, Her Carboard Lover, Angels With Broken Wings, Captain Kidd, Gay Cavalier, King of the Bandits, High Conquest, Robin Hood of Monterey, Pirates of Monterey, Dude Goes West, Malaya, We Were Strangers, Crisis, The Furies, The Torch, Bullfighter and the Lady, Mark of Renegade, Ten Tall Men, My Six Convicts, Glory Alley, Miracle of Fatima, Apache War Smoke, Bad & the Beautiful, Thunder Bay, Diamond Queen, Beneath the 12-Mile Reef, French Line, Underwater, The Racers, That Lady, Treasure of Pancho Villa, Bandido, Around the World in 80 Days, Three Violent People, The Midnight Story, Last of the Fast Guns, Appointment With a Shadow, Wild and the Innocent, The Big Circus, Guns of the Timberland, Samar, Cheyenne Autumn, The Reward, Any Gun Can Play, Christian Licorice Store, Islands in the Stream, Caboblanco, Barbarosa.
TELEVISION: Guest: High Chaparral, Bonanza, Alfred Hitchcock Presents, The FBI, Gunsmoke, The Fugitive, etc.

ROLLE, ESTHER: Actress. b. Pompano Beach, FL, Nov. 8, 1922. e. New School for Social Research. An original member of Negro Ensemble Co. in N.Y. Has appeared both off and on Bdwy (in The Blacks, Amen Corner, Blues for Mister Charlie, Don't Play Us Cheap, Member of the Wedding) and in several TV series.
PICTURES: Nothing But a Man, Cleopatra Jones, P.K. and the Kid, The Mighty Quinn, Driving Miss Daisy, House of Cards.
TELEVISION: Guest roles: N.Y.P.D., Like It Is, Darkroom, The Winners, The Grand Baby. Regular on series: One Life to Live, Maude, Good Times. Movies: I Know Why the Caged Bird Sings, Summer of My German Soldier (Emmy Award), A Raisin in the Sun, Age-Old Friends, The Kid Who Loved Christmas.

ROLLINS, HOWARD: Actor. b. Baltimore, MD, Oct. 17, 1950. e. Towson State Coll. NY stage in We Interrupt This Program, Traps, Streamers, The Mighty Gents, Medal of Honor Rag, G.R. Point.
PICTURES: Ragtime (debut, 1981; Acad. Award nom.), The House of God, A Soldier's Story, On the Block.
TELEVISION: Series: Our Street (PBS 1969–73), All My Children, Wildside, In the Heat of the Night. Mini-series: King, Roots: The Next Generation. Movies: My Old Man, Doctor's Story, He's Fired, She's Hired, The Boy King, The Children of Times Square. Johnnie Mae Gibson: FBI, With Murder in Mind. Specials: Eliza: Our Story, Dear America: Letters Home From Vietnam (reader).

ROLLINS, JACK: Producer. b. 1914. Co-founder of talent management firm Rollins, Joffe, Mora and Brezner Inc. handling careers of Woody Allen, Nichols and May, Robin Williams, Robert Klein, David Letterman, Dick Cavett, Billy Crystal.
PICTURES: Co-prod./exec.prod. with Charles Joffe: Take the Money and Run, Bananas, Everything You Always Wanted to Know About Sex..., Sleeper, Love and Death, The Front, Annie Hall, Interiors, Manhattan, Stardust Memories, Zelig, Broadway Danny Rose (also actor), The Purple Rose of Cairo, Hannah and Her Sisters, Radio Days, September, Another Woman, New York Stories (Oedipus Wrecks), Crimes and Misdemeanors, Alice, Shadows and Fog, Husbands and Wives, Manhattan Murder Mystery.
TELEVISION: Prod./exec. prod.: The Dick Cavett Show, Late Night With David Letterman.

ROMAN, LAWRENCE: Writer. b. Jersey City, NJ, May 30, 1921. e. UCLA, 1943. Author Bdwy plays: Under the Yum Yum Tree, P.S. I Love You, Alone Together. Wrote play, Buying Out, prod. in Buffalo, N.Y.; wrote play Crystal, Crystal Chandelier, (prod. in Stockbridge, Mass); Coulda, Woulda, Shoulda (prod. in Berlin, Germany), Moving Mountains.
PICTURES: Drums Across the River, Vice Squad, Naked Alibi, One Desire, Man from Bitter Ridge, Kiss Before Dying, Slaughter on Tenth Avenue, Under the Yum Yum Tree, The Swinger, Paper Lion, Red Sun, A Warm December, McQ.
TELEVISION: Movies: Anatomy of an Illness; Badge of the Assassin; Three Wishes for Jamie, Final Verdict, The Ernest Green Story.

ROMAN, RUTH: Actress. b. Boston, MA, Dec. 23, 1924. p. professionals. e. Girls H.S., Boston; Bishop Lee Dramatic Sch. Started career with little theatre groups: New Eng. Repertory Co., Elizabeth Peabody Players. Chicago Theatre includes Night of the Iguana, Two for the Season (Sarah Siddons Award). Screen debut in Universal serial, Queen of the Jungle, then minor roles; author stories, The Whip Son, The House of Seven Gables.
PICTURES: Good Sam, Belle Starr's Daughter, The Window, Champion, Barricade, Beyond the Forest, Always Leave Them Laughing, Colt .45, Three Secrets, Dallas, Strangers on a Train, Tomorrow is Another Day, Invitation, Lightning Strikes Twice, Starlift, Mara Maru, Young Man With Ideas, Blowing Wild, Far Country, Shanghai Story, Tanganyika, Down Three Dark Streets, Joe Macbeth, Bottom of the Bottle, Great Day in the Morning, Rebel in Town, Five Steps to Danger, Bitter Victory, Desert Desperadoes, Look in Any

Window, Miracle of the Cowards (Spanish), Love Has Many Faces, Impulse, The Killing Kind, The Baby, Day of the Animals, Echoes.
TELEVISION: *Series*: The Long Hot Summer, Knots Landing. *Guest*: Naked City, Route 66, The Defenders, Breaking Point, Eleventh Hour, Producers Showcase, Dr. Kildare, Murder She Wrote, Cannon, Ironside. *Movies*: The Old Man Who Cried Wolf, Incident in San Francisco, Go Ask Alice, Punch and Jody, The Sacketts.

ROMERO, CESAR: Actor. b. New York, NY, Feb. 15, 1907. e. Collegiate Sch., Riverdale Country Sch. In U.S. Coast Guard, W.W.II. In 1927 on N.Y. stage.
PICTURES: The Thin Man (debut, 1934), Cheating Cheaters, British Agent, Show Them No Mercy, Metropolitan, Cardinal Richeleu, Love Before Breakfast, 15 Maiden Lane, Armored Car, She's Dangerous, Dangerously Yours, Rendezvous, Wee Willie Winkie, Happy Landing, My Lucky Star, Five of a Kind, The Return of the Cisco Kid, The Little Princess, The Gay Caballero, Cisco Kid and the Lady, Charlie Chan at Treasure Island, Great American Broadcast, Wintertime, Coney Island, Captain from Castile, Beautiful Blonde from Bashful Bend, Deep Waters, Julia Misbehaves, That Lady in Ermine, Diamond Jim Brady, Clive of India, Weekend in Havana, Springtime in the Rockies, Tales of Manhattan, Tall, Dark and Handsome, Once a Thief, The Jungle, Lost Continent, FBI Girl, Frontier Marshall, Happy Go Lovely, Scotland Yard Inspector, Prisoners of the Casbah, Shadow Man, The Americano, Vera Cruz, The Racers, Around the World in Eighty Days, Leather Saint, Ocean's 11, Pepe, Seven Women From Hell, If a Man Answers, The Castillan, Donovan's Reef, A House is Not a Home, Two on a Guillotine, Sergeant Deadhead, Marriage on the Rocks, Batman, Hot Millions, Skidoo, Latitude Zero, A Talent for Loving, Crooks and Coronets, Target: Harry, Midas Run, The Computer Wore Tennis Shoes, Madigan's Millions, The Proud and the Damned, Soul Soldier, Now You See Him Now You Don't, The Spectre of Edgar Allan Poe, The Strongest Man in the World, Carioca Tiger, The Story of Father Kino, Lust in the Dust, Mortuary Academy, Simple Justice, Judgment Day.
TELEVISION: Series: Your Chevrolet Showroom (emcee), Passport to Danger, Take a Good Look (panelist), Batman (frequent guest), Falcon Crest. Guest on many series incl. Bonanza, Mod Squad, Fantasy Island, Murder She Wrote, Love American Style. Movie: Don't Push I'll Charge When I'm Ready.

ROMERO, GEORGE A.: Director, Writer. b. New York, NY, 1940. e. Carnegie-Mellon Univ.
PICTURES: *Dir., s.p., cameraman*: Night of the Living Dead, There's Always Vanilla, The Crazies, Jack's Wife (also ed.). *Director*: Martin (also ed., s.p., actor), Dawn of the Dead, Knightriders (also s.p.), Creepshow (also co-ed.), Day of the Dead (also s.p., edit.), Monkey Shines (also s.p.), Night of the Living Dead (s.p., co-exec. prod.), Two Evil Eyes (The Facts in the Case of M. Valdemar; also s.p.), The Dark Half (also s.p., exec. prod.).
TELEVISION: Tales from the Dark Side (exec. prod., s.p.).

ROOKER, MICHAEL: Actor. b. Jasper, AL, 1955. e. Goodman School of Drama. Studied Japanese martial art of Aikido prior to establishing himself in Chicago theatre, where he appeared in Union Boys, The Crack Walker and Moon Children.
PICTURES: Streets of Fire (debut, 1984), Light of Day, Rent-a-Cop, Eight Men Out, Mississippi Burning, Sea of Love, Music Box, Henry: Portrait of a Serial Killer, Days of Thunder, JFK, The Dark Half, Cliffhanger, Tombstone.
TELEVISION: *Movie*: Afterburn.

ROONEY, ANDREW A: Writer, Producer. b. Albany, NY, Jan. 14, 1919. e. Colgate U. Started career as writer for Arthur Godfrey then for Garry Moore, Sam Levenson, Victor Borge, wrote and produced documentaries, including Black History: Lost Stolen or Strayed (Emmy Award, 1969), An Essay on War, An Essay on Bridges, In Praise of New York City, Mr. Rooney Goes to Washington, etc. Regularly appears on 60 Minutes (CBS).

ROONEY, MICKEY: Actor. r.n. Joe Yule, Jr. b. Brooklyn, NY, Sept. 23, 1920. Son of Joe Yule & Nell Carter, vaudeville performers. U.S. Army, W.W.II. In vaudeville during early infancy with parents and others before m.p. debut and after; from age of 5 to 12 created screen version of Fontaine Fox newspaper comic character Mickey McGuire in series of short subjects of that title, also appeared in feature Orchids and Ermine. Adopting name of Mickey Rooney, ret. to vaudeville; resumed screen career 1932. Special Academy Award 1940 for Andy Hardy characterization; voted among first ten Money-Making Stars in M.P. Herald-Fame Poll. 1938–43. Broadway: Sugar Babies (debut, 1979), The Will Rogers Follies. Regional: W.C., Lend Me a Tenor. Autobiographies: i.e. (1965), Life is Too Short (1991). Honorary Academy Award, 1983.
PICTURES: Orchids and Ermine (feature debut, 1927), Emma, The Beast of the City, Sin's Pay Day, High Speed, Officer Thirteen, Fast Companions, My Pal the King, The Big Cage, The Life of Jimmy Dolan, The Big Chance, Broadway

to Hollywood, The World Changes, The Chief, Beloved, I Like It That Way, Love Birds, Half a Sinner, The Lost Jungle, Manhattan Melodrama, Upperworld, Hide-Out, Chained, Blind Date, Death on the Diamond, The County Chairman, Reckless, The Healer, A Midsummer Night's Dream, Ah Wilderness, Riff-Raff, Little Lord Fauntleroy, The Devil is a Sissy, Down the Stretch, Captains Courageous, Slave Ship, A Family Affair, Hoosier Schoolboy, Live Love and Learn, Thoroughbreds Don't Cry, You're Only Young Once, Love is a Headache, Judge Hardy's Children, Hold That Kiss, Lord Jeff, Love Finds Andy Hardy, Boys Town, Stablemates, Out West With the Hardys, The Adventures of Huckleberry Finn, The Hardys Ride High, Andy Hardy Gets Spring Fever, Babes in Arms (Acad. Award nom.), Judge Hardy and Son, Young Tom Edison, Andy Hardy Meets Debutante, Strike Up the Band, Andy Hardy's Private Secretary, Men of Boy's Town, Life Begins for Andy Hardy, Babes on Broadway, The Courtship of Andy Hardy, A Yank at Eton, Andy Hardy's Double Life, The Human Comedy (Acad. Award nom.), Girl Crazy, Thousands Cheer, Andy Hardy's Blonde Trouble, National Velvet, Love Laughs at Andy Hardy, Killer McCoy, Summer Holiday, Words and Music, The Big Wheel, Quicksand, He's a Cockeyed Wonder, The Fireball, My Outlaw Brother, The Strip, Sound Off, All Ashore, Off Limits, A Slight Case of Larceny, Drive a Crooked Road, The Atomic Kid, Bridges at Toko-Ri, The Twinkle in God's Eye, Francis in the Haunted House, The Bold and the Brave (Acad. Award nom.), Magnificent Roughnecks, Operation Mad Ball, Baby Face Nelson, Andy Hardy Comes Home, A Nice Little Bank That Should Be Robbed, The Last Mile, The Big Operator, Platinum High School, The Private Lives of Adam and Eve, Breakfast at Tiffany's, King of the Roaring Twenties, Requiem for a Heavyweight, Everything's Ducky, It's a Mad Mad Mad Mad World, Secret Invasion, 24 Hours to Kill, The Devil in Love, Ambush Bay, How to Stuff a Wild Bikini, The Extraordinary Seaman, Skidoo, The Comic, 80 Steps to Jonah, The Cockeyed Cowboys of Calico County, Hollywood Blue, B.J. Lang Presents (The Manipulator), Richard, Pulp, The Godmothers (also s.p., music), Ace of Hearts, Thunder County, That's Entertainment, Journey Back to Oz (voice), From Hong Kong With Love, Rachel's Man, Find the Lady, The Domino Principle, Pete's Dragon, The Magic of Lassie, The Black Stallion (Acad. Award nom.), Arabian Adventure, The Fox and the Hound (voice), The Emperor of Peru, The Black Stallion Returns, The Care Bears Movie (voice), Erik the Viking, My Heroes Have Always Been Cowboys, The Legend of Wolf Mountain, Little Nemo (voice), The Milky Life (La Vida Lactea), Revenge of the Red Baron.
TELEVISION: *Series*: Hey Mickey, One of the Boys, The Black Stallion. *Many specials including*: Playhouse 90, Pinocchio, Eddie, Somebody's Waiting, The Dick Powell Theater. *Movies*: Evil Roy Slade, My Kidnapper My Love, Leave 'Em Laughing, Bill (Emmy Award, 1982), Senior Trip, Bill: On His Own, It Came Upon the Midnight Clear, Bluegrass, Home for Christmas, The Gambler Returns: Luck of the Draw. Many guest appearances including The Golden Girls, The Judy Garland Show, Naked City, Wagon Train, Twilight Zone, The Lucy Show, Hollywood Squares, Night Gallery, The Love Boat.

ROOS, FRED: Producer. b. Santa Monica, CA, May 22, 1934. e. UCLA, B.A. Directed documentary films for Armed Forces Radio and Television Network. Worked briefly as agent for MCA and story editor for Robert Lippert Productions. Worked as casting dir. in 1960s and served as casting dir. on The Godfather, beginning longtime association with filmmakers Francis Coppola and George Lucas.
PICTURES: The Conversation, The Godfather Part II, Apocalypse Now, The Black Stallion, The Escape Artist (exec. prod.), The Black Stallion Returns, Hammett, One From the Heart, The Outsiders, Rumble Fish, The Cotton Club, One Magic Christmas, Seven Minutes in Heaven, Peggy Sue Got Married (special consultant), Barfly, Gardens of Stone (co-exec. prod.), Tucker: The Man and His Dream, New York Stories (Life Without Zoe), Wait Until Spring Bandini, The Godfather Part III, Hearts of Darkness: A Filmmaker's Apocalypse (exec. prod.), The Secret Garden.
TELEVISION: Series: The Outsiders (exec. prod.). Movie: Montana.

ROOT, WELLS: Writer. b. Buffalo, NY, March 21, 1900. e. Yale U. Drama ed., NY World; dramatic and film critic, Time mag.; fiction, articles, various magazines; many TV dramas, various programs.
PICTURES: I Cover the Waterfront, Tiger Shark, Bird of Paradise, Prisoner of Zenda, Magnificent Obsession, Texas Across the River.

ROSE, ALEX: Producer. r.n. Alexandra Rose. b. Jan. 20, 1946. e. U. of WI, BS. Started in m.p. distribution with Medford Films. Later became asst. sls. mgr. for New World Pictures.
PICTURES: *co-prod.*: Drive-In, I Wanna Hold Your Hand, Big Wednesday, Norma Rae, Nothing in Common (solo prod.), Overboard (co-prod.), Quigley Down Under, Frankie and Johnny.

TELEVISION: Nothing in Common (co-exec. prod. with Garry Marshall), *Pilots*: Norma Rae, Just Us Kids.

ROSE, JACK: Writer. b. Warsaw, Poland, Nov. 4, 1911. e. Ohio U. 1934, B.A. m. Audrey Mary Rose, writer, prod. Paramount Pictures, L.A.
PICTURES: Ladies Man, Sorrowful Jones, The Great Lover, It's A Great Feeling, Pale Face, My Favorite Brunette, Road to Rio, Daughter of Rosie O'Grady, Always Leave Them Laughing, On Moonlight Bay, Riding High, I'll See You in My Dreams, Room for One More, April in Paris, Trouble Along the Way, Living it Up, Seven Little Foys, Houseboat, Five Pennies, Beau James, It Started in Naples, On the Double, Papa's Delicate Condition, Who's Got the Action?, Who's Been Sleeping in My Bed?, A Touch of Class, The Duchess and the Dirtwater Fox, Lost and Found, The Great Muppet Caper.
TELEVISION: Academy Awards (1988, writer).

ROSE, REGINALD: Writer. b. New York, NY, Dec. 10, 1921. e. City Coll. of New York. Worked as clerk, publicist, Warner Bros.; adv. acct. exec., copy chief; U.S. Air Force, W.W.II; first TV play, Bus to Nowhere, 1951; since then numerous TV plays, Studio One, Playhouse 90. Creator of The Defenders, other programs.
PICTURES: Crime in the Streets, 12 Angry Men, Dino, Man of the West, The Man in the Net, Baxter, Somebody Killed Her Husband, The Wild Geese, The Sea Wolves, Whose Life Is It Anyway?, Wild Geese II, The Final Option.
TELEVISION: Dear Friends, Thunder on Sycamore Street, Tragedy in a Temporary Town, My Two Loves, The Rules of Marriage, Studs Lonigan, Escape from Sobibor.

ROSE, STEPHEN: Executive. Entered m.p. industry in 1964 with Columbia Pictures; named adv. dir. In 1970 joined Cinema V Distributing, Inc. as dir. of adv.; left in 1971 to take post at Cinemation Industries, where was named v.p. and bd. member. In 1975 joined Paramount Pictures as dir. of adv.; promoted to v.p./adv. In 1979 formed Barrich Prods. with Gordon Weaver. In Feb., 1982, rejoined Paramount as v.p., mktg; 1983, named v.p. of mktg. for Paramount; sr. v.p., mktg., 1983. Resigned in 1984 to form Barrich Marketing with Gordon Weaver.

ROSEN, ROBERT L.: Producer. b. Palm Springs, CA, Jan. 7, 1937. e. U. of Southern Calif.
PICTURES: French Connection II; Black Sunday; Prophecy; Going Ape; The Challenge; Courage (also dir.); Porky's Revenge, World Gone Wild, Dead-Bang (exec. prod.). *Exec. in chg. of prod.*: Little Big Man, Le Mans, The Reivers, Rio Lobo, Big Jake, Scrooge, Fourth War (Line Producer).
TELEVISION: Gilligan's Island, Hawaii Five-O, Have Gun Will Travel.

ROSENBERG, FRANK P.: Producer, Writer. b. New York, NY, Nov. 22, 1913. e. Columbia U., NYU. Joined Columbia 1929; writer m.p. novelizations & radio dramatizations; 1933, conceived and wrote script for first-ever ship-to-shore CBS network broadcast for Lady for a Day; exploit, mgr., 1941; apptd. national dir. adv., publicity, exploitation, Columbia Pictures, 1944. Pub. dir. M.P. Victory Loan, 1945; dir. pub. Columbia Pictures Studios, Hollywood, 1946. Resigned 1947 to enter production. Co-prod. Man Eater of Kumaon. Collab. adapt., assoc. prod. Where the Sidewalk Ends.
PICTURES: Man Eater of Kumaon, Where the Sidewalk Ends (co-adapt.), The Secret of Convict Lake, Return of the Texan, The Farmer Takes a Wife, King of the Khyber Rifles, Illegal, Miracle in the Rain, The Girl He Left Behind, One-Eyed Jacks, Critic's Choice, Madigan, The Steagle (exec. prod.), The Reincarnation of Peter Proud, Gray Lady Down.
TELEVISION: Exec. prod. and prod. for Schlitz Playhouse programs during 1957–58; prod., The Troubleshooters; exec. prod., Arrest and Trial, 1963–64; exec. prod. Kraft Suspense Theatre, 1964–65; v.p. MCA Universal 1964–9; co-exec. prod., CBS tv movie Family of Strangers.

ROSENBERG, GRANT E.: Executive. b. San Francisco, CA, 1952. e. Univ. of Cal. at Davis. Started career in research dept., NBC; 1977, joined Paramount in research and later in development; 1984, v.p., dramatic dev.; then sr. v.p., dev., for TV group, Paramount. 1985, named sr. v.p., network TV for Walt Disney Pictures; 1988, named pres., Lee Rich Productions, TV div., and exec. prod. of Molloy TV series. 1990, writer, prod., Paramount TV. Series: MacGyver (writer), Star Trek: The Next Generation (writer), Time Trax (exec. prod., creator). Writer, prod. for Lorimar TV.

ROSENBERG, RICHARD K.: Executive, Attorney. b. Paterson, NJ, Apr. 4, 1942. e. Indiana Univ. Corporation & entertainment attorney for major corps. and celebrities. Formed RKR Entertainment Group in 1977 with subsidiaries RKR Releasing, RKR Artists and RKR Productions. Subsequently consolidated into RKR Pictures Inc. Films include Alice Sweet Alice (a.k.a. Holy Terror), Hell's Angels Forever, Mother Lode, Best Revenge, The Wild Duck, Primary Motive, Fatal Past.

ROSENBERG, RICK: Producer. b. Los Angeles, CA. e. Los Angeles City Coll., UCLA. Started career in mail room of Columbia Pictures, then asst. to prod. Jerry Bresler on Major Dundee and Love Has Many Faces. Asst. to Col. v.p., Arthur Kramer. Was assoc. prod. on The Reivers and in 1970 prod. first feature, Adam at Six A.M., with Bob Christiansen, with whom co-prod. all credits listed below.
PICTURES: Adam at Six A.M., Hide in Plain Sight.
TELEVISION: Suddenly Single, The Glass House, A Brand New Life, The Man Who Could Talk to Kids, The Autobiography of Miss Jane Pittman, I Love You . . . Goodbye, Queen of the Stardust Ballroom, Born Innocent, A Death in Canaan, Strangers, Robert Kennedy and His Times, Kids Don't Tell, As Summers Die, Gore Vidal's Lincoln, Red Earth White Earth, Heist.

ROSENBERG, STUART: Director, Producer. b. New York, NY, Aug. 11, 1927. e. NYU. Emmy nom: 1963; DGA noms: 1962–5.
PICTURES: Murder, Inc. (co-dir.), Cool Hand Luke, The April Fools, Move, WUSA, Pocket Money, The Laughing Policeman (also prod.), The Drowning Pool, Voyage Of The Damned, The Amityville Horror, Love and Bullets, Brubaker, The Pope of Greenwich Village, Let's Get Harry (under pseudonym Allan Smithee), My Heroes Have Always Been Cowboys.
TELEVISION: Numerous episodes of such series as The Untouchables, Naked City, The Defenders (Emmy Award, 1963), Espionage, Chrysler Theatre, Twilight Zone, Alfred Hitchcock Theater.

ROSENFELT, FRANK E.: Executive. b. Peabody, MA, Nov. 15, 1921. e. Cornell U., B.S.; Cornell Law Sch., L.L.B. Served as atty. for RKO Radio Pictures, before joining MGM in 1955 as member of legal dept. Appt. secty. in 1966. Named v.p., gen. counsel in 1969 and pres. in 1973. In 1974 also named chief exec. officer. Bd. chmn. & chief exec. officer, MGM to 1981; now vice chmn., MGM/UA Communications Co. Member: Bd. of Governors, Academy of M.P. Arts & Sciences for 9 years. Retired from MGM/UA in Aug. 1990, now consultant to MGM-Pathe Commun. Co..

ROSENFELT, SCOTT: Producer, Director. b. Easton, PA, Dec. 20, 1955. e. NYU.
PICTURES: *Producer*: Teen Wolf, Extremities, Russkies, Mystic Pizza, Big Man on Campus (co-prod.), Home Alone, Family Prayers (dir.).

ROSENFIELD, JONAS, JR.: Executive. b. Dallas, TX, June 29, 1915. e. U. of Miami, A.B. In U.S. Navy, W.W.II. Warner Bros. advertising copy dept., 1936–40; adv. mgr. Walt Disney, 1941; a founder & pres. N.Y. Screen Publicists Guild. Advertising manager and director, 20th Cent.-Fox, 1941–1950; v.p. Italian Films Export, 1950–55; v.p. in chg. adv. pub. expl. Columbia Pictures, 1955–63; v.p. worldwide advertising, publicity and promotion, 20th Century-Fox, 1963–77; film mktg. consultant, 1977–78; lecturer in mktg., U. of Southern California, 1978–79; v.p. in chg. of worldwide mktg., Melvin Simon Productions, 1979–1981; Filmways Pictures as exec. v.p., worldwide adv./pub., promo. 1982; lecturer adjunct, U.S.C. Sch. of Cinema & TV, 1982–84; pres. American Film Marketing Association, 1983 to present.

ROSENMAN, HOWARD: Producer. b. Brooklyn, NY, Feb. 1, 1945. e. Brooklyn Col. Asst. to Sir Michael Benthall on Bdwy. show; prod., Benton & Bowles Agency; ABC-TV; RSO Prods. Now co-pres., Sandollar Prods.
PICTURES: Sparkle, The Main Event, Resurrection, Lost Angels, Gross Anatomy, True Identity, Father of the Bride, Shining Through, Straight Talk, A Stranger Among Us, Buffy the Vampire Slayer.
TELEVISION: *Movies*: Isn't It Shocking? Altogether Now, Death Scream, Virginia Hill, Killer Bees. *Specials*: Common Threads: Stories from the Quilt (co-exec. prod.), Tidy Endings.

ROSENMAN, LEONARD: Composer. b. New York, NY, Sept. 7, 1924. Winner of two Oscars: Barry Lyndon, Bound for Glory; and two Emmys: Sybil, Friendly Fire.
PICTURES: East of Eden, Cobweb, Rebel Without a Cause, Edge of the City, The Savage Eye, The Chapman Report, Fantastic Voyage, Hellfighters, Beneath the Planet of the Apes, Barry Lyndon, Birch Interval, Race With the Devil, Bound For Glory, A Man Called Horse, The Car, September 30, 1955, The Enemy of the People, The Lord of the Rings, Promises in the Dark, Prophecy, Hide in Plain Sight, The Jazz Singer, Making Love, Miss Lonely Hearts, Cross Creek, Heart of the Stag, Star Trek IV: The Voyage Home, Robocop 2.
TELEVISION: Sylvia, Friendly Fire, City in Fear, Murder in Texas, Vanished, The Wall, Miss Lonelyhearts, Celebrity, The Return of Marcus Welby MD, Heartsounds, First Steps, Promised a Miracle, Keeper of the City.

ROSENSTEIN, GERTRUDE: Director. b. New York, NY. e. Barnard Coll., B.A., Neighborhood Playhouse. exec. asst. to George Balanchine & Lincoln Kirstein, N.Y.C. Ballet. Assoc. with Gian Carlo Menotti, Festival of Two Worlds, Spoleto, Italy.

TELEVISION: Assoc. dir., NBC Opera, Emmy Awards, Kennedy Memorial Mass; dir., Concentration. TV staff dir., NBC. Now freelance director, news programs, election coverage, music and dance programs, commercials. Governor, NY Television Academy. Member: Emmy Awards committee.

ROSENTHAL, BUD: Executive. b. Brooklyn, NY, Mar. 21, 1934. e. Brooklyn Coll., B.A., 1954, NYU. U.S. Army, 1954–56; college correspondent, N.Y. Times; ent. m.p. ind. as associate editor, Independent Film Journal, 1957. Joined Columbia Pictures publicity dept. as trade paper contact and news writer, 1959 newspaper and syndicate contact 1960; national publicity mgr., Columbia Pictures Corp., 1962–67; asst. prod. Something For Everyone; pub. dir., Anderson Tapes, Such Good Friends; story ed. and casting dir., Sigma Prods., 1972–75; associate prod., Broadway play, Full Circle, 1973; assoc. prod., Rosebud, 1974; dir. intl. press relations, The Bluebird, 1975; Warner Bros. project coordinator, Superman, 1977–79; Superman II, 1980–81; Superman III, 1982–83; Columbia Pictures intl. mktg. coordinator, Ghostbusters, 1984–85; Tri-Star intl. mktg. coordinator, Labyrinth, 1986–87; Warner Bros. worldwide mktg. coordinator, Batman, 1988–89; project coordinator, Time Warner Presents The Earth Day Special, Warner Bros. Studios Rededication, Celebration of Tradition, 1990. Columbia/TriStar Intl. mktg. co-ord., Boyz N the Hood, etc; WB Intl. mktg. co-ord., Batman Returns, 1992.

ROSENTHAL, RICK: Director. b. New York, NY, June 15, 1949. Launched career as filmmaker-in-residence with New Hampshire TV Network. Moved to Los Angeles to study at American Film Institute where filmed Moonface, 1973. Theatrical feature debut: Halloween II, 1981.
PICTURES: Bad Boys, American Dreamer, Russkies, Distant Thunder.
TELEVISION: Fire on the Mountain, Code of Vengeance, Secrets of Midland Heights, Nasty Boys, Devlin. Series: Life Goes Un.

ROSENZWEIG, BARNEY: Producer. b. Los Angeles, CA, Dec. 23, 1937. e. U. of Southern California, 1959. m. actress Sharon Gless.
TELEVISION: Prod.: Daniel Boone (series), Men of the Dragon, One of My Wives Is Missing, Charlie's Angels (series), Angel on My Shoulder, American Dream (pilot), John Steinbeck's East of Eden (mini-series; Golden Globe Award). Exec. prod.: This Girl for Hire, Cagney and Lacey (series; Emmy Awards for Best Drama Series: 1985, 1986), The Trials of Rosie O'Neill (series).
PICTURES: Morituri (assoc. prod.), Do Not Disturb (assoc. prod.), Caprice (assoc. prod.), Who Fears the Devil (prod.).

ROSI, FRANCESCO: Director. b. Naples, Italy, 1922. Apprenticed as asst. to Visconti and Antonioni.
PICTURES: Red Shirts (co-dir.), The Challenge, Salvatore Giuliano, Hands Over the City, More Than a Miracle, Just Another War, Lucky Luciano, The Mattei Affair, (Christ Stopped at) Eboli, Three Brothers, Carmen, Chronicle of a Death Foretold, To Forget Palermo.

ROSS, DIANA: Singer, Actress. b. Detroit, MI, Mar. 26, 1944. Formed musical group at age 14 with two friends, Mary Wilson and Florence Ballard. In 1960 they auditioned for Berry Gordy, head of Motown Record Corp. and were hired to sing backgrounds on records for Motown acts. After completing high school, the trio was named the Supremes and went on tour with Motor Town Revue. Over period of 10 yrs. Supremes had 15 consecutive hit records and once had five consecutive records in no. one spot on charts. In 1969 Diana Ross went on her own, appearing on TV and in nightclubs.
PICTURES: Lady Sings the Blues (debut, 1972; Acad. Award nom.), Mahogany, The Wiz.
TELEVISION: Diana! (special; also exec. prod. & writer), Motown 25: Yesterday Today Forever, Motown Returns to the Apollo, Diana's World Tour.

ROSS, HERBERT: Director. b. New York, NY, May 13, 1927. m. Lee Radziwill. e. studied dance with Doris Humphrey, Helene Platova, Caird Leslie. Trained for stage with Herbert Berghof, 1946–50. As Bdwy dancer in Laffing Room Only, Beggars Holiday, Bloomer Girl, Look Ma I'm Dancing, Inside U.S.A., and with the American Ballet Theatre. Resident choreographer 1958–9 ABT for Caprichos, Concerto in D, The Maids, Tristan, Thief Who Loved a Ghost. Choreographer-Director on Broadway for A Tree Grows in Brooklyn (1951), The Gay Life, I Can Get It For You Wholesale, Tovarich, Anyone Can Whistle, Do I Hear a Waltz, On a Clear Day You Can See Forever, The Apple Tree. Also dir. revivals of Finian's Rainbow, Wonderful Town. Broadway dir.: Chapter Two. I Ought To Be in Pictures. Follies in Concert. Ent. m.p. ind. as choreographer for Carmen Jones, The Young Ones, Summer Holiday (also dir. musical sequences), Inside Daisy Clover, Dr. Doolittle, Funny Girl (also dir. musical numbers).
PICTURES: Goodbye Mr. Chips (debut, 1969), The Owl and the Pussycat, T.R. Baskin, Play It Again Sam, The Last of Sheila (also prod.), Funny Lady, The Sunshine Boys, The

Seven Percent Solution (also prod.), The Turning Point (also prod.), The Goodbye Girl, California Suite, Nijinsky (also prod.), Pennies from Heaven (also prod.), I Ought to Be in Pictures (also co-prod.), Max Dugan Returns (also prod.), Footloose, Protocol (also prod.), The Secret of My Success (also prod.), Dancers (also prod.), Steel Magnolias, My Blue Heaven (also prod.), True Colors (also prod.), Soapdish (exec. prod. only), Undercover Blues (also co-exec. prod.).
TELEVISION: Choreographer. Series: Milton Berle Show (also prod., 1952–57), Martha Raye Show, Bell Telephone Hour (also prod., dir.). Specials: Wonderful Town (also dir.), Meet Me in St. Louis, Jerome Kern Special, Bea Lillie and Cyril Ritchard Show (also dir.), The Fantastiks, The Fred Astaire Special (1963, dir.).

ROSS, KATHARINE: Actress. b. Los Angeles, CA, Jan. 29, 1943. m. actor Sam Elliott. e. Santa Rosa Coll. Joined the San Francisco Workshop, appeared in The Devil's Disciple, The Balcony. TV debut, 1962 in Sam Benedict segment.
TELEVISION: Movies: The Longest Hundred Miles, Wanted: The Sundance Woman, Murder by Natural Causes, Rodeo Girl, Murder in Texas, Marian Rose White, Shadow Riders, Travis McGee, Secrets of a Mother and Daughter, Conagher (also co-script). Guest: Ben Casey, The Bob Hope-Chrysler Theatre, The Virginian, Wagon Train, Kraft Mystery Theatre, The Lieutenant, The Road West. Series: The Colbys.
PICTURES: Shenandoah (debut, 1965), Mister Buddwing, The Singing Nun, Games, The Graduate (Golden Globe Award; Acad. Award nom.; voted Most Promising Female Newcomer), Hellfighters, Butch Cassidy and the Sundance Kid, Tell Them Willie Boy is Here, Fools, Get to Know Your Rabbit, They Only Kill Their Masters, The Stepford Wives, Voyage of the Damned, The Betsy, The Swarm, The Legacy, The Final Countdown, Wrong Is Right, Red-Headed Stranger.

ROSS, KENNETH: Writer. b. London, Sept. 16, 1941. Entered m.p. industry 1970.
TELEVISION: The Roundelay, ATV Network, 1963. The Messenger, CBC Network, 1966.
THEATRE: The Raft, London, 1964. Under The Skin, Glasgow, 1968. Mr. Kilt & The Great I Am, London, 1970.
PICTURES: Screenplays: Brother Sun, Sister Moon, Slag, The Reckless Years (also orig. story), Abelard & Heloise, The Day of the Jackal (So. Cal. M.P. Council Award; nom. for Writers' Guild, SFTA, and Golden Globe Awards), The Devil's Lieutenant, The Odessa File (nom. for Writers' Guild Award), Quest, (orig. story, s.p.), Black Sunday (Edgar Allen Poe Award, Mystery Writers of America, 1977), The Fourth War, Epiphany (orig. story, s.p.).

ROSSELLINI, ISABELLA: Actress. b. Rome, Italy, June 18, 1952. Daughter of Ingrid Bergman and Roberto Rossellini. Came to America 1972. Worked as translator for Italian News Bureau. Taught Italian at New Sch. for Social Research. Worked 3 years on second unit assignments for journalist Gianni Mina and as NY corr. for Ital. TV series, The Other Sunday. Model for Vogue, Harper's Bazaar, Italian Elle, Lancome Cosmetics.
PICTURES: A Matter of Time (debut 1976 with her mother), The Meadow, Il Papocchio, White Nights, Blue Velvet, Tough Guys Don't Dance, Siesta, Zelly and Me, Cousins, Les Dames Galantes, The Siege of Venice, Wild at Heart, Death Becomes Her, The Pickle, The Innocent, Fearless.
TELEVISION: Movies: The Last Elephant, Lies of the Twins. Guest: The Tracey Ullman Show. Special: The Gift.

ROSSO, LEWIS, T.: Executive. b. Hoboken, NJ, Feb. 3, 1909. Ent. m.p. ind. 1930; prod. & mgt. for Consolidated Film Ind., 1930–44; Republic Prod., 1944–50; prod. mgr. Republic, 1950–55; asst. sec'y and asst. treas. Republic Pictures Corp., 1959; exec. asst. to exec. prod. mgr., 20th Century-Fox Films, 1960; plant mgr., Samuel Goldwyn Studios, 1961–71; exec. admin. asst. plant mgr., The Burbank Studios, 1972–88.

ROSSOVICH, RICK: Actor. b. Palo Alto, CA, August 28, 1957. e. Calif. St. Univ. Sacramento (art history). Studied acting with coach Vincent Chase.
PICTURES: The Lords of Discipline (debut, 1983), Losin' It, Streets of Fire, The Terminator, Fast Forward, Warning Sign, Top Gun, Let's Get Harry, The Morning After, Roxanne, Paint It Black, The Witching Hour, Spellbinder, Navy SEALS, Cognac.
TELEVISION: Series: MacGruder and Loud, Sons and Daughters. Guest: Tales from the Crypt (The Switch). Special: 14 Going on 30. Movies: Deadly Lessons, The Gambler Returns: Luck of the Draw.

ROTH, BOBBY: Director, Writer, Producer.
PICTURES: The Boss' Son; Circle of Power; Independence Day; Heartbreakers.
TELEVISION: Episodes of Miami Vice, The Insiders, Crime Story. Movies: Tonight's the Night, The Man Who Fell to Earth, Dead Solid Perfect (dir., co-s.p.), Baja Oklahoma (dir., co-s.p.), The Man Inside.

ROTH, JOE: Executive, Producer, Director. b. New York, NY, 1948. Began career working as prod. assistant on commercials and feature films in San Francisco. Also ran the lights for improv group Pitchel Players. Moved with them to Los Angeles, and produced their shows incl. the $250,000 film Tunnelvision. In 1987 co-founder independent film prod. co. Morgan Creek Productions. 1989 left to become chairman of newly-formed Fox Film Corp., the theatrical film unit of 20th Century Fox Film Corp. Also named head of News Corp. unit. Resigned from Fox, Jan. 1993. Pres. & founder, Caravan Pictures.
PICTURES: *Producer*: Tunnelvision, Cracking Up, Americathon, Our Winning Season, The Final Terror, The Stone Boy, Where the River Runs Black, Bachelor Party, Off Beat, Streets of Gold (dir. debut), Revenge of the Nerds II (dir.). *Exec. prod.*: Young Guns, Dead Ringers, Skin Deep, Major League, Renegades, Coupe de Ville (dir.), Enemies: A Love Story, Pacific Heights.

ROTH, PAUL A.: Executive. b. Asheville, NC, March 28, 1930. e. U. of North Carolina, A.B. political science, 1948–51; George Washington U. Law Sch., 1951–52. U.S. Army 1952–55. Dist. Mgr. Valley Enterprises, Inc. 1955–56. Vice Pres. Roth Enterprises, Inc. 1956–65. Pres. Roth Enterprises, Inc. 1965–present. Pres., Valley Lanes Inc. 1975–present. V.P., CAPA Ltd. 1976–present. Pres., Carolina Cinema Corp., 1980–present. Pres., Thrashers Ocean Fries, 1987–present. Dir. Riggs Bank of Maryland, 1984–present. President NATO of Virginia 1971–73. Chmn. bd. NATO of Virginia, 1973–75. Member National NATO Board, 1971–present. Exec. Comm. NATO of Va. & Md., 1965–present. Variety Club Tent 11 Board Mem. 1959–65. President National NATO, 1973–75; chmn. National NATO bd. dir. 1975–77. Chmn., NATO Government Relations Committee, 1988–present. Member Foundation Motion Picture Pioneers, 1973–present. Member & advisory committee, Will Rogers Hospital, 1973–present. Trustee American Film Institute, 1973–75. Recipient: NATO Mid-Atlantic Exhibitor of the Year (1990), S.M. Hassanein Humanitarian Award at ShowEast (1991), ShoWest Award (1993).

ROTH, RICHARD A.: Producer. b. Beverly Hills, CA, 1943. e. Stanford U. Law Sch. Worked for L.A. law firm before beginning film career as lawyer and literary agent for Ziegler-Ross Agency. In 1970 left to develop s.p. Summer of '42 with Herman Raucher.
PICTURES: Summer of '42, Our Time, The Adventures of Sherlock Holmes' Smarter Brother, Julia, Outland, In Country (co-prod.).

ROTH, TIM: Actor. b. London, England, 1961. Started acting with various fringe theatre groups such as Glasgow Citizen's Theatre, The Oval House, and the Royal Court. Also on London stage in Metamorphosis.
PICTURES: The Hit, A World Apart, The Cook the Thief His Wife and Her Lover, Vincent & Theo, Rosencrantz and Guildenstern Are Dead, Jumpin at the Boneyard, Reservoir Dogs, Backsliding, Bodies Rest and Motion.
TELEVISION: *Specials/Movies* (BBC): Meantime, Made in Britain, Metamorphosis, Knuckle, Yellow Backs, King of the Ghetto, The Common Pursuit, Murder in the Heartland (U.S.).

ROTHMAN, THOMAS E: Executive. b. Baltimore, MD, Nov. 21, 1954. m. actress Jessica Harper. e. Brown U., B.A. 1976; Columbia Law Sch., J.D. 1980. Worked as law clerk with Second Circuit Court of Appeals 1981–82 before becoming partner in entertainment law firm, Frankfurt, Garbus, Klien & Selz 1982–87. In 1987 joined Columbia Pictures as exec. v.p. and asst. to pres., named exec. prod. v.p. Left in 1989 to join Samuel Goldwyn Co. as sr. v.p. and head of worldwide production.
PICTURES: Co-prod.: Down By Law, Candy Mountain.

ROTUNNO, GIUSEPPE: Cinematographer. b. Rome, Italy, March 19, 1923. Gained fame as leading cinematographer of Italian films working with Federico Fellini. Later worked in Hollywood.
PICTURES: Tosca, Monte Carlo Story, White Nights, The Naked Maja, On the Beach, Fast and Sexy, The Angel Wore Red, Five Branded Women, Rocco and His Brothers, Boccaccio '70, The Leopard, The Organizer, Juliet of the Spirits, The Bible, Anizo, Candy, Spirits of the Dead, Fellini Satyricon, The Secret of Santa Vittoria, Carnal Knowledge, Fellini's Roma, Man of La Mancha, Amarcord, Love and Anarchy, Fellini's Casanova, All Screwed Up, End of the World in Our Usual Bed in a Night Full of Rain, Orchestra Rehearsal, All That Jazz, City of Women, Popeye, Rollover, Five Days One Summer, And the Ship Sails On, American Dreamer, Desire, Nothing Left to Do But Cry, The Red Sonja, Hotel Colonial, Julia and Julia, Rent-a-Cop, Rebus, Haunted Summer, The Adventures of Baron Munchausen, Regarding Henry, Once Upon a Crime.
TELEVISION: The Scarlet and the Black.

ROUNDTREE, RICHARD: Actor. b. New Rochelle, NY, July 9, 1942. e. Southern Illinois U. Former model, Ebony Magazine Fashion Fair; joined workshop of Negro Ensemble Company, appeared in Kongi's Harvest, Man, Better Man, Mau Mau Room; played lead role in Philadelphia road company of The Great White Hope before film debut.
PICTURES: What Do You Say to a Naked Lady? (debut, 1970), Shaft, Embassy, Charley One-Eye, Shaft's Big Score, Embassy, Shaft in Africa, Earthquake, Diamonds, Man Friday, Portrait of a Hitman, Escape to Athena, Game for Vultures, An Eye for an Eye, Inchon, Q (The Winged Serpent), One Down Two to Go, The Big Score, Young Warriors, Killpoint, City Heat, Opposing Force, Jocks, Maniac Cop, Homer and Eddie, Angel III: The Final Chapter, The Party Line, Getting Even, American Cops, The Banker, Night Visitor, Crack House, Bad Jim, Lost Memories, Body of Influence, Deadly Rivals.
TELEVISION: *Series*: Shaft, Outlaws. *Movies*: Firehouse, The Fifth Missile, Christmas in Connecticut. *Mini-Series*: Roots, A.D.

ROURKE, MICKEY: Actor. b. Schenectady, NY, 1956. m. actress Carre Otis. Moved to Miami as a boy. Fought as an amateur boxer 4 years in Miami. Studied acting with Sandra Seacat while working as a nightclub bouncer, a sidewalk pretzel vendor and other odd jobs. Moved to LA, 1978. Debut: TV movie City in Fear (1978).
PICTURES: 1941 (debut, 1979), Fade to Black, Heaven's Gate, Body Heat, Diner (Natl. Society of Film Critics Award, 1982), Rumblefish, Eureka, The Pope of Greenwich Village, Year of the Dragon, 9½ Weeks, Angel Heart, A Prayer for the Dying, Barfly, Homeboy (also wrote orig. story), Francesco, Johnny Handsome, Wild Orchid, Desperate Hours, Harley Davidson and the Marlboro Man, White Sands.
TELEVISION: *Movies*: City in Fear, Rape and Marriage: The Rideout Case, Act of Love.

ROUSSELOT, PHILIPPE: Cinematographer. b. Meurthe et Moselle, France, 1945. e. Vaugirard Film Sch., Paris. Worked as camera assistant to Nestor Almendros on My Night at Maud's, Claire's Knee, Love in the Afternoon.
PICTURES: The Guinea Pig Couple, Adom ou le sang d'Abel, Paradiso, Pauline et l'ordinateur, Peppermint Soda, For Clemence, Cocktail Molotov, La Provinciale, A Girl From Lorraine, Diva (Cesar, Natl. Society of Film Critics, and Moscow Awards), The Jaws of the Wolf, The Moon in the Gutter, Thieves After Dark, The Emerald Forest, Therese (Cesar Award), Hope and Glory, Dangerous Liaisons, The Bear, We're No Angels, Too Beautiful for You, Henry and June, A River Runs Through It (Acad. Award), Sommersby.

ROWAN, DANIELLE: Executive. Began career with Paramount Pictures 1980; asst. to pres. & gen. sls. mgr. Canadian operations. 1984, transferred to N.Y. as asst. to sr. v.p., dist. 1985, appt. exec. administrator dist./mktg.

ROWE, ROY: Owner-operator, Rowe Amusement Co., Burgaw, NC. b. Burgaw, May 29, 1905. e. U. of North Carolina. Eng. instructor, private bus. coll., 1926–29; Publix Sch. for Mgrs., N.Y., 1930–31; mgr. theatres, Spartanburg, SC; Greensboro & Raleigh, NC; mgr., Warner Theatre, Pittsburgh, PA, 1931–34; city mgr. for Warner Theatres, Washington, PA, 1934–35; opened own theatres in NC 1935; member NC Senate, 1937, 1941, 1945, 1949, 1957, 1965; House of Rep., 1943; Major, Civil Air Patrol, W.W.II; pres. Carolina Aero Club, 1943–44; chmn. NC Aeornautics Comm., 1941–49; dir. Theatre Owners No. 8 & So. Car. 1943–45; pres., Theatre Owners of S.C. & N.C. 1944–45; pres., Assn. of Governing Boards of State Universities, 1964. Owned and operated motel, Carolina Beach, NC, 1965–67., Rowe Insurance Agency, 1967–69. Mem. Exec. Bd., U. of N.C. Trustees, 1969. Principal Clerk, NC Senate 1969–75. Retired. Now watercolor artist and world traveller.

ROWLAND, ROY: Director. b. New York, NY, Dec. 31, 1902. e. U. of Southern California, law. Script clerk; asst. dir.; asst. to late W. S. Van Dyke on Tarzan pictures; dir. of shorts, "How to" Benchley series; Crime Does Not Pay series. Pete Smith Specialties.
PICTURES: Think First, Stranger in Town, Lost Angel, Our Vines Have Tender Grapes, Tenth Avenue Angel, Night patrol, Ski Soldier, Boys' Ranch, Romance of Rosy Ridge, Killer McCoy, Scene of the Crime, Outriders, Excuse My Dust, Two Weeks With Love, Bugles in Afternoon, 5000 Fingers of Dr. T. Affair with a Stranger, The Moonlighter, Witness to Murder, Rogue Cop, Many Rivers to Cross, Hit the Deck, Meet Me in Las Vegas, Slander, Somewhere I'll Find Him, Gun Glory, The Seven Hills of Rome, The Girl Hunters, Gunfighters of Casa Grande, They Called Him Gringo, Tiger of the Seven Seas, Thunder Over the Indian Ocean.

ROWLANDS, GENA: Actress. b. Cambria, WI, June 19, 1934. e. U. of Wisconsin. Mother of actor Nicholas Cassavetes. Came to New York to attend American Acad. of Dramatic Arts, where met and married John Cassavetes. Made Bdwy. debut as understudy and then succeeded to role of The Girl in The Seven Year Itch. Launched as star with part in The Middle of the Night, which she played 18 mos.
PICTURES: The High Cost of Loving (debut, 1958), Lonely Are the Brave, The Spiral Road, A Child Is Waiting, Tony

Rome, Faces, Minnie and Moskowitz, A Woman Under the Influence (Acad. Award nom.), Two Minute Warning, The Brink's Job, Opening Night, Gloria (Acad. Award nom.), Tempest, Love Streams, Light of Day, Another Woman, Once Around, Ted and Venus, Night on Earth.
TELEVISION: Movies: Question of Love, Strangers: The Story of a Mother & Daughter, An Early Frost, The Betty Ford Story (Emmy Award, 1987), Montana, Face of a Stranger (Emmy Award, 1992), Crazy in Love, Silent Cries. Guest: The Philco TV Playhouse, Studio One, Alfred Hitchcock Presents, Dr. Kildare, Bonanza, The Kraft Mystery Theatre, Columbo. Series: 87th Precinct, Peyton Place.

ROWLEY, JOHN H.: Executive. b. San Angelo, TX, Oct. 6, 1917. e. U. of Texas, 1935–39. Consultant, United Artists Theatre Circuit, Inc. Southwest Div.; past president, NATO of Texas; past Int'l Chief barker, Variety Clubs Int'l; past pres., TOA; pres., Variety Foundation of Texas. Currently exec. dir. NATO of Texas.

ROZSA, MIKLOS: Composer. b. Budapest, Hungary, April 18, 1907. e. Leipzig Conservatory. Wrote great number of symphonic and chamber music works. Composed music for many m.p. Screen Composers Assn. 1956. Cesar of French Academy for Providence, 1978.
PICTURES: Knight Without Armor, Thief of Bagdad, Lydia, Sundown, That Hamilton Woman, The Jungle Book, Five Graves to Cairo, So Produly We Hail, Woman of the Town, Double Indemnity, The Killers, Madame Bovary, The Lost Weekend, The Hour Before the Dawn, Spellbound (Acad. Award), A Song to Remember, The Killers, The Strange Love of Martha Ivers, A Double Life (Acad. Award), Asphalt Jungle, Quo Vadis, Ivanhoe, Story of Three Loves, Plymouth Adventure, Young Bess, Julius Caesar, Knights of the Round Table, Crest of the Wave, Green Fire, Men of the Fighting Lady, Valley of the Kings, The King's Thief, Moonfleet, Tribute to a Bad Man, Bhowani Junction, Diane, Lust for Life, The Seventh Sin, Something of Value, Tip on a Dead Jockey, A Time to Love and a Time to Die, The World the Flesh and the Devil, Ben-Hur (Acad. Award), King of Kings, El Cid, Sodom and Gomorrah, The VIP's, The Power, The Green Berets, The Private Life of Sherlock Holmes, The Golden Voyage of Sinbad, Providence, The Private Files of J. Edgar Hoover, Fedora, Last Embrace, Time After Time, Eye of the Needle, Dead Men Don't Wear Plaid.

RUBEN, JOSEPH: Director. b. Briarcliff, NY, 1951. e. U. of Michigan, majoring in theater and film; Brandeis U., B.A. Interest in film began in high school. Bought a Super-8 camera and filmed his first movie, a teenage love story. First feature, The Sister-in-Law, a low budget feature which he wrote and dir. in 1975.
PICTURES: The Sister-in-Law (also s.p., prod.), The Pom-Pom Girls (also s.p., prod.), Joy Ride (also co-s.p.), Our Winning Season (also s.p.), G.O.R.P., Dreamscape (also co-s.p.), The Stepfather, True Believer, Sleeping With the Enemy, The Good Son.
TELEVISION: Breaking Away (pilot), Eddie Dodd.

RUBIN, STANLEY: Producer, Writer. b. New York, NY, Oct. 8, 1917; ed. UCLA, 1933–37. Phi Beta Kappa. Writer—radio, magazines, pictures, 1937–41; U.S. Army Air Force, 1942–45; writer, prod., owner, Your Show Time, Story Theatre TV series; winner of 1st Emmy awarded to filmed series: The Necklace, 1949. Producer, RKO, 20th-Fox, U.I., MGM, Paramount, Rastar.
PICTURES: The Narrow Margin, My Pal Gus, Destination Gobi, River of No Return, Destry, Francis in the Navy, Behind the High Wall, Rawhide Years, The Girl Most Likely, Promise Her Anything, The President's Analyst, Revenge, White Hunter Black Heart (co-prod.).
TELEVISION: G.E. Theatre, Ghost and Mrs. Muir, Bracken's World, The Man and the City, Executive Suite. Movies: Babe (co-prod.), And Your Name is Jonah, Don't Look Back: The Story of Satchel Page, Escape From Iran: The Canadian Caper (exec. prod.).

RUBINSTEIN, JOHN: Actor, Composer, Director. b. Los Angeles, CA, December 8, 1946. Son of concert pianist Arthur Rubinstein and dancer-writer Aniela Rubinstein. e. UCLA.
THEATER: Pippin (NY debut, 1972; Theatre World Award), Picture (Mark Taper, LA), Children of a Lesser God (Tony Award, Drama Desk, L.A. Drama Critics Awards, 1980), Fools, The Caine Mutiny Court-Martial, M. Butterfly, Kiss of the Spider Woman. Director: The Rover, Les Liaisons Dangereuses, Phantasie, Nightingale, The Old Boy.
PICTURES: Journey to Shiloh (debut, 1968), The Trouble With Girls, Getting Straight, The Wild Pack, Zachariah, The Car, The Boys From Brazil, In Search of Historic Jesus, Daniel, Someone to Watch Over Me, Another Stakeout.
TELEVISION: Series: Family, Crazy Like a Fox. Guest: The Virginian (1966), Ironside, Dragnet, Room 222, The Psychiatrist, The Mary Tyler Moore Show, Cannon, The Mod Squad, Nichols, Hawaii Five-O, Barnaby Jones, Policewoman, Barbary Coast, The Rookies, The Streets of San Francisco, Harry O, Vegas, The Class of '65, Movin' On, Stop the

Presses, Wonder Woman, Lou Grant, Fantasy Island, The Quest, Quincy, Trapper John M.D., The Love Boat, Father Dowling, The Paper Chase, Murder She Wrote. Special: Triple Play—Sam Found Out. Movies: The Marriage Proposal, God Bless the Children, A Howling in the Woods, Something Evil, All Together Now, The Gift of the Magi, Roots: The Next Generations, Just Make Me an Offer, The French Atlantic Affair, Corey: For the People, Happily Ever After, Moviola, Skokie, The Mr. and Ms. Mysteries, Killjoy, Freedom to Speak, Someone's Killing the High Fashion Models; I Take These Men, M.A.D.D.: Mothers Against Drunk Driving, Liberace, Voices Within: The Lives of Truddi Chase, In My Daughter's Name, The American Clock. Director: A Matter of Conscience, Summer Stories: The Mall.
SCORES: Films: Paddy, Jeremiah Johnson, The Candidate, Kid Blue, The Killer Inside Me. Television: All Together Now, Emily, Emily, Stalk the Wild Child, Champions: A Love Story, To Race the Wind, The Ordeal of Patty Hearst, Amber Waves, Johnny Belinda, Secrets of a Mother and Daughter, Choices of the Heart, The Dollmaker, Family (Emmy nom.), The Fitzpatricks, The Mackenzies of Paradise Cove, The New Land, For Heaven's Sake, The Lazarus Syndrome, The City Killer, China Beach.

RUBINSTEIN, RICHARD P.: Producer, Executive. b. New York, NY, June 15, 1947. e. American U. B.S. 1969, Columbia U. MBA 1971. Pres. & CEO, Laurel Entertainment, Inc.
PICTURES: Martin, Dawn Of The Dead, Knightriders, Creepshow, Day Of The Dead, Creepshow 2, Pet Sematary, Tales From the Darkside: The Movie.
TELEVISION: Exec. prod.: Series: Tales From the Darkside, Monsters, Stephen King's Golden Years. Movie: The Stand.

RUDDY, ALBERT S.: Producer. b. Montreal, Canada, March 28, 1934. e. U. of Southern California, B.S. in design, Sch. of Architecture, 1956. Exec. prod. of 1991 TV movie Miracle in the Wilderness.
PICTURES: The Wild Seed (Pennebaker), Little Fauss & Big Halsey, Making It, The Godfather, The Longest Yard, Coonskin, Matilda, The Cannonball Run, Megaforce, Lassiter, Cannonball Run II, Farewell to the King, Paramedics, Speed Zone, Impulse, Ladybugs, Bad Girls.

RUDIE, EVELYN: Actress, Singer, Songwriter. r.n. Evelyn Rudie Bernauer, b. Hollywood, Calif. March 28. e. Hollywood H.S., U.C.L.A. At 19, after childstar career in TV and films, stage debut at Gallery Theatre in Hollywood as songwriter, musical dir., choreographer and star performer: Ostrogoths and King of the Schnorrers. Currently producer, artistic dir., Santa Monica Playhouse; founder of own repertoire co., among major productions: Author! Author!, Attorney at Love, Dreamplay, The Alchemist, The Fools, Red, Dear Gabby. Screen debut as child performer Daddy Longlegs. Received Emmy Nomination for first TV leading role, Eloise, Playhouse 90, 1956. Star in Hollywood's Walk of Fame.
PICTURES: The Wings of Eagles, Gift of Love, Bye Bye Birdie. Filmdom's Famous Fives critics award, 1958.
TV: Hostess with the Mostess, Playhouse 90, Dinah Shore, Red Skelton Show, George Gobel Show, Omnibus, Matinee Theatre, Hitchcock presents, Gale Storm Show, Jack Paar, Wagon Train, G.E. Theatre, 77 Sunset Strip, etc.

RUDIN, SCOTT: Executive. b. New York, NY, July 14, 1958. Began career as prod. asst. on Bdwy. for producers Kermit Bloomgarden, Robert Whitehead; then casting director. 1984, became producer for 20th Century Fox; named exec. v.p. prod.; 1986, appt. pres. prod., 20th-Fox. Resigned 1987.
PICTURES: Prod.: I'm Dancing as Fast as I Can, Reckless, Mrs. Soffel, Flatliners (exec. prod.), Pacific Heights, Regarding Henry, Little Man Tate, The Addams Family, White Sands, Sister Act, Jennifer Eight, Life With Mikey, The Firm, Searching for Bobby Fisher, Sister Act 2.
TELEVISION: Little Gloria . . . Happy at Last (exec. prod.).

RUDOLPH, ALAN: Director, Writer. b. Los Angeles, CA, Dec., 1943. Son of Oscar Rudolph, TV director of '50s and '60s. Made his screen debut in his father's The Rocket Man (1954). Began in industry doing odd jobs in Hollywood studios. In 1969 accepted for Directors Guild assistant director's training program. Worked with Robert Altman on California Split and The Long Goodbye (asst. dir.) and co-writer on Buffalo Bill and the Indians.
PICTURES: Welcome to L.A. (debut as dir.), Remember My Name, Roadie, Endangered Species (also co-s.p.), Songwriter, Choose Me (also s.p.), Trouble in Mind (also s.p.), Made in Heaven, The Moderns (also co-s.p.), Love at Large (also s.p.), Mortal Thoughts, The Player (actor only), Equinox (also s.p.), Mrs. Parker and the Round Table (also co-s.p.).

RUEHL, MERCEDES: Actress. b. Queens, NY. Raised in Silver Spring, MD. e. College of New Rochelle, B.A. English lit. Worked for years in regional theater, mostly in classics.
THEATER: Bdwy: I'm Not Rappaport, Lost in Yonkers (Tony Award, 1991). Off-Bdwy: American Notes, The Marriage

of Bette and Boo (Obie Award), Coming of Age in Soho, Other People's Money.
PICTURES: The Warriors (debut, 1979), Four Friends, Heartburn, Radio Days, 84 Charing Cross Road, The Secret of My Success, Big, Married to the Mob, Slaves of New York, Crazy People, Another You, The Fisher King (Acad. Award, supp. actress, 1991), Lost in Yonkers, Last Action Hero.
TELEVISION: Pilot: Late Bloomer. Guest: Our Family Honor.

RUGOLO, PETE: Composer, Arranger. b. Sicily, Italy, Dec. 25, 1915. To U.S., 1919. e. San Francisco State Coll., Mills Coll., Oakland. Armed Forces, 1942–46; pianist, arr. for many orch. including Stan Kenton; m.p. and TV.
PICTURES: The Strip, Skirts Ahoy, Glory Alley, Latin Lovers, Easy to Love, Jack the Ripper, Foxtrot, Buddy, Buddy; Chu Chu and the Philly Flash.
TELEVISION: Richard Diamond, The Thin Man, Thriller, more than 25 movies.

RULE, JANICE: Actress. b. Cincinnati, OH, Aug. 15, 1931. e. Wheaton & Glenbard H.S., Glen Ellyn, IL. Dancer 4 yrs. in Chicago & New York nightclubs; stage experience in It's Great To Be Alive, as understudy of Bambi Lynn; in chorus of Miss Liberty; Broadway stage debut Picnic, 1953. Star of The Happiest Girl in the World.
PICTURES: Goodbye My Fancy (debut, 1951), Starlift, Holiday for Sinners, Rogue's March, Woman's Devotion, Gun for a Coward, Bell Book and Candle, Subterraneans, Invitation to a Gunfighter, The Chase, Alvarez Kelly, Welcome to Hard Times, The Swimmer, The Ambushers, Doctors' Wives, Gumshoe, Kid Blue, 3 Women, Missing, Rainy Day Friends, American Flyers.
TELEVISION: Movies: Shadow on the Land, Trial Run, The Devil and Miss Sarah, The Word.

RUSH, BARBARA: Actress. b. Denver, CO, Jan. 4, 1927. e. U. of California. First stage appearance at age of ten, Loberto Theatre, Santa Barbara, CA, in fantasy, Golden Ball; won acting award in coll. for characterization of Birdie (The Little Foxes); scholarship, Pasadena Playhouse Theatre Arts Coll.
STAGE: A Woman of Independent Means, 40 Carats, Same Time Next Year, Steel Magnolias.
PICTURES: The First Legion, Quebec, Molly, When Worlds Collide, Flaming Feather, Prince of Pirates, It Came From Outer Space, Taza Son of Cochise, Magnificent Obsession, Black Shield of Falworth, Captain Lightfoot, Kiss of Fire, World in My Corner, Bigger Than Life, Flight to Hong Kong, Oh Men! Oh Women!, No Down Payment, Harry Black and the Tiger, The Young Philadelphians, Bramble Bush, Strangers When We Meet, Come Blow Your Horn, Robin and the Seven Hoods, Hombre, The Man, Superdad, Can't Stop the Music, Summer Lovers.
TELEVISION: Series: Saints and Sinners, Peyton Place, The New Dick Van Dyke Show, Flamingo Road. Movies: Suddenly Single, Cutter, Eyes of Charles Sand, Moon of the Wolf, Crime Club, The Last Day, Death on the Freeway, The Seekers, Flamingo Road (pilot), The Night the Bridge Fell Down.

RUSH, HERMAN: Executive. b. Philadelphia, PA, June 20, 1929. e. Temple U., Headed Flamingo Telefilms, Inc. 1957–60; 1960–71, pres., television div. of Creative Mgt. Assoc. Pres., Herman Rush Assoc. Inc., 1971–77. In 1977–78 chmn bd., Rush-Flaherty Agency, Inc. In 1970 headed Marble Arch TV. In 1980 named pres., Columbia TV; 1984, named pres. of newly formed Columbia Pictures TV Group. In 1986, named chmn. of newly formed Coca-Cola Telecommunications, Inc. In 1988, chairman, Rush Entertainment Group; 1989, became creative consultant for CBN Producers Group. 1992, Katz/Rush Ent., partner. Co-founder, dir. of Transactional Media, Informercial and Transactional Program Production Co.

RUSH, RICHARD: Director, Producer, Writer. b. New York, NY, 1930.
PICTURES: Director: Too Soon To Love (also prod., s.p.), Of Love and Desire (also prod., s.p.), A Man Called Dagger, Fickle Finger of Fate, Thunder Alley, Hell's Angels on Wheels, Psych-Out (also s.p.), Savage Seven, Getting Straight (also prod.), Freebie and the Bean (also prod.), The Stunt Man (also prod., s.p.; Acad. Award nom. for best dir., s.p.), Air America (co-s.p.), Color of Night.

RUSSELL, CHUCK: Director. Asst. dir. and line prod. on many low-budget films for Roger Corman and Sunn Classics, including Death Race 2000.
PICTURES: Dreamscape (co-s.p., line prod.), Back to School (prod.), Nightmare on Elm Street III (dir., co-s.p.), The Blob (dir., co-s.p.).

RUSSELL, JANE: Actress. b. Bemidji, MN, June 21, 1921. e. Max Reinhardt's Theatrical Workshop & Mme. Ouspenskaya. Photographer's model.
PICTURES: The Outlaw (debut), Young Widow, Paleface, His Kind of Woman, Double Dynamite, Macao, Son of

Paleface, Montana Belle, Las Vegas Story, Road to Bali (cameo), Gentlemen Prefer Blondes, French Line, Underwater, Gentlemen Marry Brunettes, Foxfire, Tall Men, Hot Blood, Revolt of Mamie Stover, Fuzzy Pink Nightgown, Fate Is The Hunter, Waco, Johnny Reno, Born Losers, Darker Than Amber.
TELEVISION: Yellow Rose (series).

RUSSELL, KEN: Director, Producer, Writer. b. Southampton, England, July 3, 1927. e. Walthamstow Art Sch. Early career as dancer, actor, stills photographer, TV documentary filmmaker. Ent. TV ind. 1959. Made 33 documentaries for BBC-TV. Also made numerous pop videos.
TELEVISION: The Secret Life of Sir Arnold Box, Lady Chatterly's Lover, Portrait of a Soviet Composer, Elgar, A House in Bayswater, Always on Sunday, The Debussy Film, Isadora Duncan, Dantés Inferno, Song of Summer—Delius, Dance of the Seven Veils. HBO: Dust Before Fireworks, Prisoner of Honor.
PICTURES: French Dressing, Billion Dollar Brain, Women in Love, The Music Lovers (also prod.), The Devils (also prod., s.p.), The Boy Friend (also prod., s.p.), Savage Messiah (also prod.), Mahler (also s.p.), Tommy (also prod., s.p.), Lisztomania (also s.p.), Valentino, Altered States, Crimes of Passion, Gothic, Aria (sequence), Salome's Last Dance (also s.p., actor), The Lair of the White Worm (also prod., s.p.), The Rainbow (also prod., co-s.p.), The Russia House (actor only), Whore (also s.p.).

RUSSELL, KURT: Actor. b. Springfield, MA, March 17, 1951. Son of former baseball player turned actor Bing Russell (deputy sheriff on Bonanza). At 12 got lead in The Travels of Jamie McPheeters (1963–64). Starred as child in many Disney shows and films. Professional baseball player 1971–73. Host, Kurt Russell Celebrity Shoot Out, 4-day hunting tournament.
PICTURES: It Happened at the World's Fair (debut, 1963), Follow Me Boys, The One and Only Genuine Original Family Band, The Horse in the Grey Flannel Suit, The Computer Wore Tennis Shoes, The Barefoot Executive, Fools' Parade, Now You See Him Now You Don't, Charley and the Angel, Superdad, The Strongest Man in the World, Used Cars, Escape from New York, The Fox and The Hound (voice), The Thing, Silkwood, Swing Shift, The Mean Season, The Best of Times, Big Trouble in Little China, Overboard, Tequila Sunrise, Winter People, Tango and Cash, Backdraft, Unlawful Entry, Captain Ron. Tombstone.
TELEVISION: Series: Travels of Jamie McPheeters, The New Land, The Quest. Movies: Search for the Gods, The Deadly Tower, The Quest (pilot), Christmas Miracle in Caulfield U.S.A., Elvis, Amber Waves. Guest: The Fugitive, Daniel Boone, Gilligan's Island, Lost in Space, The F.B.I., Love American Style, Gunsmoke, Hawaii Five-O.

RUSSELL, THERESA: Actress. r.n. Theresa Paup. b. San Diego, CA, Mar. 20, 1957. m. dir.-cinematographer Nicolas Roeg. e. Burbank H.S. Began modeling career at 12. Studied at Actors' Studio in Hollywood.
PICTURES: The Last Tycoon (debut, 1976), Straight Time, Bad Timing/A Sensual Obsession, Eureka, The Razor's Edge, Insignificance, Black Widow, Aria, Track 29, Physical Evidence, Impulse, Whore, Kafka, Cold Heaven.
TELEVISION: Mini-Series: Blind Ambition.

RUSSO, RENE: Actress. b. California. Raised in Burbank. Worked as top fashion model for Eileen Ford Agency prior to acting.
PICTURES: Major League (debut, 1989), Mr. Destiny, One Good Cop, Freejack, Lethal Weapon 3, In the Line of Fire.

RUTHERFORD, ANN: Actress. b. Toronto, Canada, Nov. 2, 1920. Trained by mother (cousin of Richard Mansfield); with parents in stock as child; later on Los Angeles radio programs. Screen debut, 1935.
PICTURES: You're Only Young Once, Love Finds Andy Hardy, The Hardys Ride High, Andy Hardy Gets Spring Fever, Gone With the Wind, Pride and Prejudice, Laramie Trail, Whistling in Dixie, Happy Land, Bermuda Mystery, Two O'Clock Courage, Bedside Manner, The Madonna's Secret, Murder in the Music Hall, Secret Life of Walter Mitty, Operation Haylift, Adventures of Don Juan, They Only Kill Their Masters.

RYAN, ARTHUR N.: Executive. Joined Paramount in N.Y. in 1967 as asst. treas; later made dir. of admin. and business affairs, exec. asst. to Robert Evans and asst. scty. In 1970 appt. v.p.-prod. adm. In 1975 named sr. v.p. handling all prod. operations for Paramount's m.p. and TV divisions. Named asst. to the chmn. & CEO 1976; chmn. & pres. Magicam, Inc.; chmn. Fortune General Corp.; chmn. Paramount-Communications; co-chmn. of scholarship comm. of Academy of Motion Picture Arts and Sciences; trustee of Univ. Film Study Center in Boston. Joined Technicolor in August 1976 as pres., chief operating officer and director; vice chmn., 1983–85; chmn. & CEO, 1985 to date. Chmn. Technicolor Audio-Visual Systems International, Inc.; dir. Technicolor S.P.A.; dir. Technicolor, Film Intl.; and chmn. of exec. committee, Technicolor Graphics

Services, Inc.; dir., Technicolor, Inc.; chmn., Technicolor Fotografica, S.A.; Chmn. Technicolor Film Intl. Service Company, Inc.; director and Deputy Chairman Technicolor Limited; chmn. & dir., The Vidtronics Company, Inc.; chmn. & CEO, Compact Video, Inc., 1984 to date; dir, Four Star Int'l., 1983 to date; dir., MacAndrews & Forbes, Inc. 1985 to date; Permanent charities committee of the Entertainment Industry; Hollywood Canteen Foundations. Vice-chmn. & dir., Calif. Inst. of Arts. Trustee: Motion Picture & Television Fund. In 1985 named chmn., Technicolor.

RYAN, JOHN P.: Actor. b. New York, NY, July 30, 1936. e. City Col of NY.
PICTURES: The Tiger Makes Out (debut, 1967), A Lovely Way to Die, What's So Bad About Feeling Good?, Five Easy Pieces, The King of Marvin Gardens, The Legend of Nigger Charley, Cops and Robbers, Dillinger, Shamus, It's Alive, The Missouri Breaks, Futureworld, It Lives Again, The Last Flight of Noah's Ark, On the Nickel, The Postman Always Rings Twice, The Escape Artist, Breathless, The Right Stuff, The Cotton Club, Runaway Train, Avenging Force, Death Wish 4: The Crackdown, Delta Force II, Fatal Beauty, Three O'Clock High, Rent-a-Cop, Paramedics, City of Shadows, Best of the Best, White Sands, Hoffa, Star Time, Young Goodman Brown.
TELEVISION: Series: Archer. Guest: M*A*S*H, Kojak, Starsky & Hutch, Matt Helm, Matt Huston, Miami Vice. Movies: Target Risk, Death Scream, Kill Me If You Can, A Killing Affair, Houston: The Legend of Texas, Blood River, Shooting Stars.
THEATRE: NY: Duet for Three, Sgt. Musgrave's Dance, Yerma, Nobody Hears a Broken Drum, The Love Suicide at Schofield Barracks, The Silent Partner, Twelve Angry Men, Medea.

RYAN, MEG: Actress. b. Fairfield, CT, Nov. 19, 1961. e. NYU. m. actor Dennis Quaid. Supported herself, while studying journalism at NYU, by making commercials.
PICTURES: Rich and Famous (debut, 1981), Amityville 3-D, Top Gun, Armed and Dangerous, Innerspace, Promised Land, D.O.A., The Presidio, When Harry Met Sally, Joe Versus the Volcano, The Doors, Prelude to a Kiss, Sleepless in Seattle, Flesh & Bone, Significant Other.
TELEVISION: Series: One of the Boys, As the World Turns (1982–4), Wild Side.

RYAN, MITCHELL: Actor. b. Louisville, KY, Jan. 11, 1928. Entered acting following service in Navy during Korean War. Was New York stage actor working off-Bdwy. for Ted Mann and Joseph Papp; on Bdwy. in Wait Until Dark. Member of Arena Stage group in Washington.
PICTURES: Monte Walsh, The Hunting Party, My Old Man's Place, High Plains Drifter, The Friends of Eddie Coyle, ElectraGlide in Blue, Magnum Force, Labyrinth, Winter People.
TELEVISION: Series: Chase, Executive Suite, Having Babies, The Chisholms, Dark Shadows, High Performance, King Crossings. Movies: Angel City, The Five of Me, Death of a Centerfold—The Dorothy Stratten Story, Uncommon Valor, Medea, Kenny Rogers as the Gambler—The Adventure Continues, Robert Kennedy & His Times, Fatal Vision, Favorite Son, The Ryan White Story, Margaret Bourke-White.

RYDELL, MARK: Producer, Director, Actor. b. March 23, 1934. e. Juilliard Sch. of Music. Studied acting with Sanford Meisner of N.Y. Neighborhood Playhouse. Became member of Actors Studio. Was leading actor for six years on daytime CBS serial, As The World Turns. Made Broadway debut in Seagulls over Sorrento and film bow in Crime in the Streets. Went to Hollywood as TV director (Ben Casey, I Spy, Gunsmoke, etc.). Theatrical feature debut: The Fox (1968). Partner with Sydney Pollack in Sanford Prods., film, TV prod. co. Formed own production co., Concourse Productions.
PICTURES: Director: The Fox, The Reivers, The Cowboys (also prod.), Cinderella Liberty (also prod.), Harry and Walter Go To New York, The Rose, On Golden Pond, The River, Man in the Moon (prod. only), For the Boys, Intersection (also co-prod.). Actor: Crime in the Streets, The Long Goodbye, Punchline, Havana.

RYDER, WINONA: Actress. b. Winona, MN, Oct. 29, 1971. r.n. Winona Horowitz. Grew up in San Francisco. At 7, moved with family to Northern CA commune. At 13 discovered by talent scout during a performance at San Francisco's American Conservatory theatre, where she was studying, and given screen test.
PICTURES: Lucas (debut, 1986), Square Dance, Beetlejuice, 1969, Heathers, Great Balls of Fire, Welcome Home Roxy Carmichael, Edward Scissorhands, Mermaids, Night on Earth, Bram Stoker's Dracula, The Age of Innocence, House of the Spirits, Reality Bites.

S

SACKHEIM, WILLIAM B.: Producer, Writer. b. Gloversville, NY, Oct. 31, 1921. e. UCLA.
PICTURES: Art of Love, The In-Laws (co-prod.), The Competition, First Blood (co-s.p.), The Survivors (prod.), No Small Affair (prod.), The Hard Way (prod.), Pacific Heights (prod.), White Sands (prod.).
TELEVISION: The Law (Emmy Award, 1975), Gideon Oliver (series, exec. prod.), Almost Grown (exec. prod.), The Antagonists (exec. prod.), The Human Factor (exec. prod.).

SACKS, SAMUEL: Attorney, Agent. b. New York, NY, March 29, 1908. e. City Coll. of New York, St. John's Law Sch., LL.B., 1930. Admitted Calif. Bar, 1943; priv. prac., law, N.Y. 1931–42; attorney, William Morris Agency, Inc., Sept. 1942; head of west coast TV business affairs, 1948–75. bd. of dir., Alliance of Television Film Producers, 1956–60. L.A. Copyright Society Treasurer, Beverly Hills Bar Assn., Los Angeles Bar Assn., American Bar Assn.; Academy of TV Arts & Sciences; Hollywood Radio & TV Society. Pres. Adat Shalom Synagogue, 1967–69, chmn. of bd., 1969–71; pres., American Field Service West L.A. Chapter 1970–72, United Synagogue of America (Pacific Southwest region), v.p., 1974–88. Counsel, entertainment field, Simon & Sheridan, 1975–89, Los Angeles Citizens' Olympic Committee. Arbitrator for Screen Actors Guild, Assn. of Talent Agents and American Arbitration Assn. Chmn. Task Force Project Caring; board of dir., Jewish Family Service of L.A.; exec. comm., Congregational Cabinet University of Judaism, 1975 to 1990. Bd. of dirs., Friars Club, 1991–present. Council for the Caucus for Producers, Writers & Directors, 1975–present.

SAFER, MORLEY: News Correspondent. b. Toronto, Ont., 1931. e. U. of Western Ontario. Started as corresp. and prod. with Canadian Broadcasting Corp. Joined CBS News London Bureau 1964, chief of Saigon Bureau, 1965. Chief of CBS London bureau 1967–70. Joined 60 Minutes as co-editor in Dec., 1970.

SAFFLE, M. W. "BUD": Executive. b. Spokane, WA, June 29, 1923. e. U. of Washington. In service 1943–46. Started in m.p. business as booker, 1948. Entire career with Saffle Theatre Service as buyer-booker; named pres. in 1970. Also pres. of Grays Harbor Theatres, Inc., operating theatres in Aberdeen, WA. Also operates drive-in Centralia, WA. On bd. of NATO of WA for 15 yrs; pres. of same for 2 terms and secty.-treas. 6 yrs. Elected to National NATO bd. in 1972. Founder of Variety Tent 46, serving as chief barker three times.

SAFIR, SIDNEY: Executive. b. Vienna, Austria, Feb. 2, 1923. e. London U. Ent. m.p. ind. 1940, Shipman & King Cinemas; RKO Radio Picture, 1941; salesman, British Lion, 1943; European sls. mgr., Lion Int'l, 1958; gen. sls. mgr. Lion Int'l, 1960; president, Lion Int'l Inc., 1965; man. dir. Lion Int'l Ltd. 1969; dir., British Lion Films Ltd., 1972. Formed Safir Films Ltd. with his son Lawrence, 1977.

SAGANSKY, JEFF: Executive. b. 1953. Joined CBS 1976 in bdcst. finance; 1977, NBC, assoc. in pgm. development.; 1977, mgr. film pgms.; 1978, dir. dramatic dev.; 1978, v.p., dev. David Gerber Co.; 1981, returned to NBC as series dev. v.p.; 1983, sr. v.p. series programming; 1985, joined Tri-Star Pictures as pres. of production; 1989 promoted to president of Tri-Star, later that year joined CBS as entertainment division president.

SÄGEBRECHT, MARIANNE: Actress. b. Starnberg, Germany, Aug. 1945. In 1977 conceived revue Opera Curiosa, followed by stage role in Adele Spitzeder.
PICTURES: Die Schaukel (debut, 1983), Sugarbaby, Crazy Boys, Bagdad Cafe, Moon Over Parador, The War of the Roses, Rosalie Goes Shopping, Martha and I, The Milky Life (La Vida Lactea), Dust Devil.
TELEVISION: Movie: Herr Kischott.

SAINT, EVA MARIE: Actress. b. Newark, NJ, July 4, 1924. e. Bowling Green State U., Ohio. Radio, TV actress; on Broadway in Trip to Bountiful, The Lincoln Mask, Duet for One.
PICTURES: On the Waterfront (debut, 1954; Acad. Award, best supp. actress), That Certain Feeling, Raintree County, Hatful of Rain, North by Northwest, Exodus, All Fall Down, 36 Hours, The Sandpiper, The Russians Are Coming, Grand Prix, The Stalking Moon, Loving, Cancel My Reservation, Nothing in Common.
TELEVISION: Movies: Carol for Another Christmas, The Macahans, A Christmas to Remember, When Hell Was in Session, Fatal Weakness, Curse of King Tut's Tomb, Best Little Girl in the World, Splendor in the Grass, Malibu, Jane Doe, Love Leads the Way, Fatal Vision, The Last Days of Patton, A Year in the Life, Norman Rockwell's Breaking Ties, I'll Be Home for Christmas, Voyage of Terror: The Achille Lauro Affair, People Like Us (Emmy Award, 1991), Danielle Steel's Palomino, Kiss of a Killer. Series: Campus Hoopla,

Sai-Sal

One Man's Family, Moonlighting. *Guest*: Taxi. *Special*: First Woman President.

SAINT JAMES, SUSAN: Actress. b. Los Angeles, CA, Aug. 14, 1946. r.n. Susan Miller. e. Connecticut Coll. for Women. Was model for 2 years; then signed to contract by Universal Pictures.
TELEVISION: *Series*: The Name of the Game (Emmy Award, 1969), McMillan & Wife, Kate and Allie. *Movies*: Fame is the Name of the Game, Alias Smith and Jones, Once Upon a Dead Man, Magic Carpet, Scott Free, Night Cries, Desperate Women, The Girls in the Office, Sex and the Single Parent, S.O.S. Titanic, The Kid from Nowhere, I Take These Men. *Special*: A Very Special Christmas Party.
PICTURES: P.J., Where Angels Go . . . Trouble Follows, What's So Bad About Feeling Good?, Jigsaw, Outlaw Blues, Love at First Bite, How to Beat the High Cost of Living, Carbon Copy, Don't Cry It's Only Thunder.

ST. JOHN, JILL: Actress. r.n. Jill Oppenheim. b. Los Angeles, CA, Aug. 19, 1940. m. Robert Wagner. On radio series One Man's family. Television debut, A Christmas Carol, 1948.
PICTURES: Summer Love, The Remarkable Mr. Pennypacker, Holiday for Lovers, The Lost World, The Roman Spring of Mrs. Stone, Tender Is the Night, Come Blow Your Horn, Who's Minding the Store?, Who's Been Sleeping in My Bed?, Honeymoon Hotel, The Liquidator, The Oscar, Banning, Tony Rome, Eight on the Lam, The King's Pirate, Diamonds Are Forever, Sitting Target, The Concrete Jungle, The Player.
TELEVISION: *Series*: Emerald Point. *Movies*: Fame Is the Name of the Game, How I Spent My Summer Vacation, The Spy Killer, Foreign Exchange, Brenda Starr, Telethon, Hart to Hart (pilot), Rooster. *Guest*: Dupont Theatre, Fireside Theatre, Batman, The Love Boat. *Mini-Series*: Around the World in 80 Days.

ST. JOHNS, RICHARD R.: Executive Producer. b. Los Angeles, CA, Jan. 20, 1929. Son of journalist Adela Rogers St. Johns. e. Stanford U., B.A., 1953; Stanford Law Sch., J.D., 1954. Joined law firm O'Melveny & Meyers 1954, specializing in entertainment law. 1963 became partner in law firm. 1968 became sr. v.p., Filmways, Inc., becoming president and chief operating office in 1969. 1972, formed Richard R. St. Johns and Associates, independent management and packaging firm. Formed Guinness Film Group in 1975, branching out into full-scale motion picture prod.
PICTURES: *Exec. prod.*: The Uncanny, Death Hunt, Matilda, The Silent Flute (Circle of Iron), Nightwing, The Wanderers, The Mountain Men, The Final Countdown, A Change of Seasons, Dead & Buried, Death Hunt, American Pop, Venom, Fire and Ice.

SAJAK, PAT: TV Host. b. Chicago, IL, 1946. e. Columbia Coll., Chicago. Broadcasting career began as newscaster for Chicago radio station. 1968 drafted into Army, where served 4 years as disc jockey for Armed Forces Radio in Saigon, Vietnam. Moved to Nashville, where continued radio career while also working as weatherman and host of public affairs prog. for local TV station. 1977 moved to LA to become nightly weatherman on KNBC. Took over as host of daytime edition of Wheel of Fortune and later the syndicated nighttime edition (4 Emmy nom.). 1989, The Pat Sajak Show.
PICTURE: Airplane II: The Sequel.
TELEVISION: *Host*: The Thanksgiving Day Parade, The Rose Parade.

SAKS, GENE: Director, Actor. b. New York, NY, Nov. 8, 1921. e. Cornell U. Attended dramatic workshop, New School for Social Research. Active in off-Broadway in 1948–49, forming cooperative theatre group at Cherry Lane Theatre. Joined Actor's Studio, followed by touring and stock. Also appeared in live TV dramas (Philco Playhouse, Producer's Showcase). Directed many Broadway plays before turning to film direction with Barefoot in the Park (1967) President of SSDC.
BROADWAY: *Director*: Enter Laughing, Nobody Loves an Albatross, Generation, Half a Sixpence, Mame, A Mother's Kisses, Sheep on the Runway, How the Other Half Loves, Same Time Next Year, California Suite, I Love My Wife (Tony Award), Brighton Beach Memoirs (Tony Award), Biloxi Blues (Tony Award), The Odd Couple (1985), Broadway Bound, Rumors, Lost in Yonkers, Jake's Women. *Actor*: Middle of the Night, Howie, The Tenth Man, A Shot in the Dark, A Thousand Clowns.
PICTURES: *Director*: Barefoot in the Park, The Odd Couple, Cactus Flower, Last of the Red Hot Lovers, Mame, Brighton Beach Memoirs, A Fine Romance. *Actor*: A Thousand Clowns, Prisoner of Second Avenue, The One and Only, Lovesick, The Goodbye People.

SALANT, RICHARD S.: Executive. b. New York, NY, Apr. 14, 1914. e. Harvard Coll. A.B., 1931–35; Harvard Law Sch., 1935–38. Atty. Gen.'s Com. on Admin. Procedure, 1939–41; Office of Solicitor Gen., U.S. Dept. of Justice, 1941–43; U.S. Naval Res., 1943–46; assoc., Roseman, Goldmark, Colin & Kave, 1946–48; then partner, 1948–51; pres. CBS news div., 1961–64; v.p. special asst. to pres. CBS, Inc., 1951–61, 1964–66; pres., CBS news div., 1966; mem. bd. of dir., CBS, Inc. 1964–69; vice chmn., NBC bd., 1979–81; sr. adviser, 1981–83; pres. CEO, National News Council, 1983–84. Retired.

SALKIND, ALEXANDER: Producer. b. Danzig/Gdansk, of Russian extraction, June 2, 1921. Grew up in Berlin where father, Miguel, produced films. Went to Cuba with father to assist him in film production. First solo venture a Buster Keaton comedy, 1945. Returned to Europe where made many pictures in Spain, Italy, France and Hungary. TV series: Superboy.
PICTURES: Austerlitz, The Trial, The Light at the Edge of the World (exec. prod.), Kill! Kill! Kill! (with Ilya Salkind), Bluebeard, *Exec. prod.*: The Three Musketeers, The Four Musketeers, The Prince and the Pauper, Superman, Supergirl, Santa Claus: The Movie, Christopher Columbus: The Discovery.

SALKIND, ILYA: Producer. b. Mexico City, 1947. e. U. of London. Grew up in many countries where father, Alexander, produced films. First film job as production runner on The Life of Cervantes for father. Was assoc. prod. on Light at the Edge of the World.
PICTURES: The Three Musketeers, The Four Musketeers, Superman, Superman II (exec. prod.), Supergirl (exec. prod.), Superman III (exec. prod.), Christopher Columbus: The Discovery.
TELEVISION: Superboy (exec. prod.).

SALKOW, SIDNEY: Director, Writer. b. New York, NY, June 16, 1911. e. City Coll. of New York, B.A.; Harvard Law Sch. Stage dir. & prod. asst. number N.Y. dram. prods. (Dir. Bloodstream, Black Tower, etc.) and mgr. summer theatre. From 1933 variously dialogue dir., assoc. dir., writer & dir. numerous pictures Paramount, Universal, Republic, Columbia, etc.; dir. number of pictures in Lone Wolf series (for Columbia), Tillie the Toiler, Flight Lieutenant, etc. In armed service, W.W.II.
PICTURES: Millie's Daughter, Bulldog Drummond at Bay, Admiral Was a Lady, Fugitive Lady, Golden Hawk, Scarlet Angel, Pathfinder, Prince of Pirates, Jack McCall Desperado, Raiders of the 7 Seas, Sitting Bull, Robbers' Roost, Shadow of the Eagle, Las Vegas Shakedown, Toughest Man Alive, Chicago Confidential, Iron Sheriff, Great Sioux Massacre, Martin Eden.
TELEVISION: Created, prod. dir., This is Alice series for Desilu, Lassie, Fury, Wells Fargo series. Headed prod. for FF Prod. in Rome, 1967–71.

SALOMON, MIKAEL: Cinematographer. b. Copenhagen, Denmark, Feb. 24, 1945.
PICTURES: *Europe*: The Flying Devils, The Baron, Once a Cop, Early Spring, The Wolf at the Door; *U.S.*: Zelly and Me, Torch Song Trilogy, Stealing Heaven, The Abyss (Acad. Award nom.), Always, Arachnophobia, Backdraft, Far and Away, A Far Off Place (dir. only).
TELEVISION: The Man Who Broke 1,000 Chains (ACE Award), Space Rangers (dir.).

SALTER, HANS J.: Composer, Conductor. b. Vienna, Jan. 14, 1896. e. U. Acad. of Music, Vienna, Austria. Mus. dir.: Volksopera, Vienna; State Oper. Berlin; Metropole Theatre, Berlin; comp., cond., UFA, Berlin, 1929–33; European br., Universal, 1934–36; to U.S., Univ. 1938–47, 1950–52, wrote over 150 scores.
PICTURES: It Started With Eve, His Butler's Sister, Christmas Holiday, Spring Parade, First Love, Can't Help Singing, Frankenstein Meets the Wolfman, Scarlet Street, Magnificent Doll, The Spoilers, Frenchie, Flesh and Fury, Golden Horde, The Sign of the Ram, Frightened City, Ghost of Frankenstein, Black Friday, House of Frankenstein, The Wolfman, Hold That Ghost, The Invisible Man Returns, the Mummy's Hand, Man-Eater of Kumaon, This Island Earth, Tomahawk, The Battle of Apache Pass, Please Believe Me, Apache Drums, The Prince Who Was a Thief, Untamed Frontier, Lover Come Back, Thunder on the Hill, Bend of the River, Against All Flags, Black Shield of Falworth, Sign of the Pagan, Far Horizons, Man Without a Star, Wichita, Autumn Leaves, Red Sundown, Hold Back the Night, Rawhide Years, The Oklahoman, Three Brave Men, The Creature from the Black Lagoon, Pay the Devil, Law of the Trigger, Female Animal, Raw Wind in Eden, The Wild and the Innocent, Bat Masterson Story, Man in the Net, You Never Can Tell, Come September, Follow That Dream, If a Man Answers, Bedtime Story, The Warlord, Beau Geste, Return of the Gunfighter.
TELEVISION: Wichita Town, Laramie, The Law and Mr. Jones, The Virginian, Wagon Train, Lost in Space, Maya.

SALTZMAN, HARRY: Producer. Lowndes Productions, Ltd. b. October, 1915. St. John, N.B., Canada. Ent. film ind. 1945. Chmn. bd., H.M. Tenment, Ltd., London.
PICTURES: The Iron Petticoat, Look Back in Anger, The Entertainer, Saturday Night, Sunday Morning, Ipcress File, Funeral in Berlin, Billion Dollar Brain, Battle of Britain, Nijinsky (exec. prod.). Also co-producer of 10 James Bond films.

SALZBURG, JOSEPH S.: Producer, Editor. b. New York, NY, July 27, 1917. Film librarian, then rose to v.p. in chg. of prod., Pictorial Films, 1935–42; civilian chief film ed. U.S. Army Signal Corps Photo Center, 1942–44; U.S. Army Air Forces, 1944–46; prod. mgr., Pictorial Films, 1946–50; prod. mgr. Associated Artists Prod., then M.P. for TV, 1950–51; org. m.p. prod. & edit. service for theatrical, non-theatrical & TV films 1951–56; prod. mgr., dir. of films oper., official Films. Oct. 1956–59; prod. sup. tech. dir. Lynn Romero Prod. features and TV; assoc. prod. Lynn Romero Prod. TV series, Counterthrust 1959–60; v.p., sec'y, B.L. Coleman Assoc., Inc. & Newspix, Inc. 1961; pres. National Production Assoc., Inc. 1960–1962, chief of production, UPI Newsfilm, 1963–66. Prod./account exec. Fred A. Niles Comm. Center, 1966. Appt. v.p., F.A. Niles Communications Centers Inc., N.Y., 1969. In 1979 appointed in addition exec. producer & gen. mgr., F. A. Niles Communication centers Inc., N.Y. studio. 1989, elected mem. bd. dir., Florida Motion Pictures & Television Assn., Palm Beach area chap.; 1989 professor m.p. & TV prod. course at Palm Beach Comm. Coll.: Breaking into TV and Movie Making in South Florida.

SAMMS, EMMA: Actress. b. London, England, Aug. 28, 1960. Former fashion model. Has worked as commercial photographer for such magazines as Ritz, Metro, and Architectural Digest. Co-founder of charitable org. the Starlight Foundation.
TELEVISION: Series: General Hospital, Dynasty, The Colbys. Movies: Goliath Awaits, Agatha Christie's Murder in Three Acts, The Lady and the Highwayman, A Connecticut Yankee in King Arthur's Court, Bejeweled, Shadow of a Stranger. Guest: Hotel, The New Mike Hammer, Murder She Wrote, Newhart, My Two Dads.
PICTURES: Arabian Adventure (debut, 1979), The Shrimp on the Barbie, Delirious.

SAMPSON, LEONARD E.: Exhibitor. b. New York, NY, Oct. 9, 1918. e. City Coll. of New York, B.B.A., 1939. Entered m.p. industry as stagehand helper and usher, Skouras Park Plaza, Bronx 1932–36; asst. mgr. Gramercy Park, 1937–38; mgr., 5th Avenue Playhouse, 1939–41; mgr., Ascot Bronx, 1941–42. In Army 1942–46. On return entered into partnership with cousin Robert C. Spodick in Lincoln, a New Haven art house. Organized Nutmeg Theatres in 1952 in assn. with Norman Bialek, operating 6 art and conventional theatres in Conn., mainly in Westport and Norwalk. Sold Nutmeg in 1968 to Robert Smerling (now Loews Theatres). Retains partnership with Spodick in New Haven's York Sq., Built Groton, CT, Cinemas I & II in 1970 and Norwich, CT, Cinema I & II, 1976 and acquired Village Cinemas I, II & III, Mystic, in association with Spodick and William Rosen. Operated as Gemini Theatre Circuit. Acquired Westerly Cinema I, II & III, 1982. Sold Gemini Theatre Circuit to Hoyts Theatres, 1987.

SAMUELS, ABRAM: Executive. b. Allentown, PA, Sept. 15, 1920. e. Lehigh U. U.S. Army 1942–46; pres. Automatic Devices Co. 1946–76; bd. chmn. 1976–88.

SAMUELSON, DAVID W., F.R.P.S., F.B.K.S., B.S.C.: Executive. b. London, England, July 6, 1924. Son of early producer G. B. Samuelson. Joined ind. 1941 with British Movietone News. Later film cameraman, 1947. Left Movietone 1960 to join family company, Samuelson Film Service Ltd. Dir., Samuelson Group Plc, 1958–84. Past president British Kinematograph Sound & TV Soc., Past Chmn, British Board of Film Classification, London Intl. Film Sch. Author of Motion Picture Camera and Lighting Equipment, Motion Picture Camera Techniques, Motion Picture Camera Data, Samuelson Manual of Cinematography, Panaflex User's Manual and Cinematographers Computer Program. Currently consultant on technology film making, author, lecturer. Won Acad. Award for Engineering, 1980 and Acad. Award for Tech. Achievement, 1987.

SAMUELSON, PETER GEORGE WYLIE: Producer. b. London, England, October 16, 1951. e. Cambridge U., M.A., English literature. Early career as interpreter, production assistant, then prod. mgr. 1975, Return of the Pink Panther. 1979–85, exec. v.p., Interscope Communications, Inc. 1982–present, Intl. Pres., Starlight Foundation. 1986–present, pres., Film Associates, Inc. 1985–90 chmn., Samuelson Group, Inc. 1990–present, partner, New Era Prods. of Los Angeles and London.
PICTURES: Speed Merchants, High Velocity, One by One, Return of the Pink Panther, Santa Fe, A Man a Woman and a Bank, Revenge of the Nerds, Turk 182, Tom and Viv.

SAMUELSON, SYDNEY, C.B.E., B.S.C., Hon. F.B.K.S., Executive. b. London, England, Dec. 7, 1925. e. Irene Avenue Council Sch., Lancing, Sussex. Early career as cinema projectionist, 1939–42; Gaumont British News, 1942–43; Royal Air Force, 1943–47; asst. cameraman, cameraman, director/cameraman until 1960; founded Samuelson Film Service, 1955; now pres. Samuelson Group plc; Trustee and chmn. board of management, British Acad. of Film and Television Arts (chmn. of Council 1973–76). Member of Exec. Council (Pres. 1983–86; Trustee: 1982–9) Cinema and Television Benevo-

lent Fund. Member of Executive, Cinema & Television Veterans (pres. 1980–81); assoc. member, American Society of Cinematographers. Hon. Tech. Adviser, Royal Naval Film Corp. Hon. member, Guild of British Camera Technicians (1986); Member, British Society of Cinematographers (Patron, 1993; governor, 1969–79; 1st vice pres., 1976–77), Hon. Mem. for Life, Assn. of Cinema & Television Technicians, 1990. Appointed British Film Commissioner, 1991. Recipient of two British Academy Awards: Michael Balcon (19985), Fellowship (1993).

SANDA, DOMINIQUE: Actress. b. Paris, France, March 11, 1951. r.n. Dominique Varaigne. e. Saint Vincent de Paul, Paris. Was a popular model for women's magazines when cast by Robert Bresson as the tragic heroine in his Dostoyevsky adaptation Un Femme Douce (1968).
PICTURES: Un Femme Douce, First Love, The Conformist, The Garden of the Finzi-Continis, La Notte Dei Fiori, Sans Mobile Apparent, Impossible Object, The Mackintosh Man, Steppenwolf, Conversation Piece, 1900, L'Eredita Ferramonti, Damnation Alley, Beyond Good and Evil, The Song of Roland, Utopia, The Navire Night, Travels on the Sly, Caboblanco, A Room in Town, Dust of the Empire, The Way to Bresson, The Sailor 512, With All Hands, On a Moonlit Night, Warrior and Prisoners, Je Ne Vous Derangerai Plus, Moi, La Pire De Toutes, Voyage, Emile Rosen.
TELEVISION: The Sealed Train, La Naissance Du Jour, Il Decimo Clandestino, Voglia Di Vivere, Achille Lauro, Warburg, Comme Par Hazard, Non Siamo Soli, Albert Savarus.

SANDERS, JAY O.: Actor. b. Austin, TX, Apr. 16, 1953. e. SUNY/Purchase. First professional theatre experience with NY Shakespeare-in-the Park prods. of Henry V and Measure for Measure. Appeared in Abel's Sister for England's Royal Court Theatre.
PICTURES: Starting Over (debut, 1979), Hanky Panky, Eddie Macon's Run, Cross Creek, Tucker: The Man and His Dream, The Prince of Pennsylvania, Glory, Just Like in the Movies, Mr. Destiny, V.I. Warshawski, Defenseless, Meeting Venus, JFK.
TELEVISION: Series: Aftermash, Crime Story. Movies: The Day Christ Died, Living Proof: The Hank Williams Jr. Story, A Doctor's Story, Cold Sassy Tree, Hostages. Special: The Revolt of Mother. Guest: Roseanne, The Young Riders, Spenser: For Hire, Kate and Allie, Miami Vice.
THEATRE: NY: Loose Ends, The Caine Mutiny Court-Martial, Buried Child, In Trousers, Geniuses, King John, Saint Joan.

SANDERS, TERRY BARRETT: Producer, Director, Writer. b. New York, NY, Dec. 20, 1931. e. UCLA, 1951; Co-prod., photographed, A Time Out of War, 1954. Academy award best two-reel subject, and won first prize Venice Film Festival, etc.; co-wrote The Day Lincoln Was Shot, CBS-TV; s.p. the Naked and the Dead; prod. Crime and Punishment—USA., prod., co-dir. War Hunt; prod. and dir. Portrait of Zubin Mehta for U.S.I.A. Assoc. dean, Film Sch., California Inst. of the Arts. Prod.-Dir.: Four Stones for Kanemitsu (Acad. Award nom.). Prod.-Dir.-Writer: Rose Kennedy: A Life to Remember (Acad. Award nom.) Professor, UCLA. Pres., American Film Foundation.
TELEVISION: Prod. dir.: Hollywood and the Stars, The Legend of Marilyn Monroe, National Geographic Society specials, The Kids from Fame, Film Bios Kennedy Center Honors; Slow Fires; Lillian Gish: the Actor's Life for Me (Emmy Award).

SANDRICH, JAY: Director. b. Los Angeles, CA, Feb. 24, 1932. e. UCLA.
PICTURE: Seems Like Old Times.
TELEVISION: The Lily Tomlin Show (DGA Award, 1975). Movies: The Crooked Hearts, What Are Best Friends For?, For Richer For Poorer. Series: Mary Tyler Moore Show (1970–77; Emmy Awards 1971 & 1973), Soap (1977–78), Phyllis (pilot), Tony Randall Show (pilot), Bob Newhart Show (pilot), Benson (pilot), Golden Girls (pilot), Empty Nest (pilot), The Cosby Show (1985–89; Emmy Award 1985, 1986; DGA Award 1985).

SANDS, JULIAN: Actor. b. Yorkshire, Eng. 1958. e. Central School of Speech and Drama, London 1979. Formed small theater co. that played in schools and youth clubs. Professional debut in Derek Jarman's short, Broken English and one-line part in Privates on Parade. Then opposite Anthony Hopkins in British TV series A Married Man (1981).
PICTURES: Privates on Parade (debut, 1982), Oxford Blues, The Killing Fields, After Darkness, The Doctor and the Devils, A Room with a View, Gothic, Siesta, Vibes, Wherever You Are, Manika: The Girl Who Lived Twice, Warlock, Tennessee Nights, Arachnophobia, Night Sun, Impromptu, Naked Lunch, Wicked, Husbands and Lovers, Tale of a Vampire, Boxing Helena.
TELEVISION: Series: A Married Man. Movies: Romance on the Orient Express, Harem, The Room, Murder By Moonlight, Grand Isle, Crazy in Love.

SANDS, TOMMY: Singer. b. Chicago, IL, Aug. 27, 1937. e. Schools there and Houston, TX, Greenwood, LA. Father, Benny Sands, concert pianist. Started career as guitar player, singer when 5, at KWKH station, Shreveport. One of pioneers of rock music. First manager was Col. Tom Parker. Acting debut: Kraft TV show The Singin' Idol; recording contract won him million record sales of Teen Age Crush.
PICTURES: Sing Boy Sing, Mardi Gras, Love in a Goldfish Bowl, Babes in Toyland, The Longest Day, Ensign Pulver, None But the Brave, The Violent Ones.

SANFORD, ISABEL: Actress. b. New York, NY, Aug. 29, 1917. e. Textile H.S., Evander Childs H.S. Began acting in elementary school and continued through high school. Joined American Negro Theatre in the 1930's (then The Star Players) which disbanded in W.W.II. Latter associated with YWCA project and off-Bdwy. plays. Bdwy. debut in The Amen Corner.
PICTURES: Guess Who's Coming to Dinner, Pendulum, Stand Up and Be Counted, The New Centurions, Love at First Bite.
TELEVISION: *Series*: All in the Family, The Jeffersons (Emmy Award, 1981). *Movie*: The Great Man's Whiskers.

SAN GIACOMO, LAURA: Actress. b. New Jersey, 1962. e. Carnegie Melon Univ. m. actor Cameron Dye. Appeared Off-Bdwy in North Shore Fish, Beirut, The Love Talker, Italian American Reconciliation.
PICTURES: Sex Lies and Videotape (debut, 1989), Pretty Woman, Vital Signs, Quigley Down Under, Once Around, Under Suspicion, Where the Day Takes You.
TELEVISION: *Movie*: For Their Own Good.

SANSOM, LESTER A.: Producer. b. Salt Lake City, UT, Apr. 24, 1910. e. U. of Utah. Radio singer under name of Jack Allen, 1930; ent. m.p. ind. in editorial dept., Fox Film Corp., Dec. 1931; served in U.S. Navy as head of film library, Washington, DC, 1942–45; head of edit. dept. & post-prod., Allied Artists, from 1953; assoc. prod. Skabenga; prod., co-writer, Battle Flame; assoc. prod. Hell to Eternity, exec. prod. The Thin Red Line, prod. Crack in the World; prod. Bikini Paradise, Battle of the Bulge, Custer of the West, Co-prod., Krakatoa— East of Java; exec. prod. 12 + 1.

SAPERSTEIN, DAVID: Writer, Director. b. Brooklyn, NY, March 19, 1937. e. Bronx H.S. of Science, CCNY, Film Institute, Chemical Engineering. 1960–80 write, prod. and dir. documentary films, TV commercials. Also wrote lyrics and managed rhythm and blues and rock 'n roll groups. Author of novels: Cocoon, Killing Affair, Metamorphosis, Red Devil, Funerama. Assoc. Professor NYU Graduate Film & TV.
PICTURES: Cocoon (story), Killing Affair (dir., s.p.), Personal Choice (dir., s.p.), Fatal Reunion (s.p.), Queen of America (s.p.), Torch, Sara Deri, Hearts & Diamonds, Vets, Do Not Disturb, Point of Honor, Snatched, Jack in the Box, Schoolhouse, Roberto: The Roberto Clemente Story.
TELEVISION: The Vintage Years (pilot), Dance of the Athletes (dir., writer), Rodeo—A Matter of Style (dir., writer), Mama Sings, The Corky Project.

SAPERSTEIN, HENRY G.: Executive. b. Chicago, IL, June 2, 1918. e. U. of Chicago. Theatre owner, Chicago, 1943–45; pres. Television Personalities, Inc., 1955–67 Mister Magoo, Dick Tracy, TV shows, 1960–62; 1960–67 Glen Films, Inc.; prod., All-Star Golf, 1958–62; prod. Championship Bowling, 1958–60; prod. Ding Dong School, 1959–60; pres. owner, UPA Pictures, Inc. Prod.: Mr. Magoo, Dick Tracy cartoon series, Mr. Magoo's Christmas Carol, T.N.T. Show, Turnon, Tune In Drop Out. Pres. Screen Entertainment Co., Benedict Pictures Corp., United Prod. of America; pres. H. G. Saperstein & Associates. Producer: The Vaudeville Thing; Tchaikovsky Competition, Gerald McBoing Boing Show
PICTURES: *Producer*: Gay Purr-ee, What's Up Tiger Lily?, T-A-M-I, Swan Lake, Monster Zero, War of the Gargantuas, Hell in the Pacific, War of the Gargantuas.

SARA, MIA: Actress. b. Brooklyn, NY, 1968. Started doing TV commercials; landed role in soap opera, All My Children.
PICTURES: Legend (debut, 1986), Ferris Bueller's Day Off, The Long Lost Friend, Apprentice to Murder, A Row of Crows, Imagination, Any Man's Death, Shadows in the Storm, A Stranger Among Us, By the Sword.
TELEVISION: *Movies*: Queenie, Till We Meet Again, Daughter of Darkness, Blindsided, Call of the Wild. *Special*: Big Time. *Guest*: Alfred Hitchcock Presents.

SARAFIAN, RICHARD C.: Director. b. New York, NY. April 28, 1935. Studied medicine and law before entering film industry with director Robert Altman making industrial documentaries.
TELEVISION: Gunsmoke, Bonanza, Guns of Will Sonnet, I Spy Wild, Wild West; Maverick, Twilight Zone, Gangster Chronicles, Movies: Shadow on the Land, Disaster on the Coastline, Splendor in the Grass, A Killing Affair, Liberty, Golden Moment—An Olympic Love Story. As Actor: Foley Square (series).
PICTURES: Andy (debut, 1965), Run Wild Run Free, Ballad of a Badman, Fragment of Fear, Man in the Wilder-

ness, Vanishing Point, Lolly Madonna XXX, The Man Who Loved Cat Dancing, The Next Man (also prod.), Sunburn, The Bear, Songwriter (actor only), Street Justice (also actor), Crisis 2050, Truk Lagoon.

SARANDON, CHRIS: Actor. b. Beckley, WV, July 24, 1942. e. U. of West Virginia. Mem. Catholic U.'s National Players touring U.S. in Shakespeare and Moliere. Acted with Washington, D.C. improvisational theater co. and Long Wharf. Bdwy debut, The Rothschilds. Then Two Gentlemen of Verona, Censored Scenes from King Kong, Marco Polo Sings a Solo, The Devil's Disciple, The Soldier's Tale, The Woods.
PICTURES: Dog Day Afternoon (debut, 1975; Acad. Award nom.), Lipstick, The Sentinel, Cuba, The Osterman Weekend, Protocol, Fright Night, Collision Course, The Princess Bride, Child's Play, Slaves of New York, Forced March, Whispers, The Resurrected.
TELEVISION: *Series*: The Guiding Light.· *Movies*: Thursday's Game, You Can't Go Home Again, The Day Christ Died, A Tale of Two Cities, This Child Is Mine, Broken Promises, Liberty, Mayflower Madam, Tailspin: Behind the Korean Airliner Tragedy, The Stranger Within, A Murderous Affair: The Carolyn Warmus Story.

SARANDON, SUSAN: Actress. r.n. Susan Tomaling. b. New York, NY, Oct. 4, 1946. e. Catholic U. Raised in Metuchen, New Jersey. Returned to New York to pursue acting, first signing with Ford Model Agency. Made film debut in Joe (1970). Also appeared on TV in A World Apart series. Co-produced film, The Last of the Cowboys (a.k.a. The Great Smokey Roadblock).
THEATER: *NY*: An Evening With Richard Nixon And . . . , A Coupla White Chicks Sitting Around Talking, Extremities.
PICTURES: Joe (debut, 1970), Lady Liberty, Lovin' Molly, The Front Page, The Great Waldo Pepper, The Rocky Horror Picture Show, Dragonfly (One Summer Love), Checkered Flag or Crash, The Last of the Cowboys (also co-prod.), The Other Side of Midnight, Pretty Baby, King of the Gypsies, Something Short of Paradise, Loving Couples, Atlantic City (Acad. Award nom.), Tempest, The Hunger, The Buddy System, Compromising Positions, The Witches of Eastwick, Bull Durham, Sweet Hearts Dance, The January Man, A Dry White Season, Through the Wire (narrator), White Palace, Thelma & Louise (Acad. Award nom.), The Player, Light Sleeper, Bob Roberts, Lorenzo's Oil (Acad. Award nom.), The Client.
TELEVISION: *Series*: Search For Tomorrow. *Guest*: Calucci's Dept, Owen Marshall: Counsellor at Law. *Specials*: Rimers of Eldritch, June Moon, Who Am I This Time? *Mini-Series*: A.D. *Movies*: F. Scott Fitzgerald & the Last of the Belles, Mussolini: Decline and Fall of Il Duce, Women of Valor.

SARGENT ALVIN: Writer. b. Philadelphia, PA, Apr. 12, 1927. Began career as writer for TV, then turned to theatrical films.
PICTURES: Gambit (co-s.p.), The Stalking Moon, The Sterile Cuckoo, I Walk the Line, The Effect of Gamma Rays on Man-in-the-Moon Marigolds, Paper Moon (Acad. Award nom.), Love and Pain (and the whole damn thing), Julia (Acad. Award, 1977), Bobby Deerfield, Straight Time (co-s.p.), Ordinary People (Acad. Award, 1980), Nuts (co-s.p.), Dominick and Eugene (co-s.p.), White Palace (co-s.p.), What About Bob? (co-story), Other People's Money, Hero (co-story).
TELEVISION: *Movies*: Footsteps, The Impatient Heart. *Series*: The Naked City, Route 66, Ben Casey, Alfred Hitchcock Presents, The Nurses, Mr. Novak, Empire.

SARGENT, DICK: Actor. b. Carmel, CA, Apr. 19, 1930. e. Stanford Univ. Veteran of over 250 TV shows, 17 feature films and 5 TV series.
PICTURES: Bernardine, Mardi Gras, Operation Petticoat, That Touch of Mink, Captain Newman M.D., The Ghost and Mr. Chicken, The Private Navy of Sgt. O'Farrell, Hardcore. Parts: The Clonus Horror, Body Count, Teen Witch, Rock-a-Die-Baby.
TELEVISION: *Series*: One Happy Family, Broadside, The Tammy Grimes Show, Bewitched, Down to Earth. *Movies*: Melvin Purvis: G-Man, Fantasy Island (pilot), The Power Within, The Gossip Columnist, Acting on Impulse. *Mini-Series*: Rich Man Poor Man.

SARGENT, JOSEPH: Director. r.n. Giuseppe Danielle Sargente. b. Jersey City, NJ, July 25, 1925. e. studied theatre, New Sch. for Social Research 1946–49.
PICTURES: One Spy Too Many, The Hell With Heroes, Colossus: The Forbin Project, White Lightning, The Taking of Pelham One Two Three, MacArthur, Goldengirl, Coast to Coast, Nightmares, Jaws—The Revenge (also prod.).
TELEVISION: The Spy in the Green Hat, *Mini-series*: The Manions of America, James Mitchener's Space. *Movies*: The Sunshine Patriot, The Immortal (pilot), The Man, Tribes, The Marcus-Nelson Murders (Emmy award for tv movie that was pilot for Kojak series), Maybe I'll Come Home in the Spring (also prod.), The Man Who Died Twice, The Night That Panicked America, Sunshine (also prod.), Friendly Persuasion, Amber Waves, Hustling, Freedom, Tomorrow's Child,

Memorial Day, Terrible Joe Moran, Choices of the Heart (also prod.), Space, Love Is Never Silent (Emmy Award), Passion Flower, Of Pure Blood, There Must Be a Pony, The Karen Carpenter Story, Day One, The Incident, Caroline? (Emmy Award), The Last Elephant, Never Forget, Miss Rose White (Emmy Award), Somebody's Daughter (also prod.), Skylark (also prod.).

SARLUI, ED: Executive. b. Amsterdam, The Netherlands, Nov. 10, 1925. Owner, Peruvian Films, S.A.; pres., Radio Films of Peru, S.A.; pres. Bryant Films Educatoriana, S.A.; partner, United Producers de Colombia Ltd.; pres. Royal Film N.V.; pres., United Producers de Centroamerica, S.A.; pres. United Producers de Mexico, S.A.; pres., United Producers Int'l, Inc., Continental Motion Pictures, Inc. 1988, formed Cinema Corp. of America with Moshe Diamant and Elliott Kastner. Co-chmn. Epic Prods. Inc.
PICTURES: Exec. prod.: Full Moon in Blue Water, High Spirits, Teen Witch, Courage Mountain, Night Game.

SARNOFF, ROBERT W.: Executive. b. New York, NY, July 2, 1918. e. Harvard U., B.A., 1939; Columbia Law Sch. 1940. In office of Coordinator of Info., Wash., DC, Aug. 1941; the U.S. Navy, Mar. 1942; asst. to publisher, Gardner Cowles, Jr., 1945; mem. of staff Look Mag., 1946, with NBC, 1948–65; pres., Dec. 1955–58; chmn. bd., 1958; bd. of dir. RCA, 1957; chmn bd. chief exec. officer, NBC, 1958–65; pres. RCA, 1966; Chief Exec. Officer, 1968; bd. chmn., 1970–75. Mem., TV Pioneers, 1957; pres., 1952–53; International Radio & TV Society, Broadcasters Committee for Radio Free Europe. Am Home Products, Inc., dir., of Business Committee for the Arts. Chmn, past pres. council, Acad. of TV Arts & Sciences; v.p. & bd. of dir., Acad. of TV Arts & Sciences Foundation.

SARNOFF, THOMAS W.: Executive. b. New York, NY, Feb. 23, 1927. e. Phillips Acad., Andover, MA, 1939–43, Princeton U., 1943–45, Stanford U. grad. 1948, B.S. in E.E.; Grad Sch. of Bus. Admin. 1948–49. Sgt., U.S. Army Signal Corps, 1945–46; prod. & sales, ABC-TV, Hollywood, 1949–50; prod. dept. MGM, 1951–52; asst. to dir. of finance and oper., NBC, 1952–54; dir. of prod. and bus. affairs, 1954–57; vice pres., prod. and bus. affairs, 1957–60; v.p. adm. west coast, 1960–62; v.p. west coast, 1962; exec. v.p. 1965–77; bd. of dir., NBC prods 1961–77; bd of dir. Hope Enterprises 1960–75; dir. NABCAT, Inc. 1967–75; dir. Valley County Cable TV, Inc. 1969–75; Pres. NBC Entertainment Corp. 1972–77; Pres. Sarnoff International Enterprises, Inc. 1977–81; pres., Sarnoff Enter-tainment Corp., 1981–; pres., Venturetainment Corp. 1986–; Past pres. Research Foundation at St. Joseph Hospital of Burbank; past pres. Permanent Charities of the Entertain-ment Ind.; past ch. bd. of trustees, National Acad. of TV Arts and Sciences. Pres. Acad. of TV Arts & Sciences Foundation 1990–.

SARRAZIN, MICHAEL: Actor. r.n. Jacques Michel Andre Sarrazin. b. Quebec, Canada, May 22, 1940. Began acting at 17 on CBC TV; signed by Universal, 1965.
PICTURES: Gunfight in Abilene (debut, 1967), The Flim-Flam Man, The Sweet Ride, Journey to Shiloh, A Man Called Gannon, Eye of the Cat, In Search of Gregory, They Shoot Horses Don't They?, The Pursuit of Happiness, Sometimes a Great Notion, Believe in Me, The Groundstar Conspiracy, Harry in Your Pocket, For Pete's Sake, The Reincarnation of Peter Proud, The Loves and Times of Scaramouche, The Gumball Rally, Caravans, Double Negative, The Seduction, Fighting Back, Joshua Then and Now, Captive Hearts, Mascara, Keeping Track, Malarek, Lena's Holiday.
TELEVISION: Guest: Chrysler Theatre, The Virginian, World Premiere. Movies: The Doomsday Flight, Frankenstein: The True Story, Beulah Land, Passion and Paradise.

SASSOWER, HARVEY L.: Advertising director. b. New York, NY, July 28, 1945. e. City Coll. of New York, B.A., advertising. 1968 asst. to adv. mg., United Artists. 1969, asst. to adv. dir., 20th Century-Fox, 1969, appointed adv. mgr. of ABC Pictures Corp., dir. of adv., ABC Pictures, 1970; pres., Universal Spectrum, Inc. (design & adv. studio). Art director; author.

SAUL, OSCAR: Writer. b. Brooklyn, NY, Dec. 26, 1912. e. Brooklyn Coll. 1932. Co-author play, Medicine Show; m.p. ed., U.S. Public Health Svce; numerous radio and TV plays. Wrote novel The Dark Side of Love.
PICTURES: Once Upon a Time, Strange Affair, Road House, Lady Gambles, Once More My Darling, Woman in Hiding, Secret of Convict Lake, A Streetcar Named Desire, Thunder on the Hill, Affair in Trinidad, Let's Do It Again (prod.), Helen Morgan Story, Joker is Wild, Naked Maja, Second Time Around, Major Dundee, Silencers, Man and Boy, Amigos, Snowstar.
TELEVISION: A Streetcar Name Desire, many others.

SAUNDERS, WILLIAM: Executive. b. London, England, Jan. 4, 1923. e. left Upton House Central Sch. at 16. Served in British Eighth Army, 1941–47. Entered industry in 1947 as salesman with 20th Century Fox Film Co. in London; sales mgr., Anglo-Amalgamated Film Co., London, 1951–61; with

Motion Picture Producers Assoc. of Amer. as sales dir. in Lagos, Nigeria, dist. Amer. feature films to West African countries, 1962–64; joined 20th Century Fox TV Int'l., Paris as v.p. European TV sales, 1964–83; 20th Century TV Int'l., Los Angeles as sr. v.p., 1983; named exec. v.p. 1987 and president, 1988–present.

SAURA, CARLOS: Director. b. Huesca, Spain, January 4, 1932. e. educated as engineer. Worked as professional photographer from 1949. Studied at Instituto de Investigaciones y Experien-cias Cinematograficos, Madrid, 1952–57 where he then taught from 1957–64 until being dismissed for political reasons. 1957–58 dir. shorts La tarde del domingo and Cuenca.
PICTURES: Director and s.p.: Los Golfos (The Urchins), Lament for a Bandit, La caza, Peppermint frappe, Stress es tres, tres; La Madriguera, The Garden of Delights, Ana and the Wolves, Cousin Angelica (jury prize, Cannes, 1974), Cria! (special jury prize, Cannes, 1976), Elisa Vide Mia, Los ojos vendados, Mama Cumple 100 Años, Hurry, Hurry (Golden Bear, Berlin Fest., 1981), Blood Wedding, Dulces Horas, Antonieta, Carmen, El Amor Brujo, El Durado, The Dark Night.

SAVAGE, DAVID: Executive Producer, Advertising Executive. b. New York, NY, March 17, 1929. e. Rochester Inst. of Technology. In research development & testing div., Eastman Kodak Co., 2 yrs.; adv. mgr. asst. nat'l sales mgr., Official Films; org., film dept. mgr. WCBS-TV; dir. of film procurement, CBS; mgr. of film procurement, NBC; mgr. planning, mer-chandising, Recorded Tape Dept., RCA Records; promo. mgr., special products mktg. RCA Records Div.; program and marketing chmn. RCA SelectaVision group; v.p., operations, Wunderman, Rilotto, & Kline, 1970; pres., Response Indus-tries, Inc., (direct response adv. agency) 1973 which became affiliate of McCann Erickson; and was sr. v.p. of McCann Erickson Pres., Mattel Direct Marketing, 1982; v.p. and man. dir., Foote Cene Belding, subsid. Knipp-Taylor USA, 1985.

SAVAGE, FRED: Actor. b. Highland Park, IL, July 9, 1976. While in kindergarten auditioned for commercial at local community center. Didn't get the job but called back by same dir. for two more tests. Chosen for Pac-Man vitamin ad which led to 27 on-camera TV commercials and 36 voice-over radio spots.
PICTURES: The Boy Who Could Fly, The Princess Bride, Vice Versa, Little Monsters, The Wizard.
TELEVISION: Series: Morningstar/Eveningstar, The Won-der Years. Movies: Convicted: A Mother's Story, Run Till You Fall, When You Remember Me, Christmas on Division Street. Special: Runaway Ralph. Guest: The Twilight Zone.

SAVAGE, JOHN: Actor. r.n. John Youngs. b. Old Bethpage, Long Island, NY, Aug. 25, 1949. Studied at American Acad. of Dramatic Arts. In Manhattan organized Children's Theatre Group which performed in public housing. Won Drama Desk Award for performance in One Flew Over the Cuckoo's Nest (Chicago & LA).
PICTURES: Bad Company (debut, 1972), Steelyard Blues, The Killing Kind, The Sister in Law (also composed score), The Deer Hunter, Hair, The Onion Field, Inside Moves, Cattle Annie and Little Britches, The Amateur, Brady's Escape, Maria's Lovers, Salvador, Beauty and the Beast, Hotel Colonial, Soldier's Revenge, The Beat, Caribe, Do the Right Thing, Point of View, Any Man's Death, The Godfather Part III, Hunting, Primary Motive, My Forgotten Man, Shattered Image.
STAGE: Fiddler on the Roof, Ari, Siamese Connections, The Hostage, American Buffalo, Of Mice and Men.
TELEVISION: Series: Gibbsville. Movies: All the Kind Strangers, Eric (also wrote and performed songs), Turning Point of Jim Malloy, Coming Out of the Ice, The Tender Age (The Little Sister), Silent Witness, The Nairobi Affair, Desper-ate, The Burning Shore, Daybreak. Special: Date Rape (Afterschool Special).

SAVALAS, TELLY: Actor. r.n. Aristotle Savalas. b. Garden City, NY, Jan. 21, 1924. e. Columbia U., B.S. Joined Information Services of State Dept.; made exec. dir., then named sr. dir. of news, special events for ABC, where created Your Voice of America series. Acting career began with debut in Bring Home a Baby on Armstrong Circle Theatre TV.
PICTURES: The Young Savages (debut, 1961), Mad Dog Coll, Birdman of Alcatraz (Acad. Award nom.), Cape Fear, The Interns, Man from the Diner's Club, Love is a Ball, Johnny Cool, The New Interns, Greatest Story Ever Told, The Slender Thread, Genghis Khan, Battle of the Bulge, Beau Geste, Dirty Dozen, Sol Madrid, The Scalphunters, Buona Sera Mrs. Campbell, MacKenna's Gold, The Assassination Bureau, Crooks and Coronets, On Her Majesty's Secret Service, Kelly's Heroes, The Land Raiders, The Family, A Town Called Bastard, Pretty Maids All in a Row, Clay Pigeon, Pancho Villa, Redneck, Crime Boss, Sonny and Jed, A Reason to Live A Reason to Die, Horror Express, Killer Force, Lisa and the Devil (House of Exorcism), Inside Out, Beyond Reason (also dir., s.p.), Capricorn One, Beyond the Poseidon Adventure, Escape to Athena, The Muppet Movie,

Fake-Out, Cannonball Run II, The Secret of the Sahara, GoBots (voice), Faceless.
TELEVISION: *Series*: Acapulco, Kojak (Emmy Award, 1974). *Movies*: Mongo's Back in Town, Visions, The Marcus-Nelson Murders, She Cried Murder, Alcatraz: The Whole Shocking Story, Hellinger's Law, The Cartier Affair, The Dirty Dozen: The Deadly Mission, Alice in Wonderland, The Dirty Dozen: The Fatal Mission. *Host*: Return to the Titanic.

SAWELSON, MEL: Executive b. Los Angeles, CA, Sept. 5, 1929. e. U. of Southern California, 1947–48; UCLA. 1948–49. Entered M.P. industry in 1947; mgr., Acme Film Laboratories, Inc., 1952; pres. Sports-TV; 1957–59; produced, Olympic Films, International Olympic Organization, 1956; produced, Big 10 Hilites, PCC Hilites, All American Game of the Week, 1957–59; 1st m.p. lab. exec. to install videotape, 1959; created Acme-chroma process of transferring color videotape to film; pres., Acme Film & Videotape Labs., 1967–71; v.p. Consolidated Film Industries, 1971, exec. v.p. 1972; pres., Glen Glenn Sound Co., 1972.

SAWYER, DIANE: News Correspondent, Anchor. b. Glasgow, KY, Dec. 22, 1945. m. director Mike Nichols. e. Wellesley Coll. Studied law before deciding on career in TV. Former Junior Miss winner and weather reporter on a Louisville TV station before arriving in Washington, 1970. Worked for Nixon Administration in press office from 1970–74; assisted Nixon in writing memoirs, 1975–78. Joined CBS News as reporter in Washington bureau in 1978; named correspondent in 1980. Served as CBS State Dept. correspondent 1980–81. Joined Charles Kuralt as co-anchor of the weekday editions of CBS Morning News in 1981; 1984–89 correspondent on 60 Minutes; 1989, signed by ABC News as co-anchor of Primetime Live news prog. with Sam Donaldson.

SAXON, JOHN: Actor. r.n. Carmine Orrico. b. Brooklyn, NY, Aug. 5, 1936.
PICTURES: Running Wild (debut, 1955), The Unguarded Moment, Rock Pretty Baby, Summer Love, The Reluctant Debutante, This Happy Feeling, The Restless Years, The Big Fisherman, Cry Tough, Portrait in Black, The Unforgiven, The Plunderers, Posse from Hell, Mr. Hobbs Takes a Vacation, War Hunt, Evil Eye, The Cardinal, The Ravagers, The Cavern, The Appaloosa, Queen of Blood, Night Caller From Outer Space, For Singles Only, Death of a Gunfighter, Company of Killers, Joe Kidd, Enter The Dragon, Black Christmas, Mitchell, The Swiss Conspiracy, Strange Shadows in an Empty Room, Moonshine County Express, Shalimar, The Bees, The Glove, The Electric Horseman, Battle Beyond the Stars, Beyond Evil, Blood Beach, Cannibal in the Streets, Wrong Is Right, The Big Score, Nightmare on Elm Street, Prisoners of the Lost Universe, Fever Pitch, Nightmare on Elm Street 3: Dream Warriors, Criminal Act, Death House (also dir.), My Mom's a Werewolf, Aftershock, Blood Salvage, Hellmaster, Crossing the Line, Maximum Force, No Escape No Return.
TELEVISION: *Series*: The Bold Ones (The New Doctors), Falcon Crest. *Movies*: The Doomsday Flight, Winchester 73, Istanbul Express, The Intruders, Snatched, Linda, Can Ellen Be Saved?, Planet Earth, Crossfire, Strange New World, Raid on Entebbe, The Immigrants, Golden Gate, Rooster, Prisoners of the Lost Universe, Payoff, Blackmail, Genghis Khan.

SAYLES, JOHN: Writer, Director, Editor, Actor. b. Schnectady, NY, Sept. 28, 1950. e. Williams Coll., B.S. psychology, 1972. Wrote two novels: Pride of the Bimbos, 1975 and Union Dues, 1978; also The Anarchist's Convention, collection of short stories and, Thinking in Pictures: The Making of the Movie Matewan (1987). First screenplay: Piranha (1978). Wrote and directed plays off-Bdwy (New Hope for the Dead, Turnbuckle). Directed Bruce Springsteen music videos (Born in the U.S.A., I'm on Fire, Glory Days). Recipient of MacArthur Foundation Grant for genius.
PICTURES: Piranha (s.p.), Battle Beyond the Stars (s.p.), Lady in Red (s.p.), Return of the Secaucus Seven (dir., s.p., actor, editor), Alligator (s.p.), The Howling (co-s.p., actor), The Challenge (co-s.p.), Lianna (dir., s.p., actor, edit.), Baby It's You (dir., s.p.), The Brother from Another Planet (dir., s.p., edit., actor), Enormous Changes at the Last Minute (co-s.p.), The Clan of the Cave Bear (s.p.), Hard Choices (actor), Something Wild (actor), Wild Thing (s.p.), Matewan (dir., s.p., actor), Eight Men Out (dir., s.p., actor), Breaking In (s.p.), Little Vegas (actor), City of Hope (dir., s.p., edit., actor), Straight Talk (actor), Malcolm X (actor), Passion Fish (dir., s.p., edit.), Matinee (actor), My Life's in Turnaround (actor).
TELEVISION: A Perfect Match, Unnatural Causes (actor, writer), Shannon's Deal (writer). *Special*: Mountain View (Alive From Off Center).

SCACCHI, GRETA: Actress. b. Milan, Italy, Feb. 18, 1960. e. England and Australia. Acted in Bristol Old Vic Theatre in England.
PICTURES: Das Zweiter Gesicht, Heat and Dust, The Coca Cola Kid, Burke & Wills, Defence of the Realm, A Man in Love, Good Morning Babylon, White Mischief, Paura e

Amore (Fear and Love), Woman in the Moon, Presumed Innocent, Fires Within, Shattered, The Player, Turtle Beach, Salt on Our Skin, The Browning Version.
TELEVISION: *Mini-Series*: Waterfront (Australia). *Movies*: Ebony Tower, Dr. Fischer of Geneva, Camille.

SCARDINO, DON: Actor. b. Canada. On Bdwy. in Godspell, King of Hearts, Johnny No Trump, As You Like It. Director: Godspell, A Few Good Men.
PICTURES: The People Next Door, Homer, Squirm, Cruising, He Knows You're Alone.
TELEVISION: *Series*: The Guiding Light. *Dir*.: 27 Wagons Full of Cotton.

SCARWID, DIANA: Actress. b. Savannah, GA. Went to N.Y. after high school to attend American Acad. of Dramatic Arts, Pace U., 1975. Member of National Shakespeare Conservatory (Woodstock, NY) and worked in regional theatres before moving to Hollywood 1976.
PICTURES: Pretty Baby (debut, 1978), Honeysuckle Rose, Inside Moves (Acad. Award nom.), Mommie Dearest, Rumble Fish, Strange Invaders, Silkwood, The Ladies Club, Psycho III, Extremities, Heat, Brenda Starr.
TELEVISION: *Guest*: Gibbsville, Kingston: Confidential. *Mini-Series*: Studs Lonigan. *Movies*: In the Glitter Palace, The Possessed, Forever, Battered, Guyana Tragedy: The Story of Jim Jones, Desperate Lives, Thou Shalt Not Kill, A Bunny's Tale, After the Promise, Night of the Hunter, Simple Justice, Labor of Love: The Arlette Schweitzer Story.

SCHAEFER, CARL: Media Consultant, Publicist, b. Cleveland, OH, Sept. 2, 1908. e. UCLA. Contr. to mag., including Vanity Fair, Hollywood Citizen-News, 1931–35; Warner Bros., 1935.; Huesped de Honor, Mexico, 1943; OSS W.W.II, 1944–45; Int'l Comt. AMPS, chmn. 1966–67; Italian Order of Merit, 1957; Chevalier de l'ordre de la Couronne, Belgium, 1963. Pres., Foreign Trade Assn. of Southern Calif., 1954; chmn. of bd., 1955; British-American C. of C., Dir., 1962; Chevalier French Legion d'Honneur, 1955; Comm. Hollywood Museum; dir., intl. relations, Warner Bros. Seven Arts Int'l Corp., 1960; formed own firm, Carl Schaefer Enterprises, 1971. Dir. pub. rel., British-American Chamber of Commerce, 1971; dir. pub. rel. Iota Intl. Pictures, 1971; dir. pub. rel. Lyric Films Intl., 1971; bureau chief (Hollywood) Movie/TV Marketing, 1971; man. dir., Intl. Festival Advisory Council, 1971; dir. pub. rel. & adv. Francis Lederer Enterprises (Inc. American National Acad. of Performing Arts, and Canoga Mission Gallery) 1974; West Coast rep. Angelika Films of N.Y. 1974, Hwd. rep Korwitz/Geiger Products. 1975–; Hwd. corresp. Movie News, S'pore, & Femina, Hong Kong, 1974–; member Westn. Publications Assn. 1975–; field rep. Birch Records 1975; Hollywood rep Antena Magazine, Buenos Aires; dir pub rel Style Magazine. Coordinator Hollywood Reporter Annual Key Art Awards; coordinator Hollywood Reporter Annual Marketing Concept Awards; exec. comm. & historian ShoWest; Mem: National Panel of Consumer Arbitrators, 1985; Hollywood Corr., Gold Coast Times of Australia, 1986–87. Winner 1990 Key Art Award. Member: AMPAS, awarded certif. of Appreciation, 1962; charter member, Publicists Guild of America; pres. Pacific Intercollegiate Press Assn., while UCLA Daily Bruin Editor, 1930–31.

SCHAEFER, GEORGE: Director, Producer. b. Wallingford, CT, Dec. 16, 1920. e. Lafayette Coll., Yale Drama Sch. Bdwy. shows include The Linden Tree; Man and Superman; Body Beautiful, Last of Mrs. Lincoln, G.I. Hamlet, Mixed Couples, The Heiress (revival), Idiot's Delight (revival), Teahouse of the August Moon; Write Me a Murder. 1986, joined UCLA as chairman, Theatre, Film, TV.
PICTURES: Pendulum, Generation, Doctors' Wives, Once Upon a Scoundrel, Macbeth, An Enemy of the People.
TELEVISION: *Director*: Hamlet, One Touch of Venus, The Corn Is Green, The Good Fairy, The Little Foxes, Little Moon of Alban (Emmy Award, 1959), Harvey, Macbeth (Emmy Award, 1961), The Magnificent Yankee (Emmy Award, 1965), Kiss Me Kate, Elizabeth the Queen (Emmy Award, 1968), A War of Children (Emmy Award, 1973), Pygmalion, F. Scott Fitzgerald, Blind Ambition, First You Cry, Our Town, Sandburg's Lincoln, The People vs. Jean Harris, A Piano for Mrs. Cimino, The Deadly Game, Children in the Crossfire, Right of Way, Stone Pillow, Mrs. Delafield Wants to Marry, Laura Lansing Slept Here, Let Me Hear You Whisper, The Man Upstairs (also co-prod.).

SCHAFFEL, ROBERT: Producer. b. Washington, DC, March 2, 1944. Partner with Jon Voight in Voight-Schaffel Prods. Now heads Robert Schaffel Prods.
PICTURES: Gordon's War, Sunnyside, Lookin' to Get Out, Table for Five, American Anthem, Distant Thunder, Jacknife, Diggstown.

SCHATZBERG, JERRY: Director. b. New York, NY, June 26, 1927. e. student U. of Miami, 1947–48. Early career in photography as asst. to Bill Helburn 1954–56. Freelance still photographer and TV commercials dir. 1956–69. Contrib. photographs to several mags. incl. Life.

PICTURES: Puzzle of a Downfall Child (1970), Panic in Needle Park, Scarecrow, Sweet Revenge (prod.-dir.), The Seduction of Joe Tynan, Honeysuckle Rose, Misunderstood, No Small Affair, Street Smart, Reunion.
TELEVISION: Clinton and Nadine.

SCHEIDER, ROY: Actor. b. Orange, NJ, Nov. 10, 1932. e. Franklin and Marshall Coll. where he won the Theresa Helburn Acting Award twice. First professional acting in N.Y. Shakespeare Festival 1961 prod. of Romeo and Juliet. Became member of Lincoln Center Repertory Co. and acted with Boston Arts Festival, American Shakespeare Festival, Arena Stage (Wash., DC) and American Repertory Co. Appeared in documentary In Our Hands.
STAGE: Richard III, Stephen D, Sergeant Musgrave's Dance, The Alchemist, Betrayal.
PICTURES: Curse of the Living Corpse (debut, 1964), Paper Lion, Star!, Stiletto, Loving, Puzzle of a Downfall Child, Klute, The French Connection (Acad. Award nom.), The Outside Man, The French Conspiracy, The Seven Ups, Sheila Levine is Dead and Living in New York, Jaws, Marathon Man, Sorcerer, Jaws 2, Last Embrace, All That Jazz (Acad. Award nom.), Still of the Night, Blue Thunder, 2010, Mishima (narrator), The Men's Club, 52 Pickup, Cohen and Tate, Listen to Me, Night Game, The Fourth War, The Russia House, Naked Lunch, Romeo Is Bleeding.
TELEVISION: Movies: Assignment Munich, Jacobo Timerman: Prisoner Without a Name Cell Without a Number, Tiger Town, Somebody Has to Shoot the Picture, Wild Justice. Series: seaQuest DSV.Guest: Hallmark Hall of Fame, Studio One, N.Y.P.D. Special: Portrait of the Soviet Union (host).

SCHEINMAN, ANDREW: Producer. b. 1948. e. Univ. of VA, received law degree. Professional tennis player before entering film business as producer of three Charlton Heston films.
PICTURES: The Mountain Man, The Awakening, Modern Romance, Mother Lode, The Sure Thing, Stand By Me, The Princess Bride, When Harry Met Sally . . . , Misery, A Few Good Men, North.
TELEVISION: Series: Seinfeld (exec. prod.)

SCHELL, MARIA: Actress. b. Vienna, Austria, Jan. 5, 1926. Sister of Maximillian Schell. Made debut at 12 in Swiss film, The Gravel Pit. Subsequently appeared in many British and American films.
PICTURES: Angel with a Trumpet, The Magic Box, Angel-ika, So Little Time, The Heart of the Matter, The Rats, Napoleon, Gervaise, The Last Bridge, Rose Bernd, White Nights, The Brothers Karamazov, The Hanging Tree, As the Sea Rages, A Day Will Come, Cimarron, The Mark, End of Desire, Only a Woman, 99 Women, Devil By the Tail, Night of the Blood Monster, The Odessa File, Voyage of the Damned, The Twist, Superman, Just a Gigolo, 1919.
TELEVISION: (U.S.): Christmas Lilies of the Field, Inside the Third Reich, Martian Chronicles, Samson and Delilah.

SCHELL, MAXIMILIAN: Actor, Director. b. Vienna, Dec. 8, 1930. Sister is actress Maria Schell.
PICTURES: Children Mother and the General (debut, 1955), The Young Lions, Judgment at Nuremberg (Acad. Award, 1961), Five Finger Exercise, The Reluctant Saint, The Condemned of Altona, Topkapi, Return from the Ashes, The Deadly Affair, Counterpoint, The Desperate Ones, The Castle, Krakatoa East of Java, Simon Bolivar, First Love (also dir.), Trotta, Pope Joan, Paulina 1880, The Pedestrian (dir.), The Odessa File, The Man in the Glass Booth, End of the Game (dir., co-prod.), St. Ives, The Day That Shook the World, A Bridge Too Far, Cross of Iron, Julia, Players, Avalanche Express, Together?, The Black Hole, The Chosen, Marlene (dir.), Man Under Suspicion, The Rose Garden, The Freshman, Labyrinth, A Far Off Place.
TELEVISION: Shows include: Playhouse 90, Judgment at Nuremberg, The Fifth Column, The Diary of Anne Frank, Turn The Key Deftly, Phantom of the Opera, Heidi, The Assisi Underground, Peter the Great (mini-series), Young Catherine, Stalin, Miss Rose White.

SCHENCK, AUBREY: Producer. b. Brooklyn, NY, Aug. 26, 1908. e. Cornell U., NYU. With law firm of O'Brien, Driscoll & Raftery; buyer & attorney for Natl. Theatres, 1936; prod. for 20th Century-Fox 1945; exec. prod. Eagle Lion 1946; contract prod. Universal Internatl. 1948; Aubrey Schenck Productions, Inc.
PICTURES: Shock, Johnny Comes Flying Home, Strange Triangle, Repeat Performance, T-Men, Mickey, It's a Joke Son, Trapped, Port of New York, Wyoming Man, Undercover Girl, Fat Man, Target Unknown; formed own co. to prod. War Paint, Beachhead. Also: Yellow Tomahawk, Shield for Murder, Big House, U.S.A., Crime Against Joe, Emergency Hospital, Ghost Town, Broken Star, Rebels in Town, Pharaoh's Curse, Three Bad Sisters, Fort Yuma, Desert Sands, Quincannon, Frontier Scout, Black Sleep, Hot Cars, War Drums, Voodoo Island, Revolt at Fort Laramie, Tomahawk Trail, Untamed Youth, Girl in Black Stockings, Bop Girl Goes Calypso, Up Periscope, Violent Road, Reckless, Frankenstein 1970, Wild Harvest, Robinson Crusoe On Mars, Don't Worry, Ambush

Bay, Kill a Dragon, Impasse, More Dead Than Alive, Barquero, Daughters of Satan.
TELEVISION: Miami Undercover, series.

SCHEPISI, FRED: Producer, Director, Writer. b. Melbourne, Australia, Dec. 26, 1939. e. Assumption Col., Marcellin Col. Assessed student films at Melbourne's Swinburne Inst. of Tech., worked on gov. sponsored experimental Film Fund, Made TV commercials. Founded The Film House prod. co.
PICTURES: Director: The Devil's Playground (also prod., s.p.; Australian Film Inst. Award for Best Film), The Chant of Jimmie Blacksmith (also prod., s.p.; Writers Guild Award), Barbarosa, Iceman, Plenty, Roxanne, A Cry in the Dark (also co-s.p.; Australian Film Inst. Award for Best Screenplay), The Russia House (also co-prod.), Mr. Baseball (also co-prod.), Six Degrees of Separation.

SCHERICK, EDGAR J: Executive, Producer. b. New York, NY, Oct. 16, 1924. e. Harvard U.; elected to Phi Beta Kappa. Asst. dir. of radio and TV; assoc. media dir. and dir. of sports special events, Dancer-Fitzgerald-Sample ad agency, NY during 1950s. Introduced Wide World of Sports on TV through his co., Sports Programs, Inc. Was v.p. in chg. of network programming at ABC-TV. Pres. of Palomar Pictures Int'l. Now independent producer.
PICTURES: For Love of Ivy, The Birthday Party, Take the Money and Run, They Shoot Horses, Don't They?, The Killing of Sister George, Ring of Bright Water, Jenny, Sleuth, The Heartbreak Kid, Law and Disorder, The Stepford Wives, I Never Promised You a Rose Garden, The Taking of Pelham One, Two, Three, The American Success Company, I'm Dancing As Fast As I Can, Shoot the Moon, White Dog, Reckless, Mrs. Soffel.
TELEVISION: The Man Who Wanted to Live Forever (1970); The Silence; Circle of Children; Raid on Entebbe; Panic in Echo Park; Zuma Beach; An American Christmas Carol; The Seduction of Miss Leona; Revenge of the Stepford Wives; Hitler's SS; The High Price of Passion; The Stepford Children; Unholy Matrimony; Little Gloria . . . Happy at Last; On Wings of Eagles; Hands of a Stranger; Home Fires; He Makes Me Feel Like Dancin' (Emmy and Acad. Awards, 1983); Stranger on My Land (exec. prod.); And the Band Played On; The Kennedys of Massachusetts; Satin's Touch (exec. prod.), Phantom of the Opera, The Secret Life of Ian Fleming.

SCHICK, ELLIOT: Executive. b. Brooklyn, NY, Dec. 24, 1924. e. Brooklyn Coll., B.A.; New School for Social Research, drama workshop, directing 1945–46. Author of book for Ballet Theatre, Manfred; book, The Administration of the Economic and Social Council. 1942–48, prod. & dir. radio shows for WNYC, N.Y., composed and arranged music for radio and stage production; 1946–48; dialogue director, Republic Studios; 1948–50, prod. & dir. TV shows and commercials, Nova Productions; 1950–51, editor, United Nations Film Div.; 1951–53, editor, Candid Camera; 1953–55, asst. studio mgr., American Natl. Studios; 1955–56, prod. & dir. live and video tape shows for KCET; 1973–77, sprv. prod. for AIP; 1977, joined EMI Films, Inc. as v.p. prod.
PICTURES: Asst. dir.: Tora Tora Tora. Prod. mgr.: 3 in the Attic, Up in the Cellar, Bunny O'Hare, Honkers, Hickey and Boggs, Kansas City Bomber, White Lightning. Sprv. prod.: Sugar Hill, Return to Macon County, Cooley High, Future-world, Island of Dr. Moreau. Exec.-in-chg.-prod.: The Deer Hunter, Blue Skies Again, Farewell to the King. Prod.: The Earthling, Fools Die. Co-Prod.: Cherry 2000, Masters of the Universe. Exec. prod.: Marie.
TELEVISION: prod., Private Benjamin (TV series), supvr. prod., Pippin (TV).

SCHIFRIN, LALO: Composer. b. Buenos Aires, Argentina, June 21, 1932. Father was conductor of Teatro Colon in B.A. for 30 years. Schifrin studied with Juan Carlos Paz in Arg. and later Paris Cons. Returned to homeland and wrote for stage, modern dance, TV. Became interested in jazz and joined Dizzie Gillespie's band in 1962 as pianist and composer. Settled in L.A. Pres. Young Musicians Fed. Music; dir. and conductor, Paris Philharmonic 1987.
PICTURES: The Cincinnati Kid, The Liquidator, Once a Thief, Venetian Affair, Murderer's Row, Blindfold, Joy House, Cool Hand Luke, The President's Analyst, Sol Madrid, Where Angels Go—Trouble Follows, Coogan's Bluff, Hell in the Pacific, Bullitt, Beguiled, The Fox, The Brotherhood, Eye of the Cat, Kelly's Heroes, Hellstrom Chronicles, THX 1138, Dirty Harry, Joe Kidd, Prime Cut, Enter the Dragon, Charley Varrick, Magnum Force, Man on a Swing, The Four Musketeers, Voyage of the Damned, The Eagle Has Landed, Voyage of the Damned, Rollercoaster, Telefon, Nunzio, The Cat from Outer Space, The Manitou, Boulevard Nights, The Concord—Airport '79, Love and Bullets, Serial, The Big Brawl, Brubaker, Escape to Athena, The Amityville Horror, The Nude Bomb, The Competition, When Time Ran Out, Caveman, Buddy, Buddy, The Seduction, A Stranger Is Watching, Amityville II: The Possession, The Sting II, The Osterman Weekend, Sudden Impact, The Mean Season, The

New Kids, Doctor Detroit, Tank, The Silence at Bethany, The Fourth Protocol, The Dead Pool, Berlin Blues (music and songs), Return From the River Kwai, F/X 2.
TELEVISION: Mission Impossible (theme), Mannix (theme), Petrocelli (theme), Hollywood Wives, A.D., Private Sessions, Foster and Laurie, Medical Center, Petrocelli, Starsky and Hutch, Earth Star Voyager, Princess Daisy, Falcon's Gold, Kung Fu: The Movie, Original Sin, The Neon Empire, Shakedown on Sunset Strip, Little White Lies, Face to Face, El Quixote.

SCHILLER, FRED: Playwright, Screen & TV writer. b. Vienna, Austria, Jan. 6, 1924. e. Columbia Univ. (B.A.). Awarded: New York Literary Prize for McCall magazine story Ten Men and a Prayer. Member of Dramatists' Guild and Writer's Guild of America. Formerly chief corres. European Newspaper Feature Services. Honored by the U. of Wyoming and the American Heritage Center for literary achievements with a special Fred Schiller Collection for their library. Awarded the Honor Silver Cross by Austrian Govt., for literary achievements and for furthering cultural relations between Austria and U.S.
PICTURES FOR: MGM, Columbia, RKO, Republic and Henri Sokal Films, Paris.
TELEVISION: Wrote some 53 TV plays for all major networks. Only U.S. writer granted permission to adapt G.B. Shaw's play, The Inca of Perusalem, for an NBC TV special. Other Specials: Demandez Vicky! for Paris and Finder BitteMelden! for Austria.
STAGE: Come On Up (U.S.), Anything Can Happen (London), Demandez Vicky (Paris), Finder Please Return (Athens, Madrid), Finder Bitte Melden (Berlin, Baden-Baden, and Vienna). The Love Trap (Cambria Playhouse).

SCHILLER, LAWRENCE J.: Producer, Director. b. New York, NY, Dec. 28, 1936. Photojournalist with Life Magazine & Saturday Evening Post, 1958–70; collaborated on numerous books including three by Norman Mailer: The Executioner's Song, Marilyn, and The Faith of Graffiti; Muhammad Ali with Wilfrid Sheed; Minamata with Eugene Smith.
PICTURES: The Man Who Skied Down Everest (editorial concept & direction); Lady Sings the Blues, Butch Cassidy & the Sundance Kid (conceived and executed special still montages & titles); The American Dreamer (prod., dir.).
TELEVISION: Hey, I'm Alive (prod., dir.); Producer: The Trial of Lee Harvey Oswald, The Winds of Kitty Hawk, Marilyn, The Untold Story, An Act of Love, Child Bride of Short Creek, The Executioner's Song (prod., dir.), Peter the Great, Margaret Bourke-White (prod., dir.).

SCHINE, G. DAVID: Executive. b. Gloversville, NY, Sept. 11, 1927. e. Harvard U., Pres., gen. mgr. Schine Hotels 1950–63. Film exhibitor until 1966 in New York, Ohio, Kentucky, Maryland, Delaware, and West Virginia. Exec. prod. of French Connection, 1971. Writer, prod., dir. of That's Action!, 1977. Chief Exec. officer of Schine Productions (production) and Epic Productions (distribution), Visual Sciences, Inc., High Resolution Sciences, Inc., and Studio Television Services, Inc.

SCHLAIFER, CHARLES: Executive. President, Charles Schlaifer and Company, Inc., advertising agency with offices in New York and Los Angeles. b. Omaha, NB, July 1, 1909. Reporter Daily News, World-Herald, (Omaha). In 1930 appt. adv. mgr. Paramount theatres, Omaha; then of Publix theats., Omaha; then of Tri-State circuit, Neb., Iowa; 1936–42 man. dir. United Artists Theats., San Francisco; advisor, nat'l adv., United Artists prod. In 1942 appt. adv. mgr. 20th Cent.-Fox; named asst. dir. adv., publicity, & exploitation, 1944; appt. v.p. & dir. of advertising, pub., exploitation and radio, 1945. Resigned 1949, to establish own adv. agency. Pres., Charles Schlaifer & Co., Inc. (Clients incl. 20th, Paramount, Fox Theatres, Loews Theatres.) Chmn. advertising advisory council, MPAA; instructor at New School for Social Research, N.Y., on m.p.; revised m.p. adv. code; permanent chmn. first MPAA pub rel. com. Member; Nat'l Advisory Mental Health Council to U.S. Surgeon General; Founder and vice-chmn. bd. of gov., Nat'l Assn. of Mental Health. Lecturer, writer on adv. & mental health bd. of gov., Menninger Foundation; founder, co-chmn., Nat'l Mental Health Comm., secy., treas., Joint Comm. on Mental Illness & Health; expert witness Congress, govt. hearings creating National Institute of Mental Health in U.S. Public Health Service. Elected Hon. Fellow of the Amer. Psychiatric Assn., 1959; V. chmn., trustee in chg., Mental Health and Mental Retardation Facilities, NY State, 1964; secy., treas., Joint Commission Mental Health for Children; vice chmn. bd. Foundation for Child Mental Welfare, 1963. Mem. bd. trustees Research Found. 1966. Mem.: White House Conference on the Handicapped, 1952–65; elected honorary fellow, Post Graduate Psychiatric Institute, 1968. Hon. Doctor of Letters, John F. Kennedy Coll., Wahoo, Neb., 1969; Chmn. N.Y. State Health and Mental Hygiene Facilities Improvement Corp., 1970; Hon. Fellow—American Ortho Psychiatric Assoc., 1970; Hon. Fellow British Royal Society of Health. Wisdom Award Hon. Wisdom Mag., 1969; social conscience award Karen Horney Clinic, 1972. Chmn, NY

State Facilities Dev. Corp., 1973–; Advisory Council to the National Institute of Mental Health to the Surgeon General of the U.S. 1976–. Author of 4 books.

SCHLANG, JOSEPH: Executive. b. New York, NY, Feb. 24, 1911, e. NYU. Owner and leader in N.Y. real estate, and exec. dir. of many enterprises. Pres. of International Opera Co. & Opera Presentations, Inc. Produced two weekly radio programs: Opera Stars of Tomorrow and 100 & More Ways to Improve N.Y.C. since April, 1973. Opera Presentations, Inc., a non-profit corp. distributes and exhibits opera, ballet and art films throughout America and the school system. Over 100 cultural films owned by Schlang are supplied to Opera Presentations free to use.

SCHLATTER, GEORGE: Producer, Director, Writer. b. Birmingham, AL, Dec. 31, 1932. m. former actress Jolene Brand. e. Pepperdine U. on football scholarship. First industry job was MCA agent in band and act dept. Then gen. mgr. and show producer Ciro's nightclub (where he met Dick Martin and Dan Rowan). Produced shows at Frontier Hotel and Silver Slipper, Las Vegas. Sang 2 seasons St. Louis Municipal Opera Co.
TELEVISION: Created: Rowan & Martin's Laugh-In (2 Emmy Awards), Real People. Specials with Goldie Hawn, Robin Williams, Shirley MacLaine, Doris Day, John Denver, Frank Sinatra, Jackie Gleason, Danny Thomas, Bob Hope, Milton Berle, Danny Kaye, George Burns, Dinah Shore, Lucille Ball, Goldie & Liza Together, Salute to Lady Liberty, Las Vegas 75th Anniversary, Speak Up America, Real Kids, Best of Times, Look At Us, Shape of Things, Magic or Miracle. Produced and wrote first 5 years of the Grammy Awards, TV series with Dinah Shore, Judy Garland, Bill Cosby, Robin Williams, Steve Lawrence. ABC American Comedy Awards (3 years), George Schlatter's Comedy Club, George Schlatter's Funny People, Beverly Hills 75th Anniversary, Humor and the Presidency, Frank Liza & Sammy . . . The Ultimate Event, Sammy Davis Jr. 60th Anniversary Celebration (Emmy Award).

SCHLESINGER, JOHN: Director, Producer. b. London, England, Feb. 16, 1926. e. Oxford U., BBC dir. 1958–60: Wrote and dir. Terminus for British Transport Films (Golden Lion, best doc., Venice); The Class. Some episodes The Valiant Years series. Appeared as actor in films: Sailor of the King (1953), Pursuit of the Graf Spee, Brothers in Law, The Divided Heart, The Last Man to Hang, Fifty Years of Action (DGA doc.). Assoc. dir., National Theatre, London 1973–89.
PICTURES: A Kind of Loving (Golden Bear Award, Berlin 1961), Billy Liar, Darling (NY Film Critics Award, 1965), Far From the Madding Crowd, Midnight Cowboy (also co-prod.; Acad. Awards for Best Picture & Director, 1969), Sunday Bloody Sunday, Visions of Eight (sequence), The Day of the Locust, Marathon Man, Yanks, Honky Tonk Freeway, The Falcon and the Snowman (also co-prod.), The Believers (also co-prod.), Madame Sousatzka (also co-s.p.), Pacific Heights (also cameo), The Innocent.
TELEVISION: Separate Tables, An Englishman Abroad (BAFTA Award), The Lost Language of Cranes (actor only), A Question of Attribution (BAFTA Award).
OPERA: Les Contes d'Hoffmann (Royal Opera House 1981; SWET award); Der Rosenkavalier, Un Ballo in Maschera (Salzburg Fest., 1989).
THEATRE: No Why (RSC), Timon of Athens (RSC), Days in the Trees (RSC), I And Albert, Heartbreak House (NT), Julius Caesar (NT), True West (NT).

SCHLONDORFF, VOLKER: Director. b. Wiesbaden, Germany, March 31, 1939. m. dir.-actress Margarethe von Trotta. Studied in France, acquiring degree in political science in Paris. Studied at French Intl. Film Sch. (IDHEC) before becoming asst. to Jean-Pierre Melville, Alain Resnais, and Louis Malle.
PICTURES: Young Torless, A Degree of Murder, Michael Kohlhass, Baal, The Sudden Fortune of the Poor People of Kombach, Die Moral der Rugh Halbfass, A Free Woman, The Lost Honor of Katharine Blum, Le Coup de Grace, Valeska Gert, The Tin Drum, Circle of Deceit, Swann in Love, The Handmaid's Tale, Voyager (also co-s.p.).
TELEVISION: Death of a Salesman, A Gathering of Old Men.

SCHLOSSBERG, JULIAN: Producer, Distributor, Director, Radio TV Host. b. New York, NY, Jan. 26, 1942. e. N.Y. Joined ABC-TV network 1964 as asst. acct. rep.; named act. rep. 1965; 1966, joined Walter Reade Organization as asst. v.p. chg. of TV; 1969, moved to WRO Theatre Div.; 1970, joined faculty of School of Visual Arts; 1971 named v.p. of WRO Theatres; 1976, joined Paramount Pictures as v.p. in charge of feature film acquisition. Since 1978 pres. & owner of Castle Hill Productions; 1974, prod. & moderated An Evening with Joseph E. Levine at Town Hall, N.Y.; 1974–1980, host of radio show Movie Talk on WMCA (N.Y.), WMEX (Boston), WICE (Providence); 1982–83 host of syndicated TV show, Julian Schlossbergs' Movie Talk; producers' rep. for Elia Kazan, Dustin Hoffman, Elaine May, George C. Scott. Responsible

for restored version of Orson Welles' Othello, re-released in 1992.
PICTURES: Going Hollywood: The War Years, Hollywood Uncensored, Hollywood Ghost Stories, No Nukes, Going Hollywood: The 30's, 10 From Your Show of Shows, In the Spirit.
THEATRE: It Had To Be You, An Evening with Nichols and May, Rainbow Room, N.Y., Mr. Gogol and Mr. Preen.
TELEVISION: Steve Allen's Golden Age of Comedy; All the Best, Steve Allen.

SCHLOSSER, HERBERT S.: Executive. b. Atlantic City, NJ, April 21, 1926. e. Princeton U., Yale Law Sch. Joined law firm of Phillips, Nizer, Benjamin, Krim & Ballon, 1954; attorney, California National Productions (subsidiary of National Broadcasting Company) 1957; v.p. & gen. mgr., 1960; director, talent & program administration, NBC television network, 1961; v.p., talent & program admin., 1962; v.p. programs west coast, 1966–72; exec. v.p., NBC-TV, 1972; president, NBC Television Network, 1973, pres. & chief operating officer, NBC, April 1, 1974–76; Pres. & chief executive officer, 1977–78; exec. V.P. RCA 1978–85; sr. advisor, broadcasting & entertainment, Wertheim, Schroder & Co., 1986.

SCHLUSSELBERG, MARTIN: Film Executive. b. Sept. 1936. e. Yeshiva U. Booking clerk. UA. 1956; head booker, Citation Films, 1958; head booker, Desilu Dist., Co., 1961; head booker, and asst. to gen. sls. mgr., Medallion Pictures Corp., 1963; World Ent. Corp., 1966, Sales Mgr.; Crystal Pictures, 1978, sls. mgr., v.p.

SCHMIDT, WOLF: Producer, Distributor. b. Freiburg/Br., Germany, June 30, 1937. Came to U.S. 1962 as freelance journalist. Started producing in 1969, distributing independently since 1972. Now heads Kodiak Films.
PICTURES: Ski Fever (prod.), Stamping Ground (co-prod.), Young Hannah (exec. prod.), Things Fall Apart (prod.),The Passover Plot (prod.), Run For the Roses (co-prod.), Ghost Fever (exec. prod.), Defense Play (prod.), Riding the Edge (prod.), The Fourth War (prod.), Neon City (prod.)

SCHMOELLER, DAVID: Writer, Director. b. Louisville, KY, Dec. 8, 1947. e. Universidad de Las Americas, 1967–69; studied film and theater under Luis Bunuel and Alejandro Jodorowsky, U. of Texas, B.A., M.A., 1969–74. Wrote and directed 7 short films while studying at U. of Texas; won 27 intl. awards. In Hollywood spent 6 months working as intern to Peter Hyams on film, Capricorn One. Now heads own co., The Schmoeller Corp.
PICTURES: Tourist Trap (debut as dir.); The Seduction (Dir., s.p.); Crawlspace (dir., s.p.). As writer only: The Day Time Ended, The Peeper, Last Chance Romance, Thrill Palace, Warriors of the Wind (Eng. adaptation), Ghost Town (story), Catacombs (dir.), Puppet Master (dir.), The Arrival (dir.).
TELEVISION: James at 15 (s.p.); Kid Flicks (cable; s.p., prod.).
NOVEL: The Seduction.

SCHNEER, CHARLES H.: Producer, b. Norfolk, VA, May 5, 1920. e. Columbia Coll. pres., Morningside Prods. Inc. & Pictures Corp.; 1956. Founded Andor Films 1974. Chmn, Acad. of MP Arts & Sciences, London Screening Committee.
PICTURES: Prod. The 3 Worlds of Gulliver, The 7th Voyage of Sinbad, I Aim at the Stars, Face of a Fugitive, Good Day for a Hanging, Battle of the Coral Sea, Tarawa Beachhead, Mysterious Island, Jason and the Argonauts, First Men In The Moon, Half A Sixpence, Land Raiders, Valley of Gwangi, The Executioner, The Golden Voyage of Sinbad, Sinbad & The Eye of the Tiger, Clash of the Titans.

SCHNEIDER, DICK: Producer, Director. b. Cazadero, CA, Mar. 7. e. Coll. of the Pacific. U.S. Navy, W.W.II. Winner of 9 Emmys.
TELEVISION: Dough Re Mi, Wide Wide World, Colgate Comedy Hour, Beatrice Lilly & Jackie Gleason Comedy Hours, Henry Morgan Show, Kate Smith Show, Big Story, Treasury Men in Action, Doorway to Danger, Today Show, Home, Tonight Show, General Mills Circus; dir. coverage of political conventions; dir. NBC-TV coverage, Princess Margaret's wedding and Paris summit conference; dir. Eleanor Roosevelt Specials, 1959–60; Something Special 61, At This Very Moment, Inauguration, Gemini, Papal Mass for all networks at Yankee Stadium, 1965–66; 1966–67 Tonight Show, Orange Bowl, Jr. Miss Pageant; 1967–70 College Queen, Emmy Award. Prod.; Prod.-dir., NBC Expt. in TV, New Communication; prod., Big Sur; prod.-dir., Jr. Miss Pageant, 1968–69; dir. Dream House, ABC; dir. Who, What or Where, NBC; produced in 1970: Stars and Stripes; in 1972: Post Parade, Stars and Stripes 1973–75; Salute to Sir Lew; Jeopardy; NBC Star Salute, 1980; Rose Parade, 1974–87; Star Salute, 1981; UCP Telethons, 1981–91. Macy's Parade, 1965–93; 1986, People's Choice, Jeopardy. 1984–92. Photo Finish, 1990–.

SCHNEIDER, JOHN: Actor. b. Mount Kisco, NY, Apr. 8, 1954. Active in drama club in high school in Atlanta. Worked as

fashion model and played guitar singing own compositions in various Atlanta clubs. Active in local community theatre. Summer stock in New Hampshire. Bdwy debut 1991 in Grand Hotel.
PICTURES: Smokey and the Bandit, Million Dollar Dixie Deliverance, Eddie Macon's Run, The Curse, Cocaine Wars, Speed Zone, Ministry of Vengeance.
TELEVISION: Series: Dukes of Hazzard, Grand Slam. Specials: John Schneider—Back Home, Wild Jack. Movies: Dream House, Happy Endings, Stagecoach, Christmas Comes to Willow Creek, Outback Bound, Gus Brown and Midnight Brewster, Highway Heartbreaker.

SCHNEIDER, JOHN, A.: Executive. b. Chicago, IL, Dec. 4, 1926. e. U. of Notre Dame, B.S. U.S.N.R., 1943–47, Exec. assignments with CBS-TV, in Chicago and New York 1950–58; VP, gen. mgr. WCAU-TV, Philadelphia 1958–64; WCBS-TV, New York 1964–65; pres. CBS-TV Network 1965–66; pres. CBS/Broadcast Group 1966–69, 1971–77; exec. VP CBS Inc. 1969–71, TV and MP consultant 1977–79; consultant WCI, 1979; pres., CEO Warner Amex Satellite Entertainment Corp., 1980.

SCHNEIER, FREDERICK: Executive. b. New York, NY, May 31, 1927; e. NYU, 1951, bus. admin.; NYU Grad. Sch., M.B.A., 1953. Dir. sls. planning, Mutual Broadcasting System, 1947–53; media research dir., RKO Teleradio, 1953–55; RKO Teleradio Advisory Comm., 1955–56; exec. staff RKO Teleradio & dir., marketing services, 1956–58; exec. vice-pres., Showcorporation, 1958–71; v.p. TV programming, RKO General, 1972–1973; v.p.; Hemdale Leisure Corporation, 1973–79; Viacom Enterprises v.p., feature films, 1979; sr. v.p., program acquisitions & motion pictures, 1980–83; sr. v.p., acquisitions, Showtime/The Movie Channel, 1983–85; sr. v.p. program acquisitions, program enterprises, 1985–87; exec. v.p., programming; 1987–89; pres. & CEO, Viacom Pictures Inc.

SCHOEFFLING, MICHAEL: Actor. b. Philadelphia, PA. e. Temple Univ.
PICTURES: Sixteen Candles (debut, 1984), Vision Quest, Sylvester, Bellizaire the Cajun, Let's Get Harry, Slaves of New York, Longtime Companion, Mermaids, Wild Hearts Can't Be Broken.

SCHOENFELD, LESTER: Executive. b. Brooklyn, NY, Dec. 6, 1916. e. City Coll. of New York, 1934–38. Asst. mgr., Randforce Amusement, 1936–38; mgr., Rugoff & Becker circuit, 1938–47; mgr., Golden & Ambassador Theatres, 1948; print & sales dept., Film Classics, 1948–50; chg. of theatrical, non-theatrical & TV dist., Brit. Info. Serv.; est. Lester A. Schoenfeld Films, 1958; Schoenfeld Films Distributing Corp., 1960.

SCHORR, DANIEL: Television News Correspondent. b. New York, NY, Aug. 31, 1916. e. City Coll. of New York. Started with various news services and newspapers. Joined CBS in 1953 on special assignment; 1955, reopened CBS bureau in Moscow; 1958–60, roving assignment; 1960–1966, chief German Bureau; 1966–76, chief of Washington Bureau; 1979, Public Radio and TV; 1980, correspondent for Cable News Network.

SCHRADER, PAUL: Writer, Director. b. Grand Rapids, MI, July 22, 1946. m. actress Mary Beth Hurt. e. Calvin Coll. (theology & philosophy); Columbia U., UCLA, M.A., cinema. Served as film critic for L.A. Free Press and Cinema 1970–72. Former professor at Columbia U.
PICTURES: The Yakuza (co-s.p.), Taxi Driver (s.p.), Rolling Thunder (s.p.), Obsession (s.p.), Blue Collar (co-s.p., dir.) Hardcore (s.p., dir.), Old Boyfriends (co-s.p., and exec. prod.), American Gigolo (s.p., dir.), Raging Bull (co-s.p.), Cat People (dir.), Mishima (co-s.p., dir.), The Mosquito Coast (s.p.), Light of Day (dir., s.p.), The Last Temptation of Christ (s.p.), Patty Hearst (dir.), The Comfort of Strangers (dir.), Light Sleeper (dir., s.p.).

SCHRODER, RICK: Actor. b. Staten Island, NY, April 13, 1970. Started modelling while only four months; did many TV commercials before theatrical film debut in The Champ, at age eight.
PICTURES: The Champ, The Last Flight of Noah's Ark, The Earthling, Apt Pupil, Across the Tracks, There Goes My Baby.
TELEVISION: Series: Silver Spoons. Movies: Little Lord Fauntleroy, Something So Right, Two Kinds of Love, A Reason to Live, Too Young the Hero, Terror on Highway 91, Out on the Edge, A Son's Promise, The Stranger Within, Blood River, My Son Johnny, Miles From Nowhere. Mini-Series: Lonesome Dove.

SCHROEDER, BARBET: Producer, Director. b. Teheran, Iran, Aug. 26, 1941. e. Sorbonne (philosophy). Worked as a photojournalist in India and critic for Cahiers du Cinema and L'Air de Paris, 1958–63. 1963: asst. to Jean-Luc Godard on Les Carabiniers. 1964: formed own prod. co. Les Films du Losange. Prod. and acted in Rohmer's La Boulangere de

Monceau. As actor only: Paris vu par, La Bonlangire de Roberte.

PICTURES: *Producer*: La Bonlangere de Monceau (26 mins.), La Carriere de Suzanne (52 mins.), Mediterrannee, Paris Vu Par, The Collector, Tu Imagines Robinson, My Night at Maud's, Claire's Knee, Chloe in the Afternoon, Out One (co-prod.), The Mother and the Whore (co-prod.), Celine and Julie Go Boating, Flocons D'Or, The Marquise of O, Roulette Chinoise (co-prod.), The American Friend (co-prod.), Le Passe-Montagne, The Rites of Death, Perceval Le Gallois, Le Navire Night, Le Pont du Nord, Mauvaise Conduite. *Director*: More (1969), Sing-Song (documentary), La Vallee, General Idi Amin Dada (doc.), Maitresse, Koko a Talking Gorilla (doc.), Charles Bukowski (50 4-min. videos, 1982–84), Tricheurs, Barfly, Reversal of Fortune, Single White Female.

SCHUCK, JOHN: Actor. b. Boston, MA, Feb. 4, 1940. e. Denison (BA).

PICTURES: M*A*S*H, Brewster McCloud, McCabe and Mrs. Miller, Hammersmith is Out, Blade, Thieves Like Us, Butch and Sundance: The Early Days, Just You and Me Kid, Earthbound, Finders Keepers, Star Trek VI: The Voyage Home, Outrageous Fortune, The New Adventures of Pippi Longstocking, My Mom's a Werewolf, Second Sight, Dick Tracy, Star Trek VI: The Undiscovered Country.

TELEVISION: *Series*: McMillan and Wife, Holmes and Yoyo, Turnabout, The Odd Couple (1982), The Munsters Today. *Mini-Series*: Roots. *Movies*: Once Upon a Dead Man, Hunter, Till Death Us Do Part, Four Eyes and Six Guns.

THEATRE: Annie

SCHULBERG, BUDD WILSON: Writer. b. New York, NY, Mar. 27, 1914. son of B. P. Schulberg, prod. e. Dartmouth Coll. Publicist, Paramount Pictures, 1931; writer for screen from 1932. Armed services W.W.II. Syndicated newspaper columnist: The Schulberg Report.

THEATER: The Disenchanted (with Harvey Breit, 1958), What Makes Sammy Run? (bk. for musical, 1963–4).

PICTURES: A Star is Born (additional dial.), Nothing Sacred (add. dial.), Little Orphan Annie (co-s.p.), Winter Carnival (co-s.p. with F. Scott Fitzgerald), Weekend for Three (orig. and co-s.p.), City Without Men (co-story), Government Girl (adapt.), Original s.p.: On the Waterfront (Acad. Award, & Writers Guild Award, 1954), A Face in The Crowd, Wind Across the Everglades (co-s.p.), Joe Louis: For All Times (doc., Cine Golden Eagle Award, 1985).

BOOKS: *Novels*: What Makes Sammy Run?, The Disenchanted, Harder They Fall, On the Waterfront, Some Faces in the Crowd, Wind Across the Everglades, Everything That Moves, Love Action Laughter and Other Sad Tales, Sanctuary V. *Non-fiction books*: Writers in America, Moving Pictures: Memories of a Hollywood Prince, Swan Watch, Loser and Still Champion: Muhammad Ali

TELEVISION: What Makes Sammy Run?, A Question of Honor, A Table at Ciro's, Joe Louis for All Time; winner of several awards.

SCHULTZ, MICHAEL: Director, Producer. b. Milwaukee, WI, Nov. 10, 1938. e. U. of Wisconsin, Marquette U. Theatre includes The Song of the Lusitainian Bogey, Kongi's Harvest; Does a Tiger Wear a Necktie?; Operation Sidewinder, What the Winesellers Buy, The Cherry Orchard.

PICTURES: *Director*: Cooley High, Car Wash, Greased Lightning, Which Way Is Up?, Sgt. Pepper's Lonely Hearts Club Band, Scavenger Hunt, Carbon Copy, The Last Dragon, Krush Groove (also prod.), Disorderlies (also prod.), Livin' Large.

TELEVISION: *Specials*: To Be Young Gifted and Black, Ceremonies in Dark Old Men, For Us the Living, Fade Out: The Erosion of Black Images in the Media (documentary). *Movies*: Benny's Place, The Jerk Too, Timestalkers, Rock 'n' Roll Mom, Tarzan in Manhattan, Jury Duty, Dayo.

SCHULMAN, JOHN A.: Executive. b. Washington, D.C., Sept. 13, 1946. e. Yale U., 1968; law degree from Boalt Hall, U. of California, Berkeley, 1972. Founding partner in Beverly Hills law firm, Weissmann, Wolff, Bergman, Coleman & Schulman in 1981 after nine years with firm of Kaplan, Livingston, Goodwin, Berkowitz & Selvin. Joined Warner Bros. 1984 as v.p. & gen. counsel; 1989 appt. sr. v.p. and gen. counsel. 1991, exec. v.p. and gen. counsel.

SCHULTZ, DWIGHT: Actor. b. Baltimore, MD, Nov. 24, 1947. e. Townson St. Univ. Acted with Williamstown Theatre Fest. prior to NY stage work, incl. The Crucifer of Blood, The Water Engine, and Night and Day.

PICTURES: Fat Man and Little Boy, The Long Walk Home, The Temp.

TELEVISION: *Series*: The A-Team, Star Trek: The Next Generation. *Movies*: Child of Rage, When Your Love Leaves, Perry Mason: The Case of the Sinister Spirit, Perry Mason: The Case of the Musical Murder, A Woman With a Past, The Last Wish, A Killer Among Us.

SCHUMACHER, JOEL: Writer, Director. b. New York, NY, Aug. 29, 1939. Worked as design and display artist for Henri Bendel

dept. store NY while attending Parson's Sch. of Design. As fashion designer opened own boutique, Paraphernalia. Joined Revlon as designer of clothing and packaging before entering m.p. indus. as costume designer on Play It As It Lays, Sleeper, The Last of Sheila, Blume in Love, Prisoner of 2nd Avenue, Interiors.

PICTURES: *Writer*: Car Wash, Sparkle, The Wiz. *Director*: The Incredible Shrinking Woman, D.C. Cab (also s.p.), St. Elmo's Fire (also s.p.), The Lost Boys, Cousins, Flatliners, Dying Young, Falling Down, The Client.

TELEVISION: Director: *Movies*: The Virginia Hill Story (also writer), Amateur Night at the Dixie Bar & Grill (also writer). *Music video*: Devil Inside for rock group INXS (dir.). Series: 2000 Malibu Drive. *Exec. Prod.*: Slow Burn.

SCHWAB, SHELLY: Executive. Station mgr., WAGA-TV, Atlanta; various sls. & mgr. posts with CBS. Joined MCA, 1978, becoming exec. v.p., MCA-TV. 1986, appt. pres., MCA TV Enterprises, 1989 appt. pres. MCA TV.

SCHWARTZ, BERNARD: Producer. Brought to Hollywood by the late Howard Hughes to watch his film interests; Schwartz teamed with atty. Greg Bautzer to package movie deals for clients. Re-cut number of Buster Keaton's silent movies into documentary anthologies (The Golden Age of Comedy, When Comedy Was King, etc.). Subsequently made TV series, One Step Beyond, followed by The Wackiest Ship in the Army, Miss Teen International specials, etc. Named pres. Joseph M. Schenck Enterprises, for which made Journey to the Center of the Earth, Eye of the Cat, A Cold Wind in August, I Passed for White, The Shattered Room, Trackdown. Presently partnered with Alan Silverman of Essaness Theatres.

PICTURES: Coal Miner's Daughter (prod.), Road Games (exec. prod.) Psycho II (exec. prod.), St. Elmo's Fire (co-exec. prod.).

TELEVISION: Elvis and Me (co-exec. prod.).

SCHWARY, RONALD L.: Producer. b. Oregon, May 23, 1944. e. U. of Southern California. Started as movie extra before becoming asst. dir.; served as assoc. prod. on The Electric Horseman.

PICTURES: Ordinary People (Acad. Award for Best Picture, 1980), Absence of Malice, Tootsie, A Soldier's Story, Batteries Not Included, Havana, Scent of a Woman, Cops and Robbersons.

TELEVISION: Tour of Duty.

SCHWARZENEGGER, ARNOLD: Actor. b. Graz, Austria, July 30, 1947. m. NBC reporter Maria Shriver. e. U. Wisconsin, B.A. Titles: Junior Mr. Europe (at age 18), Mr. Universe (3 time winner), Mr. Olympia (7 times), Mr. Europe, Mr. World. Special Olympics weightlifting Coach (1989), Prison Weightlifting Rehabilitation Prog. Awards: Sportsman of the Year (1977, Assn. Physical Fitness Ctrs.), Golden Globe (best newcomer, 1977), ShoWest '85 Intl. Star., ShoWest Career Achievement Award, NATO Male Star of Yr. (1987),

PICTURES: Hercules in New York (debut, 1970; billed as Arnold Strong; a.k.a. Hercules Goes Bananas), The Long Goodbye, Stay Hungry, Pumping Iron, The Villain, Scavenger Hunt, Conan the Barbarian, Conan the Destroyer, The Terminator, Red Sonja, Commando, Raw Deal, Predator, The Running Man, Red Heat, Twins, Total Recall, Kindergarten Cop, Terminator 2: Judgment Day, Dave (cameo), Last Action Hero (also exec. prod.).

TELEVISION: *Movie*: The Jayne Mansfield Story. *Special*: A Very Special Christmas Party (host). *Guest*: Streets of San Francisco. *Director*: Tales from the Crypt (The Switch), Christmas in Connecticut (movie).

BOOKS: Arnold: The Education of a Bodybuilder, Arnold's Bodyshaping for Women, Arnold's Bodybuilding for Men, The Encyclopedia of Modern Bodybuilding.

SCHYGULLA, HANNA: Actress. b. Kattowitz, Germany, Dec. 25, 1943. Worked with Rainer Werner Fassbinder in Munich's Action Theater; a founder of the "anti-theatre" group.

PICTURES: Love Is Colder Than Death, Gods of the Plague, Rio Das Mortes, Beware of a Holy Whore, The Merchant of Four Seasons, The Bitter Tears of Petra Von Kant, House by the Sea, Jail Bait, Effi Briest, The Marriage of Maria Braun, Berlin Alexanderplatz, Lili Marleen, The Night of Varennes, Passion, A Labor of Love, A Love in Germany, The Delta Force, The Future Is a Woman, Forever Lulu, Miss Arizona, The Summer of Ms. Forbes, Dead Again.

TELEVISION: (U.S.): Peter the Great, Barnum, Casanova.

SCIORRA, ANNABELLA: Actress. b. New York, NY, 1964. Studied acting at HB Studio.

PICTURES: True Love (debut, 1989), Internal Affairs, Cadillac Man, Reversal of Fortune, The Hard Way, Jungle Fever, The Hand That Rocks the Cradle, Whispers in the Dark, The Night We Never Met, Mr. Wonderful, Romeo is Bleeding.

TELEVISION: *Mini-Series*: The Fortunate Pilgrim. *Movie*: Prison Stories: Women on the Inside.

THEATRE: Orpheus Descending, Bus Stop, Three Sisters, Snow Angel, Cries and Shouts, Trip Back Down, Love and Junk, Stay With Me.

SCOFIELD, PAUL: Actor. b. Hurstpierpoint, England, Jan. 21, 1922. Gained greatest fame on London stage in many Shakespeare and other plays, including Staircase, Savages, Uncle Vanya, and I'm Not Rappaport, Heartbreak House, The Government Inspector, Ring Round the Moon, The Complaisant Lover, Expresso Bongo, A Dead Secret. NY stage: A Man for All Seasons (Tony Award, 1962).
PICTURES: That Lady (debut, 1955), Carve Her Name with Pride, The Train, A Man for All Seasons (Acad. Award, 1966), Tell Me Lies, King Lear, Bartleby, Scorpio, A Delicate Balance, 1919, When the Whales Came, Henry V, Hamlet, Utz.
TELEVISION: (U.S.): Movies: Anna Karenina, The Attic: The Hiding of Anne Frank. Special: The Male of the Species (Emmy Award, 1969).

SCOGGINS, TRACY: Actress. b. Galveston, TX, Nov. 13, 1959. Studied acting at H.B. Studies, Wynn Handman Studios. Appeared on stage in L.A. in The Sicilian Bachelor.
TELEVISION: Series: Renegades, Hawaiian Heat, The Colbys. Movies: Twirl, Jury Duty, Dan Turner: Hollywood Detective. Pilots: The Naturals, High Life, Unauthorized Biographies. Guest: Hotel, Crazy Like a Fox, Dallas, Magnum P.I., The Fall Guy, Mike Hammer, The Heights.
PICTURES: Some Kind of Hero, Toy Soldier, In Dangerous Company, The Gumshoe Kid, Watchers II, Time Bomb, Silhouette, Ultimate Desires, Alien Intruder, Demonic Toys.

SCOLA, ETTORE: Director. b. Trevico, Italy, May 10, 1931. e. U. of Rome. Began career 1947 as journalist; 1950, wrote for radio shows. Then script writer 1954; debut as director, 1964. Has directed or co-directed 20 films, all of which he also scripted or co-wrote. Also has written 50 other scripts, mostly comedies, for other directors.
PICTURES: Let's Talk about Women, Economical Crisis, One Sketch, The Archdevil, Will Your Heroes Find Their Friends Who Disappeared so Mysteriously in Africa?, Inspector Pepe, Pizza Triangle, Excuse Me My Name Is Rocco Papaleo, The Greatest Evening of My Life, We All Loved Each Other so Much, Down and Dirty, Signore e Signori Buonanotte, A Special Day, Viva Italia, Chi Si Dice a Roma, The Terrace, Passion of Love, The Night of Varennes, Le Bal, Macaroni, The Family (also co-s.p.), Le Capitain Fracassa, Splendor (also s.p.), What Time is It? (also s.p.)

SCOLARI, PETER: Actor. b. New Rochelle, NY, Sept. 12, 1954.
TELEVISION: Series: Goodtime Girls, Bosom Buddies, Baby Makes Five, Newhart, Family Album. Movies: Carpool, Amazon, Fatal Confession, The Ryan White Story. Guest: Remington Steele, The Love Boat, Family Ties, The New Mike Hammer, Trying Times (Death and Taxes), Fallen Angels (I'll Be Waiting).
PICTURES: The Rosebud Beach Hotel, Corporate Affairs.

SCORSESE, MARTIN: Writer, Director, Editor. b. New York, NY, Nov. 17, 1942. Began career while film arts student at NYU, doing shorts What's A Nice Girl Like You Doing in a Place Like This? (dir., s.p.), It's Not Just You Murray and The Big Shave. Other short films: Street Scenes, Italianamerican, American Boy, Mirror Mirror, Somewhere Down the Crazy River. Dir. 2 commercials for Armani.
PICTURES: Editor: Woodstock, Medicine Ball Caravan, Unholy Rollers, Elvis on Tour. Director: Who's That Knocking at My Door? (also s.p., assoc. prod., actor), Boxcar Bertha (also actor), Mean Streets (also co-s.p., actor), Alice Doesn't Live Here Anymore, Taxi Driver (also actor), Cannonball (actor only), New York New York, The Last Waltz (also actor), Raging Bull, The King of Comedy (also actor), After Hours, 'Round Midnight (actor only), The Color of Money, The Last Temptation of Christ, New York Stories (Life Lessons), Akira Kurosawa's Dreams (actor only), GoodFellas (also co-s.p.), The Grifters (prod. only), Guilty By Suspicion (actor only), Cape Fear, Mad Dog and Glory (co-prod. only), The Age of Innocence (also co-s.p.).
TELEVISION: Amazing Stories.
THEATRE: The Act.

SCOTT, CAMPBELL: Actor. b. New York, NY, July 19, 1962. e. Lawrence Univ. Son of George C. Scott and Colleen Dewhurst. Studied with Geraldine Page and Stella Adler.
PICTURES: Five Corners (debut, 1988), From Hollywood to Deadwood, Longtime Companion, The Sheltering Sky, Dying Young, Dead Again, Singles, The Innocent, Mrs. Parker and the Round Table.
THEATRE: NY: The Last Outpost, The Real Thing, Copperhead, The Queen and the Rebels, Hay Fever, A Man For All Seasons, Long Day's Journey Into Night, Measure for Measure, Pericles, On the Bum. Regional: Romeo and Juliet, Our Town, Gillette, School for Wives, Hamlet.
TELEVISION: Mini-Series: The Kennedys of Massachusetts. Guest: Family Ties, L.A. Law. Movie: The Perfect Tribute.

SCOTT, GEORGE C.: Actor, Director. b. Wise, VA, Oct. 18, 1927. m. actress Trish VanDevere. Father of actor Campbell Scott. Served 4 years Marine Corps. e. U. of Missouri, appeared in varsity productions, summer stock, Shakespeare.
THEATRE: Off-Bdwy: Richard III (Theatre World Award), As You Like It, Children of Darkness, General Seeger, Merchant of Venice, Desire Under the Elms, Antony and Cleopatra, Wrong Turn at Lungfish. Bdwy: Comes a Day, The Andersonville Trial, The Wall, The Little Foxes, Plaza Suite, Uncle Vanya, All God's Chillun Got Wings (dir.), Death of a Salesman (also dir.), Sly Fox, Present Laughter (also dir.), The Boys in Autumn, On Borrowed Time (also dir.). L.A. stage: Wrong Turn at Lungfish.
PICTURES: The Hanging Tree (debut, 1959), Anatomy of a Murder, The Hustler, The List of Adrian Messenger, Dr. Strangelove: Or How I Learned to Stop Worrying and Love the Bomb, The Yellow Rolls Royce, The Bible, Not With My Wife You Don't, The Flim-Flam Man, Petulia, This Savage Land, Patton (Acad. Award, 1970), They Might Be Giants, The Last Run, The Hospital, The New Centurions, Rage (also dir.), Oklahoma Crude, The Day of the Dolphin, Bank Shot, The Savage Is Loose (also dir., prod.), The Hindenburg, Islands in the Stream, Crossed Swords, Movie Movie, Hardcore, The Changeling, The Formula, Taps, Firestarter, The Exorcist III, The Rescuers Down Under (voice).
TELEVISION: Series: East Side West Side, Mr. President. Movies: Jane Eyre, Fear on Trial, Oliver Twist, China Rose, A Christmas Carol, Choices, The Last Days of Patton, The Murders in the Rue Morgue, Pals, The Ryan White Story, Descending Angel, Finding the Way Home, Curacao. Mini-Series: Mussolini—The Untold Story. Guest: Major TV playhouses including DuPont Show of the Month, Playhouse 90, Hallmark Hall of Fame, Kraft Theatre, Omnibus, Armstrong Theatre, Play of the Week, NBC Sunday Showcase, Dow Hour of Great Mysteries, Esso Theatre. Specials: Power and the Glory, The Brass Bottle, The Savage Land, The Crucible, The Price (Emmy Award, 1971), Beauty and the Beast, The Andersonville Trial (dir.)

SCOTT, GORDON: Actor. r.n. Gordon M. Werschkul. b. Portland, OR, Aug. 3, 1927. e. U. of Oregon. U.S. Army, 1944–47; then worked as fireman, cowboy, life guard; signed by Sol Lesser Prod. for role of Tarzan; debut in Tarzan's Hidden Jungle (1955); since in: Tarzan and the Lost Safari, Tarzan's Greatest Adventure, Duel of the Titans, Goliath and the Vampires, The Lion of St. Mark, The Tramplers.

SCOTT, MARTHA: Actress. b. Jamesport, MO, September 22, 1916. e. U. of Michigan. In little theatres over U.S.; summer stock N.Y.; on radio with Orson Welles; Broadway debut Our Town (1938), film debut in Our Town, 1940 (Oscar nom.). Became theater producer in 1968 with Henry Fonda and Alfred De Liagre at Kennedy Center and on Bdwy (Time of Your Life, First Monday in October).
PICTURES: Our Town (debut, 1940), The Howards of Virginia, Cheers for Miss Bishop, They Dare Not Love, One Foot in Heaven, In Old Oklahoma, Hi Diddle Diddle, So Well Remembered, Strange Bargain, When I Grow Up, Desperate Hours, The Ten Commandments, Eighteen and Anxious, Sayonara, Ben-Hur, Airport 1975, Turning Point, Doin' Time on Planet Earth.
PLAYS INCLUDE: Soldier's Wife, Voice of the Turtle, The Number, Male Animal, Remarkable Mr. Pennypacker, Forty-Second Cousin, The Crucible.
TELEVISION: Movies: Beulah Land, Adam, Father Figure, Charleston, The Word, Daughter of the Street. Guest: Murder She Wrote, Hotel, A Girl's Life (pilot).

SCOTT, RIDLEY: Director, Producer. b. South Shields, Northumberland, Eng., Nov. 30, 1937. Brother of director Tony Scott. e. Royal College of Art, London. Joined newly formed Film Sch. First film: Boy on Bicycle (short). Won design scholarship in NY. Returned to London and joined BBC as set designer (Z-Cars, The Informer series). Directed almost 3,000 commercials in 18 years. Formed Percy Main Prods. Also mng. dir. of Ridley Scott Assocs.
PICTURES: The Duellists, Alien, Blade Runner, Legend, Someone to Watch Over Me (also exec. prod.), Black Rain, Thelma & Louise (also co-prod.), 1492: Conquest of Paradise (also co-prod.), The Browning Version (co-prod. only).

SCOTT, TONY: Director. Began career in TV commercials, being partnered with his brother Ridley in prod. co. Winner of numerous Clios, Gold & Silver Lions, and other awards. Entered m.p. industry 1972, directing half-hr. film, One of the Missing, for British Film Inst. and Loving Memory, 1-hr. feature for Albert Finney.
PICTURES: The Hunger, Top Gun, Beverly Hills Cop II, Revenge, Days of Thunder, The Last Boy Scout, True Romance.

SCOTT-THOMAS, KRISTIN: Actress. b. England. Lived in France since 18. e. Central School of Speech and Drama, London and Ecole Nationale des Arts et Technique de Theatre in Paris. Stage debut in La Lune Declinante Sur 4 Ou 5 Personnes Qui Danse. Other theater work in Paris.

PICTURES: Djamel Et Juliette, L'Agent Troube, La Meridienne, Under the Cherry Moon, A Handful of Dust, Force Majeure, Bille en tete, The Bachelor, Bitter Moon.

TELEVISION: L'Ami D'Enfance de Maigret, Blockhaus, Chameleon/La Tricheuse (Aust.), Sentimental Journey (Germany), The Tenth Man, Endless Game, Framed.

SCULLY, JOE: Talent Executive, Casting Director, Producer, Writer. b. Kearny, NJ, March 1, 1926. e. Goodman Memorial Theatre of the Art Inst. of Chicago, 1946. m. Penelope Gillette. Acted until 1951. CBS-TV, N.Y. Casting Dir., Danger You Are There, Omnibus, The Web, 1951–56. Wrote The Little Woman for CBS Danger Anthology Series, 1954. 1956–60, CBS-TV, Associate Prod., Studio One, Dupont Show of the Month, Playhouse 90. 1962–64, Writer for CBS Repertoire Workshop anthology series, 1963–4. CBS Stations Div. KNXT, Producer, Repertoire Workshop. 1965–70 Casting Dir. 20th Century-Fox Films. 1970–74 Independent Casting Director. 1974–75 Universal TV, Casting Dir. 1975, Member, AMPAS since 1975; NBC-TV Manager, Casting & Talent. 1978, Re-established Joe Scully-Casting, independent service to the industry. Founding member, CSA, 1982; 1983, casting director, Walt Disney Pictures. 1991 published story in Emmy Magazine: Have You Ever . . . You Know?

PICTURES: Hello Dolly, In Like Flint, Valley of the Dolls, Planet of the Apes, The Flim-Flam Man, Sounder, Lady Sings the Blues, Play It as It Lays, The Stone Killer, Parallax View, Lifeguard, Man in the Glass Booth, Middle Age Crazy, Death Wish II, Frankenweenie (short), North of Chiang Mai, Chained in Paradiso (video).

TELEVISION: Series: Peyton Place, Bonanza, Room 222, Nichols, Snoop Sisters, Columbo, Switch, McMillan & Wife, Tales of the Unexpected, Gone Are the Days (Disney Channel). Pilots: Julia, The Ghost and Mrs. Muir, The Bill Cosby Show. Movies: Thief, Missiles of October, Gone Are the Days, Earth II. Australian: Flair (mini-series), Ebb Tide (movie).

SEAGAL, STEVEN: Actor, Producer. b. Lansing, MI, April 10, 1951. m. actress Kelly LeBrock. Became skilled at martial arts at an early age, studying Aikido. Lived in Japan for 15 yrs. where he opened a martial arts academy. Opened similar academy upon his return to U.S. in Los Angeles. Was martial arts choreographer/coordinator on film The Challenge.

PICTURES: Above the Law (debut, 1988; also co-prod., co-story), Hard to Kill, Marked for Death (also co-prod.), Out for Justice (also co-prod.), Under Siege (also co-prod.), On Deadly Ground (also dir., co-prod.).

SEAGROVE, JENNY: Actress. b. Kuala Lumpur, Malaysia. e. Bristol Old Vic. Theatre Sch. Stage debut 1979. Early TV: The Brack Report, The Woman in White, Diana. Recent stage: Jane Eyre, King Lear, Present Laughter.

PICTURES: Moonlighting, Local Hero, Nate and Hayes, Appointment With Death, A Chorus of Disapproval, The Guardian, Bullseye!, Miss Beatty's Children.

TELEVISION: A Woman of Substance, Hold The Dream, In Like Flynn, Killer, Lucy Walker, Magic Moments, Some Other Spring, The Betrothed, Deadly Game, The Sign of Four, The Incident at Victoria Falls.

SECOMBE, SIR HARRY, C.B.E.: Singer, Comedian, Actor. b. Swansea, Wales, Sept. 8, 1921. m.p. debut, Penny Points to Paradise, 1951; awarded, C.B.E., 1963. 1963–64: London stage starring in Pickwick. 1965: same role New York stage. 1967–68, The Four Musketeers; 1975, The Plumber's Progress. Awarded KBE. 1991. Autobiography: Arias and Raspberries.

PICTURES: Forces Sweetheart, Down Among the Z Men, Svengali, Davy, Jet Storm, Oliver, The Bed Sitting Room, Song of Norway, Rhubarb, Doctor in Trouble, The Magnificent Seven Deadly Sins, Sunstruck.

TELEVISION: Numerous appearances, incl. own series: Secombe and Friends, The Harry Secombe Show, Secombe with Music. Also special version, Pickwick. Presenter of Tyne Tees TV's Highway since 1983. Author of Twice Brightly, Goon for Lunch, Katy and the Nurgla, Welsh Fargo, Goon Abroad, The Harry Secombe Diet Book, Harry Secombe's Highway, The Highway Companion.

SEDGWICK, KYRA: Actress. b. New York, NY, Aug. 19, 1965. e. USC. m. actor Kevin Bacon.

PICTURES: War and Love, Tai-Pan, Kansas, Born on the Fourth of July, Mr. & Mrs. Bridge, Pyrates, Singles, Heart & Souls.

TELEVISION: Movies: The Man Who Broke 1000 Chains, Lemon Sky, Miss Rose White, Family Pictures. Guest: Amazing Stories. Special: Cinder Ella: A Modern Fairy Tale.

THEATRE: NY: Time Was, Dakota's Belly Wyoming, Ah Wilderness (Theatre World Award), Maids of Honor.

SEGAL, GEORGE: Actor. b. New York, NY, Feb. 13, 1934. m. Linda Rogoff. e. Columbia U., B.A., 1955. Worked as janitor, ticket-taker, soft-drink salesman, usher and under-study at N.Y.'s Circle in the Square theatre. Acting debut: Downtown Theatre's revival of Don Juan. Formed a nightclub singing act with Patricia Scott. Record album of ragtime songs and banjo music: The Yama, Yama Man. Dir. debut: Bucks County Playhouse prod. Scuba Duba.

THEATER: The Iceman Cometh (1956 revival), Antony and Cleopatra N.Y. Shakespeare Festival, Leave It to Jane, The Premise (satiric improvisational revue), Gideon, Rattle of a Simple Man, The Knack, Requiem for a Heavyweight, The Fourth Wall (regional).

TELEVISION: Specials: Death of a Salesman, Of Mice and Men, The Desperate Hours. Guest: The Nurses, Naked City, Alfred Hitchcock Presents. Movies: Trackdown: Finding the Goodbar Killer, The Cold Room, The Zany Adventures of Robin Hood, Not My Kid, Many Happy Returns, Endless Game, Taking the Heat. Series: Take Five, Murphy's Law.

PICTURES: The Young Doctors (debut, 1961), The Longest Day, Act One, The New Interns, Invitation to a Gunfighter, Ship of Fools, King Rat, Lost Command, Who's Afraid of Virginia Woolf? (Acad. Award nom.), The Quiller Memorandum, The St. Valentine's Day Massacre, Bye Bye Braverman, No Way to Treat a Lady, The Southern Star, The Bridge at Remagen, The Girl Who Couldn't Say No, Loving, The Owl and the Pussycat, Where's Poppa?, Born to Win, The Hot Rock, A Touch of Class, Blume in Love, The Terminal Man, California Split, Russian Roulette, The Black Bird, The Duchess and the Dirtwater Fox, Fun with Dick and Jane, Rollercoaster, Who Is Killing the Great Chefs of Europe?, Lost and Found, The Last Married Couple in America, Carbon Copy, Killing 'em Softly, Stick, All's Fair, Look Who's Talking, The Clearing, For the Boys.

SEGAL, MAURICE: Publicist. b. New York, NY, July 22, 1921. e. City Coll. of New York, 1937–41. Entered m.p. ind., adv. dept., 20th Fox, 1941–42; U.S. Army 1942–46; feature writer, pub. dept., 20th Fox, April, 1946; asst. to dir., adv., pub., Century Circuit, 1947; press book dept., Paramount, 1949; trade press rep. 1950; trade press rep. RKO Radio, Nov. 1952; res. to join Richard Condon-Kay Norton, publicists, May, 1953; adv., pub. dept., U-I. Sept. 1954; asst. chge. pub. mgr., United Artists Apr. 1957. Hollywood pub.-exploit., coordinator, 1958; exec. in chg. of M.P. press dept., Universal City Studios, 1966; West Coast adv.-pub. dir., National Gen. Pictures, 1971; Pres., Maurice E. Segal Co., 1974; dir., West Coast operations, Charles Schlaifer & Co., 1976; v.p., Max Youngstein Enterprises, 1979; exec. v.p., Taft Intl. Pictures, 1980; pres. Maurice E. Segal Co., 1982.

SEIDELMAN, ARTHUR ALLAN: Director, Producer, Writer. b. New York, NY, October 11. e. Whittier Coll., B.A.; UCLA, M.A. Former staff member, Repertory Theatre of Lincoln Center and Phoenix Theatre, NY.

THEATER: Dir., Prod. (L.A.): The Beautiful People, Five Finger Exercise, The Purification, etc. Director (NY): Awakening of Spring, Hamp, Ceremony of Innocence, The Justice Box, Billy, Vieux Carre, The World of My America, Awake and Sing; The Four Seasons, Inherit the Wind, The Most Happy Fella, as well as numerous regional prods. and national tours.

PICTURES: Children of Rage (1978, dir., s.p.), Echoes, The Caller, Rescue Me.

TELEVISION: Director: Ceremony of Innocence, Family, Magnum, P.I., Murder She Wrote, Hill Street Blues, Trapper John M.D., Paper Chase, Knots Landing, Bay City Blues, Capitol News, WIOU, L.A. Law, FBI: The Untold Stories. Movies: Which Mother is Mine? A Special Gift, Schoolboy Father, A Matter of Time, I Think I'm Having a Baby, Sin of Innocence, Kate's Secret, Ceremony of Innocence, Poker Alice, The People Across the Lake, Addicted to His Love, A Friendship in Vienna, A Place at the Table, Look Away, An Enemy Among Us, Glory Years, Strange Voices, False Witness, The Kid Who Loved Christmas, Body Language.

SEIDELMAN, SUSAN: Director. b. near Philadelphia, PA, Dec.11, 1952. e. Drexel Univ. B.A. Worked at a UHF television station in Phila., NYU film school M.F.A. Debut: 28-min. student film And You Act Like One Too. Then dir. Deficit (short, funded by AFI), and Yours Truly, Andrea G. Stern.

PICTURES: Smithereens (dir., prod., co-s.p.; 1st Amer. indep. feature accepted into competition at Cannes Film Fest., 1982), Desperately Seeking Susan, Making Mr. Right, Cookie (also exec. prod.), She-Devil, The Dutch Master.

TELEVISION: Confessions of a Suburban Girl (BBC; also writer, actress).

SEINFELD, JERRY: Comedian, Actor. b. Brooklyn, NY, Apr. 29, 1954. e. Queens Col. Stand-up comic; guested on such shows as The Tonight Show, Late Night With David Letterman. Received American Comedy Award for funniest male comedy stand-up, 1988.

TELEVISION: Series: Benson, Seinfeld (also co-creator, writer). Pilot: The Seinfeld Chronicles. Special: Jerry Seinfeld - Stand-Up Confidential (also writer).

SELBY, DAVID: Actor. b. Morganstown, WV. Feb. 5, 1941. e. U. of West Virginia. Acted in outdoor dramas in home state and did regional theatre elsewhere. Was asst. instructor in lit. at Southern Illinois U.

PICTURES: Night of Dark Shadows, Up the Sandbox, Super Cops, Rich Kids, Raise the Titanic, Rich and Famous, Dying Young.

TELEVISION: *Series*: Dark Shadows, Flamingo Road, Falcon Crest. *Mini-Series*: Washington: Behind Closed Doors. *Movies*: Telethon, The Night Rider, Love for Rent, Doctor Franken, King of the Olympics: The Lives and Loves of Avery Brundage, Grave Secrets: The Legacy of Hilltop Drive, Lady Boss. *Guest*: Kojak, Doogie Howser M.D.

SELF, WILLIAM: Producer. b. Dayton, OH, June 21, 1921. e. U. of Chicago, 1943. Prod.-dir., Schlitz Playhouse of Stars, 1952–56; prod., The Frank Sinatra Show, 1957; exec. prod., CBS-TV, The Twilight Zone, Hotel De Paree. 1960–61 exec. prod., 20th Century-Fox TV. Hong Kong, Adventures in Paradise, Bus Stop, Follow The Sun, Margie; v.p. in chg. of prod., 20th Century-Fox TV, 1962; exec. vp., 1964. Pres., FOX TV 1969; v.p. 20th Century Fox Film Corp., 1969; pres. of William Self Productions, Inc., partner, Frankovich/Self Productions; 1975; vice-pres., programs, Hollywood CBS Television Network, 1976; 1977, v.p. motion pictures for television and miniseries, CBS Television Network; 1982, pres., CBS Theatrical Films. In 1985, pres., William Self Prods. in association with CBS Prods. 1990, pres. Self Productions, Inc.

TELEVISION: Movies (exec. prod.): The Tenth Man (also prod.), Sarah Plain & Tall, Skylark.

SELIG, ROBERT WILLIAM: Exhibitor. b. Cripple Creek, CO, Feb., 1910. e. U. of Denver, 1932, B.A.; doctorate, 1959. 1932 joined advertising sales div., 20th Century Fox, Denver. Founding mem. Theatre Owners of Amer. and NATO. Consultant, Pacific Theatres. Lifetime Trustee, U. of Denver. Member Kappa Sigma, Omicron Delta Kappa, Beta Gamma Sigma; Nat'l Methodist Church Foundation; Past Pres., Theatre Association of California and CEO NATO of CA; board of directors Los Angeles Chamber of Commerce; founder NATO/ShoWest Conventions. Received NATO Sherrill C. Corwin Award, 1989.

SELLECCA, CONNIE: Actress. b. Bronx, NY, May 25, 1955. m. anchor-host John Tesh.

TELEVISION: *Series*: Flying High, Beyond Westworld, The Greatest American Hero, Hotel, P.S. I Luv U. *Movies*: The Bermuda Depths (debut, 1978), Flying High (pilot), Captain America II, She's Dressed to Kill, The Last Fling, International Airport, Downpayment on Murder, Brotherhood of the Rose, Turn Back the Clock, Miracle Landing, People Like Us, A House of Secrets and Lies (also co-exec. prod.), Passport to Murder. *Specials*: The Celebrity Football Classic, Celebrity Challenge of the Sexes, Circus of the Stars.

SELLECK, TOM: Actor. b. Detroit, MI, Jan. 29, 1945. e. U. of Southern California. Grew up in Southern California. Did some modelling, appearing in several commercials before being signed to contract with 20th Century Fox. First acting job was on tv series Bracken's World.

PICTURES: Myra Breckenridge (debut, 1970), The Seven Minutes, Daughters of Satan, Terminal Island, Midway, The Washington Affair, Coma, High Road to China, Lassiter, Runaway, Three Men and a Baby, Her Alibi, An Innocent Man, Quigley Down Under, Three Men and a Little Lady, Folks!, Christopher Columbus: The Discovery, Mr. Baseball.

TELEVISION: *Series*: The Young and the Restless, The Rockford Files, Magnum, P.I. (Emmy Award, 1984). *Movies*: The Movie Murderer, A Case of Rape, Most Wanted, Superdome, Returning Home, The Sacketts, The Concrete Cowboys, Divorce Wars, Louis L'Amour's The Shadow Riders. *Exec. prod.*: B.L. Stryker (series), Revealing Evidence, The Silver Fox.

SELTZER, DAVID: Writer, Director. b. Highland Park, IL, 1940. m. flutist Eugenia Zukerman. e. Northwestern U. School for Film and Television. Moved to NY where worked on TV game show I've Got a Secret. Made short My Trip to New York. 1966 moved to LA to write for David Wolper's Incredible World of Animals. Then dir. and prod. Wolper documentaries. Worked as ghostwriter on film Willy Wonka and the Chocolate Factory.

PICTURES: *Writer*: The Hellstrom Chronicle, One Is a Lonely Number, The Omen, Damien: The Omen Part II; The Other Side of the Mountain, Six Weeks, Table for Five, Lucas (also dir.). Punchline (also dir.). Bird on a Wire, Shining Through (also dir., co-exec. prod.).

TELEVISION: National Geographic Specials (prod., dir., writer), William Holden in Unconquered Worlds (prod., dir., writer), The Underworld World of Jacques Cousteau. Movies: Writer: The Story of Eric, Green Eyes, My Father's House, Larry.

SELTZER, WALTER: Executive. b. Philadelphia, PA, Nov. 7, 1914. e. U. of Pennsylvania. Publicity mgr. for Warner Bros. Theatres, Philadelphia; Fox West Coast Theatres; with MGM 1936–39; Warner Bros., 1939–40; Columbia, 1940–41. Enlisted U.S. Marine Corps, 1941–44. Pub. dir., Hal Wallis, 1945–54; v.p. in chg. adv & pub., Hecht-Lancaster Orgn., Feb., 1954–56; assoc. prod., The Boss; partner, Glass-Seltzer,

pub. rel. firm; v.p. & exec. prod, Pennebaker Production. 1982, v.p., M.P. & TV Fund. Pres., WSP Inc.

PICTURES: One-Eyed Jacks, Shake Hands With the Devil, Paris Blues, The Naked Edge, Man in the Middle, Wild Seed, War Lord, Beau Geste, Will Penny, Number One, Darker Than Amber, The Omega Man, Skyjacked, Soylent Green, The Cay, The Last Hard Men.

SEMEL, TERRY: Executive. b. New York, NY, Feb. 24, 1943. e. Long Island Univ., B.S. Accounting 1964. Warner Bros. sales trainee 1966. Branch mgr., Cleveland, Los Angeles. V.P. Domestic sls. mgr. for CBS, 1971–73. Buena Vista as v.p., gen. sls. mgr., 1973–5. In 1975 went to Warner Bros. as pres. domestic sls. In 1978 named exec. v.p. and chief operating officer WB Inc. Named pres., Warner Bros. & COO 1980. Named Pioneer of the Year by Foundation of Motion Picture Pioneers, 1990.

SEMLER, DEAN: Cinematographer. b. Australia. Served as 2nd unit dir. and cameraman on the mini-series Lonesome Dove, Son of the Morningstar.

PICTURES: The Road Warrior, Mad Max Beyond Thunderdome, The Lighthorsemen, Cocktail, Young Guns, Farewell to the King, K-9, Dead Calm, Impulse, Young Guns II, Dances With Wolves (Acad. Award), City Slickers, The Power of One, Super Mario Bros., Last Action Hero.

SEMPLE, LORENZO, JR.: Writer.

PICTURES: Fathom, Pretty Poison, Daddy's Gone A-Hunting (with Larry Cohen), The Sporting Club, The Marriage of a Young Stockbroker, Papillon (co-s.p.), Super Cops, The Parallax View (co-s.p.), The Drowning Pool (co-s.p.), Three Days of the Condor (co-s.p.), King Kong, Hurricane (and exec. prod.), Flash Gordon, Never Say Never Again, Sheena (co-s.p.), Never Too Young to Die.

TELEVISION: *Series*: Batman (1966). *Movie*: Rearview Mirror.

SEN, BACHOO: Producer, Distributor. Entered industry 1950 in India and 1958 in U.K. Director of English Film Co. Ltd., English Film Co. (Exports) Ltd. and All-American Leisure Group, U.K. Ltd. Among 38 features produced: Her Private Hell, Loving Feeling, Love Is a Splendid Illusion, Tenderness, Adam and Nicole, The Intruders. In U.S., Nightmare Weekend. Chairman of All American Leisure Group Inc. Dir. of Bop, Inc.

SENDREY, ALBERT: Music Composer, Arranger, Conductor. b. Chicago, IL, Dec. 26, 1921. e. Trinity Coll. Music, London, U. of Southern California, Paris, & Leipzig Conservatories. Winner, Chi. Symphony Orch. prize for First Symphony, 1941; 1948, Reichhold Award Detroit Symph. Orch. for 2nd Symphony. Ohio Sesquicentenn. Award for Overture, Johnny Appleseed, 1953; French libretto: One Act Opera: The Telltale Stones, 1964; arr., Mary Martin at Radio City Music Hall, 1965. Composer, arr., orch. for many plays, films and TV. On stage was pianist/conductor for Lauritz Melchior, Kathryn Grayson, Ray Bolger, Danny Kaye, Tony Martin, Buddy Ebsen.

MEMBER: M.P. Academy, ASCAP, ASMAC, TV Academy.

BROADWAY: orch., arr.: Peter Pan, Ziegfeld Follies, New Faces, At the Grand, Pink Jungle, The Great Waltz, Turn to the Right.

PICTURES: Orch: The Yearling, Three Musketeers, Father's Little Dividend, Duchess of Idaho, Royal Wedding, Easy to Love, Great Caruso, American in Paris, Brigadoon, Athena, Finian's Rainbow, Guys and Dolls, Meet Me in Las Vegas, Opposite Sex, High Society, Raintree County, Let's Be Happy, Ride the High Country, Hallelujah Trail, The Hook, The Comancheros, Nevada Smith, The Oscar, Thoroughly Modern Millie, Hello Down There, Private Navy of Sgt. O'Farrell, Hard Times.

TELEVISION: comp. music: Laramie, Wagon Train, Ben Casey, Wolper Documentaries, Americans Abroad, J. F. Kennedy Anthology; Young Man from Boston, High Chaparral, (collab. with Harry Sukman), Bonanza (with D. Rose), The Monroes, Ken Murray's Hollywood, SWAT (collab. B. de Vorzon), Hard Times, (collab.), Napoleon and Josephine (orch.).

SENECA, JOE: Actor. Has been acting since 1973. In the 1950's was part of a satirical singing group, The Three Riffs performing at a New York club, Le Ruban Bleu. In the 1950s and '60s wrote songs. 1970–73 was a writer for Sesame Street.

THEATER: The Little Foxes (starring Elizabeth Taylor), Of Mice and Men (starring James Earl Jones), Sizwe Banzi Is Dead (Pittsburgh), Ma Rainey's Black Bottom (Yale Repertory and B'way).

PICTURES: Kramer vs. Kramer, The Verdict, Silverado, The Evil Men Do, Crossroads, School Daze, The Blob, Mississippi Masala.

TELEVISION: The Wilma Rudolph Story, Terrible Joe Moran, Solomon Northrup's Odyssey, The House of Dies Drear, Dorothy and Son (Amazing Stories), A Gathering of Old Men.

SERNAS, JACQUES: Actor, Producer. b. Lithuania, July 30, 1925. Became naturalized French citizen, studying medicine in Paris. Was amateur boxer when heard Jean Gabin needed an acting boxer for The Mirror, in which he made professional debut as actor. Has appeared in over 80 films, made in recent years primarily in Italy, now his home.
    PICTURES: Lost Youth, The Golden Salamander, Helen of Troy, Jump into Hell, The First Night, La Dolce Vita, 55 Days in Peking, F.B.I.: Operation Baalbeck (also prod.), Operation Gold in the Balearic Islands (also prod.), Super Fly TNT.
    TELEVISION: The School of the Painters of Paris (prod. only), The 18th Century Seen Through Its Famous Painters (prod. only), The Red Triangle (Ital. series).

SEYMOUR, JANE: Actress. r.n. Joyce Frankenberg. b. Hillingdon, England, Feb. 15, 1951. Dancer with London Festival Ballet at 13. On Bdwy. in Amadeus (1980). British Repetory including Canterbury, Harrogate, Sussex, Windsor.
    PICTURES: Oh! What a Lovely War (debut, 1968), The Only Way, Young Winston, Live and Let Die, Sinbad and the Eye of the Tiger, Battlestar Galactica, Oh Heavenly Dog, Somewhere in Time, Lassiter, Head Office, The Tunnel, The French Revolution, Keys to Freedom, Leather Funnel.
    TELEVISION: Series: The Onedine Line, Dr. Quinn: Medicine Woman. Movies: Frankenstein: The True Story, Captains and the Kings, Benny and Barney: Las Vegas Undercover, Seventh Avenue, Killer on Board, The Four Feathers, The Awakening Land, Love's Dark Ride, Dallas Cowboys Cheerleaders, Our Mutual Friend, East of Eden, The Scarlet Pimpernal, Phantom of the Opera, The Haunting Passion, Dark Mirror, The Sun Also Rises, Obsessed with a Married Woman, Jamaica Inn, Crossings, War and Remembrance (mini-series), The Woman He Loved, Onassis: The Richest Man in the World (Emmy Award, 1988), Jack the Ripper, Angel of Death, I Remember You, Memories of Midnight, Are You Lonesome Tonight?, Matters of the Heart, Medicine Woman, Sunstroke (also exec. prod.), Heidi, Praying Mantis.

SHABER, DAVID: Screenwriter. b. Cleveland, OH. e. Western Reserve U., Yale U., Taught at Allegheny Coll. and Smith Coll. in speech and drama dept. Prof. of screenwriting Columbia Univ. Film School. Contributor to Cosmopolitan, Life, Esquire; had several short stories in O'Henry prize collections. Also wrote dramas (Shake Hands with the Clown, The Youngest Shall Ask, Bunker Reveries, etc.). First screenplay was Such Good Friends for Otto Preminger.
    PICTURES: The Last Embrace, The Warriors, Those Lips, Those Eyes, Night Hawks, Rollover, The Hunt for Red October (uncredited), Flight of the Intruder.

SHAGAN, STEVE: Writer. b. New York, NY. Oct. 25, 1927. Apprenticed in little theatres, film lab chores, stagehand jobs. Wrote, produced and directed film short, One Every Second; moved to Hollywood in 1959. Was IATSE technician, working as grip, stagehand, electrician to support film writing. Also did freelance advertising and publicity; produced Tarzan TV show. In 1968 began writing and producing two-hour films for TV.
    PICTURES: Writer: Save the Tiger (also prod.; Acad. Award nom., WGA award, best original s.p., 1973), W.W. and the Dixie Dancekings (exec. prod.), Hustle, Voyage of the Damned (co.-s.p.; Acad. Award nom.), Nightwing (co-s.p.), The Formula (also prod.), The Sicilian.
    TELEVISION: Writer-producer: River of Mystery, Spanish Portrait, Sole Survivor, A Step Out of Line, House on Garibaldi Street (exec. prod.).
    BOOKS: Save the Tiger, City of Angels, The Formula, The Circle, The Discovery, Vendetta, Pillars of Fire, A Cast of Thousands.

SHAIMAN, MARC: Composer, Arranger. b. New Jersey, 1959. Moved to NY at 16 where he met Bette Milder; was arranger and lyricists for her stage shows and the album Thighs & Whispers. Wrote music for Saturday Night Live, musical material for Billy Crytsal for the Academy Awards. Prod. and arranger for several Harry Connick, Jr. albums. Appeared on stage in Haarlem Nocturne.
    PICTURES: Divine Madness (music dir., arranger), The Cotton Club (music sprv., arranger), Broadcast News (cameo), Big Business (music sprv., arranger), Beaches (arranger), When Harry Met Sally... (music sprv.), Misery (music), Scenes From a Mall (music, adapt.), City Slickers (music), Hot Shots (cameo), For the Boys (music sprv., arranger, co-composer), The Addams Family (music, cameo, co-wrote song "Mamuschka"), Sister Act (music, adapt.), Mr. Saturday Night (music, cameo), A Few Good Men (music), Life With Mikey (music spvr.), Sleepless in Seattle (musical spvr., co-wrote song "With a Wink and a Smile") Heart and Souls (music), For Love or Money (co-composer), Addams Family Values (music), Sister Act 2 (music, adaptations).

SHALIT, GENE: Critic. b. New York, NY, 1932. e. U. of Illinois. Started as freelance writer; joined NBC Radio Network, working on Monitor, 1968. Has been book and film critic,

sports and general columnist. Since 1973 has been featured regular on NBC Today Show. Edits newsletter Shalit's Sampler.

SHANDLING, GARRY: Actor, Comedian, Writer, Producer. b. Chicago, IL, Nov. 29, 1949. e. Univ. of AZ. Moved to LA where he became writer for such sitcoms as Sanford & Son, Welcome Back Kotter, Three's Company. Became stand-up comedian in nightclubs which led to appearances on The Tonight Show.
    TELEVISION: Series: It's Garry Shandling's Show (also exec. prod., writer; ACE Awards for Best Series & Actor), The Larry Sanders Show (also co-exec. prod., co-creator, co-writer). Specials: Garry Shandling - Alone in Las Vegas (also writer, prod.), It's Garry Shandling's Show - 25th Anniversary Special (also exec. prod., writer), Grammy Awards (host), Garry Shandling: Stand-Up (also writer). Guest: Tonight Show (also frequent guest host), Late Night With David Letterman.
    PICTURE: The Night We Never Met.

SHANLEY, JOHN PATRICK: Writer. b. New York, NY, 1950. e. NYU. Cameo appearance in 1988 film Crossing Delancey. Dir. and wrote short I am Angry.
    THEATER: Rockaway, Welcome to the Moon, Danny and the Deep Blue Sea, Savage in Limbo, Dreamer Examines His Pillow, Italian-American Reconciliation (also dir.), Beggars in the House of Plenty (also dir.).
    PICTURES: Moonstruck (Acad. Award), Five Corners (also assoc. prod.), The January Man, Joe Versus the Volcano (dir., s.p.), Alive.

SHAPIRO, KEN: Producer, Director, Writer, Actor. b. New Jersey, 1943. e. Bard Coll. Was child actor on tv and teacher in Brooklyn before opening "world's first video theatre" in East Village of Manhattan: Channel One, 90 mins. of TV lampoons and original material shown on TV monitors to live audience. Took 16 mm material on college dates with success, culminating in feature film: The Groove Tube, 1974.
    PICTURE: Modern Problems (co-s.p., dir.)

SHAPIRO, ROBERT W.: Producer. b. Brooklyn, NY, March 1, 1938. e. U. of Southern CA., Joined William Morris Agency, Inc., 1958. dir. and head of motion picture dept., William Morris Agency (UK) Ltd., 1969; man. dir., 1970. 1974 vice president, head int'l. m.p. dept., William Morris, Inc. In March, 1977 joined Warner Bros. as exec. v.p. in chg. of worldwide production. 1981, named WB pres., theatrical production div. Resigned 1983 to produce films.
    PICTURES: Pee-Wee's Big Adventure (prod.); Empire of the Sun (exec. prod.); Arthur 2 On the Rocks (prod.), There Goes My Baby (prod.).
    TELEVISION: Producer: The Summer My Father Grew Up.

SHARE, MICHAEL: Executive. Began career with Paramount Pictures 1974 as booker in Indianapolis. 1975–76 appt. salesman; 1976–77 sls. mgr. in Philadelphia; 1977, Cincinnati branch mgr.; 1980, Chicago branch mgr. 1985, promoted to v.p., eastern div.

SHARIF, OMAR: Actor. r.n. Michel Shahoub. b. Alexandria, Egypt, April 10, 1932. e. Victoria Coll., Cairo.; pres. of College Dramatic Society. m. Faten Hamama. Starred in 21 Egyptian and two French films prior to Lawrence of Arabia. Left Egypt 1964. Champion contract bridge player. 1983 made rare stage appearance in The Sleeping Prince (Chistester, then West End).
    PICTURES: The Blazing Sun (1954, debut), Our Happy Days, La Chatelane du Liban, Goha, Lawrence of Arabia, The Mameluks, The Fall of the Roman Empire, Behold a Pale Horse, Marco the Magnificent, Genghis Khan, The Yellow Rolls-Royce, Doctor Zhivago, The Poppy is Also a Flower, Night of the Generals, More Than a Miracle, Funny Girl, McKenna's Gold, The Appointment, Mayerling, Che!, The Last Valley, The Horsemen, The Burglars, The Tamarind Seed, The Mysterious Island of Captain Nemo, Juggernaut, Funny Lady, Crime and Passion, The Pink Panther Strikes Again, Ashanti, Bloodline, The Baltimore Bullet, Oh Heavenly Dog, Green Ice, Chanel Solitaire, Top Secret, The Possessed, Paradise Calling, The Blue Pyramids, Keys to Freedom, Novice, Mountains of the Moon, Michelangelo and Me, Drums of Fire, Le Guignol, The Puppet, The Rainbow Thief, Journey of Love, Mother, 588 Rue Paradis.
    TELEVISION: S*H*E, Pleasure Palace, The Far Pavilions, Peter the Great, Harem, Anastasia, Grand Larceny, Omar Sharif Returns to Egypt, The Mysteries of the Pyramids Live (host), Memories of Midnight, Mrs. 'arris Goes to Paris.

SHARP, ALAN: Writer. b. Glasgow, Scotland. Writes western screenplays.
    PICTURES: The Hired Hand, Ulzana's Raid, Billy Two Hats, Night Moves, The Osterman Weekend, Little Treasure (also dir.), Freeway, Cat Chaser (co-s.p.).
    TELEVISION: Coming Out of the Ice.

SHARP, DON: Writer, director. b. Hobart, Tasmania, Australia, Apr. 4, 1921, e. St. Virgils Col. Early career as actor in Australia. Ent. m.p. ind. in England with Group Three as screenwriter,

1951. Began directing 1955 with doc. children's films, 2nd unit work and filmed TV series.

PICTURES: The Golden Disc, The Professionals, Linda, Two Guys Abroad, Kiss of the Vampire, It's All Happening, Devil Ship Pirates, Witchcraft, Those Magnificent Men in Their Flying Machines (2nd unit), Curse of the Fly, The Face of Fu Manchu, Rasputin—The Mad Monk, Our Man in Marrakesh, The Brides of Fu Manchu, Rocket to the Moon, Taste of Excitement, The Violent Enemy, Puppet on a Chain, Psychomania, Dark Places, Callan, Hennessy, The Four Feathers, The 39 Steps, Bear Island.

TELEVISION: Ghost Squad, The Champions, The Human Jungle, The Avengers, House of Horror, Q.E.D., A Woman of Substance, Tusitala, Hold the Dream, Tears in the Rain, Act of Will.

SHATNER, WILLIAM: Actor. b. Montreal, Quebec, Mar. 22, 1931. e. McGill U. Toured Canada in various stock, repertory companies. Author: Tek War, Tek Lords, Tek Lab, Tek Vengeance, Believe.

PICTURES: The Brothers Karamazov (debut, 1958), Judgment at Nuremberg, The Explosive Generation, The Intruder, The Outrage, Incubus, White Comanche, Impulse, Big Bad Mama, The Devil's Rain, Kingdom of the Spiders, Land of No Return, Star Trek—The Motion Picture, The Kidnapping of the President, Visiting Hours, Star Trek II: The Wrath of Khan, Airplane II: The Sequel, Star Trek III: The Search for Spock, Star Trek IV: The Voyage Home, Star Trek V: The Final Frontier (also dir., orig. story), Bill & Ted's Bogus Journey (cameo), Star Trek VI: The Undiscovered Country, National Lampoon's Loaded Weapon 1.

TELEVISION: Series: For the People, Star Trek, Barbary Coast, T.J. Hooker, Rescue 911 (host). Movies: Sole Survivor, Vanished, Owen Marshall: Counselor at Law (pilot), The People, The Hound of the Baskervilles, Incident on a Dark Street, Go Ask Alice, The Horror at 37000 Feet, Pioneer Woman, Indict and Convict, Pray for the Wildcats, Barbary Coast (pilot), Perilous Voyage, The Bastard, Little Women, Crash, Disaster on the Coastliner, The Baby Sitter, Secrets of a Married Man, North Beach and Rawhide, Broken Angel, Family of Strangers. Special: The Andersonville Trial. Mini-Series: Testimony of Two Men.

THEATRE: NY: Tamburlaine the Great, The World of Susie Wong (Theatre World Award), A Shot in the Dark, l'Idiote.

SHAVELSON, MELVILLE: Writer, Director. b. Brooklyn, NY, April 1, 1917. e. Cornell U., 1937, A.B. Radio writer: We The People, Bicycle Party, 1937, Bob Hope Show, 1938–43. Screen writer; apptd. prod., Warner Bros. 1951. Conceived for TV: Make Room for Daddy, My World and Welcome To It. Author: book, How To Make a Jewish Movie. Lualda, The Great Houdinis, The Eleventh Commandment, Ike, Don't Shoot It's Only Me. Pres., Writers Guild of America, West, 1969–71, 1979–81, 1985–87; Pres., Writers Guild Foundation 1978–93.

PICTURES: Writer: Princess & the Pirate, Wonder Man, Kid From Brooklyn, Sorrowful Jones, It's a Great Feeling, Daughter of Rosie O'Grady, Always Leave Them Laughing, Where There's Life, On Moonlight Bay, I'll See You in My Dreams, Room For One More, April in Paris, Trouble Along the Way, Living It Up. Director-Writer: Seven Little Foys, Beau James, Houseboat, It Started in Naples, The Five Pennies, On the Double, The Pigeon That Took Rome (also prod.), A New Kind of Love (also prod.), Cast a Giant Shadow (also prod.), Yours Mine and Ours, The War Between Men and Women, Mixed Company.

TV FEATURES: The Legend of Valentino, The Great Houdinis, Ike, The Other Woman, Deceptions; Academy Awards, 1988, 1990 (writer).

SHAVER, HELEN: Actress. b. St. Thomas, Ontario, Canada, Feb. 24, 1951. e. Banff Sch. of Fine Arts, Alberta. Worked on stage and screen in Canada before coming to Los Angeles 1978.

PICTURES: Christina, Shoot, Starship Invasions, Outrageous!, High-Ballin', The Amityville Horror, In Praise of Older Women, Who Has Seen the Wind, Gas, Harry Tracy, The Osterman Weekend, Best Defense, Desert Hearts, The Color of Money, The Believers, The Land Before Time (voice), Bethune: The Making of a Hero, Walking After Midnight, Tree of Hands, Zebrahead, That Night, Change of Heart.

TELEVISION: Series: United States, Jessica Novak, WIOU. Movies: Lovey: Circle of Children II, Between Two Brothers, Many Happy Returns, The Park is Mine, Countdown To Looking Glass, No Blame, B.L. Stryker: The Dancer's Touch, Pair of Aces, Columbo: Rest in Peace Mrs. Columbo, Survive the Night, Poisoned By Love: The Kern County Murders, Trial & Error. Guest: Ray Bradbury Theatre, Amazing Stories.

THEATRE: Tamara, Are You Lookin'? Ghost on Fire, A Doll's House, The Master Builder, The Hostage, Jake's Women (Bdwy debut; Theatre World Award).

SHAWN, WALLACE: Playwright, Actor. b. New York, NY, Nov. 12, 1943. Son of former New Yorker editor William Shawn. e. Harvard; Oxford U. Taught English in India on a Fulbright scholarship 1965–66. English, Latin and drama teacher, NY 1968–70.

PLAYS: Our Late Night (1975, Obie Award), The Mandrake (translation), A Thought in Three Parts, Marie and Bruce, The Hotel Play, Aunt Dan and Lemon, The Fever (Obie Award: Best Play, 1991). Opera: The Music Teacher (with Allen Shawn).

THEATER: Actor: The Mandrake (1977), The Master and Margerita, Chinchilla, Aunt Dan and Lemon, The Fever.

PICTURES: Manhattan, Starting Over, All That Jazz, Strong Medicine, Simon, Atlantic City, My Dinner With Andre (also co-s.p.), A Little Sex, Lovesick, The First Time, Deal of the Century, Strange Invaders, Saigon—Year of the Cat, Crackers, The Hotel New Hampshire, The Bostonians, Micki and Maude, Heaven Help Us, Head Office, The Bedroom Window, Radio Days, Prick Up Your Ears, Nice Girls Don't Explode, The Princess Bride, The Moderns, She's Out of Control, Scenes From the Class Struggle in Beverly Hills, We're No Angels, Shadows and Fog, Mom and Dad Save the World, Nickel and Dime, The Cemetery Club, Un-Becoming Age, The Meteor Man.

SHAYE, ROBERT: Executive. b. Detroit, MI, Mar. 4, 1939. e. U. of Michigan, B.B.A.; Columbia U. Law. At 15 wrote, prod. dir. training film for father's supermarket staff. Later won first prize in Society of Cinematologists' Rosenthal Competition (best m.p. by American dir. under 25). Wrote, prod., dir., edited short films, trailers and TV commercials, including award-winning shorts, Image and On Fighting Witches (prod., dir.). Founded New Line Cinema 1967. Chmn. & CEO, New Line Cinema.

PICTURES: Prod./exec. prod.: Stunts, XTRO, Alone in the Dark, The First Time, Polyester, Critters, Quiet Cool, My Demon Lover, A Nightmare on Elm Street (parts 1,2,3,4,5,6), The Hidden, Stranded, Critters 2, Hairspray, Heart Condition, Book of Love (dir.).

TELEVISION: Freddy's Nightmare: the Series (exec. prod.).

SHEA, JOHN: Actor. b. Conway, NH, April 14, 1949. Raised in MA. e. Bates Coll., ME; Yale Drama School (1970), graduated as a director, 1973. Worked as asst. dir. Chelsea Theater; taught part-time at Pratt Inst.

THEATER: Yentl (debut 1975, Off-Bdwy and Bdwy; Theatre World Award), Sorrows of Stephen, Long Day's Journey Into Night, The Master and Margerita, Romeo and Juliet (Circle in the Sq.), American Days (Drama Desk Award), The Dining Room (Obie Award), End of the World (Bdwy), The Normal Heart (London, 1987), Animal Kingdom, Rosmersholm (La Mama).

PICTURES: Hussy, Missing, Windy City (Best Actor Montreal Film Festival), A New Life, Unsettled Land, Honeymoon (French), Stealing Home, Freejack, Honey I Blew Up the Kid, Snake Eyes.

TELEVISION: Series: WIOU, Lois and Clark. Movies: The Nativity, Family Reunion, Coast to Coast (BBC), Hitler's S.S.: Portrait in Evil, A Case of Deadly Force, The Impossible Spy, Magic Moments, Baby M (Emmy Award), Do You Know the Muffin Man, Small Sacrifices, Notorious, Ladykiller. Mini-Series: The Last Convertible, Kennedy.

SHEAFF, DONALD J.: Executive. b. Oct. 23, 1925. e. U.of California at L.A., 1948; Pierce Coll., 1957. Served 4 yrs. during W.W.II in Navy Air Corps in South Pacific. 1946, joined Technicolor Motion Picture Div. in supervisory capacity; 1957, lab. supervisor, Lookout Mountain Air Force Station, handling Top Secret film for Air Force and Atomic Energy Commission. Est. and org. the installation of Vandenberg Air Force Base Lab. facilities, which Technicolor designed. 1961 joined Panacolor Corp., 1963; joined Pacific Title and Art Studio in charge of color control for special effects and titles. Returned to Technicolor Corp. 1966, app't. Plant Mgr. of Television Div., Oct. 1966, V.P. & Gen. Mgr. of the Television Div., July, 1973 appt v.p. & gen. mgr., Motion Picture Division; 1976; mgr., special visual effects, Universal City Studios. Member: SMPTE, Nat'l Academy of Television Arts & Sciences. Has conducted scientific seminars for SMPTE.

SHEARER, HARRY: Writer, Actor. b. Los Angeles, CA, Dec. 23, 1943. e. UCLA (pol. science); grad. work in urban gov., Harvard. At 7 appeared on The Jack Benny Show. Worked as freelance journalist for Newsweek, L.A. Times and publ. articles in New West, L.A. Magazine and Film Comment. Also taught h.s. Eng. and social studies and worked in CA State Legislature in Sacramento. Founding mem. The Credibility Gap, co-wrote, co-prod. and performed on comedy group's albums (A Great Gift Idea, The Bronze Age of Radio). Co-wrote, co-prod. Albert Brooks' album A Star is Bought. Host of Le Show, L.A. radio prog. Writer-cast mem. Saturday Night Live (1979–80 & 1984–85).

THEATER: Accomplice (Pasadena Playhouse).

PICTURES: Actor: Abbott and Costello Go to Mars (debut, as child, 1953), Cracking Up, Real Life (also co-s.p.), Animalympics (voice), The Fish That Saved Pittsburgh, Serial, One-Trick Pony, The Right Stuff, This is Spinal Tap (also co-s.p.), Plain Clothes, My Stepmother is an Alien (voice), Oscar, Pure Luck, Blood & Concrete, The Fisher King, A League of Their Own.

TELEVISION: *Series*: Fernwood 2-Night (creative consultant), The Simpsons (voice). *Specials*: Likely Stories, It's Just TV, Paul Shaffer: Viva Shaf Vegas, Comedy Hour, Portrait of a White Marriage (also dir.), The Magic of Live, Spinal Tap Reunion (also co-writer).

SHEEDY, ALLY: Actress. r.n. Alexandra Sheedy. b. New York, NY, June 13, 1962. e. U. of Southern California. m. actor David Lansbury. Daughter of literary agent Charlotte Sheedy. At age 12 wrote children's book. She Was Nice to Mice; later pieces in The New York Times, The Village Voice, Ms. Published book of poetry Yesterday I Saw the Sun. Began acting in TV commercials at 15. Chicago Theatre in Wrong Turn at Lungfish, NY stage debut in Advice from a Caterpillar.
PICTURES: Bad Boys (debut, 1983), WarGames, Oxford Blues, The Breakfast Club, St. Elmo's Fire, Twice in a Lifetime, Blue City, Short Circuit, Maid to Order, Heart of Dixie, Betsy's Wedding, Only the Lonely, Home Alone 2: Lost in New York, Tattletale, The Pickle.
TELEVISION: *Movies*: The Best Little Girl in the World, The Violation of Sarah McDavid, The Day the Loving Stopped, Splendor in the Grass, Deadly Lessons, We Are the Children, Fear, The Lost Capone, Lethal Exposure, Chantilly Lace. *Guest*: Hill Street Blues, St. Elsewhere.

SHEEN, CHARLIE: Actor. r.n. Carlos Irwin Estevez. b. Los Angeles, Sept. 3, 1965. Son of Martin Sheen. Brother of actors Emilio and Ramon Sheen. Made debut as extra in TV movie, The Execution of Private Slovik (starring father) and as extra in Apocalypse Now (also starring father).
PICTURES: Grizzly II—The Predator, Red Dawn, The Boys Next Door, Lucas, Ferris Bueller's Day Off, The Wraith, Platoon, Wisdom, Three for the Road, No Man's Land, Wall Street, Never on Tuesday, Young Guns, Eight Men Out, Major League, Beverly Hills Brats, Courage Mountain, Navy Seals, Men at Work, The Rookie, Cadence, Hot Shots!, National Lampoon's Loaded Weapon 1, Hot Shots Part Deux!, Dead-Fall, The Three Musketeers.
TELEVISION: *Movies*: Silence of the Heart, Backtrack.

SHEEN, MARTIN: Actor. r.n. Ramon Estevez. b. Dayton, OH, Aug. 3, 1940. Father of actors Emilio Estevez, Charlie Sheen and Ramon Estevez. Wrote play (as Ramon G. Estevez) Down the Morning Line (prod. Public Theatre, 1969). Emmy Award as dir., exec. prod. Babies Having Babies (1986).
THEATER: The Connection (debut, 1959 with the Living Theater), Women of Trachis, Many Loves, In the Jungle of Cities, Never Live Over a Pretzel Factory, The Subject Was Roses, The Wicked Crooks, Hamlet, Romeo and Juliet, Hello Goodbye, The Happiness Cage, Death of a Salesman (with George C. Scott), Julius Caesar, The Crucible.
PICTURES: The Incident (debut, 1967), The Subject Was Roses, Catch-22, No Drums No Bugles, Rage, Pickup on 101, Badlands, The Legend of Earl Durrand, The Cassandra Crossing, The Little Girl Who Lives Down the Lane, Apocalypse Now, Eagle's Wing, The Final Countdown, Loophole, Gandhi, That Championship Season, Enigma, Man Woman and Child, The Dead Zone, Firestarter, The Believers, Siesta, Wall Street, Walking After Midnight, Da (also co-exec. prod.), Judgment in Berlin (also exec. prod.), Beverly Hills Brats, Cold Front, Beyond the Stars, The Maid, Cadence (also dir.), JFK (narrator), Hear No Evil, Hot Shots Part Deux (cameo), Gettysburg.
TELEVISION: *Series*: As the World Turns. *Movies*: Then Came Bronson, Mongo's Back in Town, Welcome Home Johnny Bristol, That Certain Summer, Letters for Three Lovers, Pursuit, Catholics, Message to My Daughter, The Execution of Private Slovik, The California Kid, The Missiles of October, The Story of Pretty Boy Floyd, Sweet Hostage, The Guardian, The Last Survivors, Blind Ambition, The Long Road Home (Emmy Award, 1981), In the Custody of Strangers, Choices of the Heart, The Atlanta Child Murders, Consenting Adult, Shattered Spirits, News at Eleven, Out of the Darkness, Samaritan, Conspiracy: The Trial of the Chicago 8, No Means No (exec. prod. only), Nightbreaker (also exec. prod.), Guilty Until Proven Innocent, The Water Engine (story), The Last P.O.W.?: The Bobby Garwood Story. *Mini-Series*: Kennedy, Queen.

SHEFFER, CRAIG: Actor. b. York, PA, 1960. e. East Stroudsberg Univ., PA. Started career in tv commercials; in soap opera, One Life to Live. On NY stage in Fresh Horses, G.R. Point, Torch Song Trilogy (Bdwy & Off-Bdwy).
PICTURES: That Was Then This Is Now (debut, 1985), Fire with Fire, Some Kind of Wonderful, Voyage of the Rock Aliens, Split Decisions, Nightbreed, Instant Karma (also exec. prod.), Blue Desert, Eye of the Storm, A River Runs Through It, Fire in the Sky, The Program, Roadflower.
TELEVISION: *Series*: The Hamptons. *Movie*: Babycakes.

SHEFFIELD, JOHN: Actor. b. Pasadena, CA, April 11, 1931. e. UCLA. Stage debut at 7 in On Borrowed Time. Created screen role of Tarzan's son in Tarzan pictures and role of Bomba in Bomba series.
PICTURES: Babes in Arms, Lucky Cisco Kid, Little Orvie, Bomba series, Million Dollar Baby, Knute Rockne, The

Golden Idol, Lord of the Jungle, Roughly Speaking, Golden Idol, Lord of the Jungle.
TELEVISION: series: Bantu the Zebra Boy.

SHEFTER, BERT: Composer, Conductor. b. Russia, May 15, 1904. e. Carnegie Inst. of Technology, Curtis Inst., Damrosch Inst. Member of piano team, Gould & Shefter, on radio & in theatres; org. own band; concert pianist; comp., cond. for many films and TV.
PICTURES: composer, conductor: Tall Texan, No Escape, Great Jesse James Raid, Sins of Jezebel, The Big Circus, The Fly, Lost World, Jack the Giant Killer, Monkey on My Back, Cattle King; Curse of the Fly, Last Man on Earth, Voyage to the Bottom of the Sea, The Bubble, Dog of Flanders.
TELEVISION: Written shows for Sunset Strip, Surfside, Hawaiian Eye, Maverick, Sugarfoot, Lawman, Bourbon St., Roaring 20's.

SHEINBERG, SIDNEY JAY: Executive. b. Corpus Christi, TX, Jan. 14, 1935. e. Columbia Coll., A.B. 1955; LL.B., 1958. Admitted to Calif. bar, 1958; assoc. in law U. of California Sch. of Law, Los Angeles, 1958–59; Joined MCA, Inc, 1959. Pres., TV div., 1971–74; exec. v.p., parent co., 1969–73. Named MCA pres. & chief oper. off., 1973.

SHELDON, DAVID: Producer, Director, Writer. b. New York, NY. e. Yale U. Sch. of Drama, M.F.A.; Principia Coll., B.A.; Actors Studio, directors unit. Directed N.Y. & L.A. companies of What the Butler Saw, Alley Oop, Jimmy Shine, From 1972–74 was exec. at American Intl. Pictures (now Orion Pictures) supervising various prod. & post-prod. aspects of such films as Dillinger, Sisters, Macon County Line, Reincarnation of Peter Proud, Slaughter, Dr. Phibes, Prod./Dir., The Gateway Playhouse in N.Y. where dir. over 50 plays and musicals. Started the Sheldon/Post Company in 1991 with Ira Post.
PICTURES: *Producer-Writer*: Grizzly, Sheba Baby, The Evil, Project: Kill. *Producer*: Just Before Dawn, Abby, Day of the Animals, The Manitou. *Director*: Lovely But Deadly. *Writer*: The Predator.

SHELDON, JAMES: Director. r.n. Schleifer. b. New York, NY. Nov. 12. e. U. of North Carolina. Page boy, NBC; announcer-writer-dir., NBC Internat'l Div.; staff dir., ABC radio; staff prod. dir., Young & Rubicam; free lance prod. dir. of many programs live tape and film, N.Y. and Hollywood.
TELEVISION: Series (prod./dir.): Mr. Peepers, Armstrong Circle Theatre, Robert Montgomery Presents, Schlitz Playhouse, West Point, Zane Grey Theatre, The Millionaire, Desilu Playhouse, Perry Mason, Twilight Zone, Route 66, Naked City, The Virginian, Alfred Hitchcock Presents, Fugitive, Espionage, Defenders, Nurses, Bing Crosby Show, Family Affair, Wonderful World of Disney, Man From UNCLE, Felony Squad, That Girl, Ironside, My World and Welcome To It, To Rome With Love, Owen Marshall, Room 222, Apple's Way, Love American Style, McMillan and Wife, Sanford and Son, Ellery Queen, Rich Man, Poor Man II, Family, MASH, Switch, Loveboat, Sheriff Lobo, Knots Landing, The Waltons, 240-Robert, Nurse, Dukes of Hazard, Todays F.B.I., McLain's Law, 7 Brides for 7 Brothers, Lottery, Partners in Crime, Jessie, Santa Barbara, Half Nelson, Stir Crazy, The Equalizer, Sledge Hammer, Cagney & Lacey. Movies: Gidget Grows Up, With This Ring, The Gossip Columnist.

SHELDON, SIDNEY: Writer, Producer, Novelist. b. Chicago, IL, Feb. 11, 1917. e. Northwestern U. Novels made into films include Other Side of Midnight, Bloodline, Naked Face. Awards: Oscar, Writers Guild, Tony, Edgar.
PICTURES: *Writer*: The Bachelor and the Bobbysoxer (Acad. Award, 1947), Easter Parade, Annie Get Your Gun, Three Guys Named Mike, Dream Wife (also dir.), Remains to Be Seen, You're Never Too Young, Pardners, The Buster Keaton Story (also prod., dir.), The Birds and the Bees, Gambling Daughters (story), Bill Rose's Jumbo.
TELEVISION: Series: Patty Duke Show (creator), I Dream of Jeannie (creator, prod.), Nancy (creator, prod.), Hart to Hart (creator). Novels made into mini-series: Rage of Angels, Master of the Game, Windmills of the Gods, If Tomorrow Comes, Memories of Midnight, The Sands of Time, Stranger in the Mirror.
NOVELS: The Naked Face, The Other Side of Midnight, A Stranger in the Mirror, Bloodline, Rage of Angels, Master of the Game, If Tomorrow Comes, Windmills of the Gods, The Sands of Time, Memories of Midnight, The Doomsday Conspiracy, The Stars Shine Down.
THEATER: Redhead (Tony Award, 1959). Alice in Arms, Jackpot, Dream With Music, Merry Widow (revision), Roman Candle.

SHELTON, RON: Writer, Director. b. Whittier, CA, Sept. 15, 1945. e. Westmont Coll., Santa Barbara, CA, 1967; U of Arizona, Tucson, AZ, 1974. For 5 years played second base for Baltimore Orioles farm team. Cleaned bars and dressed mannequins to support his art: painting and sculpture. A script he wrote, A Player to Be Named Later (which he later filmed himself as Bull Durham), attracted attention of dir. Roger Spottiswoode who directed his first two s.p.

PICTURES: The Pursuit of D. B. Cooper (assoc. prod.), Under Fire (s.p., 2nd unit dir.), The Best of Times (s.p., 2nd unit dir.), Bull Durham (dir., s.p.), Blaze (dir., s.p.), White Men Can't Jump (dir., s.p.), Blue Chips (s.p.).

SHENSON, WALTER: Producer. b. San Francisco, CA. e. Stanford U., Calif.; Ent. m.p. ind. 1941; studio exec., writing, prod., prom. shorts, trailers, Columbia; sup. publ., expl., London, Columbia European production, 1955.

PICTURES: prod.: The Mouse That Roared, A Matter of Who, The Mouse on the Moon, A Hard Day's Night, Help!, 30 is a Dangerous Age Cynthia, Don't Raise the Bridge Lower the River, A Talent for Loving, Welcome to the Club (also dir.), The Chicken Chronicles, Reuben Reuben, Echo Park.

SHEPARD, SAM: Writer, Actor. r.n. Samuel Shepard Rogers. b. Fort Sheridan, IL, Nov. 5, 1943. Grew up in California, Montana and South Dakota. Worked as stable hand, sheep shearer, orange picker in CA, a car wrecker in MA and musician with rock group Holy Modal Rounders. Lived near San Francisco, where, in addition to writing, ran a drama workshop at the U. of California at Davis. Recipient of Brandeis U. Creative Arts Citation, 1976, and American Acad. of Arts and Letters Award, 1975.

PLAYS: Icarus' Mother, Red Cross (triple bill—1966 Obie Award), La Turista (1967 Obie), Forensic and the Navigators, Melodrama Play, Tooth of Crime (1973 Obie), Back Dog Beast Bait, Operation Sidewinder, 4-H Club, The Unseen Hand, Mad Dog Blues, Shaved Splits, Rock Garden, Curse of the Starving Class (1978 Obie), Buried Child (Pulitzer Prize, 1979, Obie), Fool For Love, A Lie of the Mind.

PICTURES: Actor: Renaldo and Clara, Days of Heaven, Resurrection, Raggedy Man, Frances, The Right Stuff (Acad. Award nom.), Country, Fool for Love, Crimes of the Heart, Baby Boom, Steel Magnolias, Bright Angel, Defenseless, Voyager, Thunderheart, The Pelican Brief. Writer: Me and My Brother (co-s.p.), Zabriskie Point (co-s.p.), Oh Calcutta! (contributor), Renaldo and Clara (co-s.p.), Paris Texas, Fool for Love, Far North (also dir.), Silent Tongue (also dir.).

TELEVISION: Fourteen Hundred Thousand Blue Bitch (BBC).

SHEPHERD, CYBILL: Actress, Singer. b. Memphis, TN, Feb. 18, 1950. e. Hunter Coll., NYU, U. of Southern California. Was fashion model before acting debut in 1971 (won Model of the Year title, 1968). Debut record album, Cybill Does It . . . To Cole Porter, 1974, followed by Stan Getz: Mad About the Boy, Vanilla, Somewhere Down the Road.

PICTURES: The Last Picture Show (debut, 1971), The Heartbreak Kid, Daisy Miller, At Long Last Love, Taxi Driver, Special Delivery, Silver Bears, The Lady Vanishes, The Return, Chances Are, Texasville, Alice, Once Upon a Crime, Married to It.

TELEVISION: Series: The Yellow Rose, Moonlighting. Movies: A Guide for the Married Woman, Secrets of a Married Man, Seduced, The Long Hot Summer, Which Way Home, Memphis (also co-writer, co-exec. prod.), Stormy Weathers, Telling Secrets, There Was a Little Boy.

SHEPHERD, RICHARD: Producer. b. Kansas City, MO, June 4, 1927. e. Stanford U. In U.S. Naval Reserve, 1944–45. Entered ent. field as exec. with MCA, 1948, functioning in radio, TV, and m.p. fields until 1956, with time out for U.S. Army, 1950–52. In 1956 became head of talent for Columbia Pictures. In 1962 joined CMA talent agency on its founding, becoming exec. v.p. in chg. of m.p. div. Left to join Warner Bros. in Aug., 1972, as exec. v.p. for prod. Resigned Oct. 1, 1974 to become indep. prod. In 1976 named MGM sr. v.p. & worldwide head of theatrical prod.

PICTURES: Twelve Angry Men, The Hanging Tree, The Fugitive Kind, Breakfast at Tiffany's (prod.), Alex and the Gypsy, Robin and Marian, Volunteers, The Hunger.

SHER, LOUIS K.: Executive. b. Columbus, OH, Feb. 25, 1914. e. Ohio State U., 1933. Exec., Stone's Grills Co., 1934–37; owned & operated, Sher Vending Co., 1937–43. U.S. Army, 1943–46. V.p., Sons Bars & Grills, 1947–54; org. & pres. Art Theatre Guild, 1954; opened art theatres for first time in many cities, org. opera film series, film classic series and similar motion picture activities in many cities. Org., Film Festival at Antioch Coll., 1960; pioneer in fighting obscenity laws in Ohio; operates 10 theatres in midwest and western states. Co-producer of the musical broadway production Shenandoah and American Dance Machine. Produced film, Deathmask.

SHERAK, THOMAS: Executive. b. Brooklyn, NY June 22, 1945. e. New York Community Coll., mktg. degree. 1967–69, US Army, Specialist E5 Sgt.; 1970, began career in m.p. industry, Paramount Pictures sls. dept.; 1974, R/C Theatres, booking dept.; 1977, joined General Cinema Theatres as district film buyer; 1978, promoted to v.p., films; 1982, promoted to v.p. head film buyer; 1983, joined 20th Century Fox as pres., domestic dist. & mktg.; 1985, pres., domestic dist.; 1986,

president, domestic dist. & marketing. 1990-present, exec. v.p., 20th Century Fox.

SHERIDAN, JAMEY: Actor. b. Pasadena, CA, July 12, 1951. e. Univ. of CA, Santa Barbara.

PICTURES: Jumpin' Jack Flash (debut, 1986), The House on Carroll Street, Distant Thunder, Stanley & Iris, Quick Change, Talent for the Game, All I Want for Christmas, A Stranger Among Us, Whispers in the Dark.

TELEVISION: Series: The Doctors, Another World, Shannon's Deal. Movies: One Police Plaza, Shannon's Deal (pilot), Murder in High Places. Guest: St. Elsewhere, Spenser: For Hire.

THEATRE: NY: Just a Little Bit Less Than Normal, The Arbor, Major Barbara, One Wedding Two Rooms Three Friends, The Man Who Came to Dinner, Hamlet, Biloxi Blues, All My Sons (Tony nom.), Long Day's Journey Into Night, Ah Wilderness. Regional: Loose Ends, Deathtrap, Homesteaders.

SHERIDAN, JIM: Director, Writer. b. Dublin, Ireland, 1949. e. Univ Col. in Dublin, NYU Inst. of Films & TV. Started as director-writer at Lyric Theatre in Belfast and Abbey Theatre in Dublin; also at Project Arts Theatre (1976–80), NY Irish Arts Center (1982–7) as artistic director. Founded Children's Theatre Company in Dublin.

PICTURES: Dir.-Writer: My Left Foot, The Field, Into the West (s.p. only), In the Name of the Father. THEATRE: Writer: Mobile Homes, Spike in the First World War (Edinburgh Festival Fringe Award for best play, 1983).

SHERIDAN, NICOLLETTE: Actress. b. Worthing, Sussex, England, Nov. 21, 1963. Moved to LA in 1973. Became model in NYC before turning to acting.

TELEVISION: Series: Paper Dolls, Knots Landing. Movies: Dark Mansions, Agatha Christie's Dead Man's Folly, Jackie Collins' Lucky/Chances, Deceptions.

PICTURES: The Sure Thing (debut, 1985), Noises Off.

SHERMAN, RICHARD M.: Composer, Lyricist, Screenwriter. b. New York, NY, June 12, 1928. e. Bard Coll., B.A., 1949. Info. & Educ. Br., U.S. Army, 1953–55. Songwriter, composer, Walt Disney Prods 1960–71, then freelance. With partner-brother Robert has won 2 Acad. Awards (for song & score Mary Poppins, 1964), 9 Acad. Award nom., 2 Grammys, 17 gold and platinum albums, 1st Prize, Moscow Film Fest. (for Tom Sawyer) and a star on Hollywood Walk of Fame. Have written over 500 pub. and recorded songs. Also wrote score for Bdwy musical Over Here (1974) and songs for Disney Theme Parks.

SONGS: Things I Might Have Been, Tall Paul, Christmas in New Orleans, Mad Passionate Love, Midnight Oil, You're Sixteen, That Darn Cat, The Wonderful Thing About Tiggers, It's a Small World (after all), A Spoonful of Sugar, Super-califragilistic, Feed the Birds, Age of Not Believing, When You're Loved, Pineapple Princess, Let's Get Together, Maggie's Theme, Chim Chim Cheree (Acad. Award), Chitty Chitty Bang Bang, Winnie the Pooh, Fortuosity, Slipper and the Rose Waltz, Comedy Album: Smash Flops.

PICTURES: Nightmare, The Cruel Tower, Absent Minded Professor, The Parent Trap, Big Red, In Search of the Castaways, Moon Pilot, Bon Voyage, Legend of Lobo, Summer Magic, Miracle of the White Stallions, The Sword in the Stone, Misadventures of Merlin Jones, Mary Poppins (Acad. Award), Those Calloways, The Monkey's Uncle, That Darn Cat, Winnie the Pooh, Chitty Chitty Bang Bang, The Jungle Book, The Happiest Millionaire, The One and Only Genuine Original Family Band, The Aristocats, Bedknobs & Broomsticks, Snoopy Come Home, Charlotte's Web, Songs & S.P.: Tom Sawyer, The Slipper and the Rose, The Magic of Lassie, Huckleberry Finn, Little Nemo.

TELEVISION: Wonderful World of Color, Bell Telephone Hour, Welcome to Pooh Corner, The Enchanted Musical Playhouse, The Timberwood Tales.

SHERMAN, ROBERT B.: Composer, Lyricist, Screenwriter. b. New York, NY, Dec. 19, 1925. e. Bard Coll., B.A., 1949. U.S. Army, W.W.II, 1943–45 (purple heart). Songwriter, 1952–60; pres., Music World Corp., 1958; songwriter, composer, Walt Disney, 1971, then freelance. Hon. Phd., Lincoln Col, 1990.

SONGS: Things I Might Have Been, Tall Paul, Midnight Oil, You're Sixteen, That Darn Cat, The Wonderful Thing About Tiggers, It's a Small World (after all), A Spoonful of Sugar, Supercalifragilistic, Feed the Birds, Age of Not Believing, When You're Loved. Pineapple Princess, Let's Get Together, Maggie's Theme, Chim Chim Cheree (Acad. Award).

PICTURES: The Absent-Minded Professor, The Parent Trap, Big Red, In Search of the Castaways, Moon Pilot, Bon Voyage, Legend of Lobo, Summer Magic, Miracle of the White Stallions, The Sword in the Stone, Misadventures of Merlin Jones, Mary Poppins (Acad. Award), Those Calloways, The Monkey's Uncle, That Darn Cat, Winnie the Pooh, The Jungle Book, The Happiest Millionaire, Chitty Chitty Bang Bang, The Aristocats, Bedknobs & Broomsticks, Snoopy Come Home, Charlotte's Web, Little Nemo. Songs & S.P.:

Tom Sawyer, The Slipper and the Rose, The Magic of Lassie, Huckleberry Finn, Magic Journeys.
TELEVISION: Wonderful World of Color, Bell Telephone Hour, Welcome to Pooh Corner, The Enchanted Musical Playhouse.

SHERMAN, SAMUEL M.: Producer, Director, Writer. b. New York, NY. e. City Coll. of New York, B.A. Entered m.p. ind. as writer, cameraman, film ed., neg. & sound cutter; nat'l mag. ed., Westerns Magazine 1959; pres., Signature Films; prod., dir., TV pilot, The Three Mesquiteers, 1960; prod., Pulse Pounding Perils, 1961; helped create, ed., dir., Screen Thrills Illustrated; exec. prod., Screen Thrills; v.p., Golden Age Films, 1962; prod., Joe Franklin's Silent Screen, 1963; N.Y. rep., Victor Adamson Prods.; owns world rights; The Scarlet Letter; 1965; N.Y. rep., Tal prods., Hlywd.; adv. & pub. Hemisphere Pictures; ed., autobiog., Joe Bonomo; prod., writer, Chaplin's Art of Comedy, The Strongman; prod., Hollywood's Greatest Stuntman; story adapt., Fiend With the Electronic Brain. 1967, prod. Spanish version Chaplin Su Arte y Su Comedia; tech. consul., Hal Roach Studios, NBC, Music from the Land; 1968, N.Y. rep. East West Pict. of Hollywood. 1968, N.Y. rep., Al Adamson Prods. of Hollywood; Ed.-in-chief, bk., The Strongman. Pres., Independent-International Pictures Corp., pres., Producers Commercial Productions, Inc. Chmn. of Creditors' Committee, Allied Artists Television Corp.; president, Independent-International Entertainment, TV div. Independent-International Pictures Corp. Pres., Technovision Inc.; pres., Super Video, Inc.
PICTURES: assoc. prod.: Horror of the Blood Monsters, Blood of Ghastly Horror; prod., s.p.: Brain of Blood; prod. supervisor Dracula vs. Frankenstein; Exec. prod. Angels, Wild Women; The Naughty Stewardesses (prod., s.p.), Girls For Rent; TV special, Wild Wild World of Comedy; The Dynamite Brothers (exec. prod.); Blazing Stewardesses (prod., s.p.); Cinderella 2000 (exec. prod.); Team-Mates (also story); dir-s.p., Raiders of the Living Dead.

SHERMAN, VINCENT: Director. b. Vienna, GA, July 16, 1906. e. Oglethorpe U. B.A. Writer, actor, dialogue dir., then prod. dir.
PICTURES: Dir.: Return of Doctor X, Saturday's Children, Man Who Talked Too Much, Underground, Flight from Destiny, The Hard Way, All Through the Night, Old Acquaintances, In Our Time, Mr. Skeffington, Pillow to Post, Janie Gets Married, Nora Prentiss, The Unfaithful, Adventures of Don Juan, Somewhere in the City, Hasty Heart, Damned Don't Cry, Harriet Craig, Goodbye, My Fancy, Lone Star, Assignment—Paris; prod. dir.: Affair in Trinidad, The Young Philadelphians, The Naked Earth, Second Time Around, Ice Palace, Fever in the Blood, Garment Jungle.
TELEVISION: 35 episodes of Medical Center, Westside Medical, Baretta, Waltons, Doctors Hospital, Trapper John, Movies: The Last Hurrah, Women at West Point, The Yeagers (pilot), Bogey, The Dream Merchants, Trouble in High Timber Country, High Hopes—The Capra Years.

SHERRIN, NED: Producer, Director, Writer. b. Low Ham, Somerset, England, Feb. 18, 1931. Early career writing plays and musical plays. Prod., dir., ATV Birmingham, 1955–57; prod., Midlands Affairs, Paper Talk, etc. Joined BBC-TV 1957 and produced many TV talk programs. Novels: (with Caryl Brahms) Cindy-Ella or I Gotta Shoe (also prod. as stage play), Rappell 1910, Benbow Was His Name.
TELEVISION: England: prod.: Ask Me Another, Henry Hall Show, Laugh Line, Parasol. Assoc. prod.: Tonight series. Little Beggars, 1962; prod., creator: That Was The Week That Was, 1962–63; prod., dir.: Benbow Was His Name (co-author), 1964; Take a Sapphire (co-author), The Long Garden Party, The Long Cocktail Party. ABC of Britain revue. Prod., dir.: thrice-weekly series Not So Much a Programme, More a Way of Life, 1964–65. Appearances inc. Your Witness, Quiz of The Week, Terra Firma, Who Said That, The Rather Reassuring Programme, Song by Song, Loose Ends Radio 4.
PICTURES: prod.: The Virgin Soldiers (with Leslie Gilliat), Every Home Should Have One, Up Pompeii, Girl Stroke Boy (co-author with Caryl Brahms), Up the Chastity Belt, Rentadick, The Garnet Saga, Up the Front, The National Health, The Cobblers of Umbridge (dir. with Ian Wilson).

SHERWOOD, MADELEINE: Actress. b. Montreal, Canada, Nov. 13, 1922. e. Yale Drama Sch. Trained with Montreal Rep. and Actors Studio. Has dir. prods. at Actors Studio and regional theaters, as well as 2 AFI films Goodnight Sweet Prince and Sunday.
THEATER: The Crucible, Sweet Bird of Youth, Cat on a Hot Tin Roof, Invitation to a March, The Garden of Sweets, Camelot, Hey You, Light Man!, Brecht on Brecht, Night of the Iguana, Arturo Ui, Do I Hear a Waltz?, Inadmissible Evidence, All Over, Older People, Getting Out, The Suicide, Eclipse, Miss Edwina.
PICTURES: Baby Doll, Cat on a Hot Tin Roof, Parrish, Sweet Bird of Youth, The 91st Day, Hurry Sundown, Pendulum, Wicked Wicked, The Changeling, Resurrection, Teachers, An Unremarkable Life, Silence Like Glass.

TELEVISION: Series: The Flying Nun. Mini-Series: Rich Man Poor Man. Movies: The Manhunter, Nobody's Child, Palace Guard; many guest appearances.

SHIELDS, BROOKE: Actress. b. New York, NY, May 31, 1965. e. Princeton U. Honors in Frencn Lit. Discovered at age 11 months by photographer Francesco Scavullo to pose in Ivory Soap ads. NY stage debut 1986 Off-Bdwy in The Eden Cinema.
PICTURES: Alice Sweet Alice (a.k.a. Holy Terror; Communion; debut 1977), Pretty Baby, King of the Gypsies, Tilt, Wanda Nevada, Just You and Me Kid, The Blue Lagoon, Endless Love, Sahara, The Muppets Take Manhattan (cameo), Speed Zone (cameo), Back Street Dreams, Brenda Starr, An American Love (It.).
TELEVISION: Movies: The Prince of Central Park, Wet Gold, The Diamond Trap; and numerous specials.

SHIELDS, WILLIAM A.: Executive. b. New York, NY, 1946. e. El Camino Coll., California State Coll. at LA. Entered the motion picture industry in 1966 with Pacific Theatres, then MGM sales dept., L.A. and Denver, 1970; New World Pictures, 1972; 20th Century-Fox, Washington, 1973; New York district manager, 20th Century-Fox, 1973–75. Joined Mann Theatres Corporation of California as head booker in 1975. Gen. sls. mgr., Far West Films, 1977–79; joined Avco Embassy as Western div. mgr., promoted to asst. gen. sls. mgr., 1980; promoted to v.p-gen. sls. mgr., January, 1981. In 1983 joined New World Pictures as exec. v.p., worldwide mktg. & acquisitions. Promoted to pres., worldwide sls. & mktg., 1985. 1987, pres. CEO, New World Intl. 1989, joined Trans Atlantic Pictures as pres., CEO when company purchased assets of New World's feature film division. Sold ownership in Trans Atlantic and formed G.E.L. Prod. & Distrib., Feb. 1992. Exec. prod. Au Pair (1991); exec. in charge of prod. Death Ring (1992). Exec. prod. of Uninvited. Past chmn, American Film Mktg. Assn. (1987–91). Presently chmn. American Film Export Assn.

SHIFF, RICHARD: Executive. b. New York, NY, Mar. 3, 1942. e. Queens College, B.A., M.A., Brooklyn Col., P.D. Joined Warner Bros. as sales analyst, 1977. In 1979 named dist. coordinator; 1980, asst. dir. sls. admin. 1982, promoted to post, dir. sls. admin. 1987, v.p., theatrical sls. operations.

SHIKATA, MASAO: Executive. b. Kyoto, Japan, Apr. 22, 1918. e. Naniwa Commercial Coll. Chmn., Sansha Electric Manufacturing Co. Ltd., Tokyo and Osaka, makers of power semiconductors & applied electronic equipment; pres. Japan Motion Picture Equipment Manufacturers & Suppliers Assoc.; v.p., Japan Machinery Design Center; v.p., Japan Optical Industry Assoc.; director, Federation of Japanese Film Industries Inc.

SHINBACH, BRUCE D.: Executive. b. South Bend, IN, June 29, 1939. e. U. of Colorado, B.A., 1963; New York Inst. of Finance; Northwestern U., M.A., 1965. Stockbroker for Harris, Upham & Co., 1964, shopping center developer, Dixie Associates, 1966 to present. Pres., Monarch Theatres.

SHIRE, DAVID: Composer. b. Buffalo, NY, July 3, 1937. m. actress Didi Conn. e. Yale U., 1959, B.A. Composer of theater scores: The Sap of Life, Urban Blight, Starting Here, Starting Now; Baby, Closer Than Ever. Won Academy Award, best original song It Goes Like It Goes from Norma Rae, 1979; Acad. Award nom. I'll Never Say Goodbye from The Promise, 1979. Emmy noms. Raid on Entebbe, The Defection of Simas Kudirka, Do You Remember Love? and The Kennedys of Massachusetts. Grammy Awards for Saturday Night Fever.
PICTURES: One More Train to Rob, Summertree, Drive, He Said; Skin Game, To Find a Man, Showdown, Two People, Steelyard Blues (adapt.), Class of '44, The Conversation, The Taking of Pelham 1-2-3, The Fortune, Farewell My Lovely, The Hindenberg, All the President's Men, The Big Bus, Harry and Walter Go to New York, Saturday Night Fever (adapt. & add. music), Straight Time, The Promise, Old Boyfriends, Norma Rae, Only When I Laugh, The Night the Lights Went Out in Georgia, Paternity, The World According to Garp, Max Dugan Returns, Oh God You Devil, 2010, Fast Break, Return to Oz, Short Circuit, 'night Mother, Vice Versa, Monkey Shines, Bed and Breakfast.
TELEVISION: Series themes: Sarge, McCloud, The Practice, Sirota's Court, Joe & Sons, Lucas Tanner, Alice, Tales of the Unexpected, Brewster Place, Room for Two. Movies: Priest Killer, McCloud, Harpy, Three Faces of Love, Killer Bees, Tell Me Where It Hurts, The Defection of Simas Kudirka, Three for the Road, Amelia Earhart, Something for Joey, Raid on Entebbe, The Storyteller, Promise, Mayflower Madam, Echoes in the Darkness, Jesse, God Bless the Child, Common Ground, The Clinic, Convicted, The Women of Brewster Place, I Know My First Name is Steven, The Kennedys of Massachusetts (mini-series), The Great Los Angeles Earthquake, The Boys, Sarah: Plain and Tall, Always Remember I Love You, Paris Trout, Four Eyes, Broadway Bound, Bed of Lies, Last Wish, Alison, Habitation of Dragons, many others.

SHIRE, TALIA: Actress. b. New York, NY, April 25, 1946. Raised on road by her father, arranger-conductor Carmine Coppola, who toured with Broadway musicals. After 2 yrs. at Yale Sch. of Drama she moved to L.A. where appeared in many theatrical productions. Sister of Francis Ford Coppola.
PICTURES: The Dunwich Horror, Gas-s-s, The Christian Licorice Store, The Outside Man, The Godfather, The Godfather Part II (Acad. Award nom.), Rocky (Acad. Award nom.), Old Boyfriends, Prophecy, Rocky II, Windows, Rocky III, Rocky IV, RAD, Lionheart (co-prod.), New York Stories (Life Without Zoe), Rocky V, The Godfather III, Bed and Breakfast, Cold Heaven, DeadFall.
TELEVISION: Mini-Series: Rich Man Poor Man. Movies: Foster and Laurie, Kill Me If You Can, Daddy I Don't Like It Like This, For Richer For Poorer, Chantilly Lace. Special: Please God I'm Only 17.

SHIVAS, MARK: Producer, Director. e. Oxford.
TELEVISION: Presenter of Cinema. Producer: The Six Wives of Henry VIII, Casanova, The Edwardians, The Evacuees, The Glittering Prizes, Abide With Me, Rogue Male, .84 Charing Cross Road, The Three Hostages, She Fell Among Thieves, Professional Foul, Telford's Change, On Giant's Shoulders, & The Price, What If it's Raining?, The Story Teller. Now Head of films, BBC TV.
PICTURES: Producer: Richard's Things, Moonlighting, A Private Function, The Witches. Exec. Prod.: Bad Blood, Truly Madly Deeply, Enchanted April, The Grass Arena, Memento Mori, Great Moments in Aviation.

SHORE, DINAH: Singer. r.n. Frances Rose Shore. b. Winchester, TN, Mar. 1, 1917. e. Vanderbilt U., B.A., 1939. Became singer WNEW, N.Y., 1938; joined NBC as sustaining singer, 1938; started contract RCA-Victor, 1940; star Chamber Music Soc. of Lower Basin St. program, 1940; joined Eddie Cantor radio pgm., 1941; star own radio program, General Foods, 1943; entertained troops European Theatre of operations, 1944; radio program, Procter & Gamble. Star TV show, Chevrolet, 1951–61 (Emmy Awards, 1956, 1957); Dinah Shore Specials, 1964–65. 1969: Dinah Shore Special, Like Hep. 1970–71: Dinah's Place (Emmy, 1973, 1974), Dinah! (Emmy, 1976), Death Car on the Freeway, A Conversation With Dinah (Cable 1989).
PICTURES: Thank Your Lucky Stars, Up in Arms, Belle of the Yukon, Follow the Boys, Make Mine Music (voice), Till the Clouds Roll By, Fun and Fancy Free (voice), Aaron Slick from Punkin Crick, Oh God! (cameo).

SHORE, HOWARD: Composer, Musician. Began career as musical director for Saturday Night Live.
PICTURES: Scanners, Videodrome, The Brood, The Fly, After Hours, Heaven, Belizaire, The Cajun, Nadine, Moving, Big, Dead Ringers, The Lemon Sisters, An Innocent Man, Postcards From the Edge (musical numbers sprv.).
TELEVISION: Coca-Cola Presents Live: The Hard Rock.

SHORT, MARTIN: Actor, Comedian. b. Toronto, Can., Mar. 26, 1950. e. McMaster U. Trained as social worker but instead performed on stage in Godspell as well as in revues and cabarets in Toronto, 1973–78 including a stint as a member of the Toronto unit of the Second City comedy troupe (1977–78). Best known for comic characters he created such as nerdy Ed Grimley and lounge lizard Jackie Rogers Jr. as well as impersonations of Katharine Hepburn and Jerry Lewis on Saturday Night Live (1985–86).
PICTURES: Lost and Found, The Outsider, Three Amigos, Innerspace, Cross My Heart, Three Fugitives, The Big Picture, Pure Luck, Father of the Bride, Clifford, Captain Ron.
TELEVISION: Series: The Associates (1979), I'm a Big Girl Now, SCTV Network (Emmy Award for writing, 1983), Saturday Night Live, The Completely Mental Misadventures of Ed Grimley (cartoon series). Specials: All's Well That Ends Well, Really Weird Tales, Martin Short's Concert for the North Americas (SHO), Martin Short Goes Hollywood (HBO). Movies: The Family Man, Sunset Limousine.

SHOWALTER, MAX: Actor, composer. s.n. Casey Adams. b. Caldwell, KS, June 2, 1917. e. Caldwell H.S.; Pasadena Playhouse. Composed background music for films: Vicki, Return of Jack Slade, Bdwy. Harrigan 'n Hart (composer), Touch of the Child (lyricist-composer). Recordings incl. The Brementown Musicians, The Gold Dog (as narrator, composer, pianist and singer). On bd. of trustees: Eugene O'Neill Theatre Center, Natl. Theatre of the Deaf, Ivorytown Playhouse, Shoreline Alliance for the Arts. Gov's Bd.: Commission for the Arts.
BROADWAY: Knights of Song, Very Warm for May, My Sister Eileen, Showboat, John Loves Mary, Make Mine Manhattan, Lend an Ear, Hello Dolly!, The Grass Harp.
PICTURES: Always Leave Them Laughing, With a Song in My Heart, What Price Glory, My Wife's Best Friend, Niagara, Destination Gobi, Dangerous Crossing, Vicki, Night People, Naked Alibi, Never Say Goodbye, Bus Stop, Down Three Dark Streets, Indestructible Man, Designing Woman, Female Animal, The Monster That Challenged the World, Voice In the Mirror, The Naked and the Dead, It Happened to Jane, Elmer

Gantry, Return to Peyton Place, Summer and Smoke, Music Man, Smog, Bon Voyage, My Six Loves, Lord Love a Duck, Move Over Darling, Sex and the Single Girl, Fate Is the Hunter, How to Murder Your Wife, The Moonshine War, The Anderson Tapes, 10, Racing with the Moon, Sixteen Candles.

SHUE, ELISABETH: Actress. b. South Orange, NJ, Oct. 6, 1963. e. Harvard.
PICTURES: The Karate Kid (debut, 1984), Adventures in Babysitting, Link, Cocktail, Back to the Future Parts II & III, The Marrying Man, Soapdish, Twenty Bucks.
TELEVISION: Series: Call to Glory. Movies: Charles and Diana, Double Switch. Special: Hale the Hero.

SHULER-DONNER, LAUREN: Producer. b. Cleveland, OH. B.S. in film & bdcstg., Boston U. Began filmmaking career as ed. of educational films then camera-woman in TV prod., assoc. prod., story editor, creative affairs exec.; TV movie: Amateur Night at the Dixie Bar and Grill (prod.). Assoc. prod. on film Thank God It's Friday.
PICTURES: Mr. Mom, Ladyhawke, St. Elmo's Fire, Pretty in Pink, Three Fugitives, The Favor, Radio Flyer, Dave, Free Willy.

SHULL, RICHARD B.: Actor. b. Evanston, IL, Feb. 24, 1929. e. State U. of Iowa. B.A. drama, 1950., Kemper Mil. Sch. AA humanities, 1986. U.S. Army, 1953. 1953–56, exec. asst. prod. Gordon W. Pollock Prods.; 1954–56 stage mgr. Hyde Park Playhouse; other prod. jobs and freelance stage mgr. and dir. 1950–70. N.Y. stage debut in Wake Up, Darling (1956), also in Minnie's Boys, Goodtime Charley (Tony nom.), The Marriage of Bette and Boo (Obie Award), One of the All-Time Greats, Ain't Broadway Grand.
PICTURES: The Anderson Tapes (debut, 1971), B.S. I Love You, Such Good Friends, Hail to the Chief, Slither, Sssss, Cockfighter, The Fortune, The Black Bird, Hearts of the West, The Big Bus, The Pack, Dreamer, Wholly Moses, Heartbeeps, Spring Break, Lovesick, Unfaithfully Yours, Splash, Garbo Talks, Tune in Tomorrow, Housesitter.
TELEVISION: Series: Diana, Holmes & Yoyo. Guest: Your Hit Parade (1950), Rockford Files, Good Times, Love American Style, Hart to Hart, Lou Grant. Movies: Ziegfeld: A Man and His Women, Studs Lonigan, Will There Really Be a Morning? The Boy Who Loved Trolls, Keeping the Faith, Seize the Day.

SHURPIN, SOL: Executive. b. New York, NY, Feb. 22, 1914. e. Pace Inst., 1936. Law stenog., 1932–33; Joe Hornstein, Inc., 1933–41; National Theatre Supply, 1941–48; purchased interest in Raytone Screen Corp., became v.p., 1948; pres., Raytone, 1952; pres., Technikote Corp., which succeeded Raytone Screen, 1956–present; sole owner, Technikote Corp., 1962.

SHUTT, BUFFY: Executive. e. Sarah Lawrence Col. Joined Paramount 1973 as sect. with N.Y. pub. staff; 1975, natl. mag. contact. 1978, named dir. of pub.; later exec. dir. of pub. Promoted 1980 to v.p., pub. & promo. Resigned to join Time-Life Films as v.p. East coast prod; returned to Paramount in 1981 as sr. v.p. & asst. to pres. of Motion Picture Group. 1984, appt. exec. v.p.-mktg. for M.P. Group, Paramount. 1985, appoint. pres. of mktg. 1986, resigned. Formed Shutt-Jones Communications, 1987, marketing consultancy with Kathy Jones. 1989, appt. marketing pres., Columbia Pictures & Tri-Star Pictures. 1991, mktg. pres. of TriStar.

SIDARIS, ANDY: Producer, Director, Writer. b. Chicago, IL, Feb. 20, 1932. e. Southern Methodist U., B.A., radio-TV. Began television career in 1950 in Dallas, TX as a director at station WFAA-TV; now pres., The Sidaris Company. Won 8 Emmy Awards.
PICTURES: Dir., Stacey, The Racing Scene, M*A*S*H football sequences, Seven (prod.-dir.), Malibu Express (prod., dir., s.p.), Hard Ticket to Hawaii (dir., s.p.), Picasso Trigger (dir., s.p.), Savage Beach (dir., s.p.), Guns (dir., s.p.), Do or Die (dir., s.p.).
TELEVISION: Dir., The Racers/Mario Andretti/Joe Leonard/Al Unser, ABC's Championship Auto Racing, ABC's NCAA Game of the Week, 1968 Summer Olympics (Mexico City), 1972 Summer Olympics (Munich), 1976 Summer Olympics (Montreal), 1984 Summer Olympics (L.A.), 1964 Winter Olympics (Innsbruck), 1968 Winter Olympics (Grenoble), 1976 Winter Olympics (Innsbruck), 1980 Winter Olympics (Lake Placid), 1988 Winter Olympics (Calgary), Wide World of Sports, The Racers/Craig and Lee Breedlove, dir.: The Burt Reynolds Late Show, dir., Kojak episode, Nancy Drew episodes.

SIDNEY, GEORGE: Director, Producer. b. New York, NY, Oct. 4, 1916. Son of L. K. Sidney, veteran showman and v.p. MGM, and Hazel Mooney, actress. From 1932 at MGM as test, second unit and short subjects dir. Several Academy Awards for shorts, Our Gang Comedies, Pete Smith etc. In 1941 made feature dir., MGM. Pres., Director's Guild of America, 16 yrs; spec. presidential assignment to Atomic Energy Commission and U.S. Air Force; 1961–66, Pres., Hanna-Barbera Productions; Doctorate of Science Hanneman Medical University and Hospital. Mem. ASCAP. Pres., Directors, Inc., since 1969; v.p., Directors Foundation; v.p., D.W. Griffith Foundation; life mem., ACTT (England) and DGA. Directed U.N. special, Who Has Seen the Wind? Awarded Gold Medal for service to D.G.A. 1959, Doctorate from Collegio Barcellona 1989, Life Membership in D.G.A.

PICTURES: Free and Easy, Pacific Rendezvous, Pilot No. 5, Thousands Cheer, Bathing Beauty, Anchors Aweigh, Harvey Girls, Holiday in Mexico, Cass Timberlane, Three Musketeers, Red Danube, Key to the City, Annie Get Your Gun, Show Boat, Scaramouche, Young Bess, Kiss Me Kate, Jupiter's Darling, Eddie Duchin Story, Jeanne Eagels (also prod.), Pal Joey, Who Was That Lady? (also prod.), Pepe (also prod.), Bye Bye Birdie, A Ticklish Affair, Viva Las Vegas, The Swinger (also prod.), Half a Sixpence (also co-prod.).

SIDNEY, SYLVIA: Actress. b. New York, NY, Aug. 8, 1910. r.n. Sophia Kosow. e. Theatre Guild Sch. On stage, then screen debut in Through Different Eyes (1929).

PLAYS: Nice Women, Crossroads, Bad Girl, The Gentle People, Auntie Mame, Joan of Lorraine, Angel Street, Enter Laughing, Vieux Carre.

PICTURES: City Streets, Ladies of the Big House, Confessions of a Co-Ed, An American Tragedy, Street Scene, The Miracle Man, Merrily We Go to Hell, Madame Butterfly, Pick-Up, Jennie Gerhardt, Good Dame, Thirty Day Princess, Behold My Wife, Accent on Youth, Mary Burns—Fugitive, Trail of the Lonesome Pine, Fury, A Woman Alone, You Only Live Once, Dead End, You and Me, One Third of a Nation, The Wagons Roll at Night, Blood on the Sun, Mr. Ace, Searching Wind, Love from a Stranger, Les Miserables, Violent Saturday, Behind the High Wall, Summer Wishes Winter Dreams, Gold Told Me To (Demons), I Never Promised You a Rose Garden, Damien-Omen II, Corrupt, Hammett, Beetlejuice, Used People.

TELEVISION: Movies: Do Not Fold Spindle or Mutilate, Death at Love House, Raid on Entebbe, The Gossip Columnist, FDR—The Last Year, The Shadow Box, A Small Killing, Come Along With Me, Having It All, Finnegan Begin Again, An Early Frost, Pals. Specials: Andre's Mother, The Witching of Ben Wagner. Guest: thirtysomething.

SIEMASZKO, CASEY: Actor. b. Chicago, IL, March 17, 1961. r.n. Kazimierz Siemaszko. e. Goodman Theatre School of Drama, Chicago.

PICTURES: Class (debut, 1983), Secret Admirer, Back to the Future, Stand By Me, Gardens of Stone, Three O'Clock High, Biloxi Blues, Young Guns, Breaking In, Back to the Future Part II, Of Mice and Men.

TELEVISION: Movie: Miracle of the Heart: A Boys Town Story.

SIKKING, JAMES B.: Actor. b. Los Angeles, CA, March 5, 1934. e. UCLA, B.A. Theatre includes Waltz of the Toreadors, Plaza Suite, Damn Yankees, The Big Knife.

PICTURES: The Magnificent Seven, Von Ryan's Express, Chandler, The New Centurions, The Electric Horseman, Capricorn One, Ordinary People, Outland, The Star Chamber, Up the Creek, Star Trek III—The Search for Spock, Morons from Outer Space, Soul Man, Narrow Margin, Final Approach.

TELEVISION: Series: General Hospital, Turnabout, Hill Street Blues, Doogie Howser, M.D. Movies: The Jesse Owens Story, First Steps, Bay Coven, Brotherhood of the Rose, Too Good to be True, Desperado: Badlands Justice, Doing Time on Maple Drive. Mini-Series: Around the World in 80 Days. Specials: Tales from the Hollywood Hills (Golden Land), Ollie Hopnoodle's Haven of Bliss.

SILLIPHANT, STIRLING: Executive, Writer. b. Detroit, MI, Jan. 16, 1918. e. U. of Southern California, B.A., 1938. On pub. staff, Walt Disney Productions, Burbank 1938–41; 1941–42, exploit. & pub., Hal Horne Org. for 20th Century-Fox in New York & other key cities, 1942–43, asst. to Spyros P. Skouras. U.S. Navy, W.W.II. Since 1946, 20th-Fox; in chg. special events and promotions, June 1949; appt. Eastern pub. mgr. 1951.

PICTURES: Prod.: Joe Louis Story, Shaft. Prod.-s.p.: 5 Against the House, The Slender Thread, In the Heat of the Night (Acad. Award, 1967), Liberation of L.B. Jones. Writer: Marlowe, A Walk in the Spring Rain, Shaft in Africa, The New Centurions, Poseidon Adventure, Towering Inferno, The Killer Elite, The Enforcer, Telefon, The Swarm, Circle of Iron, When Time Ran Out, Over the Top, Catch the Heat.

TELEVISION: Series: The Naked City, Route 66, Space, Golden Gate, Fly Away Home (prod., writer), Mussolini—The Untold Story, Pearl (exec. prod., writer), Salem's Lot (exec. prod.), Welcome to Paradise (exec. prod., writer), Travis McGee, The Three Kings (prod., writer), Brotherhood of the Rose (exec. prod.).

SILVA, HENRY: Actor. b. Puerto Rico, 1928.

PICTURES: Viva Zapata, Crowded Paradise, A Hatful of Rain, The Bravados, Green Mansions, Cinderfella, Ocean's Eleven, Sergeants 3, The Manchurian Candidate, A Gathering of Eagles, Johnny Cool, The Secret Invasion, Hail Mafia, The Return of Mr. Moto, The Reward, The Hills Ran Red, The Plainsman, Matchless, Never a Dull Moment, The Animals, Man and Boy, The Italian Connection, The Kidnap of Mary Lou, Shoot, Thirst, Buck Rogers in the 25th Century, Love and Bullets, Virus, Alligator, Sharky's Machine, Wrong Is Right, Megaforce, Cannonball Run II, Lust in the Dust, Code of Silence, Alan Quartermain and the Lost City of Gold, Amazon Women on the Moon, Above the Law, Bulletproof, Dick Tracy, Fists of Steel, Trained to Kill.

TELEVISION: Movies: Black Noon, Drive Hard Drive Fast, Contract on Cherry Street, Happy. Series: Buck Rogers in the 25th Century.

SILVER, JOAN MICKLIN: Writer, Director. b. Omaha, NB, May 24, 1935. m. producer Raphael Silver. Daughter is dir. Marisa Silver. e. Sarah Lawrence Coll. Began career as writer for educational films. Original s.p., Limbo, produced by Universal Pictures. In 1972 Learning Corp. of Am. commissioned her to write and direct a 30-min. film, The Immigrant Experience. Also wrote and directed two children's films for same co; dir. & wrote short film Bernice Bobs Her Hair. First feature was Hester Street, which she wrote and directed.

THEATER: Director: Album, Maybe I'm Doing It Wrong, A . . . My Name is Alice, A . . . My Name is Still Alice (co-conceived & co-dir. with Julianne Boyd).

PICTURES: Director: Hester Street (also s.p.), Between the Lines, On the Yard (prod.), Head Over Heels (also s.p., retitled Chilly Scenes of Winter), Crossing Delancey, Loverboy, Big Girls Don't Cry . . . They Get Even.

TELEVISION: Finnegan Begin Again (dir.), The Nightingale: Faerie Tale Theatre (s.p.), Parole Board (Prison Stories: Women on the Inside), A Private Matter (dir.).

SILVER, JOEL: Producer. b. 1939. e. NYU. Made first film, a short called Ten Pin Alley; moved to Los Angeles with job as asst. to Lawrence Gordon. Named pres., Lawrence Gordon Prods.; developed with Gordon and produced and marketed Hooper, The End, The Driver, The Warriors. At Universal Pictures as prod. v.p.; supervising Smokey and the Bandit II, Xanadu. Honored 1990 as NATO/Showest's Producer of the Year. Appeared in 1988 film Who Framed Roger Rabbit.

PICTURES: Co-Producer: 48 Hrs., Streets of Fire, Brewster's Millions. Producer: Weird Science, Commando, Jumpin' Jack Flash, Lethal Weapon, The Predator, Action Jackson, Die Hard, Road House, Lethal Weapon 2, Ford Fairlane, Die Hard 2, Predator 2, Hudson Hawk, Ricochet, The Last Boy Scout, Lethal Weapon 3.

TELEVISION: Tales from the Crypt (exec. prod. & prod.; also dir. episode), Two Fisted Tales, Parker Can.

SILVER, LEON J.: Executive. b. Boston, MA, March 25, 1918. e. U. of Southern California, 1935–39. Independent prod. of short subjects, 1939; story analyst, Paramount, 1940, film writer, U.S. Army Pictorial Service, 1941–46; freelance writer, 1946; film writer. prod., U.S. Public Health Service, 1946–51, asst. chief, foreign film prod., U.S. Dept. of State, 1951–54; acting chief, domestic film prod., U.S. Information Agency, 1955. Division Chief, Worldwide Documentary Film & Television Product, U.S. Information Agency, Apr. 6, 1968, 1978 to 1979, sr. advisor IV, film production. Coordinator of TV & film, all Fed Govt. Agencies Private Industry under Exec. Office, pres. of U.S. 1980. Resigned, 1980. Now TV network writer-producer-novelist.

SILVER, MARISA: Director. b. New York, NY, April 23, 1960. Daughter of director Joan Micklin Silver and prod.-dir. Raphael Silver. e. Harvard U. where she directed short Dexter T. and edited doc. Light Coming Through: a Portrait of Maud Morgan.

PICTURES: Old Enough (prod. for $400,000) Permanent Record, Vital Signs, He Said/She Said (co-dir.).

TELEVISION: Co-dir.: A Community of Praise (an episode of PBS series Middletown, 1982).

SILVER, RAPHAEL D.: Producer. b. Cleveland, OH, 1930. e. Harvard Coll. and Harvard Graduate Sch. of Business Adm. Is pres. of Midwestern Land Devel. Corp. and Hodgson Houses, Inc. In 1973 formed Midwest Film Productions to produce Hester Street, written and directed by Joan Micklin Silver. Also distributed film independently. Also produced Between the Lines. Exec. prod. of Crossing Delancey. Directed On the Yard and a Walk on the Moon,.

SILVER, RON: Actor, Director. b. New York, NY, July 2, 1946. e. U. of Buffalo, St. John's U., Taiwan, M.A. Trained for stage at Herbert Berghof Studios and Actors Studio. N.Y. stage debut in Kasper and Public Insult, 1971. Elected pres. of Actors Equity Assn. 1991.

THEATER: El Grande de Coca Cola, Lotta, More Than You Deserve, Angel City (Mark Taper, LA), Hurlyburly, Social

Security, Hunting Cockroaches, Speed-the-Plow (Tony & Drama Desk Award), Gorilla (Chicago), Friends, And.

PICTURES: Tunnelvision, Welcome to L.A., Semi-Tough, Silent Rage, Best Friends, The Entity, Lovesick, Silkwood, Garbo Talks, Oh God! You Devil, Goodbye People, Eat and Run, Enemies A Love Story, Blue Steel, Reversal of Fortune, Mr. Saturday Night, Married to It.

TELEVISION: *Series*: Mac Davis Show, Rhoda, Dear Detective, Stockard Channing Show, Baker's Dozen. *Movies*: The Return of the World's Greatest Detective, Murder at the Mardi Gras, Betrayal, Word of Honor, The Billionaire Boys Club, Fellow Traveler, Forgotten Prisoners: The Amnesty Files, Live Wire, Blindside, Lifepod (also dir.).*Guest*: Trying Times (Drive He Said), Hill Street Blues, Wiseguy.

SILVERMAN, FRED: Producer. b. New York, NY, Sept., 1937. e. Syracuse U., Ohio State U., master's in TV and theatre arts. Joined WGN-TV, indep. sta. in Chicago. Came to N.Y. for exec. post at WPIX-TV, where stayed only six weeks CBS-TV hired him as dir. of daytime programs. Named v.p., programs 1970. In 1975 left CBS to become pres., ABC Entertainment. In 1978, named pres. and chief exec. officer of NBC. Now Pres., Fred Silverman Company, Los Angeles.

TELEVISION: Prod./exec. prod.: *Series*: Perry Mason Movies, Matlock, In the Heat of the Night, Jake and the Fatman, Father Dowling Mysteries, Dick Van Dyke Mystery Movies. *Movies*: The Astronaut, Family Flight, Man on a String, The Alpha Caper, Coffee, Tea, or Me; Outrage, The President's Plane is Missing, The FBI Story: The FBI vs. Alvin Karpis, The Last Hurrah, Young Joe: The Forgotten Kennedy, Kill Me If You Can, A Woman Called Moses, The Jesse Owens Story, First Steps, She Knows Too Much.

SILVERMAN, JIM: Executive. b. Des Moines, IA, June 26, 1950. e. U. of Hawaii, B.A., 1972; Taiwan National U., foreign language study, 1973. Exec. v.p. & co-founder, Commtron Corp., division of Bergen Brunswig Corp., 1975–83; pres. & founder, Continental Video, Inc., division of Cinema Group, Inc.

PICTURE: Prod.: Crack House.

SILVERMAN, JONATHAN: Actor. b. Los Angeles, CA, Aug. 5, 1966. e. USC, NYU.

PICTURES: Girls Just Want to Have Fun, Brighton Beach Memoirs, Caddyshack II, Stealing Home, Weekend at Bernie's, Class Action, Breaking the Rules, Life in the Food Chain (Age Isn't Everything), Little Sister, Weekend at Bernie's II.

TELEVISION: *Series*: Gimme a Break. *Movies*: Travelling Man, For Richer For Poorer, Broadway Bound, 12:01.

THEATRE: *NY*: Brighton Beach Memoirs, Biloxi Blues, Broadway Bound. *LA*: The Illusion (Dramalogue Award), Pay or Play.

SILVERMAN, RON: Producer, Writer. b. Los Angeles, CA, June 13, 1933. e. UCLA, 1951–53; U. of Arizona, 1953–55. Reporter-reviewer, Daily Variety, 1957–61; asst. to prod.-dir. Mark Robson, Red Lion Films, 20th Century-Fox, 1961–62; assoc. prod., Daystar Productions, 1961; v.p., 1964; assoc. prod. Crackerby TV series, 1965. Prod. exec., Warner Bros. TV, 1966; prod. & exec. Ted Mann Prods., 1967.

PICTURES: Buster and Billie (prod. 1974), Lifeguard, Brubaker (prod.), Krull (prod.), Shoot to Kill (co-prod.).

TELEVISION: Wild West (writer).

SILVERSTEIN, ELLIOT: Director. b. Boston, MA, Aug. 3, 1927. e. Boston Coll., Yale U. Started career on television.

PICTURES: Cat Ballou, The Happening, A Man Called Horse, Deadly Honeymoon, The Car.

TELEVISION: *Movies*: Belle Sommers, Betrayed by Innocence, Night of Courage, Fight for Life, Rich Men Single Women. *Series*: Tales From the Crypt.

SILVERSTEIN, MAURICE: Executive. b. Syracuse, NY, March 1, 1912. Booker, salesman, MGM domestic dep't; International Dep't, MGM; supervisor Southeast Asia Hdqts. Singapore, MGM, 1938–42; OWI chief, film distribution for Europe, hdqts. London, during W.W.II; asst. sales supervisor, Far East, MGM; regional director, Latin America, 1947; liaison exec. to handle independent productions MGM, 1956; vice-pres., MGM International, 1957; first vice-pres., 1958; pres., MGM International, 1963; vice-pres., parent company, Metro-Goldwyn-Mayer Inc. in charge of foreign production, 1970; Silverstein Int'l Corp., pres.

SIMMONS, ANTHONY: Director. Writer. b. London, England. e. Grad. from the LSE with LL.B. Practiced briefly as a barrister before entering the industry as writer/director of documentaries, then commercials and feature films. Awards: Grand Prix (shorts), Venice, Grand Prix, Locarno; 2 Int. Emmys, various Intl. Awards for commercials. Publications: The Optimists of Nine Elms, A Little Space for Issie Brown.

PICTURES: Sunday By the Sea, Bow Bells, Four in the Morning, The Optimists, Black Joy, Little Sweetheart.

TELEVISION: On Giant's Shoulders, Supergran and the Magic Ray, Day After the Fair, Inspector Morse, Van de Valk, Inspector Frost, The Good Guys.

SIMMONS, JEAN: Actress. b. London, England, Jan. 31, 1929. e. Aida Foster Sch., London. Screen debut 1944, at 14 in Give Us the Moon. Voted one of top ten British money-making stars in M.P. Herald-Fame Poll, 1950–51. London stage: A Little Night Music. Awards: Cannes Film Festival Homage 1988, Italian Outstanding Film Achievement Award 1989, French Govt. Commandeur de L'Ordre des Arts des Lettres. 1990.

PICTURES: Give Us the Moon (debut, 1944), Mr. Emmanuel, Meet Sexton Blake, Kiss the Bride Goodbye, Sports Day, Caesar and Cleopatra, Way to the Stars, Great Expectations, Hungry Hill, Black Narcissus, Uncle Silas, The Women In the Hall, Hamlet (Acad. Award nom., Venice Film Fest., Best Actress), Blue Lagoon, Adam and Evelyne, Trio, So Long at the Fair, Cage of Gold, The Clouded Yellow, Androcles and the Lion (U.S. film debut), Angel Face, Young Bess, Affair with a Stranger, The Actress, The Robe, She Couldn't Say No, A Bullet Is Waiting, The Egyptian, Desiree, Footsteps in the Fog, Guys and Dolls, Hilda Crane, This Could Be the Night, Until They Sail, The Big Country, Home Before Dark, This Earth Is Mine, Elmer Gantry, Spartacus, The Grass Is Greener, All the Way Home, Life at the Top, Mister Buddwing, Rough Night in Jericho, Divorce American Style, The Happy Ending (Acad. Award nom.), Say Hello to Yesterday, Mr. Sycamore, Dominique, Going Undercover, The Dawning.

TELEVISION: *Movies & Specials*: Heidi, Beggarman Thief, The Easter Promise, The Home Front, Golden Gate, Jacqueline Susann's, Valley of the Dolls 1981, A Small Killing, Inherit the Wind, Great Expectations, Sensibility and Sense, The Laker Girls, Perry Mason: The Case of Lost Love, People Like Us, December Flower. *Mini-Series*: The Dain Curse, The Thorn Birds (Emmy Award, 1983), North and South Book II. *Series*: Dark Shadows (1991).

SIMMONS, MATTY: Producer. b. Oct. 3. As bd. chmn., National Lampoon, Inc. produced National Lampoon Radio Hour, National Lampoon Lemmings, National Lampoon Show. Resigned from National Lampoon Inc. 1989. Now heads Matty Simmons Productions.

PICTURES: National Lampoon's Animal House, National Lampoon's Vacation, National Lampoon Goes to the Movies, National Lampoon's Class Reunion, National Lampoon's European Vacation, National Lampoon's Family Dies, National Lampoon's Christmas Vacation (exec. prod.).

TELEVISION: National Lampoon's Disco Beavers, National Lampoon's Class of '86 (exec. prod.), Delta House.

SIMON, MELVIN: Executive. b. New York, NY, Oct. 21, 1926. e. City Coll.of New York, B.B.A., 1949; graduate work at Indiana U. Law Sch. Owns and operates, in partnership with two brothers, over 110 shopping centers in U.S. In 1978 formed Melvin Simon Productions, privately owned corp., to finance films. Dissolved Co. in 1983.

PICTURES: Exec. Prod.: Dominique, When a Stranger Calls, The Runner Stumbles, Scavenger Hunt, Cloud Dancer, The Stunt Man, My Bodyguard, Zorro—The Gay Blade, Chu Chu and the Philly Flash, Porky's, Porky's II—The Next Day, Uforia, Wolf Lake, Porky's Revenge.

MEMBER: Friars Club; N.Y. div.; 1978, v.p., Intl. Council of Shopping Centers; 1978, commerce and industry chmn. of muscular dystrophy; mem. bd., Indiana Repertory Theatre 1978, corporate sponsor: Indianapolis 500 Festival, Indianapolis Museum of Arts, Indianapolis Children's Museum; Indianapolis Zoological Society.

SIMON, NEIL: Playwright, Screenwriter, Producer. b. Bronx, NY, July 4, 1927. e. NYU. U.S. Army Air Force, 1945–46. Wrote comedy for radio with brother, Danny, (Robert Q. Lewis Show and for Goodman Ace), also TV scripts for Sid Caesar, Red Buttons, Jackie Gleason, Phil Silvers, Garry Moore, Tallulah Bankhead Show. With Danny contributed to Bdwy revues Catch a Star (1955), and New Faces of 1956. Adapted several of own plays to screen.

PLAYS: Come Blow Your Horn, Little Me, Barefoot in the Park, The Odd Couple (Tony Award, 1965), Sweet Charity, The Star Spangled Girl, Plaza Suite, Promises Promises, Last of the Red Hot Lovers, The Gingerbread Lady, The Prisoner of Second Avenue, The Sunshine Boys, The Good Doctor, God's Favorite, California Suite, Chapter Two, They're Playing Our Song, I Ought to Be in Pictures, Fools, Little Me (revised version), Brighton Beach Memoirs, Biloxi Blues (Tony Award, 1985), The Odd Couple (female version), Broadway Bound, Rumors, Lost in Yonkers (Pulitzer Prize, Tony Award, 1991), Jake's Women, The Goodbye Girl (musical).

PICTURES: After the Fox, Barefoot in the Park (also assoc. prod.), The Odd Couple, The Out-of-Towners, Plaza Suite, Last of the Red Hot Lovers, The Heartbreak Kid, The Prisoner of Second Avenue, The Sunshine Boys, Murder by Death, The Goodbye Girl, The Cheap Detective, California Suite, Chapter Two, Seems Like Old Times, Only When I

Laugh (also co-prod.), I Ought to Be in Pictures (also co-prod.), Max Dugan Returns (also co-prod.), The Lonely Guy (adaptation), The Slugger's Wife, Brighton Beach Memoirs, Biloxi Blues (also co-prod.), The Marrying Man, Lost in Yonkers.
TELEVISION: *Specials*: The Trouble With People, Plaza Suite. *Movie*: Broadway Bound.

SIMON, PAUL: Singer, Composer, Actor. b. Newark, NJ, Oct. 13, 1941. e. Queens Coll., BA; postgrad. Brooklyn Law Sch. Teamed with Art Garfunkel in 1964, writing and performing own songs; they parted in 1970. Reunited for concert in New York, 1982, which was televised on HBO. Songs: With Garfunkel: Mrs. Robinson (Grammy Award), The Boxer, Bridge Over Troubled Water (Grammy).
PICTURES: The Graduate (songs), Annie Hall (actor), One Trick Pony (s.p., act., comp.)
TELEVISION: *Specials*: The Fred Astaire Show, The Paul Simon Special (Emmy), Home Box Office Presents Paul Simon, Graceland: The African Concert, Mother Goose Rock 'n' Rhyme, Paul Simon's Concert in the Park. *Guest*: Sesame St.
ALBUMS: *with Garfunkel*: Wednesday Morning 3 a.m., Sounds of Silence, Parsley, Sage, Rosemary and Thyme, The Graduate (Grammy), Bookends, Bridge Over Troubled Water (Grammy), Simon & Garfunkel's Greatest Hits, Concert in the Park. *Solo*: Paul Simon, There Goes Rhymin' Simon, Live Rhymin', Still Crazy After All These Years (Grammy), Greatest Hits, One Trick Pony, Hearts and Bones, Graceland (Grammy), Negotiations and Love Songs, 1971–86, The Rhythm of the Saints, Paul Simon's Concert in the Park.

SIMON, SIMONE: Actress. b. April 23, 1911, Marseilles, France. Played in many films in Europe, among them Les Beaux Jours, La Bete Humaine, and Lac aux Dames. On stage in Toi C'est Moi, and others.
PICTURES: Girl's Dormitory, Ladies in Love, Seventh Heaven, All That Money Can Buy, Cat People, Love and Hisses, Josette, Johnny Doesn't Live Here Any More, Temptation, Harbor, Lost Women, La Ronde, Le Plaisir, Double Destin, The Extra Day.

SIMPSON, DON: Producer. b. Anchorage, AL, Oct. 29, 1945. e. U. of Oregon, Phi Beta Kappa, 1967. Began career in industry as acct. exec. with Jack Woodel Agency, San Francisco, where supervised mktg. of Warner Bros. films. Recruited by WB in 1971 as mktg. exec. specializing in youth market; oversaw Woodstock, Clockwork Orange, Billy Jack, etc. Co-writer on low-budget films, Aloha, Bobby and Rose and Cannonball. Joined Paramount as prod. exec. 1975; promoted 1977 to v.p., prod. Named sr. v.p. of prod., 1980; pres. of worldwide prod., 1981. Formed Don Simpson/Jerry Bruckheimer Prods. 1983, entering into exclusive deal with Paramount to develop and produce for m.p. and TV divisions.
PICTURES: *Co-writer*: Aloha Bobby and Rose, Cannonball. *Producer*: Flashdance, Thief of Hearts, Beverly Hills Cop, Top Gun, Beverly Hills Cop II, Days of Thunder.

SIMPSON, GARRY: Producer, Director, Writer. e. Stanford U. Major shows with NBC-TV: Jimmy Durante Show, Armstrong Circle Theatre, Ed Wynn Show, Philco TV Playhouse, Ballet Theatre. Awards: Academy of TV Arts & Sci., Sylvania. Documentary film writer-producer awards: International Film & TV Festival, Chicago Film Festival, Broadcast Media Awards. Currently, independent prod.-dir.

SIMPSON, O.J.: Actor. b. San Francisco, CA, July 9, 1947. r.n. Orenthal James Simpson. e. U. of Southern California. Was star collegiate and professional football player and winner of Heisman Trophy. Began sportscasting 1969.
PICTURES: The Klansman, The Towering Inferno, Killer Force, Cassandra Crossing, Capricorn One, Firepower, Hambone & Hillie, The Naked Gun, The Naked Gun 2-1/2.
TELEVISION: *Mini-Series*: Roots. *Movies*: A Killing Affair, Goldie and the Boxer (also exec. prod.), Detour to Terror (also exec. prod.), Goldie and the Boxer Go to Hollywood (also exec. prod.), Cocaine and Blue Eyes (also exec. prod.), Student Exchange. Prod.: High Five (pilot), Superbowl Saturday Night (host & co-prod.) *Series*: First and Ten (HBO), NFL Live.

SIMS, JOAN: Actress. b. Laindon, England, May 9, 1930. e. Trained at RADA. Early career in repertory and West End Theatre.
PICTURES: Dry Rot, Off the Record, No Time for Tears, Just My Luck, The Naked Truth, The Captain's Table, Passport to Shame, Emergency Ward 10, Most of the Carry On' films, Doctor in Love, Watch Your Stern, Twice Round the Daffodils, The Iron Maiden, Nurse on Wheels, Doctor in Clover, Doctor in Trouble, The Garnett Saga, Not Now Darling, Don't Just Lie There Say Something, Love Among the Ruins, One of Our Dinosaurs Is Missing, Till Death Us Do Part, The Way of the World, Deceptions, The Fool.
TELEVISION: Over 100 shows incl. Stanley Baxter Show, Dick Emery Show, Carry on Shows, Love Among the Ruins, Born and Bred, Worzel Gummidge, Ladykillers, Crown Court,

Cockles, Fairly Secret Army, Tickle on the Tum, Miss Marple: A Murder Is Announced, Hay Fever, In Loving Memory, Drummonds, Farrington of the F.O., Dr. Who, On the Up (3 series), Boys From the Bush, Simon & the Witch, Children's TV, On the Up, Boys From the Bush, Tender Loving Care.

SINATRA, FRANK: Actor, Singer. b. Hoboken, NJ, Dec. 12, 1915. Sportswriter; then singer on radio various N.Y. stations; joined Harry James orchestra, later Tommy Dorsey. On screen as a band vocalist in Las Vegas Nights, Ship Ahoy, Reveille with Beverly. Spec. Academy Award 1945 for acting in The House I Live In, short subject on tolerance. Received Jean Hersholt Humanitarian Award, 1971.
PICTURES: Las Vegas Nights (debut, 1941), Ship Ahoy, Reveille With Beverly, Higher and Higher (acting debut, 1943), Step Lively, Anchors Aweigh, Till the Clouds Roll By, It Happened in Brooklyn, Miracle of the Bells, Kissing Bandit, Take Me Out to the Ball Game, On the Town, Double Dynamite, Meet Danny Wilson, From Here to Eternity (Acad. Award. best supporting actor, 1953), Suddenly, Young at Heart, Not as a Stranger, Tender Trap, Guys and Dolls, Man With the Golden Arm, Meet Me in Las Vegas (cameo), Johnny Concho (also prod.), High Society, Around The World in 80 Days, Pride and the Passion, The Joker is Wild, Pal Joey, Kings Go Forth, Some Came Running, A Hole in the Head, Never So Few, Can-Can, Ocean's 11, Pepe, Devil at Four O'Clock, Sergeants 3 (also prod.), The Road to Hong Kong (cameo), The Manchurian Candidate, Come Blow Your Horn, The List of Adrian Messenger, 4 for Texas, Robin and the Seven Hoods (also prod.), None But the Brave (also dir., prod.), Von Ryan's Express, Marriage on the Rocks, Cast a Giant Shadow, The Oscar (cameo), Assault on a Queen, The Naked Runner, Tony Rome, The Detective, Lady in Cement, Dirty Dingus Magee, That's Entertainment!, The First Deadly Sin (also exec. prod.), Cannonball Run II (cameo), Who Framed Roger Rabbit (voice), Listen Up.
TELEVISION: *Series*: The Frank Sinatra Show (1950–2; 1957–8); numerous specials, and guest appearances, incl. Club Oasis, Anything Goes (1954), Hollywood Palace, Our Town (1955), Frank Sinatra: A Man and His Music (Emmy Award), Magnum P.I., Sinatra: Concert for the Americas. *Movie*: Contract on Cherry Street.

SINCLAIR, ANDREW: Director, Writer. b. 1935. Early career as novelist and historian, playwright. Published 11 books in U.K., U.S. Entered m.p. industry in 1968.
PICTURES: Before Winter Comes (s.p.), Adventures in the Skin Trade (s.p.), Voyage of the Beagle (s.p.), You? (s.p.), The Breaking of Bumbo (dir., s.p.), Under Milk Wood (dir., s.p.), Malachi's Cove (prod.), Tuxedo Warrior (prod.), The Representative (s.p.), The Scarlet Letter (s.p.), Martin (s.p.), The Sword and the Grail (s.p.).

SINCLAIR, MADGE: Actress. b. Kingston, Jamaica, April 28, 1938. e. Shortwood Women's College. Worked in Jamaica as a teacher and in the insurance business before moving to NY. Chairwoman, Madge Walters Sinclair Inc., Caribbean Child Life Foundation. Awards: NAACP Image Award, 1981 and 1983, best actress in dramatic series, Trapper John M.D.; Drama-Logue Critics Award, 1986, Boseman & Lena; Mother of the Year Award, 1984. L.A. area Emmy Award, Look Away. Member: bd. of dir., Lost Angeles Theatre Center.
THEATER: Kumaliza (NYSF, debut, 1969); Iphigenia (NYSF, NY and Young Vic, London); Mod Donna, Ti-Jean and His Brothers, Blood; Division Street (Mark Taper Forum), Boesman & Lena (LA Theatre Center), Tartuffe (L.A. Theatre Center), Stars in the Morning (LATC), Piano (LATC), Jacques and His Master (LATC), Trinity (New Federal Theatre).
PICTURES: Conrack (debut, 1974), Cornbread Earl & Me, Leadbelly, I Will I Will...For Now, Convoy, Uncle Joe Shannon, Star Trek IV: The Voyage Home, Coming to America.
TELEVISION: *Series*: Grandpa Goes to Washington (1978–79), Trapper John M.D. (1980–86), O'Hara, Gabriel's Fire (Emmy Award, 1991; revamped as Pros & Cons). *Guest*: Madigan, Medical Center, The Waltons, Joe Forester, Doctor's Hospital, Executive Suite, Medical Story, Serpico, The White Shadow, All in the Family, Homeroom, Midnight Caller, Roseanne. *Mini-Series*: Roots, The Orchid House (Britain), Queen. *Movies*: I Love, You, Goodbye, One in a Million: The Ron LeFlore Story, I Know Why the Caged Bird Sings, High Ice, Jimmy B and Andre, Guyana Tragedy: The Story of Jim Jones, Victims, Look Away: The Emancipation of Mary Todd Lincoln, Divided We Stand, Jonathan: The Boy Nobody Wanted, The Man With 3 Wives.

SINDEN, DONALD: Actor. b. Plymouth, England, Oct. 9, 1923. Stage debut 1942 in fit-up shows; London stage includes There's a Girl in My Soup, The Relapse, Not Now Darling, King Lear, Othello, Present Laughter, Uncle Vanya, The School for Scandal, Two Into One, The Scarlet Pimpernel, Oscar Wilde, Major Barbara, Out of Order. Bdwy: London Assurance, Habeas Corpus. TV debut 1948; screen debut in 1953, Cruel Sea.

PICTURES: The Cruel Sea, Mogambo, A Day to Remember, You Know What Sailors Are, Doctor in the House, The Beachcomber, Mad About Men, An Alligator Named Daisy, Black Tent, Eyewitness, Tiger in the Smoke, Doctor at Large, Rockets Galore (Mad Little Island), The Captain's Table, Operation Bullshine, Your Money or Your Wife, The Siege of Sydney Street, Twice Around the Daffodils, Mix Me a Person, Decline and Fall, Villain, Rentadick, The Island at the Top of the World, That Lucky Touch, The Children.

TELEVISION: Bullet in the Ballet, Road to Rome, Dinner With the Family, Odd Man In, Love from Italy, The Frog, The Glove, The Mystery of Edwin Drood, The Happy Ones, The Comedy of Errors, The Wars of the Roses, The Red House, Blackmail, A Bachelor Gray, Our Man at St. Marks (3 series), The Wind in the Tall Paper Chimney, A Woman Above Reproach, Call My Bluff, Relatively Speaking, Father Dear Father, The 19th Hole, Seven Days in the Life of Andrew Pelham (serial), The Assyrian Rejuvenator, The Organization (serial), The Confederacy of Wives, Tell It to the Chancellor, The Rivals, Two's Company (4 series), All's Well That Ends Well, Never the Twain (11 series).

SINGER, LORI: Actress. b. Corpus Christi, TX, Nov. 6, 1962. Sister of actor Marc Singer and daughter of symphony conductor Jacques Singer. Concert cellist while in teens. Won starring role in TV series Fame (1981).

PICTURES: Footloose (debut, 1984), The Falcon and The Snowman, The Man with One Red Shoe, Trouble in Mind, Summer Heat, Made in U.S.A., Warlock, Equinox, Sunset Grill, Short Cuts.

TELEVISION: Series: Fame. Movies: Born Beautiful, Storm and Sorrow. Special: Sensibility and Sense.

SINGER, MARC: Actor. b. Vancouver, B.C., Canada, Jan. 29. Brother of actress Lori Singer. Son of symphony conductor Jacques Singer. Trained in summer stock and regional theatre.

PICTURES: Go Tell the Spartans, If You Could See What I Hear, The Beastmaster, Born to Race, A Man Called Sarge, Watchers II, Body Chemistry, Dead Space, In the Cold of the Night, Beastmaster 2, The Berlin Conspiracy, Alien Intruder.

TELEVISION: Series: The Contender, "V", Dallas. Mini-Series: 79 Park Avenue, Roots: The Next Generation. Movies: Things in Their Season, Journey from Darkness, Something for Joey, Never Con a Killer, Sergeant Matlovich vs. the U.S. Air Force, The Two Worlds of Jennie Logan, For Ladies Only, Paper Dolls, "V", Her Life as a Man, "V"—The Final Battle, Deadly Game, The Sea Wolf.

SINGLETON, JOHN: Director, Writer. b. Los Angeles, CA, Jan. 6, 1968. Entered USC's Filmic Writing Program, where he received a Robert Riskin Award and two Jack Nicholson Writing Awards. With debut feature Boyz N the Hood (1991) he became the first African-American and youngest person ever to be nominated for an Academy Award for Best Director.

PICTURES: Director-Writer: Boyz N the Hood (Acad. Award noms. for best dir. & s.p.), Poetic Justice (also co-prod.).

SINGLETON, PENNY: Actress. r.n. Dorothy McNulty. b. Philadelphia, PA, September 15, 1908. e. Columbia U. First Broadway success came as top comedienne in Good News., exec. pres. AGVA.

PICTURES: Outside of Paradise, Swing Your Lady, Men Are Such Fools, Boy Meets Girl, Mr. Chump, Mad Miss Manton, Garden of the Moon, Secrets of an Actress, Hard to Get, 28 films in Blondie series, Rocket Busters, Go West Young Lady, Footlight Glamor, Young Widow, The Best Man, Jetsons: The Movie (voice).

TELEVISION: The Jetsons (voice).

SIODMAK, CURT: Director, Writer. b. 1902. e. U. of Zurich. Engineer, newspaper reporter, writer in Berlin; novelist, including F.P.1 Does Not Answer, adapt. 1932 for Ufa. Originals and screenplays in France and England including France (Le Bal), Transatlantic Tunnel, GB.

PICTURES: Writer: Her Jungle Love, Aloma of the South Sea, Invisible Woman, Son of Dracula, The Mantrap, House of Frankenstein, Shady Lady, Beast with Five Fingers, Berlin Express, Tarzan's Magic Fountain, Four Days Leave, Bride of the Gorilla (also dir.), The Magnetic Monster (also dir.), Riders to the Stars, Creature with the Atom Brain, Earth vs. the Flying Saucers.

SKASE, CHRISTOPHER: Executive. b. Australia, 1946. Began career as reporter for Fairfax publication, Australian Financial Review. In 1970s set up investment company with about $20,000. Revived Australian TV Seven network in Melbourne and then in U.S. bought Hal Roach Studios and NY based prod.-dist. Robert Halmi which he merged into Qintex Entertainment. Qintex Entertainment produced TV mini-series Lonesome Dove.

SKELTON, RED: Actor, Comedian. r.n. Richard Skelton. b. Vincennes, IN, July 18, 1913. Joined medicine show at 10;

later in show boat stock, minstrel shows, vaudeville, burlesque, circus. On radio from 1936. Red Skelton Show, TV, (1951–71; Emmy Awards: Best Comedian, Best Comedy Writing). Received ATAS Governor's Award in 1986. Composer of music, writer of short stories and painter.

PICTURES: Having Wonderful Time (debut, 1939), Flight Command, Lady Be Good, The People vs. Dr. Kildare, Dr. Kildare's Wedding Day, Whistling in the Dark, Whistling in Dixie, Ship Ahoy, Maisie Gets Her Man, Panama Hattie, Du Barry Was a Lady, Thousands Cheer, I Dood It, Whistling in Brooklyn, Bathing Beauty, Ziegfeld Follies, Merton of the Movies, Fuller Brush Man, Southern Yankee, Neptune's Daughter, Yellow Cab Man, Three Little Words, Watch the Birdie, Excuse My Dust, Texas Carnival, Lovely to Look At, The Clown, Half a Hero, Great Diamond Robbery, Around the World in 80 Days, Public Pigeon No. 1, Ocean's 11, Those Magnificent Men in Their Flying Machines.

SKERRITT, TOM: Actor. b. Detroit, MI, Aug. 25, 1933. e. Wayne State U., UCLA. Appeared in Italian movies 1972–76. Model for Guess? jeans ads.

PICTURES: War Hunt (debut, 1962), One Man's Way, Those Calloways, M*A*S*H, Wild Rovers, Fuzz, Big Bad Mama, Thieves Like Us, The Devil's Rain, The Turning Point, Up in Smoke, Ice Castles, Alien, Savage Harvest, Silence of the North, A Dangerous Summer, Fighting Back, The Dead Zone, Top Gun, Opposing Force, Space Camp, Wisdom, Maid to Order, The Big Town, Poltergeist III, Steel Magnolias, Big Man on Campus, The Rookie, Wild Orchid II: Two Shades of Blue, Poison Ivy, Singles, A River Runs Through It, Knight Moves.

TELEVISION: Series: Ryan's Four, Cheers, Picket Fences. Movies: The Bird Men, The Last Day, Maneaters Are Loose!, The Calendar Girl Murders, Miles to Go, Parent Trap II, A Touch of Scandal, Poker Alice, Moving Target, Nightmare at Bitter Creek, The Heist, Red King White Knight, The China Lake Murders, Child of the Night, In Sickness and in Health, Getting Up and Going Home. Director: Kelly vs. Kelly (Afterschool Special).

SKOLIMOWSKI, JERZY: Director, Writer. b. Lodz, Poland, May 5, 1938. e. Warsaw U., State Superior Film Sch., Lodz, Poland. Scriptwriter for Wajda's Innocent Sorcerers (also actor), Polanski's Knife in the Water and Lomnicki's Poslizg. Author: Somewhere Close to Oneself, Somebody Got Drowned.

PICTURES: Director-Writer: Identification Marks—None (also actor, edit., art dir.), Walkover (also actor, edit.), Barrier, The Departure, Hands Up (also actor), Dialogue, The Adventures of Gerard, Deep End, King Queen Knave (dir. only), The Shout, Circle of Deceit (actor only), Moonlighting (also prod., actor), Success Is the Best Revenge, The Lightship, White Nights (actor), Big Shots (actor), Torrents of Spring (also actor), 30 Door Key (also co-s.p., prod.), The Hollow Men (prod.).

SKYE, IONE: Actress. b. London, Eng., Sept. 4, 1971. r.n. Ione Skye Leitch. Daughter of folksinger Donovan (Leitch) and sister of actor Donovan Leitch. m. singer-actor Adam Horovitz. Fashion photo of her in magazine led to audition for film River's Edge.

PICTURES: River's Edge (debut, 1987 as Ione Skye Leitch), Stranded, A Night in the Life of Jimmy Reardon, Say Anything, The Rachel Papers, Mindwalk, Wayne's World, Gas Food Lodging, Samantha, Guncrazy.

TELEVISION: Series: Covington Cross. Movies: Napoleon and Josephine. Specials: It's Called the Sugar Plum, Nightmare Classics (Carmilla).

SLATER, CHRISTIAN: Actor. b. New York, NY, Aug. 18, 1969. Mother is NY casting dir. Mary Jo Slater, father Los Angeles stage actor Michael Hawkins. Made prof. debut at 9 in The Music Man starring Dick Van Dyke in the natl. tour, then on Bdwy. Also on Bdwy in Macbeth, A Christmas Carol, David Copperfield and Merlin. Off-Bdwy in Landscape of the Body, Between Daylight and Boonville and Somewhere's Better. Also summer theatre. Directed 1992 L.A. prod. of The Laughter Epidemic.

PICTURES: The Invisible Boy, Twisted, The Legend of Billie Jean, The Name of the Rose, Tucker: The Man and His Dream, Gleaming the Cube, Heathers, The Wizard, Tales from the Dark Side: The Movie, Beyond the Stars, Young Guns II, Pump Up the Volume, Robin Hood: Prince of Thieves, Mobsters, Star Trek VI: The Undiscovered Country (cameo), Kuffs, FernGully ... The Last Rainforest (voice), Where the Day Takes You, Untamed Heart, True Romance.

TELEVISION: Soap operas: One Life to Live, All My Children, Ryan's Hope. Specials: Sherlock Holmes, Pardon Me for Living, The Haunted Mansion Mystery, Cry Wolf, The Edge (Professional Man). Movies: Living Proof: The Hank Williams Jr. Story, Desperate For Love.

SLATER, DAPHNE: Actress. b. Bayswater, London, England, March 3, 1928. e. Haberdashers' Askes Sch.; Royal Acad. of Dramatic Art. Stage debut: The Rising Generation, 1945; plays include King Lear; m.p. debut in Courtneys of Curzon

Street, 1947; TV debut for BBC in I Want to Be an Actor, 1946.

TELEVISION: Emma, Shout Aloud Salvation, All the Year Round, They Fly by Twilight, Pride and Prejudice, The Affair at Assino, Beau Brummell, Jane Eyre, Precious Bane, The Dark Is Light Enough, Mary Rose, Julius Caesar, Berkeley Square, Less Than Kind, The Burning Glass, Persuasion, The Winslow Boy, She Stoops to Conquer, Nothing to Pay, The Father, The Bald Prima Donna, The Big Breaker, The Cocktail Party, Photo Finish, The Seagull, Love Story, Emergency Ward 10, Jackanory, The First Freedom, Man of Our Times, The Jazz Age, Callan, The Piano Tuner, Happy Ever After, The Pretenders, Virtue, Elizabeth R, The Staff Room, Footprints in the Sand.

SLATER, HELEN: Actress. b. New York, NY, Dec. 19, 1963. Off-Bdwy: Responsible Parties, Almost Romance.

PICTURES: Supergirl (debut, 1984), The Legend of Billie Jean, Ruthless People, The Secret of My Success, Sticky Fingers, Happy Together, City Slickers, A House in the Hills, Betrayal of the Dove.

TELEVISION: Series: Capital News. Movies: 12:01, Chantilly Lace.

SLATZER, ROBERT FRANKLIN: Writer, Director, Producer, Author. b. Marion, OH, April 4, 1927. e. Ohio State U., UCLA, 1947. Radio news commentator sportscaster, wrote radio serials; adv. dir., Brush-Moore Newspapers; feature writer, Scripps-Howard Newspapers; adv. exec., The Columbus Dispatch; syn. columnist, NY Journal-American; wrote guest columns for Walter Winchell and Dorothy Kilgallen; author of western short stories and novels; wrote, dir., prod. industrial films, docs., sports specials and commercials; 1949–51, writer for Grand National Studios Prods, Monogram Pictures, Republic Studios, Eagle-Lion Films; 1951, publicist, Hope Enterprises; pub. dir., Paramount Pictures; 1952, personal mgr. to Marilyn Monroe, Ken Maynard, James Craig, Gail Russell and other stars; 1953, story editor and assoc. prod., Joe Palooka Productions; 1953–54, staff writer Universal Studios, RKO Radio Pictures, MGM, Columbia and Paramount Studios; 1958, formed Robert F. Slatzer Productions; 1960, exec. in chg. of prod., Jaguar Pictures Corp.; 1963–65, pres., Slatzer Oil & Gas Co.; 1966–67, bd. dir., United Mining & Milling Corp.; 1967–70, wrote and dir. feature films; 1970–74, exec., Columbia Pictures Corp.; 1974, resumed producing and financing features and television films; 1976, honored as "Fellow", Mark Twain. Inst.

PICTURES: White Gold, The Obsessed, Mike and the Heiress, Under Texas Skies, They Came To Kill, Trail of the Mounties, Jungle Goddess, Montana Desperado, Pride of the Blue, Green Grass of Wyoming, The Naked Jungle, Warpaint, Broken Lance, Elephant Walk, South of Death Valley, The Big Gusher, Arctic Flight, The Hellcats, Bigfoot, John Wayne's No Substitute for Victory', Joniko—Eskimo Boy, Operation North Slope, Claws, Don't Go West, Mulefeathers, The Unfinished, Single Room Furnished, Viva Zapata, Inchon.

TELEVISION: The Great Outdoors, Adventures of White Arrow, Let's Go Boating, The Joe Palooka Story, Amos & Andy, I Am the Law, Files of Jeffrey Jones, Fireside Theatre, The Unser Story, Year of Opportunity (Award winning spec.), The Big Ones, Ken Maynard's West, Where are They Now?, The Groovy Seven, The Untouchables, The Detectives, Wild Wild West, Wagon Train, Playhouse 90, Highway Patrol, David Frost Special, Today Show, ABC News, 20/20, Inside Edition, The Reporters, Current Affair, The Geraldo Show, Hard Copy, Larry King Show, Marilyn and Me, The Marilyn Files.

AUTHOR: (novels) Desert Empire, Rose of the Range, Rio, Rawhide Range, The Cowboy and the Heiress, Daphne, Campaign Girl, Scarlet, The Dance Studio Hucksters, Born to be Wild, Single Room Furnished, The West is Still Wild, Gusher, The Young Wildcats; (biographies) The Life and Curious Death of Marilyn Monroe, The Life and Legend of Ken Maynard, Who Killed Thelma Todd?, The Duke of Thieves, Bing Crosby—The Hollow Man, Duke: The Life and Times of John Wayne, The Marilyn Files.

SLAVIN, GEORGE: Writer. b. Newark, NJ, Mar. 2, 1916; e. Bucknell U., drama, Yale U. Has written over 300 TV episodes & pilots. WGA TV Award. Collected works at U. Wyoming. Received Stanford U, Maxwell Anderson Playwriting Award.

PICTURES: story, co-s.p., Intrigue; co-story, Woman on Pier 13; co-s.p., The Nevadan, Mystery Submarine; co-story & s.p. Peggy, Red Mountain, City of Bad Men; co-story, Weekend with Father, Thunder Bay, Rocket Man; co-story, co-s.p., Smoke Signal, Uranium Boom; co-s.p., Desert Sands, The Halliday Brand, Son of Robin Hood, Big House USA (co-s.p.), Fighting Stallions (s.p.).

SLOAN, JOHN R.: Producer. e. Merchiston Castle School, Edinburg, 1932–39; asst. dir. and prod. man. Warners, London, Hollywood; 1939–46, Army.

PICTURES: Sea Devils, The End of the Affair, Port Afrique, Abandon Ship, The Safecracker, Beyond this Place, The

Killers of Kilimanjaro, Johnny Nobody, The Reluctant Saint, The Running Man, The Last Command, To Sir With Love, Fragment of Fear, Dad's Army, Lord Jim, No Sex Please, We're British, The Odessa File, Force 10 From Navarone, The Children's Story.

SLOCOMBE, DOUGLAS: Cinematographer. b. England, Feb. 10, 1913. Former journalist. Filmed the invasion of Poland and Holland. Under contract to Ealing Studios 17 years.

PICTURES: Dead of Night, The Captive Heart, Hue and Cry, The Loves of Joanna Godden, It Always Rains on Sunday, Saraband for Dead Lovers, Kind Hearts and Coronets, Cage of Gold, The Lavender Hill Mob, Mandy, The Man in the White Suit, The Titfield Thunderbolt, Man in the Sky, Ludwig II, Lease on Life, The Smallest Show on Earth, Tread Softly, Stranger, Circus of Horrors, The Young Ones, The Mark, The L-Shaped Room, Freud, The Servant (BAFTA Award), Guns at Batashi, A High Wind in Jamaica, The Blue Max, Promise Her Anything, The Vampire Killers, Fathom, Robbery, Boom, The Lion in Winter, The Italian Job, The Music Lovers, Murphy's War, The Buttercup Chain, Travels With My Aunt (Acad. Award nom.), Jesus Christ Superstar, The Great Gatsby, Rollerball, Hedda, The Sailor Who Fell From Grace With the Sea, Nasty Habits, Julia, Close Encounters of the Third Kind, Caravans, Lost and Found, The Lady Vanishes, Nijinsky, Raiders of the Lost Ark, The Pirates of Penzance, Never Say Never Again, Indiana Jones and the Temple of Doom, Water, Lady Jane, Indiana Jones and the Last Crusade.

TELEVISION: Love Among the Ruins.

SLOTE, A. R.: Bureau Chief in Pakistan for Quigley Publications. b. Bagasra, India, June 9, 1935. e. Pakistan National H.S., Muslim Sch. and Art. Coll., Karachi. Booker, Columbia Pictures Int. Corp. Asst. mgr., Plaza Cinema, Paradise Theatres, Ltd. Editor: Filmlife, 1959–64; Karachi correspondent for Weekly Chitrali, Pakistan Daily Observer, Dhaka, 1966–70. Editor, publisher: Pakistan Filmdom, 1966; Sind Film Directory, 1981; Platinum Jubilee Film Directory, 1987. Film Page Incharge, The Star Daily of Karachi since 1971. Winner of National Film Award for Best Showbiz Journalist (1989).

SMIGHT, JACK: Director. b. Minneapolis, MN, March 9, 1926. e. U. of MN, BA. Began as disc jockey then became TV dir. of One Man's Family (1953).

PICTURES: I'd Rather Be Rich, The Third Day, Harper, Kaleidoscope, The Secret War of Harry Frigg, No Way to Treat a Lady, Strategy of Terror, The Illustrated Man, The Travelling Executioner, Rabbit Run, Airport 1975, Midway, Damnation Alley, Fast Break, Loving Couples, Number One with a Bullet, The Favorite.

TELEVISION: Series: Banacek, Columbo, Madigan. Specials: Eddie (Emmy, 1959), Roll of Thunder Hear My Cry. Movies: The Screaming Woman, Banacek: Detour to Nowhere, The Longest Night, Frankenstein—The True Story, Partners in Crime, Double Indemnity, Linda, Remembrance of Love.

SMITH, ALEXIS: Actress. b. Penticton, Canada, June 8, 1921. m. actor Craig Stevens. e. LA City Col. In summer stock British Columbia.

PICTURES: She Couldn't Say No, Flight From Destiny, Smiling Ghost, Dive Bomber, Steel Against the Sky, Gentleman Jim, Thank Your Lucky Stars, The Constant Nymph, The Doughgirls, Adventures of Mark Twain, Conflict, Rhapsody in Blue, The Horn Blows at Midnight, San Antonio, One More Tomorrow, Night and Day, Of Human Bondage, Stallion Road, The Two Mrs. Carrolls, The Woman in White, Always Together, The Decision of Christopher Blake, Whiplash, South of St. Louis, Any Number Can Play, One Last Fling, Undercover Girl, Wyoming Mail, Montana, Here Comes the Groom, Cave of the Outlaws, The Turning Point, Split Second, Sleeping Tiger, The Eternal Sea, Beau James, This Happy Feeling, The Young Phildelphians, Once is Not Enough, The Little Girl Who Lives Down the Lane, Casey's Shadow, The Trout, Tough Guys.

BROADWAY: Follies (Tony Award, 1971), The Women, Summer Brave, Platinum.

TELEVISION: Movies: A Death in California, Dress Gray, Marcus Welby M.D.: A Holiday Affair. Series: Hothouse. (Died: June 9, 1993.)

SMITH, CHARLES MARTIN: Actor, Director. b. Los Angeles, CA, Oct. 30, 1953. e. California State U. Father is animation artist Frank Smith.

PICTURES: Actor: The Culpepper Cattle Company, Fuzz, The Spikes Gang, American Graffiti, Pat Garrett and Billy the Kid, Rafferty and the Gold Dust Twins, No Deposit No Return, The Hazing, The Buddy Holly Story, More American Graffiti, Herbie Goes Bananas, Never Cry Wolf, Starman, Trick or Treat (also dir.), The Untouchables, The Experts, The Hot Spot, Deep Cover, Fifty-Fifty (also dir.).

TELEVISION: Speed Buggy (voice). Guest: The Brady Bunch, Monte Nash, Baretta, Streets of San Francisco, Petrocelli, The Rookies, Grizzly Adams, Twilight Zone, Ray

Bradbury Theatre. *Movies*: Go Ask Alice, Law of the Land, Cotton Candy, Boris and Natasha (also dir.), And the Band Played On.

SMITH, DAVID R.: Archivist. b. Pasadena, CA, Oct. 13, 1940. e. Pasadena City Coll., A.A., 1960; U. of California, Berkeley, B.A. 1962, MLS 1963. Writer of numerous historical articles. Worked as librarian at Library of Congress, 1963–65 and as reference librarian, UCLA 1965–70 before becoming archivist for The Walt Disney Co. 1970–present. Exec. dir., The Manuscript Society, 1980–; member, Society of CA Archivists, Intl. Animated Film Society (ASIFA), American Assn. of State and Local History Received service award, ASIFA, and award of distinction, Manuscript Soc, 1983. Co-Author: The Ultimate Disney Trivia Book (1992).

SMITH, HOWARD K.: News commentator. b. Ferriday, LA, May 12, 1914. e. Tulane U., 1936; Heidelberg U., Germany; Oxford U., Rhodes scholarship. United Press, London, 1939; United Press Bureau, Copenhagen; United Press, Berlin, 1940; joined CBS News, Berlin corr., 1941. Reported on occupied Europe from Switzerland to 1944; covered Nuremberg trials, 1946; ret. to U.S., moderator, commentator or reporter, CBS Reports, Face the Nation, Eyewitness to History, The Great Challenge, numerous news specials (Emmy Award, 1960 for The Population Explosion). Sunday night news analysis. CBS News Washington corr., 1957; chief corr. & mgr., Washington Bureau, 1961; joined, ABC News, Jan. 1962. News and comment, ABC news. Anchorman and commentator, ABC Evening News. Author: Last Train from Berlin, 1942, The State of Europe, 1949. Washington, D.C.—The Story of Our Nation's Capital, 1967.

SMITH, HY: Executive. b. New York, NY, June 3, 1934. e. Baruch Sch., City Coll. of New York, B.B.A. Joined Paramount Pictures 1967, foreign ad.-pub coordinator; 1969-joined United Artists as foreign ad.-pub mgr., named intl. ad.-pub dir., 1970; named v.p.; intl. adv.-pub. 1976; Appointed vice pres. worldwide advertising, publicity and promotion, 1978; 1981, named first v.p., adv./pub./promo; 1982, joined Rastar Films as v.p.s., intl. project director for Annie. 1983, joined United Intl. Pictures as sr. v.p., adv/pub, based in London. 1984, named sr. v.p., mktg.

SMITH, JACLYN: Actress. b. Houston, TX, Oct. 26, 1947. Started acting while in high school and studied drama and psychology at Trinity U. in San Antonio. Appeared in many commercials as model.
PICTURES: The Adventurers, Bootleggers, Nightkill, Deja Vu.
TELEVISION: *Series*: Charlie's Angels, Christine Cromwell. *Guest*: McCloud, Get Christy Love, The Rookies, World of Disney, Switch. *Movies*: Probe, Switch, Charlie's Angels (pilot), Escape from Bogen County, The Users, Jacqueline Bouvier Kennedy, Rage of Angels, The Night They Saved Christmas, Sentimental Journey, Florence Nightingale, Rage of Angels: The Story Continues, Windmills of the Gods, The Bourne Identity, Settle the Score, Danielle Steel's Kaleidoscope, Lies Before Kisses, The Rape of Dr. Willis, In the Arms of a Killer, Nightmare in the Daylight, Love Can Be Murder.

SMITH, JOSEPH P.: Executive. b. Brooklyn, NY, March 28, 1921. e. Columbia U. Started career Wall Street; joined RKO Radio Pictures, served in sales and managerial posts; exec. vice-pres., Lippert Productions, Hollywood; vice pres., Telepictures, Inc., formed and pres., Cinema-Vue Corp.; pres., Pathe Pictures, Inc., Pathe News, Inc.

SMITH, KURTWOOD: Actor. b. New Lisbon, WI, July 3, 1942. Starred in Oscar-nominated short 12:01 P.M.
PICTURES: Roadie (debut, 1980), Zoot Suit, Going Berserk, Staying Alive, Flashpoint, Robocop, Rambo III, True Believer, Dead Poets Society, Heart of Dixie, Quick Change, Oscar, Company Business, Star Trek VI: The Undiscovered Country, Shadows and Fog, The Crush, Heart and Souls, Fortress, Boxing Helena.
TELEVISION: *Series*: The Renegades, The New Adventures of Beans Baxter. *Movies*: Murder in Texas, Missing Pieces, The Midnight Hour, International Airport, Deadly Messages, The Christmas Gift, Doorways. *Mini-Series*: North and South Book II, The Nightmare Years. *Guest*: Stir Crazy, Stingray, Newhart, 21 Jump Street, It's Garry Shandling's Show, The Famous Teddy Z, Big Wave Daves.
THEATRE: Plymouth Rock, The Price, Faces by Chekhov, Familiar Faces, Enemy of the People, The Debutante Ball (all in Calif.), The Lucky Spot (Williamston), Signature (Poughkeepsie).

SMITH, LANE: Actor. b. Memphis, TN, Apr. 29.
TELEVISION: *Series*: V, Kay O'Brien, Good Sports, Good and Evil. *Mini-Series*: Chiefs. *Movies*: A Death in Canaan, Crash, The Solitary Man, Disaster on the Coastliner, City in Fear, Gideon's Trumpet, A Rumor of War, The Georgia Peaches, Mark I Love You, Dark Night of the Scarecrow, Prime Suspect, Thou Shalt Not Kill, Special Bulletin, Something About Amelia, Dress Gray, The Final Days, False

Arrest, Duplicates. *Specials*: Displaced Person, Member of the Wedding.
PICTURES: Network, Honeysuckle Rose, Prince of the City, Frances, Red Dawn, Places in the Heart, Weeds, Prison, Race for Glory, Air America, My Cousin Vinny, The Mighty Ducks, The Distinguished Gentleman, Son-in-Law.
THEATRE: *NY*: Visions of Kerouac, Brechtesgarten, Glengarry Glen Ross (Drama Desk Award).

SMITH, DAME MAGGIE: D.B.E. C.B.E. Actress. b. Ilford, England, Dec. 28, 1934. Early career Oxford Playhouse. With the Old Vic 1959–60. Also with Stratford Ontario Shakespeare Fest. 1975–78, & 1980. Received C.B.E. 1970; D.B.E., 1990.
THEATER: Twelfth Night (debut, 1952), Cakes and Ale, New Faces of 1956 (NY debut, as comedienne), Share My Lettuce, The Stepmother, What Every Woman Knows, Rhinoceros, The Rehearsal, The Private Ear, The Public Eye, Mary Mary, The Recruiting Officer, Othello, The Master Builder, Hay Fever, Much Ado About Nothing, Black Comedy, Miss Julie, Trelawney of the Wells, The Beaux Stratagem, The Three Sisters, Hedda Gabler, Design for Living (L.A.), Private Lives (London & NY), Slap, Peter Pan, As You Like It, Macbeth, Night and Day (London & NY), Virginia, Way of the World, Lettice and Lovage (London & NY, Tony Award), The Importance of Being Earnest.
PICTURES: Nowhere to Go (debut, 1958), Go to Blazes, The V.I.P.s, The Pumpkin Eater, Young Cassidy, Othello, The Honey Pot, Hot Millions, The Prime of Miss Jean Brodie (Acad. Award, BAFTA Award, 1969), Oh What a Lovely War, Love and Pain, Travels with My Aunt, Murder by Death, Death on the Nile, California Suite (Acad. Award, supp. actress, 1978), Clash of the Titans, Quartet, Evil Under the Sun, The Missionary, Better Late Than Never, A Private Function (BAFTA Award), Lily in Love, A Room with a View, The Lonely Passion of Judith Hearne, Romeo-Juliet (voice), Hook, Sister Act, The Secret Garden, Sister Act 2.
TELEVISION: Much Ado About Nothing, Man and Superman, On Approval, Home and Beauty, Mrs. Silly, Bed Among the Lentils, Memento Mori, Suddenly Last Summer.

SMITH, MAURICE: Producer, Director, Writer. b. London, England, May 12, 1939. e. St. Ignatius Coll. Prior to entering m.p. industry, worked in bank in England, on newspaper in Canada, pool hustler, general contractor in Los Angeles, CA.
PICTURES: The Glory Stompers, Scream Free, Cycle Savages, Hard Trail, Diamond Stud, Love Swedish Style, November Children, How Come Nobody's On Our Side, Joys of Jezebel, Screwball Hotel, Grotesque (exec. prod.).

SMITH, ROGER: Actor, Producer. b. South Gate, CA, Dec. 18, 1932. m. actress-performer Ann Margret. e. U. of Arizona. Started career at age 7, one of the Meglin Kiddies, appearing at the Mayan Theater, Wilshire, Ebell. Sings, composes, American folk songs. Producer: Ann-Margret cabaret and theater shows.
PICTURES: No Time to Be Young, Crash Landing, Operation Madball, Man of a Thousand Faces, Never Steal Anything Small, Auntie Mame, Rogues Gallery.
TELEVISION: The Horace Heidt Show, Ted Mack Original Amateur Hour, 77 Sunset Strip (series), writer, ABC-TV.

SMITH, WILLIAM: Actor. b. Columbia, MO, May 24, 1932. e. Syracuse, U., BA; UCLA, MA.
PICTURES: Darker Than Amber, C.C. and Company, The Losers, Run, Angel, Run, Blood and Guts, Seven, Fast Company, No Knife, Twilight's Last Gleaming, The Frisco Kid, Any Which Way You Can, Rumble Fish, Red Dawn, Eye of the Tiger, Commando Squad, Moon in Scorpio, Hell Comes to Frogtown, Maniac Cop, Red Nights, Nam, B.O.R.N., Action U.S.A., Deadly Breed, Evil Altar, Jungle Assault, L.A. Vice, Slow Burn, Terror in Beverly Hills, Hell on the Battleground, Forgotten Heroes, Instant Karma, Empire of Ash, Emperor of the Bronx.
TELEVISION: *Mini-Series*: Rich Man Poor Man. *Series*: Laredo, Rich Man Poor Man: Book II. *Series*: Laredo, Rich Man Poor Man: Book II, Hawaii 5-0, Wildside. *Movies*: The Over-the-Hill Gang, Crowhaven Farm, The Rockford Files (pilot), The Sex Symbol, Death Among Friends, Manhunter, The Rebels, Wild Times, The Jerk Too.

SMITROVICH, BILL: Actor. b. Bridgeport, CT, May 16, 1947. e. Univ. of Bridgeport, Smith Col. Studied acting at Actors and Directors Lab.
TELEVISION: *Series*: Crime Story, Life Goes On. *Guest*: Miami Vice. *Movies*: Born Beautiful, Muggable Mary, Gregory K, Labor of Love: The Arlette Schweitzer Story.
PICTURES: A Little Sex, Without a Trace, Splash, Maria's Lovers, Key Exchange, Silver Bullet, Band of the Hand, Manhunter, A Killing Affair, Her Alibi, Renegades, Crazy People.
THEATRE: *Bdwy*: The American Clock. *Off-Bdwy*: Never Say Die, Frankie and Johnny in the Claire de Lune, Seks. *Regional*: Requeim for a Heavyweight, Food from Trash, Of Mice and Men, The Love Suicide at Schofield Barracks.

SMITS, JIMMY: Actor. b. New York, NY, July 9, 1955. e. Brooklyn Coll., B.A.; Cornell U., M.F.A. Worked as community organizer before acting with NY Shakespeare Fest. Public Theater.
THEATER: Hamlet (NY Shakespeare Fest., 1983), Little Victories, Buck, The Ballad of Soapy Smith.
PICTURES: Running Scared (debut, 1986), The Believers, Old Gringo, Vital Signs, Fires Within, Switch, Gross Misconduct.
TELEVISION: Series: L.A. Law (Emmy Award, 1990). Pilot: Miami Vice. Movies: Rockabye, The Highwayman, Dangerous Affection, Glitz, The Broken Cord, The Tommyknockers. Specials: The Other Side of the Border (narrator).

SMOLEN, DONALD E.: Executive. b. New York, NY, Aug. 10, 1923. e. NYU, 1943; Pratt Inst., 1947, Ecole Des Beaux Arts, 1949. Art dept. Fox, 1940–41; art dept. Kayton Spiero Advtg., 1942; illustrator designer, Gilbert Miller Studios 1946–49; free lance illustrator, designer, 1951–65 servicing such accounts as UA, Fox, Warner Bros., TWA, Ford Motors; dir. of adv., UA. Resigned 1974 to form own co., Donald E. Smolen and Associates, consultant for m.p. adv.; 1975 merged to form Smolen, Smith and Connolly, advertising and marketing consultants to m.p. industry. Created ad campaigns for All the Presidents' Men, Fiddler on the Roof, Rocky, Superman, Star Wars. 1987, joined newly formed distribution arm, Kings Road Entertainment.

SMOTHERS BROTHERS: Comedians, Singers.
SMOTHERS, DICK: b. New York, NY, Nov. 20, 1939. e. San Jose State College. Film debut: The Silver Bears (1978). On Bdwy in musical I Love My Wife (1978–79).
SMOTHERS, TOM: b. New York, NY, Feb. 2, 1937. e. San Jose State College. In films Get to Know Your Rabbit, The Silver Bears, There Goes the Bride, Serial, Pandemonium. On Bdwy in musical I Love My Wife (1978–79).
Began career as coffeehouse folk singers with a bit of comic banter mixed in. After success at some of hipper West Coast clubs, appeared on Jack Paar's Tonight Show, The Jack Benny Show and as regulars on Steve Allen's show, 1961. 1962–65 had a series of popular albums. After starring in a situation comedy show, they hosted their own variety program which became progressively controversial as its topical humor began to cover the political and social turmoil of the 1960s until it was canceled by CBS in 1969.
TELEVISION: The Steve Allen Show (1961), The Smothers Brothers Show (1965–66), The Smothers Brothers Comedy Hour (1967–69), The Smothers Brothers Show (1970, ABC), The Smothers Brothers Show (1975), Fitz and Bones, The Smothers Brothers Reunion (special, 1988), The Smothers Brothers Comedy Hour.

SNELL, PETER R. E.: Producer. b. Nov. 17, 1941. Entered industry 1967. Appt. head of prod. and man. dir. British Lion 1973. Joined Robert Stigwood group 1975. Returned to indep. prod., 1978; Hennessy. Appt. chief exec., Britannic Film & Television Ltd. 1985, purchased British Lion Film Prods., Ltd. from Thorn/EMI 1986–87. 1988: Chairman and chief executive British Lion.
PICTURES: Prod.: Winters Tale, Some May Live, A Month in the Country, Carnaby 68, Subterfuge, Julius Caesar, Goodbye Gemini, Antony and Cleopatra, The Wicker Man, Hennessy, Bear Island, Mother Lode, Lady Jane, Turtle Diary, A Prayer for the Dying.
TELEVISION: A Man For All Seasons (exec. prod.), Tears in the Rain, Treasure Island (exec. prod.), The Crucifer of Blood (exec. prod.), Death Train (prod.)

SNIPES, WESLEY: Actor. b. Orlando, FL, July 31, 1962. Raise in the Bronx, NY. e. SUNY/Purchase. Appeared in Michael Jackson video Bad.
PICTURES: Wildcats (debut, 1986), Streets of Gold, Critical Condition, Major League, Mo' Better Blues, King of New York, New Jack City, Jungle Fever, White Men Can't Jump, The Waterdance, Passenger 57, Boiling Point, Rising Sun, Demolition Man.
TELEVISION: Special: Vietnam War Stories (ACE Award, 1989).
THEATRE: Bdwy: The Boys of Winter, Death and the King's Horsemen, Execution of Justice.

SNODGRESS, CARRIE: Actress. b. Chicago, IL, Oct 27, 1945. e. Northern Illinois U. and M.A. degree from the Goodman Theatre. Plays include All Way Home, Oh What a Lovely War, Caesar and Cleopatra and Tartuffe (Sarah Siddons Award, 1966), The Price, Vanities, The Curse of the Starving Class.
PICTURES: Rabbit Run, Diary of a Mad Housewife (Acad. Award nom.), The Fury, The Attic, Homework, Trick or Treats, A Night in Heaven, Pale Rider, Murphy's Law, Blueberry Hill, The Chill Factor, Nowhere to Run, Across the Tracks, Blue Sky, The Ballad of Little Jo.
TELEVISION: Movies: The Whole World is Watching, Silent Night Lonely Night, The Impatient Heart, Love's Dark Ride, Fast Friends, The Solitary Man, Nadia, The Rose and the Jackal, Woman With a Past. Guest: The Outsider, The Virginian, Judd for the Defense, Medical Center, Marcus Welby, M.D.

SNOW, MARK: Composer. b. Brooklyn, NY, 1946. e. Juilliard School of Music, 1968. As co-founder and member of New York Rock 'n' Roll Ensemble, appeared with the Boston Pops, at Carnegie Hall concerts and on the college circuit in the 1960s and 1970s.
PICTURES: Skateboard, Something Short of Paradise, High Risk, Jake Speed.
TELEVISION: Series: The Rookies, Starsky and Hutch, The Gemini Man, Family, The San Pedro Beach Bums, The Love Boat, The Next Step Beyond, Vega$, Hart to Hart, When the Whistle Blows, Dynasty, Falcon Crest, Strike Force, Cagney and Lacey, T.J. Hooker, The Family Tree, Lottery!, Double Trouble, Crazy Like a Fox, Hometown. Mini-series: Blood and Orchids. Movies: The Boy in the Plastic Bubble, Overboard, The Return of the Mod Squad, Angel City, Games Mother Never Taught You, John Steinbeck's Winter of Our Discontent, Packin' It In, I Married a Centerfold, Something About Amelia, Challenge of a Lifetime, California Girls, I Dream of Jeannie: Fifteen Years Later, Not My Kid, The Lady From Yesterday, Beverly Hills Cowgirl Blues, Acceptable Risks, News at Eleven, The Girl Who Spelled Freedom (Emmy nom.), Murder By the Book, A Hobo's Christmas, The Father Clements Story, Still Crazy Like a Fox, Cracked Up, Roman Holiday, Pals, Murder Ordained, Louis L'Amour's Down the Long Hills, The Saint, The Return of Ben Casey, Bluegrass, Alone in the Neon Jungle, Those She Left Behind, Stuck With Each Other, Settle the Score, Archie: To Riverdale and Back Again, Child of the Night, Dead Reckoning, Follow Your Heart, The Girl Who Came Between Them, The Little Kidnappers, Miracle Landing, When He's Not a Stranger, Opposites Attract, Crash: The Mystery of Flight 1501, In the Line of Duty, The Marla Hanson Story, A Woman Scorned: The Betty Broderick Story, Highway Heartbreaker, Deliver Them From Evil: The Taking of Alta View, An American Story, Telling Secrets, The Man With 3 Wives, Born Too Soon, In the Line of Duty: Ambush in Waco. Specials: Day-to-Day Affairs, Vietnam War Story.

SNYDER, TOM: Newscaster, Show host. b. Milwaukee, WI, May 12, 1936. e. Marquette U. First job in news dept. of WRIT, Milwaukee. Subsequently with WSAV-TV, Savannah; WAII-TV, Atlanta; KTLA-TV, Los Angeles; and KYW-TV, Philadelphia, before moving to KNBC in L.A. in 1970 as anchorman for weeknight newscast. Named host of NBC-TV's Tomorrow program in Oct., 1973 (Emmy Award), and moved to NY in Dec., 1974, as anchorman of one-hour segment of NewsCenter 4. In Aug., 1975, inaugurated the NBC News Update, one-minute weeknight prime time news spot. Host for Tomorrow talk show, Tom Snyder Show (ABC Radio).

SOADY, WILLIAM C.: Executive. b. Toronto, Canada, Oct. 7, 1943. Career with Universal Pictures started in 1970 when named Toronto branch mgr.; promoted to v.p. & gen. sls. mgr. of Universal Film (Canada) in 1971. Promoted to v.p. & gen. sls. mgr., Universal Pictures, 1981, in New York, relocating to L.A. in 1981. In 1983 named pres. of Universal Pictures Distribution, new domestic dist. div. of Universal; resigned Sept., 1988. Named exec. v.p. distribution, Tri-Star Pictures, 1988. Pres. of distrib. , 1992.

SOAMES, RICHARD: Executive. b. London, England, June 6, 1936. Joined Film Finances Ltd. 1972; Appt. director Film Finances Ltd., 1977: Appt. man. dir. 1979. Appt. pres. Film Finances Canada Ltd. 1982: Appt. pres., Film Finances Inc. Also formed Doric Prods., Inc.
PICTURES: The Boss's Wife, The Principal, Honey, I Shrunk the Kids, Tap.

SOBLE, RON: Actor. b. Chicago, IL, March 28, 1932. e. U. of Michigan. Served U.S. Army, 11th Airborne, in Japan. Studied acting in New York and was member of Jose Quintero's Circle in the Square Players. Acted in such plays as Romeo and Juliet, Murder in the Cathedral, The Petrified Forest; prod. assoc. on TV series Suspense and Danger, and appeared in 56 series. Co-star in The Monroes TV show.
PICTURES: Navajo Run, Al Capone, The Cincinnati Kid, True Grit, Chisum, Joe Kidd, Papillon.

SODERBERGH, STEVEN: Director, Writer, Editor. b. Georgia, Jan. 14, 1963. First major professional job was shooting concert footage for rock group Yes for Grammy-winning video, 1986.
PICTURES: Director-Editor: Sex Lies and Videotape (debut, 1989; also s.p., sound; Cannes Fest. Palme d'Or Award; Acad. Award nom. for best s.p.), Kafka, King of the Hill (also s.p.).
TELEVISION: Series: Fallen Angels (The Quiet Room).

SOHMER, STEVE: Executive. b. 1942. 1977–82, v.p., adv./promo. CBS-TV. 1982, joined NBC as v.p. of adv./creative svcs. Promoted to exec. v.p., 1984. In 1985 joined Columbia Pictures as pres. & chief oper. officer. Resigned 1987 to head Steve Sohmer Inc., creative boutique & advertising agency. 1989, named pres. and CEO Nelson Television. Author of novel Favorite Son.

PICTURES: Leonard Part 6 (exec. prod. for Bill Cosby). TELEVISION: Favorite Son (exec. prod., s.p.).

SOKOLOW, DIANE: Executive. b. New York, NY. e. Temple U. m. Mel Sokolow. 1975, v.p., East Coast operations, for Lorimar; with Warner Bros. 1977–81; served as v.p. of East Coast production. Left to form The Sokolow Co. with husband, Mel, to produce films. 1982, returned to WB as v.p., East Coast prod. 1984, joined Motown Prods. as exec. v.p.; producer, MGM-UA 1986–87. Currently co-pres. Sokolow Co. with Mel Sokolow.
PICTURE: My Son's Brother (co-prod.).
TELEVISION: Exec. Prod.: Miles from Nowhere, Trial: The Price of Passion, Lady Against the Odds, Fallen Champ, Silent Cries.

SOLO, ROBERT H.: Producer. b. Waterbury, CT, Dec. 4, 1932. e. U. of Connecticut, BA. Early career as agent with Ashley-Famous; later production as exec. asst. to Jack Warner and Walter MacEwen at Warner Bros. 1971, named WB v.p., foreign production 1974, named exec. v.p., prod. at Burbank Studio. Now indep. prod.
PICTURES: Scrooge, The Devils (co-prod.), Invasion of the Body Snatchers, The Awakening, I The Jury, Bad Boys, Colors, Above the Law (exec. prod.), Winter People, Blue Sky, Car 54 Where Are You? Body Snatchers.

SOLOMON, T. G.: Executive. b. Jan. 5. e. Louisiana State U. Past chmn. and past pres. of the National Association of Theatre Owners. Past chief barker, Variety Tent 45; past pres., Mississippi Theatre Owners; past pres., Texas Theatre Owners; chmn., Louisiana Film Commission; past pres., Louisiana Theatres Assn. Chmn. of bd., Gulf States Theatres, Inc.

SOLT, ANDREW W.: Producer, Writer, Director. b. London, Eng. December 13, 1947. e. UCLA. Nephew of Andrew Peter Solt.
PICTURES: Imagine: John Lennon, This is Elvis, It Came From Hollywood.
TELEVISION: Honeymooners' Reunion, The Muppets. . .A Celebration of 30 Years, Cousteau: Mississippi, Happy Birthday Donald Duck, America Censored, Remembering Marilyn, Great Moments in Disney Animation, ET & Friends, Disney's DTV Monster Hits, Heroes of Rock 'n Roll, Bob Hope's Christmas Tours, Disney Goes To The Oscars, Cousteau: Oasis In Space Cousteau: Odyssey, The Rolling Stones, '89.

SOLTZ, CHARLENE E.: Executive. b. New London, CT. Director of public affairs for Motion Picture Association of America, Inc. and the Motion Picture Export Association of America, Inc.

SOMERS, SUZANNE: Actress. r.n. Suzanne Mahoney. b. San Bruno, CA, Oct. 16, 1946. e. Lone Mountain, San Francisco Coll. for Women. Pursued modeling career; worked as regular on Mantrap, syndicated talk show. Did summer stock and theatrical roles. Author: Touch Me Again, Some People Live More Than Others. Biggest TV success in Three's Company series (1977–81).
PICTURES: Bullitt, Daddy's Gone A-Hunting, Fools, American Graffiti, Magnum Force, Yesterday's Hero, Nothing Personal.
TELEVISION: Guest: One Day at a Time, Lotsa Luck, The Rockford Files, Starsky & Hutch, The Rich Little Show, Battle of the Network Stars, Love Boat, Series: Three's Company, She's the Sheriff, Step by Step. Movies: Sky Heist, It Happened at Lakewood Manor (Ants), Happily Ever After, Zuma Beach, Rich Men Single Women, Keeping Secrets, Exclusive. Mini-Series: Hollywood Wives. Specials: Us Against the World, Disney's Totally Minnie.

SOMMER, ELKE: Actress. r.n. Elke Schletz. b. Berlin, Germany, Nov. 5, 1940. To Britain 1956. Ent. films in Germany, 1958, and since made films in Germany and Italy incl. Friend of the Jaguar, Traveling Luxury, Heaven and Cupid, Ship of the Dead. 1960: made debut in British films.
PICTURES: Don't Bother to Knock, The Victors, The Prize, Love the Italian Way, A Shot in the Dark, The Art of Love, The Money Trap, The Oscar, Boy Did I Get a Wrong Number, The Venetian Affair, Deadlier than the Male, Frontier Hellcat. Under contract to ABPC; The Corrupt Ones, The Wicked Dreams of Paula Schultz, They Came to Rob Las Vegas, The Wrecking Crew, Baron Blood, Zeppelin, Percy, Ten Little Indians, Lisa and the Devil, The Prisoner of Zenda, A Nightingale Sang in Berkeley Square, The Net, The Double McGuffin, Exit Sunset Blvd., The Man in Pyjamas, The Astral Factor (Invisible Strangler), Lily in Love, Himmelsheim, Severed Ties.
TELEVISION: Movies: Probe, Stunt Seven, The Top of the Hill, Inside the Third Reich, Jenny's War, Anastasia: The Mystery of Anya. Mini-Series: Peter the Great.

SOMMER, JOSEF: Actor. b. Greifswald, Germany, June 26, 1934. Raised in North Carolina. e. Carnegie-Mellon U. Studied at American Shakespeare Festival in Stratford, CT, 1962–64. US Army, 1958–60. NY stage debut in Othello, 1970.

PICTURES: Dirty Harry (debut, 1971), Man on a Swing, The Front, Close Encounters of the Third Kind, Oliver's Story, Hide in Plain Sight, Absence of Malice, Reds, Rollover, Hanky Panky, Still of the Night, Sophie's Choice (narrator), Independence Day, Silkwood, Iceman, Witness, D.A.R.Y.L., Target, The Rosary Murders, Chances Are, Dracula's Widow, Forced March, Bloodhounds of Broadway, Shadows and Fog, The Mighty Ducks.
TELEVISION: Series: Hothouse, Under Cover. Specials: Morning Becomes Electra, The Scarlet Letter, Saigon. Movies: Too Far to Go, Doctor Franken, The Henderson Monster, Sparkling Cyanide, The Betty Ford Story, A Special Friendship, Bridge to Silence, The Bionic Showdown: The Six Million Dollar Man and the Bionic Woman, Money Power Murder, Spy Games, Hostages, An American Story, Citizen Cohn, Hostages. Mini-Series: The Kennedys of Massachusetts, A Woman Named Jackie.

SONDHEIM, STEPHEN: Composer, Lyricist. b. New York, NY, March 22, 1930. e. Williams Coll. Writer for Topper TV series, 1953. Wrote incidental music for The Girls of Summer (1956), Invitation to a March (1961), Twigs (1971). Winner of 6 Grammy Awards: Cast Albums 1970, 1973, 1980 and song of the year 1975. Named Visiting Prof. of Contemporary Theater, Oxford U. 1990.
THEATER: Lyrics only: West Side Story, Gypsy, Do I Hear a Waltz?. Music and lyrics: A Funny Thing Happened on the Way to the Forum, Anyone Can Whistle, Company (Tony Award, 1971), Follies (Tony, 1972), A Little Night Music (Tony, 1973), The Frogs, Candide (new lyrics for revival), Pacific Overtures, Sweeney Todd, (Tony, 1979), Merrily We Roll Along, Sunday in the Park with George (Pulitzer Prize, 1985), Into the Woods. (Tony, 1988), Assassins. Theater anthologies of his songs: Side By Side By Sondheim; Marry Me a Little, Putting It Together.
PICTURES: West Side Story (lyrics), Gypsy (lyrics), A Funny Thing Happened on the Way to the Forum (music, lyrics), The Last of Sheila (s.p.), Stavisky (score), A Little Night Music (music, lyrics), Reds (score), Dick Tracy (music, lyrics; Acad. Award for best song: Sooner or Later)
TELEVISION: Special: Evening Primrose (music, lyrics; ABC Stage '67).

SORDI, ALBERTO: Actor. b. Rome, Italy, June 15, 1919. Won an Oliver Hardy sound-a-like contest at 13. Worked in Italian music halls before making film debut in 1938. Appeared in Fellini's early films. One of Italy's most popular film comedians, he has also had a successful career on TV with own series.
PICTURES: La Principessa Tarakanova (1938), I Vitelloni, The Sign of Venus, A Farewell to Arms, La Gran Guerra, The Best of Enemies, Tutti a Casa, Il Mafioso, Il Diavolo (To Bed or Not to Bed), Those Magnificent Men in Their Flying Machines, Le Streghe, Un Italiano in America, Viva Italia, Riusciranno i Nostri Eroi, Le Termoin, I Know That You Know That I Know (also dir.), A Taste of Life, Acquitted for Having Committed the Deed.

SORVINO, PAUL: Actor. b. New York, NY, 1939. Acted on Bdwy.; broke into films with Where's Poppa in 1970.
THEATER: Bajour, An American Millionaire, The Mating Dance, King Lear, That Championship Season.
PICTURES: Where's Poppa? (debut, 1970), The Panic in Needle Park, Made for Each Other, A Touch of Class, Day of the Dolphin, The Gambler, Shoot It Black Shoot It Blue, I Will I Will . . . For Now, Oh God, Bloodbrothers, Slow Dancing in the Big City, The Brink's Job, Lost and Found, Cruising, Reds, I The Jury, That Championship Season, Off the Wall, Very Close Quarters, Turk 182, The Stuff, A Fine Mess, Vasectomy, Dick Tracy, GoodFellas, The Rocketeer, Life in the Food Chain (Age Isn't Everything), The Firm.
TELEVISION: Series: We'll Get By, Bert D'Angelo: Superstar, The Oldest Rookie, Law and Order. Mini-Series: Seventh Avenue, Chiefs. Movies: Tell Me Where It Hurts, It Couldn't Happen to a Nicer Guy, Dummy, A Question of Honor, My Mother's Secret Life, With Intent to Kill, Surviving, Don't Touch My Daughter. Guest: Moonlighting. Special: The Last Mile.

SOTHERN, ANN: Actress. r.n. Harriet Lake. b. Valley City, ND, Jan. 22, 1909. e. Washington U. p. Annette Yde-Lake, opera singer. In m.p. since 1927. Star of 10 Maisie movies in series from 1939–47. Has recently become noted painter.
PICTURES: Broadway Nights (debut in bit part, 1927), Hearts in Exile, The Show of Shows, Hold Everything, Whoopee, Doughboys, Broadway Through a Keyhole, Let's Fall in Love, Melody in Spring, The Party's Over, The Hellcat, Blind Date, Kid Millions, Folies Bergere, Eight Bells, Hooray for Love, The Girl Friend, Grand Exit, You May Be Next, Hell Ship Morgan, Don't Gamble With Love, My American Wife, Walking on Air, The Smartest Girl in Town, Dangerous Number, Fifty Roads to Town, There Goes My Girl, Super Sleuth, Danger: Love at Work, There Goes the Groom, She's Got Everything, Trade Winds, Hotel For Women, Maisie (and subsequent series of 9 other films), Fast and Furious, Joe

and Ethel Turp Call on the President, Brother Orchid, Dulcy, Lady Be Good, Panama Hattie, Cry Havoc, Thousands Cheer, Three Hearts for Julia, April Showers, Words and Music, The Judge Steps Out, A Letter to Three Wives, Shadow on the Wall, Nancy Goes to Rio, Blue Gardenia, Lady in a Cage, The Best Man, Sylvia, Chubasco, The Killing Kind, Golden Needles, Crazy Mama, The Manitou, The Little Dragons, The Whales of August (Acad. Award. nom).
TELEVISION: *Series:* Private Secretary, Ann Sothern Show, My Mother The Car (voice of the car). *Movies:* The Outsider, Congratulations It's a Boy, A Death of Innocence, The Weekend Nun, The Great Man's Whiskers, Letter to Three Wives. *Mini-Series:* Captain and the Kings.

SOUL, DAVID: Actor. r.n. David Solberg. b. Chicago, IL, Aug. 28, 1943.
TELEVISION: *Series:* Here Come the Brides, Owen Marshall—Counselor at Law, Starsky and Hutch, Casablanca, Yellow Rose, Unsub. *Movies:* The Disappearance of Flight 412, Starsky and Hutch (pilot), Little Ladies of the Night, Salem's Lot, Swan Song (also co-prod.), Rage, Homeward Bound, The Manions of America, World War III, Through Naked Eyes, The Fifth Missile, Harry's Hong Kong, In the Line of Duty: The FBI Murders, Prime Target, So Proudly We Hail, Bride in Black, A Cry in the Wild, The Taking of Peggy Ann, Perry Mason: The Case of the Fatal Framing, Grave Secrets: The Legacy of Hilltop Drive.
PICTURES: Johnny Got His Gun, Magnum Force, Dog Pound Shuffle, The Hanoi Hilton, Appointment with Death.

SPACEK, SISSY: Actress. r.n. Mary Elizabeth Spacek. b. Quitman, TX, Dec. 25, 1949. m. director Jack Fisk. Cousin of actor Rip Torn. Attended acting classes in New York under Lee Strasberg. Had bit role in Andy Warhol's Trash. Worked as set decorator on films Death Game, Phantom of the Paradise.
PICTURES: Prime Cut, Ginger in the Morning, Badlands, Carrie, Welcome to L.A., 3 Women, Heart Beat, Coal Miner's Daughter (Acad. Award, 1980), Raggedy Man, Missing, The Man With Two Brains (voice), The River, Marie, Violets Are Blue, 'night Mother, Crimes of the Heart, The Long Walk Home, JFK, Hard Promises.
TELEVISION: *Movies:* The Girls of Huntington House, The Migrants, Katherine, A Private Matter. *Special:* Verna: USO Girl. *Guest:* The Rookies, The Waltons.

SPACEY, KEVIN: Actor. b. South Orange, NJ, July 26, 1959. Raised in southern CA. e. L.A. Valley Coll., appearing in stage productions as well as stand-up comedy clubs, before attending Juilliard Sch. of Drama. Has appeared in numerous regional and repertory productions including the Kennedy Center (The Seagull), Williamstown Theatre Fest. and Seattle Rep. Theatre, and with New York Shakespeare Fest.
THEATER: Henry IV Part I, The Robbers, Barbarians, Ghosts, Hurlyburly, Long Day's Journey into Night (with Jack Lemmon), National Anthems, Lost in Yonkers (Tony Award, 1991), Playland.
PICTURES: Heartburn (debut, 1986), Rocket Gibraltar, Working Girl, See No Evil Hear No Evil, Dad, A Show of Force, Henry and June, Glengarry Glen Ross, Consenting Adults.
TELEVISION: *Specials:* Long Day's Journey into Night, Darrow (Amer. Playhouse). *Movies:* The Murder of Mary Phagan, Fall from Grace, When You Remember Me. *Series:* Wiseguy. *Guest:* L.A. Law.

SPADER, JAMES: Actor. b. Boston suburbs, MA, Feb. 7, 1960. e. Phillips Academy. Studied acting at Michael Chekhov Studio. Has worked as soda jerk, truck driver and stable boy between acting jobs.
PICTURES: Endless Love (debut, 1981), The New Kids, Tuff Turf, Pretty in Pink, Mannequin, Baby Boom, Less Than Zero, Wall Street, Jack's Back, The Rachel Papers, Sex Lies and Videotape (Cannes Fest. Award, 1989), Bad Influence, White Palace, True Colors, Storyville, Bob Roberts, The Music of Chance, Wolf.
TELEVISION: *Series:* The Family Tree. *Movies:* Cocaine: One Man's Seduction, A Killer in the Family, Starcrossed, Family Secrets. *Pilot:* Diner.

SPANO, VINCENT: Actor. b. New York, NY, Oct. 18, 1962. While attending Stuyvesant H.S. made stage debut at 14 in The Shadow Box (Long Wharf and Bdwy).
THEATER: The Shadow Box, Balm in Gilead.
PICTURES: Over the Edge (debut, 1979), The Double McGuffin, The Black Stallion Returns, Baby It's You, Rumblefish, Alphabet City, Maria's Lovers, Creator, Good Morning Babylon, And God Created Woman, 1753: Venetian Red, High Frequency (Aquarium), Oscar, City of Hope, Alive, Indian Summer.
TELEVISION: *Series:* Search for Tomorrow. *Movies:* The Gentleman Bandit, Senior Trip, Blood Ties, Afterburn.

SPEARS, JR., HAROLD T.: Executive. b. Atlanta, GA, June 21, 1929. e. U. of Georgia, 1951. With Floyd Theatres, Lakeland, FL, since 1953; now pres.

SPECKTOR, FREDERICK: Executive. b. Los Angeles, CA, April 24, 1933. e. U. of Southern California, UCLA. M.P. agent, Ashley Famous Agency, 1962–64; Artists Agency Corp., 1964–68; exec. M.P. dept., William Morris Agency, 1968–78; exec. Creative Artists Agency, 1978–present. Trustees Council, Education First, bd. of dirs., Amer. Jewish Committee.

SPELLING, AARON: Executive. b. Dallas, TX, Apr. 22, 1928. Father of actress Tori Spelling. Was actor/writer before becoming producer at Four Star in 1957. In 1967, formed Thomas/Spelling Productions to produce TV series and movies, including Mod Squad. In 1969, formed his own co., Aaron Spelling Productions. In 1972, partnered with Leonard Goldberg to produce The Rookies, Charlie's Angels, Fantasy Island, Starsky and Hutch, Hart to Hart, T.J. Hooker, Family, and under own company banner: The Love Boat, Vega$, Dynasty, Matt Houston, Hotel, The Colbys, Life with Lucy, Nightingales, HeartBeat, Beverly Hills 90210, The Heights, Melrose Place, The Round Table, Winnetka Road, and over 111 movies for television.
PICTURES: Mr. Mom (exec. prod.), Surrender, Three O'Clock High (exec. prod.), Cross My Heart (co-exec. prod.), Satisfaction (co-prod.), Loose Cannons, Soapdish.
RECENT TELEVISION: *Exec. Prod.:* The Three Kings, Nightingales, Day One (Emmy Award), Rich Men Single Women, The Love Boat: The Valentine Voyage, Jailbirds, Back to the Streets of San Francisco, Grass Roots, Terror on Track 9.

SPENGLER, PIERRE: Producer. b. Paris, France, 1947. Went on stage at 15; returned to language studies at Alliance Française. Entered film industry as production runner and office boy. Teamed for first time with friend Ilya Salkind on The Light at the Edge of the World, produced by Alexander Salkind.
PICTURES: Bluebeard, The Three Musketeers, The Four Musketeers, Crossed Swords, Superman, Superman II, Superman III, Santa Claus: The Movie, The Return of the Musketeers.

SPENSER, JEREMY: Actor. b. Ceylon, 1937; e. Downshill Sch., Farnham, England. Ent. films 1947 in Anna Karenina.
PICTURES: It's Great To Be Young, The Prince and the Showgirl, Wonderful Things, Ferry to Hong Kong, Roman Spring of Mrs. Stone, Vengeance, King and Country, He Who Rides a Tiger, Fahrenheit 451.

SPHEERIS, PENELOPE: Director. b. New Orleans, LA, 1945. e. UCLA. Film Sch., MFA.
PICTURES: Real Life (prod. only). *Director:* The Decline of Western Civilization (also prod., s.p.), Suburbia (also s.p.), The Boys Next Door, Summer Camp Nightmare (s.p. only), Hollywood Vice Squad, Dudes, The Decline of Western Civilization—Part II: The Metal Years, Wedding Band (actress only), Wayne's World, The Beverly Hillbillies.
TELEVISION: Saturday Night Live (prod. only), Danger Theatre (co-creator, dir., co-writer). *Movie:* Prison Stories: Women on the Inside (New Chicks).

SPIEGEL, LARRY: Producer, Writer, Director. b. Brooklyn, NY. e. Ohio U. With CBS-TV; Benton & Bowles; Wells, Rich, Green; BBDO. Now heads Appledown Films, Inc.
PICTURES: Hail (s.p.), Book of Numbers (s.p.), Death Game (prod.), Stunts (prod.), Spree (dir./s.p.), Phobia (prod.), Remo Williams: The Adventure Begins (prod.), Dove Against Death (prod.).
TELEVISION: Alexander (writer, prod.), Incredible Indelible Magical Physical Mystery Trip (writer), Bear That Slept Through Christmas (writer), Never Fool With A Gypsy Ikon (writer), Mystery Trip Through Little Red's Head (writer), Planet of The Apes (animated; writer), Jan Stephenson Golf Video (prod.), Remo Williams (pilot ABC;· prod.).

SPIELBERG, STEVEN: Director, Producer. b. Cincinnati, OH, Dec. 18, 1947. e. California State Coll. m. actress Kate Capshaw. Made home movies as child; completed first film with story and actors at 12 yrs. old in Phoenix. At 13 won film contest for 40-min. war movie, Escape to Nowhere. At 16 made 140-min. film, Firelight. At California State Coll. made five films. First professional work, Amblin', 20 min. short which led to signing contract with Universal Pictures at age 20. Formed own co. Amblin Entertainment headquartered at Universal Studios. Received Irving Thalberg Memorial Award, 1987.
PICTURES: *Director:* The Sugarland Express (also story), Jaws, Close Encounters of The Third Kind (also s.p.), 1941, Raiders of the Lost Ark, E.T. The Extra-Terrestrial (also co-prod.), Twilight Zone—The Movie (sequence dir.; also co-exec. prod.), Indiana Jones and the Temple of Doom, The Color Purple (also co-prod.), Empire of the Sun (also co-prod.), Indiana Jones and the Last Crusade, Always (also co-prod.), Hook, Jurassic Park, Schindler's List (also co-prod.). *Co-Exec. Prod.:* I Wanna Hold Your Hand, Used Cars, Continental Divide, Gremlins (also cameo), The Goonies, Back to the Future, Young Sherlock Holmes, The Money Pit, An American Tail, Innerspace, Batteries Not Included, Who Framed Roger Rabbit, The Land Before Time, Dad, Back to

the Future Part II, Joe Versus the Volcano, Back to the Future Part III, Gremlins 2: The New Batch, Arachnophobia, Cape Fear, An American Tail: Fievel Goes West, The Flintstones. *Co-Prod.-Story-Screenplay:* Poltergeist. *Actor only:* The Blues Brothers, Listen Up: The Lives of Quincy Jones.

TELEVISION: *Series episodes:* Columbo, Owen Marshall: Counsellor-at-Law, The Pyschiatrist. *Movies:* Night Gallery (co-dir.), Duel, Something Evil, Savage. *Exec. Prod.:* Amazing Stories (also dir. of 2 episodes), Tiny Toon Adventures (Emmy Award, 1991), Class of '61 (movie), Family Dog (series), seaQuest DSV (series).

SPIKINGS, BARRY: Executive. b. Boston, England, Nov. 23, 1939. Ent. m.p. ind. 1973. Joint man. dir. British Lion Films Ltd., 1975. Appt. jnt. man. dir. EMI Films Ltd. 1977. 1979, appt. chmn. & chief exec., EMI Film & Theatre Corp.; chmn. & chief exec, EMI Films, Ltd., chmn. EMI Cinemas, Ltd.; chmn., Elstree Studios, Ltd.; Chmn. EMI-TV Programs, Inc., 1980; appt. chmn. chief exec., EMI Films Group, Jan. 1982; June, 1985 Barry Spikings Productions Inc. (U.S.A.); June, 1985 became director Galactic Films Inc. (with Lord Anthony Rufus Issacs); Oct., 1986, acquired Embassy Home Entertainment from Coca Cola Co., renamed Nelson Entertainment Inc., appointed pres. and chief operating officer. Sept., 1992, Pleskow/Spikings Partnership, film prod. and distrib. partnership with Eric Pleskow.

PICTURES: *Prod.:* Conduct Unbecoming, The Man Who Fell to Earth, The Deer Hunter, Texasville. *Exec. prod.:* Convoy.

SPINETTI, VICTOR: Actor. b. South Wales, Sept. 2, 1933. e. Monmouth School. Entered industry in 1955. Appeared on Broadway in Oh! What a Lovely War winning 1965 Tony Award and Theatre World Award.

PICTURES: A Hard Day's Night, The Wild Affair, Help!, The Taming of the Shrew, Can Hieronymus Merkin Ever Forget Mercy Humppe and Find True Happiness?, Under Milk Wood, The Return of the Pink Panther, The Krays.

THEATRE: *London:* Expresso Bongo, Candide, Make Me an Offer, Oh What a Lovely War, The Odd Couple, Cat Among the Pigeons, etc.

TELEVISION: The Magical Mystery Tour, Vincent Van Gogh, Paradise Club, The Attic.

SPIRA, STEVEN S.: Executive. b. New York, NY, Mar. 25, 1955. e. City Coll. of New York; Benjamin Cardozo Sch. of Law. Associated 10 years with N.Y. law firm, Monasch, Chazen & Stream. 1984, joined 20th Century Fox as sr. counsel; 1985, to Warner Bros. Now WB sr. v.p., theatrical business affairs.

SPITZ, JAMES R.: Executive. b. Milwaukee, WI, Dec. 4, 1940. Began career in industry 1962 with Warner Bros., working way thru sls. dept. and holding various positions such as booker and office mgr. in New York, San Francisco, Salt Lake City, Seattle and Kansas City. Appt. branch mgr. of WB Seattle-Portland branch; then L.A. branch mgr. Worked at United Artists 1972–77, first as L.A. branch mgr. and then western div. mgr. Joined Avco Embassy as asst. gen. sls. mgr., 1979. In 1980 left to go to Columbia Pictures as v.p. & gen. sls. mgr. In 1981 promoted to pres. of Columbia Pictures' domestic distribution.

SPIVAK, LAWRENCE E.: TV Producer, Consultant. b. New York, NY, June 11, 1900. e. AB, Harvard U. LL.D. (hon.) Wilberforce U.; Litt. D. (hon.) Suffolk U. L.H.D. (hon.) Tampa U. Began as bus. mgr., Antiques Mag., 1921–30; asst. to the pub., Hunting and Fishing, Nat. Sportsman mags., 1930–33; bus. mgr., American Mercury, 1934–39; pub., 1939–44; editor, pub., 1944–50; founder, 1941, pub. until 1954, of Ellery Queen's Mystery Mag., The Mag. of Fantasy and Science Fiction; Founder, American Mercury Library (Paperback Books) 1937; Mercury Mystery Books, Bestseller Mysteries, Jonathan Press Books; originator, co-founder, producer, moderator, program, Meet the Press (radio 1945, TV 1947). Recipient two Peabody Awards. Winner of Emmy Award for outstanding achievement in Coverage of Special Events and Honor Award from U. of Missouri for Distinguished Service in Journalism. Originated 1st series of Paperback Books in 1943 for Armed Services, which was forerunner of "The Armed Services Edition."

SPODICK, ROBERT C.: Exhibitor. b. New York, NY, Dec. 3, 1919. e. City Coll. of New York, 1940; ent. NYC m.p. ind. as errand boy Skouras Park Plaza, Bronx 1932–33; reel boy, asst. mgr., Loew's Theatres; mgr., Little Carnegie and other art theatres; exploitation man, United Artists. Acquired Lincoln, New Haven art house in 1945 in partnership with cousin Leonard E. Sampson; developed Nutmeg Theatre circuit, which was sold in 1968 to Robert Smerling. Beginning in 1970, built Groton, CT., Cinemas I and II; Norwich Cinemas I and II, Mystic Village Cinemas I, II and III, and Westerley Triple Cinemas in RI as Gemini Cinema Circuit in partnership with Sampson and William Rosen. Gemini sold to Interstate Theatres, 1986. With Sampson presently operates York Square I & II and The New Lincoln in New Haven. Pres., Allied of CT, 1962–64; Pres. NATO of Conn. 1968–73. Past

Chmn. Exec. Comm., CT Ass'n of Theatre Owners, and active member.

SPOTTISWOODE, ROGER: Director. b. England. Film editor of TV commercials and documentaries before turning to direction.

PICTURES: *Editor:* Straw Dogs, The Getaway, Pat Garrett and Billy the Kid, Hard Times, The Gambler, Who'll Stop the Rain? (assoc. prod.), Baby (exec. prod.). *Director:* Terror Train, The Pursuit of D.B. Cooper, Under Fire, The Best of Times, Shoot to Kill, Turner & Hooch, Air America, Stop Or My Mom Will Shoot.

TELEVISION: *Movies:* The Renegades, The Last Innocent Man, Third Degree Burn, And the Band Played On. *Special:* Time Flies When You're Alive.

SPRADLIN, G.D.: Actor. b. Daylight Township, Garvin County, OK, Aug. 31, 1920. e. Univ. of Oklahoma—doctor of Juris Prudence (1948). Started career as lawyer, became Independent Oil Producer. Active in local politics before turning to acting. Joined Oklahoma Repertory Theatre in 1964.

PICTURES: Will Penny (debut, 1968), Number One, Zabriskie Point, Monte Walsh, Tora! Tora! Tora!, The Hunting Party, The Godfather Part II, MacArthur, One on One, North Dallas Forty, Apocalypse Now, The Formula, Wrong Is Right, The Lords of Discipline, Tank, The War of the Roses.

TELEVISION: *Series:* Rich Man Poor Man Book II. *Mini-Series:* Space, Dream West, Nutcracker: Money Madness and Murder, Robert Kennedy and His Times, War and Remembrance. *Movies:* Dial Hot Line, Sam Hill: Who Killed the Mysterious Mr. Foster?, Oregon Trail, Maneaters Are Loose!, And I Alone Survived, Jayne Mansfield Story, Resting Place, Shoot First: A Cop's Vengeance, Telling Secrets.

SPRINGER, PAUL D.: Executive. e. Brooklyn Law Sch. Served as assoc. for N.Y. law firm, Johnson and Tannebaum. Later with legal dept. of Columbia Pictures. 1970, joined Paramount Pictures N.Y. legal dept. 1970; promoted to v.p. Theatrical Distrib. Counsel, 1979; promoted to sr. v.p., chief resident counsel, 1987, promoted to sr. v.p.s, asst. general counsel responsible for all legal functions for Paramount's distribution and marketing depts. Mem., NY and California Bars.

SPRINGFIELD, RICK: Actor, Singer, Songwriter. b. Sydney, Australia, Aug. 23, 1949.

PICTURES: Battlestar Galactica, Hard to Hold (act., addl. music).

TELEVISION: *Series:* General Hospital, Human Target. *Specials:* An Evening at the Improv, Countdown '81. *Movies:* Nick Knight, Dead Reckoning.

STACK, ROBERT: Actor. b. Los Angeles, CA, Jan. 13, 1919. e. U. of Southern California. In U.S. Armed Forces (Navy), W.W.II. Studied acting at Henry Duffy School of Theatre 6 mo. then signed a contract with Universal. National skeet champion at age 16. Autobiography: Straight Shooting.

PICTURES: First Love (debut, 1939), When the Daltons Rode, Mortal Storm, Little Bit of Heaven, Nice Girl?, Badlands of Dakota, To Be or Not To Be, Eagle Squadron, Men of Texas, Fighter Squadron, Date With Judy, Miss Tatlock's Millions, Mr. Music, Bullfighter and the Lady, My Outlaw Brother, Bwana Devil, War Paint, Conquest of Cochise, Sabre Jet, Iron Glove, High & the Mighty, House of Bamboo, Good Morning Miss Dove, Great Day in the Morning, Written on the Wind (Acad. Award nom.), The Gift of Love, The Tarnished Angels, John Paul Jones, Last Voyage, The Caretakers, Is Paris Burning?, The Corrupt Ones, Story of a Woman, 1941, Airplane!, Uncommon Valor, Big Trouble, Transformers (voice), Plain Clothes, Caddyshack II, Dangerous Curves, Joe Versus the Volcano.

TELEVISION: *Series:* The Untouchables (Emmy Award, 1960), The Name of the Game, Most Wanted, Strike Force, Unsolved Mysteries (host), Final Appeal (host). *Guest:* Playhouse 90 (Panic Button). *Movies:* The Strange and Deadly Occurance, Adventures of the Queen, Murder on Flight 502, Most Wanted (pilot), Undercover With the KKK (narrator), Midas Valley, Perry Mason: The Case of the Sinister Spirit, The Return of Eliot Ness. *Mini-Series:* George Washington, Hollywood Wives.

STAHL, AL: Executive. b. July 3, 1916. Syndicated newspaper cartoonist; asst. animator, Max Fleischer, gag ed. Terrytoons; U.S. Signal Corps; opened own studios, 1946; prod. first animated TV cartoon show; pres., Animated Prod., prod. live and animated commercials; member of bd. NTFC. Developed and built first animation camera and stand, 1950. Designed and produced opening animation for The Honeymooners, The Electric Company, Saturday Night Live. Produced over 5,000 tv spots. Prod. 50 min. documentary War and Pieces for U.S. Army Commandy of War in the Gulf, 1991.

STALLONE, SYLVESTER: Actor, Writer, Director. b. New York, NY, July 6, 1946. After high school taught at American Coll. of Switzerland instructing children of career diplomats, young royalty, etc. Returned to U.S. in 1967 and studied drama at U. of Miami, 1969. Came to New York to seek acting career, taking part-time jobs, including usher for Walter Reade Theatres. Then turned to writing, selling several TV scripts.

PICTURES: Party at Kitty and Studs, Bananas, Rebel (A Man Called Rainbo), The Lords of Flatbush (also co-s.p.), The Prisoner of 2nd Avenue, Capone, Death Race 2000, Farewell My Lovely, Cannonball, Rocky (also s.p.; Acad. Award noms. for best actor & s.p.), F.I.S.T. (also co-s.p.), Paradise Alley (also s.p., dir.), Rocky II (also s.p., dir.), Nighthawks, Victory, Rocky III (also s.p., dir.), First Blood (also co-s.p.), Staying Alive (cameo; also dir., prod., co-s.p.), Rhinestone (also co-s.p.), Rambo: First Blood Part II (also co-s.p.), Rocky IV (also dir., s.p.), Cobra (also s.p.), Over the Top (also co-s.p.), Rambo III (also co-s.p.), Lock Up, Tango and Cash, Rocky V (also s.p.), Oscar, Stop Or My Mom Will Shoot, Cliffhanger (also co-s.p.), Demolition Man.

TELEVISION: Guest: Kojak, Police Story, Dream On.

STAMOS, JOHN: Actor. b. Cypress, CA, Aug. 19, 1963. Landed role of Blackie Parrish on daytime serial General Hospital in 1982. Has toured with his own band John Stamos and the Bad Boyz.

TELEVISION: Series: General Hospital, Dreams, You Again?, Full House. Movies: Daughter of the Streets, Captive.

PICTURE: Born to Ride.

STAMP, TERENCE: Actor. b. London, England, July 23, 1939. Stage experience including Alfie on Broadway. Recent stage: Dracula, The Lady from the Sea, Airborne Symphony.

PICTURES: Billy Budd (debut 1962, Acad. Award nom.), Term of Trial, The Collector (best actor award, Cannes, 1965), Modesty Blaise, Far from the Madding Crowd, Poor Cow, Blue, Teorema, Spirits of the Dead, The Mind of Mr. Soames, A Season in Hell, Hu-Man, The Divine Nymph, Strip-Tease, Superman, Meetings with Remarkable Men, Together?, Superman II, Monster Island, Death in the Vatican, The Hit, The Company of Wolves, Link, Legal Eagles, The Sicilian, Wall Street, Young Guns, Alien Nation, Stranger in the House (also dir., co-s.p.), Genuine Risk, Beltenebros, The Real McCoy.

STANDER, LIONEL: Actor. b. New York, NY, Jan. 11, 1908. e. coll. N.Y. stage, 1952. On TV in Hart to Hart.

PICTURES: Scoundrel, Page Miss Glory, Gay Deception, Music Goes 'Round, Mr. Deeds Goes to Town, A Star Is Born, Meet Nero Wolfe, Guadalcanal Diary, Big Show-Off, Specter of the Rose, In Old Sacramento, Kid from Brooklyn, Gentleman Joe Palooka, Mad Wednesday, Call Northside 777, Unfaithfully Yours, Trouble Makers, Two Gals and a Guy, St. Benny the Dip, The Loved One, Promise Her Anything, Cul de Sac, A Dandy in Aspic, Once Upon a Time in the West, The Gang That Couldn't Shoot Straight, Treasure Island, Pulp, The Black Bird, The Cassandra Crossing, New York New York, Matilda, 1941, The Squeeze, Transformers (voice), Wicked Stepmother, Cookie, Joey Takes a Cab.

TELEVISION: Series: Hart to Hart. Pilots: The Sunshine Boys, Time of Their Lives.

STANFILL, DENNIS C: Executive. b. Centerville, TN, April 1, 1927. e. Lawrenceburg H.S.; U.S. Naval Acad., B.S., 1949; Oxford U. (Rhodes scholar) M.A., 1953; U. of South Carolina, L.H.D. (hon.). Corporate finance specialist, Lehman Brothers 1959–65; v.p. finance, Times Mirror Company, Los Angeles, 1965–69; exec. v.p. finance, 20th Century-Fox Film Corp., 1969–71, pres., 1971, chmn. bd./chief exec. officer, 1971–81; pres., Stanfill, Brown & Co., venture capital firm, 1981–90; chmn. bd./CEO, AME, Inc., 1990–2; co-chmn. bd./co-CEO, MGM, 1992–.

STANG, ARNOLD: Performer, b. Chelsea, MA, Sept. 28, 1927. Radio, 1935–50; on Bdwy, in five plays and in m.p. and short subjects; guest appearances on TV shows. Much voice-over cartoon work. Starred in 36 shorts.

TELEVISION: Series: School House, Henry Morgan Show, Doc Corkle, Top Cat (voice), Broadside. Guest: Captain Video, Milton Berle, Danny Thomas, Perry Como, Ed Sullivan, Red Skelton, Frank Sinatra, Wagon Train, Jack Benny, Johnny Carson, December Bride, Playhouse 90, Batman, Bonanza, Bob Hope, Danny Kaye, Jackie Gleason, Emergency, Feeling Good, Chico & the Man, Super Jaws & Catfish, Busting Loose, Flying High, Robert Klein Specials, Tales from the Dark Side, True Blue, Cosby Show.

PICTURES: Seven Days Leave, My Sister Eileen, Let's Go Steady, They Got Me Covered, So This is New York, Double for Della, Return of Marco Polo, Spirit of '76, Man with the Golden Arm, Dondi, The Wonderful World of the Brothers Grimm, It's a Mad Mad Mad Mad World, Pinocchio in Outer Space (voice), Alakazam the Great (voice), Hello Down There, Skidoo, The Aristocats (voice), Raggedy Ann & Andy (voice), Gang That Couldn't Shoot Straight, That's Life, Hercules in New York, Ghost Dad, Dennis the Menace.

STANLEY, KIM: Actress. r.n. Patricia Reid. b. Tularosa, NM, Feb. 11, 1925. e. U. of New Mexico. Began stage acting in college and later in stock. Worked as model in NY while training with Elia Kazan and Lee Strasberg at Actors Studio. In late 1960s and 1970s taught drama, Coll. of Santa Fe, NM.

THEATER: The Dog, Beneath the Skin (NY debut, 1948), Him, Yes Is For a Very Young Man, Montserrat, The House of Bernarda Alba, The Chase, Picnic (NY Drama Critics Award, 1953), The Traveling Lady, The Great Dreamer, Bus Stop, A Clearing in the Woods, A Touch of the Poet, A Far Country, Natural Affection, The Three Sisters.

PICTURES: The Goddess (debut, 1958), Seance on a Wet Afternoon (Acad. Award nom.), The Three Sisters, Frances (Acad. Award nom.), The Right Stuff.

TELEVISION: Specials: Clash by Night, The Travelling Lady, Cat on a Hot Tin Roof (Emmy Award, 1985). Movie: U.M.C. Guest: Ben Casey (A Cardinal Act of Mercy; Emmy Award, 1963).

STANTON, HARRY DEAN: Actor. b. West Irvine, KY, July 14, 1926. Acting debut at Pasadena Playhouse. Billed in early film appearances as Dean Stanton.

PICTURES: Revolt at Fort Laramie (debut, 1957), Tomahawk Trail, The Proud Rebel, Pork Chop Hill, The Adventures of Huckleberry Finn, A Dog's Best Friend, Hero's Island, The Man From the Diner's Club, Ride in the Whirlwind, The Hostage, A Time for Killing, Rebel Rousers, Cool Hand Luke, Day of the Evil Gun, The Miniskirt Mob, Kelly's Heroes, Cisco Pike, Two-Lane Blacktop, Face to the Wind (Cry for Me Billy), Pat Garrett and Billy the Kid, Dillinger, Where the Lilies Bloom, Cockfighter, Zandy's Bride, The Godfather Part II, Rafferty and the Gold Dust Twins, Rancho Deluxe, Farewell My Lovely, In the Shade, Win Place or Steal, The Missouri Breaks, Straight Time, Renaldo and Clara, Alien, The Rose, Wise Blood, Death Watch, The Black Marble, Private Benjamin, Escape From New York, One From the Heart, Young Doctors in Love, Christine, Repo Man, Red Dawn, The Bear, Paris Texas, The Care Bears Movie (voice), One Magic Christmas, Fool for Love, UFOria, Pretty in Pink, Slamdance, Stars and Bars, Mr. North, The Last Temptation of Christ, Dream a Little Dream, Twister, The Fourth War, Stranger in the House, Wild at Heart, Man Trouble, Twin Peaks: Fire Walk With Me.

TELEVISION: Movies: Flatbed Annie & Sweetpie: Lady Truckers, I Want to Live, Payoff, Hostages. Special: Hotel Room (Tricks).

STAPLETON, JEAN: Actress. r.n. Jeanne Murray. b. New York, NY. e. Wadleigh H.S. Summer stock in NH, ME, MA, and PA. Broadway debut in in The Summer House (1954). President, Advisory bd., Women's Research and Education Instit. (Wash., D.C.); bd.: Eleanor Roosevelt Val-kill, Hyde Park; trustee: Actors Fund of America.

THEATER: Harvey, Damn Yankees, Bells Are Ringing, Juno, Rhinoceros, Funny Girl, Arsenic and Old Lace (Bdwy and tour), Mountain Language/The Birthday Party (Obie Award), The Learned Ladies, Bon Appetit, The Roads to Home, Night Seasons, Morning's at Seven, You Can't Take It With You, The Show-Off, The Mystery of Edwin Drood (natl. tour). and extensive regional work at the Totem Pole Playhouse, Fayetteville, PA, Pocono Playhouse, Mountain Home Pa; Peterborough Playhouse, N.H. and others. Operatic debut with Baltimore Opera Co. in Candide, then The Italian Lesson and Bon Appetit. Starred in San Jose Civic Light Opera Co.'s Sweeney Todd.

PICTURES: Damn Yankees, Bells Are Ringing, Something Wild, Up the Down Staircase, Cold Turkey, Klute, The Buddy System.

TELEVISION: Series: All in the Family (3 Emmy Awards), Bagdad Cafe. Movies: Tail Gunner Joe, Aunt Mary, Angel Dusted, Isabel's Choice, Eleanor: First Lady of the World (Emmy nom.), A Matter of Sex, Dead Man's Folly, Fire in the Dark, The Habitation of Dragons. Specials: You Can't Take It With You, Grown-Ups (ACE nom.), Jack and the Beanstalk and Cinderella (Faerie Tale Theatre), Something's Afoot, Let Me Hear You Whisper, Mother Goose Rock 'n' Rhyme, Parallax Garden.

STAPLETON, MAUREEN: Actress. b. Troy, NY, June 21, 1925. Worked as a model and waitress while studying acting with Herbert Berghof in N.Y. in 1944 and became member of Actors Studio. Broadway debut, 1946, in The Playboy of the Western World. Became a star in 1951 in The Rose Tattoo.

THEATER: Anthony and Cleopatra, Detective Story, Bird Cage, The Rose Tattoo (Tony Award, 1951), The Emperor's Clothes, The Crucible, Richard III, The Seagull, 27 Wagons Full of Cotton, Orpheus Descending, The Cold Wind and the Warm, Toys in the Attic, The Glass Menagerie (1965 & 1975), Plaza Suite, Norman Is That You?, Gingerbread Lady (Tony Award, 1971), The Country Girl, Secret Affairs of Mildred Wild, The Gin Game, The Little Foxes.

PICTURES: Lonelyhearts (debut, 1958; Acad. Award nom.), The Fugitive Kind, A View from the Bridge, Bye Bye Birdie, Airport (Acad. Award nom.), Plaza Suite, Interiors (Acad. Award nom.), Lost and Found, The Runner Stumbles, The Fan, On the Right Track, Reds (Acad. Award, supp. actress, 1981), Johnny Dangerously, The Cosmic Eye (voice), Cocoon, The Money Pit, Heartburn, Sweet Lorraine, Made in Heaven, Nuts, Doin' Time on Planet Earth (cameo), Cocoon: The Return, Passed Away.

TELEVISION: *Series*: What Happened? (panelist, 1952), The Thorns. *Specials*: For Whom the Bell Tolls, Among the Paths to Eden (Emmy, 1968). *Movies*: Tell Me Where It Hurts, Queen of the Stardust Ballroom, Cat on a Hot Tin Roof, The Gathering, Letters From Frank, The Gathering Part II, The Electric Grandmother, Little Gloria—Happy at Last, Family Secrets, Sentimental Journey, Private Sessions, Liberace: Behind the Music, Last Wish, Miss Rose White.

STARGER, MARTIN: Executive. b. New York, NY, May 8, 1932. e. City Coll. of New York. Served in U.S. Army Signal Corp., where prod. training films. Joined BBDO, starting in TV prod. dept.; later made v.p. & assoc. dir. of TV. Joined ABC in 1966, as v.p. of programs, ABC-TV, East Coast. In 1968, prom. to v.p. and natl prog. dir; in 1969 named v.p. in chg. progr. Named pres., ABC Entertainment, July 17, 1972. In June, 1975 formed Marstar Productions Inc., M.P. & TV production company of which he is pres. In March 1978 formed Marble Arch Productions, of which he was pres. Formed Rule/Starger Co. with Elton Rule, 1988.
PICTURES: *Exec. prod.*: Nashville, The Domino Principle, The Muppet Movie, Raise the Titanic, Saturn 3, The Great Muppet Caper, Hard Country, The Legend of the Lone Ranger, On Golden Pond, Sophie's Choice, Barbarosa, Mask.
TELEVISION: Friendly Fire (Emmy Award, 1979), Escape from Sobibor, Earth Star Voyager, Marcus Welby, M.D., A Holiday Affair.

STARK, RAY: Producer. e. Rutgers U. Began career after W.W.II as agent handling Red Ryder radio scripts, and later literary works for such writers as Costain, Marquand and Hecht. Publicity writer, Warner Bros. Joined Famous Artists Agency, where he represented such personalities as Marilyn Monroe, Kirk Douglas and Richard Burton; in 1957, resigned exec. position to form Seven Arts Prods. with Eliot Hyman, serving as exec. v.p. and head of production until July, 1966, when he left to take on personal production projects. Founded Rastar Prods. and Ray Stark Prods. Received Irving Thalberg Award from Acad. of M.P. Arts and Sciences 1980. TV production: Barbarians at the Gate.
PICTURES: The World of Susie Wong, Night of the Iguana, This Property Is Condemned, Oh Dad Poor Dad, Reflections in a Golden Eye, Funny Girl, The Owl and the Pussycat, Fat City, The Way We Were, Summer Wishes Winter Dreams, For Pete's Sake, Funny Lady, The Sunshine Boys, Robin and Marian, Murder by Death, The Goodbye Girl, Casey's Shadow, The Cheap Detective, California Suite, The Electric Horseman, Chapter Two, Seems Like Old Times, Annie, The Slugger's Wife, Nothing in Common, Brighton Beach Memoirs, Biloxi Blues, Steel Magnolias, Revenge, Lost in Yonkers.

STARK, WILBUR: Producer, Director. b. New York, NY, Aug. 10, 1922. e. Columbia U. Started career as actor, Brooklyn Academy Players; slsm. & producer radio station WMCA-NY, 1942–46; for 18 yrs. producer-director of theatrical feature films and over 1500 live dramas and over 300 TV movies, including 81 for CBS as producer (directing over 30).
PICTURES: The Cat People (exec. consultant), The Thing (exec. prod.), My Lover My Son (prod., story), Vampire Circus (prod., story), The Love Box (prod., dir. s.p.), A Policeman's Lot (prod., dir), All I Want Is You and You . . . (prod.), The Petrified Prince (prod., dir.), The Storyteller (exec. prod.), An Act of Reprisal (prod.).
TELEVISION: *Producer*: Newsstand Theatre, Rocky King Detective, Modern Romances with Martha Scott, True Story, Col. Humphrey Flack, My Father Is a Detective, Brothers Branagan (prod.), The Object is . . . (prod.).

STARR, RINGO: O.B.E. Singer, Musician, Songwriter, Actor. r.n. Richard Starkey. b. Liverpool, England, July 7, 1940. m. actress Barbara Bach. Former member of The Beatles.
PICTURES: A Hard Day's Night, Help!, Yellow Submarine, Candy, The Magic Christian, Let It Be, 200 Motels, Blindman, The Concert for Bangladesh, Lisztomania, The Last Waltz, Sextette, The Kids Are Alright, Caveman, Give My Regards to Broad Street, Water (cameo), Walking After Midnight.
TELEVISION: *Movies*: Princess Daisy, Alice in Wonderland. *Series*: Shining Time Station

STEEL, DAWN: Executive. b. New York, NY, Aug. 19, 1946. m. producer Charles Roven. e. marketing student, Boston U. 1964–65, NYU 1966–67; sportswriter, Major League Baseball Digest and NFL/NY 1968–69; 1969–75, editor of Penthouse Magazine; Pres. Oh Dawn! merchandising co. 1979–80, v.p. merchandising Paramount Pictures; 1978–79, merchandising consult., Playboy NYC; 1980–83, v.p. prod. Paramount Pictures. Joined Columbia Pictures 1987 as president (first woman studio pres.), resigned 1990. Columbia productions incl. Ghostbusters II, When Harry Met Sally ..., Casualties of War, Postcards From the Edge, Flatliners, Awakenings. Formed Steel Pictures for the Walt Disney Co., 1990. Prod. for Disney: Honey I Blew Up the Kid, Cool Runnings, Sister Act 2. Recipient of Crystal Award (1989).

MEMBER: AMPAAS, Amer. Film Inst. (bd. 1988–90), NOW Legal Defense Fund; 1993–present, member of dean's advisory bd. at UCLA Sch. of Theatre, Film & TV.

STEELE, TOMMY: Performer. r.n. Tommy Hicks. b. London, Dec. 17, 1936. Early career Merchant Navy. First TV and film appearances, 1956. Composed and sang title song for The Shiralee. Stage musicals: Half a Sixpence, Hans Andersen, Singin' in the Rain, Some Like It Hot.
PICTURES: Kill Me Tomorrow, The Tommy Steele Story (Rock Around the World), The Duke Wore Jeans, Tommy the Toreador, Light Up the Sky, It's All Happening (The Dream Maker), The Happiest Millionaire, Half a Sixpence, Finian's Rainbow, Where's Jack?
TELEVISION: Tommy Steele Spectaculars, Richard Whittington Esquire (Rediffusion), Ed Sullivan Show, Gene Kelly in NY NY, Perry Como Show, Twelfth Night, The Tommy Steele Hour, Tommy Steele in Search of Charlie Chaplin, Tommy Steele and a Show, Quincy's Quest.

STEENBURGEN, MARY: Actress. b. Newport, AR, Feb. 8, 1953. Graduated from Neighborhood Playhouse. Received honorary doctorate degrees from Univ. of Ark. at Little Rock and Hendrix Col. in Conway, AR. On Bdwy stage 1993 in Candida.
PICTURES: Goin' South (debut, 1978), Time After Time, Melvin and Howard (Acad. Award, supp. actress, 1980), Ragtime, A Midsummer Night's Sex Comedy, Cross Creek, Romantic Comedy, One Magic Christmas, Dead of Winter, End of the Line (also exec. prod.), The Whales of August, Miss Firecracker, Parenthood, Back to the Future Part III, The Long Walk Home (narrator), The Butcher's Wife, Clifford, Philadelphia.
TELEVISION: *Mini-Series*: Tender Is the Night. *Specials*: Faerie Tale Theatre (Little Red Riding Hood), The Gift. *Movie*: The Attic: The Hiding of Anne Frank. *Series*: Back to the Future (voice for animated series).

STEIGER, ROD: Actor. b. Westhampton, NY, Apr. 14, 1925. e. Westside H.S., Newark, NJ. Served in U.S. Navy, then employed in Civil Service; studied acting at N.Y. Theatre Wing Dramatic Workshop Actors' Studio; numerous TV plays; on Broadway in ANTA prod. of Night Music.
PICTURES: Teresa (debut, 1951), On the Waterfront, The Big Knife, Oklahoma!, The Court Martial of Billy Mitchell, Jubal, The Harder They Fall, Back From Eternity, Run of the Arrow, The Unholy Wife, Across the Bridge, Cry Terror, Al Capone, Seven Thieves, The Mark, World in My Pocket, 13 West Street, Convicts 4, The Longest Day, Hands Over the City, Time of Indifference, The Pawnbroker, The Loved One, Dr. Zhivago, And There Came a Man (A Man Called John), In the Heat of the Night (Acad. Award, 1967), The Girl and the General, No Way to Treat a Lady, The Sergeant, The Illustrated Man, Three Into Two Won't Go, Waterloo, Happy Birthday Wanda June, Duck You Sucker! (A Fistful of Dynamite), The Heroes, Lolly Madonna XXX, Lucky Luciano, Mussolini: Dead or Alive (The Last Days of Mussolini), Hennessey, Dirty Hands, W.C. Fields and Me, Portrait of a Hitman (Jim Buck), Wolf Lake, F.I.S.T., Breakthrough (Sgt. Steiner), The Amityville Horror, Love and Bullets, Klondike Fever, The Lucky Star, Lion of the Desert, Cattle Annie and Little Britches, The Chosen, The Magic Mountain, The Naked Face, The Kindred, Catch the Heat, American Gothic, The January Man, Men of Respect, The Ballad of the Sad Cafe, Tennessee Waltz, Guilty as Charged, That Summer of White Roses, The Player.
TELEVISION: Many appearances in 1950s live TV including Marty. *Movies*: Jesus of Nazareth, Cook & Perry: The Race to the Pole, Sword of Gideon, Desperado: Avalanche at Devil's Ridge, Passion and Paradise, In the Line of Duty: Manhunt in the Dakotas, Sinatra. *Mini-Series*: Hollywood Wives.

STEINBERG, DAVID: Actor, Writer, Director. b. Winnipeg, Canada, Aug. 9, 1942. e. U. of Chicago; Hebrew Theological Coll. Member Second City troupe; comedian at comedy clubs: Mr. Kelly's Hungry i, Bitter End. Starred in London and Bdwy. stage prods. Bdwy. includes Little Murders; Carry Me Back to Morningside Heights.
PICTURES: The End, Something Short of Paradise, Paternity (dir.), Going Berserk (dir., co.-s.p.).
TELEVISION: *Series*: Music Scene (writer, co-host), Tonight Show (guest host), David Steinberg Show. *Special*: Second City: 25 Years in Revue. *Director*: Newhart, The Popcorn Kid, Golden Girls, One Big Family, Faerie Tale Theatre, Richard Belzer Special, Baby on Board, Annie McGuire, Seinfeld, Evening Shade, Designing Women, and many commercials.

STEINBERG, HERB: b. New York, NY, July 3, 1921. e. City Coll. of New York, 1937–41. Capt. U.S. Army, 1942–46; pub. PRC, 1946, Eagle Lion, 1946–49, Paramount 1949; pub. mgr. 1951; expl. mgr., 1954; studio adv. & pub. dir., 1958; exec. chg. of spec. proj., press dept., Universal City Studio, 1963; v.p., Universal Studio Tours, 1971; 1974 v.p., MCA Recreation Services. Appt. to California Tourism Commission, Calif.

Tourism Hall of Fame, 1984; consultant, MCA, Inc., 1987; bd. trustees, Motion Picture & TV Fund, 1987; Communications dir. Alliance of Motion Picture & Television Producers.

STEINMAN, MONTE: Executive. b. New York, NY, May 18, 1955. e. Wharton Sch. of Univ. of PA. Joined Paramount Pictures 1980 as sr. financial analyst. Series of promotions followed, culminating in appt. as dir. of financial planning of Gulf + Western's Entertainment and Communications Group, in February, 1984. In 1985, named exec. dir., financial planning. 1990, joined Viacom Intl., as mgr. financial planning. 1993, dir. financial planning, MTV Networks.

STEMBLER, JOHN H.: Executive. b. Miami, FL, Feb. 18, 1913. e. U. of Florida Law Sch., 1937. Asst. U.S. att., South. dist. of Fla., 1941; U.S. Air Force, 1941–45; pres. Georgia Theatre Co., 1957; named chmn., 1983; NATO member exec. comm. and past pres.; Major Gen. USAF (Ret); past bd. chmn., National Bank of Georgia.

STEMBLER, WILLIAM J.: Executive. b. Atlanta, GA, Nov. 29, 1946. e. Westminister Sch., 1964; U. of Florida, 1968; U. of Georgia Law Sch., 1971. 1st. lt. U.S. Army, 1971; capt., U.S. Army Reserve; resigned 1976. Enforcement atty., SEC, Atlanta office, 1972–73; joined Georgia Theatre Co., 1973; pres. 1983–86; joined United Artists Communications, Inc., 1986, as v.p.; Incorporated Value Cinemas 1988, Southern Cinemas, Inc., 1990, and Georgia Theatre Co. II in May, 1991 as its chmn. & pres.
MEMBER: bd. of dir., Merchant Bank of Atlanta; bd. of dir., & v.p., NATO, 1983–present; mbr., NATO OF GA & past-pres., 1983–85; Rotary Club of Atlanta, pres. 1991–2.

STEPHENS, ROBERT: Actor. b. Bristol, England, July 14, 1931. e. Esme Church School, Bradford. Made his stage debut at age 13; joined the Royal Court Company in 1956.
PICTURES: Circle of Deception (debut, 1961), A Taste of Honey, Pirates of Tortuga, The Inspector, The Small World of Sammy Lee, Cleopatra, Morgan!, Romeo and Juliet, The Prime of Miss Jean Brodie, The Private Life of Sherlock Holmes, The Asphyx, Travels with My Aunt, Luther, The Duellists, The Shout, Empire of the Sun, High Season, Wonderland (The Fruit Machine), Henry V, The Bonfire of the Vanities, The Pope Must Die, Afraid of the Dark, Chaplin, Searching for Bobby Fisher.
THEATRE: London: The Crucible, The Good Woman of Setzuan, The Country Wife, The Entertainer, Look After Lulu, The Wrong Side of the Park, Saint Joan, The Recruiting Officer, Royal Hunt of the Sun, The Beaux Stratagem, Armstrong's Last Goodnight, Apropos of Falling Sleet (also dir.), Murderer, Private Lives. NY: Epitaph for George Dillon, Sherlock Holmes.
TELEVISION: Vienna 1900 (series), Parnell and O'Shea, Gangsters, Softly Softly, The Holocaust (series, Vienna), Eustace and Hilda, Voyage of Charles Darwin, Kean, Office Story, Friends in Space Society, Suez, Hesther for Example, The Executioner, Eden End, Year of the French, Box of Delights (series), By the Sword Divided, Hells Bells (series), War and Remembrance, Window Sir, Lizzies Pictures (series), Fortunes of War (series), Inspector Morse, Radical Chambers, Adam Bede.

STERLING, JAN: Actress. r.n. Jane Sterling Adriance. b. April 3, 1923. e. private tutors; Fay Compton Sch. of Dramatic Art, London. N.Y. stage debut: Bachelor Born.
STAGE: Panama Hattie, Present Laughter, John Loves Mary, Two Blind Mice, Front Page, Over 21, Born Yesterday, The November People.
PICTURES: Johnny Belinda (debut, 1948), Appointment with Danger, Mystery Street, Caged, Union Station, Skipper Surprised His Wife, Big Carnival (Ace in the Hole), The Mating Season, Rhubarb, Flesh and Fury, Sky Full of Moon, Pony Express, The Vanquished, Split Second, Alaska Seas, The High and the Mighty (Acad. Award nom.), Return From the Sea, Human Jungle, Women's Prison, Female on the Beach, Man with the Gun, 1984, The Harder They Fall, Slaughter on Tenth Avenue, Kathy O', The Female Animal, High School Confidential, Love in a Goldfish Bowl, The Incident, The Angry Breed, The Minx, First Monday in October.
TELEVISION: Series: You're in the Picture (panelist, 1961), Made in America, The Guiding Light (1969–70). Mini-Series: Backstairs at the White House. Movies: Having Babies, Dangerous Company, My Kidnapper My Love.

STERLING, ROBERT: Actor. r.n. William Sterling Hart. b. Newcastle, PA, Nov. 13, 1917. e. U. of Pittsburgh. m. Anne Jeffreys, actress. Father of actress Tisha Sterling. Fountain pen salesman, day laborer, clerk, industrial branch credit mgr., clothing salesman on West Coast; served as pilot-instructor U.S. Army Corps. 3 yrs.
PICTURES: Blondie Meets the Boss, Only Angels Have Wings, Manhattan Heartbeat, Yesterday's Heroes, Gay Caballero, Penalty, I'll Wait for You, Get-Away, Ringside Maisie, Two-Faced Woman, Dr. Kildare's Victory, Johnny Eager, This Time for Keeps, Somewhere I'll Find You, Secret Heart,

Roughshod, Bunco Squad, Sundowners, Show Boat, Column South, Voyage to the Bottom of the Sea, Return to Peyton Place, A Global Affair.
TELEVISION: Series: Topper, Love That Jill, Ichabod and Me. Movies: Letters from Three Lovers, Beggarman, Thief.

STERN, ALFRED E. F.: Public relations executive. b. Boston, MA, Aug. 4. e. Boston U., BS in journalism. Reporter, editor, Lowell Sun, Quincy Patriot-Ledger, Dartmouth News; publicist, RKO Radio Pictures, 1946–54; publicity dir., 1955; West Coast publicity dir., NTA, 1958; own public relations org., Alfred E. F. Stern Co., Inc., 1960.

STERN, DANIEL: Actor. b. Bethesda, MD, Aug. 28, 1957. e. H.B. Studios. Appeared in 1984 short film Frankenweenie.
PICTURES: Breaking Away (debut, 1979), Starting Over, A Small Circle of Friends, Stardust Memories, It's My Turn, One-Trick Pony, Honky Tonk Freeway, I'm Dancing As Fast As I Can, Diner, Blue Thunder, Get Crazy, C.H.U.D., Key Exchange, The Boss' Wife, Hannah and Her Sisters, Born in East L.A., D.O.A., The Milagro Beanfield War, Leviathan, Little Monsters, Friends Lovers and Lunatics, Coupe de Ville, My Blue Heaven, Home Alone, City Slickers, Home Alone 2: Lost in New York, Rookie of the Year (also dir.).
TELEVISION: Movies: Samson and Delilah, Weekend War, The Court-Martial of Jackie Robinson. Series: Hometown, The Wonder Years (narrator).

STERN, EDDIE: Film buyer. b. New York, NY, Jan. 13, 1917. e. Columbia Sch. of Journalism. Head film buyer and booker, specializing in art theatres, for Rugoff and Becker, N.Y.; Captain, USAF; joined Wometco Ent. in 1952 as asst. to film buyer; v.p. motion picture theatre film buying and booking, Wometco Enterprises, Inc. Retired from Wometco 1985. Now handling film buying and booking for Theatres of Nassau, Ltd.

STERN, EZRA E.: Attorney. b. New York, NY, Mar. 22, 1908. e. Southwestern U. 1930, LL.B. pres., Wilshire Bar Assn. Former legal counsel for So. Calif. Theatre Owners Assn. Member: Calif. State Bar; member, Int'l Variety Clubs; former chief barker, Variety Club So. Calif. Tent 25; pres., Variety Int'l Boys' Club; board of dir., Los Angeles Metropolitan Recreation & Youth Services Council; bd. of trustees, Welfare Planning Council, Los Angeles Region; former mem. Los Angeles Area Council, Boys' Club of America; pres., Variety International Boys' Club 1976–77 and 1979–80. Member bd., Will Rogers Inst., M.P. Pioneers. 1984, honored by Variety Boys and Girls Club as founder of youth recreational facility.

STERN, STEWART: Writer. b. New York, NY, Mar. 22, 1922. e. Ethical Culture Sch., 1927–40; U. of Iowa, 1940–43. Rifle Squad Leader, S/Sgt. 106th Inf. Div., 1943–45; actor, asst. stage mgr., The French Touch, Bdwy. 1945–46; dialogue dir. Eagle-Lion Studios, 1946–48. 1948 to date: screenwriter.
TELEVISION: (Plays) Crip, And Crown Thy Good, Thunder of Silence, Heart of Darkness, A Christmas to Remember, Sybil (Emmy, 1977).
PICTURES: Teresa, Benjy (orig. s.p.) Rebel Without a Cause, The Rack, The James Dean Story, The Outsider, The Ugly American, Rachel, Rachel, The Last Movie, Summer Wishes—Winter Dreams (orig. s.p.).

STERNHAGEN, FRANCES: Actress. b. Washington, DC, Jan. 13, 1930. e. Vassar Coll., drama dept.; Perry-Mansfield School of Theatre. Studied with Sanford Meisner at Neighborhood Playhouse, NY. Was teacher at Milton Acad. in MA. Acted with Arena Stage, Washington, DC, 1953–54.
THEATER: Thieves Carnival (off-Bdwy debut, 1955), The Skin of Our Teeth, The Carefree Tree, The Admirable Bashville, Ulysses in Night Town, Viva Madison Avenue!, Red Eye of Love, Misalliance, Great Day in the Morning, The Right Honorable Gentleman, The Displaced Person, The Cocktail Party, Cock-a-Doodle Dandy, Playboy of the Western World, The Sign in Sidney Brustein's Window, Enemies, The Good Doctor (Tony Award, 1974), Equus, Angel, On Golden Pond, The Father, Grownups, Summer, You Can't Take It With You, Home Front, Driving Miss Daisy, Remembrance, A Perfect Ganesh.
PICTURES: Up the Down Staircase (debut, 1967), The Tiger Makes Out, The Hospital, Two People, Fedora, Starting Over, Outland, Independence Day, Romantic Comedy, Bright Lights Big City, See You in the Morning, Communion, Sibling Rivalry, Misery, Doc Hollywood, Raising Cain.
TELEVISION: Series: Love of Life, Doctors, Golden Years. Movies: Who'll Save Our Children?, Mother and Daughter: The Loving War, Prototype, Under One Roof, Follow Your Heart, She Woke Up, Labor of Love: The Arlette Schweitzer Story. Guest: Cheers, Tales From the Crypt.

STEUER, ROBERT B.: Executive. b. New Orleans, LA, Nov. 18, 1937. e. U. of Illinois, & 1955–57; Tulane U., 1957–59, B.B.A. Booker-Southern D.I. circuit, New Orleans, 1959; assoc., prod., Poor White Trash; 1960; v.p. Cinema Dist. America, 1961; co-prod., Flesh Eaters, Common Law Wife, 1963; Flack Black Pussy Cat, 1966; partner, gen. mgr., radio station WTVF, Mobile, 1963; dir. special projects, American Intl.

Pictures, 1967; so. div. sls. mgr., AIP, 1971; v.p. asst. gen. sls. mgr., AIP, 1974; partner, United Producers Organization, producing Screamers, 1977; v.p., sls., Ely Landau Org., 1979; v.p., gen. sls. mgr., Film Ventures Intl., 1981; exec. v.p. worldwide mktg., 1983; pres., FVI, 1986–89. 1987, exec. v.p. worldwide mktg. Film Ventures Intl; 1987–88 exec. prod. Operation: Take No Prisoners, Most Dangerous Women Alive, Tunnels, Criminal Act, Au Pair; 1989 sales consultant, 20th Century Fox, 1990–present, prods. rep.; When the Wales Came, China Cry, Twogether, Sweet and Short, Taxi to Soweto, and worldwide mktg., distrib. and sls. consultant to entertainment industry.

STEVENS, ANDREW: Actor, Director, Writer, Producer. b. Memphis, TN, June 10, 1955. Son of actress Stella Stevens. e. Antioch U., L.A., B.A. (psychology). Studied acting with Strasberg, David Craig, Vincent Chase, and Pat Randall. Began balancing work between film, TV and stage. L.A. stage includes Journey's End, Mass Appeal, Leader of the Pack, Billy Budd (also prod.), P.S. Your Cat is Dead, Bouncers (L.A. Drama Circle Critics Award).
PICTURES: Shampoo, Day of the Animals, Massacre at Central High, Las Vegas Lady, Vigilante Force, The Boys in Company C, The Fury, Death Hunt, The Seduction, Ten to Midnight, Scared Stiff, Tusks, Fine Gold, Deadly Innocents, Down the Drain, Eyewitness to Murder, The Ranch, The Terror Within, Blood Chase, Counterforce, The Terror Within II (also dir., s.p.), Red Blooded American Girl, Night Eyes (also s.p., prod.), Munchie, Double Threat, Night Eyes II (also s.p., prod.), Deadly Rivals, Night Eyes III (also s.p., dir.), Body Chemistry III (also prod.), Eyewitness to Murder.
TELEVISION: Series: Oregon Trail, Code Red, Emerald Point N.A.S., Dallas. Mini-series: Hollywood Wives, Once and Eagle. Movies: Beggarman Thief, The Rebels, The Bastard, The Last Survivors, The Oregon Trail, Secrets, Topper (also prod.), Women at Westpoint, Code Red, Miracle on Ice, Journey's End, Forbidden Love, Murder in Malibu (Columbo). Special: Werewolf of Woodstock.Guest: Adam-12, Apple's Way, The Quest, Police Story, Shazam, Hotel, Westside Medical, Murder She Wrote, Love Boat. Director: Swamp Thing (3 episodes), Silk Stalkings (also actor), General Hospital (3 eps).

STEVENS, CONNIE: Actress. r.n. Concetta Ann Ingolia. b. Brooklyn, NY, August 8, 1938. e. Sacred Heart Acad., Hollywood Professional Sch. Began career as winner of several talent contests in Hollywood; prof. debut, Hollywood Repertory Theatre's prod. Finian's Rainbow; Bdwy in Star Spangled Girl (Theatre World Award); recordings include: Kookie Kookie Lend Me Your Comb, 16 Reasons, What Did You Wanna Make Me Cry For, From Me to You, They're Jealous of Me, A Girl Never Knows.
PICTURES: Eighteen and Anxious, Young and Dangerous, Drag Strip Riot, Rock-a-Bye Baby, The Party Crashers, Parrish, Susan Slade, Palm Springs Weekend, Two on a Guillotine, Never Too Late, Way Way Out, The Grissom Gang, Scorchy, Sgt. Pepper's Lonely Hearts Club Band (cameo), Grease 2, Back to the Beach, Tapeheads.
TELEVISION: Movies: Mister Jerico, Call Her Mom, Playmates, Every Man Needs One, The Sex Symbol, Love's Savage Fury, Scruples, Bring Me the Head of Dobie Gillis. Series: Hawaiian Eye, Wendy and Me, Kraft Music Halls Presents The Des O'Connor Show, Starting from Scratch.

STEVENS, CRAIG: Actor. r.n. Gail Shikles. b. Liberty, MO, July 8, 1918. m. actress Alexis Smith. e. U. of Kansas. Played in coll. dramatics. On screen 1941 in Affectionately Yours.
PICTURES: Since You Went Away, The Doughgirls, Roughly Speaking, Too Young to Know, Humoresque, The Man I Love, That Way With Women, Night Unto Night, Love and Learn, Lady Takes a Sailor, Phone Call from a Stranger, French Line, Where the Sidewalk Ends, Duel on the Mississippi, Gunn, "S.O.B."
TELEVISION: Guest: Lux Video Theatre, Four Star Playhouse, Loretta Young Show, Schlitz Playhouse, Dinah Shore, Ernie Ford Shows, Chevy Show, Summer on Ice, The Millionaire, The Bold Ones. Series: Peter Gunn (1958–61), Man of the World (ATV England), Mr. Broadway, The Invisible Man, Dallas. Movies: The Killer Bees, The Cabot Connection, The Home Front, Supercarrier, Marcus Welby, M.D.—A Holiday Affair. Mini-Series: Rich Man Poor Man.
STAGE: Here's Love, King of Hearts, Plain and Fancy, Critics Choice, Mary Mary, Cactus Flower (natl. co.), My Fair Lady.

STEVENS, FISHER: Actor. b. Chicago, IL, Nov. 27, 1963. e. NYU. Artistic Director of Naked Angels Theatre Co. in NYC.
THEATER: NY: Torch Song Trilogy (Off-Bdwy & Bdwy), Brighton Beach Memoirs, A Perfect Ganesh.
PICTURES: The Burning, Baby It's You, The Brother From Another Planet, The Flamingo Kid, My Science Project, Short Circuit, The Boss's Wife, Short Circuit 2, Point of View, Reversal of Fortune, The Marrying Man, Mystery Date, Bob Roberts, Hero, When the Party's Over, Super Mario Bros.

TELEVISION: Series: Key West. Guest: Columbo. Special: It's Called the Sugar Plum.

STEVENS, GEORGE, JR.: Director, Writer, Producer. b. Los Angeles, CA, Apr. 3, 1932. Son of late director George Stevens. e. Occidental Coll., 1949–53, B.A. 1st Lieut. U.S. Air Force; TV dir., Alfred Hitchcock Presents, Peter Gunn, 1957–61; prod. asst. Giant Productions, 1953–54; prod. asst. Mark VII, Ltd., 1956–57; dir. M.P. Service, U.S. Information Agency 1962–67; chmn., U.S. deleg. to Film Festivals at Cannes (1962, 1964), Venice (1962, 1963), Moscow (1963); Founding director, American Film Institute, 1967–79; co-chmn., American Film Institute, 1979 to present.
PICTURES: The Diary of Anne Frank (assoc. prod.), The Greatest Story Ever Told (assoc. prod.), John F. Kennedy: Years of Lightning Day of Drums (prod.), America at the Movies (prod.), George Stevens: A Filmmaker's Journey (dir., s.p., prod.); 1988 WGA Award for TV broadcast).
TELEVISION: Specials: American Film Institute's Salutes (exec. prod./writer, 1973–93; received 1975 Emmy Award as exec. prod. of The American Film Institue Salute to James Cagney), The Stars Salute America's Greatest Movies (exec. prod.), The Kennedy Center Honors (prod./writer, 1978–92; Emmy Awards: 1984, 1986, 1989), America Entertains Vice Premier Deng (prod./writer), Christmas in Washington, (exec. prod./writer, 1982–92), Movies: The Murder of Mary Phagan (co-writer, prod., 1988; Emmy Award for prod.; also Christopher & Peabody Awards), Separate But Equal (dir., writer, co-exec. prod.; Emmy Award for exec. prod.; also Christopher Award, Ohio State Award, Paul Selvin Award by the Writers Guild of America).

STEVENS, K. T.: Actress. r.n. Gloria Wood. b. Hollywood, CA, July 20, 1919. e. U. of Southern California. Daughter of late director Sam Wood.
STAGE: You Can't Take It With You, The Man Who Came to Dinner, My Sister Eileen, Laura, Nine Girls, St. Joan, The Voice of the Turtle, The Tender Trap, The Land is Bright.
PICTURES: (debut) Peck's Bad Boy, The Great Man's Lady, Navy Blue and Gold, Address Unknown, Kitty Foyle, Port of New York, Harriet Craig, Vice Squad, Tumbleweed, Missile to the Moon, Bob and Ted and Carol and Alice, They're Playing With Fire.
TELEVISION: Series: The Young and the Restless, Paradise Bay, Days of Our Lives, General Hospital. Guest: Wagon Train, Patty Duke Show, Buck Rogers, Adam 12, Marcus Welby, Knots Landing, Perry Mason, many others.

STEVENS, LESLIE: Executive, Writer, Producer, Director. b. Washington, DC, Feb. 3, 1924. e. Westminister Sch., London, Yale Drama Sch., American Theatre Wing, N.Y. Sold first play, The Mechanical Rat at 15; wrote six plays for summer stock groups, 1941–42; U.S. Air Force, 1943; pres., exec. prod. Daystar Prods.
STAGE: Bullfight (off B'way) 1953–54; wrote, Broadway: Champagne Complex; The Lovers; The Marriage-Go-Round; The Pink Jungle, Joy Joy.
TELEVISION: For Playhouse 90: Invitation to a Gunfighter, Charley's Aunt, Rumors of Evening, The Violent Heart, Portrait of a Murderer, The Second Man; Kraft TV Theatre, Duel, Four Star Playhouse, Producers Showcase, Bloomer Girl. Series: Stoney Burke (creator, prod., dir.), Outer Limits (created, prod., dir.) It Takes a Thief (exec. prod.), McCloud (prod. writer of pilot; exec. prod. series), Men From Shiloh (exec. prod.) series; Name of the Game (exec. prod., writer, dir.), prod.-writer, pilot of Search (prod., writer of pilot; exec. prod., series creator), Movie of Today, Paperback Playhouse, Earthside Musical Base, Invisible Man (exec. prod.), Gemini Man (spv. prod. for pilot and series), Battlestar Galactica (co-prod., pilot), Buck Rogers (co-writer), The Highwayman (sprv. prod.).
PICTURES: The Left-Handed Gun 1958 (s.p.). Private Property (co-prod., dir., s.p.), The Marriage-Go-Round (s.p.), Hero's Island (prod., dir., s.p.), Battlestar Galactica (co-prod.), Buck Rogers (s.p., prod.), Three Kinds of Heat (dir., prod., s.p.).

STEVENS, MARK: Actor. r.n. Richard Stevens. b. Cleveland, OH, Dec. 13, 1922. e. privately; Beaux Arts and Sir George Williams Sch. of Fine Arts, Montreal. Had varied career before appearing on stage and radio in Canada; later joined station WAKB in Akron; then prod. mgr., WJW, Akron. Screen debut in Objective Burma. Formed Mark Stevens Prod., Mark Stevens Television Prod., 1955.
PICTURES: God Is My Co-Pilot, Pride of the Marines, Within These Walls, From This Day Forward, The Dark Corner, I Wonder Who's Kissing Her Now, The Street With No Name, The Snake Pit, Sand, Oh You Beautiful Doll, Dancing in the Dark, Between Midnight and Dawn, Please Believe Me, Target Unknown, Katie Did It, Little Egypt, Reunion in Reno, Mutiny, Big Frame, Torpedo Alley, Jack Slade, Cry Vengeance (also dir.), Timetable (also dir.), Gunsight Ridge, September Storm, Fate Is the Hunter, Frozen Alive, Sunscorched.

TELEVISION: *Series*: Martin Kane: Private Eye, Big Town (also prod., writer). *Guest*: Murder She Wrote.

STEVENS, STELLA: Actress, (Director). b. Yazoo City, MS, Oct. 1, 1937. r.n. Estelle Eggleston. Mother of actor Andrew Stevens. e. Attended Memphis State U. Modeled in Memphis when she was discovered by talent scouts. Was briefly a term contract actress at 20th Century-Fox, later under exclusive contract to Paramount, then Columbia. Director: Just For a Laugh (A.F.I. film), The American Heroine (feature length doc.), The Ranch (feature comedy).
PICTURES: Say One For Me (debut, 1959), The Blue Angel, Li'l Abner, Man Trap, Girls! Girls! Girls!, Too Late Blues, The Nutty Professor, The Courtship of Eddie's Father, Advance to the Rear, Synanon, The Secret of My Success, The Silencers, Rage, Where Angels Go Trouble Follows, How To Save A Marriage and Ruin Your Life, Sol Madrid, The Mad Room, The Ballad of Cable Hogue, A Town Called Hell, Slaughter, Stand Up & Be Counted, The Poseidon Adventure, Arnold, Cleopatra Jones and the Casino of Gold, Las Vegas Lady, Nickelodeon, The Manitou, Wacko, Chained Heat, The Longshot, Monster in the Closet, Down the Drain, Last Call, The Ranch (dir.), The Terror Within II, Eye of the Stranger, The Quest, Exiled in America, Smart Talk, The Nutty Nut.
TELEVISION: *Series*: Ben Casey, Flamingo Road, Santa Barbara. *Guest*: Bob Hope Bing Crosby Special, Frontier Circus, Johnny Ringo, Alfred Hitchcock, Love Boat, Highway to Heaven, Murder She Wrote, Martin Mull's White America, A Table at Ciros, In the Heat of the Night, Hotel, Night Court, Newhart, Dangerous Curves, The Commish. *Movies*: In Broad Daylight, Climb an Angry Mountain, Linda, The Day The Earth Moved, Honky Tonk, New Original Wonder Woman (pilot), Kiss Me Kill Me, Wanted the Sundance Woman, Charlie Cobb (pilot), The Night They Took Miss Beautiful, Murder in Peyton Place, The Jordan Chance, Cruise into Terror, New Love Boat (pilot), Friendship Secrets and Lies, Hart to Hart (pilot), The French Atlantic Affair, The Pendragon Affair (Eddie Capra Mystery pilot), Make Me an Offer, Children of Divorce, Twirl, Amazons, Women of San Quentin, No Man's Land, A Masterpiece of Murder, Fatal Confessions (Father Dowling pilot), Man Against The Mob, Jake Spanner: Private Eye.

STEVENSON, PARKER: Actor. b. Philadelphia, PA, June 4, 1953. e. Princeton U. m. actress Kirstie Alley. Began professional acting career by starring in film, A Separate Peace, while high school senior, having attracted attention through work on TV commercials.
PICTURES: A Separate Peace (debut, 1972), Our Time, Lifeguard, Stroker Ace, Stitches.
TELEVISION: *Guest*: The Streets of San Francisco, Gunsmoke. *Series*: Hardy Boys Mysteries, Falcon Crest, Probe, Baywatch. *Mini-Series*: North & South Book II, All the Rivers Run. *Movies*: This House Possessed, Shooting Stars, That Secret Sunday, Baywatch: Panic at Malibu Pier, The Cover Girl and the Cop, Are You Lonesome Tonight?, Nighttide, Shadow of a Stranger.

STEWART, DOUGLAS DAY: Writer, Director.
PICTURES: *Writer*: The Blue Lagoon, An Officer and a Gentleman. *Director-Writer*: Thief of Hearts, Listen to Me.
TELEVISION: Writer: Boy in the Plastic Bubble, The Man Who Could Talk to Kids, Murder or Mercy.

STEWART, ELAINE: Actress. b. Montclair, NJ, May 31, 1929. Usher, cashier, m.p. theatre, Montclair; model, Conover Agcy., 1948; many TV shows; screen debut in Sailor Beware (1951); Star of Tomorrow, 1954.
PICTURES: Sky Full of Moon, The Bad and the Beautiful, Desperate Search, Code Two, Slight Case of Larceny, Young Bess, Take the High Ground, Brigadoon, Adventures of Hajji Baba, Tattered Dress, Rise and Fall of Legs Diamond, Most Dangerous Man Alive.

STEWART, JAMES: Actor. b. Indiana, PA, May 20, 1908. e. Mercersburg Acad.; Princeton U. With Falmouth Stock Co., Cape Cod; on N.Y. stage in Goodbye Again; stage mgr. for Camille with Jane Cowl (Boston). In films since 1935; joined U.S. Air Force 1942, commissioned Col. 1944. Retired as Brig. Gen. Voted one of top ten money-making stars, M.P. Herald-Fame poll, 1950, 52, 54, 57; No. 1 Money-Making Star, 1955. 1968, Screen Actors Guild Award. Mem.: Bd. of Trustees, Princeton U. Trustee, Claremont Coll.; exec. bd. of Los Angeles Council of Boy Scouts of America; bd. of dirs., Project Hope. Honorary Academy Award, 1984. Author: Jimmy Stewart and His Poems (1989).
STAGE: Spring in Autumn, All Good Americans, Yellow Jack, Journey at Night, Harvey.
PICTURES: Murder Man (debut, 1935), Rose Marie, Wife vs. Secretary, Next Time We Love, Small Town Girl, Speed, Gorgeous Hussy, Born to Dance, After the Thin Man, Seventh Heaven, The Last Gangster, Navy Blue and Gold, Of Human Hearts, You Can't Take It With You, Vivacious Lady, Shopworn Angel, Made For Each Other, Ice Follies of 1939, Mr. Smith Goes to Washington, It's A Wonderful World, Destry Rides Again, Shop Around the Corner, Mortal Storm,

No Time For Comedy, The Philadelphia Story (Acad. Award, 1940), Come Live With Me, Pot O'Gold, Ziegfeld Girl, It's a Wonderful Life, Magic Town, Call Northside 777, On Our Merry Way, Rope, You Gotta Stay Happy, The Stratton Story, Malaya, Winchester '73, Broken Arrow, Harvey, The Jackpot, No Highway in the Sky, The Greatest Show on Earth, Carbine Williams, Bend of the River, The Naked Spur, Thunder Bay, The Glenn Miller Story, Rear Window, Far Country, Strategic Air Command, Man From Laramie, The Man Who Knew Too Much, The Spirit of St. Louis, Night Passage, Vertigo, Bell Book and Candle, Anatomy of a Murder, The FBI Story, The Mountain Road, Two Rode Together, The Man Who Shot Liberty Valance, Mr. Hobbs Takes a Vacation, How the West Was Won, Take Her She's Mine, Cheyenne Autumn, Dear Brigitte, Shenandoah, Flight of the Phoenix, The Rare Breed, Firecreek, Bandolero, The Cheyenne Social Club, Fool's Parade, That's Entertainment, The Shootist, Airport '77, The Big Sleep, The Magic of Lassie, An American Tail: Fievel Goes West (voice).
TELEVISION: *Series*: The Jimmy Stewart Show (1971–72), Hawkins (1973–74). *Movies*: Hawkins on Murder, Right of Way.

STEWART, JAMES L.: Executive. e. U. of Southern California, B.A. in cinema-TV and M.B.A. in finance. Worked for two years in sales for CBS Radio Network—West Coast. Spent four years with MGM in promotion and marketing. With Walt Disney Prods. for 12 years, functioning in marketing, management and administrative activities; named v.p.-corp. relations & admin. asst. to pres. In 1978 joined in formation of Aurora Pictures, of which is exec. v.p., secty., & COO.
PICTURES: Exec. Prod.: Why Would I Lie?, The Secret of NIMH, Eddie and the Cruisers, Heart Like a Wheel, East of the Sun, West of the Moon, Maxie.

STEWART, MARILYN: Marketing & Public Relations Executive. b. New York, NY. e. Hunter Coll. Entered ind. as scty. then asst. to MGM dir. of adv. Left to become prom.-pub. dir. for Verve/Folkways Records; duties also included ar and talent scouting. In 1966 joined 20th-Fox as radio/tv pub. coordinator. In 1969 went to Para. Pictures as mag. pub. coordinator; 1970 named worldwide dir. of pub. for Para., including creation of overall mkt. concepts, becoming 1st woman to be appt. to that position at major co. Campaigns included Love Story and The Godfather. In 1972 opened own consulting office specializing in m.p. marketing and p.r. Headquarters in N.Y.; repr. in L.A. Has represented The Lords of Flatbush, Bang the Drum Slowly, The Kids Are Alright, Autumn Sonata, The Tin Drum, A Cry in the Dark, The Russia House, Filmex, Michael Moriarty, Arthur Hiller, Fred Schepisi, Volker Schlondorff, Hemdale Pictures, Lucasfilm.

STEWART PATRICK: Actor. b. Mirfield, England, July 13, 1940. Trained at Bristol Old Vic Theatre School. Made professional stage debut 1959 in Treasure Island with Lincoln Rep. Co. at the Theatre Royal in Lincoln.
PICTURES: Hennessey, Hedda, Excalibur, The Pague Dogs (voice), Races, Dune, Lifeforce, Code Name: Emerald, Wild Geese II, The Doctor and the Devils, Lady Jane, L.A. Story, Gunmen, Robin Hood: Men in Tights.
TELEVISION: *Series*: Eleventh Hour (BBC), Maybury (BBC), Star Trek: The Next Generation (U.S.). *Mini-Series*: I Claudius, Smiley's People. *Movies*: Little Lord Fauntleroy, Pope John Paul II, Death Train. *BBC Specials*: Oedipus Rex, Miss Julie, Hamlet, The Devil's Disciple, Fall of Eagles, The Artist's Story, Love Girl and the Innocent, Conrad, A Walk With Destiny, Alfred the Great, The Madness, When the Actors Come, Tolstoy: A Question of Faith, The Anatomist, The Mozart Inquest.
THEATRE: NY: A Midsummer Night's Dream, A Christmas Carol. Numerous London theatre credits incl.: The Investigation, Henry V, The Caretaker, Body and Soul, Who's Afraid of Virginia Woolf?, Yonadab. Associate artist with Royal Shakespeare Co. since 1967; many appearances with them incl. Antony and Cleopatra for which he received the Olivier Award for Best Supporting Actor in 1979.

STIERS, DAVID OGDEN: Actor. b. Peoria, IL, Oct. 31, 1942. Guest conductor: 50 American orchestras incl. Chicago, San Diego, Dallas, Utah, and Chamber Orchestra of Baltimore. Resident conductor of Yaquina Chamber Orchestra in Oregon.
TELEVISION: *Series*: Doc, M*A*S*H. *Movies*: Charlie's Angels (pilot), A Circle of Children, A Love Affair: The Eleanor and Lou Gehrig Story, Sgt. Matlovich Vs. the U.S. Air Force, Breaking Up is Hard to Do, Damien: The Leper Priest, The Day the Bubble Burst, Anatomy of an Illness, The First Olympics: Athens 1896, The Bad Seed, 5 Perry Mason Movies (Shooting Star, Lost Love, Sinister Spirit, Avenging Ace, Lady in the Lake), Mrs. Delafield Wants to Marry, The Alamo: 13 Days to Glory, The Kissing Place, Final Notice, The Final Days, How to Murder a Millionaire, Wife Mother Murderer, The Last of His Tribe, Without a Kiss Goodbye. *Specials*: The Oldest Living Graduate, The Innocents Abroad, Mastergate. *Mini-Series*: North and South (also Book II).

THEATRE: *NY*: The Magic Show, Ulysses in Nighttown, The Three Sisters, Beggar's Opera, Measure for Measure.
PICTURES: Drive He Said, THX 1138, Oh God!, The Cheap Detective, Magic, Harry's War, The Man With One Red Shoe, Better Off Dead, Creator, Another Woman, The Accidental Tourist, Doc Hollywood, Beauty and the Beast (voice), Shadows and Fog.

STIGWOOD, ROBERT: Executive. b. Adelaide, Australia, April 16, 1934. e. Sacred Heart Coll. Began career as copywriter for Aust. ad agency; at 21 left home for England. Series of first jobs led to his opening a London theatrical agency. Began casting commercials for TV; prod. records for clients. Became first independent record producer in Great Britain. In mid '60s joined forces with Brian Epstein, mgr. of Beatles, to become co-mgr. of NEMS Enterprises. At Epstein's death formed own co., launching careers of such artists as Bee Gees, Cream, etc. Moved into theatre prod. in London: Hair, Jesus Christ Superstar, Pippin, Oh Calcutta!, Evita. Entered film prod. with Jesus Christ Superstar. Formed RSO Records in 1973.
PICTURES: Jesus Christ Superstar, Tommy, Saturday Night Fever, Grease, Sgt. Pepper's Lonely Hearts Club Band, Moment by Moment, Times Square (co.-prod.), The Fan, Gallipoli, Grease 2, Staying Alive.

STING: Musician, Actor. r.n. Gordon Matthew Sumner. b. Newcastle-Upon-Tyne, England, Oct. 2, 1951. e. Warwick U. A schoolteacher before helping form rock group, The Police as songwriter, singer and bass player. Broadway debut, Threepenny Opera, 1989.
PICTURES: Quadrophenia, Radio On, The Great Rock 'n' Roll Swindle, The Secret Policeman's Other Ball, Brimstone and Treacle, Dune, The Bride, Plenty, Bring on the Night, Julia and Julia, Stormy Monday, The Adventures of Baron Munchausen, Resident Alien, The Music Tells You.

STOCKWELL, DEAN: Actor. b. Hollywood, CA, Mar. 5, 1935. p. Harry and Betty Veronica Stockwell. Brother is actor Guy Stockwell. e. Long Island public schools and Martin Milmore, Boston. On stage in Theatre Guild prod. Innocent Voyage. Appeared on radio in Death Valley Days and Dr. Christian. Named in 1949 M.P. Herald-Fame Stars of Tomorrow poll; 1976 retired to Santa Monica as a licensed real estate broker but soon returned to acting.
PICTURES: The Valley of Decision (debut, 1945), Anchors Aweigh, Abbott and Costello in Hollywood, The Green Years, Home Sweet Homicide, The Mighty McGurk, The Arnelo Affair, The Romance of Rosy Ridge, Song of the Thin Man, Gentleman's Agreement, Deep Waters, Down to Sea in Ships, Boy with Green Hair, The Secret Garden, Happy Years, Kim, Stars in My Crown, Cattle Drive, Gun for a Coward, The Careless Years, Compulsion, Sons and Lovers, Long Day's Journey Into Night, Rapture, Psych-out, The Dunwich Horror, The Last Movie, The Loners, Werewolf of Washington, Won Ton Ton The Dog Who Saved Hollywood, Win Place or Steal, Tracks, She Came to the Valley, Alsino and the Condor, Human Highway (also co-dir., s.p.), Wrong Is Right, To Kill a Stranger, Paris Texas, Dune, Legend of Billie Jean, To Live and Die in L.A., Blue Velvet, Gardens of Stone, Beverly Hills Cop II, The Blue Iguana, Tucker: The Man and His Dream, Married to the Mob, Palais Royale, Limit Up, Buying Time, Time Guardian, The Player.
TELEVISION: *Series*: Quantum Leap. *Guest*: Miami Vice, Hart to Hart, Simon and Simon, The A-Team, Wagon Train, Twilight Zone, Playhouse 90, Hallmark Hall of Fame, Hunter, Police Story, Greatest Show on Earth. *Movies*: Paper Man, The Failing of Raymond, The Adventures of Nick Carter, The Return of Joe Forrester, A Killing Affair, The Gambler III: The Legend Continues, Son of the Morning Star, Backtrack, Shame, Fatal Memories. *Pilot*: Caught in the Act.

STOCKWELL, JOHN: Actor, Writer, Director. b. Galveston, TX, Mar. 25, 1961. e. Harvard, Actor's Workshop at NYU, RADA. Was guitarist with NY rock group The Brood. Theatre includes Camino Real, 3 Boys, Merry Wives of Windsor, Loot, Ah Wilderness.
PICTURES: So Fine (debut, 1981), Losin' It, Eddie and the Cruisers, Christine, City Limits, My Science Project, Dangerously Close (also co-s.p.), Top Gun, Radioactive Dreams, Under Cover (dir., co-s.p. only), Born to Ride.
TELEVISION: *Series*: The Guiding Light. *Movies*: Quarterback Princess, The Billionaire Boys Club. *Mini-Series*: North and South. *Specials*: A Family Tree (Trying Times), Eyes of the Panther (Nightmare Classics). *Pilot*: Too Good to Be True. *Guest*: Miami Vice, The Young Riders.

STODDARD, BRANDON: Executive. b. Brideport, CT, March 31, 1937. e. Yale U., Columbia Law Sch. Was program ass't. at Batton, Barton, Durstine and Osborn before joining Grey Advertising, where was successively, program operations supvr., dir. daytime programming, v.p. in chg. of TV, radio programming. Joined ABC in 1970; named v.p. daytime programs for ABC Entertainment, 1972; v.p. children's programs, 1973. Named v.p., motion pictures for TV, 1974. In 1976 named v.p., dramatic programs and m.p. for TV. In June,

1979, named pres., ABC Motion Pictures. In 1985 appt. pres., ABC Entertainment. Resigned March, 1989 to head ABC Prods. unit to create and prod. series and movies for ABC and other networks.

STOLNITZ, ART: Executive. b. Rochester, NY, March 13, 1928. e. U. of Tennessee, LL.B., 1952. U.S. Navy Air Force. Legal dept., William Morris Agency, 1953, dir. business affairs, ZIV, 1959; dir. new program development, ZIV-United Artists, 1960; literary agent, MCA, 1961; dir. business affairs, Selmur Productions, Selmur Pictures, 1963; v.p. ABC Pictures, 1969; v.p. Metromedia Producers Corporation, 1970, executive v.p. Metromedia Producers Corporation; 1975 exec. v.p. and prod. Charles Fries Prods. 1976, prod. Edgar J. Scherick Productions; 1976–77 prod., Grizzly Adams (TV); 1977; v.p. business affairs, Warner Bros.-TV; 1980, sr. v.p., business affairs; 1990, exec. v.p. business & financial affairs, Lorimar Television.

STOLOFF, VICTOR: Producer, Writer, Director, Editor. b. March 17, 1913. e. French Law U. Ac. Fines Arts. Prod. dir. writer of award winning documentaries (Warner Bros. release); Prod. dir. writer first U.S. film made in Italy, German & Rome; First U.S. film made in Egypt; Collaborator William Dieterle films; Contract writer, dir. to Sidney Buchman, Columbia, S.p.: Volcano, The Sinner, Shark Reef, Journey Around the World. Of Love and Desire (prod., s.p.); Intimacy (prod., dir.), The Washington Affair (prod., dir.), The 300 Year Weekend (dir., orig. s.p.).
TELEVISION: Ford Theatre, Lloyd Bridges series, National Velvet, High Adventure, with Lowell Thomas, Prod. on location 22, Hawaii Five-O, Why? Director (orig. s.p.) Created Woman of Russia, first of TV series. Originator, exec. prod., dir. for T.V., Vaclav Havel's play Audience, filmed in Prague, 1990.

STOLTZ, ERIC: Actor. b. American Samoa, 1961. Family moved to California when he was 8. Spent 2 years at U. of Southern California in theatre arts; left to study with Stella Adler and later William Traylor and Peggy Feury. Stage work with an American rep. co. in Scotland in Tobacco Road, You're a Good Man Charlie Brown, Working. Off-Bdwy: The Widow Claire, The American Plan, Down the Road. Broadway debut Our Town (1988, Theatre World Award, Tony nom. & Drama Desk nom.), followed by Two Shakespearean Actors.
PICTURES: Fast Times at Ridgemont High (debut, 1982), Surf II, Running Hot, The Wild Life, The New Kids, Mask, Code Name: Emerald, Some Kind of Wonderful, Lionheart, Sister Sister, Haunted Summer, Manifesto, The Fly II, Say Anything, Memphis Belle, The Waterdance, Singles (cameo), Bodies Rest & Motion (also co-prod.), Naked in New York, Killing Zoe.
TELEVISION: Many series appearances. *Movies*: The Grass is Always Greener Over the Septic Tank, The Seekers, The Violation of Sarah McDavid, Paper Dolls, Thursday's Child, A Killer in the Family, Money, The Heart of Justice, Foreign Affairs, Roommates. *Specials*: Things Are Looking Up, Sensibility and Sense, Our Town.

STONE, ANDREW L.: Producer, Director. b. California, July 16, 1902. e. U. of California. Ent. ind. 1918 at Universal San Francisco exch.; later author, prod., dir. series of pictures for Paramount; prod., dir. for Sono-Art; 1932–36. org. and oper. Race Night company; prod., dir., The Girl Said No, 1936; Stolen Heaven, Say It in French, The Great Victory Herbert, Magician Music, 1940. Dir. Stormy Weather; formed Andrew Stone Prods., 1943.
PICTURES: The Great Victor Herbert, Stormy Weather, Hi Diddle Diddle, Sensations of 1945, Bedside Manner, Bachelor's Daughter, Fun on a Weekend, Highway 301, Confidence Girl, Steel Trap, Blueprint for Murder, Night Holds Terror, Julie, Cry Terror, The Decks Ran Red, The Last Voyage, Ring of Fire, Password is Courage, Never Put It in Writing, Secret of My Success, Song of Norway, The Great Waltz.

STONE, BURTON J.: Executive. b. Feb. 16, 1928; e. Florida Southern Coll. Was film ed., Hollywood Film Co. 1951–53; serv. mgr., sales mgr. and gen. mgr., Consolidated Film Inds., 1953–61; nat'l sales mgr., Movielab, 1961–63; pres., All-service Film Laboratories, 1963; v.p. Technicolor, Inc., 1963–70. Pres., Precision Film Labs., 1972–78. Pres., Deluxe Laboratories, Inc., a wholly-owned subsidiary of 20th Century Fox, 1978–present.
MEMBER: Board of directors, Will Rogers Foundation and Motion Picture Pioneers; member Acad. of Motion Picture Arts & Sciences, American Society of Cinematographers; awarded fellowship in Society of Motion Picture & Television Engineers; past pres., Association of Cinema & Video Laboratories; awarded fellowship in British Kinematograph, Sound & Television Society.

STONE, DEE WALLACE: Actress. r.n. Deanna Bowers. b. Kansas City, MO, Dec. 14, 1948. m. actor Christopher Stone. e. U. of Kansas, theater and education. Taught high school English. Came to NY to audition for Hal Prince and spent 2 years working in commercials and industrial shows. First break in Police Story episode.

PICTURES: The Stepford Wives (debut, 1975), The Hills Have Eyes, 10, The Howling, E.T. the Extra-Terrestrial, Jimmy the Kid, Cujo, Critters, Secret Admirer, Club Life, Shadow Play, The White Dragon, Alligator II: The Return, Popcorn, Rescue Me.

TELEVISION: Series: Together We Stand, Lassie. Movies: The Sky's No Limit, Young Love First Love, The Secret War of Jackie's Girls, Child Bride of Short Creek, The Five of Me, A Whale for the Killing, Skeezer, Wait Til Your Mother Gets Home, Happy, I Take These Men, Hostage Flight, Sin of Innocence, Addicted to His Love, Stranger on My Land. Terror in the Sky, The Christmas Visitor, I'm Dangerous Tonight, Prophet of Evil: The Ervil LeBaron Story.Guest: Chips.

STONE, EZRA: Actor, Dir., Writer, Prod., Teacher, Lecturer, Farmer. b. New Bedford, MA, Dec. 2, 1917. e. American Acad. of Dramatic Arts, N.Y., 1934–35. Actor: National Junior Theatre, 1931; Broadway: Parade, Ah Wilderness, Oh Evening Star, Three Men on a Horse, Room Service, Brother Rat; created Henry Aldrich, What a Life, The Alchemist, She Stoops to Conquer; prod. asst. to George Abbott, 1935–40; created Henry Aldrich on radio's Aldrich Family, 1938; starred, prod. and staged Those Were the Days, This is the Army, USAAF, 1941–45; directed on Broadway: See My Lawyer, 1939, Reunion in New York, 1940. Has over 25 intl. film awards; Grand Prize, Barcelona Int'l Film Festival. The College of Fellows of Amer. Theatre Hon., Doctor of Fine Arts, Univ. of Missouri-Columbia.

STAGE: This Is the Army; January Thaw; At War with the Army; To Tell You the Truth; Me and Molly; Wake Up Darling; Make a Million; The Man That Corrupted Hadleyburg; The Pink Elephant; Dear Ruth; Come Blow Your Horn; God Bless Our Bank, Fallen Angels; Finishing Touches; Dracula—The Vampire King; Sweet Land (exec. prod., dir.); Centennial Celebration of Founding Newtown, PA (actor).

PICTURES: Did 300 documentary films for IBM. American Heart Assn., Chapman Coll., University of Judaism, Jewish Theological Seminary; dir. live action sequences for The Daydreamer; The Forty Million (prod., dir., co-narrator).

TELEVISION: Aldrich Family, Danny Thomas, Ed Wynn, Ezio Pinza, Martha Raye, Fred Allen, Herb Shriner, Life With Father, Sid Caesar, Joan Davis, dir. Joe and Mabel, prod., dir. Bachelor Father, Angel, The Hathaways, spec. Affairs of Antol, Shari Lewis, Bob Hope, My Living Doll, Munsters, Karen, Tammy, O.K. Crackerby, Please Don't Eat the Daisies; dir., writer Woody Allen pilot, Loredo, Pistols & Petticoats, Petticoat Junction, Phyllis Diller Show, Lost in Space, Tammy Grimes show, Julia, Flying Nun, Debbie Reynolds, The Jimmy Stewart Show, Lassie, Sandy Duncan Show, Tribute to the Lunts, Love American Style, Bob Newhart, Space Academy, Munster's Revenge, Quincy, ABC Circle Playhouse Project UFO, Actor, (PBS Paul Muni, biography film).

AUTHOR: Coming Major, 1945, co-author; Deems Taylor; Liberte, Puccini Opera, 1951; contributor to: Variety, Magazine Digest, N.Y. Post; Equity Magazine, etc. Teacher: American Acad. Dramatic Arts, assoc. dir., American Theatre Wing; American Coll. Theatre Fest., Princeton, Yale, UCLA: pres./dir., David Library of Amer. Revolution.

STONE, MARIANNE: Actress. b. London, England. Studied Royal Acad. of Dramatic Art, West End debut in The Kingmaker, 1946.

TELEVISION: Maigret, Bootsie and Snudge, Jimmy Edwards Show, Wayne and Schuster Show, Roy Hudd Show, Harry Worth Show, Steptoe and Son, Informer, Love Story, Father Dear Father, Bless This House, The Man Outside, Crown Court, Public Eye, Miss Nightingale, She, Little Lord Fauntleroy, The Secret Army (2 series), Shillingbury Tale, The Bright Side (series), Tickets for the Titanic (series), The Balance of Nature, Jaws, Hammer House of Mystery & Suspense, The Nineteenth Hole.

PICTURES: Brighton Rock, Seven Days to Noon, The Clouded Yellow, Wrong Arm of the Law, Heavens Above, Stolen Hours, Nothing But the Best, Curse of the Mummy's Tomb, Hysteria, The Beauty Jungle, A Hard Day's Night, Rattle of a Simple Man, Echo of Diana, Act of Murder, Catch Us If You Can, You Must Be Joking, The Countess from Hong Kong, The Wrong Box, To Sir With Love, The Bliss of Mrs. Blossom, Here We Go Round the Mulberry Bush, Carry on Doctor, The Twisted Nerve, The Best House in London, Oh! What a Lovely War; The Raging Moon, There's a Girl in My Soup, All the Right Noises, Assault, Carry On at Your Convenience, All Coppers Are. . ., Carry on Girls, Penny Gold, The Vault of Horror, Percy's Progress, Confessions of a Window Cleaner, Carry on Dick, That Lucky Touch, Sarah, Carry on Behind, Confessions From a Holiday Camp, The Chiffy Kids, What's Up Superdoc?; The Class of Miss McMichael, The Human Factor, Dangerous Davies, Funny Money, Terry on the Fence, Carry on Laughing.

STONE, OLIVER: Director, Writer. b. New York, NY, Sept. 15, 1946. e. Yale U., NYU, B.F.A., 1971. Teacher in Cholon,

Vietnam 1965–66. U.S. Infantry specialist 4th Class. 1967–68 in Vietnam (Purple Heart, Bronze Star with Oak Leaf Cluster honors).

PICTURES: Sugar Cookies (assoc. prod.), Seizure (dir., s.p., co-editor, 1974), Midnight Express (s.p.; Acad. Award, 1978), The Hand (dir., s.p., cameo), Conan the Barbarian (co-s.p.), Scarface (s.p.), Year of the Dragon (co-s.p.), Salvador (dir., co-s.p., co-prod.), 8 Million Ways to Die (co-s.p.), Platoon (dir., s.p., cameo; Acad. Award & DGA Award for Best Director, 1986), Wall Street (dir., co-s.p., cameo), Talk Radio (dir., co-s.p.), Born on the Fourth of July (dir., co-s.p., cameo; Acad. Award & DGA Award for Best Director, 1989), Blue Steel (co-prod.), Reversal of Fortune (co-prod.), The Doors (dir., co-s.p., cameo), Iron Maze (co-exec. prod.), JFK (dir., co-prod., co-s.p.), South Central (co-exec. prod.), Zebrahead (co-exec. prod.), Dave (actor), Heaven and Earth (dir., co-prod., s.p.), Natural Born KIllers (dir., co-prod., co-s.p.).

TELEVISION: Mini-Series: Wild Palms (co-exec. prod.)

STONE, PETER: Writer. b. Los Angeles, CA, Feb. 27, 1930. Son of film prod. John Stone and screenwriter Hilda Hess Stone. e. Bard Col., B.A. 1951; Yale U, M.F.A., 1953.

THEATER: Kean, Skyscraper, 1776 (Tony and NY Drama Critics Circle Awards, 1969), Two By Two, Sugar, Full Circle, Woman of the Year (Tony Award, 1981), My One and Only, Grand Hotel, Will Rogers Follies (Tony, Grammy and NY Drama Critics Circle Awards).

PICTURES: Charade, Father Goose (Acad. Award, 1964), Mirage, Arabesque, Secret War of Harry Frigg, Jigsaw, Sweet Charity, Skin Game, The Taking of Pelham One Two Three, 1776 (adapted own stage musical book to screen), Silver Bears, Who Is Killing the Great Chefs of Europe?, Why Would I Lie?

TELEVISION: Studio One, Brenner, Witness, Asphalt Jungle, The Defenders (Emmy, 1962). Androcles and the Lion, Adam's Rib (series), Ivan the Terrible (series), Baby on Board, Grand Larceny.

STONE, SHARON: Actress. b. Meadville, PA, March 10, 1958. e. Edinboro St. Univ. Started as model, appearing in several TV commercials.

PICTURES: Stardust Memories (debut, 1980), Deadly Blessing, Bolero, Irreconcilable Differences, King Soloman's Mines, Allan Quartermain and the Lost City of Gold, Cold Steel, Police Academy 4: Citizens on Patrol, Action Jackson, Above the Law, Beyond the Stars, Blood and Sand, Total Recall, He Said/She Said, Scissors, Year of the Gun, Basic Instinct, Diary of a Hit Man, Where Sleeping Dogs Lie, Sliver, Last Action Hero (cameo), Intersection.

TELEVISION: Series: Bay City Blues. Mini-Series: War and Remembrance. Movies: Not Just Another Affair, The Calendar Girl Murders, The Vegas Strip Wars, Tears in the Rain. Pilots: Mr. & Mrs. Ryan, Badlands 2005. Guest: T.J. Hooker, Magnum P.I.

STOPPARD, TOM: Writer, Director. b. Zlin, Czechoslovakia, July 3, 1937. r.n. Tomas Straussler. Playwright whose works include Rosencrantz and Guildenstern Are Dead, Jumpers, Travesties, The Real Thing, Hapgood, Arcadia.

PICTURES: The Romantic Englishwoman, Despair, The Human Factor, Squaring the Circle, Brazil, Empire of the Sun, The Russia House, Rosencrantz and Guildenstern Are Dead (also dir.), Billy Bathgate.

STORARO, VITTORIO: Cinematographer. b. Rome, Italy, 1940. Trained at Rome's Centro Sperimentale and began filming short films. His work as Bernardo Bertolucci's regular cameraman has won him an international reputation and award-winning work in Europe and America. Photographic consultant on Disney's 3-D short Captain Eo.

PICTURES: Giovinezza Giovinezza (Youthful Youthful), The Conformist, The Spider's Stratagem, 'Tis a Pity She's a Whore, Last Tango in Paris, Giordano Bruno, 1900, Submission, Agatha, Apocalypse Now (Acad. Award, 1979), Luna, Reds (Acad. Award, 1981), One From the Heart, Wagner, Ladyhawke, Ishtar, The Last Emperor (Acad. Award, 1987), Tucker: The Man and His Dream, New York Stories (Life Without Zoe), Dick Tracy, The Sheltering Sky.

STOREY, FREDERICK: Executive. b. Columbus, GA, Nov. 12, 1909. e. Georgia Tech. Adv. staff Atlanta Journal, 1933–38; adv. staff C. P. Clark Adv. Agcy., 1938; partner 1940; U.S. Navy, 1941–46; staff Georgia Theatre Co., 1946; v.p. 1947–52. Founded Storey Theatres Inc., Atlanta, GA; 1952, now bd. chmn. (formerly pres.) of Georgia State Theatres; dir. numerous theatre cos.; v.p. dir., Motion Picture Theatre Owners of Georgia, Dist. Alumnus award, Georgia Tech, 1979.

STORKE, WILLIAM F.: Producer. b. Rochester, NY, Aug. 12, 1927. e. UCLA, B.A. 1948. In Navy in W.W.II. First position with NBC Hollywood guest relations staff, 1948. Moved to continuity acceptance dept. as comm. editor. Prom. to asst. mgr. comm. spvr. before joining NBC West Coast sales dept., 1953. Transferred to N.Y. as prog. acct. exec., 1955; named administrator, participating prog. sales, Nov., 1957. Named

dir., participating program sales, 1959. Named dir., program adm., NBC-TV, Jan., 1964; in Feb. elected v.p., program adm. In 1967 named v.p., programs, East Coast; in 1968, appt. v.p., special programs, NBC-TV Network; 1979, pres., Claridge Group, Ltd.; exec. v.p. Entertainment Partners, Inc., N.Y., 1982–. Pres., Storke Enterprises Inc. 1988–.
TELEVISION: Producer: Oliver Twist, To Catch A King, A Christmas Carol, The Last Days of Patton, A Special Friendship, The Ted Kennedy Jr. Story, Buck James (series, exec. prod.), Old Man and the Sea, Hands of a Murderer (Sherlock Holmes).

STORM, GALE: Actress. r.n. Josephine Cottle. b. Bloomington, TX, April 5, 1922. Won a "Gateway to Hollywood" talent contest while still in high school, in 1939. Made several minor films in the 1940s including several Roy Rogers westerns, before becoming popular TV comedienne on My Little Margie (1952–55). Also launched successful recording career. Autobiography: I Ain't Down Yet (1981).
PICTURES: Tom Brown's Schooldays (debut, 1939), Smart Alecks, Foreign Agent, Nearly Eighteen, Where Are Your Children?, Revenge of the Zombies, The Right to Live, Sunbonnet Sue, Swing Parade of 1946, It Happened on Fifth Avenue, The Dude Goes West, Stampede, The Kid From Texas, Abandoned, Between Midnight and Dawn, Underworld Story, Curtain Call at Cactus Creek, Al Jennings of Oklahoma, Texas Rangers, Woman of the North Country.
TELEVISION: Series: My Little Margie, Oh Susanna.

STOSSEL, JOHN: News Correspondent. b. 1947. e. Princeton U. Started as producer-reporter with KGW-TV in Portland, OR. Joined WCBS-TV in New York as investigative reporter and consumer editor, winning 15 local Emmy Awards. In June, 1981 joined ABC-TV, appearing on Good Morning America and 20/20 as consumer editor. Also provides twice-weekly consumer reports on ABC Radio Information Network. Author: Shopping Smart (1982).

STOWE, MADELEINE: Actress. b. Los Angeles, CA, Aug. 18, 1958. e. USC. Began acting at the Solari Theatre in Beverly Hills where she appeared in The Tenth Man.
PICTURES: Stakeout (debut, 1987), Tropical Snow, Worth Winning, Revenge, The Two Jakes, Closet Land, China Moon, Unlawful Entry, The Last of the Mohicans, Another Stakeout, Short Cuts, Bad Girls.
TELEVISION: Series: The Gangster Chronicles. Movies: The Nativity, The Deerslayer, Amazons, Blood and Orchids. Mini-Series: Beulah Land.

STRADLING, HARRY, JR.: Cinematographer. b. New York, NY, Jan. 7, 1925. Son of Harry Stradling, renowned cinematographer.
PICTURES: Welcome to Hard Times, Support Your Local Sheriff, The Mad Room, Dirty Dingus Magee, Little Big Man, There Was a Crooked Man, The Late Liz, Something Big, Fools' Parade, Support Your Local Gunfighter, Skyjacked, Thumb Tripping, 1776, The Man Who Loved Cat Dancing, Nightmare Honeymoon, The Way We Were, McQ, Bank Shot, Bite the Bullet, Mitchell, Rooster Cogburn, Special Delivery, Midway, The Big Bus, The Greatest, Damnation Alley, Born Again, Convoy, Go Tell the Spartans, Prophecy, Up the Academy, Carny, S.O.B., The Pursuit of D.B. Cooper, Buddy Buddy, O'Hara's Wife, Micki and Maude, A Fine Mess, Blind Date, Caddyshack II.
TELEVISION: George Washington (mini-series).

STRAIGHT, BEATRICE: Actress. b. Old Westbury, NY, Aug. 2, 1918. Trained in classics; won Tony award early in career for best actress in Arthur Miller's The Crucible. Many films and TV programs.
THEATER: King Lear, Twelfth Night, The Possessed, Land of Fame, Eastward in Eden, The Heiress (Bdwy. & on tour), The Crucible (Tony Award), Phedra, Everything in the Garden, Ghosts, All My Sons, and regional theater (Streetcar Named Desire, Lion in Winter, Old Times).
PICTURES: Phone Call from a Stranger, Patterns, The Nun's Story, Garden Party, Network (Acad. Award, supp. actress, 1976), The Promise, Bloodline, The Formula, Endless Love, Poltergeist, Two of a Kind, Power.
TELEVISION: Series: Beacon Hill, King's Crossing, Jack and Mike. Mini-Series: The Dain Curse, Robert Kennedy and His Times. Specials: The Borrowers, Faerie Tale Theatre (The Princess and the Pea). Movies: Killer on Board, Under Siege, Run Till You Fall, People Like Us.

STRASBERG, SUSAN: Actress. b. New York, NY, May 22, 1938. e. N.Y. Parents: late Lee Strasberg, stage dir. & dir. of Actors Studio, and Paula Miller, actress. Off-Bdwy stage debut in Maya; on TV in series, The Marriage and Time, The Duchess and the Smugs, Romeo and Juliet. Starred on Bdwy in The Diary of Anne Frank (Theatre World Award), Time Remembered, Zeffirelli's Lady of the Camillias, Shadow of a Gunman. Toured in Agnes of God. Author, Bittersweet. Acting Teacher, like father.
PICTURES: The Cobweb (debut, 1955), Picnic, Stage Struck, Scream of Fear, Adventures of a Young Man, High

Bright Sun (McGuire Go Home!), The Trip, Psych-Out, Chubasco, The Name of the Game Is Kill, The Brotherhood, So Evil My Sister, Legend of Hillbilly John, And Millions Will Die, Rollercoaster, The Manitou, In Praise of Older Women, Sweet 16, The Delta Force, Bloody Birthday, Prime Suspect, The Runnin' Kind, Schweitzer, The Cherry Orchard.
TELEVISION: Movies: Marcus Welby M.D. (A Matter of Humanities), Hauser's Memory, Mr. & Mrs. Bo Jo Jones, SST-Death Flight, Beggarman, Thief, The Immigrants, Toma (pilot), Frankenstein, Rona Jaffe's Mazes and Monsters. Series: The Marriage, Toma. Guest: Murder She Wrote, Cagney and Lacy.

STRASSBERG, STEPHEN: Publicist. b. New York, NY. e. City Coll. of New York, B.S.S. Joined Loew's Inc., 1940; served in U.S. Army, WW II; publicist with Republic Pictures, 1946–49; asst. nat'l adv. dir., Film Classics, 1949–50; pub. dir., Eagle Lion Classics, 1950; publicist Lopert Films, Inc., 1951; dir. of adv., pub., Imperial Films, 1953; pub. dir., WABC, WABC-TV, N.Y., 1955; asst. dir., Press Information; ABC, 1957; dir. press info. ABC-TV Network, 1958; dir., News Information, ABC-TV Network, 1975.

STRATHAIRN, DAVID: Actor. b. San Francisco, CA, 1949. e. Williams Col.
PICTURES: Return of the Secaucus 7, Lovesick, Silkwood, Iceman, The Brother from Another Planet, When Nature Calls, Enormous Changes at the Last Minute, At Close Range, Matewan, Stars and Bars, Dominick and Eugene, Call Me, Eight Men Out, The Feud, Memphis Belle, City of Hope, Big Girls Don't Cry . . . They Get Even, A League of Their Own, Bob Roberts, Sneakers, Passion Fish, Lost in Yonkers, The Firm.
TELEVISION: Series: The Days and Nights of Molly Dodd. Movies: Day One, Son of the Morning Star, Heat Wave, Judgment, Without Warning: The James Brady Story, O Pioneers!. Guest: Miami Vice, The Equalizer.
THEATRE: Einstein and the Polar Bear, Blue Plate Special, Fen, I'm Not Rappaport, Salonika, A Lie of the Mind, The Birthday Party, Danton's Death, Mountain Language, L'Atelier, A Moon for the Misbegotten, Temptation.

STRAUSS, PETER: Actor. b. Croton-on-Hudson, NY., Feb. 20, 1947. e. Northwestern U. Spotted at N.U. by talent agent and sent to Hollywood. On stage at Mark Taper Theatre in Dance Next Door, The Dirty Man.
PICTURES: Hail Hero! (debut, 1969), Soldier Blue, The Trail of the Catonsville Nine, The Last Tycoon, Spacehunter.
TELEVISION: Movies: Man Without a Country, Attack on Terror: The FBI Versus the Ku Klux Klan, Young Joe: The Forgotten Kennedy, The Jericho Mile (Emmy Award), Angel on My Shoulder; Heart of Steel, Under Siege, A Whale for the Killing, Penalty Phase, Proud Men, Brotherhood of the Rose, Peter Gunn, 83 Hours Till Dawn, Flight of Black Angel, Fugitive Among Us, Trial: The Price of Passion, Men Don't Tell. Mini-Series: Rich Man Poor Man, Masada, Kane & Abel, Tender Is The Night.

STRAUSS, PETER E.: Executive. b. Oct. 7, 1940. e. Oberlin Coll., London Sch. of Economics, Columbia U. Sch. of Law, L.L.B., 1965. Vice pres., University Dormitory Dev. Co., 1965–68; v.p., Allart Cinema 16, 1968–69; v.p. prod., Allied Artists Pictures Corp., 1970; 1974 elected exec. v.p. Joined Rastar Films; left to become independent. 1987, pres. & CEO of The Movie Group. Pres. of the Movie Group.
PICTURE: Producer: Best of the Best, Cadence, By the Sword, Best of the Best II.

STREEP, MERYL: Actress. r.n. Mary Louise Streep. b. Summit, NJ, June 22, 1949. e. Vassar. Acted for a season with traveling theater co. in VT. Awarded scholarship to Yale Drama School, 1972, where she was cast in 12–15 roles a year. NY stage debut: Trelawny of the Wells (1975) with New York Shakespeare Fest. Appeared in 1984 documentary In Our Hands.
THEATER: Off-Broadway: 27 Wagons Full of Cotton (Theatre World Award), A Memory of Two Mondays, Secret Service, Henry V, (New York Shakespeare Fest.), Measure for Measure (NYSF), The Cherry Orchard, Happy End (Broadway debut, 1977), Taming of the Shrew (NYSF), Taken in Marriage, Alice in Concert, Isn't It Romantic?.
PICTURES: Julia (debut, 1977), The Deer Hunter, Manhattan, The Seduction of Joe Tynan, Kramer vs. Kramer (Acad. Award, supp. actress, 1979), The French Lieutenant's Woman, Still of the Night, Sophie's Choice (Acad. Award, 1982), Silkwood, Falling in Love, Plenty, Out of Africa, Heartburn, Ironweed, A Cry in the Dark, She-Devil, Postcards From the Edge, Defending Your Life, Death Becomes Her, The House of the Spirits.
TELEVISION: Mini-Series: Holocaust (Emmy Award, 1978). Movie: The Deadliest Season. Specials (PBS): Secret Service, Uncommon Women and Others, Age 7 in America (host).

STREISAND, BARBRA: Singer, Actress, Director. b. New York, NY, April 24, 1942. e. Erasmus H.S., Brooklyn. Son is actor

Jason Gould. Appeared in New York night clubs. NY stage debut: Another Evening with Harry Stoones (1961), followed by Pins and Needles. On Broadway in I Can Get It For You Wholesale, Funny Girl. Performed song Prisoner for 1978 film Eyes of Laura Mars. Appeared in 1990 documentary Listen Up.

PICTURES: Funny Girl (debut; Acad. Award, 1968), Hello Dolly!, On A Clear Day You Can See Forever, The Owl and the Pussycat, What's Up Doc?, Up the Sandbox, The Way We Were, For Pete's Sake, Funny Lady, A Star Is Born (also co-composer), exec. prod.; Acad. Award for best song: Evergreen), The Main Event (also co-prod.), All Night Long, Yentl (also dir., prod., co.s.p.), Nuts (also prod., co-composer), The Prince of Tides (also dir., co-prod.).

TELEVISION: Specials: My Name is Barbra (Emmy Award, 1965), Color Me Barbra, Belle of 14th Street, A Happening in Central Park, Barbra Streisand . . . And Other Musical Instruments, Putting It Together, One Voice. Guest: Ed Sullivan, Merv Griffin, Judy Garland Show, Saturday Night Live.

STRICK, WESLEY: Writer. b. New York, NY. e. UC at Berkeley, 1975. Was rock critic for magazines Rolling Stone, Cream, Circus.

PICTURES: True Believer, Arachnophobia, Cape Fear, Final Analysis, Batman Returns.

TELEVISION: Series: Eddie Dodd (pilot).

STRICKLAND, GAIL: Actress. b. Birmingham, AL, May 18. e. Florida St. Univ. NY Theatre includes Status Quo Vadis, I Won't Dance.

TELEVISION: Series: The Insiders, What a Country, Heart-beat. Movies: Ellery Queen, My Father's House, The Dark Side of Innocence, The Gathering, A Love Affair: The Eleanor and Lou Gehrig Story, The President's Mistress, Ski Lift to Death, Letters from Frank, King Crab, Rape and Marriage: The Rideout Case, A Matter of Life and Death, My Body My Child, Eleanor: First Lady of the World, Life of the Party: The Story of Beatrice, Starlight: The Plane That Couldn't Land, The Burden of Proof, Silent Cries, Spies.

PICTURES: The Drowning Pool, Bittersweet Love, Bound for Glory, One on One, Who'll Stop the Rain, Norma Rae, Lies, Oxford Blues, Protocol, The Man in the Moon, Three of Hearts.

STRICKLYN, RAY: Actor. b. Houston, TX, October 8, 1930. e. U. of Houston. Official U.S. representative at Edinburgh Intl. Festival (1988); and Israel Intl. Festival (1989). TV Movies: Jealousy, Danielle Steel's Secrets.

PLAYS: Broadway debut in Moss Hart's The Climate of Eden. Tours: Stalag 17, Confessions of a Nightingale. Off-B'way: The Grass Harp, Confessions of a Nightingale. Los Angeles: Confessions of a Nightingale, Vieux Carre, Compulsion, The Caretaker, Naomi Court, Bus Stop.

PICTURES: The Proud and the Profane, Crime In the Streets, Somebody Up There Likes Me, The Catered Affair, The Last Wagon, Return of Dracula, 10 North Frederick, The Remarkable Mr. Pennypacker, The Big Fisherman, Young Jesse James, The Plunderers, The Lost World, Track of Thunder, Arizona Raiders, Dogpound Shuffle.

AWARDS: Theatre World Award; 2 Hollywood Foreign Press Golden Globe noms. (10 North Frederick and The Plunderers); Best Actor Awards 1984 & 86 for Vieux Carre and Confessions of a Nightingale (LA Drama Critics, LA. Weekly Award, Drama-Logue, Robby Award, AGLA Media Award, Oscar Wilde Award).

STRINGER, HOWARD: Executive. b. Cardiff, Wales. Feb. 19, 1942. e. Oxford U., B.A., M.A., modern history/international relations. Received Army Commendation Medal for meritorious achievement for service in Vietnam (1965–67). Joined CBS, 1965, at WCBS-TV, NY, rising from assoc. prod., prod. to exec. prod. of documentary broadcasts. Served as prod., dir. and writer of CBS Reports: The Palestinians (Overseas Press Club of America, Writers Guild Awards, 1974); The Rockefellers (Emmy Award, 1973). Won 9 Emmy Awards as exec. prod., prod., writer or dir: CBS Reports: The Boston Goes to China; CBS Reports: The Defense of the United States; CBS Evening News with Dan Rather: The Beirut Bombing; The Countdown Against Cancer; The Black Family. Exec. prod., CBS Reports; exec. prod., CBS Evening News with Dan Rather, 1981–84. Appointed exec. vice pres., CBS News Division, 1984; pres., CBS News, 1986; pres., CBS/Broadcast Group, 1988.

STRITCH, ELAINE: Actress. b. Detroit, MI, Feb. 2, 1926. e. studied acting with Erwin Piscator at the New Sch. for Social Research. Major career on stage. Bdwy debut 1946 in Loco.

THEATER: Made in Heaven, Angel in the Wings, Call Me Madam, Pal Joey, On Your Toes, Bus Stop, Goldilocks, Sail Away, Who's Afraid of Virginia Woolf?, Wonderful Town, Company. London: Gingerbread Lady, Small Craft Warnings, Company.

PICTURES: The Scarlet Hour (debut, 1955), Three Violent People, A Farewell to Arms, The Perfect Furlough, Who Killed Teddy Bear?, Sidelong Glances of a Pigeon Kicker, The

Spiral Staircase, Providence, September, Cocoon: The Return, Cadillac Man.

TELEVISION: Series: Growing Paynes (1948), Pantomine Quiz (regular, 1953–55, 1958), My Sister Eileen, The Trials of O'Brien, Two's Company (London), Nobody's Perfect (London; also adapt.) The Ellen Burstyn Show. Specials: Company: the Making of the Album, Kennedy Center Tonight, Follies in Concert, Sensibility and Sense. Movies: The Secret Life of Archie's Wife, An Inconvenient Woman, Chance of a Lifetime.

STROCK, HERBERT L.: Producer, Writer, Director, Film editor. b. Boston, MA, Jan. 13, 1918. e. U. of Southern California, A.B., M.A. in cinema. Prof. of cinema, U. of Southern California, 1941. Started career, publicity leg man, Jimmy Fidler, Hollywood columnist; editorial dept., MGM, 1941–47; pres., IMPPRO, Inc., 1955–59; assoc. prod.-supv. film ed., U.A.; director: AIP, Warner Bros. independent, Phoenix Films. Pres. Herbert L. Strock Prods.

PICTURES: Storm Over Tibet, Magnetic Monster, Riders to the Stars, The Glass Wall. Director: Gog, Battle Taxi, Donovan's Brain, Rider on a Dead Horse, Devil's Messenger, Brother on the Run, One Hour of Hell, Witches Brew, Blood of Dracula, I Was a Teenage Frankenstein, The Crawling Hand; Soul Brothers Die Hard, Monstroids. Writer-film editor, Hurray for Betty Boop (cartoon). Sound Effects editor on Katy Caterpillar (cartoon feature). Editor: Night Screams, Detour. Post-prod. spvr.: King Kung Fu, Sidewalk Motel. Co-director: Deadly Presence. Editor: California Dreaming. Dir., ed.: Gramma's Gold. Prod/edit.: The Visitors.

TELEVISION: Highway Patrol, Harbor Command, Men of Annapolis, I Led Three Lives, The Veil, Dragnet, 77 Sunset Strip, Maverick, Cheyenne, Bronco, Sugarfoot, Colt 45, Science Fiction Thea., Seahunt, Corliss Archer, Bonanza, Hallmark Hall of Fame, The Small Miracle, Hans Brinker, The Inventing of America (specials); What Will We Say to a Hungry World (telethon), They Search for Survival (special), Flipper (series). Documentaries: Atlantis, Legends, UFO Journals, UFO Syndrome, Legend of the Lochness Monster, China-Mao to Now, El-Papa—Journey to Tibet. Editor: Peace Corps' Partnership in Health. L.A. Dept. of Water & Power: Water You Can Trust; Olympic Comm. Your Olympic Legacy—AAF.

STRODE, WOODY: Actor. r.n. Woodrow Strode. b. Los Angeles, 1914. Before W.W.II at UCLA. With Kenny Washington was one of first black players to integrate collegiate football. For 9 years after W.W.II was a professional wrestler. Worked for John Ford, Cecil B. DeMille, Henry Hathaway.

PICTURES: The Lion Hunters, (debut, 1951), Caribbean, City Beneath the Sea, The Gambler From Natchez, The Ten Commandments, Tarzan's Fight for Life, Pork Chop Hill, The Buccaneer, The Last Voyage, Sergeant Rutledge, Spartacus, The Sins of Rachel Cade, Two Rode Together, The Man Who Shot Liberty Valance, Tarzan's Three Challenges, Genghis Khan, 7 Women, The Professionals, Shalako, Once Upon a Time in the West, Che!, Tarzan's Deadly Silence, The Deserter, The Last Rebel, The Revengers, The Italian Connection, The Gatling Gun, Winterhawk, Oil, Kingdom of the Spiders, Jaguar Lives, Cuba Crossing, Ravagers, Vigilante, The Black Stallion Returns, Scream, Jungle Warriors, The Cotton Club, Lust in the Dust, Storyville, Posse.

TELEVISION: Movies: Breakout, Key West, A Gathering of Old Men.

STROLLER, LOUIS A.: Producer. b. Brooklyn, NY, April 3, 1942. e. Nicholas Coll. of Business Admin., BBA, 1963. Entered film business in 1963 doing a variety of jobs in local NY studios, and TV commercials. Unit manager on The Producers. Moved to L.A. in 1970s. First asst. dir. Charley, Take the Money and Run, Lovers and Other Strangers, They Might Be Giants, Man on a Swing, 92 in the Shade. Prod. mgr.: Mortadella, Sisters, Sweet Revenge, The Eyes of Laura Mars, Telefon. Assoc. prod.: Badlands, Carrie. The Seduction of Joe Tynan.

PICTURES: Exec. prod. or prod.: Simon, The Four Seasons, Venom, Eddie Macon's Run, Scarface, Sweet Liberty, Real Men, A New Life, Sea of Love, Betsy's Wedding, Back in the U.S.S.R., The Real McCoy, Carlito's Way.

TELEVISION: Half a Lifetime (exec. prod.; nom. 4 ACE Awards), Blue Ice.

STRONG, JOHN: Producer, Director, Writer, Actor. b. New York, NY, Dec. 3. e. U. of Miami, Cornell U., B.S., architectural engineering. Began acting in small role in film Duel in the Sun; on Bdwy in Annie Get Your Gun and understudy for James Dean in Immoralist. Appeared in many radio and TV serials, regular on Captain Video and the Video Ranger, later under contract as actor to Universal and Warner Bros. Member, Writers Guild America West, Directors Guild of America, Producers Guild of America, Dramatists Guild. Pres., Cinevent Corp.

PICTURES: Perilous Journey (exec. prod., writer), Eddie & the Cruisers (sprv. prod.), Heart Like a Wheel (sprv. prod.), For Your Eyes Only (s.p.), The Earthling (prod.), The Moun-

tain Men (actor, prod.), Savage Streets (prod.), Steel Justice (prod.), Knights of the City (prod.), Garbage Pail Kids (sprv. prod.), Cop (sprv. prod.), Wild Thing (sprv. prod.), Summer Heat (sprv. prod.), Teen Wolf II (sprv. prod.), Atlantic Entertainment (sprv. prod.), Show of Force (prod., s.p.), Prime Directive (prod., s.p.), Sinapore Sling (prod., s.p.), Willie Sutton Story (prod.), Bandit Queen (prod.), Fatal Charm (exec. prod.), Colors of Love (prod.), Black Ice (dir., s.p.).
TELEVISION: The John Strong Show (host, exec. prod.), The Nurse (special, writer), McCloud (prod., writer), The Thrill of the Fall (prod.), Search (prod., writer, 2nd unit dir.), Outer Limits (exec. chg. prod.), Name of the Game (exec. chg. prod.), I Spy (writer), Love American Style (writer), All in the Family (writer), Changes (prod., dir., writer), Charlie's Angels (writer), Hawaii Five O' (writer).

STROUD, DON: Actor. b. Honolulu, Hawaii, Sept. 1, 1937.
PICTURES: Games, Madigan, Journey to Shiloh, What's So Bad About Feeling Good?, Coogan's Bluff, Bloody Mama, Explosion, Angel Unchained, Tick Tick Tick, Von Richtofen and Brown, Joe Kidd, Slaughter's Big Rip-Off, Scalawag, Murph the Surf, The Killer Inside Me, The House by the Lake, The Choirboys, The Buddy Holly Story, The Amityville Horror, The Night the Lights Went Out in Georgia, Search and Destroy, Sweet Sixteen, Armed and Dangerous, Licence to Kill, Down the Drain, The Divine Enforcer.
TELEVISION: Series: Mike Hammer. Movies: Split Second to an Epitaph, Something for a Lonely Man, DA: Conspiracy to Kill, Deadly Dream, Daughters of Joshua Cabe, Rolling Man, The Elevator, Return of Joe Forrester, High Risk, Katie: Portrait of a Centerfold, Two to Tango.

STRUTHERS, SALLY: Actress. b. Portland, OR, July 28, 1947. First tv appearance was as dancer on a Herb Alpert special. Appeared on Broadway stage in Wally's Cafe.
PICTURES: The Phynx, Five Easy Pieces, The Getaway.
TELEVISION: Series: The Smothers Summer Show (1970), The Tim Conway Comedy Hour, All in the Family (Emmy Awards: 1972, 1979), Pebbles and Bamm-Bamm (voice), Flintstones Comedy Hour (voice), Gloria, 9 to 5, Dinosaurs (voice). Movies: The Great Houdinis, Aloha Means Goodbye, Hey I'm Alive, Intimate Strangers, My Husband is Missing, And Your Name is Jonah, A Gun in the House, A Deadly Silence, In the Best Interests of the Children.

STUBBS, IMOGEN: Actress. b. Newcastle-upon-Tyne, 1961. Brought up in West London on sailing barge on the Thames. Grandmother was playwright Esther McCracken. e. Exeter Coll. at Oxford U. in English. Joined Oxford U. Dramatic Society appearing in revues and at Edinburgh Festival in play called Poison. Trained for stage at Royal Acad. of Dramatic Art. Prof. stage debut in Cabaret and The Boyfriend, in Ipswich. Acted with Royal Shakespeare Co. in The Two Noble Kinsmen, The Rover, Richard II.
PICTURES: Privileged, A Summer Story, Nanou, Erik the Viking, True Colors.
TELEVISION: The Browning Version, Deadline, The Rainbow, Fellow Traveller.

STULBERG, GORDON: Executive. b. Toronto, Canada, Dec. 17, 1927. e. U. of Toronto, B.A.; Cornell Law Sch., LL.B. Was assoc. & member, Pacht, Ross, Warne & Bernhard; ent. m.p. ind. as exec. asst. to v.p., Columbia Pictures Corp., 1956–60; v.p. & chief studio admin. off., 1960–67; pres. of Cinema Center Films (div. of CBS) 1967–71; pres. 20th Century-Fox, Sept. 1971–75; 1980, named pres. & chief operating officer, PolyGram Pictures. Member of NY, Calif. bars, Chairman, American Interactive Media (Polygram subsidiary).

STYNE, JULE: Composer, Producer. r.n. Jules Stein. b. London, Eng., Dec. 31, 1905. To U.S. as a child; guest piano soloist with Chicago Symph. Orch. at 8; played with many dance bands; gen. mus. dir. Granada & Marbro Theat., Chicago; vocal coach, arranger, conductor & comp. for several m.p. studios; entertainment consult.
SONGS: I've Heard That Song Before, It's Magic, I'll Walk Alone, It's Been a Long, Long Time; Let It Snow, 3 Coins in the Fountain (Acad. Award in collab. Sammy Cahn, 1954), Make Someone Happy, Just in Time, The Party's Over, Small World, Everything's Coming Up Roses, People.
STAGE: High Button Shoes, Gentlemen Prefer Blondes, Two on the Aisle, Hazel Flagg, Peter Pan, Bells Are Ringing, Gypsy, Funny Girl, Hallelujah Baby (Tony Award), Sugar, Bar Mitzvah Boy.
PICTURES: Scores: Kid from Brooklyn, It Happened in Brooklyn, Romance on the High Seas, It's a Great Feeling, West Point Story, Meet Me After the Show, Living It Up, My Sister Eileen. Films of musicals: Bells Are Ringing, Gypsy, Funny Girl.

SUGAR, JOSEPH M.: Executive. b. New York, NY, June 4, 1922. e. NYU. Started with Republic Pictures 1938; after service, U.S. Army Air Force, went to Eagle Lion which was taken over by United Artists; 1953, U.A., N.Y., metropolitan district mgr.; 1959, Magna Pictures Corp., v.p. sls.; 1962, 20th Century-Fox, v.p. domestic distribution; 1967, Warner-7 Arts,

exec. v.p.; 1968, pres., Cinerama Rel. Corp.; 1974, formed Joe Sugar, Inc.; 1976, joined A.I.P. as exec. v.p. worldwide sls. & pres.—A.I.P. Distribution Co.—A.I.P. later became Filmways; 1983, Embassy Pictures. exec. v.p. dist; 1986, Joe Sugar, Inc. when Embassy sold to Coca Cola. Member Cinema Lodge, B'nai B'rith; A.F.I.; Motion Picture Pioneers, Variety Club.

SUGAR, LARRY: Executive. b. Phoenix, AZ, May 26, 1945. m. Bonnie Sugar. e. Cheshire Acad., 1962; CSUN, B.A., 1967; U. of Southern Calif., J.D., 1971. Writer and co-author, Calif. Primary Reading Program, 1967–68. Joined Warner Bros. as dir., legal and corp. affairs, 1971–74; 20th Century Fox legal staff, 1974–77; co-owner with Bonnie Sugar, Serendipity Prods., 1977–81; named pres., intl., Lorimar Prods. 1981–84; exec. v.p., distribution, CBS 1984–85; exec. v.p. worldwide distribution, Weintraub Entertainment Group 1987–89; formed Sugar Entertainment, chmn., 1989–1991; pres. intl., Republic Pictures, Inc. 1991–.
PICTURES: Exec. prod.: Slapstick, Steel Dawn, Options, Damned River, Fatal Sky, Graveyard Shift, Shattered, Dark Horse, Family Prayers. Prod: With Deadly Intent.

SUGARMAN, BURT: Producer. b. Beverly Hills, CA, Jan. 4. e. U. of Southern California. Chmn. & CEO, Giant Group, Ltd., diversified co. traded on NYSE. Heads Barris Industries Inc.
PICTURES: Kiss Me Goodbye, Extremities, Children of a Lesser God, Crimes of the Heart.
TELEVISION: Midnight Special, Switched on Symphony, The Mancini Generation, Johnny Mann's Stand Up and Cheer, etc.

SULLIVAN, BARRY: Actor. r.n. Patrick Barry. b. New York, NY, Aug. 29, 1912. e. NYU, Temple U. Usher in theatre.; buyer for dept. stores; N.Y. stage: The Man Who Came to Dinner, Brother Rat, Idiot's Delight, The Land is Bright, Caine Mutiny Court Martial, etc.
PICTURES: Woman of the Town, Lady in the Dark, Rainbow Island, Two Years Before the Mast, And Now Tomorrow, Duffy's Tavern, Three Guys Named Mike, Cause for Alarm, Grounds for Marriage, Life of Her Own, Nancy Goes to Rio, Inside Straight, Payment on Demand, Mr. Imperium, No Questions Asked, Unknown Man, Skirts Ahoy, Bad & the Beautiful, Jeopardy, Cry of the Hunted, China Venture, Loophole, Her 12 Men, Miami Story, Playgirl, Queen Bee, Texas Lady, Strategic Air Command, Maverick Queen, Julie, Dragon Wells Massacre, The Way to the Gold, Forty Guns, Wolf Larsen, Another Time Another Place, Purple Gang, Seven Ways from Sundown, Light in the Piazza, A Gathering of Eagles, Stage to Thunder Rock, Pyro, Man in the Middle, My Blood Runs Cold, Harlow, Planet of the Vampires, Intimacy, An American Dream, Buckskin, Tell Them Willie Boy Is Here, It Takes All Kinds, Shark!, Earthquake, The Human Factor, Take a Hard Ride, Survival, French Quarter, Oh God!, Caravans.
TELEVISION: Series: Man Called X (1955–56); Harbourmaster, The Tall Man, Road West, Rich Man Poor Man Book II. Mini-Series: Once an Eagle, Backstairs at the White House. Movies: The Immortal, Night Gallery (pilot), House on Greenapple Road, Johnny Belinda, Yuma, No Room to Run, Casino.

SULLIVAN, REV. PATRICK J., S.J., S.T.D.: Provost, Graduate Center at Tarrytown, Fordham U. b. New York, NY, March 25, 1920. e. Regis H.S.: Georgetown U., A.B.; 1943; Woodstock Coll., M.A., 1944; Fordham U. 1945–47; S.T.L. Weston Coll. 1947–51; S.T.D. Gregorian U. (Rome), 1952–54. Prof. of Theology, Woodstock Coll., 1954–57; Consultor, Pontifical Commission for Social Communications, 1968–82; Exec. Dir., U.S. Catholic Conference, Film & Broadcasting Office, 1965–80; Fordham Univ. Grad Sch. of Business, Assoc. Dean 1982–83, Dean 1983–85.

SUNSHINE, ROBERT HOWARD: Publisher. b. Brooklyn, NY, Jan. 17, 1946. e. U. of Rhode Island; Brooklyn Law Sch., 1971. Admitted to NY State Bar, 1971. President of Pubsun Corp., owner of The Film Journal. Publisher of The Film Journal. Exec. dir., Theatre Equipment Association, 1979–present; exec. dir., Variety, The Children's Charity of New York, 1975–present; secretary and exec. dir. Foundation of the Motion Picture Pioneers, 1975–present; exec. dir., Natl. Assoc. of Theatre Owners of NY State, 1985–present; Producer of Variety Telethon, 1985–present; coordinator and producer, Show East Convention; coordinator and prod., Cinema Expo Intl., Brussels, Belgium.

SURTEES, BRUCE: Cinematographer. b. Los Angeles, CA, July 23, 1937. Son of cinematographer Robert L. Surtees.
PICTURES: The Beguiled, Play Misty for Me, Dirty Harry, The Great Northfield Minnesota Raid, Conquest of the Planet of the Apes, Joe Kidd, The Outfit, High Plains Drifter, Blume in Love, Lenny (Acad. Award nom.), Night Moves, Leadbelly, The Outlaw Josey Wales, The Shootist, Three Warriors, Sparkle, Big Wednesday, Movie Movie (Baxter's Beauties of 1933), Dreamer, Escape from Alcatraz, Ladies and Gentlemen the Fabulous Stains, White Dog, Firefox, Inchon, Honkytonk Man, Bad Boys, Risky Business, Sudden Impact,

Tightrope, Beverly Hills Cop, Pale Rider, Psycho III, Out of Bounds, Ratboy, Back to the Beach, License to Drive, Men Don't Leave, Run, The Super, The Crush, That Night.

SUSCHITZKY, PETER: Cinematographer. Spent long time in Latin America as documentary cinematographer. Later made commercials in France, England, and U.S. First feature It Happened Here, 1962.
PICTURES: over 30 features including A Midsummer Night's Dream, Charlie Bubbles, Leo the Last, Privilege, That'll Be the Day, Lisztomania, The Rocky Horror Picture Show, All Creatures Great and Small (TV in U.S.), Valentino, The Empire Strikes Back, Krull, Falling in Love, In Extremis, Dead Ringers, Where the Heart Is, Naked Lunch, The Public Eye, The Vanishing, M. Butterfly.

SUTHERLAND, DONALD: Actor. b. St. John, New Brunswick, Canada, July 17, 1935. Father of actor Kiefer Sutherland. e. U. of Toronto, B.A., 1956. At 14 became a radio announcer and disc jockey. Worked in a mine in Finland. Theatre includes: The Male Animal (debut), The Tempest (Hart House Theatre, U. of Toronto), Two years at London Acad. of Music and Dramatic Art. Spent a year and a half with the Perth Repertory Theatre in Scotland, then repertory at Nottingham, Chesterfield, Bromley and Sheffield.
STAGE: August for the People (London debut), On a Clear Day You Can See Canterbury, The Shewing Up of Blanco Posnet, The Spoon River Anthology, Lolita (Bdwy debut, 1981).
PICTURES: Castle of the Living Dead (debut, 1964), The World Ten Times Over, Dr. Terror's House of Horrors, Die Die My Darling, The Bedford Incident, Promise Her Anything, The Dirty Dozen, Billion Dollar Brain, Sebastian, Oedipus the King, Interlude, Joanna, The Split, M*A*S*H, Start the Revolution Without Me, Act of the Heart, Kelly's Heroes, Alex in Wonderland, Little Murders, Klute, Johnny Got His Gun, F.T.A. (also co-prod., co-dir., co-s.p.), Steelyard Blues (also exec. prod.), Lady Ice, Alien Thunder, Don't Look Now, S*P*Y*S, The Day of the Locust, End of the Game (cameo), Casanova, The Eagle Has Landed, 1900, The Disappearance, Kentucky Fried Movie, National Lampoon's Animal House, Invasion of the Body Snatchers, Blood Relatives, The Great Train Robbery, Murder by Decree, Bear Island, A Man a Woman and a Bank, Nothing Personal, Ordinary People, Gas, Eye of the Needle, Threshold, Max Dugan Returns, Crackers, Ordeal by Innocence, Heaven Help Us, Revolution, Wolf at the Door, The Rosary Murders, Bethune: The Making of a Hero (Dr. Bethune), The Trouble With Spies, Apprentice to Murder, Lost Angels, Lock Up, A Dry White Season, Eminent Domain, Backdraft, Buster's Bedroom, JFK, Scream of Stone, Buffy the Vampire Slayer, Shadow of the Wolf, Benefit of the Doubt, Younger and Younger, Six Degrees of Separation.
TELEVISION: Specials: (British) Gore Vidal's Marching to the Sea, Albee's The Death of Bessie Smith, Hamlet at Elsinore, Gideon's Way, The Champions, Give Me Your Answer True, The Prize (narrator). Guest: The Saint, The Avengers. Movies: The Sunshine Patriot, The Winter of Our Discontent, Quicksand: No Escape, The Railway Station Man.

SUTHERLAND, KIEFER: Actor. b. Los Angeles, CA, Dec. 18, 1966. Son of actor Donald Sutherland and actress Shirley Douglas. Moved to Toronto at 10. Debut with L.A. Odyssey Theater at 9 in Throne of Straw. Worked in local Toronto theater workshops. Starring debut The Bay Boy (1984) for which he won Canadian equivalent of Acad. Award.
PICTURES: Max Dugan Returns (debut, 1983), The Bay Boy, At Close Range, Crazy Moon, Stand By Me, The Lost Boys, The Killing Time, Promised Land, Bright Lights Big City, Young Guns, 1969, Renegades, Flashback, Chicago Joe and the Showgirl, Flatliners, Young Guns II, The Nutcracker Prince (voice), Article 99, Twin Peaks: Fire Walk With Me, A Few Good Men, The Vanishing, The Three Musketeers.
TELEVISION: Movies: Trapped in Silence, Brotherhood of Justice, Last Light (also dir.). Guest: Amazing Stories (The Mission).

SUTTON, JAMES T.: Executive. b. California, Sept. 13. e. Columbia U. Film inspector, U.S. government; overseas m.p. service, WW II; co-owner, gen. mgr., Hal Davis Studios; hd. TV commercial div., Allan Sandler Films; Academy Art Pictures; pres., chmn. of bd., exec. prod., Royal Russian Studios, Inc., western hemisphere div.; pres. exec. prod. Gold Lion Prods., Inc.; pres. exec. prod. James T. Sutton-John L. Carpenter Prods.; pres., exec. dir., Airax Corp.; pres. of Skyax (div. of Airax).

SUZMAN, JANET: Actress. b. Johannesburg, South Africa, Feb. 9, 1939. e. Kingsmead Coll., U. of Witwatersrand. Trained at L.A.M.D.A. London stage debut in The Comedy of Errors. Recent stage: Another Time, Hippolytos. Director: Othello in Market Theatre and Channel 4 (TV), Death of a Salesman.
PICTURES: Nicholas and Alexandra (Acad. Award nom. 1971), A Day in the Death of Joe Egg, The Black Windmill, Nijinsky, Priest of Love, The Draughtsman's Contract, And the Ship Sails On, A Dry White Season, Nuns on the Run, Leon the Pig Farmer.
TELEVISION: The Three Sisters, Hedda Gabler, The House on Garibaldi Street (movie). The Zany Adventures of Robin Hood (movie), Miss Nightingale, Macbeth, Mountbatten—Last Viceroy of India (series), The Singing Detective (series), Clayhanger (series), The Miser, Revolutionary Witness, Saint Joan, Twelfth Night, Master Class on Shakespearean Comedy, Inspector Morse.

SVENSON, BO: Actor. b. Goteborg, Sweden, Feb. 13, 1941. e. UCLA, 1970–74. U.S. Marine Corps 1959–65.
PICTURES: Maurie (1973), The Great Waldo Pepper, Part 2: Walking Tall, Breaking Point, Special Delivery, Portrait of a Hitman, Final Chapter—Walking Tall, Our Man in Mecca, The Inglorious Bastard, North Dallas Forty, Virus, Night Warning, Thunder Warrior, Deadly Impact, Wizards of the Lost Kingdom, The Manhunt, The Delta Force, Choke Canyon, Heartbreak Ridge, War Bus 2, Silent Hero, Thunder Warrior II, White Phantom, Deep Space, Justice Done, The Train, Soda Cracker, Curse II: The Bite, Captain Henkel, Running Combat.
TELEVISION: Series: Here Come the Brides (1968–70); Walking Tall (1980–81). Movies: The Bravos, Frankenstein, You'll Never See Me Again, Hitched, Target Risk, Snowbeast, Gold of the Amazon Women, Jealousy.

SWAIM, BOB: Director, Writer. b. Evanston, IL, Nov. 2, 1943. e. Calif. State U, B.A.; L'Ecole Nationale de la Cinematographie, Paris, BTS 1969. American director who has often worked in France. Began career making shorts: Le Journal de M Bonnafous, Self Portrait of a Pornographer, Vive les Jacques. Received Cesar award French Acad. M.P., 1982; Chevalier des Arts et des Lettres 1985.
PICTURES: La Nuit de Saint-Germain-des-Pres (1977), La Balance, Half Moon Street, Masquerade, Atlantide, Da Costa.

SWALLOW, NORMAN: Producer. b. Manchester, Eng., Feb. 17, 1921. e. Manchester Grammar Sch., Keble Coll., Oxford U. British Army 1941–46; BBC as writer-prod. of doc., 1946; wrote 3 doc. films, 1948; TV as doc. prod., 1950; prods. include American Looks at Britain, with Howard K. Smith for CBS, Wilfred Pickles at Home series; orig. Speaking Personally series with appearance of people like Bertrand Russell; co-prod. TV coverage of Britain's general election, 1951; ed. prod. BBC monthly prog. Special Inquiry, 1952–56; World is Ours, 1954–56; study tour Middle East, India, Pakistan, Ceylon, 1956–57; writer, prod. Line of Defense, I Was a Stranger; asst. head films for BBC, 1957; writer-prod., On Target, 1959; apptd. chief asst. (doc. & gen.), BBC-TV, 1960; asst. editor, Panorama, BBC-TV, 1961. Joined Denis Mitchell films, May 1963; writer, prod., Pomp and Pageantry, The Right to Health, A Wedding on Saturday; The End of a Street; exec. prod., Report from Britain; writer, prod., Youth, British, Football; co-prod. This England. prod. A Railwayman for Me; co-prod. Ten Days That Shook the World. The Long Bridge; prod., dir.: The Three Happiest Years; exec. prod. Omnibus series, 1968–70. Writer, prod., dir. To Leningrad With Love; exec. prod. Omnibus Series, 1968–72. Writer, co-prod. Eisenstein. BBC-TV Head of Arts Features 1972–74. Prod.-dir. series A Lasting Joy. Exec. Prod. Granada TV since 1974 of The Christians, This England, Clouds of Glory. Winner Desmond Davis Award (UK) 1977. Exec. prod. A Conductor At Work, A Pianist At Work. Prod., A Lot of Happiness (1982 Emmy Award). Freelance producer/director since 1985. The Last Day for BBC-TV, 1986, Johnny and Alf Go Home for BBC-TV, 1989.

SWANSON, KRISTY: Actress. b. Mission Viejo, CA, 1969. Signed with modeling agency at age 9, appearing in over 30 commercials. Acting debut at 13 on Disney series Dreamfinders.
PICTURES: Pretty in Pink, Ferris Bueller's Day Off, Deadly Friend, Flowers in the Attic, Diving In, Mannequin Two on the Move, Hot Shots, Highway to Hell, Buffy the Vampire Slayer.
TELEVISION: Series: Dreamfinders, Knots Landing, Nightingales. Movies: Miracle of the Heart: A Boys Town Story, Not Quite Human.

SWAYZE, JOHN CAMERON: Reporter, Commercial spokesman. b. Wichita, KS, Apr. 4, 1906. e. U. of Kansas; Anderson-Milton Dramatic Sch. Reporter and ed., Kansas City, MO Journal-Post; news dept. KMBC, Kansas City; head of news, NBC western network, Hollywood; NBC radio news reports, N.Y.; covered political conv. TV 1948–52; began News Caravan on NBC in 1949–56; panel mem. Who Said That, 1949–51; Watch the World on NBC-TV, 1948–50; Sightseeing With The Swayzes (with family) NBC-TV, 1953; news program, ABC, 1957. Host: Circle Theatre, NBC, and panel member, To Tell the Truth, CBS. Voted best news commentator, M.P. Daily TV Poll, 1951–55.
MEMBER: Lambs Club; National Press Club, Washington, Greenwich, Conn., CC.

SWAYZE, PATRICK: Actor, Dancer. b. Houston, TX. Aug. 18, 1952. e. San Jacinto Col. m. actress-dancer Lisa Niemi. Son of choreographer Patsy Swayze (Urban Cowboy). Brother is actor Don Swayze. Began as dancer appearing in Disney on Parade on tour as Prince Charming. Songwriter and singer with 6 bands. Studied dance at Harkness and Joffrey Ballet Schs. On Bdwy. as dancer in Goodtime Charley, Grease. Co-author of play Without a Word.
PICTURES: Skatetown USA (debut, 1979), The Outsiders, Uncommon Valor, Red Dawn, Grandview USA (also choreographer), Youngblood, Dirty Dancing (also co-wrote and sang She's Like the Wind), Steel Dawn, Tiger Warsaw, Road House, Next of Kin, Ghost, Point Break, City of Joy, Father Hood.
TELEVISION: Mini-Series: North and South: Books I and II. Movies: The Comeback Kid, Return of the Rebels, The Renegades (pilot), Off Sides. Series: Renegades. Guest: M*A*S*H, Amazing Stories.

SWEENEY, D.B.: Actor. r.n. Daniel Bernard Sweeney. b. Shoreham, NY, 1961. e. NYU, 1984 B.F.A.
PICTURES: Power, Fire With Fire, Gardens of Stone, No Man's Land, Eight Men Out, Memphis Belle, Blue Desert, Sons, Leather Jackets, Heaven is a Playground, The Cutting Edge, A Day in October, Hear No Evil, Fire in the Sky.
TELEVISION: Mini-Series: Lonesome Dove. Movies: Out of the Darkness, Miss Rose White.
THEATRE: NY: The Caine Mutiny Court-Martial (Bdwy), The Seagull: The Hamptons: 1990.

SWERLING, JO: Writer. b. Russia, Apr. 8, 1897. Newspaper & mag. writer; author vaude. sketches; co-author plays, The Kibitzer, Guys and Dolls (Tony Award, 1951).
PICTURES: s.p., The Kibitzer, Guys and Dolls (co-author, orig. play); Platinum Blonde, Washington Merry-Go-Round, Dirigible, Man's Castle; collab. s.p., Whole Town's Talking; s.p., No Greater Glory, Pennies from Heaven, Double Wedding, Made for Each Other; collab. s.p., The Westerner; s.p., Confirm or Deny, Blood and Sand; collab. s.p., Pride of the Yankees; story, Lady Takes a Chance; s.p., Crash Dive, Lifeboat, Leave Her to Heaven, Thunder in the East.
TELEVISION: collab. The Lord Don't Play Favorites, NBC.

SWERLING, JO, JR.: Executive, Producer. b. Los Angeles, CA, June 18, 1931. e. UCLA, 1948–51; California Maritime Acad., 1951–54. Son of writer Jo Swerling. Active duty US Navy 1954–56. Joined Revue Prods./Universal Television, 1957–81, as prod. coordinator, assoc. prod., prod., assoc. exec. prod., exec. prod., writer, director, actor; currently sr. v.p. and supervising prod., The Cannell Studios.
TELEVISION: Series: Kraft Suspense Theater (prod.), Run for Your Life (prod., writer, Emmy, nom.), The Rockford Files (prod., writer), Cool Million (prod.), Alias Smith & Jones (assoc. exec. prod.), Baretta (prod., Emmy nom.), City of Angels (exec. prod.), Toma (exec. prod.), Jigsaw (prod.), The Bold Ones (prod., writer), Lawyers (prod., writer). Mini-series: Captains and the Kings (prod., Emmy nom.), Aspen (prod.), The Last Convertible (exec. prod., dir.). Movies: Producer: This Is the West That Was, The Whole World Is Watching, The Invasion of Johnson County, The Outsider, Do You Take This Stranger, Burn the Town Down, The Three-Thousand Mile Chase, How to Steal an Airplane. Supervising prod. Stephen J. Cannell Productions: The Greatest American Hero, Quest, The A-Team, Hardcastle & McCormick, Riptide, The Last Precinct, Hunter, Stingray, Wiseguy, 21 Jump Street, J.J. Starbuck, Sonny Spoon, The Rousters, Unsub, Booker, Top of the Hill, Broken Badges, Dead End Brattigan.

SWIFT, DAVID: Producer, Director, Writer. b. Minneapolis, MN, 1919. Served with 8th Air Force in England, W.W.II. Entered m.p. ind. in Walt Disney animation dept. After service, comedy writer for radio. Later, starting in 1949, TV drama writer for Philco Playhouse, Studio One, Kraft Theatre, Omnibus. Created Mr. Peepers, Jamie. Writer-dir. Playhouse 90, Rifleman, Wagon Train, Climax, others.
PICTURES: Director-Writer: Pollyana, The Parent Trap, The Interns, Love Is a Ball, Under the Yum Yum Tree, Good Neighbor Sam (also prod.), How to Succeed in Business Without Really Trying (also prod.). Writer: Candleshoe, Foolin' Around (also story).

SWIFT, LELA: Director.
TELEVISION: Studio One, Suspense, The Web, Justice, DuPont Show of the Week, Purex Specials For Women, (Emmy Award) Dark Shadows, Norman Corwin Presents, ABC Late Night 90 min. Specials, ABC Daytime 90 min. Play Break. Won three Emmy awards for best director of day-time serial: Ryan's Hope (1977, 1979, 1980). Monitor award for best director of a daytime serial: Ryan's Hope. 1985. 1989, The Rope (A & E).

SWINK, ROBERT E.: Film editor, Director. b. Rocky Ford, CO, June 3, 1918. Joined editorial dept., RKO Radio, 1936; appt. film ed., 1941. In U.S. Army Signal Corps, 1944–45; supv. editor, Fox studio. Edited numerous productions.

PICTURES: Detective Story, Carrie, Roman Holiday, Desperate Hours, Friendly Persuasion, The Big Country, The Diary of Anne Frank, The Young Doctors, The Children's Hour, The Best Man, The Collector, How To Steal A Million, Flim Flam Man, Funny Girl, The Liberation of L. B. Jones, The Cowboys, Skyjacked, Lady Ice, Papillion, Three the Hard Way, Rooster Cogburn, Midway, Islands in the Stream, Gray Lady Down, The Boys From Brazil, The In-Laws, Going in Style, Sphinx, Welcome Home.

SWISS, FERN: Executive. Executive director-financial planning for Motion Picture Group of Paramount Pictures. Joined co. in 1979 as financial analyst and advance to controller-TV in 1983. Named to present post, 1984.

SWIT, LORETTA: Actress. b. Passaic, NJ, Nov. 4, 1939. Stage debut in Any Wednesday. Toured in Mame for year. Arrived in Hollywood in 1971 and began TV career. Stage: Same Time Next Year (Bdwy), The Mystery of Edwin Drood, Shirley Valentine (Sarah Siddons Award).
PICTURES: Stand Up and Be Counted (debut, 1972), Deadhead Miles, Freebie and the Bean, Race with the Devil, S.O.B., Beer, Whoops Apocalypse.
TELEVISION: Series: M*A*S*H (Emmy Awards, 1980, 1982), Those Incredible Animals (host). Guest: Gunsmoke, Mannix, Hawaii Five-O, Mission: Impossible, The Doctors, Cade's County. Movies: Hostage Heart, Shirts/Skins, The Last Day, Coffeeville, Valentine, Mirror Mirror, Friendships Secrets and Lies, Cagney & Lacey, Games Mother Never Taught You, Friendships Secrets & Lies, First Affair, The Execution, Dreams of Gold: The Mel Fisher Story, Hell Hath No Fury, A Killer Among Friends. Specials: 14 Going on 30, Bob Hope, Tony Orlando, Perry Como, Best Christmas Pageant Ever, Miracle at Moreaux, My Dad Can't Be Crazy Can He?.

SWOPE, HERBERT BAYARD, JR.: Director, Producer, Commentator. b. New York, NY. e. Horace Mann Sch., Princeton U. U.S. Navy, 1941–46; joined CBS-TV as remote unit dir., 1946 directing many "firsts" in sportscasting; winner, Variety Show Management Award for sports coverage & citation by Amer. TV Society, 1948; joined NBC as dir., 1949; prod. dir., 1951; Lights Out, The Clock, The Black Robe, dir., Robt. Montgomery Presents; winner, 1952 Sylvania. TV Award Outstanding Achievement in Dir. Technique; became exec. prod., NBC-TV in charge of Wide, Wide, World; directed Helen Hayes, Billie Burke, Boris Karloff & Peter Lorre in Arsenic & Old Lace (live); also Climax. Film prod., 20th Century-Fox, Hilda Crane, Three Brave Men, True Story of Jesse James, The Bravados, The Fiend who Walked the West; 1960–62; exec. prod. 20th-Fox TV; Many Loves of Dobie Gillis, Five Fingers; dir. co-prod. on Broadway, Step On A Crack, Fragile Fox, Fair Game for Lovers. 1970–72 exec. at N.Y. Off-Track Betting Corp. 1973–74; v.p., Walter Reade Organization, Inc.; 1975–76 producer-host, This Was TV, Growth of a Giant; 1976 to present commentator-interviewer, Swope's Scope, (radio—WSBR-AM)); Critic's Views (TV: WTVJ, Ch. 5); Column: Now and Then (Palm Beach Pictorial).

SYKES, ERIC, O.B.E.: Scriptwriter, Comedian, Actor. b. Oldham, England, 1923. Early career actor; 1948 wrote first three series, BBC's Educating Archie TV comedy series for Frankie Howerd, Max Bygraves, Harry Secombe. BBC panel show member. Sykes Versus TV, The Frankie Howerd Series. Longterm contract with ATV 1956. Own BBC series 1958–78 Sykes and A . . . Specials: Silent Movies for TV, The Plank (also dir. & s.p.), If You Go Down Into the Woods Today, Rhubarb, It's Your Move, Mr. H is Late. Starred in 19th Hole in 1989.
THEATRE: Toured extensively in Big Bad Mouse. 1966–9 in America, Rhodesia, Australia, Canada, One Man Show (1982), Time and Time Again, Run for Your Wife, Two Into One, The 19th Hole, several pantomimes.
PICTURES: Watch Your Stern, Very Important Person, Invasion Quartet, Village of Daughters, Kill or Cure, Heavens Above, The Bargee, One Way Pendulum, Those Magnificent Men in Their Flying Machines, Rotten to the Core, The Liquidator, The Spy With The Cold Nose, Shalako, Monte Carlo or Bust, Theatre of Blood, Splitting Heirs, The Big Freeze.

SYLBERT, ANTHEA: Executive. b. New York, NY, Oct. 6, 1939. e. Barnard Coll., B.A.; Parsons Sch. of Design, M.A. Early career in costume design with range of Bdwy. (The Real Thing), off-Bdwy. and m.p. credits (Rosemary's Baby, F.I.S.T., Shampoo, The Fortune, A New Leaf, The Heartbreak Kid. Two A.A. nominations for creative costume designs for Julia and Chinatown. Joined Warner Bros. in October, 1977, as v.p., special projects, acting as liaison between creative executives, production dept., and creative talent producing films for company. In October, 1978, named v.p. production (projects included One Trick Pony, Personal Best, etc.). In March, 1980 appointed v.p.—production, for United Artists, working on Jinxed, Still of the Night, Yentl, etc. In 1982 became indept. prod. in partnership with Goldie Hawn (Hawn/Sylbert Movie

Co.) producing Swing Shift, Protocol, Wildcats, Overboard, My Blue Heaven, Deceived, Crisscross.

SYMS, SYLVIA: Actress. b. London, Dec. 3, 1934. e. Convent and Grammar Sch. Film debut, 1955, My Teenage Daughter.
PICTURES: No Time For Tears, Birthday Present, Woman In A Dressing Gown, Ice Cold in Alex, The Devil's Disciple, Moonraker, Bachelor of Hearts, No Trees in the Street, Ferry to Hong Kong, Expresso Bongo, Conspiracy of Hearts, The World of Suzie Wong, Flame in the Streets, Victim, Quare Fellow, Punch & Judy Man, The World Ten Times Over, East of Sudan, The Eliminator, Operation Crossbow, The Big Job, Hostile Witness, The Marauders, Danger Route, Run Wild Run Free, The Desperados, Asylum, The Tamarind Seed, Give Us This Day, There Goes the Bride, Absolute Beginners, A Chorus of Disapproval, Shirley Valentine, Shining Through, Dirty Weekend.
TELEVISION: The Human Jungle (series), Something to Declare, The Saint (series), The Baron (series), Bat Out of Hell, Department in Terror, Friends and Romans, Strange Report, Half-hour Story, The Root of All Evil, The Bridesmaid, Clutterbuck, Movie Quiz, My Good Woman, Looks Familiar, Love and Marriage, The Truth About Verity, I'm Bob, He's Dickie, Blankety Blank, The Story of Nancy Astor, Give Us a Clue, Sykes, Crown Court, A Murder Is Announced, Murder at Lynch Cross, Rockcliffes Follies, Dr. Who, Countdown, Ruth Rendell Mystery, May to December, Intimate Contact, Thatcher the Final Days, Natural Lies. Mulberry, Peak Practice.

SZABO, ISTVAN: Director. b. Budapest, Hungary, Feb. 18, 1938. e. Academy of Theatre and Film Art, Budapest, 1961. Debut Koncert (short, diploma film) 1961.
PICTURES: Variations on a Theme (short), You (short), The Age of Daydreaming, Father, Piety (short), Love Film Budapest, Why I Love It (series of shorts), 25 Fireman's Street, Premiere, Budapest Tales, City Map (short), Confidence (Silver Bear, Berlin Festival), The Green Bird, Mephisto (Best screenplay, Cannes Festival); Hungarian Film Critics Award; Academy Award, Best Foreign Film, 1982), Colonel Redl (director, co-s.p.), Tusztortenet (Stand Off) (actor only), Meeting Venus.

SZWARC, JEANNOT: Director. b. Paris, France, Nov. 21, 1939.
PICTURES: Extreme Close-Up, Bug, Jaws II, Somewhere in Time, Enigma, Supergirl, Santa Claus—The Movie, Honor Bound.
TELEVISION: Series: Ironside, To Catch a Thief, Kojak, Columbo, Night Gallery, Crime Club, True Life Stories, Twilight Zone (1986). Movies: Night of Terror, The Weekend Nun, The Devil's Daughter, You'll Never See Me Again, The Small Miracle, Lisa: Bright and Dark, A Summer Without Boys, Crime Club, Code Name: Diamond Head, Murders in the Rue Morgue.

T

MR. T: Actor. r.n. Lawrence Tero. b. Chicago, IL, May 21, 1953. Professional bodyguard when hired by Sylvester Stallone in 1980 to play prizefighter in Rocky III.
TELEVISION: Series: The A Team, T & T. Movie: The Toughest Man in the World. Guest: Silver Spoons.
PICTURES: Rocky III, D.C. Cab.

TAFFNER DONALD L.: Executive. b. New York, NY. e. St. Johns U. William Morris Agency, 1950–59; Paramount Pictures. 1959–63; D. L. Taffner Ltd., 1963–present.
TELEVISION: Prod.: Three's Company, Too Close For Comfort.

TAKEI, GEORGE: Actor. b. Los Angeles, CA, April 20, 1937. e. U. of California, UCLA. Professional debut in Playhouse 90 production while training at Desilu Workshop in Hollywood. Gained fame as Sulu in Star Trek TV series. Co-author of novel, Mirror Friend, Mirror Foe.
PICTURES: Ice Palace, A Majority of One, Hell to Eternity, PT 109, Red Line 7000, An American Dream, Walk Don't Run, The Green Berets, Star Trek—The Motion Picture, Star Trek II: The Wrath of Khan, Star Trek III: The Search for Spock, Star Trek IV: The Voyage Home, Star Trek V: The Final Frontier, Return From the River Kwai, Prisoners of the Sun, Star Trek VI: The Undiscovered Country.
TELEVISION: Series: Star Trek. Guest: Perry Mason, Alcoa Premiere, Mr. Novak, The Wackiest Ship in the Army, I Spy, Magnum PI, Trapper John M.D., Miami Vice, Murder She Wrote, McGyver, Hawaiian Eye, Californian, Hawaii 5-O, My Three Sons, John Forsythe Show, Death Valley Days, Theatre in America.

TALBOT, LYLE: Actor. r.n. Lysle Hollywood. b. Pittsburgh, PA, Feb. 8, 1902. In Army Air Corps, W.W.II. First screen appearance in Vitaphone short; then in Love Is A Racket, 1932. One of the orign. founders of Screen Actors Guild #21.

PICTURES: Up in Arms, Sensations of 1945, One Body Too Many, Dixie Jamboree, Gambler's Choice, Strange Impersonation, Vicious Circle, Mutineers, Sky Dragon, The Jackpot, Sea Tiger, Down Among the Sheltering Palms, Star of Texas, Capt. Kidd & the Slave Girl, Tobor the Great, Steel Cage, There's No Business Like Show Business, Jail Busters, Jail Bait, Sudden Danger, Plan 9 From Outer Space, High School Confidential, City of Fear, Sunrise at Campobello.
TELEVISION: Newhart (1987).
MEMBER: Masonic Lodge (Shriner), Lambs, Masquers, American Legion.

TAMBLYN, RUSS: Actor b. Los Angeles, CA, Dec. 30, 1935. e. No. Hollywood H.S. West Coast radio shows; on stage with little theatre group; song-and-dance act in Los Angeles clubs, veterans hospitals.
PICTURES: The Boy with Green Hair, Reign of Terror, Samson and Delilah, Gun Crazy, Kid from Cleveland, The Vicious Years, Captain Carey U.S.A., Father of the Bride, As Young As You Feel, Father's Little Dividend, Cave of Outlaws, Winning Team, Retreat Hell, Take the High Ground, Seven Brides for Seven Brothers, Deep in My Heart, Many Rivers to Cross, Hit the Deck, Last Hunt, Fastest Gun Alive, The Young Guns, Don't Go Near the Water, Peyton Place (Acad. Award nom.), High School Confidential, tom thumb, Cimarron, West Side Story, Wonderful World of the Brothers Grimm, How the West Was Won, Follow the Boys, The Haunting, Long Ships, Son of a Gunfighter, War of the Gargantuas, Scream Free, Dracula Vs. Frankenstein, Satan's Sadists, The Female Bunch, The Last Movie, Win Place or Steal, Murder Gang, Human Highway, Aftershock, Commando Squad, Cyclone, Necromancer, B.O.R.N., Phantom Empire, Bloodscream, Wizards of the Demon Sword, Cabin Boy.
TELEVISION: Series: Twin Peaks. Guest: Greatest Show on Earth, Burke's Law, Cade's County, The Quest, Quantum Leap.

TAMBOR, JEFFREY: Actor. b. San Francisco, CA, July 8, 1944. e. San Francisco St. (BA), Wayne St. (MA). Acted with Seattle Rep., Actors Theatre of Louisville, Loeb Drama Ctr. (Harvard), Milwaukee Rep. Theatre, Acad. Festival Theatre (Chicago), Old Globe Theatre in San Diego, South Coast Rep. Theatre. Bdwy in Measure for Measure, Sly Fox.
TELEVISION: Series: The Ropers, Hill Street Blues, 9 to 5, Mr. Sunshine, Max Headroom, Studio 5-B, American Dreamer, The Larry Sanders Show. Movies: Alcatraz: The Whole Shocking Story, A Gun in the House, The Star Maker, Take Your Best Shot, Cocaine: One Man's Seduction, Sadat, The Awakening of Candra, The Three Wishes of Billy Grier, The Burden of Proof, Honey Let's Kill the Neighbors, The Countdown Has Begun. Mini-Series: Robert Kennedy & His Times. Guest: Three's Company, M*A*S*H, Barney Miller, Tales From the Crypt, The Golden Globe, Empty Nest, Doogie Howser M.D., Equal Justice, Murder She Wrote.
PICTURES: And Justice for all, Saturday the 14th, Mr. Mom, The Man Who Wasn't There, No Small Affair, Three O'Clock High, Lisa, City Slickers, Life Stinks, Pastime, Article 99, Brenda Starr, Crossing the Bridge, The Webbers, Face Dancer, Under Pressure, A House in the Hills.

TANDY, JESSICA: Actress. b. London, Eng., June 7, 1909. m. actor-writer-dir. Hume Cronyn. On London, N.Y. stage, 1928–42.
THEATRE: N.Y. stage. A Streetcar Named Desire (Tony Award, 1948), Hilda Crane, The Four Poster, Coward In Two Keys; The Way of the World, Eve and A Midsummer Night's Dream at Stratford Festival 1976, Canada; limited tours of Many Faces of Love 1974–76 and for CBC, Canada 1977; performed in The Gin Game, Long Wharf Thea., CT, Long Day's Journey Into Night, (Canada). The Gin Game (Pulitzer Prize winning play, Tony Award, 1978), and toured with it in U.S., Toronto, London and U.S.S.R., 1979, and Long Day's Journey Into Night, Foxfire (Stratford Festival 1980, Rose Cort, Guthrie Theatre, Minneapolis 1981 and N.Y., Tony Award); The Glass Menagerie (N.Y.), Salonika, The Petition.
PICTURES: The Indiscretions of Eve, Murder in the Family, The Seventh Cross, The Valley of Decision, Dragonwyck, The Green Years, Forever Amber, A Woman's Vengeance, September Affair, The Desert Fox, The Light In The Forest, Adventures of a Young Man, The Birds, Butley, Honky Tonk Freeway, The World According to Garp, Still of the Night, Best Friends, The Bostonians, Cocoon, Batteries Not Included, The House on Carroll Street, Cocoon: The Return, Driving Miss Daisy (Acad. Award, 1989), Fried Green Tomatoes, Used People.
TELEVISION: Portrait of a Madonna (1948), The Marriage (summer comedy series with Hume Cronyn, 1954), The Fourposter, The Fallen Idol, Moon and the Sixpence, Tennessee Williams's Faces of Live, The Gin Game, Foxfire (Emmy Award, 1988), The Story Lady.

TANEN, NED: Executive. b. Los Angeles, CA, 1931. e. UCLA, law degree. Joined MCA, Inc. 1954; Appt. v.p. in 1968. Brought Uni Records, since absorbed by MCA Records, to best-seller status with such artists as Neil Diamond, Elton John, Olivia Newton-John. First became active in theatrical film prod. in

1972. In 1975 began overseeing feature prod. for Universal. In 1976 named pres. of Universal Theatrical Motion Pictures, established as div. of Universal City Studios. Left in 1982 to become independent producer. 1985, joined Paramount Pictures as pres. of Motion Picture Group. Resigned 1988 to continue as sr. advisor at Paramount. Producer: Cops and Robbersons, Guarding Tess.

TANKERSLEY, ROBERT K.: Executive. b. Decatur, IL, July 31, 1927. In U.S. Navy, 1945–46; Marine Corps, 1949–55. With Natl. Theatre Supply as salesman in Denver 13 yrs. 1959–87, pres. Western Service & Supply, Denver, theatre equip. co.; 1960–87, mgr., Tankersley Enterprises theatre equip. Also was CEO of Theatre Operators, Inc., Bozeman, Mont. Member: Theatre Equipment Assn. (past pres.), National NATO Presidents Advisory Council; Rocky Mt. Motion Picture Assn. (past pres.), SMPTE, Motion Picture Pioneers, past chief barker, Variety Club Tent #37. Colorado, Wyoming NATO (past pres.) chmn.-elect Exhibitors West.

TAPLIN, JONATHAN: Producer. b. Cleveland, OH, July 18, 1947. e. Princeton U.
PICTURES: Mean Streets, The Last Waltz, Carny (exec. prod.), Grandview U.S.A. (co-exec. prod.), Under Fire, Baby, My Science Project, Until the End of the World, K2.
TELEVISION: Shelly Duvall's Faerie Tale Theatre (6 episodes), 1968: The 25th Anniversary, The Native Americans.

TAPS, JONIE: Producer. Executive. Columbia Studio.
PICTURES: Jolson Story, Down to Earth, Thrill of Brazil. Produced: When You're Smiling, Sunny Side of Street, Sound Off, Rainbow Round My Shoulder, All Ashore, Cruisin' Down the River, Drive a Crooked Road, Three for the Show, Bring Your Smile Along, He Laughed Last, Shadow on the Window.
MEMBER: Friars Club, Hillcrest Country Club.

TARADASH, DANIEL: Writer, Director. b. Louisville, KY, Jan. 29, 1913. e. Harvard Coll., B.A., 1933; Harvard Law Sch., LL.B., 1936. Passed NY Bar, 1937; won nationwide playwriting contest, 1938; U.S. Army W.W.II. Pres. Screen Writers Branch, WGA, 1955–56; v.p., Writers Guild of America, West 1956–59; mem. Writers Guild Council, 1954–65; mem., bd. of govnrs. Motion Picture Acad. Arts & Sciences, 1964–74, 1990–3; v.p. 1968–70 and pres. 1970–73. Trustee, Producers-Writers Guild Pension plan 1960–73. chmn., 1965. Mem. Bd. of Trustees of American Film Institute 1967–69. WGA's Valentine Davies Award, 1971. Pres., Academy M.P. Arts & Sciences, 1970–73, mem. bd. trustees, Entertainment Hall of Fame Foundation. Mem., Public Media General Programs panel for the National Foundation for the Arts, Pres. Writers Guild of America, West, 1977–79. Natl. chmn., Writers Guild of America 1979–81. WGA's Morgan Cox Award, 1988. WGA's Edmund H. North Founders Award 1991. Member of jury, Gijon, Spain, Film Festival, 1991. Festival to present Taradash Screenwriting Award 1992–; USC retrospective and tribute, 1992.
PICTURES: Golden Boy, A Little Bit of Heaven, Knock on Any Door, Rancho Notorious, Don't Bother to Knock, From Here to Eternity (Acad. Award 1953), Desiree, Storm Center (also dir., co-story), Picnic, Bell Book and Candle, The Saboteur Code Name—Morituri, Hawaii (co-s.p.), Castle Keep (co-s.p.). Doctors' Wives, The Other Side of Midnight (co-s.p.).

TARNOFF, JOHN B.: Producer. b. New York, NY, Mar. 3, 1952. e. UCLA, motion pictures & TV, 1973–74; Amherst Coll., B.A., 1969–73. Named field exec. with Taylor-Laughlin Distribution (company arm of Billy Jack Enterprises) 1974; left in 1975 to be literary agent with Bart/Levy, Inc.; later with Michael Levy & Associates, Paul Kohner/Michael Levy Agency; Headed TV dept., Kohner/Levy, 1979. Joined MGM as production exec., 1979; v.p., development, 1979–80; sr. v.p. production & devel., 1981–82; exec. v.p., Kings Road Prods., 1983–84; v.p., prod., Orion Pictures Corp., 1985; exec. prod., Out of Bounds, Columbia Pictures, 1986; v.p., prod., De Laurentiis Entertainment Group, 1987. Head of production, DeLaurentiis Entertainment, Australia, 1987–88. Exec. v.p. production, Village Roadshow Pictures, 1988–. Exec. Prod.: The Delinquents, Blood Oath.

TARSES, JAY: Producer, Writer, Actor. b. Baltimore, MD, July 3, 1939. e. U. of Washington, degree in theater. Wrote and acted with little-theater co. in Pittsburgh, drove a truck in NY for Allen Funt's Candid Camera and worked in advertising and promotion for Armstrong Cork Co. in Lancaster, PA where met Tom Patchett. Formed Patchett and Tarses, stand-up comedy team that played coffeehouse circuit in the late 1960s. Later twosome became TV writing team and joined writing staff of Carol Burnett Show winning Emmy in 1972.
TELEVISION: As actor: Series: Make Your Own Kind of Music, Open All Night, The Days and Nights of Molly Dodd. Specials: Arthur Godfrey's Portable Electric Medicine Show, The Duck Factory.
With Tom Patchett: The Bob Newhart Show (exec. prod., writer), The Tony Randell Show (creator, exec. prod., writer), We've Got Each Other (creator, exec. prod.), Mary (prod.),

Open All Night (creator, prod., writer), Buffalo Bill (exec. prod., writer). Solo: The Days and Nights of Molly Dodd (creator, prod., writer), The "Slap" Maxwell Story (creator, prod., writer). Pilots: The Chopped Liver Brothers (exec. prod., writer), The Faculty (exec. prod., dir., writer).
PICTURES: Co-s.p. with Patchett: Up the Academy, The Great Muppet Caper, The Muppets Take Manhattan.

TARTIKOFF, BRANDON: Executive. b. New York, NY, Jan. 13, 1949. e. Yale U. Started TV career in 1971 in promo. dept. of ABC affiliates in New Haven, CT Joined promo. staff at ABC affiliate in Chicago. In 1976 went to New York, with ABC-TV as mgr., dramatic development; moved to NBC Entertainment in Sept., 1977, as dir., comedy programs. In 1978 appt. v.p., programs, West Coast, NBC Entertainment; 1980, named pres. of that division. Pres. NBC Entertainment since 1980. Also heads own prod. co., NBC Productions. 1990, appointed chairman of NBC Entertainment Group. 1991, appointed chmn. of Paramount Pictures. Resigned from Paramount, Oct. 1992.
PICTURES: Square Dance, Satisfaction.

TASCO, RAI: Actor, Announcer. r.n. Ridgeway Tasco. b. Boston, MA, Aug. 12, 1917. e. Boston English High. 1935. U.S. Army, 1935–45. Grad., Cambridge Sch. of Radio & TV, New York, 1950. Appeared in most TV and radio dramatic shows, and stage plays, New York and Hollywood; Broadway stage & films; dramatic instructor.

TAVERNIER, BERTRAND: Director, Writer. b. Lyon, France, April 25, 1941. After 2 yrs. of law study, quit to become film critic for Cahiers du Cinema and Cinema 60. Asst. to dir. Jean-Pierre Melville on Leon Morin Priest (1961), also worked as film publicist. Wrote film scripts and a book on the Western and a history of American cinema. Partner for 6 yrs. with Pierre Rissient in film promotion company, during which time he studied all aspects of film-making. 1963: directed episode of Les Baisers. Pres., Lumiere Inst., Lyon. Book: 50 Years of American Cinema.
PICTURES: Director-Co-Writer: The Clockmaker, Let Joy Reign Supreme, The Judge and the Assassin, Spoiled Children, Deathwatch, A Week's Vacation, Clean Slate (Coup de Torchon), Mississippi Blues (co-dir. with Robert Parrish), A Sunday in the Country, 'Round Midnight, Beatrice (dir. only), Life and Nothing But, Daddy Nostalgia, The Undeclared War (also co-prod.; co-dir. with Patrick Rutman), L627 (also prod.).
TELEVISION: Phillippe Soupault, October Country (co-dir. with Robert Parrish), Lyon, le regard interieur.

TAVIANI, PAOLO and VITTORIO: Directors, Writers. b. San Miniato, Pisa, Italy, (Paolo: Nov. 8, 1931; Vittorio: Sept. 20, 1929); e. Univ. of Pisa (Paolo: liberal arts; Vittorio: law). The two brothers always work in collaboration from script preparation through shooting and editing. 1950: With Valentino Orsini ran cine-club at Pisa. 1954: In collab. with Caesare Zavattini directed short about Nazi massacre at San Miniato. 1954–59: with Orsini made series of short documentaries (Curatorne e Montanara; Carlo Pisacane; Ville della Brianza; Lavatori della pietra; Pitori in cita; I Pazzi della domenica; Moravia, Cabunara). Worked as assistant to Rosellini, Luciano Emmer and Raymond Pellegrini. 1960: collaborated on an episode of Italy Is Not a Poor Country.
FEATURE FILMS (all by both): A Man to Burn (1962),; Matrimonial Outlaws, The Subversives, Under the Sign of Scorpio, Saint Michael Had a Rooster, Allonsanfan, Padre Padrone (Cannes Film Fest.: Grand Prix & Critics International Prize, 1977), The Meadow, The Night of the Shooting Stars (1981—Best Director Award, Natl. Society of Film Critics; Special Jury Prize, Cannes), Kaos, Good Morning Babylon.

TAYLOR, DELORES: Actress, Writer, Producer. b. Winner, SD, Sept. 27, 1939. e. U. of South Dakota, studying commercial art. m. Tom Laughlin. First TV experience was heading art dept. at RCA wholesale center in Milwaukee. Established first Montessori School in U.S. in Santa Monica for several yrs., with husband. Made feature film debut as actress in Billy Jack in 1971. Wrote s.p. with husband for that and sequels, The Trial of Billy Jack, Billy Jack Goes to Washington, under pseudonym Teresa Christina.
PICTURES: Exec. Prod., Writer: Proper Time, Young Sinners, Born Losers, The Master Gunfighter. Exec. Prod., Writer, Actress: Billy Jack, Trial of Billy Jack, Billy Jack Goes to Washington, Return of Billy Jack.

TAYLOR, DON: Actor, Director. b. Freeport, PA, Dec. 13, 1920. e. Pennsylvania State U. Appeared in Army Air Corps' Winged Victory on stage & screen; author screenplays, TV shows.
PICTURES: Actor: Girl Crazy, Winged Victory, Song of the Thing Man, The Naked City, For the Love of Mary, Battleground, Father of the Bride, Target Unknown, Father's Little Dividend, Submarine Command, Flying Leathernecks, Blue Veil, Japanese War Bride, Stalag 17, The Girls of Pleasure Island, Destination Gobi, Johnny Dark, Men of Sherwood Forest, I'll Cry Tomorrow, The Bold and the Brave, Ride the High Iron. Director: Everything's Ducky, Ride the Wild Surf,

Jack of Diamonds, Five Man Army, Escape from The Planet of the Apes, Tom Sawyer, Echoes Of A Summer, The Great Scout and Cathouse Thursday, The Island of Dr. Moreau, Damien-Omen II, The Final Countdown.

TELEVISION: *Director*: Something for a Lonely Man, Wild Women, Heat of Anger, Night Games, Honky Tonk, The Manhunter, Circle of Children, The Gift, The Promise of Love, Broken Promise, Red Flag, Drop Out Father, Listen to Your Heart, September Gun, My Wicked Wicked Ways: The Legend of Errol Flynn, Secret Weapons, Going for the Gold: The Bill Johnson Story, Classified Love, Ghost of a Chance, The Diamond Trap.

TAYLOR, ELIZABETH: Actress. b. London, Eng., Feb. 27, 1932. e. Bryon House, London. When 3 years old danced before Princess Elizabeth, Margaret Rose. Came to U.S. at outbreak of W.W.II. Author: World Enough and Time (with Richard Burton; 1964), Elizabeth Taylor (1965), Elizabeth Takes Off (1988). Initiated Ben Gurion U.—Elizabeth Taylor Fund for Children of the Negev, 1982. Co-founded American Foundation for AIDS Research, 1985. Named Comdr. Arts & Letters (France) 1985, Legion of Honor, 1987. Established the Elizabeth Taylor AIDS Foundation in 1991. Recipient of AFI Life Achievement Award (1993), Jean Hersholt Humanitarian Award (1993).

PICTURES: There's One Born Every Minute (debut, 1942), Lassie Come Home, Jane Eyre, White Cliffs of Dover, National Velvet, Courage of Lassie, Life with Father, Cynthia, A Date With Judy, Julia Misbehaves, Little Women, Conspirator, The Big Hangover, Father of the Bride, Father's Little Dividend, A Place in the Sun, Calloway Went Thataway (cameo), Love Is Better Than Ever, Ivanhoe, The Girl Who Had Everything, Rhapsody, Elephant Walk, Beau Brummell, The Last Time I Saw Paris, Giant, Raintree County, Cat on a Hot Tin Roof, Suddenly Last Summer, Butterfield 8 (Acad. Award, 1960), Cleopatra, The V.I.P.s, The Sandpiper, Who's Afraid of Virginia Woolf? (Acad. Award, 1966), The Taming of the Shrew, Doctor Faustus, Reflections in a Golden Eye, The Comedians, Boom!, Secret Ceremony, The Only Game in Town, X Y and Zee (Zee & Company), Under Milk Wood, Hammersmith Is Out, Night Watch, Ash Wednesday, The Driver's Seat, That's Entertainment!, The Blue Bird, A Little Night Music, Winter Kills, The Mirror Crack'd, Genocide (narrator), Young Toscanini, The Flintstones.

TELEVISION: *Movies*: Divorce His/Divorce Hers, Victory at Entebbe, Between Friends, Malice in Wonderland, There Must Be a Pony, Poker Alice, Sweet Bird of Youth. *Mini-Series*: North and South. *Guest*: Here's Lucy (1970 with Richard Burton), General Hospital (1981), All My Children (1983). *Specials*: Elizabeth Taylor in London, America's All-Star Salute to Elizabeth Taylor.

THEATRE: *Bdwy*: The Little Foxes (also London), Private Lives.

TAYLOR, LILI: Actress. b. Chicago, IL, 1967.
PICTURES: Mystic Pizza, Say Anything, Born on the Fourth of July, Bright Angel, Dogfight, Arizona Dream, Watch It, Household Saints, Short Cuts, Rudy.
THEATRE: *NY*: What Did He See, Aven U Boys. *Regional*: Mud, The Love Talker, Fun. *Director*: Collateral Damage.

TAYLOR, MESHACH: Actor. b. Boston, MA, Apr. 11. e. Florida A & M Univ. Hosted Chicago TV show Black Life.
TELEVISION: *Series*: Buffalo Bill, Designing Women. *Guest*: Lou Grant, Barney Miller, Melba, Golden Girls, M*A*S*H, The White Shadow, What's Happening Now, ALF. *Movies*: An Innocent Man, How to Murder a Millionaire. *Specials*: Huckleberry Finn, The Rec Room.
PICTURES: Damien: Omen II, The Howling, The Beast Within, Explorers, Warning Sign, One More Saturday Night, From the Hip, Mannequin, The Allnighter, House of Games, Welcome to Oblivion, Mannequin 2 on the Move, Class Act.
THEATRE: Streamers, Sizwe Banzi is Dead, The Island, Native Son, Wonderful Ice Cream Suit, Bloody Bess, Sirens of Titan, Night Feast, Huckleberry Finn, Cops.

TAYLOR, RENÉE: Actress, Writer. b. New York, NY, March 19, 1935. Wife of actor Joseph Bologna, with whom she collaborates in writing. Their Bdwy. plays include Lovers and Other Strangers, It Had to Be You. Actress: One of the All-Time Greats.
PICTURES: *Actress*: The Errand Boy, The Detective, The Producers, A New Leaf, Lovers and Other Strangers (also s.p.), Made for Each Other (also s.p.), Last of the Red Hot Lovers, Lovesick, It Had to Be You (also co-dir., co-s.p.), That's Adequate, White Palace, End of Innocence, Delirious, All I Want for Christmas, Forever.
TELEVISION: *Writer*: Acts of Love and Other Comedies (Emmy), Paradise, Calucci's Department, The American Dream Machine, etc. *Actress*: Series regular: Jack Paar Show, Mary Hartman Mary Hartman. Movie: Woman of the Year (also co-writer).

TAYLOR, ROD: Actor. b. Sydney, Australia, Jan. 11, 1930. e. East Sydney Fine Arts Coll. Started out as artist then turned to acting on stage. Formed own company, Rodler, Inc., for TV-film production.
PICTURES: The Sturt Expedition (debut, 1951), King of the Coral Sea, Long John Silver, Top Gun, The Virgin Queen, Hell on Frisco Bay, World Without End, The Rack, Giant, The Catered Affair, Raintree County, Step Down to Terror, Separate Tables, Ask Any Girl, The Time Machine, Seven Seas to Calais, 101 Dalmatians (voice), The Birds, A Gathering of Eagles, The V.I.P.s, Sunday in New York, Fate is the Hunter, 36 Hours, Young Cassidy, Do Not Disturb, The Glass Bottom Boat, The Liquidator, Hotel, Chuka (also prod.), Dark of the Sun, High Commissioner (Nobody Runs Forever), The Hell with Heroes, Zabriskie Point, Darker Than Amber, The Man Who Had Power Over Women, The Heroes, The Train Robbers, Trader Horn, The Deadly Trackers, Hell River, Blondy, Picture Show Man, A Time To Die, On the Run, Close Enemy.
TELEVISION: *Movies*: Powerkeg, Family Flight, The Oregon Trail, Cry of the Innocent, Jacqueline Bouvier Kennedy, Charles and Diana: A Royal Love Story, Outlaws, Danielle Steel's Palomino, Grass Roots. *Series*: Hong Kong (1960–63), Bearcats, Masquerade, The Oregon Trail, Outlaws, Falcon Crest.

TAYLOR, RONNIE: Director of Photography. b. London, England, 1924. Ent. m.p. ind. 1941 at Gainsborough Studios.
PICTURES: Tommy, The Silent Flute, Circle of Iron, Savage Harvest, Gandhi, High Road to China, The Hound of the Baskervilles, The Champions, Master of the Game (UK shoot), A Chorus Line, Foreign Body, Cry Freedom, Opera (Italy), The Experts, Sea of Love, Popcorn, The Rainbow Thief, Jewels, Age of Treason.

TAYLOR, JOHN RUSSELL: Writer, Critic. b. Dover, England, June 19, 1935. e. Cambridge U., B.A., 1956. Editor: Times Educational Supplement, London, 1959–60; film critic, The Times, London, 1962–73; art critic, 1978–; editor, Films and Filming, 1983–; prof., division of Cinema, USC, 1972–78. Member: London Film and TV Press Guild, London Critics Circle, NY Society of Cinematologists.
BOOKS: Joseph L. Mankiewicz: An Index, The Angry Theatre, Anatomy of a Television Play, Cinema Eye Cinema Ear, Shakespeare: A Celebration (cont.), New English Dramatists 8 (ed. & intr.), The Hollywood Musical, The Second Wave: Hollywood Dramatists for the 70s, Masterworks of the British Cinema, Directors and Directions: Peter Shaffer, Hitch, Cukor's Hollywood, Impressionism, Strangers in Paradise, Ingrid Bergman, Alec Guinness: A Celebration, Vivien Leigh, Hollywood 1940s, Portraits of the British Cinema.

TAYLOR-YOUNG, LEIGH: Actress. b. Washington, DC, Jan. 25, 1945. e. Northwestern U. Bdwy debut 1966 in Three Bags Full. Additional stage: The Beckett Plays (Off-Bdwy., LA), Knives, Sleeping Dogs.
PICTURES: I Love You Alice B. Toklas, The Games, The Big Bounce, The Adventurers, The Buttercup Chain, The Horsemen, The Gang That Couldn't Shoot Straight, Soylent Green, Can't Stop the Music, Looker, Secret Admirer, Jagged Edge, Honeymoon Academy, Accidents.
TELEVISION: *Series*: Peyton Place, The Devlin Connection, The Hamptons, Dallas. *Movies*: Marathon, Napoleon and Josephine: A Love Story, Perry Mason: The Case of the Sinister Spirit, Who Gets the Friends, Bonnie and McCloud. *Guest*: Civil Wars, The Young Riders, Alfred Hitchcock Presents, Spenser for Hire, Evening Shade. *Pilots*: Ghostwriter, Houston Knights.

TEAGUE, LEWIS: Director. b. 1941. e. NYU. Editor and/or 2nd unit dir. on such films as Cockfighter, Crazy Mama, Death Race 2000, Avalanche.
PICTURES: Dirty O'Neil (co-dir.); Lady in Red (also editor); Alligator; Fighting Back; Cujo; Cat's Eye; Jewel of the Nile, Collision Course, Navy SEALS.
TELEVISION: Series episodes: Alfred Hitchcock Presents, Daredevils, Shannon's Deal. Movie: T Bone N Weasel.

TELLER, IRA Executive. b. New York, NY, July 3, 1940. e. City Coll. of New York, & 1957–61; NYU Graduate Sch. of Arts, 1961–62. Publicist, Pressbook Dept., 20th Century Fox, 1961–62; asst. to adv. mgr., Embassy Pictures Corp., 1962–63; asst. adv. mgr., Columbia Pictures Corp., 1963; adv. mgr., Columbia Pictures Corp., 1964, 1964–65; asst. to chmn. of bd., Diener, Hauser, Greenthal Agy., 1966; adv. mgr., 20th Century-Fox, 1966–67; 1967, adv. dir. 20th Cent.-Fox.; dir. of adv., Nat'l General Pictures Corp., 1969; eastern dir., adv.-pub., 1972; national dir., adv-pub., 1973; Bryanston Distributors, Inc. v.p. adv.-pub., 1974; Cine Artists Pictures Corp. v.p. adv-pub., 1975; Lorimar Productions, v.p., adv.-marketing, 1976–77. 1977–present, pres. Ira Teller and Company, Inc.

TEMPLE (BLACK), SHIRLEY JANE: Actress, Diplomat. b. Santa Monica, CA, April 23, 1928. In 1932 screen debut, Red Haired Alibi. In 1933 To the Last Man; then leading figure in series of Educational shorts called Baby Burlesque and Frolics of Youth, until breakthrough role in Stand Up and Cheer, 1934, which resulted in career as child and teen star. Voted one of ten best Money-Making Stars in Motion Picture Herald-Fame Poll, 1934–39. As an adult, turned her attention to government and international issues. Republican candidate for U.S. House of Representatives, 1967. Rep. to 24th General Assembly of U.N. (1969–70). Special asst. to chmn., President's Council on the Environment (1970–72). U.S. Ambassador to Ghana (1974–76). Chief of Protocol, White House (1976–77); member of U.S. delegation on African Refugee problems, Geneva, 1981; 1987 made 1st honorary U.S. Foreign Service Rep. for State Dept.; 1989, appt. Ambassador to Czechoslovakia. Autobiography: Child Star (1988).

PICTURES: The Red-Haired Alibi (feature debut, 1932), To the Last Man, Out All Night, Mandalay, Carolina, Stand Up and Cheer, Baby Take a Bow, Now and Forever, Bright Eyes, Now I'll Tell, Change of Heart, Little Miss Marker, The Little Colonel, Our Little Girl, Curly Top, The Littlest Rebel, Captain January, Poor Little Rich Girl, Dimples, Stowaway, Wee Willie Winkle, Heidi, Rebecca of Sunnybrook Farm, Little Miss Broadway, Just Around the Corner, Little Princess, Susannah of the Mounties, The Blue Bird, Young People, Kathleen, Miss Annie Rooney. Since You Went Away, I'll Be Seeing You, Kiss and Tell, That Hagen Girl, Honeymoon, Bachelor and the Bobby-Soxer, Fort Apache, Mr. Belvedere Goes to College, Adventure in Baltimore, Story of Seabiscuit, Kiss for Corliss.

TELEVISION: Series: Shirley Temple's Storybook (host, performer).

TENNANT, VICTORIA: Actress. b. London, England, Sept. 30, 1953. e. Central Sch. of Speech & Drama. Daughter of ballerina Irina Baronova and talent agent Cecil Tennant.

PICTURES: The Ragman's Daughter, Horror Planet (Inseminoid), Strangers Kiss, All of Me, The Holocaft Covenant, Best Seller, Flowers in the Attic, Fool's Mate, The Handmaid's Tale, L.A. Story, Whispers, The Plague.

TELEVISION: Mini-Series: Voice of the Heart, Winds of War, Chiefs, War and Remembrance, Act of Will. Movies: Maigret, Dempsey, Under Siege.

THEATRE: Love Letters (Steppenwolf), Getting Married (NY).

TERRY, SIR JOHN: Film Consultant. b. London, England, 1913. e. Mill Hill Sch. Early career as solicitor. Entered m.p. ind. Film Producers Guild 1946–47; then legal dept. Rank Organisation until 1949; joined National Film Finance Corporation; its chief solicitor 1949–57; sec., 1956–57; man. dir., 1958–78.

TESICH, STEVE: Writer. b. Titovo, Utice, Yugoslavia, Sept. 29, 1942. e. Indiana U., Columbia U. Came to U.S. at age 14. While doing graduate work in Russian literature at Columbia left to begin writing. Taken up by American Place Theatre which did his play, The Carpenters, in 1970. Other plays include Division Street, Square One, The Speed of Darkness, and On the Open Road.

PICTURES: Breaking Away (Acad. Award), Eyewitness, Four Friends, The World According to Garp, American Flyers, Eleni.

TESLER, BRIAN: C.B.E. Dept. Chmn. (Holding) plc. and Chmn. LWT Programme Advisory Board from 1992. previously, chmn., Managing Director, London Weekend Television Ltd. b. London, England, 1929. e. Chiswick County School and Exeter College, Oxford. Ent. TV ind. as trainee prod., BBC. 1952–56 Prod. Light Entertainment, BBC TV. 1957–59 Prod. Light Entertainment, ATV. 1960–63 joined ABC Television as head of features and light ent. then programme controller and director of programmes. 1968 appt. dir. of programmes, Thames Television. appt. dep. chief executive LWT. 1976 appt. man. dir. LWT. 1976. appt. chmn. , 1984. Governor, Natl. Film & TV sch., British Film Inst. Dir., ITN, 1980–91. ITCA Council 1980–82. Dir., Channel 4, 1980–85. Director Services Sound and Vision Corp. Member, British Screen Advisory Council. V.P. and Fellow of Royal TV Society. Dir., Oracle Teletext Ltd., 1981–83.

TETZLAFF, TED: Director. b. Los Angeles, CA, June 3, 1903. Joined camera dept. Fox Studios, became first cameraman; dir., 1940; served in U.S. Air Corps as a Major, W.W.II.

PICTURES: Cameraman: Enchanted Cottage, Notorious. Dir.: World Premiere, Riffraff, Fighting Father Dunne, Window, Johnny Allegro, Dangerous Profession, Gambling House, White Tower, Under the Gun, Treasure of Lost Canyon, Terror on a Train, Son of Sinbad.

TEWKESBURY, JOAN: Writer, Director. b. Redlands, CA, April 8, 1936. e. U. of Southern California. Student American Sch. Dance 1947–54. Ostrich and understudy in Mary Martin's Peter Pan. Directed and choreographed Theatre prods. in L.A., London, Edinburgh Festival, Scotland. Taught dance and theory, American Sch. of Dance 1959–64; taught in theatre arts depts. of two universities: U. of Southern California, Immaculate Heart. Became script supvr. for Robert Altman on McCabe & Mrs. Miller. Off-Bdwy: Cowboy Jack Street (writer, dir.). Teacher in film dept. UCLA. Sundance advisor, 1992–93: directors lab-writers lab. American Musical Theatre Festival in Philadelphia: Chippy (dir.)

PICTURES: Thieves Like Us (co.-s.p.), Nashville, (s.p.), Old Boyfriends (dir.), Hampstead Center (doc. of Anna Freud, writer, dir.), A Night in Heaven (s.p.), The Player (actress).

TELEVISION: Series: Alfred Hitchcock Presents (dir., writer), Elysian Fields (pilot; dir., writer, exec. prod.), Almost Grown (dir.), Shannon's Deal (dir., writer). Movies: The Acorn People (dir., s.p.), The Tenth Month (dir., s.p.), Cold Sassy Tree (dir., s.p.), Sudie and Simpson (dir.), Wild Texas Wind (dir.), The Stranger (writer, dir.).

THALHIMER, JR., MORTON G.: Former Theatre Executive. b. Richmond, VA, June 27, 1924. e. Dartmouth Coll., 1948, B.A.; U. of Virginia, 1959. Naval aviator in W.W.II. Joined Century Theatres as trainee 1948; Jamestown Amusement, 1949–50. Past pres. Neighborhood Theatre, Inc. 1967–86. Charter member of Theatre Owners of America; past member and v.p. of NATO, served on finance comm. and Trade Practice comm. bd. member and past president of NATO of VA, 1973–75. Mem. Variety Club Int'l., Tent 11; patron life member, Variety Club of Israel, Tent 51.

THAXTER, PHYLLIS: Actress. b. Portland, ME, Nov. 20, 1921. e. St. Genevieve Sch., Montreal. Mother of actress Skye Aubrey.

PICTURES: Thirty Seconds Over Tokyo (debut, 1944), Bewitched, Weekend at the Waldorf, Sea of Grass, Living in a Big Way, Tenth Avenue Angel, Sign of the Ram, Blood on the Moon, Act of Violence, No Man of Her Own, The Breaking Point, Fort Worth, Jim Thorpe—All American, Come Fill the Cup, She's Working Her Way Through College, Springfield Rifle, Operation Secret, Women's Prison, Man Afraid, The World of Henry Orient, Superman.

TELEVISION: Guest: Wagon Train, Alfred Hitchcock, Twilight Zone, Purex Specials For Women, Playhouse 90, The Fugitive, Defenders. Movies: Incident in San Francisco, The Longest Night, Three Sovereigns for Sarah. Mini-Series: Once an Eagle.

THEODORAKIS, MIKIS: Composer. b. Greece, 1925.

PICTURES: Eva, Night Ambush, Shadow of the Cat, Phaedra, Five Miles to Midnight, Zorba the Greek, The Day the Fish Came Out, The Trojan Women, State of Siege, Serpico, Iphigenia.

THIGPEN, LYNNE: Actress, Singer. b. Joliet, IL, Dec. 22.

PICTURES: Godspell (debut, 1973), The Warriors, Tootsie, Streets of Fire, Sweet Liberty, Hello Again, Running on Empty, Lean on Me, Impulse, Article 99, Bob Roberts.

TELEVISION: Series: Love Sidney, The News is the News, FM. Pilot: Pottersville. Guest: The Equalizer, Gimme a Break. Movie: Rockabye.

THEATRE: NY: The Magic Show, But Never Jam Today, Tintypes, And I Ain't Finished Yet, Full Hookup, Balm in Gilead, A Month of Sundays, Fences, Boesman & Lena.

THINNES, ROY: Actor. b. Chicago, IL, April 6, 1938.

PICTURES: Journey to the Far Side of the Sun, Charlie One-Eye, Airport 75, The Hindenburg, Rush Week.

TELEVISION: Series: General Hospital (1963–65), The Long Hot Summer, The Invaders, The Psychiatrist, From Here to Eternity, One Life to Live, Falcon Crest, Dark Shadows. Movies: The Other Man, The Psychiatrist: God Bless the Children, Black Noon, The Horror at 37,000 Feet, The Norliss Tales, Satan's School for Girls, Death Race, The Manhunter, Secrets, Code Name: Diamond Head, Sizzle, The Return of the Mod Squad, Freedom, Dark Holiday, Blue Bayou, The Hand in the Glove, An Inconvenient Woman, Lady Against the Odds, Stormy Weathers. Mini-series: From Here to Eternity, Scruples.

THOMAS, BETTY: Actress. b. St. Louis, MO, July 27, 1948. e. Univ. of Ohio. Former member of Chicago's Second City improv group.

TELEVISION: Series: Hill Street Blues (Emmy Award). Movies: Outside Chance, Nashville Grab, When Your Lover Leaves, Prison for Children. Director: Doogie Howser M.D.

PICTURES: Tunnelvision, Chesty Anderson—U.S. Navy, Loose Shoes, Used Cars, Homework, Troop Beverly Hills. Director: Only You.

THOMAS, GERALD: Producer, Director. b. Hull, England, 1920. Entered m.p. industry 1946.

PICTURES: Tony Draws a Horse, Appointment With Venus, Venetian Bird, Sword and the Rose, A Day to Remember, Mad About Men, Doctor in the House, Above Us the Waves, A Novel Affair, After the Ball, Timelock, Vicious Circle, Chain of Events, Solitary Child, The Duke Wore Jeans, Carry on Sergeant, Carry on Nurse, Carry on Teacher, Please Turn Over, Carry on Constable, Watch Your Stern, No Kidding, Carry on Regardless, Raising The Wind, Twice Around the Daffodils, Carry on Cruising, The Iron Maiden, Nurse on Wheels, Call Me a Cab, Carry on Jack, Carry on Spying, Carry on Cleo, The Big Job, Carry On Cowboy, Carry on Screaming, Don't Lose Your Head, Follow That Camel, Carry on Doctor, Carry On Up The Khyber, Carry on Up the Jungle, Carry on Loving, Carry on Camping, Carry on Again, Doctor,

Carry on, Henry, Carry on at Your Convenience, Carry on Matron, Carry on Abroad, Bless This House, Carry On Girls, Carry on Dick, Carry on Behind, Carry on England, That's Carry On, Carry on Emmanuelle, The Second Victory, Carry on Columbus.

TELEVISION: Prod. and dir. Rob Roy, serial. Prod. Carry on Christmas. Prod., Carry on Laughing. Dir. Best of Carry On. Prod. Odd Man Out, (series). Dir., Carry on Laughing, Comedy Tonight (Canada), What a Carry On, Just for Laughs, Laugh With the Carry On's.

THOMAS, HARRY E.: Exhibitor. b. Monroe, LA, May 22, 1920. e. Louisiana State U., 1938–41. Psychological Branch of Army Air Force, 1942–46. Past pres., secy., and treas. of NATO of MS. Dir. of Design & Const. & Sec. Gulf State Theatres Inc. Retired 1978.

THOMAS, HENRY: Actor. b. San Antonio, TX, Sept. 8, 1971. Made film debut at the age of 9 in Raggedy Man, 1981. On stage in Artichoke, The Guardsman.

PICTURES: Raggedy Man (debut, 1981), E.T. The Extra-Terrestrial, Misunderstood, Cloak and Dagger, The Quest, Murder One, Valmont, Fire in the Sky, Legends of the Fall.

TELEVISION: Special: The Steeler and the Pittsburgh Kid. Movies: Psycho IV: The Beginning, A Taste for Killing.

THOMAS, JAY: Actor. b. New Orleans, LA, July 12, 1948. Started as stand-up comedian before pursuing acting career in NY. Appeared on NY stage with Playwrights Horizons and Off-Bdwy in Isn't It Romantic? Also morning disc jockey on L.A. radio station KPWR-FM.

TELEVISION: Series: Mork & Mindy, Cheers, Married People, Love & War. Guest: Murphy Brown (Emmy Award, 1991).

PICTURE: Straight Talk.

THOMAS, JEREMY: Producer. b. London, Eng., July 27, 1949. e. Millfield School. Son of dir. Ralph Thomas ("Doctor" comedies) and nephew of dir. Gerald Thomas ("Carry On . . ." comedies). Entered industry 1969. Worked as film ed. on Brother Can You Spare a Dime, 1974. Received Evening Standard Special Award for Outstanding Contribution to Cinema in 1990, BAFTA's Michael Balcon Award in 1991.

PICTURES: Mad Dog Morgan, The Shout, The Great Rock 'n' Roll Swindle, Bad Timing: A Sensual Obsession, Eureka, Merry Christmas Mr. Lawrence, The Hit, Insignificance, The Last Emperor (Acad. Award, 1987), Everybody Wins, The Sheltering Sky, Let Him Have It (exec. prod.), Naked Lunch, Little Buddha.

THOMAS, MARLO: Actress. b. Detroit, MI, Nov. 21, 1938. Daughter of late Danny Thomas. m. Phil Donahue. Sister of TV producer Tony Thomas. e. U. of Southern California. Started career with small TV roles, summer stock. Appeared in London stage prod. of Barefoot in the Park. Most Promising Newcomer Awards from both Fame and Photoplay for series That Girl. Conceived book, record and TV special Free to Be You and Me (Emmy Award, 1974).

THEATER: NY: Thieves, Social Security. Regional: Six Degrees of Separation.

PICTURES: Jenny, Thieves, In the Spirit.

TELEVISION: Series: The Joey Bishop Show, That Girl. Specials: Acts of Love and Other Comedies, Free To Be You and Me (also prod.; Emmy Award, 1974), The Body Human: Facts for Girls (Emmy Award, 1981), Love Sex ... and Marriage (also exec. prod.), Free to Be a Family (host, exec. prod.; Emmy Award, 1989). Movies: It Happened One Christmas (also co-prod.), The Lost Honor of Kathryn Beck (also exec. prod.), Consenting Adult, Nobody's Child (Emmy Award, 1986), Leap of Faith (co-exec. prod. only), Held Hostage: The Sis and Jerry Levin Story. Guest: Dobie Gillis, Zane Grey Theatre, Thriller.

THOMAS, PHILIP MICHAEL: Actor. b. Columbus, OH, May 26, 1949. e. Oakwood Coll.

PICTURES: Black Fist, Sparkle, The Wizard of Speed and Time.

TELEVISION: Series: Miami Vice. Movies: Toma, The Beasts Are on the Streets, This Man Stands Alone, Valentine, A Fight for Jenny, False Witness. Special: Disney's Totally Minnie, The Debbie Allen Special.

THOMAS, RALPH: Director. b. Hull, Yorkshire, England, Aug. 10, 1915. e. Tellisford Coll., Clifton and University Coll., London. Journalist in early career, entered m.p. ind. 1932 as film ed.; service with 9th Lancers, 1939–45; then film director.

PICTURES: prod.: The Clouded Yellow; Dir.: Appointment with Venus (Island Rescue), Day to Remember, Travellers' Joy, Venetian Bird, Once Upon a Dream, Doctor in the House, Mad about Men, Above Us the Waves, Doctor At Sea, Iron Petticoat, Checkpoint, Doctor at Large, Campbell's Kingdom, A Tale of Two Cities, The Wind Cannot Read, The 39 Steps, Upstairs and Downstairs, Conspiracy of Hearts, Doctors in Love, No Love for Johnnie, No, My Darling Daughter, A Pair of Briefs, The Wild & the Willing, Doctor in Distress, Hot Enough for June, The High Bright Sun, Agent

008½, Doctor in Clover, Deadlier Than the Male, Nobody Runs Forever, Some Girls Do, Doctor in Trouble, Percy, Quest, The Love Ban, Percy's Progress, A Nightingale Sang in Berkeley Square, Pop Pirates.

THOMAS, RICHARD: Actor. b. New York, NY, June 13, 1951. e. Columbia U. Made TV debut at age 7 on Hallmark Hall of Fame special The Christmas Tree. That same year appeared on Brodawy in Sunrise at Campobello.

PICTURES: Winning (debut, 1969), Last Summer, Red Sky at Morning, The Todd Killings, You'll Like My Mother, September 30, 1955, Battle Beyond the Stars.

TELEVISION: Series: One Two Three Go, As the World Turns, The Waltons (Emmy Award, 1973). Guest: Great Ghost Tales, Bonanza, Love American Style, Medical Center, Marcus Welby M.D., The F.B.I., Tales From the Crypt (Mute Witness to Murder). Movies: Homecoming, The Red Badge of Courage, The Silence, Getting Married, No Other Love, All Quiet on the Western Front, To Find My Son, Berlin Tunnel 21, Johnny Belinda Living Proof: The Hank Williams Jr. Story, Hobson's Choice, The Master of Ballantrae, Final Jeopardy, Glory Glory, Go To the Light, Common Ground, Stephen King's IT, Mission of the Shark, Yes Virginia There Is a Santa Claus, Crash Landing: The Rescue of Flight 232, I Can Make You Love Me: The Stalking of Laura Black. Specials: A Doll's House, Give Us Barabbas, HMS Pinafore, Barefoot in the Park, Fifth of July, Andre's Mother.

THEATRE: Sunrise at Campobello, Everything in the Garden, Fifth of July, The Front Page, Love Letters, Square One, The Lisbon Traviata, Danton's Death.

THOMAS, ROBERT G. ("BOB"): Producer, Director. b. Glen Ridge, NJ, July 21, 1943. e. U. of Bridgeport, Fairleigh Dickinson U. Prod. educational radio programs, 1962, WPKN-FM. Asst. stage mgr. Meadowbrook Dinner Theatre, 1963; 1964 began career as TV cameraman for NY stations. Worked both full-time and freelance for major TV and video tape studios. 1968, started Bob Thomas Productions, producing business/sales films and TV commercials. Has 8 awards from natl. film festivals; nominated for 5 Emmys for TV series called The Jersey Side he produced for WOR-TV. Inventor of Futurevision 2000 multi-imaging video system for conventions and exhibits.

PICTURES: Shorts: Valley Forge with Bob Hope, New Jersey—200 Years. Road-Eo '77.

TELEVISION: The Jersey Side (talk/entertainment), Jersey People (weekly talk/entertainment prog), Movies '89 (synd. film preview series).

THOMAS, ROBERT J. ("BOB"): Columnist, Associated Press, Hollywood. b. San Diego, CA, Jan. 26, 1922. p. George H. Thomas, publicist. e. UCLA. Joined Associated Press staff, Los Angeles, 1943; corr. Fresno, 1944; Hollywood since 1944. Writer mag. articles; appearances, radio; orig. story Big Mike.

BOOKS: author: The Art of Animation, King Cohn, Thalberg, Selznick, Winchell, Secret Boss of California; The Heart of Hollywood; Howard, The Amazing Mr. Hughes; Weekend '33; Marlon, Portrait of the Rebel as an Artist; Walt Disney, An American Original; Bud and Lou, The Abbott and Costello Story; The Road to Hollywood (with Bob Hope); The One and Only Bing, Joan Crawford; Golden Boy: The Secret Life of William Holden; Astaire: The Man, The Dancer; I Got Rhythm, The Ethel Merman Story; Liberace, Clown Prince of Hollywood (Jack L. Warner), Disney's Art of Animation.

THOMOPOULOS, ANTHONY D.: Executive. b. Mt. Vernon, NY, Feb. 7, 1938. e. Georgetown U. Began career in broadcasting at NBC, 1959, starting as mailroom clerk and moving to radio division in prod. & admin. Shortly named to post in intl. division sales, involved with programming for stations and in dev. TV systems for other nations. Joined Four Star Entertainment Corp. as dir. of foreign sales, 1964; named v.p., 1965; exec. v.p., 1969. In 1970 joined RCA SelectaVision Div. as dir. of programming. In 1971 joined Tomorrow Entertainment as v.p. In 1973 joined ABC as v.p., prime-time programs in N.Y.; 1974, named v.p., prime-time TV creative operations, ABC Entertainment. In 1975 named v.p. of special programs, ABC Entertainment; 1976 made v.p., ABC-TV, assisting pres. Frederick S. Pierce in supervising all activities of the division. In Feb., 1978 named pres. of ABC Entertainment. In June 1983 promoted to pres., ABC Broadcast Group in chg. all TV & radio operations. 1986, pres. & COO, United Artists Corp. Resigned Sept., 1988. Independent prod. with Columbia, 1989.

THOMPSON, EMMA: Actress. b. London, England, Apr. 15, 1959. e. Cambridge Univ. m. actor-director Kenneth Branagh. Daughter of actors Eric Thompson and Phyllida Law. Acted with the Footlights at the Edinburgh Fringe. At Cambridge co-wrote, co-produced, co-directed and co-starred in school's first all-female revue Woman's Hour, as well as solo show Short Vehicle.

PICTURES: Henry V, The Tall Guy, Impromptu, Dead Again, Howards End (Acad. Award, BAFTA, NY Film Critics, LA Film Critics, Golden Globe, Natl. Society of Film Critics & Natl. Board of Review Awards for Best Actress of 1992),

Peter's Friends, Much Ado About Nothing, Remains of the Day, In the Name of the Father.
TELEVISION: *Series*: Thompson (also writer). *Mini-Series*: Tutti Frutti, Fortunes of War (BAFTA Best Actress award). *Specials*: The Emma Thompson Special, The Winslow Boy, Look Back in Anger, Knuckle. *Guest*: Cheers.
THEATRE: *London*: Me and My Girl, Look Back in Anger. *Renaissance Theatre Company* (World Tour): A Midsummer Night's Dream, King Lear.

THOMPSON, J. LEE: Writer, Director, Producer. b. Bristol, England, 1914. On Brit. stage; writer of stage plays including: Murder Without Crime, Cousin Simon, Curious Dr. Robson (collab.) Thousands of Summers, Human Touch. Writer and m.p. director.
PICTURES: The Middle Watch (s.p.), For Them That Trespass (s.p.), Murder Without Crime (dir., s.p.), The Yellow Balloon, Weak and the Wicked. *Director*: As Long as They're Happy, For Better or Worse, An Alligator Named Daisy, Yield To The Night, The Good Companions (co-prod., dir.), Woman In The Dressing Gown, Ice Cold in Alex, No Trees in the Street, Tiger Bay, I Aim at the Stars, The Guns of Navarone, Taras Bulba, Cape Fear, Kings of the Sun, What A Way to Go, John Goldfarb Please Come Home, Return From the Ashes, Eye of the Devil, MacKenna's Gold, Before Winter Comes, The Chairman, Country Dance (Brotherly Love), Conquest of the Planet of the Apes, Battle for the Planet of the Apes, Huckleberry Finn, The Reincarnation of Peter Proud, St. Ives, The White Buffalo, The Greek Tycoon, The Passage, Cabo-blanco, Happy Birthday To Me, The Ambassador, 10 to Midnight, The Evil That Men Do, King Solomon's Mines, Murphy's Law, Firewalker, Death Wish IV, Messenger of Death, Kinjite.
TELEVISION: A Great American Tragedy, The Blue Knight, Widow.

THOMPSON, JACK: Actor. r.n. John Payne. b. Sydney, Australia, Aug. 31, 1940. e. Queensland U. Joined drama workshop at school; first part was in TV soap opera as continuing character. 1988, appt. to bd. of Australian Film Finance Corp. Formed Pan Film Enterprises.
PICTURES: Outback, Wake in Fright, Libido, Petersen, A Sunday Too Far Away, Caddie, Mad Dog Coll, The Chant of Jimmie Blacksmith, Breaker Morant (Australian award), The Earthling, The Club, The Man From Snowy River, Bad Blood, Merry Christmas Mr. Lawrence, Flesh + Blood, Burke & Willis, Turtle Beach, Wind, A Far Off Place, Ruby Cairo.
TELEVISION: The Last Frontier, A Woman Called Golda, Waterfront, The Letter, Beryl Markham: A Shadow on the Sun, Paradise, Last Frontier, Wreck of the Stinson.

THOMPSON, LEA: Actress. b. Rochester, MN, May 31, 1961. m. director Howard Deutch. Danced professionally since age of 14; won scholarship to Penn. Ballet Co., American Ballet Theatre, San Francisco Ballet. Gave up that career for acting. L.A. stage: Bus Stop, The Illusion.
PICTURES: Jaws 3-D (debut, 1983), All the Right Moves, Red Dawn, The Wild Life, Back to the Future, Space Camp, Howard the Duck, Some Kind of Wonderful, Casual Sex?, Going Undercover, The Wizard of Loneliness, Back to the Future Part II, Back to the Future Part III, Article 99, Dennis the Menace, The Beverly Hillbillies.
TELEVISION: *Movies*: Nightbreaker, Montana, Stolen Babies. *Guest*: Tales From the Crypt.

THOMPSON, SADA: Actress. b. Des Moines, IA, Sept. 27, 1929. e. Carnegie Inst. of Technology, Pittsburgh. First N.Y. stage appearance in Under Milkwood with Dylan Thomas. Bdwy. career has produced many awards topped by The Effects of Gamma Rays, for which he won Obie, Drama Desk, Variety Poll, and Twigs for which she won the 1972 Tony Award. Recent theater: Real Estate.
PICTURE: Desperate Characters.
TELEVISION: *Specials*: Sandburg's Lincoln, Our Town, Andre's Mother. *Movies*: The Entertainer, Princess Daisy, My Two Loves, Fatal Confession: A Father Dowling Mystery, Home Fires Burning, Fear Stalk. *Series*: Family (Emmy Award, 1978). *Mini-Series*: Queen.

THULIN, INGRID: Actress, Director. b. Solleftea, Sweden, Jan. 27, 1929. m. Harry Schein. Made acting debut at 18 at the Municipal Theatre in Norrkoping. Studied at Stockholm's Royal Dramatic Theatre. Worked with Malmo and Stockholm repertory. Appeared on Swedish stage in nearly 50 plays including Gigi, Peer Gynt, Two for the Seesaw, Twelfth Night, Miss Julie. Has directed plays and films in Stockholm. N.Y. stage debut, 1967: Of Love Remembered. Author: Somebody I Knew (1993).
PICTURES: *For Ingmar Bergman*: Wild Strawberries, Brink of Life (Best Actress Award, Cannes Film Festival), The Magician, Winter Light, The Silence, The Hour of the Wolf, The Ritual, Cries and Whispers. *Also*: Night Games, The Bathers, Adelaide, La Guerre Est Finie, The Four Horsemen of the Apocalypse, Return From Ashes, The Damned, Moses, The Cassandra Crossing, Madame Kitty, After the Rehearsal, Rabbit Face, House of Smiles.

THUNA, LEONORA: Writer, Producer. b. May 3, 1929. e. Hunter Coll., A.B., 1951. Playwright, The Natural Look (Broadway, 1967), Show Me Where the Good Times Are (1970), Let Me Hear You Smile (1973), Fugue (1987), and other plays and musicals off-Bdwy. and on tour. Librettist/Prod.: Jekyll and Hyde (musical, George Street Playhouse, New Brunswick, N.J. 1990).
TELEVISION: *Movies*: The Love Boat II (co-writer), I Know Why the Caged Bird Sings (writer), Famill Secrets (writer, co-prod.), Torch Song (writer). *Pilot*: The Natural Look (writer, prod.). *Series* (writer): episodes of Family, Lou Grant, In the Beginning, Starting Fresh (prod.), Grandpa Goes to Washington (co-exec. prod.), Angie (exec. prod.), The Goodtime Girls (co-creator & supvr. prod.). Also writer for Broadway variety special for Entertainment Channel.
PICTURE: How to Beat the High Cost of Living (story).

THURMAN, UMA: Actress. b. Boston, MA, Apr. 29, 1970. Named after a Hindu deity. Raised in Woodstock, NY and Amherst, MA where father taught Asian studies. Father's work took family to India where they lived three years. e. Professional Children's School, NY. Worked as model while still in high school.
PICTURES: Kiss Daddy Good Night, Johnny Be Good, Dangerous Liaisons, The Adventures of Baron Munchausen, Where the Heart Is, Henry and June, Final Analysis, Jennifer Eight, Mad Dog and Glory, Even Cowgirls Get the Blues.
TELEVISION: *Movie*: Robin Hood.

TICOTIN, RACHEL: Actress. b. Bronx, NY, Nov. 1, 1958. Began career as dancer with the Ballet Hispanico of New York, before becoming a production assist. on such films as The Wanderers, Dressed to Kill and Raging Bull.
PICTURES: King of the Gypsies, Fort Apache: The Bronx, Critical Condition, Total Recall, One Good Cop, FX2, Falling Down, Natural Born Killers.
TELEVISION: *Series*: For Love and Honor, Ohara, Crime and Punishment. *Movies*: Love Mary, Rockabye, When the Bough Breaks, Spies Lies and Naked Thighs, Prison Stories: Women on the Inside, Keep the Change, From the Files of Joseph Wambaugh: A Jury of One.

TIERNEY, LAWRENCE: Actor. b. Brooklyn, NY, Mar. 15, 1919. Brother of actor Scott Brady. e. Manhattan Coll. Track athlete (natl. championship Cross Country Team, N.Y. Athletic Club). On stage as actor. Screen debut 1943 in The Ghost Ship.
PICTURES: Government Girl, The Falcon Out West, Youth Runs Wild, Back to Bataan, Dillinger, Mama Loves Papa, Those Endearing Young Charms, Badman's Territory, Step By Step, San Quentin, Devil Thumbs a Ride, Born to Kill, Bodyguard, Kill or Be Killed, Best of the Bad Men, Shake-down, Greatest Show on Earth, Hoodlum, Bushwackers, Steel Cage, Female Jungle, Singing in the Dark, A Child Is Waiting, Custer of the West, Such Good Friends, Abduction, Bad, Kirlian Witness, Gloria, Arthur, Midnight, Prizzi's Honor, Silver Bullet, Murphy's Law, Tough Guys Don't Dance, Offspring, The Horror Show, Wizards of the Demon Sword, Why Me?, City of Hope, The Runestone, Reservoir Dogs.
TELEVISION: *Movies*: Terrible Joe Moran, Dillinger. *Guest*: Hill Street Blues, Star Trek: The Next Generation.

TIFFIN, PAMELA: Actress. r.n. Pamela Wonso. b. Oklahoma City, OK, Oct. 13, 1942. e. Hunter Coll., Columbia U., Loyola U, Rome Center. Studied acting with Stella Adler and Harold Clurman. Started modeling as a teenager.
PICTURES: Summer and Smoke (debut, 1961), One Two Three, State Fair, Come Fly with Me, For Those Who Think Young, The Pleasure Seekers, The Hallelujah Trail, Harper, Paranoia, Kiss the Other Sheik, Viva Max, Deaf Smith and Johnny Ears, Evil Fingers.
PLAYS: Dinner at Eight (Theatre World Award), Uncle Vanya.

TIGHE, KEVIN: Actor. b. Los Angeles, CA, Aug. 13, 1944. e. Cal. State, B.A. in psychology; USC M.F.A. in performing arts. Served in U.S. Army, 1967–9. Received N.E.A. Director's Fellowship, Seattle Rep. Theatre, 1988–9.
PICTURES: The Graduate (debut, 1967), Matewan, Eight Men Out, K-9, Lost Angels, Road House, Another 48 HRS, Bright Angel, City of Hope, Newsies, School Ties, I Love a Man in Uniform, What's Eating Gilbert Grape?
TELEVISION: *Series*: Emergency. *Guest*: Tales From the Crypt (Cutting Cards). *Movies*: Perry Mason: The Case of the Defiant Daughter, Better Off Dead, Caught in the Act.

TILLY, MEG: Actress. b. Canada, 1960. Began acting and dancing in community theatrical prods. while in high school. To New York at 16; appeared on TV in Hill Street Blues. Film debut was a few lines in Fame.
PICTURES: Fame (debut, 1980), Tex, Psycho II, One Dark Night, The Big Chill, Impulse, Agnes of God (Acad. Award nom.), Off Beat, Masquerade, The Girl in a Swing, Valmont, The Two Jakes, Leaving Normal, Body Snatchers.
TELEVISION: *Series*: Winnetka Road. *Specials*: The Trouble With Grandpa, Camilla (Nightmare Classics). *Movie*: In

the Best Interest of the Child. *Guest*: Fallen Angels (Dead-End for Delia).

TINKER, GRANT A.: Executive. b. Stamford, CT., Jan. 11, 1926. e. Dartmouth Coll., 1947. Joined NBC radio prog. dept. 1949. In 1954 with McCann-Erickson ad agency, TV dept. In 1958, Benton & Bowles Ad Agency, TV dept. From 1961–66 with NBC, v.p., programs, West Coast; v.p. in chg. of programming, N.Y., 1966–67. Joined Universal Television as v.p., 1968–69; 20th-Fox, v.p., 1969–70. Became pres. MTM Enterprises, Inc. 1970. Named NBC bd. chmn. & CEO, 1981–86. Received ATAS Governor's Award in 1987. Formed indep. prod. co. G.T.G. Entertainment, 1988.

TISCH, LAURENCE A.: Executive. b. Brooklyn, NY, March 5, 1923. e. NYU, 1941; U. of Pennsylvania Wharton Sch., 1942; Harvard Law Sch., 1946. Pres. Tisch Hotels, Inc., 1950–59; pres. Americana Hotel, Inc., Miami Beach, 1956–59; Chmn. of bd. and co-chief executive officer of Loews Corp since 1960. Also chmn. of bd. of CNA Financial Corp since 1947. President and chief executive officer and chmn. of board, CBS since 1986.

TISCH, PRESTON ROBERT: Executive. b. Brooklyn, NY, April 29, 1926. e. Bucknell U., Lewisberg, PA, 1943–44; U. of Michigan, B.A., 1948. Pres. Loew's Corporation. Postmaster General of the U.S. 1986–1988. March, 1988 returned to Loews Corp. as president and co-chief executive. Elected member of bd. CBS Inc. Sept., 1988.

TISCH, STEVE: Producer. b. Lakewood, NJ, 1949. e. Tufts U. Son of Preston Tisch. Worked during school breaks for John Avildsen and Fred Weintraub. Signed upon graduation as exec. asst. to Peter Guber, then prod. head at Columbia Pictures. Entered producer ranks with Outlaw Blues, 1977, collaborating with Jon Avnet with whom formed Tisch/Avnet Prods. Alliance with Phoenix Entertainment 1988.
PICTURES: Coast to Coast, Risky Business, Deal of the Century, Soul Man, Big Business, Hot to Trot, Heart of Dixie, Heart Condition, Bad Influence.
TELEVISION: Homeward Bound, No Other Love, Prime Suspect, Something So Right, The Burning Bed (exec. prod.), Call to Glory (series), Silence of the Heart, In Love and War (sole prod.), Evil in Clear River, Dirty Dancing (series), Out on the Edge (exec. prod.), 3,000 Miles 21 Days 10 Cents (exec. prod.), Judgment (exec. prod.), Afterburn (exec. prod.).

TOBACK, JAMES: Writer, Producer, Director. b. New York, NY, Nov. 23, 1944. e. Harvard U. Taught literature at City Coll. of New York; contributed articles and criticism to Harper's, Esquire, Commentary, etc. Wrote book Jim, on actor-athlete Jim Brown (1971). First screenplay, The Gambler, filmed in 1974.
PICTURES: The Gambler (s.p.), Fingers (s.p., dir.), Love and Money (s.p., dir., prod.), Exposed (dir., prod., s.p.), The Pick-Up Artist (dir., s.p.), The Big Bang (s.p., actor), Alice (actor), Bugsy (s.p., actor).

TOBOLOWSKY, STEPHEN: Actor. b. Dallas, TX, May 30, 1951. e. Southern Methodist Univ.
PICTURES: Swing Shift (voice), True Stories (co-s.p.), Nobody's Fool, Spaceballs, Mississippi Burning, Checking Out, Two Idiots in Hollywood (dir. & s.p.), Great Balls of Fire!, In Country, Breaking In, Bird on a Wire, Funny About Love, Welcome Home Roxy Carmichael, The Grifters, Thelma & Louise, Memoirs of an Invisible Man, Basic Instinct, Roadside Prophets, Single White Female, Sneakers, Where the Day Takes You, Sneakers, Hero, Groundhog Day, The Pickle, Josh and S.A.M., Calendar Girl.
TELEVISION: *Movies*: Last Flight Out, Marla Hanson Story, Perry Mason: The Case of the Maligned Mobster, Tagget, Deadlock, Deadly Medicine, When Love Kills: The Seduction of John Hearn. *Guest*: Crazy Like a Fox, Designing Women, L.A. Law, Days and Nights of Molly Dodd.
THEATRE: *Actor*: Whose Life Is It Anyway?, Crimes of the Heart, Godspell, Three Sisters, The Glass Menagerie, Barabass. *Director*: The Miss Firecracker Contest, The Lucky Spot, The Bridgehead (Dramalogue Award).

TODD, BEVERLY: Actress, Director, Producer. b. Chicago, IL, July 11, 1946.
PICTURES: The Lost Man, They Call Me Mister Tibbs!, Brother John, Vice Squad, Homework, The Ladies Club, Happy Hour, Baby Boom, Moving, Clara's Heart, Lean on Me.
TELEVISION: *Series*: Love of Life, Having Babies, The Redd Foxx Show. *Mini-Series*: Roots. *Movies*: Deadlock, The Ghost of Flight 401, Having Babies II, The Jericho Mile, Don't Look Back, A Touch of Scandal, A Different Affair. *Guest*: Magnum P.I., The Robert Guillaume Show, Falcon Crest, Quincy M.E., Hill Street Blues, Family, Benson, Lou Grant. *Special*: Don't Hit Me Mom (Afterschool Special).
THEATRE: *NY*: Carry Me Back to Morningside Heights, Black Visions. *Producer*: A Laugh a Tear: The Story of Black Humor in America. *Director*: I Need a Man.

TODD, RICHARD: O.B.E. Actor. b. Dublin, Ireland, June 11, 1919. e. Shrewsbury. In repertory, 1937; founder-member, Dundee

Repertory Theatre, 1939; distinguished war service, 1939–46; Dundee Repertory, 1946–48; screen debut, 1948; For Them That Trespass, 1948. 1970 Founder-Director Triumph Theatre Productions. Published autobiography, 1986, Volume II, 1989. Awarded O.B.E., 1993.
PICTURES: For Them That Trespass (debut, 1948), The Hasty Heart, Interrupted Journey, Stage Fright, Portrait of Clare, Lightning Strikes Twice, Flesh and Blood, Story of Robin Hood, 24 Hours of a Woman's Life, The Venetian Bird, Sword and the Rose, Rob Roy, Les Secrets d'Alcove, A Man Called Peter (U.S.), Virgin Queen (U.S.), Dam Busters, D-Day the Sixth of June (U.S.), Marie Antoinette, Yangtse Incident, Saint Joan, Chase a Crooked Shadow, The Naked Earth, Intent to Kill, Danger Within, Never Let Go, The Long the Short and the Tall, Don't Bother to Knock (also exec. prod.), The Hellions, The Longest Day, Crime Does Not Pay, The Boys, The Very Edge, Death Drums Along the River, Battle of the Villa Fiorita, Operation Crossbow, Coast of Skeletons, The Love-Ins, Subterfuge, Dorian Gray, Asylum, The Sky is Falling, Number One of the Secret Service, The Big Sleep, House of the Long Shadows.
TELEVISION: Wuthering Heights, Carrington V.C., The Brighton Mesmerists, Beautiful Lies, The Boy Dominic, Murder She Wrote, Virtual Murder.
STAGE: 1966–67, An Ideal Husband; Dear Octopus. Co-founder, Triumph Theatre Prods., Ltd. plays since 1970: Roar Like a Dove, Grass Is Greener, The Marquise (U.S.). Sleuth, 1972–73 (England and Australia). Murder by Numbers, The Hollow Crown (with RSC), Equus. On Approval, Quadrille, This Happy Breed, The Business of Murder, 1981–86 (London), Intent to Kill, The Woman in Black, Beyond Reasonable Doubt, Sweet Revenge.

TODMAN, HOWARD: Executive. b. New York, NY, Nov. 24, 1920. e. Hamilton Coll., 1941. Dir. business affairs, Goodson-Todman Productions; treas., Goodson-Todman Associates, inc.; v.p. & treas., Goodson-Todman Enterprises, Ltd.; Treasurer, Peak Prods., Inc.; Treas. Goodson-Todman Bcstg. Inc.; v.p. Price Productions, Inc.; v.p. Celebrity Productions, Inc.; chmn., N.Y. Cancer Crusade, radio & TV.

TOKOFSKY, JERRY H.: Executive. b. New York, NY, Apr. 14, 1936. e. NYU, B.S., journalism, 1956; New York Law, 1959. Entered William Morris Agency while at NYU 1953, working in night club dept. to live TV. Moved to Beverly Hills office, 1959. Entered m.p. div. WMA, 1960. Joined Columbia Pictures, as prod. v.p., 1963–70. Joined Paramount Pictures 1970 as prod. v.p. To MGM as prod. v.p., 1971. Now producer & exec. v.p., Zupnik Enterprises, Inc.
PICTURES: Producer: Where's Poppa, Born to Win, Paternity, Dreamscape, Fear City, Wildfire, Glengarry Glen Ross.

TOLKAN, JAMES: Actor. b. Calumet, MI, June 20, 1931. e. Univ. of Iowa. Trained with Stella Adler.
PICTURES: Stiletto, They Might Be Giants, The Friends of Eddie Coyle, Serpico, Love and Death, The Amityville Horror, Wolfen, Prince of the City, Author! Author!, Hanky Panky, Nightmares (voice), WarGames, Iceman, The River, Turk 182!, Flanagan, Back to the Future, Off Beat, Top Gun, Armed and Dangerous, Masters of the Universe, Made in Heaven, Viper, Split Decisions, True Blood, Second Sight, Back to the Future Part II, Family Business, Opportunity Knocks, Back to the Future Part III, Dick Tracy, Hangfire, Problem Child 2, Driving Me Crazy, Boiling Point.
TELEVISION: *Series*: Mary, The Hat Squad. *Movies*: Little Spies, Leap of Faith, Weekend War, The Case of the Hillside Stranglers, Sketch Artist. *Guest*: Remington Steele, Miami Vice, The Equalizer, Tales From the Crypt.
THEATRE: NY: Abe Lincoln in Illinois, Once in a Lifetime, Three Sisters, The Cannibals, Mary Stuart, The Silent Partner, 42 Seconds from Broadway, Full Circle, Macbeth, Dream of a Blacklisted Actor, Jungle of Cities, Wings.

TOLKIN, MICHAEL: Writer, Director, Producer. b. New York, NY, 1950. e. Middlebury Col, VT. Novels: The Player (1988), Among the Dead (1992).
PICTURES: Gleaming the Cube (s.p.), The Rapture (dir., s.p.), The Player (s.p., co-prod., actor; WGA Award), Deep Cover (story, co-s.p.), The New Age (dir., s.p.).

TOM, C. Y.: Cinematographer, Distributor. b. Toy Shan, Kwong Tung Providence, Southern China, Nov. 6, 1907. Graduated N.Y. Inst. of Photography, 1926. Photographed newsreels for The Great Wall Film Co. of Shanghai; 1926–29; in charge of production, Shanghai, 1929–32. Arrived in L.A. 1932. Studied production techniques in Hollywood. Toured Europe, managing Chinese vaudeville, 1935. Studio mgr. and dir. photography for the Liberal Art and Chi Ming Motion Picture Co., 1935–41. President, Chinamerica Film Exchange and Chinamerica Film Studio, Hong Kong and Shanghai. Distributor, Monogram, Film Classics and Telenews, Hong Kong, Macao and China; built Capitol Theatre, Hong Kong, 1948–59.

TOMEI, MARISA. Actress. b. Brooklyn, NY, Dec. 4, 1964. e. Boston U.
PICTURES: The Flamingo Kid (debut, 1984), Playing for Keeps, Oscar, Zandalee, My Cousin Vinny (Acad. Award, supp. actress, 1992), Chaplin, Untamed Heart, Equinox, The Paper.
TELEVISION: Series: As the World Turns, A Different World. Movie: Parker Kane.
THEATRE: Beiruit (L.A.). NY: Daughters (Theatre World Award), The Comedy of Errors, What the Butler Saw.

TOMLIN, LILY: Actress. r.n. Mary Jean Tomlin. b. Detroit, MI, Sept. 1, 1939. Wayne State U. (studied pre-med). Studied mime with Paul Curtis. Started inventing characters for comedy sketches in college, used them in cafe and night club dates in Detroit. 1965 went to NY performing skits on coffee-house circuit, landed job on The Garry Moore Show. Moved to L.A. where she appeared on The Music Scene. 1969, first appeared on Laugh-In TV series, gaining national attention with such characters as telephone operator Ernestine and child Edith Ann.
THEATER: Appearing Nightly (Special Tony Award, 1977), The Search for Signs of Intelligent Life in the Universe (1985, on Bdwy and on tour; Tony Award, best actress).
TELEVISION: Series: The Music Scene (host, 1969), Laugh-In (1969–3). Specials: Lily (Emmy Award as writer, 1974), Lily Tomlin (Emmy Award as writer, 1976), The Paul Simon Special (Emmy Award as writer, 1978), Lily—Sold Out (also exec. prod.; Emmy Award as exec.-prod., 1981), The Muppets Go to the Movies, Lily for President?, Live—and in Person, Funny You Don't Look 200, Free to Be . . . a Family. Movie: And the Band Played On.
PICTURES: Nashville, (debut, 1975; NY Film Critics Award, supp. actress; Acad Award nom.), The Late Show, Moment by Moment, Nine to Five, The Incredible Shrinking Woman, All of Me, Lily Tomlin (doc. behind the scenes of The Search for Intelligent Life), Big Business, The Search for Signs of Intelligent Life in the Universe, Shadows and Fog, The Player, Short Cuts, The Beverly Hillbillies.
RECORDS: This Is a Recording (Grammy Award, 1971), Modern Scream, And That's The Truth, Lily Tomlin On Stage.

TOPOL: Actor. b. Tel-Aviv, Israel, Sept. 9, 1935. r.n. Chaim Topol. London's West End & Manchester in Fiddler on the Roof repeating role on screen; 1989 repeated role in U.S. (Tony nom.), Canada & Japan tour.
PICTURES: Sallah, Cast a Giant Shadow, Before Winter Comes, A Talent for Loving, Fiddler on the Roof (Acad. Award nom.), Follow Me (The Public Eye), Galileo, Flash Gordon, For Your Eyes Only, Ervinka, A Dime Novel.
TELEVISION: Movies: House on Garibaldi Street, Queenie. Mini-Series: The Winds of War, War and Remembrance.

TORME, MEL: Singer, Actor. b. Chicago, IL, Sept. 13, 1925. Singing debut at age of 4; won radio audition 1933; on radio; composed song Lament to Love; with Chico Marx's orchestra as drummer, arranger & vocalist 1942; served in U.S. Army, W.W.II; org. vocal group Meltones; many recordings; night clubs, concerts.
PICTURES: Higher and Higher (debut, 1943), Pardon My Rhythm, Let's Go Steady, Janie Gets Married, Junior Miss, Night and Day, Good News, Words and Music, Duchess of Idaho, The Big Operator, Girls Town, Walk Like a Dragon, The Patsy, A Man Called Adam, The Land of No Return (Snowman), Daffy Duck's Quackbusters (voice), The Naked Gun 2-1/2.
TELEVISION: Series: TV's Top Tunes, The Judy Garland Show (musical advisor, guest), It Was a Very Good Year (host). Movie: Pray TV.

TORN, RIP: Actor. r.n. Elmore Torn, Jr. b. Temple, TX, Feb. 6, 1931. e. Texas A & M U., U. of Texas. Served in army. Signed as understudy for lead in Cat on a Hot Tin Roof on Broadway.
THEATER: Orpheus Descending, Sweet Bird of Youth (Theatre World Award), Daughter of Silence, Macbeth, Desire Under the Elms, Strange Interlude, Blues For Mr. Charlie, The Kitchen, The Deer Park (Obie Award), The Beard, The Cuban Thing, Dream of a Blacklisted Actor, The Dance of Death, Anna Christie.
PICTURES: Baby Doll (debut, 1956), A Face in the Crowd, Time Limit, Pork Chop Hill, King of Kings, Hero's Island, Sweet Bird of Youth, Critic's Choice, The Cincinnati Kid, One Spy Too Many, You're a Big Boy Now, Beach Red, Sol Madrid, Beyond the Law, Coming Apart, Tropic of Cancer, Maidstone, Payday, Slaughter, Crazy Joe, Birch Interval, The Man Who Fell to Earth, Nasty Habits, Private Life of J. Edgar Hoover, Coma, The Seduction of Joe Tynan, Heartland, One Trick Pony, First Family, A Stranger is Watching, The Beastmaster, Jinxed, Airplane II: The Sequel, Cross Creek, Misunderstood, Songwriter, Flashpoint, City Heat, Summer Rental, Beer, Extreme Prejudice, Nadine, The Telephone (also dir.), Cold Feet, Hit List, Silence Like Glass, Blind Curve, The Hunt for Red October, Defending Your Life, Beautiful Dreamers, Hard Promises, Robocop 3, Dolly Dearest, Where the Rivers Flow North.

TELEVISION: Series: The Larry Sanders Show. Movies: The President's Plane is Missing, Attack on Terror: The FBI vs. the Ku Klux Klan, Song of Myself, The Execution, Betrayal, When She Says No, The Atlanta Child Murders, J. Edgar Hoover, Sophia Loren—Her Story, Rape and Marriage—The Rideout Case, Blind Ambition, Montserrat, Laguna Heat, Steel Cowboy, Cat on a Hot Tin Roof, The King of Love, April Morning, Sweet Bird of Youth, Pair of Aces, By Dawn's Early Light, Another Pair of Aces, My Son Johnny, Death Hits the Jackpot, T Bone N Weasel, A Mother's Right: The Elizabeth Morgan Story, Dead Ahead: The Exxon Valdez Disaster.

TOTTER, AUDREY: Actress. b. Joliet, IL, Dec. 20, 1918. In many stage plays. On radio 1939–44.
PLAYS: Copperhead, Stage Door, Late Christopher Bean, My Sister Eileen.
PICTURES: Main Street After Dark (debut, 1944), Her Highness and the Bellboy, Dangerous Partners, The Sailor Takes a Wife, Adventure, The Hidden Eye, The Secret Heart, The Postman Always Rings Twice, Cockeyed Miracle, Lady in the Lake, Beginning or the End, Unsuspected, High Wall, The Saxon Charm, Alias Nick Beal, Any Number Can Play, Tension, The Set-Up, Under the Gun, The Blue Veil, Sellout, F.B.I. Girl, Assignment-Paris, My Pal Gus, Woman They Almost Lynched, Cruisin' Down the River, Man in the Dark, Mission Over Korea, Champ for a Day, Massacre Canyon, Women's Prison, A Bullet for Joey, Vanishing American, Ghost Diver, Jet Attack, Man or Gun, The Carpetbaggers, Harlow, Chubasco, The Apple Dumpling Gang Rides Again.
TELEVISION: Series: Cimarron City, Our Man Higgins, Medical Center (1972–76). Movies: The Outsider, U.M.C., The Nativity, The Great Cash Giveaway, City Killer. Guest: Murder, She Wrote.

TOWERS, CONSTANCE: Actress. b. Whitefish, MT, May 20, 1934. m. John Gavin, actor and former U.S. Ambassador to Mexico. e. Juilliard Sch. of Music. Stage work on Broadway and tour.
THEATER: Bdwy: Ari, Anya, Engagement Baby, King and I (1977–79 opp. Yul Brynner). Chicago: Steel Magnolias.
PICTURES: Horse Soldiers, Sergeant Rutledge, Fate Is the Hunter, Shock Corridor, Naked Kiss, Sylvester, Fast Forward, Nutty Nut.
TELEVISION: Series: Love Is a Many Splendored Thing, VTV, Capitol. Mini-Series: On Wings of Eagles, Sands of Time. Guest: Home Show, The Loner, Murder, She Wrote, STN, Hour Mag, MacGyver, Designing Women, Midnight Caller, Matlock, Baywatch, Prince of Bel Air.

TOWERS, HARRY ALAN: Executive, Producer. b. London, England, 1920. Prod. and wrote: 1963: Sanders of the River; 1964: Code Seven Victim Five.
PICTURES: City of Fear, Mozambique, Coast of Skeletons, Sandy the Seal, 24 Hours to Kill, The Face of Fu Manchu, Ten Little Indians, Marrakesh, Circus of Fear, The Brides of Fu Manchu, Sumuru, Five Golden Dragons, The Vengeance of Fu Manchu, Jules Verne's Rocket to the Moon, House of a Thousand Dolls, The Face of Eve, Blood of Fu Manchu, 99 Women, Girl From Rio, Marquis de Sade's Justine, Castle of Fu Manchu, Venus in Furs, Philosophy in the Boudoir, Eugenie, Dorian Gray, Count Dracula, The Bloody Judge, Black Beauty, Night Hair Child, The Call of the Wild, Treasure Island, White Fang, Death in Persepolis, Ten Little Indians, End of Innocence, Black Cobra, Black Velvet-White Silk, Night of The High Tide, King Solomon's Treasure, Shape of Things to Come, Klondike Fever, Fanny Hill, Frank and I, Black Venus, Christmas, Black Arrow, Pompeii, Love Circles, Lightning—White Stallion, Gor, Outlaw of Gor, Dragonard, Skeleton Coast, Master of Dragonard Hill, Nam, Fire With Fire, Jekyll and Hyde, River of Death, Cobra Strike, The Howling IV—The Original Nightmare, Skeleton Coast, Edge of Sanity, Ten Little Indians, Platoon Leader, Captive Rage, American Ninja III: Blood Hunt, The Fall of the House of Usher, Edgar Allan Poe's Buried Alive, Phantom of the Opera, Oddball Hall, Terror of Manhattan, The Lost World, Return to the Lost World, Black Museum, Golden Years of Sherlock Holmes, Chicago Loop, The Mangler, Harry Palmer, Beijing Express, Midnight in Moscow.

TOWNE, ROBERT: Writer, Director, Producer. b. 1936. Was member of Warren Beatty's production staff on Bonnie and Clyde and contributed to that screenplay. Also uncredited, wrote Pacino-Brando garden scene in The Godfather; script doctor on Marathon Man, The Missouri Breaks and others. Appeared as an actor under the name Edward Wain in the Last Woman on Earth and The Creature from the Haunted Sea.
PICTURES: Writer: The Last Woman on Earth (as Edward Wain), The Tomb of Ligeia, Villa Rides, Drive He Said (actor only), The Last Detail, Chinatown (Acad. Award, 1974), Shampoo (co-s.p.), The Yazuka (co-s.p.), Personal Best (also dir., prod.), Greystoke: The Legend of Tarzan (s.p., uncredited), The Pick-Up Artist (actor only), The Bedroom

Window (exec. prod. only), Tequila Sunrise (also dir.), Days of Thunder, The Two Jakes, The Firm (co-s.p.).

TOWNSEND, CLAIRE: b. New York, NY, Feb. 20, 1952. e. Princeton U. Joined 20th Century-Fox in 1976; named west coast story editor & v.p. creative affairs. Left in 1978 to go to United Artists, where named v.p. of production, responsible for managing the acquisition, development and production of feature films. Now independent producer.

TOWNSEND, ROBERT: Producer, Director, Writer, Actor. b. Chicago, IL, Feb. 6, 1957. e. attended Illinois State U. and Hunter Coll. Planned baseball career before turning to acting. Veteran of Experimental Black Actors Guild and Second City. Film debut: Cooley High (1974). TV commercials; stand-up comedy at NY Improvisation; taped Evening at the Improv.
PICTURES: *Actor:* Willie and Phil, Streets of Fire, A Soldier's Story, American Flyers, Odd Jobs, Ratboy, Hollywood Shuffle (also prod., dir., co-s.p.), Eddie Murphy Raw (dir. only), The Mighty Quinn, That's Adequate, The Five Heartbeats (also dir., exec. prod., co-s.p.), The Meteor Man (also dir., s.p., co-prod.).
TELEVISION: *Series:* Another Page (PBS series), Townsend Television. *Specials:* Robert Townsend and His Partners in Crime; Take No Prisoners: Robert Townsend and His Partners in Crime II (HBO). *Movies:* Women at West Point, Senior Trip!, In Love With an Older Woman.

TRAMBUKIS, WILLIAM J.: Executive. b. Providence, R.I., July 26, 1926. e. Mt. Pleasant Bus. Col. Began career as usher with Loew's in Providence, RI, 1941. Served 1943–46 with Navy Seabees. Recipient of Quigley Awards. Managed/supervised Loew's Theatres in several New England cities, Harrisburg, PA, Syracuse, Rochester, Buffalo, NY, Washington, DC, Richmond, Norfolk, VA, Toronto, Canada, Atlanta, GA. Appt. Loew's NorthEastern Division mgr. 1964; Loew's gen. mgr. 1975: v.p. in 1976; sr. v.p., 1985. Retired, 1987.

TRAVANTI, DANIEL J.: Actor. b. Kenosha, WI, March 7, 1940. e. U. of Wisconsin (B.A.), Loyola Marymount Univ. (M.A.), Yale Sch. of Drama. Woodrow Wilson fellow, 1961. Formerly acted as Dan Travanty. On stage in Twigs, Othello, I Never Sang for My Father, Only Kidding, The Taming of the Shrew, Les Liaisons Dangereuses.
PICTURES: St. Ives, Midnight Crossing, Millenium, Megaville.
TELEVISION: *Series:* General Hospital, Hill Street Blues (Emmy Awards, 1981, 1982; Golden Globe Award, 1981), Missing Persons. *Movies:* The Love War, Adam, Aurora, Murrow, Adam: His Song Continues, I Never Sang for My Father, Fellow Traveler, Howard Beach: Making the Case for Murder, Tagget, Eyes of a Witness, The Christmas Stallion.

TRAVERS, BILL: Actor, Producer, Director. b. Newcastle-on-Tyne, England. Jan. 3, 1922. Actor in repertory co.; London stage in Cage Me a Peacock, Damask Cheek, Square Ring, I Captured the Castle; A Cook for Mr. General (Broadway); Royal Shakespeare Theatre Co., 1962. Abraham Cochrane, Peter Pan.
PICTURES: Square Ring, Romeo and Juliet, Geordie, Footsteps in the Fog, Bhowani Junction, Barretts of Wimpole Street, Smallest Show on Earth, Seventh Sin, Passionate Summer, Bridal Path, Gorgo, The Green Helmet, Two Living—One Dead, Born Free, Duel at Diablo, A Midsummer Night's Dream, Ring of Bright Water, Boulevard du Rhum (Rum Runner), Christian the Lion, The Belstone Fox.
TELEVISION: A Cook for the General (Kraft), Episode, A Giant Is Born (U.S.), Espionage, Rawhide, CBS Voice of America (Rome), Lorna Doone, The Admirable Crichton, Lovejoy. *Producer/Director/Writer:* The Lions Are Free, An Elephant Called Slowly, The Lion at Worlds End, Christian the Lion, Wild Dogs of Africa, Baboons of Gombe, The Hyena Story, Deathtrap, Lions of the Serengeti, River of Sand, Bloody Ivory, Sexual Encounters of the Floral Kind, Lovejoy.

TRAVIS, NANCY: Actress. b. New York, NY, Sept. 21, 1961. Raised in Baltimore, MD, and Farmingham, MA. e. NYU. Attended Circle-in-the-Square Theatre school. Acted with NY Amer. Jewish Theatre before landing role in touring prod. of Brighton Beach Memoirs.
PICTURES: Three Men and a Baby (debut, 1987), Married to the Mob, Eight Men Out, Internal Affairs, Loose Cannons, Air America, Three Men and a Little Lady, Passed Away, Chaplin, The Vanishing, So I Married an Axe Murderer, Greedy.
TELEVISION: *Movies:* Malice in Wonderland, Harem, I'll Be Home for Christmas.
THEATRE: I'm Not Rappaport (Bdwy), Brighton Beach Memoirs (tour). *La Jolla Playhouse:* My Children My Africa, Three Sisters.

TRAVOLTA, JOHN: Actor. b. Englewood, NJ, Feb. 18, 1954. m. actress Kelly Preston. Quit school at 16 to pursue theatre career; first stage role in Who Will Save the Plowboy? Did off-Bdwy prod. of Rain; next to Broadway in Grease. Toured with latter for 10 months. Also in Over Here on Bdwy. with Andrew Sisters for 10 months.

PICTURES: The Devil's Rain (debut, 1975), Carrie, Saturday Night Fever (Acad. Award nom.), Grease, Moment by Moment, Urban Cowboy, Blow Out, Staying Alive, Two of a Kind, Perfect, The Experts, Look Who's Talking, Look Who's Talking Too, Shout, Look Who's Talking 3.
TELEVISION: *Series:* Welcome Back Kotter. *Movies:* The Boy in the Plastic Bubble, Chains of Gold, Boris & Natasha (cameo). *Special:* The Dumb Waiter. *Guest:* Emergency, Owen Marshall, The Rookies, Medical Center.

TREMAYNE, LES: Actor. b. London, England, Apr. 16, 1913. e. Northwestern U., Chicago Art Inst., Columbia U., UCLA. First professional appearance in British mp., 1916, with mother; stock, little theatres, vaudeville, 1925–40; entered radio field, 1930; numerous shows on all networks. Blue ribbon award for best perf. of the month for A Man Called Peter; dir. Hollywood Rep. Theatre, 1957; pres. Hollywood Actors' Council, 1951–58; chmn. Actors Div. workshop com. Acad. TV Arts & Sciences; Mem.: The Workshop Comm. of the Hollywood M.P. & TV Museum Comm. One of 17 founding members, Pacific Pioneer Broadcasters; Life member, Actor's Fund; charter/founding mem. AFTRA, Chicago local. (delegate to most conventions since 1938). mem. Local, L.A, and Natl. AFTRA bds.
SHOWS: Woman in My House, Errand of Mercy, You Are There, One Man's Family, Heartbeat Theatre, The First Nighter (lead 7 yrs.); on Broadway in Heads or Tails, Detective Story.
TELEVISION: Lux Video Theatre, 20th Century-Fox Hour, Navy Log, One Man's Family, Meet Mille, The Millionaire, The Whistler, Truth or Consequences, NBC Matinee, The Girl, O'Henry series, Rin Tin Tin, Bachelor Father, The Texan, Adventures of Ellery Queen, Court of Last Resort, Rifleman, State Trooper, Rescue 8, June Allyson-Dupont Show, Wagon Train, M Squad, Hitchcock Presents, Mr. Ed., Perry Mason.
PICTURES: The Racket, Blue Veil, Francis Goes to West Point, It Grows on Trees, I Love Melvin, Under the Red Sea, Dream Wife, War of the Worlds, Susan Slept Here, Lieutenant Wore Skirts, Unguarded Moment, Everything But the Truth, Monolith Monsters, Perfect Furlough, North by Northwest, Say One for Me, The Gallant Hours, The Angry Red Planet, The Story of Ruth, The Fortune Cookie, Daffy Duck's Movie: Fantastic Island (voice), Starchaser (voice).

TREVOR, CLAIRE: Actress. b. New York, NY, Mar. 8, 1910. e. American Acad. of Dramatic Arts; Columbia U. On Broadway in Party's Over, Whistling in the Dark, Big Two. On radio in Big Town for 4 yrs.
PICTURES: Life in the Raw (debut, 1933), Last Trail, Mad Game, Jimmy and Sally, Dante's Inferno, Dead End, The Amazing Dr. Clitterhouse, Valley of the Giants, Stagecoach, Allegheny Uprising, Dark Command, Texas, Honky Tonk, Street of Chance, Adventures of Martin Eden, Crossroads, Woman of the Town, The Desperados, Murder My Sweet, Johnny Angel, Crack-Up, Bachelor's Daughters, Born to Kill, Raw Deal, Valley of the Giants, Babe Ruth, Velvet Touch, Key Largo (Acad. Award, supp. actress, 1948), Lucky Stiff, Best of the Bad Men, Border Line, Hoodlum Empire, Hard Fast and Beautiful, My Man and I, Stop You're Killing Me, Stranger Wore a Gun, High and the Mighty, Man Without a Star, Luch Gallant, The Mountain, Marjorie Morningstar, Two Weeks in Another Town, The Stripper, How to Murder Your Wife, Capetown Affair, Kiss Me Goodbye.
TELEVISION: Dodsworth (Emmy Award), No Sad Songs for Me, Ladies in Retirement, Alfred Hitchcock Presents, The Untouchables, Love Boat, Murder She Wrote.

TREXLER, CHARLES B.: Exhibitor. b. Wadesboro, NC, Feb. 8, 1916. From 1937 to Nov. 1948 was practicing CPA except for 2 yrs. in U.S. Army in W.W.II. Joined Stewart & Everett Theatres in 1948 as controller. In March, 1953 named gen. mgr.; Jan. 1, 1954, exec. v.p., treas.; May, 1962 named pres.; Feb. 1, 1983, named bd. chmn. Former bd. chmn., NATO of North and South Carolina; v.p. & bd. mem., National NATO.

TRIKONIS, GUS: Director. b. New York, NY. Started career in chorus of West Side Story on Bdwy. Turned to directing, making low-budget weekenders (films shot in 12 days only on weekends).
PICTURES: Moonshine County Express, The Evil, Touched by Love, Take This Job and Shove It.
TELEVISION: *Movies:* The Darker Side of Terror, She's Dressed To Kill, Flamingo Road (pilot), Elvis and the Beauty Queen, Twirl, Miss All-American Beauty, Dempsey, First Affair, Malice in Wonderland, Love on the Run, Open Admissions, The Great Pretender. *Mini-Series:* The Last Convertible (co-dir.). *Episode:* Twilight Zone (1985).

TRINTIGNANT, JEAN-LOUIS: Actor. b. Aix-en-Provence, France, Dec. 11, 1930. m. Nadine Marquand, director. Theatre debut: 1951, To Each According to His Hunger. Then Mary Stuart, Macbeth (at the Comedie de Saint-Etienne). 1955 screen debut.
PICTURES: Si Tous Les Gars du Monde, La Loi des Rues, And God Created Woman, Club de Femmes, Les Liaisons Dangereuses, L'Estate Violente, Austerlitz, La Millieme Fen-

etre, Pleins Feux sur L'Assain, Coeur Battant, L'Atlantide, The Game of Truth, Horace 62, Les Sept Peches Capitaux (7 Capital Sins), Le Combat dans L'Ile, The Easy Life, II Successo, Nutty, Naughty Chateau, Les Pas Perdus, La Bonne Occase, Mata-Hari, Meurtre a L'Italienne, La Longue Marche, Le 17eme Ciel, Un Jour a Paris, Is Paris Burning?, The Sleeping Car Murders, A Man and a Woman, Enigma, Safari Diamants, Trans-Europ-Express, Mon Amour, Mon Amour, Un Homme a Abattre, La Morte Ha Fatto L'Uovo, Les Biches, Grand Silence, 2, Ma Nuit Chez Maud (My Night at Maud's), The Conformist, The Crook, Without Apparent Motive, The Outside Man, The French Conspiracy, Simon the Swiss, Agression, Les Violons du Bal, The Sunday Woman, Under Fire, La Nuit de Varennes, Long Live Life!, Next Summer, Departure, Return, The Man With the Silver Eyes, Femme Je Personne, Confidentially Yours, A Man and a Woman: 20 Years Later, La Vallee Fantome; Rendezvous, Bunker Palace Hotel.

TROELL, JAN: Writer, Director, Cinematographer, Editor. b. Limhamn, Skane, Sweden, July 23, 1931. Was teacher before entering industry. In early 60s photographed Bo Widerberg's first film, The Pram. Became apprentice in TV; made m.p. debut as director in 1965 with Stay in the Marshland.
PICTURES: Dir.-Writer-Photog.-Edit.: Here Is Your Life, Eeny Meeny Miny Mo, The Emigrants, The New Land, Zandy's Bride, Hurricane, The Flight of the Eagle, The Land of Dreams.

TRUMBULL, DOUGLAS: Cinematographer, Director, Writer. b. Los Angeles, CA, Apr. 8, 1942. Inventor Showscan Film process. President, The Trumbull Company, Inc. Did Special Effects for Universal Studios attraction Back to the Future: The Ride. Director: Showscan short films New Magic, Let's Go, Big Ball, Leonardo's Dream, Night of the Dreams, Chevy Collector.
PICTURES: Did special effects for 2001: A Space Odyssey, Silent Running (also dir.), The Andromeda Strain, Close Encounters of the Third Kind, Star Trek: The Motion Picture, Blade Runner, Brainstorm (also dir., prod.).

TUBB, BARRY: Actor. b. Snyder, TX, 1963. Former rodeo star. Studied acting at Amer. Conservatory Theatre in SF.
PICTURES: Mask, The Legend of Billie Jean, Top Gun, Valentino Returns, Warm Summer Rain, Guilty By Suspicion.
TELEVISION: Series: Bay City Blues. Guest: Hill Street Blues. Movies: Consenting Adult, The Billionaire Boys Club, Without Her Consent. Mini-Series: Lonesome Dove.
THEATRE: Sweet Sue (Bdwy), The Authentic Life of Billy the Kid.

TUCKER, MELVILLE: Executive. b. New York, NY, Mar. 4, 1916. e. Princeton U. Asst. purchasing agent Consolidated Laboratories, N.Y., 1934–36; sound effects & picture ed., Republic Productions, Inc. 1936–8; then asst. production mgr. & first asst. dir., 1938–42; served in U.S. Army 1942–46; asst. prod. Republic 1946; assoc. producer, 1947–52; prod., Universal 1952–54; prod. exec. v.p., Universal, 1955–70; production exec. U-I, 1954–71; prod.-Verdon Prods., 1971–present.
PICTURES: The Missourians, Thunder in God's Country, Rodeo King and the Senorita, Utah Wagon Train. U-I prod., 1953: Drums Across the River, Black Shield of Falworth; prod. A Warm December, Uptown Saturday Night, Let's Do It Again, A Piece of the Action, exec. prod.: Stir Crazy, Hanky Panky, Fast Forward.

TUCKER, MICHAEL: Actor. b. Baltimore, MD, Feb. 6, 1944. m. actress Jill Eikenberry. e. Carnegie Tech. Drama Sch. Worked in regional theater (Washington's Arena Stage) and with the New York Shakespeare Festival in Trelawney of the Wells, Comedy of Errors, Measure for Measure, The Merry Wives of Windsor. Also prod. revival of El Grande de Coca Cola (1986).
THEATER: Includes: Moonchildren, Modigliani, The Goodbye People, The Rivals, Mother Courage, Waiting for Godot, Oh What a Lovely War, I'm Not Rappaport (American Place Theatre).
PICTURES: A Night Full of Rain (1977), An Unmarried Woman, Eyes of Laura Mars, Diner, The Goodbye People, The Purple Rose of Cairo, Radio Days, Tin Men, Checking Out.
TELEVISION: Series: L.A. Law. Movies: Concealed Enemies, Vampire, Assault and Matrimony, Day One, Spy, Too Young to Die?, Casey's Gift: For Love of a Child, The Secret Life of Archie's Wife, In the Nick of Time, A Town Torn Apart. Specials: Love Sex. . .and Marriage, A Family Again. Guest: Hill Street Blues.

TUCKERMAN, DAVID R.: Executive. b. Perth Amboy, NJ, Nov. 9, 1946. e. Monmouth Coll., F.L.U. 1967–70; B.S.B.A. Entered industry with A.I.T. Theatres, 1967; gen. mgr.; Music Makers Theatres, 1973; v.p., Leigh Group, MMT, head film buyer, 1976; sr. v.p., MMT, 1980; Loews Film Buyer, 1986; Loews v.p. film, 1993.
MEMBER: SMPTE, Variety Int., MPBC, AFI, Motion Picture Pioneers.

TUGGLE, RICHARD: Director, Writer. b. Coral Gables, FL, Aug. 8, 1948. e. U. Virginia, B.A. 1970. Wrote screenplays before directorial debut with Tightrope, 1984.
PICTURES: Escape from Alcatraz (s.p.), Tightrope (dir., s.p.), Out of Bounds (dir.).

TUNE, TOMMY: Actor, Director, Choreographer, Dancer. b. Wichita Falls, TX, Feb. 28, 1939. e. Univ of Texas at Austin. Began professional career dancing in chorus of Bdwy. shows (Baker Street, A Joyful Noise, How Now Dow Jones, etc.). Recipient of 9 Tony Awards.
PICTURES: Hello Dolly!, The Boy Friend.
STAGE: Performer: Seesaw, My One and Only, Bye Bye Birdie (tour), Tommy Tune Tonite! (Bdwy & tour). Director and/ or choreographer: The Club, Cloud 9, The Best Little Whorehouse in Texas, Nine, A Day in Hollywood/A Night in the Ukraine, Stepping Out, My One and Only, Grand Hotel, The Will Rogers Follies.
TELEVISION: Series: Dean Martin Presents the Golddiggers; also numerous specials and Tony Award Shows.

TURMAN, LAWRENCE: Producer. b. Los Angeles, CA, Nov. 28, 1926. e. UCLA. In textile business 5 years, then joined Kurt Frings Agency; left in 1960 to form Millar-Turman Prods.
PICTURES: Prod.: The Young Doctors, I Could Go on Singing, The Best Man. Formed own prod. co., Lawrence Turman, Inc., to make The Flim-Flam Man, The Graduate, Pretty Poison (exec. prod.), The Great White Hope, The Marriage of a Young Stockbroker (also dir.), The Nickel Ride (exec. prod.), The Drowning Pool, First Love, Heroes, Walk Proud, Tribute, Caveman, The Thing, Second Thoughts (also dir.), Mass Appeal, The Mean Season, Short Circuit, Running Scared, Short Circuit 2, Full Moon in Blue Water, Gleaming the Cube, The Getaway.
TELEVISION: Co-prod. with David Foster: The Gift of Love, News at Eleven, Between Two Brothers. Prod.: The Morning After, She Lives, Unwed Father. Co-exec. prod.: Jesse.

TURNER, CLIFFORD: Producer. b. Leeds, England, 1913. Ent. m.p. industry as cutting room asst. Gaumont British. Edited number early British pictures, before going to Hollywood in 1935. Subsequently edited for Warners, Columbia, Universal, Fox. Returned to England 1948 to edit The Small Back Room. Dir. and exec. prod. since 1950 in Hollywood and NY. Formed Boulevard Film Productions Ltd., Screen Biographies Intl. Inc., Television Enterprises Inc. Four Against the Bank of England. 1972: Utrillo, Rose of Cimarron, Mystery of the General Grant; La Cicatrice, The Valadon Story, Streets of Montmartre, The Murderess, Le Nain Rouge, Victoria La Scandaleuse, Research Warning.

TURNER, FREDERICK: Executive. b. London, England. Ent. m.p. ind. 1946. Early career with Eagle-Lion before transferring to Rank Overseas Film Distributors, then Rank Film Distributors. Became financial controller and appt. managing director 1981. Currently responsible for Film Investments and Distribution, UK and Overseas, covering all media.

TURNER, JANINE: Actress. b. Lincoln, NE, Dec. 6, 1962. Raised in Texas. Studied dance, joined Forth Worth Ballet. Started modeling at age 15 in NYC, enrolled in Professional Children's School. First major acting job was on series Dallas. On stage in Full Moon and High Tide in the Ladies Room.
TELEVISION: Series: Behind the Screen, General Hospital (1982–83), Northern Exposure. Guest: The Love Boat, The A-Team, Mike Hammer.
PICTURES: Young Doctors in Love, Knights of the City, Tai-Pan, Monkey Shines, Steel Magnolias, The Ambulance, Cliffhanger.

TURNER, KATHLEEN: Actress. b. Springfield, MO, June 19, 1954. e. U. of Maryland, SMSU.
THEATRE: Bdwy: Gemini, Cat on a Hot Tin Roof (Theatre World Award). Regional: Camille (Long Wharf, CT, 1987).
PICTURES: Body Heat (debut, 1981), The Man With Two Brains, Romancing the Stone, Crimes of Passion, A Breed Apart, Prizzi's Honor, The Jewel of the Nile, Peggy Sue Got Married (Acad. Award nom.), Julia and Julia, Switching Channels, Who Framed Roger Rabbit (voice), The Accidental Tourist, The War of the Roses, V. I. Warshawski, House of Cards, Undercover Blues, Serial Mom.
TELEVISION: Series: The Doctors. Special: Dear America: Letters Home From Vietnam (reader).

TURNER, LANA: Actress. b. Wallace, ID, Feb. 8, 1921. Parents, Virgil Turner and Mildred Cowan.
PICTURES: They Won't Forget, Great Garrick, Adventures of Marco Polo, Four's a Crowd, Love Finds Andy Hardy, The Chaser, Rich Man Poor Girl, Dramatic School, Calling Dr. Kildare, These Glamour Girls, Dancing Coed. Two Girls on Broadway, We Who Are Young, Ziegfeld Girl, Dr. Jekyll and Mr. Hyde, Honky Tonk, Johnny Eager, Somewhere I'll Find You, Slightly Dangerous, The Youngest Profession (cameo), DuBarry Was a Lady (cameo), Marriage Is a Private Affair, Keep Your Powder Dry, Week-End at the Waldorf, Postman Always Rings Twice, Green Dolphin Street, Cass Timberlane,

Homecoming, Three Musketeers, Life of Her Own, Mr. Imperium, The Merry Widow, Bad & the Beautiful, Latin Lovers, Flame & the Flesh, Betrayed, The Prodigal, Sea Chase, Rains of Ranchipur, Diane, Peyton Place (Acad. Award nom.), Another Time Another Place, The Lady Takes a Flyer, Imitation of Life, Portrait in Black, By Love Possessed, Bachelor in Paradise, Who's Got the Action?, Love Has Many Faces, Madame X, The Big Cube, Persecution, Bittersweet Love, Witches' Brew.
    TELEVISION: *Series*: The Survivors, Falcon Crest. *Guest*: Love Boat.

TURNER, ROBERT EDWARD (TED): Executive. b. Cincinnati, OH., Nov. 19, 1938. e. Brown U. m. actress Jane Fonda. Began career in Savannah in family's outdoor adv. business, selling space on billboards. Bought co. in 1963 and in 1970 entered broadcasting with purchase of a failing TV station in Atlanta which he turned into WTBS, a "superstation" which in 1985 reached 80% of U.S. homes equipped with cable. 1980, established CNN a 24-hr. cable news service. Purchased MGM. Co-owner two professional sports teams in Atlanta: Braves (baseball) and Hawks (basketball). Started Turner Network Television 1988.

TURNER, TINA: Singer, Actress. r.n. Annie Mae Bullock. b. Brownsville, TX, Nov. 26, 1939. Previously married to Ike Turner and appeared with him on road in Ike and Tina Turner Revue. Many hit records. Autobiography: I Tina.
    PICTURES: Gimme Shelter, Taking Off, Soul to Soul, Tommy, Sound of the City, Mad Max Beyond Thunderdome, What's Love Got to Do With It (vocals), Last Action Hero.
    TELEVISION: *Special*: Tina—Live From Rio.

TURTURRO, JOHN: Actor. b. Brooklyn, NY, Feb. 28, 1957. e. SUNY/New Paltz; Yale Drama School, 1983. m. actress Katherine Borowitz. Worked in regional theater and off-Bdwy in Danny and the Deep Blue Sea (Obie & Theatre World Awards, 1985), Men Without Dates, Tooth of the Crime, La Puta Viva, Chaos and Hard Times, The Bald Soprano, Of Mice and Men, The Resistible Rise of Arturo Ui. Bdwy debut, Death of a Salesman (1984).
    PICTURES: Raging Bull (debut, 1980), Exterminator II, The Flamingo Kid, Desperately Seeking Susan, To Live and Die in L.A., Hannah and Her Sisters, Gung Ho, Offbeat, The Color of Money, The Sicilian, Five Corners, Do the Right Thing, Mo' Better Blues, State of Grace, Miller's Crossing, Men of Respect, Jungle Fever, Barton Fink (Cannes Film Fest. Award), Brain Donors, Mac (also dir., co-s.p.), Fearless, Being Human, Quiz Show.
    TELEVISION: *Mini-Series*: The Fortunate Pilgrim. *Movie*: Backtrack.

TUSHINGHAM, RITA: Actress. b. Liverpool, England, March 14, 1942. m. director Ousama Rawi. Student at Liverpool Playhouse.
    THEATER: The Giveaway, Lorna and Ted, Mistress of Novices, The Undiscovered Country, Mysteries.
    PICTURES: A Taste of Honey (debut, 1961), The Leather Boys, A Place to Go, Girl With Green Eyes, The Knack, Dr. Zhivago, The Trap, Smashing Time, Diamonds for Breakfast, The Guru, The Bedsitting Room, Straight on 'til Morning, Situation, Instant Coffee, The Human Factor, Rachel's Man, The Slum Boy, The Black Journal, Bread Butter and Jam, Mysteries, Felix Krull, Lady Killers, The Spaghetti Thing, Seeing Red, The Housekeeper, Resurrected, Dante and Beatrice in Liverpool, Hard Days Hard Nights, Paper Marriage, Desert Lunch.
    TELEVISION: (U.S.) Green Eyes, Bread, Sunday Pursuit, Gutt Ein Journalist, Hamburg Poison.

TUTIN, DOROTHY: Actress. b. London, Eng., Apr. 8, 1930. e. St. Catherine's Sch. Bramley, Guildford (Surrey). Stage debut in The Thistle & the Rose, 1949.
    PLAYS INCLUDE: Much Ado About Nothing, The Living Room, I Am a Camera, The Lark, Wild Duck, Juliet, Ophelia, Viola, Portia, Cressida, Rosalind, The Devils, Once More With Feeling, The Cherry Orchard, Victoria Regina-Portrait of a Queen, Old Times, Peter Pan, What Every Woman Knows, Month in the Country, Macbeth, Antony and Cleopatra, Undiscovered Country, Reflections, After the Lions, Ballerina, A Kind of Alaska, Are You Sitting Comfortably?, Chalk Garden, Brighton Beach Memoirs, Thursday's Ladies, The Browning Version, A Little Night Music, Henry VIII, Party Time, The Seagull, Getting Married.
    PICTURES: The Importance of Being Earnest, The Beggar's Opera, A Tale of Two Cities, Cromwell, Savage Messiah, The Shooting Party, Murder with Mirrors, Great Moments in Aviation.
    TELEVISION: Living Room, Victoria Regina, Invitation to a Voyage, Antigone, Colombe, Carrington V.C., The Hollow Crown, Scent of Fear, From Chekhov With Love, Anne Boleyn in The Six Wives of Henry VIII, Flotsam and Jetsam, Mother & Son, South Riding, Willow Cabins, Ghosts, Sister Dora, The Double Dealer, The Combination, La Ronde, Tales of the Unexpected, 10 Downing Street, Life After Death, King

Lear, Landscape, The Father, The Demon Lover, Robin Hood, All Creatures Great and Small, A Kind of Alaska, The Bill, Lease of Death, Anglo-Saxon Attitudes, Body and Soul.

TWAINE, MICHAEL: ·Actor, Director. b. New York, NY, Nov. 1, 1939. e. Ohio State U. Served U.S. Army. While studying with Lee Strasberg, worked as private detective, school teacher. Made stage debut City Center, 1956, in Mr. Roberts. Became village coffee house and club comedian 1968 to 1972.
    PICTURES: Marriage Italian Style (voice), American Soap, Blood Bath, F.I.S.T., Cheap Shots, Platoon (voice), Billy Bathgate (voice).
    TELEVISION: The Silent Drum, Starsky & Hutch, Wonder Woman, Streets of San Francisco, Soap, Lou Grant, Diff'rent Strokes, Nurse, Stalk the Wild Child, The Courage and the Passion, Eischied, America's Most Wanted.

TWIGGY: Actress. r.n. Leslie Hornby. b. London, England, Sept. 19, 1949. m. actor Leigh Lawson. At 17 regarded as world's leading high fashion model. Made m.p. debut in The Boy Friend, 1971. Starred in many London West End Shows, including Cinderella and Captain Beaky Presents. 1983: on Broadway in musical, My One and Only.
    TELEVISION: Hosted and starred in major American & British music shows including Twiggy (U.K.), Twiggy and Friends (U.K.), and Juke Box (U.S.); also in Pygmalion (England), Sun Child (Eng.), Young Charlie Chaplin. *Movies*: The Diamond Trap, Body Bags. *Series* (U.S.): Princesses.
    PICTURES: The Boyfriend (debut, 1971), W, There Goes the Bride, The Blues Brothers, The Doctor and the Devils, Club Paradise, Madame Sousatzka, Istanbul.

TWYMAN, ALAN P.: Executive. b. Dayton, OH, May 30, 1934. e. U. of Cincinnati. Twyman Films, Inc. sales 1958, vice pres.-pres., 1975. NAVA board of directors, 1964–69; pres. 1970, chmn. of bd., 1972. In 1983 left to form own co., Alan Twyman Presents.

TYRRELL, SUSAN: Actress. b. San Francisco, CA, 1946. Made first prof. appearance with Art Carney in summer theatre tour prod. of Time Out for Ginger. Worked in off-Bdwy. prods. and as waitress in coffee house before attracting attention in Lincoln Center Repertory Co. prods. of A Cry of Players, The Time of Your Life, Camino Real.
    THEATER: The Knack, Futz, Father's Day, A Coupla White Chicks Sitting Around Talking, The Rotten Life.
    PICTURES: Shoot Out (debut, 1971), The Steagle, Been Down So Long It Looks Like Up to Me, Shoot Out, Fat City (Acad. Award nom.), Catch My Soul, Zandy's Bride, The Killer Inside Me, Islands in the Stream, Andy Warhol's Bad, I Never Promised You a Rose Garden, Another Man Another Chance, September 30, 1955, Racquet, Loose Shoes, Forbidden Zone, Subway Riders, Night Warning, Fast-Walking, Liar's Moon, Tales of Ordinary Madness, Fire and Ice (voice), Angel, The Killers, Avenging Angel, Flesh and Blood, The Offspring, Big Top Pee-Wee, Tapeheads, The Underachievers, Far From Home, Cry-Baby, Motorama.
    TELEVISION: *Series*: Open All Night. *Movies*: Lady of the House, Midnight Lace, Jealousy, Thompson's Last Run, Poker Alice, The Christmas Star, Windmills of the Gods. *Mini-Series*: If Tomorrow Comes.

TYSON, CICELY: Actress. b. New York, NY, Dec. 19, 1933. e. NYU. Studied at Actor's Studio. Former secretary and model. Co-founder, Dance Theatre of Harlem.
    THEATER: The Blacks, Moon on a Rainbow Shawl, Tiger Tiger Burning Bright, The Corn Is Green.
    PICTURES: Odds Against Tomorrow, The Last Angry Man, A Man Called Adam, The Comedians, The Heart Is a Lonely Hunter, Sounder (Acad. Award nom.), The Blue Bird, The River Niger, A Hero Ain't Nothin' But a Sandwich, The Concorde—Airport '79, Bustin' Loose, Fried Green Tomatoes.
    TELEVISION: *Series*: East Side West Side, The Guiding Light. *Movies*: Marriage: Year One, The Autobiography of Miss Jane Pittman (Emmy Award, 1974), Just An Old Sweet Song, Wilma, A Woman Called Moses, The Marva Collins Story, Benny's Place, Playing with Fire, Acceptable Risks, Samaritan: The Mitch Snyder Story, The Women of Brewster Place, Heat Wave, The Kid Who Loved Christmas, Duplicates, When No One Would Listen. *Guest*: B.L. Stryker. *Special*: Without Borders (host). *Mini-Series*: Roots. *Pilot*: Clippers.

U

UGGAMS, LESLIE: Singer. b. New York, NY, May 25, 1943. e. Professional Children's Sch., grad., 1960. Juilliard Sch. of Music. Beg. singing career age 5. TV debut as Ethel Waters' niece on Beulah. Also on Johnny Olsen's TV kids at age 7, Your Show of Shows as singer, 1953; Recording artist for Columbia Records, Atlantic, Motown Wrote The Leslie Uggams Beauty Book (1962).

STAGE: Hallelujah Baby (Tony & Theatre World Awards, 1968), Her First Roman, Blues in the Night, Jerry's Girls, Anything Goes (natl. co. & Bdwy), Stringbean (Dallas).
PICTURES: Two Weeks in Another Town, Poor Pretty Eddie, Black Girl, Heartbreak Motel, Skyjacked.
RADIO: Peter Lind Hayes-Mary Healy Show, Milton Berle, Arthur Godfrey, Star Time.
TELEVISION: Series: Sing Along With Mitch, The Leslie Uggams Show (1969), Fantasy (Emmy Award, 1984). Guest: Beulah (1949), Kids and Company, Milton Berle Show, Name That Tune, Jack Paar Show, Garry Moore. Mini-Series: Roots, Backstairs at the White House. Movie: Sizzle. Specials: The Book of Lists (co-host). Fantasy (Emmy, 1983, host), I Love Men, 'S Wonderful, 'S Marvelous, 'S Gershwin, Sinatra and Friends, Placido Domingo Steppin' Out With the Ladies.

ULLMAN, TRACEY: Actress, Comedian, Singer. b. Hackbridge, England, Dec. 29, 1959. m. British TV prod. Allan McKeown. e. won a performance sch. scholarship at 12. Attended the Italia Conti School for 4 years. Soon after appeared on British TV and onstage in Grease and The Rocky Horror Picture Show. Also performed in improvisational play Four in a Million (1981) at the Royal Court Theatre, London (London Theatre Critics Award). Recorded gold-selling album You Broke My Heart in Seventeen Places. U.S. TV debut, the Tracey Ullman Show (debuted April, 1987).
PICTURES: Give My Regards to Broad Street, Plenty, Jumpin' Jack Flash, I Love You to Death, Happily Ever After (voice), Robin Hood: Men in Tights, Household Saints.
TELEVISION: Three of a Kind (BBC series), Tracey Ullman Show (Emmy Awards, 1989, 1990), They Don't Know (Music video), The Best of the Tracey Ullman Show (Emmy Award, 1990).
THEATRE: NY: The Taming of the Shrew, The Big Love.

ULLMANN, LIV: Actress. b. Tokyo, Japan of Norwegian parents, Dec. 16, 1939. Accompanied parents to Canada when W.W.II began and later returned to Norway. Was catapulted to fame in a succession of Swedish films directed by Ingmar Bergman. Author: Changing, (1977), Choices. Ambassador for UNICEF since 1980. Youngest person to date to receive the Order of St. Olav from the King of Norway.
THEATER: (U.S.) A Doll's House, Anna Christie, I Remember Mama (musical), Ghosts, Old Times.
PICTURES: The Wayward Girl (debut, 1959), Persona, Hour of the Wolf, Shame, The Passion of Anna, The Night Visitor, Cold Sweat, The Emigrants, The New Land, Pope Joan, Cries and Whispers, Lost Horizon, 40 Carats, Scenes From a Marriage, Zandy's Bride, The Abdication, Leonor, Face to Face, A Bridge Too Far, The Serpent's Egg, Autumn Sonata, Richard's Things, The Wild Duck, Bay Boy, Gaby—A True Story. Moscow Adieu (Donatello Award, Best Actress, 1987), A Time of Indifference, La Amiga, The Rose Garden, Mindwalk, The Ox, The Long Shadow, Sophie (dir., co-s.p. only).
TELEVISION: Lady From the Sea, Jacobo Timerman: Prisoner Without a Name Cell Without a Number.

UNDERWOOD, BLAIR: Actor. b. Tacoma, WA, Aug. 25, 1964. e. Carnegie-Mellon Univ. NY stage: Measure for Measure.
TELEVISION: Series: One Life to Live, Downtown, L.A. Law. Movies: The Cover Girl and the Cop, Heat Wave, Murder in Mississippi, Father & Son: Dangerous Relations (also assoc. prod.). Guest: Scarecrow and Mrs. King, The Cosby Show, Knight Rider, 21 Jump Street.
PICTURES: Krush Groove, Posse.

UNDERWOOD, RON: Director. b. Glendale, CA, Nov. 6, 1953. e. USC.
TELEVISION: The Mouse and the Motorcycle (Peabody Award), Runaway Ralph (Emmy nomination).
PICTURES: Tremors (also co-story), City Slickers, Heart and Souls.

UNGER, ANTHONY B.: Executive, Producer. b. New York, NY, Oct. 19, 1940. e. Duke U., U. of Southern California. Prod. ass't Third Man, TV series, 1961. v.p. Unger Productions, Inc., 1964; v.p. Landau-Unger Co., Inc., 1965; v.p. Commonwealth United Entertainment in London, 1968; pres., Unger Prods. Inc., 1978–present.
PICTURES: The Desperate Ones. The Madwoman of Chaillot, The Battle of Neretva, The Magic Christian, Julius Caesar. The Devil's Widow. Don't Look Now; Force Ten From Navarone, The Unseen; Silent Rage.

UNGER, KURT: Producer. b. Berlin, Germany, Jan. 10, 1922. Entered ind. in 1939 in charge of m.p. entertainment for British troops in Middle East. Subsequently in charge of production and distrib. for UA in Israel, Italy and England.
PICTURES: Judith, The Best House in London, Puppet on a Chain, Pope Joan, Return From the River Kwai.

UNGER, STEPHEN A.: Executive. b. New York, NY, May 31, 1946. e. NYU, Grad. Film and Television Instit. Started as independent prod. and dist. of theatrical and TV films. In June, 1978, joined Universal Pictures Intl. Sales as foreign sls. mgr.

Named v.p. Universal Theatrical Motion Pictures in 1979, responsible for licensing theatrical or TV features not handled by U.I.P. in territories outside U.S. & Canada and worldwide acquisitions. In 1980 joined CBS Theatrical Films as intl. v.p., sls.; 1982–88, pres., Unger Intl. Distributors, Inc.; 1988 joined Korn/Ferry Intl. as exec. v.p., worldwide entertainment div. Promoted to mng. dir., 1989–91. Joined Spencer Stuart Exec. Search Consultants as mng. dir., Worldwide Ent. Div. Aug., 1991.

URICH, ROBERT: Actor. b. Toronto, OH, Dec. 19, 1946. e. Florida State U., B.A., radio and TV communications; Michigan State U., M.A. Communications Mgmt. Appeared in university plays. Was sales account executive at WGN Radio, Chicago, before turning to stage acting (Ivanhoe Theatre, Chicago).
TELEVISION: Series: Bob & Carol & Ted & Alice, S.W.A.T., Soap, Tabitha, Vega$, Gavilan, Spenser For Hire, American Dreamer, Crossroads, It Had to Be You. Guest: The FBI, Gunsmoke, Kung Fu, Marcus Welby MD, The Love Boat. Movies: Killdozer, Vega$ (pilot), Leave Yesterday Behind, When She Was Bad, Fighting Back, Killing at Hell's Gate, Take Your Best Shot, Princess Daisy, Invitation to Hell, His Mistress, Scandal Sheet, Young Again, April Morning, The Comeback, She Knows Too Much, Murder By Night, Night Walk, Blind Faith, Spooner, A Quiet Little Neighborhood A Perfect Little Murder, Stranger at My Door, And Then She Was Gone, Survive the Savage Sea, Blind Man's Bluff (also co-prod.), Double Edge, Revolver, Deadly Relations, Spenser: Ceremony (also co-exec. prod.). Mini-Series: Mistral's Daughter, Amerika, Lonesome Dove.
PICTURES: Magnum Force, Endangered Species, The Ice Pirates, Turk 182.

URMAN, MARK: Executive. b. New York, NY, Nov. 24, 1952. e. Union Coll., 1973; NYU, cinema, 1973–74. m. story analyst Deborah Davis. 1973, apprentice publicist, Universal Pictures; 1973–82, United Artists intl. dept. as assoc. publicist, sr. publicist and ultimately asst. to v.p. worldwide ad-pub.; 1982–84, dir., publicity and marketing, Triumph Films (Columbia/Gaumont); 1985–86, exec. dir. East Coast pub., Columbia Pictures; 1986–89, v.p. East Coast pub., Columbia Pictures. Joined Dennis Davidson Associates as v.p., 1989; promoted to sr.v.p., 1991. Member: Motion Picture Academy.

URQUHART, ROBERT: Actor, Writer. b. Scotland, October 16, 1922. e. George Heriots, Edinburgh. Served in Merchant Navy 1938–45; stage debut, Park Theatre, Glasgow; screen debut: You're Only Young Twice, 1951.
PICTURES: Isn't Life Wonderful, The House Of The Arrow, Knights of the Round Table, Happy Ever After (Tonight's the Night), Golden Ivory, The Dark Avenger, You Can't Escape, Yangtse Incident, Curse of Frankenstein, Dunkirk, The Trouble with Eve, Danger Tomorrow, Foxhole in Cairo, Murder in Mind, The Bulldog Greed, 55 Days At Peking, The Break, Murder at the Gallup, The Syndicate, The Limbo Line, The Looking Glass War, Brotherly Love (Country Dance), Playing Away, Restless Natives, Sharma and Beyond, P'Tang Bang Clipper Bang, Kitchen Toto, Testimony.
TELEVISION: Tamer Tamed, Infinite Shoeblack, Morning Departure, The Human Touch, The Iron Harp, Sleeping Clergyman, The Naked Lady, For Services Rendered, The Bright One, Jango, Murder Swamp, She Died Young, Plane Makers (series), Reporter, Inheritors (series); Mr. Goodall (series), The Nearly Man, The Button Man, Happy Returns, Endless-Aimless, Bleak House, The Queens Arms, Shostakovich.
AUTHOR: (Wrote TV) House of Lies, End of the Tether, Landfall, The Touch of a Dead Hand.

USLAN, MICHAEL E.: Producer, Writer. b. Bayonne, NJ, June 2, 1951. e. Indiana U., A.B., M.S., J.D. Wrote 12 books, including Dick Clark's 1st 25 Years of Rock 'n' Roll; 1976–80 atty. with United Artists; Produced with Benjamin Melniker.
PICTURES: Swamp Thing (prod.), The Return of Swamp Thing, Batman (exec. prod.), Batman Returns (exec. prod.), Batman: The Animated Movie (prod.).
TELEVISION: Three Sovereigns for Sarah (exec. prod.), Dinosaucers (exec. prod., creator, writer), Swamp Thing (exec. prod. for both live-action and animated series), Fish Police (exec. prod.), South Korea cultural segments NBC Summer Olympics 1988 (exec. prod.), Television's Greatest Bits (prod., creator, writer), 1st National Trivia Quiz (prod., writer), Where in the World Is Carmen Sandiego? (animated, exec. prod.)

USTINOV, SIR PETER: Actor, Writer, Director. b. London, Eng., Apr. 16, 1921. e. Westminster Sch. In Brit. Army, W.W.II. On Brit. stage from 1937. Screen debut 1941 in Brit. picture Mein Kampf, My Crimes. Awards: 2 Acad. Awards, supp. actor; Golden Globe; 3 Emmy Awards (Specials: Life of Samuel Johnson, Barefoot in Athens, A Storm in Summer); Grammy Award for Peter and the Wolf; NY Critics Award and Donaldson Award for best foreign play (The Love of Four Colonels); British Critics Award (Romanoff and Juliet).
THEATER: Romanoff and Juliet, N.Y., London; and 17 other plays. Dir., acted, Photo Finish; wrote, Life In My Hands,

The Unknown Soldier and His Wife, Half Way Up The Tree, King Lear, Beethoven's Tenth, An Evening With Peter Ustinov.
PICTURES: Actor: The Goose Steps Out, One of Our Aircraft Is Missing, The Way Ahead (co-s.p.), School for Secrets (wrote, dir. & co-prod. only), Vice Versa (dir., s.p. only), Private Angelo (also adapt., dir., co-prod.), Odette, Quo Vadis, The Magic Box, Hotel Sahara, The Egyptian, Beau Brummell, We're No Angels, Lola Montez, The Spies, The Man Who Wagged His Tail, The Sundowners, Spartacus (Acad. Award, supp. actor, 1960), Romanoff and Juliet (also prod., s.p.), Billy Budd (also prod., dir., s.p.), Topkapi (Acad. Award, supp. actor, 1964), John Goldfarb Please Come Home, Lady L. (also dir., s.p.), The Comedians, Blackbeard's Ghost, Hot Millions, Viva Max. Hammersmith Is Out (also dir.), Robin Hood (voice), Logan's Run, Treasure of Matecumbe, One of Our Dinosaurs Is Missing, Purple Taxi, The Last Remake of Beau Geste, Doppio Delitto, Death on the Nile, Ashanti, Charlie Chan and the Curse of the Dragon Queen, Grendel Grendel Grendel (voice), The Great Muppet Caper, Evil Under the Sun, Memed My Hawk (also dir., s.p.), Appointment with Death, Lorenzo's Oil.
RECENT TV: The Well Tempered Bach, 13 at Dinner, Deadman's Folly, Peter Ustinov's Russia, World Challenge, Murder in Three Acts, The Secret Identity of Jack the Ripper (host), Around the World in 80 Days, The Mozart Mystique, Ustinov on the Orient Express.

V

VACCARO, BRENDA: Actress. b. Brooklyn, NY, Nov. 18, 1939. e. Thomas Jefferson H.S., Dallas; studied two yrs. at Neighborhood Playhouse in N.Y. Was waitress and model before landing first Bdwy. role in Everybody Loves Opal. Toured in Tunnel of Love and returned to N.Y. for role in The Affair.
THEATER: Everybody Loves Opal (Theatre World Award), The Affair, Children From Their Games, Cactus Flower (Tony Award, 1965), The Natural Look, How Now Dow Jones (Tony nom.), The Goodbye People (Tony nom.), Father's Day, The Odd Couple, Jake's Women.
PICTURES: Where It's At, Midnight Cowboy, I Love My Wife, Summertree, Going Home, Once Is Not Enough (Acad. Award nom., Golden Globe Award), Airport '77, House by the Lake, Capricorn One, Fast Charlie the Moonbeam Rider, The First Deadly Sin, Zorro the Gay Blade, Supergirl, Water, Cookie, Heart of Midnight, Ten Little Indians.
TELEVISION: Series: Sara, Dear Detective, Paper Dolls. Guest: The F.B.I., The Name of the Game, The Helen Reddy Show, The Shape of Things (special, Emmy, supp. actress, 1974), The Golden Girls, Columbo, Murder She Wrote, Flesh & Blood, Golden Girls (Emmy nom.), Civil Wars. Movies: Travis Logan D.A., What's a Nice Girl Like You . . . ?, Honor Thy Father, Sunshine, The Big Ripoff, Guyana Tragedy, The Pride of Jesse Hallam, The Star Maker, A Long Way Home, Deceptions, Julius and Ethel Rosenberg, Stolen: One Husband, Red Shoes Diaries.

VADIM, ROGER: Director, Writer. b. Paris, Jan. 26, 1928. r.n. Roger Vadim Plemiannikow. m. actress Marie-Christine Barrault.
PICTURES: Futures Vedettes (s.p.). Writer-Director: And God Created Woman, Heaven Fell That Night, Les Liaisons Dangereuses, Warrior's Rest, Vice and Virtue, La Ronde, The Game is Over. Director: Barbarella, Pretty Maids All in a Row, Don Juan, Night Games, A Faithful Woman, Hot Touch, And God Created Woman (1988).
TELEVISION: Beauty and the Beast (Faerie Tale Theatre).

VAJNA, ANDREW: Executive. b. Budapest, Hungary, Aug. 1, 1944. e. UCLA. Launched career with purchase of m.p. theaters in Far East. Founded Panasia Film Ltd. in Hong Kong. Exhibitor and dist. of feature films since 1970. Formed Carolco Service, Inc. (foreign sls. org.), with Mario Kassar 1976. Founder and Pres., American Film Mkt. Assn., 1982. Resigned from Carolco, 1989; formed independent production co., Cinergi Prods., 1990.
PICTURES: Exec. Prod.: The Silent Partner, The Changeling, Suzanne, The Amateur, Your Ticket Is No Longer Valid, Carbon Copy, First Blood, Rambo: First Blood Part II, Angel Heart, Extreme Prejudice, Red Heat, Iron Eagle II, Deepstar Six, Johnny Handsome, Air America, Total Recall, Medicine Man.

VALE, EUGENE: Writer. b. April 11, 1916. e. Zurich, Switzerland. m. Evelyn Wahl. Story and s.p., The Second Face, The Shattered Dream, 1954 SWG award nom., best written telefilm; The Dark Wave. 1957, m.p. academy award nominations.
PICTURES: A Global Affair, Francis of Assissi, The Bridge of San Luis Rey, A Family Scandal, The Thirteenth Apostle, Hold the Split Second.
TELEVISION: Four Star Playhouse, Fireside Theatre, 20th Century Fox Hour, Schlitz Playhouse, Hollywood Opening Night, NBC, Crusader, Lux Video Theatre, Danger, CBS,

Chevron Theatre, Douglas Fairbanks, Pepsi Cola Playhouse, Waterfront, Christophers, Cavalcade of America, Hallmark Hall of Fame.
AUTHOR: Technique of Screenplay Writing, The Thirteenth Apostle, Chaos Below Heaven, Passion Play.

VALENTI, JACK J.: Executive. b. Sept. 5, 1921. e. U. of Houston, B.A., 1946; Harvard U., M.B.A., bus. admin., 1948. Air force pilot in European theatre, W.W.II; adv. and pub. rel. exec. in Houston; special asst. and advisor to Pres. Lyndon B. Johnson, 1963–66, elected pres., Motion Picture Association of America, MPEA and AMPTP, since June, 1966. Named Motion Picture Pioneer of the Year, 1988.

VALENTINE, KAREN: Actress. b. Sebastopol, CA, May 25, 1947.
PICTURES: Forever Young Forever Free, Hot Lead and Cold Feet, The North Avenue Irregulars.
TELEVISION: Series: Room 222 (Emmy, 1970), Karen, Our Time (host). Guest: My Friend Tony, Hollywood Squares, Laugh-In, The Bold Ones, Sonny and Cher, Mike Hammer, Murder, She Wrote. Movies: Gidget Grows Up, The Daughters of Joshua Cabe, Coffee Tea or Me?, The Girl Who Came Gift-Wrapped, The Love Boat (pilot), Having Babies, Murder at the World Series, Return to Fantasy Island, Go West Young Girl, Muggable Mary: Street Cop, Money on the Side, Skeezer, Illusions, Jane Doe, Children in the Crossfire, He's Fired She's Hired, A Fighting Choice, Perfect People. Special: The Emancipation of Lizzie Stern (Afterschool Special).

VALLI, ALIDA: Actress. r.n. Alida von Altenburger. b. Pola, Italy, May 31, 1921. e. M.P. Acad., Rome (dramatics); m. Oscar de Mejo, pianist-composer. In Italian m.p.; won Venice Film Festival Award in Piccolo Mondo Antico (Little Old World).
PICTURES: Vita Ricomincia, Giovanna; to U.S. 1947; U.S. m.p. debut in Paradine Case, 1947, Miracle of the Bells, The Third Man, Walk Softly Stranger, White Tower, Lovers of Toledo, Stranger's Hand, The Castilian, Ophelia, Spider's Stratagem, The Cassandra Crossing, Suspiria, 1900, Luna, Le Jupon Rouge, A Notre Regrettable epoux, Inferno.

VALLONE, RAF: Actor. b. Turin, Italy, Feb. 17, 1916. e. U. of Turin. Former newspaper writer. Directed operas Norma, La Traviata, Adrianna in NY, San Francisco and Houston.
PICTURES: Bitter Rice (debut, 1949), Vendetta, Under the Olive Tree, Anna, Path of Hope, White Line, Rome 11 O'Clock, Strange Deception, Anita Garibaldi, Daughters of Destiny, Teresa Raquin, Riviera, The Secret Invasion. Two Women, El Cid, Phaedra, A View From the Bridge, The Cardinal, Harlow, Nevada Smith, Kiss the Girls and Make Them Die, The Desperate Ones, The Secret Invasion, The Italian Job, The Kremlin Letter, Cannon for Cordoba, A Gunfight, Summertime Killer, Rosebud, The Human Factor, That Lucky Touch, The Other Side of Midnight, The Devil's Advocate, The Greek Tycoon, An Almost Perfect Affair, A Time to Die, Lion of the Desert, The Godfather Part III.
TELEVISION: Fame (Hallmark Hall of Fame), Honor Thy Father, Catholics, The Scarlet and the Black, Christopher Columbus, Goya.

VAN ARK, JOAN: Actress. b. New York, NY, June 16, 1943. m. NBC news reporter John Marshall. e. Yale U of Drama. Two early appearances on Dallas led to role in spin off Knots Landing on which she has starred 13 years. Began career in touring co. then on Broadway and in London in Barefoot in the Park. Also appeared on Bdwy with the APA-Phoenix Rep. Co. in the 1970s. As a runner has competed in 12 marathons, incl. Boston Marathon. On TV also created voices for animated series Spiderwoman, Thundarr and Dingbat and the Creeps and special Cyrano de Bergerac. Estee Lauder spokesperson.
THEATER: School for Wives (Tony Award nom.; Theatre World Award), The Rules of the Game (Theatre World Award). L.A.: Cyrano de Bergerac, Ring Around the Moon, Chemin de Fer, As You Like It (L.A. Drama Critics Award). Williamstown Theatre Fest.: Night of the Iguana, The Legend of Oedipus. Off-Bdwy & L.A.: Love Letters.
PICTURE: Frogs.
TELEVISION: Series: Temperatures Rising, We've Got Each Other, Dallas, Knots Landing. Guest: The F.B.I., The Girl with Something Extra, Quark, Dallas, Quincy, Rockford Files, Rhoda. Co-host: Miss USA and Miss Universe Pageants, Battle of the Network Stars, Macy's Thanksgiving Parade, Tournament of Roses Parade. Movies: The Judge and Jake Wyler, Big Rose, Testimony of Two Men, Shell Game, The Last Dinosaur, Red Flag—The Ultimate Game, Glitter, Shakedown on the Sunset Strip, My First Love, Always Remember I Love You, The Grand Central Murders, Tainted Blood.

VANCE, LEIGH: Scriptwriter, Producer. b. Harrogate, England, March 18, 1922. e. Shrewsbury Coll. WWII RAF pilot, 1940–46. Early career: reporter, critic. Ent. TV 1951, then films, many TV scripts; 1961, won Edgar Allan Poe Award, 1969 brought to Hollywood by Paramount.
PICTURES: The Flesh Is Weak, Heart of a Child, Picadilly Third Stop, Women Shall Weep, The Shakedown, Eyes of

Youth, The Frightened City, It's All Happening Dr. Crippen, Outcast, Walk Like A Man, Crossplot, Tall Cool Girl, The Black Windmill.
TELEVISION: Mannix, Mission Impossible, many pilots and movies-of-the-week. The Avengers, The Saint, Cannon (exec. story consultant, prod.), Caribe (exec. story consultant), Bronk (prod.), Baretta (exec. prod.), Switch (exec. prod.), The Phoenix (prod.), Hart to Hart (prod.).

VAN DAMME, JEAN-CLAUDE: Actor. b. Brussels, Belgium, 1960. r.n. Jean-Claude Van Varenberg. Former European karate champion, began studying martial arts at 11 yrs. old. Won the European Professional Karate Association's middleweight championship. Ran California Gym in Brussels before coming to U.S. in 1981.
PICTURES: Rue Barbar (debut), No Retreat No Surrender, Bloodsport, Black Eagle, Cyborg, Kickboxer (also co-story), Death Warrant, Lionheart (also co-s.p., story), Double Impact (also co-prod., co-s.p., co-story, fight choreographer), Universal Soldier, Nowhere to Run, Last Action Hero (cameo), Hard Target.

VAN DEVERE, TRISH: Actress. b. Englewood Cliffs, NJ, March 9, 1945. e. Ohio Wesleyan U. m. actor George C. Scott. On Bdwy. in Sly Fox, Tricks of the Trade, etc.
PICTURES: The Landlord, Where's Poppa?, The Last Run, One Is a Lonely Number, Harry in Your Pocket, The Day of the Dolphin, The Savage Is Loose, Movie Movie, The Changeling, The Hearse, Uphill All the Way, Messenger of Death.
TELEVISION: Movies: Stalk the Wild Child, Beauty and the Beast, Sharon: Portrait of a Mistress, Mayflower—The Pilgrim's Adventure, All God's Children, Haunted, Curacao.

VAN DOREN, MAMIE: Actress. r.n. Joan Lucille Olander. b. Rowena, SD, Feb. 6, 1933. e. Los Angeles H.S. Secy. law firm, L.A.; prof. debut as singer with Ted Fio Rita orch.
THEATRE: Appeared in many stock plays incl.: Once in a Lifetime, Boy Meets Girl, Come Back Little Sheba.
PICTURES: Forbidden; All American, Yankee Pasha, Francis Joins the Wacs, Ain't Misbehavin, Second Greatest Sex, Running Wild, Star in the Dust, Untamed Youth, Girl in Black Stockings, Teachers Pet, Girls Guns and Gangsters, High School Confidential, The Beat Generation, The Big Operator, Born Reckless, Girls Town, The Private Lives of Adam and Eve, Sex Kittens Go to College, College Confidential, Vice Raid, The Candidate, Three Nuts in Search of a Bolt, Las Vegas Hillbillys, The Navy Vs. the Night Monsters, You've Got to Be Smart, Voyage to the Planet of the Prehistoric Women, Free Ride.

VAN DYKE, DICK: Actor. b. West Plains, MO, Dec., 13, 1925. Brother is actor Jerry Van Dyke. Son is actor Barry Van Dyke. Served in U.S.A.F., W.W.II. After discharge from service, opened advertising agency in Danville, IL. Teamed with friend in nightclub act called Eric and Van, The Merry Mutes, and for 4 yrs. toured country doing a routine in which they pantomimed and lip-synched to records. 1953 hosted local TV show in Atlanta, then New Orleans. 1955 to NY as host of CBS Morning show.
THEATRE: The Girls Against the Boys (Theatre World Award), Bye Bye Birdie (Tony Award, 1961), The Music Man (revival).
PICTURES: Bye Bye Birdie (debut, 1963), What a Way to Go, Mary Poppins, The Art of Love, Lt. Robin Crusoe USN, Divorce American Style, Fitzwilly, Chitty Chitty Bang Bang, Some Kind of a Nut, The Comic, Cold Turkey, The Runner Stumbles, Dick Tracy.
TELEVISION: Series: The Morning Show, CBS Cartoon Theatre (host), The Chevy Showroom, Pantomime Quiz, Laugh Line (emcee), The Dick Van Dyke Show (3 Emmy Awards: 1964, 1965, 1966), The New Dick Van Dyke Show, Van Dyke and Company (Emmy Award, 1977), The Carol Burnett Show, The Van Dyke Show. Movies: The Morning After, Drop-Out Father, Found Money, The Country Girl, Ghost of a Chance, Keys to the Kingdom, Daughters of Privilege, Diagnosis of Murder, The House on Sycamore Street, A Twist of the Knife. Pilot: Harry's Battles. Specials: The Dick Van Dyke Special, Dick Van Dyke and the Other Woman, Julie and Dick in Covent Garden, The Confessions of Dick Van Dyke, CBS Library: The Wrong Way Kid (Emmy Award, 1984).

VAN FLEET, JO: Actress. b. Oakland, CA, Dec. 30, 1919. e. Coll. of the Pacific. Neighborhood Playhouse.
THEATRE: Bdwy: Winter's Tale, Whole World Over, Closing Door, King Lear, Flight into Egypt, Camino Real, Trip to Bountiful (Tony Award), Look Homeward Angel, The Glass Menagerie, The Alligators, Oh Dad Poor Dad Mama's Hung You in the Closet and I'm Feeling So Sad.
PICTURES: East of Eden (debut; Academy Award, best supp. actress, 1955), I'll Cry Tomorrow (Look Award), The Rose Tattoo, King and Four Queens, Gunfight at the OK Corral, This Angry Age, Wild River, Cool Hand Luke, I Love You Alice B. Toklas, The Gang That Couldn't Shoot Straight, The Tenant.

TELEVISION: Specials: Cinderella, Paradise Lost. Guest: Bonanza, Mod Squad. Movies: The Family Rico, Satan's School for Girls, Power, Seize the Day.

VANGELIS: Composer, Conductor. Full name: Vangelis Papathanassiou. b. Greece, March 23, 1943. Began composing as child, performing own compositions at 6. Left Greece for Paris by late 1960s. Composed and recorded his symphonic poem Faire que ton reve soit plus long que la nuit, and album Terra. Collaborated with filmmaker Frederic Rossif for whom composed La Cantique des Creatures. Moved to London then to Greece in 1989. Formed band Formynx in Greece; then Aphrodite's Child in Paris.
PICTURES: Chariots of Fire (Acad. Award, 1981), Antarctica, Missing, Blade Runner, The Year of Living Dangerously, The Bounty, Wonders of Life, Wild and Beautiful, Nosferatu in Venice, Francesco, 1492: Conquest of Paradise.

VANOCUR, SANDER: News Commentator. b. Cleveland, OH, Jan. 8, 1928. e. Northwestern U. Began career as journalist on London staff of Manchester Guardian 1954–5; City staff, NY Times 1956–57. Joined NBC in 1957, hosting First Tuesday series. Resigned in 1971 to be correspondent of the National Public Affairs Center for PBS. TV Critic for Washington Post, 1975–7. In 1977 joined ABC News as v.p., special reporting units 1977–80. Chief overview corr. ABC news, 1980–81; sr. corr. 1981–present. Anchor: Business World.

VAN PALLANDT, NINA: Actress. b. Copenhagen, Denmark, July 15, 1932. e. U. of Southern California. Returned to Denmark where married Baron Frederik Van Pallandt with whom she had appeared as folk singer throughout Europe. Made 3 films with him; went on world tour together. Now divorced. Has appeared in New York as singer.
PICTURES: The Long Goodbye, Assault on Agathon, A Wedding, Quintet, American Gigolo, Cloud Dancer, Cutter and Bone, Asi Como Habian Sido, The Sword and the Sorcerer, Jungle Warriors, Time Out, O.C. and Stiggs.
TELEVISION: Movie: Guilty or Innocent: The Sam Shepherd Murder Case.

VAN PATTEN, DICK: Actor. b. New York, NY, Dec. 9, 1928. Sister is actress Joyce Van Patten. Father of actors James and Vincent Van Patten. Began career as child actor with Bdwy. debut at 7 yrs., playing son of Melvyn Douglas in Tapestry in Gray. Has worked since in stage, radio, TV, films.
PICTURES: Reg'lar Fellers (debut, 1941), Psychomania, Charly, Zachariah, Making It, Joe Kidd, Soylent Green, Dirty Little Billy, Westworld, Superdad, Strongest Man in the World, Gus, Treasure of Matecumbe, The Shaggy D.A., Freaky Friday, High Anxiety, Spaceballs, The New Adventures of Pippi Longstocking, Robin Hood: Men in Tights.
TELEVISION: Guest: Arnie, The Rookies, Cannon, Banyon, The Little People, The Streets of San Francisco, Hotel, Growing Pains, Love Boat, Murder She Wrote. Series: Mama, The Partners, The New Dick Van Dyke Show, When Things Were Rotten, Eight is Enough, WIOU. Specials: Jay Leno's Family Comedy Hour, A Mouse A Mystery and Me, 14 Going On 30. Movies: Hec Ramsey (pilot), The Crooked Hearts, The Love Boat (pilot), With This Ring, Diary of a Hitchhiker, Eight is Enough Reunion, Going to the Chapel, An Eight is Enough Wedding, Jake Spanner—Private Eye.
STAGE: The Lady Who Came to Stay, O Mistress Mine, On Borrowed Time, Ah, Wilderness, Watch on the Rhine, The Skin of Our Teeth, Kiss and Tell, Mister Roberts, Thieves.

VAN PATTEN, JOYCE: Actress. b. New York, NY, March 9, 1935. Brother is actor Dick Van Patten. Mother of actress Talia Balsam.
PICTURES: Reg'lar Fellers (debut, 1941), Fourteen Hours, The Goddess, I Love You Alice B. Toklas, Making It, Something Big, Thumb Tripping, The Manchu Eagle Murder Caper Mystery, Mame, The Bad News Bears, Mikey and Nicky, The Falcon and the Snowman, St. Elmo's Fire, Billy Galvin, Blind Date, Trust Me, Monkey Shines.
TELEVISION: Series: The Danny Kaye Show, The Good Guys, The Don Rickles Show, Mary Tyler Moore Hour. Guest: Brooklyn Bridge. Movies: But I Don't Want to Get Married!, Winter Kill, The Stranger Within, Let's Switch, Winner Take All, To Kill a Cop, Murder at the Mardi Gras, The Comedy Company, Eleanor: First Lady of the World, Another Woman's Child, The Demon Murder Case, In Defense of Kids, Malice in Wonderland, Under the Influence, The Haunted, Maid for Each Other. Mini-Series: The Martian Chronicles. Special: Bus Stop.
THEATRE: NY: Spoon River Anthology, Same Time Next Year, The Supporting Cast, The Seagull, I Ought to Be in Pictures, Brighton Beach Memoirs, Murder at the Howard Johnson's, Rumors, Jake's Women.

VAN PEEBLES, MARIO: Actor, Director, Producer, Writer. b. Mexico D.F., Mexico, Jan. 15, 1957. Father is filmmaker Melvin Van Peebles. e. Columbia U., B.A. economics, 1980. Studied acting with Stella Adler 1983. Served as budget analyst for NY Mayor Ed Koch and later worked as a Ford model. Directed music videos for Kid Creole and the

Coconuts, Nighttrain (dir., prod., cameo) and for film Identity Crisis. Appeared as child in father's film Sweet Sweetback's Baadasssss Song. Dir., prod. wrote and starred in short Juliet. Exec. prod. of soundtracks for Posse and Gunmen.

THEATER: Waltz of the Stork (Bdwy debut, 1984), Take Me Along, The Legend of Deadwood Dick, Champeen, Friday the 13th.

PICTURES: The Cotton Club, Delivery Boys, Exterminator II, 3:15. Rappin' (also wrote and performed 5 songs), South Bronx Heroes, Heartbreak Ridge (also songs), Last Resort, Jaws: the Revenge, Hot Shot, Identity Crisis (also s.p.), New Jack City (also dir.), Gunmen, Posse (also dir.).

TELEVISION: Series: Sonny Spoon. Guest: L.A. Law, One Life to Live, The Cosby Show, The Pat Sajack Show (guest host), In Living Color. Movies: The Cable Car Murder, Sophisticated Gents, Children of the Night (Bronze Halo Award), The Facts of Life Down Under, The Child Saver, Blue Bayou, Triumph of the Heart: The Ricky Bell Story, Stompin' at the Savoy, In the Line of Duty: Street War, Crosscurrents, Full Eclipse. Specials: American Masters: A Glory of Ghosts (Emperor Jones, All God's Chillun), Third & Oak: The Pool Hall (CBS play). Director: Sonny Spoon, 21 Jump Street, Top of the Hill, Wise Guy, Malcolm Takes a Shot (DGA nom.), Gabriel's Fire, Missing Persons, In Living Color.

VAN PEEBLES, MELVIN: Producer, Director, Writer, Composer, Editor, Actor. b. Chicago, IL, Aug. 21, 1932. e. Ohio Wesleyan U., 1953. Father of actor Mario Van Peebles. Was portrait painter in Mexico, cable car driver in San Francisco; journalist in Paris and (in 1970s) options trader on Wall Street. Dir. Funky Beat music video.

AUTHOR—BOOKS: The Big Heart, A Bear for the FBI, Le Chinois de XIV, La Permission (Story of a Three Day Pass) La Fete a Harlem, The True American, Sweet Sweetback's Baadasssss Song, Just an Old Sweet Song, Bold Money, No Identity Crisis (co-author with Mario VanPeebles).

PICTURES: The Story of a Three-Day Pass (dir., s.p., music), Watermelon Man (dir., music), Sweet Sweetback's Baadasssss Song (prod., dir., s.p., edit., music, actor), Don't Play Us Cheap (prod., dir., s.p., edit., music), Greased Lightning (co-s.p.), America (actor), O.C. and Stiggs (actor), Jaws: The Revenge (actor), Identity Crisis (prod., dir., co-edit., actor), True Identity (actor), Boomerang (actor), Posse (actor), Last Action Hero (actor).

STAGE: Bdwy (writer, prod., dir.): Ain't Supposed to Die a Natural Death, Don't Play Us Cheap, Waltz of the Stork (also actor). Off-Bdwy: Champeen, Waltz of the Stork, Kickin the Science.

TELEVISION: Author: Down Home, Just an Old Sweet Song, The Day They Came to Arrest the Book (Emmy Award). Actor: Taking Care of Terrific, Sophisticated Gents, Sonny Spoons (series). Director: Nipsey Russell at Harrah's, Vroom Vroom Vroom (also writer; German tv).

ALBUMS: Composer: Brer Soul, Watermelon Man, Sweet Sweetback's Baadasssss Song, As Serious as a Heart Attack, Don't Play Us Cheap, Ain't Suppose to Die a Natural Death, What the #*!% You Mean, I Can't Sing.

VAN PRAAG, WILLIAM: Executive, Producer, Director, Writer, Editor. Advertising Consultant. b. New York, NY, Sept. 13, 1924. e. CREI, Columbia U. U.S. Army, 1942. Paramount, 1945; Brandt Bros. Prods., 1946; NBC, 1947; v.p. Television Features, 1948. Devlpd. vidicon system in m.p. prod., 1949. Started, pres., Van Praag Prod. Inc. 1951. Formed Ernst-Van Praag, Inc. 1971, a communications and marketing counseling firm (N.Y., Brussels, Tokyo). Pres., International Film, TV and A-V Producers Assn, 1969, Creator of Van-O-Vision. Winner of commercial, short subject and feature theatrical awards. Author of Color Your Picture, Primer of Creative Editing, and Van Praag's Magic Eye. Past pres., Film Producer's Assn, mem. DGA, SAG, 771 IATSE, National Academy of TV Arts and Sciences, International Radio and TV Executive Society and Soc. of MP and TV Engineers.

VAN SANT, GUS: Director. Writer. b. Louisville, KY, 1952. Raised in Darien, CT, then moved to Oregon at age 17. e. Rhode Island Sch. of Design, where he studied painting. Went to L.A. in 1976, becoming prod. asst. to dir. Ken Shapiro. Made first low-budget film, Alice in Hollywood, which was never released. Later made commercials for NY ad agency before returning to filmmaking.

PICTURES: Mala Noche, Drugstore Cowboy (Natl. Soc. of Film Critics Awards for best dir. & s.p.; NY Film Critics & L.A. Film Critics Award for s.p.), My Own Private Idaho, Even Cowgirls Get the Blues.

VARNEY, JIM: Actor. b. Lexington, KY, June 15, 1949. Studied acting at the Barter Theatre. Performed as stand-up comedian in NY and LA. Appeared in dinner theatre productions of Death of a Salesman, Camelot, Guys and Dolls, etc. During 1970's starred as Sgt. Glory in long running series of TV commercials. Became famous with character of Ernest P. Worrell in TV commercials beginning in 1980.

PICTURES: Ernest Goes to Camp, Ernest Saves Christmas, Fast Food, Ernest Goes to Jail, Ernest Scared Stupid, Wilder Napalm, The Beverly Hillbillies.

TELEVISION: Series: The Johnny Cash Show (1976), Operation Petticoat, Pink Lady, Tom T.'s Pop Goes the Country, The Rousters, Hey Vern It's Ernest (Emmy Award, 1989). Guest: Fernwood 2-Night, Alice, America 2-Nite. Pilot: Operation Petticoat.

VAUGHN, ROBERT: Actor. b. New York, NY, Nov. 22, 1932. e. L.A. State coll., B.S. and M.A. Theatre Arts 1956; USC, Ph.D. Communications, 1970. Gained fame as Napoleon Solo in The Man From U.N.C.L.E. TV series. Author: Only Victims, 1972.

PICTURES: Hell's Crossroads, No Time to Be Young, Teenage Caveman, Unwed Mother, Good Day for a Hanging, The Young Philadelphians (Acad. Award nom.), The Magnificent Seven, The Big Show, The Caretakers, To Trap a Spy, The Spy With My Face, One Spy Too Many, The Venetian Affair, How to Steal the World, Bullitt, The Bridge at Remagen, If It's Tuesday This Must Be Belgium (cameo), The Mind of Mr. Soames, Julius Caesar, The Statue, Clay Pigeon, The Towering Inferno, The Babysitter, Lucifer Complex, Demon Seed (voice), Starship Invasions, Brass Target, Good Luck Miss Wycoff, Hangar 18, Sweet Dirty Tony, Battle Beyond the Stars, Virus, S.O.B., Superman III, Black Moon Rising, The Delta Force, Rampage, Nightstick, Hour of the Assassin, Skeleton Coast, River of Death, Captive Rage, Nobody's Perfect, Fair Trade, Edgar Allan Poe's Buried Alive, That's Adequate, C.H.U.D. II: Bud the Chud, Transylvania Twist, Going Under, Twilight Blue.

TELEVISION: Series: The Lieutenant, The Man From U.N.C.L.E., The Protectors, Emerald Point N.A.S., The A-Team, Danger Theatre. Mini-Series: Captains and the Kings, Washington: Behind Closed Doors (Emmy Award, 1978), Centennial, Backstairs at the White House, The Blue and the Gray, Evergreen. Movies: The Woman Hunter, Kiss Me Kill Me, The Islander, The Rebels, Mirror Mirror, Doctor Franken, The Gossip Columnist, City in Fear, Fantasies, The Day the Bubble Burst, A Question of Honor, Inside the Third Reich, Intimate Agony, The Return of the Man From U.N.C.L.E., International Airport, Murrow, Prince of Bel Air, Desperado, Perry Mason: The Case of the Defiant Daughter, Dark Avenger. BBC: One of Our Spies is Missing, The Spy in the Green Hat.

VELDE, JAMES R.: Executive. b. Bloomington, IL, Nov. 1, 1913. e. Illinois Wesleyan U. Entered m.p. ind. as night shipper Paramount ex. Detroit, 1934; then city salesman, office mgr. until joining Army, 1943, rejoining same ex. upon dischge., 1946; to Paramount, Washington as Baltimore city salesman, same yr.; br. mgr. Selznick Rel. Org. Pittsburgh, 1948; salesman Eagle-Lion Classics, Pittsburgh, 1949; br. mgr. ELC, Des Moines, 1949; br. mgr., ELC, Detroit, 1950; west coast dist. mgr., United Artists, April, 1951; Western div. mgr. UA, 1952; gen. sales mgr., 1956; v.p., 1958; dir., IJA, 1968; sr. v.p., 1972. Retired, 1977. Worked with Ray Stark as advisor, 1978–83.

VELJOHNSON, REGINALD: Actor. b. Queens, NY, Aug. 16, 1952. e. Long Island Inst. of Music and Arts, NYU.

TELEVISION: Series: Perfect Strangers, Family Matters. Movies: Quiet Victory: The Charlie Wedemeyer Story, The Bride in Black, Jury Duty: The Comedy, Grass Roots.

PICTURES: Wolfen (debut, 1981), Ghostbusters, The Cotton Club, Remo Williams, Armed and Dangerous, Crocodile Dundee, Die Hard, Turner & Hooch, Die Hard 2, Posse.

THEATRE: NY: But Never Jam Today, Inacent Black, World of Ben Caldwell, Staggerlee.

VENORA, DIANE: Actress. b. Hartford, CT, 1952. Member of Juilliard's Acting Company, Circle Repertory Co. and the Ensemble Studio Theatre. Theater includes A Midsummer Night's Dream, the title role in Hamlet (New York Shakespeare Festival), Uncle Vanya (at La Mama), Messiah, Penguin Toquet, Tomorrow's Monday (Circle Rep). Largo Desolato, School for Scandal, The Seagull, A Man for All Seasons, Peer Gynt (Williamstown Fest.), The Winter's Tale, Hamlet (NYSF).

PICTURES: All That Jazz, Wolfen, Terminal Choice, The Cotton Club, F/X, Ironweed, Bird (NY Film Critics Award, best supp. actress), Reversal of Fortune.

TELEVISION: Mini-series: A.D. Movie: Cook and Peary: The Race to the Pole. Special: Getting There.

VERDON, GWEN: Actress, Dancer, Choreographer. b. Culver City, CA, Jan. 13, 1925. Married to late dir.-choreographer Bob Fosse. Studied dancing with her mother, E. Belcher, Carmelita Marrachi, and Jack Cole.

THEATER: Bonanza Bound! (1947), Magdalena (asst. choreographer to Jack Cole), Alive and Kicking (1950), Can-Can (Donaldson Award and Tony Awards), Damn Yankees (Tony Award), New Girl in Town (Tony Award), Redhead (Tony Award), Sweet Charity, Children! Children!, Milliken's Breakfast Show (Waldorf Astoria, 1973), Damn Yankees (revival Westbury, Long Island, 1974), Chicago, Dancin' (asst. choreographer, prod. sprv. road co.), Sing Happy (tribute to Kander and Ebb, 1978), Parade of Stars Playing the Palace (Actors' Fund benefit, 1983), Night of 100 Stars II (1985).

PICTURES: On the Riviera (debut, 1951), David and Bathsheba, Meet Me After the Show, The Merry Widow, The I Don't Care Girl, Farmer Takes a Wife, Damn Yankees, The Cotton Club, Cocoon, Nadine, Cocoon: The Return, Alice.

TELEVISION: Guest: M*A*S*H, Fame, All My Children, Magnum P.I., The Equalizer, All is Forgiven, Dear John. Movies: Legs, The Jerk Too.

VEREEN, BEN: Singer, Dancer, Actor. b. Miami, FL, Oct. 10, 1946. e. High School of Performing Arts. On stage in Hair, Sweet Charity, Jesus Christ Superstar (Theatre World Award), Pippin (Tony Award, 1973), Grind.

PICTURES: Sweet Charity, Gasss, Funny Lady, All That Jazz, Buy and Cell, Friend to Friend, Once Upon a Forest (voice).

TELEVISION: Movies: Louis Armstrong—Chicago Style, The Jesse Owens Story, Lost in London, Intruders. Mini-Series: Roots, Ellis Island, A.D. Series: Ben Vereen . . . Comin' at Ya, Ten Speed and Brown Shoe, Webster, Zoobilee Zoo, You Write the Songs (host), J.J. Starbuck, Silk Stalkings. Specials: Ben Vereen—His Roots, Uptown—A Tribute to the Apollo Theatre.

VERHOEVEN, PAUL: Director. b. Amsterdam, The Netherlands, July 18, 1938. e. U. of Leiden, Ph.D., (mathematics and physics) where he began making films.

PICTURES: Memories of a Streetwalker, Turkish Delight, Keetje Tippel (Cathy Tippel), Soldier of Orange, Spetters, The Fourth Man, Flesh + Blood, Robocop, Total Recall, Basic Instinct.

VERNON, ANNE: Actress. r.n. Edith Antoinette Alexandrine Vignaud. b. Paris, Jan. 7, 1924. e. Ecole des Beaux Arts, Paris. Worked for French designer; screen debut in French films; toured with French theatre group; first starring role, Le Mannequin Assassine 1948. Wrote French cookbooks. Was subject of 1980 French TV film detailing her paintings, Les Peintres Enchanteurs.

PICTURES: Edouar et Caroline, Terror on a Train, Ainsi Finit La Nuit, A Warning to Wantons, Patto Col Diavolo, A Tale of Five Cities, Shakedown, Song of Paris, The Umbrellas of Cherbourg, General Della Rovere, La Rue L'Estrapade, Love Lottery.

VERNON, JOHN: Actor. b. Montreal, Canada, Feb. 24, 1932. r.n. Adolphus Raymondus Vernon Agopowicz. e. Banff Sch. of Fine Arts, Royal Acad. of Dramatic Art. Worked on London stage and radio. First film work as voice of Big Brother in 1984 (1956). Father of actress Kate Vernon.

PICTURES: 1984 (voice; debut, 1956), Nobody Waved Goodbye, Point Blank, Justine, Topaz, Tell Them Willie Boy is Here, One More Train to Rob, Dirty Harry, Fear Is the Key, Charley Varrick, W (I Want Her Dead), The Black Windmill, Brannigan, Sweet Movie, The Outlaw Josey Wales, Angela, A Special Day, The Uncanny, Golden Rendezvous, National Lampoon's Animal House, It Rained All Night the Day I Left, Crunch, Fantastica, Herbie Goes Bananas, Heavy Metal (voice), Airplane II: The Sequel, Chained Heat, Curtains, Savage Streets, Jungle Warriors, Fraternity Vacation, Doin' Time, Double Exposure (Terminal Exposure), Ernest Goes to Camp, Blue Monkey, Nightstick, Border Heat, Deadly Stranger, Dixie Lanes, Killer Klowns From Outer Space, Bail-Out, I'm Gonna Git You Sucka, Office Party, War Bus Commando, Mob Story, The Naked Truth.

TELEVISION: Series: Tugboat Annie (Canadian tv), Wojeck (Canadian tv), Delta House, Hail to the Chief. Movies: Trial Run, Escape, Cool Million, Hunter, The Questor Tapes, Mousey, The Virginia Hill Story, The Imposter, Swiss Family Robinson, The Barbary Coast, Matt Helm, Mary Jane Harper Cried Last Night, The Sacketts, The Blood of Others, Two Men (Can.), The Woman Who Sinned, The Fire Next Time. Mini-Series: The Blue and the Gray, Louisiana (Fr.). Pilots: B-Men, War of the Worlds. Guest: Tarzan, Kung Fu, Faerie Tale Theatre (Little Red Riding Hood), The Greatest American Hero, Fall Guy, Alfred Hitchcock Presents, Knight Rider, Tales From the Crypt, etc.

VERONA, STEPHEN: Director, Producer, Writer. b. Illinois, Sept. 11, 1940. e. Sch. of Visual Arts. Directed and wrote some 300 commercials (over 50 award-winners) before turning to feature films in 1972, which he wrote as well. Also dir. award-winning short subjects (featuring Barbra Streisand, The Beatles, Simon and Garfunkle and The Lovin' Spoonful). Also prod., dir. of Angela Lansbury's Positive Moves video. Is an artist whose works have been exhibited at numerous CA and NY galleries.

PICTURES: The Rehearsal (Acad. Award nom, short subj., 1971), The Lords of Flatbush (prod., co-dir., co-s.p.), Pipe Dreams (prod., dir., s.p.), Boardwalk (dir., co-s.p.), Talking Walls (dir., s.p.).

TELEVISION: Class of 1966 (prod. designer, ani. dir.); Diff'rent Strokes; The Music People; Sesame Street; Take a

Giant Step; Double Exposure; Flatbush Avenue (pilot, prod., co-s.p.).

VETTER, RICHARD: Executive. b. San Diego, CA, Feb. 24, 1928. e. Pepperdine Coll., B.A., 1950; San Diego State Coll., M.A., 1953; UCLA, Ph.D., 1959. U.S. Navy: aerial phot., 1946–48, reserve instr., San Diego County Schools, 1951–54; asst. prof., audio-vis. commun., U.C.L.A., 1960–63. Inventor, co-dev., Dimension 150 Widescreen Process. 1957–63: formed D-150 Inc., 1963; exec. v.p. mem.: SMPTE, Technical & Scientific Awards Committee, AMPAS.

VICTOR, JAMES: Actor. r.n. Lincoln Rafael Peralta Diaz. b. Santiago, Dominican Republic, July 27, 1939. e. Haaren H.S., N.Y. Studied at Actors Studio West. On stage in Bullfight, Ceremony for an Assassinated Blackman, Latina, The Man in the Glass Booth, The M.C. (1985 Drama-Logue Critics, and Cesar best actor awards), I Gave You a Calendar (1983 Drama-Logue Critics Award), I Don't Have To Show You No Stinking Badges (1986 Drama-Logue Critics Award). Member of Academy of Mo. Pic. Arts & Sciences, Actors Branch.

PICTURES: Fuzz, Rolling Thunder, Boulevard Nights, Defiance, Losin' It, Borderline; Stand and Deliver.

TELEVISION: Series: Viva Valdez, Condo, I Married Dora, Angelica Mi Vida, The New Zorro. Many appearances on specials. Movies: Robert Kennedy and His Times, Twin Detectives, Remington Steel, The Streets of L.A., I Desire, Second Serve, Grand Slam.

AWARDS: Cleo, 1975, for Mug Shot; L.A. Drama-Logue Critics Award, 1980, for Latina; Golden Eagle Award, 1981, for consistent outstanding performances in motion pictures.

VILLECHAIZE, HERVE: Actor. b. Paris, France, April 23, 1943. Sought career as artist, studying in Paris and then coming to New York to the Art Students League. Studied acting with Julie Bovasso. First film, The Guitar, shot in Spain. On Broadway in Elizabeth the First and Gloria and Esperenze. Also performed mime in N.Y. City Opera productions.

PICTURES: Hollywood Blvd. No. 2, Hot Tomorrow, The Man with the Golden Gun, Crazy Joe, The Gang That Couldn't Shoot Straight, Greaser's Palace, Seizure, The One and Only, Forbidden Zone, Malatesta's Carnival, Chappaqua, Airplane II: The Sequel, Two Moon Junction.

TELEVISION: Fantasy Island (series).

VINCENT, JR., FRANCIS T: Executive. b. Waterbury, CT, May 29, 1938. e. Williams Coll. B.A., 1960; Yale Law Sch. LL.B., 1963. Bar, CT 1963; NY, 1964; D.C. 1969. 1969–78, partner in law firm of Caplin & Drysdale, specializing in corporate banking and securities matters. 1978, assoc. dir. of, Division of Corporation Finance of Securities & Exchange Commission. Exec. v.p. of the Coca-Cola Company and pres. & CEO of its entertainment business sector. Also chmn. & CEO of Columbia Pictures Industries, Inc.; appt. pres. CEO, 1978. Mem. bd. of dir. of The Coca-Cola Bottling Co. of New York. 1987–June 1988. Rejoined law firm of Caplin & Drysdale, Washington, D.C., 1988. Trustee of Williams Coll. & The Hotchkiss Sch.

VINCENT, JAN-MICHAEL: Actor. b. Denver, CO, July 15, 1945. e. Ventura City (CA) Coll. as art major. Joined National Guard. Discovered by agent Dick Clayton. Hired by Robert Conrad to appear in his film, Los Bandidos. Signed to 6-mo. contract by Universal; for which made Journey to Shiloh. Then did pilot TV movie for 20th-Fox based on Hardy Boys series of book. Originally called self Michael Vincent; changed after The Undefeated.

PICTURES: Los Bandidos, Journey to Shiloh, The Undefeated, Going Home, The Mechanic, The World's Greatest Athlete, Buster and Billie, Bite the Bullet, White Line Fever, Baby Blue Marine, Vigilante Force, Shadow of the Hawk, Damnation Alley, Big Wednesday, Hooper, Defiance, Hard Country, The Return, The Last Plane Out, Born in East L.A., Hit List, Deadly Embrace, Demonstone, Hangfire, Raw Nerve, Alienator, In Gold We Trust, The Divine Enforcer, Sins of Desire.

TELEVISION: Guest: Lassie, Bonanza. Series: Dangerous Island (Banana Splits Hour), The Survivors, Airwolf. Movies: Tribes, The Catcher, Sandcastle, Deliver Us From Evil, Six Against the Rock, Tarzan in Manhattan. Mini-Series: The Winds of War.

VINCENT, KATHARINE: Actress. r.n. Ella Vincenti. b. St. Louis, MO, May 28, 1918.

THEATRE: Broadway shows include: Love or Bust, 1938; Could She Tell?, 1939; Banners of 1939; Czarina Smith, 1940. Numerous roadshow tours.

PICTURES: Peptipa's Waltz, 1942 (debut), Error in Her Ways, Stars and Stripes on Tour, 1943, Skin Deep, 1944, The Hungry, Voodoo Village, Welcome to Genoa, 1950, Unknown Betrayal, 1956, The Hooker, 1962 (Descanto films).

TELEVISION: The Untouchables, Moses, The Lawgiver, Dolce Far Niente (mini-series TVF Roma).

VINER, MICHAEL: Producer, Writer. b. 1945. m. actress Deborah Raffin. e. Harvard U., Georgetown U. Served as aide to Robert Kennedy; was legman for political columnist Jack

Anderson. Settled in Hollywood, where worked for prod. Aaron Rosenberg, first as prod. asst. on three Frank Sinatra films; then asst. prod. on Joaquin Murietta. In music industry was record producer, manager, executive, eventually heading own division, at MGM. Debut as writer-producer in 1976 with TV special, Special of the Stars. Theatrical film debut as prod.-co-writer of Touched by Love, 1980. Television: Windmills of the Gods (exec. prod.). Exec. Prod.: Rainbow Drive; Prod.: Memories of Midnight. President: Dove Audio.

VITALE, JOSEPH A.: Actor. b. New York, NY, Sept. 6, 1901. Singer in companies of The Student Prince, Golden Dawn, etc. In 1924, on dramatic stage (Hold on to Your Hats, Page Miss Glory, All Editions, I'd Rather Be Right, Common Ground, Thieves Fall Out, many others). Screen debut, 1943.
PICTURES: The Falcon in Mexico, None But the Lonely Heart, Lady Luck, Road to Rio, Where There's Life, The Paleface, Connecticut Yankee, Illegal Entry, Red Hot and Blue, Fancy Pants, My Friend Irma Goes West, Stop You're Killing Me, Stranger Wore a Gun, Square Jungle, Rumble On the Docks, The Lost Tribe, A Bullet for Joey, the Deerslayer, The Threat, Mr. Imperium, Apache Rifles.
TELEVISION: Climax, Lineup, Bengal Lancers, Wagon Train, Schlitz Playhouse, Cimmaron City, Telephone Time, Wyatt Earp, Rawhide, Red Skelton, The Thin Man, This Man Dawson, The Falcon, The Lone Ranger, Playhouse 90, Rin Tin Tin, Jane Wyman Theatre, Northwest Passade, Restless Gun, Waterfront, Mr. & Mrs. North, Empire, Hazel, Mr. Ed, To Rome With Love, many others; Fisherman's Wharf (pilot).

VITTI, MONICA: Actress. r.n. Maria Luisa Ceciarelli. b. Rome, Italy, Nov. 3, 1933.
PICTURES: L'Avventura, La Notte, L'Eclipse, Dragées du Poivre, The Nutty Naughty Chateau, Alta Infidelitata, The Red Desert, Le Bambole, Il Disco Volante, Modesty Blaise, Le Fate, The Chastity Belt, Girl with a Pistol, The Pacifist, The Phantom of Liberty, Duck in Orange Sauce, An Almost Perfect Affair, The Mystery of Oberwald, The Flirt, Secret Scandal (dir. debut).

VOIGHT, JON: Actor. b. Yonkers, NY. Dec. 29, 1938. e. Archbishop Stepinac H.S., White Plains, NY; Catholic U. of Amer., D.C. (B.F.A.) 1960; studied acting at the Neighborhood Playhouse and in private classes with Stanford Meisner, four yrs. THEATRE: Bdwy.: The Sound of Music (debut, 1959), That Summer That Fall (Theatre World Award), The Seagull. Off-Bdwy: A View From the Bridge (1964 revival). Regional Theatre: Romeo & Juliet, A Streetcar Name Desire, Hamlet.
TELEVISION: Special: The Dwarf (Public Broadcast Lab). Guest: Gunsmoke, Naked City, The Defenders, Coronet Blue, NYPD. Movies: Chernobyl: The Final Warning, The Last of His Tribe.
PICTURES: Hour of the Gun (debut, 1967), Fearless Frank, Midnight Cowboy, Out of It, Catch-22, The Revolutionary, Deliverance, All-American Boy, Conrack, The Odessa File, End of the Game, Coming Home (Acad. Award, 1978), The Champ, Lookin' To Get Out (also co-s.p., prod.), Table for Five (also prod.), Runaway Train, Desert Bloom, Eternity.

VOLONTE, GIAN MARIA: Actor. b. Milan, April 9, 1933. e. Rome's National Acad. of Dramatic Art, 1957 graduate. Entered on professional theatrical career, playing Shakespeare and Racine, along with modern works, Sacco and Vanzetti and The Deputy. On TV in Chekov's Uncle Vanya and Dostoyevsky's The Idiot. First major film roles in Un Uomo da Bruciare, 1961 and Il Terrorista, 1963. Called self John Welles in credits for spaghetti westerns.
PICTURES: Girl With a Suitcase, Il Terrorista, Il Peccato, A Fistful of Dollars, The Magnificent Cuckold, Le Stagioni del Nostro Amore, For a Few Dollars More, L'Armata Brancaleone, Investigation of a Citizen Above Suspicion, Red Circle, Uomini Contro, The Working Class Goes to Paradise, Wind from the East, Sacco and Vanzetti, L'Attenat, Slap the Monster on Page One, Just Another War, The Mattei Affair, The French Conspiracy, Lucky Luciano, Giordano Bruno, Todo Modo, Letters from Marusia, I Am Afraid, Eboli, Orgo, True Story of the Lady of the Camellias, The Death of Mario Ricci, Chronicle of a Death Foretold, Il Caso Moro, The Boy from Calabria, L'Oeuvre au Noir, Pestalozzi's Berg, Open Doors, Tre Colonne in Cronaca, A Simple Story.

VON ROTHKIRCH, Dr. EDWARD: Producer. b. July 30, 1919. e. Friedrich Wilhelm V., Berlin; Rockhurst Coll., Midwestern Coll. Prod. asst., research, Pan American Prod., 1941; research Pacific Films, 1942; U.S. Air Force, 1942–44; asst. prod., Pan American Productions, 1945; analyst, Cambridge Prod., 1947; assoc. prod., Pentagon Films, 1949; assoc. prod., Reelestic Pictures, 1950; assoc. prod. Cambridge-Meran Prod. Co., 1951; assoc. exec. prod., Cambridge Prod., 1954; also v.-p. Continental Prod. Services; assoc. exec. prod. Trinity Hill Productions, produced Pan-American Highway 1954, The Keepers TV series, 1953–58, Famous Women of the Bible, 1955–58; To the Stars TV series, 1954–58; also sec.-treas. Crusader Records and v.p. Orbit Records. Member of many professional societies, director Intl. Association of Independent Producers, presently exec. prod., Galaxie

Productions, and Encore Records also exec. editor, Intercontinental Media Services, Ltd.

VON SYDOW, MAX: Actor. b. Lund, Sweden, April 10, 1929. m. Keratin Olin, actress, 1951. Theatrical debut in a Cathedral Sch. of Lund prod. of The Nobel Prize. Served in the Swedish Quartermaster. Corps two yrs. Studied at Royal Dramatic Theatre Sch. in Stockholm. Tour in municipal theatres. Has appeared on stage in Stockholm, London (The Tempest, 1988). Paris and Helsinki in Faust, The Legend and The Misanthrope. 1954 won Sweden's Royal Foundation Cultural Award. Appeared on Bdwy in Duet for One.
PICTURES: Miss Julie, The Seventh Seal, Wild Strawberries, Brink of Life, The Magician, The Virgin Spring, Through a Glass Darkly, Winter Light, The Greatest Story Ever Told, The Reward, Hawaii, The Quiller Memorandum, Hour of the Wolf, Shame, The Kremlin Letter, The Passion of Anna, Night Visitor, The Touch, The Emigrants, Embassy, The New Land, Steppenwolf, Three Days of the Condor, The Ultimate Warrior, Foxtrot, Voyage of the Damned, Exorcist II: The Heretic, March or Die, Brass Target, Hurricane, Deathwatch, Flash Gordon, She Dances Alone, Victory, Conan the Barbarian, Flight of the Eagle, Strange Brew, Never Say Never Again, Target Eagle, Dreamscape, Dune, Code Name: Emerald, Hannah and Her Sisters, Duet for One, The Second Victory, Wolf at the Door, Pelle the Conqueror (Acad. Award nom.), Katinka (dir.), Awakenings, A Kiss Before Dying, Until the End of the World, Zentropa (narrator), The Bachelor, The Best Intentions, The Ox, Father, The Silent Touch, Grandfather's Journey, Needful Things.
TELEVISION: Movies—Mini-Series: Samson and Delilah, Christopher Columbus, Kojak: The Belarus File, Brotherhood of the Rose, Hiroshima: Out of the Ashes, Red King, White Knight.

VON TROTTA, MARGARETHE: Director, Writer. b. Berlin, Germany, Feb. 21, 1942. e. Studied German and Latin literature in Munich and Paris. Studied acting in Munich and began career as actress. 1970 began collaborating on Schlondorff's films as well as acting in them.
PICTURES: Actress: Schrage Vogel, Brandstifter, Gotter der Pest, Baal, Der Amerikanische Soldat, The Sudden Wealth of the Poor People of Kombach (also co-s.p.), Die Moral der Ruth Halbfass, Strohfeuer (also co-s.p.), Desaster, Ubernachtung in Tirol, etc. Dir. and co-s.p.: The Lost Honor of Katharina Blum (co-dir., co-s.p., with Schlondorff), The Second Awakening of Christa Klages, Sisters or the Balance of Happiness, Marianne and Julianne, Heller Wahn (Sheer Madness), Rosa Luxemburg, Paura e Amore (Three Sisters), The African Woman, The Long Silence.

VON ZERNECK, FRANK: Producer. b. New York, NY, Nov. 3, 1940. e. Hofstra Coll., 1962. Has produced plays in New York, Los Angeles, and on national tour and over 60 tv films and mini-series. Partner, von Zerneck/Sertner Films. Devised Portrait film genre for TV movies: Portrait of a Stripper, Portrait of a Mistress, Portrait of a Centerfold, etc.
TELEVISION: 21 Hours at Munich, Dress Gray, Miracle on Ice, Combat High, Queenie, In the Custody of Strangers, The First Time, Baby Sister, Policewoman Centerfold, Obsessive Love, Invitation to Hell, Romance on the Orient Express, Hostage Flight, Exec. prod.: The Proud Men, Man Against the Mob, To Heal a Nation, Lady Mobster, Maybe Baby, Full Exposure: the Sex Tapes Scandal, Gore Vidal's Billy the Kid, Too Young to Die, The Great Los Angeles Earthquake, The Court-Martial of Jackie Robinson, White Hot: The Mysterious Murder of Thelma Todd, Survive the Savage Sea, Opposites Attract, Menu for Murder, Battling for Baby, Woman With a Past, Jackie Collins' Lady Boss, Danger Island, The Broken Chain.
Past chmn. of California Theatre Council; former officer of League of Resident theatres; member of League of New York Theatres & Producers; Producers Guild of America; chmn's council, the Caucus for Producers, Writers, and Directors; Board of Directors, Allied Communications, Inc. Museum of Radio & Television in NYC, Hollywood Television & Radio Society, Acad. of TV Arts & Sciences, Natl. Acad. of Cable Programming. Guest faculty, American Film Inst.

W

WADLEIGH, MICHAEL: Director. b. Akron, OH, Sept. 24, 1941. e. Ohio State U., B.S., B.A., M.A., Columbia Medical Sch. Directed Woodstock (1970), Wolfen (dir., co-s.p.), Out of Order, The Village at the End of the Universe (dir., s.p.).

WAGGONER, LYLE: Actor. b. Kansas City, KS, April 13, 1935. e. Washington U., St. Louis, Was salesman before becoming actor with road co. prod. of Li'l Abner. Formed own sales-promo co. to finance trip to CA for acting career in 1965. Did commercials, then signed by 20th-Fox for new-talent school.
TELEVISION: Series: The Carol Burnett Show, The Jimmie Rodgers Show, It's Your Bet (host), Wonder Woman. Movies:

Letters from Three Lovers, The New Original Wonder Woman, The Love Boat II, The Gossip Columnist, Gridlock.
PICTURES: Love Me Deadly, Journey to the Center of Time, Catalina Caper, Surf II, Murder Weapon, Dead Women in Lingerie.

WAGNER, JANE: Writer, Director, Producer. b. Morristown, TN, Feb. 2, 1935. e. attended Sch. of Visual Arts, NY. Worked as designer for Kimberly Clark, created Teach Me Read Me sheets for Fieldcrest.
THEATRE: Bdwy.: Appearing Nitely (dir., co-writer), The Search for Signs of Intelligent Life in the Universe (dir., writer; NY Drama Desk Award & Special NY Drama Critics Award), both starring Lily Tomlin.
PICTURES: Moment by Moment (s.p., dir.), The Incredible Shrinking Woman (s.p., exec. prod.), The Search for Signs of Intelligent Life in the Universe (s.p., exec. prod.).
TELEVISION: Specials: J.T. (writer; Peabody Award), Lily (prod., co-writer; Emmy & WGA Awards), Lily Tomlin (prod., writer; Emmy Award for writing), People (prod., writer), Lily—Sold Out (exec. prod., co-writer; Emmy Award for producing), Lily for President? (exec. prod., co-writer), The Edith Ann Show (writer, exec. prod.).

WAGNER, LINDSAY: Actress. b. Los Angeles, CA, June 22, 1949. Appeared in school plays in Portland, OR; studied singing and worked professionally with rock group. In 1968 went to L.A. Signed to Universal contract in 1971.
PICTURES: Two People, Paper Chase, Second Wind, Nighthawks, High Risk, Martin's Day, Ricochet.
TELEVISION: Series: The Bionic Woman (Emmy Award, 1977), Jessie, Peaceable Kingdom. Guest: The F.B.I., Owen Marshall: Counselor at Law, Night Gallery, The Bold Ones, Marcus Welby M.D., The Six Million Dollar Man. Movies: The Rockford Files (pilot), The Incredible Journey of Dr. Meg Laurel, The Two Worlds of Jennie Logan, Callie and Son, Memories Never Die, I Want to Live, Princess Daisy, Two Kinds of Love, Passions, This Child Is Mine, Child's Cry, Convicted, Young Again, Stranger in My Bed, The Return of the Six Million Dollar Man and the Bionic Woman, Student Exchange, Evil in Clear River, The Taking of Flight 847, Nightmare at Bitter Creek, From the Dead of Night, The Bionic Showdown: The Six-Million Dollar Man and the Bionic Woman, Shattered Dreams, Babies, Fire in the Dark, She Woke Up, Treacherous Crossing, To Be the Best, A Message From Holly.

WAGNER, RAYMOND JAMES: Producer. b. College Point, NY, Nov. 3, 1925. e. Middlebury Coll., Williams Coll. Joined Young & Rubicam, Inc., as radio-TV commercial head in Hollywood, 1950–59. Head of pilot development, Universal Studios, 1960–65. V.p. of production (features) for MGM, 1972–79. Presently independent producer.
PICTURES: Prod.: Petulia, Loving (exec. prod.), Code of Silence, Rent-a-Cop, Hero and the Terror, Turner and Hooch, Run, Fifty Fifty.

WAGNER, ROBERT: Actor. b. Detroit, MI, Feb. 10, 1930. e. Saint Monica's H.S. m. Jill St. John.
PICTURES: The Halls of Montezuma (debut, 1950), The Happy Years, The Frogmen, Let's Make It Legal, With A Song in My Heart, What Price Glory, Stars and Stripes Forever, The Silver Whip, Titanic (Star of Tomorrow, 1953). Beneath the 12-Mile Reef, Prince Valiant, Broken Lance, White Feather, A Kiss Before Dying, The Mountain, Between Heaven and Hell, True Story of Jesse James, Stopover Tokyo, The Hunters, In Love and War, Say One for Me, All the Fine Young Cannibals, Sail a Crooked Ship, The Longest Day, The War Lover, The Condemned of Altona, The Pink Panther, Harper, Banning, The Biggest Bundle of Them All, Don't Just Stand There, Winning, The Towering Inferno, Midway, The Concorde—Airport '79, Curse of the Pink Panther, I Am the Cheese, Delirious, The Player, Dragon: The Bruce Lee Story.
TELEVISION: Series: It Takes A Thief, Switch, Hart to Hart, Lime Street. Movies: How I Spent My Summer Vacation, City Beneath the Sea, The Cable Car Murder, Killer by Night, Madame Sin (also exec. prod.), Streets of San Francisco (pilot), The Affair, The Abduction of St. Anne, Switch (pilot), Death at Love House, Cat on a Hot Tin Roof, The Critical List, Hart to Hart (pilot), To Catch a King, There Must Be a Pony, Love Among Thieves, Windmills of the Gods, Indiscreet, This Gun for Hire, False Arrest, Daniel Steel's Jewels, Deep Trouble. Mini-series: Pearl, Around the World in 80 Days.

WAHL, KEN: Actor. b. Chicago, IL, Feb. 14, 1953. No acting experience when cast in The Wanderers in 1978.
PICTURES: The Wanderers (debut, 1979), Fort Apache The Bronx, Race to the Yankee Zephyr, Jinxed, The Soldier, Purple Hearts, The Omega Syndrome, The Taking of Beverly Hills (also co-exec. prod.), The Favor, Back in the U.S.A.
TELEVISION: Movies: The Dirty Dozen: The Next Mission, The Gladiator. Series: Double Dare, Wiseguy.

WAITE, RALPH: Actor. b. White Plains, NY, June 22, 1929. e. Bucknell U., Yale U. Social worker, publicity director, assistant editor and minister before turning to acting. Appeared in

many Bdwy. plays, including Hogan's Goat, The Watering Place, Trial of Lee Harvey Oswald, off-Bdwy. in The Destiny of Me. Biggest success on TV in The Waltons. Is founder of the Los Angeles Actors Theatre. Wrote, produced, directed and acted in theatrical film, On the Nickel.
PICTURES: Cool Hand Luke, A Lovely Way to Die, Last Summer, Five Easy Pieces, Lawman, The Grissom Gang, The Sporting Club, Pursuit of Happiness, Chato's Land, The Magnificent Seven Ride, Trouble Man, Kid Blue, The Stone Killer, On the Nickel (also dir., prod., s.p.), Crash and Burn, The Bodyguard, Cliffhanger.
TELEVISION: Series: The Waltons, The Mississippi. Movies: The Secret Life of John Chapman, The Borgia Stick, Red Alert, Ohms, Angel City, The Gentleman Bandit, A Wedding on Waltons Mountain, Mother's Day on Waltons Mountain, A Day for Thanks on Waltons Mountain, A Good Sport, Crime of Innocence, Red Earth White Earth. Mini-series: Roots.

WAITE, RIC: Cinematographer. Photographed more than 40 movies-of-the-week for TV, 1979–83. First theatrical film, The Other Side of the Mountain, 1975.
PICTURES: Defiance, On the Nickel, The Long Riders, The Border, Tex, 48 Hrs., Class, Uncommon Valor, Footloose, Red Dawn, Volunteers, Summer Rental, Brewster's Millions, Cobra, Adventures in Babysitting, The Great Outdoors, Marked for Death, Out for Justice, Rapid Fire.
TELEVISION: Captains and the Kings (Emmy, 1977), Tail Gunner Joe, Huey P. Long, Revenge of the Stepford Wives, Baby Comes Home.

WAITS, TOM: Singer, Composer, Actor. b. Pomona, CA, Dec. 7, 1949. Recorded numerous albums and received Acad. Award nom. for his song score of One from the Heart. Composed songs for On the Nickel, Streetwise, Paradise Alley, Wolfen. Has also starred in Chicago's Steppenwolf Theatre Co.'s Frank's Wild Years (also co-wrote, wrote the music) and Los Angeles Theatre Co.'s Demon Wine. Wrote songs and music for opera The Black Rider (1990).
PICTURES: As actor: Paradise Alley (1978), Poetry in Motion, The Outsiders, Rumble Fish, The Cotton Club, Down by Law (also music), Ironweed, Candy Mountain, Big Time (also co-s.p., performer), Cold Feet, Bearskin, On a Moonlit Night (music only), The Two Jakes, Queens Logic, The Fisher King, At Play in the Fields of the Lord, Bram Stoker's Dracula, Short Cuts.

WAJDA, ANDRZE J: Director, Writer. b. Suwalki, Poland, March 6, 1926. e. Fine Arts Academy, Krakow, Poland, 1945–48; High School of Cinematography, Lodz, Poland, 1950–52. 1940–43, worked as asst. in restoration of church paintings. 1942, joined Polish gov. in exile's A.K. (Home Army Resistance) against German occupation. 1950–52, directed shorts (While You Sleep; The Bad Boy, The Pottery of Ilzecka) as part of film school degree; 1954, asst. dir. to Aleksander Ford on 5 Boys from Barska Street. Work flourished under easing of political restraints in Poland during late 1950s. 1981, concentrated on theatrical projects in Poland and film prods. with non-Polish studios. 1983, gov. dissolved his Studio X film prod. group. 1984, gov. demanded Wajda's resignation as head of filmmakers' assoc. in order to continue org.'s existence. 1989, appt. artistic dir. of Teatr Powszechny, official Warsaw theater. Also leader of the Cultural Comm. of the Citizen's Committee. June 1989, elected senator
PICTURES: Dir.-Writer: A Generation (debut, 1957); I Walk to the Sun; Kanal; Ashes and Diamonds; Lotna; Innocent Sorcerers; Samson; Lady Macbeth of Mtsensk; Warszawa (episode of Love at 20); Ashes; Gates to Paradise; Everything for Sale; Landscape After the Battle; The Wedding; Promised Land; The Shadow Line; Man of Marble; Without Anesthetic; Invitation to the Inside; The Orchestra Conductor; The Girls from Wilko; Man of Iron (Golden Palm Award, Cannes, 1981); Danton; A Love in Germany; A Chronicle of Amorous Accidents, The Possessed, Korczak.
TELEVISION: Poly-Poly; The Birch Wood; Pilate and the Others; The Dead Class; November Night; Crime and Punishment.

WALD, MALVIN: Writer, Producer. b. New York, NY, Aug. 8, 1917. e. Brooklyn Coll., B.A., J.D. Woodland U. Coll. of Law; grad. work Columbia U., NYU, U. of Southern CA. Newspaper reporter and editor, publicist, social worker, radio actor. Screenplays and original stories for Columbia, 20th-Fox, UA, MGM, WB; U.S. Air Force; tech. sgt., wrote 30 doc. films for film unit. Exec. prod., 20th Century Fox TV Doc. Unit, 1963–64 writer-prod. U.S.I.A., 1964–65; writer-prod., Ivan Tors Films, 1965–69; prof., U. of Southern California Sch. of Cinema, Television, 1986–90 bd. of dir.; Writer's Guild of America; 1983–85, Trustee, Writers Guild Foundation, edit. bd. WGA Journal, 1992; Acad. of Motion Picture Arts and Sciences, co-author of book, Three Major Screenplays. Contributor to books, American Screenwriters, Close-Ups. Published s.p., Naked City. Consultant, Natl. Endowment for Humanities and Corp. for Public Broadcasting. Visiting professor, Southern Illinois Univ. Pre-selection judge, Focus writing awards. Media & prod. consultant, Apache Mountain Spirit (PBS); playwright, ANTA-West. Co-author, L.A. Press Club 40th Anniversary Show, 1987. Dramatists Guild. Mag. articles published in Film Comment, Journal of Popular Film & TV, Journal of TV Writers Guild of America, American Heritage, Hollywood: Then and Now, Writers Digest, 1991–92.

PICTURES: The Naked City (Acad. Award nom., best story); Behind Locked Doors, The Dark Past, Ten Gentlemen from West Point, The Powers Girl, Two in a Taxi, Undercover Man, Outrage, On the Loose; (assoc. prod. and sec.-treas., Filmakers Pictures, Inc.); Battle Taxi, Man on Fire, Al Capone, Venus in Furs, In Search of Historic Jesus, Legend of Sleepy Hollow. Shorts: An Answer, Employees Only (Acad. Award nom., best sht. doc.), Boy Who Owned a Melephant (Venice Children's Film Fest. gold medal), Unarmed in Africa, The Policeman, James Weldon Johnson, Me an Alcoholic?, Problem Solving, Managerial Control.

TELEVISION: Many credits including Playhouse 90, Marilyn Monroe, Hollywood: The Golden Years, The Rafer Johnson Story, D-Day, Project: Man in Space, Tales of Hans Christian Andersen, John F. Kennedy, Biography of A Rookie, Alcoa-Goodyear Hour, Climax, Shirley Temple Storybook, Life of Riley, Peter Gunn, Perry Mason, Dobie Gillis, Combat, Moonport (U.S.I.A.; prod., writer), Daktari, (assoc. prod.) Primus, California Tomorrow (prod.), Mod Squad, Untamed World, Around the World of Mike Todd, The Billie Jean King Show, Life and Times of Grizzly Adams, Mark Twain's America, Greatest Heroes of the Bible, Littlest Hobo., Rich Little's You Asked For It, Hugh Hefner's Bunny Memories.

WALD, RICHARD C.: Executive. b. New York, NY, 1931. e. Columbia Coll., Clare Coll. (Cambridge). Joined the New York Herald Tribune in 1951 as Columbia Coll. correspondent; religion editor, political reporter; foreign correspondent (London, Bonn), 1959–63; assoc. editor, 1963–65; mgn. editor from 1965 until paper ceased publication in 1966; Sunday editor, World Journal Tribune, 1966; mgn. editor, Washington Post, 1967; vice president, Whitney Communications Corp., 1967–68; joined National Broadcasting Company as vice president, NBC News, 1968; exec. v.p., 1972; president, NBC News, 1973; sr. v.p., ABC News, 1978.

WALKEN, CHRISTOPHER: Actor. b. Astoria, NY, Mar. 31, 1943. Began career in off-Bdwy. musical Best Foot Forward (Clarence Derwent Award), starring Liza Minnelli. Continued in musicals until cast in original Bdwy. production of The Lion in Winter (Clarence Derwent Award) as King Philip. Obie Award for title role in Kid Champion and Theater World Award for performance in N.Y. City Center revival of The Rose Tattoo. Also in Hurlyburly (Bdwy.) NY Shakespeare Festival: Coriolanus, Othello. Appeared in Madonna video Bad Girl.

PICTURES: The Anderson Tapes (debut, 1971), The Happiness Cage, Next Stop Greenwich Village, The Sentinel, Annie Hall, Roseland, The Deer Hunter (Acad. Award, supp. actor, 1978), Last Embrace, Heaven's Gate, The Dogs of War, Shoot the Sun Down, Pennies from Heaven, Brainstorm, The Dead Zone, A View to a Kill, At Close Range, Deadline, The Milagro Beanfield War, Biloxi Blues, Puss in Boots, Homeboy, Communion, King of New York, The Comfort of Strangers, McBain, All-American Murder, Batman Returns, Mistress, Le Grand Pardon, True Romance, A Business Affair, Wayne's World 2.

TELEVISION: Movies: Sarah: Plain and Tall, Skylark, Scam. Special: Who Am I This Time? Guest: Saturday Night Live.

WALKER, CLINT: Actor. b. Hartford, IL, May 30, 1927. e. schools there. Joined Merchant Marine 1944, worked as sheet metal worker, carpenter, other jobs in Alton, IL; set out with wife and infant daughter for oil fields in TX; decided to try acting. Got screen test at Paramount Studios for Cecil B. De Mille; later landed contract to star in Cheyenne TV films at Warner.

PICTURES: Fort Dobbs, Yellowstone Kelly, Gold of the Seven Saints, None But the Brave, Send Me No Flowers, Maya, Night of the Grizzly, The Dirty Dozen, The Great Bank Robbery, Sam Whisky, More Dead Than Alive, The Phynx, Pancho Villa, Baker's Hawk, The White Buffalo, Hysterical.

TELEVISION: Series: Cheyenne, Kodiak. Movies: Yuma, Hardcase, The Bounty Man, Scream of the Wolf, Killdozer, Snowbeast, Mysterious Island of Beautiful Women, The Gambler Returns: Luck of the Draw. Mini-Series: Centennial.

WALKER, E. CARDON: Executive. b. Rexburg, ID, Jan. 9, 1916. e. UCLA, B.A. 1938. Four years officer, U.S. Navy, Started with Walt Disney Productions 1938; camera, story, unit director short subjects, budget control. Headed, 1950, adv. & pub. 1956, v.p. in chg. of adv. & sales. 1960 member bd. of dir. & exec. comm. 1965 v.p., mkt. 1967 exec. v.p. operations 1968, exec. v.p. and chief operating officer; pres., 1971; Nov. 1976 pres. and chief executive officer; June, 1980, named bd. chmn. & chief executive officer; May, 1983, became chmn. of exec. committee, which position he retained until Sept. 1984. Remains a board member.

WALKER, KATHRYN: Actress. b. Philadelphia, PA, Jan. 9. m. singer-songwriter James Taylor. e. Wells Coll., Harvard.

Studied acting at London Acad. of Music and Dramatic Art on Fulbright Fellowship. Stage roles include part in Private Lives with Elizabeth Taylor and Richard Burton, and Wild Honey with Ian McKellen.

PICTURES: Slap Shot, Rich Kids, Neighbors, D.A.R.Y.L., Dangerous Game, Emma and Elvis.

TELEVISION: Series: Beacon Hill. Movies: The Winds of Kitty Hawk, Too Far to Go, FDR: The Last Year, A Whale for the Killing, Family Reunion, Special Bulletin, The Murder of Mary Phagan. Mini-Series: The Adams Chronicles (Emmy Award, 1976).

WALLACE, MIKE: TV Commentator, Interviewer. b. Brookline, MA, May 9, 1918. e. U. of Michigan, 1939. Night Beat, WABD, N.Y., 1956; The Mike Wallace Interview, ABC, 1956–58; Newspaper col., Mike Wallace Asks, N.Y. Post, 1957–58; News Beat, WNTA-TV, 1959–61; The Mike Wallace Interview, WNTA-TV, 1959–61; Biography, 1962; correspondent, CBS News, 1963, CBS Radio; Personal Closeup, Mike Wallace at Large; Co-editor, 60 Minutes (Emmy Awards, 1971, 1972, 1973), CBS News.

WALLACH, ELI: Actor. b. Brooklyn, NY, Dec. 7, 1915. m. actress Anne Jackson. e. U. of Texas. Capt. in Medical Admin. Corps during W.W.II. After college acting, appeared in summer stock. Made Broadway debut in Skydrift, 1945, followed by Antony & Cleopatra, The Rose Tattoo (Tony Award), Mademoiselle Colombe, Camino Real, Teahouse of August Moon (also London), Major Barbara, Rhinoceros, Luv, Twice Around the Park, Cafe Crown, The Price. Charter member, Actors Studio in 1947.

PICTURES: Baby Doll (debut, 1956; BAFTA Award), The Line Up, The Magnificent Seven, Seven Thieves, The Misfits, Hemingway's Adventures of A Young Man, How the West Was Won, The Victors, Act One, The Moonspinners, Kisses for My President, Lord Jim, Genghis Khan, How to Steal a Million, The Good the Bad and the Ugly, The Tiger Makes Out, How to Save a Marriage and Ruin Your Life, MacKenna's Gold, A Lovely Way to Die, Ace High, The Brain, Zigzag, The People Next Door, The Angle Levine, The Adventures of Gerard, Romance of a Horse Thief, Cinderella Liberty, Crazy Joe, Stateline Motel, Don't Turn the Other Cheek, The Sentinel, Nasty Habits, The Deep, Domino Principle, Girlfriends, Movie Movie, Circle of Iron, Firepower, Winter Kills, The Hunter, The Salamander, Sam's Son, Tough Guys, Nuts, Funny, The Two Jakes, The Godfather Part III, Article 99, Mistress, Night and the City.

TELEVISION: Series: Our Family Honor. Guest: Studio One, Philco Playhouse, Playhouse 90, The Poppy Is Also a Flower (Emmy Award). Movies: Cold Night's Death, Indict and Convict, Seventh Avenue, The Pirate, Fugitive Family, Pride of Jesse Halam, Skokie, The Wall, Anatomy of an Illness, Murder: By Reason of Insanity, Something in Common, Executioner's Song, Christopher Columbus, Embassy, The Impossible Spy, Vendetta: Secrets of a Mafia Bride, Legacy of Lies, Teamster Boss: The Jackie Presser Story.

WALLACH, GEORGE: Producer, Writer, Director. b. New York, NY, Sept. 25, 1918. e. SUNY-Westbury. Actor in theatre & radio 1938–45; U.S. Navy 1942–45; supvr. radio-TV Div. of Amer. Thea. Wing 1946–48; dir., WNEW, 1946–48; prod./dir., Wendy Barrie Show, 1948–49; prod.-dir. for WNBC-WNBT, 1950; Dir., news, spec. events WNBT-WNBC, 1951–52; prod. mgr., NBC Film Div. 1953–56, appt. TV officer, U.S.I.A., 1957. Film-TV officer American Embassy, Bonn, Germany, 1961. Film-TV officer American Embassy; Tehran, Iran, 1965–66; MoPix Prod. Officer, JUSPAO, American Embassy, Saigon, 1966; prod.-dir.-wr., Greece Today, 1967–68. Exec. prod.-dir., George Wallach Productions, spec. doc., travel, and industrial films, chairman, Film-TV Dept., N.Y. Institute of Photography, 1968–75; Prof. film-TV-radio, Brooklyn Coll., 1975–80; Dir., special projects, Directors Guild of America 1978–88; presently international representative for Denver Film Festival, U.S. Contact for Moscow Film Festival, U.S. prod. for A Native for Beijing in NY, a series of 20 1 hr. programs for Beijing TV.

PICTURES: It Happened in Havana, Bwana Devil (assoc. prod., exec. mgr.).

TELEVISION: NBC-producer: Inner Sanctum, The Falcon, His Honor Homer Bell, Watch the World; dir., Wanted, CBS-TV series.

WALSH, J.T.: Actor. b. San Francisco, CA. Did not begin acting until age 30, when quit job in sales to join off-Broadway theater co.

THEATER: Glengarry Glen Ross (Drama Desk Award), Rose, Last Licks, Richard III, Macbeth, Half a Lifetime, American Clock.

PICTURES: Eddie Macon's Run, Hard Choices, Power, Hannah and Her Sisters, Tin Men, House of Games, Good Morning Vietnam, Things Change, Tequila Sunrise, Wired, The Big Picture, Dad, Crazy People, Why Me?, Narrow Margin, Misery, The Grifters, The Russia House, Backdraft, Defenseless, True Identity, Iron Maze, A Few Good Men,

Hoffa, Sniper, National Lampoon's Loaded Weapon 1, Red Rock West, Blue Chips.

TELEVISION: *Movies*: Little Gloria: Happy at Last, Jacobo Timerman: Prisoner Without a Name Cell Without a Number, Right to Kill, Tough Cookies, Windmills of the Gods, In the Shadow of a Killer.

WALSH, M. EMMET: Actor. r.n. Michael Emmet Walsh. b. Ogdensburg, NY, Mar. 22, 1935. e. Clarkson Col. (B.B.A.), Academy of Dramatic Arts (1959–61).

PICTURES: Midnight Cowboy, Stiletto, Alice's Restaurant, End of the Road, Loving, The Traveling Executioner, Little Big Man, Cold Turkey, They Might Be Giants, Escape from the Planet of the Apes, Get to Know Your Rabbit, What's Up Doc?, Kid Blue, Serpico, The Gambler, The Prisoner of 2nd Avenue, At Long Last Love, Mikey and Nicky, Nickelodeon, Bound for Glory, Airport '77, Slap Shot, Straight Time, The Fish That Saved Pittsburgh, The Jerk, Brubaker, Raise the Titanic, Ordinary People, Back Roads, Reds, Cannery Row, The Escape Artist, Blade Runner, Fast-Walking, Silkwood, Scandalous, (Raw) Courage, The Pope of Greenwich Village, Grandview USA, Missing in Action, Blood Simple, Fletch, The Best of Times, Wildcats, Critters, Back to School, Raising Arizona, Harry and the Hendersons, No Man's Land, The Milagro Beanfield War, Sunset, Clean and Sober, Sundown: The Vampire in Retreat, The Mighty Quinn, Red Scorpion, Thundergound, War Party, Catch Me If You Can, Chatta-hoochee, Narrow Margin, White Sands, Killer Image, Equi-nox, The Music of Chance, Bitter Harvest, Wilder Napalm, Cops and Robbersons.

TELEVISION: *Series*: The Sandy Duncan Show, Dear Detective, Unsub. *Movies*: Sarah T.—Portrait of a Teenage Alcoholic, Crime Club, Invasion of Johnson County, Red Alert, Superdome, A Question of Guilt, No Other Love, The Gift, Skag, City in Fear, High Noon Part II, Hellinger's Law, Night Partners, The Deliberate Stranger, Resting Place, Broken Vows, Hero in the Family, The Abduction of Kari Swenson, Murder Ordained, Brotherhood of the Rose, Love and Lies, Fourth Story, Wild Card, Four Eyes and Six-Guns. *Mini-Series*: The French-Atlantic Affair, East of Eden. *Guest*: Julia, Amy Prentiss, The Jimmy Stewart Show, Bonanza, All in the Family, Rockford Files, The Waltons, Nichols, Starsky & Hutch, Amazing Stories, Twilight Zone, The Flash, Jackie Thomas Show, Tales From the Crypt, many others. *Pilot*: Silver Fox.

THEATRE: *Broadway*: Does the Tiger Wear a Necktie?, That Championship Season. *Off-Bdwy*: The Old Glory, The Outside Man, Death of the Well Loved Boy; also summer stock and regional theatre.

WALSTON, RAY: Actor. b. New Orleans, LA, Nov. 2, 1918. Won 1956 Tony Award for Damn Yankees.

TELEVISION: *Series*: My Favorite Martian, Stop Susan Williams, Silver Spoons, Fast Times. *Guest*: You Are There, Producers Showcase, There Shall Be No Night, Studio One, Playhouse 90, Oh Madeline, Crash Course. *Movies*: Institute for Revenge, The Kid With the Broken Halo, The Fall of the House of Usher, This Girl for Hire, The Jerk Too, Amos, Red River, I Know My First Name is Steven, One Special Victory.

PICTURES: Kiss Them For Me (debut, 1957), South Pacific, Damn Yankees, Say One for Me, Tall Story, The Apartment, Portrait In Black, Convicts Four, Wives and Lovers, Who's Minding the Store?, Kiss Me Stupid, Caprice, Paint Your Wagon, The Sting, Silver Streak, The Happy Hooker Goes to Washington, Popeye, Galaxy of Terror, Fast Times at Ridgemont High, O'Hara's Wife, Private School, Johnny Dangerously, RAD, From the Hip, O.C. and Stiggs, A Man of Passion, Blood Relations, Saturday the 14th Strikes Back, Paramedics, Ski Patrol, Blood Salvage, Popcorn, The Player, Of Mice and Men.

WALTER, JESSICA: Actress. b. Brooklyn, NY, Jan. 31, 1944. m. actor Ron Leibman. e. H.S. of the Performing Arts. Studied at Bucks County Playhouse and Neighborhood Playhouse. Many TV performances plus lead in series, For the People. Broadway debut in Advise and Consent, 1961. Also, Photo Finish (Clarence Derwent Award), Night Life, A Severed Head, Rumors.

PICTURES: Lilith (debut, 1964), The Group, Grand Prix, Bye Bye Braverman, Number One, Play Misty For Me, Goldengirl, Going Ape, Spring Fever, The Flamingo Kid, Tapeheads.

TELEVISION: *Series*: For the People, Love of Life, Amy Prentiss (Emmy Award, 1975), Bare Essence, Aaron's Way, Dinosaurs (voice), The Round Table. *Movies*: The Immortal (pilot), Three's a Crowd, They Call It Murder, Women in Chains, Home for the Holidays, Hurricane, Having Babies, Victory at Entebbe, Black Market Baby, Wild and Wooly, Dr. Strange, Secrets of Three Hungry Wives, Vampire, She's Dressed to Kill, Miracle on Ice, Scruples, Thursday's Child, The Return of Marcus Welby M.D., The Execution, Killer in the Mirror. *Mini-Series*: Wheels.

WALTER, TRACEY: Actor. b. Jersey City, NJ, Nov. 25.

PICTURES: Goin' South, Blue Collar, Hardcore, The Hunter, The Hand, Raggedy Man, Honkytonk Man, Timerider, Rumble Fish, Conan the Destroyer, Repo Man, At Close Range, Something Wild, Malone, Mortuary Academy, Married to the Mob, Under the Boardwalk, Out of the Dark, Batman, Homer and Eddie, Young Guns II, The Two Jakes, Pacific Heights, The Silence of the Lambs, City Slickers, Delusion, Amos and Andrew, Philadelphia.

TELEVISION: *Series*: Best of the West, On the Air.

WALTERS, BARBARA: Broadcast Journalist. b. Boston, MA, Sept. 25, 1931. Daughter of Latin Quarter nightclub impres-sario Lou Walters. e. Sarah Lawrence Coll. Began working in TV after graduation. Joined The Today Show in 1961 as writer-researcher, making occasional on-camera appear-ances. In 1963 became full-time on camera. In April, 1974, named permanent co-host. Also hosted own prog., Not for Women Only. In 1976 joined ABC-TV Evening News, (host, 1976–78), correspondent World News Tonight (1978); corresp. 20/20 (1979–present). Host of The Barbara Walters Specials (1979–present). Author: How to Talk with Practically Anybody About Practically Anything (1970). Recipient of numerous awards incl. Emmy, Media, Peabody. Named one of women most admired by American People in 1982 & 84 Gallup Polls. Inducted into the Television Academy Hall of Fame, 1990.

WALTERS, JULIE: Actress. b. Birmingham, England, Feb. 22, 1950. Trained for 2 years to be a nurse before studying drama at Manchester Polytechnic, followed by year at Granada's Stables Theatre. Joined Everyman Theatre, Liver-pool. Also toured Dockland pubs with songs, dance and imitations.

THEATER: Breezeblock Park, Funny Perculiar, The Glad Hand, Good Fun, Educating Rita, Jumpers, Fool for Love, When I Was a Girl I Used to Scream and Shout, Frankie and Johnnie in the Claire de Lune, Macbeth, Having a Ball, The Rose Tattoo, Jumpers, Fool for Love, When I Was a Girl I Used to Scream and Shout, Frankie and Johnny.

PICTURES: Educating Rita, She'll Be Wearing Pink Py-jamas, Car Trouble, Personal Services, Prick Up Your Ears, Buster, Mack the Knife, Killing Dad, Stepping Out, Just Like a Woman, The Clothes in the Wardrobe, Wide Eyed and Legless.

TELEVISION: Unfair Exchanges, Talent, Nearly a Happy Ending, Family Man, Happy Since I Met You, The Secret Diary of Adrian Mole (series), Wood and Walters (series), Say Something Happened, Intensive Care, The Boys from the Black Stuff, Talking Heads, Victoria Wood As Seen on TV (series & special), The Birthday Party, Her Big Chance, Nearly a Happy Ending, Julie Walters & Friends (special), GBH (series), The All-Day Breakfast Show (special).

WANAMAKER, SAM: Actor, Stage producer, Film director. b. Chicago, IL, June 14, 1919. e. Drake U. On Broadway stage as actor, producer, presenter.

THEATER: 1961–62, acting on New York stage in Cafe Crown, Counterattack, This Too Shall Pass, Joan of Lorraine (also dir.), Goodbye My Fancy (also dir.), Caesar & Cleopatra (dir.), The Far Country; prod. dir. Children From Their Games, (N.Y.); Rhinoceros (Washington, D.C.). Opera prods.: King Priam, Forza Del Destino; A Case of Libel (dir.). London West End stage: Winter Journey, The Big Knife, The Threepenny Opera, The Rainmaker; 1956, acting, producing London and Liverpool stage; 1959–60, acting at Stratford-on-Avon; Foun-der and exec. dir.: Shakespeare Globe Trust. Dir. Sydney Opera House Opening, Bankside Festival (prod.), U.S. tour, Shakespeare's Globe, Aida, San Francisco Opera.

PICTURES: My Girl Tisa (debut, 1948), Give Us This Day, Mr. Denning Drives North, The Secret, The Criminal, Taras Bulba, Man in the Middle, Those Magnificent Men in Their Flying Machines, The Spy Who Came in from the Cold, Warning Shot, The Day the Fish Came Out, Danger Route, File of the Golden Goose (dir. only), The Executioner (dir. only), The Eliminator, The Chinese Visitor, Catlow, Voyage of the Damned, Sinbad and the Eye of the Tiger (dir. only), Billy Jack Goes to Washington, Private Benjamin, The Competi-tion, Irreconcilable Differences, The Aviator, Raw Deal, Superman IV, Baby Boom, Judgment in Berlin, Guilty By Suspicion, Pure Luck, City of Joy.

TELEVISION: The Big Wheel, The White Death, A Young Lady of Property (dir.), The Defenders, Oedipus Rex, Russian Self Impressions, Man of World (series), Espionage, Outer Limits. Dir. several episodes The Defenders series, Arturo Ui, War and Peace, The Ferret, Heartsounds, The Berrengers, The Ghost Writer, Sadie and Son, Deceptions, The Law, Baby Boom (series), The Shell Seekers, To Cast a Shadow, A Time to Remember, Killer Rules, Bloodlines: Murder in the Family, Wild Justice.

WANG, WAYNE: Director. b. Hong Kong, 1949. m. actress Cora Miao. e. came to U.S. to study photography at College of Arts and Crafts, Oakland, CA. With a Master's Degree in film and television, returned to Hong Kong. Worked on TV comedy series. First dir. work, as asst. dir. for Chinese sequences of Golden Needle. First film A Man, A Woman and a Killer. Won grant from AFI and National Endowment of the Arts, used to finance Chan is Missing (1982) which cost $22,000.

PICTURES: Chan is Missing (also s.p., editor, prod.), Dim Sum: A Little Bit of Heart (also prod., story), Slam Dance, Eat a Bowl of Tea, Life is Cheap . . . But Toilet Paper is Expensive (also exec. prod., story), Joy Luck Club.

WARD, BURT: Actor, Executive. b. Los Angeles, CA, July 6, 1945. Pres. of Pinnacle Associates, Inc. and the World of Earlybird, a publicly traded holding co. and a children's social value education program, respectively.

TELEVISION: Batman (co-starred as Robin 1966—68).

PICTURES: Batman, Virgin High, Kill Crazy, Hot Under the Collar, Robochic, The Dwelling.

WARD, DAVID S.: Writer, Director. b. Providence, RI, Oct. 24, 1947. e. Pomona Col. (BA), U. of Southern California where attended film school. First script was Steelyard Blues produced at Warner Bros. in 1972 by producers Michael and Julia Phillips, and Tony Bill.

PICTURES: The Sting (Acad. Award, best orig. s.p., 1973), Cannery Row (s.p., dir.), The Sting II (s.p.), The Milagro Beanfield War (co-s.p.), Major League (dir., s.p.), King Ralph (dir., s.p.), Sleepless in Seattle (co-s.p.).

WARD, FRED: Actor. b. San Diego, CA, 1943. Studied at Herbert Berghof Studio. On stage in The Glass Menagerie, One Flew over the Cuckoo's Nest, Angel City, Domino Courts.

PICTURES: Escape from Alcatraz (debut, 1979), Tilt, Carny, Southern Comfort, Timerider, The Right Stuff, Silkwood, Uncommon Valor, Swing Shift, Uforia, Secret Admirer, Remo Williams: The Adventure Begins, Off Limits, Big Business, The Prince of Pennsylvania, Tremors, Miami Blues (also co-exec. prod.), Henry and June, Thunderheart, The Player, Bob Roberts, The Dark Wind, Short Cuts.

TELEVISION: Movies: Belle Starr, Noon Wine, Florida Straits, Cast a Deadly Spell, Backtrack, Four Eyes and Six-Guns. Special: Noon Wine (Amer. Playhouse).

WARD, RACHEL: Actress. b. London, 1957. m. actor Bryan Brown. Top fashion and TV commercial model before becoming actress. Studied acting with Stella Adler and Robert Modica. On stage in Sydney in A Doll's House, Hopping to Byzantium.

PICTURES: Night School, The Final Terror, Sharky's Machine, Dead Men Don't Wear Plaid, Against All Odds, The Good Wife, Hotel Colonial, How to Get Ahead in Advertising, After Dark My Sweet, Christopher Columbus: The Discovery, Wide Sargasso Sea.

TELEVISION: Mini-series: The Thorn Birds, Shadow of the Cobra (U.K.). Movies: Christmas Lillies of the Field. Fortress, And the Sea Will Tell, Black Magic, Double Jeopardy.

WARD, SIMON: Actor. b. London, England, Oct. 19, 1941. Ent. ind. 1964.

PICTURES: If, Frankenstein Must Be Destroyed, I Start Counting, Quest for Love, Young Winston, Hitler—The Last Ten Days, The Three Musketeers, The Four Musketeers, Children of Rage, Deadly Strangers. Aces High, The Battle Flag, The Chosen, Dominique, Zulu Dawn, The Monster Club, Supergirl, Leave All Fair, Double X, Wuthering Heights.

TELEVISION: Spoiled, Chips with Everything, The Corsican Brothers, All Creatures Great and Small, Dracula, The Last Giraffe, Around the World in 80 Days.

WARD, VINCENT: Director, Writer. b. New Zealand, 1956. e. Ilam Sch. of Art. At 21 dir. & co-wrote short film A State of Siege (Hugo Award, Chicago Film Fest.)

PICTURES: In Spring One Plants Alone (Silver Hugo, Chicago Film Fest.), Vigil (Grand Prix Awards, Madrid & Prades Film Fests), The Navigator (Australian Film Awards for Best Picture & Director), Alien3 (story only), Map of the Human Heart.

WARDEN, JACK: Actor. b. Newark, NJ, Sept. 18, 1920. r.n. Jack Warden Lebzelter. With Margo Jones theatre in Dallas (rep. co.).

THEATRE: Bdwy: Golden Boy, Sing Me No Lullaby, Very Special Baby, Cages (Obie Award), Stages A View from the Bridge, The Man in the Glass Booth, The Body Beautiful. Repertory: Twelfth Night, She Stoops to Conquer, Importance of Being Earnest, Summer and Smoke, Taming of the Shrew, etc.

PICTURES: The Frogmen, You're in the Navy Now, The Man With My Face, Red Ball Express, From Here to Eternity, Edge of the City, 12 Angry Men, The Bachelor Party, Darby's Rangers, Run Silent Run Deep, The Sound and the Fury, That Kind of Woman, Wake Men When It's Over, Escape From Zahrain, Donovan's Reef, The Thin Red Line, Blindfold, Bye Bye Braverman, The Sporting Club, Summertree, Who Is Harry Kellerman?, Welcome to the Club, Billy Two Hats, The Man Who Loved Cat Dancing, The Apprenticeship of Duddy Kravitz, Shampoo (Acad. Award nom.), All the President's Men, The White Buffalo, Heaven Can Wait (Acad.

Award nom.), Death on the Nile, The Champ, Dreamer, Beyond the Poseidon Adventure, And Justice for All, Being There, Used Cars, The Great Muppet Caper, Chu Chu and the Philly Flash, Carbon Copy, So Fine, The Verdict, Crackers, The Aviator, September, The Presidio, Everybody Wins, Problem Child, Problem Child 2, Passed Away, Night and the City, Toys, Guilty As Sin.

TELEVISION: Series: Mr. Peepers, Norby, The Asphalt Jungle, The Wackiest Ship in the Army, N.Y.P.D., Jigsaw John, The Bad News Bears, Crazy Like a Fox. Guest: Philco Goodyear Producer's Showcase, Kraft. Movies: The Face of Fear, Brian's Song (Emmy Award, 1972), What's a Nice Girl Like You . . .?, Man on a String, Lt. Schuster's Wife, Remember When, The Godchild, Journey From Darkness, They Only Come Out at Night, Raid on Entebbe, Topper, A Private Battle, Hobson's Choice, Helen Keller: The Miracle Continues, Hoover vs. The Kennedys, The Three Kings, Dead Solid Perfect, Judgment. Mini-Series: Robert Kennedy and His Times, A.D.

WARNER, DAVID: Actor. b. Manchester, England, July 29, 1941. e. Royal Acad. of Dramatic Art. Made London stage debut in Tony Richardson's version of A Midsummer Night's Dream (1962). Four seasons with Royal Shakespeare Co. Theater includes Afore Night Come, The Tempest, The Wars of the Roses, The Government Inspector, Twelfth Night, I Claudius.

PICTURES: Tom Jones (debut, 1963), Morgan!, The Deadly Affair, A King's Story (voice), Work is a Four Letter Word, A Midsummer's Night Dream, The Bofors Gun, The Fixer, The Seagull, Michael Kolhaus, The Ballad of Cable Hogue, Perfect Friday, Straw Dogs, A Doll's House, From Beyond the Grave, Little Malcolm, Mr. Quilp, The Omen, Providence, The Disappearance, Cross of Iron, Silver Bears, Nightwing, The Concorde—Airport '79, Time After Time, The 39 Steps, The Island, The French Lieutenant's Woman, Time Bandits, Tron, The Man With Two Brains, The Company of Wolves, Hansel and Gretel, My Best Friend is a Vampire, Waxworks, Mr. North, Silent Night, Office Party, Hanna's War, Pulse Pounders, Keys to Freedom, Star Trek V: The Final Frontier, S.P.O.O.K.S., Tripwire, Mortal Passions, Teenage Mutant Ninja Turtles II: The Secret of the Ooze, Star Trek VI: The Undiscovered Country, Dark at Noon, Drive.

TELEVISION: Movies: S.O.S. Titantic, Desperado, A Christmas Carol, Hitler's SS—Portrait in Evil, Perry Mason: The Case of the Poisoned Pen, The Secret Life of Ian Fleming, Cast a Deadly Spell, The House on Sycamore Street, Perry Mason: The Case of the Skin-Deep Scandal, John Carpenter Presents Body Bags. Mini-Series: Holocaust, Masada (Emmy Award, 1981), Marco Polo, Wild Palms. Specials: Love's Labour's Lost, Uncle Vanya.

WARNER, JACK JR.: Producer. b. San Francisco, CA, Mar. 27, 1916. p. Jack L. Warner, and Mrs. Albert S. Rogell. e. Beverly Hills H.S.; U. of Southern California, B.A. Entered Warner New York office studying distrib. and exhib. for 1½ years. Transferred to prod. dept. at West Coast studios, then to short subject dept. as assoc. prod. As reserve officer called to active duty in 1942 and served as combat photo unit officer in 164th Signal Photo Co. for one year. Transf. to Signal Corps Photographic Center, Astoria, NY, where participated in prod. Army Signal Corps training films. Was asst. to chief of training films prod. In 1944 assigned to Hq. First U.S. Army Group to assist in planning combat photography for invasion of Europe. Until cessation of hostilities was asst. chief Photo Branch Office of Chief Signal Officer in 12th Army Group and on fall of Germany was on staff of General Eisenhower in Frankfurt as asst. and acting photo officer, Office of the Chief Signal Officer, Theatre Service Forces European Theatre (TSFET). Released from active duty April 20, 1945. Commissioned Lt. Col. Signal Corps Reserve. In 1947 with Warner Bros. Pictures Distrib. Corp., making survey of exhib. and distrib. as related to prod.; liaison between Warner and Assoc. Brit. Pictures on The Hasty Heart, 1948—49; org. Jack M. Warner Prod., Inc., 1949; first film, The Man Who Cheated Himself, distrib. by 20th Cent.-Fox; prod. dept., Warner Bros., 1951; prod. exec. Warners 1953. In charge of TV film prod. for Warners 1955; exec. in charge of television comm. and ind. film dept., Warner Bros. 1956; v.p., Warner Bros. Pictures, Inc., Jan. 1958; Warner association terminated Jan. 1959. Reactivated indep. m.p. co. Jack M. Warner Prod. to prod. feature TV and industrial films; pres., Jack Warner Prods., Inc., prod. theatrical films, 1961; prod., dir., Brushfire; Commissioned Colonel, Signal Corps. U.S. Army Reserve, 1962; 1977—78: Prod.: TV series & films for theatrical and TV, Jack Warner Pdns; writer, 1979—81. Author: Bijou Dream (novel, 1982).1983—87: writer, projected TV series and theatrical films. Completing novel and screenplay.

WARNER, MALCOLM-JAMAL: Actor. b. Jersey City, NJ, Aug. 18, 1970. Raised in Los Angeles. Was 13 years old when signed to play Bill Cosby's son on The Cosby Show.

THEATER: Three Ways Home (off-Bdwy debut, 1988).

TELEVISION: Series: The Cosby Show (also dir. episode), Here and Now. Movies: The Father Clements Story, Mother's Day.

WARREN, GENE: Executive. b. Denver, CO, Aug. 12, 1916. Pres. of Excelsior Prods., prod. co. specializing in special effects and animation. Has headed 2 other cos. of similar nature over past 20 years, functioning at various times as prod., dir., studio prod. head and writer. Producer-director of following shorts: The Tool Box, Suzy Snowflake, Santa and the Three Dwarfs, Land of the Midnight Sun and these documentaries/training films: Mariner I, Mariner III, Apollo, U.S. Navy titles.
Special effects on theatrical features incl: Black Sunday, tom thumb, The Time Machine (Acad. Award), The Wonderful World of the Brothers Grimm, 7 Faces of Dr. Lao, The Power, Legend of Hillybilly John. TV series include: The Man from Atlantis, Land of the Lost, Star Trek, Outer Limits, Twilight Zone, Mission Impossible. TV Movie: Satan's School for Girls.

WARREN, JENNIFER: Actress, Producer. b. New York, NY, Aug. 12, 1941. e. U. of Wisconsin, Madison, B.A. Grad work at Wesleyan U. Studied acting with Uta Hagen at HB Studios. As part of AFI Women's Directing Workshop, directed Point of Departure, short film which received Cine Golden Eagle and Aspen Film Festival Awards. Formed Tiger Rose Productions, indep. film-TV prod. co., 1988. Exec. prod., You Don't Have to Die (Acad. Award, doc. short, 1989).
THEATER: Scuba Duba (off-Bdwy. debut, 1967), 6 RMS RIV VU (Theatre World Award), Harvey, P.S., Your Cat Is Dead, Bdwy: Saint Joan, Volpone, Henry V (Guthrie Theatre).
PICTURES: Night Moves (debut, 1975), Slapshot, Another Man Another Chance, Ice Castles, Fatal Beauty.
TELEVISION: Series: Paper Dolls. Pilots: Double Dare, Knights of the Kitchen Table. Guest: Kojak. Movies: Banjo Hackett: Roamin' Free, Shark Kill, First You Cry, Steel Cowboy, Champions: A Love Story, Angel City, The Choice, The Intruder Within, Freedom, Paper Dolls (pilot), Confessions of a Married Man, Amazons, Full Exposure: The Sex Tape Scandal. Mini-Series: Celebrity.

WARREN, LESLEY ANN: Actress. b. New York, NY, Aug. 16, 1948. Studied acting under Lee Strasberg. Big break came in Rodgers and Hammerstein's Cinderella on TV (1964), where she was seen by Disney scout. Broadway debut in 110 in the Shade (1963), followed by Drat! The Cat! (Theatre World Award).
PICTURES: The Happiest Millionaire (debut, 1967), The One and Only Genuine Original Family Band, Pickup on 101, Harry and Walter Go to New York, Victor/Victoria (Acad. Award nom.), A Night in Heaven, Songwriter, Choose Me, Race to the Yankee Zephyr, Clue, Burglar, Cop, Worth Winning, Life Stinks, Pure Country, Color of Night.
TELEVISION: Series: Mission: Impossible (1970–71). Mini-series: 79 Park Avenue, Pearl, Evergreen. Movies: Seven in Darkness, Love Hate Love, Assignment Munich, The Daughters of Joshua Cabe, The Letters, The Legend of Valentino, Betrayal, Portrait of a Stripper, Beulah Land, Portrait of a Showgirl, A Fight for Jenny, Apology, Baja Oklahoma, Family of Spies, A Seduction in Travis County, In Sickness and in Health, Willing to Kill: The Texas Cheerleader Story. Specials: The Saga of Sonora, It's a Bird It's a Plane It's Superman, A Special Eddie Rabbit, The Dancing Princess, 27 Wagons Full of Cotton, Janie's Got a Gun, Willie Nelson: Big Six-O.

WARRICK, RUTH: Actress. b. St. Joseph, MO, June 29, 1916. Film debut in 1941: Citizen Kane.
PICTURES: Obliging Young Lady, The Corsican Brothers, Journey Into Fear, Forever and a Day, Perilous Holiday, Father of the Bride, The Iron Major, Secret Command, Mr. Winkle Goes to War, Guest in the House, China Sky, Song of the South, Driftwood, Daisy Kenyon, Arch of Triumph, The Great Dan Patch, Make Believe Ballroom, Three Husbands, Let's Dance, One Too Many, Roogie's Bump, The Great Bank Robbery, The Returning.
TELEVISION: Studio One, Robert Montgomery Presents, Lux Star Playhouse, Sometimes I Don't Love My Mother, Peyton Place—The Next Generation. Series: Peyton Place, All My Children.

WASHBURN, DERIC: Writer. b. Buffalo, NY. e. Harvard U., English lit. Has written number of plays, including The Love Nest and Ginger Anne.
PICTURES: Silent Running (co-s.p.), The Deer Hunter (co-s.p.), The Border, Extreme Prejudice.

WASHINGTON, DENZEL: Actor. b. Mt. Vernon, NY, Dec. 28, 1954. e. Fordham U., B.A., journalism. Studied acting with American Conservatory Theatre, San Francisco.
THEATER: When the Chickens Come Home to Roost (Audelco Award), Coriolanus, Spell #7, The Mighty Gents, Ceremonies in Dark Old Men, A Soldier's Play, Checkmates, Richard III.
PICTURES: Carbon Copy (debut, 1981), A Soldier's Story, Power, Cry Freedom (Acad. Award nom.), The Mighty Quinn, For Queen and Country, Glory (Acad. Award & Golden Globe, best supp. actor, 1989), Heart Condition, Mo' Better Blues, Ricochet, Mississippi Masala, Malcolm X (NY Film Critics Award, Acad. Award nom.), Much Ado About Nothing, Philadelphia, The Pelican Brief.

TELEVISION: Movies: Wilma, Flesh and Blood, License to Kill, The George McKenna Story. Series: St. Elsewhere (1982–88).

WASSERMAN, DALE: Writer, Producer. b. Rhinelander, WI, Nov. 2, 1917. Stage: lighting designer, dir., prod.; dir. for. attractions, S. Hurok; began writing, 1954. Founding member & trustee of O'Neill Theatre Centre; artistic dir. Midwest Playwrights Laboratory; member, Acad. M.P. Arts & Sciences; awards include Emmy, Tony, Critics Circle (Broadway), Outer Circle; Writers Guild.
TELEVISION: The Fog, The Citadel, The Power and the Glory, Engineer of Death, The Lincoln Murder Case, I Don Quixote, Elisha and the Long Knives, and others.
PLAYS: Livin' the Life, 998, One Flew Over the Cuckoo's Nest, The Pencil of God, Man of La Mancha, Play With Fire, Shakespeare and the Indians, Mountain High, Western Star, Green.
PICTURES: Cleopatra, The Vikings, The Sea and the Shadow, Quick Before It Melts, Mister Buddwing, A Walk with Love and Death, Man of La Mancha.

WASSERMAN, LEW: Executive. b. Cleveland, OH, March 15, 1913. National dir. advertising and publ. Music Corporation of Amer. 1936–38; v.p. 1938–39; v.p. motion picture div. 1940; Chairman of the bd., Chief Executive Officer, MCA, Inc., Universal City, CA. Received Jean Hersholt Humanitarian Award, 1973.

WASSON, CRAIG: Actor. b. Ontario, OR, March 15, 1954. Also musician/songwriter.
THEATRE: Godspell, All God's Chillun Got Wings, Death of a Salesman (also wrote incidental music), Jock, Children of Eden, M. Butterfly, Skin of Our Teeth, etc. Wrote incidental music for prod. of The Glass Menagerie.
PICTURES: Rollercoaster, The Boys in Company C (also wrote and performed song "Here I Am"), Go Tell the Spartans, The Outsider, Carny, Schizoid, Ghost Story, Four Friends, Second Thoughts (also wrote and performed music), Body Double, The Men's Club, A Nightmare on Elm Street 3, The Trackers, Moonlight Sonata, Malcolm X, Bum Rap (also wrote and performed music).
TELEVISION: Series: Phyllis (also wrote and performed orig. songs), Skag, One Life to Live. Guest: M*A*S*H, Baa Baa Black Sheep, Rockford Files, Hart to Hart, L.A. Law, Kung Fu: The Legend Continues. Movies: The Silence, Mrs. R's Daughter, Skag, Thornwell, Why Me?, Strapped. Specials: A More Perfect Union, Innocents Abroad.

WATANABE, GEDDE: Actor. b. Ogden, UT, June 26. Trained for stage at American Conservatory Theatre, San Francisco. Appeared with N.Y. Shakespeare Fest. Shakespeare in the Park series and with Pan Asian Repertory Theatre, N.Y.
THEATER: Pacific Overtures (debut, as Tree Boy, Bdwy. and on tour, 1976), Oedipus the King, Bullet Headed Birds, Poor Little Lambs.
PICTURES: Sixteen Candles (debut, 1984), Volunteers, Gung Ho, Vamp, UHF, The Spring.
TELEVISION: Series: Gung Ho. Movie: Miss America: Behind the Crown.

WATERHOUSE, KEITH: Writer. b. Leeds, England, Feb. 6, 1929. Early career as journalist, novelist. Author of There is a Happy Land, Billy Liar, Jubb, The Bucket Shop. Ent. m.p. ind. 1960.
PICTURES: s.p. (with Willis Hall): Whistle Down The Wind, A Kind of Loving, Billy Liar, Man in the Middle, Pretty Polly, Lock Up Your Daughters, The Valiant, West Eleven.
TELEVISION: (series): Inside George Webley, Queenie's Castle, Budgie, Billy Liar, There is a Happy Land, Charters and Caldicott.

WATERS, JOHN: Director, Writer. b. Baltimore, MD, Apr. 22, 1946. Renowned for elevating "bad taste" to outrageous high comedy. First short film Hag in a Black Leather Jacket (1964) shot in Baltimore, as are most of his films. Other shorts include Roman Candles, and Eat Your Makeup. Feature debut, Mondo Trasho.
PICTURES: Mondo Trasho (dir., prod., s.p., photo., edit.; film marked debut of Divine), Multiple Maniacs (dir., prod., editor, sound), Pink Flamingos (dir., prod., s.p., photo., edit.), Female Trouble (dir., s.p., photo., prod.), Desperate Living (dir., prod., s.p.), Polyester (filmed in "Odorama" complete with scratch and sniff cards, prod., dir., s.p.), Something Wild (actor only), Hairspray (dir., s.p., co-prod., actor), Homer and Eddie (actor only), Cry-Baby (dir., s.p.), Serial Mom (dir., s.p.).

WATERSTON, SAM: Actor. b. Cambridge, MA, Nov. 15, 1940. e. Yale U. Spent jr. year at Sorbonne in Paris as part of the Amer. Actors' Workshop run by American dir. John Berry. Broadway debut in Oh Dad Poor Dad . . . (1963). Film debut, The Plastic Dome of Norma Jean (made 1965; unreleased). TV debut Pound (Camera Three). Helped work in New York Shakespeare Festival prods. since As You Like It (1963).
THEATER: N.Y. Shakespeare Festival: As You Like It, Ergo, Henry IV (Part I & II), Cymbeline, Hamlet, Much Ado

About Nothing, The Tempest. *Off Bdwy*: The Knack, La Turista, Waiting for Godot, The Three Sisters. *Broadway*: The Paisley Convertible, Halfway Up the Tree, Indian, Hay Fever, The Trial of Cantonsville Nine, A Meeting by the River, Much Ado About Nothing (Drama Desk and Obie Awards), A Doll's House, Lunch Hour, Benefactors, A Walk in the Woods.

PICTURES: Fitzwilly (debut, 1967), Three, Generation, Cover Me Babe, Mahoney's Estate, Who Killed Mary What's 'er Name?, Savages, The Great Gatsby, Journey Into Fear, Rancho Deluxe, Sweet Revenge, Capricorn One, Interiors, Eagle's Wing, Sweet William, Hopscotch, Heaven's Gate, The Killing Fields, Warning Sign, Hannah and Her Sisters, Just Between Friends, A Certain Desire, The Devil's Paradise, September, Welcome Home, Crimes and Misdemeanors, The Man in the Moon, Mindwalk, A Captive in the Land, Serial Mom.

TELEVISION: *Specials*: Pound, Robert Lowell, The Good Lieutenant, Much Ado About Nothing, Oppenheimer, A Walk in the Woods. *Movies*: The Glass Menagerie, Reflections of Murder, Friendly Fire, Games Mother Never Taught You, In Defense of Kids, Dempsey, Finnegan Begin Again, Love Lives On, The Fifth Missile, The Room Upstairs, Terrorist on Trial: The United States vs. Salim Ajami, Gore Vidal's Lincoln, Lantern Hill, The Shell Seekers. *Mini-Series*: The Nightmare Years, The Civil War (voice). *Series*: Q.E.D., I'll Fly Away. *Guest*: Amazing Stories.

WATKIN, DAVID: Director of Photography. b. Margate, Eng., March 23, 1925. Entered British documentary industry in Jan., 1948. With British Transport Films as asst. cameraman, 1950–55; as cameraman, 1954–61. Feature film debut The Knack beginning long creative relationship with director Richard Lester.

PICTURES: The Knack (1965), Help!, Marat/Sade, How I Won the War, Charge of the Light Brigade, The Bed-Sitting Room, Catch-22, The Devils, The Boyfriend, The Homecoming, A Delicate Balance, The Three Musketeers, The Four Musketeers, Mahogany, To the Devil a Daughter, Robin and Marian, Joseph Andrews, Hanover Street, Cuba, That Summer, Endless Love, Chariots of Fire, Yentl, The Hotel New Hampshire, Return to Oz, White Nights, Out of Africa (Acad. Award, 1985), Moonstruck, Sky Bandits, Masquerade, The Good Mother, Last Rites, Journey to the Center of the Earth, Memphis Belle, Hamlet, The Object of Beauty, This Boy's Life.

WATKINS, GRATH: Actor. b. London, Aug. 8, 1922. e. University Coll. Sch. Served in Royal Air Force 1944–45. Entered films in 1945 with role in The Captive Heart.

PICTURES: Bedelia, Gaiety George, A Matter of Life and Death, The Hanging Judge, Goodbye Mr. Chips, Cromwell, The Rise and Fall of Michael Rimmer, Virgin Witch, Fright, Naughty, Twins of Evil, Mary Queen of Scots, Steptoe and Son, Henry VIII, Cinderella, The Omen.

TELEVISION: People in Conflict (Canada).

WATTLES, JOSHUA S.: Executive. b. New York, NY, Apr. 13, 1951. Now sr. v.p. and deputy gen. counsel also in chg. of music matters for Paramount Pictures. Previously worked with Richard Zimbert, exec. v.p. Prior to joining Para. legal dept. in 1981 was atty. in office of gen. counsel at ASCAP. Member N.Y. and Calif. Bars.

WAX, MORTON DENNIS: Public Relations Executive. b. New York, NY, March 13, 1932. e. Brooklyn Coll., 1952. President of Morton Dennis Wax & Assoc., Inc., p.r. and marketing firm servicing intl. creative marketplace, established 1956. Contrib. writer to Box Office Magazine, Film Journal. Recent articles: Creativity (Advertising Age), Rolling Stone's Marketing Through Music, Words & Music, Campaign Magazine, Songwriters Guild of America National Edition. As sect. of VPA, conceptualized intl. Monitor Award, an annual event, currently under auspices of ITS. Public relations counsel to London Intl. Advertising Awards. Member: The Public Relations Society of America, Natl. Acad. of TV Arts & Sciences, Natl. Acad. of Recording Arts & Sciences, Publishers Publicity Assoc. Creator of Brother Can You Spare a Dime Day, first natl. fund raising day for the homeless, 1993.

WAYANS, DAMON: Actor. b. New York, NY, 1960. Brother of comedian-actor Keenen Ivory Wayans. Started as stand up comedian.

TELEVISION: *Series*: Saturday Night Live (1985–6), In Living Color (also writer). *Special*: The Last Stand? (HBO). PICTURES: Beverly Hills Cop (debut, 1984), Hollywood Shuffle, Roxanne, Colors, Punchline, I'm Gonna Git You Sucka, Earth Girls Are Easy, Look Who's Talking Too (voice), The Last Boy Scout, Mo' Money (also s.p., co-exec. prod.), Last Action Hero (cameo).

WAYANS, KEENEN IVORY: Actor, Director, Writer. b. NYC, June 8, 1958. e. Tuskegee Inst. Began as stand-up comic at The Improv in NYC and L.A. Brother of comedian-actor Damon Wayans.

TELEVISION: *Series*: For Love and Honor, In Living Color (also exec. prod. & writer; Emmy Award 1990). *Guest*:

Benson, Cheers, CHiPS, A Different World. *Special*: Partners in Crime (also co-writer).

PICTURES: Star 80, Hollywood Shuffle (also co-s.p.), Eddie Murphy Raw (co-prod., co-s.p. only), I'm Gonna Git You Sucka (also dir., s.p.), The Five Heartbeats (co-s.p. only).

WAYLAND, LEN: Actor. b. California, Dec. 28. e. Junior Coll., Modesto, CA. Wrote, prod. weekly radio series 1939–41, KPAS, KTRB, Calif. Service, radar navigator, 1941–45; en. theatre, Tobacco Road, 1946; 1973, formed Len Wayland Prods. for prod. of theatrical pictures and TV series. In 1976–77: prod./dir.: Don't Let It Bother You. 1978, prod., dir., You're not there yet, for own co.

THEATRE: Played summer and winter stock 1947–49. Bdwy, Streetcar Named Desire, 1949, and tour; toured, Heaven Can Wait; My Name Is Legion; Love of Four Colonels, Stalag 17, prod., USA (off-Bdwy); A Man For All Seasons, Bdwy.

TELEVISION: A Time to Live (serial), First Love, 1955; Armstrong Circle Theatre, Justice, Sgt. Bilko, Kraft Theatre; Dr. Weaver, From These Roots. Profiles in Courage, Dr. Kildare, Gunsmoke, Slattery's People, Ben Casey, A Noise in the World, Love Is a Many Splendored Thing; Dragnet, Outsider; Ironside, Name of the Game, The Bold Ones, Daniel Boone, The Virginian, Project U.F.O., Sam (series), The Blue and the Gray, Hunter, A-Team, Dallas, Amy on the Lips, Generations (serial).

WAYNE, DAVID: Actor, r.n. Wayne David McKeekan; b. Traverse City, MI, Jan. 30, 1914. e. Western Michigan U., 1935. In 1936 appeared in Shakespearean Rep., Cleveland Expo., marionette shows.

THEATRE: *Broadway*: Finian's Rainbow (Tony Award, 1947), Mister Roberts, Teahouse of the August Moon (Tony Award, 1954), The Happy Time.

PICTURES: Portrait of Jennie (debut, 1949), Adam's Rib, The Reformer and the Redhead, My Blue Heaven, Stella, M, Up Front, As Young As You Feel, With a Song in My Heart, Wait 'Til the Sun Shines Nellie, We're Not Married, O. Henry's Full House, The Tender Trap, The Naked Hills, The Three Faces of Eve, The Sad Sack, The Last Angry Man, The Big Gamble, The Andromeda Strain, The African Elephant (narrator), Huckleberry Finn, The Front Page, The Apple Dumpling Gang, The Prize Fighter, Finders Keepers.

TELEVISION: *Series*: Norby, The Adventures of Ellery Queen, Dallas, House Calls. *Specials*: Ruggles of Red Gap, The Strawberry Blonde, The Devil and Daniel Webster, Teahouse of the August Moon (Hallmark), Arsenic and Old Lace, The Boy Who Stole the Elephants (Disney), Benjamin Franklin: The Statesman. *Guest*: Studio One, G.E. Theatre, Twilight Zone (Escape Clause), Batman, Night Gallery, Medical Center, Hawaii Five-O, Family, St. Elsewhere, Murder She Wrote, many others. *Movies*: The FBI Story: The FBI vs. Alvin Karpis - Public Enemy Number One, Ellery Queen (pilot; a.k.a. Too Many Suspects), In the Glitter Palace, Murder at the Mardi Gras, The Girls in the Office, The Gift of Love, An American Christmas Carol, Poker Alice. *Mini-Series*: Once an Eagle, Black Beauty, Loose Change.

WAYNE, JOEL: Executive. Began career with Grey Advertising; in 17 years won many awards (60 Clios, 25 N.Y. Art Director Club Awards, etc.). Was exec. v.p. & creative dir. of agency when left in 1979 to join Warner Bros. as v.p., creative adv. 1987, named sr. v.p., worldwide creative adv.

WAYNE, MICHAEL A.: Executive. r.n. Michael A. Morrison. b. Los Angeles, CA, Nov. 23, 1934. Son of late actor John Wayne. e. Loyola H.S.; Loyola U., B.B.A. Asst. dir., various companies, 1955–56; asst. dir., Revue Prods., 1956–57; pres. Batjac Prods, and Romina Prods., 1961; asst. to producer: China Doll, 1957; Escort West; The Alamo; prod.; McLintock!; co-prod., Cast Giant Shadow; prod. The Green Berets; exec. prod. Chisum; prod. Big Jake; prod. The Train Robbers; prod. Cahill, U.S. Marshall, exec. prod. McQ, Brannigan.

WAYNE, PATRICK: Actor. b. Los Angeles, July 15, 1939. e. Loyola U, 1961, BS in biology. Son of late actor John Wayne. Made film debut at age 11 in Rio Grande with father.

PICTURES: The Searchers, The Alamo, The Comancheros, McClintock, Cheyenne Autumn, Shenandoah, An Eye for an Eye, The Green Berets, The Deserter, Big Jake, The Gatling Gun, Beyond Atlantis, The Bears and I, Mustang Country, Sinbad and the Eye of the Tiger, The People Time Forgot, Rustler's Rhapsody, Young Guns, Her Alibi, Chill Factor.

TELEVISION: *Series*: The Rounders, Shirley. *Movies*: Sole Survivor, Yesterday's Child, Flight to Holocaust, The Last Hurrah, Three on a Date. *Guest*: Frank's Place.

WEAKLAND, KEVIN L.: Producer, Entertainer. b. Philadelphia, PA, Aug. 14, 1963. e. Holy Family Coll. 1977–82, entertainment consultant and actor; 1982–present, entertainment producer and financier as well as entertainer (singer-actor). Company: KLW International, Inc.

MEMBER: Association of Independent Video and Film-makers; National Academy of Video Arts & Sciences; Mid-Atlantic Arts Consortium; National Music Publishers Assn.; New Jersey Associations of Media Artists.

WEATHERS, CARL: Actor. b. New Orleans, LA, Jan. 14, 1948. e. San Diego Univ.
PICTURES: Bucktown, Friday Foster, Rocky, Close Encounters of the Third Kind, Semi-Tough, Force Ten From Navarone, Rocky II, Death Hunt, Rocky III, Rocky IV, Predator, Action Jackson, Hurricane Smith.
TELEVISION: Series: Fortune Dane, Tour of Duty. Movies: The Hostage Heart, The Bermuda Depths, Dangerous Passion, Street Justice.

WEAVER, DENNIS: Actor, Director. b. Joplin, MO, June 4, 1925. e. U. of Oklahoma, B.A., fine arts, 1948.
TELEVISION: Series: Gunsmoke (1955–64; Emmy Award, 1959), Kentucky Jones (1964–65), Gentle Ben (1967–69), McCloud (1970–76), Stone (1979–80), Emerald Point NAS (1983–84), Buck James (1987–88). Movies: McCloud: Who Killed Miss USA?, The Forgotten Man, Duel, Rolling Man, Female Artillery, The Great Man's Whiskers, Terror on the Beach, Intimate Strangers, The Islander, Ishi: The Last of His Tribe, The Ordeal of Patty Hearst, Stone (pilot), Amber Waves, The Ordeal of Dr. Mudd, The Day the Loving Stopped, Don't Go to Sleep, Cocaine: One Man's Seduction, Bluffing It, Disaster at Silo 7, The Return of Sam McCloud (also co-exec. prod.). Mini-Series: Centennial, Pearl. Special: Mastergate.
PICTURES: Horizons West, The Raiders, The Redhead From Wyoming, The Lawless Breed, Mississippi Gambler, Law and Order, It Happens Every Thursday, War Arrow, Dangerous Mission, Dragnet, Seven Angry Men, Touch of Evil, The Gallant Hours, Duel at Diablo, Way Way Out, Gentle Giant, A Man Called Sledge, What's the Matter with Helen?, Mission Batangas, Walking After Midnight.

WEAVER, FRITZ: Actor. b. Pittsburgh, PA, Jan. 19, 1926. e. U. of Chicago. On stage in Chalk Garden (Theatre World Award), Miss Lonelyhearts, All American, Shot in the Dark, Baker Street, Child's Play (Tony, 1970), The Price, The Crucible, etc.
PICTURES: Fail Safe (debut, 1964), The Maltese Bippy, A Walk in the Spring Rain, Company of Killers, The Day of the Dolphin, Marathon Man, Demon Seed, Black Sunday, The Big Fix, Jaws of Satan, Creepshow, Power.
TELEVISION: Movies: The Borgia Stick, Berlin Affair, Heat of Anger, The Snoop Sisters, Hunter, The Legend of Lizzie Borden, Captains Courageous, The Hearst and Davies Affair, A Death in California, My Name is Bill W, Ironclads, Citizen Cohn, Blind Spot. Mini-Series: Holocaust, The Martian Chronicles, Dream West, I'll Take Manhattan.

WEAVER, SIGOURNEY: Actress. r.n. Susan Weaver. b. New York, NY, Oct. 8, 1949. e. Stanford U., Yale U. Daughter of Sylvester "Pat" Weaver, former NBC pres. Mother, actress Elizabeth Inglis (one-time contract player for Warner Bros.). After college formed working partnership with fellow student Christopher Durang for off-Bdwy. improvisational productions. First professional appearance on stage in 1974 in The Constant Wife with Ingrid Bergman. Formed Goat Cay Prods.
THEATER: Off-Off-Bdwy: The Nature and Purpose of the Universe. Off-Bdwy: Titanic/Das Lusitania Songspiel (also co-writer), Gemini (by Yale class mate Albert Innaurato), Marco Polo Sings a Solo, New Jerusalem, The Merchant of Venice, Beyond Therapy. Bdwy: Hurlyburly.
PICTURES: Madman (Israeli; debut, 1976), Annie Hall, Alien, Eyewitness, The Year of Living Dangerously, Deal of the Century, Ghostbusters, One Woman or Two, Aliens, Half Moon Street, Gorillas in the Mist, Working Girl, Ghostbusters II, Alien 3 (also co-prod.), 1492: Conquest of Paradise, Dave.
TELEVISION: Series: The Best of Families (PBS), Somerset. Special: The Sorrows of Gin.

WEAVER, SYLVESTER L., JR.: Executive. b. Los Angeles, CA, Dec. 21, 1908. e. Dartmouth Coll. Daughter is actress Sigourney Weaver. CBS, Don Lee Network, 1932–35; Young & Rubicam adv. agency, 1935–38; adv. mgr., American Tobacco Co., 1938–47; v.p. Young & Rubicam, 1947–49; joined NBC as v.p., chg. TV, 1949; appt'd v.p. chg. NBC Radio & TV networks, 1952; vice-chmn. bd., NBC, Jan., 1953; pres., NBC, Dec., 1953; bd. chmn., Dec. 1955; As head of NBC during TV's formative years, Weaver is credited as the father of TV talk/service program, founding both Tonight and Today shows, also innovated the rotating multi-star anthology series, the Wide Wide World series and concept of TV "special." Own firm, 430 Park Avenue., N.Y., 1956; chmn. of bd. McCann-Erickson Corp. (Intl.), 1959; pres., Subscription TV, Inc. Comm. Consultant in Los Angeles, CA and President, Weaver Productions, Inc. On magazine series Television: Inside and Out (1981–82).
AWARDS: Emmy Trustees' and Governor's Award (1967) and Governor's Award (1983), TV Hall of Fame (1984), NAB Hall of Fame (1986).

WEBB, CHLOE: Actress. b. New York, NY. e. Boston Conservatory of Music and Drama. On stage with Boston Shakespeare Co., Goodman Theatre in Chicago and Mark Taper Forum, L.A. In Forbidden Broadway (Off-Bdwy. and L.A.) impersonating Angela Lansbury, Mary Martin and Carol Channing.
PICTURES: Sid and Nancy (debut, 1986); Twins, Heart Condition, The Belly of an Architect, Queens Logic.
TELEVISION: Guest: Remington Steele, China Beach (pilot). Series: Thicke of the Night. Special: Who Am I This Time? Movies: Lucky Day, Silent Cries.

WEBSTER, R.A.: Executive. b. Montreal, Canada, 1933. e. Bishop's Univ. (BA), Univ. of New Brunswick (BCL) and Univ. of London (LLM). Early career as barrister and solicitor. Ent. m.p. ind. 1961 as asst. company secretary, Associated British Picture Corp. 1966: booking dir., Associated British Cinemas; 1974: managing dir., Associated British Cinemas; 1979: chmn.-mgn. dir., Thorn EMI Cinemas; 1981: dir. of product acquisition, Thorn EMI Screen Entertainment; 1986: pres., theatre div., Cinema International Corp. BV (CIC).

WEDGEWORTH, ANN: Actress. b. Abilene, TX, Jan. 21, 1935. e. U. of Texas. On stage in Thieves, Blues for Mr. Charlie, Chapter Two (Tony Award, 1978), etc.
PICTURES: Bang the Drum Slowly, Scarecrow, The Catamount Killing, Law and Disorder, Dragonfly (One Summer Love), Birch Interval, Handle with Care, Thieves, No Small Affair, Sweet Dreams, The Men's Club, Made in Heaven, A Tiger's Tale, Far North, Miss Firecracker, Steel Magnolias, Green Card.
TELEVISION: Series: The Edge of Night, Another World, Somerset, Three's Company, Filthy Rich, Evening Shade. Movies: The War Between the Tates, Bogie, Elvis and the Beauty Queen, Killjoy, Right to Kill?, A Stranger Waits, Cooperstown. Pilot: Harlan & Merleen.

WEILER, GERALD E.: Producer. b. Mannheim, Germany, May 8, 1928. e. Harvard, 1946–48; Columbia, B.S., 1949–51; New York U. Grad. Sch., 1951–53. Writer, WHN, N.Y. writer, sports ed., news ed., Telenews Prod., Inc., 1948–52; asst. to prod., Richard de Rochemont, Vavin, Inc., 1952; U.S. Army, 1953–55; v.p. Vavin Inc. 1955–73; President, Weiler Communications Inc. 1973. Winner, NY "Lotto" Lottery, 1988; retired 1989.

WEILL, CLAUDIA: Director. b. New York, NY 1947. e. Radcliffe, B.A., 1969. Teacher of acting, Cornish Institute, 1983; guest lecturer on film directing, NYU and Columbia U. Winner of Donatello Award, best director, 1979; Mademoiselle Woman of the Year, 1974; AFI Independent Filmmakers Grant, 1973. Worked as prod. asst. on doc. Revolution.
THEATER: An Evening for Merlin Finch (debut, 1975, Williamstown), Stillife, Found a Peanut, The Longest Walk.
PICTURES: Doc. shorts: This Is the Home of Mrs. Levant Grahame; Roaches' Serenade. Director: The Other Half of the Sky—A China Memoir, Girlfriends, It's My Turn.
TELEVISION: The 51st State, Sesame Street, Joyce at 34, The Great Love Experiment, thirtysomething. Movie: A Child Lost Forever.

WEINBLATT, MIKE: Television Executive. b. Perth Amboy, NJ, June 10, 1929. e. Syracuse U. Served in Army as counter-intelligence agent, mostly in Japan (1952–53). Joined NBC in 1957; has headed two major TV network functions—talent/program admin. & sls. Joined network business affairs dept. in 1958 as mgr., business affairs, facilities operations; rose to post of director, pricing & financial services before moving to sales in November, 1962, as mgr., participating program sales. Named v.p., eastern sales, NBC-TV, 1968. Named v.p., talent & program admin., October, 1968; promoted to v.p. sales, February, 1973. January, 1975 named sr. v.p., sales; later became exec. v.p. Appointed exec. v.p. & gen. mgr. of NBC TV network in August, 1977. Appointed Pres., NBC Entertainment, 1978. 1980, joined Showtime/Movie Channel as pres. & chief oper. off. 1984, pres., Multi Media Entertainment. 1990, chmn. Weinblatt Communications Inc. 1991, mng. dir. Interequity Capital Corp.

WEINGROD, HERSCHEL: Writer, Producer. b. Milwaukee, WI, Oct. 30, 1947. e. U. of Wisconsin, 1965–69; London Film Sch., 1969–71.
PICTURES: Co-writer with Timothy Harris: Cheaper to Keep Her, Trading Places (BAFTA nom., best orig. s.p.; NAACP Image Award, best m.p., 1983), Brewster's Millions, My Stepmother Is An Alien, Paint It Black, Twins (People's Choice Award, best comedy 1988), Kindergarten Cop, Pure Luck, Falling Down.
TELEVISION: Street of Dreams (exec. prod.).

WEINSTEIN, HENRY T.: Executive Producer. b. New York, NY, July 12, 1924. e. City Coll. of New York, Carnegie Inst. of Technology. Dir. of: the Brattle Theatre, Theatre in the Round, Houston, Texas. Prod. for The Theatre Guild, N.Y. Producer, 20th Century-Fox, M.G.M. Exec. in chg. of prod. American Film Theatre, Skyfield Productions. Currently, v.p., creative affairs, Cannon Films.

PICTURES: Tender is the Night, Joy in the Morning, Cervantes, Madwoman of Chaillot, The Battle of Neretva, Magic Christian, A Delicate Balance, The Homecoming, The Iceman Cometh, Lost in the Stars, Butley, Luther, Rhinoceros, Galileo, The Man in the Glass Booth, In Celebration, Runaway Train, 52 Pick-Up, Texasville.
TELEVISION: Play of the Week series, prod.

WEINSTEIN, PAULA: Independent Producer. b. Nov. 19, 1945. e. Columbia U. Daughter of late prod. Hannah Weinstein. Partnered with Gareth Wigan in WW Productions at Warner Brothers. Started as theatrical agent with William Morris and International Creative Management. With Warner Brothers, 1976–78 as production v.p.; left to go to 20th Century-Fox in same capacity. Named Fox sr. v.p., worldwide prod. In 1980 appointed v.p., prod., the Ladd Company. 1981, joined United Artists as pres., motion picture div. In 1983, began own prod. company at Columbia Pictures, also serving as a consultant for Columbia. 1987, joined MGM as exec. consultant. Prod.: A Dry White Season, The Fabulous Baker Boys, The Rose and the Jackal (TV). With husband Mark Rosenberg formed Spring Creek Productions.

WEINTRAUB, FRED: Executive, Producer. b. Bronx, NY, April 27, 1928. e. U. of Pennsylvania Wharton Sch. of Business. Owner of The Bitter End Coffeehouse to 1971. Personal management, Campus Coffee House Entertainment Circuit; TV Production Hootenanny, Popendipity; syndicated TV show host: From The Bitter End; motion picture prod.; v.p., creative services, Warner Bros. 1969, exec. in chg. Woodstock; prod. motion pictures, Weintraub-Heller Productions, 1974; then Fred Weintraub Productions, which became Weintraub/Kuhn Prods. in 1990.
PICTURES: Enter The Dragon, Rage, Black Belt Jones, Truck Turner, Golden Needles, Animal Stars, Hot Potato, The Ultimate Warrior, Dirty Knights Work, Those Cuckoo Crazy Animals, Crash, Outlaw Blues, The Pack, The Promise, Tom Horn, Battle Creek Brawl, Force Five, High Road to China, Out of Control, Gymkata, Princess Academy, Born to Ride.
TELEVISION: My Father My Son (prod.) Trouble Bound, Dead Wrong, documentaries JFK Assassination, The Bruce Lee Story.

WEINTRAUB, JERRY: Producer. b. New York, NY, Sept. 26, 1937. m. former singer Jayne Morgan. Sole owner and chmn. of Management Three, representing entertainment personalities, including John Denver, John Davidson, Frank Sinatra, Neil Diamond, etc. Also involved with Intercontinental Broadcasting Systems, Inc. (cable programming) and Jerry Weintraub/Armand Hammer Prods. (production co.). 1985, named United Artists Corp. chmn. Resigned, 1986. 1987: formed Weintraub Entertainment Group.
PICTURES: Nashville, Oh God!, Cruising, All Night Long, Diner, The Karate Kid, The Karate Kid Part II, The Karate Kid Part III, Pure Country, The Firm (actor), The Next Karate Kid.

WEINTRAUB, SY: Executive. b. New York, NY, 1923. e. U. of Missouri, B.A., journalism, 1947; graduate of American Theater Wing. Started career in 1949 forming with associates a TV syndication co., Flamingo Films, Inc., which merged with Associated Artists to form Motion Pictures for Television, Inc., largest syndicator at that time. He originated Superman and Grand Ol' Opry series for TV. In 1958 bought Sol Lesser Prods., owners of film rights for Tarzan, and began producing and distributing Tarzan films through Banner Productions, Inc. Also formerly chmn. of bd. of Panavision, Inc.; bd. mem. and pres. of National General Television Corp., and pres. of KMGM-TV in Minneapolis. In 1978 named chmn. of Columbia Pictures Industries' new Film Entertainment Group, also joining office of the chief executive of CPI.

WEIR, PETER: Director, Writer. b. Sydney, Australia, Aug. 8, 1944. e. attended Scots Coll. and Sydney U. Briefly worked selling real estate, traveled to Eng. 1965. Entered Australian TV industry as stagehand 1967 while prod. amateur revues. Dir. shorts: Count Vim's Last Exercise, The Life and Times of Reverend Buck Shotte, Homeside, Incredible Floridas, What Ever Happened to Green Valley ? 1967–73.
PICTURES: First prof. credit: director-writer of Michael, an episode of the feature, Three To Go (1970). Director: The Cars that Ate Paris (also s.p., co-story; a.k.a. The Cars That Eat People), Picnic at Hanging Rock, The Last Wave (also s.p.), The Plumber (also s.p.), Gallipoli (also story), The Year of Living Dangerously (also co-s.p.), Witness, The Mosquito Coast, Dead Poets Society, Green Card (also prod., s.p.), Fearless.

WEIS, DON: Writer, Director, Producer. b. Milwaukee, WI, May 13, 1922. e. U. of Southern California.
PICTURES: (dial. dir.) Body and Soul, The Red Pony, Champion, Home of the Brave, The Men; (dir.) Letter From a Soldier, sequence in It's a Big Country, Bannerline, Just This Once, You for Me, I Love Melvin, Remains To Be Seen, A Slight Case of Larceny, Half a Hero, Affairs of Dobie Gillis, Adventures of Haiji Baba, Ride the High Iron, Catch Me If You

Can, Gene Krupa Story, Critic's Choice, Looking for Love, The King's Pirate, Repo.
TELEVISION: Dear Phoebe. Best TV director, 1956, 1958. Screen Dir. Guild, The Longest Hundred Miles, It Takes a Thief, Ironside, M*A*S*H., Happy Days, Planet of the Apes, Bronk, Petrocelli, The Magician, Mannix, Night Stalker, Barbary Coast, Courtship of Eddie's Father, Starsky & Hutch, Hawaii Five-O, Chips, Charlie's Angels, Love Boat, Fantasy Island, Remington Steele, Hill St. Blues, Murphy's Law.

WEISS, STEVEN ALAN: Executive. b. Glendale, CA, Oct. 19, 1944. e. Los Angeles City Coll., A.A., 1964; U. of Southern California, B.S., 1966; Northwestern U., B.S., 1967; LaSalle Extension U., J.D., 1970. U.S. Navy-San Diego, Great Lakes, Vallejo & Treasure Island, 1966–67; shipyard liaison officer, Pearl Harbor Naval Shipyard, U.S. Navy, 1970; gen. mgr., Adrian Weiss Prods., 1970–74; organized Weiss Global Enterprises with Adrian Weiss 1974 for production, acquisition & distribution of films. Purchased with Tom J. Corradine and Adrian Weiss from the Benedict E. Bogeaus Estate nine features, 1974. Secty./treas. of Film Investment Corp. & Weiss Global Enterprises. (Cos. own, control or have dist. rights to over 300 features, many TV series, documentaries, etc.)
MEMBER: Natl. Assn. of TV Program Executive Intl.; National Cable TV Assn.; American Film Institute.

WEISSMAN, MURRAY: Executive. b. New York, NY, Dec. 23. e. U. of Southern California. Asst. dir. of press info., CBS, 1960–66; mgr., TV press dept., Universal Studio, 1966–68; executive in charge of m.p. press dept., Universal Studios & asst. secy., Universal Pictures, 1968–76; marketing exec., Columbia Pictures, 1976–77; vice pres. of advertising & publicity, Lorimar Productions, 1977; vice pres., ICPR Public Relations Company, 1978–81; now principal, Weissman/Angellotti.

WEISSMAN, SEYMOUR J.: Executive, Producer, Director. Weissman Franz Productions. b. Brooklyn, NY, May 28, 1931. e. Kenyon Coll., Eng. Lit., A.B., 1953; U. of Southern California, cinema, 1955. Unity Films, 1954; Henry Strauss & Co., 1954; Dir. of motion pictures, White Sands Proving Grounds, N.M., 1954–55; M.P.O., 1955; Caliman Prod., 1956; prod. dir., Dynamic Films, Inc., 1958–59; prod., dir., Viston Assoc., 1959–64; dir., VPI Prods., 1966.

WEITZNER, DAVID: Executive. b. New York, NY, Nov. 13, 1938. e. Michigan State U. Entered industry in 1960 as member Columbia Pictures adv. dep't; later with Donahue and Coe as ass't exec. and Loew's Theatres adv. dep't; later with Embassy Pictures, adv. mgr.; dir. of adv. and exploitation for Palomar Pictures Corp.; v.p. in charge of adv., pub., and exploitation for ABC Pictures Corp.; v.p., entertainment/leisure div., Grey Advertising; v.p., worldwide adv., 20th Century Fox; exec. v.p. adv./pub./promo., Universal Pictures; exec. v.p., mktg. & dist., Embassy Pictures; 1985, joined 20th Century-Fox Films as pres. of mktg. 1987, pres., mktg., Weintraub Entertainment Group; 1988 joined MCA/Universal as pres. worldwide marketing, MCA Recreation Services.

WELCH, RAQUEL: Actress. r.n. Raquel Tejada. b. Chicago, IL, Sept. 5, 1940. e. La Jolla H.S. Theatre arts scholarship S.D. St. Col. Broadway debut, Woman of the Year, 1981.
PICTURES: Roustabout, A House Is Not a Home, Do Not Disturb, A Swingin' Summer, Fantastic Voyage, Shoot Loud Louder . . . I Don't Understand, One Million Years B.C., Fathom, The Oldest Profession, Bedazzled, The Biggest Bundle of Them All, The Queens, Bandolero, Lady in Cement, 100 Rifles, Flare Up, The Magic Christian, Myra Breckinridge, Restless, Hannie Caulder, Kansas City Bomber, Fuzz, Bluebeard, The Last of Sheila, The Three Musketeers, The Four Musketeers, The Wild Party, Mother Jugs & Speed, Crossed Swords, L'Animal.
TELEVISION: Special: From Raquel With Love. Movies: Legend of Walks Far Woman, Right to Die, Scandal in a Small Town, Trouble in Paradise, Tainted Blood, Judith Krantz's Torch Song. Guest: Cher, The Muppet Show, Saturday Night Live.

WELD, TUESDAY: Actress. r.n. Susan Weld. b. New York, NY, Aug. 27, 1943. m. violinist Pinchas Zuckerman. e. Hollywood Professional Sch. Began modeling at 4 yrs.
PICTURES: Rock Rock Rock (debut, 1956), Rally 'Round the Flag Boys! The Five Pennies, Because They're Young, High Time, Sex Kittens Go to College, The Private Lives of Adam and Eve, Return to Peyton Place, Wild in the Country, Bachelor Flat, Soldier in the Rain, I'll Take Sweden, The Cincinnati Kid, Lord Love a Duck, Pretty Poison, I Walk the Line, A Safe Place, Play It As It Lays, Looking for Mr. Goodbar (Acad. Award nom.), Who'll Stop the Rain, Serial, Thief, Author! Author!, Once Upon a Time in America, Heartbreak Hotel, Falling Down.
TELEVISION: Series: The Many Loves of Dobie Gillis (1959–60). Movies: Reflections of Murder, F. Scott Fitzgerald in Hollywood, A Question of Guilt, Mother and Daughter: The Loving War, Madame X, The Winter of Our Discontent,

Scorned and Swindled, Something in Common, Circle of Violence. *Special*: The Rainmaker.

WELLER, PETER: Actor. b. Stevens Point, WI, June 24, 1947. Acting since 10 years old. e. North Texas State U. Studied at American Acad. of Dramatic Arts with Uta Hagen. Member, Actor's Studio.
PICTURES: Butch and Sundance: The Early Years (debut, 1979), Just Tell Me What You Want, Shoot the Moon, Of Unknown Origin, Adventures of Buckaroo Banzai, Firstborn, Robocop, Shakedown, A Killing Affair, Leviathan, The Tunnel, Robocop 2, Cat Chaser, Naked Lunch, Fifty Fifty.
TELEVISION: *Movies*: The Man Without a Country, The Silence, Kentucky Woman, Two Kinds of Love, Apology, Women & Men: Stories of Seduction (Dust Before Fireworks), Rainbow Drive. *Guest*: Lou Grant, Exit 10.
STAGE: Sticks and Bones (moved up from understudy, Bdwy. debut), Full Circle, Summer Brave, Macbeth, The Wool-Gatherers, Rebel Women, Streamers, The Woods, Serenading Louie.

WELLS, FRANK G.: Executive. b. California, March 4, 1932. e. Pomona Coll., 1949–53; Oxford U., 1953–55; Rhodes Scholarship Jurisprudence. U.S. Army, Infantry first lieutenant, 1955–57; Stanford Law Sch. 1957–59. Joined Gang, Tyre & Brown (entertainment industry law firm) 1959; partner, 1962–69; mem., State Bar of Calif., American Bar Assoc., Los Angeles County Bar Assoc., vice chmn., Warner Bros. Inc.; 1985, pres. & COO, The Walt Disney Company.

WENDERS, WIM: Director, Writer. b. Dusseldorf, Germany, August 14, 1945. Studied film 1967–70 at Filmhochschule in Munich. Worked as film critic 1968–70 for Filmkritik and Die Suddeutsche Zeitung. In 1967 made first short films (Schauplatze) and three others before first feature, Summer in the City, in 1970.
PICTURES: *Director-Writer*: Summer in the City (also prod.), The Scarlet Letter, The Goalie's Anxiety at the Penalty Kick, Alice in the Cities, Wrong Move (dir. only), Kings of the Road (also prod.), The American Friend, Lightning Over Water (also actor), Hammett (dir. only), The State of Things, Paris Texas (dir. only), Tokyo-Ga (also edit.), Wings of Desire (also prod.), All Night Long (as actor), Notebooks on Cities and Clothes (also photog.), Until the End of the World, Faraway So Close! (also prod.).

WENDKOS, PAUL: Director. b. Philadelphia, PA, Sept. 20, 1926.
PICTURES: The Burglar, Tarawa Beachhead, Gidget, Face of a Fugitive, Battle of the Coral Sea, Because They're Young, Angel Baby, Gidget Goes to Rome, Miles to Terror, Guns of the Magnificent Seven, Cannon for Cordova, The Mephisto Waltz, Special Delivery.
TELEVISION: Hawaii 5-0 (pilot), Fear No Evil, The Brotherhood of the Bell, Travis Logan D.A., A Tattered Web, A Little Game, A Death of Innocence, The Delphi Bureau, Haunts of the Very Rich, Footsteps, The Strangers in 7-A, Honor Thy Father, Terror on the Beach, The Underground Man, The Legend of Lizzie Borden, Death Among Friends, The Death of Ritchie, Secrets, Good Against Evil, Harold Robbins' 79 Park Avenue, A Woman Called Moses, The Ordeal of Patty Hearst, Act of Violence, Ordeal of Doctor Mudd, A Cry for Love, The Five of Me, Golden Gate, Farrell for the People, Cocaine: One Man's Seduction, Intimate Agony, The Awakening of Candra, Celebrity, Scorned and Swindled, The Execution, The Bad Seed, Picking Up the Pieces, Rage of Angels: The Story Continues, Sister Margaret and the Saturday Night Ladies, Six Against the Rock, Right to Die, The Taking of Flight 847: The Uli Derickson Story, The Great Escape II: The Untold Story (co-dir.), From the Dead of Night, Cross of Fire, Blind Faith, Good Cops Bad Cops, The Chase, White Hot: The Murder of Thelma Todd, Guilty Until Proven Innocent.

WENDT, GEORGE: Actor. b. Chicago, IL, Oct. 17, 1948. e. Rockhurst Col. Joined Second City's acting troupe in 1973. Appeared in NBC pilot Nothing but Comedy.
TELEVISION: *Series*: Making the Grade, Cheers. *Guest*: Alice, Soap, Taxi, Hart to Hart, Saturday Night Live, Seinfeld. *Movies*: Oblomov (BBC), The Ratings Game.
PICTURES: My Bodyguard, Somewhere in Time, Airplane II: The Sequel, Jekyll & Hyde Together Again, The Woman in Red, Dreamscape, Thief of Hearts, No Small Affair, Fletch, House, Gung Ho, Plain Clothes, Guilty by Suspicion, Forever Young.

WERNER, PETER: Producer, Director. b. New York, NY, Jan. 17, 1947. e. Dartmouth Coll., AFI. Received Acad. Award for short subject, In the Region of Ice, 1976.
PICTURES: Don't Cry It's Only Thunder, No Man's Land.
TELEVISION: *Director*: Battered, Barnburning, Moonlighting, Aunt Mary, Hard Knox, I Married a Centerfold, Women in Song, Outlaws, Sins of the Father, LBJ: The Early Years. Men (exec. prod., dir.), The Image, Hiroshima: Out of the Ashes, D.E.A. (pilot), Ned Blessing, Doors, Middle Ages, The Good Policeman.

WERTHEIMER, THOMAS: Executive. b. 1938. e. Princeton U., B.A. 1960; Columbia U., LLB, 1963. Vice pres. business affairs subs. ABC 1964–72; joined MCA Inc 1972. Vice-pres. Universal TV dir.; corp. v.p. 1974–83; exec. v.p. 1983–director and officer of subsidiaries. Member exec. committee.

WERTMULLER, LINA: Writer, Director. b. Rome, Italy, Aug. 14, 1928. m. sculptor-set designer Enrico Job. e. Acad. of Theatre, Rome, 1951. Began working in theatre in 1951; Prod.-dir. avant-garde plays in Italy 1951–52; mem. puppet troupe 1952–62; actress, stage mgr., set designer, publicity writer, for theater, radio & TV 1952–62. Began film career as asst. to Fellini on 8½ in 1962. Following year wrote and directed first film, The Lizards. Had big TV success with series called Gian Burasca and then returned to theatre for a time. 1988, named Special Commissioner of Centro Sperimentale di Cinematografia. To date the only woman to be nominated for an Academy Award for Best Director (Seven Beauties, 1976).
PICTURES: *Director-Writer*: The Lizards (dir. debut, 1963), Let's Talk About Men, The Seduction of Mimi (Cannes Fest, best dir. award 1972), Love and Anarchy, All Screwed Up, Swept Away . . . By an Unusual Destiny in the Blue Sea of August, Seven Beauties (Acad. Award noms. for dir. & s.p., 1976), The End of the World in Our Usual Bed in a Night Full of Rain, Blood Feud, A Joke of Destiny (Lying in Wait Around the Corner Like a Bandit), A Complex Plot About Women, Sotto Sotto (Softly Softly), Summer Night With Greek Profile Almond Eyes and a Scent of Basil, The Tenth One in Hiding, On a Moonlit Night, Saturday Sunday Monday.
TELEVISION: Rita the Mosquito, Il Decimo Clandestino (Cannes Fest.).

WEST, ADAM: Actor. b. Walla Walla, WA, Sept. 19, 1929. r.n. William West Anderson. e. Whitman Col. (B.A.), Stanford Univ.
PICTURES: The Young Philadelphians, Geronimo, Soldier in the Rain, Tammy and the Doctor, Robinson Crusoe on Mars, The Outlaws Is Coming!, Mara of the Wilderness, Batman, The Girl Who Knew Too Much, Marriage of a Young Stockbroker, The Specialist, Hell River, Hooper, The Happy Hooker Goes to Hollywood, Blonde Ambition, One Dark Night, Young Lady Chatterly, Hell Raiders, Zombie Nightmare, Doin' Time on Planet Earth, Mad About You, John Travis: Solar Survivor, Maxim Xul, The New Age.
TELEVISION: *Series*: The Detectives, Batman, The Last Precinct, Danger Theatre. *Movies*: The Eyes of Charles Sands, For the Love of It, I Take These Men, Nevada Smith, Poor Devil, The Last Precinct. *Guest*: Hawaiian Eye, 77 Sunset Strip, Bonanza, The Outer Limits, Petticoat Junction, Bewitched, The Big Valley, Love American Style, Night Gallery, Mannix, Alice, Murder She Wrote, The Simpsons (voice). *Pilots*: Lookwell, 1775, Reel Life.

WEST, TIMOTHY: Actor. b. Yorkshire, England, Oct. 20, 1934. m. actress Prunella Scales. e. John Lyon Sch. Harow. Ent. ind. 1960. Began acting 1956 after two years as recording engineer. Worked in regional repertory, London's West End and for Royal Shakespeare Company. Dec., 1979 appointed artistic controller of Old Vic. Has directed extensively in theatre.
PICTURES: Twisted Nerve, The Looking Glass War, Nicholas and Alexandra, The Day of the Jackal, Hedda, Joseph Andrews, The Devil's Advocate, Agatha, The Thirty Nine Steps, Rough Cut, Cry Freedom, Consuming Passions.
TELEVISION: Edward VII, Hard Times, Crime and Punishment, Henry VIII, Churchill and the Generals, Brass, The Monocled Mutineer, The Good Doctor Bodkin Adams, What the Butler Saw, Harry's Kingdom, The Train, When We Are Married, Breakthrough at Reykjavik, Strife, A Shadow on the Sun, The Contractor, Blore, m.p., Survival of the Fittest, Oliver Twist, Why Lockerbie, Framed.

WESTCOTT, HELEN: Actress. r.n. Myrthas Helen Hickman. b. Hollywood, CA, 1929. e. Los Angeles Jr. Coll., 1946. In play The Drunkard, at 7, for 9 yrs.; many radio shows.
PICTURES: A Midsummer Night's Dream (as child), Adventures of Don Juan, Girl from Jones Beach, Mr. Belvedere Goes to College, Whirlpool, Dancing in the Dark, The Gunfighter, Three Came Home, Secret of Convict Lake, Phone Call from a Stranger, Return of Texan, With a Song in My Heart, Loan Shark, Abbott and Costello Meet Dr. Jekyl & Mr. Hyde, Charge at Feather River, Hot Blood, The Last Hurrah, I Love My Wife.

WESTON, JACK: Actor. b. Cleveland, OH, Aug. 21, 1924. r.n. Jack Weinstein. Began career in 1934 in children's division of Cleveland Playhouse. In Army in W.W.II. Success came in Broadway hit, Season in the Sun. Was frequent performer in top TV shows during 1950s. Film debut in Stage Struck in 1958.
PICTURES: Stage Struck (debut, 1958), I Want to Live!, Imitation of Life, Please Don't Eat the Daisies, All in a Night's Work, The Honeymoon Machine, It's Only Money, Palm Springs Weekend, The Incredible Mr. Limpet, Mirage, The Cincinnati Kid, Wait Until Dark, The Counterfeit Killer, The

Thomas Crown Affair, The April Fools, Cactus Flower, A New Leaf, Fuzz, Marco, Gator, The Ritz, Cuba, Can't Stop the Music, The Four Seasons, High Road to China, The Long-shot, RAD, Ishtar, Dirty Dancing, Short Circuit 2.
TELEVISION: *Guest*: Studio One, Philco Theatre, Kraft Playhouse. *Series*: Rod Browning of the Rocket Rangers, My Sister Eileen, The Hathaways, The Four Seasons. *Mini-Series*: If Tomorrow Comes, 79 Park Avenue. *Movies*: Now You See It—Now You Don't, Deliver Us From Evil, I Love a Mystery.

WESTON, JAY: Producer. b. New York, NY, March 9, 1929. e. New York U. Operated own pub. agency before moving into film prod. In 1965 launched Weston Production; sold orig. s.p., The War Horses, to Embassy Pictures; acquired and marketed other properties. Became prod. story exec. for Palomar-ABC Pictures in 1967.
PICTURES: For Love of Ivy (co-prod.), Lady Sings the Blues (co-prod.), W.C. Fields and Me, Chu Chu and the Philly Flash, Night of the Juggler, Buddy, Buddy.
STAGE: Does a Tiger Wear a Necktie (co-prod.).
TELEVISION: Laguna Heat (exec. prod.).

WETTIG, PATRICIA: Actress. b. Cincinnati, OH, Dec. 4, 1951. m. actor Ken Olin. e. Temple Univ. Studied at Neighborhood Playhouse. Began acting career with NY's Circle Repertory Company appearing in The Wool Gatherer, The Diviners and A Tale Told. Other theatre work includes The Dining Room, Talking With (LA), Threads, Innocent Thoughts, and My Mother Said I Never Should.
TELEVISION: *Series*: St. Elsewhere, thirtysomething (2 Emmy Awards). *Movies*: Silent Motive, Taking Back My Life: The Nancy Ziegenmeyer Story.
PICTURES: Guilty by Suspicion, City Slickers.

WEXLER, HASKELL: Cinematographer, Director. b. Chicago, 1926. Photographed educational and industrial films before features. Documentaries as cin. include: The Living City, The Savage Eye, T. for Tumbleweed, Stakeout on Dope Street, Brazil—A Report on Torture, Interviews With Mai Lai Veterans with Jane Fonda, Interview—Chile's President Allende, Introduction to the Enemy. Elected by Acad. Mo. Pic. Arts & Sciences to Bd. of Governors, Cinematographers Branch. 1991, elected by AMPAS to bd. of govs. - Cinematographers Branch; 1993, received lifetime achievement award from American Society of Cinematographers.
PICTURES: Studs Lonigan, Five Bold Women, The Hoodlum Priest, Angel Baby, A Face In the Rain, America America, The Best Man, The Bus (also dir., prod.), The Loved One (also co-prod.), Who's Afraid of Virginia Woolf? (Acad. Award, 1966), In the Heat of the Night, The Thomas Crown Affair, Medium Cool (also co-prod., dir., s.p.), Trial of Catonsville Nine, American Graffiti, One Flew Over the Cuckoo's Nest, Bound for Glory (Acad. Award, 1976), Coming Home, Days of Heaven (addit. photog.), No Nukes (also co-dir.), Second Hand Hearts, Richard Pryor: Live on the Sunset Strip, Lookin' to Get Out, The Man Who Loved Women, Matewan, Colors, Latino (dir., writer only), Three Fugitives, Blaze, Through the Wire, Other People's Money, Rolling Stones at the MAX, The Babe.
TELEVISION: The Kid From Nowhere.

WHALEY, FRANK: Actor. b. Syracuse, NY, 1963. e. SUNY, Albany. With his brother formed rock band the Niagaras. NY theatre: Face Divided, The Indian Wants the Bronx, The Years.
PICTURES: Ironweed (debut, 1987), Field of Dreams, Little Monsters, Born on the Fourth of July, The Freshman, Cold Dog Soup, The Doors, Career Opportunities, JFK, Back in the U.S.S.R., A Midnight Clear, Hoffa, Swing Kids.
TELEVISION: *Specials*: Soldier Boys, Seasonal Differences. *Movies*: Unconquered, Flying Blind. *Pilot*: Flipside. *Guest*: Spenser: For Hire, The Equalizer.

WHALLEY-KILMER, JOANNE: Actress. b. Manchester, England, Aug. 25, 1964. m. actor Val Kilmer. Began stage career while in teens including season of Edward Bond plays at Royal Court Theatre (Olivier Award nom.) and The Three Sisters, The Lulu Plays. NY: What the Butler Saw (Theatre World Award).
PICTURES: Dance With a Stranger, No Surrender, The Good Father, Willow, To Kill a Priest, Scandal, Kill Me Again, Navy SEALS, Crossing the Line, Shattered, Storyville, Mother's Boys, A Good Man in Africa.
TELEVISION: The Singing Detective, A Quiet Life, Edge of Darkness, A Christmas Carol, Save Your Kisses, Will You Love Me Tomorrow.

WHEATON, WIL: Actor. r.n. Richard William Wheaton III. b. Burbank, CA, July 29, 1972. Graduated L.A. Professional H.S., June, 1990. Began acting in commercials at age 7.
PICTURES: The Secret of NIMH (voice), The Buddy System, Hambone and Hillie, The Last Starfighter, Stand by Me, The Curse, Toy Soldiers, December.
TELEVISION: *Series*: Star Trek: The Next Generation. *Pilots*: Long Time Gone, 13 Thirteenth Avenue, The Man Who Fell to Earth. *Movies*: A Long Way Home (debut, 1981),

The Defiant Ones, Young Harry Houdini, The Last Prostitute. *Specials*: The Shooting, My Dad Can't Be Crazy Can He?, Lifestories (A Deadly Secret). *Guest*: St. Elsewhere, Family Ties.

WHITAKER, FOREST: Actor. b. Longview, TX, July 15, 1961. Raised in Los Angeles. e. U. of Southern California (studied voice), Music Conservatory. Former all-league defensive tackle. Stage credits include Swan, Romeo and Juliet, Hamlet, Ring Around the Moon, Craig's Wife, Whose Life Is It Anyway?, The Greeks (all at Drama Studio London), School Talk (LA), Patchwork Shakespeare (CA Youth Theatre). Beggar's Opera, Jesus Christ Superstar. Directed prods. of Look Back in Anger, Drums Across the Realm.
PICTURES: Fast Times at Ridgemont High (debut, 1982), Vision Quest, The Color of Money, Platoon, Stakeout, Good Morning Vietnam, Bloodsport, Bird (Cannes Film Fest. Award, 1988), Johnny Handsome, Downtown, Rage in Harlem (also co-prod.), Article 99, Diary of a Hit Man, Consenting Adults, The Crying Game, Body Snatchers.
TELEVISION: *Movies*: Hands of a Stranger, Criminal Justice, Last Light.*Guest*: Amazing Stories, Hill Street Blues, Cagney and Lacey, Trapper John M.D., The Fall Guy, Different Strokes. *Mini-Series*: North and South, Parts I & II.

WHITE, BETTY: Actress. b. Oak Park, IL, Jan. 17, 1924. m. late Allen Ludden. Began on radio in Blondie, The Great Gildersleeve, This Is Your F.B.I. Moved into TV with live local show, L.A.
TELEVISION: *Panelist*: Make the Connection (1955), Match Game P.M., Liar's Club. *Series*: Life with Elizabeth, Date With the Angels (1957–58), The Betty White Show (1958), The Jack Paar Show, Mary Tyler Moore Show (Emmy Awards 1975, 1976), The Pet Set, The Betty White Show (1977–8), Just Men (host, Emmy, 1983), Mama's Family, Golden Girls (Emmy, 1986), The Golden Palace. *Movies*: Vanished, With This Ring, The Best Place to Be, Before and After, The Gossip Columnist, Chance of a Lifetime. *Host*: Macy's Thanksgiving Parade for 10 yrs, Rose Parade (20 yrs.).

WHITE, JESSE: Actor. r.n. Jesse Weidenfeld. b. Buffalo, NY, Jan. 3, 1920. e. Akron, OH H.S. Did odd jobs, then salesman; radio, vaudeville, burlesque, nightclubs and little theatre work; Broadway stage debut in Moon is Down, 1942; other shows include Harvey, Born Yesterday, etc. Has appeared on numerous radio and TV shows, regular on Private Secretary, Danny Thomas, Ann Sothern Show. Best known as Maytag repairman on long-running commercial 1967–89.
PICTURES: Harvey, Death of a Salesman, Callaway Went Thataway, Million Dollar Mermaid, Witness to Murder, Forever Female, Not as a Stranger, Bad Seed, Back from Eternity, Designing Woman, Marjorie Morningstar, Legs Diamond, Fever in the Blood, Sail a Crooked Ship, It's Only Money, The Yellow Canary, It's a Mad Mad Mad Mad World, Looking For Love, A House Is Not a Home, Bless the Beasts and Children, The Cat from Outer Space, Monster in the Closet, Matinee.

WHITE, LEONARD: Producer, Director, Actor. b. Sussex, Eng. TV dir., prod., CBC-TV (Canada), T.W.W. Ltd. T.T. TV & ABC-TV; Jupiter Thea., Inc.; Crest Theatre; Royal Alexandra Thea.; Toronto Thea., 1953–57. England, Playhouse, Oxford, Perth Repertory Thea., Hornchurch, Guilford Repertory Thea. Belgrade Thea., Coventry. Actor: U.S.A. debut in A Sleep of Prisoners, 1951–52; London West End. In the White Devil, He Who Gets Slapped, Macbeth, Still She Wished for Company, Point of Departure.
PICTURES: The Dark Man, The Large Rope, River Beat, Hunted, Martin Luther, Passage Home, Breakout, Circumstantial Evidence, At the Stroke of Nine, etc.
TELEVISION: All networks, G. Britain and CBC (Canada). Prod., ABC-TV; 1960–68. Series: Inside Story, Armchair Mystery Thea., Police Surgeon, The Avengers (orig. prod.; first 40 episodes), Out of This World, Armchair Theatre, Strathblair (10 episodes). Prod., 1968–69; prod., Thames Television, 1969–70. Drama consultant CBC-TV Toronto, 1970–80 HTV (UK); 1980–87 STV (UK). 350 drama productions for ITV (UK) Network.

WHITE, ROY B.: Executive, Exhibitor. b. Cincinnati, OH, July 30, 1926. e. U. of Cincinnati. Flight engineer, U.S. Air Force during W.W.II; sales department of 20th Century-Fox, 1949–52; began in exhibition, 1952; past pres., Mid-States Theatres; chmn. R. M. White Management, Inc.; past president, National Association of Theatre Owners: past Chairman of the Board, National Association of Theatre Owners: Board of Trustees—American Film Inst.; Board of Directors NATO of Ohio, b.o.d., Motion Picture Pioneers Foundation; Will Rogers Hospital, Nat'l. Endowment for Arts.

WHITELAW, BILLIE, C.B.E., D.Litt.: Actress. b. Coventry, England, June 6, 1932. Acted on radio and television since childhood. Winner of the TV Actress of the Year and 1972, Guild Award, Best Actress, 1960. British Acad. Award 1969; U.S. National Society of Film Critics Award best supp. actress, 1968. Evening News, Best Film Actress, 1977; best

actress Sony Radio Radio Award 1987, 1989. 1988 Evening Standard Award for Best Actress.
STAGE: 3 years with National Theatre of Great Britain. England, My England (Revue). Progress to the Park, A Touch of the Poet, Othello, Trelawney of the Wells, After Haggerty, Not I, Alphabetical Order, Footfalls, Molly, The Greeks, Happy Days, Passion Play, Rockaby (also in N.Y. and Adelaide Festival), Tales from Hollywood, Who's Afraid of Virginia Woolf?
PICTURES: The Fake, The Sleeping Tiger, Make Mine Mink, Bobbikins, No Love for Johnnie, Mr. Topaze, Hell Is a City, Payroll, Charlies Bubbles, The Adding Machine, Twisted Nerve, Start the Revolution Without Me, Leo the Last, Eagle in a Cage, Gumshoe, Frenzy, Nightwatch, The Omen, Leopard in the Snow, The Water Babies, An Unsuitable Job for a Woman, The Dark Crystal (voice), Slayground, Shadey, The Chain, Maurice, The Dressmaker, Joyriders, The Krays, Freddie as F.R.O.7 (voice).
TELEVISION: Over 100 leading roles incl. No Trains to Lime Street, Lady of the Camelias, Resurrection, Beyond the Horizon, Anna Christie, You and Me, A World of Time, Dr. Jekyll and Mr. Hyde, Poet Game, Sextet (8 plays for BBC), Wessex Tales, The Fifty Pound Note, Supernatural (2 plays), Four plays by Samuel Beckett, Eustace and Hilda, The Oresteia of Aeschylus, The Haunted Man, Private Schultz, Jamaica Inn, Happy Days, Camille, Imaginary Friends, The Secret Garden, The Picnic, A Tale of Two Cities, The Fifteen Streets, Three Beckett plays, Lorna Doone, Duel of Love, A Murder of Quality, The Cloning of Joanna May, The Entertainers, Firm Friends, Skallagrigg.

WHITEMORE, HUGH: Writer. b. England, 1936. Studied acting at Royal Acad. of Dramatic Art. Has since written for television, film, theatre.
THEATER: Stevie, Pack of Lies, Breaking the Code, The Best of Friends, It's Ralph.
PICTURES: All Neat in Black Stockings, All Creatures Great and Small, Stevie, The Return of the Soldier, 84 Charing Cross Road, Utz.
TELEVISION: Cider With Rosie (Writers' Guild Award 1971), Elizabeth R (Emmy Award 1971), Country Matters (Writers' Guild Award 1972), Dummy (RAT—Prix Italia 1979), Rebecca, All For Love, A Dedicated Man, Down at the Hydro, A Bit of Singing and Dancing, Concealed Enemies (Emmy, Neil Simon Awards 1984), Pack of Lies, The Final Days, The Best of Friends.

WHITMAN, STUART: Actor. b. San Francisco, CA., Feb. 1, 1928. Army Corp. of Engineers (1945–1948), at Fort Lewis, WA; while in army, competed as light heavyweight boxer. Studied drama under G.I. Bill at Ben Bard Drama Sch. and L.A. City Coll., Performed in Heaven Can Wait and became member of Michael Chekhov Stage Society and Arthur Kennedy Group. Entered films in early 1950s. TV debut on 26 episodes Highway Patrol.
PICTURES: When Worlds Collide, The Day The Earth Stood Still, Rhapsody, Seven Men From Now, War Drums, Johnny Trouble, Darby's Rangers, Ten North Frederick, The Decks Ran Red, China Doll, The Sound and the Fury, These Thousand Hills, Hound Dog Man, The Story of Ruth, Murder Inc., Francis of Assisi, The Fiercest Heart, The Mark (Acad. Award nom.), The Comancheros, Convicts 4, The Longest Day, The Day and the Hour (Fr./It.), Shock Treatment, Rio Conchos, Those Magnificent Men In Their Flying Machines, Sands of the Kalahari, Signpost to Murder, An American Dream, The Invincible Six, The Last Escape, Captain Apache (US/Sp.), Night Of The Lepus, Welcome to Arrow Beach (Tender Flesh), Crazy Mama, Call Him Mr. Shatter, Assault on Paradise (Maniac/Ransom), Mean Johnny Barrows, Las Vegas Lady, Eaten Alive!, Tony Saitta/Tough Tony (It.), Strange Shadows In An Empty Room; Ruby; The White Buffalo; Delta Fox, Thoroughbred (Run for the Roses), Oil (It. as Red Adair), La Murjer de la Tierra Caliente (Sp./It.); Guyana: Cult of the Damned, Cuba Crossing, Jamaican Gold, The Monster Club, Demonoid, Butterfly, Treasure Of The Amazon, John Travis: Solar Survivor, Deadly Reactor, Moving Target, Mob Boss.
TELEVISION: Series: Cimarron Strip (series 1967–68). Guest: The Crowd Pleaser (Alcoa-Goodyear), Highway Patrol, Dr. Christian, Hangman's Noose (Zane Grey). Mini-Series: The Last Convertible, Hemingway. Movies: The Man Who Wanted to Live Forever, City Beneath the Sea, Revenge, The Woman Hunter, The Man Who Died Twice, Cat Creature, Go West Young Girl, The Pirate, Women in White, The Seekers, Condominium, Stillwatch, Once Upon a Texas Train.

WHITMORE, JAMES: Actor. r.n. James Allen Whitmore, Jr. b. White Plains, NY, Oct. 1, 1921. e. Yale U. In Yale Drama Sch. players; co-founder Yale radio station, 1942; U.S. Marine Corps, W.W.II; in USO, in American Wing Theatre school, in stock. Broadway debut in Command Decision, 1947. Star of Tomorrow.
PICTURES: The Undercover Man (debut, 1949), Battleground, The Asphalt Jungle, The Next Voice You Hear, Mrs.

O'Malley and Mr. Malone, Outriders, Please Believe Me, Across the Wide Missouri, It's a Big Country, Because You're Mine, Above and Beyond, The Girl Who Had Everything, All the Brothers Were Valiant, Kiss Me Kate, The Command, Them, Battle Cry, The McConnell Story, Last Frontier, Oklahoma, Crime in the Streets, Eddie Duchin Story, The Deep Six, Face of Fire, Who Was That Lady?, Black Like Me, Chuka, Waterhole No. 3, Nobody's Perfect, Planet of the Apes, Madigan, The Split, Guns of the Magnificent Seven, Tora! Tora! Tora!, Chato's Land, The Harrad Experiment, Where the Red Fern Grows, Give 'em Hell Harry, The Serpent's Egg, The First Deadly Sin, Nuts, Old Explorers, Rita Hayworth and Shawshank Redemption.
TELEVISION: Series: The Law and Mr. Jones, My Friend Tony, Temperature's Rising. Movies: The Challenge, If Tomorrow Comes, I Will Fight No More Forever, Rage, Mark I Love You, Glory! Glory!, Sky High. Mini-Series: The Word, Celebrity, Favorite Son. Special: All My Sons.

WICKES, MARY: Actress. r.n. Mary Wickenhauser. b. St. Louis, MO. e. Washington U., St. Louis (A.B., D. Arts, Hon.); postgrad, UCLA. Lecturer, seminars on acting in comedy, Coll. of Wm. & Mary, Washington U. at St. Louis, Am. Conserv. Th. in S.F. Debut at Berkshire Playhouse, Stockbridge, MA. Bd. of dir., Med. Aux Center for Health Sciences, UCLA, 1977–; L.A. Oncologic Inst., 1987–.
THEATRE: (Bdwy) Stage Door, Father Malachy's Miracle, The Man Who Came to Dinner, Jackpot, Hollywood Pinafore, Town House, Park Avenue, Oklahoma! (revival). Stock and regional theatre at Mark Taper Forum, Ahmanson and Chandler Pavillion (L.A.), Berkshire Playhouse in Stockbridge, Cape Playhouse in Dennis (MA), Amer. Conservatory Theatre (San Francisco), and many others.
PICTURES: The Man Who Came to Dinner (debut, 1941), Now Voyager, Who Done It?, Mayor of 44th Street, How's About It?, Higher and Higher, Happy Land, Rhythm of the Islands, My Kingdom for a Cook, Decision of Christopher Blake, June Bride, Anna Lucasta, Petty Girl, I'll See You in My Dreams, On Moonlight Bay, The Story of Will Rogers, Young Man With Ideas, By the Light of the Silvery Moon, Half a Hero, The Actress, White Christmas, Proud Rebel, Dance With Me Henry, Don't Go Near the Water, It Happened to Jane, Who's Minding the Store?, Sins of Rachel Cade, Cimarron (1961), The Music Man, Fate is the Hunter, Dear Heart, How to Murder Your Wife, The Trouble With Angels, The Spirit Is Willing, Where Angels Go Trouble Follows, Snowball Express, Touched By Love, Postcards from the Edge, Sister Act, Sister Act 2.
TELEVISION: Series: Halls of Ivy, Mrs. G Goes to College, Dennis the Menace, Doc, Father Dowling Mysteries. Guest: Make Room for Daddy, Lucy Show, M*A*S*H, Sigmund and the Sea Monsters, Wonderworks (The Canterville Ghost), Studio One (Mary Poppins, Miss Hargreaves, The Storm), Highway to Heaven, You Can't Take It With You, Murder She Wrote. Movies: The Monk, Willa.

WIDMARK, RICHARD: Actor. b. Sunrise, MN, Dec. 26, 1914. e. Lake Forest U. Instructor, 1938. On radio, then stage, films.
PICTURES: Kiss of Death (debut, 1947), Road House, Street With No Name, Yellow Sky, Down to the Sea in Ships, Slattery's Hurricane, Night and the City, Panic in the Streets, No Way Out, Halls of Montezuma, The Frogmen, Red Skies of Montana, Don't Bother to Knock, O. Henry's Full House, My Pal Gus, Destination Gobi, Pickup on South Street, Take the High Ground, Garden of Evil, Hell & High Water, Broken Lance, Prize of Gold, The Cobweb, Backlash, Run for the Sun, The Last Wagon, Saint Joan, Time Limit, The Law and Jake Wade, The Tunnel of Love, The Trap, Warlock, The Alamo, The Secret Ways, Two Rode Together, Judgment at Nuremberg, How the West Was Won, Flight from Ashiya, The Long Ships, Cheyenne Autumn, The Bedford Incident, Alvarez Kelly, The Way West, Madigan, Death of a Gunfighter, A Talent for Loving, The Moonshine War, When The Legends Die, Murder on the Orient Express, To the Devil—A Daughter, Twilight's Last Gleaming, The Domino Principle, Rollercoaster, Coma, The Swarm, Bear Island, National Lampoon Goes to the Movies, Hanky Panky, The Final Option, Against All Odds, True Colors.
TELEVISION: Series: Madigan. Movies: Vanished, Brock's Last Case, The Last Day, Mr. Horn, All God's Children, A Whale for the Killing, Blackout, A Gathering of Old Men, Once Upon a Texas Train, Cold Sassy Tree. Special: Benjamin Franklin.

WIESEN, BERNARD: Producer, Director, Writer, Executive. b. New York, NY. e. City Coll. of New York, B.A.; Pasadena Playhouse Coll. of Theatre, Master of Theatre Arts; Dramatic Workshop of New School.
PICTURES: Producer-Director: Fear No More. Asst. Dir. The King and I, The Left Hand of God, The Rains of Ranchipur, To Catch a Thief, The Trouble with Harry.
TELEVISION: Director: How to Marry A Millionaire, Valentine's Day. Assoc. Producer: Valentine's Day, Three on an Island, Cap'n Ahab, Sally and Sam. Assoc. Prod.: Daniel Boone. Producer/Director: Julia, Co-Producer-Director: The

Jimmy Stewart Show. Prod. Exec.: Executive Suite (pilot). Exec. Paramount TV, director of current programming. Writer: Love 4 Love, The Grand Turk.
STAGE: First Monday in October (Bdwy.)—co. prod.

WIEST, DIANNE: Actress. b. Kansas City, MO, March 28, 1948. e. U. of Maryland. Studied ballet but abandoned it for theatre. Did regional theatre work (Yale Repertory, Arena Stage) and performed with N.Y. Shakespeare Festival.
THEATER: Toured with Amer. Shakespeare Co.; Arena Stage (Heartbreak House, Our Town, The Dybbuk, Inherit the Wind). Public Theater (Ashes, Agamennon, Leave it to Beaver is Dead), Yale Rep. (Hedda Gabler, A Doll's House). NY: The Art of Dining (Obie & Theatre World Awards), Frankenstein (Bdwy), Othello, Beyond Therapy, Not About Heroes (dir.; also at Williamstown Fest.), Hunting Cockroaches, Square One, In the Summer House.
PICTURES: It's My Turn (debut, 1980), I'm Dancing as Fast as I Can, Independence Day, Footloose, Falling in Love, The Purple Rose of Cairo, Hannah and Her Sisters (Acad. Award, supp. actress, 1986), Radio Days, The Lost Boys, September, Bright Lights Big City, Parenthood (Acad. Award nom.), Cookie, Edward Scissorhands, Little Man Tate, Cops and Robbersons.
TELEVISION: Specials: Zalman or the Madness of God, Out of Our Father's House. Movies: The Wall, The Face of Rage.

WIGAN, GARETH: Executive. b. London, England, Dec. 2, 1931. e. Oxford. Agent, MCA London; 1957; John Redway & Associates, 1960; co-founder, agent Gregson & Wigan Ltd., 1961; co-founder, agent London Intl., 1968; independent prod., 1970; v.p., creative affairs, 20th Century Fox, 1975; v.p., prod., Fox, 1976; v.p., The Ladd Co., 1979–83. Company W.W. Prods. Currently exec. production consultant, Columbia Pictures.
PICTURES: Unman Wittering & Zigo; Running Scared; etc.

WIHTOL, ARN S.: Executive. b. Millville, NJ, Sept. 4, 1944. e. San Jose State. Exec. v.p., international sales, Pacific International Enterprises.
PICTURES: Production Exec. and Co-Writer: Mystery Mansion. Casting and Controller: Dream Chasers. Producer's assistant: Sacred Ground.

WILBY, JAMES: Actor. b. Rangoon, Burma, Feb. 20, 1958. Lived a nomadic childhood moving from Burma to Ceylon, then Jamaica and finally England. e. Durham U. Trained at Royal Acad. of Dramatic Art where he played Shakespearean roles and landed a part in Oxford Film Foundation's Privileged (1982). West End stage debut Another Country. Also acted in regional theater. 1988: The Common Pursuit.
PICTURES: Dreamchild (debut, 1985), Maurice, A Handful of Dust, A Summer Story, Conspiracy, The Siege of Venice, Immaculate Conception, Howards End.
TELEVISION: Dutch Girls, A Tale of Two Cities, Mother Love, Tell Me That You Love Me, Adam Bede.

WILDE, ARTHUR L.: Publicist. b. San Francisco, CA, May 27. S.F. Daily News; Matson Lines; pub. dept., Warner Bros.; 1936; dir. exploitation, CBS; pub. dir., Hal Wallis Prod.; pub. dept., Paramount; pub., Hecht-Hill-Lancaster; v.p., Arthur Jacobs, public rel.; Blowitz-Maskell Publicity Agency; pub. dir., C. V. Whitney Pictures; gen. v.p., 1958; owner, pub.-ad. agency, The Arthur L. Wilde Co., 1961–65; freelance publicist, 1965–66; pub. rel. consultant, Marineland of Florida, 1965; unit publicity dir., United Artists, National General, Paramount, 1966–69; free lance publicity, 1971; unit publicist, MGM, Paramount, United Artists, 1972–74; staff position; Features Publicity at Paramount Pictures, 1973. Freelance unit publicist again in 1976 at Universal, Paramount and Lorimar Productions. 1978–79, Columbia Pictures & Universal Studios; 1980, Marble Arch. Prods. & Northstar Intl. Pictures; 1981, studio pub. mgr., 20th Century-Fox; recently staff unit publicist for 20th-Fox; 1984–89, currently free lance unit publicist for feature films.

WILDER, BILLY: Director, Writer, Producer. r.n. Samuel Wilder. b. Austria, June 22, 1906. Newspaperman in Vienna and Berlin; then author of screen story People on Sunday (debut, 1929) followed by 10 other German films. inc. Emil and the Detectives (s.p.). French films: Mauvaise Graine (co-dir., s.p.). Adorable (s.p.). To Hollywood 1934. Head of Film Section, Psych. Warfare Div., U.S. Army, 1945, Am. Zone, Germany. American Film Institute Life Achievement Award 1987. Irving Thalberg Memorial Award 1988.
PICTURES: As co-writer: Music in the Air, Lottery Lover, Champagne Waltz (co-wrote story), Bluebeard's Eighth Wife, Midnight, Ninotchka, What a Life, Rhythm on the River (co-wrote orig. story), Arise My Love, Ball of Fire, Hold Back the Dawn.
PICTURES: As director & co-writer: The Major and the Minor, Five Graves to Cairo, Double Indemnity, The Lost Weekend (Acad. Awards for best dir. & s.p., 1945), The Emperor Waltz, A Foreign Affair, Sunset Boulevard (Acad. Award, best story and s.p., 1950). As dir.-co-s.p.-prod.: Ace in

the Hole (a.k.a. The Big Carnival), Stalag 17, Sabrina, The Seven Year Itch (dir. & co-s.p. only), The Spirit of St. Louis, Love in the Afternoon, Witness for the Prosecution (dir. & co-s.p. only), Some Like It Hot, The Apartment (Acad. Awards, best picture, dir., & original story and s.p., 1960), One Two Three, Irma La Douce, Kiss Me Stupid, The Fortune Cookie, The Private Life of Sherlock Holmes, Avanti!, The Front Page (dir. & co-s.p. only), Fedora, Buddy Buddy (dir. & co-s.p. only).

WILDER, GENE: Actor, Director, Writer. r.n. Jerry Silberman. b. Milwaukee, WI, June 11, 1935. e. U. of Iowa. Joined Bristol Old Vic company in England, became champion fencer; in NY, worked as chauffeur, fencing instructor, etc. before N.Y. off-Broadway debut in Roots.
BROADWAY: The Complaisant Lover, Mother Courage, Luv, One Flew Over the Cuckoo's Nest.
PICTURES: Bonnie and Clyde (debut, 1967), The Producers (Acad. Award nom.), Start the Revolution Without Me, Quackser Fortune Has a Cousin in the Bronx, Willy Wonka and the Chocolate Factory, Everything You Always Wanted to Know About Sex*, Rhinoceros, Blazing Saddles, The Little Prince, Young Frankenstein (also co-s.p.), The Adventure of Sherlock Holmes' Smarter Brother (also dir., s.p.), Silver Streak, The World's Greatest Lover (also dir., s.p., prod.), The Frisco Kid, Stir Crazy, Sunday Lovers (also dir. & s.p.; episode), Hanky Panky, The Woman in Red (also dir., s.p.), Haunted Honeymoon (also dir., s.p., prod.), See No Evil Hear No Evil (also co-s.p.), Funny About Love, Another You.
TELEVISION: Specials: Death of a Salesman (1966), The Scarecrow, Neil Simon Special, Anne Bancroft Special (1974), The Trouble With People, Marlo Thomas Special (1973). Movie: Thursday's Game.

WILK, TED: Theatrical agent. b. Minneapolis, MN, Jan. 5, 1908. e. U. of Michigan, 1926–30. Publix Theatres, Duluth, MN, 1930; Warner Bros., Minneapolis, 1932–33; Film Daily, Hollywood, 1934–40; U.S. Army, 1941–46; Lou Irwin agency 1946–61; Ted Wilk Agency, since 1961.

WILLIAMS, BERT: Executive, Actor. b. Newark, NJ, April 12, 1922. e. U. of Southern California. Navy, 1942–45. Summer Stock, 1940–41; world's prof. diving champion, 1945–48; star diver, Larry Crosby, Buster Crabbe, Johnny Weismuller, Dutch Smith Shows, 1945–48; writer, asst. prod., Martin Mooney Prods., PRC, Goldwyn Studios; pres., Bert Prods., Bert Williams Motion Picture Producers and Distributors, Inc. Member, M.P. Academy of Fine Arts & TV Academy of Arts & Science. Masters Outdoor & Indoor National Diving, 1985–87, 89, 90. 1989 World Masters Diving Champion; 1990 World Games Diving Champion.
THEATRE: Roadshow plays include: Cat on a Hot Tin Roof, Hamlet, Run From The Hunter, Sugar and Spice, Hope Is a Thing Called Feathers, 69 Below, Tribute.
PICTURES: Actor: Fort Apache, Rio Grande, American Bandito, Angel Baby; The Nest of the Cuckoo Birds (also prod., dir.), Around the World Under the Sea; Deathwatch 28 (s.p.), Gambit, No Secret, This Must Be the Last Day of Summer, Twenty Eight Watched (dir.), Adventure To Treasure Reef (prod., dir.), Knife Fighters (s.p.). Black Freedom; A Crime of Sex, The Masters (prod., dir.), Crazy Joe, Serpico, Lady Ice, The Klansman, Report to the Commissioner, Tracks, All the President's Men, From Noon Till Three, While Buffalo, Shark Bait (s.p.), The Big Bus, Wanda Nevada, Cuba Crossing, Sunnyside, Cuba, The Last Resort, The All Night Treasure Hunt. Tom Horn, Kill Castro, Midnight Madness, The All-American Hustler, 10 to Midnight, Police Academy 2, One More Werewolf Picture, Silent Scream, Murphy's Law, Cobra, Assassinations, Penitentiary III, Messenger of Death, Death Under the Rock, Innocent Blood, Public Access, Tropic of Desire.
TELEVISION: Flipper, Sea Hunt, Final Judgment, Project Eliminator, Speargun, Gentle Ben, The Law (pilot) and Police Story (actor). Get Christy Love, General Hospital, Columbo, Brenner for the People, Mayday 40,000 Feet, Jigsaw John (Blue Knight episode), Police Woman, Chips, Mobil One, Street Killing, East of Eden, Rose for Emily, Brett Maverick, Today's F.B.I., The Judge. Fifth St. Gym (also prod., dir., s.p.; pilot), Helter Skelter, The Green Eyed Bear, The Amazing Howard Hughes, Mike Douglas Show, Johnny Carson Show, Tales from the Dark Side, The Last Car, This Is the Life, Deadly Intentions, Divorce Court, Man Who Broke 1000 Chains, Nightmare Classics (Eye of the Panther), Man from Atlantis.

WILLIAMS, BILLY DEE: Actor. b. New York, NY, April 6, 1937. e. National Acad. of Fine Arts and Design. Studied acting with Paul Mann and Sidney Poitier at actor's workshop in Harlem. Was child actor in the Firebrand of Florence with Lotte Lenya; Broadway adult debut in The Cool World in 1961.
STAGE: A Taste of Honey, Hallelujah Baby, I Have a Dream, Fences.
PICTURES: The Last Angry Man (debut, 1959), The Out-of-Towners, The Final Comedown, Lady Sings the Blues, Hit!, The Take, Mahogany, The Bingo Long Travelling All-Stars and Motor Kings, Scott Joplin, The Empire Strikes Back,

Nighthawks, Return of the Jedi, Marvin and Tige, Fear City, Number One with a Bullet, Deadly Illusion, Batman, The Pit and the Pendulum, Driving Me Crazy, Giant Steps, Alien Intruder.
TELEVISION: *Series*: The Guiding Light, Double Dare. *Mini-Series*: Chiefs. *Movies*: Carter's Army, Brian's Song, The Glass House, Christmas Lilies of the Field, Children of Divorce, The Hostage Tower, The Imposter, Courage, Oceans of Fire, The Right of the People, Dangerous Passion, The Jacksons: An American Dream, Marked for Murder. Guest: The F.B.I., The Interns, Mission Impossible, Mod Squad, Dynasty, In Living Color.

WILLIAMS, CARA: Actress, Comedienne. r.n. Bernice Kamiat. b. Brooklyn, NY, 1925. e. Hollywood Professional Sch. Ent. ind., 20th Century Fox, child actress.
PICTURES: The Happy Land, Something for the Boys, Boomerang, Don Juan Quilligan, Sitting Pretty, The Girl Next Door, Meet Me in Las Vegas, Never Steal Anything Small, The Defiant Ones (Acad. Award nom.), The Man from the Diners' Club, Doctors' Wives, The White Buffalo.
TELEVISION: *Series*: Pete and Gladys, The Cara Williams Show, Rhoda. *Guest*: Alfred Hitchcock Presents, Desilu Playhouse, The Jackie Gleason Show, Henry Fonda Special.

WILLIAMS, CARL W.: Executive. b. Decatur, IL, March 9, 1927. e. Illinois State Normal U., B.S., 1949; UCLA, M.A., 1950. dir. adv. photo., Clark Equipment Co., 1951–54; film dir., WKAR-TV, E. Lansing, MI, 1954–56; Prod., dir., Capital Films, E. Lansing, MI, 1957; dir., A-V Laboratory, U.C.L.A., 1957–63; co-dev. Dimension 150 Widescreen process, 1957; formed D-150 Inc., 1963; Filbert Co., 1970, v.p., 1977; v.p., Cinema Equipment Sales of Calif., Inc., 1986; pres. 1992.
MEMBER: MAMPAS, SMPTE, AFI.

WILLIAMS, CINDY: Actress. b. Van Nuys, CA., Aug. 22, 1947. e. Los Angeles City Coll. Appeared in high school and college plays; first prof. role in Roger Corman's film Gas-s-s-s. Made TV debut in Room 222 and had recurring role.
PICTURES: Gas-s-s-s (debut, 1970), Beware the Blob, Drive He Said, The Christian Licorice Store, Travels with My Aunt, American Graffiti, The Conversation, Mr. Ricco, The First Nudie Musical, More American Graffiti, Uforia, Rude Awakening, Big Man on Campus, Bingo!, Father of the Bride (co-prod. only), The Leftovers.
TELEVISION: *Series*: The Funny Side, Laverne and Shirley, Normal Life, Getting By. *Guest*: The Neighbors, Barefoot in the Park, My World and Welcome to It, Love American Style, Nanny and the Professor, The Bobby Sherman Show—Getting Together.*Movies*: The Migrants, Help Wanted: Kids, Save the Dog, Tricks of the Trade, Perry Mason: The Case of the Poisoned Pen, Menu for Murder (Murder at the PTA Luncheon), Earth Angel. *Pilot*: Steel Magnolias.

WILLIAMS, ELMO: Film editor, Director, Producer. b. Oklahoma City, OK, Apr. 30, 1913. Film editor 1933–39, with British & Dominion Studio, England. Since then with RKO-Radio as film editor for numerous major productions; mgr., dir., 20th Century Fox Prod. Ltd. v.p., worldwide production, 20th Century-Fox Film 1971. President Ibex Films. Exec. v.p., Gaylord Prods., 1979; promoted to pres., worldwide prods.
PICTURES: High Noon (edit; Acad. Award, 1952), Tall Texan (dir., edit.), The Cowboy (prod., dir., edit.), 20,000 Leagues Under the Sea (edit.), Apache Kid (dir.), The Vikings (2nd unit dir., film ed.), The Big Gamble (2nd Unit dir.), The Longest Day (assoc. prod.), Zorba the Greek (exec. prod.), Those Magnificent Men in Their Flying Machines (exec. prod.), The Blue Max (exec. prod.), Tora! Tora! Tora! (prod.), Sidewinder One (edit.), Caravans (edit.), Man Woman and Child (prod.).
TELEVISION: Tales of the Vikings (co-prod., dir.).

WILLIAMS, ESTHER: Actress. b. Los Angeles, CA, Aug. 8, 1923. e. U. of Southern California. Swimmer San Francisco World's Fair Aquacade; professional model. Voted one of Top Ten Money-Making Stars in M.P. Herald-Fame poll, 1950.
PICTURES: Andy Hardy's Double Life (debut, 1942), A Guy Named Joe, Bathing Beauty, Thrill of a Romance, Ziegfeld Follies, Hoodlum Saint, Easy to Wed, Fiesta, This Time for Keeps, On an Island With You, Take Me Out to the Ball Game, Neptune's Daughter, Pagan Love Song, Duchess of Idaho, Texas Carnival, Callaway Went Thataway (cameo), Skirts Ahoy!, Million Dollar Mermaid, Dangerous When Wet, Easy to Love, Jupiter's Darling, Unguarded Moment, Raw Wind in Eden, The Big Show, The Magic Fountain.

WILLIAMS, JO BETH: Actress. b. Houston, TX, 1953. m. director John Pasquin. e. Brown U. One of Glamour Magazine's top 10 college girls, 1969–70. Acted with rep. companies in Rhode Island, Philadelphia, Boston, Washington, DC, etc. Spent over two years in New York-based daytime serials, Somerset and The Guiding Light. Film debut in Kramer Vs. Kramer, 1979.
THEATER: Ladyhouse Blues (1979), A Coupla White Chicks Sitting Around Talking, Gardenia.

PICTURES: Kramer Vs. Kramer (debut, 1979), Stir Crazy, The Dogs of War, Poltergeist, Endangered Species, The Big Chill, American Dreamer, Teachers, Desert Bloom, Poltergeist II, Memories of Me, Welcome Home, Switch, Dutch, Stop Or My Mom Will Shoot, Me Myself & I, Wyatt Earp.
TELEVISION: *Movies*: Fun and Games, The Big Black Pill, Feasting with Panthers, Jabberwocky, The Day After, Adam, Kids Don't Tell, Adam: His Song Continues, Murder Ordained, Baby M, My Name is Bill W, Child of the Night, Bump in the Night (co-exec. prod. only), Victim of Love, Jonathan: The Boy Nobody Wanted, Sex Love and Cold Hard Cash, Chantilly Lace. *Series*: Fish Police (voice).

WILLIAMS, JOHN: Composer. b. New York, NY, Feb. 8, 1932. e. UCLA, Juilliard Sch. Worked as session musician in '50s; began career as film composer in late '50s. Considerable experience as musical director and conductor as well as composer. Since 1977 conductor of Boston Pops.
PICTURES: I Passed for White, Because They're Young, The Secret Ways, Bachelor Flat, Diamond Head, Gidget Goes to Rome, The Killers, None But the Brave, John Goldfarb Please Come Home, The Rare Breed, How To Steal a Million, The Plainsman, Not with My Wife You Don't, Penelope, A Guide for the Married Man, Fitzwilly, Valley of the Dolls, Daddy's Gone A-Hunting, Goodbye Mr. Chips (mus. supvr. & dir.), The Reivers, Fiddler on the Roof (musc. dir.; Acad. Award), The Cowboys, Images, Pete 'n' Tillie, The Poseidon Adventure, Tom Sawyer (musc. supvr.), The Long Goodbye, The Man Who Loved Cat Dancing, The Paper Chase, Cinderella Liberty, Conrack, The Sugarland Express, Earthquake, The Towering Inferno, The Eiger Sanction, Jaws (Acad. Award), Family Plot, The Missouri Breaks, Midway, Black Sunday, Star Wars (Acad. Award), Raggedy Ann & Andy, Close Encounters of the Third Kind, The Fury, Jaws II, Superman, Meteor, Quintet, Dracula, 1941, The Empire Strikes Back, Raiders of the Lost Ark, Heartbeeps, E.T.: The Extra-Terrestrial (Acad. Award), Yes Giorgio, Monsignor, Return of the Jedi, Indiana Jones and the Temple of Doom, The River, SpaceCamp, The Witches of Eastwick, Empire of the Sun, The Accidental Tourist, Indiana Jones and the Last Crusade, Born on the Fourth of July, Always, Stanley & Iris, Presumed Innocent, Home Alone, Hook, JFK, Far and Away, Home Alone 2: Lost in New York, Jurassic Park.
TELEVISION: Once Upon a Savage Night, Jane Eyre (Emmy Award), Sergeant Ryker, Heidi (Emmy Award), The Ewok Adventure. Series themes: Checkmate, Alcoa Premiere, Wide Country, Lost in Space, The Time Tunnel, NBC News Theme, Amazing Stories.

WILLIAMS, OSCAR: Writer, Producer, Director. e. San Francisco State U., getting degree in film, TV. Was director's intern on The Great White Hope (directed by Martin Ritt) through the American Film Inst. For tv directed The Wack Attack.
PICTURES: The Final Comedown (s.p., prod., dir.), Black Belt Jones (s.p., assoc. prod.) Five on the Black Hand Side (dir.), Truck Turner (s.p.), Hot Potato (s.p., dir.).

WILLIAMS, PAUL: Actor, Composer. b. Omaha, NE, Sept. 19, 1940. Began career at studios as set painter and stunt parachutist. Bit and character parts in commercials followed. Became song writer, collaborating briefly with Biff Rose and later with Roger Nichols, with whom wrote several bestsellers, including We've Only Just Begun, Rainy Days and Mondays, Just an Old-Fashioned Love Song, Evergreen (Acad. Award with Barbra Streisand, 1976).
PICTURES: *As actor*: The Loved One, The Chase, Watermelon Man, Battle for the Planet of the Apes, Phantom of the Paradise (and score), Smokey and the Bandit, The Cheap Detective, The Muppet Movie (and songs), Stone Cold Dead, Smokey and the Bandit II & III, The Chill Factor, The Doors, Solar Crisis (voice). *Scores*: Cinderella Liberty, Bugsy Malone (also vocals), A Star Is Born (co-composer), Agatha, One on One, Ishtar (songs), The Muppet Christmas Carol.
TELEVISION: *Series*: Sugar Time! (songs, music spvr.). *Movies (actor)*: Flight to Holocaust, The Wild Wild West Revisted, Rooster, Night They Saved Christmas, People Like Us.

WILLIAMS, PAUL: Director. b. New York, NY, Nov. 12, 1943. e. Harvard (Phi Beta Kappa, 1965). First gained attention as director of film short, Girl, which won Golden Eagle award, made in collaboration with producer Edward R. Pressman, with whom he formed Pressman-Williams Enterprises which prod. Badlands, Phantom of the Paradise, etc.
PICTURES: Out of It (also s.p.), The Revolutionary, Dealing: or the Berkeley to Boston Forty Brick Lost Bag Blues (also s.p.), Nunzio, Miss Right (also stcry), The November Men (also actor).

WILLIAMS, RICHARD: Producer, Painter, Film animator. b. March, 1933, Toronto, Canada. Entered industry in 1955. Founded Richard Williams Animation Ltd. in 1962, having entered films by producing The Little Island (1st Prize, Venice Film Festival) in 1955. His company produces TV commercials for Eng., Amer., France and Germany, entertainment shorts and animated films. Designed animated feature titles for What's

New Pussycat?, A Funny Thing Happened On The Way To The Forum, Casino Royale, etc. (20 feature titles in 6 years). 1969: Animated sequences: Charge of the Light Brigade (Woodfall). 1971: A Christmas Carol, animated TV special for ABC-TV. Who Framed Roger Rabbit (dir. of animation).

AWARDS: at Festivals at Venice, Edinburgh, Mannheim, Montreal, Trieste, Melbourne, West Germany, New York, Locarno, Vancouver, Philadelphia, Zagreb, Hollywood, Cork, Los Angeles. 1973: Won Academy Award, best cartoon. 1989, Academy Award, BAFTA Award, AMPAS Award, special effects, also Special Achievement Awards for work over 30 years, esp. Roger Rabbit by both BAFTA and AMPAS.

WILLIAMS, ROBIN: Actor, Comedian. b. Chicago, IL, July 21, 1951. e. Claremont Men's Coll. (CA), Coll. of Marin (CA), studying acting at latter. Continued studies at Juilliard with John Houseman in New York augmenting income as a street mime. As San Francisco club performer appeared at Holy City Zoo, Intersection, The Great American Music Hall and The Boardinghouse. In Los Angeles performed as stand-up comedian at Comedy Store, Improvisation, and The Ice House. First TV appearance on 1977–8 Laugh-In specials, followed by The Great American Laugh Off. Guest on Happy Days as extraterrestrial Mork from Ork, led to own series.
TELEVISION: *Series:* The Richard Pryor Show (1977), Laugh-In (1977–8 revival; later aired as series in 1979), Mork and Mindy, Shakespeare: The Animated Tales (host). *Guest:* America Tonight, Ninety Minutes Live, The Alan Hamel Show. *Specials:* An Evening With Robin Williams, E.T. & Friends, Faerie Tale Theatre (The Frog Prince), Carol Carl Whoopi and Robin (Emmy Award, 1987), Free To Be . . . a Family, Dear America: Letters Home from Vietnam (reader), ABC Presents a Royal Gala (Emmy Award, 1988). *Movie:* Seize the Day.
PICTURES: Can I Do It . . . Til I Need Glasses?, Popeye, The World According to Garp, The Survivors, Moscow on the Hudson, The Best of Times, Club Paradise, Good Morning Vietnam (Acad. Award nom.), The Adventures of Baron Munchausen, Dead Poets Society (Acad. Award nom.), Cadillac Man, Awakenings, Dead Again, The Fisher King (Acad. Award nom.), Hook, Shakes the Clown, FernGully . . . The Last Rainforest (voice), Aladdin (voice), Toys, Being Human, Mrs. Doubtfire (also co-prod.).

WILLIAMS, ROGER: Pianist, Concert, film, TV Personality. b. Omaha, NE, Oct. 1, 1926. e. Drake U., Idaho State Coll. Hon. Ph.D. Midland and Wagner Colls. Served U.S. Navy W.W.II. Appeared as guest artist in number of films. Public debut on TV's Arthur Godfrey Talent Scouts and Chance of a Lifetime. Other TV appearances include Ed Sullivan, Hollywood Palace, Kraft Summer Series, Celanese Special. Tours in addition to U.S. and Australia. Concert Halls—Japan, Mexico, Union of South Africa. Recorded 75 Albums, Kapp (now MCA) Records, with sales over 15 million albums.

WILLIAMS, TREAT: Actor. r.n. Richard Williams. b. Rowayton, CT, Dec. 1, 1952. e. Franklin and Marshall Coll. Landed role on Bdwy. in musical, Over Here! also played leading role in Grease on Bdwy.
THEATER: Over Here, Bus Stop (Equity Library Theatre), Once in a Lifetime, The Pirates of Penzance, Some Men Need Help, Oh Hell, Oleanna.
PICTURES: Deadly Hero (debut, 1976), The Ritz, The Eagle Has Landed, Hair, 1941, Why Would I Lie?, Prince of the City, The Pursuit of D. B. Cooper, Once Upon a Time in America, Flashpoint, Smooth Talk, The Men's Club, Dead Heat, Sweet Lies, Heart of Dixie, Night of the Sharks, Russicum, Beyond the Ocean, Where the Rivers Flow North.
TELEVISION: *Movies:* Dempsey, A Streetcar Named Desire, J. Edgar Hoover, Echoes in the Darkness, Third Degree Burn, Max and Helen, Final Verdict, Till Death Us Do Part, The Water Engine, Deadly Matrimony, Bonds of Love (also co-exec. prod.). *Mini-Series:* Drug Wars: The Camarena Story. *Specials:* The Little Mermaid (Faerie Tale Theatre), Some Men Need Help. *Series:* Eddie Dodd, Good Advice. *Guest:* Tales From the Crypt.

WILLIAMS-JONES, MICHAEL: Executive. b. England, June 3, 1947. Joined United Artists as trainee, 1967; territorial mgr., South Africa, 1969; territorial mgr., Brazil, 1971; territorial mgr., England, 1976; appt. v.p., continental European mgr., 1978; sr. v.p. foreign mgr., 1979; In 1982 joined United Intl. Pictures as sr. v.p. intl. sls., based in London. 1984, named pres. UIP motion picture group; 1986, named pres. & CEO.

WILLIAMSON, FRED: Actor, Director, Writer. b. Gary, IN, March 5, 1937. e. Northwestern U. Spent 10 yrs. playing pro football before turning to acting.
PICTURES: M*A*S*H (debut, 1970), Tell Me That You Love Me Junie Moon, The Legend of Nigger Charley, Hammer, Black Caesar, The Soul of Nigger Charley, Hell Up in Harlem, That Man Bolt, Crazy Joe, Three Tough Guys, Black Eye, Three the Hard Way, Boss Nigger, Bucktown, No Way Back (also dir., prod., a.p.), Take a Hard Ride, Adios Amigo, Death Journey (also dir., prod.), Joshua, Blind Rage, Fist of Fear Touch of Death, 1990: The Bronx Warriors, One Down Two to

Go (also dir., prod., Vigilante, Warriors of the Wasteland, Deadly Impact, The Big Score (also dir.), The Last Fight (also dir.), Foxtrap (also dir., prod.), Warrior of the Lost World, Deadly Intent, Delta Force, Commando, Taxi Killer (prod.), Hell's Heroes, Justice Done (also dir.), Soda Cracker (also dir., prod.).
TELEVISION: *Series:* Julia, Monday Night Football, Half Nelson. *Guest:* Police Story, The Rookies, Lou Grant.

WILLIAMSON, NICOL: Actor. b. Hamilton, Scotland, Sept. 14, 1938. Has played many classical roles with Royal Shakespeare Co., including Macbeth, Malvolio, and Coriolanus. Starred on Broadway in Inadmissible Evidence; Rex (musical debut), Macbeth, I Hate Hamlet.
PICTURES: Inadmissible Evidence, The Bofors Gun, Laughter in the Dark, The Reckoning, Hamlet, The Jerusalem File, The Wilby Conspiracy, Robin and Marian, The Seven Percent Solution, The Goodbye Girl (cameo), The Cheap Detective, The Human Factor, Excalibur, Venom, I'm Dancing As Fast As I Can, Return to Oz, Black Widow, The Exorcist III, Apt Pupil.
TELEVISION: *Movies:* Sakharov, Passion Flower. *Mini-Series:* Lord Mountbatten, The Word, Christopher Columbus. *Specials:* Of Mice and Men (1968), Macbeth, I Know What I Meant.

WILLIAMSON, PATRICK: Executive. b. England, Oct. 1929. Joined Columbia Pictures London office 1944—career spanned advertising & publicity responsibilities until 1967 when appt. managing dir. Columbia Great Britain in 1971. Also man. dir. on formation of Columbia-Warner. Promoted to executive position in Columbia's home office, New York, April, 1973 and pres. of international operations Feb. 1974. Vice pres., Coca-Cola Export Corp., April, 1983; exec. v.p. Columbia Pictures Industries, 1985; director, CPI, 1985; exec. v.p., Coca-Cola Entertainment Business Sector, 1987; promoted to special asst. to pres. & CEO of Coca-Cola Entertainment Business Sector, July, 1987. Served on boards of Tri-Star Pictures, RCA/Columbia Home Video, RCA/Columbia Int'l. Video. 1987, named pres. Triumph Releasing Corp., a unit of Columbia Pictures Entertainment. Consultant to Sony Pictures Entertainment, 1989.

WILLIS, BRUCE: Actor. b. Germany, March 19, 1955. m. actress Demi Moore. Moved to New Jersey when he was 2. After graduating high school, worked at DuPont plant in neighboring town. First entertainment work was as harmonica player in band called Loose Goose. Formed Night Owl Promotions and attended Montclair State Coll. NJ, where he acted in Cat on a Hot Tin Roof. NY stage debut: Heaven and Earth. Member of Barbara Contardi's First Amendment Comedy Theatre; supplemented acting work by doing Levi's 501 jeans commercials and as bartender in a N.Y. nightclub, Kamikaze. Appeared as extra in film The First Deadly Sin.
THEATER: Fool for Love.
PICTURES: Blind Date, Sunset, Die Hard, In Country, Look Who's Talking, That's Adequate, Die Hard 2, Look Who's Talking Too (voice), The Bonfire of the Vanities, Mortal Thoughts, Hudson Hawk (also co-story), Billy Bathgate, The Last Boy Scout, The Player, Death Becomes Her, National Lampoon's Loaded Weapon 1, Striking Distance, Color of Night, North.
TELEVISION: *Series:* Moonlighting (Emmy Award, 1987). *Guest:* Hart to Hart, Miami Vice, Twilight Zone. *Special:* Bruce Willis: The Return of Bruno (also writer, prod.).

WILLIS, GORDON: Cinematographer. Acted two summers in stock at Gloucester, MA, where also did stage settings and scenery. Photographer in Air Force; then cameraman, making documentaries. In TV did commercials and documentaries.
PICTURES: End of the Road, Loving, The Landlord, The People Next Door, Little Murders, Bad Company, Klute, Up the Sandbox, The Paper Chase, The Godfather, The Parallax View, The Godfather Part II, The Drowning Pool, All the President's Men, September 30, 1955, Annie Hall, Comes a Horseman, Interiors, Manhattan, Stardust Memories, Pennies from Heaven, A Midsummer Night's Sex Comedy, Perfect, Zelig, Broadway Danny Rose, The Purple Rose of Cairo, The Money Pit, The Pick-Up Artist, Bright Lights Big City, Presumed Innocent, The Godfather Part III. *Director:* Windows (1980; debut).
TELEVISION: The Lost Honor of Kathryn Beck.

WILSON, ELIZABETH: Actress. b. Grand Rapids, MI, April 4, 1925.
THEATRE: *Bdwy:* Picnic (debut, 1953), The Desk Set, The Tunnel of Love, Little Murders, Big Fish Little Fish, Sheep on the Runway, Sticks and Bones (Tony Award, 1972), Uncle Vanya, Morning's at Seven, Ah! Wilderness, The Importance of Being Earnest, You Can't Take It With You. *Off-Bdwy:* Big Fish Little Fish, Sheep on the Runway, Token in Marriage (Drama Desk Award), Three Penny Opera, Salonika, Ante Room, Eh?. *Tour:* The Cocktail Hour.
PICTURES: Picnic (debut, 1955), Patterns, The Goddess, The Tunnel of Love, Happy Anniversary, A Child is Waiting,

The Birds, The Tiger Makes Out, The Graduate, Jenny, Catch-22, Little Murders, Day of the Dolphin, Man on a Swing, The Happy Hooker, The Prisoner of Second Avenue, Nine to Five, The Incredible Shrinking Woman, Grace Quigley, Where Are the Children?, The Believers, Regarding Henry, The Addams Family.
TELEVISION: *Series*: East Side West Side, Doc, Morningstar/Eveningstar, Delta. *Movies*: Miles to Go Before I Sleep, Once Upon a Family, Million Dollar Infield, Sanctuary of Fear, Morning's at Seven, Nutcracker: Money Madness and Murder (Emmy nom.), Conspiracy of Love, Skylark. *Mini-Series*: Queen. *Specials*: Patterns, Happy Endings, Morning's at Seven, You Can't Take It With You. *Guest*: U.S. Steel Hour, Maude, All in the Family, Love Sidney.

WILSON, FLIP: Performer. r.n. Clerow Wilson. b. Newark, NJ, Dec. 8, 1933. Left school at 16 to join Air Force; played clubs in FL & Bahamas until 1965 when made guest appearance on NBC.
TELEVISION: *Series*: The Flip Wilson Show (Emmy Award for writing, 1971), People Are Funny (1984, host), Charlie & Co. *Guest*: That's Life, Sammy and Company, Love American Style, Here's Lucy, The Six Million Dollar Man, 227, etc. *Specials*: Flip Wilson Special (1969), Clerow Wilson and the Miracle of P.S. 114, Clerow Wilson's Great Escape, Pinocchio, Zora is My Name.
PICTURES: Uptown Saturday Night, Skatetown USA, The Fish That Saved Pittsburgh.

WILSON, HUGH: Producer, Director, Writer. b. Miami, FL, Aug. 21, 1943. Gained fame for creating, writing, producing and directing TV series, WKRP in Cincinnati, Frank's Place and The Famous Teddy Z. Feature film dir. debut with Police Academy (1984).
PICTURES: Stroker Ace (co-s.p.). *Director-Writer*: Police Academy, Rustler's Rhapsody, Burglar, Guarding Tess.

WILSON, SCOTT: Actor. b. Atlanta, GA, 1942. Was college athlete on basketball scholarship when injured and had to leave school. Moved to L.A. and enrolled in local acting class.
PICTURES: In the Heat of the Night (debut, 1967), In Cold Blood, The Gypsy Moths, Castle Keep, The Grissom Gang, The New Centurions, Lolly Madonna XXX, The Great Gatsby, Twinkle Twinkle Killer Kane (a.k.a. The Ninth Configuration), The Right Stuff, The Aviator, On the Line, A Year of the Quiet Sun, Blue City, Malone, Johnny Handsome, The Exorcist III, Young Guns II, Femme Fatale, Pure Luck, Flesh and Bone.
TELEVISION: *Movies*: Jesse, Elvis and the Colonel.

WINCER, SIMON: Director. b. Australia. Directed over 200 hours of dramatic programs for Australian TV, including Cash and Company, Tandarra, Ryan, Against the Wind, The Sullivans, etc. Exec. prod. of The Man from Snowy River, then the top-grossing theatrical film in Australia.
PICTURES: Snapshot, Harlequin, Phar Lap, D.A.R.Y.L., The Lighthorsemen (also co.-prod.), Quigley Down Under, Harley Davidson and the Marlboro Man, Free Willy.
TELEVISION: *Movies*: The Last Frontier, Bluegrass, Lonesome Dove (Emmy Award, 1989), The Girl Who Spelled Freedom. *Series*: The Young Indiana Jones Chronicles.

WINCHELL, PAUL: Performer. b. New York, NY, Dec. 21, 1924. e. Sch. of Industrial Arts. At 13 won first prize Major Bowes Radio Amateur Hour; signed by Ted Weems; created Jerry Mahoney when 17; Host of The Bigelow Show (1948–49), ventriloquist & star own Paul Winchell-Jerry Mahoney show (1950–54). Ringmaster Circus Time and panelist on Keep Talking. Hosted film Stop! Look! and Laugh! In The Treasure Chest (TV movie, 1975). Provides voices for numerous films (The Aristocats, Winnie the Pooh, The Fox and the Hound) and Saturday morning cartoons (Dastardly and Muttley, Goober and the Ghost Chasers). In the news in 1975 as inventor of an artificial heart. Appeared in 1970 film Which Way to the Front?.

WINDOM, WILLIAM: Actor. b. New York, NY, Sept. 28, 1923.
TELEVISION: *Series*: The Farmer's Daughter, My World and Welcome to It (Emmy Award, 1970), The Girl With Something Extra, Brothers and Sisters, Murder She Wrote, Parenthood.*Movies*: Prescription: Murder, U.M.C., The House on Greenapple Road, Assault on the Wayne, Escape, A Taste of Evil, Marriage: Year One, The Homecoming, Second Chance, A Great American Tragedy, Pursuit, The Girls of Huntington House, The Day the Earth Moved, The Abduction of St. Anne, Journey from Darkness, Guilty or Innocent: The Sam Sheppard Murder Case, Bridger, Richie Brockelman: Missing 24 Hours, Hunters of the Reef, Portrait of a Rebel: Margaret Sanger, Leave 'Em Laughing, Side Show, Desperate Lives, The Rules of Marriage, Why Me?, Off Sides, Velvet, Surviving, There Must Be a Pony, Dennis the Menace, Chance of a Lifetime, Attack of the 50 Ft. Woman. *Mini-Series*: Once an Eagle, Seventh Avenue, Blind Ambition. *Guest*: Robert Montgomery Presents, Ben Casey, Lucy Show, The FBI, Gunsmoke, Partridge Family, That Girl, The Rookies, Streets of San Francisco, Barney Miller, Kojak,

Police Woman, Love Boat, St. Elsewhere, Newhart, many others.
PICTURES: To Kill a Mockingbird (debut, 1962), Cattle King, For Love or Money, One Man's Way, The Americanization of Emily, Hour of the Gun, The Detective, The Gypsy Moths, The Angry Breed, Brewster McCloud, Fool's Parade, Escape From the Planet of the Apes, The Mephisto Waltz, The Man, Now You See Him Now You Don't, Echoes of a Summer, Mean Dog Blues, Separate Ways, Last Plane Out, Grandview U.S.A., Prince Jack, Space Rage, Funland, Pinocchio and the Emperor of the Night (voice), Planes Trains and Automobiles, She's Having a Baby, Sommersby.

WINDSOR, MARIE: Actress. r.n. Emily Marie Bertelsen. b. Marysvale, UT, Dec. 11, 1922. Winner of beauty contests, including Miss Utah. Worked as telephone girl, dancing teacher. Trained for acting by Maria Ouspenskaya. Won Look Mag. Award, best supporting actress, 1957.
PICTURES: Song of the Thin Man, Unfinished Dance, On an Island With You, Three Musketeers, Kissing Bandit, Force of Evil, Oupost in Morocco, Fighting Kentuckian, Beautiful Blonde From Bashful Bend, Frenchie, Dakota L'il, Little Big Horn, Two Dollar Bettor, Hurricane Island, The Narrow Margin, Japanese War Bride, The Jungle, The Sniper, The Tall Texan, The City That Never Sleeps, The Eddie Cantor Story, Trouble Along the Way, Cat Women of the Moon, Hell's Half Acre, The Bounty Hunter, No Man's Woman, Abbott & Costello Meet the Mummy, Swamp Women, Two Gun Lady, The Killing, The Unholy Wife, The Story of Mankind, Girl in Black Stockings, Parson and the Outlaw, Island Woman, Paradise Alley, The Day Mars Invaded Earth, Critics Choice, Mail Order Bride, Bedtime Story, Chamber of Horrors, Support Your Local Gunfighter, The Good Guys and the Bad Guys, One More Train To Rob, Cahill U.S. Marshall, The Outfit, Hearts of the West, Freaky Friday, Lovely But Deadly.
TELEVISION: *Series*: Supercarrier. *Movies*: Wild Women, Manhunter, Salem's Lot, J.O.E. and the Colonel.

WINELAND, FRED L.: Theatre Executive. b. Washington, DC, 1926. e. Southeastern U., 1957. Pres., Wineland Theatres, circuit which owns and operates two Maryland drive-ins, three Maryland indoor multi-cinemas and two Virginia multi-cinemas.

WINFIELD, PAUL: Actor. b. Los Angeles, CA, May 22, 1940. e. attended U. of Portland 1957–59, Stanford U., L.A. City Coll. and UCLA. Inducted in Black Filmmakers Hall of Fame.
THEATER: Regional work at Dallas Theatre Center (A Lesson From Aloes), Goodman Theatre (Enemy of the People), Stanford Repertory Theatre and Inner City Cultural Center, L.A.; At Lincoln Center in The Latent Heterosexual, and Richard III. Broadway: Checkmates, Othello, Merry Wives of Windsor.
PICTURES: The Lost Man, RPM, Brother John, Sounder (Acad. Award nom.), Trouble Man, Gordon's War, Conrack, Huckleberry Finn, Hustle, Twilight's Last Gleaming, The Greatest, Damnation Alley, A Hero Ain't Nothin' But a Sandwich, High Velocity, Carbon Copy, Star Trek II—The Wrath of Khan, White Dog, On the Run, Mike's Murder, The Terminator, Blue City, Death Before Dishonor, Big Shots, The Serpent and the Rainbow, Presumed Innocent, Cliffhanger, Dennis the Menace.
TELEVISION: *Series*: Julia (1968–70), The Charmings, Wiseguy, 227. *Movies*: The Horror at 37,000 Feet, It's Good to Be Alive (The Fight), Green Eyes, Angel City, Key Tortuga, The Sophisticated Gents, Dreams Don't Die, Sister Sister, For Us the Living, Go Tell It on the Mountain, Under Siege, The Roy Campanella Story, Guilty of Innocence, Women of Brewster Place, Roots: The Gift, Back to Hannibal. *Mini-Series*: King, Backstairs at the White House, The Blue and the Gray, Roots: The Next Generations, Queen.

WINFREY, OPRAH: TV Talk Show Hostess, Actress, Producer. b. Kosciusko, MS, Jan. 29, 1954. e. Tennessee State U. Started as radio reporter then TV news reporter-anchor in Nashville. Moved to Baltimore in same capacity, later co-hosting successful morning talk show. Left for Chicago to host own show AM Chicago which became top-rated in only a month; expanded to national syndication in 1986. Formed own production co., Harpo Productions, Inc. in 1986 which assumed ownership and prod. of The Oprah Winfrey Show in 1988. Named Broadcaster of the Year by Intl. Radio and TV Soc., 1988. Purchased Chicago movie and TV production facility, 1988; renamed Harpo Studios. National Daytime Emmy Award, 1987, Outstanding Talk/Service Program Host.
PICTURES: The Color Purple (debut, 1985; Acad. Award nom.), Native Son, Throw Momma From the Train (cameo).
TELEVISION: *Movies*: The Women of Brewster Place (actress, co-exec. prod.), Overexposed (co-prod. only). *Series*: The Oprah Winfrey Show (Emmy Awards), Brewster Place (also exec. prod.). *Special*: Pee-wee's Playhouse Christmas Special.

WINGER, DEBRA: Actress. b. Cleveland, OH, May 17, 1955. e. California State U. Served in Israeli Army. Began career in TV series Wonder Woman.

PICTURES: Slumber Party '57 (debut, 1977), Thank God It's Friday, French Postcards, Urban Cowboy, Cannery Row, An Officer and a Gentleman, Terms of Endearment, Mike's Murder, Legal Eagles, Black Widow, Made in Heaven, Betrayed, Everybody Wins, The Sheltering Sky, Leap of Faith, Wilder Napalm, A Dangerous Woman, Shadowlands.
TELEVISION: *Movie*: Special Olympics. *Guest*: Wonder Woman, James at 16.

WINITSKY, ALEX: Producer. b. New York, NY, Dec. 27, 1924. e. NYU, BS, LLB, JD. In partnership with attorneys for 20 years with Arlene Sellers before they turned to financing and later production of films.
PICTURES: Co-prod. with Sellers: End of the Game, The Seven-Per-Cent Solution, Cross of Iron, Night Calls, Silver Bears, The Lady Vanishes, Breakthrough, Cuba, Blue Skies Again, Irreconcilable Differences, Scandalous, Swing Shift, Bad Medicine.
TELEVISION: Ford—The Man and the Machine.

WINKLER, HENRY: Actor, Producer, Director. b. New York, NY, Oct. 30, 1945. e. Emerson Coll., Yale Sch. of Drama, MA. Appeared with Yale Repertory Co.; returned to N.Y. to work in radio. Did 30 TV commercials before starring in The Great American Dream Machine and Masquerade on TV. Formed Winkler/Daniel Prod. Co. with Ann Daniel.
PICTURES: *Actor*: Crazy Joe (debut, 1974), The Lords of Flatbush, Heroes, The One and Only, Night Shift. *Exec. Prod*: The Sure Thing. *Director*: Memories of Me, Cop and a Half.
TELEVISION: *Series*: Happy Days, Ryans Four (co.-prod.), Mr. Sunshine (co-exec. prod.), McGyver (prod.), A Life Apart (prod.). *Guest*: The Mary Tyler Moore Show, The Bob Newhart Show, The Paul Sand Show, Rhoda, Laverne & Shirley.*Specials*: Henry Winkler Meets William Shakespeare, America Salutes Richard Rodgers, A Family Again (exec. prod.), Two Daddies (voice, exec. prod.) *Movies*: Katherine, An American Christmas Carol, Absolute Strangers. *Director*: A Smoky Mountain Christmas (movie), All the Kids Do It (also actor, exec. prod.; Emmy as exec. prod., 1985). *Exec. prod.*: Who Are the DeBolts—and Where Did They Get 19 Kids?, Scandal Sheet, When Your Lover Leaves, Starflight, Second Start, Morning Glory (pilot).

WINKLER, IRWIN: Producer, Director. b. New York, NY, May 28, 1931. e. NYU.
PICTURES: *Producer*: Double Trouble, Blue, The Split, They Shoot Horses Don't They?, The Strawberry Statement, Leo the Last, Believe in Me, The Gang That Couldn't Shoot Straight, The Mechanic, The New Centurions, Up the Sandbox, Busting, S*P*Y*S, The Gambler, Breakout, Peeper, Rocky (Acad. Award for Best Picture, 1976), Nickelodeon, New York New York, Valentino, Comes a Horseman, Uncle Joe Shannon, Rocky II, Raging Bull, True Confessions, Rocky III, Author! Author!, The Right Stuff, Rocky IV, Revolution, 'Round Midnight, Betrayed, Music Box, Good-Fellas, Rocky V. *Director*: Guilty by Suspicion (also s.p.), Night and the City.

WINNER, MICHAEL: Producer, Director, Writer. b. London, Eng., Oct. 30, 1935. e. Cambridge U. Ent. m.p. ind. as columnist, dir., Drummer Films. Presenter: True Crimes. Actor: For the Greater Good, Decadence, Calliope, The Full Wax.
TELEVISION: Series: White Hunter, Dick and the Duchess.
PICTURES: *Writer*: Man With A Gun. *Director-Writer*: Haunted England, Shoot to Kill, Swiss Holiday, Climb Up the Wall, Out of the Shadow, Some Like It Cool, Girls Girls Girls, It's Magic, Behave Yourself, The Cool Mikado, You Must Be Joking, West 11, The System (The Girl-Getters), I'll Never Forget What's 'is Name, The Jokers. *Director*: Hannibal Brooks (also prod., s.p.), The Games, Lawman, The Night-comers, Chato's Land, The Mechanic, Scorpio (also prod., s.p.), The Stone Killer, Death Wish, Won Ton Ton the Dog Who Saved Hollywood, The Sentinel (also prod., s.p.), The Big Sleep (also prod., s.p.), Firepower (also prod., s.p.), Death Wish II, The Wicked Lady (also prod., s.p.), Scream for Help, Death Wish III, Appointment With Death (also prod., s.p.), A Chorus of Disapproval (also prod., s.p.), Bullseye (also prod., s.p.), Dirty Weekend (also prod., s.p.).

WINNINGHAM, MARE: Actress. b. Phoenix, AZ, May 6, 1959. TV debut at age 16 as a singer on The Gong Show. Debut solo album What Might Be released in 1992.
PICTURES: One-Trick Pony, Threshold, St. Elmo's Fire, Nobody's Fool, Made in Heaven, Shy People, Miracle Mile, Turner and Hooch, Hard Promises, Wyatt Earp.
TELEVISION: *Mini-series*: The Thorn Birds, Studs Lonigan. *Movies*: Special Olympics, The Death of Ocean View Park, Amber Waves (Emmy Award), The Women's Room, Freedom, A Few Days in Weasel Creek, Missing Children: A Mother's Story. Helen Keller: The Miracle Continues, Single Bars Single Women, Love Is Never Silent, Who is Julia, A Winner Never Quits, Eye on the Sparrow, God Bless the Child, Love and Lies, Crossing to Freedom, Fatal Exposure, She Stood Alone, Those Secrets, Intruders, Better Off Dead.

WINTER, ALEX: Actor. b. London, England, July 17, 1965. e. NYU. At age 4 began studying dance. Played opposite Vincent Price in St. Louis Opera production of Oliver! Co-founder of Stern-Winter Prods. Produced videos for Red Hot Chili Peppers, Human Radio, Ice Cube, etc. Co-directed TV special Hard Rock Cafe Presents: Save the Planet.
PICTURES: Death Wish III, The Lost Boys, Haunted Summer, Bill & Ted's Excellent Adventure, Rosalie Goes Shopping, Bill & Ted's Bogus Journey, Hideous Mutant Freekz (also dir., co-s.p.).
TELEVISION: *Movie*: Gaugin the Savage. *Series*: Idiot Box (co-creator).
THEATRE: *Bdwy*: The King and I (1977 revival), Peter Pan (1979 revival). *Off-Bdwy*: Close of Play.

WINTERS, DAVID: Choreographer, Actor, Director. b. London, April 5, 1939. Acted in both Broadway and m.p. version of West Side Story (as A-rab). Directed and acted in number of TV shows. Choreography credits include films Viva Las Vegas, Billie, Send Me No Flowers, Tickle Me, Pajama Party, Girl Happy, The Swinger, Made in Paris, Easy Come, Easy Go, The Island of Doctor Moreau, Roller Boogie, A Star is Born, Blame It on the Night. Was choreographer for TV series Hullabaloo, Shindig, Donny and Marie Osmond, The Big Show, and Steve Allen Show, and TV specials starring Joey Heatherton, Nancy Sinatra, Diana Ross, Raquel Welch, Ann Margret, Lucille Ball. Pres., A.I.P. Distribution, A.I.P. Productions and A.I.P. Home Video, 1989, formed Pyramid Distributors. Features incl.: Firehead, Raw Nerve, Center of the Web, Double Vision.

WINTERS, DEBORAH: Actress. b. Los Angeles, CA. e. Professional Children's Sch., New York; began studying acting at Stella Adler's with Pearl Pearson. at age 13 and Lee Strasberg at 16. Acting debut at age 5 in TV commercials. Casting dir.: Aloha Summer (asst.), Breakdancers From Mars (assoc. prod., casting dir.), Into the Spider's Web, The Hidden Jungle, Haunted, Broken Spur, Behind the Mask (also assoc. prod.).
PICTURES: Me Natalie, Hail Hero!, The People Next Door, Kotch, Class of '44, Blue Sunshine, The Lamp, The Outing.
TELEVISION: *Special*: Six Characters in Search of an Author. *Guest*: Matt Houston, Medical Center. *Movies*: Lottery, Gemini Man. Tarantulas: The Deadly Cargo, Little Girl Lost, Space City. *Mini-Series*: The Winds of War.

WINTERS, JERRY: Producer, Director. b. Waterbury, CT, Aug. 18, 1917. e. Antioch Coll., B.A., 1940. Photog., 1940–42; U.S. Air Force, 1942–46; photog., Hollywood, 1946–47; prod. assoc. Tonight on Broadway, CBS-TV, 1949; assc. prod., College Bowl, ABC-TV, 1950–51; in charge N.Y. film prod., Television Varieties, Inc., 1951–54; Production head Eldorado Int'l Pictures Corp., 1964–67; vice president, Edutornics Corp., 1968; pres. Giralda Pros., 1971.
PICTURES: prod., Renoir; prod.-dir., Herman Melville's Moby Dick, Speak to Me Child; prod; English version, The Loves of Liszt.

WINTERS, JONATHAN: Performer. b. Dayton, OH, Nov. 11, 1925. e. Kenyon Coll.; Dayton Art Inst., B.F.A. Disc jockey, Dayton and Columbus stations; night club comedian. Performed at Blue Angel and Ruban Bleu (NY), Black Orchid (Chicago), Flamingo, Sands, Riviera (Las Vegas) and on Bdwy. in John Murray Anderson's Almanac. Author: Mouse Breath, Conformity and Other Social Ills, Winters Tales, Hang Ups (book on his paintings). Recorded 7 comedy albums.
TELEVISION: *Series*: And Here's the Show, NBC Comedy Hour, Jonathan Winters Show (1956–7), Masquerade Party (panelist), The Andy Williams Show, The Jonathan Winters Show (1967–9), Hot Dog, The Wacky World of Jonathan Winters, Mork and Mindy, Hee Haw, The Smurfs (voice of Papa Smurf), The Completely Mental Misadventures of Ed Grimley (voices), Davis Rules (Emmy Award, 1991), Fish Police (voice). *Guest*: Steve Allen Show, Garry Moore Show, Jack Paar, Omnibus, Twlight Zone, many others. *Special*: 'Tis the Season to Be Smurfy (voice). *Movies*: Now You See It—Now You Don't, More Wild Wild West.
PICTURES: It's a Mad Mad Mad Mad World (debut, 1963), The Loved One, The Russians Are Coming the Russians Are Coming, Penelope, Oh Dad Poor Dad Mama's Hung You in the Closet and I'm Feelin' So Sad, Eight on the Lam, Viva Max, The Fish That Saved Pittsburgh, The Longshot, Say Yes, Moon Over Parador.

WINTERS, SHELLEY: Actress. r.n. Shirley Schrift. b. St. Louis, MO, Aug. 18, 1922. e. Wayne U. Clerked in 5 & 10 cent store; in vaudeville; NY stage (Conquest, Night Before Christmas, Meet the People, Rosalinda, A Hatful of Rain, Girls of Summer, Minnie's Boys, One Night Stand of a Noisy Passenger. (Off-Bdwy). Autobiographies: Shelley, Also Know as Shirley (1981), Shelley II: The Middle of My Century (1989).
PICTURES: Nine Girls, Sailor's Holiday, Knickerbocker Holiday, Cover Girl, Double Life, Cry of the City, Larceny, Take one False Step, Johnny Stool Pigeon, Great Gatsby, South Sea Sinner, Winchester '73, Frenchie, Place in the Sun, He Ran All the Way, Behave Yourself, The Raging Tide,

Phone Call From a Stranger, Meet Danny Wilson, Untamed Frontier, My Man and I, Tennessee Champ, Executive Suite, Saskatchewan, Playgirl, To Dorothy a Son (Cash on Delivery), Mambo, Night of the Hunter, I Am a Camera, Big Knife, Treasure of Pancho Villa, I Died a Thousand Times, Diary of Anne Frank (Acad. Award, supp., 1959), Odds Against Tomorrow, Let No Man Write My Epitaph, Young Savages, Lolita, Chapman Report, The Balcony, Wives and Lovers, Time of Indifference, A House Is Not a Home, A Patch of Blue (Acad. Award, supp., 1965), The Greatest Story Ever Told, Harper, Alfie, Enter Laughing, The Scalphunters, Wild in the Streets, Buona Sera Mrs. Campbell, The Mad Room, How Do I Love Thee?, Bloody Mama, Flap, What's the Matter with Helen?, Who Slew Auntie Roo?, The Poseidon Adventure, Cleopatra Jones, Something to Hide, Blume in Love, Diamonds, Journey Into Fear, That Lucky Touch, Next Stop Greenwich Village, The Tenant, Tentacles, Pete's Dragon, King of the Gypsies, The Magician of Lublin, The Visitors, City on Fire, S.O.B., Over the Brooklyn Bridge, Ellie, Witchfire (also assoc. prod.), Deja Vu, Very Close Quarters, The Delta Force, The Order of Things, Purple People Eater, An Unremarkable Life, Touch of a Stranger, Stepping Out, The Pickle.

TELEVISION: *Special*: Bob Hope Chrysler Theatre: Two is the Number (Emmy, 1964). *Movies*: Revenge, A Death of Innocence, The Adventures of Nick Carter, The Devil's Daughter, Big Rose, The Sex Symbol, The Initiation of Sarah, Elvis, Alice in Wonderland. *Mini-Series*: The French Atlantic Affair.

WINTMAN, MELVIN R.: Theatre Executive. b. Chelsea, MA. e. U. of Massachusetts, Northeastern U., J.D. Major, infantry, AUS, W.W.II. Attorney. Now consultant & dir., General Cinema Corp.; formerly exec. v.p., GCC and pres., GCC Theatres, Inc., Boston. Dir. Will Rogers Memorial Fund. Former pres. Theatre Owners of New England (1969–70); past dir. NATO (1969–70); treas., Nat'l Assoc. of Concessionaires (1960).

WISDOM, NORMAN: Actor, Singer, Comedian. Musical and legit. b. London, Eng., Feb. 4, 1915. Many London West End stage shows including royal command performances. New York Broadway shows include Walking Happy and Not Now Darling. Two Broadway awards. Films include Trouble in Store, One Good Turn, Man of the Moment, Up in the World, Just My Luck, The Square Peg, There Was a Crooked Man, The Bulldog Breed, The Girl on the Boat, On the Beat, A Stitch in Time, The Early Bird, Press for Time, The Sandwich Man, What's Good for the Goose, Double X, and others mostly for the Rank Organisation and United Artists. In US: The Night They Raided Minsky's. TV musical: Androcles and the Lion.

WISE, ROBERT: Director, Producer. b. Winchester, IN, Sept. 10, 1914. e. Franklin Coll., Franklin, IN. Ent. m.p. ind. in cutting dept. RKO, 1933; sound cutter, asst. ed.; film ed., 1938; edited Citizen Kane, Magnificent Ambersons; 1944, became dir.; to 20th Century-Fox, 1949; ass'n. Mirisch Co. independent prod. 1959; assn. MGM independent prod., 1962; assn. 20th Century Fox Independent Prod. 1963. Partner, Filmakers Group, The Tripar Group.

PICTURES: Curse of the Cat People (debut as co-dir.), Mademoiselle Fifi, The Body Snatcher, Game of Death, Criminal Court, Born to Kill, Mystery in Mexico, Blood on the Moon, The Set Up, Three Secrets, Two Flags West, House on Telegraph Hill, Day the Earth Stood Still, Captive City, Something for the Birds, Destination Gobi, Desert Rats, So Big, Executive Suite, Helen of Troy, Tribute to a Bad Man, Somebody Up There Likes Me, Until They Sail, This Could Be the Night, Run Silent Run Deep, I Want to Live, Odds Against Tomorrow (also prod.), West Side Story (co-dir.; prod.; Acad. Awards for dir. & picture, 1961), Two For the Seesaw, The Haunting, The Sound of Music (also prod.; Acad. Awards for dir. & picture, 1965), The Sand Pebbles (also prod.), Star! (also prod.), The Andromeda Strain (also prod.), Two People (also prod.), The Hindenburg (also prod.), Audrey Rose, Star Trek: The Motion Picture, Wisdom (exec. prod. only), Rooftops.

WISEMAN, FREDERICK: Documentary filmmaker (prod., dir., edit). b. Boston, MA, Jan. 1, 1930. e. Williams College, B.A., 1951; Yale Law Sch., L.L.B., 1954. Member: MA Bar. Private law practice, Paris, 1956–57. Lecturer-in-Law, Boston U. Law Sch., 1959–61; Russell Sage Fdn. Fellowship, Harvard U., 1961–62; research assoc., Brandeis U., dept. of sociology, 1962–66; visiting lecturer at numerous universities. Author: Psychiatry and Law: Use and Abuse of Psychiatry in a Murder Case (American Journal of Psychiatry, Oct. 1961). Co-author: Implementation (section of report of President's Comm. on Law Enforcement and Administration of Justice). Fellow, Amer. Acad. of Arts & Sciences, 1991; John D. and Catherine T. MacArthur Foundation Fellowship, 1982–7; John Simon Guggenheim Memorial Foundation Fellowship, 1980–1. Films are distributed through his Zipporah Films, located in Cambridge, MA. Awards include 3 Emmys, Peabody Award,

Intl. Documentary Assn. Career Achievement Award, among others.

PICTURES: Titicut Follies (1967), High School, Law and Order, Hospital, Basic Training, Essene, Juvenile Court, Primate, Welfare, Meat, Canal Zone, Sinai Field Mission, Manoeuvre, Model, Seraphita's Diary, The Store, Racetrack, Deaf, Blind, Multi-Handicapped, Adjustment and Work, Missile, Near Death, Central Park, Aspen.

WISEMAN, JOSEPH: Actor. b. Montreal, Canada, May 15, 1918. Began acting in the thirties, including Bdwy. stage, radio, m.p. and later TV.

PICTURES: Detective Story (debut, 1951), Viva Zapata, Les Miserables, Champ for a Day, The Silver Chalice, The Prodigal, Three Brave Men, The Garment Jungle, The Unforgiven, Happy Thieves, Dr. No, Bye Bye Braverman, The Counterfeit Killer, The Night They Raided Minsky's, Stiletto, Lawman, The Valachi Papers, The Apprenticeship of Duddy Kravitz, Journey Into Fear, The Betsy, Buck Rogers in the 25th Century, Jaguar Lives.

STAGE: King Lear, Golden Boy, The Diary of Anne Frank, Uncle Vanya, The Last Analysis, Enemies, Detective Story, Three Sisters, Tenth Man, Incident at Vickey, Marco Williams, Unfinished Stories, many others.

TELEVISION: *Mini-Series*: QB VII, Masada, Rage of Angels. *Movies*: Pursuit, Murder at the World Series, Seize the Day, Lady Mobster. *Series*: Crime Story.

WITHERS, GOOGIE: Actress. b. Karachi, India, Mar. 12, 1917. Trained as a dancer under Italia Conti, Helena Lehmiski & Buddy Bradley; stage debut Victoria Palace in Windmill Man, 1929. Best Actress Award, Deep Blue Sea, 1954. Began screen career at 18. TV also. Theatrical tours Australia, Sun Award, Best Actress, 1974. Awarded officer of the Order of Australia (A.O.) 1980. U.S. ACE Cable award, best actress for Time After Time, 1988.

PICTURES: Haunted Honeymoon, Jeannie, One of Our Aircraft Is Missing, On Approval, Dead of Night, It Always Rains on Sunday, Miranda, Traveler's Joy, Night and the City, White Corridors, Lady Godiva Rides Again, Derby Day, Devil on Horseback, Safe Harbor, Nickel Queen.

STAGE: (Britain) Winter Journey, Deep Blue Sea, Hamlet, Much Ado About Nothing. (Australia) Plaza Suite, Relatively Speaking, Beckman Place, Woman in a Dressing Gown, The Constant Wife, First Four Hundred Years, Roar Like a Dove, The Cherry Orchard, An Ideal Husband. (London) Getting Married, Exit the King. (New York) The Complaisant Lover, Chichester Festival Theatre and Haymarket, London, in The Circle, The Kingfisher, Importance of Being Earnest, The Cherry Orchard, Dandy Dick, The Kingfisher (Australia and Middle East), Time and the Conways (Chichester), School for Scandal (London), Stardust (UK tour). 1986: The Chalk Garden, Hay Fever, Ring Round the Moon, The Cocktail Hour (UK, Australian tour), High Spirits (Aus. tour), On Golden Pond (UK tour).

TELEVISION: *Series*: Within These Walls, Time After Time, *Movies*: Hotel Du Lac, Northanger Abbey, Ending Up.

WITHERS, JANE: Actress. b. Atlanta, GA, April 12, 1927. By 1934 attracted attention as child player on screen, after radio appearance in Los Angeles and experimental pictures parts, in 1934 in Fox production Bright Eyes, Ginger; thereafter to 1942 featured or starred in numerous 20th-Fox prod. Voted Money-Making Star M.P. Herald-Fame Poll, 1937, 1938. Starred as Josephine the Plumber in Comet commercials. TV Movie: All Together Now.

PICTURES: Boy Friend, Pack Up Your Troubles, Chicken Family Wagon, Shooting High, High School, Youth Will Be Served, Girl From Avenue A, Golden Hoofs, A Very Young Lady, Her First Beau, Small Town Deb, Young America, The Mad Martindales, Johnny Doughboy, The North Star, My Best Gal, Faces in the Fog, Affairs of Geraldine, Danger Street, Giant, The Right Approach, Captain Newman M.D.

WITT, PAUL JUNGER: Producer. b. New York, NY, Mar. 20, 1943. e. Univ. of VA. Was assoc. prod., prod. and dir. for Screen Gems, starting in 1965; prod. for Spelling-Goldberg Prods., 1972; Prod.-exec. prod. for Danny Thomas Prods., 1973. With Tony Thomas became co-founder, exec. prod. of Witt/Thomas Prods., 1975.

TELEVISION: *Series*: The Rookies, Soap, It's a Living, I'm a Big Girl Now, It Takes Two, Condo, Hail to the Chief, The Golden Girls (Emmy Awards: 1986, 1987), Beauty and the Beast, Empty Nest, Blossom, Good and Evil, Herman's Head, Nurses, Woops, The John Larroquette Show. *Movies*: Brian's Song (Emmy Award: 1972), No Place to Run, Home for the Holidays, A Cold Night's Death, The Letters, Blood Sport, Remember When, The Gun and the Pulpit, Satan's Triangle, Griffin and Phoenix, High Risk, Trouble in High Timber Country.

PICTURES: Firstborn, Dead Poets Society, Final Analysis.

WIZAN, JOE: Executive. b. Los Angeles, CA, Jan. 7, 1935. e. UCLA. Started in industry as agent for William Morris Agency. Left to form London Intl. Artists, Ltd. in association with Richard Gregson, Alan Ladd, Jr. and Mike Gruskoff.

When firm dissolved joined Creative Management Associates as v.p. in chg. of creative services. In 1969 formed own indep. prod. co. 1981, named pres., CBS Theatrical Film Div. 1982, returned to 20th Century-Fox as independent producer. 1983, named pres., 20th-Fox Prods.; Resigned in 1984.
PICTURES: Jeremiah Johnson, Junior Bonner, Prime Cut, The Last American Hero, Audrey Rose, Voices, And Justice for All, Best Friends, Unfaithfully Yours, Two of a Kind, Tough Guys, Witching Hour, Split Decisions, Spellbinder (prod.), Short Time (exec. prod.).

WOLF, EMANUEL L.: Executive b. Brooklyn, NY, Mar. 27, 1927. e. Syracuse U., B.A., 1950; Maxwell Sch., Syracuse U., M.A. 1952; Maxwell Scholar in Public Admin.-Economics; Chi Eta Sigma (Econ. Hon.). 1952–55. Management consultant, exec. office of Secretary of Navy & Dept. of Interior, Wash., DC, 1956. National dir. of Program & Admin. of a Veterans Org. 1957–61. Pres. E. L. Wolf Associates, Washington, DC, 1961–Jan. 1965. Treasurer, Kalvex, Inc. Dec. 1962. Dir. Kalvex, Inc. March 1963. Dir. Allied Artists Pictures Corp., Jan. 1965. Pres. Kalvex, Inc. April 1966–present, pres. & chmn. of the Bd. Kalvex, Inc.; Chmn. of the Bd. Vitabath, Inc.; Chmn. of the Bd. Lexington Instruments; pres. & chairman of the bd. Pharmaceutical Savings Plan, Inc. Syracuse U. Corporate Advisory Board, American Committee for the Weizmann Institute of Science (Bd. of Directors). Pres. & chmn. of bd., Allied Artists Pictures Corp: January, 1976: pres., & bd. chmn. & CEO Allied Artists Industries Inc., created by Merger of Allied Artists Pictures Corp., Kalvex Inc. and PSP, Inc. 1985, formed indep. prod. co., Emanuel L. Wolf Prods.; 1986–90, pres. & chmn. of bd., Today Home Entertainment. 1991–present. Emanuel L. Wolf Prods., Inc.

WOLF, THOMAS HOWARD: TV news exec. b. New York, NY, April 22, 1916. e. Princeton U., B.A., magna cum laude, 1937. Time & Life Mag. 1937–39; 1937–39 NEA (Scripps-Howard) 1940–46; European mgr., NEA, 1942–46. War correspondent, (ETO, MTO) NBC radio correspondent, Paris, 1944–45; co-owner, pres., Information Prod., Inc. founded 1951; co-owner, chmn. Butterfield & Wolf, Inc. founded 1955; prod. CBS series Tomorrow, 1960; exec. prod., CBS daily live Calendar Show, 1961–62; sr. prod., ABC News Report, 1963; exec. prod., ABC Scope, 1964–66. v.p. dir. of TV Documentaries, 1966; v.p., dir. of TV Public Affairs, 1974; dir. TV Cultural Affairs, 1976. Pres., Wolf Communications, Inc., 1981–

WOLFSON, RICHARD: Executive. b. New York, NY, Jan. 7, 1923. e. Harvard Coll., Yale Law Sch., 1945–47, law sect'y to Justice Wiley Rutledge, U.S. Supreme Court. Law instructor at NYU Law Sch.; later received Guggenheim Fellowship; 1952, joined Wometco Ent. as counsel and asst. to pres.; named v.p. dir. in 1959 and sr. v.p. in 1962; named exec. v.p. and general counsel in 1973; named chmn., exec. comm., 1976; co-author of Jurisdiction of the Supreme Court of the United States and author of articles in various legal publications. Retired from Wometco 1982; counsel, Valdes-Fanli, Cobb, Bischoff and Kriss. Miami, FL. Treasurer & Chmn., finance committee Greater Miami Opera; dir., Eastern Natl. Bank, Miami, FL.

WOLPER, DAVID L.: Producer. b. New York, NY, Jan. 11, 1928. m. Gloria Diane Hill. e. Drake U., U. of Southern California. Treas., Flamingo Films, 1948; merged with Associated Artist to form M.P. for TV, Inc., acting as v.p. in chg. of West Coast oper., 1950; v.p. reactivated Flamingo Films, 1954; also pres. Harris-Wolper Pictures, Inc.; pres. Wolper Prod. 1958; pres. Dawn Prod.; v.p. Bd. Dir. Metromedia, 1965; pres. Wolper Pictures Ltd. 1967; ch. of bd. Wolper Prod., Inc., 1967; pres. Wolper Pictures, 1968; pres. Wolper Productions, 1970; pres. & ch. of bd. of dir. The Wolper Organization, Inc., 1971; consultant to Warner Bros. & Warner Communications, Pres., David L. Wolper Prods., Inc. 1977. Received Jean Hersholt Humanitarian Award, 1985; Intl. Documentary Assn. Career Achievement Award, 1988. Also received French Natl. Legion of Honor Medal, Lifetime Achievement Award from Producers Guild, Charles de Gaulle Centennial Medal.
TELEVISION: Specials: The Race For Space, The Making of the President (1960, 1964, 1968), National Geographic Society Specials (1965–68, 1971–75), The Rise and Fall of the Third Reich, The Undersea World of Jacques Cousteau (1967–68), George Plimpton specials (1970–72), American Heritage specials (1973–74), Primal Man specials (1973–75), Judgment specials (1974), Smithsonian Specials, Sandburg's Lincoln, The Man Who Saw Tomorrow, Opening & Closing Ceremonies: Olympic Games 1984, Liberty Weekend 1986, A Celebration of Tradition for Warner Bros. Series: Story of . . . , Biography, Hollywood and the Stars, Men in Crisis, The March of Time (1965–66), Appointment With Destiny, Get Christie Love, Chico and the Man, Welcome Back Kotter, Casablanca. Movies: The 500 Pound Jerk, I Will Fight No More Forever, Victory at Entebbe, Agatha Christie's Murder Is Easy, What Price Victory, Roots: The Gift, When You Remember Me, Dillinger, The Plot to Kill Hitler, Murder in Mississippi, Bed of Lies. Mini-Series: Roots (Emmy Award, 1977), Roots: The Next Generations, (Emmy Award, 1979),

Moviola (This Year's Blonde, The Scarlett O'Hara War, The Silent Lovers), The Thorn Birds, North & South, North & South Book II, Napoleon & Josephine: A Love Story, Queen.
PICTURES: Four Days in November, If It's Tuesday This Must Be Belgium, Say Goodbye 1971, Willie Wonka and the Chocolate Factory, Visions of Eight, Birds Do it Bees Do It, Imagine: John Lennon.

WOO, JOHN: Director. b. Guangzhou, China, 1948. e. Matteo Ricci Col, Hong Kong. Started making experimental 16 mm films in 1967. Entered film industry in 1969 as prod. asst. for Cathay Film Co., then asst. dir. 1971 joined Shaw Brothers working as asst. dir. to Zhang Che. Directorial debut 1973 with The Young Dragons.
PICTURES: The Young Dragons, The Dragon Tamers, Countdown in Kung Fu, Princess Chang Ping, From Riches to Rags, Money Crazy, Follow th Star, Last Hurrah for Chivalry, To Hell With the Devil, Laughing Times, Plain Jane to the Rescue, Sunset Warriors (Heroes Shed No Tears), The Time You Need a Friend, Run Tiger Run, A Better Tomorrow, A Better Tomorrow II, Just Heroes, The Killer, Bullet in the Head, Once a Thief, Hard Boiled, Hard Target (U.S. debut, 1993).

WOOD, ELIJAH: Actor. b. Cedar Rapids, IA, Jan. 28, 1981. Started in commercial modeling. Landed first acting job in Paula Abdul video Forever Your Girl.
PICTURES: Back to the Future Part II (debut, 1989), Internal Affairs, Avalon, Paradise, Radio Flyer, Forever Young, The Adventures of Huck Finn, The Good Son, North.
TELEVISION: Movies: Child of the Night, Day-O.

WOODARD, ALFRE: Actress. b. Tulsa, OK, Nov. 8, 1953. e. Boston U., B.A. Soon after graduation landed role in Washington, D.C. Arena Stage theater in Horatio, and Saved.
THEATER: A Christmas Carol, Bugs Guns, Leander Stillwell, For Colored Girls Who Have Considered Suicide/When the Rainbow Is Enuf, A Map of the World, A Winter's Tale, Two By South.
PICTURES: Remember My Name, Health, Cross Creek (Acad. Award nom.), Extremities, Scrooged, Miss Firecracker, Grand Canyon, The Gun in Betty Lou's Handbag, Passion Fish, Rich in Love. Heart and Souls, Crooklyn.
TELEVISION: Series: Tucker's Witch, Sara, St. Elsewhere. Guest: Palmerstown USA, What Really Happened to the Class of '65?, Hill Street Blues (Emmy Award, 1984), L.A. Law (Emmy Award, 1987). Movies: Freedom Road, Sophisticated Gents, Go Tell It on the Mountain, Sweet Revenge, Unnatural Causes, The Killing Floor, Mandela, A Mother's Courage: The Mary Thomas Story, Blue Bayou. Specials: For Colored Girls Who Haved Considered Suicide/When the Rainbow is Enuf, Trial of the Moke, Words by Heart.

WOODS, DONALD: Actor. b. Brandon, Manitoba, Canada, Dec. 2, 1906. e. UC Berkeley. Appeared in WB shorts Song of a Nation, and Star in the Night (Oscar winner, 1945).
PICTURES: Tale of Two Cities, Story of Louis Pasteur, Anthony Adverse, Forgotten Girls, Love Honor and Oh Baby, I Was a Prisoner on Devil's Island, Watch on the Rhine, Bridge of San Luis Rey, Wonder Man, Roughly Speaking, Barbary Pirate, 13 Ghosts, Kissin' Cousins, Moment to Moment; 58 other films.
STAGE: Holiday, Charley's Aunt, Dracula, Strange Interlude; Two for the Seesaw, L.A., 1961; Rosmersholm, N.Y., 1962; One by One, N.Y., 1964; Soldier, You Can't Take It With You, Chicago, 1969; Twelfth Night, Assassination 1865; Chicago, 1969–71; Perfect Gentleman, 1980.
TELEVISION: G.E. Theatre, Wind from the South, Wagon Train, Thrillers, Sunset Strip, Ben Casey, Laramie, The Rebel, The Law and Mr. Jones, The Roaring 20's, Wild Wild West, Bonanza. Series: Tammy.

WOODS, JAMES: Actor. b. Vernal UT, Apr. 18, 1947. e. Massachusetts Inst. of Technology (appeared in 36 plays at M.I.T., Harvard and Theatre Co. of Boston). Left college to pursue acting career in New York; Broadway in Borstal Boy, Conduct Unbecoming (off-Bdwy, Obie Award), Saved, Trial of the Catonsville Nine, Moonchildren (Theatre World Award), Green Julia (off-Bdwy.), Finishing Touches, etc.
PICTURES: The Visitors (debut, 1971), Hickey and Boggs, The Way We Were, The Gambler, Distance, Night Moves, Alex and the Gypsy, The Choirboys, The Onion Field, The Black Marble, Eyewitness, Fast-Walking, Split Image, Videodrome, Against All Odds, Once Upon a Time in America, Cat's Eye, Joshua Then and Now, Salvador (Acad. Award nom., Independent Film Project Spirit Award), Best Seller, Cop (also co-prod.), The Boost, True Believer, Immediate Family, The Hard Way, Straight Talk, Diggstown, Chaplin, The Getaway.
TELEVISION: Movies: Footsteps, A Great American Tragedy, Foster and Laurie, F. Scott Fitzgerald in Hollywood, The Disappearance of Aimee, Raid on Entebbe, Billion Dollar Bubble, The Gift of Love, Incredible Journey of Dr. Meg Laurel, And Your Name is Jonah, Badge of the Assassin, Promise (Emmy, Golden Globe, Golden Apple Awards), In Love and War, My Name is Bill W. (Emmy Award), Women &

Men: Stories of Seduction (Hills Like White Elephants), The Boys, Citizen Cohn. *Specials*: All the Way Home, Crimes of Passion (host). *Mini-series*: Holocaust. *Guest*: Kojak, Rockford Files, Streets of San Francisco, The Rookies, Police Story, Saturday Night Live, Dream On.

WOODWARD, EDWARD, O.B.E.: Actor, Singer. b. Croydon, England, June 1, 1930. e. Royal Acad. of Dramatic Art. As singer has recorded 11 LPs. 2 Gold Discs. Television Actor of the Year, 1969–70; also Sun Award, Best Actor, 1970, 71, 72.
THEATRE: 20 West End plays and musicals, including The Art of Living, The Little Doctor, A Rattle of a Simple Man (West End/Bdwy.), The High Bid, The Male of the Species. High Spirits (Bdwy musical), The Best Laid Plans. Recent stage: On Approval, The Wolf, Richard III, The Assassin.
TELEVISION: *Series*: Callan, Nice Work, The Equalizer (4 Emmy noms., Golden Globe Award), Over My Dead Body. *Movies/Specials*: Sword of Honour, Bassplayer and Blonde (mini-series), Saturday, Sunday, Monday, Rod of Iron, The Trial of Lady Chatterly, Wet Job—Callan Special, Churchill: The Wilderness Years, Blunt Instrument, Killer Contract, Arthur the King, Uncle Tom's Cabin, A Christmas Carol, Codename: Kyril, Hunted, The Man in the Brown Suit, Hands of a Murderer, World War II, Suspicious Circumstances.
PICTURES: Where There's a Will (debut, 1955), Becket, File on the Golden Goose, Incense for the Damned, Young Winston, Sitting Target, Hunted, Wicker Man, Callan, Stand Up Virgin Soldiers, Breaker Morant, The Appointment, The Final Option (Who Dares Wins), Champions, King David, Mister Johnson.

WOODWARD, JOANNE: Actress. b. Thomasville, GA, Feb. 27, 1930. m. Paul Newman. e. Louisiana State U. Studied at Neighborhood Playhouse Dramatic Sch. and the Actors Studio. Appeared in many TV dramatic shows.
THEATER: Picnic, The Lovers, Baby Want a Kiss, Candida, The Glass Menagerie (Williamstown, The Long Wharf).
PICTURES: Count Three and Pray (debut, 1955), A Kiss Before Dying, Three Faces of Eve (Acad. Award, 1957), No Down Payment, The Long Hot Summer, Rally 'Round the Flag Boys, The Sound and the Fury, The Fugitive Kind, From the Terrace, Paris Blues, The Stripper, A New Kind of Love, Signpost to Murder, A Big Hand for the Little Lady, A Fine Madness, Rachel Rachel (Acad. Award nom.), Winning, WUSA, They Might Be Giants, The Effect of Gamma Rays on Man-in-the-Moon Marigolds, Summer Wishes Winter Dreams (Acad. Award nom.), The Drowning Pool, The End, Harry and Son, The Glass Menagerie, Mr. and Mrs. Bridge (Acad. Award nom.), Philadelphia.
TELEVISION: *Specials*: Broadway's Dreamers: The Legacy of The Group Theater (host, co-prod.) Emmy Award, 1990), Family Thanksgiving Special (dir. only). *Movies*: Sybil, Come Back Little Sheba, See How She Runs (Emmy Award, 1978), A Christmas to Remember, The Streets of L.A., The Shadow Box, Crisis at Central High, Passions, Do You Remember Love? (Emmy Award, 1985), Foreign Affairs, Blind Spot (also co-prod.).

WOOLDRIDGE, SUSAN: Actress. b. London, England. e. Central Sch. of Speech & Drama/Ecole/Jacques LeCoq. Paris. Ent. ind. 1971.
THEATER incl.: Macbeth, School for Scandal, Merchant of Venice, The Cherry Orchard, Look Back in Anger, 'night Mother, Map of the Heart.
PICTURES: The Shout, Butley, Loyalties, Hope and Glory, How to Get Ahead in Advertising, Bye Bye Blues, Twenty-One, Afraid of the Dark, Just Like a Woman.
TELEVISION: The Naked Civil Servant, John McNab, The Racing Game, The Jewel in the Crown, The Last Place on Earth, Hay Fever, Time and the Conways, Dead Man's Folly, The Devil's Disciple, The Dark Room, Pastoralcare, The Small Assassin, A Fine Romance, Ticket to Ride, Changing Step, Pied Piper, Crimestrike, Broke, Miss Pym's Day Out, An Unwanted Woman, The Humming Bird Tree, Inspector Alleyn Mysteries, Tracey Ullman Show, Bad Company.

WOOLF, SIR JOHN: Knighted 1975. Producer. b. England, 1913. e. Institut Montana, Switzerland. Awarded U.S. Bronze star for service in WWII. Asst. dir. Army Kinematography, War Office 1944–45; Founder and chmn. Romulus Films Ltd, since 1948. Man dir. since 1967; chmn. since 1982 of British & American Film Holdings Plc; dir. First Leisure Corp. Plc since 1982. Co-founder and exec. dir., Anglia TV Group PLC, 1958–83. Member: Cinematograph Films Council, 1969–79; bd. of gov., Services Sound & Vision Corp (formerly Services Kinema Corp.) 1974–83; exec. council and trustee, Cinema and Television Benevolent Fund; Freeman, City of London, 1982; FRSA 1978. Received special awards for contribution to British film indust. from Cinematograph Exhibitors Assoc. 1969. and Variety Club of GB, 1974.
PICTURES: Prod. by Romulus Gp.: The African Queen, Pandora and the Flying Dutchman, Moulin Rouge, Beat the Devil, I Am a Camera, Carrington VC, The Bespoke Overcoat (short; Acad. Award, BAFTA Award), Story of Ester Costello, Room at the Top (BAFTA Award, best film, 1958). Wrong Arm

of the Law, The L-Shaped Room, Term of Trial, Life at the Top, Oliver! (Acad. Award, Golden Globe, best film, 1968), Day of the Jackal, The Odessa File.
TELEVISION: Prod. for Anglia TV incl-100 Tales of the Unexpected, Miss Morrison's Ghosts, The Kingfisher, Edwin, Love Song.

WOPAT, TOM: Actor. b. Lodi, WI, Sept. 9, 1951. e. U. of Wisconsin. Left school to travel for two years with rock group as lead singer and guitarist. Spent two summers at Barn Theater in MI. Came to New York; off-Bdwy. in A Bistro Car on the CNR. On Bdwy. in hit musical, I Love My Wife, City of Angels.
TELEVISION: *Series*: The Dukes of Hazzard, Blue Skies, A Peaceable Kingdom. *Movies*: Christmas Comes to Willow Creek, Burning Rage, Just My Imagination.

WORKMAN, CHUCK: Director, Writer, Producer. b. Philadelphia, PA., June 5. e. Rutgers U., B.A.; Cornell U. Pres., International Documentary Assoc. 1987–88; Member: Directors Guild of America Special Projects Comm., DGA National Board, 1987; Bd. mem.: Santa Monica Arts Fdn. Lecturer, U. of Southern California. Pres. Calliope Films, Inc. Winner Clio Award, 1969, 1970. Acad. Award, 1987.
PLAYS: Bruno's Ghost (1981, writer, dir.), Diplomacy (writer, dir.), The Man Who Wore White Shoes (writer); Bloomers (writer).
PICTURES: Monday's Child (1967, editor), Traitors of San Angel (editor), The Money (dir., s.p.), Protocol (dir., media sequences), Stoogemania (dir., co-s.p.), Precious Images (Acad. Award, Best Live Action Short, 1986; Gold Hugo Award, Cannes Film Fest., N.Y. Film Fest.), Words (Best Short, Houston Fest., N.Y. Film Fest., 1988), Pieces of Silver, Superstar (dir.-prod.).
DOCUMENTARIES: The Making of the Deep (prod., dir., writer), The Director and the Image (CINE Golden Eagle Award, 1980), The Game, The Best Show in Town (CINE Golden Eagle), And the Winner Is . . ., The Keeper of the Light.

WORONOV, MARY: Actress. b. Brooklyn, NY, Dec. 8, 1946. e. Cornell. On NY stage in In the Boom Boom Room (Theatre World Award).
PICTURES: The Chelsea Girls, Kemek: It's Controlling Your Mind, Sugar Cookies, Seizure, Cover Girl Models, Death Race 2000, Cannonball, Jackson County Jail, Hollywood Boulevard, Bad Georgia Road, Mr. Billion, The One and Only, The Lady in Red, Rock 'n' Roll High School, National Lampoon Goes to the Movies, Angel of H.E.A.T., Heartbeeps, Eating Raoul, Get Crazy, Night of the Comet, Hellhole, My Man Adam, Nomads, Movie House Massacre, Chopping Mall, Terrorvision, Black Widow, Scenes From the Class Struggle in Beverly Hills, Let It Ride, Mortuary Academy, Dick Tracy, Watchers II, Warlock, Club Fed, Where Sleeping Dogs Lie, Motorama, Hell-Rollers, Grief.
TELEVISION: *Movies*: In the Glitter Palace, Challenge of a Lifetime, Acting on Impulse.

WORTH, IRENE: Actress. b. Nebraska, June 23, 1916. e. UCLA. Formerly a teacher. Bdwy. debut in The Two Mrs. Carrolls, after which went to London where made her home. Appeared with Old Vic and Royal Shakespeare Co.; returned to U.S. to appear on Bdwy. in the Cocktail Party.
THEATER: Hotel Paradiso, Mary Stuart, The Potting Shed, Toys in the Attic, Tiny Alice (Tony Award, 1965), Sweet Bird of Youth (Tony Award, 1976), Cherry Orchard, Old Times Happy Days, Coriolanus (NY Shakespeare Fest), Lost in Yonkers (Tony Award, 1991).
PICTURES: One Night With You, Secret People, Orders to Kill (British Acad. Award, best actress), The Scapegoat, Seven Seas to Calais, King Lear, Nicholas and Alexander, Rich Kids, Eyewitness, Deathtrap, Fast Forward, Lost in Yonkers.
TELEVISION:: The Lady from the Sea, The Duchess of Malfi, The Way of the World, Prince Orestes, Forbidden, The Big Knife, The Shell Seekers.

WORTH, MARVIN: Producer, Writer. b. Brooklyn, NY. Jazz promoter and manager before starting to write special material for Alan King, Buddy Hackett, Joey Bishop, Lenny Bruce and many others.
PICTURES: *Writer*: Boys Night Out, Three on a Couch, Promise Her Anything. *Producer*: Where's Poppa?, Malcolm X (documentary), Lenny, Fire Sale, The Rose, Up the Academy, Soup for One, Unfaithfully Yours, Rhinestone, Falling in Love, Less Than Zero, Patty Hearst, Running Mates, See No Evil, Hear No Evil, Flashback.
THEATER: Lenny (prod.).
TELEVISION: Steve Allen Show, Jackie Gleason, Ray Bolger's Washington Square, Chevy Shows, General Motors' 50th Anniversary Show, Milton Berle Show, Colgate Comedy Hour, Martha Raye Show, Polly Bergen Show, Ann Sothern Show, Judy Garland Show, Get Smart.

WOWCHUK, HARRY N.: Actor, Writer, Photographer, Producer, Executive. b. Philadelphia, PA. Oct. 16, 1948. e. Santa Monica City Coll., UCLA, theater arts, 1970. Started film career as actor, stunt-driver-photographer. T.V. and commercial credits include: TV Guide, Seal Test, Camel Cigarettes, Miller High Life, American Motors, Camera V, AW Rootbeer. Former exec. v.p. International Cinema, in chg. of prod. and distribution; V.P. J. Newport Film Productions; pres., United West Productions.

PICTURES: The Lost Dutchman, Las Vegas Lady, This Is a Hijack, Tidal Wave, Tunnel Vision, Incredible 2-Headed Transplant, Jud, Bad Charleston Charlie, Some Call It Loving, Summer School Teachers, Five Minutes of Freedom, Pushing Up Daisies, Money-Marbles-Chalk, The Models, Love Swedish Style, Up-Down-Up, Sunday's Child, Soul Brothers, Freedom Riders, Perilous Journey, Claws of Death, Georgia Peaches.

WOWCHUK, NICHOLAS: Executive, Producer, Writer, Editor, Financier. b. Philadelphia, PA. e. St. Basil's Coll., UCLA. Founder-publisher: All-American Athlete Magazine; Sports and Health Digest; The Spectator. Former sports writer: Phila. Evening Public Ledger; Phila. Daily Record; Phila. Inquirer. Founder & bd. chmn.: Mutual Realty Investment Co.; Mutual Mortgage Co., Beverly Hills, CA. President: Mutual General Films, Bev. Hills, CA; Abbey Theatrical Films, N.Y.; Mutual Film Distribution Co.; Mutual Recording & Broadcasting Enterprises.

PICTURES: Exec. Prod.: Perilous Journey, Incredible 2-Headed Transplant, Pushing Up Daisies, Money-Marbles-Chalk, Five Minutes of Freedom, The Campaign, Claws of Death. Prod.: Scorpion's Web, Pursuit, Brave Men, Sea of Despair, Cossacks In Battle, The Straight White Line, Tilt, Rooster, To Live . . . You Gotta Win.

WRAY, FAY: Actress. b. Alberta, Canada, Sept. 10, 1907. On stage in Pilgrimage Play, Hollywood, 1923; m.p. debut in Gasoline Love; thereafter in many m.p. for Paramount to 1930; then in films for various Hollywood and Brit. prod. Autobiography: On the Other Hand (1989).

PICTURES: Streets of Sin, The Wedding March, The Four Feathers, The Texan, Dirigible, Doctor X, The Most Dangerous Game, The Vampire Bat, The Mystery of the Wax Museum, King Kong, The Bowery, Madame Spy, The Affairs of Cellini, The Clairvoyant, They Met in a Taxi, Murder in Greenwich Village, The Jury's Secret, Smashing the Spy Ring, Navy Secrets, Wildcat Bus, Adam Had Four Sons, Melody for Three, Not a Ladies' Man, Small Town Girl, Treasure of the Golden Condor, Queen Bee, The Cobweb, Hell on Frisco Bay, Crime of Passion, Rock Pretty Baby, Tammy and the Bachelor, Summer Love, Dragstrip Riot.

TELEVISION: Series: Pride of the Family. Movie: Gideon's Trumpet.

WRIGHT, AMY: Actress. b. Chicago, IL, Apr. 15, 1950. e. Beloit Col. Studied acting with Uta Hagen; 1976, joined Rip Torn's Sanctuary Theatre. Bdwy in Fifth of July, Noises Off.

PICTURES: Not a Pretty Picture, Girlfriends, The Deer Hunter, Breaking Away, The Amityville Horror, Heartland, Wise Blood, Stardust Memories, Inside Moves, Off Beat, The Telephone, Crossing Delancey, The Accidental Tourist, Miss Firecracker, Daddy's Dyin', Deceived, Love Hurts, Hard Promises.

TELEVISION: Movies: Trapped in Silence, Settle the Score. Special: Largo Desolato. Pilot: A Fine Romance.

WRIGHT, ROBERT C.: Executive. b. Rockville Center, NY, April 23, 1943. e. Coll. Holy Cross, B.A. history, 1965; U. of Virginia, LLB 1968. Mem. NY, VA, MA, NJ Bar. 1969, joined General Electric; lawyer in plastics div. Later moved into product & sls. management in plastics div. 1980, moved to Cox Cable as pres. Returned to GE 1983 heading small appliances div.; moved to GE Financial Services & GE Credit Corp. as pres., which posts he held when named head of NBC following purchase of NBC's parent RCA by GE. President and chief exec. off., National Broadcasting Co. (NBC), September 1986 to present.

WRIGHT, TERESA: Actress. b. New York, NY, Oct. 27, 1918.

PICTURES: The Little Foxes (debut, 1941), Pride of the Yankees, Mrs. Miniver (Acad. Award, supp. actress, 1942), Shadow of a Doubt, Casanova Brown, Best Years of Our Lives, Trouble with Women, Pursued, Imperfect Lady, Enchantment, The Capture, The Men, Something to Live For, California Conquest, Steel Trap, Count the Hours, The Actress, Track of the Cat, The Search for Bridey Murphy, Escapade in Japan, The Restless Years, Hail Hero, The Happy Ending, Roseland, Somewhere in Time, The Good Mother.

STAGE: Tours: Mary Mary, Tchin-Tchin, The Effect of Gamma Rays on Man-in-the-Moon Marigolds, Noel Coward in Two Keys, The Master Builder. Regional Theatre: Long Day's Journey into Night, You Can't Take It With You, All The Way Home, Wings. NY: Life with Father, Dark at the Top of the Stairs, Mary Mary, I Never Sang for My Father, Death of a Salesman, Ah Wilderness!, Morning's at Seven (also London).

TELEVISION: Specials: The Margaret Bourke-White Story, The Miracle Worker, The Golden Honeymoon, The Fig Tree.

Movies: Crawlspace, The Elevator, Flood, Bill-on His Own, Perry Mason: The Case of the Desperate Deception.

WUHL, ROBERT: Actor, Writer. b. Union, NJ, Oct. 9, 1951. e. Univ. of Houston. Worked as stand-up comedian and joke writer. Was story editor on series Police Squad! Appeared in 1988 Academy Award winning short Ray's Male Heterosexual Dance Hall.

PICTURES: The Hollywood Knights (debut, 1980), Flashdance, Good Morning Vietnam, Bull Durham, Batman, Blaze, Wedding Band, Mistress.

TELEVISION: Pilots: Rockhopper, Sniff. Guest: Tales from the Crypt, Moonlighting, L.A. Law, Falcon Crest. Specials: The Big Bang (also dir.), Comic Relief IV, The Earth Day Special. Writer: Police Squad, Sledge Hammer, Grammy Awards (1987–9), Academy Awards (Emmy Award, 1991).

WYATT, JANE: Actress. b. New York, NY, Aug. 12, 1910. e. Miss Chapin's Sch., Barnard Coll. m. Edgar B. Ward. Joined Apprentice Sch., Berkshire Playhouse, Stockbridge, Mass. Understudied in Tradewinds and The Vinegar Tree. Appeared in Give Me Yesterday and the Tadpole. In 1933 succeeded Margaret Sullavan in Dinner at Eight. New York stage, The Autumn Garden, 1951; other plays, The Bishop Misbehaves, Conquest, Eveningsong, The Mad Hopes, Hope for the Best, The Joyous Season For Services Rendered, Driving Miss Daisy, Love Letters.

PICTURES: Great Expectations (1934), One More River, The Luckiest Girl in the World, Lost Horizon, Kisses for Breakfast, Weekend for Three, The Navy Comes Through, The Kansan, Buckskin Frontier, The Iron Road, None But the Lonely Heart, Strange Conquest, Boomerang, Gentleman's Agreement, Pitfall, No Minor Vices, Bad Boy, Canadian Pacific, Task Force, House By the River, Our Very Own, My Blue Heaven, The Man Who Cheated Himself, Criminal Lawyer, Interlude, Two Little Bears, Never Too Late, Treasure of Matecumbe, Star Trek IV: The Voyage Home.

TELEVISION: Series: Father Knows Best (1954–59; 3 Emmy Awards: 1957, 1958, 1959). Guest: Bob Hope Chrysler Theater, The Virginian, Wagon Train, U.S. Steel Hour, Bell Telephone Hour, Confidential For Women, My Father My Mother, Star Trek, Barefoot in the Park, The Ghost and Mrs. Muir, Here Come the Brides, Love American Style, Fantasy Island, Love Boat. Movies: Katherine, Tom Sawyer; Father Knows Best Reunion, A Love Affair, Amelia Earhart, Superdome, The Nativity, The Millionaire, Missing Children—A Mother's Story, Amityville: The Evil Escapes, Neighbors, Ladies of the Corridor.

WYMAN, JANE: Actress. r.n. Sarah Jane Fulks. b. St. Joseph, MO, Jan. 5, 1917. Voted one of top ten money-making stars in M.P. Herald-Fame poll, 1954.

PICTURES: Golddiggers of 1937, My Man Godfrey, King of Burlesque, Smart Blonde, Stage Struck, King and the Chorus Girl, Ready Willing and Able, Slim, The Singing Marine, Public Wedding, Mr. Dodd Takes the Air, The Crowd Roars, Brother Rat, Wide Open Faces, The Spy Ring, He Couldn't Say No, Fools for Scandal, Kid Nightingale, Tail Spin, Private Detective, Kid from Kokomo, Torchy Plays With Dynamite, Brother Rat a Baby, An Angel From Texas, Gambling on the High Seas, Tugboat Annie Sails Again, My Love Came Back, The Body Disappears, Honeymoon for Three, Bad Men of Missouri, You're in the Army Now, Larceny, Inc., My Favorite Spy, Footlight Serenade, Princess O'Rourke, Doughgirls, Make Your Own Bed, Crime by Night, Hollywood Canteen, Lost Weekend, One More Tomorrow, Night and Day, The Yearling, Cheyenne, Magic Town, Johnny Belinda (Acad. Award, 1948), A Kiss in the Dark, The Lady Takes a Sailor, It's a Great Feeling, Stage Fright, The Glass Menagerie, Three Guys Named Mike, Here Comes the Groom, Blue Veil, Starlift, Just for You, Story of Will Rogers, Let's Do It Again, So Big, Magnificent Obsession, Lucy Gallant, All That Heaven Allows, Miracle in the Rain, Holiday for Lovers, Pollyanna, Bon Voyage, How to Commit Marriage.

TELEVISION: Series: Fireside Theatre (The Jane Wyman Show), Summer Playhouse, Falcon Crest. Movies: The Failing of Raymond, The Incredible Journey of Dr. Meg Laurel.

WYMAN, THOMAS H.: Executive. b. 1931. Joined CBS, Inc. in 1980 as pres. & chief exec. Then chmn until 1986. Prior career as chief exec. of Green Giant Co.; became v. chmn. to 1988, of Pillsbury Co. when it acquired Green Giant in 1979.

WYMORE, PATRICE: Actress. b. Miltonvale, KS, Dec. 17, 1926. p. James A. Wymore, oper. exhib. film delivery service throughout Kans.; ret. Widow of actor Errol Flynn. Began career as child performer, tent shows, county fairs, vaudeville; later, toured night clubs in middle west, own song & dance act; modelled, Chicago understudy Betty Bruce, Up in Central Park, played role Hollywood Bowl; then, N.Y. stage, Hold It! All For Love; radio & TV roles.

PICTURES: Tea for Two (debut, 1950), Rocky Mountain, I'll See You In My Dreams, Star-Lift, Big Trees, Man Behind the Gun, She's Working Her Way Through College, She's Back on Broadway, Chamber of Horrors.

WYNN, TRACY KEENAN: Writer. b. Hollywood, CA, Feb. 28, 1945. e. UCLA Theatre Arts Dept., BA in film/TV division, 1967. Fourth generation in show business: son of actor Keenan Wynn, grandson of Ed Wynn, great-grandson of Frank Keenan, Irish Shakespearean actor who made Bdwy. debut in 1880.
PICTURES: The Longest Yard, The Drowning Pool (co-s.p.), The Deep (co. s.p.).
TELEVISION: Movies: The Glass House, Tribes (also assoc. prod.: Emmy & WGA Awards), The Autobiography of Miss Jane Pittman (Emmy Award & WGA Awards), Hit Lady (dir. only), Quest, Bloody Friday (also co-prod.), Capone in Jail, Carolina Skeletons.

WYNTER, DANA: Actress. b. London, England. June 8, 1931. r.n. Dagmar Spencer-Marcus. e. North London Collegiate, Rhodes Univ. of South Africa. On stage in London; NY stage in Black Eyed Susan. Radio in England incl. Orson Welles' The Private Lives of Harry Lime. Now a freelance journalist for The Guardian (England), and such magazines as Cosmopolitan, Country Living, National Review. etc., and The Irish Times, The Irish Independent.
PICTURES: White Corridors, Col. March Investigates, Invasion of the Body Snatchers, View from Pompey's Head, D-Day: The Sixth of June, Something of Value, Fraulein, Shake Hands with the Devil, In Love and War, Sink the Bismarck, On the Double, The List of Adrian Messenger, If He Hollers Let Him Go, Airport, Santee, Le Savage (Lovers Like Us).
TELEVISION: Guest: Robert Montgomery Show, Suspense, Studio One, U.S. Steel Hour, Laura, Playhouse 90, Dick Powell Show, Wagon Train, Virginian, Burkes Law, Bob Hope Presents, Alfred Hitchcock, Twelve O'Clock High, The Rogues, Ben Casey, FBI Story, Ironside, Love Boat, My Three Sons, What's My Line?, Fantasy Island, Hart to Hart, Wild Wild West. Series: The Man Who Never Was, Dana Wynter in Ireland (exec. prod./writer/presenter). Movies: Companions in Nightmare, Any Second Now, Owen Marshall: Counselor at Law (pilot), The Connection, The Questor Tapes, The Lives of Jenny Dolan, M Station: Hawaii, The Royal Romance of Charles and Diana, The Return of Ironside. Mini-Series: Backstairs at the White House.

Y

YABLANS, FRANK: Executive. B. Brooklyn, NY, Aug. 27, 1935. Ent. m.p. ind. as Warner Bros. booker, 1957. Warner Bros. salesman in N.Y., Boston, Milwaukee, Chicago, 1957–59. Milwaukee br. mgr. Buena Vista, 1959–66. Midwest sales mgr., Sigma III, 1966. Eastern sales mgr., 1967, sales v.p. 1968. V.P. general sales mgr., Paramount Pic. Corp., 1969; v.p.-dist., April 1970; sr. v.p.-mkt., Oct., 1970; exec. v.p., April 1971; named pres. May, 1971. In Jan., 1975, became an indep. prod., his company called, Frank Yablans Presentations Inc. 1983, MGM/UA Entertainment Co. as bd. chmn. & chief oper. off. Held titles of bd. chmn. & chief exec. off. with both MGM and UA Corp when resigned, 1985. Same year teamed with PSO Delphi to form Northstar Entertainment Co.; 1986, non-exclusive deal with Empire Entertainment; 1988, non-exclusive 3-year deal with Columbia Pictures; 1989, pres. Epic Prods., pres., ceo Nova Intl. Films Inc.
PICTURES: Producer: Silver Streak (exec. prod.), The Other Side of Midnight, The Fury, North Dallas Forty (also co-s.p.), Mommie Dearest (also co-s.p.), Monsignor (co.-prod), Star Chamber, Kidco, Buy and Cell, Lisa.

YABLANS, IRWIN: Executive. b. Brooklyn, NY, July 25, 1934. Began career in industry at WB in 1956 after two-yr. stint with U.S. Army in Germany. Held m.p. sales posts in Washington, DC, Albany, Detroit, Milwaukee and Portland. In 1962 joined Paramount as L.A. mgr.; in 1964 made western sales mgr. In 1972 entered production as assoc. prod. on Howard W. Koch's Badge 373. Pres. of Compass Int'l. Pictures. Exec. v.p., low budget films, Lorimar Productions. Resigned June, 1984. In 1985 named chmn., Orion Pictures Distributing Corp. 1988: named chmn. and CEO of newly formed Epic Pictures.
PICTURES: The Education of Sonny Carson (1974). Exec. prod.: Halloween, Roller Boogie (also story), Fade To Black (also story), Seduction (prod.), Halloween II, Halloween III: Season of the Witch, Parasite, Tank, Hell Night, Prison Arena, Why Me?, Men at Work.

YATES, PETER: Producer, Director. b. Ewshoot, Eng., July 24, 1929. e. Royal Acad. of Dramatic Art. Ent. m.p. ind. as studio mgr. and dubbing asst. with De Lane Lea. Asst. dir.: The Entertainer, The Guns of Navarone, A Taste of Honey, The Roman Spring of Mrs. Stone. Stage dir.: The American Dream, The Death of Bessie Smith, Passing Game, Interpreters. Received Acad. Award noms. for Best Director/Picture (Producer): Breaking Away, The Dresser.
TELEVISION: Series: Danger Man (Secret Agent), The Saint.

PICTURES: Summer Holiday, One Way Pendulum, Robbery (also co-s.p.), Bullitt, John and Mary, Murphy's War, The Hot Rock, The Friends of Eddie Coyle, For Pete's Sake, Mother Jugs and Speed (also prod.), The Deep, Breaking Away (also prod.), Eyewitness (also prod.), Krull, The Dresser (also prod.), Eleni, Suspect, The House on Carroll Street (also prod.), An Innocent Man, Year of the Comet (also co-prod.).

YELLEN, LINDA: Producer, Director, Writer. b. New York, NY, July 13, 1949. e. Barnard Coll., B.A., Columbia U., M.F.A., Ph.D. Also lecturer Barnard Coll., Yale U., asst. professor, City U. of New York. Member: exec. council, DGA.
PICTURES: Looking Up (prod., dir.), Prospera, Come Out Come Out, Everybody Wins (prod.).
TELEVISION: Movies: Mayflower: The Pilgrims' Adventure (prod.), Playing for Time (exec. prod.; Emmy, Peabody & Christopher Awards, 1980), Hardhat and Legs (prod.), The Royal Romance of Charles and Diana (exec. prod., co-writer), Prisoner Without a Name Cell Without a Number (prod., dir., co-writer; Peabody & WGA Awards, 1985), Liberace: Behind the Music (exec. prod.), Sweet Bird of Youth (exec. prod.), Rebound (dir., co-writer), Chantilly Lace (dir., prod., writer).

YORDAN, PHILIP: Writer. b. Chicago, IL, 1913. e. U. of Illinois, B.A., Kent Coll. of Law, LL.D. Author, producer, playwright (Anna Lucasta). Began screen writing 1942 with collab. s.p. Syncopation.
PICTURES: Unknown Guest, Johnny Doesn't Live Here, When Strangers Marry, Dillinger (Acad. Award nom.), Whistle Stop, The Chase, Suspense, Anna Lucasta, House of Strangers, Edge of Doom, Detective Story (Acad. Award nom.), Mary Maru, Houdini, Blowing Wild, Man Crazy, Naked Jungle, Johnny Guitar, Broken Lance (Acad. Award for story, 1954), Conquest of Space, Man from Laramie, Last Frontier, The Harder They Fall (also prod.), Men In War (also prod.), No Down Payment (also prod.), God's Little Acre (also prod.), The Bravados, The Time Machine, The Day of the Outlaw, Studs Lonigan, King of Kings, El Cid, 55 Days at Peking, Fall of the Roman Empire, Battle of the Bulge, Royal Hunt of the Sun, Brigham, Cataclysm, Night Train to Terror, Satan's Warriors, Cry Wilderness, Bloody Wednesday (prod., s.p.), The Unholy (co-s.p.), Dead Girls Don't Dance (prod., s.p.).

YORK, MICHAEL: Actor. r.n. Michael York-Johnson. b. Fulmer, England, March 27, 1942. Early career with Oxford U. Dramatic Society and National Youth Theatre; later Dundee Repertory, National Theatre. 1992 Autobiography: Accidentally on Purpose (Simon & Schuster).
THEATER: Any Just Cause, Hamlet, Ring Round the Moon (Los Angeles), Cyrano de Bergerac. Bdwy: Outcry, Bent, The Little Prince and the Aviator, Whisper in the Mind, The Crucible, Someone Who'll Watch Over Me.
PICTURES: The Taming of the Shrew, Accident, Red and Blue, Smashing Time, Romeo and Juliet, The Strange Affair, The Guru, Alfred the Great, Justine, Something for Everyone, Zeppelin, La Poudre D'Escampette, Cabaret, England Made Me, Lost Horizon, The Three Musketeers, Murder on the Orient Express, The Four Musketeers, Conduct Unbecoming, Logan's Run, Seven Nights in Japan, The Last Remake of Beau Geste, The Island of Dr. Moreau, Fedora, The Riddle of the Sands (also assoc. prod.), Final Assignment, The White Lions, The Weather in the Streets, Success Is the Best Revenge, Dawn, Lethal Obsession (Der Joker), The Return of the Musketeers, Phantom of Death, The Secret of the Sahara, Midnight Cop, The Wanderer, The Long Shadow, Wide Sargasso Sea, Rochade, Discretion Assured.
TELEVISION: The Forsyte Saga, Rebel in the Grave, Jesus of Nazareth, True Patriot, Much Ado About Nothing. Series: Knots Landing. Movies: Great Expectations, A Man Called Intrepid, The Phantom of the Opera, The Master of Ballantrae, Space, For Those I Loved, The Far Country, Dark Mansions, Sword of Gideon, Four Minute Mile, The Lady and the Highwayman, The Heat of the Day, Till We Meet Again, Night of the Fox, A Duel of Love, The Road to Avonlea. Host: The Hunt for Stolen War Treasure.

YORK, SUSANNAH: Actress. b. London, England, Jan. 9, 1941. Ent. TV 1959. Ent. films in 1960. Wrote two books: In Search of Unicorns and Lark's Castle.
THEATER: A Cheap Bunch of Flowers, Wings of the Dove, Singular Life of Albert Nobbs, Man and Superman, Mrs. Warren's Profession, Peter Pan, The Maids, Private Lives, The Importance of Being Earnest, Hedda Gabler (New York), Agnes of God, The Human Voice. Produced The Big One, a variety show for peace, 1984. Penthesilea, Fatal Attraction, The Apple Cart, Private Treason, Lyric for a Tango, The Glass Menagerie, Streetcar Named Desire.
PICTURES: Tunes of Glory (debut, 1960), There Was a Crooked Man, Greengage Summer (Loss of Innocence), Freud, Tom Jones, The Seventh Dawn, Sands of the Kalahari, Kaleidoscope, A Man for All Seasons, Sebastian, Duffy, The Killing of Sister George, Oh What a Lovely War, The Battle of Britain, Lock Up Your Daughters, They Shoot Horses Don't They? (Acad. Award nom.), Brotherly Love

(Country Dance), Zee & Co. (X Y & Zee), Happy Birthday Wanda June, Images, The Maids, Gold, Conduct Unbecoming, That Lucky Touch, Sky Riders, The Silent Partner, Superman, The Shout, Falling in Love Again, The Awakening, Superman II, Loophole, Yellowbeard, Land of Faraway, Superman IV (voice), Prettykill, Bluebeard Bluebeard, A Summer Story, American Roulette, Diamond's Edge, Melancholia.

TELEVISION: The Crucible, The Rebel and the Soldier, The First Gentleman, The Richest Man in the World, Slaughter of St. Teresa's Day, Kiss On A Grass Green Pillow, Fallen Angels, Prince Regent, Second Chance, Betjeman's Briton, We'll Meet Again, Jane Eyre, A Christmas Carol, Star Quality, Macho, Return Journey, After the War, The Man From the Pru, The Haunting of the New, Devices and Desires, Boon, Little Women.

YORKIN, BUD: Producer, Director. r.n. Alan "Bud" Yorkin. b. Washington, PA, Feb. 22, 1926. e. Carnegie Tech., Columbia U. U.S. Navy, 1942–45; Began career in TV in NBC's engineering dept. Moved into prod., first as stage mgr., then assoc. dir. of Colgate Comedy Hour (Martin and Lewis) and dir. of Dinah Shore Show. Formed Tandem Productions with Norman Lear; 1974 formed own production co.

TELEVISION: Series director: Songs at Twilight, Martin & Lewis Show, Abbott and Costello Show, Spike Jones Show, Tony Martin Show (also prod., writer), George Gobel Show, The Ford Show Starring Tennesse Ernie Ford (also prod.). Specials (dir.): An Evening with Fred Astaire (Emmy Award, 1959), Another Evening with Fred Astaire, The Jack Benny Hour Specials (Emmy Award, 1960), Henry Fonda and the Family, We Love You Madly with Duke Ellington, TV Guide Awards Show, Bobby Darin and Friends, Danny Kaye Special, Where It's At with Dick Cavett, Many Sides of Don Rickles, Robert Young and the Family, owner. Series co-prod.: All In The Family, Sanford and Son, Maude, Good Times, What's Happening!, Carter Country, Diff'rent Strokes, Archie Bunker's Place.

PICTURES: Come Blow Your Horn (dir., co-prod., adapt.), Never Too Late (dir.), Divorce American Style (dir.), The Night They Raided Minsky's (exec. prod.), Inspector Clouseau (dir.), Start the Revolution Without Me (prod., dir.), Cold Turkey (exec. prod.), Thief Who Came to Dinner (prod., dir.), Deal of the Century (prod.), Twice in a Lifetime (prod., dir.), Arthur 2 on the Rocks (dir.), Love Hurts (prod., dir.), For the Boys (actor), Intersection (co-prod.).

YOUNG, ALAN: Actor. r.n. Angus Young. b. North Shield, Northumberland, England, Nov. 19, 1919. Cartoonist, acted first as monologist at 13 years in Canada; radio comedian 10 yrs. in Canada and U.S.; served in Canadian Navy as sub-lt. 1942–44; wrote, dir. and acted in comedy broadcasts.

PICTURES: Margie (debut, 1946), Chicken Every Sunday, Mr. Belvedere Goes to College, Aaron Slick from Punkin Crick, Androcles and the Lion, Gentlemen Marry Brunettes, Tom Thumb, Time Machine, Baker's Hawk, The Cat from Outer Space, Duck Tales: The Movie (voice).

TELEVISION: Series: The Alan Young Show (Emmy Award, 1950), Saturday Night Revue, Mr. Ed, Coming of Age. Movie: Earth Angel.

YOUNG, BURT: Actor, Writer. b. New York, NY, April 30, 1940. Worked at variety of jobs (boxer, trucker, etc.) before turning to acting and joining Actor's Studio. Appeared in off-Bdwy. plays which led to Hollywood career. On Bdwy in Cuba and His Teddy Bear.

PICTURES: Cinderella Liberty, Chinatown, The Gambler, Murph the Surf, The Killer Elite, Rocky (Acad. Award nom.), Twilight's Last Gleaming, The Choirboys, Convoy, Uncle Joe Shannon (also s.p.), Rocky II, Blood Beach, All the Marbles, Rocky III, Lookin' To Get Out, Amityville II: The Possession, Over the Brooklyn Bridge, Once Upon a Time in America, The Pope of Greenwich Village, Rocky IV, Back to School, Blood Red, Beverly Hills Brats, Last Exit to Brooklyn, Medium Rare, Betsy's Wedding, Wait Until Spring Bandini, Diving In, Backstreet Dreams, Rocky V, Bright Angel, Red American, Club Fed, Excessive Force.

TELEVISION: Series: Roomies. Guest: M*A*S*H, Baretta, Tales From the Crypt. Movies: The Great Niagara, Hustling, Serpico: The Deadly Game, Woman of the Year, Daddy I Don't Like It Like This (also s.p.), Murder Can Hurt You, A Summer to Remember, Double Deception.

YOUNG, CARROLL: Writer. b. Cincinnati, OH. e. St. Xavier Coll. Publicist for Pathe Studios, Fox West Coast Theatres, RKO Studios, MGM, 1930–35; story ed. Sol Lesser Prod., Ernst Lubitsch Prod., 1936–40; asst. to exec. prod., RKO, 1941; U.S. Army Air Force, 1942–44.

PICTURES: Tarzan Triumphs, Tarzan's Desert Mystery, Tarzan and Leopard Woman, Tarzan and Mermaids, many in Jungle Jim series, Hidden City, The Jungle, Lost Continent, Tarzan and the She-Devil, Cannibal Attack, Apache Warrior, She-Devil, The Deerslayer, Machete.

YOUNG, CHRIS: Actor. b. Chambersburg, PA, Apr. 28, 1971. Stage debut in college production of Pippin, followed by On Golden Pond.

PICTURES: The Great Outdoors (debut, 1988), Book of Love, December, The Runestone, Warlock: The Armageddon.

TELEVISION: Series: Max Headroom, Falcon Crest, Live-In, Married People. Pilot: Jake's Journey. Movies: Dance 'Til Dawn, Breaking the Silence. Special: Square One. Guest: Crime & Punishment.

YOUNG, FREDDIE: O.B.E. Cinematographer. b. England, 1902. r.n. Frederick Young. Entered British film industry in 1917. Gaumont Studio Shepherd's Bush, London as lab asst. First picture as chief cameraman, 1927 then chief cameraman to Herbert Wilcox British & Dominions Studios Elstree Herts. Army capt. Army Film prod. group directing training films 3 yrs. Invalided out. Signed with MGM British 15 yrs. Also credited as F.A. Young. BAFTA Fellowship 1972, Prix D'Honeur (Lawrence of Arabia) O.B.E. 1970.

PICTURES: Victory 1918, A Peep Behind the Scenes, The Speckled Band, Goodnight Vienna, The Loves of Robert Burns, The King of Paris, White Cargo (first British talkie), Rookery Nook, A Cuckoo in the Nest, Canaries Sometimes Sing, A Night Like This, Plunder, Thark, On Approval, Mischief, Return of the Rat, The Happy Ending, Yes, Mr. Brown; This'll Make You Whistle, That's a Good Girl, Nell Gwynne, Peg of Old Drury, The Little Damozel, Bitter Sweet, The Queen's Affair, Sport of Kings, A Warm Corner, The W Plan, Victoria the Great, Sixty Glorious Years, Goodbye Mr. Chips, Nurse Edith Cavell, The 49th Parallel, Contraband, Busman's Honeymoon, The Young Mr. Pitt, Caesar and Cleopatra, Escape, So Well Remembered, Edward, My Son; The Conspirator, The Winslow Boy, Calling Bulldog Drummond, Ivanhoe, Knights of the Round Table, Mogambo, Invitation to the Dance, Bhowani Junction, The Barretts of Wimpole Street, The Little Hut, Indiscreet, I Accuse, Inn of the Sixth Happiness, Solomon and Sheba, Betrayed, Island in the Sun, Treasure Island, Lust for Life, Macbeth, Greengage Summer, Lawrence of Arabia (Acad. Award, 1962), The Seventh Dawn, Lord Jim, The Deadly Affair, Rotten to the Core, Doctor Zhivago (Acad. Award, 1965), You Only Live Twice, The Battle of Britain, Sinful Davey, Ryan's Daughter (Acad. Award, 1970), Nicholas and Alexandra, The Asphyx, Luther, The Tamarind Seed, Permission to Kill, The Blue Bird, Seven Nights in Japan, Stevie, Bloodline, Rough Cut, Richard's Things, Invitation to the Wedding, Sword of the Valiant.

TELEVISION: Great Expectations, The Man in the Iron Mask, Macbeth (Emmy Award, 1960), Ike: The War Years, Arthur's Hollowed Ground (director).

YOUNG, IRWIN: Executive. b. New York, NY. e. Perkiomen Sch., Lehigh U., B.S., 1950. Pres., Du Art Film Laboratories, Inc.

YOUNG, KAREN: Actress. b. 1958. Trained at Image Theatre/Studio in NYC.

PICTURES: Deep in the Heart (debut, 1983), Almost You, Birdy, Nine 1/2 Weeks, Heat, Jaws the Revenge, Torch Song Trilogy, Criminal Law, Night Game, The Boy Who Cried Bitch, Hoffa.

TELEVISION: Movies: The Execution of Raymond Graham, The 10 Million Dollar Getaway, The Summer My Father Grew Up.

THEATRE: A Lie of the Mind, 3 Acts of Recognition, Five of Us, Mud People.

YOUNG, LORETTA: Actress. r.n. Gretchen Young; b. Salt Lake City, UT, Jan. 6, 1913. e. Ramona Convent, Alhambra, CA, Immaculate Heart Coll. Hollywood. After small part in Naughty But Nice, lead in Laugh Clown, Laugh. Played in almost 100 films. Autobiography: The Things I Had to Learn (1962).

PICTURES: Laugh Clown Laugh (debut, 1928), Loose Ankles, The Squall, Kismet, I Like Your Nerve, The Devil to Pay, Platinum Blonde, The Hatchet Man, Big Business Girl, Life Beings, Zoo in Budapest, Life of Jimmy Dolan, Midnight Mary, Heroes for Sale, The Devil's in Love, She Had to Say Yes, A Man's Castle, The House of Rothschild, Bulldog Drummond Strikes Back, Born to Be Bad, Caravan, The White Parade, Clive of India, Call of the Wild, Shanghai, The Crusades, The Unguarded Hour, Private Number, Ramona, Ladies in Love, Love is News, Cafe Metropolis, Wife Doctor and Nurse, Second Honeymoon, Four Men and a Prayer, Suez, Kentucky, Three Blind Mice, Wife Husband and Friend, The Story of Alexander Graham Bell, Eternally Yours, The Doctor Takes a Wife, He Stayed for Breakfast, Lady from Cheyenne, The Men in Her Life, Bedtime Story, A Night to Remember, China, Ladies Courageous, and Now Tomorrow, Along Came Jones, The Stranger, The Perfect Marriage, The Farmer's Daughter (Acad. Award, 1947), The Bishop's Wife, Rachel and the Stranger, The Accused, Mother Is a Freshman, Come to the Stable, Key to the City, Cause for Alarm, Half Angel, Paula, Because of You, It Happens Every Thursday.

TELEVISION: Series: Loretta Young Show, (NBC-TV 1953–61; 3 Emmy Awards), The New Loretta Young Show

(CBS-TV 1962); Returned to TV, 1986, in movies: Christmas Eve (1986), Lady in a Corner.

YOUNG, ROBERT: Actor. b. Chicago, IL, Feb. 22, 1907.
PICTURES: Black Camel (debut, 1931), The Sin of Madelon Claudet, Strange Interlude, The Kid From Spain, Today We Live, Men Must Fight, Hell Below, Tugboat Annie, Saturday's Millions, The Right to Romance, Carolina, Lazy River, The House of Rothchild, Spitfire, Paris Interlude, Whom the Gods Destroy, Death on the Diamond, The Band Plays On, Vagabond Lady, Calm Yourself, Red Salute, Remember Last Night?, West Point of the Air, The Bride Comes Home, It's Love Again, Secret Agent, 3 Wise Guys, The Bride Walks Out, Sworn Enemy, The Longest Night, Stowaway, Dangerous Number, Married Before Breakfast, The Emperor's Candlesticks, I Met Him in Paris, The Bride Wore Red, Navy Blue and Gold, Paradise for Three, Josette, The Toy Wife, Three Comrades, Rich Man Poor Girl, Shining Hour, Bridal Suite, Honolulu, Miracles For Sale, Maisie, Northwest Passage, The Mortal Storm, Florian, Western Union, Sporting Blood, Dr. Kildare's Crisis, The Trial of Mary Dugan, Lady Be Good, Married Bachelor, H.M. Pulham Esq., Joe Smith American, Cairo, Journey for Margaret, Slightly Dangerous, Claudia, Sweet Rosie O'Grady, The Canterville Ghost, The Enchanted Cottage, Those Endearing Young Charms, The Searching Wind, Claudia and David, Lady Luck, They Won't Believe Me, Crossfire, Relentless, Sitting Pretty, Adventure in Baltimore, That Forsyte Woman, Bride for Sale, And Baby Makes Three, The Second Woman, Half-Breed, Goodbye My Fancy, Secret of the Incas.
TELEVISION: Series: Father Knows Best (2 Emmy Awards: 1956, 1957), Window on Main Street, Marcus Welby M.D. (Emmy Award, 1970). Movies: Marcus Welby M.D. (pilot; a.k.a. A Matter of Humanities), Vanished, All My Darling Daughters, My Darling Daughters' Anniversary, Little Women, The Return of Marcus Welby M.D., Marcus Welby M.D.: A Holiday Affair.

YOUNG, ROBERT M.: Director. b. New York, NY, Nov. 22, 1924. e. Harvard.
PICTURES: Nothing But a Man (prod., co-s.p.), The Plot Against Harry (co-prod., photog.), Short Eyes, Rich Kids, One-Trick Pony, The Ballad of Gregorio Cortez (also s.p. adapt.), Alambrista! (also s.p., photog.), Extremities, Saving Grace, Dominick and Eugene, Triumph of the Spirit, Talent for the Game, American Me (co-prod. only), Children of Fate (exec. dir. & exec. prod. only), Roosters.
TELEVISION: Specials: Sit-In, Angola—Journey to a War, The Inferno (a.k.a. Cortile Cascino; also prod., writer, edit.), Anatomy of a Hospital, The Eskimo: Fight for Life (Emmy Award, 1971).

YOUNG, SEAN: Actress. b. Louisville, KY, Nov. 20, 1959. r.n. Mary Sean Young. e. Interlochen Arts Acad., MI, studied dance, voice, flute and writing. After graduating, moved to N.Y., worked as receptionist, model for 6 months and signed with ICM. Shortly after signed for film debut in Jane Austen in Manhattan (1980). On L.A. Stage in Stardust.
PICTURES: Jane Austen in Manhattan, Stripes, Blade Runner, Young Doctors in Love, Dune, Baby: The Secret of the Lost Legend, No Way Out, Wall Street, The Boost, Cousins, Fire Birds, A Kiss Before Dying, Love Crimes, Once Upon a Crime, Hold Me Thrill Me Kiss Me, Forever, Fatal Instinct, Ace Ventura.
TELEVISION: Special: Under the Biltmore Clock. Mini-Series: Tender Is the Night. Movies: Blood and Orchids, The Sketch Artist, Blue Ice.

YOUNG, TERENCE: Director. Writer. b. Shanghai, China, June 20, 1915. e. Cambridge U. Served with Guards Armoured Div., W.W.II; ent. m.p. ind. 1936 at BIP Studios. Screenwriter turned director.
PICTURES: Writer: On the Night of the Fire, On Approval, Dangerous Moonlight, Theirs is the Glory; Director: Corridor of Mirrors, One Night With You, Woman Hater, They Were Not Divided, The Valley of the Eagles, Red Beret (Paratrooper), That Lady, Safari, Zarak, Action of the Tiger, Too Hot to Handle, Black Tights, Dr. No., From Russia With Love, The Amorous Adventures of Moll Flanders, Thunderball, Triple Cross, The Rover, Wait Until Dark, Grand Slam, Mayerling (also s.p.), The Christmas Tree, Red Sun, The Valachi Papers, The Klansman, Bloodline, Inchon, The Jigsaw Man.

YOUNGSTEIN, MAX E.: Executive. b. March 21, 1913. e. Fordham U. Member New York Bar. Motion picture consultant and indep. prod. Member, Producers Guild. Pres., Max E. Youngstein Enterprises. 1940–41, dir. adv. & pub., 20th Century Fox; later dir. studio special svcs.; asst. to pres. 1942–44, US Army Signal Corps. 1945, v.p. & gen. mgr., Stanley Kramer Prods. 1946–48, dir. adv. & pub., Eagle Lion Films; v.p. chg. adv. & pub. & prod. liaison. 1949–50, dir. adv. & pub., Paramount; mem. exec. comm. & v.p. dir. dist. co. 1951–62, gen. v.p., partner, bd. mem., dir. adv. & pub., United Artists Corp. Formed UA Music Co. Pres., UA Records. 1977, consultant to Bart-Palevsky Prods. Advisor, Golden Harvest Films. Consultant, Rico-Lion. 1979, Shamrock Prods., Rank Film Distribu-

tors, Taft Bdcst. Co., Encore Prods., Bobrun Prods., Selkirk Films. 1980, named Chmn. & CEO, Taft Int'l. Pictures. 1984, Consultant, Orion, 1984 20th Century-Fox. 1985–86, pres., Great American Pictures. Consultant, H&M Trust, Color Systems Technology, Mickey Rooney Film Prods., Peachtree Prods.
PICTURES: Young Billy Young, Best of Cinerama, Man in the Middle, Fail Safe, The Money Trap, The Dangerous Days of Kiowa Jones, Welcome to Hard Times.

YULIN, HARRIS: Actor. b. Los Angeles, Nov. 5. On Bdwy. in Watch on the Rhine, A Lesson from Aloes, etc. Founder of the Los Angeles Classic Theatre.
PICTURES: End of the Road, Doc, The Midnight Man, Night Moves, Steel, Scarface, The Believers, Fatal Beauty, Candy Mountain, Bad Dreams, Judgement in Berlin, Another Woman, Ghostbusters II, Final Analysis.
TELEVISION: Specials/Movies: The Thirteenth Day—The Story of Esther, When Every Day Was the Fourth of July, Missiles of October, Conspiracy: Trial of the Chicago Seven, Last Ride of the Dalton Gang, Robert Kennedy and His Times, Tailspin: Behind the Korean Airlines Tragedy, Face of a Stranger, The Last Hit. Series: WIOU.
THEATRE: A Midsummer Night's Dream, King John, Hamlet, Julius Caesar, Tartuffe, Approaching Zanzibar, Baba Goya, Front Page, Henry V, The Visit.

Z

ZAENTZ, SAUL: Producer. b. Passaic, NJ.
PICTURES: One Flew Over the Cuckoo's Nest (Acad. Award for Best Picture, 1975), Three Warriors, The Lord of the Rings, Amadeus (Acad. Award for Best Picture, 1984), The Mosquito Coast (exec. prod.), The Unbearable Lightness of Being, At Play in the Fields of the Lord.

ZANUCK, LILI FINI: Producer, Director. b. Leominster, MA, Apr. 2, 1954. e. Northern VA Commun. Col. Worked for Carnation Co. in LA prior to entering film business. Joined Zanuck/Brown Company in 1978, working in develop. and various phases of production; 1984–present, prod. Made directorial debut 1991 with Rush. Named Producer of the Year (1985) by NATO, along with Richard D. Zanuck and David Brown; Producer of the Year (1989) by Producers Guild of America, with Zanuck.
PICTURES: Cocoon, Cocoon: The Return, Driving Miss Daisy (Acad. Award, Golden Globe & Natl. Board of Review Awards for Best Picture 1989), Rush (dir.), Rich in Love, Clean Slate.

ZANUCK, RICHARD DARRYL: Executive. b. Los Angeles, CA, Dec 13, 1934. e. Stanford U. 1952–56. f. Darryl Zanuck. Story dept., 20th Century Fox, 1954; N.Y. pub. dept., 1955; asst. to prod.: Island in the Sun, The Sun Also Rises, The Longest Day; v.p. Darryl F. Zanuck Prod. 1958; first credit as prod. Compulsion (1959); president's prod. rep., 20th Century Fox Studio, 1963; v.p. charge prod., 20th Fox; pres., 20th Fox TV exec. v.p. chge. prod., 20th Fox, 1967. 1968: Chmn. of Bd., Television div., 20th Century Fox, 1969: Pres., 20th Century Fox Film Corp. Joined Warner Bros., March 1971, as sr. exec. v.p.; Resigned July, 1972 to form Zanuck-Brown Production Company, Universal Pictures. Joined 20th Century-Fox, 1980–83. To Warner Bros., 1983. To MGM Entertainment, 1986. 1988, dissolved 16-year partnership with David Brown. Formed The Zanuck Company, Jan., 1989. Recipient: Irving Thalberg Award (1991).
PICTURES: Compulsion, The Chapman Report, Ssssssss, The Sting (Acad. Award for Best Picture, 1973), The Sugarland Express, Willie Dynamite, The Black Windmill, The Girl from Petrovka, The Eiger Sanction, Jaws, MacArthur, Jaws 2, The Island, Neighbors, The Verdict, Cocoon, Target, Cocoon: The Return, Driving Miss Daisy (Acad. Award for Best Picture, 1989), Rush, Rich in Love, Clean Slate.

ZEFFIRELLI, FRANCO: Director, Writer. b. Florence, Italy, Feb. 12, 1923. e. Florence Univ. Was stage director before entering film industry. Set designer 1949–52 for Visconti plays (A Streetcar Named Desire, The Three Sisters). Worked as asst. dir. on La Terra Trema, Bellissima, Senso. Director of operas.
PICTURES: Director-Screenplay: The Taming of the Shrew (also prod.), Romeo and Juliet, Brother Sun Sister Moon, The Champ (dir. only), Endless Love (dir. only), La Traviata (also prod. design), Otello, Young Toscanini (dir., story), Hamlet.
TELEVISION: Mini-Series: Jesus of Nazareth.

ZELNICK, STRAUSS: Executive. b. Boston, MA, June 26, 1957. e. Wesleyan U. B.A., 1979 (Summa Cum Laude); Harvard Grad. School of Business Administration, M.B.A., 1983; Harvard Law School, J.D., 1983 (Cum Laude). 1983–86, v.p., international television sales, Columbia Pictures International Corp. 1988–89, pres. & chief operating officer, Vestron, Inc.; 1989–93, pres. & chief operating officer, Fox Film Corp.

ZEMECKIS, ROBERT: Director, Writer. b. Chicago, IL, 1952. m. actress Mary Ellen Trainor. e. U. of Film Awards sponsored by

M.P. Academy of Arts & Sciences, plus 15 intl. honors. Has film editing background, having worked as cutter on TV commercials in Illinois. Also cut films at NBC News, Chicago, as summer job. After schooling went to Universal to observe on set of TV series, McCloud. Wrote script for that series in collab. with Bob Gale. Turned to feature films, directing I Wanna Hold Your Hand and co-writing s.p. with Gale and co-writing 1941 with him.
PICTURES: Director: I Wanna Hold Your Hand (also co-s.p.), 1941 (co-s.p. only), Used Cars (also co-s.p.), Romancing the Stone, Back to the Future (also co-s.p.), Who Framed Roger Rabbit, Back to the Future II & III (also story), Death Becomes Her (also co-prod.), The Public Eye (exec. prod. only), Trespass (co-s.p.).
TELEVISION: Amazing Stories, Tales From the Crypt (exec. prod.; also dir., All Through the House).

ZENS, WILL: Producer, Director. b. Milwaukee, WI, June 26, 1920. e. Marquette U., U. of Southern California, B.A., M.A. Wrote, produced and directed many TV shows. Formed Riviera Productions in 1960 to produce theatrical motion pictures.
TELEVISION: Punch & Trudy, Your Police, Aqua Lung Adventures, Teletunes, Sunday Drive.
PICTURES: Capture That Capsule, The Starfighters, To the Shores of Hell, Road to Nashville, Hell on Wheels, From Nashville with Music, Yankee Station, Help Me ... I'm Possessed!, Hot Summer in Barefoot County, The Fix, Truckin' Man, The Satan Crossing (dir., s.p.), Death on the Carrier, Terror in the Streets.

ZERBE, ANTHONY: Actor. b. Long Beach, CA, May 20, 1936. Studied at Stella Adler Theatre Studio.
PICTURES: Cool Hand Luke, Will Penny, The Liberation of L.B. Jones, The Molly Maguires, The Call Me Mister Tibbs, Cotton Comes to Harlem, The Omega Man, The Life and Times of Judge Roy Bean, The Strange Vengeance of Rosalie, The Laughing Policeman, Papillon, The Parallax View, Farewell My Lovely, Rooster Cogburn, The Turning Point, Who'll Stop the Rain, The First Deadly Sin, The Dead Zone, Off Beat, Opposing Force, Private Investigation, Steel Dawn, Listen to Me, See No Evil Hear No Evil, Licence to Kill.
TELEVISION: Series: Harry-O (Emmy Award, 1976), The Young Riders. Movies: The Priest Killer, The Hound of the Baskervilles, Snatched, She Lives, The Healers, In the Glitter Palace, KISS Meets the Phantom of the Park, Attica, The Seduction of Miss Leona, Rascals and Robbers: The Secret Adventures of Tom Sawyer and Huck Finn, A Question of Honor, The Return of the Man from U.N.C.L.E., One Police Plaza. Mini-Series: Once an Eagle, Centennial, The Chisholms, George Washington, A.D.
THEATRE: NY: Solomon's Child, The Little Foxes.

ZETTERLING, MAI: Actress, Director. b. Sweden, May 24, 1925. e. Ordtuery Sch., Theater Sch. First m.p.: Sweden, Frenzy. Has made numerous stage and screen appearances since in Sweden. British screen debut, Frieda. Since 1969 directing plays & films in Sweden. Won Golden Lion at Venice in 1964 for The War Game.
PICTURES: Bad Lord Byron, Quartet, Portrait from Life, Romantic Age, Blackmailed, Hell is Sold Out, Desperate Moment, Knock on Wood, Dance Little Lady, Prize of Gold, Seven Waves Away (Abandon Ship), The Truth About Women, Jetstorm, Faces in the Dark, Piccadilly Third Stop, Offbeat, Only Two Can Play, The Main Attraction, The Witches, Hidden Agenda, Grandfather's Journey. Director: Loving Couples, Night Games, Dr. Glas, The Girls, Visions of Eight (segment), Scrubbers.
TELEVISION: Idiot's Delight, Mayerling, Doll's House, Dance of Death, etc. dir. doc. for BBC and in Sweden. Wrote and dir. Scrubbers, Amorosa.

ZIDE, LARRY M: Executive. b. Flushing, NY, Oct. 16, 1954. 3rd generation in mp. industry. Started 1972 with American Intl. Pictures in sls. & adv.; 1973, named branch sls. mgr., Memphis. 1975, joined Dimension Pictures as print controller; 1978, formed Zica Films Co. serving m.p. industry. 1985, Zica merged with Filmtreat Intl. Corp; named pres., newly formed Filmtreat West Corp.

ZIDE, MICHAEL (MICKEY): Executive. b. Detroit, MI, May 31, 1932. Joined mp. industry with American Intl. Pictures as print controller; 1962, promoted to asst. gen. sls. mgr. Named v.p., special projects, 1970; 1972, joined Academy Pictures as v.p. of prod. Later went with Zica Film Co.; 1985, named exec. v.p., Filmtreat West Corp.

ZIEFF, HOWARD: Director. b. Los Angeles, CA, 1943. Started as artist and photographer, working as newsreel photographer for L.A. TV station. Went to N.Y. to do still photography; became top photo artist in advertising. Turned to film direction with Slither in 1972.
PICTURES: Slither, Hearts of the West, House Calls, The Main Event, Private Benjamin, Unfaithfully Yours, The Dream Team, My Girl, My Girl 2.

ZIFKIN, WALTER: Executive. b. July 16, 1936. New York, NY. e. UCLA, A.B., 1958; U. of Southern California, LL.B., 1961. CBS legal dept., 1961–63; William Morris Agency 1963–present; exec. vice-pres.; 1989 also chief operating officer.

ZIMBALIST, EFREM, JR.: Actor. b. New York, NY, Nov. 30, 1923. Son of violinist Efrem Zimbalist and opera singer Alma Gluck. Father of actress Stephanie Zimbalist. e. Fay Sch., Southboro, MA; St. Paul's, Concord, NH; Yale. Studied drama, Neighborhood Playhouse. N.Y. Stage debut, The Rugged Path. Shows with American Repertory Theatre; Henry VIII, Androcles and the Lion, What Every Woman Knows, Yellow Jack, Appeared, Hedda Gabler. Co-prod., The Medium, The Telephone, The Consul, (Critics Award, Pulitzer Prize). Screen debut, House of Strangers (1949). Gave up acting after death of his wife and served as asst. to father, Curtis Inst. of Music for 4 years. Returned to acting, stock co., Hammonton, NJ, 1954.
TELEVISION: Series: Concerning Miss Marlow, 77 Sunset Strip, The FBI, Hotel. Guest: Philco, Goodyear Playhouse, U.S. Steel Hour. Movies: Who is the Black Dahlia?, A Family Upside Down, Terror Out of the Sky, The Best Place to Be, The Gathering Part II, Baby Sister, Shooting Stars. Host: You Are the Jury. Mini-Series: Scruples.
PICTURES: House of Strangers, Bomber B-52, Band of Angels, The Deep Six, Violent Road, Girl on the Run, Too Much Too Soon, Home Before Dark, The Crowded Sky, A Fever in the Blood, By Love Possessed, Chapman Report, The Reward, Harlow (electronovision), Wait Until Dark, Airport 1975, Elmira, Hot Shots.

ZIMBALIST, STEPHANIE: Actress. b. New York, NY, Oct. 8, 1956. Daughter of actor Efrem Zimbalist Jr.
THEATER: The Cherry Orchard (Long Wharf, CT, 1984). Toured in My One and Only, The Baby Dance (New Haven).
PICTURES: The Magic of Lassie, The Awakening.
TELEVISION: Series: Remington Steele (1982–87). Mini-series: Centennial. Movies: Yesterday's Child, In the Matter of Karen Ann Quinlan, The Gathering, The Long Journey Back, Forever, The Triangle Factory Fire Scandal, The Best Place to Be, The Baby Sitter, The Golden Moment-An Olympic Love Story, Elvis and the Beauty Queen, Tomorrow's Child, Love on the Run, A Letter to Three Wives, Celebration Family, Caroline?, The Killing Mind, The Story Lady, Breaking the Silence, Sexual Advances.

ZIMBERT, RICHARD: Executive. Member, California bar. Has been with Paramount Pictures in executive capacities since 1975. In 1985 named exec. v.p. of co.

ZINNEMANN, FRED: Director. b. Vienna, Austria, Apr. 29, 1907. e. Vienna U., law. Studied violin as a boy; after law, studied photographic technique, lighting & mechanics (Paris); asst. cameraman 1 yr. Berlin; came to U.S. 1929; extra in m.p. All Quiet on the Western Front, 1930; asst. to Berthold Viertel, script clerk & asst. to Robert Flaherty, 1931; dir. Mexican documentary The Wave, 1934; short subjects dir., MGM, winning Academy Award for That Mothers Might Live, 1938; feature dir. 1942; winner of first Screen Directors' Award 1948 with The Search. 4 N.Y. Film Critics Awards; 2 Director's Guild Annual Awards; 4 Acad. Awards, 9 Acad. Award noms., 3 Golden Globe Awards. Other awards: U.S. Congressional Life Achievement Award (1987), Gold Medal City of Vienna, Donatello Award (Italy), Order of Arts & Letters (France), Golden Thistle Award (Edinburgh, Scotland), etc. Fellowships: BAFTA and BFI. Director of Acad. Award winning short Benjy (for L.A. Orthopedic Hospital, 1951). Author: My Life in the Movies (Scribner, 1992).
PICTURES: Kid Glove Killer (debut, 1942), Eyes in the Night, The Seventh Cross, Little Mister Jim, My Brother Talks to Horses, The Search, Act of Violence, The Men, Teresa, High Noon (NY Film Critics Award), Member of the Wedding, From Here to Eternity (Acad. Award, DGA & NY Film Critics Awards for best dir., 1953), Oklahoma!, A Hatful of Rain, The Nun's Story (NY Film Critics Award), The Sundowners (also prod.), Behold a Pale Horse (also prod.), A Man for All Seasons, (also prod.; Acad. Awards for best picture & dir.; DGA & NY Film Critics Awards, 1966), The Day of the Jackal, Julia, Five Days One Summer (also prod.).

ZINNEMANN, TIM: Producer. b. Los Angeles, CA. e. Columbia U. Son of dir. Fred Zinnemann. Began career industry as film editor; then asst. dir. on 20 films. Production mgr. for 5 projects; assoc. prod. on The Cowboys and Smile. Produced Straight Time for Warners with Stanley Beck.
PICTURES: A Small Circle of Friends, The Long Riders, Tex, Impulse, Fandango, Crossroads, The Running Man, Pet Sematary (exec. prod.).
TELEVISION: The Jericho Mile (ABC).

ZISKIN, LAURA: Producer. e. USC Cinema School. Worked as game show writer, development exec. before joining Jon Peters' prod. co. where she worked on A Star is Born, Eyes of Laura Mars (assoc. prod.). Formed Fogwood Films with Sally Field.

PICTURES: Murphy's Romance, No Way Out, D.O.A., The Rescue, Everybody's All American, Pretty Woman (exec. prod.), What About Bob?, The Doctor, Hero (also co-story).

ZITO, JOSEPH: Director. b. New York, NY, May 14, 1949. e. City Coll. of New York.
PICTURES: Abduction, The Prowler, Friday the 13th: The Final Chapter, Missing in Action, Invasion U.S.A., Red Scorpion, Red Palms.

ZSIGMOND, VILMOS: Cinematographer. b. Szeged, Hungary, June 16, 1930. e. National Film Sch. Began career photographing Hungarian Revolution of 1956. Later escaped from Hungary with friend Laszlo Kovacs, also a cinematographer. Winner of Academy Award and British Academy Award for cinematography, also several int'l and domestic awards as dir. of TV commercials.
PICTURES: The Time Travelers (1964), The Sadist, The Name of the Game is Kill, Futz, Picasso Summer, The Monitors, Red Sky at Morning, McCabe and Mrs. Miller, The Hired Hand, The Ski Bum, Images, Deliverance, Scarecrow, The Long Goodbye, Cinderella Liberty, The Sugarland Express, The Girl From Petrovka, Sweet Revenge, Death Riders, Obsession, Close Encounters of the Third Kind (Acad. Award, 1977), The Last Waltz, The Deer Hunter (BAFTA Award, Acad. Award nom.), Winter Kills, The Rose, Heaven's Gate, Blow Out, The Border, Jinxed, Table for Five, No Small Affair, The River (Acad. Award nom.), Real Genius, The Witches of Eastwick, Fat Man and Little Boy, The Two Jakes, Journey to Spirit Island, The Bonfire of the Vanities, The Long Shadow (dir.), Sliver, Intersection.
TELEVISION: Flesh and Blood, Stalin.

ZUCKER, DAVID: Producer, Director, Writer. b. Milwaukee, WI, Oct. 16, 1947. e. U. of Wisconsin, majoring in film. With brother, Jerry, and friend Jim Abrahams founded the Kentucky Fried Theatre in Madison in 1969, (moved theater to L.A. 1972) later wrote script for film of that name released in 1977. Trio followed this with Airplane, 1980, which they wrote and jointly directed while serving as executive producers.
PICTURES: The Kentucky Fried Movie (co-s.p., actor), Airplane! (co-s.p., co-dir., actor), Top Secret (co-dir., co-s.p.); Ruthless People (co-dir.), The Naked Gun (exec. prod., dir., co-s.p.), The Naked Gun 2½: The Smell of Fear (dir., exec. prod., co-s.p., actor), Brain Donors (co-exec. prod.).
TELEVISION: Police Squad (series), Our Planet Tonight (special).

ZUCKER, JERRY: Producer, Director. Writer. b. Milwaukee, WI, Mar. 11, 1950. e. U. of Wisconsin, majoring in education. With brother, David, and friend Jim Abrahams founded the Kentucky Fried Theatre in Madison in 1970 and wrote script for film of that name released in 1977. Trio followed this with Airplane! in 1980 which they wrote and jointly directed and served as executive producers.
PICTURES: The Kentucky Fried Movie (co-s.p., actor), Rock 'n' Roll High School (2nd unit dir.), Airplane! (co-dir., co-s.p.), Top Secret (co-dir., co-s.p.); Ruthless People (co-dir.), The Naked Gun (exec. prod., co-s.p.), Ghost (dir.), The Naked Gun AF2-1/2 (exec. co-prod.), Brain Donors (co-exec. prod.), My Life (co-prod.).
TELEVISION: Series: Police Squad! (co-exec. prod., dir.; co-wrote first episode).

ZUGSMITH, ALBERT: Producer, Director, Writer. b. Atlantic City, NJ, April 24, 1910. e. U. of Virginia. Pres. Intercontinental Broadcasting Corp.; ed. publ. Atlantic City Daily World; v.p. Smith Davis Corp.; Chmn of bd., Continental Telecasting Corp., Television Corp. of America; assoc. ed. American Press; pres. World Printing Co.; exec. CBS; pres. American Pictures Corp.; pres. Famous Players Int'l Corp.
PICTURES: Written on the Wind, Man in the Shadow, Red Sundown, Star in the Dust, Tarnished Angels, The Incredible Shrinking Man, The Girl in the Kremlin, The Square Jungle, Female on the Beach, Touch of Evil, Captive Women, Sword of Venus, Port Sinister, Invasion U.S.A., Top Banana, Paris Model, Slaughter on Tenth Avenue, The Female Animal, High School Confidential, Night of the Quarter Moon, Beat Generation, The Big Operator, Girls Town, Violated!, Platinum High School, Private Lives of Adam and Eve, Dondi, College Confidential, Confessions of an Opium Eater, The Great Space Adventure, On Her Bed of Roses, Fanny Hill, The Rapist!, Private Lives of Adam and Eve, The Beat Generation, How to Break Into the Movies, The Chinese Room, Street Girl, The President's Girl Friend, The Phantom Gunslinger, Sappho, Darling, Menage a Trois, Two Roses and a Goldenrod, The Friendly Neighbors, Why Me God?, Tom Jones Rides Again, etc.

ZUNIGA, DAPHNE: Actress. b. Berkeley, CA, 1962. e. UCLA.
PICTURES: Pranks (debut, 1982), The Initiation, Vision Quest, The Sure Thing, Modern Girls, Spaceballs, Last Rites, The Fly II, Gross Anatomy, Staying Together, Eight Hundred Leagues Down the Amazon.
TELEVISION: Movies: Quarterback Princess, Stone Pillow, Prey of the Chameleon. Series: Melrose Place. Guest: Family Ties, Nightmare Classics (Eye of the Panther).

ZWICK, EDWARD: Writer, Producer, Director. b. Chicago, IL, Oct. 8, 1952. e. Harvard U., B.A., 1974; American Film Inst. Center for Advanced Film Studies, M.F.A., 1976. Editor and feature writer, The New Republic and Rolling Stone magazines, 1972–74. Author: Literature and Liberalism (1975). Formed Bedford Falls Production Co. with Special Bulletin collaborator Marshall Herskovitz.
PICTURES: Director: About Last Night (debut, 1986), Glory, Leaving Normal, Legends of the Fall (also co-prod.).
TELEVISION: Series: Family (writer, then story editor, dir., prod., Humanitas Prize Award, 1980), thirtysomething (co-exec. prod.; Emmy Award, 1988), Dream Street (exec. prod.), Movies (dir.): Paper Dolls, Having It All, Extreme Close-Up (also co-exec. prod., co-story). Special: Special Bulletin (also co-prod., co-story; 2 Emmy Awards, also DGA, WGA & Humanitas Prize Awards, 1983).

ZWICK, JOEL: Director. b. Brooklyn, NY, Jan. 11, 1942. e. Brooklyn Coll., B.A., M.A.
THEATER: Dance with Me, Cold Storage, Esther, Cafe La Mama.
PICTURE: Second Sight.
TELEVISION: Series: Laverne and Shirley, Mork and Mindy, Angie (pilot), It's a Living, Bosom Buddies (pilot), Struck by Lightning (pilot), America 2100, Goodtime Girls, Hot W.A.C.S. (also exec. prod.), Little Darlings, Joanie Loves Chachi, Star of the Family (pilot), The New Odd Couple (also supv. prod.), Webster, Brothers (supv. prod.), Perfect Strangers (also pilot), Full House (also pilot), Family Matters (pilot), Adventures in Babysitting (pilot), Morning Glory (pilot), Up to No Good (pilot), Going Places (pilot), Hangin' With Mr. Cooper (pilot).

OBITUARIES (Sept. 1, 1992—Sept. 30, 1993)

Gary Abrahams	11/05/92	Michael Kanin	3/12/93
Dana Andrews	12/17/92	Ruby Keeler	2/28/93
Robert Blattner	10/31/92	Bernard Korbin	8/27/93
Shirley Booth	10/16/92	David A. Lipton	3/2/93
David Brian	7/15/93	Cleavon Little	10/22/92
James Bridges	6/6/93	Joseph L. Mankiewicz	2/5/93
Raymond Burr	9/12/93	George "Sparky" McFarland	6/30/93
Sammy Cahn	1/15/93	Richard Murphy	5/19/93
Cantinflas	4/20/93	Jean Negulesco	7/18/93
Bob Crosby	3/9/93	Rudolf Nureyev	1/6/93
Tad Danielewski	1/6/93	Lindsley Parsons	10/9/92
"Curly" Joe DeRita	7/3/93	Anthony Perkins	9/12/92
Jean Carmen Dillow	8/26/93	Milton Platt	11/19/92
Denholm Elliot	10/6/92	Henry Plitt	1/20/93
Kenneth Englund	8/10/93	Kate Reid	3/27/93
Gary Essert	12/16/92	Hal Roach	11/2/92
John C. Foreman	11/20/92	Will Rogers Jr.	7/10/93
Vincent Gardenia	12/9/92	Mark Rosenberg	11/6/92
George L. George	1/5/93	Steven J. Ross	12/20/92
Donald Getz	8/22/93	Richard Salant	2/16/93
Donald T. Gillin	11/30/92	Richard Sale	3/4/93
Lillian Gish	2/27/93	Ralph Serpe	10/24/92
Melvyn Gold	5/28/93	Dan Seymour	5/25/93
Mark Goodson	12/18/92	Ray Sharkey	6/11/93
Michael Gordon	4/29/93	Irene Sharaff	8/16/93
Joseph Gould	7/11/93	Anne Shirley	7/4/93
Stewart Granger	8/16/93	Alexis Smith	6/9/93
Fred Gwynne	7/2/93	Donn B. Tatum	5/31/93
Helen Hayes	3/17/93	Ann Todd	5/6/93
Audrey Hepburn	1/20/93	Diane Varsi	11/19/92
Sterling Holloway	11/22/92	Herve Villechaize	9/4/93
Cy Howard	4/29/93	Walter Waldman	7/4/93
Richard Jordan	8/30/93	Bill Williams	9/21/92

Services

Animation

CALIFORNIA

A I A PRODUCTIONS, INC., 15132 LaMaida St., Sherman Oaks, CA 91403; (818) 501-4406.

ALLEN, DAVID, PRODS., 918 W. Oak St., Burbank, CA 91506; (818) 845-9270; 848-0303; FAX: (818) 567-4954.

ANGEL ARTS DESIGN INC., 11729 King St., North Hollywood, CA 91607; (818) 763-8023.

ANGST ANIMATION POST PRODUCTION, 1308 Truitt St., Glendale, CA 91201-2341; (818) 244-6073; FAX: (818) 244-6373.

APOGEE PRODUCTIONS, INC., 6842 Valjean Ave., Van Nuys, CA 91406; (818) 989-5757; FAX: (818) 781-6671.

ARCCA ANIMATION, 279 S. Beverly Hills Dr., Suite 339, Beverly Hills, CA 90212; (310) 271-5928.

AVAILABLE LIGHT LTD., 3110 W. Burbank Blvd., Burbank, CA 91505- 2313; (818) 842-2109; FAX: (818) 842-0661.

BAER ANIMATION CO., 3765 Cahuenga Blvd. W., Studio City, CA 91604; (818) 780-8666; FAX: (818) 760-8698.

BASS/YAGER & ASSOCS., 7039 Sunset Blvd., Los Angeles, CA 90028; (213) 466-9701.

BOSUSTOW ENTERTAINMENT, 1156 Galloway St., Pacific Palisades, CA 90272; (310) 454-8843.

BRAVERMAN PRODS. INC., 3000 Olympic Blvd., #1431, Santa Monica, CA 90404; (310) 315-4710; FAX: (310) 315-4847.

BRUBAKER GROUP, THE, 10560 Dolcedo Way, Los Angeles, CA 90077; (310) 472-4766; 478-9588.

CALICO LTD., 8843 Shirley Ave., Northridge, CA 91324-3481; (818) 701-5862; FAX: (818) 772-1484.

CELESTIAL MECHANIX INC., 612 Hampton Dr., Venice, CA 90291; (310) 392-8771.

CLAMPETT, BOB, PRODS. INC., 729 Seward St., Los Angeles, CA 90038; (213) 466-0264.

COAST PRODS., 1001 N. Poinsetta Pl., Los Angeles, CA 90046-6795; (213) 876-2021.

CRUSE & COMPANY, 7000 Romaine St., Hollywood, CA 90038; (213) 851-8814; FAX: (213) 851-8788.

DIC ENTERPRISES, INC., 3601 W. Olive, Burbank, CA 91505; (818) 955-5400.

DIGITAL VISION ENTERTAINMENT, 7080 Hollywood Blvd., Los Angeles, CA 90028; (213) 462-3790.

DREAM QUEST IMAGES, 2635 Park Center Dr., Simi Valley, CA 93065; (310) 558-4051; (805) 581-2671; FAX: (805) 583-4673.

DREAMLIGHT IMAGES INC., 932 N. La Brea Ave., Suite C, Hollywood, CA 90038; (213) 850-1996.

DUCK SOUP PRODUCTIONS, 1026 Montana Ave., Santa Monica, CA 90403; (310) 451-0771; FAX: (310) 451-0114.

ENERGY PRODUCTIONS, 12700 Ventura Blvd., Studio City, CA 91604; (213) 462-3310; FAX: (213) 871-2763.

FANTASY II FILM EFFECTS, 504 S. Varney St., Burbank CA 91502; (818) 843-1413; FAX: (818) 848-2824.

FINE ARTS PRODUCTIONS, INC., 11304 Dilling St., Toluca Lake, CA 91602; (818) 506-0928; 506-0095; FAX: (818) 766-8786.

FITZGERALD, WAYNE, FILMDESIGN, INC., 6430 Sunset Blvd., #200, Hollywood, CA 90046; (213) 851-1060.

FLINT PRODUCTIONS INC., 7758 Sunset Blvd., West Hollywood, CA 90046; (213) 851-1060.

FRANKS, SYLVIA, 12056 Summit Circle, Beverly Hills, CA 90210; (310) 276-5282; FAX: (310) 276-9793.

HANNA BARBERA, 3400 W. Cahuenga Blvd., Hollywood, CA 90068; (213) 851-5000; FAX: (213) 969-1201.

HOLLYWOOD CARTOON COMPANY, THE, 12517 Chandler Blvd., #203, N. Hollywood, CA 91607; (818) 766-2447; FAX: (818) 766-9795.

INDUSTRIAL LIGHT & MAGIC, P.O. Box 2459, San Rafael, CA 94912; (415) 258-2000.

INTERACTIVE PRODUCTION ASSOCIATES, 3200 Airport Ave., Suite 20, Santa Monica, CA 90405; (310) 390-9466; FAX: (310) 390-7525.

INTROVISION SYSTEMS INC., 1011 N. Fuller Ave., Hollywood, CA 90046; (213) 851-9262; FAX: (213) 851-1649.

JEAN-GUY JACQUE & COMPANY, 13214 Moorpark, Suite 303, Sherman Oaks, CA 91423-3284; (818) 981-0596; FAX: (818) 981-1524.

KURTZ & FRIENDS, 2312 W. Olive Ave., Burbank, CA 91506; (818) 841-8188.

KUSHNER-LOCKE, INC., 10850 Wilshire Blvd., 9th Fl., Los Angeles, CA 90024; (310) 470-0400.

LANTZ, WALTER, 4444 Lakeside Dr., Suite 310, Burbank, CA 91505; (818) 569-3625.

LIMELITE, 1640 N. Gower St., Hollywood, CA 90028; (213) 856-8606; FAX: (213) 856-0698.

LITTLEJOHN, WILLIAM PRODS., INC., 23425 Malibu Colony Dr., Malibu, CA 90265; (310) 456-8620; FAX: (310) 456-2978.

LUMENI PRODUCTIONS, 1727 N. Ivar Ave., Hollywood, CA 90028; (213) 462-2110; FAX: (213) 462-8250.

MARKS COMMUNICATIONS INC., 2690 N. Beachwood Dr., Los Angeles, CA 90068; (213) 957-9904; FAX: (213) 957-9909.

MARVEL PRODS., 4640 Lankershim Blvd., #600, N. Hollywood, CA 91602; (818) 769-0400; FAX: (818) 769-1120.

FRITZ MILLER ANIMATION/GRAPHICS, 10806 Ventura Blvd., Suite 4, Studio City, CA 91604; (818) 985-6074.

NELVANA, 9000 Sunset Blvd., Suite 911, Los Angeles, CA 90069; (310) 278-8466; FAX: (213) 278-4872.

OPTICAM, INC., 810 Navy St., Santa Monica, CA 90405; (310) 453-5451.

PLAYHOUSE PICTURES, 1401 N. La Brea Ave., Hollywood, CA 90028-7505; (213) 851-2112; FAX: (213) 851-2117.

QUARTET FILMS, INC., 12345 Ventura Blvd., #M, Studio City, CA 91604; (818) 509-0100.

RUBY-SPEARS PRODUCTIONS, 3575 Cahuenga Blvd., W., Los Angeles, 90068; (213) 874-5100; FAX: (213) 851-9757.

SABAN ENTERTAINMENT, 4000 W. Alameda, 5th Fl., Burbank, CA 91505; (818) 972-4800; FAX: (818) 972-4895.

SINGLE FRAME FILMS, 437½ N. Genessee Ave., Los Angeles, CA 90036; (213) 655-2664.

SIR REEL PICTURES, 8036 Shady Glade Ave., North Hollywood, CA 91605; (818) 768-9778; FAX: (818) 504-9945.

SOUND CONCEPTS INC., 3485 Meier St., Los Angeles, CA 90066; (310) 390-7406.

SOUTH, LEONARD, PRODS., 4883 Lankershim Blvd., N. Hollywood, CA 91601-2746; (818) 760-8383; FAX: (818) 766-8301.

STIPES, DAVID, PRODUCTIONS, INC., 10665 Vanowen St., Burbank, CA 91505-1136; (818) 753-9093.

STOKES/KOHNE, 738 N. Cahuenga Blvd., Hollywood, CA 90038; (213) 469-8176; FAX: (213) 469-0377.

STUDIO PRODUCTIONS INC., 650 N. Bronson Ave., #223, Hollywood, CA 90004; (213) 856-8048; FAX: (213) 461-4202.

VIDE-U PRODUCTIONS, 1034 Shenandoah St., Los Angeles, CA 90035; (310) 657-4385.

WATERFRONT TECHNOLOGIES, 3820 Old Ranch Pkwy., #170, Seal Beach, CA 90240; (310) 799-0011; FAX: (310) 799-1092.

WONG, ARNIE, TIGERFLY INC., 735 E. Kensington Rd., Los Angeles, CA 90026; (213) 482-2335.

RICK ZETTNER & ASSOCIATES, INC., 211 N. Victory Blvd., Burbank, CA 91502; (818) 848-7673; FAX: (818) 841-1917.

LAS VEGAS

ROBERT LEONARD PRODUCTIONS ENTERTAINMENT, INC., P.O. Box 81440, Las Vegas, NV 89180; (702) 877-2449.

ORLANDO

DISNEY-MGM STUDIOS, 1675 Buena Vista Blvd., Lake Buena Vista, FL 32830-0200; (407) 560-5353, 560-5600; FAX: (407) 827-5168.

NEW YORK

APA STUDIOS INC., 230 W. 10 St., New York, NY 10014; (212) 929-9436; 675-4894.

ALEXANDER, SAM, PRODUCTIONS INC., 311 W. 43 St., New York, NY 10036; (212) 765-5180.

ANIMATED PRODUCTIONS, INC., 1600 Broadway, New York, NY 10019; (212) 265-2942; (800) 439-1360.

ANIMOTION, 501 W. Fayette St., Syracuse, NY 13204; (315) 471-3533.

BASKT, EDWARD, 160 W. 96 St., New York, NY 10025; (212) 666-2579.

BEBELL VISUAL COMMUNICATIONS, 420 E. 55th St., Suite 6U, New York, NY 10022; (212) 486-6577.

BIGMAN PICTURES, 133 W. 19 St., New York, NY 10011; (212) 242-1411.

BLECHMAN, R.O., INC., 2 W. 47 St., New York, NY 10036; (212) 869-1630.

BROADCAST ARTS, INC., 632 Broadway, 2nd floor, New York, NY 10012; (212) 254-5400.

BROADWAY VIDEO, 1619 Broadway, New York, NY 10019; (212) 265-7600.

BUNIN, ELINOR, PRODUCTIONS, INC., 870 United Nations Plaza, New York, NY 10017; (212) 688-0759.

BUZZCO ASSOCIATES, INC., 110 W. 40 St., New York, NY 10010; (212) 840-0411.

CAESAR VIDEO GRAPHICS, INC., 137 E. 25 St., New York, NY 10010; (212) 684-7673.

CHARLEX, 2. W. 45 St., New York, NY 10036; (212) 719-4600.

CLARK, IAN 229 E. 96 St., New York, NY 10028; (212) 289-0998.

COREY DESIGN STUDIO, 42 E. 23 St., New York, NY 10010; (212) 529-7238.

DARINO FILMS, 222 Park Ave. S., New York, NY 10003; (212) 228-4024.

DA SILVA ANIMATION, 311 E. 85 St., New York, NY 10028; (212) 535-5760.

DATA MOTION ARTS, INC., 231 E. 55 St., 6th Fl., New York, NY 10022; (212) 888-0400; (203) 327-3714.

EDITEL, 222 E. 44 St., New York, NY 10017; (212) 867-4600.

F-STOP STUDIO, (Gary Becker Animation/Motion Graphics), 231 W. 29 St., New York, NY 10001; (212) 239-8010.

FANTASTIC ANIMATION MACHINE, THE, INC., 1501 Broadway, New York, NY 10036; (212) 697-2525.

FILIGREE FILMS, INC., 155 Ave. of the Americas, 10th floor, New York, NY 10013; (212) 627-1770.

FOCH, BILL, GRAPHICS, 25 W. 45 St., #203, New York, NY 10036; (212) 921-9414.

FRIEDMAN, HAROLD, CONSORTIUM, 420 Lexington Ave., New York, NY 10017; (212) 697-0858.

GATI, JOHN, FILM EFFECTS, INC., 6456 83rd Place, Middle Village, NY 11379; (718) 894-5753.

R/GREENBERG ASSOC. INC., 350 W. 39 St., New York, NY 10018; (212) 239-6767; FAX: (212) 947-3769.

GROSSMAN BROS., 19 Crosby St., New York, NY 10013; (212) 925-1965.

HUBLEY STUDIO, 2575 Palisade Ave., Riverdale, NY 10463; (212) 543-5958.

ICE TEA PRODUCTIONS, 160 E. 38 St., New York, NY 10016; (212) 557-8185.

INK TANK, THE, 2 W. 47 St., New York, NY 10036; (212) 869-1630.

KIMMELMAN ANIMATION, 39 W. 38 St., New York, NY 10018; (212) 944-6611.

LANDMAN, K., INC., 156 Fifth Ave., Suite 302, New York, NY 10010; (212) 924-4254.

LIBERTY STUDIOS, INC., 238 E. 26 St., New York, NY 10010, (212) 532-1865.

LIEBMAN, JERRY, PRODUCTIONS, 76 Laight St., New York, NY 10013; (212) 431-3452.

LYONS, ROBERT, 258 17 St., Brooklyn, NY 11215; (718) 788-0335.

MAGNO SOUND & VIDEO, 729 Seventh Ave., New York, NY 10019; (212) 302-2505.

MAVERICKS MOTION GRAPHICS, 25 W. 45 St., New York, NY 10036; (212) 382-2424.

METROPOLIS GRAPHICS, 349 W. 4 St., New York, NY 10014; (212) 989-2982.

MIMONDO PRODUCTIONS LTD., 208 W. 30 St., New York, NY 10001; (212) 695-0056.

MOTIONPICKER STUDIOS, INC., (Clay Animation), 416 Ocean Ave., Brooklyn, NY 11226; (718) 856-2763.

MUSIVISION, INC., 185 E. 85 St., New York, NY 10028; (212) 860-4420.

NOYES & LAYBOURNE ENTERPRISES, INC., 51 Leonard St., New York, NY 10013; (212) 941-6030.

OVATION FILMS INC., 81 Irving Pl., New York, NY 10003; (212) 529-4111.

PAN PRODUCTIONS, 223 Water St., Brooklyn, NY, 11201; (718) 237-1945.

POLESTAR FILM & ASSOC., 231 W. 29 St., New York, NY 10001; (212) 268-2088.

RANKIN/BASS PRODUCTIONS, 24 W. 55 St., New York, NY 10019; (212) 582-4017.

REMBRANDT FILMS, 59 E. 54 St., New York, NY 10022; (212) 758-1024.

SHADOW LIGHT PRODUCTIONS, INC., 163 W. 23 St., New York, NY 10011; (212) 689-7511, 924-0105.

SPORN, MICHAEL, ANIMATION, 632 Broadway, New York, NY 10012; (212) 228-3372.

STREAMLINE FILM MANUFACTURING, 109 E. 29 St., New York, NY 10016; (212) 481-3766.

TELEZIGN, 460 W. 42 St., New York, NY 10036; (212) 279-2000.

TRANSAMERICA VIDEO SERVICES, 25 W. 45 St., New York, NY 10036; (212) 575-5082.

VIDEART OPTICALS, INC., 63 W. 38 St., New York, NY 10018; (212) 840-2163.

VIDEO WORKS, 24 W. 40 St., New York, NY 10018; (212) 869-2500.

WOO ART INTERNATIONAL, 133 W. 19 St., New York, NY 10011; (212) 989-7870.

PORTLAND, OR

WILL VINTON PRODUCTIONS, 1400 N.W. 22nd Ave., Portland, OR 97210; (503) 225-1130.

Camera Equipment

ACE CAMERA, 3506 W. Magnolia Blvd., Burbank, CA 91505; (818) 845-5711.

AMERICAN VIDEOGRAM INC., 12020 W. Pico Blvd., Los Angeles, CA 90064; (310) 477-1535; FAX: (310) 473-5299.

APOGEE PRODUCTIONS, INC., 6842 Valjean Ave., Van Nuys, CA 91406; (818) 989-5757; FAX: (818) 781-6671.

ARMISTEAD-PEARSON CAMERA RENTAL, INC., 9800 Glenhill Dr., Burbank, CA 91504; (800) 523-5045.

AUDIO VISUAL HEADQUARTERS, 2300 Gladwick, Rancho Dominguez, CA 90220; (310) 885-4200; FAX: (310) 603-0652.

BELL & HOWELL, 3333 Wilshire Blvd., Los Angeles, CA 90038.

BERC/BROADCAST EQUIPMENT RENTAL CO., 4545 Chermak St., Burbank, CA 91505-9930; (818) 841-3000; FAX: (818) 841-7919.

BEXEL CORP, 625 W. 55 St., New York, NY 10019; (212) 246-5051; FAX: (212) 246-6373.

CENTURY PRECISION OPTICS, 10713 Burbank Blvd., N. Hollywood, CA 91601; (818) 766-3715; FAX: (818) 505-9865.

CINE VIDEO, 948 N. Cahuenga Blvd., Hollywood, CA 90038; (213) 464-6200; FAX: (213) 469-8566.

CINEMA 65 RENTALS, 3750 S. Robertson Blvd., Suite 101, Culver City, CA 90232; (310) 202-6566; FAX: (310) 202-6937.

CINEMA ENGINEERING CO., 7243 Atoll Ave., N. Hollywood, CA 91605-4105; (818) 765-5340; FAX: (818) 765-5349.

CLAIRMONT CAMERA, 4040 Vineland Ave., Studio City, CA 91604; (818) 761-4440; FAX: (818) 761-0861.

GORDON, ALAN, ENTERPRISES, INC., 1430 N. Cahuenga Blvd., Hollywood, CA 90028; (213) 466-3561; FAX: (213) 871-2193.

HILL PRODUCTION SERVICE INC., 1139 N. Highland Ave., Hollywood, CA 90038; (213) 463-1182; FAX: (213) 463-1182.

MILLER PROFESSIONAL EQUIPMENT, 10816 Burbank Blvd., N. Hollywood, CA 91601; (818) 766-9451; FAX: (818) 766-0250.

MOVIE MAKERS, 7095 Hollywood Blvd., Hollywood, CA 90028; (213) 871-6882; FAX: (213) 850-5302.

PACIFIC OCEAN POST, 730 Arizona Ave., Santa Monica, CA 90401; (310) 458-3300; FAX: (310) 394-6852.

PANAVISION, INC., 18618 Oxnard St., Tarzana, CA 91356; (818) 881-1702; FAX: (818) 342-8166.

PANTHER CORP., 4242 Lankershim Blvd., N. Hollywood, CA 91602; (818) 761-5414; FAX: (818) 761-5455.

TYLER CAMERA SYSTEMS, 14218 Aetna St., Van Nuys, CA 91401; (818) 989-4420; FAX: (818) 989-0423.

UNIVERSAL FACILITIES RENTAL DIVISION, 100 Universal City Plaza, Universal City, CA 91608; (818) 777-3000.

WEXLER VIDEO, INC., 800 N. Victory Blvd., Burbank, CA 91502; (818) 846-9381; (800) 800-9383.

Casting

CALIFORNIA

BRAMSON & ASSOC., 7400 Beverly Blvd., Los Angeles, CA 90036; (213) 938-3595; FAX: (213) 938-0852.

CASTING COMPANY, THE (Janet & Michael Hirshenson), 7319 Beverly Blvd., Suite 1, Los Angeles, CA 90036; (213) 938-2170; FAX: (213) 938-6778.

CASTING SOCIETY OF AMERICA, 6565 Sunset Blvd., Suite 306, Los Angeles, CA 90028; (213) 463-1925.

CENTRAL CASTING, 2600 W. Olive Ave., Burbank, CA 91505; (818) 569-5200; FAX: (818) 845-6507.

DANIELS, GLENN, 4000 Warner Blvd., Burbank, CA 91522; (818) 954-1495.

FENTON-TAYLOR CASTING, c/o Universal Pictures, 100 Universal Plaza, Bungalow 477, Universal City, CA 91608; (818) 777-4610

FOY, NANCY, Paramount Pictures, 5555 Melrose Ave., Los Angeles, CA 90038; (213) 956-5444.

GOLDMAN, DANNY, & ASSOCIATES CASTING, 1006 N. Cole Ave., Los Angeles, CA 90038; (213) 463-1600; FAX: (213) 463-3139.

HENDERSON/HANLEY CASTING, 8125 Lankershim Blvd., N. Hollywood, CA 91605; (818) 768-2126.

LIROFF, MARCI, P.O. Box 35483, Los Angeles, CA 90035; (213) 953-7203.

NICITA, WALLY, 10000 W. Washington Blvd., Suite 3017, Culver City, CA 90232; (310) 280-6515.

PAGANO, BIALY, MANWILLER, 1680 N. Vine St., Suite 904, Los Angeles, CA 90028; (213) 871-0051.

PERLE, SALLY & ASSOCS. INC., 12178 Ventura Blvd., Studio City, CA 91604; (818) 762-8752; FAX: (818) 762-2831.

SLATER, MARY JO, CASTING, 8670 Wilshire Blvd., 2nd Fl., Beverly Hills, CA 90211; (310) 289-6148; FAX: (310) 289-0305.

STALMASTER, LYNN, & ASSOCIATES, 9911 W. Pico Blvd., Suite 1580, Los Angeles, CA 90035; (310) 552-0983.

Commercial Jingles

CALIFORNIA

ASSOCIATED PRODUCTION MUSIC, 6255 Sunset Blvd., Suite 724, Hollywood, CA 90028; (213) 461-3211; FAX: (213) 461-9102.
AUSPEX RECORDS, P.O. Box 1740,, Studio City, CA 91604; (213) 877-1078; (818) 763-1955.
BERTUS PRODUCTIONS, 22723 Berdon St., Woodland Hills, CA 91367; (818) 883-1920.
BULLETS—A TOTAL MUSIC CO., 4520 Callada Place, Tarzana, CA 91356; (818)708-7359; FAX: (818) 708-9648.
CALIFORNIA STAR PRODUCTIONS, 8843 Shirley Ave., Northridge, CA 91324; (818) 993-4584.
CREATIVE SERVICES GROUP, 5739 Babbitt Ave., Encino, CA 91316; (818) 343-7005.
DANA PRODUCTIONS, 6249 Babcock Ave., North Hollywood, CA 91606; (213) 877-9246.
ERICSON, WILLIAM, AGENCY, 1024 Mission St., South Pasadena, CA 91030; (213) 461-4969; (818) 799-2404.
RICK FLEISHMAN MUSIC, 5739 Babbitt Ave., Encino, CA 91316; (818) 343-7005; FAX: (818) 774-1299.
FULLER SOUND AV RECORDING, 1948 Riverside Dr., Los Angeles, CA 90039; (213) 660-4914.
GRAND STAFF MUSIC PRODUCTIONS, 5740 Tujunga Ave., N. Hollywood, CA 91601; (818) 760-2205.
HLC KILLER MUSIC, 6520 W. Sunset Blvd., Hollywood, CA 90028; (213) 464-6333.
HANIFAN, BRUCE, PRODUCTIONS, 9023 Beverlywood St., Los Angeles, CA 90034; (310) 559-4522.
HARK'S SOUND STUDIO, 1041 N. Orange Dr., Hollywood, CA 90038; (213) 463-3288.
CRAIG HARRIS MUSIC, P.O. Box 110, North Hollywood, CA 91603; (818) 508-8000.
HOOK, LINE & SINGERS, 10700 Ventura Blvd., Suite E., North Hollywood, CA 91604; (818) 761-7773.
INTERLOK STUDIOS, 1550 Crossroads of the World, Hollywood, CA 90028; (213) 469-3986.
L.A./NY MUSIC CO., 9034 Sunset Blvd., Suite 101, Los Angeles, CA 90069; (310) 273-1667; FAX: (310) 275-3749.
L.A. TRAX INC., 8033 N. Sunset Blvd., Suite 1010, Los Angeles, CA 90046; (213) 852-1980.
MAGID, LEE, INC., P.O. Box 532, Malibu, CA 90265; (310) 463- 5998.
MANSON, EDDY, PRODUCTIONS, INC., 7245 Hillside Ave., Suite 216, Los Angeles, CA 90046; (213) 874-9318.
NOWELS, RICK, PRODUCTIONS, 7469 Melrose Ave., Suite 33, Hollywood, CA 90046; (213) 655-7990.
ONE NOTE PRODUCTIONS, 30014 Harvester Rd., Malibu, CA 90265; (310) 457-6670.
TED PERLMAN ARRANGEMENTS, 4519 Coldwater Canyon Ave., Suite 6, Studio City, CA 91607; (818) 762-2758.
PIECE OF CAKE, INC., 4425 Clybourn Ave., North Hollywood, CA 91602; (818) 763-2087; FAX: (818) 763-2926.
RITZ & ASSOCIATES ADVERTISING, 636 N. Robertson Blvd., Los Angeles, CA 90069; (310) 652-9813.
RUSK SOUND STUDIO, 1556 N. La Brea Ave., Hollywood, CA 90028; (213) 462-6477; RAX: (213) 462-5684.
SHADOE STEVENS INC., 3575 W. Cahuenga Blvd., Los Angeles, CA 90068; (310) 274-1244.
TARTAGLIA MUSIC PRODUCTIONS, 3815 W. Olive Ave., Suite 102, Burbank, CA 91505; (818) 508-7900.
TRIANON RECORDING STUDIOS, 1435 South St., Long Beach, CA 90805; (310) 422-2095.
UNDERSCORE ASSOCIATES, 8306 Wilshire Blvd., Suite 355, Beverly Hills, CA 90211; (818) 845-4000.
WESTLAKE AUDIO, INC., 7265 Santa Monica Blvd., Los Angeles, CA 90046; (213) 851-9800.
WIRTH-HOWARD PRODUCTIONS, 5706 Ostin St., Woodland Hills, CA 91367; (818) 888-6198.
WORDS & MUSIC, 1509 Cross Roads of the World, Hollywood, CA 90028; (213) 464-3070.
Y.L.S. PRODUCTIONS, P.O. Box 34, Los Alamitos, CA 90720; (310) 430-2890; FAX: (310) 596-9563.

NEW YORK

ALEXANDER, JOHN ERIC, MUSIC INC., 311 W. 43 St., Suite 202, New York, NY 10036; (212) 581-8560.
MUSIC MAKERS, INC., 150 W. 56 St., New York, NY 10019; (212) 582-5656.
SHELTON LEIGH PALMER & CO., 19 W. 36 St., New York, NY 10018; (212) 714-1710; 967-6210.

Completion Guarantees and Bonding

CALIFORNIA

COMPLETION BOND COMPANY, INC., THE, 2121 Ave. of the Stars, Suite 830, Century City, CA 90067-5001; (310) 553-8300; FAX: (310) 553-6610.
FILM FINANCES INC., 9000 Sunset Blvd., Suite 808, Los Angeles, CA 90069; (310) 275-7323.
INTERNATIONAL FILM GUARANTORS (FIREMAN'S FUND INSURANCE CO.), Entertainment Industry Div., 10940 Wilshire Blvd., #1900, Los Angeles, CA 90024; (310) 443-9848; FAX: (310) 208-8094.
WORLDWIDE COMPLETION SERVICES, INC., 9200 Sunset Blvd., #401, Los Angeles, CA 90069, (310) 276-4084; New York office: 888 Seventh Ave., 10106, (212) 489-7666.

NEW YORK

BC BURNHAM & COMPANY, 474 Sylvan Ave., Englewood Cliffs, NJ 07632; (201) 568-9800; (212) 563-7000.
COHEN INSURANCE, 225 W. 34th St., New York, NY 10122; (212) 244-8075.
DE WITT STERN, GUTMANN & CO., 420 Lexington Ave., New York, NY 10170; (212) 867-3550.
REIFF, D. R., & ASSOCIATES, 41 W. 83 St., New York, NY 10024; (212) 877-1099.
RICHMAR BROKERAGE, 310 Northern Blvd., Great Neck, NY 11021; (718) 895-7151; (516) 829-5200.
RUBEN, ALBERT G., & CO., 48 W. 25 St., 12 Floor, New York, NY 10010; (212) 627-7400.

Consultants

CALIFORNIA

BLUE MOUNTAIN PRODUCTIONS INC., 1800 N. Highland Ave., #411, Hollywood, CA 90068; (213) 464-0871.
CORPORATE SEAL, THE, 1310 N. Cherokee Ave., Los Angeles, CA 90028; (213) 464-8357.
CREATIVE ENTERPRISE INTL. INC., 6630 Sunset Blvd., Hollywood, CA 90028; (213) 466-1237.
CAROLE LIEBERMAN (Psychiatric Script Consultant), 247 S. Beverly Dr., Beverly Hills, CA 90212; (310) 456-2458.
M 2 RESEARCH, 1020 N. La Brea Ave., Los Angeles, CA 90038; (213) 464-7414.
MARSHALL/PLUMB RESEARCH ASSOCIATES (Legal research, script clearances), 4150 Riverside Dr., Suite 212, Burbank, CA 91505; (818) 848-7071.
MIRIMAR ENTERPRISES, P.O. Box 4621, N. Hollywood, CA 91607; (818) 784-4177.
MOTION PICTURE MARINE, 616 Venice Blvd., Marina Del Rey, CA 90291; (310) 822-1100.
2nd UNIT INC., 616 Venice Blvd., Venice, CA 90291; (310) 822-8648.

NEW YORK

BENNER MEDICAL PRODUCTIONS, INC., 204 E. 77 St., New York, NY 10028; (212) 737-7402. (Medical consultants on set.)
BOOZ, ALLEN & HAMILTON INC., 101 Park Ave., New York, NY 10178; (212) 697-1900. (Strategy, reorganization for companies)
BROADCAST BUSINESS CONSULTANTS, LTD., 41 E. 42 St., New York, NY 10017; (212) 687-3525. (Talent payment and residuals.)
CONSULTANTS FOR TALENT PAYMENT INC., 22 W. 27 St., New York, NY 10001; (212) 696-1100. (Talent payment and residuals.)
DALE SYSTEM INC., 1101 Stewart Ave., Garden City, NY 11530; (516) 794-2800; 250 W. 57 St., New York, NY 10107; (212) 586-1320.
DELTA CONSULTANTS INC., 333 W. 52 St., #410, New York, NY 10019; (212) 245-2570.
DEWITT MEDIA INC., 460 Park Ave. S., 10th Fl., New York, NY 10106; (212) 545-0120 (Media consulting and buying service. Adv. planning and buying of media.)
ROSS-GAFFNEY, 21 W. 46 St., New York, NY 10036; (212) 719-2744. (Assembling production crews.)
SECOND LINE SEARCH, 330 W. 42 St., #2901, New York, NY 10036; (212) 594-5544. (Stock footage researchers.)
SOUND ENTERPRISES, 305 E. 40 St., #18G, New York, NY 10016; (212) 986-2097. (Sound recording.)

Costumes & Uniforms

NEW YORK

AAA ACADEMY TUXEDOS, Broadway & 54th St., New York, NY 10019; (212) 765-1440.

ALLAN UNIFORM RENTAL SERVICE INC., 152 E. 23 St., New York, NY 10010; (212) 529-4655.

ANIMAL OUTFITS FOR PEOPLE CO., 110 Riverside Dr., New York, NY 10024; (212) 877-5085.

CHENKO STUDIO, 130 W. 47 St., New York, NY 10036; (212) 944-0215.

COSTUME ARMOUR INC., 2 Mill St., Cornwall-on-Hudson, NY 12520; (914) 534-9120.

CREATIVE COSTUME CO., 330 W. 38 St., New York, NY 10018; (212) 564-5552.

DAVID'S OUTFITTERS, INC., 36 W. 20 St., New York, NY 10011; (212) 691-7388.

DOMSEY INTERNATIONAL SALES CORP., 431 Kent Ave., Brooklyn, NY 11211; (800) 221-RAGS; (718) 384-6000.

EAVES-BROOKS COSTUME CO., INC., 21-07 41st Ave., Long Island City, NY 11101; (718) 729-1010.

HOUSE OF COSTUMES LTD., 166 Jericho Turnpike, Mineola, NY 11501; (516) 294-0170.

IN COSTUME, 37 W. 20 St., New York, NY 10011; (212) 255-5502.

IZQUIERO STUDIOS, 118 W. 22 St., New York, NY 10011; (212) 807-9757.

LILLIAN COSTUME CO. OF L.I. INC. 226 Jericho Turnpike, Mineola, NY 11501; (516) 746-6060.

LONDON, GENE, STUDIOS, 897 Broadway, New York, NY 10003; (212) 533-4105.

RUBIE'S COSTUME CO., INC., 120-08 Jamaica Ave., Richmond Hill, Queens, NY 11418; (718) 846-1008.

WEST COAST

ADELE'S OF HOLLYWOOD, 5034 Hollywood Blvd., Los Angeles, 90027; (213) 663-2231.

AMERICAN COSTUME CORP., 12980 Raymer St., North Hollywood, CA 91605; (818) 764-2239.

BERMAN'S COSTUME CO., 2019 Stradella Rd., Los Angeles, CA 90077; (310) 472-1844.

BUENA VISTA STUDIOS, 500 S. Buena Vista St., Burbank, CA 91521; (818) 560-0044.

CALIFORNIA COSTUME/NORCOSTO, 5867 Lankershim Blvd., N. Hollywood, CA 91601; (818) 760-2911; (213) 461-6555.

CENTER THEATRE GROUP COSTUME SHOP, 3301 E. 14th St., Los Angeles, CA 90023; (213) 267-1230; FAX: (213) 267-0378.

COSTUME PLACE, THE, 4041 W. Sunset Blvd., Los Angeles, CA 90029; (213) 661-2597.

COSTUME RENTALS CO., 7007 Lankershim Blvd., North Hollywood, CA 91605; (818) 765-8877; FAX: (818) 503-1913.

ELIZABETH COURTNEY COSTUMES, 8636 Melrose Ave., Los Angeles, CA; (310) 657-4360.

DRESSED TO KILL, INC., 8762 Holloway Dr., W. Hollywood, CA 90069; (310) 652-4334; FAX: (310) 662-9274.

E. C. 2 COSTUMES, 431 S. Fairfax Ave., Los Angeles, CA 90036; (213) 934-1131; 934-1138.

EASTERN COSTUME, 12106 Sherman Way, N. Hollywood, CA 91605; (818) 604-0842; (800) 800-5744; FAX: (818) 503-1913.

FANTASY COSTUMES, 4649½ San Fernando Rd., Glendale, CA 91204; (213) 245-7367.

FORMAL TOUCH ANTIQUE TUXEDO SERVICE, 842 N. Fairfax Ave., Los Angeles, CA 90046; (213) 658-5553.

HOLLYWOOD TOYS & COSTUMES, 6562 Hollywood Blvd., Hollywood, CA 90028; (213) 465-3119.

INTERNATIONAL COSTUME, 1423 Marcellina Ave., Torrance, CA 90501; (310) 320-6392.

LUCAS, ELIZABETH, COLLECTION, 1021 Montana Ave., Santa Monica, CA 90403; (310) 451-4058.

PALACE COSTUME COMPANY, 835 N. Fairfax Ave., Los Angeles, CA 90046; (213) 651-5458; FAX: (213) 658-7133.

SOMEWHERE IN TIME COSTUMES, 98 E. Colorado Blvd., Pasadena, CA 91105; (818) 792-7503.

STUDIO WARDROBE DEPT., THE, P.O. Box 3158, Van Nuys, CA 91407; (818) 781-4267.

TUXEDO CENTER, 7360 Sunset Blvd., Los Angeles, 90046; (213) 874-4200.

URSULA'S COSTUMES INC., 9069-A Venice Blvd., Los Angeles, CA 90034; (213) 559-8210.

VALLEY STUDIO, 150 W. Cypress Ave., Suite G, Burbank, CA 91502-1742; (818) 843-1861.

WARNER BROS. STUDIOS, 4000 Warner Blvd., Burbank, CA 91522; (818) 954-6000.

WESTERN COSTUME CO., 11041 Van Owen St., N. Hollywood, CA 91605; (818) 760-0902.

Cutting Rooms

LOS ANGELES

ASTROFILM SERVICE, 932 N. La Brea Ave., Los Angeles, CA 90038; (213) 851-1673.

CREST NATIONAL FILM & VIDEOTAPE LABS, 1141 N. Seward St., Hollywood, CA 90038; (213) 466-0624; 462-6696; FAX: (213) 461-8901.

DELTA PRODUCTIONS, 3333 Glendale, Suite 3, Los Angeles, CA 90039; (213) 663-8754.

EDITING COMPANY, THE, 8300 Beverly Blvd., Los Angeles, CA 90048; (213) 653-3570.

JDH SOUND, 12156 Olympic Blvd., Los Angeles, CA 90064-1079; (310) 820-8802.

MOVIE TECH INC., 832 N. Seward St., Hollywood, CA 90038; (213) 467-8491; 467-5423; FAX: (213) 467-8471.

PRODUCTIONS WEST, 6311 Romaine St., Suite 4134, Los Angeles, CA 90038; (213) 464-0169.

TRIO VISUAL, 3040 N. Avon St., Burbank, CA 91504; (818) 567-0079.

UNIVERSAL FACILITIES RENTAL DIV., 100 Universal City Plaza, Universal City, CA 91608; (818) 777-3000; 777-2731.

NEW YORK

ANIMATED PRODS., INC., 1600 Broadway, New York, NY 10019; (212) 265-2942; (800) 439-1360.

ANOMALY FILMS, 135 Hudson St., New York, NY 10013; (212) 925-1500.

ARCHIVE FILMS, INC., 530 W. 25 St., New York, NY 10001; (212) 620-3955.

CAMERA MART, 456 W. 55 St., New York, NY 10019; (212) 757-6977.

CARTER, JOHN, ASSOCS., INC., 300 W. 55 St., #10-V, New York, NY 10019; (212) 541-7006.

CINERGY COMMUNICATIONS CORP., 321 W. 44 St., 10036; (212) 582-2900.

CUTTING EDGE ENTERPRISES, 432 W. 45 St., New York, NY 10036; (212) 541-9664.

DARINO FILMS, 222 Park Ave. S, #2A, New York, NY 10003; (212) 228-4024.

EASY EDIT, 432 W. 45 St., New York, NY 10036; (212) 541-9664.

EDITING MACHINE, THE, INC., 630 Ninth Ave., New York, NY 10036; (212) 757-5420.

FILM/VIDEO ARTS INC., 817 Broadway, 2nd floor, New York, NY 10003-4797; (212) 673-9361.

KEM EDITING SYSTEMS, INC., 653 11 Ave., New York, NY 10036; (212) 765-2868.

KOPEL FILMS INC., 311 W. 43 St., New York, NY 10036; (212) 757-4742.

MAGNO SOUND & VIDEO, 729 Seventh Ave., New York, NY 10019; (212) 302-2505.

MAYSLES FILM INC., 250 W. 54 St., New York, NY 10019; (212) 582-6050.

MULTIVIDEO GROUP LTD., THE, 50 E. 42 St., #1107, New York, NY 10017; (212) 986-1577; 972-1015.

NATIONAL BROADCASTING CO., 30 Rockefeller Plaza, #412, New York, NY 10112; (212) 664-4444.

PHANTASMAGORIA PRODS., 111 Eighth Ave., New York, NY 10011; (212) 366-0909.

REFLECTIONS XXII M.P. CO., 263 W. 54 St., New York, NY 10019; (212) 247-5370.

RICHTER PRODS., INC., 330 W. 42 St., New York, NY 10036; (212) 947-1395.

ROSS-GAFFNEY, INC., 21 W. 46 St., New York, NY 10036; (212) 719-2744.

SILVER, TONY, FILMS INC., 49 W. 27 St., New York, NY 10001; (212) 679-2200.

SOUND ONE CORP., 1619 Broadway, 8th floor, New York, NY 10019; (212) 765-4757.

TODD-AO STUDIOS EAST, 259 W. 54 St., New York, NY 10019; (212) 265-6225.

VALKHN FILMS INC., 1600 Broadway, Suite 404, New York, NY 10019; (212) 586-1603.

Editing Equipment

LOS ANGELES

AMETHYST STUDIOS, 7000 Santa Monica Blvd., Hollywood, CA 90038; (213) 467-3700.

AMPEX CORP., 340 Parkside Dr., San Fernando, CA 91340; (818) 365-8627.

ASTROFILM SERVICE, 932 N. La Brea Ave., Los Angeles, CA 90038; (213) 851-1673.

BEXEL CORP., 801 S. Main St., Burbank, CA 91506; (818) 841-5051.

BIRNS & SAWYER, INC., 1026 N. Highland Ave., Hollywood, CA 90038; (213) 466-8211; FAX: (213) 466-7049.

CALIFORNIA COMMS. INC., 6900 Santa Monica Blvd., Los Angeles, CA 90038; (213) 466-8511.

CHENOWETH FILMS, 1860 E. N. Hills Dr., La Habra, CA 90631; (310) 691-1652.

CHRISTY'S, 135 N. Victory, Burbank, CA 91502; (818) 845-1755; (213) 849-1148.

CINE MAGIC & ASSOCIATES, 11121 Salt Lake Ave., Northridge, CA 91326; (818) 845-7651.

CINEDCO, 1125 Grand Central Ave., Glendale, CA 91201-2425, (818) 502-9100; FAX: (818) 502-0052.

CINEMA PRODUCTS CORP., 3211 S. La Cienega Blvd., Los Angeles, CA 90016-3112; (310) 836-7991.

CRAIG PRODUCTIONS, 6314 La Mirada Ave., Los Angeles, CA 90038; (310) 476-7146.

EAGLE EYE FILM COMPANY, 4019 Tujunga Ave., P.O. Box 1968, Studio City, CA 91604; (818) 506-6100.

EDIQUIP, 6820 Romaine St., Hollywood, CA 90038; (213) 467-3107.

GORDON, ALAN, ENTERPRISES, INC., 1430 Cahuenga Blvd., Hollywood, CA 90028; (213) 466-3561; (818) 985-5500; FAX: (213) 871-2193.

GRASS VALLEY GROUP INC., THE, 21243 Ventura Blvd., #143, Woodland Hills, CA 91364; (818) 999-2303.

HOLLYWOOD FILM CO., 3294 E. 26th St., Los Angeles, CA 90023; (213) 462-3284; FAX: (213) 263-9665.

J & R FILM CO., INC., 6820 Romaine St., Hollywood, CA 90038; (213) 467-3107.

JACOBSON, GARY, 1248 S. Fairfax, Malibu, CA 90019; (310) 937-6588.

KEM WEST INC., 5417 N. Cahuenga Blvd., Suite A, N. Hollywood, CA 91601; (213) 850-0200.

MAGNASYNC/MOVIELA CORP. 1141 N. Mansfield Ave., Los Angeles, CA 90038; (818) 763-8441.

MARKET STREET SOUND, 73 Market St., Venice, CA 90291; (310) 396-5937; (818) 842-4441.

NEWMAN/FRANKS, 2956 Nicada Dr., Los Angeles, CA 90077; (310) 470-0140; 470-0145; FAX: (310) 470-2410.

PLASTIC REEL CORP. OF AMERICA, 8140 Webb Ave., North Hollywood, CA 91605; (818) 504-0400.

RBC ENTERPRISES, 1860 E. North Hills Dr., La Habra, CA 90631; (310) 691-1652.

ROLAND, GLENN, FILMS, 10711 Wellworth Ave., Los Angeles, CA 90024; (310) 475-0937.

RUBBER DUBBERS, INC., 626 Justin Ave., Glendale, CA 91201; (818) 241-5600; FAX: (818) 241-1366.

SPECTRA SYSTEMS, INC., 2040 N. Lincoln St., Burbank, CA 91504; (818) 842-1111.

STEENBECK INC., 9554 Vasser Ave., Chatsworth, CA 91311; (818) 998-4033; FAX: (818) 998-6992.

VIDEO SUPPORT SERVICES, 3473½ Cahuenga Blvd., W. Los Angeles, CA 90068; (213) 469-9000.

ORLANDO

POST GROUP, THE, % Walt Disney-MGM Studios, Roy O. Disney Production Center, Lake Buena Vista, FL 32830; (407) 560-5600.

NEW YORK

BROADCAST EQUIPMENT SUPPLY CORP., Box 7460, Rego Park, Queens, NY 11374; (718) 843-6839.

CAMERA MART, INC., 456 W. 55 St., New York, NY 10019; (212) 757-6977.

CAMERA SERVICE CENTER INC., 625 W. 54 St., New York, NY 10019; (212) 757-0906.

CINERGY COMMUNICATIONS, CORP., 321 W. 44 St., New York, NY 10036; (212) 582-2900.

COMPREHENSIVE SERVICE AV INC., 432 W. 45 St., New York, NY 10036; (212) 586-6161.

CUTTING EDGE, 432 W. 45 St., New York, NY 10036; (212) 541-9664.

EASY EDIT, 432 W. 45 St., New York, NY 10036; (212) 541-9664.

EDITING MACHINE, THE, 630 Ninth Ave. #1000 New York, NY 10036; (212) 757-5420.

J & R FILM CO., INC., 636 Eleventh Ave., New York, NY 10036; (212) 247-0972.

KEM EDITING SYSTEMS, 653 Eleventh Ave., New York, NY 10036; (212) 765-2868.

LAUMIC CO., INC., 306 E. 39 St., New York, NY 10016; (212) 889-3300.

MPCS VIDEO INDUSTRIES INC., 514 W. 57 St., New York, NY 10019; (212) 586-3690; (800) 223-0622.

MAYSLES FILM, INC., 250 W. 54 St., New York, NY 10019; (212) 582-6050.

MONTAGE GROUP LTD., 1 W. 85 St., New York, NY 10024; (212) 595-0400.

MOTION PICTURES ENTERPRISES, INC. 430 W. 45 St., New York, NY 10036; (212) 245-0969.

NEUMADE, P.O. Box 5001, Norwalk, CT 06856; (203) 866-7600.

PLASTIC REEL CORP. OF AMERICA, Brisbin Ave., Lyndhurst, NJ 07071; (201) 933-5100; (212) 541-6464.

ROSS-GAFFNEY INC., 21 W. 46 St., 9th floor, New York, NY 10036; (212) 719-2744.

SPERA CORP., 511 W. 33 St., New York, NY 10001-1302; (212) 629-0009.

STUDIO FILM & TAPE INC., 630 Ninth Ave., New York, NY 10036; (212) 977-9330.

Editing Services

LOS ANGELES

ACE & EDIE 2, 722 N. Seward St., Los Angeles, CA 90038; (213) 462-2185; FAX: (213) 461-4993.

ADVENTURE FILM & TAPE, 1034 N. Seward St., Hollywood, CA 90038; (213) 460-4557.

ALTER IMAGE, 1818 S. Victory Blvd., Glendale, CA 91201; (818) 244-6030.

ASTROFILM SERVICE, 932 N. La Brea Ave., Los Angeles, CA 90038; (213) 851-1673.

AVAILABLE LIGHT LTD., 3110 W. Burbank Blvd., Burbank, CA 91505; (818) 842-2109.

CFI (CONSOLIDATED FILM INDUSTRIES), 959 Seward St., Hollywood, CA 90038; (213) 462-3161; 960-7444; FAX: (213) 460-4885.

CHRISTY'S EDITORIAL FILM SUPPLY, INC., 135 N. Victory Blvd., Burbank, CA 91502; (818) 845-1755; (213) 849-1148; FAX: (213) 849-2048.

CINEASTE GROUP, THE, 812 N. Highland Ave., Hollywood, CA 90038; (213) 464-8158.

COMPACT VIDEO SERVICES, INC., 2813 W. Alameda Ave., Burbank, CA 91505; (818) 840-7000; (800) 423-2277.

CRAWFORD EDITORIAL, 2440 El Contento Dr., Hollywood, CA 90068; (213) 462-2818.

CROSS CUTS, 1330 N. Vine St., Hollywood, CA 90028; (213) 465-2292.

CULVER STUDIOS, THE, 9336 W. Washington Blvd., Culver City, CA 90230; (310) 202-3396; 836-5537.

DELTA PRODUCTIONS, 3333 Glendale Blvd., Suite 3, Los Angeles, CA 90039; (213) 663-8754.

EAGLE EYE FILM CO., 4019 Tujunga Ave., P.O. Box 1968, Studio City, CA 91604; (818) 506-6100.

ECHO FILM SERVICES, INC., 4119 Burbank Blvd., Burbank, CA 91505; (818) 841-4114.

EDITING COMPANY, THE, 8300 Beverly Blvd., Los Angeles, CA 90048; (213) 653-3570.

ELECTRONIC ARTS & TECHNOLOGY, 3655 Motor Ave., Los Angeles, CA 90034; (310) 836-2556.

FILM CORE, 849 N. Seward St., Hollywood, 90038; (213) 464-7303.

FILMSERVICE LABORATORIES, INC., 6327 Santa Monica Blvd., Los Angeles, CA 90038; (213) 464-5141.

525 POST PRODUCTION, 6425 Santa Monica Blvd., Hollywood, CA 90038; (213) 466-3348; FAX: (213) 467-1589.

FREUD & KLEPPEL INC., 6290 Sunset Blvd., #603, Los Angeles, CA 90028; (213) 469-1444.

HOLLYWOOD ASSOCIATES, INC., 359 E. Magnolia Blvd., Suite G, Burbank, CA 91502.

IMAGE TRANSFORM LAB., 4142 Lankershim Blvd., No. Hollywood, CA 91602; (818) 985-7566; (800) 423-2652.

KEM WEST, 5417 N. Cahuenga Blvd., Suite A, North Hollywood, CA 91601; (213) 850-0200.

LASER-PACIFIC MEDIA CORP., 540 N. Hollywood Way, Burbank, CA 91505; (818) 842-0777.

MATHERS, JIM, FILM COMPANY, P.O. Box 1973, Studio City, CA 91604; (818) 762-2214.

MOFFIT, WILLIAM ASSOCS., 747 N. Lake Ave., #B, Pasadena, CA 91104; (818) 791-2559.

MOVIE TECH INC., 832 N. Seward St., Hollywood, CA 90038; (213) 467-8491; 467-5423; FAX: (213) 467-8471.

PARAMOUNT STUDIO GROUP, 5555 Melrose Ave., Hollywood 90038; (213) 468-5000.

POST PLUS INC., 6650 Santa Monica Blvd., 2nd floor, Hollywood, CA 90038; (213) 463-7108.

PRO VIDEO/CINETAPE, 801 N. La Brea Ave., Los Angeles, CA 90038; (213) 934-8836; 934-8840.

PRODUCTION GROUP, THE, 1330 N. Vine St., Los Angeles, CA 90028; (213) 469-8111; FAX: (213) 462-0836.

RED CAR, 1040 N. Las Palmas Ave., Los Angeles, CA 90038; (213) 466-4467; FAX: (213) 466-4925.

REEL THING OF CALIFORNIA INC., 1253 N. Vine St., Suite 14, Hollywood, CA 90038; (213) 466-8588.

RENCHER'S EDITORIAL SERVICE, 738 Cahuenga Blvd., Hollywood, CA 90038; (213) 463-9836.

TELEVISION CENTER, 6311 Romaine St., Los Angeles, CA 90038; (213) 464-6638.

UNIVERSAL FACILITIES RENTAL DIVISION, 100 Universal City Plaza, Universal City 91608; (818) 777-3000; 777-2731.

WARNER BROS. STUDIOS, 4000 Warner Blvd., Burbank, CA 91522; (818) 954-6000.

WARNER HOLLYWOOD STUDIOS, 1041 N. Formosa Ave., W. Hollywood, CA 90046; (213) 850-2500.

WILDWOOD FILM SERVICE, 6855 Santa Monica Blvd., Suite 400, Los Angeles, CA 90038; (213) 462-6388.

WOLLIN PRODUCTION SERVICES, INC., 666 N. Robertson Blvd., Los Angeles, CA 90069; (310) 659-0175.

MIAMI

KESSER POST PRODUCTION, 21 SW 15 Rd., Miami, FL 33129; (305) 358-7900.

NEW YORK

ANIMATED PRODS., INC., 1600 Broadway, 10019; (212) 265-2942.

ANOTHER DIRECTION, 231 E. 51 St., 10022; (212) 753-8250.

BACKSTREET EDIT, INC., 49 W. 27 St., New York, NY 10001; (212) 684-5001.

BENDER EDITORIAL SERVICE, INC., 27 E. 39 St., New York, NY 10016; (212) 867- 1515.

BERT'S PLACE, 141 E. 44 St., New York, NY 10017; (212) 682-5891.

CANARICK'S, B., CO., LTD., 50 E. 42 St., New York, NY 10017; (212) 972-1015.

CHARLES, MICHAEL, EDITORIAL, 6 E. 45 St., New York, NY 10017; (212) 953-2490.

CINE METRIC, INC., 290 Madison Ave., New York, NY 10017; (212) 922-0910.

CINE TAPE, INC., 241 E. 51 St., New York, NY 10022; (212) 355-0070.

CRESCENT CUTTERS, INC., 304 E. 45 St., New York, NY 10017; (212) 687-2802.

CREW CUTS FILM & TAPE, INC., 9 E. 47 St., New York, NY 10017; (212) 371-4545.

CUT ABOVE EDITORIAL INC., A, 17 E. 45 St., New York, NY 10017; (212) 661-4949.

DJM FILMS, INC., 4 E. 46 St., New York, NY 10017; (212) 687-0111.

DEE, DAVID, 62 W. 45 St., New York, NY 10036; (212) 764-4700.

DELL, JEFF, FILM SERVICE INC., 241 E. 51 St., New York, NY 10022; (212) 371-7915.

EDITING CONCEPTS, 214 E. 50 St., New York, NY 10022; (212) 980-3340.

EDITORS, THE, 220 E. 48 St., New York, NY 10017; (212) 371-0862.

EDITOR'S GAS, 16 E. 48 St., New York, NY 10017; (212) 832-6690.

EDITORS HIDEAWAY, INC., 219 E. 44 St., New York, NY 10022; (212) 661-3850.

FILM BUILDERS, 10 E. 40 St., New York, NY 10016; (212) 683-4004.

FILM-RITE, INC., 1185 Ave. of the Americas, New York, NY 10036; (212) 575-6801.

FINAMORE, D.P., 619 W. 54 St., New York, NY 10019; (212) 582-5265.

FIRST EDITION, 5 E. 47 St., New York, NY 10017; (212) 838-3044.

FISCHER, FREDERIC, FILMS, 28 Verandah Pl., Brooklyn, NY 11201; (718) 852-2643.

GRENADIER PRODS., INC., 220 E. 23 St., New York, NY 10010; (212) 545-0388.

GROVE, ERIC, FILM, 145 Ave. of Americas, New York, NY 10013; (212) 989-5454.

HAYES, DENNIS, FILM EDITING, INC., 9 E. 40 St., New York, NY 10016; (213) 683-5080.

HORN/EISENBERG FILM & TAPE EDITING, 16 W. 46 St., New York, NY 10036; (212) 391-8166.

HOROWITZ, ROBERT, FILMS, 321 W. 44 St., New York, NY 10036; (212) 397-9380.

JPC VISUALS, 11 E. 47 St., New York, NY 10017; (212) 223-0555.

JUPITER EDITORIAL SERVICE, 201 E. 16 St., New York, NY 10003; (212) 460-5600.

KOPEL FILMS, INC., 311 W. 43 St., New York, NY 10036; (212) 757-4742.

LFR EDITORIAL, INC., 20 E. 46 St., New York, NY 10017; (212) 682-5950.

LANDA, SAUL, INC., 20 E. 46 St., New York, NY 10017; (212) 682-5950.

MAGNO SOUND & VIDEO, 729 Seventh Ave., 10019; (212) 302-2505.

MESSINA EDITORIAL, INC., 18 E. 41 St., New York, NY 10017; (212) 481-3456.

MORTY'S FILM SERVICES, LTD., 10 E. 40 St., New York, NY 10016; (212) 696-5040.

P.A.T. FILM SERVICES, 630 Ninth Ave., New York, NY 10036; (212) 247-0900.

PDR PRODUCTIONS, INC., 219 E. 44 St., New York, NY 10017; (212) 986-2020.

PALESTRINI FILM EDITING, INC., 575 Lexington Ave., New York, NY 10022; (212) 752-EDIT.

PELCO EDITORIAL INC., 757 Third Ave., New York, NY 10017; (212) 319-EDIT.

PINEYRO, GLORIA, FILM SERVICES CORP., 19 W. 21 St., New York, NY 10010; (212) 627-0707.

POWER POST PRODUCTION, 25 W. 43 St., New York, NY 10036; (212) 840-3860.

REBELEDIT, 292 Madison Ave., 26th Floor, New York, NY 10017; (212) 686-8622.

REFLECTIONS XXII M.P. CO., 263 W. 54 St., New York, NY 10019; (212) 247-5370.

RICH ENTERPRISES CORP., 208 W. 30 St., New York, NY 10001; (212) 947-3943.

ROSEBUD PRODUCTIONS, INC., 304 E. 45 St., New York, NY 10017; (212) 818-0707.

ROSS-GAFFNEY, INC., 21 W. 46 St., New York, NY 10036; (212) 719-2747; 997-1464.

SG VIDEO, 16 W. 22 St., New York, NY 10010; (212) 691-1414.

SALAMANDRA IMAGES, INC., 6 E. 39 St., New York, NY 10016; (212) 779-0707.

SANDPIPER EDITORIAL SERVICE, 298 Fifth Ave., New York, NY 10018; (212) 564-6643.

SELIGMAN, MAX, P.O. Box 710, Jackson Heights, NY 11372; (718) 803-0885.

SOLOMON, LAURENCE, FILM GROUP, 244 W. 49 St., Suite 400, New York, NY 10019; (212) 582-6246.

SPECTRUM ASSOCS. INC., 536 W. 29 St., New York, NY 10001, (212) 563-1680.

SPLICE IS NICE, 141 E. 44 St., New York, NY 10017; (212) 599-1711.

STONE CUTTERS, 422 Madison Ave., New York, NY 10017; (212) 421-9404.

STYLIANOU, MICHEL, PRODUCTIONS, NC., 265 Madison Ave., New York, NY 10016; (212) 972-8888.

SYNCROFILM SERVICES, INC., 72 W. 45 St., New York, NY 10036; (212) 719-2966.

TAKE 5 EDITORIAL SERVICES, INC., 681 Lexington Ave., New York, NY 10022; (212) 759-7404.

TAPE HOUSE INC., 216 E. 45 St., New York, NY 10017; (212) 557-4949.

TAPESTRY PRODUCTIONS, LTD., 924 Broadway, 2nd floor, New York, NY 10010; (212) 677-6007.

TRAILER SHOP, INC., THE, 21 W. 46 St., New York, NY 10036; (212) 944-0318.

TRAIMAN, HENRY, ASSOCIATES, 160 Madison Ave., New York, NY 10016; (212) 889-3400.

VALKHN FILMS INC., 1650 Broadway, New York, NY 10019; (212) 586-1603.

WACHTER, GARY, EDITORIAL, INC., 159 W. 53 St., New York, NY 10019; (212) 399-7770.

WARMFLASH PRODUCTIONS, INC., 630 Ninth Ave., New York, NY 10036; (212) 757-5969.

WILLIAMS, BILLY, EDITORIAL, 231 E. 51 St., New York, NY 10022; (212) 753-8250.

WORLD CINEVISION SERVICES, INC., 321 W. 44 St., New York, NY 10036; (212) 265-4587.

Film Preservation & Repair

ACCUTREAT FILMS, INC., 630 Ninth Ave., #1101, New York, NY 10036; (212) 247-3415.

AFD/PHOTOGRAD FILM COATING LAB, 1015 N. Cahuenga Blvd., Hollywood, CA 90038; (213) 469-8141; FAX: (213) 469-1888.

BARTCO CO., 924 N. Formosa, Hollywood, CA 90046; (213) 851- 5411.

BONDED SERVICES, 5260 Vineland Ave., N. Hollywood, CA 91601; (818) 761-4058; FAX: (818) 761-5939.

DELTA PRODUCTIONS, 3333 Glendale Blvd., Suite 3, Los Angeles, CA 90039; (213) 663-8754; FAX: (213) 663-3460.

DURAFILM CO., 137 No. La Brea Ave., Hollywood, CA 90036; (213) 936-1156.

FILM PRESERVE, 2 Depot Plaza, #202-B, Bedford Hills, NY 10507; (914) 242-9838.

FILMLIFE INCORPORATED, Filmlife Bldg., 141 Moonachie Road, Moonachie, NJ 07074; (201) 440-8500.

FILMTREAT INTERNATIONAL CORP., 42-24 Orchard St., Long Island City, NY 11101; (718) 784-4040. Y. W. Mociuk, pres.

FILMTREAT WEST CORP., 12326 Montague Lane, Pacoima, CA 91331; (818) 506-3276.

HOLLYWOOD VAULTS, 742 N. Seward St., Los Angeles, CA 90038; (213) 461-6464; (805) 569-5336; FAX: (805) 569-1675.

INTERNATIONAL CINE SERVICES, INC., 920 Allen Ave., Glendale, CA 91201; (818) 242-3839; FAX: (818) 242-1566.
PEERLESS FILM PROCESSING CORPORATION, 42-24 Orchard St., Long Island City, NY 11101; (718) 784-4040. Y. M. Mociuk, pres.
PERMAFILM NORTH AMERICA CORP., 280 High St., Milford, CT 06460; (203) 877-7746.
PRODUCERS FILM CENTER, 948 N. Sycamore Ave., Los Angeles, CA 90038; (213) 851-1122.
TITRA FILM CALIFORNIA INC., 733 Salem St., Glendale, CA 91203; (818) 244-3663, 244-3762.
WESTERN FILM INDUSTRIES, 30941 W. Agoura Rd., Suite 302, Westlake Village, CA 91361; (818) 889-7350; FAX: (818) 707-3937.

Film Processing Labs

ATLANTA

CINEFILM LABORATORY, 2156 Faulkner Rd., N.E., 30324; (404) 633-1448; (800) 633-1448.
SOUTHERN FILM LAB INC., 2050-H Chamblee Tucker Rd., Chamblee, GA 30341; (404) 458-0026.

BOSTON

CINE SERVICE LABORATORIES, INC., 1380 Soldiers Field Rd., Brighton, 02135; (617) 254-7882.
DU ART BOSTON/NEW ENGLAND, 650 Beacon St., 02215; (617) 267-8717; 969-0666.
FILM SERVICE LAB, 93 Harvey St., Cambridge, MA 02140; (617) 542-8501.
SPORTS FILM LAB, 361 W. Broadway, South Boston 02127; (617) 268-8388.

CHICAGO

ALLIED FILM & VIDEO SERVICES, 1322 W. Belmont Ave., 60657; (312) 348-0373.
ASTRO COLOR LAB, 61 W. Erie, 60610; (312) 280-5500.
CINEMA VIDEO CENTER, 211 E. Grand Ave., 60611; (312) 527-4050.
EASTMAN KODAK CO., 1331 Business Center Dr., Mt. Prospect 60056; (312) 635-5900.
FILMACK, 1327 S. Wabash, 60605; (312) 427-3395.
SPECTRUM MOTION PICTURE LAB, 399 Gundersen, Carol Stream, IL 60187; (312) 665-4242; (800) 345-6522.

COLUMBIA, SC

SOUTHEASTERN FILM COMPANY, 3604 Main St., 29203; (803) 252-3753.

COLUMBUS, OH

JOHN R. BENNETT, 2553 Cleveland Ave., 43211; (614) 267-7007.

DALLAS

ALLIED & WBS FILM & VIDEO SERVICES, 4 Dallas Communications Complex, #111, Irving 75039; (214) 869-0100.
SOUTHWEST FILM LABORATORY, INC., 3024 Fort Worth Ave., 75211; (214) 331-8347.

DAYTON, OH

VALDHERE INC., 3060 Valleywood Dr., Dayton, 45429; (513) 293-2191.

DETROIT

FILM CRAFT LAB., INC., 66 Sibley, 48201; (313) 962-2611.
MULTI-MEDIA INC., 7154 E. Nevada St., 48234; (313) 366- 5200.
PRODUCERS COLOR SERVICE, 2921 E. Grand Blvd., 48202; (313) 874-1112.
WILLIAMS SERVICE, 601 W. Fort, 48226; (313) 962-9070.

FORT LEE, NJ

LEXICHROME, INC., 2055 Center Ave., Fort Lee, NJ 07024.

HOLLYWOOD-LOS ANGELES

ALPHA CINE LABORATORY INC., 5724 W. Third St., Suite 311, Los Angeles, 90036; (213) 934-7793; FAX: (213) 934-6307.
ASHFIELD CO., 747 N. Seward St., Hollywood 90038; (213) 462-3231.
AUDIO VISUAL HEADQUARTERS CORP., 361 N. Oak, Inglewood 90302; (310) 419-4040.
BROADCAST STANDARDS, INC., 2044 Cottner Ave., Los Angeles, 90025; (310) 312-9060.
CINESERVICE, INC., 6518½ Santa Monica Blvd., Los Angeles, 90038; (213) 463-3178.
CONRAD FILM DUPLICATING COMPANY, 6750 Santa Monica Blvd., Hollywood, 90038; (213) 463-5614.
CONSOLIDATED FILM INDUSTRIES, 959 N. Seward St., Hollywood, 90038; (213) 960-7444; FAX: (213) 460-4885.
CREST NATIONAL VIDEO FILM LABS, 1141 N. Seward St., Hollywood, 90038; (213) 466-0624; 462-6696; FAX: (213) 461-8901.
DELUXE LABORATORIES, INC., 1377 N. Serrano Ave., Hollywood, 90027; (213) 462-6171; (800) 2DE-LUXE.
EASTMAN KODAK LABORATORY 1017 N. Las Palmas Ave., Los Angeles, 90038; (213) 465-7152; (800) 621-1234.
FILM TECHNOLOGY CO. INC., 726 Cole Ave., Los Angeles, 90038; (213) 464-3456
FILMSERVICE LABORATORIES, INC., 6327 Santa Monica Blvd., Hollywood, 90038; (213) 464-5141; 461-6911.
FLORA COLOR, 1715 N. Mariposa, Hollywood, CA 90027; (213) 663-2291.
FOTO-KEM FOTO-TRONICS, FILM-VIDEO LAB, 2800 W. Olive Ave., Burbank, 91505; (818) 846-3101; FAX: (818) 841-2130.
FOTORAMA, 1507 N. Cahuenga Blvd., Los Angeles, 90028; (213) 469-1578.
GETTY FILM LAB, 7641 Densmore Ave., Van Nuys, CA 91406; (818) 997-7801; (213) 873-5646; FAX: (818) 787-9359.
HOLLYWOOD FILM & VIDEO INC., 6060 Sunset Blvd., Hollywood, 90028; (213) 464-2181; FAX: (213) 464-0893.
HOLMES, FRANK, LABORATORIES, 1947 First St., San Fernando, 91340; (818) 365-4501.
IMAGE TRANSFORM LABORATORY, 3611 N. San Fernando Rd., Burbank, 91505; (818) 841-3812; FAX: (818) 841-3999.
LEXICHROME, INC., 1331 N. Formosa, Hollywood, 90046; FAX: (213) 878-0216.
METROCOLOR LAB, (div. of Lorimar Telepictures), 10202 W. Washington Blvd., Culver City, 90232-3783; (310) 280-5858; 280-8000.
MORCRAFT FILMS, 837 N. Cahuenga Blvd., Los Angeles, 90038; (213) 464-2009.
MULTI-LAB, 1633 Maria St., Burbank, 91504; (213) 465-9970.
NEWELL COLOR LAB, 221 N. Westmoreland Ave., Los Angeles, 90004; (213) 380-2980.
NEWSFILM & VIDEO LABORATORY, INC., 516 N. Larchmont Blvd., Hollywood, 90004; (213) 462-6814.
PACIFIC FILM LABORATORIES, 823 Seward, Los Angeles, 90038; (213) 461-9921; FAX: (213) 466-5047.
PACIFIC TITLE & ART STUDIO, 6350 Santa Monica Blvd., Los Angeles, 90038; (213) 464-0121; 938-3711.
PEERLESS FILM PROCESSING CORP., 920 Allen Ave., Glendale, 91201; (818) 242-2181.
RGB COLOR LAB, 816 N. Highland Ave., Los Angeles, 90038; (213) 469-1959.
SINA'S CUSTOM LAB, 3136 Wilshire Blvd., Los Angeles, 90010; (213) 381-5161.
SUPER CINE, INC., 2214 W. Olive Ave., Burbank, 91506; (818) 843-8260.
TECHNICOLOR INC., (Professional Film Division), 4050 Lankershim Blvd., North Hollywood, 91608; (818) 769-8500.
UNITED COLOR LAB. INC., 835 N. Seward, Hollywood, 90038; (213) 461-9921; 469-7291.
UNIVERSAL FACILITIES RENTAL DIVISION, 100 Universal City Plaza, Universal City, 91608; (818) 777-3000; 777-2731.
YALE LABS, 1509 N. Gordon St., Los Angeles, 90028; (213) 464-6181.

HOUSTON

PHOTOGRAPHIC LABORATORIES, THE, 1926 W. Gray, 77019; (713) 527-9300.

MEMPHIS, TN

MOTION PICTURE LABORATORIES, INC., 781 S. Main St. 38101; (901) 774-4944; (800) 444-4675.

MIAMI, FL

CONTINENTAL FILM LABS, INC., 1998 Northeast 150 St., N. Miami, 33181; (305) 949-4252; (800) 327-8296.

MILWAUKEE, WI

CENTRAL FILM LABORATORY & PHOTO SUPPLY, 1003 North Third St., 53203; (414) 272-0606.

NEW ORLEANS

PAN AMERICAN FILMS, 822 N. Rampart St., 70116; (504) 522-5364.

NEW YORK CITY

A-1 REVERSE-O-LAB INC., 333 W. 39 St., 10018; (212) 239-9530.
ACCUTREAT FILM, INC., 630 Ninth Ave., 10036; (212) 247-3415.
CINE MAGNETICS FILM & VIDEO, 298 Fifth Ave., 10016; (212) 564-6737.
DELUXE GENERAL INC., 630 Ninth Ave., 10036; (212) 489-8800.
DUART FILM LABORATORIES, 245 W. 55 St., 10019; (212) 757-4580.
GUFFANTI FILM LABORATORIES INC., 630 Ninth Ave., 10036; (212) 265-5530.
HBO STUDIO PRODS., 120A E. 23 St., 10010; (212) 512-7800.
J & D LABS INC., 12 W. 21 St., 10010; (212) 691-5613.
JAN FILM LAB, INC., 302 W. 37 St., 10018; (212) 279-5438.
LABLINK, INC., 115 W. 45 St., 10036; (212) 302-7373.
LIEBERMAN, KEN, LABORATORIES INC., 118 W. 22 St., 10011; (212) 633-0500.
MAGNO SOUND & VIDEO, 729 Seventh Ave., 10019; (212) 302-2505; FAX: (212) 819-1282.
MAGNO VISUALS, 115 W. 45 St., 10036; (212) 575-5162; 575-5159.
MILLENNIUM FILM WORK SHOP, 66 E. 4 St., 10003; (212) 673-0090.
PRECISION FILM LABS, INC., 311 W. 43 St., 10036; (212) 489-8800.
STUDIO FILM & TAPE LABS INC., 630 Ninth Ave., 10036; (212) 977-9330.
STUDIO WEST LTD., 239 W. 39 St., 10018; (212) 489-1190.
TVC IMAGE TECHNOLOGY, 311 W. 43 St., 10036; (212) 397-8600; Outside NY: (800) 225-6566.
TECHNICOLOR INC., 321 W. 44 St., 10036; (212) 582-7310.
VAN CHROMES CORP., 21 W. 46 St., 10036; (212) 302-5700.

OMAHA

CORNHUSKER FILM PROCESSING LAB, 1817 Vinton St., 68108; (402) 341-4290.

PITTSBURGH

WRS MOTION PICTURE LAB., 210 Semple St., 15213; (412) 687-3700.

PORTLAND OR

TEKNIFILM INC., 909 N.W. 19th, 97209; (503) 224-3835.

SALT LAKE CITY, UT

ALPHA CINE LAB. INC., 450 S. 900 St., #205, 84102; (801) 363-9465.

SAN FRANCISCO

DINER/ALLIED FILM & VIDEO, 620 Third St., 94107; (415) 777-1700.
HIGHLAND LABS., 840 Battery St., 94111; (415) 981-5010.
LUCASFILM LTD., P.O. Box 2009, San Rafael, CA 94912; (415) 662-1800.
MONACO LABORATORIES, INC., 234 Ninth St., 94103; (415) 864-5350.

SEATTLE, WA

ALPHA CINE LABORATORY, 1001 Lenora St., 98121; (206) 682-8230; (800) 426-7070.
FORDE MOTION PICTURE LABORATORY, 306 Fairview Ave. N., 98109; (206) 682-2510; (800) 682-2510.

SPRINGFIELD, MA

PENFIELD PRODUCTIONS LTD., 35 Springfield St., Agawarm 01001; (413) 786-4454.

TAMPA, FL

BEACON FILM LABORATORY, 8029 N. Nebraska Ave.; (813) 932-9636.

Film Storage Vaults

ATLANTA

BENTON FILM FORWARDING CO., 168 Baker St., N.W.; (404) 577-2821.

FORT LEE, NJ

BONDED FILM STORAGE, service & storage: 550 Main St., Fort Lee, NJ 07024; (212) 557-6732; (201) 944-3700.
BONDED SERVICES, exec. offices: 2050 Center Ave., 07024; (201) 592-7868; (212) 695-2034 (NY).
FORT LEE FILM STORAGE & SERVICE, 504 Jane St., 07024; (201) 944-1030.

HOLLYWOOD-LOS ANGELES

(Hollywood studios have their own storage vaults)
AMERICAN ARCHIVES, INC., 11120 Weddington St., North Hollywood, 91601; (818) 506-STOR; (818) 506-6688.
ARCHIVES FOR ADVANCED MEDIA, 3205 Burton Ave., Burbank, CA 91504; (818) 848-9766.
BELL & HOWELL RECORDS MANAGEMENT, 1025 N. Highland Ave., Los Angeles, 90038; (213) 466-9271.
BONDED SERVICES, 5260 Vineland Ave., North Hollywood, 91601; (818) 761-4058; FAX: (818) 761-5939.
BRAKEWATER TRANSPORT, INC., 8401 E. Slauson Ave., Pico Rivera, CA 90660; (310) 949-6639.
CONSOLIDATED FILM INDUSTRIES, 959 N. Seward St., Hollywood CA 90038; (213) 462-3161. (Stores only film which Consolidated Laboratory is handling.)
HACKIE, RAY, FILM SERVICE, 1720 W. Slauson Ave., Los Angeles, 90047; (213) 299-2095, 299-9596; FAX: (213) 299-9597.
HOLLYWOOD FILM CO., 5446 Carlton Way, Hollywood, 90027; (213) 462-1971; 462-3284; FAX: (213) 263-9665.
HOLLYWOOD VAULTS, INC., Vault: 742 N. Seward St., Hollywood 90038; (213) 461-6464; Office: 1780 Prospect Ave., Santa Barbara, CA 93103; (805) 569-5336; FAX: (805) 569-1657.
INTERNATIONAL CINE SERVICES, INC., 920 Allen Ave., Glendale, 91201; (818) 242-3839; FAX: (818) 242-1566.
IRON MOUNTAIN RECORDS MANAGEMENT, 1025 N. Highland Ave., Hollywood, 90038; (213) 466-9271; (213) 467-8068.
JONES, TYLIE, & ASSOC., 3519 W. Pacific Ave., Burbank, 91505; (818) 955-7600; FAX: (818) 955-8542.
PACIFIC TITLE ARCHIVES, 4800 San Vicente Blvd., Los Angeles, 90019; (213) 938-3711; FAX: (213) 938-6364; 561 Mateo St., Los Angeles, 90013; (213) 617-8650; 617-8405; FAX: (213) 617-7876; 10717 Vanowen St., N. Hollywood, 91605; (818) 760-4223; FAX: (818) 760-1704.
PRODUCERS FILM CENTER, 948 N. Sycamore Ave., Hollywood, 90038; (213) 851-1122.
S.A. GLOBEL STUDIOS, 201 N. Occidental Blvd., Los Angeles, 90026; (213) 384-3331.
TAPE-FILM INDUSTRIES (TFI), 941 N. Highland Ave., Hollywood 90038; (213) 461-3361; FAX: (213) 469-2386.
THEATRE TRANSIT, INC., 8401 E. Slauson Ave., Pico Rivera, 90660; (310) 949-6659.
VAULT WORKS, THE, 7306 Coldwater Canyon Ave., North Hollywood 91605; (818) 764-0685.

NEW YORK CITY

BONDED SERVICES, 250 W. 57 St., 10019; (212) 956-2212; 550 Main St., Ft. Lee, NJ; (201) 944-3700.
METRO BUSINESS ARCHIVES, 609 W. 51 St., 10019; (212) 489-7890.
PAT FILM SERVICES, INC., 630 Ninth Ave., 10036; (212) 247-0900.
TAPE FILM INDUSTRIES, 619 W. 54 St., 10019; (212) 708-0500.

Financing Companies & Banking Services

ANDARY, J.E., PRODUCTIONS & FINANCING, 7080 Hollywood Blvd. #114, Los Angeles, CA 90028; (213) 466-3379.

BANK OF AMERICA Entertainment Industries Division, 555 S. Flower St., Los Angeles, CA 90071; (213) 228-4096.

BANK OF BEVERLY HILLS, 9808 Wilshire Blvd., Suite 207, Beverly Hills, CA 90212; (310) 274-9240.

BANK OF CALIFORNIA Entertainment Division, 9401 Wilshire Blvd., Beverly Hills, CA 90212; (310) 273-7200; 205-3035; FAX: (310) 273-9030.

BANK OF NEW YORK, 530 Fifth Ave., New York, NY 10036; (212) 852-4098; 495-1784.

BANKERS TRUST, Media Division, 280 Park Ave., 15th floor, New York, NY 10017; (212) 250-2500.

CAMDEN ENTERTAINMENT FINANCE INC., 9454 Wilshire Blvd., #650, Beverly Hills, CA 90212; (310) 659-5317.

CHARTER FINANCIAL INC., One Rockefeller Plaza, New York, NY 10020; (212) 399-7777.

CHASE MANHATTAN BANK, N.A., Media & Communications Component, 1 Chase Manhattan Plaza, 5th floor, New York, NY 10081; (212) 552-2222; 552-4848.

CHEMICAL BANK Entertainment Industries Group, 277 Park Ave., New York, NY 10172; (212) 935-9935; 333 S. Grand Ave., Suite 2600, Los Angeles, CA 90071; (213) 253-5006.

CINEMA GROUP, 8758 Venice Blvd., Los Angeles, CA 90034; (310) 204-0102.

CINEREP SERVICES, 28 Avenue 28th, Marina Del Rey, CA 90291; (310) 305-1394.

CITICORP, USA, INC., 725 S. Figueroa St., Los Angeles, CA 90017; (213) 239-1400; 239-1800.

CITY NATIONAL BANK Entertainment Division, 400 N. Roxbury Dr., Suite 400, Beverly Hills, CA 90210; (310) 550-5696.

CONSTANT FINANCIAL SERVICES INC., 8749 Holloway Dr., Los Angeles, CA 90069; (213) 650-5227.

CROCKER BANK, THE, Entertainment Industries Group, 10100 Santa Monica Blvd., Suite 420-A, Los Angeles, CA 90067; (213) 253-3300.

DnC AMERICA BANKING CORP., 600 Fifth Ave., 16th Floor, New York, NY 10020; (212) 315-6581.

FILM CAPITAL CORP., 291 Mel Ave., #272, Palm Springs, CA 92262-4843; (619) 778-7461.

FILM FINANCES, INC., 9000 Sunset Blvd., Suite 808, Los Angeles, CA 90069; (310) 275-7323; FAX: (310) 275-1706; TELEX: 183-205.

FIRST BANK NATIONAL ASSOCIATION, Entertainment Division, 444 S. Flower St., Suite 1730, Los Angeles, CA 90017; (213) 623-8267.

FIRST CHARTER BANK Entertainment Division, 265 N. Beverly Drive, Beverly Hills, CA 90210; (310) 275-2225.

FIRST INTERSTATE BANK OF CALIFORNIA, Entertainment Division, 9601 Wilshire Blvd., Beverly Hills, CA 90210; (310) 858-5585.

FIRST LOS ANGELES BANK Entertainment Division, 9595 Wilshire Blvd., Beverly Hills, CA 90212; (310) 557-1211.

FLEET CREDIT CORPORATION, 3990 Westerly Place, Suite 100, Newport Beach, CA 92660; (714) 955-2574.

GOLCHAN, FREDERIC PRODUCTIONS, 4000 Warner Blvd. Production One, Room 104A, Burbank, CA 91505; (818) 854-2418.

HERITAGE ENTERTAINMENT, 11500 W. Olympic Blvd., Suite 300, Los Angeles, CA 90064; (310) 477-8100.

HILTON FINANCIAL GROUP, INC., 3500 W. Olive Ave., Suite 740, Burbank, CA 91505; (818) 953-4161.

IMPERIAL BANKING, Entertainment Banking, 9757 Wilshire Blvd., Beverly Hills, CA 90212; (310) 338-3139.

HORWITZ, LEWIS, ORGANIZATION, 1840 Century Park East, Los Angeles, CA 90067; (310) 275-7171.

MERCANTILE NATIONAL BANK, 1840 Century Park East, Los Angeles, CA 90067; (310) 277-2265.

METRO BANK Entertainment Division, 10900 Wilshire Blvd., 3rd floor, Los Angeles, CA 90024; (310) 824-5700.

MOTION PICTURES INVESTMENT CO., 430 S. Burnside Ave., Los Angeles, CA 90036; (213) 931-9241.

SECURITY PACIFIC BANK, 333 S. Hope St., H14-60, Los Angeles, CA 90071; (213) 362-0600.

SPECTRUM ENTERTAINMENT LTD., 8800 Sunset Blvd, Suite 302, Los Angeles, CA 90069; (310) 855-1412.

TOKAI BANK OF CALIFORNIA, 200 E. Colorado Blvd., Pasadena, CA 91105; (818) 570-6391.

TOUCHE ROSS, 1000 Wilshire Blvd., Los Angeles, CA 90017; (213) 688-0800; FAX: (213) 284-9029.

UNION BANK, 9460 Wilshire Blvd., 1st Floor, Beverly Hills, CA 90213; (310) 550-6627; 550-6522; FAX: (310) 859-3813.

WALKER CORPORATE FINANCIAL CONSULTING, P.O. Box 93-543, Sunset Station, Hollywood, CA 90093; (213) 876-6300.

WELLS FARGO BANK Entertainment Division, 9600 Santa Monica Blvd., Beverly Hills, CA 92010; (310) 285-7387; FAX: (310) 858-7924.

WESTERN SECURITY BANK, ENTERTAINMENT DIVISION, 4100 W. Alameda Ave., Toluca Lake, CA 91505; (818) 843-0707.

Lighting Equipment

CALIFORNIA

ACEY-DECY LIGHTING, 5420 Vineland Ave., N. Hollywood, CA 91601; (818) 766-9445; FAX: (818) 766-4758.

ADCO EQUIPMENT, INC., 605 Freeway at Rose Hill Rd., P.O. Box 2100, City of Industry, CA 91746; (310) 695-0748; (714) 670-0333.

AMERICAN NEONICS, INC., 5542 Satsuma Ave., North Hollywood, CA 91601; (818) 982-0316; (213) 875-1815; FAX: (818) 985-2364.

AMETRON RENTALS, 1200 N. Vine St., Hollywood, CA 90038; (213) 466-4321; FAX: (213) 871-0127.

APRICOT ENTERTAINMENT, INC., 940 N. Orange Dr., Hollywood, CA 90038; (213) 469-4000.

AUTOMATED STUDIO LIGHTING, 10848 Cantara St., Sun Valley, CA 91352; (818) 504-0500.

BARDWELL & MC ALISTER INC., 2621 Empire Ave., Burbank, CA 91504; (219) 849-5533; (818) 843-6821.

BERC (BROADCAST EQUIPMENT RENTAL COMPANY), 4545 Chermak St., Burbank, CA 91505; (818) 841-3000; (213) 464-7655; FAX: (818) 841-7919.

BERLIN LIGHTING & GENERATORS, 9315 Burnet Ave., Sepulveda, CA 91343; (818) 341-5105.

BIFROST EFFECTS/LASERFX, 6733 Sale Ave., West Hills, CA 91307; (818) 704-0423; (818) 704-4629.

BIRNS & SAWYER INC., 1026 N. Highland Ave., Hollywood, CA 90038; (213) 466-8211; FAX: (213) 466-7049.

BUENA VISTA STUDIOS, 500 S. Buena Vista St., Burbank, CA 91521; (818) 560-0044.

CALIFORNIA VIDEO CENTER, 5432 W. 102 St., Los Angeles, CA 90045; (310) 216-5400; FAX: (310) 216-5498.

CASTEX RENTALS, INC., 1044 N. Cole Ave., Los Angeles, CA 90038; (213) 462-1468.

CHINDIT EQUIPMENT CO., 717 S. Victory Blvd., Burbank, CA 91502; (818) 842-1817.

CINE VIDEO, 948 N. Cahuenga Blvd., Hollywood, CA 90038; (213) 464-6200; FAX: (213) 469-8566.

CINELEASE INC., 2020 N. Lincoln St., Burbank, CA 91504; (818) 841-8282; FAX: (818) 843-7834.

CINEVANS LOCATION EQUIPMENT, P.O. Box 2390, Toluca Lake Station, North Hollywood, CA 91602; (818) 846-5386.

CINEWORKS, 1119 N. Hudson Ave., Los Angeles, CA 90038; (213) 464-0296; FAX: (213) 464-1202.

COLORTRAN, INC., 1015 Chestnut St., Burbank, CA 91506-9983; (818) 843-1200; FAX: (818) 954-8520.

COOL-LUX LIGHTING IND., INC., 5723 Auckland Ave., North Hollywood, CA 91601; (818) 761-6116; 761-8181.

CUSTOM NEON, 2210 S. La Brea Ave., Los Angeles, CA 90016; (213) 937-NEON.

EXPENDABLE SUPPLY STORE, 7830 N. San Fernando Rd., Sun Valley, CA 91352; (818) 767-5065; (213) 875-2409; 1316 N. Western Ave., Hollywood, CA 90027; (213) 465-3191; FAX: (818) 768-2422.

EXPENDABLES PLUS (Div. of Cinelease Inc.), 2020 N. Lincoln St., Burbank, CA 91504; (818) 842-4800; FAX: (818) 954-9641.

FAX COMPANY, 1430 N. Cahuenga Blvd., Hollywood, CA 90028; (213) 466-3561; (818) 985-5500; FAX: (213) 871-2193.

FILMTRUCKS, INC., 11166 Gault St., N. Hollywood, CA 91605; (818) 764-9900; (213) 243-1500; FAX: (818) 764-4159.

FIORENTINO, IMERO, ASSOCIATES, 7060 Hollywood Blvd., Suite 1000, Los Angeles, CA 90028; (213) 467-4020.

G-FORCE INTERNATIONAL ENTERTAINMENT CORP., 279 S. Beverly Dr., Suite 1038, Beverly Hills, CA 90212; (310) 271-0700.

GMT STUDIOS, 5751 Buckingham Pkway, Unit C, Culver City, CA 90230; (310) 649-3733.

ALAN GORDON ENTERPRISES, INC., 1430 N. Cahuenga Blvd, Hollywood, CA 90028; (213) 466-3561; (818) 985-5500; FAX: (213) 871-2193.

HARRIS, DENNY, INC., OF CALIFORNIA, 12166 W. Olympic Blvd., Los Angeles, CA 90064; (310) 826-6565.

HOFFMAN VIDEO SYSTEMS, 870 N. Vine St., Hollywood, CA 90038; (213) 465-6900.

HOLLYWOOD CENTER STUDIOS INC., 1040 N. Las Palmas Ave., Los Angeles, CA 90038; (213) 469-5000; FAX: (213) 871-8105.

HOLLYWOOD RENTAL COMPANY, INC., 7848 N. San Fernando Rd., Sun Valley, CA 91352; (818) 768-8018; (213) 849-1326; FAX: (818) 768-2422.

INTER VIDEO/TRITRONICS, INC., 733 N. Victory Blvd., Burbank, CA 91502; (818) 843-3633; 569-4000; FAX: (818) 843-6884.

J & L SERVICE, 10555 Victory Blvd., North Hollywood, CA 91606; (818) 508-7780.

KEYLITE PSI, 11200 Sherman Way, Sun Valley, CA 91352; (818) 841-5483; FAX: (818) 503-9736.

L.A. MARQUEE INC., 12023 Ventura Blvd., Studio City, CA 91604; (818) 505-6572.

LASER MEDIA, INC., 6383 Arizona Circle, Los Angeles, CA 90045-1201; (310) 820-3750; FAX: (310) 207-9630.

LEE AMERICA WEST INC., 3620 Valhalla Dr., Burbank, CA 91505; (818) 848-1111; FAX: (818) 848-1381.
LEONETTI CINE RENTALS, 5609 Sunset Blvd., Los Angeles, CA 90028; (213) 469-2987; FAX: (213) 469-9223.
LEXUS LIGHTING, INC., 7562 San Fernando Rd., Sun Valley, CA 91352; (818) 768-4508.
LOWEY & CO., Castilian Dr., Hollywood, CA 90068; (213) 876-7808.
MOLE-RICHARDSON CO., 937 N. Sycamore Ave., Hollywood, CA 90038; (213) 851-0111; FAX: (213) 851-5593.
NIGHTS OF NEON, 7442 Varna Ave., N. Hollywood, CA 91605; (818) 982-3592; FAX: (818) 503-1090.
NORCOSTCO, INC., 5867 Lankershim Blvd., N. Hollywood, CA 91601; (213) 461-6555; (818) 760-2911; FAX: (818) 980-4737.
ONE PASS FILM & VIDEO, One China Basin Bldg., San Francisco, CA 94107; (415) 777-5777.
PALADIN GROUP, INC., THE, 7356 Santa Monica, Los Angeles, CA 90046; (213) 851-8222.
PALINKO'S STUDIO, 9901 Edmore Pl., Sun Valley, CA 91352; (818) 767-5925; 768-2013.
PROFESSIONAL DESIGN PRODUCTS, INC., 531 Fifth St., Unit E, San Fernando, CA 91340; (818) 898-0888; FAX: (818) 898-0199.
RALEIGH STUDIOS, 650 N. Bronson Ave., Los Angeles, CA 90004; (213) 466-3111; FAX: (213) 871-4428.
ROSCO LABORATORIES INC., 1135 N. Highland Ave., Hollywood, CA 90038; (213) 462-2233.
S.A. GLOBAL STUDIOS, 201 N. Occidental Blvd., Los Angeles, CA 90026; (213) 384-3331.
SHOTMAKER/LIGHTMAKER COMPANY, 28145 Avenue Crocker, Valencia, CA 91355; (805) 257-1444; (800) 426-6284; FAX: (805) 257-6197.
S.I.R. LIGHTING INC., 3334 LaCienega Pl., Los Angeles, CA 90016; (213) 466-3417; 466-1314.
SPRINGBOARD STUDIOS, 12229 Montague St., Arleta, CA 91331; (818) 896-4321.
STRAND LIGHTING, 18111 S. Santa Fe Ave., Rancho Dominguez, CA 90221; (310) 637-7500; FAX: (310) 632-5519.
STUDIO SPECTRUM INC., 1056 N. Lake St., Burbank, CA 91502; (818) 843-1610.
SUNDANCE, 4211 Arch Dr., Suite 201, Studio City, CA 91604; (818) 985-9740.
SUPERSTAGE, 1119 N. Hudson Ave., Los Angeles, CA 90038; (213) 464-0296.
TM MOTION PICTURE EQUIPMENT RENTALS, 7365 Greenbush Ave., North Hollywood, CA 91605; (818) 764-7479.
TELEMEDIA PRODUCTIONS, 18321 Ventura Blvd., Suite 660, Tarzana, CA 91356; (818) 708-2005.
TRIANGLE SCENERY/DRAPERY/LIGHTING CO., 1215 Bates Ave., Los Angeles, CA 90029; (213) 662-8129.
ULTRAVISION INC., 7022 Sunset Blvd., Hollywood, CA 90028; (213) 871-2727.
UNITED TELEPRODUCTION SERVICES, 15055 Oxnard St., Van Nuys, CA 91411; (818) 997-0100.
UNIVERSAL FACILITIES RENTAL DIVISION, 100 Universal City Plaza, Universal City, CA 91608; (818) 777-3000; 777-2731.
UT PHOTO SERVICE, 3088 N. Clybourn Ave., Burbank, CA 91505; (213) 245-6631; FAX: (213) 245-9008.
VALENCIA STUDIOS, THE, 28343 Avenue Crocker, Valencia, CA 91355; (805) 257-1202; (800) STA-GEIT; FAX: (805) 257-1002.
VISUAL EYES PRODUCTIONS, 2401 Main St., Santa Monica, CA 90405; (310) 392-8300; FAX: (310) 392-7480.
WARNER BROS. STUDIOS, 4000 Warner Blvd., Burbank, CA 91522; (818) 954-2677.
WHITEHOUSE AUDIO VISUAL, 2696 Lavery Ct., Unit 8, Newbury Park, CA 91320; (805) 498-4177; FAX: (805) 499-7947.

EAST COAST

ACE LIGHTING, 1 W. 19 St., New York, NY 10011; (212) 206-1475.
BARBIZON ELECTRIC, 426 W. 55 St., New York, NY 10019; (212) 586-1620; 3 Draper St., Woburn, MA 01801; (617) 935-3920; 1125 N. 53 Court, West Palm Beach, FL 33407; (407) 844-5973; 6437G General Green Way, Alexandria, VA 22312; (703) 750-3900.
BIG APPLE CINE SERVICE, 51-02 21 St., Long Island City, NY 11101; (719) 361-5508.
CAMERA MART, 456 W. 55 St., New York, NY 10019; (212) 757-6977.
CAMERA SERVICE CENTER, 625 W. 54 St., New York, NY 10019 (213) 757-0906.
CECO INTERNATIONAL CORP., 440 W. 15 St., New York, NY 10011; (212) 206-8280.
CESTARE, THOMAS, INC., 188 Herricks Rd., Mineola, NY, 11501; (516) 742-5550.
CHELSEA FILM & VIDEO, INC., 1 W. 19 St., New York, NY 10011; (212) 243-8923.
ERIK LIGHTING INC., 4077 Park Ave., Bronx, NY 10457; (212) 901-3100; (800) 858-4450.

FEATURE SYSTEMS, INC., 512 W. 36 St., New York, NY 10018; (212) 736-0447.
FIORENTINO, IMERO, ASSOCIATES, 33 W. 60 St., New York, NY 10023; (212) 246-0600.
GOBLIN MARKET FILM SERVICE, 52 St. Marks Pl., Staten Island, NY 10301; (718) 447-7157.
HOTLIGHTS, 133 W. 19 St., New York, NY 10011; (212) 645-5295.
LTM CORP. OF AMERICA, 353 W. 39 St., New York, NY 10018; (212) 268-2667.
LIBERTY LIGHTING LIMITED, 236 W. 27 St., #4A, New York, NY 10001; (212) 627-9455.
LIGHTING & PRODUCTION EQUIPMENT, INC., 1676 DeForrest Circle, Atlanta, GA 30318; (404) 352-0464.
LOCATION POWER & ILLUMINATION, 19½ Lafayette St., Saratoga Springs, NY 12866; (518) 583-3431.
LOWEL-LIGHT MANUFACTURING, 140 58 St., Brooklyn, NY 11220; (718) 921-0600.
MOVIE MOBILE, INC., 30-15 Vernon Blvd., Astoria, NY 11102; (718) 545-7200.
PARIS FILMS PRODS., 31-00 47 Ave., Long Island City, NY 11101; (718) 482-7633.
PROCAMERA & LIGHTING RENTALS, INC., 511 W. 33 St., New York, NY 10001; (212) 695-1330.
PRODUCTION ARTS LIGHTING, INC., 636 Eleventh Ave., New York, NY 10036; (212) 489-0312; FAX: (212) 245-3723.
SPARKS, R.D., LTD., 142 Washington St., Bloomfield, NJ 07003; (201) 680-9514.
STAR LIGHTING, 38-16 Skillman Ave., Long Island City, NY 11101; (212) 691-1910.
STARK LIGHTING, (914) 225-4855; (212) 867-1172.
SUN LIGHTS, 229 W. 16 St., #1-A, New York, NY, 10011; (212) 929-4345.
TELETECHNIQUES SALES AND RENTALS, 1 W. 19 St., New York, NY 10011; (212) 206-1475; 633-1868.
TIMES SQUARE THEATRICAL & STUDIO SUPPLY CORP., 318 W. 47 St., New York, NY 10036; (212) 245-4155.
XENO-LIGHTS INC., 1 Worth St., New York, NY 10013; (212) 941-9494.

Market Research

LOS ANGELES

ASI MARKET RESEARCH, INC., 2600 W. Olive Ave., Suite 700, Burbank, CA 91505; (818) 843-4400.
AMERICAN MARKETING ASSOCIATION, P.O. Box 2421, Van Nuys, CA 91404; (818) 772-0808.
BLACK & HART ASSOCIATES, 9016 Wilshire Blvd., Suite 500, Beverly Hills, CA 90211-9960; (800) AIR-MAIL.
CASSIDY-WATSON ASSOCIATES (CWA), 1614 N. Argyle Ave., Hollywood, CA 90028; (213) 462-1739.
CRA INC., DR. IRVING S. WHITE, 908 Tiverton Ave., Los Angeles, CA 90024; (310) 824-1811; FAX: 824-5543.
DMR AUDIENCE PREVIEWS & SURVEYS, P.O. Box 69556, Los Angeles, CA 90069; (310) 271-7111.
EDWARDS, ROGER M., ENTERTAINMENT RESEARCH, 636 S. Dunsmuir Ave., Los Angeles, CA 90036; (213) 936-3800.
ENTERTAINMENT DATA, INC., 8350 Wilshire Blvd., #210, Beverly Hills, CA 90210; (213) 658-8300.
FREEMAN, ALLAN, MARKETING & RESEARCH ASSOCIATES, 9696 Moorgate Rd., Beverly Hills, CA 90210; (310) 276-2140; FAX: (310) 276-8897.
GERBER, ROBIN & ASSOCIATES, INC., 15910 Ventura Blvd., Suite 706, Encino, CA 91436; (818) 501-8881; (213) 274-6014.
GLOBAL MEDIA ASSOCIATES/USA, 22837 Ventura Blvd., Suite 302, Woodland Hills, CA 91367; (818) 888-1033; Telex: 9102504157.
GOLDBERG, MAX, & ASSOCIATES, INC., 4289 Bakman Ave., Studio City, CA 91602; (818) 980-5879.
HERST ENTERTAINMENT RESOURCES, 231 N. Orchard Dr., Burbank, CA 91506; (818) 841-2545.
HILTON FINANCIAL GROUP, INC., 3500 W. Olive Ave., Suite 740, Burbank, CA 91505; (818) 953-4160.
HISPANIC ENTERTAINMENT SPECIALIST, 4418 Colfax Ave., N., Hollywood, CA 91602; (818) 766-9100.
IDC SERVICES INC., 2600 W. Olive Ave., Burbank, CA 91505; (818) 569-5100.
IMAGE ANALYSTS, P.O. Box 2787, Venice, CA 90294-2787; (310) 458-0503.
IMMEDIATO, JEFFREY & ASSOCIATES, P.O. Box 5611, Long Beach, CA 90805; (310) 422-9295.
JOYCE COMMUNICATIONS, 953 N. Highland Ave., Los Angeles, CA 90038; (213) 467-2446; FAX: (213) 467-2401.

KROWN/YOUNG & RUBICAM, (Entertainment Marketing Group), 9696 Culver Blvd., Suite 201, Culver City, CA 90232; (310) 202-8100.

LOWELL, SIGMUND, 11930 Montana Ave., Los Angeles, CA 90049; (310) 207-5947.

MANPEAL RESEARCH & CONSULTING, INC., 9624 Wendover Dr., Beverly Hills, CA 90210; (310) 278-8613.

McCANN-ERICKSON INC., 6420 Wilshire Blvd., Los Angeles, CA 90048; (213) 655-9420.

MICHAELS, HARMON, & ASSOCIATES, 16161 Nordhoff St., #11, Sepulveda, CA 91343; (818) 891-2972.

MORRIS TV & VIDEO, INC., 2730 Monterey St., Suite 105, Torrance, CA 90503; (310) 533-4800; FAX: (310) 533-1993.

MOSES, CHARLES A., 3219 W. Alameda Ave., Burbank, CA 91505; (818) 848-0513; FAX: (818) 848-4977.

NIELSEN, A.C., COMPANY, 3731 Wilshire Blvd., #940, Los Angeles, CA 90010; (213) 386-7316; FAX: (213) 386-7317.

PENLAND PRODUCTIONS, INC., 303 N. Glenoaks Blvd., Suite 780, Burbank, CA 91502; (818) 840-9461.

PROFESSIONAL RESEARCH ASSOCIATES, P.O. Box 5447, Culver City, CA 90231; (310) 394-1650.

QWEST AUDIENCE RESEARCH & DEVELOPMENT, 574 Lillian Way, Los Angeles, CA 90004; (213) 465-2696.

RADIO TV REPORTS, 6255 Sunset Blvd., #1515, Los Angeles, CA 90028; (213) 466-6124.

THE RESEARCH DEPARTMENT, 18653 Ventura Blvd., Suite 351, Tarzana, CA 91365; (818) 342-5355.

RESEARCH FRONTIERS CORPORATION, 3524 Caribeth Dr., Encino, CA 91436-4101; (818) 783-1620.

RITZ & ASSOCIATES ADVERTISING, 636 N. Robertson Blvd., Los Angeles, CA 90069; (310) 652-9813.

SNOW, JANET & ASSOCIATES, 327 Reeves Dr., Beverly Hills, CA 90212; (310) 552-0082.

TISHKOFF & ASSOCIATES, INC., 3440 Motor Ave., Ground 71. Suite, Los Angeles, CA 90034; (310) 837-0792.

VACANTI/McMAHON COMMUNICATIONS, 2700 Cahuenga Blvd., Los Angeles, CA 90068; (213) 850-1990.

VIDEO MARKETING NEWSLETTER, 1680 Vine St., Suite 820, Hollywood, CA 90028; (213) 462-6350; FAX: (213) 467-0314.

VIDEO MONITORING SERVICES OF AMERICA, 3434 W. Sixth St., Suite 401, Los Angeles, CA 90020-2536; (213) 380-5011.

VIDEO VIEWS/CINEMA SURVEY, 6777 Hollywood Blvd., Suite 206, Los Angeles, CA 90028; (213) 469-9880.

WESTERN INTERNATIONAL RESEARCH, 8544 Sunset Blvd., Los Angeles, CA 90069; (310) 854-4869.

WORLD CLASS SPORTS AGENCY, 9171 Wilshire Blvd., Suite 404, Beverly Hills, CA 90210; (310) 278-2010.

NEW YORK & EAST COAST

CERTIFIED MARKETING SERVICES, INC. (CMS), Route 9, Kinderhook, NY 12106; (518) 758-6405. (National field coverage for in-theatre research/audience reaction cards and tabulation. Trailer monitoring and tracking programs.)

GALLUP ORGANIZATION, THE, 47 Hulfish St., Princeton, NJ 08542; (609) 924-9600.

MARKET RESEARCH CORP. OF AMERICA, 4 Landmark Sq., Stamford, CT 06901; (203) 324-9600; 819 S. Wabash, Chicago, IL 60605; (708) 480-9600; 2215 Sanders Road, Northbrook, IL 60062; (708) 480-9600.

NIELSEN, A. C., CO., MEDIA RESEARCH, Nielsen Plaza, Northbrook, IL 60062, (312) 498-6300; 1290 Ave. of the Americas, New York, NY 10019, (212) 956-2500; 6255 Sunset Blvd., Los Angeles, CA 90028; (213) 466-4391.

OPINION RESEARCH CORP., P.O. Box 183, Princeton, NJ 08542-0183; (609) 924-5900.

POLITZ, ALFRED, MEDIA STUDIES, 300 Park Ave. South, New York, NY 10010; (212) 982-7600.

ROPER ORGANIZATION, THE, 205 E. 42 St., New York, NY 10017; (212) 599-0700.

SINDLINGER & CO., INC., 405 Osborne St., Wallingford, PA 19086; (215) 565-0247.

STARCH INRA HOOPER, INC., 566 East Boston Post Rd., Mamaroneck, NY 10543; (914) 698-0800.

Merchandisers

DISNEY, WALT, PRODUCTIONS, (Character Merchandising Division), 500 Park Ave., New York, NY 10022; (212) 593-8900.

LICENSING CORPORATION OF AMERICA, 1325 Ave. of Americas, New York, NY 10019; (212) 636-5600; 4000 Warner Blvd., Burbank, CA 91522; (818) 954-6640.

LUCASFILM LICENSING, P.O. Box 2009, San Rafael, CA 94912; (415) 662-1800.

Music, Music Libraries and Music Cutting

CALIFORNIA

ALSHIRE INTERNATIONAL, INC., 1015 Isabel St., P.O. Box 7107, Burbank, CA 91510; (213) 849-4671; (800) 423-2936; FAX: (818) 569-3718.

ASSOCIATED PRODUCTION MUSIC, 6255 Sunset Blvd., Suite 820, Hollywood, CA 90028; (213) 461-3211; FAX (213) 461-9102.

AUDIO ACHIEVEMENTS RECORDING STUDIO, 1327 Cabrillo Ave., Torrance, CA 90501; (310) 533-9531.

AUDIO POST, 3755 Cahuenga Blvd., West, Suite C, Studio City, CA 91604; (818) 761-5220.

BLUEFIELD MUSIC DESIGN, 2147 Holly Dr., Los Angeles, CA 90068; (213) 463-SONG.

BUZZY'S RECORDING SERVICES, 6900 Melrose Ave., Los Angeles, CA 90038; (213) 931-1867; FAX: (213) 931-9681.

CARBONE, JOEY, 5724 Third St., Suite 303, Los Angeles, CA 90036; (213) 462-3380.

CARMAN PRODUCTIONS INC., 15456 Cabrito Road, Van Nuys, CA 91406; (213) 873-7370; (818) 787-6436.

CEXTON RECORDS, 2740 S. Harbor Blvd., Suite K, Santa Ana, CA 92704; (714) 641-1074; FAX: (714) 641-1025.

CLAY, TOM, PRODUCTIONS, 6515 Sunset Blvd., Suite 201A Hollywood, CA 90028; (213) 464-6566.

CON FUOCO PRODUCTIONS & RECORDS, 6381 Hollywood Blvd., Suite 640, Los Angeles, CA 90028; (213) 461-0331.

DEBOOGEDY MUSIC, 1521 Clark Ave., Burbank, CA 91506; (818) 845-3118; (818) 763-6443.

FIDELITY RECORDING STUDIO, 4412 Whitsett Ave., Studio City, CA 91604; (818) 508-3263.

FLEISHMAN, RICK, MUSIC, 5739 Babbitt Ave., Encino, CA 91316; (818) 343-7005; FAX: (818) 774-1299.

FOUR JAYS MUSIC PUBLISHING CO., P.O. Box 50540, Santa Barbara, CA 93150; (805) 969-2504; FAX: (805) 565-3877.

FRONT ROW CENTER THEATRE MEMORABILIA, 8127 W. Third St., W. Hollywood, CA 90048; (213) 852-0149.

HANIFAN, BRUCE, PRODUCTIONS, 9023 Beverlywood St., Los Angeles, CA 90034; (310) 559-4522.

HOLLYWOOD FILM MUSIC LIBRARY, 11684 Ventura Blvd., #850, Studio City, CA 91604; (818) 985-9997.

INTERSOUND, INC., 8746 Sunset Blvd., Los Angeles, CA 90069; (310) 652-3741; Telex: 798563; Answbk: INTERSOUND INC.

MANSON, EDDY, PRODUCTIONS, INC., 7245 Hillside Ave., Suite 216, Los Angeles, CA 90046; (213) 874-9318.

MARGERY MUSIC CO., 7245 Hillside Ave., Suite 216, Los Angeles, CA 90046-2329; (213) 874-9318.

MOVIE TECH INC., 832 N. Seward St., Hollywood, CA 90038; (213) 467-8491; (213) 467-5423; FAX: (213) 467-8471.

MUSICUM LAUDE, 2988 Avenel Terrace, Los Angeles, CA 90039; (213) 660-5444.

NAMRAC MUSIC, 15456 Cabrito Road, Van Nuys, CA 91406; (213) 873-7370.

NIDA MUSIC PUBLISHING CO., 4014 Murietta Ave., Sherman Oaks, CA 91423; (818) 981-5331.

OUTLAW SOUND, 1140 N. La Brea Ave., Los Angeles, CA 90038; (213) 462-1873; FAX: (213) 856-4311.

RESEARCH VIDEO, 4900 Vineland Ave., N. Hollywood, CA 91601; (818) 509-0506; Telex: 298873; Answbk: USSM UR.

SELECTED SOUND RECORDED MUSIC LIBRARY, 6777 Hollywood Blvd., Suite 209, Hollywood, CA 90028; (213) 469-9910.

SINGING STORE U.S.A., 16851 Victory Blvd., Suite 10, Van Nuys, CA 91406; (818) 781-9098; FAX: (818) 781-8979.

SOUTHERN LIBRARY OF RECORDED MUSIC, 6777 Hollywood Blvd., Suite 209, Hollywood, CA 90028; (213) 469-9910.

STEVENS, KRIS, ENTERPRISES INC., 14241 Ventura Blvd., Suite 204, Sherman Oaks, CA 91423; (818) 981-8255; FAX: (818) 990-4350.

TOM THUMB MUSIC, Box 34485, Whitney Building, Los Angeles, CA 90034; (310) 836-4678.

TODD-AO/GLEN GLENN STUDIOS, 900 N. Seward St., Hollywood, CA 90038; (213) 469-7221.

WEAVER, ROBERT, ENTERPRISES, INC., 22723 Berdon St., Woodland Hills, CA 91367; (818) 883-1920.

WILLIAMS, MARY, MUSIC CLEARANCE CORPORATION, 6223 Selma Ave., Suite 211, Hollywood, CA 90028; (213) 462-6575; FAX: (213) 462-3433.

ZAENTZ, SAUL, COMPANY FILM CENTER, 2600 Tenth St., Berkeley, CA 94710; (415) 549-2500; (800) 227-0466; FAX: (415) 486-2015.

ZAPPA, FRANK, MUSIC, P.O. Box 5265, N. Hollywood, CA 91616; (818) 764-0800; FAX: (818) 764-4972.

NEW YORK

AJR MUSIC PRODUCTIONS, 40 Grove St. Middletown, NY 10940; (212) 724-5658.

ALEXANDER, JOHN ERIC, MUSIC, 311 W. 43 St., New York, NY 10036; (212) 581-8560.

ANTLAND PRODUCTIONS, INC., 231 E. 55th St., New York, NY 10022; (212) 371-2715.

AQUARIUS TRANSFERMATION LTD., 12 E. 46 St., New York, NY 10017; (212) 697-3636.

ASTROMUSIC, 11 Fort George Hill, Apt. 13c, New York, NY 10040; (212) 942-0004.

AUDIO DIRECTORS, INC., 325 W. 19 St., New York, NY 10011; (212) 924-5850.

BLACK, ARNOLD, PRODUCTIONS, INC., 895 West End Ave., New York, NY 10025; (212) 865-5933.

BLACKSTONE, WENDY, MUSIC, INC., 59 W. 10 St., Suite 4E, New York, NY 10011; (212) 228-4091.

BRAUNSTEIN, ALAN, MUSIC INC., 400 West 43 St., #14S, New York, NY 10036; (212) 736-0067.

CORELLI-JACOBS FILM MUSIC LIBRARY, 25 W. 45 St., New York, NY 10036; (212) 382-0220.

ELECTRO-NOVA PRODUCTIONS, 342 Madison Ave., New York, NY 10017; (212) 687-5838.

ELIAS ASSOCIATES 6 W. 20 St., New York, NY 10011; (212) 807-6151.

¼ PRODUCTIONS, 320 W. 46 St., 6th Fl., New York, NY 10036; (212) 581-4444.

GERARDI, BOB, MUSIC, 160 W. 73 St., New York, NY 10023; (212) 874-6436.

GOODMAN, TOMMY, ENTERPRISES, INC., 30 Second Ave., Nyack, NY 10960; (212) 489-1641.

HARMONIC RANCH, (Audio for Video-Sound Effects-Composer Referral Service) 59 Franklin St., New York, NY 10013; (212) 966-3141.

HASTINGS SOUND EDITORIAL INC., 119 Rosedale Ave., Hastings-on-Hudson, NY 10706; (914) 478-0227.

HILL, JOHN, MUSIC, 116 E. 37 St., New York, NY 10016; (212) 683-2273.

HOROWITZ, DAVID, MUSIC ASSOCIATES, 373 Park Ave. So., New York, NY 10016; (212) 779-3030.

IBERO-AMERICAN PRODUCTIONS, 630 Ninth Ave., New York, NY 10036; (212) 245-7826.

KAMEN AUDIO PRODUCTIONS, INC., 701 7th Ave., 6th Fl., New York, NY 10036; (212) 575-4660.

KARP, MICHAEL, MUSIC, INC., 260 W. 39 St., New York, NY 10018; (212) 840-3285.

KINGSLEY MUSIC, 201 W. 70th St., New York, NY 10023; (212) 787-4975.

LAVSKY, RICHARD, MUSIC , 16 E. 42 St., New York, NY 10017; (212) 697-9800.

LEVIN, LOUIS, MUSIC, 211 E. 53rd St., New York, NY 10022; (212) 223-0025.

LICHT, DAN, MUSIC, 112 E. 7th St., New York, NY 10009; (212) 475-2675.

LINO SOUND, Louis Lino: Original Music & Sound Design, 108 N. 6th St., Brooklyn, NY 11211; (718) 388-3314.

LITTLE GEMSTONE MUSIC, P.O. Box 1703, Fort Lee, NJ 07024; (201) 488-8562, 487-5847.

LOOK & COMPANY, 170 5th Ave., New York, NY 10010; (212) 627-3500.

MACROSE MUSIC, INC., Composer/Arranger-Fred Thaler, 353 W. 19 St., New York, NY 10011; (212) 206-1323.

MORROW, CHARLES, ASSOCIATES INC., 611 Broadway, #817, New York, NY 10012; (212) 529-4550.

MUSIC HOUSE INC., 16 E. 42 St., New York, NY 10017; (212) 697-9800.

NEWFOUND MUSIC PRODUCTIONS, INC., 250 W. 27 St., Suite 5H, New York, NY 10001; (212) 691-9667.

NORTH FORTY PRODUCTIONS, INC., 252 E. 51 St., New York, NY 10022; (212) 751-8300.

NOT JUST JINGLES, 420 W. 45 St., New York, NY 10036; (212) 246-6468.

OMNIMUSIC, 52 Main St., Port Washington, New York, NY 11050; (516) 883-0121.

PATCO RESOURCES, 799 Broadway, New York, NY 10003; (212) 505-9490.

PERFECT SOUND, 1697 Broadway, Suite 1106, New York, NY 10019; (212) 315-5852.

PICTURE SCORES, INC., 42 W. 38 St., New York, NY 10018; (212) 869-5885.

PISCES MUSIC LTD., 12 E. 46 St., New York, NY 10017; (212) 682-1860.

RADIO BAND OF AMERICA, 1350 Avenue of the Americas, New York, NY 10019; (212) 687-4800.

RIVELLINO MUSIC, 5 Palmer Ln., Thornwood, NY 10594; (914) 769-5734.

ROSS-GAFFNEY, INC., 21 W. 46 St., New York, NY, 10036; (212) 719-2744.

SCORE PRODUCTIONS, INC., 254 E. 49 St., New York, NY 10017; (212) 751-2510.

SHELTON LEIGH PALMER & CO., 19 W. 36 St., New York, NY 10018; (212) 714-1710.

SOUND PATROL, LTD., 6 E. 39 St., New York, NY 10016; (212) 213-6666.

SOUND SHOP, 321 W. 44 St., New York, NY 10036; (212) 757-5837.

SPLASH PRODUCTIONS INC., 123 W. 28th St., New York, NY 10001; (212) 695-3665.

STOCK ROCK, 421 Hudson St., #220, New York, NY 10014; (212) 989-7845.

SUNDAY PRODUCTIONS, INC., 1501 Bdwy., New York, NY 10036; (212) 302-6888.

SUTCLIFFE MUSIC INC., 8 W. 19 St., New York, NY 10011; (212) 989-9292.

TNG/EARTHLING-BOB SAKAYAMA, 110 W. 86 St., New York, NY 10024; (212) 799-4181.

ULFIK, RICK, PRODUCTIONS, 130 W. 42 St., Suite 904, New York, NY 10036; (212) 704-0888.

VALENTINO, THOMAS J., INC, 151 W. 46 St., New York, NY 10036; (212) 869-5210.

WILBUR, SANDY, MUSIC, INC., 100 Beach Ave., Larchmont, NY 10538; (914) 833-0369.

WOLOSHIN, SID, INC., 95 Madison Ave., New York, NY 10016; (212) 684-7222.

OHIO

SOUND STUDIO, THE, P.O. Box 892, Reynoldsburg, OH 43068; (614) 759-6821; FAX: (614) 759-1625.

Properties and Scenery

LOS ANGELES

ABRAHAM RUGS GALLERY, 525 N. LaCienega Blvd., Los Angeles, CA 90048; (310) 652-6520; (800) 222-RUGS.

ALLEN, WALTER, PLANT RENTALS, 4996 Melrose Ave., Los Angeles, CA 90029-3738; (213) 469-3621.

ANIMAL MAKERS, 2363 Teller Rd., Unit 106, Newbury Park, CA 91320; (805) 499-9779; FAX: (805) 499-3454.

ANTIQUARIAN TRADERS, 4851 S. Alameda St., Los Angeles, CA 90058; (213) 627-2144.

ANTIQUE & CLASSIC CAR RENTALS, 611½ W. Vernon Ave., Los Angeles, CA 90037; (213) 232-7211.

ANTIQUE GUILD, 8800 Venice Blvd., Los Angeles, CA 90034; (310) 838-3131; FAX: (310) 287-2486.

BAYBERRY CARRIAGE COMPANY, P.O. Box 4006, West Hills, CA 91308; (818) 992-8448.

BEDFELLOWS, 12250 Ventura Blvd., Sherman Oaks, CA 91604; (818) 985-0500; FAX: (818) 985-0617.

BRICK PRICE'S MOVIE MINIATURES (WONDERWORKS), 7231 Remmet Ave., #F, Canoga Park, CA 91303-1532; (818) 992-8811.

BROOK FURNITURE RENTAL, 14255 Ventura Blvd., Sherman Oaks, CA 91423; (818) 986-6500; 3281 Wilshire Blvd., Los Angeles, CA 90010; (818) 382-8262; 8549 Wilshire Blvd., Beverly Hills, CA 90210; (213) 652-6795.

BRUBAKER GROUP, THE, 10560 Dolcedo Way, Los Angeles, CA 90077; (310) 472-4766; 478-9588.

CAMERA READY CARS, 1577 Placentia, Newport Beach, CA 92663; (714) 645-4700.

CARTHAY SET SERVICES, 5907 W. Pico Blvd., Los Angeles, CA 90029; (213) 938-2101.

CINEMAFLOAT, 1624 W. Ocean Front, Newport Beach, CA 92663; (714) 675-8888.

CLASSIC CAR SUPPLIERS, 1905 Sunset Plaza Dr., W. Hollywood, CA 90069; (310) 657-7823.

CLASSIC LEASING COMPANY, 1100 Santa Monica Blvd., Santa Monica, CA 90401 (310) 393-9100.

CONTINENTAL SCENERY, 1022 N. La Brea Ave., Los Angeles, CA 90038; (213) 461-4139.

DISNEY STUDIOS, 500 S. Buena Vista St., Burbank, CA 91521; (818) 560-0044.

DOZAR OFFICE FURNITURE, 9937 Jefferson Blvd., Culver City, CA 90232; (310) 559-9292; FAX: (310) 559-9009.

ELLIS MERCANTILE CO., 169 N. La Brea Ave., Los Angeles, CA 90036; (213) 933-7334; FAX: (213) 930-1268.

EXPENDABLE SUPPLY STORE, 1316 N. Western Ave., Hollywood, CA 90027; (213) 465-3191; FAX: (818) 768-2422; 7830 N. San Fernando Rd., Sun Valley, CA 91352; (818) 767-5065; (213) 875-2409.

FILMTRIX, INC., 11054 Chandler Blvd., N. Hollywood, CA 91601; (818) 980-3700; FAX: (818) 980-3703.
FIORITTO, LARRY, SPECIAL EFFECTS SERVICES, 1067 E. Orange Grove, Burbank, CA 91501; (818) 954-9829.
GEYER, PETER, ACTION PROPS & SETS, 8235 Lankershim Blvd., Suite G, N. Hollywood, CA 91605; (818) 768-0070.
GROSH SCENIC STUDIOS, 4114 Sunset Blvd.; Los Angeles CA, 90029; (213) 662-1134.
HAND PROP ROOM, INC., 5700 Venice Blvd., Los Angeles, CA 90019; (213) 931-1534; FAX: (213) 931-2145.
HOLLYWOOD BREAKAWAY, 15125-B Califa St., Van Nuys, CA 91411; (818) 781-0621.
HOLLYWOOD CENTRAL PROPS, 7333 Radford Ave., N. Hollywood, CA 91605; (818) 765-1923.
HOLLYWOOD PICTURE VEHICLES, 7046 Darby Ave., Reseda, CA 91301; (818) 506-7562.
HORSELESS CARRIAGE CLUB OF AMERICA, 7210 Jordan Ave., Box D-76, Canoga Park, CA 91303; (818) 704-4253.
HOUSE OF PROPS, 1117 Gower St., Hollywood, CA 90038; (213) 463-3166; FAX: (213) 463-8302.
IMAGE ENGINEERING, INC., 632 N. Victory Blvd., Burbank, CA 91502; (818) 846-5865; FAX: (818) 846-5127.
INDEPENDENT STUDIO SERVICES, 11907 Wicks St., Sun Valley, CA 91352; (818) 764-0840; 768-5711.
IWASAKI IMAGES, (food replicas), 20460 Gramercy Pl., Torrance, CA 90501; (310) 328-7121.
KREISS COLLECTION, 8619 Melrose Ave., Los Angeles, CA 90069-5010; (310) 657-3990.
LAZZARINI'S S/VFX, THE CREATURE SHOP, 2554 Lincoln Blvd., Suite 1067, Marina Del Rey, CA 90291; (818) 989-0220.
MODERN PROPS, 4063 Redwood Ave., Los Angeles, CA 90066; (310) 306-1400; FAX: (213) 882-5992.
NATIONAL HELICOPTER SERVICE, 16800 Roscoe Blvd., Va Nuys, CA 91406; (818) 345-5222; FAX: (818) 782-0466.
NIGHTS OF NEON, 7442 Varna Ave., N. Hollywood, CA 91605; (818) 982-3592; FAX: (818) 503-1090.
NORCOSTCO, INC., 5867 Lankershim Blvd., N. Hollywood, CA 91601; (213) 461-6555; (818) 760-2911; FAX: (818) 980-4737.
OMEGA CINEMA PROPS., 5857 Santa Monica, Blvd., Los Angeles, 90038; (213) 466-8201; FAX: (213) 461-3643.
PROP CITY, 9336 W. Washington Blvd., Culver City, CA 90230; (310) 559-7022; 202-3350.
PROP MASTERS, INC., 420 S. First St., Burbank, CA 91502; (818) 846-3915; 846-3957; FAX: (818) 846-1278.
PROP SERVICES WEST INC., 915 N. Citrus Ave., Los Angeles, CA 90038; (213) 461-3371.
R/C MODELS, P.O. Box 6026, San Pedro, CA 90734; (310) 833-4700.
ROSCHU, 6514 Santa Monica Blvd., Los Angeles 90038; (213) 469-2749.
SARTINO, JACQUELINE, 953 N. Edinburgh Ave., Los Angeles, CA 90046; (213) 654-3326; FAX: (213) 656-6192.
SCENERY WEST, 1126 N. Citrus Ave., Hollywood, CA 90038; (213) 467-7495.
SCENIC EXPRESS, 3025 Fletcher Dr., Los Angeles, CA 90065; (213) 254-4351; FAX: (213) 254-4411.
SPECIAL EFFECTS UNLIMITED, 752 N. Cahuenga Blvd., Los Angeles, CA 90038; (213) 466-3361.
STUDIO PICTURE VEHICLES, 10901 Sherman Way, Sun Valley, CA 91352; (818) 765-1201; 781-4223.
THORNBIRD ARMS, 21626 Lassen St., Chatsworth, CA 91311; (818) 341-8227.
TRIANGLE SCENERY/DRAPERY/LIGHTING CO., 1215 Bates Ave., Los Angeles, CA 90029; (213) 662-8129.
WARNER BROS. STUDIOS, 4000 Warner Blvd., Burbank, CA 91522; (818) 954-2923; FAX: (818) 954-2677.

NEW YORK

ATI MEDICAL STUDIO PRODUCTIONS, 532 Fifth Ave., Pelham, NY 10803; (800) 257-7477.
ADVERTISING IN MOVIES INC., Kaufman Astoria Studios, 34-12 36th St., Astoria, Queens, NY 11106; (718) 729-9288.
ALTMAN LUGGAGE, 135 Orchard St., New York, NY 10002; (212) 254-7275.
ANTIQUE & CLASSIC AUTOS, (Leonard Shiller), 811 Union St., Brooklyn, NY 11215; (718) 788-3400.
ARENSON OFFICE FURNISHINGS, 315 E. 62 St., New York, NY 10021; (212) 838-8880.
ARTS & CRAFTERS INC., 175 Johnson St., Brooklyn, NY 11201; (718) 875-8151.
BROOKLYN MODEL WORKS, 60 Washington Ave., Brooklyn, NY 11205; (718) 834-1944.
CENTRAL PROPERTIES, 514 W. 49 St., 2nd Floor, New York, NY 10019; (212) 265-7767.
CENTRE FIREARMS CO, INC., 10 W. 37 St., New York, NY 10018; (212) 244-4040, 244-4044.

CINEMA GALLERIES, 517 W. 35 St., New York, NY 10001; (212) 627-1222.
CINEMA WORLD PRODUCTS, INC., 2621 Palisade Ave., Riverdale, NY 10463; (212) 548-1928.
CLASSIC CARS LEASING CO., 500 Park Ave., New York, NY 10022; (212) 752-8080.
COOPER FILM CARS, 132 Perry, New York, NY 10014; (212) 929-3909.
DARROW'S FUN ANTIQUES, 309 E. 61 St., New York, NY 10021; (212) 838-0730.
ECLECTIC/ENCORE PROPERTIES INC., 620 W. 26 St., 4th floor, New York, NY 10001; (212) 645-8880.
ENVIRION VISION, 3074 Whaleneck Dr., Merrick, NY 11566; (516) 378-2250.
FINKEL, LARRY, CENTURY SALES, 55 Spruce St., Cedarhurst, NY 11516; (516) 569-3099.
GALI KITCHEN RENTAL EQUIPMENT, INC., 404 E. 88 St., New York, NY 10028; (212) 289-5405.
HOLLAND PARADISE, 800 Sixth Ave., New York, NY 10001; (212) 684-3397.
KEMPLER CO., INC., GEORGE J., 160 Fifth Ave., New York, NY 10010; (212) 989-1180.
KUTTNER PROP RENTALS INC., 56 W. 22 St., New York, NY 10010; (212) 242-7969.
LENS & REPRO EQUIPMENT CORP., THE, 33 W. 17 St., New York, NY 10011; (212) 675-1900.
MERCURY NEON SIGN SHOP, 157 2nd Ave., New York, NY 10003; (212) 219-0542.
NICCOLINI ANTIQUES, 38 W. 21 St., New York, NY 10010; (212) 366-6766; (800) 734-9975.
PICTURE CARS, EAST, 701 Hicks St., Brooklyn, NY 11231; (718) 852-2300.
PROPS FOR TODAY, 121 W. 19 St., 3rd floor, New York, NY 10011; (212) 206-0330.
SAY IT IN NEON, INC., 288 Third Ave., Brooklyn, NY 12151; (718) 625-1481.
SCHOEPFER STUDIO, 138 W. 31 St., New York, NY 10001; (212) 736-6939.
STARBUCK STUDIO, 162 W. 21 St., New York, NY 10011; (212) 807-7299.
VISUAL SERVICES, 40 W. 72 St., New York, NY 10023; (212) 580-9551.
WAVES (Antique radios), 32 E. 13 St., New York, NY 10003; (212) 989-9284.
WEAPONS SPECIALISTS, 33 Greene St., 1-W, New York, NY 10013; (212) 941-7696.

PITTSBURGH

PARK PLACE STUDIO, 4801 Penn Ave., 15224; (412) 363-7538; FAX: (412) 363-4318.

Raw Stock Manufacturers

AGFA CORPORATION, MOTION PICTURE PRODUCTS DIVISION. (Manufacturer, distributor 35mm color, black, white raw stock.) Executive offices: 100 Challenger Rd., Ridgefield Park, NJ 07660; (201) 440-2500 or (212) 971-0260.
BRANCHES:
San Francisco, 94080; 601 Gateway Blvd., Ste. 500, South San Francisco, CA; (415) 589-0700.
Los Angeles, 90067: 1801 Century Park East, Suite 110; (213) 552-9622.
EASTMAN KODAK CO., MOTION PICTURES AUDIOVISUAL PRODUCTS DIVISION. 343 State St., Rochester, NY; Tel.: (716) 724-4000. 1901 W. 22nd St., Oakbrook, IL 60521; Tel.: (312) 654-5300. 6700 Santa Monica Blvd., Hollywood, CA, 90038; Tel.: (213) 464-6131. 1133 Ave. of the Americas, New York, NY 10036; Tel.: (212) 930-8000.
FUJI PHOTO FILM U.S.A., INC., (distributor of Fuji Professional Motion Picture Film) Northeast Region Sales & Dist. Ctr., 800 Central Blvd., Carlstadt, NJ 07072; (201) 935-6022; Corp. headquarters: 555 Taxter Rd., Elmsford, NY 10523; (914) 789-8100; (800) 241-7695.
ILFORD, INC., W. 70 Century Rd., Paramus, NJ 07653; (201) 265-6000.
3M COMPANY (MINNESOTA MINING & MANUFACTURING CO.), Photo Color Systems Division, (Manufacturer and distributor of color 35mm film, C-41 process.) 3M Center, Bldg. 223-2SE-05, St. Paul, MN 55144; (800) 654-5007.
RESEARCH TECHNOLOGY, INC., 4700 Chase Ave., Lincolnwood, IL 60646; (312) 677-3000.

Rental Studios and Production Facilities

ATLANTA

LIGHTING & PRODUCTION EQUIPMENT, INC., 1676 DeFoor Circle; 30318; (404) 352-0464.

BOSTON

CHARLES RIVER STUDIOS, 1380 Soldiers Field Rd, Boston, MA 02135; (617) 783-3535.

CHICAGO

HARPO STUDIOS, 1058 W. Washington Blvd., Chicago, IL 60607; (312) 738-3456.

LOS ANGELES

ACTORS CENTER, 11969; Ventura Blvd., Studio City, CA 91604; (818) 505-9400.

AMERICAN INSTITUTE OF VIDEO, 20850 Dearborn St., Chatsworth, CA 91311; (818) 700-8987.

ANDERSON, TOM FILMWORKS, 6382 Hollywood Blvd., Suite 308, Los Angeles, CA 90028; (213) 464-0386.

BOWEN VIDEO FACILITIES & STAGE, 760 N. Lake St., Burbank, CA 91502; (818) 504-0070.

BURBANK MEDIA CENTER, 2801 W. Olive Ave., Burbank, CA 91505; (818) 845-3531.

CBS/MTM STUDIOS, 4024 N. Radford Ave., Studio City, CA 91604; (818) 760-5000; FAX: (818) 760-5409.

CFI (CONSOLIDATED FILM INDUSTRIES), 959 Seward St., Hollywood, CA 90038; (213) 960-7444; FAX: (213) 460-4885.

CANNELL STUDIOS, THE, 7083 Hollywood Blvd., Hollywood, CA 90028; (213) 465-5800; FAX: (213) 463-4987.

CARMEN PRODUCTIONS INC., 15456 Cabrito Rd., Van Nuys, CA 91406; (213) 873-7370; (818) 787-6436.

CARTHAY STUDIOS, INC., 5907 W. Pico Blvd., Los Angeles 90035; (213) 938-2101; FAX: (213) 936-2769.

CHAPLIN STAGE, 1416 N. La Brea Ave., Hollywood, CA 90028; (213) 469-2411; 856-2682.

CINEWORKS-SUPERSTAGE, 1119 N. Hudson Ave., Los Angeles, CA 90038; (213) 464-0296; FAX: (213) 464-1202.

COMPLEX, THE, 6476 Santa Monica Blvd., Hollywood, CA 90038; (213) 465-0383, 469-5408.

CULVER STUDIOS, INC., 9336 W. Washington, Culver City, CA 90230; (310) 202-3396; 202-1234; FAX: (310) 202-3272.

DESIGN ARTS STUDIOS/THE STAGE, 1128 N. Las Palmas, Hollywood, CA 90038; (213) 464-9118.

DISNEY, WALT, STUDIOS, 500 S. Buena Vista St., Burbank, CA 91521; (818) 560-5151, 560-1000; FAX: (818) 560-1930.

EMPIRE BURBANK STUDIOS, 1845 Empire Ave., Burbank, CA 91504; (818) 840-1400; FAX: (818) 567-1062.

ERECTER SET, INC., 1150 S. La Brea Ave., Los Angeles, CA 90019; (213) 938-4762; FAX: (213) 931-9565.

GMT STUDIOS, 5751 Buckingham Parkway, Unit C, Culver City, CA 90230; (310) 649-3733.

GLENDALE STUDIOS, 1239 S. Glendale Ave., Glendale, CA 91205; (818) 552-5000; FAX: (818) 502-5311.

GROUP W. PRODUCTIONS, One Lakeside Plaza, 3801 Barham Blvd., Los Angeles, CA 90068; (213) 850-3800; FAX: (213) 850-3889.

HARBOR STAR STAGE, Bldg. 575, 399 Navy Way, Terminal Island, CA 90731; (310) 833-7023.

HARK'S SOUND STUDIOS, 1041 N. Orange Dr., Hollywood, CA 90036; (213) 463-3288.

HOLLYWOOD CENTER STUDIOS, INC., 1040 N. Las Palmas Ave., Los Angeles, CA 90038; (213) 469-5000; FAX: (213) 871-8105.

HOLLYWOOD NATIONAL STUDIOS, 6605 Eleanor Ave., Los Angeles, CA 90038; (213) 467-6272.

HOLLYWOOD STAGE, THE, 6650 Santa Monica Blvd., Los Angeles, CA 90038; (213) 466-4393.

HOLLYWOOD VIDEO STUDIOS, 505 Boccaccio, Venice, CA 90291; (310) 827-1036; FAX: (310) 305-0308.

INTER VIDEO/TRITRONICS, INC., 733 N. Victory Blvd., Burbank, CA 91502; (818) 843-3633; 569-4000; FAX: (818) 843-6884.

INTERSOUND, INC., 8746 Sunset Blvd., Los Angeles, CA 90069; (310) 652-3741; FAX: (310) 854-7290.

JOHNSON, RAY, STUDIOS, 5435 Denny St., N. Hollywood, CA 91601; (818) 508-7348.

KCET STUDIOS, 4401 Sunset Blvd., Los Angeles, CA 90027; (213) 953-5258, 666-6500; FAX: (213) 953-5496.

KITAY, BEN, STUDIOS, 1015 N. Cahuenga Blvd., Stage 15, Hollywood, CA 90038; (213) 466-9015; FAX: (213) 466-4421.

LORIMAR STUDIOS, 300 S. Lorimar Sq., Burbank, CA 91505; (818) 954-6000.

MELROSE STAGE, 4361 Melrose Ave., Los Angeles, CA 90029; (213) 660-8466.

MOLE-RICHARDSON CO., 937 N. Sycamore Ave., Los Angeles 90038; (213) 831-0111.

MORO-LANDIS, 10960 Ventura Blvd., Studio City, CA 91604; (818) 753-5081; (818) 753-5691.

MULTI-MEDIA STUDIOS, 10401 W. Jefferson Blvd., Culver City, CA 90232-1928; (310) 202-0135; FAX: (310) 202-8219.

NORTH HOLLYWOOD STAGE (ROSE & SALLMAN PRODS.), 7336 Hinds Ave., N. Hollywood, CA 91605; (818) 503-8808.

OCCIDENTAL STUDIOS, 201 N. Occidental Blvd., Los Angeles, CA 90026; (213) 384-3331; FAX: (213) 384-2684.

PARAMOUNT STUDIO GROUP, DIV., 5555 Melrose Ave., Los Angeles, CA 90038; (213) 468-5000.

PEG STUDIOS (Patchett Entertainment Group), 8621 Hayden Place, Culver City, CA 90232; (213) 202-8997.

RALEIGH STUDIOS, 650 N. Bronson Ave., Los Angeles, CA 90004; (213) 466-3111; FAX: (213) 871-4428.

REN-MAR STUDIOS, 846 N. Cahuenga Blvd., Los Angeles, CA 90038; (213) 463-0808.

SANTA CLARITA STUDIOS, 25135 Anza Dr., Santa Clarita, CA 91355; (805) 294-2000; FAX: (805) 294-2020.

S.I.R. FILM STUDIOS, INC., 3322 LaCienega Pl., Los Angeles, CA 90016; (310) 287-3600; FAX: (310) 287-3608.

SILVERLAKE ENTERTAINMENT CENTER, 2405 Glendale Blvd., Los Angeles, CA 90039; (213) 665-4187.

SONY PICTURES STUDIOS, 10202 W. Washington Blvd., Culver City, CA 90232; (310) 280-8000.

SUNSET-GOWER STUDIOS LTD., 1438 N. Gower St., Los Angeles, CA 90028; (213) 467-1001.

TELEVISION CENTER, 6311 Romaine St., Los Angeles, CA 90038; (213) 464-6638.

TWENTIETH CENTURY FOX, 10201 W. Pico Blvd., Los Angeles, CA 90035; (310) 277-2211.

UNIVERSAL CITY STUDIOS, 100 Universal City Plaza, Universal City, 91608; (818) 777-3000; 777-2731.

VPS STUDIOS, 800 N. Seward St., Hollywood, CA 90038; (213) 469-7244; FAX: (213) 463-7538.

VALENCIA STUDIOS, THE, 28343 Ave. Crocker, Valencia, CA 91355; (800) 257-1202; (800) 782-4348; FAX: (805) 257-1002.

WARNER BROS. INC., 4000 Warner Blvd., Burbank, CA 91522; (818) 954-6000, 954-2923; FAX: (818) 954-4213.

WARNER HOLLYWOOD STUDIOS, 1041 N. Formosa Ave., W. Hollywood, CA 90046; (213) 850-2837; FAX: (213) 850-2839.

WEST COAST EAST TELEVISION, 1103 W. Isabel St., Burbank, CA 91506; (818) 563-1100.

WHITEFIRE THEATRE, THE SOUNDSTAGE RENTAL, 13500 Ventura Blvd., Sherman Oaks, CA 91423; (818) 990-2324.

MIAMI

GREAT SOUTHERN STUDIOS, 15221 N.E. 21 Ave., N. Miami Beach, FL 33162; (305) 947-0430.

MIAMI FIVE, 7355 N.W. 41st St., Miami, FL 33166; (305) 593-6969.

NEW YORK

AMPS MEDIA SERVICES, P.O. Box 729, Lake Placid, NY 12946; (518) 523-2677.

ADVENTURE FILM STUDIOS, 40-13 104 St., Queens, NY 11368; (718) 478-2639.

APOLLO THEATRE TV CENTRE, 253 W. 125 St., NY, NY 10027; (212) 222-0992.

ATELIER CINEMA VIDEO STAGES, 295 W. 4 St., New York, NY 10014; (212) 243-3550.

BC STUDIOS, 152 W. 25 St., New York, NY 10001; (212) 242-4065.

BOKEN SOUND STUDIO, 513 W. 54 St., New York, NY 10019; (212) 581-5507.

BREITROSE-SELTZER STAGES, INC., 443 W. 18 St., New York, NY 10011; (212) 807-0664.

BROADWAY STUDIOS, 25-09 Broadway, Astoria, New York, NY 11106; (718) 274-9121.

CAMERA MART STAGES, 456 W. 55 St., New York, NY 10019; (212) 757-6977.

CECO INTERNATIONAL CORP., 440 W. 15 St., New York, NY 10011; (212) 206-8280.

CESTARE STUDIOS, INC., 188 Herricks Rd., Mineola, NY 11501; (516) 742-5550.

CINE STUDIO, 241 W. 54 St., New York, NY 10019; (212) 581-1916.

COMTECH, 770 Lexington Ave., New York, NY 10021; (212) 826-2935.

CORBETT & CO., 17 W. 17 St., New York, NY 10011; (212) 989-7892.

DE FILIPPO, DOM, STUDIO, 207 E. 37 St., New York, NY 10016; (212) 986-5444, 867-4220.

EMPIRE STAGES OF NY, 50-20 25 St., Long Island City, NY 11101; (718) 392-4747.

FARKAS FILMS, INC., 385 Third Ave., New York, NY 10016; (212) 679-8212.

GLOBUS STUDIOS, 44 W. 24 St., New York, NY 10011; (212) 243-1008.

HBO STUDIO PRODS., 120 E. 23 St., 10010; (212) 512-7800.

HORVATH & ASSOCIATES STUDIOS LTD., 95 Charles St., New York, NY 10014; (212) 741-0300.

KAUFMAN ASTORIA STUDIOS, 34-12 36th St., Astoria, NY 11106; (718) 392-5600; FAX: (718) 706-7733.

LRP VIDEO, 3 Dag Hammarskjold Plaza, New York, NY 10017; (212) 759-0822.

MAGNETIC IMAGE VIDEO, INC., 581 Avenue of the Americas, New York, NY 10011; (212) 337-0033.

MAGNO SOUND & VIDEO, 729 Seventh Ave., 10019; (212) 302-2505.

MIDTOWN STUDIOS, 101 Fifth Ave., New York, NY 10003; (212) 633-8484; FAX: (212) 255-3930.

MODERN TELECOMMUNICATIONS/MTI, 1 Dag Hammarskjold Pl., New York, NY 10017; (212) 355-0510.

MOTHERS SOUND STUDIO, 210 E. 5 St., New York, NY 10003; (212) 529-5097.

NATIONAL VIDEO CENTER/RECORDING STUDIOS, INC., 460 W. 42 St., New York, NY 10036; (212) 279-2000.

95TH STREET STUDIO, INC., 206 E. 95 St., New York, NY 10028; (212) 831-1946.

PHOENIX STAGES, 537 W. 59 St., New York, NY 10019; (212) 581-7670.

PRIMALUX VIDEO PRODUCTION, INC., 30 W. 26 St., New York, NY 10010; (212) 206-1402.

REEVES ENTERTAINMENT GROUP, 708 Third Ave., New York, NY 10017; (212) 599-3072.

SHINBONE ALLEY STAGE, 680 Broadway, New York, NY 10012; (212) 420-8463.

SILVERCUP STUDIOS, 42-25 21st St., Long Island City, NY 11101; (718) 784-3390; (212) 349-9600.

TELETECHNIQUES, INC., 1 W. 19 St., New York, NY 10011; (212) 206-1475.

3-G STAGE CORP., 236 W. 61 St., New York, NY 10023; (212) 247-3130.

UNITED FILM ENTERPRISES, INC., 26 W. Park Ave., Suite 107, Long Beach, NY 11561; (516)431-2687.

UNITEL VIDEO INC., 515 W. 57 St., New York, NY 10019; (212) 265-3600.

VERITAS STUDIOS, 527 W. 45 St., New York, NY 10036; (212) 581-2050.

VIDEO PLANNING INC, 250 W. 57 St., New York, NY 10019; (212) 582-5066.

NORTH CAROLINA

CAROLCO STUDIOS, 1223 N. 23 St., Wilmington, NC 28405; (919) 343-3500; (800) 462-2987.

ORLANDO

UNIVERSAL STUDIOS FLORIDA, 1000 Universal Studios Plaza, Orlando, FL 32819; (407) 363-8400.

WALT DISNEY/MGM STUDIOS, 3300 N. Bonnett Creek Rd., Lake Buena Vista, FL 32830-0200; (407) 560-5353; 560-6188.

TEMPE, AZ

WONDER BROTHERS, 2244 S. Industrial Park Ave., Tempe, AZ 85281; (602) 921-0139.

Screening Rooms

ATLANTA

CINEVISION CORP., 3300 Northeast Expwy., Bldg. 2, Atlanta 30341; (404) 455-8988; FAX: (404) 455-4066.

BOSTON

E.M. LOEW ENTERPRISES, 168 Center St. Danvers, MA 01923; (508) 777-7774.

CHICAGO

CINECENTER, 1 E. Erie, Suite 350, Chicago, IL 60611; (312) 266-6198.

HARPO STUDIOS INC., 1058 W. Washington, Chicago, IL 60607; (312) 633-1000.

LOS ANGELES

ACADEMY OF MOTION PICTURE ARTS & SCIENCES: ACADEMY LITTLE THEATER & SAMUEL GOLDWYN THEATRE, 8949 Wilshire Blvd., 3rd Floor, Beverly Hills, 90211-1972; (310) 247-3000; FAX: (213) 859-9619.

ACADEMY PLAZA THEATRE, 5230 Lankershim Blvd., N. Hollywood, CA 91601; (818) 761-0458; FAX: (818) 766-7484.

AIDIKOFF, CHARLES, SCREENING ROOM, 150 S. Rodeo Dr., #140, Beverly Hills, CA 90212; (310) 274-0866.

AMERICAN FILM INSTITUTE, 2021 N. Western Ave., Los Angeles, CA 90027; (213) 856-7600; FAX: (213) 467-4578.

BEVERLY HILLS SCREENING INC., 8949 Sunset Blvd., Suite 201, Beverly Hills, CA 90069; (310) 275-3088.

BIG TIME PICTURE COMPANY, 122101½ Nebraska Ave., Los Angeles, CA 90025; (310) 207-0921; FAX: (310) 826-0071.

CANNON SOUND STUDIOS, 640 S. San Vicente Blvd., Los Angeles, CA 90048; (213) 658-2012.

DAUGHERTY AUDIO/VIDEO DESIGN, 2172 Ridgemont, Los Angeles, CA 90046; (213) 650-5665; 718-5531.

DIRECTORS GUILD OF AMERICA, 7920 W. Sunset Blvd., Los Angeles 90046; (310) 289-2000; FAX: (310) 289-2029.

HOLLY-VINE SCREENING ROOM, 6253 Hollywood Blvd., Suite 1210, Los Angeles, CA 90028; (213) 462-3498.

HOLLYWOOD NEWSREEL SYNDICATE, INC., 1622 N. Gower St., Los Angeles, CA 90028; (213) 469-7307; FAX: (213) 469-8251.

HOLLYWOOD SCREENING ROOM, 1800 N. Highland Ave., Suite 509, Hollywood 90028; (213) 466-1888.

L'IMAGE AUDIO/VISUAL CO., 10729 Devonshire St., Suite 143, Northridge, CA 91325; (818) 368-9584.

JDH SOUND, 12156 Olympic Blvd., Los Angeles, CA 90064-1079; (310) 820-8802; FAX: (310) 207-0914.

OCCIDENTAL STUDIOS, 201 N. Occidental Blvd., Los Angeles, CA 90026; (213) 384-3331.

PREVIEW HOUSE, 7655 Sunset Blvd., Los Angeles 90046; (213) 876-6600.

RALEIGH STUDIOS, 650 N. Bronson Ave., Los Angeles, CA 90004; (213) 466-3111.

ROLAND, GLENN, FILMS, P.O. Box 341408, Los Angeles, CA 90024; (310) 475-0937.

SOUND WEST INC., 12166 Olympic Blvd., Los Angeles, CA 90064; (310) 826-6560; FAX: (310) 207-0914.

VAN DE VEER PHOTO EFFECTS, 724 S. Victory Blvd., Burbank, CA 91502; (818) 841-2512.

WARNER BROS. STUDIOS, 4000 Warner Blvd., Burbank, CA 91522; (818) 954-6000, 954-2923; FAX: (818) 954-2677.

WRITERS GUILD DOHENY PLAZA THEATER, 135 S. Doheny Dr. Beverly Hills, CA 90211; (310) 550-1000, 205-2502.

MILWAUKEE

MARCUS THEATRES, 212 W. Wisconsin Ave., 53203; (414) 272-6020.

MISSION, KS

DICKINSON OPERATING CO., 5913 Woodson Rd., Mission, KS 66202; (913) 432-2334.

NEW YORK

(All major producers-distributors have screening rooms at their home offices in New York for their own use. Most also have screening room facilities at their New York exchanges.)

BROADWAY SCREENING ROOM, THE, 1619 Broadway, 5th Floor, New York, NY 10019; (212) 307-0990.

CINE-METRIC THEATRE CORP., 290 Madison Ave., New York, NY 10017; (212) 922-0910.

MAGNO PREVIEW THEATRE, 1600 Broadway, New York, NY 10019; (212) 302- 2505.

MAGNO SOUND SCREENING ROOM, 729 Seventh Ave., New York, NY 10019; (212) 302-2505.

MOVIE MAKERS THEATRE, 311 W. 43 St., New York, NY 10036; (212) 397-9789; outside NY: (800) 225-6566.

NAVESYNC SOUND, 513 W. 54 St., New York, NY 10019; (212) 246-0100.

PRECISION FILM LABS' SCREENING THEATRE, 311 W. 43 St., New York, NY, 10036; (212) 489-8800.

TECHNICOLOR, 321 W. 44 St., New York, NY 10036; (212) 582-7310.

TODD-AO STUDIOS EAST, 259 W. 54 St., New York, NY 10019; (212) 265-6225.

SAN FRANCISCO

EXPLORATORIUM, McBEAN THEATER, THE, 3601 Lyon St., San Francisco, CA 94123; (415) 563-7337.

PACIFIC FILM ARCHIVE, 2625 Durant Ave., Berkeley, CA 94720; (510) 642-1412.
SAUL ZAENTZ CO. FILM CENTER, THE, 2600 Tenth St., Berkeley, CA 94710; (415) 549-2500.

Sound and Recording Services

HOLLYWOOD

ADVANTAGE AUDIO, 1026 Hollywood Way, Burbank, CA 91505; (818) 566-8555.
AUDIO EFFECTS COMPANY, 1600 N. Western Ave., Hollywood 90027; (213) 469-3692.
B & B SOUND STUDIOS, 3610 W. Magnolia Blvd., Burbank, CA 91505; (818) 848-4496.
BURR, WALLY, RECORDING, 1126 Hollywood Way, #203, Burbank, CA 91505; (818) 845-0500.
BUZZY'S RECORDING SERVICES, 6900 Melrose Ave., Los Angeles, CA 90038; (213) 931-1867; FAX: (213) 931-9681.
CINESOUND, 915 N. Highland Ave., Hollywood, CA 90038; (213) 464-1155; FAX: (213) 464-1820.
COMPACT VIDEO SERVICES, 2813 Alameda Ave., Burbank, CA 91505; (818) 840-7000; (800) 423-2277; FAX: (818) 846-5197.
CRYSTAL SOUND RECORDING, 1014 N. Vine St., Los Angeles, CA 90038; (213) 466-6452.
EVERGREEN RECORDING STUDIOS, 4403 W. Magnolia Blvd., Burbank, CA 91505; (818) 841-6800.
FIDELITY RECORDING STUDIO, 4412 Whitsett Ave., Studio City, CA 91604; (818) 508-3263.
FIESTA SOUND & VIDEO, 1655 S. Compton Ave., Los Angeles, CA 90021; (213) 748-2057; 748-2665.
GLEN GLENN SOUND CO., 900 N. Seward St., Hollywood, CA 90038; (213) 962-4000.
GROUP IV RECORDING, 1541 Wilcox Ave., Los Angeles, CA 90028; (213) 466-6444; FAX: (213) 466-6714.
HARK'S SOUND STUDIO, 1041 N. Orange Dr., Hollywood, CA 90038; (213) 463-3288.
INTERSOUND INC., 8746 Sunset Blvd., Los Angeles, CA 90069; (310) 652-3741; FAX: (310) 854-7290.
LARRABEE SOUND, 8811 Santa Monica Blvd., W. Hollywood, CA 90069; (213) 657-6750.
MCA/WHITNEY RECORDING, 1516 W. Glenoaks Blvd., Glenoaks, CA 91201; (818) 507-1041.
MUSIC GRINDERS STUDIOS, 7460 Melrose Ave., Los Angeles, CA 90046; (213) 655-2996.
NEW JACK SOUND RECORDERS, 1956 N. Cahuenga Blvd., Los Angeles, CA 90068; (213) 466-6141; FAX: (213) 466-3751.
PARAMOUNT RECORDING STUDIOS, 6245 Santa Monica Blvd., Hollywood, CA 90038; (213) 465-4000.
REPUBLIC SOUND STUDIOS INC., 7060 Hollywood Blvd., Los Angeles, CA 90028; (213) 462-6897.
RYDER SOUND SERVICES, INC., 1611 Vine St., Hollywood, CA 90038; (213) 469-3511.
SANTA MONICA SOUND RECORDERS, 2114 Pico Blvd., Santa Monica, CA 90405; (310) 450-3193.
SCREENMUSIC STUDIOS, 11700 Ventura Blvd., Studio City, CA 91604; (818) 753-6040.
SIGNET SOUND STUDIOS, 7317 Romaine St., Los Angeles, CA 90046; (213) 850-1515; FAX: (213) 874-1420.
SKYLINE RECORDING, 1402 Old Topanga Canyon Rd., Topanga Park, CA 90290; (310) 455-2044.
SOUND CITY, INC., 15456 Cabrito Rd., Van Nuys, CA 91406; (213) 873-2842; (818) 787-3722.
SOUND GUYS, 4063 Radford Ave., #102, Studio City, CA 91604; (818) 505-6638.
SOUND IMAGE STUDIO, 6556 Wilkinson Ave., N. Hollywood, CA 91606-2320; (818) 762-8881.
SOUND SERVICES, INC., (SSI), 7155 Santa Monica Blvd., Los Angeles, CA 90046; (213) 874-9344; FAX: (213) 850-7189.
SOUNDS UNLIMITED, P.O. Box 69C, West Hollywood, CA 90069; (310) 659-9578.
SOUNDCASTLE RECORDING STUDIO, 2840 Rowena Ave., Los Angeles, CA 90039; (213) 665-5201; FAX: (213) 662-4273.
STUDIO M PRODUCTIONS UNLIMITED, 1041 N. Orange Dr., Hollywood, CA 90038; (213) 462-7372, (800) 453-3345.
SUNSET SOUND, 6650 Sunset Blvd., Hollywood, CA 90028; (213) 469-1186.
SUNWEST RECORDING STUDIOS, 5533 Sunset Blvd., Hollywood, CA 90028; (213) 465-1000.
TELESOUND, INC., 6110 Santa Monica Blvd., Los Angeles, CA 90038; (213) 462-6981; FAX: (213) 464-1305.

TODD-AO GLEN GLENN STUDIOS, 900 N. Seward St., Hollywood, CA 90038; (213) 962-4000.
TRIANON RECORDING STUDIOS, 1435 South St., Long Beach, CA 90805; (310) 422-2095.
UNIVERSAL CITY STUDIOS, 100 Universal City Plaza, Universal City, CA 91608; (818) 777-1000.
VALENTINE RECORDING STUDIOS, 5330 Laurel Canyon Blvd., N. Hollywood, CA 91607; (818) 769-1515.
WARNER BROS. STUDIOS, 4000 Warner Blvd., Burbank, CA 91522; (818) 954-6000.
WARNER HOLLYWOOD STUDIOS, 1041 N. Formosa, Los Angeles, CA 90046; (213) 850-2500; FAX: (213) 850-2839.
WAVES SOUND RECORDERS, 1956 N. Cahuenga Blvd., Hollywood, CA 90048; (213) 466-6141; FAX: (213) 466-3751.
WESTLAKE STUDIOS, C.D. & E., 7265 Santa Monica Blvd., Los Angeles, CA 90046; (213) 851-9800; 655-0303.
WESTWORLD RECORDERS, 7118 Van Nuys Blvd., Van Nuys, CA 91405; (818) 782-8449.

NEW YORK

A & J RECORDING STUDIOS, INC., 225 W. 57 St., New York, NY 10019; (212) 247-4860.
AQUARIUS TRANSFERMATION LTD., 12 E. 46 St., New York, NY 10017; (212) 697-3636.
AUDIO DEPARTMENT, THE, 119 W. 57 St., New York, NY 10019; (212) 586-3503.
BEE VEE SOUND INC., 211 E. 43 St., #603, New York, NY 10017; (212) 949-9170.
BLANK TAPES, INC., RECORDING STUDIOS, 37 W. 20 St., New York, NY 10011; (212) 255-5313.
CP SOUND, 123 W. 18 St., New York, NY 10011; (212) 627-7700.
CINEQUIP, INC., 241 E. 51 St., New York, NY 10022; (212) 308-5100.
CORELLI-JACOBS FILM MUSIC, INC., 25 W. 45 St., New York, NY 10036; (212) 382-0220.
CREATIVE AUDIO RECORDING SERVICES, 19 W. 36 St., New York, NY 10018; (212) 714-0976.
DB SOUND STUDIOS, INC., 25 W. 45 St., New York, NY 10036; (212) 764-6000.
DOLBY LABORATORIES INC., 1350 Ave. of the Americas, 28th Floor, New York, NY 10019-4703; (212) 767-1700.
DOWNTOWN TRANSFER, 167 Perry St., New York, NY 10014; (212) 627-7728.
EAST SIDE AUDIO & VIDEO, 216 E. 45 St., New York, NY 10017; (212) 867-0730.
ELECTRONOVA PRODUCTIONS, 342 Madison Ave., New York, NY 10017; (212) 687-5838.
HIT FACTORY, THE, INC., 237 W. 54 St., 10019; (212) 664-1000.
IBERO-AMERICAN PRODUCTIONS, 630 Ninth Ave., New York, NY 10036; (212) 245-7826.
MAGNO SOUND & VIDEO, 729 Seventh Ave., 10019; (212) 302-2505.
MIX PLACE, THE, 663 Fifth Ave., New York, NY 10022; (212) 759-8311.
NATIONAL VIDEO CENTER RECORDING STUDIOS, 460 W. 42 St., New York, NY 10036; (212) 279-2000.
NAVESYNC SOUND, 513 W. 54 St., New York, NY 10019; (212) 246-0100.
NEW BREED STUDIOS, 251 W. 30 St., New York, NY 10001; (212) 714-9379.
PHOTO MAGNETIC SOUND STUDIOS, 222 E. 44 St., New York, NY 10017; (212) 687-9030.
PRINCZKO PRODUCTIONS, 9 E. 38 St., New York, NY 10016; (212) 683-1300.
ROSS-GAFFNEY, INC., 21 W. 46 St., New York, NY 10018; (212) 719-2744.
SCHWARTZ, HOWARD M., RECORDING, INC., 420 Lexington Ave., New York, NY 10017: (212) 687-4180.
SOUND ONE CORP., 1619 Broadway, New York, NY 10019; (212) 765-4757.
SOUND PATROL, LTD., 6 E. 39 St., New York, NY 10016; (212) 213-6666.
SOUND SHOP, THE, 321 W. 44 St., New York, NY 10036; (212) 757-5700.
TODD-AO STUDIOS EAST, 259 W. 54 St., New York, NY 10019; (212) 265-6225.
TOPHAM AUDIO, INC., 311 W. 43 St., #910, New York, NY 10036; (212) 586-1033; (800) 883-1033; FAX: (212) 586-0970.
TRACK TRANSFERS, INC., 45 W. 45 St., New York, NY 10036; (212) 730-1635; 730-0555.
UNITED RECORDING, 681 Fifth Ave., New York, NY 10022; (212) 751-4660.
VALENTINO, THOMAS, 151 W. 46 St., #803, New York, NY 10036; (212) 869-5210; (800) 223-6278.
VOICES, 16 E. 48 St., New York, NY 10017; (212) 935-9820.
WAREHOUSE RECORDING, 320 W. 46 St., New York, NY 10036; (212) 265-6060, 581-4444.

ORLANDO

DISNEY-MGM STUDIOS, P.O. Box 10200, 1675 Buena Vista Blvd., Lake Buena Vista, FL 32830-0200; (407) 560-7299, 560-5600.
TOPHAM AUDIO, INC., 4403 Vineland Rd., #B-3, Orlando, FL 32811; (407) 649-6444; (800) 486-6444; FAX: (407) 648-1352.

SAN FRANCISCO

DOLBY LABORATORIES, INC., Head Office & U.S. Sales, 100 Potrero Ave., 94103; (415) 558-0200; Telex: 34409.
LUCASFILM LTD. (Sprocket Systs., Inc.), P.O. Box 2009, San Rafael, CA 94912; (415) 662-1800; FAX: (415) 662-2460.
MUSIC ANNEX INC., 69 Green St., San Francisco, CA 94111; (415) 421-6622.
RUSSIAN HILL RECORDING, 1520 Pacific Ave., San Francisco, CA 94109; (415) 474-4520.
SAUL ZAENTZ FILM CENTER, THE, 2600 Tenth St., Berkeley, CA 94710; (415) 549-2500.

Special Effects

LOS ANGELES AREA

ANDERSON, HOWARD A., CO., 100 Universal City Plaza, #504-3, Universal City, CA 91608; (818) 777-2402.
APOGEE PRODS., INC., 6842 Valjean Ave., Van Nuys, CA 91406; (818) 989-5757.
APOLLO EFFECTS, LTD., 13105 Saticoy St., N. Hollywood, CA 91605-3498; (818) 982-9398.
ART F/X, 3575 Cahuenga Blvd., W., Suite 560, Los Angeles, CA 90068; (213) 876-9469.
BIFROST LASERFX EFFECTS, 6733 Sale Ave., West Hills, CA 91307; (818) 704-0423.
BOSS FILM CORP., 13335 Maxela Ave., Marina del Rey, CA 90292; (310) 823-0433.
BUENA VISTA VISUAL EFFECTS GROUP, 500 S. Buena Vista St., Burbank, CA 91521; (818) 560-5284.
CINEMA RESEARCH, 6860 Lexington Ave., Los Angeles, CA 90038; (213) 460-4111.
DIGITAL VISION ENTERTAINMENT, 7080 Hollywood, Suite 901, Los Angeles, CA 90028; (213) 462-3790.
DREAM QUEST IMAGES, 2635 Park Center Dr., Simi Valley, CA 93065; (805) 581-2671.
DREAMLIGHT IMAGES, INC., 932 N. La Brea Ave., Suite C, Hollywood, CA 90038; (213) 850-1996; FAX: (213) 850-5318.
ELIXIR STUDIOS, 6650 Santa Monica Blvd., Hollywood, CA 90038; (213) 467-1800.
ENERGY PRODUCTIONS, 12700 Ventura Blvd., Studio City, CA 91604; (818) 508-1444, (800) 462-4379.
FANTASY II FILM EFFECTS, 504 S. Varney St., Burbank, CA 91502; (818) 843-1413.
FILMTRIX, INC., 11054 Chandler Blvd., N. Hollywood, CA 91601; (818) 980-3700; FAX: (818) 980-3703.
IMAGE ENGINEERING INC., 632 N. Victory Blvd., Burbank, CA 91502; (818) 846-5865.
INTROVISION, 1011 N. Fuller Ave., Hollywood, CA 90046; (213) 851-9262.
JOHNSON, RAY, STUDIOS, 5435 Denny St., N. Hollywood, CA 91601; (818) 508-7348.
JOHNSON'S, STEVE X/FX, INC., 8010 Wheatland Ave., Unit J, Sun Valley, CA 91352; (818) 504-2177; FAX: (818) 504-2838.
LASER-PACIFIC MEDIA, 540 N. Hollywood Way, Burbank, CA 91505; (818) 842-0777.
MERLIN S/FX CO., Raleigh Studios, 5300 Melrose Ave., Hollywood, CA 90038; (213) 871-4433; FAX: (213) 871-4428.
MILLER, DAVID, STUDIO, 9043 Sunland Blvd., Sun Valley, CA 91352; (818) 768-6403.
PACIFIC TITLE & ART STUDIO, 6350 Santa Monica Blvd., Los Angeles 90038; (213) 464-0121; 938-3711.
RHYTHM AND HUES, 910 N. Sycamore Ave., Los Angeles, CA 90038; (213) 851-6500.
SPECIAL EFFECTS UNLIMITED, 752 N. Cahuenga Blvd., Los Angeles, CA 90038; (213) 466-3361.
VAN DER VEER PHOTO EFFECTS, 724 S. Victory Blvd., Burbank, CA 91342; (818) 841-2512.
VISUAL CONCEPTS ENGINEERING, 13300 Ralston Ave., Sylmar, CA 91342; (818) 367-9187.
YOUNG, GENE EFFECTS, 517 W. Windsor Rd., Glendale, CA 91204; (818) 243-8593; 848-7471.

LAS VEGAS

LEONARD, ROBERT, PRODUCTIONS, INC., P.O. Box 81440, Las Vegas, NV 89180; (702) 877-2449.

NEW YORK

APA, 230 W. 10 St., New York, NY 10014; (212) 929-9436; 675-4894.
ANIMUS FILMS, 2 W. 47 St., New York, NY 10036; (212) 391-8716.
BALSMEYER & EVERETT, 230 W. 17 St., New York, NY 10011; (212) 627-3430.
BROADCAST ARTS, INC., 632 Broadway, New York, NY 10012; (212) 254-5400.
BROOKLYN MODEL WORKS, 60 Washington Ave., Brooklyn, NY 11205; (718) 834-1944.
CACIOPPO PRODUCTION DESIGN INC., 42 E. 23 St., New York, NY 10010; (212) 777-1828.
CHARLEX, INC., 2 W. 45 St., New York, NY 10036; (212) 719-4600.
CIMMELLI INC., 16 Walter St., Pearl River, NY 10965; (914) 735-2090.
CLELAND STUDIO, INC., 122 Spring St., New York, NY 10012; (212) 431-9185.
D'ANDREA PRODUCTIONS INC., 12 W. 37 St., New York, NY 10018; (212) 947-1211.
DARINO, 222 Park Ave. South, #2A New York, NY 10003; (212) 228-4024.
DE FILIPPO, DOM, STUDIO, INC., 207 E. 37 St., New York, NY 10016; (212) 986-5444; 867-4220.
DENARO, SAL, AND PUPPETS, 174 DeGraw St., Brooklyn, NY 11231; (718) 875-1711.
EASTERN OPTICAL EFFECTS, 321 W. 44 St., #401, New York, NY 10036; (212) 541-9220.
EDITEL/NEW YORK, 222 E. 44 St., New York, NY 10017; (212) 867-4600.
EFEX SPECIALISTS, 35-39 37th St., Long Island City, NY 11101; (718) 937-2417.
EUE/SCREEN GEM PRINTS, 222 E. 44 St., New York, NY 10017; (212) 867-4030.
FANTASTIC ANIMATION MACHINE, INC., THE, 1501 Bdwy., New York, NY 10036; (212) 697-2525.
FRIEDMAN, HAROLD CONSORTIUM, 420 Lexington Ave., New York, NY 10017; (212) 697-0858.
GATI, JOHN, FILM EFFECTS, INC., 154 W. 57 St., Suite 832, New York, NY 10019; (212) 582-9060.
GEARY, MICHAEL, NEW YORK SPECIAL EFFECTS, Pier 60 N. River, New York, NY ; (212) 741-0218.
GIZMO SPECIAL EFFECTS, 111 W. 24 St., New York, NY 10011; (212) 242-1504.
GLOBUS STUDIOS, INC., 44 W. 24 St., New York, NY 10010; (212) 243-1008.
R/GREENBERG ASSOCIATES, 350 W. 39 St., New York, NY 10018; (212) 239-6767.
HOLOGRAPHIC STUDIOS, 240 E. 26 St., New York, NY 10010; (212) 686-9397.
KUNZ, PETER, CO., INC., RD1 Box 223, High Falls, NY 12440; (914) 687-0400.
LEVY, DANIEL, 408 E. 13 St., New York, NY 10009; (212) 254-8964.
LIBERTY STUDIOS, INC. 238 E. 26 St., New York, NY 10010; (212) 532-1865.
MALLIE STUDIO, INC., 40 Stevens Pl., Lawrence, NY 11559; (516) 239-8782.
MANTELL, PAUL, SPECIAL CREATIONS, 181 Hudson St., New York, NY 10013; (212) 966-9038.
OPTICAL HOUSE, INC., 25 W. 45 St., New York, NY 10036; (212) 924-9150.
PROP EFFECTS & RIGGING, 713 Snediker Ave., Brooklyn, NY 11207; (718) 272-1613.
SMA VISUAL EFFECTS CORP., 84 Wooster St., New York, NY 10012; (212) 226-7474.
SPECIAL EFFECTS UNLIMITED, 18 Euclid Ave., Yonkers, NY; (914) 965-5625.
THEATER EFFECTS, INC., 52 Cottage St., Port Chester, NY 10573; (914) 937-9266.
YURKIW LTD., 568 Broadway, New York, NY 10012; (212) 226-6338.

ORLANDO

DISNEY-MGM STUDIOS, P.O. Box 10200, 1675 Buena Vista Blvd., Lake Buena Vista, FL 32830; (407) 560-7299, 560-5600.

SAN RAFAEL

LUCASFILM, LTD. (Industrial Light & Magic), P.O. Box 2009, San Rafael, CA 94912; (415) 662-1800.

Stock-Shot Film Libraries

CHICAGO

BRITANNICA FILMS, 425 N. Michigan Ave., Chicago, IL 60611; (312) 347-7400, ext. 6512; (800) 554-9862.
FILE TAPE COMPANY, 210 E. Pearson, Chicago, IL 60611; (312) 649-0599.

HOLLYWOOD-LOS ANGELES

ACADEMY OF MOTION PICTURE ARTS & SCIENCES LIBRARY, 333 S. La Cienega Blvd., Beverly Hills, CA 90048; (310) 247-3020, 247-3000.
AFTER IMAGE INC., 6100 Wilshire Blvd., Suite 240, Los Angeles, 90048; (213) 480-1105.
AMERICAN FILM INSTITUTE LIBRARY, 2021 N. Western Ave., Los Angeles, 90027; (213) 856-7600; 856-7655.
ANDERSON, TOM, FILMWORKS, 6362 Hollywood Blvd., Suite 308, Los Angeles, 90028; (213) 464-0386.
APOLLO EFFECTS, LTD., 13105 Saticoy St., N. Hollywood, CA 91605-3498; (818) 982-9398.
ASSOCIATED MEDIA IMAGES, INC., 650 N. Bronson, Suite 300, Los Angeles, 90004; (213) 871-1340; FAX: (213) 469-6048.
BUDGET FILMS, 4590 Santa Monica Blvd., Los Angeles, 90029; (213) 660- 0187; FAX: (213) 660-5571.
BUENA VISTA STUDIOS, 500 S. Buena Vista St., Burbank, 91521; (818) 560-0044.
CAMEO FILM LIBRARY, 10620 Burbank Blvd., North Hollywood, 91601; (818) 980-8700; FAX: (818) 980-7113.
CINEMAPHILE AMALGAMATED PICTURES, P.O. Box 8054, Universal City, 91608; (213) 939-9042.
CLARK, DICK, MEDIA ARCHIVES, INC., 3003 W. Olive Ave., Burbank, CA 91505; (818) 841-3003; FAX: (818) 954-8609.
CLASSIC IMMAGES, 1041 N. Formosa Ave., W. Hollywood, CA 90046; (213) 850-2980; (800) 949-CLIP; FAX: (213) 850-2981.
CLIP JOINT FOR FILM, THE, 833-B N. Hollywood Way, Burbank, CA 91505; (818) 842-2525.
DORN, LARRY, ASSOCS., 5550 Wilshire Blvd., #306, Los Angeles, 90036; (213) 935-6266; FAX: (213) 935-9523.
DREAMLIGHT IMAGES, INC., 932 N. La Brea Ave., Suite C, Hollywood, 90038; (213) 850-1996; FAX: (213) 850-5318.
ENERGY PRODUCTIONS, 12700 Ventura Blvd., Studio City, 91604; (818) 508-1444; (800) IMA-GERY; FAX: (818) 508-1293.
ENTERPRISES PRODUCTIONS, 5912 Ramirez Canyon, Malibu, 90265-4423; (213) 457-8081.
FILM & VIDEO STOCK SHOTS, INC., 10700 Ventura Blvd., #E, Studio City, CA 91604-3561; (213) 850-1900; (818) 760-2098.
FILM BANK, 425 N. Victory Blvd., Burbank, 91502; (818) 841-9176.
FISH FILMS INC., 4548 Van Noord Ave., Studio City, 91604-1013; (818) 905-1071; FAX (818) 905-0301.
FORSHER, JAMES, COLLECTION OF ARCHIVAL FOOTAGE, 9016 Wilshire Blvd., #403, Beverly Hills, CA 90211; (213) 655-6958.
G-FORCE INTERNATIONAL ENTERTAINMENT CORP., 279 S. Beverly Dr., Suite 1038, Beverly Hills, 90212; (310) 271-0700.
GREAT WAVES FILM LIBRARY, 483 Mariposa Dr., Ventura, 93001; (805) 653-2699.
GRINBERG, SHERMAN, FILM LIBRARIES, INC., 1040 N. McCadden Pl., Hollywood, CA 90038; (213) 464-7491; FAX: (213) 462-5352.
HALICKI, H.B., PRODS., 17902 S. Vermont Ave., P.O. Box 2123, Gardena 90248; (213) 770-1744.
HERITAGE ENTERTAINMENT INC., 7920 Sunset Blvd., Suite 200, Los Angeles, 90046; (213) 850-5858.
HOLLYWOOD NEWSREEL SYNDICATE INC., 1622 N. Gower St., Hollywood, 90028; (213) 469-7307; FAX: (213) 469-8251.
IMAGE BANK WEST, THE, 4526 Wilshire Blvd., Los Angeles, 90010; (213) 930-0797; FAX: (213) 930-1089.
INTERVIDEO/TRITRONICS, INC., 733 N. Victory Blvd., Burbank 91502; (818) 843-3633; 569-4000; FAX: 843-6884.
LACY, CLAY, AVIATION INC., 7435 Valjean Ave., Van Nuys, 91406; (818) 989-2900; FAX: (818) 909-9537.
MAC GILLIVRAY FREEMAN FILM & TAPE LIBRARY, P.O. Box 205, Laguna Beach, CA 92652; (714) 494-1055; FAX: (714) 494-2079.
MAINSTREET IMAGERY, INC., 13105 Saticoy St., N. Hollywood, 91605; (818) 503-0931; FAX: (818) 982-9383.
PALISADES WILDLIFE LIBRARY, 1205 S. Ogden Dr., Los Angeles, 90019; (213) 931-6186.
PHOTO-CHUTING ENTERPRISES, 12619 S. Manor Dr., Hawthorne, 90250; (213) 678-0163.
PRODUCERS LIBRARY SERVICE, 1051 N. Cole Ave., Hollywood, 90038; (213) 465-0572; FAX: (213) 465-1671.
PYRAMID FILM & VIDEO, 2801 Colorado Ave., Santa Monica, 90404; (310) 828-7577; FAX: (310) 453-9083.

SAWADE, RON, CO., P.O. Box 1310, Pismo, CA 93448; (818) 769-1737.
STOCK HOUSE, THE, 6922 Hollywood Blvd., Suite 621, Los Angeles, 90028; (213) 461-0061; FAX: (213) 461-2457.
TURNER ENTERTAINMENT CO., 10100 Venice Blvd., Culver City, 90232; (310) 558-7300.
TWA MOVIE & TV PROMOTIONS, 5550 Wilshire Blvd., Suite 303, Los Angeles, 90036; (213) 935-6266; FAX: (213) 935-9523.
UCLA FILM & TELEVISION ARCHIVE, 1015 N. Cahvenga Blvd., Hollywood, CA 90038; (213) 466-8559; FAX: (213) 461-6317.
UNITED STATES AIR FORCE, Office of Public Affairs, Western Region, 11000 Wilshire Blvd., Suite 10114, Los Angeles, 90024; (310) 575-7522, 575-7511; FAX: (310) 473-9960.
UNITED STATES ARMY, Office of Public Affairs, 11000 Wilshire Blvd, Suite 10104, Los Angeles, 90024-3688; (310) 575-7621; FAX: (310) 473-8874.
UNIVERSAL CITY STUDIOS, 100 Universal City Plaza, Universal City, 91608; (818) 777-3000; FAX: 777-2731.
VIDEO TAPE LIBRARY LTD., 1509 N. Crescent Heights, Blvd. #2, Los Angeles, 90046; (213) 656-4330; FAX: (213) 656-8746.
WPA FILM LIBRARY, 5525 W. 159th St., Oak Forest, IL 60452; (708) 535-1540; (800) 777-2223; FAX: (708) 535-1541.
WORLDWIDE ENTERTAINMENT CORP., 5912 Ramirez Canyon, Malibu, 90265; (310) 457-8081.

MIAMI

KESSER STOCK LIBRARY, 21 SW 15 Rd., Miami, 33129; (305) 358-7900.

NEW YORK

AMERICAN MUSEUM OF NATURAL HISTORY FILM ARCHIVES, Central Park West at 79 St., 10024; (212) 769- 5419.
ARCHIVE FILM PRODUCTIONS, INC., 530 W. 25 St., 10001; (212) 620-3955; FAX: (212) 645-2137.
CHERTOK ASSOCIATES, INC., One South Franklin St., Nyack, NY 10960; (914) 358-4729; FAX: (914) 358-4732.
COE FILM ASSOCIATES, INC., 65 E. 96 St., 10128; (212) 831-5355; FAX: (212) 645-0681.
FILM PRESERVE, THE, 2 Depot Plaza, #202-B, Bedford Hills, NY 10507; (914) 242-9838.
SHERMAN GRINBERG FILM LIBRARIES, INC., 630 Ninth Ave., NY 10036; (212) 765-5170; FAX: (212) 245-2339.
HALCYON DAYS PRODUCTIONS, 12 West End Ave., 10023; (212) 397-7190.
IMAGE BANK, THE, 111 Fifth Ave., 10003; (212) 529-6700; FAX: (212) 529-8886.
IMAGEWAYS, INC. 412 W. 48 St., 10036; (212) 265-1287.
JALBERT PRODUCTIONS, INC., 775 Park Ave., Huntington, NY 11743; (516) 351-5878.
KILLIAM SHOWS, INC., 6 E. 39 St., 10016; (212) 679-8230.
MOVIETONE NEWS, INC. FILM LIBRARY, (Subsidiary of 20th Century Fox), 460 W. 54 St., 10019; (212) 408-8450.
MUSEUM OF MODERN ART FILM LIBRARY, 11 W. 53 St., 10019; (212) 245-8900.
NBC NEWS ARCHIVES, 30 Rockefeller Plaza, 10112; (212) 664-3797.
NEWSREEL ACCESS SYSTEMS, INC., 150 E. 58 St., 10155; (212) 826-2800.
PETRIFIED FILMS INC., 430 W. 14 St., Rm. 411, 10014; (212) 242-5461; FAX: (212) 691-8347.
PORT AUTHORITY OF NY & NJ, THE, 1 World Trade Center, 10048; (212) 466-7646.
PRELINGER ASSOC., INC., 430 W. 14 St., 10014; (212) 255- 8866.
SECOND LINE SEARCH, 330 W. 42 St., Room 2901, 10036; (212) 594-5544.
SPALLA, RICK, VIDEO PRODUCTIONS, 301 W. 45 St., 10036; (212) 765-4646; 462-4710.
STREAMLINE FILM ARCHIVES, 432 Park Ave. S., 10016; (212) 696-2616.
WTN-WORLDWIDE TV NEWS CORP., 1995 Broadway, 10023; (212) 362-4440.

TUCSON, AZ

SOURCE STOCK FOOTAGE, THE, 738 N. Constitution Dr., Tucson, AZ 85748; (602) 298-4810.

Stop Watches

DUCOMMUN, M., CO., 48 Main St., Warwick, NY 10990; (914) 986-5757.

MARCEL WATCH CORP., 1115 Broadway, 4th Fl., New York, NY 10010; (212) 620-8181.

SMITH TIME, P.O. Box 496, Ivy, VA 22945; (804) 977-7440.

Subtitles

CALIFORNIA

CAPTIONS, INC., 2479 Lanterman Terrace, Los Angeles, CA 90039; (213) CAP-TION; 2619 Hyperion Ave., Suite A, Los Angeles, CA 90027; (213) 665-4860.

CINETYP, INC., 843 Seward St., Hollywood, CA 90038; (213) 463-8569; FAX: (213) 463-4129.

CREST NATIONAL VIDEOTAPE FILM LABS, 1000 N. Highland Ave., Hollywood, CA 90038; (213) 466-0624; 462-6696; FAX: (213) 461-8901.

FOREIGN LANGUAGE GRAPHICS, 1010 LaLoma Rd., Los Angeles, CA 90041; (213) 256-0969.

GLOBAL LANGUAGE SERVICES, 2027 Las Lunas, Pasadena, CA 91107; (818) 792-0862; 792-0576; FAX: (818) 792-8793.

GOOSI, 14937 Ventura Blvd., #301, Sherman Oaks, CA 91403; (818) 906-9946.

HANSON, DIANE GOULLARD, 583-1/2 N. Windsor Blvd., Los Angeles, CA 90004; (213) 962-2441; FAX: (213) 957-1117.

HEADLEY INTERNATIONAL PICTURES, 738 N. Cahuenga Blvd., #F, Los Angeles, CA 90038; (213) 469-9650.

HOMER AND ASSOCIATES, INC., Sunset Gower Studios, 1420 N. Beachwood Dr., Hollywood, CA 90028; (213) 462-4710.

INTERSOUND, INC., 8746 Sunset Blvd., Los Angeles, CA 90069; (310) 652-3741; FAX: (310) 854-7290.

INTEX AUDIOVISUALS, 9021 Melrose Ave., Suite 205, Los Angeles, CA 90069; (310) 275-9571; FAX: (310) 271-1319.

LINGUATHEQUE OF L.A., 13601 Ventura Blvd., #102, Sherman Oaks, CA 91423; (818) 894-2882; FAX: (818) 893-5199.

MAINSTREET IMAGERY, INC., 13105 Saticoy St., N. Hollywood, CA 91605; (818) 503-0931.

MASTERWORDS, 1512 Eleventh St., #205, Santa Monica, CA 90401-2907; (310) 394-7998; FAX: (310) 394-7954.

P.F.M. DUBBING INTERNATIONAL, 8306 Wilshire Blvd., Suite 947, Beverly Hills, CA 90211; (310) 936-7577; FAX: (310) 936-1691.

PACIFIC TITLE & ART STUDIO, 6350 Santa Monica Blvd., Los Angeles, CA 90038; (213) 464-0121; 938-3711.

RENCHER'S EDITORIAL SERVICE, 738 Cahuenga Blvd., Hollywood, CA 90038; (213) 463-9836; FAX: (213) 469-0377.

ROLAND FRENCH TRANSLATION SERVICES, 10711 Wellworth Ave., Los Angeles, CA 90024; (310) 475-4347.

SOFTNI CORP., 2319A W. Olive Ave., Burbank, CA 91506; (818) 558-1168; FAX: (818) 558-1169.

NEW YORK

CAPTION CENTER, THE, 231 E. 55 St., New York, NY 10022; (212) 223-4930.

DEVLIN VIDEO SERVICE, 1501 Broadway, Suite 408, New York, NY 10036; (212) 391-1313.

EISENMAN, HELEN, 630 Ninth Ave., Suite 414, New York, NY 10036; (212) 757-5969; 749-3655.

FIMA NOVECK PRODUCTIONS, 161 E. 61 St., New York, NY 10021; (212) 751-2329.

RENNERT BILINGUAL TRANSLATIONS, 2 W. 45 St., 5th floor, New York, NY 10036; (212) 819-1776.

Trailers

ATLANTA

CINEMA CONCEPTS THEATRE SERVICE COMPANY, INC., 2030 Powers Ferry Rd., Atlanta, GA 30339; (404) 956-7460.

CHICAGO

FILMACK STUDIOS, 1327 S. Wabash Ave., Chicago, IL 60605; (312) 427-3395.

LOS ANGELES

ANDERSON, HOWARD A., CO., 100 Universal City Plaza, #504-3, Universal City, CA 91608; (818) 777-2402; FAX: (818) 777-7154.

AVAILABLE LIGHT LTD., 3110 W. Burbank Blvd., CA 91505; (818) 842-2109; (818) 842-0661.

BOSUSTOW VIDEO, 3000 Olympic Blvd., Santa Monica, CA 90404; (310) 315-4888; (310) 315-4800.

COMING ATTRACTIONS, 550 N. Brand Blvd., Suite 700, Glendale, CA 91203; (213) 465-4129.

CREATIVE PARTNERSHIP, INC., THE, 7525 Fountain Ave., Hollywood, CA 90046; (213) 850-5551; FAX: (213) 850-0391.

CRUSE & CO., 7000 Romaine St., Hollywood, CA 90038; (213) 851-8814; FAX: (213) 851-8788.

EMERALD LIGHT PICTURES, 2111 Woodland Way, Hollywood, CA 90068; (213) 876-9693.

FERRO, PABLO & ASSOCIATES, 1756 N. Sierra Bonita Ave., Hollywood, CA 90046; (213) 850-6193.

FOX, B.D., & FRIENDS, INC. ADVERTISING, 1111 Broadway, Santa Monica, CA 90401; (310) 394-7150; FAX: (310) 393-1569.

GLASS/SCHOOR FILMS, 565 Westbourne Dr., Los Angeles, CA 90048; (310) 854-5400; FAX: (310) 854-6781.

HOLLYWOOD NEWSREEL SYNDICATE INC., 1622 N. Gower St., Los Angeles, CA 90028; (213) 469-7307; FAX: (213) 469-8251.

HOMER & ASSOCIATES, INC., 1420 N. Beachwood Dr., Hollywood, CA 90028; (213) 462-4710.

INTEX AUDIO VISUALS, 9021 Melrose Ave., Suite 205, Los Angeles, CA 90069; (310) 275-9571; FAX: (310) 271-1319.

JKR PRODUCTIONS, INC., 12140 W. Olympic Blvd., Suite 21, Los Angeles, CA 90064; (310) 826-3666.

KALEIDOSCOPE FILMS INC., 844 N. Seward St., Hollywood, CA 90038; (213) 465-1151; FAX: (213) 871-1376.

KEY WEST EDITING, 5701 Buckingham Pkwy., Suite C, Culver City, CA 90230; (310) 645-3348.

LAJON PRODUCTIONS, INC., 2907 W. Olive Ave., Burbank, CA 91505; (818) 841-1440; FAX: (818) 841-4659.

LEE FILM DESIGN, 2293 El Contento, Hollywood, CA 90068; (213) 467-9317.

LUMENI PRODUCTIONS, 1727 N. Ivar Ave., Hollywood, CA 90028; (213) 462-2110; FAX: (213) 462-8250.

MAINSTREET IMAGERY, INC., 13105 Saticoy St., N. Hollywood, CA 91605; (818) 503-0931; FAX: (818) 982-9383.

MARS PRODUCTION CORP., 4405 Riverside Dr., Suite 305, Burbank, CA 91505; (818) 841-0101.

MERCER TITLES & OPTICAL EFFECTS LTD., 106 W. Burbank Blvd., Burbank, CA 91502; (818) 840-8866; FAX: (818) 840-8828.

MULTI-MEDIA WORKS, 7227 Beverly Blvd., Los Angeles, CA 90036; (213) 939-1185.

NATIONAL SCREEN SERVICE GROUP INC., 2001 S. La Cienega Blvd., Los Angeles, CA 90034; (310) 836-1505.

NEWMAN/FRANKS, 2956 Nicada Dr., Los Angeles, CA 90077; (310) 470-0140; 470-0145; FAX: (310) 470-2410.

RENCHER'S EDITORIAL SERVICE, 738 Cahuenga Blvd., Hollywood, CA 90038; (213) 463-9836.

RUBBER DUBBERS, INC., 626 Justin Ave., Glendale, CA 91201; (818) 241-5600; FAX: (818) 241-1366.

RUXIN, JIM, 12140 W. Olympic Blvd., Suite 21, Los Angeles, CA 90064; (310) 826-3666.

SKYLIGHT PRODUCTIONS INC., 6815 W. Willoughby Ave., Suite 201, Los Angeles, CA 90038; (213) 464-4500; FAX: (213) 463-1884.

SOUND SERVICES INC., 7155 Santa Monica Blvd., Los Angeles, CA 90046; (213) 874-9344; (818) 986-3255.

SOUTH, LEONARD, PRODUCTIONS, 4883 Lankershim Blvd., N. Hollywood, CA 91601; (818) 760-8383; FAX: (818) 760-8301.

STROCK, HERBERT L., PRODUCTIONS, 6500 Barton Ave., Los Angeles, CA 90038; (213) 461-1298.

UNIVERSAL FACILITIES RENTAL DIVISION, 100 Universal City Plaza, Universal City, CA 91608, (818) 777-3000; 777-2731.

VIDCOM ENTERTAINMENT, INC., P.O. Box 2926, Hollywood, CA 90078; (310) 301-8433.

VIDE-U PRODUCTIONS, 1034 Shenandoah St., Los Angeles, CA 90035; (310) 657-4385; FAX: (310) 657-4385.

NEW YORK CITY

ALEXANDER, JOHN ERIC, MUSIC INC., 311 W. 43 St., Suite 202, New York, NY 10036; (212) 581-8560.

DARINO FILMS, 222 Park Ave. South, New York, NY 10003, (212) 228-4024.

EAST END PRODUCTIONS, 513 W. 54 St., New York, NY 10019;(212) 489-1865.

GLASS/SCHOOR FILMS, 42 W. 38 St., New York, NY 10018; (212) 944-0140; FAX: (212) 869-1473.

R/GREENBERG ASSOCIATES INC., 350 W. 39 St., New York, NY 10018; (212) 239-6767.

NATIONAL SCREEN SERVICE GROUP CORP., 40 Rockwood Pl., Englewood, NJ 07631; (201) 871-7900.

QUARTERMOON PRODUCTIONS INC., 12 Morand Lane, Wilton, CT 06897; (203) 762-2663.

Talent and Literary Agencies

HOLLYWOOD

(City is Los Angeles, unless otherwise indicated.)

ABRAMS ARTISTS & ASSOCS., 9200 Sunset Blvd., Suite 625, 90069; (310) 859-0625; FAX: (310) 276-6193.
ABRAMS, RUBALOFF & LAWRENCE., INC., 8075 West 3rd, Suite 303, 90048; (213) 935-1700; FAX: (213) 932-9901.
ACTORS GROUP AGENCY, 8730 Sunset Blvd., Suite 220 West, 90069; (310) 657-7113; FAX: (310) 657-1756.
AGENCY FOR PERFORMING ARTS, 9000 Sunset Blvd., #1200, 90069; (310) 273-0744; FAX: (310) 275-9401.
AGENCY, THE, 10351 Santa Monica Blvd., #211, 90025; (310) 551-3000; FAX: (310) 551-1424.
AIMEE ENTERTAINMENT ASSOCIATION, 13743 Victory Blvd., Van Nuys, CA 91401; (818) 994-9354; FAX: (818) 781-9834.
ALL-STAR TALENT AGENCY, 21416 Chase St., #2, Canoga Park, CA 91304; (818) 346-4313.
ALL TALENT AGENCY, 2437 E. Washington Blvd., Pasadena, 91104; (818) 797-8202; FAX: (818) 791-5250.
ALVARADO, CARLOS, AGENCY, 8150 Beverly Blvd., Suite 308, 90048; (213) 655-7978; FAX: (213) 655-0777.
AMBROSIO/MORTIMER & ASSOCS., 9000 Sunset Blvd., Suite 702, 90069; (310) 274-4274; FAX: (310) 274-9642.
AMSEL, EISENSTADT & FRAZIER, INC., 6310 San Vicente Blvd., Suite 407, 90048; (213) 939-1188; FAX: (213) 939-0630.
ARTISTS AGENCY, THE, 10000 Santa Monica Blvd., Suite 305, 90067; (310) 277-7779; FAX: (310) 785-9338.
ARTISTS GROUP, THE, 1930 Century Park West, Suite 403, 90067; (310) 552-1100; FAX: (310) 277-9513.
ASSOCIATED TALENT INTL., 9744 Wilshire Blvd., Suite 312, Beverly Hills, 90212; (310) 271-4662.
BADGLEY/CONNOR, 9229 Sunset Blvd., #311, 90069; (310) 278-9313; FAX: (310) 278-4128.
BAUMAN, HILLER & ASSOCS., 5750 Wilshire Blvd., #512, 90036; (213) 857-6666; FAX: (213) 857-0638.
BEAKEL, DeBORD & PAUL and ASSOCS., 10637 Burbank Blvd., N. Hollywood, 91601; (818) 506-7615.
BENNETT AGENCY, 150 S. Barrington Ave., Suite 1, 90049; (310) 471-2251.
BLANCHARD, NINA, ENTERPRISES INC., 957 Cole Ave., 90038; (213) 462-7274; FAX: (213) 462-3855.
BLOOM, J. MICHAEL, 9200 Sunset Blvd., Suite 710, 90069; (310) 275-6800; FAX: (310) 275-6941.
BORINSTEIN ORECK BOGART AGENCY, 8271 Melrose Ave., Suite 110, 90046; (213) 658-7500; FAX: (213) 658-8866.
BRANDT COMPANY, 12700 Ventura Blvd., #340, Studio City, CA 91604; (818) 506-7747.
BRESLER, KELLY, KIPPERMAN, 15760 Ventura Blvd., #1730, Encino, CA 91436; (818) 905-1155.
BROWN, CURTIS, LTD., 606 N. Larchmont Blvd., #309, 90004; (213) 461-0148.
CALDER AGENCY, 17420 Ventura Blvd., Suite 4, Encino, 91316; (818) 906-2825
CAMDEN-ITG, 822 So. Robertson Blvd., #200, 90035; (310) 289-2700; FAX: (310) 286-2718.
CARROLL, WILLIAM, AGENCY, 120 S. Victory, Suite 104, Burbank, 91502; (818) 848-9948; FAX: (213) 849-2553.
CAVALERI & ASSOCIATES, 6605 Hollywood Blvd., Suite 220, 90028; (213) 461-2940; FAX: (213) 469-1213.
CENTURY ARTISTS, LTD., 9744 Wilshire Blvd., Suite 308, Beverly Hills, 90212; (310) 273-4366
CHASIN AGENCY, THE, 190 N. Canon Dr., Suite 201, Beverly Hills, CA 90210; (310) 278-7505; FAX: (310) 275-6685.
CINEMA TALENT INTL., 8033 W. Sunset Blvd., #808; 90046; (213) 656-1937; FAX: (213) 654-4678.
CIRCLE TALENT AGENCY, 433 N. Camden Dr., #400, Beverly Hills, CA 90210; (310) 285-1585.
COMMERCIALS UNLTD., INC., 7461 Beverly Blvd., Suite 400, 90036; (213) 937-2220; FAX: (213) 937-5919.
CONTEMPORARY ARTISTS LTD., 1427 Third St., #205, Santa Monica, CA 90401; (310) 395-1800.
CORALIE JR. AGENCY, 4789 Vineland Ave., #100, N. Hollywood, CA 91602; (818) 766-9501.
CRAIG AGENCY, THE, 8485 Melrose Pl., Suite E, 90069; (213) 655-0236; FAX: (213) 655-1491.
CREATIVE ARTISTS AGENCY, 9830 Wilshire Blvd., Beverly Hills, CA 90212; (310) 288-4545; FAX: (310) 288-4800.
CUMBER, LIL, ATTRACTIONS AGENCY, 6363 Sunset Blvd., Suite 701, 90028; (213) 469-1919; (213) 294-8245.

CUNNINGHAM, ESCOTT, DIPENE & ASSOC. 261 S. Robertson Blvd., Beverly Hills, 90211; (310) 855-1700; (310) 855-1011.
DIAMOND ARTISTS AGENCY, LTD., 9200 Sunset Blvd., 90069; (310) 278-8146
EMERALD ARTISTS, 6565 Sunset Blvd., #312, 90028; (213) 465-2974.
ENTERTAINMENT ENTERPRISES, 1680 Vine St., Suite 519, 90028; (213) 462-6001; FAX: (213) 462-6003.
EXCLUSIVE ARTISTS AGENCY, 2501 W. Burbank Blvd., Suite 304, Burbank, CA 91505; (818) 846-0262.
FAVORED ARTISTS, 8150 Beverly Blvd., #201, 90048; (213) 653-3191.
FELBER, WM., 2126 Cahuenga Blvd., 90068; (213) 466-7627.
FIELDS, LIANA, AGENCY, 3325 Wilshire Blvd., #749, 90010; (213) 292-8550.
FILM ARTISTS ASSOCIATES, 7080 Hollywood Blvd., Suite 704, Los Angeles, CA 90028; (213) 463-1010; FAX: (213) 463-0702.
FIRST ARTISTS AGENCY, 10000 Riverside Dr., Suite 6, Toluca Lake, CA 91602; (818) 509-9292; FAX: (818) 509-9295.
FLICK EAST-WEST TALENTS INC., 9057 Nemo St., Suite A, W. Hollywood, 90069; (310) 247-1777; FAX: (310) 858-1357.
GAGE GROUP, THE, 9255 Sunset Blvd., Suite 515, 90069; (310) 859-8777; FAX: (310) 859-8166.
GARRICK, DALE, INTL. AGENCY, 8831 Sunset Blvd., #402, 90069; (310) 657-2661.
GEDDES AGENCY, 8457 Melrose Pl., Suite 200, 90069; (213) 651-2401; FAX: (213) 253-0901.
GERLER, STEVENS, & ASSOCIATES, 3349 Cahuenga Blvd. West, Suite 1, 90068; (213) 850-7386.
GERSH AGENCY, THE, 232 N. Canon Dr., Beverly Hills, 90210; (310) 274-6611; FAX: (310) 274-3923.
GOLD, HARRY & ASSOCIATES, 3500 W. Olive, Burbank, CA 91505; (818) 972-4300.
GORFAINE/SCHWARTZ AGENCY, 3301 Barham Blvd., #201, 90068; (213) 969-1011; FAX: (213) 969-1022.
GRAY/GOODMAN, INC., 211 S. Beverly Dr., Suite 100, Beverly Hills, 90212; (310) 276-7070; FAX: (310) 276-6049.
GREEN, IVAN, AGENCY, 8383 Wilshire Blvd., Suite 1039, Beverly Hills, CA 90211; (310) 651-5377.
GROSSMAN & ASSOCIATES, 211 S. Beverly Dr., Suite 206, 90212; (310) 550-8127
HAMILBURG AGENCY, 292 S. La Cienega, Suite 312, Beverly Hills, 90211; (310) 657-1501
HECHT, BEVERLY, AGENCY, 8949 Sunset Blvd., Suite 203, 90069; (310) 278-3544
HENDERSON/HOGAN AGENCY, 247 S. Beverly Dr., #102, Beverly Hills, CA 90212; (310) 274-7815.
INNOVATIVE ARTISTS, 1999 Ave. of the Stars, Suite 2850, 90067-6082; (310) 553-5200; FAX: (310) 557-2211.
INT'L CREATIVE MANAGEMENT, 8942 Wilshire Blvd., Beverly Hills, CA 90211; (310) 550-4000; FAX: (213) 550-4108.
INTERTALENT AGENCY, 131 S. Rodeo Dr., #300, Beverly Hills, CA 90212; (310) 858-6200.
INTERNATIONAL TALENT AGENCY, 1124 W. Angelono Ave., Suite M, Burbank, 91506; (818) 842-1204.
KELMAN/ARLETTA AGENCY, 7813 Sunset Blvd., 90046; (213) 851-8822; FAX: (213) 851-4923.
KINGSLEY COLTON & ASSOCIATES, 16661 Ventura Blvd., Suite 400, Encino, CA 91436; (818) 788-6043.
KOHNER AGENCY, 9169 Sunset Blvd., 90069; (310) 550-1060; FAX: (310) 276-1088.
KOPALOFF COMPANY, THE, 1930 Century Park West, Suite 403, 90067; (310) 203-8430; FAX: (310) 277-9513.
KRAFT AGENCY, THE, 6525 Sunset Blvd., Suite 407, 90028; (213) 962-4716; FAX: (213) 962-4903.
L.A. ARTISTS, 2566 Overland Ave., Suite 620, 90064; (310) 202-0254; FAX: (310) 836-6814.
LANE, SUSAN, 14071 Windsor Pl., Santa Ana, CA 92705; (714) 731-1420; FAX: (714) 731-5223.
LANTZ OFFICE, 9255 Sunset Blvd., #505, 90069; (310) 858-1144; FAX: (310) 858-0828.
LAZAR, IRVING PAUL, 120 El Camino Dr., Suite 206, Beverly Hills, 90212; (310) 275-6153
LEADING ARTISTS, 9560 Wilshire Blvd., Suite 500, Beverly Hills, CA 90212; (310) 273-6700; FAX: (310) 247-1111.
LIGHT, ROBERT, AGENCY, 6404 Wilshire Blvd., Suite 800, 90048; (213) 651-1777; FAX: (213) 651-4933.
LYONS/SHELDON AGENCY, 8344 Melrose Ave., Suite 20, 90069; (213) 655-5100.

MARTEL AGENCY, 1680 N. Vine St., Suite 203, 90028; (213) 461-5943; FAX: (213) 461-6350.

McHUGH AGENCY, JAMES, 8150 Beverly Blvd., 90048; (213) 651-2770.

MEDIA ARTISTS GROUP, 6255 Sunset Blvd., 90028; (213) 463-5610.

METROPOLITAN TALENT, 9320 Wilshire Blvd., Suite 300, Beverly Hills, 90212; (310) 247-5500.

MISHKIN AGENCY, 2355 Benedict Canyon Dr., Beverly Hills, CA 90210; (310) 274-5261

MORRIS, WILLIAM, 151 El Camino Dr., Beverly Hills, 90212; (310) 274-7451; FAX: (310) 859-4462.

PACIFIC ARTISTS, 515 N. LaCienega Blvd., 90048; (310) 657-5990.

PRIVILEGE TALENT AGENCY, 8344 Beverly Blvd., 2nd Floor, 90048; (213) 658-8781.

PROGRESSIVE ARTISTS AGENCY, 400 S. Beverly Dr., Suite 216, Beverly Hills, CA 90212; (310) 553-8561.

ROBERTS COMPANY, THE, 10345 W. Olympic Blvd., PH, 90064; (310) 552-7800; FAX: (310) 552-9324.

ROBINSON, WEINTRAUB, GROSS & ASSOCIATES, 8428 Melrose Place, 90069; (213) 653-5802; FAX: (213) 653-9268.

ROSENBERG, MIRIAM, 8428 Melrose Pl., Suite B, 90069; (213) 653-7383.

SANDERS AGENCY LTD., 8831 Sunset Blvd., Suite 304, 90069; (310) 652-1119; FAX: (310) 652-7810.

SCHECTER, IRV, COMPANY, 9300 Wilshire Blvd., #410, Beverly Hills, CA 90212; (310) 278-8070; FAX: (310) 278-6058.

SCHWARTZ & ASSOC., DON, 8749 Sunset Blvd., 90069; (310) 657-8910.

SELECTED ARTISTS AGENCY, 3575 Cahuega Blvd., 2nd fl., 90068; (818) 905-5744.

SHAPIRA, DAVID, ASSOCIATES, INC., 15301 Ventura Blvd., Suite 345, Sherman Oaks, CA 91403; (818) 906-0322; FAX: (818) 783-2562.

SMITH, SUSAN, & ASSOCIATES, 121 N. San Vicente Blvd., Beverly Hills, 90211; (310) 852-4777.

STE REPRESENTATION LTD., 9301 Wilshire Blvd., Suite 312, Beverly Hills, CA 90210; (310) 550-3982; FAX: (310) 550-5991.

STONE/MANNERS AGENCY, 8091 Selma Ave., 90046; (213) 654-7575.

SWANSON, H.N., 8523 Sunset Blvd., 90069; (310) 652-5385.

TANNEN & ASSOC. HERB, 1800 N. Vine St., Suite 305, 90028; (213) 466-6191; FAX: (213) 466-0863.

TOBIAS, HERB & ASSOCIATES, 1901 Ave. of the Stars, Suite 840, 90067; (310) 277-6211.

TRIAD ARTISTS, 10100 Santa Monica Blvd., 16th floor, 90067; (310) 556-2727; FAX: (310) 557-0501.

TWENTIETH CENTURY ARTISTS, 14724 Ventura Blvd., Suite 401, Sherman Oaks, 91403; (818) 788-5516.

UNITED TALENT AGENCY, 9560 Wilshire Blvd., #500, Beverly Hills, CA 90212; (310) 273-6700; FAX: (310) 247-1111.

WEBB, RUTH, ENTERPRISES, INC., 7500 De Vista Dr. 90069; (213) 874-1700; FAX: (213) 874-1860.

WRITERS & ARTISTS AGENCY, 924 Westwood Blvd., Suite 900, 90024; (310) 824-6300.

NEW YORK & EAST COAST

(For New York City area telephone code is 212.)

ABRAMS ARTISTS & ASSOCIATES, INC., 420 Madison Ave., Suite 1400, 10017; 935-8980.

ACTORS GROUP AGENCY, THE, 157 W. 57 St., Suite 211, 10019; 245-2930.

AGENCY FOR THE PERFORMING ARTS, 888 Seventh Ave., 10106; 582-1500; FAX: (212) 245-1647.

AMERICAN-INT'L TALENT 303 W. 42 St., 10036; 245-8888.

ANDERSON, BEVERLY, 1501 Broadway, 10036; 944-7773.

ASSOCIATED BOOKING CORP., 1995 Broadway, 10023; 874-2400

ASTOR, RICHARD, 1697 Broadway, 10019; 581-1970

BAUMAN, HILLER & ASSOCIATES, 250 W. 57 St., #2223, 10019; 757-0098; FAX: (212) 489-8531.

BLOOM, J. MICHAEL, & ASSOC., 233 Park Ave. S., 10003; 529-6500; FAX: (212) 529-5838.

BRESLER, KELLY, KIPPERMAN, 111 W. 57 St., #1409, 10019; 265-1980; FAX: (212) 265-2671.

COLEMAN-ROSENBERG AGCY., 210 E. 58 St., 10022; 838-0734

COOPER, BILL, ASSOCS., INC., 224 W. 49 St., #411, 10019; 307-1100

CUNNINGHAM, ESCOTT, DIPENE & ASSOCIATES, 118 E. 25 St., 6 Fl., 10010; 477-1666; FAX: (212) 979-2011.

DEACY, JANE, 181 Revolutionary Rd., Scarborough, 10510; (914) 941-1414.

DEERING, DOROTHY, LITERARY AGENCY, 1507 Oakmont Dr., Acworth, GA 30102; (404) 591-2051; FAX: (404) 591-0369.

DIAMOND ARTISTS, LTD., 119 W. 57 St., 10019; 247-3025

FLICK EAST-WEST TALENTS, INC., Carnegie Hall Studio 1110, 881 Seventh Ave., 10019; 307-1850.

GAGE GROUP, THE, 315 W. 57 St., 10019; 541-5250.

GERSH AGENCY INC., THE, 130 W. 42 St., #1804, 10036; 997-1818.

HARTIG, MICHAEL, 114 E. 28 St., #203., 10016; 684-0010

HENDERSON/HOGAN AGENCY, 405 W. 44 St., 10036; 765-5190

HUNT, DIANA, 44 W. 44 St., 10036; 391-4971

INNOVATIVE ARTISTS, 130 W. 57 St., #5B, 10019; 315-4455; FAX: (212) 315-4688.

INT'L CREATIVE MANAGEMENT, 40 W. 57 St., 10019; 556-5600

JAN J. AGENCY, 213 E. 38 St., 10016; 682-0202

KROLL, LUCY, 390 West End Ave., 10024; 877-0627

LANTZ OFFICE, 888 Seventh Ave., #2500, 10106; 586-0200.

LARNER, LIONEL LTD., 130 W. 57 St., 10019; 246-3105

LEIGH, SANFORD, ENTERPRISES, LTD., 440 E. 62 St., 10021; 752-4450

LEWIS, LESTER, ASSOC., 400 E. 52 St., 10022; 758-2480

MARTINELLI, JOHN, ATTRACTIONS, 888 Eighth Ave., 10019; 586-0963

McDERMOTT, MARGE, 216 E. 39 St., 10016; 889-1583

MORRIS AGENCY, WM., 1350 Ave. of the Americas, 10019; 586-5100

OPPENHEIM-CHRISTIE ASSOC., 13 E. 37 St., 10016; 213-4330

OSCARD, FIFI AGENCY, 19 W. 44 St., 10036; 764-1100

OSTERTAG, BARNA, 211 E. 79 St., 10021; 288-3509

PREMIER TALENT AGENCY, 3 E. 54 St., 10003; 758-4900.

RYAN, CHARLES VERNON, 1841 Broadway, 10023; 245-2225

STE REPRESENTATION LTD., 888 Seventh Ave., #201, 10019; 246-1030.

SANDERS AGENCY, LTD., THE, 1204 Broadway, 10001; 779-3737.

SCHULLER TALENT, 276 Fifth Ave., 10001; 532-6005.

SILVER, MONTY, 145 W. 45 St., 10036; 391-4545.

TALENT REPS., INC., 20 E. 53 St., 10022; 752-1835

TRIAD ARTISTS, 888 Seventh Ave., Suite 1602, 10106; 489-8100.

WATERS, BOB, AGENCY, 1501 Broadway, #705, 10036; 302-8787

WOLTERS, HANNS, 10 W. 37 St., 10018; 714-0100

WRITERS & ARTISTS AGENCY, 19 W. 44 St., #1000, 10036; 391-1112.

Advertising & Publicity Representatives

HOLLYWOOD-LOS ANGELES-BEVERLY HILLS

ABRAMS, BOB, AND ASSOCIATES, 2030 Prosser Ave., Los Angeles 90025; (310) 475-7739.

BBDO, 10960 Wilshire Blvd., # 1600, Los Angeles, 90024; (213) 879-1673.

BAKER, WINOKUR, RYDER, 9348 Civic Center Dr., 4th fl., Beverly Hills, CA 90210; (310) 278-1460; FAX: (310) 278-2571.

BARLOR ASSOCIATES, 428 N. Palm Dr., BH 90210; 278-1998.

BENDER, GOLDMAN & HELPER, 11500 W. Olympic Blvd., Suite 655, Los Angeles, CA 90064; (310) 473-4147; FAX: (310) 478-4727.

BRAVERMAN-MIRISCH, INC., 1517 Schuyler Rd., Beverly Hills, CA 90210; (310) 274-5204.

BROCATO & KELMAN, INC., 8425 W. 3rd St., Los Angeles 90048; (213) 653-9595; FAX: (213) 659-1765.

DICK BROOKS UNLIMITED, 3511 Beverly Ridge Dr., Sherman Oaks, CA 91403; (310) 273-8477.

CLEIN & WHITE, 8584 Melrose Ave., W. Hollywood 90069; (310) 659-4141; FAX: (213) 659-3995.

DANCER-FITZGERALD-SAMPLE INC., 3501 Sepulveda, Torrace 90505; (310) 214-6000.

D'ARCY, MASIUS, BENTON & BOWLES, 6500 Wilshire Blvd., Los Angeles 90048; (213) 658-4500.

DAVIDSON, DENNIS, & ASSOCS. INC., 5670 Wilshire Blvd., Los Angeles 90036; 954-5858.

DELLA FEMINA TRAVISANO & PARTNERS, 5900 Wilshire Blvd., #1900, Los Angeles 90036; 937-8540.

DENTSU, YOUNG & RUBICAM, INC., 4751 Wilshire Blvd., #203, Los Angeles 90010; (213) 930-5000.

DORN, LARRY, ASSOCS. INC., 5820 Wilshire Blvd., Suite 306, Los Angeles 90036; (213) 935-6266; FAX: (213) 935-9523.

DOUGHERTY & ASSOCS. PUBLIC RELS., 139 S. Beverly Dr., Suite 311, Beverly Hills, 90212; (310) 273-8177.

GELFOND, GORDON AND ASSOCIATES, 11500 Olympic Blvd., Suite 377, Los Angeles, CA 90064; (310) 478-3600; FAX: (213) 477-4825.

GUTTMAN & PAM LTD., 118 S. Beverly Dr., Suite 201, Beverly Hills, 90212; (310) 246-4600.

HANSON & SCHWAM, 2020 Ave. of Stars, Suite 410, Los Angeles 90067; (310) 557-1199; FAX: (310) 557-9090.

LEE & ASSOCIATES, 145 S. Fairfax Ave., Los Angeles 90036; (213) 938-3300; FAX: (213) 938-3305.

LEVINE, SCHNEIDER, PUB. REL. CO., 8730 Sunset Blvd., Los Angeles, CA 90069; (310) 659-6400; FAX: (310) 659-1309.

LEWIS & ASSOCIATES, 3600 Wilshire Blvd., # 200, Los Angeles 90010; (213) 739-1000.

McKENZIE, KING & GORDON, 1680 N. Vine St., # 710, Hollywood 90028; (213) 466-3421.

MYERS, JULIAN, PUBLIC RELATIONS, 2040 Ave. of the Stars, #410, Century City, CA 90067; (213) 557-1199; FAX: (213) 557-9090.

PMK INC., 955 Carrillo Dr., Los Angeles, 90048; (213) 954-4000.

PUBLICITY WEST, 2155 Ridgemont Dr., Los Angeles, 90046; (213) 654-3816; (818) 954-1951; FAX: (213) 654-6084.

ROGERS & COWAN, 10000 Santa Monica Blvd., Suite 400, Los Angeles, 90067; (310) 201-8800; FAX: (310) 552-0412.

RUDER, FINN, INC., 3345 Wilshire Blvd., #909, Los Angeles, CA 90010; (213) 385-5271.

SAATCHI & SAATCHI, 5757 Wilshire Blvd., Los Angeles, CA; 937-2710.

SOLTERS, ROSKIN, FRIEDMAN, INC., 5455 Wilshire Blvd., # 2200, Los Angeles, CA 90036; (213) 936-7900.

NEW YORK

(Area code is 212 unless otherwise indicated.)

AYER, N.W., INC., Worldwide Plaza, 825 Eighth Ave., 10019-7498; 474-5000; FAX: (212) 474-5400.

BACKER, SPIELVOGEL, BATES, WORLDWIDE INC., 405 Lexington Ave., 8th Fl., 10174; 297-7000.

BAKER WINOKUR RYDER, 145 Sixth Ave., 10013; 206-7160.

BATTEN, BARTON, DURSTINE & OSBORN, INC., 1285 Ave. of the Americas, 10019; 459-5000.

BENDER, GOLDMAN & HELPER, 400 Madison Ave., 10017; 371-0798.

BILLINGS, MARION, PUBLICITY LTD, 250 W. 57 St., #2420, 10107; 581-4493.

CLEIN & WHITE, 33 W. 54th St., 10019; 247-4100.

COMMUNICATIONS PLUS INC., 102 Madison Ave., So., 10016; 686-9570.

DDB NEEDHAM WORLDWIDE INC., 437 Madison Ave., 10022; 415-2000.

D'ARCY, MASIUS, BENTON & BOWLES, 1675 Broadway, 10019; 468-3622.

DAVIDSON, DENNIS, & ASSOCIATES, 1776 Broadway, 10019; 246-0500.

DAVIS, AL, PUBLICITY, 12 W. 31 St., 10001; 643-1786.

DEAN, SAMANTHA, & ASSOCS., 36 W. 44 St., 10036; 391-2675.

DELLA FEMINA, McNAMEE, WCRS, INC., 350 Hudson St., 10014; 886-4100.

EISEN, MAX, 234 W. 44 St., 10036; 391-1072.

GOODMAN, FRANK, 1776 Broadway, 10019; 246-4180.

GREY ADVERTISING AGENCY, 777 Third Ave., 10017; 546-2000.

GREY ENTERTAINMENT & MEDIA, 875 Third Ave., 10022; 303-2400.

LYNN, BRUCE, PUBLICITY, 153 Waverly Pl., 10014; 691-7515.

MARDER, JONATHAN, & ASSOCS., 108 E. 38 St., Suite 18-A, New York, NY 10016; 725-4530.

McCANN-ERICKSON, INC., 750 Third, 10017; 697-6000.

OGILVY & MATHER, 450 Park Ave. S., 10016; 951-5400.

PMK (PICKWICK, MASLANSKY, KOENIGBERG) 1776 Broadway, 10019; 582-1111.

POST, MYRNA ASSOCIATES, 145 E. 49 St., 10022; 935-7122.

ROFFMAN, RICHARD H., ASSOCIATES, 697 West End Ave., 10025; 749-3647.

ROGERS & COWAN, INC., 475 Park Ave. So., 32nd Fl., 10016; 447-9630.

RUDER, FINN INC., 301 E. 57 St. 10022; 593-6400.

SAATCHI & SAATCHI ADVERTISING, 375 Hudson St., 10014-3620; 463-2000.

SELTZER, NANCY, & ASSOCS., 1775 Broadway, 10019; 307-0117.

SOLTERS, ROSKIN, AND FREIDMAN, INC., 45 W. 34 St., 10001; 947-0515.

THOMPSON, J. WALTER, 466 Lexington Ave., 10017; 210-7000.

WANG, NORMAN & GLUCK, SOPHIE, 279 Mott St., #5-F, 10012; 758-8535.

WAX, MORTON D. PUBLIC RELATIONS, 1560 Broadway, 10019; 302-5360.

WELLS, RICH, GREENE, BDDP, INC., 9 W. 57 St., 10019; 303-5000.

WOLHANDER, JOE, ASSOCIATES, INC., 11 W. 30 St., Suite 10R, 10001; 947-6015.

YOUNG & RUBICAM INTERNATIONAL, 285 Madison Ave., 10017; 210-3000.

U.S. State and City
Film Commissions

U.S. State and City Film Commissions

ALABAMA
Michael Boyer, Alabama Film Office, 401 Adams Ave., Montgomery, AL 36130; (800) 633-5898; (205) 242-4195; FAX: (205) 242-0486.

ALASKA
Mary Pignalberi, Coordinator, Alaska Film Office, Frontier Bldg., 3601 "C" St., Suite 700, Anchorage, AK 99503; (907) 562-4163; FAX: (907) 563-3575.

ARIZONA
William E. MacCallum, Director, Arizona Film Commission, 3800 N. Central Ave., Bldg. D; Phoenix, AZ 85012; (602) 280-1380; (800) 523-6695; FAX: (602) 280-1384.

City of Phoenix
Luci Marshall, Motion Picture Coordinating Office, City of Phoenix, 251 W. Washington, Phoenix, AZ 85003; (602) 262-4850; FAX (602) 534-2295.

City of Scottsdale
Jan Horne, Film Liaison, 3939 Civic Center Blvd., Scottsdale, AZ 85251; (602) 994-2636; FAX: (602) 994-7780.

City of Tucson
Tom B. Hilderband, Executive Director, Tucson Film Office, 32 N. Stone Ave., #100, Tucson, AZ 85701; (602) 791-4000; (602) 429-1000; FAX: (602) 791-4963.

ARKANSAS
William Buck, Director, AR Motion Picture Development Office, One Capitol Mall, Suite 2C-200, Little Rock, AR 72201, (501) 682-7676; FAX: (501) 682-FILM.

CALIFORNIA
Patti Stolkin Archuletta, Director, California Film Commission, 6922 Hollywood Blvd., Suite 600, Hollywood, CA 90028; (213) 736-2465; FAX: (213) 736-3159.

City of Los Angeles
Charles M. Weisenberg, Director, Motion Picture/Television Division, 6922 Hollywood Blvd., Suite 614, Hollywood, CA 90028; (213) 461-8614; FAX: (213) 237-1020.

County of Los Angeles
Stephanie Leiner, Director, 6922 Hollywood Blvd., Suite 606, Los Angeles, CA 90028; (213) 957-1000; FAX: (213) 463-0613.

City of Oakland
Jeanie Rucker, Oakland Film Office, 505 14th St., #715, Oakland, CA 94612; (510) 238-2193; FAX: (510) 238-2227.

City of San Diego
Wally Schlotter, Director, San Diego Film Commission, 402 W. Broadway, Suite 1000, San Diego, CA 92101; (619) 234-3456; FAX: (619) 234-0571.

City of San Francisco
Lorraine Rominger, Director, San Francisco Film Commission, Office of the Mayor, City Hall, Room 200, San Francisco, CA 94102; (415) 554-6144; FAX: (415) 554-6160.

City of San Jose
Joe O'Kane, Executive Director, San Jose Film & Video Commission, 333 W. San Carlos St., Suite 1000, San Jose, CA 95110; (408) 295-9600; (800) SAN-JOSE; FAX: (408) 295-3937.

County of San Mateo
Marc Chapdelaine, San Mateo County Film Commission, Seabreeze Plaza, 111 Anza Blvd., Suite 410, Burlingame, CA 94010; (415) 348-7600; (800) 288-4748; FAX: (415) 348-7687.

Monterey County
Julie Armstrong, Director, Monterey County Film Commission, P.O. Box 111, Monterey, CA 93942-0111; (408) 646-0910; FAX: (408) 655-9244.

Sonoma County
Sheree Green-Christian, Director, Sonoma County Film/Video Commission, 5000 Roberts Lake Rd., Rohnert Park, CA 94928 (707) 584-8100; FAX: (707) 584-8111.

COLORADO
Michael Klein, Director; Colorado Motion Picture & TV Commission, 1625 Broadway, Suite 1975, Denver, CO 80202; (303) 572-5444; (800) SCO-UTUS; FAX: (303) 572-5099.

Boulder County
Shelly Helmerick, Boulder County Film Commission, P.O. Box 73, Boulder CO 80306; (303) 442-1044; (800) 444-0447; FAX: (303) 938-8837.

City of Colorado Springs
Paula Vickerman, Colorado Springs Film Commission, 30 South Nevada Ave., Suite 405, Colorado Springs, CO 80903; (719) 578-6279; FAX: (719) 578-6394.

CONNECTICUT
Tricia Hood-Paesani, Director, Connecticut Film Commission, 865 Brook St., Rocky Hill, CT 06067-3405; (203) 258-4301; FAX: (203) 529-0535.

DELAWARE
Sharon Alwine, Coordinator, Delaware Development Office; 99 Kings Highway, P.O. Box 1401, Dover, DE 19903; (800) 441-8846; (302) 739-4271; FAX: (302) 739-5749.

DISTRICT OF COLUMBIA
Crystal Palmer Brazil, Director, Mayor's Office of Motion Picture/Television Development, 717 14th St. NW, 10th fl., Washington, D.C. 20005; (202) 727-6600.

FLORIDA
Wil Plymel, Florida Film Liaison Office, , Florida Dept. of Commerce, 107 W. Gaines St., Suite 466, Tallahassee, FL 32399-2000; (904) 487-1100; FAX: (904) 922-5943.

Fort Lauderdale Area/Broward County
Elizabeth Wentworth, Director, Motion Picture & TV Office, Broward Economic Development Council, 200 E. Las Olas Blvd., Suite 1850, Fort Lauderdale, FL 33301; (305) 524-3113; FAX: (305) 524-3167.

City of Jacksonville
Todd Roobin, Jacksonville Film & TV Office, 128 E. Forsyth St., Suite 505, Jacksonville, FL 32202; (904) 630-1905; FAX: (904) 630-1485.

City of Miami
Nora Swan, Coordintor, Office of Film, Video and Recording Dept. of Development, Dupont Plaza Center, 300 Biscayne Blvd. Way, Suite 400, Miami, FL 33131; (305) 579-3366; FAX: (305) 371-9710.

Miami-Dade County
Deeny Kaplan, Director, Miami-Dade Office of Film, TV & Print, 50 S.W. 32 Rd., Bldg. 9, Miami, FL 33129; (305) 857-6666; FAX: (305) 857-6890.

Ocala/Marion County
Sue Sargent-Latham, Community Liaison, Ocala/Marion County Film Commission, Economic Development Council, 110 E. Silver Springs Blvd., Ocala, FL 34470; (904) 629-2757; FAX: (904) 629-1581.

Orlando/Central Florida
Katherine Ramsberger, Director, Orlando Film Commission, 200 E. Robinson St., Suite 600, Orlando, FL 32801-1950; (407) 422-7159; FAX: (407) 843-9514.

GEORGIA
Norman Bielowicz, Director, Georgia Film & Videotape Office, 285 Peachtree Center Avenue, N.W., Suite 1000, Atlanta, GA 30303; (404) 656-7830; FAX: (404) 651-9063.

HAWAII
Georgette T. Deemer, Manager, Hawaii Film Office, P.O. Box 2359, Honolulu, HI 96804; (808) 586-2570; FAX: (808) 586-2572.

IDAHO
Peg Owens Crist, Film Promotion, Idaho Film Bureau, 700 W. State St., 2nd floor, Boise, ID 83720-2700; (208) 334-2470; (800) 942-8338; FAX: (208) 334-2631.

ILLINOIS
Suzy Kellett, Director, Illinois Film Office, James R. Thompson Center, 100 W. Randolph, Suite 3-400, Chicago, IL 60601; (312) 814-3600; FAX: (312) 814-6732.

City of Chicago
Charles Geocaris, Director, Chicago Film Offce, One North LaSalle, Suite 2165, Chicago, IL 60602; (312) 744-6415; FAX: (312) 744-1378.

INDIANA
Jane Rulon, Director, Indiana Department of Commerce Tourism & Film Development Division, 1 N. Capitol Ave., Suite 700, Indianapolis, IN 46204-2288 (317) 232-8829; FAX: (317) 232-8995.

IOWA
Wendol Jarvis, Iowa Film Office, 200 E. Grand Ave., Des Moines, IA 50309; (800) 779-FILM; FAX:(515) 242-4859.

KANSAS
Vicky Henley, Film Commissioner; Kansas Film Commission, 700 SW Harrison St., Suite 1300, Topeka, KS 66603; (913) 296-4927; FAX: (913) 296-5055.

KENTUCKY
Russ Slone, Kentucky Film Commission, 500 Mero St., Capitol Plaza Tower, 22nd floor, Frankfort, KY 40601; (502) 564-FILM; FAX: (502) 564-7588.

LOUISIANA
George J. Steiner, Jr., Director, Louisiana Film Commission, P.O. Box 44320, Baton Rouge, LA 70804-4320; (504) 342-8150; FAX: (504) 342-7988.

City of New Orleans
Kimberly Carbo, New Orleans Film Commission, City Hall, 1300 Perdido St., Rm. 1W02, New Orleans, LA 70112; (504) 565-6580; FAX: (504) 565-6588.

MAINE
D. Lea Girardin, Director, Maine Film Office, State House Station 59, 189 State St., Augusta, ME 04333; (207) 289-5707; FAX: (207) 287-5701.

MARYLAND
Jay Schlossberg-Cohen, Director, Maryland Film Commission, 601 N. Howard St., Baltimore, MD 21201; (301) 333-6633; FAX: (301) 333-6643.

MASSACHUSETTS
Linda Peterson Warren, Director, Massachusetts Film Office, 10 Park Plaza, Suite 2310, Boston, MA 02116; (617) 973-8800; FAX: (617) 973-8810.

MICHIGAN
Janet Lockwood, Michigan Film Office, 525 W. Ottawa, P.O. Box 30004, Lansing, MI 48909; (800) 477-3456; FAX: (517) 373-3872.

MINNESOTA
Randy Adamsick, Executive Director, Minnesota Film Board, 401 N. Third St., Suite 460, Minneapolis, MN 55401; (612) 332-6493; FAX: (612) 332-3735.

MISSISSIPPI
Ward Emling, Film Officer, Mississippi State Film Office, 1200 Walter Sillers Bldg., P.O. Box 849, Jackson, MS 39205-0849; (601) 359-3297; FAX: (601) 359-2832.

City of Columbus
Carolyn Denton, Director, Columbus Film Commission, P.O. Box 789, Columbus, MS 39703; (601) 329-1191; (800) 327-2686; FAX: (601) 329-8969.

City of Natchez
Connie Taunton, Natchez Film Commission, P.O. Box 1485, Natchez, MS 39120; (601) 446-6345; (800) 647-6724; FAX: (601) 442-0814.

MISSOURI

Kate Arnold-Schuck, Manager, Missouri Film Office, Harry S. Truman Bldg., Room 290, P.O. Box 1055, Jefferson City, MO 65102; (314) 751-9050; FAX: (314) 751-5160.

MONTANA

Lonie Stimac, Director, Montana Film Office, 1424 Ninth Ave., Helena, MT 59620-0401; (406) 444-2654; (800) 553-4563; FAX: (406) 444-2808.

City of Billings

Nancy Bond, Billings Film Liaison Office, P.O. Box 31177, Billings, MT 59107; (406) 245-4111.

City of Butte

Connie Kinney, Film Commissioner, Butte Film Liaison Office, 2950 Harrison Ave., Butte, MT 59701; (406) 494-5595.

City of Great Falls and Northern Montana

Cheryl Rosales (Mittal), Great Falls Film Liaison Office, (406) 761-7877 or (406) 453-5468.

NEBRASKA

Mary Ethel Emanual, Film Office, P.O. Box 94666, Lincoln NE 68509-4666, (402) 471-2593; (800) 228-4307; FAX: (402) 471-3778.

City of Omaha/Douglas County

Julie Schrier, Kathy Sheppard, Omaha Film Commission, 1819 Farnam St., #1206, Omaha, NE 68183; (402) 444-7736; FAX: (402) 444-4187.

NEVADA

Bob Hirsch, Motion Picture Division, Nevada Economic Development Commission, 3770 Howard Hughes Pkwy., Suite 295, Las Vegas, NV 89109; (702) 486-7150 (office); (702) 791-0839 (after hours and holidays); FAX: (702) 486-7372.

NEW HAMPSHIRE

Ann Kennard, Director, New Hampshire Film and Television Bureau, Box 856, Concord, NH 03302-0856; (603) 271-2598; FAX: (603) 271-2629.

NEW JERSEY

Joe Friedman, Motion Picture and Television Commission, P.O. Box 47023, 153 Halsey St., 5th fl., Newark, NJ 07101; (201) 648-6279; FAX: (201) 648-7350.

NEW MEXICO

Linda Taylor Hutchison, Director, New Mexico Film Commission, 1050 Old Pecos Trail, Santa Fe, NM 87501; (800) 545-9871 (toll-free); (505) 827-7365 (in-state).

City of Albuquerque

Victoria Dye, Special projects, Co-ordinator, Albuquerque Film and Television Commission, Albuquerque Convention & Visitor's Bureau, P.O. Box 26866, Albuquerque, NM 87125; (505) 842-9918, (800) 733-9918; FAX: (505) 247-9101.

NEW YORK

Bruce Feinberg, Commissioner, New York State Governor's Office for Motion Picture & Television Development, Pier 62, West 23 St. & Hudson River, Room 307, New York, NY 10011; (212) 929-0240; FAX: (212) 929-0506.

City of New York

Richard Brick, Director, Mayor's Office of Film, Theatre & Broadcasting, 254 W. 54 St., 13th floor, New York, NY 10019; (212) 489-6710; FAX: (212) 307-6237.

Nassau County

Debra Markowitz, Director, Nassau County Film Office, 1550 Franklin Ave., Rm. 139, Mineola, NY 11501; (516) 571-4160; FAX: (516) 571-4161.

Suffolk County

Thomas Junor, Commissioner, Suffolk County Motion Picture & TV Commission, H. Lee Dennison Bldg., Veterans Memorial Highway, Hauppauge, NY 11788; (516) 853-4800; FAX: (516) 853-4888.

NORTH CAROLINA

William Arnold, Director, North Carolina Film Commission, 430 N. Salisbury St., Raleigh, NC 27611; (919) 733-9900; (800) 232-9227; FAX: (919) 715-0151.

NORTH DAKOTA

Jeff Eslinger, Film Commissioner, North Dakota Film Office, 604 E. Blvd., Liberty Memorial Bldg., State Capitol, Bismarck, ND 58505; (701) 224-2525; (800) 435-5663; FAX: (701) 224-4878.

OHIO

Eve Lapolla, Manager, Ohio Film Bureau, 77 S. High St., 28th Floor, Columbus, OH 43266-0101; (614) 466-2284 or (800) 848-1300; FAX: (614) 644-1789.

City of Cincinnati

Lori Holladay, Exec. Director, Greater Cincinnati Film Commission, 264 McCormick Pl., Cincinnati, OH 45219; (513) 784-1744; FAX: (513) 784-1884.

OKLAHOMA

Mary Nell Clark, Director, Oklahoma Film Office, 440 S. Houston, Room 506, Tulsa, OK 74127; (800) 766-3456; (918) 581-2660; FAX: (918) 581-2844.

OREGON

David Woolson, Executive Director, Oregon Film & Video Office, Economic Development Dept., 775 Summer, N.E., Salem, OR 97310; (503) 373-1232; FAX: (503) 581-5115.

City of Portland

Keeston Lowery, Film & Video Coordinator, Portland Film & Video Office, 1220 S.W. Fifth Ave., Room 414, Portland, OR 97204; (503) 823-4046; FAX: (503) 823-3014.

PENNSYLVANIA

T. William Hanson, Film Bureau, c/o Dept. of Commerce, Forum Bldg., Suite 449, Harrisburg, PA 17120; (717) 783-FILM (3456); FAX: (717) 234-4560.

City of Philadelphia

Sharon Pinkenson, Executive Director, Film Office, Office of the City Representative, 1650 Arch St., 19th Floor, Philadelphia, PA 19103, (215) 686-2668; FAX: (215) 686-3659.

RHODE ISLAND

Richardson Smith, Director, Rhode Island Film & TV Office, 7 Jackson Walkway, Providence, RI 02903; (401) 277-3456; FAX: (401) 277-2102.

SOUTH CAROLINA

Isabel Hill, Director, South Carolina Film Office, P.O. Box 927, Columbia, SC 29202; (803) 737-0400; FAX: (803) 737-0418.

SOUTH DAKOTA

Gary Keller, Film Office Coordinator, South Dakota Film Commission, 711 E. Wells Ave., Pierre, SD 57501-3369; (605) 773-3301; (800) 952-3625; FAX: (605) 773-3256.

TENNESSEE

Dancy L. Jones, Executive Director of the Film, Entertainment & Music Commission, Rachel Jackson Bldg., 320 Sixth Ave., N., 7th floor, Nashville, TN 37243-0790; (615) 741-3456; (800) 251-8594; FAX: (615) 741-5829.

Memphis & Shelby County

Linn Sitler, Executive Director, Memphis-Shelby Co. Film/Tape/Music Commission, Beale St., Landing, 245 Wagner Pl., Suite 4, Memphis, TN 38103-3815; (901) 527-8300; FAX: (901) 527-8326.

TEXAS

Marlene Saritzky, Executive Director, Texas Film Commission, P.O. Box 13246, Austin, TX 78711; (512) 463-9200; FAX: (512) 320-9569.

City of El Paso

Susie Gaines, El Paso Film Commission, One Civic Center Plaza, El Paso, TX 79901; (915) 534-0698; (800) 351-6024; FAX: (915) 532-2963.

City of Houston

Rick Ferguson, Director, Houston Film Commission, 801 Congress, Houston, TX 77002; (800) 365-7575; (713) 227-3100 x615; FAX: (713) 227-6336.

City of Irving

Ellen Sandoloski, Director, Irving Texas Film Commission, 6309 N. O'Connor Rd., LB119, Irving, TX 75039-3510; (800) 247-8464; (214) 869-0303; FAX: (214) 869-4609.

Dallas/Fort Worth

Roger Burke, Dallas/Fort Worth Regional Film Commission, P.O. Box 610246, DFW Airport, TX 75261; (214) 621-0400; FAX: (214) 929-0916.

UTAH

Leigh von der Esch, Executive Director, Utah Film Commission, 324 South State, Suite 500, Salt Lake City, UT 84111; (801) 538-8740; (800) 453-8824; FAX: (801) 538-8886.

City of Moab

Bette L. Stanton, Executive Director, Moab Film Commission, 59 S. Main St., Moab, UT 84532; (801) 259-6388; FAX: (801) 259-6399.

Park City

Nancy V. Kolmer, Director, Park City Film Commission, P.O. Box 1630, Park City, UT 84060; (800) 453-1360; FAX: (801) 649-4132; (801) 649-6100.

VERMONT

J. Gregory Gerdel, Director, Vermont Film Bureau, Agency of Development and Community Affairs, 134 State St., Montpelier, VT 05602-3403; (802) 828-3236; (802) 828-3230; FAX: (802) 828-3233.

VIRGINIA

Rita McClenny, Director, Virginia Film Office, 1021 E. Cary St., 12th floor, Richmond, VA 23219; (804) 371-8204; FAX: (804) 786-1121.

WASHINGTON STATE

Christine Lewis, Manager, Washington State Film & Video Office, 2001 6th Ave., Suite 2700, Seattle, WA 98121; (206) 464-7148; FAX: (206) 464-5868.

WEST VIRGINIA

Jeffrey Harpold, Director, West Virginia Film Office, 2101 Washington St. East, Charleston, WV 25305; (304) 558-2286; FAX: (304) 558-0108; (800) 225-5982.

WISCONSIN

Stanley Solheim, Film Office, Department of Development, 123 W. Washington Ave., 6th floor, Madison, WI 53707; (608) 267-FILM; FAX: (608) 266-3403.

WYOMING

Bill D. Lindstrom, Manager, Wyoming Film Office, Wyoming Travel Commission, Interstate 25 at College Dr., Cheyenne, WY 82002-0660; (800) 458-6657 or (307) 777-7851; FAX: (307) 777-6904.

City of Jackson Hole

Deborah Supowit, Director/Liaison, Jackson Hole Film Commission, P.O. Box E, Jackson, WY 83001; (307) 733-3316; FAX: (307) 733-5585.

PUERTO RICO

Puerto Rico Film Institute, P.O. Box 362350, San Juan, PR 00936-2350; (809) 758-4747, ext. 2250-2255; FAX: (809) 754-9645.

VIRGIN ISLANDS

Manny Centeno, Director, Film Promotion Office, 78 Contant 1-2-3, St. Thomas VI 00802; (809) 774-8784; (809) 775-1444; FAX: (809) 774-4390.

Government Services &

Film Distributors

* **FEDERAL GOVERNMENT FILM & MEDIA SERVICES**

* **DISTRIBUTORS OF 16mm FEATURE FILMS**

* **FILM DISTRIBUTORS IN KEY CITIES**

Federal Government Film & Media Services

(All Federal Government offices are changing phone numbers over the next few years; if you have any trouble reaching the offices listed below, contact (202) 708-8100 for further information.)

EXECUTIVE DEPARTMENTS

DEPARTMENT OF AGRICULTURE

Video and Teleconference Division, Office of Public Affairs, 1614 South Bldg., USDA, Washington, DC 20250-1300; (202) 720-6072; Larry Quinn, chief of division.
Produces video, film, and teleconference presentations for use and distribution both inside and outside of the department.
(For information on obtaining USDA productions, see *National Archives and Records Administration*, below.)

DEPARTMENT OF COMMERCE

Audiovisual Section, Office of Public Affairs, 14th St., Rm. 5521, Washington, DC 20230; (202) 482-3263; Bob Amdur, section chief.
Productions of department (by individual bureaus) videos and films are contracted out; distribution is free of charge and handled by an outside company. Contact this number for more information.
International Trade Administration, Office of Service Industries, Information Industries Division, 14th St. and Constitution Ave. room H-1114, Washington, DC 20230; (202) 482-4781; John Siegmund, Senior International Trade Specialist.
Studies and reports statistics of the industry at home and abroad; the material gathered is published in department reports along with comparative information from other industries. Also concerned with promoting the industry abroad and overcoming trade barriers.
National Telecommunications and Information Administration, Main Commerce Bldg., Washington, DC 20230; (202) 482-1840; Thomas Sugrue, Asst. Secretary for Communications and Information.
Develops telecommunications policy for executive branch; conducts technical research on various aspects of telecommunications; makes and administers grants to noncommercial public telecommunications services for construction of facilities.

DEPARTMENT OF DEFENSE

Special Assistant (Audiovisual), Office of the Assistant Secretary of Defense (Public Affairs), the Pentagon, Room 2E789, Washington, DC, 20301; (703) 695-2936; Mr. Philip M. Strub, head of division.
Acts on all requests for Department of Defense assistance from the film and television industries involved in entertainment productions and documentaries not dealing specifically with news.
Broadcast-Pictorial Branch, Office of the Assistant Secretary of Defense (Public Affairs), the Pentagon, Room 2E765, Washington, DC, 20301; (703) 695-0168; Bettie Sprigg, acting branch chief.
Provides still photographs and motion media materials to non-government electronic and print news media, news documentary producers, non-entertainment oriented producers, educational institutions, and publishers.
Federal Audiovisual Contract Management Office, 601 N. Fairfax St. Room 326, Alexandria, VA 22314-2007; (703) 274-4876; Flo Bradley, Chief of FACMO; Florence Harley, Audiovisual management specialist.
Maintains lists of qualified film and video producers; contracts throughout the federal government will only be awarded to producers who appear on these lists.
MILITARY SERVICES
Secretary of the Air Force, Office of Public Affairs, SAF/PAM, the Pentagon, Room 5C879, Washington, DC 20330-1000; (703) 697-2769.
Secretary of the Army, Media Relations Division, Army Public Affairs, the Pentagon, Room 2E641, Washington, DC 20310-1500, (703) 697-2564; Col. William L. Mulvey, chief of division.
Department of the Navy, Chief of Information, Audiovisual Entertainment, the Pentagon, Room 2E352, Washington, DC 20350-1200; (703) 697-0866; Robert Manning, director.
Headquarters, U.S. Marine Corps, Media Branch Public Affairs Division, Code PAM, Washington, DC 20380; (202) 694-1492; Lt. Col. Ronald Stokes, chief of branch.
(The above public affairs offices all have regional branches; contact the Washington addresses for more information. For U.S. Coast Guard, see Dept. of Transportation.)

DEPARTMENT OF EDUCATION

Office of Public Affairs, Audiovisual Division, 400 Maryland Ave. SW, Rm. 2089, FOB #6, Washington, DC 20202; (202) 401-1576; Greg Grayson, Audiovisual officer.
Monitors all film, video, and audio materials generated by department contracts with, or grants to, companies or non-profit organizations. Distribution of these materials is through the National Audiovisual Center (see *National Archives and Records Administration*, below) or by special arrangements with producers.

Office of Special Education and Rehabilitation Services, 400 Maryland Ave. SW, Switzer Bldg., Rm. 4629, Washington, DC, 20202; (202) 205-9172; Ernie Hairston, branch chief, captioning.
This division purchases already produced films and captions them for use by the hearing impaired; contact Mr. Hairston for a catalogue of titles.

DEPARTMENT OF ENERGY

Office of Public Affairs, 1000 Independence Ave. SW, PA5, Room 8-H068, Washington, DC 20585; (202) 586-6250; Chett Gray, Public Information Specialist.
This department contracts film and video productions to a private company.

DEPARTMENT OF HEALTH AND HUMAN SERVICES

Office of Public Affairs, 200 Independence Ave. SW, room 634E, Washington, DC, 20201; (202) 690-7850.
Produces, distributes, and contracts out video and radio productions. Each of the five branches of HHS has its own public affairs and audivisual office, listed below.
Administration for Children & Family, 370 L'Enfant Promenade SW, 6th floor, Washington, DC 20447; (202) 401-9215; David Siegel, acting director.
ACF contracts to produce videos outside of the department.
Health Care Financing Administration, 200 Independence Ave. SW, Rm. 314G, Washington, DC 20201; (202) 690-6113; Maria Friedman, acting Director of Public Affairs.
Produces, distributes, and contracts out films and tapes.
Social Security Administration, Office of Public Affairs, 4200 West High Rise, 6401 Security Blvd., Baltimore, MD 21235; (401) 965-8904.
Produces and distributes films and tapes.
U.S. Public Health Service (including *Alcohol, Drug Abuse, and Mental Health Administration, Centers for Disease Control, Food and Drug Administration, Health Resources and Services Administration, Indian Health Service, National Institutes of Health*) Office of Communications, 200 Independence Ave. SW, Rm. 719H, Washington, DC 20201; (202) 690-6867; William Grigg, Director, News Division.
Produces, distributes, and contracts out films and tapes.

DEPARTMENT OF HOUSING AND URBAN DEVELOPMENT

Office of Public Affairs, HUD Bldg., 451 7th St. SW, Rm. 10132, Washington, DC 20410; (202) 708-0980.
This department occasionally contracts outside the government for video productions.

DEPARTMENT OF THE INTERIOR

Bureau of Mines,
Audiovisual Library, Cochransmill Road, P.O. Box 18070, Pittsburgh, PA 15236; (412) 892-6845; Evelyn Donnelly, librarian (for distribution and free rental of films and tapes).
Office of Public Information, Audiovisual Programs, 2401 E St. NW, Washington, DC 20241; (202) 501-9649; William Gage, Manager of Audiovisual Programs.
The bureau maintains a library of 16mm films, ¾, and ½ inch videos depicting mining, metallurgical operations, and related manufacturing processes. One branch of the program, Mineral Resource Series, is composed of broad-based documentaries directed toward a general audience; the films are produced by independent producers and industrial concerns (they do not carry trademarks, trade names, or other direct advertising). The second branch, Technology Transfer Film Program, is produced by bureau research divisions and is directed toward industry and specialized educational programs. All films and tapes are loaned free of charge (except for return postage) to educational institutions, industries, training workers, engineering and scientific societies, and civic and business associations. Information and catalogues may be obtained from both of the above addresses.

DEPARTMENT OF JUSTICE

Audiovisual Services, 10th St. and Pennsylvania Ave., Rm. 1313, Washington, DC 20530; (202) 514-4696; Mathew White, supervisor.
Records department ceremonies and functions; no distribution.

DEPARTMENT OF LABOR

Audiovisual and Photographic Services Branch, Audiovisual Division, 200 Constitution Ave. NW, N6311, Washington, DC 20210; (202) 219-7910; Stan Hankin, Executive Producer.
Produces 16mm, 35mm, and video productions and documents department ceremonies; contracts work outside the department as well.

DEPARTMENT OF STATE

International Communications and Information Policy, Department of State, Rm. 6317, Washington, DC 20520; (202) 647-5727; Bradley P. Holmes, U.S. Coordinator and Director.

Develops, implements, and oversees international communication policy for the department; acts as a liaison for other federal agencies and the private sector in international communications issues.

Office of International Trade Control, Department of State, Rm. 3831, Washington, DC 20520; (202) 647-2325; Robert L. Price, Director.

Concerned with commercial aspects of film industry, trade treaties, restrictions, quotas, copyrights, etc; call for information on specific questions.

Office of Press Relations, Department of State, Rm. 2109-A, Washington, DC 20520; (202) 647-0874; Frances Hess, Director of Staff.

Produces video documentaries on foreign policy topics; available for free educational and public distribution through the Washington office and a number of regional centers. Contact the above address for more information and a catalogue.

DEPARTMENT OF TRANSPORTATION

Federal Highway Administration, Audiovisual and Visual Aids, 400 7th St. SW, Rm. 4429, HMS22, Washington, DC 20590; (202) 366-0481; Colonel Giles, section chief.

Produces videos and films to transportation professionals; distribution is through National Audio Visual Center (see, National Archives and Records Administration, below).

National Highway and Traffic Safety Administration, Public Affairs, Audiovisual Section, 400 7th St. SW, Rm. 5232, Washington, DC 20590; (202) 366-9550; Tina Foley, Public Affairs Specialist.

Produces and distributes videos and films; also, contracts work outside of the department.

U. S. Coast Guard, Motion Picture and Television Office, 11000 Wilshire Blvd., Los Angeles, CA 90024; (310) 575-7817, FAX: (310) 575-7851; Cmdr. John McElwain, CWO Dan Dewell, Liaison Officers.

Oversees Coast Guard involvement with Motion Picture and Entertainment Television industries. Authorizes use of Coast Guard generated film and video in entertainment products.

U.S. Coast Guard, Public Affairs, Commandant (G-CP), 2100 2nd St., SW, Washington DC 20593;

Media Relations Branch, (202) 267-1587. News media and public information office. Coordinates use of Coast Guard generated film, video and photos by the news media.

Audiovisual Branch, (202) 267-0923; Contracts out for and oversees production and distribution of internal and public information audiovisual programs. Collects and catalogs Coast Guard generated film, video, and still photos.

DEPARTMENT OF TREASURY

Office of Public Affairs, 1500 Pennsylvania Ave. NW, Rm. 3442, Washington, DC 20220; (202) 622-2960; Jack De Vore, Deputy Asst. for P.A.

Productions are made by individual bureaus within the department (such as the Internal Revenue Service). Contact this address and phone number for more information.

EXECUTIVE AGENCIES

ENVIRONMENTAL PROTECTION AGENCY

Audiovisual Division, 401 M St. SW, North Conference, Washington, DC 20460; (202) 260-6735; Edward Wallace, Director.

Produces and distributes videos and films on the environment, pollution, conservation, and related subjects; contracts some productions outside of the agency. Some distribution through the National Audiovisual Center (see, National Archives and Records Administration, below); loans are mostly free of charge (videos are dubbed on to blank tapes mailed to the division).

FEDERAL COMMUNICATIONS COMMISSION

1919 M St. NW, Washington, DC 20554; (202) 632-6600.

Regulates interstate and foreign communications by television, radio, satellite, cable, wire, and microwave. Reviews applications for construction permits and licenses for such services. Selected divisions listed below; for further information, contact *Office of Public Affairs*; (202) 632-5050; Lorrie Secrest, Director.

Engineering and Technology Bureau, (202) 632-7060; Thomas Stanley, chief engineer.

Advises FCC on all technical matters and assists in development of telecommunications policy. Reviews developments in telecommunication technology. Technical library open to the public.

Mass Media Bureau, (202) 632-6460; Roy J. Stewart, chief.

Licenses, regulates, and develops audio and video services in traditional broadcasting, cable, and emerging systems including high definition television; processes applications for licensing of commercial and non-commercial television and radio broadcast equipment and facilities; handles renewals and changes of ownership; investigates public complaints.

Cable Television Branch, (202) 632-7480; Ronald Parver, chief.

Processes applications and notifications for licensing of cable television relay service stations; registers cable television systems; develops, administer, and enforces regulation of cable TV and CARS.

FEDERAL TRADE COMMISSION

6th St. and Pennsylvania Ave. NW, Washington, DC 20580; (202) 326-2180.

Administers statutes designed to promote fair competetion; institutes proceedings to prevent unfair or deceptive practices, combinations in restraint of trade, false advertising, and illegal price discrimination. Supervises associations of exporters under the Export Trade Act. (For specific bureaus or further information, contact the *Public Affairs Office* at the above address and phone number.)

LIBRARY OF CONGRESS

Copyright Office, Madison Bldg., Rm. 403, Washington, DC 20540; (202) 707-8350; Ralph Oman, Register of Copyrights.

Registers films and videos for copyrights.

Copyright Cataloging Division, Rm. 513; (202) 707-8040; William Collins, chief of division.

Supervises the preparation of the semi-annual *Catalog of Copyright Entries: Motion Pictures and Film Strips* which is distributed by the Superintendent of Documents, Government Printing Office, Washington, DC 20402. This publication contains descriptive data for all theatrical and non-theatrical films and videos registered for copyright during each six-month period.

Motion Picture, Broadcast and Recorded Sound Division of the *Research Services Department*, Madison Bldg., Rm. 338, Washington, DC 20540; (202) 707-5840; David Francis, chief of division.

Supervises the library's collection of more than 331,000 films and videos. The collection is an archive of copyright deposits plus some gift materials. It contains 35mm, 16mm, and 3/4 inch features and television programs, and some documentary, educational, scientific, religious, and industrial productions. The collection is chiefly American, but includes German, Italian, and Japanese films. The division has an entensive film and video preservation program and houses historically important films from the early days of the industry.

NATIONAL ARCHIVES AND RECORDS ADMINISTRATION

Motion Picture Sound and Video Branch, 7th St. & Pennsylvania Ave. NW, Room 2W, Washington, DC 20408; (202) 501-5449; Jack Saunders, chief of branch.

Houses one of the world's largest audiovisual archives, including more than 120,000 films and 13,000 videos; collection includes documentaries, newreels, combat films, and raw historical footage (government productions as well as gift collections from film corporations and television networks).

National Audiovisual Center, Customer Services Section, 8700 Edgeworth Dr., Capitol Heights, MD 20743-3701; (301) 763-1896; Mike Rusnak, director.

Holds relatively current collection of over 8,500 U.S. government audiovisual productions for sale and rental (available in all formats). Distributes the collections of many government departments and agencies, in addition to those specifically noted above.

Presidential Libraries Central Office, 7th St. & Pennsylvania Ave. NW, Washington, DC 20408; (202) 501-5700; John Fawcett, Director.

The eight presidential libraries, located throughout the country, can be reached from this office. Each library has extensive audiovisual materials relevant to that administration; the collection begins with President Hoover.

NATIONAL ENDOWMENT FOR THE ARTS

Media Arts Program: Film/Radio/Television, 1100 Pennsylvania Ave. NW, Washington, DC 20506; (202) 682-5452; Brian O'Doherty, director.

Provides grants to individuals and non-profit organizations for film, video, and radio productions; supports arts programming for public television and radio.

NATIONAL ENDOWMENT FOR THE HUMANITIES

Humanities Projects in Media, 1100 Pennsylvania Ave. NW, Washington, DC 20506; (202) 606-8278; James Dougherty, director.

Provides grants for non-profit media projects aimed at advancing the use and understanding of the humanities.

SECURITIES AND EXCHANGE COMMISSION

Division of Corporation Finance, 450 5th St. NW, Washington, DC 20549.

Reviews financial statements and disclosures.

Radio, Television, and Telegraph, Rm. 3113; (202) 272-2683; H. Christopher Owings, Asst., Director.

Motion Pictures, Rm. 3134; (202) 272-3275; James Daly, Asst. Director.

(For further information concerning registration of security offerings and supervision of trading, contact *Public Affairs*, (202) 272-2650.

SMITHSONIAN INSTITUTION

Film Archives, Archives Division, National Air and Space Museum, Washington, DC 20560; (202) 357-3133; Mark Taylor, Film Archivist.

Houses about 10,000 films and videos from Smithsonian, government, other museums, and industry collections.

Telecommunications Office, National Museum of American History, Rm. BB40, Washington, DC 20560; (202) 357-2984; Paul Johnson, Director.

Produces films and videos which are distributed for a fee through a private company. Contact this office for more information.

(Other museums and galleries have small archive collections; contact the *Office of Public Affairs* for more information, (202) 357-2627.)

U.S. INFORMATION AGENCY

Television and Film Service, 601 D St. NW, Rm. 5000, Washington, DC 20547; (202) 501-7806; Wm. Aemes, acting director.

USIA produces and acquires about 200 film and television documentaries annually for information and cultural programs in 117 countries. In addition, close to 350 targeted, and 150 worldwide news clips are made for use on foreign television. These are seen abroad in commercial theatres, on television, in schools and community centers, and by clubs, universities, and other audiences. Television and Film Service also certifies the exemption of import duties if a film is educational.

U.S. INTERNATIONAL TRADE COMMISSION

Office of the Secretary, 500 E Street, Rm. 112, Washington, DC 20436; (202) 205-2000; Paul Bardos, acting Secretary.

Conducts countervailing duty, anti-dumping, and patent and trademark infringement investigations; the commission is a fact-finding body which addresses business complaints, holds hearings, and makes recommendations to the Department of Commerce.

Distributors of 16mm Feature Films

Following is a listing of distributors having substantial selections of 16mm films for lease or rental. Additionally, some of the companies may have prints available for outright purchase. Inquiries for catalogs listing complete product should be made to the addresses given below.

BENCHMARK FILMS
145 Scarborough Road, Briarcliff Manor, NY 10510; (914) 762-3838.

BIOGRAPH ENTERTAINMENT
2 Depot Plaza; #202-B, Bedford Hills, NY 10507; (914) 242-9838.

BUDGET FILMS
4590 Santa Monica Blvd., Los Angeles, CA 90029; (213) 660-0187.

BUENA VISTA PICTURES DISTRIBUTION—NON-THEATRICAL
3900 West Alameda Avenue, Suite 2400, Burbank, CA 91521-0021; (818) 567-5058.

CAPITOL ENTERTAINMENT
4818 Yuma St. NW, Washington, DC 20016; (202) 363-8800.

CAROUSEL FILM, INC.
260 5th Ave., room 705, New York, NY 10001; (212) 683-1660.

CINECOM PICTURES
850 Third Ave., New York, NY 10022; (212) 319-5000.

CINEMA GUILD
1697 Broadway, New York, NY 10019; (212) 246-5522.

CIRCLE RELEASING
2445 M St., Suite 225, Washington, DC 20037; (202) 429-9044.

COLUMBIA CLASSICS
10202 West Washington Blvd., Suite 2119, Culver City, CA 90232; (310) 280-4485.

CORINTH FILMS
34 Gansevoort St., New York, NY 10014; (212) 463-0305.

DIRECT CINEMA
P.O. Box 10003, Santa Monica, CA 90410; (310) 369-4774.

EM GEE FILM LIBRARY
6924 Canby Ave., Suite 103, Reseda, CA 91335; (818) 981-5506, 881-8110.

FILM-MAKERS COOPERATIVE
175 Lexington Ave., New York, NY 10016; (212) 889-3820.

FILMS INCORPORATED
5547 N. Ravenswood Ave., Chicago, IL 60640; (312) 878-2600.

FIRST RUN/ICARUS
153 Waverly Place, New York, NY 10004; (212) 243-0600.

GOLDWYN, SAMUEL, COMPANY
10203 Santa Monica Blvd., Los Angeles, CA 90067; (310) 552-2255.

HURLOCK CINE-WORLD, INC.
P.O. Box 34619, Juneau, AK 99803; (907) 789-3995.

IFEX FILMS/INTERNATIONAL FILM EXCHANGE LTD.
201 W. 52nd St., New York, NY 10019; (212) 582-4318.

INTERAMA
301 W. 53rd St., Suite 19E, New York, NY 10019; (212) 977-4836.

IVY FILMS
725 Providence Rd., #204, Charlotte, NC 28207; (704) 333-3991.

KINO INTERNATIONAL
333 W. 39th St., Suite 503, New York, NY 10018; (212) 629-6880.

KIT PARKER FILMS
P.O. Box 16022, Monterey, CA 93942; (408) 649-5573.

MANBECK PICTURES CORP.
3621 Wakonda Dr., Des Moines, IA 50321; (515) 285-1166.

MODERN SOUND
1402 Howard St., Omaha, NE 68102; (402) 341-8476.

MUSEUM OF MODERN ART FILM LIBRARY
11 W. 53rd St., New York, NY 10019; (212) 708-9433.

NEW LINE CINEMA
888 Seventh Ave., New York, NY 10106; (212) 649-4900.

NEW YORKER FILMS
16 W. 61st St., New York, NY 10023; (212) 247-6110.

PYRAMID FILMS
2801 Colorado Ave., Santa Monica, CA 90404; (310) 828-7577, (800) 421-2304.

REPUBLIC PICTURES CORPORATION
12636 Beatrice St., Los Angeles, CA 90066; (310) 306-4040.

SWANK MOTION PICTURES
201 S. Jefferson Ave., St. Louis, MO 63103; (314) 534-6300.

THIRD WORLD NEWSREEL
335 W. 38th St., New York, NY 10018; (212) 947-9277 (feature documentaries and short fiction).

TRANS-WORLD FILMS
332 S. Michigan Ave., Chicago, IL 60604; (312) 922-1530.

Film Distributors in Key Cities

ATLANTA

Buena Vista Distribution Co., 1190 W. Druid Hill Dr., Suite T-75, 30329; (404) 634-6525. Rod Rodriguez, Div. mgr.
MGM/UA Distribution Co., 2957 Clairmont Road NE, #280, 30329; (404) 325-3470. Larry Terrell, SE reg. director.
New Line Cinema Corp., 4501 Circle 75 Parkway NW, 30339; (404) 952-0056.
Paramount Film Distributing Corp., 7000 Century Parkway, #1340, 30328; (404) 399-6121.
Triumph Releasing Corp., 3100 Breckinridge Blvd., #135, Duluth, GA 30136; (404) 564-8521. Judith Marsh, managing dir.
Twentieth Century-Fox Film Corp., 2635 Century Parkway, N.E., 30345; (404) 321-1178. Larry Jameson, Branch Mgr.
Universal Film Exchange, 6060 McDonough Dr., Norcross GA 30093; (404) 448-8032. Curtis Fainn, Mgr.
Warner Bros., 2970 Clairmont Rd., 30329; (404) 325-0301. Barry Nelson, Branch Mgr.

BOSTON

Buena Vista Distribution Co., 990 Washington St., Dedham, MA, 02026; (617) 461-0870. John Molson, Branch Mgr.
Cine Research Assoc., 32 Fisher Avenue, Roxbury, 02161; (617) 442-9756.
Cinema Booking Service of New England, PO Box 827, Needham, 02191; (617) 986-2122.
Cinema Film Consultants Inc., PO Box 331, 02199; (617) 437-7050.
Lockwood & McKinnon, Film Corp., 45 Walpole St., Norwood 02062; (617) 769-8900.
Natl. Film Service Operating Corp., 20-30 Freeport Way, Dorchester 02122; (617) 288-1600.
Paramount Film Distributing Corp., Parking Way Bldg., 10 Granite St., Quincy, 02169-9134; (617) 773-3100. Joe Rathgab.
Triumph Releasing Corp., 20 Park Plaza, #905, 02116; (617) 426-8980. John Monahan, man. dir.
Universal Film Exchanges, Inc., 44 Winchester St., 02116; (617) 426-8760. Joan Corrado.
Warner Bros. Pictures Dist. Corp., 45 Braintree Hill, Office P/C 301, 02184; (617) 848-2550. Andrew Silverman, Branch Mgr.
Zipporah Films, 1 Richdale Ave. #4, Cambridge, 02140; (617) 576-3603.

CHARLOTTE

Carolina Booking Service, 230 S. Tryon St., 28202; (704) 377-9341.
Carolina Film Service Inc., 522 Penman St., 28203; (704) 333-2115.

CHICAGO

Beacon Films, 930 Pitner Ave., Evanston, IL 60202; (800) 323-5448.
Buena Vista Distribution Co. Inc. 9700 Higgins Rd., Suite 550, Rosemont, 60018; (708) 696-0900. Rick Rice, Div. mgr.
MGM/UA Distribution Co., 6133 River Rd., Suite 900, Rosemont, 60018; (708) 518-0500.
Paramount Film Distributing Co., 8750 W. Bryn Mawr Ave., 60631; (312) 380-4560. Bob Weiss.
Triumph Releasing, 2800 River Rd., #230, Des Plaines, IL 60018; (708) 298-9080.
Twentieth Century Fox Film Corp., 1100 Woodfield Rd., Schaumburg, IL, 60173; (708) 706-9240. Bert Livingston, Div. mgr.
Warner Bros. Dist. Corp., 1111 East Touhy Ave., Des Plaines, IL 60018; (708) 296-5070. Floyd Brethour, Div. mgr.

CINCINNATI

C. J. Ruff Film Distributing Co., 1601 Harrison Ave., 45214; (513) 921-8200.

DALLAS

Buena Vista Distribution, 10300 N. Central Expressway, 75206; (214) 363-9494. Jim Nocella, Div. mgr.
Crump Distributors, Inc. 6545 Lange Circle, 75214; (214) 826-6331. Jim Crump.
MGM/UA Distribution Co., 3 Forest Plaza, 12221 Merit Drive, #1610, 75251; (214) 387-1500. Jeffrey Kaufman, SW Reg. Director.

Orion Pictures Distribution Corp., 7557 Rambler Rd., 75231; (214) 363-7600. Redmond Gautier, Div. mgr.
Paramount Film Distributing Corp., 12222 Merit Dr., Suite 840, 75251; (214) 387-4400.
Taurus Ent., 1900 S. Central Expressway, 75215; (214) 421-1900. Sara Murray, mgr.
Triumph Releasing Corp., 12770 Merit Dr., #702, 75251; (214) 770-4220.
Twentieth Century Fox Film Corp., 12222 Merit Dr., 75251; (214) 233-4571. Richard King, Div. mgr.
Universal Film Exchanges, Inc., 7502 Greenville Ave., 75231; (214) 360-0022.
Warner Bros. Distributing Corp., 8144 Walnut Hill Lane 920, 75231; (214) 691-6101. Bob Motley, Div. mgr.

DENVER

Crest Distributing Co., 1443 Larimer, 80202; (303) 571-5569.

DETROIT

DRD Distributors, 14830 Fenkell Ave., 48227; (313) 838-6006.
Natl. Film Service Operating Corp., 6111 Concord St., 48211; (313) 923-2150.

HONOLULU, HI

Pacific Motion Picture Co. Ltd., 470 N. Nimitz Hwy., 96817; (808) 531-1117.

JACKSONVILLE, FL

Clark Film Releasing, 905 North St., 32211; (904) 721-2122. Harry Clark, pres. Belton Clark, vp.

KANSAS CITY, MO

Midwest Films, 3859 W. 95th St., Shawnee Mission, KS 66206; (913) 381-2058. Gene Irwin.

LOS ANGELES

Seymour Borde Associates, 1800 N. Highland Ave., Hollywood, CA 90028; (213) 461-3936.
Buena Vista Dist. Co. Inc., 3900 W. Alameda Ave., Suite 2431, Burbank, 91521-0021; (818) 567-5000. Pat Pade, Div. mgr.
Cori Films International, 2049 Century Park E., #780, 90067; (310) 557-0173.
Crest Film Distributors, 116 N. Robertson Blvd., 90052; (310) 652-8844. J. Persell.
Crown International Pictures, 8701 Wilshire Blvd., B.H. 90211; (310) 657-6700.
MGM/UA Distribution Co., 11111 Santa Monica Blvd., 90025; (213) 444-1500. Corky Lewin, L.A. Reg. VP.
Orion Pictures Distribution Corp., 1888 Century Park E., Suite 416, Century City, 90067; (310) 282-0550.
Paramount Film Dist. Corp., 15260 Ventura Blvd., Suite 1140, Sherman Oaks, 91403; (818) 789-2900.
Toho Co. Ltd., 2049 Century Park E., 90067; (310) 277-1081.
Triumph Releasing Corp., 8671 Wilshire Blvd., 6th Fl., Beverly Hills, CA 90211; (310) 657-6410. Roger Cels, managing dir.
Twentieth Century Fox Film Corp., 15250 Ventura Blvd., Sherman Oaks, CA 91403; (818) 995-7750.
Universal Film Exchange, 8901 Beverly Blvd., 90048; (310) 550-7461.
Warner Bros. Pictures Distribution Corp., 15821 Ventura Blvd., #685, Encino, 91436; (818) 784-7494. Shirley Becker, Div. mgr.

NEW YORK

Bedford Entertainment, 101 W. 57th St., 10019; (212) 265-0680.
Buena Vista Distribution Co., 500 Park Ave., 10022; (212) 735-5421. Phil Fortune, Div. mgr.
Cinecom Entertainment, 850 Third Ave., 10022; (212) 319-5000.
Cinevista Releasing, 560 W. 43 St., 10036; (212) 947-4373.
First Run Features, 153 Waverly Place, 10011; (212) 243-0600.
Grange Communications, Inc., 45 W. 60 St., 10023; (212) 582-4261.
Gray City, Inc., 853 Broadway, 10001; (212) 473-3600.

Independent International Pictures Corp., 223 State Hwy. #18, East Brunswick, NJ 08816; (201) 249-8982.

Independent Feature Project, 132 W. 21 St., 10019; (212) 245-1622.

Italtoons Corp., 32 W. 40 St., 10018; (212) 730-0280.

MGM Distribution Co., 1350 Ave. of the Americas, 10019; (212) 708-0393. Bob Burke, NY Reg. VP.

Marvin Films, Inc., 1400 Old Country Road, Westbury, NY 11590; (516) 338-4488.

Miramax Films, 375 Greenwich St., 10013; (212) 941-3800.

Orion Pictures Distribution Corp., 304 Park Ave. S., 10010; (212) 505-0051.

Paramount Film Distributing Corp., 15 Columbus Circle, 10023; (212) 373-8000. Pam Pritzker.

Promovision International Films, Ltd., 560 W. 43 St., 10036; (212) 947-4373.

Taurus Entertainment, 113 Middle Neck Rd., Great Neck, NY 11021; (516) 829-1520.

Third World Newsreel, 335 W. 38 St., 10018; (212) 947-9277.

Toho International, 1501 Broadway, 10036; (212) 391-9058.

Triumph Releasing Corp., 711 Fifth Avenue, 10022; (212) 751-4400.

Twentieth Century Fox Film Corp., 1211 Ave. of the Americas, 3rd Fl., 10036; (212) 556-2490.

Universal Film Exchange, 445 Park Ave., 10022; (212) 759-7500. Gary Rocco, mgr.

Warner Bros. Distributing Corporation, 75 Rockefeller Plaza, 14th floor, 10019; (212) 484-6203. Robert Miller, Div. mgr.

PHILADELPHIA

Triumph Releasing Corp., 1617 John F. Kennedy Blvd., #800, 19103; (215) 568-3889; Joe Saladino, managing dir.

PITTSBURGH

Paramount Film Distributing Corp., Fulton Bldg., 107 6th St., 15222; (412) 281-9270. Kay Grotto, mgr.

SEATTLE

MGM Distribution Co., 225 108th Ave., N.E. Bellevue, WA 98004; (206) 453-1172. S. Amato, NW Sr. Sales mgr.

Northwest Diversified Entertainment, 2819 First, 98121; (206) 441-5380.

Seattle National Film Service, 900 Maynard S., 98134; (206) 682-6685.

WASHINGTON, DC

Key Theatre Ent., 1325½ Wisconsin Ave., N.W., 20007; (202) 965-4401. David Levy.

Warner Bros. Dist. Corp., 1700 Rockville Pike, Rockville, MD 20852; (301) 230-1324. Daniel Chinich, Branch Mgr.

Pictures

*   CREDITS FOR FEATURE FILMS,
     SEPTEMBER, 1992–AUGUST, 1993

CREDITS FOR FEATURE FILMS

September, 1992–August, 1993

The Adventures of Huck Finn ... Buena Vista

A Buena Vista Pictures release of a Walt Disney Pictures presentation of a Laurence Mark production. Producer: Mark. Executive Producers: Barry Bernardi, Steve White. Co-Producer: John Baldecchi. Director-Screenplay: Stephen Sommers, based on the novel "The Adventures of Huckleberry Finn" by Mark Twain. Cinematography: Janusz Kaminski. Music: Bill Conti. Editor: Bob Ducsay. In Technicolor. Running time: 106 minutes. MPAA Rating: PG. Release date: April 2, 1993.

Players: Elijah Wood, Courtney B. Vance, Jason Robards, Robbie Coltrane, Ron Perlman, Dana Ivey, Anne Heche, James Gammon, Paxton Whitehead, Tom Aldredge, Laura Bundy, Curtis Armstrong, Mary Louise Wilson, Frances Conroy, Daniel Tamberelli, Denman Anderson, Mickey Cassidy, Alex Zuckerman, Leon Russom.

Aladdin .... Buena Vista

A Buena Vista Pictures release of a Walt Disney Pictures presentation. Producers-Directors: John Musker, Ron Clements. Screenplay: Clements, Musker, Ted Elliott, Terry Rossio. Songs: Alan Menken, Howard Ashman, Tim Rice. Music: Menken. Editor: H. Lee Patterson. In Technicolor. Running time: 90 minutes. MPAA Rating: G. Release date: November 11, 1992.

Voice Cast: Scott Weinger, Robin Williams, Linda Larkin, Jonathan Freeman, Frank Welker, Gilbert Gottfried, Douglas Seale, Brad Kane, Lea Salonga.

Alive .... Buena Vista

A Buena Vista Pictures release of a Touchstone Pictures and Paramount Pictures presentation of a Kennedy/Marshall production. Producers: Robert Watts, Kathleen Kennedy. Co-Producer: Bruce Cohen. Director: Frank Marshall. Screenplay: John Patrick Shanley, based on the book by Piers Paul Read. Cinematography: Peter James. Music: James Newton Howard. Editors: Michael Kahn, William Goldenberg. In Technicolor. Running time: 126 minutes. MPAA Rating: R. Release date: January 15, 1993.

Players: Ethan Hawke, Josh Hamilton, Vincent Spano, Bruce Ramsay, John Haymes Newton, David Kriegel, Kevin Breznahan, Sam Behrens, Illeana Douglas, Jack Noseworthy, Christian Meoli, Jake Carpenter, Michael De Lorenzo, Jose Zuniga, Danny Nucci, Ele Keats, David Cubitt, Gian Di Donna, John Cassini.

Amos & Andrew .... Columbia

A Columbia Pictures release of a Castle Rock Entertainment in association with New Line Cinema presentation. Producer: Gary Goetzman. Co-Producers: Jack Cummins, Marshall Persinger. Director-Screenplay: E. Max Frye. Cinematography: Walt Lloyd. Music: Richard Gibbs. Editor: Jane Kurson. In Technicolor. Running time: 92 minutes. MPAA Rating: PG-13. Release date: March 5, 1993.

Players: Nicolas Cage, Samuel L. Jackson, Michael Lerner, Dabney Coleman, Margaret Colin, Brad Dourif, Chelcie Ross, I.M. Hobson, Jeff Blumenkrantz, Jodi Long, Todd Weeks, Giancarlo Esposito, Ron Taylor, Loretta Devine, Bob Balaban, Tracey Walter.

Another Stakeout .... Buena Vista

A Buena Vista release of a Touchstone Pictures presentation. Producers: Jim Kouf, Cathleen Summers, Lynn Bigelow. Executive Producer-Director: John Badham. Screenplay: Kouf, based on his characters. Cinematography: Roy H. Wagner. Music: Arthur B. Rubinstein. Editor: Frank Morris. In Technicolor. Running time: 109 minutes. MPAA Rating: PG-13. Release date: July 23, 1993.

Players: Richard Dreyfuss, Emilio Estevez, Rosie O'Donnell, Dennis Farina, Marcia Strassman, Cathy Moriarty, John Rubinstein, Miguel Ferrer, Sharon Maughan, Madeleine Stowe, Dan Lauria.

Army of Darkness .... Universal

A Universal Pictures release of a Dino De Laurentiis presentation of a Renaissance Pictures production. Producer: Robert Tapert. Co-Pro-

ducers: Bruce Campbell, Introvision International. Director: Sam Raimi. Screenplay: Sam Raimi, Ivan Raimi. Cinematography: Bill Pope. Music: Joseph LoDuca, Danny Elfman. Editor: Bob Murawski, R.O.C. Sandstorm. In Deluxe color. Running time: 77 minutes. MPAA Rating: R. Release date: February 26, 1993.

Players: Bruce Campbell, Embeth Davidtz, Marcus Gilbert, Ian Abercrombie, Richard Grove, Michael Earl Reid, Timothy Patrick Quill, Bridget Fonda, Patricia Tallman, Theodore Raimi.

Aspen Extreme .... Buena Vista

A Buena Vista Pictures release of a Hollywood Pictures presentation, in association with Touchwood Pacific Partners I, of a Leonard Goldberg production. Executive Producer: Fred T. Gallo. Producer: Goldberg. Director-Screenplay: Patrick Hasburg. Cinematography: Steven Fierberg. Music: Michael Convertino. Editor: Steven Kemper. In Technicolor. Running time: 117 minutes. MPAA Rating: PG-13. Release date: January 22, 1993.

Players: Paul Gross, Peter Berg, Finola Hughes, Teri Polo, William Russ, Trevor Eve, Martin Kemp, Stewart Finley-McLennan, William McNamara, Nicolette Scorsese.

Benny & Joon .... MGM

A Metro-Goldwyn-Mayer release of a Roth/Arnold production. Producers: Susan Arnold, Donna Roth. Executive Producer: Bill Badalato. Director: Jeremiah Chechik. Screenplay: Barry Berman. Story: Berman, Leslie McNeil. Cinematography: John Schwartzman. Music: Rachel Portman. Editor: Carol Littleton. In Deluxe color. Running time: 100 minutes. MPAA Rating: PG. Release date: April 16, 1993.

Players: Johnny Depp, Mary Stuart Masterson, Aidan Quinn, Julianne Moore, Oliver Platt, C.C.H. Pounder, Dan Hedaya, Joe Grifasi, William H. Macy, Liane Alexandra Curtis, Eileen Ryan, Don Hamilton, Waldo Larson.

Best of the Best 2 .... 20th Century Fox

A 20th Century Fox release presented by The Movie Group. Executive Producers: Frank Giustra, Peter E. Strauss. Producers: Strauss, Phillip Rhee. Director: Robert Radler. Screenplay: Max Strom, John Allen Nelson, based on characters created by Paul Levine. Cinematography: Fred Tammes. Music: David Michael Frank. Editor: Bert Lovitt. In Deluxe color. Running time: 100 minutes. MPAA Rating: R. Release date: March 5, 1993.

Players: Eric Roberts, Phillip Rhee, Christopher Penn, Edan Gross, Ralph Moeller, Meg Foster, Sonny Landham, Wayne Newton, Betty Carvalho, Simon Rhee, Claire Stansfield.

Bob Roberts .... Paramount

A Paramount Pictures release with Miramax Films of a Polygram/Working Title Production in association with Barry Levinson and Mark Johnson and Live Entertainment. Producer: Forrest Murray. Executive Producers: Ronna Wallace, Paul Webster, Tim Bevan. Director-Screenplay: Tim Robbins. Cinematography: Jean Lepine. Music: David Robbins. Songs: David Robbins, Tim Robbins. Editor: Lisa Churgin. In Technicolor. Running time: 102 minutes. MPAA Rating: R. Release date: September 4, 1992.

Players: Tim Robbins, Giancarlo Esposito, Ray Wise, Rebecca Jenkins, Harry J. Lenix, John Ottavino, Robert Stanton, Alan Rickman, Gore Vidal, Brian Murray, Jack Black, Matt McGrath, James Spader, Pamela Reed, Helen Hunt, Peter Gallagher, Lynne Thigpen, Kelly Willis, Anita Gillette, Susan Sarandon, Fred Ward, Fisher Stevens, Gil Robbins, John Cusack, Bob Balaban, June Stein, Allan Nicholls, Robert Hegyes, David Strathairn, Ann Talman.

Body of Evidence .... MGM

An MGM release of a Dino De Laurentiis Communications production. Executive Producers: Stephen Deutsch, Melinda Jason. Producer: De Laurentiis. Director: Uli Edel. Screenplay: Brad Mirman.

423

Cinematography: Doug Milsome. Music: Graeme Revell. Editor: Thom Noble. In Deluxe color. Running time: 99 minutes. MPAA Rating: R. Release date: January 15, 1993.

Players: Madonna, Willem Dafoe, Joe Mantegna, Anne Archer, Julianne Moore, Jurgen Prochnow, Frank Langella, Stan Shaw, Charles Hallahan, Lillian Lehman, Mark Rolston, Jeff Perry, Richard Riehle.

The Bodyguard .... Warner Bros.

A Warner Bros. release of a TIG Production in association with Kasdan Pictures. Producers: Lawrence Kasdan, Jim Wilson, Kevin Costner. Director: Mick Jackson. Screenplay: Kasdan. Cinematography: Andrew Dunn. Music: Alan Silvestri. Editor: Richard A. Harris. In Technicolor. Running time: 130 minutes. MPAA Rating: R. Release date: November 25, 1992.

Players: Kevin Costner, Whitney Houston, Gary Kemp, Bill Cobbs, Ralph Waite, Tomas Arana, Michele Lamar Richards, Mike Starr, Christopher Birt, DeVaughn Nixon, Gerry Bamman, Joe Urla, Robert Wuhl, Charles Keating, Debbie Reynolds, Bert Remsen, Ethel Ayler.

Born Yesterday .... Buena Vista

A Buena Vista Pictures release of a Hollywood Pictures presentation in association with Touchwood Pacific Partners I of a D. Constantine Conte production. Producer: Conte. Executive Producer: Stratton Leopold. Director: Luis Mandoki. Screenplay: Douglas McGrath, based on the play by Garson Kanin. Cinematography: Lajos Koltai. Music: George Fenton. Editor: Lesley Walker. In Technicolor. Running time: 101 minutes. MPAA Rating: PG. Release date: March 26, 1993.

Players: Melanie Griffith, John Goodman, Don Johnson, Edward Herrmann, Max Perlich, Michael Ensign, Benjamin C. Bradlee, Sally Quinn, William Frankfather, Fred Dalton Thompson, Celeste Yarnall, Nora Dunn, Meg Wittner, William Forward, Ted Raimi, Rondi Reed, Mary Gordon Murray, Matthew Faison, Kate McGregor-Stewart.

Bound By Honor
(Blood In Blood Out) .... Buena Vista

A Buena Vista release of a Hollywood Pictures presentation in association with Touchwood Pacific Partners I. Executive Producers: Jimmy Santiago Baca, Stratton Leopold. Producers: Taylor Hackford, Jerry Gershwin. Director: Hackford. Screenplay: Baca, Jeremy Iacone, Floyd Mutrux. Story: Ross Thomas. Cinematography: Gabriel Beristain. Music: Bill Conti. Editors: Fredric Steinkamp, Karl F. Steinkamp. In Deluxe color. Running time: 174 minutes. MPAA Rating: R. Release date: January 15, 1993.

Players: Damian Chapa, Jesse Borrego, Benjamin Bratt, Enrique Castillo, Victor Rivers, Delroy Lindo, Tom Towles, Carlos Carrarsco, Teddy Wilson, Raymond Cruz, Valente Rodriguez, Lanny Flaherty.

Bram Stoker's Dracula .... Columbia

A Columbia Pictures release of an American Zoetrope/Osiris Films production. Producers: Francis Ford Coppola, Fred Fuchs, Charles Mulvehill. Executive Producers: Michael Apted, Robert O'Connor. Director: Coppola. Screenplay: James V. Hart, based on the novel by Bram Stoker. Cinematography: Michael Ballhaus. Music: Wojciech Kilar. Editors: Nichoals C. Smith, Glen Scantlebury, Anne Goursaud. In Technicolor. Running time: 127 minutes. MPAA Rating: R. Release date: November 13, 1992.

Players: Gary Oldman, Winona Ryder, Anthony Hopkins, Cary Elwes, Keanu Reeves, Richard E. Grant, Bill Campbell, Sadie Frost, Tom Waits, Monica Bellucci, Michaela Bercu, Florina Kendrick, Jay Robinson, I.M. Hobson, Laurie Franks.

Candyman .... TriStar

A TriStar Pictures release in association with Polygram Filmed Entertainment of a Propaganda Films production. Producers: Steve Golin, Sigurjon Sighvatsson, Alan Poul. Executive Producer: Clive Barker. Director-Screenplay: Bernard Rose. Cinematography: Anthony B. Richmond. Music: Philip Glass. Editor: Dan Rae. In Deluxe color. Running time: 101 minutes. MPAA Rating: R. Release date: October 16, 1992.

Players: Virginia Madsen, Tony Todd, Xander Berkeley, Kasi Lemmons, Vanessa Williams, DeJuan Guy, Marianna Eliott, Ted Raimi, Ria Pavia, Mark Daniels, Lisa Ann Poggi.

Captain Ron .... Buena Vista

A Touchstone Pictures release in association with Touchwood Pacific Partners I of a David Permut production. Producers: Permut, Paige Simpson. Executive Producer: Ralph Winter. Director: Thom

---

Eberhardt. Screenplay: John Dwyer, Eberhardt. Story: Dwyer. Cinematography: Daryn Okada. Music: Nicholas Pike. Editor: Tina Hirsch. In Technicolor. Running time: 104 minutes. MPAA Rating: PG-13. Release date: September 18, 1992.

Players: Kurt Russell, Martin Short, Mary Kay Place, Benjamin Salisbury, Meadow Sisto, Emmanuel Logrono, Jorge Luis Ramos, J.A. Preston, Tanya Soler, Raul Estela, Dan Butler, Tom McGowan, Paul Anka, Jainardo Batista.

CB4 .... Universal

A Universal Pictures release of a Brian Grazer/Sean Daniel production. Executive Producers: Daniel, Grazer. Producer: Nelson George. Director: Tamra Davis. Screenplay: Chris Rock, George, Robert LoCash. Story: Rock, George. Cinematography: Karl Walter Lindenlaub. Music: John Barnes. Editor: Earl Watson. In Deluxe color. Running time: 86 minutes. MPAA Rating: R. Release date: March 12, 1993.

Players: Chris Rock, Allen Payne, Deezer D, Chris Elliott, Phil Hartman, Charlie Murphy, Khandi Alexander, Arthur Evans, Theresa Randle, Willard E. Pugh, Ice T, Ice Cube, Richard Gant, Stoney Jackson, La-Wanda Page.

The Cemetery Club .... Buena Vista

A Buena Vista release of a Touchstone Pictures presentation of a David Brown/Sophie Hurst/Bonnie Palef production in association with David Manson. Executive Producers: Manson, Philip Rose, Howard Hurst. Producers: Brown, Hurst, Palef. Director: Bill Duke. Screenplay: Ivan Menchell, based on his play. Cinematography: Steven Poster. Music: Elmer Bernstein. Editor: John Carter. In color. Running time: 106 minutes. MPAA Rating: PG-13. Release date: February 3, 1993.

Players: Ellen Burstyn, Olympia Dukakis, Diane Ladd, Danny Aiello, Lainie Kazan, Jeff Howell, Christina Ricci, Bernie Casey, Alan Manson, Sam Schwartz, Wallace Shawn, Louis Guss, Irma St. Paule, Alice Eisner, Lee Richardson, Allan Pinsker, Hy Anzell, Jerry Orbach.

Chaplin .... TriStar

A TriStar release of a Mario Kassar presentation of a Carolco/Le Studio Canal +/RCS Video production, produced in association with Japan Satellite Broadcasting. Producers: Richard Attenborough, Kassar. Co-Producer: Terence Clegg. Director: Attenborough. Screenplay: William Boyd, Bryan Forbes, William Goldman, based on "My Autobiography" by Charles Chaplin, and "Chaplin: His Life and Art" by David Robinson. Story: Diana Hawkins. Cinematography: Sven Nykvist. Music: John Barry. Editor: Anne V. Coates. In Technicolor. Running time: 144 minutes. MPAA Rating: PG-13. Release date: December 25, 1992.

Players: Robert Downey Jr., Dan Aykroyd, Geraldine Chaplin, Kevin Dunn, Milla Jovovich, Moira Kelly, Kevin Kline, Diane Lane, Penelope Ann Miller, Paul Rhys, John Thaw, Marisa Tomei, Nancy Travis, James Woods, Robert Stephens, Norbert Weisser, David Duchovny, Michael Blevins, Donnie Kehr, Maria Pitillo.

Cliffhanger .... TriStar

A TriStar Pictures release of a Carolco/Studio Canal+/Pioneer Production in association with RCS Video. Producers: Alan Marshall, Renny Harlin. Executive Producer: Mario Kassar. Co-Producers: Gene Patrick Hines, James R. Zatolokin, David Rotman. Co-Executive Producer: Lynwood Spinks. Director: Harlin. Screenplay: Michael France, Sylvester Stallone. Screen Story: France, based on a premise by John Long. Cinematography: Alex Thomson. Music: Trevor Jones. Editor: Frank J. Urioste. In Technicolor, Panavision. Running time: 116 minutes. MPAA Rating: R. Release date: May 28, 1993.

Players: Sylvester Stallone, John Lithgow, Michael Rooker, Janine Turner, Rex Linn, Caroline Goodall, Leon, Craig Fairbrass, Gregory Scott Cummins, Denis Forest, Michelle Joyner, Max Perlich, Paul Winfield, Ralph Waite, Trey Brownell, Zach Grenier, Bruce McGill.

Coneheads .... Paramount

A Paramount Pictures release of a Lorne Michaels production. Producer: Michaels. Executive Producer: Michael Rachmil. Director: Steve Barron. Screenplay: Tom Davis, Dan Aykroyd, Bonnie Turner, Terry Turner. Cinematographer: Francis Kenny. Music: David Newman. Editor: Paul Trejo. In Deluxe color. Running time: 86 minutes. MPAA Rating: PG. Release date: July 23, 1993.

Players; Dan Aykroyd, Jane Curtin, Michelle Burke, Michael McKean, David Spade, Chris Farley, Whip Hubley, Michael Richards, Sinbad, Phil Hartman, Adam Sandler, Shishir Kurup, Jon Lovitz, Jason Alexander, Lisa

Jane Persky, Kevin Nealon, Jan Hooks, Julia Sweeney, Ellen Degeneres, Todd Susman, Tom Arnold, Garrett Morris, Dave Thomas, Laraine Newman.

Consenting Adults .... Buena Vista

A Buena Vista release of a Hollywood Pictures presentation in associa-
tion with Touchwood Pacific Partners I. Producers: Alan J. Pakula,
David Permut. Executive Producer: Pieter Jan Brugge. Co-Producer:
Katie Jacobs. Director: Pakula. Screenplay: Matthew Chapman. Cin-
ematography: Stephen Golblatt. Music: Michael Small. Editor: Sam
O'Steen. In Technicolor. Running time: 100 minutes. MPAA Rating:
R. Release date: October 16, 1991.
*Players: Kevin Kline, Mary Elizabeth Mastrantonio, Kevin Spacey,
Rebecca Miller, Forest Whitaker, E.G. Marshall, Kimberly McCullough.*

Cop and a Half .... Universal

A Universal Pictures release of an Imagine Entertainment presenta-
tion. Producer: Paul Maslansky. Executive Producer: Tova Laiter.
Director: Henry Winkler. Screenplay: Arne Olsen. Cinematography:
Bill Butler. Music: Alan Silvestri. Editor: Daniel Hanley, Roger
Tweten. In Deluxe color. Running time: 93 minutes. MPAA Rating:
PG. Release date: April 2, 1993.
*Players: Burt Reynolds, Norman D. Golden II, Ruby Dee, Holland
Taylor, Ray Sharkey, Sammy Hernandez, Frank Sivero, Rocky Girodani.*

Crossing the Bridge .... Buena Vista

A Buena Vista Pictures release of a Touchstone Pictures presentation
of an Outlaw production. Producers: Jeffrey Silver, Robert Newmyer.
Co-Producers: Caroline Baron, Jack Binder. Director-Screenplay:
Mike Binder. Photography: Tom Sigel. Music: Peter Himmelman.
Editor: Adam Weiss. In Deluxe color. Running time: 103 minutes.
MPAA Rating: R. Release date: September 11, 1992.
*Players: Josh Charles, Jason Gedrick, Stephen Baldwin, Cheryl Pollak,
Rita Taggart, Hy Anzell, Richard Edson, Ken Jenkins, Abraham Benrubi,
David Schwimmer, Bob Nickman, James Krag, Rana Haugen, Jeffrey
Tambor, Todd Tidgewell.*

The Crush .... Warner Bros.

A Warner Bros. release of a James G. Robinson presentation of a
Morgan Creek production. Producer: Robinson. Executive Producer:
Gary Barber. Director-Screenplay: Alan Shapiro. Cinematography:
Bruce Surtees. Music: Graeme Revell. Editor: Ian Crafford. In Tech-
nicolor. Running time: 89 minutes. MPAA Rating: R. Release date:
April 2, 1993.
*Players: Cary Elwes, Alicia Silverstone, Jennifer Rubin, Amber Ben-
son, Kurtwood Smith, Gwynyth Walsh, Matthew Walker.*

The Dark Half .... Orion

An Orion Pictures release of a Dark Half production. Producer:
Declan Baldwin. Executive Producer-Director-Screenplay: George A.
Romero. Based on the novel by Stephen King. Cinematography: Tony
Pierce-Roberts. Music: Christopher Young. Editor: Pasquale Buba.
In Deluxe color. Running time: 121 minutes. MPAA Rating: R. Release
date: April 23, 1993.
*Players: Timothy Hutton, Amy Madigan, Michael Rooker, Julie Harris,
Robert Joy, Kent Broadhurst, Beth Grant, Rutanya Alda, Tom Mardiro-
sian, Glenn Colerider, Chelsea Field, Royal Dano.*

Dave .... Warner Bros.

A Warner Bros. release of a Northern Lights Entertainment/Donner/
Shuler-Donner production. Producers: Lauren Shuler-Donner, Ivan
Reitman. Executive Producers: Joe Medjuck, Michael C. Gross.
Director: Reitman. Screenplay: Gary Ross. Cinematography: Adam
Greenberg. Music: James Newton Howard. Editor: Sheldon Kahn. In
Technicolor. Running time: 110 minutes. MPAA Rating: PG-13. Re-
lease date: May 7, 1993.
*Players: Kevin Kline, Sigourney Weaver, Frank Langella, Kevin Dunn,
Ving Rhames, Ben Kingsley, Charles Grodin, Faith Prince, Laura Linney,
Bonnie Hunt, Parley Baer, Stefan Gierasch, Anna Deavere Smith, Charles
Hallahan, Tom Dugan, Larry King, Jay Leno, Arnold Schwarzenegger,
Oliver Stone, Sander Vanocur.*

Dennis the Menace .... Warner Bros.

A Warner Bros. release of a John Hughes production. Producers:
Hughes, Richard Vane. Executive Producer: Ernest Chambers. Director: Nick Castle. Screenplay: Hughes, based on characters created
by Hank Ketcham. Cinematography: Thomas Ackerman. Music:
Jerry Goldsmith. Editor: Alan Heim. In Technicolor. Running time:
96 minutes. MPAA Rating: PG. Release date: June 25, 1993.

*Players: Walter Matthau, Mason Gamble, Joan Plowright, Christopher
Lloyd, Lea Thompson, Robert Stanton, Amy Sakasitz, Kellen Hathaway,
Paul Winfield, Natasha Lyonne, Devin Ratray, Hank Johnston, Billie Bird,
Arnold Stang, Melinda Mullins.*

The Distinguished
Gentleman .... Buena Vista

A Buena Vista release of a Hollywood Pictures presentation in associa-
tion with Touchwood Pacific Parners I of a Leonard Goldberg produc-
tion. Producers: Goldberg, Michael Peyser. Executive Producer-
Screenplay: Marty Kaplan. Director: Jonathan Lynn. Story: Kaplan,
Jonathan Reynolds. Cinematography: Gabriel Beristain. Music:
Randy Edelman. Editors: Tony Lombardo, Barry B. Leirer. In Tech-
nicolor. Running time: 113 minutes. MPAA Rating: R. Release date:
December 4, 1992.
*Players: Eddie Murphy, Lane Smith, Sheryl Lee Ralph, Joe Don Baker,
Victoria Rowell, Grant Shaud, Kevin McCarthy, Charles S. Dutton, Victor
Rivers, Chi, Sonny Jim Gaines, Noble Willingham, Gary Frank, James
Garner, Della Reese.*

Dragon: The Bruce Lee Story ..... Universal

A Universal Pictures release of a Raffaella De Laurentiis production.
Producer: De Laurentiis. Executive Producer: Dan York. Director:
Rob Cohen. Screenplay: Edward Khmara, John Raffo, Cohen, based
on the book "Bruce Lee: The Man Only I Knew" by Linda Lee
Cadwell. Cinematography: David Eggby. Music: Randy Edelman.
Editor: Peter Amundson. In Fujicolor. Running time: 121 minutes.
MPAA Rating: PG-13. Release date: May 7, 1993.
*Players: Jason Scott Lee, Lauren Holly, Robert Wagner, Michael
Learned, Nancy Kwan, Kay Tong Lim, Sterling Macer, Ric Young, Sven-
Ole Thorsen, John Cheung, Ong Soo Han, Aki Aleong, Clyde Kusatsu,
Van Williams, Paul Mantee.*

Dr. Giggles .... Universal

A Universal Pictures release of a Largo Entertainment presentation in
association with JVC Entertainment of a Dark Horse production.
Producer: Stuart M. Besser. Executive Producer: Jack Roe. Director:
Manny Coto. Screenplay: Coto, Graeme Whifler. Cinematography:
Robert Draper. Music: Brian May. Editor: Debra Neil. In Deluxe
color, Super 35 Widescreen. Running time: 95 minutes. MPAA Rat-
ing: R. Release date: October 23, 1992.
*Players: Larry Drake, Holly Marie Combs, Cliff De Young, Glenn
Quinn, Keith Diamond, Richard Bradford, Michelle Johnson, John Vick-
ery, Nancy Fish.*

El Mariachi .... Columbia

A Columbia Pictures release of a Los Hooligans production. Pro-
ducers-Screenplay: Robert Rodriguez, Carlos Gallardo. Director-
Story-Editor: Rodriguez. In Technicolor. Running time: 82 minutes.
MPAA Rating: R. Release date: Feb. 26, 1993.
*Players: Carlos Gallardo, Consuelo Gomez, Reinol Martinez, Peter
Marquardt, Jaime de Hoyos, Ramiro Gomez.*

Falling Down .... Warner Bros.

A Warner Bros. release of an Arnold Kopelson production, presented
in association with Le Studio Canal+, Regency Enterprises and Alcor
Films. Producers: Kopelson, Herschel Weingrod, Timothy Harris.
Executive Producer: Arnon Milchan. Co-Producers: Dan Kolsrud,
Stephen Brown, Nana Greenwald. Director: Joel Schumacher.
Screenplay: Ebbe Roe Smith. Cinematography: Andrzej Bartkowiak.
Music: James Newton Howard. Editor: Paul Hirsch. In Technicolor.
Running time: 115 minutes. MPAA Rating: R. Release date: February
26, 1993.
*Players: Michael Douglas, Robert Duvall, Barbara Hershey, Rachel
Ticotin, Tuesday Weld, Frederic Forrest, Lois Smith, Joey Hope Singer,
Ebbe Roe Smith, Michael Paul Chan, Raymond J. Barry, D.W. Moffett,
Steve Park, Kimberly Scott, James Keane, Macon McCalman, Richard
Montoya, Bruce Beatty.*

A Far Off Place .... Buena Vista

A Buena Vista Pictures release of a Walt Disney Pictures/Amblin
Entertainment presentation in association with Touchwood Pacific
Partners I. Executive Producers: Kathleen Kennedy, Frank Marshall,
Gerald R. Molen. Producers: Eva Monley, Elaine Sperber. Director:
Mikael Salomon. Screenplay: Robert Caswell, Jonathan Hensleigh,
Sally Robinson, based on the books "A Story Like the Wind" and "A
Far Off Place" by Laurens van der Post. Cinematography: Juan Ruiz-
Anchia. Music: James Horner. Editor: Ray Lovejoy. In Technicolor,

Widescreen. Running time: 105 minutes. MPAA Rating: PG. Release date: March 12, 1993.

Players: Reese Witherspoon, Ethan Randall, Jack Thompson, Sarel Bok, Maximilian Schell, Robert Burke, Patricia Kalember, Daniel Gerroll, Miles Anderson, Fidelis Cheza.

Father Hood .... Buena Vista

A Buena Vista Pictures release of a Hollywood Pictures presentation. Producers: Nicholas Pileggi, Anant Singh, Gillian Gorfil. Executive Producer: Jeffrey Chernov. Director: Darrell James Roodt. Screenplay: Scott Spencer. Music: Patrick O'Hearn. Editor: David Heitner . In color. Running time: 94 minutes. MPAA Rating: PG-13. Release date: August 27, 1993.

Players: Patrick Swayze, Halle Berry, Sabrina Lloyd, Diane Ladd, Brian Bonsall, Michael Ironside, Adrienne Barbeau, Bob Gunton.

A Few Good Men .... Columbia

A Columbia Pictures release of a Columbia Pictures and Castle Rock Entertainment presentation of a David Brown production. Executive Producers: William Gilmore, Rachel Pfeffer. Producers: Brown, Rob Reiner, Andrew Scheinman. Director: Reiner. Screenplay: Aaron Sorkin, based on his play. Photography: Robert Richardson. Music: Marc Shaiman. Editor: Robert Leighton. In Panavision, Technicolor. Running time: 138 minutes. MPAA Rating: R. Release date: December 11, 1992.

Players: Tom Cruise, Jack Nicholson, Demi Moore, Kevin Bacon, Kiefer Sutherland, Kevin Pollak, James Marshall, J.T. Walsh, Christopher Guest, J.A. Preston, Matt Craven, Wolfgang Bodison, Xander Berkeley, Noah Wyle, Cuba Gooding Jr.

Fire in the Sky .... Paramount

A Paramount Pictures release of a Joe Wizan/Todd Black production. Producers: Wizan, Black. Executive Producer: Wolfgang Glattes. Director: Robert Lieberman. Screenplay: Tracy Torme. Based upon the book "The Walton Experience" by Travis Walton. Cinematography: Bill Pope. Music: Mark Isham. Editor: Steve Mirkovich. In Deluxe color. Running time: 108 minutes. MPAA Rating: PG-13. Release date: March 12, 1993.

Players: D.B. Sweeney, Robert Patrick, Craig Sheffer, James Garner, Henry Thomas, Bradley Gregg, Kathleen Wilhoite, Noble Willingham, Georgia Emelin, Scott MacDonald, Wayne Grace, Kenneth White, Robert Biheller.

The Firm .... Paramount

A Paramount Pictures release of a John Davis/Scott Rudin/Mirage production. Producers: Rudin, Davis, Sydney Pollack. Executive Producers: Michael Hausman, Lindsay Doran. Director: Pollack. Screenplay: David Rabe, Robert Towne, David Rayfiel. Based upon the novel by John Grisham. Cinematography: John Seale. Music: Dave Grusin. Editors: William Steinkamp, Frederic Steinkamp. In Deluxe color. Running time: 154 minutes. MPAA Rating: R. Release date: June 30, 1993.

Players: Tom Cruise, Gene Hackman, Jeanne Tripplehorn, Ed Harris, Hal Holbrook, Terry Kinney, Holly Hunter, Wilford Brimley, David Strathairn, Gary Busey, Steven Hill, Tobin Bell, Barbara Garrick, Jerry Hardin, Paul Calderon, Jerry Weintraub, Sullivan Walker, John Beal, Karina Lombard, Paul Sorvino.

Forever Young .... Warner Bros.

A Warner Bros. release of an Icon production in association with Edward S. Feldman. Producer: Bruce Davey. Executive Producers: Feldman, Jeffrey Abrams. Director: Steve Miner. Screenplay: Abrams. Cinematography: Russell Boyd. Music: Jerry Goldsmith. Editor: Jon Poll. In Technicolor. Running time: 102 minutes. MPAA Rating: PG. Release date: December 16, 1992.

Players: Mel Gibson, Jamie Lee Curtis, Elijah Wood, Isabel Glasser, George Wendt, Joe Morton, Nicolas Surovy, David Marshall Grant, Robert Hy Gorman, Millie Slavin, Michael Goorjian, Art LaFleur, J.D. Cullum, Veronica Lauren, Eric Pierpoint.

1492: Conquest of Paradise ..... Paramount

A Paramount Pictures release of a Percy Main/Legende/Cyrk production. Producers: Ridley Scott, Alain Goldman. Executive Producers: Mimi Polk Sotela, Iain Smith. Co-Producers: Marc Boyman, Roselyne Bosch, Pere Fages. Director: Scott. Screenplay: Bosch. Cinematography: Adrian Biddle. Music: Vangelis. Editors: William Anderson, Françoise Bonnot. British-French-Spanish. In Rank color, Panavision. Running time: 150 minutes. MPAA Rating: PG-13. Release date: October 9, 1992.

Players: Gerard Depardieu, Armand Assante, Sigourney Weaver, Angela Molina, Loren Dean, Fernando Rey, Michael Wincott, Tcheky Karyo, Kevin Dunn, Frank Langella, Mark Margolis, Kario Salem.

Free Willy .... Warner Bros.

A Warner Bros. release of a Le Studio Canal+, Regency Enterprises and Alcor Films presentation of a Donner/Shuler-Donner production. Producers: Jennie Lew Tugend, Lauren Shuler-Donner. Executive Producers: Richard Donner, Arnon Milchan. Co-Producers: Penelope L. Foster, Richard Solomon, Jim Van Wyck. Director: Simon Wincer. Screenplay: Keith A. Walker, Corey Blechman. Story: Walker. Cinematography: Robbie Greenberg. Music: Basil Poledouris. Editor: O. Nicholas Brown. In Panavision, Technicolor. Running time: 111 minutes. MPAA Rating: PG. Release date: July 16, 1993.

Players: Jason James Richter, Lori Petty, Jayne Atkinson, August Schellenberg, Michael Madsen, Michael Ironside, Richard Riehle, Mykelti Williamson, Michael Bacall, Danielle Harris, Keiko.

The Fugitive .... Warner Bros.

A Warner Bros. release of a Keith Barish/Arnold Kopelson production. Producer: Kopelson. Executive Producers: Barish, Roy Huggins. Co-Producer: Peter MacGregor-Scott. Director: Andrew Davis. Screenplay: Jeb Stuart, David Twohy. Story: Twohy. Based on characters created by Roy Huggins. Cinematography: Michael Chapman. Music: James Newton Howard. Editors: Dennis Virkler, David Finfer. In Technicolor. Running time: 127 minutes. MPAA Rating: PG-13. Release date: August 6, 1993.

Players: Harrison Ford, Tommy Lee Jones, Sela Ward, Julianne Moore, Joe Pantoliano, Andreas Katsulas, Jeroen Krabbe, Daniel Roebuck, L. Scott Caldwell, Tom Wood, Ron Dean, Joseph Kosala.

Groundhog Day .... Columbia

A Columbia Pictures release of a Trevor Albert production. Producers: Albert, Harold Ramis. Executive Producer: C.O. Erickson. Director: Ramis. Screenplay: Danny Rubin, Ramis. Story: Rubin. Cinematography: John Bailey. Music: George Fenton. Editor: Pembroke J. Herring. In Technicolor. Running time: 103 minutes. MPAA Rating: PG. Release date: February 12, 1993.

Players: Bill Murray, Andie MacDowell, Chris Elliott, Stephen Tobolowsky, Brian Doyle-Murray, Marita Geraghty, Angela Paton, Rick Ducommun, Rick Overton, Robin Duke, Carol Bivins, Willie Garson, Ken Hudson Campbell, Harold Ramis, Les Podewell.

Guilty As Sin .... Buena Vista

A Buena Vista Pictures release of a Hollywood Pictures presentation of a Martin Ransohoff production. Producer: Martin Ransohoff. Executive Producers: Don Carmody, Bob Robinson. Director: Sidney Lumet. Screenplay: Larry Cohen. Cinematography: Andrzej Bartkowiak. Editor: Evan Lottman. Music: Howard Shore. In Technicolor. Running time: 106 minutes. MPAA Rating: R. Release date: June 4, 1993.

Players: Rebecca De Mornay, Don Johnson, Stephen Lang, Jack Warden, Dana Ivey, Ron White, Norma Dell'Agnese, Sean McCann, Luis Guzman, Robert Kennedy, James Blendick.

Hard Target .... Universal

A Universal Pictures release of an Alphaville/Renaissance production. Producers: James Jacks, Sean Daniel. Executive Producers: Moshe Diamant, Sam Raimi, Robert Tapert. Director: John Woo. Screenplay: Chuck Pfarrer. Cinematography: Russell Carpenter. Music: Graeme Revell. Editor: Bob Murawski. In Deluxe color. Running time: 92 minutes. MPAA Rating: R. Release date: August 20, 1993.

Players: Jean-Claude Van Damme, Lance Henriksen, Yancy Butler, Arnold Vosloo, Kasi Lemmons, Wilford Brimley.

Hear No Evil .... 20th Century Fox

A 20th Century Fox release of a David Matalon production. Producer: Matalon. Executive Producer: David Streit. Director: Robert Greenwald. Screenplay: R.M. Badat, Kathleen Rowell. Story: Badat, Danny Rubin. Cinematography: Steven Shaw. Music: Graeme Revell. Editor: Eva Gardos. In Technicolor. Running time: 97 minutes. MPAA Rating: R. Release date: March 26, 1993.

Players: Marlee Matlin, D.B. Sweeney, Martin Sheen, John C. McGinley, Christina Carlisi, Greg Elam, Charley Lang, Marge Redmond, Billie Worley.

Heart and Souls .... Universal

A Universal Pictures release of an Alphaville/Stampede Entertainment production. Producers: Nancy Roberts, Sean Daniel. Director: Ron Underwood. Screenplay-Screen Story: Brent Maddock, S.S. Wilson, Gregory Hansen, Erik Hansen. Executive Producers: Cari-Esta Albert, James Jacks. Music: Marc Shaiman. Editor: O. Nicholas Brown. In Panavision, Deluxe color. Running time: 102 minutes. MPAA Rating: PG-13. Release date: August 13, 1993.

Players: Robert Downey Jr., Charles Grodin, Alfre Woodard, Kyra Sedgwick, Tom Sizemore, Elisabeth Shue, David Paymer, Bill Calvert, Lisa Lucas, Richard Portnow, Eric Lloyd, Wren T. Brown, Lorinne Dills-Vozofff, B.B. King, Marc Shaiman, Kurtwood Smith.

Hero .... Columbia

A Columbia Pictures release of a Laura Ziskin production. Producer: Ziskin. Executive Producer: Joseph M. Caracciolo. Director: Stephen Frears. Screenplay: David Webb Peoples. Story: Ziskin, Alvin Sargent, Peoples. Cinematography: Oliver Stapleton. Music: George Fenton. Editor: Mick Audsley. In Technicolor. Running time: 116 minutes. MPAA Rating: PG-13. Release date: October 2, 1992.

Players: Dustin Hoffman, Geena Davis, Andy Garcia, Joan Cusack, Kevin J. O'Connor, Maury Chaykin, Stephen Tobolowsky, Christian Clemenson, Chevy Chase, Fisher Stevens, Tom Arnold, James Madio, Susie Cusack, Cady Huffman, Richard Riehle, Daniel Leroy Baldwin, Don Yesso, Lee Wilkof, Darrell Larson, Warren Berlinger, Edward Herrmann.

Hexed .... Columbia

A Columbia Pictures release of a Price Entertainment/Brillstein-Grey production. Executive Producers: Bernie Brillstein, Howard Klein. Producers: Marc S. Fischer, Louis G. Friedman. Director-Screenplay: Alan Spencer. Cinematography: James Chressanthis. Music: Lance Rubin. Editor: Debra McDermott. In Technicolor. Running time: 90 minutes. MPAA Rating: R. Release date: January 22, 1993.

Players: Arye Gross, Claudia Christian, Adrienne Shelly, Ray Baker, R. Lee Ermey, Michael Knight, Robin Curtis, Brandis Kemp, Norman Fell, Pamela Roylance, Billy Jones, Shelley Michelle.

Hocus Pocus .... Buena Vista

A Buena Vista Pictures release of a Walt Disney Pictures presentation of a David Kirschner/Steven Haft production. Producers: David Kirschner, Steven Haft. Executive Producer: Ralph Winter. Co-Producer: Bonnie Bruckheimer. Co-Executive Producer: Mick Garris. Director: Kenny Ortega. Screenplay: Mick Garris, Neil Cuthbert. Story: Kirschner, Garris. Cinematographer: Hiro Narita. Music: Mary Vogt. Editor: Peter E. Berger. In Technicolor. Running time: 93 minutes. MPAA Rating: PG. Release date: July 16, 1993.

Players: Bette Midler, Sarah Jessica Parker, Kathy Najimy, Omri Katz, Thora Birch, Vinessa Shaw, Amanda Shepherd, Larry Bagby III, Tobias Jelinek, Stephanie Faracy, Penny Marshall, Garry Marshall, Charlie Rocket, Doug Jones, Norbert Weisser, Kathleen Freeman.

Hoffa .... 20th Century Fox

A 20th Century Fox release of an Edward R. Pressman production presented in association with Jersey Films. Producers: Edward R. Pressman, Danny DeVito, Caldecot Chubb. Executive Producer: Joseph Isgro. Co-Producer: Harold Schneider. Director: DeVito. Screenplay: David Mamet. Cinematography: Stephen H. Burum. Music: David Newman. Editors: Lynzee Klingman, Ronald Roose. In Panavision, Color. Running time: 140 minutes. MPAA Rating: R. Release date: December 25, 1992.

Players: Jack Nicholson, Danny DeVito, Armand Assante, J.T. Walsh, John C. Reilly, Frank Whaley, Kevin Anderson, John P. Ryan, Robert Prosky, Natalija Nogulich, Nicholas Pryor, Paul Guilfoyle, Karen Young, Cliff Gorman, Joanne Neer, Joe V. Greco, Bruno Kirby.

Homeward Bound:
The Incredible Journey .... Buena Vista

A Buena Vista release of a Walt Disney Pictures presentation in association with Touchwood Pacific Partners I. Executive Producers: Donald W. Ernst, Kirk Wise. Producers: Franklin R. Levy, Jeffrey Chernov. Director: DuWayne Dunham. Screenplay: Caroline Thompson, Linda Woolverton, based on the book "The Incredible Journey" by Sheila Burnford. Cinematography: Reed Smoot. Music: Bruce Broughton. Editor: Jonathan P. Shaw. In Technicolor. Running time: 84 minutes. MPAA Rating: G. Release date: February 3, 1993.

Players: Ben, Rattler, Tiki, Robert Hays, Kim Greist, Jean Smart, Benj Thall, Veronica Lauren, Kevin Chevalia; voices of Michael J. Fox, Sally Field, Don Ameche.

Home Alone 2:
Lost in New York .... 20th Century Fox

A 20th Century Fox release of a John Hughes production. Producer-Screenplay: Hughes. Executive Producers: Mark Radcliffe, Duncan Henderson, Richard Vane. Director: Chris Columbus. Cinematography: Julio Macat. Music: John Williams. Editor: Raja Gosnell. In Kodak color. Running time: 120 minutes. MPAA Rating: PG. Release date: November 20, 1992.

Players: Macaulay Culkin, Joe Pesci, Daniel Stern, Catherine O'Hara, John Heard, Devin Ratray, Hillary Wolf, Maureen Elisabeth Shay, Tim Curry, Brenda Fricker, Eddie Bracken, Dana Ivey, Rob Schneider, Leigh Zimmerman, Michael C. Maronna, Gerry Bamman, Jedediah Cohen, Kieran Culkin, Bob Eubanks, Rip Taylor, Jaye P. Morgan, Jimmie Walker, Ally Sheedy, Donald Trump, Senta Moses.

Hot Shots! Part Deux ..... 20th Century Fox

Producer: Bill Badalato. Executive Producer: Pat Proft. Director: Jim Abrahams. Screenplay: Abrahams, Proft. Cinematography: John R. Leonetti. Music: Basil Poledouris. Editor: Malcolm Campbell. In Deluxe color. Running time: 89 minutes. MPAA Rating: PG-13. Release date: May 21, 1993.

Players: Charlie Sheen, Richard Crenna, Valeria Golino, Lloyd Bridges, Brenda Bakke, Miguel Ferrer, Rowan Atkinson, Jerry Haleva, David Wohl, Mitchell Ryan, Michael Colyar, Gregory Sierra, Andreas Katsulas, Clyde Kusatsu, Bob Vila, Martin Sheen.

Husbands and Wives .... TriStar

A TriStar release of a Jack Rollins & Charles H. Joffe production. Producer: Robert Greenhut. Executive Producers: Rollins, Joffe. Co-Producers: Helen Robin, Joseph Hartwick. Director-Screenplay: Woody Allen. Cinematography: Carlo Di Palma. Editor: Susan E. Morse. In Technicolor. Running time: 108 minutes. MPAA Rating: R. Release date: September 18, 1992.

Players: Woody Allen, Judy Davis, Mia Farrow, Sydney Pollack, Liam Neeson, Lysette Anthony, Juliette Lewis, Blythe Danner, Ron Rifkin, Cristi Conaway, Timothy Jerome, Jerry Zaks, Bruce Jay Friedman, Benno Schmidt, Jeffrey Kurland (voice).

In the Line of Fire .... Columbia

A Columbia Pictures release of a Castle Rock production. Producer: Jeff Apple. Executive Producers: Wolfgang Petersen, Gail Katz, David Valdes. Director: Petersen. Screenplay: Jeff Maguire. Cinematographer: John Bailey. Music: Ennio Morricone. Editor: Anne V. Coates. In Technicolor, Panavision. Running time: 130 minutes. MPAA Rating: R. Release date: July 9, 1993.

Players: Clint Eastwood, John Malkovich, Rene Russo, Dylan McDermott, Gary Cole, Fred Dalton Thompson, John Mahoney, Greg Alan-Williams, Jim Curley, Sally Hughes, Clyde Kusatsu, Tobin Bell, Steve Hytner, John Heard, Bob Schott, Elsa Raven, Patrika Darbo.

Indecent Proposal .... Paramount

A Paramount Pictures release of a Sherry Lansing production. Producer: Lansing. Executive Producers: Tom Schulman, Alex Gartner. Co-Producer, Michael Tadross. Director: Adrian Lyne. Screenplay: Amy Holden Jones, based upon the novel by Jack Engelhart. Cinematography: Howard Atherton. Music: John Barry. Editor: Joe Hutshing. In Deluxe color. Running time: 117 minutes. MPAA Rating: R. Release date: April 7, 1993.

Players: Robert Redford, Demi Moore, Woody Harrelson, Seymour Cassel, Oliver Platt, Billy Bob Thornton, Rip Taylor, Billy Connolly, Joel Brooks, Pierre Epstein, Danny Zorn, Kevin West, Pamela Holt, Tommy Bush, Mariclare Costello, Sheena Easton, Herbie Hancock.

Indian Summer .... Buena Vista

A Buena Vista release of a Touchstone Pictures presentation of an Outlaw Production. Producers: Jeffrey Silver, Robert Newmyer. Co-Producers: Caroline Baron, Jack Binder. Director-Screenplay: Mike Binder. Cinematography: Tom Sigel. Music: Miles Goodman. Editor: Adam Weiss. In Technicolor. Running time: 97 minutes. MPAA Rating: PG-13. Release date: April 23, 1993.

Players: Alan Arkin, Matt Craven, Diane Lane, Bill Paxton, Elizabeth Perkins, Kevin Pollak, Sam Raimi, Vincent Spano, Julie Warner, Kimberly Williams, Richard Cevolleau, Anne Holloway, Robert Feldmann, Cliff Woolner.

Innocent Blood .... Warner Bros.

A Warner Bros. release of a Lee Rich production. Producers: Rich, Leslie Belzberg. Executive Producer: Jonathan Sheinberg. Director:

427

John Landis. Screenplay: Michael Wolk. Cinematography: Mac Ahlberg. Music: Ira Newborn. Editor: Dale Beldin. In Technicolor. Running time: 108 minutes. MPAA Rating: R. Release date: September 25, 1992.

Players: Anne Parillaud, Robert Loggia, Anthony LaPaglia, Don Rickles, David Proval, Rocco Sisto, Chazz Palminteri, Kim Coates, Marshall Bell, Leo Burmester, Angela Bassett, Luis Guzman, Frank Oz, Forrest J. Ackerman, Michael Ritchie, Sam Raimi, Dario Argento, Linnea Quigley, Elaine Kagan.

Jack the Bear .... 20th Century Fox

A 20th Century Fox release of an American Filmworks/Lucky Dog production. Producer: Bruce Gilbert. Director: Marshall Herskovitz. Executive Producer: Ron Yerxa. Screenplay: Steven Zaillian, based on the novel by Dan McCall. Cinematography: Fred Murphy. Music: James Horner. Editor: Steven Rosenblum. In Deluxe color, 35 Super Widescreen. Running time: 99 minutes. MPAA Rating: PG-13. Release date: April 2, 1993.

Players: Danny DeVito, Robert J. Steinmiller Jr., Miko Hughes, Gary Sinise, Art LaFleur, Stefan Gierasch, Erica Yohn, Andrea Marcovicci, Julia Louis-Dreyfus, Reese Witherspoon, Bert Remsen, Carl Gabriel Yorke, Lee Garlington, Lorinne Vozoff, Troy Slaten, Justin Mosley Spink, Jessica Steinmiller, Cliff Bemis.

Jennifer Eight .... Paramount

A Paramount Pictures release of a Scott Rudin production. Producers: Gary Lucchesi, David Wimbury. Executive Producer: Rudin. Director-Screenplay: Bruce Robinson. Cinematography: Conrad L. Hall. Music: Christopher Young. Editor: Conrad Buff. In Deluxe color. Running time: 124 minutes. MPAA Rating: R. Release date: November 6, 1992.

Players: Andy Garcia, Uma Thurman, Lance Henriksen, Kathy Baker, Graham Beckel, John Malkovich, Kevin Conway, Perry Lang, Nicholas Love, Michael O'Neill, Paul Bates, Bob Gunton, Lenny Von Dohlen, Bryan Larkin, Debbon Ayer, Eddie Korbich.

Jumpin at the Boneyard ... 20th Century Fox

A 20th Century Fox release of a Kasdan Pictures presentation. Producers: Nina R. Sadowsky, Lloyd Goldfine. Executive Producer: Lawrence Kasdan. Director-Screenplay: Jeff Stanzler. Cinematography: Lloyd Goldfine. Music: Steve Postel. Editor: Christopher Tellefsen. In DuArt color. Running time: 101 minutes. MPAA Rating: R. Release date: September 18, 1992.

Players: Tim Roth, Alexis Arquette, Danitra Vance, Samuel L. Jackson, Kathleen Chalfant, Luis Guzman, Elizabeth Bracco, Jeffrey Wright, Richard Morris, Agustin Rodriguez.

Jurassic Park .... Universal

A Universal Pictures release of an Amblin Entertainment production. Producers: Kathleen Kennedy, Gerald R. Molen. Director: Steven Spielberg. Screenplay: Michael Crichton, David Koepp, based on the novel by Crichton. Cinematography: Dean Cundey. Music: John Williams. Editor: Michael Kahn. In Deluxe color. Running time: 123 minutes. MPAA Rating: PG-13. Release date: June 11, 1993.

Players: Sam Neill, Laura Dern, Jeff Goldblum, Richard Attenborough, Bob Peck, Martin Ferrero, B.D. Wong, Joseph Mazzello, Ariana Richards, Samuel L. Jackson, Wayne Knight, Jerry Molen, Miguel Sandoval.

Last Action Hero .... Columbia

A Columbia Pictures release of a Steve Roth/Oak production. Producers: Steve Roth, John McTiernan. Co-Producers: Robert E. Relyea, Neal Nordlinger. Executive Producer: Arnold Schwarzenegger. Director: McTiernan. Screenplay: Shane Black, David Arnott. Story: Zak Penn, Adam Leff. Cinematography: Dean Semler. Music: Michael Kamen. Editor: John Wright. In Panavision, Technicolor. Running time: 130 minutes. MPAA Rating: PG-13. Release date: June 18, 1993.

Players: Arnold Schwarzenegger, Austin O'Brien, F. Murray Abraham, Art Carney, Charles Dance, Frank McRae, Tom Noonan, Robert Prosky, Anthony Quinn, Mercedes Ruehl, Sir Ian McKellen, Prof. Toru Tanaka, Joan Plowright, Keith Barish, Jim Belushi, Chevy Chase, Leeza Gibbons, Hammer, Little Richard, Robert Patrick, Maria Shriver, Sharon Stone, Jean-Claude Van Damme, Tina Turner, Melvin Van Peebles, Damon Wayans, Jason Kelly, Ryan Todd, Apollo Dukakis, Rick Ducommun, Noah Emmerich, Danny DeVito (voice).

The Last of the Mohicans . 20th Century Fox

A 20th Century Fox release from Morgan Creek Intl. Producers: Michael Mann, Hunt Lowry. Executive Producer: James G. Robin-

son. Director: Mann. Screenplay: Mann, Christopher Crowe, based on the novel by James Fenimore Cooper and the screenplay by Philip Dunne for the 1936 film. Adapted by John L. Balderston, Paul Perez, Daniel Moore. Cinematography: Dante Spinotti. Music: Trevor Jones, Randy Edelman. Editors: Dov Hoenig, Arthur Schmidt. In Deluxe color, Panavision. Running time: 111 minutes. MPAA Rating: R. Release date: September 25, 1992.

Players: Daniel Day-Lewis, Madeleine Stowe, Russell Means, Eric Schweig, Jodhi May, Steven Waddington, Wes Studi, Maurice Roeves, Patrice Chereau.

Leap of Faith .... Paramount

A Paramount Pictures release of a Michael Manheim/David V. Picker production. Producers: Manheim, Picker. Executive Producer: Ralph S. Singleton. Director: Richard Pearce. Screenplay: Janus Cercone. Cinematography: Matthew F. Leonetti. Music: Cliff Eidelman. Editors: Don Zimmerman, Mark Warner, John F. Burnett. In Deluxe color. Running time: 108 minutes. MPAA Rating: PG-13. Release date: December 18, 1992.

Players: Steve Martin, Debra Winger, Lolita Davidovich, Lukas Haas, Liam Neeson, Meat Loaf, Philip Seymour Hoffman, M.C. Gainey, La Chanze, Delores Hall, John Toles-Bey, Albertina Walker, Ricky Dillard, Vince Davis, Troy Evans, Phyllis Somerville.

Life With Mikey .... Buena Vista

A Buena Vista release of a Touchstone Pictures presentation of a Scott production. Producers: Teri Schwartz, Rubin. Director: James Lapine. Co-Producer-Screenplay: Marc Lawrence. Cinematography: Rob Hahn. Music: Alan Menken. Editor: Robert Leighton. In Technicolor. Running time: 93 minutes. MPAA Rating: PG. Release date: June 4, 1993.

Players: Michael J. Fox, Christina Vidal, Nathan Lane, Cyndi Lauper, David Krumholtz, David Huddleston, Victor Garber, Frances Chaney, Kathryn Grody, Mary Alice, Annabelle Gurwitch, Kathleen McNenny, Michael Rupert, Christine Baranski, Chris Durang, Brenda Currin, Heather MacRae, Wendy Wasserstein, Dylan Baker, Kate Burton, Jonathan Charles Kaplan, Stephen Bogardus, William Finn, Robin Byrd, Mandy Patinkin, BETTY, Sean Power, Laura Bundy, Barbara Walsh, Ruben Blades.

Lorenzo's Oil .... Universal

A Universal Pictures release of a Kennedy Miller Film. Producers: Doug Mitchell, George Miller. Executive Producer: Arnold Burk. Director: Miller. Screenplay: Miller, Nick Enright. Cinematography: John Seale. Editors: Richard Francis-Bruce, Marcus D'Arcy, Lee Smith. In Technicolor. Running time: 135 minutes. MPAA Rating: PG-13. Release date: December 30, 1992.

Players: Nick Nolte, Susan Sarandon, Peter Ustinov, Zack O'Malley Greenburg, Kathleen Wilhoite, Gerry Bamman, Margo Martindale, James Rebhorn, Ann Hearn, Maduka Steady, Mary Wakio, Don Subbaby, Colin Ward, LaTanya Richardson, Jennifer Dundas, William Cameron, Becky Ann Baker, Laura Linney, Joyce Reehling, Barbara Poitier.

Love Field .... Orion

An Orion Pictures release of a Sanford/Pillsbury production. Producers: Sarah Pillsbury, Midge Sanford. Executive Producers: Kate Guinzburg, George Goodman. Director: Jonathan Kaplan. Screenplay: Don Roos. Cinematography: Ralf Bode. Music: Jerry Goldsmith. Editor: Jane Kurson. In Technicolor. Running time: 104 minutes. MPAA Rating: PG-13. Release date: December 11, 1992.

Players: Michelle Pfeiffer, Dennis Haysbert, Stephanie McFadden, Brian Kerwin, Louise Latham, Peggy Rea, Beth Grant, Johnny Ray McGhee, Cooper Huckabee, Troy Evans, Mark Miller, Pearl Jones.

Love Potion No. 9 .... 20th Century Fox

Producer-Director-Screenplay: Dale Launer. Executive Producer: Thomas M. Hammel. Cinematography: William Wages. Music: Jed Leiber. Editor: Suzanne Pettit. In CFI color. Running time: 96 minutes. MPAA Rating: PG-13. Release date: November 13, 1992.

Players: Tate Donovan, Sandra Bullock, Mary Mara, Dale Midkiff, Hillary Bailey Smith, Dylan Baker, Blake Clark, Bruce McCarty, Rebecca Staab, Adrian Paul, Ric Reitz, Anne Bancroft.

The Lover .... MGM

A Metro-Goldwyn-Mayer release of a Claude Berri presentation of a Renn/Buriill/Films A2 co-production. Director: Jean-Jacques Annaud. Screenplay: Gerard Brach, Annaud, based on the novel by Marguerite Duras. Cinematography: Robert Fraisse. Music: Gabriel

Yared. Editor: Noelle Boisson. French. In color. Running time: 103 minutes. MPAA Rating: R. Release date: October 30, 1992.

Players: Jane March, Tony Leung, Frederique Meininger, Arnaud Giovaninetti, Melvil Poupaud, Lisa Faulkner, Xiem Mang.

Mad Dog and Glory .... Universal

A Universal Pictures release of a Martin Scorsese/Barbara De Fina production. Executive Producers: De Fina, Scorsese. Director: John McNaughton. Screenplay: Price. Cinematography: Robby Muller. Music: Elmer Bernstein. Editors: Craig McKay, Elena Maganini. In Technicolor. Running time: 96 minutes. MPAA Rating: R. Release date: March 5, 1993.

Players: Robert De Niro, Uma Thurman, Bill Murray, David Caruso, Mike Starr, Tom Towles, Kathy Baker, Derek Anunciation.

Made in America .... Warner Bros.

A Warner Bros. release of a Le Studio Canal+, Regency Enterprises and Alcor Films presentation of a Stonebridge Entertainment/Kalola Productions, Inc./Arnon Milchan Production. Producers: Milchan, Michael Douglas, Rick Bieber. Executive Producers: Nadine Schiff, Marcia Brandwynne. Co-Executive Producer: Steven Reuther. Co-Producer: Patrick Palmer. Director: Richard Benjamin. Screenplay: Holly Goldberg Sloan. Story: Brandwynne, Schiff, Sloan. Cinematography: Ralf Bode. Music: Mark Isham. Editor: Jacqueline Cambas. In Deluxe color. Running time: 111 minutes. MPAA Rating: PG-13. Release date: May 28, 1993.

Players: Whoopi Goldberg, Ted Danson, Will Smith, Nia Long, Paul Rodriguez, Jennifer Tilly, Peggy Rea, Clyde Kusatsu, David Bowe, Jeffrey Joseph, Rawley Valverde, Fred Mancuso, Charlene Fernetz, Shawn Levy, Lu Leonard.

The Magical World of Chuck Jones .... Warner Bros.

A Warner Bros. release of a Magical World Pictures/IF/X Prods. presentation. Producers: David La Lik Wong, George Daugherty. Executive Producer: Valerie Kausen. Director: Daugherty. Cinematography: Peter Bonilla. Music: Patrick Cameron. Editor: Peter E. Berger. In color. Running time: 93 minutes. MPAA Rating: PG. Release date: October 23, 1992.

Documentary featuring Chuck Jones, Joe Dante, Danny Elfman, June Foray, Friz Freleng, Whoopi Goldberg, Matt Groening, Steve Guttenberg, Ron Howard, Marian Jones, George Lucas, Roddy McDowall, Gary Rydstrom, Steven Spielberg.

Malcolm X .... Warner Bros.

A Warner Bros. release in association with Largo International N.V. of a 40 Acres and a Mule Filmworks production/a Marvin Worth production. Producers: Marvin Worth, Spike Lee. Co-Producers: Monty Ross, Jon Kilik, Preston Holmes. Director: Lee. Screenplay: Arnold Perl, Lee, based on the book "The Autobiography of Malcolm X" as told to Alex Haley. Cinematography: Ernest Dickerson. Music: Terence Blanchard. Editor: Barry Alexander Brown. In color. Running time: 203 minutes. MPAA Rating: PG-13. Release date: November 18, 1992.

Players: Denzel Washington, Angela Bassett, Albert Hall, Al Freeman Jr., Delroy Lindo, Spike Lee, Theresa Randle, Kate Vernon, Lonette McKee, Tommy Hollis, James McDaniel, Ernest Thomas, Jean La Marre, O.L. Duke, Larry McCoy, Maurice Sneed, Debi Mazar, Phyllis Yvonne Stickney, Scot Anthony Robinson, James E. Gaines, Joe Seneca, Latanya Richardson, Giancarlo Esposito, Roger Guenveur Smith, Craig Wasson, David Patrick Kelly, Shirley Stoler, Abdul Salaam El Razzac, Pee Wee Love, Beatrice Winde, John Sayles, Martin Donovan, Nick Turturro, Miki Howard, Bobby Seale, Christopher Plummer, Karen Allen, Peter Boyle, William Kunstler, Ossie Davis (voice).

The Man Without a Face ...... Warner Bros.

A Warner Bros. release of an Icon production. Producer: Bruce Davey. Executive Producer: Stephen McEveety. Director: Mel Gibson. Screenplay: Malcolm MacRury, based on the novel by Isabelle Holland. Cinematography: Donald M. McAlpine. Music: James Horner. Editor: Tony Gibbs. In Technicolor. Running time: 114 minutes. MPAA Rating: PG-13. Release date: August 25, 1993.

Players: Mel Gibson, Nick Stahl, Margaret Whitton, Fay Masterson, Geoffrey Lewis, Gaby Hoffman, Richard Masur, Michael DeLuise, Ethan Phillips, Jean De Baere, Viva, Justin Kanew, Jack De Mave, George Martin, Zach Grenier, Kelly Wood, Sean Kellman.

Manhattan Murder Mystery .... TriStar

A TriStar Pictures release of a Jack Rollins and Charles H. Joffe production. Producer: Robert Greenhut. Executive Producers: Rollins, Joffe. Director: Woody Allen. Screenplay: Allen, Marshall Brickman. Cinematography: Carlo DiPalma. Editor: Susan E. Morse. In Technicolor. Running time: 107 minutes. MPAA Rating: PG. Release date: August 18, 1993.

Players: Diane Keaton, Woody Allen, Alan Alda, Anjelica Huston, Jerry Adler, Joy Behar, Ron Rifkin, Lynn Cohen, Melanie Norris, Marge Redmond, William Addy, Aida Turturro.

Married to It .... Orion

An Orion Pictures release of a Thomas Baer production. Producer: Baer. Executive Producers: Peter V. Herald, John L. Jacobs. Director: Arthur Hiller. Screenplay: Janet Kovalcik. Cinematography: Victor Kemper. Music: Henry Mancini. Editor: Robert C. Jones. In Deluxe color. Running time: 112 minutes. MPAA Rating: R. Release date: March 26, 1993.

Players: Beau Bridges, Stockard Channing, Robert Sean Leonard, Mary Stuart Masterson, Cybill Shepherd, Ron Silver, Don Francks, Donna Vivino, Jimmy Shea, Nathaniel Moreau, Chris Wiggins, Gerry Bamman.

Matinee .... Universal

A Universal Pictures release of a Renfield production. Producer: Michael Finnell. Director: Joe Dante. Screenplay: Charlie Haas. Story: Jerico, Haas. Cinematography: John Hora. Music: Jerry Goldsmith. Editor: Marshall Harvey. In Deluxe color. Running time: 99 minutes. MPAA Rating: PG. Release date: January 29, 1993.

Players: John Goodman, Cathy Moriarty, Omri Katz, Simon Fenton, Lisa Jakub, Kellie Martin, Jesse Lee, Lucinda Jenney, James Villemaire, Robert Picardo, Jesse White, Dick Miller, John Sayles, David Clennon, Lucy Butler, Mark McCracken, William Schallert, Robert Cornthwaite, Kevin McCarthy.

The Meteor Man .... MGM

A Metro-Goldwyn-Mayer release of a Tinsel Townsend production. Producer: Loretha C. Jones. Director-Screenplay: Robert Townsend. Cinematography: John A. Alonzo. Music: Cliff Eidelman. Editors: Adam Bernardi, Richard Candib, Andrew London, Pam Wise. In Deluxe color. Running time: 100 minutes. MPAA Rating: PG. Release date: August 6, 1993.

Players: Robert Townsend, Marla Gibbs, Eddie Griffin, Robert Guillaume, James Earl Jones, Roy Fegan, Cynthia Belgrave, Marilyn Coleman, Another Bad Creation, Don Cheadle, Tiny Lister, Bobby McGee, Wallace Shawn, Stephanie Williams, Jenifer Lewis, Naughty By Nature, Cypress Hill, Biz Markie, Big Daddy Kane, Frank Gorshin, Beverly Johnson, LaWanda Page, Lela Rochon, Sinbad, Nancy Wilson, Luther Vandross, Bill Cosby, Stu Gilliam, Charlayne Woodard, Tommy R. Hicks, Faizon Love.

The Mighty Ducks .... Buena Vista

A Buena Vista release of a Walt Disney Pictures presentation in association with Touchstone Pacific Partners I of an Avnet/Kerner production. Producers: Jordan Kerner, Jon Avnet. Co-Producers: Lynn Morgan, Martin Hubert. Director: Stephen Herek. Screenplay: Steven Brill. Cinematography: Thomas Del Ruth. Music: David Newman. Editors: Larry Bock, John F. Link. In Technicolor. Running time: 105 minutes. MPAA Rating: PG. Release date: October 2, 1992.

Players: Emilio Estevez, Joss Ackland, Lane Smith, Heidi Kling, Josef Sommer, Joshua Jackson.

Mr. Baseball .... Universal

A Universal Pictures presentation of an Outlaw production in association with Pacific Artists. Producers: Fred Schepisi, Doug Claybourne, Robert Newmyer. Executive Producers: John Kao, Jeffrey Silver. Director: Schepisi. Screenplay: Gary Ross, Kevin Wade, Monte Merrick. Story: Theo Pelletier, John Junkerman. Cinematography: Ian Baker. Music: Jerry Goldsmith. Editor: Peter Honess. In Panavision, Deluxe color. Running time: 108 minutes. MPAA Rating: PG-13. Release date: October 2, 1992.

Players: Tom Selleck, Ken Takakura, Aya Takanashi, Toshi Shioya, Dennis Haysbert, Kohsuke Toyohara, Toshizo Fujiwara, Tim McCarver, Art LaFleur, Mak Takano, Leon Lee, Kenji Morinaga.

Mr. Saturday Night .... Columbia

A Columbia Pictures release of a Castle Rock Entertainment in association with New Line Cinema presentation of a Face production. Producer-Director: Billy Crystal. Executive Producers: Lowell Ganz,

Babaloo Mandel. Co-Producer: Peter Schindler. Screenplay: Crystal, Ganz, Mandel. Cinematography: Don Peterman. Music: Marc Shaiman. Editor: Kent Beyda. In Technicolor. Running time: 119 minutes. MPAA Rating: R. Release date: September 23, 1992.

Players: Billy Crystal, David Paymer, Julie Warner, Helen Hunt, Mary Mara, Jerry Orbach, Ron Silver, Sage Allen, Jason Marsden, Michael Weiner, Larry Gelman, Kay Freeman, Howard Mann, Julius Branca, Will Jordan, Jackie Gayle, Carl Ballantine, Slappy White, Richard Mehana, Conrad Janis, Tim Russ, Marc Shaiman, Jerry Lewis, Shadoe Stevens, Lindsay Crystal, Lowell Ganz, Babaloo Mandel.

The Muppet Christmas Carol ... Buena Vista
A Buena Vista Pictures release of a Walt Disney Pictures presentation from Jim Henson Productions. Producers: Brian Henson, Martin G. Baker. Co-Producer-Screenplay: Jerry Juhl. Director: Brian Henson. Cinematography: John Fenner. Music: Miles Goodman. Songs: Paul Williams. Editor: Michael Jablow. In Technicolor. Running time: 85 minutes. MPAA Rating: G. Release date: December 11, 1992.

Players: Michael Caine, Steven Mackintosh, Meredith Braun, Robin Weaver; and Kermit the Frog, Rizzo the Rat, Bean Bunny, Beaker, Belinda Cratchit (Steve Whitmire), The Great Gonzo, Robert Marley, Bunsen Honeydew, Betina Cratchit (Dave Goelz), Tiny Tim Cratchit, Jacob Marley, Ma Bear (Jerry Nelson), Miss Piggy, Fozzie Bear, Sam Eagle, Animal (Frank Oz), Peter Cratchit, Old Joe, Swedish Chef (David Rudman).

My Boyfriend's Back .... Buena Vista
A Buena Vista Pictures release of a Touchstone Pictures presentation. Producer: Sean S. Cunningham. Director: Bob Balaban. Screenplay: Dean Lorey. Cinematography: Mac Ahlberg. Music: Harry Manfredini. Editor: Michael Jablow. In color. Running time: 80 minutes. MPAA Rating: PG-13. Release date: August 6, 1993.

Players: Andrew Lowery, Traci Lind, Danny Zorn, Edward Herrmann, Mary Beth Hurt, Paul Dooley, Cloris Leachman, Matthew Fox, Austin Pendleton, Jay O. Sanders, Bob Dishy, Paxton Whitehead.

Needful Things .... Columbia
A Columbia Pictures release of a Castle Rock Entertainment presentation in association with New Line Cinema. Producer: Jack Cummins. Executive Producer: Peter Yates. Director: Fraser C. Heston. Screenplay: W.D. Richter, based on the novel by Stephen King. Cinematography: Tony Westman. Music: Patrick Doyle. Editor: Rob Kobrin. In Technicolor. Running time: 120 minutes. MPAA Rating: R. Release date: August 27, 1993.

Players: Ed Harris, Max von Sydow, Bonnie Bedelia, Amanda Plummer, J.T. Walsh, Ray McKinnon, Duncan Fraser, Valri Bromfield, Shane Meier.

Neil Simon's "Lost in Yonkers" ... Columbia
A Columbia Pictures release of a Rastar production. Producer: Ray Stark. Executive Producer: Joseph M. Caracciolo. Director: Martha Coolidge. Screenplay: Neil Simon, based on his play. Cinematography: Johnny E. Jensen. Music: Elmer Bernstein. Editor: Steven Cohen. In Technicolor. Running time: 110 minutes. MPAA Rating: PG. Release date: May 14, 1993.

Players: Richard Dreyfuss, Mercedes Ruehl, Irene Worth, Brad Stoll, Mike Damus, David Strathairn, Robert Guy Miranda, Jack Laufer, Susan Merson.

Night and the City .... 20th Century Fox
A 20th Century Fox release of a Tribeca Production in association with Penta Entertainment. Producer: Jane Rosenthal, Irwin Winkler. Executive Producers: Harry J. Ufland, Mary Jane Ufland. Co-Producer, Rob Cowan. Director: Winkler. Screenplay: Richard Price, based on the 1950 film written by Jo Eisinger, and the novel by Gerald Kersh. Cinematography: Tak Fujimoto. Music: James Newton Howard. Editor: David Brenner. In Deluxe color. Running time: 98 minutes. MPAA Rating: R. Release date: October 16, 1992.

Players: Robert De Niro, Jessica Lange, Cliff Gorman, Alan King, Jack Warden, Eli Wallach, Barry Primus, Gene Kirkwood, Pedro Sanchez.

Nowhere to Run .... Columbia
A Columbia Pictures release of an Adelson/Baumgarten production. Executive Producer: Michael Rachmil. Producers: Craig Baumgarten, Gary Adelson. Director: Robert Harmon. Screenplay: Joe Eszterhas, Leslie Bohem, Randy Feldman. Story: Eszterhas, Richard Marquand. Cinematography: David Gribble. Music: Mark Isham. Editor: Zach Staenberg, Mark Helfrich. In Technicolor. Running time: 94 minutes. MPAA Rating: R. Release date: January 22, 1993.

Players: Jean-Claude Van Damme, Rosanna Arquette, Kieran Culkin, Ted Levine, Tiffany Taubman, Edward Blatchford, Anthony Starke, Joss Ackland.

Of Mice and Men .... MGM
A Metro-Goldwyn-Mayer release of a Russ Smith/Gary Sinise production. Producers: Smith, Sinise. Executive Producer: Alan C. Blomquist. Director: Sinise. Screenplay: Horton Foote. Cinematography: Kenneth MacMillan. Music: Mark Isham. Editor: Robert L. Sinise. In Deluxe color. Running time: 110 minutes. MPAA Rating: PG-13. Release date: October 2, 1992.

Players: John Malkovich, Gary Sinise, Ray Walston, Casey Siemaszko, Sherilyn Fenn, John Terry, Richard Riehle, Alexis Arquette, Joe Morton, Noble Willingham, Joe d'Angerio, Tuck Milligan.

One Upon a Forest .... 20th Century Fox
A 20th Century Fox release of a Hanna-Barbera production in association with HTV Cymru/Wales Ltd. Producers: David Kirschner, Jerry Mills. Executive Producers: William Hanna, Paul Gertz. Director: Charles Grosvenor. Screenplay: Mark Young, Kelly Ward, from a story created by Rae Lambert. Animation Director: Dave Michener. Music: James Horner. Editor: Pat A. Foley. In CFI color. Running time: 80 minutes. MPAA Rating: G. Release date: June 19, 1993.

Voice Cast: Michael Crawford, Ben Vereen, Ellen Blain, Ben Gregory, Paige Gosney, Elizabeth Moss.

Only the Strong .... 20th Century Fox
A 20th Century Fox release of a Firestone Pictures & Davis Films presentation. Producers: Samuel Hadida, Stuart S. Shapiro, Steven G. Menkin. Executive Producer: Victor Hadida. Director: Sheldon Lettich. Screenplay: Lettich, Luis Esteban. Cinematography: Edward Pei. Music: Harvey W. Mason. Editor: Stephen Semel. In color. Running time: 96 minutes. MPAA Rating: PG-13. Release date: August 27, 1993.

Players: Mark Dacascos, Stacey Travis, Geoffrey Lewis, Paco Christian Prieto, Todd Susman, Jeffrey Anderson Gunter, Richard Coca.

Out on a Limb .... Universal
A Universal Pictures release of an Interscope Communications production. Producer: Michael Hertzberg. Executive Producers: Ted Field, Scott Kroopf, Robert W. Cort. Director: Francis Veber. Screenplay: Daniel Goldin, Joshua Goldin. Cinematography: Donald E. Thorin. Music: Van Dyke Parks. Editor: Glenn Farr. In Deluxe color. Running time: 83 minutes. MPAA Rating: PG. Release date: September 4, 1992.

Players: Matthew Broderick, Jeffrey Jones, Heidi Kling, John C. Reilly, Marian Mercer, Larry Hankin, David Margulies, Courtney Peldon, Michael Monks, Andy Kossin, Nancy Lenehan.

Passenger 57 .... Warner Bros.
A Warner Bros. release of a Lee Rich production. Producers: Lee Rich, Dan Paulson, Dylan Sellers. Executive Producer: Jonathan Sheinberg. Co-Producer: Robert J. Anderson. Director: Kevin Hooks. Screenplay: David Loughery, Dan Gordon. Story: Stewart Raffill, Gordon. Cinematography: Mark Irwin. Music: Stanley Clarke. Editor: Richard Nord. In Technicolor. Running time: 83 minutes. MPAA Rating: R. Release date: November 6, 1992.

Players: Wesley Snipes, Bruce Payne, Tom Sizemore, Alex Datcher, Bruce Greenwood, Robert Hooks, Elizabeth Hurley, Michael Horse, Marc Macaulay, Ernie Lively, Duchess Tomasello, Cameron Roberts, James Short, Joel Fogel, Jane McPherson.

The Pickle .... Columbia
Producer-Director-Screenplay: Paul Mazursky. Executive Producer: Patrick McCormick. Co-Producer-Editor: Stuart Pappe. Cinematography: Fred Murphy. Music: Michel Legrand. In Technicolor. Running time: 103 minutes. MPAA Rating: R. Release date: April 30, 1993.

Players: Danny Aiello, Dyan Cannon, Clotilde Courau, Shelley Winters, Barry Miller, Jerry Stiller, Chris Penn, Little Richard, Jodi Long, Rebecca Miller, Stephen Tobolowsky, Caroline Aaron, Linda Carlson, Ally Sheedy, Spalding Gray, Paul Mazursky, Griffin Dunne, Dudley Moore, Isabella Rossellini.

Poetic Justice .... Columbia
Producers: Steve Nicolaides, John Singleton. Director-Screenplay: Singleton. Cinematography: Peter Lyons Collister. Music: Stanley

Clarke. Editor: Bruce Cannon. In Technicolor. Running time: 110 minutes. MPAA Rating: R. Release date: July 23, 1993.

Players: Janet Jackson, Tupac Shakur, Regina King, Joe Torry, Tyra Ferrell, Roger Guenveur Smith, Maya Angelou, Q-Tip, Tone Loc, Miki Howard, Keith Washington, Mikki Val, Dina D., Baha Jackson.

Point of No Return .... Warner Bros.

A Warner Bros. release of an Art Linson production. Producer: Linson. Co-Producer: James Herbert. Director: John Badham. Screenplay: Robert Getchell, Alexandra Seros, based on the film "Nikita" by Luc Besson. Cinematography: Michael Watkins. Music: Hans Zimmer. Editor: Frank Morriss. In Panavision, Technicolor. Running time: 109 minutes. MPAA Rating: R. Release date: March 19, 1993.

Players: Bridget Fonda, Gabriel Byrne, Dermot Mulroney, Anne Bancroft, Miguel Ferrer, Harvey Keitel, Olivia D'Abo, Richard Romanus, Lorraine Toussaint, Geoffrey Lewis, Mic Rodgers, Michael Rapaport, Ray Oriel, Spike McClure, Lieux Dressler.

The Public Eye .... Universal

A Universal Pictures release of a Robert Zemeckis production. Producer: Sue Baden-Powell. Executive Producer: Zemeckis. Director-Screenplay: Howard Franklin. Cinematography: Peter Suschitzky. Music: Mark Isham. Editor: Evan Lottman. In Deluxe color. Running time: 98 minutes. MPAA Rating: R. Release date: October 16, 1992.

Players: Joe Pesci, Barbara Hershey, Stanley Tucci, Jerry Adler, Jared Harris, Richard Riehle, Timothy Hendrickson, Del Close, Gerry Becker, David Hull, Patricia Healy.

Pure Country .... Warner Bros.

A Warner Bros. release of a Jerry Weintraub production. Producer: Weintraub. Executive Producer: R.J. Louis. Director: Christopher Cain. Screenplay: Rex McGee. Cinematography: Richard Bowen. Music: Steve Dorff. Editor: Jack Hofstra. In Technicolor. Running time: 112 minutes. MPAA Rating: PG. Release date: October 23, 1992.

Players: George Strait, Lesley Ann Warrren, Isbael Glasser, Kyle Chandler, John Doe, Rory Calhoun, Molly McClure, James Terry McIlvain, Toby Metcalf, Mark Walters, Tom Christopher.

Rich in Love .... MGM

An MGM release of a Zanuck Co. production. Producers: Richard D. Zanuck, Lili Fini Zanuck. Co-Producers: David Brown, Gary Daigler. Director: Bruce Beresford. Screenplay: Alfred Uhry, based on the novel by Josephine Humphreys. Cinematography: Peter James. Music: Georges Delerue. Editor: Mark Warner. In Deluxe color. Running time: 105 minutes. MPAA Rating: PG-13. Release date: March 5, 1993.

Players: Albert Finney, Jill Clayburgh, Kathryn Erbe, Ethan Hawke, Kyle MacLachlan, Piper Laurie, Suzy Amis, Alfre Woodard.

Rising Sun .... 20th Century Fox

A 20th Century Fox release of a Walrus & Associates Ltd. production. Producer: Peter Kaufman. Executive Producer: Sean Connery. Director: Philip Kaufman. Screenplay: Philip Kaufman, Michael Crichton, Michael Backes. Based upon the novel by Michael Crichton. Cinematography: Michael Chapman. Music: Toru Takemitsu. Editors: Stephen A. Rotter, William S. Scharf. In Deluxe color. Running time: 129 minutes. MPAA Rating: R. Release date: July 30, 1993.

Players: Sean Connery, Wesley Snipes, Harvey Keitel, Cary-Hiroyuki Tagawa, Kevin Anderson, Mako, Ray Wise, Stan Egi, Stan Shaw, Tia Carrere, Steve Buscemi, Tajana Patitz, Peter Crombie, Sam Lloyd, Alexandra Powers, Daniel Von Bargen, Clyde Kusatsu, Lauren Robinson, Amy Hill, Michael Chapman.

A River Runs Through It .... Columbia

Producers: Robert Redford, Patrick Markey. Executive Producer: Jake Eberts. Director: Redford. Screenplay: Richard Friedenberg, based on the story by Norman Maclean. Cinematography: Philippe Rousselot. Music: Mark Isham. Editor: Lynzee Klingman. In Technicolor. Running time: 123 minutes. MPAA Rating: PG. Release date: October 9, 1992.

Players: Craig Sheffer, Brad Pitt, Tom Skerritt, Brenda Blethyn, Emily Lloyd, Edie McClurg, Stephen Shellen, Vann Gravage, Nicole Burdette, Susan Traylor, Joseph Gordon-Levitt, Michael Cudlitz, Rob Cox, Buck Simmonds, MacIntyre Dixon, Robert Redford (narrator).

Robin Hood:
Men in Tights .... 20th Century Fox

A 20th Century Fox release of a Brooksfilm production in association with Gaumont. Producer-Director: Mel Brooks. Executive Producer: Peter Schindler. Screenplay: Brooks, Evan Chandler, J. David Shapiro. Story: Shapiro, Chandler. Cinematographer: Michael D. O'Shea. Music: Hummie Mann. Editor: Stephen E. Rivkin. In Deluxe color. Running time: 104 minutes. MPAA Rating: PG-13. Release date: July 28, 1993.

Players: Cary Elwes, Richard Lewis, Roger Rees, Amy Yasbeck, Mark Blankfield, Dave Chappelle, Isaac Hayes, Megan Cavanagh, Eric Allan Kramer, Matthew Porretta, Tracey Ullman, Patrick Stewart, Dom De-Luise, Dick Van Patten, Robert Ridgley, Mel Brooks, Avery Schreiber, Chuck McCann, Clive Revill, Carol Arthur, Malcolm Danare, Rudy De Luca, Laurie Main, James Van Patten, David DeLuise, Tony Tanner, Ronny Graham.

Rookie of the Year .... 20th Century Fox

Producer: Robert Harper. Executive Producer: Jack Brodsky, Irby Smith. Director: Daniel Stern. Screenplay: Sam Harper. Cinematography: Jack N. Green. Music: Bill Conti. Editors: Donn Cambern, Raja Gosnell. In Technicolor. Running time: 103 minutes. MPAA Rating: PG. Release date: July 7, 1993.

Players: Thomas Ian Nicholas, Gary Busey, Albert Hall, Amy Norton, Dan Hedaya, Daniel Stern, Bruce Altman, Eddie Bracken, John Candy.

The Sandlot .... 20th Century Fox

A 20th Century Fox release of an Island World presentation. Producers: Dale de la Torre, William S. Gilmore. Executive Producers: Mark Burg, Chris Zarpas. Director: David Mickey Evans. Screenplay: Evans, Robert Gunter. Cinematography: Anthony B. Richmond. Music: David Newman. Editor: Michael A. Stevenson. In Deluxe color. Running time: 101 minutes. MPAA Rating: PG. Release date: April 7, 1993.

Players: Tom Guiry, Mike Vitar, Patrick Renna, Chauncey Leopardi, Marty York, Brandon Adams, Grant Gelt, Karen Allen, James Earl Jones, Denis Leary, Shane Obedzinski, Victor DiMattia, Art La Fleur, Marlee Shelton, Herb Muller, Maury Wills, Arliss Howard.

Sarafina! .... Buena Vista

A Hollywood Pictures and Miramax Films release of an Anant Singh production of a Distant Horizon and Ideal Films presentation in association with Videovision Enterprises, Les Films Ariane, Vanguard Films and the BBC. Executive Producers: Kirk D'Amico, Sudhir Pragjee, Helena Spring, Sanjeev Singh. Director: Darrell James Roodt. Screenplay: William Nicholson, Mbongeni Ngema. Cinematography: Mark Vicente. Music: Stanley Myers. Songs: Ngema, Hugh Masekela. Editors: Peter Hollywood, Sarah Thomas, David Heitner. French-British-South African. In Technicolor. Running time: 99 minutes. MPAA Rating: PG-13. Release date: September 18, 1992.

Players: Leleti Khumalo, Whoopi Goldberg, Miriam Makeba, John Kani, Dumisani Dlamini, Mbongeni Ngema, Sipho Kunene, Tertius Meintjes, Robert Whithead.

Scent of a Woman .... Universal

A Universal Pictures release of a City Light Films production. Producer-Director: Martin Brest. Executive Producer: Ronald L. Schwary. Screenplay: Bo Goldman. Cinematography: Donald E. Thorin. Music: Thomas Newman. Editors: William Steinkamp, Michael Tronick, Harvey Rosenstock. In Deluxe/Duart color. Running time: 155 minutes. MPAA Rating: R. Release date: December 23, 1992.

Players: Al Pacino, Chris O'Donnell, James Rebhorn, Gabrielle Anwar, Philip S. Hoffman, Richard Venture, Bradley Whitford, Rochelle Oliver, Nicholas Sadler, Margaret Eginton, Tom Riis Farrell, Gene Canfield, Frances Conroy, Ron Eldard, David Lansbury.

School Ties .... Paramount

A Paramount Pictures release of a Jaffe/Lansing production. Producers: Stanley R. Jaffe, Sherry Lansing. Executive Producer: Danton Rissner. Director: Robert Mandel. Screenplay: Dick Wolf, Darryl Ponicsan. Story: Wolf. Cinematography: Freddie Francis. Music: Maurice Jarre. Editors: Jerry Greenberg, Jacqueline Cambas. In Deluxe color. Running time: 107 minutes. MPAA Rating: PG-13. Release date: September 18, 1992.

Players: Brendan Fraser, Matt Damon, Chris O'Donnell, Randall Batinkoff, Andrew Lowery, Cole Hauser, Ben Affleck, Anthony Rapp, Amy Locane, Peter Donat, Zeljko Ivanek, Kevin Tighe, Michael Higgins, Ed Lauter, Elizabeth Franz, John Cunningham.

Searching for Bobby Fischer .... Paramount

A Paramount Pictures release of a Joel Rudin/Mirage production. Producers: Rudin, William Horberg. Executive Producer: Sydney Pollack. Co-Producer: David Wisnievitz. Director/Screenplay: Steven Zaillian, based upon the book by Fred Waitzkin. Cinematography: Conrad L. Hall. Music: James Horner. Editor: Wayne Wahrman. In color. Running time: 110 minutes. MPAA Rating: PG. Release date: August 11, 1993.

Players: Joe Mantegna, Max Pomeranc, Joan Allen, Laurence Fishburne, Ben Kingsley, David Paymer, Michael Nirenberg, Robert Stephens, Hal Scardino, Vasek Simek, William H. Macy, Dan Hedaya, Laura Linney, Anthony Heald, Steven Randazzo, Josh Mostel, Chelsea Moore, Tony Shalhoub, Tom McGowan, Austin Pendleton, Joel Benjamin.

The Secret Garden .... Warner Bros.

A Warner Bros. release of an American Zoetrope production. Producers: Fred Fuchs, Fred Roos, Tom Luddy. Executive Producer: Francis Ford Coppola. Director: Agnieszka Holland. Screenplay: Caroline Thompson. Based on the book by Frances Hodgson Burnett. Cinematography: Roger Deakins. Music: Zbigniew Preisner. Editor: Isabelle Lorente. In Technicolor. Running time: 101 minutes. MPAA Rating: G. Release date: August 13, 1993.

Players: Kate Maberly, Heydon Prowse, Andrew Knott, Maggie Smith, Laura Crossley, John Lynch, Walter Sparrow, Irene Jacobs, Frank Baker, Valerie Hill, Andrea Pickering.

Shadow of the Wolf .... Triumph

A Triumph release of a Vision International and Mark Damon presentation in association with Transfilm Inc. and Eiffel Production S.A. Producer: Claude Leger. Executive Producer: Charles L. Smiley. Co-Producer-Director: Jacques Dorfmann. Screenplay: Rudy Worlitzer, Evan Jones, based upon the novel "Agaguk" by Yves Theriault. Cinematography: Billy Williams. Music: Maurice Jarre. Editor: Francoise Bonnot. French-Canadian. In color, Cinemascope. Running time: 108 minutes. MPAA Rating: PG-13. Release date: March 5, 1993.

Players: Lou Diamond Phillips, Toshiro Mifune, Jennifer Tilly, Donald Sutherland, Bernard-Pierre Donnadieu, Nicolas Campbell, Raoul Trujillo, Qalingo Tookalak, Jobie Arnaituk.

Sidekicks .... Triumph

A Triumph Releasing Corp. release of a Gallery Films presentation. Producer: Don Carmody. Executive Producers: Chuck Norris, Jim McIngvale, Linda McIngvale. Director: Aaron Norris. Screenplay: Don Thompson, Lou Illar. Story: Illar. Cinematography: Joao Fernandes. Music: Alan Silvestri. Editors: David Rawlins, Bernard Weiser. In color. Running time: 100 minutes. MPAA Rating: PG. Release date: April 16, 1993.

Players: Jonathan Brandis, Chuck Norris, Beau Bridges, Mako, Julia Nickson-Soul, Joe Piscopo, Danica McKellar, John Buchanan, Richard Moll.

Singles .... Warner Bros.

A Warner Bros. release of an Atkinson/Knickerbocker Films production. Producers: Cameron Crowe, Richard Hashimoto. Executive Producer: Art Linson. Co-Producer-Editor: Richard Chew. Director-Screenplay: Crowe. Cinematography: Ueli Steiger. Music: Paul Westerberg. In Technicolor. Running time: 99 minutes. MPAA Rating: PG-13. Release date: September 18, 1992.

Players: Campbell Scott, Kyra Sedgwick, Bridget Fonda, Matt Dillon, Sheila Kelly, Jim True, Bill Pullman, James Le Gros, Devon Raymond, Camillo Gallardo, Ally Walker, Eric Stoltz, Jeremy Piven, Tom Skerritt, Peter Horton, Bill Smillie, Victor Garber.

Sleepless in Seattle .... TriStar

A TriStar Pictures release of a Gary Foster production. Producer: Foster. Executive Producers: Lynda Obst, Patrick Crowley. Director: Nora Ephron. Screenplay: Ephron, David S. Ward, Jeff Arch. Story: Arch. Cinematography: Sven Nykvist. Music: Marc Shaiman. Editor: Robert Reitano. In Technicolor. Running time: 104 minutes. MPAA Rating: PG. Release date: June 26, 1993.

Players: Tom Hanks, Meg Ryan, Ross Malinger, Rosie O'Donnell, Bill Pullman, Gaby Hoffman, Rob Reiner, Victor Garber, Rita Wilson, Barbara Garrick, Carey Lowell.

Sliver .... Paramount

A Paramount Pictures release of a Robert Evans Production. Producer: Evans. Executive Producers: Howard W. Koch, Jr., Joe Esz-

terhas. Co-Producer: William J. MacDonald. Director: Phillip Noyce. Screenplay: Eszterhas, based on the novel by Ira Levin. Cinematography: Vilmos Zsigmond. Music: Howard Shore. Editors: Richard Francis-Bruce, William Hoy. In Deluxe color. Running time: 106 minutes. MPAA Rating: R. Release date: May 21, 1993.

Players: Sharon Stone, Tom Berenger, William Baldwin, Polly Walker, Colleen Camp, Amanda Foreman, Martin Landau, CCH Pounder, Nina Foch, Keene Curtis, Nicholas Pryor, Anne Betancourt, Tony Peck, Frantz Turner.

Sneakers .... Universal

A Universal Pictures release of a Lawrence Lasker/Walter F. Parkes production. Producers: Parkes, Lasker. Executive Producer: Lindsley Parsons, Jr. Director: Phil Alden Robinson. Screenplay: Robinson, Lasker, Parkes. Cinematography: John Lindley. Music: James Horner. Editor: Tom Rolf. In Technicolor. Running time: 125 minutes. MPAA Rating: PG-13. Release date: September 9, 1992.

Players: Robert Redford, Sidney Poitier, River Phoenix, Dan Aykroyd, Ben Kingsley, Mary McDonnell, David Strathairn, Timothy Busfield, George Hearn, Stephen Tobolowsky, Gary Hershberger, Jojo Marr, James Earl Jones.

Sniper .... TriStar

A TriStar Pictures release of a Baltimore Pictures production. Executive Producers: Mark Johnson, Walon Green, Patrick Wachsberger. Producer: Robert L. Rosen. Director: Luis Llosa. Screenplay: Michael Frost Beckner, Crash Leyland. Cinematography: Bill Butler. Music: Gary Chang. Editor: Scott Smith. In Film House color. Running time: 98 minutes. MPAA Rating: R. Release date: January 29, 1993.

Players: Tom Berenger, Billy Zane, J.T. Walsh, Aden Young, Ken Radley, Reinaldo Arenas, Carolos Alvarez, Roy Edmonds.

So I Married an Axe Murderer .... TriStar

A TriStar Pictures release of a Fried/Woods Films production. Producers: Robert N. Fried, Cary Woods. Executive Producer: Bernie Williams. Co-Producer: Jana Sue Memel. Director: Thomas Schlamme. Screenplay: Robbie Fox. Cinematography: Julio Macat. Music: Bruce Broughton. Editors: Richard Halsey, Colleen Halsey. In Technicolor. Running time: 110 minutes. MPAA Rating: PG-13. Release date: July 30, 1993.

Players: Mike Myers, Nancy Travis, Anthony LaPaglia, Amanda Plummer, Brenda Fricker, Matt Doherty, Charles Grodin, Phil Hartman, Debi Mazar, Steven Wright, Patrick Bristow, Cintra Wilson, Greg Germann, Adele Proom, Alan Arkin.

Sommersby .... Warner Bros.

A Warner Bros. release of a Le Studio Canal+, Regency Enterprises/Alcor Films presentation of an Arnon Milchan production. Executive Producers: Richard Gere, Maggie Wilde. Producer: Milchan. Director: Jon Amiel. Screenplay: Nicholas Meyer, Sarah Kernochan. Story: Meyer, Anthony Shaffer, based on the film "The Return of Martin Guare" by Daniel Vigne, Jean-Claude Carriere. Cinematography: Philippe Rousselt. Music: Danny Elfman. Editor: Peter Boyle. In Panavision, Technicolor. Running time: 115 minutes. Rated PG-13. Release date: February 5, 1993.

Players: Richard Gere, Jodie Foster, William Windom, Lanny Flaherty, Bill Pullman, Brett Kelley, Clarice Taylor, Frankie Faison, R. Lee Ermey, Richard Hamilton, James Earl Jones, Karen Kirschenbauer, Carter McNeese, Dean Whitworth, Maury Chaykin.

Son-in-Law .... Buena Vista

A Buena Vista Pictures release of a Hollywood Pictures presentation of a Rotenberg/Lenkov production. Producers: Michael Rotenberg, Peter M. Lenkov. Executive Producer: Hilton Green. Director: Steve Rash. Screenplay: Fax Bahr, Adam Small, Shawn Schepps. Story: Patrick J. Clifton, Susan McMartin, Lenkov. Cinematography: Peter Deming. Music: Richard Gibbs. Editor: Dennis M. Hill. In Technicolor. Running time: 95 minutes. MPAA Rating: PG-13. Release date: July 2, 1993.

Players: Pauly Shore, Carla Gugino, Lane Smith, Cindy Pickett, Mason Adams, Patrick Renna, Dennis Burkley, Tiffani-Amber Thiessen, Dan Gauthier.

Son of the Pink Panther .... MGM

An MGM release of a United Artists presentation in association with Filmauro S.R.L. Producer: Tony Adams. Executive Producer: Nigel Wooll. Director/Story: Blake Edwards. Screenplay: Edwards, Madeline Sunshine, Steve Sunshine. Cinematography: Dick Bush. Music: Henry Mancini. Editor: Robert Pergament. In Deluxe color. Running time: 93 minutes. MPAA Rating: PG. Release date: August 27, 1993.

Players: Roberto Benigni, Herbert Lom, Claudia Cardinale, Shabana Azmi, Debrah Farentino, Jennifer Edwards, Robert Davi, Mark Schneider, Mike Starr, Kenny Spalding, Anton Rodgers, Burt Kwouk, Graham Stark, Oliver Cotton, Spütare Tanney, Liz Smith, Nicoletta Braschi.

South Central .... Warner Bros.

A Warner Bros. release of an Oliver Stone presentation of an Ixtlan production in association with Monument Pictures & Enchantment Films. Producers: Janet Yang, William B. Steakley. Co-Producer-Director-Screenplay: Steve Anderson, based on the novel "Crips" by Donald Bakeer. Executive Producer: Stone. Co-Executive Producers: Michael Spielberg, Brad Gilbert. Cinematography: Charlie Lieberman. Music: Tim Truman. Editor: Steve Nevius. In Deluxe color. Running time: 99 minutes. MPAA Rating: R. Release date: September 18, 1992.

Players: Glenn Plummer, Byron Keith Minns, Lexie D. Bigham, Vincent Craig Dupree, LaRita Shelby, Kevin Best, Allan Hatcher, Alvin Hatcher, Christian Coleman, Ivory Ocean, Starletta Dupois, Carl Lumbly.

Super Mario Bros. .... Buena Vista

A Buena Vista Pictures release of a Hollywood Pictures presentation of a Lightmotive/Allied Filmmakers presentation in association with Cinergi Productions. Producers: Jake Eberts, Roland Joffe. Co-Producer: Fred Caruso. Directors: Rocky Morton, Annabel Jankel. Screenplay: Parker Bennett, Terry Runte, Ed Solomon. Cinematography: Dean Semler. Music: Alan Silvestri. Editor: Mark Goldblatt. In Technicolor. Running time: 104 minutes. MPAA Rating: PG. Release date: May 28, 1993.

Players: Bob Hoskins, John Leguizamo, Dennis Hoppper, Samantha Mathis, James Stevens, Richard Edson, Fiona Shaw, Dana Kaminski, Mojo Nixon, Gianni Russo, Francesca Roberts, Lance Henriksen, Sylvia Harman, Desiree Marie Velez, Andrea Powell, Heather Pendergast, Melanie Salvatore, John Fifer.

Swing Kids .... Buena Vista

A Buena Vista Pictures release of a Hollywood Pictures presentation in association with Touchwood Pacific Partners I of a John Bard Manulis/Mark Gordon production. Producers: Gordon, Manulis. Executive Producers: Frank Marshall, Christopher Meledandri. Co-Producer: Harry Benn. Director: Thomas Carter. Screenplay: Jonathan Marc Feldman. Cinematography: Jerzy Zielinski. Music: James Horner. Editor: Michael R. Miller. In Technicolor. Running time: 113 minutes. MPAA Rating: PG-13. Release date: March 5, 1993.

Players: Robert Sean Leonard, Christian Bale, Frank Whaley, Barbara Hershey, Kenneth Branagh, Tushka Bergen, David Tom, Julia Stemberger, Jayce Bartok, Noah Wyle, Johan Leysen, Douglas Roberts, Martin Clunes, Jessica Stevenson.

The Temp .... Paramount

A Paramount Pictures release of a David Permut production. Producers: Permut, Tom Engelman. Executive Producer: Howard W. Koch, Jr. Director: Tom Holland. Screenplay: Kevin Falls. Story: Falls, Engelman. Cinematography: Steve Yaconelli. Music: Frederic Talgorn. Editor: Scott Conrad. In Deluxe color. Running time: 98 minutes. MPAA Rating: R. Release date: February 12, 1993.

Players: Timothy Hutton, Lara Flynn Boyle, Faye Dunaway, Dwight Schultz, Oliver Platt, Steven Weber, Colleen Flynn, Scott Coffey, Dakin Matthews, Maura Tierney, Lin Shaye, Michael Winters.

That Night .... Warner Bros.

A Warner Bros. release of a Le Studio Canal+, Regency Enterprises and Alcor Films presentation of an Arnon Milchan production. Producers: Arnon Milchan, Steven Reuther. Executive Producers: Julie Kirkham, Elliott Lewitt. Co-Producer: Llewellyn Wells. Director-Screenplay: Craig Bolotin. Based upon the novel by Alice McDermott. Cinematography: Bruce Surtees. Music: David Newman. Editor: Priscilla Nedd-Friendly. In color. Running time: 89 minutes. MPAA Rating: PG-13. Release date: August 6, 1993.

Players: C. Thomas Howell, Juliette Lewis, Helen Shaver, Eliza Duschku, J. Smith-Cameron, John Dossett.

There Goes the Neighborhood ... Paramount

A Paramount Pictures release of a Kings Road production. Producer: Stephen Friedman. Director-Screenplay: Bill Phillips. Cinematogra-

phy: Walt Lloyd. Music: David Bell. Editor: Sharyn L. Ross. In Panavision, Color. Running time: 88 minutes. MPAA Rating: PG-13. Release date: November 6, 1992.

Players: Jeff Daniels, Catherine O'Hara, Dabney Coleman, Hector Elizondo, Judith Ivey, Rhea Perlman, Harris Yulin.

The Thing Called Love .... Paramount

A Paramount Pictures release of a John Davis production. Producer: Davis. Director: Peter Bogdanovich. Screenplay: Carol Heikkinen. Editor: Terry Stokes. In Deluxe color. Running time: 116 minutes. MPAA Rating: PG-13. Release date: August 27, 1993.

Players: River Phoenix, Samantha Mathis, Dermot Mulroney, Sandra Bullock, Trisha Yearwood, K.T. Oslin, Anthony Clark, Webb WIlder, Deborah Allen, Jimie Dale Gilmore, Katy Moffatt, Joel Sonnier, Pam Tillis, Kevin Welch.

This Boy's Life .... Warner Bros.

A Warner Bros. release of an Art Linson production. Producer: Art Linson. Executive Producers: Peter Guber, Jon Peters. Director: Michael Caton-Jones. Screenplay: Robert Getchell, based on the book by Tobias Wolff. Cinematography: David Watkin. Music: Carter Burwell. Editor: Jim Clark. In Panavision, Technicolor. Running time: 115 minutes. MPAA Rating: R. Release date: April 9, 1993.

Players: Robert De Niro, Ellen Barkin, Leonard DiCaprio, Jonah Blechman, Eliza Duschku, Chris Cooper, Carla Gugino, Zack Ansley, Tracey Ellis, Kathy Kinney, Bobby Zameroski, Tobey Maguire, Gerrit Graham, Lee Wilkof, Tristan Tait, Travis MacDonald.

Toys .... 20th Century Fox

A 20th Century Fox release of a Baltimore Pictures production. Producers: Mark Johnson, Barry Levinson. Co-Producers: Charles Newirth, Peter Giuiliano. Director: Levinson. Screenplay: Valerie Curtin, Levinson. Cinematography: Adam Greenberg. Music: Hans Zimmer, Trevor Horn. Editor: Stu Linder. In Deluxe color. Running time: 121 minutes. MPAA Rating: PG-13. Release date: December 18, 1992.

Players: Robin Williams, Michael Gambon, Joan Cusack, Robin Wright, LL Cool J, Donald O'Connor, Arthur Malet, Jack Warden, Debi Mazar, Wendy Melvoin, Julio Oscar Mechoso, Jamie Foxx.

Trespass .... Paramount

A Universal Pictures release of a Canton/Zemeckis/Gale production. Producer: Neil Canton. Executive Producers-Screenplay: Robert Zemeckis, Bob Gale. Director: Walter Hill. Cinematography: Lloyd Ahern. Music: Ry Cooder. Editor: Freeman Davies. In Deluxe color. Running time: 101 minutes. MPAA Rating: R. Release date: December 25, 1992.

Players: Bill Paxton, Ice T, William Sadler, Ice Cube, Art Evans, De'Voreaux White, Bruce A. Young, Glenn Plummer, Stoney Jackson, T.E. Russell, Tiny Lister, John Toles-Bey, Tico Wells.

Under Siege .... Warner Bros.

A Warner Bros. release in association with Regency Enterprises, Le Studio Canal+, and Alcor Films of an Arnon Milchan production. Producers: Milchan, Steven Seagal, Steven Reuther. Executive Producers: J.F. Lawton, Gary Goldstein. Co-Producers: Jack B. Bernstein, Peter MacGregor-Scott. Director: Andrew Davis. Screenplay: Lawton. Cinematography: Frank Tidy. Music: Gary Chang. Editor: Robert A. Ferretti. In Technicolor, Panavision. Running time: 102 minutes. MPAA Rating: R. Release date: October 9, 1992.

Players: Steven Seagal, Tommy Lee Jones, Gary Busey, Erika Eleniak, Patrick O'Neal, Nick Mancuso, Andy Romano, Damian Chapa, Troy Evans, David McKnight, Bernie Casey, Michael Welden, Colm Meaney.

Untamed Heart .... MGM

Executive Producer: J. Boyce Harman, Jr. Producers: Tony Bill, Helen Buck Bartlett. Director: Bill. Screenplay: Tom Sierchio. Cinematography: Jost Vacano. Music: Cliff Eidelman. Editor: Mia Goldman. In Deluxe color. Running time: 102 minutes. MPAA Rating: PG-13. Release date: February 12, 1993.

Players: Christian Slater, Marisa Tomei, Rosie Perez, Kyle Secor, Willie Garson, James Cada, Gary Groomes, Claudia Wilkens.

Used People .... 20th Century Fox

A 20th Century Fox release from Largo Entertainment of a Lawrence Gordon presentation, in association with JVC Entertainment. Executive Producer: Lloyd Levin, Michael Barnathan. Producer: Peggy

Rajski. Director: Beeban Kidron. Screenplay-Co-Producer: Todd Graff, based on his "The Grandma Plays." Cinematography: David Watkin. Music: Rachel Portman. Editor: John Tintori. In Deluxe color. Running time: 115 minutes. MPAA Rating: PG-13. Release date: December 16, 1992.

Players: Shirley MacLaine, Kathy Bates, Marcello Mastroianni, Jessica Tandy, Marcia Gay Harden, Sylvia Sidney, Joe Pantoliano, Mathew Branton, Bob Dishy, Charles Cioffi, Louis Guss, Helen Hanft, Irving Metzman, Doris Roberts, Lee Wallace.

The Vanishing .... 20th Century Fox

A 20th Century Fox release of a Morra, Brezner, Steinberg & Tenenbaum production. Executive Producers: Peiter Jan Brugge, Lauren Weissman. Producers: Larry Brezner, Paul Schiff. Director: George Sluizer. Screenplay: Todd Graff, based on the film "Spoorloss" by Sluizer, Tim Krabbe, and on the novel "The Golden Egg" by Krabbe. Cinematography: Peter Suschitzky. Music: Jerry Goldsmith. Editor: Bruce Green. In Deluxe color. Running time: 110 minutes. MPAA Rating: R. Release date: February 5, 1993.

Players: Jeff Bridges, Kiefer Sutherland, Nancy Travis, Sandra Bullock, Park Overall, Maggie Linderman, Lisa Eichhorn, George Hearn, Lynn Hamilton.

Weekend at Bernie's II .... TriStar

A TriStar Pictures release of a Victor Drai Productions presentation of an Artim production. Producers: Drai, Joseph Perez. Executive Producer: Howard Ellis. Co-Producer: Don Carmody. Director-Screenplay: Robert Klane. Cinematographer: Edward Morey III. Music: Peter Wolf. Editor: Peck Prior. In Deluxe color. Running time: 89 minutes. MPAA Rating: PG. Release date: July 9, 1993.

Players: Andrew McCarthy, Jonathan Silverman, Terry Kiser, Barry Bostwick, Troy Beyer, Tom Wright, Steve James, Novella Nelson, Phil Coccioletti, Gary Dourdan, James Lally, Michael Rogers.

What's Love Got to Do With It .. Buena Vista

A Buena Vista release of a Touchstone Pictures presentation of a Krost/Chapin production. Producers: Doug Chapin, Barry Krost. Executive Producers: Roger Davies, Mario Iscovich. Co-Producer: Pat Kehoe. Director: Brian Gibson. Screenplay: Kate Lanier, based on the book "I, Tina" by Tina Turner and Kurt Loder. Cinematography: Jamie Anderson. Music: Stanley Clarke. Editor: Stuart Pappe. In Technicolor. Running time: 118 minutes. MPAA Rating: R. Release date: June 9, 1993.

Players: Angela Bassett, Laurence Fishburne, Vanessa Bell Calloway, Jenifer Lewis, Phyllis Yvonne Stickney, Khandi Alexander.

Wilder Naplam .... TriStar

A TriStar Pictures release of a Baltimore Pictures production. Producers: Mark Johnson, Stuart Cornfeld. Executive Producer: Barrie M. Osborne. Director: Glenn Gordon Caron. Screenplay: Vince Gilligan. Cinematography: Jerry Hartleben. Music: Michael Kamen. Editor: Artie Mandelberg. In Technicolor. Running time: 110 minutes. MPAA Rating: PG-13. Release date: August 20, 1993.

Players: Debra Winger, Dennis Quaid, Arliss Howard, M. Emmet Walsh, Jim Varney, Mimi Lieber, Marvin J. McIntyre, The Mighty Echoes, Justin LaBlanc, Lance Lee Baxley, Peter Willie.

Wind .... TriStar

A TriStar Pictures release of a Mata Yamamoto production. Producers: Yamamoto, Tom Luddy. Executive Producers: Francis Ford Coppola, Fred Fuchs. Director: Carroll Ballard. Screenplay: Rudy Wurlitzer, Mac Gudgeon. Story: Jeff Benjamin, Roger Vaughan, Kimball Livingston. Cinematography: John Toll. Music: Basil Poledouris. Editor: Michael Chandler. In Technicolor. Running time: 126 minutes. MPAA Rating: PG-13. Release date: September 11, 1992.

Players: Matthew Modine, Jennifer Grey, Cliff Robertson, Jack Thompson, Stellan Skarsgard, Rebecca Miller, Ned Vaughn, Peter Montgomery, Elmer Ahlwardt, Saylor Creswell, James Rebhorn, Michael Higgins, Mark Walsh, Kim Sheridan, Bruce Epke, Sean Leonard.

Zebrahead .... Triumph

A Triumph relase of an Ixtlan production. Producers: Jeff Dowd, Charles Mitchell, WIlliam F. Willett. Executive Producers: Oliver Stone, Janet Yang. Co-Executive Producer: Peter Newman. Director-Screenplay: Anthony Drazan. Cinematography: Maryse Alberti. Music: Taj Mahal. Editor: Elizabeth Kling. In color. Running time: 100 minutes. MPAA Rating: R. Release date: October 23, 1992.

Players: Michael Rapaport, N'Bushe Wright, Kevin Corrigan, Deshonn Castle, Ray Sharkey, Martin Priest, Shirley Benyas, Helen Shaver, Luke Reilly, Paul Butler.

Films Released in the U.S. by Independent Distributors and Classics Divisions

September, 1992–August, 1993

Key: Running time is opposite title, followed by distributor, MPAA rating (if any, in parentheses), month and year of release, director (in parentheses), and stars.

American Fabulous 105
FIRST RUN FEATURES. October, 1992. (Reno Dakota), Jeffrey Strouth.

American Heart 113
TRITON. (R) May, 1993. (Martin Bell), Jeff Bridges, Edward Furlong, Lucinda Jenney.

Amongst Friends 88
FINE LINE. (R) July, 1993. (Rob Weiss), Steve Parlavecchio, Joseph Lindsey, Patrick McGraw.

Bad Lieutenant 98
ARIES FILMS. (NC-17) November, 1992. (Abel Ferrara), Harvey Keitel, Frankie Thorn, Paul Hipp.

The Ballad of Little Jo 120
FINE LINE. (R) August, 1993. (Maggie Greenwalt), Suzy Amis, Ian McKellen, David Chung.

Benefit of the Doubt 90
MIRAMAX. (R) July, 1993. (Jonathan Heap), Donald Sutherland, Amy Irving, Graham Greene.

Bodies, Rest & Motion 93
FINE LINE. (R) April, 1993. (Michael Steinberg), Phoebe Cates, Eric Stoltz, Bridget Fonda.

Breaking the Rules 100
MIRAMAX. (PG-13) October, 1992. (Neal Israel), Jason Bateman, C. Thomas Howell, Jonathan Silverman.

Brother's Keeper 120
CREATIVE THINKING. September, 1992. (Joe Berlinger, Bruce Sinofsky), Documentary.

Butterscotch and Chocolate 87
LANG & ASSOCS. (PG-13) October, 1992. (Nate Grant), Rickey Hendon, Tony Alcantar.

By the Sword 91
MOVIE GROUP. (R) May, 1993. (Jeremy Kagan), F. Murray Abraham, Eric Roberts, Mia Sara.

Carnosaur 82
CONCORDE. (R) May, 1993. (Adam Simon), Diane Ladd, Raphael Sbarge, Jennifer Runyon.

Chain of Desire 107
MAD DOG PICTURES. (R) June, 1993. (Temistocles Lopez), Malcolm McDowell, Linda Fiorentino, Tim Guinee.

Cheatin' Hearts 90
TRIMARK. July, 1993. (Rod McCall), Sally Kirkland, James Brolin, Kris Kristofferson.

Children of the Corn II 92
DIMENSION. (R) January, 1993. (David Price), Terence Knox, Paul Scherrer, Rosalind Allen.

Claire of the Moon 107
DEMI-MONDE. October, 1992. (Nicole Conn), Trisha Todd, Karen Trumbo, Faith McDevitt.

Delivered Vacant 118
ISLET. May, 1993. (Nora Jacobson), Documentary.

Double Threat 96
PYRAMID. (R) December, 1992. (David A. Prior), Sally Kirkland, Andrew Stevens, Richard Lynch.

Emma and Elvis 105
NORTHERN ARTS. October, 1992. (Julia Reichert), Kathryn Walker, Mark Blum, Jason Duchin.

Equinox 115
I.R.S. June, 1993. (Alan Rudolph), Matthew Modine, Lara Flynn Boyle, Marisa Tomei.

Ethan Frome 99
MIRAMAX. (PG) March, 1993. (John Madden), Liam Neeson, Patricia Arquette, Joan Allen.

Excessive Force 90
NEW LINE CINEMA. (R) May, 1993. (Jon Hess), Thomas Ian Griffith, Charlotte Lewis, James Earl Jones.

Family Prayers 105
ARROW ENTERTAINMENT. (PG) March, 1993. (Scott Rosenfelt), Joe Mantegna, Anne Archer, Paul Reiser.

Fathers and Sons 100
PACIFIC PICTURES. (R) November, 1992. (Paul Mones), Jeff Goldblum, Rory Cochrane, Rocky Carroll.

Feed 76
ORIGINAL CINEMA. October, 1992. (Kevin Rafferty, James Ridgeway), Documentary.

Fifty Fifty 101
CANNON. (R) February, 1993. (Charles Martin Smith), Peter Weller, Robert Hays, Ramona Rahman.

From Hollywood to Hanoi 78
INDEPT. July, 1993. (Tiana Thi Thanh Nga), Documentary.

Frozen Assets 96
RKO. (PG-13) October, 1992. (George Miller), Shelley Long, Corbin Bernsen, Larry Miller.

The Giving 100
NORTHERN ARTS. November, 1992. (Eames Demetrios), Jeremiah Pollock, Lee Hampton, Flor Hawkins.

Glengarry Glen Ross (P) 100
NEW LINE CINEMA. (R) September, 1992. (James Foley), Al Pacino, Jack Lemmon, Ed Harris.

Happily Ever After 74
FIRST NATIONAL. (G) May, 1993. (John Howley), Animated.

Hellraiser III: Hell on Earth 93
DIMENSION. (R) September, 1992. (Anthony Hickox), Doug Bradley, Terry Farrell, Paula Marshall.

Hold Me, Thrill Me, Kiss Me 92
MAD DOG PICTURES. July, 1993. (Joel Hirshman), Adrienne Shelly, Sean Young, Max Parrish.

House of Cards 107
MIRAMAX. June, 1993. (Michael Lessac), Kathleen Turner, Tommy Lee Jones, Asha Menina.

How U Like Me Now 109
SHAPIRO GLICKENHAUS. (R) March, 1993. (Darryl Roberts), Darnell Williams, Salli Richardson, Daniel Gardner.

Hugh Hefner: Once Upon a Time 91
I.R.S. October, 1992. (Robert Heath), Documentary.

I'll Love You Forever . . . Tonight 77
HEADLINER PRODS. July, 1993. (Edgar Michael Bravo), Paul Marius, Jason Adams, David Poynter. B&W.

In the Soup 90
TRITON. October, 1992. (Alexandre Rockwell), Steve Buscemi, Seymour Cassel, Jennifer Beals. B&W.

Inside Monkey Zetterland 92
IRS. August, 1993. (Jefery Levy), Steven Antin, Patricia Arquette, Tate Donovan.

Jason Goes to Hell: The Final Friday 88
NEW LINE CINEMA. (R) August, 1993. (Adam Marcus), John D. LeMay, Kane Hodder, Allison Smith.

Joey Breaker 92
SKOURAS. (R) May, 1993. (Steven Starr), Richard Edson, Cedella Marley, Fred Fondren.

Judas Project, The 97
RS ENTERTAINMENT. (PG-13) February, 1993. (James H. Barden), John O'Banion, Ramy Zada, Jeff Corey.

Just Another Girl on the I.R.T. 92
MIRAMAX. (R) March, 1993. (Leslie Harris), Ariyan Johnson, Kevin Thigpen, Ebony Jerido.

King of the Hill 102
GRAMERCY. (PG-13) August, 1993. (Steven Soderbergh), Jesse Bradford, Jeroen Krabbe, Lisa Eichhorn.

Knight Moves (P) 96
INTERSTAR RELEASING. (R) January, 1993. (Carl Schenkel), Christopher Lambert, Diane Lane, Tom Skerritt.

Last Call at Maud's 74
MAUD'S PROJECT. March, 1993. (Paris Poirier), Documentary.

The Last Party 96
TRITON. August, 1993. (Mark Benjamin, Marc Levin), Robert Downey, Jr.

Legend of Wolf Mountain 91
HEMDALE. (PG) November, 1992. (Craig Clyde), Bo Hopkins, Mickey Rooney, Robert Z'Dar.

435

Foreign Films Released in the U.S. by Independent Distributors and Classics Divisions

September, 1992–August, 1993

Key: Running time is opposite title, followed by distributor, MPAA rating (if any), month and year of release, nationality, director (in parentheses), and stars.

Alberto Express 90
MK2. October, 1992. French-Italian. (Arthur Joffe), Sergio Castellitto, Nino Manfredi, Marie Trintignant.

American Friends 95
CASTLE HILL. April, 1993. British. (Tristam Powell), Michael Palin, Connie Booth, Trini Alvarado.

Barjo 85
MYRIAD PICTURES. July, 1993. French. (Jerome Boivin), Anne Brochet, Richard Bohringer, Hippolyte Girardot.

Becoming Colette 97
CASTLE HILL. November, 1992. German-U.S. (Danny Huston), Mathilda May, Klaus Maria Brandauer, Virginia Madsen.

The Beekeeper 120
MK2. May, 1993. Greek. (Theo Angelopoulous), Marcello Mastroianni, Nadia Mourouzi, Serge Reggiani.

Being at Home With Claude 84
STRAND RELEASING. August, 1993. French-Canadian. (Jean Boudin), Roy Dupuis, Jacques Godin, Jean-François Pichette.

Betty 103
MK2. August, 1993. French. (Claude Chabrol), Marie Trintignant, Stephane Audran, Jean-Francois Garreau.

Black to the Promised Land 75
BLUE PRODS. April, 1993. Israeli. (Madeleine Ali), Documentary.

A Breath of Life 96
SURF FILM. January, 1993. Italian. (Beppe Cino), Franco Nero, Vanessa Redgrave, Lucrezia Lante Della Rovere.

A Captive in the Land 96
NORKAT. January, 1993. Soviet-U.S. (John Berry), Sam Waterston, Aleksandr Potapov.

Careful 96
ZEITGEIST. August, 1993. Canadian. (Guy Maddin), Kyle McCulloch, Gosia Dobrowolska, Sarah Neville.

China, My Sorrow 86
MILESTONE. January, 1993. Chinese. (Dai Sijie), Guo Liang Yi, Tieu Quan Nghieu.

Close to Eden 106
MIRAMAX. October, 1992. Russian. (Nikita Mikhalkov), Bayaertu, Badema, Vladimir Gostukhin.

Colin Nutley's House of Angels 119
SONY PICTURES CLASSICS. (R) August, 1993. Swedish. (Colin Nutley), Helena Bergstrom, Rikard Wolff, Sven Wollter.

The Crying Game (P) 112
MIRAMAX. (R) November, 1992. British. (Neil Jordan), Stephen Rea, Forest Whitaker, Miranda Richardson.

Danzon 103
SONY PICTURES CLASSICS. (PG-13) September, 1992. Mexican. (Maria Novaro), Maria Rojo, Carmen Salinas, Blanca Guerra.

Dark at Noon 100
SIDERAL PRODS. August, 1993. French-Argentine. (Raul Ruiz), John Hurt, Didier Bourdon, David Warner.

Dead-Alive 97
TRIMARK. February, 1993. New Zealand. (Peter Jackson), Timothy Balme, Diana Penalver, Elizabeth Moody.

Dead Flowers 98
OAK ISLAND. April, 1993. Austrian. (Peter Ily Huemer), Kate Valk, Thierry van Werveke, Tana Schanzara.

Deadly Currents 115
NORMANDIE. October, 1992. Canadian. (Simcha Jacobovici), Documentary.

Double Edge 86
CASTLE HILL. (PG-13) September, 1992. Israeli-U.S. (Amos Kollek), Faye Dunaway, Amos Kollek, Mohammad Bakri.

The Efficiency Expert 89
MIRAMAX. (PG) November, 1992. Australian. (Mark Joffe), Anthony Hopkins, Ben Mendelsohn, Toni Collette.

Especially on Sunday 81
MIRAMAX. (R) August, 1993. Italian. (Giuseppe Tornatore), Philippe Noiret, Ornella Muti, Bruno Ganz.

The Execution Protocol 87
FIRST RUN. April, 1993. British. (Stephen Trombley), Documentary.

Female Misbehavior 80
FIRST RUN. April, 1993. German. (Monika Truet), Documentary.

A Fine Romance 82
CASTLE HILL. (PG-13) September, 1992. Italian. (Gene Saks), Julie Andrews, Marcello Mastroianni.

Flaming Ears 83
WOMEN MAKE MOVIES. January, 1993. Austrian. (Angela Hans Scheirl, Dietmar Schipek, Ursula Puerrer), Susanna Heilmayr, Ursula Puerrer.

For a Lost Soldier 93
STRAND. May, 1993. Dutch. (Roeland Kerbosch), Maarten Smit, Andrew Kelley, Jeroen Krabbe.

Forbidden Love: The Unashamed Stories of Lesbian Lives 85
WOMEN MAKE MOVIES. August, 1993. Canadian. (Aerlyn Weissman, Lynne Fernie), Documentary.

Garden of Scorpions 96
LEN FILM. March, 1993. Russian. (Oleg Kovalov). Compilation.

Get Thee Out 90
FIRST RUN FEATURES. January, 1993. Russian. (Dimitri Astrakhan), Otar Mengvinetukutsey, Elena Anisimova.

Guelwaar 115
NEW YORKER. April, 1993. Sengalese-French. (Ousmane Sembene), Omar Seck, Ndiawar Diop, Isseu Niang.

Hard-Boiled 126
GOLDEN PRINCESS/MILESTONE. April, 1993. Hong Kong. (John Woo), Chow Yun-fat, Bowie Lam, Philip Chan.

Herman 106
RKO. November, 1992. Norwegian. (Erik Gustavson), Anders Danielson Lie, Frank Robert, Elisabeth Sand.

Il Ladro di Bambini (Stolen Children) 112
GOLDWYN. March, 1993. Italian. (Gianni Amelio), Enrico LoVerso, Valentina Scalici, Florence Darel.

In Advance of the Landing 85
CINEPLEX ODEON. January, 1993. Canadian. (Dan Curtis), Documentary.

Intervista 108
CASTLE HILL. November, 1992. Italian. (Federico Fellini), Sergio Rubini, Maurizio Mein, Anita Ekberg.

Jacquot 118
SONY CLASSICS.(PG-13) June, 1993. French. (Agnes Varda), Philippe Maron, Eduoard Joubeaud, Laurent Monnier.

Jit 98
NORTHERN ARTS. March, 1993. Zimbabwe. (Michael Raeburn), Dominic Makuvachuma, Sibongile Nene.

John Lurie and the Lounge Lizards Live in Berlin 101
TELECOM JAPAN. September, 1992. Japanese. (Garret Linn), Documentary.

Johnny Stecchino 100
NEW LINE CINEMA. (R) October, 1992. Italian. (Roberto Benigni), Roberto Benigni, Nicoletta Braschi, Paolo Bonacelli.

La Vie de Boheme 100
KINO. July, 1993. French-Finnish. (Aki Kurasmaki), Matti Pellonpaa, Evelyn Didi, Andre Wilms.

The Last Butterfly 110
ARROW. August, 1993. Czech. (Karel Kachyna), Tom Courtenay, Brigitte Fossey, Ingrid Held.

The Last Days of Chez Nous 96
FINE LINE FEATURES. (R) February, 1993. Australian. (Gillian Armstrong), Lisa Harrow, Bruno Ganz, Kerry Fox.

438

Feature Pictures

* **1980–1992**

FEATURE PICTURES
January 1, 1980—August 31, 1992

For complete list of 1970's releases see Vols. 1981 through 1992. In the following listings the distributor is followed by the release date, foreign language and English subtitles (if applicable), the director (in parentheses), and cast. (CS) indicates CinemaScope; (VV) indicates VistaVision; (SS) Super-Scope; (T) Technirama; (P) Panavision; (D-150) Dimension-150; (TV) Technovision; (VS) VistaScope; (SP) Super Panavision; (3-D) Three Dimension; (TE) Techniscope; (J-D-C) J-D-C Widescreen; (T-AO) Todd AO; (WS) Widescreen—process not identified. All films are in color unless otherwise indicated.

	Length in Mins.		Length in Mins.

A

ABOUT LAST NIGHT 113
TRI-STAR. July, 1986. (Edward Zwick), Rob Lowe, Demi Moore, James Belushi.

ABOVE THE LAW 99
WARNER BROS. April, 1988. (Andrew Davis), Steven Seagal, Pam Grier.

ABSENCE OF MALICE 116
COLUMBIA. November, 1981. (Sydney Pollack), Paul Newman, Sally Field, Melinda Dillon.

ABSOLUTE BEGINNERS (TE) 107
ORION. April, 1986. (Julien Temple) Eddie O'Connell, Patsy Kensit, David Bowie.

ABSOLUTION 105
TRANS WORLD ENTERTAINMENT. February, 1988 (made, 1979). British. (Anthony Page), Richard Burton, Dominic Guard.

ABYSS, THE (WS) 140
20TH CENTURY FOX. August, 1989. (James Cameron), Ed Harris, Mary Elizabeth Mastrantonio.

ACCIDENTAL TOURIST, THE (P) 121
WARNER BROS. December, 1988. (Lawrence Kasdan), William Hurt, Kathleen Turner, Geena Davis.

ACCUSED, THE 110
PARAMOUNT. October, 1988. (Jonathan Kaplan), Kelly McGillis, Jodie Foster.

ACES: IRON EAGLE III 98
NEW LINE CINEMA/7 ARTS. June, 1992. (John Glen), Louis Gossett, Jr., Rachel McLish, Horst Buccholz.

ACROSS THE TRACKS 99
ACADEMY ENT.-DESERT PRODS. February, 1991. (Sandy Tung), Rick Schroder, Brad Pitt, Carry Snodgress.

ACT OF PIRACY 101
BLOSSOM PICTURES. March, 1990. (John "Bud" Cardos), Gary Busey, Belinda Bauer, Ray Sharkey.

ACTION JACKSON 95
LORIMAR FILM ENTERTAINMENT. February, 1988. (Craig R. Baxley), Carl Weathers, Craig T. Nelson, Vanity.

ADAM'S RIB 77
OCTOBER FILMS. May, 1992. Russian. (Vyacheslav Krishtofovich), Inna Churikova, Sveltana Ryabova, Maria Golubkina.

ADDAMS FAMILY, THE 100
PARAMOUNT. November, 1991. (Barry Sonnenfeld), Anjelica Huston, Raul Julia, Christopher Lloyd.

ADJUSTER, THE (P) 101
ORION CLASSICS. May, 1992. Canadian. (Atom Egoyan), Elias Koteas, Arsinee Khanjian, Maury Chaykin.

ADVENTURE OF THE ACTION HUNTERS, THE 80
TROMA. May, 1987. (Lee Bonner), Ronald Hunter, Sean Murphy.

ADVENTURES IN BABYSITTING 99
BUENA VISTA. July, 1987. (Chris Columbus), Elisabeth Shue, Maia Brewton.

ADVENTURES OF BARON MUNCHAUSEN, THE 125
COLUMBIA. March, 1989. British. (Terry Gilliam), John Neville, Eric Idle, Oliver Reed.

ADVENTURES OF BUCKAROO BANZAI: ACROSS THE EIGHTH DIMENSION, THE 103
20TH CENTURY FOX. August, 1984. (W.D. Richter), Peter Weller, John Lithgow, Ellen Barkin.

ADVENTURES OF FORD FAIRLANE, THE (P) 104
20TH CENTURY FOX. July, 1990. (Remy Harlin), Andrew Dice Clay, Wayne Newton, Priscilla Presley.

ADVENTURES OF MARK TWAIN 90
ATLANTIC RELEASING. January, 1986. (Will Vinton), Animated.

ADVENTURES OF MILO AND OTIS, THE (P) 76
COLUMBIA. August, 1989. Japanese. (Masanori Hata), Narrator: Dudley Moore.

ADVENTURES OF THE AMERICAN RABBIT 85
ATLANTIC RELEASING. February, 1986. Animated.

AFFENGEIL 87
FIRST RUN FEATURES. July, 1992. German. (Rosa von Praunheim), Lotte Huber, Rosa von Praunheim, Helga Sloop.

AFRAID OF THE DARK 92
FINE LINE. July, 1992. British. (Mark Peploe), James Fox, Fanny Ardant, Ben Keyworth.

AFTER DARK, MY SWEET 114
AVENUE. August, 1990. (James Foley), Jason Patric, Rachel Ward, Bruce Dern.

AFTER HOURS 97
WARNER BROS. September, 1985. (Martin Scorsese), Griffin Dunne, Rosanna Arquette, Teri Garr.

AFTER MIDNIGHT 90
MGM/UA. November, 1989. (Ken Wheat, Jim Wheat), Jillian McWhirter, Marc McClure.

AFTER THE FALL OF NEW YORK 95
ALMI PICTURES. January, 1985. Italian-French; Eng. dubbed. (Martin Dolman), Michael Sopkiw, Valentine Monnier.

AFTER THE RAIN 105
NEW CENTURY/VISTA. September, 1988. (Harry Thompson), Maruschka Paul, Ned Beatty.

AFTER THE REHEARSAL 72
TRIUMPH. June, 1984. Swedish; Eng. titles. (Ingmar Bergman), Erland Josephson, Ingrid Thulin.

AGAINST ALL ODDS 125
COLUMBIA. March, 1984. (Taylor Hackford), Rachel Ward, Jeff Bridges, James Woods.

AGENT ON ICE 97
SHAPIRO ENTERTAINMENT. May, 1986. (Clark Worswick), Tom Ormeny, Clifford David.

AGNES OF GOD 98
COLUMBIA. September, 1985. (Norman Jewison), Jane Fonda, Anne Bancroft, Meg Tilly.

AIR AMERICA (P) 112
TRI-STAR. August, 1990. (Roger Spottiswoode), Mel Gibson, Robert Downey, Jr.

AIRPLANE 88
PARAMOUNT. July, 1980. (Jim Abrahams, David & Jerry Zucker), Robert Hays, Julie Hagerty.

AIRPLANE II: THE SEQUEL 84
PARAMOUNT. December, 1982. (Ken Finkleman), Robert Hays, Julie Hagerty.

AKIRA 124
STREAMLINE. December, 1989. Japanese. (Katsuhiro Otomo), Animated.

AKIRA KUROSAWA'S DREAMS 120
WARNER BROS. August, 1990. Japanese. (Akira Kurosawa), Mitsunori Isaki, Mieko Harada, Martin Scorsese.

ALADDIN 100
CANNON GROUP. April, 1987. (Bruno Corbucci), Bud Spencer, Janet Agren.

ALAMO BAY 98
TRI-STAR. April, 1985. (Louis Malle), Amy Madigan, Ed Harris.

ALAN & NAOMI 96
TRITON. January, 1992. (Sterling VanWagenen), Lukas Haas, Vanessa Zaoui, Michael Gross.

ALCHEMIST, THE 84
EMPIRE PICTURES. January, 1986. (James Amante, Charles Band), Robert Ginty, Lucinda Dooling.

Length in Mins.

ASSAULT OF THE KILLER BIMBOS 75
EMPIRE PICTURES. May, 1988. (Anita Rosenberg), Elizabeth Kaitan, Christina Whitaker.

AT CLOSE RANGE (P) 111
ORION. April, 1986. (James Foley), Sean Penn, Christopher Walken, Mary Stuart Masterson.

AT PLAY IN THE FIELDS OF THE LORD 187
UNIVERSAL. December, 1991. (Hector Babenco), Tom Berenger, Kathy Bates, Aidan Quinn, John Lithgow.

AT THE CROSSROADS: JEWS IN EASTERN EUROPE TODAY 85
ARTHUR CANTOR FILMS. February, 1991. (Oren Rudavsky, Yale Strom). Documentary.

AT THE MAX 89
BLC GROUP/IMAX CORP. October, 1991. (Julien Temple), The Rolling Stones.

ATHENS, GA—INSIDE/OUT 82
ASA COMMUNICATIONS. May, 1987. (Tony Gayton). Documentary.

ATLANTIC CITY 105
PARAMOUNT. April, 1981. Canadian. (Louis Malle), Burt Lancaster, Susan Sarandon.

ATOMIC CAFE, THE 88
ARCHIVES PROJECT. March, 1982. (Kevin Rafferty, Jayne Loader, Pierce Rafferty). Documentary.

AU REVOIR, LES ENFANTS (Goodbye, Children) 104
ORION CLASSICS. February, 1988. French; Eng. subtitles. (Louis Malle), Gaspard Manesse, Raphael Fejto.

AURORA ENCOUNTER, THE 90
NEW WORLD PICTURES. August, 1986. (Jim McCullouch, Sr.), Jack Elam, Peter Brown.

AUSTERIA 109
AFRA FILM ENTERPRISES. March, 1988. Polish; Eng. subtitles. (Jerzy Kawalerowicz), Franciszek Peiczka, Wojciech Pszoniak.

AUTHOR! AUTHOR! 110
20TH CENTURY FOX. July, 1982. (Arthur Hiller), Al Pacino, Dyan Cannon, Tuesday Weld.

AVALON 126
TRI-STAR. October, 1990. (Barry Levinson), Aidan Quinn, Armin Mueller-Stahl, Elijah Wood.

AVANTI POPOLO 84
FILM VENTURES. April, 1989. In Arabic and Hebrew; Eng. titles. (Rafi Bukaee), Salim Daw, Suhel Hadad.

AVENGING ANGEL 93
NEW WORLD. January, 1985. (Robert Vincent O'Neil), Betsy Russell, Rory Calhoun.

AVENGING FORCE 103
CANNON GROUP. September 1986. (Sam Firstenberg), Michael Dudikoff, Steve James.

AVIATOR, THE 96
MGM/UA. March, 1985. (George Miller), Christopher Reeve, Rosanna Arquette.

AVIATOR'S WIFE, THE 104
NEW YORKER. October, 1981. French; Eng. titles. (Eric Rohmer), Philippe Marlaud, Marie Riviere.

AWAKENING, THE 100
WARNER BROS. October, 1980. (Mike Newell), Charlton Heston, Susannah York.

AWAKENINGS 121
COLUMBIA. December, 1990. (Penny Marshall), Robert De Niro, Robin Williams, Julie Kavner.

AY, CARMELA! 95
PRESTIGE. February, 1991. Spanish. (Carlos Saura), Carmen Maura, Andres Pajares, Gabin Diego.

B

BABAR: THE MOVIE 80
NEW LINE CINEMA. August, 1989. Canadian-French. (Alan Bunce), Gordon Pinsent, Elizabeth Hanna (voices).

BABE, THE 113
UNIVERSAL. April, 1992. (Arthur Hiller), John Goodman, Kelly McGillis, Trini Alvarado.

BABETTE'S FEAST 102
ORION CLASSICS. March, 1988. Danish; Eng. subtitles. (Gabriel Axel), Stephane Audran, Jean-Philippe Lafont.

BABY...SECRET OF THE LOST LEGEND 95
BUENA VISTA. March, 1985. (B.W.L. Norton), William Katt, Sean Young.

BABY BOOM 103
MGM/UA. October, 1987. (Charles Shyer), Diane Keaton, Harold Ramis, Sam Shepard.

BABY, IT'S YOU 105
PARAMOUNT. March, 1983. (John Sayles), Rosanna Arquette, Vincent Spano.

Length in Mins.

BACHELOR PARTY 106
20TH CENTURY FOX. June, 1984. (Neal Israel), Tom Hanks, Tawyn Kitaen.

BACK IN THE U.S.S.R. 89
20TH CENTURY FOX. February, 1992. (Deran Sarafian), Frank Whaley, Natalya Negoda, Roman Polanski.

BACK ROADS (P) 94
WARNER BROS. March, 1981. (Martin Ritt), Sally Field, Tommy Lee Jones.

BACK TO ARARAT 100
FIRST RUN FEATURES. May, 1989. French-Armenian-English; Eng. titles. (Pea Holmquist, Jim Downing, Suzanne Khardalian). Documentary. B&W/color.

BACK TO BACK 95
CONCORDE. January, 1990. (John Kincade), Bill Paxton, Todd Field, Apolonia Kotero.

BACK TO SCHOOL 96
ORION. June, 1986. (Alan Metter), Rodney Dangerfield, Sally Kellerman, Keith Gordon.

BACK TO THE BEACH 90
PARAMOUNT. August, 1987. (Lyndall Hobbs), Frankie Avalon, Annette Funicello.

BACK TO THE FUTURE 116
UNIVERSAL. July, 1985. (Robert Zemeckis), Michael J. Fox, Christopher Lloyd.

BACK TO THE FUTURE PART II 107
UNIVERSAL. November, 1989. (Robert Zemeckis), Michael J. Fox, Christopher Lloyd.

BACK TO THE FUTURE PART III 118
UNIVERSAL. May, 1990. (Robert Zemeckis), Michael J. Fox, Christopher Lloyd, Mary Steenburgen.

BACKDRAFT (P) 135
UNIVERSAL. May, 1991. (Ron Howard), Kurt Russell, William Baldwin, Robert De Niro.

BACKLASH 90
SAMUEL GOLDWYN CO. August, 1987. Australian. (Bill Bennett), David Argue, Gia Carides.

BACKSTREET DREAMS 104
VIDMARK. September, 1990. (Rupert Hitzig), Jason O'Malley, Brooke Shields, Burt Young.

BAD BOYS 123
UNIVERSAL. March, 1983. (Rick Rosenthal), Sean Penn, Reni Santoni, Esai Morales.

BAD DREAMS 84
20TH CENTURY-FOX. April, 1988. (Andrew Fleming), Jennifer Rubin, Bruce Abbott.

BAD GIRLS DORMITORY 95
AQUARIUS RELEASING. January, 1986. (Tim Kincaid), Carey Zuriss, Teresa Farley.

BAD GUYS 86
INTERPICTURES RELEASING. March, 1986. (Joel Silbert), Adam Baldwin, Mike Jolly.

BAD INFLUENCE 99
TRIUMPH. March, 1990. (Curtis Hanson), Rob Lowe, James Spader.

BAD MEDICINE 96
20TH CENTURY FOX. November, 1985. (Harvey Miller), Steve Guttenberg, Alan Arkin.

BAD TIMING/A SENSUAL OBSESSION 122
WORLD NORTHAL. October, 1980. British. (Nicolas Roeg), Art Garfunkel, Theresa Russell.

BAGDAD CAFE 91
ISLAND. April, 1988. West German. (Percy Adlon), Marianne Sagebrecht, C.C.H. Pounder.

BAHIA 90
ATLANTIC RELEASING. March, 1986. Portuguese; Eng. titles. (Marcel Camus), Mira Fonesca, Zen Periera.

BAIL JUMPER 96
ANGELIKA. April, 1990. (Christian Faber), Eszter Balint, B.J. Spalding, Tony Askin.

BAKAYAROO! 93
SHOCHIKU. February, 1989. In Japanese; Eng. titles. (Eriko Watanabe, Tetsuya Nakajima, Takahito Hara), Haruko Sagara, Tsuyoshi Ihara.

BALLAD OF GREGORIO CORTEZ, THE 104
EMBASSY. September, 1983. (Robert M. Young), Edward James Olmos, Tom Bower.

BALLAD OF NARAYAMA, THE 128
KINO INTL. September, 1984. Japanese; Eng. titles. (Shohei Imamura), Ken Ogata, Sumiko Sakamoto.

BALLAD OF THE SAD CAFE, THE 100
ANGELIKA. May, 1991. (Simon Callow), Vanessa Redgrave, Keith Carradine, Cork Hubbert.

BALTIMORE BULLET, THE 103
AVCO EMBASSY. April, 1980. (Robert Ellis Miller), James Coburn, Omar Sharif.

Length in Mins.

BEST FRIENDS 109
WARNER BROS. December, 1982. (Norman Jewison), Burt Reynolds, Goldie Hawn.

BEST INTENTIONS, THE 182
GOLDWYN. July, 1992. Swedish. (Bille August), Samuel Froler, Pernilla August, Max von Sydow.

BEST LITTLE WHOREHOUSE IN TEXAS, THE (P) 114
UNIVERSAL. July, 1982. (Colin Higgins), Burt Reynolds, Dolly Parton.

BEST OF THE BEST 95
TAURUS. November, 1989. (Bob Radler), Eric Roberts, James Earl Jones, Sally Kirkland.

BEST OF TIMES, THE 104
UNIVERSAL. January, 1986. (Roger Spottiswoode), Robin Williams, Kurt Russell.

BEST SELLER 110
ORION. September, 1987. (John Flynn), James Woods, Brian Dennehy.

BETRAYAL 90
20TH CENTURY FOX CLASSICS. February, 1983. British. (David Jones), Jeremy Irons, Ben Kingsley, Patricia Hodge.

BETRAYED 127
MGM/UA. August, 1988. (Constantin Costa-Gavras), Debra Winger, Tom Berenger, John Heard.

BETSY'S WEDDING 94
BUENA VISTA. June, 1990. (Alan Alda), Alan Alda, Madeline Kahn, Molly Ringwald.

BETTER OFF DEAD 98
WARNER BROS. October, 1985. (Savage Steve Holland), John Cusack, David Ogden Stiers.

BETTY BLUE 120
ALIVE FILMS. November, 1986. French; Eng. titles. (Jean-Jacques Beineix), Beatrice Dalle, Jean-Hugues Anglade.

BETWEEN WARS 97
SATORI. February, 1985. (Michael Thornhill), Corin Redgrave, Arthur Dignam.

BEVERLY HILLS BRATS 91
TAURUS. October, 1989. (Dimitri Sotirakis), Burt Young, Martin Sheen.

BEVERLY HILLS COP 105
PARAMOUNT. December, 1984. (Martin Brest), Eddie Murphy, Judge Reinhold, Ronny Cox.

BEVERLY HILLS COP II 102
PARAMOUNT. May, 1987. (Tony Scott), Eddie Murphy, Judge Reinhold.

BEYOND THE LIMIT 103
PARAMOUNT. September, 1983. (John Mackenzie), Michael Caine, Richard Gere.

BEYOND THE REEF 91
UNIVERSAL. May, 1981. (Frank C. Clark), Dayton Ka'ne, Maren Jensen.

BEYOND THE WALLS 103
WARNER BROS. February, 1985. Hebrew; Eng. titles. (Uri Barbash), Arnon Zadok, Muhamad Bakri.

BEYOND THERAPY 93
NEW WORLD PICTURES. February, 1987. (Robert Altman), Julie Hagerty, Jeff Goldblum.

BIG 102
20TH CENTURY FOX. June, 1988. (Penny Marshall), Tom Hanks, Elizabeth Perkins.

BIG BAD JOHN 92
MAGNUM ENTERTAINMENT. February, 1990. (Burt Kennedy), Jimmy Dean, Jack Elam, Ned Beatty.

BIG BAD MAMA II 83
CONCORDE. September, 1987. (Jim Wynorski), Angie Dickinson, Robert Culp.

BIG BANG, THE 81
TRITON. May, 1990. (James Toback), Emma Astner, Missy Body, Eugene Fodor.

BIG BLUE, THE (CS) 119
COLUMBIA. August, 1988. (Luc Besson), Jean-Marc Barr, Jean Reno, Rosanna Arquette.

BIG BLUE, THE 100
ANGELIKA. December, 1989. (Andrew Horn), David Brisbin, Taunie VreNon.

BIG BUSINESS 97
BUENA VISTA. June, 1988. (Jim Abrahams), Bette Midler, Lily Tomlin.

BIG CHILL, THE (P) 103
COLUMBIA. September, 1983. (Lawrence Kasdan), Kevin Kline, Tom Berenger, Glenn Close, William Hurt.

BIG DIS, THE 84
OLYMPIA. June, 1990. (Gordon Eriksen, John O'Brien), James Haig, Kevin Haig. B&W.

BIG EASY, THE 108
COLUMBIA. August, 1987. (Jim McBride), Dennis Quaid, Ellen Barkin.

Length in Mins.

BIG GIRLS DON'T CRY...THEY GET EVEN 102
NEW LINE CINEMA. May, 1992. (Joan Micklin Silver), Hillary Wolf, David Strathairn, Margaret Whitton.

BIG MAN ON CAMPUS 105
VESTRON. February, 1990. (Jeremy Paul Kagan), Allan Katz, Corey Parker, Cindy Williams.

BIG PICTURE, THE 100
COLUMBIA. September, 1989. (Christopher Guest), Kevin Bacon, Emily Longstreth, Michael McKean.

BIG RED ONE, THE 113
UNITED ARTISTS. July, 1980. (Samuel Fuller), Lee Marvin, Mark Hamill.

BIG SCORE, THE 90
ALMI PICTURES. November, 1983. (Fred Williamson), Fred Williamson, John Saxon.

BIG SHOTS 90
20TH CENTURY FOX. October, 1987. (Robert Mandel), Ricky Busker, Darius McCrary.

BIG TIME 90
ISLAND PICTURES. September, 1988. (Chris Blum), Documentary.

BIG TOP PEE-WEE 86
PARAMOUNT. July, 1988. (Randal Kleiser), Paul Reubens (Pee-Wee Herman) Kris Kristofferson, Valeria Golino.

BIG TOWN, THE 109
COLUMBIA. September, 1987. (Ben Bolt), Matt Dillon, Diane Lane, Tommy Lee Jones.

BIG TROUBLE (P) 93
COLUMBIA. May, 1986. (John Cassavetes), Peter Falk, Alan Arkin.

BIG TROUBLE IN LITTLE CHINA (P) 99
20TH CENTURY FOX. July, 1986. (John Carpenter), Kurt Russell, Kim Cattrall.

BIGGER SPLASH, A 105
BUZZY ENTERPRISES. October, 1984. David Hockney, Peter Schlesinger.

BIGGLES—ADVENTURES IN TIME 92
NEW CENTURY/VISTA FILM CO. January, 1988. British. (John Hough), Neil Dickson, Alex Hyde-White.

BIKINI ISLAND 85
CURB/ESQUIRE. July, 1991. (Anthony Markes), Holly Floria, Alicia Anne.

BIKINI SHOP, THE 99
INTERNATIONAL FILM MARKETING. February, 1987. (David Wechter), Michael David Wright, Bruce Greenwood.

BILL & TED'S BOGUS JOURNEY 95
ORION. July, 1991. (Pete Hewitt), Keanu Reeves, Alex Winter, William Sadler.

BILL & TED'S EXCELLENT ADVENTURE (P) 90
ORION. February, 1989. (Stephen Herek), Keanu Reeves, Alex Winter, George Carlin.

BILL COSBY—HIMSELF 105
20TH CENTURY FOX CLASSICS. May, 1983. (Bill Cosby), Bill Cosby.

BILLY BATHGATE 107
BUENA VISTA. November, 1991. (Robert Benton), Dustin Hoffman, Loren Dean, Nicole Kidman, Bruce Willis.

BILLY GALVIN 95
VESTRON PICTURES. February, 1987. (John Gray), Karl Malden, Lenny von Dohlen.

BILOXI BLUES (WS) 106
UNIVERSAL. March, 1988. (Mike Nichols), Matthew Broderick, Christopher Walken.

BINGO 87
TRISTAR. August, 1991. (Matthew Robbins), Cindy Williams, David Rasche, Robert J. Steinmiller, Jr.

BIRD 161
WARNER BROS. September, 1988. (Clint Eastwood), Forest Whitaker, Diane Venora.

BIRD ON A WIRE (WS) 110
UNIVERSAL. May, 1990. (John Badham), Mel Gibson, Goldie Hawn.

BIRDY 120
TRI-STAR. December, 1984. (Alan Parker), Matthew Modine, Nicolas Cage.

BLACK CAT, THE 91
WORLD NORTHAL. February, 1984. Italian; dubbed. (Lucio Fulci), Patrick Magee.

BLACK CAULDRON, THE (T) 80
BUENA VISTA. July, 1985. (Ted Berman), Animated.

BLACK LIZARD 86
CINEVISTA. September, 1991. Japanese. 1968. (Kinji Fukasaku), Akihiro Maruyama, Isao Kimura, Yukio Mishima.

BLACK MARBLE, THE (P) 113
AVCO EMBASSY. March, 1980. (Harold Becker), Robert Foxworth, Paula Prentiss.

	Length in Mins.

BLACK MOON RISING 100
NEW WORLD PICTURES. January, 1986. (Harley Cokliss), Tommy Lee Jones, Linda Hamilton.

BLACK RAIN 123
ANGELIKA. February 1990. Japanese. (Shohei Imamura), Yoshiko Tanaka,Kazuo Kitmamura.

BLACK RAIN (P) 126
PARAMOUNT. September, 1989. (Ridley Scott), Michael Douglas, Andy Garcia, Ken Takakura.

BLACK ROBE 100
GOLDWYN. October, 1991. Canadian-Australin. (Bruce Beresford), Lotheire Bluteau, Aden Young, Sandrine Holt.

BLACK STALLION RETURNS, THE 103
MGM/UA. March, 1983. (Robert Dalva), Kelly Reno, Vincent Spano.

BLACK SUN 731 103
GRAND ESSEX ENTERPRISES. March, 1989. Japanese; Eng. titles. (T.F. Mous), Wang Gan, Mei Zhao Hua.

BLACK WIDOW 103
20TH CENTURY FOX. February, 1987. (Bob Rafelson), Debra Winger, Theresa Russell.

BLADE RUNNER (P) 118
WARNER BROS. June, 1982. (Ridley Scott), Harrison Ford, Rutger Hauer.

BLAME IT ON RIO 100
20TH CENTURY FOX. February, 1984. (Stanley Donen), Michael Caine, Joseph Bologna.

BLAME IT ON THE BELLBOY 78
BUENA VISTA. March, 1992. British. (Mark Herman), Dudley Moore, Bryan Brown, Patsy Kensit.

BLAME IT ON THE NIGHT 85
TRI-STAR. November, 1984. (Gene Taft), Nick Mancuso, Byron Thames.

BLAST 'EM 100
SILENT FICTION FILMS. July, 1992. Canadian. (Joseph Blasioli), Documentary.

BLAZE 120
BUENA VISTA. December, 1989. (Ron Shelton), Paul Newman, Lolita Davidovich.

BLIND 120
ZIPPORAH FILMS. December, 1987. (Frederick Wiseman). Documentary.

BLIND DATE 99
NEW LINE CINEMA. September, 1984. (Niko Mastorakis), Joseph Bottoms, Kirstie Alley.

BLIND DATE (P) 93
TRI-STAR. March, 1987. (Blake Edwards), Kim Basinger, Bruce Willis.

BLIND FURY 85
TRI-STAR. March, 1990. (Phillip Noyce), Rutger Hauer, Brandon Call.

BLIND TRUST (POUVOIR INTIME) 90
CINEMA GROUP ENTERTAINMENT. November, 1987. French; Eng. subtitles. (Yves Simoneau), Marie Tifo, Pierre Curzi.

BLISS 111
NEW WORLD PICTURES. February, 1986. Australian. (Ray Lawrence), Barry Otto, Lynette Curran.

BLOB, THE 92
TRI-STAR. August, 1988. (Chuck Russell), Shawnee Smith, Kevin Dillon.

BLOOD & CONCRETE 98
I.R.S. September, 1991. (Jeffrey Reiner), Billy Zane, Jennifer Beals, Darren McGavin.

BLOOD DINER 90
LIGHTNING PICTURES. July, 1987. (Jackie Kong), Rick Burks, Carl Crew.

BLOOD IN THE FACE 75
FIRST RUN FEATURES. February, 1991. (Anne Bohlen, Kevin Rafferty, James Ridgeway), Documentary.

BLOOD OF HEROES, THE 90
NEW LINE CINEMA. February, 1990. (David Peoples), Rutger Hauer, Joan Chen.

BLOOD RED 91
HEMDALE. August, 1989. (Peter Masterson), Eric Roberts, Dennis Hopper.

BLOOD SALVAGE 98
PARAGON ARTS. May, 1990. (Tucker Johnston), Danny Nelson, Lori Birdsong, John Saxon.

BLOOD SIMPLE 96
CIRCLE RELEASING. January, 1985. (Joel Coen), John Getz, Frances McDormand, M. Emmet Walsh.

BLOOD WEDDING 72
LIBRA. October, 1981. Spanish; Eng. titles. (Carlos Saura), Antonio Gades, Cristina Hoyos.

	Length in Mins.

BLOODFIST 85
CONCORDE. September, 1989. (Terence Winkless), Don "The Dragon" Wilson, Joe Marie Avellana.

BLOODFIST II 88
CONCORDE. October, 1990. (Andy Blumenthal), Don Wilson, Rina Reyes.

BLOODFIST III: FORCED TO FIGHT 88
CONCORDE. January, 1992. (Francis Sassone), Don "The Dragon" Wilson, Richard Roundtree, Gregory McKinney.

BLOODHOUNDS OF BROADWAY 90
COLUMBIA. November, 1989. (Howard Brookner), Matt Dillon, Madonna, Rutger Hauer, Jennifer Grey.

BLOODSPORT 92
CANNON GROUP. February, 1988. (Newt Arnold), Jean Claude Van Damme, Donald Gibb.

BLOW OUT 108
FILMWAYS. July, 1981. (Brian DePalma), John Travolta, Nancy Allen, John Lithgow.

BLOWBACK 95
NORTHERN ARTS. August, 1991. (Marc Levin), Bruce McCarty, Jane Hamper, Eddie Figueroa.

BLUE CITY 83
PARAMOUNT. May, 1986. (Michelle Manning), Judd Nelson, Ally Sheedy.

BLUE IGUANA, THE 90
PARAMOUNT. April, 1988. (John Lafia), Dylan McDermott, Jessica Harper.

BLUE LAGOON, THE 104
COLUMBIA. June, 1980. (Randel Kleiser), Brooke Shields, Christopher Atkins.

BLUE MONKEY 98
SPECTRAFILM. September, 1987. (William Fruet), Steve Railsback, Gwynyth Walsh.

BLUE SKIES AGAIN 96
WARNER BROS. March, 1983. (Richard Michaels), Harry Hamlin, Robyn Barto, Mimi Rogers.

BLUE STEEL 102
MGM/UA. March, 1990. (Kathryn Bigelow), Jamie Lee Curtis, Ron Silver.

BLUE THUNDER 108
COLUMBIA. May, 1983. (John Badham), Roy Scheider, Warren Oates, Malcolm McDowell.

BLUE VELVET (J-D-C) 120
DE LAURENTIIS. September, 1986. (David Lynch), Kyle MacLachlan, Isabella Rossellini, Dennis Hopper.

BLUEBERRY HILL 87
MGM/UA. December, 1988. (Strathford Hamilton), Carrie Snodgress, Jennifer Rubin.

BLUES BROTHERS, THE 113
UNIVERSAL. June, 1980. (John Landis), John Belushi, Dan Aykroyd.

BOAT, THE (DAS BOOT) 150
COLUMBIA, February, 1982. German. (Wolfgang Petersen), Jurgen Prochnow, Herbert Gronemeyer.

BODY BEAT 96
VIDMARK. September, 1988. (Ted Mather), Tony Dean Fields, Galyn Gorg.

BODY CHEMISTRY 85
CONCORDE. March, 1990. (Kristine Peterson), Marc Singer, Lisa Pescia, Mary Crosby.

BODY DOUBLE 109
COLUMBIA. October, 1984. (Brian De Palma), Craig Wasson, Melanie Griffith.

BODY HEAT 113
WARNER BROS. August, 1981. (Lawrence Kasdan), William Hurt, Kathleen Turner.

BODY PARTS 88
PARAMOUNT. August, 1991. (Eric Red), Jeff Fahey, Lindsay Duncan, Brad Dourif.

BODY ROCK 93
NEW WORLD. September, 1984. (Marcelo Epstein), Lorenzo Lamas, Vicki Frederick.

BODY SLAM 89
DE LAURENTIIS. May, 1987. (Hal Needham), Dirk Benedict, Tanya Roberts.

BOGGY CREEK II 91
HOWCO INTERNATIONAL. December, 1985. (Charles B. Pierce), Charles B. Pierce, Cindy Butler.

BOLERO 173
DOUBLE 13. June, 1982. (Claude Lelouch), James Caan, Geraldine Chaplin.

BOLERO 104
CANNON FILMS. August, 1984. (John Derek), Bo Derek, George Kennedy.

BONFIRE OF THE VANITIES, THE 125
WARNER BROS. December, 1990. (Brian DePalma), Tom Hanks, Bruce Willis, Melanie Griffith.

	Length in Mins.

BOOK OF DAYS 73
STUTZ CO. February, 1990. (Meredith Monk), Gerd Wameling, Lucas Hoving.

BOOK OF LOVE 88
NEW LINE CINEMA. February, 1991. (Robert Shaye), Chris Young, Keith Coogan, John Cameron Mitchell.

BOOMERANG .... 118.
PARAMOUNT. July, 1992. (Reginald Hudlin), Eddie Murphy, Robin Givens, Halle Berry.

BOOST, THE 95
HEMDALE. December, 1988. (Harold Becker), James Woods, Sean Young.

BORDER, THE (P) 107
UNIVERSAL. February, 1982. (Tony Richardson), Jack Nicholson, Harvey Keitel.

BORDER RADIO 84
INTERNATIONAL FILM MARKETING. September, 1988. (Alison Anders, Dean Lent, Kurt Voss), Chris D. John Doe. B & W.

BORDERLINE (P) 106
ASSOCIATED FILM DIST. October, 1980. (Jerrold Freedman), Charles Bronson, Bruno Kirby.

BORN AMERICAN 95
CONCORDE-CINEMA GROUP. September, 1986. (Renny Harlin), Mike Norris, Steve Durham.

BORN IN EAST L.A. 85
UNIVERSAL. August, 1987. (Cheech Marin), Cheech Marin, Daniel Stern.

BORN OF FIRE 84
VIDMARK ENTERTAINMENT. September, 1987. (Jamil Dehlavi), Peter Firth, Suzan Crowley.

BORN ON THE FOURTH OF JULY (P) 145
UNIVERSAL. December, 1989. (Oliver Stone), Tom Cruise, Kyra Sedgwick, Willem Dafoe.

BORN TO RACE 98
MGM/UA. January, 1988. (James Fargo), Joseph Bottoms, Marc Singer.

BORN TO RIDE 88
WARNER BROS. May, 1991. (Graham Baker), John Stamos, John Stockwell, Teri Polo.

BORROWER, THE 97
CANNON. August, 1991. (John McNaughton), Tom Towles, Rae Dawn Chong, Antonio Fargas.

BOSS' WIFE, THE 83
TRI-STAR. November, 1986. (Ziggy Steinberg), Daniel Stern, Arielle Dombasle.

BOSTONIANS, THE 120
ALMI PICTURES. August, 1984. (James Ivory), Christopher Reeve, Vanessa Redgrave, Madeleine Potter.

BOUNTY, THE (J-D-C) 132
ORION PICTURES. May, 1984. (Roger Donaldson), Mel Gibson, Anthony Hopkins.

BOXER AND DEATH, THE 107
SIREN PICTURES. October, 1988. German, Czech; Eng. subtitles. (Peter Solan) Stefan Kvietik, Manfred Krug.

BOY FROM CALABRIA, A (UN RAGAZZO DI CALABRIA) 106
IFEX. November, 1987. Italian. (Luigi Comencini), Santo Polimeno, Gian Maria Volonte.

BOY IN BLUE, THE 93
20TH CENTURY FOX. January, 1986. Canadian. (Charles Jarrott), Nicolas Cage, Cynthia Dale.

BOY WHO COULD FLY, THE 114
20TH CENTURY FOX. August, 1986. (Nick Castle), Lucy Deakins, Jay Underwood.

BOY WHO CRIED BITCH, THE 105
PILGRIMS 3 CORP. October, 1991. (Juan Jose Campanella), Harley Cross, Karen Young, Jesse Bradford.

BOYFRIENDS AND GIRLFRIENDS (L'AMI DE MON AMIE) 102
ORION CLASSICS. July, 1988. French; Eng. subtitles. (Eric Rohmer), Emmanuelle Chaulet, Sophie Renoir.

BOYS NEXT DOOR, THE 88
NEW WORLD PICTURES. November, 1985. (Penelope Spheeris), Maxwell Caulfield, Charlie Sheen.

BOYZ N THE HOOD 107
COLUMBIA. July, 1991. (John Singleton), Cuba Gooding, Jr., Ice Cube, Larry Fishburne.

BRADDOCK: MISSING IN ACTION III 103
CANNON GROUP. January, 1988. (Aaron Norris), Chuck Norris, Aki Aleong.

BRADY'S ESCAPE 96
SATORI. June, 1984. Hungarian. (Pal Gabor), John Savage, Kelly Reno.

BRAIN DAMAGE 94
PALISADES ENTERTAINMENT. April, 1988. (Frank Henenlotter), Rick Herbst, Gordon MacDonald.

	Length in Mins.

BRAIN DONORS 79
PARAMOUNT. April, 1992. (Dennis Dugan), John Turturro, Mel Smith, Bob Nelson.

BRAINSTORM (P) 106
MGM/UA. September, 1983. (Douglas Trumbull), Christopher Walken, Natalie Wood.

BRANCHES OF THE TREE, THE 120
ERATO FILMS. April, 1992. Indian-French. (Satyajit Ray), Ajit Benerjee, Maradan Benerjee, Soumitra Chatterjee.

BRAVE LITTLE TOASTER, THE 89
HYPERION PICTURES. May, 1989. (Jerry Rees). Animated.

BRAVESTARR 91
TAURUS ENTERTAINMENT. September, 1988. (Tom Tataranowicz). Animated.

BRAZIL 131
UNIVERSAL. December, 1985. (Terry Gilliam), Jonathan Pryce, Robert De Niro, Kim Greist.

BREAK OF DAWN 105
CINEWEST. December, 1988. (Isaac Artenstein), Oscar Chavez. Maria Rojo.

BREAKER MORANT 108
NEW WORLD/QUARTET FILMS. February, 1981. Australian. (Bruce Beresford), Edward Woodward, Jack Thompson.

BREAKFAST CLUB, THE 97
UNIVERSAL. February, 1985. (John Hughes), Emilio Estevez, Judd Nelson, Molly Ringwald.

BREAKIN' 90
MGM/UA. May, 1984. (Joel Silberg), Lucinda Dickey, Adolfo Quinones.

BREAKIN' 2 ELECTRIC BOOGALOO 94
TRI-STAR. December, 1984. (Sam Firstenberg), Lucinda Dickey, Adolfo Quinones.

BREAKING GLASS 104
PARAMOUNT. September, 1980. British. (Brian Gibson), Phil Daniels, Hazel O'Connor.

BREAKING IN 91
SAMUEL GOLDWYN CO. October, 1989. (Bill Forsyth), Burt Reynolds, Casey Siemaszko.

BREATHLESS 100
ORION. May, 1983. (Jim McBride), Richard Gere, Valerie Kaprisky.

BREED APART, A 101
HEMDALE RELEASING. March, 1986. (Philippe Mora), Kathleen Turner, Rutger Hauer, Powers Boothe.

BRENDA STARR 87
TRIUMPH. April, 1992. (Robert Ellis Miller), Brooke Shields, Timothy Dalton, Tony Peck.

BREWSTER'S MILLIONS 97
UNIVERSAL. May, 1985. (Walter Hill), Richard Pryor, John Candy.

BRIDE, THE 118
COLUMBIA. August, 1985. (Franc Roddam), Jennifer Beals, Clancy Brown, Sting.

BRIDE OF RE-ANIMATOR 97
50TH ST. FILMS. February, 1991. (Brian Yuzna), Jeffrey Combs, Bruce Abbott, Kathleen Kinmont.

BRIEF HISTORY OF TIME, A 80
TRITON. August, 1992. British. (Errol Morris), Stephen Hawking.

BRIGHT ANGEL 94
HEMDALE. June, 1991. (Michael Fields), Dermot Mulroney, Lili Taylor, Sam Shepard.

BRIGHT LIGHTS, BIG CITY 110
MGM/UA. April, 1988. (James Bridges), Michael J. Fox, Kiefer Sutherland, Phoebe Cates.

BRIGHTNESS (YEELEN) 105
LES FILMS CISSE. August, 1988. Mali; Eng. titles. (Souleymane Cisse), Issiaka Kane, Aoua Sangare.

BRIGHTON BEACH MEMOIRS 108
UNIVERSAL. December, 1986. (Gene Saks), Blythe Danner, Jonathan Silverman, Judith Ivey.

BRIMSTONE AND TREACLE 85
UA CLASSICS. November, 1982. British. (Richard Loncraine), Sting, Denholm Elliott.

BRING ON THE NIGHT 97
SAMUEL GOLDWYN CO. November, 1985. (Michael Apted), Sting, Omar Hakim.

BRITANNIA HOSPITAL 116
UA CLASSICS. March, 1983. British. (Lindsay Anderson), Leonard Rossiter, Graham Crowden.

BROADCAST NEWS 131
20TH CENTURY FOX. December, 1987. (James L. Brooks), William Hurt, Holly Hunter, Albert Brooks.

BROADWAY DANNY ROSE 86
ORION. January, 1984. (Woody Allen), Woody Allen, Mia Farrow. B & W.

447

Length in Mins.

BROKEN MIRRORS 105
FIRST RUN FEATURES. March, 1987. Dutch; Eng. titles. (Marleen Gorris), Lineke Rijxman, Henriette Tol.

BROKEN NOSES 75
WEBER/RUSH. November, 1987. (Bruce Weber). Documentary.

BRONCO BILLY 117
WARNER BROS. June, 1980. (Clint Eastwood), Clint Eastwood, Sondra Locke.

BROTHER FROM ANOTHER PLANET, THE 110
CINECOM INTL. September, 1984. (John Sayles), Joe Morton, Daryl Edwards.

BRUBAKER 130
20TH CENTURY FOX. June, 1980. (Stuart Rosenberg), Robert Redford, Yaphet Kotto.

BUDDIES 81
NEW LINE. September, 1985. (Arthur J. Bressan, Jr.), Geoff Edholm, David Schacter.

BUDDY BUDDY (P) 98
UNITED ARTISTS. December, 1981. (Billy Wilder), Jack Lemmon, Walter Matthau.

BUDDY SYSTEM, THE 110
20TH CENTURY-FOX. January, 1984. (Glenn Jordan), Richard Dreyfuss, Susan Sarandon.

BUFFET FROID 95
INTERAMA. September, 1987. French; Eng. subtitles. (Bertrand Blier), Gerard Depardieu, Bernard Blier.

BUFFY THE VAMPIRE SLAYER 85
20TH CENTURY FOX. July, 1992. (Fran Rubel Kazui), Kristy Swanson, Donald Sutherland, Luke Perry.

BUGS BUNNY'S 3rd MOVIE: 1001 RABBIT TALES 90
WARNER BROS. November, 1982. Animated.

BUGSY 135
TRISTAR. December, 1991. (Barry Levinson), Warren Beatty, Annette Bening, Harvey Keitel, Ben Kingsley.

BULL DURHAM 108
ORION. June, 1988. (Ron Shelton), Kevin Costner, Susan Sarandon, Tim Robbins.

BULLETPROOF 94
CINETEL. May, 1988. (Steve Carver), Gary Busey, Darlanne Fluegel.

BULLIES 90
UNIVERSAL. September, 1986. Canadian. (Paul Lynch), Janet Lane-Green, Stephen Hunter.

BULLSEYE 95
CINEMA GROUP. May, 1987. Australian. (Carl Schultz), Paul Goddard, Kathryn Walker.

BULLSHOT 85
ISLAND ALIVE. August, 1985. British. (Dick Clement), Alan Shearman, Diz White.

'BURBS, THE 103
UNIVERSAL. February, 1989. (Joe Dante), Tom Hanks, Bruce Dern, Carrie Fisher.

BURGLAR 102
WARNER BROS. March, 1987. (Hugh Wilson), Whoopi Goldberg, Bobcat Goldthwait.

BURGLAR, THE (VZLOMSHIK) 89
IFEX. August, 1988. Russian; Eng. subtitles. (Valery Ogorodnikov), Oleg Yelykomov, Konstantin Kinchev.

BURIED ALIVE 94
AQUARIUS. June, 1984. Italian; dubbed. (Joe D'Amato), Kieran Canter.

BURKE AND WILLS 140
HEMDALE RELEASING. June, 1987. Australian. (Graeme Clifford), Jack Thompson, Nigel Travers.

BURNING SECRET 106
VESTRON PICTURES. December, 1988. British-U.S.-West German. (Andrew Birkin), Faye Dunaway, Klaus Maria Brandauer.

BUSINESS AS USUAL 88
CANNON RELEASING. October, 1988. British. (Lezli-An Barrett), Glenda Jackson, John Thaw.

BUSTER 103
HEMDALE. November, 1988. British. (David Green), Phil Collins, Julie Walters.

BUSTIN' LOOSE 94
UNIVERSAL. May, 1981. (Oz Scott), Richard Pryor, Cicely Tyson.

BUTCHER'S WIFE, THE 104
PARAMOUNT. October, 1991. (Terry Hughes), Demi Moore, Jeff Daniels, George Dzundza.

BUTTERFLY 107
ANALYSIS. February, 1982. (Matt Cimber), Stacy Keach, Pia Zadora, Orson Welles.

Length in Mins.

BUY & CELL 91
TRANS WORLD ENTERTAINMENT. January, 1989. (Robert Boris), Robert Carradine, Michael Winslow, Malcolm McDowell.

BUYING TIME 97
MGM/UA. May, 1989. (Mitchell Gabourie), Jeff Schultz, Page Fletcher.

BYE BYE BABY 85
SEYMOUR BORDE & ASSOCS. April, 1989. Italian. (Enrico Oldoini), Carol Alt, Brigitte Nielsen.

BYE BYE BLUES 110
CIRCLE RELEASING. March, 1990. Canadian. (Anne Wheeler), Rebecca Jenkins, Luke Reilly, Michael Ontkean.

C

C.H.U.D. 110
NEW WORLD PICTURES. July, 1984. (Douglas Cheek), John Heard, Kim Greist, Daniel Stern.

CABEZA DE VACA 111
CONCORDE. May, 1992. Mexican-Spanish. (Nicolas Eshevarria), Juan Diego, Daniel Gimenez Cacho.

CACTUS 95
SPECTRAFILM. October, 1986. British. (Paul Cox), Isabelle Huppert, Robert Menzies.

CADDIE 107
ATLANTIC. February, 1981. Australian. (Donald Crombie), Helen Morse, Takis Emmanuel.

CADDYSHACK 93
WARNER BROS. July, 1980. (Harold Ramis), Chevy Chase, Ted Knight, Rodney Dangerfield.

CADDYSHACK II 93
WARNER BROS. July, 1988. (Allan Arkush), Jackie Mason, Dyan Cannon.

CADENCE 97
NEW LINE CINEMA. January, 1991. (Martin Sheen), Charlie Sheen, Martin Sheen, Larry Fishburne.

CADILLAC MAN 97
ORION. May, 1990. (Roger Donaldson), Robin Williams, Tim Robbins.

CAGE 101
NEW CENTURY/VISTA. September, 1989. (Lang Elliott), Lou Ferrigno, Reb Brown.

CAGE/CUNNINGHAM 95
CUNNINGHAM DANCE FOUNDATION. December, 1991. (Elliot Caplan), Documentary.

CAL 102
WARNER BROS. August, 1984. British. (Pat O'Connor), Helen Mirren, John Lynch.

CALIGULA 156
PENTHOUSE FILMS. February, 1980. (Tinto Brass), Malcolm McDowell, Peter O'Toole, John Gielgud.

CALL ME 93
VESTRON PICTURES. May, 1988. (Sollace Mitchell), Patricia Charbonneau, Stephen McHattie.

CALLER, THE 98
EMPIRE PICTURES. April, 1987. (Arthur Seidelman), Malcolm McDowell, Madolyn Smith.

CALLING THE SHOTS 118
WORLD ARTISTS. October, 1988. Canadian. (Janis Cole, Holly Dale). Documentary.

CAMERON'S CLOSET 86
SVS FILMS. January, 1989. (Armand Mastroianni), Cotter Smith, Mel Harris, Tab Hunter.

CAMILA 105
EUROPEAN CLASSICS. March, 1985. Spanish; Eng. titles. (Maria Luisa Bemberg), Susu Pecoraro, Imanol Arias.

CAMILLE CLAUDEL 149
ORION CLASSICS. December, 1989. French. (Bruno Nuytten), Isabelle Adjani, Gerard Depardieu.

CAMMINA CAMMINA 150
GRANGE COMMUNICATIONS. July, 1988 (release of 1984 film). Italian; Eng. subtitles. (Ermanno Olmi), Alberto Fumagalli, Antonio Cucciarre.

CAMP AT THIAROYE, THE 157
NEW YORKER. September, 1990. French. (Ousmane Sembene, Thierno Faty Sow), Ibrahima Sane, Sijiri Bakaba.

CAMPUS MAN 94
PARAMOUNT. April, 1987. (Ron Casden), John Dye, Steve Lyon.

CAN SHE BAKE A CHERRY PIE? 90
WORLD WIDE CLASSICS. December, 1983. (Henry Jaglom), Karen Black, Michael Emil.

CANDY MOUNTAIN 91
IFEX. February, 1988. Swiss-Canadian-French. (Robert Frank, Rudy Wurlitzer), Kevin J. O'Connor, Harris Yulin.

Length in Mins.

CANNERY ROW 120
MGM/UA. February, 1982. (David S. Ward), Nick Nolte, Debra Winger.

CANNIBAL TOURS 70
DIRECT CINEMA LTD. August, 1989. (Dennis O'Rourke). Documentary.

CANNONBALL RUN, THE 95
20TH CENTURY FOX. June, 1981. (Hal Needham), Burt Reynolds, Roger Moore, Farrah Fawcett.

CANNONBALL RUN II (P) 108
WARNER BROS. June, 1984. (Hal Needham), Burt Reynolds, Dom DeLuise.

CAN'T BUY ME LOVE 94
BUENA VISTA. August, 1987. (Steve Rash), Patrick Dempsey, Amanda Peterson.

CAN'T STOP THE MUSIC (P) 118
ASSOCIATED FILM DIST. June, 1980. (Nancy Walker), Village People, Valerie Perrine.

CAPE FEAR (P) 130
UNIVERSAL. November, 1991. (Martin Scorsese), Robert De Niro, Nick Nolte, Jessica Lange, Juliette Lewis.

CAPTIVE 95
CINETEL. October, 1986. British-French. (Paul Mayerberg), Irina Brook, Oliver Reed.

CAPTIVE HEARTS 97
MGM/UA. June, 1987. (Paul Almond), Noriyuki (Pat) Morita, Chris Makepeace.

CARAVAGGIO 93
BRITISH FILM INSTITUTE. August, 1986. British. (Derek Jarman), Nigel Terry, Sean Bean.

CARBON COPY 92
EMBASSY, September, 1981. (Michael Schultz), George Segal, Susan Saint James.

CARE BEARS ADVENTURES IN WONDERLAND, THE .. 75
CINEPLEX ODEON FILMS. August, 1987. (Ray Jafelice). Animated.

CARE BEARS MOVIE, THE 75
SAMUEL GOLDWYN CO. March, 1985. Canadian. (Arna Selznick), Animated.

CARE BEARS MOVIE II: A NEW GENERATION 77
COLUMBIA. March, 1986. (Dale Schott), Animated.

CAREER OPPORTUNITIES 85
UNIVERSAL. March, 1991. (Bryan Gordon), Frank Whaley, Jennifer Connelly, Dermot Mulroney.

CAREFUL HE MIGHT HEAR YOU 116
TLC FILMS. June, 1984. Australian. (Carl Schultz), Wendy Hughes, Robyn Nevin.

CARIBE 89
MIRAMAX FILMS. May, 1988. Canadian. (Michael Kennedy), John Savage, Kara Glover.

CARMEN 99
ORION. October, 1983. Spanish; Eng. titles. (Carlos Saura), Laura del Sol.

CARMEN 152
TRIUMPH. September, 1984. French; Eng. titles. (Francisco Rossi), Julia Migenes-Johnson, Placido Domingo.

CARNY 108
UNITED ARTISTS. May, 1980. (Robert Kaylor), Gary Busey, Jodie Foster.

CASSANDRA CAT 87
CESKOSLOVENSKY FILMEXPORT. July, 1990 (release of 1963 film), Czechoslovak. (Vojtĕch Jasný), Jan Werich, Emilie Vašáryová.

CASTAWAY 117
CANNON SCREEN ENTERTAINMENT. September, 1987. (Nicolas Roeg), Oliver Reed, Amanda Donohoe.

CASTLE OF CAGLIOSTRO, THE 100
STREAMLINE. July, 1992. Japanese. (Hayao Miyazaki), Animated.

CASUAL SEX? 97
UNIVERSAL. April, 1988. (Genevieve Robert), Lea Thompson, Victoria Jackson.

CASUALTIES OF WAR (P) 113
COLUMBIA. August, 1989. (Brian DePalma), Michael J. Fox, Sean Penn.

CAT PEOPLE 118
UNIVERSAL. April, 1982. (Paul Schrader), Nastassia Kinski, Malcolm McDowell.

CATCH ME IF YOU CAN 105
MCEG. October, 1989. (Stephen Sommers), Matt Lattanzi, Loryn Locklin.

CATCH THE HEAT 87
TRANS WORLD ENTERTAINMENT. June, 1987. (Joel Silberg), David Dukes, Tiana Alexandra, Rod Steiger.

CAT'S EYE 93
MGM/UA. April, 1985. (Lewis Teague), Drew Barrymore, James Woods, Robert Hays.

Length in Mins.

CATTLE ANNIE AND LITTLE BRITCHES 97
UNIVERSAL. May, 1981. (Lamont Johnson), Burt Lancaster, John Savage, Amanda Plummer.

CAUGHT 113
WORLD WIDE PICTURES. November, 1987. (James F. Collier), John Shepherd, Amerjit Deu, Jill Ireland.

CAVE GIRL 87
CROWN INTL. May, 1985. (David Oliver), Daniel Roebuck, Cindy Ann Thompson.

CAVEMAN 91
UNITED ARTISTS. April, 1981. (Carl Gottlieb), Ringo Starr, Barbara Bach, Dennis Quaid.

CEASE FIRE 85
CINEWORLD. October, 1985. (David Nutter), Don Johnson, Lisa Blount.

CELIA 102
KIM LEWIS MARKETING. December, 1989. Australian. (Ann Turner), Rebecca Smart, Nicolas Eadie.

CENTER OF THE WEB 91
A.I.P. STUDIO. May, 1992. (David A. Prior), Robert Davi, Charlene Tilton, Tony Curtis.

CERTAIN FURY 97
NEW WORLD. February, 1985. (Stephen Gyllenhaal), Tatum O'Neal, Irene Cara.

C'EST LA VIE 97
GOLDWYN. November, 1990. French. (Diane Kurys), Nathalie Baye, Richard Berry, Julie Bataille.

CHAIR, THE 90
ANGELIKA. December, 1989. (Waldemar Korzeniowsky), James Coco, Trini Alvarado, Stephen Geoffreys.

CHALLENGE, THE 112
EMBASSY. July, 1982. (John Frankenheimer), Scott Glenn, Toshiro Mifune.

CHAMELEON STREET 98
NORTHERN ARTS. April, 1991. (Wendell B. Harris, Jr.), Wendell B. Harris, Jr., Angela Leslie.

CHAMPIONS 115
EMBASSY. April, 1984. British. (John Irvin), John Hurt, Edward Woodward.

CHAMPIONS FOREVER 90
ION PICTURES. September, 1989. (Dimitri Logothetis), Documentary.

CHAN IS MISSING 80
NEW YORKER. April, 1982. (Wayne Wang), Wood Moy, Marc Hayashi.

CHANCES ARE 108
TRI-STAR. March, 1989. (Emile Ardolino), Cybill Shepherd, Robert Downey Jr., Ryan O'Neal.

CHANEL SOLITAIRE 120
UNITED FILM DISTRIBUTION. October, 1981. U.S.-French. (George Kaczender), Marie-France Pisier, Timothy Dalton.

CHANGE OF SEASONS, A 102
20TH CENTURY FOX. December, 1980. (Richard Lang), Shirley MacLaine, Anthony Hopkins.

CHANGELING, THE 109
ASSOCIATED FILM DISTRIBUTION. March, 1980. Canadian. (Peter Medak), George C. Scott, Trish Van Devere.

CHANT OF JIMMIE BLACKSMITH, THE 124
NEW YORKER. September, 1980. Australian. (Fred Schepisi), Tommy Lewis, Freddy Reynolds.

CHARIOTS OF FIRE 123
WARNER BROS. September, 1981. British. (Hugh Hudson), Ben Cross, Ian Charleson, Ian Holm.

CHATTAHOOCHEE 97
HEMDALE. April, 1990. (Mick Jackson), Gary Oldman, Dennis Hopper.

CHATTANOOGA CHOO CHOO 102
APRIL FOOLS. May, 1984. (Bruce Bilson), Barbara Eden, George Kennedy, Joe Namath.

CHEAP SHOTS 92
HEMDALE/SELECT. November, 1991. (Jeff Ureless), Louis Zorich, David Patrick Kelly, Mary Louise Wilson.

CHEAPER TO KEEP HER 92
AMERICAN CINEMA. September, 1981. (Ken Annakin), Mac Davis, Tovah Feldshuh.

CHECK IS IN THE MAIL, THE 91
ASCOT ENTERTAINMENT. March, 1986. (Joan Darling), Brian Dennehy, Anne Archer.

CHECKING OUT 93
WARNER BROS. April, 1989. (David Leland), Jeff Daniels, Melanie Mayron.

CHEECH AND CHONG'S NEXT MOVIE 99
UNIVERSAL. July, 1980. (Thomas Chong), Richard "Cheech" Marin, Thomas Chong.

449

	Length in Mins.

CHEECH AND CHONG'S NICE DREAMS 89
COLUMBIA. June, 1981. (Thomas Chong), Richard "Cheech" Marin, Thomas Chong.

CHEECH AND CHONG'S THE CORSICAN BROTHERS . 90
ORION PICTURES. June, 1984. (Thomas Chong), Richard "Cheech" Marin, Thomas Chong.

CHEERLEADER CAMP 88
ATLANTIC RELEASING. August, 1988. (John Quinn), Betsy Russell, Leif Garrett.

CHEETAH 84
BUENA VISTA. August, 1989. (Jeff Blyth), Keith Coogan, Lucy Deakins.

CHERRY 2000 93
ORION. February, 1988. (Steve de Jarnatt), Melanie Griffith, David Andrews, Ben Johnson.

CHICAGO JOE AND THE SHOWGIRL 103
NEW LINE CINEMA. July, 1990. British. (Bernard Rose), Kiefer Sutherland, Emily Lloyd.

CHILDREN OF A LESSER GOD 110
PARAMOUNT. October, 1986. (Randa Haines), William Hurt, Marlee Matlin.

CHILDREN OF THE CORN 93
NEW WORLD PICTURES. February, 1984. (Fritz Kiersch), Peter Horton, Linda Hamilton.

CHILD'S PLAY 87
MGM/UA. November, 1988. (Tom Holland), Catherine Hicks, Chris Sarandon.

CHILD'S PLAY 2 86
UNIVERSAL. November, 1990. (John Lafia), Alex Vincent, Christine Elise, Jenny Agutter.

CHILD'S PLAY 3 90
UNIVERSAL. August, 1991. (Jack Bender), Justin Whalin, Perrey Reeves, Jeremy Sylvers.

CHINA CRY 107
PENLAND CO. November, 1990. (James E. Collier), Julia Nickson-Soul, Russell Wong, James Shigeta.

CHINA GIRL 88
VESTRON PICTURES. September, 1987. (Abel Ferrara), Russell Wong, Richard Panebianco.

CHINA RUN 92
REEL MOVIES INTL. April, 1987. (Mickey Grant). Documentary.

CHINESE GHOST STORY, A 98
GORDON'S FILMS. September, 1988. Cantonese; Eng. titles. (Ching Siu Tung), Leslie Cheung, Wong Tsu Hsien.

CHIPMUNK ADVENTURE, THE 90
SAMUEL GOLDWYN CO. May, 1987. (Janice Karmen). Animated.

CHOCOLAT 105
ORION CLASSICS. March, 1989. French; Eng. titles. (Claire Denis), Isaach de Bankolé, Giulia Boschi.

CHOCOLATE WAR, THE 100
MCEG. November, 1988. (Keith Gordon), John Glover, Ilan Mitchell-Smith.

CHOKE CANYON 94
UNITED FILM DISTRIBUTION. August, 1986. (Chuck Bail), Stephen Collins, Janet Julian.

CHOOSE ME 106
ISLAND ALIVE. November, 1984. (Alan Rudolph), Genevieve Bujold, Keith Carradine.

CHOPPER CHICKS IN ZOMBIETOWN 89
TRIAX. March, 1990. (Dan Hoskins), Jamie Rose, Catherine Carlen.

CHOPPING MALL 76
CONCORDE PICTURES. November, 1986. (Jim Wynorski), Kelli Maroney, Tony O'Dell.

CHORUS LINE, A 113
COLUMBIA. December, 1985. (Richard Attenborough), Michael Douglas, Terrence Mann.

CHORUS OF DISAPPROVAL, A 92
SOUTHGATE ENTERTAINMENT. August, 1989. British. (Michael Winner), Anthony Hopkins, Jeremy Irons.

CHOSEN, THE 108
20TH CENTURY FOX. April, 1982. (Jeremy Paul Kagan), Maximilian Schell, Rod Steiger, Barry Miller.

CHRISTINE (P) 110
COLUMBIA. December, 1983. (John Carpenter), Keith Gordon, John Stockwell.

CHRISTMAS STORY, A 94
MGM/UA. November, 1983. (Bob Clark), Melinda Dillon, Darren McGavin, Peter Billingsley.

CHRISTOPHER COLUMBUS—THE DISCOVERY (P) 121
WARNER BROS. August, 1992. (John Glen), George Corraface, Marlon Brando, Tom Selleck.

CHU CHU AND THE PHILLY FLASH 100
20TH CENTURY FOX. August, 1981. (David Lowell Rich), Alan Arkin, Carol Burnett.

	Length in Mins.

CHUCK BERRY: HAIL! HAIL! ROCK 'N' ROLL 120
UNIVERSAL. October, 1987. (Taylor Hackford), Documentary.

CINEMA PARADISO 123
MIRAMAX. February, 1990. Italian. (Giuseppe Tornatore), Philippe Noiret, Jacques Perrin.

CIRCUITRY MAN 96
SKOURAS. August, 1990. (Steve Lovy), Jim Metzler, Dennis Christopher, Dana Wheeler-Nicholson.

CITY AND THE DOGS, THE 114
CINEVISTA/PROMOVISION. January, 1987. Spanish. (Francisco J. Lombardi), Pablo Serra, Gustavo Bueno.

CITY HEAT 94
WARNER BROS. December, 1984. (Richard Benjamin), Clint Eastwood, Burt Reynolds.

CITY LIMITS 85
ATLANTIC RELEASING. September, 1985. (Aaron Lipstadt), Darrell Larson, John Stockwell.

CITY OF HOPE 130
GOLDWYN. October, 1991. (John Sayles), Vincent Spano, Joe Morton, Tony Lo Bianco, Todd Graff.

CITY OF JOY 134
TRISTAR. April, 1992. British-French. (Roland Joffé, Patrick Swayze, Om Puri, Pauline Collins.

CITY OF WOMEN 138
NEW YORKER. April, 1981. Italian. (Federico Fellini), Marcello Mastroianni, Ettore Manni.

CITY SLICKERS 110
COLUMBIA. June, 1991. (Ron Underwood), Billy Crystal, Daniel Stern, Bruno Kirby.

CITY ZERO 84
IFEX. March, 1991. Soviet. (Karen Shakhnazarov), Leonid Filatov, Oleg Basilashvili.

CLAN OF THE CAVE BEAR, THE (P) 98
WARNER BROS. January, 1988. (Michael Chapman), Daryl Hannah, Pamela Reed.

CLARA'S HEART 108
WARNER BROS. October, 1988. (Robert Mulligan), Whoopi Goldberg, Neil Patrick Harris.

CLASH OF THE TITANS 118
UNITED ARTISTS. June, 1981. British. (Desmond Davis), Harry Hamlin, Judi Bowker, Laurence Olivier.

CLASS 98
ORION. July, 1983. (John Lewis Carlino), Rob Lowe, Jacqueline Bisset, Andrew McCarthy.

CLASS ACT 98
WARNER BROS. June, 1992. (Randall Miller), Christopher "Kid" Reid, Christopher "Play" Martin, Andre Rosey.

CLASS ACTION 109
20TH CENTURY FOX. March, 1991. (Michael Apted), Gene Hackman, Mary Elizabeth Mastrantonio, Colin Friels.

CLASS ENEMY 125
TELECULTURE. July, 1984. German; Eng. titles. (Peter Stein), Greger Hansen.

CLASS OF 1999 98
TAURUS ENTERTAINMENT. May, 1990. (Mark L. Lester), Bradley Gregg, Malcolm McDowell.

CLASS OF NUKE 'EM HIGH 81
TROMA. October, 1986. (Richard Haines), Janelle Brady, Gilbert Brenton.

CLASS OF NUKE 'EM HIGH PART 2: SUBHUMANOID MELTDOWN 95
TROMA. April, 1991. (Eric Louzil), Brick Bronsky, Lisa Gaye.

CLASS RELATIONS 126
JANUS FILMS. February, 1987. German; Eng. titles. (Jean-Marie Straub/Danielle Huillet), Christian Heinisch.

CLEAN AND SOBER 124
WARNER BROS. August, 1988. (Glenn Gordon Caron), Michael Keaton, Kathy Baker, Morgan Freeman.

CLEARCUT 98
NORTHERN ARTS. August, 1992. Canadian. (Richard Bugajski), Ron Lea, Graham Greene, Michael Hogan.

CLIMB, THE 90
CINETEL. May, 1987. (Don Shebib), Bruce Greenwood, James Hurdle.

CLINIC, THE 93
SATORI. February, 1985. (David Stevens), Chris Haywood, Simon Burke.

CLOAK AND DAGGER 101
UNIVERSAL. August, 1984. (Richard Franklin), Henry Thomas, Dabney Coleman.

CLOCKWISE 96
UNIVERSAL. October, 1986. British. (Christopher Morahan), John Cleese, Alison Steadman.

	Length in Mins.

CLOSE MY EYES 109
CASTLE HILL. November, 1991. British. (Stephen Poliakoff), Alan Rickman, Clive Owen, Saskia Reeves.

CLOSET LAND 89
UNIVERSAL. March, 1991. (Radha Bharadwaj), Madeleine Stowe, Alan Rickman.

CLOWNHOUSE 84
TRIUMPH. July, 1990. (Victor Salva), Nathan Forrest Winters, Brian McHugh.

CLUB PARADISE 104
WARNER BROS. July, 1986. (Harold Ramis), Robin Williams, Peter O'Toole.

CLUE 87
PARAMOUNT December, 1985. (Jonathan Lynn), Eileen Brennan, Tim Curry, Christopher Lloyd.

COAL MINER'S DAUGHTER 125
UNIVERSAL. March, 1980. (Michael Apted), Sissy Spacek, Tommy Lee Jones, Beverly D'Angelo.

COAST TO COAST 95
PARAMOUNT. October, 1980. (Joseph Sargent), Dyan Cannon, Robert Blake.

COBRA 87
WARNER BROS. May, 1986. (George P. Cosmatos), Sylvester Stallone, Brigitte Nielsen.

COCA-COLA KID, THE 94
CINECOM INTL. July, 1985. Australian. (Dusan Makavejev), Eric Roberts, Greta Scacchi.

COCAINE WARS 85
CONCORDE-CINEMA GROUP. November, 1985. (Hector Olivera), John Schneider, Kathryn Witt.

COCKTAIL 104
BUENA VISTA. July, 1988. (Roger Donaldson), Tom Cruise, Bryan Brown, Elisabeth Shue.

COCOON (P) 117
20TH CENTURY FOX. June, 1985. (Ron Howard), Don Ameche, Wilford Brimley, Jessica Tandy.

COCOON: THE RETURN 116
20TH CENTURY FOX. November, 1988. (Daniel Petrie), Don Ameche, Wilford Brimley, Hume Cronyn.

CODE NAME: EMERALD 93
MGM/UA. September, 1985. (Jonathan Sanger), Ed Harris, Max Von Sydow.

CODE OF SILENCE 102
ORION. May, 1985. (Andy Davis), Chuck Norris, Henry Silva.

CODENAME: WILD GEESE 93
NEW WORLD PICTURES. September, 1986. West German-Italian. In English. (Anthony M. Dawson, Antonio Marghereti), Lewis Collins, Lee Van Cleef.

COHEN & TATE 85
HEMDALE. January, 1989. (Eric Red), Roy Scheider, Adam Baldwin.

COLD FEET 91
CINECOM INTL. May, 1984. (Bruce Van Dusen), Griffin Dunne, Marissa Chibas.

COLD FEET 91
AVENUE PICTURES. May, 1989. (Robert Dornhelm), Keith Carradine, Sally Kirkland, Tom Waits.

COLD HEAVEN 103
HEMDALE. May, 1992. (Nicolas Roeg), Theresa Russell, Mark Harmon, James Russo.

COLD MOON 92
GAMUONT. April, 1992. French. (Patrick Bouchitey), Jean-Francois Stevenin, Patrick Bouchitey, Jean-Pierre Bisson.

COLD STEEL 90
CINETEL FILMS. January, 1988. (Dorothy Ann Puzo), Brad Davis, Sharon Stone.

COLEGAS (EL PICO) 107
DAVID WHITTEN PROMOTIONS. August, 1987. In Spanish. (Eloy de la Iglesia), Jose Manuel Cervino, Jose Luis Manzano.

COLONEL REDL 149
ORION CLASSICS. November, 1986. German; Eng. titles. (Istvan Szabo), Klaus Maria Brandauer, Armin Muller-Stahl.

COLOR ADJUSTMENT 86
CALIFORNIA NEWSREEL. January, 1992. (Marlon T. Riggs), Documentary.

COLOR OF DESTINY, THE 104
EMBRA FILME. July, 1988. Portuguese; Eng. subtitles. (Jorge Duran), Guilherme Fontes, Norma Bengel.

COLOR OF MONEY, THE 119
BUENA VISTA. October, 1986. (Martin Scorsese), Paul Newman, Tom Cruise.

COLOR PURPLE, THE 152
WARNER BROS. December, 1985. (Steven Spielberg), Danny Glover, Whoopi Goldberg, Oprah Winfrey.

	Length in Mins.

COLORS 120
ORION. April, 1988. (Dennis Hopper), Sean Penn, Robert Duvall, Maria Conchita Alonso.

COMBAT SHOCK 96
TROMA. October, 1986. (Buddy Giovanazzo), Mitch Maglio, Asaph Livni.

COME AND SEE 142
IFEX. February, 1987. Russian; Eng. titles. (Elim Klimov), Aleksei Kravchenko, Olga Mironova.

COME BACK TO THE FIVE AND DIME, JIMMY DEAN, JIMMY DEAN 110
CINECOM INTL. November, 1982. (Robert Altman), Sandy Dennis, Cher.

COME SEE THE PARADISE 138
20TH CENTURY FOX. December, 1990. (Alan Parker), Dennis Quaid, Tamlyn Tomita, Sab Shimono.

COMEDY'S DIRTIEST DOZEN 88
ISLAND. October, 1990. (Lenny Wong), Tim Allen, John Fox, Joey Gaynor.

COMFORT AND JOY 106
UNIVERSAL. October, 1984. British. (Bill Forsyth), Bill Peterson, Eleanor David.

COMIC BOOK CONFIDENTIAL 90
CINECOM. June, 1989. Canadian. (Ron Mann, Charles Lippincott). Documentary.

COMIC MAGAZINE 120
CINECOM. January, 1987. (Yojiro Simoneau), Yuya Uchida, Yumi Asou.

COMIN' AT YA! 91
August, 1981. Italian. (Ferdinando Baldi), Tony Anthony, Gene Quintano.

COMING TO AMERICA 116
PARAMOUNT. June, 1988. (John Landis), Eddie Murphy, Arsenio Hall, James Earl Jones.

COMING UP ROSES 93
SKOURAS PICTURES. September, 1987. Welsh. (Stephen Bayly), Dafydd Hywel, Iola Gregory.

COMMANDO 88
20TH CENTURY FOX. October, 1985. (Mark L. Lester), Arnold Schwarzenegger, Rae Dawn Chong.

COMMANDO SQUAD 89
TRANS WORLD ENTERTAINMENT. June, 1987. (Fred Olen Ray), Brian Thompson, Kathy Shower.

COMMISSAR 105
IFEX. June, 1988. Russian; Eng subtitles. (Aleksandr Askoldov), Nonna Mordukova, Rolan Bykov.

COMMITMENTS, THE 118
20TH CENTURY FOX. August, 1991. British. (Alan Parker), Robert Arkins, Johnny Murphy, Andrew Strong, Angeline Ball.

COMMUNION 107
NEW LINE CINEMA. November, 1989. (Philippe Mora), Christopher Walken, Lindsay Crouse.

COMPANY BUSINESS 98
MGM. September, 1991. (Nicholas Meyer), Gene Hackman, Mikhail Baryshnikov, Kurtwood Smith.

COMPANY OF WOLVES, THE 95
CANNON FILMS. April, 1985. British. (Neil Jordan), Angela Lansbury, David Warner.

COMPERES, LES 98
EUROPEAN INTL. May, 1984. French; Eng. titles. (Francis Veber), Pierre Richard.

COMPETITION, THE 129
COLUMBIA. December, 1980. (Joel Oliansky), Richard Dreyfuss, Amy Irving.

COMPLEX WORLD 81
HEARTBREAK HITS. November, 1990. (James Wolpaw), Stanley Matis, Dan Welch.

COMPROMISING POSITIONS 98
PARAMOUNT. August, 1985. (Frank Perry), Susan Sarandon, Raul Julia.

COMRADES 180
GAVIN FILM. January, 1989. British. (Bill Douglas), Robin Soans, William Gaminara.

CONAN THE BARBARIAN 115
UNIVERSAL. May, 1982. (John Milius), Arnold Schwarzenegger, James Earl Jones.

CONAN THE DESTROYER 103
UNIVERSAL. June, 1984. (Richard Fleischer), Arnold Schwarzenegger, Grace Jones.

CONCRETE ANGELS 97
SHAPIRO ENTERTAINMENT. September, 1987. (Carlo Liconti), Joseph Dimambro, Luke McKeehan.

CONDORMAN (P) 90
BUENA VISTA. August, 1981. British. (Charles Jarrott), Michael Crawford, Oliver Reed.

Length in Mins.

CONFIDENTIALLY YOURS 111
INTERNATIONAL SPECTRAFILM. January, 1984. French; Eng. titles. (François Truffaut), Jean-Louis Trintignant, Fanny Ardant.

CONSUMING PASSIONS 98
SAMUEL GOLDWYN CO. April, 1988. British. (Giles Foster), Jonathan Pryce, Tyler Butterworth, Vanessa Redgrave.

CONTINENTAL DIVIDE 103
UNIVERSAL. September, 1981. (Michael Apted), John Belushi, Blair Brown.

CONVICTS 95
M.C.E.G. December, 1991. (Peter Masterson), Robert Duvall, Lukas Haas, James Earl Jones.

COOK, THE THIEF, HIS WIFE & HER LOVER, THE 122
MIRAMAX. April, 1990. British. (Peter Greenaway), Helen Mirren, Michael Gambon, Alan Howard.

COOKIE 93
WARNER BROS. August, 1989. (Susan Seidelman), Peter Falk, Dianne Wiest, Emily Lloyd.

COOL AS ICE 93
UNIVERSAL. October, 1991. (David Kellogg), Vanilla Ice, Kristin Minter, Michael Gross.

COOL RUNNINGS: THE REGGAE MOVIE 105
R5/S8. October, 1986. Jamaican. (Robert Mugge). Documentary.

COOL WORLD 105
PARAMOUNT. July, 1992. (Ralph Bakshi), Kim Basinger, Brad Pitt, Gabriel Byrne.

COP 110
ATLANTIC ENTERTAINMENT GROUP. January, 1988. (James B. Harris), James Woods, Lesley Ann Warren.

CORPORATE AFFAIRS 89
CONCORDE. October, 1990. (Terence H. Winkless), Peter Scolari, Mary Crosby, Chris Lemmon.

CORRUPT 99
NEW LINE CINEMA. December, 1983. Italian. (Roberto Faenza), Harvey Keitel, John Lydon.

COTTON CLUB, THE 127
ORION. December, 1984. (Francis Coppola), Richard Gere, Gregory Hines, Diane Lane.

COUCH TRIP, THE 98
ORION. January, 1988. (Michael Ritchie), Dan Aykroyd, Walter Matthau, Charles Grodin.

COUNTRY 109
BUENA VISTA. October, 1984. (Richard Pearce), Jessica Lange, Sam Shepard.

COUP DE TORCHON 128
BIOGRAPH/QUARTET/FRANK MORENO. December, 1982. French; Eng. titles. (Bertrand Tavernier), Philippe Noiret, Isabelle Huppert.

COUPE DE VILLE (WS) 99
UNIVERSAL. March, 1990. (Joe Roth), Patrick Dempsey, Daniel Stern, Alan Arkin.

COURAGE MOUNTAIN 96
TRIUMPH. February, 1990. (Christopher Leitch), Juliette Caton, Leslie Caron, Charlie Sheen.

COURIER, THE 87
VESTRON PICTURES. December, 1988. Irish. (Frank Deasy, Joe Lee), Padraig O'Loingsigh, Cait O'Riordan, Gabriel Byrne.

COUSIN BOBBY 70
CINEVISTA. May, 1992. (Jonathan Demme), Documentary.

COUSINS 110
PARAMOUNT. February, 1989. (Joel Schumacher), Ted Danson, Isabella Rossellini, Sean Young.

COVERGIRL 93
NEW WORLD PICTURES. January, 1984. (Jean-Claude Lord), Jeff Conaway, Irena Ferris.

COVERUP: BEHIND THE IRAN CONTRA AFFAIR 75
EMPOWERMENT PROJECT. August, 1988. (Barbara Trent). Documentary.

CRACK HOUSE 90
CANNON. November, 1989. (Michael Fischa), Jim Brown, Anthony Geary.

CRACK IN THE MIRROR 95
TRIAX ENTERTAINMENT. February, 1989. (Robby Benson). Robby Benson, Danny Aiello.

CRACKDOWN 87
CONCORDE. January, 1991. (Louis Morneau), Cliff De Young, Robert Beltran, Jamie Rose.

CRACKERS 92
UNIVERSAL. February, 1984. (Louis Malle), Donald Sutherland, Sean Penn.

CRAZY FAMILY, THE 106
NEW YORKER FILMS. February, 1986. Japanese; Eng. titles. (Sogo Ishii), Katsuya Kobayashi.

Length in Mins.

CRAZY MOON 87
MIRAMAX. July, 1987. Canadian. (Allan Eastman), Kiefer Sutherland, Peter Spence.

CRAZY PEOPLE 90
PARAMOUNT. April, 1990. (Tony Bill), Dudley Moore, Daryl Hannah.

CREATOR 107
UNIVERSAL. September, 1985. (Ivan Passer), Peter O'Toole, Mariel Hemingway.

CREATURE 97
CARDINAL FILM. April, 1985. (William Malone), Stan Ivar, Wendy Schaal.

CREEPSHOW 122
WARNER BROS. November, 1983. (George Romero), Hal Holbrook, Adrienne Barbeau, Leslie Nielsen.

CREEPSHOW 2 89
NEW WORLD PICTURES. May, 1987. (Michael Gornick), Lois Chiles, George Kennedy, Dorothy Lamour.

CREEPZOIDS 71
URBAN CLASSICS. September, 1987. (David De Coteau), Linnea Quigley, Ken Abraham.

CRIME ZONE 93
CONCORDE. December, 1988. (Luis Llosa), David Carradine, Peter Nelson.

CRIMES AND MISDEMEANORS 104
ORION. October, 1989. (Woody Allen), Woody Allen, Martin Landau, Alan Alda, Mia Farrow.

CRIMES OF PASSION 101
NEW WORLD. October, 1984. (Ken Russell), Kathleen Turner, Anthony Perkins, John Laughlin.

CRIMES OF THE HEART 105
DE LAURENTIIS. December, 1986. (Bruce Beresford), Diane Keaton, Jessica Lange, Sissy Spacek.

CRIMEWAVE 83
COLUMBIA. April, 1986. (Sam Raimi), Louise Lasser, Paul L. Smith.

CRIMINAL LAW 117
HEMDALE. April, 1989. (Martin Campbell), Gary Oldman, Kevin Bacon.

CRISSCROSS 100
MGM. May, 1992. (Chris Menges), Goldie Hawn, Arliss Howard, David Arnott, Keith Carradine.

CRITICAL CONDITION 100
PARAMOUNT. January, 1987. (Michael Apted), Richard Pryor, Rachel Ticotin.

CRITTERS 86
NEW LINE CINEMA April, 1986. (Stephen Herek), Dee Wallace Stone, M. Emmet Walsh.

CRITTERS 2; THE MAIN COURSE 87
NEW LINE CINEMA. April, 1988. (Mick Garris), Scott Grimes, Liane Curtis.

"CROCODILE" DUNDEE (P) 98
PARAMOUNT. September, 1986. Australian. (Peter Faiman), Paul Hogan, Linda Kozlowski.

"CROCODILE" DUNDEE II (P) 111
PARAMOUNT. May, 1988. Australian. (John Cornell), Paul Hogan, Linda Kozlowski.

CROOKED HEARTS 112
MGM. May, 1991. (Michael Bortman), Vincent D'Onofrio, Jennifer Jason Leigh, Peter Berg.

CROSS COUNTRY 107
NEW WORLD PICTURES. November, 1983. (Paul Lynch), Richard Beymer, Nina Axelrod.

CROSS CREEK 125
UNIVERSAL. September, 1983. (Martin Ritt), Mary Steenburgen, Rip Torn, Alfre Woodard.

CROSS MY HEART 96
UNIVERSAL. November, 1987. (Armyan Bernstein), Martin Short, Annette O'Toole, Paul Reiser.

CROSS MY HEART (La Fracture du Myocarde) 105
MK2. April, 1991. French. (Jacques Fansten), Sylvain Copans, Nicolas Parodi, Cecilia Rouaud.

CROSSING DELANCEY 97
WARNER BROS. August, 1988. (Joan Micklin Silver), Amy Irving, Reizl Bozyk, Peter Riegert.

CROSSING THE LINE (a.k.a. The Big Man) 93
MIRAMAX. August, 1991. British. (David Leland), Liam Neeson, Joanne Whalley-Kilmer, Ian Bannen.

CROSSOVER DREAMS 86
MIRAMAX FILMS. August, 1985. (Leon Ichaso), Ruben Blades, Shawn Elliot.

CROSSROADS 96
COLUMBIA. March, 1986. (Walter Hill), Ralph Macchio, Joe Seneca.

CRUISING 106
UNITED ARTISTS. February, 1980. (William Friedkin), Al Pacino, Paul Sorvino.

Length in Mins.

CRUSOE 95
ISLAND PICTURES. March, 1989. (Caleb Deschanel), Aidan Quinn, Adé Sapara.

CRY-BABY 89
UNIVERSAL. April, 1990. (John Waters), Johnny Depp, Amy Locane, Polly Bergen.

CRY FREEDOM (P) 157
UNIVERSAL. November, 1987. British. (Richard Attenborough), Kevin Kline, Denzel Washington, Penelope Wilton.

CRY FROM THE MOUNTAIN 90
WORLD WIDE PICTURES. November, 1985. (James F. Collier), Wes Parker, Rita Walter.

CRY IN THE DARK, A (P) 121
WARNER BROS. November, 1988. Australian. (Fred Schepisi), Meryl Streep, Sam Neill.

CRY IN THE WILD, A 81
CONCORDE. June, 1990. (Mark Griffiths), Jared Rushton, Pamela Sue Martin.

CRY OF THE OWL, THE 102
R5/S8. October, 1991. French, 1987. (Claude Chabrol), Christophe Malavoy, Mathilda May.

CRY WILDERNESS 95
VISTO INTL. February, 1987. (Jay Schlossberg-Cohen), Eric Foster, Maurice Grandmaison.

CRYSTAL HEART 103
NEW WORLD PICTURES. February, 1987. (Gil Bettman), Lee Curreri, Tawny Kitaen.

CRYSTALSTONE 103
TMS PICTURES. February, 1988. (Antonio Pelaez), Frank Grimes, Kamlesh Gupta.

CUJO 91
WARNER BROS. August, 1983. (Lewis Teague), Dee Wallace, Danny Pintauro.

CUP FINAL 107
FIRST RUN FEATURES. August, 1992. Israeli. (Eran Riklis), Moshe Ivgi, Muhamad Bacri, Suheil Haddad.

CURE IN ORANGE, THE 96
ASA COMMUNICATIONS/MOVIE VISIONS. October, 1987. (Tim Pope). Documentary.

CURLY SUE 102
WARNER BROS. October, 1991. (John Hughes), James Belushi, Alisan Porter, Kelly Lynch.

CURSE, THE (WS) 90
TRANS WORLD ENTERTAINMENT. September, 1987. (David Keith), Wil Wheaton, Claude Akins.

CURSE OF THE PINK PANTHER 110
MGM/UA. August, 1983. (Blake Edwards), David Niven, Robert Wagner.

CUT AND RUN 87
NEW WORLD PICTURES. May, 1986. (Ruggero Deadato), Lisa Blount, Leonard Mann.

CUTTER AND BONE (CUTTER'S WAY) 109
UNITED ARTISTS. March, 1981. (Ivan Passer), Jeff Bridges, John Heard.

CUTTING CLASS 90
REPUBLIC. September, 1989. (Rospo Pallenberg), Brad Pitt, Jill Schoelen, Roddy McDowall.

CUTTING EDGE, THE 101
MGM. March, 1992. (Paul M. Glaser), D.B. Sweeney, Moira Kelly, Roy Dotrice.

CYBORG 85
CANNON ENTERTAINMENT. April, 1989. (Albert Pyun), Jean-Claude Van Damme, Deborah Richter.

CYCLONE 83
CINTEL FILMS. June, 1987. (Fred Olen Ray), Heather Thomas, Jeffrey Combs.

CYRANO DE BERGERAC 138
ORION CLASSICS. November, 1990. French. (Jean-Paul Rappeneau), Gérard Depardieu, Anne Brochet, Vincent Perez.

D

D.A.R.Y.L. (P) 99
PARAMOUNT. June, 1985. (Simon Wincer), Mary Beth Hurt, Michael McKean, Barret Oliver.

D.C. CAB 99
UNIVERSAL. December, 1983. (Joel Schumacher), Adam Baldwin, Charlie Barnett, Max Gail, Mr. T.

D.O.A. 96
BUENA VISTA. March, 1988. (Rocky Morton, Annabel Jankel), Dennis Quaid, Meg Ryan.

DA 102
FILM DALLAS PICTURES. April, 1988. (Matt Clark), Barnard Hughes, Martin Sheen.

DAD 117
UNIVERSAL. October, 1989. (Gary David Goldberg), Jack Lemmon, Ted Danson, Ethan Hawke.

Length in Mins.

DADDY NOSTALGIA 105
AVENUE. April, 1991. French. (Bertrand Tavernier), Dirk Bogarde, Jane Birkin, Odette Laure.

DADDY'S BOYS 85
CONCORDE. June, 1988. (Joe Minion), Daryl Haney, Laura Burkett.

DADDY'S DYIN' . . . WHO'S GOT THE WILL? 95
MGM/UA. May, 1990. (Jack Fisk), Beau Bridges, Beverly D'Angelo.

DAFFY DUCK'S MOVIE: FANTASTIC ISLAND 78
WARNER BROS. September, 1983. (Fritz Freleng), Animated.

DAFFY DUCK'S QUACKBUSTERS 80
WARNER BROS. September, 1988. (Chuck Jones, Fritz Freleng, Robert McKimson), Animated.

DAKOTA 97
MIRAMAX. December, 1988. (Fred Holmes), Lou Diamond Phillips, Eli Cummins.

DAMNED RIVER 96
MGM/UA. October, 1989. (Michael Schroeder), Stephen Shellen, Lisa Aliff.

DANCE OF HOPE 75
FIRST RUN FEATURES. December, 1989. (Deborah Shaffer), Documentary.

DANCE TO WIN 102
MGM/UA. December, 1989. (Ted Mather), Carlos Gomez, Daniel Quinn.

DANCE WITH A STRANGER 101
SAMUEL GOLDWYN CO. August, 1985. British. (Mike Newell), Miranda Richardson, Rupert Everett.

DANCERS 99
CANNON GROUP. October, 1987. (Herbert Ross), Mikhail Baryshnikov, Alessandra Ferri.

DANCES WITH WOLVES (P) 181
ORION. November, 1990. (Kevin Costner), Kevin Costner, Mary McDonnell, Graham Greene.

DANCING IN THE DARK 98
NEW WORLD PICTURES. October, 1986. Canadian. (Leon Marr), Martha Henry, Neil Munro.

DANGEROUS LIAISONS 120
WARNER BROS. December, 1988. (Stephen Frears), Glenn Close, John Malkovich, Michelle Pfeiffer.

DANGEROUS LOVE 94
CONCORDE PICTURES. September, 1988. (Marty Ollstein), Lawrence Monoson, Brenda Bakke, Elliott Gould.

DANGEROUS MOVES 100
SPECTRAFILM. May, 1985. French; Eng. titles. (Richard Dembo), Michel Piccoli.

DANGEROUSLY CLOSE 95
CANNON FILMS. May, 1986. (Albert Pyun), John Stockwell, J. Eddie Peck.

DANIEL 130
PARAMOUNT. August, 1983. (Sidney Lumet), Timothy Hutton, Mandy Patinkin, Lindsay Crouse.

DANNY BOY 92
TRIUMPH. May, 1984. Irish. (Neil Jordan), Stephen Rhea, Marie Kean.

DANTON 136
TRIUMPH October, 1983. French; Eng. titles. (Andrzej Wajda), Gerard Depardieu, Wojciech Psznoiak.

DAREDREAMER 108
LENSMAN CO. February, 1990. (Barry Caillier), Tim Noah, Alyce LaTourelle.

DARK BACKWARD, THE 100
GREYCAT FILMS. July, 1991. (Adam Rifkin), Judd Nelson, Bill Paxton, Wayne Newton.

DARK BEFORE DAWN 95
PSM ENTERTAINMENT. September, 1988. (Robert Totten), Sonny Gibson, Doug McClure.

DARK CRYSTAL, THE (P) 94
UNIVERSAL. December, 1982. (Jim Henson, Frank Oz), Puppets.

DARK EYES (OCI CIRONIE) 118
ISLAND PICTURES. September, 1987. Italian and Russian; Eng. subtitles. (Nikita Mikhalkov), Marcello Mastroianni, Silvana Mangano.

DARK HABITS 95
CINEVISTA. May, 1988. Spanish; Eng. subtitles. (Pedro Almodovar), Cristina S. Pascual, Julieta Serrano.

DARK HORSE 90
REPUBLIC. July, 1992. (David Hemmings), Ed Begley Jr., Mimi Rogers, Ari Meyers.

DARK NIGHT 115
HORIZON PRODS. June, 1988. Chinese; Eng. subtitles. (Fred Tan), Sue Ming-Ming, Hsu Ming.

Length in Mins.

DARK OBSESSION (a.k.a. Diamond Skulls) 87
CIRCLE. June, 1991. British. (Nick Broomfield), Gabriel Byrne, Amanda Donohoe, Douglas Hodge.

DARK OF THE NIGHT 88
CASTLE HILL. May, 1986. New Zealand. (Gaylene Preston), Heather Bolton, David Letch.

DARKMAN 95
UNIVERSAL. August, 1990. (Sam Raimi), Liam Neeson, Frances McDormand.

DATE WITH AN ANGEL (J-D-C) 105
DE LAURENTIIS. November, 1987. (Tom McLouglin), Michael E. Knight, Phoebe Cates.

DAUGHTERS OF THE DUST 114
KINO INTL. January, 1992. (Julie Dash), Cora Lee Day, Alva Rodgers, Adisa Anderson.

DAY OF THE DEAD 102
UNITED FILM. July, 1985. (George A. Romero), Lori Cardile, Terry Alexander.

DAYS OF THUNDER (P) 105
PARAMOUNT. June, 1990. (Tony Scott), Tom Cruise, Robert Duvall, Nicole Kidman.

DEAD, THE 83
VESTRON PICTURES. December, 1987. (John Huston), Anjelica Huston, Donal McCann.

DEAD AGAIN 108
PARAMOUNT. August, 1991. (Kenneth Branagh), Kenneth Branagh, Emma Thompson, Derek Jacobi.

DEAD-BANG 105
WARNER BROS. March, 1989. (John Frankenheimer), Don Johnson, Penelope Ann Miller.

DEAD CALM (P) 96
WARNER BROS. April, 1989. Australian. (Phillip Noyce), Sam Neill, Nicole Kidman, Billy Zane.

DEAD-END DRIVE IN 90
NEW WORLD PICTURES. September, 1986. Australian. (Brian Trenchard-Smith), Ned Manning, Natalie McCurry.

DEAD HEAT 86
NEW WORLD PICTURES. May, 1988. (Mark Goldblatt), Treat Williams, Joe Piscopo.

DEAD MEN DON'T DIE 84
TRANS ATLANTIC. September, 1991. (Malcolm Marmorstein), Elliott Gould, Melissa Anderson, Mabel King.

DEAD MEN DON'T WEAR PLAID 89
UNIVERSAL. May, 1982. (Carl Reiner), Steve Martin, Rachel Ward. B & W.

DEAD OF WINTER 100
MGM/UA. February, 1987. (Arthur Penn), Mary Steenburgen, Roddy McDowall.

DEAD POETS SOCIETY 128
BUENA VISTA. June, 1989. (Peter Weir), Robin Williams, Robert Sean Leonard, Ethan Hawke.

DEAD POOL, THE 91
WARNER BROS. July, 1988. (Buddy Van Horn), Clint Eastwood, Patricia Clarkson.

DEAD RINGER 101
OGDEN AVE. July, 1991. (Allan Nicholls), Meat Loaf, Josh Mostel, MacIntyre Dixon.

DEAD RINGERS 115
20TH CENTURY FOX. September, 1988. Canadian. (David Cronenberg), Jeremy Irons, Genevieve Bujold.

DEAD SPACE 80
CONCORDE. January, 1991. (Fred Gallo), Marc Singer, Laura Tate.

DEAD TIME STORIES 81
BEDFORD ENTERTAINMENT. January, 1987. (Jeffrey Delman), Scott Valentine, Nicole Picard.

DEAD WOMEN IN LINGERIE 89
AFI USA. November, 1991. (Erica Fox), John Romo, Jerry Orbach, Dennis Christopher.

DEAD ZONE, THE 102
PARAMOUNT. October, 1983. (David Cronenberg), Christopher Walken, Brooke Adams.

DEADLINE 100
SKOURAS PICTURES. September, 1987. German. (Nathaniel Gutman), Christopher Walken, Hywel Bennett.

DEADLY BLESSING 102
UNITED ARTISTS. August, 1981. (Wes Craven), Maren Jensen, Susan Buckner.

DEADLY FORCE 95
EMBASSY. July, 1983. (Paul Aaron), Wings Hauser, Joyce Ingalls.

DEADLY FRIEND 99
WARNER BROS. October, 1986. (Wes Craven), Matthew Laborteaux, Kristy Swanson.

DEADLY ILLUSION 87
CINETEL. October, 1987. (William Tannen, Larry Cohen), Billy Dee Williams, Vanity.

Length in Mins.

DEAL OF THE CENTURY 98
WARNER BROS. November, 1983. (William Friedkin), Chevy Chase, Sigourney Weaver.

DEALERS 95
SKOURAS. November, 1989. British. (Colin Bucksey), Paul McGann, Rebecca DeMornay.

DEAR AMERICA: LETTERS FROM VIETNAM 87
BILL COUTURIE. October, 1987. (Bill Couturie). Documentary.

DEATH BECOMES HER 103
UNIVERSAL. July, 1992. (Robert Zemeckis), Meryl Streep, Goldie Hawn, Bruce Willis.

DEATH BEFORE DISHONOR 95
NEW WORLD PICTURES. February, 1987. (Terry Leonard), Fred Dryer, Brian Keith.

DEATH HUNT 96
20TH CENTURY FOX. May, 1981. (Peter R. Hunt), Charles Bronson, Lee Marvin.

DEATH OF A SOLDIER 93
SCOTTI PICTURES. May, 1986. Australian. (Philippe Mora), James Coburn, Bill Hunter.

DEATH OF AN ANGEL 92
20TH CENTURY FOX. March, 1986. (Petru Popescu), Bonnie Bedelia, Nick Mancuso.

DEATH SENTENCE 104
SPHINX FILMS. June, 1986. Polish; Eng. titles. (Witold Orzechowski), Doris Kunstmann.

DEATH VALLEY 87
UNIVERSAL. May, 1982. (Dick Richards), Paul Le Mat, Catherine Hicks.

DEATH WARRANT 89
MGM/UA. September, 1990. (Deran Sarafian), Jean-Claude Van Damme, Robert Guillaume, Cynthia Gibb.

DEATHWATCH 100
QUARTET FILMS. September, 1984. French-German. (Bertrand Travernier), Romy Schneider, Harvey Keitel.

DEATH WISH II 93
FILMWAYS. May, 1982. (Michael Winner), Charles Bronson, Jill Ireland.

DEATH WISH 3 90
CANNON FILMS. November, 1985. (Michael Winner), Charles Bronson, Deborah Raffin.

DEATH WISH 4: THE CRACKDOWN 99
CANNON GROUP. November, 1987. (J. Lee Thompson), Charles Bronson, Kay Lenz.

DEATHROW GAMESHOW 83
CROWN INTL. PICTURES. December, 1987. (Mark Pirro), John McCafferty, Robin Blythe.

DEATHSTALKER 80
NEW WORLD PICTURES. January, 1984. (John Watson), Richard Hill, Barbi Benton.

DEATHTRAP 116
WARNER BROS. March, 1982. (Sidney Lumet), Michael Caine, Christopher Reeve.

DEBAJO DEL MUNDO (UNDER THE EARTH) 100
NEW WORLD PICTURES. October, 1988. Argentine-Czech. In Spanish; Eng. subtitles. (Beda Docampo Feijóo and Juan Bacitista Stagnaro), Sergio Renan, Barbara Mugica.

DECEIVED 102
BUENA VISTA. September, 1991. (Damian Harris), Goldie Hawn, John Heard, Ashley Peldon.

DECEIVERS, THE 112
CINECOM PICTURES. September, 1988. British. (Nicholas Meyer), Pierce Brosnan, Saeed Jaffrey.

DECEMBER 91
I.R.S. December, 1991. (Gabe Torres), Wil Wheaton, Chris Young, Balthazar Getty, Brian Krause.

DECLINE OF THE AMERICAN EMPIRE, THE 95
CINEPLEX ODEON FILMS. November, 1986. Canadian. (Denys Arcand), Dominique Michel, Dorothee Berryman.

DECLINE OF WESTERN CIVILIZATION PART II: THE METAL YEARS, THE 90
NEW LINE CINEMA. June, 1988. (Penelope Spheeris), Joe Perry, Steven Tyler. Documentary.

DEEP BLUES 91
AFI USA. November, 1991. (Robert Mugge), Junior Kimbrough, Jessie Mae Hemphill.

DEEP COVER 110
NEW LINE CINEMA. April, 1992. (Bill Duke), Larry Fishburne, Jeff Goldblum, Victoria Dillard.

DEEP IN THE HEART 99
WARNER BROS. January, 1984. British. (Tony Garnett), Karen Young, Suzie Humphreys.

DEEPSTAR SIX 100
TRI-STAR. January, 1989. (Sean S. Cunningham), Taurean Blacque, Nancy Everhard, Greg Evigan.

	Length in Mins.

DEF BY TEMPTATION 95
TROMA. March, 1990. (James Bond III), James Bond III, Kadeem Hardison.

DEF-CON 4 88
NEW WORLD. March, 1985. (Paul Donovan), Lenore Zann, Maury Chaykin.

DEFENDING YOUR LIFE 110
WARNER BROS. March, 1991. (Albert Brooks), Albert Brooks, Meryl Streep, Rip Torn.

DEFENSE OF THE REALM 96
HEMDALE RELEASING. January, 1987. British. (David Drury), Gabriel Byrne, Greta Scacchi.

DEFENSE PLAY 93
TRANS WORLD ENTERTAINMENT. September, 1988. (Monte Markham), David Oliver, Susan Ursitti.

DEFENSELESS 104
7 ARTS-NEW LINE CINEMA. August, 1991. (Martin Campbell), Barbara Hershey, Sam Shepard, Mary Beth Hurt.

DEFIANCE 103
AMERICAN INTERNATIONAL. March, 1980. (John Flynn), Jan-Michael Vincent, Art Carney.

DELICATESSEN 100
MIRAMAX. April, 1992. French. (Jean-Pierre Jeunet, Marc Caro), Marie-Laure Dougnac, Jean Claude Dreyfus, Dominique Pinon.

DELIRIOUS 96
MGM. August, 1991. (Tom Mankiewicz), John Candy, Mariel Hemingway, Dylan Baker.

DELTA FORCE, THE 126
CANNON FILMS. February, 1986. (Menahem Golan), Chuck Norris, Lee Marvin.

DELTA FORCE 2 105
MGM/UA. August, 1990. (Aaron Norris), Chuck Norris, Billy Drago.

DELUSION 100
I.R.S. MEDIA. June, 1991. (Carl Colpaert), Jim Metzler, Jennifer Rubin, Kyle Secor.

DEMONS IN THE GARDEN 100
SPECTRAFILM. February, 1984. Spanish; Eng. titles. (Manuel Gutierrez Aracon), Angela Molina.

DEMONSTONE 88
FRIES. March, 1990. (Andrew Prowse), Jan-Michael Vincent, R. Lee Ermey.

DEPECHE MODE 101 117
WESTWOOD ONE. April, 1989. (D.A. Pennebaker, Chris Hegedus, David Dawkins), Depeche Mode.

DERANGED 81
PLATINUM PICTURES. October, 1987. (Chuck Vincent), Jane Hamilton, Paul Siederman.

DERNIER COMBAT, LE 90
TRIUMPH. June, 1984. French; Eng. titles. (Luc Besson), Pierre Jolivet.

DESERT BLOOM 104
COLUMBIA. January, 1986. (Eugene Corr), Jon Voight, Jo-Beth Williams, Annabeth Gish.

DESERT HEARTS 93
SAMUEL GOLDWYN CO. April, 1986. (Donna Deitch), Helen Shaver, Patricia Charbonneau.

DESERT WARRIOR 85
CONCORDE PICTURES. September, 1985. (Cirio H. Santiago), Gary Watkins, Laura Banks.

DESIRE & HELL AT SUNSET MOTEL 90
TWO MOON RELEASING. April, 1992. (Allen Castle), Sherilyn Fenn, Whip Hubley, David Hewlett.

DESIRE: SEXUALITY IN GERMANY, 1910–1945 87
MAYAVISION. June, 1990. British. (Stuart Marshall), Documentary.

DESPERATE HOURS 105
MGM. October, 1990. (Michael Cimino), Mickey Rourke, Anthony Hopkins, Mimi Rogers.

DESPERATELY SEEKING SUSAN 104
ORION. March, 1985. (Susan Seidelman), Rosanna Arquette, Madonna, Aidan Quinn.

DESTROYER 94
MOVIESTORE ENTERTAINMENT. April, 1988. (Robert Kirk), Deborah Foreman, Clayton Rohner.

DETECTIVE 98
SPECTRAFILM. August, 1985. French; Eng. titles. (Jean-Luc Godard), Claude Brasseur, Nathalie Baye.

DEVIL AND MAX DEVLIN, THE 96
BUENA VISTA. February, 1981. (Steven Hilliard Stern), Elliott Gould, Bill Cosby.

DEVIL IN THE FLESH 110
ORION CLASSICS. May, 1987. Italian; Eng. titles. (Marco Bellocchio), Maruschka Detmers, Federico Pitzalis.

	Length in Mins.

DIAMOND'S EDGE 83
CASTLE HILL. November, 1990. British. (Stephen Bayly), Colin Dale, Dursley McLinden, Susannah York.

DIARY FOR MY CHILDREN 106
NEW YORKER. November, 1984. Hungarian; Eng. titles. (Marta Meszaros), Zsuzsa Czinkoci.

DIARY OF A HIT MAN 91
VISION INTL. May, 1992. (Roy London), Forest Whitaker, Sherilyn Fenn, Sharon Stone.

DICE RULES 87
7 ARTS. May, 1991. (Jay Dubin), Andrew Dice Clay.

DICK TRACY 103
BUENA VISTA. June, 1990. (Warren Beatty), Warren Beatty, Madonna, Al Pacino, Charlie Korsmo.

DIE HARD (P) 131
20TH CENTURY FOX. July, 1988. (John McTiernan), Bruce Willis, Alan Rickman, Bonnie Bedelia.

DIE HARD 2 (P) 124
20TH CENTURY FOX. July, 1990. (Remy Harlin), Bruce Willis, Bonnie Bedelia.

DIE LAUGHING 108
WARNER BROS. March, 1980. (Jeff Werner), Robby Benson, Charles Durning.

DIGGSTOWN 97
MGM. August, 1992. (Michael Ritchie), James Woods, Louis Gossett, Jr., Bruce Dern.

DIM SUM: A LITTLE BIT OF HEART 88
ORION. August, 1985. (Wayne Wang), Laureen Chew, Kim Chew.

DINER 110
MGM/UA. March, 1982. (Barry Levinson), Steve Guttenberg, Daniel Stern, Kevin Bacon.

DIPLOMATIC IMMUNITY 95
FRIES ENT. April, 1991. (Peter Maris), Bruce Boxleitner, Billy Drago, Tom Breznahan.

DIRT BIKE KID, THE 90
CONCORDE-CINEMA GROUP. November, 1985. (Hoite C. Caston), Peter Billingsley, Stuart Pankin.

DIRTY DANCING 97
VESTRON PICTURES. August, 1987. (Emile Ardolino), Jennifer Grey, Patrick Swayze.

DIRTY ROTTEN SCOUNDRELS 110
ORION. December, 1988. (Frank Oz), Steve Martin, Michael Caine, Glenne Headly.

DIRTY TRICKS 91
AVCO EMBASSY. May, 1981. (Alvin Rakoff), Elliot Gould, Kate Jackson.

DISORDERLIES 96
WARNER BROS. August, 1987. (Michael Schultz), Damon Wimbley, Darren Robinson.

DISORGANIZED CRIME 101
BUENA VISTA. April, 1989. (Jim Kouf), Corbin Bernsen, Fred Gwynne, Lou Diamond Phillips.

DISTANT HARMONY 85
CIRCLE RELEASING LUCHINA LTD. PARTNERSHIP. February, 1988. (DeWitt Sage), Luciano Pavarotti.

DISTANT THUNDER 114
PARAMOUNT. November, 1988. Canadian. (Rick Rosenthal), John Lithgow, Ralph Macchio.

DISTANT VOICES, STILL LIVES 85
AVENUE. July, 1989. British. (Terence Davies), Freda Dowie, Pete Postlewaite.

DISTURBED 96
LIVE ENTERTAINMENT. November, 1990. (Charles Winkler), Malcolm McDowell, Geoffrey Lewis, Priscilla Pointer.

DIVA 123
UA CLASSICS. April, 1982. French; Eng. titles. (Jean-Jacques Beineix), Frederic Andrei, Wilhelmenia Wiggins Fernandez.

DIVINE MADNESS (P) 94
WARNER BROS. September, 1980. (Michael Ritchie), Bette Midler.

DIVINE OBSESSION 85
PANORAMA ENTERTAINMENT. March, 1990. (Yuri Sivo), Brian Benben, Deborah Farentino.

DIVING IN 92
SKOURAS. September, 1990. (Strathford Hamilton), Matt Adler, Burt Young, Matt Lattanzi.

DO OR DIE 97
MALIBU BAY. June, 1991. (Andy Sidaris), Pat Morita, Erik Estrada, Dona Speir.

DO THE RIGHT THING 120
UNIVERSAL. June, 1989. (Spike Lee), Danny Aiello, Ossie Davis, Spike Lee, John Savage.

DO YOU REMEMBER DOLLY BELL? 106
INTL. HOME CINEMA. August, 1986. Czechoslovakian; Eng. titles. (Emir Kusturica), Slavko Stimac.

Length in Mins.

DOC HOLLYWOOD 103
WARNER BROS. August, 1991. (Michael Caton-Jones), Michael J. Fox, Julie Warner, Barnard Hughes.

DOC'S KINGDOM 90
GARANCE, FILMARGEM. September, 1988. French. In English. (Robert Kramer), Paul McIsaac, Vincent Gallo.

DOCTOR, THE 124
BUENA VISTA. July, 1991. (Randa Haines), William Hurt, Elizabeth Perkins, Christine Lahti.

DOCTOR AND THE DEVILS, THE (J-D-C) 93
20TH CENTURY FOX. October, 1985. British. (Freddie Francis), Timothy Dalton, Jonathan Pryce.

DR. CALIGARI 80
STEINER. May, 1990. (Stephen Sayadian), Madeleine Reynal, Fox Harris.

DOCTOR DETROIT 89
UNIVERSAL. May, 1983. (Michael Pressman), Dan Aykroyd, Howard Hesseman.

DOG TAGS 100
CINEVEST ENTERTAINMENT. February, 1990. (Romano Scavolini), Clive Wood, Baird Stafford.

DOGFIGHT 92
WARNER BROS. September, 1991. (Nancy Savoca), River Phoenix, Lili Taylor, Richard Panebianco.

DOGS IN SPACE 108
SKOURAS. October, 1987. Australian. (Richard Lowenstein), Michael Hutchence, Saskia Post.

DOGS OF WAR, THE (P) 101
UNITED ARTISTS. February, 1981. (John Irvin), Christopher Walken, Tom Berenger.

DOIN' TIME ON PLANET EARTH 85
CANNON RELEASING. September, 1988. (Charles Matthau), Nicholas Strouse, Hugh Gillin, Adam West.

DOLLS 77
EMPIRE PICTURES. February, 1987. (Stuart Gordon) Ian Patrick Williams, Carolyn Purdy-Gordon.

DOLLY, LOTTE & MARIA 60
FIRST RUN FEATURES. September, 1988. West German. (Rosa Von Praunheim). Documentary.

DOMINICK AND EUGENE 111
ORION. March, 1988. (Robert M. Young), Tom Hulce, Ray Liotta, Jamie Lee Curtis.

DON JUAN, MY LOVE 96
IFEX. July, 1991. Spanish. (Antonio Mercero), Juan Luis Galiardo, Maria Barranco, Loles Leon.

DONA HERLINDA AND HER SON 90
CINEVISTA. April, 1986. Spanish; Eng. titles. Guadalupe Del Toro, Arturo Meza.

DON'T OPEN TILL CHRISTMAS 86
21ST CENTURY DIST. December, 1984. (Edmund Purdom), Edmund Purdom, Alan Lake.

DON'T TELL HER IT'S ME 101
HEMDALE. September, 1990. (Malcolm Mowbray), Steve Guttenberg, Shelley Long, Jami Gertz.

DON'T TELL MOM THE BABYSITTER'S DEAD 105
WARNER BROS. June, 1991. (Stephen Herek), Christina Applegate, Joanna Cassidy, Keith Coogan.

DOORS, THE (P) 135
TRISTAR. March, 1991. (Oliver Stone), Val Kilmer, Meg Ryan, Frank Whaley, Kyle MacLachlan.

DOUBLE EXPOSURE 97
CROWN INTERNATIONAL. August, 1982. (William Bryon Hillman), Michael Callan, Joanna Pettet.

DOUBLE EXPOSURE 97
UNITED FILM DIST. CO. September, 1987. (Nico Mastorakis), Mark Hennessy, Scott King.

DOUBLE IMPACT 118
COLUMBIA. August, 1991. (Sheldon Lettich), Jean-Claude Van Damme, Geoffrey Lewis, Alan Scarfe.

DOUBLE LIFE OF VERONIQUE, THE 90
MIRAMAX. November, 1991. French-Polish. (Krzysztof Kieslowski), Irene Jacob, Halina Gryglaszewska.

DOWN AND OUT IN BEVERLY HILLS 97
BUENA VISTA. January, 1986. (Paul Mazursky), Nick Nolte, Richard Dreyfuss, Bette Midler.

DOWN BY LAW 107
ISLAND PICTURES. September, 1986. (Jim Jarmusch), Tom Waits, John Lurie. B&W.

DOWN TWISTED 97
CANNON GROUP. February, 1987. (Arthur Pyun), Carey Lowell, Charles Rocket.

DOWNTOWN 96
20TH CENTURY FOX. January, 1990. (Richard Benjamin), Anthony Edwards, Forest Whitaker.

DRAGNET 106
UNIVERSAL. June, 1987. (Tom Mankiewicz), Dan Aykroyd, Tom Hanks, Alexandra Paul.

Length in Mins.

DRAGON CHOW 75
NEW YORKER FILMS. May, 1988. German, Mandarin and Urdu; Eng. subtitles. (Jan Schutte), Bhasker, Ric Young.

DRAGONSLAYER (P) 110
PARAMOUNT. June, 1981. (Matthew Robbins), Peter MacNicol, Caitlin Clarke, Ralph Richardson.

DRAUGHTSMAN'S CONTRACT, THE 103
UA CLASSICS. June, 1983. British. (Peter Greenaway), Anthony Higgins, Janet Suzman.

DREAM A LITTLE DREAM 99
VESTRON. March, 1989. (Marc Rocco), Corey Feldman, Meredith Salenger, Jason Robards.

DREAN DECEIVERS 60
FIRST RUN. August, 1992. (David Van Taylor), Documentary.

DREAM LOVER 104
MGM-UA. February, 1986. (Alan J. Pakula), Kristy McNichol, Ben Masters.

DREAM MACHINE, THE 86
INTL. CREATIVE EXCHANGE. September, 1991. (Lyman Dayton), Corey Haim, Evan Richards, Jeremy Slate.

DREAM TEAM, THE 113
UNIVERSAL. April, 1989. (Howard Zieff), Michael Keaton, Christopher Lloyd, Peter Boyle.

DREAMCHILD 93
UNIVERSAL. October, 1985. British. (Gavin Millar), Coral Browne, Ian Holm.

DREAMSCAPE 98
20TH CENTURY FOX. August, 1984. (Joseph Ruben), Dennis Quaid, Max Von Sydow, Kate Capshaw.

DRESSED TO KILL 105
FILMWAYS. July, 1980. (Brian De Palma), Michael Caine, Angie Dickinson, Nancy Allen.

DRESSER, THE 118
COLUMBIA. December, 1983. British. (Peter Yates), Albert Finney, Tom Courtenay.

DRESSMAKER, THE 92
EURO-AMERICAN FILMS. January, 1989. British. (Jim O'Brien), Joan Plowright, Billie Whitelaw.

DRIFTER, THE 90
CONCORDE PICTURES. February, 1988. (Larry Brand), Kim Delaney, Timothy Bottoms.

DRIFTING/NAGOOA 80
NU-IMAGE FILM. May, 1984. (Amos Guttman), Jonathan Sagalie.

DRIVE 87
MEGAGIANT ENT. July, 1992. (Jefery Levy), David Warner, Steven Antin, Dedee Pfeiffer.

DRIVING ME CRAZY 89
MOTION PICTURE CORP. OF AMER. November, 1991. (Jon Turtletaub), Thomas Gottschalk, Billy Dee Williams, Milton Berle.

DRIVING ME CRAZY 85
FIRST RUN FEATURES. March, 1990. British. (Nick Broomfield), André Heller, Mercedes Ellington.

DRIVING MISS DAISY 99
WARNER BROS. December, 1989. (Bruce Beresford), Morgan Freeman, Jessica Tandy.

DROP DEAD FRED 98
NEW LINE CINEMA. May, 1991. (Ate De Jong), Phoebe Cates, Rik Mayall, Marsha Mason.

DROWNING BY NUMBERS 114
PRESTIGE. April, 1991. British. (Peter Greenaway), Joan Plowright, Juliette Stevenson, Bernard Hill.

DRUGSTORE COWBOY 100
AVENUE. October, 1989. (Gus Van Sant Jr.), Matt Dillon, Kelly Lynch.

DRY WHITE SEASON, A 97
MGM/UA. September, 1989. (Euzhan Palcy), Donald Sutherland, Zakes Mokae, Marlon Brando.

DUCK TALES: THE MOVIE—TREASURE OF THE LOST LAMP 74
BUENA VISTA. August, 1990. (Bob Hathcock), Animated.

DUDES 90
NEW CENTURY/VISTA FILM. August, 1987. (Penelope Spheeris), Jon Cryer, Daniel Roebuck.

DUET FOR ONE 107
CANNON GROUP. December, 1986. British. (Andrei Konchalovsky), Julie Andrews, Alan Bates.

DUNE (T-AO) 140
UNIVERSAL. December, 1984. (David Lynch), Kyle MacLachlan, Francesa Annis, Max von Sydow.

DUNE WARRIORS 90
CONCORDE. January, 1991. (Cirio H. Santiago), David Carradine, Rick Hill, Luke Askew.

**Length
in Mins.**

DUNGEONMASTER, THE 73
EMPIRE. May, 1985. (Rosemary Turko, 6 additional dirs.),
Jeffrey Byron, Richard Moll.

DUST 87
KINO INTL. November, 1986. French-Belgian. (Marion
Hansel), Jane Birkin, Trevor Howard.

DUTCH 107
20TH CENTURY FOX. July, 1991. (Peter Faiman), Ed
O'Neill, Ethan Randall, JoBeth Williams.

DUTCH TREAT 84
CANNON GROUP. January, 1987. (Boaz Davidson), David
Landsberg, Lorin Dreyfuss.

DYING YOUNG 105
20TH CENTURY FOX. June, 1991. (Joel Schumacher), Julia
Roberts, Campbell Scott, Vincent D'Onofrio.

E

E.T. THE EXTRA-TERRESTRIAL 115
UNIVERSAL. June, 1982. (Steven Spielberg), Dee Wallace,
Henry Thomas.

EAR, THE 91
INTL. FILM EXCHANGE. March, 1992. Czech. (Karel Kachyna), Radoslav Brzobahaty, Jirina Bohdalova.

EARTH GIRLS ARE EASY 100
VESTRON. May, 1989. (Julien Temple), Geena Davis, Jeff
Goldblum.

EARTHLING THE 98
FILMWAYS. February, 1981. Australian. (Peter Collinson),
William Holden, Ricky Schroder.

EASY MONEY 95
ORION. August, 1983. (James Signorelli), Rodney Dangerfield, Joe Pesci.

EASY WHEELS 90
FRIES ENTERTAINMENT. September, 1989. (David O'Malley), Paul Le Mat, Eileen Davidson.

EAT A BOWL OF TEA 102
COLUMBIA. July, 1989. (Wayne Wang), Cora Miao, Russell
Wong.

EAT AND RUN 90
NEW WORLD PICTURES. October, 1986. (Christopher
Hart), Ron Silver, Sharon Schlarth.

EAT THE PEACH 98
SKOURAS PICTURES. July, 1987. Irish. (Peter Ormrod),
Stephen Brennan, Eamon Morrissey.

EAT THE RICH 88
NEW LINE CINEMA. October, 1987. British. (Peter Richardson), Lanah Pelly, Nosher Powell.

EATING 110
INT'L RAINBOW. November, 1990. (Henry Jaglom), Nelly
Alard, Mary Crosby, Frances Bergen.

EATING RAOUL 83
20TH CENTURY FOX INTL. CLASSICS/ QUARTET FILMS.
September, 1982. (Paul Bartel), Mary Woronov, Paul Bartel.

EBOLI 120
FRANKLIN MEDIA. March, 1980. Italian; Eng. titles. (Francesco Rossi), Gian Maria Volonte.

ECHO PARK 93
ATLANTIC RELEASING. April, 1986. (Robert Dornhelm),
Susan Dey, Tom Hulce.

ECHOES FROM A SOMBER EMPIRE 91
NEW YORKER. July, 1992. German-French. (Werner Herzog), Documentary.

ECHOES OF PARADISE 92
CASTLE HILL/TRIUMPH. March, 1989. Australian. (Phillip Noyce), Wendy Hughes, John Lone.

EDDIE AND THE CRUISERS 92
EMBASSY. September, 1983. (Martin Davidson), Tom Berenger, Michael Pare, Ellen Barkin.

EDDIE AND THE CRUISERS II: EDDIE LIVES ... 103
SCOTTI BROS. August, 1989. Canadian. (Jean-Claude Lord),
Michael Paré, Marina Orsini.

EDDIE MACON'S RUN 95
UNIVERSAL. March, 1983. (Jeff Kanew), Kirk Douglas,
John Schneider.

EDGAR ALLAN POE'S MASQUE OF THE RED DEATH . 85
CONCORDE. September, 1989. (Larry Brand), Patrick Mac-
nee, Adrian Paul.

EDGE OF SANITY 90
MILLIMETER. April, 1989. British. (Gérard Kikoine), Anthony Perkins, Glynis Barber.

EDITH AND MARCEL 140
MIRAMAX FILMS. June, 1984. French; Eng. titles. (Claude
Lelouch), Evelyn Bouix, Marcel Cerdan, Jr.

EDITH'S DIARY 108
GREENTREE PRODS. January, 1986. German; Eng. titles.
(Hans W. Geissendoerfer), Angela Winkler.

**Length
in Mins.**

EDUCATING RITA 114
COLUMBIA. September, 1983. British. (Lewis Gilbert), Michael Caine, Julie Walters.

EDWARD SCISSORHANDS 100
20TH CENTURY FOX. December, 1990. (Tim Burton),
Johnny Depp, Dianne Wiest, Winona Ryder.

EDWARD II 90
FINE LINE FEATURES. March, 1992. British. (Derek Jarman), Steven Waddington, Kevin Collins, Andrew Tiernan.

EIGHT MEN OUT 119
ORION. September, 1988. (John Sayles), John Cusack, D.B.
Sweeney, Charlie Sheen.

8 MILLION WAYS TO DIE 115
TRI-STAR. April, 1986. (Hal Ashby), Jeff Bridges, Rosanna
Arquette, Andy Garcia.

18 AGAIN! 100
NEW WORLD PICTURES. April, 1988. (Paul Flaherty),
George Burns, Charlie Schlatter.

EIGHTIES, THE 80
PARADISE FILMS. May, 1985. French; Eng. titles. (Chantal
Akerman), François Beukelaers.

84 CHARING CROSS ROAD 97
COLUMBIA. February, 1987. (David Jones), Anne Bancroft,
Anthony Hopkins.

84 CHARLIE MOPIC 95
NEW CENTURY/VISTA. March, 1989. (Patrick Duncan),
Jonathan Emerson, Nicholas Cascone.

EL AMOR BRUJO 100
ORION CLASSICS. December, 1986. Spanish; Eng. titles.
(Carlos Saura), Antonio Gades, Cristina Hoyos.

EL DEPUTADO 111
DAVID WHITTEN PROMOTIONS. November, 1985. Span-
ish; Eng. titles. (Eloy de la Iglesia), Jose Sacristan.

EL NORTE 139
CINECOM INTL./ISLAND ALIVE. January, 1984. Spanish;
Eng. titles. (Gregory Nava), Zaide Silvia Gutierrez, David
Villalpando.

ELECTRIC DREAMS 95
MGM/UA. July, 1984. (Steve Barron), Lenny Von Dohlen,
Virginia Madsen.

ELEMENT OF CRIME, THE 104
REEL MOVIES INTL. May, 1987. Danish; in English. (Lars
von Trier), Michael Elphick, Me Me Lai.

ELENI 117
WARNER BROS. November, 1985. (Peter Yates), Kate
Nelligan, John Malkovich.

ELEPHANT MAN, THE (P) 125
PARAMOUNT. October, 1980. (David Lynch), Anthony Hopkins, John Hurt. B&W.

ELIMINATORS 96
EMPIRE PICTURES. January, 1986. (Peter Manoogian), Andrew Prine, Denise Crosby.

ELLIOT FAUMAN, Ph.D. 86
TAURUS ENTERTAINMENT. March, 1990. (Ric Klass),
Randy Dreyfuss, Jean Kasem.

ELVIRA, MISTRESS OF THE DARK 96
NEW WORLD PICTURES. September, 1988. (James Signorelli), Cassandra Peterson, Edie McClurg.

EMERALD FOREST, THE (P) 113
EMBASSY. July, 1985. (John Boorman), Powers Boothe, Meg
Foster, Charlie Boorman.

EMINENT DOMAIN 107
TRIUMPH. April, 1991. Canadian-Israeli-French. (John Irvin), Donald Sutherland, Anne Archer, Paul Freeman.

EMMANUELLE 4 95
CANNON. January, 1985. French; dubbed. (Francis Gia-
cobetti), Sylvia Kristel, Mia Nygren.

EMMA'S SHADOW 98
ANGELIKA. September, 1989. Danish. (Soeren Kragh-
Jacobsen), Line Kruse, Borje Ahlstedt.

EMPEROR'S NEW CLOTHES, THE 80
CANNON GROUP. July, 1987. (David Irving), Robert Morse,
Jason Carter.

EMPIRE OF THE SUN 152
WARNER BROS. December, 1987. (Steven Spielberg), Christian Bale, John Malkovich, Miranda Richardson.

EMPIRE STATE 104
VIDMARK. April, 1988. British. (Ron Peck), Cathryn Harrison, Jason Hoganson.

EMPIRE STRIKES BACK, THE (P) 124
20TH CENTURY FOX. May, 1980. (Irvin Kershner), Mark
Hamill, Harrison Ford, Carrie Fisher.

ENCHANTED APRIL 101
MIRAMAX. July, 1992. British. (Mike Newell), Josie Lawrence, Miranda Richardson, Joan Plowright.

Length in Mins.

EXTERMINATOR 2 89
CANNON. September, 1984. (Mark Buntzman), Robert Ginty, Mario Van Peebles.

EXTRAMUROS 119
FRAMELINE. June, 1991. Spanish. (Miguel Picazo), Carmen Maura, Mercedes Sampietro, Assumpta Serna.

EXTREME PREJUDICE 104
TRI-STAR. April, 1987. (Walter Hill), Nick Nolte, Powers Boothe.

EXTREMITIES 90
ATLANTIC RELEASING. August, 1986. (Robert M. Young), Farrah Fawcett, James Russo.

EYE FOR AN EYE, AN 106
EMBASSY. August, 1981. (Steve Carver), Chuck Norris, Christopher Lee.

EYE OF THE NEEDLE 111
UNITED ARTISTS. July, 1981. (Richard Marquand), Donald Sutherland, Kate Nelligan.

EYE OF THE TIGER 90
SCOTTI BROS. November, 1986. (Richard Sarafian), Gary Busey, Yaphet Kotto.

EYES OF A STRANGER (P) 85
WARNER BROS. March, 1981. (Ken Wiederhorn), Lauren Tewes, Jennifer Jason Leigh.

EYES OF FIRE 86
AQUARIUS FILMS. April, 1986. (Avery Crounse), Dennis Lipscomb, Guy Boyd.

EYEWITNESS 102
20TH CENTURY FOX. March, 1981. (Peter Yates), William Hurt, Sigourney Weaver.

F

F/X 106
ORION. February, 1986. (Robert Mandel), Bryan Brown, Brian Dennehy.

F/X 2 107
ORION. May, 1991. (Richard Franklin), Bryan Brown, Brian Dennehy, Rachel Ticotin.

FABULOUS BAKER BOYS, THE 114
20TH CENTURY FOX. October, 1989. (Steve Kloves), Jeff Bridges, Michelle Pfeiffer, Beau Bridges.

FACES OF WOMEN 105
NEW YORKER FILMS. February, 1987. French; Eng. titles. (Desire Ecare), Eugenie Cisse Roland, Sidiki Bakaba.

FADE TO BLACK 100
AMERICAN CINEMA. October, 1980. (Vernon Zimmerman), Dennis Christopher, Tim Thomerson.

FALCON AND THE SNOWMAN, THE 131
ORION. January, 1985. (John Schlesinger), Timothy Hutton, Sean Penn.

FALLING FROM GRACE 100
COLUMBIA. February, 1992. (John Mellencamp), John Mellencamp, Mariel Hemingway, Kay Lenz.

FALLING IN LOVE 102
PARAMOUNT. November, 1984. (Ulu Grosbard), Robert De Niro, Meryl Streep.

FALSE IDENTITY 92
RKO PICTURES. June, 1990. (James Keach), Stacy Keach, Genevieve Bujold.

FAME 127
MGM/UA. May, 1980. (Alan Parker), Eddie Barth, Irene Cara, Barry Miller, Anne Meara.

FAMILY, THE (LA FAMIGLIA) 127
VESTRON PICTURES. January, 1988. Italian; Eng. subtitles. (Ettore Scola), Vittorio Gassman, Fanny Ardant.

FAMILY BUSINESS 115
TRI-STAR. December, 1989. (Sidney Lumet), Sean Connery, Dustin Hoffman, Matthew Broderick.

FAMILY BUSINESS (CONSEIL DE FAMILIE) ... 123
EUROPEAN CLASSICS. September, 1987. French; Eng. subtitles. (Constantin Costa-Gavras), Johnny Hallyday, Fanny Ardant.

FAMILY GAME 107
CIRCLE RELEASING. September, 1985. Japanese; Eng. titles. (Yoshimitsu Morita), Yusaku Matsuda, Juzo Itami.

FAMILY VIEWING 86
CINEPHILE. July, 1988. Canadian. (Atom Egoyan), Aidan Tierney, Arsinee Khankian.

FAMINE WITHIN, THE 90
DIRECT CINEMA. July, 1991. (Katherine Gilday), Documentary.

FAN, THE 95
PARAMOUNT. May, 1981. (Edward Bianchi), Lauren Bacall, James Garner, Michael Biehn.

Length in Mins.

FANDANGO 91
WARNER BROS. January, 1985. (Kevin Reynolds), Kevin Costner, Judd Nelson.

FANNY AND ALEXANDER 188
EMBASSY. June, 1983. Swedish; Eng. titles. (Ingmar Bergman), Ewa Froling, Erland Josephson.

FAR AND AWAY 138
UNIVERSAL. May, 1992. (Ron Howard), Tom Cruise, Nicole Kidman, Thomas Gibson.

FAR FROM HOME 86
VESTRON. June, 1989. (Meiert Avis), Matt Frewer, Drew Barrymore.

FAR NORTH 90
ALIVE ENTERPRISES. November, 1988. (Sam Shepard), Jessica Lange, Charles Durning.

FAR OUT MAN 85
NEW LINE CINEMA. May, 1990. (Tommy Chong), Tommy Chong, C. Thomas Howell, Shelby Chong.

FAREWELL (PROSHCHANIE) 140
INTERNATIONAL FILM EXCHANGE (IFEX). March, 1987. Russian; Eng. titles. (Elem Klimov), S. Staniuta, L. Durov.

FAREWELL TO THE KING 117
ORION. March, 1989. (John Millius), Nick Nolte, Nigel Havers.

FAST FOOD 92
FRIES ENTERTAINMENT. April, 1989. (Michael A. Simpson), Clark Brandon, Randal Patrick.

FAST FORWARD 110
COLUMBIA. February, 1985. (Sidney Poitier), John Scott Clough, Don Franklin.

FAST TALKING 93
CINECOM INTL. April, 1986. (Ken Cameron), Rod Zuanic, Toni Allaylis.

FAST TIMES AT RIDGEMONT HIGH 108
UNIVERSAL. August, 1982. (Amy Heckerling), Sean Penn, Jennifer Jason Leigh, Judge Rheinhold.

FAST-WALKING 115
PICKMAN. October, 1982. (James B. Harris), James Woods, Tim McIntire.

FAT MAN AND LITTLE BOY (P) 126
PARAMOUNT. October, 1989. (Roland Joffé), Paul Newman, Dwight Schultz, John Cusack.

FATAL ATTRACTION (aka HEAD ON) 90
GREENTREE PRODS. September, 1985. (Michael Grant), Sally Kellerman, Stephen Lack.

FATAL ATTRACTION 119
PARAMOUNT. September, 1987. (Adrian Lyne), Michael Douglas, Glenn Close.

FATAL BEAUTY 104
MGM/UA. October, 1987. (Tom Holland), Whoopi Goldberg, Sam Elliott.

FATHER 90
NORTHERN ARTS. July, 1992. Australian. (John Power), Max von Sydow, Carol Drinkwater, Julia Blake.

FATHER OF THE BRIDE 105
BUENA VISTA. December, 1991. (Charles Shyer), Steve Martin, Diane Keaton, Kimberly Williams.

FATSO 94
20TH CENTURY FOX. February, 1980. (Anne Bancroft), Dom DeLuise, Anne Bancroft.

FAVOR, THE WATCH AND THE VERY BIG FISH, THE ... 89
TRIMARK. May, 1992. British. (Ben Lewin), Bob Hoskins, Natasha Richardson, Jeff Goldblum.

FAVORITES OF THE MOON 101
SPECTRAFILM. February, 1985. French; Eng. titles. (Otor Ioseliani), Alix De Montaigu, Pascal Aubler.

FEAR 96
CINETEL FILMS. November, 1988. (Robert A. Ferretti), Cliff DeYoung, Kay Lenz.

FEAR, ANXIETY AND DEPRESSION 94
SAMUEL GOLDWYN CO. December, 1989. (Todd Solondz), Todd Solondz, Jill Wisoff.

FEAR CITY 96
CHEVY CHASE CO. February, 1985. (Abel Ferrara), Tom Berenger, Billy Dee Williams.

FEAR NO EVIL 99
AVCO EMBASSY. January, 1981. (Frank Laloggia), Stefan Arngrim, Elizabeth Hoffman.

FEDS 83
WARNER BROS. October, 1988. (Dan Goldberg), Rebecca DeMornay, Mary Gross.

FEEL THE HEAT 87
TRANS WORLD ENTERTAINMENT. June, 1987. (Joel Silberg), David Dukes, Tiana Alexandra.

459

	Length in Mins.

FLAMINGO KID, THE 100
20TH CENTURY FOX. December, 1984. (Garry Marshall), Matt Dillon, Richard Crenna, Hector Elizondo.

FLASH GORDON 113
UNIVERSAL. December, 1980. (Mike Hodges), Sam Jones, Melody Anderson, Max von Sydow.

FLASH OF GREEN, A 131
SPECTRAFILM. June, 1985. (Victor Nunez), Ed Harris, Blair Brown.

FLASHBACK 107
PARAMOUNT. February, 1990. (Franco Amurri), Dennis Hopper, Kiefer Sutherland.

FLASHDANCE 96
PARAMOUNT. April, 1983. (Adrian Lyne), Jennifer Beals, Michael Nouri.

FLASHPOINT 93
TRI-STAR. August, 1984. (William Tannen), Kris Kristofferson, Treat Williams.

FLATLINERS (P) 111
COLUMBIA. August, 1990. (Joel Schumacher), Kiefer Sutherland, Julia Roberts, Kevin Bacon.

FLESH + BLOOD (TV) 126
ORION. August, 1985. (Paul Verhoeven), Rutger Hauer, Jennifer Jason Leigh.

FLESHBURN 90
CROWN INTL. May, 1984. (George Gage), Steve Kanaly, Karen Carlson.

FLETCH 96
UNIVERSAL. May, 1985. (Michael Ritchie), Chevy Chase, Dana Wheeler-Nicholson, Tim Matheson.

FLETCH LIVES 95
UNIVERSAL. March, 1989. (Michael Ritchie), Chevy Chase, Hal Holbrook.

FLEX 87
TRIAX. May, 1990 (Pat Domenico), Harry Grant, Lorin Jean Vail.

FLIGHT OF THE INTRUDER (P) 115
PARAMOUNT. January, 1991. (John Milius), Danny Glover, Willem Dafoe, Brad Johnson.

FLIGHT OF THE NAVIGATOR 90
BUENA VISTA. July, 1986. (Randel Kleiser), Joey Cramer, Veronica Cartwright.

FLOWERS IN THE ATTIC 95
NEW WORLD PICTURES AND FRIES ENTERTAINMENT. November, 1987. (Jeffrey Bloom), Louise Fletcher, Victoria Tennant.

FLOWING 116
EAST-WEST CLASSICS. November, 1985. Japanese; Eng. titles. (Mikio Naruse), Kinuyo Tanaka.

FLY, THE 100
20TH CENTURY FOX. August, 1986. (David Cronenberg), Jeff Goldblum, Geena Davis.

FLY II, THE 105
20TH CENTURY FOX. February, 1989. (Chris Walas), Eric Stoltz, Daphne Zuniga.

FOG, THE (P) 91
AVCO EMBASSY. February, 1980. (John Carpenter), Adrienne Barbeau, Hal Holbrook, Jamie Lee Curtis.

FOLKS! 106
20TH CENTURY FOX. May, 1992. (Ted Kotcheff), Tom Selleck, Don Ameche, Anne Jackson.

FOOD OF THE GODS II 91
CONCORDE. May, 1989. Canadian. (Damian Lee), Paul Coufos, Lisa Schrage.

FOOL FOR LOVE 106
CANNON FILMS. December, 1985. (Robert Altman), Sam Shepard, Kim Basinger, Harry Dean Stanton.

FOOLIN' AROUND 101
COLUMBIA. April, 1980. (Richard T. Heffron), Gary Busey, Annette O'Toole.

FOOLS OF FORTUNE 109
NEW LINE CINEMA. September, 1990. British. (Pat O'Connor), Mary Elizabeth Mastrantonio, Iain Glen, Julie Christie.

FOOTLOOSE 106
PARAMOUNT. February, 1984. (Herbert Ross), Kevin Bacon, Lori Singer, John Lithgow.

FOR ALL MANKIND 87
APOLLO RELEASING. November, 1989. (Al Reinert), Documentary.

FOR KEEPS? 98
TRI-STAR. January, 1988. (John G. Avildsen), Molly Ringwald, Randall Batinkoff.

FOR QUEEN AND COUNTRY 106
ATLANTIC RELEASING. May, 1989. British. (Martin Stellman), Denzel Washington, Dorian Healy.

	Length in Mins.

FOR SASHA 115
MK2. June, 1992. French. (Alexandre Arcady), Sophie Marceau, Richard Berry, Fabien Orcier.

FOR THE BOYS 148
20TH CENTURY FOX. November, 1991. (Mark Rydell), Bette Midler, James Caan, George Segal.

FOR YOUR EYES ONLY (P) 128
UNITED ARTISTS. June, 1981. British. (John Glen), Roger Moore, Carole Bouquet.

FORBIDDEN DANCE, THE 97
COLUMBIA. March, 1990. (Greydon Clark), Laura Herring, Jeff James.

FORCE OF CIRCUMSTANCE 89
UPFRONT FILMS. June, 1990. (Liza Bear), Borbala Major, Jessica Stutchbury.

FORCED MARCH 104
SHAPIRO GLICKENHAUS. November, 1989. (Rick King), Chris Sarandon, Renee Soutendijk.

FORCED VENGEANCE 90
MGM/UA. August, 1982. (James Fargo), Chuck Norris, Mary Louise Weller.

FOREIGN BODY 108
ORION. September, 1986. British. (Ronald Neame), Victor Banerjee, Warren Mitchell.

FOREVER ACTIVISTS: STORIES FROM THE
VETERANS OF THE ABRAHAM LINCOLN BRIGADE ... 60
TARA RELEASING. June, 1991. (Judith Montell), Documentary.

FOREVER, LULU 85
TRI-STAR. April, 1987. (Amos Kollek), Hanna Schygulla, Deborah Harry.

FOREVER MARY 100
CINEVISTA. April, 1991. Italian. (Marco Risi), Michele Placido, Alessandro di Sanzo, Claudio Amendola.

FORGOTTEN TUNE FOR THE FLUTE, A (ZABITAYA
MELODIA DLIA FLEITI) 131
FRIES ENTERTAINMENT. December, 1988. Russian; Eng. subtitles. (Eldar Ryazanov), Leonid Filatov, Tatyana Dogileva.

FORMULA, THE 117
UNITED ARTISTS. December, 1980. (John G. Avildsen), George C. Scott, Marlon Brando.

FORT APACHE, THE BRONX 120
20TH CENTURY FOX. February, 1981. (Daniel Petrie), Paul Newman, Edward Asner, Ken Wahl.

48 HRS. 96
PARAMOUNT. December, 1982. (Walter Hill), Nick Nolte, Eddie Murphy.

FOUR ADVENTURES OF REINETTE & MARABELLE ... 95
NEW YORKER. July, 1989. French; Eng. titles. (Eric Rohmer), Joëlle Miquel, Jessica Forde.

FOUR FRIENDS 115
FILMWAYS. December, 1981. (Arthur Penn), Craig Wasson, Jodi Thelen, Jim Metzler.

FOUR SEASONS, THE 108
UNIVERSAL. May, 1981. (Alan Alda), Alan Alda, Carol Burnett, Len Cariou, Rita Moreno.

FOURTH MAN, THE 95
SPECTRAFILM. June, 1984. Dutch; Eng. titles. (Paul Verhoeven), Renee Soutendjk, Jeroen Krabbe.

FOURTH PROTOCOL, THE 119
LORIMAR PICTURES. August, 1987. British. (John Mackenzie), Michael Caine, Pierce Brosnan.

FOURTH WAR, THE 91
NEW AGE RELEASING. March, 1990. (John Frankenheimer), Roy Scheider, Jurgen Prochnow.

FOX AND THE HOUND, THE 83
BUENA VISTA. July, 1981. Animated.

FOX TRAP 85
SNIZZLEFRITZ DIST. February, 1986. (Fred Williamson), Fred Williamson, Chris Connelly.

FOXES 106
UNITED ARTISTS. March, 1980. (Adrian Lyne), Jodie Foster, Scott Baio, Cherie Currie.

FRANCES 140
UNIVERSAL. December, 1982. (Graeme Clifford), Jessica Lange, Kim Stanley, Sam Shepard.

FRANKENHOOKER 90
SHAPIRO GLICKENHAUS. June, 1990. (Frank Henenlotter), James Lorinz, Patty Mullen.

FRANKENSTEIN GENERAL HOSPITAL 92
NEW STAR ENTERTAINMENT. March, 1988. (Deborah Roberts), Mark Blankfield, Leslie Jordan.

FRANKIE AND JOHNNY 118
PARAMOUNT. October, 1991. (Garry Marshall), Al Pacino, Michelle Pfeiffer, Kate Nelligan.

461

Length in Mins.

FRANTIC 120
WARNER BROS. February, 1988. (Roman Polanski), Harrison Ford, Emmanuelle Seigner, Betty Buckley.

FRATERNITY VACATION 93
NEW WORLD. February, 1985. (James Frawley), Stephen Geoffreys, Sheree J. Wilson, Tim Robbins.

FREDDIE AS F.R.O. 7 90
MIRAMAX. August, 1992. British. (Jon Acevski), Animated.

FREDDY'S DEAD: THE FINAL NIGHTMARE (3-D) 96
NEW LINE CINEMA. September, 1991. (Rachel Talalay), Robert Englund, Lisa Zane, Lezlie Deane.

FREEDOM 100
SATORI. February, 1985. (Joseph Sargent), Jon Blake, Candy Raymond.

FREEJACK 110
WARNER BROS. January, 1992. (Geoff Murphy), Emilio Estevez, Mick Jagger, Rene Russo.

FREEWAY 91
NEW WORLD PICTURES. September, 1988. (Francis Delia), Darlanne Fluegel, James Russo.

FREEZE—DIE—COME TO LIFE 105
IFEX. December, 1990. Soviet. (Vitaly Kanevski), Pavel Nazarov, Dinara Drukarova. B&W.

FRENCH LESSON 90
WARNER BROS. February, 1986. (Brian Gilbert), Jane Snowden, Alexandre Sterling.

FRENCH LIEUTENANT'S WOMAN, THE 123
UNITED ARTISTS. September, 1981. British. (Karel Reisz), Meryl Streep, Jeremy Irons.

FRESH HORSES 105
COLUMBIA. November, 1988. (David Anspaugh), Molly Ringwald, Andrew McCarthy.

FRESHMAN, THE 102
TRI-STAR. July, 1990. (Andrew Bergman), Marlon Brando, Matthew Broderick.

FRIDA 107
NEW YORKER FILMS. June, 1987. Spanish; Eng. titles. (Paul Leduc), Ofelia Medina, Juan Jose Gurrola.

FRIDAY THE 13TH 95
PARAMOUNT. May, 1980. (Sean S. Cunningham), Betsy Palmer, Adrienne King, Kevin Bacon.

FRIDAY THE 13TH, PART 2 87
PARAMOUNT. May, 1981. (Steve Miner), Amy Steel, John Furey.

FRIDAY THE 13TH PART 3—IN 3D 96
PARAMOUNT. August, 1982. (Steve Miner), Dana Kimmell, Paul Kratka.

FRIDAY THE 13TH—THE FINAL CHAPTER (Part 4) 91
PARAMOUNT. April, 1984. (Joseph Zito), Kimberly Beck, Corey Feldman.

FRIDAY THE 13TH—A NEW BEGINNING (Part 5) 92
PARAMOUNT. March, 1985. (Danny Steinmann), John Shepard, Melanie Kinaman.

FRIDAY THE 13TH PART VI: JASON LIVES 87
PARAMOUNT. August, 1986. (Tom McLoughlin), Thom Matthews, Jennifer Cooke.

FRIDAY THE 13TH PART VII—THE NEW BLOOD 90
PARAMOUNT. May, 1988. (John Carl Buechler), Jennifer Banko, John Otrin.

FRIDAY THE 13TH PART VIII—JASON TAKES MANHATTAN 100
PARAMOUNT. July, 1989. (Rob Hedden), Jensen Daggett, Scott Reeves.

FRIED GREEN TOMATOES 133
UNIVERSAL. December, 1991. (Jon Avnet), Kathy Bates, Mary Stuart Masterson, Jessica Tandy, Mary-Louise Parker.

FRIENDS, LOVERS & LUNATICS 88
FRIES ENTERTAINMENT. November, 1989. (Stephen Withrow), Daniel Stern, Sheila McCarthy, Damir Andrei.

FRIENDSHIP'S DEATH 86
CORALIE FILMS. January, 1989. British. (Peter Wollen), Tilda Swinton, Bill Patterson.

FRIGHT NIGHT (P) 105
COLUMBIA. August, 1985. (Tom Holland), Chris Sarandon, William Ragsdale, Stephen Geoffreys.

FRIGHT NIGHT PART 2 101
NEW CENTURY/VISTA. May, 1989. (Tommy Lee Wallace), Roddy McDowall, William Ragsdale.

FRINGE DWELLERS, THE 98
ATLANTIC RELEASING. January, 1987. Australian. (Bruce Beresford), Justin Saunders, Kristina Nehm.

FROM HOLLYWOOD TO DEADWOOD 96
ISLAND. October, 1989. (Rex Pickett), Scott Paulin, Jim Haynie.

FROM RUSSIA WITH ROCK 108
INTL. FILM CIRCUIT. December, 1990. Soviet. (Marjaana Mykkanen), Documentary.

Length in Mins.

FROM THE HIP (J-D-C) 111
DE LAURENTIIS. February, 1987. (Bob Clark), Judd Nelson, Elizabeth Perkins, John Hurt.

FROM THE POLE TO THE EQUATOR (DAL POLO AT L'EQUATORE) 96
MOMA. April, 1988. German-Italian. (Yervant Gianikian, Angela Ricci). Compilation. B&W (hand tinted).

FULL FATHOM FIVE 80
CONCORDE. August, 1990. (Carl Franklin), Michael Moriarty, Diego Bertie.

FULL METAL JACKET 116
WARNER BROS. June, 1987. (Stanley Kubrick), Matthew Modine, Adam Baldwin, Arliss Howard.

FULL MOON IN BLUE WATER 90
TRANSWORLD ENTERTAINMENT. November, 1988. (Peter Masterson), Gene Hackman, Teri Garr.

FULL MOON IN NEW YORK 88
SHIOBU FILM CO. June, 1990. Chinese. (Stanley Kwan), Sylvia Chang, Maggie Cheung.

FUN DOWN THERE 85
FRAMELINE. June, 1990. (Roger Stigliano), Michael Waite, Nickolas B. Nagourney.

FUNERAL, THE (OSOSHIKI) 124
NEW YORKER FILMS. October, 1987. Japanese; Eng. titles. (Juzo Itami), Tsutomu Yamazaki, Nobuko Miyamoto.

FUNLAND 87
DOUBLE HELIX FILMS. October, 1987. (Michael Simpson), William Windom, David L. Lander.

FUNNY 81
ORIGINAL CINEMA. June, 1989. (Bran Ferren). Documentary.

FUNNY ABOUT LOVE 101
PARAMOUNT. September, 1990. (Leonard Nimoy), Gene Wilder, Christine Lahti, Mary Stuart Masterson.

FUNNY FARM 101
WARNER BROS. June, 1988. (George Roy Hill), Chevy Chase, Madolyn Smith.

FURTHER ADVENTURES OF TENNESSEE BUCK, THE ... 90
TRANS WORLD ENTERTAINMENT. April, 1988. (David Keith), David Keith, Kathy Shower.

FURY, THE 118
20TH CENTURY FOX. March, 1978. (Brian De Palma), Kirk Douglas, John Cassavetes, Amy Irving.

G

GABRIELA 102
MGM/UA CLASSICS. May, 1984. Portuguese; Eng. titles. (Bruno Barreto), Marcello Mastroianni.

GABY—A TRUE STORY 110
TRI-STAR. October, 1987. (Luis Mandoki), Norma Aleandro, Rachel Levin, Liv Ullmann.

GALLIPOLI (P) 110
PARAMOUNT. August, 1981. Australian. (Peter Weir), Mel Gibson, Mark Lee.

GAME, THE 116
AQUARIUS RELEASING. April, 1990. (Curtis Brown), Curtis Brown, Richard Lee Ross.

GANDHI 188
COLUMBIA. December, 1982. British. (Richard Attenborough), Ben Kingsley, Candice Bergen.

GANG OF FOUR, THE 150
METROPOLIS FILMS. December, 1989. French-Swiss. (Jacques Rivette), Bulle Ogier, Benoit Regent.

GARBAGE PAIL KIDS MOVIE, THE 100
ATLANTIC RELEASING. August, 1987. (Rod Amateau), Anthony Newley, Mackenzie Astin.

GARBO TALKS 103
MGM/UA. October, 1984. (Sidney Lumet), Anne Bancroft, Ron Silver, Catherine Hicks.

GARDENS OF STONE 111
TRI-STAR. May, 1987. (Francis Coppola), James Caan, Anjelica Huston, James Earl Jones, D. B. Sweeney.

GAS 94
PARAMOUNT. July, 1981. Canadian. (Les Rose), Donald Sutherland, Susan Anspach.

GAS FOOD LODGING 100
I.R.S. July, 1992. (Allision Anders), Brooke Adams, Ione Skye, Fairuza Balk.

GATE II 95
TRIUMPH. February, 1992. (Tibor Takacs), Louis Tripp, Simon Reynolds, Pamela Segall.

GENUINE RISK 87
I.R.S. RELEASING. December, 1990. (Kurt Voss), Terence Stamp, Peter Berg, Michelle Johnson.

Length in Mins.

HALLOWEEN 5: THE REVENGE OF MICHAEL MYERS . 96
GALAXY. October, 1989. (Dominique Othenin-Girard), Donald Pleasence, Danielle Harris.

HAMBONE AND HILLIE 89
NEW WORLD PICTURES. April, 1984. (Roy Watts), Lillian Gish, Timothy Bottoms.

HAMBURGER HILL 110
PARAMOUNT. August, 1987. (John Irvin), Anthony Barrile, Michael Patrick Boatman, Courtney B. Vance.

HAMBURGER . . . THE MOTION PICTURE 126
F-M ENTERTAINMENT. January, 1986. (Mike Marvin), Leigh McCloskey, Dick Butkus.

HAMLET 135
WARNER BROS. December, 1990. British. (Franco Zeffirelli), Mel Gibson, Glenn Close, Alan Bates, Paul Scofield.

HAMMETT 97
ORION/WARNER BROS. June, 1983. (Wim Wenders), Frederic Forrest, Peter Boyle, Marilu Henner.

HAND, THE 108
WARNER BROS. April, 1981. (Oliver Stone), Michael Caine, Andrea Marcovicci.

HAND THAT ROCKS THE CRADLE, THE 110
BUENA VISTA. January, 1992. (Curtis Hanson), Annabella Sciorra, Rebecca DeMornay, Matt McCoy.

HANDFUL OF DUST, A 117
NEW LINE CINEMA. June, 1988. British. (Charles Sturridge), James Wilby, Kristin Scott Thomas.

HANDMAID'S TALE, THE 109
CINECOM. March, 1990. (Volker Schlondorff), Natasha Richardson, Faye Dunaway, Aidan Quinn.

HANGFIRE 89
MOTION PICTURE CORP. OF AMERICA. January, 1991. (Peter Maris), Brad Davis, Jan-Michael Vincent, Kim Delaney.

HANGIN' WITH THE HOMEBOYS 89
NEW LINE CINEMA. May, 1991. (Joseph B. Vasquez), Doug E. Doug, Mario Joyner, John Leguizamo.

HANKY PANKY 105
COLUMBIA. June, 1982. (Sidney Poitier), Gene Wilder, Gilda Radner, Richard Widmark.

HANNA'S WAR 158
CANNON. November, 1988. (Menaham Golan), Maruschka Detmers, Ellen Burstyn.

HANNAH AND HER SISTERS 106
ORION. February, 1986. (Woody Allen), Woody Allen, Michael Caine, Mia Farrow, Dianne Wiest.

HANNAH K. 108
UNIVERSAL. September, 1983. French. (Constantin Costa-Gavras), Jill Clayburgh, Jean Yanne.

HANOI HILTON, THE 123
CANNON GROUP. March, 1987. (Lionel Chetwynd), Michael Moriarty, Jeffrey Jones.

HANUSSEN 140
COLUMBIA. March, 1989. Hungarian-W. German. (Istvan Szabo), Klaus Maria Brandauer, Erland Josephson.

HAPPY BIRTHDAY, GEMINI 107
UNITED ARTISTS. May, 1980. (Richard Benner), Madeline Kahn, Rita Moreno, David Marshall Grant.

HAPPY BIRTHDAY TO ME 108
COLUMBIA. May, 1981. Canadian. (J. Lee Thompson), Melissa Sue Anderson, Glenn Ford.

HAPPY HOUR 86
THE MOVIE STORE. May, 1987. (John De Bello), Richard Gilliland, Jamie Farr.

HAPPY NEW YEAR 85
COLUMBIA. August, 1987. (John G. Avildsen), Peter Falk, Charles Durning.

HAPPY TOGETHER 96
SEYMOUR BORDE & ASSOC. May, 1990. (Mel Damski), Patrick Dempsey, Helen Slater.

HARD CHOICES 90
LORIMAR PICTURES. May, 1986. (Rick King), Margaret Klenck, Gary McCleery.

HARD COUNTRY 104
ASSOCIATED FILM DISTRIBUTION. April, 1981. (David Greene), Jan-Michael Vincent, Kim Basinger.

HARD PROMISES 95
COLUMBIA. January, 1992. (Martin Davidson), Sissy Spacek, William Petersen, Brian Kerwin.

HARD TICKET TO HAWAII 96
MALIBU BAY FILMS. March, 1987. (Andy Sidaris), Ronn Moss, Dona Speir.

HARD TO HOLD 93
UNIVERSAL. April, 1984. (Larry Peerce), Rick Springfield, Janet Eilber.

HARD TO KILL 95
WARNER BROS. February, 1990. (Bruce Malmuth), Steven Seagal, Kelly Le Brock.

HARD TRAVELING 99
NEW WORLD PICTURES. August, 1986. (Dan Bessie), J.E. Freeman, Ellen Geer.

HARD WAY, THE 111
UNIVERSAL. March, 1991. (John Badham), Michael J. Fox, James Woods, Stephen Lang.

HARDBODIES 88
COLUMBIA. May, 1984. (Mark Griffiths), Grant Cramer, Teal Roberts.

HARDBODIES 2 88
CINTEL FILMS. October, 1986. (Mark Griffiths), Brad Zutaut, Sam Temeles.

HARDLY WORKING 91
20TH CENTURY FOX. April, 1981. (Jerry Lewis), Jerry Lewis, Susan Oliver.

HARLEM NIGHTS 115
PARAMOUNT. November, 1989. (Eddie Murphy), Eddie Murphy, Richard Pryor, Redd Foxx.

HARLEY DAVIDSON AND THE MARLBORO MAN 93
MGM. August, 1991. (Simon Wincer), Mickey Rourke, Don Johnson, Daniel Baldwin.

HARRY AND SON 117
ORION. March, 1984. (Paul Newman), Paul Newman, Robby Benson, Judith Ivey.

HARRY AND THE HENDERSONS 110
UNIVERSAL. June, 1987. (William Dear), John Lithgow, Melinda Dillon, Don Ameche.

HARRY TRACY 101
QUARTET FILMS. December, 1983. (William A. Graham), Bruce Dern, Helen Shaver.

HAUNTED HONEYMOON 82
ORION. July, 1986. (Gene Wilder), Gene Wilder, Gilda Radner, Dom DeLuise.

HAUNTED SUMMER 115
CANNON GROUP. December, 1988. (Ivan Passer), Philip Anglim, Laura Dern, Alice Krige, Eric Stoltz.

HAUNTING OF MORELLA, THE 87
CONCORDE. February, 1990. (Jim Wynorksi), David McCallum, Nicole Eggert.

HAVANA 144
UNIVERSAL. December, 1990. (Sydney Pollack), Robert Redford, Lena Olin, Alan Arkin, Raul Julia.

HAWKS 110
SKOURAS. November, 1989. British. (Robert Ellis Miller), Timothy Dalton, Anthony Edwards.

HE KNOWS YOU'RE ALONE 94
UNITED ARTISTS. September, 1980. (Armand Mastroianni), Don Scardino, Caitlin O'Hearney.

HE SAID/SHE SAID (P) 115
PARAMOUNT. February, 1991. (Ken Kwapis, Marisa Silver), Kevin Bacon, Elizabeth Perkins, Nathan Lane.

HE'S MY GIRL 104
SCOTTI BROS. ENTERTAINMENT. September, 1987. (Gabrielle Beaumont), T.K. Carter, David Hallyday.

HEAD OFFICE 90
TRI-STAR. January, 1986. (Ken Finkleman), Eddie Albert, Danny De Vito, Judge Rheinhold.

HEAR MY SONG 104
MIRAMAX. December, 1991. British-Irish. (Peter Chelsom), Ned Beatty, Adrian Dunbar, Shirley Anne Field.

HEARING VOICES 87
PHOENIX INTL. November, 1991. (Sharon Greytak), Erika Nagy, Stephen Gatta, Tim Ahern.

HEART 90
NEW WORLD PICTURES. September, 1987. (James Lemmo), Brad Davis, Francis Fisher.

HEART BEAT 109
WARNER BROS. January, 1980. (John Byrum), Nick Nolte, Sissy Spacek, John Heard.

HEART CONDITION 100
NEW LINE CINEMA. February, 1990. (James D. Parriott), Bob Hoskins, Denzel Washington.

HEART LIKE A WHEEL 113
20TH CENTURY FOX. September, 1983. (Jonathan Kaplan), Bonnie Bedelia, Beau Bridges.

HEART OF DIXIE 95
ORION. August, 1989. (Martin Davidson), Ally Sheedy, Virginia Madsen, Phoebe Cates.

HEART OF MIDNIGHT 96
SAMUEL GOLDWYN CO. March, 1989. (Matthew Chapman), Jennifer Jason Leigh, Peter Coyote.

HEART OF THE STAG 94
NEW WORLD PICTURES. July, 1984. (Michael Firth), Bruno Lawrence, Terence Cooper.

Length in Mins.

HEARTBEEPS 79
UNIVERSAL. December, 1981. (Allan Arkush), Andy Kaufman, Bernadette Peters.

HEARTBREAK HOTEL 93
BUENA VISTA. September, 1988. (Chris Columbus), David Keith, Charlie Schlatter, Tuesday Weld.

HEARTBREAK RIDGE 130
WARNER BROS. December, 1986. (Clint Eastwood), Clint Eastwood, Marsha Mason, Everett McGill.

HEARTBREAKERS 98
ORION. September, 1984. (Bobby Roth), Peter Coyote, Nick Mancuso.

HEARTBURN 108
PARAMOUNT. July, 1986. (Mike Nichols), Meryl Streep, Jack Nicholson.

HEARTS OF DARKNESS: A FILMMAKER'S APOCALYPSE 96
TRITON. November, 1991. (Fax Bahr), Documentary.

HEAT 101
NEW CENTURY/VISTA. March, 1987. (Dick Richards), Burt Reynolds, Karen Young.

HEAT AND DUST 130
UNIVERSAL. September, 1983. British. (James Ivory), Julie Christie, Greta Scacchi.

HEAT AND SUNLIGHT 92
SNOWBALL PRODS. November, 1988. (Rob Nilsson), Rob Nilsson, Consuelo Faust. B&W.

HEAT OF DESIRE 85
TRIUMPH. 1983. French; Eng. titles. (Luc Beraud) Clio Goldsmith, Patrick Dewaere.

HEATHCLIFF: THE MOVIE 73
ATLANTIC RELEASING. January, 1986. (Bruno Bianchi), Animated.

HEATHERS 102
NEW WORLD. March, 1989. (Michael Lehmann), Winona Ryder, Christian Slater.

HEAVEN 80
ISLAND PICTURES. April, 1987. (Diane Keaton). Documentary.

HEAVEN AND EARTH 105
TRITON. February, 1991. Japanese. (Haruki Kadokawa), Takaai Enoki, Masahiko Tsugawa.

HEAVEN BECOMES HELL 99
TAURUS. March, 1989. (Mickey Nivelli), Michael Walker, James Davies.

HEAVEN HELP US 104
TRI-STAR. February, 1985. (Michael Dinner), Donald Sutherland, John Heard, Andrew McCarthy.

HEAVEN IS A PLAYGROUND 111
NEW LINE CINEMA. October, 1991. (Randall Field), D.B. Sweeney, Michael Warren, Richard Jordan.

HEAVENLY BODIES 89
MGM/UA. February, 1985. (Lawrence Dane), Cynthia Dale, Richard Rebiere.

HEAVENLY KID, THE 89
ORION. July, 1985. (Cary Medoway), Lewis Smith, Jason Gedrick.

HEAVEN'S GATE (P) 205
UNITED ARTISTS. November, 1980. (Michael Cimino), Kris Kristofferson, Christopher Walken.

HEAVY METAL 92
COLUMBIA. August, 1981. (Gerald Potterton), Animated.

HEAVY PETTING 80
SKOURAS. September, 1989. (Obie Benz), Documentary.

HEIDI'S SONG 94
PARAMOUNT. November, 1982. (Robert Taylor). Animated.

HELL COMES TO FROGTOWN 96
NEW WORLD PICTURES. January, 1988. (R.J. Kizer/Donald G. Jackson), Roddy Piper, Sandahl Bergman.

HELLHOLE 95
ARKOFF INTL. March, 1985. (Pierre de Moro), Ray Sharkey, Judy Landers.

HELLO ACTORS STUDIO 165
ACTORS STUDIO. November, 1988. (Annie Tresgot). Documentary.

HELLO AGAIN 96
BUENA VISTA. November, 1987. (Frank Perry), Shelley Long, Judith Ivey, Gabriel Byrne.

HELLO MARY LOU: PROM NIGHT II 96
SAMUEL GOLDWYN CO. October, 1987. Canadian. (Bruce Pittman), Michael Ironside, Wendy Lyon.

HELLRAISER 90
NEW WORLD PICTURES. September, 1987. British. (Clive Barker), Andrew Robinson, Clare Higgins.

Length in Mins.

HENRY AND JUNE 136
UNIVERSAL. October, 1990. (Philip Kaufman), Fred Ward, Uma Thurman, Maria de Medeiros, Richard E. Grant.

HENRY IV 95
ORION. June, 1985. Italian; Eng. titles. (Marco Bellochio), Marcello Mastroianni, Claudia Cardinale.

HENRY V 137
SAMUEL GOLDWYN CO. November, 1989. British (Kenneth Branagh), Kenneth Branagh, Derek Jacobi, Paul Scofield.

HENRY: PORTRAIT OF A SERIAL KILLER 90
GREYCAT FILMS. January, 1990. (John McNaughton), Michael Rooker, Tracy Arnold, Tom Towles.

HER ALIBI 94
WARNER BROS. February, 1989. (Bruce Beresford), Tom Selleck, Paulina Porizkova.

HERCULES 99
MGM/UA. August, 1983. Italian. (Lewis Coates, Luigi Cozzi), Lou Ferrigno, Mirella D'Angelo.

HERE COME THE LITTLES 75
ATLANTIC RELEASING. May, 1985. Luxembourg. (Benjamin Deyries), Animated.

HERO AND THE TERROR 96
CANNON FILMS. August, 1988. (William Tannen), Chuck Norris, Brynn Thayer.

HERO AT LARGE 99
UNITED ARTISTS. February, 1980. (Martin Davidson), John Ritter, Anne Archer.

HEROES STAND ALONE 83
CONCORDE. September, 1989. (Mark Griffiths), Chad Everett, Bradford Dillman.

HEY BABU RIBA (BAL NA VODI) 109
ORION CLASSICS. September, 1987. Serbo-Croatian; Eng. subtitles. (Jovan Acin), Gala Videnovic, Milan Strljic.

HIDDEN, THE 96
NEW LINE CINEMA/HERON COMMUNICATIONS. October, 1987. (Jack Sholder), Michael Nouri, Kyle MacLachlan.

HIDDEN AGENDA 108
HEMDALE. November, 1990. British. (Ken Loach), Frances McDormand, Brian Cox, Brad Dourif.

HIDE IN PLAIN SIGHT (P) 93
UNITED ARTISTS. March, 1980. (James Caan), James Caan, Jill Eikenberry.

HIDING OUT 98
DE LAURENTIIS. November, 1987. (Bob Giraldi), Jon Cryer, Keith Coogan, Annabeth Gish.

HIGH FIDELITY: THE ADVENTURES OF THE GUARNERI STRING QUARTET 85
FOUR OAKS FOUNDATION. September, 1989. (Allan Miller), Documentary.

HIGH FREQUENCY 105
MCEG. May, 1989. Italian. (Faliero Rosati), Vincent Spano, Oliver Benny.

HIGH HEELS 112
MIRAMAX. December, 1991. Spanish. (Pedro Almodovar), Victoria Abril, Marisa Paredes, Miguel Bose.

HIGH HOPES 112
SKOURAS. February, 1989. British. (Mike Leigh), Philip Davis, Ruth Sheen.

HIGH POINT 86
NEW WORLD. September, 1984. Canadian. (Peter Carter), Richard Harris, Christopher Plummer.

HIGH ROAD TO CHINA (TV) 105
WARNER BROS. March, 1983. (Brian G. Hutton), Tom Selleck, Bess Armstrong.

HIGH SEASON 104
HEMDALE. March, 1988. British. (Clare Peploe), Jacqueline Bisset, James Fox.

HIGH SPIRITS 97
TRI-STAR. November, 1988. (Neil Jordan), Daryl Hannah, Peter O'Toole, Steve Guttenberg.

HIGH TIDE 104
TRI-STAR. December, 1987. Australian. (Gillian Armstrong), Judy Davis, Jan Adele.

HIGHER EDUCATION 92
PALISADES ENTERTAINMENT. January, 1988. Canadian. (John Sheppard), Kevin Hicks, Isabelle Mejias.

HIGHLANDER 111
20TH CENTURY FOX. March, 1986. (Russell Mulcahy), Christopher Lambert, Roxanne Hart, Sean Connery.

HIGHLANDER 2: THE QUICKENING (CS) 91
INTERSTAR. November, 1991. (Russell Mulcahy), Christopher Lambert, Sean Connery, Virginia Madsen.

HIGHWAY 61 102
SKOURAS. April, 1992. British-Canadian. (Bruce McDonald), Valerie Buhagiar, Don McKellar, Earl Pastko.

	Length in Mins.

	Length in Mins.

JUICE 95
PARAMOUNT. January, 1992. (Ernest Dickerson), Omar Epps, Tupac Shakur, Jermaine Hopkins.

JULIA AND JULIA 97
CINECOM. February, 1988. Italian. (Peter Del Monte), Kathleen Turner, Sting.

JULIA HAS TWO LOVERS 91
SOUTH GATE ENT. March, 1991. (Bashar Shbib), Daphna Kastner, David Duchovny, David Charles.

JUMPIN' JACK FLASH 100
20TH CENTURY FOX. October, 1986. (Penny Marshall), Whoopi Goldberg, Stephen Collins.

JUMPIN' NIGHT IN THE GARDEN OF EDEN, A 80
FIRST RUN FEATURES. March, 1988. Israeli. (Michael Goldman), Documentary.

JUNGLE FEVER 132
UNIVERSAL. June, 1991. (Spike Lee), Wesley Snipes, Annabella Sciorra, Anthony Quinn, Ossie Davis.

JUNGLE WARRIORS 93
AQUARIUS FILMS. November, 1984. (Ernst R. von Theumer), Nina Van Pallandt.

JUST A GIGOLO 105
UA CLASSICS. May, 1981. W. German. (David Hemmings), David Bowie, Kim Novak, Marlene Dietrich.

JUST BETWEEN FRIENDS 120
ORION. March, 1986. (Allan Burns), Mary Tyler Moore, Ted Danson, Christine Lahti.

JUST LIKE IN THE MOVIES 90
CABRIOLET. September, 1990. (Bram Towbin, Mark Halliday), Jay O. Saunders, Alan Ruck.

JUST ONE OF THE GUYS 100
COLUMBIA. April, 1985. (Lisa Gottlieb), Joyce Hyser, Clayton Rohner.

JUST TELL ME WHAT YOU WANT 112
WARNER BROS. February, 1980. (Sidney Lumet), Ali McGraw, Alan King.

JUST THE WAY YOU ARE 94
MGM/UA. November, 1984. (Edouard Molinaro), Kristy McNichol, Michael Ontkean.

K

K2 111
PARAMOUNT. May, 1992. British. (Franc Roddam), Michael Biehn, Matt Craven, Raymond J. Barry.

K-9 102
UNIVERSAL. April, 1989. (Rod Daniel), James Belushi, Mel Harris.

KGB: THE SECRET WAR (aka LETHAL) 89
CINEMA GROUP. November, 1985. (Dwight Little), Michael Billington, Denise DuBarry.

KAFKA 98
MIRAMAX. December, 1991. (Steven Soderberg), Jeremy Iroins, Theresa Russel, Joel Grey, Ian Holm. B&W/Color.

KAGEMUSHA (WS) 161
20TH CENTURY FOX. October, 1980. Japanese; Eng. titles. (Akira Kurosawa), Tatsuya Nakadai, Tsutomu Yamazaki.

KAMILLA 100
NEW LINE CINEMA. December, 1983. Norwegian; Eng. titles. (Vibeke Lokkeberg), Nina Knapkog.

KAMILLA AND THE THIEF 94
PENELOPE FILM. December, 1988. Norwegian-British. In English. (Grete Salomonsen), Veronica Flaat, Dennis Storhoi.

KANDYLAND 93
NEW WORLD PICTURES. September, 1987. (Robert Schnitzer), Kim Evenson, Charles Laulette.

KANGAROO 105
CINEPLEX ODEON FILMS. March, 1987. Australian. (Tim Burstall), Colin Friels, Judy Davis.

KANSAS (P) 100
TRANS WORLD ENTERTAINMENT. September, 1988. (David Stevens), Matt Dillon, Andrew McCarthy.

KAOS 118
MGM-UA CLASSICS. February, 1986. Italian; Eng. titles. (Paolo & Vittorio Taviani), Margarita Lozano.

KARATE KID, THE 126
COLUMBIA. June, 1984. (John G. Avildsen), Ralph Macchio, Noriyuki (Pat) Morita.

KARATE KID PART II, THE 113
COLUMBIA. June, 1986. (John G. Avildsen), Ralph Macchio, Noriyuki (Pat) Morita.

KARATE KID PART III, THE 111
COLUMBIA. June, 1989. (John G. Avildsen), Ralph Macchio, Noriyuki (Pat) Morita.

KARL MAY 187
GOETHE HOUSE. June, 1986. German; Eng. titles. (Hans-Jurgen Syberberg), Helmut Kaurner.

	Length in Mins.

KARMA 103
LAUSANNE. July, 1987. Vietnamese. (Ho Quang Minh). Tran Quang, Phuong Dung.

KEATON'S COP 95
CANNON. March, 1990. (Bob Burge), Lee Majors, Abe Vigoda.

KEEP, THE (P) 95
PARAMOUNT. December, 1983. (Michael Mann), Scott Glenn, Ian McKellen.

KEEPING TRACK 102
SHAPIRO ENTERTAINMENT. January, 1987. Canadian. (Robin Spry), Michael Sarrazin, Margot Kidder.

KENNY (THE KID BROTHER) 95
ASKA. November, 1988. Canadian-Japanese. In Eng. (Claude Cagnon), Kenny Easterday, Caitlin Clarke.

KEY EXCHANGE 90
20TH CENTURY FOX. August, 1985. (Barnet Kellman), Ben Masters, Brooke Adams.

KICKBOXER 105
CANNON. September, 1989. (Mark DiSalle, David Worth), Jean-Claude Van Damme, Denis Alexio.

KICKBOXER 2 90
TRIMARK. June, 1991. (Albert Pyun), Sasha Mitchell, Peter Boyle.

KILL ME AGAIN 94
MGM/UA. October, 1989. (John Dahl), Val Kilmer, Joanne Whalley-Kilmer.

KILLER KLOWNS FROM OUTER SPACE 88
TRANS WORLD ENTERTAINMENT. August, 1988. (Stephen Chiodo), Grant Cramer, Suzanne Snyder.

KILLER PARTY 91
MGM-UA. May, 1986. (William Fruet), Martin Hewitt, Ralph Seymour.

KILLING AFFAIR, A 100
HEMDALE. July, 1988. (David Saperstein), Peter Weller, Kathy Baker.

KILLING FIELDS, THE 141
WARNER BROS. November, 1984. British. (Roland Joffe), Sam Waterston, Dr. Haing S. Ngor.

KILLING HEAT 104
SATORI. October, 1984. (Michael Raeburn), Karen Black, John Thaw.

KILLING OF ANGEL STREET, THE 98
SATORI. March, 1983. Australian. (Donald Crombie) Liz Alexander, John Hargreaves.

KILLING TIME, THE 95
NEW WORLD PICTURES. October, 1987. (Rick King), Beau Bridges, Kiefer Sutherland.

KILL-OF, THE 110
CABRIOLET. October, 1990. (Maggie Greenwald), Loretta Gross, Jackson Sims.

KILLPOINT 89
CROWN INTL. March, 1984. (Frank Harris), Leo Fong, Richard Roundtree.

KINDERGARTEN, THE 143
IFEX. February, 1986. German; Eng. titles. (Yevgeny Yevtushenko), Klaus Maria Brandauer.

KINDERGARTEN COP 110
UNIVERSAL. December, 1990. (Ivan Reitman), Arnold Schwarzenegger, Penelope Ann Miller, Pamela Reed.

KINDRED, THE 91
F/M ENTERTAINMENT. January, 1987. (Jeffrey Obrow/Stephen Carpenter), David Allen Brooks, Rod Steiger.

KING DAVID 114
PARAMOUNT. March, 1985. (Bruce Beresford), Richard Gere, Edward Woodward.

KING JAMES VERSION 91
FIRST RUN FEATURES. September, 1991. (Robert Gardner), Christina Braggs, Joan Pryor, Ellwoodson Williams.

KING KONG LIVES (J-D-C) 105
DE LAURENTIIS. December, 1986. (John Guillermin), Brian Kerwin, Linda Hamilton.

KING LEAR 90
CANNON GROUP. January, 1988. (Jean-Luc Godard), Burgess Meredith, Peter Sellars.

KING OF COMEDY, THE 101
20TH CENTURY FOX. February, 1983. (Martin Scorsese), Robert De Niro, Jerry Lewis.

KING OF NEW YORK 103
NEW LINE CINEMA. September, 1990. Italian-U.S. (Abel Ferrara), Christopher Walken, Larry Fishburne, David Caruso.

KING OF THE MOUNTAIN 90
UNIVERSAL. April, 1981. (Noel Nosseck), Harry Hamlin, Joseph Bottoms.

	Length in Mins.

KING RALPH 99
UNIVERSAL. February, 1991. (David S. Ward), John Goodman, Peter O'Toole, John Hurt.

KING SOLOMON'S MINES 100
CANNON FILMS. November, 1985. (J. Lee Thompson), Richard Chamberlain, Sharon Stone.

KINJITE (FORBIDDEN SUBJECTS) 97
CANNON ENTERTAINMENT. February, 1989. (J. Lee Thompson), Charles Bronson, Perry Lopez.

KIPPERBANG 85
MGM/UA. April, 1984. British. (Michael Apted), John Albasiny, Abigail Cuttenden.

KISS, THE 101
TRI-STAR. October, 1988. (Pen Densham), Joanna Pacula, Meredith Salenger.

KISS BEFORE DYING, A 95
UNIVERSAL. April, 1991. (James Dearden), Matt Dillon, Sean Young, Max von Sydow.

KISS DADDY GOODNIGHT 80
UPFRONT FILMS. May, 1988. (Peter Ily Huemer), Uma Thurman, Paul Dillon.

KISS ME A KILLER 92
CONCORDE. April, 1991. (Marcus De Leon), Julie Carmen, Robert Beltran.

KISS ME GOODBYE 101
20TH CENTURY FOX. December, 1982. (Robert Mulligan), Sally Field, James Caan, Jeff Bridges.

KISS OF THE SPIDER WOMAN 119
ISLAND ALIVE. July, 1985. (Hector Babenco), William Hurt, Raul Julia.

KITCHEN TOTO, THE 96
CANNON GROUP. July, 1988. British. (Harry Hook), Edwin Mahinda, Bob Peck.

KNIGHTS AND EMERALDS 94
WARNER BROS. March, 1987. British. (Ian Emes), Christopher Wild, Beverly Hills.

KNIGHTS OF THE CITY 88
NEW WORLD PICTURES. February, 1986. (Dominic Orlando), Leon Isaac Kennedy, John Mengati.

KNIGHTRIDERS 145
UNITED FILM DIST. April, 1981. (George A. Romero), Ed Harris, Gary Lahti.

KORCZAK 120
NEW YORKER. April, 1991. Polish. (Andrzej Wajda), Wojtek Pszoniak, Ewa Dalkowska, Piotr Kozlowski.

KOYAANISQATSI 87
INSTITUTE FOR REGIONAL EDUCATION. 1983. (Godfrey Reggio). Time lapse non-narrative photography.

KRAYS, THE 119
MIRAMAX. November, 1990. British. (Peter Medak), Gary Kemp, Martin Kemp, Billie Whitelaw.

KRULL 117
COLUMBIA. July, 1983. (Peter Yates), Ken Marshall, Lynette Anthony.

KRUSH GROOVE 97
WARNER BROS. October, 1985. (Michael Schultz), Blair Underwood, Joseph Simmons.

KUFFS 102
UNIVERSAL. January, 1992. (Bruce A. Evans), Christian Slater, Tony Goldwyn, Milla Jovovich.

KUNG FU MASTER 80
EXPANDED ENTERTAINMENT. June, 1989. French. (Agnes Varda), Jane Birkin, Mathieu Demy.

L

L.A. STORY 95
TRI-STAR. February, 1991. (Mick Jackson), Steve Martin, Victoria Tennant, Richard E. Grant.

L'ADDITION 93
NEW WORLD PICTURES. September, 1985. French; Eng. titles. (Denis Amar), Richard Berry.

L'AMOUR PAR TERRE 126
SPECTRAFILM. September, 1986. French; Eng. titles. (Jacques Rivette), Geraldine Chaplin, Jane Birkin.

L'ARGENT 90
CINECOM. March, 1984. French; Eng. titles. (Robert Bresson), Christian Patey, Sylvie van den Elsen.

L'ETAT SAUVAGE 111
INTERAMA. January, 1984. French (Francis Girod), Marie-Christine Barrault, Claude Brasseur.

LA BALANCE 102
SPECTRAFILM. November, 1983. French; Eng. titles. (Bob Swaim), Nathalie Baye, Philippe Leotard.

	Length in Mins.

LA BAMBA 108
COLUMBIA. July, 1987. (Luis Valdez), Lou Diamond Phillips, Esai Morales.

LA BELLE NOISEUSE 240
MK2. October, 1991. French. (Jacques Ribette), Michel Piccoli, Jane Birkin, Emmanuelle Beart.

LA BOCA DEL LOBO 122
CINEVISTA INC. August, 1989. Spanish; Eng. titles. (Francisco J. Lombardi), Miguel Angel Bueno Wunder, Antonio Vega Espejo.

LA BOHÈME 106
NEW YORKER FILMS. June, 1989. Italian; Eng. titles. (Luigi Comencini), Barbara Hendricks, Luca Canonici (voice of Jose Carreras).

LA CAGE AUX FOLLES II 100
UNITED ARTISTS, February, 1981. French; Eng. titles. (Edouard Molinaro), Ugo Tognazzi, Michel Serrault

LA CAGE AUX FOLLES 3: THE WEDDING 87
TRI-STAR. January, 1986. French; Eng. titles. (Georges Lautner), Michel Serrault, Ugo Tognazzi.

LA CHEVRE 91
EUROPEAN CLASSICS. July, 1985. French; Eng. titles. (Francis Veber), Pierre Richard, Gerard Depardieu.

LA COLLECTIONEUSE 88
PATHE. April, 1981. French; Eng. titles. (Eric Rohmer), Patrick Bauchau, Haydee Politoff.

LA DISCRÈTE 95
MK2. August, 1992. French. (Christian Vincent), Fabrice Muchini, Judith Henry, Maurice Garrel.

LA GRAN FIESTA 105
ZAGA FILMS. July, 1987. Spanish; Eng. titles. (Marcos Zurinaga), Daniel Lugo, Miguelangel Suarez.

LA LECTRICE 98
ORION CLASSICS. April, 1989. French; Eng. titles. (Michel Deville), Miou-Miou, Christian Ruche.

LA NUIT DE VARENNES 133
TRIUMPH. February, 1983. French; Eng. titles. (Ettore Scola), Marcello Mastroianni, Jean-Louis Barrault.

LA VIE EST BELLE (LIFE IS ROSY) 85
LAMY FILMS. November, 1987. Belgian-Zaire-French. (Benoit Lamy, Ngangura Mweze), Papa Wemba, Krubwa Bibi.

LABYRINTH (J-D-C) 101
TRI-STAR. June, 1986. (Jim Henson), David Bowie, Jennifer Connelly.

LABYRINTH OF PASSION 100
CINEVISTA. January, 1990. Spanish. (Pedro Almodóvar), Cecilia Roth, Imanol Arias.

LADIES AND GENTLEMEN: THE FABULOUS STAINS ... 87
FILMS, INC. March, 1985. (Lou Adler), Diane Ladd, Ray Winstone.

LADIES CLUB, THE 90
NEW LINE CINEMA. April, 1986. (A.K. Allen), Karen Austin, Diana Scarwid.

LADIES ON THE ROCKS 100
NEW YORKER. February, 1985. Danish; Eng. titles. (Christian Braad Thomsen), Anne Marie Helger.

LADY BEWARE 108
SCOTTI BROS. September, 1987. (Karen Arthur), Diane Lane, Michael Woods.

LADY IN WHITE 112
NEW CENTURY/VISTA. April, 1988. (Frank LaLoggia), Lukas Haas, Len Cariou.

LADY JANE 142
PARAMOUNT. February, 1986. British. (Trevor Nunn), Helena Bonham Carter, Cary Elwes.

LADY TERMINATOR 82
STUDIO ENTERTAINMENT. June, 1989. (Jalil Jackson), Barbara Anne Constable, Christopher J. Hart.

LADYBUGS 89
PARAMOUNT. March, 1992. (Sidney J. Furie), Rodney Dangerfield, Jackée, Jonathan Brandis.

LADYHAWKE (WS) 124
WARNER BROS. April, 1985. (Richard Donner), Matthew Broderick, Rutger Hauer, Michelle Pfeiffer.

LAIR OF THE WHITE WORM, THE 93
VESTRON PICTURES. October, 1988. British. (Ken Russell), Amanda Donohoe, Hugh Grant, Catherine Oxenberg.

LAMBADA 98
WARNER BROS. March, 1990. (Joel Silberg), J. Eddie Peck, Melora Hardin.

LAND BEFORE TIME, THE 66
UNIVERSAL. November, 1988. (Don Bluth). Animated.

LAND OF THE SMALL, THE 94
NEW WORLD PICTURES. September, 1987. (Vojtech Jasny), Karen Elkin, Michael Blouin.

Length in Mins.

LAND OF PROMISE 165
TINC PRODS. February, 1988. Polish; Eng. subtitles. (Andrzej Wajda), Daniel Olbrychski, Wojciech Pszoniak.

LANDLORD BLUES 96
L.L. PICTURES. December, 1988. (Jacob Burckhardt), Mark Boone Jr.

LANDSCAPE IN THE MIST 126
NEW YORKER. September, 1990. Greek. (Theo Angelopoulos), Michalis Zeke, Tania Palaiologou.

L'ANGE 70
FIRST RUN FEATURES. March, 1991. French. (Patrick Bokanowski), Maurice Baquet, Jean-Marie Bon.

L'ANNEE DES MEDUSES 110
EUROPEAN CLASSICS. April, 1987. French; Eng. titles. (Christopher Frank), Valerie Kaprisky, Bernard Giraudeau.

LA FEMME NIKITA 117
GOLDWYN. March, 1991. French. (Luc Besson), Anne Parillaud, Jean-Hughes Anglade, Jeanne Moreau.

LAPUTA: CASTLE IN THE SKY 124
STREAMLINE PICTURES. March, 1989. Japanese. Dubbed in English. (Hayao Miyazaki). Animated.

LARKS ON A STRING 96
IFEX. February, 1991. Czechoslovakian, 1969. (Jiri Menzel), Vaclav Neckar, Rudolf Hrusinsky.

LASER MAN, THE 93
ORIGINAL CINEMA. March, 1990. (Peter Wang), Marc Hayashi, Tony Leung.

LASSITER (TV) 100
WARNER BROS. February, 1984. (Roger Young), Tom Selleck, Jane Seymour.

LAST BOY SCOUT, THE (P) 105
WARNER BROS. December, 1991. (Tony Scott), Bruce Willis, Damon Wayans, Chelsea Field.

LAST DRAGON, THE 109
TRI-STAR. March, 1985. (Michael Schultz), Taimak, Vanity.

LAST EMPEROR, THE (TV) 160
COLUMBIA. November, 1987. British-Italian. (Bernardo Bertolucci), John Lone, Joan Chen, Peter O'Toole.

LAST EMPEROR, THE 100
SOUTHERN FILMS. October, 1988. Mandarin; Eng. subtitles. (Li Han Hsiang), Tony Leung, Pan Hung.

LAST EXIT TO BROOKLYN 103
CINECOM. May, 1990. W. German-U.S. (Uli Edel), Stephen Lang, Jennifer Jason Leigh.

LAST FLIGHT OF NOAH'S ARK 97
BUENA VISTA. July, 1980. (Charles Jarrott), Elliott Gould, Ricky Schroder.

LAST MARRIED COUPLE IN AMERICA, THE 100
UNIVERSAL. February, 1980. (Gilbert Cates), George Segal, Natalie Wood.

LAST METRO, THE 133
UNITED ARTISTS. February, 1981. French; Eng. titles. (François Truffaut), Catherine Deneuve, Gerard Depardieu.

LAST MINUTE, THE 105
IFEX. February, 1988. Italian; Eng. subtitles. (Pupi Avati), Ugo Tognazzi, Lino Capolicchio.

LAST NIGHT AT THE ALAMO 80
CINECOM INTL. March, 1984. (Eagle Pennell), Sonny Davis, Lou Perry. B&W.

LAST OF THE FINEST 106
ORION. March, 1990. (John Mackenzie), Brian Dennehy, Joe Pantoliano.

LAST OF PHILIP BANTER, THE 103
CINEVISTA/PROMOVISION INTL. January, 1988. Spanish-Swiss; in English. (Herve Hachuel), Scott Paulin, Irene Miracle.

LAST RESORT 86
CONCORDE. September, 1986. (Zane Buzby), Charles Grodin, Robin Pearson Rose.

LAST RITES 103
MGM/UA. November, 1988. (Donald P. Bellisario), Tom Berenger, Daphne Zuniga.

LAST STARFIGHTER, THE (P) 100
UNIVERSAL. July, 1984. (Nick Castle), Lance Guest, Robert Preston, Dan O'Herlihy.

LAST TEMPTATION OF CHRIST, THE 164
UNIVERSAL. August, 1988. (Martin Scorsese), Willem Dafoe, Harvey Keitel, Barbara Hershey.

LAST UNICORN, THE 84
JENSEN-FARLEY. November, 1982. (Arthur Rankin Jr., Jules Bass). Animated.

LATE CHRYSANTHEMUMS 101
EAST-WEST CLASSICS. September, 1985. Japanese; Eng. titles. (Mikio Naruse), Haruko Sugimura.

LATE FOR DINNER 92
COLUMBIA. September, 1991. (W.D. Richter), Brian Wimmer, Peter Berg, Marcia Gay Harden.

Length in Mins.

LATE SUMMER BLUES 101
KINO INTERNATIONAL CORP. August, 1988. Hebrew; Eng. subtitles. (Renen Schorr), Dor Zweigenbom, Yoav Tsafir.

LATINO 105
CINECOM INTL. February, 1986. (Haskell Wexler), Annette Cardona, Robert Beltran.

LAW OF DESIRE 100
CINEVISTA. March, 1987. Spanish; Eng. titles. (Pedro Almodovar), Eusebio Poncela, Carmen Maura.

LAWNMOWER MAN, THE 108
NEW LINE CINEMA. March, 1992. (Brett Leonard), Jeff Fahey, Pierce Brosnan, Jenny Wright.

LAWS OF GRAVITY 100
RKO. August, 1992. (Nick Gomez), Adam Trese, Peter Greene, Edie Falco.

LE BAL 121
ALMI CLASSICS. March, 1984. French; Eng. titles. (Ettore Scola), Christopher Allwright, Marc Berman.

LE BEAU MARIAGE 97
UA CLASSICS. August, 1982. French; Eng. titles. (Eric Rohmer), Beatrice Romand, Andre Bussollier.

LE CAVIAR ROUGE 92
GALAXY INTERNATIONAL. March, 1988. French; Eng. subtitles. (Robert Hossein), Robert Hossein, Candice Patou.

LE SCHPOUNTZ 135
INTERAMA. April, 1989 release of 1938 film. French; Eng. titles. (Marcel Pagnol), Fernandel, Orane Demazis.

LEADER OF THE BAND 95
NEW CENTURY/VISTA. August, 1987. (Nessa Hyams), Steve Landesberg.

LEAGUE OF THEIR OWN, A (P) 128
COLUMBIA. July, 1992. (Penny Marshall), Tom Hanks, Geena Davis, Lori Petty, Madonna.

LEAN ON ME 104
WARNER BROS. March, 1989. (John G. Avildsen), Morgan Freeman, Robert Guillaume.

LEATHERFACE: TEXAS CHAINSAW MASSACRE III 81
NEW LINE CINEMA. January, 1990. (Jeff Burr), Kate Hodge, Viggo Mortensen.

LEAVING NORMAL 110
UNIVERSAL. April, 1992. (Edward Zwick), Christine Lahti, Meg Tilly, Patrika Darbo.

LEFT-HANDED WOMAN, THE 119
NEW YORKER. March, 1980. German; Eng. titles. (Peter Handke), Edith Clever, Bruno Ganz.

LEGAL EAGLES (P) 114
UNIVERSAL. June, 1986. (Ivan Reitman), Robert Redford, Debra Winger, Daryl Hannah.

LEGEND (P) 89
UNIVERSAL. April, 1986. (Ridley Scott), Tom Cruise, Mia Sara, Tim Curry.

LEGEND OF BILLIE JEAN, THE 96
TRI-STAR. July, 1985. (Matthew Robbins), Helen Slater, Keith Gordon, Christian Slater.

LEGEND OF THE LONE RANGER, THE 98
UNIVERSAL. May, 1981. (William A. Fraker), Klinton Spilsbury, Michael Horse.

LEGEND OF SURAM FORTRESS 90
IFEX. February, 1987. Georgian; Eng. titles. (Sergei Paradjanov).

LEMON SISTERS, THE 93
MIRAMAX. August, 1990. (Joyce Chopra), Diane Keaton, Carol Kane, Kathryn Grody.

LENINGRAD COWBOYS GO AMERICA 80
ORION CLASSICS. November, 1990. Finnish. (Aki Kaurismaki), Matti Pellonpaa, Heikki Keskinen.

LEONARD PART 6 85
COLUMBIA. December, 1987. (Paul Weiland), Bill Cosby, Tom Courtenay.

LEPRECHAUN 92
TRIMARK. May, 1992. (Mark Jones), Warwick Davis, Jennifer Aniston, Ken Olandt.

LES PLOUFFES 180
INTL. CINEMA CORP. November, 1985. French; Eng. titles. (Gilles Carles), Emile Genest.

LESS THAN ZERO 98
20TH CENTURY FOX. November, 1987. (Marek Kanievska), Andrew McCarthy, Jami Gertz, Robert Downey, Jr.

LET HIM HAVE IT 114
NEW LINE CINEMA. December, 1991. British. (Peter Medak), Chris Eccleston, Paul Reynolds, Tom Courtenay.

LET IT RIDE 86
PARAMOUNT. August, 1989. (Joe Pytka), Richard Dreyfuss, David Johansen, Teri Garr.

L'ETAT SAUVAGE 111
INTERAMA. January, 1990. French. (Francis Girod), Marie-Christine Barrault, Claude Brasseur.

	Length in Mins.

MAN IN THE MOON, THE 99
MGM. October, 1991. (Robert Mulligan), Reese Witherspoon, Jason London, Sam Waterston.

MAN INSIDE, THE 93
NEW LINE CINEMA. October, 1990. (Bobby Roth), Jurgen Prochnow, Peter Coyote, Nathalie Baye.

MAN IN THE SILK HAT, THE 96
KINO INTERNATIONAL. April, 1988. (Maud Linder). Documentary.

MAN LIKE EVA, A 92
PROMOVISION INTL. June, 1985. German; Eng. titles. (Radu Gabrea), Eva Mattes.

MAN OF FLOWERS 91
SPECTRAFILM. December, 1984. Australian. (Paul Cox), Norman Kaye, Alyson Best.

MAN OF MARBLE 160
NEW YORKER. January, 1981. Polish; Eng. titles. (Andrzej Wajda), Krystyna Janda, Jerzy Radziwilowicz.

MAN ON FIRE 93
TRI-STAR. October, 1987. French-Italian. (Elie Chouraqui), Scott Glenn, Jade Malle.

MAN TROUBLE 100
20TH CENTURY FOX. July, 1992. (Bob Rafelson), Jack Nicholson, Ellen Barkin, Beverly D'Angelo.

MAN UNDER SUSPICION 128
SPECTRAFILM. February, 1985. German; Eng. titles. (Norbert Kuckelmann), Maximilian Schell.

MAN WHO LOVED WOMEN, THE 110
COLUMBIA. December, 1983. (Blake Edwards), Burt Reynolds, Julie Andrews, Kim Basinger.

MAN WHO MISTOOK HIS WIFE FOR A HAT, THE 75
FILMS FOR THE HUMANITIES. August, 1988. (Christopher Rawlence), Emile Elcourt, Frederick Westcott.

MAN WHO WASN'T THERE, THE (3-D) 111
PARAMOUNT. August, 1983. (Bruce Malmuth), Steve Guttenburg, Lisa Langlois.

MAN WITH ONE RED SHOE, THE 93
20TH CENTURY FOX. July, 1985. (Stan Dragoti), Tom Hanks, Dabney Coleman.

MAN WITH THREE COFFINS, THE 105
NEW YORKER. October, 1988. South Korean; Eng. subtitles. (Lee Chang-ho), Kim Myung-kon, Lee Bo-hee.

MAN WITH TWO BRAINS, THE 93
WARNER BROS. June, 1983. (Carl Reiner), Steve Martin, Kathleen Turner, David Warner.

MAN, WOMAN AND CHILD 100
PARAMOUNT. April, 1983. (Dick Richards), Martin Sheen, Blythe Danner.

MANCHURIAN AVENGER 81
FACET FILM. April, 1985. (Ed Warnick), Bobby Kim, Bill Wallace.

MANHATTAN PROJECT, THE 117
20TH CENTURY FOX. June, 1986. (Marshall Brickman), John Lithgow, Christopher Collet.

MANHUNTER (P) 119
DE LAURENTIIS. August, 1986. (Michael Mann), William L. Petersen, Kim Greist.

MANIAC COP 85
SHAPIRO GLICKENHAUS ENTERTAINMENT. May, 1988. (William Lustig), Tom Atkins, Bruce Campbell.

MANIFESTO 94
CANNON GROUP. January, 1989. (Dusan Makevejev), Camilla Soeberg, Alfred Molina, Simon Callow, Eric Stoltz.

MANNEQUIN 89
20TH CENTURY FOX. February, 1987. (Michael Gottlieb), Andrew McCarthy, Kim Cattrall.

MANNEQUIN TWO ON THE MOVE 95
20TH CENTURY FOX. May, 1991. (Stewart Raffill) William Ragsdale, Kristy Swanson, Meshach Taylor.

MANON OF THE SPRING 113
ORION CLASSICS. November, 1987. French; Eng. subtitles. (Claude Berri), Yves Montand, Daniel Auteuil.

MAPANTSULA 105
RAY WAVE PRODS. September, 1989. South African-Australian-British. (Oliver Schmitz), Thomas Mogotlane.

MARIA'S LOVERS 103
CANNON FILMS. January, 1985. (Andrei Konchalovsky), Nastassja Kinski, John Savage, Robert Mitchum.

MARIE 108
MGM/UA. September, 1985. (Roger Donaldson), Sissy Spacek, Jeff Daniels.

MARKED FOR DEATH (WS) 96
20TH CENTURY FOX. October, 1990. (Dwight H. Little), Steven Seagal, Basil Wallace, Keith David.

MARLENE 96
ALIVE FILMS. November, 1986. German. (Maximilian Schell). Documentary on Marlene Dietrich.

MARQUIS 83
A.Y. ALLIGATOR. July, 1991. Belgian-French. (Henri Xhonneux), Philippe Bizot, Bien de Moor.

MARRIED TO THE MOB 103
ORION. August, 1988. (Jonathan Demme), Michelle Pfeiffer, Matthew Modine, Dean Stockwell.

MARRYING MAN, THE 115
BUENA VISTA. April, 1991. (Jerry Rees), Alec Baldwin, Kim Basinger, Robert Loggia, Fisher Stevens.

MARTIANS GO HOME 85
TAURUS ENTERTAINMENT. April, 1990. (David Odell), Randy Quaid, Margaret Colin.

MARTIN'S DAY 98
MGM/UA. February, 1985. (Alan Gibson), Richard Harris, Lindsay Wagner.

MARVIN AND TIGE 104
LORIMAR. December, 1983. (Eric Weston), John Cassavetes, Billy Dee Williams.

MASK 120
UNIVERSAL. March, 1985. (Peter Bogdanovich), Cher, Sam Elliott, Eric Stoltz.

MASQUERADE 91
MGM/UA. March, 1988. (Bob Swaim), Rob Lowe, Meg Tilly.

MASS APPEAL 100
UNIVERSAL. December, 1984. (Glenn Jordan), Jack Lemmon, Zeljko Ivanek.

MASS IS ENDED, THE 94
RAI/SACIS. May, 1988. Italian; Eng. subtitles. (Nanni Moretti), Nanni Moretti, Ferruccio De Ceresa.

MASTERS OF THE UNIVERSE 106
CANNON GROUP. August, 1987. (Gary Goddard), Dolph Lundgren, Frank Langella.

MATA HARI 108
CANNON. April, 1985. (Curtis Harrington), Sylvia Kristel, Christopher Cazenove.

MATADOR 115
CINEVISTA/PROMOVISION INTL. April, 1988. Spanish; Eng. subtitles. (Pedro Almodovar), Assumpta Serna, Antonio Banderas.

MATEWAN 130
CINECOM INTL. August, 1987. (John Sayles), Chris Cooper, Will Oldham, Mary McDonnell.

MATTER OF DEGREES, A 88
FOX/LORBER. September, 1991. (W. T. Morgan), Arye Gross, Judith Hoag, Tom Sizemore.

MATTER OF HEART 107
KINO INTL. October, 1986. Documentary.

MAURICE 140
CINECOM PICTURES. September, 1987. British. (James Ivory), James Wilby, Hugh Grant, Rupert Graves.

MAX DUGAN RETURNS 98
20TH CENTURY FOX. March, 1983. (Herbert Ross), Marsha Mason, Jason Robards, Matthew Broderick.

MAXIE 90
ORION. September, 1985. (Paul Aaron), Glenn Close, Mandy Patinkin.

MAXIMUM OVERDRIVE 97
DE LAURENTIIS. July, 1986. (Stephen King), Emilio Estevez, Pat Hingle.

MAY FOOLS 108
ORION CLASSICS. June, 1990. French. (Louis Malle), Michel Piccoli, Miou-Miou, Michel Duchaussoy.

McBAIN 102
SHAPIRO GLICKENHAUS. September, 1991. (James Glickenhaus), Christopher Walken, Michael Ironside, Maria Conchita Alonso.

ME AND HIM 90
COLUMBIA. August, 1989. (Doris Dorrie), Griffin Dunne, Ellen Greene.

MEAN SEASON, THE 103
ORION. February, 1985. (Philip Boros), Kurt Russell, Mariel Hemingway.

MEATBALLS PART II 96
TRI-STAR. July, 1984. (Ken Wiederhorn), Archie Hahn, John Mengatti.

MEATBALLS III 94
THE MOVIE STORE. May, 1987. (George Mendeluk), Sally Kellerman, Patrick Dempsey.

MEDICINE MAN (P) 104
BUENA VISTA. February, 1992. (John McTiernan), Sean Connery, Lorraine Bracco, Jose Wilker.

MEET THE APPLEGATES 90
TRITON. February, 1991. (Michael Lehmann), Ed Begley Jr., Stockard Channing, Dabney Coleman.

MEET THE HOLLOWHEADS 86
MOVIESTORE ENTERTAINMENT. November, 1989. (Tom Burman), John Glover, Nancy Mette.

	Length in Mins.

MISADVENTURES OF MR. WILT, THE 92
SAMUEL GOLDWYN CO. June, 1990. British (Michael Tuchner), Griff Rhys Jones, Mel Smith.

MISCHIEF 93
20TH CENTURY FOX. February, 1985. (Mel Damski), Doug McKeon, Catherine Mary Stewart.

MISERY 109
COLUMBIA. November, 1990. (Rob Reiner), James Caan, Kathy Bates, Lauren Bacall.

MISFIT BRIGADE, THE 101
TRANS WORLD ENTERTAINMENT. January, 1988. (Gordon Hessler), David Carradine, Don W. Moffett.

MISHIMA 122
WARNER BROS. September, 1985. (Paul Schrader), Japanese; Eng. titles. Ken Ogata, Masayuki Shionaya.

MISPLACED 95
SUBWAY FILMS. October, 1990. (Louis Yansen), John Cameron Mitchell, Viveca Lindfors, Elzbieta Czyzewska.

MISS FIRECRACKER 102
CORSAIR. April, 1989. (Thomas Schlamme), Holly Hunter, Mary Steenburgen, Tim Robbins.

MISS MARY 102
NEW WORLD PICTURES. November, 1986. Argentine. In English. (Maria Luisa Bemberg), Julie Christie, Sofia Viruboff.

MISS OR MYTH? 60
GOLD MOUNTAIN. June, 1987. (Geoffrey Dunn, Mark Schwartz). Documentary.

MISSING (P) 122
UNIVERSAL. February, 1982. (Constantin Costa-Gavras), Jack Lemmon, Sissy Spacek.

MISSING IN ACTION 101
CANNON GROUP. November, 1984. (Joseph Zito), Chuck Norris, M. Emmet Walsh.

MISSING IN ACTION 2—THE BEGINNING 96
CANNON GROUP. March, 1985. (Lance Hool), Chuck Norris, Soon-Teck Oh.

MISSION, THE 96
NEW LINE CINEMA. May, 1984. Farsi; Eng. titles. (Parviz Sayyad), Houshang Touzie.

MISSION, THE (J-D-C) 128
WARNER BROS. October, 1986. British. (Roland Joffe), Robert De Niro, Jeremy Irons.

MISSIONARY, THE 91
COLUMBIA. November, 1982. British. (Richard Loncraine), Michael Palin, Maggie Smith.

MISSISSIPPI BURNING 125
ORION. December, 1988. (Alan Parker), Gene Hackman, Willem Dafoe, Frances McDormand.

MISSISSIPPI MASALA 118
SAMUEL GOLDWYN CO. February, 1992. (Mira Nair), Denzel Washington, Sarita Choudhury, Roshan Seth.

MISTRESS 109
RAINBOW/TRIBECA. August, 1992. (Barry Primus), Robert Wuhl, Martin Landau, Robert De Niro.

MR. AND MRS. BRIDGE 127
MIRAMAX. November, 1990. (James Ivory), Paul Newman, Joanne Woodward, Robert Sean Leonard.

MR. DESTINY 112
BUENA VISTA. October, 1990. (James Orr), James Belushi, Michael Caine, Linda Hamilton.

MR. FROST 95
TRIUMPH. November, 1990. British-French. (Philippe Setbon), Jeff Goldblum, Kathy Baker, Alan Bates.

MR. HOOVER & I 85
TURIN FILM. April, 1990. (Emile DeAntonio), Documentary.

MISTER JOHNSON 103
AVENUE. March, 1991. British. (Bruce Beresford), Pierce Brosnan, Maynard Eziashi, Edward Woodward.

MR. LOVE 90
WARNER BROS. April, 1986. British. (Roy Battersby), Barry Jackson, Maurice Denham.

MR. MOM 91
20TH CENTURY FOX. July, 1983. (Stan Dragoti), Michael Keaton, Teri Garr.

MR. NICE GUY 92
SHAPIRO ENTERTAINMENT. September, 1987. (Henry Wolfond), Mike MacDonald, Jan Smithers.

MR. NORTH 92
SAMUEL GOLDWYN CO. July, 1988. (Danny Huston), Anthony Edwards, Robert Mitchum, Lauren Bacall.

MR. UNIVERSE 98
ZEITGEIST. March, 1990. Hungarian. (György Szomjas), Laszlo Szabo, Mickey Hargitay.

MRS. SOFFEL 110
MGM/UA. December, 1984. (Gillian Armstrong), Diane Keaton, Mel Gibson, Matthew Modine.

MISUNDERSTOOD 91
MGM/UA. March, 1984. (Jerry Schatzberg), Gene Hackman, Henry Thomas.

MIXED BLOOD 98
CINEVISTA. October, 1985. (Paul Morrissey), Marilla Pera, Richard Ulacia.

MIXUP (MELI-MELO) 65
INTERAMA. July, 1987. (Françoise Romand). Documentary.

MO' BETTER BLUES 127
UNIVERSAL. August, 1990. (Spike Lee), Denzel Washington, Joie Lee, Wesley Snipes.

MO' MONEY 89
COLUMBIA. July, 1992. (Peter Macdonald), Damon Wayans, Marlon Wayans, Stacey Dash.

MOBSTERS 104
UNIVERSAL. July, 1991. (Michael Karbelnikoff), Christian Slater, Patrick Dempsey, Richard Grieco.

MODEL COUPLE, THE 103
INDEPT. November, 1990. French. (William Klein), Anemone, Andre Dussolier.

MODERN GIRLS 84
ATLANTIC RELEASING. December, 1986. (Jerry Kramer), Daphne Zuniga, Virginia Madsen.

MODERN LOVE 109
SVS/TRIUMPH. April, 1990. (Robby Benson), Robby Benson, Karla DeVito, Burt Reynolds.

MODERN PROBLEMS 91
20TH CENTURY FOX. December, 1981. (Ken Shapiro), Chevy Chase, Patti D'Arbanville.

MODERN ROMANCE 93
COLUMBIA. March, 1981. (Albert Brooks), Albert Brooks, Kathryn Harrold.

MODERNS, THE 126
ALIVE FILMS. April, 1988. (Alan Rudolph), Keith Carradine, Linda Fiorentino.

MOM AND DAD SAVE THE WORLD 88
WARNER BROS. July, 1992. (Greg Beeman), Teri Garr, Jeffrey Jones, Jon Lovitz.

MOMMIE DEAREST 129
PARAMOUNT. September, 1981. (Frank Perry), Faye Dunaway, Diana Scarwid.

MON ONCLE D'AMERIQUE 123
NEW WORLD. December, 1980. French; Eng. titles. (Alain Resnais), Gerard Depardieu, Nicole Garcia.

MONA LISA 100
ISLAND PICTURES. June, 1986. British. (Neil Jordan), Bob Hoskins, Cathy Tyson, Michael Caine.

MONDO NEW YORK 83
FOURTH AND BROADWAY FILMS (ISLAND PICTURES). April, 1988. (Harvey Keith), Joey Arias, Rick Aviles, Charlie Barnett.

MONEY PIT, THE 91
UNIVERSAL. March, 1986. (Richard Benjamin), Tom Hanks, Shelley Long.

MONEYTREE, THE 94
BLACK SHEEP FILMS. April, 1992. (Alan Dienstag), Christopher Dienstag, Robbi Collins, Richard Roughgarden.

MONKEY GRIP 101
CINECOM INTL. November, 1983. (Ken Cameron), Noni Hazlehurst, Colin Friels.

MONKEY SHINES 115
ORION. July, 1988. (George A. Romero), Jason Beghe, John Pankow.

MONSIEUR HIRE 88
ORION CLASSICS. April, 1990. French. (Patrice Leconte), Michel Blanc, Sandrine Bonnaire.

MONSIGNOR (T) 111
20TH CENTURY FOX. October, 1982. (Frank Perry), Christopher Reeve, Genevieve Bujold.

MONSTER IN A BOX 88
FINE LINE FEATURES. May, 1992. (Nick Broomfield), Spalding Gray.

MONSTER IN THE CLOSET 87
TROMA. January, 1987. (Roger Dahlin), Donald Grant, Denise DuBarry.

MONSTER SQUAD, THE (P) 81
TRI-STAR. August, 1987. (Fred Dekker), Andre Gower, Duncan Regehr.

MONTH IN THE COUNTRY, A 96
ORION CLASSICS. February, 1988. British. (Pat O'Connor), Colin Firth, Kenneth Branagh.

MONTY PYTHON LIVE AT THE HOLLYWOOD BOWL ... 77
COLUMBIA. July, 1982. British. (Terry Hughes), Monty Python Troupe.

	Length in Mins.

MONTY PYTHON'S THE MEANING OF LIFE 103
UNIVERSAL. March, 1983. British. (Terry Jones), Graham Chapman, John Cleese.

MOON IN THE GUTTER, THE 126
TRIUMPH. September, 1983. French; Eng. titles. (Jean-Jacques Beineix), Gerard Depardieu, Nastassja Kinski.

MOON OVER PARADOR 105
UNIVERSAL. September, 1988. (Paul Mazursky), Richard Dreyfuss, Raul Julia, Sonia Braga.

MOONLIGHTING 97
UNIVERSAL CLASSICS. September, 1982. British. (Jerzy Skolimowski), Jeremy Irons, Eugene Lipinski.

MOONSTRUCK 102
MGM/UA. December, 1987. (Norman Jewison), Cher, Nicolas Cage, Olympia Dukakis.

MORGAN STEWART'S COMING HOME 96
NEW CENTURY/VISTA. February, 1987. (Paul Aaron), Jon Cryer, Lynn Redgrave.

MORNING AFTER, THE 103
20TH CENTURY FOX. December, 1986. (Sidney Lumet), Jane Fonda, Jeff Bridges.

MORONS FROM OUTER SPACE 91
UNIVERSAL. September, 1985. British. (Mike Hodges), Mel Smith, Griff Rhys Jones.

MORTAL PASSIONS 98
MGM/UA. January, 1990. (Andrew Lane), Zach Galligan, Krista Errickson.

MORTAL THOUGHTS 104
COLUMBIA. April, 1991. (Alan Rudolph), Demi Moore, Glenne Headley, Bruce Willis.

MORTUARY ACADEMY 85
TAURUS ENTERTAINMENT. May, 1988. (Michael Schroeder), Paul Bartel, Mary Woronov.

MOSCOW DOES NOT BELIEVE IN TEARS 152
IFEX. December, 1980. Russian; Eng. titles. (Vladimir Menshov), Vena Alentova, Irina Muravyova.

MOSCOW ON THE HUDSON 115
COLUMBIA. April, 1984. (Paul Mazursky), Robin Williams, Alejandro Rey, Maria Conchita Alonso.

MOSQUITO COAST, THE 117
WARNER BROS. November, 1986. (Peter Weir), Harrison Ford, Helen Mirren.

MOST BEAUTIFUL, THE 85
R5/S8 (Michael Jeck). June, 1987 release of 1944 film. Japanese. (Akira Kurosawa), Yoko Yaguchi, Takashi Shimura.

MOUNTAIN HILL MOTEL MASSACRE 96
NEW WORLD PICTURES. May, 1986. (Jim McCollough), Bill Thurman, Anna Chappell.

MOUNTAIN MEN, THE 102
COLUMBIA. July, 1980. (Richard Lang), Charlton Heston, Brian Keith.

MOUNTAINS OF THE MOON 135
TRI-STAR. February, 1990. (Bob Rafelson), Patrick Bergin, Iain Glen.

MOVERS AND SHAKERS 80
MGM/UA. May, 1985. (William Asher), Walter Matthau, Charles Grodin.

MOVING 89
WARNER BROS. March, 1988. (Alan Metter), Richard Pryor, Beverly Todd.

MOVING OUT 90
SATORI. January, 1985. (Michael Pattinson), Vince Colosimo, Maurice Devincentis.

MOVING VIOLATIONS 90
20TH CENTURY FOX. April, 1985. (Neal Israel), John Murray, Jennifer Tilly.

MOZART BROTHERS, THE 111
FIRST RUN FEATURES. September, 1987. Swedish; Eng. subtitles. (Suzanne Osten), Etienne Glaser, Philip Zanden.

MUHAMMAD ALI, THE GREATEST 120
FILMS PARIS. November, 1990. (William Klein), Documentary.

MUNCHIE 80
CONCORDE. May, 1992. (Jim Wynorski), Loni Anderson, Andrew Stevens, Jaime McEnnan.

MUNCHIES 85
CONCORDE PICTURES. March, 1987. (Bettina Hirsch), Harvey Korman, Charles Stratton.

MUPPETS TAKE MANHATTAN, THE 94
TRI-STAR. July, 1984. (Frank Oz). The Muppets, Lonny Price.

MURDER ONE 95
MIRAMAX FILMS. September, 1988. Canadian. (Graeme Campbell), Henry Thomas, James Wilder.

MURPHY'S LAW 100
CANNON FILMS. April, 1986. (J. Lee Thompson), Charles Bronson, Kathleen Wilhoite.

	Length in Mins.

MURPHY'S ROMANCE (P) 107
COLUMBIA. December, 1985. (Martin Ritt), Sally Field, James Garner.

MUSIC BOX (P) 124
TRI-STAR. December, 1989. (Costa-Gavras), Jessica Lange, Armin Mueller-Stahl, Frederic Forrest.

MUSIC TEACHER, THE 100
ORION CLASSICS. July, 1989. French; Eng. titles. (Gerard Corbiau), Jose Van Dam, Anne Roussel.

MUSIC TELLS YOU, THE 60
PENNEBAKER ASSOCS. June, 1992. (Chris Hegedus, D. A. Pennebaker), Brandford Marsalis.

MY AMERICAN COUSIN 95
SPECTRAFILM. February, 1986. Canadian. (Sandy Wilson), Margret Langrick, John Wildman.

MY BEAUTIFUL LAUNDRETTE 93
ORION CLASSICS. March, 1986. British. (Stephen Frears), Daniel Day Lewis, Saeed Jaffrey.

MY BEST FRIEND IS A VAMPIRE 100
KINGS ROAD ENTERTAINMENT. May, 1988. (Jimmy Huston), Robert Sean Leonard, Lee Anne Locken.

MY BEST FRIEND'S GIRL 99
EUROPEAN INTL. April, 1984. French; Eng. titles. (Bertrand Blier), Thierry L'hermitte.

MY BLOODY VALENTINE 91
PARAMOUNT. February, 1981. Canadian. (George Mihalka), Paul Kelman, Lori Hallier.

MY BLUE HEAVEN 95
WARNER BROS. August, 1990. (Herbert Ross), Steve Martin, Rick Moranis, Joan Cusack.

MY BODYGUARD 96
20TH CENTURY FOX. July, 1980. (Tony Bill), Chris Makepeace, Adam Baldwin, Matt Dillon.

MY CHAUFFEUR 97
CROWN INT. January, 1986. (Daniel Beaird), Deborah Foreman, Sam Jones.

MY COUSIN VINNY 119
20TH CENTURY FOX. March, 1992. (Jonathan Lynn), Joe Pesci, Marisa Tomei, Ralph Macchio.

MY DARK LADY 104
FILM GALLERY. February, 1987. (Fred A. Keller), Fred A. Keller, Lorna Hill.

MY DEMON LOVER 86
NEW LINE CINEMA. April, 1987. (Charles Loventhal), Scott Valentine, Michelle Little.

MY DINNER WITH ANDRE 110
NEW YORKER. October, 1981. (Louis Malle), Andre Gregory, Wallace Shawn.

MY FATHER'S COMING 82
TARA RELEASING. November, 1991. German. (Monika Treut), Alfred Edel, Shelley Kastner, Annie Sprinkle.

MY FATHER'S GLORY 110
ORION CLASSICS. June, 1991. French. (Yves Robert), Philippe Caubere, Nathalie Roussel.

MY FAVORITE YEAR 92
MGM/UA. October, 1982. (Richard Benjamin), Peter O'Toole, Jessica Harper, Mark Linn-Baker.

MY FIRST FORTY YEARS 106
TRI-STAR. November, 1989. Italian. (Carlo Vanzina), Carol Alt, Elliott Gould.

MY FIRST WIFE 99
SPECTRAFILM. April, 1985. Australian. (Paul Cox), John Hargreaves, Wendy Hughes.

MY FRIEND IVAN LAPSHIN 92
IFEX. May, 1987. Russian. (Alexei Gherman), Andrei Boltnev, Andrei Mironov.

MY FRIENDS NEED KILLING 72
CINEMA PRODUCERS CENTER. June, 1984. (Paul Leder), Greg Millavey.

MY GIRL 102
COLUMBIA. November, 1991. (Howard Zieff), Dan Aykroyd, Jamie Lee Curtis, Anna Chlumsky, Macaulay Culkin.

MY HEROES HAVE ALWAYS BEEN COWBOYS 106
SAMUEL GOLDWYN CO. March, 1991. (Stuart Rosenberg), Scott Glenn, Kate Capshaw, Ben Johnson.

MY LEFT FOOT 103
MIRAMAX. November, 1989. Irish. (Jim Sheridan), Daniel Day Lewis, Brenda Fricker, Ray McAnally.

MY LIFE AS A DOG 101
SKOURAS PICTURES. May, 1987. Swedish; Eng. titles. (Lasse Hallstrom), Anton Glanzelius, Tomas von Bromssen.

MY LITTLE GIRL 118
HEMDALE RELEASING. May, 1988. (Connie Kaiserman), Mary Stuart Masterson, James Earl Jones.

MY LITTLE PONY 87
DE LAURENTIIS. June, 1986. (Michael Joens). Animated.

Length in Mins.

MY MOTHER'S CASTLE 98
ORION CLASSICS. July, 1991. French. (Yves Robert), Julien Ciamaca, Philippe Caubere.

MY NEW PARTNER 107
ORION. March, 1985. French; Eng. titles. (Claude Zidi), Philippe Noiret.

MY OWN PRIVATE IDAHO 105
NEW LINE CINEMA. September, 1991. (Gus Van Sant), River Phoenix, Keanu Reeves, James Russo.

MY SCIENCE PROJECT 94
BUENA VISTA. August, 1985. (Jonathan Beteul), John Stockwell, Danielle Von Zerneck.

MY STEPMOTHER IS AN ALIEN 108
COLUMBIA. December, 1988. (Richard Benjamin), Dan Aykroyd, Kim Basinger.

MY SWEET LITTLE VILLAGE. 101
CIRCLE FILMS. January, 1987. Czechoslavakian; Eng. titles. (Jiri Menzel), Janos Ban, Marian Labuda.

MY UNCLE'S LEGACY 105
IFEX. June, 1990. Serbo-Croatian. (Krsto Papic), Davor Janjic, Alma Prica.

MYSTERY DATE 98
ORION. August, 1991. (Jonathan Wacks), Ethan Hawke, Teri Polo, B.D. Wong, Brian McNamara.

MYSTERY OF ALEXINA, THE 86
EUROPEAN CLASSICS. January, 1986. French; Eng. titles. (Rene Feret), Vuillemin, Valerie Stroh.

MYSTERY TRAIN 110
ORION CLASSICS. November, 1989. (Jim Jarmusch), Youki Kudoh, Masatoshi Nagase, Screamin' Jay Hawkins.

MYSTIC PIZZA 104
SAMUEL GOLDWYN CO. October, 1988. (Donald Petrie), Julia Roberts, Annabeth Gish, Lili Taylor.

N

NADINE 83
TRI-STAR. August, 1987. (Robert Benton), Jeff Bridges, Kim Basinger.

NAKED CAGE, THE 97
CANNON FILMS. March, 1986. (Paul Nicholas), Shari Shattuck, Angel Tompkins.

NAKED FACE, THE 103
CANNON FILMS. January, 1985. (Bryan Forbes), Roger Moore, Rod Steiger.

NAKED GUN, THE 85
PARAMOUNT. December, 1988. (David Zucker), Leslie Nielsen, George Kennedy.

NAKED GUN 2½: THE SMELL OF FEAR 85
PARAMOUNT. June, 1991. (David Zucker), Leslie Nielsen, Priscilla Presley, Robert Goulet.

NAKED LUNCH 115
20TH CENTURY FOX. December, 1991. British-Canadian. (David Cronenberg), Peter Weller, Judy Davis, Ian Holm.

NAKED OBSESSION 80
CONCORDE. January, 1991. (Dan Golden), William Katt, Rick Dean, Maria Ford.

NAKED TANGO 93
NEW LINE CINEMA. August, 1991. Argentine-U.S. (Leonard Schrader), Vincent D'Onofrio, Mathilda May, Esai Morales.

NAME OF THE ROSE, THE 130
20TH CENTURY FOX. September, 1986. (Jean-Jacques Annaud), Sean Connery, F. Murray Abraham.

NANOU 110
UMBRELLA FILMS. September, 1988. British. In French & English; Eng. titles. (Conny Templeman), Imogen Stubbs, Daniel Day-Lewis.

NARROW MARGIN (P) 97
TRI-STAR. September, 1990. (Peter Hyams), Gene Hackman, Anne Archer, James B. Sikking.

NATE AND HAYES 100
PARAMOUNT. November, 1983. (Ferdinand Fairfax), Tommy Lee Jones, Michael O'Keefe.

NATIONAL LAMPOON'S CHRISTMAS VACATION ... 97
WARNER BROS. December, 1989. (Jeremiah Chechik), Chevy Chase, Beverly D'Angelo.

NATIONAL LAMPOON'S CLASS REUNION 84
20TH CENTURY FOX. November, 1982. (Michael Miller), Gerrit Graham, Michael Lerner.

NATIONAL LAMPOON'S EUROPEAN VACATION 94
WARNER BROS. July, 1985. (Amy Heckerling), Chevy Chase, Beverly D'Angelo.

NATIONAL LAMPOON'S VACATION 100
WARNER BROS. July, 1983. (Harold Ramis), Chevy Chase, Beverly D'Angelo.

Length in Mins.

NATIVE SON 112
CINECOM. December, 1986. (Jerrold Freedman), Carroll Baker, Akousua Busia, Matt Dillon.

NATURAL, THE 134
TRI-STAR. May, 1984. (Barry Levinson), Robert Redford, Robert Duvall.

NATURAL HISTORY OF PARKING LOTS, THE 92
STRAND RELEASING. October, 1990. (Everett Lewis), Charlie Bean, B. Wyatt.

NAVIGATOR, THE 92
CIRCLE RELEASING. March, 1989. New Zealand. (Vincent Ward), Bruce Lyons, Chris Haywood.

NAVY SEALS 113
ORION. July, 1990. (Lewis Teague), Charlie Sheen, Michael Biehn.

NEAR DARK 95
DE LAURENTIIS. October, 1987. (Kathryn Bigelow), Adrian Pasdar, Jenny Wright, Lance Henriksen.

NECESSARY ROUGHNESS 108
PARAMOUNT. September, 1991. (Stan Dragoti), Scott Bakula, Hector Elizondo, Robert Loggia.

NECROPOLIS 76
EMPIRE PICTURES. May, 1987. (Bruce Hickey), LeeAnne Baker, Jacquie Fitz.

NEIGHBORS 95
COLUMBIA. December, 1981. (John G. Avildson), John Belushi, Dan Aykroyd.

NEON MANIACS 91
BEDFORD ENTERTAINMENT. November, 1986. (Joseph Mangine), Allan Hayes, Leilani Sarelle.

NEST, THE 88
CONCORDE PICTURES. January, 1988. (Terence H. Winkless), Robert Lansing, Lisa Langlois.

NEVER CRY WOLF (P) 105
BUENA VISTA. October, 1983. (Carroll Ballard), Charles Martin Smith, Brian Dennehy.

NEVER LEAVE NEVADA 88
CABRIOLET. April, 1991. (Steve Swartz), Steve Swartz, Rodney Rincon. B&W.

NEVER SAY NEVER AGAIN 137
WARNER BROS. October, 1983. British. (Irvin Kershner), Sean Connery, Kim Basinger, Max Von Sydow.

NEVER TOO YOUNG TO DIE 92
PAUL ENTERTAINMENT. June, 1986. (Gil Bettman), John Stamos, Vanity.

NEVERENDING STORY, THE (TV) 94
WARNER BROS. June, 1984. W. German-British. (Wolfgang Petersen), Noah Hathaway, Barret Oliver.

NEVERENDING STORY II: THE NEXT CHAPTER, THE .. 89
WARNER BROS. February, 1991. German. (George Miller), Jonathan Brandis, Kenny Morrison, Clarissa Burt.

NEW ADVENTURES OF PIPPI LONGSTOCKING, THE .. 100
COLUMBIA. July, 1988. (Ken Annakin), Tami Erin, Eileen Brennan.

NEW BLOOD, THE—FRIDAY THE 13TH PART VII ... 90
PARAMOUNT. May, 1988. (John Carl Buechler), Jennifer Banko, John Otrin.

NEW JACK CITY 97
WARNER BROS. March, 1991. (Mario Van Peebles), Wesley Snipes, Ice T, Mario Van Peebles, Judd Nelson.

NEW KIDS, THE 90
COLUMBIA. January, 1985. (Sean Cunningham), Shannon Presby, Lori Loughlin.

NEW LIFE, A 104
PARAMOUNT. March, 1988. (Alan Alda), Alan Alda, Ann-Margret, Hal Linden.

NEW YEAR'S DAY 87
INTERNATIONAL RAINBOW PICTURES. December, 1989. (Henry Jaglom), Maggie Jakobson, Henry Jaglom.

NEW YORK NIGHTS 100
BEDFORD. March, 1984. (Roman Vanderbes), Corinne Alphen, George Ayer.

NEW YORK STORIES 123
BUENA VISTA. March, 1989. (Martin Scorsese, Francis Coppola, Woody Allen), Nick Nolte, Talia Shire, Woody Allen.

NEWSIES (P) 121
BUENA VISTA. April, 1992. (Kenny Ortega), Christian Bale, Robert Duvall, David Moscow, Trey Parker.

NEXT OF KIN 108
WARNER BROS. October, 1989. (John Irvin), Patrick Swayze, Liam Neeson.

NEXT SUMMER 100
EUROPEAN CLASSICS. August, 1986. French; Eng. titles. (Nadine Trintignant), Fanny Ardant.

NICE GIRLS DON'T EXPLODE 92
NEW WORLD PICTURES. April, 1987. (Chuck Martinez), Barbara Harris, Michelle Meyrink.

Length in Mins.

NIGHT ANGEL 90
FRIES ENTERTAINMENT. September, 1990. (Dominique Othenin-Girard), Isa Anderson, Karen Black, Debra Feuer.

NIGHT BEFORE, THE 85
KINGS ROAD ENTERTAINMENT. March, 1988. (Thom Eberhardt), Keanu Reeves, Lori Loughlin.

NIGHT CROSSING 106
BUENA VISTA. February, 1982. British. (Delbert Mann), John Hurt, Jane Alexander.

NIGHT GAME 93
TRANS WORLD. September, 1989. (Peter Masterson), Roy Scheider, Karen Young.

NIGHT IN HAVANA: DIZZY GILLESPIE IN CUBA, A 84
CINEPHILE USA. May, 1989. (John Holland). Documentary.

NIGHT IN HEAVEN, A 83
20TH CENTURY FOX. November, 1983. (John G. Avildsen), Christopher Atkins, Lesley Ann Warren.

NIGHT IN THE LIFE OF JIMMY REARDON, A 92
20TH CENTURY FOX. February, 1988. (William Richert), River Phoenix, Ann Magnuson.

'NIGHT MOTHER 96
UNIVERSAL. September, 1986. (Tom Moore), Sissy Spacek, Anne Brancroft.

NIGHT OF THE COMET 100
ATLANTIC RELEASING. November, 1984. (Thom Eberhardt), Catherine Mary Stewart.

NIGHT OF THE CREEPS 85
TRI-STAR. August, 1986. (Fred Dekker), Jason Lively, Steve Marshall.

NIGHT OF THE DEMONS 89
INTERNATIONAL FILM MARKETING. September, 1988. (Kevin S. Tenney), Linnea Quigley, Cathy Podewell.

NIGHT OF THE LIVING DEAD 96
COLUMBIA. October, 1990. (Tom Savini), Tony Todd, Patricia Tallman, Tom Towles.

NIGHT OF THE SHOOTING STARS 106
UA CLASSICS. September, 1982. Italian; Eng. titles. (Paolo & Vittorio Taviani), Omero Antonutti, Margarita Lozano.

NIGHT OF THE WARRIOR 100
TRIMARK. June, 1991. (Rafal Zielinski), Lorenzo Lamas, Anthony Geary, Arlene Dahl.

NIGHT ON EARTH 128
FINE LINE FEATURES. May, 1992. (Jim Jarmusch), Gena Rowlands, Giancarlo Esposito, Roberto Begigni.

NIGHT PATROL 83
NEW WORLD. November, 1984. (Jackie Kong), Linda Blair, Pat Paulsen.

NIGHT SHADOWS 99
FILM VENTURES. September, 1984. (John [Bud] Cardos), Wings Hauser, Bo Hopkins.

NIGHT SHIFT (P) 105
WARNER BROS. July, 1982. (Ron Howard), Henry Winkler, Michael Keaton

NIGHT STALKER, THE 89
ALMI PICTURES. April, 1987. (Max Kleven), Charles Napier, Michelle Reese.

NIGHT THE LIGHTS WENT OUT IN GEORGIA, THE 120
AVCO EMBASSY. June, 1981. (Ronald F. Maxwell), Kristy McNichol, Dennis Quaid, Mark Hamill.

NIGHT TRAIN TO TERROR 93
VISTO INTL. May, 1985. (Five directors), John Phillip Law, Cameron Mitchell.

NIGHT VISITOR 93
MGM/UA. May, 1989. (Rupert Hitzig), Elliott Gould, Richard Roundtree.

NIGHT ZOO (UN ZOO LA NUIT) 115
FILM DALLAS. March, 1988. French; Eng. subtitles. (Jean-Claude Lauzon), Roger Le Bel, Gilles Maheu.

NIGHTBREED 100
20TH CENTURY FOX. February, 1990. (Clive Barker), Craig Sheffer, David Cronenberg.

NIGHTFALL 82
CONCORDE PICTURES. April, 1988. (Paul Mayersberg), David Birney, Sarah Douglas.

NIGHTFLYERS 89
NEW CENTURY/VISTA FILM CO. October, 1987. ("T.C. Blake", Robert Collector), Catherine Mary Stewart, Michael Praed.

NIGHTHAWKS 98
UNIVERSAL. April, 1981. (Bruce Malmuth), Sylvester Stallone, Billy Dee Williams, Rutger Hauer.

NIGHTMARE AT SHADOW WOODS 84
FILM ARTS FOUNDATION. June, 1987. (John W. Grissmer), Louise Lasser, Mark Soper.

NIGHTMARE ON ELM STREET, A 91
NEW LINE CINEMA. November, 1984. (Wes Craven), John Saxon, Ronee Blakley.

Length in Mins.

NIGHTMARE ON ELM STREET, PART 2: FREDDY'S REVENGE, A 84
NEW LINE CINEMA. November, 1985. (Jack Sholder), Mark Patton, Kim Myers.

NIGHTMARE ON ELM STREET 3: DREAM WARRIORS . 96
NEW LINE CINEMA. February, 1987. (Chuck Russell), Heather Langenkamp, Patricia Arquette.

NIGHTMARE ON ELM STREET 4: THE DREAM MASTER, A 93
NEW LINE CINEMA. August, 1988. (Renny Harlin), Robert Englund, Lisa Wilcox.

NIGHTMARE ON ELM STREET 5: THE DREAM CHILD . 89
NEW LINE CINEMA. August, 1989. (Stephen Hopkins), Robert Englund, Lisa Wilcox.

NIJINSKY 125
PARAMOUNT. March, 1980. British. (Herbert Ross), Alan Bates, George De La Pena, Leslie Browne.

NINE 1/2 WEEKS 113
MGM/UA. February, 1986. (Adrian Lyne), Mickey Rourke, Kim Basinger.

9 DEATHS OF THE NINJA 94
CROWN INTL. April, 1985. (Emmett Alston), Sho Kosugi, Brent Huff.

976-EVIL 93
NEW LINE CINEMA. March, 1989. (Robert Englund) Stephen Geoffreys, Sandy Dennis.

9 TO 5 110
20TH CENTURY FOX. December, 1980. (Colin Higgins), Jane Fonda, Lily Tomlin, Dolly Parton.

1918 91
CINECOM INTL. April, 1985. (Ken Harrison), William Converse-Roberts, Matthew Broderick.

1984 117
ATLANTIC RELEASING. January, 1985. British. (Michael Radford), Richard Burton, John Hurt.

NINETEEN NINETEEN 99
SPECTRAFILM. September, 1986. British. (Hugh Brody), Paul Scofield, Maria Schell.

1990: THE BRONX WARRIORS 84
UNITED FILM. April, 1983. Italian. (Enzo G. Castellari), Vic Morrow, Christopher Connelly.

1969 90
ATLANTIC ENTERTAINMENT GROUP. November, 1988. (Ernest Thompson), Robert Downey Jr., Kiefer Sutherland.

90 DAYS 99
CINECOM INTL. September, 1986. Canadian. (Giles Walker), Stefan Widoslawsky, Christine Pak.

NINJA III—THE DOMINATION 95
CANNON GROUP. September, 1984. (Sam Firstenberg), Lucinda Dickey, Jordan Bennett.

NINJA TURF 86
ASCOT ENTERTAINMENT. March, 1986. (Richard Park), Jun Chong, Phillip Rhee.

NINTH CONFIGURATION (a.k.a. Twinkle Twinkle Killer Kane) 118
UFD. August, 1980. (William Peter Blatty), Stacy Keach, Scott Wilson.

NO END 108
NEW YORKER FILMS. March, 1987. Polish; Eng. titles. (Krzystof Kieslowski), Grazyna Szapolowska, Jerzy Radziwilowicz.

NO FEAR, NO DIE 97
ART LOGIC. August, 1992. French. (Claire Denis), Isaach de Bankole, Alex Descas, Jean-Claude Brialy.

NO HOLDS BARRED 91
NEW LINE CINEMA. June, 1989. (Thomas J. Wright), Hulk Hogan, Kurt Fuller.

NO MAN'S LAND 110
NEW YORKER FILMS. February, 1987, French-Swiss; Eng. titles. (Alain Tanner), Hugues Quester, Myriam Mezieres.

NO MAN'S LAND 106
ORION. October, 1987. (Peter Werner), Charlie Sheen, D.B. Sweeney.

NO MERCY 105
TRI-STAR. December, 1986. (Richard Pearce), Richard Gere, Kim Basinger.

NO NUKES 103
WARNER BROS. July, 1980. (Julian Schlossberg), Jackson Browne, David Crosby.

NO PICNIC 88
GREAT JONES FILM GROUP. July, 1990. (Philip Hartman), David Brisbin, Myoshin.

NO RETREAT, NO SURRENDER 90
NEW WORLD PICTURES. May, 1986. (Corey Yuen), Kurt McKinne, Jean-Claude Van Damme.

	Length in Mins.

NO RETREAT, NO SURRENDER II 92
SHAPIRO GLICKENHAUS. January, 1989. (Corey Yuen), Loren Avedon, Max Thayer.

NO SECRETS 92
I.R.S. MEDIA. May, 1991. (Dezso Magyar), Adam Coleman Howard, Amy Locane, Traci Lind.

NO SKIN OFF MY ASS 73
STRAND. November, 1991. Canadian. (Bruce LaBruce), Bruce LaBruce, Klaus Von Brucker, G. B. Jones.

NO SMALL AFFAIR 103
COLUMBIA. November, 1984. (Jerry Schatzberg), Jon Cryer, Demi Moore.

NO SURRENDER 100
CIRCLE RELEASING. August, 1986. (Peter K. Smith), Michael Angelis, Avis Bunnage.

NO WAY OUT 116
ORION. August, 1987. (Roger Donaldson), Kevin Costner, Gene Hackman, Sean Young.

NOBODY LISTENED 117
CUBAN HUMAN RIGHTS FILM PROJECT. December, 1988. (Nestor Almendros, Jorge Ulla) Documentary.

NOBODY'S FOOL 107
ISLAND PICTURES. November, 1986. (Evelyn Purcell), Rosanna Arquette, Eric Roberts.

NOBODY'S PERFECT 89
MOVIESTORE ENTERTAINMENT. February, 1990. (Robert Kaylor), Chad Lowe, Gail O'Grady.

NOBODY'S PERFEKT 96
COLUMBIA. July, 1981. (Peter Bonerz), Gabe Kaplan, Alex Karras.

NOIR ET BLANC 80
GREYCAT FILMS. May, 1991. French. (Claire Devers), Francis Frappat, Jacques Martial.

NOISES OFF 104
BUENA VISTA. March, 1992. (Peter Bogdanovich), Michael Caine, Carol Burnett, John Ritter, Christopher Reeve.

NOMADS 95
ATLANTIC RELEASING. March, 1986. (John McTiernan), Pierce Brosnan, Lesley-Anne Down.

NORTH SHORE 92
UNIVERSAL. August, 1987. (William Phelps), Matt Adler, Gregory Harrison, Nia Peeples.

NOS AMOURS, A 102
TRIUMPH. October, 1984. French; Eng. titles. (Maurice Pialat), Sandrine Bonnaire.

NOT FOR PUBLICATION 87
SAMUEL GOLDWYN CO. November, 1984. (Paul Bartel), Nancy Allen, David Naughton.

NOT QUITE PARADISE 157
NEW WORLD PICTURES. June, 1986. (Lewis Gilbert), Sam Robards, Joanna Pacula.

NOT WITHOUT MY DAUGHTER 114
MGM. January, 1991. (Brian Gilbert), Sally Field, Alfred Molina, Sheila Rosenthal.

NOTEBOOKS ON CITIES AND CLOTHES 80
CONNOISSEUR. October, 1991. W. German. (Wim Wenders), Documentary.

NOTHING BUT TROUBLE 94
WARNER BROS. February, 1991. (Dan Aykroyd), Chevy Chase, Demi Moore, John Candy, Dan Aykroyd.

NOTHING IN COMMON 118
TRI-STAR. July, 1986. (Garry Marshall), Tom Hanks, Jackie Gleason.

NOTHING LASTS FOREVER 82
MGM/UA. September, 1984. (Tom Schiller), Zach Galligan, Apollonia Van Ravenstein.

NOWHERE TO HIDE 90
NEW CENTURY/VISTA. October, 1986. (Mario Azzopardi), Amy Madigan, Daniel Hugh Kelly.

NUDE BOMB, THE 94
UNIVERSAL. May, 1980. (Clive Donner), Don Adams, Sylvia Kristel.

NUMBER ONE WITH A BULLET 101
CANNON GROUP. January, 1987. (Jack Smight), Robert Carradine, Billy Dee Williams.

NUNS ON THE RUN 90
20TH CENTURY FOX. March, 1990. British. (Jonathan Lynn), Eric Idle, Robbie Coltrane.

NUTCRACKER PRINCE, THE 75
WARNER BROS. November, 1990. Canadian. (Paul Schibli), Animated.

NUTCRACKER: THE MOTION PICTURE, THE 84
CANNON GROUP. November, 1986. (Carroll Ballard), Hugh Bigney, Vanessa Sharp.

NUTS 116
WARNER BROS. November, 1987. (Martin Ritt), Barbra Streisand, Richard Dreyfuss.

O

	Length in Mins.

O. C. AND STIGGS 109
MGM. July, 1987. (Robert Altman), Daniel H. Jenkins, Neill Barry.

OBJECT OF BEAUTY, THE 101
AVENUE. April 1991. British. (Michael Lindsay-Hogg), John Malkovich, Andie MacDowell.

OBLOMOV 146
IFEX. March, 1981. Russian; Eng. titles. (Nikita Mikhalkov), Oleg Tabakov, Yuri Bogatryev.

OBSERVATIONS UNDER THE VOLCANO 82
TELECULTURE. November, 1984. (Christian Blackwood). Documentary.

OBSESSED 103
NEW STAR. November, 1988. Canadian. (Robin Spry), Kerrie Keane, Daniel Pilon.

OCTOPUSSY (P) 130
MGM/UA. June, 1983. British. (John Glen), Roger Moore, Maud Adams.

OF UNKNOWN ORIGIN 112
WARNER BROS. November, 1983. Canadian. (George Pan Cosmatos), Peter Weller, Jennifer Dale.

OFF BEAT 92
BUENA VISTA. April, 1986. (Michael Dinner), Judge Reinhold, Meg Tilly.

OFF LIMITS 102
20TH CENTURY FOX. March, 1988. (Christopher Crowe), Willem Dafoe, Gregory Hines, Fred Ward.

OFF THE MARK 90
FRIES ENTERTAINMENT. November, 1987. (Bill Berry), Mark Neely, Terry Farrell.

OFFICIAL STORY, THE 112
ALMI PICTURES. November, 1985. Spanish; Eng. titles. (Luis Puenzo), Norma Aleandro, Hector Alterio.

OFFICER AND A GENTLEMEN, AN 126
PARAMOUNT. July, 1982. (Taylor Hackford), Richard Gere, Debra Winger, Louis Gossett, Jr.

OFFSPRING, THE 96
TMS PICTURES. September, 1987. (Jeff Burr), Clu Gulager, Vincent Price.

OH GOD! BOOK II 94
WARNER BROS. October, 1980. (Gilbert Cates), George Burns, Suzanne Pleshette.

OH, GOD! YOU DEVIL 96
WARNER BROS. November, 1984. (Paul Bogart), George Burns, Ted Wass.

OH, HEAVENLY DOG! 103
20TH CENTURY FOX. August, 1980. (Joe Camp), Chevy Chase, Benji.

OLD ENOUGH 91
ORION CLASSICS. August, 1984. (Marisa Silver), Sarah Boyd, Rainbow Harvest.

OLD EXPLORERS 91
TAURUS ENTERTAINMENT. September, 1990. (William Pohlad), Jose Ferrer, James Whitmore.

OLD GRINGO 119
COLUMBIA. October, 1989. (Luis Peunzo), Jane Fonda, Gregory Peck, Jimmy Smits.

OLIVER & COMPANY 72
BUENA VISTA. November, 1988. (George Scribner). Animated.

OMEGA SYNDROME 88
NEW WORLD PICTURES. March, 1987. (Joseph Manduke), Ken Wahl, George DiCenzo.

ON GOLDEN POND 109
UNIVERSAL. December, 1981. (Mark Rydell), Katharine Hepburn, Henry Fonda, Jane Fonda.

ON THE BLACK HILL 116
ROXIE RELEASING. July, 1989. British. (Andrew Grieve), Mike Gwilym, Robert Gwilym.

ON THE EDGE 91
SKOURAS PICTURES. May, 1986. (Rob Nilsson), Bruce Dern, John Marley.

ON THE MAKE 95
MIRAMAX FILMS. September, 1987. (Jose Luis Borau), David Carradine, Scott Wilson.

ON THE MAKE 74
TAURUS. April, 1989. (Samuel Hurwitz), Steve Irlen, Mark McKelvey.

ON VALENTINE'S DAY 105
ANGELIKA FILMS. April, 1986. (Ken Harrison), Hallie Foote, William Converse-Roberts.

ONCE AROUND 113
UNIVERSAL. January, 1991. (Lasse Halstrom), Richard Dreyfuss, Holly Hunter, Danny Aiello.

	Length in Mins.

PACIFIC HEIGHTS 103
20TH CENTURY FOX. September, 1990. (John Schlesinger), Matthew Modine, Melanie Griffith, Michael Keaton.

PACKAGE, THE 108
ORION. August, 1989. (Andrew Davis), Gene Hackman, Tommy Lee Jones.

PACKAGE TOUR 75
NEW YORKER FILMS. January, 1987. Hungarian. (Gyula Gazdag). Documentary.

PADRE NUESTRO 90
IFEX. April, 1987. Spanish; Eng. titles. (Francisco Regueiro), Fernando Rey, Francisco Rabal.

PAIN IN THE A–, A 90
CORWIN MAHLER. August, 1980. French; Eng. titles. (Edouard Molinaro), Lino Ventura, Jacques Brel.

PAINTING THE TOWN 78
PADDED CELL. May, 1992. (Andrew Behar), Richard Osterwell.

PALE RIDER 115
WARNER BROS. June, 1985. (Clint Eastwood), Clint Eastwood, Michael Moriarty.

PANAMA DECEPTION, THE 91
EMPOWERMENT PROJECT. July, 1992. (Barbara Trent), Documentary.

PAPER MASK 105
CASTLE HILL. November, 1991. British. (Christopher Morahan), Paul McGann, Amanda Donohoe, Frederick Treves.

PAPER WEDDING, A 90
CAPITOL ENT. June, 1991. French Canadian. (Michel Brault), Genevieve Bujold, Manuel Aranguiz.

PAPERHOUSE 94
VESTRON. February, 1989. British. (Bernard Rose), Charlotte Burke, Elliott Spiers.

PARADISE 110
BUENA VISTA. September, 1991. (Mary Agnes Donoghue), Don Johnson, Melanie Griffith, Elijah Wood.

PARAMEDICS 91
VESTRON. June, 1988. (Stuart Margolin), George Newbern, Christopher McDonald.

PARENTHOOD 124
UNIVERSAL. August, 1989. (Ron Howard), Steve Martin, Mary Steenburgen, Jason Robards, Dianne Wiest.

PARENTS 82
VESTRON. January, 1989. (Bob Balaban), Randy Quaid, Mary Beth Hurt.

PARIS IS BURNING 78
OFF-WHITE PRODS. March, 1991. (Jennie Livingston), Documentary.

PARIS, TEXAS 140
20TH CENTURY FOX. November, 1984. (Wim Wenders), Harry Dean Stanton, Nastassja Kinski.

PARTING GLANCES 90
CINECOM INTL. February, 1986. (Bill Sherwood), Richard Ganoung, John Bolger.

PARTING OF THE WAYS 83
THE CINEMA GUILD. September, 1987. Spanish; Eng. subtitles. (Jesus Diaz), Veronica Lynn, Jorge Trinchet.

PARTISANS OF VILNA 130
EUROPEAN CLASSICS. September, 1986. (Josh Waletzky). Documentary.

PARTNERS 98
PARAMOUNT. April, 1982. (James Burrows), Ryan O'Neal, John Hurt.

PARTY ANIMAL, THE 78
INTL. FILM MARKETING. January, 1985. (David Beaird), Matthew Causey, Tim Carhart.

PARTY CAMP 96
LIGHTNING PICTURES. June, 1987. (Gary Graver), Andrew Ross, Kerry Brennan.

PARTY LINE 91
SVS FILMS. October, 1988. (William Webb), Richard Hatch, Shawn Weatherly.

PASCALI'S ISLAND 101
AVENUE PICTURES. July, 1988. British. (James Dearden), Ben Kingsley, Charles Dance, Helen Mirren.

PASS THE AMMO 91
NEW CENTURY/VISTA. March, 1988. (David Beaird), Tim Curry, Annie Potts.

PASSAGE TO INDIA, A 163
COLUMBIA. December, 1984. British. (David Lean), Judy Davis, Victor Banerjee, Peggy Ashcroft.

PASSED AWAY 96
BUENA VISTA. April, 1992. (Charlie Peters), Bob Hoskins, Pamela Reed, Maureen Stapleton.

PASSION 87
MGM/UA CLASSICS. October, 1983. French; Eng. titles. (Jean-Luc Godard), Isabelle Huppert.

	Length in Mins.

PASTIME 98
MIRAMAX. August, 1991. (Robin B. Armstrong), William Russ, Glenn Plummer, Noble Willingham.

PATERNITY 94
PARAMOUNT. October, 1981. (David Steinberg), Burt Reynolds, Beverly D'Angelo.

PATHFINDER (P) 88
IFEX. April, 1989. (Nils Gaup), Mille Gaup, Nils Utsi.

PATRIOT, THE 90
CROWN INTL. December, 1986. (Frank Harris), Gregg Henry, Simone Griffith.

PATRIOT GAMES (P) 117
PARAMOUNT. June, 1992. (Phillip Noyce), Harrison Ford, Patrick Bergin, Anne Archer.

PATTES BLANCHES 92
INTERAMA. May, 1989 release of 1949 film. French; Eng. titles. (Jean Grémillon), Suzy Delair, Arlette Thomas.

PATTI ROCKS 87
FILM DALLAS PICTURES. January, 1988. (David Burton Morris), Chris Mulkey, John Jenkins, Karen Landry.

PATTY HEARST 108
ATLANTIC ENTERTAINMENT. September, 1988. (Paul Schrader), Natasha Richardson, William Forsythe.

PAUL McCARTNEY'S GET BACK 89
NEW LINE CINEMA. October, 1991. British. (Richard Lester), Documentary.

PAULINE AT THE BEACH 94
ORION CLASSICS. July, 1983. French; Eng. titles. (Eric Rohmer), Amanda Langlet, Arielle Dombasle.

PEACEMAKER 90
FRIES. May, 1990. (Kevin S. Tenney), Robert Forster, Lance Edwards.

PEE-WEE'S BIG ADVENTURE 90
WARNER BROS. August, 1985. (Tim Burton), Paul Reubens, Elizabeth Daily.

PEGGY SUE GOT MARRIED 104
TRI-STAR. October, 1986. (Francis Coppola), Kathleen Turner, Nicolas Cage.

PEKING OPERA BLUES 98
GORDON'S FILMS. May, 1988. Cantonese; Eng. subtitles. (Tsui Hark), Lin Ching Hsia, Cherie Chung.

PELLE THE CONQUEROR 160
MIRAMAX FILMS. December, 1988. Danish-Swedish; Eng. subtitles. (Bille August), Max von Sydow, Pelle Hvenegaard.

PENITENT, THE 94
CINEWORLD. May, 1988. (Cliff Osmond), Raul Julia, Armand Assante.

PENITENTIARY II 103
MGM/UA. April, 1982. (Jamaa Fanaka), Leon Isaac Kennedy, Glynn Turman.

PENITENTIARY III 91
CANNON GROUP. September, 1987. (Jamaa Fanaka), Leon Isaac Kennedy, Anthony Geary.

PENN AND TELLER GET KILLED (P) 89
WARNER BROS. September, 1989. (Arthur Penn), Penn Jillette, Teller.

PENNIES FROM HEAVEN 107
MGM/UA. December, 1981. (Herbert Ross), Steve Martin, Bernadette Peters, Christopher Walken.

PEOPLE UNDER THE STAIRS, THE 102
UNIVERSAL. November, 1991. (Wes Craven), Brandon Adams, Everett McGill, Wendy Robie.

PEPI, LUCI, BOM 80
CINEVISTA. May, 1992. Spanish, 1980. (Pedro Almodovar), Carmen Maura, Felix Rotaeta, Olvido Gara "Alaska", Eva Siva.

PERFECT (P) 120
COLUMBIA. June, 1985. (James Bridges), John Travolta, Jamie Lee Curtis.

PERFECT MATCH, THE 92
SANDSTAR RELEASING. May, 1988. (Mark Deimel), Marc McClure, Jennifer Edwards.

PERFECT MODEL, THE 89
CHICAGO CINEMA ENTERTAINMENT. April, 1989. (Darryl Roberts), Stoney Jackson, Anthony Norman McKay.

PERFECT MURDER, THE 90
MERCHANT IVORY PRODS. March, 1990. British-Indian. (Zafar Hai), Naseeruddin Shan, Stellan Skarsgard.

PERFECT STRANGERS 100
ITC ENTERTAINMENT. July, 1986. (Larry Cohen), Anne Carlisle, Brad Rijn.

PERFECT WEAPON, THE 85
PARAMOUNT. March, 1991. (Mark DiSalle), Jeff Speakman, John Dye, Mako.

PERFECTLY NORMAL 104
4 SEASONS ENT. February, 1991. Canadian. (Yves Simoneau), Robbie Coltrane, Michael Riley, Deborah Duchene.

Length in Mins.

PRIVATE PROPERTY 90
CINE-CIRCLE. March, 1986. (Alan Roberts), Harlee Mc-Bride, Brett Clark.

PRIVATE SCHOOL 97
UNIVERSAL. July, 1983. (Noel Black), Phoebe Cates, Betsy Russell, Matthew Modine.

PRIVATES ON PARADE 95
ORION CLASSICS. April, 1984. British. (Michael Blakemore), John Cleese, Denis Quilley.

PRIVILEGE 103
ZEITGEIST. January, 1991. (Yvonne Rainer), Alice Spivak, Novella Nelson.

PRIZZI'S HONOR 129
20TH CENTURY FOX. June, 1985. (John Huston), Jack Nicholson, Kathleen Turner, Anjelica Huston.

PROBLEM CHILD 82
UNIVERSAL. July, 1990. (Dennis Dugan), John Ritter, Jack Warden.

PROBLEM CHILD 2 87
UNIVERSAL. July, 1991. (Brian Levant), John Ritter, Jack Warden, Laraine Newman.

PROFOUND DESIRE OF THE GODS, THE 175
EAST-WEST CLASSICS. May, 1988. Japanese; Eng. subtitles. (Shohei Imamura), Rentaro Mikuni, Choichiro Kawarazaki.

PROGRAMMED TO KILL 92
TRANS WORLD ENTERTAINMENT. May, 1987. (Allan Holzman), Robert Ginty, Sandahl Bergman.

PROJECT X 108
20TH CENTURY FOX. April, 1987. (Jonathan Kaplan), Matthew Broderick, Helen Hunt.

PROMISE, A (Ninguen No Yakusoku) 123
NEW YORKER. October, 1988. Japanese. (Yoshishige Yoshida), Choichiro, Orie Sato.

PROMISED LAND 100
VESTRON PICTURES. January, 1988. (Michael Hoffman), Jason Gedrick, Kiefer Sutherland, Meg Ryan.

PROOF 86
FINE LINE FEATURES. March, 1992. Australian. (Jocelyn Moorhouse), Hugo Weaving, Genevieve Picot, Russell Crowe.

PROSPERO'S BOOKS 129
MIRAMAX. November, 1991. British. (Peter Greenaway), John Gielgud, Michael Clark, Michael Blanc.

PROTECTOR, THE 95
WARNER BROS. August, 1985. (James Glickenhaus), Jackie Chan, Danny Aiello.

PROTOCOL 96
WARNER BROS. December, 1984. (Herbert Ross), Goldie Hawn, Chris Sarandon.

PSYCHO II 113
UNIVERSAL. June, 1983. (Richard Franklin), Anthony Perkins, Vera Miles.

PSYCHO III 96
UNIVERSAL. July, 1986. (Anthony Perkins), Anthony Perkins, Diana Scarwid.

PSYCHOS IN LOVE 87
ICN BLEECKER. May, 1987. (Gorman Bechard), Carmine Capobianco, Debi Thibeault.

PUERTO RICAN MAMBO, THE (NOT A MUSICAL) 90
CABRIOLET FILMS. March, 1992. (Ben Model), Luis Caballero.

PULSE 95
COLUMBIA. March, 1988. (Paul Golding), Cliff De Young, Roxanne Hart.

PUMP UP THE VOLUME 100
NEW LINE CINEMA. August, 1990. (Allan Moyle), Christian Slater, Annie Ross, Ellen Greene.

PUMPING IRON II: THE WOMEN 107
CINECOM INTL. May, 1985. (George Butler). Documentary.

PUMPKINHEAD 86
MGM/UA. October, 1988. (Stan Winston), Lance Henriksen, Jeff East.

PUNCHLINE 128
COLUMBIA. September, 1988. (David Seltzer), Sally Field, Tom Hanks.

PUPPET MASTER 90
JGM ENTERPRISES. January, 1990. (David Schmoeller), Paul LeMat, Irene Miracle.

PUPPETOON MOVIE, THE 80
EXPANDED ENTERTAINMENT. June, 1987. Compilation of George Pal animated shorts.

PURE LUCK 96
UNIVERSAL. August, 1991. (Nadia Tass), Martin Short, Danny Glover, Sheila Kelley.

PURPLE HAZE 97
TRIUMPH. November, 1983. (David Burton Morris), Peter Nelson, Chuck McQuarry.

Length in Mins.

PURPLE HEARTS 116
WARNER BROS. May, 1984. (Sidney J. Furie), Ken Wahl, Cheryl Ladd.

PURPLE PEOPLE EATER 92
CONCORDE PICTURES. December, 1988 (Linda Shayne), Ned Beatty, Neil Patrick Harris.

PURPLE RAIN 111
WARNER BROS. July, 1984. (Albert Magnoli), Prince, Apollonia Kotero.

PURPLE ROSE OF CAIRO, THE 82
ORION. March, 1985. (Woody Allen), Mia Farrow, Jeff Daniels, Danny Aiello.

PURSUIT OF D.B. COOPER, THE 100
UNIVERSAL. November, 1981. (Roger Spottiswoode), Robert Duvall, Treat Williams.

Q

Q&A 132
TRI-STAR. April, 1990. (Sidney Lumet), Nick Nolte, Timothy Hutton, Armand Assante.

Q: QUETZALCOATL 93
UFD. October, 1982. (Larry Cohen), David Carradine, Michael Moriarty.

QUARTET 101
NEW WORLD. October, 1981. British-French. (James Ivory), Alan Bates, Maggie Smith.

QUEEN OF HEARTS 103
CINECOM. September, 1989. British. (Jon Amiel), Vittorio Duse, Joseph Long.

QUEENS LOGIC 116
NEW LINE CINEMA. February, 1991. (Steve Rash), Kevin Bacon, Joe Mantegna, John Malkovich.

QUEST FOR FIRE (P) 97
20TH CENTURY FOX. March, 1982. French-Canadian. (Jean-Jacques Annaud), Everett McGill, Rae Dawn Chong.

QUICK CHANGE 88
WARNER BROS. July, 1990. (Howard Franklin, Bill Murray), Bill Murray, Geena Davis, Randy Quaid.

QUICKSILVER 106
COLUMBIA. February, 1986. (Tom Donnelly), Kevin Bacon, Jami Gertz.

QUIET COOL 80
NEW LINE CINEMA. November, 1986. (Clay Borris), James Remar, Adam Coleman Howard.

QUIET EARTH, THE 91
SKOURAS PICTURES. March, 1986. (Geoff Murphy), Bruno Laurence, Alison Routledge.

QUIGLEY DOWN UNDER (P) 119
MGM. October, 1990. (Simon Wincer), Tom Selleck, Alan Rickman, Laura San Giacomo.

QUILOMBO 114
NEW YORKER FILMS. March, 1986. Portuguese; Eng. titles. (Carlos Diegues). Antonio Pompeo.

R

RABID GRANNIES 83
TROMA. September, 1989. (Emmanuel Kervyn), Catherine Aymerie, Caroline Braekman.

RACE FOR GLORY 96
NEW CENTURY/VISTA. August, 1989. (Rocky Lang), Alex McArthur, Peter Berg.

RACHEL PAPERS, THE 95
MGM/UA. May, 1989. British. (Damian Harris), Dexter Fletcher, Ione Skye, James Spader.

RACHEL RIVER 90
TAURUS. January, 1989. (Sandy Smolan), Pamela Reed, Viveca Lindfors, Craig T. Nelson.

RACING WITH THE MOON 108
PARAMOUNT. March, 1984. (Richard Benjamin), Sean Penn, Elizabeth McGovern.

RAD 91
TRI-STAR. March, 1986. (Hal Needham), Bill Allen, Lori Loughlin.

RADIO DAYS 85
ORION. January, 1987. (Woody Allen), Mia Farrow, Seth Green, Julie Kavner, Dianne Wiest.

RADIO FLYER (P) 120
COLUMBIA. February, 1992. (Richard Donner), Elijah Wood, Lorraine Bracco, Joseph Mazzello.

RADIOACTIVE DREAMS (P) 98
DE LAURENTIIS. September, 1986. (Albert Pyun), John Stockwell, Michael Dudikoff.

	Length in Mins.

RAGE 91
GEL INTL. October, 1986. Italian; Spanish; dubbed in English. (Anthony Richmond = Tonino Ricci), Conrad Nicholas, Stelio Candelli.

RAGE IN HARLEM, A 115
MIRAMAX. May, 1991. (Bill Duke), Forest Whitaker, Gregory Hines, Robin Givens.

RAGE OF HONOR 91
TRANS WORLD ENTERTAINMENT. February, 1987. (Gordon Hessler), Sho Kosugi, Lewis Van Bergen.

RAGGEDY MAN 94
UNIVERSAL. September, 1981. (Jack Fisk), Sissy Spacek, Eric Roberts, Henry Thomas.

RAGGEDY RAWNEY, THE 102
L. W. BLAIR PRODS. February, 1990. British. (Bob Hoskins), Bob Hoskins, Dexter Fletcher.

RAGING BULL 128
UNITED ARTISTS. November, 1980. (Martin Scorsese), Robert De Niro, Cathy Moriarty. B&W.

RAGTIME (T-AO) 155
PARAMOUNT. November, 1981. (Milos Forman), James Cagney, Elizabeth McGovern, Howard E. Rollins, Brad Dourif.

RAIDERS OF THE LOST ARK (P) 115
PARAMOUNT. June, 1981. (Steven Spielberg), Harrison Ford, Karen Allen.

RAIN KILLER, THE 93
CONCORDE. September, 1990. (Ken Stein), Ray Sharkey, David Beecroft, Michael Chiklis.

RAIN MAN 140
MGM/UA. December, 1988. (Barry Levinson), Dustin Hoffman, Tom Cruise.

RAINBOW, THE 112
VESTRON. May, 1989. British. (Ken Russell), Sammi Davis, Paul McGann, Amanda Donohoe, Glenda Jackson.

RAINBOW BRITE AND THE STAR STEALER 97
WARNER BROS. November, 1985. (Bernard Deyries, Kimio Yabuki). Animated.

RAINY DAY FRIENDS 90
POWERDANCE CORP. July, 1986. (Gary Kent), Easi Morales, Chuck Bail.

RAISE THE RED LANTERN 125
ORION CLASSICS. March, 1992. Hong Kong-Chinese-Mandarin. (Zhang Yimou), Gong Li, Ma Jingwu, He Califei.

RAISE THE TITANIC (T) 112
ASSOCIATED FILM DIST. August, 1980. (Jerry Jameson), Jason Robards, Richard Jordan, David Selby.

RAISING ARIZONA 94
20TH CENTURY FOX. March, 1987. (Joel Coen), Nicolas Cage, Holly Hunter, Trey Wilson.

RAISING CAIN 95
UNIVERSAL. August, 1992. (Brian DePalma), John Lithgow, Lolita Davidovich, Steven Bauer.

RAMBLING ROSE 112
NEW LINE CINEMA. October, 1991. (Martha Coolidge), Laura Dern, Robert Duvall, Lukas Haas, Diane Ladd.

RAMBLIN' GAL 106
AQUARIUS. June, 1991. (Roberto Monticello), Lu Ann Horstman Person), Deborah Strang, Andrew Krawetz.

RAMBO: FIRST BLOOD PART II 95
TRI-STAR. May, 1985. (George Pan Cosmatos), Sylvester Stallone, Richard Crenna.

RAMBO III (J-D-C) 101
TRI-STAR. May, 1988. (Peter MacDonald), Sylvester Stallone, Richard Crenna.

RAN (WS) 160
ORION CLASSICS. December, 1985. Japanese; Eng. titles. (Akira Kurosawa), Tatsuya Nakadai.

RAPID FIRE 95
20TH CENTURY FOX. August, 1992. (Dwight H. Little), Brandon Lee, Powers Boothe, Nick Mancuso.

RAPPIN' 92
CANNON GROUP. May, 1985. (Joel Silberg), Mario Van Peebles, Tasia Valenza.

RAPTURE, THE 102
NEW LINE CINEMA. October, 1991. (Michael Tolkin), Mimi Rogers, David Duchovny, Patrick Bauchau.

RASPAD 103
MK2. April, 1992. Soviet. (Mikhail Belikov), Sergei Shakurov, Tatiana Kochemasova.

RATBOY 104
WARNER BROS. October, 1986. (Sondra Locke), Sondra Locke, Robert Townsend.

RATE IT X 95
INTERAMA INC. October, 1986. (Lucy Winer, Paula de Koenigsberg). Documentary.

	Length in Mins.

RAW 91
PARAMOUNT. December, 1987. (Robert Townsend), Eddie Murphy.

RAW DEAL 106
DE LAURENTIIS. June, 1986. (John Irvin), Arnold Schwarzenegger, Kathryn Harrold.

RAW NERVE 91
A.I.P. STUDIOS. May, 1991. (David A. Prior), Glenn Ford, Ted Prior, Sandahl Bergman.

RAWHEAD REX 89
EMPIRE PICTURES. January, 1987. British. (George Pavlov), David Dukes, Kelly Piper.

RAZOR'S EDGE, THE 128
COLUMBIA. October, 1984. (John Byrum), Bill Murray, Theresa Russell, Catherine Hicks.

RAZORBACK (P) 94
WARNER BROS. November, 1984. Australian. (Russell Mulcahy), Gregory Harrison, Arkie Whiteley.

RE-ANIMATOR 86
EMPIRE PICTURES. October, 1985. (Stuart Gordon), Jeffrey Combs, Bruce Abbott.

REAL GENIUS 104
TRI-STAR. August, 1985. (Martha Coolidge), Val Kilmer, Gabe Jarret.

REAL MEN 96
MGM/UA. September, 1987. (Dennis Feldman), James Belushi, John Ritter.

REBEL LOVE 80
TROMA. June, 1986. (Milton Bagby, Jr.), Jamie Rose, Terence Knox.

RECKLESS 90
MGM/UA. February, 1984. (James Foley), Aidan Quinn, Daryl Hannah.

RECORD, THE 92
ROYAL STAR PRODUCTIONS. May, 1988. German; Eng. subtitles. (Daniel Helfer), Uwe Ochsenknect, Laszlo I. Kisch. B&W.

RECRUITS 82
CONCORDE. October, 1986. (Rafal Zielinski), Steve Osmond, Doug Annear.

RED DAWN 114
MGM/UA. August, 1984. (John Milius), Patrick Swayze, C. Thomas Howell.

RED-HEADED STRANGER 105
ALIVE FILMS. February, 1987. (William Wittliff), Willie Nelson, Morgan Fairchild.

RED HEAT 103
TRI-STAR. June, 1988. (Walter Hill), Arnold Schwarzenegger, James Belushi.

RED SCORPION 102
SHAPIRO GLICKENHAUS ENTERTAINMENT. April, 1989. (Joseph Zito), Dolph Lundgren, M. Emmet Walsh.

RED SONJA 89
MGM/UA. July, 1985. (Richard Fleischer), Brigitte Nielsen, Arnold Schwarzenegger.

RED SORGHUM (Hong Gaoliang) 91
NEW YORKER. October, 1988. Mandarin; Eng. subtitles. (Zhang Yimou), Gong Li, Jiang Wen.

RED SURF 104
ARROWHEAD ENTERTAINMENT. June, 1990. (H. Gordon Boos), George Clooney, Doug Savant.

REDS 199
PARAMOUNT. December, 1981. (Warren Beatty), Warren Beatty, Diane Keaton, Maureen Stapleton.

REFLECTING SKIN, THE 93
PRESTIGE. June, 1991. British. (Philip Ridley), Viggo Mortensen, Lindsay Duncan, Jeremy Cooper.

REFORM SCHOOL GIRLS 94
NEW WORLD PICTURES. August, 1986. (Tom De Simone), Linda Carol, Wendy Williams.

REGARDING HENRY 107
PARAMOUNT. July, 1991. (Mike Nichols), Harrison Ford, Annette Bening, Bill Nunn, Mikki Allen.

REJUVENATOR, THE 86
SVS FILMS. July, 1988. (Brian Thomas Jones), Vivian Lanko, John MacKay.

RELENTLESS 90
NEW LINE. August, 1989. (William Lustig), Judd Nelson, Robert Loggia.

REMBETIKO 101
ATHOS ENTERTAINMENT. May, 1985. Greek; Eng. titles. (Costas Ferris), Sotiria Leonardou.

REMO WILLIAMS: THE ADVENTURE BEGINS 121
ORION. October, 1985. (Guy Hamilton), Fred Ward, Joel Grey.

	Length in Mins.

RIO 100 90
NEW YORKER FILMS. August, 1987. (Nelson Pereira dos Santos), Glauce Rocha, Roberto Batalin.

RISKY BUSINESS 96
WARNER BROS. August, 1983. (Paul Brickman), Tom Cruise, Rebecca DeMornay.

RITA, SUE AND BOB TOO 95
ORION CLASSICS. July, 1987. British. (Alan Clarke), Michelle Holmes, Siobhan Finneran.

RIVER, THE 122
UNIVERSAL. December, 1984. (Mark Rydell), Mel Gibson, Sissy Spacek, Scott Glenn.

RIVER OF DEATH 103
CANNON. September, 1989. (Steve Carver), Michael Dudikoff, Robert Vaughn, Donald Pleasence.

RIVER OF FIRELIES 115
SHOCHIKU COMPANY. November, 1988. Japanese; Eng. titles. (Eizo Sugawa), Takayuki Sakazume, Rentaro Mikuni.

RIVER RAT, THE 93
PARAMOUNT. September, 1984. (Tom Rickman), Tommy Lee Jones, Martha Plimpton.

RIVER'S EDGE 99
ISLAND PICTURES. May, 1987. (Tim Hunter), Crispin Glover, Keanu Reaves, Dennis Hopper.

RIVERBEND 100
PRISM ENTERTAINMENT. March, 1990. (San Firstenberg), Steve James, Margaret Avery.

ROAD HOUSE (P) 114
MGM/UA. May, 1989. (Rowdy Herrington), Patrick Swayze, Kelly Lynch, Sam Elliott.

ROAD WARRIOR, THE 94
WARNER BROS. May, 1982. Australian. (George Miller), Mel Gibson, Bruce Spence.

ROADHOUSE 66 96
ATLANTIC. July, 1984. (Mark Robinson), Willem Dafoe, Judge Reinhold, Karen Lee.

ROADIE (P) 105
UNITED ARTISTS. June, 1980. (Alan Rudolph), Meat Loaf, Kaki Hunter.

ROADSIDE PROPHETS 96
FINE LINE FEATURES. March, 1992. (Abbe Wool), John Doe, Adam Horovitz, David Anthony Marshall.

ROBIN HOOD: PRINCE OF THIEVES 141
WARNER BROS. June, 1991. (Kevin Reynolds), Kevin Costner, Morgan Freeman, Alan Rickman.

ROBOCOP 103
ORION. July, 1987. (Paul Verhoeven), Peter Weller, Nancy Allen.

ROBOCOP 2 118
ORION. June, 1990. (Irvin Kershner), Peter Weller, Nancy Allen.

ROBOT CARNIVAL 91
STREAMLINE. February, 1991. Japanese. (Various directors), Animated.

ROBOT JOX 84
TRIUMPH. November, 1990. (Stuart Gordon), Gary Graham, Anne-Marie Johnson, Paul Koslo.

ROCK-A-DOODLE 77
SAMUEL GOLDWYN CO. April, 1992. (Don Bluth), Animated.

ROCK SOUP 81
Z FILMS. April, 1992. (Lech Kowalski), Documentary.

ROCKET GIBRALTAR 100
COLUMBIA. September, 1988. (Daniel Petrie), Burt Lancaster, Suzy Amis, Patricia Clarkson.

ROCKETEER, THE (P) 108
BUENA VISTA. June, 1991. (Joe Johnston), Bill Campbell, Jennifer Connelly, Alan Arkin, Timothy Dalton.

ROCKULA 91
CANNON. February, 1990. (Luca Bercovici), Dean Cameron, Toni Basil.

ROCKY III (P) 99
MGM/UA. May, 1982. (Sylvester Stallone), Sylvester Stallone, Talia Shire.

ROCKY IV 91
MGM/UA. November, 1985. (Sylvester Stallone), Sylvester Stallone, Talia Shire.

ROCKY V 103
MGM/UA. November, 1990. (John G. Avildsen), Sylvester Stallone, Talia Shire, Burt Young.

RODRIGO D: NO FUTURE 92
KINO INTL. January, 1991. Colombian-Spanish. (Victor Manuel Gaviria), Ramiro Menese, Carlos Maria Resrepo.

ROGER CORMAN'S FRANKENSTEIN UNBOUND 85
20TH CENTURY FOX. November, 1990. (Roger Corman), John Hurt, Raul Julia, Jason Patric.

	Length in Mins.

ROGER & ME 90
WARNER BROS. December, 1989. (Michael Moore), Documentary.

ROLLING VENGEANCE 90
APOLLO PICTURES. April, 1987. (Steven H. Stern), Don Michael Paul, Lawrence Dane.

ROLLOVER (P) 118
WARNER BROS. December, 1981. (Alan J. Pakula), Jane Fonda, Kris Kristofferson.

ROMANCING THE STONE (P) 105
20TH CENTURY FOX. March, 1984. (Robert Zemeckis), Michael Douglas, Kathleen Turner, Danny DeVito.

ROMANTIC COMEDY 103
MGM/UA. October, 1983. (Arthur Hiller), Dudley Moore, Mary Steenburgen.

ROMEO & JULIA 94
KAUFMAN FILMS. February, 1992. (Kevin Kaufman), Bob Koherr, Ivana Kane, Patrick McGuinness.

ROMERO 105
FOUR SEASONS ENTERTAINMENT. August, 1989. (John Duigan), Raul Julia, Richard Jordan.

ROOFTOPS 95
NEW VISIONS. March, 1989. (Robert Wise), Jason Gedrick, Troy Beyer.

ROOKIE, THE (P) 121
WARNER BROS. December, 1990. (Clint Eastwood), Clint Eastwood, Charlie Sheen, Raul Julia, Sonia Braga.

ROOM WITH A VIEW, A 115
CINECOM INTL. March, 1986. British. (James Ivory), Maggie Smith, Helena Bonham Carter, Julian Sands.

RORRET 105
NEW YORKER. February, 1989. Italian; Eng. titles. (Fulvio Wetzl), Lou Castel, Ann Galiena.

ROSA LUXEMBURG 122
NEW YORKER FILMS. May, 1987. German; Eng. titles. (Margarethe von Trotta), Barbara Sukowa, Daniel Olbrychski.

ROSALIE GOES SHOPPING 94
FOUR SEASONS ENTERTAINMENT. February, 1990. W. German. (Percy Adlon), Marianne Sagebrecht, Brad Davis, Judge Reinhold.

ROSARY MURDERS, THE 105
NEW LINE CINEMA. August, 1987. (Fred Walton), Donald Sutherland, Charles Durning.

ROSE GARDEN, THE 112
CANNON/PATHE. December, 1989. West German-U.S. (Fons Rademakers), Liv Ullman, Maximillian Schell.

ROSE KING, THE 115
FILMVERLAG FUTURA. December, 1987. German. (Werner Schroeter), Magdelena Montezuma, Antonio Orlando.

ROSEBUD BEACH HOTEL, THE 87
ALMI PICTURES. November, 1984. (Harry Hurwitz), Colleen Camp, Peter Scolari.

ROSENCRANTZ & GUILDENSTERN ARE DEAD 118
CINECOM. February, 1991. British. (Tom Stoppard), Gary Oldman, Tim Roth, Richard Dreyfuss.

ROUGE OF THE NORTH 106
GREYCAT. December, 1991. Chinese. (Fred Tan), Hsia Wen-Shi, Msu Ming, Kao-Chich.

ROUGH CUT 111
PARAMOUNT. June, 1980. (Donald Siegel), Burt Reynolds, Lesley-Anne Down, David Niven.

'ROUND MIDNIGHT (P) 133
WARNER BROS. October, 1986. French. (Bertrand Tavernier), Dexter Gordon, François Cluzet.

ROUTE ONE/USA 255
INTERAMA. November, 1990. (Robert Kramer), Documentary.

ROVER DANGERFIELD 74
WARNER BROS. August, 1991. (Jim George, Bob Seeley), Animated.

ROXANNE (P) 107
COLUMBIA. June, 1987. (Fred Schepisi), Steve Martin, Daryl Hannah, Rick Rossovich, Shelley Duvall.

RUBIN & ED 82
I.R.S. May, 1992. (Trent Harris), Crispin Glover, Howard Hesseman, Karen Black.

RUBY 110
TRIUMPH. March, 1992. (John Mackenzie), Danny Aiello, Sherilyn Fenn, Arliss Howard.

RUDE AWAKENING 100
ORION. August, 1989. (Aaron Russo, David Greenwalt), Cheech Marin, Eric Roberts, Julie Hagerty.

RUMBLE FISH 94
UNIVERSAL. October, 1983. (Francis Coppola), Matt Dillon, Mickey Rourke. B&W.

	Length in Mins.

RUMPLESTILTSKIN 84
CANNON GROUP. April, 1987. (David Irving), Amy Irving, Billy Barty.

RUN 91
BUENA VISTA. Feburary, 1991. (Geoff Burrowes), Patrick Dempsey, Kelly Preston, Ken Pogue.

RUN OF THE HOUSE 109
ZOO PRODS. LTD. May, 1992. (James M. Felter), Alan Edwards, Lisa-Marie Felter, Harry A. Winter.

RUNAWAY (P) 100
TRI-STAR. December, 1984. (Michael Crichton), Tom Selleck, Cynthia Rhodes.

RUNAWAY TRAIN 111
CANNON FILMS. December, 1985. (Andrei Konchalovsky), Jon Voight, Eric Roberts, Rebecca DeMornay.

RUNESTONE, THE 101
HYPERION PICTURES. February, 1992. (Willard Carroll), Peter Riegert, Joan Severance, Alexander Godunov.

RUNNER, THE (DAWANDEH) 94
INTERNATIONAL HOME CINEMA. March, 1987. In Farsi. (Amir Naderi), Madjid Niroumand, Mousa Torkiradeh.

RUNNIN' KIND, THE 101
MGM/UA. September, 1989. (Max Tash), David Packer, Pleasant Gehman.

RUNNING BRAVE 105
BUENA VISTA. November, 1983. Canadian. (D.S. Everett, Donald Shebib), Robby Benson, Pat Hingle.

RUNNING HOT 95
NEW LINE CINEMA. January, 1984. (Mark Griffiths), Eric Stoltz, Stuart Margolin.

RUNNING MAN, THE 101
TRI-STAR. November, 1987. (Paul Michael Glaser), Arnold Schwarzenegger, Maria Conchita Alonso.

RUNNING ON EMPTY 116
WARNER BROS. September, 1988. (Sidney Lumet), Christine Lahti, River Phoenix, Judd Hirsch.

RUNNING SCARED (P) 106
MGM/UA. June, 1986. (Peter Hyams), Gregory Hines, Billy Crystal.

RUSH 77
CINEMA SHARES INTL. October, 1984. (Anthony Richmond, Tonino Ricci), Conrad Nichols, Gordon Mitchell.

RUSH 120
MGM. December, 1991. (Lili Fini Zanuck), Jason Patric, Jennifer Jason Leigh, Sam Elliott.

RUSSIA HOUSE, THE (TV) 123
MGM. December, 1990. (Fred Schepisi), Sean Connery, Michelle Pfeiffer, Roy Scheider.

RUSSICUM 111
TRI-STAR. November, 1989. Italian. (Pasquale Squitieri), Treat Williams, F. Murray Abraham.

RUSSKIES 99
NEW CENTURY/VISTA FILM CO. November, 1987. (Rick Rosenthal), Whip Hubley, Leaf Phoenix.

RUSTLERS' RHAPSODY 88
PARAMOUNT. May, 1985. (Hugh Wilson), Tom Berenger, G. W. Bailey.

RUTHLESS PEOPLE 93
BUENA VISTA. June, 1986. (Jim Abrahams, David Zucker, Jerry Zucker), Danny DeVito, Bette Midler.

RUTHLESS ROMANCE 140
IFEX. September, 1985. Russian; Eng. titles. (Eldar Ryazanov), Nikita Mikhalkov.

S

S.O.B. (P) 121
PARAMOUNT. July, 1981. (Blake Edwards), Julie Andrews, William Holden, Robert Preston.

SACRIFICE, THE 145
ORION CLASSICS. November, 1986. French-Swedish; Eng. titles. (Andrei Tarkovsky), Erland Josephson, Susan Fleetwood.

SAHARA 104
MGM/UA. March, 1984. (Andrew V. McLaglen), Brooke Shields, Lambert Wilson.

ST. ELMO'S FIRE (P) 108
COLUMBIA. June, 1985. (Joel Schumacher), Rob Lowe, Demi Moore, Andrew McCarthy.

SALAAM BOMBAY! 113
CINECOM. October, 1988. Indian; Eng. subtitles. (Mira Nair), Shafiq Syed, Sarfuddin Qurrassi.

SALSA 97
CANNON GROUP. May, 1988. (Boaz Davidson), Robby Rosa, Rodney Harvey.

SALOME'S LAST DANCE 89
VESTRON PICTURES. May, 1988. British. (Ken Russell), Glenda Jackson, Stratford Johns.

SALVADOR 123
HEMDALE RELEASING. March, 1986. (Oliver Stone), James Woods, James Belushi, John Savage.

SALVATION! 80
CIRCLE RELEASING CORP. May, 1987. (Beth B.), Stephen McHattie, Dominique Davalos.

SAM MARLOW, PRIVATE EYE (a.k.a. The Man With Bogart's Face) 111
20TH CENTURY FOX. October, 1980. (Andrew J. Fenady), Robert Sacchi, Franco Nero.

SAM'S SON 104
INVICTUS ENT. August, 1984. (Michael Landon), Eli Wallach, Anne Jackson.

SAMMY AND ROSIE GET LAID 100
CINECOM PICTURES. October, 1987. British. (Stephen Frears), Shashi Kapoor, Claire Bloom.

SAMUEL BECKETT: SILENCE TO SILENCE 98
RTE-TV. April, 1987. Irish. (Sean O'Mordha). Documentary.

SAND AND BLOOD 100
NEW YORKER. December, 1989. French. (Jeanne Nainchrik), Sami Frey, Patrick Catalifo.

SANS SOLEIL 100
NEW YORKER. August, 1984. French; Eng. narration. (Chris Marker).

SANSHIRO, SUAGATA PART 2 83
R5/S8. January, 1989 release of a 1945 film. Japanese; Eng. titles. (Akira Kurosawa), Susumu Fujita, Denjiro Okochi.

SANTA CLAUS: THE MOVIE (J-D-C) 112
TRI-STAR. November, 1985. (Jeannot Szwarc), David Huddleston, Dudley Moore.

SANTA FE 110
ROXIE RELEASING. July, 1988. German; Eng. subtitles. (Alex Corti), Gabriel Barylli, Doris Buchrucker.

SATAN 106
RUSSIMPEX. June, 1992. Russian. (Viktor Aristov), Sergei Kuprianov, Svetlana Bragarnik, Veniamin Malotschevski.

SATISFACTION 92
20TH CENTURY FOX. February, 1988. (Joan Freeman), Justine Bateman, Liam Neeson.

SATURDAY NIGHT AT THE PALACE 88
INTERNATIONAL FILM MARKETING. May, 1988. South African. (Robert Davies), Bill Flynn, John Kani.

SATURN 3 88
ASSOCIATED FILM DISTRIBUTION. March, 1980. (Stanley Donen), Farrah Fawcett, Kirk Douglas.

SAVAGE BEACH 95
MALIBU BAY. October, 1989. (Andy Sidaris), Dona Speir, Hope Marie Carlton.

SAVAGE HARVEST 86
20TH CENTURY FOX. May, 1981. (Robert Collins), Tom Skerritt, Michelle Phillips.

SAVAGE ISLAND 74
EMPIRE PICTURES. September, 1985. (Edward Muller, Nicholas Beardsley), Linda Blair, Anthony Steffen.

SAVAGE STREETS 93
MOTION PICTURE MARKETING. October, 1984. (Danny Steinmann), Linda Blair, John Vernon.

SAVE AND PROTECT 167
INTL. FILM CIRCUIT. July, 1992. Russian. (Aleksandr Sokurov), Cecile Zervudacki, Robert Vaab.

SAVING GRACE 112
COLUMBIA. July, 1986. (Robert M. Young), Tom Conti, Giancarlo Giannini.

SAY AMEN, SOMEBODY 100
UA CLASSICS. January, 1984. (George T. Nierenberg). Documentary.

SAY ANYTHING 100
20TH CENTURY FOX. April, 1989. (Cameron Crowe), John Cusack, Ione Skye.

SAY YES 88
CINTEL FILMS. March, 1986. (Larry Yust), Lissa Layng, Art Hindle, Jonathan Winters.

SCALPS 83
21ST CENTURY DIST. December, 1983. (Fred Olen Ray), Kirk Alyn, Carroll Borland.

SCANDAL 114
MIRAMAX. April, 1989. British. (Michael Caton-Jones), John Hurt, Joanne Whalley-Kilmer, Bridget Fonda.

SCANDALOUS 94
ORION. January, 1984. (Rob Cohen), Robert Hays, John Gielgud, Pamela Stephenson.

SCANNERS 103
AVCO-EMBASSY. January, 1981. Canadian. (David Cronenberg), Jennifer O'Neill, Stephen Lack.

Length in Mins.

SCANNERS II: THE NEW ORDER 104
TRITON. June, 1991. Canadian. (Christian Duguay, David Hewlett), Yvan Ponton, Deborah Raffin.

SCARECROW (CHUCHELA) 127
IFEX. June, 1987. Russian. (Rolan Bykov), Christina Orbakaite, Yuri Nikulin.

SCARFACE (P) 169
UNIVERSAL. December, 1983. (Brian De Palma), Al Pacino, Steven Bauer, Michelle Pfeiffer.

SCENE OF THE CRIME 90
GRANGE/KINO. January, 1987. French; Eng. titles. (Andre Techine), Catherine Deneuve, Danielle Darrieux.

SCENES FROM A MALL 87
BUENA VISTA. February, 1991. (Paul Mazursky), Bette Midler, Woody Allen.

SCENES FROM THE CLASS STRUGGLE IN BEVERLY HILLS 102
CINECOM. June, 1989. (Paul Bartel), Jacqueline Bisset, Ray Sharkey, Robert Beltran.

SCENES FROM THE GOLDMINE 99
HEMDALE. September, 1987. (Marc Rocco), Catherine Mary Stewart, Alex Rocco.

SCHOOL DAZE 120
COLUMBIA. February, 1988. (Spike Lee), Larry Fishburne, Giancarlo Esposito, Spike Lee.

SCHOOL SPIRIT 90
CONCORDE-CINEMA GROUP. October, 1985. (Alan Holleb), Tom Nolan, Elizabeth Foxx.

SCISSORS 105
DDM FILM CORP. March, 1991. (Frank De Felitta), Sharon Stone, Steve Railsback, Ronny Cox.

SCORPION 98
CROWN INTL. December, 1986. (William Rieard), Tonny Tulleners, Don Murray.

SCREEN TEST 96
CINTEL. March, 1986. (Sam Auster), Michael Allan Bloom, Monique Gabrielle.

SCROOGED 101
PARAMOUNT. November, 1988. (Richard Donner), Bill Murray, Karen Allen.

SCRUBBERS 90
ORION CLASSICS. February, 1984. British. (Mai Zetterling), Amanda York, Chrissie Cotterill.

SEA AND POISON, THE 121
GADES FILMS. July, 1987. Japanese. (Kei Kumai), Ken Watanabe, Mikio Narita.

SEA OF LOVE 113
UNIVERSAL. September, 1989. (Harold Becker), Al Pacino, Ellen Barkin, John Goodman.

SEA WOLVES THE 120
PARAMOUNT. June, 1981. (Andrew V. McLaglen), Gregory Peck, Roger Moore, David Niven.

SEARCH FOR SIGNS OF INTELLIGENT LIFE IN THE UNIVERSE, THE 110
ORION CLASSICS. September, 1991. (John Gailey), Lily Tomlin.

SEASON OF FEAR 89
MGM/UA. May, 1989. (Doug Campbell), Michael Bowen, Ray Wise.

SECOND CIRCLE, THE 92
INTL. FILM CIRCUIT. January, 1992. (Aleksandr Sokhurov), Petr Alexandrov.

SECOND HAND HEARTS 102
PARAMOUNT. May, 1981. (Hal Ashby), Robert Blake, Barbara Harris.

SECOND SIGHT 83
WARNER BROS. November, 1989. (Joel Zwick), John Larroquette, Bronson Pinchot.

SECOND THOUGHTS 109
UNIVERSAL. March, 1983. (Lawrence Turman), Lucie Arnaz, Craig Wasson.

SECOND VICTORY, THE 112
FILMWORLD. June, 1987. British. (Gerald Thomas), Anthony Andrews, Max Von Sydow, Helmut Griem.

SECRET ADMIRER 98
ORION. June, 1985. (David Greenwalt), C. Thomas Howell, Lori Loughlin, Dee Wallace Stone.

SECRET FRIENDS 97
BRIARPATCH. February, 1992. British. (Dennis Potter), Alan Bates, Gina Bellman, Frances Barber.

SECRET HONOR 90
CINECOM INTL. June, 1985. (Robert Altman), Philip Baker Hall.

SECRET OF MY SUCCESS 110
UNIVERSAL. April, 1987. (Herbert Ross), Michael J. Fox, Helen Slater, Richard Jordan.

Length in Mins.

SECRET OF NIMH, THE 83
MGM/UA. July, 1982. (Don Bluth). Animated.

SECRET OF THE SWORD, THE 87
ATLANTIC RELEASING. May, 1985. (Five directors), Animated.

SECRET PLACES 96
20TH CENTURY FOX. May, 1985. (Zelda Barron), Maria-Theres Relin, Tara MacGowran.

SECRET POLICEMAN'S OTHER BALL, THE 91
MIRAMAX. June, 1982. British. (Julian Temple, Roger Graef), John Cleese, Peter Cook, Michael Palin, Sting.

SECRETS 78
SAMUEL GOLDWYN. August, 1984. (Gavin Millar), Helen Lindsay, John Horsley.

SEDUCTION, THE 104
EMBASSY. January, 1982. (David Schmoeller), Morgan Fairchild, Michael Sarrazin.

SEDUCTION: THE CRUEL WOMEN 90
FIRST RUN FEATURES. November, 1989. German. (Elfi Mikesch), Mechthild Grossman, Udo Kier.

SEE NO EVIL, HEAR NO EVIL 103
TRI-STAR. May, 1989. (Arthur Hiller), Gene Wilder, Richard Pryor.

SEE YOU IN THE MORNING 119
WARNER BROS. April, 1989. (Alan J. Pakula), Jeff Bridges, Alice Krige.

SEEMS LIKE OLD TIMES 102
COLUMBIA. December, 1980. (Jay Sandrich), Goldie Hawn, Chevy Chase, Charles Grodin.

SENDER, THE 95
PARAMOUNT. October, 1982. British. (Roger Christian), Kathryn Harrold, Zeljko Ivanek.

SENSE OF FREEDOM, A 85
HAND MADE FILMS. October, 1985. (John MacKenzie), David Hayman, Alex Norton.

SEPTEMBER 82
ORION. December, 1987. (Woody Allen), Denholm Elliott, Dianne Wiest, Mia Farrow, Elaine Stritch.

SERA POSIBLE EL SUR 86
THE CINEMA GUILD. August, 1987. (Stefan Paul). Documentary.

SERIAL 91
PARAMOUNT. March, 1980. (Bill Persky), Martin Mull, Tuesday Weld, Sally Kellerman.

SERPENT AND THE RAINBOW, THE 98
UNIVERSAL. February, 1988. (Wes Craven), Bill Pullman, Cathy Tyson.

SESAME STREET PRESENTS: FOLLOW THAT BIRD ... 88
WARNER BROS. August, 1985. (Ken Kwapis), Caroll Spinney, Jim Henson.

SEVEN HOURS TO JUDGMENT 88
TRANS WORLD ENTERTAINMENT. September, 1988. (Beau Bridges), Beau Bridges, Ron Leibman.

SEVEN MINUTES IN HEAVEN 90
WARNER BROS. May, 1986. (Linda Feferman), Jennifer Connelly, Maddie Corman.

SEVENTH SIGN, THE (P) 97
TRI-STAR. April, 1988. (Carl Schultz), Demi Moore, Michael Biehn.

SEX APPEAL 84
SEYMOUR BORDE. May, 1986. (Chuck Vincent), Louie Bonnano, Tally Brittany.

SEX, DRUGS, ROCK & ROLL 96
AVENUE. September, 1991. (John McNaughton), Eric Bogosian.

SEX, LIES AND VIDEOTAPE 101
MIRAMAX. August, 1989. (Steven Soderbergh), James Spader, Andie MacDowell, Peter Gallagher, Laura San Giacomo.

SHADEY 90
SKOURAS PICTURES. June, 1987. British. (Philip Saville), Antony Sher, Billie Whitelaw.

SHADOW OF ANGELS 108
ALBATROS/ARTCOFILM. March, 1992. German. (Daniel Schmid), Ingrid Craven, Rainer Werner Fassbinder, Klaus Lowitsch.

SHADOW OF CHINA 100
NEW LINE CINEMA. March, 1991. Japanese. (Mitsuo Yanagimachi), John Lone, Koichi Sato, Sammi Davis.

SHADOW PLAY 95
NEW WORLD PICTURES. September, 1986. (Susan Shadburne), Dee Wallace Stone, Cloris Leachman.

SHADOWS AND FOG 86
ORION. March, 1992. (Woody Allen), Woody Allen, Mia Farrow, John Cusack, Lily Tomlin. B & W.

	Length in Mins.

SILENT MADNESS 91
ALMI PICTURES. November, 1984. (Simon Nuchtern), Belinda Montgomery.

SILENT NIGHT, DEADLY NIGHT 79
TRI-STAR. November, 1984. (Charles E. Sellier, Jr.), Lilyian Chauvan, Gilmer McCormick.

SILENT NIGHT, DEADLY NIGHT PART II 88
ASCOT ENTERTAINMENT. April, 1987. (Lee Harry), Eric Freeman, James L. Newman.

SILENT RAGE 100
COLUMBIA. April, 1982. (Michael Miller), Chuck Norris, Ron Silver.

SILK ROAD, THE 126
TRIMARK. January, 1992. Japanese, 1988. (Junya Sato), Koichi Sato, Toshiyuki Nishida.

SILKWOOD (P) 131
20TH CENTURY FOX. December, 1983. (Mike Nichols), Meryl Streep, Kurt Russell, Cher.

SILVER BULLET 95
PARAMOUNT. October, 1985. (Daniel Attias), Gary Busey, Everett McGill, Corey Haim.

SILVER CITY 110
SAMUEL GOLDWYN CO. May, 1985. Australian. (Sophie Turkiewicz), Gosia Dobrowolska, Ivar Kants.

SILVER DREAM RACER 101
ALMI FILMS. September, 1983. British. (David Wickes), David Essex, Beau Bridges.

SILVERADO (T) 132
COLUMBIA. July, 1985. (Lawrence Kasdan), Kevin Kline, Scott Glenn, Danny Glover, Kevin Costner.

SIMON 97
WARNER BROS. March, 1980. (Marshall Brickman), Alan Arkin, Madeline Kahn.

SINCERELY CHARLOTTE 92
NEW LINE CINEMA. July, 1986. French; Eng. titles. (Caroline Huppert), Isabelle Huppert.

SINFUL LIFE, A 100
NEW LINE CINEMA. June, 1989. (William Schreiner), Anita Morris, Rick Overton, Dennis Christopher.

SING 97
TRI-STAR. March, 1989. (Richard Baskin), Lorraine Bracco, Peter Dobson.

SINGING ON THE TREADMILL 91
HUNGAROFILM. July, 1987. Hungarian; Eng. titles. (Gyula Gazdag), Ewald Schorm, Lili Monori.

SINGING THE BLUES IN RED 110
ANGELIKA FILMS. January, 1988. German; Eng. subtitles. (Kenneth Loach), Gerulf Pannach, Fabienne Babe.

SINGLE WHITE FEMALE 107
COLUMBIA. August, 1992. (Barbet Schroeder), Bridget Fonda, Jennifer Jason Leigh, Steven Weber.

SISTER ACT 100
BUENA VISTA. May, 1992. (Emile Ardolino), Whoopi Goldberg, Maggie Smith, Harvey Keitel, Kathy Najimy.

SISTER, SISTER 91
NEW WORLD PICTURES. February, 1988. (Bill Condon), Eric Stoltz, Jennifer Jason Leigh.

SISTERHOOD, THE 76
CONCORDE PICTURES. January, 1988. (Cirio H. Santiago), Rebecca Holden, Chuck Wagner.

SITTING DUCKS 90
UNITED FILM DIST. April, 1980. (Henry Jaglom), Michael Emil, Zack Norman.

SIX PACK 110
20TH CENTURY FOX. July, 1982. (Daniel Petrie), Kenny Rogers, Diane Lane.

SIX WEEKS 107
UNIVERSAL. December, 1982. (Tony Bill), Dudley Moore, Mary Tyler Moore, Katherine Healy.

SIXTEEN CANDLES 93
UNIVERSAL. May, 1984. (John Hughes), Molly Ringwald, Anthony Michael Hall, Michael Schoeffling.

16 DAYS OF GLORY 145
PARAMOUNT. March, 1986. (Bud Greenspan). Documentary.

'68 99
NEW WORLD PICTURES. February, 1988. (Steven Kovacs), Eric Larson, Robert Locke.

SKI COUNTRY 93
WARREN MILLER PRODS. November, 1984. (Warren Miller), Greg Smith, Hans Fahien.

SKI PATROL 91
TRIUMPH. January, 1990. (Richard Correll), Roger Rose, T. K. Carter.

SKI SCHOOL 88
MOVIESTORE ENT. January, 1991. Canadian. (Damian Lee), Dean Cameron, Tom Breznahan, Patrick Labyorteaux.

	Length in Mins.

SKIN DEEP (P) 101
20TH CENTURY FOX. March, 1989. (Blake Edwards), John Ritter, Vincent Gardenia, Alyson Reed.

SKY BANDITS 93
GALAXY INTL. October, 1986. British. (Zoran Perisic), Scott McGinnis, Jeff Osterhage.

SKY PIRATES 86
INTERNATIONAL FILM MARKETING. May, 1988. Australian. (Colin Eggleston), John Hargreaves, Meredith Phillips.

SLACKER 97
ORION CLASSICS. July, 1991. (Richard Linklater), Richard Linklater, Rudy Basquez.

SLAM DANCE 99
ISLAND PICTURES. August, 1987. (Wayne Wang), Tom Hulce, Mary Elizabeth Mastrantonio.

SLAMMER GIRLS 80
LIGHTNING PICTURES. June, 1987. (Chuck Vincent), Devon Jenkin, Jeff Eagle.

SLAPSTICK OF ANOTHER KIND 87
INTL. FILM MKTG. March, 1984. (Steven Paul), Jerry Lewis, Madeline Kahn.

SLATE, WYN & ME 92
HEMDALE RELEASING CORPORATION. November, 1987. Australian. (Don McLennan), Sigrid Thornton, Simon Burke.

SLAUGHTER HIGH 90
VESTRON PICTURES. April, 1987. (George Dugdale, Mark Ezra, Peter Litten), Caroline Munro, Simon Scudamore.

SLAUGHTERHOUSE 85
JGM ENTERPRISES. September, 1987. (Rick Roessler), Don Barrett, Sherry Bendorf.

SLAUGHTERHOUSE ROCK 97
TAURUS ENTERTAINMENT CO. February, 1988. (Dimitri Logothetis), Toni Basil, Nicholas Celozzi.

SLAVES OF NEW YORK 121
TRI-STAR. March, 1989. (James Ivory), Bernadette Peters, Adam Coleman Howard.

SLAYGROUND 89
UNIVERSAL. February, 1984. British. (Terry Bedford), Peter Coyote, Mel Smith.

SLEAZY UNCLE, THE 105
QUARTET. February, 1991. Italian. (Franco Brusati), Vittorio Gassman, Giancarlo Giannini, Andrea Ferreol.

SLEEPAWAY CAMP 84
UNITED FILM DIST. November, 1983. (Robert Hiltzik), Mike Kellin, Felissa Rose, Christopher Collet.

SLEEPAWAY CAMP 2: UNHAPPY CAMPERS 80
DOUBLE HELIX FILMS. October, 1988. (Michael A. Simpson), Pamela Springsteen, Brian Patrick Clarke.

SLEEPING BEAUTY 90
CANNON GROUP. June, 1987. (David Irving), Morgan Fairchild, Tahnee Welch.

SLEEPING CAR, THE 87
TRIAX ENTERTAINMENT. February, 1990. (Douglas Curtis), David Naughton, Judie Aronson.

SLEEPING WITH THE ENEMY 99
20TH CENTURY FOX. February, 1991. (Joseph Ruben), Julia Roberts, Patrick Bergin, Kevin Anderson.

SLEEPWALK 75
FIRST RUN FEATURES. July, 1987. (Sara Driver), Suzanne Fletcher, Ann Magnuson.

SLUGGER'S WIFE, THE 105
COLUMBIA. March, 1985. (Hal Ashby), Michael O'Keefe, Rebecca DeMornay.

SLUGS 92
NEW WORLD PICTURES. February, 1988. Spanish. (Juan Piquer Simon), Michael Garfield, Santiago Alvarez.

SLUMBER PARTY MASSACRE II 75
CONCORDE PICTURES. October, 1987. (Deborah Brock), Crystal Bernard, Kimberly McArthur.

SLUMER PARTY MASSACRE III 77
CONCORDE. September, 1990. (Sally Mattison), Keely Christian, Brittain Frye.

SMALL CIRCLE OF FRIENDS, A 112
UNITED ARTISTS. March, 1980. (Rob Cohen), Brad Davis, Karen Allen.

SMALL TIME 88
PANORAMA. November, 1991. (Norman Loftis), Richard Barboza, Carolyn Kinebrew, Scott Ferguson.

SMASH PALACE 100
ATLANTIC. April, 1982. Australian. (Roger Donaldson), Bruno Lawrence, Anna Jemison, Greer Robson.

SMILE OF THE LAMB, THE 93
DARK HORSE FILMS. June, 1987. Hebrew; Eng. titles. (Shimon Dotan), Tuncel Curtiz, Rami Danon.

SMITHEREENS 90
NEW LINE. November, 1982. (Susan Seidelman), Susan Berman, Brad Rinn.

Length in Mins.

STORMY MONDAY 93
ATLANTIC ENTERTAINMENT GROUP. April, 1988. British. (Mike Figgis), Melanie Griffith, Tommy Lee Jones.

STORY OF BOYS AND GIRLS, THE 92
ARIES. August, 1991. Italian. (Pupi Avati), Felice Andreasi, Angiola Baggi, Davide Bechini.

STORY OF WOMEN 110
MK2/NEW YORKER. October, 1989. French. (Claude Chabrol), Isabelle Huppert, François Cluzet.

STORYVILLE 110
20TH CENTURY FOX. August, 1992. (Mark Frost), James Spader, Jason Robards, Joanne Whalley-Kilmer.

STRAIGHT OUT OF BROOKLYN 91
SAMUEL GOLDWYN CO. May, 1991. (Matty Rich), George T. Odom, Lawrence Gilliard Jr.

STRAIGHT TALK 92
BUENA VISTA. April, 1992. (Barnet Kellman), Dolly Parton, James Woods, Griffin Dunne.

STRAIGHT TO HELL 86
ISLAND PICTURES. June, 1987. (Alex Cox), Sy Richardson, Joe Strummer.

STRAND: UNDER THE DARK CLOTH 81
KINO. December, 1991. Canadian. (John Walker), Documentary.

STRANDED 80
NEW LINE CINEMA. November, 1987. (Tex Fuller), Ione Skye, Joe Morton.

STRANGE BREW 90
MGM/UA. August, 1983. (Dave Thomas, Rick Moranis), Dave Thomas, Rick Moranis.

STRANGE INVADERS (P) 93
ORION. September, 1983. (Michael Laughlin), Paul LeMat, Karen Allen.

STRANGER, THE 88
COLUMBIA. December, 1987. (Adolfo Aristarain), Bonnie Bedelia, Peter Riegert.

STRANGER, THE 120
NATL. FILM DEVELOPMENT. May, 1992. Indian. (Satyajit Ray), Deepankar De, Mamata Shankar, Utpal Dutt.

STRANGER AMONG US, A 109
BUENA VISTA. July, 1992. (Sidney Lumet), Melanie Griffith, Eric Thal, John Pankow.

STRANGER IS WATCHING, A 92
MGM/UA. January, 1982. (Sean S. Cunningham), Kate Mulgrew, Rip Torn.

STRANGER THAN PARADISE 90
SAMUEL GOLDWYN CO. October, 1984. (Jim Jarmusch), John Lurie, Eszter Balint. B&W.

STRANGERS IN GOOD COMPANY 101
FIRST RUN/CASTLE HILL. May, 1991. Canadian. (Cynthia Scott), Alice Diabo, Constance Garneau.

STRANGER'S KISS 94
ORION CLASSICS. February, 1984. (Matthew Chapman), Pete Coyote, Victoria Tennant.

STRAPLESS 103
MIRAMAX. May, 1990. British. (David Hare), Blair Brown, Bridget Fonda.

STREAMERS 118
UA CLASSICS. November, 1983. (Robert Altman), Matthew Modine, Michael Wright.

STREET ASYLUM 89
ORIGINAL CINEMA. April, 1990. (Greggory Brown), Wings Hauser, Alex Cord, G. Gordon Liddy.

STREET HUNTER 93
CDGP/21st CENTURY FILMS. November, 1990. (John A. Gallagher), Steve James, Reb Brown, John Leguizamo.

STREET OF NO RETURN 90
THUNDER FILMS. August, 1991. French-Portuguese. (Samuel Fuller), Keith Carradine, Valentina Vargas, Bill Duke.

STREET SMART 95
CANNON GROUP. March, 1987. (Jerry Schatzberg), Christopher Reeve, Morgan Freeman, Kathy Baker.

STREET SOLDIERS 98
ACADEMY ENTERTAINMENT. March, 1991. (Lee Harry), Jun Chong, Jeff Rector.

STREETS 83
CONCORDE. January, 1990. (Katt Shea Ruben), Christina Applegate, David Mendenhall.

STREETS OF FIRE 94
UNIVERSAL. June, 1984. (Walter Hill), Michael Pare, Diane Lane, Rick Moranis.

STREETS OF GOLD 95
20TH CENTURY FOX. November, 1986. (Joe Roth), Klaus Maria Brandauer, Adrian Pasdar.

STREETWALKIN' 86
CONCORDE-CINEMA GROUP. September, 1985. (Joan Freeman), Melissa Leo, Dale Midkiff.

Length in Mins.

STREETWISE 92
ANGELIKA FILMS. April, 1985. (Martin Bell). Documentary.

STRICTLY BUSINESS 83
WARNER BROS. November, 1991. (Kevin Hooks), Tommy Davidson, Halle Berry, Joseph C. Phillips.

STRIKE IT RICH 84
MILLIMETER. January, 1990. British. (James Scott), Robert Lindsay, Molly Ringwald.

STRIP JACK NAKED 96
FRAMELINE. June, 1991. British. (Ron Peck), Documentary.

STRIPES 105
COLUMBIA. June, 1981. (Ivan Reitman), Bill Murray, Harold Ramis, Warren Oates.

STRIPPED TO KILL 84
CONCORDE PICTURES. June, 1987. (Katt Shea Rubin), Kay Lenz, Greg Evigan.

STRIPPED TO KILL 2: LIVE GIRLS 82
CONCORDE. January, 1989. (Katt Shea Ruben), Maria Ford, Eb Lottimer.

STRIPPER 90
20TH CENTURY FOX. January, 1986. (Jerome Gary), Janette Boyd, Sara Costa.

STROKER ACE 96
UNIVERSAL/WARNER BROS. July, 1983. (Hal Needham), Burt Reynolds, Ned Beatty, Loni Anderson.

STUCK ON YOU 88
TROMA. October, 1983. (Michael Herz, Samuel Weil), Professor Irwin Corey.

STUDENT BODIES 86
PARAMOUNT. August, 1981. (Mickey Rose), Kristen Riter, Matthew Goldsby.

STUDENT CONFIDENTIAL 94
TROMA. June, 1988. (Richard Horian), Eric Douglas, Marlon Jackson.

STUFF, THE 88
NEW WORLD PICTURES. September, 1986. (Larry Cohen), Michael Moriarty, Andrea Marcovicci.

STUNT MAN, THE 129
20TH CENTURY FOX. October, 1980. (Richard Rush), Peter O'Toole, Steve Railsback, Barbara Hershey.

SUBURBAN COMMANDO 85
NEW LINE CINEMA. October, 1991. (Burt Kennedy), Hulk Hogan, Christopher Lloyd, Shelley Duvall.

SUBURBIA (a.k.a. The Wild Side) 94
NEW WORLD PICTURES. May, 1984. (Penelope Spheeris), Chris Pedersen, Tim O'Brien.

SUBWAY 108
ISLAND ALIVE. November, 1985. French; Eng. titles. (Luc Besson), Isabelle Adjani, Christopher Lambert.

SUBWAY TO THE STARS 105
FILMDALLAS PICTURES. March, 1988. Portuguese; Eng. subtitles. (Rodolfo Brandao), Guiherme Fontes, Milton Goncalves.

SUDDEN IMPACT (P) 117
WARNER BROS. December, 1983. (Clint Eastwood), Clint Eastwood, Sondra Locke.

SUGAR CANE ALLEY 103
ORION CLASSICS. April, 1984. French; Eng. titles. (Euzhan Palcy), Garry Cadenat.

SUGARBABY 86
KINO INTL. November, 1985. German; Eng. titles. (Percy Adlon), Marianne Sagebrecht, Eisi Gulp.

SUICIDE CLUB, THE 90
ANGELIKA FILMS. May, 1988. (James Bruce), Mariel Hemingway, Robert Joy.

SUITORS, THE 106
FIRST RUN FEATURES. May, 1989. In Farsi; Eng. titles. (Ghasem Ebrahimian), Pouran, Ali Azizian.

SULLIVAN'S PAVILION (a.k.a. The Beer Drinker's Guide to Fitness and Film Making) 83
ADIRONADACK ALLIANCE. November, 1987. (Fred G. Sullivan), Fred G. Sullivan, Polly Sullivan.

SUMMER 98
ORION CLASSICS. August, 1986. French; Eng. titles. (Eric Rohmer), Marie Riviere, Lisa Heredia.

SUMMER CAMP NIGHTMARE 87
CONCORDE PICTURES. April, 1987. (Bert Dragin), Chuck Connors, Charles Stratton.

SUMMER HEAT 90
ATLANTIC RELEASING. May, 1987. (Michie Gleason), Lori Singer, Anthony Edwards, Bruce Abbott.

SUMMER LOVERS 98
FILMWAYS. August, 1982. (Randal Kleiser), Peter Gallagher, Daryl Hannah.

	Length in Mins.

TEX 103
BUENA VISTA. July, 1982. (Tim Hunter), Matt Dillon, Jim Metzler, Meg Tilly.

TEXAS CHAINSAW MASSACRE PART 2, THE 95
CANNON FILMS. August, 1986. (Tobe Hooper), Dennis Hopper, Caroline Williams.

TEXASVILLE 123
COLUMBIA. September, 1990. (Peter Bogdanovich), Jeff Bridges, Cybill Shepherd, Timothy Bottoms.

THANK YOU AND GOODNIGHT! 77
ARIES FILMS. January, 1992. (Jan Oxenberg), Documentary.

THAT CHAMPIONSHIP SEASON 108
CANNON FILMS. December, 1982. (Jason Miller), Bruce Dern, Stacy Keach, Robert Mitchum.

THAT SINKING FEELING 82
SAMUEL GOLDWYN CO. February, 1984. Scottish; 1979. (Bill Forsyth), Robert Buchanan, John Hughes.

THAT WAS THEN . . . THIS IS NOW 102
PARAMOUNT. November, 1985. (Christopher Cain), Emilio Estevez, Craig Sheffer.

THAT'S ADEQUATE 80
SOUTH GATE ENTERTAINMENT. January, 1990. (Harry Hurwitz), Tony Randall, James Coco, Bruce Willis.

THAT'S DANCING! 105
MGM/UA. January, 1985. (Jack Haley, Jr.), Gene Kelly, Liza Minnelli.

THAT'S LIFE! (P) 102
COLUMBIA. September, 1986. (Blake Edwards), Jack Lemmon, Julie Andrews.

THELMA AND LOUISE (P) 128
MGM. May, 1991. (Ridley Scott), Susan Sarandon, Geena Davis, Harvey Keitel.

THELONIOUS MONK: STRAIGHT, NO CHASER 89
WARNER BROS. October, 1989. (Charlotte Zwerin), Documentary.

THEME, THE (TEMA) 100
IFEX. October, 1987. Russian; Eng. subtitles. (Gleb Panfilov), Inna Churikova, Mikhail Ulyanov.

THERESE 91
CIRCLE RELEASING. October, 1986. French; Eng. titles. (Alain Cavalier), Catherine Mouchet, Aurore Prieto.

THERE'S NOTHING OUT THERE 90
VALKHN FILM. January, 1992. (Rolfe Kanefsky), Craig Peck, Wendy Bednarz, Mark Collver.

THEY LIVE (P) 93
UNIVERSAL. November, 1988. (John Carpenter), Roddy Piper, Keith David.

THEY'RE PLAYING WITH FIRE 96
NEW WORLD PICTURES. May, 1984. (Howard [Hikmet] Avedis), Sybil Danning, Eric Brown.

THIEF 118
UNITED ARTISTS. March, 1981. (Michael Mann), James Caan, Tuesday Weld.

THIEF OF HEARTS (P) 99
PARAMOUNT. October, 1984. (Douglas Day Stewart), Steven Bauer, Barbara Williams.

THIN BLUE LINE, THE 106
MIRAMAX. August, 1988. (Errol Morris). Documentary.

THING, THE 108
UNIVERSAL. July, 1982. (John Carpenter), Kurt Russell, Wilford Brimley, Donald Moffat.

THINGS ARE TOUGH ALL OVER 92
COLUMBIA. August, 1982. (Tom Avildsen), Tommy Chong, Richard Marin.

THINGS CHANGE 100
COLUMBIA. October, 1988. (David Mamet), Don Ameche, Joe Mantegna.

THINK BIG 86
CONCORDE. March, 1990. (Jon Turteltaub), Peter Paul, David Paul, Martin Mull.

38: VIENNA BEFORE THE FALL 96
EAST-WEST CLASSICS. May, 1988. German; Eng. subtitles. (Wolfgang Gluck), Tobias Engel, Sunnyi Melles.

35 UP 128
SAMUEL GOLDWYN CO. January, 1992. British. (Michael Apted), Documentary.

36 FILLETTE 92
CIRCLE RELEASING. January, 1989. French; Eng. titles. (Catherine Breillat), Delphin Zentout, Etienne Chicot.

THIS IS ELVIS 109
WARNER BROS. May, 1981. (Malcolm Leo, Andrew Solt). Documentary.

THIS IS MY LIFE 95
20TH CENTURY FOX. February, 1992. (Nora Ephron), Julie Kavner, Samantha Mathis, Dan Aykroyd.

	Length in Mins.

THIS IS SPINAL TAP 82
EMBASSY. March, 1984. (Rob Reiner), Christopher Guest, Rob Reiner, Michael McKean.

THOSE GLORY, GLORY DAYS 91
CINECOM INTL. January, 1986. (Philip Savile), Julia McKenzie, Elizabeth Spriggs.

THOSE LIPS, THOSE EYES (P) 106
UNITED ARTISTS. August, 1980. (Michael Pressman), Frank Langella, Thomas Hulce.

THOU SHALT NOT KILL . . . EXCEPT 94
FILMWORLD DISTRIBUTORS. September, 1987. (Josh Becker), Brian Schulz, John Manfredi.

THOUSAND LITTLE KISSES, A 110
CINECOM INTL. July, 1985. (Mira Recanati), Dina Doronne, Rivka Neuman.

THREE AMIGOS 105
ORION. December, 1986. (John Landis), Chevy Chase, Steve Martin, Martin Short.

THREE BROTHERS 113
NEW WORLD. February, 1982. Italian; Eng. titles. (Francesco Rosi), Philippe Noiret, Charles Vanel.

THREE FOR THE ROAD 88
NEW CENTURY/VISTA. April, 1987. (Bill Norton, Jr.), Charlie Sheen, Kerri Green.

THREE FUGITIVES 96
BUENA VISTA. January, 1989. (Francis Veber), Nick Nolte, Martin Short.

THREE KINDS OF HEAT 87
CANNON GROUP. June, 1987. (Leslie Stevens), Robert Ginty, Victoria Barrett.

THREE MEN AND A BABY 102
BUENA VISTA. November, 1987. (Leonard Nimoy), Tom Selleck, Steve Guttenberg, Ted Danson.

THREE MEN AND A CRADLE 100
SAMUEL GOLDWYN CO. April, 1986. French; Eng. titles. (Coline Serreau), Roland Giraud, Michel Boujenah.

THREE MEN AND A LITTLE LADY 100
BUENA VISTA. November, 1990. (Emile Ardolino), Tom Selleck, Steve Guttenberg, Ted Danson.

3 NINJAS 84
BUENA VISTA. August, 1992. (Jon Turteltaub), Victor Wong, Michael Treanor, Max Elliott Slade.

THREE O'CLOCK HIGH 97
UNIVERSAL. October, 1987. (Phil Joanou), Casey Siemaszko, Anne Ryan.

THREE SAD TIGERS 105
INTERNATIONAL FILM CIRCUIT. December, 1989. Spanish. (Raúl Ruiz), Nelson Villagra, Shenda Román.

THRESHOLD 97
20TH CENTURY FOX. January, 1983. Canadian. (Richard Pearce), Donald Sutherland, Jeff Goldblum.

THROUGH THE WIRE 85
ORIGINAL CINEMA. April, 1990. (Nina Rosenblum), Documentary.

THROW MOMMA FROM THE TRAIN 88
ORION. December, 1987. (Danny DeVito), Danny DeVito, Billy Crystal, Anne Ramsey.

THUNDER ALLEY 111
CANNON GROUP. April, 1985. (J.S. Cardone), Roger Wilson.

THUNDERHEART 118
TRISTAR. April, 1992. (Michael Apted), Val Kilmer, Sam Shepard, Graham Greene.

THY KINGDOM COME . . . THY WILL BE DONE 107
ROXIE FILMS. January, 1988. British-U.S. (Anthony Thomas). Documentary.

TICKET TO HEAVEN 107
UA CLASSICS. November, 1981. Canadian. (Ralph L. Thomas), Nick Mancuso, Saul Rubinek, Meg Foster.

TIE ME UP! TIE ME DOWN! 105
MIRAMAX. April, 1990. Spanish. (Pedro Almodovar), Victoria Abril, Antonio Banderas.

TIGER WARSAW 92
SONY PICTURES. September, 1988. (Amin Q. Chaudhri), Patrick Swayze, Piper Laurie.

TIGER'S TALE, A 97
ATLANTIC ENTERTAINMENT. February, 1988. (Peter Douglas), Ann-Margret, C. Thomas Howell.

TIGHTROPE (P) 114
WARNER BROS. August, 1984. (Richard Tuggle), Clint Eastwood, Genevieve Bujold.

TILAI 81
NEW YORKER. October, 1990. Moore. (Idrissa Ouedraogo), Rasmane Ouedraogo, Ina Cisse.

TIM 108
SATORI. September, 1981. Australian. (Michael Pate), Piper Laurie, Mel Gibson.

	Length in Mins.			Length in Mins.

TIME BANDITS 107
   EMBASSY. November, 1981. British. (Terry Gilliam), John Cleese, Sean Connery, Shelley Duvall.

TIME GUARDIAN, THE 85
   HEMDALE. August, 1989. Australian. (Brian Hannant), Tom Burlinson, Dean Stockwell.

TIME OF DESTINY, A 118
   COLUMBIA. April, 1988. (Gregory Nava), William Hurt, Timothy Hutton.

TIME OF THE GYPSIES 142
   COLUMBIA. February, 1990. Serbo-Croatian. (Emir Kusturica), Davor Dujmovic, Bora Todorovic.

TIME TO DIE, A 91
   ALMI FILMS. September, 1983. (Matt Cimber), Edward Albert, Rod Taylor, Rex Harrison.

TIME TRACKERS 87
   CONCORDE. April, 1989. (Howard R. Cohen), Ned Beatty, Wil Shriner.

TIME WILL TELL 89
   I.R.S. May, 1992. British. (Delcan Lowney), Documentary.

TIMEBOMB 96
   MGM. September, 1991. (Avi Nesher), Michael Biehn, Patsy Kensit, Robert Culp.

TIMES OF HARVEY MILK, THE 87
   TELECULTURE. October, 1984. (Robert Epstein). Documentary.

TIMES SQUARE (P) 111
   ASSOCIATED FILM DIST. October, 1980. (Alan Moyle), Tim Curry, Trini Alvarado.

TIMES TO COME 96
   CINEVISTA. November, 1989. Spanish. (Gustavo Mosquera), Hugo Soto, Juan Leyrado.

TIN DRUM, THE 142
   NEW WORLD PICTURES. April, 1980. German; Eng. titles. (Volker Schlondorff), David Bennent, Mario Adorf.

TIN MEN 112
   BUENA VISTA. March, 1987. (Barry Levinson), Richard Dreyfuss, Danny DeVito, Barbara Hershey.

TO BE OR NOT TO BE (P) 108
   20TH CENTURY FOX. December, 1983. (Alan Johnson), Mel Brooks, Anne Bancroft, Tim Matheson.

TO DIE FOR 90
   SKOURAS. May, 1989. (Deran Sarafian), Brendan Hughes, Sydney Walsh.

TO KILL A PRIEST (P) 117
   COLUMBIA. October, 1989. French. (Agnieszka Holland), Christopher Lambert, Ed Harris.

TO LIVE AND DIE IN L.A. 116
   MGM-UA November, 1985. (William Friedkin), William L. Petersen, Willem Dafoe.

TO SLEEP WITH ANGER 100
   SAMUEL GOLDWYN CO. October, 1990. (Charles Burnett), Danny Glover, Paul Butler, Mary Alice.

TOBY McTEAGUE 95
   SPECTRAFILM. March, 1986. (Jean-Claude Lord), Yannick Bisson, Winston Recker.

TOKYO-GA 92
   GARY CITY. April, 1985. (Wim Wenders). Documentary.

TOKYO POP 97
   SPECTRAFILM. April, 1988. (Fran Rubel Kuzui), Carrie Hamilton, Yutaka Tadokoro.

TOM HORN (P) 98
   WARNER BROS. March, 1980. (William Wiard), Steve McQueen, Linda Evans.

TOMBOY 92
   CROWN INTL. January, 1985. (Herb Freed), Betsy Russell, Jerry Dinome.

TOO BEAUTIFUL FOR YOU 91
   ORION CLASSICS. March, 1990. French. (Bertrand Blier), Gérard Depardieu, Josiane Balasko, Carole Bouquet.

TOO FAR TO GO 100
   ZOETROPE. April, 1982. (Fielder Cook), Michael Moriarty, Blythe Danner.

TOO MUCH SUN 100
   NEW LINE CINEMA. January, 1991. (Robert Downey), Andrea Martin, Eric Idle, Robert Downey, Jr.

TOO OUTRAGEOUS! 100
   SPECTRAFILM. September, 1987. Canadian. (Richard Benner), Craig Russell, Hollis McLaren.

TOO SCARED TO SCREAM 104
   MOVIE STORE. January, 1985. (Tony Lo Bianco), Mike Connors, Anne Archer.

TOOTSIE (P) 116
   COLUMBIA. December, 1982. (Sydney Pollack), Dustin Hoffman, Jessica Lange, Charles Durning.

TOP GUN 110
   PARAMOUNT. May, 1986. (Tony Scott), Tom Cruise, Kelly McGillis, Val Kilmer.

TOP SECRET! 90
   PARAMOUNT. June, 1984. (Jim Abrahams, David Zucker, Jerry Zucker), Val Kilmer, Lucy Gutterbridge.

TORA-SAN GOES TO VIENNA 111
   KINO INTERNATIONAL. November, 1989. Japanese. (Yoji Yamada), Kiyoshi Atsumi, Chieko Baisho.

TORCH SONG TRILOGY 117
   NEW LINE CINEMA. December, 1988. (Paul Bogart), Harvey Fierstein, Anne Bancroft, Matthew Broderick.

TORCHLIGHT 91
   FILM VENTURES INTL. February, 1985. (Tom Wright), Pamela Sue Martin, Steve Railsback.

TORMENT 85
   NEW WORLD PICTURES. April, 1986. (Samson Aslanian), Taylor Gilbert, William Witt.

TORN APART 85
   CASTLE HILL. April, 1990. (Jack Fisher), Adrian Pasdar, Cecilia Peck.

TORRENTS OF SPRING 93
   MILLIMETER. February, 1990. Italian-French. (Jerzy Skolimowski), Timothy Hutton, Nastassja Kinski.

TOTAL RECALL 109
   TRI-STAR. June, 1990. (Paul Verhoeven), Arnold Schwarzenegger, Rachel Ticotin.

TOTO LE HEROS 90
   TRITON. March, 1992. Belgian-French-German. (Jaco Van Dormael), Michel Bouguet, Jo De Backer, Thomas Doget.

TOUCH AND GO 101
   UNIVERSAL. August, 1986. (Robert Mandel), Michael Keaton, Maria Conchita Alonso.

TOUCH OF A STRANGER 87
   RAVEN-STAR PICTURES. September, 1990. (Brad Gilbert), Shelley Winters, Anthony Nocerino.

TOUCHED 89
   INTL. FILM MKTG. October, 1983. (John Flynn), Robert Hays, Kathleen Beller.

TOUCHED BY LOVE 95
   COLUMBIA. April, 1980. (Gus Trikonis), Deborah Raffin, Diane Lane.

TOUGH ENOUGH 107
   20TH CENTURY FOX. March, 1983. (Richard Fleischer), Dennis Quaid, Carlene Watkins.

TOUGH GUYS (P) 104
   BUENA VISTA. October, 1986. (Jeff Kanew), Burt Lancaster, Kirk Douglas, Eli Wallach.

TOUGH GUYS DON'T DANCE 108
   CANNON GROUP. September, 1987. (Norman Mailer), Ryan O'Neal, Isabella Rossellini.

TOUGHER THAN LEATHER 92
   NEW LINE CINEMA. September, 1988. (Rick Rubin), Joseph Simmons, Darryl McDaniels.

TOUKI-BOUKI 95
   INTL. FILM CIRCUIT. February, 1991. French-Senegalese. (Djibril Diop Mambety), Magaye Niang, Mareme Niang.

TOUTE UNE NUIT 89
   WORLD ARTISTS RELEASING. June, 1989. French; Eng. titles. (Chantal Akerman), Aurore Clement, Paul Allio.

TOXIC AVENGER, THE 85
   TROMA. April, 1986. (Michael Herz, Samuel Weil), Andrea Maranda, Mitchell Cohen.

TOXIC AVENGER PART II 95
   TROMA. March, 1989. (Michael Herz, Lloyd Kaufman), Ron Fazio, John Altamura, Phoebe Legere.

TOXIC AVENGER PART III: THE LAST TEMPTATION OF TOXIE, THE 89
   TROMA. November, 1989. (Lloyd Kaufman, Michael Herz), Ron Fazio, John Altamura.

TOY, THE 99
   COLUMBIA. December, 1982. (Richard Donner), Richard Pryor, Jackie Gleason.

TOY SOLDIERS 91
   NEW WORLD PICTURES. May, 1984. (David Fisher), Jason Miller, Cleavon Little.

TOY SOLDIERS 112
   TRI-STAR. April, 1991. (Daniel Petrie, Jr.), Sean Astin, Wil Wheaton, Keith Coogan, Louis Gossett, Jr.

TRACK 29 86
   ISLAND PICTURES. September, 1988. British. (Nicolas Roeg), Theresa Russell, Gary Oldman.

TRADING HEARTS 88
   CINEWORLD. July, 1988. (Neil Leifer), Raul Julia, Beverly D'Angelo.

Length in Mins.

TRADING PLACES 106
PARAMOUNT. June, 1983. (John Landis), Dan Aykroyd, Eddie Murphy, Don Ameche.

TRAFFIC JAM 116
CINETEL. March, 1988. Italian-French-Spanish-West German; Eng. subtitles. (Luigi Comencini), Annie Girardot, Fernando Rey.

TRAGEDY OF A RIDICULOUS MAN 118
WARNER BROS. February, 1982. Italian; Eng. titles. (Bernardo Bertolucci), Ugo Tognazzi, Anouk Aimee.

TRAIL OF THE PINK PANTHER (P) 97
MGM/UA. December, 1982. (Blake Edwards), Peter Sellers, David Niven.

TRANSES 87
INTERFILM. January, 1985. Arabic; Eng. titles. (Ahmed el-Maanouni), Boujema Hgour.

TRANSFORMERS: THE MOVIE 86
DE LAURENTIIS. August, 1986. (Nelson Shin). Animated.

TRANSYLVANIA 6-5000 94
NEW WORLD PICTURES. November, 1985. (Rudy De-Luca), Jeff Goldblum, Joseph Bologna.

TRAP THEM AND KILL THEM 92
MEGASTAR PICTURES. February, 1984. Italian; dubbed. (Joe D'Amato = Arist De Massaccesi), Laura Gemser.

TRAVELLING NORTH 96
CINEPLEX ODEON. February, 1988. Australian. (Carl Schultz), Leo McKern, Julia Blake.

TREASURE OF THE FOUR CROWNS (3-D) 99
CANNON FILMS. January, 1983. Spanish. (Ferdinando Baldi), Tony Anthony, Ana Obregon.

TREASURE OF THE MOON GODDESS 89
ASCOT ENTERTAINMENT. January, 1988. (Joseph Louis Agraz), Asher Brauner, Don Calfa.

TREE WE HURT, THE 75
GREEK FILM CENTER. January, 1988. Greek; Eng. titles. (Dimos Avdeliodis), Yannis Avdeliodis, Nikos Mioteris.

TREMORS 96
UNIVERSAL. January, 1990. (Ron Underwood), Kevin Bacon, Fred Ward.

TRENCHCOAT 91
BUENA VISTA. March, 1983. (Michael Tuchner), Margot Kidder, Robert Hays.

TRESPASSES 100
SHAPIRO ENTERTAINMENT. January, 1987. (Loren Bivens, Adam Rourke), Robert Kuhn, Van Brooks.

TRIAL ON THE ROAD 95
IFEX. June, 1987. In Russian. (Alexei Gherman), Vladislav Zamansky, Rolan Bykov.

TRIBUTE 125
20TH CENTURY FOX. December, 1980. Canadian. (Bob Clark), Jack Lemmon, Robby Benson.

TRICK OR TREAT 97
DE LAURENTIIS. October, 1986. (Charles Martin Smith), Marc Price, Tony Fields.

TRIP TO BOUNTIFUL, THE 106
ISLAND PICTURES. December, 1985. (Peter Masterson), Geraldine Page, John Heard, Rebecca DeMornay.

TRIPLE BOGEY ON A PAR 5 HOLE 85
POE PRODS. March, 1992. (Amos Poe), Eric Mitchell, Daisy Hall, Jesse McBride.

TRIPWIRE 91
NEW LINE CINEMA. January, 1990. (James Lemmo), Terence Know, David Warner.

TRIUMPH OF THE SPIRIT 120
TRIUMPH. December, 1989. (Robert M. Young), Willem Dafoe, Edward James Olmos.

TRIUMPHS OF A MAN CALLLED HORSE 86
JENSEN FARLEY. March, 1984. (John Hough), Richard Harris, Michael Beck.

TROLL 86
EMPIRE PICTURES. January, 1986. (John Buechler), Noah Hathaway, Michael Moriarty.

TRON 96
BUENA VISTA. July, 1982. (Steve Lisberger), Jeff Bridges, Bruce Boxleitner, David Warner.

TROOP BEVERLY HILLS 105
COLUMBIA. March, 1989. (Jeff Kanew), Shelley Long, Craig T. Nelson.

TROPICAL SNOW 88
PSM ENTERTAINMENT. April, 1989. (Ciro Duran), Nick Corri, Madeleine Stowe.

TROUBLE IN MIND 111
ISLAND ALIVE. March, 1986. (Alan Rudolph), Kris Kristofferson, Keith Carradine.

TROUBLE WITH SPIES, THE 91
DE LAURENTIIS. December, 1987. (Burt Kennedy), Donald Sutherland, Ned Beatty.

Length in Mins.

TRUE BELIEVER 103
COLUMBIA. February, 1989. (Joseph Ruben), James Woods, Robert Downey Jr.

TRUE BLOOD 97
FRIES ENTERTAINMENT. May, 1989. (Frank Kerr), Jeff Fahey, Chad Lowe.

TRUE COLORS 111
PARAMOUNT. March, 1991. (Herbert Ross), John Cusack, James Spader, Imogen Stubbs, Mandy Patinkin.

TRUE CONFESSIONS 107
UNITED ARTISTS. September, 1981. (Ulu Grosbard), Robert DeNiro, Robert Duvall, Charles Durning.

TRUE IDENTITY 93
BUENA VISTA. August, 1991. (Charles Lane), Lenny Henry, Frank Langella, Charles Lane.

TRUE LOVE 103
MGM/UA. September, 1989. (Nancy Savoca), Annabella Sciorra, Ron Eldard.

TRUE STORIES 90
WARNER BROS. October, 1986. (David Byrne), David Byrne, John Goodman, Swoosie Kurtz.

TRULY, MADLY, DEEPLY 107
GOLDWYN. May, 1991. British. (Anthony Minghella), Juliette Stevenson, Alan Rickman, Michael Maloney.

TRUST 103
FINE LINE/NEW CINEMA. July, 1991. (Hal Hartley), Adrienne Shelly, Martin Donovan, Merritt Nelson.

TRUST ME 104
CINECOM. November, 1989. (Bobby Houston), Adam Ant, David Packer.

TRUTH OR DARE 118
MIRAMAX. May, 1991. (Alek Keshishian), Madonna.

TUCKER: THE MAN AND HIS DREAM (TV) 111
PARAMOUNT. August, 1988. (Francis Ford Coppola), Jeff Bridges, Joan Allen, Martin Landau.

TUFF TURF 112
NEW WORLD. February, 1985. (Fritz Kiersch), James Spader, Kim Richards.

TUNE IN TOMORROW 102
CINECOM. October, 1990. (Jon Amiel), Barbara Hershey, Keanu Reeves, Peter Falk.

TURK 182 98
20TH CENTURY FOX. February, 1985. (Bob Clark), Timothy Hutton, Robert Urich.

TURNAROUND 90
CINEMA GROUP DISTRIBUTION. April, 1987. (Ola Solum), Doug McKeon, Eddie Albert.

TURNER & HOOCH 100
BUENA VISTA. July, 1989. (Roger Spottiswoode), Tom Hanks, Mare Winningham.

TURTLE BEACH 85
WARNER BROS. May, 1992. Australian. (Stephen Wallace), Greta Scacchi, Joan Chen, Jack Thompson.

TURTLE DIARY 97
SAMUEL GOLDWYN CO. February, 1986. British. (John Irvin), Glenda Jackson, Ben Kingsley.

28 UP 133
GRANADA. October, 1985. (Michael Apted). Documentary.

TWENTY-ONE 101
TRITON. October, 1991. British. (Don Boyd), Patsy Kensit, Jack Shepherd, Patrick Ryecart.

29TH STREET 101
20TH CENTURY FOX. November, 1991. (George Gallo), Danny Aiello, Anthony LaPaglia, Lainie Kazan.

TWICE DEAD 85
CONCORDE. September, 1988. (Bert Dragin), Tom Breznahan, Jill Whitlow.

TWICE IN A LIFETIME 117
BUD YORKIN CO. October, 1985. (Bud Yorkin), Gene Hackman, Ann-Margret, Ellen Burstyn.

TWILIGHT OF THE COCKROACHES (GOKIBURI) 105
STREAMLINE. September, 1989. Japanese. (Hiroaki Yoshida), Animated.

TWILIGHT TIME 102
MGM/UA. February, 1983. (Goran Paskaljevic), Karl Malden, Mia Roth.

TWILIGHT ZONE—THE MOVIE 102
WARNER BROS. June, 1983. (John Landis, Steven Spielberg, Joe Dante, George Miller), Dan Aykroyd, Albert Brooks.

TWIN PEAKS: FIRE WALK WITH ME 134
NEW LINE CINEMA. August, 1992. (David Lynch), Sheryl Lee, Moira Kelly, Ray Wise.

TWINS 112
UNIVERSAL. December, 1988. (Ivan Reitman), Arnold Schwarzenegger, Danny DeVito.

	Length in Mins.

TWIST AND SHOUT 100
MIRAMAX FILMS. September, 1986. Danish; Eng. titles. (Billie August), Adam Tonsberg, Lars Simonsen.

TWISTED JUSTICE 94
SEYMOUR BORDE. March, 1990. (David Heavener), David Heavener, Erik Estrada.

TWISTED OBSESSION 103
IVE. (R) August, 1990. French-Italian. (Fernando Trueba), Jeff Goldblum, Miranda Richardson, Anemone.

TWISTER 94
VESTRON. June, 1989. (Michael Almereyda), Harry Dean Stanton, Suzy Amis, Crispin Glover.

TWO EVIL EYES 122
TAURUS. October, 1991. Italian. (George Romero, Dario Argento), Adrienne Barbeau, Harvey Keitel, Madeleine Potter.

TWO JAKES, THE 138
PARAMOUNT. August, 1990. (Jack Nicholson), Jack Nicholson, Harvey Keitel, Meg Tilly.

TWO LIVES OF MATTIA PASCAL, THE 120
RAI/SACIS. March, 1988. Italian; Eng. subtitles. (Mario Monicelli), Marcello Mastroianni, Senta Berger.

TWO MOON JUNCTION 104
LORIMAR. April, 1988. (Zalman King), Sherilyn Fenn, Richard Tyson.

TWO OF A KIND 87
20TH CENTURY-FOX. December, 1983. (John Herzfeld), John Travolta, Olivia Newton-John.

2010 (P) 114
MGM/UA. December, 1984. (Peter Hyams), Roy Scheider, John Lithgow.

TYPHOON CLUB 115
KUZUI ENTERPRISES. December, 1986. Japanese; Eng. titles. (Shinji Somai), Yuichi Mikami, Shigeru Kurebayashi.

U

U2: RATTLE AND HUM 99
PARAMOUNT. November, 1988. (Phil Joanou). Documentary. B & W/Color.

UHF 96
ORION. July, 1989. (Jay Levey), Weird Al Yankovic, Victoria Jackson.

UFORIA 100
UNIVERSAL. January, 1986. (John Binder), Cindy Williams, Harry Dean Stanton.

UNBEARABLE LIGHTNESS OF BEING, THE 171
ORION. February, 1988. (Phillip Kaufman), Daniel Day-Lewis, Juliette Binoche, Lena Olin.

UNBELIEVABLE TRUTH, THE 90
MIRAMAX. July, 1990. (Hal Hartley), Adrienne Shelly, Robert Burke, Gary Sauer.

UNBORN, THE 83
CONCORDE. April, 1991. (Rodman Flender), Brooke Adams, Jeff Hayenga, James Karen.

UNCLE BUCK 100
UNIVERSAL. August, 1989. (John Hughes), John Candy, Amy Madigan, Macaulay Culkin.

UNCLE MOSES 87
NATIONAL CENTER FOR JEWISH FILM. November, 1991. Yiddish, 1932. (Sidney Goldin, Aubrey Scotto), Maurice Schwartz, Zvee Scooler. B&W.

UNCOMMON VALOR 105
PARAMOUNT. December, 1983. (Ted Kotcheff), Gene Hackman, Robert Stack, Patrick Swayze.

UNDER COVER 94
CANNON GROUP. April, 1987. (John Stockwell), David Neidorf, Jennifer Jason Leigh.

UNDER FIRE 124
ORION PICTURES. October, 1983. (Roger Spottiswoode), Nick Nolte, Gene Hackman, Joanna Cassidy.

UNDER SUSPICION (P) 99
COLUMBIA. February, 1992. British. (Simon Moore), Liam Neeson, Laura San Giacomo, Kenneth, Cranham.

UNDER THE BOARDWALK 100
NEW WORLD PICTURES. April, 1989. (Fritz Kiersch), Keith Coogan, Danielle von Zerneck.

UNDER THE CHERRY MOON 98
WARNER BROS. July, 1986. (Prince), Prince, Jerome Benton. B & W.

UNDER THE RAINBOW 98
WARNER BROS. July, 1981. (Steve Rash), Chevy Chase, Carrie Fisher.

UNDER THE SUN OF SATAN 97
ALIVE. March, 1989. French; Eng. titles. (Maurice Pialat), Gerard Depardieu, Sandrine Bonnaire.

UNDER THE VOLCANO 112
UNIVERSAL. June, 1984. (John Huston), Albert Finney, Jacqueline Bisset.

UNDERTOW 95
CAPSTONE. September, 1992. (Thomas Mazziotti), Peter Dobson, Burtt Harris, Greg Mullavey.

UNFAITHFULLY YOURS 96
20TH CENTURY FOX. February, 1984. (Howard Zieff), Dudley Moore, Nastassja Kinski.

UNFINISHED BUSINESS 65
AMERICAN FILM INSTITUTE. May, 1987. Canadian. (Viveca Lindfors), Viveca Lindfors, Peter Donat.

UNFORGIVEN (P) 132
WARNER BROS. August, 1992. (Clint Eastwood), Clint Eastwood, Gene Hackman, Morgan Freeman, Richard Harris.

UNHOLY, THE 100
VESTRON PICTURES. April, 1988. (Camilio Vila), Ben Cross, Hal Holbrook.

UNIVERSAL SOLDIER (P) 104
TRISTAR. July, 1992. (Roland Emmerich), Jean-Claude Van Damme, Dolph Lundgren, Ally Walker.

UNLAWFUL ENTRY 111
20TH CENTURY FOX. June, 1992. (Jonathan Kaplan), Kurt Russell, Ray Liotta, Madeleine Stowe.

UNREMARKABLE LIFE, AN 92
SVS FILMS. October, 1989. (Amin Q. Chaudhri), Patricia Neal, Shelley Winters, Mako.

UNSUITABLE JOB FOR A WOMAN, AN 90
CASTLE HILL. April, 1985. British. (Christopher Petit), Billie Whitelaw, Paul Freeman.

UNTIL SEPTEMBER 95
MGM/UA. September, 1984. (Richard Marquand), Karen Allen, Thierry Lhermitte.

UNTIL THE END OF THE WORLD 157
WARNER BROS. December, 1991. German-French-Australian. (Wim Wenders), William Hurt, Solveig Dommartin, Sam Neil.

UNTOUCHABLES, THE 119
PARAMOUNT. June, 1987. (Brian De Palma), Kevin Costner, Sean Connery, Robert De Niro.

UP THE ACADEMY 96
WARNER BROS. June, 1980. (Robert Downey), Ron Liebman, Wendell Brown.

UP THE CREEK 99
ORION. April, 1984. (Robert Butler), Tim Matheson, Don Monahan.

UP TO A CERTAIN POINT 98
NEW YORKER. March, 1985. Spanish; Eng. titles. (Tomas Gutierra Alea), Oscar Alvarez.

UPHILL ALL THE WAY 86
NEW WORLD PICTURES. January, 1986. (Frank Q. Dobbs), Roy Clark, Mel Tillis.

URANUS 100
PRESTIGE. August, 1991. French. (Claude Berri), Philippe Noiret, Gerard Depardieu, Michel Blanc.

URBAN COWBOY (P) 135
PARAMOUNT. June, 1980. (James Bridges), John Travolta, Debra Winger, Scott Glenn.

USED CARS 111
COLUMBIA. August, 1980. (Robert Zemeckis), Kurt Russell, Jack Warden.

USED INNOCENCE 95
FIRST RUN. February, 1989. (James Benning). Documentary.

UTU 104
PICKMAN FILMS. September, 1984. (Geoff Murphy), Anzac Wallace.

V

V. I. WARSHAWSKI 89
BUENA VISTA. July, 1991. (Jeff Kanew), Kathleen Turner, Jay O. Sanders, Charles Durning.

VAGABOND 106
IFEX. May, 1986. French; Eng. titles. (Agnes Varda), Sandrine Bonnaire, Macha Meril.

VAGRANT, THE 91
MGM. May, 1992. (Chris Walas), Bill Paxton, Michael Ironside, Colleen Camp, Marc McClure.

VALENTINO RETURNS 90
SKOURAS PICTURES. July, 1989. (Peter Hoffman), Frederic Forrest, Veronica Cartwright, Barry Tubb.

VALET GIRLS 82
EMPIRE PICTURES. January, 1987 (Rafal Zielinski), Meri D. Marshall, April Stewart.

	Length in Mins.

VALLEY GIRL 95
ATLANTIC. April, 1983. (Martha Coolidge), Nicolas Cage, Deborah Foreman.

VALMONT (P) 137
ORION. November, 1989. French-British. (Milos Forman), Colin Firth, Annette Bening, Meg Telly.

VAMP 94
NEW WORLD PICTURES. July, 1986. (Richard Wenk), Chris Makepeace, Sandy Baron.

VAMPIRE'S KISS 105
HEMDALE. June, 1989. (Robert Bierman), Nicolas Cage, Maria Conchita Alonso, Jennifer Beals.

VANISHING, THE 107
TARA RELEASING. October, 1990. Dutch. (George Sluizer), Gene Bervoets, Johanna Ter Steege.

VARIETY 100
HORIZON FILMS. March, 1985. (Bette Gordon), Sandy McLeod, Will Patton.

VASECTOMY: A DELICATE MATTER 90
VANDOM INTL. PICTURES. September, 1986. (Robert Burge), Paul Sorvino, Cassandra Edwards.

VASSA 106
IFEX. November, 1983. Russian; Eng. titles. (Gleb Panfilov), Inna Churkova.

VENDETTA 88
CONCORDE PICTURES. September, 1986. (Mel Ferrer), Karen Chase, Lisa Clarson.

VENOM 94
PARAMOUNT. January, 1982. (Piers Haggard), Klaus Kinski, Oliver Reed.

VERA 87
GRANGE/KINO. October, 1987. Portuguese. (Sergio Toledo), Ana Beatriz Nogueira, Aida Leiner.

VERDICT, THE 126
20TH CENTURY FOX. December, 1982. (Sidney Lumet), Paul Newman, Charlotte Rampling.

VERONICO CRUZ 100
CINEVISTA. January, 1990. Argentine-British. (Miguel Pereira), Juan Jose Camero, Gonzalo Morales.

VERONIKA VOSS 105
UA CLASSICS. September, 1982. German; Eng. titles. (Rainer Werner Fassbinder), Rosel Zech, Hilmar Thate.

VERY MORAL NIGHT, A 99
HUNGAROFILM. March, 1989. Hungarian; Eng. titles. (Karoly Makk), Iren Psota, Margit Makay.

VERY OLD MAN WITH ENORMOUS WINGS, A 90
ORIGINAL CINEMA. December, 1990. Spanish. (Fernando Birri), Fernando Birri, Asdrubal Melendez.

VIA APPIA 90
STRAND RELEASING. August, 1992. German. (Jochen Hick), Peter Senner, Yves Jansen, Guilherme de Padua.

VIBES (P) 99
COLUMBIA. August, 1988. (Ken Kwapis), Cyndi Lauper, Jeff Goldblum.

VICE SQUAD 97
EMBASSY. January, 1982. (Gary A. Sherman), Season Hubley, Gary Swanson.

VICE VERSA 98
COLUMBIA. March, 1988. (Brian Gilbert), Judge Reinhold, Fred Savage.

VICIOUS 88
SVS FILMS. December, 1988. Australian. (Karl Zwicky), Tamblyn Lord, Craig Pearce.

VICTOR/VICTORIA (P) 133
MGM/UA. March, 1982. (Blake Edwards), Julie Andrews, Robert Preston, James Garner.

VICTORY 117
PARAMOUNT. July, 1981. (John Huston), Sylvester Stallone, Michael Caine.

VIDEODROME 88
UNIVERSAL. February, 1983. Canadian. (David Cronenberg), James Woods, Deborah Harry.

VIETNAM, TEXAS 85
TRIUMPH. June, 1990. (Robert Ginty), Robert Ginty, Haing S. Ngor.

VIEW TO A KILL, A (P) 131
MGM/UA. May, 1985. British. (John Glen), Roger Moore, Christopher Walken.

VINCENT & THEO 138
HEMDALE. November, 1990. French-British. (Robert Altman), Tim Roth, Paul Rhys, Johanna Ter Steege.

VINCENT: THE LIFE AND DEATH OF VINCENT VAN GOGH 105
ILLUMINATION FILMS. March, 1988. Australian. (Paul Cox), Voice of John Hurt.

	Length in Mins.

VIOLENCE AT NOON 99
KINO INTL./SHOCHIKU CO. November, 1988 release of 1966 film. Japanese; Eng. subtitles. (Nagisa Oshima), Seada Kawaguchi, Akiko Koyama.

VIOLETS ARE BLUE 88
COLUMBIA. April, 1986. (Jack Fisk), Sissy Spacek, Kevin Kline.

VIPER 94
FRIES DISTRIBUTION. May, 1988. (Peter Maris), Linda Purl, James Tolkan.

VIRGIN MACHINE 85
FIRST RUN FEATURES. February, 1989. German; Eng. titles. (Monika Treut), Ian Blum, Marcelo Uriona.

VIRGIN QUEEN OF ST. FRANCIS HIGH, THE 94
CROWN INTL. PICTURES. November, 1987. (Francesco Lucente), Joseph R. Straface, Stacy Christensen.

VIRUS KNOWS NO MORALS, A 82
FIRST RUN FEATURES. June, 1987. West German. (Rosa von Praunheim). Documentary.

VISION QUEST 105
WARNER BROS. February, 1985. (Harold Becker), Matthew Modine, Linda Fiorentino.

VISITING HOURS 105
20TH CENTURY FOX. May, 1982. Canadian. (Jean Claude Lord), Lee Grant, William Shatner.

VITAL SIGNS 103
20TH CENTURY FOX. April, 1990. (Marisa Silver), Adrian Pasdar, Diane Lane, Jimmy Smits.

VOICES FROM THE ATTIC 60
SIREN PICTURES. May, 1989. (Debbie Goodstein). Documentary.

VOICES FROM THE FRONT 88
FRAMELINE. March, 1992. (Robyn Hutt), Documentary.

VOICES OF "SARAFINA!" 85
NEW YORKER. February, 1989. (Nigel Noble), cast of Broadway show "Sarafina!"

VOLUNTEERS 106
TRI-STAR. August, 1985. (Nicholas Meyers), Tom Hanks, John Candy.

VOYAGE TO CYTHERA 149
GREEK FILM CENTER. March, 1989. Greek; Eng. titles. (Theo Angelopoulos), Manos Katrakis, Mary Chronopoulou.

VOYAGER 110
CASTLE HILL. January, 1992. German-French. (Volker Schlondorff), Sam Shepard, Julie Delpy, Barbara Sukowa.

VOYEUR 100
PRESTIGE. August, 1991. Dutch. (Alex Van Warmerdam), Alex Van Warmerdam, Olga Zuiderhoek.

W

WAGNER 300
ALAN LANDSBERG. December, 1983. (Tony Palmer), Richard Burton, Vanessa Redgrave, Gemma Craven.

WAIT FOR ME IN HEAVEN 111
MD WAX/COURIER. October, 1990. Spanish. (Antonio Mercero), Jose Soriano, Chus Lampreave.

WAIT UNTIL SPRING, BANDINI 100
ORION CLASSICS. June, 1990. Belgian-French-Italian. (Dominique Deruddere), Joe Mantegna, Faye Dunaway.

WAITING FOR THE LIGHT 100
TRIUMPH. November, 1990. (Christopher Monger), Shirley MacLaine, Teri Garr, Clancy Brown.

WAITING FOR THE MOON 87
SKOURAS PICTURES. March, 1987. (Jill Godmilow), Linda Hunt, Linda Bassett, Andrew McCarthy.

WALK LIKE A MAN 86
MGM. April, 1987. (Melvin Frank), Howie Mandel, Christopher Lloyd.

WALKER 95
UNIVERSAL. December, 1987. (Alex Cox), Ed Harris, Richard Masur.

WALKING THE EDGE 93
EMPIRE PICTURES. January, 1985. (Norbert Meisel), Robert Forster, Nancy Kwan.

WALL, THE 117
KINO INTL. June, 1986. Turkish; Eng. titles. (Yilmaz Guney), Tuncel Kuritz.

WALL STREET 124
20TH CENTURY FOX. December, 1987. (Oliver Stone), Charlie Sheen, Michael Douglas.

WALTZ ACROSS TEXAS 99
ATLANTIC. October, 1982. (Ernest Day), Terry Jastrow, Anne Archer.

WANNSEE CONFERENCE, THE 87
FILMS INC./REARGUARD. February, 1987. German; Eng. titles. (Heinz Schirk), Robert Artzorn, Friedrich Beckhaus.

Length in Mins.

WANTED: DEAD OR ALIVE 104
NEW WORLD PICTURES. January, 1987. (Gary Sherman), Rutger Hauer, Gene Simmons.

WAR 99
TROMA. September, 1988. (Samuel Weil, Michael Herz), Carolyn Deauchamp, Sean Bowen.

WAR AND LOVE 112
CANNON FILMS. September, 1985. (Moshe Mizrahi), Sebastian Keneas, Kyra Sedgwick.

WAR OF THE ROSES, THE 118
20TH CENTURY FOX. December, 1989. (Danny DeVito), Michael Douglas, Kathleen Turner, Danny DeVito.

WAR PARTY 96
HEMDALE. September, 1989. (Franc Roddam), Billy Wirth, Kevin Dillon.

WAR REQUIEM 92
MOVIE VISIONS. November, 1989. British. (Derek Jarman), Laurence Olivier, Nathaniel Parker.

WARGAMES 110
MGM/UA. June, 1983. (John Badham), Matthew Broderick, Dabney Coleman.

WARLOCK 102
TRIMARK. January, 1991. (Steve Miner), Julian Sands, Richard E. Grant, Lori Singer.

WARM NIGHTS ON A SLOW MOVING TRAIN 91
MILLIMETER. March, 1989. Australian. (Bob Ellis), Wendy Hughes, Colin Friels.

WARNING SIGN 100
20TH CENTURY FOX. August, 1985. (Hal Barwood), Sam Waterson, Kathleen Quinlan.

WARRIOR QUEEN 69
SEYMOUR BORDE & ASSOCIATES. January, 1987. (Chuck Vincent), Sybil Danning, Donald Pleasence.

WASH, THE 94
SKOUROS PICTURES. August, 1988. (Michael Toshkyuki Uno), Mako, Nobu McCarthy.

WATCHER IN THE WOODS, THE 84
BUENA VISTA. April, 1980. (John Hough), Bette Davis, Carroll Baker.

WATCHERS 92
UNIVERSAL. December, 1988. Canadian. (Jon Hess), Corey Haim, Barbara Williams.

WATER 95
ATLANTIC RELEASING. April, 1986. British. (Dick Clement), Michael Caine, Valerie Perrine.

WATERDANCE, THE 106
SAMUEL GOLDWYN CO. May, 1992. (Neal Jimenez, Michael Steinberg), Eric Stoltz, Helen Hunt, Wesley Snipes.

WATERWALKER 83
SHADOW DIST. January, 1987. (Bill Mason). Documentary.

WAVELENGTH 87
NEW WORLD PICTURES. October, 1983. (Mike Gray), Robert Carradine, Cherie Currie.

WAX, OR THE DISCOVERY OF TELEVISION AMONG
THE BEES 85
JASMINE TEA. August, 1992. (David Blair), David Blair, Meg Savlov.

WAXWORK 97
VESTRON PICTURES. June, 1988. (Anthony Hickox), Zach Galligan, Deborah Foreman.

WAY IT IS, THE 80
SPRING FILMS. April, 1986. (Eric Mitchell), Kai Eric, Boris Major.

WAYNE'S WORLD 95
PARAMOUNT. February, 1992. (Penelope Spheeris), Mike Myers, Dana Carvey, Rob Lowe.

WE THE LIVING (NOI VIVI) 170
ANGELIKA FILMS. November, 1988 release of 1942 film. (Goffredo Alessandrini), Alida Valli, Rossano Brazzi.

WE THINK THE WORLD OF YOU 94
CINECOM. December, 1988. British. (Colin Gregg), Alan Bates, Gary Oldman.

WEAPONS OF THE SPIRIT 90
FIRST RUN FEATURES. September, 1989. French. (Pierre Sauvage), Documentary.

WEAVERS: WASN'T THAT A TIME, THE 78
UA CLASSICS. May, 1981. (Jim Brown), Documentary.

WEDDING BAND 82
IRS MEDIA. March, 1990. (Daniel Raskov), William Katt, Joyce Hyser.

WEDDING IN GALILEE 113
KINO INTL. June, 1988. Arabic; Eng. subtitles. (Michel Khleifi), Ali M. El Akili, Makram Khouri.

WEEDS 115
DE LAURENTIIS. October, 1987. (John Hancock), Nick Nolte, Rita Taggart, Lane Smith.

Length in Mins.

WEEKEND AT BERNIE'S 97
20TH CENTURY FOX. July, 1989. (Ted Kotcheff), Andrew McCarthy, Jonathan Silverman.

WEEKEND PASS 92
CROWN INTL. February, 1984. (Lawrence Bassoff), D.W. Brown, Peter Ellenstein.

WEEKEND WARRIORS 85
THE MOVIE STORE. August, 1987. (Bert Convy), Chris Lemmon, Vic Tayback.

WEEK'S VACATION, A 102
BIOGRAPH INTL. March, 1982. French; Eng. titles. (Bertrand Tavernier), Nathalie Baye, Gerard Lanvin.

WEININGER'S LAST NIGHT 100
CINEPOOL-WEGA FILM. July, 1991. Austrian. (Paulus Manker), Paulus Manker, Hilde Sochor.

WEIRD SCIENCE 94
UNIVERSAL. August, 1985. (John Hughes), Anthony Michael Hall, Kelly LeBrock.

WELCOME HOME 96
COLUMBIA. September, 1989. (Franklin J. Schaffner), Kris Kristofferson, JoBeth Williams, Sam Waterston.

WELCOME HOME ROXY CARMICHAEL 98
PARAMOUNT. October, 1990. (Jim Abrahams), Winona Ryder, Jeff Daniels, Laila Robbins.

WELCOME IN VIENNA 127
ROXIE. January, 1988. German-British; Eng. subtitles. (Axel Corti), Gabriel Barylli, Nicolas Brieger.

WELCOME TO 18 89
AMERICAN DISTRIBUTION GROUP. November, 1986. (Terry Carr), Courtney Thorne-Smith, Mariska Hargitay.

WELCOME TO OBLIVION 89
CONCORDE. February, 1990. (Augusto Tomayo), Dack Rambo, Meshach Taylor.

WE'RE NO ANGELS (P) 108
PARAMOUNT. December, 1989. (Neil Jordan), Robert De Niro, Sean Penn.

WE'RE TALKIN' SERIOUS MONEY 95
CINETEL. May, 1992. (James Lemmo), Dennis Farina, Leo Rossi, Fran Drescher.

WEST INDIES 125
MYPHEDUH FILMS. March, 1985. French; Eng. titles. (Med Hondo), Jenny Alpha.

WETHERBY 97
MGM/UA. July, 1985. British. (David Hare), Vanessa Redgrave, Ian Holm.

WHALES OF AUGUST, THE 90
ALIVE FILMS. October, 1987. (Lindsay Anderson), Bette Davis, Lillian Gish, Vincent Price.

WHAT ABOUT BOB? 99
BUENA VISTA. May, 1991. (Frank Oz), Bill Murray, Richard Dreyfuss, Julie Hagerty.

WHAT HAPPENED TO KEROUAC? 96
NEW YORKER FILMS. May, 1986. (Richard Lerner, Lewis MacAdams). Documentary.

WHAT HAVE I DONE TO DESERVE THIS? 100
CINEVISTA. April, 1985. Spanish; Eng. titles. (Pedro Almodovar), Carmen Maura.

WHATEVER IT TAKES 93
AQUARIUS FILMS. March, 1986. (Bob Demchuk), Tom Mason, Martin Balsam.

WHEN FATHER WAS AWAY ON BUSINESS 144
CANNON FILMS. October, 1985. Yugoslavian; Eng. titles. (Emir Kusturica), Moreno E. Bartolli.

WHEN HARRY MET SALLY 95
COLUMBIA. July, 1989. (Rob Reiner), Billy Crystal, Meg Ryan.

WHEN NATURE CALLS 88
TROMA. October, 1984. (Charles Kaufman), David Orange, Barbara Marineau.

WHEN THE RAVEN FLIES 109
SWEDISH FILM INSTITUTE. April, 1985. Icelandic; Eng. titles. (Hrafn Gunnlaugsson), Jacob Thor Einarsson.

WHEN THE WHALES CAME 100
20TH CENTURY FOX. October, 1989. British. (Clive Rees), Paul Scofield, Helen Mirren.

WHEN THE WIND BLOWS 85
KINGS ROAD. March, 1988. British. (Jimmy Murakami). Animated. Voices of Peggy Ashcroft, John Mills.

WHEN TIME RAN OUT (P) 115
WARNER BROS. March, 1980. (James Goldstone), Paul Newman, William Holden.

WHERE 96
WHERE PRODS. September, 1991. Hungarian-U.S. (Gabor Szabo), Miklos Acsm. Renata Satler. B&W.

	Length in Mins.

WHERE ANGELS FEAR TO TREAD 113
FINE LINE FEATURES. February, 1992. British. (Charles Sturridge), Helena Bonham Carter, Rupert Graves, Judy Davis.

WHERE ARE THE CHILDREN? 92
COLUMBIA. January, 1986. (Bruce Malmuth), Jill Clayburgh, Max Gail.

WHERE SPRING COMES LATE 106
SHOCHIKU COMPANY. November, 1988. Japanese; Eng. subtitles. (Yoji Yamada), Chieko Baisho.

WHERE THE BOYS ARE: 1984 97
TRI-STAR. April, 1984. (Hy Averback), Lisa Hartman, Russell Todd.

WHERE THE BUFFALO ROAM 96
UNIVERSAL. April, 1980. (Art Linson), Peter Boyle, Bill Murray.

WHERE THE GREEN ANTS DREAM 100
ORION. February, 1985. German. (Werner Herzog), Bruce Spencer, Wankjuk Marika.

WHERE THE HEART IS 94
BUENA VISTA. February, 1990. (John Boorman), Dabney Coleman, Uma Thurman, Joanna Cassidy.

WHERE THE HEART ROAMS 83
FILM ARTS FOUNDATION. June, 1987. (George Paul Csicsery). Documentary.

WHERE THE RIVER RUNS BLACK 100
MGM/UA. September, 1986. (Christopher Cain), Charles Durning, Alessandro Rabelo.

WHERE'S PICONE? 112
ITALTOONS CORP. April, 1985. Italian; Eng. titles. (Nanni Loy), Giancarlo Giannini, Lina Sastri.

WHISPERS IN THE DARK 102
PARAMOUNT. August, 1992. (Christopher Crowe), Annabella Sciorra, Jamey Sheridan, Alan Alda.

WHISTLE BLOWER, THE 110
HEMDALE RELEASING. July, 1987. British. (Simon Langton), Michael Caine, James Fox.

WHITE FANG 107
BUENA VISTA. January, 1991. (Randal Kleiser), Ethan Hawke, Klaus Maria Brandauer, Seymour Cassel.

WHITE GIRL, THE 88
TONY BROWN PRODS. February, 1990. (Tony Brown), Troy Beyer, Taimak.

WHITE HUNTER, BLACK HEART 112
WARNER BROS. September, 1990. (Clint Eastwood), Clint Eastwood, Jeff Fahey, George Dzundza.

WHITE MEN CAN'T JUMP 114
20TH CENTURY FOX. March, 1992. (Ron Shelton), Wesley Snipes, Woody Harrelson, Rosie Perez.

WHITE MISCHIEF 107
COLUMBIA. April, 1988. British. (Michael Radford), Sarah Miles, Joss Ackland, Charles Dance.

WHITE NIGHTS 135
COLUMBIA. November, 1985. (Taylor Hackford), Mikhail Baryshnikov, Gregory Hines.

WHITE OF THE EYE 110
PALISADES ENTERTAINMENT. May, 1988. British. (Donald Cammell), David Keith, Cathy Moriarty.

WHITE PALACE 105
UNIVERSAL. October, 1990. (Luis Mandoki), Susan Sarandon, James Spader, Eileen Brennan.

WHITE SANDS 101
WARNER BROS. April, 1992. (Roger Donaldson), Willem Dafoe, Mary Elizabeth Mastrantonio, Mickey Rourke.

WHITE WATER SUMMER 90
COLUMBIA. July, 1987. (Jeff Bleckner), Kevin Bacon, Sean Astin.

WHITE WINTER HEAT 91
ERIC CHANDLER LTD. October, 1987. (Warren Miller). Documentary.

WHO FRAMED ROGER RABBIT 103
BUENA VISTA. June, 1988. (Robert Zemeckis), Bob Hoskins, Christopher Lloyd.

WHO'S HARRY CRUMB? 98
TRI-STAR. February, 1989. (Paul Flaherty), John Candy, Jeffrey Jones.

WHO'S THAT GIRL? 92
WARNER BROS. August, 1987. (James Foley), Madonna, Griffin Dunne.

WHOLLY MOSES (P) 105
COLUMBIA. June, 1980. (Gary Weis), Dudley Moore, James Coco, Laraine Newman.

WHOOPEE BOYS 88
PARAMOUNT. August, 1986. (John Byrum), Michael O'Keefe, Paul Rodriguez.

	Length in Mins.

WHORE 85
TRIMARK. October, 1991. (Ken Russell), Theresa Russell, Antonio Fargas, Benjamin Mouton.

WHOSE LIFE IS IT ANYWAY? (P) 118
UNITED ARTISTS. December, 1981. (John Badham), Richard Dreyfuss, John Cassavetes.

WHY ME? 88
TRIUMPH. April, 1990. (Gene Quintano), Christophe Lambert, Christopher Lloyd, Kim Greist.

WHY WOULD I LIE? 106
UNITED ARTISTS. August, 1980. (Larry Peerce), Treat Williams, Lisa Eichhorn.

WICKED LADY, THE 98
MGM/UA. October, 1983. British. (Michael Winner), Faye Dunaway, Alan Bates.

WICKED STEPMOTHER 92
MGM/UA. February, 1989. (Larry Cohen), Bette Davis, Barbara Carrera.

WILD AT HEART 124
SAMUEL GOLDWYN CO. August, 1990. (David Lynch), Nicolas Cage, Laura Dern, Willem Dafoe.

WILD DUCK, THE 96
RKR RELEASING. March, 1985. Australian. (Henri Safran), Liv Ullmann, Jeremy Irons.

WILD GEESE II 125
UNIVERSAL. October, 1985. British. (Peter Hunt), Scott Glenn, Barbara Carrera.

WILD HEARTS CAN'T BE BROKEN 89
BUENA VISTA. May, 1991. (Steve Miner), Gabrielle Anwar, Michael Schoeffling, Cliff Robertson.

WILD LIFE, THE 96
UNIVERSAL. September, 1984. (Art Linson), Christopher Penn, Eric Stoltz.

WILD ORCHID 100
TRIUMPH. April, 1990. (Zalman King), Mickey Rourke, Jacqueline Bisset, Carre Otis.

WILD PAIR, THE 88
TRANS WORLD ENTERTAINMENT. December, 1987. (Beau Bridges), Beau Bridges, Bubba Smith, Lloyd Bridges.

WILD THING 92
ATLANTIC RELEASING. April, 1987. (Max Reid), Rob Knepper, Kathleen Quinlan.

WILD WHEELS 64
TARA RELEASING. August, 1992. (Harrod Blank), Documentary.

WILDCATS 107
WARNER BROS. February, 1986. (Michael Ritchie), Goldie Hawn, Swoosie Kurtz.

WILLIE AND PHIL 116
20TH CENTURY FOX. August, 1980. (Paul Mazursky), Michael Ontkean, Ray Sharkey, Margot Kidder.

WILLOW (P) 125
MGM/UA. May, 1988. (Ron Howard), Val Kilmer, Joanne Whalley.

WILLY/MILLY 90
CONCORDE-CINEMA GROUP. May, 1986. (Paul Schneider), Pamela Segall, Eric Gurry.

WINDOW SHOPPING 96
WORLD ARTISTS. April, 1992. French. (Chantal Akerman), Miriam Boyer, John Berry, Delphine Seyrig.

WINDOWS (P) 94
UNITED ARTISTS. January, 1980. (Gordon Willis), Talia Shire, Joseph Cortese.

WINDRIDER 92
UNITED ARTISTS. June, 1987. (Vincent Monton), Tom Burlinson, Nicole Kidman.

WINDY CITY 105
WARNER BROS. September, 1984. (Armyan Bernstein), John Shea, Kate Capshaw.

WINGS OF DESIRE (DER HIMMEL UBER BERLIN) 130
ORION CLASSICS. April, 1988. German-British; Eng. subtitles. (Wim Wenders), Bruno Ganz, Solveig Dommartin. B&W/color.

WINNERS TAKE ALL 102
APOLLO PICTURES. June, 1987. (Fritz Kiersch), Don Michael Paul, Kathleen York.

WINTER FLIGHT 89
CINECOM INTL. February, 1986. (Roy Battersby), Reece Dinsdale, Nicola Cowper.

WINTER IN LISBON, THE 100
CASTLE HILL. March, 1992. Spanish-French-Portuguese. (Jose Antonio Zorrilla), Dizzy Gillespie, Christian Vadim.

WINTER OF OUR DREAMS 89
SATORI. November, 1982. Australian. (John Duigan), Judy Davis, Bryan Brown.

507

Length in Mins.

WINTER PEOPLE (P) 110
COLUMBIA. April, 1989. (Ted Kotcheff), Kurt Russell, Kelly McGillis.

WINTER TAN, A 91
CIRCLE RELEASING. October, 1988. Canadian. (Jackie Burroughs, Louis Clark, John Frizzell, John Walker, Aerlyn Weissman), Jackie Burroughs, Erando Gonzalez.

WIRED 108
TAURUS ENTERTAINMENT. August, 1989. (Larry Peerce), Michael Chiklis, Ray Sharkey, J.T. Walsh.

WISDOM 109
20TH CENTURY FOX. August, 1986. (Emilio Estevez), Demi Moore, Emilio Estevez, Tom Skerritt.

WISE BLOOD 108
NEW LINE. February, 1980. (John Huston), Brad Dourif, Daniel Shor.

WISE GUYS 91
MGM/UA. April, 1986. (Brian De Palma), Danny DeVito, Joe Piscopo.

WISECRACKS 90
ALLIANCE. June, 1992. Canadian. (Gail Singer), Documentary.

WISH YOU WERE HERE 90
ATLANTIC RELEASING. July, 1987. British. (David Leland), Emily Lloyd, Geoffrey Hutchings, Tom Bell.

WITCHES, THE 92
WARNER BROS. February, 1990. (Nicolas Roeg), Anjelica Huston, Jasen Fisher, Mai Zetterling.

WITCHES OF EASTWICK, THE (P) 118
WARNER BROS. June, 1987. (George Miller), Jack Nicholson, Cher, Susan Sarandon, Michelle Pfeiffer.

WITHNAIL & I 108
CINEPLEX ODEON FILMS. April, 1987. British. (Bruce Robinson), Richard E. Grant, Paul McGann.

WITHOUT A CLUE 106
ORION. October, 1988. British. (Thom Eberhardt), Michael Caine, Ben Kingsley.

WITHOUT A TRACE 117
20TH CENTURY FOX. February, 1983. (Stanley R. Jaffe), Kate Nelligan, Judd Hirsch.

WITHOUT WITNESS 97
IFEX. October, 1984. Russian; Eng. titles. (Nikita Mikhalkov), Irina Kouchenkok.

WITHOUT YOU I'M NOTHING 94
M.C.E.G. May, 1990. (John Boskovich), Sandra Bernhard, Joe Doe.

WITNESS 112
PARAMOUNT. February, 1985. (Peter Weir), Harrison Ford, Kelly McGillis, Lukas Haas.

WIZARD, THE 99
UNIVERSAL. December, 1989. (Todd Holland), Fred Savage, Beau Bridges.

WIZARD OF LONELINESS, THE 110
SKOURAS PICTURES. September, 1988. (Jenny Bowen), Lukas Haas, Lea Thompson.

WIZARD OF SPEED AND TIME, THE 95
SHAPIRO GLICKENHAUS. September, 1989. (Mike Jittlov) Mike Jittlov, Richard Kaye.

WOLF AT THE DOOR, THE 92
INTERNATIONAL FILM MARKETING. August, 1987. Danish-French; in English. (Henning Carlson), Donald Sutherland, Max Von Sydow.

WOLFEN (P) 115
WARNER BROS. July, 1981. (Michael Wadleigh), Albert Finney, Diane Venora.

WOMAN, HER MEN AND HER FUTON, A 90
INTERPERSONAL FILMS. July, 1992. (Mussef Sibay), Jennifer Rubin, Lance Edwards, Michael Cerveris.

WOMAN IN FLAMES, A 106
ALMI CLASSICS. February, 1984. German; Eng. titles. (Robert Van Ackeren), Gudrum Landgrebe.

WOMAN IN RED, THE 87
ORION PICTURES. August, 1984. (Gene Wilder), Gene Wilder, Charles Grodin.

WOMAN NEXT DOOR, THE 106
UA CLASSICS. October, 1981. French; Eng. titles. (François Truffaut), Gerard Depardieu, Fanny Ardant.

WOMAN'S TALE, A 94
ORION CLASSICS. December, 1991. Australian. (Paul Cox), Sheila Florance, Gosia Dobrowolska, Norman Kaye.

WOMBLING FREE 96
SATORI. February, 1984. British. (Lionel Jeffries), David Tomlinson, Frances De La Tour.

WOMEN ON THE VERGE OF A NERVOUS BREAKDOWN 88
ORION CLASSICS. November, 1988. Spanish; Eng. subtitles. (Pedro Almodóvar), Carmen Maura, Antonio Banderas.

Length in Mins.

WOMEN'S CLUB, THE 89
LIGHTNING PICTURES. September, 1987. (Sandra Weintraub), Michael Pare, Maud Adams.

WONDERLAND 103
VESTRON. April, 1989. British. (Philip Saville), Emile Charles, Tony Forsyth.

WORKING GIRL 113
20TH CENTURY FOX. December, 1988. (Mike Nichols), Harrison Ford, Sigourney Weaver, Melanie Griffith.

WORKING GIRLS 90
MIRAMAX FILMS. February, 1987. (Lizzie Borden), Louise Smith, Ellen McElduff.

WORLD ACCORDING TO GARP, THE 136
WARNER BROS. July, 1982. (George Roy Hill), Robin Williams, Mary Beth Hurt, Glenn Close.

WORLD APART, A 112
ATLANTIC RELEASING CORP. June, 1988. British. (Chris Menges), Barbara Hershey, Jodhi May.

WORLD GONE WILD 94
LORIMAR PICTURES. April, 1988. (Lee H. Katzin), Bruce Dern, Michael Pare.

WORTH WINNING 95
20TH CENTURY FOX. October, 1989. (Will Mackenzie), Mark Harmon, Madeleine Stowe.

WRAITH, THE 92
NEW CENTURY VISTA. November, 1986. (Mike Marvin), Charlie Sheen, Nick Cassavetes.

WRONG GUYS, THE 86
NEW WORLD PICTURES. May, 1988. (Danny Bilson), Louie Anderson, Richard Lewis.

WRONG IS RIGHT (P) 119
COLUMBIA. April, 1982. (Richard Brooks), Sean Connery, George Grizzard.

X

XANADU 93
UNIVERSAL. August, 1980. (Robert Greenwald), Olivia Newton-John, Gene Kelly.

Y

YAABA 90
NEW YORKER. October, 1989. Moore. (Idrissa Ouedraogo), Fatimata Sanga, Noufou Ouedraogo.

YEAR MY VOICE BROKE, THE 101
AVENUE ENTERTAINMENT. August, 1988. Australian. (John Duigan), Noah Taylor, Loene Carmen.

YEAR OF LIVING DANGEROUSLY, THE (P) 114
MGM/UA. January, 1983. Australian. (Peter Weir), Mel Gibson, Sigourney Weaver, Linda Hunt.

YEAR OF THE COMET 91
COLUMBIA. April, 1992. (Peter Yates), Penelope Ann Miller, Tim Daly, Louis Jourdan.

YEAR OF THE DRAGON 136
MGM/UA. August, 1985. (Michael Cimino), Mickey Rourke, John Lone.

YEAR OF THE GUN 111
TRIUMPH. November, 1991. (John Frankenheimer), Andrew McCarthy, Valeria Golino, Sharon Stone.

YEAR OF THE QUIET SUN, A 106
SANDSTAR RELEASING. October, 1985. Polish; Eng. titles. (Krzysztof Zanussi), Scott Wilson.

YELLOW HAIR AND THE FORTRESS OF GOLD 102
CROWN INTL. November, 1984. (Matt Cimber), Laurine Landon, Ken Roberson.

YELLOWBEARD 101
ORION. June, 1983. (Mel Damski), Graham Chapman, Peter Boyle.

YEN FAMILY, THE 113
FUJISANKEI COMMUN. INTL. August, 1991. Japanese. (Yojiri Takita), Kaori Momoi, Takeshi Kaga.

YENTL 134
MGM/UA. November, 1983. (Barbra Streisand), Barbra Streisand, Mandy Patinkin, Amy Irving.

YES, GIORGIO 111
MGM/UA. September, 1982. (Franklin J. Schaffner), Luciano Pavarotti, Kathryn Harrold.

YOR, THE HUNTER FROM THE FUTURE 88
COLUMBIA. August, 1983. Italian. (Anthony M. Dawson, Antonio Margheriti), Reb Brown, Corinne Clery.

YOU CAN'T HURRY LOVE 92
LIGHTNING PICTURES. January, 1988. (Richard Martini), David Packer, Scott McGinnis.

YOU TALKIN' TO ME? 97
MGM/UA. September, 1987. (Charles Winkler), Jim Youngs, James Noble.

*Corporate Histories
of the Major Motion Picture
Companies*

Corporate Histories of the Major Motion Picture Companies

Columbia Pictures (Sony Pictures Entertainment, Inc.)

Columbia Pictures can trace its humble beginnings back to 1920 when on Beachwood Drive near Sunset Boulevard in Hollywood there were a number of "shoestring" film companies (the area was dubbed "Poverty Row"), some of which went on to bigger things while others did not. Foremost among the former was the CBC Films Sales Co., an organization formed in 1920 by two brothers, Harry and Jack Cohn, and Joe Brandt, all of whom had worked previously together at Universal Studios. (The name CBC, made up of the initials of the last names of the triumvirate, was also called "Corned Beef & Cabbage" by wits of the day.)

In the beginning CBC was set up to make a series of shorts known as Screen Snapshots, showing the off-screen activities of movie stars and intended also to help publicize the current pictures of the stars. A second project was subsequently introduced: The Hall Room Boys, a comedy series starring the vaudeville team of Edward Flanagan and Neely Edwards. Soon the new company expanded to produce westerns and other comedy shorts, and in 1922 it produced its first feature: "More To Be Pitied Than Scorned." The film cost only $20,000 and realized sales of about $130,000. On January 20, 1924, flushed with their modest success, the owners renamed their company Columbia Pictures.

Two years later the fledgling Columbia had advanced to the point where it began to open film exchanges of its own instead of operating on a states-right basis (selling films outright to local theatres for a flat fee). 1926 was also the year in which Harry Cohn persuaded his associates to buy a small Gower Street lot with two stages and a small office building. Sam Briskin was hired as general manager.

Columbia was now going full steam ahead. In 1929 it produced its first all-talking feature: "The Donovan Affair." This low-budget murder mystery was directed by Frank Capra, who was to become a major factor in the continuing rise of Columbia Pictures.

By this time the company had opened a home office in New York, where Jack Cohn functioned as vice president and treasurer, while Harry ran the production operation on the West Coast. Inevitably there was great rivalry for control between the two brothers with Joe Brandt more often than not in the middle. In 1931 Brandt sold his interest in Columbia and retired. The next year Harry Cohn assumed the title of president, while retaining his post as production chief. (This made him the only movie mogul of the day to hold both positions at the same time.)

Harry Cohn's power over Columbia became increasingly monolithic, and he wielded it to move the company ahead at every opportunity. In 1935 he purchased a 40-acre ranch in Burbank for location filming (later this was expanded to 40 more acres). Pictures—most of them low-budget "Bs" designed for double-billing—were ground out steadily with a few "As" thrown in each year for good measure. The company's first big artistic success appeared in 1934. It was a Capra project called "It Happened One Night," and it was not only the top box office draw of its year but it won five major Academy Awards, including one for best picture.

Capra followed this triumph in the years following with such hits as "Mr. Deeds Goes to Town" (1936); "Lost Horizon" (1937); "You Can't Take It With You" (1938); and "Mr. Smith Goes to Washington" (1939).

Throughout the 40s Columbia prospered and by the end of the decade it could claim to be one of the industry's "major" studios. (Unlike the "Big Five" studios, Columbia did not own any theatres and thus did not have to suffer the traumas of reorganization under the industry's Consent Decrees which forced those studios to divest themselves of their exhibition properties.)

Big commerical hits of the period included "The Jolson Story" (1946) and "Jolson Sings Again" (1949). Columbia could also boast of a string of Oscar winners: "All the King's Men" (1949); "Born Yesterday" (1950); "From Here to Eternity" (1953) and "On the Waterfront" (1954).

In 1951 Columbia diversified into television by forming Screen Gems, a wholly-owned subsidiary set up to make programs and commercials. It became the first major studio to make "telefilms": those features designed expressly for showing on the tube. The division was the project of Ralph Cohn, son of co-founder Jack, and he turned it into an immediate financial success.

With the death of Harry Cohn in 1958 (following Jack's demise in 1956) the company's fortunes in its theatrical production division began a decline that was arrested temporarily in the 60s when the successor management—headed by veterans of the company, Abe Schneider and Leo Jaffe—made some major investments in British film production and released "Lawrence of Arabia" (1962), "A Man for All Seasons" (1966) and the musical "Oliver" (1968).

Other hits of the 60s were "Guess Who's Coming to Dinner" (1967) and "To Sir With Love," (1967); the success of these and others was attributable in large part to Mike Frankovich, who became production head in 1954. In 1968 he turned independent and was succeeded by Stanley Schneider, whose father, Abe, headed the company at the time. Another son of Abe, Bert, helped the company's fortunes vastly in 1969 when he and Robert Rafelson co-produced, "Easy Rider," one of the biggest hits in Columbia's history.

This triumph was followed, however, by a dry period during which profits fell and managerial changes abounded. Rescue from possible bankruptcy came in the person of Herbert Allen Jr., a former Wall Street banker, who bought control of Columbia and took over as president and chief executive officer. He brought in a new management team headed by Alan Hirschfield and David Begelman. Their endeavors produced such hits as "Shampoo" (1975) and "Close Encounters of the Third Kind" (1977), but Begelman left in 1978 after an embezzlement scandal and Hirschfield followed soon thereafter.

Begelman's successor as production chief was Frank Price (who had previously headed Universal Television) and under his regime the company produced such successful fims as "Kramer V. Kramer" (1979), "Tootsie" (1982), and "Ghostbusters" (1984). Price departed in 1985 and in 1986, in a surprise move, David Puttnam, an independent British producer, was signed as chairman of the company with a three-and-a-half year contract. His program of making "quality" pictures at low and medium budgets was not a success, and he was abruptly dropped in 1987. Succeeding him was Dawn Steel, who was named president.

Early in 1982 Columbia had been purchased by the Coca-Cola Company at a price of about $750,000,000. Under its aegis Columbia was one of three companies which in that same year (the others: Home Box Office and CBS, Inc.) joined forces to finance a new production company, Tri-Star Pictures. At the start it was emphasized that the new company would be separate

511

from Columbia, except that Tri-Star would use Columbia's distribution facilities under the direction of Tri-Star executives. Tri-Star's first hit was "The Natural" in 1984. Other successes have been "Rambo: First Blood Part II" (1985); "Rambo III" (1988); "Look Who's Talking" (1989) and "Total Recall" (1990). In a corporate change early in 1989 Tri-Star was made a unit of Columbia Pictures with Jeff Sagansky, president of Tri-Star, reporting to Ms. Steel.

Columbia Pictures Entertainment was formed in 1987 by the Coca-Cola Company in a restructuring of its entertainment business sector. CPE consisted of two film production companies: Columbia Pictures, first incorporated in 1924, and Tri-Star Pictures, which was formed in 1982; two television arms: Columbia Pictures Television (producer of prime time network TV series and distributor of syndicated programs) and Merv Griffin Enterprises (first-run syndication); and Loews Theatre Management Corp., a theatre circuit with some 635 screens in 180 locations.

In September, 1989, the CPE board received and accepted a $3.4 billion cash offer from the Sony Corporation of Japan to buy the company. Sony also assumed $1.3 billion in debt and purchased $100 million in preferred stock from the Coca-Cola Co., which, at the time, owned 49 per cent of Columbia. (Coca-Cola had reduced its interest in CPE when it merged Columbia Pictures with Tri-Star Pictures.) Sony had previously acquired another American show business firm, CBS Records, in 1987 and indicated it would follow the same executive staff policy at CPE as it had adopted for CBS Records—keeping Americans in charge.

To that end it went after the highly successful film producers Jon Peters and Peter Guber ("Rain Man," "Batman," etc.) and their Guber-Peters Entertainment Company. To complete the $200 million deal, Sony had first to extricate the pair from a five-year contract they had signed with Warner Bros. Under a complex agreement (which settled a $1 billion law suit brought by WB against Sony) Sony transferred to Time Warner, Inc., the parent of WB, a 50 per cent interest in the CBS Record Club; gave Time Warner the right to distribute Columbia's films and made-for-TV movies on cable, and exchanged its 35 per cent interest in Burbank Studio for the Lorimar studio lot in Culver City (formerly MGM). Sony also agreed to give Time Warner the stock that Columbia owned in Jerry Weintraub Entertainment, a film production company. (Columbia owned about 15 per cent of the publicly traded stock.) In 1991 Jon Peters resigned from his position as co-chairman, the Culver Studio lot was officially purchased for $80 million, and the company was renamed Sony Pictures Entertainment, Inc. Later that year Mark Canton left Warner Bros. to become the new chairman of Columbia Pictures.

RECENT COLUMBIA RELEASES:

1990: Awakenings, The Fifth Monkey, Flatliners, The Forbidden Dance, The Gods Must Be Crazy II, Lord of the Flies, Misery, Night of the Living Dead, Postcards From the Edge, Revenge, Sibling Rivalry, The Spirit of 76, Texasville, Time of the Gypsies.

1991: Boyz N the Hood, City Slickers, Double Impact, The Inner Circle, Late for Dinner, Men of Respect, Mortal Thoughts, My Girl, The Prince of Tides, Return to the Blue Lagoon, Stone Cold, The Taking of Beverly Hills.

1992: Bram Stoker's Dracula, Falling From Grace, A Few Good Men, Gladiator, Hard Promises, Hero, Honeymoon in Vegas, A League of Their Own, Mo' Money, Mr. Saturday Night, Radio Flyer, A River Runs Through It, Single White Female, Stephen King's Sleepwalkers, Under Suspicion, Year of the Comet.

1993: (Jan.–Oct.): The Age of Innocence, Amos and Andrew, Calendar Girl, El Mariachi, Groundhog Day, Hexed, In the Line of Fire, Last Action Hero, Lost in Yonkers, Malice, Needful Things, Nowhere to Run, The Pickle, Poetic Justice, Striking Distance.

The Walt Disney Company

It was 1923 when Walt Disney first came to Hollywood from Kansas City with his brother Roy, with whom he set up an animation studio in the back of a real estate office. Five years after that Disney introduced his most famous creation: a rodent-like creature called Mickey Mouse, who debuted in a cartoon called "Steamboat Willie" at the Colony Theatre in New York City on November 18. It was an immediate and smash hit, and Disney thereupon commenced his popular series of Silly Symphony cartoons, based on musical themes rather than animal characters, the first of which was called "The Skeleton Dance."

From 1929 through 1931 Disney distributed his product through Columbia Pictures, but he was dissatisfied with the low production advances that company paid and also with their policy of block-booking his work with cartoons made by others that he considered inferior to his. So in 1932 he turned to United Artists and provided them with about 20 cartoons per year—half of them featuring Mickey Mouse and the others in the Silly Symphony series. Production cost of the cartoons is said to have been about $50,000 each. UA paid Disney about 60 per cent of the rentals received from film exhibitors, and his gross income at the time was in the neighborhood of one and a half million dollars per year.

Disney's contract with UA expired in 1937, and he switched over to RKO Radio Pictures, for whom he produced his first feature-length cartoon, "Snow White and the Seven Dwarfs." This film played Radio City Music Hall in New York for five weeks, setting a record of two weeks more than any other film shown in the theatre to that time. "Snow White" has continued to be reissued in theatres over the years, drawing large audiences on each occasion. As of 1988 it still had not been shown on television; nor has it been put out on video cassette.

"Snow White" was followed by a series of hits, all released by RKO: "Pinnochio" (1939); "Dumbo" (1941); "Bambi" (1943); "Cinderella" (1950) and "Peter Pan" (1953), among others that were not so successful. One of the latter was "Fantasia" (1940), a boldly experimental film in which Disney sought to unite his art to the music of great composers like Beethoven and Tschaikovsky. Critical response to the picture was mixed, and the box office proved lukewarm.

RKO's financial troubles, which led to its demise in 1958, caused Walt Disney Productions to break with it in 1953 and form its own national distribution outlet. This arm of the company was name Buena Vista after the street where the Disney studio was located. First picture to be released by the new operation was "The Living Desert" (1953), which won the feature documentary Academy Award for the year and was extremely well-received by the public. "Living Desert" was an outgrowth of the True-Life Adventure shorts Disney had started in 1948.

Enormously rising costs in the production of animation films were behind the decision of the Disney people at this point to concentrate on live-action features. Once again the Disney "touch" turned to box office gold: "20,000 Leagues Under the Sea" (1954) took in over $11 million in domestic rentals, and ten years later "Mary Poppins" (1964) more than quadrupled that figure with over $45 million, to cite only two mega-hits of their time.

With Walt Disney's death in 1966, however, the company's fortunes started to falter. A string of mediocre pictures began to give the Disney "family" label a bad name, and the television programming, although often successful in the ratings, did not live up to the high standards Walt had set. One bright financial spot was to be found in the success of the company's amusement parks. Disneyland Park in Anaheim, California, opened in 1953, had been followed by Walt Disney World in Central Florida (near Orlando) in 1971. (A third park started operations in Tokyo, Japan, in 1983 and has proved similarly successful.) Roy Disney's death in 1971 had left no surviving Disney family members at the helm. This was reversed in 1983 when

Ron Miller, Walt's son-in-law, was made chief executive. It is he who assumed the difficult task of working to push the company's film products out of its founder's shadow by starting Touchstone Pictures, a subsidiary designed to make films appealing to adults without tarnishing the company's image. In 1984 Touchstone delivered "Splash," a big hit, which alone, however, could not solve the company's growing financial troubles.

A drive for new leadership from the outside was spearheaded by Roy Disney, son of Walt's brother of the same name; the second Roy owned stock but had never been given much of a hand in running company operations after the death of its founders. Offers were made to Frank Wells, a former vice chairman of Warner Bros., and Michael Eisner, who at the time was president of Paramount Pictures. The Eisner (chairman)—Wells (president) team took over in late 1984, Miller having been ousted and Roy Disney named vice chairman.

Under the new management the company has prospered in all its divisions, to wit: Touchstone's "Three Men and a Baby" racked up domestic rentals of over $160 million in 1987–88; "The Golden Girls" series on television is a consistent hit; and attendance at the three theme parks is zooming. The latter are to be joined in 1992 by a $2 billion EuroDisneyland near Paris.

Early in 1990 Disney announced a massive ten-year expansion agenda which will see it add hundreds of new rides and shows to its existing theme parks, build second attractions, in Southern California and Florida, and open new units in Tokyo and Paris. In fiscal 1989 Disney's theme parks and resorts racked up operating earnings of $785.4 million, which was 64 per cent of the company's total operating profits of $1.2 billion.

During 1990 Disney continued to do well in its motion picture division, bolstered considerably by a surprise springtime hit in "Pretty Woman" which looked to be not only the top-grossing film of 1990 but definitely the biggest hit in Disney history. Its "Dick Tracy" was one of a handful of films that passed the $100 million mark in the important summer theatrical grosses. The company's latest division, Hollywood Pictures, began in the summer of 1990 on a good note with the hit thriller "Arachnophobia," and released their biggest success "The Hand That Rocks the Cradle" in January of 1992. Certainly the studio's greatest triumph in recent years was "Beauty and the Beast" which took in over $145,000,000 at U.S. box offices and became the first animated feature to receive an Oscar nomination for Best Picture. This triumph was followed by an even more impressive run for 1992's "Aladdin" which became the first Disney release to gross more than $200 million.

In May of 1993 Disney purchased the highly successful independent distributor Miramax Films, which would continue to operate as a separate company.

RECENT DISNEY RELEASES:

1990: Arachnophobia, Betsy's Wedding, Dick Tracy, Duck-Tales: The Movie, Ernest Goes to Jail, Fire Birds, Green Card, Mr. Destiny, Pretty Woman, The Rescuers Down Under, Spaced Invaders, Stella, Taking Care of Business, Three Men and a Little Lady, Where the Heart Is.

1991: Beauty and the Beast, Billy Bathgate, Deceived, The Doctor, Ernest Scared Stupid, Father of the Bride, The Marrying Man, One Good Cop, Oscar, Paradise, The Rocketeer, Run, Scenes From a Mall, Shipwrecked, True Identity, V.I. Warshawski, What About Bob?, White Fang, Wild Hearts Can't Be Broken.

1992: Aladdin, Blame It on the Bellboy, Captain Ron, Consenting Adults, Crossing the Bridge, The Distinguished Gentleman, Encino Man, The Gun in Betty Lou's Handbag, The Hand That Rocks the Cradle, Honey I Blew Up the Kid, Medicine Man, The Mighty Ducks, The Muppet Christmas Carol, Newsies, Noises Off, Passed Away, Sarafina!, Sister Act, Straight Talk, A Stranger Among Us, 3 Ninjas.

1993 (Jan.–Oct.): The Adventures of Huck Finn, Alive, Another Stakeout, Aspen Extreme, Born Yesterday, Bound by

Honor, The Cemetery Club, Cool Runnings, A Far Off Place, Father Hood, Guilty As Sin, Hocus Pocus, Homeward Bound: The Incredible Journey, Indian Summer, The Joy Luck Club, Life With Mikey, Money for Nothing, My Boyfriend's Back, The Nightmare Before Christmas, The Program, Son-in-Law, Super Mario Bros., Swing Kids, What's Love Got to Do With It.

Metro-Goldwyn-Mayer, Inc. (formerly MGM-Pathe, MGM/UA)

United Artists was purchased by the Metro-Goldwyn-Mayer Film Company in 1981 with the then present executives retained and the former company becoming a wholly-owned subsidiary of the latter as parent. In 1983 the name of the parent company was changed to MGM/UA Entertainment Co.

In 1986 Turner Broadcasting System, purchased MGM/UA Entertainment Co. for approximately $1.5 billion and sold the UA portion to Tracinda Corporation along with the MGM motion picture and television production and distribution businesses and the home entertainment division. The MGM lot and laboratory were sold by Turner to Lorimar-Telepictures. Turner retained only the MGM film library, which includes pre-1948 name to MGM/UA Communications Co., kept the MGM and UA motion picture production and marketing entities separate (United Artists Pictures, Inc. and Metro-Goldwyn-Mayer Pictures, Inc.) and combined the two companies' television operations into one group (MGM/UA Television). Meanwhile the distribution outlet (MGM/UA Distribution Co.) remained virtually unchanged.

Histories of MGM and UA prior to their merger appear below.

Since completion of the deal with Turner, Kirk Kerkorian, the financier who controls MGM-UA, has proposed a number of other asset sales and spinoffs, none of which worked out. In one such the Qintex Group of Australia in 1989 agreed to pay $1.5 billion for the company, but the deal collapsed when Qintex could not come up with all the money. Negotiations have also been held with a number of potential acquirers, including Turner Broadcasting (again), and Pathe Communications Corporation, an entertainment company controlled by the Italian financier Giancarlo Parretti.

MGM-UA has had a few hits in recent years, including "Rain Man" and "A Fish Called Wanda," but most of its pictures have been disappointments at the box office. In 1989–90 new production activity was virtually dormant.

Pathe Communications Corporation's $1.3 billion acquisition of MGM/UA in November of 1990 was just the beginning of a new series of distribution setbacks, lawsuits and corporate problems for the eternally troubled studio. Purchased by Italian financier Giancarlo Parretti the new company was now renamed MGM-Pathe, and United Artists as distributor and/or producer of new product was now a part of history. No sooner had Parretti stepped in when the money problems began with the studio accused of non-payment by various vendors and corporations. MGM's further financial woes were reflected in its decision to yank the John Candy vehicle "Delirious" from its scheduled opening date because it could not come up with the $7 million needed to publicize the movie.

By April of 1991 Parretti was removed from his position as chairman with control given over to Alan Ladd, Jr. That month MGM-Pathe was given a $145 million loan from Credit Lyonnais, allowing them to start up film distribution after months of inactivity. When it was revealed that the parent corporation, Pathe Communications, had authorized Credit Lyonnais to put up half the company for sale, Parretti attempted to reinstate himself as studio chairman. Due to loans and transactions totalling up to $885 million Pathe Communications was some $395 million in debt to Credit Lyonnais. In May 1992 Credit Lyonnais bought up 98.5% of MGM-Pathe, thereby officially disposing of Parretti. Following this move the company was once again rechristened Metro-Goldwyn-Mayer Inc.

In July of 1993 Alan Ladd Jr. was dismissed from his position and replaced by former Paramount Pictures chairman Frank G. Mancuso. The company also revived United Artists with its August 1993 release "Son of the Pink Panther."

RECENT MGM RELEASES

1990: Blue Steel, Daddy's Dyin' . . . Who's Got the Will?, Death Warrant, Delta Force 2, Desperate Hours, Instant Karma, Mortal Passions, Quigley Down Under, The Russia House, Stanley & Iris.

1991: Company Business, Crooked Hearts, Delirious, Fires Within, Harley Davidson & the Marlboro Man, The Indian Runner, Liebestraum, Life Stinks, The Man in the Moon, Not Without My Daughter, Rush, Shattered, Thelma & Louise, Time Bomb.

1992: Crisscross, The Cutting Edge, Diggstown, The Lover, Of Mice and Men, Once Upon a Crime, The Vagrant.

1993 (Jan.–Oct.): Benny & Joon, Body of Evidence, Fatal Instinct, Flight of the Innocent, The Meteor Man, Rich in Love, Son of the Pink Panther (UA), Undercover Blues, Untamed Heart.

History of Metro-Goldwyn-Mayer

Metro-Goldwyn-Mayer, Inc., formerly known as Loew's, Inc., took its original name from its founder, the late Marcus Loew, a pioneer in the nickelodeon and arcade era of the movies. Among his early associates were Adolph Zukor and the brothers Joseph M. and Nicholas M. Schenck. For years the organization was active exclusively in film exhibition, chiefly in theatres with a mixed picture and vaudeville policy. In 1910, after several years of expansion, Marcus Loew organized Loew's Consolidated Enterprises. The next year this was succeeded by Loew's Theatrical Enterprises, extending the scope of theatre operations from New York into other cities.

By 1919, Loew's had partial or entire control of 56 theatres. Loew's, Inc., was organized in October, 1919, and acquired the stock of Loew's Theatrical Enterprises. Continuing a policy of gradual expansion of theatre interests, business had reached a point where Marcus Loew, Nicholas M. Schenck and other executives were looking about for a way of uniting their theatre interests to an active production organization. This problem was met in 1920 with the acquisition of the stock of Metro Pictures Corporation, which later turned out such films as "The Prisoner of Zenda," "Scaramouche," and "The Four Horsemen."

The move to fortify the playing schedules of the Loew's Theatres with an annual production output proved sound, and a further expansion was in order. In 1924, Marcus Loew and his associates made successful overtures for the interests in the Goldwyn Company, which had been started in 1917, and Loew's became the owner of the merged Metro-Goldwyn stock. Shortly afterwards producing assets of Louis B. Mayer Pictures, including the services of Mayer, Irving Thalberg and J. Robert Rubin were acquired by the company and the production organization controlled by Loew's took the name of Metro-Goldwyn-Mayer.

In 1936 and 1937, to simplify the corporate structure, legal control of the entire production and distribution organization was vested in Loew's, Inc., with Metro-Goldwyn-Mayer being used merely as a trade name.

On February 6, 1952 the consent decree against Loew's, Inc., was signed in New York. It provided a divorce between the producing and distributing phases of the corporation and its domestic exhibition activities and interests.

Trade practices and other provisions of the Loew's decree generally followed those of earlier decrees. Pursuant to the consent decree MGM, Inc. and its wholly owned subsidiary, Loew's Theatres, entered into a reorganization agreement providing for the transfer by MGM, Inc. of its theatre assets located in the United States and Canada and Radio Station WMGM to Loew's Theatres, Inc. in exchange for all of the issued and outstanding shares of Common Stock of Loew's Theatres, Inc. and the distribution of said shares of Common Stock to the stockholders of Metro-Goldwyn-Mayer Inc. on the basis of one share of such stock for each share of Common Stock of Metro-Goldwyn-Mayer Inc. to be thereafter outstanding. At the same time the outstanding shares of stock of Metro-Goldwyn-Mayer Inc. were reclassified by the filing of an amendment to its Certificate of Incorporation which changed each of its issued and outstanding shares of Common Stock without par value into one-half of a share of Common Stock without par value.

Among notable pictures in the company history have been "The Big Parade," silent "Ben Hur," "Grand Hotel," "Dinner at Eight," "The Thin Man," "David Copperfield," "A Tale of Two Cities," "Mutiny on the Bounty," "Captains Courageous," "Goodbye Mr. Chips," "Mrs. Miniver," "The Wizard of Oz," "Gone With the Wind," produced by David O. Selznick, released by M-G-M, "Madame Curie," "The Yearling," "Battleground," "King Solomon's Mines," "Quo Vadis," "Seven Brides for Seven Brothers," "Ben Hur" (sound), "Doctor Zhivago," "2001: A Space Odyssey," "That's Entertainment," etc.

In 1973 the company ceased distribution of its own pictures, licensing domestic distribution to United Artists and foreign distribution to CIC.

In June, 1980 the motion picture operations of MGM, Inc. were spun off to stockholders, share for share, as Metro-Goldwyn-Mayer Film Co.

Orion Pictures

Orion Pictures was formed in 1978 by members of the Management Group, a company that had been responsible for developing the film library of United Artists Corporation since 1951. The parent corporation, Filmways Inc., changed its name to Orion Pictures Corporation in 1982.

With distribution handled by Warner Bros., Orion released its first motion picture, "A Little Romance," in April of 1979. Their first substantial hit, the Dudley Moore-Julie Andrews comedy "10" premiered in the Autumn of that year. During their first 2½ years Orion produced 23 films, the most successful of which was another Dudley Moore vehicle, "Arthur" (1981). There were also four joint releases with Warner Bros.

Starting in 1982 Orion was now its own distributor scoring impressive box office returns on such films as "First Blood," "The Terminator," "Hannah and Her Sisters," "Back to School," "Throw Momma From the Train," and "Bull Durham." To further legitimize the company's position as an industry major Orion won four Academy Awards for Best Picture in a seven year span: "Amadeus" (1984), "Platoon" (1986), "Dances With Wolves" (1990), and "The Silence of the Lambs" (1991). A classics unit was also developed to handle specialized and foreign art house films. These titles included "Another Country," "Jean de Florette," "Wings of Desire," "Cyrano de Bergerac," and "Europa Europa."

Despite the enormous box office revenues taken in by both "Dances With Wolves" and "The Silence of the Lambs" Orion was facing financial hardships in the 1990's as too many failed films drained away profits. The company officially declared bankruptcy in December 1991, claiming debts of some $500 million. Several studio releases completed during that year were put on the shelf until outside financing was available.

Through a personal guarantee from its principal stockholder, John Kluge, Orion managed to stay afloat and reorganize. By mid-1993 Kluge owned 56% of the company. In 1992 both Arthur Krim, Chairman of the Board since 1978, and Eric Pleskow, who began as President and Chief Executive Officer that same year, departed, the latter replaced by Leonard White.

In the summer of 1993 a joint venture with Metromedia Co. resulted in Orion Productions Co. with the idea of financing new films. Six older titles, long in waiting, were scheduled for distribution in 1994.

RECENT ORION RELEASES

1990: Alice, Cadillac Man, Dances With Wolves, Everybody Wins, The First Power, The Hot Spot, The Last of the Finest, Love at Large, Madhouse, Mermaids, Miami Blues, Navy SEALS, Robocop 2, State of Grace.

1991: Bill & Ted's Bogus Journey, Eve of Destruction, F/X 2, Little Man Tate, Mystery Date, The Silence of the Lambs.

1992: Article 99, Love Field, Shadows and Fog.

1993: The Dark Half, Married to It, Me and the Kid, Robocop 3.

Paramount Pictures

Paramount Pictures Corp., may be said to have taken most of its origins from the activities of Adolph Zukor, who entered the amusement field in the dawn years with a penny arcade, with Hales's Tours, a motion picture exhibition device, and with nickelodeon theatres, including an early association with the late Marcus Loew in those undertakings. Mr. Zukor in 1912 formed the Engadine Corporation, to distribute an imported picture, which evolved into his Famous Players Film Company, which was to make famous plays with famous players in them. W. W. Hodkinson, emerging from General Film Company, the "trust" of the day, in 1914 formed Paramount Pictures Corporation, which took over distribution of the Zukor product and along with it the product of the Jesse L. Lasky Feature Play Company and others. This led to a course of mergers, with Mr. Zukor dominant.

Famous Players-Lasky Corporation was incorporated on July 19, 1916. In 1917 twelve producing companies merged with it. At the same time the corporation integrated production and distribution by acquiring a national distribution system through a merger with Artcraft Pictures Corporation and Paramount Pictures Corporation.

In 1919 the corporation started its theatre acquisition program. It acquired stock interest in Southern Enterprises, Inc., with 135 theatres in the South; in 1920 it acquired stock interest in New England Theatres, Inc., with 50 New England theatres; in the Butterfield Theatre Circuit with 70 theatres in Michigan about 1926; in Balaban & Katz with 50 theatres in Illinois at the same time. Later numerous theatres in the West and Middle West were acquired.

Paramount's first great star was Mary Pickford, around whom Mr. Zukor built his Famous Players. The roster of the organization has included a preponderance of the great names of the screen. "The Covered Wagon," and "The Ten Commandments" are landmarks of Paramount tradition.

In April, 1927, the corporate name was changed to Paramount Famous Lasky Corporation, and in April, 1930, to Paramount Publix Corporation. In 1933, Paramount Publix Corporation was adjudicated bankrupt in the Federal District Court for the Southern District of New York. In June, 1935, it was reorganized under Section 77B of the Bankruptcy Act under the name of Paramount Pictures, Inc.

In December, 1949, as a result of the reorganization required by the Consent Decree in the action of the Government against the major companies, Paramount split into two companies— Paramount Pictures Corporation, for production-distribution, and United Paramount Theatres, Inc., for theatre operation.

With the other studios following World War II Paramount was hurt by the decline in theatre audiences; it experimented with 3-D in 1953 and then the next year introduced a new process called VistaVision to compete with CinemaScope, which was being promoted by 20th Century Fox. First film in the process was "White Christmas," a big hit, as was Cecil B. DeMille's final spectacle, a remake of "The Ten Commandments" in

1956. VistaVision was phased out a couple of years later, however; it proved too expensive and CinemaScope had become the "norm" for the industry.

Paramount merged with Gulf & Western Industries Oct. 19, 1966, with Gulf & Western as the surviving corporation and Paramount as a subsidiary with its own management. Barney Balaban, former exhibitor who became president of Paramount in 1935, was retained in an honorary position, along with Zukor. Robert Evans, a young producer and former actor, was brought in as production head under Charles Bluhdorn, head of Gulf & Western. Bluhdorn expanded theatrical film production and increased the company's investment in TV production (an area Paramount had been slow in moving into in the 50s). Evans had great success with "Love Story" (1970) and two Francis Ford Coppola pictures, "The Godfather" (1972) and "The Godfather, Part II" (1974).

With the departure of Evans in 1975 to become an independent producer the company moved ahead under Barry Diller as chief executive officer and later under Frank Mancuso, promoted from vice president in charge of distribution to chairman of Paramount Pictures in 1984. The decade of the '80s brought the company many successes: including the "Star Trek" series; the "Indiana Jones" films; "Fatal Attraction," "Top Gun," etc.

Ned Tanen left Universal Pictures the same year to become president of Paramount. In 1987 the studio celebrated its 75th anniversary.

In 1989 Gulf and Western changed its name to Paramount Communications, Inc., around the same time that Martin S. Davis, chairman, sought to intervene in the deal for Time, Inc. to merge with Warner Communications Inc. (see Warner Bros. history). The hostile move to block that deal and allow Paramount to acquire Time instead was blocked in the courts.

Davis began streamlining Paramount Communications in order to focus on entertainment and publishing. One move was to sell off the company's financial services business, the Associates, for $3.3 billion in the fall of 1989. In the spring of 1991 Frank Mancuso was suddenly ousted from his position as chairman to be replaced by former NBC head Brandon Tartikoff.

Paramount continues to hold interests in U.S. theatres, maintaining a 50 per cent investment in Cinamerica Limited Partnership, which includes Mann Theatres in the West and Trans-Lux Theatres in the East. In Aug. 1992 the company planned to enter the theme-park business, purchasing Kings Entertainment Co. for $400 million. Brandon Tartikoff resigned in October 1992 to be replaced by Sherry Lansing.

In September 1993 Viacom Inc. offered to purchase the company for $8.2 billion in cash and stock. Viacom, which owns MTV, Nickelodeon and Showtime, planned on renaming the company Paramount Viacom International with Sumner Redstone as chairman. Soon after Barry Diller's home shopping company, QVC Network Inc., put in its bid for $9.5 million. A final agreement was expected to be reached in the Fall.

RECENT PARAMOUNT RELEASES

1990: Almost an Angel, Another 48 HRS, Crazy People, Days of Thunder, Flashback, Funny About Love, Ghost, The Godfather Part III, The Hunt for Red October, Internal Affairs, A Show of Force, Stephen King's Graveyard Shift, Tales From the Darkside: The Movie, The Two Jakes, Welcome Home Roxy Carmichael.

1991: The Addams Family, All I Want for Christmas, Body Parts, The Butcher's Wife, Dead Again, Flight of the Intruder, Frankie & Johnny, He Said/She Said, The Naked Gun 2½: The Smell of Fear, Necessary Roughness, The Perfect Weapon, Regarding Henry, Soapdish, Star Trek IV: The Undiscovered Country, Stepping Out, Talent for the Game, True Colors.

1992: Bebe's Kids, Bob Roberts, Boomerang, Brain Donors, Cool World, 1492: Conquest of Paradise, Jennifer Eight, Juice, K2, Ladybugs, Leap of Faith, Patriot Games, Pet Sematary Two, School Ties, There Goes the Neighborhood, Wayne's World, Whispers in the Dark.

1993 (Jan.–Oct.): Bopha, Coneheads, Fire in the Sky, The Firm, Indecent Proposal, It's All True, Searching for Bobby Fischer, Sliver, The Temp, The Thing Called Love.

TriStar Pictures

Tri-Star Pictures began in November of 1982 as a joint venture of three major corporatons, Columbia Pictures, CBS Television and Home Box Office, with the idea that these diverse markets—theatrical, broadcast TV and pay TV—would compliment each other. The company, headquartered in New York, was launched in the Spring of 1984 with "Where the Boys Are" followed by its first success, "The Natural" in May. Within its first year Tri-Star was considered an "instant major" being responsible for one of the year's best picture nominees at the 1984 Academy Awards: "Places in the Heart."

The company went public in 1985, the same year that CBS sold its interest in the partnership, primarily to Columbia. The next year HBO sold most of its interest thereby making Columbia Pictures' parent company, Coca-Cola the largest shareholder. In 1987 Coca-Cola merged Tri-Star with its Entertainment Business Sector, which included Columbia Pictures and Columbia Television, resulting in Columbia Pictures Entertainment. Tri-Star continued to function as a separate distributor within CPE and moved its headquarters from Manhattan to Burbank, California.

The Sony Corporation purchased Columbia Pictures Entertainment in 1989 and later renamed the parent corporation Sony Pictures Entertainment. Tri-Star, along with Columbia, moved from their headquarters in Burbank to the former MGM lot in Culver City in 1990. The following year the hyphen was dropped from the company name making it simply TriStar Pictures.

RECENT TRISTAR RELEASES:

1990: Air America, Avalon, Blind Fury, The Freshman, I Love You to Death, Jacob's Ladder, Look Who's Talking Too, Loose Cannons, Mountains of the Moon, Narrow Margin, Q&A, Side Out, Total Recall.

1991: Another You, Bingo, Bugsy, The Doors, The Fisher King, Hook, Hudson Hawk, L.A. Story, Terminator 2: Judgment Day, Toy Soldiers.

1992: Basic Instinct, Candyman, Chaplin, City of Joy, Husbands and Wives, Thunderheart, Universal Soldier, Wind.

1993 (Jan.–Oct.): Cliffhanger, Manhattan Murder Mystery, Mr. Jones, Rudy, Sleepless in Seattle, Sniper, So I Married an Axe Murderer, Weekend at Bernie's 2, Wilder Napalm.

Twentieth Century Fox

Twentieth Century Fox Film Corporation is the end result of a business begun back in the nickelodeon days of show business by William Fox. From modest beginnings it has grown to a vast company with many divisions—feature motion picture production and distribution, television production and distribution, and television stations ownership.

At the turn of the century, Mr. Fox, then in textiles, entered the arcade and nickelodeon business and became a member of the exhibition firm of Fox, Moss and Brill. His associates were B. S. Moss and Sol Brill. This association led to the establishment by Mr. Fox of a film exchange, the Greater New York Film Rental Company. In 1913 he organized the Box Office Attraction Company, later acquiring the services of Winfield Sheehan, associated with Mr. Fox for many years.

February 1, 1915, the Fox Film Corporation was founded with the intention of combining production, exhibition and distribution under one name. Film exchanges were established in a dozen cities throughout the country. Today the company has 80 domestic branches and offices located throughout the world.

In 1917, with the shift of production from the east to the west coast, Fox Films moved into its Sunset Studio in Hollywood.

When sound came to the industry, in 1926, Fox Film was able to use the pioneering efforts of Theodore Case and Earl I. Sponable, who invented Movietone, a sound-on-film process.

About 1929 there started a series of reorganizations and financial deals and involvements, principally of which was the purchase by Fox Films of control of Loew's, Inc., for approximately $44,000,000. By order of the Government, the Fox Company's ownership of Loew's was later dissolved and various banking interests acquired control of the stock in the Loew Company.

During these reorganizations, William Fox's connections with the company were discontinued. Sidney R. Kent joined the company as executive vice-president on April 1, 1932, and two weeks later became the company's president. Mr. Kent continued as president until his death, early in 1942.

In 1935, The Fox Film Corporation was merged with a major producing organization. Twentieth Century Pictures, headed by Joseph M. Schenck and the company assumed its present corporate name. This merger brought Darryl F. Zanuck into the company as vice-president in charge of production of the merged organizations. Mr. Schenck became chairman of the board and continued in that position until his resignation in June, 1942, when Wendell L. Wilkie took over the post.

Darryl F. Zanuck remained as Production Head until 1956, when he resigned to enter independent production. Buddy Adler succeeded Darryl F. Zanuck as Production Head. Upon Mr. Adler's death, Robert Goldstein and then Peter G. Levathes took over studio reins.

Following Mr. Kent's death, Spyros P. Skouras a leading theatre operator, became president. On July 25, 1962, Darryl F. Zanuck was elected president and Spyros P. Skouras was named chairman of the board, a position he held until March 1969 when he retired. Thereafter Richard D. Zanuck was named Executive Vice-President in Charge of Worldwide Producion. Within a short period of time the Zanucks turned an ailing company into one of leadership and prestige in the entertainment field. In 1969, Darryl F. Zanuck was made Chairman of the Board and Chief Executive Officer, and Richard D. Zanuck was made president.

In 1971, 20th Century-Fox Film Corporation weathered a trying proxy fight which had the resounding effect of giving the company added resolve. A new managerial team was elected by the Board of Directors which saw Dennis C. Stanfill succeeding Richard D. Zanuck as President of the company, and, shortly thereafter, elevated to the position of Chairman of the Board of Directors and the studio's Chief Executive Officer.

In June, 1972, the majority of the company's East Coast personnel consolidated with that of the West Coast, thus placing the distribution, publicity, advertising, promotion and general accounting departments all under the same roof.

Fox merged with a company owned by Marvin Davis and his family—effective June 12, 1981. In 1985 Davis sold the company to Rupert Murdoch.

In October 1985 Fox, Inc. was formed. It was a consolidation consisting of three principal operating units: Twentieth Century Fox Film Corporation, Fox Television Stations, Inc. and Fox Broadcasting Company. Then in the summer of 1989 a revamping was announced that signalled a new emphasis on motion pictures. The company appointed Joe Roth, an independent producer and director, as chairman of its major film-making unit and renamed it the Fox Film Corporation. Roth has a mandate to increase production to 30 films a year as compared to the 12 films released in 1989. Roth's appointment marks the first time a film director has run a major studio since Ernst Lubitsch headed Paramount Pictures in 1935.

Roth's first picture for Fox, "Die Hard 2," proved to be a big hit in the summer of 1990. This was followed by the gigantic success of "Home Alone" which went on to become the 2nd highest grossing film in the studio's history. Roth announced his resignation in December of 1992. His replacement, Peter Chernin, was a Fox television executive.

RECENT FOX RELEASES

1990: The Adventures of Ford Fairlane, Come See the Paradise, Die Hard 2, Downtown, Edward Scissorhands, The Exorcist III, Frankenstein Unbound, Home Alone, Marked for Death, Miller's Crossing, Nightbreed, Nuns on the Run, Pacific Heights, Predator 2, Short Time, Vital Signs, Young Guns II.

1991: Barton Fink, Class Action, The Commitments, Dutch, Dying Young, The Five Heartbeats, For the Boys, Grand Canyon, Hot Shots, Mannequin 2 on the Move, Naked Lunch, Only the Lonely, Point Break, Sleeping With the Enemy, The Super, 29th Street.

1992: Alien[3], Back in the U.S.S.R., Buffy the Vampire Slayer, FernGully . . . The Last Rain Forest, Folks!, Hoffa, Home Alone 2: Lost in New York, Jumpin' at the Boneyard, The Last of the Mohicans, Love Potion No. 9, Man Trouble, My Cousin Vinny, Night and the City, Prelude to a Kiss, Rapid Fire, Shining Through, Storyville, This is My Life, Toys, Unlawful Entry, Used People, White Men Can't Jump.

1993 (Jan.–Oct.): Best of the Best 2, The Beverly Hillbillies, Freaked, The Good Son, Hear No Evil, Hot Shots! Part Deux, Jack the Bear, Once Upon a Forest, Rising Sun, Robin Hood: Men in Tights, Rookie of the Year, The Sandlot, The Vanishing.

Universal Pictures

Universal Pictures has a history stemming from the pioneer days of the industry. The company was formed under the title "Universal" in 1912, when Carl Laemmle amalgamated Bison 101, Nestor, Powers and several other organizations, including his own Imp firm. Carl Laemmle had entered the picture business as an exhibitor, opening the White Front Theatre on Milwaukee Avenue, Chicago, February 24, 1906.

He founded Laemmle Film Service on October 1 of that year, quit the Patents Company in April, 1909, and released his first Independent Motion Picture (Imp) Company "Feature," "Hiawatha," length, 998 feet, on October 25, 1909.

In that experimental epoch, Universal launched the star system by hiring Florence Lawrence for $1,000 a week and billing her as "Queen of the Screen." The studio also produced the screen's initial "expos" film, "Traffic in Souls," first film to be reviewed by the drama critics of the daily press. Universal acquired a studio at Sunset Boulevard and Gower Street in 1914, and began making pictures in Hollywood. In 1915, production was moved to the present site, Universal City. Here appeared Wallace Reid, Lon Chaney, Mary Pickford, Rudolph Valentino and Boris Karloff, among many others.

"Foolish Wives," "first million-dollar feature," "The Hunchback of Notre Dame," "All Quiet On the Western Front," and screen dramas of like import, were filmed in the decades which followed.

On March 16, 1920, Carl Laemmle and R. H. Cochrane assumed complete control of the company.

On April 2, 1936, Universal passed under new management, with J. Cheever Cowdin as chairman of the board. On January 6, 1938, Nate J. Blumberg became president of the company.

Under the new management Universal embarked upon the policy of developing star values and was most successful during the time in the establishment of such names as Deanna Durbin, Abbott & Costello, Maria Montez, Donald O'Connor and others under contract.

During 1946, the company underwent its second transformation. Production-wise, it eliminated the production of all so-called "B" pictures, Westerns and serials, following a merger and acquisition of the assets of International Pictures Corp. of Leo Spitz and William Goetz. Mr. Spitz and Mr. Goetz became the production heads and Universal-International trademark emerged.

Secondly, Universal completed a distribution deal with the J. Arthur Rank organization for the American distribution of the top British pictures produced by the Rank affiliated companies.

The year 1946 also saw the emergence of United World Pictures, a wholly-owned Universal subsidiary, to handle production and distribution of non-theatrical films. United World acquired the Bell and Howell Filmsound Library of 6,000 subjects. It then purchased Castle Films, the largest seller of non-theatrical packaged films to the home. The year 1950 saw the resignation of J. Cheever Cowdin with Mr. Blumberg assuming full command. Alfred E. Daff, who had been foreign sales manager, assumed the top post in the foreign distribution set-up and then became director of world sales with the resignation of W. A. Scully—a post without parallel in the industry. Mr. Scully was to continue until 1954 as domestic sales consultant.

Charles J. Feldman was appointed domestic sales manager under Mr. Daff and Americo Aboaf foreign sales head.

In November, 1951 Decca Records acquired approximately 28 percent of Universal's common stock to make it the largest single stockholder in the company. For this interest Decca paid $3,773,914 for the 234,900 shares involved and the right to purchase 32,500 additional warrants, according to a report made by Milton R. Rackmil, president of Decca, to the Securities and Exchange Commission.

He reported that of these shares, 78,000 were purchased on the New York Stock Exchange, while the balance, most of which formerly was owned by the Paul G. Brown estate, was bought from Gertrude Bergman. Maurice A. Bergman, Lewis Fox Blumberg, N. J. Blumberg, Vera F. Blumberg, Alfred E. Daff, Edith Mayer Goetz, William Goetz, Doris Jean Mayer and Leo Spitz.

The warrants were purchased from N. J. Blumberg and Doris Jean Mayer, at a reported price of $5 each. The purchases on the New York Stock Exchange were made at current market prices; the purchases from the individuals named were made at prices reached as a result of negotiations. Purchase of the holdings of Spitz as executive head of production and Goetz as executive in charge of production. Their block of about 15,000 shares was acquired at approximately $15 a share. Blumberg's holdings included 15,000 shares and 32,500 warrants. In announcing the purchase, Rackmil declared, "The ownership of these shares will bring about a close association between our two companies. We have kindred interests in the entertainment business. These interests can be developed for our mutual benefit. The transaction indicates the confidence that our respective companies have in the future of the motion picture and allied industries."

In the spring of 1952, Decca Records became the controlling stockholder of Universal. Its interests were acquired partly in the open market and partly through the purchase of all J. Arthur Rank's stock in the company. As a result, Milton R. Rackmil, president of Decca Records, was made a member of the Universal board and subsequently elected president of Universal in July, 1952. In June of 1962, MCA, Inc., exchanged its common and a newly-issued preferred stock for Decca capital stock leading to a consolidation of the two companies and making Universal Pictures Company the theatrical film producing division of MCA, Inc.

In the Spring of 1964 the creation of the Universal City Studios image started with the separate motion picture and television arms. On March 25, 1966, Universal Pictures became a division of Universal City Studios, Inc., a subsidiary of MCA, Inc.

In 1982 Universal released Steven Spielberg's "E.T.: The Extra Terrestrial," which became the top-grossing film of all time, racking up over $228 million in film rentals in the domestic market. Other recent success have included the "Back to the Future" series; "Twins," "Field of Dreams," "Parenthood," "Born on the Fourth of July," "Kindergarten Cop," "Cape Fear," and "Fried Green Tomatoes."

November of 1990 saw two major events in the studio's recent history. A fire swept through the backlot in Universal City destroying acres of sets and causing millions of dollars worth of damage. Further upheaval resulted from MCA Inc.'s purchase by the Matsushita Electrical Industrial Company for an estimated $6.6 billion, the most expensive sale of an American company to the Japanese in history.

Steven Spielberg's "Jurassic Park" arrived in the summer of 1993 and quickly set box office records, grossing over $300 million. It would eventually land in the number two position on the all-time moneymakers list, right behind "E.T."

RECENT UNIVERSAL RELEASES

1990: Back to the Future Part III, Bird on a Wire, Child's Play 2, Coupe de Ville, Cry-Baby, Darkman, Ghost Dad, The Guardian, Havana, Henry and June, Jetsons: The Movie, Kindergarten Cop, Mo' Better Blues, Opportunity Knocks, Problem Child, Tremors, White Palace.

1991: An American Tail: Fievel Goes West, At Play in the Fields of the Lord, Backdraft, Cape Fear, Career Opportunities, Child's Play 3, Closet Land, Cool as Ice, Fried Green Tomatoes, The Hard Way, Jungle Fever, King Ralph, A Kiss Before Dying, Lionheart, Mobsters, Once Around, The People Under the Stairs, Problem Child 2, Pure Luck, Shout.

1992: American Me, The Babe, Beethoven, Death Becomes Her, Dr. Giggles, Far and Away, Housesitter, Kuffs, Leaving Normal, Lorenzo's Oil, Mr. Baseball, Out on a Limb, The Public Eye, Raising Cain, Scent of a Woman, Sneakers, Stop! Or My Mom Will Shoot, Trespass.

1993 (Jan.–Oct.): Army of Darkness, CB4, Cop and a Half, Dragon: The Bruce Lee Story, For Love or Money, Hard Target, Heart and Souls, Judgment Night, Jurassic Park, Mad Dog and Glory, Matinee, The Real McCoy, Splitting Heirs.

Warner Bros. Inc.

Warner Bros. Pictures, Inc. may be said to have had its origins in the 90-seat Cascade Theatre, a nickelodeon, in Newcastle, Pa., early in 1905 when Harry M. Warner set it up and brought into the business his three brothers: Sam, Albert, and Jack. Soon thereafter the brothers branched out into distribution, establishing film exchanges in Pennsylvania and Virginia. Then in 1913 they moved into film production with Warner Features.

Warner Bros., the company of the modern era, was incorporated in 1923 to produce as well as distribute. This young concern acquired its first theatre at Youngstown, Ohio, in December, 1924.

Warner Bros.' first important impress on production came in 1918 when they filmed "My Four Years in Germany," based on Ambassador James W. Gerard's book. In 1920–22 they averaged only two or three features per year, but by 1923, the year of incorporation, they released 14 pictures, including the first of the famous Rin-Tin-Tin series.

Scripts for the movies about that popular dog were provided by Darryl F. Zanuck, an ambitious writer who soon worked his way up to become the company's production chief under studio head Jack Warner. (Harry was president; Albert, treasurer; and Sam shared production responsibilities with Jack.) Zanuck stayed until 1933 and was succeeded by Hall Wallis, who held the post for the next decade.

In 1925 Warner acquired Vitagraph, Inc., which operated 34 exchanges in the U.S. and Canada, and it also bought two other concerns with foreign exchanges. That same year the company began its experiments with sound, working a year later in tandem with Western Electric to produce a sound-on-disc process (called Vitaphone) for synchronized film-sound recroding. The first Vitaphone program was premiered in August 1926; it included some musical shorts and the feature "Don Juan" with John Barrymore backed by a full musical and sound-effects track.

Success was instantaneous, so the studio produced "The Jazz Singer" for a premiere in October, 1927, which created a sensation—this in spite of the fact that it was not a full talkie having only synchronized songs and fragments of dialogue. In July 1928 Warners released "the first 100% all-talking picture," which was "Lights of New York," a one-hour feature that also broke box office records.

This bold pioneering in sound brought Warner Bros. to the forefront of the industry and inspired further expansion of its theatre holdings and studio facilities. It acquired the Stanley Company of America (a circuit with 250 theatres) in 1928 and also bought First National Pictures, which had a 135-acre studio and back lot, along with exchanges and theatres. Warners also purchased a number of leading music publishing companies to help in production of its musicals (including "Forty-Second Street," the "Gold Diggers" series, "Footlight Parade" and others.

Along with the other motion picture companies, Warners suffered a fall in profits in the early days of the Depression. Sales of some assets and theatres, along with drastic cuts in production costs, enabled the company to recover and to take advantage of the boom years when they came in the 1940s.

In 1953 the company completed the reorganization it was forced to undergo by the government's Consent Decree. Stockholders had approved a plan to separate the company into two entities: the theatres were sold to Fabian Enterprises, Inc., and the company renamed Stanley Warner Corporation. The "new" production-distribution company remained Warner Bros. Pictures, Inc. (Stockholders had received one-half share in each company for each share they held.)

By this time only three of the Warner Bros. were still living, Sam having died in 1927. In 1956 Harry M. and Albert sold their shares in the company (600,000) to an investment group headed by Serge Semenenko and Charles Allen Jr. Jack retained his shares, remaining as the largest single stockholder and becoming president of the company.

On July 15, 1967, a subsidiary of Seven Arts Productions Limited (a Canadian-based company headed by Eliot Hyman) acquired substantially all the assets and business of Warner Bros. Pictures, Inc. The company subsequently was called Warner Bros.-Seven Arts Limited. (Assets did not include the Warner pre-1948 film library of some 850 features and 1,000 shorts, which had been sold to United Artists in 1956.)

On July 8, 1969, Warner Bros.-Seven Arts was acquired by Kinney National Service, Inc., a giant conglomerate headed by Steven J. Ross, the name of which was changed in 1971 to Warner Communications, Inc. The studio reverted to its original name of Warner Bros. and appointed as its new head was Ted Ashley, a former talent agent who helped turn the film arm's fortunes around in the early 1960s with a series of successful movies including "Superman," "The Exorcist," and "All the President's Men." Robert A. Daly succeeded Ashley as Warner Bros. chairman and chief executive officer in 1980.

In 1983–84 Warner Communications survived a financial crisis which had resulted from tremendous losses experienced by a video-games subsidiary (Atari) by unloading the offending unit and concentrating on motion picture and television entertainment production, along with music recording and publishing.

In 1989 Warner Communications was acquired by Time, Inc. in an $18 billion merger that created one of the largest communications and entertainment companies in the world. Attempts to block the merger by Paramount Communications, Inc., which had offered $12.2 billion for Time, were rebuffed in the courts.

The Paramount offer would have given shareholders cash while the Time-Warner takeover involved an exchange of stock. Time-Warner, as the new company is called, consists not only of the Warner subsidiaries previously described but the Time publishing empire and these communications subsidiaries: Home Box Office, Cinemax, HBO Video, and American Television and Communications Corp.

In 1989 Warner Bros. regained full control of its Burbank Studio when it reacquired the 35 per cent interest that was owned by Columbia Pictures Entertainment. This occurred as one result of the settlement of a lawsuit WB filed against Sony Corporation, the new owner of CPE, over a five-year contract WB held with the Guber-Peters film production company. Sony wanted Jon Peters and Peter Guber to take over the helm of CPE when they purchased it in 1989. To free the two producers from their commitment to WB, Sony made an unusual settlement.

In addition to acquiring the Columbia stake in the Warner lot, WB received a 50 per cent interest in the CBS Record Club, which Sony owns, along with the right to distribute Columbia's films and made-for-TV movies on cable TV over the next decade.

Peters and Guber were instrumental in aiding Warners to rebound from a two-year box office slump in the summer of 1989 when they produced "Batman," which brought in domestic rentals of over $150 million, making it the fourth top-grossing film of all-time to that date. Warners also released "Lethal Weapon II" in the same summer; it took in almost $80 million in rentals. In early 1991 the company announced a partnership with several European entertainment companies to produce some 20 films.

Time Warner continues to hold a 50 per cent interest in Cinamerica Limited Partnership, a company which includes Mann Theatres and Festival Theatres in California and Trans-Lux Theatres in the East. In Oct. 1991, two Japanese companies, Toshiba Corp. and C. Itoh & Co., paid $500 million each for a combined 12.5% stake in the company.

In May 1993, the company created a new division, Warner Bros. Family Entertainment, to release movies aimed at the children's market. These titles included "Free Willy" and "The Secret Garden."

RECENT WARNER BROS. RELEASES

1990: Akira Kurosawa's Dreams, The Bonfire of the Vanities, GoodFellas, Graffiti Bridge, Gremlins 2: The New Batch, Hamlet, Hard to Kill, Impulse, Joe Vs. the Volcano, Lambada, Listen Up: The Lives of Quincy Jones, Memphis Belle, Men Don't Leave, My Blue Heaven, The Nutcracker Prince, Presumed Innocent, Quick Change, Reversal of Fortune, The Rookie, The Sheltering Sky, White Hunter Black Heart, The Witches.

1991: Born to Ride, Defending Your Life, Doc Hollywood, Dogfight, Don't Tell Mom the Babysitter's Dead, Guilty by Suspicion, If Looks Could Kill, JFK, The Last Boy Scout, Meeting Venus, New Jack City, Nothing But Trouble, Other People's Money, Out for Justice, Ricochet, Robin Hood: Prince of Thieves, Rover Dangerfield, Showdown in Little Tokyo, Strictly Business, Switch, Until the End of the World.

1992: Batman Returns, The Bodyguard, Christopher Columbus—The Discovery, Class Act, Final Analysis, Forever Young, Freejack, Innocent Blood, Lethal Weapon 3, The Magical World of Chuck Jones, Malcolm X, The Mambo Kings, Memoirs of an Invisible Man, Mom & Dad Save the World, Passenger 57, The Power of One, Pure Country, Singles, South Central, Stay Tuned, Turtle Beach, Under Siege, Unforgiven, White Sands.

1993 (Jan.–Oct.): Airborne, Dave, Demolition Man, Dennis the Menace, The Crush, Falling Down, Fearless, Free Willy, The Fugitive, M. Butterfly, Made in America, The Man Without a Face, Mr. Wonderful, Point of No Return, The Secret Garden, Sommersby, That Night, This Boy's Life, True Romance.

Corporations

* **STRUCTURE**

* **EXECUTIVE PERSONNEL**

Motion Picture Corporations

See also, Index: Distributors of 16mm Feature Films, Non-Theatrical Motion Pictures, Services.

ABC Distribution Co.

825 Seventh Ave., New York, NY 10019; (212) 456-1725; FAX: (212) 456-1708; 2040 Ave. of the Stars, Century City, CA 90067; (310) 557-6600; FAX: (310) 557-7925.
PRESIDENT
Archie Purvis
SENIOR VICE PRESIDENT
Joseph Y. Abrams
DIRECTOR THEATRICAL SALES AND ADVERTISING PROMOTION
June Shelley

AMC Entertainment Inc.

106 W. 14th St., Kansas City, MO 64105; (816) 221-4000. (Parent company of an exhibition conglomerate; for U.S. theatres owned see American Multi-Cinema, Inc., in theatre circuits section.)
CHAIRMAN & CEO
Stanley H. Durwood
PRESIDENT
Edward D. Durwood
SENIOR VICE PRESIDENT & COO
Philip M. Singleton

AMC FILM MARKETING, INC.

21700 Oxnard St., Suite 640, Woodland Hills, CA 91367; (818) 587-6400; FAX: (818) 587-6498.
PRESIDENT
Don Harris
SENIOR VICE PRESIDENT
Gene Goodman

ANS International

91 Fifth Ave., 5th floor, New York, NY 10003; (212) 366-1733.
PRESIDENT
Apo Oguz

ASA Communications, Inc.

24 Mt. View Circle, Amherst, MA 01002; (413) 256-8595.
PRESIDENT
David Mazor
TREASURER
Katheen Mazor
VICE PRESIDENT BUSINESS AFFAIRS
Jennie Haney
EXECUTIVE SECRETARY TO PRESIDENT
Debra Balduc
DIRECTOR CREATIVE DEVELOPMENT
Annette Tocanelli

ATA Trading Corp.

50 W. 34 St., Suite 5C-6, New York, NY 10001; (212) 594-6460; FAX: (212) 594-6461. (Film and video, foreign and domestic distribution and production of features, shorts, series, documentaries, music, children's entertainment.)
PRESIDENT
Harold G. Lewis
VICE PRESIDENT
Susan Lewis
SECRETARY
Rita Stone

Academy Entertainment

9250 Wilshire Blvd., Suite 400, Beverly Hills, CA 90212; (310) 275-2170. (Film distributor).
PRESIDENT
Trisha Robinson
VICE PRESIDENT, ACQUISITIONS, BUSINESS AFFAIRS
Brian Kandler

Alice Entertainment, Inc.

2986 Baseline Ave., Santa Ynez, CA 93460; (805) 688-1523; FAX: (805) 688-7934. Organized 1989. (Distribution of children's programming docu-dramas, action/adventure documentaries, movies for television and theatrical release; animation.)
PRESIDENT
Alice Donenfeld

Alive Films

8912 Burton Way, Beverly Hills, CA 90211; (310) 247-7800; FAX: (310) 274-7823.
CO-CHAIR
Shep Gordon
CO-CHAIR
Carolyn Pfeiffer

Amazing Movies

7471 Melrose Ave., Suite 7, Los Angeles, CA 90046; (213) 852-1396; FAX: (213) 658-7265. Organized 1984. (Producer and distributor of feature films, worldwide.)
PRESIDENT
Douglas C. Witkins
SENIOR VICE PRESIDENT
Nile Niami
VICE PRESIDENT, BUSINESS AFFAIRS
Martin Ivada
DIRECTOR OF OPERATIONS
David Gordon
BOARD OF DIRECTORS
Douglas C. Witkins (pres., CEO); Milda J. Witkins (secretary/treasurer)
BRANCH
Munich, Germany

Amblin Entertainment

100 Universal Plaza, Bungalow 477, Universal City, CA 91608; (818) 777-4600.
PRESIDENT
Steven Spielberg

American Cinema Marketing Corp.

13923 La Maida St., Sherman Oaks, CA 91423; (213) 850-6300; FAX: (213) 850-7117. Organized 1982. (Distributor.)
PRESIDENT
George Murphy
CORPORATE DIRECTOR
Jack F. Murphy

American Film Distributors

8833 W. Sunset Blvd., #305, Los Angeles, CA 90069; (310) 657-4506.
PRESIDENT
Norbert Meisel

American First Run Studios

14225 Ventura Blvd., Sherman Oaks, CA 91423; (818) 981-4950; FAX: (818) 501-6224. (Production and distribution.)

American Playhouse

1776 Broadway, New York, NY 10019; (212) 757-4300. (Produces films for theatrical distribution and public tv.).
EXECUTIVE PRODUCER
Lindsay Law

Angelika Films, Inc.

110 Greene St., Suite 1102, New York, NY 10012; (212) 274-1990; FAX: (212) 966-4957.
PRESIDENT
Joseph J.M. Saleh
CHAIRMAN
Angelika Saleh
VICE PRESIDENT, CREATIVE SERVICES
Eva D. Saleh
VICE PRESIDENT, CONTRACT SERVICES & ANCILLARY AFFAIRS
Rafael Guadalupe
VICE PRESIDENT, ACQUISITIONS
Jessica Saleh Hunt
EXECUTIVE VICE PRESIDENT, ANGELIKA FILMS INTERNATIONAL
Alex Massis

Apollo Pictures

6071 Bristol Pkwy., Culver City, CA 90230; (310) 568-8282; FAX: (310) 641-5738.
PRESIDENT AND CHIEF OPERATING OFFICER
David Smitas

Apricot Entertainment, Inc.

940 N. Orange Dr., Hollywood, CA 90038; (213) 469-4000; FAX: (213) 469-5809. Organized 1988. (Feature film financing, studio rental and theatrical film production.)
PRESIDENT
Naofumi Okamoto

Aquarius Releasing Inc.

Film Center Building, 630 Ninth Ave., 5th floor, New York, NY 10036; (212) 245-8530; FAX: (212) 397-7701. (Distribution—U.S.A. & Canada. Foreign—exhibition, production, producers' representative, live concerts.)
CHIEF EXECUTIVE OFFICER
Terry Levene
SECRETARY-TREASURER
Sarie Berenstein
PUBLICITY AND ADVERTISING DEPARTMENT
Wayne Weil
FACILITY DEPARTMENT
Bruce Grossbard
NEW YORK BRANCH MANAGER
Michael Harney

Archive Films, Inc.

530 W. 25 St., New York, NY 10001; (212) 620-3955; FAX: (212) 645-2137. Organized 1979. (Stock shot library.)

PRESIDENT
Patrick Montgomery
DIRECTOR, INTERNATIONAL OPERATIONS
Eileen Straussman

Aries Film Releasing Corp./L.P.

315 W. 57 St., Suite 609, New York, NY 10019; (212) 246-0528; FAX: (212) 247-4588. Organized 1989. (North American theatrical distribution of foreign, art and American independent motion pictures.)
PRESIDENT & CEO
Paul E. Cohen
GENERAL SALES MANAGER
T. C. Rice
DIRECTOR OF ACQUISITIONS
Gayle Gari Cohen
DIRECTOR OF DISTRIBUTION SERVICES
Elliott Schwartz
TREASURER
Oliver J. Sterling

Arista Films, Inc.

16027 Ventura Blvd., Suite 206, Encino, CA 91436; (818) 907-7660. FAX: (818) 905-6872. Telex: 4720572 ARIFILM. Organized 1974. (Motion picture distribution.)
PRESIDENT
Louis George
VICE PRESIDENT
Niki George
EXECUTIVE VICE PRESIDENT
Gene L. George

Arkoff International Pictures

Lakeside Plaza, 3801 Barham Blvd., Suite 178, Los Angeles, CA 90068; (213) 882-1161; FAX: (213) 882-1039. Organized 1981. (Production and distribution of motion pictures and TV.)
PRESIDENT & CEO
Samuel Z. Arkoff
EXECUTIVE VICE PRESIDENT
Louis S. Arkoff
SENIOR VICE PRESIDENT, DEVELOPMENT & ACQUISITIONS
Willie H. Kutner

Army Chief of Public Affairs

Los Angeles Branch: 11000 Wilshire Blvd., Suite 10104, Los Angeles, CA 90024-3688; (310) 575-7621. FAX: (310) 473-8874. (Technical advisors for West Coast entertainment industry; emphasis on motion picture and TV industries.)
CHIEF OF PUBLIC AFFAIRS
Lt. Col. Mitch Marovitz
TECHNICAL ADVISORS
Major David Georgi
PUBLIC INFORMATION OFFICER
Kathy Canham Ross

Arrow Entertainment

666 Fifth Ave., 21st floor, New York, NY 10103; (212) 974-2000. (Film distributor.)

Astron Films Corporation

360 W. 22 St., New York, NY 10011; (212) 989-6089. (Writers, producers, directors, independent financiers of feature films.)
PRESIDENT & CHAIRMAN
Jack O'Connell
CREATIVE DIRECTOR
Patricia Kay Williams

August Entertainment

838 N. Fairfax Ave., Los Angeles, CA 90046; (213) 658-8888; FAX: (213) 658-7654. (International film distribution.)
PRESIDENT
  Gregory Cascante
EXECUTIVE VICE PRESIDENTS
  H. Michael Heuser
  Eleanor Powell
CHIEF FINANCIAL OFFICER
  Elizabeth V. Davis
DIRECTOR, ADVERTISING & PUBLICITY
  Cori Cascante

Aura Entertainment Int., Inc.

322 W. 57 St., Suite 30-D, New York, NY 10019; (212) 399-9177. Organized 1985. (Sales and production/distribution organization.)
OFFICER
  John Iula

Aurora Productions, Inc.

8642 Melrose Ave., Suite 200, Los Angeles, CA 90069; (310) 854-6900; FAX: (310) 854-0583. Organized 1976. (Executive production of motion pictures.)
PRESIDENT
  William Stuart
VICE PRESIDENT, PRODUCTION & DEVELOPMENT
  Douglas S. Cook
DIRECTOR, CREATIVE AFFAIRS
  David Weisberg

Avenue Pictures

11111 Santa Monica Blvd., Suite 2110, Los Angeles, CA 90025; (310) 996-6800; FAX: (310) 473-4376. (Motion picture and television production.)
CHAIRMAN & CEO
  Cary Brokaw
PRESIDENT OF TELEVISION
  Randy Robinson
CHIEF FINANCIAL OFFICER
  Sherri L. Halfon

Batjac Productions, Inc.

9595 Wilshire Blvd., Suite 610, Beverly Hills, CA 90212-2506; (310) 278-9870; FAX: (213) 272-7381.
PRESIDENT
  Michael A. Wayne

Beck International Corp

P.O. Box 1228, Scarsdale, NY 10583; (914) 472-5930; FAX: (914) 472-6564; N.Y. FAX: (212) 391-2750.
CHAIRMAN
  Alexander Beck
PRESIDENT
  Kenneth A. Beck
VICE PRESIDENT, SECRETARY
  Felicia L. Beck-Zfira
EXECUTIVE VICE PRESIDENT, PRODUCTION
  Yaron Zfira
VICE PRESIDENT
  Shirley Beck

Bedford/Triboro Entertainment, Inc.

12 W. 27th St., New York, NY 10001; (212) 686-6116; FAX: (212) 245-8723. Organized 1979. (Production and distribution.)
PRESIDENT
  Steven D. Mackler

Best Film & Video Corp.

108 New South Rd., Hicksville, NY 11801; (516) 931-6969; FAX: (516) 931-5959. Organized 1981. (Production and distribution of product to theatrical, TV, cable, non-theatrical and home video markets.)
PRESIDENT
  Roy Winnick
MARKETING DIRECTOR
  Arlene Winnick

Big Bear Licensing Corp.

12400 Wilshire Blvd., Suite 360, Los Angeles, CA 90025; (310) 820-5161; Telex: 3719647; FAX: (310) 820-7683. Organized 1978. (Motion picture production and foreign sales.)
PRESIDENT
  Wolf Schmidt

Blossom Pictures Inc.

1414 Ave. of the Americas, 18th floor, New York, NY 10019; (212) 486-8880; FAX: (212) 753-4142. Organized 1979.
PRESIDENT
  Jerry Gruenberg
CHIEF EXECUTIVE OFFICER
  Thomas S. Gruenberg
OFFICE MANAGER
  Mary M. Gonzalez
BOARD OF DIRECTORS
  Jerry Gruenberg (pres.), Thomas S. Gruenberg, Joyce Gruenberg

Blue Ridge Entertainment

10490 Santa Monica Blvd., Los Angeles, CA 90025; (310) 474-6688; FAX: (310) 475-2677; Telex: 91024-07101. Organized 1986. (Motion picture production and international distribution.)
PRESIDENT
  Penny Karlin
CHAIRMAN & CEO
  Lamar Card
CHIEF FINANCIAL OFFICER
  Carol Beazer
VICE PRESIDENT INTERNATIONAL DIRECTOR, SALES
  Eric Saltzgaber
EXECUTIVE DIRECTOR, ACQUISITIONS/PRODUCTION
  Barbara Mannion

Blum Group, Inc., The

494 Tuallitan Road, Los Angeles, CA 90049; (310) 476-2229. Organized 1973. (Production and distribution of motion pictures.)
PRESIDENT
  Harry N. Blum
TREASURER
  Stephen L. Kadish
SECRETARY
  S. R. Blum
DIRECTOR OF MARKETING & CUSTOMER RELATIONS
  Lehoa Miller
DIRECTOR OF OPERATIONS & ADMINISTRATION
  Shobi Deuani

Boardwalk Productions

5150 Wilshire Blvd., Suite 505, Los Angeles, CA 90036; (213) 938-0109; FAX: (213) 938-5395. Organized 1961. (Motion picture production.)
PRESIDENT
  Robert P. Mulligan
VICE PRESIDENT
  Mortimer S. Rosenthal

SECRETARY
Sandy Mulligan
TREASURER
Stanley B. Broffman

Nai Bonet Enterprises Ltd.

345 W. 58 St., New York, NY 10019; (212) 581-8628. Organized 1978. (Feature film producer.)
PRESIDENT
Nai Bonet

Borde Releasing, Inc.

1800 N. Highland, Suite 311, Hollywood, CA 90028; (213) 461-3936; FAX: (213) 461-5287. (Production and distribution.)
CHIEF EXECUTIVE OFFICER
Mark Borde

Braverman Productions, Inc.

3000 Olympic Blvd., Santa Monica, CA 90404; (310) 315-4710; FAX: (310) 315-4800. (Producers of prime time specials, features, variety shows, commercials, documentaries, educational and corporate films, titles and special montages.)
PRESIDENT
Charles Braverman
DIRECTOR OF DEVELOPMENT
Diane Wynter

Bryna Company, The

141 El Camino Dr., Beverly Hills, CA 90212; (310) 274-5294; FAX: (310) 274-2537. Organized 1958.
PRESIDENT
Anne Douglas

Buena Vista Pictures

(see The Walt Disney Company)

Bill Burrud Productions

16902 Bolsa Chica, #203, Huntington Beach, CA 92649; (714) 846-7174; FAX: (714) 846-4814. Organized 1954. (Feature film and TV production of animal/wildlife/reality/human adventure documentaries/world exploration.)
PRESIDENT
John Burrud
VICE PRESIDENT IN CHARGE OF PRODUCTION
Linda Karabin-Hecomovich

Cabriolet Films Inc.

34 W. 13th St., New York, NY 10011; (212) 243-5898; FAX: (212) 794-4769. (Motion picture distributor).

Camrac Studios

1775 Kuenzli St., Reno, NV 89502; (702) 323-0965. Organized 1979. (Independent studio/location production company that specializes in all film and video formats. Productions include regional commercials, corporate presentations, and home entertainment.)
PRESIDENT
Shirley Mitchell
DIRECTOR/PRODUCER
Jim Mitchell
AFFILIATIONS
Mitchell Productions (subsidiary).

Cannell Studios, The

7083 Hollywood Blvd., Hollywood, CA 90028; (213) 465-5800; FAX: (213) 856-7454.
CHAIRMAN & CHIEF EXECUTIVE OFFICER
Stephen J. Cannell
PRESIDENT, CANNELL STUDIOS
Michael J. Dubelko
PRESIDENT, STEVE CANNELL PRODS.
Kim LeMasters
SENIOR VICE PRESIDENT
Jo Swerling, Jr.
SENIOR VICE PRESIDENT/LEGAL & BUSINESS AFFAIRS
Howard D. Kurtzman
CHIEF FINANCIAL OFFICER
Joseph C. Kaczorowski

Cannon Pictures

8200 Wilshire Blvd., Beverly Hills, CA 90211; (213) 966-5600; FAX: (213) 653-5485. (Motion picture distribution.)

Capitol Entertainment Corp.

4818 Yuma St., N.W., Washington, D.C. 20016; (202) 363-8800; FAX: (202) 363-4680. Organized 1989. (Motion picture distribution.)
PRESIDENT
Ted Goldberg
VICE PRESIDENT, SALES & MARKETING
Ronnie Cooper

Carolco Pictures Inc.

8800 Sunset Boulevard, Los Angeles, CA 90069; (310) 859-8800; FAX: (310) 657-1629. (Production of Motion Pictures.)
CHAIRMAN OF THE BOARD
Mario F. Kassar
PRESIDENT OF PRODUCTION & EXECUTIVE VICE PRESIDENT/BUSINESS AND PRODUCTION AFFAIRS
Lynwood Spinks
EXECUTIVE VICE PRESIDENT/CFO
William A. Shpall
EXECUTIVE VICE PRESIDENT/STRATEGIC OPERATIONS
Satoshi Matsumoto
SENIOR VICE PRESIDENT/GENERAL COUNSEL/CORPORATE SECRETARY
Robert W. Goldsmith
SENIOR VICE PRESIDENT/FINANCE
Karen A. Taylor

CAROLCO INTERNATIONAL N.V.

8800 Sunset Blvd., Los Angeles, CA 90069; (310) 859-8800; FAX: (310) 657-1629. (Foreign production and servicing of motion pictures.)
CHAIRMAN OF THE BOARD
Mario F. Kassar
MANAGING DIRECTOR
Gustavo G. Koeijers

CAROLCO SERVICE INC.

8800 Sunset Blvd., Los Angeles, CA 90069; (310) 859-8800; FAX: (310) 657-1629. (Foreign sales and servicing of motion pictures.)
CHAIRMAN OF THE BOARD
Mario F. Kassar
EXECUTIVE VICE PRESIDENT/BUSINESS & PRODUCTION AFFAIRS
Lynwood Spinks
EXECUTIVE VICE PRESIDENT/CFO
William A. Shpall
EXECUTIVE VICE PRESIDENT WORLDWIDE MARKETING
Andrew Fogelson
EXECUTIVE VICE PRESIDENT/STRATEGIC OPERATIONS
Satoshi Matsumoto

SENIOR VICE PRESIDENT/GENERAL COUNSEL/CORPORATE SECRETARY
Robert W. Goldsmith
SENIOR VICE PRESIDENT/FINANCE
Karen A. Taylor
SENIOR VICE PRESIDENT/WORLDWIDE THEATRICAL & TELEVISION SERVICES
Philip G. Provenzale
SENIOR VICE PRESIDENT/INTERNATIONAL SALES ADMINISTRATION
Murray Cohen
SENIOR VICE PRESIDENT/ADMINISTRATION & PERSONNEL
H. Beth Rice
SENIOR VICE PRESIDENT/CREATIVE AFFAIRS
Kathryn Sommer
SENIOR VICE PRESIDENT/BUSINESS AFFAIRS (FEATURES)
Lewis Weakland
VICE PRESIDENT/TRADEMARK/COPYRIGHT
Darnell Young
VICE PRESIDENT/MOTION PICTURE LEGAL AFFAIRS
Jeff Matloff
VICE PRESIDENT/BUSINESS AFFAIRS ADMINISTRATION
Beth Hoffman
VICE PRESIDENT/PUBLICITY
Stephanie Pond-Smith
VICE PRESIDENT, POST PRODUCTION
Noori Dehnahi

CAROLCO PRODUCTION SERVICES INC.

8800 Sunset Blvd., Los Angeles, CA 90069; (310) 859-8800; FAX: (310) 657-1629. (Production servicing of motion pictures.)
CHAIRMAN OF THE BOARD
Mario F. Kassar
PRESIDENT
Lynwood Spinks
EXECUTIVE VICE PRESIDENT/CFO
William A. Shpall
SENIOR VICE PRESIDENT/GENERAL COUNSEL/CORPORATE SECRETARY
Robert W. Goldsmith
SENIOR VICE PRESIDENT/FINANCE
Karen A. Taylor
SENIOR VICE PRESIDENT/BUSINESS AFFAIRS (FEATURES)
Lewis Weakland

CAROLCO STUDIOS INC.

1223 North 23rd Street, Wilmington, North Carolina 28405; (919) 343-3500; FAX: (919) 343-3574. (Full-service professional production facility for theatrical, television and commercial filming.)
CHAIRMAN OF THE BOARD
Mario F. Kassar
GENERAL MANAGER
Kent Swaim
PRESIDENT
Lynwood Spinks
EXECUTIVE VICE PRESIDENT/CFO
William A. Shpall
SENIOR VICE PRESIDENT/GENERAL COUNSEL/CORPORATE SECRETARY
Robert W. Goldsmith
SENIOR VICE PRESIDENT/FINANCE
Karen A. Taylor

Castle Hill Productions, Inc.

1414 Ave. of the Americas, New York, NY, 10019; (212) 888-0080; FAX: (212) 644-0956. 116 N. Robertson Blvd., Suite 505, Los Angeles, CA 90048; (310) 652-5254.
PRESIDENT
Julian Schlossberg
PRESIDENT, MARKETING & DISTRIBUTION
Mel Maron
CONTROLLER
Randall San Antonio
SENIOR ACCOUNT EXECUTIVE
Barbara Karmel
DIRECTOR, SALES SERVICES
Milly Sherman

NATIONAL
Ivory Harris
MANAGER, ADVERTISING/SALES SERVICES
David Wright
DIRECTOR, NON-THEATRICAL SALES
Lester Schoenfeld

Castle Rock Entertainment

335 N. Maple Dr., Suite 135, Beverly Hills, CA 90210; (310) 285-2300; FAX: (310) 285-2345.
PRINCIPALS & CO-FOUNDERS
Alan Horn
Glenn Padnick
Andrew Scheinman
Martin Shafer
Rob Reiner
SENIOR VICE PRESIDENT & GENERAL COUNCIL
Gregory M. Paul
VICE PRESIDENT & CHIEF FINANCIAL OFFICER
Al Linton
VICE PRESIDENT, BUSINESS AFFAIRS
Jess Wittenberg
VICE PRESIDENT, PUBLICITY & PROMOTION
John DeSimio
VICE PRESIDENT, PHYSICAL PRODUCTION
Jeff Stott
VICE PRESIDENT, PRODUCTION
Liz Glotzer
VICE PRESIDENT, LEGAL AFFAIRS
Julia Bingham
VICE PRESIDENT, TV PRODUCTION
Robin Green
VICE PRESIDENT, FIRST RUN SYNDICATION
Al Burton

Certified Reports Inc. (CRI) East

Kinderhook, NY 12106; (518) 758-6400; FAX: (518) 758-6451. (Theatre checking open and blind nationwide.)
CHAIRMAN OF BOARD
Jack J. Spitzer
PRESIDENT
Bill Smith
VICE PRESIDENT
Frank Falkenhainer
VICE PRESIDENT, ADMINISTRATION & FINANCE
Michael F. Myers

CERTIFIED REPORTS INC. (CRI) WEST

9846 White Oak Ave., Suite 202, Northridge, CA 91325; (818) 727-0929; FAX: (818) 727-7426.
VICE PRESIDENT
Elizabeth Stevens

Chartoff Productions

1250 Sixth St., Suite 201, Santa Monica, CA 90401; (310) 319-1960; FAX: (310) 319-3469. (Producer.)
PRINCIPAL
Robert Chartoff

Cinecom Entertainment Group, Inc.

c/o October Films, Inc., 45 Rockefeller Plaza, 30th floor, New York, NY 10111; (212) 332-2488; FAX: (212) 332-2499. Organized 1982. (Motion picture distribution and production.)
CHAIRMAN & CO-CHIEF EXECUTIVE OFFICER
Stephen Swid
PRESIDENT & CO-CHIEF EXECUTIVE OFFICER
Amir J. Malin
DIRECTOR OF SPECIAL PROJECTS
Linda Duchin
CORPORATE CONTROLLER
Daniel Lieblein

Cinema Guild

1697 Broadway, Suite 506, New York, NY 10019; (212) 246-5522; FAX: (212) 246-5525.
PRESIDENT
  Philip S. Hobel
VICE PRESIDENT & GENERAL MANAGER
  Gary Crowdus
VICE PRESIDENT
  Mary Ann Hobel

Cinematograph

13 Edsal Ave., Nanuet, NY 10954-2504; (914) 623-8609; and (201) 461-6258. Organized 1975. (Motion picture and television production.)
PRESIDENT
  Victor Eisenberg

Cinemax Marketing and Distribution Corporation (The Arthur Manson Organization)

1370 Avenue of the Americas, New York, NY 10019; (212) 581-6285. (Producer's marketing and distribution consultants; creative presentation and maximization of potential for motion pictures.)
PRESIDENT
  Arthur Manson

Cine-Media International, Ltd.

One Transglobal Square, P.O. Box 7005, Long Beach, CA 90807; (213) 426-3622. Organized 1975. (Production and distribution of theatrical motion pictures and television films.) A subsidiary of Transglobal Industries and Subsidiaries, Inc.
PRESIDENT & CHIEF EXECUTIVE OFFICER
  J. Bond Johnson, Ph.D.
VICE PRESIDENT
  Rudolph A. Maglin
SECRETARY
  Ruth Johnson
TREASURER
  Lenore Maglin
EXECUTIVE PRODUCER
  Frank Capra, Jr.
CREATIVE CONSULTANT
  Chester Dent
DIRECTOR OF PRODUCTION
  Travis Edward Pike
DIRECTOR OF FINANCE
  William A. Becker, CPA
GENERAL COUNSEL
  Stuart I. Berton, Esq.

CineTel Films Inc.

8255 Sunset Blvd., Lost Angeles, CA 90046; (213) 654-4000; FAX: (213) 650-6400.
PRESIDENT & CHIEF EXECUTIVE OFFICER
  Paul Hertzberg
EXECUTIVE VICE PRESIDENT
  Lisa Hansen
CHIEF FINANCIAL OFFICER
  Nick Gorenc
DISTRIBUTION CONSULTANT
  Milton Goldstein
VICE PRESIDENT OF CREATIVE AFFAIRS
  Catalaine Knell
VICE PRESIDENT OF BUSINESS AFFAIRS
  Richard K. Rosenberg
DIRECTOR, INTERNATIONAL DISTRIBUTION
  Marcy Rubin

Cinetrust Entertainment Corp.

Fox Plaza, 2121 Ave. of the Stars, 6th floor, Los Angeles, CA 90067; (310) 551-6504; FAX: (310) 551-6622; Telex: 698218 HOC LSA. (Worldwide film and TV distribution and marketing.)
PRESIDENT & CHIEF EXECUTIVE OFFICER
  Kelly Ross
CO-CHAIRMAN, CHIEF OPERATING OFFICER
  Gabriel E. Gyorffy

Cinevest Entertainment Group Inc.

450 Seventh Ave., Suite 2702, New York, NY 10123; (212) 465-0866; FAX: (212) 465-2166. (Domestic and foreign motion picture distribution, production and sales.)
PRESIDENT
  Arthur Schweitzer
OPERATIONS MANAGER
  Carmen Dixon

Cinevista, Inc.

560 W. 43 St., Suite 8-J, New York, NY 10036-4310; (212) 947-4373; FAX: (212) 947-0644. Organized 1980. (Domestic distribution specializing in independent and foreign feature films. Video and international sales.)
PRESIDENT
  Rene Fuentes-chao
VICE PRESIDENT, SALES AND MARKETING
  John R. Tilley

Cineworld Corporation

2670 N.E. 24 St., Pompano Beach, FL 33064; (305) 781-2627; FAX: (305) 781-2627. (Distribution, production, international co-production, financing and packaging.)
PRESIDENT
  John F. Rickert
SECRETARY/TREASURER
  Ildiko M. Rickert

Circle Releasing Corp.

1101 N. 23rd St., NW, Washington, D.C. 20037; (202) 331-3838; FAX: (202) 429-9043. Organized 1984. (Distribution and production.)
CO-CHAIRMAN
  Ted Pedas
CO-CHAIRMAN
  James Pedas
PRESIDENT
  Ben Barenholtz
VICE PRESIDENT, GENERAL SALES MANAGER
  Fran Spielman
VICE PRESIDENT, MARKETING & DEVELOPMENT
  George Pelecanos
GENERAL COUNSEL
  William Durkin

Dick Clark Film Group, Inc.

(A subsidiary of Dick Clark Productions, Inc.)
3003 W. Olive Ave., Burbank, CA 91510; (818) 841-3003. Organized 1990. (Production of films for theatres and television.)
CHAIRMAN & CEO
  Dick Clark
PRESIDENT & COO
  Francis C. La Maina
SENIOR VICE PRESIDENT
  Neil Stearns

Woody Clark Productions, Inc.

P.O. Box 10407, Piedmont, CA 94610; (510) 451-1668. Organized 1979. (Production of features and education/business documentaries.)
CHAIRMAN & PRESIDENT
  Woodrow W. Clark Jr., Ph.D.

526

PRODUCERS
Hobart Swan
Douglas Pray
Chien Ei Yu
TOKYO PRODUCER
Mike Barlow

Cobra Media, Inc.

650 Bronson Ave., Hollywood, CA 90004; (213) 466-3388. Organized 1981. (Motion picture distribution for U.S.A. and Canada for all media.)
PRESIDENT
Herman Cohen
VICE PRESIDENT
Didier Chatelain
ADVERTISING & PUBLICITY CONSULTANT
Spence Steinhurst
SALES EXECUTIVE
Terry Mize

Herman Cohen Productions

650 N. Bronson Ave., Hollywood, CA 90004; (213) 466-3388. (Motion picture production.)
PRESIDENT
Herman Cohen
EXECUTIVE VICE PRESIDENT
Didier Chatelain

Columbia Pictures

(see Sony Pictures Entertainment, Inc.)

Communications and Entertainment Corp.

800 Third Ave., 29th fl., New York, NY 10022; (212) 486-3999. (International distribution and financing of theatrical films.)
CHIEF EXECUTIVE OFFICER
N. Norman Muller
PRESIDENT
Thomas W. Smith
VICE PRESIDENT/CHIEF FINANCIAL OFFICER
Jay M. Behling
EXECUTIVE VICE PRODUCER
Jeffrey Konvitz

ODYSSEY DISTRIBUTORS LTD.

6500 Wilshire Blvd., Suite 400, Los Angeles, CA 90048; (213)655-9333. (International film distribution company.)
PRESIDENT
Peter Elson

ODYSSEY ENTERTAINMENT LTD.

6500 Wilshire Blvd., Suite 400, Los Angeles, CA 90048; (213) 655-9335.
PRESIDENT
Robert Meyers

Concorde

11600 San Vicente Blvd., Los Angeles, CA 90049; (310) 820-6733; FAX: (310) 207-6826. Studios located at 600 S. Main St., Venice, CA 90291. (Producers and distributors of feature films.)
PRESIDENT
Roger Corman
EXECUTIVE VICE PRESIDENT
Julie Corman
VICE PRESIDENT, DEVELOPMENT
Robert Kershner

VICE PRESIDENT OF PRODUCTION
Mike Elliott
VICE PRESIDENT OF FINANCE
Goly Jamshidi
VICE PRESIDENT OF ANCILLARY RIGHTS
Pamela A. Abraham
VICE PRESIDENT, WORLDWIDE DISTRIBUTION
Minard Hamilton
VICE PRESIDENT, DOMESTIC DISTRIBUTION
William H. Bromiley
DIRECTOR OF INTERNATIONAL MARKETING SERVICES
Peter Shiau
DIRECTOR OF ADVERTISING AND PUBLICITY
Michelle Burkowski
DIRECTOR OF LEGAL AND BUSINESS AFFAIRS
Edward Reilly

Consolidated Film Industries

959 N. Seward St., Hollywood, CA 90038-2595; (213) 960-7444; FAX: (213) 460-4885. (Wholly-owned subsidiary of Continental Graphics. Post production, especially film processing and tape transfers.)
PRESIDENT
Jesse T. Ellington
SENIOR VICE PRESIDENT & TREASURER
Kent Cooper
EXECUTIVE VICE PRESIDENT, FILM LABORATORY
George Hutchison
VICE PRESIDENT, SALES AND MARKETING
Michael Papadaki
VICE PRESIDENT, ENGINEERING
John Baptista
VICE PRESIDENT, HUMAN RESOURCES
Joseph A. Aredas
GENERAL MANAGER, VIDEOTAPE
George Anderson
CONTROLLER
Richard Marcus
BUSINESS AFFAIRS DIRECTOR
Stanley Salter
ASSISTANT TO PRESIDENT
Berneice Herbers

Continental Film Group, Ltd.

Park St., Sharon, PA 16146-3090; (412) 981-3456; FAX: (412) 981-2668; Telex: 4796638 CFG UI. Organized 1985. (Production company.)
PRESIDENT & CHIEF EXECUTIVE OFFICER
Amin Q. Chaudhri
VICE PRESIDENT IN CHARGE OF DEVELOPMENT
Asha N. Chaudhri
ASSISTANT TO THE PRESIDENT/CEO
Maraline Kubik
BOARD OF DIRECTORS
Amin Q. Chaudhri, Robert Holof, Navin Desai

Continental Film Studios, Ltd.

Park St., Sharon, PA 16146-3090; (412) 981-3456; FAX: (412) 981-2668; Telex: 4796638 CFG UI. Organized 1988.
PRESIDENT & CHIEF EXECUTIVE OFFICER
Amin Q. Chaudhri
VICE PRESIDENT
Navin Desai
SECRETARY
Jenny Chrisinger
VICE PRESIDENT IN CHARGE OF DEVELOPMENT
Asha N. Chaudhri
ASSISTANT TO THE PRESIDENT
Maraline Kubik

Coproducers Corporation

2670 N.E. 24 St., Pompano Beach, FL 33064; (305) 781-2627; FAX: (305) 781-2627. (Distribution, production, international co-production, financing and packaging.)

PRESIDENT
John F. Rickert
SECRETARY/TREASURER
Ildiko M. Rickert

Corinth Films, Inc.

34 Gansvoort St., New York, NY 10014; (212) 463-0305.

PRESIDENT
John M. Poole
EXECUTIVE VICE PRESIDENT
Peter J. Meyer
VICE PRESIDENT, TECHNICAL OPERATIONS
Richard Evangelista

Thomas Craven Film Corp.

5 W. 19 St., New York, NY 10011; (212) 463-7190; FAX: (212) 627-4761. Organized 1951. (Producers of documentary, industrial, educational, government, and technical films as well as TV featurettes.)

PRESIDENT
Michael Craven
VICE PRESIDENT
Ernest Barbieri

Crazy Horse Productions, Inc.

2718 Second St., Santa Monica, CA 90405; (310) 396-4923; FAX: (310) 823-5183. (Motion picture production and distribution.)

Crest Film Distributor, Inc.

116 N. Robertson Blvd., Suite 505, Los Angeles, CA 90048; (310) 652-8844; FAX: (310) 652-5595. (Distributor of motion pictures theatrically.)

PRESIDENT
Jerry Percell

Bing Crosby Productions, Inc.

610 S. Ardmore Ave., Los Angeles, CA 90005; (213) 487-7150.

PRESIDENT
Nicholas D. Trigony
VICE PRESIDENT
John R. Dillon
VICE PRESIDENT & TREASURER
John G. Boyette

Crown International Pictures

8701 Wilshire Blvd., Beverly Hills, CA 90211; (310) 657-6700; FAX: (310) 657-4489; Telex: 140709 CROWN INTL. Organized 1959.

PRESIDENT & CEO
Mark Tenser
VICE PRESIDENT, INTERNATIONAL SALES
Herb Fletcher
VICE PRESIDENT, BUSINESS AFFAIRS
Scott E. Schwimer
VICE PRESIDENT, HOME VIDEO/PAY-TV AND WORLDWIDE
ACQUISITIONS
Lynette Prucha
VICE PRESIDENT, FINANCE & ADMINISTRATION
James Boyd
CONTROLLER
Willie De Leon
DIRECTOR, INTERNATIONAL SALES
D. Paul Zito
DIRECTOR, PUBLICITY & ADVERTISING
Lisa Agay
PRODUCER
Marilyn J. Tenser

Crystal Pictures, Inc.

1560 Broadway, New York, NY 10036; (212) 840-6181; FAX: 840-6182. Cable: CRYSPIC NEW YORK. Telex: 620852. (Importers and exporters of theatrical and TV films, shorts and documentaries, film financing and specialized distribution, domestic and foreign; syndication and distribution of U.S. and foreign feature films to TV and cable world-wide.)

PRESIDENT
Joshua Tager
GENERAL SALES MANAGER
Sidney Tager

Curb/Esquire Films

3907 W. Alameda Ave., Suite 102, Burbank, CA 91505; (818) 843-2872; FAX: (818) 566-1719.

PRESIDENT
Carole Curb
CHAIRPERSON
Mike Curb

Dale System, Inc., Theatre Division

1101 Stewart Ave., Garden City, NY 11530; (516) 794-2800. FAX: (516) 542-1063. (Nationwide system for testing honesty and efficiency of theatre personnel through use of checkers, undercover operatives and polygraph examinations. Evaluates procedures, eliminates loss.)

PRESIDENT
Harvey Yaffe
VICE PRESIDENTS
William Shaw, Anthony Sorrentino
TREASURER
Alan Lowell
THEATRE DIVISION DIRECTOR
Helen Robin
BRANCH OFFICES
New Haven, Boston, Rochester, Miami, New York.

Davnor Productions, Ltd.

2 Depot Plaza, Suite 202B, Bedford Hills, NY 10507; (914) 242-9838; FAX: (914) 242-9854. Organized 1986.

PRESIDENT
Robert A. Harris
EAST COAST LIAISON
Joanne Lawson

Curt Deckert Associates, Inc.

18061 Darmel Place, Santa Ana, CA 92705; (714) 639-0746; FAX: (714) 978-1187. Organized 1976. (Technical management consultants; development of optical-photographic special effects equipment and other related systems involving optical technology and R&D consulting.)

PRESIDENT
Curt Deckert

Walt Disney Company, The

500 S. Buena Vista St., Burbank, CA 91521; (818) 560-1000; FAX: (818) 840-5737. 500 Park Ave., New York, NY 10022; (212) 593-8900. (Motion Picture and television producer and distributor. Also see separate section for corporate history.)

CHAIRMAN OF THE BOARD & CHIEF EXECUTIVE OFFICER
Michael D. Eisner
PRESIDENT & CHIEF OPERATING OFFICER
Frank G. Wells
VICE CHAIRMAN OF THE BOARD
Roy E. Disney

EXECUTIVE VICE PRESIDENT, STRATEGIC PLANNING AND
DEVELOPMENT
  Lawrence P. Murphy
EXECUTIVE VICE PRESIDENT LAW AND HUMAN
RESOURCES
  Sanford Litvack
EXECUTIVE VICE PRESIDENT & CHIEF FINANCIAL OFFICER,
EURODISNEY
  Michael J. Montgomery
EXECUTIVE VICE PRESIDENT, ADMINISTRATION &
WORLDWIDE CORPORATE BUSINESS AFFAIRS
  Joe Shapiro
SENIOR VICE PRESIDENT & CHIEF FINANCIAL OFFICER
  Richard D. Nanula
VICE PRESIDENT, PLANNING AND CONTROL
  John Garand
VICE PRESIDENT & CORPORATE SECRETARY
  Doris A. Smith

THE WALT DISNEY STUDIOS

500 South Buena Vista Street, Burbank, CA 91521;
(818) 560-5151.
CHAIRMAN
  Jeffrey Katzenberg
PRESIDENT
  Richard Frank
EXECUTIVE VICE PRESIDENT
  Helene Hahn
EXECUTIVE VICE PRESIDENT, FINANCE & CHIEF FINANCIAL
OFFICER
  Chris McGurk
EXECUTIVE VICE PRESIDENT
  W. Randolph Reiss
VICE PRESIDENTS, COUNSEL
  Peter F. Nolan
  Joseph M. Santaniello

BUENA VISTA PICTURES MARKETING

500 South Buena Vista Street, Burbank, CA 91521;
(818) 560-5151.
PRESIDENT, WORLDWIDE MARKETING
  Robert B. Levin
SENIOR VICE PRESIDENT, MEDIA
  Bobbi Blair
SENIOR VICE PRESIDENT, CREATIVE SERVICES
  Robert Jahn
SENIOR VICE PRESIDENT, DOMESTIC MARKETING
  Gary Kalkin
VICE PRESIDENT, CREATIVE FILM SERVICES
  Peter Adee
VICE PRESIDENT, CREATIVE FILM SERVICES
  Oren Aviv
VICE PRESIDENT, PROMOTIONS
  Brett Dicker
VICE PRESIDENT, SPECIAL MARKETING
  Alan Dinwiddie
VICE PRESIDENT, MEDIA
  Mary Beth Garber
VICE PRESIDENT, PRINT ADVERTISING
  Hy Levine
VICE PRESIDENT, RESEARCH
  Dana Lombardo
VICE PRESIDENT, CREATIVE FILM SERVICES
  Constance Mantle
VICE PRESIDENT, FINANCE (MARKETING & DISTRIBUTION)
  Robert D. Murphy
VICE PRESIDENT, PUBLICITY
  Terry Press
VICE PRESIDENT, PUBLICITY
  Louise Spencer
VICE PRESIDENT, CREATIVE PRINT SERVICES
  Fred Tio

WALT DISNEY PICTURES AND
  TOUCHSTONE PICTURES

500 South Buena Vista Street, Burbank, CA 91521;
(818) 560-1000.
PRESIDENT TOUCHSTONE PICTURES AND WALT DISNEY
PICTURES
  David Hoberman

PRESIDENT, FEATURE ANIMATION
  Peter Schneider
EXECUTIVE VICE PRESIDENT, PRODUCTION, TOUCHSTONE
PICTURES
  Donald DeLine
EXECUTIVE VICE PRESIDENT, PRODUCTION, WALT DISNEY
PICTURES
  David E. Vogel
SENIOR VICE PRESIDENT IN CHARGE OF BUSINESS & LEGAL
AFFAIRS, TOUCHSTONE PICTURES, WALT DISNEY PICTURES,
FEATURE ANIMATION
  Robert Osher
SENIOR VICE PRESIDENT, MUSIC
  Chris Montan
SENIOR VICE PRESIDENT, MOTION PICTURE PRODUCTION
  Bruce Hendricks
SENIOR VICE PRESIDENT PRODUCTION, TOUCHSTONE
PICTURES
  Jane Goldenring
SENIOR VICE PRESIDENT, TOUCHSTONE PICTURES
  Bridget Johnson
SENIOR VICE PRESIDENT, BUSINESS AFFAIRS
  Robert J. DeBitetto
SENIOR VICE PRESIDENT, MOTION PICTURE & TELEVISION
POST-PRODUCTION
  David McCann
VICE PRESIDENT, PRODUCTION & FINANCE (FEATURE
ANIMATION)
  Tim Engel
VICE PRESIDENT, OPERATIONS—FEATURE ANIMATION
  Michael Laney
VICE PRESIDENT, FEATURE ANIMATION, DEVELOPMENT
  Thomas Schumacher
VICE PRESIDENT, PRODUCTION FINANCE
  Paul Steinke
VICE PRESIDENT PRODUCTION, WALT DISNEY PICTURES
  Bernie Goldman
VICE PRESIDENT, PRODUCTION, WALT DISNEY PICTURES
  Michael Roberts
VICE PRESIDENT, PRODUCTION, WALT DISNEY PICTURES
  Mireille Soria
VICE PRESIDENT PRODUCTION, TOUCHSTONE PICTURES
  Stephen Gelber
VICE PRESIDENT PRODUCTION, TOUCHSTONE PICTURES
  Gaye Hirsch
VICE PRESIDENT PRODUCTION, TOUCHSTONE PICTURES
  Alexandra Schwartz
VICE PRESIDENT, MUSIC BUSINESS & LEGAL AFFAIRS
  Kevin W. Breen
VICE PRESIDENT, PARTICIPATION & RESIDUALS
  William Clark
VICE PRESIDENT, BUSINESS AND LEGAL AFFAIRS, THEME
PARK PRODUCTIONS
  Merritt D. Farren
VICE PRESIDENT, THEATRICAL ANIMATION, BUSINESS
AFFAIRS
  Steven W. Gerse
VICE PRESIDENT, LABOR RELATIONS
  Robert W. Johnson
VICE PRESIDENT, NEW TECHNOLOGY & DEVELOPMENT
  Bob Lambert
VICE PRESIDENT, PLANNING & ANALYSIS
  Rob Moore
VICE PRESIDENT, LEGAL AFFAIRS
  Katie O'Connell
VICE PRESIDENT, MUSIC
  Matt Walker
DIRECTOR, BUSINESS AFFAIRS
  Paul H. Green
DIRECTOR, BUSINESS AFFAIRS
  Laura Fox
DIRECTOR OF PRODUCTION/WALT DISNEY PICTURES
  Brian Snedeker
DIRECTOR OF PRODUCTION/WALT DISNEY PICTURES
  Steve Tao
DIRECTOR OF PRODUCTION/TOUCHSTONE PICTURES
  Todd Garner
DIRECTOR OF PRODUCTION/TOUCHSTONE PICTURES
  Christina Steinberg
CREATIVE EXECUTIVES
  Robin Claire
  Peter Egan
  Jordi Ros
  Matt West
SENIOR ATTORNEY
  Sylvia J. Krask

529

HOLLYWOOD PICTURES

500 South Buena Vista Street, Burbank, CA 91521; (818) 560-6990.

PRESIDENT
  Ricardo Mestres
SENIOR VICE PRESIDENT, BUSINESS & LEGAL AFFAIRS
  Bernadine Brandis
SENIOR PRESIDENT, PRODUCTION
  Dan Halsted
SENIOR VICE PRESIDENT, PRODUCTION
  Charles Hirschhorn
SENIOR VICE PRESIDENT, MUSIC
  Chris Montan
VICE PRESIDENT, PRODUCTION
  Chip Diggins
VICE PRESIDENT, MOTION PICTURE PRODUCTION
  Sam Mercer
VICE PRESIDENT, PRODUCTION
  Mike Stenson
VICE PRESIDENT, CASTING
  Leslee Feldman
DIRECTOR, MUSIC
  William Green
DIRECTOR OF CREATIVE AFFAIRS
  Scott Immergut
DIRECTOR OF CREATIVE AFFAIRS
  Gail Lyon
DIRECTOR OF CREATIVE AFFAIRS
  Jay Stern
CREATIVE EXECUTIVE
  Charles Gold
CREATIVE EXECUTIVE
  Henry Huang
CREATIVE EXECUTIVE
  Tracey Kemble
CREATIVE EXECUTIVE
  Jim Wedaa
VICE PRESIDENT, LEGAL AFFAIRS
  Steve Bardwil
VICE PRESIDENT, PRODUCTION RESOURCES
  Scott Dorman
VICE PRESIDENT, BUSINESS AFFAIRS
  Art Frazier
VICE PRESIDENT, BUSINESS AFFAIRS
  Jane Garzilli
VICE PRESIDENT, BUSINESS AFFAIRS
  Paul Lamori
VICE PRESIDENT, BUSINESS AFFAIRS
  James Lefkowitz
VICE PRESIDENT, PRODUCTION FINANCE
  Paul Steinke

BUENA VISTA PICTURES DISTRIBUTION

3900 West Alameda Avenue, Tower Building, Suite 2400, Burbank, CA 91521-0021; (818) 567-5000.

PRESIDENT
  Richard W. Cook
SENIOR VICE PRESIDENT & GENERAL SALES MANAGER
  Phil Barlow
VICE PRESIDENT—ASSISTANT GENERAL SALES MANAGER/ EAST & CANADA
  Charles Viane
VICE PRESIDENT—ASSISTANT GENERAL SALES MANAGER/ WEST
  Roger Lewin
VICE PRESIDENT, GENERAL COUNSEL
  Robert Cunningham
VICE PRESIDENT, EAST/NEW YORK
  Phil Fortune
VICE PRESIDENT, FINANCE (MARKETING & DISTRIBUTION)
  Robert D. Murphy
VICE PRESIDENT, SOUTHWEST/DALLAS
  Jim Nocella
VICE PRESIDENT, WEST/LOS ANGELES
  Pat Pade
VICE PRESIDENT, NON-THEATRICAL
  Linda Palmer
VICE PRESIDENT, MIDWEST/CHICAGO
  Rick Rice
VICE PRESIDENT, SOUTHEAST/ATLANTA
  Rod Rodriguez

VICE PRESIDENT, OPERATIONS
  Anne Waldeck
VICE PRESIDENT, MIDWEST/CHICAGO
  Rick Rice
VICE PRESIDENT, SOUTHEAST/ATLANTA
  Rod Rodriguez
VICE PRESIDENT, OPERATIONS
  Anne Waldeck
Production Division: 333 North Glenoaks Boulevard, Suite 201, Burbank, California 91501 (818) 955-6850
SENIOR VICE PRESIDENT/PRODUCTION & FINANCE
  Sandra Rabins

BUENA VISTA PICTURES DISTRIBUTION CANADA, INC.

1235 Bay Street, Suite 502, Toronto, Ontario, Canada M5R 3K4.

MANAGING DIRECTOR, CANADA
  Peter Wertelecky

BUENA VISTA INTERNATIONAL

500 South Buena Vista Street, Burbank, California 91521 (818) 560-1000

PRESIDENT, INTERNATIONAL THEATRICAL DISTRIBUTION & WORLDWIDE VIDEO
  William M. Mechanic
PRESIDENT, BUENA VISTA WORLDWIDE MARKETING
  Robert Levin
PRESIDENT, BUENA VISTA INTERNATIONAL
  Mark Zoradi
SENIOR VICE PRESIDENT, THEATRICAL DISTRIBUTION & MARKETING
  Kevin Hyson
SENIOR VICE PRESIDENT, BUSINESS & LEGAL AFFAIRS
  Lawrence Kaplan
VICE PRESIDENT, PUBLICITY
  Hilary Clark
VICE PRESIDENT, MARKETING, JAPAN
  Tateo Ikunaga
VICE PRESIDENT, LATIN AMERICA & THE CARIBBEAN
  Diego Lerner
VICE PRESIDENT, FINANCE & ADMINISTRATION
  Greg Probert
VICE PRESIDENT AND GENERAL MANAGER, GERMANY
  Wofgang Braun
VICE PRESIDENT AND GENERAL MANAGER, SWEDEN
  Eric Broberg
VICE PRESIDENT AND GENERAL MANAGER, U.K.
  Danial Battsek
VICE PRESIDENT AND GENERAL MANAGER, AUSTRIA
  Ferdinand Morawetz
VICE PRESIDENT & GENERAL MANAGER, SOUTH KOREA
  S.I. Kim
VICE PRESIDENT, DUBBING PRODUCTIONS
  Jeffrey S. Miller
VICE PRESIDENT DISTRIBUTION, EUROPE
  Stuart Salter
VICE PRESIDENT & GENERAL MANAGER, SPAIN
  F. Javier Vasallo
VICE PRESIDENT AND GENERAL MANAGER, ITALY
  Filippo Roviglioni
VICE PRESIDENT AND GENERAL MANAGER, SPAIN
  F. Javier Vasallo
VICE PRESIDENT AND GENERAL MANAGER, SWITZERLAND
  Dr. Adriano Vigano
VICE PRESIDENT AND GENERAL MANAGER, BENELUX
  Paul Zonderland

BUENA VISTA INTERNATIONAL TELEVISION

350 South Buena Vista Street, Burbank, CA 91521; (818) 560-1000.

PRESIDENT TELEVISION/LONDON
  Etienne de Villiers
VICE PRESIDENT SALES & MARKETING/LONDON
  Ed Borgerding
VICE PRESIDENT & GENERAL MANAGER/LONDON
  John Elia

VICE PRESIDENT MARKETING/LONDON
Selby Hall
VICE PRESIDENT DISTRIBUTION/CANADA
Orest Olijnyk
VICE PRESIDENT BUSINESS AFFAIRS/LONDON
Sally Davies

BUENA VISTA PRODUCTIONS— INTERNATIONAL

350 South Buena Vista Street, Burbank, CA 91521; (818) 560-1000.

SENIOR VICE PRESIDENT INTERNATIONAL PROGRAMMING/ LONDON
David Simon
VICE PRESIDENT PROGRAMMING/AUSTRIALIA, CANADA, LATIN AMERICA, FAR EAST
David Snyder
VICE PRESIDENT PROGRAMMING/JAPAN
Ryuichi Okumura

BUENA VISTA PRODUCTIONS

500 South Buena Vista Street, Burbank, CA 91421; (818) 560-2125.

SENIOR VICE PRESIDENT PROGRAMMING
Amy Sacks
VICE PRESIDENT PRODUCTION & PROGRAMMING
Mary Kellogg-Joslyn
VICE PRESIDENT PRODUCTION
Hayma (Screech) Washington

BUENA VISTA VISUAL EFFECTS

500 South Buena Vista Street, Burbank, CA 91421; (818) 560-2735.

VICE PRESIDENT, VISUAL EFFECTS, WALT DISNEY PICTURES
Harrison Ellenshaw
VICE PRESIDENT, ADMINISTRATION, VISUAL EFFECTS, WALT DISNEY PICTURES
Ray Scalice

WALT DISNEY TELEVISION AND TOUCHSTONE TELEVISION

500 South Buena Vista Street, Burbank, CA 91521; (818) 560-5000

EXECUTIVE VICE PRESIDENT, NETWORK TELEVISION
Dean Valentine
SENIOR VICE PRESIDENT, NETWORK TELEVISION
Laurie Younger
SENIOR VICE PRESIDENT, CURRENT NETWORK TELEVISION
John Litvack
SENIOR VICE PRESIDENT, MOVIES FOR TELEVISION
Sheri Singer
VICE PRESIDENT, CURRENT COMEDY NETWORK TELEVISION
Lance Taylor
VICE PRESIDENT, DEVELOPMENT, NETWORK TELEVISION
David Kissinger
SENIOR VICE PRESIDENT, TELEVISION PRODUCTION
Mitch Ackerman
VICE PRESIDENT, VIDEOTAPE PRODUCTION
Ted Kaye
VICE PRESIDENT, TV PRODUCTION FINANCE
Walter O'Neal
VICE PRESIDENT, POST PRODUCTION, TELEVISION
Grady Jones
VICE PRESIDENT, TELEVISION CASTING
Eugene Blythe
SENIOR VICE PRESIDENT, MARKETING
Carole Black
VICE PRESIDENT, ADVERTISING/PUBLICITY/PROMOTION
Marian Effinger
VICE PRESIDENT, NETWORK TELEVISION LEGAL AFFAIRS
Jeffrey Paule
VICE PRESIDENT, NETWORK TELEVISION BUSINESS AFFAIRS
Scottye Hedstrom

VICE PRESIDENT, NETWORK TELEVISION BUSINESS AFFAIRS
Rosalind Marks
VICE PRESIDENT, NETWORK TELEVISION FINANCE
Joanna Spak
VICE PRESIDENT, RESEARCH
Joanne Burns
VICE PRESIDENT, LABOR RELATIONS
Robert W. Johnson
VICE PRESIDENT, PARTICIPATION & RESIDUALS
William Clark
VICE PRESIDENT, PAY TELEVISION SALES & ADMINISTRATION
Wendy Ferren

BUENA VISTA TELEVISION

500 South Buena Vista Street, Burbank, CA 91521; (818) 560-5000

PRESIDENT
Robert Jacquemin
SENIOR VICE PRESIDENT, SALES
Janice Marinelli-Mazza
VICE PRESIDENT/GENERAL SALES MANAGER, EAST COAST
Tom Cerio
VICE PRESIDENT/GENERAL SALES MANAGER, WEST COAST
Jim Paker
SENIOR VICE PRESIDENT/GENERAL MANAGER
Mark Zoradi
SENIOR VICE PRESIDENT, PROGRAMMING
Amy Sacks
VICE PRESIDENT, PRODUCTION
Mary Kellogg-Joslyn
VICE PRESIDENT, PRODUCTION
Screech Washington
SENIOR VICE PRESIDENT, SALES
Mort Marcus
VICE PRESIDENT/EASTERN REGIONAL MANAGER
Lloyd Komeser
VICE PRESIDENT/SOUTHEAST REGIONAL MANAGER
John Bryan
VICE PRESIDENT/MIDWEST REGIONAL MANAGER
John Rouse
VICE PRESIDENT/OPERATIONS AND SALES DEVELOPMENT
Helen Faust
SENIOR VICE PRESIDENT, AD SALES
Mike Shaw
VICE PRESIDENT, AD SALES—MIDWEST
Jim Engleman
VICE PRESIDENT, AD SALES
Norman Lesser
VICE PRESIDENT, AD SALES
Howard Levy
SENIOR VICE PRESIDENT, PROGRAMMING
Amy Sacks
VICE PRESIDENT, PRODUCTION
Mary Kellogg-Joslyn
VICE PRESIDENT, PRODUCTION
Screech Washington
SENIOR VICE PRESIDENT, MARKETING
Carole Black
VICE PRESIDENT, CREATIVE SERVICES
Sal Sardo
VICE PRESIDENT, PUBLICITY
Marian Effinger
VICE PRESIDENT, MARKETING
Mark Workman
VICE PRESIDENT, RESEARCH
Joanne Burns
SENIOR VICE PRESIDENT, BUSINESS AFFAIRS
Kenneth D. Werner
VICE PRESIDENT, FINANCE & ADMINISTRATION
Andrew Lewis
VICE PRESIDENT, AFFILIATE RELATIONS
Sharon Yokoi

DISNEY CONSUMER PRODUCTS

500 South Buena Vista Street, Burbank, CA 91521; (818) 560-1000

PRESIDENT—DISNEY CONSUMER PRODUCTS
Barton K. Boyd

THE DISNEY CHANNEL

3800 West Alameda Avenue, Burbank, CA 91505; (818) 569-7500

PRESIDENT
John F. Cooke
SENIOR VICE PRESIDENT, ORIGINAL PROGRAMMING
Stephen D. Fields
SENIOR VICE PRESIDENT, SALES & AFFILIATE MARKETING
Mark A. Handler
SENIOR VICE PRESIDENT, BUSINESS & LEGAL AFFAIRS
Frederick Kuperberg
SENIOR VICE PRESIDENT, FINANCE/ADMINISTRATION
Patrick T. Lopker
SENIOR VICE PRESIDENT, PROGRAMMING
Bruce N. Rider
SENIOR VICE PRESIDENT, NEW BUSINESS DEVELOPMENT
Winifred B. Wechsler
SENIOR VICE PRESIDENT, CONSUMER MARKETING
Thomas J. Wszalek

BUENA VISTA HOME VIDEO

500 South Buena Vista Street, Burbank, CA 91521; (818) 560-1000

PRESIDENT, INTERNATIONAL THEATRICAL & WORLDWIDE VIDEO
William M. Mechanic
PRESIDENT, DOMESTIC HOME VIDEO
Ann Daly
PRESIDENT, INTERNATIONAL HOME VIDEO
Michael Orlin Johnson
SENIOR VICE PRESIDENT, DOMESTIC SALES
Richard E. Longwell
SENIOR VICE PRESIDENT, INTERNATIONAL MARKETING
Robin Miller Jay
SENIOR VICE PRESIDENT, BUSINESS & LEGAL AFFAIRS
John J. Reagan
SENIOR VICE PRESIDENT, WORLDWIDE PAY TV
Hal Richardson

HOLLYWOOD RECORDS

500 South Buena Vista Street, Burbank, CA 91521; (818) 560-1000

PRESIDENT
Peter Paterno
EXECUTIVE VICE PRESIDENT
Wesley Hein
EXECUTIVE VICE PRESIDENT & GENERAL MANAGER
Brad Hunt
SENIOR VICE PRESIDENT, PROMOTIONS
Brenda Romanom

WALT DISNEY IMAGINEERING

1401 Flower Street, Glendale, CA 91221; (818) 544-6500

PRESIDENT
Marty Sklar
EXECUTIVE VICE PRESIDENT
Stanley (Mickey) Steinberg

WALT DISNEY RECORDS

500 South Buena Vista Street, Burbank, CA 91521; (818) 560-1000 (A division of Disney Consumer Products.)

VICE PRESIDENT
Mark Jaffe
VICE PRESIDENT, MARKETING
Liz Kalodner

WALT DISNEY PUBLISHING

500 South Buena Vista Street, Burbank, CA 91521; (818) 560-1000; 114 Fifth Avenue, New York, NY 10011; (212) 633-4400.

VICE PRESIDENT & EDITOR-IN-CHIEF, DISCOVER MAGAZINE (CA)
Paul Hoffman

EDITOR-IN-CHIEF, DISNEY ADVENTURES MAGAZINE (CA)
Tommi Lewis
VICE PRESIDENT, MAGAZINE PUBLISHING (CA)
John Skipper
VICE PRESIDENT, DISNEY LICENSED PUBLISHING (CA)
Jan Smith
VICE PRESIDENT, DISNEY ART EDITIONS (CA)
Wayne Smith
SENIOR VICE PRESIDENT, DIRECT RESPONSE & EDUCATION (CA)
Charles P. Wickham
SENIOR VICE PRESIDENT, DISNEY PUBLISHING (NY)
Michael Lynton
VICE PRESIDENT & PUBLISHER, DISNEY PRESS/HYPERION BOOKS FOR CHILDREN
Elizabeth Gordon
VICE PRESIDENT & PUBLISHER HYPERION PRESS (General Interest, Adult Fiction and Non-Fiction)
Robert Miller
PRESIDENT AND EDITOR-IN-CHIEF
Jake Winebaum

Dubie-Do Productions, Inc.

New York City: (212) 765-4240 or 1 Laurie Dr., Englewood Cliffs, NJ 07632; (201) 568-4214; FAX: (201) 568-4240. (Production of motion pictures for theatres and TV.)

PRESIDENT
Richard S. Dubelman

EMI Films, Inc.

640 San Vicente Blvd., Los Angeles, CA 90048; (213) 960-4600. Organized 1971. (Motion picture production and distribution.)

CHAIRMAN AND CHIEF EXECUTIVE OFFICER
Gary Dartnall
PRESIDENT AND CHIEF OPERATING OFFICER
Barr B. Potter
VICE PRESIDENT MARKETING & DISTRIBUTION
Michael Bromhead
FINANCE DIRECTOR
Bob Edwards

Eagle Productions, U.S.A.

P.O. Box 67, Galway, NY 12074; (518) 372-3900. Chicago office: 5052 North Menard Ave., Chicago, IL 60630; (312) 545-8393; FAX: (518) 399-3277; Direct FAX: (518) 384-2001.

PRESIDENT AND CHIEF EXECUTIVE OFFICER
Tadeusz A. J. E. Czolowski
VICE PRESIDENT—PRODUCTION
T. K. Czolowski
VICE PRESIDENT—PUBLIC RELATIONS
J. St. Thomas
VICE PRESIDENT—MUSIC DIVISION
T. X. D. Rinkus
VICE PRESIDENT MUSIC DIVISION OPERATIONS
Michael P. Czolowski

Eastman Kodak Company

343 State St., Rochester, NY 14650; (716) 724-4000; 1901 W. 22nd St., Oakbrook, IL 60522-9004; (312) 218-5175; 6700 Santa Monica Boulevard, Hollywood, CA 90038; (213) 464-6131; 1133 Ave. of the Americas, New York, NY 10036; (212) 930-8000; Williams Square, 5221 N. O'Connor Blvd., Irving, TX 75039-3798; (214) 506-9700; 4 Concourse Parkway, Suite 300, Atlanta, GA 30328; (404) 392-6841; 1122 Mapunapuna St., Honolulu, Hawaii 96817; (808) 833-1661. (Motion picture film offices & laboratories.)

CHAIRMAN, PRESIDENT & CHIEF EXECUTIVE OFFICER
Kay R. Whitmore
PRESIDENT, KODAK IMAGING GROUP
Dr. Leo J. Thomas
VICE PRESIDENT & GENERAL MANAGER, MOTION PICTURE & TELEVISION IMAGING DIVISION
Henry D. Petit

GENERAL MANAGER, MARKETING & VICE-PRESIDENT,
MOTION PICTURE & TELEVISION, IMAGING DIVISION
Robert Woolman

East-West Classics

225 Greenbank Ave., Piedmont, CA 94611-4131; Tel. & FAX: (510) 655-6333. Organized 1985. (Theatrical, non-theatrical, TV & video distribution.)
CEO/OWNER
Audie E. Bock

Electric Shadow Productions, Inc.

8522 National Blvd., Culver City, CA 90232; (310) 836-9977; FAX: (310) 836-5501.
PRESIDENT, CREATIVE & CORPORATE DEVELOPMENT
Anne Marie Gillen
PRESIDENT
Shannon Silverman
CHAIR
Sarah Duvall

Energy Productions, Timescape Image Library

12700 Ventura Blvd., 4th Fl., Studio City, CA 91604; (818) 508-1444; (800)IMA-GERY; FAX: (818) 508-1293. (Stock footage library.)
CHIEF EXECUTIVE OFFICERS
Louis Schwartzberg
Jan Ross
Craig Robin

Entertainment Data, Inc.

8350 Wilshire Blvd., Suite 210, Beverly Hills, CA 90211; (213) 658-8300. Organized 1976. (Provides daily box office information for distribution and exhibition. On-line access to current and historical data. Release schedule services updated weekly.)
PRESIDENT
Marcy Polier
SENIOR VICE PRESIDENT
Philip Garfinkle
BRANCHES
Los Angeles, Washington D.C., San Francisco, New York, Dallas, Chicago, Toronto, Atlanta, London

Entertainment Productions, Inc.

2210 Wilshire Blvd., Suite 744, Santa Monica, CA 90403; (310) 456-3143. Organized 1971. (Produces motion picture and television productions for worldwide markets, including home video, cable, theatrical, etc.)
PRESIDENT
Edward Coe

Epic Productions, Inc.

3330 Cahuenga Blvd. W., Suite 500, Los Angeles, CA 90068; (213) 969-2800; FAX: (213) 969-8211. (Feature film production and distribution.)
CHIEF EXECUTIVE OFFICER
John Peters
PRESIDENT OF DOMESTIC MARKETING, DISTRIBUTION & HOME VIDEO
Elliot Slutzky
VICE PRESIDENT/CONTROLLER
Carl Law
LEGAL/BUSINESS AFFAIRS
Jeff Hagedorn
SENIOR VICE PRESIDENT, MARKETING & DISTRIBUTION
David Garber
VICE PRESIDENT, INTERNATIONAL SALES/ADMINISTRATION
Paul Woolley

VICE PRESIDENT, HOME VIDEO
Jeff Fink

Expanded Entertainment

28024 Dorothy Dr., Agoura Hills, CA 91301; (818) 991-2884; FAX: (818) 991-3773. Telex: 247770 ANIM UR. (Specializes in compilations of animated short subjects.)
PRESIDENT
Terry Thoren
DIRECTOR OF ACQUISITIONS
Benjamin G. Levy

Jerry Fairbanks Productions

P.O. Box 50553, Santa Barbara, CA 93150; (805) 969-7001. (Producer of theatrical short subjects and features, commercial and television films.)
EXECUTIVE PRODUCER
Jerry Fairbanks
PRODUCTION SUPERVISOR
William R. Lieb

WESTERN AUDIO VISUAL ENTERPRISES

P.O. Box 50553, Santa Barbara, CA 93150; (805) 969-7001. (Motion picture print distribution center.)
OWNER
Jerry Fairbanks

YUKON PICTURES, INC.

P.O. Box 50553, Santa Barbara, CA 93150; (805) 969-7001. (Theatrical feature production and distribution.)
PRESIDENT
Jerry Fairbanks

Falcon Productions, Inc.

725 Market St., Wilmington, DE 19801; (302) 454-3863. (Producer.)
PRESIDENT
John W. Hulme

Film Corporation of America, Inc.

A division of Shepard & Company, Inc. 1735 York Ave., New York, NY 10128; (212) 876-2330; FAX: (212) 427-8387. Production offices: 125 North Main St., Port Chester, NY 10573; (914) 937-1603; FAX: (914) 937-8496. (International and domestic production and distribution company.)
CHAIRMAN
C.M. Shepard
PRESIDENT
Steve Florin
CHIEF FINANCIAL OFFICER
Mark Kain
EXECUTIVE VICE PRESIDENT PRODUCTION
Peter Malcolm
PERSONNEL
Norman Hascoe

Film World Entertainments, Inc.

6311 Romaine St., Suite 7309, Hollywood, CA 90038; (213) 466-0676; FAX: (213) 856-0107. Organizied 1985. (Distributor.)
PRESIDENT
Robert F. Burkhardt

Filmart Enterprises, Ltd.

Park Street, Sharon, PA 16146; (412) 981-3456; FAX: (412) 981-2852. (Production company.)
PRESIDENT
Amin Q. Chaudhri

VICE PRESIDENT
  Jenny Chrisinger
VICE PRESIDENT OF CREATIVE AFFAIRS
  Maraline Kubik

Films Around the World, Inc.

342 Madison Ave., Suite 812, New York, NY 10173; (212) 752-5050; FAX: (212) 838-9642. Organized 1931.
PRESIDENT
  Alexander W. Kogan, Jr.
VICE PRESIDENT
  Barry Tucker
PRESIDENT, TELEVISION DIVISION/SALES MANAGER
  Beverly Partridge
VICE PRESIDENT, TELEVISION DIVISION
  Deborah Dave

Filmworld International Productions, Inc.

PRESIDENT AND CHIEF EXECUTIVE OFFICER
  Alexander W. Kogan, Jr.

Films Incorporated

5547 N. Ravenswood Ave., Chicago, IL 60640; (312) 878-2600; (800) 323-4222, ext. 42. (Distributor of 16 and 35mm films and licenses public performance video.)
PRESIDENT, ENTERTAINMENT DIVISION
  Allen J. Green

Filmtreat International Corp.

42-44 Orchard St., Long Island City, NY 11101; (718) 784-4040; FAX: (718) 784-4766. (Motion picture film care and rejuvenation.)
PRESIDENT
  Y. W. Mociuk
VICE PRESIDENT
  Sam Borodinsky
GENERAL MANAGER
  Kathi G. Weiss

FILMTREAT WEST CORP.

12326 Montague Lane, Pacoima, CA 91331; (818) 890-3456; FAX: (818) 890-0235.
PRESIDENT
  Larry Zide
VICE PRESIDENT
  Mickey Zide

Filmworld Distributors, Inc.

342 Madison Ave., Suite 812, New York, NY 10173; (212) 599-9500; FAX: (212) 599-6040. (Motion picture distributor.)
PRESIDENT
  Alexander W. Kogan, Jr.

Fireside Entertainment Corporation

1650 Broadway, Suite 1001, New York, NY 10019; (212) 489-8160. Organized 1986. (Production of film and television programming.)
PRODUCER
  Steven S. Schwartz

First Cinema Ventures, Inc.

1250 Sixth Street, Suite 200, Santa Monica CA 90401; (310) 394-8847; FAX: (310) 823-5183. Organized 1985. (Film production and distribution.)
PRESIDENT
  Lon J. Kerr

First Run Features

153 Waverly Place, New York, NY 10014; (212) 243-0600; FAX: (212) 989-7649. Organized 1980. (Distributor of foreign films and documentaries in theatrical and non-theatrical markets; distributor of home videos in North America.)
PRESIDENT
  Seymour Wishman
VICE PRESIDENT, THEATRICAL SALES & MARKETING
  Marc A. Mauceri
VICE PRESIDENT, RETAIL HOME VIDEO SALES
  Lisa Burkin

Forty Acres & a Mule Filmworks

124 Dekalb Ave., Brooklyn, NY 11217; (718) 624-3703; FAX:(718) 624-2008. (Motion picture production.)
ADMINISTRATIVE DIRECTOR
  Desiree Jellerette

Four Point Entertainment, Inc.

3375 Cahuenga Blvd., W., Suite 600, Los Angeles, CA 90068-1303; (213) 850-1600; FAX: (213) 850-6709. (Television and motion picture production.)
PRESIDENT
  Ron Ziskin
CHAIRMAN
  Shukri Ghalayini

Fox Inc.

10201 W. Pico Blvd., Los Angeles, CA 90035; P.O. Box 900, Beverly Hills, CA 90213; (310) 277-2211. Parent company of Fox Broadcasting Company, Fox Television Stations, Inc., Fox Film Corporation (see separate listings).
CHAIRMAN AND CHIEF EXECUTIVE OFFICER
  Rupert Murdoch
EXECUTIVE VICE PRESIDENT
  George Vradenburg
CHIEF OPERATING OFFICER
  Chase Carey
EXECUTIVE VICE PRESIDENT
  Tom Sherak
SENIOR VICE PRESIDENT, EMPLOYEE RELATIONS
  Dean Ferris
SENIOR VICE PRESIDENT, GENERAL COUNSEL
  David Handleman
SENIOR VICE PRESIDENT, FINANCE
  Harvey Finkel
SENIOR VICE PRESIDENT
  Andrew Setos
VICE PRESIDENT, CORPORATE COMMUNICATIONS
  Dennis E. Petroskey
VICE PRESIDENT, LABOR RELATIONS
  Pamela DiGiovanni
VICE PRESIDENT, LEGAL AFFAIRS
  Daphne Gronich
SENIOR VICE PRESIDENT, ASSISTANT GENERAL COUNSEL
  Mary Anne Harrison
VICE PRESIDENT, COMPENSATION/BENEFITS
  Lynn Franzoi

TWENTIETH CENTURY FOX

P.O. Box 900, Beverly Hills, CA 90213; (310) 277-2211; Telex: 6-74875. New York Office: 1211 Ave. of the Americas, New York, NY 10036; (212) 556-2400. (Producer and distributor.)
(See corporate history in separate section.)
CHIEF EXECUTIVE OFFICER & OWNER
  Rupert Murdoch
CHAIRMAN
  Peter Chernin
PRESIDENT AND CHIEF OPERATING OFFICER
  Strauss Zelnick
SENIOR VICE PRESIDENT, CONTROLLER
  Harvey Finkel

EXECUTIVE VICE PRESIDENT, STUDIO LEGAL AFFAIRS,
DEPUTY GENERAL COUNSEL
    Lyman S. Gronemeyer
SENIOR VICE PRESIDENT, LEGAL AFFAIRS AND ASSISTANT
GENERAL COUNSEL
    Michael Doodan
VICE PRESIDENT, TAXES
    Earl Hammond
VICE PRESIDENT, PARTICIPATIONS
    Steve Kaplan
VICE PRESIDENT, PERSONNEL
    Leslee Perlstein
VICE PRESIDENT, MANAGEMENT INFORMATION SYSTEMS
    Alec Peterson
DATE AND PLACE OF INCORPORATION
    As Fox Film Corp., February 1, 1915, New York. Succeeded by Twentieth Century-Fox Film Corp., July 22, 1952, Delaware. (See separate listing for parent company Fox Inc.)

MOTION PICTURE DIVISION

PRODUCTION
PRESIDENT OF WORLDWIDE PRODUCTION
    Tom Jacobson
SENIOR VICE PRESIDENTS, PRODUCTION
    Elizabeth Gabler, Susan Cartsonis
EXECUTIVE VICE PRESIDENT, BUSINESS AFFAIRS
    Melinda Benedek
SENIOR VICE PRESIDENT, POST-PRODUCTION
    Gary Gerlich
SENIOR VICE PRESIDENT, FEATURE PRODUCTION
    Jon Landau
SENIOR VICE PRESIDENT, PRODUCTION
    Michael London
SENIOR VICE PRESIDENT, MUSIC
    Elliot Lurie
VICE PRESIDENT, BUSINESS AFFAIRS
    Daphne Gronich
SENIOR VICE PRESIDENT, PRODUCTION
    Susan Cartsonis
SENIOR VICE PRESIDENT, PRODUCTION
    Riley Ellis
VICE PRESIDENT, TALENT ADMINISTRATION
    Susan McIntosh

MARKETING AND DISTRIBUTION (Domestic)

Home Office: P.O. Box 900, Beverly Hills, CA 90213; (213) 277-2211.

PRESIDENT, DOMESTIC DISTRIBUTION AND MARKETING
    Thomas Sherak
EXECUTIVE VICE PRESIDENT, GENERAL SALES MANAGER
    Richard Myerson
SENIOR VICE PRESIDENT, MARKETING
    Geoffrey Ammer
SENIOR VICE PRESIDENT, GENERAL SALES MANAGER, EAST REGION
    Bruce Snyder
EXECUTIVE VICE PRESIDENT, MARKETING
    Andrea Jaffe
VICE PRESIDENT, SALES OPERATIONS AND ADMINISTRATION
    Harvey Applebaum
VICE PRESIDENT, GENERAL MANAGER, CANADA FOX
    Tony Ciancatottia
VICE PRESIDENT, NATIONAL PUBLICITY
    Michael Russell
SENIOR VICE PRESIDENT, LICENSING & MERCHANDISING
    Albert Ovadia
SENIOR VICE PRESIDENT, CREATIVE MARKETING
    Chris Pula
VICE PRESIDENT, SOUTHERN DIVISION MANAGER
    Richard King
VICE PRESIDENT, WESTERN DIVISION MANAGER
    James Naify
VICE PRESIDENT, SALES, NEW YORK, DIVISION SALES MANAGER
    Ron Polon
VICE PRESIDENT, SALES ADMINISTRATION/BRANCH OPERATIONS
    Morris Stermer
SENIOR VICE PRESIDENT, MEDIA
    Nancy Utley-Jacobs

DOMESTIC BRANCHES

ATLANTA, GA 30345-1347—Suite 990, 2635 Century Pkwy., NE: (404) 321-1178. Larry Jameson.
BOSTON, MA 02116—Suite 1101, 545 Boylston St.; (617) 267-4800. Carl Bertolino.
CHICAGO, IL 60173 (Schaumburg)—Suite 100, 1100 Woodfield Rd.; (312) 843-3640. Robert Kaplowitz.
DALLAS, TX 75215—Suite 460, 12222 Merit Dr.; (214) 392-0101. Woodrow Townsend.
NEW YORK 10019—8th floor, 40 W. 57 St.; (212) 977-5500. Robert Polon.
LOS ANGELES, CA 91403 (Sherman Oaks)—Suite 700, 15250 Ventura Blvd., (818) 995-7750. Donna Wolfe.
WASHINGTON, DC 20005-1872—Suite 329, 1156 15 St., NE; (202) 223-6320. Francis X. Gormley.
CANADA
TORONTO M5V 2T3 Ontario—6th floor., 720 King St.; (416) 366-9941. Dave Forget.

INTERNATIONAL DISTRIBUTION

FOX INTERNATIONAL CORPORATION

P.O. Box 900, Beverly Hills, CA 90213; (213) 277-2211; Telex: 6-74875.

International Division

PRESIDENT, INTERNATIONAL DISTRIBUTION AND MARKETING
    Walter Senior
SENIOR VICE PRESIDENT, EUROPE, MIDDLE EAST AND AFRICA
    Jorge G. Canizares
VICE PRESIDENT, INTERNATIONAL ADVERTISING, PUBLICITY AND PUBLICITY
    Joel Coler

FOREIGN BRANCHES AND MANAGERS

Great Britain and Eire

Fox Film Co., Ltd., 31-32 Soho Square, London, WIV 6AP, England. Telex: 27869 CENTFOX F. Cables: CENTFOX LONDON WI (Distribution) Telephone: 01 437 7766. TWENIFOX LONDON (Production) Night Line: 437 2755; Gerard Lefebre, dir. UK; Colin Hankins, dir. pub.-adv.; Sye Blackmore, media relations coordinator.
Dublin Branch
Prosperity Chambers, 5/7 Upper O'Connell Street, Dublin 1, Telephone; dublin (00017) 43068 Brendan McCaul, mgr.
Twentieth Century-Fox Productions Ltd., 31-32 Soho Square, London WIV 6AP. Tim Hampton, mgr. dir.

CONTINENTAL DIVISION

20th Century Fox, 23 Rue de Marignan, 75008, Paris, France. P.O. Box 188 75363, Paris. CEDEX 08. Marc Bernard, dir. adv.-pub.; Elisabeth Gagarine, asst. to Bernard. Tel.: (331) 4256-4483. Telex: 643027 FOXCONT.

Austria

Vienna—Centfox-Film Ges, M.B.H., 35 Neubaugasse, 1071 Vienna; Roman Hoerman, Manager.

Belgium

Brussels—Twentieth Century-Fox Film Belge S.A., Chaussee de Haecht 67, 1030 Brussels; George Buyse, manager.

Denmark

Columbia-Fox, 13 Hauchsvej, DK-1825 Copenhagen V; Jorgen Nielsen, manager.

France

Twentieth Century-Fox France Inc.
Lyons—11 Place Bellecour, M. Bonny, sales rep.
Marseille—75 Blvd. de la Liberation, 13001 Marseille, Yves Rouquette, manager.
Paris (Head Office)—23 Rue de Marignan, 75008 Paris, Robert Balk, Managing Director; Henri Ruimy, Mid-East Supervisor; Gerard Perrousset, Administrative manager; Claude Venin, adv. mgr.; Alain Roulleau, pub. mgr.
Paris (Exchange)—160 Rue Oberkampf, Paris, Henri Ruimy, Regional dir., Near East.

Finland

Oy Fox Films AB Kaisaniemenkatu 2 b, 00100, Helsinki, Finland. Jukka Makela, mgr. dir. Tel.: (3580) 650011. Telex: 1001658 KINOSTO.

Germany

Twentieth Century-Fox of Germany GMBH, Hainer weg 37/53, D-6000 Frankfurt/M. 70 Werner Kaspers, General manager; R. Behrhardt, chief of administration; Sales Manager, Walter Schweer.

Berlin—Kurfürstendamm 52, D-1000 Berlin 15., Gunter Grunberg, manager.

Düsseldorf—Garaf-Adolf-Strasse 108, D-4000, Dusseldorf 1., Albert-Ernst Tobias, manager.

Frankfurt/Main—Taunusstrasse 40-42, D-6000, Frankfurt/M. 1, Walter Schweer, sales mgr.

Hamburg—Klosterwall 4 (City-Hof), D-2000 Hamburg 1., Eberhard Woehlert, manager.

Munich—Lenbachplatz 3, D-8000 München 2, Kurt Schreiber, manager.

Greece

Spentzos Film Ltd., 9-13 Gravias St., Athens, Greece 106.78. George Spentzos. Tel.: (301) 3639-463.

Holland

Amsterdam—Netherlands Fox Film Corporation B.V., Van Eeghenstraat 98, 1071 GL, Amsterdam, Netherlands. Tel.: 763534. Telex: 10787 (HOLEX NL). Jim W. Stalknecht, mgr. dir. & financial controller.

Italy

20th Century-Fox Italy, Inc., Via Palestro 24, 00185 Rome, Gaetano Scaffidi, general manager.

Ancona—Via Marsala 15, Enzo Porcarelli, agent.
Rome—Via dei Mille 34, Roberto Balmas, agent.
Bologna—Via Amendola 12/C, Oscar Palmirani, agent.
Catania—Via De Felice 60, Edoardo Cumitini.
Florence—Via Fiume 14, Alfredo Lasagni.
Genoa—Via Fiasella 62-64/r, Mario Gavanna, Agent.
Milan—Via Spoerga 20, Lucio Umberto Vicini.
Naples—Piazza Gesu Nuovo 33, Antonio Stella.
Padua—Via Triesta 6—Francesco Miola.
Turin—Via Pomba 20—Massimo Eieuteri.

Norway

Oslo—Kommunenes Film Central A/S Nedre Vollgt 9, Oslo 1 Knut G. A. Bohrvim, Managing Director

Portugal

Lisbon—Filmes Castello Lopes, Lda., Praca Marques de Pombal, nno. 6-1°, Lisbon 1, Gerard Castello Lopes & Jose Manuel Castello Lopes, Directors.

Spain

Hispano Foxfilm S.A.E., Plaza del Callao, 4–5°, 28013 Madrid, Spain, Benjamin Benhamou, managing director.

Barcelona—Paeso de Garcia, 77, Barcelona 8, Raimundo Bartra, manager.

Valencia—Gran Via Germanias, 53, Valencia 6., Enrique Manes, manager.

Bilbao—Ercilla, 20, Bilbao, Emilio Acha, manager.

Sevilla—Santa Mará de Gracia, 3, Sevilla, Enrique Gutierrer, manager.

La Coruna—J. L. Perez de Cepeda, 15, La Coruna, Luis Carames, agent.

Balearic Islands—Exclusivas Films Baleares, Via Roma, 3, Palma de Mallorca, Rafael Salas, agent.

Canary Islands—Doctor Juan de Padilla, 24 Las Palmas de Gran Canaria, Jesús Rodrúquez Doreste, agent.

Sweden

Stockholm—AB Fox Film, S-117 88, Stockholm, Sweden Soder Malarstrand 27. Bengt Bengtson, Managing Director & Home Office Representative.

Switzerland

Geneva—20th Century-Fox Film Corporation, Societe d'Exploitation pour la Suisse, 2 Place du Cirque, P.O. Box 121, 1211 Geneva 8, Jean-Pierre Reyren, manager.

NEAR EAST

Egypt

Cairo—20th Century-Fox Import Corp., 11, Sarai Saray el-Ezbekieh, P.O. Box 693, Cairo, Egypt, Antoine Zeind, manager.

Israel

Tel Aviv—Albert D. Matalon & Co., Ltd., 15 Hess Street (P.O. Box 4388) Amnon Matalon, General manager.

Lebanon

Beirut—Michael Haddad, Les Films de Georges Haddad & Co., rue Principale, Wake Amchit Bldg., Jounieh. P.O. Box 4680. Beirut, Lebanon.

AUSTRALIA AND NEW ZEALAND

Australia

Fox Columbia Film Distributors Pty Ltd., 6th floor, 600 George St., Sydney, N.S.W. 2000. G.P.O. Box 3342, Sydney, N.S.W. 2001. Telephone: 235 7877 Cable: COLUMFILM Telex: 26278 Direct: 011-61-2-235-7877; Peter Wilkinson, Managing Director; Barry M. Cooper, Sales Manager; Ann Yorke, Director of Advertising.

BRANCHES

Melbourne—140 Bourke St., Richmond, Melbourne, VIC 3000; Frank Henley., G.P.O. Box 1710, Melbourne, VIC, 3000.

Brisbane—Cnr. Manning & Melbourne Sts., South Brisbane, Queensland 4101 P.O. Box 189, Brisbane, Old 4001, Sonny Schattling, manager.

Adelaide—159 Helifax St., Adelaide, S.A. 5000, Russell Anderson, manager

Perth—90 Burswood Rd., Victoria Park, Perth, W.A. Australia 6100.

New Zealand

Auckland—Amalgamated Film Distribution, P.O. Box 6445, Wellesley St., Auckland, Alan L. Flyger, manager.

AFRICA

Republic of South Africa

Johannesburg—Twentieth Century-Fox Film (S.A.) (Pty) Ltd., 11th floor, Kalhof, 112 Pritchard St., Johannesburg 2001, Transvaal, South Africa, P.O. Box 1100 Johannesburg 2000, Geoffrey B. Rawsthorne, managing director.

FAR EASTERN DISTRICT

Hong Kong—Fox Columbia Film Distributors, No. 11, Canton Rd., Tsimashatsui, Kowloon, Hong Kong; TST Box 98407, Tsimashatsui Post Office, Kowloon, Hong Kong, Eddie Chau, manager.

India

20th Century-Fox Corporation (India) Pvt. Ltd., Metro House, 3rd Floor, Mahatma Gandhi Rd., Bombay 400 020., G.P.O. 765, Bombay 1., Pakka V. Prabhu, managing director.

Calcutta—19 Jawaharlal Nehru Rd., Calcutta 13, S. M. Karnad, manager.

Madras—1/17H Mount Rd., Madras 2, T. C. Krishnan, manager.

New Delhi—Plaza Theatre Bldg., Connaught Circus, New Delhi, J. Noronha, manager.

Japan

Twentieth Century-Fox (Far East), Inc., Fukide Bldg., 1–13, Toranomon 4-chome, Minato-ku, tokyo 105; Yoshitsugu Fukada, General manager, Noriyoshi Matsumoto, asst. gen. mgr. & dir. publ-mktg.

BRANCHES

Fukuoka—1–18, Tenjin 4-chome, Chuo-Ku, Fukuoka 810; K. Nishimura, Manager.

Osaka—Chiyoda Bldg., Nishi Bekkan (2nd fl.), 5–8, Umeda 2-chome, Kita-ku, Osaka 530, K. Hiromoto, Manager.

Sapporo—No. 1, Nishi 1-chome, Minami 1-Jo, Chuo-Ku, Sapporo 060; I. Kamada, Manager.

Pakistan

Karachi—Twentieth Century-Fox Pakistan Inc., 207 Hotel Metropole, Club Rd., Karachi 17, G.P.O Box 3734, Karachi, Zahid Nayeem, general manager.

Lahore—Twentieth Century-Fox Pakistan Inc., 43 Shahran E. Quaid E Azam, Lahore G.P.O. Box 75, Lahore, A.H. Rizvi Shah, branch manager.

Republic of the Philippines

Manila—20th Century-Fox Films Philippines Inc., Penthouse, Avenue Theatre Bldg., Rizal Ave., Manila, P.O. Box 423, Manila, Rodrigo Dulfo, home office rep.

Manila—Mever Films, Inc., Penthouse, Avenue Theatre Bldg., Rizal Ave., Manila, P.O. Box 3174, Manila Philippines, John Litton, president (agent).

Singapore—20th Century-Fox Film (East) Private Ltd., 83 Victoria St. (1st floor) P.O. Box 141 Queen St., PostOffice, Singapore, Rep. of Singapore, John Foo, Managing Director.

Malaysia

Kuala Lumpur Branch Office, Twentieth Century-Fox Film (Malaya) Sendirian Berhad, 22 Jalan Padang Walter Grenier, off Japan Imbi, Kuala Lumpur 06-23, West Malaysia. Malaysia Branch, Kwi Leong Lim, Manager; Singapore—John Foo, Manager.

Taiwan

Taipei—Twentieth Century-Fox Inc. USA (Taiwan Branch), 109, G-Mei St., 3rd floor, K. K. Poon, manager.

Thailand

Bangkok—Twentieth Century-Fox Thailand Inc., South-East Insurance Bldg.—6th floor, 315 Silom Rd., P.O. Box 2492, Bangkok 5, William Blamey, manager.

LATIN AMERICAN DIVISION

Argentina

Columbia Pictures of Argentina, Inc., Fox Film De La Argentina, Warner Bros. South, Inc. S.A.—mailing address: Columbia-Fox, Lavalle 1878, Buenos Aires, Argentina, Alberto Liferoff, general manager, Jorge A. Mozuc, admin. manager.

Bahia Blanca—Disciba S.R.L., Soler 346, Bahia Blanca, Pcia de Buenos Aires

Cordoba—Distribuidora Parana S.R.L., Lima 346, Cordoba.

Rosario—Distribuidora Panama S.R.L., Maipu 973 Rosario, Pcia de Santa Fe.

Sante Fe—Distribuidora Panama S.R.L., Hipolito Yrigoyen 2564 Santa Fe, Pcia de Santa Fe.

Mendoza—Mitre 1623—Mendoza, Mendoza.

Tucuman—Discinor S.R.L., Jujuy 120, San Miguel De Tucuman, Tucuman

Bolivia

La Paz—Distribuidores Asociados De Peliculas LTDA., Av. Montes 768, 3er, Piso-Edificio De Col., Mailing Address: Casilla 4709, La Paz, Bolivia, Licnio Manay, manager.

Brazil

Fox Film do Brazil (S.A.): Harry Anastassiadi, general manager; Rua Joaquim Silva 98, 6°/7° ands., Lapa ZC-06, Caixa Postal 989-ZC-00, 20241 Rio de Janeiro, RJ. Belo Horizonte, MG.—José Dinez, branch manager, Rua Aarão Reis Sala 204. Caixa Postal 486, 30.000 Belo Horizonte, MG.

Botucatú—Araujo & Passos, Rua Joao Passos 702, Caixa Postal 38 and 72, 18600 Botucatú, São Paulo, (agent).

Curitiba—Fama Films S.A., Rua Barão do Rio Branco 370/1°, Caixa Postal 994, Curitiba, Paraná (agent).

Porto Alegre—Dist. Filmes Wermar Ltda. Rua Siqueira Campos 820, Porto Alegre, Rio Grande do Sul (agent).

Recife—União Cinematográfica Brasileira, S.A., Rua Aurora 175, Bioco A, Ed. Duarte Coelho, 3°andar, Caixa Postal 27, Recife, Pernambuco (agent).

Rubeira/to Preto—Cinefilmes Distrib. Import. Cinematográfica Ltda., Rua Duque de Caxias 639/2°andar, Caixa Postal 305, Ribeirão Preto, São Paulo (agent).

São José do Rio Preto—Agência de Filmes Rio Preto Ltda., Rua Col. Spinola 3054, Caixa Postal 190, São José do Rio Preto, São Paulo (agent).

Salvador—Art Films, S.A., Rua Lopes Cardoso 41, 2°andar 40.000 Salvador, Bahia (Agent).

Brazil-Joint Operation—Columbia-Fox Servicos de Distribuição de Filmes Ltda. (For information only. Do not address mail to the service company in Rio de Janeiro.) Harry Anastassiadi, Fox Rep., William E. Hummel, Columbia Rep.

Chile

Santiago—Columbia Pictures of Chile, Inc. Asociacion Twentieth Century Fox Chile, Inc., Huerfanos 786, Of. 210, Santiago, Casilla 9003 or Casilla 3770, Arthur Ehrlich, Manager; Arturo Parra, sales manager.

Colombia

Bogotá—Fox-Columbia Pictures of Colombia, Inc., Carrera 5 No. 22-85, 5o. Piso, Apartado Aéreo 3892, Bogotá, D.E., Colombia, S.A., Mauro Lara, general manager.

Barranquilla—Fox Columbia Pictures of Colombia, Inc., Calle 53 No. 52-68, 2o Piso, Apartado Aéreo 380, Barranquilla, Colombia, S.A. Efrain Gomez, branch manager.

Cali—Fox Columbia Pictures of Colombia, Inc., Carrera 4 No. 14-45, Apartado Aéreo 138, Cali, Colombia, S.A., Mario Perlaza, branch manager.

Mexico

20th Century Fox Films de Mexico, S.A., Queretaro 65B, 06700 Mexico, D.F., Apartado Postal 373, Mexico D.F. (Z.P.1) Mexico, Michel Rosen-

thal, gen. mgr.; Javier Lopez, sls. mgr. Tel.: (525) 584-6635. Telex: 17-71002 CFOXME.

Monterrey—Peliculas de La Sultana, S.A. Calle General Trevino No. 831 Pte. Monterrey, N.L., Zacarias Cobas, Agent.

Guadalajara—Peliculas Naçionales E. Internacionales de Guadalajara, S.A., Av. Libertad 1047, Guillermo Quezada, manager.

Merida—Agencia Distibuidora de Peliculas, Calle 60 No. 492, Merida, Yuc., Juan Gene Anay, manager.

Torreon—Distribuidora de Peliculas Jose Ignacio Maynez, J.A. de La Fuenta 244 Sur, Torreon, Coah., Jose Ignacio Maynez, manager.

Panama

Columbia Pictures of Panama, Inc., Twentieth Century-Fox Film, S.A., Via Espana Entre Calles 46 y 50 Este, Apartado 4492, Panama 5, Rep. de Panama, managing director joint oper., Paul Branca.

Costa Rica—Discine, S.A., Apartado Postal 1147, San Jose, Costa Rica, Alvaro Rovira Guido, agent.

Guatemala—Cadena Cinematografica Guatemalteca, 7a. Ave. 19-28 Zona 1, Guatemala, Guatemala, Rodolfo Rosenberg, agent.

Nicaragua—Distribuidora de Peliculas, Cortes-Hernandez, Apartado 3941, Managua, Nicaragua, Aginadack Cortes, agent.

Honduras—Hugo R. Erazo, Apartado 299, Tegucigalpa, Honduras, agent.

El Salvador—Julio Suvillaga Z., Apartado 19 (Sucursal del Centro), San Salvador, El Salvador, agent.

Peru

Lima—Twentieth Century-Fox Peruna S.A., Jr. Lampa 1115, Of. 1002, Lima 1, Peru, Casilla Postal 2532 & 6085, Lima 1, Peru, Tomas Rios De Armero, managing director.

Puerto Rico

San Juan—Twentieth Century-Fox Puerto Rico Inc., Metro Building, 1255 Ponce de Leon Ave., P.O. Box "S" 422 San Juan, Puerto Rico 00902, Luis Rodriguez, managing director.

Uruguay

Montevideo—Horacio Hermida Limitada, Soriano 1263, Montevideo, Uruguay, Horacio D. Hermida, agent.

Venezuela

Caracas—M.D.F., S.R.L., Edificio Teatro Las Palmas (Piso 4°), Av. Principal de las Palmas, Caracas (1050, Venezuela), P.O. Box 2008, Caracas, Venezuela, J. Alberto Liberoff, representative.

TWENTIETH TELEVISION CORP.

PRODUCTION DIVISION

PRESIDENT, NETWORK TV
Steve Bell
CHAIRMAN
Lucie Salhany
PRESIDENT, PRODUCTION, NETWORK TV
Peter Roth
SENIOR VICE PRESIDENT, CREATIVE AFFAIRS
Jeffrey Kramer
EXECUTIVE VICE PRESIDENT, TV BUSINESS AFFAIRS
David Freedman
EXECUTIVE VICE PRESIDENT, PRODUCTION AND FINANCE—TV
Charles Goldstein
SENIOR VICE PRESIDENT, BUSINESS AFFAIRS
Gary Newman
SENIOR VICE PRESIDENT, PROGRAMS
Ken Horton
VICE PRESIDENT, PRODUCTION MANAGEMENT
Bob Gros
VICE PRESIDENT, TAPE PRODUCTION
Joel Hornstock
VICE PRESIDENT, TELEVISION POST PRODUCTION
Edward Nassour
VICE PRESIDENT, BUSINESS AFFAIRS
David Robinson
VICE PRESIDENT, PRODUCTION LEGAL AFFAIRS
Walter Swanson

DOMESTIC SYNDICATION

PRESIDENT, DOMESTIC SYNDICATION
Greg Meidel
EXEC. VICE PRESIDENT, ADMINISTRATION AND OPERATIONS
Leonard J. Grossi
EXECUTIVE VICE PRESIDENT, GENERAL SALES MANAGER
Ken Solomon

EXECUTIVE VICE PRESIDENT, PROGRAMMING
Peter Marino
SENIOR VICE PRESIDENT, SALES, WESTERN DIVISION SALES
MANAGER
Tony Bauer
SENIOR VICE PRESIDENT, SALES, EASTERN REGIONAL SALES
MANAGER
Dan Greenblatt
SENIOR VICE PRESIDENT, SALES DEVELOPMENT AND FEATURE
FILM PLANNING
Joseph Greene
VICE PRESIDENT, NORTHEASTERN DIVISION SALES
Ted Baker
VICE PRESIDENT, TELEVISION BUSINESS AFFAIRS
Benson H. Begun
VICE PRESIDENT, WESTERN DIVISION SALES
John Campagnolo
SENIOR VICE PRESIDENT, ADVERTISING/PROMOTION/PUBLICITY
David LaFountaine
VICE PRESIDENT, CENTRAL DIVISION SALES
Dennis Juravic
VICE PRESIDENT, DOMESTIC ADVERTISER SALES
Matthew Jacobson
VICE PRESIDENT, SOUTHEASTERN DIVISION SALES
Michael Newsom
VICE PRESIDENT, SOUTHWESTERN DIVISION SALES
Vic Zimmerman
VICE PRESIDENT, STRATEGIC PLANNING AND ADMINISTRATION
Robert Fleming

INTERNATIONAL SYNDICATION

PRESIDENT, INTERNATIONAL SYNDICATION
James Gianopulos
VICE PRESIDENT, AUSTRALIA AND FAR EAST TERRITORIES
Tom Warne
SALES MANAGER, FRANCE
Gerard Grant
VICE PRESIDENT, LATIN AMERICA
Elie Wahba
VICE PRESIDENT, EUROPE/U.K./AFRICA
Malcolm Vaughan
MANAGER, MEXICO/CENTRAL AMERICA
Gustavo Montaudon
DIRECTOR, SALES LONDON
Steve Cornish

VIDEO AND PAY TELEVISION

EXECUTIVE VICE PRESIDENT
Jim Griffiths
VICE PRESIDENT, PAY TV
Ken Bettsteller

Fox Lorber

419 Park Ave. So., 20th floor, New York, NY 10016; (212) 686-6777; (Motion Picture and television distribution.)
PRESIDENT & CEO
Richard Lorber
COO
Kiyoshi Watanabe
SENIOR VICE PRESIDENT, U.S. THEATRICAL & VIDEO
DISTRIBUTION
Michael Olivieri
DIRECTOR, INTERNATIONAL SALES
Sheri Levine
ASSOCIATE DIRECTOR, INTERNATIONAL SALES
Nickie Stienmann
MANAGER, INTERNATIONAL SALES
Nancy Silverstone
MANAGER, ACQUISITIONS
Krysanne Katsoolis

Fries Entertainment, Inc.

6922 Hollywood Blvd., Hollywood, CA 90028; (213) 466-2266; FAX: (213) 466-9407; Telex: 401 954 FDC.
CHAIRMAN OF THE BOARD, PRESIDENT AND CHIEF
EXECUTIVE OFFICER
Charles W. Fries
VICE PRESIDENT, DEVELOPMENT
Chris Fries

CHIEF FINANCIAL OFFICER
Neal Smaler
VICE PRESIDENT, DOMESTIC SALES
Mike Murashko
INTERNATIONAL SALES AGENT
Anthony Gunnane

Full Moon Entertainment

3030 Anrita St., Los Angeles, CA 90065; (213) 341-5959; FAX: (213) 341-5960.
CHAIRMAN OF THE BOARD & CEO
Charles Band
EXECUTIVE VICE PRESIDENT
Debra Dion
PRESIDENT, INTERNATIONAL
Peter Wetherell

Gades Films International, Ltd.

315 E. 65 St., Suite 6A, New York, NY 10021; (212) 439-0102; Telex: 234963; Fax (212) 737-8207. Organized 1964. (Representation of foreign film producers, acquisition of films, co-production and packaging.)
PRESIDENT
Gabriel Desdoits
VICE PRESIDENT
France Desdoits

Geffen Film Company, The

9130 Sunset Blvd., Los Angeles, CA 90069; (310) 278-9010. (Motion picture production.)
PRESIDENT
Bonnie Lee
EXECUTIVE, CREATIVE AFFAIRS
Priscilla Coen

Gladden Entertainment Corp.

10100 Santa Monica Blvd., Suite 600, Los Angeles, CA 90067; (310) 282-7500.
CHAIRMAN OF THE BOARD
Bruce McNall
PRESIDENT & CEO
David Begelman
VICE PRESIDENT, FINANCE
Nora Rothrock
VICE PRESIDENT, CHIEF FINANCIAL OFFICER
Susan Waks

Go! Film Enterprises

6000 Carlton Way, Hollywood, CA 90028; Phone & FAX: (213) 463-2666. (Motion picture production and post-production.)
PRESIDENT
Sergei Goncharoff

Frederic Golchan Productions

9255 Doheny Rd., Suite 1106, Los Angeles, CA 90069; (310) 858-4939; FAX: (310) 858-7698; 5555 Melrose Ave., Dreier 112, Hollywood, CA 90038; (213) 956-3004; FAX: (213) 956-1012.
PRESIDENT
Frederic A. Golchan

Golden Harvest Films, Inc.

9884 Santa Monica Blvd., Beverly Hills, CA 90212; (310) 203-0722; FAX: (310) 556-3214. Organized 1981. (Producer of motion pictures.)
SENIOR VICE PRESIDENT, PRODUCTION
Thomas K. Gray

538

VICE PRESIDENT, ADMINISTRATION
Marlene Pivnick
DIRECTOR OF DEVELOPMENT
Peter D. Steinbroner

Milt Goldstein Enterprises, Inc.

8255 Sunset Blvd., Los Angeles, CA 90046-2432; (213) 848-3691; FAX: (213) 650-6400. Organized 1985. (Producer and distributor.)
PRESIDENT
Milton Goldstein

Samuel Goldwyn Company, The

10203 Santa Monica Blvd., Suite 500, Los Angeles, CA 90067; (310) 552-2255; FAX: (213) 284-8493. East Coast office: 888 7th Ave., #2901, New York, NY 10108; (212) 315-3030; FAX: (212) 307-6051. (Producer and distributor of motion pictures.)
CHIEF EXECUTIVE OFFICER & CHAIRMAN
Samuel Goldwyn Jr.
PRESIDENT, CHIEF OPERATING OFFICER
Meyer Gottlieb
SENIOR VICE PRESIDENT, BUSINESS AFFAIRS
Norman Flicker
SENIOR VICE PRESIDENT & CHIEF FINANCIAL OFFICER
Hans W. Turner
PRESIDENT, WORLDWIDE PRODUCTION
Tom Rothman
PRESIDENT, TELEVISION
Richard Askin
PRESIDENT, INTERNATIONAL SALES & OPERATIONS
Steven Bickel
VICE PRESIDENT, ADVERTISING
Daniel Gelfand
VICE PRESIDENT, ACQUISITIONS & PRODUCTION
Howard Cohen
VICE PRESIDENT, WORLDWIDE MARKETING
Richard Bornstein
VICE PRESIDENT, PUBLICITY
Michelle Abbrecht
VICE PRESIDENT, PLANNING & ADMINISTRATION
Mary Ann Halford

Mark Goodson Productions

375 Park Ave., New York, NY 10152; (212) 751-0600; FAX: (212) 319-0013. 5750 Wilshire Blvd., Suite 475W, Los Angeles, CA 90036; (213) 965-6500. (Producer.)
CHIEF OFFICER
Jonathan Goodson
EXECUTIVE VICE PRESIDENT
Giraud Chester
VICE PRESIDENT—FINANCE
Alan R. Sandler

Bert I. Gordon Films

9640 Arby Drive, Beverly Hills, CA 90210; FAX: (310) 274-2368.
PRESIDENT
Bert I. Gordon

Gordon Films, Inc.

119 W. 57 St., New York, NY 10019; (212) 757-9390; FAX: (212) 757-9392. Organized 1949. (Producers and distributors.)
PRESIDENT
Richard Gordon
VICE PRESIDENT
Joseph R. Cattuti
TREASURER
Richard Gordon

Gramercy Pictures

9247 Alden Dr., Beverly Hills, CA 90210; (310) 777-1960; FAX: (310) 777-1966. NY: 825 Eighth Ave., New York, NY 10019; (212) 333-8562; FAX: (212) 333-1420. (Motion picture production and distribution.)
PRESIDENT
Russell Schwartz
SENIOR VICE PRESIDENT OF PUBLICITY
Claudia Gray
VICE PRESIDENT, DISTRIBUTION
Paul Rosenfeld

Grand Am Motion Pictures, Ltd.

6649 Odessa Ave., Van Nuys, CA 91406; (818) 780-7100; FAX: (818) 997-3064.
PRESIDENT
Sidney Niekerk
VICE PRESIDENT, BUSINESS AFFAIRS
Bruce Kassman
INTERNATIONAL SALES
Dani Duran

Earl Greenburg Organization, The

Transactional Media International, 345 N. Maple, #205, Beverly Hills, CA 90210; (310) 657-2225. Organized 1988. (Produces television and motion pictures.)
PRESIDENT
Earl Greenburg

Greycat Films

3829 Delaware Lane, Las Vegas, NV 89109; (702) 737-0670; FAX: (702) 734-3628. (A division of Filmcat Inc.)
CO-PRESIDENTS
David Whitten
Suzanne Bowers Whitten

Group 1 International Distribution Organization Ltd., The (Group 1 Films)

9230 Robin Dr., Los Angeles, CA 90069; (310) 550-7280; FAX: (310) 550-0830. Organized 1964. (Production and distribution of feature films, TV specials and TV series.)
PRESIDENT AND CHIEF EXECUTIVE OFFICER
Brandon Chase
VICE PRESIDENT, FINANCIAL AFFAIRS
Frederick Goode
SENIOR VICE PRESIDENT, SALES
Jack Leff
FOREIGN SALES DIRECTOR
Marianne Chase
DIRECTOR OF ACQUISITIONS
Lee Beale
NEW PROJECTS MANAGER
Dan Ellman
PRODUCTION SUPERVISOR
Max Baum

HKM Films

1641 North Ivar Ave., Hollywood, CA 90028; (213) 465-9191; FAX: (213) 465-4203.
PRODUCER
Tom Mickel
DIRECTORS
Graham Henman
Michael Karbelnikoff
PRODUCER
Ron Altbach
DEVELOPMENT
Roger Soffer

Hanover Security Reports, Inc.

952 Manhattan Beach Blvd., Suite 250, Manhattan Beach, CA 90266; (310) 545-9891; (800) 634-5560; FAX: (310) 545-7690.
EXECUTIVE VICE PRESIDENT
Nancy Stein

Headliner Productions

2238 Redondo Beach Blvd., Torrance, CA 90504; (310) 327-0729; FAX: (310) 327-8996. (Motion picture producer and distributor.)
PRESIDENT
Dale Gasteiger Sr.
EXECUTIVE VICE PRESIDENT
Gregory Hatanaka

Hemdale Pictures Corporation

7966 Beverly Blvd., Los Angeles, CA 90048; (213) 966-3700; FAX: (213) 651-1551; (213) 651-5167. Telex: 6831949 Hemdale USA. (Producer and distributor.)
CHAIRMAN
John Daly
PRESIDENT
Derek Gibson
SENIOR VICE PRESIDENT, FINANCE
René Rousselet
EXECUTIVE VICE PRESIDENT, INTERNATIONAL
Kathy Morgan
DIRECTOR TECHNICAL SERVICES
Heather Probert
PRESIDENT—HEMDALE RELEASING CORP.
Tom Ortenberg

Hollywood Film Archive

8344 Melrose Ave., Hollywood, CA 90069; (213) 933-3345. Organized 1972. (Compiles and publishes motion picture reference information; also does legal, historical, production and copyright research.)
PRESIDENT
D. Richard Baer

Hollywood Pictures

(see The Walt Disney Company)

Home Box Office, Inc.

1100 Ave. of the Americas, New York, NY 10036; (212) 512-1000. West Coast: 2049 Century Park E., Suite 4100, Los Angeles, CA 90067; (213) 201-9200. (A subsidiary of Time-Warner, Entertainment Co.)
CHAIRMAN & CHIEF EXECUTIVE OFFICER
Michael Fuchs
PRESIDENT & COO
Jeff Bewkes
EXECUTIVE VICE PRESIDENT, HBO ENTERPRISES
Lee de Boer
SENIOR VICE PRESIDENT, CORPORATE COMMUNICATIONS
Richard Plepler

Hope Productions

3122 Arrowhead Dr., Hollywood, CA 90068; (213) 469-5596; FAX: (213) 466-3624. Incorporated 1957. (Producer and distributor of motion pictures.)
PRESIDENT
Mark Hope
TREASURER
Nancy Chu
VICE PRESIDENT
Tommy Yao
SECRETARY
Margot Hope

Hurlock Cine-World, Inc.

P.O. Box 34619, Juneau, AK 99803; (907) 789-3995. Organized 1969. (Distributor.)
PRESIDENT & TREASURER
Roger W. Hurlock
VICE PRESIDENT & SECRETARY
Mary L. Hurlock

IFEX International, Inc.

159 W. 53 St., New York, NY 10019-6050; (212) 582-4318; FAX: (212) 956-2257. (International distributor of theatrical, educational and television films. A subsidiary of Guild Entertainment Europe, Kft.)
PRESIDENT & CEO
Gerald J. Rappoport
CHAIRMAN OF THE BOARD
Thomas Hedman
VICE PRESIDENT, BUSINESS AFFAIRS
Beulah Rappoport
VICE PRESIDENT INTERNATIONAL
Dorothy Clark

INI Entertainment Group, Inc.

11150 Olympic Blvd., Suite 700, Los Angeles, CA 90064; (310) 479-6755; FAX: (310) 479-3475.
CHAIRMAN & CEO
Irv Holender
EXECUTIVE VICE PRESIDENT
Sy Samuels
VICE PRESIDENT & CFO
Michael Ricci
EXECUTIVE VICE PRESIDENT
Stephanie Zill

IRS Media

3939 Lankershim Blvd., Universal City, CA 91604; (818) 505-0555; FAX: (818) 505-1318.
CHAIRMAN
Miles Copeland
PRESIDENT
Paul Colichman

ITC Entertainment Group

12711 Ventura Blvd., Studio City, CA 91604; (818) 760-2110; FAX: (818) 506-8189.
PRESIDENT & CEO
Jules Haimovitz

DOMESTIC TELEVISION

EXECUTIVE VICE PRESIDENT, DOMESTIC TELEVISION
Michael Russo
VICE PRESIDENT, WESTERN REGION & PROGRAM DEVELOPMENT
Matt Cooperstein
VICE PRESIDENT, DOMESTIC TELEVISION, NORTHEAST REGION
Richard Easthouse
EXECUTIVE VICE PRESIDENT & GENERAL MANAGER, ITC DOMESTIC HOME VIDEO
Vallery Kountze

INTERNATIONAL DISTRIBUTION

SENIOR EXECUTIVE VICE PRESIDENT, INTERNATIONAL
James P. Marrinan
DIRECTOR, INTERNATIONAL SALES ADMINISTRATION
Valerie Bisson-Goldberg
VICE PRESIDENT, WORLDWIDE MARKETING
Lori Shackel
VICE PRESIDENT, INTERNATIONAL THEATRICAL SALES
Faye Beland

Acquisitions
SENIOR VICE PRESIDENT, WORLDWIDE ACQUISITIONS
  Paul Almond
MANAGER, INTERNATIONAL THEATRICAL DISTRIBUTION
  Wendy Reeds
Business and Legal Affairs
EXECUTIVE VICE PRESIDENT AND GENERAL COUNSEL
  John Huncke
SENIOR VICE PRESIDENT, BUSINESS AND LEGAL AFFAIRS
  Edward Gilbert
MANAGER, BUSINESS AND LEGAL AFFAIRS
  Seth Zachary
New York office: 115 E. 57th St., New York, NY 10022; (212)
371-6660.
EXECUTIVE VICE PRESIDENT, INTERNATIONAL SALES
  Armando Nunez
London office: 24 Nutford Place, London, England W1H 5YN;
(44) 1-262-3262.
SENIOR VICE PRESIDENT, INTERNATIONAL SALES
  Lynden Parry
DIRECTOR, EASTERN HEMISPHERE SALES
  Adrian Howells
VICE PRESIDENT HOME VIDEO, INTERNATIONAL SALES
  Martin Goldthorpe
PRODUCT MANAGER HOME VIDEO, INTERNATIONAL SALES
  Claire Throup

Image Organization, Inc.

9000 Sunset Blvd., Suite 915, Los Angeles, CA 90069;
(310) 278-8751; FAX: (310) 278-3967; Organized 1987.
(International distribution of motion pictures, home video
and television.)

CHAIRMAN & CHIEF EXECUTIVE OFFICER
  Pierre David
CO-CHAIRMAN
  Rene Malo (Montreal Office)
PRESIDENT
  Lawrence Goebel
SENIOR VICE PRESIDENT, WORLDWIDE DISTRIBUTION &
MARKETING
  Meyer Schwarzstein
VICE PRESIDENT, TELEVISION SALES
  Marie-Claude Poulin (Montreal Office)
CONTROLLER
  Carol Deisel Allison
VICE PRESIDENT OF INTERNATIONAL SERVICES
  William Lee Matis
VICE PRESIDENT, PRODUCTION
  Noel A. Zanitsch
DIRECTOR OF OPERATIONS
  Adele Yoshioka
BOARD OF DIRECTORS
  Pierre David, Rene Malo
BRANCHES
  Los Angeles, Montreal

Imagine Entertainment

1925 Century Park East, 23rd fl., Los Angeles, CA
90067; (310) 277-1665; FAX: (310) 785-0107. (Motion picture production.)

PRODUCER
  Brian Grazer
DIRECTOR
  Ron Howard
VICE PRESIDENT, ADMINISTRATION
  Robin Barris
PRESIDENT OF PRODUCTION
  David Friendly
SENIOR VICE PRESIDENT, PRODUCTION
  Karin Kehela
SENIOR VICE PRESIDENT, MARKETING
  Michael Rosenberg
VICE PRESIDENT, PRODUCTION
  Michael Bostick
DIRECTOR OF DEVELOPMENT
  Christine Harper
STORY EDITOR
  Bess Walkes

Imperial Entertainment Corp.

4640 Lankershim Blvd., 4th fl., No. Hollywood, CA
91602; (818) 762-0005; FAX: (818) 762-0006. Organized
1987. (Film production, finance and distribution worldwide
and video distribution in U.S.)

PRESIDENT
  Sunil R. Shah
EXECUTIVE VICE PRESIDENT
  Sundip R. Shah
EXECUTIVE VICE PRESIDENT, PRODUCTION
  Ash R. Shah
VICE PRESIDENT, PRODUCTION
  Eric Karson
VICE PRESIDENT OF FINANCE & OPERATIONS
  Juan C. Collas

Independent-International Pictures Corp.

Executive Plaza, 223 Route 18, East Brunswick, NJ
08816; (908) 249-8982; FAX: (908) 249-6550. Organized
1968. (Motion picture and television production and distribution.)

PRESIDENT
  Samuel M. Sherman
CHAIRMAN OF THE BOARD
  Dan Q. Kennis
EXECUTIVE VICE PRESIDENT
  Al Adamson

Interama Inc.

301 W. 53rd St., Suite 19E, New York, NY 10019; (212)
977-4830; FAX: (212) 581-6582. Organized 1981. (Motion
Picture, non-theatrical and video distribution.)

PRESIDENT
  Nicole Jouve

International Cine Services, Inc.

920 Allen Ave., Glendale, CA 91201; (818) 242-3839;
242-3857; FAX: (818) 242-1566. (Theatrical, non-theatrical and television distribution. Motion picture and element
storage.)

MANAGER
  Sandi Tirado

International Film Circuit

P.O. Box 1151, Old Chelsea Station, New York, NY
10011; (212) 779-0660; FAX: (212) 779-9129. (Motion picture distributor.)

PRESIDENT
  Wendy Lidell

International Rainbow Pictures

9165 Sunset Blvd., Suite 300, Los Angeles, CA 90069;
(310) 271-0202. (Film production.)

PRESIDENT
  Michael Jaglom
VICE PRESIDENT
  Henry Jaglom
BOARD OF DIRECTORS
  Henry Jaglom, Michael Jaglom
BRANCHES
  New York: 888 Seventh Ave., 34th floor, NY, NY 10106

International Research & Evaluation (IRE)

21098 IRE Control Ctr., Eagan, MN 55121-0098; (612)
888-9635; FAX: (612) 888-9124. Organized 1972. (Market

research, including probes, surveys, studies and information.)
RESEARCH DIRECTOR
Randall L. Voight
DIRECTORS
Ronald D. Olson, Sharon W. King, Norman Begley

Inter-Ocean Film Sales, Ltd.

6100 Wilshire Blvd., Suite 1500, Los Angeles, CA 90048; (213) 932-0500; FAX: (213) 932-0238. Organized 1978. (World sales organization and packagers.)
CO-CHAIRPERSONS
Anne Kopelson, Arnold Kopelson

Interscope Communications

10900 Wilshire Blvd., #1400, Los Angeles, CA 90024; (213) 208-8525; FAX: (310) 208-1197. (Film production.)
CEO & CHARIMAN
Ted Field
PRESIDENT & COO
Robert Cort
SENIOR PRODUCTION EXECUTIVES
David Madden
Scott Kroopf
SENIOR VICE PRESIDENT
Michael Helfant

InterStar Releasing

6800 College Blvd., Overland Park, KS 66211; (913) 338–3880. Organized 1990. *Branch:* 3801 Barham Blvd., Los Angeles, CA 90068. A division of Group W Prods. (a Westinghouse Company.)
PRESIDENT
Jeff Simmons
VICE PRESIDENT, MARKETING
George Kieffer
VICE PRESIDENT, DISTRIBUTION
Gene Irwin
VICE PRESIDENT, GENERAL SALES MANAGER
Ed Kershaw

Island Pictures, Inc.

8920 Sunset Blvd., 2nd Floor, Los Angeles, CA 90069; (310) 276-4500; FAX: (310) 271-7840; Telex: 691223. (Producer-distributor.)
PRESIDENT
Mark Burg
VICE PRESIDENT, OPERATIONS
Dan Genetti
PUBLICITY
Heather Parton

Italtoons Corp.

32 W. 40 St., New York, NY 10018; (212) 730-0280; FAX: (212) 730-0313.
PRESIDENT
Giuliana Nicodemi
GENERAL MANAGER
Ken Priester
SALES & ACQUISITIONS
Luisa Rivosecchi

J & M Entertainment

1289 Sunset Plaza Dr., Los Angeles, CA 90069; (213) 652-7733; FAX: (213) 652-0816; 2 Dorset Sq., London, NWI 6PU, ENGLAND; 071 723 6544. Organized 1976. (International distribution.)

CO-CHAIRMEN & CEO
Julia Palau
Michael Ryan
EXECUTIVE VICE PRESIDENT, HEAD OF BUSINESS AFFAIRS
Tony Miller
HEAD OF SALES & MARKETING
Peter Rogers
TECHNICAL DIRECTOR
Linda Deacy
VICE PRESIDENT, HEAD OF ACQUISITIONS
Karen Roberts
BOARD OF DIRECTORS
Julia Palau, Michael Ryan, Peter Rogers, Tony Miller, Linda Deacy
BRANCHES
London, Los Angeles

JEF Films Inc.

Film House, 143 Hickory Hill Circle, Osterville, MA 02655-1322; (508) 428-7198; FAX: (508) 428-7198. Organized 1973. (Produces and distributes in the following media: television (network & syndication), motion pictures, home video, pay per view, non-theatrical. Also stock footage library of 30,000 films.)
CHIEF EXECUTIVE OFFICER
Jeffrey H. Aikman
VICE PRESIDENT
Elsie Aikman
SALES MANAGER
Jo-Anne Polak
PROMOTIONS MANAGER
Janie Barber
BOARD OF DIRECTORS
Jeffrey H. Aikman, Elsie Aikman, Don Aikman, Janie Barber, Jo-Anne Polak

J.E.R. Pictures, Inc.

165 W. 46 St., Suite 507, New York, NY 10036; (212) 921-4290; FAX: (212) 391-0681. Organized 1952. (Distribution and worldwide production.)
PRESIDENT
Jerome Balsam
VICE PRESIDENTS
Rita Balsam, Mark Balsam

Jagfilms

9165 Sunset Blvd., Suite 300, Los Angeles, CA 90069; (310) 271-0202. Organized 1985. (Film production.)
PRESIDENT
Henry Jaglom
VICE PRESIDENT
Judith Wolinsky
BOARD OF DIRECTORS
Henry Jaglom, Judith Wolinsky
BRANCHES
New York: 888 Seventh Ave., 34th floor, NY, NY 10106

Jalbert Productions

775 Park Ave., Suite 230, Huntington, NY 11743; (516) 351-5878; FAX: (516) 351-5875. Organized 1970. (Television sports and specials; TV syndication, distribution, feature film production; television commercial production; corporate motivational films; film and tape distribution; stock film library.)
PRESIDENT
Joe Jay Jalbert
DIRECTORS
Ken Bernardini
Doug Copsey
SYNDICATION MANAGERS
Robin Parker
Carol Randel

Jalem Productions, Inc.

141 El Camino, Suite 201, Beverly Hills, CA 90212; (310) 278-7750. (Motion picture production.)
PRESIDENT
Jack Lemmon
VICE PRESIDENT
Connie McCauley

Janus Films Co.

#1 Bridge St., Irvington, NY 10533; (914) 591-5500; FAX: (914) 591-6484.
CHAIRMAN
William Becker
MANAGING DIRECTOR
Jonathan Turell

KLW International, Inc.

279 S. Beverly Dr., Suite 844, Los Angeles, CA 90212; (213) 203-9856. Organized 1982. (Entertainment investment). Branches in Beverly Hills, CA; Las Vegas, NV; Atlantic City, NJ.
PRESIDENT AND CHAIRMAN OF THE BOARD
Kevin L. Weakland

Paul Kagan Associates, Inc.

126 Clock Tower Place, Carmel, CA 93923-8734; (408) 624-1536; FAX: (408) 625-3225. (Research and analysis of entertainment and media industries.)
PRESIDENT
Paul Kagan

Kalish/Davidson Marketing Inc.

5670 Wilshire Blvd., Suite 700, Los Angeles, CA 90036; (213) 954-5820; FAX: (213) 954-5822. (Entertainment/leisure advertising and marketing; producer representation.)
CHAIRMAN
Dennis Davidson
PRESIDENT, CHIEF EXECUTIVE OFFICER
Eddie Kalish
SENIOR VICE PRESIDENT
Patti Stern
VICE PRESIDENT
Jill Jones
MANAGER, CREATIVE SERVICES
Molly Crafts
MANAGER, FINANCE & OPERATIONS
Glenys Thompson
BOARD OF DIRECTORS
Dennis Davidson, Eddie Kalish, A.B.J. Franklin
BRANCH
London

Kaufman Astoria Studios

34-12 36th St., Astoria, NY 11106; (718) 392-5600; FAX: (718) 706-7733. (Full-service production complex for feature films, TV commercials, television production, video and music.)
CHAIRMAN OF THE BOARD & PRESIDENT
George S. Kaufman
SENIOR EXECUTIVE VICE PRESIDENT & CHIEF OPERATING OFFICER
Hal G. Rosenbluth
DIRECTOR OF REAL ESTATE
Jay H. Schecter
STAGE MANAGER
Thomas James

Killiam Shows, Inc.

(a subsidiary of Worldview Entertainment Inc.) 6 E. 39 St., New York, NY 10016; (212) 679-8230; FAX: (212) 686-0801. Organized 1950. (Production and distribution of television/feature films; extensive collection of restored silent films.)
CHAIRMAN/CEO
Sandra J. Birnhak
PRESIDENT
Glenn E. Shealey
VICE PRESIDENT, INTERNATIONAL DISTRIBUTION
Marcy Stuzin
DIRECTOR OF NON-THEATRICAL DISTRIBUTION
Todd Quillio

Kinderhook Research, Inc.

P.O. Box 589, Kinderhook, NY 12106; (518) 758-1492; FAX: (518) 758-9896. (Distributor/exhibitor open and blind checking; housekeeping/integrity surveys: industry research.)
PRESIDENT
Andrea Koppel

Kings Road Entertainment, Inc.

1901 Ave. of the Stars, Suite 605, Los Angeles, CA 90067; (310) 552-0057; FAX: (310) 277-4468. (Producer.)
CHAIRMAN & CHIEF EXECUTIVE OFFICER
Stephen Friedman
VICE PRESIDENT, FINANCE
Suzanne L. Jealous
VICE PRESIDENT, DEVELOPMENT
Shane Stallings

Kino International Corp.

333 W. 39 St., Suite 503, New York, NY 10018; (212) 629-6880. Organized 1977. (Motion picture distribution.)
PRESIDENT
Donald Krim
GENERAL MANAGER
Gary Palmucci

Lajon Productions, Inc.

705 S. Victory Blvd., Burbank, CA 91502; (818) 841-1440; FAX: (818) 841-4659. (Producers of feature films, theatrical trailers, television programs; full facilities, video editing, digital post sound, Foley/ADR/EFX/DIA mixing.)
PRESIDENT
Lawrence Appelbaum
CREATIVE VICE PRESIDENT
Joseph H. Earle
PRODUCTION VICE PRESIDENT
Phillip Raves

Largo Entertainment

10201 W. Pico Blvd., Los Angeles, CA 90035; (310) 203-3600; FAX: (310) 203-4133. Organized 1989. (Motion Picture production and distribution.)
CHAIRMAN/CEO
Lawrence Gordon
PRESIDENT/COO
Joseph Cohen
PRESIDENT OF PRODUCTION
Lloyd Levin
EXECUTIVE IN CHARGE OF PHYSICAL PRODUCTION
Gene Levy
SENIOR VICE PRESIDENT/BUSINESS & LEGAL AFFAIRS
Nicholas Laterza
SENIOR VICE PRESIDENT/FINANCE
Steven Blume
PRESIDENT, DOMESTIC MARKETING & DISTRIBUTION
Richard Ingber
SENIOR VICE PRESIDENT, PRODUCTION
Michael Barnathan
PRESIDENT OF LARGO INTERNATIONAL, N.V.
Jean Louis Rubin

Laurel Entertainment, Inc.

928 Broadway, New York, NY 10010; (212) 674- 3800; FAX: (212) 777-6426.
CHAIRMAN AND PRESIDENT
Richard P. Rubinstein
EXECUTIVE VICE PRESIDENT, CHIEF FINANCIAL OFFICER
Virginia M. McGuire
EXECUTIVE VICE PRESIDENT, PRODUCTION
Mitchell Galin
SENIOR VICE PRESIDENT, PRODUCTION
Michael Gornick
VICE PRESIDENT, PRODUCTION ADMINISTRATION
Diane Vilagi
SENIOR STORY EDITOR
Neal Stevens
DIRECTOR OF DEVELOPMENT
Sheila Gaffney
SENIOR VICE PRESIDENT, DEVELOPMENT
Roseanne Leto

Dan Leeds Productions

810 Pirates Cove, Mamaroneck NY 10543; (914) 698-0561. (Producer of theatrical & TV films.)
PRESIDENT
Dan Leeds
VICE PRESIDENT/SECRETARY
P. C. Leeds
TREASURER
Edward Cohen

Levy-Gardner-Laven Productions, Inc.

9595 Wilshire Blvd., Suite 610, Beverly Hills, CA 90212; (310) 278-9820; FAX: (310) 278-2632.
PRESIDENT
Jules V. Levy
SECRETARY, TREASURER & VICE PRESIDENT
Arthur Gardner
VICE PRESIDENT
Arnold Laven

Lexington Group, Ltd., The

250 W. 49th St., New York, NY 10019; (212) 757-6366; FAX: (212) 757-6369. (Motion picture production and distribution; video retailing.)
CHAIRMAN
Michael S. Landes
PRESIDENT, RKO WARNER VIDEO, INC.
Michael Dougherty

Liberty Studios, Inc.

238 E. 26 St., New York, NY 10010; (212) 532-1865. Organized 1961. (Complete live action and special effects production. Owns and operates fully equipped sound stages, editing/optical facilities, cameras, lighting, grip and sound equipment, equipment transfer trucks for sound stage as well as location shooting.)
PRESIDENT, PRODUCER/DIRECTOR
Anthony Lover

Lightstorm Entertainment, Inc.

919 Santa Monica Blvd., Santa Monica, CA 90401; (310) 587-2500.
DIRECTOR
James Cameron
EXECUTIVE VICE PRESIDENT
Rae Sanchini
COO
Matt Saver
COF
Carol Henry
CREATIVE EXECUTIVE
Stacy Maez

Lirol Productions

6335 Homewood Ave., Hollywood, CA 90028; (213) 467-8111; FAX: (213) 462-1842. Organized 1958. (Production of TV programming, commercials, educational, industrial, documentary, sports, governmental films and videotape.) A division of the Lirol Corporation.
PRESIDENT/CEO
Frederic Rheinstein
VICE PRESIDENTS
Duke Gallagher, Linda Rheinstein

Lorimar Television

(see Warner Bros. Inc.)

Lucasfilm, Ltd.

P.O. Box 2459, San Rafael, CA 94912; (415) 662-1800. Incorporated 1977. (Motion picture and television production.)
CHAIRMAN OF THE BOARD AND CHIEF EXECUTIVE OFFICER
George W. Lucas, Jr.
VICE PRESIDENT AND GENERAL MANAGER—LICENSING DIVISION
Howard L. Roffman

LUCASARTS ENTERTAINMENT COMPANY

P.O. Box 2459, San Rafael, CA 94912; (415) 662-1800. (Entertainment products and services.)
VICE PRESIDENT, BUSINESS GROUP (VICE PRESIDENT, BUSINESS AFFAIRS GENERAL COUNSEL)
Lindsley Parsons, Jr.
GENERAL COUNSEL
Jim Kennedy
VICE PRESIDENT, CHIEF FINANCIAL OFFICER
Denise Jaqua
VICE PRESIDENT AND GENERAL MANAGER—SKYWALKER SOUND SOUTH
Bob Coleman
GENERAL MANAGER SKYWALKER SOUND NORTH
Kiki Morris
VICE PRESIDENT AND GENERAL MANAGER—INDUSTRIAL LIGHT & MAGIC
Jim Morris

MCA Inc.

100 Universal City Plaza, Universal City, CA 91608; (818) 777-9755; FAX: (818) 777-8216; 445 Park Ave., New York, NY 10022; (212) 759-7500.
CHAIRMAN OF THE BOARD & CHIEF EXEC. OFFICER
Lew R. Wasserman
PRESIDENT & CHIEF OPERATING OFFICER
Sidney Jay Sheinberg
EXECUTIVE VICE PRESIDENTS
Thomas Wertheimer, Charles S. Paul, Thomas P. Pollock
VICE PRESIDENTS
Richard E. Baker, Ron Bension, Phyllis Grann, Harold M. Haas, Robert D. Hadl, David Hancock, Christine Hanson, Stuart Mandel, Michael Samuel, Daniel E. Slusser, George Smith, Lawrence D. Spungin, Alvin N. Teller.
VICE PRESIDENT & SECRETARY
Michael Samuel
VICE PRESIDENT & TREASURER
Harold M. Haas
VICE PRESIDENT & CFO
Richard E. Baker
VICE PRESIDENT, FINANCIAL OPERATIONS
David Hancock
BOARD OF DIRECTORS
Charles S. Paul, Thomas P. Pollock, Thomas Wertheimer, Lew R. Wasserman, Sidney J. Sheinberg, Masahiko Hirata, Yoichi Morishita, Tsuzo Murase, Keiya Toyonaga, Atsuro Uede, Mamoru Furuichi.

PRINCIPAL SUBSIDIARIES & DIVISIONS

MCA Motion Picture Group: Universal Pictures Production, Universal Pictures Marketing, Universal Pictures Distribution

544

MCA Television Group: Universal Television, MCA TV, MCA TV International, MCA Television Entertainment

MCA Home Entertainment Group: MCA Home Video, MCA/Universal Home Video, Universal Pay-Per-View, Universal Pay Television, Universal Non-Theatrical

MCA Music Entertainment Group: MCA Records, Uni Distributing (Records and Home Video), MCA Records International, MCA Music Publishing, MCA Concerts, GRP Records, Geffen Records, Facility Merchandising, Inc., Winterland Productions

MCA Consumer Products Group: *Spencer Gifts:* Retail Stores. *MCA Publishing Group:* Book Publishing: G.P. Putnam's Sons, Berkley Publishing Group, Jove Publications.

MCA Development Group: Universal City Real Estate Development, MCA Real Estate Services, City Walk.

MCA Enterprises: MCA Enterprises International

MCA Recreation Services Group: Universal Studios Hollywood, Universal Studios Florida, Yosemite Park and Curry Co., Victoria Station Restaurant.

MK2 Productions, Inc.

250 W. 57 St., #701, New York, NY 10019; (212) 265-0453; FAX: (212) 397-0544. Organized 1989. (Film distribution, exhibition and co-production.)

CHAIRMAN
Marin Karmitz
PRESIDENT
Derval Whelan

Magno Sound & Video

729 Seventh Ave., New York, NY 10019; (212) 302-2505; FAX: (212) 819-1282. (Complete post-production facility.)

PRESIDENT
Robert Friedman
VICE PRESIDENT
David Friedman

Malibu Bay Films

9229 Sunset Blvd., Suite 202, Los Angeles, CA 90069; (310) 278-5056; FAX: (310) 278-5058. (Television and theatrical motion picture production.)

PRESIDENT
Andrew Sidaris
OFFICERS
Arlene Sidaris, Drew Sidaris

Manbeck Pictures Corp.

3621 Wakonda Dr., Des Moines, IA 50321-2132; (515) 285-1166. Organized 1966. (Distributor of 16mm classic films from the 1920s–1946. Some titles on VHS-video tape.)

PRESIDENT
Earl "Buck" Manbeck, Jr.

Manhattan Project, Ltd., The

888 7th Avenue, 30th Floor, New York, NY 10106; (212) 621-4850; FAX: (212) 621-4855. Organized 1988. (Motion picture production company.)

PRESIDENT
David Brown
VICE PRESIDENT, CREATIVE AFFAIRS
Kit Golden

Marine Corps Public Affairs-Los Angeles

11000 Wilshire Blvd., Suite 10117, Los Angeles, CA 90024; (310) 575-7272; FAX: (310) 575-7274. Organized 1948. (Provides technical aid and support to the motion picture and television industries, including script review, stock footage, on-base locations, equipment and Marine "extras.")

DIRECTOR (OFFICER IN CHARGE)
Lt. Col. Jerry Broeckert

Marvin Films

2 Heitz Pl., Hicksville, NY 11801; (516) 931-3456; FAX: (516) 931-3496.

PRESIDENT
Marvin Friedlander

Matthau Company, The

1999 Ave. of the Stars, Suite 2100, Los Angeles, CA 90067; (213) 557-2727. Organized 1981. (Motion picture production company.)

CHAIRMAN
Walter Matthau
CEO & PRESIDENT
Charles Matthau
VICE PRESIDENT, CREATIVE AFFAIRS
Laura Sutton
DIRECTOR OF OPERATIONS
Carrie Wysocki
CREATIVE EXECUTIVES
Lexi Ashton, Richard Conner
OPERATIONS
Gretchen Parker

Media Source Talent Data

11104 La Maida, Suite 4, North Hollywood, CA 91601; (818) 763-9992; FAX: (818) 769-4119. Organized 1982. (Consultants to TV, radio, feature film and entertainment print media.)

PRESIDENT
Gary G. Goldsberry
VICE PRESIDENT
Cos D. R. Goldsberry

Merchant Ivory Productions

250 W. 57 St., New York, NY 10107; (212) 582-8049.
PRESIDENT
James Ivory
VICE PRESIDENT AND TREASURER (U.S.)
Ismail Merchant
SECRETARY (U.S.)
Donald Rosenfeld

Metro-Goldwyn-Mayer Inc.

2500 Broadway St., Santa Monica, CA 90404-3061; (310) 449-3000; FAX: (310) 449-3100; 1350 Avenue of the Americas, New York, NY 10019; (212) 708-0300. (See separate section for corporate history.)

CHAIRMAN OF THE BOARD AND CHIEF EXECUTIVE OFFICER
Frank Mancuso
PRESIDENT, MGM PICTURES
Michael E. Marcus
EXECUTIVE VICE PRESIDENTS
Michael S. Hope, A. Robert Pisano
CHIEF OPERATING OFFICER
Jay Kanter
EXECUTIVE VICE PRESIDENT AND CHIEF FINANCIAL OFFICER
Thomas P. Carson
EXECUTIVE VICE PRESIDENT
Trevor Fetter
EXECUTIVE VICE PRESIDENT, GENERAL COUNSEL AND SECRETARY
William Allen Jones
SENIOR VICE PRESIDENT AND CONTROLLER
Kathleen Coughlan
SENIOR VICE PRESIDENT—LABOR RELATIONS
Benjamin B. Kahane

SENIOR VICE PRESIDENT—CORPORATE LEGAL AFFAIRS
  Sally Suchil
VICE PRESIDENT AND ASSISTANT SECRETARY
  Maria C. Angeletti
VICE PRESIDENT—MANAGEMENT INFORMATION SERVICES
  John Sanders

UNITED ARTISTS PICTURES

PRESIDENT
  John Calley

BOARD OF DIRECTORS

Jay Kanter, Alan Ladd, Jr., Charles R. Meeker III, Gui-Etienne Dufour, Alexis Wolkenstein, Sean Geary, Brad Wechsler, Bahman Naraghi, Rene Claude Jouannet

MGM TELEVISION PRODUCTION GROUP, INC.

(a division of Metro-Goldwyn-Mayer Inc.)
CHAIRMAN AND CHIEF EXECUTIVE OFFICER
  David Gerber
VICE PRESIDENT—COMEDY DEVELOPMENT
  Hank Cohen
VICE PRESIDENT—BUSINESS AFFAIRS
  Sheldon Perry
VICE PRESIDENT—POST PRODUCTION
  Andy Gonzales
VICE PRESIDENT—CURRENT PROGRAMMING
  Ron Levinson
VICE PRESIDENT—FINANCIAL ADMINISTRATION
  Thomas Malanga
VICE PRESIDENT—POST PRODUCTION
  Bruce Pobjoy
VICE PRESIDENT—ADVERTISING AND PUBLICITY
  Kim Reed
VICE PRESIDENT—MOVIES FOR TELEVISION, LONG FORM
  Teri Rawson
VICE PRESIDENT—SENIOR PRODUCTION COUNSEL
  Marcia Spielholz
VICE PRESIDENT AND SECRETARY
  Maria C. Angeletti
VICE PRESIDENT, HOME VIDEO
  George Feltenstein

Miracle Films

6311 Romaine St., Suite 7309, Hollywood, CA 90038; (213) 466-0676; FAX: (213) 856-0107. Organized 1972. (Distributor.)
PRESIDENT
  Robert F. Burkhardt

Miramax Films Corp.

375 Greenwich St., New York, NY 10013; (212) 941-3800; FAX: (212) 941-3949.
PRINCIPALS
  Bob Weinstein, Harvey Weinstein
SENIOR VICE PRESIDENT, BUSINESS & LEGAL AFFAIRS
  John Logigin
SENIOR VICE PRESIDENT OF MARKETING
  Gerry Rich
SENIOR VICE PRESIDENT OF DISTRIBUTION
  Marty Zeidman
CHIEF FINANCIAL OFFICER
  Irwin Reiter

Mirisch Corporation of California, The

100 Universal City Plaza, Universal City, CA 91608; (818) 777-1271; FAX: (818) 777-0668.
CHAIRMAN OF THE BOARD & CHIEF EXECUTIVE OFFICER
  Marvin E. Mirisch
PRESIDENT AND CHIEF PRODUCTION OFFICER
  Walter Mirisch

Modern Talking Picture Service, Inc.

General offices: 5000 Park St. N., St. Petersburg, FL 33709-2254; (813) 541-7571. Organized 1937.
CHIEF EXECUTIVE OFFICER
  Eugene Cafiero
VICE PRESIDENT/CHIEF FINANCIAL OFFICER
  P. Roger Byer

BOOKING CENTER

St. Petersburg, FL 33709—5000 Park St. N.; Outside of Florida call (800) 237-8913; Florida residents call 813-541-7571; FAX: (813) 546-9323.

Moonlight Productions

3361 St. Michael Ct., Palo Alto, CA 94306; (415) 961-7440; FAX: (415) 961-7440. Organized 1971. (Producer and distributor of undersea environmental films—16mm, color, optical sound; undersea stock shot library.)
SOLE OWNER
  Dr. Lee Tepley

Morgan Creek Productions

1875 Century Park East, Suite 200, Los Angeles, CA 90067; (310) 284-8884; FAX: (310) 282-8794. Organized 1988. Branch Office: %Harbor Industries, 10 E. Lee St., Suite 2705, Baltimore, MD 21202; (410) 752-6688; FAX: (410) 539-0404.
CHAIRMAN/CEO
  James G. Robinson
CHIEF OPERATING OFFICER/PRESIDENT, INTERNATIONAL
  Gary Barber
VICE PRESIDENT, MARKETING
  Gloria LaMont
SENIOR VICE PRESIDENT, PRODUCTION
  Larry Katz
VICE PRESIDENT, BUSINESS AFFAIRS-FINANCE
  Gary Stutman
SENIOR VICE PRESIDENT, PRODUCTION
  Jonathan Zimbert
VICE PRESIDENT, INTERNATIONAL
  Ken Shapiro
VICE PRESIDENT, PUBLICITY & PROMOTION
  Terry Curtin
VICE PRESIDENT, CREATIVE AFFAIRS
  Cathy Rabin
VICE PRESIDENT, POST-PRODUCTION
  Jody Levin

Milton I. Moritz Company, Inc., The

856 Malcolm Ave., Garden Suite, Los Angeles, CA, 90024; (213) 470-9122. (Producers' sales and marketing representation.)
PRESIDENT
  Milton I. Moritz

Morris Projects, Inc./ Cine Qua Non

P.O. Box 6130, Sarasota, FL 34278-6130; (813) 388-2441; FAX: (813) 388-4473. (Distributor of foreign-language feature films. Film buying agency.)

Motion Picture Corp. of America

1401 Ocean Ave., #301, Santa Monica, CA 90401; (310) 319-9500; FAX: (310) 319-9501. (Motion picture producer and distributor).

Movie Group, The

1900 Ave. of the Stars, Suite 1425, Los Angeles, CA 90067; (310) 556-2830; FAX: (310) 277-1490. Organized 1987. (International distribution.)

PRESIDENT
Peter E. Strauss
EXECUTIVE VICE PRESIDENTS
Jed Daly, Chris Bialek
CHIEF FINANCIAL OFFICER
Ann Oliver
VICE PRESIDENTS
Barry Gray, Deborah Scott, Chris Bialek
AFFILIATION
American Film Marketing Assoc.

Moviestore Entertainment, Inc.

11111 Santa Monica Blvd., Los Angeles, CA 90025; (310) 478-4230; FAX: (310) 478-2538. Organized 1981. (Distributor.)
PRESIDENT & CHIEF EXECUTIVE OFFICER
Kenneth M. Badish
EXECUTIVE VICE PRESIDENT
Laurie J. Halloway
DIRECTOR OF FINANCE
Kenneth R. Halloway
DIRECTOR OF INTERNATIONAL SALES & ACQUISITIONS
Joseph M. Drake
MANAGER OF FINANCE
Rolando G. Bartolome
MANAGER OF BUSINESS AFFAIRS
DeAnn Dawson
MANAGER, OPERATIONS
Lisa Zenoff
MANAGER OF DEVELOPMENT
Lori Lieberman
ASSISTANT TO BUSINESS AFFAIRS
Linda Reed

National Film Service, Inc.

902 E. Hazelwood Ave., P.O. Box L, Rahway, NJ 07065; (908) 396-9080; FAX: (908) 396-9099. (Physical distribution and warehousing of motion picture film.)
PRESIDENT
Mark Frysztacki
EXECUTIVE VICE PRESIDENT/TREASURER
Arnold Brown
VICE PRESIDENT
John H. Vickers
SECRETARY
Herb Rosenberg
VICE PRESIDENT OF OPERATIONS
Ed McCauley
ASSISTANT SECRETARY/CONTROLLER
Pat Raia

BRANCHES

ALBANY, NY: Wesco Film Service, 24 N. Third St. (rear), 12204-1621; (518) 434-1289; FAX: (518) 426-3501. Contact: John Pemberton.

ATLANTA, GA: Benton Film Forwarding Co., 168 Baker St., N.W., 30313-1891; (404) 577-2821; FAX: (404) 681-1593. Lucy Drake.

BOSTON, MA: NFS Operating Corp., 20-30 Freeport Way, Dorchester, MA 02122-2832; (617) 288-1600; FAX: (617) 288-7481. Jimmie Choukas.

BUFFALO, NY: Wesco Film Service, 108 Gruner Rd., 14227-1071; (716) 897-0467; FAX: (716) 897-0761. Bob Neffke.

BUTTE, MT: NFS Operating Corp., 150 W. Parkmont, 59071; (406) 494-3434; FAX: (406) 494-5598. Ted Bartscher.

CHARLOTTE, NC: Carolina Film Service, Inc., 522 Penman St., 28230; (703) 333-2115; FAX: (704) 343-1062. Mabel Winn, Don Trivette.

CHICAGO, IL: Highway Film Service, 4343 S. Tripp Ave., 60632-4318; (312) 254-8100; FAX: (312) 254-0421. Larry Lippert.

DALLAS, TX: Central Shipping & Inspection, 2500 S. Harwood St., 75215; (214) 421-5411; FAX: (214) 421-7021. Dennis Garrett.

CINCINNATI, OH: Highway Film Service, 421 Bauer St., 45214-2898; (513) 621-4240; FAX: (513) 621-4242. Marc Steinmetz.

CLEVELAND, OH: Cleveland Film Service Inc., 1625 E. 45th St., 44103-2316, (216) 431-9491; FAX: (216) 431-6791. John Remec.

DENVER, CO: Denver Shipping & Inspection, 5355 Harrison St., 80216-2439; (303) 296-3793; FAX: (303) 296-3794. Alan Castle.

DES MOINES, IA: Iowa Film Depot, 3123 Delaware Ave., 50313-4703; (515) 265-1469; FAX: (515) 262-9718. Robert Boots.

DETROIT, MI: NFS Operating Corp., 6111 Concord Ave., 48211-2497; (313) 923-9040. Terry McCauley, Kathie Gladden.

INDIANAPOLIS, IN: Highway Film Service, 6245 Morenci Trail, 46268-2558; (317) 297-7055: FAX: (317) 293-1932. Leslie Macke, Terri Mauer.

JACKSONVILLE, FL: Jacksonville Film Service, 2208 W. 21st St., 32209-4111; (904) 355-5477; FAX: (904) 632-1342. Bert Benton, Claude Hembree.

KANSAS CITY, MO: Highway Film Service, 1717 No. Topping St., 64120-1225; (816) 483-3638; FAX: (816) 483-1357. Conrad York, Lloyd Askren.

LOS ANGELES, CA: Gilboy, Inc., 8401 Slauson Ave., P.O. Box 97, Pico Rivera, CA, 90660-0097; (313) 949-9397; FAX: (313) 942-1822. Rodger Hinter, Pat Hanna.

MEMPHIS, TN: Memphis Film Service, Inc., 3931 Homewood Rd., 38181; (901) 794-6601; FAX: (901) 362-6793. Mike Fitzmorris, A.S. Crews.

MILWAUKEE, WI: Milwaukee Film Center, Inc., 333 N. 25th St., 53233-2590; (414) 344-0300, FAX: (414) 344-2828. Charles Trampe, Marke Trampe.

MINNEAPOLIS, MN: Independent Film Service Inc., 245 2nd Ave. N., 55401-1621; (612) 332-2203; FAX: (612) 333-0939. Jim Perrin.

NEW HAVEN, CT: New Haven Film Service, 90 Woodmont Rd., P.O. Box 3158, Milford, CT, 06460-0958; (203) 878-1465. Bill Rosen, Ralph Cocco.

NEW ORLEANS, LA: Film Inspection Service, Inc., 2411 Edenborn Ave., Metairie, LA, 70004-1266; (504) 833-5552; FAX: (504) 837-0925. D.M. Brandon, Charles Walton.

OKLAHOMA CITY, OK: Oklahoma City Ship. & Inspect., 809 S. West 7th St., 73109; (405) 235-2553; FAX: (405) 235-2554. Charles Baird, Rosemary Flowers.

OMAHA, NE: Omaha Film Depot, 1441 N. 11th St., 68102-4202; (402) 342-6576; FAX: (402) 342-1930. Charles Janousek.

PHILADELPHIA, PA: International Film Service, 130 Ferry Ave., Camden, NJ 08104-1985; (609) 962-6800; FAX: (609) 962-6051. David Adleman, John Abruzzese.

PITTSBURGH, PA: Pittsburgh Film Service, Bldg. 16, Nichol Ave., McKees Rocks, PA 15136-2678; (412) 771-2665; (412) 771-2822. George Callahan IV, Jesse Palmino.

PORTLAND, OR: Northwest Film Group, Inc., 716 N.E. Lawrence, 97232; (503) 234-6202; FAX: (503) 234-6224. Chip Blake.

ST. LOUIS, MO: Kahan Film Distributors, 3974 Page Ave., St. Louis, MO 63113-3432; (314) 371-6572; FAX: (314) 371-6574. Meyer Kahan.

SALT LAKE CITY, UT: NFS Operating Corp., 190 N. 649 W., N. Salt Lake, UT 84054-2713; (801) 292-7626 FAX: (801) 292-7785. Rulon Hammer.

SAN FRANCISCO, CA: NFS Operating Corp., 701 Bradford Way, Union City, CA 94587-3605; (510) 471-9400; FAX: (510) 471-8447. Jack Thompson.

SEATTLE, WA: Northwest Film Group, Inc. 214 - 21st St., S.E., Auburn, WA 98002; (206) 939-1533; FAX: (206) 735-9219. Virginia Armbrust.

WASHINGTON, D.C.: Highway Film Service, 15113 Old Marlboro Pike, Up. Marlboro, MD 20772-3129; (301) 952-1320; FAX: (301) 627-0532. Brad Buchanan.

National Lampoon

10850 Wilshire Blvd., Los Angeles, CA 90024; (310) 474-5780. Organized 1969. (Production of motion pictures, television and magazine publishing.)
CHAIRMAN OF THE BOARD & CEO
Jim Jimirro

National Research Group, Inc., The

7046 Hollywood Blvd., Los Angeles, CA 90028; (213) 856-4400. (Industry market research.)

CO-CHAIRMEN
Joseph Farrell, Catherine Paura
PRESIDENT
Michael Edison

National Screen Service Group, Inc.

40 Rockwood Pl., Englewood, NJ 07631; (201) 871-7900; FAX: (201) 871-7914. (Distributor of trailers, specialty and standard accessories, promotional materials.)

PRESIDENT
Peter Koplik
VICE PRESIDENT, DISTRIBUTION
Mitchell Wilen
TREASURER
Ronald Seitenbach

DOMESTIC BRANCHES & MANAGERS

KANSAS CITY, MO 64108: 1800 Baltimore Ave., (816) 842-5893; FAX: (816) 842-4553: Branch Mgr.: Eric Allen
LOS ANGELES 90034: 2001 S. LaCienega Blvd., (310) 836-1505; FAX: (310) 836-9878: Vice President, Distribution: Mitchell Wilen; Print Control: Mona Spicer
ENGLEWOOD, NJ 07631: 40 Rockwood Pl., (201) 871-7979; FAX: (201) 871-7914: Branch Mgr.: Spencer Jones

New Line Cinema Corporation

888 Seventh Ave., 20th Fl., New York, NY 10106, (212) 649-4900; FAX: (212) 649-4966. *Los Angeles:* 116 North Robertson Blvd., 2nd Fl., Los Angeles, CA 90048, (310) 854-5811. *Atlanta:* 4501 Circle 75 Parkway, Atlanta, GA 30339, (404) 952-0056. *Dallas:* 6060 North Central Expressway, Dallas, TX 75206, (214) 696-0755. Organized 1967. (Distribution & production of theatrical and non-theatrical motion pictures, lecture bureau.)

CHAIRMAN & CHIEF EXECUTIVE OFFICER
Robert Shaye
PRESIDENT & CHIEF OPERATING OFFICER
Michael Lynne
SENIOR VICE PRESIDENT & TREASURER
Stephen Abramson
SENIOR VICE PRESIDENT, BUSINESS AFFAIRS
Benjamin Zinkin
SENIOR VICE PRESIDENT, DOMESTIC DISTRIBUTION & THEATRICAL MARKETING
Mitchell Goldman
SENIOR VICE PRESIDENT, FINE LINE FEATURES
Ira Deutchman
SENIOR VICE PRESIDENT, INTERNATIONAL
Rolf Mittweg
SENIOR VICE PRESIDENT, PRODUCTION
Sara Risher
VICE PRESIDENT, PARTICIPATIONS & CONTRACT ADMINISTRATION
Susannah Juni
SENIOR VICE PRESIDENT, HOME VIDEO & ACQUISITIONS
Stephen Einhorn
VICE PRESIDENT, CONTROLLER
Tracy Adler
SENIOR VICE PRESIDENT, TELEVISION
Robert Friedman
VICE PRESIDENT, BUSINESS DEVELOPMENT
Jim Rosenthal
VICE PRESIDENT, BUSINESS AFFAIRS
Margaret Blatner
VICE PRESIDENT, BUSINESS AFFAIRS
Phillip Rosen
VICE PRESIDENT, FINANCE
Michael Spatt

VICE PRESIDENT, ADMINISTRATION
Marsha Hook-Haygood
VICE PRESIDENT, MANAGEMENT INFORMATION SYSTEMS
Richard Rippetoe
VICE PRESIDENT, NEW BUSINESS DEVELOPMENT
Michele Gotlib
DIRECTOR OF THEATRICAL ACCOUNTING
Joseph Adamo
DIRECTOR OF MIS/EAST COAST
Gordon Grant
VICE PRESIDENT, CONTRACTS ADMINISTRATION
Sonya Thompsen
DIRECTOR, ROYALTY ACCOUNTING
Arnold Adirim
DIRECTORS, ROYALTIES & PARTICIPATION
Dominique Smith, Georgina Cruz Tighe
DIRECTOR, SYSTEMS DEVELOPMENT
Tom Yip
DIRECTOR, ADMINISTRATION/WEST COAST
Janice Stahl
DIRECTOR, ADMINISTRATION/EAST COAST
Steve Harris

NEW LINE PRODUCTIONS, INC.

CHAIRPERSON
Sara Risher
EXECUTIVE VICE PRESIDENT, CREATIVE DEVELOPMENT
Michael De Luca
SENIOR VICE PRESIDENT, POST-PRODUCTION
Joseph Fineman
SENIOR VICE PRESIDENT OF CREATIVE AFFAIRS
Janet Grillo
SENIOR VICE PRESIDENT, PRODUCTION
Deborah Moore
VICE PRESIDENT, PRODUCTION - EAST COAST/SENIOR VICE PRESIDENT, MUSIC
Toby Emmerich
VICE PRESIDENTS, PRODUCTION
Cindy Hornickel, Kevin Moreton, Phillip Goldfine, Aaron Meyerson
STORY EDITOR, EAST COAST
G. Wyck Godfrey
EXECUTIVE STORY EDITOR, WEST COAST
Janis Chaskin
PRODUCTION CONTROLLER
Paul Prokop
VICE PRESIDENT, POST PRODUCTION
Evan Edelist
PRODUCTION ACQUISITIONS EXECUTIVE
Carla Fry

NEW LINE DISTRIBUTION, INC.

PRESIDENT AND CHIEF OPERATING OFFICER
Mitchell Goldman
EXECUTIVE VICE PRESIDENT & GENERAL SALES MANAGER
Al Shapiro
VICE PRESIDENT, CENTRAL DIVISION MANAGER
Steve Friedlander
VICE PRESIDENT, SALES ADMINISTRATION
David Keith
VICE PRESIDENT, SOUTHERN DIVISION MANAGER
John Trickett
VICE PRESIDENT, SOUTHEASTERN DIVISION MANAGER
Don Osley
VICE PRESIDENT, WESTERN DIVISION MANAGER
Lawrence Levy
DIRECTOR, NATIONAL PRINT CONTROL
Gisela Corcoran
EASTERN DIVISION MANAGER
Jonathan Beal
DIRECTOR, THEATRICAL FINANCIAL SERVICES
Timothy Mason

NEW LINE INTERNATIONAL RELEASING, INC.

PRESIDENT
Rolf Mittweg
SENIOR VICE PRESIDENT, SALES AND MARKETING
Camela Galano
SENIOR VICE PRESIDENT, SALES AND ADMINISTRATION
Nestor Nieves
DIRECTOR, CONTRACTS ADMINISTRATION
Ralpho Borgos
DIRECTOR, INTERNATIONAL SERVICING
Scott Spadafora

DIRECTOR, MARKETING & PUBLICITY
Terri Grochowski
VICE PRESIDENT, FINANCE
David Burkhardt

NEW LINE MARKETING, INC.

PRESIDENT
Christopher Pula
SENIOR VICE PRESIDENT, MEDIA/CO-OP ADVERTISING
Diana Charbanic
SENIOR VICE PRESIDENT, PUBLICITY & PROMOTION
Christina Kounelias
VICE PRESIDENT, CO-OP ADVERTISING
Susan Russell
DIRECTOR, CREATIVE SERVICES
Aimee Pitta
VICE PRESIDENT OF NATIONAL PROMOTIONS
Mary Goss
DIRECTOR, PRODUCT PLACEMENT
Tony Hoffman
VICE PRESIDENT, FINANCE MARKETING
Rob Kobus
VICE PRESIDENT, PUBLICITY/EAST COAST
Mary K. Donovan
DIRECTOR, CO-OP ADVERTISING
Kirk Barnett
MANAGER, NATIONAL PROMOTIONS
Anne Marie Scibelli
VICE PRESIDENT, CORPORATE RESEARCH
Karen Hermelin
DIRECTOR, PUBLICITY & PROMOTIONS/EAST COAST
Dana Laufer
DIRECTOR, MARKETING
Linda Videtti
DIRECTOR OF PUBLICITY, WEST COAST
Mark Cheatham
DIRECTOR OF PHOTOGRAPHY
Helene Steel
DIRECTOR, FIELD PUBLICITY AND PROMOTIONS
Elisa Greer
MANAGER, CO-OP ADVERTISING
Darla Eady

NEW LINE HOME VIDEO, INC.

PRESIDENT & CEO
Stephen Einhorn
SENIOR VICE PRESIDENT, SALES & MARKETING
Michael A. Karaffa
VICE PRESIDENT & DIRECTOR, SALES
Kevin Kasha

NEW LINE TELEVISION

PRESIDENT
Robert Friedman
SENIOR VICE PRESIDENT, PRODUCTION/DEVELOPMENT
Sasha Emerson
SENIOR VICE PRESIDENT, SALES
David Spiegelman

FINE LINE FEATURES

888 Seventh Ave., 20th fl., New York, NY 10106; (212) 649-4900.
PRESIDENT
Ira Deutchman
SENIOR VICE PRESIDENT, MARKETING
Elizabeth Manne
DIRECTOR, CO-OP ADVERTISING
Brian Caldwell
DIRECTOR, FIELD PUBLICITY & PROMOTIONS
Sara Eaton
MANAGER, POST PRODUCTION SERVICES
Jack Deutchman

New Yorker Films

16 W. 61 St., New York, NY 10023; (212) 247-6110; FAX: (212) 307-7855. (Motion picture distribution.)
PRESIDENT
Daniel Talbot
VICE PRESIDENT
Jose Lopez

Noble Productions, Inc.

1615 S. Crest Dr., Los Angeles, CA 90035; (310) 552-2934; Telex: 3715907-NOBLEFILM; FAX: (310) 552-3508.
CHAIRMAN AND PRESIDENT
Ika Panajotovic
SECRETARY
Elena Panajotovic

Norkat Company, Ltd., The

280 S. Beverly Dr., Suite 306, Beverly Hills, CA 90212; (310) 276-6741; Telex: 752 356 NORKAT; FAX: (310) 276-3427.
PRESIDENT
Norman B. Katz
VICE PRESIDENT
Dorothea A. Katz

Northern Arts Entertainment

Northern Arts Studios, Williamsburg, MA 01096-0201; (413) 268-9301; FAX: (413) 268-9309. (Motion picture producers and distributors.)
CHAIRMAN
John Lawrence Re
PRESIDENT
David Mazor
VICE PRESIDENT, ACQUISITIONS
Alison Brantley

Nova Entertainment

3330 Cahuenga Blvd. W., Los Angeles, CA 90068; (213) 850-5200; FAX: (213) 850-1099. (Motion picture production and distribution.)
CHAIRMAN OF THE BOARD
William Rifkin

October Films

45 Rockefeller Plaza, Suite 3014, New York, NY 10011; (212) 332-2480. (Motion picture producer and distributor.)
CO-CHAIRMEN
Jeff Lipsky, Bingham Ray

Omega Entertainment, Ltd.

8760 Shoreham Dr., Los Angeles, CA 90069; (310) 855-0516 ; Telex: 291991 OMPC UR; FAX: (310) 650-0325. Organized 1976. (Production and distribution.)
PRESIDENT & CHIEF EXECUTIVE OFFICER
Nico Mastorakis
VICE PRESIDENT, SALES
Carole Mishkind
EXECUTIVE VICE PRESIDENT
Isabelle Mastorakis Thompson
VICE PRESIDENT, PRODUCTION
Christy L. Pokarney

Original Cinema, Inc.

419 Park Ave. South, 20th fl., New York, NY 10016; (212) 545-0177. Boston: 117 Valley St., Beverly Farms, MA 01915. Organized 1987. (Marketing and distribution.)
CEO/PRESIDENT
Stephen Gang
VICE PRESIDENT, MARKETING & DISTRIBUTION
Tom Prassis

Orion Pictures Corporation

304 Park Ave. South, New York, NY 10010; (212) 505-0051; 1888 Century Park E., Los Angeles, CA 90067; (310) 282-0550.

PRESIDENT & CHIEF EXECUTIVE OFFICER
   Leonard White
SENIOR VICE PRESIDENT, BUSINESS AFFAIRS, WORLDWIDE
DISTRIBUTION
   Kimberle Lynch
SENIOR VICE PRESIDENT, CHIEF FINANCIAL OFFICER
   Cynthia Friedman
EXECUTIVE VICE PRESIDENT, GENERAL COUNSEL AND
SECRETARY
   John W. Hester
EXECUTIVE VICE PRESIDENT
   Silvia K. Merkle
VICE PRESIDENT AND TREASURER
   Gregory A. Arvensen
VICE PRESIDENT AND CONTROLLER
   Mark Belzowski
VICE PRESIDENT, BUSINESS AND LEGAL AFFAIRS
   Barbara Custer
VICE PRESIDENT, BUSINESS AFFAIRS
   Rhonda Gale
VICE PRESIDENT, BUSINESS AFFAIRS
   Debra Roth
VICE PRESIDENT, ADMINISTRATION
   Cathy Houser
VICE PRESIDENT, PRODUCTION FINANCE
   Julie Landau

ORION CLASSICS

(A division of Orion Pictures Corporation) 1888 Century
Park East, Los Angeles, CA 90067; (310) 282-0550.
VICE PRESIDENT
   John Hegeman

ORION PICTURES INTERNATIONAL

(A division of Orion Pictures Corporation) 304 Park Ave.
South, New York, NY 10010; (212) 505-0051.
PRESIDENT
   Diane Keating
SENIOR VICE PRESIDENT, TELEVISION
   Kathleen Hricik
VICE PRESIDENT, TELEVISION SALES AND ADMINISTRAION
   Robert Davie

ORION TELEVISION ENTERTAINMENT

(A division of Orion Pictures Corporation) 1888 Century
Park East, Los Angeles, CA 90067; (310) 282-0550.
EXECUTIVE VICE PRESIDENT DOMESTIC TELEVISION
DISTRIBUTION
   Joseph D. Indelli

ORION PICTURES DISTRIBUTION
CORPORATION

1888 Century Park East, Los Angeles, CA 90067; (310)
282-0550.
PRESIDENT
   Leonard White
EXECUTIVE SENIOR VICE PRESIDENT
   John Hester
SENIOR VICE PRESIDENT, CORPORATE MARKETING
   Susan Blodgett
SENIOR VICE PRESIDENT DISTRIBUTION
   John Jay Peckos
VICE PRESIDENT, NATIONAL PUBLICITY & PROMOTIONS
   Gail Block
VICE PRESIDENT, DOMESTIC DISTRIBUTION
   John Hegeman
VICE PRESIDENT SALES, SOUTHERN DIVISION
   Emmet Nicaud
VICE PRESIDENT, FINANCE & ADMINISTRATION
   Robert M. Mott
VICE PRESIDENT, MEDIA SERVICES
   Denise Quon
BRANCH OFFICES

DALLAS: Emmet Nicaud (v.p. sls., Southern Division); 7557 Rambler
Rd., Suite 670, Dallas, TX 75231; (214) 363-7600.

LOS ANGELES: Bob Wood (division manager); 1888 Century Park East,
Los Angeles, CA 90067; (310) 282-0550.
NEW YORK: Sheila DeLoach (division mgr.); 304 Park Ave. South, New
York, NY 10010; (212) 505-0051

ORION HOME ENTERTAINMENT
CORPORATION

1888 Century Park East, Los Angeles, CA 90067; (310)
282-0550.
CHAIRMAN OF THE BOARD & CHIEF EXECUTIVE OFFICER
   Leonard White
SENIOR VICE PRESIDENT, MARKETING
   Susan Blodgett
VICE PRESIDENT, ADMINISTRATION
   Gerald Sobczak

ORION HOME VIDEO

(A Division of Orion Home Entertainment Corporation);
1888 Century Park East, Los Angeles, CA 90067; (310)
282-0550. Branch: 35796 Veronica, Livonia, MI 48150
(313) 464-1515.
SENIOR VICE PRESIDENT
   Herb Dorfman
VICE PRESIDENT, SPECIAL MARKETS
   Betsy Caffrey

Overseas Filmgroup, Inc.

8800 Sunset Blvd., Suite 302, Los Angeles, CA 90069;
(310) 855-1199; FAX: (310) 855-0719.
CHAIRMAN
   Robert Little
PRESIDENT
   Ellen Little
CHIEF OPERATING OFFICER
   William Lischak
VICE PRESIDENT, CREATIVE AFFAIRS
   Liz McDermott
VICE PRESIDENT INTERNATIONAL SALES
   Richard Guardian
DIRECTOR, INTERNATIONAL TV SALES
   Bryan Hambleton
DIRECTOR, INTERNATIONAL SALES
   Maura Hoy
VICE PRESIDENT, PUBLICITY & MARKETING
   Ilyanne Morden-Kichaven

Earl Owensby Studios, Inc.

P.O. Box 184, 1048 Boiling Springs Rd., Shelby, NC
28150; (704) 487-0500. Organized 1973. (Motion picture
production and development.)
PRESIDENT & CHIEF EXECUTIVE OFFICER
   Eugene J. Kimling
EXECUTIVE VICE PRESIDENT
   Dennis Owensby
VICE PRESIDENT, DEVELOPMENT
   Debra Franklin
SECRETARY
   John Whiteheart
CONTROLLER
   John Whiteheart
PRODUCTION MANAGER
   Mike Allen
DIRECTOR UNDERWATER FILMING
   Al Giddings

P. C. Films Corp.

60 E. 42 St., Suite 2320, New York, NY 10165; (212)
599-0487; FAX: (212) 573-6141. Organized 1967. (Production and distribution.)
CONTACT
   Carl I. Kaminsky

Pacific International Enterprises, Inc.

1133 S. Riverside, Medford, OR 97501; (503) 779-0990; FAX: (503) 779-8880. Organized 1969. (Motion picture production and distribution.)

PRESIDENT/PRODUCER
Arthur R. Dubs
VICE PRESIDENT
Arn Wihtol
SECRETARY-TREASURER
Barbara J. Brown
DIRECTOR OF MEDIA
Paul Blumer
CONTROLLER/OFFICE MANAGER
Andy Gough

Pakula Productions, Inc.

330 W. 58 St., New York, NY 10019; (212) 664-0640. Organized 1969. (Motion picture and television production.)

PRESIDENT
Alan J. Pakula

Palisades Communications, Inc.

145 E. 57 St., New York, NY 10022; (212) 980-4800; FAX: (212) 980-8188. Organized 1993. (Producer-distributor and worldwide sales group. Also produces TV infomercials.)

PRESIDENT
Walter Manley
EXECUTIVE VICE PRESIDENT
Pat Hart
SALES MANAGER
Richard DeCroce

Paragon Arts International

6777 Hollywood Blvd., Suite 520, Los Angeles, CA 90028; (213) 465-5355; FAX: (213) 465-9029.

CEO
Walter Josten
PRESIDENT
John McHugh
SUPERVISING PRODUCER
Jeff Geoffray

Paramount Communications, Inc.

New-York (Home Office): 15 Columbus Circle, New York, NY 10023-7780; (212) 373-8000. West Coast: 5555 Melrose Ave., Los Angeles, CA 90038-3197; (213) 956-5000. (Producer and distributor.)

CHAIRMAN & CHIEF EXECUTIVE OFFICER
Martin S. Davis
PRESIDENT & COO
Stanley R. Jaffe
EXECUTIVE VICE PRESIDENT, CHIEF ADMINISTRATIVE OFFICER, GENERAL COUNSEL & SECRETARY
Donald Oresman
EXECUTIVE VICE PRESIDENT & CHIEF FINANCIAL OFFICER
Ronald L. Nelson
SENIOR VICE PRESIDENT, GOVERNMENT RELATIONS
Lawrence Levinson
SENIOR VICE PRESIDENT & SENIOR TAX COUNSEL
Eugene I. Meyers
SENIOR VICE PRESIDENT, CORPORATE COMMUNICATIONS
Jerry Sherman
VICE PRESIDENT, INSURANCE & NATIONAL PURCHASING
Peter A. Butler
SENIOR VICE PRESIDENT & DEPUTY GENERAL COUNSEL
Earl H. Doppelt
VICE PRESIDENT & TREASURER
Michael B. Estabrooks
VICE PRESIDENT, INTERNAL AUDIT & SPECIAL PROJECTS
Rudolph L. Hertlein
VICE PRESIDENT, ACCOUNTING & SYSTEMS
Raymond M. Nowak

PARAMOUNT PICTURES

CHAIRMAN
Sherry Lansing
EXECUTIVE VICE PRESIDENT
William Bernstein
EXECUTIVE VICE PRESIDENT, CHIEF FINANCIAL & ADMINISTRATIVE OFFICER
Patrick B. Purcell
EXECUTIVE VICE PRESIDENT, GENERAL COUNSEL
Richard Zimbert
SENIOR VICE PRESIDENT, TREASURER
Alan Bailey
SENIOR VICE PRESIDENT, MANAGEMENT INFORMATION SYSTEMS
Warren Ferriter
SENIOR VICE PRESIDENT, CONTRACT ACCOUNTING
Allen Gottlieb
SENIOR VICE PRESIDENT, HUMAN RESOURCES
William Hawkins
SENIOR VICE PRESIDENT, INDUSTRIAL RELATIONS
Stephen Koppekin
SENIOR VICE PRESIDENT, ASSISTANT GENERAL COUNSEL
Paul Springer
SENIOR VICE PRESIDENT, FINANCE
Stephen P. Taylor
SENIOR VICE PRESIDENT, DEPUTY GENERAL COUNSEL
J. Jay Rakow
VICE PRESIDENT, MOTION PICTURE PLANNING
Mark Badagliacca
VICE PRESIDENT, CONTRACT ACCOUNTING
Carmen Desiderio
VICE PRESIDENT, HUMAN RESOURCES
JoAnne Adams Griffith
VICE PRESIDENT, ADMINISTRATION
Rosemary Di Pietra
VICE PRESIDENT, MANAGEMENT INFORMATION SYSTEMS, WEST COAST
Gary Naiman
VICE PRESIDENT, EMPLOYEE RELATIONS LEGAL SERVICES
Rina Roselli
VICE PRESIDENT, CORPORATE CONTROLLER
Thomas A. Zimmerman

MOTION PICTURE GROUP

PRESIDENT, WORLDWIDE DISTRIBUTION
Barry London
PRESIDENT, PRODUCTION
John Goldwyn
SENIOR VICE PRESIDENT, BUSINESS AFFAIRS & ACQUISITIONS
Richard Fowkes
SENIOR VICE PRESIDENT, BUSINESS AFFAIRS
Gregory Gelfan
SENIOR VICE PRESIDENT, LEGAL AFFAIRS
Robert Cohen
VICE PRESIDENT, ACQUISITIONS
John Ferraro
VICE PRESIDENT, BUSINESS AFFAIRS, MUSIC
Kevin Koloff
VICE PRESIDENT, MUSIC LEGAL AFFAIRS
Linda Wohl

DOMESTIC DISTRIBUTION DIVISION

PRESIDENT
Wayne Lewellen
EXECUTIVE VICE PRESIDENT, GENERAL SALES MANAGER
Gino Campagnola
SENIOR VICE PRESIDENT, SALES OPERATIONS
Steve Rapaport
VICE PRESIDENT, SOUTHERN DIVISION
Royce Brimage
VICE PRESIDENT, EXHIBITOR SERVICES
Alan Cordover
VICE PRESIDENT, EASTERN DIVISION
Mike Share
VICE PRESIDENT, SALES ADMINISTRATION
Bernard Spannagel
VICE PRESIDENT, MIDWESTERN DIVISION
Robert Weiss
VICE PRESIDENT, WESTERN DIVISION
Clark Woods

DOMESTIC BRANCHES AND MANAGERS

Eastern Division

NEW YORK—15 Columbus Circle, 22nd Floor, New York, NY 10023, Pam Pritzker, District Manager.

BUFFALO/ALBANY, Steve Toback, Branch Manager.

WASHINGTON, D.C.—Parkingway Building, 10 Granite Street, Quincy, MA, 02269-9134, Claudia Ungar.

BOSTON/NEW HAVEN—Parkingway Building, 10 Granite Street, Quincy, MA, 02269-9134, Joe Rathgeb.

CINCINNATI/CLEVELAND—Parkingway Building, 10 Granite Street, Quincy, MA, 02269-9134, Victoria Burns.

PHILADELPHIA—15 Columbus Circle, 22nd Floor, New York, NY, 10023, Ralph Garman.

PITTSBURGH—Fulton Building, 107 6th Street, Pittsburgh, PA, 15222, Kaye Grotto.

Midwestern Division

CHICAGO—8750 West Bryn Mawr Avenue, Suite 890, Chicago, IL, 60631, Bruce Placke.

DETROIT—8750 West Bryn Mawr Avenue, Suite 890, Chicago, IL, 60631, Peter Fleisher.

KANSAS CITY/ST. LOUIS—8750 West Bryn Mawr Avenue, Suite 890, Chicago, IL, 60631, Scott Huneryager.

DES MOINES/MILWAUKEE—8750 West Bryn Mawr Avenue, Suite 890, Chicago, IL, 60631, John Slama.

INDIANAPOLIS—8750 West Bryn Mawr Avenue, Suite 890, Chicago, IL, 60631, Susan Puhl.

MINNEAPOLIS—8750 West Bryn Mawr Avenue, Suite 890, Chicago, IL, 60631, Jeremy Devine.

Southern Division

ATLANTA—7000 Central Parkway, Suite 1340, Atlanta, GA, 30328, John Hersker.

JACKSONVILLE—7000 Central Parkway, Suite 1340, Atlanta, GA, 30328, Norman Shindler.

CHARLOTTE—7000 Central Parkway, Suite 1340, Atlanta, GA, 30328, Buddy Williams.

DALLAS/OKLAHOMA CITY/NEW ORLEANS/MEMPHIS—12222 Merit Drive, Suite 840, Dallas, TX, 75251, Don Wallace.

PUERTO RICO—Miramar Plaza Building, 954 Ponce de Leon Avenue, Suite 201, San Juan, PR, 00907, Nestor Rivera.

Western Division

LOS ANGELES—15260 Ventura Boulevard, Suite 1140, Sherman Oaks, CA, 91403, Robert Box.

SAN FRANCISCO—15260 Ventura Boulevard, Suite 1140, Sherman Oaks, CA, 91403, Larry St. John

SEATTLE/PORTLAND—15260 Ventura Boulevard, Suite 1140, Sherman Oaks, CA, 91403, Ron Etchie

DENVER/SALT LAKE CITY—15260 Ventura Boulevard, Suite 1140, Sherman Oaks, CA, 91403, Jackie Rouleau.

Canadian Division

TORONTO—146 Bloor Street West, Toronto, Ontario, M5S 1M4, Bob Cowan.

MONTREAL—5887 Monkland Avenue, Montreal, Quebec, H4A 1G6, Lise Bertrand.

WINNIPEG—1109 17th Avenue, S.W., Calgary, Alberta, T2T 0B5, Blain Covert.

CALGARY/VANCOUVER—1109 17th Avenue S.W., Calgary, Alberta, T2T 0B5, Chris Sullivan.

ST. JOHN—146 Bloor Street West, Toronto, Ontario, M5S 1M4, Jean White.

INTERNATIONAL DISTRIBUTION DIVISION

VICE PRESIDENT (LONDON)
Luigi Luraschi

MARKETING DIVISION

PRESIDENT, WORLDWIDE MARKETING
Arthur Cohen
EXECUTIVE VICE PRESIDENT, NATIONAL ADVERTISING/PROMOTION
Thomas Campanella

EXECUTIVE VICE PRESIDENT, MARKETING/CREATIVE AFFAIRS
Nancy Goliger
EXECUTIVE VICE PRESIDENT, CREATIVE ADVERTISING
Michael Camp
SENIOR VICE PRESIDENT, WORLDWIDE PUBLICITY
Cheryl Boone Isaacs
VICE PRESIDENT, INTERNATIONAL MARKETING
Leslie Pound
VICE PRESIDENT, PROMOTION
Lisa Di Mario
VICE PRESIDENT, EAST COAST PUBLICITY
John Kelley
VICE PRESIDENT, MARKETING SERVICES
Jerry A. Meadors
VICE PRESIDENT, PUBLICITY
Blaise J. Noto
VICE PRESIDENT, NATIONAL ADVERTISING
Susan Wrenn
VICE PRESIDENT, ADMINISTRATION
Leslie Anderson

PRODUCTION DIVISION

SENIOR VICE PRESIDENT, MUSIC
Harlan Goodman
SENIOR VICE PRESIDENT, PRODUCTION
Michelle Manning
SENIOR VICE PRESIDENT, PRODUCTION
Karen Rosenfelt
SENIOR VICE PRESIDENT, FEATURES PRODUCTION
Michael Tadross
VICE PRESIDENT, FEATURES PRODUCTION MANAGEMENT
Larry Albucher
VICE PRESIDENT, FEATURES PRODUCTION ADMINISTRATION
Jeffrey Coleman
VICE PRESIDENT, CASTING (FEATURES)
Nancy Foy
VICE PRESIDENT, PRODUCTION
Donald Granger
VICE PRESIDENT, PRODUCTION
Bob Jaffe
VICE PRESIDENT, PRODUCTION
Tom Levine

TELEVISION GROUP

PRESIDENT
Kerry McCluggage
EXECUTIVE VICE PRESIDENT, TELEVISION GROUP
Richard Lindheim
SENIOR VICE PRESIDENT, MEDIA RELATIONS
John A. Wentworth
VICE PRESIDENT, CONTROLLER
Alan C. Fels
VICE PRESIDENT, MEDIA RELATIONS
Trisha Cardoso

DOMESTIC TELEVISION DIVISION

PRESIDENT
Steven Goldman
PRESIDENT, CREATIVE AFFAIRS & FIRST RUN PROGRAMMING
Frank Kelly
SENIOR VICE PRESIDENT, BUSINESS AFFAIRS/FINANCE
Robert Sheehan
EXECUTIVE VICE PRESIDENT
Joel Berman
EXECUTIVE VICE PRESIDENT, MARKETING
Meryl Cohen
SENIOR VICE PRESIDENT, EASTERN REGIONAL MANAGER
Dick Montgomery
SENIOR VICE PRESIDENT, CENTRAL REGIONAL MANAGER
Gerald Noonan
SENIOR VICE PRESIDENT, SOUTHERN REGIONAL MANAGER
Al Rothstein
VICE PRESIDENT, FINANCE
Karen Kanemoto
SENIOR VICE PRESIDENT, LEGAL & BUSINESS AFFAIRS
Bruce Pottash

HOME VIDEO DIVISION

PRESIDENT
Robert Klingensmith

PRESIDENT, DOMESTIC HOME VIDEO
  Eric Doctorow
EXECUTIVE VICE PRESIDENT
  Timothy Croft
EXECUTIVE VICE PRESIDENT, BUSINESS AFFAIRS/FINANCE,
VIDEO/MOTION PICTURE MARKETING
  Jack Waterman
SENIOR VICE PRESIDENT, ADVERTISING & SALES
PROMOTION
  Hollace Brown
SENIOR VICE PRESIDENT, SALES
  Jack Kanne
SENIOR VICE PRESIDENT, MARKETING
  Alan Perper
VICE PRESIDENT, BUSINESS AFFAIRS (ACQUISTIONS)
  Jonathan Bader
VICE PRESIDENT, FINANCE
  Gari Ann Douglass
VICE PRESIDENT, CREATIVE SERVICES
  Sandra Forney
VICE PRESIDENT, OPERATIONS
  Harold Fraser
VICE PRESIDENT, ADVERTISING
  Lynn Johnson
VICE PRESIDENT, LEGAL AFFAIRS
  Steven Madoff

STUDIO GROUP

PRESIDENT
  Earl Lestz
VICE PRESIDENT, FACILITY OPERATIONS
  Rae Ann Del Pozzo
VICE PRESIDENT, PLANNING & DEVELOPMENT
  Christine Essel
VICE PRESIDENT, STUDIO ADMINISTRATION
  Larry Owens
VICE PRESIDENT, LEGAL SERVICES
  Nathan Smith

OPERATIONS DIVISION

SENIOR VICE PRESIDENT
  David Mannix
VICE PRESIDENT
  Richard Nelson

POST PRODUCTION DIVISION

SENIOR VICE PRESIDENT
  Paul Haggar
VICE PRESIDENT
  Fred Chandler

VIDEOTAPE OPERATIONS DIVISION

SENIOR VICE PRESIDENT
  Thomas Bruehl

THEATRICAL EXHIBITION GROUP

PRESIDENT
  Larry Gleason

FAMOUS MUSIC PUBLISHING

CHAIRMAN & CEO
  Irwin A. Robinson
PRESIDENT
  Ira Jaffe
EXECUTIVE VICE PRESIDENT, FINANCE & ADMINISTRATION
  Sidney Herman

Tom Parker Motion Pictures

3941 S. Bristol, Suite 285, Santa Ana, CA 92704; (714)
545-2887; FAX: (714) 545-9775.
PRESIDENT
  Tom Parker

Pathe Pictures, Inc.

161 W. 54 St., New York, NY 10019-5318; (212) 247-
4767; FAX: (212) 956-3153. Organized 1959. (Producer

and distributor of features, documentaries, educational
films and children's programs.)
PRESIDENT
  Joseph P. Smith
VICE PRESIDENT, SECRETARY & TREASURER
  Samuel A. Costello
VICE PRESIDENT & GENERAL COUNSEL
  James J. Harrington
DIRECTOR OF OPERATIONS
  Joseph A. Volatile
BOARD OF DIRECTORS
  Joseph P. Smith, Samuel A. Costello, James J. Harrington

Peerless Film Processing Corporation

42-24 Orchard St., Long Island City, NY 11101; (718)
784-4040. (Protective and preservative film treatments;
film reconditioning, incl. Peer-Renu for shrunken originals,
scratch removal, rehumidification, repairs, cleaning, distri-
bution servicing of film libraries and TV shows of films.)
Domestic and foreign licenses.
PRESIDENT
  Y. W. Mociuk
EXECUTIVE VICE PRESIDENT
  Sam Borodinsky

Penthouse Films International, Ltd.

1965 Broadway, New York, NY 10023-5965; (212) 496-
6100. Organized 1975. (Feature film production.)
CHAIRMAN AND PRESIDENT
  Bob Guccione
EXECUTIVE VICE PRESIDENT
  David J. Myerson
DIRECTOR OF PUBLICITY
  Catherine Jarrat Koatz

Persky-Bright Organization

7 E. 84 St., New York, NY 10028; (212) 570-5656. Orga-
nized 1973. (Finances and produces feature motion pic-
tures.)
PARTNERS
  Lester Persky, Richard S. Bright
PRODUCTION EXECUTIVE
  Tomlinson Dean
DIRECTOR OF ADMINISTRATION
  Margaret Murphy

Lester Persky Productions, Inc.

935 Bel Air Rd., Los Angeles, CA 90077; (213) 476-
9697; FAX: (213) 476-6665; 150 Central Park South, New
York, NY 10019; (212) 246-7700.
PRESIDENT, EXECUTIVE PRODUCER
  Lester Persky
VICE PRESIDENT
  Tomlinson Dean
STORY EDITOR
  Adam Peck
CONTROLLER
  Camille Pollock

Pickman Film Corporation, The

2 Sutton Place South, Suite 18-A, New York, NY 10022;
(212) 755-5668.
PRESIDENT
  Jerome Pickman
VICE PRESIDENT/ADMINISTRATION
  Barbara Herburger

Pike Productions, Inc.

11 Clarke St., P.O. Box 300, Newport, RI 02840; (401)
846-8890; FAX: (401) 847-0070. Organized 1958. (Pro-

duction of trailers, radio & television campaigns for features; custom trailers & headers for theatres.)
PRESIDENT
James A. Pike
SALES MANAGER
Cornelia M. Pike
GRAPHIC DESIGN
Earl Davis
DIRECTOR OF PHOTOGRAPHY
Gregory M. Pike
DIRECTOR OF RECORDING
Peter Schillereff
DISTRIBUTION
Kaththea A. Sias

Planet 3 Entertainment Inc.

1847 Centinela Ave., Santa Monica, CA 90404; (310) 828-2232. (TV & film production.)
PRESIDENT
John C. Luma

Pleskow/Spikings Partnership

345 North Maple Dr., Suite 300, Beverly Hills, CA 90210; (310) 205-8333; FAX: (310) 205-8396. Organized September, 1992. (Formed as partnership between Eric Pleskow and Barry Spikings to produce motion pictures for theatrical release.)
PARTNERS
Eric Pleskow, Barry P. Spikings, Richard A. Hess

Premiere, Ltd.

204 Brazilian Ave., Suite 200, Palm Beach, FL 33480; (407) 659-1660. Organized 1986. (Motion picture development.)
PRESIDENT
James J. McNamara

Otto Preminger Films, Ltd.

201 E. 69 St., Suite 11F, New York, NY 10021; (212) 535-6001; FAX: (212) 772-1068. (Distributor; motion picture and television production.)
PRESIDENT
Hope B. Preminger
VICE PRESIDENT
Valerie Robins

Edward R. Pressman Film Corp.

445 N. Bedford Dr., PH, Beverly Hills, CA 90210; (310) 271-8383; FAX: (310) 271-9497. Organized 1969. (Film production.)
PRESIDENT
Edward R. Pressman
VICE PRESIDENT
Michael Radiloff
SENIOR VICE PRESIDENT, PRODUCTION
Anne Templeton
EXECUTIVE VICE PRESIDENT
Neil Friedman

Prism Pictures Corp.

1888 Century Park E., Suite 350, Los Angeles, CA 90067; (310) 277-3270; FAX: (310) 203-8036. Organized 1992. (Film production, cable, broadcast, syndication TV.)
CHAIRMAN OF THE BOARD
Barry Collier
CHIEF FINANCIAL OFFICER
Earl Rosenstein
PRESIDENT
Barbara Javitz

VICE PRESIDENT, BUSINESS AFFAIRS
Cynthia Berry Meyer
VICE PRESIDENT, ACQUISITIONS & ANCILLARY SALES
Gary Rubin
VICE PRESIDENT, INTERNATIONAL SALES
Liz Mackiewicz

Producer's Distribution Company

8833 Sunset Blvd., Suite 303, Los Angeles, CA 90069; (213) 657-8620. Organized 1986. (Motion picture production and distribution.)
OWNER
Ray Axelrod

Producers Entertainment

9150 Wilshire Blvd., #205, Beverly Hills, CA 90212; (310) 285-0400; FAX: (310) 281-2585. Organized 1989. (Producer of TV movies and mini-series, motion pictures.)
CHAIRMAN & CEO
Harvey Bibicoff

Promark Entertainment Group

3599 Cahuenga Blvd. W., 3rd fl., Los Angeles, CA 90068; (213) 878-0404; FAX: (213) 878-0486. Organized 1986. (International distribution and production.)
PRESIDENT
Carol M. Rossi
VICE PRESIDENT, INTERNATIONAL DISTRIBUTION
David T. Carson
VICE PRESIDENT, PRODUCTION
Steve Beswick
DIRECTOR, INTERNATIONAL SALES
Jody Jamal-Eddine
DIRECTOR, DISTRIBUTION
Susan Pritchard
ASST. TO PRESIDENT
Kate Hise
CONTROLLER
Linda C. LaFrenais

Propaganda Films

940 N. Mansfield Ave., Los Angeles, CA 90038; (213) 462-6400; FAX: (213) 463-7874.
PRINCIPALS
Joni Sighvatsson
Steve Golin

Quartet Films, Inc.

1414 Ave. of the Americas, New York, NY 10019; (212) 888-0080. Organized 1977. (Motion picture distribution.)
PRESIDENT
Julian Schlossberg
VICE PRESIDENT
Meyer Ackerman
PRESIDENT, MARKETING & DISTRIBUTION
Mel Maron
DIRECTOR, THEATRICAL DISTRIBUTION
Ivory Harris
DIRECTOR OF ADVERTISING
David Wright

RGH International Film Enterprises, Inc.

8831 W. Sunset Blvd., Los Angeles, CA 90069; (310) 652-2893; FAX: (310) 652-6237.
PRESIDENT
Robert G. Hussong
EXECUTIVE ASSISTANT
Frank McClane
VICE PRESIDENT
Adriana Shaw

RKO Pictures

551 Madison Ave., 14th fl., New York, NY 10022; (212) 644-0600; 1801 Avenue of the Stars, Suite 448, Los Angeles, CA 90067; (310) 277-0707.

CHAIRMAN & CEO
Ted Hartley
EXECUTIVE VICE PRESIDENT, CORPORATE DEVELOPMENT
Mitch Blumberg
EXECUTIVE VICE PRESIDENT, ENTERTAINMENT DIVISION
Kim Snyder

Carl Ragsdale Associates, Ltd.

4725 Stillbrooke, Houston, TX 77035; (713) 729-6530. (Producers of films for industry, television and government.)

PRESIDENT
Carl V. Ragsdale
BRANCH OFFICES
4801 Mass. Ave., NW, Suite 400, Washington, DC 20016, Arthur Neuman, Exec. Prod. in charge. Tel: (202) 364-0197; 16036 Tupper St. Sepulveda, CA 91343, Tel: (213) 894-6291. Exec. Prod. in charge: Frank Coghlan; Piazza Cairoli, 113 Roma, Italy 00186, Tel: 654-5182, Douglas R. Fleming, Exec. Prod. in charge.

Rank Precision Industries

RANK CINTEL LTD.

(Manufacturer of telecine equipment for broadcast and film/tape transfer.) Watton Road, Ware, Hertfordshire SG12 OAE. Tel.: 0920 463939. Telex: 81415. FAX: 0920 460803.

MANAGING DIRECTOR
Jack R. Brittain

RANK TAYLOR HOBSON LTD.

(Manufacturer of precision measurement equipment, professional cine lenses.) P.O. Box 36, 3 New Star Rd., Thurmaston Lane, Leicester, LE3 7JQ. Tel: 0533 763771. Telex: 34411. FAX: 0533 740167.

MANAGING DIRECTOR
Richard Freeman

RANK PRECISION INDUSTRIES GmbH (West German Office)

(Marketing of motion picture camera lenses.) Postfach 4827, Kreuzberger Ring 6 6200 Wiesbaden, West Germany; Tel.: 49 611 700874. Telex: 04186175. FAX: 49611 702495.

GESCHAFTSFUHRER
H-U Rathgeber

RANK CINTEL INC.

(Marketing of telecine equipment.) 25358 Avenue Stanford, Valencia, CA 91355; (805) 294-2310; FAX: (805) 294-1019.

EXECUTIVE VICE PRESIDENT
Arnold Taylor

RANK TAYLOR HOBSON K.K. (Japanese Office)

(Marketing of professional cine lenses.) Kokodokan Buildings, 9-13, 4-chome, Chuo-Ku, Ginza, Tokyo 336, Japan; Tel.: 813 3545 1451. Telex: 7227684. FAX: 813 3545 6522.

PRESIDENT
K. Fujimoto

International Division

DELUXE FILM LABORATORIES

1377 North Serrano Ave., Hollywood, CA 90027; Tel: 0101 213 462 6171. FAX: 0101 213 461 0608.

PRESIDENT
Bud Stone

THE FILM HOUSE GROUP

Film House Laboratory, 380 Adelaide St., West Toronto, Ontario M5V 1R7, Canada. Tel: 0101 416 364 4321. FAX: 0101 416 364 3601.

PRESIDENT
Cyril Drabinsky

RANK FILM LABORATORIES LTD.

(Processing of color and black and white film for cinema and television.) North Orbital Rd., Denham, Uxbridge, Middx. UB9 5HQ. Tel: 0895 832323. Telex: 934704. FAX: 0895 833617.

MANAGING DIRECTOR
James Downer
DIRECTOR, SALES TELEVISION
David Dowler
SALES CONTROLLER, THEATRICAL
Peter MacCrimmon

STRAND LIGHTING, INC.

(Marketing of lighting and lighting control equipment.) P.O. Box 9004, 18111 Santa Fe Ave., Rancho Dominquez, CA 90221; (310) 637-7500. FAX: (310) 632 5519. Telex: 200473.

PRESIDENT
Gene Griffiths

STRAND LIGHTING LTD. (U.K. office)

(Manufacturer and supplier of lighting and lighting control equipment.) Grant Way, Off Syon Lane, Isleworth, Middx. TW7 5QD. Tel.: 081 560 3171. Telex: 27976. FAX: 081 490 0002.

MANAGING DIRECTOR
Christopher Waldron

STRAND LIGHTING CANADA (Canadian office)

(Marketing of lighting and lighting control equipment.) 2430 Lucknow Dr., Mississauga, Ontario, L5S IV3, Canada; 0101 416 677-7130. Telex: 06968646. FAX: 0101 416 677 6859.

PRESIDENT
Mrs. D. Appleton

STRAND LIGHTING FRANCE S.A. (French office)

(Marketing of lighting and lighting control equipment.) B.P. 101, 26 Villa Des Fleurs, 92400 Courbevoie, Cedex, France. Tel.: 010 331 478 86666. Telex: 214593. FAX: 010 331 433 37175.

GENERAL MANAGER
B. Bouchet

STRAND LIGHTING ASIA LIMITED (Hong Kong office)

(Marketing of lighting and lighting control equipment.) 802 Houston Centre, 63 Mody Road, Tsimshatsui East,

Kowloon, Hong Kong. Tel.: 010 852 3 685161. Telex: 44953. FAX: 010 852 3 694890.
MANAGING DIRECTOR
P. O'Donnell

RANK LIGHTING S.r.L. (Italian office)

(Marketing of lighting and lighting control equipment.) Via delle Gardenie 33, (Pontina Vecchia KM 33400) 00040 Pomezia, Roma Italy; Tel.: 010 396 914 7123. FAX: 010 396 914 7136.

STRAND LIGHTING GmbH (West German office)

(Marketing of lighting and lighting control equipment.) P.O. Box 4527, 3300 Braunschweig, West Germany. Tel.: 010 49 533 130 080. Telex: 95641. FAX: 010 49 5331 78883.
GENERAL MANAGER
I.C. HADDON

Rankin/Bass Productions

24 W. 55 St., New York, NY 10019; (212) 582-4017. (Producer.)
CHAIRMAN
Arthur Rankin, Jr.
PRESIDENT
Jules Bass
VICE PRESIDENT
Lee Dannacher

Rapid Film Group

P.O. Box 691725, West Hollywood, CA 90069; (213) 466-0801; FAX: (213) 466-5980. Organized 1986. (International motion picture licensing/distribution.)
PRESIDENT
Adam M. Fast

Rapid Film Technique

42-24 Orchard St., Long Island City, NY 11101; (718) 784-4544; FAX: (718) 784-4766. (Film reconditioning, rejuvenation inspection, repair.)
PRESIDENT
Y.W. Mociuk
EXECUTIVE VICE PRESIDENT
Sam Borodinsky

RAPID FILM DISTRIBUTORS

(Film and videotape shipping, distribution, storage.)

Rastar Productions, Inc.

335 N. Maple Dr., #356, Beverly Hills, CA 90210; (310) 247-0130; FAX: (310) 247-9120.
CHAIRMAN OF THE BOARD
Ray Stark
PRESIDENT
Marykay Powell
EXECUTIVE VICE PRESIDENT
Robert A. Mirisch
EXECUTIVE VICE PRESIDENT, MARKETING
Don Safran
VICE PRESIDENT OF DEVELOPMENT
Paul Rosenberg

Reel Movies International, Inc.

8235 Douglas, Suite 770, Dallas, TX 75225; (214) 363-4400; FAX: (214) 739-FILM(3456). Organized 1981.
PRESIDENT
Tom T. Moore

Reeltime Distributing Corp.

353 W. 48 St., New York, NY 10036; (212) 582-5380; FAX: (212) 581-2731. Organized 1979. (Film production and distribution.)
PRESIDENT
Roberta Findlay

Republic Pictures Corporation

12636 Beatrice St., P.O. Box 66930, Los Angeles, CA 90066-0930, (310) 306-4040; FAX: (310) 301-0142. Republic Pictures Productions, 350 S. Beverly Blvd., #200, Beverly Hills, CA 90212; (310) 552-7100.
CHAIRMAN OF THE BOARD & CEO
Russell Goldsmith
EXECUTIVE VICE PRESIDENT & PRESIDENT, HOME ENTERTAINMENT GROUP
Steven Beeks
EXECUTIVE VICE PRESIDENT, REPUBLIC PICTURES PRODUCTION
Ellen Endo-Dizon
SENIOR VICE PRESIDENT—ACQUISTIONS
Mel Layton
SENIOR VICE PRESIDENT—CHIEF FINANCIAL OFFICER
David Kirchheimer
VICE PRESIDENT, HOME VIDEO
Phil Kromnick
VICE PRESIDENT—INTERNATIONAL TV
Lawrence Garrett
SENIOR VICE PRESIDENT—MARKETING
Glenn Ross

REPUBLIC PICTURES PRODUCTIONS

350 S. Beverly Blvd., #200, Beverly Hills, CA 90212; (310) 552-7100.

Rhapsody Films

30 Charlton St., New York, NY 10014; (212) 243-0152. (Film production and distribution.)
PRESIDENT
Bruce Ricker

Lee Rich Productions

4000 Warner Blvd., Bldg. 81, Room 200, Burbank, CA 91522; (818) 954-3556. Organized 1988. (Independent motion picture and television production.)
PRESIDENT, MOTION PICTURES
Gary Foster
VICE PRESIDENT, MOTION PICTURES
Josie Rosen

Riviera Productions

31628 Saddletree Dr., Westlake Village, CA 91361; (818) 889-5778. Branches: 340 Westmoor, Brookfield, WI. Organized 1953. (Producer.)
EXECUTIVE PRODUCER
F. W. Zens
ASSOCIATE PRODUCERS
Jan Elblein, Robert Zens

Rob-Rich Films, Inc.

%Sidney Ginsberg, 4463 Winners Circle, Suite 1426, Sarasota, FL 34238; (813) 925-1672. Organized 1977. (Production and distribution of motion pictures.)
PRESIDENT
Sidney Ginsberg
VICE PRESIDENT, SECRETARY & TREASURER
Nelly M. Ginsberg

Rocket Pictures

9560 Wilshire Blvd., #330, Beverly Hills, CA 90212; (213) 550-3300. (Motion picture producers.)

Roxie Releasing

3125 16th St., San Francisco, CA 94103; (415) 431-3611; FAX: (415) 431-2822. (Film distributors.)

PRESIDENT
Bill Banning

Royal Pictures

19619 E. 17 Place, Aurora, CO 80011; (303) 367-4948. (Motion picture distributor.)

GENERAL MANAGER
James Lowry
MARKETING DIRECTOR
Ron Gordon

Sandollar Productions, Inc.

8730 Sunset Blvd., Penthouse West, Los Angeles, CA 90069; (310) 659-5933; FAX: (310) 659-0433. Organized 1985. (Develops and produces projects for motion pictures and television.)

OWNERS
Sandy Gallin
Dolly Parton
PRESIDENT/PRODUCER
Carol Baum

Saturn Productions, Inc.

1697 Broadway, Suite 1105, New York, NY 10019; (212) 489-2460; FAX: (212) 397-0665. (A division of Telefilm Co., Inc.)

PRESIDENT
Tom Ward

Savoy Pictures

152 W. 57th St., New York, NY 10019; (212) 247-5810. Organized 1993. (Motion picture producer and distributor.)

Schwartzberg & Company

12700 Ventura Blvd., 4th fl., Studio City, CA 91604; (818) 508-1444; FAX: (818) 508-1293. (Film and commercial production, specializing in the integration of live action and special effects.)

CHIEF EXECUTIVE OFFICERS
Louis Schwartzberg
Jan Ross
Craig Robin

Screenvision Cinema Network

275 Madison Ave., New York, NY 10016; (212) 818-0180; FAX: (212) 818-0186. California office: 9454 Wilshire Blvd., Beverly Hills, CA 90212; (213) 276-7394. Detroit office: 400 Maple, Birmingham, MI 48009; (313) 433-3555. Organized 1976. (National screen advertising.) A joint venture of Mediavision, Inc., Paris, France and F.T.T.L. Media Co., New York.

PRESIDENT & CEO
Dennis Fogarty
SENIOR VICE PRESIDENT, OPERATIONS
George Mamantov
SENIOR VICE PRESIDENT—EAST
Anne-Marie Marcus
VICE PRESIDENT–WEST
Susan Garber
NORTH EAST ACCOUNT MANAGER
Gaye Murtagh

MIDWEST ACCOUNT MANAGER
Denise Campbell

Shapiro Glickenhaus Entertainment

12001 Ventura Place, Suite 404, Studio City, CA 91604; (818) 766-8500; FAX: (818) 766-7873.

CHAIRMAN
James M. Glickenhaus
PRESIDENT & CHIEF EXECUTIVE OFFICER
Leonard Shapiro
EXECUTIVE VICE PRESIDENT, CHIEF OPERATING OFFICER
Alan Solomon
EXECUTIVE IN CHARGE OF PRODUCTION
Frank Isaac

Showscan Corporation

3939 Landmark St., Culver City, CA 90232; (310) 558-0150; FAX: (310) 559-7984. (Producer, distributor and exhibitor of films made in the Showscan process.)

CHAIRMAN
William Eberle
EXECUTIVE VICE PRESIDENT
Jack Ottaway
VICE PRESIDENT, BUSINESS AFFAIRS
Catherine Lemon
SECRETARY
James Sorenson

Silver Lion Films

715 Broadway, Suite 310, Santa Monica, CA 90401; (310) 393-9177; FAX: (310) 458-9372. (Motion picture production.)

PRODUCER
Lance Hool
EXECUTIVE PRODUCER
Conrad Hool
DEVELOPMENT
Jeanmarie Pla

Silver Screen Management, Inc.

936 Broadway, 5th fl., New York, NY 10010; (212) 995-7600; FAX: (212) 677-1562. (An entertainment finance company.)

PRESIDENT
Roland W. Betts
EXECUTIVE VICE PRESIDENT
Tom A. Bernstein
SENIOR VICE PRESIDENT
Barbara Stubenrauch
FIRST VICE PRESIDENT
Tim Brennan

Silverfilm Productions, Inc.

600 Madison Ave., New York, NY 10022; (212) 355-0282; FAX: (212) 421–8254. Organized 1974. (Motion picture production.)

PRESIDENT
Raphael Silver
VICE PRESIDENT
Joan Micklin Silver
VICE PRESIDENT, DEVELOPMENT
Barbara Schock

Silverman Entertainment Enterprises

3510 Shoreheights Dr., Malibu, CA 90265; (310) 459-8278. Organized 1988. (Motion picture production.)

PRESIDENT
Jim Silverman

Silverstein International Corp.

200 W. 57 St., New York, NY 10019; (212) 541-6620; FAX: (212) 586-0085; Telex: 236747. Organized 1970. (Production and distribution of motion pictures.)
PRESIDENT
Maurice Silverstein

Skouras Pictures

335 N. Maple Dr., #248, Beverly Hills, CA 90210; (310) 285-5455; FAX: (310) 285-5466.
PRESIDENT & CHIEF EXECUTIVE OFFICER
Dimitri T. Skouras
EXECUTIVE VICE PRESIDENT & CHIEF OPERATING OFFICER
Jeffrey Holmes
VICE PRESIDENT, THEAREICAL
Marc Halperin
VICE PRESIDENT, CORPORATE PROJECTS
B. J. Miller
VICE PRESIDENT, ACQUISITIONS
Marjorie Skouras
PRESIDENT, SKOURAS HOME VIDEO
Danny Kopels
VICE PRESIDENT, FINANCE & ADMINISTRATION
Joanne Lawrence
DIRECTOR, PRINT OPERATIONS & CO-OP ADVERTISING
Jeff McFarland

Sony Pictures Entertainment, Inc.

10202 W. Washington Blvd., Culver City, CA 90232; (310) 280-8000; FAX: (310) 204-1300. 3400 Riverside Dr., Burbank, CA 91505; (818) 972-7000; FAX: (818) 972-0234. 711 Fifth Ave., New York, NY 10022, (212) 751-4400.

CORPORATE OFFICERS

CHAIRMAN OF THE BOARD AND CHIEF EXECUTIVE OFFICER
Peter Guber
PRESIDENT AND CHIEF OPERATING OFFICER, FILMED ENTERTAINMENT GROUP
Alan J. Levine
EXECUTIVE VICE PRESIDENT AND CHIEF FINANCIAL OFFICER
Abbott L. Brown
EXECUTIVE VICE PRESIDENT
Lawrence J. Ruisi
EXECUTIVE VICE PRESIDENT
Paul Michael Schaeffer
SENIOR VICE PRESIDENT
Ben Feingold
SENIOR VICE PRESIDENT AND CONTROLLER
Edgar H. Howells, Jr.
SENIOR VICE PRESIDENT AND GENERAL COUNSEL
Ronald N. Jacobi
SENIOR VICE PRESIDENT
Kenneth S. Williams
VICE PRESIDENT
Don DeMesquita
VICE PRESIDENT
Susan Jameson
VICE PRESIDENT AND TREASUR
Joe Kraft
VICE PRESIDENT
Lucy Wander-Perna

CORPORATE DEPARTMENT HEADS

EXECUTIVE VICE PRESIDENT, LEGAL, AND DEPUTY GENERAL GOUNSEL
Beth Berke
EXECUTIVE VICE PRESIDENT, LABOR RELATIONS AND LITIGATION
Joel Grossman
EXECUTIVE VICE PRESIDENT, LEGAL
Jared Jussim
EXECUTIVE VICE PRESIDENT AND GENERAL MANAGER, SONY PICTURES STUDIOS
Arnie Shupack
SENIOR VICE PRESIDENT, LEGAL, TRISTAR PICTURES
Liz Aschenbrenner

SENIOR VICE PRESIDENT, LEGAL, COLUMBIA PICTURES TELEVISION
Greg Boone
SENIOR VICE PRESIDENT
Barbara Cline
SENIOR VICE PRESIDENT, CORPORATE COMMUNICATIONS
Don DeMesquita
SENIOR VICE PRESIDENT, CORPORATE DEVELOPMENT
Ben Feingold
SENIOR VICE PRESIDENT, CORPORATE AFFAIRS
Susan Jameson
SENIOR VICE PRESIDENT, FINANCE, MOTION PICTURE GROUP
Shelly Rabinowitz
SENIOR VICE PRESIDENT AND CONTROLLER, COLUMBIA PICTURES TELEVISION
Joe Stevens
SENIOR VICE PRESIDENT, HUMAN RESOURCES
Lucy Wander-Perna
VICE PRESIDENT, TAXES
Bob Moses
VICE PRESIDENT, AUDIT
John Reith

Sony Pictures Entertainment Motion Picture Group

(A Sony Pictures Entertainment Company.)
10202 W. Washington Blvd., Culver City, CA 90232; (310) 280-8000.
PRESIDENT
Jon Dolgen

COLUMBIA PICTURES

10202 W. Washington Blvd., Culver City, CA 90232; (310) 280-8000; FAX: (310) 204-1300.

EXECUTIVE

CHAIRMAN
Mark Canton

PRODUCTION

PRESIDENT OF PRODUCTION
Michael Nathanson
EXECUTIVE VICE PRESIDENT, PRODUCTION
Amy Pascal
EXECUTIVE PRODUCTION CONSULTANT
Gareth P. Wigan
EXECUTIVE VICE PRESIDENT, PRODUCTION
Teddy Zee
SENIOR VICE PRESIDENT, PRODUCTION
Barry Josephson
VICE PRESIDENT, PRODUCTION
Stephanie Allain
VICE PRESIDENT, PRODUCTION
Jerry Greenberg
VICE PRESIDENT, PRODUCTION
Kevin Jones

MARKETING

EXECUTIVE VICE PRESIDENT, PRESIDENT, MARKETING AND DISTRIBUTION
Sid Ganis
EXECUTIVE VICE PRESIDENT, CREATIVE ADVERTISING
Marc Shmuger
SENIOR VICE PRESIDENT, MEDIA ADVERTISING
John Butkovich
SENIOR VICE PRESIDENT, RESEARCH
Ariel Diaz
SENIOR VICE PRESIDENT, MARKETING
Joseph Foley
SENIOR VICE PRESIDENT, PUBLICITY, PROMO/FIELD OPS
Mark Gill
VICE PRESIDENT, PUBLICITY
Marcy Granata
VICE PRESIDENT, EAST COAST PUBLICITY
Steve Klain
VICE PRESIDENT, PUBLICITY
Sandra O'Neill

VICE PRESIDENT, PUBLICITY
Doug Taylor
VICE PRESIDENT, NATIONAL PROMOTIONS
Diane Salerno

DISTRIBUTION

EXECUTIVE VICE PRESIDENT, PRESIDENT, MARKETING AND
DISTRIBUTION
Sid Ganis
PRESIDENT, DOMESTIC DISTRIBUTION
Jeffrey Blake
VICE PRESIDENT, ADMINISTRATION & OPERATIONS
Mark L. Zucker
DIVISION MANAGER, WEST COAST
Allen Elrod
DIVISION MANAGER, CENTRAL
Daniel Marks
DIVISION MANAGER, EAST COAST
Jay Sands
DIVISION MANAGER, SOUTH
Terry Tharpe

OTHER DEPARTMENTS

PRESIDENT, PRODUCTION ADMINISTRATION
Gary Martin
EXECUTIVE VICE PRESIDENT, MUSIC
Michael Dilbeck
EXECUTIVE VICE PRESIDENT, SPE MUSIC GROUP
Robert Holmes
EXECUTIVE VICE PRESIDENT, BUSINESS AFFAIRS
Gary Schrager
EXECUTIVE VICE PRESIDENT, POST PRODUCTION
James Honore
SENIOR VICE PRESIDENT, BUSINESS AFFAIRS
Alan Krieger
SENIOR VICE PRESIDENT, BUSINESS AFFAIRS
Darrell Walker
VICE PRESIDENT, GENERAL MANAGER, MERCHANDISING
Lester Borden
VICE PRESIDENT, BUSINESS AFFAIRS
Philip Elway
VICE PRESIDENT, PRODUCTION ADMINISTRATION
Bill Ewing
VICE PRESIDENT, OPERATIONS
Bryan Lee
VICE PRESIDENT, BUSINESS AFFAIRS CONTRACT
ADMINISTRATION
Thomas Stack
VICE PRESIDENT, CORPORATE STRATEGY AND PLANNING
Mindy Tucker

DOMESTIC BRANCH OFFICES

Western Division
Sony Studios, 10202 West Washington Blvd., Culver City, CA
90232; (310) 280-8000. Allen Elrod, Western Division Manager;
David Garel, Western District Manager.
Eastern Division
711 5th Ave., New York, NY 10022; (212) 751-4400. Jay Sands,
Eastern Division Manager; Jim Amos, Eastern District Manager.
Central Division
Sony Studios, 10202 West Washington Blvd., Culver City, CA
90232; (310) 280-8000. Daniel Marks, Central Division Manager;
David Knopf, Central District Manager.
Southern Division
3100 Breckinridge Blvd., #135, Duluth, GA 30136; (404)
564-8521. Terry Tharpe, Southern Division Manager; Sherman Wood,
Southern District Manager.

TRI STAR PICTURES

(A Sony Pictures Entertainment Company) 10202 West
Washington Blvd., Culver City, CA 90232; (310) 280-7700;
FAX: (310) 280-1577.

EXECUTIVE

CHAIRMAN
Mike Medavoy
VICE CHAIRMAN
Kenneth Lemberger
PRESIDENT
Marc Platt

PRODUCTION

PRESIDENT, PRODUCTION
Stacey Lassally
SENIOR VICE PRESIDENT, PRODUCTION
Michael Besman
SENIOR VICE PRESIDENT, PRODUCTION
Christopher Lee
SENIOR VICE PRESIDENT, PRODUCTION
Kevin Misher
VICE PRESIDENT, PRODUCTION
Amy Bosley

MARKETING

PRESIDENT, MARKETING
Buffy Shutt
EXECUTIVE VICE PRESIDENT, MARKETING
Kathy Jones
VICE PRESIDENT, RESEARCH
Ariel Diaz
SENIOR VICE PRESIDENT, MARKETING
Edward Egan
SENIOR VICE PRESIDENT, MEDIA
Mark Kristol
SENIOR VICE PRESIDENT, CREATIVE ADVERTISING
William Loper
SENIOR VICE PRESIDENT, PUBLICITY/PROMO/FIELD OPS
Edward Russell
VICE PRESIDENT, FIELD OPERATIONS
Rhonda Bryant
VICE PRESIDENT, PUBLICITY/SPECIAL PROJECTS
Hollace Davids
VICE PRESIDENT, PUBLICITY
Jamie Geller-Hawtof
VICE PRESIDENT, EAST COAST PUBLICITY
Dennis P. Higgins
VICE PRESIDENT, NATIONAL PROMOTIONS
Diane Salerno
VICE PRESIDENT, MEDIA
Mark Wood

DISTRIBUTION

PRESIDENT, DOMESTIC DISTRIBUTION
William C. Soady
SENIOR VICE PRESIDENT, GENERAL SALES MANAGER
Robert Capps
VICE PRESIDENT, DIVISION MANAGER WEST
Rory Bruer
VICE PRESIDENT, DIVISION MANAGER EAST
John Colloca
VICE PRESIDENT, EXHIBITOR RELATIONS
Ted Hatfield
VICE PRESIDENT, DIVISION MANAGER SOUTH
Joseph W. Kennedy
VICE PRESIDENT, DIVISION MANAGER CENTRAL
Jack Simmons

Other Departments

PRESIDENT, PRODUCTION ADMINISTRATION
Gary Martin
SENIOR VICE PRESIDENT, MUSIC
Michael Dilbeck
EXECUTIVE VICE PRESIDENT, BUSINESS AFFAIRS
Robert Geary
EXECUTIVE VICE PRESIDENT, SPE MUSIC GROUP
Robert Holmes
SENIOR VICE PRESIDENT, POST PRODUCTION
James Honore
EXECUTIVE VICE PRESIDENT, PHYSICAL PRODUCTION
Ron Lynch
SENIOR VICE PRESIDENT, LEGAL AFFAIRS
Liz Aschenbrenner
SENIOR VICE PRESIDENT, BUSINESS AFFAIRS
Gary A. Hirsch
SENIOR VICE PRESIDENT, POST PRODUCTION
Sol Lomita
SENIOR VICE PRESIDENT, BUSINESS AFFAIRS
Glenn Meredith
VICE PRESIDENT, OPERATIONS AND BUSINESS AFFAIRS
Paul D. Smith
VICE PRESIDENT, LEGAL ADMINISTRATION
Cassandra Barbour
VICE PRESIDENT, GENERAL MANAGER, MERCHANDISING
Lester Borden

VICE PRESIDENT, LEGAL AFFAIRS
Jon Gibson
VICE PRESIDENT, BUSINESS AFFAIRS ADMINISTRATION
Mark Horowitz
VICE PRESIDENT, BUSINESS AFFAIRS
John Levy

DOMESTIC BRANCH OFFICES

Western Division
Studio Plaza 3400 Riverside Dr., Burbank, CA 91505 (818)
972-7000. Rory Bruer, Vice President, Western Division Manager;
Adrian Smith, Western District Manager.
Eastern Division
711 5th Ave., New York, NY 10022; (212) 751-4400. John Colloca,
Vice President, Eastern Division Manager; Stephen Saphos, Eastern
District Manager.
Central Division
2800 River Road #210, Des Plaines, IL 60018; (708) 699-0550.
Jack Simmons, Vice President, Central Division Manager; Gary
DiFranco, Central District Manager.
Southern Division
Northcreek Place I, 9461 LBJ Freeway, Suite 128-C, Dallas, TX
75243; (214) 669-0602. Joseph W. Kennedy, Vice President, Southern
Division Manager; Julianne McNeel, Southern District Manager.

SONY PICTURES CLASSICS

550 Madison Ave., 8th floor, New York, NY 10022;
(212)833-8833.
CO-PRESIDENTS
Michael Barker
Tom Bernard
Marcie Bloom
VICE PRESIDENT, OPERATIONS
Grace Murphy

TRIUMPH RELEASING CORPORATION

3801 Barham Blvd., 3rd fl., Los Angeles, CA 90068;
(213)882-1177.
PRESIDENT
David Saunders
SENIOR VICE PRESIDENT, OPERATIONS & ADMINISTRATION
Shelly Riney
VICE PRESIDENT, BRANCH ADMINISTRATION
Al Cameron
VICE PRESIDENT, GENERAL SALES MANAGER
Dan Marks
VICE PRESIDENT, FINANCIAL SERVICES
Robert Moulton
VICE PRESIDENT, DOMESTIC DISTRIBUTION OPERATIONS
Conrad K. Steely
DIRECTOR, PRINT OPERATIONS
Michael Jones

Sony Pictures Entertainment Television Group

(A Sony Pictures Entertainment Company)
10202 W. Washington Blvd., Culver City, CA 90232;
(310) 280-8000.
PRESIDENT
Mel Harris
EXECUTIVE VICE PRESIDENT
Andrew J. Kaplan
SENIOR VICE PRESIDENT, PRODUCTION, MULTI-CAMERA
Edward Lammi
SENIOR VICE PRESIDENT, RESEARCH
David Mumford
SENIOR VICE PRESIDENT, PRODUCTION, SINGLE CAMERA
William F. Phillips
VICE PRESIDENT, PUBLICITY
Libby Gill
VICE PRESIDENT, OPERATIONS
Richard Glosser
VICE PRESIDENT, TELEVISION MUSIC
Robert Hunka

COLUMBIA PICTURES TELEVISION

3400 Riverside Dr., Burbank, CA 91505; (818) 972-
7000.
PRESIDENT
Scott Siegler
EXECUTIVE VICE PRESIDENT, BUSINESS AFFAIRS
Don Loughery
EXECUTIVE VICE PRESIDENT, CREATIVE AFFAIRS
Jeff Wachtel
SENIOR VICE PRESIDENT, CURRENT PROGRAMS
Jeanie Bradley
SENIOR VICE PRESIDENT, BUSINESS AFFAIRS
Richard Frankie
SENIOR VICE PRESIDENT, TALENT & CASTING
Rick Jacobs
VICE PRESIDENT, PRODUCTION OPERATIONS
David Holman
SENIOR VICE PRESIDENT, DRAMA
Jeff Kline
VICE PRESIDENT, POST PRODUCTION
Christina Friedgen
VICE PRESIDENT, COMEDY DEVELOPMENT
Michael Hanel
VICE PRESIDENT, COMEDY DEVELOPMENT
Mindy Schultheis
VICE PRESIDENT, BUSINESS AFFAIRS
James Goodman
VICE PRESIDENT, FILM PRODUCTION
John Morrissey
VICE PRESIDENT, RESEARCH
Douglas Roth
VICE PRESIDENT, BUSINESS AFFAIRS
Sander Schwartz
VICE PRESIDENT, TECHNICAL OPERATIONS
Phil Squyres

TRISTAR TELEVISION

9336 West Washington Blvd., Culver City, CA 90232;
(310) 202-1234.
PRESIDENT
Jon Feltheimer
EXECUTIVE VICE PRESIDENT, BUSINESS AFFAIRS
Sandra Stern
EXECUTIVE VICE PRESIDENT, SERIES PROGRAMMING
Eric Tannenbaum
EXECUTIVE VICE PRESIDENT, MOVIES AND MINI-SERIES
Helen Verno
SENIOR VICE PRESIDENT, LEGAL
Mary O'Hare
SENIOR VICE PRESIDENT, BUSINESS AFFAIRS
Debbie Stasson
VICE PRESIDENT, PRODUCTION
Andy House
VICE PRESIDENT, SERIES PROGRAMMING
Helene Michaels
VICE PRESIDENT, BUSINESS AFFAIRS
Bob Chasin
VICE PRESIDENT, MOVIES AND MINI-SERIES
Deborah Service
VICE PRESIDENT, CREATIVE AFFAIRS
Jacqueline Lyons

Spectromedia Entertainment

P.O. Box 2397, Oxnard, CA 93034-2397; (805) 984-
3525. (Motion picture and television production; personal
management; home video sub-distribution, sound stages,
state of the art digital on-line/off-line video editing and
video duplication.)
PRESIDENT
William Byron Hillman
VICE PRESIDENT
Louis Alexander
SECRETARY
Kristy Kay
TREASURER
Los Vallow
ACQUISITIONS
Henry Hiller
CREATIVE CONSULTANT
Jessica Lee

PUBLICITY
Hank Hiller
STILL PHOTOGRAPHY & POST LAYOUTS
Paul Lester
MUSIC PRODUCTION
Jack Goga

Spelling Entertainment Inc.

Wilshire Court, 5700 Wilshire Blvd., 5th floor, Suite 575, Los Angeles, CA 90036; (213) 965-5700; FAX: (213) 965-5895. Organized 1965. (Development and production of all forms of TV programming as well as the production of feature films.)
CHAIRMAN OF THE BOARD & CHIEF EXECUTIVE OFFICER
Aaron Spelling
PRESIDENT & CHIEF EXECUTIVE OFFICER
Russell Goldsmith
VICE CHAIRMAN SPELLING TELEVISION INC.
E. Duke Vincent
SENIOR VICE PRESIDENT & CHIEF FINANCIAL OFFICER
Tom Carson
SENIOR VICE PRESIDENT, BUSINESS & LEGAL AFFAIRS
Peter Bachmann
VICE PRESIDENT & SECRETARY
Renate Kamer
VICE PRESIDENT, BUSINESS AFFAIRS
Barbara Rubin
VICE PRESIDENT, TALENT
Tony Shepherd
SENIOR VICE PRESIDENT DEVELOPMENT SPELLING TELEVISION
Marcia Basichis
VICE PRESIDENT, SPECIAL SERVICES
Keith Nicol
BOARD OF DIRECTORS
Aaron Spelling, Wayne Huizenga, Steve Berrard, Craig Lindner, George Castrucci, John Lawrence, John Muething, Al Martinelli, Ron Lightstone

Star Globe Productions

1901 Avenue of the Stars, Suite 1774, Los Angeles, CA 90067; (310) 553-5541. Organized 1984. (Feature film and video production.)
PRESIDENT
C. K. Hobson
VICE PRESIDENT
Terence Hobson
TREASURER
Jerry Mosley

Strand Releasing

8033 Sunset Blvd., Suite 4002, Los Angeles, CA 90046; Phone & FAX: (213) 937-4500. (Motion picture distribution and production.)
PARTNERS
Jon Gerrans, Marcus Hu, Mike Thomas

Streamline Pictures

2908 Nebraska Ave., Santa Monica, CA 90404; (310) 998-0070; FAX: (310) 998-1145. (Specializes in distribution of animated films.)
PRESIDENT
Carl Macek

Sugar Entertainment

1800 Century Park East, 6th floor, Los Angeles, CA 90067; (310) 843-0936; FAX: (310) 553-9895. Organized 1989. (Foreign sales, marketing and film and TV production.)
CHAIRMAN & CEO
Larry Sugar
EXECUTIVE VICE PRESIDENT
Bonnie Sugar

Tara Releasing

124 Belvedere St., Suite 5, San Rafael, CA 94901; (415) 454-5838; FAX: (415) 454-5977. Organized 1982. (Film marketing and distribution.)
PRESIDENT
Guy Cables
PUBLICTY/MARKETING DIRECTOR
Rama Wiener
AFFILIATIONS
Creative Exposure, Libra Films, Parliment Films.

Taurus Entertainment Co.

113 Middle Neck Rd., Great Neck, NY 11021; (516) 829-1520; FAX: (516) 487-9796. 6671 Sunset Blvd., Suite 1514, Hollywood, CA 90028; (213) 957-1704; FAX: (213) 957-0164.
CHAIRMAN
Stanley G. Dudelson
CEO
James Dudelson
COO
Robert Dudelson
VICE PRESIDENT, BUSINESS AFFAIRS
Tina Pasternak

Taurus Film Co.

8033 Sunset Blvd., Box #93, Los Angeles, CA 90046; (213) 650-5646; FAX: (213) 650-2006. Organized 1964.
DIRECTOR
Michael F. Goldman

Technicolor, Inc.

4050 Lankershim Blvd., North Hollywood, CA 91608; (818) 769-8500; FAX: (818) 769-8186.
CHAIRMAN OF THE BOARD & CHIEF EXECUTIVE OFFICER & PRESIDENT
Thomas E. Epley
SENIOR VICE PRESIDENT & CHIEF FINANCIAL OFFICER
John C. Siciliano
GENERAL COUNSEL & SECRETARY
John H. Oliphant

TECHNICOLOR WORLDWIDE PROFESSIONAL FILM

4050 Lankershim Blvd., N. Hollywood, CA 91608; (818) 769-8500; FAX: (818) 761-4835.
PRESIDENT
Ronald W. Jarvis

TECHNICOLOR, VIDEO SERVICES

3233 East Mission Oaks Blvd., Camarillo, CA 93012; (805) 445-1122.
PRESIDENT
Emmet M. Murphy

Telemated Motion Pictures

137 S.W. 54 St., Cape Coral, FL 33914; (813) 542-9131. (Producer of documentaries, industrial, corporate image, sales promotion, training, public relations and educational films.)
PRODUCER-DIRECTOR
Saul Taffet

Bob Thomas Productions, Inc.

60 E. 42 St., New York, NY 10165; (212) 221-3602. Branch office: 2 Franklin Ct., Montville, NJ 07045 (201)

335-9100. Organized 1968. (Motion picture and television producer.)
PRESIDENT
Robert G. Thomas

Todd-AO Corporation, The

900 & 1021 N. Seward St., Hollywood, CA 90038; (213) 962-4000; 172 Golden Gate Ave., San Francisco, CA 94102; (415) 928-3200; NY: 259 W. 54th St., New York, NY 10019; (212) 265-6225. Organized 1953. (Operator of sound recording studios.)
PRESIDENT
Robert A. Naify
SENIOR EXECUTIVE VICE PRESIDENT
Salah Hassanein
EXECUTIVE VICE PRESIDENT
Buzz Knudson
EXECUTIVE VICE PRESIDENT
J.R. DeLang
CFO & SENIOR VICE PRESIDENT
Ronald Zimmerman
SENIOR VICE PRESIDENT
Chris Jenkins
SECRETARY
Dan R. Malstrom
CONTROLLER
Silas R. Cross

Toho Co., Ltd.

1501 Broadway, Suite 2005, New York, NY 10036; (212) 391-9058; FAX: (212) 840-2823. 2049 Century Park E., Suite 490, Los Angeles, CA 90067; (310) 277-1081; FAX: (310) 277-6351. (Exporters and importers of films & film distribution; theatrical production.)
NEW YORK REPRESENTATIVE
Shozo Watanabe
LOS ANGELES REPRESENTATIVE
Junro Otagawa
Yukio Kotaki

TOHO INTERNATIONAL, INC.

1501 Broadway, Suite 2005, New York, NY 10036.
NEW YORK REPRESENTATIVE
Kazuto Ohira

Touchstone Pictures

(see Walt Disney Company)

Townhouse Films, Inc.

411 E. 53 St., PHC, New York, NY 10022; (212) 838-8113; FAX: (212) 838-1127.
PRESIDENT
Romano Vanderbes
HEAD OF DISTRIBUTION AND FINANCE
John Maddocks
PUBLIC RELATIONS
Patricia Baum
ADMINISTRATIVE ASSISTANT
Stella Kim

TransAtlantic Entertainment

10351 Santa Monica Blvd., Suite 200, Los Angeles, CA 90025; (310) 772-7300; FAX: (310) 772-0610. Organized 1990. (Film and television production and distribution.)
CHAIRMAN OF THE BOARD
Robert M. Bennett
PRESIDENT & CEO
Paul Rich

Transcontinental Pictures Industries

650 N. Bronson Ave., Suite 207, Hollywood, CA 90004; (213) 464-2279; FAX: (213) 464-3212.

CHIEF EXECUTIVE OFFICER
Israel Shaked
PRESIDENT
Gordon Guiry
VICE PRESIDENT, ACQUISITIONS
Robert Kilgore
VICE PRESIDENTS
Brian Hanes
Bruce Hansen

Transvue Pictures Corp.

5131 Colbath Ave., Sherman Oaks, CA 91423; (818) 990-5600. Organized 1970. (World-wide distribution and production of motion pictures.)
PRESIDENT
Herbert B. Schlosberg
VICE PRESIDENT
J. B. Schlosberg
SECRETARY
K. Galloway
TREASURER
Herbert B. Schlosberg
DIRECTOR OF PUBLICITY AND PROMOTION
Sue Madison

TriStar Pictures

(See Sony Pictures Entertainment.)

Triax Entertainment Group, Inc.

1901 Ave. of the Stars, Suite 1551, Los Angeles, CA 90067; (213) 785-9014; FAX: (310) 785-9018. (World-wide distribution of motion pictures.)
PRESIDENT/CEO
David J. Miller
DIRECTOR, SALES & ACQUISITIONS
Bryan Ellenburg
ASSISTANT TO THE PRESIDENT
Lona Chiang
VICE PRESIDENT OF FINANCE/CFO
Steven J. Herskovitz

Tribeca Productions

375 Greenwich St., New York, NY 10013; (212) 941-4040; FAX: (212) 941-4044. Organized 1988. (Feature film production.)
PRESIDENT
Jane Rosenethal
AFFILIATION
TriStar Pictures

Trident Releasing

8401 Melrose Pl. 2nd Floor, Los Angeles, CA 90069; (213) 655-8818. Organized 1988. (Sales agents for international motion pictures, television and financiers.)
PRESIDENTS
Jean Ovrum, Victoria Plummer

Trimark Pictures

(a division of Traimark Holdings, Inc.) 2644 30th St., Santa Monica, CA 90405; (310) 314-2000; FAX: (310) 392-0252. (Motion picture producer and distributor).
CHAIRMAN
Mark Amin
PRESIDENT, CEO
Roger Burlage
EXECUTIVE VICE PRESIDENT
Sam Pirnazar
SENIOR VICE PRESIDENT
Barry Barnholtz

SENIOR VICE PRESIDENT, INTERNATIONAL SALES
Sergio Aguero
SENIOR VICE PRESIDENT, DOMESTIC DISTRIBUTION
Tim Swain
SENIOR VICE PRESIDENT, TRIMARK TELEVISION
Armando Nunez
EXECUTIVE OF TRIMARK INTERACTIVE
Kelly Flock
VICE PRESIDENT, MARKETING
Gina Draklich
VICE PRESIDENT, PUBLICITY
David Bowers
VICE PRESIDENT, DOMESTIC VIDEO
Terry Siebert

Triton Pictures

9000 Sunset Blvd., Suite 711, Los Angeles, CA 90069; (310) 275-7779; FAX: (310) 275-7334.
PRESIDENT & CEO
Jonathan Dana
SENIOR VICE PRESIDENT, MARKETING & DISTRIBUTION
Robert Berney
EXECUTIVE VICE PRESIDENT
Jeff Ivers
SENIOR VICE PRESIDENT, ACQUISITIONS & DEVELOPMENT
Robert Rock

Triumph Releasing Corporation

(See entry under Sony Pictures Entertainment, Inc.)

Troma, Inc.

733 Ninth Ave., New York, NY 10019; (212) 757-4555. Organized 1974. (Producer and distributor.)
PRESIDENT
Lloyd Kaufman
VICE PRESIDENT
Michael Herz
DIRECTOR OF THEATRICAL DISTRIBUTION
Carl Morano
DIRECTOR OF ANCILLARY SALES, WORLDWIDE
Jeffrey Sass
DIRECTOR OF BUSINESS AFFAIRS
David Greenspan
DIRECTOR OF MARKETING
Steve Gaul
DIRECTOR OF INTERNATIONAL SALES
Carl Morano
DIRECTOR OF FILM ACQUISITIONS
Maris Herz
FILM AND PRODUCT EVALUATOR
Pat Kaufman
COMPTROLLER
Maria Fridmanovich
FINANCIAL
Ira Kanarick and Gary Moscowitz
LEGAL
Stanley L. Kaufman, Roger Kirby

Twentieth Century Fox Film Corporation

(see Fox, Inc.)

21st Century Film Corporation

11080 W. Olympic Blvd., Los Angeles, CA 90064; (310) 914-0500; (310) 479-0882. Organized 1989. (Foreign motion picture distribution.)
CHAIRMAN OF THE BOARD & CHIEF EXECUTIVE OFFICER
Menahem Golan
PRESIDENT
Ami Artzi
BOARD OF DIRECTORS
Menahem Golan, Ami Artzi

UPA Pictures, Inc.

14101 Valleyheart Dr. 200, Sherman Oaks, CA 91423, (818) 990-3800; FAX: (818) 990-4854. Incorporated 1945.

PRESIDENT
Henry G. Saperstein

United Artists Pictures

(see Metro-Goldwin-Mayer Inc.)

United Film Enterprises, Inc.

120 W. Park Ave., Suite 3-F, Long Beach, NY 11561; (516) 431-2687. FAX: (516) 431-2805. (Representing major motion picture and television producers, studios and export companies. Also, acting as purchasing agent for motion picture distributors in various countries.)
PRESIDENT
Munio Podhorzer
VICE PRESIDENT, SECRETARY & TREASURER
Nathan Podhorzer

United International Pictures

(A subsidiary of United International Pictures B.V., Postbus 9255, 1006 AG Amsterdam, The Netherlands) UIP House, 45 Beadon Rd., Hammersmith, London W6 0EG, England; (081) 741-9041. Telex 8956521. FAX: (081) 748-8990.
PRESIDENT & CHIEF EXECUTIVE OFFICER
Michael Williams-Jones
SENIOR VICE PRESIDENT MARKETING
Hy Smith
SENIOR VICE PRESIDENT FINANCE & ADMINISTRATION
Peter Charles
SENIOR VICE PRESIDENT GENERAL COUNSEL
Brian Reilly
VICE PRESIDENT INTERNATIONAL PUBLICITY
Anne Bennett
VICE PRESIDENT ADVERTISING
Gina Stroud
VICE PRESIDENT INTERNATIONAL SALES—SPECIAL MARKETS
Michael Macclesfiled
VICE PRESIDENT, EUROPE
Tony Themistocleous
VICE PRESIDENT INTERNATIONAL SALES
Andrew Cripps
VICE PRESIDENT SALES—LATIN AMERICA
Michael Murphy
PRESIDENT UIP PAY-TV GROUP
Drew Kaza

HISTORY: United International Pictures B.V., a Dutch company, was formed in 1981, for the purpose of distributing internationally feature motion pictures produced and/or acquired by MGM-UA, Paramount Pictures and Universal and is wholly owned by affiliates of those companies. The Motion Picture Group has assumed, with limited exception, the theatrical/non-theatrical distribution activities previously conducted by Cinema International Corporation N.V. and United Artists Corporation. The Pay-TV Group, formed in 1983, is responsible for the planning and coordination of the three producers' foreign pay television activities.

Universal Pictures

(A division of Universal City Studios, Inc., Subsidiary of MCA, Inc.)
445 Park Ave., New York, NY 10022; (212) 759-7500. 100 Universal City Plaza, Universal City, CA 91608; (818) 777-1000; FAX: (818) 777-6280. Cable: Unifilman. (Producer and distributor.)
(See separate section for corporate history.)
CHAIRMAN, MCA MOTION PICTURE GROUP
Thomas Pollock
SENIOR VICE PRESIDENT, MCA MOTION PICTURE GROUP
Joseph A. Fischer
SENIOR VICE PRESIDENT, MCA MOTION PICTURE GROUP
Fred Bernstein
VICE PRESIDENT, MCA MOTION PICTURE GROUP
Ann Busby
VICE PRESIDENT, FINANCE
James Burk

SENIOR VICE PRESIDENT LEGAL & BUSINESS AFFAIRS
  Jon Gumpert
VICE PRESIDENT, BUSINESS AFFAIRS
  Gerald Barton

UNIVERSAL PICTURES PRODUCTION

PRESIDENT
  Casey Silver
SENIOR VICE PRESIDENT, PRODUCTION & POST
PRODUCTION
  Donna Smith
SENIOR VICE PRESIDENT, PRODUCTION
  Thomas W. Craig
EXECUTIVE VICE PRESIDENT, PRODUCTION
  Hal Lieberman

UNIVERSAL PICTURES MARKETING

SENIOR VICE PRESIDENT, MARKETING
  Perry Katz
SENIOR VICE PRESIDENT, MARKETING, NATIONAL
PUBLICITY & PROMOTION
  Bruce Feldman
SENIOR VICE PRESIDENT, PUBLICITY, PROMOTION &
MARKETING
  Anthony Evergates-Price
VICE PRESIDENT, MEDIA AND CO-OP ADVERTISING
  Vic Fondrk
VICE PRESIDENT, NATIONAL PROMOTION & FIELD
OPERATIONS
  John Polwrek
VICE PRESIDENT, PUBLICITY & PROMOTION/SPECIAL
PROJECTS
  Daniel Wheatcroft
VICE PRESIDENT, PLANNING & FINANCE
  Charlotte Reith
VICE PRESIDENT, NATIONAL PUBLICITY
  Alan Sutton

UNIVERSAL PICTURES DISTRIBUTION

PRESIDENT
  Fred Mound
SENIOR VICE PRESIDENT DISTRIBUTION/MARKETING
LIASION
  Nikki Rocco
VICE PRESIDENT & DIVISIONAL MANAGER
  Dave Richoux
VICE PRESIDENT & DIVISIONAL MANAGER
  Jack Finn
VICE PRESIDENT, DIVISIONAL MANAGER
  Nicholas C. Carpou
VICE PRESIDENT, DIVISIONAL MANAGER
  Mark T. Gaines
VICE PRESIDENT/GENERAL MANAGER—UNIVERSAL FILMS
CANADA
  Eugene Amodeo
NEW YORK METROPOLITAN DISTRICT MANAGER
  Albert Quaedvlieg
VICE PRESIDENT BRANCH OPERATIONS MANAGER
  Joe Sackatile
MANAGER PRINT CONTROL
  Harold Goldberg
DIRECTOR, EXHIBITOR RELATIONS
  Steve Ellman
MANAGER, CONTRACT PLAYDATE DEPARTMENT
  Ben Grant

DIVISION MANAGERS AND BRANCHES

Nicholas Carpou: 100 Universal City Plaza, Universal City, CA 91608,
(818) 777-4266; (Albany, Buffalo, Cincinnati, Salt Lake City, Denver).
Jack Finn: 8901 Beverly Blvd., Los Angeles, CA 90048; (213) 550-7461.
(Los Angeles, Portland, Seattle, Philadelphia, Washington, D.C., Boston,
New Haven, Puerto Rico). Mark Gaines: P.O. Box 5000, 6060 Mc-
Donough Dr., Norcross, GA 30091-5000; (404) 448-8032. (Atlanta,
Charlotte, Jacksonville, Dallas, Kansas City, Memphis, New Orleans,
Oklahoma City). Albert Quaedvlieg: 445 Park Avenue, New York, NY
10022, (212) 605-2826; (New York, Pittsburgh). Dave Richoux: P.O. Box
8622, 618 Lamont Rd., Elmhurst, IL 60126; (708) 279-9200. (Chicago,
Cleveland, Des Moines, Omaha, Detroit, Indianapolis, Milwaukee, Min-
neapolis, St. Louis, San Francisco.)

UNIVERSAL TELEVISION

(A division of Universal City Studios) 100 Universal City
Plaza, Universal City Studios, Universal City, CA 91608;
(818) 777-1000. (Producer of TV films.)
PRESIDENT
  Tom Thayer
EXECUTIVE VICE PRESIDENT, ADMINISTRATION - MCA
TELEVISION GROUP
  Ed Masket
EXECUTIVE VICE PRESIDENT IN CHARGE OF PRODUCTION
  Earl Bellamy
EXECUTIVE VICE PRESIDENT, CREATIVE AFFAIRS
  Ned Nalle
VICE PRESIDENT, CURRENT PROGRAMMING
  Peter Jankowski
SENIOR VICE PRESIDENT, DRAMATIC DEVELOPMENT
  Dan Filie
VICE PRESIDENT, TV CASTING
  Nancy McLeod-Perkins
SENIOR VICE PRESIDENT, PUBLICITY, PROMOTION &
ADVERTISING
  Robert Crutchfield

Valentino, Thomas J., Inc.

500 Executive Blvd., P.O. Box 534, Elmsford, New York,
NY 10523-0534; (212) 869-5210. (Sound effects, theatri-
cal and industrial film production music and audio casette
duplication.)
PRESIDENT
  Thomas J. Valentino, Jr.

Valiant International Pictures

4774 Melrose Ave., Hollywood, CA 90029; (213) 665-
5257; FAX: (213) 665-6473. (Production and distribution.)
PRESIDENT
  Harry Novak
VICE PRESIDENT
  Ivan Levitan
SECRETARY TREASURER
  Carmen Novak
SALES-MARKETING
  Ashley Schneider

Vanguard Films

135 E. 65 St., 4th Floor, New York, NY 10021; (212)
517-4333; FAX: (212) 734-3609. Organized 1981, as The
Program Development Co. Inc. (Television and film pro-
duction.)
PRESIDENT
  John H. Williams

Ventura Entertainment Group Ltd.

9150 Wilshire Blvd., #205, Beverly Hills, CA 90212;
(310) 285-0400. Organized 1988. (Television, motion pic-
ture, and commercial production.)
CHAIRMAN OF BOARD
  Harvey Bibicoff
EXECUTIVE VICE PRESIDENT
  Jonathan Axelrod

Veritas Productions, Inc.

New York City, (212) 765-4240 or 1 Laurie Dr., Englewood Cliffs, NJ 07632; (201) 568-4214; FAX: (201) 568-
4240. (Production of motion pictures for theatres and TV.)
PRESIDENT
  Richard S. Dubelman

Vidmark Entertainment

2901 Ocean Park Blvd., Suite 123, Santa Monica, CA
90405; (310) 399-8877; FAX: (310) 399-3828. Organized

1984. (Domestic and international video and theatrical distributors.)
CHAIRMAN
Mark Amin
EXECUTIVE VICE PRESIDENT
Sam Pirnazar
SENIOR VICE PRESIDENT
Barry Barnholtz
VICE PRESIDENT, INTERNATIONAL DIVISION
Penny Karlin
VICE PRESIDENT, SALES & MARKETING
Robert Wittenberg
DIRECTOR OF MARKETING
Gina Draklich
MANAGER OF ACQUISITIONS
David Tripet
BOARD OF DIRECTORS
Johan Wassenaar, Mark Amin, Barry Barnholtz, Sam Pirnazar, Roger Burlige

Vision International

3330 W. Cahuenga Blvd. 400, Los Angeles, CA 90068; (213) 969-2900; FAX: (213) 851-7212. (Subsidiary of Epic Productions, foreign sales.)
CHAIRMAN
Mark Damon
PRESIDENT
Etchie Stroh

Warner Bros. Inc.

(A subsidiary of Time Warner, Inc.) 75 Rockefeller Plaza, New York, NY 10019; (212) 484-8000; 640 Fifth Ave., New York, NY 10019; (212) 903-5500; 4000 Warner Blvd., Burbank, CA 91522; (818) 954-6000.
(See separate section for corporate history.)
CHAIRMAN OF THE BOARD AND CHIEF EXECUTIVE OFFICER
Robert A. Daly
PRESIDENT & CHIEF OPERATING OFFICER
Terry Semel
EXECUTIVE VICE PRESIDENT
Barry M. Meyer
EXECUTIVE VICE PRESIDENT, BUSINESS & ACQUISITIONS
James R. Miller
EXECUTIVE VICE PRESIDENT, MARKETING & PLANNING
Sanford E. Reisenbach
EXECUTIVE VICE PRESIDENT, CORPORATE PROJECTS
Charles D. McGregor
EXECUTIVE VICE PRESIDENT & TREASURER
Ralph Peterson
EXECUTIVE VICE PRESIDENT & GENERAL COUNSEL
John Schulman
SENIOR VICE PRESIDENT, TV PUBLICITY, PROMOTION & PUBLIC RELATIONS
Barbara S. Brogliatti

PRODUCTION

PRESIDENT, THEATRICAL PRODUCTION
Bruce Berman
EXECUTIVE VICE PRESIDENT, PRODUCTION
Lucy Fisher
EXECUTIVE VICE PRESIDENT, PRODUCTION
Lisa Henson
SENIOR VICE PRESIDENT, PRODUCTION
Bill Gerber
SENIOR VICE PRESIDENT, PRODUCTION
Lance Young
SENIOR VICE PRESIDENT, PRODUCTION
William Young
VICE PRESIDENT, PRODUCTION
Robert Guralnick
VICE PRESIDENT, PRODUCTION
Diana Rathburn
VICE PRESIDENT, PRODUCTION
Bob Brassel
VICE PRESIDENT, PRODUCTION
Tom Lassally
VICE PRESIDENT, CREATIVE AFFAIRS
Lorenzo Di Bonaventura

VICE PRESIDENT, CREATIVE AFFAIRS
Courtney Valenti
EXECUTIVE PRODUCTION MANAGER
Tom Joyner
EXECUTIVE PRODUCTION MANAGER
Kurt Neuwman
EXECUTIVE PRODUCTION MANAGER
Dirk Petersmann
EXECUTIVE PRODUCTION MANAGER
Phil Rawlins
SENIOR VICE PRESIDENT, TELEVISION PRODUCTION
Steve J. Papazian
VICE PRESIDENT, CREATIVE AFFAIRS, EAST COAST
Susan Dalsimer
STORY EDITOR
John Schimel
STORY SUPERVISOR
Diane Bellis
VICE PRESIDENT, TALENT
Marion Dougherty
VICE PRESIDENT, WORLDWIDE ACQUISITIONS
Mitch Horwits
VICE PRESIDENT, FILM ACQUISITION
Diane Maddox
VICE PRESIDENT, POST PRODUCTION
Fred Talmage
VICE PRESIDENT, FEATURE ESTIMATING
Amy Rabins

ADVERTISING & PUBLICITY

PRESIDENT, WORLDWIDE THEATRICAL ADVERTISING & PUBLICITY
Robert G. Friedman
SENIOR VICE PRESIDENT, WORLDWIDE CREATIVE ADVERTISING
Joel Wayne
SENIOR VICE PRESIDENT, SPECIAL PROJECTS
Joe Hyams
VICE PRESIDENT, MEDIA
John Jacobs
SENIOR VICE PRESIDENT, WORLDWIDE MARKET RESEARCH
Richard Del Belso
VICE PRESIDENT, CREATIVE ADVERTISING
Michael Smith
VICE PRESIDENT, PUBLICITY & PROMOTION
Charlotte Kandel
VICE PRESIDENT & ASSISTANT TO THE PRESIDENT, WORLDWIDE ADVERTISING & PUBLICITY SERVICES
Lori Drazen
VICE PRESIDENT, PUBLICITY
John Dartigue
VICE PRESIDENT, PUBLICITY
Dawn McElwaine
VICE PRESIDENT, NATIONAL PUBLICITY
Carl Samrock
VICE PRESIDENT, NATIONAL FIELD ACTIVITIES
Stuart Gottesman
VICE PRESIDENT OF CO-OPERATIVE ADVERTISING
Richard Kallet
DIRECTOR OF NATIONAL PROMOTION
Lynn Smith
SOUTHWEST PROMOTION AND SPECIAL EVENTS DIRECTOR
Ernie Grossman
DIRECTOR OF MEDIA
Sandra Finkel
DIRECTOR OF ADMINISTRATION, WORLDWIDE ADVERTISING AND PUBLICITY
Dennis Tange
DIRECTOR OF GRAPHIC ARTS
Kirk Freeman
DIRECTOR OF MEDIA CONTRACTS AND CONTROL
Louise Hays
VICE PRESIDENT, MARKETING RESEARCH
Daniel P. Rosen
VICE PRESIDENT, EAST COAST ADVERTISING & PUBLICITY
Don Buckley
EAST COAST PUBLICITY DIRECTOR
Mark Reina
DIRECTOR, MARKETING RESEARCH
Barbara Gross
DIRECTOR, WORLDWIDE ADVERTISING AND PUBLICITY SERVICES
Elizabeth Maffei

DIRECTOR, WORLDWIDE ADVERTISING & PUBLICITY
SERVICES
Patricia Tange
MANAGER, FILM & TAPE, T.V. ADVERTISING & PUBLICITY
SERVICES
Bruce Szeles
MANAGER, WORLDWIDE ADVERTISING AND PUBLICITY
SERVICES
Christine Cunningham
MANAGER, WORLDWIDE ADVERTISING & PUBLICITY
SERVICES
Francine Rudin
MANAGER, WEST COAST PUBLICITY
Vivian Boyer
MANAGER OF PROMOTION
Mary Murphy
RADIO AND TV PUBLICITY
Bob Frederick
DIRECTOR, PUBLICITY
Nancy Kirkpatrick
PHOTO EDITOR
Jess M. Garcia
STAFF PUBLICISTS
Diane Sponsler
Diane Gursky
Stacy Ivers
Kathleen Eichen
Ron Chan
Dennise Stires
Valerie Scott
Catherine Ortiz
STAFF PUBLICIST, INTERNATIONAL
Helen Rhodes
EAST COAST SENIOR PUBLICIST
Sandy Thompson
EAST COAST SENIOR PUBLICIST
Willa Clinton
PUBLICIST
Catherine Ortiz

DISTRIBUTION (Domestic)
PRESIDENT, DOMESTIC THEATRICAL DISTRIBUTION
D. Barry Reardon
SENIOR VICE PRESIDENT, GENERAL SALES MANAGER
Daniel R. Fellman
VICE PRESIDENT, BRANCH OPERATIONS
Howard Welinsky
VICE PRESIDENT, SALES OPERATIONS
Don Tannenbaum
VICE PRESIDENT, SALES OPERATIONS
Richard A. Schiff
VICE PRESIDENT OF PRINT CONTROL
Nancy Sams
DIRECTOR OF NON-THEATRICAL SALES
Bill Grant

DOMESTIC BRANCHES AND MANAGERS

ATLANTA: 30345-3127—2200 Century Pkwy., N.E., 780, Barry Nelson
BOSTON: 02184-1763—45 Braintree Hill Office Park 301, Andrew Silverman
CHICAGO: 60018-5899—1111 E. Touhy Ave., 440, Des Plaines, IL. Sam Rosenfeld
DALLAS: 75231-4316—8144 Walnut Hill Lane 920, Jackie Stanley
NEW YORK: 10019-6908—75 Rockefeller Plaza 14, Charles Barcellona
LOS ANGELES: 91436-2915—15821 Ventura Blvd., 685, Encino, Shirley Becker
WASHINGTON, DC: 20852-1631—1700 Rockville Pike 545, Rockville, MD, Daniel Chinich

INTERNATIONAL DISTRIBUTION
PRESIDENT, INTERNATIONAL SALES
Wayne Duband
EXECUTIVE VICE PRESIDENT, INTERNATIONAL THEATRICAL
DIVISION
Richard J. Fox
VICE PRESIDENT, INTERNATIONAL ADVERTISING AND
PUBLICITY
Rick Markovitz
VICE PRESIDENT, ADMINISTRATION
Peter Howard

VICE PRESIDENT AND SUPERVISOR, EUROPE, MIDDLE EAST
AND AFRICA
Frank Pierce
VICE PRESIDENT AND SUPERVISOR, LATIN AMERICAN
REGION
Redo Farah
VICE PRESIDENT, EUROPEAN ADVERTISING & PUBLICITY
Julian Senior
VICE PRESIDENT, BUSINESS AFFAIRS
Eric Senat
DIRECTOR, INTERNATIONAL PUBLICITY
Juliana Olinka
DIRECTOR OF ADVERTISING AND PUBLICITY, FAR EAST
Joyce Simpson
DIRECTOR, INTERNATIONAL ADVERTISING & PUBLICITY
Margarita Talleda
SENIOR VICE PRESIDENT, INTERNATIONAL THEATRICAL
DISTRIBUTION
Edward E. Frumkes
DIRECTOR OF ADMINISTRATION
Tony Dambriunas
MANAGER, INTERNATIONAL ADVERTISING & PUBLICITY
BUDGETING
Yolanda Exparza
STAFF PUBLICIST
Margie Matteson

INTERNATIONAL OFFICES, DISTRIBUTORS AND MANAGERS

Argentina
Joseph Ambar, Warner rep.; Vicente Vigo, gen. mgr., Dardo Ferrari, ad/pub mgr.
Tucuman 1938. *Buenos Aires 1051*; Tel.: 54 145 60947; FAX: 54 1 953 7678.

Australia
VILLAGE ROADSHOW CORP. LTD. D. Graham Burke, managing director; Alan Finney, gen. mgr.
206 Bourke St., *Melbourne VIC 3000*; Tel.: 61 3 667 6666; FAX: 61 3 663 1972; Telex: AA 32502.

Austria
WARNER BROS FILMVERLEIH 6ES, M.B.H. Rudolph Prochazka, gen. mgr.
Zieglergasse 10., *Vienna 1070*; Tel.: 43 222 932254; FAX: 43 222 939462; Telex: 132943 WACO A.

Belgium
WARNER BROS., Bruno Mertens, gen. mgr., John Delville, adv. mgr.
Boulevard Lambermont 440, *Brussels, 1030*; Tel.: 32 2 242 5894; FAX: 32 2 245 1709; Telex: TBA.

Bolivia
Licnio Manay, managing dir., Avenida Montes 768. 4er. Piso, Edificio de col, La Paz; Tel.: 591 2 320244; Telex: 2650.

Brazil
WARNER BROS. (SOUTH) INC., Albert S. Salem, mgr., Frederico Schiffer, ad/pub mgr.
Rua Senador Dantas, 19, 10 Andar, 20031 Rio de Janeiro, RJ: Tel.: 55 21 262 9002; FAX: 55 21 262 0195; Telex: 2123232.

Chile
Arthur Ehrlich, manager.
Huerfanos 786, Oficina 210, Santigo, Tel.: 56 2 332 503; FAX: 56 2 397 921; Telex: 340665 FCSTGO CK.

Colombia
JOSEPH & CIA REPRESENTACIONES ELEPHANT S. EN.C. Jaime Joseph, president.
Calle 96 No. 12-10, Bogota; Tel.: 57 1 610 2041; FAX: 57 1 610 2020;.

Denmark
WARNER BROS. (D) A/S WARNER & METRONOME FILM ApS, Susan Schyberg, manager; Lis Lund, pub. mgr.
Sondermarksvej 16, DK 2500 Copenhagen/Valby; Tel.: 45 31 46 8822; FAX: 45 3144 0604: Telex: 19497.

Finland
WARNER BROS. (FINLAND) OY, Aune Turja, Manager, Elisa Tornquist, pub. mgr.
Lastenkodinkija 1, 00180 Helsinki 10; Tel.: 358 0 694 0522; FAX: 358 0 694 1259; Telex: 122530.

France
WARNER BROS. (TRANSATLANTIC). INC. Steve Rubin, director; Sybill Mellion, ad/pub. mgr.

80, Avenue D'Iena 75116 Paris; Tel.: 33 1 4723 0700; FAX: 33 1 4070 9156; Telex: 640103 F.

Germany

WARNER BROS. FILM GmbH. Kurt Silberschneider, general manager; Klaus Dahm, pub. dir.
Rosenheimerstrasse 143B, 8000 Munich 80; Tel.: 49 89 418 0090; FAX: 49 89 418 00945; Telex: 5213749.

Greece

VICTOR G. MICHAELIDES A.E. CO, George Michaelides, managing dir.
96 Akadimias Street, GR 10677 Athens; Tel.: 30 1 362 3801; FAX: 30 1 360 3611; Telex: 215083.

Holland

WARNER BROS. (HOLLAND) Jean Heijl, managing dir.; San Fu Malta pub. mgr.
1803 DeBoelelaan 16 3H, 1083 HJ Amsterdam; Tel.: 31 20 464 766; FAX: 3120 449 001; Telex: 10685.

Hong Kong

WARNER BROS. (FAR EAST) INC. Hayward Pan, gen. mgr.
Siberian Fur Bldg., 8th Floor; 38–40 Haiphong Rd., Tsimshatsui, Kowloon; Tel.: 852 3739 39635; FAX: 852 3 723 3002; Telex: 31819.

India

WARNER BROS. (F.E.), INC. Lance Colamco, Mgr, director.
Eros Cinema Bldg., 42 M. Karve Rd., Bombay 400020 Tel.: 91 22 222 083; Telex: 113194.

Israel

E. GILAD & CO. (Distributor), Ephraim Gilad, manager.
Hayarden St. 11, Hayarden St. No 11, Tel Aviv 63905; Tel.: 972 3 659 191, Telex: 34180.

Italy

WARNER BROS. ITALIA S.p.A., Bernhard Weinreich, gen. mgr.
Via Varese, 16/B, 00185 Rome; Tel.: 39 6 493 191; FAX: 39 6 675 1022; Telex: 622421.

Jamaica

RUSSGRAM INVESTMENTS LTD., (Distributor), A. Russell Graham.
1A South Camp Rd., Kingston; Tel.: 809 928 1240. Telex: 2188.

Japan

WARNER BROS. (JAPAN), INC. William Ireton, managing dir.; Shoji Sato, dir. of marketing.
2-4 Kyobashi 3-chome, Chuo-ku, *Tokyo*; Tel.: 81 3 281 4531; FAX: 81 3281 4537; Telex: j 26670.

Lebanon

JOSEPH CHACRA & SONS. (Warner distributor), Joseph Chacra.
Antranik Kazandjian Bldg., Horch Tabet-Kamille Shamoune St., Sin El-Fil; Tel.: 495 745; Telex: 446 90.

Mexico

WARNER BROS. (MEXICO), Jean Pierre Leleu, Warner representative.
%Indiefilms, S.A. de C.V., Roberto Gayol #51, Col. del Ville 03100, Tel.: 905 575 0782; FAX: 905 575 0782; Telex: 1764407.

New Zealand

WARNER BROS. (N.Z.) LTD. John Steedman, managing dir., Peter Downer, pub. dir.
56 Hopetown St., 8th Floor, Aucleland; Tel.: 64 9 775 223; FAX: 64 9 392 795; Telex: 2618.

Norway

WARNER BROS. (NORWAY) A/S Jon Narvestad, general mgr., Lillemor Korsell, pub. mgr.
Oscargate 55, 0258 Oslo 2; Tel.: 47 2 43 1800; FAX: 47 2 55 4683; Telex: 78356 WARBROS.

Panama

WARNER BROS. (SOUTH), INC., Miquel Joseph, manager.
Calle 45-10 Bella Vista. Panama City; Tel.: 507 64 2606; FAX: 507 63 7512; Telex: 3129.

Peru

WARNER BROS. (SOUTH), INC. Anibal Codebo, general manager.
Nicolas de Pierola #938, Lima 1, Tel.: 51 14 277 131; Telex: 25201 or 20338.

Philippines

WARNER BROS. (F.E.), INC., Lucas Pasiliao, general manager.
PPL Bldg., Room 311, 1000 United Nations Ave., Central P.O. Box 2489, Metro Manila 2801; Tel.: 63 2 596 991; FAX: 63 2 586 215; Telex: 27491, or 65071.

Portugal

Ricardo Avila, general mgr.
Avenida Duque de Loule, 90-3 Esq. Lisbon 1000; Tel.: 3511 557 795; FAX: 351 1 575 389; Telex: 13047.

Puerto Rico

WARNER BROS. (SOUTH), R. Lopez de Pedro, manager.
Wometco Bldg., Ponce de Leon Ave., 1606 Stop 23, Santurce 00909; Tel. 809 725 5795; FAX: 809 725 7275; Telex: 0351.

Singapore

WARNER BROS. (F.E.), INC. Michael Huang, general mgr.
112, Middle Rd. 04-02, ʻMidland House, Sinapore 0718; Tel.: 65 337 5060; FAX: 65 339 1709, Telex: 22151.

South Africa

%United International Picture, Castrol House, 7 Junction Ave., Parktown, 2193 Johannesburg; Tel.: 27 11 725 4980; FAX: 2711 484 3339; Telex: 422868. (Distribution), Peter Dignan, managing dir.; Helena Nossel, pub. dir.
Johannesburg—160 Main St.

Spain

WARNER ESPANOLA, S.A. (Distribution), Ed Weinberg, Warner Rep.; Juan Falceto, pub. mgr.
Manuel Montilla 1, 28016 Madrid; Tel.: 34 1 250 6200; FAX 34 1 457 8874; Telex: 43888.

Sweden

WARNER BROS. SWEDEN AB. Rolf Eriksson, general mgr.; Peter Jansson, publicity mgr.
Hornsbruksgatan 19, 3rd floor, S-117 34 (Stockholm), Tel.: 46 8 58 6482; Telex: 11163 UNIPAC.

Switzerland

Hans-Ueli Hasler, managing dir.; Michel Hangartner, project mgr.
Nuschelerstrasse 31, 8001 Zurich, Tel.: 41 1221 3633 FAX: 41 1 211 0 689; Telex: 812480.

Taiwan

WARNER BROS. (F.E.), INC. Kimball P. Liang, Manager.
24 Kai Fang St., Section 2, 3rd Floor, Taipei, 10011, Tel.: 886 2 311 3238; FAX: 886 2311 8526; Telex: 12584.

Thailand

WARNER BROS. (F.E.), INC. Philip Lau, manager.
315 Silom Rd., Bangkok 10500; Tel.: 66 2 33 30920; FAX: 66 2 23 64834; Telex: 82857 FOXWB.

Trinidad

U.I.P. CORP. (Distributor), Mausley Ellis, managing director.
Film Center, St. James, *Port of Spain*; Tel.: 809 62 24671, FAX: 809 62 22517.

United Kingdom

Maj-Britt Kirchner, managing dir.; Frank Sagnier, dir. of ad/pub.
135 Wardour St., London WIV 4AP; Tel.: 44 1 734 8400; FAX: 44 1 437 5521; Telex: 8955617 or 22653.

Uruguay

HORACIO HERMIDA LIMITADA, Horacio Hermida, manager.
Soriance 1263. *Montevideo*; Tel.: 598-2 903044; Telex: 22364.

Venezuela

%DIFOX (Distributor), Augusto Bogni Warner Rep.
Avenida Las Palmas, Edificio Teatro Las Palmas, 4 Piso, Caracas. 1050; Tel.: 58 2 781 7586; FAX: 58 2 782 5087; Telex: 21233.

ADMINISTRATION

SENIOR VICE PRESIDENT, CORPORATE CONTROLLER
Ed Romano
SENIOR VICE PRESIDENT, INDUSTRIAL RELATIONS
Alan H. Raphael
SENIOR VICE PRESIDENT, HUMAN RESOURCES
Adrienne J. Gary
VICE PRESIDENT, LABOR RELATIONS
J. R. Ballance
DIRECTOR, LABOR RELATIONS
Julie Yanow
VICE PRESIDENT, STRATEGIC PLANNING
Steven R. Koltai
PRESIDENT, CONSUMER PRODUCTS
Dan Romanelli
PRESIDENT, WORLDWIDE RETAIL
Peter Starrett

VICE PRESIDENT, CASTING ADMINISTRATION
  Pat Hopkins
VICE PRESIDENT, CREDIT & TITLE ADMINISTRATION
  Norma Fuss

THEATRICAL LEGAL

VICE PRESIDENT & GENERAL COUNSEL, THEATRICAL
LEGAL
  Jeremy Williams
VICE PRESIDENT/DEP. GEN. COUNSEL, THEATRICAL LEGAL
  Sheldon Presser
VICE PRESIDENT, DEPUTY GENERAL COUNSEL
  Mary Ledding
SENIOR THEATRICAL COUNSEL
  Sherri Ralph
SENIOR VICE PRESIDENT, SPECIAL PROJECTS
  Stephen Ross
ASSOCIATE GENERAL COUNSEL
  Donna Josephson
ATTORNEY
  Pamela Kirsh
VICE PRESIDENT, THEATRICAL LEGAL
  Jack Sattinger
SENIOR MOTION PICTURE COUNSEL
  Marshall Silverman
ATTORNEYS
  David Read
  Alex Alben
  Judith Merians
VICE PRESIDENT, ANTI-PIRACY
  Molly Kellogg
VICE PRESIDENT, EAST COAST COUNSEL
  Stephen R. Langenthal
DIRECTOR OF LEGAL AFFAIRS–THEATRICAL
  Michele Moore

BUSINESS AFFAIRS

SENIOR VICE PRESIDENT, THEATRICAL BUSINESS AFFAIRS
  Steven S. Spira
VICE PRESIDENT, BUSINESS AFFAIRS
  Dan Furie
VICE PRESIDENT, BUSINESS AFFAIRS
  Patti Connolly
VICE PRESIDENT, BUSINESS AFFAIRS
  Virginia Tweedy

MUSIC

PRESIDENT, MUSIC
  Gary Le Mel
VICE PRESIDENT, MUSIC ADMINISTRATION
  Bill Schrank
VICE PRESIDENT, BUSINESS AFFAIRS, MUSIC
  Keith Zajic
VICE PRESIDENT, MUSIC
  Doug Frank
DIRECTOR OF MUSIC ADMINISTRATION
  Richard C. Harris

CORPORATE FILM VIDEO SERVICES

VICE PRESIDENT, CORPORATE FILM VIDEO SERVICES
  William J. Sullivan
VICE PRESIDENT OPERATIONS, CORPORATE FILM/VIDEO
SERVICES
  Peter R. Gardiner
DIRECTOR OF FILM OPERATIONS AND ASSET MANAGEMENT
  Pamela Tarrabe

ADMINISTRATIVE SERVICES

VICE PRESIDENT, ADMINISTRATIVE SERVICES
  Sebastian Pasqua

ACCOUNTING

VICE PRESIDENT & ASST. CORPORATE
  Michael Goodnight
VICE PRESIDENT, PARTICIPATIONS AND RESIDUALS
  Michael G. Edwards
VICE PRESIDENT AND ASSISTANT CORPORATE CONTROLLER
  Taylor E. Metters
VICE PRESIDENT, FINANCIAL INVESTMENTS
  Robert Fisher

ASSISTANT TREASURER
  Henry Cole
VICE PRESIDENT, PRODUCTION ACCOUNTING
  Lawrence W. Schneider
VICE PRESIDENT, CORPORATE ACCOUNTING
  Joseph Friscia
VICE PRESIDENT TAXES
  John Therrien
DIRECTOR, AUDIT AND ADVISORY SERVICES
  Mike Kory
PAYROLL MANAGER
  Phillip T. Dunne
TV CREDIT COLLECTION MANAGER
  Martin Javitz

WARNER HOME VIDEO

PRESIDENT, HOME VIDEO
  Warren N. Lieberfarb
EXECUTIVE VICE PRESIDENT & GENERAL MANAGER
  Ed Byrnes
VICE PRESIDENT WORLDWIDE PLANNING & OPERATIONS
  James Cardwell
VICE PESIDENT MARKETING & DEVELOPMENT
  Barbara O'Sullivan
VICE PRESIDENT, SALES
  David Mount
VICE PRESIDENT, WORLDWIDE VIDEO ACQUISITIONS
  Elyse Eisenberg
VICE PRESIDENT, INTERNATIONAL MARKETING
  Brian Jamieson
DIRECTOR, PUBLICITY & PROGRAM PLANNING
  Michael Finnegan
DIRECTOR, PUBLICITY & PROMOTION
  Don Keefer
DIRECTOR OF PRODUCTION
  Lewis Ostrover

WARNER BROS. ANIMATION

PRESIDENT
  Jean MacCurdy
VICE PRESIDENT OF PRODUCTION & ADMINISTRATION,
CLASSIC
ANIMATION
  Kathleen Helppie
VICE PRESIDENT, ANIMATION PRODUCTION MANAGEMENT
  Tim Sarnoff

DOMESTIC PAY-TV, ADMINISTRATION
& NETWORK FEATURES

  75 Rockefeller Plaza, New York, NY 10019; (212) 484-8000;
FAX: (212) 397-0728.
PRESIDENT FEATURES
  Edward Bleier
VICE PRESIDENT, FINANCIAL AFFAIRS
  J. T. Shadoan
VICE PRESIDENT, MARKETING
  Eric Frankel
VICE PRESIDENT, SALES PLANNING & BUSINESS AFFAIRS
  Jeffrey Calman
DIRECTOR, FINANCIAL AFFAIRS
  Tony Cocchi
ADVERTISING, PUBLICITY & PROMOTION
  Gary Hahn
MANAGER, PROGRAMMING & INVENTORY
  Stacey Nagel Galper

Warner Bros. Television

  4000 Warner Blvd., Burbank, CA 91522; (213) 843-
6000, FAX: (818) 954-4539; 75 Rockefeller Plaza, New
York, NY 10019; (212) 484-8000.
PRESIDENT
  Leslie Moonves
EXECUTIVE VICE PRESIDENT, BUSINESS AND FINANCIAL
AFFAIRS
  Art Stolnitz
SENIOR VICE PRESIDENT, CREATIVE AFFAIRS
  Tony Jonas

SENIOR VICE PRESIDENT, MOVIES & MINI-SERIES
Gregg Maday
SENIOR VICE PRESIDENT, TALENT AND CASTING
Barbara Miller
SENIOR VICE PRESIDENT, NETWORK PRODUCTION
Bob Rosenbaum
SENIOR VICE PRESIDENT, CURRENT PROGRAMMING
David Sacks
SENIOR VICE PRESIDENT, STUDIO GENERAL COUNSEL
Paul Stager
SENIOR VICE PRESIDENT, BUSINESS AFFAIRS
Julie Waxman
VICE PRESIDENT, NETWORK PRODUCTION
Andrew Ackerman
VICE PRESIDENT, DRAMA DEVELOPMENT
Billy Campbell
VICE PRESIDENT, BUSINESS AFFAIRS
Karen Cease
VICE PRESIDENT, ADMINISTRATION
Geriann Geraci
VICE PRESIDENT, BUSINESS AFFAIRS
Wilt Haff
VICE PRESIDENT, COMEDY DEVELOPMENT
David Janollari
VICE PRESIDENT, NETWORK PRODUCTION
Henry Johnson
VICE PRESIDENT, CASTING
John Levey
VICE PRESIDENT, TALENT AND CASTING
Irene Mariano
VICE PRESIDENT, BUSINESS AFFAIRS
Irwin Moss
VICE PRESIDENT, BUSINESS AFFAIRS
Roni Mueller
VICE PRESIDENT, NETWORK PRODUCTION
Patrick Newcomb
VICE PRESIDENT, CURRENT PROGRAMS
Steve Pearlman
VICE PRESIDENT, PRODUCTION CONTROL/ESTIMATING
Dorothy Relyea
VICE PRESIDENT, POST-PRODUCTION
Ted Rich
VICE PRESIDENT, LABOR RELATIONS
Alan Saxe
VICE PRESIDENT, TELEVISION MUSIC
Greg Sill
VICE PRESIDENT, CURRENT PROGRAMMING
Paul Alan Smith
VICE PRESIDENT, PUBLICITY
David Stapf
VICE PRESIDENT, BUSINESS AFFAIRS
Nancy Tellem
VICE PRESIDENT, NETWORK PRODUCTION
Judith Zaylor
VICE PRESIDENT, TELEVISION LEGAL
Barbara Zuckerman

TELEPICTURES PRODUCTIONS

PRESIDENT
Jim Paratore
SENIOR VICE PRESIDENT
Bruce Rosenblum
VICE PRESIDENT
Kevin Fortson

Warner Bros. Studios Facilities

4000 Warner Boulevard, Burbank, CA 91522; (818) 954-6000; FAX: (818) 954-4213.
PRESIDENT
Gary Credle
SENIOR VICE PRESIDENT, ADMINISTRATION & STUDIO
SERVICES
Jon C. Gilbert
VICE PRESIDENT, LEGAL/BUSINESS AFFAIRS
Jeff Nagler
VICE PRESIDENT, LABOR RELATIONS
Hank Lachmund
SENIOR VICE PRESIDENT, PRODUCTION SERVICES
Ron Stein
VICE PRESIDENT, OPERATIONS
Robert S. Pincus

VICE PRESIDENT, FINANCE
Gordon Wood
VICE PRESIDENT, POST PRODUCTION SERVICES
Thomas McCormack

Warner Hollywood Studios

1041 N. Formosa Ave., West Hollywood, CA 90046; (213) 850-2500; FAX: (213) 850-2650.
VICE PRESIDENT & GENERAL MANAGER
Jack P. Foreman
VICE PRESIDENT STUDIO OPERATIONS
Donald Daves
VICE PRESIDENT TECHNICAL OPERATIONS
Curt Belhmer
VICE PRESIDENT—CONTROLLER
Donald Putrimas

MD Wax/Courier Films

1560 Broadway, Suite 907, New York, NY 10036; (212) 302-5360; FAX: (212) 302-5364. (The distribution of high quality, subtitled foreign films in the English-speaking world, including the U.S. and Canada.)
PRESIDENT
Morton D. Wax

Weiss Global Enterprises

2055 Saviers Rd., Suite 12, Oxnard, CA 93033; (805) 486-4495; FAX: (805) 487-3330. Cable: WEISSPICT Mailing address: P.O. Box 20360, Oxnard, CA 93034-0360. (Producer of feature films, owner-distributor of 120 full-length features; television distributor of features.)
PRESIDENT–TREASURER
Adrian Weiss
SECRETARY
Ethel L. Weiss
VICE PRESIDENT
Karen Engelhardt
INFORMATION SERVICES
Alex Gordon

West Side Studios

(formerly A.I.P. Studios) 10726 McCune Ave., Los Angeles, CA 90034; (310) 559-8805; FAX:(310) 559-8849.
CHAIRMAN
David Winters
PRESIDENT
Diane Daou
VICE PRESIDENT, FINANCE
Michael Vaccaro

Winkler Films, Inc.

211 S. Beverly Dr., #200, Beverly Hills, CA 90212; (310) 858-5780; FAX: (310) 858-5799. (Producer.)
PRINCIPAL & CEO
Irwin Winkler
PRESIDENT
Rob Cowan
VICE PRESIDENT, CREATIVE AFFAIRS
Nelson McCormick
CREATIVE EXECUTIVE
Janet Crosby

Wolper Organization Inc., The

4000 Warner Blvd., Burbank, CA 91522; (818) 954-1707; FAX: (818) 954-4380.
CHAIRMAN
David L. Wolper
SENIOR VICE PRESIDENT
Auriel K. Sanderson
PRESIDENT
Mark M. Wolper

VICE PRESIDENT, DEVELOPMENT
  Nancy McCabe
VICE PRESIDENT, DEVELOPMENT
  Marci Pool

Women's Film Company, The

9165 Sunset Blvd., Suite 300, Los Angeles, CA 90069; (310) 271-0202. (Film production.)
PRESIDENT
  Henry Jaglom
VICE PRESIDENT
  Judith Wolinsky
BOARD OF DIRECTORS
  Henry Jaglom, Judith Wolinsky
BRANCHES
  New York: 888 Seventh Ave., 34th floor, New York, NY 10106

World Wide Pictures

1201 Hennepin Ave., Minneapolis, MN 55403; (612) 338-3335. (Producer of feature films for theatrical release and distributor of same as well as 16mm prints, video-cassettes, and films for television; a unit of the Billy Graham Organization.)
CHAIRMAN
  Billy Graham
SECRETARY
  John R. Corts
DIRECTOR OF OPERATIONS
  Ken Engstrom

Saul Zaentz Company Film Center, The

2600 Tenth St., Berkeley, CA 94710; (510) 486-2100; FAX: (510) 486-2115. (Motion picture rental of complete post-production facilities.)

PRESIDENT
  Saul Zaentz
EXECUTIVE VICE PRESIDENT
  Roy Segal
FACILITY MANAGER
  Scott Roberts
DIRECTOR OF OPERATIONS
  Steve Shurtz

Zanuck Company, The

202 N. Canon Dr., Beverly Hills, CA 90210; (213) 274-0261; FAX: (310) 273-9217. Organized 1989. (Production of theatrical motion pictures.)
PARTNERS
  Richard D. Zanuck
  Lili F. Zanuck

Zeitgeist Films Ltd.

247 Centre St., 2nd fl., New York, NY 10013; (212) 274-1989; FAX: (212) 274-1644. Organized 1988. (Distribution of independent films.)
VICE PRESIDENTS
  Emily Russo
  Nancy Gerstman

Zupnik Enterprises

5530 Wisconsin Ave., #900, Chevy Chase, MD 20815; (310) 654-4117. Organized 1983. (Feature film production.)
PRESIDENT
  Stanley R. Zupnik
EXECUTIVE VICE PRESIDENT
  Bernard Sanker

Non-Theatrical
Motion Pictures

* **PRODUCERS**

* **DISTRIBUTORS**

* **SERVICES**

* **LIBRARIES**

Producers, Distributors, Libraries of Non-Theatrical Motion Pictures

Following is a list of producers, distributors and film libraries handling educational, entertainment and advertising pictures mainly for non-theatrical distribution to schools, clubs, civic organizations, teaching groups and other units, as well as television. Other sources of such films include most large manufacturing and public utility companies, trade associations in various industries, medical and public health societies and agencies, social service groups, educational organizations, museums, and state universities. Many of these supply films free or merely at a charge for transportation.

Academy Film Productions, Inc.
3918 West Estes Aves., Lincolnwood, IL 60645; (708) 674-2122. Bernard Howard, exec. prod. (Producers of motion pictures and videotapes, slide-films, slides and wide screen presentations for business, TV, conventions, meetings, audio-visual sales aids for industry.)

Cameron Productions
222 Minor Ave. N., Seattle, WA 98109-5436; (206) 623-4103; FAX: (206) 623-7256. (16mm, 35mm, video production for public relations, marketing, advertising and aerial productions.)

Carousel Films, Inc.
260 Fifth Ave., New York, NY 10001; (212) 683-1660; FAX: (212) 683-1662. (Distribution of educational and documentary films and videos to schools, libraries, industry.)

Cavalcade Productions, Inc.
7360 Potter Valley Rd., Ukiah, CA 95482-9208; (707) 743-1168; FAX: (707) 743-1903. (Motion picture and videotape production.)

Continental Film Productions Corp.
4220 Amnicola Highway, P.O. Box 5126, Chattanooga, TN 37406; (615) 622-1193; FAX: (615) 629-0853. (Producers of 16mm and 35mm motion pictures, video tapes, slides and multi-media presentations for business and industry.

Thomas Craven Film Corporation
5 W. 19 St., 3rd floor, New York, NY 10011-4216; (212) 463-7190; FAX: (212) 627-4761. (Production of television, industrial, public information, training and educational films and programming, theatrical featurettes and promos; videotape production and editing services; programming for cable television systems.)

Custom Films/Video, Inc.
11 Cob Dr., Westport, CT 06880; (203) 226-0300; FAX: (203) 227-9405. (Film and video production for sports, industry, broadcast and cable TV.)

Walt Disney, Non-Theatrical
3900 W. Alameda Ave., Suite 2477, Burbank, CA 91521-0021; (818) 567-5058; FAX: (818) 972-9447. (Distributes 16mm animation and features.)

William Ditzel Productions
933 Shroyer Rd., Dayton, OH 45419-3633; (513) 298-5381; (Script and produce motion pictures and video programs; produce print communications.)

Documentary Films, Inc.
159 W. 53 St., Suite 19-B, New York, NY 10019; (212) 582-4318, FAX: (212) 956-2257. NY Telex: 420748. (Distributor of feature and short documentary films to theatres, television, and non-theatrical markets.)

Ebbets Field Productions, Ltd.
P.O. Box 42, Wykagyl Station, New Rochelle, NY 10804; (914) 636-1281. (Researches, creates, writes, produces films and videotape for business, industry, education, government, TV. Also writing and directing films for theatrical, cable and TV.)

Edward Feil Productions
4614 Prospect Ave., Cleveland, OH 44103; (216) 881-0040. (Producers of industrial, institutional, education promotion and geriatric films and videos.)

Film Effects
221 Dufferin St., Suite 201A, Toronto, Ont., M6K 1Y9; (416) 538-6000. (Opticals, animation and special effects, 35mm and 16mm opticals, animation, and special effects.)

Films For Educators/Films For TV
420 E. 55 St., Suite 6-U, New York, NY 10022; (212) 486-6577; FAX: (212) 980-9826. (Distributes feature documentaries (including health and environmental) shorts and classic motion pictures to libraries, schools, TV—worldwide.)

Films Incorporated
National Sales Office: 5547 N. Ravenswood Ave., Chicago, IL 60640; (312) 878-2600; (800) 323-4222, ext. 42. (Distributes 16mm and 35mm film and licenses public performance video.)

Gifford Animation, Inc.
134 Sisson Rd., Harwichport, MA 02646; (508) 432-4711. (Creative service and production of animated films.)

Goldsholl Film Group
420 Frontage Rd., Northfield, IL 60093; (708) 446-8300; FAX: (708) 446-8320. (Producers of motion pictures for business, industry, TV and education. Also 3D graphics, motion control, clay animation, stop motion, and cel animation.)

Hanna-Barbera Productions, Inc.
3400 Cahuenga Blvd., Hollywood, CA 90068; (213) 851-5000; FAX: (213) 969-1201. (Motion picture production—live action and animation—for industry, theatre and television.)

Hardcastle Films & Video

7319 Wise Ave., St. Louis, MO 63117; (314) 647-4200; FAX: (314) 647-4201. (Production in film and video; post-production facilities; equipment rental.)

Hartley Film Foundation, Inc.

59 Cat Rock Rd., Cos Cob, CT 06807-1799; (203) 869-1818, FAX: (203) 869-1905. (Produces and distributes films on parapsychology, the human potential, and Eastern philosophy.)

Harvest A-V Company

98 Riverside Dr., New York, NY 10024; (212) 873-6900. (Distribution of safety films for industry, governments, and education.)

Hurlock Cine-World, Inc.

Box 34619, Juneau, AK 99803-4619; (907) 789-3995. (Non-theatrical 16mm foreign feature film distributor.)

IFEX Films/IFEX International.

159 W. 53 St., Suite 19-B, New York, NY 10019; (212) 582-4318; FAX: (212) 956-2257. (Exclusive distributor of a collection of feature films, documentaries, and short subjects)

Ivy Film

725 Providence Rd., Charlotte, NC 28207-2248. (704) 335-0672; FAX: (704) 335-0672. (Exclusive distributors world-wide of over 500 feature films and 1000 short subjects from the libraries of M.& A. Alexander Inc., Crystal Pictures, Inc., and other independents. Licenses and sells feature films, TV shows, short subjects, video-cassettes, video cartridges throughout the world.)

J P I and Associates

16301 W. 54th Ave., Golden, CO 80403; (303) 278-8380. (3 camera, mobile video-tape van for TV commerical and industrial production, sports broadcasts, etc. Complete 16mm motion picture production and edit capability.)

Hugh & Suzanne Johnston, Inc.

16 Valley Rd., Princeton, NJ 08540; (609) 924-7505. (Design and production of educational, television and sponsored motion picture films; specialized film promotion and distribution services.)

Walter J. Klein Company, Ltd.

6311 Carmel Rd., Box 2087, Charlotte, NC 28247-2087; (704) 542-0735; FAX: (704) 542-0735. (Production and free distribution of sponsored films for industry, TV, government, associations; complete film facilities on 2-acre lot. Founder of IQ, the trade society of world non-theatrical film production houses.)

Curt Lowey and Associates Inc.

925 Westchester Ave., White Plains, NY 10604; (914) 948-6500. (Script, design, and produce multimedia programs, business meetings, slide presentations and collateral materials.)

MPO Videotronics, Inc.

619 W. 54 St., New York, NY 10019; (212) 708-0550; FAX: (212) 397-0866. (Manufacturer of portable integrated video playback system for sales, training, and P.O.P.)

MRC Films, Inc.

21 W. 46 St., New York, NY 10036; (212) 730-7705; (Production of motion picture and video programs for TV, government, & industry. Also consultants for "in-plant" film units, providing script, editing, animation, recording and production completion services.)

Manbeck Pictures Corp.

3621 Wakonda Dr., Des Moines, IA 50321-2132; (515) 285-1166. (Distributor of features and shorts, sound and silent film classics.)

Marathon International Productions, Inc.

Box BJ, Amagansett, NY 11930; (516) 267-7770; FAX: (516) 267-7771. (Public information films, television films, worldwide news service, company newsreels, special events coverage for industry.)

Mass Media Ministries, Inc.,

Mass Media Building, 2116 N. Charles St., Baltimore, MD 21218. (410) 727-3270; FAX: (410) 727-8192. (Rents and sells religious and educational films and videos.)

Lee Mendelson Film Productions, Inc.

1440 Chapin Ave., Burlingame, CA 94010; (415) 342-8284; FAX: (415) 342-6170. (Network TV and animation specials.)

Mode-2 Productions, Inc.

7115 Church Ave., Pittsburgh, PA 15202; (412) 766-1722. (Produces 16mm and 35mm advertising, industrial, educational films, TV.)

Modern Talking Picture Service, Inc.

5000 Park St., N., St. Petersburg, FL 33709; (813) 541-7571; FAX: (813) 546-9323. (Distributor of corporate sponsored films/videos to schools, universities, resorts and special interest groups, both free loan and sales. TV distribution/monitoring/tracking of VNRs, PSAs and extended-length productions via satellite, cable and broadcast programming. Support services include promotions, duplication, sales, and creative.)

Monumental Films & Recordings, Inc.

2160 Rockrose Ave., Baltimore, MD 21211; (301) 462-1550; FAX: (301) 462-1551. (Scripting, motion picture services, editorial services, narration and commercials, industrial, commercial and educational films and videos, sound recordings.)

Byron Morgan Associates

P.O. Box 1293, Lake Arrowhead, CA 92352-1293; (909) 337-3219. (Motion picture writing, audiovisual, TV writing, direction and production for government, education, industry, public relations, government, TV and entertainment industry.)

Jack Moss Communications Inc.

7696-B Lexington Club Blvd., Delray Beach, FL 33446; (407) 499-5770. (Scripts and production for videotapes, films, multi-media for sales meetings, training, selling, commercials and television.)

NFL Films, Inc.

330 Fellowship Rd., Mt. Laurel, NJ 08054; (609) 778-1600. (Complete film and video production company including location/studio crews, location digital

video shooting, film processing, film to tape transfer, music scoring, computer animation, and digital video post-production services.)

National Television News
13691 W. Eleven Mile Rd., Oak Park, MI 48237; (313) 541-1440. 6133 Kentland Ave., Woodland Hills, CA 91367; (818) 883-6121. (Videotape for education, TV, sales promotion, public relations.)

Pace Films, Inc.
411 E. 53 St., New York, NY 10022; (212) 755-5486. (Production of features, documentaries and distribution.)

Penfield Productions, Inc.
35 Springfield St., Agawam, MA 01001; (413) 786-4454. (Produces commercial and television films, slidefilms, and video.)

Pilot Productions, Inc.
2123 McDaniel Ave., Evanston, IL 60201-2126; (708) 328-3700; FAX: (708) 328-3761. (Video, computer slides, for sales and training presentations.)

Pinnn Audio Visual
954 W. Washington Blvd., Chicago, IL 60607; (312) 421-7560; FAX: (312) 421-7632. (Complete developers and producers of slides, film and video for industry, business and education; full in-house facilities, sound studio; meeting planning and staging; slides, film, video and sound duplication.)

Playhouse Pictures
1401 N. La Brea Ave., Hollywood, CA 90028; (213) 851-2112; FAX: (213) 851-2117. (Animation specialists in industrial, educational, entertainment and TV commercials.)

Ross Roy Inc.
100 Bloomfield Hills Pkwy., Bloomfield Hills, MI 48304; (313) 433-6000. (Produces print and broadcast advertising as well as video tapes, interactive videodiscs, sound slide-films, sales meetings, industrial theatre presentations.)

Snazelle Film Group Ltd.
155 Fell St., San Francisco, CA 94102; (415) 431-5490; FAX: (415) 552-9474. (TV film commercial production company)

Snyder Films & Video
1419 First Ave. S., Fargo, ND 58103; (701) 293-3600. (35mm and 16mm motion picture, Betacam SP video production.)

Spots Alive Consultants, Inc.
Spring Valley Rd., Ossining, NY 10562; (914) 941-7043. (Cost management in broadcast production, motion picture filming and video tape. Provides support in preparation, estimate review and post audits.)

Swain Film & Video
1185 Cattleman Rd., Sarasota, FL 34232-2813; (813) 371-2360; FAX: (813) 377-1459. (Production of videotape and motion pictures for business, industry, education and entertainment.)

Swank Motion Pictures, Inc.
National headquarters: 201 S. Jefferson Ave., St. Louis, MO 63103; (314) 534-6300; FAX: (314) 289-2187. Regional offices: 350 Vanderbilt Motor Parkway, Hauppauge, NY 11788-4753, (516) 434-1560; 910 Riverside Dr., Elmhurst, IL 60126-4967, (312) 833-0061; 201 S. Jefferson Ave., St. Louis, MO 63103-2579, (314) 534-6300; 6767 Forest Lawn Dr., Hollywood, CA 90068-1095, (213) 851-6300. (Distributes public performance 16mm and videocassettes to colleges and universities, hospitals, correctional institutions, public libraries and other non-theatrical situations.)

TFI
(A division of MPO.)
619 W. 54 St., New York, NY 10019; (212) 708-0550; FAX: (212) 977-9458. (On behalf of major TV advertisers, distributes commercials to TV stations and networks according to media schedules. On behalf of motion picture industry, distributes film trailers, advertising and promotional materials, press kits, etc. Provides post-production services.)

T.H.A. Media Distributors Ltd.
1100 Homer St., Vancouver, B.C., Canada V6B 2X6; (604) 687-4215; FAX: (604) 688-8349. (Non-theatrical and television distribution.)

TR Productions, Inc.
1031 Commonwealth Ave., Boston, MA 02215-1094; (617) 783-4844. (Producers of motion pictures, computer graphics, and multi-image sound/slide productions for business, government, and education; audio recording, sound tracks, and radio spots; industrial videotape.)

Tel-Air Interest, Inc.
1755 N.E. 149th St., Miami, FL 33181; (305) 944-3268; FAX: (305) 944-1143. (TV and motion picture production, documentary, music and sports specials for syndication and cable, film and video editing, cinematography and videography.)

Trans World Films, Inc.
332 S. Michigan Ave., Chicago, IL 60604-4382; (312) 922-1530; (800) 432-2241; FAX: (312) 427-4550. Richard S. Greene, pres. (Non-theatrical 16mm foreign feature film classics and video distributor.)

Robert Warner Productions
P.O. Box 880, East Hampton, NY 11937-0701; (516) 324-1050. (Live, film and tape programs and commercials.)

West Glen Communications, Inc.
1430 Broadway, New York, NY 10018; (212) 921-2800; FAX: (212) 944-9055. (A full service production and distribution facility specializing in sponsored free loan films and videos for broadcast, cable, motion picture theatres, community groups, schools, colleges, trade groups, professional audiences, and resorts. Also offers videos for sale and rental.)

Wexler Film Productions, Inc.
801 N. Seward St., Los Angeles, CA 90038-3601; (213) 462-6349. (Educational and medical-educational film and video. Specialized services of 16mm, 35mm, and video production, color printing, animation and equipment design.)

574

Theatre Circuits

Theatre Circuits

These listings embrace companies operating four or more theatres and are arranged alphabetically by corporate names. Circuits in Canada are in the section on Canada. Buying and Booking Services follow the Independent Theaters section.

A

Absher Enterprises, Inc.

295 North Arnold Ave., Prestonburg, KY 41653; (606) 886-6397.

J. ABSHER, owner.
KENTUCKY—GOODY: South Side Theatre (4); PIKEVILLE: Plaza Cinemas 2; PRESTONBURG: Strand 2 Theatre; SOMERSET: Showplace Cinemas (4).

Ackerman Theatres

163 Amsterdam Ave., Suite 149, New York, NY 10023; (212) 595-2141; FAX: (212) 595-2979.

MEYER ACKERMAN, pres.; J. ROBERT TOLCHIN, v.p.; COREY GREENBERG, treas.; BRIAN ACKERMAN, secty.
NEW YORK—NEW YORK CITY: Eastside Playhouse, 86th St. East Twin, 57th St. Playhouse, 68th St. Playhouse; STATEN ISLAND: Hylan Twin Cinema, Hylan Plaza 5-plex, Staten Island 10-Plex; WESTCHESTER: Cinema 100 Twin, Rye Ridge Twin, Fine Arts.

Act III Theatres

919 S.W. Taylor, Suite 900, Portland, OR 97205; (503) 221-0213. FAX: (503) 228-5032.

WALT AMAN, pres. & CFO; BOB LENIHAN, v.p. & head film buyer; BILL SPENCER, v.p. & film settlements; TIMOTHY G. WOOD, v.p., opns.; TIM REED, v.p. real estate & facilities; ROBERT PERKINS III, Nat'l mgr. of concessions and purchasing; RANDY BLAUM, Natl. dir. mktg. publicity & promotions.

Santikos/Presidio Theatres

MARK REIS, div. mgr.
TEXAS—AUSTIN: Arbor 7, Lakecreek 8, Aquarius 4, Lakehills 4, Lincoln 6, Northcross 6, Riverside 8, South Park 3, Southwood 2, Village 4, Westgate 3, Westgate 8; SAN ANTONIO: Central Park Fox 4, South Park 4, Northwest 14, Galaxy 14, Ingram Square 8, Windsor Mall 5, Century South 8, Mission D.I. 4, Westlakes 9, Embassy 14, Crossroads 6, Bandera 6, Nakoma 8, Rolling Oaks 6.

Luxury Theatres

STEVE GUFFEY, div. mgr.
ALASKA—ANCHORAGE: Denali, Fireweed, Polar, Totem; FAIRBANKS: Goldstream, KENAI: Kambe.
IDAHO—COEUR D'ALENE: Coeur d'Alene, Showboat V; LEWISTON: Orchards Tri Cinemas, Liberty.
OREGON—ALBANY: Albany; BEAVERTON: Beaverton D.I., Valley Tri, Westgate; BEND: Bend Tri Cinemas, Mountain View Cinemas, Tower Twin; COOS BAY: Egyptian; CORVALLIS: Ninth Street, Whiteside; EUGENE: Cinema World, McDonald; GRANTS PASS: Rogue, Redwood D.I.; GRESHAM: Gresham Quad; HILLSBORO: Town; HOOD RIVER: Trail Twin; McMINNVILLE: McMinnville; NORTH BEND: Pony IV Cinemas; PORTLAND: Broadway Metroplex, Clackamas, Eastgate, 82nd Ave. Cinemas, Foster D.I., Fox, Guild, Hollywood Cinemas, Jantzen Cinemas, Lloyd Cinemas, Lloyd Mall Cinemas, Mall 205 Cinemas, Music Box, Southgate, Tanasbourne, Tigard, Washington Square Cinemas; ROSEBURG: Garden Valley, Harvard Tri Cinemas, Starlite; SALEM: Capitol, Elsinore, Keizer Tri Cinemas, Lancaster Mall Cinemas, South Salem D.I., Southgate Cinemas; SPRINGFIELD: Springfield.
WASHINGTON—ABERDEEN: Southshore Mall Cinemas, Harbor D.I.; BELLINGHAM: Bellis Fair Mall, Sehome; BREMERTON: Redwood Plaza Quad; CENTRALIA: Fox; CHEHALIS: Cinema 3; EVERETT: Everett 9; KELSO: Three Rivers; KENNEWICK: Columbia Center, Clearwater; KENT: Kent VI Cinemas; LACEY: Lacey; LONGVIEW: Longview Triangle; OLYMPIA: State; PUYALLUP: Puyallup; RICHLAND: Uptown, Metro; SEATTLE: Alderwood, Crossroads, Parkway; SILVERDALE: Silverdale Cinemas; SPOKANE: East Sprague 6, Eastside, Fox Triplex, Lincoln Heights, Lyons, Newport, No. Cedar D.I., North Division; VANCOUVER: Cascade Park, Hazel Dell 3, Vancouver Plaza 10.

Allen Theatres, Inc.

P.O. Drawer 1500, 208B West Main St., Farmington, NM 87401; (505) 325-9313; FAX: (505) 326-2647.

LARRY F. ALLEN, pres.; LANE E. ALLEN, v.p.; BOYD F. SCOTT, sec.-treas. LARRY F. ALLEN, film buyer.
COLORADO—CORTEZ: Fiesta Twin, Arroyo D.I.
NEW MEXICO—ALAMOGORDO: Cinema 5; CARLSBAD: Mall Cinema 3; CLOVIS: Hilltop Twin, North Plains 4; FARMINGTON: Allen, Apache Twin D.I., Cameo, Centennial Twin, Animas Cinema IV; GALLUP: Aztec 5, Rio West Twin; HOBBS: Broadmoor, Cinema 3; LAS CRUCES: Video 4, Rio Grande, Cinema 8, Aggie D.I.; PORTALES: Tower Twin; ROSWELL: Cinema 4, Del Norte Twin, Plains Park Twin.

American Multi-Cinema, Inc.
(An AMC Entertainment Corp.)

106 West 14th St., Suite 1700, Kansas City, MO 64105; (816) 221-4000.

STANLEY H. DURWOOD, chm., & CEO; EDWARD D. DURWOOD, pres. & vice-chmn., PHILIP M. SINGLETON, sr. v.p. & COO; PETER C. BROWN, sr. v.p. & CFO.
AMC FILM MARKETING: DON HARRIS, pres.; GENE GOODMAN, sr. v.p.; JOE SABATINO, v.p.; NOEL KENDALL, v.p.
ARIZONA—CHANDLER: Laguna Village (10); GLENDALE: Gateway Village (10); MESA: Fiesta Village (6), Sunvalley (10), Three Fountains (4); PHOENIX: Bell Plaza (8), Metro Village (6), Town & Country (6); TEMPE: Lakes (6); TUCSON: Cineworld (4), El Con (6), Valencia (4).
CALIFORNIA—BAKERSFIELD: Stockdale (6); BURBANK: Burbank (14); CERRITOS: Alondra (6); CHINO: Chino Town Square (10); COLMA: Serramonte (6); ENCINITAS: Wiegand Plaza (8); FULLERTON: Fullerton (10); HAWTHORNE: Hawthorne (6); HERMOSA BEACH: Hermosa Beach (6); INDUSTRY: Puente East (4), Puente West (6), Puente Plaza (10); LONG BEACH: Marina Pacifica (6), Pine Square (16); LOS ANGELES: Carousel (4), Century City (14), Media Center (4),Old Pasadena (8); MILPITAS: Milpitas (10); MONTEBELLO: Montebello (10); MOUNTAIN VIEW: Old Mill (6); ORANGE: Orange (6); SAN BERNARDINO: Commercenter (6); SAN DIEGO: Fashion Valley (4); SAN FRANCISCO: Kabuki (8); SAN JOSE: Oakridge (6), Saratoga (6); SANTA ANA: Main Place (6); SANTA MONICA; Santa Monica (7); SANTEE: Santee Village (8); SUNNYVALE: Sunnyvale (6); TORRANCE: Rolling Hills (6); VALLEJO: Vallejo Plaza (6); VICTORVILLE: Victor Valley (10).
COLORADO—AURORA: Buckingham Square (4), Buckingham Village (6), Seven Hills (10); COLORADO SPRINGS: Tiffany Square (6); DENVER: Tiffany Plaza (6), Tivoli (12); GLENDALE: Colorado Plaza (6); LITTLETON: Southbridge (4); WESTMINSTER: Westminster Mall (6), Westminster (5).
DELAWARE—NEWARK: Cinema Center (3); WILMINGTON: Concord (2).
DISTRICT OF COLUMBIA—WASHINGTON, D.C.: Union Station (9).
FLORIDA—ALTAMONTE SPRINGS: Interstate (6); BRANDON: Regency (8); CLEARWATER: Clearwater (5), Countryside (6), Tri-City (8); DAVIE: Ridge Plaza (8); DAYTONA: Volusia Square (8); DAYTONA BEACH: Daytona (6); FORT LAUDERDALE: Coral Ridge (10); GAINESVILLE: Oaks (10); HOLLYWOOD: Sheridan (7); HOLLYWOOD BEACH: Oceanwalk (10); JACKSONVILLE: Regency Mall (8), Regency Square (6); LAKE BUENA VISTA: Pleasure Island (10); LAKELAND: Merchants Walk (10); MERRITT ISLAND: Merritt Square 1-6, Merritt Square 7-12; MIAMI: Mall of the Americas (8), Bakery Centre (7), Cocowalk (8), Kendall (10), Marina (8), Omni (10), South Dade (8); ORANGE PARK: Orange Park (5); ORLANDO: Fashion Village (8); SARASOTA: Sarasota (12); SEMINOLE: Seminole (8), Seminole Mall (2); ST. PETERSBURG: Crossroads (8), Tyrone Square (6); TAMPA: Horizon Park (4), Twin Bays (4), Varsity (6), Old Hyde Park (7); WEST PALM BEACH: Cross Country (8), Mizner Park (8).
GEORGIA—ATLANTA: Galleria (8), Phipps Plaza (12), Tower Place (6); KENNESHAW: Cobb Place (5); TUCKER: Northlake Festival (8).
ILLINOIS—CARBONDALE: University Place (8); HOFFMAN ESTATES: Barrington Square (6); NAPERVILLE: Ogden (6).
KANSAS—KANSAS CITY: Indian Springs North (4), Indian Springs South (6); OVERLAND PARK: Oak Park (12).
LOUISIANA—BOSSIER CITY: Bossier (6); METAIRIE: Galleria (8); SHREVEPORT: St. Vincent (6).

MARYLAND—GREENBELT: Academy (8), Academy (6); LaVALE: Country Club (6); NEW CARROLLTON: Carrollton (6); OXON HILL: Rivertowne (12); SILVER SPRING: City Place (10).

MASSACHUSETTS—HADLEY: Hampshire (6), Mountain Farms (4).

MICHIGAN—BIRMINGHAM: Maple (3); DEARBORN: Westborn (2); DETROIT: Bel-Air Centre (10); FARMINGTON HILLS: Old Orchard (3); GROSSE POINT WOODS: Woods (6); HARPER WOODS: Eastland (7); LANSING: Elmwood (8); LIVONIA: Laurel Park (10); Wonderland (6); MADISON HEIGHTS: Abbey (8); OAK PARK: Towne (4); OKEMOS: Meridian (14); ROCHESTER: Hampton (4); SOUTHFIELD: Southfield City (12); STERLING HEIGHTS: Sterling Center (10); TAYLOR: Southland (4); WEST BLOOMFIELD TOWNSHIP: Americana Way (6).

MISSOURI—HAZELWOOD: Village (6); KANSAS CITY: Bannister Square (4), Metro North (12), Township (6), Ward Parkway (12); LEE'S SUMMIT: Summit (4); ST. ANN: Northwest (10); ST. CHARLES: Regency (4); ST. LOUIS: Esquire (7), Crestwood (5), Galleria (6).

NEBRASKA—OMAHA: Westroads (8).

NEW JERSEY—DELRAN: Millside (4); DEPTFORD: Deptford (8); LAWRENCEVILLE: Quaker Bridge (4); MARLTON: Marlton (8); MORRISTOWN: Headquarters (10); ROCKAWAY: Rockaway (12); VINELAND: Cumberland (2), Vineland (4).

NEW YORK—AMHERST: Maple Ridge (8); CHEEKTOWAGA: Como (8), Holiday (6).

OHIO—COLUMBUS: Eastland Center (8), Eastland Plaza (6); DUBLIN: Dublin Village (14); TOLEDO: Franklin (6), North Towne (5), Southwyck (8), Southwyck (3); WESTERVILLE: Westerville (6).

OKLAHOMA—NORMAN: Robinson Crossing (6); OKLAHOMA CITY: Memorial Square (4), Northwest (8).

PENNSYLVANIA—ALLENTOWN: Tilghman Plaza (8); BRYN MAWR: Bryn Mawr (2); CORNWELL HEIGHTS: Premiere (2), Woodhaven (4); DOYLESTOWN: Barn (5); EASTON: 25th St. Cinema (4); EXTON: Exton (2); HARRISBURG: East (5); LANCASTER: Eden (2); Wonderland (4); MECHANICSBURG: Hampden Center (8); MEDIA: Granite Run (8); PHILADELPHIA: Andorra (8), Midtown (2), Olde City (2), Orleans (8), Walnut (3); QUAKERTOWN: Quakertown (6); SPRINGHOUSE: 309 Cinema (9); WAYNE: Anthony Wayne (2), Gateway (3), WESTCHESTER: Painters Crossing (9); WHITEHALL: Plaza (2); YORK: York (4).

TEXAS—ARLINGTON: Forum (6), Green Oaks (8); DALLAS: Prestonwood (5), Glen Lakes (8); FT. WORTH: Hulen Village (10), Sundance (11); HIGHLAND PARK: Highland Park Village (4); HOUSTON: Alameda East (5), Commerce Park (8), Festival (6), Greens Crossing (4), Greenway (3), Meyer Park (14), North Oaks (6), Southway (6), Town & Country (10), Westchase (5), Willowbrook (8); HUMBLE: Deerbrook (8); IRVING: Irving (6); MESQUITE: Towne Crossing (8); PLANO: Central Park (7); SAN ANTONIO: Rivercenter (9).

VIRGINIA—ARLINGTON: Courthouse Plaza (8); BAILEYS CROSSROADS: Skyline (12); DALE CITY: Potomac Mills (10); HAMPTON: Coliseum (4), Newmarket (4); NEWPORT NEWS: Patrick Henry (7); NORFOLK: Circle (10); VIRGINIA BEACH: Lynnhaven (8).

WASHINGTON—FEDERAL WAY: Center Plaza (6), SeaTac (6); TACOMA: Narrows Plaza (8).

DIVISION OFFICES: American Multi-Cinema, Inc.

Clearwater, FL 34621, Northside Square, 29399 U.S. Highway 19 North, Suite 503; Voorhes, NJ 08043, Main St., Plaza 10000, 5th floor; Kansas City, MO, 64105, 1221 Baltimore; Los Angeles, CA, 90067, Suite 1020, Two Century Plaza, 2049 Century Park East.

Apex Cinemas

4818 Yuma St., N.W., Washington, DC 20016; (202) 244-7700; FAX: (202) 363-4680.

RON GOLDMAN, pres. & owner.
MARYLAND—ANNAPOLIS: Annapolis Mall 4, Annapolis Harbour 9; PRINCE FREDERICK: Calvert Village 5; WHEATON: Aspen Hill 4.
VIRGINIA—FAIRFAX: Cinema 7.

Art Theatre Guild, Inc.

Home Office: P.O. Box 146, Scottsdale, AZ 85252; (602) 947-2426.

LOUIS K. SHER, pres.; ROBERT J. SHER, secty-treas.
ARIZONA—SCOTTSDALE: Kiva.
OHIO—COLUMBUS: Bexley I & II; DAYTON: Art I & II; TOLEDO: Westwood; YOUNGSTOWN: Foster.

Associated Theatres, Inc. & Associated Theatres Home Video

7009 University, Des Moines, IA 50311; (515) 255-0275. FAX: (515) 255-1078.

PETER J. FREDERICK, pres. & CEO; JEANNE K. FREDERICK, v.p.; JOHN BRAND, district mgr.; ELEANOR JACKSON, office mgr.; DAVE NESBIT, video mgr.

IOWA—ANAMOSA: Jones County Cinema; ATLANTIC: Frederick 2; AUDUBON: Rose; CLARINDA: Caprice; CLEAR LAKE: Lake; CRESTON: Strand; DENISON: Donna Reed; DEWITT: Opera House; GREENFIELD: Grand; GRINNELL: Cinema; HAMPTON: Windsor; HARLAN: Harlan; HOLSTEIN: State; IDA GROVE: King; KNOXVILLE: Village 2; LAMONI: Coliseum; MISSOURI VALLEY: Rialto; MT. PLEASANT: Temple 2; MT. VERNON: Odeum; OSKALOOSA: Penn Center 2; RED OAK: Grand; SHENANDOAH: Page 2; TIPTON: Hardacre; WASHINGTON: State; WINTERSET: Iowa.

NEBRASKA—COZAD: Rialto; NORFOLK: Kings 4; O'NEILL: Picture Show; BROKEN BOW: Tiffany.

SOUTH DAKOTA—GREGORY: Hipp, Hilltop D.I.; VIBORG: Lund; WINNER: Ritz, Pix D.I.

Associated Theatres of Kentucky

4050 Westport Rd., Suite 201, Louisville, KY 40207; (502) 893-8811; FAX: (502) 894-8823.

HENRY I. SAAG, pres.; ALVIN D. YOUNGER, v.p. & secty.; JOHN D. SAAG, treas.; KAREN COSSON, dir. of optns.
INDIANA—MADISON: Madison 6.
KENTUCKY—LOUISVILLE: Dixie Dozen 12, South Park D.I., Vogue.
WEST VIRGINIA—WESTON: Weston 4.

B

B & B Theatres

Box 171, 119 West 2nd, Salisbury, MO 65281; (816) 388-5219. Kansas Office: Box 388, 202 S. Washington, Iola, KS 66749; (316) 365-5701.

ELMER BILLS, BOB BAGBY, STERLING BAGBY, owners.
KANSAS—ARKANSAS CITY: Buford Cinema 3; CHANUTE: Chanute Cinema 2; COFFEYVILLE: Coffeyville Cinema 2; EL DORADO: El Dorado Embassy 2; INDEPENDENCE: Independence Cinema 3; IOLA: Iola Cinema 2; Iola 54 D.I.; McPHERSON: McPherson Cinema 3; PARSONS: Parsons Cinema 3; RUSSELL: Russell Dream Cinema; WINFIELD: Winfield Cinema 3.
MISSOURI—BROOKFIELD: Cedar Cinema; CARROLLTON: Carrollton Uptown Theatre; CARTHAGE: Carthage Cinema (2); FULTON: Fulton Cinema 2; HANNIBAL: Hannibal Cinema 5; LEBANON: Ritz 4; MARSHALL: Marshall Cinema 3; MOBERLY: Moberly Cinema, State 2; SALISBURY: Salisbury Lyric; WAYNESVILLE: Cinema 4.
OKLAHOMA—BLACKWELL: Sundowner; PONCA CITY: Plaza Twin.

Blumenfeld San Francisco Theatres

1521 Sutter St., San Francisco, CA 94109; (415) 563-6200; FAX: (415) 563-6210.

ALLAN BLUMENFELD, chief executive; ROBERT BLUMENFELD, booker & supervision; NATHAN BLUMENFELD, purchasing agent; MAX BLUMENFELD, advertising.
CALIFORNIA—FAIRFAX: Fairfax; LARKSPUR: Lark; SAN JOSE: Meridian 6; SAN FRANCISCO: Regency I, Regency 2, Royal, Alhambra, Castro.

Bowman Theatres

318 Main St., Savanna, IL 61074; (815) 273-7121.

DENNIS O. BOWMAN, pres.; ROLAND VINER, film buyer.
ILLINOIS—DIXON: Plaza Cinema 3; ROCHELLE: Hub 2; SAVANNA: Times Twin; STERLING: Midway D.I.

C

CDB Theatres

Drawer BF, Beckley, WV 25802-2854; (304) 255-4036. FAX: (304) 877-5537.

CURTIS McCALL, owner.
WEST VIRGINIA—BECKLEY: Crossroads Cinema 6, Showplace Cinemas 6; FAIRLEA: Seneca Showcase (2); RAINELLE: Curdanbri Twin Cinemas; SUMMERSVILLE: Merchants Walk Cinemas (4).

CTS Heaston Theatres, Inc.

9333 N. Meridian St., Suite 300, Indianapolis, IN 46260; (317) 846-9333.

MORRIS CANTOR, pres.; LEONARD CANTOR, v.p.
INDIANA—CARMEL: Woodland 2; INDIANAPOLIS: Greenbriar 2; South Keystone 2.

Carmike Cinemas

Home Office: 1301 First Ave., P.O. Box 391, Columbus, GA 31902-0391; (404) 576-3400. FAX: (404) 576-3441.

C. L. PATRICK, SR., chm.; MICHAEL W. PATRICK, pres. & CEO; JOHN O. BARWICK, III, v.p.-finance, treas. & CFO; ANTHONY J. RHEAD, v.p. film; FRED VAN NOY, v.p., gen. mng.; P. LAMAR FIELDS, v.p., dvlpmt.; LARRY M. ADAMS, v.p., info. systems & sec.; H. MADISON SHIRLEY, v.p., concessions & asst. sec.; MARILYN GRANT, v.p. adv.

EASTERN DIVISION

GEORGIA—ALBANY: Carmike Eight; Georgia Four; AMERICUS: Cinema Twin; CALHOUN: Martin Triple; CARTERSVILLE: Plaza Twin; COLUMBUS: Carmike Seven; Columbus Square Eight, Peachtree Triple, Plaza Triple; CORDELE: Martin Triple; DALTON: Martin Triple; DOUGLAS: Martin Twin; FITZGERALD: Capri Twin; FT. OGLETHORPE: Southgate Five; MILLEDGEVILLE: Carmike Six.

NORTH CAROLINA—ASHEBORO: Cinema Twin; ASHEVILLE: Biltmore Twin, Mall Twin; BOONE: Appalachian Twin, Chalet Triple; BURLINGTON: Park Twin; CAROLINA BEACH: Cinema Four; CARY: Waverly Place 6; CHAPEL HILL: Ram Triple; CHARLOTTE: Park Terrace Triple, Town Cinema Six, University Six; DUNN: Plaza Twin; DURHAM: Carmike 7, Center Four, South Square Four, Willowdaile Eight, YorkTown Twin; EDEN: Kingsway 4; ELIZABETH CITY: Gateway Twin; FAYETTEVILLE: Bordeaux Triple, Carmike Six; FOREST CITY: Cinema Four; GASTONIA: Eastridge Four; GOLDSBORO: Berkely Four, Eastgate Twin; GREENSBORO: Circle 6, Quaker Twin; GREENVILLE: Buccaneer Triple, Carolina Four, Park, Plaza Cinema Three; HAVELOCK: Cinema Six; HENDERSON: Cinema; HICKORY: Terrace Four; HIGH POINT: Capri Triple, Carmike 8, Martin Twin; JACKSONVILLE: Brynn Marr Triple, Cardinal Four, Carmike Seven, Cinema Six, Northwoods Twin; KINSTON: Mall Twin, Plaza Twin; LAURINBURG: Cinema Twin; LENOIR: Westgate Twin; LEXINGTON: Cinema Four; LINCOLNTON: Cinema Four; MATTHEWS: Festival 10; MOREHEAD CITY: Cinema Triple, Morehead Twin; MORGANTON: Mimosa Twin, Studio Twin; NEW BERN: Cinema Triple; NORTH WILKSBORO: Mall Twin, West Park Twin; RALEIGH: Carmike Seven, Six Forks Six, South Hills Twin, Terrace Twin, Tower Merchants 6, Tower Twin; ROANOKE RAPIDS: Cinema Twin; ROCKINGHAM: Plaza Twin; ROCKY MOUNT: Cardinal Triple, Englewood Twin, Golden East Four; SANFORD: Kendale Twin; SHELBY: Cinema Four, Mall Four; SOUTHERN PINES: Cinema Four, Town & Country Twin; STATESVILLE: Gateway Four, Newtowne Twin; WASHINGTON: Cinema Triple; WILMINGTON: Cinema Six, Independence Mall Triple, Long Leaf Twin, New Center Triple; WILSON: Gold Park Twin, Parkwood Triple; WINSTON-SALEM: Marketplace 6, Reynolda Triple, Thruway Twin.

SOUTH CAROLINA—AIKEN: Cinema Triple, Mark Twin; CHARLESTON: Carmike Six, Ultravision Four; CHESTER: Cinema Twin; CLEMSON: Astro Triple; COLUMBIA: Carmike 10; FLORENCE: Magnolia Triple; GREENVILLE: Camelot Four; GREENWOOD: Apollo 2, Crosscreek Triple; HARTSVILLE: Cinema Twin; LAURENS: Oaks Twin; MT. PLEASANT: Carmike Triple; MYRTLE BEACH: Dunes Cinema Four, Myrtle Cinema Ten; N. MYRTLE BEACH: Briarcliff Six, Ocean Cinema Triple; ORANGEBURG: Cinema Triple; ROCK HILL: Cinema Seven; SUMTER: Cinema 2, Palmetto Twin; SURFSIDE: Deerfield Triple.

VIRGINIA—BLACKSBURG: Capri Twin; BRISTOL: Bristol 6; CHARLOTTESVILLE: Carmike Six, Terrace Triple; DANVILLE: Plaza Twin, Riverside Twin; LYNCHBURG: Carmike Eight; NEWPORT NEWS: Beechmont Twin; SALEM: Valley Eight; WILLIAMSBURG: Carmike Four.

WESTERN DIVISION

ALABAMA—ANNISTON: Carmike Six, Plaza Six; AUBURN: Cinema Four; BIRMINGHAM: Bama Six, Carmike Ten, Colonnade Ten; CULLMAN: Town Square Triple; DECATUR: Century 8; DOTHAN: Circle Four; FLORENCE: Capri Four, Hickory Hills 6; GADSDEN: Mall Triple; HUNTSVILLE: University Six; MOBILE: Bell Air Cinemas, Carmike 10, Dauphin Six, Springdale 6, Village Six; MONTGOMERY: Carmike 8, Eastdale Eight, Movies Four, Twin Oaks Four; MUSCLE SHOALS: Cinema Twin; OPELIKA: Carmike Seven; PHENIX CITY: Phenix Twin; PRATTVILLE: Movies Twin; SYLACAUGA: Plaza Twin; TALLADEGA: Martin Triple; TUSCALOOSA: Bama Six.

ARKANSAS—FT. SMITH: Carmike Eight; N. LITTLE ROCK: Carmike 7.

FLORIDA—PANAMA CITY: Florida Triple, Mall 4, PENSACOLA: Mariner 4.

KENTUCKY—BOWLING GREEN: Greenwood 6, Martin Twin, Plaza Six; HOPKINSVILLE: Martin Five; MADISONVILLE: Martin Four.

NEW MEXICO—ARTESIA: Cinema Twin.

OKLAHOMA—ARDMORE: Carmike Five; BARTLESVILLE: Eastland Four, Penn Twin; CUSHING: Dunkin; DUNCAN: Carmike Six; ELK CITY: Westland; EL RENO: Cinema; ENID: Oakwood Five, Video Twin; LAWTON: Showcase Twin, Video Triple; MUSKOGEE: Carmike Six; PONCA CITY: North Park Four; SHAWNEE: Cinema Centre 8, Hornbeck Twin; STILLWATER: Carmike Six, Satellite Twin.

TENNESSEE—ATHENS: Plaza Twin; CHATTANOOGA: Eastridge Six, Four Square Three, Northgate 8; CLARKSVILLE: Carmike Eight, Cinema Five, Martin Four; CLEVELAND: Carmike Four, Village Twin; COOKEVILLE: Highland Four, Varsity Twin; CROSSVILLE: Capri Twin; DYERSBURG: Martin Triple; FRANKLIN: Williamson Eight; GREENEVILLE: Capri Twin; JOHNSON CITY: Johnson City 8; KINGSPORT: Fort Henry Five, Martin Twin, Terrace Twin; KNOXVILLE: Commons Six, Kingston Four; LEBANON: Martin Triple; MARYVILLE: FootHills Eight; MORRISTOWN: Capri Four, College Square 6; MURFREESBORO: Carmike Six, Stone River 6; NASHVILLE: Belcourt Twin, Bell Road Triple, Belle Forge Ten, Bellevue Four, Brentwood Triple, Carmike Six, Cinema North Six, Cinema South Four, Fountain Sq. 14, Galleria 10, Hermitage Four, Hickory Mall Triple, Lions Head Five, Madison, Plaza, Rivergate Eight; SPRINGFIELD: Cinema.

TEXAS—ALBILENE: Park Central 6; AMARILLO: Cinema 2; BEAUMONT: Colonnade Four; BORGER: Morley Twin; COLLEGE STATION: Cinema 3, Post Oak 3; CONROE: Woodcreek Four; DENTON: Cinema 5; LAKE GREENVILLE: Rolling Hills Four; JACKSONVILLE: Cinema Triple; LAKE JACKSON: Brasoz Mall Triple, Cinema 4; LONGVIEW: Cinema Twin, Martin Twin, Northloop Six; LUFKIN: Angelina Twin, Cinema Four, Towne Square Four; NACOGDOCHES: Carmike Six, Carmike Seven & Eight; ORANGE: Cinema Twin; PLAINVIEW: Granada Twin; PT. ARTHUR: Central Mall Four; SILSBEE: Pines. TYLER: Gaslite 4, Southloop 4, Times Square 5; WACO: Cinema Twin, Waco Square 6; WITCHITA FALLS: Century City 6, Cinema 4, Sikes 6.

MID-WESTERN DIVISION

COLORADO—ASPEN: Stage 3; COLORDAO SPRINGS: Chapel Hills 9, Citadel Terrace 6; DURANGO: Gaslight Twin; FT. COLLINS: Creger Plaza 4, University Mall Triple; GLENWOOD SPRINGS: Mall 3; GRAND JUNCTION: Carmike 7; GREELY: Carmike 5; PUEBLO: Southside 4; VAIL: Crossroads 4.

IDAHO—BLACKFOOT: Plaza Twin; BOISE: Five Mile Plaza 4; CHUBBUCK: Starlite 3; IDAHO FALLS: Rio Theatre, Yellowstone 3; MOSCOW: Kenworthy, Nuar Theatre, University 4; POCATELLO: Alameda 3; REXBURG: Holiday 3, Westwood.

ILLINOIS—COLLINSVILLE: Petite 4; GALESBURG: Cinema 2; McCOMB: Cinema 2.

IOWA—CEDAR RAPIDS: Carmike 7, Collins Rd. 5, Lindale Mall 6, Stage 4, Westdale 4; COUNCIL BLUFFS: Mall of the Bluffs 5; DES MOINES: Century 6, Fleur 4, Forum 4, Valley 3, Value Cinema 7, Westwood 6; DUBUQUE: Cinema Center 8, Kennedy Mall 6; SIOUX CITY: Plaza 1 & 2, Riviera 2, Southern Hills 12.

MINNESOTA—ALBERT LEA: Mall 3; AUSTIN: Oakpark 3, Sterling 3; FAIRMONT: Fair Mall; MANKATO: Cinema 4, Mall 4; OWATONNA: Cameo 3; RED WING: Chief 3; ROCHESTER: Apache 4, Barclay Square 6, Cinema 3, Galleria 6; WINONA: Cinema 4; WORTHINGTON: Northland 3.

MONTANA—BILLINGS: Carmike 7, Cine 7, Rimrock 5, World West Twin; BOZEMAN: Campus Square 3, Ellen, Rialto; BUTTE: Plaza 6; GREAT FALLS: Cine 4, Twilite Twin, Village Twin; HELENA: Circus Twin, Gaslight 3, Sky Hi D.I.; MISSOULA: Cine 3, Village 6.

NEBRASKA—GRAND ISLAND: Conestoga 4, Island Twin; HASTINGS: Imperial 3; KEARNEY: Hilltop 4; OMAHA: Orchard Plaza 4.

NORTH DAKOTA—DICKINSON: Cine 3; MINOT: Cinema 5, Cinema 7.

SOUTH DAKOTA—RAPID CITY: Carmike 7; SIOUX FALLS: Carmike 7; WATERTOWN: Plaza 2.

UTAH—LOGAN: Cache Valley 3; OGDEN: City Sq. 4, Riverdale 4; OREM: Carillon Sq. 4; PROVO: Academy, Central Sq. 4; SALT LAKE CITY: Cottonwood 4, Creekside 3, Flick Twin, Plaza 5400 Six, Villa Theatre.

WASHINGTON—PULLMAN: Audian, Cordova, Old Post Office.

WISCONSIN—APPLETON: Fox River 10; BELOIT: Prairie 5; DELAVAN: Delavan 2; EAU CLAIRE: Oakwood Mall 6; FRANKLIN: 41 D.I. 4; GREEN BAY: Bay 3; LACROSSE: Valley 6; LAKE GENEVA: Geneva 4; MADISON: University Sq. 4; MARSHFIELD: Marshfield 3; RICE-LAKE: Cine 3; STEVENS POINT: Stevens Point 5; SUPERIOR: Mariner 4; WAUSAU: Wausau Theatre 5.

WYOMING—CASPER: Beverly 2, East ridge 4; CHEYENNE: Cole Square 3, Frontier 6; ROCK SPRINGS: White Mountain 2.

Carolina Cinemas Corp. (Roth Theatres)

P.O. Box 79, Columbia, SC 29202; (803) 798-1014. FAX: (803) 731-1262.

PAUL A. ROTH, pres.; IRWIN R. COHEN, sr. v.p.; MICHAEL E. ROWAN, v.p. of finance; CLYDE ELLISOR, ad/pub/promo dir.; WILLIAM JONES, distr. mgr.; MARK MADISON, film buyer.
NORTH CAROLINA—ASHEVILLE: Merrimon Theatres 2, Asheville West Theatres 2.
SOUTH CAROLINA—COLUMBIA: Columbia East 4, Dutch Square 3, Gamecock 2; ORANGEBURG: Camelot 4; SUMTER: Movies 3.

Central States Theatre Corp.

505 Fifth Ave., Insurance Exchange Bldg., Des Moines, IA 50309; (515) 243-5287.

MYRON BLANK, pres., treas.; JACQUELINE BLANK, v.p., asst. sec.; ARTHUR STEIN, JR., general manager; R.D. JACKSON, sec., asst. treas.

IOWA—AMES: Ames, Century 3, Mall 2, Varsity, Ranch D.I.; BURLINGTON: West 2, Palace 2, Drive-In; CEDAR FALLS: Cinema 4, Hillcrest 2 I, Drive-In; COUNCIL BLUFFS: Drive-In; DES MOINES: S.E. 14th St. D.I.; FORT DODGE: Cinema 4; CENTERVILLE: Majestic; CHARLES CITY: Charles; CLINTON: Capri III, Cinema I; IOWA CITY: Coral 4, Englert 2, Cinema 2, Campus 3; MASON CITY: Cinema V, Drive-In; NEWTON: Capitol 2; OTTUMWA: Capri V, Drive-In; FAIRFIELD: CoEd 2.

NEBRASKA—COLUMBUS: Center 4; FREMONT: Cinema 3; KEARNEY: World 2, Drive-In; NORFOLK: Cinema 3.

Chakeres Theatres

State Theatre Bldg., 19 Fountain Ave., Springfield, OH 45501; (513) 323-6447; FAX: (513) 325-1100.

M. H. CHAKERES, pres. & chm.; PAULINE CHAKERES, exec. v.p.; HARRY CHAKERES, v.p.; PHILIP CHAKERES, v.p.; EDWARD SCHUERMAN, film buyer; DOROTHY HART, booker; PAUL RAMSEY, dir. of adv.; ELDEN PADEN, compt.

OHIO—CELINA: Celina 5, Lake D.I.; DAYTON: Kettering Cinemas 1 & 2, Melody 49 D.I. 1 & 2, Belmont Auto; FAIRBORN: Fairborn Cinemas 1 & 2, Skyborn D.I.; HILLSBORO: Colony Cinema; NEW CARLISLE: Park Layne D.I.; PIQUA: Piqua 36 D.I.; PORTSMOUTH: Scioto Breeze D.I. 1 & 2; SIDNEY: Sidney Cinemas 1-3; SPRINGFIELD: Cinemas 7, Upper Valley Mall Cinemas 5, Regent Cinemas 1 & 2; Melody Cruise-In 1 & 2; URBANA: Urbana Cinemas 1 & 2; WILMINGTON: Plaza Cinemas 5, Wilmington D.I.

KENTUCKY—FRANKFORT: Brighton Park Cinemas 2, Franklin Square Cinemas 6; LEXINGTON/WINCHESTER: Skyvue Twin D.I.; MOREHEAD: University Cinema, Trail Cinema.

Cinamerica Corporation (formerly Mann Theatres)

Suite 200, 9200 Sunset Blvd., Los Angeles, CA, 90069; P.O. Box 60909, Terminal Annex, Los Angeles, CA, 90060; (310) 273-3336. FAX: (310) 276-6445.

KEN CROWE, exec. v.p.; BEN LITTLEFIELD, exec. v.p.; MIKE PADE, exec. dir. of film.

ALASKA—ANCHORAGE: University Sixplex; EAGLE RIVER: Valley River Sixplex.

ARIZONA—TUCSON: Park Mall Fourplex.

CALIFORNIA—AGOURA HILLS: Agoura Hills 8; ARROYO GRANDE: Festival Tenplex; BAKERSFIELD: Crest Drive-In Twin; CITY OF INDUSTRY: Puente Hills 6; CLOVIS: Regency Sixplex; CULVER CITY: Culver Plaza 6; FRESNO: Festival Sixplex, Fig Garden Fourplex; GLENDALE: Exchange 8; GLENDORA: Glendora 6; HAYWARD: Festival Nineplex; HOLLYWOOD: Chinese 3, Vogue; LA JOLLA: University Towne Center Sixplex; LARKSPUR: Festival Fourplex; MANHATTAN BEACH: Manhattan Village 6; MARTINEZ: Contra Costa Fiveplex; MODESTO: Festival Tenplex; MONROVIA: Huntington Oaks Sixplex; NATIONAL CITY: Plaza Bonita Sixplex; OCEANSIDE: El Camino Sixplex; PASADENA: Hastings Ranch Triplex; SAN DIEGO: Bernardo 6, Grove 9, Cinema 21, Hazard Center 7, Rancho Bernardo Sixplex, Sports Arena Sixplex, Valley Circle; SAN LUIS OBISPO: Fremont; SAN RAMON: Crow Canyon Sixplex; SANTA FE SPRINGS: Santa Fe Springs 8; SANTA MONICA: Criterion 6; SIMI VALLEY: Sycamore Plaza 6; STOCKTON: Festival Fourplex, Regency Fourplex; TARZANA: Valley West Sixplex; THOUSAND OAKS: Conejo Twin; TORRANCE: Del Amo 9, Old Towne Sixplex; VALENCIA: Mann Tenplex; VENTURA: Buenaventura Sixplex; VISALIA: Fox Triplex, Sequoia Triplex; WALNUT CREEK: Festival Fiveplex; WESTWOOD: Bruin, Mann Fourplex, National, Plaza, Regent, Village.

COLORADO—AURORA: Aurora Mall Triplex, Aurora Plaza 6; BOULDER: Arapahoe Village 4, Fox; DENVER: Century 21, Cherry Creek 8, Tamarac Square Sixplex; ENGLEWOOD: Arapahoe East Fourplex; LAKEWOOD: Green Mountain Sixplex, Union Square Sixplex, LITTLETON: Festival 6, Kipling Place Sixplex, Southwest Plaza Fiveplex; NORTHGLENN: Northglenn Sixplex.

Cinema Entertainment Corp.

Box 1126, St. Cloud, MN 56302; (612) 251-9131; FAX: (612) 251-1003.

ROBERT A. ROSS, pres.; EDWARD VILLATA, gen. mgr.; ANTHONY D. TILLEMANS, v.p.; DAVID M. ROSS, sec.; GEORGE R. BECKER, treas.; STANLEY McCULLOCH, booker.

IOWA—WATERLOO: Crossroads 10.

MINNESOTA—BEMIDJI: Amigo 5; BRECKENRIDGE: Cinema 4; DULUTH: Cinema 8; FARIBAULT: Cinema 6; ST CLOUD: Crossroads 6, Parkwood 8, Cinema Arts 3; MOORHEAD: Safari 7; VIRGINIA: Cinema 4.

NORTH DAKOTA—FARGO: West Acres 5, West 3, Century 7.

WISCONSIN—HUDSON: Southside Cinema 4.

Cinema World

107 Sixth Street, Pittsburgh, PA 15222; (412) 232-0042; FAX: (412) 232-0052.

JEFFREY G. LEWINE, pres.; ANTHONY J. CRISAFIO, COO; PATRICK J. COREY, v.p.-opns.; VINCE PORCO, v.p.-construction.

OHIO—EAST LIVERPOOL: Skyview; FINDLAY: Cinema World Findlay, Twin Palace; MANSFIELD: Cinema World Mansfield; MT. VERNON: Colonial; SANDUSKY: Cinema World Sandusky, Mall Sandusky; ST. CLAIRSVILLE: Cinema World St. Clairsville; STEUBENVILLE: Cinema World Steubenville.

PENNSYLVANIA—PITTSBURGH: Monroeville, Mt. Lebanon, Norwin, Rainbow, Southland, Squirrel Hill, Village; MONACA: Movie World; GREENSBURG: Cinema World Greensburg, Westmoreland Mall, Greengate Mall, Cinema III; LATROBE: Laurel 30; ERIE: Cinema World Erie, Plaza Erie; CRANBERRY: Cranberry Mall, Oil City; BUTLER: Cinema World Butler, Plaza Butler; EDINBORO: Cinema World Edinboro; SHARON: Hermitage Plaza; WASHINGTON: Cinema 19, Washington Mall; STATE COLLEGE: Cinema World 5, Cinema World 6, Movies, State Twin.

WEST VIRGINIA—CLARKSBURG: Cinema World 6; MORGANTOWN: Morgantown Mall, Warner.

CinemaCal Enterprises, Inc.

1130 Burnett Ave., Suite J, P.O. Box 27848, Concord, CA 94527; (510) 685-6650. FAX: (510) 685-6507.

DALE DAVISON, pres., CEO; LOU LENCIONI III, v.p., head film buyer; RON DUNNING, v.p., opns.; SHEILA LUSK, v.p., finance; MAURICE L'ESTRANGE, v.p., adv.; PAT PETERSEN, admin. asst.

CALIFORNIA—MONTEREY: Galaxy 6; MORGAN HILL: Cinema 6, Granada 1 & 2; PANORAMA CITY: Americana 5; STOCKTON: Royal 4, Sherwood Plaza 1 & 2; VACAVILLE: Galaxy 8.

Cinemark Theatres

7502 Greenville Ave., Suite 800, LB9, Dallas, TX 75231; (214) 696-1644; FAX: (214) 696-3946. Buying & Booking Office: same as above except phone: (214) 692-1425, 692-1471, 692-1419. FAX: (214) 696-3946.

PAUL BROADHEAD, bd. chm.; LEE ROY MITCHELL, vice chmn. & CFO; TANDY MITCHELL, exec. v.p., ALAN STOCK, pres.; TED CONLEY, head film buyer, South; KEN HIGGINS, head film buyer, East/intl.; FRED KUNKEL, head film buyer/West; TOM OWENS, v.p., domestic dvlpmt.; JEFF STEDMAN, CFO; OSCAR MONTEMAYOR, dir., intl. dvlpmt.; STEVE SCHREIBER, v.p., real estate; ROBERT CARMONY, dir. thea. opns.; RON REID, construction dir.,; LOYD GIBBONS, construction project mgr.; PAM KENNEDY, interior design dir.; MICHAEL SENIO, dir. concessions; LYNN NORTON, dir. adv., West; GARY GIBBS, gen. counsel; RANDY HESTER, dir. corp. develop.; PHIL ZACHERETTI, dir. of adv., East.

ALABAMA—MOBILE: Festival Movies 10.

ARIZONA—KINGMAN: The Movies 4.

ARKANSAS—CONWAY: Cinema 6; LITTLE ROCK: Tandy 10.

CALIFORNIA—CHICO: Movies 10; HANFORD: Movies 4, Movies 8; LOS ANGELES AREA: CATHEDRAL CITY: Movies 10; CHINO: Movies 8; HEMET: Holiday Cinema 4, Movies 10; LANCASTER: Movies 3, Movies 4, Movies 6, Movies 12; PALMDALE: Movies 8, VICTORVILLE: Movies 7, Movies 10; REDDING: Movies 8; SAN FRANCISCO AREA: DANVILLE: Blackhawk Movies 7; WOODLAND: County Fair Movies 5; YUBA CITY: Yuba City 8.

DELAWARE—WILMINGTON: Movies 10.

FLORIDA—ORLANDO: Movies 12; TALLAHASSEE: Movies 8.

GEORGIA—ATLANTA AREA: FAYETTEVILLE: Movies 10; DUBLIN: Westgate Cinema 4.

ILLINOIS—JOLIET: Movies 8.

INDIANA—CLARKSVILLE: Greentree 4, Greentree 10; INDIANAPOLIS: Greenwood Corners Movies 8, Washington Market Movies 8; SOUTH BEND: Movies 10; TELL CITY: Twin 2.

KANSAS—KANSAS CITY AREA: OVERLAND PARK: Park 10.

KENTUCKY—ASHLAND: Town Cinema 10; CORBIN: Cinema 4; DANVILLE: Cinema 4; HARLAN: Cinema 4; LEXINGTON: Green 8, Man o' War 8; LOUISVILLE: Village 8; MAYSVILLE: Cinema 4; MIDDLESBORO: Cinema 4; PADUCAH: Kentucky Oaks 12; RICHMOND: Movies 8.

LOUISIANA—MONROE: Cinema 3, Cinema 10.

MICHIGAN—DETROIT AREA: LIVONIA: Terrace Cinema 4, ROSEVILLE: Macomb 4; SOUTHFIELD: Tel-Ex Cinema 4; WARREN: Universal Mall Movies 16.

MINNESOTA—MANKATO: Movies 8; MINNEAPOLIS AREA: Crystal Movies 10.

MISSISSIPPI—TUPELO: Movies 8.

NEBRASKA—OMAHA: Stockyards Movies 8.

NEW JERSEY—SOMERDALE: Movies 10.

NEW MEXICO—ALBUQUERQUE: Movies 8, Westside 8.

NEW YORK—SYRACUSE: Movies 10.

NORTH CAROLINA—ASHEBORO: Randolph Cinema 5; GREENSBORO: Brassfield 10; SALISBURY: Mall Cinema 6.

OHIO—ALLIANCE: Carnation Cinema 8; BOWLING GREEN: Woodland Mall Cinema 8; CANTON: Movies 4, Movies 10; CLEVELAND AREA: WILLOUGHBY HILLS: Movies 10; COLUMBUS: Carriage Place Movies 12, Mill Run Movies 12; MANSFIELD: Richland 3, Springfield Square 10; PIQUA: Miami Valley Cinema 6; SANDUSKY: Movies 10; WOOSTER: Movies 10; YOUNGSTOWN AREA: BOARDMAN: Movies 10; ZANESVILLE: Colony Square 10.

OKLAHOMA—ADA: North Hills 12; TULSA: Movies 8; TULSA AREA: BROKEN ARROW: Cinema 8, SAND SPRINGS: Cinema 8.

OREGON—MEDFORD: Movies 4, Movies 5; MEDFORD AREA: WHITE CITY: Movies 6; SPRINGFIELD/EUGENE: Gateway Movies 12.

SOUTH CAROLINA—CHARLESTON AREA: SUMMERVILLE: Movies 8.

TENNESSEE—KNOXVILLE: Movies 10; LA FOLLETTE: Movies 2; OLIVER SPRINGS: Tri County Cinema 3; ONEIDA: Cinema 3.

TEXAS—AUSTIN AREA: PFLUGERVILLE: Movies 12, ROUND ROCK: Movies 8, Wells Branch Movies 8; BIG SPRINGS: Movies 4; CLEBURNE: Cinema 6; COLLEGE STATION: Movie 16; CORPUS CHRISTIE: Dollar Cinema 7; CORSIDANA: Cinema 4; DALLAS AREA: ARLINGTON: Movies 8, CARROLLTON: Movies 8, GARLAND: Hollywood USA 15, GRAND PRAIRIE: Movies 16, LANCASTER: Movies 8, LEWISVILLE: Movies 8, Movies 12, MESQUITE: Big Town Cinema 9, PLANO: Movies 10, ROCKWALL: Movies 10; DEL RIO: Cinema 3; FT. WORTH: Wedgwood 4; FT. WORTH AREA: N. RICHMOND HILLS: Movies 8; HOUSTON: Bear Creek 6, Eastway 4, Northwest Village 6, Village 6, Windchimes 8; HOUSTON AREA: BAY CITY: Cinema 4, CONROE: Pine Hollow 6, KATY: Mason Park 8, MISSOURI CITY: Central 6, PASADENA: Movies 12, Southmore 6, ROSENBERG: Randall 4, TEXAS CITY: Movies 12, LUBBOCK: Movies 12, Slide Road Movies 4, South Plains Cinema 4; PARIS: Movies 2; PLAINVIEW: Town Centre Movies 6; RIO GRANDE VALLEY AREA: BROWNSVILLE: Amigo Land 2, Movies 10, Northpark Cinema 3, Sunrise Cinema 3, KINGSVILLE: Cinema 2, McALLEN: Cinema 2, Main Place 6, Movies 10; PHARR: Movies 8; WESLACO: Palm Plaza 2; SAN ANTONIO: McCreless 9, Movies 16; SHERMAN: Cinema 4, Cinema 7, Midway Movies 5; STEPHENVILLE: Cinema 6; TEXARKANA: Movies 8; VICTORIA: Cinema 4, Playhouse Cinema 4, Salem Cinema 6.

UTAH—LAYTON: Layton Hills 6, Movies 10; OGDEN: Newgate 4; PARK CITY: Holiday Village Cinema 3; PROVO: Movies 8; SALT LAKE CITY AREA: SANDY: Movies 9, SUGARHOUSE: Movies 10, WEST VALLEY CITY: Valley Fair 9.

VIRGINIA—LYNCHBURG: Movies 10; NORFOLK AREA: CHESAPEAKE: Movies 10; RICHMOND AREA: MECHANICSVILLE: Movies 14.

WISCONSIN—MILWAUKEE: Southgate Movies 10.

Cineplex Odeon Corporation (U.S.)

The following circuits are wholly owned U.S. subsidiaries of the Cineplex Odeon Corporation, 1303 Yonge Street, Toronto, Ontario M4T 2Y9; (416) 323-6600

Senator E. LEO KOLBER, Chairman; ALLEN KARP, pres. & CEO; NEIL BLATT, exec. v.p., film; HOWARD LICHTMAN, exec. v.p., mktg. & communications; ELLIS JACOB, exec. v.p. & chief financial officer; ROBERT TOKIO, exec. v.p.; IRWIN COHEN, sr. v.p., thea. opns.; JERRY BULGER, v.p. pub. affairs; No. Amer. thea. opns.; BILL HERTING, v.p. film, south div.; MICHAEL HERMAN, sr. v.p., corp. affairs; JEFFREY KENT, v.p. finance, theatres; SHAUNA KING, v.p. film central & western divisions; MICHAEL MCCARTNEY, sr. v.p. U.S. film div.; WILLIAM SNELLING, sr. v.p. adv.; DAN MCGRATH, Controller.

Regional Cineplex Odeon U.S. Executive Offices

LOS ANGELES: 1925 Century Park East, Suite 300, Los Angeles, CA 90067; (310) 551-2500.

NEW YORK: 241 East 34th Street, New York, NY 10016; (212) 679-2000.

CHICAGO: 70 E. Lake St., Suite 1600, Chicago, IL 60601-5905; (312) 726-5300.

WASHINGTON, D.C.: 1101 23rd Street N.W., Washington, D.C. 20037; (202) 331-7471.

ATLANTA: 1572 Holcomb Bridge Road, Roswell, GA 30076; (404) 992-8119.

HOUSTON: 1450 West Gray, Houston, TX 77019; (713) 524-8731.

DALLAS: 12801 North Central Expressway, Suite 1515, Dallas, TX 75243; (214) 991-0020.

SEATTLE: 18421 Alderwood Mall Blvd., Lynnwood, WA 98036; (206) 771-9011.

ARIZONA—TUCSON: Catalina 6, Crossroads 6, El Dorado 6, Foothills 7, Scottsdale Galleria 7.

CALIFORNIA—DALY CITY: Plaza 2; LOS ANGELES: Beverly Centre 13, Century Plaza 4, Fairfax Triple, Showcase, Universal City (18 screens); MARINA DEL REY: Marine Marketplace 6; SANTA MONICA: Broadway 4 Cinemas; RICHMOND: Hilltop 8; SAN FRANCISCO: Northpoint.

DISTRICT OF COLUMBIA—WASHINGTON: Avalon 2, Dupont 5, Embassy, Wisconsin Ave. (6), Jenifer 2, MacArthur Theatre (3), Outer Circle (2), Tenley 3, Uptown, West End 7.

FLORIDA—BRANDON: Plitt 4-plex; CLEARWATER: Countryside Village (4), Main Street 5, Sunshine Mall (5); JACKSONVILLE: Baymeadows 8, Mandarin 6; OCALA: Springs (3); ORLANDO: Hoffner Centre 6, Plaza 2, Sandlake 7, University 8; PENSACOLA: Plaza 3; TAMPA: Hillsboro (8), Main Street 16, University Collection (6).

GEORGIA—CONYERS: Conyers 8; CUMMING: Cumming 3; DECATUR: Market Square (4); DORAVILLE: Fridays Plaza (6); DOUGLASVILLE: Douglasville 3, Douglasville Exchange (3); DULUTH: Mall-Corners VI; GRIFFIN: Griffin 4; LaGRANGE: LaGrange Cinema 6; LAWRENCEVILLE: Lawrenceville 4; MARIETTA: Merchant's Exchange (5), Towne Centre (6); MORROW: Southlake Triple, Southlake Festival 6; PEACHTREE CITY: Westpark Walk (3); ROSWELL: Brannon Square (2), Holcomb Woods (6); SNELLVILLE: Snellville 5; STONE MOUNTAIN: Festival Cinema 6, Memorial Drive 5, Memorial Drive 4, Memorial Square (6), Stonemount (2).

IDAHO—BOISE: Egyptian, 8th St. Marketplace (2), Northgate Cinemas (6), Towne Square Cinemas (6); NAMPA: Nampa Cinemas (6).

ILLINOIS—ARLINGTON HEIGHTS: Ridge Cinemas 8, Town 'n Country (6); AURORA: Fox Valley 10, West Plaza 3, Westridge Court (3); BLOOMINGDALE: Stratford Square 8, Bloomingdale Court (6); CALUMET CITY: River Oaks 12; CARPENTERSVILLE: Springhill Mall 6; CHICAGO: Bricktown Square (6), Broadway (Lakeshore), Biograph 3, Burnam Plaza 5, Chestnut Station (5), Chicago Ridge (4), Commons (4), Lincoln Village 3, Lincoln Village 6, McClurg (3), Plaza (3), 900 North Michigan (2), Water Tower 7; CREST HILL (JOLIET): Hillcrest (2); DOWNERS GROVE: Grove Cinemas (5); HOMEWOOD: Diana 4; NILES: Golf Mill (3), Golf Glen (6); NORTHBROOK: Edens 2; NORTH RIVERSIDE: North Riverside Theatres (6); OAKBROOK: Oakbrook (3), Oakbrook Mall (4); ORLAND PARK: Orland Square 8; SCHAUMBURG: Schaumberg (9); Woodfield 9; ST. CHARLES: Foxfield 3). St. Charles (3); VERNON HILLS: Hawthorne Quad, Rivertree Court (8); WHEATON: Rice Lake 10.

MARYLAND—BOWIE: Market Place 6; GAITHESBERG: Rio 8 Cinemas; GAITHERSBURG: Lake Forest (5); St. Charles Town (9); KENSINGTON: White Flint (5); MARLOW HEIGHTS: Marlow (6); WALDORF: Waldorf North 4, Waldorf South 5; WHEATON: Wheaton Plaza 4.

MINNESOTA—EDINA: Edina 4, Yorktown 3; MINNEAPOLIS: Skyway 6; MINNETONKA: Ridge Square 3, Westwind 3; PLYMOUTH: Willow Creek 8; ST. LOUIS PARK: Knollwood 4.

NEW JERSEY—BLOOMFIELD: Royal Twin; CRANFORD: Cranford Twin; JERSEY CITY: Newport Centre (9); MENLO PARK: Menlo Park 12; MILBURN: Milburn Twin; PARAMUS: Paramus Rt. #4 (10), Paramus Rt. #17 (2); RIDGEWOOD: Warner Quad; UNION: Union Twin.

NEW YORK—NEW YORK CITY: BROOKLYN: Metro 4, Alpine (7), Fortway (5), Kenmore Quad, Kings Plaza Quad, Kingsway 5-plex; MANHATTAN: 23rd St. (3), Baronet, Cinema 3, Coronet, Ziegfield, 34th St., Manhattan I & II, Waverly, National Twin, Bay Cinema, Greenwich Twin, Carnegie Hall, Metro (2), Regency, Chelsea 9, Park & 86th 2, 62nd & Broadway, 1st & 62nd, Beekman, Olympia Twin, Plaza, Worldwide Cinemas (3), 59th St. East,; FRESH MEADOWS: Meadows 7, City Cinema 5; HUNTINGTON: Shore Quad, Whitman; LAKE GROVE: Mall Smithhaven Theatre 4; LAWRENCE: Lawrence Triplex; NANUET: Nanuet 5-plex; ROCKVILLE CENTER: Fantasy (5), Rockville Twin; GLEN COVE: Glen Cove 6; PORT WASHINGTON: Soundview 6, Islip Cinema, Hampton Arts Twin, Mattituck 8.

TEXAS—BAYTOWN: Cinema 6, Goose Creek Cinema (6), Plitt Cinema 5, HOUSTON: Plitt (5), Cinema 7 West Oaks (7), Presidio Square (6), River Oaks (12), Sharpstown Center (8), Spectrum (9), RICHARDSON: Promenade 6; TEMPLE: Cinema 5, Plitt 6; WACO: Cinema 3 & 4.

UTAH—MIDVALE: Family Center 4; NORTH SALT LAKE CITY: Trolley North 3; ODGEN: Cinedome 2, Wilshire 3; OREM: University 4; SALT LAKE CITY: Broadway 6, Crossroads 3, Holladay Center 6, Midvalley Cinemas 6, Trolley Corners 3, Trolley Square Mall 4; SANDY: South Towne Centre 10.

VIRGINIA—ALEXANDRIA: Old Town (2); ARLINGTON: Shirlington (7); FAIRFAX: Fair City Mall (6); LAKERIDGE: Tackett's Mills (4); MANASSAS: Manassas Mall (7); VIENNA: Tysons Centre (4).

WASHINGTON—BELLEVUE: Factoria Cinemas (8), John Danz; LYNWOOD: Grand Cinemas Alderwood 8, SEATTLE: Cinerama, City Centre Cinemas (2), Lewis & Clark (7), Newmark Square 5, Northgate, Oak Tree Cinemas (6), South Centre, Uptown (3); TACOMA: Tacoma

Central Cinemas 6, Tacoma Mall Twin, Tacoma South Cinemas (4), Tacoma West Cinemas (5); KIRKLAND: Kirkland Park Place 6, Lakewood 6, Totem Lake 3.

City Cinemas

1001 Third Ave., New York, NY 10022; (212) 758-5600; FAX: (212) 832-1518. (An affiliate of Pacific Theatres of So. Calif.).

JAMES J. COTTER, chm. & CEO; JEROME A. FORMAN, pres.; HERB MILLMAN, v.p., optns.; LINDA HOGARTY, adv.

NEW YORK—NEW YORK CITY: Cinema 1, Cinema 2, Cinema 3rd Ave., 86th St. East 1 & 2, 57th St. Playhouse, Murray Hill 4, 68th St. Playhouse, Sutton 1 & 2, Village East Cinemas 7.

Clark Theatres

P.O. Box 570, Enterprise, AL 36331; (205) 347-1129.

MACK CLARK, JR., owner.

ALABAMA—ANDALUSIA: Martin Twin Cinema; ENTERPRISE: Cinema I&II, Cinema III&IV, College Cinema 3; OZARK: Twin Cinemas 2.

Classic Cinemas

936 Warren Ave. Downers Grove, IL 60515; (708) 968-1600. FAX: (708) 968-1626. (A division of Tivoli Enterprises, Inc.)

WILLIS JOHNSON, pres.; CHRISTOPHER JOHNSON, v.p.; SHIRLEY JOHNSON, secty.

ILLINOIS—CARPENTERSVILLE: Cinema 5; DOWNERS GROVE: Tivoli, Tivoli South; ELK GROVE VILLAGE: Elk Grove; ELMHURST: York; FREEPORT: Lindo; HANOVER PARK: Tradewinds; KANKAKEE: Meadowview, Paramount; OAK PARK: Lake; PARK FOREST: Centre Cinema; ST. CHARLES: Arcada; WOODSTOCK: Woodstock.

Cobb Theatres

Executive Office: 924 Montclair Road, Birmingham, AL 35213; (205) 591-2323; FAX: (205) 591-7715. Booking Office: 2400 Herodian Way, Suite 125, Smyrna, GA 30080-2906.

R. C. COBB, pres.; R. M. COBB, exec. v.p.; J. R. COBB, exec. v.p., JUDITH BLANK, contr.; MILT DALY, v.p. opns.; R. M. ZEITZ, dir. adv.; JERRY BRAND, film buyer; WES CLINE, dir. real estate.

ALABAMA—BIRMINGHAM: Centerpoint 6, Galleria 10, Festival 12, Hoover Square 8, Midfield 6, Wildwood 14; HUNTSVILLE: Cinema 8, Madison Square 12; JASPER: Movies 4; SELMA: Cahaba Twin; TUSCALOOSA: Fox 10.

ARKANSAS—FAYETTEVILLE: Fiesta Square 10; ROGERS: Mall 6.

FLORIDA—BELLEVIEW: Belleview Twin; BOYNTON BEACH: Boynton 8; BRADENTON: Bradenton 8, DeSoto Square 6, Oakmont 8; CAPE CORAL: Coralwood 14; FT. MYERS: Edison Park 8, Bell Tower East 6, Bell Tower North 6, Bell Tower West 6; FT. PIERCE: Sabal Palm 6; GREEN ACRES CITY: Lakeworth 8; JUPITER: Jupiter 14; KEY WEST: Cinema 6; KISSIMMEE: Osceola Square West 6, Osceola Square East 6; LARGO: Largo Mall 8; MELBOURNE: Oaks 10, Roxy 10; NAPLES: Pavilion 10, Towne Centre 6; PINELLAS PARK: Pinella 3, Pinellas 6; PORT CHARLOTTE: Cinema Centre 8; PORT RICHEY: Embassy 6, Gulfside 10; ST. AUGUSTINE: Mall 6; SARASOTA: Cinema 10, Gulfgate 8, Parkway 8; STUART: Martin Square, Regency Square 8; SUNRISE: Sawgrass 18; TAMPA: Eastlake 3, Northdale 6, University Square 4; VENICE: Venetian 6; VERO BEACH: Vero 6; WINTER HAVEN: Springhlake 10.

GEORGIA—CARROLLTON: Mall 6.

MISSISSIPPI—JACKSON: Metro Center 4.

SOUTH CAROLINA—COLUMBIA: Capital 8.

Consolidated Amusement Co., Ltd.

P.O. Box 30548, Honolulu, HI 96820.

HAWAII—ISLAND OF HAWAII: (Hilo) Prince Kuhio Twin; Waiakea Triplex, (Kona) Hualalai Triplex; ISLAND OF OAHU: Aikahi Twin, Cinerama, Kahala Eight-Plex, Kam D.I. Twins, Kapiolani, Koko Marina, Kuhio Twins, Marina Twins, Mililani Tri-Plex, Pearlridge Fourplex, Pearlridge West 12-Plex, Varsity Twins, Waikiki Twins, Waikiki #3; ISLAND OF MAUI: Maui Theatre, Kukui Mall Four-Plex; ISLAND OF KAUAI: Plantation Cinema Twins.

Consolidated Theatres/The Stone Group

1130 East Third St., Suite 490, Charlotte, NC 28204; (704) 375-1741. FAX: (704) 375-1743.

HERMAN A. STONE, pres.; H. AUBREY STONE, JR., v.p.

NORTH CAROLINA—CHARLOTTE: Arboretum Cinemas; MONROE: Union Square Cinemas.

SOUTH CAROLINA—LEXINGTON: Pastime Cinemas.

Co-op Theatres of Michigan

21751 W. 9 Mile Rd., Suite 112, Southfield, MI 48075; (313) 356-4343.

K.J. GUIBORD, pres.

MICHIGAN—AUGUSTA: Park; CLARE: Ideal; EAST TAWAS: Family; GRAYLING: Rialto; MARSHALL: Bogar; MUSKEGON: Harbor 1 & 2; OSCODA: Lake; PAW PAW: Strand; THREE RIVERS: Riviera.

Crown Cinema Corporation

406 West 34th St., Kansas City, MO 64111; (816) 753-2355. FAX: (816) 931-6021.

RICHARD M. DURWOOD, pres.; BRENT HUDSON, controller; HAL McCLURE, head film buyer; JACKIE DIXON, secty.; HAROLD SAWTELLE, dir. operations.

KANSAS—EMPORIA: Flint Hills, Petitie Twin 2; GARDEN CITY: Sequoyah 2, State; GREAT BEND: Village 3; HUTCHINSON: Cinema Twin, Mall Cinema 4; JUNCTION CITY: Westside 2; LAWRENCE: Cinema Twin, Hillcrest 5, Varsity; LEAVENWORTH: Landing 4; LIBERAL: Southgate 4; TOPEKA: Gage 4, Boulevard 3, West Ridge 8; WICHITA: Cinema East 6, Cinema West 4, Pawnee 4.

MISSOURI—CHILLICOTHE: Ben Bolt; COLUMBIA: Campus 2, Cinema, Mall 4; JEFFERSON CITY: Ramada 4, Capital 4; JOPLIN: Joplin 6; KANSAS CITY: Blue Ridge East 5, Blue Ridge West 6, Blue Springs 8, Chouteau 4, Red Bridge 4, Seville 4, Truman Corners 4, Watts Mill 4; ROLLA: Forum 2, Ritz, Uptown; ST. JOSEPH: Hillcrest 4, Plaza 8; WARRENSBURG: Campus 2.

OHIO—HEATH: Indian Mound 6; NEWARK: Newark 4.

Crown Theatres

301 Merritt 7 Corporate Park, Norwalk, CT 06851; (203) 846-8800; FAX: (203) 846-9828.

DANIEL M. CROWN, pres.; FRANK THIEL, CFO; STEVE GOULD, dir. adv.; THOMAS BECKER, gen. mgr. theatres.

CONNECTICUT—DANBURY: Cine 3, Palace 3, Cinema 1 & 2; GREENWICH: Plaza 3; STAMFORD: Landmark Square Cinemas 3, Avon 2, Ridgway 2; TRUMBULL: Trumbull Cinemas 3.

NEW YORK—NEW YORK CITY: Gotham.

D

DeAnza Drive-Ins

1615 Cordova St., Los Angeles, CA 90007; (213) 734-9951.

WILLIAM H. OLDKNOW, pres.; JOSEPH PIETROFORTE, gen. mgr.

ARIZONA—TUSCON: DeAnza 4, Apache 2.

CALIFORNIA—POMONA: Mission 4; RUBIDEOUX: Rubideoux 2; SAN DIEGO: South Bay 3; VAN BUREN: Van Buren 3.

GEORGIA—ATLANTA: Starlite 6.

UTAH—SALT LAKE CITY: Redwood 6.

Dickinson Operating Co., Inc.

5913 Woodson Road, Mission, KS 66202; (913) 432-2334; FAX: (913) 432-9507.

WOOD DICKINSON, pres./bd. chmn.; GEORGIA DICKINSON, bd. chmn. emeritus; SCOTT DICKINSON, v.p.; PATTI DICKINSON, v.p., comm. rltns.; STEVE TAUL, treas./asst. sec.; STEVE KRUEGER, sec.; FRANK TORCHIA, v.p./head film buyer.

ILLINOIS—QUINCY: Quincy Mall Cinema 3.

KANSAS—HAYS: Fox 2; LAWRENCE: Dickinson Cinema 6; NEWTON: Fox; OLATHE: Olathe Landing 8; OVERLAND PARK: Metcalf 2, Glenwood 4, South Glen 12; PITTSBURG: Mall Cinema 4; SALINA: Central Mall 4, Vogue, Midstates 2, Sunset Plaza 2; TOPEKA: Fox Whitelakes 4; WICHITA: Mall Cinema 4, Northrock 6.

MISSOURI—BRANSON: Tablerock 4; COLUMBIA: Biscayne 3, Forum 8; GLADSTONE: Gladstone 4; INDEPENDENCE: Noland Fashion Square 6; JOPLIN: Eastgate Cinema 5, Northpark 4, Northpark Mall 5; KANSAS CITY: Antioch 2, Dickinson Cinema 6, Plaza 3; ST. JOSEPH: Trail; SPRINGFIELD: Century 21, Dickinson 8, Fremont 3, Town & Country 6, Tower, Northtown 4; WEBB CITY: Webb City D.I.

OKLAHOMA—MUSKOGEE: Arrowhead Mall Cinema 6.

Dipson Theatres, Inc.

P.O. Box 579, Batavia, NY 14021; (716) 343-2700.
BERNARD CLEMENT, pres.; WILLIAM GILLILAND, v.p.; MARK
CLEMENT, v.p.; BONNIE CLEMENT, sec. treas.
NEW YORK—BATAVIA: Cinemas I & II, Mall I & II; BUFFALO:
Amherst 3, North Park Cinema; DUNKIRK: Cine I & II; ELMIRA:
Heights; HORNELL: Cinemas Three; JAMESTOWN: Wintergarden;
LAKEWOOD: Chautauqua Mall Cinemas I & II, Lakewood Cinema 6;
SALAMANCA: Cinema I & II.
PENNSYLVANIA—BRADFORD: Cinemas I & II.

Douglas Theatre Co.

P.O. Box 81848, Lincoln, NE 68501; (402) 474-4909.
NEBRASKA—BELLEVUE: South Cinema 7, Southroads 4; LIN-
COLN: Cinema Twin, East Park 3, Douglas 3, Edgewood 3, Lincoln 3,
Plaza 4, Stuart; OMAHA: Cinema Center Complex 8, Maplewood Twin,
Q Cinema 9, Park 4, Millard 4.

E

Eastern Federal Corp.

513 S. Tryon St., Charlotte, NC 28202; (704) 377-3495;
FAX: (704) 358-8427.
IRA S. MEISELMAN, pres.; PAUL E. LLOYD, v.p. & treas.; P. E.
LLOYD, secty; GEORGE ROYSTER, secty.; JACK DURELL, film
buyer; CECIL ALLEN, dir. of adv.-pub./v.p. optns.
FLORIDA—JACKSONVILLE: Cedar Hills I & 2, Royal Palm 1, 2 &
3; TALLAHASSEE: Miracle Five, Oak Lake 6; GAINESVILLE: Royal
Park 1, 2, 3 & 4; ORLANDO: Orange Blossom 1 & 2, Conway 1 & 2;
PANAMA CITY: Regency Six; FORT MYERS: South Pointe 6; FORT
WALTON BEACH: Sun Plaza 4; PORT ORANGE: Port Orange 6; PORT
ST. LUCIE: Village Green 6.
NORTH CAROLINA—CHARLOTTE: Delta 6, Movies 8, Regency
Four, Manor 1 & 2, Park 51-6; CHAPEL HILL: Movies at Timberlyne 6,
Plaza 3; CORNELIUS: Movies on the Lake; LUMBERTON: Town &
Country 1, 2, 3 & 4; WINSTON-SALEM: North Point 5.
SOUTH CAROLINA—COLUMBIA: The Movies at Polo Road 8.

Edwards Theatres

300 Newport Center Drive, Newport Beach, CA 92660;
(714) 640-4603; FAX: (714) 721-7170.
JAMES EDWARDS 3d, pres. & chief operating officer; JAMES ED-
WARDS, SR., chm.; JOAN EDWARDS RANDOLPH, exec. v.p.; DON
C. BARTON, dir. of operations; FRANK HAFFAR, v.p. & chief admin.
officer; MARCELLA SHELDON, chief corp. secty.
CALIFORNIA—ALHAMBRA: Alhambra Place, Atlantic Palace;
ANAHEIM: Anaheim Hills Festival; ARCADIA: Edwards Drive-In;
AZUSA: Azusa D.I., Foothill Center; BREA: Brea Plaza; CARLSBAD:
La Costa; CORONA: Corona 11, Corona West End 8; COSTA MESA:
Cinema, Harbor Twin, Cinema Center 4, Mesa, South Coast Plaza 1 & 2,
South Coast Plaza 3, Triangle Square, Town Center; DEL MAR: Del Mar,
Flower Hill Twin; EL MONTE: El Monte Cinemas; EL TORO: Saddle-
back 123, Saddleback 456, El Toro; ESCONDIDO: Carousel 6, Vineyard;
FONTANA: Inland Impire Center; FOUNTAIN VALLEY: Fountain Val-
ley, Family Four-Orange Coast Cinemas; HUNTINGTON BEACH: Hunt-
ington Twin, Charter Centre, Huntington Pierside; IRVINE: University,
Woodbridge; LAGUNA BEACH: South Coast Laguna; LAGUNA
NIGUEL: Ocean Ranch Cinemas, Rancho Niguel; LA MIRADA: Gate-
way Plaza; LAVERNE: Laverne; MIRA MESA: Mira Mesa 4, Mira Mesa
7; MISSION VIEJO: Crown Valley, Trabuco Hills, Mission Viejo Mall
Cinemas; MONTEREY PARK: Monterey Mall; MORENO VALLEY:
Festival, Towngate; NEWPORT BEACH: Island, Newport Cinema, Lido;
POWAY: Poway Cinemas; SAN JUAN CAPISTRANO: Franciscan Plaza;
SAN LUIS OBISPO: Madonna Plaza, Mission; SIMI VALLEY: Moun-
taingate Plaza 7; RANCHO CALIFORNIA: Rancho California; RAN-
CHO CUCAMONGA: Rancho Cucamonga, Terra Vista Town Center;
SAN LUIS OBISPO: Fremont; SAN MARCOS: San Marcos; SANTA
ANA: Hutton Center, Bristol IV, South Coast Village; SANTA CLARITA:
Valencia; SANTA MARIA: Santa Maria; STANTON: Village Center;
TEMPLE CITY: Temple; TUSTIN: Tustin Market Place; UPLAND:
Upland 8, Mountain Green; WESTMINISTER: Mall, Twin, Westminster 10.

Enea Bros. Enterprises

6670 Amador Plaza Rd., Dublin, CA 94568; (510)
828-4401.
JOHN ENEA, JR., pres.; ROBERT ENEA, v.p.

CALIFORNIA—CARMEL: Village Theatre; CONCORD: Capri 3;
DUBLIN: Dublin Cinema 6; LIVERMORE: Vine Theatre 2; PACIFIC
GROVE: Lighthouse Cinema 4; PLEASANTON: Galaxy 8.
HAWAII—KUKUI: Grove 3.

Entertainment Management Corp.

807 Washington St., Stoughton, MA 02072 (617) 341-
2800. FAX: (617) 341-4170.
BILL HANNEY, pres.; KEITH ASH, dir. opns.; MIKE HARMON,
dist. mng.; JOAN OVERSTREET, adm.; TERESA ABBETT, public
adm.; CASSANDRA CAST, mktg. & conc.
MASSACHUSETTS—BUZZARDS BAY: Buzzards Bay Cinemas 4;
EAST BRIDGEWATER: Cinema 6; SCITUATE: Scituate Playhouse (4);
SHARON: Cinema 8; SOUTH DENNIS: Cinema 12; STOUGHTON:
Stoughton Cinema Pub.
RHODE ISLAND—EAST PROVIDENCE: Cinemas (10).

F

Floyd Theatres

4226 Old Highway 37, P.O. Box 1528, Lakeland, FL
33802; (813) 646-2436. FAX: (813) 647-2721.
HAROLD T. SPEARS, JR., pres.
FLORIDA—ARCADIA: Arcadia Twin 1 & 2; BRADENTON: Cortez
Twin; BRANDON: Brandon Twin 1 & 2; BROOKSVILLE: Brooksville
Twin 1 & 2; DADE CITY: Joylan D.I., Pasco Twin 1 & 2; DAYTONA: Big
Tree Twin 1 & 2; EUSTIS: Plaza Twin 1 & 2; FERNANDINA BEACH:
Island Twin 1 & 2; FORT MYERS: Northside Twin D.I.; LAKELAND:
Palm Cinema 1, 2, & 3, Silvermoon D.I.; LAKE WALES: Plaza Twin 1 &
2; LARGO: Ulmerton Cinema 9; LOCKHART: Rimar D.I.; PALATKA:
Plaza Twin 1 & 2; PINELLAS PARK: Mustang D.I.; PLANT CITY: Lake
Walden Cinema 8; SANFORD: Movieland D.I.; SARASOTA: Teatro
Theatre; ST. PETERSBURG: 28th St. D.I.; SEBRING: Fairmount Cin-
ema VI; Lake Shore Cinema 8; TALLAHASSEE: Mugs & Movies 1 & 2;
TAMPA: Funlan D.I.; TARPON SPRINGS: Mall Twin 1 & 2, Midway
D.I.; WINTER GARDEN: Starlite D.I.; WINTER HAVEN: Boulevard
Triple 1, 2, & 3, Continental Twin 1 & 2, Havendale D.I.
GEORGIA—STATESBORO: Statesboro Cinema 9; TIFTON: Tifton
Cinema 6.

Fox Theatres Corp.

16 Angelica St., P.O. Box 1499, Reading, PA 19611; (215)
374-4904. FAX: (212) 374-7121.
DONALD M. FOX, pres.; WILLIAM E. YERGEY, dir.; theater opera-
tions; WENDY MOORE, dir., M.I.S.; TIMOTHY TROUT, control.
DELAWARE—DOVER: Fox Theatres 6, Movies 6.
FLORIDA—POMPANO BEACH: Fox Festival 8; SUNRISE: Fox
Sunrise 8.
MARYLAND—OCEAN CITY: Sun & Surf Cinemas 4, Fox Gold
Coast 4, Fox White Marlin 5.
PENNSYLVANIA—HANOVER: Fox Theatres 4; LEBANON: Fox
Theatres 2, Howard Cinemas 4; POTTSTOWN: Fox Coventry 8, Fox
North-End 2; POTTSVILLE: Fox Theatres 2, Deer Lake D.I.; READ-
ING: Fox Berkshire 3, Fox East 4, Fox Fairgrounds 5, Sinking Spring
D.I.; SUNBURY: Fox Theatres 4.

Frank Theatres, Inc.

P.O. Box 33, Pleasantville, NJ 08232; (609) 641-3581.
NEW JERSEY—ABSECON: Absecon 8; ATLANTIC CITY: Towne
16 (Pleasantville), Point 4 (Somers Point); HAMMONTON: Route 30 (6);
LONG BEACH ISLAND & MANAHAWKIN: Harbor Twin (Manahaw-
kin), Colony 4 (Brant Beach), Beach 4 (Beach Haven Park), Colonial Twin
(Beach Haven); NORTH CAPE MAY: Cape May 8; OCEAN CITY:
Moorlyn (4), Strand 5; STONE HARBOR: Harbor Twin; VENTNOR:
Ventor 3; WILDWOOD AREA: Strand 4, Ocean Twin, Shore 4, Beach
Twin (Cape May), Penn Twin (Pennsville).

Fridley Theatres

1321 Walnut St. Des Moines, IA 50309; (515) 282-9287.
IOWA—ALGONA: Algona; ANKENY: Paramount 5; BOONE:
Boone; CARROLL: Carroll 2; CHEROKEE: American; CLARION: Clar-
ion; DECORAH: Riviera 3; DES MOINES: River Hills, Riviera, Sierra 3;
EMMETSBURG: Riviera; ESTHERVILLE: Grand 3; HUMBOLDT: Hu-
mota; INDIANOLA: Paramount 3; IOWA FALLS: Metropolitan 2;
JEFFERSON: Sierra; LAKE CITY: Capri; MANCHESTER: Castle;

MARSHALLTOWN: Orpheum 2, Plaza 2; MUSCATINE: Plaza 4, Riviera; NEVADA: Camelot; OELWEIN: Paramount 2; PERRY: Grand 3; SPENCER: Spencer 3; STORM LAKE: Vista 3; WEBSTER CITY: Webster.

NEBRASKA—GRAND ISLAND: Grand; HASTINGS: Rivoli; McCook: Cinema 3.

G

GKC Theatres

500 First National Bank Bldg., Springfield IL 62701; (217) 753-0018.

GEORGE G. KERASOTES, chm. & pres.; DALE J. GARVEY, exec. v.p. optns.; MARSHALL N. SELKIRK, exec. v.p., finance; DANIEL J. ROGERS, exec. v.p., film; ROGER FORD, exec. v.p., purchasing.

ILLINOIS—BLOOMINGTON/NORMAL: University Cinemas 5, College Hills Cinemas 4, Parkway Cinemas 8; CHAMPAIGN/URBANA: Coed Cinemas 4, Country Fair Cinemas 7, Urbana Cinemas 2; DECATUR: Hickory Point Cinemas 8; DEKALB: Campus Cinemas 4, Carrol Cinemas 2, DeKalb Cinemas 2; KEWANEE: Wanee Cinemas 2; LASALLE: Illinois Valley Cinemas 2, Showplace Cinemas 2; LINCOLN: Lincoln Cinemas 2; MORRIS: Morris Cinemas 2; OTTAWA: Roxy Cinemas 2; PEORIA: Landmark Mall Cinemas 8, Metro Cinemas 4, Sunnyland 8, Westlake Cinemas 5; PERU: Peru Mall Cinemas 6; PONTIAC: Crescent Cinemas 2; PRINCETON: Apollo Cinemas 2; STERLING: Sterling Cinemas 2; STREATOR: Majestic Cinemas 2.

INDIANA—ELKHART: Concord Cinemas 2, Encore Park Cinemas 8.

MICHIGAN—ALPENA: State Cinemas 2; BATTLE CREEK: Towne Cinemas 8; BIG RAPIDS: Big Rapids Cinemas 4; HILLSDALE: Dawn Cinema; JACKSON: Plaza Cinemas 7, Westwood Cinemas 2; LUDINGTON: Lyric Cinema 4; PORT HURON: Birchwood Cinemas 10; SAGINAW: Fashion Square Cinemas 10; TRAVERSE CITY: Grand Traverse Cinemas 8, State Cinemas 2, Traverse Bay 2.

General Cinema Theatres

1280 Boylston St., Chestnut Hill, MA 02167; (617) 277-4320; FAX: (617) 277-8875.

(A subsidiary of Harcourt General Inc.)

PAUL R. DEL ROSSI, pres.; JAMES C. THARP, sr. v.p.—film & marketing; JAY SHAPIRO, sr. v.p. dvlp.; ROBERT PAINTER, sr. v.p. opns.; KIRK SESSIONS, v.p. opns.; VICTOR GATTUSO, v.p. opns.; KEVIN FRABOTTA, v.p. opns.; ALAN DeLEMOS, v.p.—film; ROBERT MILLER, v.p.—film mktg.; JOHN LEONARD, v.p.—theatre mktg; PAUL MUCCI, v.p. finance; JOHN TOWNSEND, v.p.—construction; ILENE McCUNE, v.p.—human.

ARIZONA—PHOENIX: Bell Towne Centre 8, Paradise Valley Mall 7, Westridge 6.

CALIFORNIA—COLTON: Rancho 6; DUBLIN: Dublin Place 6; FAIRFIELD: Solano Mall 6; FREMONT: Femont Hub 8; HAYWARD: Southland 5; LOS ANGELES: Avco 3, Beverly Connection 6, Fallbrook 7, Glendale Central 5, Hollywood Galaxy 6, Northridge 8, Santa Anita 4, Sherman Oaks 5; MONTCLAIR: Montclair Plaza 8; REDONDO BEACH: Galleria at South Bay 6; SACRAMENTO: Birdcage Walk 6; SAN MATEO: Fashion Island Mall 6, Hillsdale 4.

DELAWARE—WILMINGTON: Christiana Mall 5.

FLORIDA—FT. LAUDERDALE: Coral Square 8, Deerfield Mall 8, Fountains 8, Mission Bay Plaza 8, Pembroke Pines 8; MIAMI: Cinema 10, Hialeah 8, Intracoastal 8, Riviera 8; ORLANDO: Altamonte 8, Altamonte Mall 2, Colonial Promenade 6, Fashion Square 6, Lake Mary Centre 8; WEST PALM BEACH: PGA 6.

GEORGIA—ATHENS: Georgia Square 6; ATLANTA: Akers Mill Square 4, Gwinnett Place 6, Hairston Village 8, Merchants Walk 8, Perimeter Mall 4, Sandy Springs 8; AUGUSTA: Regency Exchange 8, Regency Mall 3.

ILLINOIS—CHAMPAIGN: Market Place 4; CHICAGO: Deerbrook 4, Ford City 14, Lincoln Mall 3, Randhurst 4, Woodgrove Festival 6, Yorktown 6; DECATUR: Northgate Mall 2; JOLIET: Jefferson Square 3, Louis Joliet Mall 3; WAUKEGAN: Lakehurst 12.

INDIANA—FT. WAYNE: Coldwater Crossing 8, Glenbrook 3, Northwood Park 2; GARY: Griffith Park 2, Ridge Plaza 2, Southlake Mall 9; INDIANAPOLIS: Castleton Square 3, Clearwater Crossing 12, Eastgate Mall 6, Glendale 6, Greenwood Park 7, Lafayette Square 2, Speedway 2, Washington Square 2; SOUTH BEND: University Park East 6, University Park West 3; VALPARISO: County Seat 6.

KANSAS—WICHITA: Towne Square 6, Towne West Square 5.

LOUISIANA—ALEXANDRIA: Alexandria 6; LAFAYETTE: Acadiana Mall 5; LAKE CHARLES: Prien Lake Mall 3; NEW ORLEANS: Esplanade Mall 9, Lakeside 8, North Shore Square 6.

MAINE—PORTLAND: Maine Mall 7.

MARYLAND—BALTIMORE: Columbia City 3, Security Square 8, Towson Commons 8, York Road 2.

MASSACHUSETTS—BOSTON: Braintree 10, Chestnut Hill 5, Westgate Mall 7, Hanover Mall 4, Northshore 3, Framingham 6; NO. DARTMOUTH: North Dartmouth Mall 8; TYNGSBORO: Tyngsboro.

MICHIGAN—DETROIT: Canton 6, Novi Town Center 8; KALAMAZOO: Maple Hill Mall 3; LANSING: Lansing Mall West 6.

MINNESOTA—MINNEAPOLIS: Centennial Lakes 8, Mall of America 14, Northtown 4, Shelard Park 5, Southtown 2; ST. PAUL: Burnhaven 8, Har Mar 11.

NEW JERSEY—ASBURY PARK: Seaview Square 2; BRIDGEWATER: Bridgewater Commons 7; CAMDEN: Deptford Mall 6; MORRIS COUNTY: Morris County Mall 2; RARITAN: Somerville Circle 3; SHREWSBURY: Shrewsbury Plaza 3; SOMERSET: Rutgers 6; TOMS RIVER: Ocean County Mall 3; TRENTON: Mercer Mall 7; WATCHUNG: Blue Star 4; WEST ORANGE: Essex Green 3.

NEW MEXICO—ALBUQUERQUE: Park Square 3, San Mateo 8.

NEW YORK—BRONX: Bay Plaza 10; BUFFALO: Market Arcade 8, McKinley Mall 6, Thruway Mall 8, University 8, Walden Galleria 12; HARTSDALE: Hartsdale 4; NIAGARA FALLS: Summit Park 6; PEEKSKILL: Westchester Mall 4; ROCHESTER: Marketplace 7, Pittsford Plaza 6; YONKERS: Central Plaza 4.

NORTH CAROLINA—CHARLOTTE: Charlottetown 4, Eastland 3, SouthPark 3, Tower Place Festival 8; FAYETTEVILLE: Cross Creek Mall 3, Cross Pointe 6; GREENSBORO: Four Seasons Town Centre 4; RALEIGH: Pleasant Valley Promenade 7; WINSTON-SALEM: Hanes Mall 4.

OHIO—AKRON: Chapel Hill Mall 5, Plaza, 8, West Market Plaza 7; CANTON: Canton Centre 8; CINCINNATI: Gold Circle 2; CLEVELAND: Erie Commons 8, Parmatown 5, Randall Park Mall 3, Ridge Park Square 8, Southgate 3, Westgate Mall 6, Westwood Town Center 6; COLUMBUS: Northland 8, Westland 8; ELYRIA: Midway Mall 8.

OKLAHOMA—OKLAHOMA CITY: Brixton Square 8, Crossroads 8, Penn Square Mall 8, Quail Springs; TULSA: Eastland Mall 6, Eton Square 6, Woodland Hills 6.

PENNSYLVANIA—ALLENTOWN: Lehigh Valley Mall 8; ERIE: Millcreek Mall 9; PHILADELPHIA: Franklin Mills 10, Northeast 4, Plymouth Meeting 2; SCRANTON: Viewmont Mall 5; WILKES-BARRE: Wyoming Valley Mall 7.

RHODE ISLAND—PROVIDENCE: Lincoln Mall 4, Warwick Mall 3.

SOUTH CAROLINA—CHARLESTON: Citadel Mall 6, Northwoods Mall 8; COLUMBIA SC: Bush River Mall 8, Columbia Mall 3.

TENNESSEE—MEMPHIS: Hickory Ridge Mall 4, Mall of Memphis 5, Raleigh 6.

TEXAS—AUSTIN: Barton Creek 5, Great Hills 8, Highland 10; BEAUMONT: Gateway Plaza 2, Parkdale Mall 3; DALLAS: Carrollton Centre 6, Collin Creek 6, Furneaux Creek 7, Galleria 5, Irving Mall 7, Northpark East 2, Northpark West 2, Prestonwood 4, Red Bird Mall 10, Richardson 6, Richardson Square 3, Town East 6, Town East Mall 5, EL PASO: Cielo Vista Mall 10, Park 6, Sunland Park Mall 6; FT. WORTH: Arlington Park 8, Central Park 8, Cinema V 5, North Hills 7, Ridgmar Town Square 6; HOUSTON: Baybrook Mall 4, Copperfield 6, Deerbrook Commons 6, Galleria 4, Greenspoint Mall 5, Gulfgate Mall 4, Meyerland 3, Northline Mall 4, Point NASA 6, West Oaks Central 6, Willowbrook Mall 6; MIDLAND: Midland Park Mall 4, North Park 4.

VIRGINIA—LYNCHBURG: River Ridge Mall 4; NORFOLK: Janaf Plaza 8; ROANOKE: Tanglewood Mall 3, Valley View 6; SPRINGFIELD: Springfield Mall 10.

WASHINGTON—EVERETT: Everett Mall 10; FEDERAL WAY: Gateway Center 8; RENTON: Renton Village 6; SEATTLE: Aurora 3; SILVERDALE: Kitsap Mall 6; TACOMA: Lincoln Plaza 8.

WEST VIRGINIA—HUNTINGTON: Huntington Mall 6.

General Theatres Co.

23811 Chagrin Blvd., Beachwood, OH 44122; (216) 464-4366; FAX: (216) 464-4368.

LEONARD L. MISHKIND, pres; NORMAN BARR, gen. mgr.

OHIO—CLEVELAND: Detroit Twin, Parma Triple, Berea Triple; ORRVILLE: Orr Twin; TIFFIN: Tiffin Drive In.

Goodrich Quality Theaters, Inc.

3565 29th Street, SE, Grand Rapids, MI 49512; (616) 949-8760.

ROBERT EMMETT GOODRICH, pres. & secty.; WILLIAM T. McMANNIS, v.p. & gen. mgr.; ROSS C. PETTINGA, CFO; WANDA HOLST, film buyer; LISA THORNHILL, mkt. mgr.; RONALD B. MUSCOTT, contr.; MARTIN S. BETZ, Indiana/Illinois dist. mgr.; REED L. SIMON, Michigan dist. mgr.

INDIANA—ANDERSON: Applewood 9; LAFAYETTE: Eastside 10, Market Square 2, Tippecanoe 4; LOGANSPORT: Cass 3.

ILLINOIS—CHAMPAIGN: Savoy 14; PEORIA: Willow Knolls 14.

MICHIGAN—ANN ARBOR: Ann Arbor 1 & 2; BATTLE CREEK: W. Columbia 6; BAY CITY: Bay City 6, Hampton 6; CADILLAC: Cadillac 1 & 2; GRAND RAPIDS: 29th St. Quad 6; HOLLAND: Holland 7; JACKSON: Jackson 8; PORT HURON: Krafft 8; SAGINAW: 99¢ Quad, Saginaw 8.

H

Harkins Theatres

8350 E. McDonald, Suite 2, Scottsdale, AZ 85250; (602) 955-2233.

583

DAN HARKINS, pres. & owner; WAYNE KULLANDER, v.p.; KAREN HARKINS, sec./treas; LOU LENCIONI, film buyer.
ARIZONA—PHOENIX: Arcadia 8, Bell Tower 8, Camelview Luxury 6, Camelback Mall 3, Centerpoint Luxury 11, Christown 5, Cine Capri, Cornerstone 6, Fashion Square Luxury 7, Fiesta 5, Metrocenter 3, Poca Fiesta 4, Shea Plaza 2, Southwest 8, Thomas Mall 2, Tower Plaza 2, Tricity 5.

Holiday Amusement Co.

1600 Central Parkway, Cincinnati, OH 45210; (513) 381-1111.

JOANNE B. COHEN, pres.; SHIRLEY JONES, PAMM SANDLIN, bookers/buyers.
KENTUCKY—BELLEVUE: Marianne Cinema.
OHIO—CINCINNATI: Hollywood Cinema 1 & 2, Mt. Healthy D.I., Mt. Lookout Cinema, Westwood Cinemas I & II, Dent D.I.; HAM-ILTON: Acme D.I., Colonial D.I., Court, Holiday D.I., Village Cinema 'n' Draft House; LANCASTER: Plaza D.I.

Hoyts Cinemas Corporation

One Exeter Plaza, Boston, MA 02116-2836; (617) 267-2700. FAX: (617) 262-0707.

PETER IVANY, Chairman U.S. & Australia; MORRIS ENGLANDER, pres. & COO; JUDSON PARKER, sr. v.p. film; JAMES FITZGERALD, CFO; DANIEL VIERIA, v.p. operations.
CONNECTICUT—DAYVILLE: Dayville 3; EAST MANCHESTER: East Manchester Cinemas 6; ENFIELD: Cine Enfield 8; GROTON: Groton Cinemas 6; HARTFORD: Cine 4; MADISON: Madison Cinemas 2; MERIDEN: Meriden Cinemas 10; MYSTIC: Mystic Village Cinemas 3; NEW CANAAN: Playhouse 2; NORWICH: Norwich Cinemas 2; SAY-BROOK: Saybrook Cinemas 2, Saybrook Cinemas 4: STRATFORD: Cinemas 6; WATERBURY: Mall View Plaza 10, Naugatuck Valley Mall 4; WATERFORD: Waterford Cinemas 8; WILLIMANTIC: Jillson Sq. 6.
GEORGIA—ATLANTA: Midtown Cinemas 8, Tara Theatre 4; ROSEWELL: Rosewell Mall 10.
MAINE—AUBURN: Auburn Plaza 10; BANGOR: Bangor Cinemas 10; BIDDEFORD: Cine 8; ELLSWORTH: Maine Coast Cinemas 2; PORTLAND: Clarks Pond Cinema 8, Nickelodeon Cinemas 6; WATER-VILLE: Cinema Center 6.
MARYLAND—FREDERICK: Francis Scott Key 3, Frederick 6, Frederick Towne Mall 2, Westridge Mall 2, Westridge Mall 6; HAGERS-TOWN: Longmeadow Cinemas 3; LAUREL: Laurel Lakes 12; SALIS-BURY: The Center at Salisbury 10, Movies 4; WESTMISTER: Cranberry Mall Cinemas 9.
MASSACHUSETTS—ACTON: Acton Cinemas 4; FRANKLIN: Franklin Cinemas 6; GREAT BARRINGTON: Mahaiwe Theatre: HAR-WICH: Harwich Cinemas 6; HYANNIS: Airport Cinema 8, Cape Cod Mall Cinema 1 & 2, Cape Cod Mall Cinema 3 & 4; MASHPEE: Mashpee Cinemas 6; MILFORD: Milford Cinema Centre 495; PITTSFIELD: Berkshire Mall 10; PLYMOUTH: Independence Mall 10; TAUNTON: Silver City Galleria 10, Taunton Cinemas 8.
MICHIGAN—MONROE: Frenchtown Square Mall 8.
NEW HAMPSHIRE—KEENE: Keene Cinema 6; PORTSMOUTH: Newington Mall Cine 8.
NEW YORK—ALBANY: Cine 10, Crossgates 12; AUBURN: Finger Lakes Cinema 4; CLIFTON PARK: Clifton Country Mall 6; EAST GREENBUSH: Rensselaer Cinemas 8; ELMIRA: Arnot Mall 10; GLENS FALLS: Aviation 8, Route 9 Cinemas 5; ITHACA: Ithaca Cinemas 7; KINGSTON: Hudson Valley Mall 6; LATHAM: Latham Mall 9; NEW-BURGH: Newburgh Cinema 10; ONEONTA: South Side Mall 4; PLATTSBURGH: Champlain Center North 8; POUGHKEEPSIE: Galle-ria Cinema 8, South Hills Mall Cine 8; ROCHESTER: Cine Greece 8; SARATOGA: Saratoga Cinemas 6, Wilton Mall 8; SYRACUSE: Carousel Center Mall 12; UTICA: Riverside Mall 8, Sangertown Square 9; WATER-TOWN: Salmon Run Mall 8.
OHIO—CLEVELAND: Tower City 11; LANCASTER: River Valley 10; NEW PHILADELPHIA: New Town Mall 8.
RHODE ISLAND—WESTERLY: Westerly Cinemas 3.

J

Jeraco Theatres

7 Riverview St., South Glen Falls, NY 12803; (518) 793-1932.

JERRY ARATARE, owner; JIM BRUMAGHIM, partner.
MASSACHUSETTS—NORTH ADAMS: Heritage Cinema
NEW YORK—GLENS FALLS: Cinematheque, Empire Theatre; HUDSON FALLS: Tufco Theatre.

Johnson Theatres

1102 C St., Schuyler, NE 68661; (402) 352-3866.

DONALD JOHNSON, owner.
NEBRASKA—DAVID CITY: 4th St. Theatre; LYNCH: Lynn Theatre; NELIGH: New Moon Theatre, Starlite D.I.; O'NEILL: Royal Theatre, O'Neill D.I.; SCHUYLER: Sky Twin Theatre, Sky Way D.I.

Joy's Theatres, Inc.

P.O. Box 785, Metairie, LA 70004; (504) 834-8510.

JOY N. HOUCK, pres.
LOUISIANA—ALEXANDRIA: Dollar Cinema 6; KENNER: Joy's Cinema 8; LAFAYETTE: Dollar Cinema 4; METAIRIE: Panorama 6; SHREVEPORT: Joy's Cinema 7, Joy's Quail Creek Cinema 4; NEW ORLEANS: Joy Pitt Cinema 4.
TEXAS—TEXARKANA: Cinema City 6.

K

K/B Cinemas

2 Wisconsin Circle, 7th fl, Chevy Chase, MD 20815; (301) 961-1545.

DISTRICT OF COLUMBIA—WASHINGTON: Cerberus 3, The Cinema, Fine Arts, Foundry 7, Janus 3, Paris 3.
MARYLAND—BETHESDA: Georgetown 2, Montgomery Mall 3; LAUREL: Laurel 6; ROCKVILLE: Congressional 5.

Kent Theatres, Inc.

2870 University Blvd. W., Jacksonville, FL 32217; (904) 731-9616; FAX: (904) 739-2752. Booking Office: 1681 Sacketts Dr., Lawrenceville, GA 30243.

FREDERICK H. KENT, chmn. bd.; J. CLEVELAND KENT, pres.; JOHN B. KENT, v.p. and gen. counsel; NORMA F. KENT, sec.; JOANN GREEN, asst. secty.; ROBERT M. K. LOCKWOOD, treas.; JOANN GREEN, asst. secty.; ROBERT M. FULFORD, v.p., finance, comptroller; MICHAEL SPIVEY, v.p. & gen. mng., optns.
FLORIDA—GAINESVILLE: Plaza 3; JACKSONVILLE: Normandy 2, St. Johns 8; JACKSONVILLE BEACH: Pablo 5; LAKELAND: Lake-land Square 10; NEPTUNE BEACH: Neptune 3; MELBOURNE: Palms 8; PALM BAY: Palm Bay 10; TALLAHASSEE: Cinema 2, Parkway 5.

Kerasotes Theatres

Kerasotes Building, 104 N. 6th Street, Springfield, IL 62701; (217) 788-5200. FAX: (217) 788-5207.

JOHN G. KERASOTES, sec/treas.; DENIS KERASOTES, v.p./con-troller; ANTHONY L. KERASOTES, v.p./film; DEAN KERASOTES, v.p./optns.; JOHN G. MILLER, gen. mgr.; DEBORAH TROESCH, data processing dir.; PAT REMBUSCH, head film buyer; CLIFF METGER, concession spvr.; TIM JOHNSON, asst. gen. mgr.; FRED WALRAVEN, projection spvr.; CHUCK SHOEMAKER, facilities; RACHEL HASEN-YAGER, adv. dir.; KELLY RUFA, adv.; DANNY OWEN, video; BARRY TESTER, booker; SANDY CONSTANT, booker; SUE BAPST, asst. Controller; District Managers: ROGER WEDEKIND (Eastern); CLYDE COSTIN (Southern).
ILLINOIS—ALTON: Eastgate 6; BELLEVILLE: Quad, Ritz; BEN-TON: Toler Cinema 2; CANTON: Garden 2; CARBONDALE: Saluki 2, Varsity 3, Fox Eastgate 3; CENTRALIA: Illinois 2; CHARLESTON: Will Rogers 2; CHILLICOTHE: Town 2; DANVILLE: Times, Village Mall Cinema 6; GALESBURG: West 2, Sandburg Mall 2; GRANITE CITY: Nameoki 2; HIGHLAND: Lory 2; JACKSONVILLE: Times 2, Illinois 2; JERSEYVILLE: Stadium 2; MACOMB: Illinois 2; MARION: Town & Country 4; MATTOON: Cinema 3, Time 2; MONMOUTH: Rivoli 2; MT. VERNON: Granada 2, Stadium 2; MURPHYSBORO: Liberty; PARIS: Paris 2; PEKIN: Pekin Mall Cinema 2; QUINCY: Adams Cinema 2, State, Quincy Showcase 6; RANTOUL: Wings Cinema 2; ROCKFORD: Bel-ford Indoor 4, Belford Outdoor 2, Cherryvale 7, Colonial Village 5, Machesney Park 10, North Towne 6; ROXANA: Cine; SALEM: Salem 2; SPRINGFIELD: Fox Town & Country 2, Capital City Cinema, Esquire 4, Showplace 8, White Oaks Cinema 6; TAYLORVILLE: Cinema 2.
INDIANA—ANDERSON: Showplace 4, Mounds Mall 2; BLOOM-INGTON: Showplace 6, Indiana 2, Von Lee 3, Village 2, College Mall Cinema 4; COLUMBUS: Columbus Center Cinema 5, Crump Theatre, Courthouse 2; FORT WAYNE: Gateway 3; KOKOMO: Kokomo Mall Cinema 8, Markland Mall Cinema 5; LA PORTE: La Porte Cinema 4; MARION: Movies 4, Park Mall 2; MICHIGAN CITY: Dunes Plaza Cinema 6, Marquette 3; MUNCIE: Dollar Cinema 2, Muncie Mall Cin-ema 3, Northwest Plaza Cinema 8; NEW CASTLE: Castle; PERU: Eastwood Cinema 2; PRINCETON: Princeton 4; RICHMOND: Cinema

6, Mall Cinema 2, Sidewalk Cinema 2; SALEM: Hoosier Cinema 2; SOUTH BEND: Town & Country 3, Scottsdale Mall 6; TERRE HAUTE: Honey Creek Mall Cinema 3, Towne South Cinema 3, Meadows Cinema 2, Plaza North Cinema 2; VINCENNES: Plaza 2, Showplace 3; WASHINGTON: Indiana 2.
IOWA—KEOKUK: Plaza Cinema 3.
MISSOURI—BONNE TERRE: Bonne Terre Cinema 2; CAPE GIRARDEAU: Broadway Theatre, Town Plaza Cinema 5; DEXTER: Town & Country 2; FLAT RIVER: Movies 2; KENNETT: Cinema; POPLAR BLUFF: Rodgers 2, Mansion Mall Cinema 2; SULLIVAN: Meramec Cinema 2.

Klein Theatres

4 Normanskill Blvd., Delmar, NY 12054; (518) 439-8113; FAX: (518) 439-8114.

MORRIS H. KLEIN, treas.
NEW YORK—COXSACKIE: Hi-Way D.I.; GLENMONT: Jericho D.I.; HUDSON: Hudson Studio Theatre, Fairview Cinema 3.

Klotz, Jane M., Booking

9801 Tribonian Drive, Fort Washington, MD 20744; (301) 567-4503, 567-1775.

JANE M. KLOTZ, booker & owner.
MARYLAND—POCOMOKE CITY: Marva.
VIRGINIA—LEXINGTON: Hull's; ONANCOCK: Roseland; RICHLANDS: Richlands Mall Two.
WEST VIRGINIA—HOT SPRINGS: Homestead; WHITE SULPHUR SPRINGS: Greenbrier.

L

Laemmle Theatres

11523 Santa Monica Blvd., Los Angeles, CA 90025; (310) 478-1041; FAX: (310) 312-0382.

ROBERT and GREGORY LAEMMLE, chief officers.
CALIFORNIA—BEVERLY HILLS: Music Hall; ENCINO: Town Center 5; LOS ANGELES: Grande 4; PASADENA: Esquire, Colorado; SANTA MONICA: Monica 4-plex; WEST HOLLYWOOD: Sunset 5; WEST LOS ANGELES: Royal.

Lakes & Rivers Cinemas

3989 Central Avenue NE, Columbia Heights, MN 55421; (612) 781-8858; FAX: (612) 781-8044.

JAMES H. PAYNE, pres., film buyer; STEVE TRIPP, gen. mgr.
MINNESOTA—DETROIT LAKES: Washington Square 5; FERGUS FALLS: Westridge Twin; FOREST LAKE: Lake 5.
WISCONSIN—ST. CROIX FALLS: Falls 3.
MICHIGAN—HOUGHTON: Copper Country Cinema 3.

Landmark Theatre Corporation

Home Office: 2222 S. Barrington Ave., Los Angeles, CA 90064; (310) 473-6701.

STEPHEN A. GILULA, pres.; GARY MEYER, film consultant/buyer; GARY P. CANN, sr. v.p., finance; BERT MANZARI, sr. v.p., film; PAUL S. RICHARDSON, sr. v.p., opns. & acquisitions; JANET HUGHES, v.p., admin.; DAVID SWANSON, v.p. mktg.
CALIFORNIA—BERKELEY: U.C. Berkeley; CORONA DEL MAR: Port; LOS ANGELES: Goldwyn Pavilion Cinemas IV, Nuart, NuWilshire 2; MENLO PARK: Park, Guild; PALO ALTO: Aquarius 2, Varsity, Palo Alto Square 1; SACRAMENTO: Tower 3; SAN DIEGO: Cove, Guild, Hillcrest 5, Ken, Park; SAN FRANCISCO: Bridge, Clay, Gateway, Lumiere 3, Opera Plaza 4; SOUTH PASADENA: Rialto.
COLORADO—DENVER: Chez Artiste 3, Esquire 2, Mayan 3.
LOUISIANA—NEW ORLEANS: Prytania, Canal Place Cinemas 4.
MINNESOTA—MINNEAPOLIS: Uptown.
OHIO—CLEVELAND: Centrum 3.
TEXAS—DALLAS: Inwood 3; HOUSTON: River Oaks 3, Saks Cinemas 2.
WASHINGTON—SEATTLE: Broadway Market 4, Crest Cinema Center 4, Egyptian, Guild 45th Theatre 2, Harvard Exit 2, Metro Cinemas 10, Neptune, Seven Gables, Varsity 3.
WISCONSIN—MILWAUKEE: Downer 2, Oriental 3.

Litchfield Theatres Ltd.

P.O. Box 2189, Pawleys Island, SC 29585; (803) 237-4600. FAX: (803) 237-8802; (803) 237-1807.

STEPHEN L. COLSON, pres.; U.S. EADDY, exec. v.p.; J. JACK JORDAN, dir., mktg. & adv.; FRANK JONES, buyer & booker; LARRY VAUGHN, buyer & booker; RAY DUNLAP, dir., tech. svcs.
FLORIDA—GAINESVILLE: Butler Plaza (10); INVERNESS: Citrus (6); JACKSONVILLE: Litchfield (10); ORLANDO: Lake Mary (10), UC 6 (7); PENSACOLA: Cordova (3), Cordova Mall (4).
GEORGIA—ATLANTA AREA: Austell Road (10), Litchfield—Riverdale (10); SAVANNAH: Eisenhower, Victory Square (9).
NORTH CAROLINA—BOONE: New Market (7); FAYETTEVILLE: Omni (8); GREENSBORO: Litchfield (7); MT. AIRY: Mayberry (5); WILSON: Litchfield (6).
OKLAHOMA—EDMOND: Kickingbird (6); OKLAHOMA CITY: Windsor Hills (10).
SOUTH CAROLINA—COLUMBIA: Litchfield (7); MURRELL'S INLET: Inlet Square (7); MYRTLE BEACH: Pottery (6); SPARTANBURG: Converse (6), Westgate (6).
VIRGINIA—CHESTER: Chester (6).

Lockwood & McKinnon Co.

45 Walpole St., Suite 6, Norwood, MA 02062; (617) 769-8900; FAX: (617) 769-1340.

ROGER A. LOCKWOOD, GORDON McKINNON, chief officers.
FLORIDA—POMPANO: Cinema 4.
NEW YORK—FISHKILL: Movies 4.

Loeks, Jack, Theatres

1400 28th Street, S.W., Grand Rapids, MI 49509; (616) 532-6302. FAX: (616) 532-3660.

JOHN D. LOEKS, chmn. & chief exec. off.; JOHN D. LOEKS, JR., pres. & COO; RON VAN TIMMEREN, exec. v.p.; ROGER LUBS, v.p. optns.; NANCY HAGAN, treas.
MICHIGAN—GRAND HAVEN: Grand; GRAND RAPIDS: Studio 28 (20 screen), Alpine 4; KALAMAZOO: Plaza 2, Eastowne 5; MT. PLEASANT: Cinema 4, Ward, Broadway; MUSKEGON: Cinema 12, Getty 4 D.I., New Plaza 2; ST JOSEPH: Southtown Twin Theatre.

Loeks Star Theatres

3020 Charlevoix Dr. S.E., Grand Rapids, MI 49546; (616) 940-0866; FAX: (616) 940-0046.

Loeks Michigan Theatres, Inc., general partner, and Star Theatres, Inc., general partner. Officers: BARRIE LOEKS; pres., Loeks Michigan; JAMES LOEKS, chmn., Loeks Michigan.
MICHIGAN—CLINTON TOWNSHIP: Star Gratiot 10; GRAND RAPIDS: Star Grand Rapids 10; HOLLAND: Star Holland 8; LINCOLN PARK: Star Lincoln Park 8; MADISON HEIGHTS: Star John R 10; ROCHESTER HILLS: Star Rochester Hills, Star Winchester 8; TAYLOR: Star Taylor 8.

Loews Theatre Management Corp.

(A Sony Pictures Entertainment Company)
711 Fifth Ave., New York, NY 10022-3109; (212) 702-6200.
BARRIE LAWSON LOEKS and JIM LOEKS, chairmen; ROBERT SMERLING, pres.; SEYMOUR SMITH, exec. v.p. & gen. counsel; CHARLES GOLDWATER, sr. v.p. & gen. mgr.; TRAVIS REID, sr. v.p. & head film buyer; JOHN WALKER, sr. v.p., finance; DORIAN BROWN, sr. v.p., corp. develop. & admin.; MARC PASUCCI, v.p., adv. & publicity; PETER BRADY, v.p., construction; FRED GABLE, v.p., concessions; PETER FOURNIER, v.p., personnel & admin.; KENNETH R. BENJAMIN, v.p., real estate, DAVID TUCKERMAN, v.p. film.
CONNECTICUT—BRISTOL: Bristol 8; BROOKFIELD: Fine Arts 2; DANBURY: Danbury 1; FAIRFIELD: Community 2, County 1; GREENWICH: Greenwich 2; NORWALK: Norwalk 1&2; TORRINGTON: Holiday 6; WESTPORT: Fine Arts 1&2, Fine Arts 3, Fine Arts 4, Post 1; WILTON: Wilton 1.
FLORIDA—PEMBROKE PINES: Pembroke Pines 4.
ILLINOIS—CHICAGO: Double Drive-In 3, Esquire 6, Fine Arts 4, Hyde Park 4, Pipers Alley 4, Webster 2; CICERO: Bel-Air Drive-In 3; EVANSTON: Evanston 5; EVERGREEN: Evergreen 4; HILLSIDE: Hillside Mall 3, Hillside Square 6; LANSING: River Run 8; NORRIDGE: Norridge 10; ROLLING MEADOWS: Rolling Meadows 9; SKOKIE: Old Orchard 4; WHEELING: Twin Drive-In 3.
INDIANA—CLARKSVILLE: River Falls 10; INDIANAPOLIS: Cherry Tree 10, College Park 10, Greenwood 9, Lafayette Square 8, Norgate 4; MERRILLVILLE: Merrillville 10, Y&W Drive-In 3.
KENTUCKY—ASHLAND: Midtown 3; FLORENCE: Florence 9; LEXINGTON: Fayette 3, Lexington Mall 2, Northpark 10, Southpark 6, LOUISVILLE: Oxmoor 5; STONY BROOK: Stony Brook 10.
MARYLAND—BALTIMORE: Greenspring 3, Northpoint 4, Reistertown 5, Rotunda 2, BEL AIR: Campus Hills 7, Hartford 2; BELTSVILLE: Center Park 8; COLUMBIA: Columbia Palace 9; CROFTON: Crofton 4; GAITHERSBURG: Montogomery 2, GERMANTOWN: Germantown 6;

GLEN BURNIE: Glen Burnie 7; LEXINGTON PARK: Lexington Park 6; OWINGS MILLS: Valley Centre 9; PASADENA: Jumpers 7 Cinema; TIMONIUM: Timonium 3, Yorkridge 4; WHEATON: Wheaton Plaza 11.

MASSACHUSETTS—BOSTON: Copley Place 11, Nickelodeon 5, Cheri 4, Charles 3, Cinema 57; BROCKTON: Brockton 4; CAMBRIDGE: Janus 1, Harvard Square 5, Fresh Pond 10; DANVERS: Liberty Tree Mall 2, Danvers 6; FALL RIVER: Habour Mall 8; LEOMINSTER: Leominster 12; NATICK: Natick 6; SALEM: Salem 3; SOMERVILLE: Somerville 12.

NEW HAMPSHIRE—CONCORD: Merrimack 6; LEBANON: Lebanon 6.

NEW JERSEY—BRICK: Cinema Center 5, Circle 5; EAST BRUNSWICK: Route 18 Twin; EAST HANOVER: Metroplex 12; EATONTOWN: Community Twin; EDGEWATER: Showboat Quad; FREEHOLD: Freehold Metroplex 8, Freehold 6, Route 9 Quad; HOWELL: Cinema Centre 4; MOUNTAINSIDE: Mountainside 9; NEWARK: Newark Metroplex 6; OCEAN TOWNSHIP: Middlebrook 2; RAMSEY: Interstate Twin; RED BANK: Red Bank 2; RIDGEFIELD PARK: Ridgefield Park 12; SECAUCUS: Plaza 8, Meadow 6; TOMS RIVER: Seacourt 10, Dover 2; WAYNE: Wayne 8.

NEW YORK—BAYSHORE: South Shore Mall 2; BAYSIDE: Bay Terrace 2; BINGHAMTON: Cameo 1, Cinema 1&2, Crest 1; BRONX: Paradise Quad; BROOKLYN: Georgetown 2, Oriental 3; CAMILLUS: Camillus Mall 1&2, Camillus Mall 3-6; CLAY: Great Northern 6, Penn Can Mall 3; DEWITT: Shoppingtown 4; ELMHURST: Elmwood 4; ELMIRA: Elmira 3; ENDICOTT: Town Endicott 1, Cinema Endicott 1; FAYETTEVILLE: Fayetteville Mall 6; FOREST HILLS: Trylon 1; GARDEN CITY: Roosevelt Field 8; JOHNSON CITY: Airport Drive-In 1, Oakdale Mall 3; LEVITTOWN: Nassau Metroplex 10; MANHATTAN: Tower East 1, New York Twin, Columbus Circle 1, Astor Plaza 1, Orpheum 7, 84th Street 6, Showplace 3, State Theatre Fine Arts 1, Festival 1, Village 7, 19th Street 6; MIDDLETOWN: Middletown 10, Galleria Metroplex 10; ROCHESTER: Pittsford 2, Pittsford 1, Ridge Road Twin, Towne Quad; SCHENECTADY: Mowhawk Mall 7, Rotterdam Square 6; STONYBROOK: Stonybrook 5; VESTAL: Town Square Mall 9; WEBSTER: Webster 12.

OHIO—AKRON: State Cuyahoga Twin; CINCINNATI: Tri-County 5, Kenwood Town Center 5, Northgate 7, Kenwood 2, Covedale 2; CLEVELAND: East 8, Cedar Center 2, Yorktown Twin 2; COLUMBUS: Continent 9, Southland 3, Westerville 2; DAYTON: Salem Avenue 3, Salem Mall 4, Beaver Valley 6; MILFORD: Cinema 275 East 4.

PENNSYLVANIA—STROUDSBURG: Stroud 7.

TEXAS—ARLINGTON: Lincoln Square 10, 20 & 287 Six; DALLAS: Park Central 4; FORT WORTH: Cityview 8; HOUSTON: Southpoint 5, Saks 2, Memorial City 8, Easton Commons 8, Westwood Mall 3; PLANO: Preston Park 6, Chisholm 5; SPRING: Spring 10; STAFFORD: Southwest Sixplex; WEBSTER: Bay Area 6.

VERMONT—BURLINGTON: Nickelodeon 6.

VIRGINIA—ARLINGTON: Pentagon City 6; CHARLOTTESVILLE: Greenbrier 2; HARRISONBURG: Valley Mall 4, Loews 1-2-3; HERNDON: Worldgate 9; MANASSAS: Manassas Movies 4; McLEAN: Tysons 8.

Logan Luxury Theatres Corp.

209 N. Lawler St., Mitchell, SD 57301; (605) 996-5444; FAX: (605) 996-2857.

JEFF LOGAN, pres.; LINDA LOGAN, v.p.; JIM WILSON, booker.
SOUTH DAKOTA—HURON: Twin State 1 & 2; MITCHELL: Roxy Cinema 4, Starlite D.I., State.

M

MJR Theatres, Inc.

13671 West Eleven Mile Road, Oak Park, MI 48237; (313) 548-8282; FAX: (313) 548-4706.

MICHAEL R. MIHALICH, pres.
MICHIGAN—ADRIAN: Cinema Adrian 6; ALLEN PARK: Allen Park 5; ANN ARBOR: Fox Village 4; LIVONIA: Livonia Mall Cinema 3; ROYAL OAK: Main Theatre 4; WATERFORD: Waterford Cinema 1&2.

Malco Theatres, Inc.

5851 Ridgeway Center Parkway, Memphis, TN 38120; (901) 761-3480; FAX: (901) 681-2044.

M. A. LIGHTMAN, bd. chm.; RICHARD L. LIGHTMAN, bd. chm.; STEPHEN P. LIGHTMAN, pres.; BILL BLACKBURN, v.p.; HERBERT R. LEVY, v.p. & secty., ROBERT LEVY, v.p. adv.; JIMMY TASHIE, v.p. opns.; JOHN LIGHTMAN, v.p.
ARKANSAS—BLYTHEVILLE: Malco Twin; FAYETTEVILLE: Mall Twin, Razorback Six; FORT SMITH: Mall Trio, Malco Quartet, Malco Twin, JONESBORO: Malco Cinema 10, Plaza Twin; ROGERS: Malco Twin; SPRINGDALE: Springdale Twin.

KENTUCKY—OWENSBORO: Mall Twin, Plaza Twin, Owensboro Cinema 8.
MISSISSIPPI—COLUMBUS: Cinema 3, Malco Twin, Mall, Varsity Twin; TUPELO: Tupelo Cinema 10.
MISSOURI—SIKESTON: Malco Trio, Mall.
TENNESSEE—JACKSON: Malco Cinema 8; MEMPHIS: Winchester Court 8, Germantown Cinema 9, Highland Quartet, Bartlett Cinema 10; Malco's Ridgeway Four, Southwest Twin D.I., Summer Quartet D.I., Appletree 12, Forest Hill Cinema 8.

Mann Theatres, Inc.

704 Hennepin Ave., Minneapolis, MN 55403; (612) 332-3305.

STEPHEN MANN, pres.; BENJIE MANN, v.p.; MARVIN MANN, sec.-treas.; STEPHEN MANN, film buyer & booker.
MINNESOTA—BRAINERD: Westgate Cinema 3, Westport 3; GRAND RAPIDS: Central Square Cinema 3; HIBBING: Irongate Cinema 3; MAPLE GROVE: Cinema 10; MINNEAPOLIS: Apache 6, Boulevard 2, Heights, Suburban World, Village 4; ST. PAUL: Cina 5, Cottage Grove 3, Cottage View D.I., Galtier 4, Grandview 2, Highland 2, Maple Leaf D.I., Signal Hills 5; STILLWATER: Mall 5.

Manos Enterprises, Inc.

31 North Maple Avenue, Greensburg, PA 15601; (412) 837-2710; FAX: (412) 834-1875.

T. M. MANOS, pres.; ALEXANDER MANOS, exec. v.p.; DONALD WOODWARD, v.p., film buyer; MADELINE MANGERY, secty./treas.
MARYLAND—HAGERSTOWN: Valley Mall, I, II & III.
NEW YORK—OLEAN: Cinema Five.
PENNSYLVANIA—ALTOONA: Cinema I, II, III, IV, Park Hills Theatres; CHAMBERSBURG: Cinemas IV, Southgate 4; DUBOIS: Cinemas Five; INDIANA: Cinemas IV, Regency Mall Cinemas; KITTANNING: Cinemas Four; LATROBE: Hi-Way D.I.; UNIONTOWN: Quad 40 Cinemas, Laurel Mall Cinemas; VANDERGRIFT: Cinema I, II, III; WARREN: Cinemas III.
VIRGINIA—WINCHESTER: Apple Blossom Center Cinema, Cinemas VI, Camelot I & II.
WEST VIRGINIA—BLUEFIELD: Cinema VIII, Blue Prince; ELKINS: Twin Cinema.

March Theatres

P.O. Box 509, Spirit Lake, IA 51360; (712) 332-2784.

JACK P. MARCH, pres. & film buyer; JANE MARCH, v.p.; PETER MARCH, sec. & treas.
IOWA—LeMARS: Royal Twin I & II; SPIRIT LAKE: Royal.
NEBRASKA—WAYNE: Twin.
SOUTH DAKOTA—VERMILLION: Coyote, Vermillion.

Marcus Theatres Corporation

250 E. Wisconsin Ave., Suite 1650, Milwaukee, WI 53202-4222; (414) 272-5120.

STEVE MARCUS, chmn; BRUCE J. OLSON, pres.; MICHAEL KOMINSKY, exec. v.p. & film buyer; MICHAEL OGRODOWSKI, v.p. & booker; RICK NEALS, v.p. & film booker; DON PERKINS, v.p., MARK GRAMZ, v.p.
WISCONSIN—APPLETON: Marc 3, Valley Fair 6; BEAVER DAM: Wisconsin 4; CEDARBURG: Rivoli; GREEN BAY: Bay Park Square 3, Marc 8, Stadium 4; GURNEE: Gurnee 10; LA CROSSE: Cinema 4, King 3; MADISON: Eastgate 14, Point 10, Southtown 5, Westgate 3, West Towne 3, Point 10; MENOMONIE: State 2; MILWAUKEE AREA: South Shore 10, North Shore 10, Grand 2, Marc 5, Northtown 8, Prospect 3, Skyway 6, Southtown 6, Tosa, Westown 10, West Point 8, Starlite (2); NEENAH: Neenah; OSHKOSH: Cinema 10; RACINE: Regency Mall 6, Westgate 5; RIPON: Campus; SHEBOYGAN: Marc 8, Plaza 8 (2); STEVENS POINT: Campus 4; WAUSAU: Crossroads 4.

Melrose Associates, Inc.

120 Fulton St., Boston, MA 02109; (617) 523-2900.

MAINE—AUGUSTA: State Street (5); BRUNSWICK: Cooks Corner (4); WESTBROOK: Cine City Five (5).
MASSACHUSETTS—ACTON: Acton (4); BELLINGHAM: Bellingham D.I.; CANTON: Blue Hills D.I., Boro D.I.; CHELMSFORD: Route 3 Cinemas 6; DORCHESTER: Park Theatre; FRANKLIN: Cinema Theatre; FOXBORO: Orpheum Cinemas (3), Oxford D.I.; HAVERHILL: Cinema 495 Four, Riverview D.I.; LITTLETON: Flick Twin Theatre; LOWELL: Lowell D.I.; MIDDLEBORO: Meadowbrook D.I.; MIDDLETON: Route 114 Twin D.I.; NORTH ATTLEBORO: Tri-Boro Twin; NORTH WILBRAHAM: Parkway D.I.; PITTSFIELD: Cinema Center 8, Paris;

RAYNHAM: Chalet Twin, Route 24 Twin Cinemas, Raynham D.I.; SAL-ISBURY: Route 95 Theatre (6); SHREWSBURY: Edgemere D.I.
NEW HAMPSHIRE—GILFORD: Lake Region Twin Cinema; NORTH CONWAY: Mt. Vally Mall Cinema (4); ROCHESTER: Lilac Mall Theatre (4).
RHODE ISLAND—LONSDALE: Lonsdale Twin D.I.; NEWPORT: Holiday Theatre, Newport D.I., Starlight Twin D.I.; PROVIDENCE: Four Seasons Cinema Five (5); SMITHFIELD: Apple Valley Cinemas Four; WAKEFIELD: Campus Cinema.

Merrill Theatre Corporation

1210 Williston Road, South Burlington, VT 05403; (802) 863-4825; FAX: (802) 864-7698.

MERRILL G. JARVIS, pres.; LUCILLE A. JARVIS, v.p.
VERMONT—BURLINGTON: Ethan Allen Cinemas 4; NEWPORT: Merrill's Showplace 3; SOUTH BURLINGTON: Century Plaza 3, Merrill's Cinema 9, Merrill's Showcase 5.

Metropolitan Theatres Corp.

8727 West Third St., Los Angeles CA 90048; (213) 858-2805.

BRUCE C. CORWIN, pres.; ALLEN GILBERT, exec. v.p.; CANDACE CRAWFORD, v.p. finance; LEW O'NEIL, sr. v.p., film buyer.
CALIFORNIA—LOS ANGELES: Campus, Los Angeles, Olympic, Orpheum, Panorama, Park I & II (Huntington Park), State; PALM DESERT: Cinema 3, Town Center Cinema 10; PALM SPRINGS: Courtyard Ten; SANTA BARBARA-GOLETA: Arlington Center for the Performing Arts, Cinema I & II, Fairview I & II, Fiesta 5, Granada I, II & III, Metro 4, Plaza de Oro I & II, Riviera, Santa Barbara D.I. I & II; SIMI VALLEY: Simi D.I.
MICHIGAN—ALBION: Bohm Theatre (3); COLDWATER: Main Theatre (4); DEARBORN: Camelot Theatre (3); MANISTEE: Vogue Theatre (2); RIVERVIEW: Showboat Theatre (5).

Midcontinent Theatre Co.

(A subsidiary of Midcontinent Media, Inc.)
%Terrace Theatre Bldg., 3508 France Ave. North, Robbinsdale, MN 55422; (612) 521-0776. FAX: (612) 521-0580.

LARRY KIRSCHENMANN, v.p.; DWIGHT GUNDERSON, gen. mgr.
MINNESOTA—COON RAPIDS: Spring Brook 4; HUTCHINSON: State Triple; NEW ULM: Cinema 3; ROBBINSDALE: Terrace 3; WILLMAR: Kandi-4.
NORTH DAKOTA—DEVILS LAKE: Lake 3; BISMARCK: Plaza Triple, Gateway 8; GRAND FORKS: Plaza Twin, Colony Twin, Empire, Cinema International, Columbia Mall 4, Midco 10.
SOUTH DAKOTA—ABERDEEN: Midco 5; SIOUX FALLS: Empire 6, West Mall Seven.

Milgram Theatres Inc.

G.S.B. Bldg., Belmont & City Line Aves., Suite 412, Bala Cynwyd, PA 19004; (215) 664-3900; FAX: (215) 664-3903.

WILLIAM MILGRAM, pres.; HENRY MILGRAM, exec. vice pres.; ROBERT MILGRAM, v.p.
NEW JERSEY—BAYVILLE: Friendly Twin; GLASSBORO: Glassboro; MT. EPHRAIM: Harwan; NORTHFIELD: Tilton 6; PITMAN: Broadway; WESTMONT: Westmont Twin.
PENNSYLVANIA—ALLENTOWN: Broad, Valley; EPHRATA: Main 2; HAZELTON: Churchill 7; HUNTINGDON: Cinema, Village; LAKE HARMONY: Galleria; LEBANON: Key D.I.; LEWISBURG: Campus; LEWISTOWN: Midway D.I.; LOCK HAVEN: Roxy, MARIETTA: Marietta; MT. POCONO: Casino; NEW CUMBERLAND: Shore D.I., West Shore; NEW HOLLAND: Ritz; PHILADELPHIA: Merlin, Yeadon; PHOENIXVILLE: Colonial; SCRANTON: Ritz; THORNDALE: Thorndale; WILKES BARRE: Gateway Cinemas 5.

Mini Cinemas, Inc.

3075 West Liberty Ave., Pittsburgh, PA 15216; (412) 561-0408.

MICHAEL CARDONE, pres. CEO.
PENNSYLVANIA—PITTSBURGH: Plaza 2, South Hills, Twin Hi-Way D.I.

Mini Theatres

534 Broadhollow Rd., Suite 430, Melville, NY 11747; (516) 293-3456; FAX: (516) 293-3490.

MARTY GOLDMAN and HAROLD S. LAGER, partners.
CONNECTICUT—CANAAN: Colonial; SPRINGDALE: State Cinema.
MASSACHUSETTS—FAIRHAVEN: Bijou; GREENFIELD: Cinema Six; MARTHA'S VINEYARD: Capawock, Island, Strand; NORTH ADAMS: Cinema Six; RAYNHAM: Bijou Twin; SOUTH HADLEY: Tower Twin.
NEW HAMPSHIRE—BEDFORD: Bedford Mall 8; HOOKSETT: West River Rd. Cinema 12; LACONIA: Colonial Five; MANCHESTER: South Willow St. Cinema Nine; NASHUA: Nashua Mall 8; PORTSMOUTH: Cinema Four (5 screens); SOMERSWORTH: Tri-City Cinema Four; WEIRS BEACH: Weirs Twin D.I.
NEW YORK—ALBANY: Madison Cinema; ALEXANDRIA BAY: Bay D.I.; AVERILL PARK: Hollywood D.I.; CANANDAIGUA: Movie Time 10; CANTON: American; CATSKILL: Community Twin; CHATHAM: Crandell Cinema; CLINTON: Clinton Cinema; COBLESKILL: Movieplex Six Eight; GLENS FALLS: Glen Twin D.I.; GREENVILLE: Greenville D.I.; HANCOCK: Capitol Cinema; HUNTER: Hunter; ITHACA: State Twin; LAKE PLACID: Palace Triple: LITTLE FALLS: Valley Twin; LOWVILLE: Town Hall, Valleybrook D.I.; MALONE: Plaza; MALTA: Malta D.I.; MASSENA: Massena, 56 Auto D.I.; NORTH HOOSICK: Hatheway D.I.; OGDENSBURG: Cinema Twin; OLD FORGE: Strand; ONEIDA: Glenwood Movieplex 7; PAINTED POST: Crystal Cinema Eight; POTSDAM: Roxy Twin; SARANAC LAKE: Berkeley Twin; TANNERSVILLE: Orpheum; THOUSAND ISLAND: Thousand Island Cinema; TUPPER LAKE: State; UNADILLA: Unadilla D.I.
PENNSYLVANIA—JOHNSTOWN: New Westwood Plaza Twin.
RHODE ISLAND—NARRAGANSETT: Pier Cinema Twin; NEWPORT: Jane Pickens.
VERMONT—BURLINGTON: Century Plaza Three, Merrill's Cinema Nine, Merrills Showcase Five, Ethan Allen Quad; NEWPORT: Showplace Cinema Three; RUTLAND: Plaza Cinema Twin, Studio Cinema Twin, Westway Quad.

Movie City

P.O. Box 315, Atlantic Highlands, NJ 07716; (908) 291-0099; FAX: (908) 291-0099.

EDWARD GRANT, pres.; HOWARD GRANT, v.p.; MILDRED GRANT, treas.; JANE FABRICI, sec.
NEW JERSEY—EAST BRUNSWICK: Movie City 5; EDISON: Movie City 6; TEANECK: Movie City 3; WOODRBIDGE: Movie City 5.

Moyer Theatres

1953 N.W. Kearney, Portland, OR 97209. (503) 226-2735. FAX: (503) 295-1210.

LARRY R. MOYER, pres. & COO; CHRIS MOYER, v.p. finance; LARRY R. MOYER JR., v.p. operations.
OREGON—EUGENE: West 11th Movieland (6 screens); PORTLAND: Rose Moyer Cinemas (6); WILSONVILLE: Grand Parkway 3.
WASHINGTON—VANCOUVER: Vancouver Mall Cinema (4); OLYMPIA: Capitol Mall Cinema (4).

Muvico Theatres

255 Commercial Blvd., Ste. 200, Lauderdale-by-the-Sea, FL 33308; (305) 493-7700; FAX: (305) 493-7724.

A. HAMID HASHEMI, pres.; ROBERT R. CALEFE, sr. v.p.
FLORIDA—CORAL SPRINGS: Muvico Coral Springs 6; DELRAY BEACH: Delway 10; NORTH MIAMI: California Club (6); TAMPA: Muvico Britton 8.

N

National Amusements, Inc.

200 Elm St., P.O. Box 9126, Dedham, MA 02026; (617) 461-1600. FAX: (617) 326-1306.

SUMNER M. REDSTONE, chmn. of bd.; IRA A. KORFF, CEO; JEROME MAGNER, sr. v.p. finance treas.; WILLIAM J. TOWEY, sr. v.p., opns.; EDGAR A. KNUDSON, sr. v.p. adv. & pub.
CONNECTICUT—BERLIN: Showcase 12; HARTFORD: Showcase 10; MILFORD: Showcase 5, Milford Fourplex; NEWINGTON: Newington 3; NORTH HAVEN: Showcase 8; ORANGE: Showcase 7.

ILLINOIS— MILAN: Showcase 11; MOLINE: Parkway, Sierra, Supersaver 6.

IOWA—DAVENPORT: Showcase 10.

KENTUCKY—ERLANGER: Showcase 9; LOUISVILLE: Showcase 13.

MASSACHUSETTS—ALLSTON: Allston 2; BROOKLINE: Circle 7; DEDHAM: Showcase 12; LAWRENCE: Showcase 10; REVERE: Showcase 14; SEEKONK: Showcase 10; SPRINGFIELD: Showcase 14; WOBURN: Showcase 10; WORCESTER: Lincoln Plaza 3, Showcase 4, White City 3, Webster Square 2.

MICHIGAN—ANN ARBOR: Showcase 14; AUBURN HILLS: Showcase 14; DEARBORN: Dearborn 8; FLINT: Courtland Center 2, Showcase 14; GRAND RAPIDS: Showcase 10; HARPER WOODS: Beacon Manor 4; PONTIAC: Showcase 10, Summit Place 3; STERLING HEIGHTS: Showcase 15; WESTLAND: Quo Vadis 6, Showcase 8.

NEW HAMPSHIRE—SALEM: Salem Tri.

NEW JERSEY—ATCO: Multiplex 14; HAZLET: Multiplex 12; SAYERVILLE: Amboy Multiplex 14.

NEW YORK—BRONX: Concourse Plaza 10, Whitestone Multiplex 14; COMMACK: Commack Multiplex 15; HAWTHORNE: All Westchester Sawmill Multiplex 10; MEDFORD: Brockhaven Multiplex 14; VALLEY STREAM: Green Acres 6, Sunrise Multiplex 14.

OHIO—CINCINNATI: Showcase 12, Eastgate Mall 7; DAYTON: Beaver Creek 7, Centerville 6, Cinema North 5, Dayton Mall 8, Page Manor 2, Huber Heights 12, Cross Pointe 2, Southtown 2; SPRINGDALE: Showcase 9; TOLEDO: Franklin Park 5, Showcase, Super Cinemas 10.

PENNSYLVANIA—PITTSBURGH: Showcase East 8; Showcase West 12, Showcase North 11, Supersaver 8.

RHODE ISLAND—WARWICK: Showcase 12.

VIRGINIA—MOUNT VERNON: Mt. Vernon Multiplex 10; MERRIFIELD: Lee Highway Multiplex 14, Reston Multiplex 11.

National Theatre Corp.

5915 Landerbrook Dr., Suite 200, Cleveland, OH 44124-4034; (216) 461-2707.

BLAIR MOONEY, pres. & CEO; RUSSELL WINTNER, exec. v.p. & COO; CHARLES TAMME, gen. mgr.; GERD JAKUSZEIT, dir. of oper.

OHIO—AKRON: Akron Cine Six, Montrose Movies 8; CLEVELAND: Severance Movies 8, Great Northern 7, Great Lakes Mall 9; Memphis D.I. 3, Brookgate 5, Garfield 5; DEFIANCE: Northtowne Movies 5; DELAWARE: Delaware Square Movies 5; MARION: Southland Mall 4; NILES: Movie World 6, Boulevard Centre Movies 6; TIFFIN: Tiffin Movies 4; YOUNGSTOWN: Cinema South 10.

Neighborhood Entertainment, Inc.

1510 E. Ridge Rd., Richmond, VA 23229; P.O. Box 71270, Richmond 23255-1270; (804) 282-0303; FAX: (804) 282-0478.

FRANK W. NOVAK, JR., pres. & CEO; W. ROY TOMPKINS III, v.p.-optns., asst. sec.; DAVID H. LEVY, v.p. sec. & treas.; RAY BENTLEY, v.p.-adv. & publicity; BOB TESSIER, head film buyer.

MARYLAND—FREDERICK: Holiday 2.

VIRGINIA—CHARLOTTESVILLE: Seminole Square 4; CHESAPEAKE: Greenbrier 4; COLONIAL HEIGHTS: Southpark 6; DALE CITY: Dale 2; FALLS CHURCH: Loehmanns 2; FARMVILLE: Longwood Village 3; FRANKLIN: Armory Drive 3; FREDERICKSBURG: Spotsylvania 4; HAMPTON: Riverdale 3; HOPEWELL: Crossings 2; NEWPORT NEWS: Newmarket 4; NORFOLK: Little Creek 3, Terrace 2; PETERSBURG: Crater 8; PORTSMOUTH: Plaza 3; RICHMOND: Cloverleaf 8, Genito Forest 9, Ridge 7, Westhampton 2, Westover, Willow Lawn 4; ROANOKE: Terrace 2, Towers 3; SOUTH HILL: South Hill 2; VIRGINIA BEACH: Pembroke Mall 8.

Nelson-Ferman Theatres

%Cinema 10, Rt. 10, Succasunna, NJ 07876; (201) 584-0788.

NEW JERSEY—CLIFTON: Allwood (6); EMERSON: Emerson Quad; SUCCASUNNA: Cinema 10 Tenplex; WASHINGTON TOWNSHIP: Washington Triple Cinema.

NEW YORK—NEW CITY: Cinema 6.

Noret Theatres

2726 82nd St., Lubbock, TX 79423; (806) 745-1693; FAX: (806) 745-0952.

TEXAS—AMARILLO: Showplace 4; AUSTIN: Showplace 6; LAMESA: The Movies 1 & 2; LUBBOCK: Cinema West, Showplace 6, Winchester Twin; SAN ANGELO: Village Cinema 1 & 2; SNYDER: Cinema 1 & 2.

B. L. Nutter Theatres

P.O. Box 44, Putnam, CT 06260; (401) 568-5298.

(Operating Imperial Cinema Corp. and Nutter Theatre Management Associates)

BRUCE L. NUTTER, pres. & treas.; BRUCE L. NUTTER, gen. mgr.; CHRISTINE E. NUTTER, v.p. & asst. gen. mgr.

CONNECTICUT—HARTFORD: Colonial; PUTNAM: Royale Deluxe Theatre I & II.

MASSACHUSETTS—PALMER: Imperial Cinema; SPENCER: Imperial Cinema; WINCHENDON: Capitol.

RHODE ISLAND—PROVIDENCE: New Imperial Art Cinema; WEST GLOCESTER: Cold Springs Theatre I & II.

P

P & G Theatres

8725 Flower Ave., Silver Spring, MD 20901; (301) 588-1667.

P. SANCHEZ, owner; PAT CURTIS, head booker; LE PHAM, office mgr.

MARYLAND—CAMP SPRINGS: Andrews Manor (2); GAITHENSBURG: Montgomery Village (3); GREENBELT: Old Greenbelt; LAUREL: Laurel Towne Center (2); RIVERDALE: Riverdale Plaza; SILVER SPRING: Flower Theatre (4).

VIRGINIA—HERNDON: Herndon Twin.

Pacific Theatres

120 North Robertson Boulevard, Los Angeles, CA 90048; (310) 657-8420. FAX: (310) 855-9837, (310) 652-2439.

MICHAEL R. FORMAN, bd. chm.; JEROME A. FORMAN, pres.; JAMES J. COTTER, exec. v.p., finance; JAY SWERDLOW, exec. v.p. & gen. mgr.; JIM HUDSON, v.p. & finance; CHAN WOOD, exec. v.p. & head film buyer; IRA LEVIN, v.p. & legal counsel; DON IMMENSCHUH, v.p. theat. opns.; MILTON I. MORITZ, v.p. adv. & p.r.; DAN CHERNOW, v.p., gov. affairs & asst. gen. mgr.; MICHAEL COLLINS, v.p. purchasing & snack bar sls.

Drive-in Theatres

CALIFORNIA—BUENA PARK: Buena Park 3; CHATSWORTH: Winnetka 6; COMPTON: Compton; CULVER CITY: Studio; EL MONTE: El Monte; FRESNO: Woodward Park 4; GARDENA: Vermont Triplex; CITY OF INDUSTRY: Vineland Fourplex; LOMA LINDA: Tri City; LONG BEACH: Los Altos Triplex; ORANGE: Orange Twin; OXNARD: Sky-View Twin; PICO RIVERA: Fiesta Four; SANTA FE SPRINGS: Norwalk; SOUTH GATE: South Gate; VAN NUYS: Van Nuys 3; VENTURA: 101 Triplex; WESTCHESTER: Centinela; WESTMINSTER: Hi-Way 39 Four.

Walk-in Theatres

CALIFORNIA—CARMEL MOUNTAIN: Carmel Mountain 10; CITY OF COMMERCE: Commerce 7; EAGLE ROCK: Eagle Rock 4; GLENDALE: Regency, Roxy; HOLLYWOOD: El Capitan, Hollywood Pacific Triplex, Pacific's Cinerama Dome; HUNTINGTON PARK: Warner 2; LA JOLLA: La Jolla Village Four; LAKEWOOD: Lakewood Center Four, Lakewood Center South 9, Regency 8; LA MESA: Grossmont 4, Grossmont Trolley 8 Cinemas; NORTHRIDGE: Northridge 6; ONTARIO: Ontario 10; OXNARD: Carriage Square 5; PASADENA: Hastings 5; SAN BERNARDINO: Inland Cinema 5; SAN DIEGO: Cinerama 6, Clairemont Twin, Center Three; SANTA FE SPRINGS: Pacific 3; SHERMAN OAKS: Pacific 4; SWEETWATER: Sweetwater 6; WESTWOOD: Crest; WOODLAND HILLS: Topanga 3.

Pacific Theatres of N. California

21 Tamal Vista Blvd., Suite 135, Corte Madera, CA 94925-1144; (415) 927-0262; FAX: (415) 927-7436.

CALIFORNIA—ALBANY: Albany (2); BERKELEY: Act (2), Berkeley California (3), Fine Arts, Oaks (2), Shattuck (8); CORTE MADERA: Cinema; MILL VALLEY: Sequoia Twin; NOVATO: Rowland Plaza; OAKLAND: Piedmont; PETALUMA: Petaluma (8); SAN RAFAEL: Regency (6); SAUSALITO: Marin.

Patriot Cinemas, Inc., The

350 Lincoln St., Hingham, MA 02043; (617) 749-7963; FAX: (617) 749-7974.

PHILIP J. SCOTT, pres.; DAVID A. KIOLBASA, v.p.; EDITH L. SCOTT, v.p.; PETER WRIGHT, booker; DAVID A. SCOTT, off mgr. & treas.

MASSACHUSETTS—FALMOUTH: Falmouth Mall Cinemas 6; HINGHAM: Loring Cinema; NORTH WEYMOUTH: Harborlight Cinemas 8; SOUTH WEYMOUTH: Cameo Theatres 2.

Peterson Theatres, Inc.

P.O. Box 866907, Plano, TX 75086; (212) 618-4466; FAX: (214) 618-6521.

RICHARD W. PETERSON, pres.; JANIECE W. PETERSON, v.p.; BRIAN A. SHARP, office mgr.; B.J. SMITH, film buyer.
TEXAS—DALLAS: Astro 3 D.I., Casa Linda 4, West End Cinema 10.

Piedmont Theatres

3700 South Blvd., Charlotte, NC 28217; (704) 527-7200.

JERRY L. THEIMER, pres.
NORTH CAROLINA—BOONE: Flick 2; CHARLOTTE: Tryon Mall Fourplex, Queen Park Six Plex Indoor; CONCORD: Clearsprings 6; FAYETTEVILLE: Sycamore 5; GASTONIA: Watertower 4.
SOUTH CAROLINA—CHARLESTON: Fox IV.
VIRGINIA—LYNCHBURG: Fort Cinema Fourplex.

Plitt Amusement Co.

9059 90th St. N.W., P.O. Box 2239, Oak Harbor, WA 98277; (206) 675-0746; FAX: (206) 675-9402. L.A. Office: 1801 Century Park E., Suite 1225, Los Angeles, CA 90067, (213) 553-2364; FAX: (213) 201-9164.

RAYMOND C. FOX, pres.; SAM M. PLITT, v.p. & dir. optns.; SANDRA J. ANDRE, v.p., sec. treas.
WASHINGTON—ELLENSBURG: Liberty 3; MOSES LAKE: Lake Cinema 4; MT. VERNON: Cinema 5, College Tri 3; OAK HARBOR: Plaza 3; WALLA WALLA: Jefferson Park 3, Plaza Twin 2, Poplar Street 3.

Q

Queens Circuit Management Corp.

P.O. Box 120, Corona A Station, Corona, NY 11368-2395; (718) 478-9200.

ROLAND C. HASSANEIN, film buyer & gen. mgr.
NEW YORK—CORONA: Plaza Twin; JACKSON HEIGHTS: Colony Theatre Twin, Jackson Triplex; RIDGEWOOD: Ridgewood Fiveplex.

R

R/C Theatres Management Corp.

(An Etmac Co.) 231 West Cherry Hill Ct., Box 1056, Reisterstown, MD 21136-1056; (301) 526-4774. FAX: (301) 526-6871.

IRWIN R. COHEN, pres. & chief exec. officer; J. WAYNE ANDERSON, pres. of operations; SCOTT R. COHEN, pres. of film; DAVID G. PHILLIPS, v.p. opns.; LYNNE LOCKE MUSKA, v.p., finance; JAN S. ANDERSON, v.p. film; Division Managers: Philip Ridenour (Maryland), William Menke (Va.).
MARYLAND—ARBUTUS: Hollywood Twin Cinema; CAMBRIDGE: Dorchester Sq. Movies 4; EASTON: Easton Movies 4; ELDERSBURG: Carrolltowne Movies 6; FROSTBURG: Frostburg Cinema 4; HAGERSTOWN: Hagerstown Movies 10, Long Meadow Triple Cinema; REISTERSTOWN: Village Cinema 3.
PENNSYLVANIA—CARLISLE: Mall Cinema 8; GETTYSBURG: Majestic Cinema 3.
VIRGINIA—CHRISTIANSBURG: New River Valley Mall 8; COVINGTON: Covington Movies 3; CULPEPER: Regal Twin Cinema, State Theatre; FREDERICKSBURG: Movies of Fredericksburg 10, Virginians Cinema 4; LEESBURG: Tally Ho Twin Cinema; LEXINGTON: State Cinema 3; NORFOLK (Naval Base): Main Gate 10; STAFFORD: Aquia Town Center Movies 10; STAUNTON: Staunton Mall 6; VIRGINIA BEACH: Surf-N-Sand 8; WAYNESBORO: Wayne Twin Cinema; WILLIAMSBURG: Movies 7 at Williamsburg Sq.

RTC Theatres & Associates

805 Fletcher Lane, Hayward, CA 94544; (415) 886-7727; FAX: (415) 886-7751.

LAWRENCE E. MARTIN, pres.
CALIFORNIA—SAN LEANDRO: Bal; VISALIA: Visalia, Mooney D.I. 1 & 2; SALINAS: Fox; SAN FRANCISCO: Tower.

Redwood Theatres, Incorporated

5725 Paradise Dr., Suite 350, Corte Madera, CA 94925; Tel.: (415) 924-0656. FAX: (415) 924-6152.

RICHARD MANN, pres.; GEORGE VOGAN, v.p.; T. TAWARA, secty.-treas.; LILLIAN JOHNS, asst. secty.-treas.
CALIFORNIA—AUBURN: Auburn Cinemas 1 & 2, State 1 & 2; EUREKA: Eureka 1, 2 & 3, State 1, 2, & 3, The Movies 4; JACKSON: Jackson Cinemas 1, 2, 3, & 4; PLACERVILLE: Cinema 4, Empire 2; RED BLUFF: Riverside Plaza Cinemas 6; SONORA: Cinema 5; UKIAH: Ukiah 6; WOODLAND: State 1, 2 & 3.
OREGON—KLAMATH FALLS: Pelican Cinemas 1, 2, 3, & 4.

Regal Cinemas, Inc.

7132 Commercial Park Dr., Knoxville, TN 37918; (615) 922-1123; FAX: (615) 922-6085.

MICHAEL L. CAMPBELL, pres. chmn.; R. NEAL MELTON, v.p.-sec.; ROBERT ENGEL, v.p. film, adv.; MARK JARVIS, v.p., operations; KEITH THOMPSON, v.p.-dvlpmt; LEWIS FRAZER, CFO; GREGORY DUNN, v.p.-.concessions & mktg.; ROGER FRAZEE, dir. equip. & maintenance; LISA DEPEW, asst. controller; RHONDA MELTON, co-op adv.; SUSAN D. MILAM, exec. asst.; JAN FRAZEE, exec. asst.-optns.; MICHAEL KIVETT, dist. spv.-Northeast; DEAN DUNCAN, district supervisor-central; LEON HURST, dist. spv.-south; CHRIS BLEVINS, dist. spvr.-No. Central; PHILIP D. BORACK, BARRY STEINBERG, film buyers; ED MYERS, dir., mgmt. info. syst.
ALABAMA—DECATUR: Gateway 4, River Oaks Mall 8; GADSEN: Rainbow 8.
DELAWARE—WILMINGTON AREA: Peoples Plaza 13.
GEORGIA—ATLANTA AREA: Lawrenceville Towne Center 10, Lithonia Covington Square 8, Marietta Regal 10, Norcross Peachtree 10; AUGUSTA: Augusta Village 8; MACON: Rivergate 10; ST. MARYS: Kings Bay 6.
INDIANA—FORT WAYNE: Coventry 8, Holiday 8, Georgetown Square 2, Quimby Village 2.
LOUISIANA—SHREVEPORT: South Park Mall 8.
OHIO—CINCINNATI: Norwood Central Parke 11; CLEVELAND: Hudson 10, Macedonia 10, Westlake Promenade 10; CLEVELAND AREA: Brunswick 8, Solon Commons 10; LIMA: American Mall 2, Eastgate 4, Lima Center 3, Regal 7; LORAIN: Sheffield Centre 10; MARIETTA: Lafayette Center 7.
PENNSYLVANIA—BUTLER: Moraine Pointe 10; PHILADELPHIA AREA: Huntingdon Valley 14.
TENNESSEE—CHATTANOOGA: Hamilton Place Mall 9, Hamilton Place 8, Northgate Crossing 6; JACKSON: Regal Movies 6; KNOXVILLE: Downtown West 8, East Towne Crossing 8, East Towne Mall 7; MEMPHIS: Southbrook 7; NASHVILLE AREA: Hendersonville Indian Lake 10, Hermitage Courtyard 8, Nippers Corner 10; TULLAHOMA: Regal Cinema 8.
WEST VIRGINIA—PARKERSBURG: Grand Central Mall 5, Towne Square 6.

Regency Caribbean Cinemas

1512 Fernandez Juncos Ave., 3rd floor, San Juan, PR 00910; (809) 727-7137.

VICTOR CARRADY, pres.; ROBERT CARRADY, v.p.
DOMINICAN REPUBLIC—LA ROMANA: Papagayo; SANTO DOMINGO, Cinema Centro 9, Diana, Manzana 2, Max, Santiago 5.
PUERTO RICO—BAYAMON: Rio Hondo 10; CAGUAS: Plaza Centro 5; GUAYNABO: Cinema 4, Guaynabo 3; PONCE: Plaza Del Caribe 6, Ponce 3; SAN JUAN: Fine Arts, Metro 3, Fajardo 6, Humacao 5, Yauco 4; TRUJILLO ALTO: Trujillo Alto 3.
U.S. VIRGIN ISLANDS—ST. THOMAS: Four Winds 4, Cinema 3.

Roth Theatres (North Carolina, South Carolina)

912 Thayer Ave., Silver Spring, MD 20910; (301) 587-8450. FAX: (301) 587-8454.

PAUL A. ROTH, pres.; MICHAEL E. ROWAN, sr. v.p., finance; JOAN B. ROTH, v.p.; MARC MADISON, film buyer; FRANK COLLELI, gen. mgr; CLYDE ELLISOR, mktg.; BOB JONES, div. mgr.
NORTH CAROLINA—ASHEVILLE: Merrimon, Asheville West.

SOUTH CAROLINA—COLUMBIA: Dutch Square, Gamecock, Columbia-East; SUMTER: Movies 1-2-3; ORANGEBURG: Camelot.

S

Schulman Theatres, Inc.

2000 East 29th St., Bryan, TX 77806.

TEXAS—BRYAN: Manor East III, Schulman Six; COLLEGE STATION: Plaza Three; CROCKETT: Ritz; PALESTINE: Schulman 2; WACO: Schulman Five, Ivy Twin Cinema.

SoCal Cinemas, Inc.

13 Corporate Plaza, Newport Beach, CA 92660; (714) 640-2370.

ART SANBORN, chm; BRUCE SANBORN, pres.; GARY RICHARDSON, gen. mgr.
CALIFORNIA—ANAHEIM HILLS: Cinemapolis (13); BLUE JAY VILLAGE: Blue Jay Cinema (4); CARLSBAD: Plaza Camino Real Cinema (4); LAGUNA HILLS: Laguna Hills Mall Cinema (3); LOS ANGELES: University Cinema (3); MORENO VALLEY: Canyon Springs Cinema (3); OCEANSIDE: Town & Country Cinema (3); RIVERSIDE: Canyon Crest Cinema (9); TEMECULA: Temeku Cinema (7), Tower Cinema (2); WEST COVINA: Fox Theatre (3), Eastland Theatre (5), Wescove Cinema (3).

Standard Theatres, Inc.

19065 North Hills Dr., P.O. Box 632, Brookfield, WI 53008-0632; (414) 784-1450.

JOHN F. LING, pres.
WISCONSIN—BELOIT: Prairie Cinema Triple; DELAVAN: Delavan Twin; GREEN BAY: Bay Triple; LAKE GENEVA: Geneva Twin; MILWAUKEE: 41 Twins Outdoor.

State Theatre Company

P.O. Box 77, Brookings, SD 57006; (605) 692-6821. FAX: (605) 642-7811.

DICK PETERSON, owner.
MINNESOTA—MOORHEAD: Safari 7.
SOUTH DAKOTA—BROOKINGS: Showcase Cinema 1-2-3, PIERRE: State 1-2-3.

Storey Theatres Inc.

572 Morosgo Drive N.E. Atlanta, GA 30324; (404) 266-2800.

FREDERICK G. STOREY, chmn.; JAMES H. EDWARDS, pres. & CEO; RICK ADAMS, exec. v.p. & COO; DAVID E. TROGLIN, v.p., secty. treas.; ROBERT P. SEDLAK, v.p., film buyer.
GEORGIA—ATLANTA: Delk Ten, National Seven, North 85 Twin D.I., Shannon Seven, 12 Oaks Four, Town 12; GAINESVILLE: Blueridge Triple, Lakeshore Four.

Super Saver Cinema Ltd.

109 North Oregon, Suite 1000, El Paso, TX 79912; (915) 532-1943; FAX: (915) 542-2945.

LLOYD CURLEY, pres. & CEO; JIM McKENNA, sr. v.p., COO; DAVID HOOVER, v.p., construction; LOIS HUFNAGEL, asst. v.p., theatre optns.; KATHLEEN GILLMAN, purchas. dir.
ARIZONA—MESA: Superstation Springs 8, Town Center 8; PHOENIX: Bell Rd. 8, Palm Glen 8.
CALIFORNIA—FREMONT: Gateway Plaza 7; NORWALK: Norwalk Square 8; POMONA: Indian Hills 8; SEAL BEACH: Rossmoor 7.
COLORADO—ARVADA: Arlington Square 8; AURORA: Aurora Plaza 8; COLORADO SPRINGS: Citadel 8; DENVER: Bear Valley 8; THORNTON: Pinnacle 8.
FLORIDA—MIAMI: Westbird 8.
NEBRASKA—OMAHA: Westwood 8.
NEW YORK—BUFFALO: Elmwood 8.
OHIO—CINCINNATI: Biggs 8, Forest Fair 8; COLUMBUS: Glengary 8, Scarborough 8.
OKLAHOMA—OKLAHOMA CITY: Lakeshore 8, Mall 31 (7), Shields Plaza 8; TULSA: Mall 31 (7).

Syndicate Theatres, Inc.

55½ E. Court Street, Franklin, IN 46131; (317) 736-7144.

TRUEMAN T. REMBUSCH, pres.; MICHAEL REMBUSCH, v.p.; MARY AGNES REMBUSCH, treas.; NANCY GILLILAND, booker.
INDIANA—BATESVILLE: Gibson; CRAWFORDSVILLE: Ben Hur D.I.; FRANKLIN: Artcraft; HUNTINGTON: Huntington, Huntington D.I.; WABASH: Eagles, 13-24 D.I.; MADISON: Ohio I-II, Skyline D.I.

Syufy Enterprises

150 Golden Gate Ave., San Francisco, CA 94102; (415) 885-8400.

ARIZONA—GLENDALE: Glendale 9 D.I.; TEMPE: Scottsdale 6 D.I.; TUCSON: Century Gateway 12, Century Park 12.
CALIFORNIA—ALAMEDA: Island Auto; BURLINGAME: Hyatt Cinema, Burlingame 4 D.I.; CARSON: Southbay 6 D.I.; CITRUS HEIGHTS: Sunrise 9; CONCORD: Solano 2 D.I.; DALY CITY: Geneva 4 D.I.; FREMONT: Cinedome 8; MOUNTAIN VIEW: Century Cinema 10; NAPA: Cinedome 8 Complex; NEWARK: Cinedome Sevenplex; NORTH HOLLYWOOD: Century 7; OAKLAND: Century 8, Coliseum 4 D.I.; ORANGE: Cinedome 11, City Center 4, Stadium 8 D.I.; PINOLE: Century 10 Complex; PLEASANT HILL: Century Fiveplex; REDWOOD: Century Park 12; SACRAMENTO: Capitol Fourplex, State Sixplex, Sacramento 6 D.I., 49er 6 D.I., Century 6 Complex; SALINAS: Century Park 7, Northridge Eightplex; SAN FRANCISCO: Cinema 21, Empire 3, Presidio; SOUTH SAN FRANCISCO: Century Plaza 8; SAN JOSE: Century Almaden 5, Century 21, Century 22 Triplex, Century 23 Twin, Century 24 Twin, Century 25 Twin, Century Berryessa 10, Capitol 6 D.I., UNION CITY: Union City 6 D.I.; VALLEJO: Cinedome 8; VENTURA: Century 8.
NEVADA—HENDERSON: Cinedome 12; LAS VEGAS: Century Desert 12; Cinedome Sixplex, Las Vegas 4 D.I., Parkway Triplex, Redrock 11; RENO: Century 11, Cine Old Towne Triplex; SPARKS: El Rancho 4 D.I.
NEW MEXICO—ALBUQUERQUE: Albuquerque 6 D.I.
UTAH—SALT LAKE CITY: Century 21-23 Triplex, Century 24-29 Twin.

T

TMI Theatres

P.O. Box 2076, Deland, FL 32721; (904) 736-6830; FAX: (904) 738-2596.

FLORIDA—DELAND: Deland Cinema, Victoria Square 6; ORANGE CITY: Showcase 2; PALM CITY: Payless at Martin Downs 4.
PENNSYLVANIA—BUTLER: Penn Cinemas 2, Pioneer D.I. 3; CLARION: Orpheum Cinema 2; Garby Cinema 2; MEADVILLE: Meadville Cinema 4.

Teicher Theatres, Inc.

11 West Main St., Troy, OH 45373; (513) 339-5029.

ALAN TEICHER, pres.; JOYCE TEICHER, v.p.
OHIO—GREENVILLE: Wayne Cinema 2; TROY: Mayflower Twin, WAPAKONETA: Wapa Cinema.

Theatre Management, Inc.

P.O. Box 2076, Deland, FL 32721; (904) 736-6830; FAX: (904) 738-2596.

FLORIDA—DELAND: Deland Cinema, Victoria Square 6; ORANGE CITY: Showcase 2; PALM CITY: Martin Downs 4.
PENNSYLVANIA—BUTLER: Penn Twin, Pioneer D.I., CLARION: Clarion Theatres 4; MEADVILLE: Meadville 4.

Trad-A-House Corporation (O'Neil Theatres)

1926 C Corporate Square Dr., Slidell, LA 70458; (504) 641-4720; FAX: (504) 641-4709.

TIM O'NEIL, JR., pres.; TIM O'NEIL III, v.p.; BETTY O'NEIL, secty.-treas.
FLORIDA—DESTIN: Destin Cinema 6; HOLLYWOOD: Taft-Hollywood Plaza Cinema 12. PANAMA CITY BEACH: Edgewater Cinema 6.
GEORGIA—ATLANTA: Northeast Plaza Cinema 12.
LOUISIANA—COVINGTON: Holiday Cinema 10; CROWLEY: Crowley Cinema 4; MANDEVILLE: Causeway Cinema 4; SLIDELL: The Movies 8.

MISSISSIPPI—HATTIESBURG: Broadacres Cinema 6; PICA-YUNE: River Ridge Cinema 4; WAVELAND: Choctow Cinema 4.
NEW HAMPSHIRE—LONDONBERRY: Appletree Cinema 4.
TENNESSEE—FRANKLIN: Watson Glen Cinema 10.

U

United Artists Theatre Circuit, Inc.

9110 E. Nichols Ave., #200, Englewood, CO 80112; (303) 792-3600.

Regional Offices: Western: 21700 Oxnard St., #1000, Woodland Hills CA 91367; Eastern: 1400 Old Country Rd., #300, Westbury, NY 11590; Central: 1900 S. Central Expressway, Dallas, TX 75215.

STEWART D. BLAIR, chmn. & CEO; PETER WARZEL, COO & pres.; KURT HALL, exec. v.p. & CFO; HAL CLEVELAND, exec. v.p., domestic oper.; THOMAS ELLIOT, exec. v.p., dvlpmt.; HANK LIGHT-STONE, exec. v.p., film; JOSEPH R. CROTTY, exec. v.p., intl. de-vlpmnt.; DENNIS DANIELS, exec. v.p., dom. oper.; JIM RUYBAL, exec. v.p., corp. oper.; GENE HARDY, sr. v.p.-legal; JUDY PAQUET, sr. v.p., FIS; BILL QUIGLEY, sr. v.p., mktg.; ERIK LOMIS, sr. v.p.-film; STEVEN KOETS, sr. v.p.-tax; BRUCE TAFFET, sr. v.p., concessions.

ARIZONA—CHANDLER: Chandler Park 10; FLAGSTAFF: Flag East 2, University Plaza Theatres 3, Orpheum 1; GLENDALE: Bell Park Cinemas 6; MESA: Westwood Cinemas 2, Valvista 10; PHOENIX: UA Cinemas 6, Metro Park 8, Westridge Park 6; SCOTTSDALE: UA 5 Scottsdale, UA Pavillion 11.

ARKANSAS—LITTLE ROCK: UA Cinema 150 1, UA Cinema City 7, UA Univ Quartet, UA Park Plaza 7, Lakewood Village 8; MAGNO-LIA: Cameo Trio 3.

CALIFORNIA—ANDERSON: Gateway 4; APTOS: Aptos Twin 2; BAKERSFIELD: UA Movies 6, UA East Hills; BERKELEY: UA 7 Berkeley; BREA: UA Movies 4, UA Cinema 4 Brea; BUENA PARK: UA Buena Park 8; CAMPBELL: UA Pruneyard 3; CAPITOLA: Golden Bough, 41st Avenue Playhouse 3; CARMEL: Carmel Crossroad Center 2; CERRITOS: UA 4 Cerritos, UA Twin Cerritos 2; CHICO: UA Cinema 3-Chico, El Rey, Senator 4; CHULA VISTA: UA Chula Vista 6; CITRUS HEIGHTS: Sunrise 4, UA the Movies; CLOVIS: UA 8 Clovis, UA Sierra Vista; COLMA: Movies at Colma 6; EMERYVILLE: Movies at Em-eryville 10; ESCONDIDO: UA 8 Escondido; FRESNO: UA Cinemas 4 Fresno, Movies at Fresno 4, Manchester Mall Cine 2; GRANADA HILLS: UA Granada Hills 7; GRASS VALLEY: Del Oro Grass Valley 3, Grass Valley Cinema 2; HAYWARD: UA 6 Hayward CA; LAKEWOOD: UA Lakewood 6; LONG BEACH: UA Movies Long Beach 6; LOS ANGELES: UA Westwood 3; MARINA DEL REY: UA 6 Marina Del Rey; MERCED: UA 4 Merced, UA Regency Merced 7; MONTCLAIR: UA 6 Montclair; MONTEREY: UA Regency Monterey 1, UA State Monterey 3; NORTH HOLLYWOOD: UA Movies 6; ORANGE: UA City Cinema 6; PASADENA: UA Movies 6; REDDING: Cascade 4; RED-WOOD CITY: UA 6 Redwood City; RIVERSIDE: UA 6 Riverside, UA Tyler Cinema 4; ROHNERT PARK: Empire 4; SACRAMENTO: Arden Fair 6; SAN DIEGO: Glasshouse 6 San Diego, Horton Plaza 7; SAN FRANCISCO: UA Cinema Stonestown 2, Alexandria 3, Coronet 1, UA Galaxy 4, Metro 1, Vogue 1; SANTA CRUZ: Del Mar, Rio, UA S. Cruz 2; SANTA MARIA: Santa Maria 3; SANTA ROSA: Santa Rosa 6, UA 5 Santa Rosa, Coddingtown 4; THOUSAND OAKS: UA 5 Thousand Oaks; TORRANCE: Del Amo 6; WOODLAND HILLS: UA 6 Woodland Hills.

COLORADO—ARVADA: Cooper 6; AURORA: Cooper 5; BOUL-DER: Flatirons, Village 4; CANON CITY: Royal Gorge Twin 2; COLO-RADO SPRINGS: Rustic Hills Twin 2, Hancock Plaza 4, Cinema 70 3-Plex, Academy 6, Aircadia D.I. 1; DENVER: Continental, Target Village 3; ENGLEWOOD: Cinderella Twin D.I. 2, UA Greenwood Plaza; FORT COLLINS: Campus West Twin 2, Foothills Twin 2, Arbor Cinema 4; GLENDALE: UA Twin; GRAND JUNCTION: Mesa Twin 2, UA Colorado West 4; GREELEY: Cooper Twin 2, Greeley Mall Twin 2, Bittersweet 4-Plex; LITTLETON: Cooper 7; LONGMONT: Movies 3-Plex, Courtyard 4-Plex; LOVELAND: Orchards Twin 2; PUEBLO: Pueblo Mall 3, Cinema Twin 2, Mesa D.I. 1; THORTON: North Star D.I. 1, Thornton Town Ctr.

DELAWARE—CLAYMONT: Eric Tri-State 5.

FLORIDA—APOPKA: Movies at Wekiva 8; BOCA RATON: Town Center Boca Raton 7; BOYNTON BEACH: Boynton Beach 9; CLEAR-WATER: Movies at Clearwater 8; DAYTONA BEACH: Volusia 1-3, Cin-ema 6; HIALEAH: Movies at Hialeah 14; JACKSONVILLE: Regency Square 12, The Movies at Orange Park 7, Movies at Mandarin Landing 8; JENSEN BEACH: Movies at Treasure Coast 6; LAKE CITY: Cinema 90 6; LAUDERHILL: Movies at Lauderhill 13; MARGATE: Movies at Mar-gate 8; MARY ESTHER: Santa Rosa 3; MIAMI: Movies at the Falls 7; OCALA: Cinemas West 5; ORANGE CITY: Market Place 8; ORLANDO: Florida Mall 7, Lake Howell Square 8, Movies at Republic Square 8; PALM BEACH GARDENS: Market Place, Promenade Plaza 8; PEM-BROKE PINES: Movies at Pembroke Pines 9; PENSACOLA: University 6; PINELLAS PARK: Movies at Pinellas Park 12; PLANTATION: Planta-tion Ft. Laud. 7; POMPANO BEACH: Hibiscus Plaza 6; TALLA-HASSEE: Capitol 6; TAMPA: Mission Bell 8; WEST PALM BEACH: Mall Cinema 4, Village Green 6, Movies at River Bridge 8, Wellington Market Place.

GEORGIA—ATLANTA: Lenox Square Theatres 6, CNN Cinemas 6, Midtown 8, Tara Theatre; AUGUSTA: National Hills Cinemas 3, Masters Cinemas 7, Daniel Village Cinemas 2; DECATUR: South Dekalb 4; DULUTH: Gwinnett Mall 12; GRIFFIN: Parkwood Cinemas 3; MACON: Riverside Cinemas 4, Macon Mall 4, Westgate Theatre 6; MORROW: Southlake 8; NORCROSS: Greens Corner Cinemas 5; ROME: Litch Cinemas 4; SAVANNAH: Abercorn 6, Tara 4, Roswell 10; UNION CITY: Shannon 8; WARNER ROBINS: Parkway Cinemas 5.

IDAHO—BOISE: Fairvu 3-Plex, Overland Park 3, Plaza Twin 2, Fairvu D.I. 1; IDAHO FALLS: Idaho Falls 4.

KANSAS—SHAWNEE: Trailridge 3.

LOUISIANA—ALEXANDRIA: Westgate Cinema 8; BASTROP: Washington Square 4; BATON ROUGE: Essen Mall Cinema 6, Bon Marche Twin 2, Bon Marche 11, University Cinema 4, Siegen Village 10; BOGULUSA: Trackside Cinema 5; HOUMA: Plaza Cinema 4, Houma Twin 2, Southland Cinema 4; KENNER: West Esplanade 8; LAFAY-ETTE: Northgate Cinema 8, Westwood Theatre 1; LAKE CHARLES: Charles Cinema 3, Oak Park 6; LEESVILLE: Lee Hills Cinema 4; NEW IBERIA: Bayou Landing 6; NEW ORLEANS: Belle Promenade 10, Eastlake Plaza 8, Plaza Cinema 4, Village Aurora Cinemas 6; OPELOU-SAS: St. Landry 4, Vista Village 4; SHREVEPORT: Eastgate 4.

MARYLAND—BALTIMORE: Golden Ring 9, Movies at Harbor Park 9, UA Westview; BETHESDA: Bethesda 4; GLEN BURNIE: Movies at Marley Station 8; ROCKVILLE: UA Theatre Rockville 10.

MICHIGAN—ANN ARBOR: The Movies Briarwood 7, Fox Village 4; BENTON HARBOR: UA 5 Benton Harbor; DEARBORN: Fairlane 10; FARMINGTON: UA West River; GRAND RAPIDS: Woodland 6, North Kent Mall 8; KALAMAZOO: West Main 7; LANSING: Spartan 3; MIDLAND: Midland Plaza 2; NOVI: 12 Oaks 5; PORTAGE: Movies at Portage 10; STERLING HEIGHTS: Movies Lakeside 4; TROY: Oakland 5.

MINNESOTA—BROOKLYN CENTER: Brookdale 8; BURNS-VILLE: UA 4 Burnsville, Burnsville Mall 4; DULUTH: Movies at Miller Hill 3; EDEN PRAIRIE: UA 5 Eden Prairie West, Eden Prairie East 4; MAPLEWOOD: UA 6 Maplewood, Maplewood #Two 6; MINNE-APOLIS: Saint Anthony Main 5; ROSEVILLE: Movies at Pavillon Pl 7.

MISSISSIPPI—BILOXI: Surfside Cinema 4, Edgewater Mall 2, Edgewater Mall 3 & 4; BROOKHAVEN: Westbrook Cinema 4; FLO-WOOD: UA Parkway Place; GAUTIER: Singing River 4, Singing River 5; GREENVILLE: Cinema I-82 4, Plaza Twin 2; GREENWOOD: High-land Park 3; HATTIESBURG: Cloverleaf 3; JACKSON: Ellis Isle 4; LAUREL: Sawmill Square 5; McCOMB: Camelia Cinema 4; MERID-IAN: College Park Cinema 3, R & S Cinema 5; NATCHEZ: Natchez Mall Cinema 4; OXFORD: Cine 4; RIDGELAND: Northpark 10; VICKS-BURG: Pemberton Square 4.

MISSOURI—KANSAS CITY: Bannister Mall 5.

NEBRASKA—LINCOLN: Copper 1, Plaza 4-Plex, State Theatre, Cinema Twin 2.

NEVADA—LAS VEGAS: Sunrise 7, Cinema 8, Paradise Cinemas 6; RENO: Granada 4; SPARKS: Reno/Sparks Cinemas 2.

NEW JERSEY—LAWRENCEVILLE: Eric Lawrenceville; MID-DLETOWN: UA 7 Middletown; MOORESTOWN: Eric Moorestown 2; PENNSAUKEN: Eric Pennsauken 5; PRINCETON: Eric Garden 2, Movies at Princeton Market Fair 9; TOTOWA: Cinema 46 3; UPPER MONTCLAIR: Bellevue Montclair 1; WAYNE: Wayne 4; WESTFIELD: Rialto; WESTWOOD: The Movies at Pascack 4.

NEW MEXICO—ALBUQUERQUE: Coronado 6, Del Norte 4, N. Plaza 5, UA Four Hills 12, Winrock 6, UA at High Ridge 8; SANTA FE: Lensic, Movies Twin 2, Cinema 6.

NEW YORK—BABYLON: Babylon LI 3; BAYSIDE: Bayside 4; BRONX: Interboro Bronx 4; BRONXVILLE: Bronxville 3; BROOKLYN: Marboro Brooklyn 4, Movies at Brooklyn Sheepshead 9; CORAM: Coram 10; DOUGLASTON: Movieworld Douglaston 7; EASTHAMPTON: Easthampton 5; EAST MEADOW: Meadowbrook LI 6; FLUSHING: UA Quartet Flushing 4; FOREST HILLS: Midway 4 Queens, Forest Hills 2, Continental 1 & 2 2, Continental 3 (1); GREAT NECK: Squire Great Neck 3; LARCHMONT: Larchmont Playhouse 2; LINDENHURST: Linden-hurst; LONG ISL. CITY: Astoria 6; LYNBROOK: Lynbrook 4; MAMA-RONECK: Mamaroneck Playhouse 4; MANHASSET: Manhasset 3; MASSAPEQUA: Sunrise Massapequa 4; NEW CITY: Cinema 304 2; NEW YORK: Criterion Center 7, Gemini 2, UA East Theatre, Movieland 8th St 3; NORTHPORT: Northport; OZONE PARK: Crossbay, Ozone Park; PATCHOGUE: Movies at Patchogue 13; SMITHTOWN: Smith-town; SOUTHAMPTON: Southampton Theatre 5; SPRING VALLEY: Spring Valley 11; STATEN ISLAND: Hylan Plaza, Movies at Staten Island 10; SYOSSET: Syosset 3; WESTBURY: Westbury D.I. 3; WEST-HAMPTON BEACH: Westhampton 1; WOODBURY: UA Cinema 150; YONKERS: Movieland Yonkers 6; YORKTOWN HEIGHT: Jefferson Valley 7.

NORTH CAROLINA—ALBEMARLE: Eastgate 5; ASHEVILLE: Beaucatcher, Biltmore Square Cinemas; CARY: Imperial 4; CONCORD: Carolina Mall 8; GASTONIA: Litch Cinemas 4; GOLDSBORO: Litch Cinemas 4; HICKORY: Crown IV Cinemas 4; KENDERSONVILLE: 4 Seasons 4; LUMBERTON: Cinema IV 4; RALEIGH: Mission Valley 5; WILMINGTON: College Road 6.

OKLAHOMA—LAWTON: Cache Cinemas 8; MIDWEST CITY: Almonte 6-Plex, Heritage Park, Heritage Plaza; NORMAN: Village 6-Plex; TULSA: Fontana 6, Parklane 2, UA Promenade 4, UA Annex 7.

PENNSYLVANIA—ALLENTOWN: Allentown 4; ARDMORE: Ard-more 2; CAMP HILL: Camp Hill Twin PA 2, UA 4 Capital Ct; CLIFTON HEIGHTS: Clifton Heights 2; CONCORDVILLE: Concordville 4; EASTON: Easton 4; FAIRLESS HILLS: Penn Jersey 3, Fairless Hills 3; FEASTERVILLE: Feasterville 4; FRACKVILLE: Schuykill 4; FRAZER: Frazer 2; HARRISBURG: Eric Colonial Park Mall, Eric East Park, Eric Union Deposit; HOLMES: Eric Macdade Mall 4; JENKINTOWN:

591

Baederwood 2; KING OF PRUSSIA: Eric Plaza 2, Eric King 2, Eric Queen 4; LANCASTER: Eric Lancaster Twin 2, Pacific Lancaster 4; LANGHORNE: Eric Lincoln Plaza 2; MONTGOMERYVILLE: Eric Montgomeryville 7; MUNCY: Lycoming 4; PHILADELPHIA: Cheltenham Square 8, Eric Rittenhouse 3, Sameric 4, Sam's Place 2, Campus 3, Chestnut Hill 2, Eric's Place; SCRANTON: Eric Scranton 8; UPPER DARBY: Barclay Square 2, Movies at 69th Street; WEST GOSHEN: Eric West Goshen 2; WILLIAMSPORT: Loyal Plaza 5; WYNNEWOOD: Eric Wynnewood; YORK: Delco Plaza York 5, Movies at York Mall 2.

SOUTH CAROLINA—ANDERSON: Market Place 6, Mall 2; EASLEY: Colony 2; FLORENCE: Capri 3, Crown, Julia 4; GREENVILLE: Bijou 8, Haywood Cinemas 10; N. CHARLESTON: Aviaton Ave 8.

TEXAS—ABILENE: UA Cinema 10; AMARILLO: UA Amarillo 6, Westgate 6 Mall; ARLINGTON: UA Bowen 8; BEAUMONT: Phelan 6; BEDFORD: UA Bedford 10; CORPUS CHRISTI: UA Corpus Christi 6, UA 4 Corpus Christi, The Movies Padre Staples 6; DALLAS: UA Cine Theat 1 & 2, Walnut Hill 6, Prestonwood 5, Plaza & Park Lane 8; DENTON: UA Golden Triangle 4; DUNCANVILLE: UA Cinema South 8; EL PASO: Country Club Twin 2, Towne East 4, Northgate 2, Cinemas 6-Plex; FT WORTH: Hulen 10, Las Vegas Trail 8; GARLAND: UA North Star 8; HURST: UA Hurst 6; LAREDO: Plaza 3, UA Del Norte 4; LUBBOCK: South Plain 4; MESQUITE: Town East 6; MIDLAND: UA 4; MINERAL WELLS: UA Cinemas 1 2 3 3; ODESSA: Northpark 6, Winwood 3, UA Permian 4; PLANO: Berkeley Square 8; PORT ARTHUR: UA Cinema 6; SAN ANGELO: Southwest 7 Cinema, UA Sunset 4; SHERMAN: UA Cinemas 4; SWEETWATER: Texas 1 & 2.

VIRGINIA—FAIRFAX: Movies at Fair Oaks 8; RICHMOND: Midlothian 6, West Tower 6, Chesterfield Mall 9; VIRGINIA BEACH: UA 5 Lynnhaven VA, Lynnhaven Mall 6, UA Kempsriver 7.

WEST VIRGINIA—CHARLESTON: Kanawha 9; TEAYS: Putnam Village 3.

WISCONSIN—FOX POINT: Brown Port 2; GREENFIELD: Spring Mall 4; JANESVILLE: UA Cine 3; KENOSHA: Kensha 5; MILWAUKEE: Northridge 6, Mill Road 6, Loomis 4.

PUERTO RICO—CAROLINA: UA 6 Carolina PR; SAN JUAN: UA Cinema 150 San Juan 5; SANTURCE: Paramount 3.

W

Wehrenberg Theatres, Inc.

1215 Des Peres Road, St. Louis, MO 63131; (314) 822-4520; FAX: (314) 822-8032.

RONALD P. KRUEGER, pres.; JOHN LOUIS, exec. v.p.; CHARLES NICKS, v.p. & CFO; DOUG WHITFORD, film buyer; CLYDE PATTON, dir., facilities; CLAY REED, dir., operations.

ARIZONA—FLAGSTAFF: Flag East, Flagstaff Mall Twin, Greentree 3, Orpheum, University; PRESCOTT: Plaza West, Marina Twin.

ILLINOIS—ALTON: Alton Twin; FAIRVIEW HEIGHTS: St. Clair 10 Cine.

MISSOURI—CAPE GIRARDEAU: West Park 4 Cine; OSAGE BEACH: Osage Village 4 Cine; ST. LOUIS: St. Charles 10 Cine, Chesterfield 4, Ciné, Eureka 6, Clarkson 6, Jamestown Twin Cine, Lindbergh 8 Cine, Mid Rivers 6 Cine, Kenrick 8, Creve Coeur, Westport 1 & 2, Des Peres 4 Cine, Ronnie's 8 Cine, Halls Ferry 14 Cine, Shady Oak Theatre, 66 D.I., North Twin D.I., Union Station 10 Cine, Keller 8 Cine, North West Plaza 8; SPRINGFIELD: Battlefield 6 Ciné.

Western Massachusetts Theatres, Inc.

265 State St., Springfield, MA 01103; (413) 737-4347.

RONALD I. GOLDSTEIN, pres.

MASSACHUSETTS—AMHERST: Amherst Cinema; CHICOPEE: Rivoli; GREENFIELD: Garden 7; NORTHAMPTON: Calvin; SPRINGFIELD: Bing; WARE: Casino 2.

VERMONT—BRATTLEBORO: First Cinema 3.

Wisper & Wetsman, Inc.

P.O. Box 3032-282, Birmingham, MI 48012; (313) 642-5100 or 564-6800.

WM. M. WETSMAN, pres.

INDIANA—(WLZ Amusement Co.) INDIANAPOLIS: Twin D.I. East & West.

MICHIGAN—HOWELL: Howell; LAPEER: Pix.

Wometco Theatres

2121 Ponce De Leon Blvd., Suite 920, Coral Gables, FL 33134; (305) 443-5577; FAX: (305) 443-8088.

JACK CROSBY, chmn. bd.; FRANK J. MORENO, pres. & COO; JON C. WRAY, SR., v.p. oprs.; CARL DREW, v.p. & controller; EDU-ARDO LLAUGER, v.p., Puerto Rico; JOH ELTZ, dir. concession; FELIX POUSA, dir. construction; KELLY PALMER, film buyer.

FLORIDA—BOCA RATON: Shadowood 12; CORAL GABLES: Miracle 4; MIAMI BEACH: Byron-Carlyle 7, Bay Harbor 4; MIAMI LAKES: Miami Lakes 10 Theatres; NORTH MIAMI BEACH: 163rd St. Triple; OCALA: Boulevard 6; ORLANDO: Park 11; SOUTH DADE: Kendall 9, Miller Square 8, University 7; SUNRISE: Weston 8; WEST HOLLYWOOD: Florida 4.

BAHAMAS—FREEPORT: Columbus Twin.

PUERTO RICO—BAYAMON: Cinema Centro 6; CAYEY: Cayey 4; HATILLO: Plaza del Norte 6; HATO REY: Plaza de las Americas 5; RIO PIEDRAS: Senorial 4; MAYAGUEZ: Mayaguez 6.

Y

Yakima Theatres, Inc.

P.O. Box 50, Yakima, WA 98907; (509) 248-1360; FAX: (509) 453-3074.

MICHAEL M. MERCY, pres.; EARL BARDEN v.p.

WASHINGTON—WENATCHEE: Columbia Cinema Fiveplex; YAKIMA: Mercy Sixplex, Uptown Plaza 4, Cinema West Triplex.

Theatres by Market

Major Theatre Circuits within Major North American Markets

The following tabulation presents by key metropolitan cities circuit theatres arranged alphabetically by town, and within each town alphabetically by theatre name. Market areas are those covered by key city television and radio stations and, to some extent, newspapers. Over 2,400 circuit theatres are clustered in and around the 50 top U.S. and Canadian metropolitan markets.

New York

AMC

Deptford 8	Deptford	NJ
Headquarters 10	Morristown	NJ
Rockaway 12	Rockaway	NJ
Maple Ridge 8	Amherst	NY

Ackerman Theatres

East Side Playhouse	New York	NY
86th St. East Playhouse	New York	NY
Hylan Twin	Staten Island	NY
Hylan Plaza 5-Plex	Staten Island	NY
Staten Island 10-Plex	Staten Island	NY
Ryeridge Twin	Rye	NY
Fine Arts	Westchester	NY
Cinema 100 Twin	White Plains	NY

Cineplex

Royal Twin	Bloomfield	NJ
Cranford Twin	Cranford	NJ
Newport Centre 9	Jersey City	NJ
Menlo Park 12	Menlo Park	NJ
Milburn Twin	Milburn	NJ
Paramus Rt. #17 3	Paramus	NJ
Paramus Rt. #4 10	Paramus	NJ
Warner Quad	Ridgewood	NJ
Union Twin	Union	NJ
Alpine 7	Brooklyn	NY
Fortway 5	Brooklyn	NY
Kenmore Quad	Brooklyn	NY
Kings Plaza Quad	Brooklyn	NY
Kingsway 5-plex	Brooklyn	NY
Metro 4	Brooklyn	NY
City Cinema 5	Fresh Meadows	NY
Meadows 7	Fresh Meadows	NY
Glen Cove 7	Glen Cove	NY
Shore Quad	Huntington	NY
Whitman	Huntington	NY
Lawrence Triple	Lawrence	NY
Nanuet 5-plex	Nanuet	NY
1st & 62nd	New York	NY
23rd Street 3	New York	NY
34th St.	New York	NY
59th St. East	New York	NY
62nd & Broadway	New York	NY
Baronet	New York	NY
Bay Cinema	New York	NY
Beekman	New York	NY
Carnegie Hall	New York	NY
Chelsea 9	New York	NY
Cinema 3	New York	NY
Coronet	New York	NY
Greenwich Twin	New York	NY
Mall Smithhaven Theatre 4	New York	NY
Manhattan I & II	New York	NY
Metro 2	New York	NY
National Twin	New York	NY
Olympia Twin	New York	NY
Park & 86th 2	New York	NY
Plaza	New York	NY

Regency	New York	NY
Waverly	New York	NY
Worldwide Cinemas 3	New York	NY
Ziegfeld	New York	NY
Hampton Arts Twin	Port Washington	NY
Islip Cinema	Port Washington	NY
Mattituck 8	Port Washington	NY
Soundview 6	Port Washington	NY
Fantasy 5	Rockville Center	NY
Rockville Twin	Rockville Center	NY

City Cinemas

Cinema 1	New York	NY
Cinema 2	New York	NY
Cinema 3rd Ave	New York	NY
86th St. East 1 & 2	New York	NY
57th St. Playhouse	New York	NY
Murray Hill 4	New York	NY
68th St. Playhouse	New York	NY
Sutton 1 & 2	New York	NY
Village East Cinemas 7	New York	NY

General Cinema

Seaview Square 2	Asbury Park	NJ
Bridgewater Commons 7	Bridgewater	NJ
Brunswick Square 2	East Brunswick	NJ
Morris County Mall 2	Morris County	NJ
Somerville Circle 3	Raritan	NJ
Shrewsbury Plaza 3	Shrewsbury	NJ
Rutgers 6	Somerset	NJ
Ocean County Mall 3	Toms River	NJ
Totowa 2	Totowa	NJ
Blue Star 4	Watchung	NJ
Essex Green 3	West Orange	NJ
Bay Plaza 10	Bronx	NY
Hartsdale 4	Hartsdale	NY
Westchester Mall 4	Peekskill	NY
Central Plaza 4	Yonkers	NY

Hoyts

Galleria Cinema 8	Poughkeepsie	NY
South Hills Mall Cine 8	Poughkeepsie	NY

Loew's

Greenwich 2	Greenwich	CT
Cinema Center 5	Brick	NJ
Circle 5	Brick	NJ
Route 18 (2)	East Brunswick	NJ
Metroplex 12	East Hanover	NJ
Community 2	Eatontown	NJ
Showboat 4	Edgewater	NJ
Freehold 5	Freehold	NJ
Freehold Metroplex 8	Freehold	NJ
Cinema Center 4	Howell	NJ
Movie Twin 2	Long Beach	NJ
Route 9 Quad (4)	Morganville	NJ
Mountainside 9	Mountainside	NJ
Interstate 2	Ramsey	NJ
Red Bank 2	Red Bank	NJ
Meadowlands 6	Secaucus	NJ
Meadows Plaza 8	Secaucus	NJ
Dover 2	Toms River	NJ

Seacourt 10	Toms River	NJ
Wayne 8	Wayne	NJ
South Shore 2	Bayshore	NY
Paradise 4	Bronx	NY
Georgetown 2	Brooklyn	NY
Oriental 3	Brooklyn	NY
Roosevelt Field 8	Garden City	NY
Nassau Metroplex 10	Levittown	NY
Galleria Metroplex 10	Middletown	NY
19th Street East 6	New York	NY
84th Street 6	New York	NY
Astor Place 1	New York	NY
Columbus Circle 1	New York	NY
Festival	New York	NY
Fine Arts	New York	NY
New York 2	New York	NY
Orpheum 7	New York	NY
Showplace 3	New York	NY
State 4	New York	NY
Tower East 1	New York	NY
Village 7	New York	NY
Bay Terrace 2	Queens	NY
Elmwood 4	Queens	NY
Trylon 1	Queens	NY
Stonybrook 3	Stonybrook	NY

Milgram
Friendly Twin	Bayville	NJ
Westmont Twin	Westmont	NJ

Mini
State Cinema	Springdale	CT

National Amusement
Multiplex 12	Hazlet	NJ
Amboy Multiplex 14	Sayerville	NJ
Concourse Plaza 10	Bronx	NY
Whitestone Multiplex 14	Bronx	NY
Commack Multiplex 15	Commack	NY
All Westchester 10	Hawthorne	NY
Brockhaven Multiplex 14	Medford	NY
Green Acres 6	Valley Stream	NY
Sunrise Multiplex 14	Valley Stream	NY

UA
Eric Lawrenceville	Lawrenceville	NJ
Middletown 7	Middletown	NJ
Cinema 46 (3)	Totowa	NJ
Bellevue Montclair 3	Upper Montclair	NJ
Wayne 4	Wayne	NJ
Rialto	Westfield	NJ
The Movies at Pascack 4	Westwood	NJ
Babylon 3	Babylon	NY
Bayside 4	Bayside	NY
Interboro Bronx 4	Bronx	NY
Bronxville 3	Bronxville	NY
Brooklyn Sheepshead 9	Brooklyn	NY
Marboro Brooklyn 4	Brooklyn	NY
Coram 10	Coram	NY
Movieworld Douglaston 7	Douglaston	NY
Meadowbrook 6	East Meadow	NY
Easthampton 5	Easthampton	NY
Quartet Flushing 4	Flushing	NY
Continental 2	Forest Hills	NY
Continental 3 (1)	Forest Hills	NY
Forest Hills 2	Forest Hills	NY
Midway 4 Queens	Forest Hills	NY
Squire Great Neck 3	Great Neck	NY
Larchmont Playhouse	Larchmont	NY
Lindenhurst	Lindenhurst	NY
Astoria 6	Long Island City	NY
Lynbrook 4	Lynbrook	NY
Mamaroneck Playhouse 4	Mamaroneck	NY
Manhasset 3	Manhasset	NY

Sunrise Massapequa 9	Massapequa	NY
Cinema 304 (2)	New City	NY
Criterion Center 7	New York	NY
Gemini 2	New York	NY
Movieland 8th St. 3	New York	NY
UA East Theatre	New York	NY
Newburgh 10 Cinemas	Newburgh	NY
Northport	Newburgh	NY
Crossbay	Ozone Park	NY
Ozone Park	Ozone Park	NY
Movies at Patchogue 13	Patchogue	NY
Smithtown	Smithtown	NY
Southampton Theatre 5	Southampton	NY
Spring Valley 11	Spring Valley	NY
Hylan Plaza	Staten Island	NY
Staten Island 11	Staten Island	NY
Syosset 3	Syosset	NY
Westbury D.I. 3	Westbury	NY
Westhampton 1	Westhampton	NY
UA Cinema 150	Woodbury	NY
Movieland Yonkers 6	Yonkers	NY
Jefferson Valley 7	Yorktown Heights	NY

Los Angeles

AMC
Burbank 10	Burbank	CA
Alondra 6	Cerritos	CA
Chino Town Square 10	Chino	CA
Serramonte 6	Colma	CA
Fullerton 10	Fullerton	CA
Hawthorne 6	Hawthorne	CA
Hermosa Beach 6	Hermosa Beach	CA
Puente Hills East 4	Industry	CA
Puente Hills West	Industry	CA
Puente Plaza 10	Industry	CA
Fashion Square 4	La Habra	CA
Marina Pacifica 6	Long Beach	CA
Pine Square 16	Long Beach	CA
Carousel 4	Los Angeles	CA
Century City 14	Los Angeles	CA
Media Center 4	Los Angeles	CA
Old Pasadena 8	Los Angeles	CA
Milpitas 10	Milpitas	CA
Orange 6	Orange	CA
Commercenter 6	San Bernardino	CA
Main Place 6	Santa Ana	CA
Santa Monica 7	Santa Monica	CA
Rolling Hills 6	Torrance	CA
Victor Valley 10	Victorville	CA

Cinamerica
Agoura Hills 8	Agoura Hills	CA
Puente Hills 6	Industry	CA
Culver Plaza 6	Culver City	CA
Exchange 8	Glendale	CA
Glendora 6	Glendora	CA
Chinese 3	Hollywood	CA
Vogue	Hollywood	CA
Manhattan Village 8	Manhattan Beach	CA
Huntington Oaks Sixplex	Monrovia	CA
Hasting Ranch Triplex	Pasadena	CA
Sante Fe Springs 8	Santa Fe Springs	CA
Criterion 6	Santa Monica	CA
Sycamore Plaza 6	Simi Valley	CA
Valley West Fourplex	Tarzana	CA
Conejo Twin	Thousand Oaks	CA
Del Amo 9	Torrance	CA
Old Towne Sixplex	Torrance	CA
Mann Tenplex	Valencia	CA
Buenventura Sixplex	Ventura	CA
Bruin	Westwood	CA
Mann Fourplex	Westwood	CA
National Plaza	Westwood	CA

Regent	Westwood	CA
Village	Westwood	CA

Cinemark

Movies 10	Cathedral City	CA
Movies 8	Chino	CA
Holiday Cinema 4	Hemet	CA
Movies 10	Hemet	CA
Movies 12	Lancaster	CA
Movies 3	Lancaster	CA
Movies 4	Lancaster	CA
Movies 6	Lancaster	CA
Movies 8	Palmdale	CA
Movies 10	Victorville	CA
Movies 7	Victorville	CA

Cineplex

Beverly Centre 13	Los Angeles	CA
Century Plaza 4	Los Angeles	CA
Fairfax Triple	Los Angeles	CA
Showcase	Los Angeles	CA
Universal City 18	Los Angeles	CA
Marine Marketplace 6	Marina Del Rey	CA
Broadway 4 Cinemas	Santa Monica	CA

Edwards

Alhambra Palace	Alhambra	CA
Atlantic Palace	Alhambra	CA
Anaheim Hills Festival	Anaheim	CA
Edwards Drive-In	Arcadia	CA
Azusa D.I.	Azusa	CA
Foothill Center	Azusa	CA
Brea Plaza	Brea	CA
La Costa	Carlsbad	CA
Corona 11	Corona	CA
Cinema	Costa Mesa	CA
Corona West End	Corona	CA
Cinema Center 4	Costa Mesa	CA
Harbor Twin	Costa Mesa	CA
Mesa	Costa Mesa	CA
South Coast Plaza 1 & 2	Costa Mesa	CA
Triangle Sq	Costa Mesa	CA
Town Center	Costa Mesa	CA
El Monte Cinemas	El Monte	CA
El Toro 123	El Toro	CA
Saddleback 456	El Toro	CA
Inland Empire Center	Fontana	CA
Fountain Valley	Fountain Valley	CA
Charter Centre	Huntington Beach	CA
Family Four-Orange Coast Cinemas	Huntington Beach	CA
Huntington Pierside	Huntington Beach	CA
Huntington Twin	Huntington Beach	CA
University	Irvine	CA
Woodbridge	Irvine	CA
South Coast Laguna	Laguna Beach	CA
Ocean Ranch Cinema	Laguna Niguel	CA
Rancho Niguel	Laguna Niguel	CA
Gateway Plaza	Laguna Niguel	CA
Laverne	Laverne	CA
Crown Valley	Mission Viejo	CA
Mission Viejo Mall Cinema	Mission Viejo	CA
Trabuco Hills	Mission Viejo	CA
Monterey Mall	Monterey Park	CA
Festival	Moreno Valley	CA
Festival	Moreno Valley	CA
Towngate	Moreno Valley	CA
Island	Newport Beach	CA
Lido	Newport Beach	CA
Newport Cinema	Newport Beach	CA
Rancho California	Rancho California	CA
Rancho Cucamonga	Rancho Cucamonga	CA
Terra Vista Town Center	Rancho Cucamonga	CA
Franciscan Plaza	San Juan Capistrano	CA

Bristol IV	Santa Ana	CA
Hutton Center	Santa Ana	CA
South Coast Village	Santa Ana	CA
Valencia	Santa Clarita	CA
Mountaingate Plaza 7	Simi Valley	CA
Village Center	Stanton	CA
Temple	Temple City	CA
Market Place	Tustin	CA
Tustin	Tustin	CA
Upland 8	Upland	CA
Mountain Green	Upland	CA
Mall	Westminster	CA
Twin	Westminster	CA
Westminster 10	Westminster	CA

General Cinema

Rancho 6	Colton	CA
Avco 3	Los Angeles	CA
Beverly Connection 6	Los Angeles	CA
Fallbrook 7	Los Angeles	CA
Glendale Central 5	Los Angeles	CA
Hollywood Galaxy	Los Angeles	CA
Northridge 3	Los Angeles	CA
Santa Anita 4	Los Angeles	CA
Sherman Oaks 5	Los Angeles	CA
Montclair Plaza 8	Montclair	CA
Galleria at South Bay 6	Redondo Beach	CA
In Land 2	San Bernardino	CA

Laemmle

Music Hall	Beverly Hills	CA
Town Centers	Beverly Hills	CA
Grande 4	Los Angeles	CA
Colorado	Pasadena	CA
Esquire	Pasadena	CA
Monica 4-plex	Santa Monica	CA
Sunset 5	West Hollywood	CA
Royal	West Los Angeles	CA

Landmark

Port	Corona Del Mar	CA
Goldwyn Pavilion 4	Los Angeles	CA
NuWilshire 2	Los Angeles	CA
Nuart	Los Angeles	CA
Rialto	South Pasadena	CA

Metropolitan

Campus	Los Angeles	CA
Los Angeles	Los Angeles	CA
Olympic	Los Angeles	CA
Orpheum	Los Angeles	CA
Panorama	Los Angeles	CA
Park 1 & 2 (Huntington Park)	Los Angeles	CA
State	Los Angeles	CA
Cinema 3	Palm Desert	CA
Town Center Cinema 10	Palm Desert	CA
Courtyard 10	Palm Springs	CA
Arlington Center	Santa Barbara	CA
Cinema 1 & 2	Santa Barbara	CA
Fairview 1 & 2	Santa Barbara	CA
Fiesta 5	Santa Barbara	CA
Granada 1, 2 & 3	Santa Barbara	CA
Metro 4	Santa Barbara	CA
Plaza de Oro 1 & 2	Santa Barbara	CA
Riviera	Santa Barbara	CA
Santa Barbara D.I. 1 & 2	Santa Barbara	CA
Simi D.I.	Simi Valley	CA

Pacific

Buena Park 3	Buena Park	CA
Winnetka	Chatsworth	CA
Commerce 7	City of Commerce	CA
Vineland Fourplex	City of Industry	CA

Compton	Compton	CA
Studio	Culver City	CA
Eagle Rock 4	Eagle Rock	CA
El Monte	El Monte	CA
Vermont Triplex	Gardena	CA
Regency	Glendale	CA
Roxy	Glendale	CA
El Capitan	Hollywood	CA
Hollywood Pacific Triplex	Hollywood	CA
Pacific's Cinerama Dome	Hollywood	CA
Vine	Hollywood	CA
Warner 2	Huntington Park	CA
Lakewood Center Four	Lakewood	CA
Lakewood Center South 9	Lakewood	CA
Regency 8	Lakewood	CA
Tri City	Loma Linda	CA
Los Altos Triplex	Long Beach	CA
Northridge 6	Northridge	CA
Ontario 10	Ontario	CA
Orange Twin	Orange	CA
Carriage Square 5	Oxnard	CA
Sky-View Twin	Oxnard	CA
Hastings 5	Pasadena	CA
Fiesta Four	Pico Rivera	CA
Inland Cinema 5	San Bernardino	CA
Norwalk	Santa Fe Springs	CA
Pacific 3	Santa Fe Springs	CA
Pacific 4	Sherman Oaks	CA
Southgate	South Gate	CA
Van Nuys 3	Van Nuys	CA
101 Triplex	Ventura	CA
Centinela	Westchester	CA
Hi-way 39 (4)	Westminster	CA
Crest	Westwood	CA
Topanga 3	Woodland Hills	CA

SoCal

Cinemapolis 13	Anaheim Hills	CA
Blue Jay Cinema 4	Blue Jay Village	CA
Laguna Hills Mall Cinema 3	Laguna Hills	CA
University Cinema 3	Los Angeles	CA
Canyon Springs Cinema 7	Moreno Valley	CA
Canyon Crest Cinema 9	Riverside	CA
Fox Theatre 3	West Covina	CA
Eastland Theatre 5	West Covina	CA
Wescove Cinema 3	West Covina	CA

Syufy ·

Southbay 6 D.I.	Carson	CA
Century 7	North Hollywood	CA
Cinedome 11-plex	Orange	CA
City Center 4	Orange	CA
Stadium 8 D.I.	Orange	CA
Century 8	Ventura	CA

UA

Cinema 8	Brea	CA
UA Movies 4	Brea	CA
Buena Park 8	Buena Park	CA
Cerritos 4	Cerritos	CA
UA Twin Cerritos	Cerritos	CA
Movies at Colma 6	Colma	CA
Granada Hills 7	Granada Hills	CA
Lakewood 6	Lakewood	CA
Movies Long Beach 6	Long Beach	CA
Westwood 3	Los Angeles	CA
Marina Del Rey 6	Marina Del Rey	CA
Montclair 6	Montclair	CA
Movies	North Hollywood	CA
City Cinema 6	Orange	CA
Movies 6	Pasadena	CA

Riverside 6	Riverside	CA
Tyler Cinema 4	Riverside	CA
Thousand Oaks 5	Thousand Oaks	CA
Del Amo 6	Torrance	CA
Woodland Hills 6	Torrance	CA

Chicago

AMC

Barrington Square 6	Hoffman Estates	IL
Ogden 6	Naperville	IL

Cinemark

Movies 8	Joliet	IL

Cineplex

Ridge Cinemas 8	Arlington Heights	IL
Town n' Country 6	Arlington Heights	IL
Fox Valley 10	Aurora	IL
West Plaza 3	Aurora	IL
River Oaks 12	Calumet City	IL
Springhill Mall 6	Carpentersville	IL
900 North Michigan 2	Chicago	IL
Biograph 3	Chicago	IL
Bricktown Square 6	Chicago	IL
Broadway (Lakeshore)	Chicago	IL
Burnam Plaza 5	Chicago	IL
Chestnut Station 5	Chicago	IL
Chicago Ridge 4	Chicago	IL
Commons 4	Chicago	IL
Lincoln Village 3	Chicago	IL
Lincoln Village 6	Chicago	IL
McClurg 3	Chicago	IL
Plaza 3	Chicago	IL
Water Tower 7	Chicago	IL
Hillcrest 2	Crest Hill	IL
Downers Grove Cinemas 5	Downers Grove	IL
Diana 4	Homewood	IL
Round Lake Twin	Lake Beach	IL
Golf Glen 6	Niles	IL
Golf Mill 3	Niles	IL
Ednes 2	Northbrook	IL
Oakbrook 3	Oakbrook	IL
Oakbrook Mall 4	Oakbrook	IL
Orland Square 8	Orland Park	IL
Woodfield 9	Schaumburg	IL
Foxfield 3	St. Charles	IL
St. Charles 3	St. Charles	IL
Hawthorne Quad	Vernon Hills	IL
Rivertree Court 8	Vernon Hills	IL
Rice Lake 10	Wheaton	IL

Classic Cinemas

Cinema 5	Carpentersville	IL
Tivoli	Downer's Grove	IL
Tivoli South	Downer's Grove	IL
Elk Grove	Elk Grove Vill.	IL
York	Elmhurst	IL
Meadowview	Kankakee	IL
Paramount	Kankakee	IL
Lake	Oak Park	IL
Centre Cinema	Park Forest	IL
Woodstock	Woodstock	IL

GKC

Campus Cinemas 8	Dekalb	IL
Carrol Cinemas 2	Dekalb	IL
Dekalb Cinemas 2	Dekalb	IL
Illinois Valley Cinemas 2	Lasalle	IL
Showplace Cinemas 2	Lasalle	IL
Morris Cinemas 2	Morris	IL
Roxy Cinemas 2	Ottawa	IL
Peru Mall Cinemas 4	Peru	IL

Crescent Cinemas 2	Pontiac	IL
Majestic Cinemas 2	Streator	IL

General Cinema

Deerbrook 4	Chicago	IL
Ford City 14	Chicago	IL
Lincoln Mall 3	Chicago	IL
Randhurst 4	Chicago	IL
Woodgrove Festival 6 ..	Chicago	IL
Yorktown 6	Chicago	IL
Jefferson Square 3	Joliet	IL
Louis Joliet Mall 3	Joliet	IL
Lakehurst 12	Waukegan	IL
Griffith Park 2	Gary	IN
Ridge Plaza 2 ...	Gary	IN
Southlake Mall 9	Gary	IN
University Park East 6 .	South Bend	IN
University Park West 3 .	South Bend	IN
County Seat 6	Valparaiso	IN

Kerasotes

Granada 2	Mount Vernon	IL
Stadium 2	Mount Vernon	IL
Belford Indoor 4	Rockford	IL
Belford Outdoor 2	Rockford	IL
Cherryvale 7	Rockford	IL
Colonial Village 5	Rockford	IL
Machesney Park 10	Rockford	IL
North Towne 6	Rockford	IL
La Porte Cinema 4	La Porte	IN
Dunes Plaza Cinema 6	Michigan City	IN
Marquette 3	Michigan City	IN
Scottsdale Mall 6	South Bend	IN
Town & Country 3	South Bend	IN

Loew's

Double Drive-In 3	Chicago	IL
Esquire 6	Chicago	IL
Fine Arts 4	Chicago	IL
Hyde Park 4	Chicago	IL
Pipers Alley 4	Chicago	IL
Webster 8	Chicago	IL
Bel-Air Drive in 3	Cicero	IL
Evanston 5	Evanston	IL
Evergreen 4	Evergreen	IL
Hillside Mall 3	Hillside	IL
Hillside Square 6	Hillside	IL
River Run 8	Lansing	IL
Norridge 10	Norridge	IL
Rolling Meadows 9	Rolling Meadows ..	IL
Old Orchard 4	Skokie	IL
Twin Drive-In 3	Wheeling	IL
Merrillville 10	Merrillville	IN
Y&W Drive-In 3	Merrillville	IN

UA

Machesney Park 10	Rockford	IL

San Francisco-Oakland

AMC

Old Mill 6	Mountain View	CA
Kabuki 8	San Francisco	CA
Oakridge 6	San Jose	CA
Saratoga 6	San Jose	CA
Sunnyvale 6	Sunnyvale	CA
Vallejo Plaza 6	Vallejo	CA

Blumenfeld Theatres

Fairfax	Fairfax	CA
Lark	Larkspur	CA
Meridian 6	San Jose	CA
Regency 1	San Francisco	CA
Regency 2	San Francisco	CA

Royal	San Francisco	CA
Alhambra	San Francisco	CA
Castro	San Francisco	CA

Cinamerica

Festival Nineplex	Hayward	CA
Festival Fourplex	Larkspur	CA
Contra Costa Fiveplex ..	Martinez	CA
Crow Canyon Sixplex ..	San Ramon	CA
Festival Fiveplex	Walnut Creek	CA

Cineplex

Plaza 2	Daly City	CA
Hilltop 8	Richmond	CA
Northpoint	San Francisco	CA

General Cinema

Dublin Place 6	Dublin	CA
Solano Mall 6	Fairfield	CA
Fremont Hub 8	Fremont	CA
Southland 5	Hayward	CA
Fashion Island Mall 6 ..	San Mateo	CA
Hillsdale 4	San Mateo	CA

Landmark

U.C. Berkeley	Berkeley	CA
Guild	Menlo Park	CA
Park	Menlo Park	CA
Aquarius 2	Palo Alto	CA
Palo Alto Square 2	Palo Alto	CA
Varsity	Palo Alto	CA
Bridge	San Francisco	CA
Clay	San Francisco	CA
Gateway	San Francisco	CA
Lumiere	San Francisco	CA
Oper Plaza	San Francisco	CA

Pacific of N. Calif

Albany	Albany	CA
Act 2	Berkeley	CA
Berkeley California	Berkeley	CA
Fine Arts 2	Berkeley	CA
Oaks 2	Berkeley	CA
Shattuck 8	Berkeley	CA
Cinema	Corte Madera	CA
Sequoia Twin	Mill Valley	CA
Rowland	Novato	CA
Piedmont	Oakland	CA
Petaluma 8	Petaluma	CA
Regency 6	San Rafael	CA
Marin	Sausalito	CA

Syufy

Island Auto	Alameda	CA
Burlingame 4 D.I.	Burlingame	CA
Hyatt Cinema	Burlingame	CA
Solano Twin 2 D.I.	Concord	CA
Geneva 4 D.I.	Daly City	CA
Cinedome 8	Fremont	CA
Century Cinema 10	Mountain View	CA
Cinedome 8 Complex ...	Napa	CA
Cinedome Sevenplex ...	Newark	CA
Century 8	Oakland	CA
Coliseum 4 D.I.	Oakland	CA
Century 10 Complex ...	Pinole	CA
Century Fivecomplex ..	Pleasant Hill	CA
Century Park 12	Redwood City	CA
Century Park 7	Salinas	CA
Northridge Eightplex ...	Salinas	CA
Cinema 21	San Francisco	CA
Empire 3	San Francisco	CA
Presido	San Francisco	CA
Capitol 6 D.I.	San Jose	CA
Century 21	San Jose	CA
Century 22 Triplex	San Jose	CA
Century 23 Twin	San Jose	CA

Century 24 Twin	San Jose	CA
Century 25 Twin	San Jose	CA
Century Almaden 5	San Jose	CA
Century Berryessa	San Jose	CA
Century Plaza 8	South San Francisco	CA
Union City 6 D.I.	Union City	CA
Cinedome 8	Vallejo	CA
Triplex	Vallejo	CA

UA

Aptos Twin 2	Aptos	CA
Berkeley 7	Berkeley	CA
Pruneyard 3	Campbell	CA
41st Avenue Playhouse 3	Capitola	CA
Golden Bough	Capitola	CA
Movies at Emeryville 10	Emeryville	CA
Hayward 6	Hayward	CA
Redwood City 6	Redwood City	CA
Empire 4	Rohnert Park	CA
Alexandria 3	San Francisco	CA
Cinema Stonestown 2	San Francisco	CA
Coronet 1	San Francisco	CA
Galaxy 4	San Francisco	CA
Metro	San Francisco	CA
Vogue	San Francisco	CA
Del Mar	Santa Cruz	CA
Rio	Santa Cruz	CA
S. Cruz 2	Santa Cruz	CA
Coddingtown 4	Santa Rosa	CA
Santa Rosa 5	Santa Rosa	CA
Santa Rosa 6	Santa Rosa	CA

Toronto

Cineplex

410 & 7 Centre 4	Brampton	ON
Centennial 3	Brampton	ON
Cinemas 3	Brantford	ON
Odeon 2	Brantford	ON
Cineplex 6	Burlington	ON
Showcase Cinema 6	Burlington	ON
Twin Cinema	Cambridge	ON
Stone Road Mall 5	Guelph	ON
Centre Mall 8	Hamilton	ON
Fairway Center 5	Kitchener	ON
Frederick Mall 2	Kitchener	ON
Erin Mills 5	Mississauga	ON
South Common Mall 7	Mississauga	ON
Niagara Square 3	Niagara Falls	ON
Seneca 2	Niagara Falls	ON
Oakville Mews 5	Oakville	ON
Pendale 2	St. Catharines	ON
Town 2	St. Catharines	ON
Canada Square 8	Toronto	ON
Carlton 9	Toronto	ON
Eaton Center 17	Toronto	ON
Fairview 6	Toronto	ON
Finch 3	Toronto	ON
Humber 2	Toronto	ON
Hyland 2	Toronto	ON
Madison 5	Toronto	ON
Market Square 6	Toronto	ON
Scarborough Town Ctr. 12	Toronto	ON
Sherway 9	Toronto	ON
Varsity 2	Toronto	ON
Warden Woods 8	Toronto	ON
Woodbine Center 6	Toronto	ON
Woodside 3	Toronto	ON
York 2	Toronto	ON
Seaway 2	Welland	ON

Famous

Gateway 6	Brampton	ON
Market Square 3	Brantford	ON

Burlington Mall 3	Burlington	ON
Jackson Square 6	Hamilton	ON
Lime Ridge Cinema 4	Hamilton	ON
Capitol 2	Kitchener	ON
Kings College 4	Kitchener	ON
Square 4	Mississauga	ON
Sussex Centre 4	Mississauga	ON
Glenway 5	Newmarket	ON
Town Centre 6	Oakville	ON
Centre 8	Oshawa	ON
Lincoln Mall 3	St. Catharines	ON
Pen Centre 3	St. Catharines	ON
Fiesta Mall 4	Stoney Creek	ON
Bayview Village 4	Toronto	ON
Capitol	Toronto	ON
Cedarbrae 8	Toronto	ON
Centerpoint 2	Toronto	ON
Cumberland 4	Toronto	ON
Hollywood North	Toronto	ON
Hollywood South	Toronto	ON
Sheraton Center 2	Toronto	ON
Sheridan 4	Toronto	ON
Skyway 6	Toronto	ON
Uptown 3	Toronto	ON
Uptown Backstage 2	Toronto	ON
Victoria Terrace 6	Toronto	ON
Westwood 3	Toronto	ON
Yorkdale 6	Toronto	ON

Philadelphia

AMC

Cinema Center 3	Newark	DE
Concord 2	Wilmington	DE
Millside 4	Delran	NJ
Quaker Bridge 4	Lawrenceville	NJ
Marlton 8	Marlton	NJ
Cumberland 2	Vineland	NJ
Vineland 4	Vineland	NJ
Tilghman Plaza 8	Allentown	PA
Bryn Mawr 2	Bryn Mawr	PA
Premiere 2	Cornwell Hghts	PA
Woodhaven 4	Cornwell Hghts	PA
Exton 2	Exton	PA
Hampden Center 8	Mechanicsburg	PA
Granite Run 8	Media	PA
Andorra 8	Philadelphia	PA
Midtown 2	Philadelphia	PA
Olde City 2	Philadelphia	PA
Orleans 8	Philadelphia	PA
Walnut 3	Philadelphia	PA
Quakertown 6	Quakertown	PA
Anthony Wayne 2	Wayne	PA
Gateway 3	Wayne	PA
Painters Crossing 9	West Chester	PA
Plaza 2	Whitehall	PA

Cinemark

Movies 10	Wilmington	DE

Fox

Fox Theatres 6	Dover	DE
Movies 6	Dover	DE
Fox Berkshire 3	Reading	PA
Fox East 4	Reading	PA
Fox Fairgrounds 5	Reading	PA
Sinking Spring D.I.	Reading	PA

General Cinema

Christiana Mall 5	Wilmington	DE
Deptford Mall 6	Camden	NJ
Echelon Mall 4	Camden	NJ
Mercer Mall 7	Trenton	NJ
Lehigh Valley Mall 8	Allentown	PA
Franklin Mills 10	Philadelphia	PA

Northeast 4 . . . . Philadelphia . . . . PA
Plymouth Meeting 2 . . . Philadelphia . . . . PA

Loew's
Middlebrook 2 . . . . Ocean Township . . . NJ
Ridgefield Park 12 . . . . . Ridgefield . . . . NJ

Milgram
Glassboro . . . . Glassboro . . . . NJ
Harwan . . . . Mount Ephraim . . . . NJ
Tilton 6 . . . . Northfield . . . . NJ
Broadway . . . . Pitman . . . . NJ
Broad . . . . Allentown . . . . PA
Valley . . . . Allentown . . . . PA
Merlin . . . . Philadelphia . . . . PA
Ritz 5 . . . . Philadelphia . . . . PA
Yeadon . . . . Philadelphia . . . . PA
Thorndale . . . . Thorndale . . . . PA

National Amusement
Multiplex 14 . . . . Atco . . . . NJ

Regal
Peoples Plaza 13 . . . . . . Wilmington . . . . DE

UA
Eric Tri-State 5 . . . . Claymont . . . . DE
Eric Moorestown 2 . . . . Moorestown . . . . NJ
Eric Pennsauken 5 . . . . . Pennsauken . . . . NJ
Eric Garden 2 . . . . Princeton . . . . NJ
Princeton Market Fair 9 Princeton . . . . NJ
Allentown 4 . . . . Allentown . . . . PA
Ardmore 4 . . . . Ardmore . . . . PA
Concordville 4 . . . . Concordville . . . . . . PA
Easton 4 . . . . Easton . . . . PA
Fairless Hills 3 . . . . Fairless Hills . . . . . . PA
Penn Jersey 4 . . . . Fairless Hills . . . . . . PA
Frazer 2 . . . . Frazer . . . . PA
Eric Macdale Mall 4 . . . Holmes . . . . PA
Baederwood 2 . . . . Jenkintown . . . . PA
Eric King 2 . . . . King of Prussia . . . . PA
Eric Plaza 2 . . . . King of Prussia . . . . PA
Eric Queen 4 . . . . King of Prussia . . . . PA
Eric Montgomeryville 7 Montgomeryville . . . PA
Campus 3 . . . . Philadelphia . . . . PA
Cheltenham Square 8 . . Philadelphia . . . . PA
Chestnut Hill 2 . . . . Philadelphia . . . . PA
Eric Rittenhouse 3 . . . . . Philadelphia . . . . PA
Eric's Place . . . . Philadelphia . . . . PA
Sam's Place 2 . . . . Philadelphia . . . . PA
Sameric 4 . . . . Philadelphia . . . . PA
Barclay Sq 2 . . . . Upper Darby . . . . . . PA
Movies at 69th St . . . . . Upper Darby . . . . . . PA
Eric West Goshen 2 . . . . West Goshen . . . . . . PA
Eric Wynnewood . . . . . . Wynnewood . . . . PA

Montreal

Cineplex
Berri 5 . . . . Montreal . . . . QE
Bonaventure 2 . . . . Montreal . . . . QE
Centreville 9 . . . . Montreal . . . . QE
Cote de Neiges 7 . . . . . . Montreal . . . . QE
Cremazie . . . . Montreal . . . . QE
Dauphin 2 . . . . Montreal . . . . QE
Decarie Square 2 . . . . . . Montreal . . . . QE
Desjardins 4 . . . . Montreal . . . . QE
Egyptien 3 . . . . Montreal . . . . QE
Le Faubourg 4 . . . . Montreal . . . . QE
Capital . . . . Sherbrooke . . . . QE

Famous
Centre Eaton 6 . . . . Montreal . . . . QE
Loew's 5 . . . . Montreal . . . . QE
Palace 6 . . . . Montreal . . . . QE

Parisien 7 . . . . Montreal . . . . QE
Versailles 7 . . . . Montreal . . . . QE
Carrefour de L'Estrie 3 Sherbrooke . . . . QE

Dallas-Forth Worth

AMC
Forum 6 . . . . Arlington . . . . TX
Green Oaks 8 . . . . Arlington . . . . TX
Glen Lakes 8 . . . . Dallas . . . . TX
Prestonwood 5 . . . . Dallas . . . . TX
Hulen Village 10 . . . . . . Ft. Worth . . . . TX
Sundance 11 . . . . Ft. Worth . . . . TX
Irving 6 . . . . Irving . . . . TX
Towne Crossing 8 . . . . . Mesquite . . . . TX
Central Park 7 . . . . Plano . . . . TX

Carmike
Rolling Hills Four . . . . . Lake Greenville . . . . TX
Gaslight 4 . . . . Tyler . . . . TX
Southloop 4 . . . . Tyler . . . . TX
Times Square 5 . . . . Tyler . . . . TX
Cinema Twin . . . . Waco . . . . TX
Waco Square 6 . . . . Waco . . . . TX

Cinemark
Cinema 4 . . . . Arlington . . . . TX
Movies 8 . . . . Carrollton . . . . TX
Cinema 6 . . . . Cleburne . . . . TX
Cinema 4 . . . . Corsicana . . . . TX
Wedgwood 4 . . . . Ft. Worth . . . . TX
Hollywood USA 15 . . . . Garland . . . . TX
Movies 16 . . . . Grand Prairie . . . . . . TX
Movies 8 . . . . Lancaster . . . . TX
Movies 8 . . . . Lewisville . . . . TX
Movies 12 . . . . Lewisville . . . . TX
Big Town Cinema 9 . . . Mesquite . . . . TX
Movies 8 . . . . N. Richland Hills . . TX
Movies 10 . . . . Rockwall . . . . TX
Movies 10 . . . . Rockwall . . . . TX
Midway Movies . . . . Sherman . . . . TX
Cinema 6 . . . . Stephenville . . . . TX

Cineplex
Promenade 6 . . . . Richardson . . . . TX
Cinema 3 & 4 . . . . Waco . . . . TX

General Cinema
Carrolton Centre 6 . . . . . Dallas . . . . TX
Collin Creek 6 . . . . Dallas . . . . TX
Furneaux Creek 7 . . . . . Dallas . . . . TX
Galleria . . . . Dallas . . . . TX
Irving Mall 7 . . . . Dallas . . . . TX
Northpark East 2 . . . . . . Dallas . . . . TX
Northpark West 2 . . . . . . Dallas . . . . TX
Prestonwood 4 . . . . Dallas . . . . TX
Red Bird Mall 10 . . . . . Dallas . . . . TX
Richardson 6 . . . . Dallas . . . . TX
Richardson Square 3 . . . Dallas . . . . TX
Town East 6 . . . . Dallas . . . . TX
Town East Mall 5 . . . . . Dallas . . . . TX
Arlington Park 8 . . . . . . Ft. Worth . . . . TX
Central Park 8 . . . . Ft. Worth . . . . TX
Cinema V 5 . . . . Ft. Worth . . . . TX
North Hills 7 . . . . Ft. Worth . . . . TX
Ridgmar Town Square 6 Ft. Worth . . . . TX

Landmark
Inwood 3 . . . . Dallas . . . . TX

Loew's
20 & 287 (6) . . . . Arlington . . . . TX
Lincoln Square 10 . . . . . Arlington . . . . TX
Park Central 4 . . . . Dallas . . . . TX
Cityview 8 . . . . Fort Worth . . . . TX

| Chisholm Plano 5 ..... | Plano .... | TX |
| Preston Park 5 .... | Plano .... | TX |

UA

Bowen 8	Arlington	TX
Bedford 10	Bedford	TX
Cine Theat 1 & 2	Dallas	TX
Plaza Park Lane 8	Dallas	TX
Prestonwood 5	Dallas	TX
Walnut Hill 6	Dallas	TX
Cinema South 8	Duncanville	TX
Holen 10	Ft. Worth	TX
Las Vegas Trial 8	Ft. Worth	TX
North Star 8	Garland	TX
Hurst 6	Hurst	TX
Town East 6	Mesquite	TX
Cinemas 1, 2, 3 (3)	Mineral Wells	TX
Berkeley Square 8	Plano	TX
UA Cinemas 4	Sherman	TX

Houston

AMC

Highland Park Village 4	Highland Park	TX
Alameda East 5	Houston	TX
Commerce Park 8	Houston	TX
Festival 6	Houston	TX
Greens Crossing 6	Houston	TX
Greenway 3	Houston	TX
Meyer Park 14	Houston	TX
North Oaks 6	Houston	TX
Southway 6	Houston	TX
Town & Country 10 ...	Houston	TX
Westchase 5	Houston	TX
Willowbrook 8	Houston	TX
Deerbrook 8	Humble	TX

Carmike

Colonnade Four	Beaumont	TX
Cinema 3	College Station	TX
Movies 16	College Station	TX
Post Oak 3	College Station	TX
Woodcreek Four	Conroe	TX
Brazos Mall Triple	Lake Jackson	TX
Cinema 4	Lake Jackson	TX
Cinema Twin	Orange	TX
Pines	Silsbee	TX

Cinemark

Cinema 4	Bay City	TX
Pine Hollow 6	Conroe	TX
Bear Creek 6	Houston	TX
Eastway 4	Houston	TX
Northwest Village 6	Houston	TX
Village 6	Houston	TX
Windchimes 8	Houston	TX
Mason Park 8	Katy	TX
Central 6	Missouri City	TX
Movies 12	Pasadena	TX
Southmore 6	Pasadena	TX
Randall 8	Rosenberg	TX
Movies 12	Texas City	TX
Slide Road Movies 4 ...	Texas City	TX
South Plains Cinema 4 .	Texas City	TX
Cinema 4	Victoria	TX
Playhouse Cinema	Victoria	TX
Salem Cinema 6	Victoria	TX

Cineplex

Goose Creek Cinema 6	Baytown	TX
Plitt Cinema 5	Baytown	TX
Cinema 7 West Oaks ...	Houston	TX
Plitt 4	Houston	TX
Presidio Square 6	Houston	TX

River Oaks 12	Houston	TX
Sharpstown Center 8 ...	Houston	TX
Spectrum 9	Houston	TX
Promenade 6	Lake Jackson	TX

General Cinema

Gateway Plaza 2	Beaumont	TX
Parkdale Mall 3	Beaumont	TX
Baybrook Mall 4	Houston	TX
Cooperfield 6	Houston	TX
Deerbrook Commons 6 .	Houston	TX
Galleria 4	Houston	TX
Greenspoint Mall 5	Houston	TX
Gulfgate Mall 4	Houston	TX
Meyerland 3	Houston	TX
Northline Mall 4	Houston	TX
Point NASA 6	Houston	TX
West Oaks Central 6 ...	Houston	TX
Willowbrook Mall 6 ...	Houston	TX

Landmark

| River Oaks 3 .... | Houston .... | TX |

Loew's

Easton Commons 8	Houston	TX
Memorial City 8	Houston	TX
Saks Center 2	Houston	TX
South West 6	Houston	TX
Southpoint 5	Houston	TX
Southwest 6	Houston	TX
Spring 10	Houston	TX
Westwood Mall 3	Houston	TX

UA

| Phelan 6 .... | Beaumont .... | TX |
| Cinema 6 .... | Port Arthur ...... | TX |

Detroit

AMC

Maple 3	Birmingham	MI
Westborn 2	Dearborn	MI
Bel-Air Centre 10	Detroit	MI
Old Orchard 3	Farmington Hills ...	MI
Woods 6	Grosse Pointe Woods	MI
Eastland 7	Harper Woods	MI
Elmwood 8	Lansing	MI
Laurel Park 10	Livonia	MI
Wonderland 6	Livonia	MI
Abbey 4	Madison Heights ...	MI
Towne 4	Oak Park	MI
Meridian 14	Okemos	MI
Hampton 4	Rochester	MI
Southfield City 12	Southfield	MI
Sterling Center 10	Sterling Heights	MI
Southland 4	Taylor	MI
American West 6	W. Bloomfield	MI

Cinemark

Terrace Cinema 4	Livonia	MI
Macomb 4	Roseville	MI
Tel-Ex Cinema 4	Southfield	MI
Universal Mall		
Movies 16	Warren	MI

GKC

Genesse Valley		
Cinemas 6	Flint	MI
Birchwood Cinemas 10	Port Huron	MI

General Cinema

Canton 6	Detroit	MI
Novi Town Center 8 ...	Detroit	MI
Lansing Mall West 6 ...	Lansing	MI

Goodrich

Ann Arbor 1 & 2	Ann Arbor	MI
Kraft 8	Port Huron	MI

Hoyts

Frenchtown Square Mall 8	Monroe	MI

MJR Theatres

Allen Park 5	Allen Park	MI
Fox Village 7	Ann Arbor	MI
Livonia Mall Cinema 8	Livonia	MI
Main Theatre 4	Royal Oak	MI
Waterford Cinema 1 & 2	Waterford	MI

National Amusement

Showcase 14	Ann Arbor	MI
Showcase 14	Auburn Hills	MI
Dearborn 8	Dearborn	MI
Courtland Center 2	Flint	MI
Showcase 14	Flint	MI
Beacon East 4	Harper Woods	MI
Showcase 10	Pontiac	MI
Summit Place 3	Pontiac	MI
Showcase 15	Sterling Heights	MI
Quo Vadis 6	Westland	MI
Showcase 8	Westland	MI

Loeks Star

Star Gratiot 10	Clinton Twsp	MI
Star Lincoln Park 8	Lincoln Park	MI
Star John R 10	Madison Hts	MI
Star Rochester Hills 8 ..	Rochester Hills	MI
Star Winchester 8	Rochester Hills	MI
Star Taylor 8	Taylor	MI

UA

Fox Village 4	Ann Arbor	MI
The Movies Briarwood 7	Ann Arbor	MI
Fairlane 10	Dearborn	MI
West River	Farmington	MI
Spartan 3	Lansing	MI
12 Oaks 5	Novi	MI
Movies Lakeside 4	Sterling Heights	MI
Oakland 5	Troy	MI

Washington, D.C.

AMC

Union Station 9	Washington	DC
Academy 6	Greenbelt	MD
Academy 8	Greenbelt	MD
Carollton 6	New Carrollton	MD
Rivertowne 12	Oxon Hill	MD
City Place 10	Silver Spring	MD
Courthouse Plaza 8	Arlington	VA
Potomac Mills 10	Dale City	VA

Cineplex

Avalon 2	Washington	DC
Dupont 5	Washington	DC
Embassy	Washington	DC
Jennifer 2	Washington	DC
MacArthur Theatre 3 ...	Washington	DC
Outer Circle 2	Washington	DC
Tenley 3	Washington	DC
Uptown	Washington	DC
West End 7	Washington	DC
Wisconsin Avenue 6 ...	Washington	DC
Rio 8 Cinemas	Gaithersberg	MD
St. Charles Town 9	Gaithersberg	MD
Beltway Plaza 2	Gaithersburg	MD
Lake Forest 5	Gaithersburg	MD
White Flint 5	Kensington	MD
Marlow 6	Marlow Heights	MD

Waldorf North 4	Waldorf	MD
Waldorf South 5	Waldorf	MD
Wheaton Plaza 4	Wheaton	MD
Old Town 2	Alexandria	VA
Shirlington 7	Arlington	VA
Fair City Mall 6	Fairfax	VA
Manassas Mall 7	Manassas	VA
Tysons Centre 4	Vienna	VA

Hoyts

Francis Scott Key 3	Frederick	MD
Frederick 6	Frederick	MD
Frederick Town Mall 2 .	Frederick	MD
Westridge Mall 2	Frederick	MD
Westridge Mall 6	Frederick	MD

K.B.

Cerberus 3	Washington	DC
Cinema	Washington	DC
Fine Arts	Washington	DC
Foundry 7	Washington	DC
Janus 3	Washington	DC
Paris 3	Washington	DC
Georgetown 2	Bethesda	MD
Montgomery Mall 3 ...	Bethesda	MD
Congressional 5	Rockville	MD

Loew's

Center Park 8	Beltsville	MD
Montgomery 2	Gaithersburg	MD
Germantown 6	Germantown	MD
Jumpers 7	Pasadena	MD
Wheaton Plaza 11	Wheaton	MD
Pentagon City 6	Arlington	VA
Worldgate 9	Herndon	VA
Manassas 4	Manassas	VA
Tysons 8	Tysons Corner	VA

National Amusement

Mt. Vernon Multiplex 10	Mount Vernon	VA

Neighborhood

Holiday 2	Frederick	MD
Dale 2	Dale City	VA·
Loehmanns 2	Falls Church	VA
Spotsylvania 4	Fredericksburg	VA

R/C

Movies Fredericksburg 10	Fredericksburg	VA
Virginians Cinema 4 ...	Fredericksburg	VA
Tally Ho Twin Cinema .	Leesburg	VA
Aquia Town Movies 10	Stafford	VA

UA

Bethesda	Bethesda	MD
Rockville 10	Rockville	MD
Movie at Fair Oaks 8 ..	Fairfax	VA

Boston

General Cinema

Braintree 10	Boston	MA
Burlington Mall 4	Boston	MA
Chestnut Hill 5	Boston	MA
Framingham 6	Boston	MA
Hanover Mall 4	Boston	MA
Northshore 3	Boston	MA
Westgate Mall 7	Boston	MA
Tyngsboro	Tyngsboro	MA

Hoyts

Acton Cinemas 4	Acton	MA
Franklin Cinemas 6	Franklin	MA
Harwich Cinemas 6	Harwich	MA
Airport Cinema 8	Hyannis	MA

Cape Cod Mall Cinema 1 & 2	Hyannis	MA
Cape Cod Mall Cinema 3 & 4	Hyannis	MA
Milford Cinema Centre 495	Milford	MA
Independence Mall 10 ..	Plymouth	MA

Loew's

Charles 3	Boston	MA
Cheri 4	Boston	MA
Cinema 57	Boston	MA
Copley Place 11	Boston	MA
Nickelodeon 5	Boston	MA
Brockton 4	Brockton	MA
Fresh Pond 10	Cambridge	MA
Harvard Square	Cambridge	MA
Janus 1	Cambridge	MA
Danvers 6	Danvers	MA
Liberty Tree 2	Danvers	MA
Natick 6	Lexington	MA
Salem 3	Salem	MA

Melrose

Acton 4	Acton	MA
Bellingham D.I.	Bellingham	MA
Blue Hills D.I.	Canton	MA
Boro D.I.	Canton	MA
Route 3 Cinemas 6	Chelmsford	MA
Park Theatre	Dorchester	MA
Orpheum Cinemas 3 ...	Foxboro	MA
Oxford D.I.	Foxboro	MA
Cinema Theatre	Franklin	MA
Cinema 495 (4)	Haverhill	MA
Review D.I.	Haverhill	MA
Flick Twin Theatre	Littleton	MA
Lowel D.I.	Lowell	MA
Route 114 Twin D.I. ...	Middleton	MA
Tri-boro Twin	North Attleboro	MA
Chalet Twin	Raynham	MA
Raynham D.I.	Raynham	MA
Route 24 Twin Cinemas	Raynham	MA

Mini

Concord	Concord	MA
South Willow St. Cinema 9	Manchester	MA
Bijou Twin	Raynham	MA

National Amusement

Allston 2	Allston	MA
Circle 7	Brookline	MA
Showcase 12	Dedham	MA
Showcase 10	Lawrence	MA
Showcase 14	Revere	MA
Showcase 10	Woburn	MA

Vancouver

Cineplex

Station Square 5	Burnaby	BC
Pinetree 6	Coquitlam	BC
Granville 7	Vancouver	BC
Oakridge 3	Vancouver	BC
Park & Tilford 6	Vancouver	BC
Royal Centre 10	Vancouver	BC

Famous

Station Square 7	Burnaby	BC
Eagle Ridge 6	Coquitlam	BC
Willowbrook 6	Langley	BC
Fiesta 2	Nanaimo	BC
Esplanade 6	North Vancouver ...	BC
Guildford 4	Surrey	BC
Capitol 6	Vancouver	BC
Vancouver Centre 2	Vancouver	BC
Park Royal Triple	West Vancouver	BC

Atlanta

AMC

Galleria 8	Atlanta	GA
Phipps Plaza (12)	Atlanta	GA
Tower Place 6	Atlanta	GA
Cobb Place 8	Kenneshaw	GA

Carmike

Plaza Twin	Cartersville	GA
Martin Twin	Douglas	GA

Cinemark

Movies 10	Fayetteville	GA

Cineplex

Conyers 8	Conyers	GA
Cumming 3	Cumming	GA
Market Square 4	Decatur	GA
Fridays Plaza 6	Doraville	GA
Douglasville 3	Douglasville	GA
Douglasville Exchange 3	Douglasville	GA
Mall-Corners 6	Duluth	GA
Griffin 4	Griffin	GA
LaGrange Cinema 6 ...	LaGrange	GA
Lawrenceville 4	Lawrenceville	GA
Merchant's Exchange 5	Marietta	GA
Towne Centre 6	Marietta	GA
Southlake Festival 6 ...	Morrow	GA
Southlake Triple	Morrow	GA
Westpark Walk 3	Peachtree City	GA
Brannon Square 2	Roswell	GA
Holcomb Woods 6	Roswell	GA

Cobb

Mall 6	Carrollton	GA

General Cinema

Georgia Square 9	Athens	GA
Akers Mill Square 4 ...	Atlanta	GA
Gwinnett Place 6	Atlanta	GA
Hairston Village 8	Atlanta	GA
Merchants Walk 8	Atlanta	GA
Perimeter Mall 4	Atlanta	GA
Sandy Springs 8	Atlanta	GA

Hoyts

Tara Theatre 4	Atlanta	GA
Roswell Mall 10	Roswell	GA

Litchfield

Austell Road 10	Atlanta	GA
Litchfield	Atlanta	GA
Riverdale 10	Atlanta	GA

Regal

Lawrenceville Town 10	Atlanta	GA
Lithonia Covington Sq. 8	Atlanta	GA
Marietta Regal 10	Atlanta	GA
Rivergate 10	Macon	GA
Norcross Peachtree 10 ..	Norcross	GA

UA

CNN Cinemas 6	Atlanta	GA
Lenox Square Theatres 6	Atlanta	GA
Midtown 8	Atlanta	GA
Tara Theatre	Atlanta	GA
South Dekalb 4	Decatur	GA
Gwinnett Mall 12	Duluth	GA
Parkwood Cinemas 3 ...	Griffin	GA

Westgate Theatre 6	Macon	GA
Southlake 8	Morrow	GA
Greens Corner		
Cinemas 5	Norcross	GA
Litch Cinemas 4	Rome	GA
Roswell 10	Roswell	GA
Shannon 8	Union City	GA

Cleveland

Cinema World
Cinema World Mansfield	Mansfield	OH
Cinema World Sandusky	Sandusky	OH
Mall Sandusky	Sandusky	OH

Cinemark
Carnation Cinema 8 ...	Alliance	OH
Movies 4	Canton	OH
Movies 10	Canton	OH
Richland 3	Mansfield	OH
Springfield Square 10 ..	Mansfield	OH
Movies 10	Sandusky	OH
Movies 10	Willoughby	OH
Movies 10	Wooster	OH

General Cinema
Chapel Hill Mall 5	Akron	OH
Plaza 8	Akron	OH
West Market Plaza 7 ...	Akron	OH
Canton Centre 8	Canton	OH
Erie Commons 8	Cleveland	OH
Parmatown 5	Cleveland	OH
Randall Park Mall 3 ...	Cleveland	OH
Ridge Park Square 8 ...	Cleveland	OH
Southgate 3	Cleveland	OH
Westgate Mall 6	Cleveland	OH
Westwood Town		
Center 6	Cleveland	OH
Midway Mall 8	Elyria	OH

Hoyts
Tower City 11	Cleveland	OH

Loew's
Cedar Center 2	Cleveland	OH
East 8	Cleveland	OH
State Cuyahoga Twin 2 .	Cleveland	OH
Yorktown 2	Cleveland	OH

Regal
Hudson 10	Cleveland	OH
Macedonia 10	Cleveland	OH
Westlake Promenade ...	Cleveland	OH
Brunswick 8	Cleveland	OH
Solon Commons 8	Cleveland	OH
Sheffield Center 10	Lorain	OH

Miami-Ft. Lauderdale

AMC
Ridge Plaza 8	Davie	FL
Coral Ridge 10	Fort Lauderdale	FL
Sheridan 7	Hollywood	FL
Oceanwalk 10	Hollywood Beach ..	FL
Bakery Centre 7	Miami	FL
Cocowalk 8	Miami	FL
Kendall 10	Miami	FL
Mall of the Americas 8	Miami	FL
Marina 8	Miami	FL
Omni 10	Miami	FL
South Dade 8	Miami	FL
Cross Country 8	West Palm Beach ..	FL
Mizner Path 8	West Palm Beach ..	FL

Cobb
Belleview Twin	Belleview	FL
Boynton 8	Boynton Beach ...	FL
Lakeworth 8	Green Acres City ..	FL
Jupiter 14	Jupiter	FL
Martin Square	Stuart	FL
Regency Square 8	Stuart	FL
Sawgrass 18 .:.......	Sunrise	FL

Fox
Fox Sunrise 8	Sunrise	FL

General Cinema
Coral Square 8	Fort Lauderdale	FL
Deerfield Mall 8	Fort Lauderdale	FL
Fountains 8	Fort Lauderdale	FL
Galleria	Fort Lauderdale	FL
Mission Bay Plaza 8 ...	Fort Lauderdale	FL
Pembroke Pines 8	Fort Lauderdale	FL
The 4	Fort Lauderdale	FL
Cinema 10	Miami	FL
Hialeah 8	Miami	FL
Intracoastal 8	Miami	FL
Riveria 5	Miami	FL
PGA 6	West Palm Beach ..	FL

UA
Town Center at Boca 7	Boca Raton	FL
Boynton Beach 9	Boynton Beach	FL
Movies at Hialeah 14 .	Hialeah	FL
Treasure Coast 6	Jensen Beach	FL
Movies at Lauderhill 13	Lauderhill	FL
Movies at Margate 8 ..	Margate	FL
Movies at the Falls 7 ...	Miami	FL
Promenade Plaza 8	Palm Beach	FL
Plantation Ft. Laud. 7 ..	Plantation	FL
Hibiscus Plaza 6	Pompano Beach ...	FL
Mall Cinema 4	West Palm Beach ..	FL
River Bridge 8	West Palm Beach ..	FL
Village Green 6	West Palm Beach ..	FL
Wellington Market Place	West Palm Beach ..	FL

Wometco
Shadowood 12	Boca Raton	FL
Miracle 4	Coral Gables	FL
Bay Harbor 4	Miami Beach	FL
Byron-Carlyle 7	Miami Beach	FL
Miami Lakes 10		
Theatres	Miami Lakes	FL
163rd St. Triple	North Miami Beach	FL
Kendall 9	South Dade	FL
Miller Square 8	South Dade	FL
University 7	South Dade	FL
Weston 8	Sunrise	FL
Florida 4	West Hollywood ...	FL

Baltimore

Cineplex
Market Place 6	Bowie	MD

General Cinema
Columbia City 3	Baltimore	MD
Perring Plaza 2	Baltimore	MD
Security Square 7	Baltimore	MD
Towson Commons 8 ...	Baltimore	MD
York Road 2	Baltimore	MD

Hoyts
Laurel Lakes 12	Laurel	MD
Cranberry Malls		
Cinemas 9	Westmister	MD

K.B.

Laurel 6	Laurel	MD

Loew's

Greenspring 3	Baltimore	MD
Northpoint 4	Baltimore	MD
Reisterstown 5	Baltimore	MD
Rotunda 2	Baltimore	MD
Campus Hills 7	Bel Air	MD
Hartford 2	Bel Air	MD
Columbia 10	Columbia	MD
Glen Burnie 7	Glen Burnie	MD
Crofton 4	Odenton	MD
Valley Centre 9	Owings Mills	MD
Jumpers 7	Pasadena	MD
Yorkridge 4	Pikesville	MD
Timonium 3	Timonium	MD

R/C

Hollywood Twin Cinemas	Arbutus	MD
Carrolltowne Movies 6	Eldersburg	MD
Village Cinema 3	Reisterstown	MD

UA

Golden Ring 9	Baltimore	MD
Movies at Harbor Park 9	Baltimore	MD
Marley Station 9	Glen Burnie	MD

Seattle-Tacoma

AMC

Center Plaza 6	Federal Way	WA
Sea Tac 6	Federal Way	WA
Narrows Plaza 8	Tacoma	WA

Act III

Harbor D.I.	Aberdeen	WA
Southshore Mall Cinemas	Aberdeen	WA
Redwood Plaza Quad	Bremerton	WA
Fox	Centralia	WA
Cinema 3	Chehalis	WA
Everett 9	Everett	WA
Kent VI Cinemas	Kent	WA
Lacey	Lacey	WA
State	Olympia	WA
Puyallup	Puyallup	WA
Alderwood	Seattle	WA
Crossroads	Seattle	WA
Parkway	Seattle	WA
Silverdale Cinemas	Silverdale	WA

Cineplex

Factoria Cinemas 8	Bellevue	WA
John Danz	Bellevue	WA
Kirkland Park Place 6	Kirkland	WA
Lakewood 6	Kirkland	WA
Totem Lake 3	Kirkland	WA
Grand Cinemas Alderwood 8	Lynnwood	WA
Cinerama	Seattle	WA
City Centre Cinemas 2	Seattle	WA
Lewis & Clark 7	Seattle	WA
Newmark Square 5	Seattle	WA
Northgate	Seattle	WA
Oak Tree Cinemas 6	Seattle	WA
South Centre	Seattle	WA
Uptown 3	Seattle	WA
Tacoma Central Cinemas 6	Tacoma	WA
Tacoma Mall Twin	Tacoma	WA
Tacoma South Cinemas 4	Tacoma	WA
Tacoma West Cinemas 5	Tacoma	WA

General Cinema

Everett Mall 10	Everett	WA
Gateway Center 8	Federal Way	WA
Renton Village 8	Renton	WA
Aurora 3	Seattle	WA
Kitsap Mall 6	Silverdale	WA
Lincoln Plaza 8	Tacoma	WA

Landmark

Broadway Market 4	Seattle	WA
Crest Cinema Center 4	Seattle	WA
Egyptian	Seattle	WA
Guild 45th Theatre 2	Seattle	WA
Harvard Exit 2	Seattle	WA
Metro Cinemas 10	Seattle	WA
Neptune	Seattle	WA
Seven Gables	Seattle	WA
Varsity 3	Seattle	WA

San Diego

AMC

Wiegand Plaza 8	Encinitas	CA
Fashion Valley 4	San Diego	CA
Santee Village 8	Santee	CA

Cinamerica

University Town Sixplex	La Jolla	CA
Plaza Bonita Sixplex	National City	CA
El Camino Eightplex	Oceanside	CA
Bernardo 6	San Diego	CA
Cinema 21	San Diego	CA
Grove 9	San Diego	CA
Hazard Center 7	San Diego	CA
Rancho Bernardo Sixplex	San Diego	CA
Sports Arena Sixplex	San Diego	CA
Valley Circle	San Diego	CA

Edwards

Flower Hill Twin	Del Mar	CA
Carousel 6	Escondido	CA
Vineyard	Escondido	CA
Poway Cinemas	Poway	CA
San Marcos	San Marcos	CA

Landmark

Cove	San Diego	CA
Guild	San Diego	CA
Hillcrest 5	San Diego	CA
Ken	San Diego	CA
Park	San Diego	CA

Pacific

La Jolla Village Four	La Jolla	CA
Grossmont 4	La Mesa	CA
Grossmont Trolley 8	La Mesa	CA
Center Three	San Diego	CA
Cinerama 6	San Diego	CA
Clairemont Twin	San Diego	CA

SoCal

Plaza Camino Real Cinema 4	Carlsbad	CA
Town & Country Cinema 3	Oceanside	CA
Temeku Cinema 7	Temecula	CA
Tower Cinema 2	Temecula	CA

UA

Chula Vista 6	Chula Vista	CA
Escondido 8	Escondido	CA
Glasshouse 6	San Diego	CA
Horton Plaza 7	San Diego	CA

Minneapolis-St. Paul

Carmike

Mall 3	Albert Lea	MN
Cinema 4	Mankato	MN
Mall 4	Mankato	MN
Cameo 3	Owatonna	MN
Chief 3	Red Wing	MN
Apache 4	Rochester	MN
Barclay Square 6	Rochester	MN
Cinema 3	Rochester	MN
Galleria 6	Rochester	MN
Cinema 4	Winona	MN

Cinemark

Crystal Movies 10	Minneapolis	MN
Movies 8	Mankato	MN

Cineplex

Edina 4	Edina	MN
Yorktown 3	Edina	MN
Skyway 6	Minneapolis	MN
Ridge Square 3	Minnetonka	MN
Westwind 3	Minnetonka	MN
Willow Creek 8	Plymouth	MN
Knollwood 4	St. Louis Park	MN

General Cinema

Centennial Lakes 8	Minneapolis	MN
Mall of America 14	Minneapolis	MN
Northtown 4	Minneapolis	MN
Shelard Park 5	Minneapolis	MN
Southtown 2	Minneapolis	MN
Burnhaven 8	Saint Paul	MN
Har Mar 11	Saint Paul	MN

Landmark

Uptown	Minneapolis	MN

Mann

Cinema 10	Maple Grove	MN
Apache 6	Minneapolis	MN
Boulevard 2	Minneapolis	MN
Heights	Minneapolis	MN
Suburban World	Minneapolis	MN
Village 4	Minneapolis	MN
Cina 5	Saint Paul	MN
Cottage Grove 3	Saint Paul	MN
Cottage View D.I.	Saint Paul	MN
Galtier 4	Saint Paul	MN
Grandview 2	Saint Paul	MN
Highland 2	Saint Paul	MN
Maple Leaf D.I.	Saint Paul	MN
Signal Hills 5	Saint Paul	MN
Mall 5	Stillwater	MN

Midcontinent

Spring Brook 4	Coon Rapids	MN
State Triple	Hutchinson	MN
Cinema 3	New Ulm	MN
Terrace 3	Robbinsdale	MN
Kandi 4	Willmar	MN

UA

Brookdale 8	Brooklyn Center	MN
Burnsville 4	Burnsville	MN
Burnsville Mall 4	Burnsville	MN
Eden Prairie East 4	Eden Prairie	MN
Eden Prairie West 5	Eden Prairie	MN
Maplewood #Two 6	Maplewood	MN
Maplewood 6	Maplewood	MN
Saint Anthony Main 5	Minneapolis	MN
Movies at Pavillon Pl 7	Roseville	MN

Tampa-St. Petersburg

AMC

Regency 8	Brandon	FL
Clearwater 5	Clearwater	FL
Countryside 6	Clearwater	FL
Tri-City	Clearwater	FL
Merchants Walk 10	Lakeland	FL
Crossroads 8	Saint Petersburg	FL
Tyrone Square 6	Saint Petersburg	FL
Sarasota 12	Sarasota	FL
Seminole 8	Seminole	FL
Seminole Mall 2	Seminole	FL
Horizon Park 4	Tampa	FL
Old Hyde Park 7	Tampa	FL
Twin Bays 4	Tampa	FL
Varsity 6	Tampa	FL

Cineplex

Plitt 4-plex	Brandon	FL
Countryside Village 4	Clearwater	FL
Main Street 5	Clearwater	FL
Sunshine Mall 5	Clearwater	FL
Hillsboro 8	Tampa	FL
Main Street 6	Tampa	FL
University Collection 6	Tampa	FL

Cobb

Bradenton 8	Bradenton	FL
DeSoto Square 6	Bradenton	FL
Oakmont 8	Bradenton	FL
Coralwood 14	Cape Coral	FL
Cinema Centre 8	Charlotte	FL
Lakeland Square 10	Lakeland	FL
Largo Mall 8	Largo	FL
Embassy 6	Port Richey	FL
Gulfside 10	Port Richey	FL
Cinema 10	Sarasota	FL
Gulfgate 8	Sarasota	FL
Parkway 8	Sarasota	FL
Eastlake 3	Tampa	FL
Northdale 6	Tampa	FL
University Square 4	Tampa	FL
Venetian 6	Venice	FL
Springlake 10	Winter Haven	FL

Floyd Theatres

Arcadia Twin 1 & 2	Arcadia	FL
Cortez Twin	Bradenton	FL
Brandon Twin 1 & 2	Brandon	FL
Brooksville Twin 1 & 2	Brooksville	FL
Joylan D.I.	Dade City	FL
Pasco Twin 1 & 2	Dade City	FL
Northside Twin D.I.	Fort Myers	FL
Palm Cinema 1, 2, & 3	Lakeland	FL
Silvermoon D.I.	Lakeland	FL
Plaza Twin 1 & 2	Lake Wales	FL
Ulmeron Cinema 9	Largo	FL
Rimar D.I.	Largo	FL
Plaza Twin 1 & 2	Palatka	FL
Mustang D.I.	Pinellas Park	FL
Lake Walden Cinema 8	Plant City	FL
Teatro Theatre	Sarasota	FL
28th St. D.I.	St. Petersburg	FL
Fairmount Cinema VI	Sebring	FL
Lake Shore Cinema 8	Sebring	FL
Funlan D.I.	Tampa	FL
Mall Twin 1 & 2	Tarpon Springs	FL
Midway D.I.	Tarpon Springs	FL

General Cinema

Gateway 2	Saint Petersburg	FL

Litchfield

Citrus 6	Inverness	FL
Cordova 3	Pensacola	FL
Cordova Mall 4	Pensacola	FL

Loew's

Pembroke Pines 4	Pembroke Pines	FL

UA

Movies at Clearwater 8	Clearwater	FL
Cinema 90 (6)	Lake City	FL
Santa Rosa 3	Mary Esther	FL
Cinemas West 5	Ocala	FL
Pembroke Pines 9	Pembroke Pines	FL
University 6	Pensacola	FL
Pinellas Park 12	Pinellas Park	FL
Capitol 6	Tallahassee	FL
Mission Bell 8	Tampa	FL

Wometco

Boulevard 6	Ocala	FL

Pittsburgh

Cinema World

Cinema World Butler	Butler	PA
Plaza Butler	Butler	PA
Cinema III	Greensburg	PA
Cinema World Greensburg	Greensburg	PA
Greengate Mall	Greensburg	PA
Westmoreland Mall	Greensburg	PA
Laurel 30	Latrobe	PA
Movie World	Monaca	PA
Monroeville	Pittsburgh	PA
Mt. Lebanon	Pittsburgh	PA
Norwin	Pittsburgh	PA
Rainbow	Pittsburgh	PA
Southland	Pittsburgh	PA
Squirrel Hill	Pittsburgh	PA
Village	Pittsburgh	PA
Hermitage Plaza	Sharon	PA
Cinema 19	Washington	PA
Washington Mall	Washington	PA

National Amusement

Showcase East 8	Pittsburgh	PA
Showcase North 11	Pittsburgh	PA
Showcase West 12	Pittsburgh	PA
Supersaver 8	Pittsburgh	PA

Regal

Moraine Pointe 10	Butler	PA

St. Louis

AMC

Village 6	Hazelwood	MO
Northwest 7	St. Ann	MO
Regency 8	St. Charles	MO
Crestwood 5	St. Louis	MO
Esquire 7	St. Louis	MO
Galleria 6	St. Louis	MO

Kerasotes

Eastgate 6	Alton	IL
Quad	Belleville	IL
Ritz	Belleville	IL
Nameoki 2	Granite City	IL
Lory 2	Highland	IL
Stadium 2	Jerseyville	IL
Bonne Terre Cinema 2	Bonne Terre	MO
Town Plaza Cinema 5	Cape Girardeau	MO
Movies 2	Flat River	MO
Meramec Cinema 2	Sullivan	MO

Wehrenberg

Alton Twin	Alton	IL
St. Clair 10 Cine	Fairview Heights	IL
West Park 4 Cine	Cape Girardeau	MO
66 D.I.	St. Louis	MO
Battlefield 6 Cine	St. Louis	MO
Chesterfield 4	St. Louis	MO
Cine	St. Louis	MO
Clarkson 6	St. Louis	MO
Creve Coeur	St. Louis	MO
Des Peres 4 Cine	St. Louis	MO
Eureka 6	St. Louis	MO
Halls Ferry 14	St. Louis	MO
Jamestown Twin Cine	St. Louis	MO
Keller 8 Cine	St. Louis	MO
Kenrick 8	St. Louis	MO
Lindbergh 8 Cine	St. Louis	MO
Mid River 6 Cine	St. Louis	MO
North Twin D.I.	St. Louis	MO
North West Plaza 8	St. Louis	MO
Ronnie's 8 Cine	St. Louis	MO
Shady Oak Theatre	St. Louis	MO
St. Charles 10 Cine	St. Louis	MO
Union Station 10 Cine	St. Louis	MO
Westport 1 & 2	St. Louis	MO

Phoenix

AMC

Laguna Village 10	Chandler	AZ
Gateway Village 10	Glendale	AZ
Fiesta Village 6	Mesa	AZ
Sunvalley 10	Mesa	AZ
Three Fountains	Mesa	AZ
Bell Plaza 8	Phoenix	AZ
Metro Village 6	Phoenix	AZ
Town & Country 6	Phoenix	AZ
Lakes	Tempe	AZ

General Cinema

Bell Towne Centre 8	Phoenix	AZ
Paradise Valley Mall 7	Phoenix	AZ
Westridge 6	Phoenix	AZ

Harkins

Arcadia 8	Phoenix	AZ
Bell Tower 8	Phoenix	AZ
Camelview Luxury 2	Phoenix	AZ
Camelback Mall 3	Phoenix	AZ
Centerpoint Luxury 11	Phoenix	AZ
Christown 5	Phoenix	AZ
Cine Capri	Phoenix	AZ
Cornerstone 4	Phoenix	AZ
Fashion Sq. Luxury	Phoenix	AZ
Fiesta 5	Phoenix	AZ
Metrocenter 3	Phoenix	AZ
Poca Fiesta 4	Phoenix	AZ
Shea Plaza 5	Phoenix	AZ
Southwest 8	Phoenix	AZ
Thomas Mall 2	Phoenix	AZ
Tricity 5	Phoenix	AZ

Syufy

Glendale 9 D.I.	Glendale	AZ
Scottsdale 6 D.I.	Tempe	AZ

UA

Chandler Park 10	Chandler	AZ
Bell Park Cinemas 6	Glendale	AZ
Valvista 10	Mesa	AZ
Westwood Cinemas 2	Mesa	AZ
Metro Park 8	Phoenix	AZ

UA Cinemas 6	Phoenix	AZ
Westridge Park 6	Phoenix	AZ
Pavillion 11	Scottsdale	AZ
Scottsdale 5	Scottsdale	AZ

Wehrenberg

Marina Twin	Prescott	AZ
Plaza West	Prescott	AZ

Sacramento-Stockton

Cinamerica

Festival Tenplex	Modesto	CA
Festival Fourplex	Stockton	CA
Regency Fourplex	Stockton	CA

Cinemark

County Fair Movies 5	Woodland	CA
Yuba City 8	Yuba	CA

General Cinema

Birdcage Walk 6	Sacramento	CA

Landmark

Tower 3	Sacramento	CA

Redwood

Auburn Cinemas 1 & 2	Auburn	CA
State 1 & 2	Auburn	CA
Jackson Cinemas 1-4	Jackson	CA
Cinema 4	Placerville	CA
Empire 2	Placerville	CA
Cinema 5	Sonora	CA

Syufy

Cinedome 9	Citrus Heights	CA
49er 6 D.I.	Sacramento	CA
Capitol Fourplex	Sacramento	CA
Century 6 Complex	Sacramento	CA
Sacramento 6 D.I.	Sacramento	CA
State Sixplex	Sacramento	CA

UA

Sunrise 4	Citrus Heights	CA
UA The Movies	Citrus Heights	CA
Del Oro Grass Valley 3	Grass Valley	CA
Merced 4	Merced	CA
Regency Merced 7	Merced	CA
Arden Fair 6	Sacramento	CA

Denver

AMC

Buckingham Square 4	Aurora	CO
Buckingham Village 6	Aurora	CO
Seven Hills 10	Aurora	CO
Tiffany Square 6	Colorado Springs	CO
Tiffany Plaza 6	Denver	CO
Tivoli 12	Denver	CO
Colorado Plaza 6	Glendale	CO
Southbridge	Littleton	CO
Westminster 5	Westminster	CO
Westminster Mall 6	Westminster	CO

Carmike

Chapel Hill 9	Colorado Springs	CO
Citadel Terrace 6	Colorado Springs	CO
Creger Plaza 4	Ft. Collins	CO
University Mall	Ft. Collins	CO

Cinamerica

Aurora Mall Triplex	Aurora	CO
Aurora Plaza 6	Aurora	CO
Arapahoe Village 4	Boulder	CO

Fox	Boulder	CO
Century 21	Denver	CO
Cherry Creek 8	Denver	CO
Tamarac Square Sixplex	Denver	CO
Arapahoe East Fourplex	Englewood	CO
Green Mountain Sixplex	Lakewood	CO
Union Square Sixplex	Lakewood	CO
Festival 6	Littleton	CO
Kipling Place Sixplex	Littleton	CO
Southwest Plaza Fiveplex	Littleton	CO
Northglenn Sixplex	Northglenn	CO

Landmark

Chez Artiste 3	Denver	CO
Esquire 3	Denver	CO
Mayan 2	Denver	CO

UA

Cooper 6	Arvada	CO
Cooper 5	Aurora	CO
Flatirons	Boulder	CO
Village 4	Boulder	CO
Royal Gorge Twin 2	Canon City	CO
Academy 6	Colorado Springs	CO
Aircadia D.I.	Colorado Springs	CO
Cinema 70 3-Plex	Colorado Springs	CO
Hanock Plaza 4	Colorado Springs	CO
Rustic Hills Twin 2	Colorado Springs	CO
Continental	Denver	CO
Target Village 3	Denver	CO
Cinderella Twin D.I. 2	Englewood	CO
Greenwood Plaza	Englewood	CO
Arbor Cinema 4	Fort Collins	CO
Campus West Twin 2	Fort Collins	CO
Foothills Twin 2	Fort Collins	CO
UA Twin	Glendale	CO
Bittersweet 4-Plex	Greeley	CO
Cooper Twin 2	Greeley	CO
Greeley Mall Twin 2	Greeley	CO
Cooper 7	Littleton	CO
Courtyard 4-Plex	Longmont	CO
Orchards Twin 2	Loveland	CO
Cinema Twin 2	Pueblo	CO
Mesa D.I.	Pueblo	CO
Pueblo Mall 3	Pueblo	CO
North Star D.I. 1	Thorton	CO
Thorton Town Center	Thorton	CO

Cincinnati

Chakeres

Belmont Auto	Dayton	OH
Kettering Cinemas 1 & 2	Dayton	OH
Melody 49 D.I. 1 & 2	Dayton	OH
Fairborn Cinemas 1 & 2	Fairborn	OH
Skyborn D.I.	Fairborn	OH
Colony Cinema	Hillsboro	OH
Park Layne D.I.	New Carlisle	OH
Sidney Cinemas 1-3	Sidney	OH
Plaza Cinemas 5	Wilmington	OH
Wilmington D.I.	Wilmington	OH

General Cinema

Gold Circle 2	Cincinnati	OH

Loew's

Florence 9	Florence	KY
Covedale 2	Cincinnati	OH
Kenwood 2	Cincinnati	OH
Kenwood Center Town 5	Cincinnati	OH
Northgate 7	Cincinnati	OH
Beaver Valley 6	Dayton	OH

608

Salem Ave 3	Dayton	OH
Salem Mall 4	Dayton	OH
Cinema 275 East 4	Milford	OH

National Amusement

Showcase 9	Erlanger	KY
Eastgate Mall 7	Cincinnati	OH
Showcase 12	Cincinnati	OH
Beaver Creek 7	Dayton	OH
Centerville 6	Dayton	OH
Cinema North 5	Dayton	OH
Cross Pointe 12	Dayton	OH
Dayton Mall 8	Dayton	OH
Huber Heights 12	Dayton	OH
Page Manor 2	Dayton	OH
Southtown 2	Dayton	OH
Showcase 9	Springdale	OH

Regal

Norwood Central Parke 11	Cincinnati	OH

Kansas City

AMC

Indian Springs North 4	Kansas City	KS
Indian Springs South 6	Kansas City	KS
Oak Park 12	Overland Park	KS
Bannister Square 6	Kansas City	MO
Crown Center 6	Kansas City	MO
Metro North 12	Kansas City	MO
Ward Parkway 12	Kansas City	MO
Summit 4	Lee's Summit	MO

Crown Corp

Cinema Twin	Lawrence	KS
Hillcrest 5	Lawrence	KS
Landing 4	Leavenworth	KS
Blue Ridge East 5	Kansas City	MO
Blue Ridge West 6	Kansas City	MO
Blue Springs 8	Kansas City	MO
Chouteau 4	Kansas City	MO
Red Bridge 4	Kansas City	MO
Seville 4	Kansas City	MO
Truman Corners 4	Kansas City	MO
Watts Mill 4	Kansas City	MO
Hillcrest 4	St. Joseph	MO
Plaza 8	St. Joseph	MO
Campus 2	Warrensburg	MO

Dickinson

Dickinson Cinema 6 ...	Lawrence	KS
Olathe Landing 8	Olathe	KS
Glenwood 4	Overland Park	KS
Metcalf 2	Overland Park	KS
South Glen 12	Overland Park	KS
Gladstone 4	Gladstone	MO
Noland Fashion Square 6	Independence	MO
Antioch 2	Kansas City	MO
Dickinson Cinema 6 ...	Kansas City	MO
Plaza 3	Kansas City	MO
Trail	St. Joseph	MO

UA

Trailridge 3	Shawnee	KS
Bannister Mall 5	Kansas City	MO

Milwaukee

Carmike

Prairie 5	Beloit	WI
Delavan 2	Delavan	WI
41 D.I.	Franklin	WI

Geneva 4	Lake Geneva	WI
University Sq. 4	Madison	WI

Landmark

Downer 2	Milwaukee	WI
Oriental 3	Milwaukee	WI

Marcus

Wisconsin 4	Beaver Dam	WI
Rivoli	Cedarburg	WI
Eastgate 14	Madison	WI
Point 10	Madison	WI
Southtown 5	Madison	WI
West Towne 3	Madison	WI
Westgate 3	Madison	WI
Grand 2	Milwaukee	WI
Marc 5	Milwaukee	WI
North Shore 8	Milwaukee	WI
Northtown 8	Milwaukee	WI
Prospect 3	Milwaukee	WI
Skyway 6	Milwaukee	WI
South Shore 10	Milwaukee	WI
Southtown 6	Milwaukee	WI
Starlite 2	Milwaukee	WI
Tosa	Milwaukee	WI
West Point 8	Milwaukee	WI
Westtown 10	Milwaukee	WI
Regency Mall 6	Racine	WI
Westgate 5	Racine	WI
Marc 8	Sheboygan	WI
Plaza 8 (2)	Sheboygan	WI

UA

Brown Port 2	Fox Point	WI
Spring Mall 4	Greenfield	WI
UA Cine 3	Janesville	WI
Kenosha 5	Kenosha	WI
Loomis 4	Milwaukee	WI
Mill Road 6	Milwaukee	WI
Northridge 6	Milwaukee	WI

Portland, OR

Act III/Luxury

Beaverton D.I.	Beaverton	OR
Valley Tri	Beaverton	OR
Westgate	Beaverton	OR
Gresham Quad	Gresham	OR
Town	Hillsboro	OR
Trail Twin	Hood River	OR
McMinnville	McMinnville	OR
82nd Ave. Cinemas	Portland	OR
Broadway Metroplex ...	Portland	OR
Clackamas	Portland	OR
Eastgate	Portland	OR
Foster D.I.	Portland	OR
Fox	Portland	OR
Guild	Portland	OR
Hollywood Cinemas ...	Portland	OR
Jantzen Cinemas	Portland	OR
Lloyd Cinemas	Portland	OR
Lloyd Mall Cinemas ...	Portland	OR
Mall 205 Cinemas	Portland	OR
Music Box	Portland	OR
Southgate	Portland	OR
Tanasbourne	Portland	OR
Tigard	Portland	OR
Washington Square Cinemas	Portland	OR
Capitol	Salem	OR
Elsinore	Salem	OR
Keizer Tri Cinemas	Salem	OR
Lancaster Mall Cinemas	Salem	OR
South Salem D.I.	Salem	OR
Southgate Cinemas	Salem	OR

Cascade Park	Vancouver	WA
Hazel Dell	Vancouver	WA
Vancouver Plaza 10	Vancouver	WA

Orlando-Daytona Beach

AMC

Interstate 6	Altamonte Springs	FL
Volusia Square 8	Daytona	FL
Daytona 6	Daytona Beach	FL
Oaks 10	Gainesville	FL
Pleasure Island 10	Lk. Buena Vista	FL
Merritt Square 12	Merritt Island	FL
Orange Park 5	Orange Park	FL
Fashion Village 8	Orlando	FL

Cineplex

Hoffner Centre 6	Orlando	FL
Plaza 2	Orlando	FL
Sandlake 7	Orlando	FL
University 8	Orlando	FL

Cobb

Osceola Square East 6	Kissimmee	FL
Osceola Square West 6	Kissimmee	FL
Oaks 10	Melbourne	FL
Roxy 10	Melbourne	FL

Eastern Federal

Royal Park 1, 2, 3, & 4	Gainesville	FL
Conway 1 & 2	Orlando	FL
Northgate 1, 2, 3 & 4	Orlando	FL
Orange Blossom 1 & 2	Orlando	FL
Port Orange 6	Port Orange	FL

Floyd Theatres

Big Tree Twin 1 & 2	Daytona	FL
Plaza Twin 1 & 2	Eustis	FL
Island Twin 1 & 2	Fernandina Beach	FL
Movieland D.I.	Sanford	FL
Starlite D.I.	Winter Garden	FL
Boulevard Triple 1, 2 & 3	Winter Haven	FL
Continental Twin 1 & 2	Winter Haven	FL
Havendale D.I.	Winter Haven	FL

General Cinema

Altamonte 8	Orlando	FL
Altamonte Mall 2	Orlando	FL
Colonial Promenade 6	Orlando	FL
Fashion Square 6	Orlando	FL
Lake Mary Centre 8	Orlando	FL

Litchfield

Butler Plaza 10	Gainesville	FL
Litchfield 10	Jacksonville	FL
Lake Mary 10	Orlando	FL
UC 6 7	Orlando	FL

UA

Movies at Wekiva	Apopka	FL
Volusia 1-3	Daytona Beach	FL
Mandarin Landing 8	Jacksonville	FL
Regency Square 12	Jacksonville	FL
The Movies at Orange Sq. 7	Jacksonville	FL
Market Place 8	Orange City	FL
Florida Mall 7	Orlando	FL
Lake Howell Square 8	Orlando	FL
Movies at Republic Sq. 8	Orlando	FL

Wometco

Park 11	Orlando	FL

Hartford-New Haven

Hoyts

East Manchester Cinemas 6	East Manchester	CT
Cine Enfield 8	Enfield	CT
Cinemas 6	Groton	CT
Cine 4	Hartford	CT
Madison Cinemas 2	Madison	CT
Meriden Cinemas 10	Meriden	CT
Mystic Village Cinemas 3	Mystic	CT
Playhouse 2	New Canaan	CT
Norwich Cinemas 2	Norwich	CT
Saybrook Cinemas 2	Saybrook	CT
Saybrook Cinemas 4	Saybrook	CT
Cinemas 6	Stratford	CT
Mall View Plaza 10	Waterbury	CT
Naugatuck Valley Mall 4	Waterbury	CT
Waterford Cinemas 8	Waterford	CT
Jillson Sq.	Willimantic	CT

Loew's

Bristol 8	Bristol	CT
Fine Arts 2	Brookfield	CT
Community 2	Fairfield	CT
County 1	Fairfield	CT
Norwalk 1 & 2	Norwalk	CT
Norwalk 2	Norwalk	CT
Holiday 6	Torrington	CT
Fine Arts 1 & 2	Westport	CT
Fine Arts 3	Westport	CT
Fine Arts 4	Westport	CT
Post 1	Westport	CT
Wilton 1	Westport	CT

National Amusement

Showcase 12	Berlin	CT
Showcase 10	Hartford	CT
Milford Fourplex	Milford	CT
Showcase 5	Milford	CT
Newington 3	Newington	CT
Showcase 8	North Haven	CT
Showcase 7	Orange	CT

Columbus

AMC

Eastland Center 8	Columbus	OH
Eastland Plaza 6	Columbus	OH
Westerville 6	Westerville	OH

Chakeres

Cinemas 7	Springfield	OH
Melody Cruise-In 1 & 2	Springfield	OH
Regent Cinemas 1 & 2	Springfield	OH
Upper Valley Mall Cin. 5	Springfield	OH

Cinema World

Colonial	Mt. Vernon	OH

Cinemark

Carriage Place Movies 12	Columbus	OH
Mill Run Movies 12	Columbus	OH
Colony Square 10	Zanesville	OH

Crown Corp

Indian Mound 6	Heath	OH
Newark 4	Newark	OH

General Cinema

Northland 8	Columbus	OH
Westland 8	Columbus	OH

Loew's

Continent 9	Columbus	OH
SouthLand 3	Columbus	OH
Westerville 2	Columbus	OH

Charlotte

Carmike

Cinema Twin	Asheboro	NC
Park Terrace Triple	Charlotte	NC
Town Cinema Six	Charlotte	NC
University Six	Charlotte	NC
Eastridge Four	Gastonia	NC
Circle 6	Greensboro	NC
Quaker Twin	Greensboro	NC
Terrace Four	Hickory	NC
Capri Triple	High Point	NC
Carmike 8	High Point	NC
Martin Twin	High Point	NC
Cinema Four	Lexington	NC
Cinema Four	Lincolnton	NC
Festival 10	Matthews	NC
Plaza Twin	Rockingham	NC
Kendale Twin	Sanford	NC
Cinema Four	Southern Pines	NC
Town & Country Twin	Southern Pines	NC
Gateway Four	Statesville	NC
Newtowne Twin	Statesville	NC
Marketplace 6	Winston-Salem	NC
Reynolds Triple	Winston-Salem	NC
Thruway Twin	Winston-Salem	NC

Cinemark

Randolph Cinema 5	Asheboro	NC
Brassfield 10	Greensboro	NC
Mall Cinema 6	Salisbury	NC

Eastern Federal

Delta 6	Charlotte	NC
Manor 1 & 2	Charlotte	NC
Movies 8	Charlotte	NC
Park 51-6	Charlotte	NC
Regency Four	Charlotte	NC
Movies on the Lake	Cornelius	NC
North Point 5	Winston-Salem	NC

General Cinema

Charlottetown 4	Charlotte	NC
Eastland 3	Charlotte	NC
SouthPark 3	Charlotte	NC
Tower Place Festival 8	Charlotte	NC
Four Seasons Town 4	Greensboro	NC
Hanes Mall 4	Winston-Salem	NC

Litchfield

Litchfield 7	Greensboro	NC

UA

Eastgate 5	Albemarle	NC
Carolina Mall 8	Concord	NC
Litch Cinemas 4	Gastonia	NC
Crown 4 Cinemas 6	Hickory	NC

Raleigh-Durham

Carmike

Ram Triple	Chapel Hill	NC
Plaza Twin	Dunn	NC
Carmike 7	Durham	NC
Center Four	Durham	NC
South Square Four	Durham	NC
Willowdaile Eight	Durham	NC
York Town Twin	Durham	NC
Bordeaux Triple	Fayetteville	NC
Carmike 6	Fayetteville	NC
Berkely Four	Goldsboro	NC
Eastgate Twin	Goldsboro	NC
Cinema	Henderson	NC
Cinema Twin	Laurinburg	NC
Carmike 7	Raleigh	NC
Six Forks Six	Raleigh	NC
South Hills Twin	Raleigh	NC
Terrace Twin	Raleigh	NC
Tower	Raleigh	NC
Cardinal Triple	Rocky Mount	NC
Englewood Twin	Rocky Mount	NC
Golden East Four	Rocky Mount	NC
Gold Park Twin	Wilson	NC
Parkwood Triple	Wilson	NC

Eastern Federal

Plaza 3	Chapel Hill	NC
Movies at Timberlyne 6	Chapel Hill	NC

General Cinema

Cross Creek Mall 3	Fayetteville	NC
Cross Pointe 6	Fayetteville	NC
Pleasant Valley 7	Raleigh	NC

Litchfield

Omni 8	Fayetteville	NC
Litchfield 6	Wilson	NC

UA

Imperial 4	Cary	NC
Litch Cinemas 4	Goldsboro	NC
Mission Valley 5	Raleigh	NC

Norfolk-Virginia Beach

AMC

Coliseum 4	Hampton	VA
Newmarket 4	Hampton	VA
Patrick Henry 7	Newport News	VA
Circle 10	Norfolk	VA
Lynnhaven 8	Virginia Beach	VA

Carmike

Beechmont Twin	Newport News	VA
Carmike Four	Williamsburg	VA

Cinemark

Movies 10	Chesapeake	VA
Movies 14	Mechanicsville	VA

General Cinema

Janaf Plaza 8	Norfolk	VA

Litchfield

Chester 6	Chester	VA

Neighborhood

Greenbrier 4	Chesapeake	VA
Southpark 6	Colonial Height	VA
Armory Drive 3	Franklin	VA
Riverdale 3	Hampton	VA
Crossings 2	Hopewell	VA
Newmarket 4	Newport News	VA
Crater 8	Norfolk	VA
Little Creek 3	Norfolk	VA
Terrace 2	Norfolk	VA
Plaza 3	Portsmouth	VA
Cloverleaf 8	Richmond	VA
Genito Forest 9	Richmond	VA
Ridge 7	Richmond	VA
Westhampton 2	Richmond	VA
Westover	Richmond	VA
Willow Lawn 4	Richmond	VA
Pembroke Mall 8	Virginia Beach	VA

R/C

Surf-N-Sand 8	Virginia Beach	VA
Movies 7 at Williamsburg	Williamsburg	VA

UA

Chesterfield Mall 9	Richmond	VA
Midlothian 6	Richmond	VA
West Tower 6	Richmond	VA
Kempsriver 7	Virginia Beach	VA
UA 5 Lynnhaven	Virginia Beach	VA

Indianapolis

Cinemark

Greenwood Corners Mov. 8	Indianapolis	IN
Washington Market Mov. 8	Indianapolis	IN

General Cinema

Castleton Square 3	Indianapolis	IN
Clearwater Crossing 12	Indianapolis	IN
Eastgate Mall 6	Indianapolis	IN
Glendale 6	Indianapolis	IN
Greenwood Park 7	Indianapolis	IN
Lafayette Square 5	Indianapolis	IN
Speedway 2	Indianapolis	IN
Washington Square 2 ...	Indianapolis	IN

Goodrich

Applewood 9	Anderson	IN
Eastside 10	Lafayette	IN
Market Square 2	Lafayette	IN
Tippecanoe 4	Lafayette	IN

Kerasotes

Mounds Mall 2	Anderson	IN
Showplace 4	Anderson	IN
College Cinema Mall 4	Bloomington	IN
Indiana 2	Bloomington	IN
Showplace 6	Bloomington	IN
Village 2	Bloomington	IN
Von Lee 3	Bloomington	IN
Kokomo Mall Cinema 8	Kokomo	IN
Dollar Cinema 7	Muncie	IN
Muncie Mall Cinema 3	Muncie	IN
Northwest Plaza Cinema 8	Muncie	IN

Loew's

Cherry Tree 10	Indianapolis	IN
College Park 10	Indianapolis	IN
Greenwood 9	Indianapolis	IN
Lafayette Square 8	Indianapolis	IN
Norgate 4	Indianapolis	IN

San Antonio

AMC

Rivercenter 9	San Antonio	TX

Act III

Aquarius 4	Austin	TX
Arbor 7	Austin	TX
Lakecreek 8	Austin	TX
Lakehills 4	Austin	TX
Lincoln 6	Austin	TX
Northcross 6	Austin	TX
Riverside 8	Austin	TX
South Park 3	Austin	TX
Southwood 2	Austin	TX
Westgate 3	Austin	TX
Westgate 8	Austin	TX

Village 4	Austin	TX
Bandera 6	San Antonio	TX
Central Park Fox 4	San Antonio	TX
Century South 8	San Antonio	TX
Crossroads 6	San Antonio	TX
Embassy 14	San Antonio	TX
Galaxy 14	San Antonio	TX
Ingram Square 8	San Antonio	TX
Mission D.I. 4	San Antonio	TX
Nakoma 8	San Antonio	TX
Northwest 14	San Antonio	TX
Rolling Oaks 6	San Antonio	TX
South Park 3	San Antonio	TX
Westlakes 9	San Antonio	TX
Windsor Mall 5	San Antonio	TX

Cinemark

Movies 12	Pflugerville	TX
Movies 8	Round Rock	TX
Wells Branch Movies 8	Round Rock	TX
McCreless 9	San Antonio	TX
Movies 16	San Antonio	TX

General Cinema

Barton Creek 5	Austin	TX
Great Hills 8	Austin	TX
Highland 10	Austin	TX

Nashville

Carmike

Carmike Eight	Clarksville	TN
Cinema Five	Clarksville	TN
Martin Four	Clarksville	TN
Williamson Eight	Franklin	TN
Martin Triple	Lebanon	TN
Carmike Six	Murfreesboro	TN
Stone River 6	Murfreesboro	TN
Belcourt Twin	Nashville	TN
Bell Road Triple	Nashville	TN
Belle Forge Ten	Nashville	TN
Bellevue Four	Nashville	TN
Brentwood Triple	Nashville	TN
Carmike Six	Nashville	TN
Cinema North Six	Nashville	TN
Cinema South Four	Nashville	TN
Fountain Sq. 14	Nashville	TN
Galleria 10	Nashville	TN
Hermitage Four	Nashville	TN
Hickory Mall Triple	Nashville	TN
Lions Head Five	Nashville	TN
Madison	Nashville	TN
Plaza	Nashville	TN
Rivergate Eight	Nashville	TN
Cinema	Springfield	TN

Regal

Hendersonville Indian 10	Nashville	TN
Hermitage Courtyard 8	Nashville	TN
Nippers Corner 10	Nashville	TN

Buffalo-Niagara Falls

AMC

Como 8	Cheektowaga	NY
Holiday 6	Cheektowaga	NY

General Cinema

Market Arcade 8	Buffalo	NY
Mckinley Mall 6	Buffalo	NY
Thruway Mall 8	Buffalo	NY
University 8	Buffalo	NY
Walden Galleria 12	Buffalo	NY
Summit Park 6	Niagara Falls	NY

Marketplace 7	Rochester	NY
Pittsford Plaza 6	Rochester	NY

Hoyts
Cine Greece 8	Rochester	NY

Loew's
Pittsford 1	Rochester	NY
Pittsford 2	Rochester	NY
Towne 4	Rochester	NY
Webster 12	Rochester	NY

Mini
Movieplex 59 Eight	Dunkirk	NY

New Orleans

AMC
Galleria 8	Metairie	LA

General Cinema
Esplanade Mall 9	New Orleans	LA
Lake Side 5	New Orleans	LA
North Shore Square 6	New Orleans	LA

Landmark
Canal Place Cinemas 4	New Orleans	LA
Prytania	New Orleans	LA

UA
Bon Marche 11	Baton Rouge	LA
Bon Marche Twin 2	Baton Rouge	LA
Essen Mall Cinema 6	Baton Rouge	LA
Siegen Village 10	Baton Rouge	LA
University Cinema 4	Baton Rouge	LA
Houma Twin 2	Houma	LA
Plaza Cinema 4	Houma	LA
Southland Cinema 4	Houma	LA
West Esplanade 8	Kenner	LA
Belle Promenade 10	New Orleans	LA
Eastlake Plaza 8	New Orleans	LA
Village Aurora Cinemas 6	New Orleans	LA

Memphis

General Cinema
Hickory Ridge Mall 4	Memphis	TN
Mall of Memphis 5	Memphis	TN
Raleigh 6	Memphis	TN

Malco
Appletree 12	Memphis	TN
Bartlett Cinema 10	Memphis	TN
Forest Hill Cinema 8	Memphis	TN
Germantown Cinema 9	Memphis	TN
Highland Quartet	Memphis	TN
Malco's Ridgeway Four	Memphis	TN
Southwest Twin D.I.	Memphis	TN
Summer Quartet D.I.	Memphis	TN
Winchester Court 8	Memphis	TN

Regal
Southbrook 7	Memphis	TN

Providence-New Bedford

General Cinema
No. Dartmouth Mall 8	North Dartmouth	MA
Lincoln Mall 4	Providence	RI
Warwick Mall 3	Providence	RI

Hoyts
Mashpee Cinemas 5	Mashpee	MA
Silver City Galleria 10	Taunton	MA
Taunton Cinemas 8	Taunton	MA
Westerly Cinemas 3	Westerly	RI

Loew's
Habour Mall 8	Fall River	MA
Somerville 12	Somerville	MA
Meadowbrook D.I.	Middleboro	MA

Melrose
Newport D.I.	Newport	RI
Starlight Twin D.I.	Newport	RI
Four Seasons Cinema 5	Providence	RI
Apple Valley Cinemas Four	Smithfield	RI
Campus Cinema	Wakefield	RI

Mini
Bijou	Fairhaven	MA
Pier Cinema Twin	Narragansett	RI
Jane Pickens	Newport	RI

National Amusement
Showcase 10	Seekonk	MA
Showcase 12	Warwick	RI

Salt Lake City-Ogden

Carmike
Cache Valley	Logan	UT

Cinemark
Layton Hills 6	Layton	UT
Movies 10	Layton	UT
Newgate 4	Ogden	UT
Holiday Village Cinema 3	Park City	UT
Movies 8	Provo	UT
Movies 9	Sandy	UT
Movies 10	Sugarhouse	UT
Valley Fair 9	West Valley City	UT

Cineplex
Family Center 4	Midvale	UT
Trolley North 3	North Salt Lake City	UT
Cinedome 2	Ogden	UT
Wilshire 3	Ogden	UT
University 4	Orem	UT
Broadway 6	Salt Lake City	UT
Crossroads 3	Salt Lake City	UT
Holladay Center 6	Salt Lake City	UT
Midvalley Cinemas 6	Salt Lake City	UT
Trolley Corners 3	Salt Lake City	UT
Trolley Square Mall 4	Salt Lake City	UT
South Towne Centre 10	Sandy	UT

Syufy
Century 21-23 Triplex	Salt Lake City	UT
Century 241-29 Twin	Salt Lake City	UT

Oklahoma City

AMC
Robinson Crossing 6	Norman	OK
Memorial Square 8	Oklahoma City	OK
Northwest 8	Oklahoma City	OK

Carmike
Dunkin	Cushing	OK
Carmike Six	Duncan	OK
Cinema	El Reno	OK
Oakwood Five	Enid	OK

Video Twin	Enid	OK
Showcase Twin	Lawton	OK
Video Triple	Lawton	OK
Carmike Six	Stillwater	OK
Satellite Twin	Stillwater	OK

General Cinema
Brixton Square 8	Oklahoma City	OK
Crossroads 8	Oklahoma City	OK
Penn Square Mall	Oklahoma City	OK
Quail Springs	Oklahoma City	OK

Litchfield
Kickingbird 6	Edmond	OK
Windsor Hills 10	Oklahoma City	OK

UA
Cache Cinemas 8	Lawton	OK
Almonte 6 plex	Midwest City	OK
Heritage Park	Midwest City	OK
Heritage Plaza	Midwest City	OK
Village 6-Plex	Norman	OK

Louisville

Chakeres
Brighton Park Cinemas 2	Frankfort	KY
Franklin Square Cin. 6	Frankfort	KY
Trail Cinema	Morehead	KY
University Cinema	Morehead	KY

Cinemark
Greentree 10	Clarksville	IN
Greentree 4	Clarksville	IN
Village 8	Louisville	KY
Movies 8	Richmond	KY

Loew's
River Falls 10	Clarksville	IN
Oxmoor 5	Louisville	KY
Stonybrook 10	Stonybrook	KY

National Amusement
Showcase 13	Louisville	KY

Birmingham

Carmike
Carmike Six	Anniston	AL
Plaza Six	Anniston	AL
Cinema Four	Auburn	AL
Bama Six	Birmingham	AL
Carmike Ten	Birmingham	AL
Colonnade Ten	Birmingham	AL
Town Square Triple	Cullman	AL
Plaza Twin	Sylacauga	AL
Martin Triple	Talladega	AL
Bama Six	Tuscaloosa	AL

Cobb
Centerpoint 6	Birmingham	AL
Cinema City 8	Birmingham	AL
Festival 12	Birmingham	AL
Galleria 10	Birmingham	AL
Hoover Square 6	Birmingham	AL
Wildwood 14	Birmingham	AL
Fox 10	Tuscaloosa	AL

Grand Rapids-Battle Creek

GKC
Towne Cinemas 8	Battle Creek	MI
Plaza Cinemas 7	Jackson	MI

West Cinemas 2	Jackson	MI

General Cinema
Maple Hill Mall 3	Kalamazoo	MI

Goodrich
W. Columbia 6	Battle Creek	MI
29th St. Quad 6	Grand Rapids	MI
Holland 7	Holland	MI
Jackson 8	Jackson	MI

National Amusement
Showcase 10	Grand Rapids	MI

UA
Benton Harbor 5	Benton Harbor	MI
North Kent Mall 8	Grand Rapids	MI
Woodland 6	Grand Rapids	MI
West Main 7	Kalamazoo	MI
Movies at Portage 10	Portage	MI

Albany-Schenectady-Troy

Hoyts
Berkshire Mall 10	Pittsfield	MA
Cine 10	Albany	NY
Crossgates 12	Albany	NY
Clifton County Mall 6	Clifton Park	NY
Aviaton 8	Glens Falls	NY
Route 9 Cinemas 5	Glens Falls	NY
Hudson Valley Mall 6	Kingston	NY
Latham Mall 9	Latham	NY
South Side Mall 4	Oneonta	NY
Saratoga Cinemas 6	Saratoga	NY
Wilton Mall 8	Saratoga	NY

Loew's
Mohawk Mall 7	Schenectady	NY
Rotterdam 6	Schenectady	NY

Melrose
Cinema Center 8	Pittsfield	MA
Paris	Pittsfield	MA

Mini
Cinema 6	North Adams	MA
Madison Cinemas	Albany	NY
Hollywood D.I.	Averill Park	NY
Community Twin	Catskill	NY
Crandell Cinema	Chatham	NY
Clinton Cinema	Clinton	NY
Park	Cobleskill	NY
Glen Twin D.I.	Glens Falls	NY
Hunter	Hunter	NY
Valley Twin	Little Falls	NY
Malta D.I.	Malta	NY
Hatheway D.I.	North Hoosick	NY
Orpheum	Tannersville	NY

Harrisburg-Lancaster

AMC
East 5	Harrisburg	PA
Eden 2	Lancaster	PA
Wonderland 4	Lancaster	PA
York 4	York	PA

Fox
Fox Theatres 4	Hanover	PA
Fox Theatres 2	Lebanon	PA
Howard Cinemas 2	Lebanon	PA
Fox Coventry 8	Pottstown	PA
Fox North-End 2	Pottstown	PA
Deer Lake D.I.	Pottsville	PA

| Fox Theatres 2 .... | Pottsville .... | PA |
| Fox Theatres 4 .... | Sunbury .... | PA |

Milgram

Main 2	Ephrata	PA
Key D.I.	Lebanon	PA
Marietta	Marietta	PA

R/C

| Majestic Cinema 3 .... | Gettysburg .... | PA |

UA

Camp Hill Twin 2	Camp Hill	PA
UA 6 Capitol Ct.	Camp Hill	PA
Eric Lancaster Twin 2 ..	Lancaster	PA
Pacific Lancaster	Lancaster	PA
Delco Plaza 5	York	PA
Movies at York Mall 2 .	York	PA

Independent Theatres

* **NAME**

* **LOCATION**
      (Alphabetically by State & Town)

* **OWNER**

* **NUMBER OF SCREENS**

Buying and Booking Services

Theatre Equipment Suppliers

Independent Theatres

Drive-in theatres are indicated by a filled circle (•). In the case of drive-ins, seats refers to car capacity.

Name	Address	City & Zip	Owner	Screens	Seats
ALABAMA					
Mall Garden 1 & 2	850 Highway 43 So.	Albertville 35950	Hammonds-Lawler	1	
Playhouse Cinemas	722 Cherokee Road	Alexander City 35010	H. Legg	2	
Strand Theatre	1710 Trussell Road	Alexander City 35010	H. Peters	1	
Grand Bijou Theatre	2304 10th Terrace SIC	Birmingham 35205	R. Whorton	1	
Ritz Theatre	P.O. Box 188	Centerville 35042	T. Hellums	1	
Eastern Shore Cinema	Hwy. 98., PO Box 8	Daphne 36551	R. Cummings	1	
Dixie Theatre	Box 246	Haleyville 35565	J. Gunter	1	
•Havala Drive-in	P.O. Box 246	Haleyville 35565	J. Gunter	1	
Locke Theatre	233 Commerce	Jackson 36545	M. Denton	1	
Strand Theatre	20 Main Street	Montevallo 35115	C. Love	1	
Cinema Twin Theatre	P.O. Box 129	Rainsville 35986	L. Kilgore	2	
•Kings Drive-in	Route 7	Russellville 35653	A. King	1	200
ALASKA					
Capri Cinema	3425 E. Tudor Road	Anchorage 99507	Silver Screen Mgmt. Corp.	1	90
Cyrano's Cinema	413 D St.	Anchorage 99501	Silver Screen Mgmt. Corp.	1	35
ARIZONA					
Movieola Theatre	1389 East Hwy. 89A	Cottonwood 86326	D. Olds	1	252
Alco Theatre	111 San Antonio	Douglas 85607	R. Kroft	2	
Valley West Cinema 5	5720 W. Hayward	Glendale 85301	V.W. Operating Co.	3	
Cinema Theatre	2130 McCulloch Blvd.	Lake Havasu City 86403	K Standal	1	
Payson Picture Show	213 E. Cedar Lane	Payson 85541	L. Bevell	1	
Gila Twin	1914 W. Thatcher Blvd.	Safford 85546	Fountain Cinemas Inc.	2	
Flicker Shack Theatre	P.O. Box	Sedona 86336	M. Child	1	
Sho Lo Theatre	Box 219	Show Low 85901	I. Rawlings	2	
R & M Cinema	300 E. Wilcox	Sierra Vista 85635	M. Kroft	7	586
Wickenburg Theatre	East Center St.	Wickenburg 85358	W. Way	1	
ARKANSAS					
Landers Theatre	332 E. Main	Batesville 72501	P. Landers	1	
Melba Theatre	Main St.	Batesville 72501	D. Reynolds	1	
Main Theatre	P.O. Box 386	Berryville 72616	K. Clark	1	
Savage Theatre	P.O. Box 388	Booneville 72927	J. McNutt	1	
Garden Oaks Twin Cinema	Garden Oaks	S/C Camden 71701	Union Cinema Corp.	2	500
•Queen Twin Drive-In	P.O. Box	DeQueen 71832	D. Stearns	1	
El Dorado Cinema	1936 Northwest Ave.	El Dorado 71730	Union Cinema Corp.	3	980
•112 Drive-In	Highway 112	Fayetteville 72702	J. Terry	1	
Ark Union Theatre	University of Arkansas	Fayetteville 72701		1	
•Sunset Drive-in	P.O. Box 472	Hamburg 71646	R. Carpenter	1	
Marcus Twin Cinemas Theatre	P.O. Box 430	Hope 71801	D. Murphy	2	
Center Theatre		Kensett 72082	N. Byrd	1	
•Kenda Drive-In	Box 355	Marshall 72650	K. Sanders	1	
Drew Theatre	Box 593	Monticello 71655	J. Williams	1	
Marie's Mountain View Theatre	Box 168	Mountain View 72560	A. Clemons	1	
•Mountain View Drive-In	P.O. Box 76	Mountain View 72560	R. Thompson	1	
•Howard Auto Drive-In	P.O. Box 835	Nashville 71852	J. Johnson	1	
Village 1-2 Theatres		Newport 72112	W. Beard	2	
Carolyn Theatre	Box 179	Piggott 72454	J. Staples	1	
Pickwood 7 Cinemas	P.O. Box 218	Russellville 72801	J. Lowrey	7	
Springs Cinema	P.O. Box 598	Siloam Springs 72761	D. Smith	2	
Stuttgart Twin Cinemas		Stuttgart 72160	Union Cinema Corp.	2	
Maxie Theatre	Highway 63S	Trumann 72472	J. Noel	1	
Scott Theatre	P.O. Box 657	Waldron 72958	K. Hines	1	
CALIFORNIA					
Niles Theater	127 S. Main	Alturas 96101	F. Ertle	1	449
Brookhurst 4	2299 W. Ball Rd.	Anaheim 92804		4	
Villa Park Twin Cinema	2400 E. Lincoln Ave.	Anaheim 92806		2	
Arcata & Minor Theatre	1036 G Arc	Arcata 95521	Minor Theatre Co.	4	
Ponderosa Pines Theatre	Box 314	Bass Lake 93604	B. Paul	1	
Pacific Film Archive	2625 Durant Ave.	Berkeley 94720	Univ. of California	1	
Beverly Canon Theatre	205 N. Canon Dr.	Beverly Hills 90210	R. Solari	1	
Bishop Twin Theatre	237 N. Main St.	Bishop 93514	B. Hilborn	2	540
Camarillo Cinemas 3 Theatre	390 N. Lantana St.	Camarillo 93010	Chealin Inc.	3	
Plaza 4 Theatres	2501 Winchester Blvd.	Campbell 95008	J. Gunsky	4	
Capitola Theatre	120 Monterey Ave.	Capitola 95010	A. Jacobs	1	500
Carlsbad Theatre	2822 State St.	Carlsbad 92008	R. Normandin	10	
Plaza Theatre	4916 Carpinteria Ave.	Carpinteria 93013	P. Wheeler	1	
•Ceres Drive-in	P.O. Box 503	Ceres 94307	Maestri	1	
Chester Theatre & Video	Hwy. 36 Main St.	Chester 96020	R. Killian	1	
Vogue Theatre	226 Third Ave.	Chula Vista 91911	P. Upham	1	
Clearlake Cinema	Box 2586	Clearlake 95422	J. Wilder	2	

Name	Address	City & Zip	Owner	Screens	Seats
Colfax Cinema	48 College Park	Colfax 95616	W. Jacob	1	240
Capri Theatre	1653 Willow Pass Rd.	Concord 94520	D. Cooper	3	700
Rodgers Theatre	P.O. Box 255	Corning 96021	W. Rodgers	1	
Oaks Theatres	21275 Stevens Creek	Cupertino 95014	San Carlos Cinemas	5	732
Family Twin Cinema	9823 Walker	Cypress 90630	V. Chang	2	
The Theatre	11705 Palm Dr.	Desert Hot Springs 92240	E. Primack	1	
Avenue Theatre	11022 Downey Ave.	Downey 90241	E. Chang	1	
New Boulevard	4549 Whittier Blvd.	East Los Angeles 90022		1	
•Aero Drive-in	1470 East Broadway	El Cajon 92021	D. Bernard	1	
Crest Theatre	723 Main St.	El Centro 92243	Gallery Cinemas USA Inc.	1	924
Fox Theatre	139 S. 7th St.	El Centro 92243	Gallery Cinemas USA Inc.	1	790
La Paloma Theatre	471 First St.	Encinitas 92024	A. Largent	1	400
The Cinema Store Theatre	17281 Ventura Blvd.	Encino 91316	D. Klass	1	
Avery Memorial Theatre	430 Main St.	Etna 96027	J. Reynolds	1	
•Chief Auto Movie	P.O. Box 48	Fairfield 94533	H. Tegtmeier	1	
Chief Cinemas Four Theatres	P.O. Box 48	Fairfield 94533	H. Tegtmeier	4	
Fairfield Cinema I & II	P.O. Box 48	Fairfield 94534	H. Tegtmeier	2	
Fall River Theatre	P.O. Box 142	Fal River Mill 96028	Leatham	1	
Mission Theatre	231 N. Main St.	Fallbrook 92028	D. Mitterling	1	
Towne Theatre	338 Central Ave.	Fillmore 93015	H. Graves	1	
•Bel Air Drive-in	15895 Valley Blvd	Fontana 92335	B. Poynter	1	
Fortuna Theatre	1241 Main St.	Fortuna 95540	T. Ostrow	1	
Family Four	17161 Brookhurst St.	Fountain Valley 92708	J. Randolph	4	
Tower Theatre	1201 N. Wishon	Fresno 93728	R. Glaspey	1	
Garberville Theatre	766 Redwood Drive	Garberville 95440	S. Burke	1	
Town Plaza Cinema Theatre	705 First Street	Gilroy 95020	Rak Cinemas	1	
Pacific Regency Theatre	210 S. Brand Blvd.	Glendale 91204	Satalino	1	
Butte Theatre	P.O. Box 842	Gridley 95948	J. Santos	1	
Hanford Theatre	326 N. Irwin	Hanford 93230	J. Humason	1	1055
Metro 4 Cinemas Theatre	123 7th Street	Hanford 93230	G. Culver	4	
Movies 1-4 Theatres	136 N. 11th Avenue	Hanford 93232	Entmnt. Ctrs	4	
Hemet Theatre	220 E. Florida Ave.	Hemet 92343		1	
Highland 3 Theatres	5604 N. Figueroa	Highland Park 90042	A. Akarakian	3	
Granada Theatre	336 Fifth Avenue	Holliston 95023	J. Mahew	1	
Los Feliz Theatre	1822 N. Vermont Ave.	Hollywood 90027		1	
Swank Motion Pictures	6767 Forest Lawn Dr.	Hollywood 90068	R. Thomas	1	
Rustic Theatre	542900 North Circle	Idyllwild 92349	Bronson	1	
Star Theatre	145 N. First Street	La Puente 91744	M. Tocoline	1	260
•Lakeport Auto Movies	P.O. Box 669	Lakeport 95433	H. Tegtmeier	1	
Lakeport Twin Theatres	P.O. Box 669	Lakeport 95453	H. Tegtmeier & Reese	2	
Grove Theatre	242 S. Elmwood	Lindsay 93247	D. Johnson	1	
Gemini Twin Cinema	1028 N. H Street	Lompoc 93436	Los Padres Theatres	2	
Lompoc Theatre	112 ½ North Street	Lompoc 93436	Nichols	1	
The Movies	227 E. Barton Avenue	Lompoc 93436	Los Padres Theatres	4	
Art Theatre	2025 E. 4th Street	Long Beach 90812	H. Linn	1	
Ackerman Grand Ballroom Theatre	308 Westwood Blvd.	Los Angeles 90024	UCLA	1	1000
Eagle Theatre	4884 Eagle Rock Blvd.	Los Angeles 90041	Cinema Showcase, Inc.	1	700
Four Star Theatre	5112 Wilshire Blvd.	Los Angeles 90036	C. Attorney	1	
Gordon Theatre	614 N. La Brea	Los Angeles 90036	S. Kurstin	1	
UCLA Melnitz Theatre	405 Hilgard Ave.	Los Angeles 90024	UCLA	1	200
Los Gatos Theatre	41 N. Santa Cruz Ave.	Los Gatos 95030	I. Shwartz	1	
Malibu Cinema	3822 Cross Creek Rd.	Malibu 90265	D. O'Meara	2	
Valley Cinemas	P.O. Box 967	Manteca 95336	E. Fonseca	4	
•Marysville Drive-in	5575 Chestnut Road	Marysville 95901	R Golding	1	474
Peachtree 4 Cinemas	6000 Lindhurst	Marysville 95901	Korte/Bentz	4	
Tower Theatre	103 D Street	Marysville 95901	F. Mejia	1	
Guild Theatre	949 El Camino Real	Menlo Park 94027	Renaissance	1	
Park Theatre	1275 El Camino Real	Menlo Park 94027	Renaissance	1	
College Green Cinema 1 & 2	100 W. Olive	Merced 95340	Schesnewski	2	
Off Center Cinema	777 Edgewood Ave.	Mill Valley 94941	R. McClay	1	
Dream Theatre	301 Prescott Avenue	Monterey 93940	Harris J. & Weber A.	2	220
The Bay Theatre	464 Morro Bay Blvd.	Morro Bay 93442	J. Jannopoulos	1	
Bay Theatre	330 National Avenue	National City 92050	R. Topete	1	
Nevada Theatre	401 Broad Street	Nevada City 95959	M. Getz	1	
Peppertree Cinema 5 Theatre	10155 Reseda Blvd.	Northridge 91324	Livingston	5	
Sausalito Theatre	1613 Center Road	Novato 94947	M. Seely	1	
Paramount Theatre	2025 Broadway	Oakland 94612	City of Oakland	1	2998
Studio I Theatre	3440 Foothill Blvd.	Oakland 94601	R. Dominic	1	
Ojai Playhouse	145 East Ojai Avenue	Ojai 93023	K. Al Awar	1	
Seavue Twin Cinemas Theatre	520 Palmetto	Pacifica 94044	B. Rau	2	
Aquarius 1 & 2 Theatres	430 Emerson	Palo Alto 94030	B. Myron	2	
Varsity Theatre	456 University Ave.	Palo Alto 94301	Lutz & Corbin	1	
Pine Ridge Theatre	5990 Foster Road	Paradise 95969	Harrison	1	
Academy 6	1003 E. Colorado Blvd.	Pasadena 91106		6	
Cinema 21 Theatre	845 E. Washington Blvd.	Pasadena 91104	H. Berk	1	500
Perris Theatre	279 South D Street	Perris 92370	City of Perris	1	
Phoenix Theatre	205 Washington Street	Petaluma 94952	K. Frankel	1	
Washington Sq. Cinemas I & II	219 S. McDowell Blvd.	Petaluma 94952	Lazzarini & Foster	4	
Arena Theatre	214 Main Point	Arena 95468	R. Earlygrow	1	
•Porterville Drive-in	P.O. Box 990	Porterville 93257	Vermay Corp	2	550
Porter 3 Theatres	36 E. Mill Avenue	Porterville 93258	W. Ward	3	
Poway Theatre	12845 Poway Rd. Ste. 204	Poway 92064	P. Upham	1	300
Town Hall Theatre	469 Main Street	Quincy 95971	Plumas City Arts Comm.	1	
Ramona Twin Cinemas	626 Main Street	Ramona 92065	Cook/Long	2	360
•Redding Drive-in	897 North Market St.	Redding 96049	R. Golding	1	600
Tarantino's Theatres, Inc.	355 Palomar Dr.	Redwood City 94062	J. Tarantino	1	
Harding Plaza Cinema	212 Harding Blvd.	Roseville 95678	Korte/Bentz	1	241
Colonial Theatre	3522 Stockton Blvd.	Sacramento 95820	Bengelachal	1	
Crest Theatre	1013 K Street	Sacramento 95814	L. Garcia	1	975
•Skyview Drive-in	N. Sandburn	Salinas 93902	N. Martins	1	
Family Twin	2373 N. Sterling Ave.	San Bernardino 92404	F. Carvajal	2	

618

Name	Address	City & Zip	Owner	Screens	Seats
Century Twin Cinemas	4370 54th Street	San Diego 92115	P. Upham	2	
Oakwood Apts. Theatre	3883 Ingraham St.	San Diego 92109	R & B Mgmt.	1	
Canyon Theatre	165 San Dimas Canyon	San Dimas 91773	G. Harvey	1	
Gateway Theatre	215 Jackson Street	San Francisco 94111	Tillamany	1	
New Strand Theatre	1127 Market Street	San Francisco 94103	C. Marishita	1	
Red Vic Movie House	1659 Haight Street	San Francisco 94117	Victorian Movie House Col	1	
Roxie Theatre	3110 16th Street	San Francisco 94103	W. Banning	1	
St. Francis 1 & 2 Theatres	965 Market Street	San Francisco 94103	H. Ho	2	
York Theatre	2789 24th Street	San Francisco 94110	Aphrodite, Inc.	1	900
Kuo Hwa Theatre	330 W. Las Tunas	San Gabriel 91776	Chou	1	
Almaden Twin Theatre	5655 Gallup Dr.	San Jose 95118	J. Gunsky	2	
Burbank Theatre	552 S. Bascom Avenue	San Jose 95128	A. Shushtak	1	
Camera 3 Theatre	288 S. Second Street	San Jose 95113	Camera One Media Corp.	1	
Camera One Theatre		San Jose 95113	Camera One Media Corp.	1	
Campbell Plaza Theatre	P.O. Box 6395	San Jose 95150	J. Gunsky	6	1989
•Capitol Drive-In	3630 Hillcap Ave.	San Jose 95136		1	
Cine Mexico Theatre	1191 E. Santa Clara St.	San Jose 95116	J. Borges	1	700
Studio Theatre	396 S. First Street	San Jose 95113	Frangel Entps. Inc.	1	
Towne 3 Theatre	1433 The Alameda	San Jose 95126		3	
Palm Theatre	817 Palm Street	San Luis Obispo 93401	J. Dee	2	
Rainbow Theatre	967 Osos Street	San Luis Obispo 93401	J. Dee	1	
•Sunset Drive-in	255 Elks Lane	San Luis Obispo 93401	L. Rodkey	1	400
Victoria Street Theatre	33 W. Victoria Street	Santa Barbara 93101	Lmtd. Partnership	1	
•Skyview Drive-in 1-2	2260 Soquel Drive	Santa Cruz 95062	N. Martins	2	1062
Aero Theatre	1328 Montana Avenue	Santa Monica 90403	S. Allen	1	650
•Santee Drive-in	10990 Woodside Avenue	Santee 92071	J. Poynter	1	
Scotts Valley 1 & 2 Theatres	222 Mt. Hermon Road	Scotts Valley 95060	G. Culver	2	
Bay Theatre	340 Main Street	Seal Beach 90740	Loderhouse Enterprises	1	
Los Pinos Theatre	9325 Longbeach Blvd.	Southgate 90280		1	
New Allen Theatre	3809 Tweedy Blvd.	Southgate 90280	Vega/Varela	1	
Stanton Theatre	11300 Beach Blvd.	Stanton 90680	R. Anthony	1	845
Sierra Theatre	P.O. Box 31	Susanville 96130	C. Smith	2	
Melody 1 & 2 Theatre	1792 Moorpark Road	Thousand Oaks 91360	Chealin, Inc.	2	
American Legion Theatre	P.O. Box 157	Twain Harte 95383	Legion Post	1	
•Smith Ranch Drive-in	4584 Adobe Rd.	Twentynine Palms 92277	A. Clemons	1	
Ventura Theatre	26 S. Chestnut Street	Ventura 93002	A. Elardo	1	
Fox Theatre	304 Main Street	Watsonville 95076	H. Garcia	1	
Galaxy 3	475 Union St.	Watsonville 95076	Silver Screen Amuse.	3	600
Whittier Village 3	7038 Greenleaf Ave.	Whittier 90602		3	
Noyo Twin Cinema	57 W. Commercial St.	Willits 95490	Cinema Centre Films	1	

COLORADO

Name	Address	City & Zip	Owner	Screens	Seats
Grove Theatre	Box 1327	Alamosa 81101	Murphy	1	
Rialto Theatre	Box 1327	Alamosa 81101	Murphy	1	387
Isis Theatre	Box 180	Aspen 81612	D. Linza	1	
Playhouse Theatre	P.O. Box 1884	Aspen 81612	D. Swales	1	
Sands Theatre	211 Clayton	Brush 80723	J. Machetta	1	
Pearl Theatre		Buena Vista 81211	J. Groy	1	
Crystal Theatre	427 Main Street	Carbondale 81623	R. Ezra	1	
Wells Theatre	170 S. 1st Cheyenne	Wells 80810	K. Thyne	1	
Fine Arts Center Theatre	30 W. Dale Street	Colorado Springs 80903	Co. Spgs. Fine Arts Ctr.	1	
Princess Theatre	218 Elk Avenue	Crested Butte 81224	S. Glazer	1	
•Big Sky Drive-in		Delta 81416	S. Dewsnup	1	
Aztlan Theatre	974 Santa Fe Dr.	Denver 80404	T. Correa	1	
Lake Twin Cinema	154 Dillon Mall	Dillon 80435	D. Virgak	2	
•Rocket Drive-in	P.O. Box 3181	Durango 81301	Scales Family	1	300
Plains Theatre	P.O. Box 755	Eads 81036	J. Gardner	1	321
Stanley Village Cinemas	543 Big Thompson Hwy	Estes Park 80517	R. Pratt	3	
Flager Cinema	Box 2	Flager 80815	J. Witt	1	
Rialto Theatre	337 Denver	St. Florence 81226	T. Martinez	1	
•Holiday Twin Drive-In	2206 South Overland Tr.	Fort Collins 80521	W. Webb	2	
Cover Theater	314 Main Fort	Morgan 80701	M. Boehm	2	
•Valley Drive-in		Fort Morgan 80701	M. Boehm	1	300
•Holiday Twin Drive-in 1-2	P.O. Box 1822	Ft Collins 80522	W. Webb	2	
The Springs Theatre	915 Grand Avenue	Glenwood Springs 81601	J. Buxman	1	
Cinema 25	1204 North 25th Street	Grand Junction 81501	J. Houle	1	
Flicka 1 & 2 Theatres	Box 276	Gunnison 81230	L. Steele	2	
Chaka Theatre	Box 328	Julesburg 80737	De Castro	1	
Moutaineer Movie Theatre	P.O. Box 280	Lake City 81235	P. Virden	1	120
Lincoln Theatre	245 E. Ave.	Limon 80828	M. Steele	1	
Southglenn Cinemas 7	6840 South Race Street	Littelton 80122	R. Miller	7	
Capitol Theatre	Main Street	Manassa 81141	M. Peterson	1	
Center Cinema	121 Davis St.	Monte Vista 81144	E. Bohn	1	
•Star Drive-in	2830 West U.S. 160	Monte Vista 81144	G. Kelloff	1	150
Vali Theatre	2839 West U.S. 160	Monte Vista 81144	G. Kelloff	1	
•Star Drive-in	P.O. Box 86	Montrose 81401	G. De Vries	1	
Liberty Theatre	418 Main St.	Pagosa Springs 81147	D. Wood	1	
Bear Theatre	Box 15	Paonia 81428	C. Bear	1	
Campus Theatre	402 Prospect	Rangely 81648	J. Sell	1	
Rifle Creek Theatre	132 E. 4th	Rifle Creek 81650	Pratt	1	
Carlos Beaubien Theatre	401 Church Pl.	San Luis 81152	C. Attencio	1	118
Capitol Theatre	P.O. Box 34	Springfield 81073	R. Ruby	1	310
•Kar Vu Drive-in	Hwy 287	Springfield 81073	R. Ross	1	165
•Starlight Twin Drive-in	P.O. Box 369	Sterling 80751	Wolfenbarge	2	
Moon Theatre	P.O. Box 6	Stratton 80836	M. Koons	1	206
Fox Theatre	423 W. Main, Box 788	Trinidad 81082	J. Sawaya	1	
Fox Theatre	715 Main St.	Walsenburg 81089	S. Sawaya	1	
Gold Hill Twin Cinemas	P.O. Box 5050	Woodland Park 80866	S. Pratt	2	
Cliff Theatre	420 Main St.	Wray 80758	Palmrose	1	
Yuma Theatre	311 S. Albany St.	Yuma 80759	H. Long	1	

Name	Address	City & Zip	Owner	Screens	Seats
		CONNECTICUT			
Avon Park 1 & 2 Theatres	22 Waterville Rd.	Avon 06001	Keppner	2	
Avon Twin Theatre	Box 416	Avon 06001	S. Stieber	2	
Downtown Studio Cinema	275 Fairfield Ave.	Bridgeport 06603	G. Christ	1	
Cinestudio Theatre	300 Summit St.	Hartford 06106	Film Society	1	489
State Twin Theatre	100 Main St.	Jewett City 06351	L. McComber	2	480
Hansfiod Drive in Theatre	228 Stafford Road	Mansfield Center 06250		1	
Capitol Theatre	350 Main St.	Middleton 06457	N. Saraceno	1	
Capitol Theatre	26 Daniel St.	Milford 06460	M. Arjo	1	
Milford Pub & Cinema	201 Cherry St.	Milford 06460		2	
Cine 1-4	Middletown Ave.	New Haven 06513		4	
Bank Street Theatre	48 Bank St.	New Milford 06776	Bank St. Entrps.	2	
Newington Theatre	40 Cedar St.	Newington 06111	C. Tolis	1	
Edmond Town Hall Theatre	45 Main St.	Newton 06470	Town of Newton	1	
•Pleasant Valley Drive-In	P.O. Box 45 Rte. 181	Pleasant Valley 06063	B. Miller	1	250
Sono Cinema	15 Washington St.	South Norwalk 06854	J. Bedusa	1	300
Village Cinema Theatre	118 Suffield Village	Suffield 06078	J. Coatti	1	
Holiday Cinemas 6-Plex	McDermott Ave.	Torrington 06790	R. Laflamme	6	
Elm 1 & 2	924 South Quaker Lane	West Hartford 06110	CT Theatre Circuit	2	945
Forest Theatre 2	Forest Rd.	West Haven 06516	Terrazzano	1	
Strand Theatre	364 Main St.	Winsted 06098	J. Cremin	1	
		DISTRICT OF COLUMBIA			
AFI Theatre Kennedy Center		Washington 20566	American Film Institute	1	
Biograph Theatre	2819 M Street NW	Washington 20007	Rubin/Poryles	1	270
Key Theatre	1222 Wisconsin Ave. NW	Washington 20007	S. Levy	4	
		DELAWARE			
Midway Palace	29 Midway S/C/Rte. 1	Rehobuth Beach 19971	R. Derrickson	8	
		FLORIDA			
Chief Theatre	Box 644	Chiefland 32626	G. Parker	1	
Vance Theatre	Box 568	Chipley 32428	R. Sapp	1	
Clewiston Theatre	3030 W. Sugarland Hwy	Clewiston 33440		1	
Pines Theatre and Pub	1314 Dixon Blvd.	Cocoa Beach 32922		1	
El Teatro Carrusel	235 Alcazar Ave.	Coral Gables 33134	N. Chediak	1	
Crestiview Triplex Theatre	P.O. Box 55	Crestview 32536	E. Neutzling	3	
Fox Theatre	P.O. Box 428	Crestview 32536	N. Robinson	1	
Arcade Twin Theatre	2269 First St.	Fort Myers 33901	O. Rusnell	2	
•Thunderbird Twin Drive-in	3121 West Sunrise Blvd	Ft Lauderdale 33311	P. Henn	6	
Gateway Cinema IV	1820 E. Sunrise Blvd.	Ft. Lauderdale 33304	S. Dreier	4	
Mercede Cinema 4 Theatres	1870 N. University Dr.	Ft. Lauderdale 33322	S. Dreier	4	
Cinema & Drafthouse	3210 S.W. 35th Blvd.	Gainesville 32608	Gainesville Entertainment	1	
Hollywood Cinema Theatre	1710 Harrison St.	Hollywood 33020	A. Weinstock	1	
Pembroke Pines Cinema 1-2	1788 N. University Dr.	Hollywood 33024	J. Cassuto	2	
Arcade Theatre	P.O. Box S	Immokalen 33934	L. Sapp	1	
Five Points Theatre	1028 Park St.	Jacksonville 32204	M. Skinner	1	
Murray Hill Theatre	932 S. Edgewood Ave.	Jacksonville 32205	E. Robinson	1	
San Marco Theatre	1196 San Marco Blvd.	Jacksonville 32207	S. Ventura	1	
Midget Theatre	Box 1297	Jasper 32052	J. Jones	1	
Inverary 3 Theatres	5570 W. Oakland Park Blvd	Lauderhill 33313	M. Wurtzburg	3	
Enzian Theatre	1300 S. Orlando Ave.	Maitland 32751	C. Tiedtke	1	
Marti Triplex Theatres	420 S.W. 8th Ave.	Miami 33130	E. Capote	3	
Lincoln Theatre	555 Lincoln Rd.	Miami Beach 33139	M. Ovedia	1	
Smyrna Theatre	Box 428 New	Smyrna Beach 32069	S. Peterson	1	
Palm Plaza Twin Cinema	1147 E. John Sims Pkwy.	Niceville 32578		2	
Southland Cinema Theatre	12615 W. Dixie Hwy.	North Miami 33161	D. Amikam	1	
•Ocala Drive-in	4850 South Pine Avenue	Ocala 34480	Williams & Tomlinson	1	300
Brahman Theatre	1500 S. Parrott Ave.	Okeechobee 33472	R. Hales	1	
O. Henry's Drafthouse	200 Harrison Ave.	Panama City 32401	H. Pflegl	1	
Cinema Tavern Theatre	3940 Durango Dr.	Pensacola 32504	R. Estrada	1	
Perry Twin Cinemas	P.O. Box 838	Perry 32347	R. Long	3	
Margate Twin Cinemas	199 S. State Rd., # 7	Pompano Beach 33068	J. Wright	2	
Sarasota Film Society	P.O. Box 6130	Sarasota 34236	S. Morris	3	500
•301 Drive-in	U.S. 301	Starke 32091	V. Spaeks	1	
Florida Theatre	101 W. Call Street	Starke 32091	V. Sparks	1	
Great American Cin. Pub.	4421 N. Hubert	Tampa 33614	J. Paleveda	1	
Tampa Pitcher Show	14416 N. Dale Mabry	Tampa 33618	Tampa Pitcher Show	1	
Miracle City Cinemas	2500 S. Washington	Titusville 32780	Royal Cinemas	2	
Aloma Cinema & Draft House	2155 Aloma Avenue	Winter Park 32792	K. Stuarts	1	
		GEORGIA			
Abrams Alps Cinema	Alps Shopping Ctr.	Athens 30604	Alps Cinema Inc.	1	300
Georgia Theatre II	Beechwood Shop Center	Athens 30604	B. Stembeck	8	
Buford Highway Twin	5805 Buford Highway	Atlanta		2	
Cinema & Grill	7270 Roswell Rd.	Atlanta 30350	Cinema & Drafthouse Inc.	2	450
Fox Theatre	660 Peachtree Street	Atlanta 30305	Atlanta Landmarks	1	
Greenbriar Theatre	Greenbriar Mall	Atlanta 30331		3	
Lefont Garden Hills Cinema	2835 Peachtree Rd.	Atlanta 30305		1	
Plaza Theatre	1049 Ponce de Leon Ave.	Atlanta 30306	Lefont	3	
Blue Ridge Twin Cinema	P.O. Box 1022	Blue Ridge 30513	R. McNelley	2	400
•Swan Drive-in	P.O. Box 275	Blue Ridge 30513	J. Jones	1	
Bone Theatre	Box 607	Butler 31006	L. Bone	1	
Zebulon Theatre	207 N. Broad Street	Cairo 31728	D. Bearden	1	450

Name	Address	City & Zip	Owner	Screens	Seats
•Commerce Drive-in	Route #2 Box 52	Commerce 30529	N. Smith	1	
East Towne Twin Cinema		East Ellijay 30539	R. McNelley	2	400
Town Square Cinema	123 S. Jefferson	Eatonton 31024	D. Bridges	1	
Fayette Place Cinema	Highway 85	Fayetteville 30214		3	
Parkwood Cinema Triple	P.O. Box 591	Griffin 30223	J.A. Theatres	3	
Thompson Theatre	237 Commerce Street	Hawkinsville 31036	S. Lester	1	
The Theatre	206 Century Center	Hazlehurst 31539	W. Thompson	1	
Hillcrest Twin Cinema	1314 Brookwood Avenue	Jackson 30233	D. Ralph	2	
Maddox Theatre	226 S. Main Street	Jasper 30143	M. Maddox	1	
Main Street Theatre	P.O. Box 495	Jasper 30143	S. Middendorf	1	
Strand Cinema Twin Theatres	169 W. Cherry Street	Jesup 31545	B. Sowell	2	
Franklin Plaza Cinema	1033 Franklin Rd.	Marietta 30067		3	
Town & Country Theatre	1387 Rosewell Rd.	Marietta 30062		3	
Hargrove Theatre	Broad Street	Sparta 31087		1	
Civic Cinema	Box 407	Swainsboro 30401	B. Sowell	1	
Ritz Theatre	112 S. Church Street	Thomastown 30286	Odom/Brown	1	
Cinema Twin 1-2 Theatres	104 Cobb Street	Thomson 30824	P. Farr	2	
Knox Theatre	311 Norwood	Warrenton 30828	J. Jackson	1	

HAWAII

Name	Address	City & Zip	Owner	Screens	Seats
World Square Theatre	Box 709	Kealakekua 96750	A. Grodzinsky	1	

IDAHO

Name	Address	City & Zip	Owner	Screens	Seats
Walker Theatre	214 Grand Avenue	Arco 83213	H. Walker	1	
Flicks Twin	646 Fulton St.	Boise 83702	C. Skinner	2	291
Rex Theatre	Rt. 4, Box 626	Bonners Ferry 83805	L. Mace	1	
Linden 3 Theatres	P.O. Box 1223	Caldwell 83605	Cornwell	3	
Cascade Theatre	Star Route	Cascade 83611	D. Gleason	1	
•Coeur D Alene Drive-in	No. 3555 Government Way	Coeur D'Alene 83814	T. Moyer	1	
•Spud Drive-in	P.O. Box 158	Driggs 83422	R. Wood	1	150
Gooding Theatre	841 Main St.	Gooding 83330	B. Ward	1	400
Rex Theatre	2122 E. 1750 S	Gooding 83330	T. Dye	1	
Grace Theatre	Box 307	Grace 83241	C. Simmons	1	
Blue Fox Theatre	Box 307	Grangeville 83530	A. Wagner	1	
•Sky Vu Drive-in	435 Fanning Avenue	Idaho Falls 83401	K. Ellis	1	
Magic Lantern Cinema	Box 238	Ketchum 83340	R. Kessler	1	
The Valley Theatre	54 N. Main St.	Malad 83252	M. Evans	1	
Micro Moviehouse	230 W. Third St.	Moscow 83843	Suto/Ball	1	
Oakley Playhouse	North Blaine St.	Oakley 83346	K. Severe	1	
•Parma Motor-Vu	P.O. Box 338	Parma 83660	Cornwell	1	
Pond Student Union Theatre	Idaho State University	Pocatello 83209	D. DeTienne	1	425
Starlite Cinema 1-2-3 Theatres	P.O. Box 5430	Pocatello 83201	Essaness Theatres	3	
•Sunset Drive-in	P.O. Box 5397	Pocatello 83201	R. Morris	1	
Virginia Family Theatre	752 E. 1200 N.	Shelley 83274	D. Browning	1	
Idanha Theatre	75 S. Main St.	Soda Springs 83201	J. Bowen	2	

ILLINOIS

Name	Address	City & Zip	Owner	Screens	Seats
Aledo Opera House Theatre	108 S.E. Second Avenue	Aledo 61231	R. Maynard	1	500
Rodgers Theatre	119 W. Vienna	Anna 62906	M. McSparin	1	325
R Theatre Box 3		Auburn 62615	R. Mitchell	1	
•Hi-Lite 30 Drive-In	9 S. 307 Hill Ave.	Aurora 60504	Parkside Inc.	1	700
Hi-Lite 30 Indoor Theatre	9 S. 307 Hill Ave.	Aurora 60504	Parkside, Inc.	1	900
Paramount Arts Centre	23 E. Galena Blvd.	Aurora 60506	Aurora Civic Center	1	
1888 Catlow Theatre	116 W. Main Street	Barrington 60010	E. Skehan	1	
Lincoln Theatre	103 E. Main Street	Belleville 62220	R. Wright	3	
•Avon Drive-in	Route 50	Breese 62230	Gramann	1	
Pickwick Buffalo Grove	1000 Lake Cook Rd.	Buffalo Grove 60089	D. Vlahakis	4	1225
Marvel Cinema	228 W. Main Street	Carlinville 62626	N. Paul	2	
•French Village Drive In Theatre	8601 St. Claire Ave.	Caseyville 62220	R. Wright	1	
400 Theatre	6746 N. Sheridan Rd.	Chicago 60626	Entertainment Group	2	
Adelphi Theatre	7074 N. Clark Street	Chicago 60626	Donnelly Theatre Corp.	1	850
Davis Theatre	4614 N. Lincoln Avenue	Chicago 60625	F & F Mgt.	4	
Hub Theatre	1746 W. Chicago Avenue	Chicago 60622	R. Rabiela	1	
Patio Theatre	6008 Irving Park Blvd.	Chicago 60634	A. Kouvalis	1	
Village Theatre	1548 N. Clark Street	Chicago 60610	Taylor	4	650
Nortown Theatre	1107 Halsted St.	Chicago Heights 60411	F. Mikos	1	
Western Heights Cinema I-VIII	1301 Hilltop	Chicago Heights 60411	M. Crescenzo	8	
Olympic Theatre	6131 W. Cermak Road	Cicero 60650	G. Nikolopas	2	
Grand Theatre	220 E. Main Street	Duquoin 62832	B. Ivy	1	
Palace Theatre	122 W. Main, Box 753	Elmwood 61529	V. Reynolds	1	
Town Theatre	120 E. North	Flora 62839	J. Philips	1	
Geneva Theatre	319 W. State Street	Geneva 60134	T. Burnidge	2	780
•Harvest Moon Drive-in	Rte 475	Gibson City 60936	Cliffordorr	1	
Canna Theatre	110 E. Chestnut	Gillespie 62033	L. Pianfetti	1	268
Glenwood Theatre	183 Rd. & Halsted Sts.	Glenwood 60425	Barcikowski & Schlaffer	1	
•Grayslake Outdoor	Route 120 Box 247	Grays Lake 60030	H. Ryan	1	
Hinsdale Theatre	20 E. First St.	Hinsdale 60521		1	
Lorraine Theatre	324-326 Main Street	Hoopeston 60942	A. Nelson	1	
•Skyway Drive-in	504 North 9th Avenue	Hoopeston 60942	R. & B. Sanders	1	
La Grange Theatre	84 S. La Grange Rd.	La Grange 60525	Bischof	3	
Illinois Vall. Cinema 1 & 2	700 First Street	La Salle 61301	J. Hurley	2	
Morton Grove Theatre	7300 Dempster Ave.	Morton Grove 60053	F & F Mgt.	4	
Mundelein Cinema	155 N. Seymour	Mundelein 60060	L. Marubio	1	
State Theatre	153 W. Elm Street	Nashville 62263	Nashville Theatre Corp.	1	360
•Fairview Drive-in	Route #5	Newton 62448	D. Boldrey	1	
Roseland Theatre	Box 526	Pana 62557	R. Tanner	1	
Pickwick Theatre	5 S. Prospect Avenue	Park Ridge 60068	D. Vlahakis	4	2114

Name	Address	City & Zip	Owner	Screens	Seats
Zoe Cinema	209 N. Madison St.	Pittsfield 62363	T. Gates	1	
Second Reel Cinema	Box 5285 Clock Tower Inn	Rockford 61125	J. Kitterman	1	
Schuyville Theatre	116 E. Lafayette	Rushville 62681	Grate Enterprises	1	
Salem Theatre	Box 487	Salem 62881	L. Cluster	1	
Springfield Theatre Center	101 E. Lawrence Ave.	Springfield 62704	L. Troesch	1	
Sycamore Theatre	420 W. State St.	Sycamore 60178	T. Burnidge	3	800
Liberty Theatre	Box 172	Vandalia 62471	B. Tanner	1	
Gem Theatre	17 N. Main Street	Villa Grove 61956	K. Kleinschmidt	1	286
Valley Forge Cinema	Valley Forge S/C	Washington 61571	V. Reynolds	1	
Bon-Air Theatre	213 W. Walnut	Watseka 60970	F. Mathewson	1	300
Watseka Theatre	218 E. Walnut	Watseka 60970	R. Merrill	1	
Academy Theatre	202 N. Genesse	Waukegan 60085	G. Kallianis	1	
Wheaton Theatre	123 N. Hale	Wheaton 60187	T. Loftus	4	720
Mar Theatre	121 S. Main Street	Wilmington 60481	C. Smith	1	
Winnetka Community House	620 Lincoln Avenue	Winnetka 60093	WCH, Inc.	1	
Countryside Cinema 1 & 2	550 Countryside Drive	Yorkville 60560	National Care, Inc.	2	

INDIANA

Name	Address	City & Zip	Owner	Screens	Seats
Strand Theatre	P.O. Box 39	Angola 46703	D. Thompson	1	
Northway Cinemas 1 & 2	P.O. Box 388	Auburn 46706	D. John	2	
Brookville Theatre & Video	16 W. Fifth	Brookville 47012	D. Derenski	1	
Crown Theatre	19 N. Court Street	Crown Point 46307	J. Paunicka	1	
Concord 2	3701 S. Main St.	Elkhart 46515	Miller Theatres	2	
Embassy Theatre	1107 S. Harrison Street	Fort Wayne 46802	Embassy Theatre Found.	1	2746
•Georgetown Drive-in	8200 State Road 64	Georgetown 47122	B. Powell	1	300
Northgate Cinema	1021 N. State	Greenfield 46140	A. Strahl	1	
•Starlite Drive-in Theatre	P.O. Box 17	Harrodsburg 47434	C. Stewart	1	400
Art Theatre	230 Main St./PO Box 31	Hobart 46342	E. Prusiecki	1	525
•Twin Aire Drive-in Eastside	2463 Hoyt Avenue	Indianapolis 46204	W.L.Z. Amuse	2	
Vogue Theatre	6259 N. College Avenue	Indianapolis 46220	S. Ross	1	600
Melody Drive-In Theatre	R.R. 3, Box 7444	Knox 46534	F. Heise	1	
State Theatre 1 & 2	321 E. Market Street	Logansport 46947	W. Ritchie	2	
Palo Theatre	133 Mill Street	Lowell 46356	C. Beier	1	
Marengo Theatre	Bradley Street	Marengo 47140	K.E.P. Development	1	
Cinema 37 Theatres	1910 Morton Avenue	Martinsville 46151	C. Martens	1	352
•Mechanicsburg Drive-in	Route 1	Mechanicsburg 46071	Professional Book Co.	1	250
•Holiday Drive-in	RR 4	Mitchell 47446	Limberry	1	
Orpheum Theatre	714 Main Street	Mitchell 47446	Ferrel/Arnold	1	
•Monticello Drive-in	P.O. Box 251	Monticello 47960	J. Eubanks	1	470
Twin Lakes 1 & 2 Theatre	107 Main St.	Monticello 47960	C. Ryan	2	
Mooresville Cinema	376 S. Indiana Street	Mooresville 46158	J. Perry	1	280
Gayble Theatre	Rt. 3, Box 428 North	Judson 46366	M. Woytinek	1	
Rees Theatre	100 N. Michigan Street	Plymouth 46563	J. Housouer	1	
•Tri Way Drive-in	Old Road 31 North	Plymouth 46563	J. Housouer	1	
Times Cinema 1 & 2 Theatre	618 Main Street	Rochester 46975	K. Hoff	2	234
•Holiday Drive-In	Jct 231 & 66	Rockport 47635	D. Mosely	4	900
•Salem Drive-In	107 Macon Ave.	Salem 47617	H.&Y. Schwoeble	1	460
Scott Theatre	RR #3	Scottsburg 47170	P. West	1	
Jackson Park Cinemas	P.O. Box 762	Seymor 47274	Bowman & Cartmel	2	443
Tivoli Theatre	26 N. Washington St	Spencer 47460	WR Theatres	1	300
Pickwick Theatre	108 W. Main Street	Syracuse 46567	D. Wright	1	
Diana Theatre	137 E. Jefferson	Tipton 46072	J. Paikos	1	404
•Forty-Niner Drive-In Theatre	North State Road 49	Valparaiso 46383	B. Shinabarger	1	428
Lake 1 & 2 Theatres	P.O. Box 976	Warsaw 46580	Lake Theatre	2	
•Lincoln Dale Drive-in	221 North Columbia St.	Warsaw 46580	R. Patterson	2	800
•Warsaw Drive-in	2180 E. Old Rd. #30	Warsaw 46580	Lake Theas.	1	
Isis Theatre	Box 362	Winamac 46996	W. Doty	1	

IOWA

Name	Address	City & Zip	Owner	Screens	Seats
W. Barbary Coast Opera House	115 Benton Ave., E	Albia 52531	D. Walker	1	500
Algona Theatre	216 E. State	Algona 50511	P. Frederick	1	
King Theatre	720 12th Street	Belle Plaine 52208	J. Mansfield	1	
Iowa Theatre	107 S. Washington	Bloomfield 52537	Davis County Council	1	300
American Theatre	1101 Nodaway St.	Corning 50841	C. Ambrose	1	
Wayne Theatre	P.O. Box 32	Corydon 50060	M. Nessen	1	
Cresco Theatre	115 Second Ave., W.	Cresco 52136	G. Compston	1	
Varsity Theatre	1207 25th Street	Des Moines 50311	B. Mahon	1	472
Opera Theatre	716 Sixth Avenue	Dewitt 52742	D. Prichard	1	238
Cinema Center	8 P.O. Box 3127	Dubuque 52004	N. Yiannis	8	
Circle Theatre	108 Main Street	Elkader 52043	D. Wellendorf	1	
Grand Theatre	1031 Central Ave.	Estherville 51334	L. Kozak	2	
Harlan Theatre	621 Court Street	Harlan 51537	A. Woodraska	1	
Met Theatre	515 Washington Street	Iowa Falls 50126	J. March	1	
Village 1 & 2	212 E. Robinson	Knoxville 50138	C. Schwanebeck	2	365
Mills Entertainment	216 W. Main Street	Lake Mills 50450	A. Skellenger	1	251
Royal Twin Theatres	P.O. Box 1028	Le Mars 51031	T. March	2	
Idle Hour Theatre	208 N. Main	Leon 50144	W. Lindsey	1	
•61 Drive-in	P.O. Box 857	Maquokata 52060	D. Voy	1	180
Voy 3-Plex Theatres	207 S. Main	Maquoketa 52060	D. Voy	3	
Pioneer Theatre	P.O. Box 555	Milford 51351	Crystal Theatres Ltd.	1	
Princess Theatre	101 W. Monroe	Mt. Ayr 50854	T. Greene	1	
Odeum Theatre	P.O. Box 206	Mt. Vernon 52314	L. Hylbak	1	
•Valle Drive-In	P.O. Box 1243	Newton 50208	Perry Th. Co.	1	
Iowa Theatre	Box 245	Onawa 51040	F. Rash	1	
Lyric Theatre	118 S. Fillmore Street	Osceola 50213	R. Clark	1	
Wonderland Theatre	110 S. Main	Paullina 51046	Coppaullina	1	
Holland Theatre	P.O. Box 294	Pella 50219	Pella Theatre Corp.	1	
Rapids Theatre	RFD #2	Rock Rapids 51246	R. Kahl	1	
Iowa Theatre	923 Third Avenue	Sheldon 51201	D. Dummett	1	206

Name	Address	City & Zip	Owner	Screens	Seats
Max Theatre	338 Ninth Street	Sibley 51249	L. Pedley	1	
Story Theatre/Grand Opera House	512 Broad Street	Story City 50248	T. Thorson	1	388
Hardacre Theatre	Box 271	Tipton 52772	S. Clark	1	375
Traer Chamber Theatre	516 Second Avenue	Traer 50675	Chamber of Commerce	1	180
Rialto Theatre	P.O. Box 82	Villisca 50864	M. Lapley	1	
Strand Theatre	111 E. Third Street	West Liberty 52776	D. Horton	1	

KANSAS

Name	Address	City & Zip	Owner	Screens	Seats
Plaza Theatre	408 N.W. Second	Abilene 67410	C. Strowig	1	
Anthony Theatre	P.O. Box 251	Anthony 67003	B. Ash	1	
Royal Movie Theatre Inc.	612 Commercial Street	Atchison 66002	K. Nagel	2	230
Jayhawk Theatre	420 Main Street	Atwood 67730	City of Atwood	1	
Augusta Theatre	Box 608	Augusta 67010	Augusta Arts Council	1	657
Mainstreet Theatre	117 West Main	Beloit 67420	J. Weide	1	
Midland Theatre	212 W. 8th Street	Coffeyville 67337	P. Richardson	1	
Colby Theatres	355 N. Franklin Ave.	Colby 67701	D. Phillips	2	
Apollo Theatre 1 & 2	229 W. Sixth St.	Concordia 66901	R. Smith	2	
Derby Cinema	824 Nelson Drive	Derby 67037	R. Jones	1	
•Star Vu Drive-in		El Dorado 67042	S. Fowler	1	300
Fox Twin Cinema	113 S. Main	Ft. Scott 66701	J. Novak	2	350
Twilight Theatre	134 S. Main	Greensburg 67054	C. Spainhour	1	
Arrow Twin Theatres	729 Oregon	Hiawatha 66434	C. Holthaus	2	
Midway Theatre	217 A N. Pomeroy	Hill City 67642	S. Schulz	1	
•Boulevard Drive-in	1051 Merriam Lane	Kansas City 66103	Potter & Lux	1	
Eagle Theatre	237 N. Main	Kingman 67068	S. Meade	1	
Palace Theatre	P.O. Box 304	Kinsley 67547	Palace Theatre Inc.	1	
Liberty Hall	642 Massachusetts St.	Lawrence 66044	C. Oldfather	1	
Roach Theatre	104 W. Lincoln	Lincoln 67455	V. Finch	1	
Jarvis Theatre	P.O. Box 401	Ness City 67560	D. Jarvis	1	
•Star Drive-in	608 East Cedar	Ness City 67560	Rupp J&L	1	
Sunflower Theatre	P.O. Box 6	Oberlin 67749	J. Sullivan	1	
Majestic Theatre	724 4th St.	Phillipsburg 67661	D. Shelton	1	
Scott City Uptown Theatre	420 Main	Scott City 67871	D. Kite	1	
Strand Theatre	Box 1	Sharon Springs 67758	R. Koons	1	
Fine Arts Theatre	5909 Johnson Dr.	Shawnee Mission 66202	B. Mossman	1	
Center Theatre	217 S. Main St.	Smith Center 66967	C.T. Inc.	1	209
Ritz Theatre	112 Broadway	Stafford 67578	F. Smiley	1	
Uptown Theatre	501 Cottonwood	Strong City 66869	D. Doolittle	1	
The Movies	200 N. Main	Ulysses 67880	R. Dudley	1	
Regent Theatre	114 W. Lincoln	Wellington 67152	K. Brown	1	
Circle Cine Theatre	2570 S. Seneca	Wichita 67217	B. Clark	1	
•Landmark Twin In Drive-in	3900 South Hydraulic	Wichita 67202	Landmark	2	1300

KENTUCKY

Name	Address	City & Zip	Owner	Screens	Seats
•Tri-City Drive-in		Beaver Dam 42320	D. Moseley	1	
Corbin Cinemas 1-4	P.O. Box 172	Corbin 40701	Carnahan-Hu	1	
Drift Theatre	P.O. Box 74	Drift 41619	S. Hall	1	
Pastime Theatre	Shelby St.	Falmouth 41040	M. Goldberg	1	
Cinema 1-3 Theatres	P.O. Box 445	Glasgow 42141	W. Aspley	3	
The Movies Theatre	Box 540	Hagerhill 41222	H. Short	1	
Old Orchard Cinemas	1800 Cinema Dr.	Henderson 42420	J. Scott	4	
Alice Theatre	Route 4, Box 612	Leitchfield 42754	R. McCoy	1	
Floyd Theatre	2011 S. Brook St.	Louisville 40208	H. Adams	1	
Green Grass Theatre		Louisville	B. Powell	1	
•Cardinal Drive-in	P.O. Box 473	Mayfield 42066	D. Jones	1	
Mayfield Twin Cinema	P.O. Box 473	Mayfield 42066	D. Jones	2	
•Judy Drive-in	606 Brookmead	Mount Sterling 40353	J. Baker	1	300
Cheri III Theatre	1008 Cestnut	Murray 42071	Murray Theatres	3	
Cine Central	641 N. Central Center	Murray 42071	Murray Theatres	2	
•Bourbon Drive-in	P.O. Box 409	Paris 40361	E. Earlywine	1	
Family Theatre	113 Mutayone Ave.	Providence 42450	C. Puckett	2	
•Buccaneer Drive-in		Richmond 40475	H. Roaden	1	
Towne Cinema	Main St.	West Liberty 41472	L. Franklin	1	200
•New Dixie Drive-In	P.O. Box 179	Williamsburg 40769	Byrd	1	225

LOUISIANA

Name	Address	City & Zip	Owner	Screens	Seats
Broadmoor Theatre	9810 Florida Blvd.	Baton Rouge 70815	J. Ogden	4	1000
Chalmette Cine 1-2-3-4-5-6	8700 W. Judge Perez	Chalmette 70043	J. Costello	6	
Twin Cinema #1 Theatre	P.O. Box 898	Covington 70433	P. Salles	1	
Jet Cinema	P.O. Box 2080	Galliano 70345	Jet Cinema, Inc.	2	
Pringle Theatre	1214 Seventh Avenue	Glemora 71433	W. Pringle	1	
Coles Cinema	P.O. Box 232	Kentwood 70444	R. Coleman	1	
Mansfield Theatre	Box 820	Mansfield 71052	M. Adkison	1	
Many Twin Cinema	P.O. Box 1568	Many 71449	J. Cole	2	
Parkway Cinema 4	1011 Keyser Avenue	Natchitoches 71457	Don Theatres	4	
Saenger Theatre	143 N. Rampart Street	New Orleans 70112	K. Turner	2	
Fiske Cinema	P.O. Box 684	Oak Grove 71263	J. Laughlin	1	
Village Cinema	P.O. Box 457	Ruston 71270	Don Theatres	2	

MAINE

Name	Address	City & Zip	Owner	Screens	Seats
Criterion Theatre	P.O. Box 242	Bar Harbor 04609	B. Johnson	1	
Towne Green Cinema	P.O. Box 82	Blue Hill 04614	J. Gilmore	1	
Magic Lantern Theatre	PO Box 328	Bridgton 04009	Down East Inc.	2	250
Eveningstar Cinema	149 Maine St.	Brunswick 04011	C. Melick	1	126

623

Name	Address	City & Zip	Owner	Screens	Seats
State Twin Cinema	Main Street	Calais 04619	F.Freda	1	
Caribou Theatre	126 Sweden St.	Caribou 04736	M. Bernard	1	
Lincoln Theatre	Elm Street	Damariscotta 04543	Mid-coast Shop. Ctr.	1	240
Grand Auditorium Hancock County	Main Street	Ellsworth 04605	D. Cadigan	1	
Century Theatre	Hall Street	Fort Kent 04743	Ouellette	1	
Temple Twin Theatre	Market Square	Houlton 04730	J.Lyford	2	
Lincoln Theatre	817 Main Street	Lincoln 04457	P. Quirion	1	
Fox Cinema Theatre	1 Fox Street	Madawaska 04756	R. Pelletiee	1	
Millbridge Theatre	Main Street	Millbridge 04658	R. Parsons	1	
Opera House Theatre	219 Main Street	Norway 04268	J. Beckerley	1	
Temple Theatre	PO Box 296 Temple Ave.	Ocean Park 04063	Ocean Park Assn.	1	500
Leavitt Theatre	P.O. Box 351	Ogunquit 03907	P. Clayton	1	
Ogunquit Square Theatre	P.O. Box 144	Ogunquit 03907	G. Cookson	1	
Pittsfield Community	P.O. Box 579	Pittsfield 04967	Town of Pittsfield	1	279
Movies on Exchange St.	10 Exchange Street	Portland 04101	S. Halpert	1	145
Sanford Twin Cinema	277A Main Street	Sanford 04073	RPW Theatres	2	
Skowhegan Cinema	Box 522	Skowhegan 04976	C. Perry	1	
Stonington Opera House	Russ Hill	Stonington 04681	M. Connors	1	
Waldo Theatre	Main Street, PO Box 662	Waldoboro 04572	Nicolaisen	6	
Railroad Sq. Cinema	Box 945	Walterville 04901	RSC	1	
•Prides Corner Drive-in	651 Bridgton Rd Rt 302	Westbrook 04092	A. Tevanian	1	

MARYLAND

Name	Address	City & Zip	Owner	Screens	Seats
Baltimore Film Forum	10 Art Museum Drive	Baltimore 21218	Baltimore Art Museum	1	
•Bengies Drive-in	3417 Eastern Blvd	Baltimore 21220	Vogel	1	750
Charles Theatre	1711 N. Charles Street	Baltimore 21201	S. Levy	1	
Hillendale Cinemas	1045 Taylor Ave.	Baltimore 21286	T. Kefaber	1	
Lincoln Theatre	2912 Lightfoot Dr.	Baltimore 21209	Flaks	1	
Patterson	3136 Eastern	Baltimore 21224	F. Durkee	2	
Senator Theatre	5904 York Rd.	Baltimore 21212	T. Kefaber	1	
Westview Theatre	6026 Balt. Natl. Pike	Baltimore 21228	G. Brehm	10	
Bethesda Theatre	7719 Wisconsin Avenue	Bethesda 20814	P. Carney	1	400
Chester Theatre	P.O. Box 449	Chestertown 21620	C. Prince	1	
•Bel Air Drive-in	1920 Churchville Rd	Churchville 21028	R. Wagner	1	
Hoff Theatre	Stamp Student Union	College Park 21228	Univ. of Maryland	1	
Druid Theatre	9840 Main Street	Damascus 20872	D. Crate	1	
Avalon Theatre	Dover & Harrison Sts.	Easton 21601	Hanks	1	
Maryland Theatre	21 S. Potomac St.	Hagerstown 21740	M.D. Theatre Assn.	1	
Ye Olde Family Theatre	Leonardtown Square	Leonardstown 20650	Van-Kess	1	
Mid Towns Cinemas	Rt. 135 Mid Towns Plaza	Oakland 21550	L. Holler	2	
Olney 9 Cinemas	18167 Town Center Drive	Olney 20832	Holiday Prods. Inc.	9	
Marva Theatre #2	Market St.	Pocomoke City 21851	J. Clarke	1	
Liberty Cinema	8632 Liberty	Randallstown 21133	T. Herman	1	
Riverdale Cinema	5617 Riverdale Road	Riverdale 20840	P. Sanchez	2	600
American Pike Theatre	12109 Rockville Pike	Rockville 20852	Holiday Prods Inc.	1	
Wheaton Plaza 3 Theatres	Wheaton Plaza Shop. Ctr.	Wheaton 20902	L. Heon	3	

MASSACHUSSETTS

Name	Address	City & Zip	Owner	Screens	Seats
Amherst Theatre	30 Amity Street	Amherst 01002	R. Goldstein	1	
Regent Theatre	7 Medford Street	Arlington 02174	H. Capra	1	
Studio Cinema Theatre	376 Trapelo Road	Belmont 02178	S. Myerson	1	
Cabot Street	Cinmea 286 Cabot Street	Beverly 01915	W. Bull	1	
Larcom Theatre	13 Wallis Street	Beverly 01915	Abracadabra Ltd.	1	
Esquire Theatre	120 Fulton Street	Boston 02109		1	
Museum of Fine Arts	465 Huntington Ave.	Boston 02176		1	
Brockton East Cinemas	758 Crescent St.	Brockton 02402	R. Wedge	6	
Coolidge Corner Moviehouse	290 Harvard Ave.	Brookline 02146	J. Freed	1	
Brattle Theatre	40 Brattle Street	Cambridge 02138	Running Arts, Inc.	1	250
•Chelmsford Drive-in	P.O. Box 147	Chelmsford 01824	Carpenter	1	
Rivoli Theatre	41 Springfield Street	Chicopee 01013	R. Goldstein	1	
Island Theatre	P.O. Box 98	Edgartown 02539	R. Lockwood	1	
Gardner 1 & 2 Theatres	34 Parker Street	Gardner 01440	M. Fideli	2	
•Mohawk Drive-In		Gardner 01440	M. Fedeli	1	
Town Hall Cinema	6 Walker Street	Lenox 01240	N. Thaw	1	
Fine Arts Theatre I, II & III	19-21 Summer Street	Maynard 01754		3	670
Elm Draughthouse Theatre	35 Elm Street	Milbury 01527	R. McCrohon	1	
Gaslight Theatre	North Union Street	Nantucket 02554	R. Mitchell	1	
Zeiterion Theatre	684 Purchase Street	New Bedford 02740	R. Freedman	1	
•Coury's Drive-In	838 Curran Highway	North Adams 01247	Coury	1	
Heritage N. Adams Inn	40 Main St.	North Adams 01247	R. Asper	1	
Pleasant St. Theatre	27 Pleasant St.	Northampton 01060	R. Pini	2	189
Little Six Cinema	13 Broadway	Rockport 01966	D. Morton	6	
•Edgemere Drive-In	Route 20	Shrewsbury 01545	Route 20 Associates	1	1600
Casino Theatre	P.O. Box 315	Siasconset 02564	Siaconset Casino Ass.	1	250
Somerville Theatre	55 Davis Square	Somerville 02143	G. Daly	1	
•Wellfleet Drive-In	P.O. Box 811	Wellfleet 02667	Jentz	i	700
West Newton Cine 1-2-3	1296 Washington Street	West Newton 02165	D. Bramante	3	
Westboro Cinema	18 Lyman Street	Westboro 01581	A. Edmonds	2	372
Images Cinema	50 Spring Street	Williamstown 01267	D. Fisher	1	191
Wollaston Theatre	14 Beale Street	Wollaston 02170	A. Chandler	1	1050

MICHIGAN

Name	Address	City & Zip	Owner	Screens	Seats
Michigan Theatre	603 E. Liberty Street	Ann Arbor 48104	Michigan Theat. Fdtn.	1	
State Theatre	233 S. State St.	Ann Arbor 48104	Aloma Entertainment	1	
Beaverton Gem Theatre	205 Tonkin Street	Beaverton 48612	J. Methner	1	
Bellaire Theatre	219 N. Bridge	Bellaire 49615	L. Dawson	1	

Name	Address	City & Zip	Owner	Screens	Seats
Berkley Theatre	2990 W. 12 Mile Road	Berkley 48072	R. Komer	1	850
Boyne Cinema Theatre	216 S. Lake Street	Boyne City 49712	T. Toomey	1	
Cass Theatre	6464 Main Street	Cass City 48726	R. Hendrick	1	
•Cheboygan Drive-In	1122 Shore Dr.	Cheboygan 49721	R.J. Theatres, Inc.	1	
Chesterfield Cinema	3 33125 23 Mile Rd.	Chesterfield 48047		3	
Clio Cinema	2143 W. Vienna Rd.	Clio 48420	D. West	1	
•Capri Drive-In	1455 W. Chicago Rd.	Coldwater 49036	J. Magocs	2	1200
Crystal Theatre	114 Main Street	Crystal 48818	K. McQueen	1	
Fox Theatre	2211 Woodward Avenue	Detroit 48201	Olympia Arenas, Inc.	1	
Rennaissance Center 4	Tower 200 Rennaisance Ctr	Detroit 48226		4	
Stratford Theatre	4751 W. Vernor Hwy.	Detroit 48209	Johnson Theatre, Inc.	1	
Eastwood Theatre	21145 Gratiot Ave.	East Detroit 48021	I. Belinsky	1	
Farmington Civic 2	33332 Grand River	Farmington 48336		2	
Capitol Theatre	140 E. Second Street	Flint 48502	W. Etherly	1	
•U.S. 23 Drive-In	G5200 Fenton Rd.	Flint 48507	Warrinton	1	
Ford-Tel 4	Telford Center	Ford		4	
Gaylord Theatre	115 E. Main Street	Gaylord 49735	H. Farber	1	
Community Theatre	52 Carrington	Harbor Beach 48441	J. Swartz	1	
Alco Theatre	P.O. Box 547	Harrisville 48740	J. Swise	1	
Cinema Theatre	213 W. State Street	Hastings 49058	S. Johnson	1	
Hillman Theatre	430 N. State	Hillman 49746	W. Watkins	1	
•Cherry Bowl Drive-In	9812 Honor Hwy	Honor 49640	T. Kenney	1	300
Copper Theatre	510 Shelden Avenue	Houghton 49931	Copper Theatres	1	
Pines Theatre	4673 Houghton Lake Dr.	Houghton Lake 48629	C. Huddy	1	
Plaza Cinema Theatre	U.S. #2 West	Iron River 49935	L. Anceli	1	
Keego Twin	3040 Orchard Lake Rd.	Keego Harbor 48320		2	
Odeon Southside	3500 S. Cedar Street	Lansing 48910	Odeon Corp.	4	460
Odeon Theatre	300 N. Clippert Street	Lansing 48912		1	
Playhouse Theaters	2415 Gratiot Blvd.	Marysville 48040	R. Querciagrossa	3	640
Studio M 123 Theatres	2926 Midland Road	Midland 48640	J. Rapanos	3	
Denniston Cinema 3	6495 N. Monroe Street	Monroe 48161	J. Sterling	3	900
River City Twin Cinemas 1 & 2	393 N. Telegraph Road	Monroe 48161	B. Cole	2	
The Rex Theatre	235 W. Main St.	Morenci 49256	E. Chase	1	225
Gaslight Cinema	302 Petoskey Street	Petoskey 49770	J. Patterson	1	
Penn Theatre	P.O. Box 537	Plymouth 48170	S. Smith	1	
McMorran Place Theatre	701 McMorran Blvd.	Port Huron 48060	McMorran	1	
Rogers Theatre	245 N. Third Street	Rogers City 49779	R. Vogelheim	1	400
Court Theatre	1216 Court Street	Saginaw 48602	L. Eischer	1	
•Hi-Way Drive-In	2887 E. Sanick	Sandusky 48471	S. Fetting	1	200
Sanilac Theatre	31 E. Lincoln	Sandusky 48471	S. Fetting	1	361
Midway Theatre	Box 116	Spalding 49886	A. Perry	1	
Show Theatre	220 N. State Street	St. Ignace 49781	G. Law	1	
Bay Theatre	214 St. Joseph	Suttons Bay 49682	R. Bahle	1	285
Milford Cinema	8581 Cooley Beach Dr.	Union Lake 48085		1	
•Ford Wyoming Drive-In	P.O. Box 220	Wayne 48184	Ford-Wyoming Inc.	8	2600
State-Wayne	35310 Michigan Ave.	Wayne 48184		4	
West Branch Cinema	210 W. Houghton	West Branch 48661	West Branch Cinema, Inc.	1	
Pigeon Theatre	112 S. Kalamazoo	White Pigeon 49099	J. Herring	1	360

MINNESOTA

Name	Address	City & Zip	Owner	Screens	Seats
Orpheum Theatre	305 W. Main St.	Ada 56510	T. Rocker	1	
Rialto Theatre	220 Minnesota Ave.,	N. Aitkin 56431	K. Peysar	1	
Midway Mall Cinema 5	2910 S. Broadway St.	Alexandria 56308	Tentelino Enterprises	3	1160
Anoka Cinema	420 E. Main	Anoka 55303	Continental Cinema	2	424
Apple Valley 6	7200 147th St.	Apple Valley 55124	Guetschoff	6	
Lido Theatre	309 W. Main Street	Arlington 55307	P. Vossen	1	
Tacora Theatre	Box 142	Aurora 55705	D. Rudolph	1	300
Grand Theatre	106 N. Main	Baudette 56623		1	
•Cisco Drive-In	Highway 2W	Bemidji 56601	B. Woodard	1	
De Marce Theatre	1320 Atlantic Avenue	Benson 56215	L. Demarce	1	
Blackduck		Blackduck 56630	R. Moore	1	
•65 Hi Drive-In	10100 Central Ave. NE	Blaine 55434	I. Braverman	1	
Buffalo Cinema	100 NE 1st Ave.	Buffalo 55313	Cinema Business Corp.	3	510
Cinema 5	130 Main St. N	Cambridge 55008	Guetschoff	5	
Canby Theatre	109 St. Olaf Ave. N.	Canby 56220	J. Alley	1	600
Chaska		Chaska 55318	M. Deleuhry	1	
Comet Theatre	River St. & Second Ave.	Cook 55723	D. Nakari	1	
Grand Theatres 1 & 2	124 E. 2nd Street	Crookston 56716	J. Northern States Amuse.	2	
Dock 1 & 2 Cinema	3675 Parkway	Deephaven 55391	H. Arent	1	
Delano	Hwy 12	Delano 55328	Muller	3	
Washington Square Cinemas		Detroit Lakes 56501	Muller	5	
East Bethel Theatre		East Bethel	J. Payne	1	
Elk River Cinema		Elk River 55330	Muller	6	
State Theatre	238 E. Sheridan St.	Ely 55731	Guetschoff	5	
Excelsior Dock	26 Water St.	Excelsior 55331		1	
Forest Lake 5	119 Lake St. NE	Forest Lake 55025	H. Arendt	3	
Lesdan Theatre	105 W. First Street	Fosston 56542	J. Payne	5	
•75 Hi Drive-In		Hallock	J. Winter	1	
JEM	Box 656	Harmony 55939		1	
Hastings 7		Hastings	Guetschoff	7	
Cine 1-2 Theatres	1319 Third Street	International Falls 56649	R. Hanover	2	612
State Theatre	600 2nd St.	Jackson 56143	J. Matuska	1	
•Vali Hi Drive-In	11260 Hudson Blvd.	Lake Elmo 55042	R. O'Neil	1	
LeSueur Theatre	209 S. Main	LeSueur 56058	J. Edwards	1	274
Hollywood	210 N. Sibley Ave.	Litchfield 55355	D. Lutz	1	
Falls	115 1st Street SE	Little Falls 56345		4	
•Long Drive-In	Hwy 71 N.	Long Prairie 56347		1	
Palace Theatre	104 E. Main St.	Luverne 56156	M. DeBates	1	441
Madelia	117 W. Main St.	Madelia 56062	E. Christensen	1	
Grand	310 6th St.	Madison 56256		1	
•Star Drive-In		Mahnomen		1	

Name	Address	City & Zip	Owner	Screens	Seats
Plaza	1793 Beam Ave.	Maplewood 55109	Williams & Moen	2	
Marshall Cinema 3	230 W. Lyon	Marshall 56258	S. Hiller	3	
Milaca Theatre	160 S. Central	Milaca 56353	B. Gorecki	1	
Film in the Cities		Minneapolis		1	
Parkway Theatre	4814 Chicago Ave.	Minneapolis 55417	W. Irvine	1	
Riverview	3800 42nd Ave. So.	Minneapolis 55406	Williams & Moen	1	
Univ. of Minn. Film Society	425 Ontario SE	Minneapolis 55414	MN Film Center	2	
Plaza Theatre	Southtown	Montevideo 56265	Vonderhahr	3	
Monticello 1-2 Theatres	Route #1	Monticello 55362	A. Muller	2	
Lake Theatre	Fourth & Elm	Moose Lake 55767	W. Lower	1	
Morris	12 E. 6th Street	Morris 56267	Curt Barber	1	
Cinema & Drafthouse	Winnetka Rd.	New Hope 55427	B. Minnette	2	
Family Theatre	628 Main St.	North Branch 55056		1	
Park Theatre	107 S. Main St.	Park Rapids 56470	J. Wasche	2	427
Koronis Cinema 1 & 2	209 Washburne Ave.	Paynesville 56362	P. Schoell	2	210
Comet Theatre	Main St.	Perham 56573	J. Wasche	1	300
Quarry Twin	204 E. Main St.	Pipestone 56164	L. Elliott	2	
Strand 2		Princeton		1	
Falls 1&2 Theatre	Box 454	Redwood Falls 56283		1	
Roseville 4	1211 Larpenter Ave.	Roseville 55113	Guetschoff	4	
Vogue	309 N. Commercial	Sandstone 55072	J. Petersen	1	
Main Street Theatre	319 Main St.	Sauk Centre 56378	R. Douvier	1	
Roso Theatre	310 N. Main	Sauk Centre 56378	R. Douvier	1	
Shakopee Town	1116 Shakopee Town Sq.	Shakopee 55379	Guetschoff	6	
Sherburn Theatre	116 N. Main	Sherburn 56171		1	
St. James Cinema		St. James		1	
Staples Cinema	204 4th St. NE	Staples 56479	G. Rosenthal	1	
Galaxy Twin	Box 337	Thief River Falls 56701	J. Hickerson	2	
Cozy Theatre	223 Jefferson St.	Wadena 56482		1	
State Theatre	P.O. Box 40	Walker 56484	Bresley/Bauer	1	
• Sky Vu Drive-In		Warren		1	
Flame Theatre	25 W. Franklin	Wells 56097	K. Pillars	1	
Gopher Theatre	907 Broadway	Wheaton 56296		1	
State Theatre	926 4th Ave	Windom 56101		1	
State Theatre	88 E. Fourth St.	Zumbrota 55992	R. Mowry	1	

MISSISSIPPI

Name	Address	City & Zip	Owner	Screens	Seats
Star Theatre	600 S. Beach Blvd.	Bay St. Louis 39520	W. Schultz	1	250
The Silver Screen	2650 Beach Blvd.	Biloxi 39531	Silver Screen Th., Inc.	3	
Ritz Theatre	Route 1, Box 7	Crenshaw 38621	P. Henderson	1	
Broad Country Cinema III	Box 511	Magee 39111	B. McCall	3	
Cine Theatre	125 E. Bankhead Street	New Albany 38652	H. Stephens	1	450
Roxy Twin Theatres	Box 421	Newton 39345	M. Connett	2	
Hoka Cinema	304 S. 14th	Oxford 38655	R. Shapiro	1	
Trace Theatre	728 Main Street	Port Gibson 39150	E. Doss	1	
New Dixie Theatre	106 S. Main St.	Ripley 38663	D. Wells	1	
Tobie Twin Cinema	218 E. Main Street	Senatobia 38668	P. Maxey	2	
Cinema 12 Four	Highway 12 & Spring St.	Starkville 39759	C. Riekhof	4	650
Plaza Twin Cinema	P.O. Box 688	Yazoo City 39194	G. Twiner	2	390

MISSOURI

Name	Address	City & Zip	Owner	Screens	Seats
Princess Theatre	14 W. Olive	Aurora 65605	D. Gold	1	
• Sunset Drive-In	1601 E. Church	Aurora 65605	L. Marks	1	300
Avalon Theatre	Box 475	Ava 65608	H. Pettit	1	
T.J. State Theatre	209 W. Church, PO Box 87	Bowling Green 63334	T. Gates	1	
• Highway 65 Drive-In	P.O. Box 174	Buffalo 65622	De Jarnette	1	200
• Sky Vue Drive-In		Butler 64730	G. Snitz	1	
Ritz Theatre	311 N. Main Street	Cameron 64429	W. West	1	
Crest Cinema II & Video	212 N. Washington	Clinton 64735	R. Follmer	2	
Forsyth Theatre	P.O. Box 308	Forsyth 65653	W. Pinet	1	
Sunderman Theatre House	Court Square	Fredericktown 63645	R. Sunderman	1	
Davis Theatre	Box 487	Higginsville 64037	T White	1	
• Sunset Drive-In		Houston 65483	Wyatt	1	
• Twin Drive-In 1 & 2	Kentucky Rd.	Independence 64050	Twin DI Theatres	1	
• I 70 Drive-In	8701 U.S. Hwy 40	Kansas City 64129	Stone Enter.	1	
Old Chelsea Theatre	200 W. Fourth Street	Kansas City 64105	New Brighton Theatres	1	
Baldwin Hall Theatre	16 Overbrook	Kirksville 63501	S. Paulding	1	
• Barco Drive-In	57 SE 25th Lane	Lamar 64759	B. Felts	1	400
• Mini 5 Drive-In		Lebanon 65536	C. Burton	1	
Star Theatre	268 N. Jefferson	Lebanon 65536	C. Burton	1	
• Macon Drive-In	RR 63	Macon 63552	O. Arnold	1	
Uptown Theatre	104 N. Kansas Avenue	Marceline 64658	B. Fogleson	1	
Cherokee Theatre	815 E. Third Street	Milan 63556	H. Helton	1	
Strand Theatre	308 South Hickory	Mount Vernon 65712	C. Ruble	1	
Paradise Theatre	408 Armour Rd. N.	Kansas City 64116	F. Henderson	1	
Twin Fox Theatre	110 S. Main Street	Nevada 64772	J. Novak	2	332
Walt Theatre	Box 77	New Haven 63068	M. Hebbeler	1	
Ozark Theatre	P.O. Box 294	Noel 64854	J. Carroll	1	
Civic Theatre	P.O. Box 350	Osceola 64776	D. Dysart	1	
Melinda Theatre	Star Route	Piedmont 63957	L. Ross	1	
• Pinehill Drive-In		Piedmont 63957	L. Ross	1	
• Owen Drive-In Theatre	P.O. Box 223	Seymour 65746	H. Owen	1	75
St. Andrews Cinema	2025 Golfway St.	Charles 63301	Beta Theatre Co.	1	
Avalon Theatre	4225 S. Kings Hwy.	St. Louis 63109	C. Tsvis	1	
Cross Keys Cinema	Lindebergh-New Hills	St. Louis 63136		1	
Hi-Pointe Theatre	1001 McCausland Avenue	St. Louis 63117	G. James	1	500
Kirkwood Cinema	338 S. Kirkwood Rd.	St. Louis 63122		1	
Melvin Theatre	2912 Chippewa	St. Louis 63118	H. Carnell	1	
Ste. Genevieve Cinemas 1 & 2	Pointe Bass Plaza	Ste. Genevieve 63670	J. Mattler	2	418

Name	Address	City & Zip	Owner	Screens	Seats
Roxy Theatre & Video	228 N. Van Buren	Warsaw 65335	R. Follmer	1	
Cinema 1 Plus 1 Plus 1	1900 Hwy. 100 E.	Washington 63090	D. Mittler	3	
Glass Sword Cinema 3	Route 1, Box 37	West Plains 65775	G. York	3	673

MONTANA

Name	Address	City & Zip	Owner	Screens	Seats
Washoe Theatre	305 Main Street	Anaconda 59711	J. Lussy	1	
Lake Theatre	Box Q	Baker 59513	W. Flint	1	
Park Theatre	313 N. Piegan Street	Browning 59417	Kingston	1	
Roxy Theatre	Box 782	Choteau 59422	L. Schilling	1	
Orpheum Theatre	P.O. Box/#7, 4th St SE	Conrad 59425	Larcon Theatres	1	
State Theatre	111 East Main	Cut Bank 59427	Larcon Theatres	1	
Rialto Theatre	418 Main	Deer Lodge 49722	H. Hansen	1	700
Big Sky Cinema I & II	560 N. Montana Street	Dillon 59725	H. Pickerill	2	472
Madison Theatre	115 Main Street	Ennis 59729	J. Armitage	1	250
Majestic Theatre	P.O. Box L	Eureka 59917	C. Pershall	1	
Roxy Theatre	981 Main Street	Forsyth 59327	M. Blakesley	1	
Terry's II Theatres	620 Second Ave. S.	Glasgow 59230	P. Terry	2	
Rose Theatre	215 N. Merrill Ave.	Glendive 59330	L. Moore	1	
Centre Cinema & Video	Box 437	Hardin 59034	D. Smith	1	256
Grand Theatre	P.O. Box 368	Harlem 59526	W. Hays	1	
Harlo Theatre	20 N. Central	Harlowton 59036	Booster Club	1	140
Second Story Cinema	9 Placer	Helena 59601	Film Society	1	
Rio Theatre	Box 375	Jordan 59337	N. Murnion	1	
Laurel Movie Haus	13 First Avenue	Laurel 59044	T. Kilpatrick	1	
•Westernaire Drive-In	219 West Main	Lewiston 59457	J. Campbell	1	195
Judith Theatre	219 W. Main	Lewistown 59457	J.Campbell	1	
•Libby Drive-In	604 Mineral Ave.	Libby 59923	Huber, L & E	1	
Villa Theatre	P.O. Box 820	Malta 59538	R. Pancake	1	
Crystal Theatre	515 S. Higgins	Missoula 59801	J. Laakso	1	160
•Go West Drive-in	P.O. Box 7277	Missoula 59807	W. Simons	1	
Llano Theatre	304 Clayton	Plains 58959	W. Ekstrom	1	
Orpheum Theatre	119 S. Main Street	Plentywood 59254	G. Nielsen	1	
Showboat Cinema	416 Main Street	Polson 59860	H. Pickerill	2	
Silver Screen Theatre	309 Main St.	Roundup 59072	K. Zieske	1	
Park Theatre	Box 187	Saint Ignatius 59865	W. Mitchell	1	
Roxy Theatre	P.O. Box 868	Shelby 59474	Larcon Theatres	1	
Center Theatre	Box 1113	Sidney 59270	L. Stoops	1	
Strand Theatre	P.O. Box 700	Superior 59872	Jensen Enterprises	1	300
Rex Theatre	P.O. Box 278	Thompson Falls 59873	H. Jensen	1	
Chalet Theatre	P.O. Box D	W. Yellowstone 59758	G. Yarbrough	1	
Strand Theatre	P.O. Box 783	White Slphr Spgs 59645	T. Barth	1	162
Mountain Cinemas	P.O. Box 1491	Whitefish 59937	H. Pickerill	2	

NEBRASKA

Name	Address	City & Zip	Owner	Screens	Seats
Royal Theatre	S. Star Rte. Box 36	Ainsworth 69210	D. Cole	1	
Blair Twin Theatre	South Highway 30	Blair 68008	P. Frederick	2	
State Theatre	706-C Avenue	Central City 68826	K. Blodgett	1	
Star Theatre	321 Center Avenue	Curtis 69025	Star Theatres, Inc.	1	200
Rosebowl Theatre	R.R. 1, Box 113	Franklin 68939	A. Smith	1	
Rialto II Theatre	160 N. Ninth Street	Geneva 68361	City of Geneva	1	
K-K Appliance	East Highway 30	Gothenburg 69138	Gothenburg	1	
Sun Theatre	421 West Avenue	Holdrege 68949	E. Braner	1	
Imperial Theatre	P.O. Box 1128	Imperial 69033	A. Daugherty	1	
Joyo Theatre	Box 29138	Lincoln 68529	D. Montgomery	1	313
•Pineview Drive-In		Long Pine 69217	D. Cole	1	
Nile Theatre	1433 Center	Mitchell 69537	M. Burton	1	
Dundee Theatre	4952 Dodge Street	Omaha 68132	D. Moran	1	
Roxie Theatre	P.O. Box 6	Randolph 68771	L. Leise	1	
Grand Theatre	317 Grand Avenue	Ravenna 68869	R. Vogt	1	
Rivoli Theatre	533 Main Street	Seward 68434	J. Wiseheart	1	
Carlin Theatre	P.O. Box 28	Spalding 68665	P. Carlin	1	276
Jewell Theatre	P.O. Box 178	Valentine 69201	S. Dredge	1	
Empress Theatre	P.O. Box 157	Verdigree 68783	I. Prokap	1	
Legion Theatre	P.O. Box 195	Wallace 69169	Legion Post	1	
Gay Theatre	310 Main Street	Wayne 68787	J. March	1	

NEVADA

Name	Address	City & Zip	Owner	Screens	Seats
Incline Village Theatre	P.O. Box 15	Crystal Bay 89402	R. Tamblyn	1	
Fallon Theatre	71 S. Maine Street	Fallon 89406	R. Erickson	2	
Meadowdale Theatres	P.O. Box 6	Gardnerville 89410	W. Tomerlin	2	
Cactus Theatre	P.O. Box 1252	Hawthorne 89415	M. Rogers	1	210
El Rancho Theatre	3008 Holly Hill	Las Vegas 89104	E. Escobedo	1	
Four Star Theatre	112 N. Fourth Street	Las Vegas 89101	E. Glass	1	
Gem Theatre	1025 Main Street	Pioche 89043	D. Christian	1	
High Sierra Theatre	Box C	Stateline 89449	B. Retzer	1	
Nevada Theatre	P.O. Box 263	Wells 89835	P. Moschetti	1	

NEW HAMPSHIRE

Name	Address	City & Zip	Owner	Screens	Seats
Bedford Mall Cinema	Everett Tpk	Bedford 03110	Canad Inc.	1	
Cinema 93 Theatre	12 Loudon Road	Concord 03301	B. Steelman	1	
Concord Theatre	18½ S. Main St.	Concord 03301		1	
Majestic Theatre	36 Main St.	Conway 03818	T. Goodman	1	
Tri City Cinemas	Tri City Plaza	Dover 03820	Canad, Inc.	4	700
Cinema 1-2-3 Theatres	Lakes Region Mall	Guilford 03246	D. Dirian	3	
Hampton Cinema Six	P.O. Box 1259	Hampton 03842	M. Tinios	6	

627

Name	Address	City & Zip	Owner	Screens	Seats
Casino Theatre	Ocean Boulevard	Hampton Beach 03842	F. Shaake	1	
•Midway Drive-In	Box 594	Littleton 03561	R. Morneau	1	
Cinema IV	Appletree Mall	Londonderry		4	
S. Willow St. Cinemas	1279 S. Willow St.	Manchester 03103	Canad Inc.	9	
•Milford Twin Drive-In	Box 101	Milford 03055	R. Scharmett	2	
Canad Nashua Mall	Everett Tpk at Broad St.	Nashua 03060	Canad Inc.	3	
Scenic Theatre	21 Depot Street	Pittsfield 03263	A. Dame	1	
Canad Cinema	Lafayette Rd.	Portsmouth 03801		1	
Lafayette Road Cinema	581 Lafayette Road	Portsmouth 03801	Canad Inc.	5	
Tri City Plaza Cinemas	High Street	Somersworth	Canad Inc.	2	
•Milford Drive-in Theatre 1 & 2	Rt. 101A A	West Milford 03055		2	
Town Hall Theatre	P.O. Box 7	Wilton 03086	D. Markaverich	1	
•Northfield Drive-In	Northfield Rd.	Winchester 03470	M. Shakaer	1	450
•Meadows Drive-In	P.O. Box 44 Route 135	Woodsville 03785	L. Tegu	1	400

NEW JERSEY

Name	Address	City & Zip	Owner	Screens	Seats
Strathmore Twin	Rt. 34	Aberdeen 07747		2	
Lincoln Cinema Five	832 Kearney Ave.	Arlington 07032	S. Papas	5	
Atlantic Triple	82 First Avenue-Box 269	Atlantic Highlands 07716	L. Edwards	3	600
Bergenfield Cinema 5	58 S. Washington Ave.	Bergenfield 07621	Clearview Cinemas Corp.	5	
Berkley Heights Cinema	450 Springfield Ave.	Berkley Heights 07922	S. Goldstein	1	346
Bernardsville Cinema	5 Mine Brook Road	Bernardsville 07924	Clearview Cinemas Corp.	1	
Center Theatre	562 Bloomfield Ave.	Bloomfield 07003		1	
Brook Cinema	10 Hamilton St.	Bound Brook 08805	I. Muthu	1	
Cinema 23 Fiveplex	State Hwy. No. 23	Cedar Grove 07009	Kin-Mall Cinemas	5	
Chatham	Shunpike Road	Chatham 07928		1	
Cinema 206	Chester Spngs. S/C	Chester 07930		2	
Allwood Sixplex	96 Market St.	Clifton 07012		6	
Clifton Quad	Main & Clifton Ave.	Clifton 07014		4	
Closter Cinema	130 Closter Plaza	Closter 07624	Clearview Cinemas Corp.	1	
Dunellen	458 North Ave. Rte 28	Dunellen		1	
The Movies	Brunswick Sq.	East Brunswick 08816		2	
Elmora	144 Elmora	Elizabeth 07202		1	
Liberty Theatre	1121 Elizabeth Ave.	Elizabeth 07201	F. Bravo	3	600
Emerson Quad Theatre	346 Kinderkamack	Emerson 07630	D. Sanders	4	
Hyway Theatres		Fairlawn		5	
Cinema Plaza	Hwy. 202 & 31	Flemington 08822		5	
Hunterdon Theatre	Hwy. 31	Flemington 08822		1	
Galaxy Theatre	7000 Blvd.	East Guttenberg 07093		3	
Mall Theatre	Route No. 57	Hackettstown 07840		2	
Hawthorne Theatre	300 Lafayette Ave.	Hawthorne 07506	J. Sayegh	5	
Hoboken Cinemas #1-2	5 Marine View Plaza	Hoboken 07030	V. Orjelick	2	
Castle Twin	1115 Clinton Avenue	Irvington 07109		2	
Movie City	675 Rte. 1	Iselin 08830		5	1180
Hudson Mall Cinemas	State Hwy. 440 So.	Jersey City 07305		4	
Kendall Park Cinema	27 Kendall Park S/C	Kendall Park 08824		7	
Kin-Mall Theatres	25 Kinnelon Rd.	Kinnelon 07405	Kin-Mall Cinemas	8	
Meadtown	Route 23	North Kinnelon 07405	Kin-Mall Cinemas	1	
Linden Quad	400 Wood Avenue	Linden 07036	Kin-Mall Cinemas	5	
Colony Theatres		Livingston		3	
Madison Triplex	14 Lincoln Pl.	Madison 07940	Clearview Cinemas Corp.	3	
Maplewood	155 Maplewood Ave.	Maplewood 07040		3	
Clairidge Triple Cinema	486 Bloomfield Ave.	Montclair 07042	P. Petersen	3	
Wellmont Theatre	400 Bloomfield Ave.	Montclair 07042		3	
Lumberton Cinema	Rt. 38 Eayerstown Rd.	Mt. Molly 08060	D. Saunders	2	
Newton Twin	234 Spring	Newton 07860		2	
Little Art Theatre	750 Pasadena Ave.	Northfield 08225	L. Rickert	1	
Franklin Triplex Theas	510 Franklin Ave.	Nutley 07110	P. Vivian	3	
Cinema 35 Theatre	65 West Route 4	Paramus 07652	Hudson Amusements	1	
Fabian	45 Church Street	Paterson 07505		1	
Broadway Theatre	South Broadway	Pitman 08071	C. Platt	1	
Colonial Twin	245 Wanague Ave.	Pompton Lakes 07442		2	
Ramsey Theatre	125 E. Main St.	Ramsey 07446	P. Vivian	1	
Rialto	172 Main Street	Ridgefield Park 07660		1	
Montgomery Center Theatre	Highway #206	Rocky Hill 08553	R. Piechota	2	
New Park Theatre	23 Westfield Ave. W.	Roselle Park 07204	TLN Corp.	5	975
William Center Twin	Williams Plaza	Rutherford 07070		2	
Sparta Theatre	25 Centre	Sparta 07871		2	
Tenafly Cinema 4	4 ½ W. Railroad Ave.	Tenafly 07670	Clearview Cinemas Corp.	4	
Five Points Cinema	327 Chestnut St.	Union 07083		2	350
Lost Picture Show	23955 Springfield Ave.	Union 07083		1	
Summit Quad	1214 Summit Ave.	Union City 07087		4	
Washington Twin Cinema	163 E. Washington	Washington 07882		2	
Washington Triple Cinema		Washington Township		3	
Mayfair Theatre	6405 Park Ave. West	New York 07093	Hong Sheng Co. Inc.	3	
Rialto 3	250 E. Broad St.	Westfield 07090		3	
Westfield Twin	138 Westfield	Westfield 07090	D. Horn	2	635
Hanover Twin Cinema	Sykesville Road	Wrightstown 08562	T. Miller	2	

NEW MEXICO

Name	Address	City & Zip	Owner	Screens	Seats
Far North Cinema 4 Th	6300 San Mateo N.E.	Albuquerque 87109	R. Garner	4	
•Sunset Drive-In	1700 Arenal Rd. S.W.	Albuquerque 87105	D. Armino	1	
Cuba Cinema	Box 1537	Cuba 87013	J. Hodovance	1	200
Deming Cinema 3 Theatres	111 W. Pine	Deming 88030	C. Childers	3	
Coronado Theatre	324 E. Second	Lordsburg 88045	W. Gavin	1	
Resort Theatre	P.O. Box 227	Reserve 87830	G. McCarty	1	
Jean Cocteau Theatre	418 Montezuma Street	Santa Fe 87501	L. Cohn	1	
•Yucca Drive-In	P.O. Box 575	Santa Fe 87501	Winoko Corp.	1	

628

Name	Address	City & Zip	Owner	Screens	Seats
Pecos Theatre	219 4th Street	Santa Rosa 88435	R. Sanchez	1	
El Rio Theatre	P.O. Box 147	Truth or Consequence 87901	J. Whetzel	1	

NEW YORK

Name	Address	City & Zip	Owner	Screens	Seats
Madison Theatre	1036 Madison Ave.	Albany 12208	B. Rosenblatt	1	
Spectrum Cinemas	290 Delaware Avenue	Albany 12209	Spectrum Cinema Corp.	3	
•Orleans Drive-In	Route 31	Albion 14411	W. Baker	1	
•Allegany Drive-In		Allegany 14706	Bordonaro	1	2435
Auburn Cinema 1 & 2	Grant Avenue	Auburn 13021	D. Martini	2	
•Hollywood Drive-In	RR 4 Box 44	Averill Park 12018	F. Fisher	1	474
Grand Ave Twin	1841 Grand Ave.	Baldwin 11510	G.G. Theatres	2	300
Bedford Playhouse	Rt. 22	Bedford 10506	R. Lesser	2	500
Bellmore Theatre	222 Pettit Ave.	Bellmore 11710		2	600
Mid Island Theatre	4045 Hempstead Tpke.	Bethpage L.I. 11714		1	
Cameo Theatre	63 Main Street	Brewster 10509	M. Abrams	1	
Allerton Triplex	744 Allerton Ave.	Bronx 10467	W. Quinn	2	
New Riverdale Twin	5683 Riverdale Ave.	Bronx 10471		3	
New American Quad	1450 East Avenue	Bronx 10461		2	
The Dale	189 W. 231 St.	Bronx 10463	Lesser	4	
Brooklyn Center Cinema	Campus Road & Hillel Pl.	Brooklyn 11210	F. Angel	2	412
Brooklyn Heights Twin	70 Henry St.	Brooklyn 11201	Bklyn Bridge Cinemas	1	
Canarsie Triplex	9310 Avenue L	Brooklyn 11236		2	400
Cobble Hill Fiveplex	265 Court St.	Brooklyn 11231		3	
Commodore Twin Theatre	329 Broadway	Brooklyn 11211		5	
New Kent Twin	1170 Coney Island Avenue	Brooklyn 11230	J. Crespi	2	
Plaza Twin Cinema	314 Flatbush Avenue	Brooklyn 11226	E. Steinberg	2	
Community	373 Main St.	Catskill 12414	R. Ardala	2	
Centereach Theatre	1970 Middle Country Rd.	Centereach 11720	T. Thornton	2	734
•Border Drive-In	Route 9	Champlain 12919	C. Harbula	1	
Chester 6		Chester 10918	A. Bruce	6	
Pine Cinema	1850 Route 112	Coram 11727	S. Epstein	4	
•Delevan Drive-In	Route 16	Delevan 14042	G. Mendola	1	
State Theatre	72 Second Street	Deposit 13754	Deposit Community Theatre	1	
•Fair Oaks Drive-In		Fair Oaks 10919	Lesser	1	
N. Shore Towers Cinema	272-40 Grand Cent. Park	Floral Park 11005	J. Aidela	1	
Main Street Quad	7266 Main St.	Flushing 11367		4	
Utopia Twin	18702 Union Turnpike	Flushing 11366		2	
Franklin Quad	989 Hempstead Turnpike	Franklin Square 13057		4	
•Greenville Drive-In	Route #32	Greenburgh 12083	Greenville Eleven	1	
Village Cinema	211 Front Street	Greenport 11944	Village Cinema Circuit	4	
Hamilton Cinema	7 Lebanon Street	Hamilton 13346	A. Shepherd	1	300
Village Cinema	Seven 145 N. Franklin Ct.	Hempstead 11550	Village Cinema Circuit	7	
Hunter	Main St.	Hunter 12442	T. Thornton	1	229
•Hyde Park Drive-In	Rte. 9	Hyde Park 12538		1	
Roosevelt Fourplex		Hyde Park		4	
Cinemapolis 1 & 2	171 E. State St.	Ithaca 14850	L. Cohen	2	289
Cornell Cinema	104 Willard Straight	Ithaca 14853	Cornell Univ.	2	760
Fall Creek Pictures	1201 N. Tioga St.	Ithaca 14850	L. Cohen	3	306
Hudson Valley Mall Sixplex		Kingston 12401		6	
Palace	26 Main St.	Lake Placid 12946	Reg. Clark	3	572
Levittown Twin	3080 Hempstead Tpke.	Levittown 11756		2	
Liberty Triplex	P.O. Box 525	Liberty 12754	J. Illiparampil	3	900
•Transit Drive-In	6655 Transit Rd.	Lockport 14094	M. Cohen	1	900
Park Avenue Twin	179 E. Park Ave.	Long Beach 11561		2	
Malverne Twin Cinema	350 Hempstead Ave.	Malverne 11565	Cinematique	2	
Mattituck Twin Theatre	Route 25 Mattituck	Mattituck 11952	Puma	2	
•Middletown Drive-In	R.D. 4	Middletown 10940		1	
Moviehouse		Millerton 12546		1	
Monroe		Monroe 10950		1	
Mall Quad		Monticello 12701	Florin-Creative	4	
Mt. Kisco Cinema	144 Main St.	Mt. Kisco 10549	R. Lasser	5	600
Herrick Twin	3324 Hillside Ave	New Hyde Park 11040	G.G. Theatres	2	450
New Paltz Quad	Rte. 299 New Paltz Plaza	New Paltz 12516	Florin-Creative	4	
Angelika 57th	225 W. 57th St.	New York 10019	Angelika Film	1	
Angelika Film Center	18 West Houston St.	New York 10012	Angelika Film	6	
Art East Cinema	First Ave. & 61st	New York 10021		1	
Cinema Village	12th Street 22 E. 12th Street	New York 10003	Cinemart Cinemas Corp.	1	300
Embassy 1	Broadway & 46th Sts.	New York 10036	Guild Enterprises	1	500
Embassy 2-3-4	7th Ave. & N. 47th St.	New York 10036	Guild Enterprises	3	1057
Essex Theatre	375 Grand Street	New York 10010	G. Zicos	1	
Film Forum	209 W. Houston Street	New York 10014	Film Forum	3	472
Grammercy Theatre	127 East 23rd St	New York 10011		1	
Guild Theatre	Rockefeller Plaza	New York 10020	Guild Enterprises	1	
Harlem Victoria 5	235 W. 125th St.	New York 10027		5	
Joseph Papp Public Theatre	425 Lafayette St.	New York 10003		1	
Lincoln Plaza Cinemas 6	30 Lincoln Plaza	New York 10023	New York Cinemas	6	1100
New Coliseum	701 W. 181st St.	New York 10033		4	
Nova Theatre	3589 Broadway	New York 10031	J. Nova	2	
Quad Cinema	34 W. 13th St.	New York 10011		4	550
Theatre 80 St. Marks	80 St. Marks Place	New York 10003	R. Aidala	1	
Cinema East	Rte. 59	Nyack 10960		2	
Cinema Twin Theatres	NY St. Rts. Big N Shp.	Oneida 13421	C. Zurich	2	
•El Rancho Drive-In	Rte. #5	Palatine Brdg. 13428	Hallmark	1	
Central		Pearl River 10965		1	
Beach Quad Cinema	Beach Shopping Center	Peekskill 10566	D. Horn	4	965
•Silver Lake Drive-In	P.O. Box 26	Perry 14530	J. Stefanon	1	400
Port Jefferson Twin	Rt. 112	Port Jefferson 11776		2	
Port Washington 7-Plex	116 Main St.	Port Washington 11050	G.G. Theatres	7	1120
Cinema 8	Galleria Mall	Poughkeepsie 12701		8	
SUNY at Purchase Film Series	Campus Center N.	Purchase 10577	State Univ.	1	
Cinemart Twin	106-03 Metropolitan Ave.	Queens 11385	Cinemart Cinema Corp.	2	950

629

Name	Address	City & Zip	Owner	Screens	Seats
•Glen Twin Drive-In	P.O. Box 4079	Queensbury 12804	J. Gardner	2	
Lyceum Theatre	139 S. Broadway	Red Hook 12571	Florin-Creative	6	
Drake Theatre	62-90 Woodhaven Blvd.	Rego Park 11374		2	
Upstate Films	Montgomery St.	Rhinebeck 12572	S. Leiber	2	
The Little Theatre	240 East Avenue	Rochester 14604	W. Coppard	3	678
Surfside Twin Theatre	103-22 Rockaway Beach	Rockaway Park 11694	H. Elgart	2	
Roscoe Theatre	Broad Street	Roscoe 12776	J. Amback	1	
Rosendale Theatre	Main Street	Rosendale 12472	A. Cacchio	1	
Roslyn Twin Theatre	20 Tower Place	Roslyn 11576	Lesser	2	
Sag Harbor Cinema	Main Street	Sag Harbor L.I. 11963	G. Mallow	1	
Orpheum Theatre	P.O. Box 113	Saugerties 12477	T. Thornton	1	600
Sayville Triplex	Railroad Ave.	Sayville 11782		3	
Southampton Cinemas Theatre	43 Hill Street	Southampton L.I. 11968	H. Karlin	3	
Cinema 59	Rte. 59	Spring Valley 10977		2	
Lafayette		Suffern 10901		1	
Center Twin Theatre	42-17 Queens Blvd.	Sunnyside 11104	S. Epstein	2	
Genesee Theatre	2182 W. Genesee St.	Syracuse 13215	D. Martini	1	
Westcott Cinema	524 Westcott St.	Syracuse 13202	Westcott Cinema Inc.	1	575
State Theatre	Park St.	Tupper Lake 12986	J.S. Cinema	1	
Walton	30 Gardner St.	Walton 13850	P & P Enterprises	1	
•Warwick Drive-In	Rte 94	Warwick 10990	Seeber	1	
South Bay Cinemas	495 Montauk Hwy.	West Babylon 11704	JHL Assoc.	4	
West Islip Cinemas	444 Union Blvd.	West Islip 11795	WITC Corp.	2	
Salisbury Theatre	610 Old Country Road	Westbury 11590	Salisbury Thea. Corp.	1	

NORTH CAROLINA

Name	Address	City & Zip	Owner	Screens	Seats
Andrews Twin Cinema		Andrews 28901	R. McNelley	2	400
•Belmont Drive-In	314 McAdenville Road	Belmont 28012	W. Lawing	1	
•Bessemer City Drive-In	Box 664	Bessemer City 28016	R. Stinette	1	
Gem Theatre	Box 1501	Bryson City 28713	M. Mangan	1	
Terrace Theatre	Huffman Mill Rd.	Burlington 27215	H. Bennett	5	982
Yancey 1 & 2 Theatre	P.O. Box 775	Burnsville 28714	B. Mandala	2	
Varsity Theatres	121 E. Franklin St.	Chapel Hill 27514	C.H. Cinema Corp.	2	
Charlotte Cinema	4120 E. Independence Blvd	Charlotte 28205	S. Kamin	1	
State Theatre	P.O. Box 572	Cornelius 28031	J. Ritchie	1	
Riverview Cinema	5200 Roxboro Rd.	Durham 27704	C. Mabe	1	
Fontana Movie Theatre	Fontana Resort	Fontana 28733	D. Fetch	1	
Carolina Theatre	310 S. Greene St.	Greensboro 27401	United Arts Council	1	1091
•Raleigh Road Outdoor	P.O. Box 1412	Henderson 27536	E. Lyles	1	265
Highlands Theatre	Box 725	Highlands 28741	Schiffi	1	
Gem Theatre	111 W. First St.	Kannapolis 28081	Whitley/Scarboro/Rutledge	1	912
Louisburg Theatre	109 W. Nash St.	Louisburg 27549	W. Pernell	1	250
Ye Olde Pioneer Theatre (est. 1918)	111 Budleigh St.	Manteo 27954	H. Creef	1	315
Mars Theatre	P.O. Box 339	Mars Hill 28754	C. McFarland	1	365
Mayberry Cinema 3	3 Fowler Road	Mt. Airy 27030	Johnson J. & B.	3	
Henn Theatre	P.O. Box 398	Murphy 28906	P. Henn	1	
Orpheum Theatre	129 Williamsboro St.	Oxford 27565	C. Batchelor	1	
Rowan Cinema	Statesville Blvd.	Salisbury 28144	T. James	3	
Tryon Theatre	127 Trade St.	Tryon 28782	B. Flood	1	350
Ansonia Theatre	112 S. Rutherford	Wadesboro 28170	B. Craft	1	
•Bel Air Drive-In	Box 307	Walkertown 27051	P. McGee	1	
•Waynesville Drive-In	Box 77	Waynesville 28786	J. Clark	1	
Cinema III Theatres	627 S. Madison	Whiteville 28472	J. Fisher	3	350

NORTH DAKOTA

Name	Address	City & Zip	Owner	Screens	Seats
Ash Theatre	P.O. Box 444	Ashley 58413	L. Schnabel	1	198
Bijou Theatre	82 S.E. First	Beach 58621	L. Walz	1	300
Grand Theatres	1486 Interstate Loop	Bismarck 58501	J. Brekke	3	
Grand Theatre	Box 418	Carrington 58421	R. Kuss	1	
Fargo Theatre	314 Broadway	Fargo 58107	Fargo Theatre Mgmt. Co.	1	870
Forman	40 Main Street	Forman 58032	P. Tuchscher	1	
•Stardust 17 Drive-In	Hiway 17 West	Grafton 58237	Henriksen	1	300
Strand I & II	P.O. Box 72	Grafton 58237	Red River Enterprises	2	
Halliday Theatre	Box 2	Halliday 58636	J. Bohrer	1	
Central Cinema Theatre	810 Lincoln Ave.	Harvey 58341	Harvey Redev. Corp.	1	
Cinema Twin	Highway 200 East	Hazen 58545	L. Keim	2	400
Mayer Theatre	412 Wash	Hebron 58638	A. Mayer	1	
Bison Twin Theatres	Buffalo Mall	Jamestown 58401	L. Keim	2	430
Cinema Twin	Jamestown Mall	Jamestown 58401	L. Keim	2	500
Roxy Theatre	714-Third Street	Langdon 58249	J. Dunford	1	
Avalon Theatre	208 Towner Avenue	Larimore 58251	E. Sickles	1	
Delchar Theatre	20 W. Main	Mayville 58257	S. Larson	1	
Page Theatre	P.O. Box 141	Page 58064	Page Jaycees	1	
Curt's Theatre	106 Main Avenue	Rolla 58367	C. Bonn	1	
•Lake Park Drive-In		Willston 58801	J. Snyder	1	
Dakota Theatre	16 N. Fifth Street	Wishek 58495	L. Schauer	1	

OHIO

Name	Address	City & Zip	Owner	Screens	Seats
Akron Civic Theatre	182 S. Main Street	Akron 44308	E. Patti	1	
Mount Union Theatre	1745 S. Union Street	Alliance 44601	P. Honaker	1	
•Pymatuning Lake Drive-In	5863 Beach St.	Andover 44003	E. Leonhard	1	
•Magic City Drive-In	5602 S. Cleveland-Mass.	Barberton 44203	G. Greive	1	700
West Theatre	1017 Wooster Rd. West	Barberton 44203	G. Greive	1	700
Brunswick Cinema	1480 Pearl Road	Brunswick 44212	P. Pyros	1	
MNC's Bryan Bijou Theatre	140 South Lyn Street	Bryan 43506	M. Sobieck	3	400
Belden Village Twin Cinemas	6404 Market St.	Canton 44718	E. Pollak	4	

Name	Address	City & Zip	Owner	Screens	Seats
Circle Mall Cinemas	3911 Everhard Rd. N.W.	Canton 44079	H. Poulos	4	
Palace Theatre	605 N. Market Street	Canton 44702	Canton Palace Assn.	1	
Geauga Cinema	101 Water Street	Chardon 44024	L. Dolan	1	
•Mayfield Road Drive-In	P.O. Box 368	Chardon 44026	Maisano	1	
Emery Theatre	1112 Walnut Street	Cincinnati 45210	Univ. of Cincinnati	1	1376
Cleveland Cinematheque	11141 E. Boulevard	Cleveland 44106	Cleve. Institute Art	2	700
Cleveland Museum of Art	11150 E. Boulevard	Cleveland 44106	Cleveland Museum of Art	2	920
Lakeshore 1-3 Theatre	22624 Lakeshore Blvd.	Cleveland 44123	A. Saluan	3	
Flickers Cinema Pub	5227 Bethel Centre	Columbus 43220	G. Ackerman	3	
Flickers East Cinema Pub	4501 Refugee Road	Columbus 43232	G. Ackerman	3	
Graceland Cinema 1&2	230 Graceland Blvd.	Columbus 43214	G. Ackerman	2	
Ohio Theatre	39 E. State Street	Columbus 43215	D. Streigig	1	
Palace Theatre	55 E. State Street	Columbus 43215	K. LeVegue	1	
•South Drive-In 1 & 2	3050 South High St.	Columbus 43207	Rainbow Ent.	1	
MNC's Valentine Theatre 1 & 2	602 Clinton Street	Defiance 43512	M. Sobieck	2	700
Lorain Twin Cinema	119 Foxhill	Elyria 44035	J. Cooper	2	
Colony Theatre	Box 31	Gallipolis 45631	H. Wheeler	1	
Spring Valley Cinema	531 Jackson Pike	Gallipolis 45631	W. Duerson	3	
Garrettsville Twin 1 & 2	8009 State St.	Garrettsville 44231	R. Doane	2	
•Skyway Drive-In	426 Fourth Street	Gibsonburg 43420	J. Binder	1	
•Ranch Drive-In	P.O. Box 7	Greenfield 45123	Teicher	1	
Markay Theatre	Main Street	Jackson 45640	Jackson Bact. Inc.	2	
Elder Theatre	106 W. Pike St.	Jackson Center 45334	R. Miller	1	400
Plaza 1 & 2	University Shpg. Ctr.	Kent 44240	Ohio Movies	2	
Duncan Theatre	110 N. Main St.	Killbuck 44637	H. Yoder	1	
•Skyview Drive-In	315 Timberlane Dr.	Lancaster 43130	C. Crum	1	400
Frontier Theatres	2100 Harding Hwy	Lima 45804	R. Heitmeyer	4	
•Sharon Drive-In	2951 West Elm Street	Lima 45805	J. Schrider	1	
Lorain Twin Cinema	119 Foxhill Lane #4C	Lorain 44055	J. Cooper	2	
Palace Theatre	60305 Broadway	Lorain 44502	J. Handyside	1	
Ohio Theatre	156 N. Water	Loudonville 44842	H. Yoder	1	
Renaissance Theatre	138 Park Ave.	W Mansfield 44902	T. Miller	1	
•Sunset Drive-In	1155 Laurelwood Rd.	Mansfield 44907	H. Nusbaum	1	
•Starlite Drive-In	1889 State Rte 127	Maria Stein 45860	E. Hyman	1	
Palace Theatre	276 W. Center	Marion 43302	Palace Cultural Assn.	1	
McArthur Twin Cinema	112 N. Market St.	McArthur 45651	D. Burton	2	255
Opera House Theatre	15 W. Main St.	McConnellsville 43756	G.Finley	1	
•Starglow Drive-In	2835 Cincinnati-Dayton	Middletown 45042	E. Cox	1	
Crescent Theatre	131 E. Fourth St.	Minster 45365	R. Knostman	1	
Capitol Theatre	22 W. High St.	Mt. Gilead 83338	Staiger/Hupfer	1	
•33 Drive-In	Route 1	Nelsonville 45764	E. Edwards	1	520
•Auto Rama Twin Drive-In	33395 Lorain Rd.	North Ridgeville 44039	T. Sherman	2	1200
•Starview Drive-In	2883 US Hwy 20W	Norwalk 44857	S. Steel	1	
Towne & Country Theatre	55 E. Main St.	Norwalk 44857	T & C Players	1	
Cinema 20	1469 Mentor Ave.	Painesville 44077	Hall/Ryan	1	
•Sandusky Drive-In	P.O. Box 550	Sandusky 44870	Seitz Amusements	1	350
Sandusky State Theatre	109 Columbus Ave.	Sandusky 44870	Sandusky State Theatres	1	
Parkland Theatre	6636 Hillside Ave.	Saylor Park 45233	B. Bauaer	1	
•Auto-Vue Drive-In	P.O. Box 92	Sidney 45365	Negelspach	1	
St. Mary's Theatre	119 W. Spring St.	St. Mary's 45885	R. Knotsman	1	
•Winter Drive-In 1 & 2	Route 43	Steubenville 43952	Skirball	1	
Strongsville Cinema 1 & 2	14781 Pearl Rd.	Strongsville 44136	A. Goisios	2	
The Ritz Theatre	30 S. Washington	Tiffin 44883	Tiffin Theatres Inc.	1	1000
Fox Theatre	3725 Williston Rd.	Toledo 43619	JR Denniston Theatre Co.	2	725
•Van Del Drive-In	19986 E. Ridge Road	Van Wert 45891	T. Epps	1	
•Blue Sky Drive-In	959 Broad St.	Wadsworth 44261	G. Greive	1	600
Great Oaks Cinema	179 Great Oaks Trail	Wadsworth 44281	G. Greive	2	600
•Elm Road Twin Drive-In	1895 Elm Road	Warren 44446	M. Hreno	2	
•Star Auto	1150 N. Shoop	Wauseon 43567	R. Wyse	1	
Wheelersburg Cinema	8805 Ohio River Rd.	Wheelersburg 45694	W. Duerson	6	
Uptown Theatre	2730 Market St.	Youngstown 44507	S. Foster	1	

OKLAHOMA

Name	Address	City & Zip	Owner	Screens	Seats
Rialto 1 & 2 Theatres	516 Flynn St.	Alva 73717	J. Jones	2	
Pastime Theatre	201 N. High	Antlers 74523	G. Poole	1	
Thompson Theatre	Box 6	Atoka 74525	C. Henderson	1	
Camelot Theatre	P.O. Box 836	Boise City 73933	J. James	1	
•51 Drive-In	14007 71st St. NE	Broken Arrow 74012	B. Stevens	1	
H & S Theatre	816 Manvel	Chandler 74834	H. Wakely	1	
Gentry Theatre	214 W. Gentry	Checotah 74426	G. Crumpler	1	
Rook Theatre	P.O. Box 530	Cheyenne 73628	G. Kirk	1	
Southland Twin Theatre	P.O. Box 427	Chickasha 73534	M. Wells	2	416
Wigwam Theatre	P.O. Box 385	Coalgate 74538	J. Hickman	1	
Palace Theatre	P.O. Box 427	Duncan 73534	M. Wells	1	525
Royal Theatre	109 N. Main St.	Fairview 73737	J. Adamson	1	
•Beacon Drive-In	P.O. Box 337	Guthrie 73044	M. Powell, Jr.	1	80
Ortman Theatre	Box 37	Hennessey 73742	G. Ortman	1	
New Ritz Theatre	108 Plaza	Madill 73446	G. Smith	1	
Thunderbird Twin Cinema	1603 E. Steveowens	Miami 74354	J. Leak	2	
•Chief Drive-In Theatre	P.O. Box 427	Nennekah 73534	M. Wells	1	200
Crystal Theatre	401 W. Broadway	Okemah 74859	M. Smyth	1	
Tower Theatre	425 N.W. 23rd	Oklahoma City 73101	G. Shanbour	1	
Royal Twin Theatre & Video	119 E. Paul	Pauls Valley 73075	M. Brewer	2	
•Tee Pee Drive-In	Hwy. 66 West	Sapulpa 74066	J. Malone	1	
•Tahlequah Drive-In	311 South Morris	Tahlequah 74464	B. Ukena	1	
Ritz Theatre	P.O. Box 628	Talihina 74571	F. Wright	1	
The Cinema	1 William Ctr. Forum	Tulsa 74172	Trammell Crow	1	
89er Theatre		Watonga 73772	D. Collier	1	
Key Theatre	115 N. Wewoka	Wewoka 74884	J. Horn	1	
Lakeside Triple Theatres	P.O. Box 571	Woodward 73801	D. Terry	3	

Name	Address	City & Zip	Owner	Screens	Seats

OREGON

Name	Address	City & Zip	Owner	Screens	Seats
Eltrym Theatre	1809 First St.	Baker City 97814	Western Amusement	1	
Aloha Theatre	18295 SW Tualatin Hwy	Beaverton 97006	Family Theatre	1	
Chinook Theatre	P.O. Box 6097	Brockings 97415	R. Beem	1	
• Frontier Drive-In	28569 Redwood Hwy	Cave Junction 97523	L. Musil	1	
Liberty Playhouse	212 S. Main St.	Condon 97823	J. Steisver	1	
Egyptian Theatre	229 S. Broadway	Coos Bay 97420	T. McSwain	1	
Opera House	8th & Albany	Elgin 97827	C. McLaughlin	1	
OK Theatre	208 W. Main	Enterprise 97828	R. Ford	1	
Bijou Theatre	492 E. 13th Ave.	Eugene 97401	M. Lamont	2	
Mt. Hood Theatre	401 E. Powell Blvd.	Gresham 97030		1	
Valley Theatre	Rt. 1 Box 67	Halfway 97834	R. Peer	1	
Wilderness Theatre	P.O. Box 309	John Day 97845	D. Elliott	1	
Lake Twin Cinema	106 N. State St.	Lake Oswego		3	
Alger Theatre	Box 31	Lakeview 97630	R. Alger	1	
Kuhn Theatre	668 Main	Lebanon 97355	D. Saunders	1	
Bijou Theatre	Box 354	Lincoln City 97367	J. Mace	1	
Movie House Theatre	Box 1	Moro 97039	D. Healey	1	
Centre 1 & 2 Theatre	Box 449	Ontario 97914	H. Matthews	2	600
Pix Theatre	358 S. Oregon St.	Ontario 97914	J. Ross	1	
• Oregon City Drive-in Theatre	18955 S. South End Rd.	Oregon City 97503		1	
Cinema Tri-Plex Theatre	P.O. Box 430	Pendleton 97801	L. Spiess	3	
Avalon 1 & 2 Theatre	3451 S.E. Belmont St.	Portland 97214	J. McKee	2	
Cinema 21	616 NW 21st Ave.	Portland 97209		1	
Cinemagic	2021 SE Hawthorne Blvd.	Portland 97214		1	
Clinton Street Cinema	2522 Clinton St.	Portland 97202	Clinton St. Collective	1	
Emerald City Theatre	1732 N. Blandena	Portland 97217	J. News	1	
Joy Theatre	11959 SW Pacific Hwy.	Portland 97223	Family Theatre	1	
Laurelhurst Theatre	2735 E. Burnside St.	Portland 97214		5	
Milwaukie Tri Cinema	11011 SE Main St.	Portland 97222	Family Theatre	1	
Moreland Theatre	6712 SE	Portland 97202		1	
Mt. Tabor Tri-Cinema	4811 S.E. Hawthorne	Portland 97215	S. Donkin	2	
New St. Johns Theatre	8704 N. Lombard St.	Portland 97203		1	
Roseway Theatre	7229 NE Sandy Blvd.	Portland 97213		1	
Sellwood Theatre	1323 Se Tacoma St.	Portland 97202	Family Theatre	1	
Salem Cinema	445 High S.E.	Salem 97308	L. Miles	1	165
Sherwood Oriental Theatre	125 N.W. First St.	Sherwood 97140	Rothschild/Stoller	1	
Palace Theatre	P.O. Box 176	Silverton 97381	Paulson & Rasmussen	1	480
Star Cinema	350 N. Third Ave.	Stayton 97383	J. Lane	1	427
Cascade Cinema 1-2 Theatre	3817 W. 10th St.	The Dalles 97058	L. Moyer	2	
Granada	223 E. Second St.	The Dalles 97058		1	
Joy Theatre	11959 S.W. Pacific Hwy.	Tigard 97223	Kerchinsky	1	
Tualatin Twin Cinema	8345 SW Nyberg Rd.	Tualatin 97062	Family Theatre	2	
Joy Theatre	715 Bridge St.	Veronia 97064	J. Thomas	1	
• Woodburn Drive-In	P.O. Box 591	Woodburn 97071	L. Stitt	1	

PENNSYLVANIA

Name	Address	City & Zip	Owner	Screens	Seats
Mr. Bill Roach Theatre	2146 Maplewood Ave.	Abington 19001	B. Roach	1	
19th Street Theatrre	525 N. 19th St.	Allentown 18104	H. Heydt	1	
Franklin	425 Tilghman St.	Allentown 18103	A. Moffa	1	479
Pitt Theatre	P.O. Box 246	Bedford 15522	J. Cessna	1	400
• Super 71 A & B Drive-in		Belle Vernon 15012	V. Castelli	2	
Strand Theatre	114 E. Front St.	Berwick 18603	M. Trautman	1	
Boyd Theatre	40 Bethlehem Plaza	Bethlehem 18018	Valley Theatres	1	1040
Capitol Twin Theatre	E. Main St.	Bloomsburg 17815	M. Trautman	2	
State Theatre	61 N. Reading Ave.	Boyertown 19512	R. Ritner	1	300
• Malden Drive-In	380 Old National Pike	Brownsville 15417	A. Shashura	1	
• Circle Drive-In	12 Salem Avenue	Carbondale 18407	M. Delfino	1	
• Sunset Drive-In	4235 Sunset Pike	Chambersburg 17201	H. Kagan	1	
Cheswick Quad	Pittsburgh Street	Cheswick 15024	J. Mulone	4	
Ritz Twin Theatres	111 E. Market St.	Clearfield 16830	R. Knepp	2	
• Super 322 Drive-In	Woodland & digler Hwy.	Clearfield 16830	Favuzza	1	
Iris Theatre	157 W. Adams St.	Cochranton 16314	J. Motzing	1	
State Theatre	421 Locust St.	Columbia 17512	M. Warren	1	
• Dependable Drive-In	9 Clinton Rd.	Coraopolis 15108		1	
• Corry Drive-In	RD #3	Corry 16407	Kirsch Ths.	1	
Coudersport Theatre	Main Street	Coudersport 16915	J. Rigas	1	
• Haars Drive-In	185 Logan Rd.	Dillsburg 17019	V. Harr	1	
Dubois Playhouse Theatre	8 N. Brady St.	Dubois 15801	J. Test	1	
Edensburg Cinema Theatre	129 S. Center	Edensburg 15931	D. Persio	1	
• Peninsula Twin Drive-In	303 Peninsula Drive	Erie 16505	Cinemette	2	
• Route 222 Drive-In	RD #2	Fleetwood 19522	Angstadt & Wolfe	1	150
Waterworks Cinemas	Waterworks Mall	Fox Chapel 15238		8	
Glen Theatre	37 Manchester St.	Glen Rock 17327	F. Strausbaugh	1	150
• Halifax Drive-In	Route 147	Halifax 17032	M. Trautman	1	
Harmar Cinemas	2583 Freeport Rd.	Harmarville 15238		6	
• Laurel Drive-In	R.D. 1	Hazleton 18201	F. Sacco	1	
The Movies	1154 Main St.	Hellertown 18055	E. Koffler	1	
Hershey Lodge Cinema	W. Chocolate Ave	Hershey 17033	Herco, Inc.	1	
• Maple Drive-In	Route 6	Honesdale 18431	M. Delfino	1	
Huntingdon Cinema	717 Washington Street	Huntingdon 16652	D. Peoples	1	
Lamp Theatre	220 Main Street	Irwin 15642	A. Beters	1	
Merlin Theatre	212 Old York Td.	Jenkintown 19046	P. Merlin	1	
Strand Cinemas I & II	32 N. Whiteoak Street	Kutztown 19530	P. Angstadt	2	
• Key Drive-In	15th Ave. & E. Lehman	Lebanon 17042	J. Weber	1	
• Mahoning Valley Drive-In	Road #2	Lehighton 18235	J. Farruggio	1	
Campus Theatre	413 Market Street	Lewisburg 17837	J. Stiefel	1	650
• Midway Drive-In	Route 322	Lewistown 17044	F. Royer	1	
Ligonier Theatre	210 W. Main Street	Ligonier 15658	A. Troil Jr.	1	
• Port Drive-In	Rd. # 1	Linden 17744	J. Farruggio	1	

Name	Address	City & Zip	Owner	Screens	Seats
Roxy Theatre	314 E. Main Street	Lock Haven 17745	J. Stiefel	1	450
Marietta Theatre	130 W. Market Street	Marietta 17547	D. Kalmbach	1	
Tri State 1-2 Theatres	Route 6 & 209	Matamoras 18336	M. Tonkin	2	
Parkway Theatre	644 Broadway	McKees Rocks 15136	I. Gasper	1	
Eastland Theatre		McKeesport 15132		2	
Rainbow Village Cinema Triplex	White Oaks Shop. Ctr.	McKeesport 15132	G. Monezis	3	
Media Theatre	104 E. State St.	Media 15131	T. Berezowski	2	
Elks Theatre	Emaus & Union Sts.	Middletown 17057	J. Crist	1	
Colonnade Theatre	Center Street	Millersburg 17061	M. Trautman	1	
Montrose Pump n Pantry Theatre	18 Public Avenue	Montrose 18801	Pump n Pantry Stores	1	228
Casino Theatre	Belmont Ave.	Mt. Pocono 18344	G. Litz	1	300
Ritz Theatre	9 Main Street	Muncy 17756	D. Wilt	1	
Narberth Theatre	129 N. Narberth Avenue	Narberth 19072	Narberth Theatre Inc.	1	
•Skyline Drive-In	1707 Audley Ave.	New Castle 16105	Ohio Movies	1	
West Shore Theatre	317 Bridge Street	New Cumberland 17070	F. Bollen	1	
Ritz Theatre	132 E. Main Street	New Holland 17557	R. Peters	1	
Newtown Theatre	120 N. State Street	Newtown 18940	M. Farruggio	1	
•Cumberland Drive-In	Route 1	Newville 17241	D. Mowery	1	
Roxy Theatre	2004 Main Street	Northampton 18067	Roxy Mgt. Co.	1	561
•Point Drive-In	Rd. #1 Box 334G	Northumberland 17857	Sports Set	1	
•Shankweiler Drive-In	Rd. 1	Orefield 18069	R. Malkames	1	
Capital Theatre	N. 52nd St.	Philadelphia 19131	P. Kleiman	1	
Ritz Five	214 Walnut St.	Philadelphia 19106		5	
Ritz at the Bourse	Fourth St.	Philadelphia 19106		5	
Roxy Theatre	2023 Sansom St.	Philadelphia 19103	M. Raab	2	270
Colonial Theatre	227 Bridge St.	Phoenixville 19460	S. LaRosa	1	
Beehive Big Screen	3807 Forbes Ave.	Pittsburgh 15213	S. Zumoff	1	
Bellvue Theatre	609 Lincoln Ave	Pittsburgh 15202		4	
Hollywood Theatre	Potomac Ave.	Pittsburgh 15216		1	
Manor Cinema	1729 Murray Ave.	Pittsburgh		4	
Oaks Cinema	310 Allegheny River Bl.	Pittsburgh 15139		1	
Pittsburgh Playhouse	Craft Ave.	Pittsburgh		2	
Regent Square	1035 S. Braddock St.	Pittsburgh 15218		1	
Rex Theatre	1602 E. Carson St.	Pittsburgh 15203		1	
Waterworks Cinemas	Waterwork Mall	Pittsburgh 14122	N. Mulone	10	2160
Reality Theatre	Main Street	Robertsdale 16674	M. O'Hagan	1	
356 Cinemas	718 S. Pike Road	Sarver 16055	J. Mulone	4	
Sayre Theatre	205 S. Elmer Avenue	Sayre 18840	S. Freedman	1	
Ritz Courtyard Cinema	222 Wyoming Avenue	Scranton 18503	A. Clay	1	586
Sellersville Cinema	24W Temple Avenue	Sellersville 18960	P. Maclay	1	325
Victoria Theatre	46 W. Independence St.	Shamokin 17872	J. Mattox	1	2000
Broad Theatre	24 W. Broad St.	Souderton 18964	M. Kerver	1	
•Temple Drive-In	1670 N. Atherton St.	State College 16801	Eds Discount	1	
Foxmoor Cinemas	Foxmoor S/C Box 6M E.	Stroudsburg 18301		5	1000
Keystone Theatre	601 Main St.	Towanda 18848	Bradford Cty. Reg. Arts Cnl	1	500
Tremont Theatre	135 E. Main Street	Tremont 17891	P. Knapp	1	
Majestic Theatre	29 W. Broad St. W.	Hazleton 18201	G. Litz	1	650
•Bucks County Drive-In	401 Easton Rd.	Warrington 18976		1	
Watson Theatre	131 Main Street	Watsonville 17777	R. Deibler	1	
Waynesburg Theatre & Arts Center	40 W. High Street	Waynesburg 15370	R. Kuger	1	
Arcadia Theatre	50 Main Street	Wellsboro 16901	R. Dunham	1	600
•Wysox Drive-In	Route 6	Wysox 18854	Buffington	1	
Yeadon Theatre	Church Lane & Bailey Rd.	Yeadon 19051	Yeadon Theatre Co.	1	

RHODE ISLAND

Name	Address	City & Zip	Owner	Screens	Seats
Empire Theatre	P.O. Box 46	Block Island 02807	M. Huggins	1	
Park Cinemas I, II & III	848 Park Ave.	Cranston 02910	S.S.C. Cinemas	3	770
Greenwich Cinema	11 Pricewood Drive	East Greenwich 02818	S. Erinakes	1	
Starcase Triplex Theatres	1346 W. Main Road	Middletown 02840	S. Erinakes	3	
Pier Cinema 1 & 2 Theatre	Pier Village Mall	Narragansett 02882	W. Rosen	2	
Jane Pickens Theatre	49 Touro Road	Newport 02840	J. Jarvis	1	
Opera House Cinema	19 Touro Street	Newport 02840	SSC Cinemas	3	
•Rustic Drive-In		No. Smithfield 02876	Hallmark	1	
Avon Cinema Theatre	260 Thayer Street	Providence 02906	E. Dulgarian	1	
Cable Car Cinema	204 S. Main Street	Providence 02906	R. Bilodeau	1	
Meadowbrook Cinema	2452 Warwick Avenue	Warwick 02889	B. Vanasse	3	
Palace Theatre	85 Washington Street	West Warwick 02893	J. Tavone	1	
Stadium Theatre	Monument Square	Woonsocket 02895	A. Darman	1	

SOUTH CAROLINA

Name	Address	City & Zip	Owner	Screens	Seats
Belvedere Cinema	North Main Street	Anderson 29621	H. Cochran	1	
Osteen Twin 1 Theatre	P.O. Box 1506	Anderson 29621	P. Osteen	1	
Village Cinema	P.O. Box 408	Anderson 29622	C. Bolt	4	
Little Theatre	160 Main Street	Bamberg 29003	D. Cole	1	
Plaza 8 Theatres	U.S. Hwy. 21 & 170	Beaufort 29902	P. Trask	5	
Little Theatre	506 Dekalb Street	Camden 29020	G. Coan	1	
Darlington Cinema	118 Pearl Street	Darlington 29532	M. Watkins	1	
Main Street Cinemas	3000 Main Street	Hilton Head Island 29926	W. Harn	3	
The Island Theatre	Coligny Plaza	Hilton Head Island 29928	W. Harn	1	
•East Main Drive-In	P.O. Box 939	Lake City 29560	W. Funk	1	
Crown Twin Theatre	Westgate Shopping Ctr	Lancaster 29720	D. Watson	2	
Mini Cinema Theatre	Box 3435 Cherry Rd.	Rock Hill 29730	R. Turnbull	1	
Cook Theatre	Box 56	Walterboro 29488	H. Cook	1	

Name	Address	City & Zip	Owner	Screens	Seats

SOUTH DAKOTA

Name	Address	City & Zip	Owner	Screens	Seats
Lorain Theatre	RRA Box 5	Armour 57313	C. Farke	1	
Strand Theatre	703 Main	Britton 57430	I. Besse	1	
Hamlin County Dakota Cinema	Box 101	Bryant 57221	L. Klungseth	1	195
State Theatre	108 S. Main	Chamberlain 57325	J. Buche	1	246
Dells Theatre	511 4th Street	Dell Rapids 57022	J. King	1	400
Lyric Theatre	805 G Avenue	Eureka 57437	D. Lapka	1	297
Mix Theatre	P.O. Box 280	Lake Andes 57101	M. Durham	1	
Palace Theatre	209 Main Street	Lemmon 57638	P. Priest	1	
West Twin 1-2 Theatres	Box 361	Madison 57042	Prostrollo	2	
Inland Theatre	Box 608	Martin 57551	P. Nelson	1	
Mill Theatres 1-2-3	316 S. Main Street	Milbank 57252	N. Bagaus	3	
Mac Theatre	311 Main Street	Mobridge 57601	R. Maier	1	476
•Pheasant Drive-In	Box 217	Mobridge 57601	R. Maier	1	
Cinema Theatre	P.O. Box 37	Redfield 57469	T. Gallup	1	
•Pheasant City Drive-In	625 East Third St.	Redfield 57469	T. Gallup	1	
Star Theatre	P.O. Box 259	Selby 57472	D. Marin	1	
•Winner Drive-In	P.O. Box 562	Winner 57580	H. Fast	1	

TENNESSEE

Name	Address	City & Zip	Owner	Screens	Seats
American Cinema Twin	Whiteway Shop. Ctr	Athens 37303	P. Goddard	2	
•Midway Drive-In	2137 Highway 30	E Athens 37303	T. Epps	1	
•Beacon Drive-In	Rte. 666 Box 2	Bristol 37620	A. Leonard	1	
•Green Hills	Drive-In RR 1	Carthage 37030	T. Parker	1	
Cinema 1 & 2 Theatre	Box 3206	Cleveland 37311	C. Benton	2	
Shady Brook Cinema	P.O. Box 419	Columbia 38402	H. Vinson	6	
Richland Park Cinema	Route 1 Box 567	Dayton 37321	B. Matherly	1	
•Broadway Drive-In	3020 Highway 70	W Dickson 37055	Armstrong	1	
•Dunlap Drive-In	Box 178	Dunlap 37327	L. Boston	1	
Bonnie Kate Twin Theatre	P.O. Box 466	Elizabethton 37643	R. Glover	2	
•Stateline Drive-In	Route 8 Box 598	Elizabethton 37643	E. Bolling	1	
Cinema 1 & 2	Box 100	Erwin 37650	J. Hendren	1	400
Lincoln Twin Theatres	Box 604	Fayetteville 37334	J. Rhoton	2	
•Sumner Drive-In	1401 Nashville Pike	Gallatin 37066	H. Smith	1	
Northgate Crossing Cinemas	622 Northgate Mall	Hixson 37343	J. Ellis	4	
Capri Cinema	5304 Kingston Pike	Knoxville 37919	J. Simpson	1	
Tennessee Theatre	604 S. Gay Street	Knoxville 37902	Dick Bdcstg. Co.	1	1500
Terrace Tap House Theatre	315 Mohican Drive	Knoxville 37901	J. Simpson	2	
Fare 4 Theatres	5117 Old Summer Road	Memphis 38122	A. Keshani	1	
Strand Theatre	7979 Wilkersonville Rd.	Millington 38053	C. Sim	1	
Cinema One Theatre	726 S. Tennessee Blvd.	Murfreesboro 37130	H. Christian	1	
•Woodzo Drive-In	Box 87	Newport 37821	H. Smith	1	
Roane Theatre	106 W. Richmond St.	Rockwood 37854	F. Wodall	1	
Southgate Cinemas	411 Florence Road	Savannah 38372	G. Adams	3	
Capri Twin Theatre	201 Depot St.	Shelbyville 37160		2	
Fair Theatre & Lobby Video	112 E. Market Street	Somerville 38608	N. Fair	1	365
•Sparta Drive-In	Box 187	Sparta 38583	Mid. Tenn. Am.	1	
Capitol Theatre	P.O. Box 837	Union City 38261	Scarborough	1	
Merlu Theatre	Rt. #3	Waverly 37185	L. Curtis	1	
•Valley Drive-In	P.O. Box 330	Waverly 37185	N. Flexer	1	
Wayne Theatre	P.O. Box 717	Waynesboro 38485	H. Corn	1	
•Cross Roads Drive-In	R.F.D. 2	Whitwell 37397	R. Reeves	1	
•Family Drive-In	Box 523	Winchester 37398	Cumberland	1	
•Lake Country Drive-In		Wynnburg 38077	D. Scott	1	

TEXAS

Name	Address	City & Zip	Owner	Screens	Seats
Paramount Theatre	352 Cypress Street	Abilene 79601	Paramount Comm.	1	
•Park Drive-In	P.O. Box 3654	Abilene 79601	J. Mitchell	1	
Westgate Cinema 1 & 2 Theatre	100 Westgate S/C	Abilene 79605		2	
•Buckhorn Drive-In	Box 1170	Alice 78332	Noret Theas.	1	
Rangra Theatres	109 E. Holland	Alpine 79830	A. Rangra	2	375
Cinema IV Theatres	Athens Center	Athens 75751	Mitchell Theatres	4	
Tower Theatre	814 Chestnut Street	Bastrop 78602	S. Tabor	2	
Regal Twin Theatre	206 S. Fifth St.	Brownfield 79316	S. Jones	2	
Victoria Theatre	1244 E. 14th Street	Brownsville 78521	R. Ruenes	1	
Nueces Theatre	P.O. Box 166	Camp Wood 78833	J. Hodges	1	
Palace Theatre	Box 1146	Canadian 79014	R. Talley	1	
Plaza Theatre	119 N. Buffalo	Canton 75103	T. Honea	1	
Varsity Theatre	2302 Fourth Ave.	Canyon 79015	B. Poff	1	
Plaza Theatre	1115 W. Fourth Street	Carrollton 75006	Lowrey	1	700
Carthage Twin Cinema	1120 W. Panola	Carthage 75633	D. Bates	2	
Palace Theatre	200 Main	Childress 79201	R. Nies	1	
Cliftex Theatre	306 W. Fifth Street	Clifton 76634	J. Morgan	1	
Memorial Student Center	Box J-1	College Station 77844	Texas A&M Univ.	1	
Cinema 76	Box 596	Copperas Cove 76522	Whatley Theatres	1	
Cove Theatre	P.O. Box 1043	Copperas Cove 76522	K. Hall	1	
Cinema IV	1803 W. Seventh	Corsicana 75110	Trans Texas	4	
Guild Theatre	1220 E. Valverde	Crystal City 78839	Luna Theatres	1	
Morris Theatre	P.O. Box P	Daingerfield 75638	W. Bass	2	460
Mission Theatre	409 Denrock	Dalhart 79022	D. Gilbert	2	450
Evelyn Twin Theatre	P.O. Box 476	Dumas 79029	R. Nies	2	
Eagle Pass Cinema 3 Theatre	455 Bibb Street	Eagle Pass 78852	C. Brill	3	
Iris Theatre	P.O. Box 1042	Eagle Pass 78852	H. Munoz	1	
Majestic Theatre	P.O. Box 705	Eastland 76448	Eastland Fine Arts	1	825
Rivas Cinema	P.O. Box 681	Eden 76837	S. Rivas	1	
•Ascarate Drive-In	6701 Delta Dr.	El Paso 79905	D. Pierce	1	
•Cinema Park Drive-In	10676 Montana	El Paso 79935	Flw. Theatre	3	
Pioneer Theatre	113 E. Rice Street	Falfurrias 78355	G. Vela	1	

Name	Address	City & Zip	Owner	Screens	Seats
•Mansfield 1 & 2 Drive-In ...	2935 E. Seminary Dr.	Fort Worth 76119	J. Mitchell	2	
Seventh Street Theatre	3128 W. Seventh Street	Fort Worth 76107	B. Milligan	1	
Ganado Theatre	Rt. 1 Box 32	Ganado 77962	A. Svoboda	1	
Walnut Twin Theatre	3310 W. Walnut	Garland 75042	D. Christenson	2	200
Cinema I & II	P.O. Box 726	Giddings 78942	Pearce/Johnson	2	514
Cozy Theatre	108 E. Commerce	Gladewater 75647	A. Gaston	1	
•Brazos Drive-In		Granbury 76048	Johnson	1	
Show Theatre	P.O. Box 218	Grand Saline 75140	Adrian	1	
Briargrove III Theatres	6100 Westheimer	Houston 77057	Dollar Cinema	1	
Garden Oaks	3732 N. Shepherd Drive	Houston 77018	Zarzana Theatres	1	
Jewel Theatre	P.O. Box 98	Humble 77338	Ivy H.D.	1	
Cinema 1-2-3 Theatres	Univ. Hts. Shopping Ctr.	Huntsville 77340	G. Palmer	3	
Chateau 3 Theatre	P.O. Box 150517	Irving 75015	Meagher	3	
Texan Theatre	648 E. Main St.	Junction 76849	J. Evans	1	
Cole-Rosenberg Theatre	Box 303	La Grange 78945	G. Rainosek	1	
Cinema I & II Theatres	310 This Way Lake	Jackson 77566	J. Huebel	2	600
Lake I & II Theatres	3 Circle Way	Lake Jackson 77566	J. Huebel	2	850
Marble Theatre	218 Main St.	Marble Falls 78654	G. Spitzer	1	
Marshall Twin Cinema	1901 E. Travis	Marshall 75670	W. Bass	2	
Odeon Theatre	P.O. Box 43	Mason 76856	T. Hooten	1	
Select Theatre	P.O. Box 645	Mineola 75773	Lake Country Playhouse	1	
SFA Theatre	2210 North Street	Nacogdoches 75961	W. Matterson	1	
Grandview Cinema	2760 N. Grandview	Odessa 79760	Hodge Assoc.	1	
Cinema 1 & 2 Theatre	3330 W. Bowling Lane	Orange 77636	Cine Mark	2	
El Capitan Theatre	P.O. Box 801	Pharr 78577	R. Benitez	1	
Plestex Theatre	P.O. Box 24	Pleasanton 78064	G. Talley	3	
Hollywood Theatre	1510 Trinity	Port Arthur 77640	L. Fontana	1	
Twin Dolphin Cinemas	P.O. Box 989	Port Lavaca 77979	D. Walraven	2	
Rig Theatre	P.O. Box 361	Premont 78375	R. Schultz	1	
Cinema 35 Theatre	P.O. Box 634	Rockport 78382	Dinger	1	
Roma Theatre	P.O. Box 131	Roma 78584	E. Ramirez	1	
•Mission Drive-In 4	3100 Roosevelt	San Antonio 78214	Santikos	4	
Cozy Theatre	607 Lyons Avenue	Schulenburg 78956	B. Pettit	1	
Palace Twin Theatre	314 S. Austin Street	Seguin 78156	G. Roscoe, Mrs.	2	
Texas Theatre	217 N. Main Street	Shamrock 79079	A. Boyter	1	
Plaza Twin Theatre	1717 Cumberland	Vernon 76384	S. Barton	2	848
Weatherford Theatres	111 College St.	Weatherford 76086	A.B. Cinema	4	
Palace Theatre	109 E. Post Office St.	Weimar 78962	H. Michna	1	
Majestic Theatre	136 W.N. Commerce	Wills Point 75169	K. Lybrand	1	
Grand Theatre	P.O. Box 191	Yoakum 77995	M. Picha	1	

UTAH

Name	Address	City & Zip	Owner	Screens	Seats
Towne Cinemas 1 & 2	120 W. Main St.	American Fork 84003	R. Vance	2	
Cinema Theatre	Box 112	Beaver 84713	E. Dewsnup	1	
Wayne Theatre	Box 205	Bicknell 84715	S. Brinkerhoff	1	315
San Juan Theatre	120 W. Center St.	Blanding 84511	J. Slavens	1	
Queen Theatre	460 West 500 South	Bountiful 84010	R. Miller	1	
Roy Theatre	956 E. 800 South	Bountiful 84010	B. Call	1	
Capitol Theatre I & II	53 S. Main St.	Brigham City 84302	R. Walker	2	
Cedar Cinema Twin Theatre	Box 366	Cedar City 84720	J. Sawyers	5	
T & T Twin Theatre	420 E. Topaz Blvd.	Delta 84624	C. Tolbert	2	
Esquire Theatre	Box 382	East Carbon 84520	T. Dickerson	1	
Towne Theatre	21 N. Main	Ephraim 84627	R. Anderson	1	414
Avon Theatre	94 S. Main St.	Heber 84032	S. Zimmerman	1	
Butch Cassidy Cinema	163 N. Main	Huntington 84528	S. Parker	1	
Kanab Theatre	29 W. Center	Kanab 84741	P. Roundy	1	
Cinemas Five	4140 West 5415	South Kearns 84118	R. Miller	5	
Utah Theatre	18 W. Center St.	Logan 84321	K. Hansen	1	
The Movies	P.O. Box 489	Monticello 84535	G. Young	1	
•Basin Drive-In Theatre	680 N. State	Mt. Pleasant 84647	R. Anderson	1	200
Cinedome North Theatre	1481 W. Riverdale Rd.	Ogden 84403	D. Tulles	1	
Country Club Theatre	3930 Washington Blvd.	Ogden 84403	J. Cuculich	1	
•Motor Vu Drive-In	5368 So. 1050 West	Ogden 84403	H. Coleman	1	
•North Star Drive-In	2131 N. Highway 89	Ogden 84404	W. Webb	1	
Scera Theatre	745 S. State St.	Orem 84057	Scera Corp.	1	
•Timpanogos Drive-In	614 N. 1200	W. Orem 84057	W. Bunting	1	
Huish Theatre	98 W. Utah Ave.	Payson 84651	P. Mower	1	
Walker Cinemas 4	1776 S. Highway 89	Perry 84302	R. Walker	4	
•Motor Vu	1645 N. Carbondale Rd.	Price 84501	S.Dewsnup	1	
Webbs Family Theatre	126 S. 100	East Providence 84332	S. Webb	1	
•Pioneer Twin Drive-In	Box 241	Provo 84603	M. Cox	2	
Varsity Theatre	Rm. 218 Bldg. ELWC	Provo 84603	B. Young Univ.	1	415
Roosevelt Twin Theatre	P.O. Box 2139	Roosevelt 84066	J. Chasel	2	
Avalon Theatre	3605 S. State	Salt Lake City 84115	A. Proctor	1	500
National Guard Theatre	765 N. 220 West	Salt Lake City 84116	P. Dell	1	
Sandy Starship	5239 Green Pine Rd.	Salt Lake City 84123	R. Miller	4	
•Valley View Drive-In	3646 View Crest Crcl.	Salt Lake City 84117	W. Webb	1	700
Main Family Theatre	141 N. Main	Smithfield 84335	K. Hansen	1	
Main Street Movie	165 North Main Street	Spanish Fork 84660	D. Dunn	1	
•Art City Drive-In	720 North Main	Springfield 84663	W. Webb	1	
Ritz Theatre	107 N. Main St.	Tooele 84074	Ritz Mgt. Corp.	2	
•Sunset Drive-In	Box 910	Vernal 84078	Shiner Bros.	1	
Sunset Theatre	P.O. Box 910	Vernal 84078	Shiner Bros.	1	
Tri Cinema Theatre	P.O. Box 910	Vernal 84078	Shiner Bros.	3	
•Valley Vu Drive-In	3555 S. 4800 West	West Valley City 84120	W. Webb	1	

VERMONT

Name	Address	City & Zip	Owner	Screens	Seats
Memorial Theatre	Main Street	Barton 05822	Barton Village Inc.	1	
New Faces Cinema	The Square Bellows	Falls 05101	Town of Rickingham	1	

Name	Address	City & Zip	Owner	Screens	Seats
Cinema 1-2-3 Theatre	Rt. 67 A	Bennington 05201	G. Couture	2	
Harte Theatre	P.O. Box 524	Bennington 05201	G. Houran	1	
•Randall Drive-In	Rte 12	Bethel 05032	Osterberg	1	180
Nickelodeon 6 Plex Theatre	222 Colleg St.	Burlington 05401	J. Tranum	6	
•Fairlee Drive-In	Rte 5, Box 31	Fairlee 05045	R. Herb	1	350
Capitol Theatre	93 State St.	Montpelier 05602	F. Bashara	5	
Savoy Theatre	26 Main St.	Montpelier 05602	R. Winston	1	
Bijou Theatre	Portland St.	Morrisville 05661	J. McKinley	1	
Cinema Theatre	Main Street	Newport 05855	Graphic	1	
Merrills Showplace 1-2-3	East Main St.	Newport 05855	M. Jarvis	3	
Elray Theatre	26 Main St.	Springfield 05156	R. Ellis	2	300
•St. Albans Drive-In		St. Albans 05478	P. Gamache	1	500
Welden Theatre 3	17 Prospect St.	St. Albans 05478	P. Gamache	3	500
Star Theatre	18 Eastern Ave.	St. Johnsbury 05819	Recreation Inc.	1	
Stowe Cinema	Box 1287	Stowe 05672	V. Buonano	1	

VIRGINIA

Name	Address	City & Zip	Owner	Screens	Seats
Fox Chase Cinema	4621 Duke St.	Alexandria 22304	Rubin/Poryles	3	620
Arlington Cinema'n' Drafthouse	2903 Columbia	Pike Arlington		1	
Idle Hour Theatre	P.O. Box 245	Belle Haven 23306	R. Pase	1	400
•Central Drive-In		Blackwood 24222	J. Kiser	1	
Palace Theatre	303 Mason Ave.	Cape Charles 23310	T. Savage	1	
Movie Palace	110 E. Main St.	Charlottesville 22901	A. Martin	2	
Vinegar Hill Theatre	220 W. Market St.	Charlottesville 22901	A. Porotti	1	220
Mecca Theatre	P.O. Box 185	Chase City 23924	J. McNeer	1	
Lee Cinema	1215 E. Lee Highway	Chillhowie 24319	J. Maxey	2	
Ballou Park Twin Theatres	150 Tunstall Rd.	Danville 24541	W. Headley	2	
Ewing Theatre	P.O. Box 254	Ewing 24248	D. Howard	1	
•Fork Union Drive-In	Route 612	Fork Union 23055	F. White	1	
Hillside Cinema	#1-2 Box 449 Rt. 14	Gloucester 23061	Jennings/Mullins	2	
Elkhorn City Cinema	P.O. Box 125	Haysi 24256	L. Mullens	1	
Henrico Theatre	305 E. Nine Mile Rd.	Highland Springs 23075	C. Horne	1	
Fairfax Theatre	Main Street	Kilmarnock 22482	Jennigs/Mullins	1	
•Hulls Drive-In	Rt. #5	Lexington 24450	S. Hull	1	
Page Theatre	33 E. Main St.	Luray 22825	J. Spencer	2	
Village Theatre	9310 Warwick Blvd.	Newport News 23601	J. Gordon	1	400
Roseland Theatre	48 Market St./P.O. 178	Onancock 23417	Onancock Theatre Corp.	1	349
Commmodore Theatre	421 High St.	Portsmouth 23704	F. Schoenfeld	1	
Radford Theatre	1043 Norwood St.	Radford 24141	F. Kirk	1	509
Richland Mall Twin Theatres	P.O. Box 1440	Richlands 24641	K. Davis	2	
Hippodrome Theatre	528 N. Second St.	Richmond 23219	J. Stalling	1	
Cinema 1 & 2 Inc.	Rt 2, Box 336, Hwy 58	E South Boston 24592	M. Day	2	450
Daw Theatre	P.O. Box 1025	Tappahannock 22560	W. Cleaton	1	396
Williamsburg Theatre	Duke of Gloucester St.	Williamsburg 23185	Col. Williamsburg Fdn.	1	538
Wytheville Cinema 1 & 2	720 E. Monroe St.	Wytheville 24382	B. Shope	2	

WASHINGTON

Name	Address	City & Zip	Owner	Screens	Seats
Olympic Theatre	107 N. Olympic Ave.	Arlington 98223	Pappas & Pappas	1	
•White Elephant Drive-In	1 502 State St.	Centralia 98531	W. Slusher	2	
•Auto View Drive-In	112 North Main St.	Colville 99114	Jest Ths.	1	
Sunset Theatre	P.O. Box 827	Connell 99326	Palace Theatre Corp.	1	
Village Cinema	515 River Dr.	Coulce Dam 99116	K. Schmidt	1	
Edmonds Theatre	415 Main St.	Edmonds 98020	Aeries II, Inc.	2	300
Elma Theatre	113 N. 4th St.	Elma 98541	D. Lund	1	600
Harbor Mall Cinema Theatre	14511 Sherman Dr. N.W.	Gig Harbor 98335	J. Walston	1	
Clyde Theatre	P.O. Box 199	Langley 98260	S. Willeford	1	
G Theatre	P.O. Box 568	Mossyrock 98564	D. Shriver	1	
Roxy Theatre	P.O. Box 214	Newport 99156	R. Bishop	1	
Omak Theatre	Box W	Omak 98841	L. Lassila	1	
Seeley Theatre	P.O. Box 887	Pomeroy 99347	Lucck & Compt.	1	
Plaza Twin Theatre	820 Bay St.	Port Orchard 98366	P.O. Improvement Corp.	2	325
•Rodeo Triplex Drive-In	7369 State Hwy. 3 SW	Port Orchard 98366	Finely McCoy	3	
•Wheel In Motor Movie	210 Theatre Rd.	Port Townsend 98368	R. Wiley	1	150
•Big Bear Drive-In	P.O. Box 25	Poulsbo 98370	J. Lilquist	1	
Liberty Theatre	116 W. Main St.	Puyallup 98371		1	
Willapa Theatre	P.O. Box 191	Raymond 98577	Tambellini	1	
Roxy Theatre	504 Third St.	S Renton 98055	C. Olosky	1	
Ritz Theatre	107 E. Main St.	Ritzville 99169	D. Gesche	1	
Roslyn Theatre	4 Dakota St.	Roslyn 98941	J. Donaldson	1	
Egyptian Theatre	801 E. Pine	Seattle 98122	McDonald	1	
Market Theatre	1428 Post Alley	Seattle 98101	A. Broroder	1	
Village Cinema	142 Mountain View Dr.	Sequim 98382	F. Torrence	1	191
Franklin Plaza Theatre	517 W. Franklin	Shelton 98584	R. Nye	1	
Bijou Theatre	2611 N. Proctor	Tacoma 98407	S. Mayo	1	
Liberty Theatre Inc.	857 142 St. So.	Tacoma 98444	W. Dunwoody	1	
Recreation Systems Ltd.	Fifth Ave.S.Box 193	Taholah 98587	Pickernell	1	
Cascade Park Cinemas	S.E. 411 Chkalov Dr.	Vancouver 98684	J. Thrift	4	
Cascade Theatres	7302 E. 18th St.	Vancouver 98661		1	
Island Theatre	Box 491	Vashon 98070	J. Stoltz	1	
Liberty Cinemas	P.O. Box 2506	Wentachee 98807	Sun Basin	5	1300
•Country Drive-In	8301 Tieton Drive	Yakima 98908	J. Anderson	2	650
•Fruitvale Drive-In Triple	P.O. Box 1551	Yakima 98901	W. Davidson	3	

WEST VIRGINIA

Name	Address	City & Zip	Owner	Screens	Seats
•Pipe Stem Drive-In		Athens 25873	R.Warden	1	
Star Theatre	Rt. 3, Box 191	Berkeley Springs 25411	Mozier/Soronen	1	325

Name	Address	City & Zip	Owner	Screens	Seats
Kanawha Theatre	601 57th St. NE	Charleston 25304	D. Corder	1	
Robinson Grand Theatre	444 W. Pike Street	Clarksburg 26301	M. Stout	1	
•Craigsville Drive-In		Craigsville 26205	J. Hanna	1	225
Manos Theatre	14 E. Main	Grafton 26354	J. Henderson	1	
Kingwood Cinema 1&2 Theatre	Kingwood Shopping Center	Kingwood 26537	R. Snyder	2	
Seneca Showcase 1 & 2	Rt. 219 Greenbriar Mall	Lewisburg 24901	C. McCall	2	
Berkley Plaza	Seven Berkley Place S/C	Martinsburg 24134	E. Costolo, Jr.	7	
•Meadowbridge Drive-In	P.O. Box 291	Meadowbridge 25976	H. McClanahan	1	
Strand Theatre	Fifth & Jefferson St.	Moundsville 26041	Ramser	1	175
Mt. Hope Theatre	531 Main Street	Mt. Hope 25880	F. Bonifacio	1	
•Jungle Drive-In	RR 1	Parkersburg 26101	C. Westbrook	1	
Seneca Theatre	Main Street	Petersburg 26847	G. Michael	1	
•Pineville Drive-In		Pineville 28474	P. Warden	1	
Cherry River Cinema	Cherry River Shop.Pl.	Richwood 26261	J. Chapman	1	
South C Cinema	205 D Street	S. Charleston 25303	R. Colan	1	
Shepherdstown Opera House	131 W. German St.	Shepherdstown 25443		1	
Robey Theatre	P.O. Box 869	Spencer 25276	M. Burch	1	
•Valley Drive-In	P.O. Box 188 St.	Albans 25177	W. Erwin	1	
Cinderella Theatre	P.O. Box 220	Williamson 25661	S. Kapourales	1	

WISCONSIN

Name	Address	City & Zip	Owner	Screens	Seats
•1329 Drive-In	P.O. Box 86	Abbotsford 54405	D.& L. Hodd	1	250
Abby Theatre	P.O. Box 86	Abbotsford 54405	D.& L. Hodd	1	386
Adams Theatre	157 S. Main Street	Adams 53910	A. Davidson	1	
Towne Movie House	524 Second Street	Algoma 54201	G. Goebel	1	
Amery Theatre	228 N. Keller Avenue	Amery 54001	M. Schanon	1	266
Bay Theatre	420 Main Street	Ashland 54806	A. Bergman	3	
Blaine Theatre	102 East Oak	Boscobel 53805	J. Thiele	1	365
Norton Cinema 1 Theatre	26 N. Madison Street	Chilton 53014	J. Norton	1	
Cornell Theatre	Box 325	Cornell 54732	J. Harvatine	1	
Isle Theatre	1345 2nd Ave.	Cumberland 54829	D. Long	1	230
Dodge Theatre	205 N. Iowa Street	Dodgeville 53533	J. Blabaum	1	
Eagle Theatre	218 E. Wall Street	Eagle River 53521	Conway Theatres	1	
Vilas Cinema 1-3	216 E. Wall	Eagle River 54521	S. Conway	3	
Gilman Theatre	North Main Street	Gilman 54433	T. Romig	1	
Budget Cinemas-South	4475 S. 108th Street	Greenfield 53228	B.C., Inc.	2	
Mall Cinemas	2500 Milton Ave.	Janesville 53545	B. Porchetta	3	
Rock Theatres	1620 Newport Ave.	Janesville 53547	B. Porchetta	7	
•Hiway 18 Drive-In		Jefferson	Mescop Inc.	1	
Market Square Theatres	8600 Sheridan Rd.	Kenosha 53719	Square Duck Corp	2	
Fredric March Play Crcl/WI Un.Thtr	800 Langdon Street	Madison 53706	Univ. of WI	1	1468
Hilldale Theatre	702 N. Midvale Blvd.	Madison 53705	Madison 20th Theatres	2	747
Majestic Theatre	115 King St.	Madison 53703	Madison 20th Theatres	1	
Orpheum Theatre	216 State St.	Madison 53705	Madison 20th Theatres	2	2050
•Cinema 2 Outdoor		Manispique	Mescop Inc.	1	
Gail Theatre	101 W. State Box 42	Mauston 53948	R. Kitson	1	
Cinema North 1 & 2 Theatres	910 W. Broadway	Medford 54451	D. Deda	2	
Cosmo Theatre	813 E. Main Street	Merrill 54452	O. Settele	2	
Avalon Theatre	2473 S. Kinnickinnic	Milwaukee 53207	E. Levin	1	1300
Budget Cinemas-North	7222 W. Good Hope	Milwaukee 53203	B.C., Inc.	2	
Times Cinema	5905 W. Vliet St.	Milwaukee 53208	S. Levin	1	467
•Sky Vue Drive-In	P.O. Box 297	Monroe 53566	R. Goetz	1	
Cinemas North	205 N. Lake	Phillips 54555	D. Deda	1	
Center Cinema Theatre	192 S. Central Ave.	Richland Center 53581	W. Muth	2	
•Starlite Drive-In		Richmond Center	Mescop Inc.	1	
Falls Theatre	105 S. Main Street	River Falls 54022	S. McCulloch	1	
•Skyway Drive-In		Sister Bay	Mescop Inc.	1	
Palace Theatre	238 Walnut Street	Spooner 54801	G. Clayton	1	
Cinema Cafe	255 E. Main Street	Stoughton 53589	D. Lange	1	
Donna Theatre	P.O. Box 289	Sturgeon Bay 54235	G. Goebel	2	
•Dells Drive-In	P.O. Box 383	Wisconsin Dells 53965	D. Legros	1	200
Lakeland Cinemas	Hwy. 51	Woodruff 54568	Conway Theatre	3	500

WYOMING

Name	Address	City & Zip	Owner	Screens	Seats
Ford Theatre	Box 1210	Afton 83110	D. Horseley	1	
Flick Theatre	Box 314	Big Piney 83113	C. Smith	1	
Evanston Valley Cinema	45 E. Aspen Grove Dr.	Evanston 82930	D. Coleman	4	
Sky Hi Theatres		Gillette 82716	L. Steele	2	
Movie Machine	P.O. Box 3681	Jackson Hole 83001	F. Londy	6	
•Drive-In	P.O. Box 815	Lovell 82431	L. Bischoff	1	
Hyart Theatre	Box 815	Lovell 82431	H. Bischoff	1	
Vali Cinema Theatre	204 N. Bent	Powell 82435	A. Mercer	1	
•Vali Drive-In	Box 271	Powell 82435	A. Mercer	1	190
Movies 3	1720 Edinburgh	Rawlins 82301	R. Pryde	3	
Cinema Theatre	P.O. Box 607	Rock Springs 82901	K. Hiatt	1	
Centennial Twin Theatres	36 E. Alger Street	Sheridan 82801	R. Campbell	2	
•Skyline Drive-In	Box C	Sheridan 82801	R. Campbell	1	
Ritz Theatre	309 Arapahoe	Thermopolis 82443	D. Kraske	1	192
Wyoming Theatre	126 E. 20th Avenue	Torrington 82240	R. Heyl	2	426
Cinema West Theatre	Box 576	Wheatland 82201	S. Reichhardt	1	

Buying and Booking Services

This listing is comprised of companies servicing 15 or more screens.

Affiliated Theatres Corp.

2 Barry St., Randolph, MA 02368; (617) 986-2122.
ALAN HOCHBERG, pres.

Ashurst Agency

215 Huntcliff Court, Fayetteville, GA 30214; (404)
461-9851; FAX: (404) 719-1565.
ANNETTE ASHURST, owner.

Bendheim Booking—Buying Service

% Neighborhood Entertainment, 1510 East Ridge Rd.,
P.O. Box 71270, Richmond, VA 23255; (804) 282-0303;
FAX: (804) 282-0478.
FRANK NOVAK JR., pres. & CEO; ROBERT TESSIER, head film
buyer.

California Booking

Box 11, Agoura, CA 91301; (818) 991-8593; FAX: (818)
991-8898.
CAROL COMBS, owner.

Capitol Service

10624 N. Port Washington Rd., Mequon, WI 53092;
(414) 241-4545; FAX: (414) 241-4301.
DEAN FITZGERALD.

Carolina Booking Service

250 Cabarrus Ave., P.O. Box 994, Concord, NC 28026;
(704) 788-3366.
BILL CLINE, owner.

Cinema Booking Service of New England, Inc.

P.O. Box 827, Needham, MA 02192; (617) 986-2122.
STANTON DAVIS, pres.

Cinema Film Consultants, Inc.

Box 331, Boston, MA 02199; (617) 437-7050; FAX: (617)
437-7538.
RICHARD MYERSON, MARTIN ZIDES, owners.

Cinema Service

6060 N. Central Expwy., #462, Dallas, TX 75206; (214)
692-7555; FAX: (214) 692-7559.
TIM PATTON, pres.

Cinema Service, Inc.

15840 Ventura Blvd., Suite 308, Encino, CA 91436;
(818) 995-8737.
ENNIS ADKINS, pres.; WILL VINER, v.p.

Cinema Services Film Booking

Roxbury Mall, Box 654, Succasunna, NJ 07876; (201)
584-8160.
CRAIG ZELTNER, owner.

Clark Theatre Service, Inc.

29501 Greenfield Rd., Suite 214, Southfield, MI 48076;
(313) 559-9464.
ROBERT HINES, pres.; PATRICK SAMMON, v.p.; GAIL PAVKO-
VICH, booker.

Complete Booking Service

4 Woodlawn Green, Ste. 150, Charlotte, NC 28217;
(704) 522-0777; FAX: (313) 559-9467.
BILL VANDERHORST, owner, KATHIE VANDERHORST, secty.

Consolidated Theatre Service, Inc.

9333 N. Meridian St., Suite 300, Indianapolis, IN 46260;
(317) 846-9333; FAX: (317) 846-9382.
MORRIS CANTOR, buyer & booker; LEONARD CANTOR, buyer &
booker; NORMA MESALAM, office mgr. & cashier.

Continental Film Service

2425 Cleveland Ave., #125, Santa Rosa, CA 95403;
(707) 523-1592; FAX: (707) 523-1799.
RICHARD GAMBOGI, owner.

Co-Operative Theatres of Ohio, Inc.

5915 Landerbrook Dr., Suite 200, Mayfield Heights, OH
44124; (216) 461-2700; FAX: (216) 461-6411.
DAVID BEAUPAIN, pres.; JOHN KNEPP, v.p.; FRANCES VOLAN,
booker.

Creative Entertainment Consultants

1600 Broadway, Suite 601, New York, NY 10019; (212)
333-7770; FAX: (212) 333-7904.
LARRY LAPIDUS, pres., NICK GUADAGNO, exec. vice pres.

Couch Booking Service

Box 763302, Dallas, TX 75376; (214) 330-9976.
LEON COUCH, owner.

Dalrymple Theatre Service

4208 Overlook Dr., Bloomington, MN 55437; (612)
888-0041.
DON DALRYMPLE, owner.

Douglas Theatre Co.

P.O. Box 81848, Lincoln, NE 68501; (402) 474-4909.
DAVE LIVINGSTON, pres.

Epperson Theatre Service

1917 Cecelia Circle, Salt Lake City, UT 84121; (801) 278-3986.
DICK EPPERSON, owner.

Eddy G. Erickson Booking Service

3405 Jubilee Trail, Dallas, TX 75229; (214) 352-3821.
EDDY G. ERICKSON, owner.

Exhibitors Service, Inc.

5757 Century Blvd., #514, Los Angeles, CA 90045; (310) 649-4811.

Film Booking Office Corporation

Northcreek Place 1, 9461 LBJ Freeway, Suite 206, Dallas, TX 75243; (214) 234-6192; FAX: (214) 234-8571.
JOHN SHAW, pres.; JANINE BRADFORD, v.p.

Film Service Theatre Group

3487 W. 2100 South, #204, Salt Lake City, UT 84119-1162; (801) 973-3227; FAX: (801) 973-3364.
DAVID SHARP, pres. (Theatrical Div.)

Florin-Creative Film Services

125 North Main St., Port Chester, NY 10573; (914) 937-1603; (914) 937-8496.
STEVEN FLORIN, pres.

Forman & United Theatres

Box 1649, Bothell, WA 98041-1649; (206) 488-0944; FAX: (206) 488-9318.
MICHAEL FORMAN, owner.

Guyett Booking Service

P.O. Box 6346, Shawnee Mission, KS 66206-1934; (913) 648-5189.
HAROLD P. GUYETT, film buyer & booker.

Independent Film Services

221 East 68 Terrace, Kansas City, MO 64113; (816) 363-4993.
BRADFORD BILLS, owner.

Independent Theatre Booking Service

4523 Park Rd., #A-105, Charlotte, NC 28209; (704) 529-1200.
ROBERT SMITH, owner.

Independent Theatre Service

5225 Touhy Ave., Skokie, IL 60077; (708) 675-8232.
DELLA M. GALLO, owner.

Johnson Theatre Service

936 Warren Ave., Downers Grove, IL 60516; (708) 515-9333; FAX: (708) 968-1626.
BRIAN BOYLAN, contact.

Jane M. Klotz Booking

9801 Tribonian Drive, Fort Washington, MD 20744; (301) 567-4503.
HARLEY DAVIDSON, pres.; JANE M. KLOTZ, mgr. & booker.

Lesser Theatre Service

110 Greene St., Suite 802, New York, NY 10012; (212) 925-4776; FAX: (212) 941-6719.
RON LESSER, pres.; ROB LAWINSKI, film buyer.

MJR Theatre Service, Inc.

13671 West Eleven Mile Rd., Oak Park, MI 48237; (313) 547-8282; FAX: (313) 548-4706.
MICHAEL R. MIHALICH, pres.

Marcus Theatres Corporation

212 W. Wisconsin Ave., Milwaukee, WI 53203; (414) 272-6026.
MICHAEL KOMINSKY, exec. v.p. & film buyer.

McCulloch Theatre Service

704 Hennepin Ave., Minneapolis, MN 55403; (612) 333-2281.
STAN McCULLOCH, owner.

Mescop, Inc.

P.O. Box 303, Sussex, WI 53089; (414) 251-6808.
JAMES FLORENCE, pres. & buyer; LINDA WITTMANN, PATRICIA B. FLORENCE, bookers.

Milgram Theatres, Inc.

1616 Walnut St., Suite 2000, Philadelphia, PA 19103; (215) 985-4900; FAX: (215) 985-4934.
WILLIAM MILGRAM, pres.; HANK MILGRAM, exec. v.p.; ROBERT MILGRAM, v.p.

Mini Theatres

534 Broadhollow Rd., Suite 430, Melville, NY 11747; (516) 293-FILM; FAX: (516) 293-3490.
HAROLD S. LAGER, MARTY GOLDMAN, partners.

Morris Projects, Inc.

P.O. Box 6130, Sarasota, FL 34278-6130; (813) 388-2441; FAX: (813) 388-4473.
SUE MORRIS, principal.

Motion Picture Counseling

1010 B. St., #210; San Rafael, CA 94901; (415) 459-3456.
RON LITVIN, owner.

Norris Booking Agency

P.O. Box 8824, Jacksonville, FL 32239; (904) 641-0019.
REX NORRIS, owner.

Northwest Diversified Entertainment

2819 First Ave., Suite 240, Seattle, WA 98121; (206) 441-5380.
BENJAMIN L. HANNAH, pres.; VICTORIA HAWKER, film buyer.

Preferred Booking Service

1601 Harrison Ave., Cincinnati, OH 45214-1401; (513) 921-8266; FAX: (513) 921-8206.
FRED SCHWEITZER, owner.

Philbin Cinema Service Inc.

4700 S. 900 E, Suite 9B, Salt Lake City, UT 84117; (801) 263-3725.
TOM PHILBIN, owner.

Professional Service for the Booking & Buying of Film

37 Norman Dr., Framingham, MA 01701; (508) 872-9389.
HENRY SCULLY, owner.

R/C Theatres Booking Service

(An Etmac Co.) 231 West Cherry Hill Ct., Box 1056, Reisterstown, MD 21136-1056; (301) 526-4774; FAX: (301) 526-6871.
IRWIN R. COHEN, pres.; SCOTT R. COHEN, head of film negotiations; JAN S. ANDERSON, sr. booker.
See listing under Theatre Circuits.

Roxy Management Company, Inc.

2004 Main Street, Northampton, PA 18067; (215) 262-7699.
RICHARD C. WOLFE, pres.; LEE J. STEIN, v.p.

Saffle United Theatre Service

P.O. Box 1649, Bothell, WA 98041; (206) 488-0944; FAX: (206) 488-9318.
BUD SAFFLE, dir.; DOROTHEA MAYES, booker.

Theatre Management Assoc.

53 Carlton Pl., Passaic, NJ 07055; (201) 471-3002; FAX: (201) 471-3004.
RUDY DeBLASIO, pres., RICK SULLIVAN, vice pres.

Theatre Service Network

P.O. Box 190, 217 S. Bridge St., Yorkville, IL 60560; (708) 553-0588; FAX: (708) 553-0594.
BUCK KOLKMEYER, pres.; STEVE FELPERIN, v.p.

Triangle Theatre Service, Inc.

1170 Broadway, New York, NY 10001; (212) 679-6400.
IRVING DOLLINGER and RICHARD DOLLINGER, owners.

Tri-State Theatre Service, Inc.

Film Arts Building, 636 Northland Blvd., Cincinnati, OH 45240; (513) 851-5700; FAX: (513) 851-5708.
PHIL BORACK, pres.; BARRY STEINBERG, v.p.

Turbyfill Booking Service

P.O. Box 16126, Jacksonville, FL 32216; (904) 725-7590.
EARL TURBYFILL, owner.

Twin State Booking Service

3600 Johnny Cake Lane, Charlotte, NC 28226; (704) 554-5949.
R.T. BELCHER, owner.

Viking Film Service

1228 Wagon Wheel Road, Hopkins, MN 55343; (612) 933-7271.
JOHN R. KELVIE, booking and buying.

Vonderhaar Cinema Marketing

P. O. Box 222, Osseo, MN 55369; (612) 424-7617.
MIKE VONDERHAAR, owner.

Walker Theatre Service

350 South 400 East, #222W, Salt Lake City, UT 84111; (801) 521-0335.
BARRY WALKER, owner.

Wilson Theatre Service

22035 167th St., Big Lake, MN 55309; (612) 263-3800.
JIM WILSON, owner.

Theatre Equipment Suppliers

A S C TECHNICAL SERVICES CORP.
(formerly Altec Service Corp.) Exec. Offices: P.O. Box 860706, Plano, TX 75086; (214) 422-2160. (Sound service, booth maintenance, equipment sales.)

AMERICAN DESK MANUFACTURING
Public Seating Division, P.O. Box 6107, Temple, TX 76503; (817) 773-1776. (Theatre seating.)

APPLIED LIGHTING SYSTEMS
407 Old County Rd., Belmont, CA 94002; (415) 595-5496.

ASSIGNED SEATING, INC.
102 N. California Ave., City of Industry, CA 91744; (213) 583-5073; FAX: (818) 968-5316. (Manufactures theatre seats.)

BEVELITE-ADLER
103 Mensing Way, Cannon Falls, MN 55009; (800) LETTERS; FAX: (507) 263-4887. (Marquee letters, etc.)

CEMCORP (CONSOLIDATED ENGINEERING & MANUFACTURING CORP.)
110 Industry Lane, P.O. Box 296, Forest Hill, MD 21050; (410) 838-0036, 879-3022; FAX: (410) 838-8079. (Manufactures and designs ticket issuing equipment.)

CINEMA EQUIPMENT SALES OF CALIFORNIA, INC.
3151 Cahuenga Blvd. West, Suite 110, Los Angeles, CA 90068; (213) 874-0188; FAX: (213) 874-0667.

CINEMA FILM SYSTEMS
791 N. Benson Ave., Suite E, Upland, CA 91786; (714) 931-9318; FAX: (714) 949-8815. Midwestern Office: 3840 S. Helena, Aurora, CO 80013; (303) 699-7477; FAX: (303) 680-6071. Eastern/International: P.O. Box 6, Westhampton, NY 11977; (516) 288-3330; FAX: (516) 288-6005.

DILLINGHAM TICKET COMPANY
781 Ceres Ave., Los Angeles, CA 90021-0519; (213) 627-6916; FAX: (213) 623-2758.

DOLBY LABORATORIES, INC.
100 Potrero Ave., San Francisco, CA 94103; (415) 558-0200; FAX: (415) 863-1373. (Theatre sound equipment.)

EPRAD INC.
2541 Tracy Rd., Northwood, OH 43619-1097, or P.O. Box 73, Rossford, OH 43460-0073; (419) 666-3266; FAX: (419) 666-6534. (Theatre equipment and accessories, incl. amplifiers, speakers, etc.)

ELECTROFEX
24307 Magic Mountain Pkwy., Suite 272, Valencia, CA 91355; (805) 250-0055; FAX: (805) 250-1844. (Lighting.)

GLATZ-JACOBSON THEATRE DESIGN CONSULTANTS
9961 W. 86th Place, Arvada, CO 80005; (303) 421-9516. (Theatre design, decorating; also consultants.)

HALGO SPECIALTIES
16760 Stagg St., Suite 209, Van Nuys, CA 91406; (818) 366-0744; FAX: (818) 780-3486. (Projection screens.)

HARRAH'S THEATRE SERVICE & SUPPLY, INC.
25613 Dollar St., Unit 1, Hayward, CA 94544; (510) 881-4989; FAX: (818) 767-0540.

HURLEY SCREEN CORP.
(A subsidiary of CEMCORP, see above address.)

INDIANA CASH DRAWER COMPANY
P.O. Box 236, Shelbyville, IN 46176; (317) 398-6643.

INTERNATIONAL CINEMA EQUIPMENT
100 N.E. 39th St., Miami, FL 33137-3632; (305) 573-7339; FAX: (305) 573-8101.

JET SPRAY CORP.
P.O. Box 8250, 825 University Ave., Norwood, MA 02062; (617) 769-7500; FAX: (617) 769-2368. (Visual display, beverage dispensers, etc.)

KONETA MATTING DIVISION
7090 Lunar Dr., Wapakoneta, OH 45895; (419) 738-2155. (Entrance mats, matting.)

LA VEZZI PRECISION, INC.
999 Regency Dr., Glendale Height, IL 60139-2281; (708) 582-1230; FAX: (708) 582-1238. (Manufacturers of parts for projectors, soundheads.)

LIBERTY THEATRICAL DECOR
P.O. Box 2122, Castro Valley, CA 94546; (510) 889-6945.

MANKO SEATING CO.
(Division of Manko Fabrics Co., Inc.) 50 W. 36 St., New York, NY 10018; (212) 695-7470; FAX: (212) 563-0840. (Manufacturing seat covers and backs.)

MARBLE COMPANY, INC., THE
P.O. Box 160030, 421 Hart Lane, Nashville, TN 37216; (615) 227-7772; (800) 759-5905; FAX: (615) 228-1301. (Projection room supplies and equipment.)

MIRACLE RECREATION EQUIPMENT CO.
P.O. Box 420, Hwy. 60 & Bridle Lane, Monett, MO 65708; (417) 235-6917; (800) 523-4202; FAX: (417) 235-3551. (Drive-in playground equipment.)

MULONE, NICK & SON
100 Highland Ave., Cheswick, PA 15024; (412) 274-6646, 274-5994; FAX: (412) 274-4808. (Screen frames, masking.)

NATIONAL CINEMA SUPPLY
P.O. Box 151167, Tampa, FL 33684; (813) 884-7855; FAX: (813) 884-7855. (Theatre equipment, concession stands, etc.)

NATIONAL TICKET COMPANY
P.O. Box 547, Shamokin, PA 17872-0547; (717) 672-2900; FAX: (800) 829-0888.

NEUMANDE PRODUCTS CORP.
200 Connecticut Ave., Norwalk, CT 06854; (203) 866-7600; FAX: (203) 866-7522. (Projection booth equipment.)

NOVELTY SCENIC STUDIOS
40 Sea Cliff Ave., Glen Cove, NY 11542; (718) 895-8668; (516) 671-5940; FAX: (516) 674-2213. (Stage curtains, drapes, wall coverings.)

PACER/C.A.T.S.
355 Inverness Drive S., Englewood, CO 80122; (303) 649-9818; FAX: (303) 643-3814. (Technology for theatre management systems.)

641

PASKAL LIGHTING

6820 Romaine St., Hollywood, CA 90038; (213) 466-5233; FAX: (213) 466-1071.

PEREY MANUFACTURING

655 Washington Blvd., Suite 704, Stamford, CT 06901; (203) 961-8444; FAX: (203) 961-8855.

PROCTOR COMPANIES

2335 S. Inca, Denver, CO 80223; (303) 934-5455; FAX: (303) 934-6236. (Concession counters, wallcovering.)

PROJECTED SOUND, INC.

469 Avon Ave., Plainfield, IN 46168; (317) 839-4111; FAX: (317) 839-2476.

S&K THEATRICAL DRAPERIES

7313 Varna Ave., North Hollywood, CA 91605; (818) 503-0596; FAX: (818) 503-0599.

SCHNEIDER

400 Crossways Dr., Woodbury, NY 11797-2009; (516) 496-8500; FAX: (516) 496-8524. (Projection lenses.)

SCHULT DESIGN & DISPLAY

13910 Century Lane, Grandview, MO 64030-3920; (816) 966-8998; (800) 783-8998; FAX: (816) 966-0990. (Slide projector sales & installation.)

SELBY INDUSTRIES INC.

P.O. Box 267, Richfield, OH 44286; (216) 659-6631; (800) 647-6224; FAX: (216) 659-4112. (Drive-in designs, box offices, etc.)

SOUNDFOLD, INC.

Box 2125, Dayton, OH 45429-0125; (513) 228-3773, 293-2671; FAX: (513) 293-9542. (Accoustical wallcovering, carpets, screen and stage services.)

SPERLING, LARRY, ECONO-PLEAT (EASTWEST CARPET MILLS)

2664 S. LaCienega Blvd., Los Angeles, CA 90034; (310) 559-7847; FAX: (310) 559-6357. (Manufacturers of accoustical fabric wallcoverings.)

STEIN INDUSTRIES

22 Sprague Ave., Amityville, NY 11701; (516) 789-2222; FAX: (516) 789-8888. (Concession stands, theatre lobby fixtures, etc.)

STEVENS CARPET/J P S CARPET CORP.

1185 Avenue of the Americas, New York, NY 10036; (212) 642-1160; FAX: (212) 642-1108.

STEWART FILMSCREEN CORP.

1161 W. Sepulveda Blvd., Torrance, CA 90502; (310) 326-1422; (800) 762-4999; FAX: (310) 326-6870.

STRAND LIGHTING

20 Bushes Lane, Elmwood Park, NJ 07407; (201) 791-7000; (800) 352-6745; FAX: (201) 791-3167.

TECHNIKOTE CORP.

63 Seabring St., Brooklyn, NY 11231; (718) 624-6429; FAX: (718) 624-0129. (Theatre screens.)

THEATRE EQUIPMENT ASSOCIATION

244 W. 49 St., Suite 200, New York, NY 10019; (212) 246-6460; FAX: (212) 265-6428.

TRIANGLE SCENERY DRAPERY & LIGHTING CO.

1215 Bates Ave., Los Angeles, CA 90029; (213) 662-8129; FAX: (213) 662-8129.

ULTRA-STEREO LABS INC.

18730 Oxnard St., Suite 208, Tarzana, CA 91356; (818) 609-7405; FAX: (818) 609-7408.

WAGNER ZIP-CHANGE

3100 Hirsch St., Melrose Park, IL 60160-1799; (708) 681-4100; (800) 323-0744; FAX: (800) 243-4924. (Marquee letters and background.)

XETRON DIVISION

10 Saddle Rd., Cedar Knolls, NJ 07927; (201) 267-8200; FAX: (201) 267-4903. (Film presentation equipment, incl. projectors, consoles, etc.)

Motion Picture
Organizations

* **PRODUCER-DISTRIBUTOR, EXHIBITOR, VARIETY & FILM CLUBS**

* **GUILDS AND UNIONS**

Producer-Distributor, Exhibitor, Variety & Film Clubs

Academy of Motion Picture Arts and Sciences

Executive Offices: 8949 Wilshire Blvd., Beverly Hills, CA 90211; (310) 247-3000. Library: 333 S. La Cienega Blvd., Beverly Hills, CA 90211; (310) 247-3020. (Organized June, 1927; Membership 5,127.)

PRESIDENT
Robert Rehme
FIRST VICE PRESIDENT
Donn Cambern
VICE PRESIDENT
Alan Bergman, Arthur Hamilton
TREASURER
Fay Kanin
SECRETARY
Frank Mancuso
EXECUTIVE DIRECTOR
Bruce Davis
LEGAL COUNSEL
John B. Quinn
BOARD OF GOVERNORS
Saul Bass, Carl Bell, Peter E. Berger, Alan Bergman, Ashley Boone, Robert F. Boyle, Albert Brenner, Bruce Broughton, Donn Cambern, Gilbert Cates, Allen Daviau, June Foray, Sid Ganis, Arthur Hamilton, Arthur Hiller, Cheryl Boone Isaacs, Norman Jewison, Fay Kanin, Hal Kanter, Howard W. Koch, Jack Lemmon, Marvin Jay Levy, Karl Malden, Frank G. Mancuso, Roddy McDowall, Donald O. Mitchell, Robert Rehme, Donald C. Rogers, Tom Rolf, Kay Rose, Daniel Taradash, Haskell Wexler, Charles F. Wheeler, Jerry Wunderlich, Saul Zaentz, Richard D. Zanuck

Afram Films, Inc.

1133 Avenue of the Americas, New York, NY 10036; (212) 840-6161; FAX: (212) 391-9239.

PRESIDENT
William M. Murray
VICE PRESIDENT
Norman Alterman
SECRETARY
Hillel Gedrich
TREASURER
Ralph R. Martens
ASSISTANT SECRETARY
Wilma C. Weglein
ASSISTANT TREASURER
Kevin Kirchoff
MEMBERS
Columbia Pictures Industries, Inc.; MGM, Inc.; Paramount Pictures Corp.; 20th Century Fox International Corp.; Universal International Films, Inc.; Warner Bros. International, a division of Warner Bros. Inc.

Alliance of Motion Picture and Television Producers

15503 Ventura Blvd., Encino, CA 91436-3140. (818) 995-3600. (Membership: Major studios, independent production companies, and film processing laboratories.)

PRESIDENT
J. Nicholas Counter III
SENIOR VICE PRESIDENT, LEGAL & BUSINESS AFFAIRS
Carol A. Lombardini
CHIEF FINANCIAL OFFICER
Kathy Grotticelli
VICE PRESIDENT, LEGAL AFFAIRS
Helayne Antler

American Cinematheque

1717 N. Highland Ave., Suite 814, Hollywood, CA 90028; (213) 461-9622; FAX: (213) 461-9737; Program Information: (213) 466-FILM. Organized 1984. (Celebrates the moving picture in all its forms through public film and video exhibition.)

CHAIRMAN
Sydney Pollack
PRESIDENT
Peter J. Dekom
EXECUTIVE DIRECTOR
Barbara Zicka Smith
BOARD OF DIRECTORS
Charles Champlin, Peter J. Dekom, William J. Doyle, David Geffen, Lawrence Gordon, Brian Grazer, Buck Henry, Godfrey Isaac, Julie Smith Kellner, Leonard Levy, Barry London, David Morse, George E. Moss, Sanford P. Paris, Michael John Pittas, Sydney Pollack, Elisabeth Pollon, Stephen A. Rodriguez, Joe Roth, Sigurjon Sighvatsson, Barbara Zicka Smith, Bette L. Smith, Robert L. Stein, Saul Zaentz

American Film Institute, The

The John F. Kennedy Center for the Performing Arts, Washington, DC 20566; (202) 828-4000; FAX: (202) 659-1970. (A national trust dedicated to preserving the hertiage of film and television; to identifying, developing and training creative individuals; and to presenting the moving image as an art form.)

DIRECTOR
Jean Firstenberg
DEPUTY DIRECTOR
James Hindman

NEW YORK OFFICE

1180 Avenue of the Americas, 10th Floor, New York, NY 10036; (212) 398-6890; FAX: (212) 790-4897.

CALIFORNIA CAMPUS

2021 N. Western Ave., P.O. Box 27999, Los Angeles, CA 90027; (213) 856-7600; FAX: (213) 467-4578.

BOARD OF TRUSTEES
Fred Pierce, chairman; George Stevens, Jr., co-chm.; Charlton Heston, pres.; Charles W. Fries; Howard Stringer, Liener Temerlin, vice-chmn.; Elizabeth Taylor, honorary trustee; Merv Adelson, Debbie Allen, Jon Avnet, Jeanine Basinger, Robert M. Bennett, Jeff Berg, James Billington, Richard Brandt, Daniel Burke, Mark Canton, Peter Chernin, Martha Coolidge, Robert A. Daly, Suzanne de Passe, John DiBiaggio, Jean Firstenberg, Michael Forman, Richard Frank, Michael Fuchs, Ina Ginsburg, Suzanne Lloyd Hayes, Lawrence Herbert, Dominique Heriard-Dubreuil, Gale Ann Hurd, Gene F. Jankowski, Robert L. Johnson, Fay Kanin, Lawrence Kasdan, Jerry Katzman, Sherry Lansing, Frank Mancuso, Marsha Mason, Ron Meyer, Michael Nesmith, Mace Neufeld, Daniel Petrie, Tom Pollock, Kelly Rose, Jill Sackler, Vivian Sobchack, Steven Spielberg, Helen Stansbury, Charles Steinberg, Gordon Stulberg, Brandon Tartikoff, Anthony Thomopoulos, Jack Valenti, Irwin Winkler, Robert Wise, David L. Wolper, Robert C. Wright, Bud Yorkin.

American Film Marketing Assn.

12424 Wilshire Blvd., Suite 600, Los Angeles, CA 90025; (310) 447-1555; FAX: (310) 447-1666. (Trade organization formed in 1980, now totalling 110 companies engaged in the sale of independently produced films to the international market. Sponsors the American Film Market in the spring.)

CHAIRMAN OF BOARD
Michael F. Goldman
PRESIDENT
Jonas Rosenfield

ABC Distribution, Co., 825 Seventh Ave., 5th Fl., New York, NY 10019

ADN Associates Ltd., 8 Cleveland Gardens, London W2 6HA United Kingdom

Alice Entertainment, Inc., 2986 Baseline Ave., Santa Ynez, CA 93460

Allied Vision Ltd., Avon House, The Glassworks, 3-4 Ashland Place, London, WIM 3JH, United Kingdom

American First Run, 14225 Ventura Blvd., Sherman Oaks, CA 91423

Angelika Films, Inc., 110 Greene St., #1102, New York, NY 10012

Arista Films, Inc., 16027 Ventura Blvd., #206, Encino, CA 91436

Atlas International, Rumfordstrasse 29-31, 8000, Munich 5, Germany

Australian Film Commission, 8 West St., N. Sydney, NSW, 2060, Australia

Australian Film Finance Corp. Pty. Ltd., 130 Elizabeth St., GPO Box 3886, Sydney NSW 2001, Australia

Bank of America NT & SA, 2049 Century Park East, Suite 300, Los Angeles, CA 90067

Banque Paribas, 2029 Century Park E., #3900, Los Angeles, CA 90067

Beyond Films, Ltd., 1875 Century Park E., Suite 1300, Los Angeles, CA 90067

Big Bear Licensing Corp., 11075 Santa Monica Blvd., #200, Los Angeles, CA 90025

Blue Ridge Entertainment, 10490 Santa Monica Blvd., Los Angeles, CA 90025

Broadstar Entertainment Corp., 6464 Sunset Blvd., PH1130 Hollywood, CA 90028

Carolco Services, Inc., 8800 Sunset Blvd., Los Angeles, CA 90069

Chemical Bank, 1800 Century Park East, Suite 400, Los Angeles, CA 90067

CineTelFilms, Inc., 8255 W. Sunset Blvd., Los Angeles, CA 90046-2432

Cinetrust Ent. Corporation, 2121 Ave. of the Stars, 6th floor, Los Angeles, CA 90067

Cinevest Entertainment, 450 Seventh Ave. #2702, New York, NY 10123

Coment Funding Corp., 800 Third Ave., 29th fl., New York, NY 10022

Concorde-New Horizons Corp., 11600 San Vicente Blvd., Los Angeles, CA 90049

Cori International: Film & Television, 19 Albermarle St., London W1, United Kingdom

Credit Du Nord, D.O.F.I., 6/8 Blvd. Haussmann, 75009 Paris, France

Credit Lyonnais Bank Nederland, Coolsingel 49, 3012 AA Rotterdam, Netherlands

Crown International Pictures, Inc., 8701 Wilshire Blvd., Beverly Hills, CA 90211

Curb Org., 3907 W. Alameda Ave., Suite 102, Burbank, CA 91505

Davian Intl., Ltd., 144 Boundry St., 1st floor, Kowloon, Hong Kong

De Nationale Investeringsbank N.V., Carnegieplein 4, P.O. Box 380, 2501 BH The Hague, Netherlands

Dino DeLaurentiis Communications, 8670 Wilshire Blvd., Beverly Hills, CA 90211

Distant Horizon Ltd., 84-86 Regent St., #508, London WIR 5PF United Kingdom

Double Helix Films, Inc., 7135 Hollywood Blvd., #104, Los Angeles, CA 90046

Film Four International, 60 Charlotte St., London WIP 2AX United Kingdom

Film World Entertainment/Miracle Films, 6311 Romaine St., #7309, Hollywood, CA 90038

Filmark International Ltd., Garley Bldg., #1401, 233-239 Nathan Rd., Kowloon, Hong Kong

Filmexport Group SRL, Via Polonia 7-9, 00198 Rome, Italy

Films (Guernsey) Limited, 40 Queen Anne's Gate, London SW1H 9AP, United Kingdom

First Charter Bank, 265 N. Beverly Dr., Beverly Hills, CA 90210

Fries Distribution Co., 6922 Hollywood Blvd., Hollywood, CA 90028

Full Moon Entertainment, 3030 Andrita St., Los Angeles, CA 90065

GEL Distribution, 11075 Santa Monica Blvd., #200, Los Angeles, CA 90025

Goldcrest Films & Television, 36/44 Brewer St., London W1R 3HP United Kingdom

Golden Harvest/Golden Comm, 9884 Santa Monica Blvd., Beverly Hills, CA 90212-1670

Samuel Goldwyn Company, 10203 Santa Monica Blvd., #500, Los Angeles, CA 90067

Grand Am Ltd., 6649 Odessa Ave., Van Nuys, CA 91406

Hemdale Pictures Corp., 7966 Beverly Blvd., Los Angeles, CA 90048

Hills Entertainment Group, Lappersveld 68, Hilversum, 1213 VB, Netherlands

IFD Films & Arts Ltd., Suite 1208, 12th fl., 233-239 Nathan Rd., Kowloon, Hong Kong

I.N.I. Entertainment Group Inc., 11150 Olympic Blvd., Suite #700, Los Angeles, CA 90064

I.R.S. Media International, 3939 Lankershim Blvd., Universal City, CA 91604

ITC Entertainment Group, 12711 Ventura Blvd., 3rd fl., Studio City, CA 91604

Image Organization Inc., 9000 Sunset Blvd., #915, Los Angeles, CA 90069

Imperial Bank/Lewis Horwitz Org., 1840 Century Park E., Los Angeles, CA 90067

Imperial Entertainment B.V., 4640 Lankershim Blvd., 4th Floor, N. Hollywood, CA 91602

Ing Bank, Postbus 1800, Locatie Code HE0401, Amsterdam 1000 BV, Netherlands

Inter-Ocean Film Sales, Ltd., 6100 Wilshire Blvd., #1500, Los Angeles, CA 90048

J & M Entertainment, 1289 Sunset Plaza Dr., Los Angeles, CA 90069

Kings Road Entertainment, 1901 Ave. of the Stars, Suite 605, Los Angeles, CA 90067.

Largo Entertainment, 10201 W. Pico Blvd., Los Angeles, CA 90035

The Robert Lewis Co., 8755 Shoreham Dr., #303, Los Angeles, CA 90069

Lone Star Pictures Intl., 4826 Greenville Ave., Dallas, TX 75206

L-Way Entertainment, 9044 Melrose Ave., 3rd fl., Los Angeles, CA 90069

M.C.E.G./Sterling Entertainment, 2121 Ave. of the Stars, #2630, Los Angeles CA 90067

Majestic Films & Television, P.O. Box 13, Gloucester Mansions, Cambridge Circus, London WC2H 8HD United Kingdom

Manley Productions Inc., 111 W. 57 St., #1401, New York, NY 10019

Mayfair Entertainment Intl., 13 Tottenham Mews, London WIP 9PJ, United Kingdom

Media Home Entertainment, 11933 Darlington Ave., Suite 1, Los Angeles, CA 90049

Melrose Entertainment, Inc., 8200 Wilshire Blvd., Beverly Hills, CA 90212

Mercantile National Bank, 1840 Century Park East, 3rd Floor, Los Angeles, CA 90067

Metro-Goldwyn-Mayer, 2500 Broadway St., Santa Monica, CA 90404-3061

Miramax Intl., 7920 Sunset Blvd., Suite 230, Los Angeles, CA 90046

Moonstone Entertainment, 9242 Beverly Blvd., Suite 230, Beverly Hills, CA 90210

Morgan Creek International Inc., 1875 Century Park E., #200, Los Angeles, CA 90067

Motion Picture Corp. of America, 1401 Ocean Ave., 3rd fl., Santa Monica, CA 90401

Movie Acquisition Corp. Ltd., 167/169 Wardour St., London W1V 3TA, United Kingdom

The Movie Group Inc., 1900 Ave. of the Stars, #1425, Los Angeles, CA 90067

The Movie House Sales Co. Ltd., ⁹⁄₁ Farenam St., 2nd fl., London, W1V 3AH United Kingdom

New Line Cinema Corp., 116 N. Robertson, Suite 200, Los Angeles, CA 90048

New World Intl., 1440 S. Sepulveda Blvd., Los Angeles, CA 90025-3458

New Zealand Film Commission, P.O. Box 11-546, 36 Allen St., Wellington, New Zealand

Noble Productions, 1615 South Crest Drive, Los Angeles, CA 90035

The Norkat Co. Ltd., 280 S. Beverly Dr., #306, Beverly Hills, CA 90212

Norstar Entertainment, 86 Bloor St. W, #500, Toronto, Ontario M5S 1M5

North American Releasing, 808 Nelson St., #2105, Vancouver, BC V6Z 2H2, Canada

Odyssey Distributors Ltd., 6500 Wilshire Blvd., #400, Los Angeles, CA 90048

Omega Entertainment Ltd., 8760 Shoreham Drive, Los Angeles, CA 90069

Overseas Filmgroup, Inc., 8800 Sunset Blvd., #302, Los Angeles, CA 90069

P.C. Films Corp., 60 E. 42nd St., #2320, New York, NY 10165

Paul International, Inc., 9903 Santa Monica Blvd., #333, Beverly Hills CA 90067

Penta Intl. Ltd., 8 Queen St., London WIX 7PH, United Kingdom

Playpont Films, Ltd., 1-2 Ramilies St., London WIV 1DF United Kingdom

Promark Entertainment Group, The Promark Center West, 3599 Cahuenga Blvd. W, #300, Los Angeles, CA 90068
Puzon Creative Entertainment, 462 Regina Blvd., Escolta, Manila, 3679 Phillipines
Quixote Productions, 8033 Sunset Blvd., #93, Los Angeles, CA 90046-2427
Rank Film Distributors, 127 Wardour St., London W1V 4AD United Kingdom
Rapi Films, Cikini 217, Jakarta, Indonesia
Reel Movies International, 8235 Douglas Ave., #770, Dallas, TX 75225
Republic Pictures Intl., 12636 Beatrice St., Los Angeles, CA 90066
SC Entertainment Intl., 434 Queen St. E., Toronto, Ont. M5A IT5 Canada
Saban Pictures Intl., 4000 W. Alameda Ave., Burbank, CA 91505
Safir Films, Ltd., 49 Littleton Rd., Harrow, Middlesex HA1 3SY, United Kingdom
The Sales Company, 62 Shaftesbury Ave., London W1V 7AA, United Kingdom
Scotti Bros. Pictures, 2114 Pico Blvd., Santa Monica, CA 90405
Shapiro/Glickenhaus Entertainment, 12001 Ventura Pl., #404, Studio City, CA 91604
Silver Star Film Corp., 8833 W. Sunset Blvd., #305, Los Angeles, CA 90069
Smart Egg Pictures, 62 Brompton Rd., London SW3 1BW, United Kingdom
Spelling Films International, 5700 Wilshire Blvd., #575, Los Angeles, CA 90036
Stairway Intl. Corp., 2100 Century Park West, Los Angeles, CA 90067
The Summit Group, 1528-D Cloverfield Blvd., Santa Monica, CA 90404-2916
Sunny Film Inc., 315 Bedok Rd., Singapore 1646
Telefilm Canada, 9350 Wilshire Blvd., #400, Beverly Hills, CA 90212
Trans Atlantic Entertainment, 1440 S. Sepulveda Blvd.#118, Los Angeles, CA 90025
Trimark Pictures, 2644 30th St., Santa Monica, CA 90405-3009
Troma, Inc., 733 Ninth Ave., New York, NY 10019
Turner Pictures Worldwide, 1888 Century Park East, 12th Floor, Los Angeles, CA 90067
21st Century Film Corp., 11080 N. Olympic Blvd., Los Angeles, CA 90064
Universal City Studios Inc., 100 Universal City Plaza, Suite 500/06, Universal City, CA 91608
Viacom Pictures Inc., 10 Universal Plaza, 31st fl. Universal City, CA 91608-1097
Vision International, 1875 Century Park E., #450, Los Angeles, CA 90067
West Side Studios, 10726 McCune Ave., Los Angeles, CA 90034
World Films Inc., 8920 Sunset Blvd., 2nd fl., Los Angeles, CA 90069
World Media Sales, Doetinchempad 27, 1324 JW Almere, Netherlands
World Trade Bank N.A., 9944 Santa Monica Blvd., Beverly Hills, CA 90212-1691

American Humane Association

L.A. office: 15503 Ventura Blvd., Encino, CA 91436; (818) 501-0123; National Headquarters: 63 Inverness Dr., East, Englewood, CO 80112; (303) 695-0811. (Organized 1877; Liaison with the television and motion picture industry as supervisors of animal action in television and motion picture production.)
NATIONAL PRESIDENT
Jack Jones
VICE PRESIDENT
Chuck Granoski
TREASURER
Harold Dates
DIRECTOR—L.A. OFFICE
Betty Denny Smith

American Motion Pictures Export Company Inc.

1133 Avenue of the Americas, New York, NY 10036; (212) 840-6161; FAX: (212) 391-9239.
PRESIDENT
William M. Murray
VICE PRESIDENTS
Norman Alterman, A. Stephen Clug, Frederic Hirsch
SECRETARY
Hillel Gedrich
TREASURER
Ralph R. Martens
ASSISTANT SECRETARY
Wilma C. Weglein

ASSISTANT TREASURER
Kevin Kirchoff
MEMBERS
Buena Vista International Inc.; Columbia Pictures Industries, Inc.; MGM, Inc.; Paramount Pictures Corp.; 20th Century Fox International Corp; Universal International Films, Inc.; Warner Bros. International, a division of Warner Bros. Inc.

American Society of Composers, Authors and Publishers (ASCAP)

One Lincoln Plaza, New York, NY 10023; (212) 595-3050. (Organized February 13, 1914; Membership: 30,400 Music Writers, 12,400 Publishers.)
PRESIDENT
Morton Gould
VICE PRESIDENTS
Marilyn Bergman, Jay Morgenstern
SECRETARY
Arthur Hamilton
TREASURER
Arnold Broido
ASSISTANT SECRETARY
Elie Siegmeister
ASSISTANT TREASURER
John McKellen
COUNSEL
Bernard Korman
MANAGING DIRECTOR
Gloria Messinger
WESTERN REGIONAL DIRECTOR
Todd Brabec, ASCAP, 6430 Sunset Boulevard, Hollywood, CA 90028
SOUTHERN REGIONAL EXECUTIVE DIRECTOR
Connie Bradley, ASCAP, Two Music Square W., Nashville, TN 37203

Asian Cinevision, Inc.

32 East Broadway, New York, NY 10002; (212) 925-8685; FAX: (212) 925-8157. (A not-for-profit organization dedicated to encouraging the creation and presentation of Asian and Asian American media arts. Current programs include film exhibitions; media services (information and referral); archive library; publications; and production services: video documentation editing, duplication, transfer, screening)
EXECUTIVE DIRECTOR
Peter Chow

Association of Cinema & Video Laboratories, Inc.

7095 Hollywood Blvd., #751, Hollywood, CA 90028; correspondence only—no phone number. (Organized 1953 to provide its members with the opportunity to discuss and exchange ideas in connection with the technical, administrative and managerial problems of motion pictures, as well as opportunities in the operation of a film and video laboratory. Publishes ACVL Handbook.)
PRESIDENT
James A. Merkle, Allied Film & Video
FIRST VICE PRESIDENT
Frank Ricotta, Technicolor
SECOND VICE PRESIDENT
Gail Ringer, Ringer Video
TREASURER
Richard Vedvick, Forde Motion Picture Labs
SECRETARY
George Hutchison, Consolidated Film Industries

Association of Film Commissioners International

%Utah Film Commission, 324 South State, Suite 500, Salt Lake City, UT 84114; (801) 538-0540; FAX: (801)

538-8778.(Organized 1975; Acts as a liaison between the visual communications industry and local governments or organizations to facilitate on-location production, to stimulate economic benefit for member governments.)

PRESIDENT
 Leigh von der Esch, Utah Film Office
VICE PRESIDENT
 Luci Marshall, Phoenix Motion Picture Office
 Mary Stricklin, Alabama Film Office
SECRETARY
 Linda Taylor Hutchison, New Mexico Film
TREASURER
 Eve Lapolla, Ohio Film Commission
BOARD OF DIRECTORS
 Lori Holladay, Cincinnati Film Office; Charles Geocaris, Chicago Film Office; Isabel Hill, South Carolina Film Office; Joe O'Kane, San Jose Film & Video Commission; David Parker, Calgary Film Services; Gail Thomson, Ontario Film Development Corporation.

Association of Independent Video & Filmmakers, Inc.

625 Broadway, New York, NY 10012; (212) 473-3400. (A national membership organization dedicated to the growth of independent media through advocacy and professional services.)

EXECUTIVE DIRECTOR
 Ruby Lerner
MEMBERSHIP/PROGRAMMING DIRECTOR
 Katherine Smith
FESTIVAL BUREAU DIRECTOR
 Kathryn Bowser

BMI (Broadcast Music, Inc.)

320 W. 57 St., New York, NY 10019; (212) 586-2000; 8730 Sunset Blvd., 3rd fl. West, Los Angeles, CA 90069; (310) 659-9109; 10 Music Square E., Nashville, TN 37203; (615) 259-3625; 79 Marylebone Rd., London NW1 5HN, England; 011-4471-935-9517.

CHAIRMAN OF THE BOARD
 James G. Babb
PRESIDENT & CHIEF EXECUTIVE OFFICER
 Frances W. Preston
SENIOR VICE PRESIDENT AND GENERAL COUNSEL
 Marvin Berenson
SENIOR VICE PRESIDENT & CHIEF FINANCIAL OFFICER
 Fred Willms
SENIOR VICE PRESIDENT, PERFORMING RIGHTS, WRITER/ PUBLISHER RELATIONS
 Del Bryant
SENIOR VICE PRESIDENT, OPERATIONS
 Richard Mark
VICE PRESIDENT, CORPORATE RELATIONS
 Robbin Ahrold
SENIOR VICE PRESIDENT, INTERNATIONAL
 Ekke Schnabel
SENIOR VICE PRESIDENT & SPECIAL COUNSEL
 Theodora Zavin
SENIOR VICE PRESIDENT, LICENSING
 John M. Shaker
VICE PRESIDENT, NASHVILLE
 Roger Sovine
VICE PRESIDENT, WRITER/PUBLISHER RELATIONS, CALIFORNIA
 Rick Riccobono
VICE PRESIDENT, WRITER/PUBLISHER RELATIONS, NEW YORK
 Charles S. Feldman
VICE PRESIDENT, GENERAL LICENSING
 Tony Annastas
VICE PRESIDENT, HUMAN RESOURCES & SECRETARY
 Edward W. Chapin
VICE PRESIDENT, EUROPEAN WRITER/PUBLISHER RELATIONS
 Philip R. Graham
VICE PRESIDENT, SPECIAL COUNSEL
 Joe A. Moscheo, II
VICE PRESIDENT, RESEARCH & INFORMATION
 Alan H. Smith

VICE PRESIDENT, TELECOMMUNICATIONS
 Larry Sweeney

Council on International Non-Theatrical Events (CINE)

1001 Connecticut Ave. N.W., Suite 638, Washington, DC 20036; (202) 785-1136, 785-1137; FAX: (202) 785-4114.
Organized 1957, CINE (A non-profit association) selects and enters television documentaries, theatrical short subjects, educational, religious, industrial, scientific and similar classes of film and television productions in approximately 120 international film & video(s) competitions held abroad each year. Professional films retained for festival entry receive the CINE Golden Eagle and amateur films, the CINE Eagle. Annually (in the Spring) diplomatic officials in Washington, DC present international honors received by CINE films at festivals and competitions held abroad. Deadline dates for receipt of forms: Feb. 1 and Aug. 1.

PRESIDENT
 Alan Rettig
CHAIRMAN OF THE EXECUTIVE COMMITTEE
 S. Paul Klein
FIRST VICE PRESIDENT
 Dr. Frank Frost
EXECUTIVE DIRECTOR
 Richard Calkins

Department of Communication of the National Council of Churches of Christ in the USA

475 Riverside Dr., Room 856, New York, NY 10115; (212) 870-2574; FAX: (212) 870-2030.

CHAIRPERSON
 Roger Burgess
DIRECTOR OF COMMUNICATION
 J. Martin Bailey
DIRECTOR OF ELECTRONIC MEDIA
 David W. Pomeroy

Exhibitor Relations Co., Inc.

116 N. Robertson Blvd., Suite 606, Los Angeles, CA 90048; (310) 657-2005; FAX: (310) 657-7283.
PRESIDENT
 John N. Krier

Film Society of Lincoln Center

70 Lincoln Center Plaza, New York, NY 10023-6595; (212) 875-5610; FAX: (212) 875-5636. (Organized 1969; An arts organization sponsoring film programs, e.g., The New York Film Festival and publisher of Film Comment magazine. Also owner of Walter Reade Theatre at Lincoln Center.)

CHAIRMAN
 Julien J. Studley
PRESIDENT
 Roy L. Furman
EXECUTIVE DIRECTOR
 Joanne Koch
EXECUTIVE PRODUCER/PROGRAMMING
 Wendy Keys
PROGRAM DIRECTOR
 Richard Peña

Foundation of the Motion Picture Pioneers, Inc., The

244 W. 49 St., Suite 305, New York, NY 10019; (212) 247-5588; FAX: (212) 265-6428.

PRESIDENT
 Bruce Corwin
CHAIRMAN OF BOARD
 Robert Rehme
EXECUTIVE VICE PRESIDENT
 A. Alan Friedberg
VICE PRESIDENTS
 Dan Fellman, Larry Gleason, Frank Mancuso, Joel Resnick
SECRETARY
 Robert Sunshine

French Film Office/Unifrance Film International

745 Fifth Ave., Suite 1512, New York, NY 10151; (212) 832-8860; FAX: (212) 755-0629. (Organized 1956; promotes French films in U.S.)
EXECUTIVE DIRECTOR FOR THE U.S.
 Catherine Verret

French Film Office for Los Angeles

10990 Wilshire Blvd., #300, Los Angeles, CA 90024; (310) 479-0643; FAX: (310) 479-8331. (Organized 1981.)
DIRECTOR
 Benoit Caron

Friars Club

57 E. 55 St., New York, NY 10022; (212) 751-7272.
ABBOT
 Frank Sinatra
DEAN
 Jack L. Green
PRIOR
 Freddie Roman
SCRIBE
 Bob Fitzsimmons
TREASURER
 Robert W. Sarnoff
EXECUTIVE DIRECTOR
 Jean-Pierre L. Trebot
DIRECTOR OF SPECIAL EVENTS
 David W. Tebet
HONORARY OFFICERS
ABBOT EMERITUS
 Milton Berle
SCRIBE EMERITUS
 Red Buttons
PROCTOR
 George Burns
PROCTOR
 Buddy Hackett
HERALD
 Paul Anka
MONITOR
 Alan King
HISTORIAN
 Bernard M. Kamber
HISTORIAN EMERITUS
 Howard Cosell
MONK
 Robert Merrill
SAMARITAN
 Norman King
LYRICIST
 Sammy Cahn
BIOGRAPHER
 Joey Adams
SQUIRE
 Henny Youngman
KNIGHT
 Gene Baylos
KNIGHT
 Louis Brandt
KNIGHT
 Tom Jones
ARCHIVIST
 James W. Grau
CHRONOLOGIST
 Al Rylander

Friars Club of California, Inc.

9900 Santa Monica Blvd., Beverly Hills, CA 90212; (213) 553-0850; 879-3375. (Organized 1947.)
PRESIDENT
 Saul H. Burakoff
FIRST VICE PRESIDENT
 Irwin M. Schaeffer
SECOND VICE PRESIDENT
 Edward G. Lewis
SECRETARY
 Norman Edell
TREASURER
 Gary G. Cohen
ASSISTANT SECRETARY/TREASURER
 David Daar

Independent Feature Project, The

132 W. 21 St., 6th floor, New York, NY 10011-3203; (212) 243-7777; FAX: (212) 243-3882. (Organized 1979; Not-for-profit membership organization which provides information and support services to independent filmmakers.)
EXECUTIVE DIRECTOR
 Catherine Tait
MARKET CO-DIRECTORS
 Jane Wright, Rachel Shapiro
BOARD OF DIRECTORS
 Doro Bachrach (pres., The Noon Wine Co.); Michael Barker (co-pres., Sony Pictures Classics); Richard Brick (NYC Mayors Office of Film, Theatre, Broadcasting); Ralph Donnelly (pres., City Cinemas); Charles Lane (Memory Lane Entertainment); Jeff Lipsky (October Films); Richard Pena (prog. dir., Film Soc. of Lincoln Ctr.); Sandra Schulberg (mng. dir., American Playhouse/Abroad); Thomas Selz (Frankfort, Garbus, Klein & Selz); Nancy Sher (Arts Channel, Tuscon, AZ); Raphael Silver (chairman, Silverfilm Productions); Nancy Tennenbaum (Nancy Tennenbaum Films); Cara White (Clein & White); Irwin Young (chairman of board, DuArt Film Laboratories Inc.)

Independent Feature Project/West

5550 Wilshire Blvd., Suite 204, Los Angeles, CA 90036; (213) 937-4379; FAX: (213) 937-4038. (Organized 1980; Supports, promotes and honors American independent films by a variety of services, programs, screenings, and magazine: "Filmmaker: The Magazine of Independent Film.")
CHAIRMAN
 Jonathan Wacks
PRESIDENT
 Cathy Main
VICE PRESIDENT
 Theodore Thomas
CHIEF FINANCIAL ADVISOR
 Caldecot Chubb
SECRETARY/TREASURER
 Steve Bannon
EXECUTIVE DIRECTOR
 Dawn Hudson
BOARD OF DIRECTORS
 Allison Anders, Gregg Araki, Jesse Beaton, Barbara Boyle, Peter Broderick, Charles Burnett, Julie Carmen, Ira Deutchman, Carl Franklin, Geoffrey Gilmore, Michael Helfant, Jeff Kleeman, Kaz Kuzuy, Carol Munday Lawrence, Jeanne Lucas, Carole Markin, Peter McCarthy, Peggy Rajski, Charles Ries, Sara Risher, Midge Sanford, Ella Taylor.
AFFILIATIONS
 American Cinemateque, Film Form, Black Filmmakers Foundation, AAPAA, Writers Guild of America/West, HAMAS, NAMAC, AFI, Sundance Institute, Women in Film, Behind the Lens, UCLA Film and TV Archives

International Documentary Association

1551 S. Robertson Blvd., Suite 201, Los Angeles, CA 90035-4233; (310) 284-8422; FAX: (310) 785-9334. (Organized 1982; Non-profit assn. which promotes the documentary film.)

PRESIDENT
Jon Wilkman
VICE PRESIDENT
Mel Stuart
SECOND VICE PRESIDENT
Ann Hassett
SECRETARY
Lisa Leeman
TREASURER
Lance Williams
EXECUTIVE DIRECTOR
Betsy A. McLane
BOARD OF DIRECTORS
Marshall Flaum, Alex Gibney, Gary Glaser, Lorraine Gray, Ann Hassett, Gabor Kalman, Lisa Leeman, Elena Minor, Kerry Neal, Tom Neff, Stephen Peck, Brenda Reiswerg, Marilyn Ryan, Rich Samuels, Doug Stewart, Mel Stuart, Richard Wells, Jon Wilkman, Lance Williams, Jessica Yu; Henry Breitrose (Stanford), Henry Hampton (Boston), Richard Kilberg (New York), Lourdes Portillo (San Francisco), Michael Rabiger (Chicago), Harry Rasky (Toronto), Robert Richter (New York), Louise Rosen (London), Marc Weiss (New York), Frederick Wiseman (Boston)

Japan Society/Film Center

333 E. 47 St., New York, NY 10017; (212) 832-1155; FAX: (212) 755-6752. (Organized 1971; Promotes Japanese culture through exhibiting Japanese films and films on Japan.)

DIRECTOR, FILM CENTER
Dr. Kyoko Hirano
FILM PROGRAM ASSISTANT
Robert Lazzaro

Motion Picture and Television Fund

23388 Mulholland Drive, Woodland Hills, CA 91364; (818) 876-1888. Hollywood Office: Bob Hope Health Center, 335 N. LaBrea Ave., Los Angeles, CA 90036; (213) 937-7250.

PRESIDENT
Roger H. Davis
FIRST VICE PRESIDENT
Chester L. Migden
SECOND VICE PRESIDENT
Frank I. Davis
THIRD VICE PRESIDENT
Janet Leigh Brandt
FOURTH VICE PRESIDENT
Marshall Wortman
TREASURER
Roger Mayer
SECRETARY
Irma Kalish
CHIEF EXECUTIVE OFFICER
William F. Haug
DIRECTOR OF PROFESSIONAL SERVICES
Timothy M. Lefevre, M.D.
CHIEF FINANCIAL OFFICER
Frank Guarrera
GROUP DIRECTOR, THE FOUNDATION
Ann Thompson-Haas

Motion Picture Association of America, Inc.

15503 Ventura Blvd., Encino, CA 91436.; (818) 995-6600.

SENIOR VICE PRESIDENT AND DIRECTOR, WORLDWIDE ANTI-PIRACY
William M. Baker
SENIOR VICE PRESIDENT AND GENERAL COUNSEL
William Billick
SENIOR VICE PRESIDENT, WEST COAST ADMINISTRATION
Bethlyn Hand
SENIOR VICE PRESIDENT AND CHIEF FINANCIAL OFFICER
John J. Collins
VICE PRESIDENT, WORLDWIDE MARKET RESEARCH
Robert A. Franklin

Advertising Administration
DIRECTOR
Bethlyn Hand
ASSOCIATE DIRECTOR
Marilyn Gordon
Classification and Rating Administration
CHAIRMAN
Richard D. Heffner

Motion Picture Export Association of America, Inc.

15503 Ventura Blvd., Encino, CA 91436.

SENIOR VICE PRESIDENT AND GENERAL COUNSEL
William Billick
SENIOR VICE PRESIDENT AND DIRECTOR, WORLDWIDE ANTI-PIRACY
William M. Baker
SENIOR VICE PRESIDENT AND CHIEF FINANCIAL OFFICER
John C. Collins
SENIOR VICE PRESIDENT, INTERNATIONAL DEPARTMENT
William M. Murray
VICE PRESIDENT, LEGAL
Walid Nasser

Museum of Modern Art, Department of Film

11 W. 53 St., New York, NY 10019; (212) 708-9600; FAX: (212) 708-9531. (Organized May, 1935.)

DIRECTOR
Mary Lea Bandy
CURATOR
Adrienne Mancia
CURATOR
Laurence Kardish
CIRCULATING FILM LIBRARIAN
William Sloan

National Association of Concessionaires

35 E. Wacker Dr., Chicago, IL 60601; (312) 236-3858; FAX: (312) 236-7809. (Organized 1944.)

EXECUTIVE DIRECTOR
Charles A. Winans
PRESIDENT
William P. Rector
BOARD CHAIRMAN
Vince Pantuso
COMMUNICATIONS DIRECTOR
Mandy Pava
VICE PRESIDENTS
Gary Horvath, Norman Chesler, Peter Leyh, David Scoco
TREASURER
Skip Stefansen
DIRECTORS—DIVERSIFIED OPERATORS
Stan Briggs, Thomas P. Keon, Craig Trimble, Randy Ziegler
DIRECTOR—THEATRE CONCESSION OPERATORS
Bruce Taffett
DIRECTOR—EQUIPMENT MANUFACTURERS
Dan Gallery
DIRECTOR—SUPPLIERS
Bruce Proctor
DIRECTOR—JOBBER/DISTRIBUTOR
Libby Mauro
DIRECTORS-AT-LARGE
Chris Bigelow, Phil Blavat, Bill Chaplain, Jim Conlan, Len Gold, R. Evan Gordon Jr., David Tomber.
REGIONAL VICE PRESIDENTS
Jeff Dodge, John Evans, Jr., Frank Liberto, Roger Marrelli, Nancy Pantuso, Luella Pappas, Dee Sexton, Bill Wells
LIFETIME honorary members board of directors
Louis L. Abramson, Larry Blumenthal, Nat Buchman, Sydney Spiegel, Van Myers
COUNCIL OF PAST PRESIDENTS
Andrew S. Berwick, Jr., Shelley Feldman, Doug Larson, Julian Lefkowitz, Jack Leonard, Philip L. Lowe, Edward S. Redstone, Vernon B. Ryles, Jr.

National Association of Theatre Owners, Inc.

4605 Lankershim Blvd., Suite 340, N. Hollywood, CA 91602 (818) 506-1778; FAX: (818) 506-0269.
PRESIDENT
William F. Kartozian
CHAIRMAN OF THE BOARD
Jerome Forman
CHAIRMAN OF THE FINANCE COMMITTEE
Irwin R. Cohen
TREASURER
Irwin R. Cohen
SECRETARY
Thomas Becker
EXECUTIVE DIRECTOR
Mary Ann Grasso
BOARD OF DIRECTORS
EXECUTIVE COMMITTEE: Thomas Becker, CT; Irwin R. Cohen, Reisterstown, MD; Ken Crowe, Los Angeles, CA; Edward Durwood, Kansas City, MO; Jerome Forman, Los Angeles, CA; Steve Gilula, CA; Allen Karp, Toronto, Canada; Barry Lawson, Loeks, NY; Lee Roy Mitchell, Dallas, TX; Ira A. Korff, Dedham, MA; Judson Parker, Boston, MA; Pete Warzel, Englewood, CO.
DIRECTORS-AT-LARGE: Meyer Ackerman, New York, NY; Walter Aman, Portland, OR; J. Wayne Anderson, Reisterstown, MD; Thomas Becker, Norwalk, CT; Byron Berkley, TX; Myron Blank, Des Moines, IA; Tobey Brehm, Ellicott, MD; H. Donald Busch, Philadelphia, PA; Ross Campbell, Sheridan, WY; Michael Campbell, Knoxville, TN; Michael Chakeres, Springfield, OH; Hal Cleveland, Englewood, CO; Irwin A. Cohen, Toronto, Ontario; Irwin R. Cohen, Reisterstown, MD; Scott Cohen, Reisterstown, MD; Bruce Corwin, Los Angeles, CA; Ken Crowe, Los Angeles, CA; Ed Durwood, Kansas City, MO; Richard Durwood, Kansas City, MO; Morris Englander, Boston, MA; Jerome Forman, Los Angeles, CA; Donald Fox, Reading, PA; Richard Fox, Reading, PA; A. Alan Friedberg, Secaucus, NJ; Jack Fuller, Jr., Columbia, SC; Darrell Gabel, Lander, WY; Steve Gilula, Los Angeles, CA; Bernard Goldberg, Jamaica, NY; Marvin Goldman, Washington, D.C.; Charles Goldwater, Secaucus, NJ; Robert Goodrich, Kentwood, MI; Jerome Gordon, Newport News, VA; Malcolm C. Green, Boston, MA; W. D. Gross, Juneau, AK; Vince Guzzo, Kansas City, MO; Larry Hanson, Marshfield, WI; Dan Harkins, Scottsdale, AZ; Philip Harris, Oakland, CA; Salah Hassanein, Woodbury, NY; Derek Hyman, Huntington, WV; Larry Jacobson, Kansas City, MO; Allen Karp, Toronto, Ontario; Beth Kerasotes, Springfield, IL; George Kerasotes, Springfield, IL; Ira A. Korff, Dedham, MA; Ronald Krueger, St. Louis, MO; Barrie Lawson Loeks, New York, NY; Ron Leslie, Prairie Village, KS; Howard Lichtman, Toronto, Canada; Richard Lightman, Memphis, TN; Hank Lightstone, Englewood, CO; Ben Littlefield, Los Angeles, CA; Jack Loeks, Wyoming, MI; Jim Loeks, New York, NY; John Loeks, Jr., Wyoming, MI; Jerome Magner, Dedham, MA; T. M. Manos, Greensburg, PA; Ben Marcus, Milwaukee, WI; Steve Marcus, Milwaukee, WI; Mike Mercy, Yakima, WA; Lee Roy Mitchell, Dallas, TX; Larry Moyer, Portland, OR; Frank Novak, Richmond, VA; Richard Orear, Kansas City, MO; Judson Parker, Boston, MA; Sperie Perakos, New Britain, CT; Ayron Pickerill, Polson, MT; Sumner Redstone, Dedham, MA; Joel Resnick, Springfield; Julian Rifkin, Duxbury, MA; Larry Roper, Twin Falls, ID; Paul Roth, Silver Spring, MD; John Rowley, Dallas, TX; Greg Rutkowski, Los Angeles, CA; Arthur Sanborn, Newport Beach, CA; Jerry Siegel, Westbury, NY; Bob Smerling, New York, NY; Seymour Smith, New York, NY; T. G. Solomon, New Orleans, LA; Arthur Stein, Des Moines, IA; William Stembler, Atlanta, GA; John Stembler, Sr., Atlanta, GA; William Towey, Boston, MA; John Treadwell, Dallas, TX; Peter Walch, Switzerland; TimWarner, Los Angeles, CA; Pete Warzel, Englewood, CO; Roy B. White, Naples, FL; Russell Wintner, Cleveland, OH

ARIZONA THEATRE OWNERS ASSOCIATION

3227 E. Bell Rd., Suite 252
Phoenix, AZ 85032

NATO OF CALIFORNIA/NEVADA

Tim Warner, Pres.
116 N. Robertson Blvd., Suite F
Los Angeles, CA 90048

NATO OF COLORADO AND WYOMING

Darrell Gabel (Wyoming)
855 S. 9th
Lander, WY 82520

CONNECTICUT ASSOC. OF THEATRE OWNERS

Steve Menschell, Pres.
164 E. Center St.
Manchester, CT 06040

NATO OF DISTRICT OF COLUMBIA

Ted Pedas, Pres.
9310 Warwick Blvd.
Newport News, VA 23601

NATO OF FLORIDA

Bill Korenbrot, Pres.
2528 Leeward Way
Winter Park, FL 32792

NATO OF IDAHO

Larry Roper, Pres.
P.O. Box "T"
Twin Falls, ID 83301

NATO OF KENTUCKY

Donal W. Jones, Pres.
P.O. Box 473
Mayfield, KY 42066

LOUISIANA ASSOC. OF THEATRE OWNERS

Dennis Guidry, Pres.
1250 Mass St.
New Orleans, LA 70119

MID-ATLANTIC NATO
(Maryland, Virginia, Washington D.C.)

Barbara Kimmitt, Chmn.
9310 Warwick Blvd.
Newport News, VA 23601

UNITED MOTION PICTURE ASSOC. OF MISSOURI & KANSAS

Darryl Smith, Pres.
Box 22473
Kansas City, MO 64113

MONTANA ASSOCIATION OF THEATRE OWNERS

Dione Smith, Pres.
P.O. Box 437
Hardin, MT 59034

THEATRE OWNERS OF NEW ENGLAND

William Towey, Pres.
One Exeter Plaza, 7th fl.
Boston, MA 02116

NATO OF NEW JERSEY

Jesse Sayegh, Pres.
P.O. Box 407, % Cinema 23
Cedar Grove, NJ 07009

NATO OF NEW YORK STATE

Jerry Siegel, Pres.
244 West 49th St., Suite 200
New York, NY 10019

NATO OF NORTH CENTRAL STATES

Larry Kirschenmann, Pres.
3508 France Ave. N.
Robbinsdale, MN 55422

NATO OF OHIO

Russell J. Wintner, Pres.
14 Troy Rd., Suite 124
Delaware, OH 43015

NATO OF PENNSYLVANIA

H. Donald Busch, Pres.
111 Chestnut Street
Philadelphia, PA 19106

NATO OF TEXAS

John H. Rowley, Exec. Dir.
12201 Merit Dr., Suite 720
Dallas, TX 75251

MOTION PICTURE EXHIBITORS OF WASHINGTON, NORTHERN IDAHO & ALASKA

Alan Blangy, Pres.
P.O. Box 2714
Kirkland, WA 98083

NATO OF WISCONSIN & UPPER MICHIGAN

Dean Fitzgerald, Pres.
212 W. Wisconsin Ave., Suite 210
Milwaukee, WI 53203

National Board of Review of Motion Pictures, Inc.

P.O. Box 589, New York, NY 10021; (212) 628-1594. (Organized March, 1909; Publisher of Films in Review, sponsor of the D.W. Griffith Awards.)
PRESIDENT
  Inez S. Glucksman
VICE PRESIDENT
  Ross Claiborne
EDITOR
  Robin Little

National Independent Theatre Exhibitors Association

1311 Scurry, P.O. Box 3553, Big Spring, TX 79720. (915) 263-8511.

PRESIDENT
  Robert E. Hutte
PRESIDENT EMERITUS
  Tom Patterson

National Music Publishers' Association, Inc.

205 E. 42 St., 18th fl., New York, NY 10017; (212) 370-5330.
CHAIRMAN
  Irwin Z. Robinson
PRESIDENT & CHIEF EXECUTIVE OFFICER
  Edward P. Murphy
VICE PRESIDENTS
  Ralph Peer II, Leon J. Brettler, William Lowery
TREASURER
  Stanley Mills

New York Women in Film

274 Madison Ave., Suite 1202, New York, NY 10016-0701; (212) 679-0870; FAX: (212) 679-0899. Organized in 1977. Serves as a networking, educational, and informational organization for professional women in film and television.
PRESIDENT
  Beth Dembitzer
VICE PRESIDENTS
  Sandra Colony, Barbara Moss, Joy Pereths
SECRETARY
  Lisa Hackett Stafford
TREASURER
  Becky Hrdy
BOARD OF DIRECTORS
  Susan Dworkin, Harlene Freezer, Ellen Geiger, Beth George, Barbara R. Goodman, Karen L. King, Eileen Newman, Amy Schewel, Dana Thrush, Vivian Treves, Helen Whitney
LEGAL COUNSEL
  Marsha Brooks
EXECUTIVE DIRECTOR
  Phyllis Schwartz
OFFICE MANAGER
  Rosemary Riccio
OFFICE COORDINATOR
  Jana Siciliano
CHAPTERS
  Atlanta, Baltimore, Boston, Chicago, Dallas, Los Angeles, Orlando, San Francisco, Washington, D.C., Jamaica, London, Melbourne, Sydney, Toronto, Vancouver

Permanent Charities Committee of the Entertainment Industries

11132 Ventura Blvd., Suite 401, Studio City, CA 91604-3156; (818) 760-7722; FAX: (818) 760-7898. (A donor federation within the entertainment industries supporting community wide charities.)
CHAIRMAN OF THE BOARD
  Daniel E. Slusser
PRESIDENT AND CHIEF EXECUTIVE OFFICER
  Lisa Paulsen
FIRST VICE PRESIDENT
  Earl Lestz
SECOND VICE PRESIDENT
  Harry Floyd
SECRETARY
  William K. Howard
TREASURER
  Robert S. Colbert, CPA
VICE PRESIDENT OF ADMINISTRATION & FINANCE
  Irwin J. Kaplan
VICE PRESIDENT, DEVELOPMENT
  Lance L. Keene
VICE PRESIDENT OF COMMUNICATIONS AND CORPORATE RELATIONS
  Danielle M. Guttman

SESAC Inc.

156 W. 56 St., New York, NY 10019; (212) 586-3450; FAX: (212) 397-4682. (One of the world's foremost music licensing organizations. A special projects department handles scoring for motion pictures, slide films, syndicated TV series and agency produced commercials; programming or background music and premium albums.)
CHAIRMEN
Freddie Gershon, Stephen Swid, Ira Smith
PRESIDENT & CEO
Vincent Candilora

Society of Composers & Lyricists

400 South Beverly Dr., Suite 214, Beverly Hills, CA 90212; (310) 281-2812; FAX: (310) 474-8992. (Approx. 350 members. Organization formed to support and promote the exchange of information among members in the composing field and filmmakers.)
PRESIDENT
Richard Bellis
VICE PRESIDENT
Brad Fiedel
SECRETARY/TREASURER
Bruce Babcock
ADMINISTRATOR
D. J. Olsen
ADVISORY BOARD
Alan Bergman, Marilyn Bergman, Bill Conti, Quincy Jones, Henry Mancini, Peter Matz, David Raksin, Lalo Schifrin, Patrick Williams
BOARD OF DIRECTORS
David Bell, Charles Bernstein, Jane Brockman, Bruce Broughton, John Cacavas, Alf Clausen, John Debney, James Di Pasquale, Ron Grant, Arthur Hamilton, Lee Holdridge, Don Peake, Ron Ramin, Nan Schwartz Mishkin, Dennis Spiegel, Shirley Walker, Gary Woods

Society of Motion Picture and Television Engineers

595 W. Hartsdale Ave. , White Plains, NY 10607; (914) 761-1100; FAX: (914) 761-3115. (Organized 1916; Membership: 9,700.)
PRESIDENT
Blaine Baker
PAST PRESIDENT
Maurice L. French
EXECUTIVE VICE PRESIDENT
Irwin W. Young
ENGINEERING VICE PRESIDENT
Stanley N. Baron
EDITORIAL VICE PRESIDENT
Frank J. Haney
FINANCIAL VICE PRESIDENT
Richard K. Schafer
CONFERENCE VICE PRESIDENT
L. John Spring Jr.
SECRETARY/TREASURER
Bernard L. Dickens
EXECUTIVE DIRECTOR
Lynette Robinson

Theatre Equipment Association

Office of the Executive Director: 244 W. 49 St., New York, NY 10019; (212) 246-6460; FAX: (212) 265-6428.
PRESIDENT
Terry Yushchyshn
VICE PRESIDENT
Ioan Allen
SECRETARY
Don Marcus
TREASURER
Dan Taylor
EXECUTIVE DIRECTOR
Robert Sunshine
CHAIRMAN OF THE BOARD
John Wilmers

United States Catholic Conference, Department of Communication, Office for Film & Broadcasting

Suite #1300, 1011 First Ave., New York, NY 10022; (212) 644-1894; FAX: (212) 644-1886.
DIRECTOR, OFFICE FOR FILM & BROADCASTING
Henry Herx

The Department of Communication of the U.S. Catholic Conference (the public policy agency of the Catholic Bishops of America) addresses the Church's apostolate in and through the print and electronic media. It provides advice and technical assistance on more than 40 radio and network television programs a year.

The Department also publishes a weekly guide to current films and television programs that appear in 100 plus papers of the Catholic Press in the United States. In this activity the Department reviews all current nationally-released theatrical films, and provides information about resources for film utilization and education (16mm films, books, magazines, festivals). The critical reviews are addressed to the moral, as well as the aesthetic dimensions of motion pictures, and are the result of a consensus based on the reactions of the Department's professional staff and Board of Consultors. All films reviewed are also classified according to the Department's rating system. In addition, this weekly service carries information and evaluative studies on trends and issues pertinent to television and motion picture with an emphasis on educational material.

The Department also plays a liaison role for the USCC with the film and broadcasting industries, national media, and religious agencies and organizations. It is a member of OCIC and UNDA, the international Catholic organizations for film and broadcasting, respectively. Consultation and information services are also provided for the Pontifical Commission for Social Communications and the communication offices of national episcopal offices throughout the world.

With staff assistance, the episcopal members of the Communication Committee administer funds raised through the Catholic Communication Campaign, an annual collection. These funds are used to support a variety of media programs, projects, and studies in this country and the Third World.

Variety Clubs International

International Office: 1560 Broadway, Suite 1209, New York, NY 10036 (212) 704-9872; FAX: (212) 704-9875. (Organized October 10, 1927; Membership: 15,000.)
PRESIDENT
John Ratcliff
CHAIRMAN OF THE BOARD
Jarvis Astaire
INTERNATIONAL CHAIRMAN
Monty Hall, O.C.
PAST PRESIDENTS
George W. Eby; Robert R. Hall, O.C.; Salah M. Hassanein; Eric D. Morley; Ralph W. Pries; Stanley J. Reynolds; Burton Robbins; John H. Rowley; Michael Samuelson; Joseph Sinay
VICE PRESIDENTS
Peter J. Barnett; Vincent Catarella; Tom Fenno; Michael Forman; Frederick M. Friedman; Anthony Hasham; Tony Hatch; Fred Levin; Julia Morley; George Pitman; Michael Reilly; Jody Reynolds, Bruce Rosen; Frank Strean; John R. Weber.
PRESIDENT'S COUNCIL
Samuel Z. Arkoff; Monty Berman, MBE; Trevor Chinn, CVO; Fred Danz; Phillip Isaacs; Lou Lavinthal; Frank Mancuso; Hank Milgram; Carl L. Patrick; Ric R. Roman; Zollio Volchnok.
TREASURER
Bernard Myerson
INTERNATIONAL COUNSELLOR
Robert R. Hall, Q.C.

TENT No. 1: Variety Club of Pittsburgh, Warner Center, 332 Fifth Ave., Pittsburgh, PA 15222; (412) 281-1163.
TENT No. 4: Variety Club of St. Louis, 425 Woods Mill Rd. S., #190, Chesterfield, MO 63017; (314) 821-8184.
TENT No. 5: Variety Club of Detroit, Cranbrook Centre, 30161 Southfield Rd., Southfield, MI 48076; (313) 258-5511.
TENT No. 6: Variety Club of Northern Ohio, 3201 Carnegie Ave., Cleveland, OH 44115 (216) 361-3201.
TENT No. 7: Variety Club of Buffalo, 195 Delaware Ave., Buffalo, NY 14202; (716) 854-7577.
TENT No. 8: Variety Club of Greater Kansas City, P.O. Box 36083, Kansas City, MO 64111; (816) 474-6427.
TENT No. 10: Variety Club of Indiana, P.O. Box 277, Shelbyville, IN 46176; (317) 398-7318.
TENT No.11: Variety Club of Greater Washington, DC, %Variety Clubs Intl., 1560 Bdwy., Suite 1209, New York, NY 10036.
TENT No. 12: Variety Club of Minnesota, 391 E. River Rd., Minneapolis, MN 55455; (612) 624-6900.
TENT No. 13: The Children's Charity of Philadelphia, Warwick Hotel, 17th & Locust, Philadelphia, PA 19103; (215) 735-0803.
TENT No. 14: The Children's Charity of Wisconsin, 750 North 18th St., Milwaukee, WI 53233; (414) 344-7211.
TENT No. 15: Variety Club of Iowa, 505 Fifth Ave., #310, Des Moines, IA 50309; (515) 243-4660.
TENT No. 16: Variety Club of Nebraska, 9100 F. Street, Omaha, NE 68127; (402) 331-4313.
TENT No. 17: Variety Club of Northern Texas, 6060 N. Central Expwy., #543, Dallas, TX 75206; (214) 368-7449.
TENT No. 19: Variety Club of Maryland, 3404 Keyser Rd., Baltimore, MD 21208; (410) 653-8668.
TENT No. 20: Variety Club of Memphis, P.O. Box 1523, Memphis, TN 38101; (901) 274-2220.
TENT NO. 21: Variety Club of Atlanta, 2970 Clairmont Rd., #1050, Atlanta, GA 30329; (404) 633-5775.
TENT No. 22: Variety Club of Oklahoma, P.O. Box 32823, Oklahoma City, OK 73123; (405) 236-1733.
TENT No. 23: Variety Club of New England, Sheraton Boston Hotel, 39 Dalton St., Boston, MA 02199; (617) 437-9500.
TENT No. 25: Variety Children's Charities of Southern California, 8455 Beverly Blvd., #303., Los Angeles, CA 90048; (213) 655-1547.
TENT No. 26: Variety Children's Charities, Illinois, 185 N. Wabash St., #800, 1040, Chicago, IL 60601; (312) 855-0885.
TENT No. 27: Variety Club of Grand Rapids, P.O. Box 2293, Grand Rapids, MI 49501; (616) 538-2877.
TENT No. 28: Variety Club of Ontario, The King Edward Hotel, 37 King St. East, Suite 300, Toronto, Ont. M5C 1E9 Canada; (416) 367-2828.
TENT No. 29: Variety Club of Mexico, Liga Periferico Sur 4903, Col. Parques Del Perdregal, Mexico City, Mexico C.P. 14010; (525) 665-4246.
TENT No. 32: Variety Club of Northern California, 582 Market St., Suite 101, San Francisco, Ca 94104, (415) 781-3894.
TENT No. 33: Variety Club of Florida, 17070 Collins Ave., Suite 205, Miami Beach, FL 33160, (305) 945-7750.
TENT No. 34: Variety Club of Houston, 3701 Kirby, #1090, Houston, TX 77098; (713) 524-2878.
TENT No. 35: Variety/The Children's Charity, 244 W. 49 St., Room 200, New York, NY 10019, (212) 247-5588.
TENT No. 36: Variety Club of Great Britain, 32 Welbeck Street, London, UK/W1M 7PG, (71) 935-4466.
TENT No. 37: Variety Club of Colorado, %Hank Lightstone, 9110 E. Nichols Ave., #200, Englewood, CO 80112; (303) 792-3600.
TENT No. 39: Variety Club of Southern Nevada, 301 N. Fremont-Fitzgeralds Hotel, 12th fl., Las Vegas, NV 89101, (702) 382-7692.
TENT No. 41: Variety Club of Ireland, 10 Merrion Sq., Dublin 2, Ireland; (353) 616355.

TENT No. 45: Variety Club of New Orleans, P.O. Box 546 Metairie, LA 70004; (504) 837-5413.
TENT No. 46: Variety Club of Pacific Northwest, %Variety Clubs Intl., 1560 Bdwy., #1209, New York, NY 10036.
TENT No. 47: Variety Club of British Columbia, 1250 Homer St., Vancouver, B.C. V6B 2Y5 Canada; (609) 669-2313.
TENT No. 50: Variety Club of Hawaii, 1517 Kapiolani Blvd., #200, Honolulu, HI 96814; (808) 955-5106.
TENT No. 51: Variety Club of Israel, 26, Yirmiyahu St., Tel Aviv, 62594 Israel 03-5467715-6.
TENT No. 52: Variety Club of Jersey, Maufant Variety Youth Centre, Grand Route de St. Martin, Jersey, St. Martin, JE3 6JB Channel Islands; 0534-56937.
TENT No. 53: Variety Club of Puerto Rico, P.O. Box 13564, Santurce, Puerto Rico 00908; (809) 793-0666.
TENT No. 54: Soleil D'enfance, 46 Rue de Seine, Paris, France 75006; (14) 407-2828.
TENT No. 56: Variety Club of Australia, Private Bag 1044 Rozelle, Sydney, N.S.W., 2039 Australia, (2) 555-1977.
TENT No. 58: Variety Club of Manitoba, 611 Wellington Crescent, Winnipeg, R3M 0A7 Manitoba, Canada, (204) 284-3911.
TENT No. 59: Variety Club of Arizona, 10595 No. Tatum, #E-146, Paradise Valley, AZ 85253; (602) 451-9377.
TENT No. 60: Variety Club of Utah, 135 Young Oaks Road, Salt Lake City, UT 84108; (801) 582-0537.
TENT No. 61: Variety Club of Southern Alberta, #202 Sony Bldg., 110 Eleven Ave. S.E., Calgary, Alberta, T2G 0X6, Canada; (403) 261-0061.
TENT No. 62: Variety Club of Switzerland, Stampfenbach Strass 69, Zurich, SWITZ 8035; 411-363-63-23.
TENT No. 63: Variety Club of Northern Alberta, 10712 176 St., Edmonton, Alberta T5S 1G7 Canada; (403) 448-9544.
TENT No. 65: Variety Club of Palm Beach, 339K, Royal Poinciana Plaza, Palm Beach, FL 33480, (407) 833-8309.
TENT No. 66: Variety Children's Charities of the Desert (Palm Springs), 1043 So. Palm Canyon Drive, Palm Springs, CA 92264; (619) 320-1177.
TENT No. 67: Variety Club of Quebec, 4670 St. Catherine Street W., #301, Westmount, Que., CAN H32155; (514) 932-0748.
TENT No. 68: Variety Club of New Zeland, P.O. Box 446, Auckland 1, New Zealand; (649) 302-2005.
TENT No. 70: Variety Club of Orlando, 2943 Eagle Lake Dr., Orlando, FL 32837; (407) 240-4770.

Will Rogers Memorial Fund

785 Mamaroneck Ave., White Plains, NY 10605; (914) 761-5550; FAX: (914) 761-1513.

PRESIDENT
Fred Mound
EXECUTIVE VICE PRESIDENT
Ralph E. Donnelly
CHAIRMAN OF THE BOARD
Jerry Forman
HONORARY CHAIRMEN
Salah M. Hassanein, Bernard Myerson, Frank G. Mancuso
TREASURER
Charles R. Hacker
SECRETARY
Seymour H. Smith
EXECUTIVE DIRECTOR
Martin Perlberg

Women in Communications, Inc.

2101 Wilson Blvd., #417, Arlington, VA 22201; (703) 528-4200; FAX: 528-4205. (Organized 1909; Promotes advancement of women in communication, protects First Amendment, encourages professionalism in the field.)

PRESIDENT
Anne S. Greenberg
EXECUTIVE DIRECTOR
Roni D. Posner
BRANCHES
Over 187 chapters.

Women in Film

6464 Sunset Blvd., #530, Hollywood, CA 90028; (213) 463-6040. (Non-profit organization formed in 1973 by professional women in the motion picture and television industries; purpose is to serve as a support group and

653

to improve the employment, position and depiction of women in film and television.)

PRESIDENT EMERITUS—FOUNDER
  Tichi Wilkerson-Kassel
EXECUTIVE DIRECTOR
  Harriet Silverman

Women in Show Business

P.O. Box 2535, Toluca Lake, CA 91610; (310) 271-3415; FAX: (818) 994-6181. (A philanthropic organization composed of women in the entertainment industry providing funds for reconstructive and restorative surgery for needy children.)

PRESIDENT
  Scherr Lillico
EXECUTIVE VICE PRESIDENT/WAYS & MEANS
  Pia Botz
EXECUTIVE VICE PRESIDENT/PHILANTHROPY
  Franceska Del-Colle
FIRST VICE PRESIDENT/PROGRAM
  Veronica Murdock
SECOND VICE PRESIDENT/MEMBERSHIP
  Barbara Bandy
RECORDING SECRETARY
  Beth Stoulil
CORRESPONDING SECRETARY
  Leah Bernstein
TREASURER
  Joyce Via

Guilds and Unions

Actor's Equity Association (AAAA-AFL-CIO-CLC)

165 W. 46 St., New York, NY 10036; (212) 869-8530; FAX: (212) 719-9815. Ann Sebastian, San Francisco, CA 94104; George Ives, 6430 Sunset Blvd., Hollywood, CA 90028; Fergus Currie, 203 N. Wabash Ave., Chicago, IL 60601. (Organized May 26, 1913; Membership 38,000.)

PRESIDENT
 Ron Silver
FIRST VICE PRESIDENT
 Patrick Quinn
SECOND VICE PRESIDENT
 Richard Warren Pugh
THIRD VICE PRESIDENT
 Arne Gundersen
FOURTH VICE PRESIDENT
 Werner Klemperer
RECORDING SECRETARY
 Lynn Archer
TREASURER
 Conard Fowkes
EXECUTIVE SECRETARY
 Alan Eisenberg
COUNSEL
 Spivak, Lipton, Watanabe, Spivak
MIDWEST REGIONAL V.P.
 Madeleine Fallon
WESTERN REGIONAL V.P.
 Jacque Lynn Colton

American Cinema Editors

1041 N. Formosa Ave., W. Hollywood, CA 90046; (213) 850-2900; FAX: (213) 850-2922. (Organized November 28, 1950; Membership: 350.)

PRESIDENT
 Michael Hoggan
VICE PRESIDENT
 Douglas Ibold
SECRETARY
 George Hively
TREASURER
 Jack Tucker

American Federation of Musicians (AFL-CIO)

1501 Broadway, New York, NY 10036; (212) 869-1330; FAX: (212) 764-6134. (Organized October, 1896; Membership: 200,000.)

PRESIDENT
 Mark Tully Massagli, Suite 600, Paramount Bldg., 1501 Broadway, New York, NY 10036. (212) 869-1330.
VICE PRESIDENT
 Steve Young, 375 Concord Ave., Belmont, MA 02178.
CANADA VICE PRESIDENT
 Ray Petch, 75 The Donway West, Suite 1010, Don Mills, Ontario, Canada M3C 2E9.
SECRETARY-TREASURER
 Stephen R. Sprague, 1501 Broadway, New York, NY 10036.
EXECUTIVE BOARD
 Kenneth B. Shirk, Sam Folio, Thomas C. Bailey, Thomas F. Lee, Raymond M. Hair, Jr.
PRESIDENT & SECRETARY-TREASURER EMERITUS
 J. Martin Emerson

American Guild of Musical Artists, Inc. (AFL-CIO, AAAA)

1727 Broadway, New York, NY 10019-5284; (212) 265-3687; FAX: (212) 262-9088. (Organized 1936; Membership 5,500.)

PRESIDENT
 Regina Resnik
FIRST VICE PRESIDENT
 Gerald Otte
SECOND VICE PRESIDENT
 Chester Ludgin
THIRD VICE PRESIDENT
 Eugene Lawrence
FOURTH VICE PRESIDENT
 Barbara Bystrom
FIFTH VICE PRESIDENT
 Franco Gentilesca
TREASURER
 William Cason
RECORDING SECRETARY
 Yolanda Antoine
NATIONAL EXECUTIVE SECRETARY
 Louise J. Gilmore
ASSOCIATE NATIONAL EXECUTIVE SECRETARY
 Alan Olsen
ASSISTANT TO THE EXECUTIVE SECRETARY
 Thomas Jamerson
COUNSEL
 Becker, London & Kossow
CO-DIRECTORS OF MEMBERSHIP
 Dolores Galdi-Sirianni, Linda Landi
FINANCIAL SECRETARY
 Grace Pedro
DIRECTOR OF PUBLIC RELATIONS
 Michael Rubino
ADMINISTRATOR FOR DANCE
 Alexander Dubé

CANADA: Christopher Marston, 260 Richmond St. E., Toronto, Ontario M5A 1P4, (416) 867-9156; CHICAGO: Barbara J. Hillman, Cornfield & Feldman, 343 S. Dearborn St., 13th Floor, Chicago, IL 60604, (312) 922-2800; NEW ENGLAND: Robert M. Segal, 11 Beacon St., Boston, MA 02108 (617) 742-0208; NEW ORLEANS: Rosemary LeBoeuf, 4438 St. Peter St., New Orleans, LA 70119, (504) 486-9410; NORTHWEST: Carolyn Carpp, 11021 NE 123rd Lane, Apt. C114, Kirkland, WA 98034, (206) 820-2999; PHILADELPHIA: Gail Lopez-Henriquez, 400 Market St., Philadelphia, PA 19106, (215) 925-8400; SAN FRANCISCO: Harry Polland, Donald Tayer, Ann Sebastian, 235 Pine St., Suite 1100, San Francisco, CA 94104, (415) 986-4060; TEXAS: Benny Hopper, 3915 Fairlakes Dr., Dallas, TX 75228; (214) 279-4720; WASHINGTON D.C.: Eleni Kallas, 16600 Shea Lane, Gaithersburg, MD 20877, (301) 869-8266.

American Guild of Variety Artists (AAAA AFL-CIO)

184 Fifth Ave., New York, NY 10010; (212) 675-1003. L.A.: 4741 Laurel Canyon Blvd., #208, N. Hollywood, CA 91607; (818) 508-9984; FAX: (818) 508-3029. (Organized July 14, 1939; Registered Membership: 78,000; Active Membership: 5,000.)

HONORARY PRESIDENT
 George Burns
HONORARY FIRST VICE PRESIDENT
 Rip Taylor
HONORARY SECOND VICE PRESIDENT
 Johnny Miles
HONORARY THIRD VICE PRESIDENT
 Gloria DeHaven
PRESIDENT
 Rod McKuen
EXECUTIVE VICE PRESIDENT
 Eileen Collins
SECRETARY-TREASURER
 Frances Gaar
REGIONAL VICE PRESIDENTS
 Ron Chisholm, David Cullen, Bobby Faye, Doris George, Wayne Hermans, Elaine Jacovini-Gonella, Deedee Knapp, Howard Kolins, Eddie Lane, Tina Marie, Angela Martin, Brad McDonald, Thomas Merriweather, Scott Senatore, Susan Streater

American Society of Cinematographers, Inc.

1782 N. Orange Dr., Hollywood, CA 90028; (213) 876-5080; FAX: (213) 876-4973. (Organized 1919; Membership: 286.)
PRESIDENT
William A. Fraker
FIRST VICE PRESIDENT
Victor Kemper
SECOND VICE PRESIDENT
Woody Omens
TREASURER
Harry Wolf
SECRETARY
Howard Anderson, Jr.

Art Directors

LOCAL 876 (IATSE) (See IATSE)

Associated Actors and Artistes of America (AAAA)-AFL-CIO

165 W. 46 St., New York, NY 10036; (212) 869-0358; FAX: (212) 869-1746. (Organized July 18, 1919; Membership: 85,000.)
PRESIDENT
Theodore Bikel
VICE PRESIDENTS
Kendall Orsatti, Sanford I. Wolfe, Rod McKuen
TREASURER
Willard Swire
EXECUTIVE SECRETARY
John C. Hall, Jr.
AFFILIATES
Actors' Equity Association, American Federation of Television and Radio Artists, American Guild of Musical Artists, American Guild of Variety Artists, Hebrew Actors Union, Italian Actors Union, Screen Actors Guild, Screen Extras Guild.

Associated Musicians of Greater New York

LOCAL 802 AFM (New York)
322 W. 48 St., New York, NY 10036; (212) 245-4802; FAX: (212) 489-6030. (Organized August 27, 1921; Membership: 15,000.)
PRESIDENT
William Moriarty
VICE PRESIDENT
Florence Nelson
SECRETARY
Martin Lambert
TREASURER
Erwin Price

Association of Film Craftsmen

Local No. 531 (NABET, AFL-CIO) 2501 W. Burbank Blvd., Suite 301, Burbank, CA 91505; (818) 563-3772; FAX: (818) 563-4172.
BUSINESS MANAGER
Ronald W. DeVall

Association of Talent Agents

9255 Sunset Blvd., Suite 318, Los Angeles, CA 90069-3381; (310) 274-0628; FAX: (310) 274-5063. (Organized April, 1937, as Artists' Managers Guild—official organization of talent agents in Hollywood.)
EXECUTIVE DIRECTOR
Chester L. Migden
FIRST VICE PRESIDENT
Sandy Bresler

VICE PRESIDENT
Nina Blanchard
VICE PRESIDENT
Sid Craig
VICE PRESIDENT
T. J. Escott
VICE PRESIDENT
Sonjia Warren Brandon
SECRETARY-TREASURER
Margaret Henderson

Authors' Guild, Inc.

330 W. 42 St., New York, NY 10036-6902; (212) 563-5904; FAX: (212) 564-8363. (Membership: 6,500.)
PRESIDENT
Mary Pope Osborne
VICE PRESIDENT
Sidney Offit
SECRETARY
Letty Cottin Pogrebin
TREASURER
Paula J. Giddings
EXECUTIVE DIRECTOR
Robin Davis Miller

Authors League of America, Inc., The

Authors League, 330 W. 42 St., New York, NY 10036; (212) 564-8350. (Membership: 15,000.)
PRESIDENT
Garson Kanin
VICE PRESIDENT
Robert Anderson
SECRETARY
Eve Merriam
TREASURER
Gerold Frank
ADMINISTRATOR
Robin Davis Miller

Broadcasting Studio Employees

LOCAL 782 (IATSE) (See IATSE)

Catholic Actors Guild of America

1501 Broadway, Suite 510, New York, NY 10036; (212) 398-1868. (Organized April, 1914; Membership: 700.)
PRESIDENT
William J. O'Malley
VICE PRESIDENT
Hildegarde
TREASURER
Martin Kiffel

Directors Guild of America, Inc. (DGA)

National Office, 7920 Sunset Blvd., Los Angeles, CA 90046; (310) 289-2000, (213) 851-3671; FAX: (213) 289-2029; 110 West 57 St., New York NY 10019; (212) 581-0370; 520 N. Michigan Ave., Suite 1026, Chicago, IL 60611; (312) 644-5050.
PRESIDENT
Arthur Hiller
NATIONAL VICE PRESIDENT
Yael Woll
VICE PRESIDENTS
Gene Reynolds, Larry Auerbach, Jack Shea, Jane Schimel, Burt Bluestein, Max Schindler
SECRETARY/TREASURER
Sheldon Leonard
ASSISTANT SECRETARY TREASURER
Marilyn Jacobs-Furey
EXECUTIVE DIRECTOR
Glenn J. Gumpel

656

Dramatists Guild, Inc., The

234 W. 44 St., New York, NY 10036; (212) 398-9366; FAX: (212) 944-0420. (Membership: 813 Active; 5,656 Associate; 350 Subscribing.)

PRESIDENT
Peter Stone
VICE PRESIDENT
Terrence McNally
SECRETARY
Arthur Kopit
TREASURER
Richard Lewine
EXECUTIVE DIRECTOR
Andrew Farber
COUNSEL
Cahill Gordon & Reindel

Episcopal Actors Guild of America, Inc.

1 E. 29 St., New York, NY 10016; (212) 685-2927. (Organized 1926; 750 members.)

HONORARY PRESIDENTS
PRESIDING BISHOP
The Right Reverend Edmond L. Browning
BISHOP OF NEW YORK
The Right Reverend Richard F. Grein
PRESIDENT
Barnard Hughes
VICE PRESIDENTS
Rev. Norman J. Catir, Jr., Warden of the Guild
Joan Fontaine
Mike Mearian
Cliff Robertson
RECORDING SECRETARY
Joan Warren
TREASURER
Edward Crimmins
EXECUTIVE SECRETARY
Lon C. Clark
EXECUTIVE ASSISTANT
Michelle Trudeau

Exhibition Employees

LOCAL 829 (IATSE) (See IATSE)

Film Exchange Employees, Back Room, Locals (IATSE)

(See IATSE)

Film Exchange Employees, Front Office

LOCAL F-45 (IATSE) (See IATSE)

First Aid Employees

LOCAL 767 (IATSE) (See IATSE)

Hollywood Film & Broadcasting Labor Council

1427 N. LaBrea Ave., Los Angeles, CA 90028; (213) 851-0220; FAX: (213) 851-9062. (Organized September, 1947; incorporated November 1948.)

PRESIDENT
Wm. K. Howard
VICE PRESIDENTS
Nick Long
Ken Orsatti
TREASURER
Gene Allen
SECRETARY
H. O'Neil Shanks

International Alliance of Theatrical Stage Employes & Moving Picture Machine Operators of the U.S. and Canada (AFL-CIO)

1515 Broadway, Suite 601, New York, NY 10036-5741; (212) 730-1770; FAX: (212) 921-7699. (Organized nationally, July 17, 1893; internationally, October 1, 1902.)

INTERNATIONAL PRESIDENT
Alfred W. Di Tolla
GENERAL SECRETARY-TREASURER
Thomas C. Short
FIRST VICE PRESIDENT
Frank A. Hobbs, Niles, IL
SECOND VICE PRESIDENT
John J. Nolan, Paramus, NJ
THIRD VICE PRESIDENT
John J. Ryan, Burtonsville, MD
FOURTH VICE PRESIDENT
Edward C. Powell, San Rafael, CA
FIFTH VICE PRESIDENT
Michael W. Proscia, North Bergen, NJ
SIXTH VICE PRESIDENT
Alan L. Cowley, West Hill, Ont.
SEVENTH VICE PRESIDENT
Nick Long, San Dimas, CA
EIGHTH VICE PRESIDENT
Daniel J. Kerins, Chicago, IL
NINTH VICE PRESIDENT
Rudy N. Napoleone, Albuquerque, NM
TENTH VICE PRESIDENT
Carmine A. Palazzo, CA
INTERNATIONAL TRUSTEES
Michael J. Sullivan, Hartford, CT; Nels L. Hansen, Las Vegas, NV; Ada S. Philpot, San Francisco, CA.

The Alliance is comprised of approximately 800 local unions covering the United States, Canada and Hawaii.

PRODUCTION

AFFILIATED PROPERTY CRAFTSMEN LOCAL 44 (IATSE—AFL-CIO), HOLLYWOOD

11500 Burbank Blvd., N. Hollywood, CA 91605; (818) 769-1739. (Organized May 15, 1939.)

ART DIRECTORS, LOCAL 876 (IATSE) HOLLYWOOD

11365 Ventura Blvd., #315, Studio City, CA 91604; (818) 762-9995. (Chartered January 7, 1960.)

COSTUME DESIGNERS GUILD LOCAL 892

13949 Ventura Blvd., Suite 309, Sherman Oaks, CA 91423; (818) 905-1557.

FIRST AID EMPLOYEES, LOCAL 767 (IATSE), LOS ANGELES

2611 Taffrail Lane, Oxnard, CA 93035; (805) 984-7918. (Chartered Oct. 30, 1942.)

INTERNATIONAL PHOTOGRAPHERS OF THE MOTION PICTURE INDUSTRIES (Cameramen) IPMPI LOCAL 666, CHICAGO

327 S. La Salle St., Suite 1122, Chicago, IL 60604; (312) 341-0966. (Chartered Jan. 1, 1929.)

MOTION PICTURE STUDIO CARTOONISTS, LOCAL 839 (IATSE), HOLLYWOOD

4729 Lankershim Blvd., N. Hollywood, CA 91602-1864; (818) 766-7151. (Chartered Jan. 18, 1952.)

MOTION PICTURE SCRIPT SUPERVISORS AND PRODUCTION OFFICE COORDINATORS LOCAL 161

505 Eighth Ave., 16th fl., New York, NY 10018; (212) 695-6248.

MOTION PICTURE SET PAINTERS & SIGN WRITERS, LOCAL 729 (IATSE), HOLLYWOOD

11365 Ventura Blvd., Suite 202, Studio City, CA 91604-3138; (818) 984-3000. (Chartered Aug. 1, 1953.)

MOTION PICTURE STUDIO ELECTRICAL LIGHTING TECHNICIANS, LOCAL 728 (IATSE), AND M.P.M.O. of U.S. AND CANADA-A.F.L.-C.I.O.

14629 Nordhoff St., Panorama City, CA 91402; (818) 891-0728. (Chartered May 15, 1939.)

MOTION PICTURE STUDIO ARTS CRAFTSPERSONS. (Illustrators and Matte Artists) LOCAL 790 (IATSE), HOLLYWOOD

13949 Ventura Blvd., Suite 301, Sherman Oaks, CA 91423; (818) 784-6555. (Chartered April 17, 1945.)

MOTION PICTURE STUDIO GRIPS, LOCAL 80 (IATSE), HOLLYWOOD

6926 Melrose Ave., Los Angeles, CA 90038-3393; (213) 931-1419. (Organized May 15, 1939.)

MOTION PICTURE STUDIO TEACHERS AND WELFARE WORKERS, LOCAL 884 (IATSE) HOLLYWOOD

P.O. Box 461467, Los Angeles, CA 90046. (Chartered September 1, 1960.)

PAINTERS & SCENIC ARTISTS, LOCAL 921 (I.A.T.S.E.) NEW ENGLAND AREA

815 Washington St., Suite 3, Newtonville, MA 02160-1625; (617) 244-8719.

PRODUCTION·OFFICE COORDINATORS & ACCOUNTANTS GUILD LOCAL 717

13949 Ventura Blvd., Suite 306, Sherman Oaks, 91423; (818) 906-9986.

PUBLICISTS, LOCAL 818 (IATSE) HOLLYWOOD

13949 Ventura Blvd., Suite 302, Sherman Oaks, 91423; (818) 905-1541. (Chartered July 11, 1955.)

RADIO AND TELEVISION SOUND EFFECTS, LOCAL 844 (IATSE), NEW YORK

Box 637, Ansonia Station, New York, NY 10023; (212) 887-3920. (Chartered July 17, 1952.)

SCENIC ARTISTS, LOCAL 816 (IATSE), LOS ANGELES

13949 Ventura Blvd., Suite 202 Sherman Oaks, CA 91423; (818) 906-7822. (Chartered March 31, 1949.)

SCRIPT SUPERVISORS, LOCAL 871 (IATSE), HOLLYWOOD

7061 B Hayvenhurst Ave., Van Nuys, CA 91406; (818) 782- 7063. (Chartered January 1, 1958.)

SET DESIGNERS AND MODEL MAKERS, LOCAL 847 (IATSE), HOLLYWOOD

13949 Ventura Blvd., Suite 301, Sherman Oaks, 91423; (818) 784-6555. (Chartered Nov. 14, 1952.)

STORY ANALYSTS, LOCAL 854 (IATSE), HOLLYWOOD

13949 Ventura Blvd., Suite 301, Sherman Oaks, 91423; (818) 784-6555. (Chartered Oct. 18, 1954.)

MOTION PICTURE STUDIO MECHANICS, LOCAL 476 (IATSE), CHICAGO

6309 N. Northwest Hwy., Chicago, IL 60631; (312) 775-5300 (Chartered Feb. 2, 1931.)

STUDIO MECHANICS, LOCAL 52 (IATSE-AFL), NEW YORK

326 W. 48 St., New York, NY 10036; (212) 399-0980. (Organized 1924.)

STUDIO MECHANICS, LOCAL 485 (I.A.T.S.E.) TUCSON

P.O. Box 3518, Tucson, AZ 85271; (602) 832-9470.

STUDIO MECHANICS, LOCAL 477 (I.A.T.S.E.) N. MIAMI

8025 N.W. 36th St., N. Miami, FL 33161; (305) 594-8585.

STUDIO MECHANICS, LOCAL 479 (I.A.T.S.E.) ATLANTA

1874 Piedmont Ave., N.E., Suite 490-D, Atlanta, GA 30324; (404) 885-9134.

STUDIO MECHANICS, LOCAL 812 (I.A.T.S.E.) DETROIT

20017 Van Dyke, Detroit, MI 48234; (313) 368-0825.

STUDIO MECHANICS, LOCAL 487 (I.A.T.S.E.) MID-ATLANTIC AREA

222 St. Paul Place, Suite 505, Baltimore, MD 21202; (410) 685-4141.

STUDIO MECHANICS, LOCAL 481 (I.A.T.S.E.) NEW ENGLAND AREA

P.O. Box 614, Milton, VT 05468; (802) 893-7067.

STUDIO MECHANICS, LOCAL 480 (I.A.T.S.E.) SANTA FE

P.O. Box 20790, Albuquerque, NM 87154; (505) 268-1796.

STUDIO MECHANICS, LOCAL 209 (I.A.T.S.E.) OHIO

Western Reserve Bldg., 1468 W. 9th St., Suite 435, Cleveland, OH 44113; (216) 621-9537.

STUDIO MECHANICS, LOCAL 484 (I.A.T.S.E.) TEXAS

114 Wilshire Court, Irving, TX 75061-2959; (214) 824-0249.

TELEVISION BROADCASTING STUDIO EMPLOYEES, LOCAL 794 (IATSE), NEW YORK

P.O. Box 154, Lenox Hill Sta., New York, NY 10021; (212) 452-3686. (Chartered June 7, 1945.)

DISTRIBUTION

FILM EXCHANGE EMPLOYEES, BACK ROOM, LOCAL B-61 (IATSE), LOS ANGELES

2034 North Brighton, No. C, Burbank, CA 94102; (818) 841-5994. (Chartered May 1, 1937.)

COMBINED FILM EXCHANGE EMPLOYEES, FRONT OFFICE, LOCAL F-45 (IATSE), CHICAGO

%G. R. Kuehnl, Apt. 1611, 5455 Sheridan Rd., Chicago, IL 60640. (Chartered Sept. 4, 1942.)

In addition to the above, there are 34 locals of Back Room Employees and 29 locals of Front Office Employees in the other exchange cities.

MOTION PICTURE HOME OFFICE AND FILM EXCHANGE EMPLOYEES, LOCAL H-63 (IATSE), NEW YORK

1515 Broadway, New York, NY 10036; (212) 730-1770. (Chartered Mar. 19, 1945.)

EXHIBITION

AMUSEMENT AREA EMPLOYEES, LOCAL B-192 (IATSE) LOS ANGELES

3518 Cahuenga Blvd., West, Suite 206, Los Angeles, CA 90068; (213) 849-1826.(Chartered Oct. 1, 1965.)

EXHIBITION EMPLOYEES, LOCAL 829 (IATSE), NEW YORK

150 E. 58 St., New York, NY 10022; (212) 752-4428/9. (Chartered Dec. 11, 1950.)

PROJECTIONISTS & VIDEO TECHNICIANS LOCAL 110 (IATSE), CHICAGO

980 N. Michigan Ave., #1350, Chicago, IL 60611; (312) 787-0220. (Chartered Feb. 4, 1915.)

OPERATORS LOCAL 150 (IATSE), LOS ANGELES

1545 N. Verdugo Rd., Suite 9, Glendale, CA 91208; (818) 240-5644. (Chartered July 16, 1908.)

PROJECTIONISTS & VIDEO TECHNICIANS LOCAL 306 (IATSE), NEW YORK

229 W. 42 St., 3rd fl., New York, NY 10036; (212) 764-6270. (Organized July, 1913.)

STAGE EMPLOYEES, LOCAL 4 (IATSE), BROOKLYN

2917 Glenwood Rd., Brooklyn, NY 11210; (718) 252-8777. (Chartered April 8, 1888.)

STAGE EMPLOYEES, LOCAL 2 (IATSE), CHICAGO

20 No. Wacker Dr., Suite 722, Chicago, IL 60606; (312) 236-3457. (Chartered July 17, 1893.)

STAGE EMPLOYEES, LOCAL 33 (IATSE), LOS ANGELES

1720 W. Magnolia Blvd., Burbank, CA 91506; (818) 841-9233. (Chartered Mar. 1, 1896.)

STAGE EMPLOYEES, LOCAL 1 (IATSE),NEW YORK

320 W. 46 St., New York, NY 10036; (212) 333-2500. (Chartered July 17, 1893.)

THEATRE EMPLOYEES, LOCAL B-46 (IATSE), CHICAGO

980 N. Michigan Ave. Suite 1350, Chicago, IL 60611; (312) 787-0220. (Chartered May 1, 1937.)

THEATRE EMPLOYEES, LOCAL B-183 (IATSE), NEW YORK

319 W. 48 St., New York, NY 10036; (212) 586-9620. (Chartered May 6, 1942.)

THEATRICAL WARDROBE ATTENDANTS, LOCAL 769 (IATSE), CHICAGO

9115 S. Roberts Rd., Chicago, IL 60457; (708) 599-9436.

THEATRICAL WARDROBE ATTENDANTS, LOCAL 768 (IATSE), LOS ANGELES

13949 Ventura Blvd., Suite 307, Sherman Oaks, 91423; (818) 789-8735.(Chartered Dec. 3, 1942.)

THEATRICAL WARDROBE ATTENDANTS, LOCAL 764 (IATSE), NEW YORK

1501 Broadway, Room 1313, New York, NY 10036; (212) 221-1717. (Chartered Sept. 4, 1942.)

TREASURERS AND TICKET SELLERS, LOCAL 750 (IATSE), CHICAGO

446 N. Edgewood, LaGrange Park, IL 60525; (708) 579-9381. (Chartered Aug. 1, 1941.)

CAMERAPERSONS, LOCAL 659 (IATSE), LOS ANGELES

7715 Sunset Blvd., Suite 300 Hollywood, CA 90046; (213) 876-0160. (Organized 1928.)

CAMERAPERSONS, LOCAL 644 (IATSE), NEW YORK

505 Eight Ave., 16th Floor, New York, NY 10018; (212) 244-2121. (Organized Nov. 15, 1926.)

INTERNATIONAL SOUND TECHNICIANS OF THE MOTION PICTURE BROADCAST AND AMUSEMENT INDUSTRIES, LOCAL 695 (IATSE-AFL), LOS ANGELES

5439 Cahuenga Blvd., No. Hollywood, CA 91601; (818) 985-9204. (Organized Sept. 15, 1930.)

LABORATORY TECHNICIANS, LOCAL 780 (IATSE), CHICAGO

327 S. La Salle St., Room 1717, Chicago, IL 60604; (312) 922-7105. (Chartered Nov. 10, 1944.)

LABORATORY TECHNICIANS, LOCAL 683 (IATSE-AFL-CIO), LOS ANGELES

2600 W. Victory Blvd., Burbank, CA 91505; (818) 955-9720 or (213) 935-1123. (Organized Sept. 29, 1919.)

LABORATORY TECHNICIANS, LOCAL 702 (IATSE-AFL), NEW YORK

1515 Broadway, Suite 601, New York, NY 10036; (212) 869-5540. (Organized September, 1937.)

MAKE-UP ARTISTS & HAIR STYLISTS, LOCAL 706 (IATSE), HOLLYWOOD

11519 Chandler Blvd., North Hollywood, CA 91601; (213) 877-2776.

MAKE-UP ARTISTS AND HAIR STYLISTS, LOCAL 798 (IATSE), NEW YORK

31 W. 21 St., 8th fl., New York, NY 10010; (212) 627-0660. (Chartered Feb. 18, 1949.)

MOTION PICTURE COSTUMERS, LOCAL 705 (IATSE-AFL), HOLLYWOOD

1427 N. La Brea Ave., Hollywood, CA 90028; (213) 851-0220. (Chartered Nov. 1, 1937.)

MOTION PICTURE CRAFTS SERVICE LOCAL 727 (IATSE), HOLLYWOOD

14629 Nordhoff St., Panorama City, CA 91402; (818) 891-0717. (Organized May 15, 1939.)

MOTION PICTURE AND VIDEO EDITORS GUILD, LOCAL 776 (IATSE), LOS ANGELES

7715 Sunset Blvd. #220, Hollywood CA 90046; (213) 876-4770. (Chartered Aug. 2, 1944.)

MOTION PICTURE & VIDEO TAPE EDITORS, LOCAL 771 (IATSE), NEW YORK

353 W. 48 St., 5th fl., New York, NY 10036; (212) 581-0771. (Chartered Aug. 18, 1943.)

TREASURERS AND TICKET SELLERS, LOCAL 857 (IATSE), LOS ANGELES

13949 Ventura Blvd., Suite 303, Sherman Oaks, CA 91423; (818) 990-7107. (Chartered June 1, 1955.)

TREASURERS AND TICKET SELLERS, LOCAL 751 (IATSE), NEW YORK

1500 Broadway, Rm. 2011, New York, NY 10036; (212) 302-7300. (Chartered Aug. 1, 1941.)

International Brotherhood of Electrical Workers (AFL-CIO, CFL)

1125 15th St., N.W., Washington, DC 20005; (202) 833-7000. (Organized November 28, 1891; Membership over 1 million.)

INTERNATIONAL PRESIDENT
John J. Barry, 1125 15th St., N.W., Washington, DC 20005.

INTERNATIONAL SECRETARY
Jack Moore, 1125 15th St. N.W., Washington, DC 20005.
INTERNATIONAL TREASURER
Thomas Van Arsdale, 158-11 Harry Van Arsdale Jr. Ave., Flushing, NY 11365.
DISTRICT OFFICES
Willowdale, Ont. M2N 5Y1 CANADA, 45 Sheppard Ave. East, Suite 401; Ken Woods.
Quincy, MA: Batterymarch Park, 02169, Paul A. Loughran.
Albany, NY: 16 Computer Dr. West, Suite C, 12205; Donald J. Funk.
Cincinnati, OH: 7710 Reading Rd., Suite 9, 45237; Paul J. Witte.
Birmingham, AL: No. 2 Metroplex Dr., Suite 304, 35209-6899; Wade H. Gurley.
Lombard, IL: 2200 S. Main St., Suite 303, 60148; James P. Conway.
Oklahoma City, OK: 4400 Will Rogers Pkwy. #309, 73108; Orville A. Tate, Jr.
Idaho Falls, ID: 330 Shoup Ave., Suite 204, P.O. Box 51216, 83405; Jon Walters.
Walnut Creek, CA: 150 N. Wiget Lane, Suite 100, 94598-2494; S. R. McCann.
Rosemont, IL: 10400 W. Higgins Rd., Suite 110, 60018-3736; Norman D. Schwitalla.
Springfield, MO: 300 So. Jefferson, Suite 300, 65806; Ray Edwards.
Chattanooga, TN: 500 Franklin Bldg., Suite 500, 37411; Carl Lansden.

IBEW LOCAL 349 (FILM)

1657 N.W. 17th Ave., Miami FL 33135; (305) 325-1330. (Organized April 24, 1904.)
BUSINESS MANAGER
Art Fernandez

IBEW LOCAL 40 (FILM)

5643 Vineland Ave., North Hollywood, CA 91601; (818) 762-4239. (Organized March 5, 1923.)
BUSINESS MANAGER
Russell J. Bartley

International Photographers of the Motion Picture Industries

IPMPI LOCALS (See IATSE)

International Sound Technicians of the Motion Picture Broadcast and Amusement Industries

LOCAL 695 (IATSE-AFL) (See IATSE)

Laboratory Technicians

LOCALS 683, 702 and 780, (IATSE) (See IATSE)

Make-Up Artists & Hair Stylists

LOCALS 706 and 798 (IATSE) (See IATSE)

Motion Picture Costumers

LOCAL 705 (IATSE) (See IATSE)

Motion Picture Crafts Service

LOCAL 727 (IATSE) (See IATSE)

Motion Picture & Video Editors

LOCALS 771 and 776 (IATSE) (See IATSE)

Motion Picture Home Office Employes

LOCAL H-63 (IATSE) (See IATSE)

Motion Picture Screen Cartoonists

LOCALS 839 (IATSE) (See IATSE)

Motion Picture Set Painters

LOCAL 729 (IATSE) (See IATSE)

Motion Picture Studio Electrical Technicians

LOCAL 728 (IATSE) (See IATSE)

Musicians Union, (Local 47, AFM, AFL-CIO)

817 Vine St., Hollywood, CA 90038; (213) 462-2161; FAX: (213) 461-5260. (Organized October 30, 1894; Membership: 11,000.)

PRESIDENT
 Bill Peterson
VICE PRESIDENT
 Richard Totusek
SECRETARY
 Serena Kay Williams
TREASURER
 Chase Craig
TRUSTEES
 Roy D'Antonio, Hal Espinosa, Vince Trombetta
DIRECTORS
 William (Buddy) Collette, Art Davis, Vince DiBari, Lyle (Spud) Murphy, Abe Most, Tommy Oliver

NABET 531/Association of Film Craftsmen

Local No. 531 (NABET, AFL-CIO, CLC) 945 Front St., Suite 201, San Francisco, CA 94111; (415) 956-5758; FAX: (415) 398-3162.

FIELD REPRESENTATIVE
 Randall White

Producers Guild of America

400 S. Beverly Dr., Suite 211, Beverly Hills, CA 90212; (310) 557-0807. (Organized 1950; Membership: 400.)

PRESIDENT
 Leonard B. Stern
VICE PRESIDENT
 Stanley Rubin
SECRETARY
 Bernard Wiesen
TREASURER
 George Sunga
EXECUTIVE DIRECTOR
 Charles B. FitzSimons

Projectionists, IATSE & MPMO Locals

(See IATSE)

Publicists Guild, Inc.

LOCAL 818 (IATSE) (See IATSE)

Radio & Television Sound Effects

LOCAL 844 (IATSE) (See IATSE)

Scenic Artists

LOCAL 816 (IATSE) (See IATSE)

Screen Actors Guild (AAAA-AFL-CIO)

National Headquarters: 5757 Wilshire Blvd., Los Angeles, CA 90036; (213) 465-4600; FAX: (213) 856-6603. Branches—*New York*, 1515 Broadway, 44th Floor, New York, NY 10036, (212) 944-1030; John McGuire; *Arizona*, 1616 East Indian School Rd., Suite 330, Phoenix, AZ 85016, (602) 265-2712; *Boston*, 11 Beacon St., Rm. 512, Boston, MA 02108, (617) 742-2688; *Chicago*, 307 North Michigan Ave., Chicago, IL 60601, (312) 372-8081; *Colorado, Nevada, New Mexico, Utah*, 950 South Cherry Street, Suite 502, Denver, CO 80222, (303) 757-6226; *Dallas*, 6060 N. Central Expressway, #302, LB 604, Dallas, TX 75206, (214) 363-8300; *Detroit*, 28690 Southfield Rd., #290 A&B, Lathrup Village, MI 48076, (313) 559-9450; *Florida*, 2299 Douglas Road, Suite 200, Miami, FL 33145, (305) 444-7677; *Georgia*, 455 E. Paces Ferry Rd., NE, #334, Atlanta, GA 30305, (404) 239-0131; *Hawaii*, 949 Kapiolani Boulevard, Suite 105, Honolulu, HI 96814, (808) 538-6122; *Houston*, 2650 Fountainview, Suite 326, Houston, TX 77057, (713) 972-1806; *Nashville*, P.O. Box 121087, Nashville, TN 37212, (615) 327-2958; *Philadelphia*, 230 South Broad Street, 10th Floor, Philadelphia, PA 19102, (215) 545-3150; *San Diego*, 7827 Convoy Court, #400, San Diego, CA 92111, (619) 278-7695; *San Francisco*, 235 Pine St., 11th fl., San Francisco, CA 94104, (415) 391-7510; *Washington, DC-Baltimore*, 5480 Wisconsin Avenue, Suite 201, Chevy Chase, MD 20815, (301) 657-2560. (Organized July 1933; Membership: 75,000.)

PRESIDENT
 Barry Gordon
PRESIDENT EMERITUS
 Leon Ames
FIRST VICE PRESIDENT
 Joe Ruskin
SECOND VICE PRESIDENT
 Paul Hecht
THIRD VICE PRESIDENT
 Richard Masur
FOURTH VICE PRESIDENT
 Jerry Sroka
FIFTH VICE PRESIDENT
 Mary Seibel
SIXTH VICE PRESIDENT
 Chuck Dorsett
SEVENTH VICE PRESIDENT
 Bruce McLaughlin
EIGHTH VICE PRESIDENT
 Barbara DeKins
NINTH VICE PRESIDENT
 Christina Belford
TENTH VICE PRESIDENT
 Maureen Donnelly
ELEVENTH VICE PRESIDENT
 Larry Keith
RECORDING SECRETARY
 Angel Tompkins
TREASURER
 Nicholas Pryor

NATIONAL EXECUTIVE STAFF

NATIONAL EXECUTIVE DIRECTOR
 Ken Orsatti
ASSOCIATE NATIONAL EXECUTIVE DIRECTOR
 John McGuire
PUBLIC RELATIONS DIRECTOR
 Mark Locher
COUNSEL
 Leo Geffner
DIRECTOR OF FINANCE
 Gerald Wilson
DIRECTOR OF ADMINSTRATION
 Clinta Dayton

Screen Composers of America

2451 Nichols Canyon Rd., Los Angeles CA 90046-1798; (213) 876-6040.

PRESIDENT
  Herschel Burke Gilbert
VICE PRESIDENT
  John Parker
SECRETARY
  Frank DeVol
TREASURER
  Nathan Scott

Screen Writers' Guild, Inc.

(See Writers Guild of America.)

Script Supervisors

LOCAL 871 (IATSE) (See IATSE)

Set Designers and Model Makers

LOCAL 847 (IATSE) (See IATSE)

Society of Motion Picture Art Directors

LOCAL 876 (IATSE) (See IATSE)

Stage Employees

LOCALS 1, 2, 4, and 33 (IATSE) (See IATSE)

Story Analysts

LOCAL 854 (IATSE) (See IATSE)

Studio Grips

LOCAL 80 (IATSE) (See IATSE)

Studio Mechanics

LOCALS 52 and 476 (IATSE) (See IATSE)

Studio Projectionists

LOCAL 165 (IATSE) (See IATSE)

Studio Property Craftsmen

LOCAL 44 (IATSE) (See IATSE)

Stuntmen's Association

4810 Whitsett Ave., North Hollywood, CA 91607; (818) 766-4334; (213) 462-2301 (service.) (Organized 1961.)
PRESIDENT
  Carl Ciarfalio

Theatre Authority, Inc.

16 E. 42 St., Suite 202, New York, NY 10017-6907; (212) 682-4215; FAX: (212) 682-8407. (Organized May 21, 1934.)

EXECUTIVE DIRECTOR
  Helen Leahy
PRESIDENT
  Jane Powell
FIRST VICE PRESIDENT
  John H. Sucke
SECOND VICE PRESIDENT
  Terry Walker
THIRD VICE PRESIDENT
  Robert Bruyr
FOURTH VICE PRESIDENT
  Rod McKuen
RECORDING SECRETARY
  Alan D. Olsen
TREASURER
  Joan Greenspan
ADVISORY COMMITTEE
  Julie Andrews, Harry Belafonte, Joey Bishop, Ellen Burstyn, Billy Davis Jr., Patty Duke, Richard Dysart, Barbara Feldon, Joan Fontaine, John Forsythe, Robert Goulet, Charlton Heston, Jerome Hines, Bob Hope, Barnard Hughes, Jack Jones, Alan King, Werner Klemperer, Angela Lansbury, Jerry Lewis, Dean Martin, Marilyn McCoo, Estelle Parsons, Gregory Peck, Jane Powell, Tony Randall, Lou Rawls, Debbie Reynolds, Tony Roberts, Dinah Shore, Frank Sinatra, Barbra Streisand, Nancy Wilson

Theatre Employees

LOCALS B-46 and B-183 (IATSE) (See IATSE)

Theatrical Wardrobe Attendants

LOCALS 764, 768 and 769 (IATSE) (See IATSE)

Treasurers and Ticketsellers

LOCALS 750, 751 and 857 (IATSE) (See IATSE)

Writers Guild of America

NATIONAL CHAIRMAN
  Edward Adler

WRITERS GUILD OF AMERICA, EAST, INC.

555 W. 57 St., New York, NY 10019; (212) 767-7800; FAX: (212) 582-1909.
PRESIDENT
  Herb Sargent
VICE PRESIDENT
  Claire Labine
SECRETARY-TREASURER
  Jane C. Bollinger
EXECUTIVE DIRECTOR
  Mona Mangan

WRITERS GUILD OF AMERICA, WEST, INC.

8955 Beverly Blvd., West Hollywood, CA 90048; (310) 550-1000; FAX: (310) 550-8185.
PRESIDENT
  Del Reisman
VICE PRESIDENT
  Carl Gottlieb
SECRETARY-TREASURER
  Ann Marcus
EXECUTIVE DIRECTOR
  Brian Walton

The Press

* **TRADE PUBLICATIONS**

Trade Publications

Quigley Publishing Company

Publishers of Motion Picture Almanac (Annual), Television & Video Almanac (Annual). 159 W. 53 St., New York, NY 10019; (212) 247-3100; FAX: (212) 489-0871.
PRESIDENT AND PUBLISHER
  Martin Quigley, Jr.
BUSINESS MANAGER
  Jim Moser
EDITOR
  Barry Monush
EDITORIAL ASSISTANTS
  Theresa Webster
  Yvonne Delaney

LONDON BUREAU
William Pay, Manager and London Editor; 15 Samuel Rd., Langdon Hills, Basildon, Essex, SS16 6E2 England. Tel.: 268-417-055.

CANADIAN BUREAU
Patricia Thompson, Editor; Box 152, Station R, Toronto, Ont., M4G 3Z3, Canada. Tel: (416) 696-2382.

FOREIGN CORRESPONDENTS
CHILE: Alan Hootnick, Lo Arcaya 1963, Vitacura, Santiago, Chile; 56-2-218-4085; FAX: 56-2-215-1802.
EGYPT: Ahmed Sami, 77 Abdel Aziz Fahmy Str., 4th fl. (Apt. 23), Abbassia, Cairo; Tel: 2477000; FAX: 2918059.
GREECE: Rena Velissariou, 32, Kolokotroni Str., AgUia Paraskevi, Attikis, Athens 153 42, Greece; Tel: 65 67 665.
INDIA: B. D. Garga, 11 Verem Villas, Reis Magos, Bardez, Goa 403114 India. FAX: 91-832-43433.
PAKISTAN: A. R. Slote, P.O. Box 7426, Karachi, 74400, Pakistan.
SRI LANKA: Chandra Perera, 437 Pethiyagoda, Kelaniya, Sri Lanka.
SWITZERLAND: Gabriella Broggi, Via E. Maraini 20B, 6900 Massagno, Switzerland; Tel: (091) 56 29 10.

Motion Picture Almanac

(Annually) 159 W. 53 St., New York, NY 10019; (212) 247-3100; FAX: (212) 489-0871.
EDITOR
  Barry Monush
BRITISH EDITOR
  William Pay
CANADIAN EDITOR
  Patricia Thompson

Television & Video Almanac

(Annually) 159 W. 53 St., New York, NY 10019; (212) 247-3100; FAX: (212) 489-0871.
EDITOR
  Barry Monush
BRITISH EDITOR
  William Pay
CANADIAN EDITOR
  Patricia Thompson

Academy Players Directory

(Tri-Annual directory published by the Academy of Motion Picture Arts & Sciences.) 8949 Wilshire Blvd., Beverly Hills, CA 90211-1972; (310) 247-3000; FAX: (310) 859-9619.
EDITOR
  Patricia L. Citrano

The American Cinematographer

(Monthly on the 1st—Semi-technical) Published by American Society of Cinematographers, Inc., P.O. Box 2230, Hollywood, CA 90078; (213) 969-4333; FAX: (213) 876-4973.
EDITOR
  David Heuring

ASSOCIATE EDITOR
  Stephen Pizzello
ACCOUNTING
  Barbara Prevedel
CIRCULATION MANAGER
  Patty Armacost
ADVERTISING MANAGER
  Angie Gollmann
EDITORIAL ADVISORY COMMITTEE
  Charles Wheeler, chairman; Philip Lathrop, co-chairman; Stephen Burum, Allen Daviau, Linwood Dunn, Woody Omens.

American Cinemeditor

(American Cinema Editors) 17337 Ventura Blvd., #226, Encino, CA 91316-3955; (818) 907-7351.

American Premiere Magazine

(Bi-monthly) 8421 Wilshire Blvd., Penthouse, Beverly Hills, CA 90211; (213) 852-0434.
PUBLISHER & EDITOR
  Susan Royal
ASSISTANT EDITOR
  Dawn Brooks

Annual Index to Motion Picture Credits

(Annual) %Academy of Motion Picture Arts and Sciences, 8949 Wilshire Blvd., Beverly Hills, CA 90211; (310) 247-3000; FAX: (310) 859-9351. (Organized 1976. Film credits reference book. Annual compilation of feature film credits for films that open in Los Angeles. Indexed by film name, crafts, distributors, individual names.)
EXECUTIVE DIRECTOR
  Bruce Davis
EDITOR
  Byerly Woodward

AV Guide: The Learning Media Newsletter

(Monthly) 380 Northwest Highway, Des Plaines, IL 60016-2282; (708) 298-6622; FAX: (708) 390-0408. (Comprehensive coverage of trends, materials, equipment across the learning media field, for anyone involved in learning processes.)
PUBLISHER
  H. S. Gillette
EDITOR
  Natalie Ferguson
CIRCULATION DIRECTOR
  Linda Lambdin

Back Stage/Shoot

(Weekly covering commercial production and advertising, published Friday.) 1515 Broadway, New York, NY 10036; (212) 764-7300; FAX: (212) 967-6786; 6715 Sunset Blvd., Los Angeles, CA 90028; (213) 957-3046; FAX: (213) 957-5766; 205 W. Randolph St., Chicago, IL 60606; (312) 236-9102; FAX: (312) 236-0054; 9543 Harding Ave., Miami Beach, FL 33154; (305) 865-8223; FAX: (305) 865-5010.
PUBLISHERS
  Roberta Griefer
EDITOR
  Peter Caranicas

Back Stage /Shoot Commercial Production Directory

(Annually, May) 1515 Broadway, 12th fl., New York, NY 10036; (212) 536-1440; FAX: (212) 536-5321.
EDITOR
  Theresa Piti

Billboard

(International music/record tape/video cassette/video disc newsweekly with readership comprising retailers/ wholesalers of prerecorded entertainment software, recording/playback equipment, record programmers for radio, discotheques, jukeboxes, music publishers, record producers/manufacturers; buyers/sellers of performing talent, artists, song writers/composers.) 5055 Wilshire Blvd., Los Angeles, CA 90036; (213) 525-2300; 1515 Broadway, New York, NY 10036; (212) 764-7300, FAX: (212) 536-5358; 49 Music Square W., Nashville, TN 37203; (615) 321-4290; 806 15 St., N.W., Washington, DC 20005; (202) 783-3282.
PUBLISHER
  Howard Lander
MANAGING EDITOR
  Ken Schlager
DIRECTOR OF SALES
  Gene Smith

Boxoffice

(Film Monthly), 6640 Sunset Blvd., #100, Hollywood, CA 90028; (213) 465-1186; FAX: (213) 465-5049.
PUBLISHER
  Robert L. Deitmeier
EDITOR/ASSOCIATE PUBLISHER
  Harley Lond
NATIONAL AD DIRECTOR
  Robert Vale
  Published by RLD Communications, Inc., 203 N. Wabash Ave., Chicago, IL 60605

Celebrity Bulletin

(A chronicle of the day-to-day activities of celebrities in New York, Hollywood, London, Paris and Rome. Published daily.) 1780 Broadway, New York, NY 10019; (212) 757-7979; 8833 Sunset Blvd., Los Angeles, CA 90069, (310) 652-1700; FAX: (310) 652-9244.
EDITOR
  Bill Murray

Celebrity Register

(A biographical index, published every two years) 1780 Broadway, Suite 300, New York, NY 10019; (212) 757-7979; FAX: (212) 397-4626.
PUBLISHER
  Gale Research
EDITOR
  Vicki Bagley

Celebrity Service International Contact Book

(Published by Celebrity Service International). 1780 Broadway, Suite 300, New York, NY 10019; (212) 757-7979; FAX: (212) 397-4626.
EDITORS
  Vicki Bagley
  Mark Kerrigan

Classic Images

P.O. Box 809, Muscatine, IA 52761; (319) 263-2331. Organized 1962. (Disseminates news of classic films to collectors.)
EDITOR
  Bob King
AFFILIATIONS
  Parent company, Muscatine Journal, a division of Lee Enterprises.

Costume Designers Guild Directory

(Annually) %Costume Designers Guild, 13949 Ventura Blvd., #309, Sherman Oaks, CA 91423; (818) 905-1557; FAX: (818) 905-1560.

Daily Variety

(Daily) 5700 Wilshire Blvd., Suite 120, Los Angeles, CA 90036; (213) 857-6600; FAX: (213) 857-0494. (Reports on motion picture, television, homevideo, pay-TV, cable, radio, theatre, nightclubs.
SPECIAL EDITIONS EDITOR
  Peter P. Pryor
MANAGING EDITOR
  Jonathan Taylor
NATIONAL SALES MANAGER
  Katherine Silver
PRODUCTION MANAGER
  Bob Butler

Editor & Publisher

(Weekly) 11 W. 19 St., New York, NY 10011; (212) 675-4380; FAX: (212) 929-1259.
PRESIDENT & EDITOR
  Robert U. Brown
MANAGING EDITOR
  John P. Consoli

Entertainment Data, Inc.

8350 Wilshire Blvd., Suite 210, Beverly Hills, CA 90211; (213) 658-8300; FAX: (213) 658-6650. (Weekly release schedule, overnight grosses, on-line database, U.S., U.K., Germany, custom research).
PRESIDENT
  Marcy Polier
SENIOR VICE PRESIDENT
  Philip Garfinkle
VICE PRESIDENT
  Deborah Hanauer
VICE PRESIDENT-FINANCE & ADMINISTRATION
  Marshall Aster
VICE PRESIDENT-OPERATIONS
  Thomas V. Borys
MANAGING DIRECTION-EDI EUROPE
  Stephen Perrin

Film & Video Magazine

(Monthly) 8455 Beverly Blvd., #508, Los Angeles, CA 90048-3416; (213) 653-8053; FAX: (213) 653-8190. (International film and video production magazine). Organized 1983. ISSN 1041-1933.
PUBLISHER/EDITOR
  David Swartz
ASSOCIATE PUBLISHER/MANAGING EDITOR
  Paula Swartz
DIRECTOR OF ADVERTISING
  Steven Rich
SENIOR EDITORS
  Keith Lissak, Katharine Stalter
ASSOCIATE EDITORS
  Robin Franks, Emily Siskin
CIRCULATION DIRECTOR
  Robin Franks

Film Journal, The

(Monthly) 244 W. 49 St., Suite 200, New York, NY 10019; (212) 246-6460; FAX: (212) 265-6428.
PUBLISHER-EDITOR
Robert H. Sunshine
ADVERTISING DIRECTOR/ASSOCIATE PUBLISHER
Jimmy Sunshine
MANAGING EDITOR
G. Kevin Lally
ASSOCIATE EDITORS
Ed Kelleher, Mitch Neuhauser
WEST COAST EDITOR
Myron Meisel
CIRCULATION MANAGER
Michelle Suede

Film Quarterly

(Quarterly.) Editorial, sales, and advertising office: University of California Press, 2120 Berkeley Way, Berkeley, CA 94720; (415) 642-4191; FAX: (415) 642-9917. (A critical journal of motion pictures and their related arts; successor to *The Quarterly of Film, Radio, and Television* and *The Hollywood Quarterly*.)
EDITOR
Ann Martin
Published by University of California Press

Films in Review

(Published by National Board of Review) P.O. Box 589, New York, NY 10021; (212) 628-1594.
EDITOR
Robin Little

Hollywood Creative Directory

3000 Olympic Blvd., Santa Monica, CA 90404; (310) 315-4815. Organized 1987. Film and TV directories and reference books covering such subjects as production companies, agents, distributors, directors, writers & their credits.

Hollywood Reporter, The

(Film, TV, entertainment daily) 5055 Wilshire Blvd., Los Angeles, CA 90036; (213) 525-2000, FAX: (213) 525-2377 (editorial), (213) 525-2019 (advertising); special issues: (213) 525-2189. 1501 Broadway, New York, NY 10036; (212) 536-5344 (main no.), (212) 536-5325 (editorial); FAX: (212) 536-5345.
PUBLISHER AND EDITOR-IN-CHIEF
Robert J. Dowling
EDITOR
Alex Ben Block
MANAGING EDITOR
Glenn Abel
ASSOCIATE PUBLISHER DIRECTOR OF SALES
Lynne Segall
MANAGER, PROMOTIONS & PUBLIC RELATIONS
C. G. O'Connor
BUREAUS
WASHINGTON, DC: 806 15th Street, NW, Suite 421, Washington DC 20005 (202) 737-2828; FAX: (202) 737-3833.
LONDON: 23 Ridgemount St., London, England WC1E 7AH; Tel: 071-323-6686; FAX: 071-323-2314, 071-323-2316. Telex: 94016522 (HREP G) FAX: 01-437-0029.

I.A.T.S.E. Official Bulletin

(Quarterly) 1515 Broadway, Suite 601, New York, NY 10036; (212) 730-1770; FAX: (212) 921-7699.
EDITOR
Thomas C. Short
ASSISTANT EDITOR
Karen A. Pizzuto

International Documentary

1551 S. Robertson Blvd., Suite 201, Los Angeles, CA 90035; (310) 284-8422; FAX: (213) 785-9334. (Promotes documentary film and filmmakers). Organized 1982.
EDITOR
Nancy Wilkman

Journal of Syd Cassyd Archives: Hollywood Report

(Quarterly) 917 S. Tremaine Ave., Hollywood, CA 90019; (213) 939-2345.
FOUNDER
Syd Cassyd

Millimeter

(A monthly magazine covering the motion picture and television production industries.) Headquarters: 826 Broadway, New York, NY 10003; (212) 477-4700; Fax: (212) 228-5859.; West Coast Office: 5358 Melrose Ave., #219 West, Hollywood, CA 90038; (213) 960-4050; FAX: (213) 960-4059.
PUBLISHER
Sam Kintzer
EDITOR
Alison Johns

Pacific Coast Studio Directory

(3 times per year) P.O. Box V, Pine Mountain, CA 93222-4921; (805) 242-2722; FAX: (805) 242-2724.
PUBLISHER
Jack Reitz

Performance Magazine

(Weekly) 2049 Century Park E., Suite 1100, Century City, CA 90067; (310) 552-3118; FAX: (310) 286-1990.
PUBLISHER
Don Waitt
L.A. SENIOR EDITOR
Stann Findelle
MANAGING EDITOR
Carol Noel

Premiere Magazine

(Monthly) K-III Magazine Corp., 2 Park Ave., 4th Floor, New York, NY 10016; (212) 725-7926, FAX: (212) 725-3442; 1990 S. Bundy Dr., #340, Los Angeles, CA 90025; (310) 207-2682.
EDITOR/PUBLICATION DIRECTOR
Susan Lyne
EXECUTIVE EDITORS
Peter Briskind, Christopher Connelly, Deborah Pines
WEST COAST EDITOR
Nancy Griffin

Producer's Master-Guide, The

(Annual) Published by BPI Communications, Inc., 1515 Broadway, 15th fl., New York, NY 10036; (800) 622-6112. International standard reference guide for producers in the motion picture, television, commercials, cable and videotape industries in the U.S., Canada, the Caribbean Islands, Mexico, United Kingdom, Australia, Philippines and Israel.
PUBLISHER AND EDITOR
Shmuel Bension

Reel Directory, The

(Annual guide to Northern California film/video production resources) P.O. Box 866, Cotati, CA 94931; (707) 584-8083.

PUBLISHER & EDITOR
Bonnie Carroll

SMPTE (Society of Motion Picture and Television Engineers) Journal

(Technical monthly) 595 W. Hartsdale Ave., White Plains, NY 10607; (914) 761-1100; FAX: (914) 761-3115.

EDITOR/PUBLISHER
Jeffrey B. Friedman

Screen Actor

(Quarterly) 7065 Hollywood Blvd., Hollywood, CA 90028-6065; (213) 856-6650; FAX: (213) 856-6802.

EDITOR
Mark Locher
ASSOCIATE EDITOR
Harry Medved

Screen World

(Annual) Published by Applause Theatre Books, 211 W. 71st., New York, NY 10023; (212) 496-7511. (An illustrated listing of film releases in the U.S. each year, Academy Award winners, promising personalities, and other data)

EDITOR
John Willis
ASSOCIATE EDITOR
Barry Monush

Seven Arts Press, Inc.

6253 Hollywood Blvd., Hollywood, CA 90028-5360; P.O. Box 649; Los Angeles, CA 90078-0649; (213) 469-1095. (Publishes books on entertainment industry—Entertainment Industry Series, Film Superlist Series.)

VICE PRESIDENT
Joseph Yore

Variety

(International entertainment business weekly, published Mondays) Reed Publishing, Inc., 475 Park Ave. S., New York, NY 10016; (212) 779-1100; FAX: (212) 779-0026; 5700 Wilshire Blvd., Suite #120, Los Angeles, CA 90036, (213) 857-6600; FAX: (213) 857-0494;*Washington D.C.*: 1483 Chain Bridge Rd., McLean, VA 22101, (703) 448-0510, FAX: (703) 827-8214; *Chicago*: P.O. Box 535, Lake Bluff, IL 60044, (708) 615-9742, FAX: (708) 615-9743; *Paris*: 33 Champs Elysees, 75008 France; Phone 43-55-07-43; *Rome:* Lungotevere Flaminio 22, Rome 00196 Italy; Phone: 361-3103; *London:* 34/35 Newman St., W1P 3PD England, (071) 637-3663; *Madrid:* Calle Lagasca, 104, 28006, Madrid, Spain; Phone: 359-6667; *Sydney, Australia:* 1-7 Albion Place, N.S.W. 2000, Phone: (02)

267-3124; *Toronto:* 74 Albany Ave., Toronto, Ont. Canada, M5R 3C3; Phone: (416) 461-5164; *Stockholm:* Travargatan 33, 17539 Jarfalla, Sweden; Phone: (46-8) 580-30392; *Munich:* Richard Strauss Str. 73, D/8000 Munich 80, Germany; Phone: (89) 39-26-94; *Tokyo:* Phone: (81-3) 3211-3161; *Berlin*: Phone: (30) 312-37-93.

VICE PRESIDENT, GENERAL MANAGER
Neal Vitale
VICE PRESIDENT, PUBLISHING OPERATIONS
Gerard A. Byrne
VICE PRESIDENT, EDITORIAL DIRECTOR
Peter Bart
MANAGING EDITOR
Max Alexander
FOREIGN EDITOR
Elizabeth Guider

Who's Who In The Motion Picture Industry

(Semi-annually) Packard Publishing, P.O. Box 2187, Beverly Hills, CA 90213; (310) 854-0276; FAX: (310) 659-1960.

PUBLISHER & EDITOR
Rodman W. Gregg

GREAT BRITAIN

Image Technology

(10 times per year) Journal of the British Kinematograph, Sound and Television Society, 549 Victoria House, Vernon Place, London, WC1B 4DJ, England; 071 242-8400; FAX: 071-405 3560.

Screen International

Published by EMAP Business Publishing. (Weekly, covering news, reviews, comment and pictures of the film and television industries.) 33-39 Bowling Green Lane, London, ECIR ODA, England; Tel: 071 837-1212; FAX: 071 278-7671.

PUBLISHING DIRECTOR
Steve Buckley
EDITOR
Oscar Moore

FRANCE

Le Film Français

(Weekly French motion picture trade magazine) 103 Blvd. St. Michel, Paris, France, 75005. U.S. office: 1144 Coronado Terrace, Los Angeles, CA 90026; Phone & FAX: (213) 413-8320.

PUBLISHER
Claude Pommereau
EDITOR
Marie-Claude Arbaudie
U.S. EDITOR
Patricia Saperstein

The Industry in
Great Britain and Ireland

* INDUSTRY DEVELOPMENTS OF YEAR

* PRODUCTION, DISTRIBUTION AND SERVICE
  COMPANIES AND PERSONNEL

* TRADE ORGANIZATIONS

* GOVERNMENT FILM DEPARTMENTS

* STUDIOS AND LABORATORIES

* CHIEF THEATRE CIRCUITS

* BRITISH-BASED SERVICES

* TRADE PUBLICATIONS

* HOME VIDEO DISTRIBUTORS

British Year in Review

DESPITE the continuing economic recession, and expanding competition from satellite television, with its pay-TV movie channels, the BBC (British Broadcasting Corporation), commercial TV channels and home video, the indications are that 1993 attendances in UK cinemas will be the highest in twelve years. Attendances are averaging two million per week, more than 100 million annually; a scale unmatched by any other European country. Gross annual box office revenue, from some 1,600 screens at over 500 sites, is estimated at £256 million ($384 million). Average revenue per admission is £2.78 ($4.17).

Since 1985, cinema owners have injected £561 million ($841 million) into refurbishing existing cinemas and building new complexes—offering a wider choice of films. Warner Bros. Theatres UK, for instance, is scheduled to open a further eight new sites over the next eighteen months, including a nine-screen multiplex in London's West End. Other major operators in these fields include MGM Cinemas, Odeon, United Cinemas International and National Amusements (UK); roughly one third of UK screens are now purpose-built multiplexes, where films enjoy considerably longer runs than was previously possible. This investment has undoubtedly helped the stabilization of cinema audiences after many years of steady decline. With good product and the up-and-coming generation of cinemagoers—over 55% of the UK audience is aged between 15 and 24, compared to 37% in the US—new audiences have been created, thereby preserving the image that the cinema is still the best place to see a film.

Hollywood films still dominate the UK market. A recent survey showed that, in one year, of the 229 films released in the UK 24 were from France, 28 from Britain and 142 from the USA. Of the 20 co-productions, the USA and UK were each involved with some six partnerships.

Violence has been the main preoccupation of the British Board of Film Classification (BBFC). Its annual report revealed that cuts for excessive violence, the use of easily imitable weapons, or unarmed combat techniques, were made in 13 cinema films. Another point to emerge was the extent to which classification and consumer advice are replacing censorship as the predominant method of media regulation in most countries. Indeed, the BBFC remains one of the few classification bodies anywhere in the world that continues to cut violent material for adult audiences. The report adds that the balance between freedom of expression and the need to protect society from those who might be aroused or encouraged by such material is hard to maintain.

Following the success of such titles as "Basic Instinct", "Hook" and "Lethal Weapon 3"—each grossing over £12 million ($18 million) on their initial release—the tables below show the top films for the first half of 1993. Moreover, this was before "Jurassic Park" hit British screens in July where, within twelve days, it became the UK's eighth biggest grosser of all time, taking more than £1 million ($1.5 million) on each day of its release, with a predicted gross of £30 million ($45 million).

However, competition for the cinema from television, home video and cable remains fierce. As a consequence, the CEA (Cinema Exhibitors Association) retains its two-year holdback of feature films being screened on television/video. This restriction has, over recent years, been relaxed so that any cinema film, on a budget not exceeding £4 million ($6 million), may now be screened on television immediately after its release if those responsible for its marketing decide that this is appropriate.

The CEA also acted swiftly to counter local producers' lobbying of the government for financial support in their "struggle for survival." Many industry observers, indeed, believe that British producers should be attracting more private finance by concentrating on films that have commercial appeal in overseas markets. Support from the government to help stimulate more UK investment in British production and lure back the American majors remains limited. In answering the producers' claims, the CEA said that it is a myth to suggest that UK exhibitors are biased against UK productions. No British film, made for and offered to cinemas, was denied access to screens. Faced with a choice of product, cinema operators will often opt for a British production, but, ultimately, it is the public who decides on the success or failure of any particular film. The producers' submission that a per cent levy on cinema admissions would not erode overall income despite an acknowledged possible corresponding shortfall in admissions, is erroneous. The proposed "blockbuster" tax would inevitably be passed on to cinema operators and to ticket prices, with the same detrimental effect on admissions.

However, British producers struggle on. The number of films—21 features—started in the first half of 1993 is comparable to the same period the previous year. In addition, Rank Film Distributors have signed a five-year production pact with Gladden, MGM and Live, as well as co-financing, with Fine Line Features, John Irvin's £5 million ($7.5 million) period film, "Widow's Peak." Hammer Film Productions will produce, in 1994, a series of remakes of Hammer titles for Warner Bros. Also, television's Channel Four and the BBC continue to support British feature production.

As the Industry mourns the loss of Elstree Studios, and as commentators, such as Michael Winner, continue to "lament the failure of British producers," one may be forgiven for thinking that the Industry in Britain is as good as dead. Optimism, however, springs eternal, and, if work is done to encourage greater investment, to retain and expand the youth audience, and to win back lapsed cinema-goers—so that Joe Public "goes to the pictures" more often than twice a year as at present—then the Industry will remain a lucrative one.

—WILLIAM PAY

Top Box-Office Films, January–June 1993

Odeon (Rank)	MGM	UCI
Dracula	The Bodyguard	The Bodyguard
A Few Good Men	Indecent Proposal	Dracula
The Jungle Book	Dracula	A Few Good Men
Groundhog Day	Forever Young	Indecent Proposal
Honey, I Blew Up the Kid	Sommersby	Home Alone 2
Indecent Proposal	The Jungle Book	Forever Young
Mr. Nanny	Under Siege	Sommersby
Forever Young	A Few Good Men	Under Siege
Sommersby	Honey, I Blew Up the Kid	Jungle Book
Chaplin	Scent of a Woman	Sister Act

British Board of Film Classification Statistics for 1992

Classification Categories	Total number and percentage of films in each categrory	Number and percentage of films classified only after cuts
'U'	21 (6.6%)	1 (4.8%)
'PG'	81 (25.4%)	8 (9.9%)
'12'	32 (10%)	4 (12.5%)
'15'	113 (35.4%)	7 (6.1%)
'18'	72 (22.6%)	8 (11.1%)
'R18'	—	—
Rejected	—	—
TOTAL	319 (100%)	28 (8.8%)

Analysis of UK Multi-Screen Cinemas

	Sites	%	Screens	%
Single Screens	322	46	322	17
2 Screens	116	17	232	13
3 Screens	117	17	351	19
4 Screens	35	5	140	8
5 Screens	24	3	120	6
6 Screens	23	3	138	7
7 Screens	9	1	63	3
8 Screens	10	1	80	4
9 Screens	5	1	45	2
10 Screens	19	3	190	10
11 Screens	3	1	33	2
12 Screens	7	1	84	5
13 Screens	1	*	13	1
14 Screens	3	1	42	2
Total	694	100	1,853	100

Seating Capacity of UK Screens

	1–500	501–1,000	1,001–1,500	1,501–2,000	2,000
Single Screens	248	62	6	5	1
2 Screens	206	21	2	2	1
3 Screens	290	55	6	—	—
4 Screens	127	12	1	—	—
5 Screens	105	14	1	—	—
6 Screens	128	8	1	1	—
7 Screens	60	3	—	—	—
8 Screens	80	—	—	—	—
9 Screens	43	2	—	—	—
10 Screens	189	1	—	—	—
11 Screens	33	—	—	—	—
12 Screens	82	2	—	—	—
13 Screens	12	1	—	—	—
14 Screens	41	1	—	—	—
Total	1,644	182	17	8	2

Source: Cinema Advertising Association

UK Cinema Exhibitors Statistics

		Sites (number)	Screens (number)	Total no. of admissions (millions)	Gross box office takings (£million)	Amount paid out for films (£million)	Revenue per admission (£millions)	Revenue per screen (£thousand)
1987		492	1035	66.8	123.8	45.1	1.85	118.7
1988		495	1117	75.2	142.2	55.1	1.89	126.9
1989		481	1177	82.9	169.5	65.4	2.04	143.7
1990 p		496	1331	78.6	187.7	69.5	2.39	143.8
1991 p		491	1420	83.5	219.3	76.1	2.63	153.3
1992 p		484	1488	83.2	227.0	77.2	2.73	152.8
1987	Q1	501	1050	19.8	37.1	14.6	1.87	35.3
	Q2	492	1035	13.1	24.8	8.0	1.89	23.7
	Q3	492	1039	17.7	32.2	11.9	1.82	31.1
	Q4	492	1048	16.2	29.8	10.7	1.84	28.5
1988	Q1	508	1121	20.1	38.0	15.1	1.89	35.1
	Q2	495	1117	15.2	28.8	10.5	1.89	25.8
	Q3	491	1123	18.5	33.5	12.6	1.81	29.9
	Q4	501	1195	21.3	41.9	16.8	1.96	36.1
1989	Q1	474	1155	24.4	49.3	20.0	2.02	44.0
	Q2	481	1177	14.5	29.6	9.8	2.04	25.4
	Q3	479	1184	22.6	45.4	18.2	2.01	38.8
	Q4	479	1208	21.4	45.1	17.4	2.11	38.2
1990	Q1	474	1276	21.6	47.9	17.9	2.22	39.7
	Q2	496	1331	17.1	40.8	13.9	2.39	31.9
p	Q3	494	1361	19.2	46.4	17.5	2.41	34.5
p	Q4	496	1402	20.7	52.6	20.3	2.54	38.1
1991 p	Q1	493	1399	23.2	58.5	21.9	2.52	41.8
p	Q2	491	1420	20.6	55.9	19.4	2.71	39.6
p	Q3	491	1460	22.9	59.4	21.6	2.59	41.3
p	Q4	487	1479	16.7	45.5	13.2	2.72	31.0
1992 p	Q1	492	1499	22.4	60.4	20.3	2.70	40.5
p	Q2	484	1488	18.9	52.6	18.4	2.78	35.2
p	Q3	478	1478	20.7	57.1	19.8	2.76	38.5
p	Q4	477	1480	21.2	56.9	18.7	2.69	38.5
1993 p	Q1	476	1479	22.7	63.1	21.7	2.78	42.7

Source: Central Statistical Office.

The Industry in Britain and Ireland— Production, Distribution, Service Companies

Abbey Films Ltd.
Film House, 35 Upper Abbey Street, Dublin 1, Ireland. Tel: Dublin 723922. FAX: 723687.
DIRECTORS
K. Anderson, L. Ward, A. Ryan

ADN Associates/Hollywood Classics
Tel: 071 262 4646; FAX: 071 262 3242.
CONTACT
Pano AlaFouzo, Joe Dreier

AGFA-GEVAERT LTD. (Motion Picture Division)
27 Great West Road, Brentford, Middlesex; TW8 9AX. Tel: 081 231 4310; FAX: 081 231 4315.
DIVISIONAL MANAGER, Motion Picture Division
Ken Biggins, MBKS
PRODUCT MANAGER, Motion Picture Division:
Peter Dimbleby, MBKS

All American Leisure Group Inc.
Production Office: 6 Woodland Way, Petts Wood, Kent BR5 1ND. Tel: 0689 871535. FAX: 0689 871519. *Corporate Office*: Suite 1, 370 Minorca Avenue, Coral Gables, (MIAMI) FL 33134, Tel: (305) 443-5444; FAX: (305) 443-4446.
CONTACT
Bachoo Sen

Allied Stars
55 Park Lane, London, W1Y 3DH. Tel: 071 493 1050. FAX: 071 499 5889.
DIRECTORS
Chairman: Dodi Fayed
President: Luke Randolph

Allied Vision Ltd.
3-4 Ashland Place, London, W1M 3JH. Tel: 071 224 1992. Telex: 22721 HGENTS. FAX: 071 224 1110.
MANAGING DIRECTOR
Peter McRae

Amy International Productions Ltd.
24 Park Ave., Wraysbury, Middx. TW19 5ET. Tel: 0784 483131/483288. FAX: 0784 483812.

Andor Films Ltd.
8 Ilchester Place, London, W14 8AA. Tel: 071 602 2382. FAX: 071 602 1047.
DIRECTORS
Stanley H. Munson, Charles H. Schneer (U.S.) Managing
DATE OF INCORPORATION
1975

Angels & Bermans
Head Office 119 Shaftesbury Avenue, London, WC2H 8AE. Tel: 071 836 5678; FAX: 071 240 9527.
CHAIRMAN
Tim Angel

SALES DIRECTOR
Ron Mawbey
Main Costume Store: 40 Camden Street, London, NW1 OEN. Tel: 071 387 0999; FAX: 071 383 5603.
PRODUCTION DIRECTOR
Richard Green
Angels & Bermans (Paris): AKA Traonouez, 196 Boulevard Voltaire, 75011 Paris, France. Tel: (1) 43 67 43 92; FAX: (1) 43 67 16 16.
CONTACT
Kristyn Ohanian

Angle Films Limited
25 Blenheim Crescent, London, W11 2EF. Tel: 071 229 6034; FAX: 071 727 8498.
CONTACT
Rex Pyke

Antelope Films Ltd.
3 Fitzroy Square, London, W1P 5AH. Tel: 071 387 4454. Telex: 266205. AFL G. FAX: 071 388 9935.
CONTACT
Mick Csaky

Anvil Film and Recording Group Ltd.
Denham Studios, North Orbital Road, Denham, Uxbridge, Middlesex, UB9 5HH. Tel: 0895 833522. Telex: 934704. FAX: 0895 835006.
CONTACTS
R. W. Keen (Production), Ken Somerville, C. Eng. M.I.E.R.E. and Alan Snelling (Sound and post prod.)

Artificial Eye Film Co.
211 Camden High Street, London, NW1 7BT. Tel: 071 267 6036 and 071 482 3981. Telex: 8951182 GECOMS. FAX: 071 267 6499.
CONTACT
Pamela Engel

Arts Council of Great Britain
14 Great Peter Street, London, SW1P 3NQ. Tel: 071 973 6443. FAX: 071 973 6581.
HEAD OF FILM, VIDEO AND BROADCASTING DEPARTMENT
Rodney Wilson

Richard Attenborough Productions Ltd.
Beaver Lodge, The Green, Richmond, Surrey, TW9 1NQ. Tel: 081 940 7234. Telex: 266446 BAPUG. FAX: 081 940 4741.
DIRECTORS
Lord Richard Attenborough, CBE, Lady Attenborough, J.P., Richard Blake, Claude Fielding

Australian Film Commission
2nd Floor, Victory House, 99-101 Regent Street, London, WIR 7HB. Tel: 071 734 9383; FAX: 071 434 0170.
DIRECTOR OF MARKETING
Sue Murray

Autocue Ltd.

Autocue House, 265 Merton Road, London, SW18 5JS. Tel: 081 870 0104. Telex: Autocue Telexir 885039 Autocu G. FAX: 081 874 3726.
CONTACTS
Mick Gould, Sarah Lewis

Avton Communications and Entertainment, Inc.

19 Watford Road, Radlett, Herts., WD7 8LF. Tel: 092385 3255. FAX 0923 855757.
CONTACT
Tony Klinger

AZ Productions Ltd.

Lorrimer House, 47 Dean Street, London, W.1. Tel: 071 437 7349.

BBC Enterprises LTd.

Woodlands, 80 Wood Lane, London, W12 0TT. Tel: 081 576 2000. FAX: 081 749 0538. Telex: 934678.
CHIEF EXECUTIVE
James Arnold-Baker

Jane Balfour Films Ltd.

Burghley House, 35 Fortress Road, London, NW5 1AD. Tel: 071 267 5392. FAX: 071 261 4241.

Beaconsfield Films, Ltd.

52 Queen Anne Street, London, W1M 9LA. Tel: 071 935 1186. Date of incorporation: March 21, 1951.
DIRECTORS
Peter Rogers, Mrs. B. E. Rogers, G. E. Malyon

BFI Film & Video Library

21 Stephen Street, London, W1P 1PL. Tel: 071 255 1444. Telex: 27624.
HEAD OF DISTRIBUTION SERVICES
Heather Stewart

Blue Dolphin Film Distributors Ltd.

(Blue Dolphin Film Productions Ltd.)
15-17 Old Compton Street, London, W1V 6JR. Tel: 071 439 9511. Telex: 928152. CRAWFI/G. FAX: 071 287 0370.

Bop Motion Pictures Ltd.

6 Woodland Way, Petts Wood, Kent BR5 IND. Tel: 0689 871535/871519. FAX: 0689 871519.
DIRECTORS
Bachoo Sen, John C. Broderick

Bordeaux Films Int. Ltd.

22 Soho Square, London, W1V 5FJ. Telex: 296588. Tel: 081 959 8556.
MANAGING DIRECTOR
K. Barakat

Box, Sydney, Associates, Ltd.

52 Queen Anne Street, London, W1M 9LA; Tel 071 935 1186.
DIRECTORS
Mrs. B. E. Rogers, G. E. Malyon

Bright Star

Reuters Television Ltd., 40 Cumberland Avenue, London, NW10 7EH. Tel: 081 965 7733. Telex: 22678. FAX: 081 965 0620.

British Lion

Pinewood Studios, Pinewood Road, Iver, Bucks., SL0 0NH. Tel: 0753 651 700. Telex 847505. FAX: 0753 656391.
CHAIRMAN AND CHIEF EXECUTIVE
Peter R. E. Snell

British Movietonews, Ltd.

North Orbital Road, Denham, Nr. Uxbridge, Middlesex, UB9 5HQ. Tel: 0895 833071; FAX: 0895 834893. London Office: 76 Old Compton Street, London, W1V 5PA. Tel: 071-437 7766.
MANAGING DIRECTOR
Barry S. Florin
LIBRARIAN
Barbara Heavens

British Sky Broadcasting Ltd.

6 Centaurs Business Park, Grant Way, Isleworth, Middx. TW7 5QD. Tel: 071 705 3000. FAX: 071 705 3030.
CHIEF EXECUTIVE
Sam Chisholm
HEAD OF PROGRAMS
David Elstein
HEAD OF ACQUISITIONS
Jeremy Boulton

British Screen Finance Ltd.

14-17 Wells Street, London, W1P 3FL. Tel: 071 323 9080; FAX: 071 323 0092.
CHIEF EXECUTIVE
Simon Perry

British Transport Films

(Archive and Library)
18-20 St. Dunstan's Road, London, SE25 6EU. Tel: 081 771 6522; FAX: 081 653 9773.
PROPRIETOR
Barry Coward

British Universities Film & Video Council

55 Greek St., London, W1V 5LR. Tel: 071 734 3687; FAX: 071 287 3914.
DIRECTOR
Murray Weston

Broughton House

3rd fl., 6-8 Sackville St., London W1X 1DD. Tel: 071 287 4601. FAX: 071 287 9652.

Bryanston Films Ltd.

Stratton House, Picadilly, London, W1X 6AS. Tel: 071 629 8886.
DIRECTORS
John T. Davey, F.C.A., Colin S. Wills, M.A., F.C.A.

Burrill Productions

19 Cranbury Rd., London SW6 2NS. Tel: 071 736 8673. FAX: 071 731 3921.
CONTACT
Timothy Burrill

Buena Vista Productions Ltd.

Beaumont House, Kensington Village, Avonmore Road, London, W14 8TS. Tel: 071 605 2400; FAX: 071 605 2597.
MANAGING DIRECTOR
David Simon

CFS Conference Centre Ltd.

22-25 Portman Close, Baker Street, London, W1A 4BE. Tel: 071 486 2881. Telex: 24672. FAX: 071 486 4152.

CIC Theatres

Lee House, 90 Great Bridgwater Street, Manchester M1 5JW. Tel: 061 455 4000; FAX: 061 455 4079.
CONTACT
Ian Riches

C.T.S. Studios Ltd.

Engineers Way, Wembley, Middlesex HA9 0DR. Tel: 081 903 4611; FAX: 081 903 7130.
CONTACT
Anne Henry

Campbell Connelly & Co. Ltd.

(Shapiro Berstein & Co. Ltd.)
(Music Publishers) 8-9 Frith Street, London, W1V 5TZ. Tel: 071 434 0066; Telex: 21892; FAX: 071 439 2848.
COPYWRIGHT-LICENSING MANAGER
Mick Booth

Cannon Film Distributors LTD

(Cannon Music Ltd)
84-86 Regent Street, London, W1R 5PF. Tel: 071 915 1717; FAX: 071 734 8411.
CONTACT
Jonathan Cocker

Capitol Films Ltd.

15 Portland Place, London, W1N 3AA. Tel: 071 872 0154; FAX: 071 636 6691.
CONTACTS
Sharon Harel, Jane Barclay

Carlton Communications PLC

15 St. George Street, London, W1R 9DE. Tel: 071 499 8050; FAX: 071 895 9575.
CHAIRMAN
Michael Green
MANAGING DIRECTOR
June de Holler

Castle Communications PLC

A29 Barwell Business Park, Leatherhead Road, Chessington, Surrey KT9 2NY. Tel: 081 974 1021. FAX: 081 974 2674.

Castle Target International

(Castle Premier Releasing Ltd.)
A29 Barwell Business Park, Leatherhead Road, Chessington, Surrey KT9 2NY. Tel: 081 974 1021. FAX: 081 974 2674.

Cattermoul Film Service

(Cecil Cattermoul Ltd.)
69 New Oxford Street, London, WC1A 1DG. Tel: 071 379 4361 and 071 379 4038. Telex: 268312 WESCOM G ATTN. CATTERMOUL. FAX: 071 240 4895.
DIRECTOR
Marina Cattermoul (Mrs.)

Roger Cherrill Ltd.

65-66 Dean Street, London, W1V 6PL. Tel: 071 437 7972. FAX: 071 437 6411.
CONTACT
Brian Hickin

Chrysalis Group PLC

Bramley Road, London, W1O 6SP. Tel: 071 221 2213; FAX: 071 221 6286.

Ci By Sales

10 Stephen Mews, London, W1P 1PP. Tel: 071 333 8877; FAX: 071 333 8878.

Cine-Lingual Sound Studios Ltd.

27/29 Berwick Street, London, W1V 3RF. Tel: 071 437 0136. FAX: 071 439 2012.
DIRECTORS
A. Anscombe, P. J. Anscombe, M. Anscombe, D. J. Old, D. J. Newman

Cinema Verity Ltd.

The Mill House, Millers Way, 1A Shepherds Bush Road, London, W6 7NA. Tel: 081 749 8485. FAX: 081 743 5062.
EXECUTIVE PRODUCER
Verity Lambert

Cinesound Effects Library Ltd.

Imperial Studios, Maxwell Road, Elstree Way, Boreham Wood, Herts.. Tel: 081 953 5837, 5545, 4904, 1587. FAX: 081 207 1728.
CONTACT
Angela Marshall

Herman Cohen Productions

88 Peterborough Road, London, S.W.11

Clip Joint

(Film Archive Library)
4 Aldred Road, London NW6 IAN. Tel: 071 794 3666. FAX: 071 431 4132.

Columbia Pictures Corporation Ltd

19-23 Wells Street, London W1P 3FP. Tel: 071 580 2090. Telex: 263392 COLPIC G. Fax: 071 528 8980.
DIRECTORS
Nicholas Bingham, Martin Blakstad, Edward J. Katz (USA), Lester McKellar, J. Edward Shugrue (USA)

Columbia Tri-Star Films (U.K.)

19/23 Wells Street, London, W1P 3FP. Tel: 071 580 2090. Telex 263392 Colpic G. FAX: 071 436 0323.
MANAGING DIRECTOR U.K.
James Katz

Columbia Tri-Star Films (Ireland)

54 Middle Abbey St., Dublin, Ireland; Tel: 01 38 72 4151.
BRANCH MANAGER
Gerry Mulcahy

674

Completion Bond Co Inc.
Pinewood Studios, Iver, Bucks., SL0 0NH. Tel: 0753 651700, 0753 652099.

CONTACT
John L. Hargreaves

Contemporary Films
24, Southwood Lawn Road, Highgate, London, N6 5SF. Tel: 081 340 5715. FAX: 081 348 1238.

CONTACT
Kitty Cooper

Cori Film Distributors
19 Albemarle Street, London, W1X 3HA. Tel: 071 493 7920. Telex: 299968 CORMAN. FAX: 071 493 8088.

CONTACTS
Marie Hoy, Fiona Mitchell

Crews Employment Agency
111 Wardour Street, London, W1V 4AY. Tel: 071 437 0350/0810/0721. FAX: 071 494 4644.

CONTACTS
Lynda Loakes, Shirley Hinds

Curzon Film Distributors Ltd.
38 Curzon Street, London, W1Y 8EY. Tel: 071 965 0565. Telex: 21612. FAX: 071 499 2018.

DIRECTORS
R. C. Wingate, G. Biggs, D. Kiernam, J. Gamble, R. Cossey

Cygnet Ltd.
Communications Business Centre, Blenheim Road, High Wycombe, Bucks., HP12 3RS. Tel: 0494 450541. FAX: 0494 462154.

MANAGING DIRECTOR
D. N. Plunket

Dee and Co. Ltd.
Suite 204, Canalot, 222 Kensal Road, London, W10 5BN. Tel: 081 960 2712. FAX: 081 960 2728. Telex: 94012826-DECO G.

De Lane Lea Sound Centre
75 Dean Street, London, W1V 5HA. Tel: 071 439 1721. FAX: 071 437 0913.

CONTACT
Richard Paynter

Walt Disney Company Ltd.
Beaumont House, Kensington Village, Avonmore Road, London, W14 8TS. Tel: 071 605 2400; FAX: 071 605 2593.

MANAGING DIRECTOR
Etienne de Villiers

Distant Horizon Ltd.
84-86 Regent Street, London, W1R 5PF. Tel: 071 734 8690. FAX: 071 734 8691.

Dolby Laboratories Inc.
346 Clapham Road, London, SW9 9AP. Tel: 071 720 1111. Telex: 919109. FAX: 071 720 4118.

CONTACT
Catherine Unwin

Dolphin International Film Distributors Ltd.
81 Piccadilly, London, W.1. Tel: 071 493 8811.

Drummer Films Ltd.
14 Haywood Close, Pinner, Middx. HA5 3LQ. Tel: 081 866 9466. FAX: 081 866 9466.

PRODUCER
Martin M. Harris (Man. Dir.)

Duck Lane Film Productions Ltd.
8 Duck Lane, London, W1V 1FL. Tel: 071 439 3912. FAX: 071 437 2260.

DIRECTOR
Rigby Andrews

ECO Ltd.
9-10 Westgate Street, Cardiff, CF1 1DA, Wales. Tel: 0222 373321. FAX: 0222 341391.

CONTACT
John Cross

Educational and Television Films, Ltd.
247a Upper Street, London, N1 IRU. Tel: 071 226 2298.

GENERAL MANAGER
Stanley Forman

English Film Co. (Exports) Ltd.
6 Woodland Way, Petts Wood, Kent BR5 IND. Tel: 0689 871535. FAX: 0689 871519.

CONTACT
Bachoo Sen

Enigma Productions
13-15 Queen's Gate Place Mews, London, SW7 5BG. Tel: 071 581 0238.

DIRECTORS
David Puttnam, Steve Norris

Entertainment Film Distributors Ltd. (Entertainment Film Productions Ltd.)
27 Soho Square, London, W1V 5FL. Tel: 071 439 1606. Telex: 262428 ENTVIF. FAX: 071 734 2483.

DIRECTORS
Michael L. Green, Trevor H. Green, Nigel Green

Eon Productions, Ltd.
2 South Audley Street, London, W1Y 6AJ. Tel: 071 493 7953. Cables: Brocfilm, London, W1. FAX: 01408 1236.

DIRECTORS
M. G. Wilson, F. B. Coote, R. A. Barkshire

Eureka Location Management
51 Tonsley Hill, London, SW18 1BW. Tel: 081 870 6569; FAX: 081 871 2158.

HEAD OF OPERATIONS
Suzannah Holt

Europa Films, Ltd.
Registered Office: Park House 158/160, Arthur Road, Wimbledon Park, London, S.W.19.

DIRECTORS
Hugh Stewart, Michael M. Stewart

675

Euston Films

365 Euston Road, London, NW1 3AR. Tel: 071 387 0911. FAX: 071 388 2122.
DIRECTOR OF PRODUCTION
Bill Launder

Eyeline Film Facilities/Video 77 Ltd.

77 Dean Street, London, W1V 6LP. Tel: 071 734 3391. Telex: 265361. FAX: 071 437 2095.
DIRECTORS
Harold Orton, Jacki Roblin

F.I.L.M.S. Ltd.

40 Queen Anne's Gate, London, SW1H 9AP.

Film and General Productions Ltd.

10 Pembridge Place, London, W2 4XB. Tel: 071 221 1141. FAX: 071 792 1167.
DIRECTORS
Clive Parsons, Davina Belling, Richard Whatmore

Film Four International

60 Charlotte Street, London, W1P 2AX. Tel: 071 631 4444. Telex: 892355. FAX: 071 580 2622.
DIRECTOR OF SALES
Bill Stephens
FILM SALES MANAGER
Heather Playford-Denman

FTS Bonded

Heston Industrial Estate, Aerodrome Way, Cranford Lane, Hounslow, TW5 9QN, Middlesex. Tel: 081 897 7973. Telex: 21747 FILMBO G. FAX: 081 897 7979.
SALES DIRECTOR
John Reeves

Film Booking Offices Ltd.

211 The Chambers, Chelsea Harbour, London, SW10 OXF. Tel: 071 734 5298. FAX: 071 352 4182.
DIRECTORS
B. G. Sammes, F. B. Perham

Film Finances, Ltd.

1/11 Hay Hill, Berkeley Square, London, W1X 7LF. Tel: 071 629 6557. FAX: 071 491 7530. Telex: 298060 (filfin); and Film Finances Inc., Suite 808, 9000 Sunset Boulevard, Los Angeles, CA 90069, U.S.A.. Tel: (213) 275-7323. Telex: 183205 (Filfns Inc. LSA).
DIRECTORS
Richard M. Soames (Man. Dir. Film Finances Ltd., Pres. Film Finances Inc.), Graham J. Easton

Filmarketeers Ltd.

81 Piccadilly, London, W1V 9HB. Tel: 071 491 2767. Telex: 299565. FAX: 071 629 1803.
DIRECTORS
S. Shorr, I. Hamaoui

Filmverhuurkantoor De Dam B.V.

59 Warwick Square, London, SW1V 2AL. Tel: 071 233 6034; FAX: 071 233 6036.
CONTACT
Moses Rothman

First Independent Films Ltd.

69 New Oxford St., London, WC1A 1DG. Tel: 071 528 7767. FAX: 071 528 7772.
MANAGING DIRECTOR
Michael Myers

First Leisure Corporation

7 Soho Street, London, W1V 5FA. Tel: 071 437 9727. FAX: 071 439 0088.
PRESIDENT
Lord Delfont
CHAIRMAN
Lord Rayne
CONTACT
D. W. Wright

Bryan Forbes Ltd.

Seven Pines, Wentworth, Surrey. FAX: 0344 845174.

Mark Forstater Productions Ltd.

Unit 66, Pall Mall Deposit, 124-128 Barlby Road, London, W1O 6BL. Tel: 081 964 1888; FAX: 081 960 9819.
CHAIRMAN
Mark Forstater

Four Star Films, Ltd.

52 Queen Anne Street, London, W1M 9LA. Tel: 071 935 1186. Date of incorporation: October, 1958.
DIRECTORS
N. Butt, G. Golledge

Fowler-Chapman Co. Ltd., The

28 Saint Mary le Park Court, Albert Bridge Road, London, SW11 4PJ. Tel: 071 223 0034. FAX: 0892 784023.
MANAGING DIRECTOR
Roy Fowler

Foxwell Film Productions Ltd.

99 Aldwych, London, W.C.2. Date of incorporation: January 13, 1949.
DIRECTORS
Ivan Foxwell, A. G. Cotterell

Frontroom Films Ltd.

1 The Barton, Mill Road, Countess Wear, Exeter, Devon EX2 6LD. Tel: 0392 70985. FAX: 0392 431405.
CONTACTS
John Davies, Robert Smith

Fuji Photo Film (UK) Ltd.

Fuji Film House, 125 Finchley Road, Swiss Cottage, London, NW3 6JH. Tel: 071 586 5900. Telex: 8812995. FAX: 071 722 4259.
MANAGING DIRECTOR
S. Takekoshi
GENERAL MANAGER
D. R. Anderson
GENERAL SALES MANAGER
E. J. Mould

GFD Communications

42 Pearse Street, Dublin 2, Ireland. Tel: Dublin 713455. FAX: 713749.
DIRECTORS
C. M. Anderson, R. J. Whitty

G.H.W. Productions, Ltd.

52 Queen Anne Street, London, W1M 9LA. Tel: 071 935 1186.

DIRECTORS
Peter Rogers, Betty E. Box, O.B.E., G. E. Malyon

G.W. Films, Ltd.

41 Montpelier Walk, London, SW7 IJH. Tel: 071 589 8829. FAX: 071 584 0024.

DIRECTORS
Lord Brabourne, Richard Goodwin

Gainsborough (Film & TV) Pictures Ltd.

8 Queen Street, Mayfair, London, W17 XPH. Tel: 071 049 1925. FAX: 071 408 2042.

Gala Film Distributors Ltd.

26 Danbury St., Islington, London, N18JU. Tel: 071 226 5085. FAX: 071 226 5897.

MANAGING DIRECTOR & CHIEF EXECUTIVE
Kenneth Rive

Gannet Films Ltd.

Eton Cottage, 88 Gresham Road, Staines, Middx. TW18 2AE. Tel: 0784 453912.

DIRECTORS
Bob Kellett, Anne Kellett
SECRETARY
B. C. Stebbings

Garrett, James, & Partners, Ltd.

25 Bruton Street, London, W1X 7DB. Tel: 071 499 6452. Telex: 261163. FAX: 071 409 1797.

DIRECTORS
J. L. M. P. Garrett (Chmn.), M. Gilmour (Managing), D. T. Cromwell (Production Dir.), M. Garrett

General Screen Enterprises

Highbridge Estate, Oxford Road, Uxbridge, Middlesex, UB8 1LX. Tel: 0895 231931. FAX: 0895 235335.

DIRECTOR AND GENERAL MANAGER
Fred Chandler

William Gilbert Associates Ltd.

16 Brook Mews North, London W23 BW. Tel: 071 258 3620. FAX: 071 723 5100. Telex: 264826 RKOINT G.

DIRECTORS
William G. Gilbert
(Managing) M. Gilbert

Ginger Films Productions Ltd.

39-41 Hanover Steps, St. Georges Fields, Albion Street, London, W2 2YG. Tel: 071 402 7543. Telex: 896559 Gecoms G. FAX: 071 262 5736.

CONTACT
Brian Jackson

Goldcrest Films and Television Ltd.

65-66 Dean Street, London, W1V 6PL. Tel: 071 437 8696; Telex: 267458 Goldcr; FAX: 071 437 4448.

CHIEF EXECUTIVE
John Quested

Golden Square Films Ltd.

Pinewood Studios, Iver heath, Bucks. SL0 0NH. Tel: 0753 656842. FAX: 0753 656475. Telex: 846606.

CHAIRMAN
John Chambers

Grade Company

Embassy House, 3 Audley Square, London, W1Y 5DR. Tel: 071 409 1925. FAX: 071 408 2042. 8 Queen St., Mayfair, London W1X 7PH

CONTACT
Lord Grade

Granada Group, PLC.

36, Golden Square, London, W1R 4AH. Tel: 01 734 8080. Telex: 27937. FAX: 01 734 8080.

DIRECTORS
Alex Bernstein (Chairman), G. J. Robinson (Chief Executive), J. Ashworth, A. W. Clements, P. J. Davis, Mark Littman, QC., I. A. Martin, A. Quinn, G. M. Wallace (Finance Director)
SECRETARY
G. J. Parrott, FCIS

Guest, Val, Productions, Ltd.

1033 Sierra Way, Palm Springs, CA 92264 USA. Tel: (619) 323-4127; FAX: (619) 320-5130.

DIRECTORS
Val Guest, John A. Maeer

Guild Entertainment Limited

Crown House, 2 Church Street, Walton-on-Thames, Surrey, KT12 2QS. Tel: 081 546 3377. Telex: 269651. FAX: 081 546 4568.

Guild Film Distribution Ltd.

Kent House, 14-17 Market Pl., Great Titchfield St., London W1N 8AR. Tel: 071 323 5151. FAX: 071 631 3568

CONTACT
Thomas Hedman

Hammer Film Productions, Ltd.

Elstree Studios, Boreham Wood, Herts. WD6 1J9. Tel: 081 953 1600. FAX: 081 905 1127.

DIRECTORS
Roy Skeggs, Timothy L. Kirby, Sir John Terry, Arthur Buck
DATE OF INCORPORATION
February 12, 1949

HandMade Films (Distributors) Ltd.

26 Cadogan Square, London, SW1X 0JP. Tel: 071 584 8345/4131. FAX: 071 584 7338.

DIRECTORS
Denis O'Brien, Gareth Jones

Harkness Screens Ltd.

Gate Studios, Station Road, Boreham Wood, Herts., WD6 1DQ. Tel: 081 953 3611. Cables: Screens, London. Telex: 8955602 Perlux G. FAX: 081 207 3657. INT. FAX: 441 207 3657.

Hemdale Holdings

21 Albion Street, London, W2 2AS. Tel: 071 724 1010. Telex: 25558. HEMHOL. FAX: 071 724 9168.

DIRECTORS
J. Daly, A. D. Kerman, D. Gibson

Jim Henson Productions

1 (B) Downshire Hill, Hampstead, London, NW3 1NR. Tel: 071 431 2818; FAX: 071 431 3737.

High Point Films & Television Ltd.

118-120 Great Titchfield Street, London, W1P 7AJ.

Hit Entertainment PLC

The Pump House, 13-16 Jacobs Well Mews, London, W1H 5PD. Tel: 071 224 1717; FAX: 071 224 1719.

Holdsworth, Gerard, Productions Ltd.

31 Palace Street, London, SW1E 5HW. Tel: 071 828 1671. FAX: 071 931 9200.
DIRECTORS
P. H. Filmer-Sankey, A. M. V. Brunker

IAC Film Sales

P.O. Box 99 c, Esher, Surrey KT10 9NF. Tel: 081 941 8699. FAX: 081 941 8622.
MANAGING DIRECTOR
Guy Collins
DIRECTOR OF SALES
Penny Wolf

ICA Projects

12 Carlton House Terrace, London, SW1Y 5AH. Tel: 071 930 0493. FAX: 071 873 0051.
CONTACT
Simon Field

ITC Entertainment Group Ltd.

24 Nutford Place, London, W.1. Tel: 071 262 3262. Telex: 912121. FAX: 071 724 0160.
SENIOR VICE PRESIDENT INTERNATIONAL
Lynden Parry

ITV Network Acquisitions

ITV Network Centre, 200 Gray's Inn Road, London, WC1X 8MF. Tel: 071 843 8120; Telex: 262988; FAX: 071 843 8160.
CONTROLLER OF ACQUISITIONS
Pat Mahoney

Inimitable Ltd.

Greenman, Highmoor, Henley-on-Thames, Oxfordshire RG9 5DH. Tel: 0491 641140. FAX: 0491 641080.
CONTACT
Gerry Anderson

Initial Films & TV Ltd.

Suite 12, 10-16 Rathbone St., London W1P 1AA. Tel: 071 637 8251.
MANAGING DIRECTOR
Eric Feliner

Island Pictures

22 St. Peters Square, London, W6 9NW. Tel: 081 741 1511.

J & M Entertainment

2 Dorset Square, London, NW1 6PU. Tel: 071 723 6544. Telex: 298538. FAX: 071 724 7541.
CONTACTS
Julia Palau, Michael Ryan

Brian Jackson Films Ltd.

39-41 Hanover Steps, St. Georges Fields, Albion Street, London, W2 2YG. Tel: 071 402 7543. Telex: 896559 Gecoms G. FAX: 071 262 5736.
CONTACT
Brian Jackson

Jaras Entertainments Ltd.

Broughton House, 3rd fl., 6–8 Sackville St., London W1X 1DD. Tel: 071 287 4601. FAX: 071 287 9652.

Kavur Productions Ltd.

14 Lownes Square, London, SW1X 9HB. Tel: 071 235 4602. FAX: 071 235 5215.

Kenilworth Film Productions Ltd.

41 Montpelier Walk, London, SW7 1JH. Tel: 071 589 8829. FAX: 071 584 0024.
DIRECTORS
Lord Brabourne, Richard Goodwin

Kettledrum Films Ltd.

37 Connaught Square, London, W.2. Tel: 071 262 0077.

Kimpton Walker Plc.

47/49 Acre Lane, London, SW2 5TN. Tel: 071 737 3317. Telex: 27789. FAX: 071 274 4534.
CONTACT
Catherine Bendall

Kodak Limited

Motion Picture and Television Imaging, Kodak House, P.O. Box 66, Station Road, Hemel Hempstead, Herts., HP1 1JU. Tel: 0442 61122; FAX: 0442 844458.
BUSINESS MANAGER
Geoff. Cadogan
SALES MANAGER
Bob Mayson

K-Tel Motion Pictures

(K-Tel International (UK) Ltd.)
620 Western Avenue, London, W.3. Tel: 081 992 8000.

Lambeth Productions

Twickenham Film Studios, St. Margarets, Twickenham, Middx. TW1 2AW. Tel: 081 892 4477. FAX: 081 891 0168. Telex: 8814497 TWICKSTG.
DIRECTORS
Sir Richard Attenborough, C.B.E., Lady Attenborough, J.P., Richard Blake, Claude Fielding, Diana Hawkins, Terry Clegg.

Liberty Films

4th Floor, The Forum, 74-80 Camden Street, London, NW1 0JL. Tel: 071 387 5733. FAX: 071 383 95368.
CONTACTS
Teresa Kelleher, John Kelleher

Limelight Films

3 Bromley Place, London, W1P 5HB. Tel: 071 255 3939. FAX: 071 436 4334.
CONTACT
Sally Woodward

678

London Film Productions Ltd.

Kent House, 14-17 Market Place, Great Titchfield Street, London, W1N 8AR. Tel: 071 323 5251. FAX: 071 436 2834.
CONTACT
J. Eliasch

London Independent Producers Ltd.

52 Queen Anne Street, London, W1M 9LA. Tel: 071 935 1186.
DIRECTORS
William MacQuitty, Mrs. B. E. MacQuitty, Ralph Thomas, Leonora Dossett
SECRETARY
G. Golledge
DATE OF INCORPORATION
February 3, 1950

Lucida Productions Ltd.

53 Greek Street, London, WIV 5LR. Tel: 071 437 1140; FAX: 071 287 5335.
DIRECTORS
Paul Joyce, Chris Rodley

Lumiere Pictures Ltd.

167-169 Wardour Street, London, WIV 3TA. Tel: 071 413 0838; FAX: 071 734 1509.
CHIEF EXECUTIVE
Jean Cazes
HEAD OF SALES
Ralph Camp, Christopher Cary

MTM Ardmore Studios Ltd.

Herbert Road, Bray, Co. Wicklow, Ireland. Tel: Dublin 862971. FAX: Dublin 861894. Telex: 91504 PATT E1.

MTV Europe

20-23 Mandela St., London NW1 0DU. Tel: 071 383 4250. FAX: 071 388 2064.

Mainline Pictures

37 Museum Street, London, WC1A 1LP. Tel: 071 242 5523.

Majestic Films and Television International

P.O. Box 13, Gloucester Mansions, Cambridge Circus, London, WC2H 8XD. Tel: 071 836 8630. FAX: 071 836 5819. Telex: 46601 BTGKA G.
CHIEF EXECUTIVE
Guy East

Management Company Entertainment Group Inc.

Portobello Dock, 328 Kensal Road, London W10 5XJ. Tel: 071 968 8888. FAX: 071 968 8537.

Manifesto Film Sales

3rd Floor, 10 Livonia Street, London, W1V 3PH. Tel: 071 439 2424. FAX: 071 437 9964.
CONTACT
John Durie

Mayfair Entertainment UK Ltd.

9 St. Martin's Court, London, WC2N 4AJ. Tel: 071 895 0328. FAX: 071 895 0329.
CHAIRMAN
Roger Wingate
MANAGING DIRECTOR
John Hogarth
DIRECTOR
Anne Boyle

Media Releasing Distributors Ltd.

27 Soho Square, London, W1V 5FL. Tel: 071 437 2341. Telex: 943763 CROCOM G (MRD). FAX: 071 734 2483.
DIRECTORS
Trevor H. Green, J. Green

Medusa Communications Ltd.

Regal Chambers, 51 Bancroft, Hitchin, Herts., SG5 1LL. Tel: 0462 421818. FAX: 0462 420393.
CHAIRMAN
David Hodgins
EXECUTIVE DIRECTOR
Stephen Rivers

Merchant-Ivory Productions

46 Lexington Street, London W1P 3LH. Tel: 071 437 1200. FAX: 071 734 1579.
CONTACTS
Ismail Merchant, James Ivory

Mersham Productions Ltd.

41 Montpelier Walk, London, SW7 1JH. Tel: 071 589 8829. FAX: 071 584 0024.
DIRECTORS
Lord Brabourne, Michael-John Knatchbull, Richard Goodwin

Metro Tartan Ltd.

79 Wardour Street, London, WIV 3TH. Tel: 071 734 8508; FAX: 071 287 2112.

Metrocolor London Ltd.

91-95 Gillespie Road, London, N5 1LS. Tel: 071 226 4422. Telex: 28463. METLON; and 22 Soho Square, London, W1V 5FL. Tel: 071 437 7811. FAX: 071 359 2353.
DIRECTORS
K. B. Fraser, S. Ross (USA), M. Meltzer (USA), S. B. Graber (USA), E. O. Denault (USA), A. D. Bruno (USA), B. E. Compton, E. G. West.

Metro-Goldwyn-Mayer Cinemas Ltd.

84-86 Regent Street, London, W1R 5PA. Tel: 071 915 1717. FAX: 071 734 8410.
DIRECTORS
Alan Ladd Jnr., Charles Meeker, Ken Meyer, Tom Carson, Martin Evans, Sanford Lieberson, Brian Yell

Miracle Communications Ltd.

69 New Oxford Street, London, WC1A 1DG. Tel: 071 379 5006. FAX: 071 528 7772.

Molliko Films (London) Ltd.

16-18 New Bridge Street, London, EC4V 6AU. Tel: 071 262 0638. Cables: Umeshmalik, London, E.C.4.
CHAIRMAN AND MAN. DIR.
Umesh Mallik, B.A., India
SECRETARY
J. R. F. Williamson, M.B.E., F.C.A.

DIRECTOR-PRODUCTION
Bina Chatterjee (Miss)
GENERAL MANAGER IN INDIA
P.C. Mallik, BSC, B.L.
SCRIPT EDITOR
Janet Bennett

Moving Picture Company

25 Noel Street, London, W1V 3RD. Tel: 071 434 3100.
FAX: 071 437 3951.
CONTACT
David Jeffers

Museum of the Moving Image

South Bank, Waterloo, London, SE1 8XT. Tel: 071 928
3535. FAX: 071 928 7938.
CONTROLLER
Adrian Wootton, BFI South Bank
CURATOR
Leslie Hardcastle, OBE

Namara Films Ltd.

45 Poland Street, London, W1V 4AV. Tel: 071 439 6480.
EXECUTIVE PRODUCER
Naim Attallah

National Film Board of Canada

1 Grosvenor Square, London, WIX OAB. Tel: 071 258
6482; FAX: 071 258 6532.

National Screen

15 Wadsworth Road, Greenford, Middlesex, UB6 7JN.
Tel: 081 998 2851. FAX: 081 997 0840 and 2 Wedgwood
Mews, 12-13 Greek Street, London, W1V 6BH. Tel: 071
437 4851. FAX: 071 287 0328.
DIRECTORS
John Mahony, Brian McIlmail, Norman Darkins

New World Trans Atlantic Pictures (UK) Ltd.

27 Soho Square, London, W1V 5FL. Tel: 071 434 0497.
FAX: 071 434 0490.

Nelson Entertainment

8 Queen Street, London, W1X 7PH. Tel: 071 493 3362.
FAX: 071 409 0503. Telex: 8950483 NELSON G.

Omandry International Ltd.

1 Fernsleigh Close, Chalfont St. Peter Gerrards Cross,
Bucks., SL9 0HR. Tel: 0494 87 4149 Telex: 837225 Exant
G. Altn. Omandry.
DIRECTORS
F. S. Poole, F. C. Poole, H. F. Poole.

Optical Film Effects Ltd.

Pinewood Studios, Iver Heath, Bucks., SL0 0NH. Tel:
0753 655486. Telex: 847505 Pinew G. FAX: 0753 656844.
DIRECTORS
R. W. Field, R. A. Dimbleby

Orion Pictures International Inc.

5–8 Warwick St., London, W1R 5RA. Tel: 071 753 8753.
Telex: 894030. FAX: 071 753 8754.
DIRECTORS
Eric Pleskow (Chm.) (U.S.), Stuart Salter (Man.), Malcolm Farrer-Brown

CONTACT
Stuart Salter

Overview Films Ltd.

16 Brook Mews North, London, W2 3BW. Tel: 071 258
3620. FAX: 071 723 5100. Telex: 2 64826 RKOINT 6.
CONTACT
William G. Gilbert

Oxford Scientific Films

Lower Road, Long Hanborough, Oxon OX8 8LL. Tel:
0993 881881. FAX: 0993 882808, and 10 Poland Street,
London, W1. Tel: 071 494 0720. FAX: 071 287 9125.
MANAGING DIRECTOR
Karen Goldie-Morrison

Palomar Pictures International (U.K.) Ltd.

5 Chancery Lane, Clifford's Inn, London, EC4A 1BU.

David Paradine Productions Ltd.

115-123, Bayham Street, London, NW1 0AG. Tel: 071
482 2898. FAX: 071 482 0871.

Paramount British Pictures, Ltd.

Twickenham Film Studios Ltd., The Barons, St. Margaret's, Twickenham, Middx. TW1 2AW. Tel: 081 892 4477.
Telex: 8814497. FAX: 081 891 0168.

Paramount Pictures (UK) Ltd.

UIP House, 45 Beadon Road, Hammersmith, London,
W6 0EG. Tel: 081 741 9041.

Park Entertainment Ltd.

1-2 Bromley Place, London, W1P 5HB. Tel: 071 637
7651. Telex: 264639. FAX: 071 436 5387.

Pearl & Dean Ltd.

Woolverstone House, 61-62 Berners Street, London,
WIP 3AE. Tel: 071 636 5252; FAX: 071 637 3191.
MANAGING DIRECTOR
Peter Howard Williams

Penta International

8 Queen Street, London, W1X 7PH. Tel: 071 409 3532.
FAX: 071 499 9885.

Perforated Front Projection Screen Co. Ltd.

182, High Street, Cottenham, Cambridge, CB4 4RX.
Tel: Cottenham 50139.
DIRECTOR
F. E. J. Witchalls
DATE OF INCORPORATION
January, 1931

Phoenix Films Ltd.

6 Flitcroft St., London WC2 8DJ. Tel: 071 836 5000. FAX:
071 836 3060.
DIRECTORS
Lewis More O'Ferrall, Alan Taylor

Plato Films Ltd.

247a Upper Street, London, N1 1RU. Tel: 071 226 2298.
GENERAL MANAGER
Stanley Forman

Playpont Films Ltd.

1-2 Ramillies Street, London, W1V 1DF. Tel: 071 734 7792. FAX: 071 734 9288.
MANAGING DIRECTOR
Don Getz
BUSINESS AFFAIRS MANAGER
Ellen Trost

Polygram Video International

347-353 Chiswick High Road, Chiswick, London, W4 4HS. Tel: 081 994 9199. FAX: 081 742 5577.
MANAGING DIRECTOR
David Rozalla

Polygram International

30 Berkeley Square, London, WIX 5HA. Tel: 071 493 8800. Telex: 263872.

Portman Zenith

43-45 Dorset Street, London, W1Y 4AB. Tel: 071 224 3344. FAX: 071 224 1057.
DIRECTORS
Victor Glynn, John Hall, John Sivers, Simon Cox, Andrew Warren, Richard Leworthy, Scott Meek, Ian Squires

Portobello Productions

56 Long Acre, Covent Garden, London WC2E 9JL. Tel: 071 379 5566. FAX: 071 379 5599. Telex: 268388 PORTO G.
EXECUTIVE PROD./DIR.
Eric Abraham

Post Office Film & Video Unit

(Archival Material) 130 Old Street, London EC1V 9PQ.

Premiere Films

Pinewood Studios, Iver Heath, Bucks., SLO ONH. Tel: 0753 650001; FAX: 0753 656861.

Productions Associates (UK) Ltd.

"The Stable Cottage," Pinewood Studios, Iver Heath, Bucks.; SL0 0NH. Tel: 071 486 9921. Telex: 847505. FAX: 0753 656844.

Prominent Features Ltd.

Prominent Studios, 68A Delancey Street, London, NW1 7RY. Tel: 071 284 0242. FAX: 071 284 1004.
DIRECTORS
Steve Abbott, Terry Gilliam, Eric Idle, Anne James, Terry Jones, Michael Palin

Python (Monty) Pictures Ltd.

Prominent Studios, 68A Delancey Street, London, NW1 7RY. Tel: 071 284 0242. FAX: 071 284 1004.
DIRECTORS
John Cleese, Terry Gilliam, Eric Idle, Terry Jones, Michael Palin

Q Film Productions Ltd.

Rosehill House, Rose Hill, Nr. Burnham, Bucks. SL1 8NN. Tel: 068 605129
DIRECTORS
I. E. L. Shand, D. J. Bennet, F. Shand

Quigley Publications

15 Samuel Road, Langdon Hills, Basildon, Essex, SS16 6EZ. Tel: 0268 417055.
UK MANAGER
William Pay

Qwertyuiop Productions Ltd.

118-120 Wardour Street, London, W1 4BT. Tel: 071 437 3224. FAX: 071 437 3674.
MANAGING DIRECTOR
David Land

Rank Organisation Plc, The

6 Connaught Place, London, W2 2EZ. Tel: 071 706 1111. Telex: 263549. FAX: 071 262 9886. Date of incorporation: February 20, 1937.
DIRECTORS
Sir Leslie Fletcher (Chairman), Michael B. Gifford (Managing Director and Chief Executive), David V. Atterton, Sir Arthur Bryan, Angus Crichton-Miller, James Daly, Michael Jackaman, Sir Denis Mountain, Bt., The Hon. Sir Angus Ogilvy, Anthony W. Stenham, Douglas M. Yates, Nigel V. Turnbull (Finance Director), J. F. Garrett.
SECRETARY
Brian C. Owers

Film and Television Division

DELUXE FILM LABORATORIES

1377 North Serrano Ave., Hollywood, CA 90027. Tel: 0101 213 462 6171. FAX: 0101 213 461 0608.
PRESIDENT
Bud Stone

THE FILM HOUSE GROUP

Film House Laboratory, 380 Adelaide Street West Toronto, Ontario MSV 1R7, Canada. Tel: 0101 416 364 4321. FAX: 0101 416 364 3601.
PRESIDENT
Cyril Drabinsky

ODEON CINEMAS LTD.

(Management of Odeon Cinemas.)
439-445 Godstone Road, Whyteleafe, Surrey. Tel: 088362 3355; FAX: 0883 626717; Telex: 262305 088362 6044. And 54 Whitcomb Street, London, WC2H 7DN. Tel: 071 839 6373. FAX: 071 321 0357.
MANAGING DIRECTOR
Laurie Clarke

PINEWOOD STUDIOS LTD.

(Film and TV studios and also the sale of goods and services relating to the manufacture of cinematograph and television films.)
Pinewood Road, Iver, Buckinghamshire SL0 0NH. Tel: (Iver) 651700. Telex: 847505. FAX: 0753 656844.
MANAGING DIRECTOR
Stephen Jaggs

RANK BRIMAR LTD.

(Manufacturer of advanced cathode ray tubes for radar and telecines).

Greenside Way, Middleton, Manchester M24 1SN. Tel: 061 681 7072. Telex: 665326. FAX: 061 682 3818.

MANAGING DIRECTOR
Dr. Richard Fenby

RANK CINTEL LTD.

(Manufacturer of telecine equipment for broadcast and film/tape transfer.) Watton Road, Ware, Hertfordshire SG12 OAE. Tel: 0920 3939. Telex: 81415. FAX: 0920 60803.

MANAGING DIRECTOR
Jack R. Brittain

RANK FILM LABORATORIES LTD.

(Processing of colour and black and white film for cinema and television.)

North Orbital Road, Denham, Uxbridge, Middlesex, UB9 5HQ. Tel. (0895) 832323. FAX: 0895 833617. Telex 934704.

MANAGING DIRECTOR
James Downer
DIRECTOR OF SALES
David Dowler
SALES CONTROLLER, THEATRICAL
Peter MacCrimmon

RANK FILM DISTRIBUTORS LTD.

(Distribution of cinematograph films.)

127 Wardour Street, London, W1V 4AD. Tel: 071 437 9020. Telex: 262556. FAX: 071 434 3689.

MANAGING DIRECTOR
Frederick Turner

RANK PRECISION INDUSTRIES LTD.

Watton Road, WARE, Herts, SG12 OAE. Tel: 0920 3929. FAX: 0920 461137.

MANAGING DIRECTOR
Peter W. B. Paxtan

RANK TAYLOR HOBSON LTD.

(Manufacturer of precision measurement equipment, professional cine lenses.)

P.O. Box 36, 1 New Star Road, Thurmaston Lane, Leicester LE3 7JQ. Tel: 0533 763771. Telex: 342338; FAX: 0533 740167.

MANAGING DIRECTOR
Richard Freeman

RANK VIDEO SERVICES LTD.

(Operation of video and broadcast facilities and video cassette duplication.)

Phoenix Park Great West Road, Brentford, Middlesex, TW8 9PL. Tel: 081 568 4311. Telex: 22345. FAX: 081 847 4032.

MANAGING DIRECTOR
Hugh Corrance

RANK VIDEO SERVICES AMERICA INC.

Corporate Centre, 540 Lake Cook Road, Suite 200, Deerfield, Illinois 60015, U.S.A. Tel: 0101 708 291 1150; FAX: 0101 708 480 6077.

PRESIDENT & CHIEF EXECUTIVE OFFICER
Philip Clement

STRAND LIGHTING LTD.

Grant Wayoff Syon Lane, Isleworth, Middx. TW7 5QD. Tel: 081 560 3171. FAX: 081 490 0002.

MANAGING DIRECTOR
Christopher Waldron

Recorded Picture Co. Ltd.

8-12 Broadwick St., London, W1V 1FH. Tel: 071 439 0607. FAX: 071 434 1192.

DIRECTORS
Jeremy Thomas, Hercules Bellville, Chris Auty

Red Rooster Film & Television Entertainment

29 Floral Street, London, WC2E 9DP. Tel: 071 379 7727; FAX: 071 379 5756.

Rediffusion Films Ltd.

P.O. Box 451, Buchanan House, 3 St. James's Square, London, SW1Y 4LS. Tel: 071 925 0550. Telex: 919673. Cables: Rediffuse. FAX: (Group 3) 071 839 7135.

Reuters Television Ltd.

40 Cumberland Avenue, London, NW10 7EH. Tel: 081 965 7733. FAX: 081 965 0620.

DIRECTOR
Enrique Jara
HEAD OF NEWS
Stephen Claypole
MANAGER, Facilities
Howard Barrow

Peter Rogers Productions Ltd.

Pinewood Studios, Iver Heath, Bucks SL0 0NH. Tel: 0753 651700. FAX: 0753 656844.

EXECUTIVE PRODUCER
Peter Rogers

Romulus Films, Ltd.

214, The Chambers, Chelsea Harbour, London, SW10 0XF. Tel: 071 376 3791. FAX: 071 352 7457.

DIRECTORS
Sir John Woolf (Chairman), Lady Woolf, J. C. Woolf, M.A., C. E. Fielding

Royal Society for the Protection of Birds (RSPB)

Film and Video Unit, The Lodge, Sandy, Beds. SG19 2DL. Tel: 0767 680551. Telex: 82469 RSPB. FAX: 0767 692365.

CONTACT
Colin Skevington

Safir Films Ltd.

22 Soho Square, London, WIV 5FJ. Tel: 071 734 5085/6; FAX: 071 734 1329. Cables: Safirfilm, London, W.I.

DIRECTORS
Doris Safir, Lawrence Safir, Sidney Safir

Salamander Film Productions Ltd.

Seven Pines, Wentworth, Surrey. FAX: 0344 845174.

DIRECTORS
Bryan Forbes, Nanette Forbes, John L. Hargreaves

Sales Company, The

62 Shaftesbury Ave., London, W1V 7AA. Tel: 071 434 9061. FAX: 071 494 3293.

CONTACT
Alison Thompson

Scimitar Films Ltd.

6-8 Sackville Street, London, W1X 1DD. Tel: 071 734 8385. FAX: 071 602 9217.

DIRECTORS
Michael Winner, M.A. (Cantab), John Fraser, M.A. (Oxon), M.Phil

Scorer Films

53 Harrington Gardnes, London, SW7 4JZ. Tel: 071 244 6436.

Scott Free Enterprises Ltd.

6-10 Lexington St., London, W1R 36S. Tel: 071 437 7426.

Shand Pictures Ltd.

Rosehill House, Rose Hill Nr. Burnham, Bucks SL1 8NN. Tel: 068 605129.

DIRECTORS
I. E. L. Shand, D. J. Bennett, F. Shand

Shepperton Studios

Studios Road, Shepperton, Middx. TW17 0QD. Tel: 09325 62611. FAX: 0932 568989.

CONTACT
Paul Oliver

Siege Productions Ltd.

17 Adam's Row, London, W.1. Tel: 071 493 4441-2.

MANAGING DIRECTOR
Peter Fetterman

Skreba Films Ltd.

5a Noel St., London, W1V 3RB. Tel: 071 437 6492. FAX: 071 437 0644.

Smart Egg Pictures

62 Brompton Road, London, SW3 1BW. Tel: 071 581 1841. Telex: 27786 GZOM G. FAX: 071 581 8998.

Sovereign Pictures Inc.

10 Greek Street, London, W1V 5LE. Tel: 071 494 1010. FAX: 071 494 3949. Telex: 261564 SOVE G.

Sovexport Film

24 HIllway, Highgate, London, N6 6QA. Tel: 081 340 1223. FAX: 081 348 1390.

CONTACT
Sergei I. Kuzmenko

The Robert Stigwood Organisation Ltd.

118-120 Wardour Street, London. Tel: 071 437 2512. Telex: 264267.

DIRECTORS
Robert Stigwood, David Land, David Herring

TKO Communications Ltd.

P.O. Box 130, Hove, East Sussex, BN3 6QV. Tel: 0273 550088. FAX: 0273 540969.

DIRECTORS
J. S. Kruger, R. Kruger

Target International Ltd.

A29 Barwell Business Park, Leatherhead Road, Chessington Castle, Surrey KT9 2NY. Tel: 081 974 1021. FAX: 081 974 2674.

Tartan Films Ltd.

40 Bernard St., London, WC1N 1LG. Tel: 071 837 3377. FAX: 071 833 4102.

CONTACT
Hamish McAlpine

Technicolor Ltd.

(Subsidiary of Carlton Communication Plc.)
Bath Road, P.O. Box No. 7, West Drayton, Middlesex, UB7 0DB. Tel: 081 759 5432; Telegraphic and Cable Address: Technicolor, West Drayton. Telex: 22344. FAX: 081 897 2666.

DIRECTORS
Ashley Hopkins (Managing Director & Chief Executive Officer), S. T. Baxter, D. Abdoo, G. Filardi (Italy).
DATE AND PLACE OF INCORPORATION
July 22, 1935, London
CAPITAL
Authorized G £1,100,000
ISSUED
£1,100,000 in shares of 25 p each

Telefilm Canada

London, W1R 5LE. Tel: 071 437 8308. Telex: 923 753. FAX: 071 734 8586.

Tiliris Film Productions

13A, Fitzgeorge Ave., London W14 0SY. Tel: 071 602 2824. FAX: 071 371 4709.

Titan International Productions Ltd.

185A Newmarket Road, Norwich, Norfolk, NR4 6AP. Tel: 0603 51139.

DIRECTORS
P. Newbrook, B.S.C., E. Newbrook

Troy Films, Ltd.

%Film Rights Ltd., Hammer House, 113 Wardour Street, London, W1V 4EH. Tel: 071 437 7151.

DIRECTORS
Michael Anderson, Maurice Lambert

Twentieth Century Fox Film Co., Ltd.

20th Century House, 31-32 Soho Square, London, W1V 6AP. Tel: 071 437 7766. FAX: 071 434 2170.

DIRECTORS
S. Moore, P. Livingstone
SECRETARY
P.L. Higginson
DATE OF INCORPORATION
March 29, 1916
SHARES
100,000 Ordinary of £1 each. Fully paid

Twentieth Century Fox Productions, Ltd.

31/32 Soho Square, London, W1V 6AP. Tel: 071 437 7766. FAX: 071 434 2170.
DIRECTORS
P. Higginson, S. Moore

Twickenham Film Studios Ltd.

St. Margarets, Twickenham, Middlesex, TW1 2AW. Tel: 081 892 4477. Telex.: 8814497, TWIKST G. FAX: 081 891 0168.
DIRECTORS
G. Coen, G. Humphreys, M. Landsberger, N. Daou, Stephen J. Mullens
SECRETARY
A. Boys
CAPITAL
£251650

Tyburn Productions Ltd.

Pinewood Studios, Iver Heath, Bucks. Tel: 0753 651700. Telex: 847505. FAX: 0753 656844.
DIRECTORS
Kevin Francis, Gillian Garrow
CHIEF EXECUTIVE
Kevin Francis
DIRECTOR OF RESEARCH AND DEVELOPMENT
Gillian Garrow
CONTROLLER OF LEGAL AND BUSINESS AFFAIRS
Brett A. Vautier
MUSIC SUPERVISOR
Philip Martell
ACCOUNTS CONTROLLER
Alan Mabbott
TECHNICAL SUPERVISOR
Annie Wallbank
ADMINISTRATOR
Annette Pearse

United Artists Screen Entertainment Ltd.

84-86 Regent Street, London, W1R 5PF. Tel: 071 915 1717. FAX: 071 734 8411.
DIRECTORS
Alan Ladd, Jr., Charles Meeker, Sanford Lieberson, Ken Meyer, Brian Yell
CONTACT IN LONDON
Sandy Lieberson

United Cinemas International UK, Ltd.

Lee House, 90 Great Bridgewater Street, Manchester, MI 5JW. Tel: 061 455 4000; FAX: 061 455 4079.
CONTACT
Ian Riches

United International Pictures

(A subsidiary of UNITED INTERNATIONAL PICTURES B.V., Postbus 9255, 1006 AG Amsterdam, The Netherlands.)
UIP House, 45 Beadon Road, Hammersmith, London, W6 0EG. Tel: 081 741 9041. Telex: 8956521. FAX: 081 748 8990. (Distribution.)
PRESIDENT AND CHIEF EXECUTIVE OFFICER
Michael Williams-Jones
SENIOR VICE PRESIDENTS
Brian Reilly (general counsel), Hy Smith (marketing), Peter Charles (finance & administration), Andrew Cripps (intl. sales)
MARKETING/SALES EXECUTIVES
Anne Bennett (VP publicity); Mark deQuervain (v.p. promotions); Michael Macclesfield (VP sales—special markets); Michael Murphy (VP sales—Latin America); Tony Themistocleous (VP sales—Europe); Gina Stroud (VP advertising).
SENIOR EXECUTIVE/GENERAL MANAGER–PAY-TV GROUP
Andrew Kaza

United International Pictures (UK)

Mortimer House, 37-41 Mortimer Street, London, W1A 2JL. Tel: 071 636 1655. Telex.: 261818. FAX: 071 637 4043.
MANAGING DIRECTOR
Christopher Hedges

Universal Pictures Ltd.

% UIP House, 45 Beadon Rd., Hammersmith, London, W6 0EG. Tel: 081 563 4329. FAX: 081 563 4331.

Video Collection International

Strand House, Caxton Way, Watford, WD1 8VF. Tel: 0923 55558.

Visual Programme Systems Ltd.

Sardinia House, 52 Lincoln's Inn Fields, London, WC2A 2L2. Tel: 071 405 0438. FAX: 071 831 9668.
CONTACT
Bernard Gilinsky

Walport International Ltd.

(Subsidiary of B.E.T. Security & Communications)
Walport House, 62/66 Whitfield Street, London, W1P 6JH. Tel: 071 631 4373. Cables: Sewalport, London, W.1. Telex: 261567. FAX: 071 636 0631.
DIRECTORS
C.D. Ring (chmn.), C. Welsh (managing)

Warfield Productions Ltd.

2 South Audley Street, London, W1Y 5DQ. Tel: 071 493 7953. Cables: Brocfilm London W.1.

Warner Bros. Distributors Ltd.

135 Wardour Street, London, W1V 4AP. Tel: 071 437 5600. Telex: 22653. FAX: 071 465 4869.
DIRECTORS
R. Fox, C. Young, E. Savat, W. Duband, C. Lima

Warner Bros. Operational Division

135 Wardour Street, London, W1V 4AP. Tel: 071 734 8400. FAX: 071 437 2950.
MANAGING DIRECTOR
Maj-Britt Kirchner

Warner Bros. Productions Ltd.

Warner Suite, Pinewood Studios, Iver Heath, Bucks., SL0 0NH. Tel: 0753 654545.
DIRECTORS
R. D. Button (Managing), E. H. Senat, A. R. Parsons

Welbeck Film Distributors, Ltd.

52 Queen Anne Street, London, W1M 9LA. Tel: 071 935 1186.
DIRECTORS
Mrs. B. E. Rogers, R. P. Thomas, J. Thomas

West One Film Producers Ltd.

% Cooper Murray, Princess House, 50-60 Eastcastle Street, London, W1A 4BY. Tel: 071 436 4773. FAX: 071 436 1889. Date and place of incorporation: London, January 30, 1964.

DIRECTOR
Anthony Simmons
SECRETARY
S. Simmons

Michael White Productions Ltd.

13 Duke St., St. James', London, SW1Y 6DB. Tel: 01 839 3971. FAX: 01 839 3836.
DIRECTORS
Michael S. White, Louise M. White

Richard Williams Animation Ltd.

Richard Williams Studio, The Forum, 74-80 Camden Street, London NW1 0EG. Tel: 071 383 3831. FAX: 071 383 3263.
DIRECTOR
Richard Williams

Winkast Film Productions Ltd.

Pinewood Studios, Iver Heath, Bucks, SL0 0NH. Tel: 0753 651700. FAX: 0753 652525.
DIRECTORS
Cassian Elwes, George Pappas
CONTACT
Chantal Ribeiro

Working Title Films Ltd.

1 Water Lane, Kentish Town Road, London, NW1 8NZ. Tel: 071 911 6100. Telex: 914106. FAX: 071-911 6150/1.
CONTACTS
Tim Bevan, Eric Fellner

World Film Services Ltd.

12-14 Argyll Street, London, WIV 1AB. Tel: 071 734 3536; FAX: 071 437 4098.
DIRECTORS
John Heyman (chairman), John Chambers (managing), Michael Simkins

Worldmark Productions, Ltd.

The Old Studio, 18 Middle Row, London, W10 5AT. Tel: 081 960 3251. FAX: 081-960 6150.
DIRECTOR
Drummond Challis

World Wide Group Ltd.

21-25 St. Anne's Court, London, W1V 3AW. Tel: 071 434 1121. FAX: 071 734 0619.
CONTACTS
R. King, R. Townsend, Brian Redhead, C. Courtenay Taylor

Christopher Young Films Ltd.

102 Brandon Street, London, SE17 IAL. Tel: 071 708 0820.

Zenith Group

43-45 Dorset Street, London W1H 4AB. Tel: 071 224 2440. FAX: 071 224 3194.
DIRECTOR OF PRODUCTION
Scott Meek

British Trade Organizations, and Government Units

Amalgamated Engineering & Electrical Union (EETPU Section)

Hayes Court, West Common Road, Bromley, BR2 7AU. Tel: 081 462 7755; FAX: 081 462 4959.
(Representing electrical electronic/lighting operatives engaged in studio production, electrical maintenance and location lighting.)
GENERAL SECRETARY
Paul Gallagher

Association of Professional Recording Services Ltd.

2 Windsor Square, Silver Sheet, Reading, Berks. RG1 2TH. Tel: 0734 756218. FAX: 0734 756216.
CHIEF EXECUTIVE
Philip Vaughan

British Academy of Film and Television Arts

195 Piccadilly, London, W1V 9LG. Tel: 071 734 0022. FAX: 071 734 1792.
PRESIDENT
H. R. H. The Princess Royal
VICE PRESIDENTS
Lord Richard Attenborough, C.B.E., David Puttnam
CHAIRMAN
Ted Childs
DIRECTOR
Tony Byrne
HON. TREASURER
Ronnie Kennedy
The British Academy of Film and Television Arts exists in order to promote, improve, and advance original and creative work amongst people engaged in film and television production.

British Actors' Equity Association

(Incorporating the Variety Artistes' Federation)
Guild House, Upper St. Martin's Lane, London, WC2 9EG. Tel: 071 379 6000; FAX: 071 379 7001.
PRESIDENT
Jeffry Wickham
GENERAL SECRETARY
Ian McGarry
VICE PRESIDENTS
Dave Eager and Helen Lambert

British Board of Film Classification

3, Soho Square, London, W1V 5DE. Tel: 071 439 7961; FAX: 071 287 0141.
PRESIDENT
Earl of Harewood
DIRECTOR
James Ferman

British Federation of Film Societies

21 Stephen Street, London, W1P 1PL. Tel: 071 255 1444. FAX: 071 255 2315.

British Film Commission

70 Baker Street, London W1M 1DJ. Tel: 071 224 5000. FAX: 071 224 1013.
COMMISSIONER
Sydney Samuelson

British Film Designers Guild

24 St. Anselm's Place, London, W1Y 1FG. Tel: 071 499 4336.
EXECUTIVE CONSULTANT
John French

British Kinematograph, Sound, and Television Society

M6-M14 Victoria House, Vernon Place, London, WC1B 4DF. Tel: 071 242 8400. FAX: 071 405 3560.
HON. SECRETARY
Ray Clipson
Founded in 1931, the Society was incorporated in 1946 to service the industries of its title encouraging technical and scientific progress. To further these aims, the Society disseminates to its Members information on technical developments within these industries, arranges technical lectures, international conferences and demonstrations, and encourages the exchange of ideas. The broad nature of its purpose is made possible by the subscriptions of its Members and by its freedom from political or commercial bias. The *BKSTS Journal*, "Image Technology," and Cinema Technology are published and sent free to members.

British Music Information Centre

(Reference library of works by 20th century British composers.)
10 Stratford Place, London, W1N 9AE. Tel: 071 499 8567; FAX: 071 499 4795.
CENTRE MANAGEMENT
Tom Morgan/Matthew Greenall

British Society of Cinematographers, Ltd.

(To promote and encourage the pursuit of the highest standards in the craft of motion picture photography)
Tree Tops, 11 Croft Road, Chalfont St. Peter Gerrards Cross, Bucks., SL9 9AE. Tel: 0753 888052; FAX: 0753 891486.
PRESIDENT
Harvey Harrison
SECRETARY & TREASURER
Frances Russell

British Videogram Association Ltd.

22 Poland Street, London, W1V 3DD. Tel: 071 437 5722. FAX: 071 437 0477.
DIRECTOR GENERAL
Norman Abbott

Broadcasting Entertainment and Theatre Cinematograph Union

111 Wardour Street, London, W1V 4BE. Tel: 071 437 8506. FAX: 071 437 8268.

Central Casting, Ltd.

Licensed annually by the Dept. of Employment.
162-170 Wardour Street, London, W1V 3AT. Tel: 071 437 1881. FAX: 071 437 2614.
DIRECTORS
R. McCallum, T. Burrill, G. Smith, M. O'Sullivan, J. Sargent, B.T. Yeoman, J. Woodward

Children's Film & Television Foundation, Ltd.

Elstree Studios, Boreham Wood, Herts., WD6 1JG. Tel: 081 953 0844. FAX: 081 207 0860.

CHIEF EXECUTIVE AND SECRETARY
Stanley T. Taylor, FCIS
DATE OF INCORPORATION
July 18, 1951
(Non-profit company set up by the six trade associations for the purpose of ensuring the production, distribution and exhibition of entertainment films specially suited for children.)

Cinema Advertising Association, Ltd.

127 Wardour Street, London, W1V 4AD. Tel: 071 439 9531. FAX: 071 439 2395.

SECRETARY
Paul Butler
PRINCIPAL OBJECTS
The CAA is a trade association of cinema and theatre screen advertising contractors operating in the United Kingdom and Eire. It is responsible for ensuring that commercials exhibited on cinema screens conform to the Code of Advertising Practice and that professional standards are both met and maintained by the cinema advertising industry. The association also conducts research into the cinema medium and its audiences and publishes booklets providing information on cinema.
Membership is confined to firms and companies engaged in the buying and selling of screen space for advertising purposes.

Cinema and Television Benevolent Fund

(Founded 1924)
22 Golden Square, London, WIR 4AD. Tel: 071 437 6567. FAX: 071 437 7186.

EXECUTIVE DIRECTOR
P. J. C. Ratcliffe, O.B.E.
APPEALS AND PUBLIC RELATIONS OFFICER
Sandra Bradley
The Fund gives relief by financial grants and allowances to needy members or ex-members of the Film Industry or Independent Television, and their widows; maintenance and education of orphans and relief in sickness, unemployment or old age and generally to assist those in distress. Convalescence is available to assist in recovery after illness or operations at "Glebelands," Wokingham, Berkshire. Admission for convalescence and other information on CTBF, free upon application.

Cinema Exhibitors' Association

22 Soho Square, London, WIR 3PA. Tel: 071 734 9551. FAX: 071 734 6147.

OFFICERS
President—I. N. Riches, United Cinemas International (UK) Ltd., Parkside House, 51-53 Brick Street, London W1Y 7DU. (071-409 1346)
Vice-Presidents—J. Maynard, The Rank Organisation, 439-445 Godstone Road, Whyteleafe, Surrey CR3 OYG. (0883 623355). R. C. Warbey, MGM Cinemas, 84-86 Regent Street, London W1R 5FP. (071 915 1717)
Immediate Past President—M. J. Vickers, 6 Ryders Avenue, Westgate-on-Sea, Kent CT8 8LN. (0843 834609)
Honorary Treasurer—B. J. F. Bull, 1 Teamans Row, Morganstown, Radyr, Cardiff. (0222 522606)
Chief Executive—John Wilkinson, CEA, 22 Soho Square, London, WIR 3PA (071 734 9551, FAX: 071 734 6147)

DELEGATES
Birmingham, Midlands & North Staffordshire Branch—M. P. Jervis, Kings Cinema Screens 1, 2, 3, Kings Square, West Bromwich, Staffs. (021-553 0030).
Devon, Cornwall & West of England Branch—P. J. Hoare, Alexandra Theatre, Newton Abbott, Devon. (0626 65368)
London Regional Branch—C. Green, Regal Cinema, Hans Place, Cromer, Norfolk NR27 9EQ (0263 513311) G. Worley, The Riverside Theatre, Quayside, Woodbridge, Suffolk IP12 1BH. (0394 380571) Mrs. D. Dowson, Coronet Cinema, Notting Hill Gate, London W11 3LB (071 221 0123) K.R. Markwick, Hallmark Cinemas, Picture House, High Street, Uckfield, Essex TN22 1AS. (0825 763822)
Deputy: G. F. Mintern, "Encore", 49 The Close, Grey's Road, Henley-on-Thames, Oxon, RG9 1SR. (0491 575698)

Manchester & Northern Counties Branch—G. B. Henshaw, Cine City, Wilmslow Road, Withington, Manchester M20 9BG. (061-445 0368) J. S. Downs, Cosmo Leisure Group, Central Hall, 62/4 Market Street, Stalybridge, Cheshire SK15 2AB. (061 338 7953)
Scottish Branch—D. M. Cameron, Dominion Cinema, Newbattle Terrace, Morningside, Edinburgh (031 447 2660)
South Wales & Monmouthshire Branch—S. Reynolds, Scala Cinema, Pontypool, Gwent (0495 756038).

CIRCUIT DELEGATES
MGM Cinemas—84-86 Regent Street, London W1R 5PF. (071-915 1717). B. C. Jenkins, S. A. Hall, M. Evans, J. Sturdy, G. Rymer, K. Pullinger, B. Smith, R. Wallis, J. H. Osborne, A. McCann, T. Reade, J. Nunes, D. Wright, R. Newcombe
Odeon Cinemas—54 Whitcomb Street, London WC2H 7DN (071-839 6373) 439-445 Godstone Road, Whyteleafe, Surrey, CR3 OYG (0883 623355). L. R. Clarke (Whyteleafe), S. Fishman (Whitcomb Street), M. G. Walker (Whyteleafe), N. J. A. Pidgeon (Whyteleafe), M. Archibald (Whitcomb Street), D. Morton (Whyteleafe), A. Robertshaw (Whyteleafe), M. Fisher, Rank Theatres Training School, Kingswest, West Street, Brighton, Sussex, A. Williams, Odeon Theatre, Leicester Square, London W.C.2.
United Cinemas International (UK)—Parkside House, 51-53 Brick Street, London W1Y 7DU (071 409 1346). Bridgewater House, P.O. Box No. 168, Whitworth Street, Manchester (061 236 5660). I. N. Riches (Brick Street), Miss F. Skeffington (Brick Street), A. McNair (Brick Street), G. Laurence (Manchester), S. Knibbs (Manchester).
National Amusements (UK) Ltd.—200 Elm Street, Dedham, Massachusetts 02026, UNITED STATES OF AMERICA (0101 617 461 1600). Showcase Cinema, Redfield Road, Lenton, Nottingham NG7 2UW. (0602 862508). Ira A. Korff (USA), J. Bilsborough (Nottingham).
Warner Bros. Theatres (UK)—135 Wardour Street, London W1V 4AP (071-437 5600). S. Wiener, P. Dobson.
CAC Leisure PLC.—Regent House, 76 Renfield Street, Glasgow G2 INQ (041-332 0606). P.O. Box 21, 23/25 Huntly Street, Inverness IV1 1LA (0463 237611). I. Cluley, 16 Locarno Road, Acton, London, W3 6RG (081-993 1511), A. Macgregor (Glasgow).
Apollo Leisure Group—424 Woolton Road, Liverpool L25 6AQ (051-708 6672) Boar's Hill, P.O. 16, Oxford OX1 5JB (0865 730066). G. S. Lipson (Liverpool), J. Merryweather, 199 Glenfield Road, Leicester LE3 6DL. (0257 471012)
CEA Branch Secretaries
Birmingham, Midlands & North Staffordshire Branch–Victoria Playhouse Group, 8 Gate Lane, Sutton Coldfield, West Midlands, B73 5TT. (021 355 5032), S. W. Clarke.
Devon, Cornwall & West of England Branch–6 Elmside, Willand Old Village, Nr. Cullompton, Devon EX15 2RN. (0884 33398), L. G. Vearncombe.
London Regional Branch–Capitol Cinema (Ward End) Ltd., 6 Russell Court, Russell Terrace, Leamington Spa CV31 1EY. (0926 422157), Mrs. J. G. M. Rabbitts.
Manchester & Northern Counties Branch–Cheshire County Cinemas Ltd., Plaza Buildings, Witton Street, Northwich, Cheshire CW9 5EA. (0606 48375), R. I. Godfrey.
Scottish Branch–30-34 Reform Street, Dundee, Fife. DD1 1RJ (0382 29222), N. J. A. Robertson, Messrs. Blackadder, Reid, Johnston.
South Wales & Monmouthshire–Scala Cinema, Pontypool, Gwent. (0495 756038), S. Reynolds.

Composers' Guild of Great Britain

34 Hanway Street, London, W1P 9DE. Tel: 071 436 0007. FAX: 071 436 1913. (Objects: to further artistic and professional interests of its members.)

PRESIDENT
Sir Peter Maxwell Davies, C.B.E.
GENERAL SECRETARY
Heather Rosenblatt

Critics' Circle

(Film Section)
CHAIRMAN
George Perry, 7 Ruehampton Lane, London, SW15 5LS.
HON. SECRETARY
John Marriott, 73 Hornsey Lane, Highgate, London, N6 5LQ.

Directors Guild of Great Britain

Suffolk House, 1-8 Whitfield Place, London, W1P 55F. Tel: 071 383 3858. FAX: 071 383 5173.

Edinburgh and Lothian Screen Industries Office

Filmhouse, 88 Lothian Road, Edinburgh EH3 9BZ, Scotland. Tel: 031 228 5960; FAX: 031 228 5967.
The regional film commission for Edinburgh and the Lothians, providing location help and advice, permits and red-tape cutting service.

Entertainment Agents' Association (Great Britain)

54 Keyes House, Dolphin Square, London, SW1V 3NA. Tel: 071 834 0515. FAX: 071 821 0261.
PRESIDENT
Kenneth Earle
SECRETARY
Ivan Birchall
OBJECTS
Founded in 1927, the Association is a professional trade organisation for agents in all fields of the entertainment industry.

Federation Against Copyright Theft (FACT)

7 Victory Business Centre, Worton Road, Isleworth, Middx., TW7 6ER. Tel: 081 568 6646. Fax: 081 560 6364.
DIRECTOR GENERAL
R. Dixon

Film Artistes' Association

(Trade Union No. 1990) F.A.A. House, 61 Marloes Road, London, W8 6LE. Tel: 071 937 4567; FAX: 071 937 0790.
GENERAL SECRETARY
George Avory

Film Censor's Office

16 Harcourt Terrace, Dublin 2, Republic of Ireland. Tel: 01 676 1985
CONTACT
Sheamus Smith

Guild of British Camera Technicians

5-11 Taunton Road, Metropolitan Centre, Greenford, Middx., UB6 8UQ. Tel: 081 578 9243. FAX: 081 575 5972.
CONTACT
Penny Burnham

Guild of British Film Editors

Travair, Spurlands End Road, Great Kingshill, High Wycombe, Bucks., HP15 6HY. Tel: 0494 712313. FAX: 02406 3563.
HON. SECRETARY
Alfred E. Cox
HON. TREASURER
Gillian Dearberg
OBJECTS
To ensure that the true value of film and sound editing is recognized not only by those engaged in it but by the whole of the film industry as an important part of the creative and artistic aspect of film production.

Guild of Film Production Executives

Pinewood Studios, Iver, Bucks. Tel: 0753 651700.
PRESIDENT
Ian Lewis

HON. SECRETARY
Denis Holt

Guild of Film Production Accountants and Financial Administrators

Twickenham Film Studios, St. Margarets, Twickenham, Middx., TW1 2AW. Tel: 081 892 4477. Telex: 884497 TWIKST G. FAX: 081 891 5574.
PRESIDENT
John Sargent
HON. SECRETARY
Maurice Landsberger

Independent Film Distributors' Association

%Connoisseur Video Ltd., 10A Stephen Mews, London, WIA 0AX. Tel: 071 957 8957; FAX: 071 957 8968.

Independent Programme Producers' Association

50-51 Berwick Street, London, W1A 4RD. Tel: 071 439 7034. FAX: 071 494 2700.
DIRECTOR
Margaret Windam Heffernan

International Animated Film Association

61 Railwayside, Barnes, London, SW13 0PQ. Tel: 081 878 4040; FAX: 081 675 8499.
VICE PRESIDENT
Pat Raine Webb
OBJECTS
Include the promotion of animation in all its apsects; economics, creativity and the expansion of its scope and uses. It provides partronage to many festivals including major international animated film festivals in Europe, North America and Asia.

International Association of Broadcasting Manufacturers

4-B, High St., Burnham, Slough SL1 7JH. Tel: 0628 667633. FAX: 0628 665882.
CHAIRMAN
Tom McGann
SECRETARY
Claude Guillaume
TREASURER
Dan Anco
ADMINISTRATOR
Alan Hirst
SECRETARIAT
Ken Walker
OBJECTS
The IABM was formed in 1976 with the purpose of fostering and coordinating the wide common interests of manufacturers of sound and television equipment and associated products worldwide.

International Visual Communications Association (IVCA)

Bolsover House, 5-6 Clipstone Street, London, W1P 7EB. Tel: 071 580 0962. FAX: 071 436 2606.
EXECUTIVE DIRECTOR
Stuart Appleton

Irish Actors Equity Group

Liberty Hall, Dublin 1, Republic of Ireland. Tel: 8740081. FAX: 8743691.
GROUP SECRETARY
Gerard Browne

Irish Film Institute

6 Eustace St., Dublin 2, Republic of Ireland. Tel: 01 679 5744. FAX: 01 679 9657.

Mechanical-Copyright Protection Society, Ltd. (MCPS)

Elgar House, 41 Streatham High Road, London, SW16 1ER. Tel: 081 769 4400. FAX: 081 769 8792. Telex: 946792 MCPS G.

OBJECTS
MCPS is an organisation of music publishers and composers, which collects and distributes 'mechanical' royalties due from the recording of their copyright musical works. These royalties accrue from the recording of music onto CD's, discs, cassettes, videos, advertising, audio-visual and broadcast productions.
MCPS is able to offer free advice on the recording of copyright music and is able to arrange the licences required for the use of music in a wide range of productions.

CUSTOMER SERVICE ADVISOR
Andy Armour

Motion Picture Export Association of America, Inc.

162-170 Wardour Street, London, W1V 3AT. Tel: 071 437 2282. FAX: 071 439 1885.

VICE PRESIDENT AND MANAGING DIRECTOR
Harlan G. Moen
DEPUTY DIRECTORS
Frank Tonini, Georg Eriksson.

Musicians' Union

60-62 Clapham Road, London, SW9 0JJ. Tel: 071 582 5566. FAX: 071 582 9805.

GENERAL SECRETARY
Dennis Scard

PACT Ltd.

(Producers Alliance for Cinema and Television)
Gordon House, Greencoat Place, London, SW1P 1PH. Tel: 071 233 6000. FAX: 071 233 8935.

CHIEF EXECUTIVE
John Woodward
MEMBERSHIP OFFICER
Martin Hart

The Performing Right Society Ltd. (PRS)

29/33 Berners Street, London, W1P 4AA. Tel: 071 580 5544. Telex: 892678 PRSLONG. FAX: 071 631 4138.

CHIEF EXECUTIVE
Edward McLean
PUBLIC AFFAIRS CONTROLLER
Terri Anderson
(Representing the composers and publishers of music.)

The Personal Managers' Assn. Ltd.

Rivercroft, One Summer Road, East Molesey, Surrey KT8 9LX. Tel: 081 398 9796. FAX: 081 398 9796.

SECRETARY
Angela Adler
An association of the principal personal managers who represent stars, feature players, authors, writers, producers, directors and technicians.

St. Paul Book and Media Centre

5A-7 Royal Exchange Square, Glasgow, G1 3AH, Scotland. Tel: 041 226 3391.

Educational and religious videos and 35mm filmstrips/audio-visual materials.

Scientific Film Association

%British Universities Film & Video Council, 55 Greek Street, London, W1V 5LR. Tel: 071 734 3687. FAX: 071 287 3914.

SECRETARY
Murray Weston

Screen Advertising World Association Ltd.

103A Oxford Street, London, W1R 1TF. Tel: 071 734 7621.

SECRETARY GENERAL
Charles Sciberras

Society of Film Distributors Ltd.

22 Golden Square, London, W1R 3PA. Tel: 071 437 4383. FAX: 071 734 0912.

PRESIDENT
James Higgins, M.B.E.
GENERAL SECRETARY
D. C. Hunt
SFD COUNCIL MEMBERS
Buena Vista Int. (UK) Ltd., Columbia Tri-Star Films UK, First Independent Films Ltd., Entertainment Film Dist. Ltd., Gala Film Dist., Guild Film Dist. Ltd., Mayfair Entertainment UK LTD, Rank Film Dist. Ltd., Twentieth Century Fox Film Co. Ltd., United International Pictures (UK), Warner Bros. Ltd.

Sound & Communications Industries Federation

4-B High Street, Burnham, Slough SL1 7JH. Tel: 0628 667633. FAX: 0628 665882.

CHIEF EXECUTIVE
Ken Walker, M.B.E.

Variety Club of Gt. Britain (Tent No. 36)

32 Welbeck Street, London, W1M 7PG. Tel: 071 935 4466. FAX: 071 487 4174.

Purposes: The purpose of association is to provide a means by which persons of good moral character and reputation engaged in the motion picture, theatrical, amusement, sports and allied industries, wherever situated, may associate in friendly relationship, and by such association support worthy children's charitable projects, foster high ideals and ethics in the motion picture, theatrical, amusement, sports and allied industries.

The Writers' Guild of Great Britain

430 Edgware Road, London, W2 1EH. Tel: 071 723 8074. FAX: 071 706 2413.

PRESIDENT
Alan Plater
HON. TREASURER
Cecil Howard
GENERAL SECRETARY
Alison Gray
The Writers Guild of Great Britain is the TUC affiliated union which is the recognised representative body for negotiating agreements for screenwriters in film, television, and radio as well as in the field of theatre and of publishing. As well as negotiating industrial agreements, the Guild represents writers wherever their interests need to be represented.

Government Divisions On Film Affairs

Australian Film Commission

2nd Floor, Victory House, 99-101 Regent Street, London, W1R 7HB. Tel: 071 734 9383. FAX: 071 434 0170.

British Council Events Section

Film, TV and Video Department, 11 Portland Place, London, W1N 4EJ. Tel: 071 389 3063/4. FAX: 071 389 3041. Telex: 8952201 BRICON G.

FESTIVALS OFFICERS
Kevin Franklin, Sativant Gill
OTHER EVENTS
Geraldine Higgins, Jo Maurice

British Film Institute (BFI)

21 Stephen Street, London, W1P 1PL. Tel: 071 255 1444. FAX: 071 436 7950. Telex: 27624 BFILDNG.

The BFI exists to encourage the development of film, television and video in the United Kingdom and to promote knowledge, understanding and enjoyment of the culture of the moving image. The Board of Governors is appointed by the Minister for National Heritage. Two are selected by a poll of the membership. The BFI's divisions and departments include BFI on the South Bank (National Film Theatre, Museum of the Moving Image and London Film Festival); Research (Research and Education, Book Publishing and the monthly 'Sight and Sound' magazine); the National Film and Television Archive including the BFI Stills, Posters and Designs collection; Exhibition and Distribution; Library and Information Services; Planning Unit; and BFI Production.

CHAIRMAN
Jeremy Thomas
DIRECTOR
Wilf Stevenson

British Film Commission

70 Baker Street, London, W1M 1DJ. Tel: 071 224 5000. FAX: 071 224 1013.

COMMISSIONER
Sydney Samuelson
CHIEF EXECUTIVE
Andrew Patrick

British Screen Advisory Council

93 Wardour Street, London, W1V 3TE. Tel: 071 413 8009. FAX: 071 734 5122.

CHAIRMAN
Lord Richard Attenborough
HONORARY PRESIDENT
Lord Wilson of Rievaulx

DEPUTY CHAIRMEN
Michael Deeley, John Hawkins, Colin Leventhal
ADMINISTRATOR
Lisa Prime

Central Office of Information

Hercules Road, London, SE1 7DU. Tel: 071 928 2345. FAX: 071 261 8874.

DIRECTOR OF FILMS, TELEVISION AND RADIO DIVISION
Malcolm Nisbet

Department of National Heritage Media Division (Films)

2-4 Cockspur Street, London, SWIY 5DH. Tel: 071 211 6000; FAX: 071 211 6210.

National Film and Television School

Beaconsfield Studios, Station Road, Beaconsfield, Bucks., HP9 1LG. Tel: 0494 671234. FAX: 0494 674042
DIRECTOR
Henning Camre

The Services Sound & Vision Corporation

Chalfont Grove, Narcot Lane, Gerrards Cross, Bucks., SL9 8TN. Tel: 02407 4461. Telegrams: Serkincor, Gerrards Cross. Telex: 837254. FAX: 02407 2982.

PATRON
H.R.H. The Princess Margaret
BOARD OF MANAGEMENT CHAIRMAN
Group Captain G. H. Pirie, C.U.O. C.B.E. D.L.
MANAGING DIRECTOR
Alan H. Protheroe, C.B.E., T.D., F.B.I.M.
ASSISTANT DIRECTOR (Marketing)
Renate Foster
PURCHASING MANAGER
Anne Eva
(All film matters for the Army, Royal Air Force and U.K. Shore Establishments of the Royal Navy are handled by the SSVC. The Corporation produces training films and film strips for the Army, and distributes and exhibits training and entertainment films to the Forces throughout the world. Under the terms of its charter the facilities and services of the Corporation may also be used for the production or exhibition of training or educational films for any Government department.)

690

British and Irish Studio Facilities, Laboratories and Video Services

Studio Facilities

ABBEY ROAD STUDIOS., 3 Abbey Road, St. John's Wood, London, NW8 9AY. Tel: 071 286 1161. FAX: 071 289 7527.

ANVIL FILM AND RECORDING GROUP LTD., Denham Studios, North Orbital Road, Denham, Nr. Uxbridge, Middlesex, UB9 5HH. Tel: 0895 833522. Telex: 934704 FAX: 0895 833617.

BRAY STUDIOS., Windsor Road, Windsor, Berks SL4 5UG. Tel: 0628 22111. FAX: 0628 770381. 4 Stages total 23,600 square feet. All depts., theatre, workshops bar and catering. Contact: Karen Jones.

CARLTON BROADCAST FACILITIES., St. John's Wood Terrace, London NW8 6PY. Tel: 071 722 8111. FAX: 071 483 4264. Sound stage. (63 × 32 × 25). Cyclorama 16 ft. high. Managing Director: Andrew Jones.

CENTRAL TELEVISION STUDIOS., Lenton Lane, Nottingham NG7 2NA. Tel: 0602 863322. FAX: 0602 435142. Contact: Nic Beeby.

CHANNEL 4 TELEVISION., 60 Charlotte Street, London, WIP 2AX. Tel: 071 631 4444. FAX: 071 637 1495. Contact: Diana Brown.

DE LANE LEA SOUND CENTRE., 75 Dean Street, London, W1V 5HA. Tel: 071 439 1721. FAX: 071 437 0913. Contact: Richard Paynter.

FOUNTAIN TELEVISION., 128 Wembley Park Drive, Wembley, Middx., HA9 8HQ. Tel: 081 900 1188. FAX: 081 900 2860. Contact: Brianan Dolan.

HALLIFORD FILM STUDIOS LTD., Manygate Lane, Shepperton, Middlesex, TW17 9EG. Tel: 0 932 226341. FAX: 0932 246336., 2 stages (60 × 60; 60 × 40) totalling 6,000 square feet. Studio Manager: Allan dÁguiar.

HILLSIDE STUDIOS, Merry Hill Road, Bushey, Watford, WD2 1DR. Tel: 081 950 7919; FAX: 081 950 1437. Contact: Dave Hillier.

LIMEHOUSE. (Limehouse Television Ltd.), The Trocadero, 19 Rupert Street, London, W1V 7FS. Tel: 071 287 3333. FAX: 071 287 1998. Contact: A. Goddard.

MTM ARDMORE STUDIOS CTD., Herbert Road Bray, Co. Wicklow, Ireland. Tel: 0404 416 2971. FAX: 0404 416 1894. Telex: 91504 PATT EI.

PINEWOOD STUDIOS., Iver Heath, Bucks. SL0 0NH. Tel: 0753 651700. Telex: 847505 Pine w G. FAX: 0753 656844. Managing Director: Stephen Jaggs. 17 stages, exterior lot (72 acres) and largest outdoor tank in Europe; sound and projection department; 5 theatres, 50 cutting rooms.

SHEPPERTON STUDIOS, Studios Road, Shepperton, Middlesex, TW17 0QD. Tel: 09325 62611. Contact: Paul Olliver. FAX: 0932 568989. 12 sound stages, 3 silent stages.

TWICKENHAM, St. Margarets, Twickenham, Middx., TW1 2AW. Tel: 081 892 4477, Cables: Twikstudios, Twickenham. Telex: 8814497 TWIKST G. Owned by Twickenham Film Studios, Ltd.—Three stages. RCA sound. Recording and dubbing theatre with 36 in-put 6 track stereo rock and roll. High speed (6 times). Directors: G. Coen, G. Humphreys, M. Landsberger, N. Daou, Stephen J. Mullens. Executive Director: G. Coen.

JOHN WOODSOUND LTD., St. Martin's Studios, Greenbank Road, Ashton-upon-Mersey, Sale, Cheshire, M33 5PN. Tel: 061 905 2077. FAX: 061 905 2382. Contact: John Wood.

Film and Video Services

BUCKS MOTION PICTURE LABORATORIES LTD., 714 Banbury Avenue, Slough, Berks., SL1 4LH. Tel: 0753 576611. FAX: 0753 691762. Also West End pickup and delivery at Roger Cherrills, 65-66 Dean Street, London, W1V 5HD. Contacts: Harry Rushton, Mike Bianchi.

COLOUR FILM SERVICES LTD., 10 Wadsworth Road, Perivale, Greenford, Middx. UB6 7JX. Tel: 081 998 2731. FAX: 081 997 8738. Telex: 24672. HEAD OFFICE: 22-25 Portman Close, London, W1A 4BE. Tel: 071 486 2881. Telex: 24672.

FILMATIC LABORATORIES LTD., 16 Colville Road, London, W11 2BS. Tel: 071 221 6081. FAX: 071 229 2718. Chairman & Managing Director: D. L. Gibbs. Assistant Managing Director: I. Magowan.

METROCOLOR LONDON, LTD., 91/95 Gillespie Road, Highbury, London, N5 1LS. Tel: 071 226 4422; Telex 28463. Also 22 Soho Square, London, W1V 5FL. Tel: 071 437 7811. Telex 28463. FAX: 071 359 2353. Managing Director: Brian Compton.

RANK FILM LABORATORIES, Denham, Uxbridge, Middlesex, UB9 5HQ. Telex: 934704. Tel: 0895 832323. FAX: 0895 833617. Managing Director: J. W. Downer. Director of Sales: David Dowler. Sales Controller, Theatrical: Peter MacCrimmon.

RANK VIDEO SERVICES LTD., Phoenix Park, Great West Road, Brentford, Middlesex, TW8 9PL. Tel: 081 568 4311. Telex: 22345.

STUDIO FILM & VIDEO LABORATORIES, LTD., 8-14 Meard Street, London, W1V 3HR. Tel: 071 437 0831. FAX: 071 734 1834. Managing Director: Ray Adams.

TECHNICOLOR LTD., P.O. Box 7 Bath Road, West Drayton, Middlesex, UB7 0DB. Tel: 081 759 5432. Telex: 22344. FAX: 081 897 2666. Managing Director: Ashley Hopkins.

Costume Suppliers

ANGELS & BERMANS, 119 Shaftesbury Avenue, London, WC2H 8AE. Tel: 071 836 5678. FAX: 071 240 9527. Chairman: Tim Angel. Sales Director: Ron Mawbey.

ART & ARCHERY, The Coach House, London Road, Ware, Herts, SG12 9QU. Tel: 0920 460335. FAX: 0920 461044. Contact: Terry Goulden.

CARLO MANZI RENTALS, 32-33 Liddell Road, London, NW6 2EW. Tel: 071 625 6391. FAX: 071 625 5386.

COSPROP LTD., 26-28 Rochester Place, London, NW1 9JR. Tel: 071 485 6731. FAX: 071 485 5942. Contact: Bernie Chapman.

THE COSTUME STUDIO, 6 Penton Grove, Off White Lion Street, London, N1 9HS. Tel: 071 388 4481. FAX: 071 837 5326. Contact: Rupert Clive, Richard Dudley.

Exhibition Circuits

ABBEY FILMS LTD, 135 Upper Abbey Street, Dublin 1. Tel: Dublin 723922. FAX: Dublin 723687. Managing Director: Leo Ward.

APOLLO LEISURE GROUP, 424 Woolton Road, Liverpool L25 6AQ. Tel: 051 708 6672. Contacts: G. S. Lipson, J. Merryweather

CAC LEISURE Plc., Regent House, 76 Reinfield Street, Glasgow G2 1NQ, Scotland. Tel: 041 332 0606. Contacts: I. Cluley, A. Macgregor

CIC THEATRES, Lee House, 90 Great Bridgewater Street, Manchester MI 5JW. Tel: 061 455 4000. FAX: 061 455 4079. Contact: Ian Riches.

FOCUS CINEMAS LTD., 147-149 Wardour Street, London, W1V 3TB. Tel: 071 434 1961.

GALLERY CINEMAS, Nightingale House, 65 Curzon Steet, London, W1Y 7PE. Tel: 071 629 9642.

KINE SUPPLIES (BIRMINGHAM) LTD., Regal Buildings, Augusta Place, Leamington Spa CV32 5EP. Tel: 0926 22157.

KINGSWAY ENTERTAINMENTS LTD., 110/112 Rosslyn Street, Kirkealdy, Scotland. Tel: Kirkcaldy 52323.

MGM CINEMAS LTD., 84-86 Regent Street, London, W1R 5PA. Tel: 071 915 1717. FAX: 071 734 8410.

NATIONAL AMUSEMENTS (UK), 200 Elm Street, Dedham, MA 02026, USA. Tel: 0101 617 461 1600. And: Showcase Cinema, Redfield Rd., Lenton, Nottingham, NG7 2UW. Tel: 0602 862508. Contacts: Ira A. Korff (USA), J. Bilsborough.

ODEON CINEMAS, 439-445 Godstone Road, Whyteleafe, Surrey, CR3 0YG. Tel: 0883 623355. Telex: 262 305. FAX: 0883 626717 and 54 Whitcomb Street, London, WC2H 7DN. Tel: 071 839 6373. FAX: 071 321 0357. Managing Director: Laurie Clarke. Bookings Director: S. Fishman.

RECORDED CINEMAS, 155-157 Oxford St., London, W1R 1TB. Tel: 071 734 7477.

UNITED CINEMAS INTERNATIONAL UK Lee House, 90 Great Bridgewater Street, Manchester, MI 5JW. Tel: 061 455 4000. FAX: 061 455 4079. Contact: Ian Riches.

WARNER BROS. THEATRES UK, 135 Wardour Street, London, W1V 4AP. Tel: 071 437 5600. Contacts: S. Wiener, P. Dobson.

Central London Cinemas

BARBICAN CENTRE CINEMA, Silk Street, Barbican, London, EC2Y 8DS. Tel: 071 638 4141.

CANNON EDGWARE ROAD, Edgware Road NW1. Tel: 071 723 5901.

CORONET NOTTINGHILL GATE, 103 Notting Hill Gate, London, W11 3LB. Tel: 071 727 6705.

CURZON MAYFAIR, Curzon Street W1. Tel: 071 499 3737.

CURZON PHOENIX, Charing Cross Road WC1. Tel: 071 240 9661.

CURZON WEST END, Shaftesbury Avenue W1. Tel: 071 439 4805.

EMPIRE LEICESTER SQUARE, Leicester Square WC2. Tel: 081 200 0200.

ICA CINEMA, The Mall, London, SWIY 5A11. Tel: 071 930 0493. FAX: 071 873 0051.

LUMIERE, St. Martin's Lane WC2. Tel: 071 836 0691.

MGM BAKER STREET, Marylebone Road NW1. Tel: 071 935 9772.

MGM COVENTRY STREET, 13 Coventry Street, London, WIV 7FE. Tel: 071 434 0034.

MGM CHELSEA, Kings Road SW3. Tel: 071 352 5096.

MGM FULHAM ROAD, Fulham Road SW10. Tel: 071 370 2636/ 0265.

MGM HAYMARKET, Haymarket SW1. Tel: 071 839 1528.

MGM OXFORD STREET, Oxford Street W1. Tel: 071 636 0310.

MGM PANTON STREET, SW1. Tel 071 930 0632.

MGM PICCADILLY, Piccadilly W1. Tel: 071 437 3561.

MGM SHAFTESBURY AVENUE, Shaftesbury Avenue W1. Tel: 071 836 8861/8606.

MGM TOTTENHAM COURT ROAD, Tottenham Court Road W1. Tel: 071 636 6148.

MGM TROCADERO, London, W.1. Tel: 071 434 0031.

MINEMA, 45 Knightsbridge, SW3. Tel: 071 235 4225.

MEZZANINE LEICESTER SQUARE, Leicester Square, WC2. Tel: 071 930 6111.

ODEON HAYMARKET, Haymarket W1. Tel: 071 839 7697.

ODEON HIGH STREET KENSINGTON, Kensington High Street W8. Tel: 071 602 6644.

ODEON LEICESTER SQUARE, Leicester Square WC2. Tel: 071 930 6111.

ODEON LEICESTER SQUARE THEATRE, Leicester Square WC2. Tel: 071 930 5252/7615.

ODEON MARBLE ARCH, Marble Arch W1. Tel: 071 723 2011.

PLAZA, Lower Regent Street W1. Tel: 081 200 0200.

PREMIERE SWISS CENTRE, Leicester Square WC2. Tel: 071 439 4470.

PRINCE CHARLES, Leicester Square WC2. Tel: 071 437 8181.

RENOIR, Brunswick Square WC1. Tel: 071 837 8402.

SCREEN ON THE GREEN, Islington Green N1. Tel: 071 226 3520.

WARNER WEST END, Leicester Square WC2. 071 439 0791.

WHITELEYS UCI BAYSWATER, Queensway W2. Tel: 071 229 4149.

Public Relations, Publicity Marketing Services

BLUE DOLPHIN FILMS, 40 Langham Street, London, WIN 5RG. Tel: 071 255 2494. FAX: 071 580 7670.

BURNUP SERVICE LTD., 15 Samuel Road, Langdon Hills, Basildon, Essex, SS16 6EZ, England. Tel: 0268 417055.

MAX CLIFFORD ASSOCIATES, 109 New Bond Street, London. W1Y 9AA. Tel. 071 408 2350. FAX: 071 409 2294.

CORBETT & KEENE, 122 Wardour St., London W1V 3TD. Tel: 071 494 3478. FAX: 071 734 2024.

CONSOLIDATED COMMUNICATIONS MANAGEMENT, 1-5 Poland Street, London, WIV 3DG. Tel: 071 287 2087. FAX: 071 734 0772.

NAMARA COWAN LTD, 45 Poland Street, London, W1V 3DF. Tel: 071 434 3871. Telex: 919034. FAX: 071 439 6489.

CREATIVE PARTNERSHIP, 19 Greek Street, London, W.1. Tel: 071 439 7762. FAX: 071 437 1467.

DENNIS DAVIDSON ASSOCIATES LTD., Royalty House, 72-74 Dean Street, London, W1V 5HB. Tel: 071 439 6391. Telex: 24148 DADASS G. FAX: 071 437 6358.

CLIFFORD ELSON PUBLICITY LTD., 223 Regent Street, London, W1R 7DG. Tel: 071 495 4012. FAX: 071 495 4175.

EDELMAN PUBLIC RELATIONS Kings Gate House, 536 Kings Road, London, SW10 0TE, Tel: 071 835 1222. FAX: 071 351 7676.

FEREF ASSOCIATES LTD., 14/17 Wells MEWS, London, W1A 1ET. Tel: 071 580 6546. FAX: 071 631 3156.

MARGARET GARDNER CONSULTANTS, 1 Brighton Road, Redhill, Surrey, RH1 6PW. Tel: 071 584 6700. FAX: 071 581 9823.

SUE HYMAN ASSOCIATES LTD., 70 Chalk Farm Road, London, N.W.1 8AN. Tel: 071 485 8489. FAX: 071 267 4715.

IMPRESSION MEDIA & PUBLIC RELATIONS, Premier House, 77 Oxford St., London, W1R 1RB. Tel: 071 439 1188. FAX: 071 734 8367.

INTERMARK PUBLIC RELATIONS LTD., 91 Regent Street, London, W1R 7TB. Tel: 071 937 1284. FAX: 071 734 1014.

JAC PUBLICITY & MARKETING CONSULTANTS LTD. 113 Wardour Street, London, W.1. Tel: 071 734 6965. Telex: 28553 JAC PUB.G. FAX: 071 439 1400.

CAROLYN JARDINE PUBLICITY, 2nd fl., 3 Richmond Bldgs., London, W1V 5EA. Tel: 071 287 6661. FAX: 071 437 0499.

RICHARD LAVER PUBLICITY, 3 Troy Court, High Street Kensington, London, W.8. 7RA. Tel: 071 937 7322. FAX: 071 937 8670.

MEDIA RELATIONS LTD., Judy Tarlo Division, Glen House, 125 Old Brompton Road, London SW7 3RP. Telephone: 071 835 1000. FAX: 071 373 0265.

PEARTREE ASSOCIATES LTD., Cloister Court, 22 Farringdon Lane, London, ECIR 3AV. Tel: 071 250 0292. FAX: 071 250 3031.

ROGERS & COWAN INTERNATIONAL, 43 King Street, Covent Garden, London, WC2E 8RJ. Tel: 071 411 3000. FAX: 071 411 3020. Contacts: Phillip Symes, Brian Daly.

JUDY TARLO DIVISION Media Relations Ltd., Glen House, 125 Old Brompton Road, London, SW7 3RP. Tel: 071 835 1000. FAX: 071 373 0265.

PETER THOMPSON ASSOCIATES, 134 Great Portland Street, London, WIN 5PH. Tel: 071 436 5991. FAX: 071 436 0509.

TOWN HOUSE PUBLICITY, 45 Islington Park Street, London, N1 1QB. Tel: 071 226 7450. FAX: 071 359 6026.

WINSOR BECK PUBLIC RELATIONS, Network House, 29-39 Stirling Road, London, W3 8DJ. Tel: 081 993 7506. FAX: 081 993 8276.

Trade Publications

Broadcast

Published weekly by EMAP Media Ltd., 33-39 Bowling Green Lane, London, EC1R 0DA. Tel: 071 837 9263; FAX: 071 837 8250.

ASSOCIATE EDITOR
Quentin Smith

Eyepiece

Journal of the Guild of British Camera Technicians, 5-11 Taunton Road, Metropolitan Centre, Greenford, Middx., UB6 8UQ. Tel: 081-578 9243. FAX: 081-575 5972.

EDITORS
Charles Hewitt
Kerry Anne Burrows
ADVTG. MANAGER
Ron Bowyer

Image Technology

Journal of the British Kinematograph, Sound and Television Society. M6-M14 Victoria House, Vernon Place, London, WC1B 4DF. Tel.: 071-242 8400. FAX: 071-405 3560. 10 issues per year

EDITOR
John Gainsborough

Screen Digest

Published monthly by Screen Digest Ltd., 37 Gower Street, London, WC1E 6HH. Tel: 071 580 2842; FAX: 071 580 0060.

EDITORIAL CHAIRMAN
John Chittock, O.B.E.
EDITOR
David Fisher

Screen International

Published weekly by EMAP Media covering news, reviews, comment and pictures of the film and television industries. 33-39 Bowling Green Lane, London, EC1R 0DA. Tel: 071 837 1212; FAX: 071 837 8326.

EDITOR
Oscar Moore

Televisual

Published monthly by the Centaur Group, St. Giles House, 50 Poland Street, London, W1V 4AX. Tel: 071-439 4222. FAX: 071-287 0768.

PUBLISHER
Tim Macpherson
EDITOR
Mundy Ellis

Financial Services and Funding

ARTS COUNCIL FILMS, 14 Great Peter Street, London, SW1P 3NQ. Tel: 071 973 6454. FAX: 071 973 6581.

BARCLAYS BANK PLC, The Media Section, Barclays Business Centre, 27 Soho Square, London, W1A 4WA. Tel: 071 439 6851. FAX: 071 434 9035.

BRITISH & COMMONWEALTH MERCHANT BANK PLC., 62 Cannon Street, London, EC4N 6AE. Tel: 071 248 0900. FAX: 071 528 8444. Telex: 884040 BCMB G.

BRITISH SCREEN FINANCE LTD., 14/17 Wells Street, London, W1P 3FL. Tel: 071 323 9080. FAX: 071 323 0092.

COMPLETION BOND COMPANY INC., Pinewood Studios, Iver Heath, Bucks: SL0 0NH. Tel: 0753 651700. FAX: 0753 655697. CONTACT: John L. Hargreaves.

CONSOLIDATED ARTISTS, Strachans Somerville, Phillips Street, St. Helier, Jersey, Channel Islands. Tel: 0534 71505. FAX: 0534 23902.

CONTRACTS INTERNATIONAL LTD., 13-14 Golden Square, London, W1R 3AG. Tel: 071 287 5800. FAX: 071 287 3779. Telex: 295835.

ERNST & YOUNG, Beckett House, 1 Lambeth Palace Road, London, SE1 7EU. Tel: 071 928 2000. FAX: 071 401 2136.

EUROPEAN SCRIPT FUND, 39c Highbury Place, London, N5 1QP. Tel: 071 226 9903. FAX: 071 354 2706.

FILM FINANCES LTD., 1/11 Hay Hill, Berkeley Square, London, W1X 7LF. Tel: 071 629 6557. Telex: 298060 FILFIN G. FAX: 071 491 7530.

FILM TRUSTEES LTD., Swan House, 52 Poland Street, London, W1V 3DF. Tel: 071 439 8541. FAX: 071 495 3223. Telex: 23788.

FILMAKER COMPLETION (UK) LTD., Millard House, Cutler Street, London, E1 7DJ. Tel: 071 283 3951. Telex: 8956132 ROBTAY G. FAX: 071 621 0140.

INTERNATIONAL COMPLETION INC., Pinewood Studios, Pinewood Road, Iver Heath, Bucks: SL0 0NH. Tel: 0753 651 700. FAX: 0753 656 564.

INVESTORS LEASE MANAGEMENT GROUP, Economist's Bldg., 268 St. James St., London, SW1A 1HA. Tel: 071 839 2336. FAX: 071-930 3793.

J & M ENTERTAINMENT, 2 Dorset Square, London, NW1 6PU. Tel: 071 723 6544. FAX: 071 724 7541.

KMPG PEAT MARWICK, 1 Puddle Dock, Blackfriars, London, EC4V 3PD. Tel: 071 236 8000. FAX: 071 248 6552.

GUINNESS MAHON & CO. LTD., 32 St. Mary at Hill, London, EC3P 3AJ. Tel: 071 623 9333. FAX: 071 283 4811.

MANDEMAR FINANCE LTD., 113-117 Wardour St., London W1V 3TD. Tel: 071 434 9729. FAX: 071-734 4970.

MEDIA GUARANTORS INTERNATIONAL INC., 38 Dover St., London, W1X 3PB. Tel: 071 491 7311. FAX: 071 493 6729.

SAMUEL MONTAGU & CO. LTD., 10 Lower Thames Street, London EC3R 6AE. Tel: 071 260 9000. FAX: 071 488 1630.

MOTION PICTURE GUARANTORS LTD., Production Centre, 40-44 Clipstone St., London, W1P 7EA. Tel: 071 323 3220. FAX: 071 637 2590.

ONE WORLD COMMUNICATIONS, 1 Wardour Mews, London, W1V 3FF. Tel: 071 437 8381.

PARMEAD INSURANCE BROKERS, LTD., Artillery House, 35 Artillery Lane, London, E1 7LR. Tel: 081 467 8656.

PERFORMANCE GUARANTEES LTD., (AUSTRALIA) PTY LTD., 113-117 Wardour St., London, W1V 3TD. Tel: 071 434 9729. FAX: 071 734 4970.

PIERSON, HELDRING & PIERSON, 99 Gresham Street, London, EC2V 7PH. Tel: 071 696 0500. FAX: 071 600 1732. Telex: 885119.

PRODUCTION PROJECTS FUND, BFI, 29 Rathbone Place, London, W1P 1AG. Tel: 071 636 5587. FAX: 071 780 9456.

RUBEN SEDGWICK INSURANCE SERVICES, Pinewood Studios, Pinewood Road, Iver, Bucks: SL0 0NH. Tel: 011 44 753 654 555. Telex: 851 848708 SEDFOR G. FAX: 011 44 753 653 152.

SCOTTISH FILM PRODUCTION FUND, 74 Victoria Crescent Road, Glasgow, G12 9JN. Tel: 041 337 2526. FAX: 041 337 2562.

SPECTRUM ENTERTAINMENT GROUP PLC, The Pines, 11 Putney Hill, London, SW15 6BA. Tel: 081 780 2525. FAX: 081 780 1671. Telex: 262433.

STOY HAYWARD, 8 Baker Street, London, W1M 1DA. Tel: 071 486 5888. FAX: 071 487 3686. Contact: Carl Williams.

TOUCHE ROSS, Hill House, 1 Little New Street, London, EC4A 3TR. Tel: 071 936 3000. FAX: 071 538 8517.

UBA LTD., Pinewood Studios, Pinewood Road, Iver Heath, Bucks SL0 0NH. Tel: 0753 656699. FAX: 0753 656844.

UNITED MEDIA LTD., 2nd fl., Broadwick House, 8-12 Broadwick St., London, W1V 4EQ. Tel: 071 434 3501. FAX: 071 734 8893.

WASA FILM FINANCE CORP. LTD., 49 Park Lane, London, W1V 4EQ. Tel: 071 491 2822. FAX: 071 493 3710.

WILLIS WRIGHTSON LONDON LTD., Willis Wrightson House, Wood Street, Kingston-upon-Thames, Surrey KT1 1UG. Tel: 071 860 6000. Telex: 929606. FAX: 081 943 4297.

British-Based Equipment Companies and Services

ABEKAS COX ELECTRONICS

Hanworth Trading Estate, Feltham TW13 6DH. Tel: 081 894 5622. FAX: 081 898 0298.

ACMADE INTERNATIONAL LTD.

Shepperton Studios, P.O. Box 64, Studios Road, Shepperton, Middx. TW17 0QD. Tel: 0932 562611. FAX: 0932 568414.

ADVENT COMMUNICATIONS LTD.

Watermeadow House, Watermeadow Chesham, Bucks. HP5 1LF. Tel: 0494 774400. Telex: 838870 G.

AEG-TELEFUNKEN (UK) LTD.

217 Bath Road, Slough, Berks. SL1 4AW. Tel: 2-872101.

AGFA-GEVAERT LTD.
Motion Picture Division

27 Great West Road, Brentford, Middlesex TW8 9AX. Tel: 081 231 4310. FAX: 081 231 4315.

AKG ACOUSTICS LTD.

191 The Vale, London, W3 7QS. Tel: 081 749 2042.

AMEK SYSTEMS AND CONTROLS LIMITED

Islington Mill, James Street, Salford M3 5HW. Tel: 061 834 6747. Telex: 668127.

AMPEX INTERNATIONAL

Acre Road, Reading, RG2 0QR. Tel: 0734 875200. FAX: 0734 866693.

AMS NEVE PLC

Billington Road, Burnley, Lancs. BB11 5ES. Tel: 0282 57011. FAX: 0282 39542.

AMSTRAD PLC

Brentwood House, 169 Kings Road, Brentwood, Essex. CM14 4EF. Tel: 0277 228888.

ARRI (G.B.) LTD.

The Movie House, 1-3 Airlinks, Spitfire Way, Heston, Middlesex. Tel: 081 848 8881. FAX: 081 561 1312.

ASTON ELECTRONIC DEVELOPMENTS LIMITED

125 Deepcut Bridge Road, Deepcut, Camberley, Surrey. Tel: 02516 6221.

AUDIENCE SYSTEMS LTD.

Wahington Road, West Wilts. Trading Estate, Westbury, Wilts. BA13 4JP. Tel: 0373 865050.

AUDIO ENGINEERING LTD.

33 Endell St., London, WCZ. Tel: 071 836 9373.

AUDIO SYSTEMS COMPONENTS LTD.

1 Comet House, Calleva Park, Aldermaston, Reading, Berks. RG7 4QW. Tel: 07356 79565. FAX: 07356 71000.

AUDIX LTD.

Station Road, Wenden, Saffron Walden, Essex.

AUDIO KINETICS

Kinetic House, Theobald St., Boreham Wood, Herts. Tel: 081 953 8118.

AVS BROADCAST

Venture House, Davis Road, Chessington, Surrey KT9 1TT. Tel: 081 391 5678. FAX: 081 391 5409. Telex: 267439 AVS.

AV DISTRIBUTORS (LONDON) LTD.

21-22 St. Albans Place, Upper Street, Islington Green London N1 0NX. Tel: 071 226 1508.

BAL COMPONENTS LTD.

Bermuda Road, Nuneaton, Warwickshire, CV10 7QF. Tel: 0203 341111. Telex: 311563.

DAVID BAYLISS LTD.

Telegraph House, Royal Crescent Formby L37 6BT. Tel: 07048 79686. FAX: 07048 78608.

BAUCH SYSTEMS

49 Theobald Street, Boreham Wood, Herts. WD6 4RZ. Tel: 081 953 0091. Telex: 27502. FAX: 081 847 5803.

BELL THEATRE SERVICES LTD.

9-17 Park Royal Road, London, NW10 7LQ. Tel: 081 963 0354. FAX: 081 963 0622.

BLITZ VISION

Unit 2, 5 Garner Close, Grecaine Estate, Watford, Herts., WD2 4JL. Tel: 0923 819401.

ROBERT BOSCH LTD.

Broadwater Park, Denham, Uxbridge, Middx. UB9 5HJ. Tel: 0895 73750. FAX: 0895 73055.

BOSE (UK) LTD.

Trinity Trading Estate, Sittingbourne, Kent, ME10 2PD. Tel: 0795 75341. FAX: 0795 27227.

BOSTON INSULATED WIRE (UK) LTD.

1 Canbury Park Road, Kingston-upon-Thames, Surrey. Tel: 081 546 3384.

BRABURY ELECTRONICS LTD.

Smirham Bridge, Hungerford, Berks. RG17 1OQU. Tel: 04 886 5511.

C.A.T.S. UK LTD.

Eagle House, 108-110 Jermyn Street, London, SW1Y 6HB. Tel: 071 930 2294.

CFS EQUIPMENT LTD.

10 Wadsworth Road, Perivale, Greenford, Middx. UB6 7JX. Tel: 081 998 2731. Telex: 24672.

CP CASES

Worton Hall Industrial Estate, Worton Road, Isleworth, Middx. TW7 6ER. Tel: 081 568 1881. FAX: 081 568 1141.

CALDER EQUIPMENT LTD.

Batford Mill Industrial Estate, Lower Luton Rd., Harpenden, Herts. AL5 5 BZ. Tel: 05827 64331.

CAMERON VIDEO SYSTEMS LTD.

Burnfield Road, Glasgow G46 7TH, Scotland. Tel: 041 633 0077. FAX: 041 633 1745.

CANFORD AUDIO

Crowther Road, Washington, Tyne & Wear NE38 0BW. Tel: 091 415 0205. Telex: 538202 CANFRD G. FAX: 091 416 0392.

CANON (U.K.) LTD.

TV Products Dept., Canon House, 2 Manor Rd., Wallington, Surrey. SM6 0BW. Tel: 081 773 3173. FAX: 081 773 2851.

CARLTON COMMUNICATIONS, PLC.

15 St. George Street, London, W1R 9DE. Tel: 071 499 8050. FAX: 071 895 9575.

CEL ELECTRONICS LTD.

Chroma House, Shire Hill, Saffron Walden, Essex CB11 3AQ. Tel: 0799 23817. Telex: 817807 CHROMA G. FAX: 0799 28081.

CHRIS JAMES & CO. LTD.

Unit 7, North Western Commercial Centre, 75 Broadfield Lane, York Way, London, NW1 9YJ. Tel: 071 284 2221.

CHYRON GROUP

Dancon House, North Circular Road, London, NW10 75S. Tel: 081 965 6599. FAX: 081 965 3690.

CINE-EUROPE LTD.

7 Silver Road, White City Industrial Park, Wood Lane, London, W12 75G. Tel: 081 743 6762. FAX: 081 749 3501.

CINEMA SUPPLY AND DESIGN (UK) LTD.

13 Carters Lane, Kiln Farm, Milton Keynes, MK11 3ER. Tel: 0908 260666. FAX: 0908 567 989.

CINEVIDEO LTD.

7 Silver Road, White City Industrial Park, Wood Lane, London W12 7SG. Tel: 081 743 3839. Telex: 915 282 CINEGP G. FAX: 081 749 3501.

CONVERGENCE EDITING

(A division of Paltex Int.)
7 Airlinks, Spitfire Way, Heston, Middx. TW5 9NR. Tel: 081 759 3891. FAX: 081 561 1122.

COX ASSOCIATES LTD.

Cox House, Amberley Way, Hounslow, Middlesex TW4 6BH. Tel: 081 570 8283. Telex: 946441 COXAL G.

CROMA RESEARCH LTD.

Croma House, North Way, Walworth Industrial Estate, Andover, Hants SP10 5AZ. Tel: 0264 332132. Telex: 477407.

DESISTI LIGHTING (UK) LTD.

15 Old Market Street, Thetford, Norfolk IP24 2EQ. Tel: 0842 752909. FAX: 0842 753746.

DOLBY LABORATORIES INC.

346 Clapham Road, London SW9 9AP. Tel: 071 720 1111. Telex: 919109. FAX: 071 720 4118.

PHILLIP DRAKE ELECTRONICS LTD.

37 Broadwater Road, Welwyn Garden City, Herts AL7 3AX. Tel: 0707 333866. Telex: 25415 DRAKE G.

EDRIC AUDIO VISUAL LTD.

34-36 Oak End Way, Gerrards Cross, Bucks. SL9 8BR. Tel.: 02813 84646 and 86521.

EDS PORTAPROMPT LTD.

Lane End Road Sands, High Wycombe, Bucks HP12 4JQ. Tel: 0494 450414. Telex: 848314 CHACOM G. ATTN EDS. FAX: 0494 37591.

ELECTROSONIC LTD.

Hawley Mill, Hawley Rd., Dartford, Kent DA2 75Y. Tel: 0322 222211.

ELF AUDIO VISUAL LTD.

836 Yeovil Road, Trading Estate, Slough, Berks. Tel: 75 36123.

ENGLISH ELECTRIC VALVE COMPANY LIMITED

Chelmsford, Essex CM1 2QU. Tel: 0245 493493.

FILM CLINIC

8-14 Meard Street, London, W1V 3HR. Tel: 071 734 9235. FAX: 071 734 9471.

FILM STOCK CENTRE

68-70 Wardour Street, London, W1V 3HP. Tel: 071 734 0038.

FILMLAB SYSTEMS INTERNATIONAL LTD.

PO Box 297, Stokenchurch, High Wycombe HP14 3RH. Tel: 0494 485271. FAX: 0494 483079.

FUJI PHOTO FILM (UK) LTD.

Fuji Film House, 125 Finchley Road, Swiss Cottage, London, NW3 6JH. Tel: 071 586 5900. Telex: 8812995. FAX: 071 722 4259.

FUTURE FILM DEVELOPMENTS

11 The Green, Brill, Aylesbury HP18 9RU. Tel: 0844 238444. FAX: 0844 238106.

GE THORN LAMPS LTD.

Miles Road, Mitcham, Surrey CR4 3YX. Tel: 081 640 1221. FAX: 081 640 9760.

GEC CABLE SYSTEMS

P.O. Box 53. Copesewood. COVENTRY CV3 1HJ. Tel: 0203 433184. Telex: 31361 GECTEL G.

GEC (LAMPS AND LIGHTING) LTD.

PO Box 17, East Lane, Wembley, Middlesex HA9 7PG. Tel: 081 904 4321.

GML

143-145 Cardiff Road. Reading, Berks. RG1 8JF. Tel: 0734 584948. Telex: 847109 GUNML G.

GORDON AUDIO VISUAL LTD.

28 Market Place, Oxford Circus, London W1N 8PH. Tel: 071 580 9191.

GTE LIGHTING LTD.

Otley Rd., Charleston, Shipley, West Yorkshire. Tel: 0274 595921.

G2 SYSTEMS

5 Mead Lane, Farnham, Surrey GU9 7DY. Tel: 0252 737151. FAX: 0252 737147.

HARKNESS SCREENS AND HALL STAGE LTD.

The Gate Studios, Station Road, Boreham Wood, Herts. WD6 1DQ. Tel: 081 953 3611. Telex: 8955602 Perlux G. Cables: Screens London. FAX: 081 207 3657. Int. FAX: 44 1 207 3657.

HARMAN (AUDIO) UK LTD.

Mill Street, Stough, BERKS. SL2 5DD. Tel: 0753 76911.

HARMAN (AUDIO) UK LTD.

Mill Street, Slough, Berks. Tel: 0753 76911. FAX: 0753 35306.

HAYDEN LABORATORIES LTD.

Chiltern Hill, Chalfont St. Peter, Bucks. 9UG. Tel: 0753 888447. FAX: 0753 880109.

HITACHI DENSHI (UK) LTD.

13-14 Garrick Industrial Centre, Irving Way, Hendon, London, NW9 6A2. Tel: 081 202 4311. FAX: 081 202 2451.

HOLMES PHOTOGRAPHIC (LOWEL)

Unit 3, Kennet Enterprise Centre, Charnham Lane, Hungerford, Berks. RG17 0EY. Tel: 0488 85244. FAX: 0488 85248.

I.C. EQUIPMENT LTD.

Unit 1-3, The Robert Elliot Center, 1 Old Nichol Street, Shoreditch, London, E2 7HR. Tel: 071 739 4800. FAX: 071 729 2554.

IAN P. KINLOCH AND COMPANY LIMITED

3 Darwin Close, Reading, Berkshire, RG2 0TB. Tel: 0734 311030. Telex: 846787 IPK Co.

ICON SOFTWARE

Icon House, 376-378 Chiswick High Road, London, W4 5TF. Tel: 081 742 8770; FAX: 081 742 8772.

IKEGAMI ELECTRONICS

61 High Street, Kingston-upon-Thames, Surrey, KT1 1LO. Tel: 081 546 7772. Telex: 897005 ITCG.

INTERACT SYSTEMS LTD.

185 Ebberns Road, Hemel Hempstead, Herts: HP3 9RD. Tel: 0442 254110. FAX: 0442 232011.

INTERNATIONAL VIDEO CORPORATION (UK) LTD.

10 Portman Road, Reading, Berks, RG3 1JR. Tel: 0734 585421.

JVC PROFESSIONAL PRODUCTS (UK) LTD.

Alperton House, Bridgewater Road, Wembley, Middx. HA0 1EG. Tel: 081 902 8812. FAX: 081 900 0941.

JEMANI LTD.

Southampton House, 192-206 York Road, Battersea, London, SW11 3SA. Tel: 071 924 3887. FAX: 071 228 0451.

KODAK LIMITED

Motion Picture and Television Imaging, P.O. Box 66, Kodak House, Station Road, Hemel Hempstead, Herts. HP1 1JU. Tel: 0442 61122. FAX: 0442 844458.

LEE LIGHTING LTD.

Wycombe Road, Wembley, Middx., HA0 1QD. Tel: 081 900 2900.

LEE FILTERS LTD.

Walworth Industrial Estate, Andover, Hants. SP10 5AN Tel: 0264 366245. FAX: 0264 355058.

MALHAM PHOTOGRAPHIC EQUIPMENT LTD.

65-67 Malham Road, London, SE23 1AJ. Tel: 081 699 0917. FAX: 081 699 4291.

MARCONI COMMUNICATION SYSTEMS LTD.

Marconi House, New Street, Chelmsford, Essex CM1 1PL. Tel: 0245 353221.

MITCHELL CAMERAS

Wycombe Road, Wembley, Middx. HA0 1QN. Tel: 081 903 7933. FAX: 081 902 3273.

NEILSON-HORDELL LTD.

11 Central Trading Estate, Staines, Middlesex TW18 4UU. Tel: 0784 456456. FAX: 0784 459657.

OPTEX

22-26 Victoria Road, New Barnet, Herts. EN4 9PF. Tel: 081 441 2199. FAX: 081 449 3646.

OSRAM (GEC) LTD.

P.O. Box 17, East Lane, Wembley, Middlesex HA9 7PG. Tel: 081 904 4321.

OTARI ELECTRIC (UK) LTD.

22 Church Street, Slough, Berks, SL1 1PT. Tel: 0753 822381. FAX: 0753 83707.

P.A.G. FILM LTD., & P.A.G. POWER LTD.

565 Kingston Road, London SW20 85A. Tel: 081 543 3131.

PANASONIC BROADCAST EUROPE

107-109 Whitby Road, Slough, Berks. SL1 3DR. Tel: 0753 521626. FAX: 0753 512673.

PANDORA'S OTHER BOX LTD.

208A Main Road, Sutton-at-Hone, Dartford, Kent DA4 9HP. Tel: 0322 866 245.

PANAVISION U.K.

Wycombe Rd., Stonebridge Park, Wembley, Middx. HA0 1QN. Tel: 081 903 7933. FAX: 081 902 3273.

PEC VIDEO

2-4 Dean Street, London W1V 5RN. Tel: 071 437 4633. FAX: 071 287 0492.

PERFECTONE PRODUCTS SA.

Ladbroke Films Ltd., 4 Kensington Park Gardens, London, W11 3HB. Tel: 071 727 3541.

PHILIPS LIGHTING LTD.

City House, 420-430 London Road, Croydon, Surrey CR9 3QR. Tel: 081 689 2166. FAX: 081 665 5102.

PHOTOMEC (LONDON) LTD.

Valley Road Industrial Estate, St. Albans, AL3 6NU, Herts. Tel: 0727 50711. FAX: 0727 43991.

QUANTEL

31 Turnpike Road, Newbury, Berks: RG13 2NE. Tel: 0635 48222. FAX: 0635 31776.

RPS BROADCAST FACILITIES

10 Giltway, Giltbrook. Nottingham NG16 2GN. Tel: 0602 384103.

RTI (UK) LTD.

Unit 6, Swan Wharf Business Centre, Waterloo, Middx. UB8 2RA. Tel: 0895 52191. FAX: 0895 74692.

RADAMEC EPO LTD.

Bridge Road, Chertsey, Surrey, KT16 8LJ. Tel: 0932 561181. FAX: 0932 568775. Telex: 929945 RADEPO G.

RANK CINTEL

Watton Road, Ware, Hertfordshire SC12 0AE. Tel: 0920 463939. FAX: 0920 60803.

RANK FILM LABORATORIES LTD.

North Orbital Road, Denham, Uxbridge, Middlesex UB9 5HQ Tel: 0895 832323 Telex: 934704 FAX: 0895.833617.

RANK TAYLOR HOBSON LTD.

P.O. Box 36, 2 New Star Rd., Leicester LE4 7JQ. Tel: 0533 763771. FAX: 0533 740167.

RANK VIDEO SERVICES LTD.

Phoenix Park, Great West Road, Brentford, Middlesex TW8 9PL. Tel: 081-568 4311; Telex 22345; FAX: 081 847 4032.

PHILIP RIGBY AND SONS LTD.

14 Creighton Avenue, Muswell Hill, London, N10 1NU. Tel: 081 883 3703. FAX: 081 444 3620.

RONFORD-BAKER ENGINEERING CO. LTD.

Braziers, Oxhey Lane, Watford, Herts. WD1 4RJ. Tel: 081 428 5941. FAX: 081 428 4743.

ROSCOLAB LTD.

Blanchard Works, Kangley Bridge Road, Sydenham, London SE26 5AQ. Tel: 081 659 2300. FAX: 081 659 3153.

SAMUELSON FILM SERVICE LONDON LTD.

21 Derby Rd., Metropolitan Centre, Greenford, Middx. UB6 8UQ. Tel: 081 578 7887. FAX: 081 578 2733.

MICHAEL SAMUELSON LIGHTING LTD.

Pinewood Studios, Iver Heath, Bucks. SL0 0NH. Tel: 0753 631133. FAX: 0753 630485.

SCREEN SUBTITLING SYSTEM LTD.

The Old Rectory, Church Lane, Claydon, Ipswich, Suffolk, IP6 0EG. Tel: 0473 831700.

SCREENTECH

23 Wrotham Road, Gravesend, Kent DA11 0PA. Tel: 0474 333111. FAX: 0474 328184. Telex: 966475 VACORP.

SELTECH/SONDOR

Bourne End Business Centre, Cores End Road, Bourne End, Bucks. SL8 5AT. Tel: 06285 29131. FAX: 06285 27468.

SHURE ELECTRONICS LTD.

Eccleston Road, Maidstone, Kent, ME15 6AU. Tel: 0622 59881.

SIGMA FILM EQUIPMENT LTD.

Unit K, Chantry Lane Industrial Estate, Storrington, West Sussex, RH20 4AD. Tel: 0903 743382. FAX: 0903 745038.

SOLID STATE LOGIC

Begbroke, Oxford OX5 IRU. Tel: 0865 842300. FAX: 0865 842118.

SONY BROADCAST INTERNATIONAL

Jay Close, Viables, Basingstoke, Hants. RG22 4SB. Tel: 0256 55011. FAX: 0256 474585.

SOUND ASSOCIATES LTD.

56 Ayres Street, London, SW1 1EU. Tel: 071 403 5348. FAX: 071 403 5394.

SPACEWARD MICROSYSTEMS LTD.

The Old School, Haddenham, Cambridge CB6 3XA. Tel: 0353 741 222.

STRAND LIGHTING

Grant Way (off Syon Lane) Isleworth, Middlesex TW7 5QD. Tel: 081 560 3171. FAX: 081 490 0002.

SURVEY & GENERAL INSTRUMENT CO. LTD.

Fircroft Way, Edenbridge, Kent TN8 6HA. Tel: 0732 864111. Telex: 95527 OPTSLS G.

SYLVANIA LIGHTING

Otley Road, Charlestown Shipley, West Yorkshire, BD17 7SN. Tel: 0274 595921.

SYSTEM VIDEO LTD.

Venture House, Davis Rd., Chessington, Surrey KT9 1TT. Tel: 081 391 5678. FAX: 081 391 5522.

TECHNOVISION CAMERAS LTD.

Unit 4 St. Margarets Business Centre, Drummond Place, Twickenham, Middlesex TW1 1JN. Tel: 081 891 5961. FAX: 081 744 1154.

TELEFEX LTD.

1 Brentford Business Centre, Commerce Road, Brentford, Middx. Tel: 081 569 9595.

THOMSON VIDEO EQUIPMENT (UK)

18 Horton Road, Datchet, Berks. Tel: 0753 681 122. FAX: 0753 681 196.

TOPHAM FILM & ENG. LTD.

316-318 Latimer Road, London, W1O 6QN. Tel: 081 960 0123.

3M UNITED KINGDOM PLC

3M House, P.O. Box 1, Bracknell, Berkshire RG12 1JU. Tel: 0344 58571.

VALIANT ELECTRICAL WHOLESALE CO.

20 Lettice Street, Fulham, London SW6. Tel: 071 736 8115. FAX: 071 731 3339.

VAN DIEMEN FILMS LTD.

Bridge House, Branksome Park Road, Camberley, Surrey, GU15 2AQ. Tel: 0276 61222. FAX: 0276 61549.

VARIAN TVT LTD.

(Subsidiary of Varian Associates Inc. of California) P.O. Box 41, Coldhams Lane, Cambridge CB1 3JU. Tel: 0223 245115. Telex: 81342 VARTVTG. FAX: 0223 214632.

VG ELECTRONICS LTD.

Theaklen Drive, Hastings, East Sussex, TN34 1YQ. Tel: 0424 446888. Telex: 957357 VGELEC. FAX: 0424 435699.

VINTEN BROADCAST LTD.

Western Way, Bury St. Edmunds, Suffolk IP33 3TB. Tel: 0284 752121. FAX: 0284 750560.

VISTEK ELECTRONICS LTD.

Unit C, Wessex Road, Bourne End, Bucks. SL8 5DT. Tel: 06285 31221. Telex: 846077.

WESTAR SALES & SERVICES LTD.

Unit 7, Cowley Mill Trading Estate, Longbridge Way, Uxbridge, Middlesex UB8 2YG. Tel: 0895 34429. Telex: 8954 169.

WILMAC LTD.

Pine Lodge, Gannock Park, Deganwy, Conwy, Gwynedd. LL31 9P2. Tel: 0492 83757.

WINSTED

Units 3/4, Wassage Way, Hampton Lovett Industrial, Estate, Droitwich WR9 10NX. Tel: (0905) 770276. Telex: 334007 WINSTD G.

MEL WORSFOLD LTD.

66 Carlyle Rd., Ealing, London, W5 4BL. Tel: 081 568 7884. FAX: 081 569 8846.

WOTAN LAMPS LTD.

1 Gresham Way, Durnsford Road, London, SW19 8HU. Tel: 081 947 1261. FAX: 081-947 5132.

ZONAL LTD.

Holmethorpe Avenue, Redhill, Surrey, RH1 2NX. Tel: 0737 767171. FAX: 0737 767610.

Home Video Distributors

ABBEY HOME ENTERTAINMENTS, 106 Harrow Road, London, W12. Tel: 071 262 1012. Contact: Anne Miles.

BBC VIDEO, Woodlands, 80 Wood Lane, London, W12. Tel: 081 743 5588. Contact: Mike Diprose.

BECKMANN HOME VIDEO, Britannia House, 1-11 Glenthorne Road, Hammersmith, London, W6 OLF. Tel: 081 748 9898. FAX: 081 748 4250.

TERRY BLOOD DISTRIBUTION, 18-20 Rosevale Road, Parkhouse Industrial Estate, Newcastle-under-Lyme, Staffs. ST5 7QT. Tel: 0782 566566. Contact: D. A. McWilliam.

BUENA VISTA HOME VIDEO, Beaumont House, Kensington Village, Avonmore Road, London, W14 8TS. Tel: 071 605 2400. Contact: Phil Jackson.

CIC VIDEO, Glenthorne House, 5-17 Hammersmith Grove, London, W6 0ND. Tel: 081 846 9433. Contact: Graham Gutteridge.

CASTLE COMMUNICATIONS, 29 Barwell Business Park, Leatherhead Road, Chessington, Surrey, KT9 2NY. Tel: 081 974 1021. Contact: P. Gardiner.

CENTRAL TELEVISION ENTERPRISES, Hesketh House, 43-45 Portman Square, London, W1H 9FG. Tel: 071 486 6688. Contact: Lesley Fromant.

CHRYSALIS HOME VIDEO LTD., The Chrysalis Bldg., Bramley Rd., London, W10 6SP. Tel: 071 221 2213. Contact: Tina Lorenzo.

COLUMBIA TRISTAR HOME VIDEO, Horatio House, 77-85 Fulham Palace Road, London, W6 8JA. Tel: 081 748 6000. Contact: Cees Zwaard.

ENTERTAINMENT UK, Blyth Road, Hayes, Middx., UB4 1DN. Tel: 081 848 7511. Contact: Eddie Cunningham.

FIRST INDEPENDENT FILMS LTD., 69 New Oxford St., London WC1 1DG. Tel: 071 5287768. Contact: Ed Ramsey.

FOXVIDEO, 31-32 Soho Square, London, W1V 6AP. Tel: 071 753 8686. Contact: Stephen Moore.

GMH ENTERTAINMENTS, 22 Manasty Road, Orton Southgate, Peterborough, PE2 6UP. Tel: 0733 233464. Contact: Iain Muspratt.

GUILD HOME VIDEO LTD., Crown House, 2 Church Street, Walton-on-Thames, Surrey KT12 2QS. Tel: 081 546 3377. Contact: Nick Hill.

MANGA ENTERTAINMENT LTD., 40 St. Peters Road, London, W6 9BD. Tel: 081 748 9000. Contact: Andy Frain.

MGM/UA HOME VIDEO (UK) LTD., 84-86 Regent Street, London, W1R 5PF. Tel: 071 915 1717. FAX: 071 734 8411. Contact: Vanessa Bathfield

ODHAMS LEISURE GROUP, 6 Morris Close Park Farm, Industrial Estate, Wellingborough, Northants., NN8 6XF. Tel: 0933 402321. Contact: D. C. Rees.

ODYSSEY VIDEO, 15 Dufours Place, London, W1V 1FE. Tel: 071 437 8251. Contact: Adrian Munsey.

PICKWICK GROUP LTD., The Water Front, Elstree Road, Elstree, Herts., WD6 3EE. Tel: 081 207 6207. Contact: Gary LeCount.

POLYGRAM VIDEO LTD., P.O. Box 1425, Chancellors House, 72 Chancellors Rd., Hammersmith, London, W6 9QB. Tel: 081 846 8515. Contact: Peter Smith.

SCREEN ENTERTAINMENT, P.O. Box 161 Radlett, Herts. WD7 8ED. Tel: 0923 858043. Contact: Carey Budnick.

SONY MUSIC ENTERTAINMENT U.K. LTD., 17-19 Soho Square, London, W1V 6HE. Tel: 071 734 8181. Contact: David Black.

THAMES VIDEO LTD., Broom Road, Teddington Lock, Middx., TW11 9NT. Tel: 081 977 3252. Contact: Katherine Senior.

VIDEO COLLECTION INTERNATIONAL, Strand UCI, Caxton Way, Watford, Herts. WD1 8UF. Tel: 0923 255558. Contact: Paddy Toomey.

VISION VIDEO LTD., Atlantic House, 1 Rockley Road, London, W14 ODL. Tel: 081 740 5500. Contact: Johnny Fewings.

WARNER HOME VIDEO, 135 Wardour Street, London, W1V 4AP. Tel: 071 494 3441. Contact: Mike Heap.

The Industry in Canada

* **YEAR IN REVIEW**

* **PRODUCTION COMPANIES AND PERSONNEL**

* **STUDIO FACILITIES AND LABORATORIES,
    SOUND TRANSFER & MIXING**

* **DISTRIBUTION COMPANIES**

* **FILM CARRIERS**

* **CHIEF EXHIBITION CIRCUITS**

* **INDEPENDENT BOOKING COMPANIES**

* **GOVERNMENT AGENCIES—FEDERAL
    AND PROVINCIAL**

* **TRADE ASSOCIATIONS**

Canadian Year in Review

The recession is still affecting moviegoing in Canada and proving to be deeper and longer-lasting than anyone had predicted. Less people are going out to watch the big screens, and the box office appears to be dropping anywhere from 10–15 percent. A number of independent distribution companies have disappeared including Cinéphile and Brightstar Films in Toronto plus two western Canada groups—Festival Films, sold to C/FP Distribution, and Nova Entertainment, purchased by Malofilm Distribution in Montréal. Another important Montréal-based distribution company, Cinema Plus, declared bankruptcy.

At mid-1993 Paragon Entertainment, a leading production company, received conditional approval for shares to be traded publicly on the Toronto Stock Exchange. A few weeks later Alliance Communications, the largest production and distribution company in the country, announced that it intended to sell shares publicly on the Toronto Stock Exchange and filed a prospectus with the Ontario Securities Commission.

"Shadow of the Wolf", a Canada/France co-production, topped the box office with an accumulated gross of close to $C3 million. This arctic adventure epic cost a reputed $C31 million making it the most expensive movie ever made here. According to statistics rounded up by PLAYBACK magazine (a trade paper published out of Toronto every two weeks), for the period January 1 to December 31, 1992 box office receipts recorded by distributors showed that other top grossers were Jean-Claude Lauzon's "Léolo" ($C635,000—around $C500,000 of this in the province of Québec), David Cronenberg's "Naked Lunch" ($C600,000), Jean Beaudin's "Being At Home With Claude" ($C588,000—most of this in Québec) and Bruce McDonald's "Highway 61" ($C525,000). These receipts are considered to be respectable returns for indigenous product.

Cineplex Odeon is one of the largest theatre circuits in North America with 1,614 screens in 363 locations (both Canada and USA). It is an Ontario corporation, and expects to conduct approximately one-third of its 1993 operations in Canada. The Hon. Leo Kolber, Chairman, and Allen Karp, President and CEO, in a joint letter to shareholders in the 1992 Annual Report, stated that the Corporation had a positive cash flow for the first time since it began the restructing process in 1989. The Canadian circuit reported an increase in attendence of 4.2% over 1991, and concession revenues also rose by 4.2%. Total revenues (Canada and US) were $US518.7 million, down from $US538.2 million in 1991, due to price reductions, theatre sales and a lower value for the Canadian dollar. Despite $US19.6 million less in revenue in 1992, the Corporation reduced its net loss to $US41.3 million, which represents a 46.5% improvement on the 1991 net loss of $US77.2 million. In addition, the Corporation also cut its general and administrative expenses by 12.9%, after a reduction of 18.4% in 1991. The first quarter of 1993 showed a reduced net loss of $US10.8 million on revenues of $US116.6 million, compared to a net loss of $US13.9 million on revenus of $US129.9 million in the first quarter of 1992. General and administrative expenses were reduced to $US4.2 million in the first quarter of 1993, a 10.6% decrease compared to the first quarter of

1992. For the first quarter of 1993 attendance increased 3.3% at Canadian theatres compared to the same period in 1992, and the concession revenue increased by 10.5% over the same period in 1992. At mid-1993 admission prices in Canada were holding at $C8 for adults in major cities, and $C4 in smaller venues. There are special concessions for youths, children and seniors, and half-price regular adult admission applies on Tuesdays in many locations.

Famous Players operates at 124 locations with 482 screens, and is holding its adult admission price at $C8.

Don Haig, head of the National Film Board's Prairie Region and Michael Francis, chairman of British Columbia Film announced "Next Wave." This joint program is designed to encourage recent graduates from BC film study programs, or other collectives, to form teams to produce first low-budget dramatic feature films. Funding is by way of cash, services and facilities from the two partners worth up to $C15,000 per project, and the use of "low cost technologies" is encouraged. Hard on the heels of this project Haig, British Columbia Film and Telefilm Canada announced a further joint venture to fund low-budget features by emerging BC filmmakers. New Views III has evolved through a pilot program over the past two years, and will provide a first or second time filmmaker with 100% of the financing for a feature film up to a maximum of $C1 million.

The 1993–94 Action Plan for the administration of Telefilm Canada's funds and programs published in early 1993 took into account the already announced federal budget cuts faced by it and other cultural agencies—10% in program plus 3% in administrative for 1993 and 1994. In 1992–93 Telefilm's government appropriation was $C145.1 million, and in 1993–94 the Corporation expected to receive only $C132.4 million. However, its estimated budget for 93/94 amounts to $C148.9 million, with the difference to be covered by expected revenues of $C15 million ($C6.5 million net) and $C10 million carried over from the previous fiscal year. But the federal budget, in April 1993, then took back an extra $7.5 million (approx.) from revenue. It's a serious situation and one in which Telefilm will find it difficult to maintain its level of support to the industry over the past number of years.

Canadian films selected for Toronto's 1993 Festival of Festivals include David Wellington's "I Love a Man in Uniform" and Denys Arcand's first feature in English "Unidentified Human Remains and the True Nature of Love."

The U.S. films well-received at the Canadian box office included "A Few Good Men," "Scent of a Woman," "The Bodyguard," "Lorenzo's Oil," "Bram Stoker's Dracula," "A League of Their Own," "Unforgiven," "Dragon: The Bruce Lee Story," "Dave," "In The Line of Fire," "Indecent Proposal," "The Firm," "Made in America," "Cliffhanger," "Free Willy," "Sleepless in Seattle" and "Jurassic Park" (of course!). Two from the U.K. went over well, "The Crying Game" a spectacular (and unexpected) success and Branagh's "Much Ado About Nothing." Australia's "Strictly Ballroom" also scored.

—PATRICIA THOMPSON

Production Companies and Personnel

Abaton Pictures Inc.

185 Grace St., Toronto, Ont. M6G 3A7; (416) 537-2641; FAX: (416) 588-6125.
PRESIDENT
Ian McDougall

ABCO Film

A division of ABCO Trading Ltd.
1967 First Ave., Vancouver, B.C. V6J 1G2; (604) 731-0234; FAX: (604) 737-6851.
PRESIDENT
Mark Abedi

ABS Productions Limited

196 Joseph Zatzman Dr., Dartmouth, N.S. B3B 1N4; (902) 468-4336.
PRESIDENT
Robert G. Sandoz
TECHNICAL DIRECTOR
A. J. McKay

The Ace Film Co.

1040 Hamilton St., Ste. 402, Vancouver, B.C. V6B 2R9; (604) 682-0001; FAX: (604) 682-7346.
EXECUTIVE PRODUCER
Parker Jefferson

ACPAV

1050 boul. René-Lévesque est, bureau 200, Montréal, Qué. H2L 2L6; (514) 849-2281; FAX: (514) 849-9487.
PRODUCERS
Marc Daigle, François Dupuis, René Gueissaz, Bernadette Payeur, Marcel G. Sabourin

Allan King Associates Limited

965 Bay St., #2209, Toronto, Ont. M5S 2A3; (416) 964-7284.
PRESIDENT
Allan King

Allegro Films Inc.

2187 rue Larivière, Montréal, Qué. H2K 2A3; (514) 288-9408; FAX: (514) 288-5735.
Tom Berry, Franco Battista

Alliance Communications Corporation

920 Yonge St., Ste. 400, Toronto, Ont. M4W 3C7; (416) 967-1174; FAX: (416) 960-0971; 355 Place Royale, Montréal, Qué. H2Y 2V3; (514) 844-3132; FAX: (514) 284-2340; 301 North Canon Dr., Ste. 318, Beverly Hills, CA 90210; (310) 275-5501; FAX: (310) 275-5502. 40 rue Boissiere, 75116 Paris, France. 011 331 47 55 44 49; FAX: 011 331 47 55 94 83.
CHAIRMAN & CEO
Robert Lantos
VICE CHAIRMAN
Jay Firestone

Alligator Films

132 MacDonnell Ave., Toronto, Ont. M6R 2A5; (416) 534-7320.
PRODUCER/DIRECTOR
Bill Sweetman

Arto-Pelli Motion Pictures Inc.

18 Gloucester Lane, 3rd Fl., Toronto, Ont. M4Y 1L5; (416) 928-0164; FAX: (416) 928-3399.
PRODUCER
Stavros C. Stavrides
DEVELOPMENT
Athena Anders

Aska Film Productions Inc.

1600 ave. De Lorimier, Ste. 211, Montréal, Qué. H2K 3W5; (514) 527-6679; FAX: (514) 527-5921.
Claude Gagnon, Yuri Yoshimura-Gagnon

Asterisk Film & Videotape Productions Ltd.

72 Coolmine Rd., Toronto, Ont. M6J 3E9; (416) 532-4439; FAX: (416) 536-0645.
David Springbett, Heather MacAndrew

Astral Communications Inc.

An Astral Communications Company
2100 rue Ste-Catherine ouest, bureau 900, Montréal, Qué. H3H 2T3; (514) 939-5000; FAX: (514) 939-1515.
CHAIRMAN, PRESIDENT & CEO
Harold Greenberg
PRESIDENT
Stuart H. Cobbett
VICE-CHAIRMAN OF THE BOARD
Anmdré Bureau

Astral Communications Inc.

An Astral Communications Company
2100 rue Ste-Catherine ouest, bureau 900, Montréal, Qué. H3H 2T3; (514) 939-5000; FAX: (514) 939-1515. BCE Place, 181 Bay St., Ste. 100, Toronto, Ont. M5J 2T3; (416) 956-2000; FAXL (416) 956-2020.
CHAIRMAN
Harold Greenberg
EXECUTIVE VICE PRESIDENT
Sidney Greenberg
SENIOR VICE PRESIDENT, PACKAGING & DISTRIBUTION
Stephen Greenberg
VICE PRESIDENT, PROGRAM DEVELOPMENT & FINANCING
David Patterson

Atlantis Films Limited

65 Heward Ave., Toronto, Ont. M4M 2T5; (416) 462-0246.
Michael MacMillan, Seaton McLean, Peter Sussman, Ted Riley
505 - 1681 Chestnut St., Vancouver, B.C. V6J 4M6; (604) 737-7410; FAX: (604) 737-7462.
Bill Gray

Barna-Alper Productions Inc.

165 Danforth Ave., Ste. 201, Toronto, Ont. M4K 1N2; (416) 463-5142; FAX: (416) 463-1999.

Laszlo Barna, Laura Alper

Beacon Group Productions Ltd.

1285 W. Pender St., 9th Fl., Vancouver, B.C. V6E 4B1; (604) 684-6440; FAX: (604) 684-9272.

PRESIDENT & CEO
A. Grant Allen
SENIOR VICE PRESIDENT/CREATIVE PLANNING
Sean Allen

Beaver Creek Pictures

81 Main St., Unionville, Ont. L3R 2E6; (416) 477-3821; FAX: (416) 470-0410.

PRODUCER/DIRECTOR
Conrad Beaubien
EXECUTIVE PRODUCERS
Jane Beaubien, Eric Douglas

Blokland Pictures Corporation

4200 Dundas St. W., #1, Toronto, Ont. M8X 1Y6. (416) 234-8654; FAX: (416) 234-5190.

PRESIDENT
Jim Blokland

Bongard Films Inc.

59 Mutual St., Toronto, Ont. M5B 2A9; (416) 368-4593.

PRODUCER/DIRECTOR
Ralph Bongard
POST-PRODUCTION
Bob Buchan cfe

Bootleg Film Corporation

188 Spadina Ave., Ste. 705, Toronto, Ont. M5T 3A4; (416) 947-0147.

Milan Cheylow, Lori Lanses

Breakthrough Films & Television Inc.

179 Mavety St., Toronto, Ont. M6P 2M1; (415) 766-6588; FAX: (416) 769-1436.

DIRECTORS/PRODUCERS
Ira Levy
Peter Williamson

Brian Avery Audio

65 Hilton Ave., Toronto, Ont. M5R 3E5; (416) 538-3103.

Brian Avery

Brian Bobbie Productions Ltd.

1007 Broadview Ave., Toronto, Ont. M4K 2S1; (416) 467-9595; FAX: (416) 467-9782.

Brian Bobbie, Janice Bobbie

Bridge Film Productions Inc.

44 Charles St. W., Ste. 2518, Toronto, Ont. M4Y 1R7; (416) 927-0663.

Brigitte Berman

Bruce A. Raymond Productions Limited

11 Soho St., Ste. 202, Toronto, Ont. M5T 1Z6; (416) 340-0130; FAX: (416) 340-0135.

PRESIDENT
Bruce Raymond

Calgary Television Centre (CKKX)

222-23 St. N.E., Calgary, Alta. T2E 7N2; (403) 235-7733.

Kim Corrigall

Cambium Film & Video Productions Ltd.

141 Gerrard St. E., Toronto, Ont. M5A 2E3; (416) 964-8750; FAX: (416) 964-1980.

PRODUCERS/DIRECTORS
Bruce Glawson, Arnie Zipursky
VICE-PRESIDENT/PRODUCTION
Julie Quesnelle

Camera One Films Ltd.

81 MacLean Ave., Toronto, Ont. M4E 2Z8; (416) 694-9591.

PRODUCER/DIRECTOR
Elias Petras

Canamedia Productions Ltd.

125 Dupont St., Toronto, Ont. M5R 1V4; (416) 324-9190; FAX: (416) 967-6162.

PRESIDENT
Les Harris

Cannell Films Ltd.

555 Brooksbank Ave., N. Vancouver, B.C. V7J 3S5; (604) 983-5000; FAX: (604) 983-5198.

VICE-PRESIDENT & GENERAL MANAGER
Stephen Sassen

Carota Films Ltd.

Blue Cross Centre, Ste. 710, 644 Main St., Moncton, N.B. E1C 1E2; (506) 853-3073; FAX: (506) 853-5032.

Karen Carota, Peter Wood

Champlain Productions Inc.

4 Westmount Sq., Ste. 200, Westmount, Qué. H3Z 2S6; (514) 933-1161; FAX: (514) 933-1706.

CHAIRMAN
Adrien Pouliot
PRESIDENT & GENERAL MANAGER
Tom Froundjian

CHECK-HIT-OUT PRODUCTIONS

3726 blvd. St-Laurent, Montréal, Qué. HH2X, 2V8; (514) 843-4725; FAX: (514) 843-4631.

Claude Chamberlan
112 Mercer St., Ste. 5R, New York, NY 10021; Tel. & FAX: (212) 925-1575.

Chetwynd Productions Inc.

82 Pricefield Rd., Toronto, Ont. M4W 1Z9; Tel. & FAX: (416) 975-1827.

PRODUCER
Robin Chetwynd

Christopher Chapman Ltd.

415 Merton St., Toronto, Ont. M4S 1B4; (416) 487-3005.

PRESIDENT
Christopher Chapman

Chumcity

299 Queen St. W., Toronto, Ont. M5V 1Z5; (416) 591-5757; FAX: (416) 340-7005.

PRESIDENT/EXECUTIVE PRODUCER
Moses Znaimer
VICE-PRESIDENT & GENERAL MANAGER
Ron Waters

Cinak Ltée

C.P. 360, Bedford, Qué. J0J 1A0; (514) 248-3295.
PRÉSIDENT
Jean Pierre Lefebvre

Cinar Films Inc.

1207 rue St-André, Montréal, Qué. H2L 3S8; (514) 843-7070; FAX: (514) 843-7080.
Ron Weinberg, Micheline Charest

Cineflix Inc.

238 Davenport Rd., Ste. 190, Toronto, Ont. M5R 1J6; Tel & FAX: (416) 531-2612. 5578 Esplanade Ave., Montréal, Qué. H2T 3A1; (514) 278-3140; FAX: (514) 270-3165.
Rebecca Yates, Glen Salzman

Cinegroup

242 Delaware Ave., Toronto, Ont. M6H 2T6; (416) 536-0655.
Barry Greenwald

Cinema Espranca International

96 Spadina Ave., Ste. 301, Toronto, Ont. M5V 2J6; (416) 865-1225; FAX: (416) 865-9223.
PRESIDENT & CEO
André Bennett
CHAIR & CONTROLLER
Maria Pimentel

Cinepix Inc.

8275 rue Mayrand, Montréal, Qué. H4P 2C8; (514) 342-2340; FAX: (514) 342-1922.
CHAIRMAN
J. Dunning
PRESIDENT
A. Link

Cineroutes Productions

345 Bain Ave., Toronto, Ont. M4J 1B9; (416) 466-7379.
Anthony Azzopardi

Cinevideo Plus

2100 rue Ste-Catherine ouest, Ste. 810, Montréal, Qué. H3H 2T3; (514) 937-7986; FAX: (514) 937-8332.
PRÉSIDENTE/DIRECTEUR GÉNÉRAL
Justine Héroux

Citadel Communications Limited

1652 Barrington St., Halifax, N.S. B3J 2A2; (902) 421-1326; FAX: (902) 423-0484.
WRITER/PRODUCER
Barry Cowling
DIRECTOR/PRODUCER
Terry Fulmer

Comedia Productions Inc.

17 Isabella St. E., Toronto, Ont. M4Y 1M7; (416) 929-3456; FAX: (416) 929-5029.
PRESIDENT
W. Paterson Ferns

Co-Producers Fund of Canada Limited

49 Don River Blvd., Toronto, Ont. M2N 2M8; (416) 222-8491; FAX: (416) 789-2037.
PRESIDENT
Tad Jaworski

Crone Films Ltd.

8175 Pasco Rd., W. Vancouver, B.C. V7W 2T5; (604) 921-6500.
Robert Crone csc

1640 Bayview Ave., Ste. 1222, Toronto, Ont. M4G 4E9; (416) 399-5787.
David Crone

Curlcom Inc.

600 Euclid St., Whitby, Ont. L1N 5C2; (416) 683-7766; FAX: (416) 666-8316.
PRESIDENT
E. G. (Ted) Curl

Cutaway Productions Ltd.

258 Wallace Ave., Ste. 204, Toronto, Ont. M6P 3M9; (416) 537-6501; FAX (416) 537-7044.
PRESIDENT
Tom Gregor
VICE-PRESIDENT
Vladimir Kabelik

Cyclops Communications Corporation

44 Gibson Ave., Toronto, Ont. M5R 1T5; (416) 927-8942; FAX: (416) 926-9878.
PRESIDENT
Samuel C. Jephcott

Dakota Films

1926 Tupper Ave., Ste. 200, Montréal, Qué. H3H 1N5; (514) 937-8522.
Steven Woloshen

Damberger Film & Cattle Co.

9120-80th Ave., Edmonton, Alta. T6C 0T8; (403) 466-4259.
PRODUCER/WRITER/DIRECTOR
Francis Damberger

David Latchman Productions Inc.

131 Bloor St. W., Ste. 1107, Toronto, Ont. M5S 1R1; (416) 961-3001; FAX: (416) 961-3895.
David Latchman

David Mackay Ltd.

23 Fraser Ave., Toronto, Ont. M6K 1Y7; (416) 538-7625; FAX (416) 538-3775.
Judith Mackay

Domino Film & Television International Ltd.

44 ave Arlington, Montréal, Qué. H3Y 2W4; (514) 933-8359; FAX: (514) 933-6659.

Doomsday Studios Limited

212 James St., Ottawa, Ont. K1R 2W4; (613) 230-9769; FAX: (613) 230-6004.

Ramona Macdonald

Dormont Studios Inc.

2297 ave. Oxford, Montréal, Qué. H4A 2X7; (514) 484-0714. 75 Orchard Park Blvd., Toronto, Ont. M4L 3E3; (416) 698-4482.

Peter Benison csc

Ego Film Arts

80 Niagara St., Toronto, Ont. M5V 1C5; (416) 365-2137; FAX: (416) 369-9093.

DIRECTOR/PRODUCER
Atom Egoyan
CONTACT
Simone Urdl

Enchanted Pictures Inc.

119 Yorkville Ave., Toronto, Ont. M5R 1C4; (416) 964-0798; FAX: (416) 964-1289.

Stephen Clerk

Equus Film Productions Inc.

174 Fulton Ave., Toronto, Ont. M4K 1Y3; (416) 429-7399; FAX: (416) 696-9108.

Keith Lock

Excalibur Pictures Inc.

2105-808 Nelson St., Vancouver, B.C. V6Z 2H2; (604) 681-2165; FAX: (604) 681-5538.

PRESIDENT
Lloyd A. Simard

La Fabrique d'Images Limitée

318 rue Sherbrooke est, Montréal, Qué. H2X 1E6; (514) 282-1505.

PRODUCERS
Denis Martel, Christiane Hamelin, Michel Raymond, Claude Landry, Louis Morin
DIRECTORS
Jacques Fournier, Marc S. Grenier, Michel Poulette, Jean-François Pouliot, Maryse Raymond, Karim Waked

Film Arts Limited

424 Adelaide St. E., Toronto, Ont. M5A 1N4; (416) 368-9925; FAX: (416) 364-1310.

PRESIDENT
Thomas Berner

Filmline International Inc.

410 St. Nicholas, Ste. 600, Montréal, Qué. H2Y 2P5; (514) 288-5888; FAX: (514) 288-8083.

Nicolas Clermont

Les Films 1608 Inc.

970 Chemin St-Louis, Sillery, Qué. G1S 1C7; (418) 683-2543; FAX: (418) 683-1105.

Nicholas Kinsey, André Tousignant

Filmwest Associates

2399 Hayman Rd., Kelowna, B.C. V1Z 1Z7; (604) 769-3399; FAX: (604) 769-5599.

George Christoff, Merrie Christoff

The Film Works Ltd.

194 Sherbourne St., #1, Toronto, Ont. M5A 2R7; (416) 360-7968; FAX: (416) 360-8569.

Eric Jordan, Paul Stephens

Fundamentally Film Inc.

349 St. Clair Ave., W., Ste. 107, Toronto, Ont. M5P 1N3; Tel. & FAX: (416) 928-1992.

Ron Singer, Joel Green

Genesis Communications Corp.

753 Crystal Ct., North Vancouver, B.C. V7R 2B6; (604) 987-9956; FAX: (604) 689-5536.

PRESIDENT
Pamela Nichol

Glen-Warren Entertainment

9 Channel Nine Ct., Scarborough, Ont. M1S 4B5; Box 9, Stn. O, Toronto, Ont., M4A 2M9; (416) 291-7571; FAX: (416) 299-2067.

PRESIDENT
Allan P. Chapman
GENERAL SALES MANAGER
Wilfred Copeland

Great North Productions Inc.

11523-100 Ave., #012, Edmonton, Alta. T5K 0J8; (403) 482-2022; FAX: (403) 482-3036.

Andy Thomson

HBW Film Productions Inc.

1725-10th Ave., S.W., Ste. 308, Calgary, Alta. T3C 0K1; (403) 228-1900; FAX: (403) 228-1110.

PRINCIPAL
Helene B. White

Heartstar Productions Ltd.

345 Carlaw Ave., 3rd Fl., Toronto, Ont. M4M 2T2; (416) 778-8612; FAX: (416) 778-8617; Los Angeles: Tel. & FAX (310) 854-5646.

PRODUCER/UNIT PRODUCTION MANAGER
John Danylkiw

Henry Less Productions Inc.

27 Government Rd., Toronto, Ont. M8X 1V6; (416) 236-5004.

Henry Less, Debra Gjendem

High Road Productions Inc.

52R Badgerow Ave., Toronto, Ont. M4M 1V4; (416) 461-3089.

Paul Jay, Joan Hutton

Hobel-Leiterman Productions Ltd.

14 Birch Ave., Toronto, Ont.; (416) 968-0577.

Douglas Leiterman, Beryl Fox

Humewood Communications Corporation

62 Humewood Dr., Toronto, Ont. M6C 2W4; (416) 658-2929; FAX: (416) 658-3176.
PRESIDENT
Dan Johnson

Image Canada Limited

957 Broadview Ave., Ste. A, Toronto, Ont. M4K 2R5; (416) 422-1270; FAX: (416) 422-4678.
Roger Pyke

Imagex Ltd.

5662 Cornwallis St., #306, Halifax, N.S. B3K 1B6; (902) 422-4000; FAX: (902) 422-4427.
PRESIDENT
Christopher Zimmer

Imax Corporation

45 Charles St. E., Toronto, Ont. M4Y 1S2; (416) 960-8509; FAX: (416) 960-8596.
PRESIDENT & CEO
Robert Kerr
PRODUCERS
Graeme Ferguson, Roman Koiter, Sally Dundas, Toni Myers

Technology Centre, 2525 Speakman Dr., Sheridan park, Mississauga, Ont. L5K 1B1, Oakville; (416) 855-1379; FAX: (416) 855-2606.
MANAGER, FILM TECHNOLOGY
Gord Harris

Independent Pictures Inc.

18 Gloucester St., 4th Fl., Toronto, Ont. M4Y 1L5; (416) 960-6310; FAX: (416) 960-8463.
PRESIDENT
Peter O'Brian

Indigo Films Inc.

464 Oakwood Ave., Toronto, Ont. M6E 2W6; (416) 652-6770; FAX: (416) 6551-7191.
PRODUCER
Brian Ferstman

Insight Production Company Ltd.

489 King St. W., Ste. 401, Toronto, Ont. M5V 1L3; (416) 596-8118; FAX: (416) 596-8270.
EXECUTIVE PRODUCER
John M. Brunton

Intercom Films Limited

1231 Yonge St., Ste. 200, Toronto, Ont. M4T 2T8; (406) 923-9008.
PRESIDENT
Gilbert W. Taylor
VICE-PRESIDENT
Glenn Frost

International Rocketship Ltd.

1778 West 2nd Ave., Vancouver, B.C. V6J 1H6; (604) 738-1778.
PRODUCER
Michael van den Bos

Investigative Productions Inc.

490 Adelaide St., W., Ste. 302, Toronto, Ont. M5V 1T2; (416) 594-0580; FAX: (416) 594-1691.

PRESIDENT
Peter Raymont

Jenfilms Inc.

366 Adelaide St. W., Ste. 706, Toronto, Ont. M5V 1R9; (416) 599-5901; FAX: (416) 599-9631.
Paul de Silva

Jillian Film & Investment Corporation

53 Hillholm Rd., Toronto, Ont. M5P 1M4; (416) 486-5498; FAX: (416) 486-7984.
Victor Solnicki, Jill Solnicki

John McGreevy Productions

36 Roxborough St. E., Toronto, Ont. M4W 1V6; (416) 922-8625; FAX: (416) 922-8624.
PRESIDENT
John McGreevy

John M. Eckert Productions Limited

385 Carlton St., Toronto, Ont. M5A 2M3; (416) 960-4961; FAX: (416) 960-4961.
John M. Eckert

Katherine Smalley Productions

368 Brunswick Ave., Toronto, Ont. M5R 2Y9; (416) 961-8907; FAX: (416) 324-8253.
PRESIDENT
Katherine Smalley

Keg Productions Ltd.

1231 Yonge St., Ste. 201, Toronto, Ont. M4T 2T8; (416) 924-2186; FAX: (416) 924-6115.
PRESIDENT
Ralph C. Ellis
MANAGING DIRECTOR
R. Stephen Ellis

Kelly Duncan Productions Inc.

1027 Davie St., Ste. 595, Vancouver, B.C. V6E 4L2; (604) 684-5714.
PRESIDENT
Kelly Duncan

Kerrigan Productions Inc.

3471 ave. Hingston, Montréal, Qué. H4A 2J5; (514) 486-8456.
DIRECTOR
Bill Kerrigan
WRITER
Louise Roy

Kicking Horse Productions

10022-103 St., 2nd Fl., Edmonton, Alta. T5J 0X2; (403) 426-6441; FAX: (403) 426-7835.
PRESIDENT
Grace Gilroy
VICE-PRESIDENT
Arvi Liimatainen

Kono Films Productions

81 Claremont Ave., Winnipeg, Man. R2H 1W1; (204) 237-5649; FAX: (204) 237-1563.
PRESIDENT
Charles Konowal

Lauron Productions

56 Shaftesbury Ave., Toronto, Ont. M4T 1A3; (416) 967-6503; FAX: (416) 967-1292.

Ronald Lillie, William Johnston, Antony Armstrong

Lawrence Hertzog Productions Limited

62 Charles St. E., Toronto, Ont. M4Y 1T1; (416) 921-9300.

Lindisfarne Productions Inc.

3627-114 A St., Edmonton, Alta. T6J 1N2; Tel. & FAX: (403) 434-6348.

WRITER/PRODUCER
Fred Keating

Lindum Films Inc.

67 Majory Ave., Toronto, Ont. M4M 2Y2; (416) 461-2305; FAX: (416) 533-2463.

WRITER/DRIECTOR/PRODUCER
Peter Blow

Lorenzo Orzari Productions

5135 Jean Talon E., #704, Montréal, Qué. H1S 2Z5, (514) 329-5412.

WRITER/PRODUCER/DIRECTOR
Lorenzo Orzari

Makin' Movies Inc.

843 Manning Ave., Toronto, Ont. M6G 2X1; (416) 534-5077.

Maureen Judge, Martin Waxman

Mako Films Ltd.

70 East Beaver Creek Rd., Richmond Hill, Ont. L4B 3B2; (416) 882-9600; FAX: (416) 882-9605.

John Stoneman, B.Sc., M.Sc., csc

Malofilm Production Inc.

3575 boul. St-Laurent, bur. 650, Montréal, Qué. H2X 2T7; (514) 844-4555; Telex: 055-61301; FAX: (514) 844-1471.

PRESIDENT
René Malo
2221 Yonge St., Ste. 100, Toronto, Ont. M4S 2B4; (416) 480-0453; FAX: (416) 480-0501.

Massey Productions Ltd.

339-163 W. Hastings St., Vancouver, B.C. V6B 1H5; (604) 682-6803; FAX: (604) 683-2423.

Raymond Massey.

Max Film Inc.

5130 boul. St-Laurent, 4e étage, Montréal, Qué. H2T 1R8; (514) 272-4425; FAX: (514) 274-0214.

Roger Frappier

Michael Mills Productions Limited

4492 Ste-Catherine W., Montréal, Qué. H3Z 1R7; (514) 931-7117; FAX: (514) 931-7099.

PRESIDENT
Michael Mills

My Country Productions Inc.

21 Sackville St., Toronto, Ont. M5A 3E1; (416) 868-1972.

Pierre Berton, Elsa Franklin

Nelvana Limited

32 Atlantic Ave., Toronto, Ont. M6K 1X8; (416) 588-5571; FAX: (416) 588-5588.

PRODUCERS
Patrick Loubert, Michael Hirsh, Clive A. Smith

Nemesis Productions

317 Adelaide St. W., Main Fl., Toronto, Ont. M5V 1P9; (416) 323-0577.

Jacques Holender

New Communication Concepts Ltd.

5-23260 Dyke Rd., Richmond, B.C. V6V 1E2; (604) 526-3351; FAX: (604) 526-3351.

PRESIDENT
Keith Cutler
VICE-PRESIDENT
Dixie Cutler

Norstar Entertainment Inc.

86 Bloor St. W., 5th Fl., Toronto, Ont. M5S 1M5; (416) 961-6278; FAX: (416) 961-5608.

PRESIDENT, CHAIRMAN & C.E.O.
Peter R. Simpson

North American Pictures Ltd.

8216 Forest Grove Dr., Burnaby, B.C. V5A 4G9; (604) 621-2165; FAX: (604) 681-5538.

PRESIDENT
Lloyd A. Simandl

Northern Lights Entertainment Corp.

1020 Mainland St., Ste. 110, Vancouver, B.C. V6B 2T4; (604) 684-2888; FAX: (604) 681-3299.

Werner Aellen

Northern Outlaw Productions Inc.

105 Harbord St., 2nd F., Toronto, Ont. M5S 1G7; (416) 925-5005; FAX: (416) 925-8770.

Peter Gentile, Stuart Clarfield

Northland Pictures

Box 549, Adelaide St., Toronto, Ont. M5C 2J6; (416) 591-7766/465-0955.

Colin Strayer

O'B & D FILMS

125 Alcorn Ave., Toronto, Ont. M4V 1E5; (416) 944-3047; FAX: (416) 323-3480.

PRODUCERS
Tim O'Brien, Greg Dummett

October Films Inc.

67 Brookfield St., Toronto, Ont. M6J 3A8; (416) 532-6253.

Bruno Lazaro Pacheco

One-Six Productions

60 Normandy Blvd., Toronto, Ont. M4L 3K3; (416) 691-7743.
Peter Sawade

Opal Productions

84 Delemere Ave., Toronto, Ont. M6N 1Z7; (416) 769-4597; FAX: (416) 604-8196.
PRODUCER/CINEMATOGRAPHER
Ihor George Lomaga
WRITER/DIRECTOR
Natalie Pawlenko

Open City Productions Ltd.

54 Mansfield Ave., Toronto, Ont. M6J 2B2; (416) 532-6892.
PRESIDENT
Andrew Johnson

The Original Motion Picture Company

326½ Bloor St. W., Toronto, Ont. M5S 1W5; (416) 979-2518; FAX: (416) 944-8475.
John Board

The Owl Centre for Children's Film and Television

56 The Esplanade, Ste. 213, Toronto, Ont. M5E 1A7; (416) 863-1661; FAX: (416) 868-6009.
EXECUTIVE PRODUCER
Annabel Slaight
PROJECT CO-ORDINATOR
Wayne Arron

Paragon Entertainment Corporation

119 Spadina Ave., Ste. 900, Toronto, Ont. M5V 2L1; (416) 977-2929; FAX: (416) 977-0489.
CHAIRMAN & C.E.O.
Jon Slan
PRESIDENT
Richarde Borchiver

The Partners' Film Company Limited

508 Church St., Toronto, Ont. M4Y 2C8; (416) 966-3500; FAX: (416) 966-5058.
GENERAL MANAGER/PRESIDENT
Donald McLean

Patterson-Partington International TV Productions

206 Laird Dr., Ste.200, Toronto, Ont. M4G 3W4; (416) 696-9633; FAX (416) 696-9640.
Carol Patterson, Lawrence Partington

Peter Gerretsen Productions Ltd.

118 Castlefield Ave., Toronto, Ont. M4R 1G4; (416) 484-9671.
WRITER/DIRECTOR
Peter Gerretsen
PRODUCER
Patricia Gerretsen

Peter Hitchcock Productions Inc.

17 Poplar Plains Rd., Toronto, Ont. M4V 2M7; (416) 921-1021; FAX: (416) 921-1189.

PRODUCER/DIRECTOR
Peter Hitchcock

Picture Plant Ltd.

P.O. Box 2465, Stn.M#306, Halifax, N.S. B3J 3E8; (902) 423-3901; FAX: (902) 422-5704.
PRESIDENT
William MacGillivray

Pierre Sarrazin Productions Inc.

42 Bernard Ave., Toronto, Ont. M5R 1R2; (416) 324-9254.
Pierre Sarrazin, Suzette Couture

Playing with Time Inc.

935 Queen St. E., Toronto, Ont. M4M 1J6; (416) 466-6170.
EXECUTIVE OFFICERS
Kit Hood, Linda Schuyler

Points East Productions Inc.

161 Maypoint Rd., Charlottetown, P.E.I. C1A 1X6; (902) 892-9819; FAX: (902) 368-3798.
PRODUCER
Jack McAndrew

Primedia Entertainment Inc.

17 Isabella St., Toronto, Ont. M4Y 1M7; (416) 929-3456; FAX (416) 929-5029.
PRESIDENT
W. Patson Ferns

Producer's Network & Lightscape Inc.

Ste. B-216, Cinevillage, 65 Heward Ave., Toronto, Ont. M4M 2T5; (416) 462-9741; FAX: (416) 462-3236.
Philip Jackson, Tim Richardson

Les Productions du Verseau Inc.

225, rue Roy est, bur. 200, Montréal, Qué. H2W 1M5; (514) 848-9814; FAX: (514) 848-9908.

Productions Grand Nord Quebec Inc.

La Maison Premier Plan, Ste., 121, 1600 ave de Lorimier, Montréal, Qué. H2K 3W5; (514) 521-7433; FAX: (514) 522-3013.
Ian McLaren

Les Productions La Fete Inc.

225 est, rue Roy, Ste. 203, Montréal, Qué. H2W 1M5; (514) 848-0417; FAX: (514) 848-0064.

Productions Pax

3781 de Bullion, Montréal, Qué. H2W 2C9; (514) 844-7077.
Tanya Tree, Erica Pomerance

Les Productions Prisma Inc.

5253 ave. du Parc, Ste. 330, Montréal, Qué. H2V 4P2; (514) 277-6686; FAX: (514) 277-8910.
PRODUCTEUR EXÉCUTIF
Claude Godbout

Provifilms Inc.

810 Chatelaine, Laval, Qué. H7W 4H9; Tel. & FAX: (514) 688-9443.
Maurice Attias

PTV Productions Inc.

125 Dupont St., 2nd Ftr., Toronto, Ont. M5R 1V4; (416) 975-9768; FAX: (416) 972-6261.
PRESIDENT
Bill Nemtin

Quest Film Productions Ltd.

1272 Redpath Cr., Montréal, Qué. H3G 2K1; (514) 849-7921.
PRESIDENT
Paul Almond

The Radio Telegraphic Co. Inc.

3340 Norwood Ave., N. Vancouver, B.C. V7N 3P3; (604) 984-9065.
Phillip Borsos

Rebelfilms, Inc.

345 Adelaide St. W., Ste. 608, Toronto, Ont. M5V 1R5; Tel. & FAX: (416) 593-1616.
PRESIDENT
Jeremy Podeswa

Red Snapper Films Ltd.

2125 Brunswick St., Halifax, N.S. B3K 2Y4; (902) 422-2427; FAX: (902) 492-2125.
PRESIDENT
Lulu Keating

Rhombus Media Inc.

489 King St. W., Ste. 102, Toronto, Ont. M5V 1L3; (416) 971-7856; FAX: (416) 971-9647.
Niv Fichman, Barbara Willis Sweete, Larry Weinstein, Sheena Macdonald

Riffraff Films Inc.

209 Adelaide St. E., Ste. 300, Toronto, Ont. M5A 1M8; (416) 777-1890; FAX: (416) 777-1891.
Alexandra Raffé

Rose Films Inc.

Head office: C.P. 40, Saint-Paul d'Abbotsford, Qué. J0E 1A0; (514) 379-5304. Production offices: 86 rue de Brésoles, Montréal, Qué. H2Y 1V5; (514) 285-8901; FAX: (514) 285-8936.
Claude Fournier, Marie-José Raymond

Rose & Ruby Productions Inc.

33 Howard St., Toronto, Ont. M4X 1J6; (416) 961-0555; FAX: (416) 961-4234.
PRESIDENT
Damian Lee

R.S.M. Productions Internationales Inc.

720 Montpellier, Ste. 509, Ville St. Laurent, Qué. H4L 5B5; (514) 748-2678; FAX: (514) 744-2087.
PRODUCER/DIRECTOR
Rafik M. Murad

Rudy Inc.

Corporate office: 40 Glengarry Ave., Toronto, Ont. M5M 1C9; (416) 489-7115. Production office: 31 Lawrence Ave. W., Toronto, Ont. M5M 1A3; (416) 489-7760; FAX: (416) 489- 7760.
Rudy Buttignol, Howard Hutton, Buffy Jeffs

Salish Park Productions Inc.

811 Beach Ave., #208, Vancouver, B.C. V6Z 2B5; (604) 681-8311.
Les Weinstein

S. Banks (In-Television) Limited

20 Holly St., Ste. 300, Toronto, Ont. M4S 3B1; (416) 484-8000; FAX: (416) 484-8001.
PRESIDENT
Sydney Banks

SC Entertainment International

434 Queen St. E., Toronto, Ont. M4A 1T5; (416) 363-6060; FAX: (416) 363-2305.
CO-CHAIRMEN
Nicolas Stiliadis, Syd Cappe

Schulz Films Inc.

50 Russell Hill Rd., Toronto, Ont. M4V 2T2; Bob Schulz (416) 961-3000/483-6495; FAX: (416) 923-2561.

SDA Productions Ltee.

1425 ouest boul. René-Lévesque, 10e étage, Montréal, Qué. H3G 1T7; (514) 866-1761.
PRÉSIDENT
François Champagne

Shane Lunny Productions Inc.

560 Beatty St., Ste. 305, Vancouver, B.C., V6B 2L3; (604) 669-0333/1-800-663-0668.
PRESIDENT
Shane Lunny

Slikk Systems Inc.

35 Turnberry Cres., Unionville, Ont. L3R 0R6; (416) 940-5555; FAX: (416) 940-9079.
Marco Bianco

Soma: Film & Video

345 Carlaw Ave., Ste. 200, Toronto, Ont. M4M 2T1; (416) 466-0822.
PRESIDENT
Deepak Sahasrabudhe
VICE-PRESIDENT
Susan Millar

Spectrum Films

Box 5613, Stn. A, Toronto, Ont. M5W 1N8; (416) 363-2340.
Holly Dale, Janis Cole

Sphinx Productions

24 Mercer St., Toronto, Ont. M5V 1H3; (416) 971-9131; FAX: (416) 971-6014.
Ron Mann

Sullivan Films Inc.

16 Clarence Sq., Toronto, Ont. M5V 1H1; (416) 597-0029; FAX: (416) 597-0320; Telex: 06-218692.
PRESIDENT
Kevin Sullivan
DIRECTOR CREATIVE DEVELOPMENT
Deborah Nathan

Sunrise Films Limited

160 Perth Ave., Toronto, Ont. M6P 3X5; (416) 535-2900; FAX: (416) 535-0311.
Paul Saltzman, Steve Levitan

Tamarac Filmworks Ltd.

3495 W. 28th Ave., Vancouver, B.C. V6S 1R8; (604) 737-7260.
PRESIDENT/PRODUCER
Alyson Drysdale

Telescene Film Group Inc.

5510 Ferrier St., Montréal, Qué. H4P 1M2; (514) 737-5512; FAX: (514) 737-7945.
PRÉSIDENT
Robin Spry

Three Blondes Inc.

72 Rusholme Rd., Toronto, Ont. M6R 3H6; (416) 537-8348; FAX: (416) 534-6542.
Annette Mangaard

Triangle Films

1303 Greene Ave., Ste. 100, Westmount, Qué. H3Z 2A7; (514) 846-1940; FAX: (416) 846-1550.
PRESIDENT
Debbie Travis
GENERAL MANAGER
Hans Rosenstein

Tricord Film & Television Corp.

141 Drakefield Rd., Markham, Ont. L3P 1G9; (416) 472-0535; FAX: (416) 472-0448.
Karen Pascal

Trillium Pictures

950 Kingsmere Ave., Ottawa, Ont. K2A 3K4; (613) 722-1437.
Robert A. Evans

Twin Dragon Film Productions Ltd.

6347 Yonge St., North York, Ont. M2M 3X7; (416) 229-1280; FAX: (416) 229-2425.
PRESIDENT
Michael McNamara
VICE PRESIDENT
Martin McNamara

USA Atlantis Media Inc.

1329 Palisades Beach Rd., Santa Monica, CA 90401; (310) 917-5540; FAX: (310) 917-5543.
Peter Sussman

Ventura Pictures Inc.

185 Grace St., Toronto, Ont. M6G 3A7; (416) 537-2641; FAX (416) 588-8125.
PRESIDENT
Ian McDougall

Venture Entertainment Group Inc.

P.O. Box 36, Stn. Q, Toronto, Ont. M4T 2L7; (416) 486-1992.
PRESIDENT & CHIEF OPERATING OFFICER
Jerry Appleton

Vintage Visuals

1133 Harwood St., #302, Vancouver, B.C. V6E 1R6; (604) 688-5985.
George C. Koller, Wendy M. Ennion

Vos Productions Inc.

209 Adelaide St. E., Ste. 300, Toronto, Ont. M5A 2M8; (416) 777-1890; FAX: (416) 777-1891.
Patricia Rozema, Alexandra Raffé

Wacko Entertainment Corporation

46 Stan Wright Industrial Park, P.O. Box 1651, Jasper, Alta. T0E 1E0; (403) 852-5212; FAX: (403) 852-4702.
PRESIDENT
Wendy Wacko

Wheeler-Hendren Enterprises Ltd.

R.R.#1, 212 Sunset Dr., R.M.D. Ganges, B.C. V0S 1E0; (604) 537-9916; FAX: (604) 537-9463.
PRODUCER/DIRECTOR/WRITER
Anne Wheeler
ASSOCIATE PRODUCER
Garth Hendren

Why Not Productions Inc.

700 King St. W., Ste. 606, Toronto, Ont. M5V 2T6; (416) 594-0059; FAX: (416) 594-0550.
PRESIDENT
Barbara Barde

David Winning

Groundstar Entertainment Corp., 918-16 Ave. N.W., Ste. 4001, Calgary, Alta. T2M 0K3; (403) 284-2889; FAX: (403) 282-7797.

Yellowknife Films Inc.

Box 2562, Yellowknife, NWT X1A 2P9; (403) 873-8610; FAX: (403) 872-9405.
Alan Booth

Yorktown Productions Ltd.

18 Gloucester St., Toronto, Ont. M4Y 1L5; (416) 923-2787.
PRESIDENT
Norman Jewison

Zero Patience Productions Limited

56 The Esplanade, Ste. 505, Toronto, Ont. M5E 1A7; (416) 203-2866; FAX: (416) 203-2867.
John Greyson, Louise Garfield, Anna Stratton

Studio Facilities

Allarcom Studios

5305 Allard Way, Edmonton, Alta. T6H 5B8; (403) 436-1250; FAX: (403) 438-8495.
CONTACT
Doug Steeden

International Versioning Centre Inc.

634 Jefferson Ave., Unit 5, Toronto, Ont. M6K 3H3; (416) 539-8000; FAX: (416) 539-8110.
PRESIDENT
Réjean Myre

North Shore Studios

555 Brooksbank Ave., N. Vancouver, B.C. V7J 3S5; (604) 983-5555; FAX: (604) 983-5554.
GENERAL MANAGER
Ralph Alderman

Panavision (Canada) Corp.

2170 ave. Pierre-Dupuy, Montréal, Qué. H3C 3R4; (514) 866-7262; FAX: (514) 866-2297.
STUDIO RENTALS
Jean Marc Herbert

Studioasis Media Corporation

793 Pharmacy Ave., Toronto, Ont. M1L 3K2; (416) 285-1111; FAX: (416) 285-9617.
STUDIO MANAGER
Gord Brodie

Studio Image

P.O. Box 3500, Stn. C, Montréal, Qué. H2L 4Z3; (514) 526-2881; FAX: (514) 526-3740.
CONTACT
Joanne Pichette

23 FPS

23 Fraser Ave., Toronto, Ont. M4K 1Y7; (416) 535-3522.
STUDIO MANAGER
Jim Hardie

Wallace Avenue Studios Inc.

258 Wallace Ave., Toronto, Ont. M6P 3M9; (416) 537-3471; FAX: (416) 532-3132.
VICE-PRESIDENT/MARKETING
Lillyann D. Goldstein
STUDIO MANAGER
Mary Snidero

Post-Production

Calgary Television Centre (CKKX)

222-23rd. St. N.E., Calgary, Alta. T2E 7N2; (403) 235-7733.
Kim Corrigall

Cinar Films Inc.

1207, rue St. André, Montréal, Qué. H2L 3S8; (514) 843-7070; FAX: (514) 843-7080.
Ron Weinberg, Micheline Charest

Laboratoire Kineco Inc.

608 Côte de l'Aqueduc, C.P. 368, Québec, Qué. G1K 6W8; (418) 527-1742; FAX: (418) 527-6822.
Pierre Rochette

McClear Pathé Recording and Post-Production Services

225 Mutual St., Toronto, Ont. M5B 2B4; (416) 977-9740; FAX: (416) 977-7147.
SENIOR MIXERS
Joe Grimaldi, Austin Grimaldi
STUDIO MANAGER
Jane Rowan

Prisma-Light Ltd.

762 Queen St. W. Toronto, Ont. M6J 1E9; (416) 367-5825.
PRESIDENT
Vladimir Czyzewski
VICE-PRESIDENT
Mark Wright

Zaza Sound Productions Ltd.

322 Dufferin St., Toronto, Ont. M6K 1Z6; (416) 534-4211; FAX: (416) 534-9520.
Paul Zaza, John Gare

Laboratories, Sound Transfer & Mixing

Alpha Cine Service

A division of Tegra Industries Inc.
916 Davie St., Vancouver, B.C. V6Z 1B8; (604) 688-7757; FAX: (604) 688-0127.
LAB MANAGER
Alex Clarkson

Bellevue Pathé Québec Inc.

An Astral Communications Company.
2000 ave. Northcliffe, Montréal, Qué. H4A 3K5; (514)
484-1186; FAX: (514) 484-2815; Telex: 055-67147.
VICE-PRESIDENT AND GENERAL MANAGER
Normand McKay

Brock Sound Post Audio

576 Manning Ave., Toronto, Ont. M6G 2V9; (416)
538-2563; FAX: (416) 593-7301.
MANAGER
Brock Fricker

Comfort Sound Recording Studio

26 Soho St., Ste. 390, Toronto, Ont. M5T 1Z7; (416)
593-7992; FAX: (416) 593-7301.
MANAGER
Doug McClement

Film House

Laboratory: 380 Adelaide St. W., Toronto, Ont. M5V
1R7; (416) 364-4321.
VICE-PRESIDENT & MANAGER
Paul Norris

Sound Studios: 424 Adelaide St. E., Toronto, Ont. M5A
1N4; (416) 364-4321.
VICE-PRESIDENT & DIRECTOR OF AUDIO POST
Tom Allwood

The Fine Print

77 Mowat Ave., Toronto, Ont. M6K 3E3; (416) 535-5227.
Hratch Keoshkerian

Gastown Film Labs

52 W. 2nd Ave., Vancouver, B.C. V5Y 1B3; (604)
875-9600; FAX: (604) 875-1347.
GENERAL MANAGER
Dave Hardon

Manta Eastern Sound

311 Adelaide St. E., Toronto, Ont. M5A 1N2; (416)
863-9316.
VICE PRSIDENT & GENERAL MANAGER
Kevin Evans
VICE PRESIDENT, OPERATIONS
Sy Potma

Master's Workshop

A division of Magnetic Enterprises Inc.
306 Rexdale Blvd., Unit 7, Rexdale, Ont. M9W 1R6;
(416) 741-1312; FAX: (416) 741-1894.
VICE-PRESIDENT & GENERAL MANAGER
Bob Predovich

Mastertrack Ltd.

35-A Hazelton Ave., Toronto, Ont. M5R 2E3; (416)
922-4004; FAX: (416) 922-8634.
Ken Burgess, Jim McBride, Paul Hopkins, Terry Wedel

Medallion/PFA

111 Peter St., 9th Fl., Toronto, Ont. M5V 2H1; (416)
593-0556; FAX: (416) 593-7201.
PRESIDENT
Michael Flanagan

Real to Reel Sound Studios

379 Shuter St., Toronto, Ont. M5A 1X3; (416) 360-7836.
ENGINEER/MANAGER
Neil Splitter

Sonolab Inc.

1500 Papineau St., Montréal, Qué. H2K 4L9; (514)
527-8671; FAX: (514) 526-5346.
GENERAL MANAGER
Pierre Mercier

Soundhouse Inc.

409 King St. W., Toronto, Ont. M5V 1K1; (416) 598-2260.
George Novotny

Soundmix Ltd.

22 Boston Ave., Toronto, Ont. M4M 2T9; (416) 461-2550.
Terry Cooke, David Cooke

Sound Techniques

181 Carlaw Ave., Toronto, Ont. M4M 2S1; (416) 778-4973.
PRESIDENT
Larry Johnson

Spence-Thomas Productions

45 Charles St. E., Toronto, Ont. M4Y 1S2; (416) 961-
3911; FAX: (416) 925-4802.
PRESIDENT
Patrick Spence-Thomas

Spot Film and Video

23 Fraser Ave., Toronto, Ont. M4K 1Y7; (416) 535-3522;
FAX: (416) 535-1041.
PRESIDENT
Michael Smith

Studio Saint-Charles

85 Grant St., Longueuil, Qué. J4H 3H4; (514) 674-4927,
526-6043; FAX: (514) 674-6929.
GENERAL MANAGER
Lucie Theriault

Distribution Companies

ACTION FILM LIMITEE, 467 est, boul. St-Joseph, Montréal, Qué. H2J 1J8; (514) 845-5572; FAX: (514) 286-2313. André Monette.

ADFILMS, 250 Merton St., 4th. Fl., Toronto, Ont. M4S 1B1; (416) 483-3551; FAX: (416) 483-2401. President: Fred T. Stinson.

ALLIANCE RELEASING, 920 Yonge St., Ste 400, Toronto, Ont. M4W 3C7; (416) 967-1141; FAX: (416) 967-4358. 355 Place Royale, Montréal, Qué. H2Y 2V3; (514) 844-3132; FAX: (514) 284-2340. President: Victor Loewy.

ASKA FILM DISTRIBUTION INC., 1600 ave. De Lorimier, Ste. 211, Montréal, Qué. H2K 3W5; (514) 521-0623; FAX: (514) 521-6174. Claude Gagnon, Luc Déry.

ASTRAL DISTRIBUTION. An Astral Communications Company. BCE Place, 181 Bay St., Ste. 101, P.O. Box 787, Toronto, Ont. M5J 2T3; (416) 956-2000; FAX: (416) 956-2020. President: Irving Ivers.

ATLANTIS RELEASING INC., Cinevillage, 65 Heward Ave., Toronto, Ont. M4M 2T5; (416) 462-0246; FAX: (416) 462-0254. Contact: Ted Riley.

BELLEVUE FILM DISTRIBUTORS LIMITED, 40 Lesmill Rd., Don Mills, Ont. M3B 2T5; (416) 449-9322. President: Herbert S. Mathers; Vice-President: H. Paul Wroe.

BONDED SERVICES INTERNATIONAL LIMITED, 288 Judson St., Unit 10, Toronto, Ont. M8Z 5T6; (416) 252-5081; FAX: (416) 252-3955. 781 King St. W., Toronto, Ont. M5V 1N4; (416) 368-1740; FAX: (416) 368-7075. Vice-President: Dan Armstrong.

BRIGHTSTAR DISTRIBUTION, 8 King St. E., Ste. 1708, Toronto, Ont. M5C 1B5; (416) 862-1555; FAX: (416) 862-2204. President: Orval Fruitman.

BUENA VISTA PICTURES DISTRIBUTION CANADA, INC. Distributors of Walt Disney Pictures, Touchstone Pictures and Hollywood Pictures. 1235 Bay St., Ste. 502, Toronto, Ont. M5R 3K4; (416) 964-9275; FAX: (416) 964-8537. General Manager: Peter Wertelecky.

C/FP DISTRIBUTION INC., 146 Bloor St. W., 3rd. Flr., Toronto, Ont. M5S 1P3; (416) 944-0104; FAX: (416) 944-2212. 8275 rue Mayrand, Montréal, Qué. H4P 2C8; (514) 342-2340; FAX: (514) 342-1922. President & CEO: André Link.

C/FP DISTRIBUTION LTD., 146 Bloor St. W., Ste. 204, Toronto, Ont. M5S 1P3; (416) 944-0104; FAX: (416) 944-2212. 815 Hornby St., Ste. 606, Vancouver, B.C. V6Z 2E6; (604) 684-0017; FAX: (604) 684-0071. President: Jeff Sackman.

CHARLES CHAPLIN ENTERPRISES INC., 318 Hillhurst Blvd., Toronto, Ont. M6B 1N2; (416) 781-0131/2010; FAX: (416) 366-6503; Cable: Chaplinent. President: Charles S. Chaplin.

CINAR FILMS INC., 1207 rue St. André, Montréal, Qué. H2L 3S8; (514) 843-7070; FAX: (514) 843-7080. Micheline Charest, Ron Weinbefg, Louise Fournier.

CINE 360 INC., 810 Chatelaine, Laval, Qué. H7W 4H9; (514) 686-1940; FAX: (514) 688-9443. Maurice Attias.

CINEMA ESPERANCA INTERNATIONAL, 96 Spadine Ave., Ste. 301, Toronto, Ont. M5V 2J6; (416) 865-1225; FAX: (416) 865-9223. President & C.E.O.: André Bennett; Chair & Controller: Marie Pimentel.

CINEPLEX ODEON FILMS CANADA INC., 1303 Yonge St., Toronto, Ont. M4T 2Y9; (416) 323-6600; FAX: (416) 323-6711; Cable: CINELAW. Vice-President: Paul Gardner.

COLUMBIA TRI-STAR FILMS OF CANADA. A division of Columbia Pictures Industries Inc. 1300 Yonge St., Ste. 606, Toronto, Ont. M4T-2W3; (416) 922-5740. Canadian General Manager: Michael Skewes; Branch Manager: Michael Brooker. Branches: 522-11th. Ave. S.W., Ste. 202, Calgary, Alta. T2R 0C8; (403) 262-8711. 2388 est rue Beaubien, Montréal, Qué. H2G 1N2; (514) 376-8551.

CREATIVE EXPOSURE, 2236 Queen St. E., Toronto, Ont. M4E 1G2; Tel. & Fax: (416) 690-0775. President: Tom Litvinskas.

CRESWIN FILM DISTRIBUTORS LTD., 18 Corwin Cr., Downsview, Ont. M3H 2A1; (416) 633-9079; FAX: (416) 638-5282. President: Larry Rittenberg.

DISTRIBUTION CINE GROUP, 1151 Alexandre-DeSve, Montréal, Qué. H2L 2T7; (514) 524-7567; FAX: (514) 524-1997. Contact: Hubert Gariépy.

FILM 2000, 2222 René-Levesque W., Ste. 1, Montréal, Qué. H3H 1R6; (514) 939-0781; FAX: (514) 939-0445. President: Claire Costom.

LES FILMS DU CREPUSCULE INTERNATIONAL, 55 ouest Mont-Royal, bur. 302, Montréal, Qué. H2T 2S5; (514) 849-2477; FAX: (514) 849-5859; Président: Louis Dussault.

FILMS TRANSIT INC., 402 est, rue Notre-Dame, Montréal, Qué. H2Y 1C8; (514) 844-3358; FAX: (514) 844-7298. Président: Jan Röfekamp.

FRANCE FILM COMPANY/COMPAGNE FRANCE FILM, 505 est rue Sherbrooke, Ste. 2401, Montréal, Qué. H2L 4N3; (514) 844-0680. Président, Directeur général: Pierre René.

JASMINE TEA FILMS INC. 83 Rameau Dr., Unit 5, Willowdale, Ont. M2H 1T6; (416) 493-3548; FAX: (416) 493-9117. President: Russel Chan.

KALEIDOSCOPE ENTERTAINMENT INC., 23 Lesmill Rd., Ste. 300, Don Mills, Ont. M3B 3P6; (416) 443-9200; Telex: 06-986562; FAX: (416) 443-8685. President: F.J. Braun; Vice-President: Randy H. Zalken.

LAPOINTE FILMS INTERNATIONAL INC., 450 rue Isabey, Saint-Laurent, Qué. H4T 1V3; (514) 521-7884; FAX: (514) 524-6435. Présidente: Diane Lapointe.

LIBRA FILMS, 96 Spadina Ave., Ste. 302, Toronto, Ont. M5V 2J6, (416) 203-2171; FAX:(416) 203-2173. President: Ron McCluskey.

MALOFILM DISTRIBUTION INC., 3575 boul. St-Laurent, bur. 650, Montréal, Qué. H2X 2T7; (514) 844-4555; FAX: (514) 844-1471. Président du conseil: René Malo. Vice-pré: François Macerola. 2221 Yonge St., Ste. 100, Toronto, Ont. M4S 2B4, (416) 480-0453; FAX: (416) 480-0501. Director of Sales & Acquisitions: Jim Murphy.

MAX FILMS DISTRIBUTION INC., 5130 St. Laurent Blvd, Montréal, Qué. H2T 1R8; (514) 272-4425; FAX: (514) 274-0214. Pierre Latour.

MGM/UA CLASSICS OF CANADA, 720 King St. W., Ste. 611, Toronto, Ont. M5V 2T3; (416) 856-9579. 1590 Mont Royal E., #301, Montréal, Qué. H2J 1Z2; (514) 525-6663.

MGM/UA DISTRIBUTION COMPANY 720 King St. W., Ste. 611, Toronto, Ont. M5V 2T3; (416) 865-9579. President: Jack Foleoy; Vice-President & General Manager: Don Popow. Branches: 1590 Mt. Royal E., #301, Montréal, Qué. H2J 1Z2; (514) 525-6663. Branch Manager: Robert Montplaisir. 720 King St. W., Ste. 611, Toronto, Ont. M5V 2T3; (416) 856-9579. Branch Manager: Joe Corsico.

NORSTAR RELEASING, 86 Bloor St. W., 5th. Fl., Toronto, Ont. M5S 1M5; (416) 961-6278; FAX: (416) 961-5608. President, Chairman & CEO: Peter R. Simpson.

PARAGON-INTERNATIONAL, 119 Spadina Ave., Ste. 900, Toronto, Ont. M5V 2L1; (416) 595-6300; FAX: (416) 977-0489. President: Ismé Bennie.

PARAMOUNT FILMS (CANADA) INC., 146 Bloor St. W., Toronto, Ont. M5S 1M4; (416) 922-3600; FAX: (416) 922-0287. President: Gino Campagnola. Branches: 146 Bloor St. W., Toronto, Ont. M5S 1M4; (416) 969-9901; FAX: (416) 922-0287. 1432 rue de Bleury, 2nd Fl., Montréal, Qué. H4A 2J1; (514) 286-9186; FAX (514) 286-5100.

PICTURE PLANT RELEASING LTD., P.O. Box 2465, Stn. M, Halifax, N.S. B3J 3E8; (902) 423-3901; FAX: (902) 422-5704. President: William D. MacGillivray.

RITTER ENTERPRISES LTD., 44 Arlington Ave., Montréal, Qué. H3Y 2W4; (514) 933-8359; FAX: (514) 933-6659, President: George Ritter.

THE ROKE ENTERTAINMENT GROUP, 522-11th. Ave. S.W., Calgary, Alta. T2R 0C8; (403) 264-4660; FAX: (403) 264-6571. Hector Ross, Frank Kettner, Syd Sniderman.

SULLIVAN FILMS DISTRIBUTION INC., 16 Clarence Sq., Toronto, Ont. M5V 1H1; (416) 597-0029; Telex: 06-218692; FAX: (416) 597-0320. President: Trudy Grant.

TRIANGLE FILMS, 1303 Greene Ave., Ste. 100, Westmount, Qué. H3Z 2A7; (514) 846-1940; FAX: (514) 846-1550. President: Debbie Travis; General Manager: Hans Rosenstein.

TWENTIETH CENTURY FOX FILM CORPORATION, 920 Yonge St., Ste. 218, Toronto, Ont. M4W 3C7; Sales: (416) 921-0001. Advertising: (416) 921-6179. Publicity: (416) 921-2506; FAX: (416) 921-9062. Vice-President & General Manager: Buddy Golden. Branch Manager: Dave Forget.

UNIVERSAL FILMS (CANADA), MCA Bldg., 2450 Victoria Pk. Ave., Willowdale, Ont. M2J 4A2; (416) 491-3000; FAX: (416) 491-2857. Vice-President & General Manager: Eugene Amodeo. Branches: 2450 Victoria Pk. Ave., Willowdale, Ont. M2J 4A2. Toronto Branch Manager: Peter Doody. 10500 Côte-de-Liesse, Ste. 145, Lachine, Qué. H8T 1A4; (514) 636-4886. Manager, 35mm: Jean Paul Hurtibise.

WARNER BROS. CANADA, 4576 Yonge St., 2nd. Fl., North York, Ont. M2N 6P1; (416) 250-8930. President & Canadian Division Manager: Philip R. Carlton. Branch: 5890 ave Monkland, Ste. 107, Montréal, Qué. H4A 1G2; (514) 481-2763. Manager: Francine Loranger.

WINNIPEG FILM GROUP DISTRIBUTION OFFICE, 304-100 Arthur St., Winnipeg, Man. R3B 1H3; (204) 942-6795; FAX: (204) 942-1555. Contact: Terry Coles.

Chief Exhibition Circuits

Cineplex Odeon Corporation

1303 Yonge St., Toronto, Ont. M4T 2Y9; (416) 323-6600; Telecopier: (416) 323-6677; Cable: CINELAW.

SENATOR E. LEO KOBLER: chmn.; ALLEN KARP: pres. & C.E.O; NEIL A. BLATT: exec. v.p., film; ELLIS JACOB: exec. v.p. & chief financial officer; HOWARD LICHTMAN, exec. v.p., marketing & communications; ROBERT J. TOKIO: exec. v.p.; MICHAEL HERMAN: sr. v.p., gen. counsel & secretary; STEPHEN F. BROWN: v.p., taxation & treasurer; SAM DIMICHELE: v.p.; JAMES VASSOS: v.p., business affairs & corporate controller.

North American Theatres Division: IRWIN COHEN: sr. v.p., operations; ERIC BAUMAN: sr. v.p., film, Canada; CLAUDE CHABOT: sr. v.p. & gen. mgr., Québec; ERIC BALL, sr. v.p., Canadian opns.; BILL SNELLING: sr. v.p., advertising; JERRY BULGER: v.p., publicity & promotions; MICHAEL KENNEDY: v.p., film & development; JEFFREY KENT: v.p., finance, theatres; BEN KUTNER: v.p., Canadian advertising; BILL HERTING: v.p., exhibition, southern division; SHAUNA KING: v.p., western & central division; KEN NACCARI: regional film buyer & director advertising.

BRITISH COLUMBIA: BURNABY: Station Square (5); CLEARBROOK: Clearbrook (6); COQUITLAM: Pinetree (6); KAMLOOPS: Odeon (4); NORTH DELTA: Scott 72 (4); PRINCE GEORGE: Odeon (3); SURREY: Hillcrest Drive-In (1); VANCOUVER: Granville Cinemas (7), Oakridge (3), Park & Tilford (6); Royal Centre (10); VICTORIA: Odeon (3), Towne (1).

ALBERTA: CALGARY: Cineplex Esso Plaza (9), Corral Drive-In (1), London Town Square (6), Marlborough (3), North Hill (1), Northland Village (5), Showcase Grand (4), Southland (4), Towne Cinema Centre (2), Westbrook (3); EDMONTON: Eaton Centre (9), Jasper Cinema Centre (2), Millwoods Drive-In (2), Twin Drive-In (2), Westmall 6 (6), West Edmonton Mall 8 (8), Westmount (4), Whitemud Crossing (6); LETHBRIDGE: Park Place (6); ST. ALBERT: Cineplex Village Tree (12).

SASKATCHEWAN: REGINA: Cinema 6 Drive-In (2), Coronet (6); SASKATOON: Pacific (4), Towne (2).

MANITOBA: WINNIPEG: Garrick (4), Grant Park (4), Odeon Drive-In (1), Towne 8 (8).

ONTARIO: BRAMPTON: Centennial (3), 410 & 7 Centre (4); BRANTFORD: Cinemas 3 (3), Odeon (2); BURLINGTON: Cineplex (6), Showcase (6); CAMBRIDGE: Twin (2); GUELPH: Stone Mall Road (5); HAMILTON: Centre Mall (8); KINGSTON: Cataraqui (6); KITCHENER: Fairway Centre (5), Frederick Mall (2), Hyland (1); LONDON: Galleria (4), Huron Market Place (4), Westmount (2); MISSISSAUGA: Erin Mills (5), South Common Mall (7); NIAGARA FALLS: Niagara Square (3), Seneca (2); OAKVILLE: Oakville Mews (5); OTTAWA: Elmdale (2), Kanata (4), Orleans Town Centre (6), St. Laurent (2), Somerset (1), Vanier (7), Westgate (3), World Exchange (3); RICHMOND HILL: Hillcrest (5); ST. CATHARINES: Can-View Drive-In (4), Pendale (2); SARNIA: Odeon (4); SUDBURY: Odeon (2); THORNHILL: Promenade (6); THUNDER BAY: Cineplex (8), Cumberland (5), Victoria (2); TORONTO: Canada Square (4), Carlton (9), Eaton Centre (17), Fairview (6), Finch (1), Humber (2), Hyland (1), Madison (5), Market Square (6), Scarborough Town Centre (12), Sherway Cinemas (9), Varsity (2), Warden Woods (8), Woodbine (3), Woodside (3), York (2); WATERLOO: Waterloo (1); WELLAND: Seaway (2); WHITBY: Champlain Mall (6); WINDSOR: Glade Place (3), Odeon (1), Palace (4).

QUEBEC: BOUCHERVILLE: Odeon Drive-In (1); BROSSARD: Odeon (3); CHICOUTIMI: Place du Royaume (3); LAVAL: Carrefour (6), Cinema 2000 (2), Laval Drive-In (4); LONGUEUIL: Place Longueuil (2); MONTRÉAL: Berri (5), Centreville (9), Complex Desjardins (4), Côte des Neiges (7), Crémazie (1), Dauphin (2), Decarie Square (2), Desjardins (4); Egyptien (3), Le Faubourg (4); POINTE-CLAIRE: Pointe-Claire (6); QUEBEC: Beauport Drive-In (3), de la Colline Drive-In (2), de Paris (3), Place Charest (8); SHERBROOKE: Capital (1); TROIS-RIVIERES: Trois-Rivieres Drive-In (2); WESTMOUNT: Atwater (3).

Empire Theatres Limited

115 King St., Stellarton, N.S. B0K 1S0; (902) 755-4440; FAX: (902) 755-6477. President: Stuart G. Fraser. Regional Office: 650 Portland St., Dartmouth, N.S. B2W 6A3; (902) 434-4114; FAX: (902) 434-6933; Telex: 019-21578. General Manager, Operations/Publicity/Promotions: Dean S. Leland.

NEW BRUNSWICK: FREDERICTON: Nashwaaksis (2); Plaza (4); MONCTON: Riverview Twin (2); SAINT JOHN: King Square (1), Parkway Twin (2), Place 400 Twin (2).

NOVA SCOTIA: AMHERST: Paramount (2); BEDFORD: Empire Four (4); BRIDGEWATER: Southshore (2); DARTMOUTH: Empire (6); HALIFAX: Oxford (1); NEW GLASGOW: Aberdeen Mall (4), Empire Drive-In (1); SYDNEY: Sydney Triple (3); TRURO: Centennial (3); YARMOUTH: Twin (2).

PRINCE EDWARD ISLAND: CHARLOTTETOWN: Charlottetown Mall (5).

NEWFOUNDLAND: CORNER BROOK: Millbrook (2); ST. JOHN'S: Avalon Mall (5), Topsail (3).

Famous Players Inc.

146 Bloor St. W., Toronto, Ont. M5S 1P3; (416) 964-5800; FAX: (416) 964-3924.

JOSEPH PEIXOTO: pres.; JOHN BAILEY: exec. v.p.; TON KARS: exec. v.p. & treasurer; MICHAEL SCHER: v.p., gen. counsel & secretary; BRIAN HOLBERTON: v.p., theatre operations; JOE STREBINGER: v.p., film; KEITH HARDING: v.p., threatre & merchandising;

Other information: BELEN CROUTCH: dir. of finance & controller.

BRITISH COLUMBIA: BURNABY: Station Square (7); COQUITLAM: Eagle Ridge (6); KELOWNA: Orchard Park (2); LANGLEY: Willowbrook (6); NORTH VANCOUVER: Esplanade (6); PRINCE GEORGE: Parkwood (1), PRINCE RUPERT: Prince Rupert (3); RICHMOND: Richmond Centre (6), Richport (2); SURREY: Guildford (4); VANCOUVER: Capitol (6), Vancouver Centre (2); VERNON: Polson Place (2); VICTORIA: Capitol (6), Coronet (1), University (4).

ALBERTA: CALGARY: Banker's Hall (5), Calgary Place (3), Market Mall (8), Palliser Square (2), South Centre (7), Sunridge (5); EDMONTON: Capitol Square (4), Gateway (8), Londonderry (2), Paramount (1), West Mall (5), Westmount Centre (4); LETHBRIDGE: Centre Cinema (2), College Mall (1), Paramount (2); RED DEER: Park Plaza (7).

SASKATCHEWAN: PRINCE ALBERT: Prince Albert (4), Pines Drive-In (1); REGINA: Cornwall Centre (4); SASKATOON: Capitol Four (4), Midtown (2).

MANITOBA: WINNIPEG: Garden City (6), Kildonan Place (6); Northstar (2), Polo Park (1), Portage Place (3), St. Vital (6).

ONTARIO: BELLEVILLE: Quinte Mall (2); BRAMPTON: Gateway (6); BRANTFORD: Market Square (3); BURLINGTON: Burlington Mall (3); CHATHAM: Capitol (2), GLOUCESTER: Gloucester 5 (5); HAMILTON: Jackson Square (6), Lime Ridge (4); KINGSTON: Capitol (7); KITCHENER: Capitol (2), Kings College (1); LONDON: Capitol (7), London Mews (6); MARKHAM: Markville (4); MISSISSAUGA: Square One (4), Sussex Centre (4); NEWMARKET: Glenway (5); OAKVILLE: Town Centre (6); OSHAWA: Centre (8); OTTAWA: Airport Drive-In (3), Britannia (6), Britannia Drive-In (2), Capitol Square (3), Elgin (2), Place de Ville (2), Rideau Centre (3); PICKERING: Town Centre (3); RICHMOND HILL: Parkway (6); ST. CATHARINES: Lincoln Mall (3), Pen Centre (3); SARNIA: Lambton 5 (5); STONEY CREEK: Fiesta Mall (4); SUDBURY: City Centre (3), Super Mall (3); THUNDER BAY: Capitol (2), Paramount (2); TIMMINS: Victory (2); TORONTO: Bayview Village (4), Capitol (1), Cedarbrae (8), Centrepoint (3), Cumberland (4), Eglinton (1), Hollywood North & South (2), Plaza (2), Regent (1), Runnymede (2), Sheraton Centre (2), Sheridan (4), Skyway (6), Uptown (3), Uptown Backstage (2), Victoria Terrace (6), Westwood (2), Yorkdale (6); WINDSOR: Devonshire (3), Parkway (5); WOODBRIDGE: 400 Drive-In (3), 7 & 27 Drive-In (2).

QUEBEC: DORVAL: Dorval (4); GATINEAU: Les Promenades (4); GREENFIELD PARK: Greenfield Park (3); LAVAL: Cinemas Laval (12); MONTREAL: Centre Eaton (6), Ciné du Parc (3), Cinéma V (2), Imperial (1), Loew's (5), Palace (6), Parisien (7), Versailles (6); POINTE CLAIRE: Famous Players (8); QUEBEC CITY: Les Galéries Capitale (6); STE.-FOY: Ste.-Foy (3); SHERBROOKE: Carrefour de l'Estrie (3).

NEW BRUNSWICK: MONCTON: Paramount (2); SAINT JOHN: Paramount (2).

NOVA SCOTIA: DARTMOUTH: Penhorn (5); HALIFAX: Park Lane (8).

Festival Cinemas

2236 Queen St., E., Toronto, Ont., M4E 1G2; (416) 690-0667; FAX: (416) 690-0755.

PRINCIPALS: Tom Litvinskas, Jerry Szczur.

ONTARIO: TORONTO: Bloor (1), Fox (1), Kingsway (1), Paradise (1), Revue (1).

Landmark Cinemas of Canada Ltd.

522-11th Ave., S.W., 4th Flr., Calgary, Alta. T2R 0C8; (403) 262-4255; Telecopier: (403) 266-1529.

DIRECTORS: Hector H. Ross, Philip H. May, Frank Kettner, Charles D. K. May, Barry Myers, Brian F. McIntosh.
HECTOR H. ROSS, chmn.; BRIAN F. MCINTOSH: pres.; PHILIP H. MAY: secty.; FRANK KETTNER: sr. v.p.; CHARLES D. K. MAY: sr. v.p.; BARRY MYERS: sr. v.p.
BRITISH COLUMBIA: ABBOTSFORD: Towne Cinema '4' (4); CRANBROOK: Armond Theatre (1); FORT ST. JOHN: Lido Theatre (1); KELOWNA: Uptown Cinema Centre (2); PENTICTON: Pen-Mar Cinema Centre (4).
YUKON: WHITEHORSE: Yukon Cinema Centre (2), Qwanlin Cinema Centre (2).
ALBERTA: BANFF: Lux Cinema Centre (4); BROOKS: Oasis Theatre (1); CAMROSE: Bailey Theatre (1); DRUMHELLER: Napier Theatre (1); EDSON: Nova Theatre (1); GRANDE PRAIRIE: Jan Cinema Centre (1), Prairie Cinema Centre (2); HINTON: Roxy Theatre (1); MEDICINE HAT: Monarch Theatre (1), Towne Cinema Centre (3); REDCLIFF: Gemini Drive-In (1); RED DEER: Uptown Cinema Centre (4); SHERWOOD PARK: Sword & Shield Cinema Centre (4); STETTLER: Jewel Theatre (1).
SASKATCHEWAN: WEYBURN: Soo (1); YORKTON: Tower Theatre (1).
MANITOBA: BRANDON: Towne (1); SELKIRK: Garry Theatre (1).

Magic Lantern Theatres

10510-121 St., P.O. Box 3707, Stn. D, Edmonton, Alta. T5L 4J7, (403) 482-1611; FAX: (403) 482-3520.

TOM HUTCHINSON: pres; BILL BOOTH: secty.
BRITISH COLUMBIA: FERNIE: Vogue (1).
NORTH WEST TERRITORY: YELLOWKNIFE: Capitol Twin (2).
ALBERTA: EDMONTON: Garneau (1); FORT SASKATCHEWAN: Gemini (2); PEACE RIVER: Cinema 72 (1); PONOKA: Capitol (1); ST. PAUL: Elite (1); SPRUCE GROVE: Magic Lantern (1); WHITECOURT: Vista (1).

SASKATCHEWAN: NORTH BATTLEFORD: Capitol (1), Frontier Twin (2).

Ontario Theatre Group

672 Mt. Pleasant Rd., Toronto, Ont. M4S 2N3; (416) 481-1186.

NORMAN STERN: pres; PETER SOROK: secty.-treas.; CHRISTINE LUDWIG: Acctg.; SHELLIE GOLDBERG: adm. & booking; DALE DOODY: film opns.; DUDLEY DUMOND: theatre opns.
ONTARIO: BELLEVILLE: Bellestar (3); BROCKVILLE: Parkedale (2); CORNWALL: Brookdale (3); GEORGETOWN: Cinema (3); HAMILTON: Westdale (1); NAPANEE: Drive-In (1); NORTH BAY: Champlain (2), Gateway (1); OWEN SOUND: Owen Sound Cinema (3); PEMBROKE: Algonquin (4); PETERBOROUGH: Lansdowne (5), Trent (2); SAULT STE. MARIE: Station Cinema (5).

Stinson Theatres Ltd.

Box 142, Barrie, Ont. L4M 4S9; (705) 726-8190.

ROBERT STINSON: pres.; CATHY WATSON: booker & buyer.
ONTARIO: BARRIE: Barrie Triple Drive-In (3), Imperial (8); CHATHAM: Cinema Six (6); COLLINGWOOD: Cinema Four (4), Collingwood Drive-In (1); HUNTSVILLE: Capitol (2), Huntsville Drive-In (1); ORANGEVILLE: Uptown (2); ORILLIA: Orillia Cinema Four (4); OWEN SOUND: Twin Drive-In (2); TIMMINS: Cinema Six (6).

Tarrant Enterprises Limited

R.R.#1, dar Valley, Ont. L0G 1E0; (416) 888-1490; FAX: (416) 473-6162.

JUNE TARRANT: pres.
ONTARIO: GUELPH: 3-Star (6); LISTOWEL: Capitol (1); NEWMARKET: Film Factory (6); ST. THOMAS: Capitor (3); TRENTON: Centre (3).

Independent Booking Companies

PRAIRIE ALLIED BOOKING ASSOCIATION A division of Theatre Agencies Ltd., 522-11th. Ave. S.W., Calgary, Alta. T2R 0C8; (403) 264-4660; Telecopier: (403) 264-6571. Hector Ross, Frank Kettner, Syd Sniderman, Ellen Smeltzer.

WEST COAST THEATRE SERVICE LTD., 302-788 Beatty St., Vancouver, B.C. V6B 1A2; (604) 669-4738; Telecopier: (604) 669-9640. Hector Ross, Doug Isman.

Film Carriers

EMERY WORLDWIDE, Pearson International Airport, P.O. Box 251, Toronto AMF, Mississauga, Ont. L5P 1B1; Information: (416) 676-2831; Sales & Information: (416) 676-2737. Sales Manager: Barbara Williams; Branches: Calgary (403) 221-1980, Dorval, (514) 636-1333; Halifax, (902) 873-3545; Ottawa, (613) 733-9650; Regina, (306) 352-9046; Saskatoon, (306) 931-1110; Vancouver, (604) 273-9077; Winnipeg, (204) 788-0204.
MAVETY FILM DELIVERY, 40 Lesmill Rd., Don Mills, Ont. M3B 2T5; (416) 447-5169. General Manager: William Pfaff.
PREFERRED SERVICE CUSTOMS BROKERS INC., P.O. Box 23925, Airport Postal Outlet, Richmond, B.C. V7B 1Y1; (604) 270-6607; FAX: (604) 270-8983. Jack Peterson.
VICTORIA FILM SERVICES LIMITED, 40 Lesmill Rd., Don Mills,

Ont. M3B 2T5; (416) 449-8597. President: Paul Wroe; Canadian General Manager: Jim Matsumoto. Branches: 1644 W. 75th. Ave., Vancouver, B.C. V6P 6G2; (604) 263-2551. Manager: Rick Williston. 3904-1st. St. N.E., Calgary, Alta. T2E 3E3; (403) 276-6696. Manager: Susan Piotrowski. 2315 Logan Ave., Winnipeg, Man. R2R 2S7; (204) 633-1203. Manager: Ben Adleman. 708 rue Walnut, Montréal, Qué. H4C 2M4; (514) 931-6212. Manager: SUZIE BERGERON. 55 Bentley St., St. John, N.B. E2K 1B2; (506) 634-1018. Manager: Kevin McDermott.
HENRY WEINER LTD., 1243 Islington Ave., Ste. 1200, Toronto, Ont. M8X 1Y9; (416) 596-8500; FAX: (416) 596-0558. Airport Office: Cargo Bldg. B., Ste. 201, Pearson International Airport, Toronto; (416) 676-2850; FAX: (416) 673-8058.

Government Agencies—Federal and Provincial

FEDERAL

The National Film Board of Canada

Head Office: 179 Rideau St., Mercury Court, Ottawa, Ont. K1A 0M9. Operational Headquarters: 3155 Chemin Côte de Liesse Rd., St. Laurent, Qué. H4N 2N4; Postal address: P.O. Box 6100, Stn. A, Montréal, Qué. H3C 3H5; (514) 283-9000; (514) 496-1646.

GOVERNMENT FILM COMMISSIONER AND CHAIRMAN OF THE NATIONAL FILM BOARD OF CANADA
Joan Pennefeather (514) 283-9244
DIRECTOR GENERAL, ENGLISH PROGRAM
Barbara Janes (514) 283-9501
DIRECTOR GENERAL, FRENCH PROGRAM
Robert Forget (514) 283-9285
DIRECTOR GENERAL, SERVICES AND TRAINING
Marcel Carrière (514) 283-9148
DIRECTOR GENERAL, ADMINISTRATION, FINANCE AND HUMAN RESOURCES
Gilles Roy (514) 283-9831
DIRECTOR OF COMMUNICATIONS
Jean-Claude Mahé (514) 283-9247
DIRECTOR, PLANNING AND EVALUATION
Claude Parent (514) 283-9251
DIRECTOR, INTERNATIONAL PROGRAM
Howard Krosnick (514) 283-9438
DIRECTOR, CORPORATE AFFAIRS
Michelle D'Auray (613) 992-3615
DIRECTOR, EMPLOYMENT EQUITY
Suzanne Chevigny (514) 283-9391
SECRETARY TO THE BOARD OF TRUSTEES
Mireille Kermoyan (514) 283-9252

English Program Branch Centres
Atlantic Centre: 5475 Spring Garden Rd., 2nd Fl., Halifax, N.S. B3J 1G2; (902) 426-1739. Head: Marilyn Belec.
Ontario Centre: 150 John St., Toronto, Ont. M5V 3C3; (416) 973-3012. Chief: Dennis Murphy
Prairie Centre: 245 Main St., Winnipeg, Man. R3C 1A7; (204) 983-2818. Head: Ches Yetman.
North West Centre: Canada Place, 9700 Jaspar Ave., Ste. 120, Edmonton, Alta. T5J 4C3; (403) 495-3015. Head: Graydon McCrea.
Pacific Centre: 1045 Howe St., Ste. 100, Vancouver, B.C. V6Z 2B1; (604) 666-5410. Head: Don Haig.
U.S. Office: 1251 Avenue of the Americas, 16th Fl., New York, N.Y. 10020; (212) 586-5131. Sales Manager: Jane Gutteridge.

Statistics Canada

Education, Culture and Tourism Division, Culture Section, R. H. Coats Bldg., 17th Fl., Ottawa, Ont. K1A 0T6; (613) 951-6862. Director: Kathleen K. Campbell.

Telefilm Canada

Head Office: Tour de la Banque Nationale, 600 ouest de la Gauchetière, 14e étage, Montréal, Qué. H3B 4L8; (514) 283-6363; Telex: 055-60998; FAX: (514) 283-8212.
Offices: 2 Bloor St. W., 22nd Fl., Toronto, Ont. M4W 3E2; (416) 973-6436; Telex: 06-218344; FAX: (416) 973-8606. 2525 Artillery Place, Ste. 220, Halifax, N.S. B3J 1J2; (902) 426-8425; FAX: (902) 426-4445. 350-375 Water St., Vancouver, B.C. V6B 5C6; (604) 666-1566; FAX: (604) 666-7754.
U.S. Office: 9350 Wilshire Blvd., Ste. 400, Beverly Hills, CA 90212; (310) 859-0268; FAX: (310) 276-4741.

BOARD OF DIRECTORS
Chairman/President: Harvey A. Corn; Vice-Chairman: André Provost. Members: Walter Gray, Marcelle Lean, Joan Pennefather

(Government Film Commissioner), Paulette Sonier-Rioux, Nancy Gay-Rotstein.
EXECUTIVE MANAGEMENT
EXECUTIVE DIRECTOR
Pierre DesRoches
FINANCING & ADMINISTRATION
DIRECTOR, FINANCING & ADMINISTRATION
Jean-Paul Paré
CONTROLLER
Lisa Scardocchio
MANAGER, FINANCIAL PLANNING & CONTRACTS ADMINISTRATION
Danny Chalifour
DIRECTOR, INFORMATION SYSTEMS
Gilles Gagné
DIRECTOR, LEGAL SERVICES
John Pelletier
MANAGER, LEGAL SERVICES (Montréal)
Marie-Céline Drapeau
PRODUCTION & DEVELOPMENT
DIRECTOR, PRODUCTION & DEVELOPMENT
Peter Katadotis
MONTRÉAL
DIRECTOR, OPERATIONS
Louis Laverdiére
MANAGER, CREATIVE AFFAIRS
Myrianne Pavlovic
MANAGER, BUSINESS AFFAIRS
Suzanne Laverdiére
PROJECT CO-ORDINATOR
Diane Ste-Marie
TORONTO
DIRECTOR, OPERATIONS
Bill House
MANAGER, CREATIVE AFFAIRS
Elke Town
MANAGER, BUSINESS AFFAIRS
Steve Ord
PROJECT CO-ORDINATOR
Helen Paul
VANCOUVER
DIRECTOR, OPERATIONS
John Taylor
MANAGER, BUSINESS AFFAIRS
Janine Boyd
MANAGER, CREATIVE AFFAIRS
Pamela Hawthorn
PROJECT CO-ORDINATOR
Colleen Siemens
HALIFAX
MANAGER, OPERATIONS
Ralph Holt
DISTRIBUTION, MARKETING & FESTIVALS
DIRECTOR, DISTRIBUTION, MARKETING & FESTIVALS
Noel Cormier
DIRECTOR, DISTRIBUTION & MARKETING (Montréal)
Ann Picard
DIRECTOR, DISTRIBUTION & MARKETING (Toronto)
Ted East
MANAGER, FESTIVALS' BUREAU
Jean Lefebvre
INTERNATIONAL AFFAIRS
MANAGER, COPRODUCTIONS
Deborah Drisdell
LOS ANGELES
DIRECTOR
Sam Wendel
PARIS
DIRECTOR
Pierre Lampron
LONDON
DIRECTOR
Bob Linnell
POLICY, PLANNING & RESEARCH
DIRECTOR, POLICY, PLANNING & RESEARCH
Robert Armstrong
COMMUNICATIONS
DIRECTOR, COMMUNICATIONS
Pierre Pontbriand

718

DIRECTOR, HUMAN & MATERIAL RESOURCES
    Marcel Choquette
MANAGER, MATERIAL RESOURCES
    Johanne Laurin

PROVINCIAL

BRITISH COLUMBIA

Ministry of Tourism and Ministry Responsible for Culture, Parliament Bldgs., Victoria, B.C. V8V 1X4; (604) 356-1793. Director, Cultural Services Branch: Richard Brownsey.

B.C. Film Fund, 555 Brooksbank Ave., N. Vancouver, B.C. V7J 3S5; (604) 983-5400; FAX: (604) 983-5401. Chairman & C.E.O.: Wayne Sterloff.

British Columbia Film Commission, 601 W. Cordova St., Vancouver, B.C. V6B 1G1; (604) 660-2732; FAX: (604) 660-4790. Director: Dianne Neufeld; Manager, Location/Production Services: Mark DesRochers.

Victoria and Vancouver Island Film Commission, 525 Fort St., Victoria, B.C. V8W 1E8; (604) 386-3976. Chairman: Brian Small.

ALBERTA

Alberta Culture & Multiculturalism, 418 Legislature Bldg., Edmonton, Alta. T5K 2B6; (403) 427-4928. Minister: Hon. Dianne Mirosh; Arts Branch, Cultural Development Division: 3rd Fl., Beaver House, 10158-103 St., Edmonton, Alta. T5J OX6; (403) 427-6315. Director: Dr. Clive Padfield.

Alberta Economic Development, Film Industry Development, 10th Fl., Sterling Pl., 9940-106th. St., Edmonton, Alta. T5K 2P6; (403) 427-2005; FAX: (403) 427-5924. Film Commissioner: William D. Marsden.

Alberta Motion Picture Development Corporation, Ste. 690, The Phipps McKinnonBldg., 10020-101A Ave., Edmonton, Alta T5J 3G2; (403) 424-8855; FAX: (403) 424-7669. General Manager: Garry S. Toth.

SASKATCHEWAN

The Saskatchewan Film and Video Corporatin (SaskFilm), 1840 McIntyre St., Regina, Sask. S4P 2P9; (306) 347-3456; FAX: (306) 359-7768. Executive Director: Gerri Cooke.

MANITOBA

Manitoba Cultural Industries Development Office (CIDO), 333-93 Lombard Ave., Winnipeg, Man. R3B 3B1; (204) 947-2040. Acting General Manager: Carole Vivier.

ONTARIO

Ministry of Culture, Tourism and Recreation, 77 Bloor St. W., Toronto, Ont. M7A 2R9; (416) 965-6487. Deputy Minister: Dr. Elaine Todres; Culture Division, Assistant Deputy Minister: Jane Marlatt (416) 314-7262; Heritage, Arts & Cultural Policy, Branch Director: Robert Montgomery (416) 314-7115.

Ontario Film Development Corporation, 175 Bloor St. E., North Tower, Ste. 300, Toronto, Ont. M4W 3R8; (416) 314-6858; FAX: (416) 314-6876.

QUEBEC

Ministere des Affaires Culturelles, Direction des arts d'interprétation, du disque et des variétiés, 225 est Grande-Allée, 3e étage, Bloc "B", Québec, Qué. G1R 5G5; (418) 644-7198; FAX: (418) 644-4080. Directeur: Claude Roy.

Sogic Generale des Industries Culturelles Quebec (SOGIC), 1755 est boul. René Lévesque est, bur. 200, Montréal, Qué. (514) 873-7768; FAX: (514) 873-4388.

NEW BRUNSWICK

N.B. Film & Video Commission, Tourism/Recreation/Heritage, P.O. Box 12345, Fredericton, N.B. E3B 5C3; (506) 453-2553/after hours 458-5512; FAX: (506) 453-2416. Commissioner: Ted Bringloe.

NOVA SCOTIA

Government of Nova Scotia, Dept. of Tourism and Culture, P.O. Box 456, Halifax, N.S. B3J 2R5; (902) 424-5929. Cultural Industries Officer: Peggy Walt.

Nova Scotia Film Development Corporation, 1724 Granville St., Halifax, N.S., B3J 1X5; (902) 424-7177; FAX: (902) 424-0617. Location Services (902) 424-7185; FAX: (902) 424-0563. Helen Wickwire Foster.

NEWFOUNDLAND

Government of Newfoundland, Cultural Affairs, P.O. Box 1854, St. John's, Nfld. A1C 5P9; (709) 576-3650.

Trade Associations

Academy of Canadian Cinema and Television

158 Pearl St., Toronto, Ont. M5H 1L3; (416) 591-2040; FAX: (416) 591-2157. 3375 boul. St-laurent, bur. 709, Montréal, Qué. H2X 2T7; (514) 849-7448; FAX: (514) 849-5069. 1120 Hamilton St., Ste. 404, Vancouver, B.C. V6B 2S2; (604) 684-4528; FAX: (604) 684-4574. 1652 Barrington St., Halifax, N.S. B3J 2A2; (902) 425-0489; FAX: (902) 425-8851. 1223 Wilshire Blvd., Ste. 435, Santa Monica, CA 90403; (310) 392-0955.

CHAIR
Ann Medina
NATIONAL VICE-CHAIRMAN
Cyril Drabinsky
EXECUTIVE DIRECTOR
Maria Topalovich

Alliance of Canadian Cinema, Television and Radio Artists (ACTRA) (CLC, FIA, IAWG)

National Office, 2239 Yonge St., Toronto, Ont. M4S 2B5; (416) 489-1311.
BOARD OF DIRECTORS
PRESIDENT
Alexander (Sandy) Crawley
PERFORMERS
Dan MacDonald
WRITERS
Jack Gray

Association des Producteurs de Films et de Video du Québec (APFVQ)

740 St-Maurice, bur. 201, Montréal, Qué. H3C 1L5; (514) 397-8600; FAX: (514) 392-0232.
PRESIDENTE/DIRECTRICE-GENERALE
Louise Baillargeon

The Association of Canadian Film Craftspeople (ACFC)

Head Office, Cinevillage, 65 Heward Ave., Ste. 105, Toronto, Ont. M4M 2T5 (416) 462-0211, FAX: (416) 462-3248.
CONTACT
Donato L. Baldassarra

Association Quebecoise des Realisateurs et Realisatrices de Cinema et de Television

740 St-Maurice, bur. 201, Montréal, Qué. H3C 1L5; (514) 397-8600; FAX: (514) 392-0232.
PRESIDENTE/DIRECTRICE-GENERALE
Louise Baillargeon

The Association of Television Producers and Directors

2 Carlton St., Ste 1319, Toronto, Ont. M5B 1J3; (416) 593-1414.

PRESIDENT
Arnold Amber
EXECUTIVE DIRECTOR
Kathy Viner

Camera Guild of Canada

181 Carlaw Ave., Ste. 201, Toronto, Ont. M4M 2S1; (416) 462-1022.

Canadian Actors' Equity Association

260 Richmond St., E., Toronto, Ont. M5A 1P4 (416) 867-9165, FAX: (416) 867-9246.
EXECUTIVE DIRECTOR
Christopher Marston

Canadian Cable Television Association

360 Albert St., Ste. 1010, Ottawa, Ont. K1R 7X7; (613) 232-7800.
PRESIDENT, C.E.O.
Ken Stein

Canadian Film & Television Production Association (CFPTA)

175 Bloor St. E., Ste. 806, Toronto, Ont. M4W 3R8; (416) 927-8942; FAX: (416) 922-4038.
PRESIDENT
Sandra Macdonald

Canadian Independent Film Caucus (CIFC)

65 Heward Ave., Bldg. A, Toronto, Ont. M4M 2T5; (416) 469-2596.
EXECUTIVE CO-ORDINATOR
Avrel Fisher

Canadian Motion Picture Distributors Association (CMPDA)

22 St. Clair Ave. E., Ste. 1703, Toronto, Ont. M4T 2S4; (416) 961-1888; FAX: (416) 968-1016.
PRESIDENT
Millard S. Roth
BOARD OF DIRECTORS
Millard S. Roth, Bernard Mayer, Eric Pertsch, Phil Carlton, Ron Suter

Canadian Picture Pioneers

21 Dundas Sq., Ste. 1210, Toronto, Ont. M5B 1B7; (416) 368-1139; FAX: (416) 368-1130.
NATIONAL EXECUTIVE
PRESIDENT
Michael Taylor
VICE-PRESIDENT
Philip Carlton
SECRETARY-TREASURER
John Freeborn
DIRECTORS
John Bailey, Eric Bauman, Irving Ivers, Denise James, Gary Martin, Roly Rickard, Norman Stern, Brian Stewart, Chris Sullivan, Paul Wroe

720

Canadian Society of Cinematographers (CSC)

89 Pinewood Tr., Mississauga, Ont. I5G 2L2; (416) 271-4684, FAX: (416) 271-7360.
GENERAL ENQUIRIES
Jennifer Hietala

Canadian Women in Radio and Television

95 Barber Greene Rd., Ste. 104, Don Mills, Ont. M3C 3E9; (416) 446-5353; FAX: (416) 446-5354.
EXECUTIVE DIRECTOR
Shari Adamek

Casting Directors of Canada (CDC)

%73 Berkeley St., Toronto, Ont. M5A 2W5; (416) 866-8339; FAX: (416) 366-4412/972-9036.
CO-CHAIR
Jann Stefoff, Ross Clydesdale

Directors Guild of Canada Inc.

National Office: 367 Bloor St. E., Ste. 401, Toronto, Ont. M4W 1H7; (416) 972-0098. Administrative Co-ordinator: Leah Bazian. Vancouver: (604) 688-2976; Calgary: (403) 237-0689; Toronto (416) 351-8200; Montréal: (514) 989-1714; Halifax: (902) 492-3424.

The Guild of Canadian Film Composers

Canadian Music Centre, 20 St. Joseph St., Toronto, Ont. M4Y 1J9; (416) 961-6601.
PRESIDENT
Paul Hoffert

The Motion Picture Foundation of Canada

22 St. Clair Ave. E., Ste. 1603, Toronto, Ont. M4T 2S4; (416) 961-1888; Telecopier: (416) 968-1016.
PRESIDENT
Millard S. Roth

Motion Picture Theatre Associations of Canada

1303 Yonge St., 1st Flr., Toronto, Ont. M4T 2Y9; (416) 323-7214; FAX: (416) 323-6607.
EXECUTIVE DIRECTOR
Dina Lebo
PRESIDENT
Stuart G. Fraser

National Association of Canadian Film and Video Distributors

62 Humewood Dr., Toronto, Ont. M6C 2W4; (416) 658-2929; FAX: (416) 658-3176.
CHAIRMAN
Victor Loewy
EXECUTIVE DIRECTOR
Dan Johnson

SOCAN/Society of Composers, Authors and Music Publishers of Canada (formerly CAPAC and PROCAN)

41 Valleybrook Dr., Don Mills, Ont. M3B 2S6; (416) 445-8700, FAX: (416) 445-7108.
GENERAL MANAGER
Michael Rock

Union Des Artistes

1290 rue Saint-Denius, 6e Étage, Montréal, Qué. (514) 288-6682, FAX: (514) 288-7150. Président: Serge Turgeon, Directeur-générale: Serge Demers. Section de Toronto (416) 967-4408, FAX: (416) 967-6898, Marco Dufour; Section de Hull-Ottawa (819) 778-2658, FAX: (819) 770-8678, Jacques Dupont; Section de Québec (418) 523-4241, Louise Piché.

Writers Guild of Canada (WGC)

35 McCaul St., 3rd Flr. North, Toronto, Ont. M5T, 1V7; (416) 979-7907; FAX: (416) 979-9273; 1-800-567-9974.
EXECUTIVE DIRECTOR
Margaret Collier

Box Office Statistics

The latest information released by Statistics Canada, a federal government agency is for 1990–91.

Number of theatres: There were 633 regular motion picture theatres (650 in 1989–90) plus 109 drive-in theatres (123 in 1989–90), making a total of 742 motion picture theatres (773 in 1989–90).

Number of screens: The number of regular motion picture screens was 1565 (1555 in 1989–90) plus 148 drive-in screens (168 in 1989–90), for a total of 1713.

Box office: Receipts from admissions increased by 3% to $C439 million, and total attendance decreased by 4% to 79 million. The national average ticket price rose 7% to $C5.92, an increase of C40 cents from 1989–90.

Expense/Profit ratio: Total revenue increased by 4% for regular theatres to $C560 million—the lowest increase in the last 5 years and compared to an increase of 13% in 1989–90. Total revenue for drive-ins decreased by 12% compared to an increase of 9% in 1989–90. Total expenses for all theatres increased by 4% compared to an increase of 13% for 1898–90. The ratio of profits to total revenues remained at 14%, since both total expenses and total revenues increased at the same rate.

The
World Market

* THE INDUSTRY IN SELECT FOREIGN COUNTRIES

The Industry in Select Foreign Countries

ARGENTINA

Population: 33.1 million.
Number of Cinema Screens: 342 in 1992, a drastic drop from the 915 reported in 1985.
Annual admissions: 12,000,000.
Top Ten Box Office Films of 1992: 1.) Sister Act, 2.) Basic Instinct, 3.) Home Alone 2, 4.) Universal Soldier, 5.) Dracula, 6.) Fried Green Tomatoes, 7.) L'Amant, 8.) The Hand That Rocks the Cradle, 9.) Unforgiven, 10.) Mediterraneo.
Trends: The Instituto Nacional de Cine (the Argentine Film Institute) has big plans for putting the country's film industry back on the map. An influx of fresh funds are expected to be generated from the controversial 10% tax on box office receipts, home video and TV revenues. Though this has been met with much resistance, the Institute's income has doubled from $4.3 million to $8 million. Hoping to take in over $25 million for 1993, a bankroll is being allotted for loans to Argentine filmmakers, aggressive promotion/marketing techniques, future publications and the possibility of staging a 1994 international film festival. 22 new projects have been given credits from $300,000 to $600,000 per film. Top producers have received loans up to $700,000 for a $1.2 million budgeted film.
Distributors: Aranjuez, Lavalle 2018 1051 Buenos Aires. Tel:(1) 951 3206, 953 5560. FAX: (1) 951 3206. Contact: Liliana Caceres; Argentina Sono Film Saci, Lavalle 1975 1051 Buenos Aires. Tel: (1) 49 0216/19. FAX: (1) 814 4063, 372 8132. Contact: Carlos L. Mentasti; Prodifilms S.A, 2025 Corrientes Avenue, 5th "A" 1045 Buenos Aires. Tel: 9532795 951 1389. FAX: (1) 953 4991. Contact: Alvaro Martinez Toledo.
Equipment—Sales and Rental: Gustavo S.M. Montrasi Equipos Y Servicios Para Cine Y T.V., 14 de Julio 556, 1427 Buenos Aires. Tel: (1) 552 5442/553 4731. FAX: (1) 554 0459. Contact: Gustavo S.M. Montrasi.
Organizations and Associations: Fundacion Cinemateca Argentina, Argentinian Cinematheque Foundation. Corrientes 2092, Piso 2 1045 Buenos Aires. Tel: (1) 953 3755, 953 7163. FAX: (1) 951 8558. Telex: 24569 Sicvil Ar. att. Cinemateca. Contact: Paulina Fernandez Jurado.

AUSTRALIA

Population: 17.4 million.
Number of screens: 840 commercial, 55 non-commercial.
Annual admissions for 1992: 45,491,000.
Top Ten Box Office Films of 1992: 1) Strictly Ballroom; 2) Basic Instinct; 3) Lethal Weapon 3; 4) Hook; 5) Beauty and the Beast; 6) Batman Returns; 7) Wayne's World; 8) Sister Act; 9) Father of the Bride; 10) Cape Fear.
Top Five Domestic Films of 1992: 1) Strictly Ballroom; 2) Romper Stomper; 3) Black Robe; 4) Blinky Bill; 5) Spotswood.
Trends: The Federal Government Trade Development Group has allocated $A300,000 ($214,000) towards marketing for foreign film and T.V. production. Pacific Film and the T.V. commission have estimated that $70 million worth of international and local production will take place between 1993–1994. Private investors are being sought for funding, as producer Phillip Emanuel allotted $A53 ($37 million) for film production with the Film Finance Corp (FFC), the main source of production funding, as its principal backer. Rothschild Inc. is creating a fund to cover four to six projects valued between $7 and $14 million.
The most attractive offer being made is the 10BA tax policy, offering investors 100% in deductions and structured returns, on the money they invest in films. $A80 to $A90 million ($63 to $65 million) is expected to be raised through tax concessions, for production funding.
Though Paul Hogan plans to shoot the film, "Lightning Jack" in the United States, he is seeking $24.5 million from Aussie investors. Using a tax structure that's less restrictive in terms of residency, this is still considered the most expensive film ever funded.
Roadshow Film Distributors is now the only major film buyer as Hoyts Distribution, the second largest distributor, reported losses of $A133 million ($94 million) during their last fiscal year. As a result, Hoyts Distribution is undergoing restructuring and has slowed down operations, distributing only the titles it currently has in its library.
Film Australia, the government's production house, is considering going private as the Liberal/National Party is considering cuts as high as $A100 million ($67.5 million) from its budget. This includes film subsidies which would represent a $6.8 million loss for 1993–1994. Meanwhile the Western Australian Film Council is looking for a commitment of $1.6 million (up $700,000) in funding. The Australian Film Commission, however, will receive an additional $2.5 million over the next few years, specifically for development and production support, and the backing of low budget films. The New South Wales Film and TV Office received a $700,000 grant this fiscal year for a one-shot production investment fund. The Office has a track record which includes helping six films with combined budgets of $13 million and attracting foreign investments worth $5.2 million. It is expected to infuse $18 million into the state's economy and create 700 jobs. Looking to increase its $315,000 fund by 20% is the

Pacific Film & TV Commission's Queensland international marketing division. The Film Development Office is seeking $700,000 to start a production investment fund to supplement a $7 million revolving three year fund implemented last year, which to date has lent $1.1 million to two film projects.
$4.2 million will be allocated to production funding over the next three years, via the state's Lotteries' Fund.
Distributors: Theatrical: Beyond Films Ltd, 1st fl., 53-55 Brisbane St., Surry Hills, NSW 2010. Tel: (02) 281 1266; Boulevard Films, 110-114 Errol St., No. Melbourne VIC 3051. Tel: (03) 329-2399; Film Australia PTY Ltd., Eaton Rd., Linfield, NSW 2070. Tel: (02) 413-8777; Hoyts Distribution, Level 6, 505 George St, Sydney, NSW 2000; Kim Lewis Marketing, 257 Coventry St., So. Melbourne, VIC 3205. Tel: (03) 690 2414; M C Stuart and Associates, 88 Highett Street, Richmond, VIC 3121. Tel: (03) 429 8666; New Vision Film Distributors, 2nd Floor, 252 Bay Street, Port Melbourne, VIC 3207. Tel: (03) 646 5555; Palace Entertainment, 233 Whitehorse Rd., Balwyn, VIC 3103. Tel: (03) 817 6421; Paramount Pictures/Paramount Television Distributors, Suite 3209, Australia Square, Sydney, NSW 2000. Tel: (02) 247 9367; Premium Films, 92 Bay St., Port Melbourne, Victoria 3207. Tel: (03) 645 1612; Quality Films, 405-411 Sussex St., Sydney, NSW 2000. Tel: (02) 212 2313; R A Becker and Co Pty Ltd, 4 21 Chandos Street, St. Leonards, NSW 2065. Tel: (06) 248 0851; Sharmill Films, South Yarra Business Centre, Suite 4, 200 Toorak Road, South Yarra, VIC 3141. Tel: (03) 826-9077; South Australian Film Corporation, 3 Butler Drive, Westside Commerce Centre, 113 Tapleys Hill Road, Hendon, SA 5014. Tel: (08) 348-9300; United International Pictures (UIP), 5th Floor, 208 Clarence Street, Sydney, NSW 2000. Tel: (02) 264 7444; United International Pictures (UIP), 54 Berwick St., Fortitude Valley, QLD 4006. Tel: (07) 252-5786; Valkyrie Films, 166 Glebe Point Road, Glebe, NSW 2037. Tel: (02) 552 2456; Virgin Vision Australia, 99 Victoria St., Potts Point, NSW 2011. Tel: (02) 368 1700; The Walt Disney Company, Castlereagh Street, Sydney, NSW 2000. Tel: (02) 267 8942; Warner Bros (Australia) Pty Ltd, Level 22, 8-20 Napier Street, North Sydney, NSW 2060. Tel: (02) 957 3899.
Organizations: Government and Industry: Actors Equity of Australia, 101/245 Chalmers St, Redfern NSW 2016. Tel: (02) 318 2066; Advertising Federation of Australia Ltd., 140 Arthur St., North Sydney, NSW. Born 2065. Tel: (02) 957 3077; Australian Broadcasting Tribunal, 76 Berry Street, North Sydney, NSW 2060. Tel: (02) 959 7811; Australian Cinematographers Society, PO Box 207, Cammeray, NSW 2062. Tel: (02) 901 3310; Australian Copyright Council, Suite 3, 245 Chalmers St, Redfern, NSW 2016. Tel: (02) 318 1788; Australian Film Commission, 8 West Street, North Sydney, NSW 2060. Tel: (02) 925 7333; Australian Film Institute, 49 Eastern Road, South Melbourne, VIC 3205. Tel: (03) 696 1844; Australian Screen Directors Association, PO Box 161, Sydney, NSW 2037. Tel: (02) 552 1726; Australian Theatrical and Amusement Employees Association, Suite 5. 245 Chalmers Street, Redfern, NSW 2016. Tel: (02) 698 3557; Department of Arts, Sport, the Environment, & Tourism, PO Box 787, Canberra, ACT 2600. Tel: (06) 274 1111; Film and Literature Board of Review, Level 1, 255 Elizabeth St., Sydney, NSW 2000. Tel: (02) 581 7000; Film Australia PTY Ltd., Eaton Rd., Linfield, NSW 2070. Tel: (02) 413 8777; Film and Television Institute (WA) Inc, 92 Adelaide Street, Fremantle, WA 6160. Tel: (09) 335 1055; Film and Video Library of Queensland, 130 Margaret Street, Pamphlett Place, Brisbane, QLD 4000. Tel: (07) 224 7936; Film Victoria, 4th Floor, 49 Spring Street, Melbourne, VIC 3000. Tel: (03) 651 4089; Motion Picture Distributors Assn. of Australia, 2nd fl., 302 Pitt St., Sydney, NSW 2000. Tel: (02) 267 3118; Motion Picture Exhibitors Assn., PO Box 216, Spring Hill, QLD 4006. Tel: (07) 397 5644; Musicians Union of Australia, Suite 506, 3 Smail Street, Ultimo 2007, NSW. Tel: (02) 281 0355; National Film and Sound Archive, McCoy Circuit, PO Box 2002, Canberra City, ACT 2601. Tel: (06) 267 1711; National Library of Australia, Film and Video Lending Collection, Parkes Place, Canberra, ACT 2600. Tel: (06) 262 1361; New South Wales Film and Television Office, GPO Box 1744, Sydney, NSW 2000. Tel: (02) 380 5599; Office of Film and Literature Classification, Level 1, 255 Elizabeth Street, Sydney, NSW 2000. Tel: (02) 581 7000; Screen Production Association, Suite 2, 144 Riley St., East Sydney, NSW 2010. Tel: (02) 360 4900; South Australian Film and Video Centre, 113 Tapley's Hill Road, Hendon, SA 5014. Tel: (08) 348 9355; South Australian Film Corporation, 3 Butler Drive, Westside Commerce Centre, Tapleys Hill Road, Hendon, SA Born 5014. Tel: (08) 348 9300; South Australian Motion Pictures Exhibitors Association, 248 Flinders Street, Adelaide, SA 5000. Tel: (08) 223 1066; Video Industry Distributors Association, 2/302 Pitt Street, Sydney, NSW 2000. Tel: (02) 264 3411; Western Australian Film Council, Suite 8, 336 Churchill Avenue, Subiaco, WA 6008. Tel: (09) 382 2500.

BELGIUM AND LUXEMBOURG

In an effort to keep film production within the confines of Luxembourg, the government has amended previous tax shelter laws, allowing for as much as an 80% tax break for shooting in-studio. Though the strategy behind this move is to give original shareholders a 25%–28% return on their investment, foreign investors will feel the pinch. Foreign film and TV producers spent some $33 million over the past few years as the rate of film production has grown rapidly. French and German industries are known to receive substantial government subsidies, as recently demonstrated by the government's 1993 budget totaling 200 Belgian francs ($6 million). Though hundreds of producers across the country have previously enjoyed good co-production relationships with foreign countries, relations might become strained at the government's latest behest. The French Language Commission insists that all subsidized films have to be spoken in French.

The industry is looking well as ticket admission sales have risen 3.6% to $5.1 million and multiplex construction is on the rise.

BRAZIL

Population: 145,200,000 million.
Number of screens: 1,200, in 1991.
Annual admissions: Figures not available.

With rampant financial and political woes, the country's film industry is desperately looking for an escape hatch. Theatrical attendance has plummeted and local production has ceased entirely. There are roughly 360 hardtops that account for an 88% revenue with an occupancy rate of 18%, though more affluent areas show a rate of 45%. The minimum wage is $70 a month, making the average $3.00 ticket price à luxury item. Still, exhibitor/distributor majors are hopeful as about 25 new screens are expected to open. Several independent companies are holding their own with a 20% share in the market and all are working feverishly to provide hardtops with latest releases.

CHILE

Population (census 1992): 13,231,803.
Number of Screens in Chile: 121 (in 1992), 150 in 1991 and 1990), 173 (in 1989). Santiago: 46 (in 1992), 31 (in 1991), 35 (in 1990), and 55 (in 1989). Regions: 75 (in 1992), 119 (in 1991), 115 (in 1990), 118 (in 1989).
Total Cinema Attendance: 8,156,213 (in 1992), 9,585,463 (in 1991), 11,017,087 (in 1990). Santiago: 5,015,587 (in 1992), 5,440,718 (in 1991), 5,256,661 (in 1990). Regions: 3,140,626 (in 1992), 4,144,745 (in 1991), 5,760,426 (in 1990).
Average Annual Attendance Per Screen: National: 67,407 (in 1992), 63,903 (in 1991), 73,447 (in 1990). Santiago: 109,035 (in 1992), 175,507 (in 1991), 150,190 (in 1990). Regions: 41,875 (in 1992), 34,830 (in 1991), 50,090 (in 1990).
Average Number of Seats Per Cinema: 600.
Average Ticket Prices (1st run): US$4.50 (in 1992) US$4.00 (in 1991), US$1.50 (in 1988).
Number of Films Released in Chile: 194 (in 1992), 218 (in 1991), 236 (in 1990). All films are subtitled in Spanish.
Most-Attended Film in 1992: "Basic Instinct". In the 1st-half of 1993, the most-attended was "The Bodyguard" (272,669 spectators in Santiago), followed by "Home Alone 2" (131,581).

Cinema attendance declined by 14.9% in 1992, continuing a trend which began about five years ago. This trend apparently coincides with the massive increase in TV ownership (now 92% of homes as compared to only 78% ten years ago) and VCR ownership (now 25% as compared to practically nil ten years ago).

However, this decline has been more than compensated by the increase in ticket prices. In the last four years, prices (equivalent in dollars) have tripled. Attendance has declined by only 38%.

Chile's capital, Santiago, has 39.1% of the nation's total population, but accounts for 61.5% of total national cinema attendance. Santiago's share of the market has been increasing significantly. The rate of decline in attendance in the Regions is much more pronounced than in Santiago. Attendance in Santiago dropped by 7.8%, but in the Regions, the drop was 24.2%.

In the near future, there will be several multiscreen complexes constructed in the suburban shopping malls in Santiago. Nightlife in the downtown is dying, and the downtown screens now show mostly sex-and-violence and second-run films. The population of Santiago is very scattered and cut off, with shopping malls eating up the lion's share of all retail business.

Censorship: The Consejo de Calificacion Cinematografica, under the jurisdiction of the federal Ministry of Education, classifies films as either: "All Ages"; "Over 14"; "Over 18" or "Over 21". In 1993, the age of majority was finally lowered to 18, and therefore the Consejo will soon be overhauling their entire system of classification.
Principal Theatre Circuit: Conate S.A.: La Capitania 1200, Las Condes, Santiago. Ph: 220-3086.
Principal Distributors: Arthur Ehrlich: Huerfanos 786, Suite 210, Santiago. Ph: 633-2503. FAX: 639-7921. Rep. for: 20th Century Fox Chile Inc./Warner Bros. (South) Inc.; Columbia Pictures; Tri-Star; Hollywood Pictures; Touchstone Pictures; Orion. Chilefilms: La Capitania 1200, Las Condes, Santiago. Tel: 220-3086.
Chilean Film Industry: The Association of Producers formed an umbrella organization, "Cine Chile", which negotiated a US$6 million line of credit with the state-owned Banco del Estado de Chile for the purpose of financing the production of Chilean films. Also, the federal government export development agency, ProChile, is now promoting Chile as a location for films, and is assisting Chilean producers in making contacts abroad. Cine Chile S.A.: Huerfanos 878, suite 918, Santiago. Ph:

633-3948. FAX: 632-5342. Miguel Littin, Pres., Joaquin Kaulen, gen. mgr. Filmocentro: Gerona 3450, Santiago. Ph: 225-2203. FAX: 209-1671. Eduardo Larrain, producer. Silvio Caiozzi Productions: Federico Froebel 1755, Santiago. Ph: 209-9031. FAX: 204-8988. Silvio Caiozzi, pres., Lupe Bornand, exec. prod.

Locations Services: Alan Hootnick, Film & Television Commission of Chile, Clasificador 125, Santiago. FAX: 231-8946. Telex: 340 412 PBVTR CK. ProChile: Alameda 1315, 2nd floor, Santiago. Ph: 696-0043. FAX: 696-0639. Angel Gallardo, sector services. Chilean Trade Bureau, Los Angeles: Patricio DeGregorio, trade commissioner. 510 W. 6th St., suite 1206, Los Angeles, CA 90014. Ph: (213) 624-6302. FAX: (213) 489-9889.

—ALAN HOOTNICK

CHINA

After 40 years the China Film Distribution and Exhibition Company will no longer monopolize the industry, allowing 16 other production studios to deal directly with local distributors and theaters, granting them a greater share in revenues. The reforms have allowed studios the option of selling abroad directly, stabilized production to 150 feature films annually, developing a stronger foreign market and eased control over the cost of theater admission. The newly created Shanghai Film Development Company, under the auspices of the Film Bureau, is to be the center of production, distribution and sales, though each producer is responsible for profits and losses.

Also in the making is the Beijing Film City, a joint effort by Beijing Film Studio and the Heavenly Steed Tourist Company. This will contribute greatly to the nation's economy as plans include making full use of all its facilities for filming and development as a major tourist attraction.

Effective measures had to be taken to combat the drop in revenues in the film industry. The 15%, 360 million yuan ($63.2 million) decrease was due to not only a reduction in ticket prices and poor quality of locally produced movies, but a change in lifestyle as well as augmented video piracy. A slight reprieve was provided by two local films, which together topped admissions off at 90 million and grossed around $37 million yuan ($650,000).

Exhibitors have spent 2.5 million yuan ($4 million) in cinema renovations as a method for regaining their audiences while the government has spent 100 million yuan ($1.8 million) in the Sichuan province alone.

CZECHOSLOVAKIA

Population: 15,600,000, two-thirds live in the Czech Republic.
Theatres: Approx. 2,000.
Admissions 1992: 41,000,000.
Top Ten Box Office Films of 1992: 1) Black Barrons; 2) Home Alone; 3) The Friend in the Rain II; 4) Kindergarten Cop; 5) Terminator 2; 6) Hot Shots; 7) Basic Instinct; 8) Picking Violetts by Dynamite; 9) Alien 3; 10) Gone With the Wind.

Distributors: Artemis, Masarykova 179/656, PO Box 1 400 13 Ustí nad Labem. Tel: 47 62049. FAX: 47 62049. Director: Dr. Jiří Kostner; Atrakt, Pod Záhradami 20 841 02 Bratislava. Tel: 7 1 50690, 7 1 53225. FAX: 7 53225, 766 254. Director: Dr. Igor Ličko; Davay, Trnavská 67 821 01 Bratislavia. Tel: 7 294 645, 294 743, 294 683, 294 685. FAX: 7 294 677. Director: Miroslav Kubala; Filmexport Prague, Na Moráni 5 Prague 2. Tel: 2 29 86 20. FAX: 2 29 33 12. Telex: 122 259. Cable: Eximpfilms. Contact: Ing. Martin Papunšek; Hollywood Classic Entertainment, Krizeneckcho Nam. 332-FSB 152 53 Prague 5. Tel: 2 590 706. FAX: 2 590 706. Contact: Mitch Berman; Interama, V Jame 5 110 00 Prague 1. Mileticova 1 821 08 Bratislava. Tel: 2 2350473, 7 61140. FAX: 2 2369332, 7 63044. Contact: Michael Malek; Intersonic Taunus Productions, Asmolovova 36 842 25 Bratislava. Tel: 7 72 20 70. FAX: 7 72 20 70. Director: Ing. Ivan Lacho; KF A.S, Jindřišská 34 112 07 Prague 1. Tel: 2 628 0374, 644 5118. FAX: 2 545 480. Telex: 122 080. Contact: Jan Knoflíčck; Lars, Spartakiádní, Blok A. Východní Tribuna Prague 6. Tel: 2 527 412. FAX: 2 522 194. Directors: Dr. Miloš Toms, Ing. Petr Hájek; Lucerna Film, Národní Třída 28 110 00 Prague 1. Tel: 2 261 341. FAX: 2 236 6903. Directors: Jan Jíra, Dr. Svatava Peschková, Video; Morava Film, Jesuitská 1 601 56 Brno. Tel: 5 26321 5. Director: Miroslav Kavka; Slovenska Pozicovna Filmov, Priemyselna 1 82460 Bratislava. Tel: 7 211301. FAX: 7 215685. Director: Ing. Emilia Sebova; Space Film, Karlovo Náměstí 19 120 00 Prague 2. Tel: 2 204 687, 204 820. FAX: 2 202 723. Director: Ing. Petr Zenkl; Transpress, Starochodovská 1098, PO Box 62 149 00 Prague 4. Tel: 2 763 161. FAX: 2 766 995. Director: Ing. Jaromír Nejedlý.

Organizations and Associations: Authors' Production and Distribution, PO Box 60 101 00 Prague 10. Tel: 2 729 204, 530 842. FAX: 2 725 453. Director: Michal Podhradský; Český Filmový Svaz (Czech Film Association), Pod Nuselskými schody 3 120 00 Prague 2. Tel: 2 691 03 10. Director: Pavel Kačírek; Charlie Centrum, Spitálska 4 811 08 Bratislava. Tel: 7 593 96. FAX: 7 551 39. Director: Eva Ďurníkova; Filmový Podnik Hl.M. Prahy, Vodičkova 30 110 00 Prague 1. Tel: 2 235 09 69. Director: Miroslav Mařik; Filmový Prumysl (Equipment), Kříženeckého nám. 322 152 53 Prague 5. Tel: 2 54 25 39. FAX: 2 54 25 39. Director: Miloš Lisý; Independent TV & Film Production Association, Hellichova 1 118 00 Prague 1. Tel: 2 536 020. FAX: 2 536 020. Director: Richard Kraus, Managing Director; National Film Archive, Narodni Třída č.40 110 00 Prague 1. Tel: 2 260 087. Director: Vladimir Opéla; Slovak Film Institute

National Cinematographic Centre, Grosslingova 32 811 09 Bratislava, CSFR (Slovakia). Tel: 7 517 89, 572 32, 49 99 29. FAX: 7 594 61. Contacts: Dr. Martin Smatlak, Dr. Viera Duricova, Head of International Department, Director: PhDr. Martin Smatlak, President of SFI-NCC; Slovensky Filmovy Ustav, ul. Cervenej armády 32 811 09 Bratislava. Tel: 7 555 31, 7 551 39, 7 572 32, 7 53489. FAX: 7 551 39. Director: PhDr. Martin Šmatlák t.č. 7 517 89, 7 499 929; Správa Kín Hlavného Mesta Bratislavy, Hviezdoslavove nám. 14 811 02 Bratislava. Tel: 7 333 44 75. FAX: 7 33 53 28. Director: JUDr. Pavel Zrínyi.

Studios: Bucfilm, Kříženeckého Nám. 322 152 53 Prague 5. Tel: 2 590 672 direct, 2 541 641, 545 444, 537 373 ext. 3062 3064. FAX: 2 590 315. Directors: Jaroslav Bouček, Jana Tomsová, Martin Mikuláš; Jam Media S.R.O., Nerudova Street No. 19 Prague 1, 118 00. Tel: 2 53 26 83. FAX: 2 53 26 83. Contact: Petr Rožánck, Dipl. Ing. Director: Vladimír Chrenovský, Dipl. Ing., General Director; KF A.S, Jindřišská 34 112 07 Prague 1. Tel: 2 628 0374, 644 5118. FAX: 2 545 480. Telex: 122 080. Contact: Mr. Jan Knoflíček, Chairman and CEO. Directors: Mr. Jan Knoflíček, General Director; Ms. Hana Jelínková, Economic Director; Mr. Jaroslav Karlíček, Technical Director; Dr. Zdeněk Ježek, Foreign Affairs.

DENMARK

Population: 5,150,000
Number of screens in 1991: 177.
Annual Admissions in 1991: 9.7 million.
Top Ten Foreign Films of 1992: 1) Lethal Weapon III; 2) Hot Shots; 3) Basic Instinct; 4) Hook; 5) Beauty and the Beast; 6) Cape Fear; 7) The Last Boy Scout; 8) Far and Away; 9) The Prince of Tides; 10) Wayne's World.
Trends: The merger between Egmont Foundation and Nordisk Film Foundation, two Scandinavian giants, has clearly placed Metronome as number two in the film and TV production, exhibition and theatrical/homevideo distribution market in Denmark. Cinema admission has been as low as 9.2 million and Metronome experts blame this on the merger.

The Danish Film Institute has propposed a small hike on TV license fees, believing this could provide as much as $18 million towards cinema production. Currently, the DFI provides production subsidies totaling $13.5 million annually.
Distributors: Constantin A/S, Skelbikgade 1, DK-1717 Copenhagen V. Tel: 33 25 24 24. FAX: 33 25 07 07. Directors: Peter Philipsen, Lejf Bernt, Kim Philipsen; Dan Ina Film, Huset. Rådhusstræde 13, 2. floor, DK-1466 Kobenhavn K. Tel: 33 32 40 77. FAX: 33 32 50 77. Director: Børge Nielsen. Director: Børge Nielsen; Dansk Management Center (DMC), Kristianiagade 7, DK-2100 Copenhagen Ø. Tel: 31 38 97 77. Contact: Michael Meinhardt; Klip, Niels Hemmingsensgade 20, DK-1153 Copenhagen K. Tel: 33 13 43 78. FAX: 33 91 52 42. Contact: Frans Rasmussen; Nordisk Film TV-Distribution AB, Box 9011, Söderhälarstrand 27, 10271 Stockholm, Sweden. Tel: +46 8 6690550. FAX: +46 8 841312. Director: C. G. Anderson; Pathe-Nordisk Film Distributio, Skelbikgade 1, DK-1717 Copenhagen V. Tel: 31 23 24 88. FAX: 31 23 04 15. Telex: 15286 filmko dk. Director: Peter Philipsen; Regina Film, Bregnegaardsvej 7, DK-2920 Charlottenlund. Tel: 31 62 96 40. Contact: Leo Schou; Scanbox Denmark, Hirsemarken 3, DK-3520 Farum. Tel: 44 99 62 00. FAX: 42 95 17 86. Contact: Kurt Wellejus; Sonet/Dansk Film APS, Sondermarksvej 16, DK-2500 Valby. Tel: 31 46 77 55. FAX: 36 44 09 69. Contact: Henrik Fabricius Bjerre; United International Pictures, Hauchsvej 13, DK-1825 Copenhagen V. Tel: 31 31 23 30. FAX: 31 23 34 20. Telex: 22402 UIPIC DK. Director: Anne-Grete Wezelenburg; Warner & Metronome Film, Søndermarksvej 16, DK-2500 Valby. Tel: 31 46 88 22. FAX: 36 44 06 04. Contact: Karin Bommesen.
Organizations and Associations: Association of Children's Film, Niels Hemmingsensgade 20, DK-1153 Coopenhagen K. Tel: 3315 6760. FAX: 3391 5242. Contact: Lis Lorentzen. Director: Søren K. Lauridsen, Chairman; Association of Danish Film DIS, Bulowsvej 50A, DK 1870, Fredericksberg C. Tel: 35 36 56 16, 31 31 23 30. FAX: 31 35 57 58. Directors: Johan Schluter, Anne-Frete Wezelenburg; The Danish Film Museum, Store Søndervoldstræde 4, DK-1419 Copenhagen K. Tel: 31 517 65 00. FAX: 31 517 13 12. Director: Ib Monty; Danish Film Institute Workshop, Vesterbrogade 24, DK-1620 Copenhagen V. Tel: 31 24 16 24. FAX: 31 24 44 19. Contact: Dino Raymond Hansen.
Studios: Columbus Film Video A.M.B.A, Islands Brygge 16-18, DK-2300 Copenhagen S. Tel: 31 57 81 20. FAX: 31 57 80 22. Director: Bjarne Eskildsen, Managing Director; Dansk Kinematograf A/S, Rath-sacksvej 13, DK-1862 Frederiksberg C. Tel: 31 31 16 36. FAX: 31 24 81 38. Contact: Jorgen Sondergaard.

EGYPT

Population: 60,00,000.
Number of cinemas: 202 in both 1992 and 1993.
Admission price: (in Egyptian pounds) Top: $7.00, low of $3.00.
Admission tax: 25%.
Number of films produced locally: 62 features.
Number of films imported: 300. For each imported film the country pays about 200 Egyptian pounds, as importation tax, plus 300 as release tax (payable to the Egyptian censorship dept.) for a period of 3 years.
Government film organizations: Ministry of Culture is under the guidance of Mr. Farouk Hosny, attached to the ministry: 1) The Censorship dept, headed by Mr. Hamdy Serour. (The Gresham-Bulding, Talat Harb

Str, Cairo); 2) The National Film center, headed by Hashem El Nahas (Al Ahram Road, Giza Egypt), attached to the Film Center: a) Cairo International Film Festival, b) Six production units for producing documentaries, experimental films, and cartoons, c) The Visual images technical center. (36, Sherif Str., Cairo); 3) Misr Co. for Theaters and Film Distribution. (87 Ramses Str., Cairo). Headed by Moustafa Eid; 4) Misr Co. For Studio & Film Productions. (art city, Al Ahram Road Giza, Egypt) Headed by Saad Abdel Rahman.
The Ministry of Culture also controls the academy of arts, to which the following institutes are attached: a) The high cinema institute, b) Theatrical arts institute, c) Conservatory & The Ballet and Dance institute. The academy of arts is headed by Dr. Fawzy Fahmy (Gamal El Din-Al Afghany str., Al Ahram Road, Giza, Egypt), d) The Egyptian Opera House (El Gezira, Kasr El Nil, Cairo).
The Egyptian Studios (controlled by Ministry of Culture): 1) Misr Studios (five stages) Al Ahram Road, Giza, Egypt, 2) Al Ahram Studios (five stages) Al Ahram Road, Giza, Egypt, 3) El Nil Studios (one stage) Al Ahram Road, Giza, Egypt, 4) Galal Studios (two stages) Hadaiek El Kobba, Cairo, 5) Nassibian Studios (one stage) El Fagala, Cairo.
Free Film Centers: The Catholic Film Center, 9, Adly str., Cairo, The American Center,** Part of the American Embassy, Cairo, The British Center,** Part of the British Embassy, Cairo, Center Cultural France, One at Al Mounira, Cairo, and at Hiliopolice.
**Both the American and British Centers have film libraries.
Principal Production Companies and Distributors: 1) Artist Unity, Farid Shawki 16, Adly Str., Cairo; 2) Aflam Farid Shawki, Farid Shawki 36, Sherif Str., Cairo; 3) Aflam Galal, Nader Galal 85, Ramses St., Cairo; 4) Alamia T.V. & Cinema, Hussein Kalla-41, Guizira elwosta, Zamalek, Cairo; 5) Aflam Misr Alamia, Yousef Shahin 35, Champlion St., Cairo; 6) Badie sobhi, Badie Sobhi 12, Soliman Elhalabi St., Cairo; 7) El-Leithy Films, Ihab El-Leithy 37, Kasr El-Nil St., Cairo; 8) Gamal El-Leithy, Gamal El-Leithy 11, Saray El-Azbakia St., Cairo; 9) Manar Film, Atef Ibrahim, 11, Saray El-Azbakia St., Cairo; 10) Tamido Film, Medhat Sherif 4, Zaki St., Orabi, Cairo; 11) Nasr Film, Mohamed Hassan 33, Orabi St., Cairo; 12) Kasr El-Nil International Ahmed Sami, (Ahmed Sami & Co.) 4, Hussein Almimar St., Kasr El Nil, Cairo. Tel. 5745416, FAX: 2918059; 13) Ceneral Film, Nagib Spiro, 85, Ramses St., Cairo; 14) Misr El-Arabia, Wasef Faiez 12, Soliman Elhalabi St., Cairo; 15) Hany Film, Zaki Guirges 4, Soliman Elhalabi St., Cairo; 16) Soat El-Fann, D. Abdel Wahab 16, Adly St., Cairo; 17) Osiris Film, Omran Ali 87, Ramses St., Cairo; 18) Masr El-Guidida, Salah Kharma, 36, Orabi St., Cairo.
** (Note) By the Law, all and any film producer is intitled to work as a distributor of his, or others' productions.
Foreign Distributors: MGM—Cairo/Egypt 35, Talat Harb St., Cairo.
Producers rendering services and handling foreign productions: Mr. Ahmed Sami, 77, Abdel Aziz Fahmy Str., (4th floor appt. 23) Tel: 2477000; 4, Hussein El Mimar Str., (1st floor appt. 4) Kasr El Nil, Cairo. Tel: 5745416 FAX: 2918059.

—AHMED SAMI

FRANCE

Population: 56,300,000
Cinema screens: Approx. 4,530
Admissions: 117,500,000 1991; down 4.3 million since 1990 and 11.2 million since 1987.
Top Ten Box Office Films of 1992: 1) Basic Instinct (US: $27 mill.); 2) Lethal Weapon 3 (US/Warner: $26m); 3) Hook (US/Col.: $20.5m); 4) L'Amant (Fr.–Brit./AMLF: $19m); 5) 1492: Conquest of Paradise (Fr.–Brit.–Span./Gaumont: $16.8 m); 6) Beauty and the Beast (US/Warner: $16.5m); 7) JFK (US/Warner: $15.7 m); 8) Indochine (Fr./Bac: $15m); 9) Le Zebre (Fr./Bac: $11.1m); 10) High Heels (Fr.–Span./UGC: $8.7m).
Trends: The Centre National de Cinematographie's budget has been increased by 7.5% equaling $2.1 billion francs ($400 million) for several new ambitious projects, while Cinematheque Operations' budget slightly increased to $3.7 million francs ($6.5 million) for 1993. A 5.5% increase generated from taxes and the Ministry of Culture provide $38 million francs ($7.6 million) for film distribution and theatre renovations, while $10 million has been allotted for nitrate to safe stock transfer.
Distributors: Alpha International, 18 rue Pasteur, 94800 Villejuif. Tel: (1) 46 77 80 85. FAX: (1) 46 78 18 38. Contact: Danielle Bourdekas; Amaya Distribution S.A, 25 rue Petit Muse, 75004 Paris. Tel: (1) 40 27 07 01. FAX (1) 42 77 60 56. Contact: Patricia de Wilde; Ariane Films, 15 rue de Colonel Pierre Avia, 75015 Paris. Tel: (1) 46 62 17 77. FAX: (1) 46 62 17 97. Director: Leslie Grunberg, President CEO; BAC Films, 5 rue Pelouze, 75008 Paris. Tel: (1) 44 70 92 30. FAX: (1) 4470 90 70. Contact: Jean Labadie; Carlton Film Export, 53 avenue Gambetta, 92400 Courbevoie. Tel: (1) 46 67 77 27. FAX: (1) 47 68 70 17. Telex: 6165054 F GRKATZ. Contact: Raoul Katz; Centre National de Documentation Pédagogique, 29 rue d'Ulm, 75230 Paris. Tel: (1) 46 34 90 00. FAX: (1) 46 34 55 44. Contacts: Françoise Blime; Michele Cohen; Cine Saison (Saison Corp Cinema Department), 1 rue François ler, 75008 Paris. Tel: (1) 42 89 77. FAX: (1) 42 89 54 06. Contact: Edith Grant; Cinemadis Films, 78 Champs-Elysees, 75008 Paris. Tel: (1) 45 62 82 87, 45 62 90 06. FAX: (1) 42 89 21 98. Contact: Jean Luret; Cinexport, 76-78 avenue des Champs-Elysees, 75008 Paris. Tel: (1) 45 62 49 45. FAX: (1) 45 63 82 26. Director: Anne-Marie Rombourg-Caraco, Directrice; Cythere Films, 34 Champs-Elysees, 75008 Paris. Tel: (1) 42 89 07 67. FAX: (1) 42 56 07 73. Contact: Claude Makovski; Dathanna International, 41 boulevard de Magenta, 75010 Paris. Tel: (1) 42 49 61 69. FAX: (1) 42 38 12 27. Telex: 250 303 F (DATHANNA). Director: Stephanie Gillet; Elixir Productions, PO Box 56, 06602 Antibes. Tel: 93 34 89 48. FAX: 93 34 24 49. Contact: Milan

Ostojic; Eurocine, 33 Champs-Elysees. 75008 Paris. Tel: (1) 42 25 64 92. FAX: (1) 42 25 73 38. Contact: Daniel Lesouer; Films de la Caverne, 7 rue des Algues-Marines, 34250 Palavas les Flots. Tel: 67 68 36 07. FAX: 75 04 87 87. Contact: Pierre Guy; Formavision, 7 rue de Cardinal Mercier, 75009 Paris. Tel: (1) 45 26 87 00. FAX: (1) 42 81 02 29. Contact: Lucien Hodebourg; Gaumont, 30 avenue Charles de Gaulle, 92200 Neuilly. Tel: (1) 46 43 20 00. FAX: (1) 46 43 20 26. Director: Nicolas Seydoux; GMT Productions, 27 rue Marbeuf, 75008 Paris. Tel: (1) 42 89 32 10. FAX: (1) 42 89 31 09. Contact: Jean-Pierre Guerin; Impex Films, 102 Champs-Elysees, 75008 Paris. Tel: (1) 45 62 20 60. FAX: (1) 42 89 33 62. Directors: Andre Samarcq, Verónique Samarcq; Jeck Film, 5 rue Rene Boulanger, 75010 Paris. Tel: (1) 42 40 78 00. FAX: (1) 48 03 02 64. Contact: Koukou Chanska. Director: Noëlle Gidon-Capelle; Les Films Christiane Kieffer, 28 avenue Charles de Gaulle, 92200 Neuilly-sur-Seine. Tel: 46 24 00 11. FAX: 46 24 12 97. Telex: 614 591. Contact: Christiane Kieffer; Les Films du Scorpion SA, 53 avenue Gambetta, 92400 Courbevoie. Tel: (1) 46 67 77 27, (1) 46 67 78 28. FAX: (1) 47 68 70 17. Telex: 616 054. F. Gr. KATZ. Contact: Alain Katz, President; Les Films Number One, 16 avenue Hoche, 75008 Paris. Tel: (1) 45 63 44 02. FAX: (1) 42 89 19 21. Contact: Pierre Kalfon; Les Films Singuliers Sarl, 20 rue Michelet, 93100 Montreuil. Tel: (1) 42 87 02 02, 42 87 59 08. FAX: (1) 42 87 01 89. Contact: Michel M. Poirier; Les Grands Films Classiques, 49 avenue Théophile Gautier, 75016 Paris. Tel: (1) 45 24 43 24. FAX: (1) 45 25 49 73. Telex: 640 207 GRANFIM F. Contact: Pascal Bonnetête; Long Island International, 82 rue Lauriston, 75116 Paris. Tel: (1) 47 04 29 50. FAX: (1) 47 04 40 51. Telex: 6 80 822 F. Director: Bernard Majani; Metropolitan Filmexport, 1 rue Lord Byron, 75008 Paris. Tel: (1) 45 63 45 60. FAX: (1) 45 63 53 37. Contact: David Hadida; Michel M. Poirier, 20 rue Michelet, 93100 Montreuil. Tel: (1) 42 87 02 02, 42 87 59 08. FAX: (1) 42 87 01 89. Director: Michel M. Poirier; MK2 Diffusion, 55 rue Traversiere, 75012 Paris. Tel: (1) 43 07 92 74. FAX: (1) 43 41 32 30. Telex: 214 720 MKPRO F. Director: Marin Karmitz, President; Mygale Films, 1 rue Damremont, 75018 Paris. Tel: (1) 42 26 12 26. Contact: James L. Frachon; Outsider Diffusion, 63 rue Pascal, 75013 Paris. Tel: (1) 43 35 81 74. FAX: (1) 47 07 10 49. Director: Laurent Geissmann; P.M.M.P. (Phillippe Mounier Marketing Production), 39 rue Vineuse, 75116 Paris. Tel: (1) 47 04 40 88. FAX: (1) 47 04 40 98. Director: Philippe Mounier; Pendulum Pictures, Ltd., 14 rue des Courtures, St. Gervais, 75003 Paris. Tel: 42 78 86 30. FAX: 42 74 14 93; Peri Productions, %Riethof, 95 rue de la Pompe, 75016 Paris. Tel: (1) 45 53 65 93. FAX: (1) 45 53 65 24. Contact: Peter Riethof, President; Point Du Jour, 38 rue Croix des Petits Champs, 75001 Paris. Tel: (1) 47 03 40 00. FAX: (1) 47 03 39 48. Contact: Fabrice Blancho; Revcom International/Les Films Ariane, 15 rue du Colonel Pierre Avia, 75015 Paris. Tel: (1) 46 62 17 77. FAX: (1) 46 62 17 92. Director: Leslie Grunberg; Vauban Productions, 9 avenue Franklin D. Roosevelt, Paris 75008. Tel: (1) 42 25 66 04. FAX: (1) 49 53 04 91. Contacts: Robert Velaise, James Velaise. Directors: Robert Velaise, James Valaise; Yves Witner S.A, 41 rue de Sèvres, 92100 Boulogne. Tel: 46 04 01 71. FAX: 46 04 00 41. Contact: Mllse. Sabine Gérmont, Attacheé de Direction. Director: Mr. Yves Witner.

Exhibitors: Cine Saison (Saison Corp Cinema Department), 1 rue François ler, 75008 Paris. Tel: (1) 42 89 50 77. FAX: (1) 42 89 54 06. Contact: Edith Grant; Federation Nationale des Cinemas Français (FNCF), 10 rue de Marignan, 75008 Paris. Tel: (1) 43 59 16 76. FAX: (1) 40 74 08 64. Director: Jean Labe, President; Gaumont, 30 avenue Charles de Gaulle, 92200 Neuilly. Tel: (1) 46 43 20 00. FAX: (1) 46 43 20 26. Director: Nicolas Seydoux; MK2 Diffusion, 55 rue Traversiere, 75012 Paris. Tel: (1) 43 07 92 74. FAX: (1) 43 41 32 30. Telex: 214 720 MKPRO F. Director: Marin Karmitz, President; Pendulum Pictures, Ltd., 14 rue des Courtures, St. Gervais, 75003 Paris. Tel: 42 78 86 30. FAX: 42 74 14 93; Union Internationale des Cinemas, 10 rue de Marignan, 75008 Paris. Tel: (1) 43 59 16 76. FAX: (1) 40 74 08 64. Contact: Veronique Bagnes.

Organizations and Associations: Academie des Arts et Techniques du Cinema, 19 avenue du President Wilson, 75116 Paris. Tel: (1) 47 23 72 33. FAX: (1) 40 70 02 91. Director: Daniel Toscan du Plantier, président. French Animation Association, 4 avenue du Nord, 78310 Maurepas. Tel: (1) 30 50 52 74. FAX: (1) 30 51 60 92. Director: President; Bureau de Liaison Europeen du Cinema, %Federation Internationale des Associations de Distributeurs de Films, Boulevard Malesherbes 43, 75008 Paris. Tel: (1) 42 66 05 32. FAX: (1) 42 66 96 92. Contact: Gilbert Gregoire, Président Adjoint de la Fiad; Chambre Syndicale des Producteurs & Exportateurs de Films Français, 5 rue de Cirque, 75008 Paris. Tel: (1) 42 25 70 63. FAX: (1) 42 25 94 27. Director: Alain Poiré, President; Federation Internationales des Associations de Distributeurs Films, 43 boulevard Malesherbes, 75008 Paris. Tel: (1) 42 66 05 32. FAX: (1) 42 66 96 92. Director: M. Luc Hemelaer. National Federation of Film Distributors, 43 boulevard Malesherbes, 75008 Paris. Tel: (1) 42 66 05 32. FAX: (1) 42 66 96 92. Director: M. Nicolas Seydoux; Federation of Théatre Cinema and Audiovisual Unions, 14-16 rue des Lilas, 75015 Paris. Tel: (1) 42 40 14 95. FAX: (1) 42 40 90 20. Director: Jean Voirin, Secrétaire Général. French Union of Actors, 21 bis rue Victor Masse, 75009 Paris. Tel: (1) 42 85 88 11. FAX: (1) 45 26 47 21. Director: François Parrot, Délégué Général. Union of Film Producers, 1 Pl des Deux Ecus, 75001 Paris. Tel: (1) 40 28 01 38. FAX: (1) 42 21 17 00. Contact: Berthemy Bruno.

Production Houses—Theatrical/Television: Acta Production, 12 rue Neuve Thierry, 92410 Ville S'Avray. Tel: 47 50 79 99. Contact: Michel Patient, Director. Director: Michel Patient; Alexandre Film, 14 rue Marignan, 75008 Paris. Tel: (1) 45 62 02 04. FAX: (1) 42 89 26 89. Directors: Alexandre Arcady, Diane Kurgs; Alizes, 19 rue Bassano, 75116 Paris. Tel: (1) 47 23 90 35. FAX: (1) 47 20 19 36. Director: Denis Karvil; Alpha International, 18 rue Pasteur, 94800 Villejuif. Tel: (1) 46 77 80 85. FAX: (1) 46 78 18 38. Contact: Danielle Bourdekas; American European Entertainment, 18 rue Beaujon, 75008 Paris. Tel: (1) 42 56 45 05. FAX: (1) 42 56 11 42. Contact: Bill Harper; Ariane Films, 15 rue de Colonel Pierre Avia, 75015 Paris. Tel: (1) 46 62 17 77. FAX: (1) 46 62 17 97. Director: Leslie Grunberg; AS Productions, 29 rue de Marignan, 75008 Paris. Tel: (1) 42 25 18 49. FAX: (1) 42 25 75 13. Contact: Alain Siritzky; Barnaba Films, 4 rue du Colonel Driant, 75001 Paris. Tel: (1) 42 21 00 27. FAX: (1) 40 39 05 48. Telex: 240 396. Contact: Musa Turincev; Bay Vista, Studios la Victorine, 16 avenue Edouard Grinda, 06200 Nice. Tel: 93 71 01 40. FAX: 93 71 04 60. Director: Antoine Sabarros; Belbo Films, 46 rue de Provence, 75009 Paris. Tel: (1) 48 78 40 04. FAX: (1) 42 85 27 50. Contact: Anne Lieske; Camera One, 11 du Bac, 75007 Paris. Tel: (1) 45 49 42 46. FAX: (1) 45 49 38 09. Contact: Michel Seydoux; Cameras Continentales, 25 rue Petit Musc. Tel: (1) 40 27 99 00. FAX: (1) 42 72 83 10. Director: Alain Moreau; Centre Europeen Cinematographique Rone-Alpes, 8 Place Lazare-Goujon, 69627 Villeur Banne Cedex. Tel: 78 03 30 91. FAX: 78 03 30 92. Contact: Marie Pascale Osterrieth; Centre National de Documentation Pèdagogique, 29 rue d'Ulm, 75230 Paris. Tel: (1) 46 34 90 00. FAX: (1) 46 34 55 44. Contact: Françoise Blime; Chrysalide Films, 7 rue Castéja, 92100 Boulogne. Tel: (1) 46 94 65 00. FAX: (1) 46 94 65 99. Contact: Monique Annaud-Baltzer; Cine Saison (Saison Corp Cinema Department), 1 rue François Ier, 75008 Paris. Tel: (1) 42 89 50 77. FAX: (1) 42 89 54 06. Contact: Edith Grant; Cinemadis Films, 78 Champs-Elysees, 75008 Paris. Tel: (1) 45 62 82 87, 45 62 90 06. FAX: (1) 42 89 21 98. Contact: Jean Luret; Cineteve, 4 Quai des Célestins, 75004 Paris. Tel: (1) 48 04 30 00. FAX: (1) 48 04 70 33. Director: Fabiènne Servan Schreiber; Compagnie Lyonnaise de Cinema, 274 Cours Emile Zola, 69100 Villeurbanne. Tel: 78 84 87 98. FAX: 78 84 98 25. Contact: Daniel Charrier; Cousteau Society, The, 25 avenue de Wagram, 75017 Paris. Tel: (1) 40 53 63 00. FAX: (1) 40 53 63 03. Telex: 641 856 F REQUINS. Director: Capt. J. Y. Cousteau, President; Creativity & Development, 1 rue Rene Anjolvy, 94250 Gentilly. Tel: 49 69 00 10. FAX: 49 69 01 05. Telex: 634 975. Contact: Anne Magnol & Donald Lawrie; Cythere Films, 34 Champs-Elysees, 75008 Paris. Tel: (1) 42 89 07 67. FAX: (1) 42 56 07 73. Contact: Claude Makovski; D+ Productions S.A.R.L. (Dee Productions Ltd.), 101 R. du FG, Saint Denis, 75010 Paris. Tel: (1) 40 22 05 49. FAX: (1) 40 22 93 60. Contact: Françoise de Leu; Dathanna International, 41 boulevard de Magenta, 75010 Paris. Tel: (1) 42 49 61 69. FAX: (1) 42 38 12 27. Telex: 250 303 F (DATHANNA). Director: Stephanie Gillet; Davis Films, 116 bis Champs-Elysees, 75008 Paris. Tel: (1) 45 61 90 45. FAX: (1) 45 63 77 31. Contact: Mr. Samuel Hadida; DEMD Productions, 38 rue René Boulanger, 75010 Paris. Tel: (1) 42 40 88 50. FAX: (1) 42 40 97 40. Contact: Caroline Hertman; Ecofilm, Studios de la Victorine, 16 avenue Edouard Grinda, 06200 Nice. Tel: 93 18 06 55, 93 72 54 54. FAX: 93 18 06 56. Director: Jeannine Kadow; Eighties Productions, 22 Galerie Saint-Marc., 75002 Paris. Tel: (1) 40 39 05 71. FAX: (1) 40 39 98 65. Contact: Michel Propper. Director: Michel Propper; Elixir Productions, PO Box 56, 06602 Antibes. Tel: 93 34 89 48. FAX: 93 34 24 49. Contact: Milan Ostojic; Entracte, 13 rue Deparcieux, 75014 Paris. Tel: (1) 43 35 35 51. FAX: (1) 43 22 34 60. Contact: Gérard Bellanger; Erato Films, 10 rue Affre, 75018 Paris. Tel: (1) 49 25 89 00. FAX: (1) 49 25 89 09. Contact: Daniel Toscan du Plantier; Eurocine, 33 Champs-Elysees, 75008 Paris. Tel: (1) 42 25 64 92. FAX: (1) 42 25 73 38. Contact: Daniel Lesouer; Fildebroc, 101-103 rue Gallieni, 92100 Boulògne. Tel: (1) 46 03 61 88. FAX: (1) 46 03 61 31. Contact: Michelle de Broca; Films et Son, 44 rue Michel Gachet, 13007 Marseille. Tel: (1) 91 52 07 63. Contact: Jean-Pierre Beulaygue; Films Princesse, 19 rue Bassano, 75116 Paris. Tel: (1) 47 20 28 74. FAX: (1) 47 20 19 36. Director: Pierre Roitfeld; FR 3 Films Production, 42 avenue d'Iena, 75116 Paris. Tel: (1) 47 23 86 10. Director: Mr. Hervé Bourges; Gaumont, 30 avenue Charles de Gaulle, 92200 Neuilly. Tel: (1) 46 43 20 00. FAX: (1) 46 23 20 26. Director: Nicolas Seydoux; GMT Productions, 27 rue Marbeuf, 75008 Paris. Tel: (1) 42 89 32 10. FAX: (1) 42 89 31 09. Contact: Jean-Pierre Guerin; Gross National Productions Ltd., B.P. 56, Antibes, 06602 Cedex. Tel: 93 34 89 48. FAX: 93 34 24 49. Contact: Milan Ostojic; Institut National de L'Audiovisuel, 4 avenue de l'Europe, 94366 Bry sur Marne. Tel: 49 83 20 00. FAX: 49 83 25 84. Director: Georges Fillioud; Jeck Film, 5 rue Rene Boulanger, 75010 Paris. Tel: (1) 42 40 78 00. FAX: (1) 48 03 02 64. Contact: Koukou Chanska; JKL International, 2 rue Constantin Pecquer, 75018 Paris. Contact: Roger Kay, Director; JSSK Productions, 5 rue Cugnot, 75018 Paris. Contact: John Simenon; Juana Production, 3 rue Haddad Simon, 06400 Cannes. Tel: 93 43 30 28. FAX: 93 38 24 55. Telex: 470 764 MESSAG. Contact: André Mallet; Labrador Films, 53 avenue Gambetta, 92400 Courbevoie. Tel: (1) 46 67 78 28. FAX: (1) 47 68 70 17. Telex: 616054 F GRKATZ. Contact: Alain Katz; Les Editions Thanatos, 4 Impasse Des Pientres, 112 rue de Saint-Denis, 75002 Paris. Tel: (1) 42 33 43 16. FAX: (1) 42 33 52 75. Contact: Jose Benazeraf; Les Films 13, 15 avenue Hoche, 75008 Paris. Tel: 42 25 00 89. FAX: (1) 42 25 64 90. Director: Claude Lelouch; Les Films Christiane Kieffer, 28 avenue Charles de Gaulle, 92200 Neuilly-sur-Seine. Tel: 46 24 00 11. FAX: 46 24 12 97. Telex: 614 591. Contact: Christiane Kieffer; Les Films de la Cassine, 101 rue Saint-Dominique, 75007 Paris. Tel: (1) 47 53 04 23. FAX: (1) 47 05 81 10. Contact: Eve Vercel; Les Films du Scorpion SA, 53 avenue Gambetta, 92400 Courbevoie. Tel: (1) 46 67 77 27, (1) 46 67 78 28. FAX: (1) 47 68 70 17. Telex: 616 054, F. GR. KATZ. Contact: Alain Katz, President; Les Films Number One, 16 avenue Hoche, 75008 Paris. Tel: (1) 45 63 44 02. FAX: (1) 42 89 19 21. Contact: Pierre Kalfon; Les Films Singuliers Sarl, 30 rue Michelet, 93100 Montreuil. Tel: (1) 42 87 02 02, 42 87 59 08. FAX: (1) 42 87 01 89. Contact: Michel M. Poirier; Les Productions du 3Ème Étage, 22 Galerie Saint-Marc, 75002 Paris. Tel: (1) 40 39 05 71. FAX: (1) 40 39 98 65. Contact: Michel Propper; LMK Images, 55 rue Traversiere, 75012 Paris. Tel: (1) 43 47 55 20. FAX: (1) 43 47 44 05. Director: Yves Eudes; Mainstream SA, 34 rue Poncelet, 75017 Paris. Tel: (1) 44 40 05 55. FAX: (1) 47 63 07 62. Contact: Alexandre Heylen; Maki Films, 59 rue des Trois Freres, 75118 Paris. Tel: (1) 43 06 22 29. FAX: (1) 45 66 72 50. Contact: Eddy Matalon; MK2 Diffusion, 55 rue Traversiere, 75012 Paris. Tel: (1) 43 07 92 74. FAX: (1) 43 41 32 30. Telex:

214 720 MKPRO F. Director: Marin Karmitz; P.M.M.P. (Philippe Mounier Marketing Production), 39 rue Vineuse, 75116 Paris. Tel: (1) 47 04 40 88. FAX: (1) 47 04 40 98. Director: Philippe Mounier; Pendulum Pictures, Ltd., 14 rue des Courtures, St. Gervais, 75003 Paris. Tel: 42 78 86 30. FAX: 42 74 14 93; Peri Productions, %Riethof, 95 rue de la Pompe, 75016 Paris. Tel: (1) 45 53 65 93. FAX: (1) 45 53 65 24. Contact: Peter Riethof; Pixibox, 26 rue Berthollet, 94110 Arcueil. Tel: (1) 49 85 17 18. FAX: (1) 49 85 16 96. Contact: Patricia Evrard; Point du Jour, 38 rue Croix des Petits Champs, 75001 Paris. Tel: (1) 47 03 40 00. FAX: (1) 47 03 39 48. Contact: Fabrice Blancho; Procidis, 35 rue Marbeuf, 75008 Paris. Tel: (1) 43 59 66 74. FAX: (1) 42 25 84 23. Contact: Michéle Fourniols; Productions Jacques Roitfeld, 19 rue de Bassano, 75116 Paris. Tel: (1) 47 20 28 74. FAX: (1) 47 20 19 36 Contact: Vladimir Roitfeld; Revcom International/ Les Films Ariane, 15 rue du Colonel Pierre Avia, 75015 Paris. Tel: (1) 46 62 17 77. FAX: (1) 46 62 17 92. Director: Leslie Grunberg; S.F.P. Productions, 35 rue des Alouettes, 75019 Paris. Tel: (1) 40 03 58 28. FAX: (1) 42 03 18 35. Telex: 240 888. Contact: Claude Charlotte Levy; Société Nouvelle de Cinématographie, 23 avenue de Neuilly, 75116 Paris. Tel: (1) 40 67 77 77. FAX: (1) 40 67 74 10. Contact: Jean-Michel Kerdraon; Sogeav Ohra, 21 Avenue du Maine, 75015 Paris. Tel: 45 49 92 30. FAX: 45 44 00 40. Director: Izza Genini; Star Productions, 27 rue du jeu des Enfants, 6700 Strasbourg. Tel: 88 32 21 38. FAX: 88 75 59 16. Contact: Rene Letzgus; Studio Herwey, 11 rue Pasteur, 01000 Bourg-en-Bresse. Tel: (74) 22 63 04. Telex: 375 819. Contact: Dominique Cauquy; Su Ma Fa Productions, 16 avenue Hoche, 75008 Paris. Tel: (1) 42 89 23 00. FAX: (1) 42 89 23 00. Director: Michel Loulergue; Telema, 26 rue Danton, 92300 Levallois-Perret. Tel: 47 58 67 30. FAX: 47 58 81 16. Contact: Charles Gassot; Tilt Productions, 14 rue Manblanc, 75015 Paris. Tel: (1) 48 28 34 44. FAX: (1) 48 28 65 12. Director: Xavier Conture, Chairman; Vauban Productions, 9 avenue Franklin D. Roosevelt, Paris 75008. Tel: (1) 42 25 66 04. FAX: (1) 49 53 04 91. Contact: Robert Velaise; Veo_2 Max Film Productions, 39 rue Durantin, 75018 Paris. Tel: (1) 42 58 38 58. FAX: (1) 42 58 38 57. Contact: Christian Zerbib; Viaduc Productions, 16 rue de Sevres, Paris 75007. Tel: (1) 45 48 96 44. Contact: Leo Fuchs.

Studios: Caiman, 30 boulevard dela Bastille, 75012 Paris. Tel: (1) 43 44 11 22. FAX: (1) 43 44 79 30. Director: Denise Fremond; Elixir Productions, PO Box 56, 06602 Antibes. Tel: 93 34 89 48. FAX: 93 34 24 49. Contact: Milan Ostojic; Exposure, 1 bis rue des Epinettes, 94410 Saint-Maurice. Tel: (1) 48 93 45 01. FAX: (1) 48 93 17 17. Contact: Claude Copin; Films et Son, 44 rue Michel Gachet, 13007 Marseille. Tel: (1) 91 52 07 63. Contact: Jean-Pierre Beulaygue; Le Studio, 36 rue du fer a Moulin, 75005 Paris. Tel: (1) 43 37 80 96. FAX: (1) 47 07 22 98. Contact: Mike or Patricia; Paris Studio Billancourt, 50 Quai du Point-du-Jour, 92100 Boulogne-Billancourt. Tel: 46 09 93 24. FAX: 46 20 24 71. Director: M. J. Pierre Alessandri; Savoie Film Production, 74250 Viuz-en-Sallaz. Tel: 50 36 80 60. FAX: 50 36 83 07. Contact: Robert Pellet. Director: Robert Pellet; Studios Eclair (Groupe Tectis), 2 rue du Bac, 92158 Suresnes Cedex. Tel: (1) 40 99 50 40. FAX: (1) 42 04 72 01. Director: Philippe Dormoy; Studios La Victorine Côte D'Azur, 16 avenue Edouard Grinda, 06200 Nice. Tel: 93 72 54 54. FAX: 93 71 91 73. Telex: 970 056. Director: Marc Galerne.

GERMANY

Population: 80,000,000.

Number of Screens: 3,686 (3,237 in former West Germany; 449 in five eastern states).

Admissions: Approx. 104 million in 1992, down from 120 million in 1991.

Top Ten Films of 1992 (with distributor and admissions): 1) Basic Instinct (Scotia: 4,512,595); 2) Hot Shots (Fox: 3,930,873); 3) Hook (Columbia: 3,417,000); 4) Rescuers Down Under (Warner: 3,080,776); 5) JFK (Warner: 2,923,551); 6) Otto—Der Liebesfilm (Tobis: 2,820,441); 7) Beethoven (UIP: 2,316,416); 8) Lethal Weapon 3 (Warner: 2,264,494); 9) My Girl (Columbia: 2,206,000); 10) Curly Sue (Warner: 2,113,012).

Trends: Marketing costs have risen to $700,000 for film distribution and advertising. Meanwhile, American films have contributed as much as 85%, over $980 million marks (about $650 million), to box office receipts. Overall, admissions have climbed 7.5% and cinema house construction and renovations by major exhibs are totaling approximately $175 million.

Distributors: ABF-Film GmbH, Rudolf Breitscheidstr 21, 6092 Kelsterbach/Main. Tel: 06107 46 78, 57 88. Contact: Hans-Günter Schweikart. Graf Adolfstr 108, 4000 Düsseldorf 1. Tel: 0211 35 80 15/6; Accord Filmverleih GmbH, Weselerstr 65, 4000 Düsseldorf 1. Tel: 0211 62 06 40; AKK Sendezentrale GmbH & Co. KG, Turmstr 8, 6700 Ludwigshafen. Tel: 06211 5981 230. FAX: 06211 5981 189. Contact: Ulrich Best; Alhambra Filmverleih GmbH, Friedrich Ebertstr 12, 4000 Düsseldorf. Tel: 0211 35 29 72. Contact: Toni Schröder; Ampex Europa GmbH, Stefan George Ring 20, 8000 Munich 81. Tel: 089 93 20 39. FAX: 089 930 31 57; Ariola-Eurodisc GmbH, Carl Berteismannstr 161, Postfach 3306, 4830 Gütersloh 1. Tel: 05241 80 51 51. Telex: 933787; Ascot Filmverleih GmbH, Leopoldstr 62, D-8000 Munich 40. Tel: 089 39 69 29. FAX: 089 33 18 19. Contact: Dr. Klaus Fischer; Atelier Film, Schusterstr 35, 8000 Munich 71. Tel: 089 790 00 55. Telex: 523975 loco d.; Basis-Film Verleih, Güntzeistr 60, 1000 Berlin 31. Tel: 030 853 30 35; Bavaria Film GmbH, Bavariafilmplatz 7, 8022 Geiselgasteig. Tel: 089 64 99 0. FAX: 089 69 92 50 7. Telex: 523254 bavat d. Contact: Felix Neunterling; Chronos Filmverleih GmbH, Schopenhauerstr 50, 1000 Berlin 38. Tel: 030 803 30 51 2. Telex: 181511. Director: Bengt von zur Mühlen; Cinema Filmverleih GmbH, Braystr 20, 8000 Munich 80. Tel: 089 47 20 61. Telex: 5213591; Compact Film GmbH, Grünwalderstr 149, 8000 Munich 90. Tel: 089 64 00 86. Contact: Peter Michael Bonitz; Connexion Film Vertriebs and Produktions GmbH & Co. KG, Harvestehuder Weg 45, Postfach 13 22 21, 2000 Hamburg 13. Tel: 040 41 17 93 00. FAX: 040 41 17 93 99. Contact: Willi Baer; Contact Filmverleih GmbH, Hüttenstr. 40, 4000 Düsseldorf 1. Tel: 0211 37 40 24/5. Contact: Barbara Seelk; Delta Filmverleih GmbH, Rosenheimerstr 2, 8000 Munich 80. Tel: 089 48 30 35. FAX: 089 48 36 52; Edition Manfred Salzgeber, Motzstraße 9, W-1000 Berlin 30. Tel: 030 215 32 09. FAX: 030 215 43 48. Contact: Manfred Salzgeber; EMI Electrola GmBH, Maarweg 149, 5000 Cologne 30. Tel: 0221 490 20. FAX: 0221 497 23 35. Telex: 8881290. Director: Friedrich E. Wottawa; Endfilm, Am Vogelherd 4, D-8401 Bach. Tel: 09482 33 77. FAX: 09482 33 78. Contact: Christian Meinke. Director: Christian Meinke; Ernst Klett Verlag Für Wissen Und Bildung, Rotebühlstr 77, Postfach 106016, 7000 Stuttgart 10. Tel: 0711 66 72 0. FAX: 0711 667 25 05; Esplanade Filmverleih, Mannheimerstr 15, 6000 Frankfurt/Main. Tel: 069 23 13 21. FAX: 069 25 22 37; Ewald Paikert OHG, Konkordiastr 13, 4000 Düsseldorf. Tel: 0211 39 40 32. Contacts: Hans Paikert, Dieter Paikert; EX Picturis Filmdistribution, Fidicinstr 40, 1000 Berlin 61. Tel: 030 691 60 08/9. FAX: 030 692 95 75. Telex: 186794. Cable: EXPIC D. Directors: Christopher Fritze, Managing Director, Peter Rommel, Head of sales; Futura/ Filmverlag Der Autoren, Rambergstr 5, 8000 Munich 40. Tel: 089 38 17 00 0. FAX: 089 38 17 00 20. Telex: 5 215 637. Directors: Theo Hinz, Antonio Exacoustos Jr.; GBM Verlag Bilding Und Medien GmbH, Schwedenstr 10 8137 Berg 2 Starnberger See. Tel 08151 511 56. Director: Karl F. Soost; Germania Filmverleih, Blissestr 38-40, 1000 Berlin 31. Tel: 030 821 30 72. Contact: G. Lehmann; Herzog Filmverleih, Geschwister Schollstr 18, 8022 Grünwald. Tel: 089 64 91 56; Highlight Filmverleih, Herkomerplatz 2, 8000 Munich 80. Tel: 089 92 69 66 02. FAX: 089 98 15 43. Contact: Jasna Vavra; Hunter-Mondial Filmverleih GmbH, Hohe Pforte 4-6, 5000 Cologne 1. Tel: 0221 21 00 41; Iltis Filmverleih GmbH, Schollstr 2, 8035 Gauting. Tel: 089 850 54 68; Impuls Filmverleih Und Vertriebs GmbH, Harvestehuder Weg 88, 2000 Hamburg 13. Tel: 040 411 79 350. FAX: 040 411 79 359. Contact: Edmund Mattig; Inter-Pathé GmbH & Co. KG, Bolongarostr 141, 6230 Frankfurt/Main 80. Tel: 069 30 40 43, 31 56 80. FAX: 069 31 10 91. Director: Paul Schmitt; Keryx Film, Immenried 97, 7964 Kisslegg 2. Tel: 07563 22 21, 82 88. FAX: 07563 85 67. Contact: Werner Forster; Kinemathek IM Ruhrgebiet, Amtsgerichtsstr 32, D-4100 Duisburg 13. Tel: 203 8 99 03. FAX: 203 8 83 09. Contact: Paul Hofmann; Kinowelt, Pfisterstr 11, 8000 Munich 2. Tel: 089 296963. FAX: 089 221491. Directors: Thomas Häberle, Rainer Kölmel; Kirch-group, Robert-Bürkle-str 2, W-8045 Ismaning. Tel: 089 950 88 323. FAX: 089 950 88 330. Contact: Gottfried Zmeck; Klasing & Co. GmbH, Siekerwass 21, 34800 Bielefeld 1. Tel: 0521 5590. Telex: 3932934. Contact: Konrad Delius; Kora Filmverleih, Leopoldstr 65, 8000 Munich 40. Tel: 089 33 44 09. Contact: Georg Kormann; Kuchenreuther Filmverleih GmbH, Leopoldstr 80, 8000 Munich 40. Tel: 089 33 22 24. Contact: Herr Fuchs; Landesfilmdienst Bayern EV, Dietlindenstr 18, 8000 Munich 40. Tel: 089 34 70 65. FAX: 089 34 70 67. Director: Walter Thomas; Luxmeta Filmverleih GmbH, Baverische Str 5, 1000 Berlin 15. Tel: (030) 8819081; Mahlzahn Film, Hüttenstr 6, 4000 Düsseldorf 1. Tel: 0211 38 18 35. Contact: Klaus Manizann; Mercator Filmverleih GmbH, Wertherstr 73, Postfach 101950, 4800 Bielefeld 1. Tel: 521 12 40 61. FAX: 521 13 10 10. Contact: Dieter Gaus; Merkur Film Agency GmbH, Inderstorferstr 57, 8000 Munich 21. Tel: 089 580 30 51. Telex: 5216092 mefi d. Director: Gudrun Fleck; Metropol Filmverleih GmbH, Wiktonastr 34, 8000 Münich 40. Tel: 089 39 30 96. FAX: 089 39 63 03. Telex: 5218055 met d. Contact: Edmund Mattig; Movie Filmverleih GmbH & Co. KG (MFV), Graf Adolfstr 108, 4000 Düsseldorf 1. Tel: 0211 37 35 51. Contact: Josy Müller; NDR International, Gazellenkamp 57, 2000 Hamburg 54. Tel: 040 413 53 81. FAX: 040 56 38 26. Telex: 211849. Director: Heinz-Günter Sass; Neue Constantin Film, Kaiserstr 39, 8000 Münich 40. Tel: 089 38 60 90. FAX: 089 38 60 92 42. Telex: 522975 filma d. Contact: Herman Weigel; Neue Herzog Filmverleih GmbH, Alte Pasingerstr 108, 8032 Gräteifing. Tel: 089 88 36 73. Contact: Gunter Otto; Noris Filmverleih, Bauvereinsstr 51, 8500 Nürnberg 20. Tel: 0911 55 17 17; Obelisk Film GmbH, Odeonsplatz 8, 8000 Munich 22. Tel: 089 228 36 71. Contact: Klaus Langemeyer; Okular Filmverleih GmbH, Ottostr 72, 8012 Ottobrunn. Tel: 089 609 41 41, 609 96 96; P. H Knipp Film, Seestr 60, 8137 Berg/Strarberger See. Tel: 08151 510 91. FAX: 08151 510 31. Telex: 5270282 knipp d.; Pandora Film, Hamburgeralle 45, 6000 Frankfurt/ Main 90. Tel: 069 77 90 94. FAX: 069 70 74 03 3. Telex: 41 70 666 pan d. Directors: Reinhard Brundig, Karl Baumgartner; Primodessa Film, Cuvilliesstr 8, 8000 Munich 80. Tel: 089 98 25 68. Contact: Michael Fengler; Progress Film-Verleih GmbH, Burgstr 27, 0-1020 Berlin. Tel: 030 280 51 10. FAX: 030 282 91 57. Telex: 114175 pfv dd.; Progress Filmverleih, Burgstr 27, 0 1020 Berlin. Tel: 030 80 51 10. Telex: 114175. Director: Hans Müller; Reinhard Berg Filmproduktion, Körnerstr 5, 6200 Wiesbaden. Tel: 06121 30 59 19; Ribu Filmproduktion GmbH & Co., Averhoffstr 10, 2000 Hamburg 76. Tel: 040 220 12 21. FAX: 040 220 12 28; Ring Film Verleih, Schwalbenstr 13, 8012 Ottobrunn. Tel: 089 609 41 41. Contact: Peter Koch; Saarfilm Verleihagentur GmbH, Grülingstr 115, 6600 Saarbrücken 2. Tel: 0681 477 61. Contacts: Karl Jung, Heinrich Gard; Scotia International, Possartstr 14, 8000 Munich 80. Tel: 089 41 30 900. FAX: 089 470 63 20. Telex: 524783. Cable: SCOTD. Contact: Stanley Lawson; Selleng Filmagentur, Lietzenburgerstr 51, 1000 Berlin 30. Tel: 030 213 67 88. Contact: Gerda Seileng; Springer-Verlag GmbH & Co. KG, Heidelbergerplatz 3, 1000 Berlin 33, Tel: 030 82 07 1. Telex: 183319. Director: Heinz Götze; Stern Filmverleih GmbH, Dacnauerstr 16, 8000 Münich 2. Tel: 089 59 45 84. Contact: H.-W. Büche; Telcast International Filmproduction GmbH, Osterwaldstr 10, 8000 Munich 40. Tel: 089 361 89 44. FAX: 089 361 37 60. Contact: Andrea Kreuzhage; Tobis Filmkunst GmbH & Co., Pacelliallee 47, 1000 Berlin 33. Tel: 030 839 00 70, FAX: 030 831 66 41. Contact: Kilian Rebentrost; Traumfabrik, Theaterplatz 1, 4300 Essen 1. Tel: 0201 23 68 02; Unidoc Film GmbH, Braunschweigerstr

20, 4600 Dortmund 1. Tel: 0231 838 01 46. Contact: Joachim Winderlich; United International Pictures GmbH, Stresemannallee 13, 6000 Frankfurt/Main 70. Tel: 069 63 70 96. FAX: 069 63 41 64. Telex: 412097. Contact: Fred Sorg; Universum Film GmbH (UFA), Berg am Laimstr 47, Postfach 801929, 8000 Munich 80. Tel: 089 413 63 47. FAX: 089 40 57 00. Telex: 524830. Director: Bernd Tietze, Managing Director; Verlag Das Freie Buch GmbH, Tulbeckstr 4, 8000 Munich 2. Tel: 089 502 48 34. Director: Stefan Eggerdinger, Managing Director; Verlag E S Mittler & Sohn GmbH, Steintorwall 17, Postfach 2352, 4900 Herford. Tel: 05221 599 10. FAX: 05221 59 91 25. Telex: 934801; Vestischer Medien Verlag (VMV), Scheideweg 120, 4390 Gladbeck. Tel: 02043 647 74. Contact: Karlheinz Schneizer; VPS Film-Entertainment Film-Verwertungsgesellschaft MBH, Saarstr 7, 8000 Munich 40. Tel: 089 38 60 10. FAX: 089 308 51 41. Telex: 17898142. Director: Rüdiger von Spies; VVL Filmvertrieb GmbH, Kreittmaystr 32, D-8000 München 2. Tel: 089 123 60 01. FAX: 089 123 81 87. Contact: Alexander Welzhafer; Wara Film Und Ton GmbH & Co. KG, Wittekindstr 15, 5000 Cologne 41. Tel: 0221 44 50 07; Zukunft Film, Postfach 1548, 7180 Crailsheim. Tel: 07951 267 30. Contact: Peter Wagner.

Exhibitors: Aktualitäten Kino Betriebs GmbH & Co. (AKI), Im Hauptbannhof, 6000 Frankfurt/Main. Tel: 069 23 21 65; Blue Movie Bar Und Filmstudio GmbH & Co. KG, Mergenthalerstr 1, 2300 Flensburg. Tel: 0461 996 60; Broadway Kino GmbH, Enrenstr 11, 5000 Cologne 1. Tel: 0221 32 33 34; Cannon Cinema GmbH, Moritzstr 6, 6200 Wiesbaden. Tel: 06121 30 00 34. Director: Manfred Ewert; City Filmtheaterbetriebs GmbH, Sonnenstr 12, 8000 Munich 2. Tel: 089 59 19 83; Colm Filmtheaterbetriebs GmbH, Alte Poststr 3, 7000 Stuttgart 1. Tel: 0711 29 22 45/6. Director: Friedl Colm; Colonia Filmtheaterbetriebs/Krüger & Co. KG, Hohenzollernring 48, 5000 Cologne 1. Tel: 0221 21 79 97; Erasmus Kinoverwaltung, Grimmstr 30A, 7000 Stuttgart 1. Tel: 0711 65 04 00. FAX: 0711 657 25 30; Filmmuseum Potsdam, Am Marstall, 0-1560 Potsdam. Tel: 0331 2 35 35. Contact: Dorett Molitor, Dr. Barbel Dalichow; Filmtheaterbetriebe Georg Reiss GmbH, Sophienstr 1, 8000 Munich 2. Tel: 089 55 21 650. FAX: 089 55 21 65 25; FWU Institut für Film und Bild, Bavaria-Film-Platz 3, PO Box 260, 8022 Geiselgasteig. Tel: 089 64 97 0. FAX: 089 64 97 36 0. Contact: Nicola C. Wagenhals; Georg Reiss Filmtheaterbetriebs GmbH, Königsplatz 53, 3500 Kassel. Tel: 0561 72 90 90; Goldermann & Riech Theatergesellschaft, Friedrich Eberstr 59, 400 Düsseldorf 1. Tel: 0211 35 00 01; Hansa Filmtheaterbetriebs GmbH & Co. KG, Hohenzollernring 48, 5000 Cologne 1. Tel: 0221 21 79 97; Heinz Riech Filmtheaterbetriebs, Gänsestr 6-8, 4410 Warendorf 2. Tel: 02581 40 43; Hohenzollern Filmtheaterbetriebs GmbH & Co. KG, Hohenzollernring 48, 5000 Cologne 1. Tel: 0221 21 79 97; KG Filmtheater AM Zoo/Thomas & Co., Kurfurstendamm 33, 1000 Berlin 15. Tel: 030 883 60 86; Krugmann & Weischer/Mundsburger Kinobetriebsgesellschaft, Hamburgerstr 152, Postfach 761149, 2000 Hamburg 76. Tel: 040 29 11 11; Liselotte Jaeger Filmtheaterbetriebs, Holzgraben 26, 6000 Frankfurt. Tel: 069 28 52 05; Mertz OHG/EM Filmtheaterbetriebe, Königstr 22, 7000 Stuttgart. Tel: 0711 22 60 76; Olympic Filmtheaterbetriebs/Heinz Riech & Sohn OHG, Graf Adolfstr 96, 4000 Düsseldorf 1. Tel: 0211 16 90 60. Contact: Herr Riech; Palast Betriebe/Schmid & Theile KG, Lautenschlagerstr 3, 7000 Stuttgart 1. Tel: 0711 22 41 89; Peter H. Vollmann, Schuchardtweg 9, 1000 Berlin 39. Tel: 4930 805 48 29. FAX: 4930 805 52 58. Contact: Peter H. Vollmann; Polygon Filmtheaterbetriebs KG/Krüger & Co., Hohenzollernring 48, 5000 Cologne 1. Tel: 0221 21 79 97; UCI, Bongardstr 16-18, 4630 Bochum. Tel: 0234 605 36. FAX: 0234 641 99. Director: Raymond Smith; UFA Theatre AG, Graf Adolfstr 96, 4000 Düsseldorf 1. Tel: 0211 16 90 60. Contact: Herr Pflughaupt; Yorck Kino GmbH, Rankestr 31, 1000 Berlin 31. Tel: 030 211 10 87.

Organizations and Associations: Federal Film Archive, Potsdamerstr 1, Postfach 320, 5400 Koblenz. Tel: 0261 505 0. FAX: 0261 50 52 26. Telex: 261852 BARCHKO D.; Federal Ministry for the Interior Film Section, Postfach 170290, 5300 Bonn 1. Tel: 0228 681 55 66/67 69. Contact: Detlet Flotho; Federal Union of Film and Television Directors in Germany, Adelheidstr 7, 8000 Munich 40. Tel: 089 271 63 80. Contact: Eberhard Hauff; German Cinematheque, Pommernallee 1, 1000 Berlin 19. Tel: 030 303 07; German Institute for Film Information, Schaumainkal 41, 6000 Frankfurt/Main 70. Tel: 069 61 70 45/6. FAX: 069 62 00 60. Telex: 41806639. Director: Eberhard Spiess; German Institute for Film Information/Film Archive, Langenbeckstr 9, Postfach 5129, 6200 Wiesbaden. Tel: 06121 37 01 62. Telex: 4186639; Export-Union Des Deutschen Films EV, Türkenstr 93, Cable: EXU D. D-8000. München 40, Tel: 089 39 00 95/6. FAX: 089 39 52 23. Telex: 5215627. Cable: EXU D. Contact: Dr. Thomas Müller; Saarbrücken Film Office, Berliner Promenade 7, 6600 Saarbrücken. Tel: 0681 39 92 97. FAX: 0681 394 52; Institute for Film and the Visual Arts in Education, Bavariatfilmplatz 3, 8022 Geiselgasteig. Tel: 089 64 97-1. FAX: 089 649 73 00. Telex: 5218598. Director: Dieter Kamm; Kölner Filmhaus, Cologne Film House, Luxemburgerstr 72, 5000 Cologne. Tel: 0221 41 73 44; Baden-Württemburg Provincial Film Service, Wolframstr 20, 7000 Stuttgart 1. Tel: 0711 25 10 12. FAX: 0711 256 94 00; Bavarian Provincial Film Service, Dietlinderstr 18, 8000 Munich 40. Tel: 089 34 70 65; Berlin Provincial Film Service, Bismarckstr 80, 1000 Berlin 12. Tel: 030 313 80 55; Lower Saxony Regional Film Service, Podbielskistr 30, 3000 Hannover 1. Tel: 511 62 78 42. FAX: 511 66 77 92. Director: Alexander Geistlinger; North Rhine-Westphalia Provincial Film Service, Schimerstr 80, 4000 Düsseldorf 1. Tel: 0211 36 05 56; Rhineland-Pfalz Provincial Film Service, Deutschhausplatz, Postfach 3004, 6500 Mainz 1. Tel: 06131 23 46 41; Schleswig-Holstein Provincial Film Service, Thormannplatz 20-22, 2370 Rendsburg. Tel: 04331 763 88; Ruhr Film Centre, In der Lake 12, 5810 Witten/Ruhr. Tel: 0234 26 09 09; The European Institute for the Media, Kaistrasse 13, D-4000 Dusseldorf. Tel: 211 90 10 40. FAX: 211 90 10 456. Contact: Nenad Pejic; Union of German Film Exporters Tegernseer Landstr 75, 8000 Munich 90. Tel: 089 692 06 60. FAX: 089 692 09 10. Contact: Lothar Wedel. Directors: Dieter Menz, Paul de Rooy; Union of German Film Exporters, Tegernseer Landstr 75, 8000 Munich 90. Tel: 089 692 06 60. FAX: 089 692 09 10.

Studios: AKK Sendezentrale GmbH & Co. KG, Turmstr 8, 6700 Ludwigshafen. Tel: 06211 5981 230. FAX: 06211 5981 189. Contact: Ulrich Best; Berliner Union-Film GmbH & Co. Studio KG, Oberlandstraß 26-35. W-1000 Berlin 42. Tel: 030 757820. FAX: 030 75782200. Telex: 184233 ustud-d. Contact: Bernhard Reicherts; Cine Group Studio and Service GmbH, Primelweg 10-12, 8192 Geretsried. Tel: 08171 63102. FAX: 08171 64539. Contact: Dipl Ing Endres; Drefa Filmatoller GmbH Dresden, Kesselsdorferstr 208, O-8038 Dresden. Tel: 0351 438 52 00. FAX: 0351 438 42 09. Contact: Bernd Loidl; Fernsehstudio Berlin Eiswerder GmbH, Eiswerderstr 18, Gebaude 122, 1000 Berlin 20. Tel: 030 335 80 45. FAX: 030 335 80 05. Telex: 186 633. Cable: FSE D. Contact: Dieter Franke; Hansa Tonstudios Gebr. Meisel GmbH, Köthenerstr 38, 1000 Berlin 61. Tel: 030 1 261 18 11. FAX: 262 8806. Contact: Matthias Härtl; Kubitsch Studio Gesellschaft M, Elisabethstr 84, 4000 Dusseldorf 1. Tel: 0211 34 50 41. FAX: 0211 31 30 58. Contact: Brigitte Freinstein; Publicom GmbH, Paul-Grunerstr 68, D-7010 Leipzig. Tel: 0341 39 12 177. FAX: 0341 39 12 177. Contact: Mr. Hirsch; RNF-Studios, Rhein-Neckar Fernsehen GmbH, Dudenstr 12-26, 6800 Mannheim 1. Tel: 0621 39202. FAX: 0621 392 2700. Contact: Richard Kaczmarzik; Studio Hamburg Atelier GmbH, Jenfelder Allee 80, 2000 Hamburg 70. Tel: 040 66 88 0. FAX: 040 66 56 01. Telex: 214 218 sth d. Contact: H. C. Möller; Touchdown Studios, Kirchbergstrasse 25, 84002 Kranzberg. Tel: 081 66 36 77. FAX: 040 66 56 01. Telex: 0214218. Director: Terry Drivas; UBU Production, Silcherstr 25, 8000 Munich 40. Tel: 089 353 46 3. FAX: 089 359 36 84. Director: Mr. Jean Uliczay; Voss and Partner GmbH, Königsbergerstr 1, W-4000 Düsseldorf 1. Tel: 0211 97 38 0. FAX: 0211 97 38 200. Contact: Christian Koehler.

GREECE

Population: 10,000,000.

Number of Theaters in Operation: 233, including five first run cinemas in Athens equipped with air condition which operate all year round. The number of open-air theatres operating during the summer months has dropped from nearly 1,000 to 179 in the Athens, Pireaus Suburbs and Attica areas.

Seating Capacity: Approximately 180,000.

Annual Attendance: No official figure available.

Admission Prices: Drs. 1,200 (U.S. $5.50).

Gross Box Office Receipts: No official figure available.

Admission Tax: 12%, but a portion of this tax (55%) is returned back to the exhibitors releasing native films.

Total Number of Films Released: 150 during the 1992–93 season.

Number of Local Films Produced: 12.

Censorship Regulations: Only for films for children under 13 or 17 is it necessary to get a respective license from the Ministry of the Presidency.

Trends: The downward slide in attendance continued this year with a 20% decrease against the results of the previous year. Only the open-air theatres did better than the previous summer, due to the efforts of their owners and the support of the local press, to survive.

Top Films of the Year: Home Alone 2, Alien 3, Fried Green Tomatoes, Hoffa, Toys, Unlawful Entry, Used People, A Stranger Among Us, White Men Can't Jump, Dead Liquor (Greek).

Local Film Production: The Greek Film Center is the main sponsor of local film production receiving Drs. 900,000,000 ($400,000) in financial support from the Ministry of Culture. As of 1993, 1.6% of the gross advertising revenue of all TV channels will go to support local film production. It is understood, of course, that said films will be telecast after their theatrical release.

Greek Production Companies: Apart from the Greek Film Center and the Television Organization (ERT) which partially finance a number of domestic films, the only production companies in operation are the George Karayannis Company, 16-18 Skalidi Str., Athens, Greca Films, 28 Em. Benaki Str., Athens, Mary Paris Co., and Finos Films.

Principal Distributors: A new importing and distribution company was established this year by George V. Michaelides, George S. Skouras and Zenos Panayotides under the trade mark ROSEBUD with head offices at 96 Academias Str., Athens 106 77. They will import and distribute independent American and European Films. ELKE, Academias Str. 96, Athens 106 77, is responsible for distributing films of Warner Bros., Goldcrest, Carolco, Lorimar, Globo, Rank, Thames International, Worldvision, etc., General Manager: George Michaelides.

United International Pictures (U.I.P.) 4, Gamveta Str. Athens 106 78, distributing films of MGM, Paramount, United Artists, Universal. General Manager, John Takaziades.

Spentzos Films S.A., 9-13 Gravias Str. Athens distributing films of 20th Century Fox, New Line Cinema and other independent films. General Manager, George Spentzos.

Prooptiki S.A., 40-42 Kolettis Str. Athens 106 82, distributing films of Columbia, Orion, Touchstone, Walt Disney, Tri-Star Cannon, General Manager, Pantelis Metropoulos.

Nea Kinissi 9-13, 9-13 Gravias Str. Athens, 106 78 distributing films of Dino de Laurentiis Entertainment Group, Atlantic International and European Films. General Manager, Antonis Karatzopoulos.

Government Film Organizations: Motion Picture Directorate by the Ministry of Culture, 12 Aristidou Str. Athens 106 72. Greek Film Center, 10 Panepistimiou Str., Athens 101 83. Thessaloniki Film Festival, 36 Sina Str., Athens 106 72. Drama Film Festival, Drama, Greece. Helliniki Teniotheke (Greek Film Archives), 1 Kanari Str., Athens 106 82.

Film Industry Associations: Panhellenic Federation of Film Exhibitors 96, Academias Str., Athens 106 77. Greek Directors Guild, 11 Tositsa Str., Athens 106 83. Greek Actors Guild, 13 Kaningos Str., Athens 106 82.

—RENA VELISSARIOU

HONG KONG

Population: 5,800,000.
Number of screens: 158
Admissions in 1992: 46 million.
Top Ten Box Office Films of 1992 (all from Hong Kong except where noted): 1) Justice, My Foot! (HK$49,884,734); 2) All's Well End's Well (HK$48,992,188); 3) Royal Tramp (HK$40,862,831); 4) Royal Tramp II (HK$36,583, 964); 5) Now You See Love . . . Now You Don't (HK$36,475,536); 6) The Magic Touch (HK$39,399,307); 7) Swordsman II (HK$34,462,861); 8) The Twin Dragons (HK$33,225,134); 9) Super Cop (HK$32,609,783); 10) Fight Back to School II (HK$31,635,680).
Trends: The Asia Pacific Film & Cinemas Conference sees the film industry strengthening by leaps and bounds as multiplex development proves to be a major contributing factor towards increased box office receipts. Though copyright infringements and poor marketing techniques have yet to be overcome, Hong Kong released 1,200 films with admissions totaling 50 million. This has been very encouraging following the 1992 record with box office revenues reaching HK$1.6 billion ($205 million). As for other Southeastern countries, they are faring equally as well. *Singapore* is releasing 800 films annually with over 80 multiplexes and box office receipts totaling $60 million. *Malaysia* with 252 multi sites has a strong international flavor, screening over 700 films. Admissions are up to 65 million, grossing MR$250 million ($125 million). *The Phillipines* has also been enjoying good foreign relations as they have imported 70% of the 400 films released. With 1,484 screens, admissions have topped 128 million with revenues of $85 million. *Thailand* is holding is own with 130 sites and plans are in the making for an additional 10 sites. They are releasing close to 400 films a year, 83 of which are from the U.S.
Distributors: Asia Television Limited, 81 Broadcast Drive, Kowloon. Tel: 338 7123. FAX: 338 4347. Telex: HX44680. Cable: ASIATV. Director: Lim Por Yen, Chairman and Chief Executive Officer; Capital Artists Limited, No. 1, Leighton Road, Causeway Bay. Tel: 833 9192. FAX: 832 5055. Telex: 62770 TVE HX. Contact: Mrs. Gilky Wan Leung; Golden Communications Co. Ltd., 8 Hammer Hill Road, Kowloon. Tel: 352 8222. FAX: 351 1683. Telex: 44848 GOHAR HX. Cable: GOLDENSUN. Directors: Raymond Chow, Chairman; Leonard Ho, President; Golden Harvest (International) Limited, 8 Hammer Hill Road, Kowloon. Tel: 352 8222. FAX: 351 1683. Telex: 44848 GOHAR HX. Cable: GOLDENSUN. Directors: Raymond Chow, Chairman; Leonard Ho, President; Golden Princess Amusement Co. Ltd., 6th Floor, 742-744 Nathan Road, Kowloon. Tel: 391 9988. FAX: 789 1365. Telex: 40888 KDGRP HX. Cable: HUNGYUFAT. Contact: David Pang; In-Gear Film Distribution (Int.) Co., 14th Floor, 206-208 Prince Edward Road, Kowloon. Tel: 380 5216. Tel: 397 1452. Contact: Rover Tang; Skynox International Ltd., Room 3, 81F, James Lee Mansion, 33-35 Carnarvon Road. Tsimshatsui, Kowloon. Tel: 723 1336. FAX: 723 0085. Contact: Ricky Uy; William Hay & Co. Ltd., 5th Floor Rear, 234 Nathan Road. Tel: 368 8319. FAX: 311 6727. Contact: Mr. Mok, Managing Director. Director: William Hay.
Organizations and Associations: Government and Ind Organisations, 13/F, Tung Wul Commercial Centre, 27 Prat Avenue, Tsim Sha Tsul, Kowloon. Tel: 311 2692, 311 2678. FAX: 311 1178. Contact: Dionne Wong.
Studios: Golden Harvest (International) Limited, 8 Hammer Hill Road, Kowloon. Tel: 352 8222. FAX: 351 1683. Telex: 44848 GOHAR HX. Cable: GOLDENSUN. Directors: Raymond Chow, Chairman; Leonard Ho, President.

HUNGARY

Population: 10,450,000.
Number of screens: 1,025.
Annual theatrical admissions: 21,457,000.
Trends: The state funded Hungarian Motion Picture Foundation has become the savior of the film industry, pumping new life into production with a 1993 budget of 831 million forints ($10 million). In addition, an extra 350 million forints ($4.2 million) has come from the Culture Ministry. As the state funded Hungrofilms has been dismembered and state facility grant Mafilm declared bankrupt, non-profit Magyar Filmunio has emerged to coordinate international promotions. With Mafilms debts totaling 650 million forints ($7.8 million), it was sold off for 415 million ($5 million). Magyar was capitalized at 1 million forints ($12,000) with running cost at around 18 million forints ($210,000). These funds have been provided by the HMPF. However lucrative the HMPF subsidies may be, the average feature budget cost roughly 35 million forints ($420,000) to produce.
Distributors: Alkotok Studioja, Nagydiofa u. 32 Budapest VII. Tel: 1 1225 283; Budapest Filmstudió Vállalat, Róna utca 174 Budapest 1145, Pob 69 Budapest 1441. Tel: 1 2518 568. FAX: 1 2510 478. Contact: Judith Ujvári; Cinemagyar KFT (Hungarofilm EX), Bathori Utca 10 H-1054 Budapest. Tel: 1 1531 317, 1 1114 614. Tel: 1 1531 317. Telex: 22-5768. Director: Judith Sugar; Duna, Steindl ut. 6, 1054 Budapest. Tel: 1 1329 931. FAX: 1 1313 135. Contact: Ms. Gabriella Jancso; Fokusz, Andrassy 108 1062 Budapest. Tel: 1 1415 886; Gordiusz, Nepstadion u. 97 1143

Budapest. Tel: 1 1429 599. FAX: 1 1428 977. Contact: Mr. Istvan Turbuk; Intercom, Karolina 65 1113 Budapest. Tel: 1 8697 676. FAX: 1 1666 377. Contact: Dr. Andras Kalman; Mokep, Fiumei ut. 25 Budapest. Tel: 1 1135 241. FAX: 1 1337 163. Contact: Mr. Zoltan Kiss; Novofilm, Varosmajor u. 20 H-1122. Budapest. Tel: 1 1555 440, 1 1759 005, 1 1752 057, 1 1552 621, 1 2026 080, 1 2027 252. FAX: 1 1559 177. Contact: Judit Kiss; Novoplasztik, Ulloi ut. 59 Budapest 1X. Tel: 1 1333 487; Pannonia Film Company, Huvosvolgyi ut 64 H-1021 Budapest. Tel: 1 1763 409, 1 1763 333. FAX: 1 1763 409. Director: Lorand Poich; Saldo Studio, Paulay Ede u. 13 1061 Budapest. Tel: 1 1226 256; Sekkelweis U. 2, Budapest V. Tel: 1 1379 617; Vico Torokvesz U. 38/A, 1022 Budapest. Tel: 1 1154 035. FAX: 1 1154 039. Contact: Mr. Janos Fenyo; Zoom, Keleti Kanoly 28/A 1024 Budapest. Tel: 1 1254 115. Contact: Mr. Lazlo Bednavick.
Organizations and Associations: Association of Cinemas of Hungary, Egyetem ter. 5. Tel: 1 1179 025. Contact: Laszlo Hamvas; Film Distributors Association, Frangepan u. 56 1135 Budapest. Tel: 1 1402 922. Contact: Gyorgy Pinke; Guild of Feature Film Directors, Varosligeti fasor 38 1068 Budapest. Tel: 1 1211 120. Contact: Janos Rozsa; Hungarian Federation of Film Societies, Róna Utca 174 Budapest H-1145. Tel: 1 1843 337, 1 2515 666/388. FAX: 1 2512 896. Telex: 22 6860. Contact: Agnes Erdólyi Z; Hungarian Film Institute, Stefania ut. 97 1145 Budapest. Tel: 1 1429 599. Contact: Ms. Vera Gyurey.

INDIA

Population: 850 million
Number of Theatres in Operation: 12,985 permanent and touring theatres (as against last year's 12,933), a slight increase mainly in the southern region, although a number of show places in major cities continue to make way for commercial complexes. Audience attendance (estimated at about 90 million weekly) has shown a downtrend.
Production: India continues to produce the largest number of films in the world with 836 feature films in 1992 (though less than the previous year's 910) a decline of almost 8%. Production takes place at in three major centres of production—Bombay, Madras and Calcutta—in 21 languages.
Export: The export of Indian films, which had been declining for some time with the advent of video and attendant piracy, has lately been looking up. Indian films are exported to UK, Singapore, Gulf countries, Fiji, Indonesia, Malaysia, USA, Mauritius, Canada and Kenya, all of which have sizeable Indian population.
Principal Importers: The Indian government's recent trade liberalization policy, eliminating stringent control on the import of foreign films, has opened up the market which augurs well for world cinema, particularly established organizations like the MPEAA (Motion Picture Export Association of America) and independent importers. Approximately 170 films will be brought into the country during the current year, marking an increase of 50% compared to last year. It is believed that MPEAA members will import about 80 films while the balance will be taken up by non-resident Indians (NRIs) and independent companies.
Principal Distributors of American Films: Allied Arts of India Inc., Metro House, M.G. Road, Bombay 400020; Columbia Films of India Ltd., Metro House, M.G. Road, Bombay 20; Metro-Goldwyn-Mayer India Ltd., Metro House, M.G. Road, Bombay 20; Paramount Films of India Ltd., Hague Bldg., Sprott Road, Bombay 20; 20th Century Fox Corp (India) Ltd., Metro House, M.G. Road, Bombay 20; United Artists Corp, Metro House, M.G. Road, Bombay 20; Universal Pictures India P Ltd., Hague Bldg., Sprott Road, Bombay 20; Warner Bros. (F.D.) Inc., Eros Theatre Bldg., 42 M. Karve Road, Bombay 20.
Censorship: Films can only be exhibited in India after having been certified by the Central Board of Film Certification. The Board has headquarters at Bombay and regional offices in Madras and Calcutta. All members of the Board are appointed by the Government.
The Board grants 'A' certificates for exhibition restricted to Adults above 18 years and 'U' certificates for unrestricted exhibition. The Board has 2 other categories for certificates 'UA' and 'S'. 'UA' is the category or rating between Universal and Adults, and is actually the equivalent of an American PG. The 'S' rating is described as "a certificate for public exhibition restricted to members of any profession or class of persons." The Board can refuse or ask for modifications before issuing a certificate.
Principal Exporters: Name and address followed by Cablegram: Asian Film Corporation—Alankar Cinema Bldg, Room No. 9—4th floor S.V.P. Road, Bombay 400 004—GODSON; A.G. Enterprise—Lotia Palace, 373 Linking Rd, Khar, Bombay—AGFILCO; Asia Films—315 G. New Charni Rd, Bombay 4—HANDRILL; Bombay United Traders—25/26 Kailash Darshan, Kennedy Bldg, Bombay 7—GOLDCOIN; C. A. Corporation—Hanuman Bldg, 3rd floor, Kalbadevi, Pickett Rd, Bombay 400 002—CHANDUFILM; Bajaj Bros (P) Ltd—Round Bldg, 3rd floor, Kalbadevi, Bombay—2 PRITPAL; Chabria Enterprises—301 Grand Canyon, 87 Pali Hill, Bombay 50—TRESSA; Chandra Bros—5th floor, Naaz Bldg, Lamington Rd, Bombay 4—CEE CHANDRA; Neptune Enterprises 4th flr, Everest Bldg, Tardeo, Bombay—34; Hinar Corpn—13 Pancheel, Waterfield Rd, Bandra, Bombay 50; Ellora Films—E. Naaz Bldg, Lamington Rd, Bombay—4 SHOWARTS; International Film Distributors—S. Feltham House, 2nd floor, 10 Graham Road, Bombay 38—SALVANI BROS; Krishna Film Distributors—541, Tardeo Airconditioned Market, Bombay 34—KISHOJAY; Rajshri Productions (P) Ltd—Bhavana, 422 V. Savarkar Road, Prabhadevi, Bombay 400 002—RAVIPIC; Trimurti Films P Ltd—B-11 Commerce Centre, Tardeo, Bombay 34—DEEWAR.
Trade Associations: Film Federation of India—91 Walkeshwar Rd, Bombay 400006; Indian Motion Picture Producer's Association—Sand-

hurst Building, S.V.P. Road, Bombay 400004; Eastern India Motion Picture Association—98E Chowringhee Square, Calcutta; South India's Film Chamber of Commerce—122 Mount Rd, Madras—600002; All India's Film Council—Shantashree, Rajkamal Kala Mandir Parel, Bombay 400001; The Indian Motion Picture Distributor's Association— 33 Vijay Chambers, Tribhuvan Road, Bombay 400 004; Federation of Film Societies of India—C 7 Bharat Bhavan—3 Chittaranjan Avenue, Calcutta 72; Indian Film Exporters Association—5C Everest Building Tardeo, Bombay 34; Indian Documentary Producers Association—305 Famous Cine Bldg Mahalaxmi, Bombay 400018; Kinematographe Renter's Society P Ltd—Haroon Bldg, P. Nariman St. Bombay 1; Cinematograph Exhibitor's Association of India—Flat 22-23B—1st floor, Vellard View, Tardeo Road, Bombay 400 034.

—B. D. GARGA

IRELAND

Population: 3,654,886.
Number of Screens in 1992: 203.
Annual Admissions in 1992: £7.9 million.
Top Ten Box Office Films of 1992: 1) Basic Instinct; 2) Lethal Weapon 3; 3) Far and Away; 4) Into the West; 5) Cape Fear; 6) Batman Returns; 7) My Girl; 8) JFK; 9) Sister Act; 10) Hook.
Distributors: 20th Century-Fox Film Co. Ltd., 1st Fl. 5 O'Connell St. Upp, Dublin 1. Tel: (1) 743068. FAX: (1) 743069. Contact: Brendan McCaul; Abbey Films Ltd., 35 Abbey Street Upper, Dublin 1. Tel: (1) 723922. FAX: (1) 723687. Contact: Leo Ward; Columbia Tri-Star Films, 24 Merchants Court, Merchants Quay, Dublin 8. Tel: (1) 6798234. FAX: (1) 6798237. Contact: Gerry Mulcahy; Dublin Film Distributors Co. Ltd., 53 Abbey Street Middle, Dublin 1. Tel: (1) 748214. FAX: (1) 534373. Contact: Gerry MacGuinness; GFD Film Library, Academy House, 42 Pearse Street, Dublin 2. Tel: (1) 713455. FAX: (1) 713749. Contact: Conor Anderson; Irish Film Centre Cinemas, 6 Eustace Street, Dublin 2. Tel: (1) 679 5744. FAX: (1) 679 9657. Contact: Niamh O'Sullivan; Light House Cinema Co. Ltd., The, 1 Suffolk Street, Dublin 2. Tel: (1) 6792644. FAX: (1) 6795744. Contact: Neil Connolly; United International Pictures (UIP), D'Olier Chambers, D'Olier Street, Dublin 2. Tel: (1) 6792668. FAX: (1) 6798801. Contact: Paddy Kelly, Manager; Warner Brothers Pictures, 2nd Fl., Russell Hse. Russell Court, Dublin 2. Tel: (1) 784000. Contact: Terry Molloy.
Exhibitors: Abbey Films Ltd., 35 Abbey Street Upper, Dublin 1. Tel: (1) 723922. FAX: (1) 723687. Contact: Leo Ward, Director; Adelphi Carlton Ltd., 98 Middle Abbey Street, Dublin 1. Tel: (1) 730786, 732909. Contact: Michael Hussey; Dublin Cinema Group, 35 Upper Abbey Street, Dublin 1. Tel: (1) 723922. FAX: (1) 723687. Directors: Leo Ward, Kevin Anderson, Paul Anderson, Paul Ward; Independent Cinemas Association, Classic Cinema, Harolds Cross, Dublin 6. Tel: (1) 975324. FAX: (1) 970920. Contact: Albert Kelly; Irish Film Centre Cinemas, 6 Eustace Street, Dublin 2. Tel: (1) 679 5744. FAX: (1) 679 9657. Director: Michael Hannigan, Cinema Director; Light House Cinema Co. Ltd., The, 1 Suffolk Street, Dublin 2. Tel: (1) 6792644. FAX: (1) 6795744. Contacts: Neil Connolly, David Kavanagh, Directors; United Cinemas International, The Square, Town Centre, Dublin 24. Tel: (1) 598170. FAX: (1) 598174. Directors: Brendan Quigley (Tallaght), Manager, Karl Milne (Coolock).
Organizations and Associations: Arts Council, The, 70 Merrion Square, Dublin 2. Tel: (1) 611840. FAX: (1) 761302. Director: Paul Freaney, Film Officer; Federation of Irish Film Societies, IFC, 6 Eustace Street, Dublin 2. Tel: (1) 778788 (Ext 281). FAX: (1) 679 9657. Contact: Brenda Gannon; Film Appeals Board, 16 Harcourt Terrace, Dublin 2. Tel: (1) 761985. FAX: (1) 761898. Contact: John F Carroll, Chairman; Film Base, The Irish Film Centre, 6 Eustace Street, Dublin 2. Tel: (1) 679 6716. FAX: (1) 679 6717. Contact: Danette Hamill; Film Censor's Office, 16 Harcourt Terrace, Dublin 2. Tel: (1) 761985. Contact: Sheamus Smith, Official Censor; Film Makers Ireland, IFC, 6 Eustace Street, Dublin 2. Tel: (1) 778788. FAX: (1) 679 9657. Contact: Paddy Barrett; Irish Actors' Equity, Liberty Hall, Dublin 1. Tel: (1) 743560, 743761. Contact: Gerald Browne; Irish Film Institute, 6 Eustace Street, Dublin 2. Tel: (1) 6795744. FAX: (1) 6799657. Contact: David Kavanagh; SIPTU (Services Industrial Professional Technical Union) Film & Broadcasting Branch, 30 Parnell Square, Dublin 1. Tel: (1) 733 977. Contact: Frances O'Brien.

ISRAEL

Population: 5,005,000.
Number of Screens: 212
Annual theatrical admissions for 1992: 13,000,000
Top ten box office films of 1992: 1) Basic Instinct 2) Lethal Weapon 3; 3) Cape Fear; 4) Beauty and the Beast; 5) The Prince of Tides; 6) Patriot Games; 7) Hot Shots!; 8) Hook; 9) Beethoven; 10) Frankie and Johnny.
Organizations: Cinema Owners Assoc., 16 Pinsker St., 634121 Tel Aviv. Tel: (3) 295138; Israel Film & TV Producers Assoc., P.O. Box 22372 Tel Aviv. Tel: (3) 293241; Israel Film Centre, 30 Gershon Agron St., P.O. Box 299, 94190 Jerusalem. Tel: (2) 210297; Israel Film Institute, National Council of Culture & Art, 7 Rothschild, Tel Aviv. Tel: (3) 656293; Israel Film Service, Ministry of Education & Culture, Hakirya Romema, P.O. Box 13240, 91138 Jerusalem. Tel: (2) 532163.
Distributors: Theatrical Argo Films Ltd, 43 Ben Yehuda St, 63341 Tel Aviv. Tel: (3) 228251; Forum Film Ltd., 11 Pinsker St., 63421, Tel Aviv.

Tel: (3) 5286211; Shapira Films, 34 Allenby Rd, PO Box 4842, 63325 Tel Aviv. Tel: (3) 5102530; Shoval Film Prod., 32 Allenby St., Tel Aviv. Tel: (3) 659288; Tamuz Films, 5 Pinsker St, Tel Aviv. Tel: (3) 201512. Fax: (3) 281564.

ITALY

Population: 57,600,000.
Number of Cinema Screens: 1,500.
Number of Admissions: $86.5 million in 1992, down from $90.2 million in 1991.
Trends: A sharp drop in the lira is forcing the Italian film industry to drastically reduce orders for American films. Distributors, rather than abide by contracts to purchase imported products, are instead paying penalties and refocusing to produce or co-produce medium-budget films in Europe. However, Warner Brothers grossed $70 million for the 1992–1993 movie going season, securing a 26.4% share in 99 principal cities. At the same time, American companies are being induced to produce in Italy, using Italian film studios. Government subsidies, totaling $650 million annually have been withdrawn since the elimination of the Ministry of Tourism and Entertainment. The average cost of producing an Italian films is $2.7 billion lire (about $1.8 million).
Distributors: Airone Cinematografica, Largo Olgiata 15, 00123 Rome. Tel: (06) 37 89 550. FAX: (06) 37 88 200. Contact: Z Belli; Avofilm SRL, Via C. Ravizza 20, 20149 Milan. Tel: (02) 480 127 07/17/27. FAX: (02) 480 127 37. Contact: Alessandro Bulath; CDI (Compagnia Distribuzione Internazionale), Largo Amilcare Ponchielli 6, 00198 Rome. Tel: (06) 8540542/8541464. FAX: (06) 8541691. Contact: Monica Girolami; Cecchi Gori Group, Via Barnaba Oriani 91, 00197 Rome. Contact: Mario Cecchi Gori; Chance Film SRL, Via G. Mercalli 19, 00197 Rome. Tel: (06) 8085041. FAX: (06) 8070506. Director: Massimo Civilotti; Cine Decima SRL, Via della Marffca 23, 00162 Rome. Tel: (06) 86897829. FAX: (06) 86897779. Contact: Sergío Bergonzelli; Columbia Tristar Films Italia SRL, Via Palestro 24, 00185 Rome. Tel: (06) 494 1196/494 1197. FAX: (06) 446 9936. Telex: 39 (6) 610 199. Director: Ricardo Avila; Croce Del Sud Cinematografica, Via Sangemini 78, 00135 Rome. Tel: (06) 3071291. FAX: (06) 65741918. Contact: F Santini; Eagle Pictures SRL, Via M Buonarroti 5, 20149 Milan. Tel: (02) 4814169, 48194522. FAX: (02) 4813389. Director: Stafano Dammicco; Federazione Italiana Cineforum (Italian Cineforum Federation), Via Pascoli 3, 24100 Bergamo. Tel: 035 244703. Telex: 35 233129. Contact: Bruno Fornara; Flying Colours Films, Via E. Ximenes 21, 00197 Rome. Tel: (06) 3215589. Fax: (06) 320423. Contact: Giuseppe Massaro; Lucky Red, Lungoteuere Marzio 10, 00186 Rome. Tel: (06) 6832451/2/3. FAX: (06) 6865083. Via Antonio Baiamonti 10, 00195 Rome. Tel: (06) 3252296. FAX: (02) 3252310. Contact: Kermit Smith; Movietime, Via Nicola Ricciotti 11, 00195 Rome. Tel: (06) 3226709. FAX: (06) 3725224. Contact: Stefano Libassi; Pegaso Inter-Communication SRL, Largo Generale Gonzaga del Vodice 4, 00195 Rome. Tel: (06) 36 12 534, 32 00 830. FAX: (06) 36 13 251. Director: Maurizio Castellano; Penta Distribuzione, Via Aurelia Antica 422, 00165 Rome. Tel: (06) 663 901. FAX: (06) 6639040. Contact: Massimo Fasoli; Quantum Image SRL, Via Fontana 16, 20122 Milan. Tel: (02) 5458621. FAX: (02) 5458915. Contact: Giovanni Della Rossa. Director: Giovanni Della Rossa, Managing Director; Silvio Berlusconi Communications, Corporate Headquarters, Palazzo Michelangelo, Via Cassanese 224, 20090 Segrate (MI). Tel: (02) 21621. FAX: (02) 21628951. Director: Carlo Bernasconi; Stardust SRL, SS 229 KM.18, 28010 Vaprio d'Agogna (NO). Tel: 0321 996441. FAX: 0321 996454. Contact: Claudio Minotti; Starlight SRL, Via Bellerio 30, 20161 Milan. Tel: (02) 6466441. FAX: (02) 6466444. Contact: Nadia Preatoni.
Exhibitors: Federazione Italiana Cineforum (Italian Cineforum Federation), Via Pascoli 3, 24100 Bergamo. Tel: 035 244703. Telex: 035 233129. Contact: Bruno Fornara; Raffaele Guadagno, Testione Cinema President srl, Largo Augusto 1, 20122 Milan. Tel: (02) 760 21410. FAX: (02) 760 222 23.
Organizations and Associations: Cine Decima SRL, Via della Marffca 23, 00162 Rome. Tel: (06) 86897829. FAX: (06) 86897779. Contact: Sergío Bergonzelli; Federazione Italiana Cineclub (F.E.D.I.C.) Italian Federation of Film Club), Via Muggia 10, 00185 Rome. Tel: (06) 358 1056. Contact: Giorgio Garibaldi; Sacis, Via Tomacelli 139, 00106 Rome. Tel: (06) 680041. FAX: (06) 6878824. Telex: 624487. Contact: Giovanni Celsi.
Studios: Cinecitta, Via Tuscolana, 1055, 00173 Rome. Tel: (06) 72 29 31. FAX: 722 21 55; CTC SPA, V le delle Legioni Romane, 43, 20147 Milan. Tel: 40 30 61-404 66 17. FAX: 48 70 04 76; De Angelis Studio, Via Cicerone, 17, 20162 Milan. Tel: 642 41 83-647 04 04; Etabeta, Via delle Vigne Nuove, 70, 00139 Rome. Tel: 81 70 941-30 09 345; Icet Studios, Via P Rossi, 3, 20093 Cologno Monzese (MI). Tel: 25 39 00 86-27 30 06 41. FAX: 254 40 73; Icet Studios SRL, Via P. Rossi 3, 20093 Cologno Monzese. Tel: (02) 2543184. FAX: (02) 27300641. Contact: Francesco Corti; Movie People, V le Berbera, 49, 20162 Milan. Tel: 647 22 00-66 10 09 32. FAX: 66 10 09 38.

JAPAN

Population: 124,400,000.
Number of Theatre Screens: 1,744.
Admissions in 1992: 125,600,000.
Top Ten Box Office Films in 1992: 1) Final Analysis; 2) Hook; 3) Alien

3; 4) JFK; 5) Beauty and the Beast; 6) Patriot Games; 7) Hot Shots!; 8) The Lover; 9) Lethal Weapon 3; 10) Twin Peaks.

Trends: Drive-in theatres with start-up costs of approximately $40 million yen ($333,000) have become the latest rage. Idle land and extremely low-budget operations have attributed to their success. Monthly revenues are projected at $50,000 with land owners receiving 10%. Resort Hotels as well as Toyota Motor Co. have recently opened their own theatres.

Major Japanese distributors have been reluctant to build more indoor theatres due to the strict fire laws and high cost of space, even though other countries have proven attendance has doubled with increased multiplex construction.

Distributors: ASCH Pictures, 12 Mori Bldg SF. 1-17-3 Toranomon, Minato-ku, Tokyo 105. Tel: 03 3581 9501. FAX: 03 3581 9510. Contact: Kaz Yamahana; Disc Center Co. Ltd., C.P.O. Box 874, Osaka 530-91. Tel: 06 323 6350. FAX: 06 323 0249. Contact: Yasutoshi Gotoh; Gaga Communications Inc., Step Roppongi Bldg., 6-8-10 Roppongi, Minato-ku, Tokyo 106. Tel: 3 5410 3500. FAX: 3 5410 3558. Director: Tetsu Fujimura, President & CEO; Media International Corporation, 2-14-5 Akasaka, Minato-ku, Tokyo 107. Tel: 03 5561 9571. FAX: 03 5561 9550/49. Telex: 2423313 KMEDIA. Contact: Mr. Yasuo Katayama; Mitsubishi Corporation, 3-1, Marunouchi 2-Chome, Chiyoda-ku, Tokyo 100-86. Tel: 3 3210 7795. FAX: 3 3210 7397. Telex: MCTOK A J33333 (ATTN:JE-Z). Contact: Ichisuke Kato; New Select Co. Ltd., Nakamura Bldg., 7th Floor, 5-9-13 Ginza, Chuo-ku. Tel: 03 3573 7571. FAX: 03 3572 0139. Director: Akira Sugiyama, Representative Director; Toho International Co., Ltd. (a division of Toho Co., Ltd.), 1-8-1, Yurakucho, Chiyoda-ku, Tokyo 100. Tel: 03 3213 6821. FAX: 03 3213 6825. Director: Isao Matsuoka, President; Toho Towa Company Limited, 6-4, Ginza 2-Chome, Chuo-ku, Tokyo 104. Tel: 3 3562 0109. FAX: 3 3535 3656. Telex: J24141. Directors: Harumasa Shirasu, President; Terumasa Yamashita, Vice President; Tokyo Broadcasting System Inc., 5-3-6 Akasaka Minato-ku, Tokyo 107. Tel: 03 3584 3111. FAX: 03 3505 1584. Contact: Yoshihide Tanimoto; TV Man Union Inc., 30-13 Motoyoyogi-Cho, Shibuya-ku, Tokyo. Tel: 3 5478 1611. FAX: 3 5478 8141. Telex: 2422774 TV MANJ. Director: Yutako Shigenobu; World Television Corporation, 6F 8-10ban Bldg., 8-10-8 Ginza, Chuo-ku, Tokyo 104. Tel: 3 3571 8047. FAX: 3 3572 2307. Telex: J25640 WORLDTYO. Contact: Toyohisa.

Studios: Imagica Corporation, 2-14-1, Higashigotanda, Shinagawa-ku, Tokyo 141. Tel: 3 3280 1280. FAX: 3 3280 1364. Contact: Koji Ichihashi, Manager, International Department; Nikkatsu Corporation, 3-28-12, Hongou, Bunkyo-ku, Tokyo. Tel: 03 5689 1019. FAX: 03 5689 1043. Telex: J26627 NIKKATSU. Contact: Kiyohiko Shoji.

Production Houses—Theatrical/Television: Avaco Creative Studios Inc., 2-3-18 Nishi-Waseda Shinjuku-ku, Tokyo 169. Tel: 03 3203 4181. FAX: 03 3207 1398. Director: Futoshi Ota, Executive Director; Itami Films Inc., Shuuwa Mamiana Residence, 303 Azabudai 3-Chome, Minato-ku, Tokyo 107. Director: Juzo Itami; Kiroku Eigasha Production Inc., 12-1 Yoyogi 2-Chome, Shibuya-ku, Tokyo 151. Tel: 03 3370 3386. FAX: 03 3370 3469. Contact: Chaco Nakajima; Nikkatsu Corporation, 3-28-12, Hongou, Bunkyo-ku, Tokyo. Tel: 03 5689 1019. FAX: 03 5689 1043. Telex: J26627 NIKKATSU. Contact: Kiyohiko Shoji; Telecom Japan International Inc., 80 St. Marks Place, New York, NY 10003, USA. Tel: (212) 254-2845. FAX: (212) 254-7845. Directors: Taku Nishimae, Producer; Tom Nagae, Producer/Director; The Seiyu Ltd., Film Making Division, Hanzomon Murayama Bldg., 3-7-1-Kojimachi, Chiyoda-ku, Tokyo 102. Tel: 03 5276 2403. FAX: 03 5276 2166. Director: Kazuo Kuro; TV Man Union Inc., 30-13 Motoyoyogi-Cho, Shibuya-ku, Tokyo. Tel: 3 5478 1611. FAX: 3 5478 8141. Telex: 2422774 TV MANJ. Director: Yutako Shigenobu; World Television Corporation, 6F 8-10ban Bldg., 8-10-8 Ginza, Chuo-ku, Tokyo 104. Tel: 3 3571 8047. FAX: 3 3572 2307. Telex: J25640 WORLDTYO. Contact: Toyohisa.

MEXICO

Population: 86,235,000.
Number of screens: 1,769 in 1991.
Annual admissions: 197 million in 1990; 36.28 million in Mexico City in 1991.

Trends: After a decade of crisis which culminated in a series of movie theaters closing, decreases in box office receipts and financial production woes, the film industry is having a reversal of fortune. With a slide in film production from 150 to 40 films a year, new strategies for boosting production were devised by establishing several new funding sources. The country's official financing and development agency is Nacional Financiera. $345,600 has been raised by the Association of Mexican Film Producers, with individual contributions of $12,800 from its 27 members in the form of dues to the Independent Producers Credit Union, supervised by the Mexican Banking Commission. A camaraderie between producers, distributors, exhibitors and unions along with government support is expected to put the industry back on its feet, creating Mexican films of greater substance.

Efforts are also being made for co-production ventures with Canada and Hollywood. Goals in raising ticket prices to $3.00–$3.50 have been reached though a recent hike already rose prices to 6,000 pesos ($2.00). This comes after a government policy that set ticket prices at $1.00, believing cheap entertainment should be provided to the people.

The Mexican Film Institute, Imcine, was able to put $300,000 up front for each of its 11 features and, in the end, spent $5.5 million out of its $11 million stipend.

NETHERLANDS

Population: 15 million
Admissions: 13.7 million in 1992.
Number of screens: 418.
Top Ten Box Office Films of 1992: 1) Flodder Does Manhattan (UIP: admissions 1,470,387); 2) Basic Instinct (Concorde: 1,228,847); 3) Lethal Weapon 3 (Warner: 637,797); 4) Boomerang (UIP: 453,173); 5) Beauty and the Beast (Warner: 434,847); 6) Cape Fear (UIP: 416,171); 7) Beethoven (UIP: 404,409); 8) The Bodyguard (Warner: 366,486); 9) Hook (Columbia/TriStar: 353,422); 10) Hot Shots (CNR Film Releasing: 342,579).

Trends: The Dutch Culture Ministry has postponed its $8.5 million national film subsidy, which is to include provisions for increased international training and facilities for training young filmmakers. The Ministry has been the primary source of funding, previously allocating a total of $7.8 million for its two agencies, with $4.5 million for production of commercial features and $3.3 million for the Film Fund, which produces arthouse documentaries and shorts. These two agencies are expected to merge with subsidies totaling $12.5 million by 1996.

Though ticket sales were down, a total of $114 million in box office receipts were divided between seven key distributors in 1991. Cannon Group Netherlands, owner of the largest share of hardtops in key cities (98%) put together a $63 million package to build eight new theatres, plus renovate existing sites.

Distributors: Argus Film, PO Box 18269, 1001 ZD Amsterdam. Tel: 20 6254585. FAX: 20 6268978. Telex: 11084 NL. Director: Rob Langestraat; Arthur V Oster NV, 16 Van Engelenweg—Willemstad—Curacao—Netherlands Antilles. Tel: 599 9 372733/372828. FAX: 599 9 372386. Director: Arthur V Oster; Atlantis Releasing BV, Tesselschadestraat 4-12, 1054 ET Amsterdam. Tel: 20 6184011. FAX: 20 6188719. Contact: Wendy Bernfeld; Bioscoop Exploitatie Minerva BV, PO Box 7220, 1007 JE Amsterdam. Tel: 20 6446823. FAX: 20 6448 946. Contact: W. Ruyters; Buena Vista International (Netherlands), Florapark 7, PO Box 891, 2003 RW Haarlem. Tel: 23 421034. FAX: 23 422079. Director: Paul Zonderland; Cine Artists Corporation, Postbus 6121, 1005 EC Amsterdam. Tel: 020 6128802. FAX: 020 6833529. Contact: Cor Dekkers, Chairman. Director: Cor Dekkers; Cinema Europe, Oranje Nassaulaan 53, PO Box 5242, 1007 AE Amsterdam. Tel: 20 6767841. FAX: 20 671 4968. Director: Cor Koppies; Cinemien Film and Video Distributors, Entrepotdok 66, 1018 AD Amsterdam. Tel: 020 6258357, 6381170. FAX: 020 6209857. Director: Phil van der Linden; CNR Film Releasing, Amstellandlaan 78, PO Box 237, 1380 AE Weesp. Tel: 2940 61853. FAX: 2940 31835. Director: Marleen Pagrach, Managing Director; Concorde Film, Lange Voorhout 35, 2514 EC Den Haag. Tel: 70 3605810/3924571. FAX: 70 3604925. Telex: 34568 COFIL NL. Director: Robbert Wijsmuller; Contact Film Cinematheek, Prinsengracht 676, 1017 KX Amsterdam. Tel: 20 6232510, 6264743. Directors: Gerard Huisman, Jef Hartisuiker; Excalibur (Benelux), Utrechtseweg 340, PO Box 261, 3730 AG De Bilt. Tel: 30 205654. FAX: 30 205877. Contact: Karolien van Lieshout; Gofilex Film, PO Box 334, 3430 AH Nieuwegein. Tel: 3402 70922. FAX: 3402 70283; Melior Films, Steynlaan 8, 1217 JS Hilversum. Tel: 35 45542. FAX: 35 235906. Director: Menno van der Molen; Meteor Film BV, Prinsengracht 546, 1017 KK Amsterdam. Tel: 020 6233858. FAX: 020 6252981. Contact: San Fu Maltha; Shooting Star Film Company Amsterdam, Singel 395, 1012 WN Amsterdam. Tel: 20 6247272. FAX: 20 6268533. Contact: Daphni Gapellaa; Stichting Stemra, Prof. E. M. Meijerslaan 3, 1183 AV Amstelveen. Tel: 20 5407911. FAX: 20 5407496; Twin Film, Sarphatistraat 183, 1018 GG Amsterdam. Tel: 20 6228206. FAX: 20 6248729. Director: Dick de Jonge, Managing Director; United International Pictures (Netherlands), Willemsparkweg 112, 1071 HN Amsterdam. Tel: 20 6622991. FAX: 20 6623240. Director: Max van Praag; Warner Bros. (Holland) BV, De Boelelaan 16 III, 1083 HY Amsterdam. Tel: 20 5411211. FAX: 20 6449001. Contact: Paulette Buenting; World Cinema, Oranje Nassaulaan 53, PO Box 5242, 1007 AE Amsterdam. Tel: 20 6767841. FAX: 20 6714968. Director: Cor Koppies; World Media Sales (USA), 662 W. Huntington Drive, Suite 518, Monrovia, CA 91016. Tel: (818) 446-5333. Fax: (818) 795-4473. Contact: Steve Hawkins.

Exhibitors: Association of Film Theatres, Prinsengracht 770, 1017 LE Amsterdam. Tel: 20 6267602. FAX: 20 6389282. Contact: Gerard Bunnik; Bioscoop Exploitatie Minerva BV, PO Box 7220, 1007 JE Amsterdam. Tel: 20 6446823. FAX: 20 6448946. Contact: W. Ruyters; Bioscooponderneming A. F. Wolff, Ondegracht 154, PO Box 777, 3500 AT Utrecht. Tel: 30 331312. FAX: 30 315227. Director: J. Ph. Wolff; Cannon Cinema Group, De Lairessestraat 111-115, 1075 HH Amsterdam. Tel: 20 5751751. FAX: 20 6622085. Director: Wim van Wouw; Jogchem's Theatres, PO Box 127, 3750 GC Bunschoten. Tel: 3499 84884. FAX: 3499 84908.

Organizations: Dutch Independent Filmmakers Assoc., P.O.Box 17408, 1001 JK Amsterdam. Tel: (20) 6205578; The Filmmakers Society of the Netherlands, P.O. Box 381. 1000 AN Amsterdam. Tel: (20) 6765088; Association for Film & Television Makers, Donker Curtiusstraat 7-414, 1051 JL Amsterdam. Tel: (20) 6881670.

NEW ZEALAND

Population: 3,500,000.
Number of theatre screens: 175.
Theatrical admissions for 1992: 6.7 million.
Top Ten Box Office Films of 1992: 1) Hook; 2) The Commitments; 3) Basic Instinct; 4) Batman Returns; 5) Beauty and the Beast; 6) The

Addams Family; 7) Lethal Weapon 3; 8) Fried Green Tomatoes; 9) Wayne's World; 10) Far and Away.

Trends: In Auckland an increase in new and improved multiplexes is once again resulting in increased box office receipts, as revenues were well over $NZ35 million ($19 million), 4% higher than 1991 figures. Wider openings, longer runs and flexibility have all yielded greater returns, as Warner Brothers billings are up 17%.

Two newcomers are investing heavily into indie-multiplexes with the latest in facilities and technology. The Bridgeway Groups, Rialto, has opened three new screens as part of a $NZ30 million ($16.5 million) development while Village Forces has spent $3.7 million on an eight screen multiplex.

A restructuring amongst all major distributors which include Disney, Warner Bros., Columbia, TriStar and their respective exhibitors has not affected the use of multiplexes. Distributors have not been choosey over who is the owner as long as the deal is right.

In Wellington quality cost effective production, along with a favorable exchange rate and an established independent film industry, has combined budget estimates exceeding $NZ100 million ($55 million). However, the NZ Film Commission (NZFC) has only $3.4 million to invest and is planning to concentrate on four to six low budget films as opposed to major productions.

Using various strategic moves, the NZFC has invested $275,000 in several seasoned producers and has been successful in attracting private investors, such as the Wellington Company, which made an investment pledge of more than $500,000.

Distributors: Endeavour Entertainment Ltd., PO Box 68-445, Newton, Auckland. Tel: 09 378 1900. FAX: 09 378 1905. Contact: John Barnett; Everard Films Ltd., PO Box 3664, Auckland 1. Tel: 09 302 1193. FAX: 09 302 1192. Contact: Mark Croft; First Training, PO Box 17096, Auckland. Tel: 09 579 1332. FAX: 09 579 5113. Contact: John Davies; Hoyts Entertainment (NZ) Ltd., PO Box 6923, Auckland. Tel: 09 309 0955. Contact: Joseph Moodabe; New Zealand Federation of Film Societies Inc., PO Box 9544, Te Aro, Wellington. Tel: 04 385 0162. FAX: 04 801 7304. Director: Bill Gosden; Pacer Kerridge Film Distributors Ltd., PO Box 1159, Auckland. Tel: 09 379 6780. FAX: 09 307 0041. Contact: Mr. Kerry Robins; Top Shelf Productions, PO Box 9101, Wellington. Tel: 04 382 8364. FAX: 04 801 6920. Contact: Vincent Burke; United International Pictures, PO Box 105263, Auckland. Tel: 09 379 6269. FAX: 09 379 6271. Contact: Timothy Ord; Video Marketing (NZ) Ltd., PO Box 25156, Auckland. Tel: 09 575 8238. FAX: 09 575 8238; Warner Bros (NZ) Ltd., PO Box 8687, Mt. Eden, Auckland. Tel: 09 377 5223. FAX: 09 309 2795.

Exhibitors: Endeavour Entertainment Ltd., PO Box 68-445, Newton, Auckland. Tel: 09 378 1900. FAX: 09 378 1905. Contact: John Barnett; Hoyts Entertainment (NZ) Ltd., PO Box 6445, Auckland. Tel: 09 303 2739. FAX: 09 307 0011. Contact: Joseph Moodabe; Pacer Kerridge Cinemas Ltd., PO Box 1159, Auckland. Tel: 09 379 6780. FAX: 09 307 0041. Contact: Marie Davis; Wellington Film Society Inc., PO Box 1584, Wellington. Tel: 04 384 6817. FAX: 04 384 6248. Contact: Bill Gosden.

Industry Organizations: Chief Censor of Films, 1 Fairway Dr., P.O. Box 46-009, Lower Hutt, Tel: (04) 5673 242; Film Censorship Board of Review, P.O. Box 805, Wellington, Tel: (04) 495 7900; Independent Producers and Directors Guild Inc., P.O. Box 3969. Wellington, Tel: (025) 425 426; National Distribution Union, Private Bag 68902, Newton, Auckland. Tel: 3780 220; National Film Library, Private Bag 36, Newmarket, Auckland. Tel: 09 523 1091; New Zealand Academy of Motion Pictures, Contact: Jane Gilbert, P.O. Box 1722, Wellington. Tel: (04) 852 904; New Zealand Film Archive, 82 Tory St., P.O. Box 9544, Wellington. Tel: 04 384 7647; New Zealand Film Commission, 36 Allen St., P.O. Box 11-546, Wellington. Tel: (4) 3859-754.

NORWAY

Trends: Boosting box office receipts by 30% over previous years were American films, which have proven to be a large draw. Though Municipal Cinemas, a major exhibitor, also focused on other foreign films including 3 Italian, 1 Spanish and 1 British, they put most of their money on 4 major U.S. films. 1991 showed only one Norwegian film with a gross of more than 8.1 million kroner ($1.4 million), more than eight other local items combined. Even with censorship and poor marketing, U.S. films are still pre-eminent.

New long term strategies and proper divestment of funds means the future is looking bright for the film industry, according to the Norwegian Film Institute (NFI). State subsidies were increased from $7.7 million to $9.3 million. Of this amount, Nordisk Film, the government controlled agency, received $4 million with NFI and its production committee receiving the balance. However, the new Cinema & TV Fund will make possible another $3.7 million.

Merging seems to be the strategy of choice, as the NFI joins forces with the National Film Board of Norway in an effort to upgrade its foreign marketing skills. The Oslo-based Nordic Screen Development formed from the combining of Filmeffekt and Moland Film, the country's biggest commercial producer, featured its first major production in Norway, Denmark and Sweden on February 4, 1993.

PAKISTAN

Population: The population of Pakistan is 118.81 million, plus 3.3 million Afghan refugees who have lived in various parts of this country for over 14 years.

Number of theatres in operation: 726, including about a dozen equipped with 70mm/Todd-AO (but not a single 70mm release for approximately a decade) and touring talkies (over 250). Over two dozen houses were closed down in various parts of the country during the last year for different reasons, including video competition, high tax rates and the price increase of land in big cities. In Karachi, the biggest city of Pakistan with a population of over 10 million, there are 63 cinemas, including two drive-ins. Only five screens imported films exclusively. Foreign films are being shown in domestic houses as well, but for only about 15% of their playing time.

Number of admissions: An average of 4.6% of the people in villages visit cinemas, while in cities and towns 15.7% go to movies. Fifty percent of those who attend movies once a week are between 11 and 29 years of age. 23% are between 30 and 50 years of age. Barely 27% in cities and 5% in villages visit cinemas once a week or less. The number of admission is not maintained either by the authorities or cinemas; however, according to the estimates, between 300,000 and 400,000 people visit an A class cinema in a big city every year.

Gross Box Office Receipts: Entertainment tax is levied by provincial governments. Punjab and Sindh levy this tax at the rate of 65% and 55% on cinema admission prices, while Baluchistan and NWFP (Sarhad) levy fixed capacity rate between 37.5 to 50%. The rates of entertainment tax on other recreations are lower, such as 10% on stage shows and 25% on amusement parks. The estimated gross box office collection for 1992/93 was Rs.543 million, as against Rs.536 million in 1991/92, minus entertainment tax.

Admission prices: The highest rate of admission (including tax) for a balcony seat is Rs.30 in some of the A-1 cinemas, situated in Cantonment areas of Karachi and Lahore. The others, situated in Municipal limits, charge between Rs.10 and Rs.20 by non-airconditioned and airconditioned cinemas, respectively. Cinemas of suburbs and villages charge even less.

Local Production: In spite of high production costs, video piracy, daily telecasts of feature films, dish antennas and political disturbances, the number of films released during 1992 was 94, as compared to 12 in 1991. Not a single co-production was financed during the year under review. However, "Raaz", a co-production with Dubai was released, while "Tilasmi Jazira" (Mysterious Island) is still under production, due to latest political developments in Russia. The legal exhibition of Indian films have been banned since 1965, but the latest films on video are openly available throughout the country. They are smuggled in from Dubai, etc. Most video shops depend on these films.

The Government of Pakistan has finally recognized the film industry as an 'Industry' and offered facilities enjoyed by other industries such as loans, concessions in taxes and import duties on equipment. To protect the rights of filmmakers, the Government also approved the amendments in the existing Copyright Act, under which a violator will be sentenced to jail for three years and will have to pay a fine of Rs.100,000.

Import of foreign films: The Government has privatized the import of foreign films, which used to be the monopoly of the National Film Development Corporation Ltd. (NAFDEC). As compared to 86 films during 1991/92, the import has gone up to 98 during 1992/93, from Hong Kong, Singapore and West. Smuggling and piracy of foreign films has also increased. These films are shown under different (censored) titles in parts of the country. A party even dared to "import" and release "Rambo—III", but failed.

According to law all the cinema houses cannot screen imported films. There are classifications—Foreign and Pakistani cinemas. A foreign house is permitted to exhibit imported films up to 85% of its playing time and must run Pakistani productions the remaining 15%. On the other hand, a Pakistani house has to screen domestic productions 85% of the playing time, but can show imported films in the remaining 15%.

Censorship regulations: There are four Boards—The Central Board of Film Censors with its head office in Islamabad and branches at Lahore, Karachi and Peshaware (opened this year). They examine domestic films while Islamabad certifies imported pictures and films rejected by branches. However, all the certificates are issued from the head office. All the Boards are comprised of lawyers, journalists, doctors, judges, and other representatives of the community. Pakistan Television and Shalimar Television have separate censor boards, for programs shown on mini screens. Films full of vulgarity and violence are not allowed to be screened. Importers pay more attention to Karate, horror, science fiction and terrorism. Bond and Rambo are still the most popular subjects in Pakistan.

Filmmakers in Pakistan also stress on action thrillers, but the trend is being changed slowly to romantic and socials, as people are tired of seeing violence and crime in movies.

Top Ten Films of the Year: The percentage of successful Pakistani films maintained status-quo during the year 1992/93; about half a dozen films proved successful at the box office. Like last year, actor Sultan Rahi remained on the top by working in 26 pictures.

The following are the top grossing imported films of the year 1992/93: "Total Recall"—Rs.1,160,622; "Universal Soldier"—Rs.1,097,932; "Crystal Hunt"—Rs.892,991; "Stone Age Warrior"—Rs.790,662; "In the Line of Action"—Rs.718,777; "Dragon From Russia"—Rs.690,684; "Rambo—III"—Rs.569,808; and "Cyborg–R.R."—Rs.759,832. These are the box office collections of the first screening at Karachi during the year 1992.

Taxes: The Pakistan film industry is one of the heaviest taxed business. Cinema houses pay 27 different taxes, including show tax, publicity tax, property tax, and fire tax. Producers and distributors (including importers) pay registration fees, import duty, and sales tax among other things.

Government Film Organizations: The Central Board of Film Censor, Street No.55-F, Blue Area, Islamabad; The Ministry of Culture, Tourism,

Sports (Cultural Division), Islamabad; The National Film Development Corporation Ltd., NAFDEC Complex, Blue Area, Islamabad.

Trade Associations: Pakistan Film Producers' Association, Regal Cinema Building, The Mall, Lahore; Pakistan Film Distributors' Association, Geeta Bhawan, Lakshmi Chowk, Lahore; Pakistan Film Exhibitors' Association, Lyric Cinema Building, Aga Khan Road, Karachi; Pakistan Motion Picture Investors' Association, Lyric Cinema Building, Aga Khan Road, Karachi; Karachi Film Journalists' Association, Lyric Cinema Building, Aga Khan Road, Karachi.

—A. R. SLOTE

PHILIPPINES

Trends: Tagalog (Filipino) Films with 60% of the local market cornered, is casting its sights towards foreign films due to some radical changes in the distributor/exhibitor industry. The most significant change has been the demise of two of the biggest theatrical circuits, Greater Manila Theaters Assn. (GMTA) and the Metro Manila Theaters Assn. (MMTA), which controlled nearly all bookings. Their domination was usurped by tycoon Henry Sy, whose emerging chain of large malls-cum-multiplexes forced the competition to slash booking fees from 10% to 1%. Sy's SM City, Centerpoint and SM Mega Mall (with 12 screens) were responsible for boosting Warner Brothers revenues by 70% when they decided to do business with this new rival, forcing exhibitors to increase admission prices. Flexibility on run and booking dates with the three SM theaters netted Warner Brothers 85%–90% for the "The Last Boy Scout".

Jemah Films, an independent distributor has found good fortune in foreign films as they grossed $7.5 million pesos ($306,000) with "Dances With Wolves".

POLAND

Population: 40 million.
Number of theatre screens: Approximately 1,195 as of 1992.
Annual admissions: 15,000,000.
Top Ten Box Office Films of 1992: 1) Terminator II (Imperial: Admissions 472,000); 2) The Silence of the Lambs (Syrena: 541,000); 3) Hook (Syrena: 510,000); 4) Alien 3 (Syrena: 311,000); 5) Basic Instinct (Imperial: 227,000); 6) Europe, Europe (Film Art Found: 377,000); 7) Hot Shots (Syrena: 227,000); 8) Pump Up the Volume (Film Art Found: 259,000); 9) The Doors (Imperial: 195,000); 10) Snow White and the Seven Dwarfs (294,000).

Distributors: Apollo-Film State Film Distributor, Pychowicka 7, PO Box 186, 30960 Krakow. Tel: 12 671355/67 1663. FAX: 12 227564/671552. Director: Wit Dudek; Film Distribution Agency, Trebacka 3, 00074 Warsaw. Tel: 2 6352038/200231 Ext. 617. FAX: 2 6351543. Director: Goloniewski Andrzej; Film Polski, Mazowiecka 618 00048 Warsaw. Tel: 22 260849/268455. FAX: 22 275784. Telex: 813640 FILM PL. Director: Leon Warecki; Filmservice Ltd., Szkolna 2, Suite 4, 00950 Warsaw. Tel: 22 261427/265031 Ext. 462. Director: Surowka Andrzej; Guild Entertainment Ltd., Stoleczna Str. 16, 01590 Warsaw. Tel: 22 336892. FAX: 22 335497. Director: Martin Gasinski; Imperial Entertainment, Kolska Str. 12 01045 Warsaw. Tel: 22 387300/389500/387475. FAX: 22 386902/387302. Director: Marek Bryll; Intercom, Kolska Str. 12 01045 Warsaw. Tel: 22 389500/389902/387585. FAX: 22 387302. Director: Marek Bryll; International Vision Arts, Karolewska Str. 1, 90560 Lodž. Tel: 371777. FAX: 371763; Jandar, Sucholeska 15 Street, 62002 Poznań-Suchyłaś. Tel: 61 125459. FAX: 61 125465; MS-Film Production, Malej Laki 5, Suite 12, 02793 Warsaw. Tel: 22 705056. FAX: 22 405935. Director: Michal Szczerbic; Muvi Entertainment Group, Rozbrat Str. 44 Warsaw. Tel: 22 292664. FAX: 22 295911; Neptun Film, Piwna 22123, 80831 Gdansk. Tel: 58 213744. Director: Jerzy Martyś; Odra-Film State Film Distributor, Boguslawskiego 14, 50023 Wroclaw. Tel: 71 37091/359223/37090. FAX: 71 441088. Director: Jucha Kazimierz; Olech International, Grundwaldzka 135 80365 Gdansk. Tel: 58 477350/531288. FAX: 58 531245; Pleograf, Pl. Mirowski 14 00135 Warsaw. Tel: 22 205126. FAX: 22 208542. Contact: Jan Mogielnicki; POKO S.C, Chelmzynska, 135 Warsaw. Tel: 22 171300/241762. FAX: 22 241762; Raven, Starowislna Str. 27, 31038 Krakow. Tel: 012 211841. FAX: 012 211841. Telex: 0326564. Director: Ing. Janusz Leszczynski; Silesia-Film, Head Office: Plebiscytowa 36 40 041 Katowice. Trade Office: al. Ujazdowskie 20/10 Warsaw. Tel: 22 628 45 18. FAX: 22 628 45 18; Starcut Film-Poland, 6 Wybickiego Str, 84230 Rumia. Tel: 58 218325. FAX: 58 206646. Contact: Czestaw Żegar; Syrena Entertainment Group, Marszalkowska 115, 00102 Warsaw. Tel: 22 209053/200301 Ext. 390. FAX: 22 273500/268563. Telex: 816926. Contact: Slawomir Salomon; Vision, Rydygiera 7, 01793 Warsaw. Tel: 22 390753. FAX: 22 391367. Telex: 812 392 PL. Director: Wlodezimierz Otulak.

Organizations and Associations: Federation of Film Trade Guilds, Pulawska 61 02595 Warsaw. Tel: 2 6284855. FAX: 22 455586. Telex: 814620 PPROF PL. Contact: M Maciej Putowski. Director: Krzysztof Gradowski, General Delegate; Film Producers' Agency Ltd. of Film Production Agency, Wisniowa 56 02520 Warsaw. Tel: 22 486831/495032. FAX: 22 455586. Telex: 814220 PPROF PL. Director: Lojek Stefan; Film Production Agency, Pulawska 61 02595 Warsaw. Tel: 22 455316/455324. FAX: 22 455586. Telex: 814610. Director: Szwajkowski Boguslaw; Polish Federaion of Film Societies, PO Box 120, Plocka 16/34, 01138 Warsaw.

Tel: 22 321187/323709. Director: Trzos Rastawiecki Andrzej; Polish Film and TV Director's Guild, Pulawska 67 02595 Warsaw. Tel: 22 455316. FAX: 22 455316. Director: Krysztof Garadowski; Polish Screenwriters Guild, Al. Jerozolimskie 49m 4100697 Warsaw. Tel: 2 6281158. Director: Maciej Karpinski; Private Film Producers Club, Walbrzyska 14116 02738 Warsaw. Tel: 22 432861/430081–85 Ext. 252. Director: Malgorzata Potocka; State Committee of Polish Cinematography, Krakowskie Przedmiescie 15/17 00071 Warsaw. Tel: 22 263449. FAX: 22 261782. Telex: 813762 BWZ PL. Director: Waldemar Dabrowski; The Association of Polish Film Producers and Production Managers, Pulawska 61 02595 Warsaw. Tel: 22 455586/416591. Director: Barbara Pec Ślesicka; The Association of Polish Filmmakers, Krakowskie Przedmiescie 21/23, 00071 Warsaw. Tel: 22 276785/263096. FAX: 2 6351927. Director: Jan Kidawa Blonski; The National Film Library, PO Box 65, Pulawska 61, 00975 Warsaw. Tel: 22 454041 Ext. 230. FAX: 22 455074. Director: Waldemar Piatek.

PORTUGAL

Population: 10,240,000
Number of screens: 291 in 1992.
Annual admissions: 12 million.
Exhibitors: Atlanta Filmes, Av.D. Carlos I 72 D 3 Apt, Lisbon. Tel: (1) 67 48 41; Columbia & Warner Filmes de Portugal Lda, Av. Duque de Loulé 90 3 Apt Esq, 1000 Lisbon. Telex: 13047 COLWAR P. Tel: (1) 57 20 07, 55 77 95; Filmes Castello Lopes, Praca Marqués de Pombal 6 1 Apt. 1298, Lisbon Codex. Tel: (1) 56 33 66; Filmes Lusomundo, Praca da Alegria 22 1 Apt, 1200 Lisbon. FAX: (1) 346 53 49. Tel: (1) 347 45 61.

RUSSIA

Number of Cinema Screens: 120,000.
Annual Admissions: 2 billion.
Trends: The Russian and Commonwealth of Independent States film industry is currently in a state of flux. After producing some 1,550 films between 1990–1992, only 150 features were scheduled for a 1993 release. With an exchange rate of 600 rubles to the dollar, the estimated cost of a single production is $10,000–16,666 rubles ($6–7 million). These costs are somewhat staggering for Russian producers who therefore are looking for low budget features ranging between $500,000 to 1 million rubles (833–11,666).

Box office revenues have decreased dramatically, the blame being placed on the recent surge of violent content, according to Moscow film critics.

Exhibitors: 12A Film Studios, 12a Chistopolny Boulevard, 101 000 Moscow. Tel: 095 924 29 95. FAX: 095 200 32 03. Telex: 411 574 Rolan SU. Contact: Alexander Mikhailov; Kinomekhanik, Ul. B. Ordinka, 43, 109017 Moscow. Tel: 233 31 85. Contact: Martos Tamara.

Organizations and Associations: ASK-Association of Joint Film-initiatives, Smolensky Blvd 17, 119 121 Moscow. Tel: 095 244 0042. FAX: 095 230 2200. Telex: 411 939 EKRAN. Director: Rustam Ibragimbekov, President; ASKIN (Association of Cinema Distributors and Exhibitors), Maly Gnezdnikovski Pereulok, 103 009 Moscow. Tel: 095 229 0054, 229 2426. FAX: 095 229 8716. Director: Ismail Tagi-Bade; Association of Independent Cinema, Bolshaya Ordynka Street 43, 109 017 Moscow. Tel: 095 231 7690, 233 3016. FAX: 095 233 3016. Director: Andrei Razumovsky, President; Confederation of Film-Makers Unions, Vasily-evskaya Street 13, 123 825 Moscow. Tel: 095 250 4114. FAX: 095 200 4284. Telex: 411 939 EKRANSY. Director: Rustam Ibragimbekov; Film-Photo Scientific and Research Institute (NIKFI), Leningradsky Prospect 47, 125 167 Moscow. Tel: 095 157 2923. FAX: 095 157 0966. Telex: 411 058 FILM SU. Director: Eleonora Vinogradova; Filmexport, Lesnaya Street 27, 125 047 Moscow. Tel: 095 251 3614. FAX: 095 251 2910. Director: Galina Podgornaya; Russian Film-Makers Union, Vasilyevskaya Street 13, 123 285 Moscow. Tel: 095 215 1440, 251 5370. FAX: 095 973 2020. Telex: 411 939 EKRAN SU. Director: Sergei Soloviev, Chairman; Society of Friends of Cinema (ODK), Konstantin Simonov Street 5, Cor. 3, Apt. 41, 125 167 Moscow. Tel: 095 151 0474. Director: Boris Omarov, President; Studio Contact, Eisenstein Ul 8, 129 226 Moscow. Tel: 095 181 18 41, 925 28 44. FAX: 095 975 22 30. Telex: 911596 STAR SU. Director: Vladimir Gramatikov.

SPAIN

Population: 39,000,000
Number of cinema screens: 1,773.
Admissions in 1992: 78.5 million.
Trends: An agreement between the Spanish Film Institute (ICAA) and Caja de Madrid, a savings and loan institute, have established a low interest credit line for film productions. Allotted for non and subsidized productions is a total of approximately $8.2 million with a maximum amount of $860,000 for individual projects. Interest rates are about 14%.

U.S. majors are finding it harder to distribute their films as a new bill requires, for every two U.S. films released, they must also distribute one Spanish film or EC film in its original undubbed version. As a financial safeguard, the bill also requires the Spanish or EC film to gross $250,000 prior to the release of one U.S. film and gross $500,000 before the release of the second. However, in 1991 only 17 Spanish films grossed over $300,000 and the revenue was lower in 1992. Hollywood majors are disputing the fair trade legalities of this bill and have a case pending in Luxembourg, before the EC court.

A private trade agreement, without government intervention, has been made in the best interest of the smaller exhibitors, giving them a flat-price booking rate of $600 per film, offering a free choice of films and without block-booking.

Production Companies: Iberoamericana Films (also distributor), Velázquez 12, Madrid 28001. Tel: 431-4246; El Desco, Ruiz Perello 15 Bajo Centro, Madrid 280048. Tel: 255-0106; Multivideo, Luna 15, Madrid 28004. Tel: 542-1552; Elfas Querejeta P.C., Maestro Lasalle 21, Madrid 28016. Tel: 345-7139; Arsenal Films, Ronda Sant Pere, Barcelona 08010. Tel: (3) 268-1233; Distar Group (also distributor), Caídos de la División Azul, 22-B, Madrid 28016. Tel: 250-3900; Figaro Films, Consejo de Cien 303, Barcelona 08007. Tel: 323-5654; Ion Producciones, Avda, Alfonso XIII, 62, Madrid 28016. Tel: 413-8237; Sabre Films, Ayala 13, Madrid 28001. Tel: 435-9680; Bocangel 28, Madria 28028. Tel: 255-1807; Impala, Manuel Motilla 1, Madrid 28016. Tel: 250-6200.

Distributors: Araba Films, Orellana 4, 2.Izda, Madrid 28004. Tel: 308-4788; C.B. Films, Diagonal 407, Barcelona 08008. Tel: (3) 416 09 54; Filmayer, Martires de Alcalá 4, Madrid 28015. Tel: (1) 248 92 05; Golem Distribucion, Avda, de Bayona 52, Pamplona 31008. Tel: (48) 260243; Alta Films, Martín de les Heros 12, Madrid 28008. Tel: 542-2702; Surffilms, Zurbano 74, Madrid 28010. Tel: 442-2944; Ivex Films, Paseo San Gervasio 16, Barcelona 08022. Tel: 418-4858; Izaro Films, Raimundo Ferníndez Villaverde 65, Madrid 28003. Tel: 555-8041; Lauren Films, Balmes 87, Barcelona 08008. Tel: 323-5300; Musidora Films, Princesa 17, Madrid 28008. Tel: 541-6869.

SRI LANKA

Population: 17.5 million
Number of Cinemas: 340 in both 1992 and 1993.
Number of Admissions: 32,872,754 in 1993; 27,605,949 in 1992.
Gross Box Office Receipts: Rs. 267,775,375 ($5,583,232) in 1993; Rs. 250,808,060 ($5,832,745.50) in 1992. Admission increased by 13% in 1993, compared to 1992. The prices of tickets remain the same as in 1992.
Admission Prices: Rs. 27.50, 18.50, 15.50, 12.50, and 9.00.
Admission Tax: 25% entertainment tax on admission tickets and an additional tax levy of Rs. 2/- on all classes of tickets are charged to assist all Local Film Producers and the Sinhala Film industry.
Number of Films Produced Locally: 27 in Sinhala, 1 English and 3 Foreign films.
Number of Sinhala Films Exhibited in 1993: 24 films.
Number of Films Imported in 1993: 62 in English from U.S.A., U.K., Hong Kong; 14 in Tamil from India; 4 Hindi from India.
Number of People Viewing Daily: 44,159 Sinhala Films; 22,991 in Tamil; 33,310 in English and Hindi.
Average Cost of Local Productions: Rs. 1,000,000 to 2,000,000. (US $20,883 to $41,666) for black and white films; Rs. 3,000,000 to 7,000,000 ($62,500 to $145,834) for colour film production.
(All above statistics are calculated according to present exchange rates prevailing in Sri Lanka—U.S. $1.00–Rs. 48.00.)

The President of Sri Lanka recommended that the Cabinet of Ministers stop immediately the outright sale of the National Film Corporation headquarters building, Colombo, to a foreign Embassy in Colombo for Rs. 65,000,000 ($1,354,167). The entire film industry opposed the sale. No alternative office space has been given to the N.F.C. The industry considers the present location the most convenient one in Columbo, as this area is earmarked for educational, cultural and scientific purposes. Further the sister institutions such as the Sri Lanka Broadcasting Corporation, Sri Lanka Rupavahini Corporation (National Television), Sri Lanka Television Training Institute are located in close proximitiy to the National Film Corporation.

The Cultural and Information Minister said that it was not his intention to impose a total ban on "X-Rated (Adults Only)" films, but to minimize the number of such films produced, and currently being screened at cinemas. The decision will seriously limit the scope of film making and drastically affect the growing Sinhala film industry, for film makers will be compelled not to tackle adult themes.

Importers and exhibitors of English language films complained that the National Film Corporation (NFC) is attempting to take on the duties of an additional censor board, restricting some categories of Hollywood films. The Sri Lankan moviegoers have been enjoying popular quality films from U.S.A., U.K., France, Italy, Germany, and other leading film making countries for over 70 years. When this type of film ceased to be imported in 1971, protests were raised throughout the press. The Government of 1970–77 did not allow the free import of films. In 1977 the government again allowed the free flow of English language films. Imported films then suffered similar restrictions in the late 80's. The Government has subsequently restored the liberalized import of English language films and it has been going on without restrictions since then.

A film that has been produced and acted by a leading film personality is virtually running to empty houses. A cinema owner reported to the NFC that their daily income from this particular film is not sufficient to meet the daily electricity bills.

In 1992 the Chairman of the National Film Corporation, Dr. S. G. Samarasinghe, proposed a private company to handle scripts for new films and the channeling of loans to the new Sinhala films produced in Sri

Lanka. In 1993 Sri Lanka produced a record number of quality films which have no chance of exhibition for two to three years. There is a record number of pot boilers churned out; double the number of quality films. The Government offered concessions and tax exemptions to exhibitors to build new cinemas but found their investments would not bring sufficient returns to justify their investments. Not one cinema was built under this scheme. Ceylon Theatres, a long standing pioneer exhibiting company, and Batik textile exporter enterpreuner, Mr. Buddhi Keerthisena, had already commenced building two cinema complexes in Colombo with shopping arcades, film studios, and three cinemas in each complex.

Government Organizations: Sri Lanka National Film Corporation: Chairman and Chief Executive: Dr. S. G. Samarasinghe, 225 Bauddhaloka Mawatha, Colombo 7, Tel: 580247; Sri Lanka Rupavahini Corporation (National Television Network), Chairman: Mr. Peter Jayasekera, Torrington Square, Colombo 7: Tel: 580131, 580123-36 (14 lines); Independent Television Network (ITN), Chairman and Competent Authority: Air Commander A. P. Samarakone, I.T.N. Studios, Wickramasingh pura, Kotte Sri Lanka, Tel: 565491; Sri Lanka Broadcasting Corporation (SLBC), Torrington Square, Colombo 7 Chairman: Mr. Kumar Abeysinghe .SLAS, Tel: 596439, 597491, 597500. Ministry under which all the above Corporations function: Ministry of Cultural Affairs and Information: Hon. W. J. M. Lokubandara; Ministry of State for Information: Mr. A. J. Ranasinghe; Secretary: Mr. K. A. S. Gunasekera. Ministry Office: Malay Street, Colombo 2, Tel: 31747, 31748, 31749. Government Film Unit, Kirillapone, Colombo 6. Department of Information-Director of Information: Dr. Sunanda Madduma Bandara, Insurance Building, Vauxhall Street, Colombo 2, Sri Lanka. Tel: 22200. Information Officer: Mrs. Kusum Rodrigo. Distributor of Films: National Film Corporation, 225 Bauddhhloka Mawatha, Colombo. Private TV Networks: MTV Network, Pannipitiya, Sri Lanka. Teleshan TV Network, Vogue Building, 528 Galle Road, Colombo 3. Tel: 575436.

Principal Private Production Companies: Telecine Ltd., 34 Hyde Park Corner, Colombo 2, Tel: 23909; Ceylon Theatres Ltd., 8 Sir. Cittampalam Gardiner Mawatha, Colombo 2; Cine Lanka Ltd., Dickmans Road, Colombo; Film Lanka Ltd., 2nd Division Maradana, Colombo 10. Cinetra, 437 Pethiyagoda, Kelaniya. Tel: 521885. Telex: 22973 VITHY CE. Telefax: 449427 VITHY COM. Attn: Chandra S. Perera.

Film Equipment Hire Service: "FILMTEL", 81/3 Isipathana Mawatha, Colombo 5, Tel: 585573, Telex: 21537—Metalix Ce–Attn. Filtel; Film Location Service (Pvt) Ltd., 35/3 Guildford Cresent, Colombo 7. Tel: 697717.

Liaison Services for Foreign Film Producers: Producers of films for foreign exhibition and television, news, documentary, commercials, features, photo safari tours, liaisoning for foreign productions, location scouting, and joint film production ventures and location facilities. Services based on Sri Lanka background, etc. Cinetra–Telecinex Ltd., 437 Pethiyagoda, Kelaniya, Sri Lanka, Tel: 521885, Telex: 22973 VITHY CE. Telefax: 449427 or 446045 VITHTHY COM, Attn. Chandra S. Perera.

Film Laboratory Services: Colour and Black & White Processing: Sarasavi Studios, Dalugama, Kelaniya, Sri Lanka; Government Film Unit Laboratory, Kirillapone, Colombo 6, Sri Lanka.

—CHANDRA S. PERERA

SWEDEN

Trends: Svensk filmindustri (SF), a subsidiary of the Bonnier media group, showed profits of at least $80 million kronor ($14.3 million) for 1992, doubling that of 1991, which is impressive after a loss of $9 million in 1990. This has paved the way to expanding the 190-screen circuit by adding eight new screens in Northern Sweden and building a 15 to 25 screen complex in Central Stockholm, all for 1993. Meanwhile, SF's chief rival, Sandrews, who operates 98 screens in 21 cities, with a 10-plex in Stockholm handling admissions over 500,000, has obtained a very lucrative agreement with U.S. companies.

"House of Angels", a film by British filmmaker Colin Nutley, which was budgeted at 15 to 16 million kronor ($2.7 million), made a hefty contribution to Svensk theaters throughout the country (though SF refused to fund production) raising admissions to over 940,000 and bringing generous returns to this industry giant.

SWITZERLAND

Population: 6,874,000
Number of Theatres in Operation: 398, down from 401 in 1992.
Number of Imported Films: 343 against 339 in 1991; 205 of them were made in the USA, 46 came from France, 26 from Germany, 10 from Italy, 13 from Great Britain, and the remaining 43 from several different countries.

Box Office Hits: US films did best at the box office, followed by France and Germany, while Swiss, Italian and British films had less success.
Associations: Schweiz. Kino-Verband and Schweizerischer Filmverleihverband have now joined forces under the name "Pro Cinema" sharing the same address: Postfach, 3001 Berne.
Swiss Film Archives: Cinemathèque Suisse, Allée Ernest Ansermet 3, 1003 Lausanne.
Federal Film Aid: Nearly all Swiss films receive funding from the Federal Cultural Office (and Swiss television). In 1992, federal aid to

cinemas totalled 11,200 million Sfr. (up from 10,200 million Sfr. in 1991). 73.52% hereof went to production and merit prizes, 24.55% to marketing and promotion, 1 million Sfr. were allotted for the formation and development of beginners, while 1.94% went towards distribution. Furthermore, 1,300 million Sfr. were granted to the Swiss cinémathèque in Lausanne.

The department examined 461 requests for federal film aid and accepted 167; 281 more did not meet the minimal quality standards required and were rejected. 26 out of 77 submitted scripts were okayed.

—GABRIELLA BROGGI

TURKEY

Population: Approx. 58 million.
Turkish Films Made in 1992: 25.
Theatre Screens: 83 (in Istanbul); 29 (in Ankara); 18 (in Izmir).
Average Ticket Price: 30,000 Turkish lire ($3.30).

Though the number of existing cinemas have fallen to 83 in Istanbul and 18 in Izmir, ticket prices have risen from $1,500 Turkish lire to $30,000 (about $3.20). Production costs have escalated more than 60% and producers are seeking foreign backers.